PETERSON'S GRADUATE PROGRAMS IN BUSINESS, EDUCATION, HEALTH, INFORMATION STUDIES, LAW & SOCIAL WORK

2011

PETERSON'S
Publishing

About Peterson's Publishing

To succeed on your lifelong educational journey, you will need accurate, dependable, and practical tools and resources. That is why Peterson's is everywhere education happens. Because whenever and however you need education content delivered, you can rely on Peterson's to provide the information, know-how, and guidance to help you reach your goals. Tools to match the right students with the right school. It's here. Personalized resources and expert guidance. It's here. Comprehensive and dependable education content—delivered whenever and however you need it. It's all here.

For more information, contact Peterson's, 2000 Lenox Drive, Lawrenceville, NJ 08648; 800-338-3282 Ext. 54229; or find us online at www.petersonspublishing.com.

Stephen Clemente, Managing Director, Publishing and Institutional Research; Bernadette Webster, Director of Publishing; Jill C. Schwartz, Editor; Ken Britschge, Research Project Manager; Courtney Foust, Amy L. Weber, Research Associates; Phyllis Johnson, Programmer; Ray Golaszewski, Manufacturing Manager; Linda M. Williams, Composition Manager; Karen Mount, Danielle Vreeland, Shannon White, Client Relations Representatives

ISSN 1088-9442
ISBN-13: 978-0-7689-2857-0
ISBN-10: 0-7689-2857-5

Printed in the United States of America

10 9 8 7 6 5 4 3 2 1   13 12 11

Forty-fifth Edition

By producing this book on recycled paper (40% post consumer waste) 200 trees were saved.

CONTENTS

ACADEMIC AND PROFESSIONAL PROGRAMS IN THE HEALTH-RELATED PROFESSIONS

ACADEMIC AND PROFESSIONAL PROGRAMS IN LAW

ACADEMIC AND PROFESSIONAL PROGRAMS IN LIBRARY AND INFORMATION STUDIES

ACADEMIC AND PROFESSIONAL PROGRAMS IN THE MEDICAL PROFESSIONS AND SCIENCES

A Note from the Peterson's Editors

The six volumes of Peterson's *Graduate and Professional Programs*, the only annually updated reference work of its kind, provide wide-ranging information on the graduate and professional programs offered by accredited colleges and universities in the United States, U.S. territories, and Canada and by those institutions outside the United States that are accredited by U.S. accrediting bodies. More than 44,000 individual academic and professional programs at more than 2,200 institutions are listed. Peterson's *Graduate and Professional Programs* have been used for more than forty years by prospective graduate and professional students, placement counselors, faculty advisers, and all others interested in postbaccalaureate education.

Graduate & Professional Programs: An Overview contains information on institutions as a whole, while the other books in the series are devoted to specific academic and professional fields:

Graduate Programs in the Humanities, Arts & Social Sciences
Graduate Programs in the Biological Sciences
Graduate Programs in the Physical Sciences, Mathematics, Agricultural Sciences, the Environment & Natural Resources
Graduate Programs in Engineering & Applied Sciences
Graduate Programs in Business, Education, Health, Information Studies, Law & Social Work

The books may be used individually or as a set. For example, if you have chosen a field of study but do not know what institution you want to attend or if you have a college or university in mind but have not chosen an academic field of study, it is best to begin with the Overview guide.

Graduate & Professional Programs: An Overview presents several directories to help you identify programs of study that might interest you; you can then research those programs further in the other books in the series by using the Directory of Graduate and Professional Programs by Field, which lists 500 fields and gives the names of those institutions that offer graduate degree programs in each.

For geographical or financial reasons, you may be interested in attending a particular institution and will want to know what it has to offer. You should turn to the Directory of Institutions and Their Offerings, which lists the degree programs available at each institution. As in the Directory of Graduate and Professional Programs by Field, the level of degrees offered is also indicated.

All books in the series include advice on graduate education, including topics such as admissions tests, financial aid, and accreditation. **The Graduate Adviser** includes two essays and information about accreditation. The first essay, "The Admissions Process," discusses general admission requirements, admission tests, factors to consider when selecting a graduate school or program, when and how to apply, and how admission decisions are made. Special information for international students and tips for minority students are also included. The second essay, "Financial Support," is an overview of the broad range of support available at the graduate level. Fellowships, scholarships, and grants; assistantships and internships; federal and private loan programs, as well as Federal Work-Study; and the GI bill are detailed. This essay concludes with advice on applying for need-based financial aid. "Accreditation and Accrediting Agencies" gives information on accreditation and its purpose and lists institutional accrediting agencies first and then specialized accrediting agencies relevant to each volume's specific fields of study.

With information on more than 44,000 graduate programs in 500 disciplines, Peterson's *Graduate and Professional Programs* give you all the information you need about the programs that are of interest to you in three formats: **Profiles** (capsule summaries of basic information), **Displays** (information that an institution or program wants to emphasize), and **Close-Ups** (written by administrators, with more expansive information than the **Profiles**, emphasizing different aspects of the programs). By using these various formats of program information, coupled with **Appendixes** and **Indexes** covering directories and subject areas for all six books, you will find that these guides provide the most comprehensive, accurate, and up-to-date graduate study information available.

Find Us on Facebook® and Follow Us on Twitter™

Join the grad school conversation on Facebook® and Twitter™ at www.facebook.com/usgradschools and www.twitter.com/usgradschools. Peterson's expert resources are available to help you as you search for the right graduate program for you.

Peterson's publishes a full line of resources with information you need to guide you through the graduate admissions process. Peterson's publications can be found at college libraries and career centers and your local bookstore or library—or visit us on the Web at www.petersonspublishing.com. Peterson's books are now also available as eBooks.

Colleges and universities will be pleased to know that Peterson's helped you in your selection. Admissions staff members are more than happy to answer questions, address specific problems, and help in any way they can. The editors at Peterson's wish you great success in your graduate program search!

THE GRADUATE ADVISER

The Admissions Process

Generalizations about graduate admissions practices are not always helpful because each institution has its own set of guidelines and procedures. Nevertheless, some broad statements can be made about the admissions process that may help you plan your strategy.

Factors Involved in Selecting a Graduate School or Program

Selecting a graduate school and a specific program of study is a complex matter. Quality of the faculty; program and course offerings; the nature, size, and location of the institution; admission requirements; cost; and the availability of financial assistance are among the many factors that affect one's choice of institution. Other considerations are job placement and achievements of the program's graduates and the institution's resources, such as libraries, laboratories, and computer facilities. If you are to make the best possible choice, you need to learn as much as you can about the schools and programs you are considering before you apply.

The following steps may help you narrow your choices.

- Talk to alumni of the programs or institutions you are considering to get their impressions of how well they were prepared for work in their fields of study.
- Remember that graduate school requirements change, so be sure to get the most up-to-date information possible.
- Talk to department faculty members and the graduate adviser at your undergraduate institution. They often have information about programs of study at other institutions.
- Visit the Web sites of the graduate schools in which you are interested to request a graduate catalog. Contact the department chair in your chosen field of study for additional information about the department and the field.
- Visit as many campuses as possible. Call ahead for an appointment with the graduate adviser in your field of interest and be sure to check out the facilities and talk to students.

General Requirements

Graduate schools and departments have requirements that applicants for admission must meet. Typically, these requirements include undergraduate transcripts (which provide information about undergraduate grade point average and course work applied toward a major), admission test scores, and letters of recommendation. Most graduate programs also ask for an essay or personal statement that describes your personal reasons for seeking graduate study. In some fields, such as art and music, portfolios or auditions may be required in addition to other evidence of talent. Some institutions require that the applicant have an undergraduate degree in the same subject as the intended graduate major.

Most institutions evaluate each applicant on the basis of the applicant's total record, and the weight accorded any given factor varies widely from institution to institution and from program to program.

The Application Process

You should begin the application process at least one year before you expect to begin your graduate study. Find out the application deadline for each institution (many are provided in the **Profile** section of this guide). Go to the institution's Web site and find out if you can apply online. If not, request a paper application form. Fill out this form thoroughly and neatly. Assume that the school needs all the information it is requesting and that the admissions officer will be sensitive to the neatness and overall quality of what you submit. Do not supply more information than the school requires.

The institution may ask at least one question that will require a three- or four-paragraph answer. Compose your response on the assumption that the admissions officer is interested in both what you think and how you express yourself. Keep your statement brief and to the point, but, at the same time, include all pertinent information about your past experiences and your educational goals. Individual statements vary greatly in style and content, which helps admissions officers differentiate among applicants. Many graduate departments give considerable weight to the statement in making their admissions decisions, so be sure to take the time to prepare a thoughtful and concise statement.

If recommendations are a part of the admissions requirements, carefully choose the individuals you ask to write them. It is generally best to ask current or former professors to write the recommendations, provided they are able to attest to your intellectual ability and motivation for doing the work required of a graduate student. It is advisable to provide stamped, preaddressed envelopes to people being asked to submit recommendations on your behalf.

Completed applications, including references, transcripts, and admission test scores, should be received at the institution by the specified date.

Be advised that institutions do not usually make admissions decisions until all materials have been received. Enclose a self-addressed postcard with your application, requesting confirmation of receipt. Allow at least ten days for the return of the postcard before making further inquiries.

If you plan to apply for financial support, it is imperative that you file your application early.

ADMISSION TESTS

The major testing program used in graduate admissions is the Graduate Record Examinations (GRE) testing program, sponsored by the GRE Board and administered by Educational Testing Service, Princeton, New Jersey.

The Graduate Record Examinations testing program consists of a General Test and eight Subject Tests. The General Test measures critical thinking, verbal reasoning, quantitative reasoning, and analytical writing skills. It is offered as an Internet-based test (iBT) in the United States, Canada, and many other countries.

The typical computer-based General Test consists of one 30-minute verbal reasoning section, one 45-minute quantitative reasoning sections, one 45-minute issue analysis (writing) section, and one 30-minute argument analysis (writing) section. In addition, an unidentified verbal or quantitative section that doesn't count toward a score may be included and an identified research section that is not scored may also be included.

The Subject Tests measure achievement and assume undergraduate majors or extensive background in the following eight disciplines:

- Biochemistry, Cell and Molecular Biology
- Biology
- Chemistry
- Computer Science
- Literature in English
- Mathematics
- Physics
- Psychology

The Subject Tests are available three times per year as paper-based administrations around the world. Testing time is approximately 2 hours and 50 minutes. You can obtain more information about the GRE by visiting the ETS Web site at www.ets.org or consulting the *GRE Information and Registration Bulletin*. The *Bulletin* can be obtained at many undergraduate colleges. You can also download it from the ETS Web site or obtain it by contacting Graduate Record Examinations, Educational Testing Service, P.O. Box 6000, Princeton, NJ 08541-6000; phone: 609-771-7670.

If you expect to apply for admission to a program that requires any of the GRE tests, you should select a test date well in advance of the

application deadline. Scores on the computer-based General Test are reported within ten to fifteen days; scores on the paper-based Subject Tests are reported within six weeks.

Another testing program, the Miller Analogies Test (MAT), is administered at more than 500 Controlled Testing Centers, licensed by Harcourt Assessment, Inc., in the United States, Canada, and other countries. The MAT computer-based test is now available. Testing time is 60 minutes. The test consists of 120 partial analogies. You can obtain the *Candidate Information Booklet,* which contains a list of test centers and instructions for taking the test, from http://www.milleranalogies.com or by calling 800-622-3231 (toll-free).

Check the specific requirements of the programs to which you are applying.

How Admission Decisions Are Made

The program you apply to is directly involved in the admissions process. Although the final decision is usually made by the graduate dean (or an associate) or the faculty admissions committee, recommendations from faculty members in your intended field are important. At some institutions, an interview is incorporated into the decision process.

A Special Note for International Students

In addition to the steps already described, there are some special considerations for international students who intend to apply for graduate study in the United States. All graduate schools require an indication of competence in English. The purpose of the Test of English as a Foreign Language (TOEFL) is to evaluate the English proficiency of people who are nonnative speakers of English and want to study at colleges and universities where English is the language of instruction. The TOEFL is administered by Educational Testing Service (ETS) under the general direction of a policy board established by the College Board and the Graduate Record Examinations Board.

The TOEFL iBT assesses the four basic language skills: listening, reading, writing, and speaking. It was administered for the first time in September 2005, and ETS continues to introduce the TOEFL iBT in selected cities. The Internet-based test is administered at secure, official test centers. The testing time is approximately 4 hours. Because the TOEFL iBT includes a speaking section, the Test of Spoken English (TSE) is no longer needed.

The TOEFL is also offered in the paper-based format in areas of the world where Internet-based testing is not available. The paper-based TOEFL consists of three sections—listening comprehension, structure and written expression, and reading comprehension. The testing time is approximately 3 hours. The Test of Written English (TWE) is also given. The TWE is a 30-minute essay that measures the examinee's ability to compose in English. Examinees receive a TWE score separate from their TOEFL score. The *Information Bulletin* contains information on local fees and registration procedures.

Additional information and registration materials are available from TOEFL Services, Educational Testing Service, P.O. Box 6151, Princeton, New Jersey 08541-6151. Phone: 609-771-7100. Web site: www.toefl.org.

International students should apply especially early because of the number of steps required to complete the admissions process. Furthermore, many United States graduate schools have a limited number of spaces for international students, and many more students apply than the schools can accommodate.

International students may find financial assistance from institutions very limited. The U.S. government requires international applicants to submit a certification of support, which is a statement attesting to the applicant's financial resources. In addition, international students *must* have health insurance coverage.

Tips for Minority Students

Indicators of a university's values in terms of diversity are found both in its recruitment programs and its resources directed to student success. Important questions: Does the institution vigorously recruit minorities for its graduate programs? Is there funding available to help with the costs associated with visiting the school? Are minorities represented in the institution's brochures or Web site or on their faculty rolls? What campus-based resources or services (including assistance in locating housing or career counseling and placement) are available? Is funding available to members of underrepresented groups?

At the program level, it is particularly important for minority students to investigate the "climate" of a program under consideration. How many minority students are enrolled and how many have graduated? What opportunities are there to work with diverse faculty and mentors whose research interests match yours? How are conflicts resolved or concerns addressed? How interested are faculty in building strong and supportive relations with students? "Climate" concerns should be addressed by posing questions to various individuals, including faculty members, current students, and alumni.

Information is also available through various organizations, such as the Hispanic Association of Colleges & Universities (HACU), and publications such as *Diverse Issues in Higher Education* and *Hispanic Outlook* magazine. There are also books devoted to this topic, such as *The Multicultural Student's Guide to Colleges* by Robert Mitchell.

Financial Support

The range of financial support at the graduate level is very broad. The following descriptions will give you a general idea of what you might expect and what will be expected of you as a financial support recipient.

Fellowships, Scholarships, and Grants

These are usually outright awards of a few hundred to many thousands of dollars with no service to the institution required in return. Fellowships and scholarships are usually awarded on the basis of merit and are highly competitive. Grants are made on the basis of financial need or special talent in a field of study. Many fellowships, scholarships, and grants not only cover tuition, fees, and supplies but also include stipends for living expenses with allowances for dependents. However, the terms of each should be examined because some do not permit recipients to supplement their income with outside work. Fellowships, scholarships, and grants may vary in the number of years for which they are awarded.

In addition to the availability of these funds at the university or program level, many excellent fellowship programs are available at the national level and may be applied for before and during enrollment in a graduate program. A listing of many of these programs can be found at the Council of Graduate Schools' Web site: http://www.cgsnet.org. There is a wealth of information in the "Programs" and "Awards" sections.

Assistantships and Internships

Many graduate students receive financial support through assistantships, particularly involving teaching or research duties. It is important to recognize that such appointments should not be viewed simply as employment relationships but rather should constitute an integral and important part of a student's graduate education. As such, the appointments should be accompanied by strong faculty mentoring and increasingly responsible apprenticeship experiences. The specific nature of these appointments in a given program should be considered in selecting that graduate program.

TEACHING ASSISTANTSHIPS

These usually provide a salary and full or partial tuition remission and may also provide health benefits. Unlike fellowships, scholarships, and grants, which require no service to the institution, teaching assistantships require recipients to provide the institution with a specific amount of undergraduate teaching, ideally related to the student's field of study. Some teaching assistants are limited to grading papers, compiling bibliographies, taking notes, or monitoring laboratories. At some graduate schools, teaching assistants must carry lighter course loads than regular full-time students.

RESEARCH ASSISTANTSHIPS

These are very similar to teaching assistantships in the manner in which financial assistance is provided. The difference is that recipients are given basic research assignments in their disciplines rather than teaching responsibilities. The work required is normally related to the student's field of study; in most instances, the assistantship supports the student's thesis or dissertation research.

ADMINISTRATIVE INTERNSHIPS

These are similar to assistantships in application of financial assistance funds, but the student is given an assignment on a part-time basis, usually as a special assistant with one of the university's administrative offices. The assignment may not necessarily be directly related to the recipient's discipline.

RESIDENCE HALL AND COUNSELING ASSISTANTSHIPS

These assistantships are frequently assigned to graduate students in psychology, counseling, and social work, but they may be offered to students in other disciplines, especially if the student has worked in this capacity during his or her undergraduate years. Duties can vary from being available in a dean's office for a specific number of hours for consultation with undergraduates to living in campus residences and being responsible for both counseling and administrative tasks or advising student activity groups. Residence hall assistantships often include a room and board allowance and, in some cases, tuition assistance and stipends. Contact the Housing and Student Life Office for more information.

Health Insurance

The availability and affordability of health insurance is an important issue and one that should be considered in an applicant's choice of institution and program. While often included with assistantships and fellowships, this is not always the case and, even if provided, the benefits may be limited. It is important to note that the U.S. government requires international students to have health insurance.

The GI Bill

This provides financial assistance for students who are veterans of the United States armed forces. If you are a veteran, contact your local Veterans Administration office to determine your eligibility and to get full details about benefits. There are a number of programs that offer educational benefits to current military enlistees. Some states have tuition assistance programs for members of the National Guard. Contact the VA office at the college for more information.

Federal Work-Study Program (FWS)

Employment is another way some students finance their graduate studies. The federally funded Federal Work-Study Program provides eligible students with employment opportunities, usually in public and private nonprofit organizations. Federal funds pay up to 75 percent of the wages, with the remainder paid by the employing agency. FWS is available to graduate students who demonstrate financial need. Not all schools have these funds, and some only award them to undergraduates. Each school sets its application deadline and work-study earnings limits. Wages vary and are related to the type of work done. You must file the Free Application for Federal Student Aid (FAFSA) to be eligible for this program.

Loans

Many graduate students borrow to finance their graduate programs when other sources of assistance (which do not have to be repaid) prove insufficient. You should always read and understand the terms of any loan program before submitting your application.

FEDERAL DIRECT LOANS

Federal Direct Stafford Loans. The Federal Direct Stafford Loan Program offers low-interest loans to students with the Department of Education acting as the lender.

There are two components of the Federal Stafford Loan program. Under the *subsidized* component of the program, the federal government pays the interest on the loan while you are enrolled in graduate school on at least a half-time basis, during the six-month grace period after you drop below half-time enrollment, as well as during any period of deferment. Under the *unsubsidized* component of the program, you pay the interest on the loan from the day proceeds are issued. Eligibility for the federal subsidy is based on demonstrated financial need as determined by the financial aid office from the information you provide on the FAFSA. A cosigner is not required, since the loan is not based on creditworthiness.

Although *unsubsidized* Federal Direct Stafford Loans may not be as desirable as *subsidized* Federal Direct Stafford Loans from the student's perspective, they are a useful source of support for those who may not qualify for the subsidized loans or who need additional financial assistance.

Graduate students may borrow up to $20,500 per year through the Direct Stafford Loan Program, up to a cumulative maximum of $138,500, including undergraduate borrowing. This may include up to $8500 in *subsidized* Direct Stafford Loans annually, depending on eligibility, up to a cumulative maximum of $65,500, including undergraduate borrowing. The amount of the loan borrowed through the *unsubsidized* Direct Stafford Loan Program equals the total amount of the loan (as much as $20,500) minus your eligibility for a *subsidized* Direct Loan (as much as $8500). You may borrow up to the cost of attendance at the school in which you are enrolled or will attend, minus estimated financial assistance from other federal, state, and private sources, up to a maximum of $20,500.

Direct Stafford Loans made on or after July 1, 2006, carry a fixed interest rate of 6.8% both for in-school and in-repayment borrowers.

A fee is deducted from the loan proceeds upon disbursement. Loans with a first disbursement on or after July 1, 2010 have a borrower origination fee of 1 percent. The Department of Education offers a 0.5 percent origination fee rebate incentive. Borrowers must make their first twelve payments on time in order to retain the rebate.

Under the *subsidized* Federal Direct Stafford Loan Program, repayment begins six months after your last date of enrollment on at least a half-time basis. Under the *unsubsidized* program, repayment of interest begins within thirty days from disbursement of the loan proceeds, and repayment of the principal begins six months after your last enrollment on at least a half-time basis. Some borrowers may choose to defer interest payments while they are in school. The accrued interest is added to the loan balance when the borrower begins repayment. There are several repayment options.

Federal Perkins Loans. The Federal Perkins Loan is available to students demonstrating financial need and is administered directly by the school. Not all schools have these funds, and some may award them to undergraduates only. Eligibility is determined from the information you provide on the FAFSA. The school will notify you of your eligibility.

Eligible graduate students may borrow up to $6000 per year, up to a maximum of $40,000, including undergraduate borrowing (even if your previous Perkins Loans have been repaid). The interest rate for Federal Perkins Loans is 5 percent, and no interest accrues while you remain in school at least half-time. There are no guarantee, loan, or disbursement fees. Repayment begins nine months after your last date of enrollment on at least a half-time basis and may extend over a maximum of ten years with no prepayment penalty.

Federal Direct Graduate PLUS Loans. Effective July 1, 2006, graduate and professional students are eligible for Graduate PLUS loans. This program allows students to borrow up to the cost of attendance, less any other aid received. These loans have a fixed interest rate of 7.9 percent, and interest begins to accrue at the time of disbursement. The PLUS loans do involve a credit check; a PLUS borrower may obtain a loan with a cosigner if his or her credit is not good enough. Grad PLUS loans may be deferred while a student in school and for the six months following a drop below half-time enrollment. For more information, contact your college financial aid office.

Deferring Your Federal Loan Repayments. If you borrowed under the Federal Direct Stafford Loan Program, Federal Direct Loan Program, or the Federal Perkins Loan Program for previous undergraduate or graduate study, your repayments may be deferred when you return to graduate school, depending on when you borrowed and under which program.

There are other deferment options available if you are temporarily unable to repay your loan. Information about these deferments is provided at your entrance and exit interviews. If you believe you are eligible for a deferment of your loan repayments, you must contact your lender or loan servicer to request a deferment form. The deferment must be filed prior to the time your repayment is due, and it must be refiled when it expires if you remain eligible for deferment at that time.

SUPPLEMENTAL (PRIVATE) LOANS

Many lending institutions offer supplemental loan programs and other financing plans, such as the ones described here, to students seeking additional assistance in meeting their education expenses. Some loan programs target all types of graduate students; others are designed specifically for business, law, or medical students. In addition, you can use private loans not specifically designed for education to help finance your graduate degree.

If you are considering borrowing through a supplemental or private loan program, you should carefully consider the terms and be sure to "read the fine print." Check with the program sponsor for the most current terms that will be applicable to the amounts you intend to borrow for graduate study. Most supplemental loan programs for graduate study offer unsubsidized, credit-based loans. In general, a credit-ready borrower is one who has a satisfactory credit history or no credit history at all. A creditworthy borrower generally must pass a credit test to be eligible to borrow or act as a cosigner for the loan funds.

Many supplemental loan programs have minimum and maximum annual loan limits. Some offer amounts equal to the cost of attendance minus any other aid you will receive for graduate study. If you are planning to borrow for several years of graduate study, consider whether there is a cumulative or aggregate limit on the amount you may borrow. Often this cumulative or aggregate limit will include any amounts you borrowed and have not repaid for undergraduate or previous graduate study.

The combination of the annual interest rate, loan fees, and the repayment terms you choose will determine how much you will repay over time. Compare these features in combination before you decide which loan program to use. Some loans offer interest rates that are adjusted monthly, some quarterly, some annually. Some offer interest rates that are lower during the in-school, grace, and deferment periods and then increase when you begin repayment. Some programs include a loan "origination" fee, which is usually deducted from the principal amount you receive when the loan is disbursed and must be repaid along with the interest and other principal when you graduate, withdraw from school, or drop below half-time study. Sometimes the loan fees are reduced if you borrow with a qualified cosigner. Some programs allow you to defer interest and/or principal payments while you are enrolled in graduate school. Many programs allow you to capitalize your interest payments; the interest due on your loan is added to the outstanding balance of your loan, so you don't have to repay immediately, but this increases the amount you owe. Other programs allow you to pay the interest as you go, which reduces the amount you later have to repay. The private loan market is very competitive, and your financial aid office can help you evaluate these programs.

Applying for Need-Based Financial Aid

Schools that award federal and institutional financial assistance based on need will require you to complete the FAFSA and, in some cases, an institutional financial aid application.

If you are applying for federal student assistance, you **must** complete the FAFSA. A service of the U.S. Department of Education, the FAFSA is free to all applicants. Most applicants apply online at www.fafsa.ed.gov. Paper applications are available at the financial aid office of your local college.

After your FAFSA information has been processed, you will receive a Student Aid Report (SAR). If you provided an e-mail address on the FAFSA, this will be sent to you electronically; otherwise, it will be mailed to your home address.

Follow the instructions on the SAR if you need to correct information reported on your original application. If your situation changes after you file your FAFSA, contact your financial aid officer to discuss amending your information. You can also appeal your financial aid award if you have extenuating circumstances.

If you would like more information on federal student financial aid, visit the FAFSA Web site or download the most recent version of *Funding Education Beyond High School: The Guide to Federal Student Aid* at http://studentaid.ed.gov/students/publications/student_guide/index.html. This guide is also available in Spanish.

The U.S. Department of Education also has a toll-free number for questions concerning federal student aid programs. The number is 1-800-4-FED AID (1-800-433-3243). If you are hearing impaired, call toll-free, 1-800-730-8913.

Summary

Remember that these are generalized statements about financial assistance at the graduate level. Because each institution allots its aid differently, you should communicate directly with the school and the specific department of interest to you. It is not unusual, for example, to find that an endowment vested within a specific department supports one or more fellowships. You may fit its requirements and specifications precisely.

Accreditation and Accrediting Agencies

Colleges and universities in the United States, and their individual academic and professional programs, are accredited by nongovernmental agencies concerned with monitoring the quality of education in this country. Agencies with both regional and national jurisdictions grant accreditation to institutions as a whole, while specialized bodies acting on a nationwide basis—often national professional associations—grant accreditation to departments and programs in specific fields.

Institutional and specialized accrediting agencies share the same basic concerns: the purpose an academic unit—whether university or program—has set for itself and how well it fulfills that purpose, the adequacy of its financial and other resources, the quality of its academic offerings, and the level of services it provides. Agencies that grant institutional accreditation take a broader view, of course, and examine university-wide or college-wide services with which a specialized agency may not concern itself.

Both types of agencies follow the same general procedures when considering an application for accreditation. The academic unit prepares a self-evaluation, focusing on the concerns mentioned above and usually including an assessment of both its strengths and weaknesses; a team of representatives of the accrediting body reviews this evaluation, visits the campus, and makes its own report; and finally, the accrediting body makes a decision on the application. Often, even when accreditation is granted, the agency makes a recommendation regarding how the institution or program can improve. All institutions and programs are also reviewed every few years to determine whether they continue to meet established standards; if they do not, they may lose their accreditation.

Accrediting agencies themselves are reviewed and evaluated periodically by the U.S. Department of Education and the Council for Higher Education Accreditation (CHEA). Recognized agencies adhere to certain standards and practices, and their authority in matters of accreditation is widely accepted in the educational community.

This does not mean, however, that accreditation is a simple matter, either for schools wishing to become accredited or for students deciding where to apply. Indeed, in certain fields the very meaning and methods of accreditation are the subject of a good deal of debate. For their part, those applying to graduate school should be aware of the safeguards provided by regional accreditation, especially in terms of degree acceptance and institutional longevity. Beyond this, applicants should understand the role that specialized accreditation plays in their field, as this varies considerably from one discipline to another. In certain professional fields, it is necessary to have graduated from a program that is accredited in order to be eligible for a license to practice, and in some fields the federal government also makes this a hiring requirement. In other disciplines, however, accreditation is not as essential, and there can be excellent programs that are not accredited. In fact, some programs choose not to seek accreditation, although most do.

Institutions and programs that present themselves for accreditation are sometimes granted the status of candidate for accreditation, or what is known as "preaccreditation." This may happen, for example, when an academic unit is too new to have met all the requirements for accreditation. Such status signifies initial recognition and indicates that the school or program in question is working to fulfill all requirements; it does not, however, guarantee that accreditation will be granted.

Institutional Accrediting Agencies—Regional

MIDDLE STATES ASSOCIATION OF COLLEGES AND SCHOOLS
Accredits institutions in Delaware, District of Columbia, Maryland, New Jersey, New York, Pennsylvania, Puerto Rico, and the Virgin Islands.
Dr. Elizabeth Sibolski, Acting President
Middle States Commission on Higher Education
3624 Market Street, Second Floor West
Philadelphia, Pennsylvania 19104
Phone: 267-284-5000
Fax: 215-662-5501
E-mail: info@msche.org
Web: www.msche.org

NEW ENGLAND ASSOCIATION OF SCHOOLS AND COLLEGES
Accredits institutions in Connecticut, Maine, Massachusetts, New Hampshire, Rhode Island, and Vermont.
Barbara E. Brittingham, Director
Commission on Institutions of Higher Education
209 Burlington Road, Suite 201
Bedford, Massachusetts 01730-1433
Phone: 781-271-0022
Fax: 781-271-0950
E-mail: CIHE@neasc.org
Web: www.neasc.org

NORTH CENTRAL ASSOCIATION OF COLLEGES AND SCHOOLS
Accredits institutions in Arizona, Arkansas, Colorado, Illinois, Indiana, Iowa, Kansas, Michigan, Minnesota, Missouri, Nebraska, New Mexico, North Dakota, Ohio, Oklahoma, South Dakota, West Virginia, Wisconsin, and Wyoming.
Dr. Sylvia Manning, President
The Higher Learning Commission
230 South LaSalle Street, Suite 7-500
Chicago, Illinois 60604-1413
Phone: 312-263-0456
Fax: 312-263-7462
E-mail: smanning@hlcommission.org
Web: www.ncahigherlearningcommission.org

NORTHWEST COMMISSION ON COLLEGES AND UNIVERSITIES
Accredits institutions in Alaska, Idaho, Montana, Nevada, Oregon, Utah, and Washington.
Dr. Sandra E. Elman, President
8060 165th Avenue, NE, Suite 100
Redmond, Washington 98052
Phone: 425-558-4224
Fax: 425-376-0596
E-mail: selman@nwccu.org
Web: www.nwccu.org

SOUTHERN ASSOCIATION OF COLLEGES AND SCHOOLS
Accredits institutions in Alabama, Florida, Georgia, Kentucky, Louisiana, Mississippi, North Carolina, South Carolina, Tennessee, Texas, and Virginia.
Belle S. Wheelan, President
Commission on Colleges
1866 Southern Lane
Decatur, Georgia 30033-4097
Phone: 404-679-4500
Fax: 404-679-4558
E-mail: questions@sacscoc.org
Web: www.sacsoc.org

WESTERN ASSOCIATION OF SCHOOLS AND COLLEGES
Accredits institutions in California, Guam, and Hawaii.
Ralph A. Wolff, President and Executive Director
Accrediting Commission for Senior Colleges and Universities
985 Atlantic Avenue, Suite 100
Alameda, California 94501
Phone: 510-748-9001
Fax: 510-748-9797
E-mail: www.wascsenior.org
Web: www.wascweb.org/contact

Institutional Accrediting Agencies—Other

ACCREDITING COUNCIL FOR INDEPENDENT COLLEGES AND SCHOOLS
Albert C. Gray, Ph.D., Executive Director and CEO
750 First Street, NE, Suite 980
Washington, DC 20002-4241
Phone: 202-336-6780
Fax: 202-842-2593
E-mail: info@acics.org
Web: www.acics.org

DISTANCE EDUCATION AND TRAINING COUNCIL (DETC)
Accrediting Commission
Michael P. Lambert, Executive Director
1601 18th Street, NW, Suite 2
Washington, DC 20009
Phone: 202-234-5100
Fax: 202-332-1386
E-mail: detc@detc.org
Web: www.detc.org

Specialized Accrediting Agencies

[Only *Graduate & Professional Programs: An Overview* of *Peterson's Graduate and Professional Programs* Series includes the complete list of specialized accrediting groups recognized by the U.S. Department of Education and the Council on Higher Education Accreditation (CHEA). The list in this book is abridged.]

ACUPUNCTURE AND ORIENTAL MEDICINE
Dort S. Bigg, J.D., Executive Director
Accreditation Commission for Acupuncture and Oriental Medicine
Maryland Trade Center #3
7501 Greenway Center Drive, Suite 760
Greenbelt, Maryland 20770
Phone: 301-313-0855
Fax: 301-313-0912
E-mail: info@acaom.org
Web: www.acaom.org

BUSINESS
Jerry Trapnell, Executive Vice President/Chief Accreditation Officer
AACSB International--The Association to Advance Collegiate Schools of Business
777 South Harbour Island Boulevard, Suite 700
Tampa, Florida 33602
Phone: 813-769-6500
Fax: 813-769-6559
E-mail: jerryt@aacsb.edu
Web: www.aacsb.edu

CHIROPRACTIC
Lee Van Dusen, President
Council on Chiropractic Education (CCE)
Commission on Accreditation
8049 North 85th Way
Scottsdale, Arizona 85258-4321
Phone: 480-443-8877
Fax: 480-483-7333
E-mail: cce@cce-usa.org
Web: www.cce-usa.org

CLINICAL LABORATORY SCIENCES
Dianne M. Cearlock, Ph.D., Chief Executive Officer
National Accrediting Agency for Clinical Laboratory Sciences
5600 N. River Road, Suite 720
Rosemont, Illinois 60018-5119
Phone: 773-714-8880
Fax: 773-714-8886
E-mail: dcearlock@naacls.org
Web: www.naacls.org

CLINICAL PASTORAL EDUCATION
Teresa E. Snorton, Executive Director
Accreditation Commission
Association for Clinical Pastoral Education, Inc.
1549 Claremont Road, Suite 103
Decatur, Georgia 30033-4611
Phone: 404-320-1472
Fax: 404-320-0849
E-mail: acpe@acpe.edu
Web: www.acpe.edu

DENTISTRY
Anthony Ziebert, Director
Commission on Dental Accreditation
American Dental Association
211 East Chicago Avenue, Suite 1900
Chicago, Illinois 60611
Phone: 312-440-4643
E-mail: accreditation@ada.org
Web: www.ada.org

HEALTH SERVICES ADMINISTRATION
Commission on Accreditation of Healthcare Management Education (CAHME)
John S. Lloyd, President and CEO
2111 Wilson Boulevard, Suite 700
Arlington, Virginia 22201
Phone: 703-351-5010
Fax: 703-991-5989
E-mail: info@cahme.org
Web: www.cahme.org

LAW
Hulett H. Askew, Consultant on Legal Education
American Bar Association
321 North Clark Street, 21st Floor
Chicago, Illinois 60654
Phone: 312-988-6738
Fax: 312-988-5681
E-mail: askewh@staff.abanet.org
Web: www.abanet.org/legaled/

LIBRARY
Karen O'Brien, Director
Office for Accreditation
American Library Association
50 East Huron Street
Chicago, Illinois 60611
Phone: 800-545-2433 Ext. 2432
Fax: 312-280-2433
E-mail: accred@ala.org
Web: www.ala.org/accreditation/

MEDICAL ILLUSTRATION
Commission on Accreditation of Allied Health Education Programs (CAAHEP)
Kathleen Megivern, Executive Director
1361 Park Street
Clearwater, Florida 33756
Phone: 727-210-2350
Fax: 727-210-2354
E-mail: mail@caahep.org
Web: www.caahep.org

MEDICINE

Liaison Committee on Medical Education (LCME)

In odd-numbered years beginning each July 1, contact:
Barbara Barzansky, Ph.D., LCME Secretary
American Medical Association
Council on Medical Education
515 North State Street
Chicago, Illinois 60654
Phone: 312-464-4933
Fax: 312-464-5830
E-mail: cme@aamc.org
Web: www.ama-assn.org

In even-numbered years beginning each July 1, contact:
Dan Hunt, M.D., LCME Secretary
Association of American Medical Colleges
2450 N Street, NW
Washington, DC 20037
Phone: 202-828-0596
Fax: 202-828-1125
E-mail: dhunt@aamc.org
Web: www.lcme.org

NATUROPATHIC MEDICINE

Daniel Seitz, J.D., Ed.D., Executive Director
Council on Naturopathic Medical Education
P.O. Box 178
Great Barrington, Massachusetts 01230
Phone: 413-528-8877
Fax: 413-528-8880
E-mail: council@cnme.org
Web: www.cnme.org

NURSE ANESTHESIA

Francis R. Gerbasi, Executive Director
Council on Accreditation of Nurse Anesthesia Educational Programs
American Association of Nurse Anesthetists
222 South Prospect Avenue, Suite 304
Park Ridge, Illinois 60068
Phone: 847-692-7050 Ext. 1154
Fax: 847-692-6968
E-mail: fgerbasi@aana.com
Web: www.aana.com

NURSE EDUCATION

Jennifer L. Butlin, Director
Commission on Collegiate Nursing Education (CCNE)
One Dupont Circle, NW, Suite 530
Washington, DC 20036-1120
Phone: 202-887-6791
Fax: 202-887-8476
E-mail: jbutlin@aacn.nche.edu
Web: www.aacn.nche.edu/accreditation

NURSE MIDWIFERY

Mary Brucker, Chair
Accreditation Commission for Midwifery Education
American College of Nurse-Midwives
Nurse-Midwifery Program
8403 Colesville Road, Suite 1550
Silver Spring, Maryland 20910
Phone: 240-485-1800
Fax: 240-485-1818
E-mail: mary_brucker@baylor.edu
Web: www.midwife.org/acme.cfm

Jo Anne Myers-Ciecko, MPH, Executive Director
Midwifery Education Accreditation Council
P.O. Box 984
La Conner, Washington 98257
Phone: 360-466-2080
Fax: 480-907-2936
E-mail: info@meacschools.org
Web: www.meacschools.org

NURSE PRACTITIONER

Susan Wysocki, RNC, NP, President and CEO
National Association of Nurse Practitioners in Women's Health
Council on Accreditation
505 C Street, NE
Washington, DC 20002
Phone: 202-543-9693 Ext. 1
Fax: 202-543-9858
E-mail: info@npwh.org
Web: www.npwh.org

NURSING

Sharon J. Tanner, Ed.D., RN, Executive Director
National League for Nursing Accrediting Commission (NLNAC)
3343 Peachtree Road, NE, Suite 500
Atlanta, Georgia 30326
Phone: 404-975-5000
Fax: 404-975-5020
E-mail: nlnac@nlnac.org
Web: www.nlnac.org

OCCUPATIONAL THERAPY

Neil Harvison, Ph.D., OTR/L
Director of Accreditation and Academic Affairs
The American Occupational Therapy Association
4720 Montgomery Lane
P.O. Box 31220
Bethesda, Maryland 20824-1220
Phone: 301-652-2682 Ext. 2912
Fax: 301-652-7711
E-mail: accred@aota.org
Web: www.aota.org

OPTOMETRY

Joyce L. Urbeck, Administrative Director
Accreditation Council on Optometric Education
American Optometric Association (AOA)
243 North Lindbergh Boulevard
St. Louis, Missouri 63141
Phone: 314-991-4000 Ext. 246
Fax: 314-991-4101
E-mail: ACOE@aoa.org
Web: www.theacoe.org

OSTEOPATHIC MEDICINE

Konrad C. Miskowicz-Retz, Ph.D., CAE
Director, Department of Education
Commission on Osteopathic College Accreditation
American Osteopathic Association
142 East Ontario Street
Chicago, Illinois 60611
Phone: 312-202-8048
Fax: 312-202-8202
E-mail: kretz@osteopathic.org
Web: www.osteopathic.org

PHARMACY

Peter H. Vlasses, Executive Director
Accreditation Council for Pharmacy Education
20 North Clark Street, Suite 2500
Chicago, Illinois 60602-5109
Phone: 312-664-3575
Fax: 312-664-4652
E-mail: csinfo@acpe-accredit.org
Web: www.acpe-accredit.org

PHYSICAL THERAPY
Mary Jane Harris, Director
Department of Accreditation
Commission on Accreditation in Physical Therapy Education
(CAPTE)
American Physical Therapy Association (APTA)
1111 North Fairfax Street
Alexandria, Virginia 22314
Phone: 703-706-3245
Fax: 703-684-7343
E-mail: accreditation@apta.org
Web: www.apta.org

PHYSICIAN ASSISTANT STUDIES
John E. McCarty, Executive Director
Accreditation Review Commission on Education for the
Physician Assistant, Inc. (ARC-PA)
12000 Findley Road, Suite 150
Johns Creek, Georgia 30097
Phone: 770-476-1224
Fax: 770-476-1738
E-mail: johnmccarty@arc-pa.org
Web: www.arc-pa.org

PODIATRIC MEDICINE
Alan R. Tinkleman, Executive Director
Council on Podiatric Medical Education (CPME)
American Podiatric Medical Association
9312 Old Georgetown Road
Bethesda, Maryland 20814-1621
Phone: 301-571-9200
Fax: 301-571-4903
E-mail: artinkleman@apma.org
Web: www.cpme.org

PUBLIC HEALTH
Laura Rasar King, M.P.H., CHES, Executive Director
Council on Education for Public Health
800 Eye Street, NW, Suite 202
Washington, DC 20001-3710
Phone: 202-789-1050
Fax: 202-789-1895
E-mail: Lking@ceph.org
Web: www.ceph.org

REHABILITATION EDUCATION
Marvin D. Kuehn, Executive Director
Council on Rehabilitation Education (CORE)
Commission on Standards and Accreditation
1699 Woodfield Road, Suite 300
Schaumburg, Illinois 60173
Phone: 847-944-1345
Fax: 847-944-1346
E-mail: sdenys@cpcredentialing.com
Web: www.core-rehab.org

SOCIAL WORK
Judith Bremner, Interim Director of Accreditation
Commission on Accreditation
Council on Social Work Education
1725 Duke Street, Suite 500
Alexandria, Virginia 22314
Phone: 703-683-8080
Fax: 703-683-8099
E-mail: jbermner@cswe.org
Web: www.cswe.org

SPEECH-LANGUAGE PATHOLOGY AND AUDIOLOGY
Patrima L. Tice, Director of Credentialing
American Speech-Language-Hearing Association
ACouncil on Academic Accreditation in Audiology and Speech-
Language Pathology
2200 Research Boulevard
Rockville, Maryland 20850-3289
Phone: 301-897-5700
Fax: 301-571-0457
E-mail: ptice@asha.org
Web: www.asha.org/academic/accreditation/default.htm

TEACHER EDUCATION
James G. Cibulka, President
National Council for Accreditation of Teacher Education
2010 Massachusetts Avenue, NW, Suite 500
Washington, DC 20036-1023
Phone: 202-466-7496
Fax: 202-296-6620
E-mail: ncate@ncate.org
Web: www.ncate.org

Frank B. Murray, President
Teacher Education Accreditation Council (TEAC)
Accreditation Committee
One Dupont Circle, Suite 320
Washington, DC 20036-0110
Phone: 202-831-0400
Fax: 202-831-3013
E-mail: teac@teac.org
Web: www.teac.org

VETERINARY MEDICINE
Elizabeth Sabin, Director
Education and Research Division
American Veterinary Medical Association (AVMA)
Council on Education
1931 North Meacham Road, Suite 100
Schaumburg, Illinois 60173
Phone: 847-925-8070 Ext. 6674
Fax: 847-925-9329
E-mail: info@avma.org
Web: www.avma.org

How to Use These Guides

As you identify the particular programs and institutions that interest you, you can use both the *Graduate & Professional Programs: An Overview* volume and the specialized volumes in the series to obtain detailed information.

- *Graduate Programs in the Physical Sciences, Mathematics, Agricultural Sciences, the Environment & Natural Resources*
- *Graduate Programs in Engineering & Applied Sciences*
- *Graduate Programs the Humanities, Arts & Social Sciences*
- *Graduate Programs in the Biological Sciences*
- *Graduate Programs in Business, Education, Health, Information Studies, Law & Social Work*

Each of the specialized volumes in the series is divided into sections that contain one or more directories devoted to programs in a particular field. If you do not find a directory devoted to your field of interest in a specific volume, consult "Directories and Subject Areas" (located at the end of each volume). After you have identified the correct volume, consult the "Directories and Subject Areas in This Book" index, which shows (as does the more general directory) what directories cover subjects not specifically named in a directory or section title.

Each of the specialized volumes in the series has a number of general directories. These directories have entries for the largest unit at an institution granting graduate degrees in that field. For example, the general Engineering and Applied Sciences directory in the *Graduate Programs in Engineering & Applied Sciences* volume consists of **Profiles** for colleges, schools, and departments of engineering and applied sciences.

General directories are followed by other directories, or sections, that give more detailed information about programs in particular areas of the general field that has been covered. The general Engineering and Applied Sciences directory, in the previous example, is followed by nineteen sections with directories in specific areas of engineering, such as Chemical Engineering, Industrial/Management Engineering, and Mechanical Engineering.

Because of the broad nature of many fields, any system of organization is bound to involve a certain amount of overlap. Environmental studies, for example, is a field whose various aspects are studied in several types of departments and schools. Readers interested in such studies will find information on relevant programs in the *Graduate Programs in the Biological Sciences* volume under Ecology and Environmental Biology; in the *Graduate Programs in the Physical Sciences, Mathematics, Agricultural Sciences, the Environment & Natural Resources* volume under Environmental Management and Policy and Natural Resources; in the *Graduate Programs in Engineering & Applied Sciences* volume under Energy Management and Policy and Environmental Engineering; and in the *Graduate Programs in Business, Education, Health, Information Studies, Law & Social Work* volume under Environmental and Occupational Health. To help you find all of the programs of interest to you, the introduction to each section within the specialized volumes includes, if applicable, a paragraph suggesting other sections and directories with information on related areas of study.

Directory of Institutions with Programs in Business, Education, Health, Information Studies, Law & Social Work

This directory lists institutions in alphabetical order and includes beneath each name the academic fields in which each institution offers graduate programs. The degree level in each field is also indicated, provided that the institution has supplied that information in response to Peterson's Annual Survey of Graduate and Professional Institutions. An M indicates that a master's degree program is offered; a D indicates that a doctoral degree program is offered; a P indicates that the first professional degree is offered; an O signifies that other advanced degrees (e.g., certificates or specialist degrees) are offered; and an * (asterisk) indicates that a **Close-Up** and/or **Display** is located in this volume. See the index, "Close-Ups and Displays," for the specific page number.

Profiles of Academic and Professional Programs in the Specialized Volumes

Each section of **Profiles** has a table of contents that lists the Program Directories, **Displays**, and **Close-Ups.** Program Directories consist of the **Profiles** of programs in the relevant fields, with **Displays** following if programs have chosen to include them. **Close-Ups,** which are more individualized statements, again if programs have chosen to submit them, are also listed.

The **Profiles** found in the 500 directories in the specialized volumes provide basic data about the graduate units in capsule form for quick reference. To make these directories as useful as possible, **Profiles** are generally listed for an institution's smallest academic unit within a subject area. In other words, if an institution has a College of Liberal Arts that administers many related programs, the **Profile** for the individual program (e.g., Program in History), not the entire College, appears in the directory.

There are some programs that do not fit into any current directory and are not given individual **Profiles**. The directory structure is reviewed annually in order to keep this number to a minimum and to accommodate major trends in graduate education.

The following outline describes the **Profile** information found in the guides and explains how best to use that information. Any item that does not apply to or was not provided by a graduate unit is omitted from its listing. The format of the **Profiles** is constant, making it easy to compare one institution with another and one program with another.

Identifying Information. The institution's name, in boldface type, is followed by a complete listing of the administrative structure for that field of study. (For example, University of Akron, Buchtel College of Arts and Sciences, Department of Theoretical and Applied Mathematics, Program in Mathematics.) The last unit listed is the one to which all information in the **Profile** pertains. The institution's city, state, and zip code follow.

Offerings. Each field of study offered by the unit is listed with all postbaccalaureate degrees awarded. Degrees that are not preceded by a specific concentration are awarded in the general field listed in the unit name. Frequently, fields of study are broken down into subspecializations, and those appear following the degrees awarded; for example, "Offerings in secondary education (M.Ed.), including English education, mathematics education, science education." Students enrolled in the M.Ed. program would be able to specialize in any of the three fields mentioned.

Professional Accreditation. Some **Profiles** indicate whether a program is professionally accredited. Because it is possible for a program to receive or lose professional accreditation at any time, students entering fields in which accreditation is important to a career should verify the status of programs by contacting either the chairperson or the appropriate accrediting association.

Jointly Offered Degrees. Explanatory statements concerning programs that are offered in cooperation with other institutions are included in the list of degrees offered. This occurs most commonly on a regional basis (for example, two state universities offering a cooperative Ph.D. in special education) or where the specialized nature of the institutions encourages joint efforts (a J.D./M.B.A. offered by a law school at an institution with no formal business programs and an institution with a business school but lacking a law school). Only programs that are truly cooperative are listed; those involving only

limited course work at another institution are not. Interested students should contact the heads of such units for further information.

Part-Time and Evening/Weekend Programs. When information regarding the availability of part-time or evening/weekend study appears in the **Profile**, it means that students are able to earn a degree exclusively through such study.

Postbaccalaureate Distance Learning Degrees. A postbaccalaureate distance learning degree program signifies that course requirements can be fulfilled with minimal or no on-campus study.

Faculty. Figures on the number of faculty members actively involved with graduate students through teaching or research are separated into full-and part-time as well as men and women whenever the information has been supplied.

Students. Figures for the number of students enrolled in graduate and professional programs pertain to the semester of highest enrollment from the 2009–10 academic year. These figures are broken down into full-and part-time and men and women whenever the data have been supplied. Information on the number of matriculated students enrolled in the unit who are members of a minority group or are international students appears here. The average age of the matriculated students is followed by the number of applicants, the percentage accepted, and the number enrolled for fall 2009.

Degrees Awarded. The number of degrees awarded in the calendar year is listed. Many doctoral programs offer a terminal master's degree if students leave the program after completing only part of the requirements for a doctoral degree; that is indicated here. All degrees are classified into one of four types: master's, doctoral, first professional, and other advanced degrees. A unit may award one or several degrees at a given level; however, the data are only collected by type and may therefore represent several different degree programs.

Degree Requirements. The information in this section is also broken down by type of degree, and all information for a degree level pertains to all degrees of that type unless otherwise specified. Degree requirements are collected in a simplified form to provide some very basic information on the nature of the program and on foreign language, thesis or dissertation, comprehensive exam, and registration requirements. Many units also provide a short list of additional requirements, such as fieldwork or an internship. For complete information on graduation requirements, contact the graduate school or program directly.

Entrance Requirements. Entrance requirements are broken down into the four degree levels of master's, doctoral, first professional, and other advanced degrees. Within each level, information may be provided in two basic categories: entrance exams and other requirements. The entrance exams are identified by the standard acronyms used by the testing agencies, unless they are not well known. Other entrance requirements are quite varied, but they often contain an undergraduate or graduate grade point average (GPA). Unless otherwise stated, the GPA is calculated on a 4.0 scale and is listed as a minimum required for admission. Additional exam requirements/recommendations for international students may be listed here. Application deadlines for domestic and international students, the application fee, and whether electronic applications are accepted may be listed here. Note that the deadline should be used for reference only; these dates are subject to change, and students interested in applying should always contact the graduate unit directly about application procedures and deadlines.

Expenses. The typical cost of study for the 2009–10 academic year is given in two basic categories: tuition and fees. Cost of study may be quite complex at a graduate institution. There are often sliding scales for part-time study, a different cost for first-year students, and other variables that make it impossible to completely cover the cost of study for each graduate program. To provide the most usable information, figures are given for full-time study for a full year where available and for part-time study in terms of a per-unit rate (per credit, per semester hour, etc.). Occasionally, variances may be noted in tuition and fees for reasons such as the type of program, whether courses are taken during the day or evening, whether courses are at the master's or doctoral level, or other institution-specific reasons. Expenses are usually subject to change; for exact costs at any given time, contact your chosen schools and programs directly. Keep in mind that the tuition of Canadian institutions is usually given in Canadian dollars.

Financial Support. This section contains data on the number of awards administered by the institution and given to graduate students during the 2009–10 academic year. The first figure given represents the total number of students receiving financial support enrolled in that unit. If the unit has provided information on graduate appointments, these are broken down into three major categories: fellowships give money to graduate students to cover the cost of study and living expenses and are not based on a work obligation or research commitment, research assistantships provide stipends to graduate students for assistance in a formal research project with a faculty member, and teaching assistantships provide stipends to graduate students for teaching or for assisting faculty members in teaching undergraduate classes. Within each category, figures are given for the total number of awards, the average yearly amount per award, and whether full or partial tuition reimbursements are awarded. In addition to graduate appointments, the availability of several other financial aid sources is covered in this section. Tuition waivers are routinely part of a graduate appointment, but units sometimes waive part or all of a student's tuition even if a graduate appointment is not available. Federal Work-Study is made available to students who demonstrate need and meet the federal guidelines; this form of aid normally includes 10 or more hours of work per week in an office of the institution. Institutionally sponsored loans are low-interest loans available to graduate students to cover both educational and living expenses. Career-related internships or fieldwork offer money to students who are participating in a formal off-campus research project or practicum. Grants, scholarships, traineeships, unspecified assistantships, and other awards may also be noted. The availability of financial support to part-time students is also indicated here.

Some programs list the financial aid application deadline and the forms that need to be completed for students to be eligible for financial awards. There are two forms: FAFSA, the Free Application for Federal Student Aid, which is required for federal aid, and the CSS PROFILE®.

Faculty Research. Each unit has the opportunity to list several keyword phrases describing the current research involving faculty members and graduate students. Space limitations prevent the unit from listing complete information on all research programs. The total expenditure for funded research from the previous academic year may also be included.

Unit Head and Application Contact. The head of the graduate program for each unit is listed with academic title and telephone and fax numbers and e-mail address if available. In addition to the unit head, many graduate programs list a separate contact for application and admission information, which follows the listing for the unit head. If no unit head or application contact is given, you should contact the overall institution for information on graduate admissions.

Displays and Close-Ups

The **Displays** and **Close-Ups** are supplementary insertions submitted by deans, chairs, and other administrators who wish to offer an additional, more individualized statement to readers. A number of graduate school and program administrators have attached a **Display** ad near the **Profile** listing. Here you will find information that an institution or program wants to emphasize. The **Close-Ups** are by their very nature more expansive and flexible than the **Profiles**, and the administrators who have written them may emphasize different aspects of their programs. All of the **Close-Ups** are organized in the same way (with the exception of a few that describe research and training opportunities instead of degree programs), and in each one you will find information on the same basic topics, such as programs of study, research facilities, tuition and fees, financial aid, and application procedures. If an institution or program has submitted a **Close-Up**, a boldface cross-reference appears below its **Profile**. As with the **Displays**, all of the **Close-Ups** in the guides have been submitted by choice; the absence of a **Display** or **Close-Up** does not reflect any type of editorial judgment on the part of Peterson's, and their presence in the guides should not be taken as an indication of status, quality, or approval. Statements regarding a university's objectives and accomplishments are a reflection of its own beliefs and are not the opinions of the Peterson's editors.

Appendixes

This section contains two appendixes. The first, "Institutional Changes Since the 2010 Edition," lists institutions that have closed, merged, or

changed their name or status since the last edition of the guides. The second, "Abbreviations Used in the Guides," gives abbreviations of degree names, along with what those abbreviations stand for. These appendixes are identical in all six volumes of **Peterson's Graduate and Professional Programs**.

Indexes

There are three indexes presented here. The first index, "Close-Ups and Displays," gives page references for all programs that have chosen to place **Close-Ups** and **Displays** in this volume. It is arranged alphabetically by institution; within institutions, the arrangement is alphabetical by subject area. It is not an index to all programs in the book's directories of **Profiles**; readers must refer to the directories themselves for **Profile** information on programs that have not submitted the additional, more individualized statements. The second index, "Directories and Subject Areas in Other Books in This Series", gives book references for the directories in the specialized volumes and also includes cross-references for subject area names not used in the directory structure, for example, "Computing Technology (see Computer Science)." The third index, "Directories and Subject Areas in This Book," gives page references for the directories in this volume and cross-references for subject area names not used in this volume's directory structure.

Data Collection Procedures

The information published in the directories and **Profiles** of all the books is collected through Peterson's Annual Survey of Graduate and Professional Institutions. The survey is sent each spring to more than 2,200 institutions offering postbaccalaureate degree programs, including accredited institutions in the United States, U.S. territories, and Canada and those institutions outside the United States that are accredited by U.S. accrediting bodies. Deans and other administrators complete these surveys, providing information on programs in the 500 academic and professional fields covered in the guides as well as overall institutional information. While every effort has been made to ensure the accuracy and completeness of the data, information is sometimes unavailable or changes occur after publication deadlines. All usable information received in time for publication has been included. The omission of any particular item from a directory or **Profile** signifies either that the item is not applicable to the institution or program or that information was not available. **Profiles** of programs scheduled to begin during the 2010–11 academic year cannot, obviously, include statistics on enrollment or, in many cases, the number of faculty members. If no usable data were submitted by an institution, its name, address, and program name appear in order to indicate the availability of graduate work.

Criteria for Inclusion in This Guide

To be included in this guide, an institution must have full accreditation or be a candidate for accreditation (preaccreditation) status by an institutional or specialized accrediting body recognized by the U.S. Department of Education or the Council for Higher Education Accreditation (CHEA). Institutional accrediting bodies, which review each institution as a whole, include the six regional associations of schools and colleges (Middle States, New England, North Central, Northwest, Southern, and Western), each of which is responsible for a specified portion of the United States and its territories. Other institutional accrediting bodies are national in scope and accredit specific kinds of institutions (e.g., Bible colleges, independent colleges, and rabbinical and Talmudic schools). Program registration by the New York State Board of Regents is considered to be the equivalent of institutional accreditation, since the board requires that all programs offered by an institution meet its standards before recognition is granted. A Canadian institution must be chartered and authorized to grant degrees by the provincial government, affiliated with a chartered institution, or accredited by a recognized U.S. accrediting body. This guide also includes institutions outside the United States that are accredited by these U.S. accrediting bodies. There are recognized specialized or professional accrediting bodies in more than fifty different fields, each of which is authorized to accredit institutions or specific programs in its particular field. For specialized institutions that offer programs in one field only, we designate this to be the equivalent of institutional accreditation. A full explanation of the accrediting process and complete information on recognized institutional (regional and national) and specialized accrediting bodies can be found online at www.chea.org or at www.ed.gov/admins/finaid/accred/index.html.

DIRECTORY OF INSTITUTIONS WITH PROGRAMS IN BUSINESS, EDUCATION, HEALTH, INFORMATION STUDIES, LAW & SOCIAL WORK

ABILENE CHRISTIAN UNIVERSITY

Accounting	M
Communication Disorders	M
Curriculum and Instruction	M
Education—General	M
Educational Leadership and Administration	M
Family Nurse Practitioner Studies	M,O
Higher Education	M
Human Resources Development	M
Human Services	M,O
Management Information Systems	M
Nursing and Healthcare Administration	M,O
Nursing Education	M,O
Nursing—General	M,O
Social Work	M
Special Education	M

ACADEMY FOR FIVE ELEMENT ACUPUNCTURE

Acupuncture and Oriental Medicine	M

ACADEMY OF ART UNIVERSITY

Advertising and Public Relations	M

ACADEMY OF CHINESE CULTURE AND HEALTH SCIENCES

Acupuncture and Oriental Medicine	M

ACADEMY OF ORIENTAL MEDICINE AT AUSTIN

Acupuncture and Oriental Medicine	M

ACADIA UNIVERSITY

Counselor Education	M
Curriculum and Instruction	M
Education—General	M
Educational Leadership and Administration	M
Educational Media/ Instructional Technology	M
Kinesiology and Movement Studies	M
Mathematics Education	M
Recreation and Park Management	M
Science Education	M
Social Sciences Education	M
Special Education	M

ACUPUNCTURE & INTEGRATIVE MEDICINE COLLEGE, BERKELEY

Acupuncture and Oriental Medicine	M

ACUPUNCTURE AND MASSAGE COLLEGE

Acupuncture and Oriental Medicine	M

ADAMS STATE COLLEGE

Counselor Education	M
Education—General	M
Physical Education	M
Special Education	M

ADELPHI UNIVERSITY

Accounting	M
Art Education	M
Business Administration and Management— General	M
Communication Disorders	M,D
Community Health	M,O
Early Childhood Education	M,O
Education—General	M,D,O
Educational Leadership and Administration	M,O
Educational Media/ Instructional Technology	M,O
Electronic Commerce	M
Elementary Education	M
English as a Second Language	M,O
Finance and Banking	M
Health Education	M,O

Human Resources Management	M,O
Management Information Systems	M
Marketing	M
Nursing—General	M,D,O
Physical Education	M,O
Public Health—General	O
Reading Education	M
Secondary Education	M
Social Work	M,D
Special Education	M,O

ADLER GRADUATE SCHOOL

Business Administration and Management— General	M,O
Counselor Education	M,O
Organizational Management	M,O

AIR FORCE INSTITUTE OF TECHNOLOGY

Logistics	M,D
Management Information Systems	M

ALABAMA AGRICULTURAL AND MECHANICAL UNIVERSITY

Business Administration and Management— General	M
Communication Disorders	M
Counselor Education	M,O
Early Childhood Education	M,O
Education—General	M,O
Educational Leadership and Administration	M,O
Elementary Education	M,O
Human Resources Management	M,O
Marketing	M
Music Education	M
Physical Education	M
Secondary Education	M,O
Social Work	M
Special Education	M,O
Vocational and Technical Education	M

ALABAMA STATE UNIVERSITY

Accounting	M
Allied Health—General	D
Business Administration and Management— General	M
Counselor Education	M,O
Early Childhood Education	M,O
Education—General	M,D,O
Educational Leadership and Administration	M,D,O
Educational Media/ Instructional Technology	M,O
Educational Policy	M,D,O
Elementary Education	M,O
English Education	M,O
Health Education	M
Mathematics Education	M,O
Physical Education	M
Physical Therapy	D
Science Education	M,O
Secondary Education	M,O
Social Sciences Education	M,O
Special Education	M

ALASKA PACIFIC UNIVERSITY

Business Administration and Management— General	M
Education—General	M
Elementary Education	M
Environmental Education	M
Health Services Management and Hospital Administration	M
Investment Management	M,O
Middle School Education	M

ALBANY COLLEGE OF PHARMACY AND HEALTH SCIENCES

Health Services Research	P,M
Pharmacy	P,M*

ALBANY LAW SCHOOL

Law	P,M

ALBANY MEDICAL COLLEGE

Allopathic Medicine	P
Bioethics	M,O
Nurse Anesthesia	M
Physician Assistant Studies	M

ALBANY STATE UNIVERSITY

Accounting	M
Business Administration and Management— General	M
Counselor Education	M
Early Childhood Education	M
Education—General	M,O
Educational Leadership and Administration	M,O
English Education	M
Family Nurse Practitioner Studies	M
Health Education	M
Health Services Management and Hospital Administration	M
Human Resources Management	M
Mathematics Education	M
Middle School Education	M
Music Education	M
Nursing Education	M
Nursing—General	M
Physical Education	M
Science Education	M
Special Education	M

ALBERT EINSTEIN COLLEGE OF MEDICINE

Allopathic Medicine	P

ALBERTUS MAGNUS COLLEGE

Business Administration and Management— General	M

ALBRIGHT COLLEGE

Early Childhood Education	M
Education—General	M
Elementary Education	M
English as a Second Language	M
Special Education	M

ALCORN STATE UNIVERSITY

Agricultural Education	M,O
Business Administration and Management— General	M
Counselor Education	M,O
Education—General	M,O
Elementary Education	M,O
Health Education	M,O
Nursing—General	M
Physical Education	M,O
Secondary Education	M,O
Special Education	M,O
Vocational and Technical Education	M,O

ALDERSON-BROADDUS COLLEGE

Physician Assistant Studies	M

ALFRED UNIVERSITY

Business Administration and Management— General	M
Counselor Education	M,D,O
Education—General	M
Mathematics Education	M
Reading Education	M

ALLEN COLLEGE

Acute Care/Critical Care Nursing	M
Adult Nursing	M
Family Nurse Practitioner Studies	M
Gerontological Nursing	M
Health Education	M
Nursing and Healthcare Administration	M

Nursing—General	M
Psychiatric Nursing	M

ALLIANT INTERNATIONAL UNIVERSITY–FRESNO

Education—General	M
Educational Leadership and Administration	D
English as a Second Language	M,D,O

ALLIANT INTERNATIONAL UNIVERSITY–IRVINE

Education—General	M,O
Educational Leadership and Administration	M,D,O
Educational Media/ Instructional Technology	M,O
Educational Psychology	M,D,O
English as a Second Language	M,D
Higher Education	M,D,O
Multilingual and Multicultural Education	M,O
Special Education	M,O

ALLIANT INTERNATIONAL UNIVERSITY–LOS ANGELES

Business Administration and Management— General	D
Education—General	M
Educational Leadership and Administration	M,D,O
Educational Psychology	M,D,O
Higher Education	M,D,O
Student Affairs	M,D,O

ALLIANT INTERNATIONAL UNIVERSITY–MÉXICO CITY

Business Administration and Management— General	M
Education—General	M
International Business	M

ALLIANT INTERNATIONAL UNIVERSITY–SACRAMENTO

Education—General	M

ALLIANT INTERNATIONAL UNIVERSITY–SAN DIEGO

Business Administration and Management— General	M,D
Education—General	M,O
Educational Leadership and Administration	M,D,O
Educational Psychology	M,D,O
English as a Second Language	M,D,O
Finance and Banking	M,D
Higher Education	M,D,O
International Business	M,D
Management Information Systems	M,D
Management Strategy and Policy	M,D
Marketing	M,D
Student Affairs	M,D,O
Sustainability Management	M,D

ALLIANT INTERNATIONAL UNIVERSITY–SAN FRANCISCO

Business Administration and Management— General	M
Education—General	M,O
Educational Leadership and Administration	M,D,O
Educational Psychology	M,D,O
Higher Education	M,D,O
Multilingual and Multicultural Education	M,O
Special Education	M,O
Sustainability Management	M

ALVERNIA UNIVERSITY

Business Administration and Management— General	M
Education—General	M
Occupational Therapy	M

Organizational Management	D
Urban Education	M

ALVERNO COLLEGE

Adult Education	M
Business Administration and Management— General	M
Education—General	M
Educational Leadership and Administration	M
Educational Media/ Instructional Technology	M
Nursing—General	M
Reading Education	M
Science Education	M

AMBERTON UNIVERSITY

Business Administration and Management— General	M
Human Resources Development	M
Human Resources Management	M

THE AMERICAN COLLEGE

Business Administration and Management— General	M
Finance and Banking	M
Organizational Management	M

AMERICAN COLLEGE OF ACUPUNCTURE AND ORIENTAL MEDICINE

Acupuncture and Oriental Medicine	M

AMERICAN COLLEGE OF HEALTHCARE SCIENCES

Allied Health—General	M

AMERICAN COLLEGE OF THESSALONIKI

Business Administration and Management— General	M,O
Entrepreneurship	M,O
Finance and Banking	M,O
Marketing	M,O

AMERICAN COLLEGE OF TRADITIONAL CHINESE MEDICINE

Acupuncture and Oriental Medicine	M,D,O

AMERICAN GRADUATE UNIVERSITY

Business Administration and Management— General	M,O
Project Management	M,O

AMERICAN INTERCONTINENTAL UNIVERSITY (TX)

Business Administration and Management— General	M

AMERICAN INTERCONTINENTAL UNIVERSITY BUCKHEAD CAMPUS

Accounting	M
Business Administration and Management— General	M
Finance and Banking	M
Marketing	M

AMERICAN INTERCONTINENTAL UNIVERSITY DUNWOODY CAMPUS

International Business	M
Management Information Systems	M

AMERICAN INTERCONTINENTAL UNIVERSITY–LONDON

Business Administration and Management— General	M
International Business	M

Management Information Systems	M

AMERICAN INTERCONTINENTAL UNIVERSITY ONLINE

Accounting	M
Business Administration and Management— General	M
Curriculum and Instruction	M
Education—General	M
Educational Leadership and Administration	M
Educational Measurement and Evaluation	M
Educational Media/ Instructional Technology	M
Finance and Banking	M
Health Services Management and Hospital Administration	M
Human Resources Management	M
Industrial and Manufacturing Management	M
International Business	M
Marketing	M
Project Management	M

AMERICAN INTERCONTINENTAL UNIVERSITY SOUTH FLORIDA

Accounting	M
Business Administration and Management— General	M
Educational Media/ Instructional Technology	M
Finance and Banking	M
Human Resources Management	M
International Business	M
Marketing	M

AMERICAN INTERNATIONAL COLLEGE

Accounting	M
Business Administration and Management— General	M
Counselor Education	M,D,O
Early Childhood Education	M,D,O
Education—General	M,D,O
Educational Leadership and Administration	M,D,O
Educational Psychology	M,D
Elementary Education	M,D,O
Finance and Banking	M
Hospitality Management	M
Human Resources Development	M
International Business	M
Management Information Systems	M
Marketing	M
Middle School Education	M,D,O
Nonprofit Management	M
Nursing and Healthcare Administration	M
Nursing Education	M
Nursing—General	M
Occupational Therapy	M
Organizational Management	M
Physical Therapy	D
Reading Education	M,D,O
Secondary Education	M,D,O
Special Education	M,D,O
Taxation	M

AMERICAN JEWISH UNIVERSITY

Business Administration and Management— General	M
Education—General	M
Nonprofit Management	M
Social Work	M

AMERICAN PUBLIC UNIVERSITY SYSTEM

Business Administration and Management— General	M
Logistics	M
Public Health—General	M

Sports Management	M
Transportation Management	M

AMERICAN SENTINEL UNIVERSITY

Business Administration and Management— General	M
Health Services Management and Hospital Administration	M
Management Information Systems	M
Nursing—General	M

AMERICAN UNIVERSITY

Accounting	M
Business Administration and Management— General	M,D,O
Curriculum and Instruction	M,O
Early Childhood Education	M,O
Education—General	M,O
Elementary Education	M,O
English as a Second Language	M,O
Entrepreneurship	M
Exercise and Sports Science	M
Finance and Banking	M,D,O
Health Education	M,O
International and Comparative Education	M
International Business	M,O
Law	P,M,O
Legal and Justice Studies	M,D,O
Management Information Systems	M,O
Marketing Research	M
Marketing	M
Nonprofit Management	M,D,O
Organizational Management	M
Real Estate	M
Secondary Education	M,O
Special Education	M
Supply Chain Management	M
Taxation	M,O

THE AMERICAN UNIVERSITY IN CAIRO

Business Administration and Management— General	M,O
English as a Second Language	M,O
Foreign Languages Education	M

THE AMERICAN UNIVERSITY IN DUBAI

Business Administration and Management— General	M
Finance and Banking	M
Health Services Management and Hospital Administration	M
International Business	M
Marketing	M

THE AMERICAN UNIVERSITY OF ATHENS

Business Administration and Management— General	M

AMERICAN UNIVERSITY OF BEIRUT

Allopathic Medicine	P,M
Business Administration and Management— General	M
Education—General	M
Environmental and Occupational Health	M
Epidemiology	M
Health Education	M
Nursing—General	M
Public Health—General	M

THE AMERICAN UNIVERSITY OF PARIS

Business Administration and Management— General	M
International Business	M
Law	M

AMERICAN UNIVERSITY OF PUERTO RICO

Art Education	M
Education—General	M
Elementary Education	M
Physical Education	M
Science Education	M
Special Education	M

AMERICAN UNIVERSITY OF SHARJAH

Business Administration and Management— General	M
English as a Second Language	M

AMRIDGE UNIVERSITY

Organizational Behavior	P,M,D
Organizational Management	P,M,D

ANAHEIM UNIVERSITY

Business Administration and Management— General	M,O
English as a Second Language	M,O
Sustainability Management	M,O

ANDERSON UNIVERSITY (IN)

Accounting	M,D
Business Administration and Management— General	M,D
Education—General	M

ANDERSON UNIVERSITY (SC)

Business Administration and Management— General	M
Education—General	M

ANDOVER NEWTON THEOLOGICAL SCHOOL

Religious Education	P,M,D

ANDREW JACKSON UNIVERSITY

Business Administration and Management— General	M
Entrepreneurship	M
Finance and Banking	M
Health Services Management and Hospital Administration	M
Hospitality Management	M
Human Resources Management	M
International Business	M
Marketing	M

ANDREWS UNIVERSITY

Accounting	M
Allied Health—General	M
Curriculum and Instruction	M,D,O
Education—General	M,D,O
Educational Leadership and Administration	M,D,O
Educational Psychology	M,D
Elementary Education	M,D,O
English as a Second Language	M,D,O
English Education	M,D,O
Finance and Banking	M
Foreign Languages Education	M,D,O
Human Services	M
Nursing—General	M
Physical Therapy	D
Reading Education	M
Religious Education	M,D,O
Science Education	M,D,O
Secondary Education	M,D,O
Social Sciences Education	M,D,O

Social Work — M
Special Education — M,D,O

ANGELO STATE UNIVERSITY
Accounting — M
Adult Nursing — M
Business Administration and Management— General — M
Counselor Education — M
Curriculum and Instruction — M
Education—General — M
Educational Leadership and Administration — M,O
Educational Measurement and Evaluation — M
Higher Education — M
Kinesiology and Movement Studies — M
Medical/Surgical Nursing — M
Nursing Education — M
Physical Therapy — D
Reading Education — M

ANNA MARIA COLLEGE
Art Education — M
Business Administration and Management— General — M,O
Early Childhood Education — M,O
Education—General — M,O
Elementary Education — M,O
English Education — M,O
Environmental and Occupational Health — M

ANTIOCH UNIVERSITY LOS ANGELES
Business Administration and Management— General — M
Education—General — M
Human Resources Development — M
Organizational Management — M

ANTIOCH UNIVERSITY MIDWEST
Business Administration and Management— General — M
Education—General — M

ANTIOCH UNIVERSITY NEW ENGLAND
Business Administration and Management— General — M
Early Childhood Education — M
Education—General — M
Educational Leadership and Administration — M
Elementary Education — M
Environmental Education — M
Foundations and Philosophy of Education — M
Organizational Management — M,O
Science Education — M
Sustainability Management — M

ANTIOCH UNIVERSITY SANTA BARBARA
Education—General — M
Organizational Management — M

ANTIOCH UNIVERSITY SEATTLE
Business Administration and Management— General — M
Education—General — M
Organizational Management — M

APPALACHIAN SCHOOL OF LAW
Law — P

APPALACHIAN STATE UNIVERSITY
Accounting — M

Business Administration and Management— General — M
Communication Disorders — M
Counselor Education — M
Curriculum and Instruction — M
Educational Leadership and Administration — M,D,O
Educational Media/ Instructional Technology — M,O
Elementary Education — M
English Education — M
Exercise and Sports Science — M
Foreign Languages Education — M
Higher Education — M,O
Home Economics Education — M
Library Science — M,O
Mathematics Education — M
Middle School Education — M
Music Education — M
Reading Education — M
Science Education — M
Social Sciences Education — M
Social Work — M
Special Education — M
Student Affairs — M
Vocational and Technical Education — M

AQUINAS COLLEGE
Business Administration and Management— General — M
Education—General — M

AQUINAS INSTITUTE OF THEOLOGY
Health Services Management and Hospital Administration — P,M,D,O

ARCADIA UNIVERSITY
Art Education — M,D,O
Business Administration and Management— General — M
Community Health — M
Computer Education — M,D,O
Early Childhood Education — M,D,O
Education—General — M,D,O
Educational Leadership and Administration — M,D,O
Educational Media/ Instructional Technology — M,D,O
Educational Psychology — M,D,O
Elementary Education — M,D,O
English Education — M,D,O
Environmental Education — M,D,O
Health Education — M
Mathematics Education — M,D,O
Music Education — M,D,O
Physical Therapy — D
Reading Education — M,D,O
Science Education — M,D,O
Secondary Education — M,D,O
Social Sciences Education — M,D,O
Special Education — M,D,O

ARGOSY UNIVERSITY, ATLANTA
Accounting — M,D
Business Administration and Management— General — M,D*
Counselor Education — M,D,O
Education—General — M,D,O
Educational Leadership and Administration — M,D,O*
Educational Media/ Instructional Technology — M,D,O
Elementary Education — M,D,O
Finance and Banking — M,D
Health Services Management and Hospital Administration — M,D
Higher Education — M,D,O
International Business — M,D
Management Information Systems — M,D
Marketing — M,D
Secondary Education — M,D,O

ARGOSY UNIVERSITY, CHICAGO
Accounting — M,D
Adult Education — M,D,O
Business Administration and Management— General — M,D
Community College Education — M,D,O
Counselor Education — D
Education—General — M,D,O*
Educational Leadership and Administration — M,D,O
Elementary Education — M,D,O
Finance and Banking — M,D
Health Services Management and Hospital Administration — M,D
Higher Education — M,D,O
International Business — M,D
Management Information Systems — M,D
Marketing — M,D
Organizational Behavior — D
Organizational Management — D
Secondary Education — M,D,O
Sustainability Management — M,D

ARGOSY UNIVERSITY, DALLAS
Accounting — M,D,O
Business Administration and Management— General — M,D,O*
Counselor Education — D
Education—General — M,D*
Educational Leadership and Administration — M,D
Finance and Banking — M,D,O
Health Services Management and Hospital Administration — M,D,O
Higher Education — M,D
International Business — M,D,O
Management Information Systems — M,D,O
Marketing — M,D,O
Sustainability Management — M,D,O

ARGOSY UNIVERSITY, DENVER
Accounting — M,D
Business Administration and Management— General — M,D*
Community College Education — M,D
Counselor Education — M,D
Education—General — M,D*
Educational Leadership and Administration — M,D
Educational Media/ Instructional Technology — M,D
Elementary Education — M,D
Finance and Banking — M,D
Health Services Management and Hospital Administration — M,D
Higher Education — M,D
International Business — M,D
Management Information Systems — M,D
Marketing — M,D
Organizational Management — M,D
Sustainability Management — M,D

ARGOSY UNIVERSITY, HAWAI'I
Accounting — M,D,O
Adult Education — M,D
Business Administration and Management— General — M,D,O*
Education—General — M,D*
Educational Leadership and Administration — M,D
Elementary Education — M,D
Finance and Banking — M,D,O
Health Services Management and Hospital Administration — M,D,O
Higher Education — M,D

International Business — M,D,O
Management Information Systems — M,D,O
Marketing — M,D,O
Organizational Management — D
Secondary Education — M,D
Sustainability Management — M,D,O

ARGOSY UNIVERSITY, INLAND EMPIRE
Accounting — M,D
Business Administration and Management— General — M,D*
Community College Education — M,D
Education—General — M,D
Educational Leadership and Administration — M,D*
Elementary Education — M,D
Finance and Banking — M,D
Health Services Management and Hospital Administration — M,D
Higher Education — M,D
International Business — M,D
Management Information Systems — M,D
Marketing — M,D
Organizational Management — M,D
Secondary Education — M,D
Sustainability Management — M,D

ARGOSY UNIVERSITY, LOS ANGELES
Accounting — M,D
Business Administration and Management— General — M,D*
Community College Education — M,D
Education—General — M,D*
Educational Leadership and Administration — M,D
Elementary Education — M,D
Finance and Banking — M,D
Health Services Management and Hospital Administration — M,D
Higher Education — M,D
International Business — M,D
Management Information Systems — M,D
Marketing — M,D
Organizational Management — M,D
Secondary Education — M,D
Sustainability Management — M,D

ARGOSY UNIVERSITY, NASHVILLE
Accounting — M,D
Business Administration and Management— General — M,D*
Counselor Education — D
Education—General — M,D,O
Educational Leadership and Administration — M,D,O*
Educational Media/ Instructional Technology — M,D,O
Elementary Education — M,D,O
Finance and Banking — M,D
Health Services Management and Hospital Administration — M,D
Higher Education — M,D,O
International Business — M,D
Management Information Systems — M,D
Marketing — M,D
Secondary Education — M,D,O

ARGOSY UNIVERSITY, ORANGE COUNTY
Accounting — M,D,O
Business Administration and Management— General — M,D,O*

---

*M—master's degree; P—first professional degree; D—doctorate; O—other advanced degree; *—Close-Up and/or Display*

Community College Education	M,D
Education—General	M,D*
Educational Leadership and Administration	M,D
Educational Media/ Instructional Technology	M,D
Elementary Education	M,D
Finance and Banking	M,D,O
Health Services Management and Hospital Administration	M,D,O
Higher Education	M,D
International Business	M,D,O
Management Information Systems	M,D,O
Marketing	M,D,O
Organizational Management	D
Secondary Education	M,D
Sustainability Management	M,D,O

ARGOSY UNIVERSITY, PHOENIX

Accounting	M,D
Adult Education	M,D,O
Business Administration and Management— General	M,D*
Community College Education	M,D,O
Education—General	M,D,O*
Educational Leadership and Administration	M,D,O
Educational Media/ Instructional Technology	M,D,O
Elementary Education	M,D,O
Finance and Banking	M,D
Health Services Management and Hospital Administration	M,D
Higher Education	M,D,O
International Business	M,D
Management Information Systems	M,D
Marketing	M,D
Secondary Education	M,D,O
Sustainability Management	M,D

ARGOSY UNIVERSITY, SALT LAKE CITY

Accounting	M,D
Business Administration and Management— General	M,D*
Counselor Education	M,D
Education—General	M,D*
Educational Leadership and Administration	M,D
Finance and Banking	M,D
Health Services Management and Hospital Administration	M,D
International Business	M,D
Management Information Systems	M,D
Marketing	M,D
Sustainability Management	M,D

ARGOSY UNIVERSITY, SAN DIEGO

Accounting	M,D
Business Administration and Management— General	M,D*
Community College Education	M,D
Education—General	M,D*
Educational Leadership and Administration	M,D
Elementary Education	M,D
Finance and Banking	M,D
Higher Education	M,D
International Business	M,D
Management Information Systems	M,D
Marketing	M,D
Organizational Management	M,D
Secondary Education	M,D

ARGOSY UNIVERSITY, SAN FRANCISCO BAY AREA

Accounting	M,D

Business Administration and Management— General	M,D*
Community College Education	M,D
Education—General	M,D*
Educational Leadership and Administration	M,D
Educational Media/ Instructional Technology	M,D
Elementary Education	M,D
Finance and Banking	M,D
Health Services Management and Hospital Administration	M,D
Higher Education	M,D
International Business	M,D
Management Information Systems	M,D
Marketing	M,D
Organizational Management	M,D
Secondary Education	M,D
Sustainability Management	M,D

ARGOSY UNIVERSITY, SARASOTA

Accounting	M,D,O
Business Administration and Management— General	M,D,O*
Counselor Education	M,D,O
Education—General	M,D,O*
Educational Leadership and Administration	M,D,O
Educational Media/ Instructional Technology	M,D,O
Elementary Education	M,D,O
Finance and Banking	M,D,O
Health Services Management and Hospital Administration	M,D,O
Higher Education	M,D,O
International Business	M,D,O
Management Information Systems	M,D,O
Marketing	M,D,O
Organizational Management	M,D,O
Secondary Education	M,D,O
Sustainability Management	M,D,O

ARGOSY UNIVERSITY, SCHAUMBURG

Accounting	M,D,O
Business Administration and Management— General	M,D,O*
Community College Education	M,D,O
Counselor Education	M,D,O
Education—General	M,D,O*
Educational Leadership and Administration	M,D,O
Elementary Education	M,D,O
Finance and Banking	M,D,O
Health Services Management and Hospital Administration	M,D,O
Higher Education	M,D,O
International Business	M,D,O
Management Information Systems	M,D,O
Marketing	M,D,O
Secondary Education	M,D,O
Sustainability Management	M,D,O

ARGOSY UNIVERSITY, SEATTLE

Accounting	M,D
Adult Education	M,D
Business Administration and Management— General	M,D*
Community College Education	M,D
Education—General	M,D*
Educational Leadership and Administration	M,D
Educational Media/ Instructional Technology	M,D
Elementary Education	M,D
Finance and Banking	M,D

Health Services Management and Hospital Administration	M,D
Higher Education	M,D
International Business	M,D
Management Information Systems	M,D
Marketing	M,D
Organizational Management	M,D
Secondary Education	M,D
Sustainability Management	M,D

ARGOSY UNIVERSITY, TAMPA

Accounting	M,D
Business Administration and Management— General	M,D*
Community College Education	M,D,O
Counselor Education	M,D,O
Education—General	M,D,O*
Educational Leadership and Administration	M,D,O
Elementary Education	M,D,O
Finance and Banking	M,D
Health Services Management and Hospital Administration	M,D
Higher Education	M,D,O
International Business	M,D
Management Information Systems	M,D
Marketing	M,D
Organizational Management	M,D
Secondary Education	M,D,O
Sustainability Management	M,D

ARGOSY UNIVERSITY, TWIN CITIES

Accounting	M,D
Business Administration and Management— General	M,D*
Education—General	M,D,O*
Educational Leadership and Administration	M,D,O
Educational Media/ Instructional Technology	M,D,O
Elementary Education	M,D,O
Finance and Banking	M,D
Health Services Management and Hospital Administration	M,D
Higher Education	M,D,O
International Business	M,D
Management Information Systems	M,D
Marketing	M,D
Organizational Management	M,D
Secondary Education	M,D,O
Sustainability Management	M,D

ARGOSY UNIVERSITY, WASHINGTON DC

Accounting	M,D,O
Business Administration and Management— General	M,D,O*
Community College Education	M,D,O
Counselor Education	M,D
Education—General	M,D,O*
Educational Leadership and Administration	M,D,O
Elementary Education	M,D,O
Finance and Banking	M,D,O
Health Services Management and Hospital Administration	M,D,O
Higher Education	M,D,O
International Business	M,D,O
Management Information Systems	M,D,O
Marketing	M,D,O
Organizational Management	M,D,O
Secondary Education	M,D,O
Sustainability Management	M,D,O

ARIZONA SCHOOL OF ACUPUNCTURE AND ORIENTAL MEDICINE

Acupuncture and Oriental Medicine	M

ARIZONA STATE UNIVERSITY

Accounting	M,D
Business Administration and Management— General	M,D
Communication Disorders	M,D
Community Health Nursing	M,D,O
Community Health	M,D,O
Counselor Education	M
Curriculum and Instruction	M,D
Education—General	M,D,O
Educational Leadership and Administration	M,D,O
Educational Media/ Instructional Technology	M,D
Educational Psychology	M,D
Elementary Education	M,D,O
English as a Second Language	M,D
Exercise and Sports Science	M,D
Finance and Banking	M,D
Foundations and Philosophy of Education	M
Health Services Management and Hospital Administration	M,D
Higher Education	M
Kinesiology and Movement Studies	D
Law	P,M
Legal and Justice Studies	P,M,D
Management Information Systems	M,D
Marketing	M,D
Music Education	M,D
Nonprofit Management	M,D
Nursing Education	M,D,O
Nursing—General	M,D,O
Physical Education	M,D,O
Psychiatric Nursing	M,D,O
Public Health—General	M,D,O
Recreation and Park Management	M,D
Secondary Education	M,D,O
Social Work	M,D
Special Education	M,D,O
Supply Chain Management	M,D
Transportation Management	M,O
Travel and Tourism	M,D

ARKANSAS STATE UNIVERSITY— JONESBORO

Accounting	M
Agricultural Education	M,O
Business Administration and Management— General	M,O
Business Education	M,O
Communication Disorders	M
Community College Education	M,D,O
Counselor Education	M,O
Curriculum and Instruction	M,D,O
Early Childhood Education	M,O
Education of the Gifted	M,D,O
Education—General	M,D,O
Educational Leadership and Administration	M,D,O
Educational Measurement and Evaluation	M,O
Electronic Commerce	M
Elementary Education	M,O
English Education	M,O
Exercise and Sports Science	M,O
Foundations and Philosophy of Education	M,D,O
Health Education	M,D,O
Management Information Systems	M
Mathematics Education	M
Middle School Education	M,O
Music Education	M,O
Nurse Anesthesia	M
Nursing—General	M

Physical Education	M,O
Physical Therapy	M,D,O
Reading Education	M,O
Science Education	M,O
Social Sciences Education	M,O
Social Work	M
Special Education	M,D,O
Student Affairs	M,O

ARKANSAS TECH UNIVERSITY

Curriculum and Instruction	M,O
Education—General	M,O
Educational Leadership and Administration	M,O
English as a Second Language	M
English Education	M,O
Nursing—General	M
Secondary Education	M,O
Student Affairs	M,O

ARMSTRONG ATLANTIC STATE UNIVERSITY

Adult Education	M
Athletic Training and Sports Medicine	M
Business Education	M
Communication Disorders	M
Curriculum and Instruction	M
Early Childhood Education	M
Education—General	M
Elementary Education	M
English Education	M
Exercise and Sports Science	M
Health Services Management and Hospital Administration	M
Mathematics Education	M
Middle School Education	M
Nursing—General	M
Physical Therapy	D
Public Health—General	M
Science Education	M
Secondary Education	M
Social Sciences Education	M
Special Education	M

ART ACADEMY OF CINCINNATI

| Art Education | M |

ASBURY THEOLOGICAL SEMINARY

| Religious Education | M,D,O |

ASBURY UNIVERSITY

Educational Leadership and Administration	M
English as a Second Language	M
Mathematics Education	M
Reading Education	M
Science Education	M
Social Sciences Education	M
Social Work	M
Special Education	M

ASHLAND THEOLOGICAL SEMINARY

| Counselor Education | P,M,D,O |

ASHLAND UNIVERSITY

Business Administration and Management— General	M
Curriculum and Instruction	M
Education—General	M,D
Educational Leadership and Administration	M,D
Educational Media/ Instructional Technology	M
Exercise and Sports Science	M
Foundations and Philosophy of Education	M
Physical Education	M
Reading Education	M
Special Education	M
Sports Management	M
Student Affairs	M

ASPEN UNIVERSITY

Business Administration and Management— General	M,O
Finance and Banking	M,O
Management Information Systems	M,O
Project Management	M,O

ASSUMPTION COLLEGE

Accounting	M,O
Business Administration and Management— General	M,O
Finance and Banking	M,O
Human Resources Management	M,O
International Business	M,O
Marketing	M,O
Nonprofit Management	M,O
Special Education	M,O

ATHABASCA UNIVERSITY

Adult Education	M
Allied Health—General	M,O
Business Administration and Management— General	M,O
Counselor Education	M,O
Distance Education Development	M,O
Education—General	M,O
Nursing and Healthcare Administration	M,O
Nursing—General	M,O
Organizational Management	M
Project Management	M,O

ATLANTA'S JOHN MARSHALL LAW SCHOOL

| Law | P |

ATLANTIC INSTITUTE OF ORIENTAL MEDICINE

| Acupuncture and Oriental Medicine | M |

ATLANTIC UNION COLLEGE

| Education—General | M |

A.T. STILL UNIVERSITY OF HEALTH SCIENCES

Allied Health—General	M,D
Athletic Training and Sports Medicine	M,D
Communication Disorders	M,D
Health Education	M,D
Health Services Management and Hospital Administration	M,D
Kinesiology and Movement Studies	M,D
Occupational Therapy	M,D
Oral and Dental Sciences	P,O
Osteopathic Medicine	P,M
Physical Therapy	M,D
Physician Assistant Studies	M,D
Public Health—General	M,D

AUBURN UNIVERSITY

Accounting	M
Adult Education	M,D,O
Business Administration and Management— General	M,D
Business Education	M,D,O
Communication Disorders	M,D
Curriculum and Instruction	M,D,O
Early Childhood Education	M,D,O
Education—General	M,D,O
Educational Leadership and Administration	M,D,O
Educational Media/ Instructional Technology	M,D,O
Educational Psychology	M,D,O
Elementary Education	M,D,O
English Education	M,D,O
Exercise and Sports Science	M,D,O
Finance and Banking	M

Foreign Languages Education	M,D,O
Health Education	M,D,O
Health Promotion	M,D,O
Higher Education	M,D,O
Human Resources Management	M,D
Kinesiology and Movement Studies	M,D,O
Management Information Systems	M,D
Mathematics Education	M,D,O
Music Education	M,D,O
Nursing—General	M,O
Pharmaceutical Sciences	M,D
Pharmacy	P
Physical Education	M,D,O
Reading Education	M,D,O
Science Education	M,D,O
Secondary Education	M,D,O
Social Sciences Education	M,D,O
Special Education	M,D
Veterinary Medicine	P
Veterinary Sciences	M,D

AUBURN UNIVERSITY MONTGOMERY

Business Administration and Management— General	M
Counselor Education	M,O
Early Childhood Education	M,O
Education—General	M,O
Educational Leadership and Administration	M,O
Elementary Education	M,O
Physical Education	M,O
Reading Education	M,O
Secondary Education	M,O
Special Education	M,O

AUGSBURG COLLEGE

Business Administration and Management— General	M
Community Health Nursing	M
Education—General	M
Nursing—General	M
Organizational Management	M
Physician Assistant Studies	M
Social Work	M
Transcultural Nursing	M

AUGUSTANA COLLEGE

| Nursing—General | M |
| Sports Management | M |

AUGUSTA STATE UNIVERSITY

Business Administration and Management— General	M
Counselor Education	M
Curriculum and Instruction	M
Education—General	M,O
Educational Leadership and Administration	M,O
Health Education	M
Physical Education	M
Secondary Education	M,O
Special Education	M,O

AURORA UNIVERSITY

Business Administration and Management— General	M
Curriculum and Instruction	M,D
Education—General	M,D
Educational Leadership and Administration	M,D
Leisure Studies	M
Reading Education	M,D
Social Work	M

AUSTIN COLLEGE

Art Education	M
Education—General	M
Elementary Education	M
Middle School Education	M
Music Education	M

| Physical Education | M |
| Secondary Education | M |

AUSTIN PEAY STATE UNIVERSITY

Business Administration and Management— General	M
Clinical Laboratory Sciences/Medical Technology	M
Community Health	M
Counselor Education	M,O
Curriculum and Instruction	M,O
Education—General	M,O
Educational Leadership and Administration	M,O
Elementary Education	M,O
Exercise and Sports Science	M
Health Education	M
Music Education	M
Nursing and Healthcare Administration	M
Nursing Education	M
Nursing Informatics	M
Nursing—General	M
Public Health—General	M
Reading Education	M
Secondary Education	M,O
Social Work	M
Special Education	M,O

AVE MARIA SCHOOL OF LAW

| Law | P |

AVERETT UNIVERSITY

Art Education	M
Business Administration and Management— General	M
Curriculum and Instruction	M
Education—General	M
Elementary Education	M
English Education	M
Health Education	M
Mathematics Education	M
Physical Education	M
Reading Education	M
Science Education	M
Social Sciences Education	M
Special Education	M

AVILA UNIVERSITY

Accounting	M
Business Administration and Management— General	M
Education—General	M,O
English as a Second Language	M,O
Finance and Banking	M
Health Services Management and Hospital Administration	M
International Business	M
Management Information Systems	M
Marketing	M
Nonprofit Management	M,O
Organizational Management	M,O
Project Management	M,O

AZUSA PACIFIC UNIVERSITY

Business Administration and Management— General	M
Counselor Education	M
Curriculum and Instruction	M
Education—General	M,D
Educational Leadership and Administration	M,D
Educational Media/ Instructional Technology	M
English as a Second Language	M,D
Higher Education	M,D
Human Resources Development	M
International Business	M
Library Science	M
Management Strategy and Policy	M

Multilingual and
  Multicultural Education — M
Music Education — M
Nonprofit Management — M
Nursing Education — M,D
Nursing—General — M,D
Organizational
  Management — M
Physical Education — M
Physical Therapy — D
Religious Education — M
Special Education — M
Student Affairs — M

BABSON COLLEGE

Accounting — M,O
Business Administration
  and Management—
  General — M,O*
Entrepreneurship — M,O

BAKER COLLEGE CENTER FOR GRADUATE STUDIES—ONLINE

Accounting — M,D
Business Administration
  and Management—
  General — M,D
Finance and Banking — M,D
Health Services
  Management and
  Hospital Administration — M,D
Human Resources
  Management — M,D
Management Information
  Systems — M,D
Marketing — M,D

BAKER UNIVERSITY

Business Administration
  and Management—
  General — M
Education—General — M,D

BAKKE GRADUATE UNIVERSITY

Business Administration
  and Management—
  General — M,D
Entrepreneurship — M,D

BALDWIN-WALLACE COLLEGE

Accounting — M
Business Administration
  and Management—
  General — M
Education—General — M
Educational Leadership
  and Administration — M
Educational Media/
  Instructional Technology — M
Entrepreneurship — M
Health Services
  Management and
  Hospital Administration — M
Human Resources
  Management — M
International Business — M
Reading Education — M
Special Education — M

BALL STATE UNIVERSITY

Accounting — M
Actuarial Science — M
Adult Education — M,D
Advertising and Public
  Relations — M
Art Education — M
Business Administration
  and Management—
  General — M
Business Education — M
Communication Disorders — M,D
Curriculum and Instruction — M,O
Education—General — M,D,O
Educational Leadership
  and Administration — M,D,O
Educational Psychology — M,D,O
Elementary Education — M,D
English as a Second
  Language — M,D
Exercise and Sports
  Science — D
Foundations and
  Philosophy of Education — D
Health Education — M
Health Promotion — M

Higher Education — M,D
Mathematics Education — M
Music Education — M,D
Nursing—General — M
Physical Education — M,D
Science Education — M,D
Secondary Education — M
Special Education — M,D,O
Vocational and Technical
  Education — M

BANK STREET COLLEGE OF EDUCATION

Early Childhood Education — M
Education—General — M*
Educational Leadership
  and Administration — M
Elementary Education — M
Foundations and
  Philosophy of Education — M
Maternal and Child Health — M
Mathematics Education — M
Middle School Education — M
Multilingual and
  Multicultural Education — M
Museum Education — M
Reading Education — M
Special Education — M

BAPTIST BIBLE COLLEGE OF PENNSYLVANIA

Counselor Education — M
Religious Education — P,M,D

BAPTIST THEOLOGICAL SEMINARY AT RICHMOND

Religious Education — P,D

BARD COLLEGE

Education—General — M

BARRY UNIVERSITY

Accounting — M
Acute Care/Critical Care
  Nursing — M,O
Athletic Training and
  Sports Medicine — M
Business Administration
  and Management—
  General — M,O
Communication Disorders — M
Counselor Education — M,D,O
Curriculum and Instruction — D,O
Distance Education
  Development — O
Early Childhood Education — M,D,O
Education of the Gifted — M,D,O
Education—General — M,D,O
Educational Leadership
  and Administration — M,D,O
Educational Media/
  Instructional Technology — M,D,O
Elementary Education — M,D,O
English as a Second
  Language — M,D,O
Exercise and Sports
  Science — M
Family Nurse Practitioner
  Studies — M,O
Finance and Banking — O
Health Services
  Management and
  Hospital Administration — M,O
Higher Education — M,D
Human Resources
  Development — M,D
Human Resources
  Management — O
International Business — O
Kinesiology and
  Movement Studies — M
Law — P
Management Information
  Systems — O
Marketing — O
Nurse Anesthesia — M
Nursing and Healthcare
  Administration — M,D,O
Nursing Education — M,O
Nursing—General — M,D,O
Occupational Therapy — M
Physician Assistant
  Studies — M
Podiatric Medicine — P
Public Health—General — M

Reading Education — M,D,O
Social Work — M,D
Special Education — M,D,O
Sports Management — M

BASTYR UNIVERSITY

Acupuncture and Oriental
  Medicine — M,D,O
Naturopathic Medicine — D

BAYAMÓN CENTRAL UNIVERSITY

Accounting — M
Business Administration
  and Management—
  General — M
Counselor Education — M
Early Childhood Education — M
Education—General — M
Educational Leadership
  and Administration — M
Elementary Education — M
Finance and Banking — M
Marketing — M
Special Education — M

BAYLOR COLLEGE OF MEDICINE

Allopathic Medicine — P
Clinical Laboratory
  Sciences/Medical
  Technology — M,D
Nurse Anesthesia — M
Physician Assistant
  Studies — M

BAYLOR UNIVERSITY

Accounting — M
Allied Health—General — M,D
Business Administration
  and Management—
  General — M
Communication Disorders — M
Curriculum and Instruction — M,D,O
Education—General — M,D,O
Educational Leadership
  and Administration — M,O
Educational Psychology — M,D,O
Emergency Medical
  Services — D
Exercise and Sports
  Science — M,D
Family Nurse Practitioner
  Studies — M
Health Education — M,D
Health Services
  Management and
  Hospital Administration — M
Law — P
Management Information
  Systems — M
Maternal and Child/
  Neonatal Nursing — M
Nursing and Healthcare
  Administration — M
Nursing—General — M
Physical Education — M,D
Physical Therapy — M,D
Social Work — M

BAY PATH COLLEGE

Educational Leadership
  and Administration — M
Entrepreneurship — M
Higher Education — M
Management Information
  Systems — M
Nonprofit Management — M
Occupational Therapy — M

BELHAVEN UNIVERSITY (MS)

Business Administration
  and Management—
  General — M
Education—General — M
Elementary Education — M
Multilingual and
  Multicultural Education — M
Secondary Education — M

BELLARMINE UNIVERSITY

Business Administration
  and Management—
  General — M
Early Childhood Education — M
Education—General — M

Educational Leadership
  and Administration — M
Family Nurse Practitioner
  Studies — M,D
Management Information
  Systems — M
Middle School Education — M
Nursing and Healthcare
  Administration — M,D
Nursing Education — M,D
Nursing—General — M,D
Physical Therapy — M,D
Reading Education — M
Secondary Education — M
Special Education — M

BELLEVUE UNIVERSITY

Business Administration
  and Management—
  General — M,D
Counselor Education — M,D
Educational Media/
  Instructional Technology — M,D
Health Services
  Management and
  Hospital Administration — M
Human Services — M
Management Information
  Systems — M
Public Health—General — M,D

BELLIN COLLEGE

Nursing and Healthcare
  Administration — M
Nursing Education — M
Nursing—General — M

BELMONT UNIVERSITY

Allied Health—General — P,M,D
Business Administration
  and Management—
  General — M
Early Childhood Education — M
Education—General — M
Elementary Education — M
English Education — M
Mathematics Education — M
Middle School Education — M
Music Education — M
Nursing—General — M
Occupational Therapy — M,D
Pharmacy — P
Physical Therapy — D
Science Education — M
Secondary Education — M
Social Sciences Education — M
Special Education — M
Sports Management — M

BEMIDJI STATE UNIVERSITY

Education—General — M
Exercise and Sports
  Science — M
Mathematics Education — M
Science Education — M
Special Education — M
Vocational and Technical
  Education — M

BENEDICTINE COLLEGE

Business Administration
  and Management—
  General — M
Educational Leadership
  and Administration — M

BENEDICTINE UNIVERSITY

Accounting — M
Business Administration
  and Management—
  General — M
Curriculum and Instruction — M
Education—General — M
Educational Leadership
  and Administration — M,D
Elementary Education — M
Entrepreneurship — M
Exercise and Sports
  Science — M
Finance and Banking — M
Health Education — M
Health Promotion — M
Health Services
  Management and
  Hospital Administration — M

Higher Education	D
Human Resources Management	M
International Business	M
Logistics	M
Management Information Systems	M
Marketing	M
Organizational Behavior	M
Organizational Management	M,D
Public Health—General	M
Reading Education	M
Science Education	M
Secondary Education	M
Special Education	M

BENNINGTON COLLEGE

Allied Health—General	O
Art Education	M
Early Childhood Education	M
Education—General	M
Elementary Education	M
English Education	M
Foreign Languages Education	M
Mathematics Education	M
Multilingual and Multicultural Education	M
Music Education	M
Science Education	M
Secondary Education	M
Social Sciences Education	M

BENTLEY UNIVERSITY

Accounting	M,D
Business Administration and Management—General	M,D,O
Finance and Banking	M
Marketing	M
Taxation	M

BERNARD M. BARUCH COLLEGE OF THE CITY UNIVERSITY OF NEW YORK

Accounting	M,D
Business Administration and Management—General	M,D,O
Educational Leadership and Administration	M,O
Entrepreneurship	M,D
Finance and Banking	M,D
Health Services Management and Hospital Administration	M
Higher Education	M
Human Resources Management	M,D
International Business	M
Management Information Systems	M,D
Management Strategy and Policy	M,D
Marketing	M,D
Nonprofit Management	M
Organizational Behavior	M,D
Organizational Management	M,D
Quantitative Analysis	M
Taxation	M

BERRY COLLEGE

Business Administration and Management—General	M
Curriculum and Instruction	O
Early Childhood Education	M
Education—General	M,O
Educational Leadership and Administration	O
Middle School Education	M
Reading Education	M
Secondary Education	M

BETHANY UNIVERSITY

Education—General	M
Educational Leadership and Administration	M

BETHEL COLLEGE

Business Administration and Management—General	M
Education—General	M
Nursing—General	M

BETHEL SEMINARY

Religious Education	P,M,D,O

BETHEL UNIVERSITY (MN)

Business Administration and Management—General	M
Education—General	M,D,O
Educational Leadership and Administration	M,D,O
Higher Education	M,O
Nursing Education	M,O
Nursing—General	M,O
Organizational Management	M
Reading Education	M,D,O
Secondary Education	M,D,O
Special Education	M,D,O

BETHEL UNIVERSITY (TN)

Education—General	M
Educational Leadership and Administration	M
Elementary Education	M
English Education	M
Physical Education	M
Science Education	M
Social Sciences Education	M
Special Education	M

BIOLA UNIVERSITY

Business Administration and Management—General	M
Education—General	M
English as a Second Language	M,D,O
Organizational Management	M
Religious Education	P,M,D

BIRMINGHAM-SOUTHERN COLLEGE

Business Administration and Management—General	M

BISHOP'S UNIVERSITY

Education—General	M,O
English as a Second Language	M,O

BLACK HILLS STATE UNIVERSITY

Business Administration and Management—General	M
Curriculum and Instruction	M
Management Strategy and Policy	M

BLESSING-RIEMAN COLLEGE OF NURSING

Nursing—General	M

BLOOMSBURG UNIVERSITY OF PENNSYLVANIA

Adult Nursing	M
Athletic Training and Sports Medicine	M
Business Administration and Management—General	M
Business Education	M
Communication Disorders	M,D
Community Health	M
Counselor Education	M
Curriculum and Instruction	M
Early Childhood Education	M
Education—General	M
Educational Media/ Instructional Technology	M
Elementary Education	M
Exercise and Sports Science	M
Family Nurse Practitioner Studies	M

Health Physics/ Radiological Health	M
Nursing and Healthcare Administration	M
Nursing—General	M
Reading Education	M
Science Education	M
Special Education	M
Student Affairs	M

BLUFFTON UNIVERSITY

Business Administration and Management—General	M
Education—General	M
Organizational Management	M

BOB JONES UNIVERSITY

Accounting	P,M,D,O
Business Administration and Management—General	P,M,D,O
Counselor Education	P,M,D,O
Curriculum and Instruction	P,M,D,O
Educational Leadership and Administration	P,M,D,O
Elementary Education	P,M,D,O
English Education	P,M,D,O
Mathematics Education	P,M,D,O
Music Education	P,M,D,O
Secondary Education	P,M,D,O
Social Sciences Education	P,M,D,O
Special Education	P,M,D,O
Student Affairs	P,M,D,O

BOISE STATE UNIVERSITY

Accounting	M
Art Education	M
Business Administration and Management—General	M
Counselor Education	M
Curriculum and Instruction	D
Early Childhood Education	M
Education—General	M,D
Educational Leadership and Administration	M,D
Educational Media/ Instructional Technology	M
Exercise and Sports Science	M
Management Information Systems	M
Music Education	M
Public Health—General	M
Reading Education	M
Science Education	M,D
Social Work	M
Special Education	M
Sports Management	M
Taxation	M

BORICUA COLLEGE

Human Services	M

BOSTON COLLEGE

Accounting	M
Adult Nursing	M,D
Business Administration and Management—General	M
Community Health Nursing	M,D
Curriculum and Instruction	M,D,O
Early Childhood Education	M
Education—General	M,D,O
Educational Leadership and Administration	M,D,O
Educational Measurement and Evaluation	M,D
Educational Psychology	M,D
Elementary Education	M
English Education	M,D
Finance and Banking	M,D
Foreign Languages Education	M
Forensic Nursing	M,D
Gerontological Nursing	M,D
Higher Education	M,D
Law	P
Maternal and Child/ Neonatal Nursing	M,D

Mathematics Education	M
Medical/Surgical Nursing	M,D
Nurse Anesthesia	M,D
Nursing—General	M,D
Organizational Behavior	D
Organizational Management	D
Pediatric Nursing	M,D
Psychiatric Nursing	M,D
Reading Education	M,O
Religious Education	P,M,D,O
Science Education	M,D
Secondary Education	M
Social Sciences Education	M
Social Work	M,D
Special Education	M,O

THE BOSTON CONSERVATORY

Music Education	M,O

BOSTON UNIVERSITY

Accounting	D
Actuarial Science	M
Advertising and Public Relations	M
Allied Health—General	M,D,O
Allopathic Medicine	P
Art Education	M
Athletic Training and Sports Medicine	D
Bioethics	M
Business Administration and Management—General	M,D
Communication Disorders	M,D,O
Counselor Education	M,O
Curriculum and Instruction	M,D,O
Dental Hygiene	P,M,D,O
Dentistry	P,M,D,O
Early Childhood Education	M,D,O
Education—General	M,D,O
Educational Leadership and Administration	M,O
Educational Media/ Instructional Technology	M,D,O
Electronic Commerce	M
Elementary Education	M
English as a Second Language	M,O
English Education	M,O
Entrepreneurship	M
Environmental and Occupational Health	M,D
Epidemiology	M,D
Finance and Banking	P,M,D
Foreign Languages Education	M
Health Education	M,O
Health Law	M
Health Promotion	M,D
Health Services Management and Hospital Administration	M,D
Human Resources Management	M,O
Industrial and Manufacturing Management	D
International and Comparative Education	M
International Business	M
International Health	M,D,O
Investment Management	M
Law	P,M
Legal and Justice Studies	M
Management Information Systems	D
Management Strategy and Policy	M
Marketing	M,D
Maternal and Child Health	M,D
Mathematics Education	M,D,O
Multilingual and Multicultural Education	M,O
Music Education	M,D
Nonprofit Management	M
Occupational Therapy	M
Oral and Dental Sciences	P,M,D,O
Organizational Behavior	D
Pharmaceutical Sciences	M
Physical Education	M,D,O
Physical Therapy	D
Project Management	M
Public Health—General	P,M,D,O

Reading Education	M,D,O
Rehabilitation Sciences	D
Science Education	M,D,O
Social Sciences Education	M,D,O
Social Work	M,D
Special Education	M,D,O
Taxation	P,M
Travel and Tourism	M

BOWIE STATE UNIVERSITY

Business Administration and Management— General	M
Counselor Education	M
Education—General	M
Educational Leadership and Administration	M,D
Elementary Education	M
Family Nurse Practitioner Studies	M
Human Resources Development	M
Management Information Systems	M,O
Nursing and Healthcare Administration	M
Nursing Education	M
Nursing—General	M
Reading Education	M
Secondary Education	M
Special Education	M

BOWLING GREEN STATE UNIVERSITY

Accounting	M
Art Education	M
Business Administration and Management— General	M
Business Education	M
Communication Disorders	M,D
Counselor Education	M
Curriculum and Instruction	M
Early Childhood Education	M
Education of the Gifted	M
Educational Leadership and Administration	M,D,O
Educational Media/ Instructional Technology	M
Foreign Languages Education	M
Higher Education	D
International and Comparative Education	M
Kinesiology and Movement Studies	M
Leisure Studies	M
Mathematics Education	M,D
Music Education	M,D
Organizational Management	M
Public Health—General	M
Reading Education	M,O
Recreation and Park Management	M
Science Education	M
Special Education	M
Sports Management	M
Student Affairs	M
Vocational and Technical Education	M

BRADLEY UNIVERSITY

Accounting	M
Business Administration and Management— General	M
Counselor Education	M
Curriculum and Instruction	M,O
Education—General	M,D,O
Educational Leadership and Administration	M
Nurse Anesthesia	M
Nursing and Healthcare Administration	M
Nursing—General	M
Physical Therapy	D

BRANDEIS UNIVERSITY

Business Administration and Management— General	M
Elementary Education	M
Entrepreneurship	M
Finance and Banking	M,D

Health Education	D
Health Services Management and Hospital Administration	M
Human Services	M
International Business	M,D
International Health	M
Management Information Systems	M,O
Nonprofit Management	M
Project Management	M,O
Religious Education	M
Secondary Education	M

BRANDON UNIVERSITY

Counselor Education	M,O
Curriculum and Instruction	M,O
Education—General	M,O
Educational Leadership and Administration	M,O
Music Education	M
Special Education	M,O

BRENAU UNIVERSITY

Accounting	M
Business Administration and Management— General	M
Early Childhood Education	M,O
Education—General	M,O
Family Nurse Practitioner Studies	M
Health Services Management and Hospital Administration	M
Middle School Education	M,O
Nursing and Healthcare Administration	M
Nursing Education	M
Occupational Therapy	M
Organizational Management	M
Project Management	M
Secondary Education	M,O
Special Education	M,O

BRESCIA UNIVERSITY

Business Administration and Management— General	M
Curriculum and Instruction	M

BRIAR CLIFF UNIVERSITY

Education—General	M
Human Resources Management	M
Nursing—General	M

BRIDGEWATER STATE UNIVERSITY

Accounting	M
Art Education	M
Business Administration and Management— General	M
Counselor Education	M,O
Early Childhood Education	M
Education—General	M,O
Educational Leadership and Administration	M,O
Educational Media/ Instructional Technology	M
Elementary Education	M
Finance and Banking	M
Health Promotion	M
Mathematics Education	M
Physical Education	M
Reading Education	M,O
Science Education	M
Secondary Education	M
Social Sciences Education	M
Social Work	M
Special Education	M

BRIERCREST SEMINARY

Business Administration and Management— General	M
Organizational Management	M

BRIGHAM YOUNG UNIVERSITY

Accounting	M
Art Education	M

Athletic Training and Sports Medicine	M,D
Business Administration and Management— General	M
Communication Disorders	M
Education—General	M,D,O
Educational Leadership and Administration	M
Educational Media/ Instructional Technology	M,D
Educational Psychology	M,D
English as a Second Language	M,O
Exercise and Sports Science	M,D
Family Nurse Practitioner Studies	M
Finance and Banking	M
Foreign Languages Education	M
Foundations and Philosophy of Education	M
Health Education	M
Health Promotion	M,D
Human Resources Management	M
Law	P,M
Management Information Systems	M
Mathematics Education	M
Music Education	M
Nonprofit Management	M
Nursing—General	M*
Reading Education	M
Recreation and Park Management	M
Religious Education	M
Science Education	M,D
Social Work	M
Special Education	M,D,O

BROCK UNIVERSITY

Accounting	M
Allied Health—General	M,D
Business Administration and Management— General	M
Education—General	M,D
English as a Second Language	M
Legal and Justice Studies	M

BROOKLYN COLLEGE OF THE CITY UNIVERSITY OF NEW YORK

Accounting	M
Art Education	M,O
Communication Disorders	M,D
Community Health	M
Counselor Education	M,O
Early Childhood Education	M
Education—General	M,O
Educational Leadership and Administration	M
Elementary Education	M
English Education	M,O
Environmental Education	M
Exercise and Sports Science	M
Foreign Languages Education	M,O
Health Education	M,O
Health Services Management and Hospital Administration	M
Mathematics Education	M,O
Middle School Education	M
Multilingual and Multicultural Education	M
Music Education	M,D,O
Organizational Behavior	M
Physical Education	M,O
Public Health—General	M
Science Education	M,O
Secondary Education	M,O
Social Sciences Education	M,O
Special Education	M
Sports Management	M

BROOKLYN LAW SCHOOL

Law	P

BROWN UNIVERSITY

Allopathic Medicine	P
Community Health	M,D

Education—General	M
Elementary Education	M
English Education	M
Epidemiology	M,D
Health Services Research	M,D
Multilingual and Multicultural Education	M,D
Public Health—General	M
Science Education	M
Secondary Education	M
Social Sciences Education	M
Urban Education	M

BRYAN COLLEGE

Business Administration and Management— General	M

BRYANT UNIVERSITY

Accounting	M
Business Administration and Management— General	M
Taxation	M

BRYN MAWR COLLEGE

Social Work	M,D

BUCKNELL UNIVERSITY

Counselor Education	M
Curriculum and Instruction	M
Education—General	M
Educational Leadership and Administration	M
Educational Measurement and Evaluation	M
Reading Education	M

BUENA VISTA UNIVERSITY

Counselor Education	M
Curriculum and Instruction	M
Education—General	M
English as a Second Language	M

BUFFALO STATE COLLEGE, STATE UNIVERSITY OF NEW YORK

Adult Education	M,O
Art Education	M
Business Education	M
Communication Disorders	M
Early Childhood Education	M
Educational Leadership and Administration	O
Educational Media/ Instructional Technology	M
Elementary Education	M
English Education	M
Human Resources Management	M,O
Mathematics Education	M
Multilingual and Multicultural Education	M
Reading Education	M
Science Education	M
Social Sciences Education	M
Special Education	M
Student Affairs	M
Vocational and Technical Education	M

BUTLER UNIVERSITY

Business Administration and Management— General	M
Counselor Education	M
Education—General	M
Educational Leadership and Administration	M
Elementary Education	M
Music Education	M
Pharmaceutical Sciences	P,M
Pharmacy	P,M
Physician Assistant Studies	P,M
Reading Education	M
Secondary Education	M
Special Education	M

CABRINI COLLEGE

Education—General	M
Organizational Management	M

CALDWELL COLLEGE

Accounting	M
Business Administration and Management—	
General	M
Counselor Education	M
Curriculum and Instruction	M
Educational Leadership and Administration	M
Special Education	M

CALIFORNIA BAPTIST UNIVERSITY

Athletic Training and Sports Medicine	M
Business Administration and Management—	
General	M
Counselor Education	M
Curriculum and Instruction	M
Education—General	M
Educational Leadership and Administration	M
Educational Media/ Instructional Technology	M
English as a Second Language	M
English Education	M
Exercise and Sports Science	M
Kinesiology and Movement Studies	M
Multilingual and Multicultural Education	M
Music Education	M
Nursing—General	M
Physical Education	M
Reading Education	M
Special Education	M
Sports Management	M
Vocational and Technical Education	M

CALIFORNIA COAST UNIVERSITY

Business Administration and Management—	
General	M
Curriculum and Instruction	M,D
Education—General	M,D
Educational Leadership and Administration	M,D
Educational Psychology	M,D
Human Resources Management	M
Marketing	M
Organizational Management	M,D

CALIFORNIA COLLEGE OF THE ARTS

Finance and Banking	M
Organizational Management	M

CALIFORNIA INTERCONTINENTAL UNIVERSITY

Business Administration and Management—	
General	M,D
Entertainment Management	M
Entrepreneurship	M,D
Finance and Banking	M,D
Health Services Management and Hospital Administration	M,D
Human Resources Management	M,D
International Business	M,D
Management Information Systems	M,D
Marketing	M,D
Organizational Management	M,D
Project Management	M,D
Quality Management	M,D

CALIFORNIA INTERNATIONAL BUSINESS UNIVERSITY

Business Administration and Management—	
General	M,D

CALIFORNIA LUTHERAN UNIVERSITY

Business Administration and Management—	
General	M,O
Counselor Education	M
Education—General	M,D
Educational Leadership and Administration	M,D
Elementary Education	M,D
Entrepreneurship	M,O
Finance and Banking	M,O
Higher Education	M,D
International Business	M,O
Management Information Systems	M,O
Marketing	M,O
Middle School Education	M,D
Organizational Behavior	M,O
Reading Education	M
Special Education	M

CALIFORNIA NATIONAL UNIVERSITY FOR ADVANCED STUDIES

Business Administration and Management—	
General	M

CALIFORNIA POLYTECHNIC STATE UNIVERSITY, SAN LUIS OBISPO

Business Administration and Management—	
General	M
Education—General	M
Industrial and Manufacturing Management	M
Kinesiology and Movement Studies	M
Taxation	M

CALIFORNIA SCHOOL OF PODIATRIC MEDICINE AT SAMUEL MERRITT COLLEGE

Podiatric Medicine	P

CALIFORNIA STATE POLYTECHNIC UNIVERSITY, POMONA

Business Administration and Management—	
General	M
Education—General	M
Kinesiology and Movement Studies	M

CALIFORNIA STATE UNIVERSITY, BAKERSFIELD

Business Administration and Management—	
General	M
Counselor Education	M
Curriculum and Instruction	M
Early Childhood Education	M
Education—General	M,O
Educational Leadership and Administration	M
Educational Media/ Instructional Technology	M
Health Services Management and Hospital Administration	M
Mathematics Education	M
Middle School Education	M
Multilingual and Multicultural Education	M
Nursing—General	M
Reading Education	M,O
Secondary Education	M
Social Work	M
Special Education	M
Student Affairs	M

CALIFORNIA STATE UNIVERSITY CHANNEL ISLANDS

Business Administration and Management—	
General	M
Educational Leadership and Administration	M

CALIFORNIA STATE UNIVERSITY, CHICO

Business Administration and Management—	
General	M
Communication Disorders	M
Curriculum and Instruction	M
Education—General	M
Foreign Languages Education	M
Health Services Management and Hospital Administration	M
Kinesiology and Movement Studies	M
Mathematics Education	M
Multilingual and Multicultural Education	M
Nursing—General	M
Reading Education	M
Recreation and Park Management	M
Science Education	M
Social Sciences Education	M
Social Work	M
Special Education	M

CALIFORNIA STATE UNIVERSITY, DOMINGUEZ HILLS

Business Administration and Management—	
General	M
Computer Education	M,O
Counselor Education	M
Curriculum and Instruction	M
Education—General	M,O
Educational Leadership and Administration	M
English as a Second Language	M,O
Health Education	M
International and Comparative Education	M
Mathematics Education	M
Multilingual and Multicultural Education	M
Nursing—General	M
Occupational Therapy	M
Physical Education	M
Physician Assistant Studies	M
Quality Management	M
Social Work	M
Special Education	M

CALIFORNIA STATE UNIVERSITY, EAST BAY

Accounting	M
Communication Disorders	M
Counselor Education	M
Early Childhood Education	M
Education—General	M
Educational Leadership and Administration	M,D
Educational Media/ Instructional Technology	M
Entrepreneurship	M
Finance and Banking	M
Health Services Management and Hospital Administration	M
Human Resources Management	M
Industrial and Manufacturing Management	M
International Business	M
Marketing	M
Physical Education	M
Reading Education	M
Recreation and Park Management	M
Social Work	M
Special Education	M
Taxation	M
Travel and Tourism	M

CALIFORNIA STATE UNIVERSITY, FRESNO

Accounting	M
Business Administration and Management—	
General	M

Communication Disorders	M
Counselor Education	M
Curriculum and Instruction	M
Early Childhood Education	M
Education—General	M,D
Educational Leadership and Administration	M,D
English as a Second Language	M
Exercise and Sports Science	M
Family Nurse Practitioner Studies	M
Health Promotion	M
Health Services Management and Hospital Administration	M
Kinesiology and Movement Studies	M
Mathematics Education	M
Music Education	M
Nursing Education	M
Nursing—General	M
Physical Therapy	M,D
Public Health—General	M
Reading Education	M
Social Sciences Education	M
Social Work	M
Special Education	M

CALIFORNIA STATE UNIVERSITY, FULLERTON

Accounting	M
Advertising and Public Relations	M
Business Administration and Management—	
General	M
Communication Disorders	M
Counselor Education	M
Educational Leadership and Administration	M,D
Educational Media/ Instructional Technology	M
Electronic Commerce	M
Elementary Education	M
English as a Second Language	M
Entrepreneurship	M
Finance and Banking	M
International Business	M
Management Information Systems	M
Marketing	M
Mathematics Education	M
Middle School Education	M
Multilingual and Multicultural Education	M
Music Education	M
Nursing—General	M
Physical Education	M
Public Health—General	M
Reading Education	M
Science Education	M
Secondary Education	M
Social Work	M
Special Education	M
Taxation	M
Travel and Tourism	M

CALIFORNIA STATE UNIVERSITY, LONG BEACH

Art Education	M
Athletic Training and Sports Medicine	M
Business Administration and Management—	
General	M
Communication Disorders	M
Counselor Education	M
Education—General	M,D
Educational Leadership and Administration	M,D
Educational Psychology	M,D
English as a Second Language	M
Exercise and Sports Science	M
Health Education	M
Health Services Management and Hospital Administration	M
Higher Education	M
Hospitality Management	M

---

*M—master's degree; P—first professional degree; D—doctorate; O—other advanced degree; *—Close-Up and/or Display*

Kinesiology and Movement Studies	M
Leisure Studies	M
Logistics	M
Mathematics Education	M
Nursing—General	M
Physical Education	M
Physical Therapy	M
Recreation and Park Management	M
Science Education	M
Secondary Education	M
Social Work	M
Special Education	M
Sports Management	M
Student Affairs	M

CALIFORNIA STATE UNIVERSITY, LOS ANGELES

Accounting	M
Art Education	M
Business Administration and Management— General	M
Communication Disorders	M
Counselor Education	M,D
Education—General	M,D
Elementary Education	M
Finance and Banking	M
Health Education	M
Health Services Management and Hospital Administration	M
International Business	M
Kinesiology and Movement Studies	M
Management Information Systems	M
Marketing	M
Music Education	M
Nursing—General	M
Physical Education	M
Reading Education	M
Secondary Education	M
Social Work	M
Special Education	M,D
Taxation	M

CALIFORNIA STATE UNIVERSITY, MONTEREY BAY

Business Administration and Management— General	M
Education—General	M
Educational Media/ Instructional Technology	M
Management Information Systems	M

CALIFORNIA STATE UNIVERSITY, NORTHRIDGE

Art Education	M
Business Administration and Management— General	M
Communication Disorders	M
Counselor Education	M
Curriculum and Instruction	M
Early Childhood Education	M
Education—General	M,D
Educational Leadership and Administration	M,D
Educational Media/ Instructional Technology	M
Educational Psychology	M
Elementary Education	M
English Education	M
Environmental and Occupational Health	M
Health Services Management and Hospital Administration	M
Hospitality Management	M
Industrial Hygiene	M
Kinesiology and Movement Studies	M
Mathematics Education	M
Multilingual and Multicultural Education	M
Music Education	M
Physical Therapy	M
Public Health—General	M
Reading Education	M
Recreation and Park Management	M

Science Education	M
Secondary Education	M
Social Work	M
Special Education	M
Taxation	M
Travel and Tourism	M

CALIFORNIA STATE UNIVERSITY, SACRAMENTO

Accounting	M
Business Administration and Management— General	M
Communication Disorders	M
Counselor Education	M
Curriculum and Instruction	M
Early Childhood Education	M
Education—General	M
Educational Leadership and Administration	M
English as a Second Language	M
Foreign Languages Education	M
Human Resources Development	M
Human Resources Management	M
Human Services	M
Management Information Systems	M
Multilingual and Multicultural Education	M
Nursing—General	M
Physical Education	M
Reading Education	M
Real Estate	M
Recreation and Park Management	M
Social Work	M
Special Education	M
Vocational and Technical Education	M

CALIFORNIA STATE UNIVERSITY, SAN BERNARDINO

Business Administration and Management— General	M
Counselor Education	M
Curriculum and Instruction	M
Education—General	M,D
Educational Leadership and Administration	M,D
Educational Media/ Instructional Technology	M
Elementary Education	M
English as a Second Language	M,D
English Education	M,D
Environmental Education	M
Health Education	M
Health Services Management and Hospital Administration	M
Kinesiology and Movement Studies	M
Mathematics Education	M
Multilingual and Multicultural Education	M
Nursing—General	M
Public Health—General	M
Reading Education	M
Science Education	M
Secondary Education	M
Social Sciences Education	M,D
Social Work	M
Special Education	M
Vocational and Technical Education	M

CALIFORNIA STATE UNIVERSITY, SAN MARCOS

Business Administration and Management— General	M
Education—General	M

CALIFORNIA STATE UNIVERSITY, STANISLAUS

Business Administration and Management— General	M
Community College Education	M,D

Counselor Education	M,D,O
Curriculum and Instruction	M,O
Education—General	M,D,O
Educational Leadership and Administration	M,D
Educational Media/ Instructional Technology	M,D
Elementary Education	M,O
English as a Second Language	M,O
Finance and Banking	M
International Business	M
Middle School Education	M,O
Multilingual and Multicultural Education	M,O
Physical Education	M
Reading Education	M,O
Secondary Education	M,O
Social Work	M
Special Education	M,D

CALIFORNIA UNIVERSITY OF PENNSYLVANIA

Athletic Training and Sports Medicine	M
Business Administration and Management— General	M
Communication Disorders	M
Counselor Education	M
Education—General	M
Educational Leadership and Administration	M
Elementary Education	M
Exercise and Sports Science	M
Legal and Justice Studies	M
Reading Education	M
Rehabilitation Sciences	M
Secondary Education	M
Social Work	M
Special Education	M
Sports Management	M
Vocational and Technical Education	M

CALIFORNIA WESTERN SCHOOL OF LAW

Accounting	P,M
Law	P,M

CALUMET COLLEGE OF SAINT JOSEPH

Educational Leadership and Administration	M
Quality Management	M

CALVIN COLLEGE

Curriculum and Instruction	M
Education—General	M
Educational Leadership and Administration	M
Reading Education	M
Special Education	M

CALVIN THEOLOGICAL SEMINARY

Religious Education	P,M,D

CAMBRIDGE COLLEGE

Business Administration and Management— General	M
Counselor Education	M,D,O
Curriculum and Instruction	M,D,O
Early Childhood Education	M,D,O
Education—General	M,D,O
Educational Leadership and Administration	M,D,O
Educational Measurement and Evaluation	M,D,O
Educational Media/ Instructional Technology	M,D,O
Elementary Education	M,D,O
English as a Second Language	M,D,O
Entrepreneurship	M
Health Education	M,D,O
Health Promotion	M,D,O
Health Services Management and Hospital Administration	M
Home Economics Education	M,D,O
Mathematics Education	M,D,O
Middle School Education	M,D,O

Nonprofit Management	M
Organizational Management	M
Reading Education	M,D,O
School Nursing	M,D,O
Science Education	M,D,O
Social Sciences Education	M,D,O
Special Education	M,D,O

CAMERON UNIVERSITY

Business Administration and Management— General	M
Education—General	M
Educational Leadership and Administration	M
Entrepreneurship	M

CAMPBELLSVILLE UNIVERSITY

Business Administration and Management— General	M
Curriculum and Instruction	M
Education—General	M
Music Education	M
Social Work	M
Special Education	M

CAMPBELL UNIVERSITY

Business Administration and Management— General	M
Counselor Education	M
Education—General	M
Educational Leadership and Administration	M
Elementary Education	M
English Education	M
Law	P
Mathematics Education	M
Middle School Education	M
Pharmaceutical Sciences	P,M
Pharmacy	P,M
Physical Education	M
Religious Education	P,M,D
Secondary Education	M
Social Sciences Education	M

CANADIAN COLLEGE OF NATUROPATHIC MEDICINE

Naturopathic Medicine	D*

CANADIAN MEMORIAL CHIROPRACTIC COLLEGE

Acupuncture and Oriental Medicine	O
Chiropractic	P,O

CANADIAN SOUTHERN BAPTIST SEMINARY

Religious Education	P,M

CANISIUS COLLEGE

Accounting	M
Business Administration and Management— General	M
Communication Disorders	M
Counselor Education	M
Early Childhood Education	M
Education—General	M
Educational Leadership and Administration	M
Elementary Education	M
Health Promotion	M
International Business	M
Marketing	M
Middle School Education	M
Physical Education	M
Reading Education	M
Rehabilitation Sciences	M
Secondary Education	M
Special Education	M
Sports Management	M
Student Affairs	M

CAPE BRETON UNIVERSITY

Art Education	M,O
Business Administration and Management— General	M
Counselor Education	M,O
Curriculum and Instruction	M,O
Education—General	M,O

Educational Media/	
Instructional Technology	M,O

CAPELLA UNIVERSITY

Accounting	M,D,O
Adult Education	M,D,O
Business Administration and Management—	
General	M,D,O
Curriculum and Instruction	M,D,O
Education—General	M,D,O
Educational Leadership and Administration	M,D,O
Educational Media/ Instructional Technology	M,D,O
Educational Psychology	M,D,O
Elementary Education	M,D,O
Environmental and Occupational Health	M,D
Finance and Banking	M,D,O
Health Services Management and Hospital Administration	M,D,O
Higher Education	M,D,O
Human Resources Management	M,D,O
Human Services	M,D,O
Management Information Systems	M,D,O
Marketing	M,D,O
Middle School Education	M,D,O
Multilingual and Multicultural Education	M,D,O
Nonprofit Management	M,D,O
Nursing Education	M,D
Organizational Management	M,D,O
Project Management	M,D,O
Reading Education	M,D,O

CAPITAL UNIVERSITY

Business Administration and Management—	
General	M
Law	P,M
Legal and Justice Studies	M
Music Education	M
Nursing and Healthcare Administration	M
Nursing—General	M
Taxation	M

CAPITOL COLLEGE

Business Administration and Management—	
General	M
Management Information Systems	M

CARDINAL STRITCH UNIVERSITY

Business Administration and Management—	
General	M
Computer Education	M
Education—General	M,D
Educational Leadership and Administration	M,D
Educational Media/ Instructional Technology	M
English as a Second Language	M
Nursing—General	M
Reading Education	M
Special Education	M
Sports Management	M
Urban Education	M,D

CARIBBEAN UNIVERSITY

Curriculum and Instruction	M,D
Early Childhood Education	M,D
Education—General	M,D
Educational Leadership and Administration	M,D
Elementary Education	M,D
English Education	M,D
Foreign Languages Education	M,D
Gerontological Nursing	M,D
Human Resources Management	M,D
Mathematics Education	M,D
Pediatric Nursing	M,D
Physical Education	M,D

Science Education	M,D
Social Sciences Education	M,D
Special Education	M,D

CARLETON UNIVERSITY

Business Administration and Management—	
General	M,D
Legal and Justice Studies	M,O
Social Work	M

CARLOS ALBIZU UNIVERSITY

Communication Disorders	M,D

CARLOS ALBIZU UNIVERSITY, MIAMI CAMPUS

Business Administration and Management—	
General	M,D
Education of the Gifted	M,D
English as a Second Language	M,D
Entrepreneurship	M,D
Nonprofit Management	M,D
Organizational Management	M,D
Special Education	M,D

CARLOW UNIVERSITY

Art Education	M
Business Administration and Management—	
General	M
Counselor Education	M
Early Childhood Education	M
Education—General	M
Educational Leadership and Administration	M
Educational Media/ Instructional Technology	M
Elementary Education	M
Family Nurse Practitioner Studies	M,D
Nonprofit Management	M
Nursing and Healthcare Administration	M,D
Nursing—General	M,D
Organizational Management	M
Secondary Education	M
Special Education	M

CARNEGIE MELLON UNIVERSITY

Accounting	D
Business Administration and Management—	
General	M,D
Education—General	M,D
Electronic Commerce	M
Entertainment Management	M
Entrepreneurship	D
Finance and Banking	D
Health Services Management and Hospital Administration	M
Industrial and Manufacturing Management	M,D
Management Information Systems	M,D
Marketing	D
Music Education	M
Organizational Behavior	D

CARROLL UNIVERSITY

Education—General	M
Physical Therapy	M,D

CARSON-NEWMAN COLLEGE

Counselor Education	M
Curriculum and Instruction	M
Education—General	M
Educational Leadership and Administration	M
Elementary Education	M
English as a Second Language	M
Family Nurse Practitioner Studies	M
Nursing Education	M
Nursing—General	M
Secondary Education	M

CARTHAGE COLLEGE

Art Education	M,O
Counselor Education	M,O
Education of the Gifted	M,O
Education—General	M,O
Educational Leadership and Administration	M,O
English Education	M,O
Reading Education	M,O
Science Education	M,O
Social Sciences Education	M,O

CASE WESTERN RESERVE UNIVERSITY

Accounting	M,D
Acute Care/Critical Care Nursing	M,D
Adult Nursing	M,D
Allopathic Medicine	P
Anesthesiologist Assistant Studies	M
Art Education	M
Bioethics	M
Business Administration and Management—	
General	M,D
Clinical Research	M
Communication Disorders	M,D
Community Health Nursing	M
Dentistry	P
Epidemiology	M,D
Family Nurse Practitioner Studies	M,D
Finance and Banking	M,D
Gerontological Nursing	M,D
Health Services Research	M,D
Human Resources Management	M
Industrial and Manufacturing Management	M,D
Law	P,M
Legal and Justice Studies	P,M
Logistics	M,D
Management Information Systems	M,D
Management Strategy and Policy	M
Marketing	M,D
Maternal and Child/ Neonatal Nursing	M,D
Medical/Surgical Nursing	M,D
Music Education	M,D
Nonprofit Management	M,O
Nurse Anesthesia	M
Nurse Midwifery	M,D
Nursing Informatics	M
Nursing—General	M,D
Oral and Dental Sciences	M,O
Organizational Behavior	M
Pediatric Nursing	M,D
Psychiatric Nursing	M,D
Public Health—General	M
Quality Management	M,D
Social Work	M,D
Supply Chain Management	M
Women's Health Nursing	M,D

CASTLETON STATE COLLEGE

Curriculum and Instruction	M
Education—General	M,O
Educational Leadership and Administration	M,O
Reading Education	M,O
Special Education	M,O

CATAWBA COLLEGE

Education—General	M
Elementary Education	M

THE CATHOLIC UNIVERSITY OF AMERICA

Adult Nursing	M,D,O
Business Administration and Management—	
General	M
Clinical Laboratory Sciences/Medical Technology	M,D
Community Health Nursing	M,D,O

Community Health	M,D,O
Curriculum and Instruction	M,D,O
Education—General	M,D,O
Educational Leadership and Administration	P,M,D,O
Educational Psychology	M,D,O
Family Nurse Practitioner Studies	M,D,O
Gerontological Nursing	M,D,O
Human Resources Management	M*
Information Studies	M
International Health	M,D,O
Law	P
Legal and Justice Studies	D,O
Library Science	M
Medical Imaging	M,D
Music Education	M,D,O
Nursing Education	M,D,O
Nursing—General	M,D,O
Pediatric Nursing	M,D,O
Psychiatric Nursing	M,D,O
Religious Education	P,M,D,O
Secondary Education	M,D,O
Social Work	M,D
Special Education	M,D,O

CEDAR CREST COLLEGE

Education—General	M

CEDARVILLE UNIVERSITY

Education—General	M

CENTENARY COLLEGE

Accounting	M
Business Administration and Management—	
General	M
Education—General	M
Educational Leadership and Administration	M
Special Education	M

CENTENARY COLLEGE OF LOUISIANA

Business Administration and Management—	
General	M
Curriculum and Instruction	M
Education—General	M
Educational Leadership and Administration	M
Elementary Education	M
Secondary Education	M

CENTRAL CONNECTICUT STATE UNIVERSITY

Actuarial Science	M,O
Advertising and Public Relations	M,O
Art Education	M,O
Business Administration and Management—	
General	M,O
Business Education	M,O
Counselor Education	M,O
Early Childhood Education	M
Education—General	M,D,O
Educational Leadership and Administration	M,D,O
Educational Media/ Instructional Technology	M
Elementary Education	M,O
English as a Second Language	M,O
Exercise and Sports Science	M,O
Foreign Languages Education	M,O
Foundations and Philosophy of Education	M
Industrial and Manufacturing Management	M,O
Information Studies	M
Logistics	M,O
Music Education	M,O
Nurse Anesthesia	M,O
Physical Education	M,O
Reading Education	M,O
Science Education	M,O
Secondary Education	M
Special Education	M,O

Supply Chain
 Management | M,O
Vocational and Technical
 Education | M,O

CENTRAL EUROPEAN UNIVERSITY

Business Administration
 and Management—
 General | M
Finance and Banking | M
International Business | M,D
Law | M,D
Legal and Justice Studies | M,D
Management Information
 Systems | M
Marketing | M
Real Estate | M

CENTRAL METHODIST UNIVERSITY

Counselor Education | M
Education—General | M
Nursing and Healthcare
 Administration | M
Nursing—General | M

CENTRAL MICHIGAN UNIVERSITY

Accounting | M
Adult Education | M
Business Administration
 and Management—
 General | M,O
Communication Disorders | M,D
Community College
 Education | M
Counselor Education | M
Curriculum and Instruction | M,D,O
Early Childhood Education | M,O
Education—General | M,D,O
Educational Leadership
 and Administration | M,D,O
Educational Media/
 Instructional Technology | M,D,O
Elementary Education | M,O
English as a Second
 Language | M
Exercise and Sports
 Science | M
Finance and Banking | M
Health Services
 Management and
 Hospital Administration | M,D,O
Higher Education | M,D,O
Hospitality Management | M
Human Resources
 Management | M,O
Industrial and
 Manufacturing
 Management | M
International Business | M,O
International Health | D,O
Leisure Studies | M
Logistics | M,O
Management Information
 Systems | M,O
Marketing | M
Mathematics Education | M,D
Middle School Education | M
Music Education | M
Physical Education | M
Physical Therapy | M,D
Physician Assistant
 Studies | M,D
Reading Education | M,O
Recreation and Park
 Management | M,O
Rehabilitation Sciences | M,D
Science Education | M
Secondary Education | M,O
Special Education | M
Sports Management | M,O
Student Affairs | M,D,O

CENTRAL STATE UNIVERSITY

Education—General | M

CENTRAL WASHINGTON UNIVERSITY

Accounting | M
Counselor Education | M
Education—General | M
English as a Second
 Language | M
Exercise and Sports
 Science | M

Home Economics
 Education | M
Reading Education | M
Special Education | M

CHADRON STATE COLLEGE

Business Administration
 and Management—
 General | M
Business Education | M,O
Counselor Education | M,O
Education—General | M,O
Educational Leadership
 and Administration | M,O
Elementary Education | M,O
English Education | M,O
Secondary Education | M,O
Social Sciences Education | M,O

CHAMINADE UNIVERSITY OF HONOLULU

Business Administration
 and Management—
 General | M
Education—General | M
Social Sciences Education | M

CHANCELLOR UNIVERSITY

Business Administration
 and Management—
 General | M

CHAPMAN UNIVERSITY

Business Administration
 and Management—
 General | M
Communication Disorders | M
Counselor Education | M,O
Curriculum and Instruction | M,D
Education—General | M,D,O
Educational Leadership
 and Administration | M,O
Educational Psychology | M,O
Elementary Education | M,O
Environmental Law | P,M
Law | P,M
Physical Therapy | D
Reading Education | M,O
Secondary Education | M
Special Education | M,O
Taxation | P,M

CHARLES DREW UNIVERSITY OF MEDICINE AND SCIENCE

Allopathic Medicine | P
Public Health—General | M

CHARLESTON SOUTHERN UNIVERSITY

Accounting | M
Business Administration
 and Management—
 General | M
Education—General | M
Educational Leadership
 and Administration | M
Elementary Education | M
Finance and Banking | M
Health Services
 Management and
 Hospital Administration | M
Management Information
 Systems | M
Organizational
 Management | M
Secondary Education | M

CHARLOTTE SCHOOL OF LAW

Law | P

CHATHAM UNIVERSITY

Accounting | M
Art Education | M
Business Administration
 and Management—
 General | M
Early Childhood Education | M
Education—General | M
Elementary Education | M
English Education | M
Environmental Education | M
Mathematics Education | M
Nursing and Healthcare
 Administration | M,D
Nursing Education | M,D

Nursing—General | M,D
Occupational Therapy | M,D
Physical Therapy | D
Physician Assistant
 Studies | M
Science Education | M
Secondary Education | M
Social Sciences Education | M
Special Education | M

CHESTNUT HILL COLLEGE

Early Childhood Education | M
Education—General | M
Educational Leadership
 and Administration | M
Educational Media/
 Instructional Technology | M,O
Elementary Education | M
Human Services | M,O
Secondary Education | M

CHEYNEY UNIVERSITY OF PENNSYLVANIA

Adult Education | M
Early Childhood Education | O
Education—General | M,O
Educational Leadership
 and Administration | M,O
Elementary Education | M
Special Education | M

THE CHICAGO SCHOOL OF PROFESSIONAL PSYCHOLOGY

Counselor Education | M,D

CHICAGO STATE UNIVERSITY

Counselor Education | M
Early Childhood Education | M
Education—General | M,D
Educational Leadership
 and Administration | M,D
Educational Media/
 Instructional Technology | M
Elementary Education | M
Foundations and
 Philosophy of Education | M
Higher Education | M,D
Library Science | M
Middle School Education | M
Multilingual and
 Multicultural Education | M
Physical Education | M
Reading Education | M
Secondary Education | M
Social Work | M
Special Education | M
Vocational and Technical
 Education | M

CHRISTIAN BROTHERS UNIVERSITY

Business Administration
 and Management—
 General | M,O
Curriculum and Instruction | M
Education—General | M
Educational Leadership
 and Administration | M
Finance and Banking | M,O
Project Management | M,O

CHRISTOPHER NEWPORT UNIVERSITY

Art Education | M
Computer Education | M
Education—General | M
Elementary Education | M
English Education | M
Foreign Languages
 Education | M
Mathematics Education | M
Music Education | M
Science Education | M
Social Sciences Education | M

THE CITADEL, THE MILITARY COLLEGE OF SOUTH CAROLINA

Business Administration
 and Management—
 General | M
Counselor Education | M,O
Education—General | M,O
Educational Leadership
 and Administration | M,O
Elementary Education | M

English Education | M
Health Education | M
Mathematics Education | M
Physical Education | M
Reading Education | M
Science Education | M
Secondary Education | M
Social Sciences Education | M
Student Affairs | M

CITY COLLEGE OF THE CITY UNIVERSITY OF NEW YORK

Early Childhood Education | M
Education—General | M,O
Educational Leadership
 and Administration | M,O
English Education | M,O
Mathematics Education | M,O
Middle School Education | M,O
Multilingual and
 Multicultural Education | M
Reading Education | M
Science Education | M
Secondary Education | M,O
Social Sciences Education | M,O
Special Education | M

CITY UNIVERSITY OF NEW YORK SCHOOL OF LAW AT QUEENS COLLEGE

Law | P

CITY UNIVERSITY OF SEATTLE

Accounting | M,O
Business Administration
 and Management—
 General | M,O
Curriculum and Instruction | M,O
Education—General | M,O
Educational Leadership
 and Administration | M,O
Educational Media/
 Instructional Technology | M,O
Elementary Education | M,O
Finance and Banking | M,O
International Business | M,O
Management Information
 Systems | M,O
Marketing | M,O
Organizational
 Management | M,O
Project Management | M,O
Reading Education | M,O
Special Education | M,O
Sustainability
 Management | M,O

CLAFLIN UNIVERSITY

Business Administration
 and Management—
 General | M
Education—General | M

CLAREMONT GRADUATE UNIVERSITY

Business Administration
 and Management—
 General | M,D,O*
Education—General | M,D,O
Educational Leadership
 and Administration | M,D,O
Educational Measurement
 and Evaluation | M,D,O
Electronic Commerce | M,D,O
Health Promotion | M,D
Higher Education | M,D,O
Human Resources
 Development | M,D,O
Human Resources
 Management | M
Information Studies | M,D,O
Management Information
 Systems | M,D,O
Management Strategy and
 Policy | M,D,O
Public Health—General | M,D
Special Education | M,D,O
Student Affairs | M,D,O
Urban Education | M,D,O

CLAREMONT MCKENNA COLLEGE

Finance and Banking | M*

CLAREMONT SCHOOL OF THEOLOGY

Religious Education	M,D

CLARION UNIVERSITY OF PENNSYLVANIA

Business Administration and Management—General	M
Communication Disorders	M
Curriculum and Instruction	M
Early Childhood Education	M
Education—General	M,O
Elementary Education	M
English Education	M
Library Science	M,O
Nursing—General	M
Reading Education	M
Rehabilitation Sciences	M
Science Education	M
Social Sciences Education	M
Special Education	M
Vocational and Technical Education	M

CLARK ATLANTA UNIVERSITY

Accounting	M
Business Administration and Management—General	M
Counselor Education	M
Curriculum and Instruction	M
Education—General	M,D,O
Educational Leadership and Administration	M,D,O
Educational Psychology	M
Social Work	M,D

CLARKE COLLEGE

Business Administration and Management—General	M
Early Childhood Education	M
Education—General	M
Educational Leadership and Administration	M
Educational Media/Instructional Technology	M
Family Nurse Practitioner Studies	M,O
Nursing and Healthcare Administration	M,O
Nursing Education	M,O
Nursing—General	M,O
Physical Therapy	D
Reading Education	M
Special Education	M

CLARKSON COLLEGE

Adult Nursing	M,O
Family Nurse Practitioner Studies	M,O
Nursing and Healthcare Administration	M,O
Nursing Education	M,O
Nursing—General	M,O

CLARKSON UNIVERSITY

Business Administration and Management—General	M
Physical Therapy	D

CLARK UNIVERSITY

Accounting	M
Business Administration and Management—General	M
Education—General	M
Finance and Banking	M
Health Services Management and Hospital Administration	M
International Business	M
Management Information Systems	M
Marketing	M

CLAYTON STATE UNIVERSITY

Business Administration and Management—General	M
Education—General	M

English Education	M
Health Services Management and Hospital Administration	M
Mathematics Education	M
Nursing—General	M

CLEARWATER CHRISTIAN COLLEGE

Educational Leadership and Administration	M

CLEARY UNIVERSITY

Accounting	M,O
Business Administration and Management—General	M,O
Finance and Banking	M,O
Nonprofit Management	M,O
Organizational Management	M,O

CLEMSON UNIVERSITY

Accounting	M
Agricultural Education	M
Business Administration and Management—General	M
Counselor Education	M
Curriculum and Instruction	D
Early Childhood Education	M
Education—General	M,D,O
Educational Leadership and Administration	M,D,O
Elementary Education	M
English Education	M
Human Resources Development	M
Marketing	M
Mathematics Education	M
Middle School Education	M
Nursing—General	M,D
Reading Education	M
Real Estate	M
Recreation and Park Management	M,D
Science Education	M
Secondary Education	M
Social Sciences Education	M
Special Education	M
Travel and Tourism	M,D
Veterinary Sciences	M,D

CLEVELAND CHIROPRACTIC COLLEGE–KANSAS CITY CAMPUS

Chiropractic	P
Health Promotion	M

CLEVELAND CHIROPRACTIC COLLEGE–LOS ANGELES CAMPUS

Chiropractic	P
Health Promotion	M

CLEVELAND STATE UNIVERSITY

Accounting	M
Adult Education	M,O
Allied Health—General	M
Art Education	M
Bioethics	M,O
Business Administration and Management—General	M,D
Communication Disorders	M
Community Health Nursing	M
Counselor Education	M,D,O
Early Childhood Education	M
Education of Students with Severe/Multiple Disabilities	M
Education—General	M,D,O
Educational Leadership and Administration	M,D,O
English as a Second Language	M
Exercise and Sports Science	M
Finance and Banking	M,D,O
Foreign Languages Education	M
Forensic Nursing	M
Health Education	M

Health Services Management and Hospital Administration	M
Human Resources Management	M
Industrial and Manufacturing Management	D
International Business	M,D,O
Law	P,M
Management Information Systems	M,D
Marketing	M,D,O
Mathematics Education	M
Medical Imaging	M
Medical Physics	M
Middle School Education	M
Music Education	M
Nonprofit Management	M,D,O
Nursing Education	M
Nursing—General	M
Occupational Therapy	M
Physical Education	M
Physical Therapy	D
Physician Assistant Studies	M,D
Public Health—General	M
Real Estate	M,D,O
Science Education	M
Social Work	M
Special Education	M
Sports Management	M
Student Affairs	M,O
Taxation	M
Urban Education	D

COASTAL CAROLINA UNIVERSITY

Accounting	M
Business Administration and Management—General	M
Education—General	M
Educational Leadership and Administration	M
Secondary Education	M

COE COLLEGE

Education—General	M

COLGATE UNIVERSITY

Secondary Education	M

THE COLLEGE AT BROCKPORT, STATE UNIVERSITY OF NEW YORK

Accounting	M
Community Health	M
Counselor Education	M,O
Curriculum and Instruction	M
Education—General	M,O
Educational Leadership and Administration	O
English Education	M
Foreign Languages Education	M,O
Health Education	M
Health Services Management and Hospital Administration	M,O
Leisure Studies	M
Mathematics Education	M
Middle School Education	M
Multilingual and Multicultural Education	M,O
Nonprofit Management	M,O
Physical Education	M
Reading Education	M
Recreation and Park Management	M
Science Education	M
Social Sciences Education	M
Social Work	M
Sports Management	M

COLLEGE FOR FINANCIAL PLANNING

Finance and Banking	M

COLLEGE OF CHARLESTON

Accounting	M
Business Administration and Management—General	M
Early Childhood Education	M

Education—General	M,O
Elementary Education	M
English as a Second Language	O
Foreign Languages Education	M
Legal and Justice Studies	M,O
Management Information Systems	M
Mathematics Education	M
Music Education	M
Science Education	M
Special Education	M

THE COLLEGE OF IDAHO

Education—General	M

COLLEGE OF MOUNT ST. JOSEPH

Art Education	M
Early Childhood Education	M
Education—General	M
Educational Leadership and Administration	M
Middle School Education	M
Multilingual and Multicultural Education	M
Music Education	M
Nursing—General	M
Organizational Management	M
Physical Therapy	D
Reading Education	M
Religious Education	M,O
Secondary Education	M

COLLEGE OF MOUNT SAINT VINCENT

Adult Nursing	M,O
Education—General	M,O
Educational Media/Instructional Technology	M,O
Family Nurse Practitioner Studies	M,O
Gerontological Nursing	M,O
Middle School Education	M,O
Multilingual and Multicultural Education	M,O
Nursing and Healthcare Administration	M,O
Nursing Education	M,O
Nursing—General	M,O
Urban Education	M,O

THE COLLEGE OF NEW JERSEY

Counselor Education	M
Early Childhood Education	M
Education—General	M,O
Educational Leadership and Administration	M,O
Elementary Education	M
English as a Second Language	M,O
Health Education	M
International and Comparative Education	M,O
Nursing—General	M,O
Physical Education	M
Reading Education	M
Secondary Education	M
Special Education	M,O

THE COLLEGE OF NEW ROCHELLE

Acute Care/Critical Care Nursing	M,O
Art Education	M
Early Childhood Education	M
Education of the Gifted	M,O
Education—General	M,O
Educational Leadership and Administration	M,O
Elementary Education	M
English as a Second Language	M,O
Family Nurse Practitioner Studies	M,O
Human Resources Development	M
Multilingual and Multicultural Education	M,O
Nursing and Healthcare Administration	M,O
Nursing Education	M,O

Nursing—General M,O
Reading Education M
Special Education M

COLLEGE OF NOTRE DAME OF MARYLAND

Business Administration
and Management—
General M
Education—General M
Educational Leadership
and Administration M,D
English as a Second
Language M
Nonprofit Management M

COLLEGE OF SAINT ELIZABETH

Business Administration
and Management—
General M
Education—General M,D,O
Educational Leadership
and Administration M,D,O
Educational Media/
Instructional Technology M,D,O
Health Services
Management and
Hospital Administration M
Higher Education M,O
Nursing—General M
Student Affairs M,O

COLLEGE OF ST. JOSEPH

Business Administration
and Management—
General M
Counselor Education M
Education—General M
Elementary Education M
English Education M
Reading Education M
Secondary Education M
Social Sciences Education M
Special Education M

COLLEGE OF SAINT MARY

Education—General M
Educational Leadership
and Administration M
Educational Measurement
and Evaluation M
English as a Second
Language M
Health Education D
Nursing—General M
Occupational Therapy M
Organizational
Management M

THE COLLEGE OF SAINT ROSE

Accounting M
Art Education M,O
Business Administration
and Management—
General M
Business Education M,O
Communication Disorders M
Counselor Education M
Curriculum and Instruction M,O
Early Childhood Education M,O
Education—General M,O
Educational Leadership
and Administration M,O
Educational Media/
Instructional Technology M,O
Educational Psychology M,O
Elementary Education M,O
Multilingual and
Multicultural Education M,O
Music Education M,O
Nonprofit Management O
Reading Education M,O
Secondary Education M,O
Special Education M,O
Student Affairs M,O

THE COLLEGE OF ST. SCHOLASTICA

Business Administration
and Management—
General M,O
Education—General M,O
Educational Media/
Instructional Technology M

Exercise and Sports
Science M
Management Information
Systems M,O
Nursing—General M,O
Occupational Therapy M
Physical Therapy D

COLLEGE OF SANTA FE

Business Administration
and Management—
General M
Counselor Education M
Curriculum and Instruction M
Education—General M
Educational Leadership
and Administration M
Finance and Banking M
Human Resources
Management M
Multilingual and
Multicultural Education M
Special Education M

COLLEGE OF STATEN ISLAND OF THE CITY UNIVERSITY OF NEW YORK

Adult Nursing M,O
Business Administration
and Management—
General M
Education—General M,O
Educational Leadership
and Administration O
Elementary Education M
Gerontological Nursing M,O
Middle School Education M
Nursing Education O
Nursing—General M,O
Secondary Education M
Special Education M

COLLEGE OF THE HUMANITIES AND SCIENCES, HARRISON MIDDLETON UNIVERSITY

Education—General M,D
Legal and Justice Studies M,D
Science Education M,D

THE COLLEGE OF WILLIAM AND MARY

Accounting M
Business Administration
and Management—
General M
Counselor Education M,D
Curriculum and Instruction M,D
Education of the Gifted M
Education—General M,D,O
Educational Leadership
and Administration M,D
Educational Media/
Instructional Technology M,D
Educational Policy M,D
Elementary Education M
English Education M
Foreign Languages
Education M
Law P,M
Mathematics Education M
Reading Education M
Science Education M
Secondary Education M
Social Sciences Education M
Special Education M

COLLÈGE UNIVERSITAIRE DE SAINT-BONIFACE

Education—General M

COLORADO CHRISTIAN UNIVERSITY

Business Administration
and Management—
General M
Curriculum and Instruction M
Education—General M

THE COLORADO COLLEGE

Art Education M
Education—General M
Elementary Education M
English Education M
Foreign Languages
Education M

Mathematics Education M
Music Education M
Science Education M
Secondary Education M
Social Sciences Education M

COLORADO SCHOOL OF TRADITIONAL CHINESE MEDICINE

Acupuncture and Oriental
Medicine M

COLORADO STATE UNIVERSITY

Accounting M
Adult Education M,D
Advertising and Public
Relations M,D
Business Administration
and Management—
General M
Community College
Education M,D
Counselor Education M,D
Education—General M,D
Educational Leadership
and Administration M,D
Environmental and
Occupational Health M,D
Exercise and Sports
Science M,D
Finance and Banking M
Foreign Languages
Education M
Management Information
Systems M
Occupational Therapy M
Organizational
Management M
Recreation and Park
Management M,D
Social Work M
Student Affairs M,D
Sustainability
Management M
Veterinary Medicine P
Veterinary Sciences M,D
Vocational and Technical
Education M,D

COLORADO STATE UNIVERSITY–PUEBLO

Art Education M
Business Administration
and Management—
General M
Education—General M
Educational Media/
Instructional Technology M
Foreign Languages
Education M
Health Education M
Music Education M
Nursing—General M
Physical Education M
Special Education M

COLORADO TECHNICAL UNIVERSITY COLORADO SPRINGS

Accounting M,D
Business Administration
and Management—
General M,D
Finance and Banking M,D
Human Resources
Management M,D
Industrial and
Manufacturing
Management M,D
Logistics M,D
Marketing M,D
Project Management M,D

COLORADO TECHNICAL UNIVERSITY DENVER

Accounting M
Business Administration
and Management—
General M
Finance and Banking M
Human Resources
Management M
Industrial and
Manufacturing
Management M
Marketing M
Project Management M

COLORADO TECHNICAL UNIVERSITY SIOUX FALLS

Business Administration
and Management—
General M
Health Services
Management and
Hospital Administration M
Human Resources
Management M
Management Information
Systems M
Organizational
Management M
Project Management M

COLUMBIA COLLEGE (MO)

Business Administration
and Management—
General M
Education—General M

COLUMBIA COLLEGE (SC)

Education—General M
Elementary Education M
Organizational Behavior M,O

COLUMBIA COLLEGE CHICAGO

Education—General M
Elementary Education M
English Education M
Entertainment
Management M
Multilingual and
Multicultural Education M
Urban Education M

COLUMBIA INTERNATIONAL UNIVERSITY

Counselor Education M,D,O
Curriculum and Instruction M,D,O
Early Childhood Education M,D,O
Education—General M,D,O
Educational Leadership
and Administration M,D,O
Educational Media/
Instructional Technology M,D,O
Elementary Education M,D,O
English as a Second
Language M,D,O
Higher Education M,D,O
Multilingual and
Multicultural Education M,D,O
Religious Education P,M,D,O
Special Education M,D,O

COLUMBIA SOUTHERN UNIVERSITY

Business Administration
and Management—
General M,D
Electronic Commerce M
Environmental and
Occupational Health M
Finance and Banking M
Health Services
Management and
Hospital Administration M
Hospitality Management M
Human Resources
Management M
International Business M
Marketing M

COLUMBIA UNIVERSITY

Accounting M,D
Actuarial Science M
Acute Care/Critical Care
Nursing M,O
Adult Nursing M,O
Allopathic Medicine P,M
Bioethics M
Business Administration
and Management—
General M,D
Community Health M,D
Dentistry P
Entrepreneurship M
Environmental and
Occupational Health M,D
Epidemiology M,D
Family Nurse Practitioner
Studies M,O
Finance and Banking M,D
Gerontological Nursing M,O

Health Services
  Management and
  Hospital Administration — M
Human Resources
  Management — M
Information Studies — M
International Business — M
Kinesiology and
  Movement Studies — M,D
Law — P,M,D
Marketing — M,D
Maternal and Child Health — M
Maternal and Child/
  Neonatal Nursing — M,O
Medical Physics — M,D,O
Medical/Surgical Nursing — M,O
Nonprofit Management — M
Nurse Anesthesia — M,O
Nurse Midwifery — M
Nursing—General — M,D,O*
Occupational Therapy — M,D
Oncology Nursing — M,O
Oral and Dental Sciences — M,D,O
Pediatric Nursing — M,O
Pharmaceutical
  Administration — M
Physical Therapy — D
Psychiatric Nursing — M,O
Public Health—General — M,D
Real Estate — M
Science Education — M,D,O
Social Work — M,D
Sports Management — M
Sustainability
  Management — M
Women's Health Nursing — O

COLUMBUS STATE UNIVERSITY

Art Education — M
Business Administration
  and Management—
  General — M
Counselor Education — M,D,O
Curriculum and Instruction — M,D,O
Early Childhood Education — M,O
Education—General — M,D,O
Educational Leadership
  and Administration — M,D,O
English Education — M,O
Health Services
  Management and
  Hospital Administration — M,O
Mathematics Education — M,O
Middle School Education — M,O
Music Education — M,O
Physical Education — M,O
Science Education — M,O
Secondary Education — M,O
Social Sciences Education — M,O
Special Education — M,O

CONCORDIA COLLEGE

Education—General — M
Foreign Languages
  Education — M

CONCORDIA UNIVERSITY (CA)

Business Administration
  and Management—
  General — M
Curriculum and Instruction — M
Education—General — M
Educational Leadership
  and Administration — M
Physical Education — M
Sports Management — M

CONCORDIA UNIVERSITY (CANADA)

Accounting — M,D,O
Adult Education — M,O
Art Education — M,D
Aviation Management — M,D,O
Business Administration
  and Management—
  General — M,D,O
Education—General — M,D,O
Educational Media/
  Instructional Technology — M,D,O
English as a Second
  Language — M,O
Exercise and Sports
  Science — M

Health Services
  Management and
  Hospital Administration — M,D,O
Investment Management — M,D,O
Mathematics Education — M,D
Organizational
  Management — M
Sports Management — M,D,O
Transportation
  Management — M,D,O

CONCORDIA UNIVERSITY (MI)

Curriculum and Instruction — M
Educational Leadership
  and Administration — M
Organizational
  Management — M

CONCORDIA UNIVERSITY (OR)

Business Administration
  and Management—
  General — M
Curriculum and Instruction — M
Education—General — M
Educational Leadership
  and Administration — M
Elementary Education — M
Secondary Education — M

CONCORDIA UNIVERSITY CHICAGO

Business Administration
  and Management—
  General — M
Counselor Education — M,O
Curriculum and Instruction — M
Early Childhood Education — M,D
Education—General — M
Educational Leadership
  and Administration — M,D,O
Educational Media/
  Instructional Technology — M
Elementary Education — M
Exercise and Sports
  Science — M
Human Services — M
Reading Education — M
Religious Education — M
Secondary Education — M

CONCORDIA UNIVERSITY, NEBRASKA

Early Childhood Education — M
Education—General — M
Educational Leadership
  and Administration — M
Elementary Education — M
Reading Education — M
Religious Education — M
Secondary Education — M

CONCORDIA UNIVERSITY, ST. PAUL

Business Administration
  and Management—
  General — M
Curriculum and Instruction — M,O
Early Childhood Education — M,O
Education—General — M,O
Educational Leadership
  and Administration — M,O
Health Services
  Management and
  Hospital Administration — M
Human Resources
  Management — M
Organizational
  Management — M
Reading Education — M,O
Religious Education — M,O
Special Education — M,O
Sports Management — M,O

CONCORDIA UNIVERSITY TEXAS

Education—General — M

CONCORDIA UNIVERSITY WISCONSIN

Art Education — M
Business Administration
  and Management—
  General — M
Counselor Education — M

Curriculum and Instruction — M
Early Childhood Education — M
Education—General — M
Educational Leadership
  and Administration — M
Environmental Education — M
Family Nurse Practitioner
  Studies — M
Finance and Banking — M
Gerontological Nursing — M
Health Services
  Management and
  Hospital Administration — M
Human Resources
  Management — M
Human Services — M,D
International Business — M
Management Information
  Systems — M
Marketing — M
Nursing Education — M
Nursing—General — M
Occupational Therapy — M
Physical Therapy — M,D
Reading Education — M
Rehabilitation Sciences — M
Special Education — M
Student Affairs — M

CONCORD LAW SCHOOL

Law — P

CONCORD UNIVERSITY

Educational Leadership
  and Administration — M
Health Promotion — M
Reading Education — M
Social Sciences Education — M

CONSERVATORIO DE MUSICA

Music Education — M

CONVERSE COLLEGE

Art Education — M,O
Curriculum and Instruction — O
Early Childhood Education — M,O
Education of the Gifted — M
Education—General — M,O
Educational Leadership
  and Administration — M,O
Elementary Education — M
English Education — M
Mathematics Education — M
Music Education — M
Science Education — M
Secondary Education — M
Social Sciences Education — M
Special Education — M

COPPIN STATE UNIVERSITY

Adult Education — M
Curriculum and Instruction — M
Education—General — M
Family Nurse Practitioner
  Studies — M,O
Human Services — M
Nursing—General — M,O
Reading Education — M
Special Education — M

CORBAN UNIVERSITY

Business Administration
  and Management—
  General — M
Education—General — M
Nonprofit Management — M

CORCORAN COLLEGE OF ART AND DESIGN

Art Education — M

CORNELL UNIVERSITY

Accounting — D
Adult Education — M,D
Agricultural Education — M,D
Business Administration
  and Management—
  General — M,D
Curriculum and Instruction — M,D
Education—General — M,D
Epidemiology — M,D
Facilities Management — M
Finance and Banking — D

Foreign Languages
  Education — M,D
Health Services
  Management and
  Hospital Administration — M,D
Hospitality Management — M,D
Human Resources
  Management — M,D
Information Studies — D
Law — P,M,D
Marketing — D
Mathematics Education — M,D
Organizational Behavior — M,D
Real Estate — M
Science Education — M,D
Social Work — M,D
Veterinary Medicine — P

CORNELL UNIVERSITY, JOAN AND SANFORD I. WEILL MEDICAL COLLEGE AND GRADUATE SCHOOL OF MEDICAL SCIENCES

Epidemiology — M
Health Services Research — M

CORNERSTONE UNIVERSITY

Business Administration
  and Management—
  General — M,O
Education—General — M,O
English as a Second
  Language — M,O

COVENANT COLLEGE

Education—General — M

CREIGHTON UNIVERSITY

Allied Health—General — P,M,D
Allopathic Medicine — P
Business Administration
  and Management—
  General — M
Counselor Education — M
Dentistry — P
Education—General — M
Educational Leadership
  and Administration — M
Elementary Education — M
Law — P,M,O
Management Information
  Systems — M
Nursing—General — M,D
Occupational Therapy — D
Pharmaceutical Sciences — M,D
Pharmacy — P
Physical Therapy — D
Secondary Education — M
Special Education — M
Student Affairs — M

CUMBERLAND UNIVERSITY

Business Administration
  and Management—
  General — M
Education—General — M
Human Resources
  Management — M
Organizational
  Management — M

CURRY COLLEGE

Business Administration
  and Management—
  General — M,O
Education—General — M,O
Educational Leadership
  and Administration — M,O
Educational Measurement
  and Evaluation — M,O
Elementary Education — M,O
Finance and Banking — M,O
Foundations and
  Philosophy of Education — M,O
Reading Education — M,O
Special Education — M,O

DAEMEN COLLEGE

Adult Nursing — M,D,O
Business Administration
  and Management—
  General — M
Early Childhood Education — M
Education—General — M

*M—master's degree; P—first professional degree; D—doctorate; O—other advanced degree; *—Close-Up and/or Display*

International Business — M
Medical/Surgical Nursing — M,D,O
Middle School Education — M
Nursing and Healthcare
  Administration — M,D,O
Nursing Education — M,D,O
Nursing—General — M,D,O
Physical Therapy — D,O
Physician Assistant
  Studies — M
Special Education — M

DAKOTA STATE UNIVERSITY

Education—General — M
Educational Media/
  Instructional Technology — M

DAKOTA WESLEYAN UNIVERSITY

Curriculum and Instruction — M
Education—General — M
Educational Leadership
  and Administration — M
Secondary Education — M

DALHOUSIE UNIVERSITY

Allopathic Medicine — P,M,D
Business Administration
  and Management—
  General — M,O
Communication Disorders — M,D
Community Health — M
Electronic Commerce — M,D
Epidemiology — M
Finance and Banking — M
Health Education — M
Health Services
  Management and
  Hospital Administration — M,D
Information Studies — M
Kinesiology and
  Movement Studies — M
Law — M,D
Leisure Studies — M
Library Science — M
Management Information
  Systems — M
Nursing—General — M,D
Occupational Therapy — M
Oral and Dental Sciences
Physical Therapy — M
Social Work — M

DALLAS BAPTIST UNIVERSITY

Accounting — M
Business Administration
  and Management—
  General — M
Counselor Education — M
Curriculum and Instruction — M
Education—General — M
Educational Leadership
  and Administration — M
Electronic Commerce — M
Elementary Education — M
English as a Second
  Language — M
Entrepreneurship — M
Finance and Banking — M
Health Services
  Management and
  Hospital Administration — M
Higher Education — M
Human Resources
  Management — M
International Business — M
Kinesiology and
  Movement Studies — M
Management Information
  Systems — M
Marketing — M
Nonprofit Management — M
Project Management — M
Reading Education — M
Religious Education — M
Secondary Education — M

DALLAS THEOLOGICAL SEMINARY

Religious Education — M,D,O

DANIEL WEBSTER COLLEGE

Aviation Management — M
Business Administration
  and Management—
  General — M

DANIEL WEBSTER COLLEGE–PORTSMOUTH CAMPUS

Business Administration
  and Management—
  General — M

DARTMOUTH COLLEGE

Allopathic Medicine — P
Business Administration
  and Management—
  General — M
Health Services
  Management and
  Hospital Administration — M,D
Health Services Research — M,D
Pharmaceutical Sciences — D
Public Health—General — M

DAVENPORT UNIVERSITY

Accounting — M
Business Administration
  and Management—
  General — M
Finance and Banking — M
Health Services
  Management and
  Hospital Administration — M
Human Resources
  Management — M
Management Strategy and
  Policy — M
Marketing — M
Public Health—General — M

DAVENPORT UNIVERSITY

Accounting — M
Business Administration
  and Management—
  General — M
Finance and Banking — M
Health Services
  Management and
  Hospital Administration — M
Human Resources
  Management — M
Management Strategy and
  Policy — M
Public Health—General — M

DAVENPORT UNIVERSITY

Accounting — M
Business Administration
  and Management—
  General — M
Finance and Banking — M
Health Services
  Management and
  Hospital Administration — M
Human Resources
  Management — M
Public Health—General — M

DEFIANCE COLLEGE

Adult Education — M
Business Administration
  and Management—
  General — M
Education—General — M
Health Services
  Management and
  Hospital Administration — M
Management Strategy and
  Policy — M
Physical Education — M
Secondary Education — M
Special Education — M

DELAWARE STATE UNIVERSITY

Adult Education — M
Art Education — M
Business Administration
  and Management—
  General — M
Curriculum and Instruction — M
Education—General — M,D
Educational Leadership
  and Administration — M,D
Exercise and Sports
  Science — M
Foreign Languages
  Education — M
Mathematics Education — M
Nursing—General — M
Reading Education — M
Science Education — M,D

Social Work — M
Special Education — M

DELAWARE VALLEY COLLEGE

Accounting — M
Business Administration
  and Management—
  General — M
Curriculum and Instruction — M
Educational Leadership
  and Administration — M
Educational Media/
  Instructional Technology — M
International Business — M

DELTA STATE UNIVERSITY

Accounting — M
Aviation Management — M
Business Administration
  and Management—
  General — M
Counselor Education — M,D
Education—General — M,D,O
Educational Leadership
  and Administration — M,D,O
Elementary Education — M,D,O
English Education — M
Family Nurse Practitioner
  Studies — M
Health Services
  Management and
  Hospital Administration — M
Higher Education — D
Marketing — M
Mathematics Education — M
Nursing Education — M
Nursing—General — M
Physical Education — M
Recreation and Park
  Management — M
Science Education — M
Secondary Education — M,O
Social Sciences Education — M
Special Education — M

DEPAUL UNIVERSITY

Accounting — M
Actuarial Science — M,O
Adult Education — M
Adult Nursing — M
Advertising and Public
  Relations — M
Business Administration
  and Management—
  General — M
Counselor Education — M,D
Curriculum and Instruction — M,D
Education—General — M,D
Educational Leadership
  and Administration — M,D
Electronic Commerce — M,D
Elementary Education — M,D
Entrepreneurship — M
Finance and Banking — M,O
Health Law — P,M,O
Health Services
  Management and
  Hospital Administration — M,O
Human Resources
  Management — M
Human Services — M,D
Industrial and
  Manufacturing
  Management — M
International Business — M
Law — P,M
Management Information
  Systems — M,D
Management Strategy and
  Policy — M
Marketing — M
Mathematics Education — M,O
Multilingual and
  Multicultural Education — M,D
Music Education — M,O
Nonprofit Management — M,O
Nurse Anesthesia — M
Nursing—General — M
Physical Education — M,D
Project Management — M,D
Reading Education — M,D
Real Estate — M
Secondary Education — M,D
Special Education — M,D

Taxation — M
Urban Education — M,D

DESALES UNIVERSITY

Accounting — M
Adult Nursing — M
Business Administration
  and Management—
  General — M
Education—General — M
Educational Media/
  Instructional Technology — M
Elementary Education — M
English as a Second
  Language — M
Family Nurse Practitioner
  Studies — M
Finance and Banking — M
Health Services
  Management and
  Hospital Administration — M
Management Information
  Systems — M
Marketing — M
Mathematics Education — M
Nurse Midwifery — M
Nursing Education — M
Nursing—General — M
Physician Assistant
  Studies — M
Project Management — M
Special Education — M

DES MOINES UNIVERSITY

Health Services
  Management and
  Hospital Administration — M
Osteopathic Medicine — P
Physical Therapy — D
Physician Assistant
  Studies — M
Podiatric Medicine — P
Public Health—General — M

DEVRY UNIVERSITY (AZ)

Business Administration
  and Management—
  General — M,O

DEVRY UNIVERSITY (CA)

Business Administration
  and Management—
  General — M,O

DEVRY UNIVERSITY (CO)

Business Administration
  and Management—
  General — M,O

DEVRY UNIVERSITY (FL)

Business Administration
  and Management—
  General — M,O

DEVRY UNIVERSITY (GA)

Business Administration
  and Management—
  General — M,O

DEVRY UNIVERSITY (IL)

Accounting — M
Business Administration
  and Management—
  General — M
Finance and Banking — M
Human Resources
  Management — M
Management Information
  Systems — M
Project Management — M

DEVRY UNIVERSITY (IN)

Business Administration
  and Management—
  General — M,O

DEVRY UNIVERSITY (MD)

Business Administration
  and Management—
  General — M,O

DEVRY UNIVERSITY (MO)

Business Administration and Management— General	M,O

DEVRY UNIVERSITY (NC)

Business Administration and Management— General	M,O

DEVRY UNIVERSITY (NV)

Business Administration and Management— General	M,O

DEVRY UNIVERSITY (OH)

Business Administration and Management— General	M,O

DEVRY UNIVERSITY (OR)

Business Administration and Management— General	M,O

DEVRY UNIVERSITY (PA)

Business Administration and Management— General	M,O

DEVRY UNIVERSITY (TX)

Business Administration and Management— General	M,O

DEVRY UNIVERSITY (UT)

Business Administration and Management— General	M

DEVRY UNIVERSITY (VA)

Business Administration and Management— General	M,O

DEVRY UNIVERSITY (WA)

Business Administration and Management— General	M,O

DEVRY UNIVERSITY (WI)

Business Administration and Management— General	M,O

DOANE COLLEGE

Business Administration and Management— General	M
Counselor Education	M
Curriculum and Instruction	M
Education—General	M
Educational Leadership and Administration	M

DOMINICAN COLLEGE

Allied Health—General	M,D
Business Administration and Management— General	M
Education—General	M
Elementary Education	M
Family Nurse Practitioner Studies	M
Nursing—General	M
Occupational Therapy	M
Physical Therapy	M,D
Special Education	M

DOMINICAN UNIVERSITY

Accounting	M
Business Administration and Management— General	M
Curriculum and Instruction	M
Early Childhood Education	M
Education—General	M
Educational Leadership and Administration	M
Elementary Education	M
English as a Second Language	M

Information Studies	M,D,O
Library Science	M,D,O
Organizational Management	M
Reading Education	M
Social Work	M
Special Education	M

DOMINICAN UNIVERSITY OF CALIFORNIA

Business Administration and Management— General	M
Education—General	M,O
International Business	M
Management Strategy and Policy	M
Nursing Education	M
Nursing—General	M
Occupational Therapy	M
Public Health—General	M
Special Education	O
Sustainability Management	M

DONGGUK ROYAL UNIVERSITY

Acupuncture and Oriental Medicine	M

DORDT COLLEGE

Education—General	M

DOWLING COLLEGE

Aviation Management	M,O
Business Administration and Management— General	M,O
Early Childhood Education	M,O
Education of the Gifted	M,O
Education—General	M,O
Educational Leadership and Administration	M,O
Educational Media/ Instructional Technology	M,O
Educational Psychology	M,O
Elementary Education	M,O
Finance and Banking	M,O
Health Services Management and Hospital Administration	M,O
Human Resources Management	M,O
Marketing	M,O
Middle School Education	M,O
Project Management	M,O
Quality Management	M,O
Reading Education	M,O
Secondary Education	M,O
Special Education	M,O

DRAKE UNIVERSITY

Business Administration and Management— General	M
Education—General	M,D,O
Law	P

DREW UNIVERSITY

Bioethics	M,D,O
Education—General	M
Foreign Languages Education	M
Mathematics Education	M
Science Education	M
Social Sciences Education	M

DREXEL UNIVERSITY

Accounting	M,D,O
Allied Health—General	M,D,O
Allopathic Medicine	P
Business Administration and Management— General	M,D,O
Curriculum and Instruction	M
Education—General	M,D,O
Educational Leadership and Administration	M,D
Educational Media/ Instructional Technology	M,D
Emergency Medical Services	M
English as a Second Language	M,D,O

Epidemiology	M,D,O
Finance and Banking	M,D,O
Higher Education	M
Hospitality Management	M
Information Studies	M*
International and Comparative Education	M
Library Science	M,D,O
Management Strategy and Policy	M,D,O
Marketing	M,D,O
Nurse Anesthesia	M
Nursing—General	M
Organizational Behavior	M,D,O
Physical Therapy	M,D,O
Physician Assistant Studies	M
Project Management	M
Public Health—General	M,D,O
Quantitative Analysis	M,D,O
Real Estate	M
Sports Management	M
Veterinary Sciences	M

DRURY UNIVERSITY

Business Administration and Management— General	M
Education of the Gifted	M
Education—General	M
Educational Media/ Instructional Technology	M
Elementary Education	M
Human Services	M
Mathematics Education	M
Middle School Education	M
Reading Education	M
Secondary Education	M
Special Education	M

DUKE UNIVERSITY

Acute Care/Critical Care Nursing	M,D,O
Adult Nursing	M,D,O
Allopathic Medicine	P
Business Administration and Management— General	M,D
Clinical Laboratory Sciences/Medical Technology	M
Clinical Research	M
Education—General	M
Environmental and Occupational Health	M,D,O
Family Nurse Practitioner Studies	M,D,O
Gerontological Nursing	M,D,O
Health Services Management and Hospital Administration	O
International Health	M
Law	P,M,D
Maternal and Child/ Neonatal Nursing	M,D,O
Nurse Anesthesia	M,D,O
Nursing and Healthcare Administration	M,D,O
Nursing Education	M,D,O
Nursing Informatics	M,D,O
Nursing—General	D
Oncology Nursing	M,D,O
Pediatric Nursing	M,D,O
Physical Therapy	D
Physician Assistant Studies	M

DUQUESNE UNIVERSITY

Accounting	M
Allied Health—General	M,D
Bioethics	M,D,O
Business Administration and Management— General	M*
Communication Disorders	M,D
Community Health	M
Counselor Education	M,D
Curriculum and Instruction	M,O
Early Childhood Education	M
Education—General	M,D,O
Educational Leadership and Administration	M,D,O
Educational Media/ Instructional Technology	M,D

Elementary Education	M
English as a Second Language	M,D
English Education	M
Family Nurse Practitioner Studies	M,O
Foreign Languages Education	M
Forensic Nursing	M,O
Foundations and Philosophy of Education	M
Health Services Management and Hospital Administration	M,D
International Business	M
Law	P,M
Management Information Systems	M
Management Strategy and Policy	M
Mathematics Education	M
Medicinal and Pharmaceutical Chemistry	M,D
Music Education	M,O
Nursing Education	M
Nursing—General	M,D,O
Occupational Therapy	M,D
Organizational Management	M
Pharmaceutical Administration	M
Pharmaceutical Sciences	M,D*
Pharmacy	P
Physical Therapy	M,D
Physician Assistant Studies	M,D
Reading Education	M
Rehabilitation Sciences	M
Science Education	M
Secondary Education	M
Social Sciences Education	M
Special Education	M
Sports Management	M
Sustainability Management	M

D'YOUVILLE COLLEGE

Business Administration and Management— General	M
Chiropractic	P
Community Health Nursing	M,O
Education—General	M,O
Educational Leadership and Administration	D
Elementary Education	M,O
Family Nurse Practitioner Studies	M,O
Health Education	D
Health Services Management and Hospital Administration	M,D,O
International Business	M
Nursing and Healthcare Administration	M,O
Nursing Education	M,O
Nursing—General	M,O*
Occupational Therapy	M
Physical Therapy	M,D,O
Physician Assistant Studies	M
Secondary Education	M,O
Special Education	M,O

EARLHAM COLLEGE

Education—General	M

EAST CAROLINA UNIVERSITY

Accounting	M
Adult Education	M,O
Allied Health—General	M,D
Allopathic Medicine	P
Business Administration and Management— General	M,D,O*
Communication Disorders	M,D
Counselor Education	M,O
Curriculum and Instruction	M
Education—General	M,D,O
Educational Leadership and Administration	M,D,O

---

*M—master's degree; P—first professional degree; D—doctorate; O—other advanced degree; *—Close-Up and/or Display*

Educational Media/ Instructional Technology	M,O
Elementary Education	M
English Education	M
Environmental and Occupational Health	M
Exercise and Sports Science	M,D
Health Education	M
Leisure Studies	M
Library Science	M,O
Logistics	M,D,O
Management Information Systems	M,D,O
Mathematics Education	M
Medical Physics	M,D
Middle School Education	M
Music Education	M
Nursing—General	M,D
Occupational Therapy	M
Physical Therapy	M,D
Physician Assistant Studies	M
Public Health—General	M
Reading Education	M
Recreation and Park Management	M
Rehabilitation Sciences	M
Science Education	M
Social Sciences Education	M
Social Work	M
Special Education	M
Vocational and Technical Education	M

EAST CENTRAL UNIVERSITY

Counselor Education	M
Education—General	M
Human Resources Management	M

EASTERN CONNECTICUT STATE UNIVERSITY

Early Childhood Education	M
Education—General	M
Educational Media/ Instructional Technology	M
Elementary Education	M
Organizational Management	M
Reading Education	M
Science Education	M
Secondary Education	M

EASTERN ILLINOIS UNIVERSITY

Accounting	M,O
Art Education	M
Business Administration and Management— General	M,O
Communication Disorders	M
Counselor Education	M
Early Childhood Education	M
Education—General	M,O
Educational Leadership and Administration	M,O
Elementary Education	M
Exercise and Sports Science	M
Kinesiology and Movement Studies	M
Mathematics Education	M
Middle School Education	M
Special Education	M
Student Affairs	M

EASTERN KENTUCKY UNIVERSITY

Agricultural Education	M
Allied Health—General	M
Art Education	M
Business Administration and Management— General	M
Business Education	M
Communication Disorders	M
Community Health	M
Counselor Education	M
Curriculum and Instruction	M
Education—General	M
Educational Leadership and Administration	M
Elementary Education	M
English Education	M
Environmental and Occupational Health	M

Family Nurse Practitioner Studies	M
Health Education	M
Health Promotion	M
Health Services Management and Hospital Administration	M
Higher Education	M
Home Economics Education	M
Library Science	M
Mathematics Education	M
Music Education	M
Nursing—General	M
Occupational Therapy	M
Physical Education	M
Recreation and Park Management	M
Science Education	M
Secondary Education	M
Social Sciences Education	M
Special Education	M
Sports Management	M
Vocational and Technical Education	M

EASTERN MENNONITE UNIVERSITY

Business Administration and Management— General	M
Education—General	M

EASTERN MICHIGAN UNIVERSITY

Accounting	M
Adult Nursing	M,O
Art Education	M
Athletic Training and Sports Medicine	M,O
Business Administration and Management— General	M,O
Clinical Research	M,O
Communication Disorders	M
Counselor Education	M,O
Curriculum and Instruction	M
Developmental Education	M,O
Early Childhood Education	M
Education—General	M,D,O
Educational Leadership and Administration	M,D,O
Educational Measurement and Evaluation	M,O
Educational Media/ Instructional Technology	M,O
Educational Psychology	M,O
Electronic Commerce	M,O
Elementary Education	M
English as a Second Language	M,O
English Education	M,O
Entrepreneurship	M,O
Exercise and Sports Science	M
Finance and Banking	M,O
Foundations and Philosophy of Education	M
Health Education	M
Health Promotion	M,O
Health Services Management and Hospital Administration	M,O
Hospitality Management	M,O
Human Resources Management	M,O
Human Services	M,O
International Business	M,O
Kinesiology and Movement Studies	M
Management Information Systems	M,O
Marketing	M,O
Mathematics Education	M
Middle School Education	M
Multilingual and Multicultural Education	M,D,O
Music Education	M
Nonprofit Management	M,O
Nursing and Healthcare Administration	M,O
Nursing Education	M,O
Occupational Therapy	M
Organizational Management	M,O
Physical Education	M
Quality Management	M,O

Reading Education	M
Science Education	M
Secondary Education	M
Social Work	M
Special Education	M,O
Sports Management	M
Supply Chain Management	M,O
Travel and Tourism	M,O
Vocational and Technical Education	M

EASTERN NAZARENE COLLEGE

Early Childhood Education	M,O
Education—General	M,O
Educational Leadership and Administration	M,O
Elementary Education	M,O
English as a Second Language	M,O
Middle School Education	M,O
Reading Education	M,O
Secondary Education	M,O
Special Education	M,O

EASTERN NEW MEXICO UNIVERSITY

Business Administration and Management— General	M
Communication Disorders	M
Counselor Education	M
Education—General	M
Human Services	M
Physical Education	M
Special Education	M

EASTERN OREGON UNIVERSITY

Education—General	M
Elementary Education	M
Secondary Education	M

EASTERN UNIVERSITY

Business Administration and Management— General	M
Counselor Education	M,O
Education—General	M,O
Health Education	M
Health Services Management and Hospital Administration	M
Multilingual and Multicultural Education	M
Nonprofit Management	M
Organizational Management	M,D
School Nursing	M,O

EASTERN VIRGINIA MEDICAL SCHOOL

Allopathic Medicine	P
Medical/Surgical Nursing	O
Physician Assistant Studies	M
Public Health—General	M
Vision Sciences	O

EASTERN WASHINGTON UNIVERSITY

Adult Education	M
Business Administration and Management— General	M
Communication Disorders	M
Computer Education	M
Counselor Education	M
Curriculum and Instruction	M
Dental Hygiene	M
Early Childhood Education	M
Education—General	M
Educational Leadership and Administration	M
Educational Media/ Instructional Technology	M
Elementary Education	M
English as a Second Language	M
Exercise and Sports Science	M
Foreign Languages Education	M
Foundations and Philosophy of Education	M
Mathematics Education	M

Music Education	M
Nursing Education	M
Nursing—General	M
Occupational Therapy	M
Physical Education	M
Physical Therapy	D
Reading Education	M
Social Work	M
Special Education	M
Sports Management	M

EAST STROUDSBURG UNIVERSITY OF PENNSYLVANIA

Communication Disorders	M
Community Health	M
Education—General	M
Educational Media/ Instructional Technology	M
Elementary Education	M
Exercise and Sports Science	M
Health Education	M
Hospitality Management	M
Physical Education	M
Public Health—General	M
Reading Education	M
Rehabilitation Sciences	M
Science Education	M
Secondary Education	M
Social Sciences Education	M
Special Education	M
Sports Management	M
Travel and Tourism	M

EAST TENNESSEE STATE UNIVERSITY

Accounting	M
Allied Health—General	M,D,O
Allopathic Medicine	P
Art Education	M
Business Administration and Management— General	M,O
Communication Disorders	M,D
Community Health	M,O
Counselor Education	M
Curriculum and Instruction	M
Early Childhood Education	M
Education—General	M,D,O
Educational Leadership and Administration	M,D,O
Educational Media/ Instructional Technology	M
Elementary Education	M
Environmental and Occupational Health	M
Epidemiology	M,O
Exercise and Sports Science	M
Finance and Banking	M
Health Services Management and Hospital Administration	M,D,O
Nursing—General	M,D,O
Physical Education	M
Physical Therapy	D
Public Health—General	M,O
Reading Education	M
Secondary Education	M
Social Work	M
Special Education	M,D
Sports Management	M
Vocational and Technical Education	M

EAST WEST COLLEGE OF NATURAL MEDICINE

Acupuncture and Oriental Medicine	M

ECOLE HÔTELIÈRE DE LAUSANNE

Hospitality Management	M

EDGEWOOD COLLEGE

Accounting	M
Business Administration and Management— General	M
Education—General	M,D,O
Educational Leadership and Administration	M,D,O
Nursing—General	M
Special Education	M,D,O

EDINBORO UNIVERSITY OF PENNSYLVANIA

Communication Disorders	M
Counselor Education	M,O
Developmental Education	M,O
Early Childhood Education	M,O
Education—General	M,O
Educational Leadership and Administration	M,O
Educational Psychology	M,O
Elementary Education	M,O
Family Nurse Practitioner Studies	M,O
Nursing Education	M,O
Nursing—General	M,O
Reading Education	M,O
Social Work	M
Special Education	M,O

EDWARD VIA VIRGINIA COLLEGE OF OSTEOPATHIC MEDICINE

Osteopathic Medicine	P

ELIZABETH CITY STATE UNIVERSITY

Education—General	M
Educational Leadership and Administration	M
Elementary Education	M

ELIZABETHTOWN COLLEGE

Occupational Therapy	M

ELMHURST COLLEGE

Accounting	M
Business Administration and Management—General	M
Educational Leadership and Administration	M
Nursing—General	M
Special Education	M
Supply Chain Management	M

ELMS COLLEGE

Communication Disorders	M,O
Early Childhood Education	M,O
Education—General	M,O
Elementary Education	M,O
English as a Second Language	M,O
English Education	M,O
Foreign Languages Education	M,O
Nursing and Healthcare Administration	M
Nursing Education	M
Nursing—General	M
Reading Education	M,O
Science Education	M,O
Secondary Education	M,O
Special Education	M,O

ELON UNIVERSITY

Business Administration and Management—General	M
Education of the Gifted	M
Education—General	M
Elementary Education	M
Law	P
Physical Therapy	D
Special Education	M

EMBRY-RIDDLE AERONAUTICAL UNIVERSITY (FL)

Aviation Management	M
Business Administration and Management—General	M

EMBRY-RIDDLE AERONAUTICAL UNIVERSITY WORLDWIDE

Aviation Management	M,O
Business Administration and Management—General	M
Education—General	M
Logistics	M
Project Management	M
Supply Chain Management	M

EMERSON COLLEGE

Advertising and Public Relations	M
Communication Disorders	M
International Business	M
Marketing	M

EMMANUEL COLLEGE (UNITED STATES)

Business Administration and Management—General	M,O
Education—General	M,O
Educational Leadership and Administration	M,O
Elementary Education	M,O
Human Resources Management	M,O
Pharmaceutical Administration	M,O
Secondary Education	M,O

EMMANUEL SCHOOL OF RELIGION

Religious Education	P,M,D

EMORY & HENRY COLLEGE

Education—General	M
Organizational Management	M
Reading Education	M

EMORY UNIVERSITY

Accounting	D
Acute Care/Critical Care Nursing	M
Adult Nursing	M
Allied Health—General	M,D
Allopathic Medicine	P
Anesthesiologist Assistant Studies	M
Business Administration and Management—General	M,D
Clinical Laboratory Sciences/Medical Technology	M,D
Clinical Research	M
Education—General	M,D,O
Environmental and Occupational Health	M
Epidemiology	M,D
Family Nurse Practitioner Studies	M
Finance and Banking	D
Gerontological Nursing	M
Health Education	M
Health Physics/Radiological Health	D
Health Promotion	M
Health Services Management and Hospital Administration	M,D
Health Services Research	M,D
International Health	M
Law	P,M,O
Management Information Systems	D
Marketing	D
Middle School Education	M,D,O
Nurse Anesthesia	M,D
Nurse Midwifery	M
Nursing and Healthcare Administration	M
Nursing—General	M,D*
Organizational Management	D
Pediatric Nursing	M
Physical Therapy	D
Physician Assistant Studies	M
Public Health—General	M,D,O
Secondary Education	M,D,O
Vision Sciences	M
Women's Health Nursing	M

EMPEROR'S COLLEGE OF TRADITIONAL ORIENTAL MEDICINE

Acupuncture and Oriental Medicine	M,D

EMPORIA STATE UNIVERSITY

Business Administration and Management—General	M
Business Education	M
Counselor Education	M
Curriculum and Instruction	M
Early Childhood Education	M
Education of the Gifted	M
Education—General	M,O
Educational Leadership and Administration	M
Educational Media/Instructional Technology	M
Elementary Education	M
English as a Second Language	M
Information Studies	M,D,O
Library Science	M,D,O
Music Education	M
Physical Education	M
Reading Education	M
Secondary Education	M
Social Sciences Education	M
Special Education	M

ENDICOTT COLLEGE

Art Education	M
Business Administration and Management—General	M
Distance Education Development	M
Early Childhood Education	M
Elementary Education	M
Hospitality Management	M*
Management Information Systems	M
Organizational Management	M
Reading Education	M
Special Education	M
Sports Management	M

ERIKSON INSTITUTE

Early Childhood Education	M,D
English as a Second Language	M,O

EVANGEL UNIVERSITY

Counselor Education	M
Education—General	M
Educational Leadership and Administration	M
Organizational Management	M
Reading Education	M
Secondary Education	M

EVEREST UNIVERSITY (Clearwater, FL)

Business Administration and Management—General	M

EVEREST UNIVERSITY (Jacksonville, FL)

Business Administration and Management—General	M

EVEREST UNIVERSITY (Melbourne, FL)

Business Administration and Management—General	M

EVEREST UNIVERSITY (Orlando, FL)

Business Administration and Management—General	M

EVEREST UNIVERSITY (Orlando, FL)

Accounting	M
Business Administration and Management—General	M
Human Resources Management	M
International Business	

EVEREST UNIVERSITY (Pompano Beach, FL)

Business Administration and Management—General	M

EVEREST UNIVERSITY (Tampa, FL)

Accounting	M
Business Administration and Management—General	M
Human Resources Management	M
International Business	M

EVERGLADES UNIVERSITY

Business Administration and Management—General	M

THE EVERGREEN STATE COLLEGE

Education—General	M
English as a Second Language	M
Mathematics Education	M

EXCELSIOR COLLEGE

Business Administration and Management—General	M
Nursing and Healthcare Administration	O
Nursing—General	M

FACULTAD DE DERECHO EUGENIO MARÍA DE HOSTOS

Law	P

FAIRFIELD UNIVERSITY

Accounting	M,O
Business Administration and Management—General	M,O
Counselor Education	M,O
Education—General	M,O
Educational Media/Instructional Technology	M,O
Elementary Education	M,O
English as a Second Language	M,O
Family Nurse Practitioner Studies	M,O
Finance and Banking	M,O
Foundations and Philosophy of Education	M,O
Health Services Management and Hospital Administration	M,O
Human Resources Management	M,O
Human Services	M,O
International Business	M,O
Management Information Systems	M,O
Marketing	M,O
Multilingual and Multicultural Education	M,O
Nurse Anesthesia	M,O
Nursing and Healthcare Administration	M,O
Nursing—General	M,O
Psychiatric Nursing	M,O
Secondary Education	M,O
Special Education	M,O
Taxation	M,O

FAIRLEIGH DICKINSON UNIVERSITY, COLLEGE AT FLORHAM

Accounting	M
Business Administration and Management—General	M,O
Education—General	M,O

---

*M—master's degree; P—first professional degree; D—doctorate; O—other advanced degree; *—Close-Up and/or Display*

Educational Leadership and Administration	M
Educational Media/ Instructional Technology	M,O
Entrepreneurship	M,O
Finance and Banking	M,O
Health Services Management and Hospital Administration	M
Hospitality Management	M
Human Resources Management	M
International Business	M,O
Marketing	M,O
Organizational Behavior	M,O
Organizational Management	M,O
Reading Education	M,O
Sustainability Management	O
Taxation	M,O

FAIRLEIGH DICKINSON UNIVERSITY, METROPOLITAN CAMPUS

Accounting	M,O
Business Administration and Management— General	M,O
Clinical Laboratory Sciences/Medical Technology	M
Curriculum and Instruction	M
Education—General	M,O
Educational Leadership and Administration	M
Educational Media/ Instructional Technology	M,O
Electronic Commerce	M
Entrepreneurship	M,O
Finance and Banking	M,O
Foundations and Philosophy of Education	M
Health Services Management and Hospital Administration	M
Hospitality Management	M
Human Resources Management	M,O
International Business	M
Management Information Systems	M,O
Marketing	M,O
Multilingual and Multicultural Education	M
Nonprofit Management	M
Nursing—General	M,D,O
Pharmaceutical Administration	M,O
Reading Education	M,O
Science Education	M
Special Education	M
Sports Management	M
Taxation	M

FAIRMONT STATE UNIVERSITY

Business Administration and Management— General	M
Distance Education Development	M
Education—General	M
Educational Leadership and Administration	M
Human Services	M
Nursing and Healthcare Administration	M
Nursing Education	M
Nursing—General	M
Reading Education	M
Special Education	M

FASHION INSTITUTE OF TECHNOLOGY

Business Administration and Management— General	M
Marketing	M

FAULKNER UNIVERSITY

Law	P

FAYETTEVILLE STATE UNIVERSITY

Business Administration and Management— General	M

Educational Leadership and Administration	M,D
Elementary Education	M
Middle School Education	M
Reading Education	M
Secondary Education	M
Social Sciences Education	M
Social Work	M

FELICIAN COLLEGE

Accounting	M
Adult Nursing	M,O
Business Administration and Management— General	M*
Education—General	M,O*
Educational Leadership and Administration	M,O
Elementary Education	M,O
Entrepreneurship	M
Family Nurse Practitioner Studies	M,O*
Nursing Education	M,O
Nursing—General	M,O
Religious Education	M,O
School Nursing	M,O
Special Education	M,O

FERRIS STATE UNIVERSITY

Allied Health—General	M
Business Administration and Management— General	M
Curriculum and Instruction	M
Developmental Education	M
Education—General	M
Educational Leadership and Administration	M
Educational Media/ Instructional Technology	M
Electronic Commerce	M
Elementary Education	M
Human Services	M
Management Information Systems	M
Nursing and Healthcare Administration	M
Nursing Education	M
Nursing Informatics	M
Nursing—General	M
Optometry	P
Pharmacy	P
Quality Management	M
Reading Education	M
Special Education	M

FIELDING GRADUATE UNIVERSITY

Educational Leadership and Administration	M,D,O
Educational Media/ Instructional Technology	M,D,O
Organizational Management	M,D,O

FITCHBURG STATE UNIVERSITY

Accounting	M
Art Education	M,O
Business Administration and Management— General	M
Counselor Education	M
Curriculum and Instruction	M
Early Childhood Education	M
Educational Leadership and Administration	M,O
Educational Media/ Instructional Technology	M,O
Elementary Education	M
English Education	M,O
Forensic Nursing	M,O
Higher Education	M,O
Human Resources Management	M
Middle School Education	M
Science Education	M,O
Secondary Education	M
Social Sciences Education	M,O
Special Education	M
Vocational and Technical Education	M

FIVE BRANCHES UNIVERSITY: GRADUATE SCHOOL OF TRADITIONAL CHINESE MEDICINE

Acupuncture and Oriental Medicine	M

FIVE TOWNS COLLEGE

Music Education	M,D

FLORIDA AGRICULTURAL AND MECHANICAL UNIVERSITY

Accounting	M
Adult Education	M,D
Allied Health—General	M
Business Administration and Management— General	M
Business Education	M
Counselor Education	M,D
Early Childhood Education	M
Education—General	M,D
Educational Leadership and Administration	M,D
Elementary Education	M
English Education	M
Finance and Banking	M
Health Education	M
Law	P
Management Information Systems	M
Marketing	M
Mathematics Education	M
Medicinal and Pharmaceutical Chemistry	M,D
Nursing and Healthcare Administration	M
Nursing—General	M
Pharmaceutical Administration	M,D
Pharmaceutical Sciences	M,D
Pharmacy	P,D
Physical Education	M
Physical Therapy	M
Public Health—General	M
Recreation and Park Management	M
Science Education	M
Secondary Education	M
Social Sciences Education	M
Social Work	M
Vocational and Technical Education	M

FLORIDA ATLANTIC UNIVERSITY

Accounting	M,D
Adult Education	M,D,O
Art Education	M
Business Administration and Management— General	M,D,O
Communication Disorders	M
Counselor Education	M,D,O
Curriculum and Instruction	M,D,O
Early Childhood Education	M,D,O
Education—General	M,D,O
Educational Leadership and Administration	M,D,O
Elementary Education	M
English as a Second Language	M,D,O
English Education	M
Entrepreneurship	M,D
Environmental Education	M
Exercise and Sports Science	M
Finance and Banking	M,D
Foundations and Philosophy of Education	M
Health Promotion	M
Higher Education	M,D,O
International Business	M,D
Management Information Systems	M
Multilingual and Multicultural Education	M,D,O
Nonprofit Management	M
Nursing—General	M,D,O
Reading Education	M
Social Work	M
Special Education	M,D
Taxation	M
Travel and Tourism	M,O

FLORIDA COASTAL SCHOOL OF LAW

Law	P

FLORIDA COLLEGE OF INTEGRATIVE MEDICINE

Acupuncture and Oriental Medicine	M

FLORIDA GULF COAST UNIVERSITY

Accounting	M
Allied Health—General	M,D
Business Administration and Management— General	M
Counselor Education	M
Curriculum and Instruction	M
Early Childhood Education	M
Education—General	M
Educational Leadership and Administration	M
Educational Media/ Instructional Technology	M
Elementary Education	M
English Education	M
Nursing—General	M
Occupational Therapy	M
Physical Therapy	M,D
Reading Education	M
Social Work	M
Special Education	M
Taxation	M

FLORIDA HOSPITAL COLLEGE OF HEALTH SCIENCES

Nurse Anesthesia	M

FLORIDA INSTITUTE OF TECHNOLOGY

Accounting	M
Business Administration and Management— General	M*
Computer Education	M,D,O
Electronic Commerce	M
Elementary Education	M,D,O
Environmental Education	M,D,O
Finance and Banking	M
Health Services Management and Hospital Administration	M*
Human Resources Management	M
Logistics	M
Management Information Systems	M
Marketing	M
Mathematics Education	M,D,O
Organizational Behavior	M,D
Project Management	M
Quality Management	M
Science Education	M,D,O
Supply Chain Management	M
Transportation Management	M

FLORIDA INTERNATIONAL UNIVERSITY

Accounting	M
Adult Education	M,D
Allopathic Medicine	P
Art Education	M,D
Athletic Training and Sports Medicine	M
Business Administration and Management— General	M,D
Communication Disorders	M
Counselor Education	M
Curriculum and Instruction	M,D,O
Early Childhood Education	M,D
Education—General	M,D,O
Educational Leadership and Administration	M,D,O
Educational Media/ Instructional Technology	M,D,O
Elementary Education	M,D
English as a Second Language	M,D,O
English Education	M,D
Environmental and Occupational Health	M,D
Epidemiology	M,D
Exercise and Sports Science	M
Finance and Banking	M
Foreign Languages Education	M,D,O
Health Promotion	M,D
Health Services Management and Hospital Administration	M,D

Higher Education	D
Hospitality Management	M
Human Resources Development	M,D
Human Resources Management	M
International and Comparative Education	M,D
International Business	M
Law	P
Leisure Studies	M
Management Information Systems	M
Mathematics Education	M,D
Music Education	M
Nursing—General	M,D
Occupational Therapy	M
Physical Education	M,D,O
Physical Therapy	D
Public Health—General	M,D
Reading Education	M,D
Real Estate	M
Recreation and Park Management	M
Science Education	M,D
Social Sciences Education	M,D
Social Work	M,D
Special Education	M,D,O
Sports Management	M
Taxation	M
Urban Education	M

FLORIDA MEMORIAL UNIVERSITY

Business Administration and Management—General	M
Education—General	M
Elementary Education	M
Reading Education	M
Special Education	M

FLORIDA SOUTHERN COLLEGE

Accounting	M
Business Administration and Management—General	M*
Education—General	M
International Business	M
Nursing—General	M

FLORIDA STATE UNIVERSITY

Accounting	M,D
Art Education	M,D,O
Business Administration and Management—General	M,D
Communication Disorders	M,D
Counselor Education	M,D,O
Distance Education Development	M,D,O
Early Childhood Education	M,D,O
Education—General	M,D,O
Educational Leadership and Administration	M,D,O
Educational Measurement and Evaluation	M,D,O
Educational Media/ Instructional Technology	M,D,O
Educational Policy	M,D,O
Educational Psychology	M,D,O
Elementary Education	M,D,O
English Education	M,D,O
Environmental Law	P,M
Exercise and Sports Science	M,D
Family Nurse Practitioner Studies	M,D,O
Finance and Banking	M,D
Foundations and Philosophy of Education	M,D,O
Health Education	M,D
Health Services Management and Hospital Administration	M,D,O
Higher Education	M,D,O
Human Resources Development	M,D,O
Information Studies	M,D,O
Insurance	M,D
International and Comparative Education	M,D,O
Law	P,M
Library Science	M,D,O

Management Information Systems	M,D
Management Strategy and Policy	M,D
Marketing	M,D
Mathematics Education	M,D,O
Music Education	M,D
Nursing Education	M,D,O
Nursing—General	M,D,O
Organizational Behavior	M,D
Physical Education	M,D
Public Health—General	M
Reading Education	M,D,O
Recreation and Park Management	M,D
Science Education	M,D,O
Social Sciences Education	M
Social Work	M,D
Special Education	M,D,O
Sports Management	M,D
Taxation	M,D

FONTBONNE UNIVERSITY

Accounting	M
Business Administration and Management—General	M
Communication Disorders	M
Computer Education	M
Education—General	M
Special Education	M
Taxation	M

FORDHAM UNIVERSITY

Accounting	M
Adult Education	M,D,O
Business Administration and Management—General	M
Counselor Education	M,D,O
Curriculum and Instruction	M,D,O
Early Childhood Education	M,D,O
Education—General	M,D,O
Educational Leadership and Administration	M,D,O
Educational Psychology	M,D,O
Elementary Education	M,D,O
English as a Second Language	M,D,O
Finance and Banking	M
Human Resources Management	M,D,O
Law	P,M
Management Information Systems	M
Marketing	M
Multilingual and Multicultural Education	M,D,O
Reading Education	M,D,O
Religious Education	M,D,O
Secondary Education	M,D,O
Social Work	M,D
Special Education	M,D,O
Taxation	M

FORT HAYS STATE UNIVERSITY

Business Administration and Management—General	M
Communication Disorders	M
Counselor Education	M
Education—General	M,O
Educational Leadership and Administration	M,O
Educational Media/ Instructional Technology	M
Health Education	M
Nursing—General	M
Physical Education	M
Special Education	M

FORT VALLEY STATE UNIVERSITY

Counselor Education	M,O
Environmental and Occupational Health	M
Public Health—General	M

FRAMINGHAM STATE UNIVERSITY

Business Administration and Management—General	M
Curriculum and Instruction	M
Early Childhood Education	M

Educational Leadership and Administration	M
Educational Media/ Instructional Technology	M
Elementary Education	M
English as a Second Language	M
English Education	M
Foreign Languages Education	M
Health Education	M
Health Services Management and Hospital Administration	M
Human Resources Management	M
Mathematics Education	M
Nursing and Healthcare Administration	M
Nursing Education	M
Nursing—General	M
Reading Education	M
Social Sciences Education	M
Special Education	M

FRANCISCAN UNIVERSITY OF STEUBENVILLE

Business Administration and Management—General	M
Curriculum and Instruction	M
Education—General	M
Educational Leadership and Administration	M
Nursing—General	M

FRANCIS MARION UNIVERSITY

Business Administration and Management—General	M
Early Childhood Education	M
Education—General	M
Elementary Education	M
Health Services Management and Hospital Administration	M
Secondary Education	M
Special Education	M

FRANKLIN PIERCE LAW CENTER

Law	P,M,O

FRANKLIN PIERCE UNIVERSITY

Business Administration and Management—General	M,D,O
Education—General	M,D,O
Health Services Management and Hospital Administration	M,D,O
Human Resources Management	M,D,O
Management Information Systems	M,D,O
Management Strategy and Policy	M,D,O
Nursing—General	M,D,O
Physical Therapy	M,D,O
Physician Assistant Studies	M,D,O
Sports Management	M,D,O

FRANKLIN UNIVERSITY

Business Administration and Management—General	M
Marketing	M

FREED-HARDEMAN UNIVERSITY

Accounting	M
Business Administration and Management—General	M
Counselor Education	M,O
Curriculum and Instruction	M,O
Education—General	M,O
Educational Leadership and Administration	M,O
Management Strategy and Policy	M
Special Education	M,O

FRESNO PACIFIC UNIVERSITY

Business Administration and Management—General	M
Counselor Education	M
Curriculum and Instruction	M
Education of Students with Severe/Multiple Disabilities	M
Education—General	M
Educational Leadership and Administration	M
Educational Media/ Instructional Technology	M
Elementary Education	M
English as a Second Language	M
Kinesiology and Movement Studies	M
Mathematics Education	M
Middle School Education	M
Multilingual and Multicultural Education	M
Reading Education	M
Science Education	M
Secondary Education	M
Special Education	M
Student Affairs	M

FRIENDS UNIVERSITY

Business Administration and Management—General	M
Education—General	M
Elementary Education	M
Health Services Management and Hospital Administration	M
Human Resources Development	M
Industrial and Manufacturing Management	M
Law	M
Management Information Systems	M
Secondary Education	M

FRONTIER SCHOOL OF MIDWIFERY AND FAMILY NURSING

Family Nurse Practitioner Studies	M,O
Nurse Midwifery	M,O
Nursing—General	M,O
Women's Health Nursing	M,O

FROSTBURG STATE UNIVERSITY

Business Administration and Management—General	M
Counselor Education	M
Curriculum and Instruction	M
Education—General	M
Educational Leadership and Administration	M
Educational Media/ Instructional Technology	M
Elementary Education	M
Reading Education	M
Recreation and Park Management	M
Secondary Education	M
Special Education	M

FULL SAIL UNIVERSITY

Business Administration and Management—General	M
Educational Media/ Instructional Technology	M
Entertainment Management	M
Marketing	M

FURMAN UNIVERSITY

Curriculum and Instruction	M
Early Childhood Education	M
Education—General	M
Educational Leadership and Administration	M
English as a Second Language	M

*M—master's degree; P—first professional degree; D—doctorate; O—other advanced degree; *—Close-Up and/or Display*

Reading Education	M
Special Education	M

GALLAUDET UNIVERSITY

Communication Disorders	M,D,O
Counselor Education	M
Early Childhood Education	M,D,O
Education of Students with Severe/Multiple Disabilities	M,D,O
Educational Leadership and Administration	M,D,O
Educational Measurement and Evaluation	M,O
Elementary Education	M,D,O
International and Comparative Education	M,O
Leisure Studies	M
Secondary Education	M,D,O
Social Work	M
Special Education	M,D,O

GANNON UNIVERSITY

Accounting	O
Business Administration and Management— General	M,O
Counselor Education	M,O
Curriculum and Instruction	M
Early Childhood Education	M
Education—General	M,D,O
Educational Leadership and Administration	M,D,O
Educational Media/ Instructional Technology	M,O
English as a Second Language	O
Environmental and Occupational Health	O
Environmental Education	M
Family Nurse Practitioner Studies	M,O
Finance and Banking	O
Human Resources Management	O
Investment Management	O
Marketing	O
Medical/Surgical Nursing	M,O
Nurse Anesthesia	M,O
Nursing and Healthcare Administration	M,O
Nursing—General	M,O
Occupational Therapy	M
Organizational Management	D
Physical Therapy	D
Physician Assistant Studies	M
Reading Education	M,O
Science Education	M

GARDNER-WEBB UNIVERSITY

Business Administration and Management— General	M
Curriculum and Instruction	D
Education—General	M,D
Educational Leadership and Administration	M,D
Elementary Education	M
English Education	M
Exercise and Sports Science	M
Middle School Education	M
Nursing—General	M,O
Physical Education	M
Religious Education	P,D

GARRETT-EVANGELICAL THEOLOGICAL SEMINARY

Religious Education	P,M,D

GENEVA COLLEGE

Business Administration and Management— General	M
Counselor Education	M
Education—General	M
Educational Leadership and Administration	M
Higher Education	M
Organizational Management	M
Reading Education	M
Special Education	M

GEORGE FOX UNIVERSITY

Business Administration and Management— General	M,D
Counselor Education	M,O
Curriculum and Instruction	M,D,O
Education—General	M,D,O
Educational Leadership and Administration	M,D,O
Educational Media/ Instructional Technology	M,D,O
English as a Second Language	M
Finance and Banking	M,D
Higher Education	M,D,O
Human Resources Management	M,D
Marketing	M,D
Multilingual and Multicultural Education	M
Organizational Management	M,D
Reading Education	M,D,O
Secondary Education	M,D,O

GEORGE MASON UNIVERSITY

Accounting	M
Advertising and Public Relations	M,O
Art Education	M
Business Administration and Management— General	M
Community College Education	D,O
Community Health	M,O
Counselor Education	M,D
Curriculum and Instruction	M
Education—General	M,D,O
Educational Leadership and Administration	M
Educational Measurement and Evaluation	M
Educational Psychology	M
Electronic Commerce	M,D,O
English as a Second Language	M,D,O
Entrepreneurship	M,O
Epidemiology	M,O
Exercise and Sports Science	M
Foreign Languages Education	M
Forensic Nursing	M,D,O
Health Promotion	M
Higher Education	D,O
Human Resources Management	M
International Health	M,O
Law	P,M
Logistics	M
Management Information Systems	M,D,O
Music Education	M,D,O
Nonprofit Management	M,D,O
Nursing and Healthcare Administration	M,D,O
Nursing Education	M,D,O
Nursing—General	M,D,O
Organizational Management	M
Public Health—General	M,O
Real Estate	M
Rehabilitation Sciences	M,O
Social Work	M
Special Education	M
Taxation	M
Transportation Management	M

GEORGETOWN COLLEGE

Education—General	M
Reading Education	M
Special Education	M

GEORGETOWN UNIVERSITY

Acute Care/Critical Care Nursing	M
Advertising and Public Relations	M,D
Allopathic Medicine	P
Business Administration and Management— General	M

English as a Second Language	M,D,O
Epidemiology	M
Family Nurse Practitioner Studies	M
Finance and Banking	D
Health Law	P,M,D
Health Physics/ Radiological Health	M
Health Promotion	M,D
Human Resources Management	M,D
Industrial and Manufacturing Management	D
International Business	P,M,D
International Health	P,M,D
Law	P,M,D
Legal and Justice Studies	P,M,D
Multilingual and Multicultural Education	M,D,O
Nurse Anesthesia	M
Nurse Midwifery	M
Nursing Education	M
Nursing—General	M
Public Health—General	M,D
Real Estate	M,D
Sports Management	M,D
Taxation	P,M,D

THE GEORGE WASHINGTON UNIVERSITY

Accounting	M,D
Adult Nursing	M,D,O
Allopathic Medicine	P
Business Administration and Management— General	M,D,O*
Communication Disorders	M
Counselor Education	M,D,O
Curriculum and Instruction	M,D,O
Early Childhood Education	M
Education—General	M,D,O
Educational Leadership and Administration	M,D,O
Educational Media/ Instructional Technology	M
Educational Policy	M,D
Elementary Education	M
Environmental and Occupational Health	M
Epidemiology	M,D
Exercise and Sports Science	M
Family Nurse Practitioner Studies	M,D,O
Finance and Banking	M,D
Health Services Management and Hospital Administration	M,D,O
Health Services Research	M,D,O
Higher Education	M,D,O
Hospitality Management	M,O
Human Resources Development	M,D,O
Human Resources Management	M,D
International and Comparative Education	M
International Business	M,D
International Health	M
Investment Management	M,D
Law	P,M,D
Legal and Justice Studies	M,O
Management Information Systems	M,D
Management Strategy and Policy	M,D
Marketing	M,D
Museum Education	M
Nonprofit Management	M
Nursing and Healthcare Administration	M,D,O
Nursing—General	M,D,O
Organizational Management	M,D
Physical Therapy	D
Physician Assistant Studies	M
Project Management	M,D
Public Health—General	M,O
Real Estate	M,D
Secondary Education	M
Special Education	M,D,O
Sports Management	M,O
Travel and Tourism	M,O

GEORGIA CAMPUS– PHILADELPHIA COLLEGE OF OSTEOPATHIC MEDICINE

Osteopathic Medicine	P

GEORGIA COLLEGE & STATE UNIVERSITY

Accounting	M
Adult Nursing	M
Business Administration and Management— General	M
Curriculum and Instruction	M,O
Early Childhood Education	M,O
Education—General	M,O
Educational Leadership and Administration	M,O
Educational Media/ Instructional Technology	M,O
Exercise and Sports Science	M
Family Nurse Practitioner Studies	M
Health Education	M
Health Promotion	M
Health Services Management and Hospital Administration	M
Kinesiology and Movement Studies	M
Logistics	M
Management Information Systems	M
Middle School Education	M,O
Music Education	M
Nursing and Healthcare Administration	M
Nursing—General	M
Physical Education	M
Recreation and Park Management	M
Secondary Education	M,O
Special Education	M,O

GEORGIA INSTITUTE OF TECHNOLOGY

Accounting	M,D,O
Business Administration and Management— General	M,D,O
Electronic Commerce	M,O
Entrepreneurship	M
Finance and Banking	M,D,O
Health Physics/ Radiological Health	M,D
Health Services Management and Hospital Administration	M
International Business	M,O
Management Information Systems	M,D,O
Management Strategy and Policy	M,D,O
Marketing	M,D,O
Medical Physics	M,D
Organizational Behavior	M,D,O

GEORGIAN COURT UNIVERSITY

Accounting	M,O
Business Administration and Management— General	M,O
Education—General	M
Educational Leadership and Administration	M,O
Educational Psychology	M,O
Religious Education	M,O

GEORGIA SOUTHERN UNIVERSITY

Accounting	M
Allied Health—General	M,D,O
Art Education	M
Business Administration and Management— General	M
Business Education	M
Community Health Nursing	M,D,O
Community Health	M,D
Counselor Education	M,O
Curriculum and Instruction	D
Early Childhood Education	M,D,O
Education—General	M,D,O
Educational Leadership and Administration	M,D,O

Educational Media/ Instructional Technology	M
Elementary Education	M
English Education	M
Environmental and Occupational Health	M,D
Epidemiology	M,D
Family Nurse Practitioner Studies	M,O
Foreign Languages Education	M
Health Education	M,D
Health Services Management and Hospital Administration	M,D
Higher Education	M
Kinesiology and Movement Studies	M
Mathematics Education	M
Middle School Education	M
Nursing—General	M,D,O
Physical Education	M
Public Health—General	M,D
Reading Education	M
Recreation and Park Management	M
Science Education	M
Secondary Education	M
Social Sciences Education	M
Special Education	M
Sports Management	M
Vocational and Technical Education	M
Women's Health Nursing	M,D,O

GEORGIA SOUTHWESTERN STATE UNIVERSITY

Business Administration and Management— General	M
Early Childhood Education	M,O
Education—General	M,O
Health Education	M,O
Middle School Education	M,O
Physical Education	M,O
Reading Education	M,O
Secondary Education	M,O
Special Education	M,O

GEORGIA STATE UNIVERSITY

Accounting	M,D,O
Actuarial Science	M
Adult Nursing	M,D,O
Allied Health—General	M,D,O
Art Education	M,D,O
Athletic Training and Sports Medicine	M
Business Administration and Management— General	M,D
Communication Disorders	M
Counselor Education	M,D,O
Early Childhood Education	M,D,O
Education of Students with Severe/Multiple Disabilities	
Education—General	M,D,O
Educational Leadership and Administration	M,D,O
Educational Measurement and Evaluation	M,D
Educational Media/ Instructional Technology	M,D,O
Educational Policy	M,D,O
Educational Psychology	M,D
English as a Second Language	M,D,O
English Education	M,D,O
Entrepreneurship	M,D
Exercise and Sports Science	M
Family Nurse Practitioner Studies	M,D,O
Finance and Banking	M,D,O
Foundations and Philosophy of Education	M,D
Health Education	M
Health Promotion	M,D,O
Health Services Management and Hospital Administration	M
Human Resources Management	M,D
Human Services	M

Insurance	M,D,O
International Business	M
Kinesiology and Movement Studies	D
Law	P
Management Information Systems	M,D
Management Strategy and Policy	M,D
Marketing	M,D
Mathematics Education	M,D,O
Middle School Education	M,O
Music Education	M,D,O
Nonprofit Management	M,D,O
Nursing—General	M,D,O
Organizational Management	M,D
Pediatric Nursing	M,D,O
Physical Education	M
Physical Therapy	D
Psychiatric Nursing	M,D,O
Public Health—General	M,D,O
Quantitative Analysis	M,D
Reading Education	M,D,O
Real Estate	M,D,O
Science Education	M,D,O
Secondary Education	M,D,O
Social Sciences Education	M,D,O
Social Work	M
Special Education	M,D
Sports Management	M
Taxation	M
Women's Health Nursing	M,D,O

GLOBAL UNIVERSITY

Religious Education	P,M

GLOBE UNIVERSITY

Business Administration and Management— General	M
Health Services Management and Hospital Administration	M
Management Information Systems	M

GODDARD COLLEGE

Business Administration and Management— General	M
Education—General	M
Health Promotion	M
Sustainability Management	M

GOLDEN GATE BAPTIST THEOLOGICAL SEMINARY

Early Childhood Education	P,M,D,O
Educational Leadership and Administration	P,M,D,O

GOLDEN GATE UNIVERSITY

Accounting	M,D,O
Advertising and Public Relations	M,D,O
Business Administration and Management— General	M,D,O
Environmental Law	P,M,D
Finance and Banking	M,D,O
Human Resources Management	M,D,O
International Business	M,D,O
Law	P,M,D
Legal and Justice Studies	P,M,D
Management Information Systems	M,D,O
Marketing	M,D,O
Taxation	P,M,D,O

GOLDEY-BEACOM COLLEGE

Business Administration and Management— General	M
Finance and Banking	M
Human Resources Management	M
International Business	M
Management Information Systems	M
Marketing	M
Taxation	M

GOLDFARB SCHOOL OF NURSING AT BARNES-JEWISH COLLEGE

Adult Nursing	M,O
Health Services Management and Hospital Administration	M,O
Maternal and Child/ Neonatal Nursing	M,O
Nurse Anesthesia	M,O
Nursing Education	M,O
Nursing—General	M,O
Oncology Nursing	M,O

GONZAGA UNIVERSITY

Accounting	M
Business Administration and Management— General	M
Education—General	M
Educational Leadership and Administration	M,D
English as a Second Language	M
Law	P
Nurse Anesthesia	M
Nursing—General	M
Organizational Management	M
Reading Education	M
Special Education	M
Sports Management	M

GOODING INSTITUTE OF NURSE ANESTHESIA

Nurse Anesthesia	M

GORDON COLLEGE

Education—General	M
Music Education	M

GOSHEN COLLEGE

Environmental Education	M
Family Nurse Practitioner Studies	M
Nursing and Healthcare Administration	M
Nursing—General	M

GOUCHER COLLEGE

Education—General	M

GOVERNORS STATE UNIVERSITY

Accounting	M
Business Administration and Management— General	M
Communication Disorders	M
Early Childhood Education	M
Education—General	M
Educational Leadership and Administration	M
Educational Media/ Instructional Technology	M
Health Services Management and Hospital Administration	M
Legal and Justice Studies	M
Management Information Systems	M
Nursing—General	M
Occupational Therapy	M
Physical Therapy	M,D
Reading Education	M
Social Work	M
Special Education	M

GRACELAND UNIVERSITY (IA)

Education—General	M
Educational Leadership and Administration	M
Educational Media/ Instructional Technology	M
Family Nurse Practitioner Studies	M,O
Nursing Education	M,O
Nursing—General	M,O
Special Education	M

GRADUATE INSTITUTE OF APPLIED LINGUISTICS

Multilingual and Multicultural Education	M,O

GRADUATE SCHOOL AND UNIVERSITY CENTER OF THE CITY UNIVERSITY OF NEW YORK

Accounting	D
Business Administration and Management— General	D
Communication Disorders	D
Educational Psychology	D
Finance and Banking	D
Management Information Systems	D
Nursing—General	D
Organizational Behavior	D
Physical Therapy	D
Public Health—General	D
Social Work	D
Urban Education	D

GRAMBLING STATE UNIVERSITY

Counselor Education	M,D
Curriculum and Instruction	M,D
Developmental Education	M,D
Education—General	M,D
Educational Leadership and Administration	M,D
Educational Media/ Instructional Technology	M,D
Family Nurse Practitioner Studies	M,O
Health Services Management and Hospital Administration	M
Higher Education	M,D
Human Resources Management	M
Mathematics Education	M,D
Nursing Education	M,O
Nursing—General	M,O
Reading Education	M,D
Science Education	M,D
Social Sciences Education	M
Social Work	M
Sports Management	M
Student Affairs	M,D

GRAND CANYON UNIVERSITY

Accounting	M
Adult Nursing	M
Business Administration and Management— General	M
Counselor Education	M
Curriculum and Instruction	M,D
Education—General	M,D
Educational Leadership and Administration	M,D
Elementary Education	M,D
Family Nurse Practitioner Studies	M
Finance and Banking	M
Health Services Management and Hospital Administration	M
Management Information Systems	M
Marketing	M
Nursing and Healthcare Administration	M
Nursing Education	M
Nursing—General	M
Organizational Management	M,D
Secondary Education	M,D
Special Education	M,D

GRAND RAPIDS THEOLOGICAL SEMINARY OF CORNERSTONE UNIVERSITY

Religious Education	P,M

GRAND VALLEY STATE UNIVERSITY

Accounting	M
Adult Education	M,O
Allied Health—General	M,D
Business Administration and Management— General	M
Curriculum and Instruction	M
Early Childhood Education	M,O
Education—General	M,O

---

*M—master's degree; P—first professional degree; D—doctorate; O—other advanced degree; *—Close-Up and/or Display*

Educational Leadership and Administration	M,O
Educational Media/ Instructional Technology	M,O
Elementary Education	M,O
English as a Second Language	M,O
English Education	M
Health Services Management and Hospital Administration	M,D
Higher Education	M,O
Management Information Systems	M
Middle School Education	M,O
Nursing and Healthcare Administration	M,D
Nursing Education	M,D
Nursing—General	M,D
Occupational Therapy	M
Physical Therapy	D
Physician Assistant Studies	M
Reading Education	M
Secondary Education	M,O
Social Work	M
Special Education	M
Taxation	M

GRAND VIEW UNIVERSITY

Business Administration and Management— General	M
Education—General	M
Nursing—General	M
Organizational Management	M

GRANTHAM UNIVERSITY

Adult Nursing	M
Business Administration and Management— General	M
Health Services Management and Hospital Administration	M
Management Information Systems	M
Nursing and Healthcare Administration	M
Nursing Education	M
Nursing Informatics	M
Organizational Management	M
Project Management	M

GRATZ COLLEGE

Education—General	M
Religious Education	M,D,O
Social Work	M,O

GREEN MOUNTAIN COLLEGE

Business Administration and Management— General	M

GREENSBORO COLLEGE

Education—General	M
Elementary Education	M
English as a Second Language	M
Special Education	M

GREENVILLE COLLEGE

Education—General	M
Elementary Education	M
Secondary Education	M

GWYNEDD-MERCY COLLEGE

Adult Nursing	M
Business Administration and Management— General	M
Counselor Education	M
Education—General	M
Educational Leadership and Administration	M
Family Nurse Practitioner Studies	M
Gerontological Nursing	M
Nursing—General	M
Oncology Nursing	M
Pediatric Nursing	M
Reading Education	M
Special Education	M

HAMLINE UNIVERSITY

Business Administration and Management— General	M,D,O
Education—General	M,D
English as a Second Language	M,D
Environmental Education	M,D
Law	P,M
Nonprofit Management	M,D,O
Reading Education	M,D
Science Education	M,D

HAMPTON UNIVERSITY

Adult Nursing	M
Business Administration and Management— General	M
Communication Disorders	M
Community Health Nursing	M
Counselor Education	M
Early Childhood Education	M
Education—General	M
Elementary Education	M
Gerontological Nursing	M
Medical Physics	M,D
Middle School Education	M
Music Education	M
Nursing—General	M
Pediatric Nursing	M
Physical Therapy	D
Psychiatric Nursing	M
Secondary Education	M
Special Education	M
Student Affairs	M
Women's Health Nursing	M

HANNIBAL-LAGRANGE COLLEGE

Education—General	M
Reading Education	M

HARDING UNIVERSITY

Accounting	M
Art Education	M,O
Business Administration and Management— General	M
Communication Disorders	M
Counselor Education	M,O
Early Childhood Education	M,O
Education—General	M,O
Educational Leadership and Administration	M,O
Elementary Education	M,O
English as a Second Language	M,O
English Education	M,O
Foreign Languages Education	M,O
Health Education	M,O
Health Services Management and Hospital Administration	M
Home Economics Education	M,O
International Business	M
Mathematics Education	M,O
Organizational Management	M
Pharmacy	P
Physician Assistant Studies	M
Reading Education	M,O
Science Education	M,O
Secondary Education	M,O
Social Sciences Education	M,O
Special Education	M,O

HARDIN-SIMMONS UNIVERSITY

Business Administration and Management— General	M
Counselor Education	M
Education of the Gifted	M
Education—General	M
Family Nurse Practitioner Studies	M
Kinesiology and Movement Studies	M
Maternal and Child/ Neonatal Nursing	M
Music Education	M
Nursing—General	M
Physical Therapy	D

Reading Education	M
Recreation and Park Management	M
Science Education	M,D

HARRISBURG UNIVERSITY OF SCIENCE AND TECHNOLOGY

Educational Media/ Instructional Technology	M
Entrepreneurship	M
Health Services Management and Hospital Administration	M
Management Information Systems	M
Project Management	M

HARVARD UNIVERSITY

Accounting	D
Allopathic Medicine	P,D
Art Education	D
Business Administration and Management— General	M,D,O
Communication Disorders	D
Curriculum and Instruction	D
Dentistry	P,M,D,O
Education—General	M,D
Educational Leadership and Administration	M,D
Educational Measurement and Evaluation	D
Educational Media/ Instructional Technology	M,O
Educational Policy	M
Educational Psychology	M
Environmental and Occupational Health	M,D
Epidemiology	M,D
Foundations and Philosophy of Education	M,O
Health Promotion	M,D
Health Services Management and Hospital Administration	M,D
Higher Education	D
Industrial and Manufacturing Management	D
International and Comparative Education	M
International Health	M,D
Law	P,M,D
Legal and Justice Studies	P
Management Strategy and Policy	D
Marketing	D
Mathematics Education	M,O
Medical Physics	D
Multilingual and Multicultural Education	D
Oral and Dental Sciences	M,D,O
Organizational Behavior	D
Public Health—General	M,D*
Reading Education	M
Science Education	M
Urban Education	D

HASTINGS COLLEGE

Education—General	M

HAWAI'I PACIFIC UNIVERSITY

Accounting	M
Business Administration and Management— General	M*
Community Health Nursing	M
Electronic Commerce	M
English as a Second Language	M*
Family Nurse Practitioner Studies	M
Finance and Banking	M
Human Resources Management	M
International Business	M
Management Information Systems	M*
Marketing	M
Nursing—General	M
Organizational Management	M*
Secondary Education	M

Social Work	M
Travel and Tourism	M

HEBREW COLLEGE

Early Childhood Education	M,O
Education—General	M,O
Middle School Education	M,O
Music Education	M,O
Religious Education	M,O
Special Education	M,O

HEBREW UNION COLLEGE– JEWISH INSTITUTE OF RELIGION (CA)

Education—General	M,D,O
Religious Education	M,D,O
Social Work	M,O

HEBREW UNION COLLEGE– JEWISH INSTITUTE OF RELIGION (NY)

Education—General	M
Religious Education	M

HEC MONTREAL

Accounting	M,O
Business Administration and Management— General	M,D,O
Electronic Commerce	M,O
Finance and Banking	M,O
Human Resources Management	M
Industrial and Manufacturing Management	M
International Business	M
Logistics	M
Management Information Systems	M
Management Strategy and Policy	M
Marketing	M
Organizational Management	M
Supply Chain Management	O
Taxation	M,O

HEIDELBERG UNIVERSITY

Business Administration and Management— General	M
Education—General	M
Music Education	M

HENDERSON STATE UNIVERSITY

Business Administration and Management— General	M
Counselor Education	M
Curriculum and Instruction	M
Early Childhood Education	M
Education—General	M,O
Educational Leadership and Administration	M,O
Middle School Education	M
Physical Education	M
Reading Education	M
Special Education	M
Sports Management	M

HENDRIX COLLEGE

Accounting	M

HERITAGE UNIVERSITY

Counselor Education	M
Education—General	M
Educational Leadership and Administration	M
English as a Second Language	M
Multilingual and Multicultural Education	M
Reading Education	M
Science Education	M
Special Education	M

HIGH POINT UNIVERSITY

Business Administration and Management— General	M
Educational Leadership and Administration	M
Elementary Education	M

Exercise and Sports
Science M
Nonprofit Management M
Special Education M

HODGES UNIVERSITY

Business Administration
and Management—
General M
Education—General M
Law M
Management Information
Systems M

HOFSTRA UNIVERSITY

Accounting M
Art Education M,D
Business Administration
and Management—
General M
Business Education M
Communication Disorders M,D
Community Health M
Counselor Education M,O
Early Childhood Education M,D,O
Education of the Gifted M,O
Education—General M,D,O
Educational Leadership
and Administration M,D,O
Educational Media/
Instructional Technology M,O
Elementary Education M,O
English as a Second
Language M,O
English Education M,D
Entertainment
Management M
Exercise and Sports
Science M
Finance and Banking M
Foreign Languages
Education M
Foundations and
Philosophy of Education M,O
Health Education M
Health Services
Management and
Hospital Administration M
Human Resources
Management M
International Business M
Law P,M
Legal and Justice Studies P,M
Management Information
Systems M
Marketing Research M
Marketing M
Mathematics Education M,D
Middle School Education O
Multilingual and
Multicultural Education M,D,O
Music Education M
Physical Education M,D
Quality Management M
Reading Education M,D,O
Real Estate M
Science Education M,D
Secondary Education M,O
Social Sciences Education M,D,O
Special Education M,D,O
Sports Management M
Taxation M

HOLLINS UNIVERSITY

Education—General M
Legal and Justice Studies M,O

HOLY FAMILY UNIVERSITY

Business Administration
and Management—
General M
Community Health
Nursing M
Education—General M
Educational Leadership
and Administration M
Elementary Education M
Finance and Banking M
Health Services
Management and
Hospital Administration M
Human Resources
Management M

Management Information
Systems M
Nursing and Healthcare
Administration M
Nursing Education M
Nursing—General M
Reading Education M
Secondary Education M
Special Education M

HOLY NAMES UNIVERSITY

Business Administration
and Management—
General M
Community Health
Nursing M,O
Education—General M,O
Educational Psychology M,O
English as a Second
Language M,O
Family Nurse Practitioner
Studies M,O
Finance and Banking M
Marketing M
Music Education M,O
Nursing and Healthcare
Administration M,O
Nursing Education M,O
Nursing—General M,O
Special Education M,O
Sports Management M
Urban Education M,O

HOOD COLLEGE

Accounting M
Business Administration
and Management—
General M
Curriculum and Instruction M,O
Early Childhood Education M,O
Education—General M,O
Educational Leadership
and Administration M,O
Elementary Education M,O
Finance and Banking M
Human Resources
Management M
Management Information
Systems M
Marketing M
Mathematics Education M,O
Middle School Education M,O
Reading Education M,O
Science Education M,O
Secondary Education M,O
Special Education M,O

HOPE INTERNATIONAL UNIVERSITY

Business Administration
and Management—
General M
Education—General M
Educational Leadership
and Administration M
International Business M
Nonprofit Management M

HOUSTON BAPTIST UNIVERSITY

Accounting M
Business Administration
and Management—
General M
Counselor Education M
Curriculum and Instruction M
Education—General M
Educational Leadership
and Administration M
Educational Measurement
and Evaluation M
English as a Second
Language M
Health Services
Management and
Hospital Administration M
Human Resources
Management M
Reading Education M

HOWARD PAYNE UNIVERSITY

Educational Leadership
and Administration M

HOWARD UNIVERSITY

Accounting M
Allopathic Medicine P,D
Business Administration
and Management—
General M
Communication Disorders M,D
Counselor Education M,O
Dentistry P,O
Early Childhood Education M,O
Education—General M,D,O
Educational Leadership
and Administration M,D,O
Educational Psychology M,D,O
Elementary Education M
Exercise and Sports
Science M
Family Nurse Practitioner
Studies M,O
Finance and Banking M
Health Education M
Human Resources
Management M
International Business M
Law P,M
Leisure Studies M
Management Information
Systems M
Marketing M
Multilingual and
Multicultural Education M,D
Music Education M
Nursing—General M,O
Oral and Dental Sciences P,O
Pharmacy P
Physical Education M
Public Health—General M
Reading Education M,O
Secondary Education M,O
Social Work M,D
Special Education M,O
Sports Management M
Supply Chain
Management M

HULT INTERNATIONAL BUSINESS SCHOOL (UNITED STATES)

Business Administration
and Management—
General M
Entrepreneurship M
Finance and Banking M
International Business M
Marketing M

HUMBOLDT STATE UNIVERSITY

Athletic Training and
Sports Medicine M
Business Administration
and Management—
General M
Education—General M
English Education M
Exercise and Sports
Science M
Kinesiology and
Movement Studies M
Physical Education M
Physical Therapy M
Social Work M

HUMPHREYS COLLEGE

Law P

HUNTER COLLEGE OF THE CITY UNIVERSITY OF NEW YORK

Accounting M
Adult Nursing M
Communication Disorders M
Community Health
Nursing M
Community Health M
Counselor Education M
Early Childhood Education M,O
Education of Students with
Severe/Multiple
Disabilities M
Education—General M,O
Educational Leadership
and Administration O
Elementary Education M
English as a Second
Language M

English Education M
Environmental and
Occupational Health M
Epidemiology M
Foreign Languages
Education M
Gerontological Nursing M
Health Services
Management and
Hospital Administration M
Mathematics Education M
Multilingual and
Multicultural Education M
Music Education M
Nursing—General M,O
Psychiatric Nursing M,O
Public Health—General M
Reading Education M,O
Science Education M,O
Secondary Education M
Social Sciences Education M
Social Work M,D
Special Education M

HUNTINGTON UNIVERSITY

Education—General M

HUSSON UNIVERSITY

Business Administration
and Management—
General M
Community Health
Nursing M,O
Counselor Education M
Family Nurse Practitioner
Studies M,O
Health Services
Management and
Hospital Administration M
Nonprofit Management M
Nursing—General M,O
Occupational Therapy M
Physical Therapy D
Psychiatric Nursing M,O

ICR GRADUATE SCHOOL

Science Education M

IDAHO STATE UNIVERSITY

Allied Health—General M,D,O
Business Administration
and Management—
General M,O
Communication Disorders M,D,O
Community Health O
Counselor Education M,D,O
Curriculum and Instruction M,O
Dental Hygiene M
Dentistry O
Education—General M,D,O
Educational Leadership
and Administration M,D,O
Educational Media/
Instructional Technology M,D,O
Elementary Education M,O
English as a Second
Language M,D,O
Health Education M
Health Physics/
Radiological Health M,D
Management Information
Systems M,O
Mathematics Education M,D
Medicinal and
Pharmaceutical
Chemistry M,D
Nursing—General M,O
Occupational Therapy M
Oral and Dental Sciences O
Pharmaceutical
Administration P,M,D
Pharmaceutical Sciences M,D
Pharmacy P,M,D
Physical Education M
Physical Therapy D
Physician Assistant
Studies M
Public Health—General M,O
Reading Education M,O
Secondary Education M,O
Special Education M,D,O
Vocational and Technical
Education M

---

*M—master's degree; P—first professional degree; D—doctorate; O—other advanced degree; *—Close-Up and/or Display*

ILLINOIS COLLEGE OF OPTOMETRY

Optometry	P

ILLINOIS INSTITUTE OF TECHNOLOGY

Business Administration and Management— General	M,D,O
Environmental and Occupational Health	M
Finance and Banking	P,M,O
Health Physics/ Radiological Health	M,D
Human Resources Development	M,D
Industrial and Manufacturing Management	M
Law	P,M
Management Information Systems	M,D
Marketing	M,O
Mathematics Education	M,D
Medical Imaging	M,D
Nonprofit Management	M
Science Education	M,D
Sustainability Management	M,O
Taxation	P,M

ILLINOIS STATE UNIVERSITY

Accounting	M
Business Administration and Management— General	M
Communication Disorders	M
Curriculum and Instruction	M,D
Education—General	M,D
Educational Leadership and Administration	M,D
Educational Policy	M,D
Educational Psychology	M,D,O
Family Nurse Practitioner Studies	M,D,O
Health Education	M
Higher Education	M,D
Management Information Systems	M
Mathematics Education	D
Nursing—General	M,D,O
Physical Education	M
Reading Education	M
Social Work	M
Special Education	M,D
Student Affairs	M

IMCA–INTERNATIONAL MANAGEMENT CENTRES ASSOCIATION

Business Administration and Management— General	M

IMMACULATA UNIVERSITY

Advertising and Public Relations	M
Counselor Education	M,D,O
Educational Leadership and Administration	M,D,O
Elementary Education	M,D,O
Multilingual and Multicultural Education	M
Nursing—General	M
Organizational Management	
Secondary Education	M,D,O
Special Education	M,D,O

INDEPENDENCE UNIVERSITY

Business Administration and Management— General	M
Community Health Nursing	M
Community Health	M
Gerontological Nursing	M
Health Promotion	M
Health Services Management and Hospital Administration	M
Nursing and Healthcare Administration	M
Nursing—General	M
Public Health—General	M

INDIANA STATE UNIVERSITY

Athletic Training and Sports Medicine	M
Business Administration and Management— General	M
Community Health	M
Counselor Education	M,D,O
Curriculum and Instruction	M,D
Early Childhood Education	M
Education—General	M,D,O
Educational Leadership and Administration	M,D,O
Educational Media/ Instructional Technology	M,D
Elementary Education	M
English as a Second Language	M,O
English Education	M
Environmental and Occupational Health	M
Exercise and Sports Science	M
Health Education	M
Health Promotion	M
Higher Education	M,D,O
Home Economics Education	M
Human Resources Development	M
Mathematics Education	M
Multilingual and Multicultural Education	M,O
Nursing—General	M
Physical Education	M
Science Education	M,D
Sports Management	M
Student Affairs	M,D,O
Vocational and Technical Education	M

INDIANA TECH

Accounting	M
Business Administration and Management— General	M
Health Services Management and Hospital Administration	M
Human Resources Development	M
Human Resources Management	M
International Business	D
Marketing	M
Organizational Management	M
Science Education	M

INDIANA UNIVERSITY BLOOMINGTON

Art Education	M,D,O
Athletic Training and Sports Medicine	M,D
Business Administration and Management— General	M,D
Communication Disorders	M,D
Counselor Education	M,D,O
Curriculum and Instruction	M,D,O
Education—General	M,D,O
Educational Leadership and Administration	M,D,O
Educational Measurement and Evaluation	M,D,O
Educational Media/ Instructional Technology	M,D,O
Educational Policy	M,D,O
Educational Psychology	M,D,O
Elementary Education	M,D,O
English as a Second Language	M,D
Exercise and Sports Science	M,D
Finance and Banking	M,D,O
Foreign Languages Education	M,D
Foundations and Philosophy of Education	M,D,O
Health Education	M,D
Health Promotion	M,D
Higher Education	M,D,O
Information Studies	M,D,O
International and Comparative Education	M,D,O

Kinesiology and Movement Studies	M,D
Law	P,M,D,O
Leisure Studies	M,D,O
Library Science	M,D,O
Management Information Systems	M,D,O
Mathematics Education	M,D,O
Multilingual and Multicultural Education	M,D
Nonprofit Management	M,D,O
Optometry	P,M,D
Physical Education	M,D
Public Health—General	M,D
Reading Education	M,D,O
Recreation and Park Management	M,D,O
Science Education	M,D,O
Secondary Education	M,D,O
Social Sciences Education	M,D,O
Special Education	M,D,O
Sports Management	M,D,O
Sustainability Management	M,D,O
Travel and Tourism	M,D,O

INDIANA UNIVERSITY EAST

Education—General	M
Social Work	M

INDIANA UNIVERSITY KOKOMO

Business Administration and Management— General	M
Education—General	M
Elementary Education	M

INDIANA UNIVERSITY NORTHWEST

Accounting	M,O
Business Administration and Management— General	M,O
Education—General	M
Elementary Education	M
Health Services Management and Hospital Administration	M,O
Human Services	M,O
Nonprofit Management	M,O
Secondary Education	M
Social Work	M

INDIANA UNIVERSITY OF PENNSYLVANIA

Adult Education	M,D
Business Administration and Management— General	M
Communication Disorders	M
Counselor Education	M
Curriculum and Instruction	M,D
Education—General	M,D,O
Educational Leadership and Administration	M,D,O
Educational Media/ Instructional Technology	M,D
Educational Psychology	M,O
Elementary Education	M
English as a Second Language	M,D
English Education	M,D
Environmental and Occupational Health	M
Exercise and Sports Science	M
Facilities Management	M
Health Education	M
Health Services Management and Hospital Administration	M,D
Higher Education	M
Human Resources Development	M
Mathematics Education	M
Music Education	M
Nursing—General	M
Physical Education	M
Reading Education	M
Special Education	M
Sports Management	M

INDIANA UNIVERSITY–PURDUE UNIVERSITY FORT WAYNE

Adult Nursing	M,O

Business Administration and Management— General	M
Communication Disorders	M
Counselor Education	M,O
Education—General	M,O
Educational Leadership and Administration	M,O
Elementary Education	M
English as a Second Language	M,O
English Education	M,O
Facilities Management	M
Nursing and Healthcare Administration	M,O
Nursing Education	M,O
Nursing—General	M,O
Organizational Management	M,O
Secondary Education	M
Special Education	M,O
Women's Health Nursing	M,O

INDIANA UNIVERSITY–PURDUE UNIVERSITY INDIANAPOLIS

Accounting	M
Acute Care/Critical Care Nursing	M,D
Adult Education	M
Adult Nursing	M,D
Allopathic Medicine	P,M,D
Art Education	M
Bioethics	M,O
Business Administration and Management— General	M
Community Health Nursing	M,D
Computer Education	M,O
Counselor Education	M,O
Curriculum and Instruction	M,O
Dentistry	P,M,D,O
Early Childhood Education	M,O
Education—General	M,O
Educational Leadership and Administration	M,O
English as a Second Language	M,O
English Education	M
Epidemiology	M
Family Nurse Practitioner Studies	M,D
Foreign Languages Education	M,O
Health Education	M,D
Health Services Management and Hospital Administration	M
Higher Education	M,O
Law	P,M,D
Library Science	M
Maternal and Child/ Neonatal Nursing	M,D
Mathematics Education	M
Nonprofit Management	M
Nursing—General	M,D
Occupational Therapy	M,D
Pediatric Nursing	M,D
Physical Education	M
Physical Therapy	M,D
Psychiatric Nursing	M,D
Public Health—General	M
Reading Education	M,O
Rehabilitation Sciences	M,D
Social Work	M,D,O
Special Education	M,O
Student Affairs	M,O
Women's Health Nursing	M,D

INDIANA UNIVERSITY SOUTH BEND

Accounting	M
Art Education	M
Business Administration and Management— General	M
Counselor Education	M
Education—General	M
Elementary Education	M
Health Services Management and Hospital Administration	M,O
Management Information Systems	M
Nonprofit Management	M,O
Secondary Education	M

Social Work	M
Special Education	M

INDIANA UNIVERSITY SOUTHEAST

Business Administration and Management— General	M
Counselor Education	M
Education—General	M
Elementary Education	M
Finance and Banking	M
Secondary Education	M

INDIANA WESLEYAN UNIVERSITY

Accounting	M
Business Administration and Management— General	M
Community Health Nursing	M,O
Counselor Education	M
Curriculum and Instruction	M
Education—General	M
Human Resources Management	M
Nursing and Healthcare Administration	M,O
Nursing Education	M,O
Nursing—General	M,O
Organizational Management	D

INSTITUTE FOR CHRISTIAN STUDIES

Education—General	M,D

INSTITUTE FOR CLINICAL SOCIAL WORK

Social Work	D

INSTITUTE OF CLINICAL ACUPUNCTURE AND ORIENTAL MEDICINE

Acupuncture and Oriental Medicine	M

INSTITUTE OF PUBLIC ADMINISTRATION

Health Services Management and Hospital Administration	M,O

INSTITUT FRANCO-EUROPÉEN DE CHIROPRATIQUE

Chiropractic	P

INSTITUTO CENTROAMERICANO DE ADMINISTRACIÓN DE EMPRESAS

Business Administration and Management— General	M
Finance and Banking	M

INSTITUTO TECNOLOGICO DE SANTO DOMINGO

Allopathic Medicine	P,M
Business Administration and Management— General	M
Education—General	M
Finance and Banking	M
Human Resources Management	M
International Business	M
Marketing	M
Organizational Management	M
Social Sciences Education	M
Supply Chain Management	M
Taxation	M

INSTITUTO TECNOLÓGICO Y DE ESTUDIOS SUPERIORES DE MONTERREY, CAMPUS CENTRAL DE VERACRUZ

Business Administration and Management— General	M
Education—General	M
Educational Leadership and Administration	M

Educational Media/ Instructional Technology	M
Electronic Commerce	M
Finance and Banking	M
International Business	M
Management Information Systems	M
Marketing	M

INSTITUTO TECNOLÓGICO Y DE ESTUDIOS SUPERIORES DE MONTERREY, CAMPUS CHIHUAHUA

International Business	M,O

INSTITUTO TECNOLÓGICO Y DE ESTUDIOS SUPERIORES DE MONTERREY, CAMPUS CIUDAD DE MÉXICO

Business Administration and Management— General	M,D
Education—General	M,D
Educational Media/ Instructional Technology	M,D
Finance and Banking	M,D
International Business	M,D
Law	P
Management Information Systems	M,D
Quality Management	M,D

INSTITUTO TECNOLÓGICO Y DE ESTUDIOS SUPERIORES DE MONTERREY, CAMPUS CIUDAD JUÁREZ

Business Administration and Management— General	M
Education—General	M
Educational Leadership and Administration	M
Educational Media/ Instructional Technology	M,D
Electronic Commerce	M
Management Information Systems	M
Quality Management	M

INSTITUTO TECNOLÓGICO Y DE ESTUDIOS SUPERIORES DE MONTERREY, CAMPUS CIUDAD OBREGÓN

Business Administration and Management— General	M
Developmental Education	M
Education—General	M
Finance and Banking	M
Management Information Systems	M
Marketing	M
Mathematics Education	M

INSTITUTO TECNOLÓGICO Y DE ESTUDIOS SUPERIORES DE MONTERREY, CAMPUS CUERNAVACA

Business Administration and Management— General	M
Finance and Banking	M
Human Resources Management	M
International Business	M
Marketing	M

INSTITUTO TECNOLÓGICO Y DE ESTUDIOS SUPERIORES DE MONTERREY, CAMPUS ESTADO DE MÉXICO

Business Administration and Management— General	M,D
Education—General	M,D
Educational Leadership and Administration	M,D
Educational Media/ Instructional Technology	M,D
Electronic Commerce	M,D
Finance and Banking	M,D

Industrial and Manufacturing Management	M,D
Management Information Systems	M,D
Marketing	M,D
Quality Management	M,D

INSTITUTO TECNOLÓGICO Y DE ESTUDIOS SUPERIORES DE MONTERREY, CAMPUS GUADALAJARA

Business Administration and Management— General	M
Finance and Banking	M

INSTITUTO TECNOLÓGICO Y DE ESTUDIOS SUPERIORES DE MONTERREY, CAMPUS IRAPUATO

Business Administration and Management— General	M,D
Education—General	M,D
Educational Leadership and Administration	M,D
Educational Media/ Instructional Technology	M,D
Electronic Commerce	M,D
Finance and Banking	M,D
Industrial and Manufacturing Management	M,D
International Business	M,D
Library Science	M,D
Management Information Systems	M,D
Marketing Research	M,D
Quality Management	M,D

INSTITUTO TECNOLÓGICO Y DE ESTUDIOS SUPERIORES DE MONTERREY, CAMPUS LAGUNA

Business Administration and Management— General	M
Management Information Systems	M

INSTITUTO TECNOLÓGICO Y DE ESTUDIOS SUPERIORES DE MONTERREY, CAMPUS LEÓN

Business Administration and Management— General	M

INSTITUTO TECNOLÓGICO Y DE ESTUDIOS SUPERIORES DE MONTERREY, CAMPUS MONTERREY

Business Administration and Management— General	M,D
Finance and Banking	M
International Business	M
Marketing	M
Science Education	M,D

INSTITUTO TECNOLÓGICO Y DE ESTUDIOS SUPERIORES DE MONTERREY, CAMPUS QUERÉTARO

Business Administration and Management— General	M

INSTITUTO TECNOLÓGICO Y DE ESTUDIOS SUPERIORES DE MONTERREY, CAMPUS SONORA NORTE

Business Administration and Management— General	M
Education—General	M

INSTITUTO TECNOLÓGICO Y DE ESTUDIOS SUPERIORES DE MONTERREY, CAMPUS TOLUCA

Business Administration and Management— General	M

INTER AMERICAN UNIVERSITY OF PUERTO RICO, AGUADILLA CAMPUS

Accounting	M
Business Administration and Management— General	M
Educational Leadership and Administration	M
Elementary Education	M
Finance and Banking	M
Human Resources Management	M
Management Information Systems	M
Marketing	M

INTER AMERICAN UNIVERSITY OF PUERTO RICO, ARECIBO CAMPUS

Accounting	M
Acute Care/Critical Care Nursing	M
Adult Nursing	M
Business Administration and Management— General	M
Community Health Nursing	M
Counselor Education	M
Curriculum and Instruction	M
Education—General	M
Educational Leadership and Administration	M
Elementary Education	M
English as a Second Language	M
Finance and Banking	M
Foreign Languages Education	M
Human Resources Management	M
Mathematics Education	M
Medical/Surgical Nursing	M
Nurse Anesthesia	M
Nursing—General	M
Science Education	M
Social Sciences Education	M

INTER AMERICAN UNIVERSITY OF PUERTO RICO, BARRANQUITAS CAMPUS

Accounting	M
Business Administration and Management— General	M
Curriculum and Instruction	M
Education—General	M
Educational Leadership and Administration	M
Elementary Education	M
Finance and Banking	M
Library Science	M

INTER AMERICAN UNIVERSITY OF PUERTO RICO, BAYAMÓN CAMPUS

Electronic Commerce	M
Human Resources Management	M

INTER AMERICAN UNIVERSITY OF PUERTO RICO, GUAYAMA CAMPUS

Early Childhood Education	M
Elementary Education	M

INTER AMERICAN UNIVERSITY OF PUERTO RICO, METROPOLITAN CAMPUS

Accounting	M
Athletic Training and Sports Medicine	M
Business Administration and Management— General	M
Business Education	M
Clinical Laboratory Sciences/Medical Technology	M
Counselor Education	M,D
Curriculum and Instruction	M,D
Education—General	M,D

*M—master's degree; P—first professional degree; D—doctorate; O—other advanced degree; *—Close-Up and/or Display*

Educational Leadership
and Administration — M,D
Educational Media/
Instructional Technology — M
Elementary Education — M
English as a Second
Language — M
Exercise and Sports
Science — M
Finance and Banking — M
Health Education — M
Higher Education — M
Human Resources
Development — M
Human Resources
Management — M
Industrial and
Manufacturing
Management — M
International Business — M
Management Information
Systems — M
Marketing — M
Mathematics Education — M
Music Education — M
Physical Education — M
Religious Education — D
Science Education — M
Social Work — M
Special Education — M
Vocational and Technical
Education — M

INTER AMERICAN UNIVERSITY OF PUERTO RICO, PONCE CAMPUS

Accounting — M
Elementary Education — M
English as a Second
Language — M
Finance and Banking — M
Human Resources
Management — M
Marketing — M
Mathematics Education — M
Science Education — M
Social Sciences Education — M

INTER AMERICAN UNIVERSITY OF PUERTO RICO, SAN GERMÁN CAMPUS

Accounting — M,D
Business Administration
and Management—
General — M,D
Business Education — M
Counselor Education — M,D
Curriculum and Instruction — D
Educational Leadership
and Administration — M,D
Elementary Education — M
English as a Second
Language — M
Entrepreneurship — D
Finance and Banking — M,D
Human Resources
Development — M,D
Human Resources
Management — M,D
Industrial and
Manufacturing
Management — M,D
International Business — M,D
Kinesiology and
Movement Studies — M
Library Science — M
Management Information
Systems — M,D
Marketing — M,D
Music Education — M
Physical Education — M
Science Education — M
Special Education — M

INTER AMERICAN UNIVERSITY OF PUERTO RICO SCHOOL OF LAW

Law — P

INTER AMERICAN UNIVERSITY OF PUERTO RICO SCHOOL OF OPTOMETRY

Optometry — P

INTERNATIONAL BAPTIST COLLEGE

Education—General — M

INTERNATIONAL COLLEGE OF THE CAYMAN ISLANDS

Business Administration
and Management—
General — M
Business Education — M
Human Resources
Management — M

INTERNATIONAL TECHNOLOGICAL UNIVERSITY

Business Administration
and Management—
General — M
Industrial and
Manufacturing
Management — M

INTERNATIONAL UNIVERSITY IN GENEVA

Business Administration
and Management—
General — M
Finance and Banking — M
International Business — M
Investment Management — M
Marketing — M

THE INTERNATIONAL UNIVERSITY OF MONACO

Business Administration
and Management—
General — M
Entrepreneurship — M
Finance and Banking — M
International Business — M
Marketing — M

IONA COLLEGE

Accounting — M,O
Advertising and Public
Relations — M
Business Administration
and Management—
General — M,O*
Education—General — M
Educational Leadership
and Administration — M
English Education — M
Finance and Banking — M,O
Foreign Languages
Education — M
Health Services
Management and
Hospital Administration — M,O
Human Resources
Management — M,O
International Business — M,O
Marketing — M,O
Mathematics Education — M
Reading Education — M
Science Education — M
Social Sciences Education — M

IOWA STATE UNIVERSITY OF SCIENCE AND TECHNOLOGY

Accounting — M
Agricultural Education — M,D
Business Administration
and Management—
General — M,D
Counselor Education — M,D
Curriculum and Instruction — M,D
Educational Leadership
and Administration — M,D
Educational Measurement
and Evaluation — M,D
Educational Media/
Instructional Technology — M,D
Elementary Education — M,D
Foundations and
Philosophy of Education — M,D
Higher Education — M,D
Home Economics
Education — M,D
Hospitality Management — M,D
Human Resources
Development — M,D
Kinesiology and
Movement Studies — M,D
Management Information
Systems — M
Mathematics Education — M,D
Special Education — M,D

Transportation
Management — M
Veterinary Medicine — P,M
Veterinary Sciences — M,D
Vocational and Technical
Education — M,D

ITHACA COLLEGE

Accounting — M
Allied Health—General — M,D
Business Administration
and Management—
General — M
Communication Disorders — M
Elementary Education — M
English Education — M
Exercise and Sports
Science — M
Foreign Languages
Education — M
Health Education — M
Mathematics Education — M
Music Education — M
Occupational Therapy — M
Physical Education — M
Physical Therapy — M,D
Science Education — M
Secondary Education — M
Social Sciences Education — M
Sports Management — M

ITT TECHNICAL INSTITUTE (IN)

Business Administration
and Management—
General — M

JACKSON STATE UNIVERSITY

Accounting — M
Business Administration
and Management—
General — M,D
Communication Disorders — M
Counselor Education — M,O
Early Childhood Education — M,D,O
Education—General — M,D,O
Educational Leadership
and Administration — M,D,O
Educational Media/
Instructional Technology — M,D,O
Elementary Education — M,D,O
English Education — M
Health Education — M
Mathematics Education — M
Music Education — M
Physical Education — M
Science Education — M,D
Secondary Education — M,D,O
Social Work — M,D
Special Education — M,O
Vocational and Technical
Education — M

JACKSONVILLE STATE UNIVERSITY

Business Administration
and Management—
General — M
Counselor Education — M
Early Childhood Education — M
Education—General — M,O
Educational Leadership
and Administration — M,O
Educational Media/
Instructional Technology — M
Elementary Education — M
Health Education — M
Nursing—General — M
Physical Education — M
Reading Education — M
Secondary Education — M
Special Education — M

JACKSONVILLE UNIVERSITY

Business Administration
and Management—
General — M
Computer Education — M
Early Childhood Education — M,O
Education—General — M,O
Educational Media/
Instructional Technology — M
Elementary Education — M
Mathematics Education — M
Music Education — M
Nursing—General — M

Oral and Dental Sciences — O
Reading Education — M

JAMES MADISON UNIVERSITY

Accounting — M
Art Education — M
Business Administration
and Management—
General — M
Communication Disorders — M,D
Early Childhood Education — M
Educational Leadership
and Administration — M
Elementary Education — M
Health Education — M
Kinesiology and
Movement Studies — M
Middle School Education — M
Music Education — M,D
Nursing—General — M
Occupational Therapy — M
Physician Assistant
Studies — M
Reading Education — M
Secondary Education — M
Special Education — M
Vocational and Technical
Education — M

JEFFERSON COLLEGE OF HEALTH SCIENCES

Nursing and Healthcare
Administration — M
Nursing Education — M
Nursing—General — M
Occupational Therapy — M
Physician Assistant
Studies — M

THE JEWISH THEOLOGICAL SEMINARY

Religious Education — M,D*

JEWISH UNIVERSITY OF AMERICA

Religious Education — M,D

JOHN BROWN UNIVERSITY

Business Administration
and Management—
General — M
Counselor Education — M
Higher Education — M
International Business — M

JOHN CARROLL UNIVERSITY

Accounting — M
Business Administration
and Management—
General — M
Counselor Education — M,O
Early Childhood Education — M
Education—General — M
Educational Leadership
and Administration — M
Educational Psychology — M
Middle School Education — M
Nonprofit Management — M
Science Education — M
Secondary Education — M

JOHN F. KENNEDY UNIVERSITY

Business Administration
and Management—
General — M,O
Education—General — M
Health Education — M
Human Resources
Development — M,O
Law — P
Organizational
Management — M,O

JOHN JAY COLLEGE OF CRIMINAL JUSTICE OF THE CITY UNIVERSITY OF NEW YORK

Legal and Justice Studies — M,D
Organizational Behavior — M,D

JOHN MARSHALL LAW SCHOOL

International Business — P,M
Law — P,M
Legal and Justice Studies — P,M
Management Information
Systems — P,M

Real Estate — P,M
Taxation — P,M

THE JOHNS HOPKINS UNIVERSITY

Acute Care/Critical Care
  Nursing — M,O
Adult Education — M,O
Adult Nursing — M,O
Allopathic Medicine — P
Bioethics — M,D
Business Administration
  and Management—
  General — M,O
Clinical Research — M,D
Community Health
  Nursing — M
Community Health — M,D
Counselor Education — M,O
Curriculum and Instruction — M,O
Early Childhood Education — M,D,O
Education of the Gifted — M,D,O
Education—General — M,D,O
Educational Leadership
  and Administration — M,D,O
Educational Media/
  Instructional Technology — M,D,O
Educational Psychology — M,O
Elementary Education — M,O
English as a Second
  Language — M,D,O
English Education — M,O
Environmental and
  Occupational Health — M,D
Epidemiology — M,D
Family Nurse Practitioner
  Studies — M,O
Finance and Banking — M,O
Foreign Languages
  Education — M,O
Health Education — M,D
Health Services
  Management and
  Hospital Administration — M,D,O
Health Services Research — M,D
Human Resources
  Development — M,O
International Health — M,D
Investment Management — M,O
Management Information
  Systems — M,O
Marketing — M
Mathematics Education — M,O
Nursing and Healthcare
  Administration — M
Nursing—General — M,D,O
Pediatric Nursing — M,O
Pharmaceutical Sciences — M
Public Health—General — M,D
Reading Education — M,D,O
Real Estate — M
Science Education — M,O
Secondary Education — M,O
Social Sciences Education — M,O
Special Education — M,D,O
Urban Education — M,O
Women's Health Nursing — M,O

JOHNSON & WALES UNIVERSITY

Accounting — M
Education—General — M
Educational Leadership
  and Administration — D
Elementary Education — D
Finance and Banking — M
Higher Education — D
Hospitality Management — M
International Business — M
Marketing — M
Organizational
  Management — M
Secondary Education — D

JOHNSON BIBLE COLLEGE

Education—General — M
Educational Media/
  Instructional Technology — M

JOHNSON STATE COLLEGE

Counselor Education — M
Curriculum and Instruction — M
Education of the Gifted — M
Education—General — M,O
Educational Psychology — M
Reading Education — M

Science Education — M
Secondary Education — M,O
Special Education — M

JONES INTERNATIONAL UNIVERSITY

Accounting — M
Adult Education — M
Business Administration
  and Management—
  General — M
Curriculum and Instruction — M
Distance Education
  Development — M
Education—General — M
Educational Leadership
  and Administration — M
Educational Media/
  Instructional Technology — M
Elementary Education — M
Entrepreneurship — M
Finance and Banking — M
Health Services
  Management and
  Hospital Administration — M
Higher Education — M
Organizational
  Management — M
Project Management — M
Secondary Education — M

THE JUDGE ADVOCATE GENERAL'S SCHOOL, U.S. ARMY

Law — M

JUDSON UNIVERSITY

Education—General — M
Organizational
  Management — M
Reading Education — M

KANSAS CITY UNIVERSITY OF MEDICINE AND BIOSCIENCES

Bioethics — M
Osteopathic Medicine — P

KANSAS STATE UNIVERSITY

Accounting — M
Adult Education — M,D
Business Administration
  and Management—
  General — M
Communication Disorders — M
Counselor Education — M,D
Curriculum and Instruction — M,D
Early Childhood Education — M
Education—General — M,D
Educational Leadership
  and Administration — M,D
Higher Education — M,D
Hospitality Management — M,D
Human Services — M
Industrial and
  Manufacturing
  Management — M
Kinesiology and
  Movement Studies — M
Marketing — M
Music Education — M
Special Education — M,D
Student Affairs — M,D
Veterinary Sciences — M
Vocational and Technical
  Education — M,D

KANSAS WESLEYAN UNIVERSITY

Business Administration
  and Management—
  General — M
Sports Management — M

KAPLAN UNIVERSITY, DAVENPORT CAMPUS

Business Administration
  and Management—
  General — M
Education—General — M
Educational Leadership
  and Administration — M
Educational Media/
  Instructional Technology — M
Entrepreneurship — M
Finance and Banking — M

Health Services
  Management and
  Hospital Administration — M,O
Higher Education — M
Human Resources
  Management — M
International Business — M
Law — M
Legal and Justice Studies — M,O
Logistics — M
Management Information
  Systems — M
Marketing — M
Mathematics Education — M
Nursing and Healthcare
  Administration — M
Nursing Education — M
Nursing—General — M
Organizational
  Management — M
Project Management — M
Reading Education — M
Science Education — M
Secondary Education — M
Special Education — M
Student Affairs — M
Supply Chain
  Management — M

KEAN UNIVERSITY

Accounting — M
Adult Education — M
Art Education — M
Business Administration
  and Management—
  General — M
Communication Disorders — M
Community Health
  Nursing — M
Community Health — M
Computer Education — M
Counselor Education — M
Curriculum and Instruction — M
Early Childhood Education — M
Education—General — M
Educational Leadership
  and Administration — M,D
Educational Psychology — M
English as a Second
  Language — M
Exercise and Sports
  Science — M
Foreign Languages
  Education — M
Health Services
  Management and
  Hospital Administration — M
International Business — M
Management Information
  Systems — M
Mathematics Education — M
Multilingual and
  Multicultural Education — M
Nonprofit Management — M
Nursing and Healthcare
  Administration — M
Nursing—General — M
Occupational Therapy — M
Reading Education — M
School Nursing — M
Science Education — M
Social Work — M
Special Education — M
Urban Education — D

KEENE STATE COLLEGE

Counselor Education — M,O
Curriculum and Instruction — M,O
Education—General — M,O
Educational Leadership
  and Administration — M,O
Special Education — M,O

KEISER UNIVERSITY

Business Administration
  and Management—
  General — M
Education—General — M
Educational Leadership
  and Administration — M,D
International Business — M
Marketing — M
Physician Assistant
  Studies — M

KELLER GRADUATE SCHOOL OF MANAGEMENT

Business Administration
  and Management—
  General — M,O

KELLER GRADUATE SCHOOL OF MANAGEMENT

Business Administration
  and Management—
  General — M

KENNESAW STATE UNIVERSITY

Accounting — M
Business Administration
  and Management—
  General — M,D
Early Childhood Education — M
Education—General — M,D,O
Educational Leadership
  and Administration — M,D,O
Educational Media/
  Instructional Technology — M
Elementary Education — M
English as a Second
  Language — M
English Education — M
Exercise and Sports
  Science — M
Health Services
  Management and
  Hospital Administration — M
Mathematics Education — M
Middle School Education — M
Nursing—General — M,D
Secondary Education — M
Social Work — M
Special Education — M

KENT STATE UNIVERSITY

Accounting — M,D
Adult Nursing — M,D
Art Education — M
Athletic Training and
  Sports Medicine — M
Business Administration
  and Management—
  General — M*
Communication Disorders — M,D
Computer Education — M
Counselor Education — M,D,O
Curriculum and Instruction — M,D,O
Early Childhood Education — M
Education of the Gifted — M
Education—General — M,D,O
Educational Leadership
  and Administration — M,D,O
Educational Measurement
  and Evaluation — M,D,O
Educational Media/
  Instructional Technology — M
Educational Psychology — M,D
English as a Second
  Language — M,D
English Education — M,D
Exercise and Sports
  Science — M,D
Family Nurse Practitioner
  Studies — M,D
Finance and Banking — D
Foreign Languages
  Education — M,D
Foundations and
  Philosophy of Education — M,D,O
Gerontological Nursing — M,D
Health Education — M,D
Higher Education — M,D,O
Hospitality Management — M
Human Services — M,D,O
Library Science — M
Management Information
  Systems — D
Marketing — D
Middle School Education — M
Music Education — M,D
Nursing and Healthcare
  Administration — M,D
Nursing—General — M,D
Pediatric Nursing — M,D
Physical Education — D
Psychiatric Nursing — M,D
Reading Education — M

Recreation and Park
  Management — M
Secondary Education — M
Special Education — M,D,O
Sports Management — M
Student Affairs — M
Travel and Tourism — M
Vocational and Technical
  Education — M,O
Women's Health Nursing — M,D

KENT STATE UNIVERSITY AT STARK

Business Administration
  and Management—
  General — M

KENTUCKY STATE UNIVERSITY

Accounting — M
Business Administration
  and Management—
  General — M
Finance and Banking — M
Human Resources
  Development — M
Management Information
  Systems — M
Marketing — M
Nonprofit Management — M
Special Education — M

KETTERING UNIVERSITY

Business Administration
  and Management—
  General — M
Industrial and
  Manufacturing
  Management — M

KEUKA COLLEGE

Business Administration
  and Management—
  General — M
Early Childhood Education — M
Nursing—General — M
Occupational Therapy — M

KING COLLEGE

Business Administration
  and Management—
  General — M

KING'S COLLEGE

Business Administration
  and Management—
  General — M
Health Services
  Management and
  Hospital Administration — M
Physician Assistant
  Studies — M
Reading Education — M

KUTZTOWN UNIVERSITY OF PENNSYLVANIA

Art Education — M,O
Business Administration
  and Management—
  General — M
Counselor Education — M
Curriculum and Instruction — M,O
Early Childhood Education — M,O
Education—General — M,O
Educational Leadership
  and Administration — M
Educational Media/
  Instructional Technology — M,O
Elementary Education — M,O
English Education — M,O
Library Science — M,O
Mathematics Education — M,O
Music Education — O
Reading Education — M
School Nursing — M,O
Science Education — M,O
Secondary Education — M,O
Social Sciences Education — M,O
Social Work — M
Special Education — M,O

LAGRANGE COLLEGE

Curriculum and Instruction — M
Education—General — M
Middle School Education — M

Organizational
  Management — M
Secondary Education — M

LAKE ERIE COLLEGE

Business Administration
  and Management—
  General — M
Curriculum and Instruction — M
Education—General — M
Educational Leadership
  and Administration — M
Health Services
  Management and
  Hospital Administration — M
Reading Education — M

LAKE ERIE COLLEGE OF OSTEOPATHIC MEDICINE

Health Education — P,M,O
Osteopathic Medicine — P,M,O
Pharmacy — P,M,O

LAKE FOREST GRADUATE SCHOOL OF MANAGEMENT

Business Administration
  and Management—
  General — M

LAKEHEAD UNIVERSITY

Education—General — M,D
Exercise and Sports
  Science — M
Health Services Research — M
Kinesiology and
  Movement Studies — M
Social Work — M

LAKELAND COLLEGE

Accounting — M
Business Administration
  and Management—
  General — M
Counselor Education — M
Education—General — M
Finance and Banking — M
Health Services
  Management and
  Hospital Administration — M
Project Management — M

LAMAR UNIVERSITY

Accounting — M
Business Administration
  and Management—
  General — M
Communication Disorders — M,D
Counselor Education — M,D,O
Education—General — M,D,O
Educational Leadership
  and Administration — M,D,O
Educational Media/
  Instructional Technology — M,D,O
Entrepreneurship — M
Finance and Banking — M
Health Services
  Management and
  Hospital Administration — M
Kinesiology and
  Movement Studies — M
Management Strategy and
  Policy — M
Music Education — M
Nursing and Healthcare
  Administration — M
Nursing Education — M
Nursing—General — M
Special Education — M,D

LANCASTER BIBLE COLLEGE & GRADUATE SCHOOL

Counselor Education — M
Special Education — M

LANCASTER THEOLOGICAL SEMINARY

Religious Education — P,M,D,O

LANDER UNIVERSITY

Curriculum and Instruction — M
Education—General — M
Elementary Education — M

LANGSTON UNIVERSITY

Education—General — M
Elementary Education — M
English as a Second
  Language — M
Multilingual and
  Multicultural Education — M
Physical Therapy — D
Urban Education — M

LA ROCHE COLLEGE

Human Resources
  Management — M,O
Nurse Anesthesia — M
Nursing and Healthcare
  Administration — M
Nursing Education — M
Nursing—General — M

LA SALLE UNIVERSITY

Business Administration
  and Management—
  General — M,O
Communication Disorders — M
Education—General — M
Educational Media/
  Instructional Technology — M
Nursing—General — M,O

LASELL COLLEGE

Advertising and Public
  Relations — M,O
Business Administration
  and Management—
  General — M,O
Hospitality Management — M,O
Human Resources
  Management — M,O
Marketing — M,O
Nonprofit Management — M,O
Project Management — M,O
Sports Management — M,O

LA SIERRA UNIVERSITY

Accounting — M,O
Advertising and Public
  Relations — M
Business Administration
  and Management—
  General — M,O
Counselor Education — M,O
Curriculum and Instruction — M,D,O
Education—General — M,D,O
Educational Leadership
  and Administration — M,D,O
Educational Psychology — M,O
Finance and Banking — M,O
Human Resources
  Management — M,O
Marketing — M,O
Religious Education — P,M

LAURA AND ALVIN SIEGAL COLLEGE OF JUDAIC STUDIES

Religious Education — M

LAURENTIAN UNIVERSITY

Business Administration
  and Management—
  General — M
Nursing—General — M
Public Health—General — D
Science Education — O
Social Work — M

LAWRENCE TECHNOLOGICAL UNIVERSITY

Business Administration
  and Management—
  General — M,D
Educational Media/
  Instructional Technology — M
Industrial and
  Manufacturing
  Management — M,D
Management Information
  Systems — M,D
Science Education — M

LEBANESE AMERICAN UNIVERSITY

Business Administration
  and Management—
  General — M
Pharmacy — P

LEBANON VALLEY COLLEGE

Business Administration
  and Management—
  General — M
Music Education — M
Physical Therapy — D
Science Education — M

LEE UNIVERSITY

Counselor Education — M
Education—General — M,O
Educational Leadership
  and Administration — M,O
Elementary Education — M,O
Music Education — M
Secondary Education — M,O
Special Education — M,O

LEHIGH UNIVERSITY

Accounting — M
Business Administration
  and Management—
  General — M,D,O
Counselor Education — M,D,O
Curriculum and Instruction — M,D,O
Education—General — M,D,O
Educational Leadership
  and Administration — M,D,O
Educational Media/
  Instructional Technology — M,D,O
Elementary Education — M,D,O
English as a Second
  Language — M,O
Finance and Banking — M
Human Services — M,D,O
International and
  Comparative Education — M,O
Project Management — M,D,O
Quantitative Analysis — M
Secondary Education — M,D,O
Special Education — M,D,O
Student Affairs — M,D,O
Supply Chain
  Management — M,D,O

LEHMAN COLLEGE OF THE CITY UNIVERSITY OF NEW YORK

Accounting — M
Adult Nursing — M
Business Education — M
Communication Disorders — M
Counselor Education — M
Early Childhood Education — M
Education—General — M
Elementary Education — M
English as a Second
  Language — M
English Education — M
Gerontological Nursing — M
Health Education — M
Health Promotion — M
Maternal and Child/
  Neonatal Nursing — M
Mathematics Education — M
Multilingual and
  Multicultural Education — M
Music Education — M
Nursing—General — M
Pediatric Nursing — M
Reading Education — M
Recreation and Park
  Management — M
Science Education — M
Social Sciences Education — M
Special Education — M

LE MOYNE COLLEGE

Business Administration
  and Management—
  General — M
Early Childhood Education — M,O
Education—General — M,O
Educational Leadership
  and Administration — M,O
Elementary Education — M,O
English Education — M,O
Middle School Education — M,O
Nursing and Healthcare
  Administration — M,O
Nursing Education — M,O
Nursing—General — M,O
Physician Assistant
  Studies — M
Secondary Education — M,O

Social Sciences Education	M,O
Special Education	M,O

LENOIR-RHYNE UNIVERSITY

Accounting	M
Athletic Training and Sports Medicine	M
Business Administration and Management— General	M
Counselor Education	M
Early Childhood Education	M
Education—General	M
Entrepreneurship	M
Occupational Therapy	M

LESLEY UNIVERSITY

Art Education	M,D,O
Computer Education	M,D,O
Curriculum and Instruction	M,D,O
Early Childhood Education	M,D,O
Education—General	M,D,O
Elementary Education	M,D,O
Environmental Education	M,D,O
Middle School Education	M,D,O
Reading Education	M,D,O
Science Education	M,D,O
Special Education	M,D,O

LETOURNEAU UNIVERSITY

Business Administration and Management— General	M
Curriculum and Instruction	M
Education—General	M
Educational Leadership and Administration	M
Management Strategy and Policy	M

LEWIS & CLARK COLLEGE

Communication Disorders	M
Early Childhood Education	M
Education—General	M
Educational Leadership and Administration	M,D
Elementary Education	M
Environmental Law	P,M
Law	P,M
Middle School Education	M
Secondary Education	M
Special Education	M

LEWIS UNIVERSITY

Accounting	M
Adult Nursing	M
Aviation Management	M
Business Administration and Management— General	M
Counselor Education	M
Curriculum and Instruction	M
Education—General	M,D,O
Educational Leadership and Administration	M,D,O
Educational Media/ Instructional Technology	M
Electronic Commerce	M
Elementary Education	M
English as a Second Language	M
Environmental and Occupational Health	M
Finance and Banking	M
Health Services Management and Hospital Administration	M
Human Resources Management	M
International Business	M
Management Information Systems	M
Marketing	M
Mathematics Education	M
Nursing and Healthcare Administration	M
Nursing Education	M
Nursing—General	M
Organizational Management	M
Project Management	M
Reading Education	M
Science Education	M

Secondary Education	M
Social Sciences Education	M
Special Education	M
Student Affairs	M

LIBERTY UNIVERSITY

Business Administration and Management— General	M
Counselor Education	M,D,O
Curriculum and Instruction	M,D,O
Early Childhood Education	M,D,O
Education of the Gifted	M,D,O
Education—General	M,D,O
Educational Leadership and Administration	M,D,O
Elementary Education	M,D,O
Law	P
Nursing—General	M,D
Reading Education	M,D,O
Secondary Education	M,D,O
Special Education	M,D,O

LIFE CHIROPRACTIC COLLEGE WEST

Chiropractic	P

LIFE UNIVERSITY

Chiropractic	P
Exercise and Sports Science	M

LIM COLLEGE

Business Administration and Management— General	M
Entrepreneurship	M

LINCOLN CHRISTIAN SEMINARY

Religious Education	P,M,D

LINCOLN MEMORIAL UNIVERSITY

Business Administration and Management— General	M
Counselor Education	M,O
Curriculum and Instruction	M,O
Education—General	M,O
Educational Leadership and Administration	M,O
English Education	M,O
Family Nurse Practitioner Studies	M
Law	P
Nurse Anesthesia	M
Nursing—General	M
Osteopathic Medicine	P

LINCOLN UNIVERSITY (CA)

Business Administration and Management— General	M,D
Finance and Banking	M,D
Human Resources Management	M,D
International Business	M,D
Investment Management	M,D
Management Information Systems	M,D

LINCOLN UNIVERSITY (MO)

Accounting	M,O
Business Administration and Management— General	M,O
Counselor Education	M,O
Educational Leadership and Administration	M,O
Elementary Education	M,O
Entrepreneurship	M,O
Secondary Education	M,O
Special Education	M,O

LINCOLN UNIVERSITY (PA)

Business Administration and Management— General	M
Early Childhood Education	M
Elementary Education	M
Finance and Banking	M
Human Resources Management	M

Human Services	M
Reading Education	M

LINDENWOOD UNIVERSITY

Accounting	M
Business Administration and Management— General	M,O
Education—General	M,D,O
Educational Leadership and Administration	M,D,O
Educational Media/ Instructional Technology	M,D,O
Entrepreneurship	M
Finance and Banking	M
Health Services Management and Hospital Administration	M,O
Human Resources Management	M,O
International Business	M
Management Information Systems	M,O
Marketing	M,O
Sports Management	M

LIPSCOMB UNIVERSITY

Accounting	M
Business Administration and Management— General	M
Curriculum and Instruction	M
Education—General	M
Educational Leadership and Administration	M
Educational Media/ Instructional Technology	M
English as a Second Language	M
Finance and Banking	M
Health Services Management and Hospital Administration	M
Mathematics Education	M
Nonprofit Management	M
Pharmacy	P
Special Education	M
Sports Management	M
Sustainability Management	M

LOCK HAVEN UNIVERSITY OF PENNSYLVANIA

Education—General	M
Elementary Education	M
Physician Assistant Studies	M

LOGAN UNIVERSITY–COLLEGE OF CHIROPRACTIC

Chiropractic	P,M

LOMA LINDA UNIVERSITY

Adult Nursing	M
Allied Health—General	M,D
Allopathic Medicine	P,M,D
Bioethics	M,O
Communication Disorders	M
Counselor Education	M,D,O
Dentistry	P,M,O
Environmental and Occupational Health	M
Epidemiology	M,D,O
Gerontological Nursing	M
Health Education	M,D
Health Promotion	M,D
Health Services Management and Hospital Administration	M
International Health	M
Nursing and Healthcare Administration	M
Nursing—General	M
Occupational Therapy	M,D
Oral and Dental Sciences	M,O
Pediatric Nursing	M
Pharmacy	P
Physical Therapy	M,D
Physician Assistant Studies	M
Public Health—General	M,D,O
Social Work	M,D

LONG ISLAND UNIVERSITY AT RIVERHEAD

Counselor Education	M,O
Early Childhood Education	M
Education—General	M,O
Elementary Education	M
Reading Education	M
Special Education	M

LONG ISLAND UNIVERSITY, BRENTWOOD CAMPUS

Counselor Education	M
Early Childhood Education	M
Education—General	M
Reading Education	M
Special Education	M

LONG ISLAND UNIVERSITY, BROOKLYN CAMPUS

Accounting	M
Adult Nursing	M,O
Athletic Training and Sports Medicine	M
Business Administration and Management— General	M
Communication Disorders	M
Community Health	M
Counselor Education	M,O
Education—General	M,O
Educational Leadership and Administration	M
Educational Media/ Instructional Technology	M
Elementary Education	M
English as a Second Language	M
English Education	M
Exercise and Sports Science	M
Health Education	M
Health Services Management and Hospital Administration	M
Human Resources Management	M
Mathematics Education	M
Multilingual and Multicultural Education	M
Nursing and Healthcare Administration	M
Nursing—General	M,O
Pharmaceutical Administration	M
Pharmaceutical Sciences	M,D
Physical Education	M
Physical Therapy	D
Reading Education	M
Special Education	M
Taxation	M

LONG ISLAND UNIVERSITY, C.W. POST CAMPUS

Accounting	M,O
Allied Health—General	M,O
Art Education	M
Business Administration and Management— General	M,O
Clinical Laboratory Sciences/Medical Technology	M
Communication Disorders	M
Computer Education	M
Counselor Education	M
Early Childhood Education	M
Education—General	M,D,O
Educational Leadership and Administration	M,D,O
Educational Media/ Instructional Technology	M
Elementary Education	M
English as a Second Language	M
English Education	M
Family Nurse Practitioner Studies	M,O
Finance and Banking	M,O
Foreign Languages Education	M
Health Services Management and Hospital Administration	M,O

*M—master's degree; P—first professional degree; D—doctorate; O—other advanced degree; *—Close-Up and/or Display*

Information Studies M,D,O
International Business M,O
Library Science M,D,O
Management Information
  Systems M,O
Marketing M,O
Mathematics Education M
Medicinal and
  Pharmaceutical
  Chemistry M
Middle School Education M
Multilingual and
  Multicultural Education M
Music Education M
Nonprofit Management M,O
Nursing—General M,O
Perfusion M
Reading Education M
Science Education M
Secondary Education M
Social Work M
Special Education M
Taxation M,O

LONG ISLAND UNIVERSITY, ROCKLAND GRADUATE CAMPUS

Business Administration
  and Management—
  General M,O
Counselor Education M
Early Childhood Education M
Educational Leadership
  and Administration M,O
Elementary Education M
Entrepreneurship M,O
Finance and Banking M,O
Health Services
  Management and
  Hospital Administration M,O
Pharmaceutical Sciences M
Reading Education M
Secondary Education M
Special Education M

LONG ISLAND UNIVERSITY, WESTCHESTER GRADUATE CAMPUS

Business Administration
  and Management—
  General M
Counselor Education M
Early Childhood Education M,O
Education—General M,O
Educational Psychology M
Elementary Education M,O
English as a Second
  Language M,O
Information Studies M
Library Science M
Multilingual and
  Multicultural Education M,O
Reading Education M,O
Secondary Education M,O
Special Education M,O

LONGWOOD UNIVERSITY

Business Administration
  and Management—
  General M
Communication Disorders M
Counselor Education M
Education—General M
Educational Leadership
  and Administration M
Educational Media/
  Instructional Technology M
Elementary Education M
English Education M
Reading Education M
Secondary Education M
Special Education M

LORAS COLLEGE

Educational Leadership
  and Administration M
Special Education M

LOUISIANA STATE UNIVERSITY AND AGRICULTURAL AND MECHANICAL COLLEGE

Accounting M,D
Agricultural Education M,D
Business Administration
  and Management—
  General M,D

Business Education M,D
Communication Disorders M,D
Counselor Education M,D,O
Education—General M,D,O
Educational Leadership
  and Administration M,D,O
Educational Measurement
  and Evaluation M,D,O
Educational Media/
  Instructional Technology M,D,O
Elementary Education M,D,O
Finance and Banking M,D
Higher Education M,D,O
Home Economics
  Education M,D
Human Resources
  Development M,D
Information Studies M
International and
  Comparative Education M,D
Kinesiology and
  Movement Studies M,D
Law M
Library Science M
Management Information
  Systems M,D
Marketing D
Medical Physics M,D
Music Education M,D
Secondary Education M,D,O
Social Work M,D
Veterinary Medicine P
Veterinary Sciences M
Vocational and Technical
  Education M,D

LOUISIANA STATE UNIVERSITY HEALTH SCIENCES CENTER

Adult Nursing M,D
Allied Health—General M
Allopathic Medicine P,M
Communication Disorders M,D
Community Health
  Nursing M,D
Dentistry P
Nurse Anesthesia M,D
Nursing—General M,D
Occupational Therapy M
Physical Therapy D

LOUISIANA STATE UNIVERSITY HEALTH SCIENCES CENTER AT SHREVEPORT

Allopathic Medicine P

LOUISIANA STATE UNIVERSITY IN SHREVEPORT

Business Administration
  and Management—
  General M
Curriculum and Instruction M
Education—General M
Educational Leadership
  and Administration M
Health Promotion M
Health Services
  Management and
  Hospital Administration M
Human Services M
Kinesiology and
  Movement Studies M
Public Health—General M

LOUISIANA TECH UNIVERSITY

Accounting M,D
Business Administration
  and Management—
  General M,D
Business Education M,D
Communication Disorders M
Counselor Education M,D
Curriculum and Instruction M,D
Education—General M,D
Educational Leadership
  and Administration M,D
English Education M,D
Exercise and Sports
  Science M
Finance and Banking M,D
Foreign Languages
  Education M,D
Health Education M,D
Marketing M,D
Mathematics Education M,D
Physical Education M,D

Science Education M,D
Secondary Education M,D
Social Sciences Education M,D
Special Education M,D

LOURDES COLLEGE

Education—General M
Educational Media/
  Instructional Technology M
Organizational
  Management M

LOYOLA MARYMOUNT UNIVERSITY

Bioethics M
Business Administration
  and Management—
  General M
Counselor Education M
Early Childhood Education M
Education—General M,D
Educational Leadership
  and Administration M,D
Elementary Education M
English as a Second
  Language M
Law P,M
Mathematics Education M
Multilingual and
  Multicultural Education M
Reading Education M
Religious Education M
Secondary Education M
Special Education M
Taxation P,M
Urban Education M

LOYOLA UNIVERSITY CHICAGO

Accounting M
Acute Care/Critical Care
  Nursing M,O
Adult Nursing M,O
Allopathic Medicine P
Business Administration
  and Management—
  General M
Counselor Education M,O
Curriculum and Instruction M,D
Education—General M,D,O
Educational Leadership
  and Administration M,D,O
Educational Measurement
  and Evaluation M,D
Educational Media/
  Instructional Technology M
Educational Policy M,D
Educational Psychology M
Elementary Education M
Environmental and
  Occupational Health M,O
Family Nurse Practitioner
  Studies M,O
Finance and Banking M
Health Law P,M,D
Health Services
  Management and
  Hospital Administration M,O
Higher Education M,D
Human Resources
  Management M
Law P,M,D
Legal and Justice Studies M,O
Management Information
  Systems M
Marketing M
Mathematics Education M
Nursing and Healthcare
  Administration M,O
Nursing Informatics M,O
Nursing—General M,D
Oncology Nursing M,O
Public Health—General M
Reading Education M
Religious Education M,O
Science Education M
Secondary Education M
Special Education M
Women's Health Nursing M

LOYOLA UNIVERSITY MARYLAND

Accounting M
Business Administration
  and Management—
  General M
Communication Disorders M,O

Counselor Education M,O
Curriculum and Instruction M,O
Early Childhood Education M,O
Education—General M,O
Educational Leadership
  and Administration M,O
Educational Media/
  Instructional Technology M
Finance and Banking M
International Business M
Management Information
  Systems M
Marketing M
Reading Education M,O
Special Education M,O

LOYOLA UNIVERSITY NEW ORLEANS

Adult Nursing M,D
Business Administration
  and Management—
  General M
Counselor Education M
Family Nurse Practitioner
  Studies M,D
Health Services
  Management and
  Hospital Administration M,D
Law P,M
Nursing—General M,D

LUTHER RICE UNIVERSITY

Religious Education P,M,D

LYNCHBURG COLLEGE

Business Administration
  and Management—
  General M
Counselor Education M
Curriculum and Instruction M
Education—General M
Educational Leadership
  and Administration M
English Education M
Nursing and Healthcare
  Administration M,D
Nursing Education M,D
Nursing—General M,D
Physical Therapy M,D
Reading Education M
Science Education M
Special Education M

LYNDON STATE COLLEGE

Counselor Education M
Curriculum and Instruction M
Education—General M
Reading Education M
Science Education M
Special Education M

LYNN UNIVERSITY

Aviation Management M
Business Administration
  and Management—
  General M
Education of the Gifted M,D
Education—General M,D
Educational Leadership
  and Administration M,D
Hospitality Management M
International Business M
Investment Management M
Marketing M
Special Education M,D
Sports Management M

MADONNA UNIVERSITY

Adult Nursing M
Business Administration
  and Management—
  General M
Education—General M
Educational Leadership
  and Administration M
English as a Second
  Language M
Health Services
  Management and
  Hospital Administration M
Hospice Nursing M
International Business M
Nursing and Healthcare
  Administration M
Nursing—General M

Quality Management	M
Reading Education	M
Special Education	M

MAHARISHI UNIVERSITY OF MANAGEMENT

Accounting	M,D
Business Administration and Management— General	M,D
Education—General	M
Elementary Education	M
Secondary Education	M
Sustainability Management	M,D

MAINE MARITIME ACADEMY

International Business	M,O
Logistics	M,O
Supply Chain Management	M,O
Transportation Management	M,O

MALONE UNIVERSITY

Business Administration and Management— General	M
Counselor Education	M
Curriculum and Instruction	M
Education—General	M
Educational Media/ Instructional Technology	M
Family Nurse Practitioner Studies	M
Nursing—General	M
Reading Education	M
Special Education	M

MANHATTAN COLLEGE

Counselor Education	M,O
Early Childhood Education	M
Education—General	M,O
Educational Leadership and Administration	M,O
Special Education	M

MANHATTANVILLE COLLEGE

Art Education	M
Early Childhood Education	M
Education—General	M
Educational Leadership and Administration	M
Elementary Education	M
English as a Second Language	M
English Education	M
Exercise and Sports Science	M
Finance and Banking	M
Foreign Languages Education	M
Human Resources Development	M
International Business	M
Management Strategy and Policy	M
Marketing	M
Mathematics Education	M
Middle School Education	M
Music Education	M
Organizational Management	M
Reading Education	M
Science Education	M
Secondary Education	M
Social Sciences Education	M
Special Education	M
Sports Management	M

MANSFIELD UNIVERSITY OF PENNSYLVANIA

Art Education	M
Education—General	M
Elementary Education	M
Information Studies	M
Library Science	M
Nursing—General	M
Organizational Management	M
Secondary Education	M

MAPLE SPRINGS BAPTIST BIBLE COLLEGE AND SEMINARY

Religious Education	P,M,D,O

MARIAN UNIVERSITY (IN)

Education—General	M

MARIAN UNIVERSITY (WI)

Adult Nursing	M
Business Administration and Management— General	M
Education—General	M,D
Educational Leadership and Administration	M,D
Nursing Education	M
Nursing—General	M
Organizational Management	M
Quality Management	M

MARIETTA COLLEGE

Education—General	M
Physician Assistant Studies	M

MARIST COLLEGE

Business Administration and Management— General	M,O
Education—General	M,O
Educational Psychology	M,O
Industrial and Manufacturing Management	M,O
Management Information Systems	M,O

MARLBORO COLLEGE

Business Administration and Management— General	M
Computer Education	M
Education—General	M
Health Services Management and Hospital Administration	M
Sustainability Management	M

MARQUETTE UNIVERSITY

Accounting	M
Adult Nursing	M,D,O
Advertising and Public Relations	M
Business Administration and Management— General	M
Communication Disorders	M
Dentistry	P
Education—General	M,D,O
Entrepreneurship	O
Foreign Languages Education	M
Gerontological Nursing	M,D,O
Human Resources Development	M
Human Resources Management	M
Law	P
Maternal and Child/ Neonatal Nursing	M,D,O
Mathematics Education	M,D
Nurse Midwifery	M,D,O
Nursing—General	M,D,O
Oral and Dental Sciences	M
Pediatric Nursing	M,D,O
Physical Therapy	D
Physician Assistant Studies	M

MARSHALL UNIVERSITY

Adult Education	M
Allopathic Medicine	P
Business Administration and Management— General	M,D,O
Communication Disorders	M
Counselor Education	M,O
Early Childhood Education	M
Education—General	M
Educational Leadership and Administration	M,D,O

Elementary Education	M
Exercise and Sports Science	
Health Education	M
Health Services Management and Hospital Administration	M,D
Human Resources Management	M
Nursing—General	M
Reading Education	M,O
Secondary Education	M
Special Education	M
Sports Management	M
Vocational and Technical Education	M

MARTIN LUTHER COLLEGE

Curriculum and Instruction	M
Education—General	M
Educational Leadership and Administration	M
Special Education	M

MARY BALDWIN COLLEGE

Education—General	M
Elementary Education	M
Middle School Education	M

MARYGROVE COLLEGE

Education—General	M
Educational Leadership and Administration	M
Elementary Education	M
Human Resources Management	M
Legal and Justice Studies	M
Reading Education	M
Secondary Education	M
Urban Education	M

MARYLAND INSTITUTE COLLEGE OF ART

Art Education	M

MARYLHURST UNIVERSITY

Business Administration and Management— General	M
Education—General	M
Finance and Banking	M
Health Services Management and Hospital Administration	M
Marketing	M
Nonprofit Management	M
Organizational Behavior	M
Real Estate	M

MARYMOUNT UNIVERSITY

Allied Health—General	M,D,O
Business Administration and Management— General	M,O
Counselor Education	M
Education—General	M
Educational Leadership and Administration	M,O
Elementary Education	M
English as a Second Language	M
Family Nurse Practitioner Studies	M,D,O
Health Promotion	M
Health Services Management and Hospital Administration	M,O
Human Resources Management	M,O
Legal and Justice Studies	M,O
Management Information Systems	M,O
Nursing Education	M,D,O
Nursing—General	M,D,O
Organizational Management	M,O
Physical Therapy	D
Project Management	M,O
Secondary Education	M
Special Education	M

MARYVILLE UNIVERSITY OF SAINT LOUIS

Accounting	M,O
Actuarial Science	M
Adult Nursing	M,D
Allied Health—General	M,D,O
Art Education	M,D
Business Administration and Management— General	M,O
Business Education	M,O
Early Childhood Education	M,D
Education of the Gifted	M,D
Education—General	M,D
Educational Leadership and Administration	M,D
Educational Psychology	M,D
Electronic Commerce	M,O
Elementary Education	M,D
English Education	M,D
Environmental Education	M,D
Family Nurse Practitioner Studies	M,D
Marketing	M,O
Middle School Education	M,D
Nursing Education	M,D
Nursing—General	M,D
Occupational Therapy	M
Physical Therapy	D
Reading Education	M,D
Secondary Education	M,D

MARYWOOD UNIVERSITY

Art Education	M
Business Administration and Management— General	M
Communication Disorders	M
Counselor Education	M,O
Early Childhood Education	M
Education—General	M
Educational Leadership and Administration	M,D
Educational Media/ Instructional Technology	M,O
Electronic Commerce	M,O
Elementary Education	M
Exercise and Sports Science	M
Finance and Banking	M
Health Education	D
Health Services Management and Hospital Administration	M
Higher Education	M,D
Investment Management	M
Kinesiology and Movement Studies	M
Library Science	M,O
Management Information Systems	M
Music Education	M
Nonprofit Management	M
Nursing and Healthcare Administration	M
Physician Assistant Studies	M
Reading Education	M
Secondary Education	M
Social Work	M,D
Special Education	M

MASSACHUSETTS COLLEGE OF ART AND DESIGN

Art Education	M
Education—General	M

MASSACHUSETTS COLLEGE OF LIBERAL ARTS

Curriculum and Instruction	M
Education—General	M
Educational Leadership and Administration	M
Reading Education	M
Special Education	M

MASSACHUSETTS COLLEGE OF PHARMACY AND HEALTH SCIENCES

Community Health	M
Health Services Management and Hospital Administration	M

*M—master's degree; P—first professional degree; D—doctorate; O—other advanced degree; *—Close-Up and/or Display*

Nursing—General — M
Oral and Dental Sciences — M
Pharmaceutical Sciences — M,D
Pharmacy — P
Physician Assistant
  Studies — M

MASSACHUSETTS INSTITUTE OF TECHNOLOGY

Business Administration
  and Management—
    General — M,D
Communication Disorders — D
Logistics — M,D
Medical Physics — D
Real Estate — M

MASSACHUSETTS MARITIME ACADEMY

Facilities Management — M

MASSACHUSETTS SCHOOL OF LAW AT ANDOVER

Law — P

MAYO MEDICAL SCHOOL

Allopathic Medicine — P

MAYO SCHOOL OF HEALTH SCIENCES

Nurse Anesthesia — M
Physical Therapy — D

MCDANIEL COLLEGE

Counselor Education — M
Curriculum and Instruction — M
Educational Leadership
  and Administration — M
Educational Media/
  Instructional Technology — M
Elementary Education — M
Human Resources
  Development — M
Human Services — M
Library Science — M
Physical Education — M
Reading Education — M
Secondary Education — M
Special Education — M

MCGILL UNIVERSITY

Accounting — M,D,O
Allopathic Medicine — M,D
Bioethics — M,D,O
Business Administration
  and Management—
    General — M,D,O
Communication Disorders — M,D
Community Health — M,D,O
Curriculum and Instruction — M,D,O
Dentistry — P,M,D,O
Education—General — M,D,O
Educational Leadership
  and Administration — M,D,O
Educational Psychology — M,D,O
Entrepreneurship — M,D,O
Environmental and
  Occupational Health — M,D,O
Epidemiology — M,D,O
Family Nurse Practitioner
  Studies — M,D,O
Finance and Banking — M,D,O
Foreign Languages
  Education — M,D,O
Foundations and
  Philosophy of Education — M,D,O
Health Services
  Management and
  Hospital Administration — M,D,O
Industrial and
  Manufacturing
  Management — M,D,O
Information Studies — M,D,O
International Business — M,D,O
Kinesiology and
  Movement Studies — M,D,O
Law — P,M,D,O
Library Science — M,D,O
Management Information
  Systems — M,D,O
Management Strategy and
  Policy — M,D,O
Marketing — M,D,O
Medical Physics — M,D
Music Education — M,D

Nursing—General — M,D,O
Oral and Dental Sciences — M,D,O
Physical Education — M,D,O
Rehabilitation Sciences — M,D,O
Social Work — M,D,O
Transportation
  Management — M,D

MCKENDREE UNIVERSITY

Business Administration
  and Management—
    General — M
Education—General — M
Educational Leadership
  and Administration — M
Higher Education — M
Human Resources
  Management — M
International Business — M
Music Education — M
Nursing and Healthcare
  Administration — M
Nursing Education — M
Nursing—General — M
Special Education — M

MCMASTER UNIVERSITY

Business Administration
  and Management—
    General — M,D
Health Physics/
  Radiological Health — M,D
Health Services Research — M,D
Human Resources
  Management — M,D
Kinesiology and
  Movement Studies — M,D
Management Information
  Systems — D
Medical Physics — M,D
Nursing—General — M,D
Occupational Therapy — M
Physical Therapy — M
Rehabilitation Sciences — M,D
Social Work — M

MCNEESE STATE UNIVERSITY

Accounting — M
Business Administration
  and Management—
    General — M
Counselor Education — M
Curriculum and Instruction — M
Early Childhood Education — M
Education—General — M
Educational Leadership
  and Administration — M,O
Educational Media/
  Instructional Technology — M,O
Elementary Education — M
Exercise and Sports
  Science — M
Family Nurse Practitioner
  Studies — M
Health Promotion — M
Music Education — M
Nursing and Healthcare
  Administration — M
Nursing Education — M
Nursing—General — M
Science Education — M
Secondary Education — M
Special Education — M

MEDAILLE COLLEGE

Business Administration
  and Management—
    General — M
Curriculum and Instruction — M
Education—General — M
Elementary Education — M
Organizational
  Management — M
Reading Education — M
Secondary Education — M
Special Education — M

MEDICAL COLLEGE OF GEORGIA

Acute Care/Critical Care
  Nursing — M
Adult Nursing — M
Allied Health—General — M
Allopathic Medicine — P
Clinical Research — M,O
Dentistry — P

Family Nurse Practitioner
  Studies — M
Nurse Anesthesia — M
Nursing and Healthcare
  Administration — M
Nursing—General — D
Oral and Dental Sciences — M,D
Pediatric Nursing — M

MEDICAL COLLEGE OF WISCONSIN

Allopathic Medicine — P
Bioethics — M,O
Clinical Laboratory
  Sciences/Medical
  Technology — M,D
Community Health — M,D,O
Environmental and
  Occupational Health — M
Epidemiology — M
Public Health—General — M,D,O

MEDICAL UNIVERSITY OF SOUTH CAROLINA

Adult Nursing — M,D
Allied Health—General — M,D
Allopathic Medicine — P
Clinical Research — M
Dentistry — P
Epidemiology — M,D
Family Nurse Practitioner
  Studies — M,D
Health Services
  Management and
  Hospital Administration — M,D
Health Services Research — M
International Health — M
Maternal and Child/
  Neonatal Nursing — M
Medical Imaging — D
Medicinal and
  Pharmaceutical
  Chemistry — D
Nurse Anesthesia — M
Nursing and Healthcare
  Administration — M
Nursing Education — M
Nursing—General — D
Occupational Therapy — M
Pediatric Nursing — D
Pharmacy — P
Physical Therapy — D
Physician Assistant
  Studies — M
Rehabilitation Sciences — D

MEHARRY MEDICAL COLLEGE

Allopathic Medicine — P
Community Health — M
Dentistry — P
Environmental and
  Occupational Health — M
Health Services
  Management and
  Hospital Administration — M

MEMORIAL UNIVERSITY OF NEWFOUNDLAND

Adult Education — M,D,O
Business Administration
  and Management—
    General — M
Clinical Research — M
Community Health — M,D,O
Curriculum and Instruction — M,D,O
Education—General — M,D,O
Educational Leadership
  and Administration — M,D,O
Educational Media/
  Instructional Technology — M,D,O
Educational Psychology — M,D,O
Epidemiology — M,D,O
Exercise and Sports
  Science — M
Kinesiology and
  Movement Studies — M
Nursing—General — M,O
Pharmaceutical Sciences — M,D
Physical Education — M
Social Work — M

MEMPHIS COLLEGE OF ART

Art Education — M

MERCER UNIVERSITY

Allopathic Medicine — P,M
Business Administration
  and Management—
    General — M
Curriculum and Instruction — M,D,O
Early Childhood Education — M,D,O
Education—General — M,D,O
Educational Leadership
  and Administration — M,D,O
Law — P
Middle School Education — M,D,O
Nursing—General — M,D,O
Pharmaceutical Sciences — P,M,D
Pharmacy — P,M,D
Reading Education — M,D,O
Secondary Education — M,D,O

MERCY COLLEGE

Accounting — M
Allied Health—General — M,D,O
Business Administration
  and Management—
    General — M
Communication Disorders — M
Counselor Education — M,O
Early Childhood Education — M
Education—General — M,O
Educational Leadership
  and Administration — M,O
Electronic Commerce — M
Elementary Education — M
English as a Second
  Language — M
Health Services
  Management and
  Hospital Administration — M
Human Resources
  Management — M,O
Middle School Education — M
Multilingual and
  Multicultural Education — M,O
Nursing and Healthcare
  Administration — M
Nursing Education — M
Nursing—General — M
Occupational Therapy — M
Organizational
  Management — M
Physical Therapy — M,D
Physician Assistant
  Studies — M
Reading Education — M
Secondary Education — M
Special Education — M,O
Urban Education — M

MERCYHURST COLLEGE

Educational Leadership
  and Administration — M,O
Multilingual and
  Multicultural Education — M,O
Organizational
  Management — M,O
Special Education — M,O

MEREDITH COLLEGE

Business Administration
  and Management—
    General — M
Education—General — M

MERITUS UNIVERSITY

Business Administration
  and Management—
    General — M
Health Services
  Management and
  Hospital Administration — M
Human Resources
  Management — M
International Business — M
Management Information
  Systems — M
Marketing — M

MERRIMACK COLLEGE

Education—General — M

MESA STATE COLLEGE

Business Administration
  and Management—
    General — M
Education—General — M

Educational Leadership
and Administration — M
English as a Second
Language — M
Nursing—General — M,D

MESSIAH COLLEGE

Art Education — M
Counselor Education — M,O

METHODIST UNIVERSITY

Business Administration
and Management—
General — M
Physician Assistant
Studies — M

METROPOLITAN COLLEGE OF NEW YORK

Business Administration
and Management—
General — M
Elementary Education — M

METROPOLITAN STATE UNIVERSITY

Adult Nursing — M,D
Business Administration
and Management—
General — M,O
Community Health
Nursing — M,D
Family Nurse Practitioner
Studies — M,D
Gerontological Nursing — M,D
Information Studies — M,O
Management Information
Systems — M,O
Nonprofit Management — M,O
Nursing and Healthcare
Administration — M,D
Nursing—General — M,D
Project Management — M,O
Women's Health Nursing — M,D

MGH INSTITUTE OF HEALTH PROFESSIONS

Allied Health—General — M,D,O
Communication Disorders — M,O
Gerontological Nursing — M,D,O
Medical Imaging — O
Nursing Education — M,D,O
Nursing—General — M,D,O
Pediatric Nursing — M,D,O
Physical Therapy — M,D,O
Psychiatric Nursing — M,D,O
Reading Education — M,O
Women's Health Nursing — M,D,O

MIAMI UNIVERSITY

Accounting — M
Art Education — M
Business Administration
and Management—
General — M
Communication Disorders — M,D
Curriculum and Instruction — M
Early Childhood Education — M
Education—General — M,D,O
Educational Leadership
and Administration — M,D
Educational Media/
Instructional Technology — M,O
Educational Psychology — M,O
Elementary Education — M
Exercise and Sports
Science — M
Higher Education — M,D
Mathematics Education — M
Music Education — M
Reading Education — M
Secondary Education — M
Special Education — M,O
Student Affairs — M,D

MICHIGAN SCHOOL OF PROFESSIONAL PSYCHOLOGY

Educational Psychology — M,D

MICHIGAN STATE UNIVERSITY

Accounting — M,D
Adult Education — M,D,O

Advertising and Public
Relations — M,D
Allopathic Medicine — P
Business Administration
and Management—
General — M,D
Clinical Laboratory
Sciences/Medical
Technology — M
Communication Disorders — M,D
Counselor Education — M,D,O
Curriculum and Instruction — M,D,O
Education—General — M,D,O
Educational Leadership
and Administration — M,D,O
Educational Measurement
and Evaluation — M,D,O
Educational Media/
Instructional Technology — M,D,O
Educational Policy — D
Educational Psychology — M,D,O
English as a Second
Language — M,D
Epidemiology — M,D
Finance and Banking — M,D
Foreign Languages
Education — D
Higher Education — M,D,O
Hospitality Management — M
Human Resources
Management — M,D
Kinesiology and
Movement Studies — M,D
Management Information
Systems — M,D
Marketing — M,D
Mathematics Education — M,D
Music Education — M,D
Nursing—General — M,D
Osteopathic Medicine — P
Public Health—General — M
Reading Education — M
Recreation and Park
Management — M,D
Science Education — M,D
Social Sciences Education — M,D
Social Work — M
Special Education — M,D,O
Supply Chain
Management — M,D
Veterinary Medicine — P
Veterinary Sciences — M,D

MICHIGAN STATE UNIVERSITY COLLEGE OF LAW

Law — P,M
Legal and Justice Studies — P,M

MICHIGAN TECHNOLOGICAL UNIVERSITY

Business Administration
and Management—
General — M
Science Education — M
Sustainability
Management — O

MICHIGAN THEOLOGICAL SEMINARY

Religious Education — P,M,O

MID-AMERICA CHRISTIAN UNIVERSITY

Business Administration
and Management—
General — M
Organizational
Management — M

MIDAMERICA NAZARENE UNIVERSITY

Business Administration
and Management—
General — M
Education—General — M
Educational Media/
Instructional Technology — M
English as a Second
Language — M
Finance and Banking — M
International Business — M
Nonprofit Management — M

Organizational
Management — M
Special Education — M

MIDDLE TENNESSEE SCHOOL OF ANESTHESIA

Nurse Anesthesia — M

MIDDLE TENNESSEE STATE UNIVERSITY

Accounting — M
Aviation Management — M
Business Administration
and Management—
General — M
Business Education — M
Counselor Education — M,O
Curriculum and Instruction — M,O
Early Childhood Education — M,O
Education—General — M,D,O
Educational Leadership
and Administration — M,O
Educational Media/
Instructional Technology — M,O
Elementary Education — M,O
English as a Second
Language — M,O
Exercise and Sports
Science — M,D
Family Nurse Practitioner
Studies — M,O
Foreign Languages
Education — M
Health Education — M
Health Services
Management and
Hospital Administration — O
Management Information
Systems — M
Management Strategy and
Policy — M
Marketing — M
Mathematics Education — M
Middle School Education — M,O
Nursing—General — M,O
Physical Education — M
Reading Education — M,D
Recreation and Park
Management — M
Science Education — M
Secondary Education — M,O
Social Work — M
Special Education — M,O
Vocational and Technical
Education — M

MIDWAY COLLEGE

Business Administration
and Management—
General — M
Organizational
Management — M

MIDWEST COLLEGE OF ORIENTAL MEDICINE

Acupuncture and Oriental
Medicine — M,O

MIDWESTERN BAPTIST THEOLOGICAL SEMINARY

Religious Education — P,M,D,O

MIDWESTERN STATE UNIVERSITY

Business Administration
and Management—
General — M
Counselor Education — M
Curriculum and Instruction — M
Education—General — M
Educational Leadership
and Administration — M
Educational Media/
Instructional Technology — M
Family Nurse Practitioner
Studies — M
Health Physics/
Radiological Health — M
Health Services
Management and
Hospital Administration — M
Human Resources
Development — M

Kinesiology and
Movement Studies — M
Nursing Education — M
Nursing—General — M
Reading Education — M
Special Education — M

MIDWESTERN UNIVERSITY, DOWNERS GROVE CAMPUS

Allied Health—General — M,D
Occupational Therapy — M
Osteopathic Medicine — P
Pharmacy — P
Physical Therapy — D
Physician Assistant
Studies — M

MIDWESTERN UNIVERSITY, GLENDALE CAMPUS

Allied Health—General — P,M,D,O
Bioethics — M,O
Dentistry — P
Health Education — M
Nurse Anesthesia — M
Occupational Therapy — M
Optometry — P
Osteopathic Medicine — P
Pharmacy — P
Physician Assistant
Studies — M
Podiatric Medicine — P

MIDWEST UNIVERSITY

English as a Second
Language — P,M,D

MIDWIVES COLLEGE OF UTAH

Nurse Midwifery — M

MILLERSVILLE UNIVERSITY OF PENNSYLVANIA

Art Education — M
Early Childhood Education — M
Education of the Gifted — M
Education—General — M
Elementary Education — M
English Education — M
Foundations and
Philosophy of Education — M
Mathematics Education — M
Nursing—General — M
Reading Education — M
Social Work — M
Special Education — M
Sports Management — M
Vocational and Technical
Education — M

MILLIGAN COLLEGE

Business Administration
and Management—
General — M
Education—General — M
Occupational Therapy — M

MILLIKIN UNIVERSITY

Business Administration
and Management—
General — M
Nursing and Healthcare
Administration — M
Nursing Education — M
Nursing—General — M

MILLSAPS COLLEGE

Accounting — M
Business Administration
and Management—
General — M

MILLS COLLEGE

Art Education — M,D
Business Administration
and Management—
General — M
Curriculum and Instruction — M,D
Early Childhood Education — M,D
Education—General — M,D
Educational Leadership
and Administration — M,D
Elementary Education — M,D
English Education — M,D

Foreign Languages
Education — M,D
Health Education — M,D
Mathematics Education — M,D
Science Education — M,D
Secondary Education — M,D
Social Sciences Education — M,D

MILWAUKEE SCHOOL OF ENGINEERING

Business Administration
and Management—
General — M
Clinical Laboratory
Sciences/Medical
Technology — M
Industrial and
Manufacturing
Management — M
International Business — M
Marketing — M
Nursing—General — M
Perfusion — M

MINNESOTA STATE UNIVERSITY MANKATO

Allied Health—General — M,D,O
Art Education — M
Business Administration
and Management—
General — M
Communication Disorders — M
Community Health — M
Counselor Education — M,D,O
Curriculum and Instruction — M,O
Early Childhood Education — M,O
Education of the Gifted — M,O
Education—General — M,D,O
Educational Leadership
and Administration — M
Educational Media/
Instructional Technology — M,O
Elementary Education — M,O
English as a Second
Language — M,O
English Education — M,O
Family Nurse Practitioner
Studies — M,D
Health Education — M
Human Services — M
Management Information
Systems — M,O
Mathematics Education — M
Multilingual and
Multicultural Education — M,O
Nursing—General — M,D
Physical Education — M,O
Science Education — M
Secondary Education — M,O
Social Sciences Education — M
Social Work — M
Special Education — M,O
Student Affairs — M,D,O

MINNESOTA STATE UNIVERSITY MOORHEAD

Communication Disorders — M
Counselor Education — M
Curriculum and Instruction — M
Education—General — M,O
Educational Leadership
and Administration — M,O
Human Services — M,O
Nursing Education — M
Nursing—General — M,O
Reading Education — M
Special Education — M

MINOT STATE UNIVERSITY

Business Administration
and Management—
General — M
Communication Disorders — M
Early Childhood Education — M
Education of Students with
Severe/Multiple
Disabilities — M
Elementary Education — M
Management Information
Systems — M
Mathematics Education — M
Music Education — M
Science Education — M
Special Education — M

MISERICORDIA UNIVERSITY

Allied Health—General — M,D
Business Administration
and Management—
General — M
Communication Disorders — M
Curriculum and Instruction — M
Education—General — M
Nursing—General — M
Occupational Therapy — M,D
Organizational
Management — M
Physical Therapy — M,D

MISSISSIPPI COLLEGE

Accounting — M,O
Advertising and Public
Relations — M
Art Education — M,D,O
Business Administration
and Management—
General — M,O
Business Education — M,D,O
Computer Education — M,D,O
Counselor Education — M,O
Curriculum and Instruction — M,D,O
Education—General — M,D,O
Educational Leadership
and Administration — M,D,O
Elementary Education — M,D,O
English as a Second
Language — M
English Education — M,D,O
Finance and Banking — M,O
Health Services
Management and
Hospital Administration — M
Higher Education — M,D,O
Kinesiology and
Movement Studies — M
Law — P,O
Legal and Justice Studies — M,O
Mathematics Education — M,D,O
Music Education — M
Science Education — M,D,O
Secondary Education — M,D,O
Social Sciences Education — M,D,O
Special Education — M,D,O

MISSISSIPPI STATE UNIVERSITY

Accounting — M,D
Agricultural Education — M,D
Business Administration
and Management—
General — M,D
Community College
Education — M,D,O
Counselor Education — M,D,O
Curriculum and Instruction — M,D,O
Education—General — M,D,O
Educational Leadership
and Administration — M,D,O
Educational Media/
Instructional Technology — M,D,O
Educational Psychology — M,D,O
Elementary Education — M,D,O
Exercise and Sports
Science — M
Finance and Banking — M,D
Foreign Languages
Education — M
Human Resources
Development — M,D,O
Kinesiology and
Movement Studies — M
Management Information
Systems — M,D
Marketing — M,D
Physical Education — M
Project Management — M
Secondary Education — M,D,O
Special Education — M,D,O
Sports Management — M
Student Affairs — M,D,O
Taxation — M,D
Veterinary Medicine — P
Veterinary Sciences — M,D
Vocational and Technical
Education — M,D,O

MISSISSIPPI UNIVERSITY FOR WOMEN

Communication Disorders — M,O
Curriculum and Instruction — M
Education of the Gifted — M

Education—General — M
Health Education — M
Nursing—General — M,O

MISSISSIPPI VALLEY STATE UNIVERSITY

Education—General — M
Elementary Education — M
Environmental and
Occupational Health — M

MISSOURI BAPTIST UNIVERSITY

Business Administration
and Management—
General — M,O
Counselor Education — M,O
Education—General — M,O
Educational Leadership
and Administration — M,O

MISSOURI SOUTHERN STATE UNIVERSITY

Business Administration
and Management—
General — M
Dental Hygiene — M
Early Childhood Education — M
Education—General — M
Educational Media/
Instructional Technology — M
Nursing—General — M

MISSOURI STATE UNIVERSITY

Accounting — M
Agricultural Education — M
Art Education — M
Business Administration
and Management—
General — M
Communication Disorders — M,D
Counselor Education — M
Curriculum and Instruction — M
Early Childhood Education — M
Educational Leadership
and Administration — M,O
Educational Media/
Instructional Technology — M
Elementary Education — M,O
Family Nurse Practitioner
Studies — M
Foreign Languages
Education — M
Health Promotion — M
Health Services
Management and
Hospital Administration — M
Management Information
Systems — M
Music Education — M
Nurse Anesthesia — M
Nursing Education — M
Nursing—General — M
Physical Education — M
Physical Therapy — D
Physician Assistant
Studies — M
Project Management — M
Public Health—General — M
Reading Education — M
Science Education — M
Secondary Education — M,O
Social Sciences Education — M
Social Work — M
Special Education — M,D
Sports Management — M
Student Affairs — M

MISSOURI UNIVERSITY OF SCIENCE AND TECHNOLOGY

Mathematics Education — M,D

MOLLOY COLLEGE

Accounting — M
Adult Nursing — M,O
Business Administration
and Management—
General — M
Education—General — M,O
Family Nurse Practitioner
Studies — M,O
Finance and Banking — M
Nursing and Healthcare
Administration — M,O
Nursing Education — M,O
Nursing Informatics — M,O

Nursing—General — M,O
Pediatric Nursing — M,O
Psychiatric Nursing — M,O
Social Work — M

MONMOUTH UNIVERSITY

Accounting — M,O
Adult Nursing — M,O
Advertising and Public
Relations — M,O
Business Administration
and Management—
General — M,O
Education—General — M,O
Educational Leadership
and Administration — M,O
Elementary Education — M,O
English as a Second
Language — M,O
Family Nurse Practitioner
Studies — M,O
Forensic Nursing — M,O
Health Services
Management and
Hospital Administration — M,O
Nursing and Healthcare
Administration — M,O
Nursing Education — M,O
Nursing—General — M,O
Psychiatric Nursing — M,O
Reading Education — M,O
School Nursing — M,O
Secondary Education — M,O
Social Work — M,O
Special Education — M,O

MONROE COLLEGE

Business Administration
and Management—
General — M

MONTANA STATE UNIVERSITY

Accounting — M
Adult Education — M,D,O
Agricultural Education — M
Counselor Education — M
Curriculum and Instruction — M,D,O
Education—General — M,D,O
Educational Leadership
and Administration — M,D,O
Exercise and Sports
Science — M
Family Nurse Practitioner
Studies — M,O
Health Education — M
Health Promotion — M
Higher Education — M,D,O
Home Economics
Education — M
Mathematics Education — M,D
Nursing Education — M,O
Nursing—General — M,O
Psychiatric Nursing — M,O
Veterinary Sciences — M,D

MONTANA STATE UNIVERSITY BILLINGS

Advertising and Public
Relations — M
Athletic Training and
Sports Medicine — M
Counselor Education — M
Curriculum and Instruction — M
Early Childhood Education — M
Education—General — M,O
Educational Media/
Instructional Technology — M
Health Services
Management and
Hospital Administration — M
Human Services — M
Physical Education — M
Reading Education — M
Secondary Education — M
Special Education — M
Sports Management — M

MONTANA STATE UNIVERSITY– NORTHERN

Counselor Education — M
Education—General — M

MONTANA TECH OF THE UNIVERSITY OF MONTANA

Industrial Hygiene — M
Project Management — M

MONTCLAIR STATE UNIVERSITY

Accounting	M,O
Advertising and Public Relations	M
Art Education	M,O
Business Administration and Management—General	M,O
Communication Disorders	M,D
Community Health	M,O
Counselor Education	M,D,O
Curriculum and Instruction	M,D,O
Early Childhood Education	M,O
Education of Students with Severe/Multiple Disabilities	M,O
Education—General	M,D,O
Educational Leadership and Administration	M,D,O
Educational Media/Instructional Technology	M,O
Educational Psychology	M,O
Elementary Education	M,O
English as a Second Language	M,O
English Education	M,O
Environmental and Occupational Health	M,D,O
Exercise and Sports Science	M,O
Finance and Banking	M,O
Foundations and Philosophy of Education	M
Health Education	M,O
Home Economics Education	M,O
International Business	M,O
Law	M
Legal and Justice Studies	M,O
Management Information Systems	M,O
Marketing	M,O
Mathematics Education	M,D,O
Middle School Education	M,D,O
Music Education	M,O
Physical Education	M,O
Reading Education	M,O
Science Education	M,D,O
Social Sciences Education	M,O
Special Education	M,O
Sports Management	M,O

MONTEREY INSTITUTE OF INTERNATIONAL STUDIES

Business Administration and Management—General	M
English as a Second Language	M*
Foreign Languages Education	M
International Business	M*

MONTREAT COLLEGE

Business Administration and Management—General	M
Education—General	M
Elementary Education	M

MOORE COLLEGE OF ART & DESIGN

Art Education	M

MORAVIAN COLLEGE

Allied Health—General	M
Business Administration and Management—General	M
Curriculum and Instruction	M
Human Resources Development	M
Human Resources Management	M
Nursing and Healthcare Administration	M
Nursing Education	M
Nursing—General	M
Supply Chain Management	M

MOREHEAD STATE UNIVERSITY

Adult Education	M,O

Art Education	M
Business Administration and Management—General	M
Business Education	M,O
Counselor Education	M,O
Curriculum and Instruction	M,O
Education of the Gifted	M,O
Education—General	M,O
Educational Leadership and Administration	M,O
Educational Media/Instructional Technology	M,O
Elementary Education	M,O
English Education	M,O
Exercise and Sports Science	M
Foreign Languages Education	M
Health Education	M
Higher Education	M,O
International and Comparative Education	M
Management Information Systems	M
Mathematics Education	M
Middle School Education	M,O
Music Education	M
Physical Education	M
Reading Education	M,O
Science Education	M
Secondary Education	M,O
Social Sciences Education	M,O
Special Education	M,O
Sports Management	M
Vocational and Technical Education	M

MOREHOUSE SCHOOL OF MEDICINE

Allopathic Medicine	P
Clinical Research	M
Epidemiology	M
Health Education	M
Health Promotion	M
Health Services Management and Hospital Administration	M
International Health	M
Public Health—General	M

MORGAN STATE UNIVERSITY

Business Administration and Management—General	D
Community College Education	D
Education—General	M,D
Educational Leadership and Administration	M,D
Elementary Education	M
Higher Education	D
Mathematics Education	M,D
Middle School Education	M
Nursing—General	M,D
Public Health—General	M,D
Science Education	M,D
Secondary Education	M
Social Work	M,D
Transportation Management	M
Urban Education	M,D

MORNINGSIDE COLLEGE

Education—General	M
Special Education	M

MORRISON UNIVERSITY

Business Administration and Management—General	M

MOUNTAIN STATE UNIVERSITY

Allied Health—General	M
Family Nurse Practitioner Studies	M,O
Management Strategy and Policy	M
Nurse Anesthesia	M,O
Nursing and Healthcare Administration	M,O
Nursing Education	M,O
Nursing—General	M,O

Organizational Management	D
Physician Assistant Studies	M

MOUNT ALOYSIUS COLLEGE

Business Administration and Management—General	M
Education—General	M

MOUNT CARMEL COLLEGE OF NURSING

Adult Nursing	M
Nursing and Healthcare Administration	M
Nursing Education	M
Nursing—General	M

MOUNT IDA COLLEGE

Business Administration and Management—General	M

MOUNT MARTY COLLEGE

Business Administration and Management—General	M
Nurse Anesthesia	M

MOUNT MARY COLLEGE

Business Administration and Management—General	M
Counselor Education	M
Education—General	M
Health Education	M
Occupational Therapy	M

MOUNT MERCY COLLEGE

Business Administration and Management—General	M
Education—General	M
Reading Education	M
Special Education	M

MOUNT SAINT MARY COLLEGE

Adult Nursing	M,O
Business Administration and Management—General	M
Early Childhood Education	M,O
Education—General	M,O
Elementary Education	M,O
Family Nurse Practitioner Studies	M,O
Finance and Banking	M
Middle School Education	M,O
Nursing and Healthcare Administration	M,O
Nursing Education	M,O
Nursing—General	M,O
Reading Education	M,O
Secondary Education	M,O
Special Education	M,O

MOUNT ST. MARY'S COLLEGE

Adult Nursing	M
Business Administration and Management—General	M
Community Health	M
Education—General	M
Educational Leadership and Administration	M
Elementary Education	M
Nursing and Healthcare Administration	M
Nursing Education	M
Nursing—General	M
Physical Therapy	D
Secondary Education	M
Special Education	M

MOUNT ST. MARY'S UNIVERSITY

Business Administration and Management—General	M
Education—General	M

MOUNT SAINT VINCENT UNIVERSITY

Adult Education	M
Curriculum and Instruction	M
Education—General	M
Educational Psychology	M
Elementary Education	M
English as a Second Language	M
Foundations and Philosophy of Education	M
Middle School Education	M
Reading Education	M
Special Education	M

MOUNT SINAI SCHOOL OF MEDICINE OF NEW YORK UNIVERSITY

Allopathic Medicine	P
Bioethics	M
Clinical Research	M,D
Community Health	M,D

MOUNT VERNON NAZARENE UNIVERSITY

Business Administration and Management—General	M
Education—General	M

MULTNOMAH UNIVERSITY

Counselor Education	M
Education—General	M
English as a Second Language	M

MURRAY STATE UNIVERSITY

Accounting	M
Agricultural Education	M
Business Administration and Management—General	M
Communication Disorders	M
Counselor Education	M,O
Early Childhood Education	M
Education—General	M,D,O
Educational Leadership and Administration	M,O
Elementary Education	M,O
English as a Second Language	M
Environmental and Occupational Health	M
Exercise and Sports Science	M
Family Nurse Practitioner Studies	M
Human Services	M
Industrial Hygiene	M
Leisure Studies	M
Middle School Education	M,O
Music Education	M
Nurse Anesthesia	M
Nursing—General	M
Physical Education	M,O
Reading Education	M,O
Secondary Education	M,O
Special Education	M
Vocational and Technical Education	M

MUSKINGUM UNIVERSITY

Education—General	M

NAROPA UNIVERSITY

Counselor Education	M
Education—General	M
Recreation and Park Management	M

NATIONAL AMERICAN UNIVERSITY

Business Administration and Management—General	M

NATIONAL COLLEGE OF MIDWIFERY

Nurse Midwifery	M,D

---

*M—master's degree; P—first professional degree; D—doctorate; O—other advanced degree; *—Close-Up and/or Display*

NATIONAL COLLEGE OF NATURAL MEDICINE

Acupuncture and Oriental Medicine	M
Naturopathic Medicine	D

THE NATIONAL GRADUATE SCHOOL OF QUALITY MANAGEMENT

Business Administration and Management— General	M
Electronic Commerce	M
Quality Management	M

NATIONAL-LOUIS UNIVERSITY

Adult Education	M,D,O
Business Administration and Management— General	M
Community College Education	M,D,O
Counselor Education	M
Curriculum and Instruction	M,D,O
Developmental Education	M,O
Early Childhood Education	M,O
Education—General	M,D,O
Educational Leadership and Administration	M,D,O
Educational Media/ Instructional Technology	M,O
Educational Psychology	M,D,O
Elementary Education	M
English Education	M,O
Human Resources Development	M
Human Resources Management	M
Human Services	M
Mathematics Education	M,O
Reading Education	M,D,O
Science Education	M,O
Secondary Education	M
Special Education	M,O

NATIONAL UNIVERSITY

Accounting	M
Business Administration and Management— General	M
Communication Disorders	M
Counselor Education	M
Education—General	M
Educational Leadership and Administration	M
Educational Media/ Instructional Technology	M
Electronic Commerce	M
Finance and Banking	M
Health Services Management and Hospital Administration	M
Human Resources Management	M
Human Services	M
International Business	M
Management Information Systems	M
Marketing	M
Multilingual and Multicultural Education	M
Organizational Management	M
Special Education	M

NATIONAL UNIVERSITY OF HEALTH SCIENCES

Acupuncture and Oriental Medicine	P,M,D
Chiropractic	P,M,D*
Naturopathic Medicine	P,M,D

NAVAL POSTGRADUATE SCHOOL

Business Administration and Management— General	M
Human Resources Development	M
Management Information Systems	M,O

NAZARENE THEOLOGICAL SEMINARY

Religious Education	P,M,D

NAZARETH COLLEGE OF ROCHESTER

Art Education	M
Business Administration and Management— General	M
Business Education	M
Communication Disorders	M
Early Childhood Education	M
Education—General	M
Educational Media/ Instructional Technology	M
Elementary Education	M
English as a Second Language	M
Gerontological Nursing	M
Human Resources Management	M
Middle School Education	M
Music Education	M
Nursing—General	M
Physical Therapy	M,D
Reading Education	M
Social Work	M

NEBRASKA METHODIST COLLEGE

Health Promotion	M
Health Services Management and Hospital Administration	M
Nursing—General	M

NEBRASKA WESLEYAN UNIVERSITY

Nursing—General	M

NEUMANN UNIVERSITY

Education—General	M,D
Management Strategy and Policy	M
Nursing—General	M
Physical Therapy	D
Sports Management	M

NEW ENGLAND COLLEGE

Accounting	M
Business Administration and Management— General	M
Education—General	M
Educational Leadership and Administration	M
Health Services Management and Hospital Administration	M
Higher Education	M
Human Services	M
Management Strategy and Policy	M
Marketing	M
Nonprofit Management	M
Project Management	M
Recreation and Park Management	M
Special Education	M
Sports Management	M

THE NEW ENGLAND COLLEGE OF OPTOMETRY

Optometry	P,M
Vision Sciences	P,M

NEW ENGLAND LAWÛBOSTON

Law	P,M

NEW ENGLAND SCHOOL OF ACUPUNCTURE

Acupuncture and Oriental Medicine	M

NEW JERSEY CITY UNIVERSITY

Accounting	M
Allied Health—General	M
Art Education	M
Business Administration and Management— General	M
Community Health	M
Early Childhood Education	M
Educational Leadership and Administration	M
Educational Media/ Instructional Technology	M
Educational Psychology	M,O
Elementary Education	M
English as a Second Language	M
Finance and Banking	M
Health Education	M
Health Services Management and Hospital Administration	M
Mathematics Education	M
Multilingual and Multicultural Education	M
Music Education	M
Reading Education	M
Secondary Education	M
Special Education	M
Urban Education	M

NEW JERSEY INSTITUTE OF TECHNOLOGY

Business Administration and Management— General	M
Management Information Systems	M,D
Transportation Management	M,D

NEWMAN THEOLOGICAL COLLEGE

Educational Leadership and Administration	M,O
Religious Education	M,O

NEWMAN UNIVERSITY

Business Administration and Management— General	M
Curriculum and Instruction	M
Education—General	M
Educational Leadership and Administration	M
English as a Second Language	M
Finance and Banking	M
International Business	M
Management Information Systems	M
Nurse Anesthesia	M
Organizational Management	M
Social Work	M

NEW MEXICO HIGHLANDS UNIVERSITY

Business Administration and Management— General	M
Counselor Education	M
Curriculum and Instruction	M
Education—General	M
Educational Leadership and Administration	M
Exercise and Sports Science	M
Health Education	M
Human Resources Management	M
International Business	M
Management Information Systems	M
Nonprofit Management	M
Social Work	M
Special Education	M
Sports Management	M

NEW MEXICO INSTITUTE OF MINING AND TECHNOLOGY

Science Education	M

NEW MEXICO STATE UNIVERSITY

Accounting	M
Adult Nursing	M,D
Agricultural Education	M
Business Administration and Management— General	M,D
Communication Disorders	M,D
Community Health Nursing	M,D
Community Health	M
Counselor Education	M,D,O
Curriculum and Instruction	M,D,O
Education—General	M,D,O
Educational Leadership and Administration	M,D

NEW ORLEANS BAPTIST THEOLOGICAL SEMINARY

Health Education	M
Marketing	D
Medical/Surgical Nursing	M,D
Multilingual and Multicultural Education	M,D
Music Education	M
Nursing and Healthcare Administration	M,D
Nursing—General	M,D
Psychiatric Nursing	M,D
Public Health—General	M
Social Work	M
Special Education	M,D

Religious Education	P,M,D

THE NEW SCHOOL: A UNIVERSITY

English as a Second Language	M
Finance and Banking	M,D
Nonprofit Management	M
Organizational Management	M

NEW YORK CHIROPRACTIC COLLEGE

Acupuncture and Oriental Medicine	M
Chiropractic	P*
Health Physics/ Radiological Health	M

NEW YORK COLLEGE OF HEALTH PROFESSIONS

Acupuncture and Oriental Medicine	M

NEW YORK COLLEGE OF PODIATRIC MEDICINE

Podiatric Medicine	P

NEW YORK COLLEGE OF TRADITIONAL CHINESE MEDICINE

Acupuncture and Oriental Medicine	M

NEW YORK INSTITUTE OF TECHNOLOGY

Accounting	M,O
Business Administration and Management— General	M,O
Counselor Education	M
Distance Education Development	M,O
Education—General	M,O
Educational Leadership and Administration	O
Educational Media/ Instructional Technology	M,O
Elementary Education	M
Finance and Banking	M,O
Human Resources Management	M,O
International Business	M,O
Management Information Systems	M,O
Marketing	M,O
Occupational Therapy	M
Osteopathic Medicine	P
Physical Therapy	M,D
Physician Assistant Studies	M

NEW YORK LAW SCHOOL

Law	P,M*
Taxation	P,M

NEW YORK MEDICAL COLLEGE

Allopathic Medicine	P
Communication Disorders	M
Environmental and Occupational Health	M,O
Epidemiology	M
Health Education	O
Health Promotion	M
Health Services Management and Hospital Administration	M,D,O
Industrial Hygiene	O
International Health	O
Physical Therapy	D
Public Health—General	M,D,O

NEW YORK UNIVERSITY

Program	Degree
Accounting	M,D
Acute Care/Critical Care Nursing	M,O
Adult Nursing	M,O
Advertising and Public Relations	M
Allopathic Medicine	P
Art Education	M
Bioethics	M
Business Administration and Management—General	P,M,D,O
Business Education	M,O
Clinical Research	P,M,D
Communication Disorders	M,D
Community Health	M,D
Counselor Education	M,D,O
Curriculum and Instruction	M,D,O
Dentistry	P
Early Childhood Education	M,D
Education—General	M,D,O
Educational Leadership and Administration	M,D,O
Educational Media/Instructional Technology	M,D,O
Educational Policy	M,D
Educational Psychology	M,D
Elementary Education	M,D
English as a Second Language	M,D,O
English Education	M,D,O
Environmental and Occupational Health	M,D
Environmental Education	M
Epidemiology	M,D
Finance and Banking	M,D,O
Foreign Languages Education	M,D,O
Foundations and Philosophy of Education	M,D
Gerontological Nursing	M,O
Health Education	M,D
Health Promotion	M,D,O
Health Services Management and Hospital Administration	M,O
Higher Education	M,D
Hospitality Management	M,D,O
Human Resources Development	M,O
Human Resources Management	M,D,O
International and Comparative Education	M,D,O
International Business	M,D
International Health	M,D
Kinesiology and Movement Studies	M,D,O
Law	P,M,D,O
Legal and Justice Studies	M,D
Management Information Systems	M,D,O
Management Strategy and Policy	M,D,O
Marketing	M,D,O
Mathematics Education	M
Medical Imaging	P,M,D
Multilingual and Multicultural Education	M,D,O
Music Education	M,D,O
Nonprofit Management	M,D,O
Nurse Midwifery	M,O
Nursing Education	M,O
Nursing Informatics	M,O
Nursing—General	M,D,O
Occupational Therapy	M,D
Oral and Dental Sciences	M,D,O
Organizational Behavior	M,D
Organizational Management	M,D
Pediatric Nursing	M,O
Physical Therapy	M,D,O
Psychiatric Nursing	M,O
Public Health—General	M,D
Quantitative Analysis	M,D,O
Reading Education	M
Real Estate	M,O
Science Education	M
Social Sciences Education	M,D,O
Social Work	M,D*
Special Education	M,D
Sports Management	M
Student Affairs	M,D
Taxation	P,M,D,O
Travel and Tourism	M,O

NIAGARA UNIVERSITY

Program	Degree
Business Administration and Management—General	M
Counselor Education	M,O
Early Childhood Education	M,O
Education—General	M,O
Educational Leadership and Administration	M,O
Elementary Education	M,O
Foundations and Philosophy of Education	M
Middle School Education	M,O
Reading Education	M
Secondary Education	M,O
Special Education	M,O

NICHOLLS STATE UNIVERSITY

Program	Degree
Business Administration and Management—General	M
Counselor Education	M
Curriculum and Instruction	M
Education—General	M
Educational Leadership and Administration	M
Mathematics Education	M

NICHOLS COLLEGE

Program	Degree
Business Administration and Management—General	M
Sports Management	M

THE NIGERIAN BAPTIST THEOLOGICAL SEMINARY

Program	Degree
Religious Education	P,M,D,O

NIPISSING UNIVERSITY

Program	Degree
Education—General	M,O

NORFOLK STATE UNIVERSITY

Program	Degree
Early Childhood Education	M
Education of Students with Severe/Multiple Disabilities	M
Education—General	M
Educational Leadership and Administration	M
Music Education	M
Secondary Education	M
Social Work	M,D
Special Education	M
Urban Education	M

NORTH CAROLINA AGRICULTURAL AND TECHNICAL STATE UNIVERSITY

Program	Degree
Adult Education	M,D
Agricultural Education	M
Art Education	M
Business Administration and Management—General	M,D
Counselor Education	M,D
Education—General	M
Educational Leadership and Administration	M,D
Educational Media/Instructional Technology	M
Elementary Education	M
English Education	M
Environmental and Occupational Health	M
Health Education	M
Human Resources Development	M,D
Mathematics Education	M
Organizational Management	M,D
Physical Education	M
Reading Education	M
Science Education	M
Social Sciences Education	M
Social Work	M
Vocational and Technical Education	M,D

NORTH CAROLINA CENTRAL UNIVERSITY

Program	Degree
Business Administration and Management—General	M
Communication Disorders	M
Counselor Education	M
Curriculum and Instruction	M
Education—General	M
Educational Leadership and Administration	M
Educational Media/Instructional Technology	M
Elementary Education	M
Information Studies	M
Law	P
Library Science	M
Mathematics Education	M
Middle School Education	M
Physical Education	M
Recreation and Park Management	M
Special Education	M
Sports Management	M

NORTH CAROLINA STATE UNIVERSITY

Program	Degree
Accounting	M
Adult Education	M,D
Agricultural Education	M,O
Business Administration and Management—General	M
Business Education	M
Community College Education	M,D
Counselor Education	M,D
Curriculum and Instruction	M,D
Developmental Education	M,D,O
Education—General	M,D,O
Educational Leadership and Administration	M,D
Educational Measurement and Evaluation	D
Educational Media/Instructional Technology	M,D
Elementary Education	M
English Education	M
Entrepreneurship	M
Epidemiology	M,D
Higher Education	M,D
Human Resources Development	M
Mathematics Education	M,D
Middle School Education	M
Nonprofit Management	M,D,O
Recreation and Park Management	M,D
Science Education	M,D
Secondary Education	M
Social Sciences Education	M
Social Work	M
Special Education	M
Sports Management	M,D
Supply Chain Management	M
Travel and Tourism	M,D
Veterinary Medicine	P,M
Veterinary Sciences	M,D

NORTH CENTRAL COLLEGE

Program	Degree
Business Administration and Management—General	M
Curriculum and Instruction	M
Education—General	M
Educational Leadership and Administration	M
Management Information Systems	M
Nonprofit Management	M

NORTHCENTRAL UNIVERSITY

Program	Degree
Business Administration and Management—General	M,D,O
Education—General	M,D,O

NORTH DAKOTA STATE UNIVERSITY

Program	Degree
Adult Education	M,D,O
Agricultural Education	M

(continued top of next column)

Program	Degree
Business Administration and Management—General	M
Counselor Education	M,D
Education—General	M,D,O
Educational Leadership and Administration	M,O
Exercise and Sports Science	M
Logistics	M,D
Mathematics Education	M,D,O
Music Education	M,D,O
Nursing—General	M,D
Pharmaceutical Sciences	M,D
Physical Education	M
Science Education	M,D,O
Social Sciences Education	M,D,O
Sports Management	M
Transportation Management	M,D
Veterinary Sciences	M,D
Vocational and Technical Education	M,D,O

NORTHEASTERN ILLINOIS UNIVERSITY

Program	Degree
Accounting	M
Business Administration and Management—General	M
Counselor Education	M
Education of the Gifted	M
Education—General	M
Educational Leadership and Administration	M
English Education	M
Finance and Banking	M
Human Resources Development	M
Marketing	M
Mathematics Education	M
Multilingual and Multicultural Education	M
Reading Education	M
Special Education	M
Urban Education	M

NORTHEASTERN OHIO UNIVERSITIES COLLEGE OF MEDICINE AND PHARMACY

Program	Degree
Allopathic Medicine	P
Pharmacy	P

NORTHEASTERN STATE UNIVERSITY

Program	Degree
Accounting	M
Business Administration and Management—General	M
Communication Disorders	M
Counselor Education	M
Early Childhood Education	M
Education—General	M
Educational Leadership and Administration	M
Educational Media/Instructional Technology	M
Finance and Banking	M
Foundations and Philosophy of Education	M
Health Education	M
Higher Education	M
Industrial and Manufacturing Management	M
Mathematics Education	M
Optometry	P
Reading Education	M
Science Education	M

NORTHEASTERN UNIVERSITY

Program	Degree
Accounting	M
Acute Care/Critical Care Nursing	M,O
Allied Health—General	P,M,D,O
Business Administration and Management—General	M,O
Communication Disorders	M,D
Counselor Education	M,O
Entrepreneurship	M
Exercise and Sports Science	M

---

*M—master's degree; P—first professional degree; D—doctorate; O—other advanced degree; *—Close-Up and/or Display*

Health Services
　Management and
　　Hospital Administration　　M,D,O
Law　　P
Legal and Justice Studies　　M,D
Management Information
　Systems　　M,D
Maternal and Child/
　Neonatal Nursing　　M,O
Nurse Anesthesia　　M,O
Nursing and Healthcare
　Administration　　M
Nursing—General　　M,O
Pediatric Nursing　　M,O
Pharmaceutical Sciences　　P,M,D
Physical Therapy　　D
Physician Assistant
　Studies　　M
Psychiatric Nursing　　M,O
Public Health—General　　M,
Student Affairs　　M,O

NORTHERN ARIZONA UNIVERSITY

Allied Health—General　　M,D,O
Business Administration
　and Management—
　General　　M
Communication Disorders　　M
Community College
　Education　　M,D,O
Counselor Education　　M,D,O
Curriculum and Instruction　　M,D,O
Early Childhood Education　　M
Education—General　　M,D,O
Educational Leadership
　and Administration　　M,D,O
Educational Media/
　Instructional Technology　　M,D,O
Educational Psychology　　M,D,O
Elementary Education　　M
English as a Second
　Language　　M,D,O
English Education　　M,D,O
Family Nurse Practitioner
　Studies　　M,O
Foreign Languages
　Education　　M
Foundations and
　Philosophy of Education　　M,D,O
Health Services
　Management and
　　Hospital Administration　　O
Higher Education　　M,D,O
Mathematics Education　　M,O
Multilingual and
　Multicultural Education　　M,D,O
Nursing Education　　M,O
Nursing—General　　M,O
Physical Therapy　　D,O
Public Health—General　　O
Science Education　　M,O
Secondary Education　　M
Special Education　　M,D,O
Student Affairs　　M,D,O
Vocational and Technical
　Education　　M,D,O

NORTHERN ILLINOIS UNIVERSITY

Accounting　　M
Adult Education　　M,D
Business Administration
　and Management—
　General　　M
Communication Disorders　　M,D
Counselor Education　　M,D
Curriculum and Instruction　　M,D
Early Childhood Education　　M,D
Education—General　　M,D,O
Educational Leadership
　and Administration　　M,D,O
Educational Media/
　Instructional Technology　　M,D
Educational Psychology　　M,D,O
Elementary Education　　M,D
Foundations and
　Philosophy of Education　　M,D,O
Higher Education　　M,D
Industrial and
　Manufacturing
　Management　　M
Law　　P
Management Information
　Systems　　M
Nursing—General　　M
Physical Education　　M
Physical Therapy　　M

Public Health—General　　M
Reading Education　　M,D
Secondary Education　　M,D
Special Education　　M,D
Sports Management　　M
Taxation　　M

NORTHERN KENTUCKY UNIVERSITY

Accounting　　M,O
Advertising and Public
　Relations　　M,O
Business Administration
　and Management—
　General　　M,O
Counselor Education　　M
Education—General　　M,D,O
Educational Leadership
　and Administration　　M,D,O
Entrepreneurship　　M,O
Finance and Banking　　M,O
International Business　　M,O
Law　　P
Marketing　　M,O
Nonprofit Management　　M,O
Nursing—General　　M,O
Organizational
　Management　　M
Project Management　　M,O
Special Education　　M,O
Student Affairs　　M,O
Taxation　　M,O

NORTHERN MICHIGAN UNIVERSITY

Counselor Education　　M
Education—General　　M,O
Educational Leadership
　and Administration　　M,O
Elementary Education　　M
Exercise and Sports
　Science　　M
Nursing—General　　M
Reading Education　　M,O
Science Education　　M
Secondary Education　　M
Special Education　　M

NORTHERN STATE UNIVERSITY

Counselor Education　　M
Education—General　　M
Educational Leadership
　and Administration　　M
Educational Media/
　Instructional Technology　　M
Elementary Education　　M
English Education　　M
Health Education　　M
Physical Education　　M
Reading Education　　M
Secondary Education　　M
Special Education　　M

NORTH GEORGIA COLLEGE & STATE UNIVERSITY

Art Education　　M,O
Early Childhood Education　　M,O
Education—General　　M,O
Educational Leadership
　and Administration　　M,O
English Education　　M,O
Family Nurse Practitioner
　Studies　　M
Mathematics Education　　M,O
Middle School Education　　M,O
Nursing—General　　M
Physical Education　　M,O
Physical Therapy　　D
Science Education　　M,O
Secondary Education　　M,O
Social Sciences Education　　M,O
Special Education　　M,O

NORTH GREENVILLE UNIVERSITY

Human Resources
　Management　　M

NORTH PARK UNIVERSITY

Adult Nursing　　M
Business Administration
　and Management—
　General　　M
Education—General　　M

Nursing and Healthcare
　Administration　　M
Nursing—General　　M

NORTHWEST CHRISTIAN UNIVERSITY

Business Administration
　and Management—
　General　　M
Counselor Education　　M
Education—General　　M

NORTHWESTERN HEALTH SCIENCES UNIVERSITY

Acupuncture and Oriental
　Medicine　　M
Chiropractic　　P
Rehabilitation Sciences　　O

NORTHWESTERN OKLAHOMA STATE UNIVERSITY

Counselor Education　　M
Education—General　　M
Elementary Education　　M
Reading Education　　M
Secondary Education　　M

NORTHWESTERN POLYTECHNIC UNIVERSITY

Business Administration
　and Management—
　General　　M

NORTHWESTERN STATE UNIVERSITY OF LOUISIANA

Adult Education　　M
Business Education　　M
Counselor Education　　M,O
Curriculum and Instruction　　M
Early Childhood Education　　M
Education—General　　M,O
Educational Leadership
　and Administration　　M,O
Educational Media/
　Instructional Technology　　M,O
Elementary Education　　M,O
English Education　　M
Health Education　　M
Home Economics
　Education　　M
Mathematics Education　　M
Middle School Education　　M
Nursing—General　　M
Reading Education　　M,O
Science Education　　M
Secondary Education　　M,O
Social Sciences Education　　M
Special Education　　M,O
Student Affairs　　M,O

NORTHWESTERN UNIVERSITY

Accounting　　D
Advertising and Public
　Relations　　M
Allopathic Medicine　　P
Business Administration
　and Management—
　General　　M
Clinical Research　　M,O
Communication Disorders　　M,D*
Education—General　　M,D*
Educational Media/
　Instructional Technology　　M,D
Electronic Commerce　　M
Elementary Education　　M
Finance and Banking　　D
Higher Education　　M
Kinesiology and
　Movement Studies　　D
Law　　P,M,O
Management Information
　Systems　　M
Management Strategy and
　Policy　　D
Marketing　　M,D
Music Education　　M,D
Organizational Behavior　　M,D
Organizational
　Management　　M,D
Physical Therapy　　D
Project Management　　M
Public Health—General　　M
Quality Management　　M
Rehabilitation Sciences　　D
Secondary Education　　M

Special Education　　M,D
Sports Management　　M
Taxation　　P,M

NORTHWEST MISSOURI STATE UNIVERSITY

Accounting　　M
Agricultural Education　　M
Business Administration
　and Management—
　General　　M
Counselor Education　　M
Early Childhood Education　　M
Education—General　　M,O
Educational Leadership
　and Administration　　M,O
Educational Media/
　Instructional Technology　　M
Elementary Education　　M,O
English as a Second
　Language　　M,O
English Education　　M
Health Education　　M
Health Services
　Management and
　　Hospital Administration　　M
Higher Education　　M
Management Information
　Systems　　M
Mathematics Education　　M
Middle School Education　　M
Music Education　　M
Physical Education　　M
Quality Management　　M,O
Reading Education　　M
Recreation and Park
　Management　　M
Science Education　　M
Secondary Education　　M,O
Social Sciences Education　　M
Special Education　　M

NORTHWEST NAZARENE UNIVERSITY

Business Administration
　and Management—
　General　　M
Counselor Education　　M
Curriculum and Instruction　　M
Education—General　　M
Educational Leadership
　and Administration　　M
Reading Education　　M
Social Work　　M
Special Education　　M

NORTHWEST UNIVERSITY

Business Administration
　and Management—
　General　　M
Education—General　　M
Organizational
　Management　　M

NORTHWOOD UNIVERSITY

Business Administration
　and Management—
　General　　M

NORWICH UNIVERSITY

Business Administration
　and Management—
　General　　M
International Business　　M
Management Information
　Systems　　M
Nursing and Healthcare
　Administration　　M
Nursing Education　　M
Organizational
　Management　　M
Science Education　　M

NOTRE DAME COLLEGE (OH)

Accounting　　M,O
Business Administration
　and Management—
　General　　M,O
Education—General　　M,O
Finance and Banking　　M,O
Management Information
　Systems　　M,O
Reading Education　　M,O
Special Education　　M,O

NOTRE DAME DE NAMUR UNIVERSITY

Business Administration and Management— General	M
Education—General	M,O
Educational Leadership and Administration	M,O
English as a Second Language	M,O
Finance and Banking	M
Human Resources Management	M
Marketing	M
Reading Education	M,O
Special Education	M,O

NOVA SOUTHEASTERN UNIVERSITY

Accounting	M,D
Adult Education	D
Allied Health—General	M,O
Art Education	M,O
Business Administration and Management— General	M,D
Communication Disorders	M,D
Computer Education	M,D,O
Counselor Education	M
Curriculum and Instruction	M,O
Dentistry	P,M
Distance Education Development	M,O
Early Childhood Education	M,O
Education of the Gifted	M,O
Education—General	M,D,O
Educational Leadership and Administration	M,D,O
Educational Media/ Instructional Technology	M,D,O
Elementary Education	M,O
English as a Second Language	M,O
English/Education	M,O
Entrepreneurship	M
Environmental Education	M,O
Finance and Banking	M,D
Health Education	M,D
Health Law	M
Higher Education	D
Human Resources Management	M,D
Human Services	M,D
International Business	M,D
Law	P,M,O
Legal and Justice Studies	M,O
Management Information Systems	M,D
Marketing	D
Mathematics Education	M,O
Multilingual and Multicultural Education	M,O
Nursing—General	M,D
Occupational Therapy	M,D
Optometry	P,M
Organizational Management	D
Osteopathic Medicine	P,M,O
Pharmacy	P
Physical Therapy	D
Physician Assistant Studies	M
Public Health—General	M
Reading Education	M,O
Real Estate	M
Science Education	M,O
Secondary Education	M,O
Social Sciences Education	M,O
Special Education	M,D,O
Sports Management	M,O
Student Affairs	M
Taxation	M
Urban Education	M,O
Vision Sciences	P,M
Vocational and Technical Education	D

NYACK COLLEGE

Accounting	M
Business Administration and Management— General	M
Education—General	M
Elementary Education	M
Organizational Management	M
Special Education	M

OAKLAND CITY UNIVERSITY

Business Administration and Management— General	M
Education—General	M,D
Educational Leadership and Administration	M,D

OAKLAND UNIVERSITY

Accounting	M,O
Adult Nursing	M
Allied Health—General	M,D,O
Business Administration and Management— General	M,O
Early Childhood Education	M,D,O
Education—General	M,D,O
Educational Leadership and Administration	M,D,O
Educational Media/ Instructional Technology	O
English as a Second Language	M,O
Entrepreneurship	M,O
Environmental and Occupational Health	M
Exercise and Sports Science	M,O
Family Nurse Practitioner Studies	M,O
Finance and Banking	M,O
Foundations and Philosophy of Education	M
Gerontological Nursing	M,O
Health Promotion	O
Higher Education	M,D,O
Human Resources Development	M
Human Resources Management	M,O
Industrial and Manufacturing Management	M,O
International Business	M,O
Management Information Systems	M,O
Marketing	M,O
Maternal and Child Health	M,D,O
Mathematics Education	M,D,O
Medical Physics	M,D
Music Education	M,D
Nurse Anesthesia	M,O
Nursing Education	M,O
Nursing—General	M,D,O
Physical Therapy	M,D
Reading Education	M,D,O
Secondary Education	M
Special Education	M,O

OBERLIN COLLEGE

Early Childhood Education	M
Education—General	M
Middle School Education	M

OCCIDENTAL COLLEGE

Education—General	M
Elementary Education	M
English Education	M
Foreign Languages Education	M
Mathematics Education	M
Science Education	M
Secondary Education	M
Social Sciences Education	M

OGI SCHOOL OF SCIENCE & ENGINEERING AT OREGON HEALTH & SCIENCE UNIVERSITY

Business Administration and Management— General	M,O
Environmental and Occupational Health	M,D
Health Services Management and Hospital Administration	M,O

OGLALA LAKOTA COLLEGE

Business Administration and Management— General	M
Educational Leadership and Administration	M

OGLETHORPE UNIVERSITY

Early Childhood Education	M
Education—General	M

OHIO COLLEGE OF PODIATRIC MEDICINE

Podiatric Medicine	P

OHIO DOMINICAN UNIVERSITY

Business Administration and Management— General	M
Education—General	M
English as a Second Language	M

OHIO NORTHERN UNIVERSITY

Law	P,M
Pharmacy	P

THE OHIO STATE UNIVERSITY

Accounting	M
Agricultural Education	M,D
Allied Health—General	M
Allopathic Medicine	P
Art Education	M,D
Business Administration and Management— General	M,D
Communication Disorders	M,D
Dentistry	P,M
Education—General	M,D
Educational Leadership and Administration	M,D
Educational Policy	M,D
Finance and Banking	M,D
Health Services Management and Hospital Administration	M,D
Hospitality Management	M,D
Human Resources Management	M,D
Law	P,M
Logistics	M
Management Information Systems	M,D
Medicinal and Pharmaceutical Chemistry	M,D
Nursing—General	M,D
Occupational Therapy	M
Optometry	P
Oral and Dental Sciences	D
Pharmaceutical Administration	M,D
Pharmaceutical Sciences	M,D
Pharmacy	P
Physical Education	M,D
Physical Therapy	M
Public Health—General	M,D
Social Work	M,D
Veterinary Medicine	P
Veterinary Sciences	M,D

THE OHIO STATE UNIVERSITY AT LIMA

Early Childhood Education	M
Education—General	M
Middle School Education	M
Social Work	M

THE OHIO STATE UNIVERSITY AT MARION

Early Childhood Education	M,D
Education—General	M,D
Middle School Education	M,D
Nursing—General	M,D
Social Work	M,D

THE OHIO STATE UNIVERSITY– MANSFIELD CAMPUS

Early Childhood Education	M
Middle School Education	M
Social Work	M

THE OHIO STATE UNIVERSITY– NEWARK CAMPUS

Early Childhood Education	M
Education—General	M
Middle School Education	M
Social Work	M

OHIO UNIVERSITY

Athletic Training and Sports Medicine	M
Business Administration and Management— General	M
Communication Disorders	M,D
Computer Education	M,D
Counselor Education	M,D
Curriculum and Instruction	M,D
Early Childhood Education	M
Education—General	M,D
Educational Leadership and Administration	M,D
Educational Measurement and Evaluation	M,D
Educational Media/ Instructional Technology	M,D
English as a Second Language	M
Exercise and Sports Science	M,D
Family Nurse Practitioner Studies	M
Finance and Banking	M
Health Services Management and Hospital Administration	M
Higher Education	M,D
Mathematics Education	M,D
Middle School Education	M,D
Multilingual and Multicultural Education	M,D
Music Education	M,O
Nursing and Healthcare Administration	M
Nursing Education	M
Nursing—General	M
Osteopathic Medicine	P
Physical Education	M
Physical Therapy	D
Reading Education	M,D
Recreation and Park Management	M
Science Education	M
Secondary Education	M,D
Social Sciences Education	M,D
Social Work	M
Special Education	M,D
Sports Management	M
Student Affairs	M,D

OHIO VALLEY UNIVERSITY

Education—General	M

OKLAHOMA CITY UNIVERSITY

Accounting	M
Business Administration and Management— General	M
Early Childhood Education	M
Education—General	M
Educational Psychology	M
Elementary Education	M
English as a Second Language	M
Finance and Banking	M
Health Services Management and Hospital Administration	M
International Business	M
Law	P
Management Information Systems	M
Marketing	M
Nonprofit Management	M
Nursing—General	M,D

OKLAHOMA STATE UNIVERSITY

Accounting	M,D
Agricultural Education	M,D
Business Administration and Management— General	M,D*
Communication Disorders	M
Curriculum and Instruction	M,D

*M—master's degree; P—first professional degree; D—doctorate; O—other advanced degree; *—Close-Up and/or Display*

Education—General	M,D,O
Educational Leadership and Administration	M,D
Educational Psychology	M,D,O
Finance and Banking	M,D
Health Education	M,D,O
Higher Education	M,D
Hospitality Management	M,D
Management Information Systems	M,D
Marketing	M,D
Mathematics Education	M,D
Music Education	M
Quantitative Analysis	M,D
Veterinary Medicine	P
Veterinary Sciences	M,D

OKLAHOMA STATE UNIVERSITY CENTER FOR HEALTH SCIENCES

Osteopathic Medicine	P

OLD DOMINION UNIVERSITY

Accounting	M
Allied Health—General	M,D
Athletic Training and Sports Medicine	M
Business Administration and Management—General	M,D
Business Education	M,D
Communication Disorders	M
Community College Education	M,D
Counselor Education	M,D,O
Curriculum and Instruction	M,D
Dental Hygiene	M
Early Childhood Education	M,D
Education—General	M,D,O
Educational Leadership and Administration	M,D,O
Educational Media/Instructional Technology	M,D
Elementary Education	M
Environmental and Occupational Health	M
Exercise and Sports Science	M
Family Nurse Practitioner Studies	M
Finance and Banking	M,D
Health Promotion	M
Health Services Research	D
Higher Education	M,D,O
International Business	M
Kinesiology and Movement Studies	D
Library Science	M
Management Information Systems	M
Marketing	D
Middle School Education	M
Music Education	M
Nurse Anesthesia	M
Nurse Midwifery	M
Nursing Education	M
Nursing—General	M,D
Physical Education	M
Physical Therapy	D
Public Health—General	M
Reading Education	M,D
Recreation and Park Management	M
Science Education	M
Secondary Education	M
Special Education	M,D
Sports Management	M
Travel and Tourism	M
Vocational and Technical Education	M,D
Women's Health Nursing	M

OLIVET COLLEGE

Education—General	M

OLIVET NAZARENE UNIVERSITY

Business Administration and Management—General	M
Curriculum and Instruction	M
Education—General	M
Educational Leadership and Administration	M
Elementary Education	M
Library Science	M

Organizational Management	M
Reading Education	M
Secondary Education	M

ORAL ROBERTS UNIVERSITY

Accounting	M
Business Administration and Management—General	M
Curriculum and Instruction	M,D
Education—General	M,D
Educational Leadership and Administration	M,D
Entrepreneurship	M
Finance and Banking	M
Higher Education	M,D
International Business	M
Marketing	M
Nonprofit Management	M
Religious Education	P,M,D

OREGON COLLEGE OF ORIENTAL MEDICINE

Acupuncture and Oriental Medicine	M,D

OREGON HEALTH & SCIENCE UNIVERSITY

Allopathic Medicine	P
Community Health Nursing	M,O
Dentistry	P,O
Epidemiology	M
Family Nurse Practitioner Studies	M,O
Gerontological Nursing	O
Nurse Anesthesia	M
Nurse Midwifery	M,O
Nursing Education	M,O
Nursing—General	M,D,O
Oral and Dental Sciences	P,M,O
Psychiatric Nursing	M,O

OREGON STATE UNIVERSITY

Adult Education	M
Agricultural Education	M
Business Administration and Management—General	M,O
Counselor Education	M,D
Education—General	M,D
Educational Leadership and Administration	M
Elementary Education	M
Environmental and Occupational Health	M
Exercise and Sports Science	M,D
Health Physics/Radiological Health	M,D
Health Promotion	M,D
Health Services Management and Hospital Administration	M,D
Kinesiology and Movement Studies	M
Mathematics Education	M,D
Music Education	M
Pharmaceutical Sciences	P,M,D
Pharmacy	P,M,D
Public Health—General	M,D
Reading Education	M
Science Education	M,D
Student Affairs	M
Veterinary Medicine	P
Veterinary Sciences	D

OREGON STATE UNIVERSITY–CASCADES

Education—General	M

OTTAWA UNIVERSITY

Business Administration and Management—General	M
Counselor Education	M
Curriculum and Instruction	M
Early Childhood Education	M
Education—General	M
Educational Leadership and Administration	M
Educational Media/Instructional Technology	M
Elementary Education	M

Finance and Banking	M
Human Resources Development	M
Human Resources Management	M
Marketing	M
Special Education	M

OTTERBEIN UNIVERSITY

Adult Nursing	M,O
Business Administration and Management—General	M
Education—General	M
Family Nurse Practitioner Studies	M,O
Nursing and Healthcare Administration	M,O
Nursing—General	M,O

OUR LADY OF HOLY CROSS COLLEGE

Counselor Education	M
Curriculum and Instruction	M
Education—General	M
Educational Leadership and Administration	M

OUR LADY OF THE LAKE COLLEGE

Nurse Anesthesia	M
Nursing and Healthcare Administration	M
Nursing Education	M
Nursing—General	M
Physician Assistant Studies	M

OUR LADY OF THE LAKE UNIVERSITY OF SAN ANTONIO

Accounting	M
Business Administration and Management—General	M
Communication Disorders	M
Counselor Education	M
Curriculum and Instruction	M
Early Childhood Education	M
Education—General	M,D
Educational Leadership and Administration	M
Educational Media/Instructional Technology	M
Elementary Education	M
English as a Second Language	M
English Education	M
Finance and Banking	M
Health Services Management and Hospital Administration	M
Management Information Systems	M
Mathematics Education	M
Middle School Education	M
Multilingual and Multicultural Education	M
Nonprofit Management	M
Organizational Management	M,D
Reading Education	M
Science Education	M
Secondary Education	M
Social Work	M
Special Education	M
Vocational and Technical Education	M

OXFORD GRADUATE SCHOOL

Organizational Management	M,D

PACE UNIVERSITY

Accounting	M
Art Education	M,O
Business Administration and Management—General	M,D,O
Curriculum and Instruction	M,O
Early Childhood Education	M,O
Education—General	M,O
Educational Leadership and Administration	M,O
Electronic Commerce	M,D,O
Elementary Education	M,O

Environmental Law	P,M,D
Family Nurse Practitioner Studies	M,D,O
Finance and Banking	M
Health Services Management and Hospital Administration	M
International Business	M
Investment Management	M
Law	P,M,D*
Legal and Justice Studies	P,M,D
Management Information Systems	M
Management Strategy and Policy	M
Marketing Research	M
Marketing	M
Nonprofit Management	M
Nursing and Healthcare Administration	M,D,O
Nursing Education	M,D,O
Nursing—General	M,D,O
Physician Assistant Studies	M
Reading Education	M,O
Special Education	M,O
Taxation	M

PACIFIC COLLEGE OF ORIENTAL MEDICINE

Acupuncture and Oriental Medicine	M,D

PACIFIC COLLEGE OF ORIENTAL MEDICINE-CHICAGO

Acupuncture and Oriental Medicine	M

PACIFIC COLLEGE OF ORIENTAL MEDICINE-NEW YORK

Acupuncture and Oriental Medicine	M

PACIFIC LUTHERAN UNIVERSITY

Business Administration and Management—General	M
Curriculum and Instruction	M
Education—General	M
Educational Leadership and Administration	M
Family Nurse Practitioner Studies	M
Nursing and Healthcare Administration	M
Nursing—General	M

PACIFIC STATES UNIVERSITY

Accounting	M,D
Business Administration and Management—General	M,D
Finance and Banking	M,D
International Business	M,D
Management Information Systems	M,D
Real Estate	M,D

PACIFIC UNION COLLEGE

Education—General	M

PACIFIC UNIVERSITY

Early Childhood Education	M
Education—General	M
Elementary Education	M
Health Services Management and Hospital Administration	M
Middle School Education	M
Occupational Therapy	M
Pharmacy	P
Physical Therapy	D
Physician Assistant Studies	M
Secondary Education	M
Special Education	M

PALM BEACH ATLANTIC UNIVERSITY

Business Administration and Management—General	M
Counselor Education	M
Education—General	M

Organizational Management	M
Pharmacy	P

PALMER COLLEGE OF CHIROPRACTIC

Chiropractic	P
Clinical Research	M

PARKER COLLEGE OF CHIROPRACTIC

Chiropractic	P

PARK UNIVERSITY

Business Administration and Management— General	M
Education—General	M
Educational Leadership and Administration	M
Entrepreneurship	M
Health Services Management and Hospital Administration	M
International Business	M
Law	M
Management Information Systems	M
Middle School Education	M
Multilingual and Multicultural Education	M
Nonprofit Management	M
Secondary Education	M
Special Education	M

PENN STATE DICKINSON SCHOOL OF LAW

Law	P,M

PENN STATE GREAT VALLEY

Business Administration and Management— General	M
Education—General	M

PENN STATE HARRISBURG

Business Administration and Management— General	M
Education—General	M,D

PENN STATE HERSHEY MEDICAL CENTER

Allopathic Medicine	P,M,D
Health Services Research	M
Public Health—General	M
Veterinary Sciences	M

PENN STATE UNIVERSITY PARK

Agricultural Education	M,D
Business Administration and Management— General	M,D
Communication Disorders	M,D
Counselor Education	M,D
Curriculum and Instruction	M,D
Education—General	M,D
Educational Media/ Instructional Technology	M,D
Educational Policy	M,D
Educational Psychology	M,D
Health Services Management and Hospital Administration	M,D
Hospitality Management	M,D
Human Resources Development	M,O
Human Resources Management	M,O
Industrial and Manufacturing Management	M
Kinesiology and Movement Studies	M,D
Leisure Studies	M,D
Nursing—General	M,D
Quality Management	M
Recreation and Park Management	M,D
Special Education	M,D
Veterinary Sciences	D
Vocational and Technical Education	M,D

PEPPERDINE UNIVERSITY

Business Administration and Management— General	M
Education—General	M,D
Educational Leadership and Administration	M,D
Educational Media/ Instructional Technology	M,D
Finance and Banking	M
International Business	M
Law	P
Organizational Management	M

PERU STATE COLLEGE

Curriculum and Instruction	M
Education—General	M
Entrepreneurship	M
Organizational Management	M

PFEIFFER UNIVERSITY

Business Administration and Management— General	M
Education—General	M
Elementary Education	M
Health Services Management and Hospital Administration	M
Organizational Management	M
Religious Education	M

PHILADELPHIA BIBLICAL UNIVERSITY

Curriculum and Instruction	M
Education—General	M
Educational Leadership and Administration	M
Organizational Management	M

PHILADELPHIA COLLEGE OF OSTEOPATHIC MEDICINE

Osteopathic Medicine	P
Physician Assistant Studies	M*

PHILADELPHIA UNIVERSITY

Business Administration and Management— General	M
Finance and Banking	M
Health Services Management and Hospital Administration	M
International Business	M
Marketing	M
Nurse Midwifery	M,O
Occupational Therapy	M
Physician Assistant Studies	M
Taxation	M

PHILLIPS GRADUATE INSTITUTE

Counselor Education	M
Organizational Behavior	M,D

PHILLIPS THEOLOGICAL SEMINARY

Business Administration and Management— General	P,M,D
Higher Education	P,M,D
Religious Education	P,M,D
Social Work	P,M,D

PIEDMONT COLLEGE

Business Administration and Management— General	M
Curriculum and Instruction	M,O
Early Childhood Education	M,O
Education—General	M,O
Secondary Education	M,O

PIKEVILLE COLLEGE

Osteopathic Medicine	P

PITTSBURG STATE UNIVERSITY

Accounting	M
Art Education	M
Business Administration and Management— General	M
Community College Education	O
Counselor Education	M
Early Childhood Education	M
Education—General	M,O
Educational Leadership and Administration	M,O
Educational Media/ Instructional Technology	M
Elementary Education	M
Higher Education	M,O
Human Resources Development	M
Music Education	M
Nursing—General	M
Physical Education	M
Reading Education	M
Secondary Education	M
Special Education	M
Vocational and Technical Education	M,O

PLYMOUTH STATE UNIVERSITY

Adult Education	D
Athletic Training and Sports Medicine	M
Business Administration and Management— General	M
Counselor Education	M
Education—General	O
Educational Leadership and Administration	M
Elementary Education	M
English Education	M
Health Education	M
Mathematics Education	M
Middle School Education	M
Reading Education	M
Science Education	M
Secondary Education	M
Special Education	M,D,O

POINT LOMA NAZARENE UNIVERSITY

Business Administration and Management— General	M
Education—General	M,O
Nursing—General	M

POINT PARK UNIVERSITY

Business Administration and Management— General	M
Curriculum and Instruction	M
Education—General	M
Educational Leadership and Administration	M
Organizational Management	M

POLYTECHNIC INSTITUTE OF NYU

Business Administration and Management— General	M,D,O
Electronic Commerce	M,D,O
Entrepreneurship	M,D,O
Finance and Banking	M,O
Human Resources Management	M,D,O
Management Information Systems	M,D,O
Organizational Behavior	M,O
Project Management	M,D,O
Transportation Management	M

POLYTECHNIC INSTITUTE OF NYU, WESTCHESTER GRADUATE CENTER

Business Administration and Management— General	M
Finance and Banking	M,O

POLYTECHNIC UNIVERSITY OF PUERTO RICO

Business Administration and Management— General	M
Industrial and Manufacturing Management	M
International Business	M

POLYTECHNIC UNIVERSITY OF THE AMERICAS–MIAMI CAMPUS

Business Administration and Management— General	M

POLYTECHNIC UNIVERSITY OF THE AMERICAS–ORLANDO CAMPUS

Business Administration and Management— General	M

PONCE SCHOOL OF MEDICINE

Allopathic Medicine	P
Epidemiology	M,D
Public Health—General	M,D

PONTIFICAL CATHOLIC UNIVERSITY OF PUERTO RICO

Accounting	M
Business Administration and Management— General	M,D
Business Education	M,D
Clinical Laboratory Sciences/Medical Technology	O
Counselor Education	M
Curriculum and Instruction	M,D
Education—General	M,D
Educational Leadership and Administration	D
Educational Psychology	M
English as a Second Language	M
Finance and Banking	M
Human Resources Management	M
Human Services	M,D
International Business	M
Law	P
Management Information Systems	M
Marketing	M
Medical/Surgical Nursing	M
Nursing—General	M
Psychiatric Nursing	M
Religious Education	M
Social Work	M

PONTIFICIA UNIVERSIDAD CATOLICA MADRE Y MAESTRA

Allopathic Medicine	P
Business Administration and Management— General	M
Finance and Banking	M
Human Resources Management	M
Insurance	M
International Business	M
Law	M
Logistics	M
Marketing	M

PORTLAND STATE UNIVERSITY

Adult Education	M,D
Business Administration and Management— General	M,D,O
Communication Disorders	M
Counselor Education	M,D
Curriculum and Instruction	M,D
Early Childhood Education	M,D
Education—General	M,D
Educational Leadership and Administration	M,D
Educational Media/ Instructional Technology	M,D

Educational Policy	M,D
Elementary Education	M,D
English as a Second Language	M
Finance and Banking	M
Foreign Languages Education	M
Health Education	M,O
Health Promotion	M,O
Health Services Management and Hospital Administration	M
Higher Education	M,D
Human Resources Management	M
Industrial and Manufacturing Management	M,D
International Business	M
Mathematics Education	M,D
Music Education	M
Public Health—General	M,O
Reading Education	M,D
Science Education	M,D
Secondary Education	M,D
Social Sciences Education	M
Social Work	M,D
Special Education	M,D

POST UNIVERSITY

Business Administration and Management—General	M
Education—General	M
Educational Media/Instructional Technology	M
Entrepreneurship	M
Finance and Banking	M
Human Services	M
Marketing	M

PRAIRIE VIEW A&M UNIVERSITY

Accounting	M
Business Administration and Management—General	M
Counselor Education	M,D
Curriculum and Instruction	M
Education—General	M,D
Educational Leadership and Administration	M,D
Family Nurse Practitioner Studies	M
Health Education	M
Legal and Justice Studies	M,D
Management Information Systems	M,D
Nursing and Healthcare Administration	M
Nursing Education	M
Nursing—General	M
Physical Education	M
Special Education	M

PRATT INSTITUTE

Art Education	M,O
Facilities Management	M
Information Studies	M,O*
Library Science	M,O
Special Education	M

PRESCOTT COLLEGE

Counselor Education	M,D
Early Childhood Education	M,D
Education—General	M,D
Educational Leadership and Administration	M,D
Elementary Education	M,D
Environmental Education	M,D
Leisure Studies	M
Secondary Education	M,D
Special Education	M,D

PRINCETON UNIVERSITY

Finance and Banking	M

PROVIDENCE COLLEGE

Accounting	M
Business Administration and Management—General	M
Counselor Education	M
Education—General	M
Educational Leadership and Administration	M

Elementary Education	M
Entrepreneurship	M
Finance and Banking	M
International Business	M
Marketing	M
Mathematics Education	M
Nonprofit Management	M
Quantitative Analysis	M
Reading Education	M
Secondary Education	M
Special Education	M

PROVIDENCE COLLEGE AND THEOLOGICAL SEMINARY

English as a Second Language	P,M,D,O
Religious Education	P,M,D,O
Student Affairs	P,M,D,O

PURDUE UNIVERSITY

Agricultural Education	M,D,O
Art Education	M,D,O
Business Administration and Management—General	M,D
Communication Disorders	M,D
Counselor Education	M,D,O
Curriculum and Instruction	M,D,O
Education of the Gifted	M,D,O
Education—General	M,D,O
Educational Leadership and Administration	M,D,O
Educational Media/Instructional Technology	M,D,O
Educational Psychology	M,D,O
Elementary Education	M,D,O
English Education	M,D,O
Epidemiology	M,D
Exercise and Sports Science	M,D
Finance and Banking	M
Foreign Languages Education	M,D,O
Foundations and Philosophy of Education	M,D,O
Health Promotion	M,D
Higher Education	M,D,O
Home Economics Education	M,D,O
Hospitality Management	M,D
Human Resources Management	M,D
Industrial and Manufacturing Management	M
International Business	M
Mathematics Education	M,D,O
Medicinal and Pharmaceutical Chemistry	M,D
Organizational Behavior	D
Pharmaceutical Administration	M,D,O
Pharmaceutical Sciences	M,D
Pharmacy	P
Physical Education	M,D
Public Health—General	M,D
Reading Education	M,D,O
Science Education	M,D,O
Social Sciences Education	M,D,O
Special Education	M,D,O
Travel and Tourism	M,D
Veterinary Medicine	P
Veterinary Sciences	M,D
Vocational and Technical Education	M,D,O

PURDUE UNIVERSITY CALUMET

Accounting	M
Business Administration and Management—General	M
Counselor Education	M
Education—General	M
Educational Leadership and Administration	M
Educational Media/Instructional Technology	M
Human Services	M
Mathematics Education	M
Nursing—General	M
Science Education	M
Special Education	M

PURDUE UNIVERSITY NORTH CENTRAL

Education—General	M
Elementary Education	M

QUEENS COLLEGE OF THE CITY UNIVERSITY OF NEW YORK

Accounting	M
Art Education	M,O
Communication Disorders	M
Counselor Education	M
Early Childhood Education	M,O
Education—General	M,O
Educational Leadership and Administration	O
Elementary Education	M,O
English as a Second Language	M
English Education	M,O
Exercise and Sports Science	M
Foreign Languages Education	M,O
Home Economics Education	M
Information Studies	M,O
Library Science	M,O
Mathematics Education	M,O
Multilingual and Multicultural Education	M,O
Music Education	M,O
Reading Education	M
Science Education	M,O
Secondary Education	M,O
Social Sciences Education	M,O
Special Education	M

QUEEN'S UNIVERSITY AT KINGSTON

Allopathic Medicine	P
Business Administration and Management—General	M
Education—General	M,D
Entrepreneurship	M
Epidemiology	M,D
Exercise and Sports Science	M,D
Family Nurse Practitioner Studies	M,D,O
Finance and Banking	M
Health Services Management and Hospital Administration	M,D
Information Studies	M,D
Law	P,M
Legal and Justice Studies	M,D
Marketing	M
Nursing—General	M,D,O
Occupational Therapy	M,D
Pediatric Nursing	M,D,O
Pharmaceutical Sciences	M,D
Physical Therapy	M,D
Project Management	M
Public Health—General	M,D
Rehabilitation Sciences	M,D
Women's Health Nursing	M,D,O

QUEENS UNIVERSITY OF CHARLOTTE

Business Administration and Management—General	M
Education—General	M
Educational Leadership and Administration	M
Elementary Education	M
Nursing and Healthcare Administration	M
Nursing—General	M
Reading Education	M

QUINCY UNIVERSITY

Business Administration and Management—General	M
Counselor Education	M
Curriculum and Instruction	M
Education—General	M
Educational Leadership and Administration	M
Human Resources Management	M
Reading Education	M
Special Education	M

QUINNIPIAC UNIVERSITY

Adult Nursing	M,O
Advertising and Public Relations	M
Allied Health—General	M,D,O
Business Administration and Management—General	M
Clinical Laboratory Sciences/Medical Technology	M
Education—General	M
Elementary Education	M
English Education	M
Family Nurse Practitioner Studies	M,O
Finance and Banking	M
Foreign Languages Education	M
Health Law	P,M
Health Physics/Radiological Health	M
Health Services Management and Hospital Administration	M
International Business	M
Investment Management	M
Law	P,M
Management Information Systems	M
Marketing	M
Mathematics Education	M
Middle School Education	M
Nursing—General	M,O
Occupational Therapy	M
Organizational Management	M
Perfusion	M
Physical Therapy	M,D
Physician Assistant Studies	M
Science Education	M
Secondary Education	M
Social Sciences Education	M
Supply Chain Management	M

RADFORD UNIVERSITY

Adult Nursing	M
Business Administration and Management—General	M
Communication Disorders	M
Counselor Education	M
Education—General	M
Educational Leadership and Administration	M
Family Nurse Practitioner Studies	M
Gerontological Nursing	M
Music Education	M
Nurse Midwifery	M
Nursing—General	M
Occupational Therapy	M
Reading Education	M
Social Work	M
Special Education	M
Student Affairs	M

RAMAPO COLLEGE OF NEW JERSEY

Educational Media/Instructional Technology	M
Nursing Education	M
Nursing—General	M

RANDOLPH COLLEGE

Curriculum and Instruction	M
Education—General	M
Special Education	M

REFORMED THEOLOGICAL SEMINARY–JACKSON CAMPUS

Religious Education	P,M,D,O

REGENT'S AMERICAN COLLEGE LONDON

Business Administration and Management—General	M
Finance and Banking	M
Human Resources Management	M
International Business	M

Management Information Systems	M
Marketing	M

REGENT UNIVERSITY

Business Administration and Management—General	M,D,O
Counselor Education	M,D,O
Education—General	M,D,O
Educational Leadership and Administration	M,D,O
Elementary Education	M,D,O
English as a Second Language	M,D,O
Entrepreneurship	M,D,O
Health Services Management and Hospital Administration	M
Law	P,M
Legal and Justice Studies	P,M
Management Strategy and Policy	M,D,O
Mathematics Education	M,D,O
Organizational Management	M,D,O
Religious Education	M,D,O
Special Education	M,D,O
Student Affairs	M,D,O

REGIS COLLEGE (MA)

Education—General	M
Elementary Education	M
Family Nurse Practitioner Studies	M,D,O
Health Services Management and Hospital Administration	M,D,O
Nursing Education	M,D,O
Nursing—General	M,D,O
Quality Management	M
Reading Education	M
Special Education	M

REGIS UNIVERSITY

Accounting	M,O
Adult Education	M,O
Allied Health—General	P,M,D,O
Business Administration and Management—General	M,O
Curriculum and Instruction	M,O
Early Childhood Education	M,O
Education—General	M,O
Educational Leadership and Administration	M,O
Educational Media/Instructional Technology	M,O
Electronic Commerce	M,O
Elementary Education	M,O
English as a Second Language	M,O
Family Nurse Practitioner Studies	P,M,D,O
Finance and Banking	M,O
Foundations and Philosophy of Education	M,O
Health Education	P,M,D,O
Health Services Management and Hospital Administration	P,M,D,O
Human Resources Management	M,O
Industrial and Manufacturing Management	M,O
International Business	M,O
Legal and Justice Studies	M,O
Management Information Systems	M,O
Marketing	M,O
Maternal and Child/Neonatal Nursing	P,M,D,O
Nonprofit Management	M,O
Nursing and Healthcare Administration	P,M,D,O
Nursing—General	P,M,D,O
Organizational Management	M,O
Pharmacy	P,M,D,O
Physical Therapy	P,M,D,O
Physician Assistant Studies	P,M,D,O
Project Management	M,O

Reading Education	M,O
Science Education	M,O
Secondary Education	M,O
Special Education	M,O

REINHARDT UNIVERSITY

Business Administration and Management—General	M
Early Childhood Education	M
Education—General	M
Music Education	M

RENSSELAER AT HARTFORD

Business Administration and Management—General	M

RENSSELAER POLYTECHNIC INSTITUTE

Business Administration and Management—General	M,D
Entrepreneurship	M

RESEARCH COLLEGE OF NURSING

Family Nurse Practitioner Studies	M
Nursing Education	M
Nursing—General	M

RHODE ISLAND COLLEGE

Accounting	M,O
Art Education	M
Counselor Education	M,O
Early Childhood Education	M
Education—General	D
Educational Leadership and Administration	M,O
Elementary Education	M
English as a Second Language	M
English Education	M
Finance and Banking	M,O
Foreign Languages Education	M
Health Education	M,O
Mathematics Education	M
Music Education	M
Nursing—General	M
Physical Education	M,O
Reading Education	M
Secondary Education	M
Social Sciences Education	M
Social Work	M
Special Education	M,O
Vocational and Technical Education	M

RHODE ISLAND SCHOOL OF DESIGN

Art Education	M

RHODES COLLEGE

Accounting	M

RICE UNIVERSITY

Business Administration and Management—General	M
Education—General	M
Science Education	M,D

THE RICHARD STOCKTON COLLEGE OF NEW JERSEY

Business Administration and Management—General	M
Education—General	M
Educational Media/Instructional Technology	M
Nursing—General	M
Occupational Therapy	M
Physical Therapy	D

RIDER UNIVERSITY

Accounting	M
Business Administration and Management—General	M
Business Education	O
Counselor Education	M,O

Curriculum and Instruction	M,O
Education—General	M,O
Educational Leadership and Administration	M,O
Elementary Education	O
English as a Second Language	O
English Education	O
Foreign Languages Education	O
Mathematics Education	O
Organizational Management	M
Reading Education	M,O
Science Education	O
Social Sciences Education	O
Special Education	M,O

RIVIER COLLEGE

Business Administration and Management—General	M
Counselor Education	M,D,O
Curriculum and Instruction	M,D,O
Early Childhood Education	M,D,O
Education—General	M,D,O
Educational Leadership and Administration	M,D,O
Elementary Education	M,D,O
Family Nurse Practitioner Studies	M
Foreign Languages Education	M
Management Information Systems	M
Nursing Education	M
Nursing—General	M
Reading Education	M,D,O
Social Sciences Education	M
Special Education	M,D,O

ROBERT MORRIS UNIVERSITY

Business Administration and Management—General	M
Business Education	M,D,O
Education—General	M,D,O
Educational Leadership and Administration	M,D,O
Human Resources Management	M
Management Information Systems	M,D
Nonprofit Management	M
Nursing—General	M,D
Organizational Management	M,D
Project Management	M,D
Taxation	M

ROBERT MORRIS UNIVERSITY ILLINOIS

Accounting	M
Business Administration and Management—General	M
Finance and Banking	M
Human Resources Management	M
Management Information Systems	M

ROBERTS WESLEYAN COLLEGE

Business Administration and Management—General	M,O
Counselor Education	M
Early Childhood Education	M,O
Education—General	M,O
Health Services Management and Hospital Administration	M
Human Services	M
Management Strategy and Policy	M,O
Marketing	M,O
Middle School Education	M,O
Nonprofit Management	M,O
Nursing and Healthcare Administration	M
Nursing Education	M
Nursing—General	M,O
Reading Education	M,O
Secondary Education	M,O

Social Work	M
Special Education	M,O
Urban Education	M,O

ROCHESTER COLLEGE

Religious Education	M

ROCHESTER INSTITUTE OF TECHNOLOGY

Accounting	M
Art Education	M
Business Administration and Management—General	M
Clinical Laboratory Sciences/Medical Technology	M
Finance and Banking	M
Health Services Management and Hospital Administration	M,O
Hospitality Management	M
Human Resources Development	M
Industrial and Manufacturing Management	M
International Business	M
Management Information Systems	M
Secondary Education	M
Special Education	M
Sustainability Management	D
Travel and Tourism	M

ROCKFORD COLLEGE

Business Administration and Management—General	M
Education—General	M
Elementary Education	M
Reading Education	M
Secondary Education	M
Special Education	M

ROCKHURST UNIVERSITY

Business Administration and Management—General	M
Communication Disorders	M
Education—General	M
Occupational Therapy	M
Physical Therapy	D

ROCKY MOUNTAIN COLLEGE

Accounting	M
Educational Leadership and Administration	M
Physician Assistant Studies	M

ROGER WILLIAMS UNIVERSITY

Education—General	M
Elementary Education	M
Law	P
Reading Education	M

ROLLINS COLLEGE

Business Administration and Management—General	M
Counselor Education	M
Education—General	M
Elementary Education	M
English Education	M
Entrepreneurship	M
Finance and Banking	M
Human Resources Development	M
Human Resources Management	M
International Business	M
Marketing	M
Mathematics Education	M
Music Education	M
Secondary Education	M

ROOSEVELT UNIVERSITY

Accounting	M
Actuarial Science	M

Business Administration and Management—	
General	M
Counselor Education	M
Early Childhood Education	M
Education—General	M,D
Educational Leadership and Administration	M
Elementary Education	M
Hospitality Management	M
Human Resources Development	M
Human Resources Management	M
International Business	M
Management Information Systems	M
Music Education	M,O
Organizational Management	M,D
Reading Education	M
Real Estate	M,O
Secondary Education	M
Special Education	M

ROSALIND FRANKLIN UNIVERSITY OF MEDICINE AND SCIENCE

Allied Health—General	M,D,O
Allopathic Medicine	P
Health Education	M
Health Services Management and Hospital Administration	M,O
Medical Physics	M
Nurse Anesthesia	M
Physical Therapy	M,D
Physician Assistant Studies	M
Podiatric Medicine	P
Women's Health Nursing	M,O

ROSEMONT COLLEGE

Business Administration and Management—	
General	M
Counselor Education	M
Curriculum and Instruction	M
Elementary Education	M
Human Services	M

ROWAN UNIVERSITY

Accounting	M
Advertising and Public Relations	M
Business Administration and Management—	
General	M
Counselor Education	M
Curriculum and Instruction	M
Education—General	M,D,O
Educational Leadership and Administration	M,D,O
Elementary Education	M
English as a Second Language	O
Entrepreneurship	M
Finance and Banking	M
Foreign Languages Education	M
Health Promotion	M
Higher Education	M
Library Science	M
Management Information Systems	M
Marketing	M
Multilingual and Multicultural Education	O
Project Management	M
Reading Education	M
Secondary Education	M
Special Education	M

ROYAL MILITARY COLLEGE OF CANADA

Business Administration and Management—	
General	M

ROYAL ROADS UNIVERSITY

Advertising and Public Relations	O
Business Administration and Management—	
General	M,O
Environmental Education	M,O

Health Services Management and Hospital Administration	O
Hospitality Management	M,O
Human Resources Management	M,O
Project Management	O
Travel and Tourism	M,O

RUSH UNIVERSITY

Acute Care/Critical Care Nursing	M,D,O
Adult Nursing	M,D,O
Allopathic Medicine	P
Bioethics	M,O
Clinical Laboratory Sciences/Medical Technology	M
Communication Disorders	M,D
Community Health Nursing	M,D,O
Family Nurse Practitioner Studies	M,D,O
Gerontological Nursing	M,D,O
Health Services Management and Hospital Administration	M,D
Maternal and Child/ Neonatal Nursing	M,D,O
Medical Physics	M,D
Medical/Surgical Nursing	M,D,O
Nurse Anesthesia	M,D,O
Nursing—General	M,D,O
Occupational Therapy	M
Pediatric Nursing	M,D,O
Pharmaceutical Sciences	M,D
Psychiatric Nursing	M,D,O

RUTGERS, THE STATE UNIVERSITY OF NEW JERSEY, CAMDEN

Business Administration and Management—	
General	M
Educational Leadership and Administration	M
Educational Policy	M
Law	P
Physical Therapy	D

RUTGERS, THE STATE UNIVERSITY OF NEW JERSEY, NEWARK

Accounting	M,D,O
Adult Nursing	M
Business Administration and Management—	
General	M,D,O
Community Health Nursing	M
Family Nurse Practitioner Studies	M
Finance and Banking	M,D,O
Gerontological Nursing	M
Health Services Management and Hospital Administration	M,D
Human Resources Management	M,D
International Business	M,D
Law	P
Management Information Systems	M,D
Management Strategy and Policy	M
Marketing	M,D
Maternal and Child/ Neonatal Nursing	M
Nursing—General	M
Organizational Management	D
Psychiatric Nursing	M
Supply Chain Management	D
Taxation	M

RUTGERS, THE STATE UNIVERSITY OF NEW JERSEY, NEW BRUNSWICK

Developmental Education	M
Early Childhood Education	M,D
Education—General	M,D
Educational Leadership and Administration	M,D

Educational Measurement and Evaluation	M
Educational Policy	D
Educational Psychology	M,D
Elementary Education	M,D
English as a Second Language	M,D
English Education	M
Foreign Languages Education	M,D
Foundations and Philosophy of Education	M,D
Human Resources Management	M,D*
Information Studies	M,D
Legal and Justice Studies	D
Library Science	M,D
Mathematics Education	M,D
Medicinal and Pharmaceutical Chemistry	M,D
Multilingual and Multicultural Education	M,D
Music Education	M,D,O
Pharmaceutical Sciences	M,D
Pharmacy	P,M,D
Public Health—General	M,D
Quality Management	M,D
Reading Education	M,D
Science Education	M,D
Social Sciences Education	M,D
Social Work	M,D
Special Education	M,D

SACRED HEART UNIVERSITY

Accounting	M
Business Administration and Management—	
General	M
Education—General	M,O
Educational Leadership and Administration	M,O
Educational Media/ Instructional Technology	M,O
Elementary Education	M,O
Exercise and Sports Science	M,D
Family Nurse Practitioner Studies	M,D
Finance and Banking	M
Health Services Management and Hospital Administration	M,D
Management Information Systems	M,O
Marketing	M
Nursing and Healthcare Administration	M,D
Nursing—General	M,D
Occupational Therapy	M
Physical Therapy	M,D
Reading Education	M,O
Secondary Education	M,O

SAGE GRADUATE SCHOOL

Adult Nursing	M,O
Art Education	M
Business Administration and Management—	
General	M
Community Health Nursing	M
Community Health	M
Counselor Education	M,O
Education—General	M,D,O
Educational Leadership and Administration	D
Elementary Education	M
English Education	M
Family Nurse Practitioner Studies	M,O
Finance and Banking	M
Gerontological Nursing	M,D,O
Health Education	M
Health Services Management and Hospital Administration	M,D,O
Human Resources Management	M
Management Strategy and Policy	M
Marketing	M
Mathematics Education	M
Nursing and Healthcare Administration	M,D,O
Nursing Education	D

Nursing—General	M,D,O
Occupational Therapy	M
Organizational Management	M,O
Physical Therapy	D
Psychiatric Nursing	M,O
Reading Education	M
Social Sciences Education	M
Special Education	M

SAGINAW VALLEY STATE UNIVERSITY

Business Administration and Management—	
General	M
Distance Education Development	M
Early Childhood Education	M
Education—General	M,O
Educational Leadership and Administration	M,O
Educational Media/ Instructional Technology	M
Elementary Education	M
Family Nurse Practitioner Studies	M
Health Services Management and Hospital Administration	M
Middle School Education	M
Nursing and Healthcare Administration	M
Nursing—General	M
Occupational Therapy	M
Physical Education	M
Reading Education	M
Science Education	M
Secondary Education	M
Special Education	M

ST. AMBROSE UNIVERSITY

Accounting	M
Business Administration and Management—	
General	M,D
Education—General	M
Educational Leadership and Administration	M
Health Services Management and Hospital Administration	M,D
Human Resources Management	M,D
Nursing—General	M
Occupational Therapy	M
Organizational Management	M
Physical Therapy	D
Social Work	M
Special Education	M

SAINT ANTHONY COLLEGE OF NURSING

Nursing—General	M

ST. AUGUSTINE'S SEMINARY OF TORONTO

Religious Education	P,M,O

ST. BONAVENTURE UNIVERSITY

Business Administration and Management—	
General	M
Counselor Education	M,O
Early Childhood Education	M
Education—General	M,O
Educational Leadership and Administration	M,O
Middle School Education	M
Reading Education	M
Secondary Education	M
Special Education	M

ST. CATHERINE UNIVERSITY

Education—General	M
Information Studies	M
Library Science	M
Nursing—General	M,D
Occupational Therapy	M
Organizational Management	M
Physical Therapy	D
Public Health—General	M
Social Work	M

ST. CLOUD STATE UNIVERSITY

Business Administration and Management—	
General	M
Communication Disorders	M
Counselor Education	M
Curriculum and Instruction	M
Education—General	M,D,O
Educational Leadership and Administration	M,D
Educational Media/ Instructional Technology	M
English as a Second Language	M
Exercise and Sports Science	M
Higher Education	M,D
Music Education	M
Nonprofit Management	M
Physical Education	M
Social Work	M
Special Education	M
Sports Management	M
Student Affairs	M

ST. EDWARD'S UNIVERSITY

Accounting	M,O
Business Administration and Management—	
General	M,O
Education—General	M,O
Educational Leadership and Administration	M,O
Educational Media/ Instructional Technology	M,O
Finance and Banking	M,O
Human Resources Management	M,O
Human Services	M,O
International Business	M,O
Management Information Systems	M,O
Marketing	M,O
Organizational Management	M
Project Management	M
Sports Management	M,O
Student Affairs	M

SAINT FRANCIS MEDICAL CENTER COLLEGE OF NURSING

Maternal and Child/ Neonatal Nursing	M,D,O
Medical/Surgical Nursing	M,D,O
Nursing Education	M,D,O
Nursing—General	M,D,O

SAINT FRANCIS UNIVERSITY

Business Administration and Management—	
General	M
Education—General	M
Educational Leadership and Administration	M
Health Education	M
Human Resources Management	M
Occupational Therapy	M
Physical Therapy	D
Physician Assistant Studies	M
Reading Education	M

ST. FRANCIS XAVIER UNIVERSITY

Adult Education	M
Curriculum and Instruction	M
Education—General	M
Educational Leadership and Administration	M

ST. JOHN FISHER COLLEGE

Business Administration and Management—	
General	M
Education—General	M,D,O
Educational Leadership and Administration	M,D
Elementary Education	M
English Education	M
Family Nurse Practitioner Studies	M,O
Foreign Languages Education	M

Human Resources Development	M
Mathematics Education	M
Middle School Education	M
Nursing Education	M,O
Nursing—General	M,D,O
Pharmacy	P
Reading Education	M
Science Education	M
Social Sciences Education	M
Special Education	M,O

ST. JOHN'S UNIVERSITY (NY)

Accounting	M,O
Actuarial Science	M
Business Administration and Management—	
General	M,O
Communication Disorders	M,D,O
Counselor Education	M,O
Early Childhood Education	M
Education—General	M,D,O
Educational Leadership and Administration	M,D,O
Elementary Education	M
English as a Second Language	M
Finance and Banking	M,O
Information Studies	M,O
Insurance	M
International Business	M,O
Law	P
Legal and Justice Studies	M
Library Science	M,O
Management Information Systems	M,O
Marketing	M,O
Multilingual and Multicultural Education	M,O
Pharmaceutical Administration	M
Pharmaceutical Sciences	M,D
Pharmacy	P
Quantitative Analysis	M,O
Reading Education	M
Secondary Education	M
Special Education	M
Sports Management	M
Taxation	M,O

SAINT JOSEPH COLLEGE

Business Administration and Management—	
General	M
Counselor Education	M
Education—General	M
Nursing—General	M
Special Education	M

ST. JOSEPH'S COLLEGE, LONG ISLAND CAMPUS

Accounting	M
Business Administration and Management—	
General	M,O
Early Childhood Education	M
Health Services Management and Hospital Administration	M,O
Human Resources Management	M,O
Nursing—General	M
Organizational Management	M,O
Reading Education	M
Special Education	M

ST. JOSEPH'S COLLEGE, NEW YORK

Accounting	M
Business Administration and Management—	
General	M*
Early Childhood Education	M
Education—General	M*
Health Services Management and Hospital Administration	M
Human Services	M
Nursing—General	M*
Reading Education	M
Special Education	M

SAINT JOSEPH'S COLLEGE OF MAINE

Business Administration and Management—	
General	M
Education—General	M
Health Services Management and Hospital Administration	M
Nursing and Healthcare Administration	M,O
Nursing Education	M,O
Nursing—General	M,O
Quality Management	M

SAINT JOSEPH'S UNIVERSITY

Accounting	M
Adult Education	M,O
Business Administration and Management—	
General	M,O
Education—General	M,D
Educational Leadership and Administration	M,D
Educational Media/ Instructional Technology	M,D
Elementary Education	M,D
Environmental and Occupational Health	M,O
Finance and Banking	M
Health Education	M,O
Health Services Management and Hospital Administration	M,O
Human Resources Management	M
Human Services	M,O
International Business	M
Law	M,O
Management Strategy and Policy	M
Marketing	M,O
Nurse Anesthesia	M,O
Organizational Management	M,D,O
Reading Education	M,D
School Nursing	M,O
Secondary Education	M,D
Special Education	M,D

ST. LAWRENCE UNIVERSITY

Counselor Education	M,O
Education—General	M,O
Educational Leadership and Administration	M,O

SAINT LEO UNIVERSITY

Accounting	M
Business Administration and Management—	
General	M
Curriculum and Instruction	M,O
Education of the Gifted	M,O
Education—General	M,O
Educational Leadership and Administration	M,O
Educational Media/ Instructional Technology	M,O
Health Services Management and Hospital Administration	M
Higher Education	M,O
Human Resources Management	M
Marketing	M
Reading Education	M,O
Social Work	M
Sports Management	M

ST. LOUIS COLLEGE OF PHARMACY

Pharmacy	P

SAINT LOUIS UNIVERSITY

Accounting	M
Allied Health—General	M,D,O
Allopathic Medicine	P
Athletic Training and Sports Medicine	M,D
Bioethics	D,O
Business Administration and Management—	
General	M

Communication Disorders	M
Community Health	M
Counselor Education	M,D,O
Curriculum and Instruction	M,D
Dentistry	M
Education—General	M,D
Educational Leadership and Administration	M,D,O
Finance and Banking	M
Foundations and Philosophy of Education	M,D
Health Services Management and Hospital Administration	M,D
Higher Education	M,D,O
International Business	M,D
Law	P,M
Nursing—General	M,D,O
Occupational Therapy	M
Oral and Dental Sciences	M
Organizational Management	M,D,O
Physical Therapy	M,D
Physician Assistant Studies	M
Public Health—General	M,D
Social Work	M
Special Education	M,D
Student Affairs	M,D,O

SAINT MARTIN'S UNIVERSITY

Business Administration and Management—	
General	M
Counselor Education	M
Education—General	M
Educational Leadership and Administration	M
English as a Second Language	M
Reading Education	M
Special Education	M
Vocational and Technical Education	M

SAINT MARY-OF-THE-WOODS COLLEGE

Management Strategy and Policy	M

SAINT MARY'S COLLEGE OF CALIFORNIA

Business Administration and Management—	
General	M
Counselor Education	M
Curriculum and Instruction	M
Early Childhood Education	M
Education—General	M
Educational Leadership and Administration	M
Exercise and Sports Science	M
Kinesiology and Movement Studies	M
Reading Education	M
Special Education	M
Sports Management	M

ST. MARY'S COLLEGE OF MARYLAND

Education—General	M

SAINT MARY'S UNIVERSITY (CANADA)

Business Administration and Management—	
General	M,D

ST. MARY'S UNIVERSITY (UNITED STATES)

Accounting	
Business Administration and Management—	
General	M
Counselor Education	D
Education—General	M,O
Educational Leadership and Administration	M,O
Finance and Banking	M
Human Services	M,D,O
International Business	M

Law	P
Reading Education	M

SAINT MARY'S UNIVERSITY OF MINNESOTA

Business Administration and Management— General	M
Education of the Gifted	M,O
Education—General	M,O
Educational Leadership and Administration	M,D,O
Elementary Education	M,O
Environmental and Occupational Health	M
Health Services Management and Hospital Administration	M
Human Resources Management	M
International Business	M
Nurse Anesthesia	M
Organizational Management	M
Project Management	M,O
Reading Education	M,O
Religious Education	M
Secondary Education	M,O
Special Education	M,O

SAINT MICHAEL'S COLLEGE

Art Education	M,O
Business Administration and Management— General	M,O
Curriculum and Instruction	M,O
Education—General	M,O
Educational Leadership and Administration	M,O
Educational Media/ Instructional Technology	M,O
English as a Second Language	M,O
Reading Education	M,O
Special Education	M,O

ST. NORBERT COLLEGE

Education—General	M

ST. PETERSBURG THEOLOGICAL SEMINARY

Religious Education	P,M,D

SAINT PETER'S COLLEGE

Accounting	M
Adult Nursing	M,D
Business Administration and Management— General	M
Curriculum and Instruction	M,O
Education—General	M,D,O
Educational Leadership and Administration	M,D,O
Elementary Education	M,O
Finance and Banking	M
Health Services Management and Hospital Administration	M
International Business	M
Management Information Systems	M
Marketing	M
Nursing and Healthcare Administration	M,D
Nursing—General	M,D
Reading Education	M
Special Education	M

SAINTS CYRIL AND METHODIUS SEMINARY

Religious Education	P,M

ST. THOMAS AQUINAS COLLEGE

Business Administration and Management— General	M
Education—General	M,O
Educational Leadership and Administration	M,O
Elementary Education	M,O
Finance and Banking	M
Marketing	M
Middle School Education	M,O
Reading Education	M,O

Secondary Education	M,O
Special Education	M,O

ST. THOMAS UNIVERSITY

Accounting	M,O
Business Administration and Management— General	M,O
Counselor Education	M,O
Education of the Gifted	M,D,O
Education—General	M,D,O
Educational Leadership and Administration	M,D,O
Educational Media/ Instructional Technology	M,D,O
Elementary Education	M,D,O
English as a Second Language	M,D,O
Health Services Management and Hospital Administration	M,O
Human Resources Management	M,O
International Business	M,O
Law	P,M
Reading Education	M,D,O
Special Education	M,D,O
Sports Management	M,O
Taxation	P,M

SAINT VINCENT COLLEGE

Curriculum and Instruction	M
Education—General	M
Educational Leadership and Administration	M
Educational Media/ Instructional Technology	M
Environmental Education	M
Nurse Anesthesia	M
Nursing and Healthcare Administration	M
Special Education	M

ST. VLADIMIR'S ORTHODOX THEOLOGICAL SEMINARY

Religious Education	P,M,D

SAINT XAVIER UNIVERSITY

Adult Nursing	M,O
Business Administration and Management— General	M,O
Communication Disorders	M
Community Health Nursing	M,O
Counselor Education	M
Curriculum and Instruction	M,O
Early Childhood Education	M,O
Education—General	M,O
Educational Leadership and Administration	M,O
Electronic Commerce	M,O
Elementary Education	M,O
Family Nurse Practitioner Studies	M,O
Finance and Banking	M,O
Health Services Management and Hospital Administration	M,O
Marketing	M,O
Nonprofit Management	M,O
Nursing and Healthcare Administration	M,O
Nursing—General	M,O
Psychiatric Nursing	M,O
Public Health—General	M,O
Reading Education	M,O
Secondary Education	M,O
Special Education	M,O
Travel and Tourism	M,O

SALEM COLLEGE

Early Childhood Education	M
Education—General	M
Elementary Education	M
English as a Second Language	M
Middle School Education	M
Reading Education	M
Secondary Education	M
Special Education	M

SALEM INTERNATIONAL UNIVERSITY

Business Administration and Management— General	M

Curriculum and Instruction	M
Education—General	M
Educational Leadership and Administration	M
International Business	M

SALEM STATE COLLEGE

Art Education	M
Business Administration and Management— General	M
Counselor Education	M
Early Childhood Education	M
Educational Leadership and Administration	M
Educational Media/ Instructional Technology	M
Elementary Education	M
English as a Second Language	M
English Education	M
Higher Education	M
Mathematics Education	M
Middle School Education	M
Nursing—General	M
Occupational Therapy	M
Physical Education	M
Reading Education	M
Science Education	M
Secondary Education	M
Social Work	M
Special Education	M

SALISBURY UNIVERSITY

Accounting	M
Business Administration and Management— General	M
Education—General	M
Educational Leadership and Administration	M
English as a Second Language	M
Mathematics Education	M
Nursing—General	M
Reading Education	M
Social Work	M

SALUS UNIVERSITY

Communication Disorders	D
Optometry	P
Physician Assistant Studies	M
Rehabilitation Sciences	M,O
Special Education	M,O
Vision Sciences	M,O

SALVE REGINA UNIVERSITY

Business Administration and Management— General	M,O
Health Services Management and Hospital Administration	M,O
Human Resources Development	M,O
Human Resources Management	M,O
Legal and Justice Studies	M

SAMFORD UNIVERSITY

Business Administration and Management— General	M
Early Childhood Education	M,D,O
Education of the Gifted	M,D,O
Education—General	M,D,O
Educational Leadership and Administration	M,D,O
Elementary Education	M,D,O
Family Nurse Practitioner Studies	M,D
Law	P,M
Music Education	M
Nurse Anesthesia	M,D
Nursing and Healthcare Administration	M,D
Nursing Education	M,D
Nursing—General	M,D
Pharmacy	P
Secondary Education	M,D,O

SAM HOUSTON STATE UNIVERSITY

Accounting	M

Business Administration and Management— General	M
Counselor Education	M,D
Curriculum and Instruction	M
Education—General	M,D
Educational Leadership and Administration	M,D
Educational Media/ Instructional Technology	M
Finance and Banking	M
Kinesiology and Movement Studies	M
Library Science	M
Music Education	M
Reading Education	M,D
Special Education	M,D

SAMRA UNIVERSITY OF ORIENTAL MEDICINE

Acupuncture and Oriental Medicine	M,D

SAMUEL MERRITT UNIVERSITY

Family Nurse Practitioner Studies	M,O
Nurse Anesthesia	M,O
Nursing and Healthcare Administration	M,O
Nursing—General	M,O
Occupational Therapy	M
Physical Therapy	D
Physician Assistant Studies	M

SAN DIEGO STATE UNIVERSITY

Accounting	M
Advertising and Public Relations	M
Business Administration and Management— General	M
Communication Disorders	M,D
Counselor Education	M
Curriculum and Instruction	M
Education—General	M,D
Educational Leadership and Administration	M
Educational Media/ Instructional Technology	M,D
Elementary Education	M
Emergency Medical Services	M,D
English as a Second Language	M,O
Entrepreneurship	M
Environmental and Occupational Health	M,D
Epidemiology	M,D
Exercise and Sports Science	M
Finance and Banking	M
Health Physics/ Radiological Health	M
Health Promotion	M,D
Health Services Management and Hospital Administration	M,D
Higher Education	M
Human Resources Management	M
Industrial and Manufacturing Management	M
International Business	M
International Health	M,D
Kinesiology and Movement Studies	M
Management Information Systems	M
Marketing	M
Mathematics Education	M,D
Multilingual and Multicultural Education	M,D
Music Education	M
Nursing—General	M
Pharmaceutical Administration	M
Physical Education	M
Public Health—General	M,D
Reading Education	M
Science Education	M,D
Secondary Education	M
Social Work	M

Special Education	M
Sports Management	M

SAN FRANCISCO STATE UNIVERSITY

Adult Education	M,O
Business Administration and Management— General	M
Clinical Laboratory Sciences/Medical Technology	M
Communication Disorders	M
Early Childhood Education	M
Education—General	M,D,O
Educational Leadership and Administration	M,O
Educational Media/ Instructional Technology	M,O
Elementary Education	M
English as a Second Language	M
English Education	M,O
Family Nurse Practitioner Studies	M
Health Education	M
Kinesiology and Movement Studies	M
Legal and Justice Studies	M,O
Leisure Studies	M
Mathematics Education	M
Music Education	M
Nonprofit Management	M
Nursing and Healthcare Administration	M
Nursing Education	M
Nursing—General	M
Physical Therapy	M,D
Public Health—General	M
Reading Education	M,O
Recreation and Park Management	M
Secondary Education	M
Social Work	M
Special Education	M,D,O

SAN JOAQUIN COLLEGE OF LAW

Law	P

SAN JOSE STATE UNIVERSITY

Accounting	M
Business Administration and Management— General	M
Communication Disorders	M
Counselor Education	M
Curriculum and Instruction	M,O
Education—General	M,O
Educational Leadership and Administration	M
Elementary Education	M,O
English as a Second Language	M,O
Gerontological Nursing	M,O
Health Education	M,O
Higher Education	M
Industrial and Manufacturing Management	M
Information Studies	M,D
Kinesiology and Movement Studies	M
Library Science	M,D
Management Information Systems	M
Mathematics Education	M
Nursing and Healthcare Administration	M,O
Nursing Education	M,O
Nursing—General	M,O
Occupational Therapy	M
Public Health—General	M,O
Quality Management	M
Reading Education	M,O
Recreation and Park Management	M
Science Education	M
Secondary Education	O
Social Work	M,O
Special Education	M
Student Affairs	M
Taxation	M
Transportation Management	M

SAN JUAN BAUTISTA SCHOOL OF MEDICINE

Allopathic Medicine	P

SANTA CLARA UNIVERSITY

Accounting	M
Business Administration and Management— General	M
Counselor Education	M
Curriculum and Instruction	M
Early Childhood Education	M,O
Education—General	M,O
Educational Leadership and Administration	M
Entrepreneurship	M
Finance and Banking	M
Higher Education	M
International Business	M
Law	P,M,O
Management Information Systems	M
Marketing	M
Organizational Management	M
Reading Education	M
Special Education	M,O
Supply Chain Management	M

SARAH LAWRENCE COLLEGE

Education—General	M
Public Health—General	M

SAVANNAH COLLEGE OF ART AND DESIGN

Advertising and Public Relations	M
Education—General	M

SAVANNAH STATE UNIVERSITY

Business Administration and Management— General	M
Social Work	M

SAYBROOK UNIVERSITY

Organizational Behavior	M,D
Organizational Management	M,D

SCHILLER INTERNATIONAL UNIVERSITY (GERMANY)

Business Administration and Management— General	M
International Business	M
Management Information Systems	M

SCHILLER INTERNATIONAL UNIVERSITY

Business Administration and Management— General	M
International Business	M

SCHILLER INTERNATIONAL UNIVERSITY (SPAIN)

Business Administration and Management— General	M
International Business	M

SCHILLER INTERNATIONAL UNIVERSITY

Business Administration and Management— General	M
International Business	M

SCHILLER INTERNATIONAL UNIVERSITY (UNITED KINGDOM)

Hospitality Management	M
International Business	M
Management Information Systems	M
Travel and Tourism	M

SCHILLER INTERNATIONAL UNIVERSITY (UNITED STATES)

Business Administration and Management— General	M
Finance and Banking	M
Hospitality Management	M
International Business	M
Management Information Systems	M
Travel and Tourism	M

SCHOOL OF THE ART INSTITUTE OF CHICAGO

Art Education	M

SCHOOL OF VISUAL ARTS (NY)

Art Education	M

SCHREINER UNIVERSITY

Education—General	M

SEATTLE INSTITUTE OF ORIENTAL MEDICINE

Acupuncture and Oriental Medicine	M

SEATTLE PACIFIC UNIVERSITY

Adult Nursing	M,O
Business Administration and Management— General	M
Counselor Education	M,D,O
Curriculum and Instruction	M
Educational Leadership and Administration	M,D,O
English as a Second Language	M
Family Nurse Practitioner Studies	M,O
Gerontological Nursing	M,O
Management Information Systems	M
Nursing and Healthcare Administration	M,O
Nursing Education	M,O
Nursing Informatics	M,O
Nursing—General	M,O
Reading Education	M
Secondary Education	M,O

SEATTLE UNIVERSITY

Accounting	M
Adult Education	M,O
Business Administration and Management— General	M,O
Community Health Nursing	M
Counselor Education	M,O
Curriculum and Instruction	M,O
Education—General	M,D,O
Educational Leadership and Administration	M,D,O
English as a Second Language	M,O
Finance and Banking	M,O
Law	P,O
Nonprofit Management	M
Nursing and Healthcare Administration	M
Nursing—General	M
Organizational Management	M,O
Psychiatric Nursing	M
Reading Education	M,O
Special Education	M,O
Sports Management	M

SETON HALL UNIVERSITY

Accounting	M,O
Adult Nursing	M,D
Advertising and Public Relations	M
Allied Health—General	M,D
Athletic Training and Sports Medicine	M
Business Administration and Management— General	M,O
Communication Disorders	M
Education—General	M,D,O
Educational Leadership and Administration	D,O
Educational Measurement and Evaluation	M,D,O
Educational Media/ Instructional Technology	M
Finance and Banking	M
Gerontological Nursing	M,D
Health Law	P,M
Health Services Management and Hospital Administration	M,D,O
Higher Education	D
International Business	M,O
Law	P,M
Marketing	M
Multilingual and Multicultural Education	O
Museum Education	M
Nonprofit Management	M,O
Nursing and Healthcare Administration	M,D
Nursing Education	M,D
Nursing—General	M,D
Occupational Therapy	M
Pediatric Nursing	M,D
Physical Therapy	D
Physician Assistant Studies	M
School Nursing	M,D
Sports Management	M
Student Affairs	M
Taxation	M,O

SETON HILL UNIVERSITY

Business Administration and Management— General	M
Education—General	M
Elementary Education	M,O
Entrepreneurship	M
Physician Assistant Studies	M
Special Education	M,O

SHASTA BIBLE COLLEGE

Educational Leadership and Administration	M
Religious Education	M

SHAWNEE STATE UNIVERSITY

Curriculum and Instruction	M
Education—General	M
Occupational Therapy	M

SHAW UNIVERSITY

Curriculum and Instruction	M

SHENANDOAH UNIVERSITY

Allied Health—General	M,D,O
Athletic Training and Sports Medicine	M
Business Administration and Management— General	M
Education—General	M,D,O
Educational Leadership and Administration	M,D,O
Elementary Education	M,D,O
English as a Second Language	M,D,O
Family Nurse Practitioner Studies	M,D,O
Middle School Education	M,D,O
Music Education	M,D,O
Nurse Midwifery	M,D,O
Nursing Education	M,D,O
Nursing—General	M,D,O
Occupational Therapy	M
Pharmacy	P
Physical Therapy	D
Physician Assistant Studies	M
Psychiatric Nursing	M,D,O
Reading Education	M,D,O
Secondary Education	M,D,O
Special Education	M,D,O

SHEPHERD UNIVERSITY

Curriculum and Instruction	M

M—master's degree; P—first professional degree; D—doctorate; O—other advanced degree; *—Close-Up and/or Display

SHERMAN COLLEGE OF STRAIGHT CHIROPRACTIC

Chiropractic	P

SHIPPENSBURG UNIVERSITY OF PENNSYLVANIA

Business Administration and Management— General	M,O
Counselor Education	M,O
Curriculum and Instruction	M
Early Childhood Education	M
Education—General	M,O
Educational Leadership and Administration	M
Elementary Education	M
English Education	M
Foreign Languages Education	M
Higher Education	M
Mathematics Education	M
Middle School Education	M
Organizational Management	M
Reading Education	M
Science Education	M
Social Work	M,O
Special Education	M
Student Affairs	M,O

SHORTER UNIVERSITY

Business Administration and Management— General	M
Curriculum and Instruction	M

SIENA HEIGHTS UNIVERSITY

Early Childhood Education	M
Education—General	M
Educational Leadership and Administration	M
Elementary Education	M
Mathematics Education	M
Middle School Education	M
Reading Education	M
Secondary Education	M

SIERRA NEVADA COLLEGE

Education—General	M
Elementary Education	M
Secondary Education	M

SILICON VALLEY UNIVERSITY

Business Administration and Management— General	M

SILVER LAKE COLLEGE

Business Administration and Management— General	M
Education—General	M
Educational Leadership and Administration	M
Music Education	M
Organizational Behavior	M
Special Education	M

SIMMONS COLLEGE

Business Administration and Management— General	M,O
Counselor Education	M,D,O
Education—General	M,D,O
Educational Leadership and Administration	M,D,O
Educational Media/ Instructional Technology	M,D,O
Elementary Education	M,O
English as a Second Language	M,O
Health Education	M,D,O
Health Promotion	M,O
Health Services Management and Hospital Administration	M,O
Information Studies	M,D
Library Science	M,D
Middle School Education	M,O
Nursing—General	M,D,O
Physical Therapy	D
Secondary Education	M,O
Social Work	M,D,O
Special Education	M,D,O
Urban Education	M,O

SIMON FRASER UNIVERSITY

Actuarial Science	M,D
Art Education	M,D
Business Administration and Management— General	M,D
Community Health	M
Counselor Education	M
Curriculum and Instruction	M,D
Education—General	M,D
Educational Leadership and Administration	M,D
Educational Media/ Instructional Technology	M,D
Educational Psychology	M,D
English as a Second Language	M
Finance and Banking	M,D
Foundations and Philosophy of Education	M,D
International Business	M,D
Kinesiology and Movement Studies	M,D
Mathematics Education	M,D
Public Health—General	M

SIMPSON COLLEGE

Education—General	M
Secondary Education	M

SIMPSON UNIVERSITY

Education—General	M
Educational Leadership and Administration	M

SINTE GLESKA UNIVERSITY

Education—General	M
Elementary Education	M

SIT GRADUATE INSTITUTE

Business Administration and Management— General	M
Education—General	M
English as a Second Language	M
Entrepreneurship	M
Foreign Languages Education	M
International and Comparative Education	M
International Business	M
Organizational Management	M

SLIPPERY ROCK UNIVERSITY OF PENNSYLVANIA

Counselor Education	M
Education—General	M
Educational Leadership and Administration	M
Elementary Education	M
Environmental Education	M
Mathematics Education	M
Physical Education	M
Physical Therapy	D
Reading Education	M
Science Education	M
Secondary Education	M
Special Education	M
Sports Management	M
Student Affairs	M

SMITH COLLEGE

Education—General	M
Elementary Education	M
English Education	M
Exercise and Sports Science	M
Foreign Languages Education	M
Mathematics Education	M
Middle School Education	M
Science Education	M
Secondary Education	M
Social Sciences Education	M
Social Work	M,D
Special Education	M

SOJOURNER-DOUGLASS COLLEGE

Human Services	M
Reading Education	M
Urban Education	M

SOKA UNIVERSITY OF AMERICA

English as a Second Language	O
Foreign Languages Education	O

SONOMA STATE UNIVERSITY

Business Administration and Management— General	M
Counselor Education	M
Curriculum and Instruction	M
Education—General	M
Educational Leadership and Administration	M
Elementary Education	M
Family Nurse Practitioner Studies	M
Kinesiology and Movement Studies	M
Special Education	M

SOUTH BAYLO UNIVERSITY

Acupuncture and Oriental Medicine	M

SOUTH CAROLINA STATE UNIVERSITY

Allied Health—General	M
Business Education	M
Communication Disorders	M
Counselor Education	M
Early Childhood Education	M
Education—General	M
Educational Leadership and Administration	D,O
Elementary Education	M
English Education	M
Entrepreneurship	M
Home Economics Education	M
Human Services	M
Mathematics Education	M
Science Education	M
Secondary Education	M
Social Sciences Education	M
Special Education	M
Vocational and Technical Education	M

SOUTH DAKOTA STATE UNIVERSITY

Counselor Education	M
Curriculum and Instruction	M
Education—General	M,D
Educational Leadership and Administration	M
Health Education	M
Hospitality Management	M,D
Nursing—General	M,D
Pharmaceutical Sciences	M,D
Pharmacy	P
Physical Education	M
Recreation and Park Management	M
Veterinary Sciences	M,D

SOUTHEASTERN BAPTIST THEOLOGICAL SEMINARY

Religious Education	P,M,D

SOUTHEASTERN LOUISIANA UNIVERSITY

Business Administration and Management— General	M
Communication Disorders	M
Counselor Education	M
Curriculum and Instruction	M
Education—General	M,D
Educational Leadership and Administration	M,D
Educational Media/ Instructional Technology	M,D
Elementary Education	M
English Education	M
Health Education	M
Kinesiology and Movement Studies	M
Nursing—General	M
Reading Education	M
Special Education	M

SOUTHEASTERN OKLAHOMA STATE UNIVERSITY

Aviation Management	M
Business Administration and Management— General	M
Counselor Education	M
Education—General	M
Educational Leadership and Administration	M
Management Information Systems	M
Mathematics Education	M
Reading Education	M

SOUTHEASTERN UNIVERSITY (FL)

Business Administration and Management— General	M
Counselor Education	M
Education—General	M
Educational Leadership and Administration	M
Elementary Education	M
Human Services	M

SOUTHEAST MISSOURI STATE UNIVERSITY

Accounting	M
Business Administration and Management— General	M
Communication Disorders	M
Counselor Education	M,O
Educational Leadership and Administration	M,O
Elementary Education	M
English as a Second Language	M
Entrepreneurship	M
Exercise and Sports Science	M
Finance and Banking	M
Foundations and Philosophy of Education	M
Health Services Management and Hospital Administration	M
Higher Education	M,O
Industrial and Manufacturing Management	M
International Business	M
Leisure Studies	M
Middle School Education	M
Music Education	M
Nursing—General	M
Science Education	M
Secondary Education	M
Special Education	M
Sports Management	M

SOUTHERN ADVENTIST UNIVERSITY

Accounting	M
Acute Care/Critical Care Nursing	M
Adult Nursing	M
Business Administration and Management— General	M
Counselor Education	M
Education—General	M
Educational Leadership and Administration	M
Family Nurse Practitioner Studies	M
Finance and Banking	M
Health Services Management and Hospital Administration	M
Marketing	M
Nonprofit Management	M
Nursing and Healthcare Administration	M
Nursing—General	M
Reading Education	M
Recreation and Park Management	M
Religious Education	M

SOUTHERN ARKANSAS UNIVERSITY–MAGNOLIA

Business Administration and Management— General	M

Counselor Education	M
Curriculum and Instruction	M
Education—General	M
Educational Leadership and Administration	M
Elementary Education	M
English as a Second Language	M
Kinesiology and Movement Studies	M
Library Science	M
Middle School Education	M
Psychiatric Nursing	M
Reading Education	M
Secondary Education	M

SOUTHERN BAPTIST THEOLOGICAL SEMINARY

Religious Education	P,M,D

SOUTHERN CALIFORNIA COLLEGE OF OPTOMETRY

Optometry	P

SOUTHERN CALIFORNIA UNIVERSITY OF HEALTH SCIENCES

Acupuncture and Oriental Medicine	M
Chiropractic	P

SOUTHERN COLLEGE OF OPTOMETRY

Optometry	P

SOUTHERN CONNECTICUT STATE UNIVERSITY

Art Education	M
Business Administration and Management—General	M
Communication Disorders	M
Counselor Education	M,O
Education—General	M,D,O
Educational Leadership and Administration	M,D,O
Educational Measurement and Evaluation	M
Elementary Education	M,O
English as a Second Language	M
Environmental Education	M,O
Exercise and Sports Science	M
Foundations and Philosophy of Education	M,D,O
Health Education	M
Information Studies	M,O
Leisure Studies	M
Library Science	M,O
Multilingual and Multicultural Education	M
Nursing and Healthcare Administration	M
Nursing Education	M
Nursing—General	M
Physical Education	M
Public Health—General	M
Reading Education	M,O
Recreation and Park Management	M
Science Education	M,O
Social Work	M
Special Education	M,O

SOUTHERN EVANGELICAL SEMINARY

Religious Education	P,M,O

SOUTHERN ILLINOIS UNIVERSITY CARBONDALE

Accounting	M,D
Business Administration and Management—General	M,D
Communication Disorders	M
Community Health	M
Counselor Education	M,D
Curriculum and Instruction	M,D
Education—General	M,D
Educational Leadership and Administration	M,D

Educational Measurement and Evaluation	M,D
Educational Psychology	M,D
English as a Second Language	M
Health Education	M,D
Health Law	M
Health Services Management and Hospital Administration	M
Higher Education	M
Law	P,M
Legal and Justice Studies	M
Music Education	M
Physical Education	M
Physician Assistant Studies	M
Recreation and Park Management	M
Social Work	M
Special Education	M
Vocational and Technical Education	M,D

SOUTHERN ILLINOIS UNIVERSITY EDWARDSVILLE

Accounting	M
Art Education	M
Business Administration and Management—General	M
Communication Disorders	M
Curriculum and Instruction	M
Dentistry	P
Education—General	M,O
Educational Leadership and Administration	M,O
Educational Media/ Instructional Technology	M,O
English as a Second Language	M,O
English Education	M,O
Family Nurse Practitioner Studies	M,O
Finance and Banking	M
Foreign Languages Education	M
Foundations and Philosophy of Education	M
Health Education	M
Kinesiology and Movement Studies	M
Management Information Systems	M
Marketing Research	M
Mathematics Education	M
Music Education	M,O
Nurse Anesthesia	M,O
Nursing and Healthcare Administration	M,O
Nursing Education	M,O
Nursing—General	M,O
Pharmacy	P
Project Management	M
Reading Education	M,O
Science Education	M
Secondary Education	M
Social Sciences Education	M
Social Work	M
Special Education	M,O
Taxation	M

SOUTHERN METHODIST UNIVERSITY

Accounting	M
Advertising and Public Relations	M
Business Administration and Management—General	M
Counselor Education	M,O
Education of the Gifted	M,D,O
Education—General	M,D,O
Entrepreneurship	M
Facilities Management	M,D
Finance and Banking	M
Law	P,M,D
Management Information Systems	M
Management Strategy and Policy	M
Marketing	M
Multilingual and Multicultural Education	M,D,O

Music Education	M,O
Taxation	P,M,D

SOUTHERN NAZARENE UNIVERSITY

Business Administration and Management—General	M
Curriculum and Instruction	M
Education—General	M
Educational Leadership and Administration	M
Nursing and Healthcare Administration	M
Nursing Education	M
Nursing—General	M

SOUTHERN NEW HAMPSHIRE UNIVERSITY

Accounting	M,D,O
Business Administration and Management—General	M,D,O
Business Education	M,O
Community Health	M,O
Computer Education	M,O
Curriculum and Instruction	M,O
Education—General	M,O
Educational Leadership and Administration	M,O
Elementary Education	M,O
English as a Second Language	M,O
Finance and Banking	M,D,O
Hospitality Management	M,D,O
Human Resources Development	M,O
Human Resources Management	M,D,O
International Business	M,D,O
Management Information Systems	M,D,O
Marketing	M,D,O
Nonprofit Management	M,D,O
Organizational Management	M,D,O
Project Management	M,D,O
Secondary Education	M,O
Special Education	M,O
Sports Management	M,D,O
Taxation	M,D,O
Vocational and Technical Education	M,O

SOUTHERN OREGON UNIVERSITY

Business Administration and Management—General	M
Early Childhood Education	M
Education—General	M
Educational Leadership and Administration	M
Elementary Education	M
Environmental Education	M
Foreign Languages Education	M
Reading Education	M
Secondary Education	M
Special Education	M

SOUTHERN POLYTECHNIC STATE UNIVERSITY

Accounting	M,O
Business Administration and Management—General	M,O
Educational Media/ Instructional Technology	M,O
Quality Management	M,O

SOUTHERN UNIVERSITY AND AGRICULTURAL AND MECHANICAL COLLEGE

Business Administration and Management—General	M
Counselor Education	M
Education—General	M,D
Educational Leadership and Administration	M
Educational Media/ Instructional Technology	M
Elementary Education	M

Family Nurse Practitioner Studies	M,D,O
Gerontological Nursing	M,D,O
Law	P
Mathematics Education	D
Nursing and Healthcare Administration	M,D,O
Nursing Education	M,D,O
Nursing—General	M,D,O
Recreation and Park Management	M
Science Education	D
Secondary Education	M
Special Education	M,D

SOUTHERN UNIVERSITY AT NEW ORLEANS

Social Work	M

SOUTHERN UTAH UNIVERSITY

Accounting	M
Business Administration and Management—General	M
Education—General	M
Exercise and Sports Science	M

SOUTHERN WESLEYAN UNIVERSITY

Business Administration and Management—General	M
Education—General	M

SOUTH TEXAS COLLEGE OF LAW

Law	P

SOUTH UNIVERSITY (AL)

Business Administration and Management—General	M
Health Services Management and Hospital Administration	M

SOUTH UNIVERSITY (FL)

Business Administration and Management—General	M
Health Services Management and Hospital Administration	M

SOUTH UNIVERSITY (GA)

Anesthesiologist Assistant Studies	M*
Business Administration and Management—General	M
Entrepreneurship	M
Hospitality Management	M*
Pharmacy	P*
Physician Assistant Studies	M*
Sustainability Management	M

SOUTH UNIVERSITY (SC)

Business Administration and Management—General	M
Health Services Management and Hospital Administration	M
Pharmacy	P*

SOUTH UNIVERSITY

Business Administration and Management—General	M

SOUTH UNIVERSITY

Business Administration and Management—General	M

SOUTHWEST ACUPUNCTURE COLLEGE

Acupuncture and Oriental Medicine	M

---

*M—master's degree; P—first professional degree; D—doctorate; O—other advanced degree; *—Close-Up and/or Display*

SOUTHWEST BAPTIST UNIVERSITY

Business Administration and Management— General	M
Education—General	M,O
Educational Leadership and Administration	M,O
Health Services Management and Hospital Administration	M
Physical Therapy	D

SOUTHWEST COLLEGE OF NATUROPATHIC MEDICINE AND HEALTH SCIENCES

Naturopathic Medicine	D*

SOUTHWESTERN ADVENTIST UNIVERSITY

Accounting	M
Business Administration and Management— General	M
Curriculum and Instruction	M
Education—General	M
Educational Leadership and Administration	M
Finance and Banking	M
Reading Education	M

SOUTHWESTERN ASSEMBLIES OF GOD UNIVERSITY

Curriculum and Instruction	M
Education—General	M
Educational Leadership and Administration	M
Religious Education	M
Secondary Education	M

SOUTHWESTERN BAPTIST THEOLOGICAL SEMINARY

Religious Education	M,D,O

SOUTHWESTERN COLLEGE (KS)

Business Administration and Management— General	M
Curriculum and Instruction	M
Education—General	M
Organizational Management	M
Special Education	M

SOUTHWESTERN LAW SCHOOL

Law	P,M

SOUTHWESTERN OKLAHOMA STATE UNIVERSITY

Allied Health—General	M
Art Education	M
Business Administration and Management— General	M
Counselor Education	M
Early Childhood Education	M
Education—General	M
Educational Leadership and Administration	M
Educational Measurement and Evaluation	M
Elementary Education	M
English Education	M
Kinesiology and Movement Studies	M
Mathematics Education	M
Music Education	M
Pharmacy	P
Recreation and Park Management	M
Science Education	M
Secondary Education	M
Social Sciences Education	M
Special Education	M

SOUTHWEST MINNESOTA STATE UNIVERSITY

Business Administration and Management— General	M
Education—General	M
Special Education	M

SPALDING UNIVERSITY

Adult Nursing	M
Business Administration and Management— General	M
Counselor Education	M
Education—General	M,D
Educational Leadership and Administration	M,D
Elementary Education	M
Family Nurse Practitioner Studies	M
Middle School Education	M
Nursing and Healthcare Administration	M
Nursing—General	M
Occupational Therapy	M
Pediatric Nursing	M
Secondary Education	M
Social Work	M
Special Education	M

SPERTUS INSTITUTE OF JEWISH STUDIES

Nonprofit Management	M
Religious Education	M

SPRING ARBOR UNIVERSITY

Business Administration and Management— General	M
Education—General	M
Nursing—General	M
Organizational Management	M
Special Education	M

SPRINGFIELD COLLEGE

Athletic Training and Sports Medicine	M,D
Counselor Education	M,O
Early Childhood Education	M
Education—General	M
Educational Leadership and Administration	M
Elementary Education	M
Exercise and Sports Science	M,D
Health Education	M,D,O
Health Promotion	M,D
Health Services Management and Hospital Administration	M
Human Services	M
Occupational Therapy	M,O
Organizational Management	M
Physical Education	M,D,O
Physical Therapy	D
Physician Assistant Studies	M
Recreation and Park Management	M
Secondary Education	M
Social Work	M
Special Education	M
Sports Management	M,D,O
Student Affairs	M,O

SPRING HILL COLLEGE

Business Administration and Management— General	M
Early Childhood Education	M
Education—General	M
Elementary Education	M
Foundations and Philosophy of Education	M
Nursing—General	M
Secondary Education	M
Social Sciences Education	M

STANFORD UNIVERSITY

Allopathic Medicine	P
Art Education	M,D
Business Administration and Management— General	M,D
Computer Education	M,D
Curriculum and Instruction	M,D
Education—General	M,D
Educational Leadership and Administration	M,D
Educational Measurement and Evaluation	M,D
Educational Psychology	D
English Education	M,D
Epidemiology	M,D
Foreign Languages Education	M
Foundations and Philosophy of Education	M,D
Health Services Research	M
Higher Education	M,D
International and Comparative Education	M,D
Law	P,M,D
Mathematics Education	M,D
Science Education	M,D
Social Sciences Education	M,D

STATE UNIVERSITY OF NEW YORK AT BINGHAMTON

Accounting	M,D
Business Administration and Management— General	M,D
Early Childhood Education	M
Education—General	M,D
Educational Leadership and Administration	M
English Education	M
Finance and Banking	M,D
Foreign Languages Education	M
Foundations and Philosophy of Education	D
Health Services Management and Hospital Administration	M,D
Legal and Justice Studies	M,D
Mathematics Education	M
Nursing—General	M,D,O
Reading Education	M
Science Education	M
Secondary Education	M
Social Sciences Education	M
Social Work	M
Special Education	M
Student Affairs	M

STATE UNIVERSITY OF NEW YORK AT FREDONIA

Accounting	M
Business Administration and Management— General	M
Communication Disorders	M
Education—General	M,O
Educational Leadership and Administration	O
Elementary Education	M
English as a Second Language	M
Music Education	M
Reading Education	M
Science Education	M
Secondary Education	M

STATE UNIVERSITY OF NEW YORK AT NEW PALTZ

Accounting	M
Art Education	M
Business Administration and Management— General	M
Communication Disorders	M
Counselor Education	M
Early Childhood Education	M
Education—General	M,O
Educational Leadership and Administration	M,O
Elementary Education	M
English as a Second Language	M
English Education	M
Multilingual and Multicultural Education	M
Reading Education	M
Science Education	M
Secondary Education	M
Social Sciences Education	M
Special Education	M

STATE UNIVERSITY OF NEW YORK AT OSWEGO

Agricultural Education	M
Art Education	M

STATE UNIVERSITY OF NEW YORK AT PLATTSBURGH

Business Administration and Management— General	M
Business Education	M
Education—General	M,O
Educational Leadership and Administration	O
Elementary Education	M
Human Services	M
Reading Education	M
Secondary Education	M
Special Education	M
Vocational and Technical Education	M

STATE UNIVERSITY OF NEW YORK AT PLATTSBURGH

Communication Disorders	M
Counselor Education	M,O
Curriculum and Instruction	M
Educational Leadership and Administration	O
Elementary Education	M
English Education	M
Foreign Languages Education	M
Mathematics Education	M
Organizational Management	M
Reading Education	M
Science Education	M
Secondary Education	M
Social Sciences Education	M
Special Education	M

STATE UNIVERSITY OF NEW YORK COLLEGE AT CORTLAND

Early Childhood Education	M
Education—General	M,O
Educational Leadership and Administration	O
English as a Second Language	M
English Education	M
Exercise and Sports Science	M
Foreign Languages Education	M
Health Education	M
Mathematics Education	M
Physical Education	M
Reading Education	M
Recreation and Park Management	M
Science Education	M
Secondary Education	M
Social Sciences Education	M
Special Education	M
Sports Management	M

STATE UNIVERSITY OF NEW YORK COLLEGE AT GENESEO

Accounting	M
Business Administration and Management— General	M
Communication Disorders	M
Early Childhood Education	M
Education—General	M
Elementary Education	M
Multilingual and Multicultural Education	M
Reading Education	M
Secondary Education	M

STATE UNIVERSITY OF NEW YORK COLLEGE AT OLD WESTBURY

Accounting	M

STATE UNIVERSITY OF NEW YORK COLLEGE AT ONEONTA

Counselor Education	M,O
Education—General	M,O
Educational Media/ Instructional Technology	M,O
Educational Psychology	M,O
Elementary Education	M
Home Economics Education	M
Middle School Education	M
Reading Education	M
Secondary Education	M
Special Education	M,O

STATE UNIVERSITY OF NEW YORK COLLEGE AT POTSDAM

Computer Education	M
Curriculum and Instruction	M
Early Childhood Education	M
Educational Media/ Instructional Technology	M
Elementary Education	M
Management Information Systems	M
Mathematics Education	M
Middle School Education	M
Music Education	M
Organizational Management	M
Reading Education	M
Science Education	M
Secondary Education	M
Social Sciences Education	M
Special Education	M

STATE UNIVERSITY OF NEW YORK COLLEGE OF ENVIRONMENTAL SCIENCE AND FORESTRY

Recreation and Park Management	M,D

STATE UNIVERSITY OF NEW YORK COLLEGE OF OPTOMETRY

Optometry	P
Vision Sciences	M,D

STATE UNIVERSITY OF NEW YORK DOWNSTATE MEDICAL CENTER

Allopathic Medicine	P,M
Community Health	M
Family Nurse Practitioner Studies	M,O
Medical/Surgical Nursing	M,O
Nurse Anesthesia	M
Nurse Midwifery	M,O
Nursing—General	M,O
Public Health—General	M*

STATE UNIVERSITY OF NEW YORK EMPIRE STATE COLLEGE

Business Administration and Management— General	M
Education—General	M

STATE UNIVERSITY OF NEW YORK INSTITUTE OF TECHNOLOGY

Accounting	M
Adult Nursing	M,O
Business Administration and Management— General	M
Family Nurse Practitioner Studies	M,O
Gerontological Nursing	M,O
Health Services Management and Hospital Administration	M
Nursing and Healthcare Administration	M,O
Nursing Education	M,O
Nursing—General	M,O

STATE UNIVERSITY OF NEW YORK MARITIME COLLEGE

Transportation Management	M

STATE UNIVERSITY OF NEW YORK UPSTATE MEDICAL UNIVERSITY

Allopathic Medicine	P
Clinical Laboratory Sciences/Medical Technology	M
Family Nurse Practitioner Studies	M,O
Nursing—General	M,O
Physical Therapy	D

STEPHEN F. AUSTIN STATE UNIVERSITY

Accounting	M
Agricultural Education	M
Athletic Training and Sports Medicine	M

Business Administration and Management— General	M
Communication Disorders	M
Counselor Education	M
Early Childhood Education	M
Education—General	M,D
Educational Leadership and Administration	M,D
Elementary Education	M
Kinesiology and Movement Studies	M
Marketing	M
Mathematics Education	M
Secondary Education	M,D
Social Work	M
Special Education	M

STEPHENS COLLEGE

Business Administration and Management— General	M
Counselor Education	M
Curriculum and Instruction	M

STETSON UNIVERSITY

Accounting	M
Business Administration and Management— General	M
Counselor Education	M
Education—General	M
Educational Leadership and Administration	M
Law	P,M
Reading Education	M

STEVENS INSTITUTE OF TECHNOLOGY

Business Administration and Management— General	M
Electronic Commerce	M,O
Entrepreneurship	M,O
Finance and Banking	M
Human Resources Management	M
Industrial and Manufacturing Management	M
International Business	M
Logistics	M,D,O
Management Information Systems	M,D,O
Management Strategy and Policy	M
Pharmaceutical Sciences	M,O
Project Management	M,O
Quality Management	M,O

STONY BROOK UNIVERSITY, STATE UNIVERSITY OF NEW YORK

Adult Nursing	M,O
Allopathic Medicine	P
Business Administration and Management— General	M,O
Community Health	M,D
Computer Education	M
Dentistry	P,O
Educational Leadership and Administration	M,O
Educational Media/ Instructional Technology	M,O
English as a Second Language	M
English Education	M,D,O
Environmental and Occupational Health	M,O
Family Nurse Practitioner Studies	M,O
Finance and Banking	M,O
Foreign Languages Education	M,O
Health Services Management and Hospital Administration	M,D,O
Human Resources Management	M,O
Management Information Systems	M,D,O
Marketing	M,O
Maternal and Child/ Neonatal Nursing	M,O

Mathematics Education	M,O
Medical Physics	M,D
Nurse Midwifery	M,O
Nursing—General	M,D,O
Occupational Therapy	M,D,O
Oral and Dental Sciences	P,M,D,O
Pediatric Nursing	M,O
Physical Education	M,O
Physical Therapy	M,D,O
Physician Assistant Studies	M,D,O
Psychiatric Nursing	M,O
Public Health—General	M
Science Education	M,D,O
Social Sciences Education	M,O
Social Work	M,D
Women's Health Nursing	M,O

STRATFORD UNIVERSITY

Accounting	M
Business Administration and Management— General	M
Entrepreneurship	M
Management Information Systems	M

STRAYER UNIVERSITY

Accounting	M
Business Administration and Management— General	M
Education—General	M
Educational Media/ Instructional Technology	M
Finance and Banking	M
Health Services Management and Hospital Administration	M
Hospitality Management	M
Human Resources Management	M
Management Information Systems	M
Marketing	M
Supply Chain Management	M
Taxation	M
Travel and Tourism	M

SUFFOLK UNIVERSITY

Accounting	M,O
Adult Education	M,O
Advertising and Public Relations	M
Business Administration and Management— General	M,O
Counselor Education	M,O
Education—General	M,O
Educational Leadership and Administration	M,O
Entrepreneurship	M,O
Finance and Banking	M,O
Foundations and Philosophy of Education	M,O
Health Education	M
Health Law	P,M
Health Services Management and Hospital Administration	M,O
Human Resources Development	M,O
International Business	M,D,O
Law	P,M
Management Strategy and Policy	M,O
Marketing	M,O
Middle School Education	M,O
Nonprofit Management	M,O
Organizational Behavior	M,O
Organizational Management	M,O
Secondary Education	M,O
Taxation	M,O

SULLIVAN UNIVERSITY

Business Administration and Management— General	P,M
Management Information Systems	P,M

SUL ROSS STATE UNIVERSITY

Art Education	M
Business Administration and Management— General	M
Counselor Education	M
Education—General	M
Educational Leadership and Administration	M
Educational Measurement and Evaluation	M
Elementary Education	M
Multilingual and Multicultural Education	M
Physical Education	M
Reading Education	M
Secondary Education	M

SWEDISH INSTITUTE, COLLEGE OF HEALTH SCIENCES

Acupuncture and Oriental Medicine	M

SWEET BRIAR COLLEGE

Education—General	M

SYRACUSE UNIVERSITY

Accounting	M,D
Advertising and Public Relations	M
Art Education	M,O
Business Administration and Management— General	M,D
Communication Disorders	M,D
Counselor Education	M,D,O
Curriculum and Instruction	M,D,O
Early Childhood Education	M
Education of Students with Severe/Multiple Disabilities	M
Education—General	M,D,O
Educational Leadership and Administration	M,D,O
Educational Measurement and Evaluation	M,D,O
Educational Media/ Instructional Technology	M,O
English as a Second Language	M
English Education	M,D
Entrepreneurship	M
Exercise and Sports Science	M
Finance and Banking	M,D
Foundations and Philosophy of Education	M,D
Health Services Management and Hospital Administration	O
Higher Education	M,D
Human Resources Development	D
Human Services	O
Industrial and Manufacturing Management	D
Information Studies	M,D*
Law	P
Library Science	M,O
Management Information Systems	M,D,O
Management Strategy and Policy	D
Marketing	M,D
Mathematics Education	M,D
Music Education	M
Organizational Behavior	D
Quantitative Analysis	D
Reading Education	M,D
Science Education	M,D
Social Sciences Education	M
Social Work	M
Special Education	M,D
Student Affairs	M
Supply Chain Management	M,D
Sustainability Management	O

TABOR COLLEGE

Accounting	M

M—master's degree; P—first professional degree; D—doctorate; O—other advanced degree; *—Close-Up and/or Display

Business Administration
and Management—
General | M

TAI SOPHIA INSTITUTE

Acupuncture and Oriental
Medicine | M,O

TARLETON STATE UNIVERSITY

Accounting | M
Agricultural Education | M
Business Administration
and Management—
General | M
Counselor Education | M,O
Curriculum and Instruction | M
Education—General | M,D,O
Educational Leadership
and Administration | M,D,O
Finance and Banking | M
Human Resources
Management | M
Management Information
Systems | M
Music Education | M
Physical Education | M
Secondary Education | M,O
Special Education | M,O

TAYLOR COLLEGE AND SEMINARY

English as a Second
Language | P,M,O

TAYLOR UNIVERSITY

Business Administration
and Management—
General | M*
Higher Education | M
International Business | M
Management Strategy and
Policy | M

TEACHERS COLLEGE, COLUMBIA UNIVERSITY

Adult Education | M,D
Art Education | M,D
Communication Disorders | M,D
Computer Education | M
Counselor Education | M,D
Curriculum and Instruction | M,D
Dentistry | M
Early Childhood Education | M,D
Education of Students with
Severe/Multiple
Disabilities | M
Education of the Gifted | M,D
Education—General | M,D,O
Educational Leadership
and Administration | M,D
Educational Measurement
and Evaluation | M,D
Educational Media/
Instructional Technology | M,D
Educational Policy | M,D
Educational Psychology | M,D
Elementary Education | M
English as a Second
Language | M,D
English Education | M,D
Foreign Languages
Education | M,D
Foundations and
Philosophy of Education | M,D
Health Education | M,D
Higher Education | M,D
International and
Comparative Education | M,D
Kinesiology and
Movement Studies | M,D
Mathematics Education | M,D
Multilingual and
Multicultural Education | M
Music Education | M,D
Nursing and Healthcare
Administration | M,D
Nursing Education | M,D
Physical Education | M,D
Public Health—General | M,D
Reading Education | M
Religious Education | M,D
Science Education | M,D
Social Sciences Education | M,D
Special Education | M,D,O

Student Affairs | M,D
Urban Education | D

TÉLÉ-UNIVERSITÉ

Distance Education
Development | M,D
Finance and Banking | M,D

TEMPLE BAPTIST SEMINARY

Religious Education | P,M,D

TEMPLE UNIVERSITY

Accounting | M,D
Actuarial Science | M
Allied Health—General | M,D
Allopathic Medicine | P
Art Education | M
Business Administration
and Management—
General | M,D
Communication Disorders | M
Community Health | M
Dentistry | P
Early Childhood Education | M,D
Education—General | M,D
Educational Leadership
and Administration | M,D
Educational Psychology | M,D
Elementary Education | M,D
English as a Second
Language | M,D
English Education | M,D
Entrepreneurship | D
Environmental and
Occupational Health | M
Epidemiology | M
Finance and Banking | M,D
Foreign Languages
Education | M,D
Health Education | M
Health Services
Management and
Hospital Administration | M
Hospitality Management | M,D
Human Resources
Management | M,D
Insurance | D
International Business | M,D
Kinesiology and
Movement Studies | M,D
Law | P,M,D
Legal and Justice Studies | P,M,D
Leisure Studies | M
Management Information
Systems | M,D
Management Strategy and
Policy | D
Marketing | M,D
Mathematics Education | M,D
Medicinal and
Pharmaceutical
Chemistry | M,D
Music Education | M,D
Nursing—General | M
Occupational Therapy | M
Oral and Dental Sciences | M,O
Pharmaceutical
Administration | M
Pharmaceutical Sciences | M,D
Pharmacy | P
Physical Education | M
Physical Therapy | D
Podiatric Medicine | P
Public Health—General | M,D
Reading Education | M,D
Recreation and Park
Management | M
Science Education | M,D
Social Work | M
Special Education | M,D
Sports Management | M,D
Taxation | P,M,D
Travel and Tourism | M
Urban Education | M,D
Vocational and Technical
Education | M,D

TENNESSEE STATE UNIVERSITY

Allied Health—General | M,D
Business Administration
and Management—
General | M
Communication Disorders | M
Counselor Education | M,D
Curriculum and Instruction | M,D

Education—General | M,D,O
Educational Leadership
and Administration | M,D,O
Elementary Education | M,D
Exercise and Sports
Science | M
Family Nurse Practitioner
Studies | M
Music Education | M
Nursing Informatics | M
Nursing—General | M
Physical Education | M
Physical Therapy | M,D
Special Education | M,D

TENNESSEE TECHNOLOGICAL UNIVERSITY

Accounting | M
Business Administration
and Management—
General | M
Curriculum and Instruction | M,O
Early Childhood Education | M,O
Education of the Gifted | D
Education—General | M,D,O
Educational Leadership
and Administration | M,O
Educational Measurement
and Evaluation | D
Educational Psychology | M,D,O
Elementary Education | M,O
Family Nurse Practitioner
Studies | M
Finance and Banking | M
Health Education | M
Human Resources
Management | M
Insurance | M
International Business | M
Kinesiology and
Movement Studies | M
Library Science | M
Management Information
Systems | M
Management Strategy and
Policy | M
Nursing and Healthcare
Administration | M
Nursing Education | M
Nursing Informatics | M
Nursing—General | M
Physical Education | M
Reading Education | M,D,O
Secondary Education | M,O
Special Education | M,O
Student Affairs | M,O

TENNESSEE TEMPLE UNIVERSITY

Curriculum and Instruction | M
Education—General | M
Educational Leadership
and Administration | M

TEXAS A&M HEALTH SCIENCE CENTER

Dental Hygiene | M
Dentistry | P
Environmental and
Occupational Health | M
Epidemiology | M
Health Education | M
Health Services
Management and
Hospital Administration | M
Oral and Dental Sciences | P,M,D,O
Public Health—General | M

TEXAS A&M INTERNATIONAL UNIVERSITY

Accounting | M
Business Administration
and Management—
General | M
Counselor Education | M
Curriculum and Instruction | M,D
Early Childhood Education | M,D
Education—General | M,D
Educational Leadership
and Administration | M
Finance and Banking | M
Foreign Languages
Education | M,D
International Business | M
Management Information
Systems | M

Multilingual and
Multicultural Education | M,D
Nursing—General | M
Reading Education | M,D
Special Education | M

TEXAS A&M UNIVERSITY

Accounting | M,D
Agricultural Education | M,D
Business Administration
and Management—
General | M,D
Counselor Education | M,D
Curriculum and Instruction | M,D
Education of the Gifted | M,D
Education—General | M,D
Educational Leadership
and Administration | M,D
Educational Measurement
and Evaluation | M,D
Educational Media/
Instructional Technology | M,D
Educational Psychology | M,D
English Education | M,D
Epidemiology | M,D
Finance and Banking | M,D
Foundations and
Philosophy of Education | M,D
Health Education | M,D
Health Physics/
Radiological Health | M,D
Human Resources
Development | M,D
Human Resources
Management | M,D
Industrial and
Manufacturing
Management | M,D
Kinesiology and
Movement Studies | M,D
Management Information
Systems | M,D
Marketing | M,D
Mathematics Education | M,D
Multilingual and
Multicultural Education | M,D
Nonprofit Management | M,O
Physical Education | M,D
Public Health—General | M,D
Reading Education | M,D
Real Estate | M
Recreation and Park
Management | M,D
Science Education | M,D
Special Education | M,D
Urban Education | M,D
Veterinary Medicine | P,M
Veterinary Sciences | M

TEXAS A&M UNIVERSITY–COMMERCE

Agricultural Education | M
Business Administration
and Management—
General | M
Counselor Education | M,D
Curriculum and Instruction | M,D
Early Childhood Education | M,D
Education—General | M,D
Educational Leadership
and Administration | M,D
Educational Media/
Instructional Technology | M,D
Elementary Education | M,D
English as a Second
Language | M,D
English Education | M,D
Exercise and Sports
Science | M,D
Health Education | M,D
Health Promotion | M,D
Higher Education | M,D
Kinesiology and
Movement Studies | M,D
Multilingual and
Multicultural Education | M,D
Music Education | M
Physical Education | M,D
Reading Education | M,D
Secondary Education | M,D
Social Sciences Education | M
Social Work | M
Special Education | M,D

TEXAS A&M UNIVERSITY–CORPUS CHRISTI

Accounting | M

Peterson's Graduate Programs in Business, Education,
Health, Information Studies, Law & Social Work 2011

Business Administration
and Management—
  General — M
Counselor Education — M,D
Curriculum and Instruction — M,D
Early Childhood Education — M,D
Education—General — M,D
Educational Leadership
and Administration — M,D
Educational Media/
  Instructional Technology — M,D
Elementary Education — M
Family Nurse Practitioner
  Studies — M
Health Services
  Management and
  Hospital Administration — M
International Business — M
Kinesiology and
  Movement Studies — M,D
Mathematics Education — M
Nursing and Healthcare
  Administration — M
Nursing—General — M
Reading Education — M,D
Secondary Education — M
Special Education — M

TEXAS A&M UNIVERSITY–KINGSVILLE

Adult Education — M
Agricultural Education — M
Business Administration
and Management—
  General — M
Communication Disorders — M
Counselor Education — M
Early Childhood Education — M
Education—General — M,D
Educational Leadership
and Administration — M,D
Elementary Education — M
English as a Second
  Language — M
Foreign Languages
  Education — M
Health Education — M
Higher Education — D
Kinesiology and
  Movement Studies — M
Multilingual and
  Multicultural Education — M,D
Music Education — M
Reading Education — M
Secondary Education — M
Special Education — M

TEXAS A&M UNIVERSITY–TEXARKANA

Accounting — M
Adult Education — M
Business Administration
and Management—
  General — M
Curriculum and Instruction — M
Education—General — M
Educational Leadership
and Administration — M
Educational Media/
  Instructional Technology — M
Special Education — M

TEXAS CHIROPRACTIC COLLEGE

Chiropractic — P

TEXAS CHRISTIAN UNIVERSITY

Accounting — M
Adult Nursing — M,D
Advertising and Public
  Relations — M
Allied Health—General — M,D
Business Administration
and Management—
  General — M,D
Communication Disorders — M
Counselor Education — M,O
Curriculum and Instruction — M
Education—General — M,D,O
Educational Leadership
and Administration — M,D,O
Educational Psychology — M,D,O
Elementary Education — M
International Business — M

Kinesiology and
  Movement Studies — M
Middle School Education — M
Music Education — M,D,O
Nurse Anesthesia — M
Nursing—General — M,D
Pediatric Nursing — M,D
Science Education — M,D
Secondary Education — M
Special Education — M

TEXAS COLLEGE OF TRADITIONAL CHINESE MEDICINE

Acupuncture and Oriental
  Medicine — M

TEXAS SOUTHERN UNIVERSITY

Business Administration
and Management—
  General — M
Counselor Education — M,D
Curriculum and Instruction — M,D
Education—General — M,D
Educational Leadership
and Administration — M,D
Health Education — M
Higher Education — M,D
Human Services — M
Law — P
Management Information
  Systems — M
Multilingual and
  Multicultural Education — M,D
Pharmacy — P,M,D
Physical Education — M
Secondary Education — M,D
Transportation
  Management — M

TEXAS STATE UNIVERSITY–SAN MARCOS

Accounting — M
Adult Education — M,D
Agricultural Education — M
Allied Health—General — M,D
Athletic Training and
  Sports Medicine — M
Business Administration
and Management—
  General — M
Communication Disorders — M
Counselor Education — M
Developmental Education — M,D
Early Childhood Education — M
Education—General — M,D,O
Educational Leadership
and Administration — M,D
Elementary Education — M
Health Education — M
Health Services
  Management and
  Hospital Administration — M
Health Services Research — M
Legal and Justice Studies — M
Leisure Studies — M
Management Information
  Systems — M
Mathematics Education — M,D
Multilingual and
  Multicultural Education — M
Music Education — M
Physical Education — M
Physical Therapy — D
Reading Education — M
Recreation and Park
  Management — M
Science Education — M
Secondary Education — M
Social Sciences Education — D
Social Work — M
Special Education — M
Vocational and Technical
  Education — M

TEXAS TECH UNIVERSITY

Accounting — M,D
Agricultural Education — M,D
Art Education — M,D
Business Administration
and Management—
  General — M,D
Counselor Education — M,D
Curriculum and Instruction — M,D
Education—General — M,D

Educational Leadership
and Administration — M,D
Educational Media/
  Instructional Technology — M,D
Educational Psychology — M,D
Elementary Education — M,D
English Education — M,D
Entrepreneurship — M
Exercise and Sports
  Science — M
Finance and Banking — M,D
Health Services
  Management and
  Hospital Administration — M,D
Higher Education — M,D
Home Economics
  Education — M,D
Hospitality Management — M,D
Industrial and
  Manufacturing
  Management — M,D
International Business — M
Law — P
Management Information
  Systems — M,D
Marketing — M,D
Multilingual and
  Multicultural Education — M,D
Music Education — M,D
Quantitative Analysis — M,D
Reading Education — M,D
Secondary Education — M,D
Special Education — M,D
Taxation — M,D

TEXAS TECH UNIVERSITY HEALTH SCIENCES CENTER

Acute Care/Critical Care
  Nursing — M,D,O
Allied Health—General — M,D
Allopathic Medicine — P
Athletic Training and
  Sports Medicine — M
Communication Disorders — M,D
Family Nurse Practitioner
  Studies — M,D,O
Gerontological Nursing — M,D,O
Health Services
  Management and
  Hospital Administration — M
Nursing and Healthcare
  Administration — M,D,O
Nursing Education — M,D,O
Nursing—General — M,D,O
Occupational Therapy — M
Pediatric Nursing — M,D,O
Pharmaceutical Sciences — M,D
Physical Therapy — M,D
Physician Assistant
  Studies — M
Rehabilitation Sciences — D

TEXAS WESLEYAN UNIVERSITY

Business Administration
and Management—
  General — M
Counselor Education — M,D
Education—General — M,D
Health Services
  Management and
  Hospital Administration — M
Law — P
Nurse Anesthesia — M,D

TEXAS WOMAN'S UNIVERSITY

Acute Care/Critical Care
  Nursing — M,D
Adult Nursing — M,D
Allied Health—General — M,D
Business Administration
and Management—
  General — M
Communication Disorders — M
Community Health — M,D
Counselor Education — M,D
Curriculum and Instruction — M,D
Early Childhood Education — M,D
Education—General — M,D
Educational Leadership
and Administration — M,D
Elementary Education — M,D
Exercise and Sports
  Science — M

Family Nurse Practitioner
  Studies — M,D
Health Education — M,D
Health Services
  Management and
  Hospital Administration — M,D
Kinesiology and
  Movement Studies — M,D
Library Science — M,D
Mathematics Education — M
Nursing and Healthcare
  Administration — M,D
Nursing Education — M,D
Nursing—General — M,D
Occupational Therapy — M,D
Pediatric Nursing — M,D
Physical Therapy — M,D
Reading Education — M,D
Science Education — M,D
Special Education — M,D
Women's Health Nursing — M,D

THOMAS COLLEGE

Business Administration
and Management—
  General — M
Business Education — M
Computer Science — M
Human Resources
  Management — M

THOMAS EDISON STATE COLLEGE

Business Administration
and Management—
  General — M
Distance Education
  Development — O
Educational Leadership
and Administration — M
Educational Media/
  Instructional Technology — O
Epidemiology — O
Human Resources
  Management — M,O
Nursing Education — O
Nursing—General — M
Organizational
  Management — O

THOMAS JEFFERSON SCHOOL OF LAW

Law — P

THOMAS JEFFERSON UNIVERSITY

Allopathic Medicine — P
Clinical Laboratory
  Sciences/Medical
  Technology — M
Clinical Research — O
Epidemiology — M
Health Services
  Management and
  Hospital Administration — M
Health Services Research — O
Nursing—General — M
Occupational Therapy — M
Pharmacy — P
Physical Therapy — M,D
Public Health—General — M

THOMAS M. COOLEY LAW SCHOOL

Law — P,M
Taxation — P,M

THOMAS MORE COLLEGE

Business Administration
and Management—
  General — M
Education—General — M

THOMAS UNIVERSITY

Business Administration
and Management—
  General — M
Education—General — M
Human Services — M
Nursing—General — M

M—master's degree; P—first professional degree; D—doctorate; O—other advanced degree; *—Close-Up and/or Display

THOMPSON RIVERS UNIVERSITY

Business Administration and Management—	
General	M
Education—General	M
Social Work	M

THUNDERBIRD SCHOOL OF GLOBAL MANAGEMENT

Business Administration and Management—	
General	M
International Business	M

TIFFIN UNIVERSITY

Business Administration and Management—	
General	M
Sports Management	M

TOURO COLLEGE

Acupuncture and Oriental Medicine	M,D
Communication Disorders	M,D
Law	P,M
Occupational Therapy	M
Physical Therapy	M,D
Public Health—General	M,D

TOURO UNIVERSITY

Education—General	P,M,D
Osteopathic Medicine	P,M,D
Pharmacy	P,M,D
Physical Therapy	P,M,D
Physician Assistant Studies	P,M,D
Public Health—General	P,M,D

TOWSON UNIVERSITY

Accounting	M
Advertising and Public Relations	O
Allied Health—General	M
Art Education	M,O
Business Administration and Management—	
General	M
Communication Disorders	M,D
Early Childhood Education	M,O
Education—General	M
Educational Media/ Instructional Technology	M,D
Elementary Education	M
Environmental and Occupational Health	D
Health Services Management and Hospital Administration	O
Human Resources Development	M
Kinesiology and Movement Studies	M
Management Information Systems	D,O
Management Strategy and Policy	O
Mathematics Education	M
Music Education	M,O
Nursing Education	M,O
Nursing—General	M,O
Occupational Therapy	M
Organizational Behavior	O
Physician Assistant Studies	M
Reading Education	M,O
Religious Education	M
Science Education	M
Secondary Education	M
Special Education	M

TRADITIONAL CHINESE MEDICAL COLLEGE OF HAWAII

Acupuncture and Oriental Medicine	M

TREVECCA NAZARENE UNIVERSITY

Business Administration and Management—	
General	M
Counselor Education	M,D
Curriculum and Instruction	M
Education—General	M,D
Educational Leadership and Administration	M,D

Educational Media/ Instructional Technology	M
Elementary Education	M
English as a Second Language	M
Library Science	M
Organizational Management	M
Physician Assistant Studies	M
Reading Education	M
Secondary Education	M
Vocational and Technical Education	M

TRINITY BAPTIST COLLEGE

Education—General	M
Educational Leadership and Administration	M
Religious Education	M
Special Education	M

TRINITY INTERNATIONAL UNIVERSITY

Bioethics	M
Business Administration and Management—	
General	P,M,D,O
Education—General	M
Educational Leadership and Administration	M
Law	P
Religious Education	P,M,D,O

TRINITY LUTHERAN SEMINARY

Religious Education	P,M

TRINITY UNIVERSITY

Accounting	M
Business Administration and Management—	
General	M
Education—General	M
Educational Leadership and Administration	M
Health Services Management and Hospital Administration	M

TRINITY (WASHINGTON) UNIVERSITY

Business Administration and Management—	
General	M
Counselor Education	M
Curriculum and Instruction	M
Early Childhood Education	M
Education—General	M
Educational Leadership and Administration	M
Elementary Education	M
English as a Second Language	M
English Education	M
Human Resources Management	M
Nonprofit Management	M
Organizational Management	M
Public Health—General	M
Reading Education	M
Secondary Education	M
Social Sciences Education	M
Special Education	M

TRINITY WESTERN UNIVERSITY

Business Administration and Management—	
General	M
Educational Leadership and Administration	M,O
English as a Second Language	M
Health Services Management and Hospital Administration	M,O
International Business	M
Nonprofit Management	M,O
Organizational Management	M,O

TRI-STATE COLLEGE OF ACUPUNCTURE

Acupuncture and Oriental Medicine	M,O

TROY UNIVERSITY

Accounting	M
Adult Education	M
Adult Nursing	M,D
Art Education	M
Business Administration and Management—	
General	M
Computer Education	M
Counselor Education	M,O
Early Childhood Education	M,O
Education of the Gifted	M
Education—General	M,O
Educational Leadership and Administration	M,O
Educational Media/ Instructional Technology	M
Elementary Education	M,O
English Education	M
Exercise and Sports Science	M
Family Nurse Practitioner Studies	M,D
Finance and Banking	M
Foundations and Philosophy of Education	M
Health Services Management and Hospital Administration	M
Higher Education	M
Hospitality Management	M
Human Resources Management	M
International Business	M
Management Information Systems	M
Maternal and Child Health	M,D
Mathematics Education	M
Music Education	M
Nonprofit Management	M
Nursing Informatics	M,D
Nursing—General	M,D
Organizational Management	M
Physical Education	M
Reading Education	M
Science Education	M
Secondary Education	M
Social Sciences Education	M
Social Work	M,O
Sports Management	M

TRUMAN STATE UNIVERSITY

Accounting	M
Communication Disorders	M
Education—General	M

TUFTS UNIVERSITY

Allopathic Medicine	P
Clinical Research	M,D
Dentistry	P
Early Childhood Education	M,D,O
Education—General	M,D,O
Environmental and Occupational Health	M,D
Epidemiology	M,D,O
International and Comparative Education	M,D
International Business	M,D
International Health	M,D
Management Strategy and Policy	O
Middle School Education	M,D
Nonprofit Management	O
Occupational Therapy	M,D,O
Oral and Dental Sciences	M,O
Public Health—General	M
Secondary Education	M,D
Veterinary Medicine	P,M,D

TUI UNIVERSITY

Adult Education	M
Business Administration and Management—	
General	M,D
Clinical Research	M,D,O
Early Childhood Education	M
Education—General	M,D
Educational Leadership and Administration	M,D
Educational Media/ Instructional Technology	M,D
Environmental and Occupational Health	M,D,O
Finance and Banking	M,D

Health Education	M,D,O
Health Services Management and Hospital Administration	M,D,O
Higher Education	M,D
Human Resources Management	M,D
International Business	M,D
International Health	M,D,O
Legal and Justice Studies	M,D,O
Logistics	M,D
Management Information Systems	M,D,O
Marketing	M,D
Nursing and Healthcare Administration	M,D,O
Project Management	M,D
Public Health—General	M,D,O
Quality Management	M,D,O
Reading Education	M

TULANE UNIVERSITY

Allopathic Medicine	P
Business Administration and Management—	
General	M,D
Environmental and Occupational Health	M,D
Epidemiology	M,D
Health Education	M
Health Services Management and Hospital Administration	M,D
International Health	M,D
Law	P,M,D
Maternal and Child Health	M,D
Public Health—General	M,D,O
Social Work	M

TUSCULUM COLLEGE

Adult Education	M
Education—General	M
Organizational Management	M

TUSKEGEE UNIVERSITY

Veterinary Medicine	P,M
Veterinary Sciences	P,M

UNIFORMED SERVICES UNIVERSITY OF THE HEALTH SCIENCES

Environmental and Occupational Health	M,D
Family Nurse Practitioner Studies	M
International Health	M,D
Medical/Surgical Nursing	M
Nurse Anesthesia	M
Nursing—General	M
Psychiatric Nursing	M
Public Health—General	M,D

UNION COLLEGE (KY)

Education—General	M
Educational Leadership and Administration	M
Elementary Education	M
Health Education	M
Middle School Education	M
Music Education	M
Physical Education	M
Reading Education	M
Secondary Education	M
Special Education	M

UNION COLLEGE (NE)

Physician Assistant Studies	M

UNION GRADUATE COLLEGE

Bioethics	M,O
Business Administration and Management—	
General	M,O
Education—General	M,O
Educational Leadership and Administration	M,O
English Education	M,O
Finance and Banking	M,O
Foreign Languages Education	M,O
Health Law	M,O

Health Services
  Management and
  Hospital Administration M,O
Human Resources
  Management M,O
Mathematics Education M,O
Middle School Education M,O
Science Education M,O
Social Sciences Education M,O

UNION INSTITUTE & UNIVERSITY

Art Education M
Counselor Education M,O
Early Childhood Education M
Education—General M,D,O
Educational Leadership
  and Administration M,D,O
Educational Psychology M
Elementary Education M
English Education M
Health Promotion M
Higher Education D
Mathematics Education M
Middle School Education M
Reading Education M,O
Science Education M
Social Sciences Education M
Special Education M,O

UNION THEOLOGICAL SEMINARY AND PRESBYTERIAN SCHOOL OF CHRISTIAN EDUCATION

Religious Education M

UNION UNIVERSITY

Business Administration
  and Management—
  General M
Education—General M,D,O
Educational Leadership
  and Administration M,D,O
Family Nurse Practitioner
  Studies M,D,O
Higher Education M,D,O
Nurse Anesthesia M,D,O
Nursing and Healthcare
  Administration M,D,O
Nursing Education M,D,O
Nursing—General M,D,O

UNITED STATES INTERNATIONAL UNIVERSITY

Business Administration
  and Management—
  General M
Finance and Banking M
Management Information
  Systems M
Management Strategy and
  Policy M
Marketing M

UNITED STATES SPORTS ACADEMY

Athletic Training and
  Sports Medicine M
Exercise and Sports
  Science M
Physical Education M
Sports Management M,D

UNIVERSIDAD ADVENTISTA DE LAS ANTILLAS

Curriculum and Instruction M
Education—General M
Educational Leadership
  and Administration M
English as a Second
  Language M
Secondary Education M

UNIVERSIDAD AUTONOMA DE GUADALAJARA

Advertising and Public
  Relations M,D
Allopathic Medicine P
Business Administration
  and Management—
  General M,D
Education—General M,D
Environmental and
  Occupational Health M,D
International Business M,D

Law M,D
Legal and Justice Studies M,D
Marketing Research M,D
Mathematics Education M,D

UNIVERSIDAD CENTRAL DEL CARIBE

Allopathic Medicine P,M

UNIVERSIDAD CENTRAL DEL ESTE

Allopathic Medicine P
Business Administration
  and Management—
  General P,M,D
Dentistry P,M,D
Educational Policy P,M,D
Finance and Banking P,M,D
Higher Education P,M,D
Human Resources
  Development P,M,D
Law P
Public Health—General P,M,D

UNIVERSIDAD DE CIENCIAS MEDICAS

Allopathic Medicine P,M,O
Community Health P,M,O
Environmental and
  Occupational Health P,M,O
Health Services
  Management and
  Hospital Administration P,M,O
Pharmacy P,M,O

UNIVERSIDAD DE IBEROAMERICA

Acute Care/Critical Care
  Nursing P,M,D
Allopathic Medicine P,M,D
Educational Psychology P,M,D
Health Services
  Management and
  Hospital Administration P,M,D

UNIVERSIDAD DE LAS AMERICAS, A.C.

Business Administration
  and Management—
  General M
Education—General M
Finance and Banking M
Marketing Research M
Organizational Behavior M
Quality Management M

UNIVERSIDAD DE LAS AMÉRICAS–PUEBLA

Business Administration
  and Management—
  General M
Clinical Laboratory
  Sciences/Medical
  Technology M
Education—General M
Finance and Banking M
Industrial and
  Manufacturing
  Management M

UNIVERSIDAD DEL ESTE

Accounting M
Adult Education M
Business Administration
  and Management—
  General M
Electronic Commerce M
Elementary Education M
English as a Second
  Language M
Foreign Languages
  Education M
Human Resources
  Management M
Management Information
  Systems M
Management Strategy and
  Policy M
Multilingual and
  Multicultural Education M
Social Work M
Special Education M

UNIVERSIDAD DEL TURABO

Accounting M
Adult Nursing M
Athletic Training and
  Sports Medicine M
Business Administration
  and Management—
  General M,D
Communication Disorders M
Counselor Education M
Curriculum and Instruction M,D
Early Childhood Education M
Education—General M,D,O
Educational Leadership
  and Administration M,D,O
English as a Second
  Language M
Family Nurse Practitioner
  Studies M
Health Promotion M
Human Resources
  Management M
Human Services M
Information Studies M
Library Science M,O
Logistics M
Management Information
  Systems M,D
Marketing M
Naturopathic Medicine D
Nursing—General M
Physical Education M
Project Management M
Quality Management M
Special Education M

UNIVERSIDAD FLET

Education—General M

UNIVERSIDAD IBEROAMERICANA

Advertising and Public
  Relations P,M
Allopathic Medicine P
Dentistry P,M
Educational Leadership
  and Administration P,M
Human Resources
  Development P,M
Law P,M
Marketing P,M
Special Education P,M

UNIVERSIDAD METROPOLITANA

Accounting M,O
Business Administration
  and Management—
  General M,O
Curriculum and Instruction M
Early Childhood Education M
Education—General M
Educational Leadership
  and Administration M
Environmental Education M
Finance and Banking M
Human Resources
  Management M
International Business M
Leisure Studies M
Management Information
  Systems M
Marketing M
Physical Education M
Recreation and Park
  Management M
Special Education M

UNIVERSIDAD NACIONAL PEDRO HENRIQUEZ URENA

Allopathic Medicine P
Business Administration
  and Management—
  General P,M,D
Dentistry P
Project Management P,M,D
Veterinary Medicine P,M,D

UNIVERSITÉ DE MONCTON

Business Administration
  and Management—
  General M
Counselor Education M
Education—General M

Educational Leadership
  and Administration M
Educational Psychology M
Social Work M

UNIVERSITÉ DE MONTRÉAL

Acute Care/Critical Care
  Nursing D
Allopathic Medicine P,D
Bioethics M,D,O
Clinical Laboratory
  Sciences/Medical
  Technology D
Communication Disorders M,O
Community Health M,D,O
Curriculum and Instruction M,D,O
Dental Hygiene O
Education—General M,D,O
Educational Leadership
  and Administration M,D,O
Educational Psychology M,D,O
Electronic Commerce M,D
Environmental and
  Occupational Health M
Health Physics/
  Radiological Health D
Health Services
  Management and
  Hospital Administration M,O
Human Services D
Information Studies M,D
Kinesiology and
  Movement Studies M,D,O
Law P,M,D,O
Library Science M,D
Maternal and Child/
  Neonatal Nursing D
Nurse Anesthesia D
Nursing—General M,D,O
Occupational Therapy O
Optometry O
Oral and Dental Sciences M,O
Pharmaceutical Sciences M,D,O
Physical Education M,D,O
Physical Therapy D
Public Health—General M,D,O
Social Work O
Taxation P,M,D,O
Veterinary Medicine D
Veterinary Sciences M,D
Vision Sciences M,D,O

UNIVERSITÉ DE SHERBROOKE

Accounting M
Allopathic Medicine P
Business Administration
  and Management—
  General P,M,D,O
Clinical Laboratory
  Sciences/Medical
  Technology M,D
Education—General M,O
Educational Leadership
  and Administration M
Elementary Education M,O
Finance and Banking M
Health Law P,M,D,O
Higher Education M,O
International Business M
Kinesiology and
  Movement Studies M,O
Law P,M,D,O
Management Information
  Systems M,O
Marketing M
Organizational Behavior M
Physical Education M,O
Social Work M
Special Education M,O
Taxation M,O

UNIVERSITÉ DU QUÉBEC À CHICOUTIMI

Business Administration
  and Management—
  General M
Education—General M,D
Project Management M

UNIVERSITÉ DU QUÉBEC À MONTRÉAL

Accounting M,O
Actuarial Science O

M—master's degree; P—first professional degree; D—doctorate; O—other advanced degree; *—Close-Up and/or Display

Business Administration
and Management—
  General   M,D,O
Education—General   M,D,O
Environmental and
  Occupational Health   O
Environmental Education   M,D,O
Finance and Banking   O
Kinesiology and
  Movement Studies   M
Law   O
Management Information
  Systems   M
Project Management   M,O
Social Work   M

UNIVERSITÉ DU QUÉBEC À RIMOUSKI

Business Administration
and Management—
  General   M,O
Education—General   M,D,O
Nursing—General   M,O
Project Management   M,O

UNIVERSITÉ DU QUÉBEC À TROIS-RIVIÈRES

Accounting   M
Business Administration
and Management—
  General   M,D
Chiropractic   P
Education—General   M,D
Educational Leadership
  and Administration   O
Educational Psychology   M,D
Finance and Banking   O
Leisure Studies   M,O
Nursing—General   M,O
Physical Education   M
Travel and Tourism   M,O

UNIVERSITÉ DU QUÉBEC, ÉCOLE NATIONALE D'ADMINISTRATION PUBLIQUE

International Business   M,O

UNIVERSITÉ DU QUÉBEC EN ABITIBI-TÉMISCAMINGUE

Business Administration
and Management—
  General   M
Education—General   M,D,O
Project Management   M,O
Social Work   M

UNIVERSITÉ DU QUÉBEC EN OUTAOUAIS

Accounting   M,O
Adult Education   O
Education—General   M,D,O
Educational Psychology   M
Finance and Banking   M,O
Nursing—General   M,O
Project Management   M,O
Social Work   M

UNIVERSITÉ LAVAL

Accounting   M,O
Advertising and Public
  Relations   O
Allopathic Medicine   P,O
Anesthesiologist Assistant
  Studies   O
Business Administration
and Management—
  General   M,D,O
Communication Disorders   M
Community Health   M,D,O
Counselor Education   M,D
Curriculum and Instruction   M,D
Dentistry   P
Education—General   M,D,O
Educational Leadership
  and Administration   M,D,O
Educational Measurement
  and Evaluation   M,D,O
Educational Media/
  Instructional Technology   M,D
Educational Psychology   M,D
Electronic Commerce   M,O
Emergency Medical
  Services   O
Entrepreneurship   M,O

Environmental and
  Occupational Health   O
Epidemiology   M,D
Facilities Management   M,O
Finance and Banking   M,O
Health Physics/
  Radiological Health   O
International Business   M,O
Kinesiology and
  Movement Studies   M,D
Law   M,D,O
Legal and Justice Studies   O
Management Information
  Systems   M,O
Marketing   M,O
Music Education   M,D
Nursing—General   M,D,O
Oral and Dental Sciences   M,O
Organizational
  Management   M,O
Pharmaceutical Sciences   M,D,O
Social Work   M,D

UNIVERSITY AT ALBANY, STATE UNIVERSITY OF NEW YORK

Accounting   M
Business Administration
and Management—
  General   M
Counselor Education   M,D,O
Curriculum and Instruction   M,D,O
Education—General   M,D,O
Educational Leadership
  and Administration   M,D,O
Educational Measurement
  and Evaluation   M,D,O
Educational Media/
  Instructional Technology   M,D,O
Educational Psychology   M,D,O
Environmental and
  Occupational Health   M,D
Epidemiology   M,D
Finance and Banking   M
Health Services
  Management and
  Hospital Administration   M
Human Resources
  Management   M
Information Studies   M,O
Marketing   M
Mathematics Education   M,D
Public Health—General   M,D
Reading Education   M,D,O
Science Education   M,D
Social Work   M,D
Special Education   M
Taxation   M

UNIVERSITY AT BUFFALO, THE STATE UNIVERSITY OF NEW YORK

Accounting   M,D,O
Adult Nursing   M,D,O
Allied Health—General   M,D,O
Allopathic Medicine   P
Business Administration
and Management—
  General   M,D,O
Clinical Laboratory
  Sciences/Medical
  Technology   M
Communication Disorders   M,D
Community Health   M,D
Counselor Education   M,D,O
Dentistry   P,M,D,O
Early Childhood Education   M,D,O
Education of the Gifted   M,D,O
Education—General   M,D,O
Educational Leadership
  and Administration   M,D,O
Educational Psychology   M,D,O
Electronic Commerce   M,D,O
Elementary Education   M,D,O
English as a Second
  Language   M,D,O
English Education   M,D,O
Epidemiology   M,D
Exercise and Sports
  Science   M,D
Finance and Banking   M,D,O
Foreign Languages
  Education   M,D,O
Higher Education   M,D,O
Human Resources
  Management   M,D,O
Information Studies   M,O
International Business   M,D,O

Law   P,M
Library Science   M,O
Logistics   M,D,O
Management Information
  Systems   M,D,O
Mathematics Education   M,D,O
Medicinal and
  Pharmaceutical
  Chemistry   M,D
Multilingual and
  Multicultural Education   M,D,O
Music Education   M,D,O
Nurse Anesthesia   M,D,O
Nursing—General   M,D,O
Occupational Therapy   M
Oral and Dental Sciences   M,D
Pharmaceutical Sciences   M,D
Pharmacy   P
Physical Therapy   D
Psychiatric Nursing   M,D,O
Public Health—General   M,D
Reading Education   M,D,O
Rehabilitation Sciences   M,D,O
Science Education   M,D,O
Social Sciences Education   M,D,O
Social Work   M,D
Special Education   M,D,O
Student Affairs   M,D,O

THE UNIVERSITY OF AKRON

Accounting   M
Business Administration
and Management—
  General   M
Communication Disorders   M,D
Counselor Education   M,D
Education—General   M,D
Educational Leadership
  and Administration   M,D
Electronic Commerce   M
Elementary Education   M,D
Entrepreneurship   M
Exercise and Sports
  Science   M
Finance and Banking   M
Health Services
  Management and
  Hospital Administration   M
Higher Education   M
Human Resources
  Management   M
International Business   M
Law   P,M
Management Information
  Systems   M
Marketing   M
Music Education   M
Nursing—General   M,D
Physical Education   M
Public Health—General   M,D
Secondary Education   M,D
Social Work   M
Special Education   M
Supply Chain
  Management   M
Taxation   M
Vocational and Technical
  Education   M

THE UNIVERSITY OF ALABAMA

Accounting   M,D
Advertising and Public
  Relations   M
Business Administration
and Management—
  General   M,D
Communication Disorders   M
Community Health   M
Counselor Education   M,D,O
Education of the Gifted   M,D,O
Educational Leadership
  and Administration   M,D,O
Elementary Education   M,D,O
English as a Second
  Language   M,D
Exercise and Sports
  Science   M,D
Finance and Banking   M,D
Health Education   M,D
Health Promotion   M,D
Higher Education   M,D
Hospitality Management   M
Information Studies   M,D
Kinesiology and
  Movement Studies   M,D
Law   P,M

Library Science   M,D
Marketing   M,D
Music Education   M,D,O
Nursing—General   M,D
Physical Education   M,D
Quality Management   M
Secondary Education   M,D,O
Social Work   M,D
Special Education   M,D,O
Sports Management   M,D
Taxation   M,D

THE UNIVERSITY OF ALABAMA AT BIRMINGHAM

Accounting   M
Allied Health—General   M,D
Allopathic Medicine   P
Art Education   M
Business Administration
and Management—
  General   M,D
Counselor Education   M
Dentistry   P
Early Childhood Education   M,D
Education—General   M,D,O
Educational Leadership
  and Administration   M,D,O
Elementary Education   M
Environmental and
  Occupational Health   D
Epidemiology   D
Health Education   M,D
Health Promotion   D
Health Services
  Management and
  Hospital Administration   M,D
Nurse Anesthesia   M
Nursing—General   M,D
Occupational Therapy   M
Optometry   P
Oral and Dental Sciences   M
Physical Education   M,D
Physical Therapy   D
Physician Assistant
  Studies   M
Public Health—General   M,D
Secondary Education   M
Special Education   M
Vision Sciences   M,D

THE UNIVERSITY OF ALABAMA IN HUNTSVILLE

Accounting   M,O
Acute Care/Critical Care
  Nursing   M,D,O
Business Administration
and Management—
  General   M
English as a Second
  Language   M,O
Family Nurse Practitioner
  Studies   M,D,O
Finance and Banking   M,O
Health Services
  Management and
  Hospital Administration   M,D,O
Human Resources
  Management   M
Logistics   M
Management Information
  Systems   M,O
Marketing   M
Nursing Education   M,D,O
Nursing—General   M,D,O
Project Management   M
Supply Chain
  Management   M
Taxation   M,O
Vision Sciences   M,D

UNIVERSITY OF ALASKA ANCHORAGE

Adult Education   M
Business Administration
and Management—
  General   M
Counselor Education   M
Early Childhood Education   M,O
Education—General   M,O
Educational Leadership
  and Administration   M,O
Family Nurse Practitioner
  Studies   M,O
Logistics   M,O
Nursing Education   M,O

Nursing—General	M,O
Project Management	M
Psychiatric Nursing	M,O
Public Health—General	M
Social Work	M,O
Special Education	M,O

UNIVERSITY OF ALASKA FAIRBANKS

Business Administration and Management— General	M
Counselor Education	M
Curriculum and Instruction	M,D,O
Education—General	M,D,O
Elementary Education	M,D,O
English Education	M,D,O
Finance and Banking	M
Multilingual and Multicultural Education	M,D,O
Music Education	M
Reading Education	M,D,O
Secondary Education	M,D,O

UNIVERSITY OF ALASKA SOUTHEAST

Business Administration and Management— General	M
Early Childhood Education	M
Education—General	M
Educational Media/ Instructional Technology	M
Elementary Education	M
Secondary Education	M

UNIVERSITY OF ALBERTA

Accounting	D
Adult Education	M,D,O
Business Administration and Management— General	M,D
Clinical Laboratory Sciences/Medical Technology	M,D
Communication Disorders	M,D
Community Health	M,D
Counselor Education	M,D
Dental Hygiene	O
Dentistry	P
Educational Leadership and Administration	M,D,O
Educational Media/ Instructional Technology	M,D
Educational Policy	M,D,O
Educational Psychology	M,D
Elementary Education	M,D
English as a Second Language	M,D
Environmental and Occupational Health	M,D
Epidemiology	M,D
Exercise and Sports Science	M,D
Finance and Banking	M,D
Health Physics/ Radiological Health	M,D
Health Promotion	M,O
Health Services Management and Hospital Administration	M,D
Health Services Research	M,D
Information Studies	M
International Business	M
International Health	M,D
Law	P,M
Library Science	M
Marketing	D
Maternal and Child/ Neonatal Nursing	P
Medical Physics	M,D
Multilingual and Multicultural Education	M
Nursing—General	M,D
Occupational Therapy	M,D
Oral and Dental Sciences	M,D
Organizational Management	D
Pharmaceutical Sciences	M,D
Pharmacy	M,D
Physical Education	M,D
Physical Therapy	M,D
Public Health—General	M,D

Recreation and Park Management	M,D
Rehabilitation Sciences	D
Secondary Education	M,D
Special Education	M,D
Sports Management	M
Vision Sciences	M,D

THE UNIVERSITY OF ARIZONA

Accounting	M
Agricultural Education	M
Allopathic Medicine	P
Art Education	M
Business Administration and Management— General	M,D
Communication Disorders	M,D
Education—General	M,D,O
Educational Leadership and Administration	M,D,O
Educational Psychology	M,D,O
English as a Second Language	M,D
English Education	D
Epidemiology	M,D
Family Nurse Practitioner Studies	M,D,O
Finance and Banking	M,D
Higher Education	M,D
Information Studies	M,D
Law	P,M
Library Science	M,D
Management Information Systems	M
Management Strategy and Policy	D
Marketing	M,D
Multilingual and Multicultural Education	M,D,O
Music Education	M,D
Nursing—General	M,D,O
Perfusion	M,D
Pharmaceutical Sciences	M,D
Pharmacy	P
Public Health—General	M,D
Reading Education	M,D,O

UNIVERSITY OF ARKANSAS

Accounting	M
Agricultural Education	M
Business Administration and Management— General	M,D
Communication Disorders	M
Counselor Education	M,D,O
Curriculum and Instruction	D
Early Childhood Education	M
Education—General	M,D,O
Educational Leadership and Administration	M,D,O
Educational Measurement and Evaluation	M,D
Educational Media/ Instructional Technology	M
Educational Policy	D
Elementary Education	M,O
Health Education	M,D
Higher Education	M,D,O
Industrial and Manufacturing Management	M
Kinesiology and Movement Studies	M,D
Law	P,M
Management Information Systems	M
Mathematics Education	M
Middle School Education	M,D,O
Nursing—General	M
Physical Education	M
Recreation and Park Management	M,D
Secondary Education	M,O
Social Work	M
Special Education	M
Vocational and Technical Education	M,D

UNIVERSITY OF ARKANSAS AT LITTLE ROCK

Accounting	M,O
Adult Education	M
Allied Health—General	M
Art Education	M

Business Administration and Management— General	M,O
Counselor Education	M
Early Childhood Education	M
Education of the Gifted	M
Education—General	M,D,O
Educational Leadership and Administration	M,D,O
Educational Media/ Instructional Technology	M
English as a Second Language	M
Foreign Languages Education	M
Higher Education	D
Law	P
Management Information Systems	M,O
Middle School Education	M
Nonprofit Management	O
Reading Education	M
Secondary Education	M
Social Work	M
Special Education	M,O
Taxation	M,O

UNIVERSITY OF ARKANSAS AT MONTICELLO

Education—General	M
Educational Leadership and Administration	M

UNIVERSITY OF ARKANSAS AT PINE BLUFF

Education—General	M
Elementary Education	M
Physical Education	M
Science Education	M
Secondary Education	M
Social Sciences Education	M

UNIVERSITY OF ARKANSAS FOR MEDICAL SCIENCES

Allopathic Medicine	P
Communication Disorders	M,D
Environmental and Occupational Health	M,O
Health Promotion	D
Health Services Research	D
Nursing—General	D
Pharmaceutical Administration	M
Pharmaceutical Sciences	M
Pharmacy	P,M

UNIVERSITY OF ATLANTA

Business Administration and Management— General	P,M,D,O
Educational Leadership and Administration	P,M,D,O
Health Services Management and Hospital Administration	P,M,D,O
Law	P,M,D,O
Management Information Systems	P,M,D,O
Project Management	P,M,D,O

UNIVERSITY OF BALTIMORE

Accounting	M,O
Business Administration and Management— General	M,O
Finance and Banking	M
Health Services Management and Hospital Administration	M
Human Services	M
Law	M
Legal and Justice Studies	M
Management Information Systems	M,O
Marketing	M
Taxation	P,M

UNIVERSITY OF BRIDGEPORT

Acupuncture and Oriental Medicine	M
Business Administration and Management— General	M

Chiropractic	P
Computer Education	M,O
Dental Hygiene	M
Early Childhood Education	M,O
Education—General	M,D,O
Educational Leadership and Administration	D,O
Elementary Education	M,O
Human Resources Development	M
Human Services	M
International and Comparative Education	M,O
Naturopathic Medicine	D
Reading Education	M,O
Secondary Education	M,O
Student Affairs	M

THE UNIVERSITY OF BRITISH COLUMBIA

Accounting	D
Adult Education	M,D
Allopathic Medicine	P,M
Art Education	M,D
Business Administration and Management— General	M,D
Business Education	M,D
Communication Disorders	M,D
Curriculum and Instruction	M,D
Dentistry	P
Early Childhood Education	M,D
Education—General	M,D,O
Educational Leadership and Administration	M,D
Educational Measurement and Evaluation	M,D,O
Educational Policy	M,D
English as a Second Language	M,D
Environmental and Occupational Health	M,D
Epidemiology	M,D
Finance and Banking	D
Foundations and Philosophy of Education	M,D
Health Services Management and Hospital Administration	M,D
Higher Education	M,D
Home Economics Education	M,D
Information Studies	M,D
International Business	D
Kinesiology and Movement Studies	M,D
Law	M,D
Library Science	M,D
Management Information Systems	D
Management Strategy and Policy	D
Marketing	D
Mathematics Education	M,D
Music Education	M,D
Nurse Anesthesia	M,D
Nursing—General	M,D
Occupational Therapy	M
Oral and Dental Sciences	M,D,O
Organizational Behavior	D
Pharmaceutical Sciences	P,M,D
Pharmacy	P,M,D
Physical Education	M,D
Public Health—General	M,D
Quantitative Analysis	M,D
Reading Education	M,D
Rehabilitation Sciences	M,D
Science Education	M,D
Social Sciences Education	M,D
Social Work	M,D
Special Education	M,D,O
Transportation Management	D
Vocational and Technical Education	M,D

UNIVERSITY OF CALGARY

Allopathic Medicine	P
Business Administration and Management— General	M,D
Community Health	M,D,O
Curriculum and Instruction	M,D,O
Education of the Gifted	M,D,O

M—master's degree; P—first professional degree; D—doctorate; O—other advanced degree; *—Close-Up and/or Display

Educational Leadership and Administration	M,D,O
Educational Measurement and Evaluation	M,D,O
Educational Media/ Instructional Technology	M,D,O
Educational Psychology	M,D
English as a Second Language	M,D,O
Environmental Law	M,O
Epidemiology	M,D
Exercise and Sports Science	M,D
Foreign Languages Education	M,D,O
Foundations and Philosophy of Education	M,D,O
Health Education	M,D
Higher Education	M,D,O
Kinesiology and Movement Studies	M,D
Law	P,M,O
Legal and Justice Studies	M,O
Management Strategy and Policy	M,D
Nursing—General	M,D,O
Social Work	M,D,O
Special Education	M,D
Vocational and Technical Education	M,D,O

UNIVERSITY OF CALIFORNIA, BERKELEY

Accounting	D,O
Allopathic Medicine	
Business Administration and Management— General	M,D,O
Clinical Research	O
Education—General	M,D,O
English as a Second Language	O
Environmental and Occupational Health	M,D
Epidemiology	M,D
Facilities Management	O
Finance and Banking	D,O
Health Services Management and Hospital Administration	D
Human Resources Management	O
Industrial and Manufacturing Management	D
Information Studies	M,D
International Business	O
Law	P,M,D
Legal and Justice Studies	D
Management Information Systems	O
Marketing	D,O
Mathematics Education	M,D
Optometry	P,O
Organizational Behavior	D
Project Management	O
Public Health—General	M,D
Real Estate	D
Science Education	M,D
Social Work	M,D
Special Education	M,D
Sustainability Management	O
Vision Sciences	M,D

UNIVERSITY OF CALIFORNIA, DAVIS

Allopathic Medicine	P
Business Administration and Management— General	M
Clinical Research	M
Curriculum and Instruction	M,D
Education—General	M,D
Educational Psychology	M,D
Epidemiology	M,D
Exercise and Sports Science	M
Law	P,M
Maternal and Child Health	M
Transportation Management	M,D
Veterinary Medicine	P
Veterinary Sciences	M,O

UNIVERSITY OF CALIFORNIA, HASTINGS COLLEGE OF THE LAW

Law	P,M

UNIVERSITY OF CALIFORNIA, IRVINE

Allopathic Medicine	P
Business Administration and Management— General	M,D
Education—General	M,D
Educational Leadership and Administration	M,D
Elementary Education	M,D
Epidemiology	M,D
Foreign Languages Education	M,D
Secondary Education	M,D

UNIVERSITY OF CALIFORNIA, LOS ANGELES

Allopathic Medicine	P
Business Administration and Management— General	M,D*
Clinical Research	M
Community Health	M,D
Dentistry	P,O
Education—General	M,D
Educational Leadership and Administration	D
English as a Second Language	M,D,O
Environmental and Occupational Health	M,D
Epidemiology	M,D
Health Services Management and Hospital Administration	M,D
Information Studies	M,D,O
Law	P,M,D
Library Science	M,D,O
Medical Physics	M,D
Nursing—General	M,D
Oral and Dental Sciences	M,D
Public Health—General	M,D
Science Education	M,D
Social Work	M,D
Special Education	D

UNIVERSITY OF CALIFORNIA, RIVERSIDE

Business Administration and Management— General	M
Curriculum and Instruction	M,D
Education—General	M,D
Educational Leadership and Administration	M,D
Educational Policy	M,D
Educational Psychology	M,D
Higher Education	M,D
Multilingual and Multicultural Education	M,D
Reading Education	M,D
Special Education	M,D

UNIVERSITY OF CALIFORNIA, SAN DIEGO

Allopathic Medicine	P
Business Administration and Management— General	M
Clinical Research	M
Communication Disorders	D
Education—General	M,D
Epidemiology	D
Health Law	M
Health Services Management and Hospital Administration	M
Law	M
Legal and Justice Studies	M
Mathematics Education	D
Pharmacy	P
Public Health—General	D
Science Education	D

UNIVERSITY OF CALIFORNIA, SAN FRANCISCO

Allopathic Medicine	P
Dentistry	P
Medicinal and Pharmaceutical Chemistry	D

Nursing—General	M,D
Oral and Dental Sciences	M,D
Pharmaceutical Sciences	D
Pharmacy	P
Physical Therapy	M,D

UNIVERSITY OF CALIFORNIA, SANTA BARBARA

Education—General	M,D
Educational Leadership and Administration	M,D
Educational Measurement and Evaluation	M,D
International and Comparative Education	M,D
Quantitative Analysis	M,D
Special Education	M,D
Transportation Management	M,D

UNIVERSITY OF CALIFORNIA, SANTA CRUZ

Education—General	M,D
Educational Policy	M,D
Finance and Banking	M
Mathematics Education	M,D
Reading Education	M,D
Science Education	M,D
Social Sciences Education	M

UNIVERSITY OF CENTRAL ARKANSAS

Accounting	M
Business Administration and Management— General	M
Communication Disorders	M,D
Counselor Education	M
Early Childhood Education	M
Education—General	M,O
Educational Leadership and Administration	M,O
Educational Media/ Instructional Technology	M
Family Nurse Practitioner Studies	M
Foreign Languages Education	M
Health Education	M
Kinesiology and Movement Studies	M
Library Science	M
Mathematics Education	M
Medical Physics	M
Music Education	M
Nursing—General	M
Occupational Therapy	M
Physical Therapy	D
Reading Education	M
Special Education	M
Student Affairs	M

UNIVERSITY OF CENTRAL FLORIDA

Accounting	M
Actuarial Science	M,O
Adult Nursing	M,D,O
Art Education	M
Business Administration and Management— General	M,D,O
Communication Disorders	M,D,O
Community College Education	M,D,O
Counselor Education	M,D,O
Curriculum and Instruction	M,D,O
Early Childhood Education	M
Education of the Gifted	M,D,O
Education—General	M,D,O
Educational Leadership and Administration	M,D,O
Educational Media/ Instructional Technology	M,D,O
Elementary Education	M,D
English as a Second Language	M,O
English Education	M
Entrepreneurship	M,O
Exercise and Sports Science	M,O
Family Nurse Practitioner Studies	M,D,O
Health Services Management and Hospital Administration	M,O

Higher Education	D
Hospitality Management	M
International and Comparative Education	M,D,O
Management Information Systems	M
Marketing	D
Mathematics Education	M,D,O
Middle School Education	M
Nonprofit Management	M,O
Nursing and Healthcare Administration	M,D,O
Nursing Education	M,D,O
Nursing—General	M,D,O
Pediatric Nursing	M,D,O
Physical Education	M,O
Physical Therapy	D
Reading Education	M,O
Real Estate	M
Science Education	M,D,O
Social Sciences Education	M,D
Social Work	M,O
Special Education	M,D,O
Sports Management	M
Taxation	M
Travel and Tourism	M
Urban Education	M,D,O
Vocational and Technical Education	M

UNIVERSITY OF CENTRAL MISSOURI

Accounting	M
Business Administration and Management— General	M
Communication Disorders	M
Counselor Education	M,D,O
Curriculum and Instruction	M,D,O
Education—General	M,D,O
Educational Leadership and Administration	M,D,O
Educational Media/ Instructional Technology	M,D,O
Elementary Education	M,D,O
English as a Second Language	M
Environmental and Occupational Health	M
Exercise and Sports Science	M
Finance and Banking	M
Foundations and Philosophy of Education	M,D,O
Human Services	M,D,O
Industrial and Manufacturing Management	M,D
Industrial Hygiene	M
Library Science	M,D,O
Management Information Systems	M
Management Strategy and Policy	M
Marketing	M
Nursing—General	M
Physical Education	M
Reading Education	M,D,O
Secondary Education	M,D,O
Special Education	M,D,O
Student Affairs	M,D,O
Vocational and Technical Education	M,D,O

UNIVERSITY OF CENTRAL OKLAHOMA

Adult Education	M
Business Administration and Management— General	M
Communication Disorders	M
Computer Education	M
Counselor Education	M
Early Childhood Education	M
Education—General	M
Educational Leadership and Administration	M
Educational Media/ Instructional Technology	M
Elementary Education	M
English as a Second Language	M
Health Education	M
Higher Education	M
Home Economics Education	M

Mathematics Education	M
Music Education	M
Reading Education	M
Secondary Education	M
Special Education	M

UNIVERSITY OF CHARLESTON

Accounting	M
Business Administration and Management— General	M
Legal and Justice Studies	M
Pharmacy	P

UNIVERSITY OF CHICAGO

Allopathic Medicine	P
Business Administration and Management— General	M,D
Health Promotion	M,D
International Business	M
Law	P,M,D
Medical Physics	D
Science Education	D
Social Work	M,D
Vision Sciences	D

UNIVERSITY OF CINCINNATI

Accounting	M,D
Acute Care/Critical Care Nursing	M,D
Adult Education	M,D,O
Adult Nursing	M,D
Allopathic Medicine	P,M
Art Education	M
Business Administration and Management— General	M,D
Communication Disorders	M,D,O
Community Health Nursing	M,D
Counselor Education	M,D,O
Curriculum and Instruction	M,D
Early Childhood Education	M
Education—General	M,D,O
Educational Leadership and Administration	M,D,O
Elementary Education	M
English as a Second Language	M,D,O
Environmental and Occupational Health	M,D
Epidemiology	M,D
Finance and Banking	D
Foundations and Philosophy of Education	M,D
Health Education	M,D
Health Physics/ Radiological Health	M
Industrial and Manufacturing Management	D
Industrial Hygiene	M,D
Law	P
Management Information Systems	M,D
Marketing	M,D
Maternal and Child/ Neonatal Nursing	M,D
Mathematics Education	M,D
Medical Imaging	D
Medical Physics	M
Music Education	M
Nurse Anesthesia	M,D
Nurse Midwifery	M,D
Nursing and Healthcare Administration	M,D
Nursing—General	M,D
Occupational Health Nursing	M,D
Organizational Management	M
Pediatric Nursing	M,D
Pharmaceutical Sciences	M,D
Pharmacy	P
Psychiatric Nursing	M,D
Quantitative Analysis	M,D
Reading Education	M,D
Rehabilitation Sciences	M,D
Science Education	M,D,O
Secondary Education	M
Social Sciences Education	M,D,O
Social Work	M

Special Education	M,D
Women's Health Nursing	M,D

UNIVERSITY OF COLORADO AT BOULDER

Accounting	M,D
Business Administration and Management— General	M*
Communication Disorders	M,D
Curriculum and Instruction	M,D
Education—General	M,D
Educational Measurement and Evaluation	D
Educational Psychology	M,D
Entrepreneurship	M,D
Finance and Banking	M,D
Kinesiology and Movement Studies	M,D
Law	P
Management Information Systems	M,D
Marketing	M,D
Medical Physics	M,D
Multilingual and Multicultural Education	M,D
Music Education	M,D
Organizational Management	M,D

UNIVERSITY OF COLORADO AT COLORADO SPRINGS

Adult Nursing	M,D
Business Administration and Management— General	M
Community Health Nursing	M,D
Counselor Education	M,D
Curriculum and Instruction	M,D
Education—General	M,D
Educational Leadership and Administration	M,D
Family Nurse Practitioner Studies	M,D
Forensic Nursing	M,D
Human Services	M,D
Maternal and Child/ Neonatal Nursing	M,D
Nursing and Healthcare Administration	M,D
Nursing—General	M,D
Special Education	M,D
Women's Health Nursing	M,D

UNIVERSITY OF COLORADO DENVER

Accounting	M
Allopathic Medicine	P
Business Administration and Management— General	M
Clinical Laboratory Sciences/Medical Technology	M,D
Counselor Education	M,O
Curriculum and Instruction	M
Dentistry	P
Early Childhood Education	M
Education—General	M,D,O
Educational Leadership and Administration	M,D,O
Educational Media/ Instructional Technology	M
English as a Second Language	M,O
English Education	M,O
Epidemiology	D
Finance and Banking	M
Health Education	D
Health Services Management and Hospital Administration	M,D
Health Services Research	D
International Business	M
Management Information Systems	M,D
Marketing	M
Nursing—General	D
Pediatric Nursing	M
Pharmaceutical Sciences	P
Pharmacy	P,D
Physical Therapy	D

Physician Assistant Studies	M
Public Health—General	M
Special Education	M

UNIVERSITY OF CONNECTICUT

Accounting	M,D
Actuarial Science	M,D
Adult Education	M,D
Agricultural Education	M,D,O
Allied Health—General	M
Business Administration and Management— General	M,D*
Clinical Research	M
Communication Disorders	M,D
Counselor Education	M,D,O
Education of the Gifted	M,D,O
Education—General	M,D,O
Educational Leadership and Administration	D,O
Educational Measurement and Evaluation	M,D,O
Educational Media/ Instructional Technology	M,D,O
Educational Psychology	M,D,O
Elementary Education	M,D,O
English Education	M,D,O
Environmental and Occupational Health	M
Exercise and Sports Science	M,D
Finance and Banking	M,D,O
Foreign Languages Education	M,D,O
Foundations and Philosophy of Education	D
Health Services Management and Hospital Administration	M,D
Higher Education	M
Human Resources Development	M
Human Resources Management	M
Law	P
Leisure Studies	M,D
Marketing	M,D
Mathematics Education	M,D,O
Medicinal and Pharmaceutical Chemistry	M,D
Multilingual and Multicultural Education	M,D,O
Music Education	M,D,O
Nonprofit Management	M,O
Nursing—General	M,D,O
Oral and Dental Sciences	M
Pharmaceutical Sciences	M,D
Pharmacy	P
Physical Therapy	D
Public Health—General	M
Quantitative Analysis	M,O
Reading Education	M,D,O
Science Education	M,D
Secondary Education	M,D,O
Social Sciences Education	M,D,O
Special Education	M,D,O

UNIVERSITY OF CONNECTICUT HEALTH CENTER

Allopathic Medicine	P
Clinical Research	M
Dentistry	P,O
Oral and Dental Sciences	M,D*
Public Health—General	M

UNIVERSITY OF DALLAS

Accounting	M
Business Administration and Management— General	M
Entertainment Management	M
Finance and Banking	M
Health Services Management and Hospital Administration	M
Human Resources Management	M
International Business	M
Logistics	M
Management Information Systems	M

Management Strategy and Policy	M
Marketing	M
Organizational Management	M
Project Management	M
Sports Management	M
Supply Chain Management	M

UNIVERSITY OF DAYTON

Accounting	M
Art Education	M
Business Administration and Management— General	M
Counselor Education	M,O
Early Childhood Education	M
Education—General	M,D,O
Educational Leadership and Administration	M,D,O
Educational Media/ Instructional Technology	M
Electronic Commerce	M
Entrepreneurship	M
Exercise and Sports Science	M,D
Finance and Banking	M
Industrial and Manufacturing Management	M
International Business	M
Law	P,M
Management Information Systems	M
Management Strategy and Policy	M
Marketing	M
Middle School Education	M
Music Education	M
Physical Education	M,D
Physical Therapy	M,D
Reading Education	M
Secondary Education	M
Special Education	M
Student Affairs	M,O

UNIVERSITY OF DELAWARE

Accounting	M
Adult Nursing	M,O
Agricultural Education	M
Business Administration and Management— General	M,D*
Business Education	M,D
Curriculum and Instruction	M,D,O
Education—General	M,D,O
Educational Leadership and Administration	M,D,O
English as a Second Language	M,D,O
Entrepreneurship	M,D
Exercise and Sports Science	M
Family Nurse Practitioner Studies	M,O
Finance and Banking	M
Foreign Languages Education	M
Gerontological Nursing	M,O
Health Promotion	M
Higher Education	M,D,O
HIV/AIDS Nursing	M,O
Hospitality Management	M
Kinesiology and Movement Studies	M,D
Management Information Systems	M
Maternal and Child/ Neonatal Nursing	M,O
Multilingual and Multicultural Education	M,D,O
Music Education	M
Nonprofit Management	M,D
Nursing and Healthcare Administration	M,O
Nursing—General	M,O
Oncology Nursing	M,O
Pediatric Nursing	M,O
Physical Therapy	D
Psychiatric Nursing	M,O
Women's Health Nursing	M,O

UNIVERSITY OF DENVER

Accounting	M

*M—master's degree; P—first professional degree; D—doctorate; O—other advanced degree; *—Close-Up and/or Display*

Adult Education	M,D,O
Advertising and Public Relations	M
Business Administration and Management—General	M,O
Curriculum and Instruction	M,D,O
Education—General	M,D,O
Educational Leadership and Administration	M,D,O
Educational Measurement and Evaluation	M,D,O
Educational Psychology	M,D,O
Electronic Commerce	M
Finance and Banking	M
Higher Education	M,D,O
Human Resources Management	M,O
Information Studies	M,O
International Business	M
Law	P,M
Legal and Justice Studies	M,O
Library Science	M,D,O
Management Information Systems	M
Management Strategy and Policy	M,O
Marketing	M
Music Education	M,O
Organizational Management	M,O
Project Management	M,O
Real Estate	M
Social Work	M,D,O
Taxation	M

UNIVERSITY OF DETROIT MERCY

Allied Health—General	M,O
Business Administration and Management—General	M,O
Computer Education	M
Counselor Education	M
Curriculum and Instruction	M
Dentistry	P
Education—General	M
Educational Leadership and Administration	M
Family Nurse Practitioner Studies	M,O
Health Services Management and Hospital Administration	M
Law	P
Management Information Systems	M
Mathematics Education	M
Nurse Anesthesia	M
Oral and Dental Sciences	M,O
Physician Assistant Studies	M
Special Education	M

UNIVERSITY OF DUBUQUE

Business Administration and Management—General	M

UNIVERSITY OF EVANSVILLE

Business Administration and Management—General	M
Education—General	M,D
Health Services Management and Hospital Administration	M
Nursing—General	M
Physical Therapy	D

THE UNIVERSITY OF FINDLAY

Athletic Training and Sports Medicine	M
Business Administration and Management—General	M
Early Childhood Education	M
Education—General	M
Educational Leadership and Administration	M
Educational Media/Instructional Technology	M
Elementary Education	M
English as a Second Language	M
Finance and Banking	M

Human Resources Management	M
International Business	M
Marketing	M
Multilingual and Multicultural Education	M
Occupational Therapy	M
Pharmacy	P
Physical Therapy	M
Special Education	M

UNIVERSITY OF FLORIDA

Accounting	M,D
Advertising and Public Relations	M
Agricultural Education	M,D
Allied Health—General	M,D
Allopathic Medicine	P
Art Education	M,D
Athletic Training and Sports Medicine	M,D
Business Administration and Management—General	M,D,O
Clinical Research	M
Communication Disorders	M,D
Counselor Education	M,D,O
Curriculum and Instruction	M,D,O
Dentistry	P,O
Early Childhood Education	M,D,O
Education—General	M,D,O
Educational Leadership and Administration	M,D,O
Educational Measurement and Evaluation	M,D,O
Educational Psychology	M,D,O
Electronic Commerce	M
Elementary Education	M,D,O
English as a Second Language	M,D,O
English Education	M,D,O
Entrepreneurship	M,D,O
Environmental and Occupational Health	M
Environmental Law	P,M,D
Epidemiology	M
Exercise and Sports Science	M,D
Finance and Banking	M,D,O
Foundations and Philosophy of Education	M,D,O
Health Education	M,D,O
Health Services Management and Hospital Administration	M,D
Health Services Research	M,D
Higher Education	M,D,O
Human Resources Management	M
Insurance	M,D,O
International Business	P,M,D
Kinesiology and Movement Studies	M,D
Law	P,M,D
Management Information Systems	M,D
Management Strategy and Policy	M
Marketing	M,D
Mathematics Education	M,D,O
Medical Imaging	M,D
Medicinal and Pharmaceutical Chemistry	P,M,D
Multilingual and Multicultural Education	M,D,O
Music Education	M,D
Nursing—General	M,D
Occupational Therapy	M
Oral and Dental Sciences	M,D,O
Pharmaceutical Administration	M,D
Pharmaceutical Sciences	D
Pharmacy	P
Physical Education	M,D
Physical Therapy	D
Physician Assistant Studies	M
Public Health—General	M
Quantitative Analysis	M
Reading Education	M,D,O
Real Estate	M,D,O
Recreation and Park Management	M,D
Rehabilitation Sciences	D
Science Education	M,D,O

Social Sciences Education	M,D,O
Special Education	M,D,O
Sports Management	M,D
Student Affairs	M,D,O
Supply Chain Management	M,D
Taxation	P,M,D
Veterinary Medicine	P
Veterinary Sciences	M,D,O

UNIVERSITY OF GEORGIA

Accounting	M
Adult Education	M,D,O
Agricultural Education	M
Art Education	M,D,O
Business Administration and Management—General	M,D
Communication Disorders	M,D,O
Counselor Education	M,D,O
Early Childhood Education	M,D,O
Education—General	M,D,O
Educational Leadership and Administration	M,D,O
Educational Media/Instructional Technology	M,D,O
Educational Policy	M,D,O
Educational Psychology	M,D,O
Elementary Education	M,D,O
English Education	M,D,O
Environmental and Occupational Health	M,D
Foreign Languages Education	M,D,O
Foundations and Philosophy of Education	M,D,O
Health Education	M,D
Health Promotion	M,D
Higher Education	D
Human Resources Management	M,D,O
Kinesiology and Movement Studies	M,D
Law	P,M
Leisure Studies	M,D,O
Marketing Research	M
Mathematics Education	M,D,O
Middle School Education	M,D,O
Music Education	M,D,O
Nonprofit Management	M,O
Pharmaceutical Sciences	M,D,O
Pharmacy	P
Physical Education	M,D
Reading Education	M,D,O
Science Education	M,D,O
Social Sciences Education	M,D,O
Social Work	M,D,O
Special Education	M,D,O
Student Affairs	M,D,O
Veterinary Medicine	P,M
Veterinary Sciences	M,D
Vocational and Technical Education	M,D,O

UNIVERSITY OF GREAT FALLS

Education—General	M
Human Services	M
Secondary Education	M

UNIVERSITY OF GUAM

Business Administration and Management—General	M
Counselor Education	M
Education—General	M
Educational Leadership and Administration	M
English as a Second Language	M
Reading Education	M
Secondary Education	M
Social Work	M
Special Education	M

UNIVERSITY OF GUELPH

Acute Care/Critical Care Nursing	M,D,O
Anesthesiologist Assistant Studies	M,D,O
Business Administration and Management—General	M,D
Emergency Medical Services	M,D,O
Epidemiology	M,D

Hospitality Management	M
Medical Imaging	M,D,O
Organizational Management	M
Veterinary Medicine	M,D,O
Veterinary Sciences	M,D,O
Vision Sciences	M,D,O

UNIVERSITY OF HARTFORD

Accounting	M,O
Business Administration and Management—General	M
Community Health Nursing	M
Counselor Education	M,O
Early Childhood Education	M
Education—General	M,D,O
Educational Leadership and Administration	D,O
Educational Media/Instructional Technology	M
Elementary Education	M
Music Education	M,D,O
Nursing Education	M
Nursing—General	M
Organizational Behavior	M
Physical Therapy	M,D
Taxation	M,O

UNIVERSITY OF HAWAII AT HILO

Education—General	M
Foreign Languages Education	M,D

UNIVERSITY OF HAWAII AT MANOA

Accounting	M,D
Adult Nursing	M,D,O
Allopathic Medicine	P
Business Administration and Management—General	M
Communication Disorders	M
Community Health Nursing	M,D,O
Curriculum and Instruction	M,D
Early Childhood Education	M
Education—General	M,D,O
Educational Leadership and Administration	M,D
Educational Media/Instructional Technology	M,D
Educational Policy	D
Educational Psychology	M,D
English as a Second Language	M,D,O
Entrepreneurship	M
Epidemiology	M,D,O
Family Nurse Practitioner Studies	M,D,O
Finance and Banking	M,D
Foreign Languages Education	M,D,O
Foundations and Philosophy of Education	M,D
Human Resources Management	M
Information Studies	M,O
International Business	M,D
Kinesiology and Movement Studies	M,D
Law	P,M,O
Library Science	M,O
Management Information Systems	M,D,O
Marketing	M,D
Nursing and Healthcare Administration	M,D,O
Nursing—General	M,D,O
Organizational Behavior	M
Organizational Management	M,D
Public Health—General	M,D,O
Real Estate	M
Social Work	M,D
Special Education	M,D
Taxation	M
Travel and Tourism	M

UNIVERSITY OF HOUSTON

Accounting	M,D
Advertising and Public Relations	M
Art Education	M,D

Business Administration and Management—	
General	M,D
Communication Disorders	M
Curriculum and Instruction	M,D
Early Childhood Education	M,D
Education of the Gifted	M,D
Education—General	M,D
Educational Leadership and Administration	M,D
Educational Media/ Instructional Technology	M,D
Educational Psychology	M,D
Elementary Education	M,D
English as a Second Language	M,D
Exercise and Sports Science	M,D
Finance and Banking	M,D
Foundations and Philosophy of Education	M,D
Health Education	M,D
Higher Education	M,D
Hospitality Management	M
Kinesiology and Movement Studies	M,D
Law	P,M
Logistics	M
Management Information Systems	M,D
Marketing	M,D
Mathematics Education	M,D
Multilingual and Multicultural Education	M,D
Optometry	P
Pharmaceutical Administration	P,M,D
Pharmacy	P,M,D
Physical Education	M,D
Project Management	M
Reading Education	M,D
Science Education	M,D
Secondary Education	M,D
Social Sciences Education	M,D
Social Work	M,D
Special Education	M,D
Vision Sciences	M,D

UNIVERSITY OF HOUSTON–CLEAR LAKE

Accounting	M
Business Administration and Management—	
General	M
Counselor Education	M
Curriculum and Instruction	M
Early Childhood Education	M
Education—General	M,D
Educational Leadership and Administration	M,D
Educational Media/ Instructional Technology	M
Exercise and Sports Science	M
Finance and Banking	M
Foundations and Philosophy of Education	M
Health Services Management and Hospital Administration	M
Human Resources Management	M
Library Science	M
Management Information Systems	M
Multilingual and Multicultural Education	M
Reading Education	M

UNIVERSITY OF HOUSTON–DOWNTOWN

Curriculum and Instruction	M
Elementary Education	M
Multilingual and Multicultural Education	M
Secondary Education	M
Urban Education	M

UNIVERSITY OF HOUSTON–VICTORIA

Accounting	M
Business Administration and Management—	
General	M

Counselor Education	M
Curriculum and Instruction	M
Education—General	M
Educational Leadership and Administration	M
Entrepreneurship	M
Finance and Banking	M
International Business	M
Marketing	M
Nursing—General	M
Special Education	M

UNIVERSITY OF IDAHO

Accounting	M
Adult Education	M,O
Agricultural Education	M
Art Education	M
Business Administration and Management—	
General	M
Counselor Education	M
Curriculum and Instruction	M
Education—General	M,D,O
Educational Leadership and Administration	M,O
English as a Second Language	M
Law	P
Physical Education	M
Recreation and Park Management	M
Special Education	M
Veterinary Sciences	M,D
Vocational and Technical Education	M,O

UNIVERSITY OF ILLINOIS AT CHICAGO

Accounting	M
Acute Care/Critical Care Nursing	M
Adult Nursing	M
Allied Health—General	M,D
Allopathic Medicine	P
Business Administration and Management—	
General	M,D
Community Health Nursing	M
Community Health	M,D
Curriculum and Instruction	M,D
Dentistry	P
Education—General	M,D
Educational Leadership and Administration	M,D
Educational Policy	M,D
Educational Psychology	D
Elementary Education	M,D
English as a Second Language	M
English Education	M,D
Environmental and Occupational Health	M,D
Epidemiology	M,D
Family Nurse Practitioner Studies	M
Gerontological Nursing	M
Health Education	M
Health Services Management and Hospital Administration	M,D
Health Services Research	M,D
Kinesiology and Movement Studies	M,D
Management Information Systems	M,D
Maternal and Child/ Neonatal Nursing	M
Mathematics Education	M
Multilingual and Multicultural Education	M,D
Nurse Midwifery	M
Nursing and Healthcare Administration	M
Nursing—General	M,D
Occupational Health Nursing	M
Occupational Therapy	M,D
Oral and Dental Sciences	M,D
Pediatric Nursing	M
Pharmaceutical Administration	M,D
Pharmaceutical Sciences	M,D
Pharmacy	P,D

Physical Therapy	M,D
Psychiatric Nursing	M
Public Health—General	M,D
Quantitative Analysis	M,D
Reading Education	M,D
Real Estate	M
School Nursing	M
Secondary Education	M,D
Social Work	M,D
Special Education	M,D
Urban Education	M,D
Women's Health Nursing	M

UNIVERSITY OF ILLINOIS AT SPRINGFIELD

Accounting	M
Business Administration and Management—	
General	M
Education—General	M
Educational Leadership and Administration	M
Human Services	M
Legal and Justice Studies	M
Management Information Systems	M
Public Health—General	M

UNIVERSITY OF ILLINOIS AT URBANA–CHAMPAIGN

Accounting	M,D
Actuarial Science	M,D
Advertising and Public Relations	M
Agricultural Education	M,D
Allopathic Medicine	P
Art Education	M,D
Business Administration and Management—	
General	M,D
Communication Disorders	M,D
Community Health	M,D
Counselor Education	M,D,O
Curriculum and Instruction	M,D,O
Education of Students with Severe/Multiple Disabilities	M,D,O
Education—General	M,D,O
Educational Leadership and Administration	M,D,O
Educational Policy	M,D
Educational Psychology	M,D,O
English as a Second Language	M,D
Finance and Banking	M,D
Foreign Languages Education	M,D
Higher Education	M,D,O
Human Resources Development	M,D,O
Human Resources Management	M,D*
Information Studies	M,D,O
Kinesiology and Movement Studies	M,D
Law	P,M,D
Leisure Studies	M,D
Library Science	M,D,O
Mathematics Education	M,D
Music Education	M,D,O
Public Health—General	M,D
Rehabilitation Sciences	M,D
Science Education	M,D
Social Work	M,D
Special Education	M,D,O
Taxation	M,D
Veterinary Medicine	P
Veterinary Sciences	M,D
Vocational and Technical Education	M,D,O

UNIVERSITY OF INDIANAPOLIS

Art Education	M
Business Administration and Management—	
General	M,O
Curriculum and Instruction	M
Education—General	M
Educational Leadership and Administration	M
Elementary Education	M
English Education	M
Foreign Languages Education	M

Mathematics Education	M
Nurse Midwifery	M
Nursing and Healthcare Administration	M
Nursing Education	M
Nursing—General	M
Occupational Therapy	M,D
Physical Education	M
Physical Therapy	M,D
Science Education	M
Secondary Education	M
Social Sciences Education	M

THE UNIVERSITY OF IOWA

Accounting	M,D
Actuarial Science	M,D
Allopathic Medicine	P
Art Education	M,D
Business Administration and Management—	
General	M,D
Clinical Research	M,D
Communication Disorders	M,D
Community Health	M,D
Counselor Education	M,D
Curriculum and Instruction	M,D
Dentistry	P,M,D,O
Developmental Education	M,D
Early Childhood Education	M,D
Education—General	M,D,O
Educational Leadership and Administration	M,D,O
Educational Measurement and Evaluation	M,D,O
Educational Policy	M,D,O
Educational Psychology	M,D,O
Elementary Education	M,D
English Education	M,D
Environmental and Occupational Health	M,D,O
Epidemiology	M,D
Exercise and Sports Science	M,D
Finance and Banking	M,D
Foreign Languages Education	M,D
Foundations and Philosophy of Education	M,D,O
Health Services Management and Hospital Administration	M,D
Higher Education	M,D,O
Information Studies	M
Investment Management	M
Law	P,M
Leisure Studies	M
Library Science	M
Marketing	M,D
Mathematics Education	M,D
Nursing—General	M,D
Oral and Dental Sciences	M,D,O
Pharmacy	M,D
Physical Education	M,D
Physical Therapy	D
Physician Assistant Studies	M
Public Health—General	M,D,O
Recreation and Park Management	M
Rehabilitation Sciences	D
Science Education	M,D
Secondary Education	M,D
Social Sciences Education	M,D
Social Work	M,D
Special Education	M,D
Sports Management	M
Student Affairs	M,D

THE UNIVERSITY OF KANSAS

Accounting	M
Allied Health—General	M,D,O
Allopathic Medicine	P,M,D
Art Education	M
Business Administration and Management—	
General	M,D
Clinical Research	M
Communication Disorders	M,D
Community Health Nursing	M,D,O
Curriculum and Instruction	M,D
Education—General	M,D,O
Educational Leadership and Administration	M,D

Educational Measurement and Evaluation	M,D
Educational Policy	D
Educational Psychology	M,D
Facilities Management	M,D,O
Family Nurse Practitioner Studies	M,D,O
Foundations and Philosophy of Education	D
Health Education	M,D,O
Health Services Management and Hospital Administration	M,D
Higher Education	M,D
Law	P
Management Information Systems	M
Medicinal and Pharmaceutical Chemistry	M,D
Music Education	M,D
Nurse Anesthesia	M
Nurse Midwifery	M,D,O
Nursing and Healthcare Administration	M,D,O
Nursing—General	M,D,O
Occupational Therapy	M,D
Organizational Management	M,D,O
Pharmaceutical Sciences	M
Physical Education	M,D
Physical Therapy	D
Psychiatric Nursing	M,D,O
Public Health—General	M
Rehabilitation Sciences	M,D
Special Education	M,D

UNIVERSITY OF KENTUCKY

Accounting	M
Allied Health—General	M,D
Allopathic Medicine	P
Art Education	M
Business Administration and Management— General	M,D
Clinical Laboratory Sciences/Medical Technology	M,D
Communication Disorders	M
Curriculum and Instruction	M,D
Dentistry	P
Early Childhood Education	M,D
Education—General	M,D,O
Educational Leadership and Administration	M,D,O
Educational Measurement and Evaluation	M,D
Educational Media/ Instructional Technology	M,D
Educational Policy	M,D
Educational Psychology	M,D,O
Exercise and Sports Science	M,D
Foreign Languages Education	M
Health Physics/ Radiological Health	M
Health Promotion	M,D
Health Services Management and Hospital Administration	M
Higher Education	M,D
Hospitality Management	M
International Business	M
Kinesiology and Movement Studies	M,D
Law	P
Library Science	M
Medical Physics	M
Middle School Education	M,D
Music Education	M,D
Nursing—General	M,D
Oral and Dental Sciences	M
Pharmaceutical Sciences	M,D
Pharmacy	P
Physical Therapy	M
Physician Assistant Studies	M
Public Health—General	M
Rehabilitation Sciences	D
Social Work	M,D
Special Education	M,D
Veterinary Sciences	M,D
Vocational and Technical Education	M

UNIVERSITY OF LA VERNE

Accounting	M
Business Administration and Management— General	M,O
Counselor Education	M,O
Education—General	M,O
Educational Leadership and Administration	M,D,O
Finance and Banking	M
Health Services Management and Hospital Administration	M,O
Health Services Research	M
International Business	M
Law	P
Management Information Systems	M
Marketing	M
Multilingual and Multicultural Education	O
Nonprofit Management	M,O
Organizational Management	M,O
Reading Education	M,O
Special Education	M
Student Affairs	M

UNIVERSITY OF LETHBRIDGE

Accounting	M,D
Business Administration and Management— General	M,D
Education—General	M,D
Educational Leadership and Administration	M,D
Exercise and Sports Science	M,D
Finance and Banking	M,D
Human Resources Management	M,D
International Business	M,D
Kinesiology and Movement Studies	M,D
Management Information Systems	M,D
Management Strategy and Policy	M,D
Nursing—General	M,D

UNIVERSITY OF LOUISIANA AT LAFAYETTE

Business Administration and Management— General	M
Communication Disorders	M,D
Counselor Education	M
Curriculum and Instruction	M
Education of the Gifted	M
Education—General	M,D
Educational Leadership and Administration	M,D
Music Education	M
Nursing—General	M

UNIVERSITY OF LOUISIANA AT MONROE

Business Administration and Management— General	M
Communication Disorders	M
Counselor Education	M
Curriculum and Instruction	M,D
Education of the Gifted	M,D
Education—General	M,D,O
Educational Leadership and Administration	M,D
Educational Measurement and Evaluation	M,D
Elementary Education	M,D
Exercise and Sports Science	M
Middle School Education	M
Pharmaceutical Sciences	M
Pharmacy	D
Reading Education	M,D
Secondary Education	M

UNIVERSITY OF LOUISVILLE

Accounting	M
Adult Nursing	M,D
Allopathic Medicine	P
Art Education	M,D

Business Administration and Management— General	M
Clinical Research	M,D,O
Communication Disorders	M,D
Community Health	M
Counselor Education	M,D
Curriculum and Instruction	M,D
Dentistry	P,M
Early Childhood Education	M,D
Education—General	M,D,O
Educational Leadership and Administration	M,D,O
Educational Psychology	M,D
Elementary Education	M,D
Entrepreneurship	M,D
Environmental and Occupational Health	M,D,O
Epidemiology	M,D
Exercise and Sports Science	M
Family Nurse Practitioner Studies	M,D
Health Education	M,D
Health Promotion	M,D,O
Health Services Management and Hospital Administration	M,D,O
Higher Education	M,D,O
Human Resources Development	M,D,O
Human Resources Management	M,D
Law	P
Logistics	M,D,O
Maternal and Child/ Neonatal Nursing	M,D
Middle School Education	M,D
Music Education	M,D
Nonprofit Management	M,D
Nursing—General	M,D
Oral and Dental Sciences	P,M
Physical Education	M
Psychiatric Nursing	M,D
Public Health—General	M,D
Reading Education	M,D
Secondary Education	M,D
Social Work	M,D,O
Special Education	M,D
Sports Management	M
Student Affairs	M,D
Supply Chain Management	M,D,O

UNIVERSITY OF MAINE

Accounting	M
Business Administration and Management— General	M
Communication Disorders	M
Counselor Education	M,D,O
Curriculum and Instruction	M
Education—General	M
Educational Leadership and Administration	M,D,O
Educational Media/ Instructional Technology	M
Elementary Education	M,O
Foreign Languages Education	M
Higher Education	M,D,O
Kinesiology and Movement Studies	M
Management Information Systems	M
Nursing—General	M,O
Physical Education	M
Reading Education	M,D,O
Science Education	M,O
Secondary Education	M,O
Social Sciences Education	M,O
Social Work	M
Special Education	M,O
Sustainability Management	M

UNIVERSITY OF MAINE AT FARMINGTON

Education—General	M
Educational Leadership and Administration	M
Educational Media/ Instructional Technology	M
Reading Education	M

UNIVERSITY OF MANAGEMENT AND TECHNOLOGY

Business Administration and Management— General	M,D,O
Management Information Systems	M,O
Project Management	M,D,O

UNIVERSITY OF MANITOBA

Adult Education	M
Business Administration and Management— General	M,D
Community Health	M,D,O
Counselor Education	M
Curriculum and Instruction	M
Dentistry	P
Education—General	M,D
Educational Leadership and Administration	M
Educational Psychology	M
English as a Second Language	M
English Education	M
Foundations and Philosophy of Education	M
Higher Education	M
Kinesiology and Movement Studies	M
Law	M
Nursing—General	M
Occupational Therapy	M,D
Oral and Dental Sciences	M,D
Pharmaceutical Sciences	M,D
Physical Education	M
Physical Therapy	M,D
Recreation and Park Management	M
Rehabilitation Sciences	M,D
Social Work	M,D
Special Education	M

UNIVERSITY OF MARY

Business Administration and Management— General	M
Curriculum and Instruction	M
Early Childhood Education	M
Education—General	M
Educational Leadership and Administration	M
Family Nurse Practitioner Studies	M
Health Services Management and Hospital Administration	M
Higher Education	M
Human Resources Management	M
Management Strategy and Policy	M
Nursing and Healthcare Administration	M
Nursing Education	M
Nursing—General	M
Occupational Therapy	M
Physical Therapy	D
Project Management	M
Reading Education	M
Special Education	M

UNIVERSITY OF MARY HARDIN-BAYLOR

Accounting	M
Business Administration and Management— General	M
Counselor Education	M
Education—General	M,D
Educational Leadership and Administration	M,D
Educational Psychology	M,D
Exercise and Sports Science	M,D
Management Information Systems	M
Nursing—General	M
Reading Education	M,D

UNIVERSITY OF MARYLAND, BALTIMORE

Allopathic Medicine	P

Clinical Laboratory Sciences/Medical Technology	M
Clinical Research	M,D
Community Health Nursing	M
Dental Hygiene	M
Dentistry	P,M,O
Epidemiology	M,D
Gerontological Nursing	M.
Health Services Research	M,D
Law	P
Maternal and Child/ Neonatal Nursing	M
Medical/Surgical Nursing	M
Nurse Midwifery	M
Nursing and Healthcare Administration	M
Nursing Education	M
Nursing—General	M,D
Oral and Dental Sciences	P,M,D,O
Pediatric Nursing	M
Pharmaceutical Administration	M,D
Pharmaceutical Sciences	D
Pharmacy	P,M,D
Physical Therapy	D
Psychiatric Nursing	M
Rehabilitation Sciences	D
Social Work	M,D

UNIVERSITY OF MARYLAND, BALTIMORE COUNTY

Art Education	M
Curriculum and Instruction	M,D,O
Distance Education Development	M,O
Early Childhood Education	M
Education—General	M,D,O
Educational Media/ Instructional Technology	M,O
Educational Policy	M,D
Elementary Education	M
English as a Second Language	M,O
English Education	M
Epidemiology	M,O
Foreign Languages Education	M
Health Education	M,O
Health Services Management and Hospital Administration	M,D,O
Human Services	M,D
Legal and Justice Studies	M,D
Mathematics Education	M
Multilingual and Multicultural Education	M,D
Music Education	M
Nonprofit Management	M,O
Reading Education	M,D,O
Science Education	M
Secondary Education	M
Social Sciences Education	M

UNIVERSITY OF MARYLAND, COLLEGE PARK

Advertising and Public Relations	M,D
Business Administration and Management— General	M,D
Communication Disorders	M,D
Counselor Education	M,D,O
Curriculum and Instruction	M,D,O
Early Childhood Education	M,D
Education—General	M,D,O*
Educational Leadership and Administration	M,D,O
Educational Measurement and Evaluation	M,D
Educational Media/ Instructional Technology	M,D,O
Educational Policy	M,D
Educational Psychology	M,D
English as a Second Language	M,D,O
Environmental and Occupational Health	M,D
Epidemiology	M,D
Foreign Languages Education	M,D
Foundations and Philosophy of Education	M,D,O

Health Education	M,D
Health Services Management and Hospital Administration	M,D
Higher Education	M,D
Information Studies	M,D
International and Comparative Education	M,D
Kinesiology and Movement Studies	M,D
Law	
Library Science	
Maternal and Child Health	M,D
Music Education	M,D
Public Health—General	M,D
Reading Education	M,D,O
Real Estate	M
Secondary Education	M,D,O
Social Work	
Special Education	M,D,O
Student Affairs	M,D,O
Veterinary Medicine	P
Veterinary Sciences	M,D

UNIVERSITY OF MARYLAND EASTERN SHORE

Counselor Education	M
Education—General	M
Educational Leadership and Administration	D
Organizational Management	D
Physical Therapy	D
Rehabilitation Sciences	M
Special Education	M
Vocational and Technical Education	M

UNIVERSITY OF MARYLAND UNIVERSITY COLLEGE

Accounting	M,O
Business Administration and Management— General	M,D,O
Community College Education	D
Distance Education Development	M,O
Education—General	M
Educational Leadership and Administration	D
Finance and Banking	M,O
Health Services Management and Hospital Administration	M,O
International Business	M,O
Management Information Systems	M,O

UNIVERSITY OF MARY WASHINGTON

Business Administration and Management— General	M
Education—General	M
Management Information Systems	M

UNIVERSITY OF MASSACHUSETTS AMHERST

Accounting	M
Art Education	M
Business Administration and Management— General	M,D
Communication Disorders	M,D
Community Health	M,D
Counselor Education	M,D,O
Early Childhood Education	M,D,O
Education—General	M,D,O
Educational Leadership and Administration	M,D,O
Educational Measurement and Evaluation	M,D,O
Educational Media/ Instructional Technology	M,D,O
Educational Policy	M,D,O
Elementary Education	M,D,O
English as a Second Language	M,D,O
Environmental and Occupational Health	M,D
Epidemiology	M,D

Foreign Languages Education	M
Health Education	M,D
Health Services Management and Hospital Administration	M,D
Higher Education	M,D,O
Hospitality Management	M
International and Comparative Education	M,D,O
Kinesiology and Movement Studies	M,D
Multilingual and Multicultural Education	M,D,O
Nursing—General	M,D
Public Health—General	M,D
Reading Education	M,D,O
Science Education	M,D,O
Secondary Education	M,D,O
Special Education	M,D,O
Sports Management	M,D
Travel and Tourism	M

UNIVERSITY OF MASSACHUSETTS BOSTON

Business Administration and Management— General	M
Counselor Education	M,O
Curriculum and Instruction	M
Education—General	M,D,O
Educational Leadership and Administration	M,D,O
Elementary Education	M,D,O
English as a Second Language	M
Foreign Languages Education	M
Health Services Management and Hospital Administration	M,D,O
Higher Education	M,D,O
Human Services	M
Multilingual and Multicultural Education	M
Nursing—General	M,D
Secondary Education	M,D,O
Special Education	M
Urban Education	M,D,O

UNIVERSITY OF MASSACHUSETTS DARTMOUTH

Accounting	M,O
Adult Nursing	M,D,O
Art Education	M
Business Administration and Management— General	M,O
Community Health Nursing	M,D,O
Education—General	M,O
Electronic Commerce	M,O
Elementary Education	M,O
Finance and Banking	M,O
Law	P
Marketing	M,O
Mathematics Education	D
Middle School Education	M,O
Nursing—General	M,D,O
Organizational Management	M,O
Secondary Education	M,O
Supply Chain Management	M,O

UNIVERSITY OF MASSACHUSETTS LOWELL

Allied Health—General	M,D,O
Business Administration and Management— General	M,O
Clinical Laboratory Sciences/Medical Technology	M,O
Curriculum and Instruction	M,D,O
Education—General	M,D,O
Educational Leadership and Administration	M,D,O
Entrepreneurship	M,O
Epidemiology	M,D,O
Family Nurse Practitioner Studies	M
Gerontological Nursing	M,O

Health Physics/ Radiological Health	M
Health Promotion	D
Health Services Management and Hospital Administration	M,O
Industrial Hygiene	M,D,O
Mathematics Education	M,D,O
Medical/Surgical Nursing	M,D,O
Music Education	M
Nursing and Healthcare Administration	D
Nursing Education	M,D,O
Nursing—General	M,D,O
Physical Therapy	D
Psychiatric Nursing	M,O
Public Health—General	M,O
Reading Education	M,D,O
Science Education	M,D,O

UNIVERSITY OF MASSACHUSETTS WORCESTER

Acute Care/Critical Care Nursing	M,D,O
Adult Nursing	M,D,O
Allopathic Medicine	P
Clinical Research	M,D
Epidemiology	D
Family Nurse Practitioner Studies	M,D,O
Gerontological Nursing	M,D,O
Health Services Research	D
Medical Physics	D
Nursing Education	M,D,O
Nursing—General	M,D,O

UNIVERSITY OF MEDICINE AND DENTISTRY OF NEW JERSEY

Adult Nursing	M,D,O
Allied Health—General	M,D,O
Allopathic Medicine	P
Clinical Laboratory Sciences/Medical Technology	M,D
Dentistry	P,M,O
Epidemiology	M,D,O
Family Nurse Practitioner Studies	M,D,O
Health Education	M,D
Health Physics/ Radiological Health	M
Health Services Management and Hospital Administration	M
Kinesiology and Movement Studies	M,D
Medical Imaging	M
Nurse Anesthesia	M,D,O
Nurse Midwifery	M,O
Nursing Informatics	M
Nursing—General	M,O
Occupational Health Nursing	M,D,O
Oral and Dental Sciences	P,M,O
Osteopathic Medicine	P
Physical Therapy	M,D
Physician Assistant Studies	M
Public Health—General	M,D,O
Transcultural Nursing	D
Women's Health Nursing	M,D,O

UNIVERSITY OF MEMPHIS

Accounting	M,D
Adult Education	M,D
Business Administration and Management— General	M,D
Communication Disorders	M,D
Counselor Education	M,D
Curriculum and Instruction	M,D
Early Childhood Education	M,D
Education—General	M,D,O
Educational Leadership and Administration	M,D
Educational Measurement and Evaluation	M,D
Educational Media/ Instructional Technology	M,D
Educational Psychology	M,D
Elementary Education	M,D
English as a Second Language	M,D,O

*M—master's degree; P—first professional degree; D—doctorate; O—other advanced degree; *—Close-Up and/or Display*

Environmental and Occupational Health	M
Epidemiology	M
Exercise and Sports Science	M
Finance and Banking	M,D
Health Promotion	M
Health Services Management and Hospital Administration	M
Higher Education	M,D
International Business	M,D
Law	P
Leisure Studies	M
Management Information Systems	M,D
Marketing	M,D
Middle School Education	M,D
Music Education	M,D
Nonprofit Management	M
Nursing—General	M,O
Physical Education	M
Public Health—General	M
Reading Education	M,D
Real Estate	M,D
Secondary Education	M,D
Special Education	M,D
Supply Chain Management	M,D
Taxation	M

UNIVERSITY OF MIAMI

Accounting	M
Acute Care/Critical Care Nursing	M,D
Adult Nursing	M,D
Advertising and Public Relations	M,D
Allopathic Medicine	P
Athletic Training and Sports Medicine	M
Business Administration and Management— General	M
Counselor Education	M,O
Early Childhood Education	M,D,O
Education—General	M,D,O*
Educational Measurement and Evaluation	M,D
Environmental and Occupational Health	M
Epidemiology	D
Exercise and Sports Science	M,D
Family Nurse Practitioner Studies	M,D
Finance and Banking	M
Higher Education	M,D,O
International Business	M
Law	P,M
Management Information Systems	M
Marketing	M
Mathematics Education	D
Multilingual and Multicultural Education	D
Music Education	M,D,O
Nurse Anesthesia	M,D
Nurse Midwifery	M,D
Nursing—General	M,D
Physical Therapy	D
Public Health—General	M
Reading Education	D
Science Education	D
Special Education	D
Sports Management	M
Taxation	M

UNIVERSITY OF MICHIGAN

Acute Care/Critical Care Nursing	M
Adult Nursing	M,O
Allopathic Medicine	P
Business Administration and Management— General	D
Clinical Research	M
Community Health Nursing	M,O
Computer Education	M,D
Curriculum and Instruction	M,D
Dental Hygiene	M
Dentistry	P
Early Childhood Education	M,D
Education—General	M,D

Educational Leadership and Administration	M,D
Educational Measurement and Evaluation	M,D
Educational Media/ Instructional Technology	M,D
English as a Second Language	M,D
English Education	M,D
Environmental and Occupational Health	M,D
Epidemiology	M,D
Family Nurse Practitioner Studies	M,O
Foreign Languages Education	M,D
Foundations and Philosophy of Education	M,D
Gerontological Nursing	M
Health Physics/ Radiological Health	M,D,O
Health Promotion	M,D
Health Services Management and Hospital Administration	M,D
Higher Education	M,D
Industrial Hygiene	M,D
Information Studies	M,D
International Health	M,D
Kinesiology and Movement Studies	M,D
Law	P,M,D
Library Science	M,D
Mathematics Education	M,D
Medical/Surgical Nursing	M
Medicinal and Pharmaceutical Chemistry	D
Multilingual and Multicultural Education	M,D
Music Education	M,D,O
Nurse Midwifery	M,O
Nursing and Healthcare Administration	M
Nursing—General	M,D,O
Occupational Health Nursing	M,O
Oral and Dental Sciences	M,D
Pediatric Nursing	M,O
Pharmaceutical Administration	D
Pharmaceutical Sciences	D
Pharmacy	P
Psychiatric Nursing	M
Public Health—General	M,D
Reading Education	M,D
Real Estate	M,O
Science Education	M,D
Social Sciences Education	M,D
Social Work	M,D
Sports Management	M,D
Taxation	P,M,D

UNIVERSITY OF MICHIGAN–DEARBORN

Accounting	M
Business Administration and Management— General	M
Curriculum and Instruction	D
Education—General	M,D
Educational Leadership and Administration	M,D
Educational Measurement and Evaluation	M,O
Educational Psychology	D
Finance and Banking	M
International Business	M
Management Information Systems	M
Marketing	M
Nonprofit Management	M,O
Science Education	M
Special Education	M,D
Supply Chain Management	M
Urban Education	D

UNIVERSITY OF MICHIGAN–FLINT

Business Administration and Management— General	M
Education—General	M
Educational Media/ Instructional Technology	M
Elementary Education	M

Health Education	M
Nurse Anesthesia	M
Nursing—General	D
Physical Therapy	D
Reading Education	M
Special Education	M

UNIVERSITY OF MINNESOTA, DULUTH

Allopathic Medicine	P*
Business Administration and Management— General	M
Communication Disorders	M
Education—General	D
Music Education	M
Pharmacy	M,D
Social Work	M

UNIVERSITY OF MINNESOTA, TWIN CITIES CAMPUS

Accounting	M,D
Adult Education	M,D,O
Adult Nursing	M
Agricultural Education	M,D
Allopathic Medicine	P
Art Education	M,D,O
Business Administration and Management— General	M,D*
Business Education	M,D
Clinical Research	M
Communication Disorders	M,D
Community Health Nursing	M
Community Health	M
Counselor Education	M,D,O
Curriculum and Instruction	M,D,O
Dentistry	P
Early Childhood Education	M,D,O
Education of the Gifted	M,D,O
Education—General	M,D,O
Educational Leadership and Administration	M,D
Educational Measurement and Evaluation	M,D
Educational Media/ Instructional Technology	M,D,O
Educational Policy	M,D,O
Educational Psychology	M,D,O
Elementary Education	M,D,O
English as a Second Language	M
English Education	M
Environmental and Occupational Health	M,D,O
Environmental Education	M,D,O
Epidemiology	M,D
Exercise and Sports Science	M,D,O
Family Nurse Practitioner Studies	M
Finance and Banking	M,D
Foreign Languages Education	M
Foundations and Philosophy of Education	M,D,O
Gerontological Nursing	M
Health Services Management and Hospital Administration	M,D
Health Services Research	M,D
Higher Education	M,D
Human Resources Development	M,D,O
Human Resources Management	M,D
Industrial and Manufacturing Management	D
Industrial Hygiene	M,D
International and Comparative Education	M,D
International Health	M,D
Kinesiology and Movement Studies	M,D
Law	P,M
Leisure Studies	M,D
Logistics	D
Management Information Systems	M,D
Management Strategy and Policy	D
Marketing	M,D
Maternal and Child Health	M
Mathematics Education	M

Medical Physics	M,D*
Medicinal and Pharmaceutical Chemistry	M,D
Multilingual and Multicultural Education	M
Nurse Anesthesia	M
Nurse Midwifery	M
Nursing and Healthcare Administration	M
Nursing—General	M,D
Occupational Health Nursing	M,D
Oral and Dental Sciences	M,D,O
Pediatric Nursing	M
Pharmaceutical Administration	M,D
Pharmaceutical Sciences	M,D
Pharmacy	P,M,D
Physical Education	M,D,O
Physical Therapy	D
Psychiatric Nursing	M
Public Health—General	M,D,O
Reading Education	M,D,O
Recreation and Park Management	M,D
Science Education	M
Social Sciences Education	M
Social Work	M,D
Special Education	M,D,O
Sports Management	M,D,O
Student Affairs	M,D,O
Supply Chain Management	M
Taxation	M
Veterinary Medicine	P
Veterinary Sciences	M,D
Vocational and Technical Education	M,D,O
Women's Health Nursing	M

UNIVERSITY OF MISSISSIPPI

Accounting	M,D
Art Education	M
Business Administration and Management— General	M,D
Communication Disorders	M
Counselor Education	M,D,O
Curriculum and Instruction	M,D,O
Education—General	M,D,O
Educational Leadership and Administration	M,D,O
Exercise and Sports Science	M,D
Higher Education	M,D,O
Law	P
Legal and Justice Studies	M
Leisure Studies	M,D
Management Information Systems	M,D
Medicinal and Pharmaceutical Chemistry	M,D
Pharmaceutical Administration	M,D
Pharmaceutical Sciences	M,D
Pharmacy	P
Recreation and Park Management	M,D
Social Work	M
Student Affairs	M,D,O
Taxation	M,D

UNIVERSITY OF MISSISSIPPI MEDICAL CENTER

Allied Health—General	M
Allopathic Medicine	P
Clinical Laboratory Sciences/Medical Technology	M,D
Dentistry	P,M,D
Maternal and Child Health	M
Nursing—General	M,D
Occupational Therapy	M
Oral and Dental Sciences	M,D
Physical Therapy	M

UNIVERSITY OF MISSOURI

Accounting	M,D
Adult Education	M,D,O
Agricultural Education	M,D,O
Allopathic Medicine	P
Art Education	M,D,O

Business Administration and Management— General	M,D
Business Education	M,D,O
Communication Disorders	M
Curriculum and Instruction	M,D,O
Early Childhood Education	M,D,O
Education of the Gifted	M,D
Education—General	M,D,O
Educational Leadership and Administration	M,D,O
Educational Media/ Instructional Technology	M,D,O
Educational Psychology	M,D,O
Elementary Education	M,D,O
English Education	M,D,O
Exercise and Sports Science	M,D
Foreign Languages Education	M,D,O
Health Education	M,D,O
Health Physics/ Radiological Health	M,D
Health Services Management and Hospital Administration	M
Higher Education	M,D,O
Hospitality Management	M,D
Information Studies	M,D,O
Law	P,M
Library Science	M,D,O
Mathematics Education	M,D,O
Medical Physics	M,D
Music Education	M,D,O
Nursing—General	M,D
Occupational Therapy	M
Physical Therapy	M
Public Health—General	M
Reading Education	M,D,O
Recreation and Park Management	M
Science Education	M,D,O
Social Sciences Education	M,D,O
Social Work	M
Special Education	M,D
Veterinary Medicine	P
Veterinary Sciences	M,D
Vocational and Technical Education	M,D,O

UNIVERSITY OF MISSOURI–KANSAS CITY

Accounting	M,D
Adult Nursing	M,D
Allopathic Medicine	P
Business Administration and Management— General	M,D
Curriculum and Instruction	M,D,O
Dental Hygiene	P,M,D,O
Dentistry	P,M,D,O
Education—General	M,D,O
Educational Leadership and Administration	M,D,O
Entrepreneurship	M,D
Family Nurse Practitioner Studies	M,D
Law	P,M
Maternal and Child/ Neonatal Nursing	M,D
Music Education	M,D
Nursing and Healthcare Administration	M,D
Nursing Education	M,D
Nursing—General	M,D
Oral and Dental Sciences	P,M,D,O
Pediatric Nursing	M,D
Pharmaceutical Sciences	P,M,D
Pharmacy	P,M,D
Reading Education	M,D,O
Social Work	M
Special Education	M,D,O
Taxation	P,M
Women's Health Nursing	M,D

UNIVERSITY OF MISSOURI–ST. LOUIS

Accounting	M,O
Adult Education	M,D,O
Business Administration and Management— General	M,O
Counselor Education	M,D
Curriculum and Instruction	M,O

Early Childhood Education	M,O
Education—General	M,D,O
Educational Leadership and Administration	M,D,O
Educational Measurement and Evaluation	M,D,O
Educational Psychology	D,O
Elementary Education	M,O
English as a Second Language	M,O
Family Nurse Practitioner Studies	M,D,O
Finance and Banking	M,O
Health Services Management and Hospital Administration	M,O
Higher Education	M,D,O
Human Resources Development	M,O
Human Resources Management	M,O
Industrial and Manufacturing Management	M,O
Logistics	M,D,O
Management Information Systems	M,D
Marketing	M,O
Middle School Education	M,O
Music Education	M
Nonprofit Management	M,O
Nursing Education	M,D,O
Nursing—General	M,D,O
Optometry	P
Quantitative Analysis	M,O
Reading Education	M,O
Secondary Education	M,O
Social Work	M,O
Special Education	M,O
Supply Chain Management	M,D,O
Vision Sciences	M,D

UNIVERSITY OF MOBILE

Business Administration and Management— General	M
Education—General	M
Nursing—General	M

THE UNIVERSITY OF MONTANA

Accounting	M
Business Administration and Management— General	M
Counselor Education	M,D,O
Curriculum and Instruction	M,D
Education—General	M,D,O
Educational Leadership and Administration	M,D,O
English Education	M
Exercise and Sports Science	M
Health Education	M
Health Promotion	M
Law	P
Mathematics Education	M,D
Music Education	M
Pharmaceutical Sciences	M,D
Pharmacy	P,M,D
Physical Education	M
Physical Therapy	D
Public Health—General	M,O
Recreation and Park Management	M,D
Social Work	M

UNIVERSITY OF MONTEVALLO

Communication Disorders	M
Counselor Education	M
Education—General	M,O
Educational Leadership and Administration	M,O
Elementary Education	M
Secondary Education	M

UNIVERSITY OF NEBRASKA AT KEARNEY

Art Education	M
Business Administration and Management— General	M
Communication Disorders	M
Counselor Education	M,O

Curriculum and Instruction	M
Education—General	M,O
Educational Leadership and Administration	M,O
Educational Media/ Instructional Technology	M
Exercise and Sports Science	M
Foreign Languages Education	M
Music Education	M
Physical Education	M
Reading Education	M
Science Education	M
Special Education	M

UNIVERSITY OF NEBRASKA AT OMAHA

Accounting	M
Business Administration and Management— General	M
Communication Disorders	M
Counselor Education	M
Education—General	M,D,O
Educational Leadership and Administration	M,D,O
Educational Media/ Instructional Technology	M,O
Educational Psychology	M,D,O
Elementary Education	M
English as a Second Language	M,O
Foreign Languages Education	M
Health Education	M
Management Information Systems	M,D,O
Physical Education	M
Reading Education	M
Recreation and Park Management	M
Secondary Education	M
Social Work	M
Special Education	M
Urban Education	M,O

UNIVERSITY OF NEBRASKA–LINCOLN

Accounting	M,D
Actuarial Science	M
Adult Education	M,D,O
Advertising and Public Relations	M,D
Agricultural Education	M
Business Administration and Management— General	M,D
Communication Disorders	M,D
Curriculum and Instruction	M,D,O
Distance Education Development	M
Early Childhood Education	M,D
Educational Leadership and Administration	M,D,O
Educational Measurement and Evaluation	M,D,O
Educational Psychology	M,D,O
Exercise and Sports Science	M,D
Finance and Banking	M,D
Health Education	M
Health Promotion	M,D
Home Economics Education	M,D
Law	P,M
Legal and Justice Studies	M
Management Information Systems	M
Marketing	M,D
Music Education	M
Special Education	M,D,O
Veterinary Sciences	M,D
Vocational and Technical Education	M,D,O

UNIVERSITY OF NEBRASKA MEDICAL CENTER

Allied Health—General	M,D,O
Allopathic Medicine	P,O
Clinical Laboratory Sciences/Medical Technology	M,O
Dentistry	P,M,D,O

Nursing—General	M,D
Perfusion	M
Pharmaceutical Sciences	M,D
Pharmacy	P
Physical Therapy	D
Physician Assistant Studies	M
Public Health—General	M

UNIVERSITY OF NEVADA, LAS VEGAS

Accounting	M
Allied Health—General	M,D
Business Administration and Management— General	M
Community Health	M,O
Counselor Education	M,O
Curriculum and Instruction	M,D
Early Childhood Education	M,D,O
Education—General	M,D,O
Educational Leadership and Administration	M,D
Educational Media/ Instructional Technology	M,D,O
Educational Psychology	M,D,O
Environmental and Occupational Health	M
Exercise and Sports Science	M
Family Nurse Practitioner Studies	M,D,O
Health Physics/ Radiological Health	M
Health Promotion	M
Health Services Management and Hospital Administration	M
Hospitality Management	M,D,O
Kinesiology and Movement Studies	M
Law	P
Leisure Studies	M
Management Information Systems	M
Nonprofit Management	M,D,O
Nursing Education	M,D,O
Nursing—General	M,D,O
Physical Education	M,D
Physical Therapy	D
Social Work	M,O
Special Education	M,D,O
Sports Management	M,D

UNIVERSITY OF NEVADA, RENO

Accounting	M
Business Administration and Management— General	M
Communication Disorders	M,D
Counselor Education	M,D,O
Curriculum and Instruction	D
Education—General	M,D,O
Educational Leadership and Administration	M,D,O
Educational Psychology	M,D,O
Elementary Education	M
English as a Second Language	M
Environmental and Occupational Health	M,D
Finance and Banking	M
Foreign Languages Education	M
Legal and Justice Studies	M,D
Management Information Systems	M
Mathematics Education	M
Nursing—General	M
Public Health—General	M,D
Reading Education	M,D
Secondary Education	M
Social Work	M
Special Education	M,D

UNIVERSITY OF NEW BRUNSWICK FREDERICTON

Business Administration and Management— General	M
Education—General	M,D
Entrepreneurship	M
Exercise and Sports Science	M

*M—master's degree; P—first professional degree; D—doctorate; O—other advanced degree; *—Close-Up and/or Display*

Health Services Research	M
Law	P
Marketing	M,D
Nursing Education	M
Nursing—General	M
Physical Education	M
Recreation and Park Management	M
Sports Management	M

UNIVERSITY OF NEW BRUNSWICK SAINT JOHN

Business Administration and Management—General	M
Electronic Commerce	M
International Business	M

UNIVERSITY OF NEW ENGLAND

Curriculum and Instruction	M
Education—General	M
Educational Leadership and Administration	M,O
Educational Measurement and Evaluation	M
Nurse Anesthesia	M
Occupational Therapy	M
Osteopathic Medicine	P
Pharmacy	P
Physical Therapy	D
Physician Assistant Studies	M
Public Health—General	M,O
Reading Education	M
Social Work	M,O

UNIVERSITY OF NEW HAMPSHIRE

Accounting	M
Business Administration and Management—General	M,O
Communication Disorders	M,O
Counselor Education	M,O
Early Childhood Education	M
Education—General	M,D,O
Educational Leadership and Administration	M,O
Elementary Education	M
English Education	M,D
Environmental Education	M
Higher Education	M
Kinesiology and Movement Studies	M
Legal and Justice Studies	M
Logistics	M,D
Mathematics Education	M,D,O
Music Education	M
Nursing—General	M,O
Occupational Therapy	M,O
Public Health—General	M,O
Reading Education	M
Recreation and Park Management	M
Science Education	M,D
Secondary Education	M,O
Social Work	M,O
Special Education	M,O

UNIVERSITY OF NEW HAVEN

Accounting	M,O
Business Administration and Management—General	M,O
Education—General	M
Environmental and Occupational Health	M,O
Facilities Management	M,O
Finance and Banking	M,O
Health Services Management and Hospital Administration	M,O
Human Resources Management	M,O
Industrial Hygiene	M
International Business	M,O
Management Strategy and Policy	M,O
Marketing	M,O
Organizational Management	M,O
Sports Management	M,O
Taxation	M

UNIVERSITY OF NEW MEXICO

Accounting	M

Allopathic Medicine	P
Art Education	M
Business Administration and Management—General	M
Clinical Laboratory Sciences/Medical Technology	M
Communication Disorders	M
Counselor Education	M,D
Dental Hygiene	M
Early Childhood Education	D
Education—General	M
Educational Leadership and Administration	M,D,O
Educational Media/Instructional Technology	M,D,O
Educational Psychology	M,D
Elementary Education	M
Exercise and Sports Science	D
Finance and Banking	M
Foundations and Philosophy of Education	M,D
Health Education	M
Human Resources Management	M
International Business	M
Law	P
Management Information Systems	M
Management Strategy and Policy	M
Marketing	M
Multilingual and Multicultural Education	D
Nursing—General	M,D
Occupational Therapy	M
Organizational Management	M
Pharmaceutical Sciences	M,D
Pharmacy	P
Physical Education	M,D
Physical Therapy	M
Public Health—General	M
Secondary Education	M
Special Education	M,D,O
Taxation	M

UNIVERSITY OF NEW ORLEANS

Accounting	M
Business Administration and Management—General	M
Counselor Education	M,D,O
Curriculum and Instruction	M,D,O
Education—General	M,D,O
Educational Leadership and Administration	M,D,O
Finance and Banking	M,D
Health Services Management and Hospital Administration	M
Hospitality Management	M
Special Education	M,D,O
Taxation	M
Travel and Tourism	M

UNIVERSITY OF NORTH ALABAMA

Business Administration and Management—General	M
Counselor Education	M
Education—General	M,O
Educational Leadership and Administration	O
Elementary Education	M,O
Nursing—General	M
Secondary Education	M
Special Education	M

THE UNIVERSITY OF NORTH CAROLINA AT CHAPEL HILL

Accounting	M,D
Adult Nursing	M,D,O
Allied Health—General	M,D
Allopathic Medicine	P
Athletic Training and Sports Medicine	M
Business Administration and Management—General	M,D
Communication Disorders	M,D
Community Health Nursing	M

Counselor Education	M
Curriculum and Instruction	M,D
Dental Hygiene	M,D
Dentistry	P
Early Childhood Education	M,D
Education—General	M,D
Educational Leadership and Administration	M,D
Educational Measurement and Evaluation	M,D
Educational Psychology	M,D
English as a Second Language	M
English Education	M
Environmental and Occupational Health	M,D
Epidemiology	M,D
Exercise and Sports Science	M
Family Nurse Practitioner Studies	M,D,O
Finance and Banking	D
Foreign Languages Education	M
Health Education	M,D
Health Promotion	M
Health Services Management and Hospital Administration	M,D
Industrial Hygiene	M,D
Information Studies	M,D,O
Kinesiology and Movement Studies	M,D
Law	P
Leisure Studies	M
Library Science	M,D,O
Management Information Systems	D
Management Strategy and Policy	D
Marketing	D
Maternal and Child Health	M,D
Mathematics Education	M
Music Education	M
Nursing and Healthcare Administration	M,D,O
Nursing—General	M,D,O
Occupational Health Nursing	M
Occupational Therapy	M,D
Oral and Dental Sciences	M,D
Organizational Behavior	D
Pediatric Nursing	M,D,O
Pharmaceutical Sciences	M,D
Physical Education	M
Physical Therapy	M,D
Psychiatric Nursing	M,D,O
Public Health—General	M,D
Reading Education	M,D
Recreation and Park Management	M
Science Education	M
Secondary Education	M
Social Sciences Education	M
Social Work	M,D
Sports Management	M
Women's Health Nursing	M,D,O

THE UNIVERSITY OF NORTH CAROLINA AT CHARLOTTE

Accounting	M
Adult Education	D
Adult Nursing	M
Art Education	M
Business Administration and Management—General	M,D
Counselor Education	M,D
Curriculum and Instruction	M,D,O
Education of the Gifted	M,D
Education—General	M
Educational Leadership and Administration	M,D,O
Educational Media/Instructional Technology	M,D,O
Elementary Education	M
English as a Second Language	M
English Education	M
Exercise and Sports Science	M
Foreign Languages Education	M
Health Services Management and Hospital Administration	M

Health Services Research	D
Kinesiology and Movement Studies	M
Marketing	M
Mathematics Education	M
Middle School Education	M
Music Education	M
Nurse Anesthesia	M
Nursing—General	M
Public Health—General	M
Reading Education	M
Secondary Education	M
Social Work	M
Special Education	M,D
Sports Management	M

THE UNIVERSITY OF NORTH CAROLINA AT GREENSBORO

Accounting	M,O
Adult Education	M,D,O
Adult Nursing	M,D,O
Business Administration and Management—General	M,O
Communication Disorders	M,D
Community Health	M,D
Counselor Education	M,D,O
Curriculum and Instruction	M,D,O
Early Childhood Education	M,D,O
Education—General	M,D,O
Educational Leadership and Administration	M,D,O
Educational Measurement and Evaluation	D
Educational Media/Instructional Technology	M,D,O
Elementary Education	D
English as a Second Language	M,D,O
English Education	M,D
Exercise and Sports Science	M,D
Finance and Banking	M,O
Foreign Languages Education	M,D,O
Gerontological Nursing	M,D,O
Higher Education	D
Information Studies	M
Library Science	M
Management Information Systems	M,D,O
Marketing	M,D
Mathematics Education	M,D,O
Middle School Education	M,D,O
Multilingual and Multicultural Education	M,D,O
Music Education	M,D
Nonprofit Management	M,O
Nurse Anesthesia	M,D,O
Nursing and Healthcare Administration	M,D,O
Nursing Education	M,D,O
Nursing—General	M,D,O
Reading Education	M,D,O
Recreation and Park Management	M
Science Education	M,D,O
Social Sciences Education	M,D,O
Social Work	M
Special Education	M,D,O
Supply Chain Management	M,D,O
Taxation	M,O

THE UNIVERSITY OF NORTH CAROLINA AT PEMBROKE

Art Education	M
Business Administration and Management—General	M
Counselor Education	M
Education—General	M
Educational Leadership and Administration	M
Elementary Education	M
English Education	M
Mathematics Education	M
Middle School Education	M
Music Education	M
Physical Education	M
Reading Education	M
Science Education	M
Social Sciences Education	M

THE UNIVERSITY OF NORTH CAROLINA WILMINGTON

Accounting	M

Business Administration and Management—General M
Curriculum and Instruction M
Education—General M,D
Educational Leadership and Administration M,D
Educational Media/Instructional Technology M
Elementary Education M
Environmental Education M
Family Nurse Practitioner Studies M
Middle School Education M
Nursing Education M
Nursing—General M
Reading Education M
Social Work M

UNIVERSITY OF NORTH DAKOTA

Accounting M
Allopathic Medicine P
Business Administration and Management—General M
Clinical Laboratory Sciences/Medical Technology M
Communication Disorders M,D
Early Childhood Education M
Education—General M,D,O
Educational Leadership and Administration M,D,O
Educational Measurement and Evaluation D
Educational Media/Instructional Technology M
Elementary Education M,D
Kinesiology and Movement Studies M
Law P
Music Education M,D
Nursing—General M,D
Occupational Therapy M
Physical Therapy M,D
Physician Assistant Studies M
Reading Education M
Secondary Education D
Social Work M
Special Education M,D

UNIVERSITY OF NORTHERN BRITISH COLUMBIA

Community Health M,D,O
Education—General M,D,O
Social Work M,D,O

UNIVERSITY OF NORTHERN COLORADO

Communication Disorders M,D
Counselor Education M,D
Early Childhood Education M,D
Education—General M,D,O
Educational Leadership and Administration M,D,O
Educational Measurement and Evaluation M,D
Educational Media/Instructional Technology M,D
Educational Psychology M,D
Exercise and Sports Science M,D
Family Nurse Practitioner Studies M,D
Foreign Languages Education M
Health Education M
Higher Education D
Library Science M
Mathematics Education M,D
Music Education M,D
Nursing Education M,D
Nursing—General M,D
Physical Education M,D
Public Health—General M
Reading Education M
Science Education M,D
Special Education M,D
Sports Management M,D
Student Affairs D

UNIVERSITY OF NORTHERN IOWA

Accounting M

Art Education M
Business Administration and Management—General M
Communication Disorders M
Community Health M,D
Counselor Education M,D
Curriculum and Instruction M,D
Early Childhood Education M
Education—General M,D,O
Educational Leadership and Administration M,D
Educational Media/Instructional Technology M
Educational Psychology M,O
Elementary Education M
English as a Second Language M
Health Education M,D
Higher Education M
Leisure Studies M,D
Mathematics Education M
Middle School Education M
Music Education M
Nonprofit Management M
Physical Education M
Reading Education M
Rehabilitation Sciences M,D
Science Education M
Social Work M
Special Education M,D
Sports Management M,D
Student Affairs M
Vocational and Technical Education M,D

UNIVERSITY OF NORTH FLORIDA

Accounting M
Adult Education M
Allied Health—General M,D,O
Business Administration and Management—General M
Communication Disorders M
Community Health M,O
Counselor Education M
Education—General M,D
Educational Leadership and Administration M,D
Educational Media/Instructional Technology M,D
Elementary Education M
English as a Second Language M
Health Services Management and Hospital Administration M,O
Health Services Research M,O
Nursing—General M,D,O
Physical Therapy D
Public Health—General M,O
Reading Education M
Secondary Education M
Special Education M

UNIVERSITY OF NORTH TEXAS

Accounting M,D
Art Education M,D,O
Business Administration and Management—General M,D
Communication Disorders M,D
Community Health M,D
Computer Education M,D
Counselor Education M,D,O
Curriculum and Instruction M,D
Early Childhood Education M,D,O
Education—General M,D,O
Educational Leadership and Administration M,D
Educational Measurement and Evaluation D
Educational Media/Instructional Technology M,D
Educational Psychology M
Finance and Banking M,D
Higher Education M,D,O
Hospitality Management M
Information Studies M,D
International and Comparative Education M,D
Kinesiology and Movement Studies M
Leisure Studies M,O

Library Science M,D
Management Information Systems M,D
Marketing D
Music Education M,D
Quantitative Analysis M,D
Reading Education M,D
Real Estate M,D
Recreation and Park Management M,O
Rehabilitation Sciences M
Secondary Education M,D
Special Education M,D,O
Taxation M,D
Vocational and Technical Education M,D

UNIVERSITY OF NORTH TEXAS HEALTH SCIENCE CENTER AT FORT WORTH

Community Health M,D
Environmental and Occupational Health M,D
Epidemiology M,D
Health Services Management and Hospital Administration M,D
Osteopathic Medicine P,M
Physician Assistant Studies M
Public Health—General M,D
Science Education M,D

UNIVERSITY OF NOTRE DAME

Accounting M
Business Administration and Management—General M
Education—General M
Law P,M,D
Nonprofit Management M
Taxation M

UNIVERSITY OF OKLAHOMA

Accounting M
Adult Education M,D
Advertising and Public Relations M
Business Administration and Management—General M,D*
Counselor Education M
Curriculum and Instruction M,D,O
Early Childhood Education M,D,O
Education—General M,D,O
Educational Leadership and Administration M,D
Educational Psychology M,D
Elementary Education M,D,O
English Education M,D,O
Environmental and Occupational Health M,D
Exercise and Sports Science M,D
Foundations and Philosophy of Education M,D
Health Services Management and Hospital Administration M
Higher Education M,D
Human Services M
Information Studies M,O
International Business M
Law P
Library Science M,O
Management Information Systems M
Management Strategy and Policy M
Mathematics Education M,D,O
Multilingual and Multicultural Education M,D,O
Music Education M,D
Organizational Behavior M
Reading Education M,D,O
Science Education M,D,O
Secondary Education M,D,O
Social Sciences Education M,D,O
Social Work M
Special Education M,D

UNIVERSITY OF OKLAHOMA HEALTH SCIENCES CENTER

Allied Health—General M,D,O

Allopathic Medicine P
Communication Disorders M,D,O
Dentistry P,O
Environmental and Occupational Health M,D
Epidemiology M,D
Health Education D
Health Physics/Radiological Health M,D
Health Promotion M,D
Health Services Management and Hospital Administration M,D
Medical Physics M,D
Nursing—General M
Occupational Therapy M
Oral and Dental Sciences M
Pharmaceutical Sciences M,D
Pharmacy P
Physical Therapy M
Public Health—General M
Reading Education M,D,O
Rehabilitation Sciences M
Special Education M,D,O

UNIVERSITY OF OKLAHOMA—TULSA

Allopathic Medicine P
Community Health P
Educational Leadership and Administration D
Health Services Management and Hospital Administration M
Music Education O
Nursing—General M,O
Organizational Management M
Physician Assistant Studies M
Public Health—General M

UNIVERSITY OF OREGON

Accounting M,D
Business Administration and Management—General M,D
Education—General M,D
Finance and Banking D
Law P,M
Management Information Systems M
Marketing D
Music Education M,D
Quantitative Analysis M

UNIVERSITY OF OTTAWA

Allopathic Medicine P,M,D
Business Administration and Management—General M*
Communication Disorders M
Community Health M,D,O
Education—General M,D,O
Electronic Commerce M,D,O
Epidemiology M
Finance and Banking D,O
Health Services Management and Hospital Administration M
Health Services Research D,O
Kinesiology and Movement Studies M
Law M,D
Music Education M,O
Nursing—General M,D,O
Project Management M,O
Public Health—General D
Rehabilitation Sciences M
Social Work M

UNIVERSITY OF PENNSYLVANIA

Accounting M,D
Acute Care/Critical Care Nursing M
Adult Nursing M
Allopathic Medicine P,O
Business Administration and Management—General M,D
Dentistry P
Education—General M,D
Educational Leadership and Administration M,D

Educational Measurement and Evaluation	M,D
Educational Media/ Instructional Technology	M
Educational Policy	M,D
Elementary Education	M
English as a Second Language	M,D
Epidemiology	M,D
Family Nurse Practitioner Studies	M,O
Finance and Banking	M,D
Health Services Management and Hospital Administration	M,D
Insurance	M,D
International and Comparative Education	M,D
International Business	M
Law	P,M,D
Legal and Justice Studies	M,D
Management Information Systems	M,D
Marketing	M,D
Maternal and Child/ Neonatal Nursing	M,O
Medical Physics	M,D
Multilingual and Multicultural Education	M,D
Nurse Anesthesia	M
Nurse Midwifery	M
Nursing and Healthcare Administration	M,D
Nursing—General	M,D,O
Occupational Health Nursing	M
Oncology Nursing	M
Organizational Behavior	M
Organizational Management	M
Pediatric Nursing	M
Psychiatric Nursing	M
Reading Education	M,D
Real Estate	M,D
Secondary Education	M
Social Work	M,D*
Veterinary Medicine	P
Women's Health Nursing	M

UNIVERSITY OF PHOENIX

Accounting	M
Adult Education	M
Business Administration and Management— General	M,D
Community Health	M
Computer Education	M
Curriculum and Instruction	M,D
Early Childhood Education	M
Education—General	M,D
Educational Leadership and Administration	M,D
Educational Media/ Instructional Technology	M,D
Elementary Education	M
English as a Second Language	M
English Education	M
Health Services Management and Hospital Administration	D
Higher Education	D
Human Resources Management	M
Management Information Systems	M
Marketing	M
Mathematics Education	M
Nursing—General	M,D
Organizational Management	D
Secondary Education	M
Special Education	M

UNIVERSITY OF PHOENIX– ATLANTA CAMPUS

Accounting	M
Business Administration and Management— General	M
Health Services Management and Hospital Administration	M
Human Resources Management	M
International Business	M

Management Information Systems	M
Marketing	M
Nursing Education	M
Nursing—General	M

UNIVERSITY OF PHOENIX– AUGUSTA CAMPUS

Accounting	M
Business Administration and Management— General	M
Health Services Management and Hospital Administration	M
Human Resources Management	M
International Business	M
Management Information Systems	M
Marketing	M
Nursing Education	M
Nursing—General	M

UNIVERSITY OF PHOENIX–AUSTIN CAMPUS

Accounting	M
Business Administration and Management— General	M
Curriculum and Instruction	M
Education—General	M
Electronic Commerce	M
Health Services Management and Hospital Administration	M
Human Resources Management	M
International Business	M
Management Information Systems	M
Marketing	M

UNIVERSITY OF PHOENIX–BAY AREA CAMPUS

Accounting	M
Adult Education	M
Business Administration and Management— General	M
Curriculum and Instruction	M
Education—General	M
Electronic Commerce	M
Elementary Education	M
Family Nurse Practitioner Studies	M
Health Services Management and Hospital Administration	M
Human Resources Management	M
International Business	M
Management Information Systems	M
Marketing	M
Nursing Education	M
Nursing—General	M
Secondary Education	M

UNIVERSITY OF PHOENIX– BIRMINGHAM CAMPUS

Accounting	M
Business Administration and Management— General	M
Community Health	M
Health Services Management and Hospital Administration	M
Human Resources Management	M
International Business	M
Management Information Systems	M
Marketing	M
Nursing Education	M
Nursing—General	M

UNIVERSITY OF PHOENIX– BOSTON CAMPUS

Business Administration and Management— General	M
International Business	M

Management Information Systems	M

UNIVERSITY OF PHOENIX– CENTRAL FLORIDA CAMPUS

Accounting	M
Business Administration and Management— General	M
Computer Education	M
Curriculum and Instruction	M
Early Childhood Education	M
Education—General	M
Educational Leadership and Administration	M
Elementary Education	M
Health Services Management and Hospital Administration	M
Human Resources Management	M
International Business	M
Management Information Systems	M
Marketing	M
Mathematics Education	M
Nursing Education	M
Nursing—General	M
Secondary Education	M

UNIVERSITY OF PHOENIX– CENTRAL MASSACHUSETTS CAMPUS

Business Administration and Management— General	M
Education—General	M

UNIVERSITY OF PHOENIX– CENTRAL VALLEY CAMPUS

Accounting	M
Business Administration and Management— General	M
Community Health	M
Computer Education	M
Curriculum and Instruction	M
Education—General	M
Elementary Education	M
Health Services Management and Hospital Administration	M
Human Resources Management	M
International Business	M
Management Information Systems	M
Marketing	M
Nursing—General	M
Secondary Education	M

UNIVERSITY OF PHOENIX– CHARLOTTE CAMPUS

Accounting	M
Allied Health—General	M
Business Administration and Management— General	M
International Business	M
Management Information Systems	M
Nursing—General	M

UNIVERSITY OF PHOENIX– CHATTANOOGA CAMPUS

Accounting	M
Business Administration and Management— General	M
Community Health	M
Curriculum and Instruction	M
Education—General	M
Educational Leadership and Administration	M
Elementary Education	M
Health Services Management and Hospital Administration	M
Human Resources Management	M
International Business	M
Management Information Systems	M
Marketing	M
Secondary Education	M

UNIVERSITY OF PHOENIX– CHEYENNE CAMPUS

Business Administration and Management— General	M
Health Services Management and Hospital Administration	M
Human Resources Management	M
International Business	M
Management Information Systems	M
Marketing	M
Nursing Education	M
Nursing—General	M

UNIVERSITY OF PHOENIX– CHICAGO CAMPUS

Business Administration and Management— General	M
Electronic Commerce	M
Human Resources Management	M
International Business	M
Management Information Systems	M

UNIVERSITY OF PHOENIX– CINCINNATI CAMPUS

Accounting	M
Business Administration and Management— General	M
Electronic Commerce	M
Health Services Management and Hospital Administration	M
Human Resources Management	M
International Business	M
Management Information Systems	M
Marketing	M
Nursing—General	M

UNIVERSITY OF PHOENIX– CLEVELAND CAMPUS

Accounting	M
Business Administration and Management— General	M
Health Services Management and Hospital Administration	M
Human Resources Management	M
International Business	M
Management Information Systems	M
Marketing	M
Nursing—General	M

UNIVERSITY OF PHOENIX– COLUMBIA CAMPUS

Business Administration and Management— General	M

UNIVERSITY OF PHOENIX– COLUMBUS GEORGIA CAMPUS

Accounting	M
Business Administration and Management— General	M
Electronic Commerce	M
Health Services Management and Hospital Administration	M
Human Resources Management	M
International Business	M
Management Information Systems	M
Marketing	M
Nursing—General	M

UNIVERSITY OF PHOENIX– COLUMBUS OHIO CAMPUS

Accounting	M
Business Administration and Management— General	M

Management Information
  Systems | M
Marketing | M
Secondary Education | M

UNIVERSITY OF PHOENIX–METRO DETROIT CAMPUS

Accounting | M
Business Administration
  and Management—
    General | M
Education—General | M
Educational Leadership
  and Administration | M
Elementary Education | M
Human Resources
  Management | M
International Business | M
Management Information
  Systems | M
Marketing | M
Nursing Education | M
Nursing—General | M
Secondary Education | M
Special Education | M

UNIVERSITY OF PHOENIX–MINNEAPOLIS/ST. LOUIS PARK CAMPUS

Accounting | M
Business Administration
  and Management—
    General | M
Family Nurse Practitioner
  Studies | M
Health Services
  Management and
  Hospital Administration | M
Human Resources
  Management | M
International Business | M
Marketing | M
Nursing Education | M
Nursing—General | M

UNIVERSITY OF PHOENIX–NASHVILLE CAMPUS

Business Administration
  and Management—
    General | M
Curriculum and Instruction | M
Education—General | M
Educational Leadership
  and Administration | M
Elementary Education | M
Health Services
  Management and
  Hospital Administration | M
Human Resources
  Management | M
Management Information
  Systems | M
Secondary Education | M

UNIVERSITY OF PHOENIX–NEW MEXICO CAMPUS

Accounting | M
Business Administration
  and Management—
    General | M
Counselor Education | M
Curriculum and Instruction | M
Education—General | M
Educational Leadership
  and Administration | M
Electronic Commerce | M
Elementary Education | M
Health Services
  Management and
  Hospital Administration | M
Human Resources
  Management | M
International Business | M
Management Information
  Systems | M
Marketing | M
Nursing Education | M
Nursing—General | M
Secondary Education | M

UNIVERSITY OF PHOENIX–NORTHERN NEVADA CAMPUS

Accounting | M

Business Administration
  and Management—
    General | M
Curriculum and Instruction | M
Education—General | M
Educational Leadership
  and Administration | M
Elementary Education | M
Health Services
  Management and
  Hospital Administration | M
Human Resources
  Management | M
International Business | M
Management Information
  Systems | M
Marketing | M
Nursing Education | M
Nursing—General | M
Secondary Education | M

UNIVERSITY OF PHOENIX–NORTHERN VIRGINIA CAMPUS

Accounting | M
Business Administration
  and Management—
    General | M
Education—General | M
Educational Leadership
  and Administration | M
Electronic Commerce | M
Health Services
  Management and
  Hospital Administration | M
Human Resources
  Management | M
International Business | M
Management Information
  Systems | M
Marketing | M
Nursing—General | M

UNIVERSITY OF PHOENIX–NORTH FLORIDA CAMPUS

Accounting | M
Business Administration
  and Management—
    General | M
Computer Education | M
Curriculum and Instruction | M
Early Childhood Education | M
Education—General | M
Educational Leadership
  and Administration | M
Elementary Education | M
Health Services
  Management and
  Hospital Administration | M
Human Resources
  Management | M
International Business | M
Management Information
  Systems | M
Marketing | M
Mathematics Education | M
Nursing Education | M
Nursing—General | M
Secondary Education | M

UNIVERSITY OF PHOENIX–NORTHWEST ARKANSAS CAMPUS

Accounting | M
Business Administration
  and Management—
    General | M
Health Services
  Management and
  Hospital Administration | M
Human Resources
  Management | M
International Business | M
Management Information
  Systems | M
Marketing | M
Nursing Education | M
Nursing—General | M

UNIVERSITY OF PHOENIX–OKLAHOMA CITY CAMPUS

Accounting | M
Business Administration
  and Management—
    General | M
Electronic Commerce | M

Health Services
  Management and
  Hospital Administration | M
Human Resources
  Management | M
International Business | M
Management Information
  Systems | M
Marketing | M
Nursing—General | M

UNIVERSITY OF PHOENIX–OMAHA CAMPUS

Accounting | M
Adult Education | M
Business Administration
  and Management—
    General | M
Computer Education | M
Curriculum and Instruction | M
Education—General | M
Educational Leadership
  and Administration | M
Elementary Education | M
English as a Second
  Language | M
English Education | M
Health Services
  Management and
  Hospital Administration | M
Human Resources
  Management | M
International Business | M
Management Information
  Systems | M
Marketing | M
Mathematics Education | M
Secondary Education | M
Special Education | M

UNIVERSITY OF PHOENIX–OREGON CAMPUS

Accounting | M
Business Administration
  and Management—
    General | M
Curriculum and Instruction | M
Early Childhood Education | M
Education—General | M
Elementary Education | M
Health Services
  Management and
  Hospital Administration | M
Human Resources
  Management | M
International Business | M
Management Information
  Systems | M
Marketing | M
Middle School Education | M
Secondary Education | M

UNIVERSITY OF PHOENIX–PHILADELPHIA CAMPUS

Accounting | M
Business Administration
  and Management—
    General | M
Health Services
  Management and
  Hospital Administration | M
Human Resources
  Management | M
International Business | M
Management Information
  Systems | M
Marketing | M
Nursing Education | M
Nursing—General | M

UNIVERSITY OF PHOENIX–PHOENIX CAMPUS

Education—General | M
Educational Leadership
  and Administration | M
Elementary Education | M
Health Education | M
Health Services
  Management and
  Hospital Administration | M
Nursing Education | M
Nursing—General | M
Secondary Education | M
Special Education | M

UNIVERSITY OF PHOENIX–PITTSBURGH CAMPUS

Accounting | M
Business Administration
  and Management—
    General | M
Electronic Commerce | M
Health Services
  Management and
  Hospital Administration | M
Human Resources
  Management | M
International Business | M
Management Information
  Systems | M
Marketing | M
Nursing Education | M

UNIVERSITY OF PHOENIX–PUERTO RICO CAMPUS

Accounting | M
Business Administration
  and Management—
    General | M
Early Childhood Education | M
Education—General | M
Educational Leadership
  and Administration | M
Health Services
  Management and
  Hospital Administration | M
Human Resources
  Management | M
International Business | M
Marketing | M

UNIVERSITY OF PHOENIX–RALEIGH CAMPUS

Accounting | M
Business Administration
  and Management—
    General | M
Electronic Commerce | M
Health Services
  Management and
  Hospital Administration | M
Human Resources
  Management | M
International Business | M
Management Information
  Systems | M
Marketing | M

UNIVERSITY OF PHOENIX–RICHMOND CAMPUS

Accounting | M
Business Administration
  and Management—
    General | M
Curriculum and Instruction | M
Educational Leadership
  and Administration | M
Health Services
  Management and
  Hospital Administration | M
Human Resources
  Management | M
Human Services | M
International Business | M
Management Information
  Systems | M
Marketing | M
Nursing Education | M
Nursing—General | M

UNIVERSITY OF PHOENIX–SACRAMENTO VALLEY CAMPUS

Accounting | M
Adult Education | M,O
Business Administration
  and Management—
    General | M
Curriculum and Instruction | M,O
Education—General | M,O
Elementary Education | M,O
Family Nurse Practitioner
  Studies | M
Health Services
  Management and
  Hospital Administration | M
Human Resources
  Management | M
International Business | M
Management Information
  Systems | M

Health Services
  Management and
  Hospital Administration   M
Human Resources
  Management   M
International Business   M
Management Information
  Systems   M
Marketing   M
Nursing—General   M

UNIVERSITY OF PHOENIX–DALLAS CAMPUS

Accounting   M
Business Administration
  and Management—
  General   M
Curriculum and Instruction   M
Education—General   M
Electronic Commerce   M
Health Services
  Management and
  Hospital Administration   M
Human Resources
  Management   M
International Business   M
Management Information
  Systems   M
Marketing   M

UNIVERSITY OF PHOENIX–DENVER CAMPUS

Accounting   M
Business Administration
  and Management—
  General   M
Curriculum and Instruction   M
Education—General   M
Educational Leadership
  and Administration   M
Electronic Commerce   M
Elementary Education   M
Health Services
  Management and
  Hospital Administration   M
Human Resources
  Management   M
International Business   M
Management Information
  Systems   M
Marketing   M
Nursing—General   M
Secondary Education   M

UNIVERSITY OF PHOENIX–DES MOINES CAMPUS

Accounting   M
Business Administration
  and Management—
  General   M
Health Services
  Management and
  Hospital Administration   M
Human Resources
  Management   M
International Business   M
Management Information
  Systems   M
Marketing   M

UNIVERSITY OF PHOENIX–EASTERN WASHINGTON CAMPUS

Accounting   M
Business Administration
  and Management—
  General   M
Health Services
  Management and
  Hospital Administration   M
Human Resources
  Management   M
Management Information
  Systems   M
Marketing   M

UNIVERSITY OF PHOENIX–FAIRFIELD COUNTY CAMPUS

Business Administration
  and Management—
  General   M

UNIVERSITY OF PHOENIX–HARRISBURG CAMPUS

Accounting   M
Business Administration
  and Management—
  General   M
Health Services
  Management and
  Hospital Administration   M
Human Resources
  Management   M
International Business   M
Management Information
  Systems   M
Marketing   M
Nursing Education   M
Nursing—General   M

UNIVERSITY OF PHOENIX–HAWAII CAMPUS

Accounting   M
Business Administration
  and Management—
  General   M
Community Health   M
Curriculum and Instruction   M
Education—General   M
Educational Leadership
  and Administration   M
Elementary Education   M
Family Nurse Practitioner
  Studies   M
Health Services
  Management and
  Hospital Administration   M
Human Resources
  Management   M
International Business   M
Management Information
  Systems   M
Marketing   M
Nursing Education   M
Nursing—General   M
Secondary Education   M
Special Education   M

UNIVERSITY OF PHOENIX–HOUSTON CAMPUS

Accounting   M
Business Administration
  and Management—
  General   M
Curriculum and Instruction   M
Education—General   M
Electronic Commerce   M
Health Services
  Management and
  Hospital Administration   M
Human Resources
  Management   M
International Business   M
Management Information
  Systems   M
Marketing   M

UNIVERSITY OF PHOENIX–IDAHO CAMPUS

Accounting   M
Business Administration
  and Management—
  General   M
Curriculum and Instruction   M
Education—General   M
Educational Leadership
  and Administration   M
Elementary Education   M
Health Services
  Management and
  Hospital Administration   M
Human Resources
  Management   M
International Business   M
Management Information
  Systems   M
Marketing   M
Nursing Education   M
Nursing—General   M
Secondary Education   M

UNIVERSITY OF PHOENIX–INDIANAPOLIS CAMPUS

Accounting   M

Business Administration
  and Management—
  General   M
Education—General   M
Elementary Education   M
Health Services
  Management and
  Hospital Administration   M
Human Resources
  Management   M
International Business   M
Management Information
  Systems   M
Marketing   M
Nursing Education   M
Nursing—General   M
Secondary Education   M

UNIVERSITY OF PHOENIX–JERSEY CITY CAMPUS

Accounting   M
Business Administration
  and Management—
  General   M
Health Services
  Management and
  Hospital Administration   M
Human Resources
  Management   M
International Business   M
Management Information
  Systems   M
Marketing   M

UNIVERSITY OF PHOENIX–KANSAS CITY CAMPUS

Accounting   M
Business Administration
  and Management—
  General   M
Education—General   M
Educational Leadership
  and Administration   M
Health Services
  Management and
  Hospital Administration   M
Human Resources
  Management   M
International Business   M
Marketing   M
Nursing—General   M

UNIVERSITY OF PHOENIX–LAS VEGAS CAMPUS

Accounting   M
Allied Health—General   M
Business Administration
  and Management—
  General   M
Curriculum and Instruction   M
Education—General   M
Educational Leadership
  and Administration   M
Elementary Education   M
Health Services
  Management and
  Hospital Administration   M
Human Resources
  Management   M
International Business   M
Management Information
  Systems   M
Marketing   M
Nursing Education   M
Nursing—General   M

UNIVERSITY OF PHOENIX–LITTLE ROCK CAMPUS

Business Administration
  and Management—
  General   M

UNIVERSITY OF PHOENIX–LOUISIANA CAMPUS

Accounting   M
Business Administration
  and Management—
  General   M
Curriculum and Instruction   M
Early Childhood Education   M
Education—General   M

Health Services
  Management and
  Hospital Administration   M
Human Resources
  Management   M
International Business   M
Management Information
  Systems   M
Marketing   M
Nursing—General   M

UNIVERSITY OF PHOENIX–LOUISVILLE CAMPUS

Business Administration
  and Management—
  General   M
Electronic Commerce   M
Health Services
  Management and
  Hospital Administration   M

UNIVERSITY OF PHOENIX–MADISON CAMPUS

Accounting   M
Business Administration
  and Management—
  General   M
Health Services
  Management and
  Hospital Administration   M
Human Resources
  Management   M
International Business   M
Management Information
  Systems   M
Marketing   M

UNIVERSITY OF PHOENIX–MADISON CAMPUS

Accounting   M
Business Administration
  and Management—
  General   M
Electronic Commerce   M
Health Services
  Management and
  Hospital Administration   M
Human Resources
  Management   M
International Business   M
Management Information
  Systems   M
Marketing   M

UNIVERSITY OF PHOENIX–MARYLAND CAMPUS

Accounting   M
Business Administration
  and Management—
  General   M
Electronic Commerce   M
Health Services
  Management and
  Hospital Administration   M
Human Resources
  Management   M
Human Services   M
International Business   M
Management Information
  Systems   M
Marketing   M
Nursing Education   M
Nursing—General   M

UNIVERSITY OF PHOENIX–MEMPHIS CAMPUS

Accounting   M
Business Administration
  and Management—
  General   M
Curriculum and Instruction   M
Education—General   M
Educational Leadership
  and Administration   M
Electronic Commerce   M
Elementary Education   M
Health Services
  Management and
  Hospital Administration   M
Human Resources
  Management   M
International Business   M

*M—master's degree; P—first professional degree; D—doctorate; O—other advanced degree; *—Close-Up and / or Display*

Marketing	M
Nursing Education	M
Nursing—General	M
Secondary Education	M,O

UNIVERSITY OF PHOENIX–ST. LOUIS CAMPUS

Accounting	M
Business Administration and Management— General	M
Health Services Management and Hospital Administration	M
Human Resources Management	M
International Business	M
Management Information Systems	M
Marketing	M
Nursing—General	M

UNIVERSITY OF PHOENIX–SAN ANTONIO CAMPUS

Accounting	M
Business Administration and Management— General	M
Curriculum and Instruction	M
Electronic Commerce	M
Health Services Management and Hospital Administration	M
Human Resources Management	M
International Business	M
Management Information Systems	M
Marketing	M

UNIVERSITY OF PHOENIX–SAN DIEGO CAMPUS

Accounting	M
Business Administration and Management— General	M
Computer Education	M
Curriculum and Instruction	M
Education—General	M
Elementary Education	M
English as a Second Language	M
Health Services Management and Hospital Administration	M
Human Resources Management	M
International Business	M
Management Information Systems	M
Marketing	M
Nursing Education	M
Nursing—General	M
Secondary Education	M

UNIVERSITY OF PHOENIX–SAVANNAH CAMPUS

Accounting	M
Business Administration and Management— General	M
Health Services Management and Hospital Administration	M
Human Resources Management	M
International Business	M
Management Information Systems	M
Marketing	M
Nursing Education	M
Nursing—General	M

UNIVERSITY OF PHOENIX–SOUTHERN ARIZONA CAMPUS

Accounting	M
Adult Education	M,O
Business Administration and Management— General	M
Counselor Education	M,O
Curriculum and Instruction	M,O
Education—General	M,O

Educational Leadership and Administration	M,O
Educational Psychology	M,O
Elementary Education	M,O
Family Nurse Practitioner Studies	M,O
Health Services Management and Hospital Administration	M,O
Human Resources Management	M
International Business	M
Management Information Systems	M
Marketing	M
Secondary Education	M,O
Special Education	M,O

UNIVERSITY OF PHOENIX–SOUTHERN CALIFORNIA CAMPUS

Adult Education	M
Computer Education	M
Curriculum and Instruction	M
Early Childhood Education	M
Education—General	M
Educational Leadership and Administration	M
English as a Second Language	M
English Education	M
Family Nurse Practitioner Studies	M
Mathematics Education	M
Nursing Education	M
Nursing—General	M
Special Education	M

UNIVERSITY OF PHOENIX–SOUTHERN COLORADO CAMPUS

Accounting	M
Business Administration and Management— General	M
Curriculum and Instruction	M,O
Education—General	M,O
Educational Leadership and Administration	M,O
Elementary Education	M,O
Health Education	M
Health Services Management and Hospital Administration	M
Human Resources Management	M
International Business	M
Management Information Systems	M
Marketing	M
Nursing—General	M
Secondary Education	M,O

UNIVERSITY OF PHOENIX–SOUTH FLORIDA CAMPUS

Accounting	M
Business Administration and Management— General	M
Computer Education	M
Curriculum and Instruction	M
Early Childhood Education	M
Education—General	M
Educational Leadership and Administration	M
Elementary Education	M
Health Services Management and Hospital Administration	M
Human Resources Management	M
International Business	M
Management Information Systems	M
Marketing	M
Mathematics Education	M
Nursing Education	M
Nursing—General	M
Secondary Education	M

UNIVERSITY OF PHOENIX–SPRINGFIELD CAMPUS

Accounting	M
Business Administration and Management— General	M

Computer Education	M
Curriculum and Instruction	M
Education—General	M
Educational Leadership and Administration	M
English as a Second Language	M
English Education	M
Health Services Management and Hospital Administration	M
Human Resources Management	M
International Business	M
Management Information Systems	M
Marketing	M
Mathematics Education	M
Nursing—General	M

UNIVERSITY OF PHOENIX–TULSA CAMPUS

Accounting	M
Business Administration and Management— General	M
Health Services Management and Hospital Administration	M
Human Resources Management	M
International Business	M
Management Information Systems	M
Marketing	M
Nursing—General	M

UNIVERSITY OF PHOENIX–UTAH CAMPUS

Accounting	M
Business Administration and Management— General	M
Curriculum and Instruction	M
Education—General	M
Educational Leadership and Administration	M
Elementary Education	M
Health Services Management and Hospital Administration	M
Human Resources Management	M
International Business	M
Management Information Systems	M
Marketing	M
Nursing Education	M
Nursing—General	M
Secondary Education	M
Special Education	M

UNIVERSITY OF PHOENIX–VANCOUVER CAMPUS

Accounting	M
Business Administration and Management— General	M
Computer Education	M
Curriculum and Instruction	M
Education—General	M
Educational Leadership and Administration	M
Health Services Management and Hospital Administration	M
Human Resources Management	M
International Business	M
Management Information Systems	M
Marketing	M
Nursing—General	M

UNIVERSITY OF PHOENIX–WESTERN WASHINGTON CAMPUS

Accounting	M
Business Administration and Management— General	M
Health Services Management and Hospital Administration	M

Human Resources Management	M
International Business	M
Management Information Systems	M
Marketing	M
Nursing Education	M
Nursing—General	M

UNIVERSITY OF PHOENIX–WEST FLORIDA CAMPUS

Accounting	M
Business Administration and Management— General	M
Computer Education	M
Curriculum and Instruction	M
Early Childhood Education	M
Education—General	M
Educational Leadership and Administration	M
Educational Media/ Instructional Technology	M
Elementary Education	M
Health Services Management and Hospital Administration	M
Human Resources Management	M
International Business	M
Management Information Systems	M
Marketing	M
Mathematics Education	M
Nursing Education	M
Nursing—General	M
Secondary Education	M

UNIVERSITY OF PHOENIX–WICHITA CAMPUS

Business Administration and Management— General	M

UNIVERSITY OF PITTSBURGH

Accounting	M,D
Acute Care/Critical Care Nursing	M,D
Adult Nursing	M,D
Allopathic Medicine	P
Athletic Training and Sports Medicine	M
Bioethics	M
Business Administration and Management— General	M,D,O
Clinical Laboratory Sciences/Medical Technology	D
Clinical Research	M,D,O
Communication Disorders	M,D
Community Health	M,D,O
Dentistry	P,M,O
Early Childhood Education	M
Education—General	M,D
Educational Leadership and Administration	M,D
Educational Measurement and Evaluation	M,D
Educational Policy	D
Elementary Education	M
English as a Second Language	O
English Education	M,D
Environmental and Occupational Health	M,D,O
Environmental Law	M,O
Epidemiology	M,D
Exercise and Sports Science	M,D
Family Nurse Practitioner Studies	M,D
Finance and Banking	M,D,O
Foreign Languages Education	M,D
Foundations and Philosophy of Education	M,D
Health Education	M,D,O
Health Law	M,O
Health Promotion	M,D,O
Health Services Management and Hospital Administration	M,D,O
Higher Education	M,D

Human Resources Management	M,D,O
Information Studies	M,D,O
International and Comparative Education	M,D
International Business	M
International Health	M,D,O
Law	P,M,O
Legal and Justice Studies	M,O
Library Science	M,D,O
Management Information Systems	M,D,O
Management Strategy and Policy	M,O
Marketing	M,D,O
Maternal and Child/ Neonatal Nursing	M,D
Mathematics Education	M,D
Nonprofit Management	M
Nurse Anesthesia	M,D
Nursing and Healthcare Administration	M,D
Nursing Education	M,D
Nursing—General	M,D
Occupational Therapy	M
Oral and Dental Sciences	M,O
Organizational Behavior	M,D,O
Pediatric Nursing	M,D
Pharmaceutical Administration	P,M,D
Pharmaceutical Sciences	M,D
Pharmacy	P
Physical Therapy	M,D
Physician Assistant Studies	M
Psychiatric Nursing	M,D
Public Health—General	M,D,O
Quantitative Analysis	D
Reading Education	M,D
Rehabilitation Sciences	M,D,O
Science Education	M,D
Secondary Education	M,D
Social Sciences Education	M,D
Social Work	M,D,O
Special Education	M,D

UNIVERSITY OF PORTLAND

Business Administration and Management— General	M
Education—General	M
Nursing—General	M,D

UNIVERSITY OF PRINCE EDWARD ISLAND

Education—General	M
Educational Leadership and Administration	M
Epidemiology	M,D
Veterinary Medicine	P
Veterinary Sciences	M,D

UNIVERSITY OF PUERTO RICO, MAYAGÜEZ CAMPUS

Agricultural Education	M
Business Administration and Management— General	M
English Education	M
Finance and Banking	M
Human Resources Management	M
Industrial and Manufacturing Management	M

UNIVERSITY OF PUERTO RICO, MEDICAL SCIENCES CAMPUS

Acute Care/Critical Care Nursing	M
Allied Health—General	M,D,O
Allopathic Medicine	P
Clinical Laboratory Sciences/Medical Technology	M,O
Clinical Research	M,O
Communication Disorders	M,D
Community Health Nursing	M
Dentistry	P
Environmental and Occupational Health	M,D
Epidemiology	M
Family Nurse Practitioner Studies	M

Health Education	M
Health Promotion	O
Health Services Management and Hospital Administration	M
Health Services Research	M
Industrial Hygiene	M
Maternal and Child Health	M
Nurse Anesthesia	M
Nurse Midwifery	M,O
Nursing—General	M
Occupational Therapy	M
Oral and Dental Sciences	O
Pharmaceutical Sciences	P,M
Pharmacy	P,M
Physical Therapy	M
Psychiatric Nursing	M
Public Health—General	M
Special Education	O

UNIVERSITY OF PUERTO RICO, RÍO PIEDRAS

Accounting	M,D
Business Administration and Management— General	M,D
Counselor Education	M,D
Curriculum and Instruction	M,D
Early Childhood Education	M
Education—General	M,D
Educational Leadership and Administration	M,D
Educational Measurement and Evaluation	M
English as a Second Language	M
Exercise and Sports Science	M
Finance and Banking	M,D
Foreign Languages Education	M,D
Human Resources Management	M,D
Industrial and Manufacturing Management	M,D
Information Studies	M,O
International Business	M,D
Law	P,M
Library Science	M,O
Marketing	M,D
Mathematics Education	M,D
Quantitative Analysis	M,D
Science Education	M,D
Social Sciences Education	M,D
Social Work	M,D
Special Education	M

UNIVERSITY OF PUGET SOUND

Counselor Education	M
Education—General	M
Elementary Education	M
Occupational Therapy	M
Physical Therapy	D
Secondary Education	M

UNIVERSITY OF REDLANDS

Business Administration and Management— General	M
Communication Disorders	M
Education—General	M,D,O
Management Information Systems	M

UNIVERSITY OF REGINA

Adult Education	M
Business Administration and Management— General	M,O
Curriculum and Instruction	M
Education—General	M,D
Educational Leadership and Administration	M
Educational Psychology	M
Human Resources Development	M
Human Resources Management	M,O
International Business	M,O
Kinesiology and Movement Studies	M,D
Social Work	M,D

UNIVERSITY OF RHODE ISLAND

Accounting	M,D
Adult Education	M,D
Business Administration and Management— General	M,D
Clinical Laboratory Sciences/Medical Technology	M,D
Communication Disorders	M
Education—General	M,D
Elementary Education	M,D
Exercise and Sports Science	M
Family Nurse Practitioner Studies	M,D
Finance and Banking	M,D
Gerontological Nursing	M,D
Health Education	M
Human Resources Management	M
Industrial and Manufacturing Management	M,D
Information Studies	M
Library Science	M
Marketing	M,D
Medicinal and Pharmaceutical Chemistry	M,D
Music Education	M,D
Nursing and Healthcare Administration	M,D
Nursing Education	M,D
Nursing—General	M,D
Pharmaceutical Sciences	M,D
Pharmacy	M,D
Physical Education	M
Physical Therapy	D
Psychiatric Nursing	M,D
Reading Education	M,D
Recreation and Park Management	M
Secondary Education	M,D
Special Education	M,D
Student Affairs	M
Supply Chain Management	M,D

UNIVERSITY OF RICHMOND

Business Administration and Management— General	M
Law	P

UNIVERSITY OF RIO GRANDE

Art Education	M
Education—General	M
Mathematics Education	M
Reading Education	M
Special Education	M

UNIVERSITY OF ROCHESTER

Acute Care/Critical Care Nursing	M,D,O
Adult Nursing	M,D,O
Allopathic Medicine	P
Business Administration and Management— General	M,D
Education—General	M,D
Entrepreneurship	M
Epidemiology	M,D
Family Nurse Practitioner Studies	M,D,O
Gerontological Nursing	M,D,O
Health Education	M,D,O
Health Promotion	M,D,O
Health Services Management and Hospital Administration	M,D,O
Health Services Research	M,D,O
Maternal and Child/ Neonatal Nursing	M,D,O
Music Education	M,D
Nursing and Healthcare Administration	M,D,O
Nursing—General	M,D,O
Oral and Dental Sciences	M
Pediatric Nursing	M,D,O
Psychiatric Nursing	M,D,O
Public Health—General	M,D

UNIVERSITY OF ST. AUGUSTINE FOR HEALTH SCIENCES

Occupational Therapy	M,D
Physical Therapy	M,D,O

UNIVERSITY OF ST. FRANCIS (IL)

Adult Nursing	M,D
Allied Health—General	M,D
Business Administration and Management— General	M
Business Education	M
Curriculum and Instruction	M
Education—General	M
Educational Leadership and Administration	M
Elementary Education	M
English Education	M
Family Nurse Practitioner Studies	M,D
Health Services Management and Hospital Administration	M
Mathematics Education	M
Nursing—General	M,D
Physician Assistant Studies	M
Reading Education	M
Science Education	M
Secondary Education	M
Social Sciences Education	M
Social Work	M
Special Education	M

UNIVERSITY OF SAINT FRANCIS (IN)

Allied Health—General	M
Business Administration and Management— General	M
Counselor Education	M
Education—General	M
Nursing—General	M
Physician Assistant Studies	M
Special Education	M

UNIVERSITY OF SAINT MARY

Business Administration and Management— General	M
Curriculum and Instruction	M
Education—General	M
Special Education	M

UNIVERSITY OF ST. MICHAEL'S COLLEGE

Religious Education	P,M,D,O

UNIVERSITY OF ST. THOMAS (MN)

Accounting	M
Business Administration and Management— General	M*
Curriculum and Instruction	M,D,O
Early Childhood Education	M,O
Education of the Gifted	M,O
Education—General	M,D,O
Educational Leadership and Administration	M,D,O
Educational Media/ Instructional Technology	M,D,O
Educational Policy	M,D,O
Elementary Education	M,O
Health Services Management and Hospital Administration	M
Human Resources Development	M,D,O
Human Resources Management	M,D,O
Industrial and Manufacturing Management	M,O
Law	P
Management Information Systems	M,O
Multilingual and Multicultural Education	M,O
Music Education	M
Organizational Management	M,D,O
Reading Education	M,O
Real Estate	M
Religious Education	M
Secondary Education	M,O
Social Work	M
Special Education	M,O
Student Affairs	M,D,O

UNIVERSITY OF ST. THOMAS (TX)

Business Administration and Management— General	M
Education—General	M

UNIVERSITY OF SAN DIEGO

Accounting	M,O
Adult Nursing	M,D
Business Administration and Management— General	M,O
Communication Disorders	M
Counselor Education	M
Curriculum and Instruction	M
Education—General	M,D,O
Educational Leadership and Administration	M,D,O
English as a Second Language	M
Family Nurse Practitioner Studies	M,D
Gerontological Nursing	M,D
Higher Education	M,D,O
Law	P,M,O
Legal and Justice Studies	P,M,O
Mathematics Education	M
Nonprofit Management	M,D,O
Nursing and Healthcare Administration	M,D
Nursing—General	M,D
Pediatric Nursing	M,D
Psychiatric Nursing	M,D
Reading Education	M
Science Education	M
Special Education	M
Supply Chain Management	M,O
Taxation	P,M,O

UNIVERSITY OF SAN FRANCISCO

Business Administration and Management— General	M
Counselor Education	M,D
Curriculum and Instruction	M,D
Education—General	M,D
Educational Leadership and Administration	M,D
Educational Media/ Instructional Technology	M,D
Electronic Commerce	M
English as a Second Language	M,D
Entrepreneurship	M
Family Nurse Practitioner Studies	D
Finance and Banking	M
Health Services Management and Hospital Administration	M
International and Comparative Education	M,D
International Business	M
Investment Management	M
Law	P,M
Management Information Systems	M
Marketing	M
Multilingual and Multicultural Education	M,D
Nonprofit Management	M
Nursing and Healthcare Administration	D
Nursing—General	M,D
Organizational Management	M
Project Management	M
Reading Education	M,D
Religious Education	M,D
Sports Management	M

UNIVERSITY OF SASKATCHEWAN

Accounting	M
Allopathic Medicine	P
Business Administration and Management— General	M
Community Health	M,D
Curriculum and Instruction	M,D,O
Dentistry	P
Education—General	M,D,O

Educational Leadership and Administration	M,D,O
Educational Psychology	M,D,O
Epidemiology	M,D
Finance and Banking	M
Foundations and Philosophy of Education	M,D,O
Health Services Management and Hospital Administration	M
International Business	M,D
Kinesiology and Movement Studies	M,D,O
Law	P,M
Marketing	M
Nursing—General	M
Organizational Behavior	M
Pharmaceutical Sciences	M,D
Special Education	M,D,O
Sustainability Management	M
Veterinary Medicine	P,M,D
Veterinary Sciences	M,D

THE UNIVERSITY OF SCRANTON

Accounting	M
Adult Nursing	M,O
Business Administration and Management— General	M
Counselor Education	M
Curriculum and Instruction	M
Early Childhood Education	M
Education—General	M
Educational Leadership and Administration	M
Elementary Education	M
English as a Second Language	M
Family Nurse Practitioner Studies	M,O
Finance and Banking	M
Health Services Management and Hospital Administration	M
Human Resources Development	M
Human Resources Management	M
International Business	M
Management Information Systems	M
Marketing	M
Nurse Anesthesia	M,O
Nursing—General	M,O
Occupational Therapy	M
Organizational Management	M
Physical Therapy	M,D
Reading Education	M
Secondary Education	M
Special Education	M

UNIVERSITY OF SIOUX FALLS

Business Administration and Management— General	M
Education—General	M,O
Educational Leadership and Administration	M,O
Educational Media/ Instructional Technology	M,O
Reading Education	M,O

UNIVERSITY OF SOUTH AFRICA

Accounting	M,D
Acute Care/Critical Care Nursing	M,D
Adult Education	M,D
Business Administration and Management— General	M,D
Counselor Education	M,D
Curriculum and Instruction	M,D
Education—General	M,D
Educational Leadership and Administration	M,D
Educational Media/ Instructional Technology	M,D
Educational Psychology	M,D
English as a Second Language	M,D
Environmental Education	M,D

Foundations and Philosophy of Education	M,D
Health Education	M,D
Health Services Management and Hospital Administration	M,D
Human Resources Development	M,D
International and Comparative Education	M,D
Law	M,D
Logistics	M,D
Management Information Systems	M
Marketing	M,D
Maternal and Child/ Neonatal Nursing	M,D
Mathematics Education	M,D
Medical/Surgical Nursing	M,D
Nurse Midwifery	M,D
Public Health—General	M,D
Quantitative Analysis	M,D
Real Estate	M,D
Science Education	M,D
Social Work	M,D
Travel and Tourism	M,D
Vocational and Technical Education	M,D

UNIVERSITY OF SOUTH ALABAMA

Accounting	M
Adult Nursing	M,D
Allied Health—General	M,D
Allopathic Medicine	P
Business Administration and Management— General	M
Communication Disorders	M,D
Community Health Nursing	M,D
Counselor Education	M,D
Early Childhood Education	M,D
Education—General	M,D,O
Educational Leadership and Administration	M,O
Educational Media/ Instructional Technology	M,D
Elementary Education	M,O
Environmental and Occupational Health	M
Exercise and Sports Science	M
Health Education	M
Leisure Studies	M
Management Information Systems	M
Maternal and Child/ Neonatal Nursing	M,D
Nursing—General	M,D
Occupational Therapy	M
Physical Education	M
Physical Therapy	D
Physician Assistant Studies	M
Reading Education	M,O
Recreation and Park Management	M
Science Education	M,O
Secondary Education	M,O
Special Education	M,O

UNIVERSITY OF SOUTH CAROLINA

Accounting	M
Acute Care/Critical Care Nursing	M,O
Adult Nursing	M
Allopathic Medicine	P
Art Education	M,D
Business Administration and Management— General	M,D
Business Education	M,D
Communication Disorders	M,D
Community Health Nursing	M
Counselor Education	D,O
Curriculum and Instruction	D
Early Childhood Education	M,D
Education—General	M,D,O
Educational Leadership and Administration	M,D,O
Educational Measurement and Evaluation	M,D

Educational Media/ Instructional Technology	M
Educational Psychology	M,D
Elementary Education	M,D
English as a Second Language	M,D,O
English Education	M,D
Entertainment Management	M
Environmental and Occupational Health	M,D
Epidemiology	M,D
Exercise and Sports Science	M,D
Family Nurse Practitioner Studies	M
Foreign Languages Education	M,D
Foundations and Philosophy of Education	D
Health Education	M,D,O
Health Promotion	M,D,O
Health Services Management and Hospital Administration	M,D
Higher Education	M
Hospitality Management	M
Human Resources Management	M
Industrial Hygiene	M,D
Information Studies	M,D,O
International Business	M
Law	P
Library Science	M,D,O
Mathematics Education	M,D
Medical/Surgical Nursing	M
Music Education	M,D,O
Nurse Anesthesia	M
Nursing and Healthcare Administration	M
Nursing—General	M,O
Pediatric Nursing	M
Pharmaceutical Sciences	M,D
Pharmacy	P
Physical Education	M,D
Psychiatric Nursing	M,O
Public Health—General	M
Reading Education	M,D
Rehabilitation Sciences	M,O
Science Education	M,D
Secondary Education	M,D
Social Sciences Education	M,D
Social Work	M,D
Special Education	M,D
Sports Management	M
Student Affairs	M
Travel and Tourism	M
Women's Health Nursing	M

UNIVERSITY OF SOUTH CAROLINA AIKEN

Education—General	M
Educational Media/ Instructional Technology	M
Elementary Education	M

UNIVERSITY OF SOUTH CAROLINA UPSTATE

Early Childhood Education	M
Education—General	M
Elementary Education	M
Special Education	M

THE UNIVERSITY OF SOUTH DAKOTA

Accounting	M
Allied Health—General	M,D
Allopathic Medicine	P
Business Administration and Management— General	M
Communication Disorders	M,D
Counselor Education	M,D,O
Curriculum and Instruction	M,D,O
Education—General	M,D,O
Educational Leadership and Administration	M,D,O
Educational Media/ Instructional Technology	M,O
Educational Psychology	M,D,O
Elementary Education	M
Health Education	M
Law	P
Occupational Therapy	M

Physical Education	M
Physical Therapy	D
Physician Assistant Studies	M
Secondary Education	M
Special Education	M

UNIVERSITY OF SOUTHERN CALIFORNIA

Accounting	M
Advertising and Public Relations	M
Allopathic Medicine	P
Business Administration and Management— General	M,D
Clinical Research	M,D,O
Counselor Education	M
Dentistry	P
Education—General	M,D
Educational Leadership and Administration	D
Educational Policy	D
Educational Psychology	D
English as a Second Language	M
Epidemiology	M,D
Health Promotion	M
Health Services Management and Hospital Administration	M,O
Health Services Research	D
Higher Education	D
International Health	M
Kinesiology and Movement Studies	M,D
Law	P,M
Medical Imaging	M,D
Multilingual and Multicultural Education	D
Music Education	M,D,O
Occupational Therapy	M,D
Oral and Dental Sciences	M,D,O
Organizational Management	M
Pharmaceutical Sciences	M,D,O*
Pharmacy	P
Physical Therapy	D
Physician Assistant Studies	M
Public Health—General	M*
Quantitative Analysis	M,D
Real Estate	M,O
Social Work	M,D
Student Affairs	M
Supply Chain Management	M,D,O
Taxation	M
Urban Education	D

UNIVERSITY OF SOUTHERN INDIANA

Business Administration and Management— General	M
Education—General	M
Elementary Education	M
Health Services Management and Hospital Administration	M
Industrial and Manufacturing Management	M
Nursing—General	M,D
Occupational Therapy	M
Secondary Education	M
Social Work	M

UNIVERSITY OF SOUTHERN MAINE

Adult Education	M,O
Adult Nursing	M,O
Business Administration and Management— General	M
Counselor Education	M,O
Education of the Gifted	M
Education—General	M,D,O
Educational Leadership and Administration	M,O
Educational Psychology	M,O
English as a Second Language	M,O
Family Nurse Practitioner Studies	M,O

Finance and Banking	M
Health Services Management and Hospital Administration	M,O
Law	P
Medical/Surgical Nursing	M,O
Middle School Education	M,O
Nonprofit Management	M,O
Nursing—General	M,O
Occupational Therapy	M
Psychiatric Nursing	M,O
Reading Education	M,O
Social Work	M
Special Education	M
Sports Management	M,O
Taxation	M

UNIVERSITY OF SOUTHERN MISSISSIPPI

Accounting	M
Adult Education	M,D,O
Adult Nursing	M,D
Advertising and Public Relations	M,D
Art Education	M
Business Administration and Management— General	M
Clinical Laboratory Sciences/Medical Technology	M
Communication Disorders	M,D
Community College Education	M,D,O
Community Health Nursing	M,D
Counselor Education	M,D,O
Curriculum and Instruction	M,D,O
Early Childhood Education	M,D,O
Education of the Gifted	M,D,O
Education—General	M,D,O
Educational Leadership and Administration	M,D,O
Educational Measurement and Evaluation	M,D,O
Elementary Education	M,D,O
Environmental and Occupational Health	M
Epidemiology	M
Exercise and Sports Science	M,D
Family Nurse Practitioner Studies	M,D
Foreign Languages Education	M
Health Education	M
Health Services Management and Hospital Administration	M
Higher Education	M,D,O
Leisure Studies	M,D
Library Science	M,O
Management Information Systems	M
Maternal and Child/ Neonatal Nursing	M,D
Mathematics Education	M,D
Music Education	M,D
Nursing and Healthcare Administration	M,D
Nursing—General	M,D
Physical Education	M,D
Psychiatric Nursing	M,D
Public Health—General	M
Reading Education	M,D,O
Recreation and Park Management	M,D
Science Education	M,D
Secondary Education	M,D,O
Social Sciences Education	M,D,O
Social Work	M
Special Education	M,D,O
Sports Management	M,D
Student Affairs	M,D,O
Vocational and Technical Education	M

UNIVERSITY OF SOUTHERN NEVADA

Business Administration and Management— General	M
Oral and Dental Sciences	O
Pharmacy	P

UNIVERSITY OF SOUTH FLORIDA

Accounting	M,D

Adult Education	M,D,O
Business Administration and Management— General	M,D
Communication Disorders	M,D
Community College Education	M,D,O
Community Health	M,D
Counselor Education	M,D,O
Curriculum and Instruction	M,D,O
Early Childhood Education	M,D,O
Education of the Gifted	M,D
Education—General	M,D,O*
Educational Leadership and Administration	M,D,O
Educational Measurement and Evaluation	M,D,O
Educational Media/ Instructional Technology	M,D,O
Elementary Education	M,D,O
English as a Second Language	M,D,O
English Education	M,D,O
Entrepreneurship	M,O
Environmental and Occupational Health	M,D
Epidemiology	M,D
Exercise and Sports Science	M
Finance and Banking	M,D
Foreign Languages Education	M,D,O
Health Services Management and Hospital Administration	M,D
Higher Education	M,D,O
Information Studies	M
International Health	M,D
Library Science	M
Management Information Systems	M,D
Marketing	M,D
Mathematics Education	M,D,O
Music Education	M,D
Nursing—General	M,D
Physical Education	M
Physical Therapy	M,D
Public Health—General	M,D
Reading Education	M,D,O
Real Estate	M,D
Science Education	M,D
Secondary Education	M,D,O
Social Sciences Education	M,D,O
Social Work	M,D
Special Education	M,D
Student Affairs	M,D,O
Vocational and Technical Education	M,D,O

THE UNIVERSITY OF TAMPA

Accounting	M
Adult Nursing	M
Business Administration and Management— General	M
Curriculum and Instruction	M
Education—General	M
Entrepreneurship	M
Family Nurse Practitioner Studies	M
Finance and Banking	M
International Business	M
Management Information Systems	M
Marketing	M
Mathematics Education	M
Nonprofit Management	M
Nursing—General	M
Science Education	M
Social Sciences Education	M

THE UNIVERSITY OF TENNESSEE

Accounting	M,D
Adult Education	M,D
Advertising and Public Relations	M,D
Agricultural Education	M
Art Education	M,D,O
Athletic Training and Sports Medicine	M,D
Bioethics	M,D
Business Administration and Management— General	M,D
Communication Disorders	M,D,O
Community Health	M,D

Counselor Education	M,D,O
Curriculum and Instruction	M,D,O
Early Childhood Education	M,D,O
Education—General	M,D,O
Educational Leadership and Administration	M,D,O
Educational Measurement and Evaluation	M,D,O
Educational Media/ Instructional Technology	M,D,O
Educational Psychology	M,D,O
Elementary Education	M,D,O
English as a Second Language	M,D,O
English Education	M,D,O
Exercise and Sports Science	M,D,O
Finance and Banking	M,D
Foreign Languages Education	M,D,O
Foundations and Philosophy of Education	M,D,O
Health Education	M
Health Promotion	M
Health Services Management and Hospital Administration	M
Hospitality Management	M
Human Resources Development	M
Industrial and Manufacturing Management	M,D
Kinesiology and Movement Studies	M,D
Law	P
Leisure Studies	M,D
Logistics	M,D
Marketing	M,D
Mathematics Education	M,D,O
Multilingual and Multicultural Education	M,D,O
Music Education	M
Nursing—General	M,D
Public Health—General	M
Reading Education	M,D,O
Recreation and Park Management	M,D
Science Education	M,D,O
Secondary Education	M,D,O
Social Sciences Education	M,D,O
Social Work	M,D
Special Education	M,D,O
Sports Management	M,D
Student Affairs	M
Transportation Management	M,D
Travel and Tourism	M
Veterinary Medicine	P

THE UNIVERSITY OF TENNESSEE AT CHATTANOOGA

Accounting	M
Athletic Training and Sports Medicine	M
Business Administration and Management— General	M
Counselor Education	M
Education—General	M,D,O
Educational Leadership and Administration	M,D,O
Educational Media/ Instructional Technology	O
Elementary Education	M,O
Family Nurse Practitioner Studies	M,O
Music Education	M
Nonprofit Management	M,O
Nurse Anesthesia	M,O
Nursing and Healthcare Administration	M,O
Nursing Education	M,O
Nursing—General	M,O
Physical Education	M
Physical Therapy	D
Project Management	M,O
Quality Management	M,O
Secondary Education	M,O
Special Education	M,O

THE UNIVERSITY OF TENNESSEE AT MARTIN

Business Administration and Management— General	M

Counselor Education	M
Education—General	M
Educational Leadership and Administration	M

THE UNIVERSITY OF TENNESSEE HEALTH SCIENCE CENTER

Allied Health—General	M,D
Allopathic Medicine	P,M,D
Dentistry	P,M,O
Nursing—General	M,D
Oral and Dental Sciences	P,M,O
Pharmaceutical Sciences	M,D
Pharmacy	P,M,D
Physical Therapy	M,D

THE UNIVERSITY OF TEXAS AT ARLINGTON

Accounting	M,D
Business Administration and Management— General	M,D*
Curriculum and Instruction	M,D
Education—General	M,D
Educational Leadership and Administration	M,D
English as a Second Language	M
Exercise and Sports Science	M,D
Family Nurse Practitioner Studies	M,D
Finance and Banking	M,D
Health Services Management and Hospital Administration	M
Human Resources Management	M
Logistics	M
Management Information Systems	M,D
Marketing Research	M
Marketing	M,D
Music Education	M
Nursing and Healthcare Administration	M,D
Nursing Education	M,D
Nursing—General	M,D
Physical Education	M,D
Quantitative Analysis	M,D
Real Estate	M,D
Social Work	M,D
Taxation	M

THE UNIVERSITY OF TEXAS AT AUSTIN

Accounting	M,D
Actuarial Science	M,D
Advertising and Public Relations	M,D
Art Education	M
Business Administration and Management— General	M,D
Communication Disorders	M,D
Counselor Education	M,D
Curriculum and Instruction	M,D
Education—General	M,D
Educational Leadership and Administration	M,D
Educational Psychology	M,D
Entrepreneurship	M
Finance and Banking	D
Foreign Languages Education	M,D
Health Education	M,D
Industrial and Manufacturing Management	D
Information Studies	M,D
Kinesiology and Movement Studies	M,D
Law	P,M,O
Management Information Systems	D
Marketing	D
Mathematics Education	M,D
Nursing—General	M,D
Pharmaceutical Sciences	M,D
Pharmacy	P
Science Education	M,D
Social Work	M,D
Special Education	M,D

Supply Chain Management	D

THE UNIVERSITY OF TEXAS AT BROWNSVILLE

Business Administration and Management— General	M
Community Health Nursing	M
Counselor Education	M
Curriculum and Instruction	M
Early Childhood Education	M
Education—General	M
Educational Leadership and Administration	M
Educational Media/ Instructional Technology	M
English as a Second Language	M
Multilingual and Multicultural Education	M
Reading Education	M
Special Education	M

THE UNIVERSITY OF TEXAS AT DALLAS

Accounting	M,D
Business Administration and Management— General	M,D*
Communication Disorders	M,D
Electronic Commerce	M
Entrepreneurship	M
Finance and Banking	M,D
Health Services Management and Hospital Administration	M
International Business	M,D
Law	M,D
Management Information Systems	M,D
Marketing	D
Mathematics Education	M
Organizational Behavior	D
Organizational Management	M
Project Management	M
Quantitative Analysis	D
Science Education	M
Supply Chain Management	M
Taxation	M

THE UNIVERSITY OF TEXAS AT EL PASO

Accounting	M
Allied Health—General	D
Art Education	M
Business Administration and Management— General	M,D,O
Communication Disorders	M
Counselor Education	M
Curriculum and Instruction	M,D
Education—General	M,D
Educational Leadership and Administration	M,D
Educational Measurement and Evaluation	M
Educational Psychology	M
English as a Second Language	M,O
English Education	M,D,O
Family Nurse Practitioner Studies	M,D,O
Health Education	M
Health Promotion	M
Health Services Management and Hospital Administration	M,D,O
International Business	M,D,O
Kinesiology and Movement Studies	M
Mathematics Education	M
Multilingual and Multicultural Education	M,D,O
Music Education	M
Nursing and Healthcare Administration	M,D,O
Nursing—General	M,D,O
Occupational Therapy	M
Physical Therapy	M
Public Health—General	M

Reading Education	M,D
Science Education	M
Social Work	M
Special Education	M

THE UNIVERSITY OF TEXAS AT SAN ANTONIO

Accounting	M,D
Business Administration and Management— General	M,D
Counselor Education	M,D
Curriculum and Instruction	M
Early Childhood Education	M
Educational Leadership and Administration	M,D
Educational Media/ Instructional Technology	M
English as a Second Language	M,D
Finance and Banking	M,D
Health Education	M
Health Promotion	M
International Business	M,D
Kinesiology and Movement Studies	M
Management Information Systems	M,D
Marketing	M,D
Multilingual and Multicultural Education	M,D
Organizational Management	M,D
Reading Education	M
Social Work	M
Special Education	M
Taxation	M,D

THE UNIVERSITY OF TEXAS AT TYLER

Business Administration and Management— General	M
Early Childhood Education	M
Educational Leadership and Administration	M
Environmental and Occupational Health	M
Family Nurse Practitioner Studies	M,D
Health Education	M
Health Services Management and Hospital Administration	M
Human Resources Development	M,D
Industrial and Manufacturing Management	M,D
Kinesiology and Movement Studies	M
Nursing and Healthcare Administration	M,D
Nursing Education	M,D
Nursing—General	M,D
Reading Education	M
Special Education	M
Vocational and Technical Education	M,D

THE UNIVERSITY OF TEXAS HEALTH SCIENCE CENTER AT HOUSTON

Allopathic Medicine	P
Dentistry	P,M
Medical Physics	M,D
Nursing—General	M,D
Public Health—General	M,D,O

THE UNIVERSITY OF TEXAS HEALTH SCIENCE CENTER AT SAN ANTONIO

Allopathic Medicine	P,M
Clinical Laboratory Sciences/Medical Technology	M
Communication Disorders	M
Dental Hygiene	M
Dentistry	P,M,O
Medical Physics	M,D
Nursing—General	M,D
Occupational Therapy	M
Oral and Dental Sciences	M,O
Physical Therapy	M

Physician Assistant Studies	M

THE UNIVERSITY OF TEXAS MEDICAL BRANCH

Allied Health—General	M,D
Allopathic Medicine	P
Clinical Laboratory Sciences/Medical Technology	M,D
Community Health	M,D
Nursing—General	M,D
Occupational Therapy	M
Physical Therapy	M,D
Physician Assistant Studies	M
Public Health—General	M

THE UNIVERSITY OF TEXAS OF THE PERMIAN BASIN

Accounting	M
Business Administration and Management— General	M
Counselor Education	M
Early Childhood Education	M
Education—General	M
Educational Leadership and Administration	M
English as a Second Language	M
Foundations and Philosophy of Education	M
Kinesiology and Movement Studies	M
Reading Education	M
Special Education	M

THE UNIVERSITY OF TEXAS–PAN AMERICAN

Accounting	M
Adult Nursing	M
Business Administration and Management— General	M,D
Communication Disorders	M
Counselor Education	M
Early Childhood Education	M
Education of the Gifted	M
Education—General	M,D
Educational Leadership and Administration	M,D
Educational Measurement and Evaluation	M
Educational Psychology	M
Elementary Education	M
English as a Second Language	M
Family Nurse Practitioner Studies	M
Finance and Banking	D
International Business	D
Kinesiology and Movement Studies	M
Management Information Systems	D
Marketing	D
Mathematics Education	M
Multilingual and Multicultural Education	M
Music Education	M
Nursing—General	M
Occupational Therapy	M
Pediatric Nursing	M
Reading Education	M
Secondary Education	M
Social Work	M
Special Education	M

THE UNIVERSITY OF TEXAS SOUTHWESTERN MEDICAL CENTER AT DALLAS

Allopathic Medicine	P
Physical Therapy	D
Physician Assistant Studies	M

THE UNIVERSITY OF THE ARTS

Art Education	M
Museum Education	M
Music Education	M

*M—master's degree; P—first professional degree; D—doctorate; O—other advanced degree; *—Close-Up and/or Display*

UNIVERSITY OF THE CUMBERLANDS

Early Childhood Education	M
Education—General	M,O
Educational Leadership and Administration	M
Elementary Education	M
Middle School Education	M
Reading Education	M
Secondary Education	M
Special Education	M

UNIVERSITY OF THE DISTRICT OF COLUMBIA

Business Administration and Management— General	M
Communication Disorders	M
Counselor Education	M
Early Childhood Education	M
Education—General	M
Law	P
Mathematics Education	M
Special Education	M

UNIVERSITY OF THE INCARNATE WORD

Accounting	M
Adult Education	M,D,O
Business Administration and Management— General	M,O
Early Childhood Education	M,D
Education—General	M,D
Educational Leadership and Administration	M,D
Educational Media/ Instructional Technology	M,D,O
Elementary Education	M
Entrepreneurship	M,D
Health Promotion	M
Health Services Management and Hospital Administration	M,O
Higher Education	M,D
International Business	M,O
Kinesiology and Movement Studies	M,D
Multilingual and Multicultural Education	M,D
Nursing—General	M
Optometry	P
Organizational Management	M,D,O
Pharmacy	P
Physical Education	M,O
Project Management	M,O
Reading Education	M,D
Science Education	M
Secondary Education	M
Special Education	M,D
Sports Management	M,O

UNIVERSITY OF THE PACIFIC

Business Administration and Management— General	M
Communication Disorders	M
Curriculum and Instruction	M,D
Education—General	M,D,O
Educational Leadership and Administration	M,D
Educational Psychology	M,D,O
Exercise and Sports Science	M
Law	P,M,D
Legal and Justice Studies	P,M,D
Music Education	M
Pharmaceutical Sciences	M,D
Pharmacy	P
Physical Therapy	M,D
Special Education	M,D
Taxation	P,M,D

UNIVERSITY OF THE SACRED HEART

Accounting	M,O
Advertising and Public Relations	M
Business Administration and Management— General	M,O
Early Childhood Education	M,O
Education—General	M,O

(continued)

Educational Media/ Instructional Technology	M
English Education	M,O
Environmental and Occupational Health	M
Foreign Languages Education	M,O
Human Resources Management	M
Legal and Justice Studies	M
Management Information Systems	M
Marketing	M
Mathematics Education	M,O
Nonprofit Management	M
Occupational Health Nursing	M
Taxation	M

UNIVERSITY OF THE SCIENCES IN PHILADELPHIA

Health Services Management and Hospital Administration	M,D
Medicinal and Pharmaceutical Chemistry	M,D
Pharmaceutical Administration	M
Pharmaceutical Sciences	M,D
Public Health—General	M,D

UNIVERSITY OF THE SOUTHWEST

Business Administration and Management— General	M
Counselor Education	M
Curriculum and Instruction	M
Early Childhood Education	M
Education—General	M
Educational Leadership and Administration	M
Educational Measurement and Evaluation	M
English as a Second Language	M
Multilingual and Multicultural Education	M
Reading Education	M
Special Education	M

UNIVERSITY OF THE VIRGIN ISLANDS

Business Administration and Management— General	M
Education—General	M
Mathematics Education	M

UNIVERSITY OF THE WEST

Business Administration and Management— General	M
Finance and Banking	M
International Business	M
Management Information Systems	M
Nonprofit Management	M

THE UNIVERSITY OF TOLEDO

Accounting	M
Adult Nursing	M,O
Art Education	M
Business Administration and Management— General	M,D
Business Education	M
Communication Disorders	M
Counselor Education	M,D,O
Curriculum and Instruction	M,D,O
Early Childhood Education	M,O
Education of the Gifted	D,O
Education—General	M,D,O
Educational Leadership and Administration	M,D,O
Educational Measurement and Evaluation	M,D
Educational Media/ Instructional Technology	M,D,O
Educational Psychology	M,D
Elementary Education	D,O
English as a Second Language	M,O
English Education	M

(continued)

Environmental and Occupational Health	M,O
Epidemiology	M,O
Exercise and Sports Science	M,D
Family Nurse Practitioner Studies	M,O
Finance and Banking	M
Foreign Languages Education	M
Foundations and Philosophy of Education	M,D
Health Education	M,D
Health Physics/ Radiological Health	M
Health Services Management and Hospital Administration	M,O
Higher Education	M,D
Human Resources Management	M
Industrial and Manufacturing Management	M,D
International Business	M
International Health	M,O
Law	P
Leisure Studies	M
Management Information Systems	M
Marketing	M
Mathematics Education	M
Medical Physics	M
Medicinal and Pharmaceutical Chemistry	M,D
Middle School Education	M
Music Education	M
Nursing Education	M,O
Nursing—General	M,O
Occupational Therapy	D
Oral and Dental Sciences	M
Pediatric Nursing	M,O
Pharmaceutical Administration	M
Pharmaceutical Sciences	M
Physical Education	M
Physical Therapy	M,D
Physician Assistant Studies	M
Public Health—General	M,O
Science Education	M
Secondary Education	M,D,O
Social Sciences Education	M
Social Work	M
Special Education	M,D,O
Vocational and Technical Education	M,O

UNIVERSITY OF TORONTO

Accounting	M,D
Allopathic Medicine	P,M,D
Bioethics	M,D
Business Administration and Management— General	M,D
Communication Disorders	M,D
Dentistry	P
Education—General	M,D
Human Resources Management	M,D
Information Studies	M,D,O
Law	P,M,D
Library Science	M,D,O
Music Education	M,D
Nursing—General	M,D
Oral and Dental Sciences	M,D
Pharmaceutical Sciences	M,D
Physical Education	M,D
Public Health—General	M,D
Rehabilitation Sciences	M,D
Social Work	M,D

UNIVERSITY OF TULSA

Accounting	M
Business Administration and Management— General	M
Communication Disorders	M
Education—General	M
Elementary Education	M
Environmental Law	P,M,O
Finance and Banking	M
Health Law	P,M,O
International Business	M
Investment Management	M

(continued)

Law	P,M,O
Management Information Systems	M
Mathematics Education	M
Science Education	M
Secondary Education	M
Taxation	M

UNIVERSITY OF UTAH

Accounting	M,D
Allopathic Medicine	P
Art Education	M
Business Administration and Management— General	M,D
Clinical Laboratory Sciences/Medical Technology	M
Communication Disorders	M,D
Counselor Education	M,D
Early Childhood Education	M,D
Education—General	M,D
Educational Leadership and Administration	M,D
Educational Media/ Instructional Technology	M,D
Educational Psychology	M,D
Elementary Education	M,D
Exercise and Sports Science	M,D
Finance and Banking	M,D
Foreign Languages Education	M,D
Foundations and Philosophy of Education	M,D
Gerontological Nursing	M,O
Health Education	M,D
Health Promotion	M,D
Health Services Management and Hospital Administration	M
Law	P,M
Leisure Studies	M,D
Medical Physics	D
Medicinal and Pharmaceutical Chemistry	M,D
Nursing—General	M,D
Occupational Therapy	M,D
Pharmaceutical Sciences	M
Pharmacy	P
Physical Therapy	D,O
Physician Assistant Studies	M
Public Health—General	M,D
Reading Education	M,D
Real Estate	M
Recreation and Park Management	M,D
Science Education	M,D
Secondary Education	M,D
Social Work	M,D
Special Education	M,D

UNIVERSITY OF VERMONT

Accounting	M
Allied Health—General	M,D
Allopathic Medicine	P
Business Administration and Management— General	M
Clinical Laboratory Sciences/Medical Technology	M,D
Counselor Education	M
Curriculum and Instruction	M
Education—General	M,D
Educational Leadership and Administration	M,D
Foreign Languages Education	M
Mathematics Education	M,D
Nursing—General	M
Physical Therapy	D
Reading Education	M
Science Education	M,D
Social Work	M
Special Education	M

UNIVERSITY OF VICTORIA

Art Education	M,D
Business Administration and Management— General	M
Counselor Education	M,D

Curriculum and Instruction — M,D
Early Childhood Education — M,D
Education—General — M,D
Educational Leadership
  and Administration — M,D
Educational Measurement
  and Evaluation — M,D
Educational Psychology — M,D
English Education — M,D
Environmental Education — M,D
Family Nurse Practitioner
  Studies — M,D
Foreign Languages
  Education — M
Foundations and
  Philosophy of Education — M,D
Kinesiology and
  Movement Studies — M
Law — P,M
Leisure Studies — M
Mathematics Education — M,D
Medical Physics — M,D
Music Education — M,D
Nursing and Healthcare
  Administration — M,D
Nursing Education — M,D
Nursing—General — M,D
Physical Education — M
Reading Education — M,D
Science Education — M,D
Social Sciences Education — M,D
Social Work — M
Special Education — M,D
Vocational and Technical
  Education — M,D

UNIVERSITY OF VIRGINIA

Accounting — M
Acute Care/Critical Care
  Nursing — M,D
Allopathic Medicine — P,M,D
Bioethics — M
Business Administration
  and Management—
  General — M,D
Clinical Research — M
Communication Disorders — M
Community Health — M,D
Counselor Education — M,D,O
Curriculum and Instruction — M,D,O
Early Childhood Education — M,D
Education of the Gifted — M,D,O
Education—General — M,D,O
Educational Leadership
  and Administration — M,D,O
Educational Measurement
  and Evaluation — M,D,O
Educational Media/
  Instructional Technology — M,D,O
Educational Psychology — M,D,O
Elementary Education — M,D,O
English Education — M,D,O
Finance and Banking — M
Foreign Languages
  Education — M,D,O
Health Education — M,D
Health Services
  Management and
  Hospital Administration — M
Health Services Research — M
Higher Education — M,D,O
Kinesiology and
  Movement Studies — M,D
Law — P,M,D,O
Management Information
  Systems — M
Marketing — M
Mathematics Education — M,D,O
Nursing and Healthcare
  Administration — M,D
Nursing—General — M,D
Physical Education — M,D
Psychiatric Nursing — M,D
Public Health—General — M,D
Reading Education — M,D,O
Science Education — M,D,O
Social Sciences Education — M,D,O
Special Education — M,D,O
Student Affairs — M,D,O

UNIVERSITY OF WASHINGTON

Accounting — M,D
Allopathic Medicine — P
Bioethics — M

Business Administration
  and Management—
  General — M,D
Business Education — M,D
Clinical Laboratory
  Sciences/Medical
  Technology — M
Clinical Research — M,D
Communication Disorders — M,D
Community Health — M,D
Curriculum and Instruction — M,D
Dentistry — P
Education—General — M,D,O
Educational Leadership
  and Administration — M,D
Educational Measurement
  and Evaluation — M,D
Educational Media/
  Instructional Technology — M,D
Educational Policy — M,D
Educational Psychology — M,D
English as a Second
  Language — M,D
English Education — M,D
Environmental and
  Occupational Health — M,D
Epidemiology — M,D
Finance and Banking — M,D
Foundations and
  Philosophy of Education — M,D
Health Services
  Management and
  Hospital Administration — M
Health Services Research — M,D
Higher Education — M,D
International Business — M,D,O
International Health — M,D
Law — P,M,D
Legal and Justice Studies — P,M,D
Library Science — M,D
Logistics — O
Maternal and Child Health — M,D
Mathematics Education — M,D
Medicinal and
  Pharmaceutical
  Chemistry — D
Multilingual and
  Multicultural Education — M,D
Music Education — M,D
Nursing—General — M,D,O
Occupational Therapy — M,D
Oral and Dental Sciences — P,M,D
Pharmaceutical Sciences — M,D
Pharmacy — P,M,D
Physical Education — M,D
Physical Therapy — M,D
Reading Education — M,D
Rehabilitation Sciences — M,D
Science Education — M,D
Social Sciences Education — M,D
Social Work — M,D
Special Education — M,D
Taxation — P,M,D
Transportation
  Management — O
Veterinary Sciences — M

UNIVERSITY OF WASHINGTON, BOTHELL

Business Administration
  and Management—
  General — M
Education—General — M
Educational Leadership
  and Administration — M
Middle School Education — M
Nursing—General — M
Secondary Education — M

UNIVERSITY OF WASHINGTON, TACOMA

Accounting — M
Business Administration
  and Management—
  General — M
Education—General — M
Educational Leadership
  and Administration — M
Elementary Education — M
Finance and Banking — M
Middle School Education — M
Nursing—General — M
Science Education — M
Secondary Education — M

Social Work — M
Special Education — M

UNIVERSITY OF WATERLOO

Accounting — M,D
Actuarial Science — M,D
Business Administration
  and Management—
  General — M
Entrepreneurship — M
Finance and Banking — M,D
Health Education — M,D
Kinesiology and
  Movement Studies — M,D
Leisure Studies — M,D
Optometry — M,D
Public Health—General — M
Recreation and Park
  Management — M,D
Taxation — M,D
Travel and Tourism — M
Vision Sciences — M,D

THE UNIVERSITY OF WEST ALABAMA

Adult Education — M
Athletic Training and
  Sports Medicine — M
Counselor Education — M
Early Childhood Education — M
Education—General — M
Educational Leadership
  and Administration — M
Educational Media/
  Instructional Technology — M
Elementary Education — M
English Education — M
Foundations and
  Philosophy of Education — M
Mathematics Education — M
Physical Education — M
Science Education — M
Secondary Education — M
Social Sciences Education — M
Special Education — M

THE UNIVERSITY OF WESTERN ONTARIO

Allopathic Medicine — P,M
Business Administration
  and Management—
  General — M,D
Communication Disorders — M
Curriculum and Instruction — M
Dentistry — P
Education—General — M
Educational Policy — M
Educational Psychology — M
Entrepreneurship — M,D
Epidemiology — M,D
Finance and Banking — M,D
Health Services
  Management and
  Hospital Administration — M,D
Information Studies — M,D
International Business — M,D
Kinesiology and
  Movement Studies — M,D
Law — P,M,O
Library Science — M,D
Management Strategy and
  Policy — M,D
Marketing — M,D
Nursing—General — M,D
Occupational Therapy — M
Oral and Dental Sciences — M
Physical Therapy — M,O
Special Education — M

UNIVERSITY OF WEST FLORIDA

Accounting — M
Business Administration
  and Management—
  General — M
Community Health — M
Counselor Education — M
Curriculum and Instruction — D,O
Early Childhood Education — M
Educational Leadership
  and Administration — M,D,O
Educational Media/
  Instructional Technology — M,D
Elementary Education — M

English as a Second
  Language — M
Environmental and
  Occupational Health — M
Exercise and Sports
  Science — M
Health Education — M
Leisure Studies — M
Management Strategy and
  Policy — M
Middle School Education — M
Nursing and Healthcare
  Administration — M
Pharmaceutical
  Administration — M
Physical Education — M
Public Health—General — M
Reading Education — M
Science Education — M
Secondary Education — M
Social Work — M
Special Education — M
Student Affairs — M
Vocational and Technical
  Education — M

UNIVERSITY OF WEST GEORGIA

Accounting — M
Art Education — M,O
Business Administration
  and Management—
  General — M
Business Education — M,O
Communication Disorders — M,O
Counselor Education — M,D,O
Early Childhood Education — M,O
Education—General — M,D,O
Educational Leadership
  and Administration — M,O
Educational Measurement
  and Evaluation — D
Educational Media/
  Instructional Technology — M,O
English Education — M,O
Foreign Languages
  Education — M,O
Health Services
  Management and
  Hospital Administration — M,O
Mathematics Education — M,O
Middle School Education — M
Music Education — M
Nursing Education — M,O
Nursing—General — M,O
Physical Education — M
Reading Education — M,O
Science Education — M,O
Secondary Education — M,O
Social Sciences Education — M,O
Special Education — M,O

UNIVERSITY OF WINDSOR

Business Administration
  and Management—
  General — M
Education—General — M,D
Kinesiology and
  Movement Studies — M
Legal and Justice Studies — M
Nursing—General — M
Social Work — M

UNIVERSITY OF WISCONSIN– EAU CLAIRE

Adult Nursing — M
Business Administration
  and Management—
  General — M*
Communication Disorders — M
Education—General — M
Elementary Education — M
Family Nurse Practitioner
  Studies — M
Library Science — M
Nursing and Healthcare
  Administration — M
Nursing Education — M
Nursing—General — M
Reading Education — M
Secondary Education — M
Special Education — M

*M—master's degree; P—first professional degree; D—doctorate; O—other advanced degree; *—Close-Up and/or Display*

UNIVERSITY OF WISCONSIN–GREEN BAY

Business Administration and Management—General	M
Education—General	M
Social Work	M

UNIVERSITY OF WISCONSIN–LA CROSSE

Athletic Training and Sports Medicine	M
Business Administration and Management—General	M*
Community Health	M
Education—General	M
Elementary Education	M
Exercise and Sports Science	M
Health Education	M
Nurse Anesthesia	M
Occupational Therapy	M
Physical Education	M
Physical Therapy	M,D
Physician Assistant Studies	M
Public Health—General	M
Recreation and Park Management	M
Rehabilitation Sciences	M
Secondary Education	M
Special Education	M
Sports Management	M
Student Affairs	M

UNIVERSITY OF WISCONSIN–MADISON

Accounting	M,D
Actuarial Science	M
Allopathic Medicine	P
Art Education	M,D
Business Administration and Management—General	M
Clinical Research	M,D
Communication Disorders	M,D
Community Health	M,D
Counselor Education	M
Curriculum and Instruction	M,D
Education—General	M,D,O
Educational Leadership and Administration	M,D,O
Educational Policy	M,D,O
Educational Psychology	M,D
Entrepreneurship	M
Epidemiology	M,D
Finance and Banking	M,D
Foreign Languages Education	M,D
Health Services Research	M,D
Human Resources Management	M,D
Information Studies	M,D
Insurance	M,D
Investment Management	D
Kinesiology and Movement Studies	M,D
Law	P,M,D
Legal and Justice Studies	M,D
Library Science	M,D
Management Information Systems	D
Management Strategy and Policy	M
Marketing Research	M
Marketing	D
Mathematics Education	M,D
Medical Physics	M,D
Music Education	M,D
Nursing—General	D
Occupational Therapy	M,D
Pharmaceutical Administration	M,D
Pharmaceutical Sciences	M,D
Pharmacy	P
Real Estate	M,D
Rehabilitation Sciences	M
Science Education	M,D
Social Work	M,D
Special Education	M,D
Supply Chain Management	M
Taxation	M

Veterinary Medicine	P
Veterinary Sciences	M,D

UNIVERSITY OF WISCONSIN–MILWAUKEE

Adult Education	D
Allied Health—General	M,D,O
Art Education	M
Business Administration and Management—General	M,D,O
Clinical Laboratory Sciences/Medical Technology	M
Communication Disorders	M,O
Counselor Education	M,D
Curriculum and Instruction	M,D
Early Childhood Education	M,D
Education—General	M,D,O
Educational Leadership and Administration	M,D,O
Educational Measurement and Evaluation	M,D
Educational Media/ Instructional Technology	D
Educational Psychology	M,D
Elementary Education	M
Family Nurse Practitioner Studies	M,D,O
Foundations and Philosophy of Education	M,D
Health Education	M,D,O
Higher Education	M,O
Human Resources Development	M,O
Information Studies	M,D,O
International Business	M,O
Investment Management	M,D,O
Kinesiology and Movement Studies	M
Library Science	M,D,O
Middle School Education	M
Multilingual and Multicultural Education	D
Music Education	M,O
Nonprofit Management	M,D
Nursing—General	M,D,O
Occupational Therapy	M,O
Physical Therapy	D
Public Health—General	M,D,O
Reading Education	M
Real Estate	M,O
Recreation and Park Management	M,O
Secondary Education	M
Social Work	M,D,O
Special Education	M,D,O
Taxation	M,D,O
Urban Education	M,D

UNIVERSITY OF WISCONSIN–OSHKOSH

Adult Nursing	M
Business Administration and Management—General	M*
Counselor Education	M
Curriculum and Instruction	M
Early Childhood Education	M
Education—General	M
Educational Leadership and Administration	M
Family Nurse Practitioner Studies	M
Health Services Management and Hospital Administration	M
International Business	M
Mathematics Education	M
Nursing—General	M
Reading Education	M
Social Work	M
Special Education	M

UNIVERSITY OF WISCONSIN–PARKSIDE

Business Administration and Management—General	M*

UNIVERSITY OF WISCONSIN–PLATTEVILLE

Adult Education	M
Counselor Education	M
Education—General	M

Elementary Education	M
English Education	M
Middle School Education	M
Project Management	M
Secondary Education	M
Vocational and Technical Education	M

UNIVERSITY OF WISCONSIN–RIVER FALLS

Agricultural Education	M
Business Administration and Management—General	M
Communication Disorders	M
Counselor Education	M,O
Education—General	M
Elementary Education	M
English as a Second Language	M
Mathematics Education	M
Reading Education	M
Science Education	M
Social Sciences Education	M

UNIVERSITY OF WISCONSIN–STEVENS POINT

Advertising and Public Relations	M
Business Administration and Management—General	M
Communication Disorders	M,D
Counselor Education	M
Education—General	M
Educational Leadership and Administration	M
Elementary Education	M
Health Promotion	M
Music Education	M
Reading Education	M
Science Education	M
Special Education	M

UNIVERSITY OF WISCONSIN–STOUT

Education—General	M,O
Human Resources Development	M
Industrial Hygiene	M
Vocational and Technical Education	M,O

UNIVERSITY OF WISCONSIN–SUPERIOR

Art Education	M
Counselor Education	M
Curriculum and Instruction	M
Education—General	M
Educational Leadership and Administration	M,O
Reading Education	M
Special Education	M

UNIVERSITY OF WISCONSIN–WHITEWATER

Accounting	M
Business Administration and Management—General	M*
Business Education	M
Communication Disorders	M
Counselor Education	M
Curriculum and Instruction	M
Education—General	M
Educational Leadership and Administration	M
Environmental and Occupational Health	M
Finance and Banking	M
Higher Education	M
Human Resources Management	M
International Business	M
Marketing	M
Reading Education	M
Secondary Education	M
Special Education	M
Supply Chain Management	M

UNIVERSITY OF WYOMING

Accounting	M
Adult Education	M,D,O

Business Administration and Management—General	M
Communication Disorders	M
Community Health	M,D
Counselor Education	M,D
Curriculum and Instruction	M,D
Distance Education Development	M,D,O
Educational Leadership and Administration	M,D,O
Educational Media/ Instructional Technology	M,D,O
Exercise and Sports Science	M
Finance and Banking	M
Health Education	M
Health Promotion	M
Kinesiology and Movement Studies	M
Law	P
Mathematics Education	M,D
Music Education	M
Nursing—General	M
Pharmacy	P
Physical Education	M
Science Education	M
Social Work	M
Special Education	M,D,O
Student Affairs	M,D

UPPER IOWA UNIVERSITY

Accounting	M
Business Administration and Management—General	M
Educational Leadership and Administration	M
Finance and Banking	M
Higher Education	M
Human Resources Management	M
Human Services	M
International Business	M
Organizational Management	M
Quality Management	M

URBANA UNIVERSITY

Business Administration and Management—General	M
Education—General	M
Nursing—General	M

URSULINE COLLEGE

Art Education	M
Business Administration and Management—General	M
Early Childhood Education	M
Education—General	M
Educational Leadership and Administration	M
Mathematics Education	M
Medical/Surgical Nursing	M,D
Middle School Education	M
Nursing and Healthcare Administration	M,D
Nursing Education	M,D
Nursing—General	M,D
Reading Education	M
Science Education	M
Social Sciences Education	M
Special Education	M

UTAH STATE UNIVERSITY

Accounting	M
Agricultural Education	M
Business Administration and Management—General	M
Business Education	M,D
Communication Disorders	M,D,O
Counselor Education	M,D
Curriculum and Instruction	D
Education—General	M,D,O
Educational Measurement and Evaluation	M,D
Educational Media/ Instructional Technology	M,D,O
Elementary Education	M
Health Education	M
Home Economics Education	M

Human Resources Management	M
Management Information Systems	M,D
Multilingual and Multicultural Education	M
Physical Education	M
Recreation and Park Management	M,D
Secondary Education	M
Special Education	M,D,O
Veterinary Sciences	M,D
Vocational and Technical Education	M

UTAH VALLEY UNIVERSITY

Education—General	M
Nursing—General	M

UTICA COLLEGE

Accounting	M
Education—General	M,O
Health Services Management and Hospital Administration	M
Occupational Therapy	M
Physical Therapy	D

VALDOSTA STATE UNIVERSITY

Business Administration and Management— General	M
Counselor Education	M,O
Early Childhood Education	M,O
Educational Leadership and Administration	M,D,O
Information Studies	M
Library Science	M
Middle School Education	M,O
Reading Education	M,O
Secondary Education	M,O
Social Work	M
Special Education	M,O

VALLEY CITY STATE UNIVERSITY

Education—General	M
Educational Media/ Instructional Technology	M
English as a Second Language	M
Library Science	M
Vocational and Technical Education	M

VALPARAISO UNIVERSITY

Business Administration and Management— General	M,O
Education—General	M
English as a Second Language	M,O
Finance and Banking	M
International Business	M
Law	P,M
Legal and Justice Studies	O
Management Information Systems	M
Nursing Education	M,O
Nursing—General	M,O
Sports Management	M

VANCOUVER ISLAND UNIVERSITY

Business Administration and Management— General	M

VANDERBILT UNIVERSITY

Acute Care/Critical Care Nursing	M,D
Adult Nursing	M,D
Allopathic Medicine	P,M,D
Business Administration and Management— General	M
Clinical Research	M
Communication Disorders	M,D
Counselor Education	M
Education—General	M,D*
Educational Leadership and Administration	M,D
Educational Measurement and Evaluation	M,D
Educational Policy	M,D

Elementary Education	M
English Education	M
Family Nurse Practitioner Studies	M,D
Finance and Banking	M
Foreign Languages Education	M,D
Gerontological Nursing	M,D
Higher Education	M,D
Human Resources Development	M,D
International and Comparative Education	M,D
Law	P,M,D
Maternal and Child/ Neonatal Nursing	M,D
Medical Physics	M
Medical/Surgical Nursing	M,D
Multilingual and Multicultural Education	M,D
Nurse Midwifery	M,D
Nursing and Healthcare Administration	M,D
Nursing Informatics	M,D
Nursing—General	M,D
Organizational Management	M,D
Pediatric Nursing	M,D
Psychiatric Nursing	M,D
Public Health—General	M
Reading Education	M
Science Education	M,D
Secondary Education	M
Special Education	M,D
Urban Education	M
Women's Health Nursing	M,D

VANDERCOOK COLLEGE OF MUSIC

Music Education	M

VANGUARD UNIVERSITY OF SOUTHERN CALIFORNIA

Business Administration and Management— General	M
Education—General	M

VAUGHN COLLEGE OF AERONAUTICS AND TECHNOLOGY

Aviation Management	M

VERMONT LAW SCHOOL

Environmental Law	M,O
Law	P,O
Legal and Justice Studies	M,O

VILLANOVA UNIVERSITY

Accounting	M
Adult Nursing	M,D,O
Business Administration and Management— General	M
Counselor Education	M*
Education—General	M*
Educational Leadership and Administration	M
Elementary Education	M
Family Nurse Practitioner Studies	M,D,O
Finance and Banking	M
Health Services Management and Hospital Administration	M,D,O
Higher Education	M
Human Resources Development	M
International Business	M
Law	P
Management Information Systems	M
Marketing	M
Nurse Anesthesia	M,D,O
Nursing and Healthcare Administration	M,D,O
Nursing Education	M,D,O
Nursing—General	M,D,O
Pediatric Nursing	M,D,O
Secondary Education	M
Taxation	M

VIRGINIA COLLEGE AT BIRMINGHAM

Business Administration and Management— General	M

VIRGINIA COMMONWEALTH UNIVERSITY

Accounting	M,D
Adult Education	M
Adult Nursing	M,D,O
Advertising and Public Relations	M
Allied Health—General	D
Allopathic Medicine	P
Art Education	M
Athletic Training and Sports Medicine	M
Business Administration and Management— General	M,O
Clinical Laboratory Sciences/Medical Technology	M,D
Community Health	D
Counselor Education	M
Curriculum and Instruction	M,O
Dentistry	P,M
Early Childhood Education	M,O
Education—General	M,D,O
Educational Leadership and Administration	D
Educational Measurement and Evaluation	D
Educational Policy	D
Educational Psychology	D
Environmental and Occupational Health	M
Epidemiology	D
Exercise and Sports Science	M
Family Nurse Practitioner Studies	M,O
Finance and Banking	M
Health Physics/ Radiological Health	D
Health Services Management and Hospital Administration	M,D
Health Services Research	D
Human Resources Development	M
Insurance	M
Management Information Systems	M,D
Marketing	O
Medical Physics	M,D
Middle School Education	M,O
Music Education	M
Nonprofit Management	O
Nurse Anesthesia	M,D
Nursing and Healthcare Administration	M,D,O
Nursing—General	M,D,O
Occupational Therapy	M,D
Pediatric Nursing	M,D,O
Pharmaceutical Sciences	P,M,D
Pharmacy	P
Physical Education	M,D
Physical Therapy	M,D
Psychiatric Nursing	M,D,O
Quantitative Analysis	M
Reading Education	M
Real Estate	M,O
Recreation and Park Management	M
Rehabilitation Sciences	D
Secondary Education	M,O
Social Sciences Education	M,O
Social Work	M,D
Special Education	M,D
Taxation	M
Urban Education	D
Women's Health Nursing	M,D,O

VIRGINIA INTERNATIONAL UNIVERSITY

Accounting	M,O
Business Administration and Management— General	M,O
English as a Second Language	M,O
Finance and Banking	M,O

Health Services Management and Hospital Administration	M,O
Human Resources Management	M,O
International Business	M,O
Logistics	M,O
Management Information Systems	M
Marketing	M,O

VIRGINIA POLYTECHNIC INSTITUTE AND STATE UNIVERSITY

Accounting	M,D
Acute Care/Critical Care Nursing	M,D
Adult Education	M,D
Agricultural Education	M,D
Business Administration and Management— General	M,D
Counselor Education	M,D,O
Curriculum and Instruction	M,D,O
Distance Education Development	M,O
Educational Leadership and Administration	D,O
Educational Measurement and Evaluation	D
Educational Media/ Instructional Technology	M,D,O
Educational Psychology	M,D,O
English Education	M,D,O
Finance and Banking	M,D
Foreign Languages Education	M
Health Education	M,D,O
Higher Education	M,D,O
Hospitality Management	M,D
Human Resources Development	M,D
Logistics	M,D
Management Information Systems	M,D,O
Marketing	M,D
Mathematics Education	M,D,O
Nonprofit Management	M,O
Physical Education	M,D,O
Quantitative Analysis	M,O
Recreation and Park Management	M,D
Special Education	D,O
Travel and Tourism	M,D
Veterinary Medicine	P
Veterinary Sciences	M,D
Vocational and Technical Education	M,D,O

VIRGINIA STATE UNIVERSITY

Community Health	M,D
Education—General	M,O
Educational Leadership and Administration	M
Health Education	M,D
Mathematics Education	M
Vocational and Technical Education	M,O

VITERBO UNIVERSITY

Business Administration and Management— General	M
Education—General	M
Nursing—General	M

WAGNER COLLEGE

Accounting	M
Business Administration and Management— General	M
Early Childhood Education	M
Education—General	M,O
Educational Leadership and Administration	O
Elementary Education	M
Family Nurse Practitioner Studies	O
Finance and Banking	M
Health Services Management and Hospital Administration	M
International Business	M
Marketing	M

*M—master's degree; P—first professional degree; D—doctorate; O—other advanced degree; *—Close-Up and / or Display*

Middle School Education — M
Nursing—General — M
Physician Assistant
  Studies — M
Reading Education — M
Secondary Education — M

WAKE FOREST UNIVERSITY

Accounting — M
Allopathic Medicine — P
Business Administration
  and Management—
    General — M
Counselor Education — M
Education—General — M
Entrepreneurship — M
Exercise and Sports
  Science — M
Finance and Banking — M
Health Services
  Management and
  Hospital Administration — M
Health Services Research — M
Industrial and
  Manufacturing
  Management — M
Law — P,M,D
Marketing — M
Secondary Education — M
Taxation — M

WALDEN UNIVERSITY

Accounting — M,D
Adult Education — M,D,O
Business Administration
  and Management—
    General — M,D
Clinical Research — M,D
Community College
  Education — M,D,O
Community Health — M,D
Counselor Education — M,D
Curriculum and Instruction — M,D,O
Distance Education
  Development — M,D,O
Early Childhood Education — M,D,O
Education—General — M,D,O
Educational Leadership
  and Administration — M,D,O
Educational Measurement
  and Evaluation — M,D,O
Educational Media/
  Instructional Technology — M,D,O
Elementary Education — M,D,O
Entrepreneurship — M,D
Epidemiology — M,D
Finance and Banking — M,D
Health Promotion — M,D
Health Services
  Management and
  Hospital Administration — M,D,O
Higher Education — M,D,O
Human Resources
  Management — M,D
Human Services — M,D
International Business — M,D
Law — M,D,O
Management Information
  Systems — M,D
Marketing — M,D
Mathematics Education — M,D,O
Middle School Education — M,D,O
Nonprofit Management — M,D,O
Nursing and Healthcare
  Administration — M,O
Nursing Education — M,O
Nursing Informatics — M,O
Nursing—General — M,O
Organizational
  Management — M,D,O
Project Management — M,D,O
Public Health—General — M,D
Quantitative Analysis — M,D
Reading Education — M,D,O
Science Education — M,D,O
Social Work — M,D
Special Education — M,D,O
Supply Chain
  Management — M,D
Sustainability
  Management — M,D

WALLA WALLA UNIVERSITY

Curriculum and Instruction — M
Education—General — M

Educational Leadership
  and Administration — M
Reading Education — M
Social Work — M
Special Education — M

WALSH COLLEGE OF ACCOUNTANCY AND BUSINESS ADMINISTRATION

Accounting — M
Business Administration
  and Management—
    General — M
Finance and Banking — M
Management Information
  Systems — M
Taxation — M

WALSH UNIVERSITY

Business Administration
  and Management—
    General — M
Counselor Education — M
Education—General — M
Physical Therapy — D

WARNER PACIFIC COLLEGE

Business Administration
  and Management—
    General — M
Education—General — M
Organizational
  Management — M

WARNER UNIVERSITY

Business Administration
  and Management—
    General — M
Education—General — M

WASHBURN UNIVERSITY

Business Administration
  and Management—
    General — M
Curriculum and Instruction — M
Education—General — M
Educational Leadership
  and Administration — M
Law — P
Reading Education — M
Social Work — M
Special Education — M

WASHINGTON ADVENTIST UNIVERSITY

Business Administration
  and Management—
    General — M
Nursing and Healthcare
  Administration — M
Nursing—General — M

WASHINGTON AND LEE UNIVERSITY

Law — P,M

WASHINGTON STATE UNIVERSITY

Accounting — M,D
Business Administration
  and Management—
    General — M,D*
Curriculum and Instruction — M,D
Education—General — M,D,O
Educational Leadership
  and Administration — M,D
Educational Psychology — M,D,O
Elementary Education — M,D
English Education — M,D
Exercise and Sports
  Science — M,D
Finance and Banking — M,D
Foreign Languages
  Education — M
Health Services
  Management and
  Hospital Administration — M
Higher Education — M,D,O
Industrial and
  Manufacturing
  Management — M,D
Insurance — D
International Business — M,D,O
Management Information
  Systems — M,D
Marketing — M,D

Mathematics Education — M,D
Multilingual and
  Multicultural Education — M,D
Music Education — M
Pharmacy — P
Reading Education — M,D
Real Estate — D
Secondary Education — M,D
Sports Management — M,D,O
Student Affairs — M,D,O
Taxation — M
Veterinary Medicine — P
Veterinary Sciences — M,D

WASHINGTON STATE UNIVERSITY SPOKANE

Communication Disorders — M
Education—General — M,O
Educational Leadership
  and Administration — M,O
Exercise and Sports
  Science — M
Health Services
  Management and
  Hospital Administration — M
Nursing—General — M
Pharmacy — P

WASHINGTON STATE UNIVERSITY TRI-CITIES

Business Administration
  and Management—
    General — M
Counselor Education — M,D
Education—General — M,D
Educational Leadership
  and Administration — M,D
Nursing—General — M
Reading Education — M,D
Secondary Education — M,D

WASHINGTON STATE UNIVERSITY VANCOUVER

Business Administration
  and Management—
    General — M
Education—General — M,D
Nursing—General — M

WASHINGTON UNIVERSITY IN ST. LOUIS

Accounting — M
Allied Health—General — M,D,O
Allopathic Medicine — P
Business Administration
  and Management—
    General — M,D
Clinical Research — M
Communication Disorders — M,D
Education—General — M,D
Educational Measurement
  and Evaluation — D
Elementary Education — M
Finance and Banking — M
Kinesiology and
  Movement Studies — D
Law — P,M,D
Occupational Therapy — M,D
Physical Therapy — D,O
Public Health—General — M,D
Secondary Education — M
Social Work — M,D*
Special Education — M,D
Supply Chain
  Management — M

WAYLAND BAPTIST UNIVERSITY

Business Administration
  and Management—
    General — M
Education—General — M
Educational Leadership
  and Administration — M
Educational Media/
  Instructional Technology — M
Health Services
  Management and
  Hospital Administration — M
Higher Education — M
Human Resources
  Management — M
International Business — M
Management Information
  Systems — M

Organizational
  Management — M
Special Education — M

WAYNESBURG UNIVERSITY

Business Administration
  and Management—
    General — M,D
Education—General — M,D
Educational Media/
  Instructional Technology — M,D
Finance and Banking — M,D
Health Services
  Management and
  Hospital Administration — M,D
Human Resources
  Management — M,D
Medical/Surgical Nursing — M,D
Nursing and Healthcare
  Administration — M,D
Nursing Education — M,D
Nursing Informatics — M,D
Nursing—General — M,D
Organizational
  Management — M,D
Special Education — M,D

WAYNE STATE COLLEGE

Business Administration
  and Management—
    General — M
Business Education — M
Counselor Education — M
Curriculum and Instruction — M
Early Childhood Education — M
Education—General — M,O
Educational Leadership
  and Administration — M,O
Elementary Education — M
English as a Second
  Language — M
English Education — M
Exercise and Sports
  Science — M
Home Economics
  Education — M
Mathematics Education — M
Music Education — M
Organizational
  Management — M
Physical Education — M
Science Education — M
Social Sciences Education — M
Special Education — M
Sports Management — M
Vocational and Technical
  Education — M

WAYNE STATE UNIVERSITY

Accounting — M,D
Acute Care/Critical Care
  Nursing — M
Adult Education — M,D,O
Adult Nursing — M
Advertising and Public
  Relations — M,D
Allopathic Medicine — P
Art Education — M,D,O
Business Administration
  and Management—
    General — M,D*
Business Education — M,D,O
Clinical Laboratory
  Sciences/Medical
  Technology — M,O
Communication Disorders — M,D
Community Health
  Nursing — M
Community Health — M,O
Counselor Education — M,D,O
Curriculum and Instruction — M,D,O
Early Childhood Education — M,D,O
Education—General — M,D,O*
Educational Leadership
  and Administration — M,D,O
Educational Measurement
  and Evaluation — M,D,O
Educational Media/
  Instructional Technology — M,D,O
Educational Policy — M,D,O
Educational Psychology — M,D,O
Elementary Education — M,D,O
English Education — M,D,O
Environmental and
  Occupational Health — M,O

Foreign Languages Education	M,D,O
Foundations and Philosophy of Education	M,D,O
Health Education	M,D,O
Health Physics/ Radiological Health	M,D
Higher Education	M,D,O
Human Services	O
Information Studies	
Kinesiology and Movement Studies	M
Law	P,M,D
Library Science	M,O
Maternal and Child/ Neonatal Nursing	M,O
Mathematics Education	M,D,O
Medical Physics	M,D
Medicinal and Pharmaceutical Chemistry	P,M,D
Multilingual and Multicultural Education	M,D,O
Music Education	M,O
Nurse Anesthesia	M,O
Nursing Education	M,O
Nursing—General	D
Occupational Therapy	M
Pediatric Nursing	M,O
Pharmaceutical Administration	P,M,D,O
Pharmaceutical Sciences	P,M,D,O
Pharmacy	P,M,D,O
Physical Education	M
Physical Therapy	M
Physician Assistant Studies	M
Psychiatric Nursing	M,O
Public Health—General	M,O
Reading Education	M,D,O
Recreation and Park Management	M
Rehabilitation Sciences	M,O
Science Education	M,D,O
Secondary Education	M,D,O
Social Sciences Education	M,D,O
Social Work	M,D,O
Special Education	M,D,O
Sports Management	M
Taxation	M,D
Vocational and Technical Education	M,D,O

WEBBER INTERNATIONAL UNIVERSITY

Accounting	M
Business Administration and Management— General	M*
Sports Management	M

WEBER STATE UNIVERSITY

Accounting	M
Athletic Training and Sports Medicine	M
Business Administration and Management— General	M
Curriculum and Instruction	M
Education—General	M
Health Services Management and Hospital Administration	M
Legal and Justice Studies	M

WEBSTER UNIVERSITY

Advertising and Public Relations	M
Business Administration and Management— General	M,D,O
Early Childhood Education	M
Education—General	M,O
Educational Leadership and Administration	M,O
Educational Media/ Instructional Technology	M,O
English as a Second Language	M
Finance and Banking	M
Health Services Management and Hospital Administration	M,D,O

Human Resources Development	M,D,O
Human Resources Management	M,D,O
International Business	M
Legal and Justice Studies	M
Management Information Systems	M,D,O
Marketing	M,D,O
Mathematics Education	M,O
Music Education	M
Nonprofit Management	M,D,O
Nurse Anesthesia	M
Nursing—General	M,O
Organizational Management	M
Quality Management	M,D,O
Social Sciences Education	M,O
Special Education	M,O

WESLEYAN COLLEGE

Business Administration and Management— General	M
Early Childhood Education	M
Education—General	M

WESLEY BIBLICAL SEMINARY

Religious Education	P,M

WESLEY COLLEGE

Business Administration and Management— General	M
Education—General	M
Nursing—General	M

WEST CHESTER UNIVERSITY OF PENNSYLVANIA

Business Administration and Management— General	M,O
Communication Disorders	M,O
Community Health	M,O
Counselor Education	M,O
Early Childhood Education	M,O
Education—General	M,O
Educational Media/ Instructional Technology	M,O
Elementary Education	M,O
English as a Second Language	M,O
Entrepreneurship	M,O
Environmental and Occupational Health	M,O
Exercise and Sports Science	M,O
Foreign Languages Education	M,O
Health Education	M,O
Health Services Management and Hospital Administration	M,O
Human Resources Management	M,O
Kinesiology and Movement Studies	M,O
Management Information Systems	M,O
Marketing	M
Music Education	M,O
Nonprofit Management	M,O
Nursing and Healthcare Administration	M,O
Nursing Education	M,O
Nursing—General	M,O
Physical Education	M,O
Public Health—General	M,O
Reading Education	M,O
School Nursing	M,O
Science Education	M,O
Secondary Education	M,O
Social Sciences Education	M,O
Social Work	M
Special Education	M,O
Sports Management	M,O

WESTERN CAROLINA UNIVERSITY

Accounting	M
Business Administration and Management— General	M
Communication Disorders	M

Community College Education	M
Counselor Education	M
Education—General	M,D,O
Educational Leadership and Administration	M,D,O
English as a Second Language	M
Entrepreneurship	M
Health Services Management and Hospital Administration	M
Higher Education	M
Human Resources Development	M
Music Education	M
Nursing Education	M,O
Nursing—General	M,O
Physical Education	M
Physical Therapy	M
Project Management	M
Social Work	M

WESTERN CONNECTICUT STATE UNIVERSITY

Accounting	M
Adult Nursing	M
Business Administration and Management— General	M
Counselor Education	M
Curriculum and Instruction	M
Education—General	M,D
Educational Leadership and Administration	D
Educational Media/ Instructional Technology	M
English as a Second Language	M
English Education	M
Health Services Management and Hospital Administration	M
Mathematics Education	M
Music Education	M
Nursing—General	M
Reading Education	M
Science Education	M
Secondary Education	M
Special Education	M

WESTERN GOVERNORS UNIVERSITY

Business Administration and Management— General	M
Education—General	M,O
Educational Leadership and Administration	M,O
Educational Measurement and Evaluation	M,O
Educational Media/ Instructional Technology	M,O
English Education	M,O
Higher Education	M,O
Management Information Systems	M
Management Strategy and Policy	M
Mathematics Education	M,O
Science Education	M,O

WESTERN ILLINOIS UNIVERSITY

Accounting	M
Business Administration and Management— General	M
Communication Disorders	M
Counselor Education	M
Distance Education Development	M,O
Education—General	M,D,O
Educational Leadership and Administration	M,D,O
Educational Media/ Instructional Technology	M,O
Elementary Education	M
Foundations and Philosophy of Education	M
Health Education	M,O
Health Services Management and Hospital Administration	M,O

Kinesiology and Movement Studies	M
Nonprofit Management	M,O
Reading Education	M
Recreation and Park Management	M
Special Education	M
Sports Management	M
Student Affairs	M
Travel and Tourism	M

WESTERN INTERNATIONAL UNIVERSITY

Business Administration and Management— General	M
Finance and Banking	M
International Business	M
Management Information Systems	M
Management Strategy and Policy	M
Marketing	M
Organizational Behavior	M
Organizational Management	M

WESTERN KENTUCKY UNIVERSITY

Art Education	M
Business Administration and Management— General	M
Business Education	M,O
Communication Disorders	M
Counselor Education	M,O
Early Childhood Education	M
Educational Leadership and Administration	M,O
Educational Media/ Instructional Technology	M
Educational Psychology	M,O
Elementary Education	M,O
English as a Second Language	M
English Education	M
Health Services Management and Hospital Administration	M
Middle School Education	M,O
Music Education	M
Nursing—General	M
Physical Education	M
Public Health—General	M
Reading Education	M
Recreation and Park Management	M
Science Education	M
Secondary Education	M,O
Social Work	M
Special Education	M
Student Affairs	M,O

WESTERN MICHIGAN UNIVERSITY

Accounting	M
Art Education	M
Athletic Training and Sports Medicine	M
Business Administration and Management— General	M
Communication Disorders	M,D
Counselor Education	M,D
Educational Leadership and Administration	M,D,O
Educational Measurement and Evaluation	M,D,O
Educational Media/ Instructional Technology	M,D,O
English Education	M,D
Exercise and Sports Science	M
Finance and Banking	M
Health Education	D
Health Services Management and Hospital Administration	M,D,O
Human Resources Development	M,D
Mathematics Education	M,D
Music Education	M
Nonprofit Management	M,D,O
Nursing—General	M
Occupational Therapy	M

Physical Education	M
Physician Assistant Studies	M
Reading Education	M,D
Rehabilitation Sciences	M
Science Education	M,D*
Social Work	M
Special Education	M,D
Sports Management	M
Vocational and Technical Education	M

WESTERN NEW ENGLAND COLLEGE

Accounting	M
Business Administration and Management— General	M
Elementary Education	M
English Education	M
Law	P,M
Mathematics Education	M
Sports Management	M

WESTERN NEW MEXICO UNIVERSITY

Business Administration and Management— General	M
Counselor Education	M
Education—General	M
Educational Leadership and Administration	M
Elementary Education	M
English as a Second Language	M
Multilingual and Multicultural Education	M
Occupational Therapy	M
Reading Education	M
Secondary Education	M
Social Work	M
Special Education	M

WESTERN OREGON UNIVERSITY

Early Childhood Education	M
Education—General	M
Educational Media/ Instructional Technology	M
Health Education	M
Mathematics Education	M
Multilingual and Multicultural Education	M
Science Education	M
Secondary Education	M
Social Sciences Education	M
Special Education	M

WESTERN SEMINARY

Human Resources Development	M

WESTERN STATES CHIROPRACTIC COLLEGE

Chiropractic	P

WESTERN STATE UNIVERSITY COLLEGE OF LAW

Law	P

WESTERN UNIVERSITY OF HEALTH SCIENCES

Allied Health—General	M,D
Dentistry	P
Family Nurse Practitioner Studies	M
Health Education	M
Nursing—General	M
Optometry	P
Osteopathic Medicine	P
Pharmaceutical Sciences	M
Pharmacy	P
Physical Therapy	D
Physician Assistant Studies	M
Veterinary Medicine	P

WESTERN WASHINGTON UNIVERSITY

Adult Education	M
Business Administration and Management— General	M
Communication Disorders	M
Counselor Education	M

Education of the Gifted	M
Education—General	M
Educational Leadership and Administration	M
Elementary Education	M
Environmental Education	M
Exercise and Sports Science	M
Higher Education	M
Physical Education	M
Science Education	M
Secondary Education	M

WESTFIELD STATE COLLEGE

Counselor Education	M
Early Childhood Education	M
Education—General	M,O
Educational Leadership and Administration	M,O
Educational Media/ Instructional Technology	M
Elementary Education	M
Physical Education	M
Reading Education	M
Secondary Education	M
Special Education	M
Vocational and Technical Education	M,O

WEST LIBERTY UNIVERSITY

Education—General	M

WESTMINSTER CHOIR COLLEGE OF RIDER UNIVERSITY

Music Education	M

WESTMINSTER COLLEGE (PA)

Counselor Education	M,O
Education—General	M,O
Educational Leadership and Administration	M,O
Reading Education	M,O

WESTMINSTER COLLEGE (UT)

Accounting	M,O
Business Administration and Management— General	M,O
Education—General	M
Family Nurse Practitioner Studies	M
Nurse Anesthesia	M
Nursing Education	M
Nursing—General	M
Public Health—General	M

WEST SUBURBAN COLLEGE OF NURSING

Nursing—General	M

WEST TEXAS A&M UNIVERSITY

Accounting	M
Business Administration and Management— General	M
Communication Disorders	M
Counselor Education	M
Curriculum and Instruction	M
Education—General	M
Educational Leadership and Administration	M
Educational Measurement and Evaluation	M
Educational Media/ Instructional Technology	M
Exercise and Sports Science	M
Finance and Banking	M
Nursing—General	M
Reading Education	M
Special Education	M

WEST VIRGINIA SCHOOL OF OSTEOPATHIC MEDICINE

Osteopathic Medicine	P

WEST VIRGINIA UNIVERSITY

Accounting	M
Agricultural Education	M,D
Allopathic Medicine	P
Art Education	M
Athletic Training and Sports Medicine	M,D

Business Administration and Management— General	M
Communication Disorders	M,D
Community Health	M
Counselor Education	M
Curriculum and Instruction	M,D
Dentistry	P
Early Childhood Education	M,D
Education of Students with Severe/Multiple Disabilities	M,D
Education of the Gifted	M,D
Education—General	M,D
Educational Leadership and Administration	M,D
Educational Media/ Instructional Technology	M,D
Educational Psychology	M
Elementary Education	M
English as a Second Language	M
Environmental and Occupational Health	D
Environmental Education	M,D
Exercise and Sports Science	M,D
Health Education	M,D
Health Promotion	M,D
Higher Education	M,D
Human Services	M
Industrial Hygiene	M
Law	P
Legal and Justice Studies	M
Marketing	M
Mathematics Education	M,D
Medicinal and Pharmaceutical Chemistry	M,D
Music Education	M,D
Nursing—General	M,D,O
Occupational Therapy	M
Oral and Dental Sciences	M
Pharmaceutical Administration	M,D
Pharmaceutical Sciences	M,D
Pharmacy	P,M,D
Physical Education	M,D
Physical Therapy	D
Public Health—General	M
Reading Education	M
Recreation and Park Management	M
Secondary Education	M,D
Social Work	M
Special Education	M,D
Sports Management	M,D

WEST VIRGINIA WESLEYAN COLLEGE

Athletic Training and Sports Medicine	M
Business Administration and Management— General	M
Education—General	M
Nursing—General	M

WHEATON COLLEGE

Education—General	M
Elementary Education	M
English as a Second Language	M,O
Religious Education	M
Secondary Education	M

WHEELING JESUIT UNIVERSITY

Accounting	M
Business Administration and Management— General	M
Nursing—General	M
Organizational Management	M
Physical Therapy	D

WHEELOCK COLLEGE

Early Childhood Education	M
Education—General	M
Educational Leadership and Administration	M
Elementary Education	M
Reading Education	M
Social Work	M
Special Education	M

WHITTIER COLLEGE

Education—General	M
Educational Leadership and Administration	M
Elementary Education	M
Law	P,M
Legal and Justice Studies	P,M
Secondary Education	M

WHITWORTH UNIVERSITY

Counselor Education	M
Education of the Gifted	M
Education—General	M
Educational Leadership and Administration	M
Elementary Education	M
International Business	M
Secondary Education	M
Special Education	M

WICHITA STATE UNIVERSITY

Accounting	M
Allied Health—General	M,D
Business Administration and Management— General	M
Communication Disorders	M,D
Counselor Education	M,O
Curriculum and Instruction	M
Education of the Gifted	M
Education—General	M,D,O
Educational Leadership and Administration	M,D,O
Educational Psychology	M,O
Exercise and Sports Science	M
Family Nurse Practitioner Studies	M,D
Human Services	M
Music Education	M
Nurse Midwifery	M,D
Nursing and Healthcare Administration	M,D
Nursing—General	M,D
Physical Therapy	D
Physician Assistant Studies	M
Social Work	M
Special Education	M
Sports Management	M

WIDENER UNIVERSITY

Accounting	M
Adult Education	M,D
Business Administration and Management— General	M
Counselor Education	M,D
Early Childhood Education	M,D
Education—General	M,D
Educational Leadership and Administration	M,D
Educational Media/ Instructional Technology	M,D
Educational Psychology	M,D
Elementary Education	M,D
English Education	M,D
Foundations and Philosophy of Education	M,D
Health Education	M,D
Health Law	P,M,D
Health Services Management and Hospital Administration	M
Human Resources Management	M
Law	P,M,D
Mathematics Education	M,D
Middle School Education	M,D
Nursing—General	M,D,O
Physical Therapy	D
Reading Education	M,D
Science Education	M,D
Social Sciences Education	M,D
Social Work	M,D
Special Education	M,D
Taxation	M

WILFRID LAURIER UNIVERSITY

Business Administration and Management— General	M,D
Foundations and Philosophy of Education	M

Kinesiology and Movement Studies	M
Physical Education	M
Social Work	M,D

WILKES UNIVERSITY

Accounting	M
Business Administration and Management—General	M
Computer Education	M,D
Distance Education Development	M,D
Education—General	M,D
Educational Leadership and Administration	M,D
Educational Measurement and Evaluation	M,D
Educational Media/Instructional Technology	M,D
Elementary Education	M,D
English Education	M,D
Entrepreneurship	M
Finance and Banking	M
Higher Education	M,D
Human Resources Management	M
International Business	M
Marketing	M
Mathematics Education	M
Nursing—General	M
Pharmacy	P
Science Education	M,D
Secondary Education	M,D
Social Sciences Education	M,D
Special Education	M,D

WILLAMETTE UNIVERSITY

Business Administration and Management—General	M
Education—General	M
Law	P,M

WILLIAM CAREY UNIVERSITY

Art Education	M,O
Business Administration and Management—General	M
Education of the Gifted	M,O
Education—General	M,O
Elementary Education	M,O
English Education	M,O
Nursing—General	M
Secondary Education	M,O
Social Sciences Education	M,O
Special Education	M,O

WILLIAM HOWARD TAFT UNIVERSITY

Education—General	M
Law	P,M
Legal and Justice Studies	P,M
Taxation	P,M

WILLIAM MITCHELL COLLEGE OF LAW

Law	P

WILLIAM PATERSON UNIVERSITY OF NEW JERSEY

Business Administration and Management—General	M
Communication Disorders	M
Counselor Education	M
Education—General	M
Educational Leadership and Administration	M
Nursing—General	M
Reading Education	M
Special Education	M

WILLIAM WOODS UNIVERSITY

Curriculum and Instruction	M,O
Educational Leadership and Administration	M,O
Elementary Education	M,O
Health Services Management and Hospital Administration	M,O
Human Resources Development	M,O

Physical Education	M,O
Secondary Education	M,O
Special Education	M,O

WILMINGTON COLLEGE

Education—General	M
Reading Education	M
Special Education	M

WILMINGTON UNIVERSITY

Adult Nursing	M
Business Administration and Management—General	M
Counselor Education	M
Education of the Gifted	M
Education—General	M
Educational Leadership and Administration	M,D
Educational Media/Instructional Technology	M
Elementary Education	M
Family Nurse Practitioner Studies	M
Finance and Banking	M
Health Services Management and Hospital Administration	M
Human Resources Management	M
Human Services	M
Logistics	M
Management Information Systems	M
Nursing—General	M
Organizational Management	M
Reading Education	M
Secondary Education	M
Special Education	M
Transportation Management	M
Vocational and Technical Education	M
Women's Health Nursing	M

WILSON COLLEGE

Education—General	M
Elementary Education	M
Secondary Education	M

WINGATE UNIVERSITY

Business Administration and Management—General	M
Education—General	M
Educational Leadership and Administration	M
Elementary Education	M
Pharmacy	P
Physical Education	M
Sports Management	M

WINONA STATE UNIVERSITY

Adult Nursing	M,D,O
Counselor Education	M
Education—General	M
Educational Leadership and Administration	M,O
Family Nurse Practitioner Studies	M,D,O
Nursing and Healthcare Administration	M,D,O
Nursing Education	M,D,O
Nursing—General	M,D,O
Recreation and Park Management	M,O
Special Education	M
Sports Management	M,O

WINSTON-SALEM STATE UNIVERSITY

Business Administration and Management—General	M
Elementary Education	M
Management Information Systems	M
Nursing—General	M
Occupational Therapy	M
Physical Therapy	M

WINTHROP UNIVERSITY

Art Education	M
Business Administration and Management—General	M
Counselor Education	M
Education—General	M
Educational Leadership and Administration	M
Middle School Education	M
Music Education	M
Physical Education	M
Project Management	M,O
Reading Education	M
Secondary Education	M
Social Work	M
Special Education	M

WITTENBERG UNIVERSITY

Education—General	M

WOODBURY UNIVERSITY

Business Administration and Management—General	M
Organizational Management	M
Real Estate	M

WORCESTER POLYTECHNIC INSTITUTE

Business Administration and Management—General	M,O
Management Information Systems	M,D,O
Marketing	M,O
Organizational Management	M,O

WORCESTER STATE COLLEGE

Accounting	M
Business Administration and Management—General	M
Communication Disorders	M
Community Health Nursing	M
Early Childhood Education	M
Education—General	M,O
Educational Leadership and Administration	M,O
Elementary Education	M
English Education	M
Foreign Languages Education	M
Health Education	M
Health Services Management and Hospital Administration	M
Middle School Education	M
Nonprofit Management	M
Occupational Therapy	M
Organizational Management	M
Reading Education	M,O
Secondary Education	M
Social Sciences Education	M
Special Education	M

WORLD MEDICINE INSTITUTE OF ACUPUNCTURE AND HERBAL MEDICINE

Acupuncture and Oriental Medicine	M

WRIGHT STATE UNIVERSITY

Accounting	M
Acute Care/Critical Care Nursing	M
Adult Education	O
Adult Nursing	M
Allopathic Medicine	P
Business Administration and Management—General	M
Business Education	M
Community Health Nursing	M
Computer Education	M
Counselor Education	M
Curriculum and Instruction	M,O
Early Childhood Education	M

Education of the Gifted	M
Education—General	M,O
Educational Leadership and Administration	M,O
Elementary Education	M
English as a Second Language	M
Family Nurse Practitioner Studies	M
Finance and Banking	M
Health Education	M
Health Promotion	M
Health Services Management and Hospital Administration	M
Higher Education	M,O
International and Comparative Education	M
International Business	M
Library Science	M
Logistics	M
Management Information Systems	M
Marketing	M
Mathematics Education	M
Medical Physics	M
Middle School Education	M
Music Education	M
Nursing and Healthcare Administration	M
Nursing—General	M
Pediatric Nursing	M
Physical Education	M
Project Management	M
Public Health—General	M
Recreation and Park Management	M
School Nursing	M
Science Education	M
Secondary Education	M
Special Education	M
Supply Chain Management	M
Vocational and Technical Education	M

XAVIER UNIVERSITY

Business Administration and Management—General	M
Counselor Education	M
Early Childhood Education	M
Education—General	M
Educational Leadership and Administration	M
Elementary Education	M
Finance and Banking	M
Health Law	M
Health Services Management and Hospital Administration	M
Human Resources Development	M
International Business	M
Management Information Systems	M
Management Strategy and Policy	M
Marketing	M
Multilingual and Multicultural Education	M
Nursing and Healthcare Administration	M
Nursing Education	M
Nursing Informatics	M
Nursing—General	M
Occupational Therapy	M
Reading Education	M
Religious Education	M
Secondary Education	M
Special Education	M
Sports Management	M

XAVIER UNIVERSITY OF LOUISIANA

Counselor Education	M
Curriculum and Instruction	M
Education—General	M
Educational Leadership and Administration	M
Pharmacy	P

YALE UNIVERSITY

Accounting	D

*M—master's degree; P—first professional degree; D—doctorate; O—other advanced degree; *—Close-Up and/or Display*

Allopathic Medicine	P
Business Administration and Management—	
General	M,D*
Environmental and Occupational Health	M,D
Epidemiology	M,D
Finance and Banking	D
Health Services Management and Hospital Administration	M,D
International Health	M
Law	P,M,D
Marketing	D
Nursing—General	M,D,O
Physician Assistant Studies	M,O
Public Health—General	M,D

YESHIVA UNIVERSITY

Accounting	M
Educational Leadership and Administration	M,D,O
Law	P,M
Religious Education	M,D,O
Social Work	M,D

YORK COLLEGE OF PENNSYLVANIA

Business Administration and Management—	
General	M
Education—General	M
Nursing—General	M

YORK UNIVERSITY

Business Administration and Management—	
General	M,D*
Education—General	M,D
Finance and Banking	M,D
Human Resources Management	M,D
International Business	M,D
Kinesiology and Movement Studies	M,D
Law	P,M,D
Nursing—General	M
Social Work	M,D

YO SAN UNIVERSITY OF TRADITIONAL CHINESE MEDICINE

Acupuncture and Oriental Medicine	M

YOUNGSTOWN STATE UNIVERSITY

Accounting	M
Business Administration and Management—	
General	M,O
Counselor Education	M
Curriculum and Instruction	M
Early Childhood Education	M
Education of the Gifted	M
Education—General	M,D
Educational Leadership and Administration	M,D
Educational Media/ Instructional Technology	M
Finance and Banking	M
Foundations and Philosophy of Education	M,D
Health Services Management and Hospital Administration	M
Human Services	M
Marketing	M
Mathematics Education	M
Middle School Education	M
Music Education	M
Nursing—General	M
Physical Therapy	D
Reading Education	M
Science Education	M
Secondary Education	M
Special Education	M

ACADEMIC AND PROFESSIONAL PROGRAMS IN BUSINESS

Section 1
Business Administration and Management

This section contains a directory of institutions offering graduate work in business administration and management, followed by in-depth entries submitted by institutions that chose to prepare detailed program descriptions. Additional information about programs listed in the directory but not augmented by an in-depth entry may be obtained by writing directly to the dean of a graduate school or chair of a department at the address given in the directory.

For programs offering related work, see also in this book Sections 2–18 and *Education (Business Education), Health Services, Nursing (Nursing and Healthcare Administration),* and *Sports Management.* In the other guides in this series:

Graduate Programs in the Humanities, Arts & Social Sciences

See *Art and Art History (Arts Administration), Economics, Family and Consumer Sciences (Consumer Economics), Political Science and International Affairs, Psychology (Industrial and Organizational Psychology),* and *Public, Regional, and Industrial Affairs (Industrial and Labor Relations)*

Graduate Programs in the Physical Sciences, Mathematics, Agricultural Sciences, the Environment & Natural Resources

See *Environmental Sciences and Management (Environmental Management and Policy)* and *Mathematical Sciences*

Graduate Programs in Engineering & Applied Sciences

See *Computer Science and Information Technology, Civil and Environmental Engineering (Construction Engineering and Management), Industrial Engineering,* and *Management of Engineering and Technology*

CONTENTS

Program Directory

Close-Ups and Displays

Business Administration and Management—General

Adelphi University, School of Business, Graduate Opportunity for Accelerated Learning MBA Program, Garden City, NY 11530-0701. Offers accounting (MBA); finance (MBA). *Accreditation:* AACSB. Part-time and evening/weekend programs available. *Students:* 4 full-time (3 women), 25 part-time (13 women); includes 11 minority (8 African Americans, 1 Asian American or Pacific Islander, 2 Hispanic Americans), 1 international. Average age 35. In 2009, 14 master's awarded. *Entrance requirements:* For master's, GMAT, 2 letters of recommendation. Additional exam requirements/recommendations for international students: Required—TOEFL (minimum score 550 paper-based; 213 computer-based; 80 iBT). *Application deadline:* For fall admission, 4/1 for international students; for spring admission, 11/1 for international students. Applications are processed on a rolling basis. Application fee: $50. Electronic applications accepted. *Expenses:* Tuition: Full-time $28,340; part-time $830 per credit. Required fees: $600; $250 per credit. Full-time tuition and fees vary according to course load and program. *Financial support:* Research assistantships with full and partial tuition reimbursements, career-related internships or fieldwork, Federal Work-Study, institutionally sponsored loans, scholarships/grants, and unspecified assistantships available. Financial award application deadline: 3/1; financial award applicants required to submit FAFSA. *Faculty research:* Capital market, executive compensation, business ethics, classical value theory, labor economics. *Unit head:* Rakesh Gupta, Chairperson, 516-877-4670, Fax: 516-877-4607, E-mail: gradbusinquiries@adelphi.edu. *Application contact:* Christine Murphy, Director of Admissions, 516-877-3050, Fax: 516-877-3039, E-mail: graduateadmissions@adelphi.edu.

Adelphi University, School of Business, MBA Program, Garden City, NY 11530-0701. Offers finance (MBA); management information systems (MBA); management/human resource management (MBA); marketing/e-commerce (MBA). *Accreditation:* AACSB. Part-time and evening/weekend programs available. *Students:* 77 full-time (30 women), 183 part-time (91 women); includes 56 minority (29 African Americans, 17 Asian Americans or Pacific Islanders, 10 Hispanic Americans), 81 international. Average age 30. In 2009, 64 master's awarded. *Degree requirements:* For master's, capstone course. *Entrance requirements:* For master's, GMAT, 2 letters of recommendation. Additional exam requirements/recommendations for international students: Required—TOEFL (minimum score 550 paper-based; 213 computer-based; 80 iBT). *Application deadline:* For fall admission, 4/1 for international students; for spring admission, 11/1 for international students. Applications are processed on a rolling basis. Application fee: $50. Electronic applications accepted. *Expenses:* Tuition: Full-time $28,340; part-time $830 per credit. Required fees: $600; $250 per credit. Full-time tuition and fees vary according to course load and program. *Financial support:* Research assistantships with full and partial tuition reimbursements, career-related internships or fieldwork, Federal Work-Study, institutionally sponsored loans, scholarships/grants, and unspecified assistantships available. Financial award application deadline: 3/1; financial award applicants required to submit FAFSA. *Faculty research:* Supply chain management, distribution channels, productivity benchmark analysis, data envelopment analysis, financial portfolio analysis. *Unit head:* Rakesh Gupta, 516-877-4670, Fax: 516-877-4607, E-mail: gradbusinquiries@adelphi.edu. *Application contact:* Christine Murphy, Director of Admissions, 516-877-3050, Fax: 516-877-3039, E-mail: graduateadmissions@adelphi.edu.

Adler Graduate School, Program in Adlerian Studies, Richfield, MN 55423. Offers art therapy specialization (MA); clinical counseling track (MA); coaching and consulting in organizations (Certificate); management consulting and organizational leadership (MA); marriage and family track (MA); non-clinical Adlerian studies track (MA); personal and professional life coaching (Certificate); school counseling (MA). Part-time and evening/weekend programs available. *Degree requirements:* For master's, thesis or alternative, 500-700 hour internship (depending on license choice). *Entrance requirements:* For master's, minimum undergraduate GPA of 3.0, 12 credits of course work in psychology or related field.

Alabama Agricultural and Mechanical University, School of Graduate Studies, School of Business, Department of Management and Marketing, Huntsville, AL 35811. Offers MBA. Part-time and evening/weekend programs available. *Degree requirements:* For master's, comprehensive exam, thesis optional. *Entrance requirements:* For master's, GMAT, minimum undergraduate GPA of 2.5. Additional exam requirements/recommendations for international students: Required—TOEFL (minimum score 500 paper-based; 173 computer-based; 61 iBT). Electronic applications accepted. *Faculty research:* Consumer behavior of blacks, small business marketing, economics of education, China in transition, international economics.

Alabama State University, School of Graduate Studies, College of Business Administration, Montgomery, AL 36101-0271. Offers M Acc. *Accreditation:* ACBSP. Part-time programs available. *Entrance requirements:* For master's, GMAT, graduate writing competency test. Additional exam requirements/recommendations for international students: Required—TOEFL (minimum score 500 paper-based; 173 computer-based).

Alaska Pacific University, Graduate Programs, Business Administration Department, Program in Business Administration, Anchorage, AK 99508-4672. Offers business administration (MBA); health services administration (MBA). Part-time and evening/weekend programs available. *Degree requirements:* For master's, capstone course. *Entrance requirements:* For master's, GMAT or GRE General Test, minimum GPA of 3.0.

Albany State University, College of Business, Program in Business Administration, Albany, GA 31705-2717. Offers MBA. *Expenses:* Tuition, state resident: full-time $2970; part-time $162 per credit hour. Tuition, nonresident: full-time $12,168; part-time $676 per credit hour. Required fees: $962; $75 per credit hour.

Albertus Magnus College, Program in Leadership, New Haven, CT 06511-1189. Offers MA. *Faculty:* 4 full-time (2 women). *Students:* 1 (woman) full-time, 32 part-time (23 women); includes 12 minority (9 African Americans, 1 Asian American or Pacific Islander, 2 Hispanic Americans). *Degree requirements:* For master's, thesis optional. *Entrance requirements:* For master's, interview. *Unit head:* Dr. Howard Fero, Director, 203-977-7100, Fax: 203-777-2112, E-mail: hfero@albertus.edu. *Application contact:* Joseph Chadwick, Director of Program Development, 203-777-0800 Ext. 114, Fax: 203-777-2112.

Albertus Magnus College, Program in Management, New Haven, CT 06511-1189. Offers business administration (MBA); management (MSM). Program also offered in East Hartford, CT. Evening/weekend programs available. *Faculty:* 16 full-time (7 women), 36 part-time/adjunct (14 women). *Students:* 247 full-time (133 women); includes 98 minority (73 African Americans, 2 American Indian/Alaska Native, 3 Asian Americans or Pacific Islanders, 20 Hispanic Americans). Average age 35. 90 applicants, 78% accepted, 66 enrolled. In 2009, 233 master's awarded. *Degree requirements:* For master's, thesis. *Entrance requirements:* For master's, 3 years of management or related experience, minimum GPA of 2.5. Additional exam requirements/recommendations for international students: Required—TOEFL. *Application deadline:* Applications are processed on a rolling basis. Application fee: $75. *Financial support:* Available to part-time students. *Unit head:* Dr. John Donohue, Vice President, Academic Affairs, 203-773-8068, Fax: 203-773-8525, E-mail: jdonohue@albertus.edu. *Application contact:* Amy Kwiatkowski, Director of Program Development, 203-777-0800 Ext. 123, Fax: 203-777-2112, E-mail: akwiatkowski@albertus.edu.

Alcorn State University, School of Graduate Studies, School of Business, Natchez, MS 39122-8399. Offers MBA.

Alfred University, Graduate School, College of Business, Alfred, NY 14802-1205. Offers business administration (MBA). *Accreditation:* AACSB. Part-time programs available. *Entrance requirements:* For master's, GMAT. Additional exam requirements/recommendations for international students: Required—TOEFL (minimum score 590 paper-based; 243 computer-based; 90 iBT), IELTS (minimum score 6.5). Electronic applications accepted. *Expenses:* Tuition: Full-time $33,296; part-time $708 per credit hour. Required fees: $880; $144 per year. Full-time tuition and fees vary according to program. *Faculty research:* Regional economic development, activity-based costing, nonprofit consumer behavior.

Alliant International University–Los Angeles, Marshall Goldsmith School of Management, Business Division, Alhambra, CA 91803-1360. Offers DBA.

Alliant International University–México City, Marshall Goldsmith School of Management, Mexico City, Mexico. Offers international business administration (MIBA); international relations (MA). Part-time and evening/weekend programs available. *Entrance requirements:* For master's, GMAT, minimum GPA of 3.0. Additional exam requirements/recommendations for international students: Required—TOEFL (minimum score 550 paper-based; 213 computer-based), TWE (minimum score 5). Electronic applications accepted. *Faculty research:* Environmental impact and business in Mexico.

Alliant International University–San Diego, Marshall Goldsmith School of Management, Business and Management Division, San Diego, CA 92131-1799. Offers business administration (MBA); information and technology management (DBA); international business (MIBA, DBA), including finance (DBA), marketing (DBA); strategic business (DBA); sustainable management (MBA); MBA/MA; MBA/PhD. Part-time and evening/weekend programs available. *Degree requirements:* For doctorate, thesis/dissertation. *Entrance requirements:* For master's, GMAT, minimum GPA of 3.0; for doctorate, GMAT, minimum GPA of 3.3. Additional exam requirements/recommendations for international students: Required—TOEFL (minimum score 550 paper-based; 213 computer-based), TWE (minimum score 5). Electronic applications accepted. *Faculty research:* Consumer behavior, international business, strategic management, information systems.

Alliant International University–San Francisco, Marshall Goldsmith School of Management, Presidio School of Management, San Francisco, CA 94133-1221. Offers sustainable management (MBA).

Alvernia University, Graduate Studies, Department of Business, Reading, PA 19607-1799. Offers MBA. *Accreditation:* ACBSP. Part-time and evening/weekend programs available. *Degree requirements:* For master's, thesis optional. *Entrance requirements:* For master's, GMAT, GRE, or MAT. Electronic applications accepted.

Alverno College, School of Business, Milwaukee, WI 53234-3922. Offers MBA. Evening/weekend programs available. *Faculty:* 4 full-time (1 woman), 2 part-time/adjunct (both women). *Students:* 94 full-time (88 women), 2 part-time (both women); includes 25 minority (8 African Americans, 2 American Indian/Alaska Native, 3 Asian Americans or Pacific Islanders, 12 Hispanic Americans), 1 international. Average age 34. 66 applicants, 55% accepted, 30 enrolled. In 2009, 27 master's awarded. *Entrance requirements:* For master's, 3 or more years relevant work experience. Additional exam requirements/recommendations for international students: Required—TOEFL. *Application deadline:* For fall admission, 7/15 priority date for domestic and international students; for spring admission, 12/15 priority date for domestic and international students. Applications are processed on a rolling basis. Application fee: $50. Electronic applications accepted. *Expenses:* Contact institution. *Financial support:* Federal Work-Study available. Support available to part-time students. Financial award application deadline: 4/15; financial award applicants required to submit FAFSA. *Unit head:* William McEachern, MBA Program Director, 414-382-6238, E-mail: william.mceachern@alverno.edu. *Application contact:* Carolyn Wise, Graduate Recruiter, 414-382-6045, Fax: 414-382-6354, E-mail: carolyn.wise@alverno.edu.

Amberton University, Graduate School, Department of Business Administration, Garland, TX 75041-5595. Offers general business (MBA); management (MBA). Part-time and evening/weekend programs available. *Entrance requirements:* For master's, minimum GPA of 3.0.

The American College, Richard D. Irwin Graduate School, Bryn Mawr, PA 19010-2105. Offers financial services (MSFS); leadership (MSM). Part-time and evening/weekend programs available. Postbaccalaureate distance learning degree programs offered (minimal on-campus study). Electronic applications accepted. *Faculty research:* Retirement counseling, social security, aging, family composition, inflation.

American College of Thessaloniki, Department of Business Administration, Pylea, Greece. Offers banking and finance (MBA); entrepreneurship (MBA, Certificate); finance (Certificate); management (MBA, Certificate); marketing (MBA, Certificate). Part-time and evening/weekend programs available. *Faculty:* 6 full-time (1 woman), 10 part-time/adjunct (2 women). *Students:* 6 full-time (3 women), 44 part-time (30 women), 17 international. 25 applicants, 96% accepted, 24 enrolled. *Degree requirements:* For master's, thesis. *Entrance requirements:* For master's, bachelor's degree. *Application deadline:* For fall admission, 9/30 priority date for domestic students; for spring admission, 2/18 priority date for domestic students. Applications are processed on a rolling basis. Application fee: $70. Electronic applications accepted. *Unit head:* Dr. Nikolaos Kourkoumelis, Chair, Business Division, 30-310-398386, E-mail: nikolaos@act.edu. *Application contact:* Elli Konstantinou, Director of Student Recruitment, 30-310-398238, E-mail: elli@act.edu.

American Graduate University, Program in Acquisition Management, Covina, CA 91724. Offers MAM, Certificate. Part-time programs available. Postbaccalaureate distance learning degree programs offered (no on-campus study). *Faculty:* 2 full-time (1 woman), 15 part-time/adjunct (2 women). *Students:* 350 part-time. In 2009, 188 master's, 10 Certificates awarded. *Entrance requirements:* Additional exam requirements/recommendations for international students: Required—TOEFL. *Application deadline:* Applications are processed on a rolling basis. Application fee: $50. Electronic applications accepted. *Expenses:* Tuition: Part-time $275 per credit. *Unit head:* Paul McDonald, President, 626-966-4576 Ext. 1006, E-mail: paulmcdonald@agu.edu. *Application contact:* Marie Sirney, Admissions Director, 626-966-4576 Ext. 1003, Fax: 626-915-1709, E-mail: mariesirney@agu.edu.

American Graduate University, Program in Business Administration, Covina, CA 91724. Offers MBA. Part-time programs available. Postbaccalaureate distance learning degree programs offered (no on-campus study). *Faculty:* 2 full-time (1 woman), 15 part-time/adjunct (2 women). *Students:* 252 part-time. In 2009, 25 master's awarded. *Entrance requirements:* Additional exam requirements/recommendations for international students: Required—TOEFL. *Application deadline:* Applications are processed on a rolling basis. Application fee: $50. Electronic applications accepted. *Expenses:* Tuition: Part-time $275 per credit. *Unit head:* Paul McDonald, President, 626-966-4576 Ext. 1006, E-mail: paulmcdonald@agu.edu. *Application contact:* Marie J. Sirney, Executive Vice President, 626-966-4576, Fax: 626-915-1709, E-mail: mariesirney@agu.edu.

American Graduate University, Program in Contract Management, Covina, CA 91724. Offers MCM, Certificate. Part-time programs available. Postbaccalaureate distance learning degree programs offered (no on-campus study). *Faculty:* 2 full-time (1 woman), 15 part-time/adjunct (2 women). *Students:* 229 part-time. In 2009, 61 master's awarded. *Entrance requirements:* Additional exam requirements/recommendations for international students: Required—TOEFL. *Application deadline:* Applications are processed on a rolling basis. Application fee: $50. Electronic applications accepted. *Expenses:* Tuition: Part-time $275 per credit. *Unit head:* Paul McDonald, President, 626-966-4576 Ext. 1006, E-mail: paulmcdonald@agu.edu. *Application contact:* Marie Sirney, 626-966-4576 Ext. 1003, Fax: 626-915-1709, E-mail: mariesirney@agu.edu.

American InterContinental University, School of Business, Houston, TX 77042. Offers management (MBA).

American InterContinental University Buckhead Campus, Program in Business Administration, Atlanta, GA 30326-1016. Offers accounting and finance (MBA); management (MBA); marketing (MBA). Evening/weekend programs available. Postbaccalaureate distance learning degree programs offered. *Entrance requirements:* For master's, minimum cumulative undergraduate GPA of 2.0. Additional exam requirements/recommendations for international students: Required—TOEFL (minimum score 530 paper-based; 230 computer-based). Electronic applications accepted. *Faculty research:* Leadership management, international advertising.

American InterContinental University–London, Program in Business Administration, London, United Kingdom. Offers international business (MBA). *Degree requirements:* For master's, thesis optional. *Entrance requirements:* For master's, interview, professional experience. Additional exam requirements/recommendations for international students: Required—TOEFL or IELTS recommended. Electronic applications accepted.

American InterContinental University Online, Program in Business Administration, Hoffman Estates, IL 60192. Offers accounting and finance (MBA); finance (MBA); healthcare management (MBA); human resource management (MBA); international business (MBA); management (MBA); marketing (MBA); operations management (MBA); organizational psychology and development (MBA); project management (MBA). Evening/weekend programs available. Postbaccalaureate distance learning degree programs offered (no on-campus study). *Entrance requirements:* Additional exam requirements/recommendations for international students: Required—TOEFL (minimum score 550 paper-based; 213 computer-based). Electronic applications accepted.

American InterContinental University South Florida, Program in International Business, Weston, FL 33326. Offers accounting and finance (MBA); human resource management (MBA); management (MBA); marketing (MBA). Part-time and evening/weekend programs available. Postbaccalaureate distance learning degree programs offered. Electronic applications accepted.

American International College, School of Business Administration, Springfield, MA 01109-3189. Offers MBA, MPA, MS, MSAT. Part-time and evening/weekend programs available. Postbaccalaureate distance learning degree programs offered (minimal on-campus study). *Faculty:* 9 full-time (1 woman), 24 part-time/adjunct (8 women). *Students:* 111 full-time (49 women), 94 part-time (45 women); includes 42 minority (31 African Americans, 1 American Indian/Alaska Native, 2 Asian Americans or Pacific Islanders, 8 Hispanic Americans), 8 international. Average age 37. 71 applicants, 68% accepted, 42 enrolled. In 2009, 57 master's awarded. *Degree requirements:* For master's, comprehensive exam (for some programs), thesis (for some programs). *Entrance requirements:* For master's, GMAT, BA or BS, minimum GPA of 2.75. Additional exam requirements/recommendations for international students: Required—TOEFL (minimum score 550 paper-based; 213 computer-based; 80 iBT). *Application deadline:* For fall admission, 4/1 priority date for domestic and international students; for spring admission, 12/1 priority date for domestic and international students. Applications are processed on a rolling basis. Application fee: $50. *Expenses:* Tuition: Full-time $12,510; part-time $695 per credit hour. Required fees: $35 per term. *Financial support:* Career-related internships or fieldwork and traineeships available. Financial award application deadline: 4/1; financial award applicants required to submit FAFSA. *Unit head:* Dr. Lea Johnson, Dean, 413-205-3230, Fax: 413-205-3943, E-mail: john.rogers@aic.edu. *Application contact:* Barbara Z. Benoit, Director of Graduate Admissions, 413-205-3700, Fax: 413-205-3051, E-mail: barbara.benoit@aic.edu.

American Jewish University, Graduate School, David Lieber School of Graduate Studies, Program in Business Administration, Bel Air, CA 90077-1599. Offers general nonprofit administration (MBA); Jewish nonprofit administration (MBA). Part-time and evening/weekend programs available. *Degree requirements:* For master's, thesis, internship. *Entrance requirements:* For master's, GMAT or GRE General Test, interview, minimum undergraduate GPA of 3.0. Additional exam requirements/recommendations for international students: Required—TOEFL (minimum score 550 paper-based; 247 computer-based).

American Public University System, AMU/APU Graduate Programs, Charles Town, WV 25414. Offers air warfare (MA Military Studies); American Revolution (MA Military Studies); business administration (MBA); Civil War (MA Military Studies); criminal justice (MA); defense management (MA Military Studies); emergency and disaster management (MA); environmental policy and management (MS); fire science management (MA); global engagement (MA); history (MA); homeland security (MA); humanities (MA); intelligence (MA Military Studies, MA Strategic Intelligence); international peace and conflict resolution (MA); international relations and conflict resolution (MA); joint warfare (MA Military Studies); land warfare international perspective (MA Military Studies); management (MA); military history (MA); military leadership (MA Military Studies); national security studies (MA); naval warfare international (MA Military Studies); naval warfare US (MA Military Studies); political science (MA); public administration (MA); public health (MA); security management (MA); space studies (MS); special ops/LIC (MA Military Studies); sports management (MA); transportation and logistics management (MA); transportation management (MA); unconventional warfare (MA Military Studies); World War II (MA Military Studies). Programs offered via distance learning only. Part-time and evening/weekend programs available. Postbaccalaureate distance learning degree programs offered (no on-campus study). *Students:* 788 full-time (330 women), 6,916 part-time (2,050 women); includes 1,767 minority (908 African Americans, 70 American Indian/Alaska Native, 223 Asian Americans or Pacific Islanders, 566 Hispanic Americans), 77 international. Average age 35. *Degree requirements:* For master's, comprehensive exam or practicum. *Entrance requirements:* For master's, bachelor's degree or equivalent, minimum GPA of 2.7 in last 60 hours of course work. *Application deadline:* Applications are processed on a rolling basis. Application fee: $0. Electronic applications accepted. *Financial support:* Applicants required to submit FAFSA. *Faculty research:* Military history, criminal justice, management performance, national security. *Unit head:* Dr. Frank McCluskey, Provost, 877-468-6268, Fax: 304-724-3780. *Application contact:* Terry Grant, Director of Enrollment Management, 877-468-6268, Fax: 304-724-3780, E-mail: info@apus.edu.

American Sentinel University, Graduate Programs, Englewood, CO 80112. Offers business administration (MBA); business intelligence (MS); computer science (MSCS); health information management (MS); healthcare (MBA); information systems (MSIS); nursing (MSN). Part-time and evening/weekend programs available. Postbaccalaureate distance learning degree programs offered (no on-campus study). *Entrance requirements:* Additional exam requirements/recommendations for international students: Required—TOEFL (minimum score 600 paper-based; 215 computer-based). Electronic applications accepted.

American University, Kogod School of Business, Master of Business Administration Program, Washington, DC 20016-8044. Offers accounting (MBA); consulting (MBA), including information technology, international business, management; corporate finance: commercial banking (MBA); corporate finance: corporate financial management (MBA); corporate finance: investment banking (MBA), including corporate finance and private equity, trading and selling; entrepreneurship (MBA); global emerging markets (MBA), including business, finance, information technology; international trade and global supply chain management (MBA); leadership (MBA); marketing management (MBA); marketing research (MBA); real estate (MBA); MBA/JD; MBA/LL M. Part-time and evening/weekend programs available. *Faculty:* 14 full-time (6 women). *Students:* 133 full-time (56 women), 121 part-time (48 women); includes 54 minority (23 African Americans, 1 American Indian/Alaska Native, 16 Asian Americans or Pacific Islanders, 14 Hispanic Americans), 43 international. Average age 29. 539 applicants, 51% accepted, 86 enrolled. In 2009, 114 master's awarded. *Entrance requirements:* For master's, GMAT. Additional exam requirements/recommendations for international students: Required—TOEFL. *Application deadline:* For fall admission, 2/1 priority date for domestic students; for spring admission, 10/1 priority date for domestic students. Applications are processed on a rolling basis. Application fee: $100. *Expenses:* Contact institution. *Financial support:* In 2009–10, 19 students received support; fellowships, research assistantships with partial tuition reimbursements available, career-related internships or fieldwork, Federal Work-Study, and institutionally sponsored loans available. Support available to part-time students. Financial award application deadline: 2/1. *Faculty research:* Information technology, decision-aiding methodology, negotiation. *Unit head:* Dr. Stevan Holmberg, Chair, 202-885-6193, E-mail: sholmbe@american.edu. *Application contact:* Shannon Demko, Associate Director of Graduate Admissions, 202-885-1994, Fax: 202-885-1108, E-mail: demko@american.edu.

American University, School of Public Affairs, Department of Public Administration, Washington, DC 20016-8070. Offers advanced organization development (Certificate); fundamentals of organization development (Certificate); key executive leadership (MPA); leadership for organizational change (Certificate); non-profit management (Certificate); organization development (MSOD); organizational change (Certificate); public administration (MPA, PhD); public financial management (Certificate); public management (Certificate); public policy (MPP); public policy analysis (Certificate); LL M/MPA; MPA/JD; MPP/JD; MPP/LLM. Part-time and evening/weekend programs available. *Faculty:* 23 full-time (9 women), 13 part-time/adjunct (4 women). *Students:* 184 full-time (117 women), 252 part-time (165 women); includes 109 minority (68 African Americans, 3 American Indian/Alaska Native, 25 Asian Americans or Pacific Islanders, 13 Hispanic Americans), 23 international. Average age 31. 843 applicants, 71% accepted, 156 enrolled. In 2009, 172 master's, 4 doctorates awarded. *Degree requirements:* For master's, comprehensive exam; for doctorate, comprehensive exam, thesis/dissertation. *Entrance requirements:* For master's, GRE, statement of purpose; 2 recommendations; for doctorate, GRE, 3 recommendations; for Certificate, bachelor's degree. Additional exam requirements/recommendations for international students: Required—TOEFL. *Application deadline:* For fall admission, 2/1 for domestic students; for spring admission, 11/1 for domestic students. Application fee: $55. *Expenses:* Tuition: Full-time $22,266; part-time $1237 per credit hour. Required fees: $430. Tuition and fees vary according to program. *Financial support:* Fellowships, research assistantships, teaching assistantships, career-related internships or fieldwork, Federal Work-Study, and institutionally sponsored loans available. Financial award application deadline: 2/1. *Faculty research:* Urban management, conservation politics, state and local budgeting, tax policy. *Unit head:* Dr. Howard McCurdy, Chair, 202-885-6236, E-mail: mccurdy@american.edu. *Application contact:* Dr. Howard McCurdy, Chair, 202-885-6236, E-mail: mccurdy@american.edu.

The American University in Cairo, Graduate Studies and Research, School of Business, Economics and Communication, Department of Management, Cairo, Egypt. Offers MBA, MPA, Diploma. *Accreditation:* AACSB. Part-time programs available. *Entrance requirements:* For master's, English entrance exam, GMAT. Electronic applications accepted. *Faculty research:* Privatization, public sector management, Islamic banking, information systems management, role of private sector in economic development.

The American University in Dubai, Master in Business Administration Program, Dubai, United Arab Emirates. Offers general (MBA); healthcare management (MBA); international finance (MBA); international marketing (MBA); management of construction enterprises (MBA). Part-time and evening/weekend programs available. *Degree requirements:* For master's, thesis optional. *Entrance requirements:* For master's, GMAT, Interview. Additional exam requirements/recommendations for international students: Required—TOEFL (minimum score 550 paper-based; 213 computer-based; 79 iBT). Electronic applications accepted.

The American University of Athens, School of Graduate Studies, Athens, Greece. Offers biomedical sciences (MS); business (MBA); business communication (MA); computer sciences (MS); engineering and applied sciences (MS); politics and policy making (MA); systems engineering (MS); telecommunications (MS). *Entrance requirements:* For master's, resume, 2 recommendation letters. Additional exam requirements/recommendations for international students: Required—TOEFL (minimum score 550 paper-based; 213 computer-based). *Faculty research:* Nanotechnology, environmental sciences, rock mechanics, human skin studies, Monte Carlo algorithms and software.

American University of Beirut, Graduate Programs, Olayan School of Business, Beirut, Lebanon. Offers business administration (MBA); executive business administration (EMBA). Part-time and evening/weekend programs available. *Degree requirements:* For master's, one foreign language, comprehensive exam, project. *Entrance requirements:* For master's, GMAT, letters of recommendation. Additional exam requirements/recommendations for international students: Required—TOEFL (minimum score 600 paper-based; 250 computer-based; 100 iBT), IELTS (minimum score 7.5). *Faculty research:* Capital acquisition, mergers and acquisition, corporate governance, financial reporting, international trade.

The American University of Paris, Graduate Programs, Paris, France. Offers cross-cultural and sustainable business management (MA); cultural translation (MA); global communications (MA); global communications and civil society (MA); international affairs, conflict resolution and civil society development (MA); Middle East and Islamic studies (MA); Middle East and Islamic studies and international affairs (MA); public policy and international affairs (MA); public policy and international law (MA). *Faculty:* 14 full-time (3 women). *Students:* 143 full-time (109 women). 71 applicants, 92% accepted, 34 enrolled. *Degree requirements:* For master's, thesis. *Entrance requirements:* For master's, minimum undergraduate GPA of 3.0. *Application deadline:* For fall admission, 4/15 priority date for international students; for spring admission, 11/15 priority date for international students. Applications are processed on a rolling basis. Application fee: $75. Tuition charges are reported in euros. *Expenses:* Tuition: Full-time 23,460 euros. *Financial support:* Scholarships/grants available. Financial award applicants required to submit FAFSA. *Unit head:* Celeste Schenk, President, 33 1-40620659, E-mail: president@aup.fr. *Application contact:* International Admissions Counselor, 33 1-40620720, Fax: 33 1-47053432, E-mail: admissions@aup.edu.

American University of Sharjah, Graduate Programs, Sharjah, United Arab Emirates. Offers business (EMBA, GEMPA, MBA); chemical engineering (MS Ch E); civil engineering (MSCE); computer engineering (MS); electrical engineering (MSEE); mechanical engineering (MSME); mechatronics engineering (MS); public administration (MPA); teaching English to speakers of other languages (MA); translation and interpreting (MA); urban planning (MUP). Part-time and evening/weekend programs available. *Faculty:* 59 full-time (4 women), 5 part-time/adjunct (1 woman). *Students:* 101 full-time (44 women), 218 part-time (95 women). Average age 27. 184 applicants, 83% accepted, 92 enrolled. In 2009, 97 master's awarded. *Entrance requirements:* For master's, GMAT (MBA). Additional exam requirements/recommendations for international students: Required—TOEFL (minimum score 550 paper-based; 213 computer-based; 80 iBT), TWE (minimum score 5). *Application deadline:* For fall admission, 7/30 priority date for domestic students, 7/15 priority date for international students; for spring admission, 12/31 priority date for domestic students, 12/16 for international students. Applications are processed on a rolling basis. Application fee: $300. Electronic applications accepted. Tuition charges are reported in United Arab Emirates dirhams. *Expenses:* Tuition: Part-time 3250 United Arab Emirates dirhams per credit hour. *Financial support:* In 2009–10, 63 students received support, including 28 research assistantships with tuition reimbursements available, 35 teaching assistantships with tuition reimbursements available. *Faculty research:* Chemical engineering, civil engineering, computer engineering, electrical engineering, linguistics, translation. *Unit head:* Ghada S. Sami, Admissions Manager, 971-65151006 Ext. 1006, Fax: 971-65151020, E-mail: graduateadmission@aus.edu. *Application contact:* Ghada S. Sami, Admissions Manager, 971-65151006 Ext. 1006, Fax: 971-65151020, E-mail: graduateadmission@aus.edu.

Anaheim University, Programs in Business Administration, Anaheim, CA 92806-5150. Offers online global (MBA); online green (MBA); professional (MBA); sustainable management (Certificate, Diploma). Postbaccalaureate distance learning degree programs offered.

Anderson University, College of Business, Anderson, SC 29621-4035. Offers MBA. *Accreditation:* ACBSP.

Anderson University, Falls School of Business, Anderson, IN 46012-3495. Offers accountancy (MA); business administration (MBA, DBA). *Accreditation:* ACBSP.

Business Administration and Management—General

Andrew Jackson University, Brian Tracy College of Business and Entrepreneurship, Birmingham, AL 35244. Offers entrepreneurship (MBA); finance (MBA); health services management (MBA); hospitality and tourism management (MBA); human resource management (MBA); international business (MBA); management (MBA); marketing (MBA). Part-time and evening/weekend programs available. Postbaccalaureate distance learning degree programs offered (no on-campus study). *Entrance requirements:* For master's, course work in calculus, statistics, macroeconomics. Additional exam requirements/recommendations for international students: Required—TOEFL (minimum score 550 paper-based; 213 computer-based). Electronic applications accepted.

Angelo State University, College of Graduate Studies, College of Business, Department of Management and Marketing, San Angelo, TX 76909. Offers business administration (MBA). *Accreditation:* ACBSP. Part-time and evening/weekend programs available. *Faculty:* 6 full-time (1 woman). *Students:* 13 full-time (5 women), 22 part-time (5 women); includes 7 minority (2 African Americans, 1 Asian American or Pacific Islander, 4 Hispanic Americans), 4 international. Average age 28. 19 applicants, 100% accepted, 15 enrolled. In 2009, 17 master's awarded. *Entrance requirements:* For master's, GMAT. Additional exam requirements/recommendations for international students: Required—TOEFL or IELTS. *Application deadline:* For fall admission, 7/15 priority date for domestic students, 6/10 for international students; for spring admission, 12/1 priority date for domestic students, 11/1 for international students. Applications are processed on a rolling basis. Application fee: $40 ($50 for international students). Electronic applications accepted. *Expenses:* Tuition, state resident: full-time $3396; part-time $142 per credit hour. Tuition, nonresident: full-time $10,152; part-time $423 per credit hour. Required fees: $1786; $36.25 per credit hour. $494 per semester. Full-time tuition and fees vary according to course load, degree level and program. *Financial support:* In 2009–10, 21 students received support. Career-related internships or fieldwork, Federal Work-Study, and scholarships/grants available. Support available to part-time students. Financial award application deadline: 3/1; financial award applicants required to submit FAFSA. *Unit head:* Dr. Tom F. Badgett, Department Head, 325-942-2383 Ext. 225, Fax: 325-942-2384, E-mail: tom.badgett@angelo.edu. *Application contact:* Dr. Carol B. Diminnie, Graduate Advisor, 325-942-2383 Ext. 229, Fax: 325-942-2194, E-mail: carol.diminnie@angelo.edu.

Anna Maria College, Graduate Division, Program in Business Administration, Paxton, MA 01612. Offers MBA, AC. Part-time and evening/weekend programs available. *Degree requirements:* For master's, capstone project. *Entrance requirements:* For master's, minimum GPA of 2.7. Additional exam requirements/recommendations for international students: Required—TOEFL (minimum score 500 paper-based). Electronic applications accepted. *Faculty research:* Management organization.

Antioch University Los Angeles, Graduate Programs, Program in Organizational Management, Culver City, CA 90230. Offers human resource development (MA); leadership (MA); organizational development (MA). Part-time and evening/weekend programs available. *Entrance requirements:* For master's, interview. Additional exam requirements/recommendations for international students: Required—TOEFL. *Faculty research:* Systems thinking and chaos theory, technology and organizational structure, nonprofit management, power and empowerment.

Antioch University Midwest, Graduate Programs, Individualized Liberal and Professional Studies Program, Yellow Springs, OH 45387-1609. Offers liberal and professional studies (MA), including counseling, creative writing, education, film studies, liberal studies, management, modern literature, psychology, theatre, visual arts. Part-time and evening/weekend programs available. Postbaccalaureate distance learning degree programs offered (minimal on-campus study). *Faculty:* 1 full-time (0 women), 2 part-time/adjunct (1 woman). *Students:* 23 full-time (13 women), 41 part-time (30 women); includes 13 minority (11 African Americans, 2 Hispanic Americans). Average age 40. 21 applicants, 76% accepted, 15 enrolled. In 2009, 24 master's awarded. *Degree requirements:* For master's, thesis or alternative. *Entrance requirements:* For master's, resume, 2 letters of reference. *Application deadline:* For fall admission, 8/1 for domestic students; for winter admission, 12/1 for domestic students; for spring admission, 3/10 for domestic students. Applications are processed on a rolling basis. Application fee: $50. Electronic applications accepted. *Expenses:* Contact institution. *Financial support:* Federal Work-Study available. Financial award applicants required to submit FAFSA. *Unit head:* Dr. Jon Saari, Chair, 937-769-1879, Fax: 937-769-1807, E-mail: jsaari@antioch.edu. *Application contact:* Seth Gordon, Assistant Director of Admissions, 937-769-1800 Ext. 1825, Fax: 937-769-1804, E-mail: sgordon@antioch.edu.

Antioch University Midwest, Graduate Programs, Program in Management, Yellow Springs, OH 45387-1609. Offers MA. Part-time and evening/weekend programs available. *Faculty:* 1 full-time (0 women), 7 part-time/adjunct (2 women). *Students:* 39 full-time (21 women), 5 part-time (2 women); includes 21 minority (20 African Americans, 1 Hispanic American). Average age 38. 16 applicants, 88% accepted, 13 enrolled. In 2009, 24 master's awarded. *Entrance requirements:* For master's, 2 letters of reference, resume. *Application deadline:* For fall admission, 9/1 for domestic students; for winter admission, 12/1 for domestic students; for spring admission, 3/10 for domestic students. Applications are processed on a rolling basis. Application fee: $50. Electronic applications accepted. *Expenses:* Contact institution. *Financial support:* Federal Work-Study available. Financial award applicants required to submit FAFSA. *Unit head:* Michael Robinson, Director, 937-769-1862, Fax: 937-769-1805, E-mail: mrobinson@antioch.edu. *Application contact:* Rob McLaughlin, Enrollment Services Manager, 937-769-1816, Fax: 937-769-1804, E-mail: rmclaughlin@antioch.edu.

Antioch University New England, Graduate School, Department of Organization and Management, Program in Organizational and Environmental Sustainability (Green MBA), Keene, NH 03431-3552. Offers MBA. Part-time programs available. *Entrance requirements:* For master's, GRE, resume, 3 letters of recommendation. Additional exam requirements/recommendations for international students: Required—TOEFL (minimum score 600 paper-based; 250 computer-based).

Antioch University Seattle, Graduate Programs, Center for Creative Change, Seattle, WA 98121-1814. Offers environment and community (MA); management (MS); organizational psychology (MA); strategic communications (MA); whole system design (MA). Evening/weekend programs available. Electronic applications accepted. *Expenses:* Contact institution.

Appalachian State University, Cratis D. Williams Graduate School, Program in Business Administration, Boone, NC 28608. Offers MBA. *Accreditation:* AACSB. Part-time programs available. Postbaccalaureate distance learning degree programs offered (no on-campus study). *Faculty:* 49 full-time (17 women). *Students:* 41 full-time (12 women), 18 part-time (4 women), 1 international. 73 applicants, 88% accepted, 32 enrolled. In 2009, 14 master's awarded. *Degree requirements:* For master's, comprehensive exam. *Entrance requirements:* For master's, GMAT, 3 letters of recommendation. Additional exam requirements/recommendations for international students: Required—TOEFL (minimum score 550 paper-based; 230 computer-based; 79 iBT), IELTS (minimum score 6.5). *Application deadline:* For fall admission, 3/1 for domestic students, 2/1 for international students; for spring admission, 7/1 for international students. Applications are processed on a rolling basis. Application fee: $50. Electronic applications accepted. *Expenses:* Tuition, state resident: full-time $2960. Tuition, nonresident: full-time $14,051. Required fees: $2320. *Financial support:* In 2009–10, 10 research assistantships (averaging $8,000 per year) were awarded; fellowships, teaching assistantships, career-related internships or fieldwork, Federal Work-Study, scholarships/grants, and unspecified assistantships also available. Financial award application deadline: 4/1; financial award applicants required to submit FAFSA. *Unit head:* Dr. Joseph Cazier, Director and Assistant Dean, College of Business, 828-262-2922, E-mail: cazierja@appstate.edu. *Application contact:* Sandy Krause, Director of Admissions, 828-262-2130, Fax: 828-262-2709, E-mail: krausesl@appstate.edu.

Aquinas College, School of Management, Grand Rapids, MI 49506-1799. Offers M Mgt. Part-time and evening/weekend programs available. *Faculty:* 9 full-time (5 women), 45 part-time/adjunct (30 women). *Students:* 9 full-time (5 women), 45 part-time (30 women); includes 2 minority (1 African American, 1 Asian American or Pacific Islander), 1 international. Average age 35. In 2009, 26 master's awarded. *Entrance requirements:* For master's, GMAT, minimum undergraduate GPA of 2.75, 2 years of work experience. Additional exam requirements/recommendations for international students: Required—TOEFL (minimum score 550 paper-based; 213 computer-based). *Application deadline:* Applications are processed on a rolling basis. *Expenses:* Contact institution. *Financial support:* In 2009–10, 26 students received support. Scholarships/grants available. Support available to part-time students. Financial award application deadline: 3/15; financial award applicants required to submit FAFSA. *Unit head:* Cynthia VanGelderen, Dean, 616-632-2922, Fax: 616-732-4489, E-mail: vangecyn@aquinas.edu. *Application contact:* Lynn Atkins-Rykert, Executive Assistant, 616-632-2924, Fax: 616-732-4489, E-mail: atkinlyn@aquinas.edu.

Arcadia University, Graduate Studies, Program in Business Administration, Glenside, PA 19038-3295. Offers MBA. *Accreditation:* ACBSP. *Students:* 105 part-time (66 women); includes 30 minority (25 African Americans, 5 Asian Americans or Pacific Islanders), 1 international. Average age 31. In 2009, 52 master's awarded. Application fee: $50. *Expenses:* Tuition: Full-time $30,450; part-time $620 per credit hour. Required fees: $165. Tuition and fees vary according to program. *Unit head:* Dr. Tony Muscia, Executive Director, 215-579-2789. *Application contact:* Office of Enrollment Management, 215-572-2910, Fax: 215-572-4049, E-mail: admiss@arcadia.edu.

Argosy University, Atlanta, College of Business, Atlanta, GA 30328. Offers accounting (DBA); corporate compliance (MBA); customized professional concentration (MBA, DBA); finance (MBA); healthcare administration (MBA); information systems (DBA); information systems management (MBA); international business (MBA, DBA); management (MBA, MSM, DBA); marketing (MBA, DBA).

See Close-Up on page 197.

Argosy University, Chicago, College of Business, Chicago, IL 60601. Offers accounting (DBA); customized professional concentration (MBA, DBA); finance (MBA); fraud examination (MBA); global business sustainability (DBA); healthcare administration (MBA); information systems (DBA); information systems management (MBA); international business (MBA, DBA); management (MBA, MSM, DBA); marketing (MBA, DBA); organizational leadership (Ed D); public administration (MBA); sustainable management (MBA). Postbaccalaureate distance learning degree programs offered (minimal on-campus study).

See Close-Up on page 199.

Argosy University, Dallas, College of Business, Farmers Branch, TX 75244. Offers accounting (DBA, AGC); corporate compliance (MBA, Graduate Certificate); customized professional concentration (MBA); finance (MBA, Graduate Certificate); fraud examination (MBA, Graduate Certificate); global business sustainability (DBA, AGC); healthcare administration (Graduate Certificate); healthcare management (MBA); information systems (MBA, DBA, AGC); information systems management (Graduate Certificate); international business (MBA, DBA, AGC, Graduate Certificate); management (MBA, DBA, AGC, Graduate Certificate); marketing (MBA, DBA, AGC, Graduate Certificate); public administration (MBA, Graduate Certificate); sustainable management (MBA, Graduate Certificate).

See Close-Up on page 201.

Argosy University, Denver, College of Business, Denver, CO 80231. Offers accounting (DBA); corporate compliance (MBA); customized professional concentration (MBA, DBA); finance (MBA); fraud examination (MBA); global business sustainability (DBA); healthcare administration (MBA); information systems (DBA); information systems management (MBA); international business (MBA, DBA); management (MBA, MSM, DBA); marketing (MBA, DBA); organizational leadership (Ed D); public administration (MBA); sustainable management (MBA).

See Close-Up on page 203.

Argosy University, Hawai'i, College of Business, Honolulu, HI 96813. Offers accounting (DBA); corporate compliance (MBA); customized professional concentration (MBA, DBA); finance (MBA, Certificate); fraud examination (MBA); global business sustainability (DBA); healthcare administration (MBA, Certificate); information systems (DBA); information systems management (MBA, Certificate); international business (MBA, DBA, Certificate); management (MBA, MSM, DBA); marketing (MBA, DBA, Certificate); organizational leadership (Ed D); public administration (MBA); sustainable management (MBA).

See Close-Up on page 205.

Argosy University, Inland Empire, College of Business, San Bernardino, CA 92408. Offers accounting (DBA); corporate compliance (MBA); customized professional concentration (MBA, DBA); finance (MBA); fraud examination (MBA); global business sustainability (DBA); healthcare administration (MBA); information systems (DBA); information systems management (MBA); international business (MBA, DBA); management (MBA, MSM, DBA); marketing (MBA, DBA); organizational leadership (Ed D); public administration (MBA); sustainable management (MBA).

See Close-Up on page 207.

Argosy University, Los Angeles, College of Business, Santa Monica, CA 90045. Offers accounting (DBA); corporate compliance (MBA); customized professional concentration (MBA, DBA); finance (MBA); fraud examination (MBA); global business sustainability (DBA); healthcare administration (MBA); information systems (DBA); information systems management (MBA); international business (MBA, DBA); management (MBA, MSM, DBA); marketing (MBA, DBA); organizational leadership (Ed D); public administration (MBA); sustainable management (MBA).

See Close-Up on page 209.

Argosy University, Nashville, College of Business, Nashville, TN 37214. Offers accounting (DBA); customized professional concentration (MBA, DBA); finance (MBA); healthcare administration (MBA); information systems (MBA, DBA); international business (MBA, DBA); management (MBA, MSM, DBA); marketing (MBA, DBA).

See Close-Up on page 211.

Argosy University, Orange County, College of Business, Orange, CA 92868. Offers accounting (DBA, Adv C); corporate compliance (MBA); customized professional concentration (MBA, DBA); finance (MBA, Certificate); fraud examination (MBA); global business sustainability (DBA); healthcare administration (MBA, Certificate); information systems (DBA, Adv C, Certificate); information systems management (MBA); international business (MBA, DBA, Adv C, Certificate); management (MBA, MSM, DBA, Adv C); marketing (MBA, DBA, Adv C, Certificate); organizational leadership (Ed D); public administration (MBA, Certificate); sustainable management (MBA).

See Close-Up on page 213.

Argosy University, Phoenix, College of Business, Phoenix, AZ 85021. Offers accounting (DBA); corporate compliance (MBA); customized professional concentration (MBA, DBA); finance (MBA); fraud examination (MBA); global business sustainability (DBA); healthcare administration (MBA); information systems (DBA); information systems management (MBA); international business (MBA, DBA); management (MBA, DBA); marketing (MBA, DBA); public administration (MBA); sustainable management (MBA).

See Close-Up on page 215.

Argosy University, Salt Lake City, College of Business, Draper, UT 84020. Offers accounting (DBA); corporate compliance (MBA); customized professional concentration (MBA, DBA); finance (MBA); fraud examination (MBA); global business sustainability (DBA); healthcare administration (MBA); information systems (DBA); information systems management (MBA); international business (MBA, DBA); management (MBA, DBA); marketing (MBA, DBA); public administration (MBA); sustainable management (MBA).

See Close-Up on page 217.

Argosy University, San Diego, College of Business, San Diego, CA 92108. Offers accounting (DBA); corporate compliance (MBA); customized professional concentration (MBA, DBA); finance (MBA); fraud examination (MBA); global business sustainability (DBA); information systems (DBA); information systems management (MBA); international business (MBA, DBA);

management (MBA, MSM, DBA); marketing (MBA, DBA); organizational leadership (Ed D); public administration (MBA).

See Close-Up on page 219.

Argosy University, San Francisco Bay Area, College of Business, Alameda, CA 94501. Offers accounting (DBA); corporate compliance (MBA); customized professional concentration (MBA, DBA); finance (MBA); fraud examination (MBA); global business sustainability (DBA); healthcare administration (MBA); information systems (DBA); information systems management (MBA); international business (MBA, DBA); management (MBA, MSM, DBA); marketing (MBA, DBA); organizational leadership (Ed D); public administration (MBA); sustainable management (MBA).

See Close-Up on page 221.

Argosy University, Sarasota, College of Business, Sarasota, FL 34235. Offers accounting (DBA, Adv C); corporate compliance (MBA, DBA, Certificate); customized professional concentration (MBA, DBA); finance (MBA, Certificate); fraud examination (MBA, Certificate); global business sustainability (DBA, Adv C); healthcare administration (MBA, Certificate); information systems (DBA, Adv C, Certificate); information systems management (MBA); international business (MBA, DBA, Adv C, Certificate); management (MBA, MSM, DBA, Adv C, Certificate); marketing (MBA, DBA, Adv C, Certificate); organizational leadership (Ed D); public administration (MBA, Certificate); sustainable management (MBA, Certificate).

See Close-Up on page 223.

Argosy University, Schaumburg, College of Business, Schaumburg, IL 60173-5403. Offers accounting (DBA, Adv C); customized professional concentration (MBA, DBA); finance (MBA, Certificate); fraud examination (MBA); global business sustainability (DBA); healthcare administration (MBA, Certificate); information systems (DBA, Adv C, Certificate); information systems management (MBA); international business (MBA, DBA, Adv C, Certificate); management (MBA, MSM, DBA, Adv C, Certificate); marketing (MBA, DBA, Adv C, Certificate); organizational leadership (Ed D); public administration (MBA); sustainable management (MBA).

See Close-Up on page 225.

Argosy University, Seattle, College of Business, Seattle, WA 98121. Offers accounting (DBA); corporate compliance (MBA); customized professional concentration (MBA, DBA); finance (MBA); fraud examination (MBA); global business sustainability (DBA); healthcare administration (MBA); information systems (DBA); information systems management (MBA); international business (MBA, DBA); management (MBA, MSM, DBA); marketing (MBA, DBA); organizational leadership (Ed D); public administration (MBA); sustainable management (MBA).

See Close-Up on page 227.

Argosy University, Tampa, College of Business, Tampa, FL 33607. Offers accounting (DBA); corporate compliance (MBA); customized professional concentration (MBA, DBA); finance (MBA); fraud examination (MBA); global business sustainability (DBA); healthcare administration (MBA); information systems (DBA); information systems management (MBA); international business (MBA, DBA); management (MBA, MSM, DBA); marketing (MBA, DBA); organizational leadership (Ed D); public administration (MBA); sustainable management (MBA).

See Close-Up on page 229.

Argosy University, Twin Cities, College of Business, Eagan, MN 55121. Offers accounting (DBA); customized professional concentration (MBA, DBA); finance (MBA); fraud examination (MBA); global business sustainability (DBA); healthcare administration (MBA); information systems (DBA); information systems management (MBA); international business (MBA, DBA); management (MBA, MSM, DBA); marketing (MBA, DBA); organizational leadership (Ed D); public administration (MBA); sustainable management (MBA).

See Close-Up on page 231.

Argosy University, Washington DC, College of Business, Arlington, VA 22209. Offers accounting (DBA); customized professional concentration (MBA, DBA); finance (MBA); fraud examination (MBA); global business sustainability (DBA); healthcare administration (MBA); information systems (DBA); information systems management (MBA); international business (MBA, DBA, Certificate); management (MBA, MSM, DBA); marketing (MBA, DBA, Certificate); organizational leadership (Ed D); public administration (MBA); sustainable management (MBA).

See Close-Up on page 233.

Arizona State University, Graduate College, W.P. Carey School of Business, Program in Applied Leadership and Management, Tempe, AZ 85287. Offers MALM. Part-time and evening/weekend programs available. *Entrance requirements:* For master's, GRE or GMAT, minimum undergraduate GPA of 3.0, 2 letters of recommendation. Additional exam requirements/recommendations for international students: Required—TOEFL (minimum score 550 paper-based; 213 computer-based; 83 iBT). Electronic applications accepted. *Expenses:* Contact institution.

Arizona State University, Graduate College, W.P. Carey School of Business, Program in Business Administration, Tempe, AZ 85287. Offers agribusiness (PhD); business administration (MBA); finance (MBA, PhD); health sector management (MBA); information systems (PhD); management (MBA, PhD); marketing (MBA, PhD); supply chain management (MBA, PhD); JD/MBA; MBA/M Arch; MBA/MHSM. *Accreditation:* AACSB. *Degree requirements:* For master's, thesis optional; for doctorate, thesis/dissertation. *Entrance requirements:* For master's, GMAT.

Arizona State University, Graduate College, W.P. Carey School of Business, Program in Commerce, Tempe, AZ 85287. Offers MS. *Entrance requirements:* For master's, GMAT or GRE, minimum cumulative GPA of 3.5, resume, 1 letter of recommendation. Electronic applications accepted.

Arkansas State University—Jonesboro, Graduate School, College of Business, Department of Economics and Finance, Jonesboro, State University, AR 72467. Offers business administration (MBA). *Accreditation:* AACSB. Part-time programs available. *Faculty:* 7 full-time (0 women). *Students:* 52 full-time (15 women), 105 part-time (45 women); includes 15 minority (9 African Americans, 1 American Indian/Alaska Native, 2 Asian Americans or Pacific Islanders, 3 Hispanic Americans), 45 international. Average age 28. 156 applicants, 87% accepted, 79 enrolled. In 2009, 55 master's awarded. *Degree requirements:* For master's, comprehensive exam, thesis or alternative. *Entrance requirements:* For master's, GMAT, appropriate bachelor's degree, letters of reference. Additional exam requirements/recommendations for international students: Required—TOEFL (minimum score 550 paper-based; 213 computer-based; 79 iBT), IELTS (minimum score 6). *Application deadline:* For fall admission, 7/15 for domestic students, 7/1 for international students; for spring admission, 12/1 for domestic students, 11/13 for international students. Applications are processed on a rolling basis. Application fee: $30 ($40 for international students). Electronic applications accepted. *Expenses:* Contact institution. *Financial support:* In 2009–10, 31 students received support. Career-related internships or fieldwork, scholarships/grants, and unspecified assistantships available. Financial award application deadline: 7/1; financial award applicants required to submit FAFSA. *Unit head:* Dr. Jeffrey Pittman, Chair, 870-972-2280, Fax: 870-972-3863, E-mail: pittman@astate.edu. *Application contact:* Dr. Andrew Sustich, Dean of the Graduate School, 870-972-3029, Fax: 870-972-3857, E-mail: sustich@astate.edu.

Arkansas State University—Jonesboro, Graduate School, College of Business, Department of Management and Marketing, Jonesboro, State University, AR 72467. Offers business administration education (SCCT); business technology education (SCCT). *Accreditation:* NCATE. Part-time programs available. *Faculty:* 8 full-time (3 women). *Students:* 2 part-time (1 woman); includes 1 minority (Asian American or Pacific Islander). Average age 30. *Degree requirements:* For SCCT, comprehensive exam. *Entrance requirements:* For degree, GRE General Test or MAT, interview, master's degree, official transcript, immunization records. Additional exam requirements/recommendations for international students: Required—TOEFL (minimum score 550 paper-based; 213 computer-based; 79 iBT), IELTS (minimum score 6). *Application deadline:* For fall admission, 7/15 for domestic students, 7/1 for international students; for spring admission, 12/1 for domestic students, 11/13 for international students. Applications are processed on a rolling basis. Application fee: $30 ($40 for international students). Electronic applications accepted. *Expenses:* Contact institution. *Financial support:* Career-related internships or fieldwork, scholarships/grants, and unspecified assistantships available. Financial award application deadline: 7/1; financial award applicants required to submit FAFSA. *Unit head:* Dr. Gail Hudson, Chair, 870-972-3430, Fax: 870-972-3833, E-mail: ghud@astate.edu. *Application contact:* Dr. Andrew Sustich, Dean of the Graduate School, 870-972-3029, Fax: 870-972-3857, E-mail: sustich@astate.edu.

Ashland University, Dauch College of Business and Economics, Ashland, OH 44805-3702. Offers MBA. *Accreditation:* ACBSP. Part-time and evening/weekend programs available. *Faculty:* 18 full-time (5 women), 18 part-time/adjunct (4 women). *Students:* 306 full-time (133 women), 295 part-time (155 women); includes 103 minority (78 African Americans, 7 American Indian/Alaska Native, 10 Asian Americans or Pacific Islanders, 8 Hispanic Americans), 72 international. Average age 33. 239 applicants, 97% accepted, 153 enrolled. In 2009, 177 master's awarded. *Degree requirements:* For master's, thesis optional. *Entrance requirements:* For master's, 2 years of full-time work experience. Additional exam requirements/recommendations for international students: Required—TOEFL. *Application deadline:* For fall admission, 8/1 priority date for domestic students; for spring admission, 12/1 priority date for domestic students. Applications are processed on a rolling basis. Application fee: $30. Electronic applications accepted. *Expenses:* Contact institution. *Financial support:* In 2009–10, 213 students received support. Tuition waivers (partial) and unspecified assistantships available. Financial award application deadline: 4/15; financial award applicants required to submit FAFSA. *Faculty research:* Human resource management, statistical analysis, global business issues, organizational development, government and business. Total annual research expenditures: $36,410. *Unit head:* Dr. Beverly Heimann, Chair, 419-289-5216, E-mail: bheimann@ashland.edu. *Application contact:* Stephen W. Krispinsky, Executive Director of MBA Program, 419-289-5236, Fax: 419-289-5910, E-mail: skrispin@ashland.edu.

Aspen University, Program in Business Administration, Denver, CO 80246. Offers business administration (MBA); finance (MBA); information management (MBA); project management (MBA, Certificate). Part-time and evening/weekend programs available. Postbaccalaureate distance learning degree programs offered (no on-campus study). *Entrance requirements:* Additional exam requirements/recommendations for international students: Required—TOEFL (minimum score 530 paper-based; 71 computer-based). Electronic applications accepted.

Assumption College, Graduate School, Department of Business Studies, Worcester, MA 01609-1296. Offers accounting (MBA); business administration (CAGS); finance/economics (MBA); general business (MBA); human resources (MBA); international business (MBA); management (MBA); marketing (MBA); nonprofit leadership (MBA). Part-time and evening/weekend programs available. *Faculty:* 6 full-time (1 woman), 14 part-time/adjunct (2 women). *Students:* 19 full-time (11 women), 127 part-time (68 women); includes 22 minority (13 African Americans, 3 Asian Americans or Pacific Islanders, 6 Hispanic Americans). Average age 27. 88 applicants, 99% accepted. In 2009, 40 master's, 2 other advanced degrees awarded. *Entrance requirements:* For master's, 3 letters of recommendation, resume; for CAGS, 3 letters of recommendation, resume, essay. Additional exam requirements/recommendations for international students: Required—TOEFL (minimum score 540 paper-based; 200 computer-based; 76 iBT), IELTS (minimum score 6). *Application deadline:* For fall admission, 6/1 priority date for domestic students, 5/1 priority date for international students; for spring admission, 11/1 priority date for domestic students, 9/1 priority date for international students. Applications are processed on a rolling basis. Application fee: $30. Electronic applications accepted. *Expenses:* Tuition: Part-time $503 per credit. Required fees: $20 per semester. One-time fee: $100 part-time. Part-time tuition and fees vary according to campus/location. *Financial support:* In 2009–10, 47 students received support. Application deadline: 6/1. *Faculty research:* Workplace diversity, dynamics of team interaction, utilization of leased employees. *Unit head:* Michael Lewis, Director, 508-767-7372, Fax: 508-767-7252, E-mail: jhunter@assumption.edu. *Application contact:* Adrian O. Dumas, Director of Graduate Enrollment Management and Services, 508-767-7365, Fax: 508-767-7030, E-mail: adumas@assumption.edu.

Athabasca University, Centre for Innovative Management, St. Albert, AB T8N 1B4, Canada. Offers business administration (MBA); information technology management (MBA), including policing concentration; management (GDM); project management (MBA, GDM). Part-time and evening/weekend programs available. Postbaccalaureate distance learning degree programs offered (no on-campus study). *Faculty:* 9 full-time (6 women), 2 part-time/adjunct (0 women). *Students:* 898 part-time. Average age 36. 297 applicants, 33 enrolled. In 2009, 179 master's, 180 other advanced degrees awarded. *Degree requirements:* For master's, thesis or alternative, applied project. *Entrance requirements:* For master's, 3-8 years of managerial experience, 3 years with undergraduate degree, 5 years managerial experience with professional designation, 8-10 years management experience (on exception). *Application deadline:* For fall admission, 6/15 for domestic and international students; for winter admission, 10/15 for domestic and international students; for spring admission, 2/15 for domestic and international students. Applications are processed on a rolling basis. Application fee: $200. Electronic applications accepted. *Expenses:* Contact institution. *Financial support:* Scholarships/grants available. *Faculty research:* Human resources, project management, operations research, information technology management, corporate stewardship, energy management. *Unit head:* Dr. Alexander Kondra, Dean, 780-418-6582, E-mail: alexk@athabascau.ca. *Application contact:* Shannon Oscroft, Receptionist and Customer Service Representative, 780-459-1144, E-mail: shannono@athabascau.ca.

Auburn University, Graduate School, College of Business, Department of Management, Auburn University, AL 36849. Offers human resource management (PhD); management (MS, PhD); management information systems (MS, PhD). *Accreditation:* AACSB. Part-time programs available. *Faculty:* 34 full-time (7 women), 5 part-time/adjunct (0 women). *Students:* 12 full-time (4 women), 12 part-time (2 women); includes 3 minority (1 African American, 2 Asian Americans or Pacific Islanders), 5 international. Average age 34. 137 applicants, 28% accepted, 20 enrolled. In 2009, 9 master's, 6 doctorates awarded. *Degree requirements:* For master's, thesis (for some programs); for doctorate, thesis/dissertation. *Entrance requirements:* For master's, GMAT, GRE General Test (MS); for doctorate, GMAT, GRE General Test. Additional exam requirements/recommendations for international students: Required—TOEFL. *Application deadline:* For fall admission, 7/7 for domestic students; for spring admission, 11/24 for domestic students. Applications are processed on a rolling basis. Application fee: $50 ($60 for international students). Electronic applications accepted. *Expenses:* Tuition, state resident: full-time $6240. Tuition, nonresident: full-time $18,720. International tuition: $18,938 full-time. Required fees: $492. Tuition and fees vary according to course load, program and reciprocity agreements. *Financial support:* Teaching assistantships, Federal Work-Study available. Support available to part-time students. Financial award application deadline: 3/15; financial award applicants required to submit FAFSA. *Unit head:* Dr. Sharon Oswald, Head, 334-844-4071. *Application contact:* Dr. George Flowers, Dean of the Graduate School, 334-844-2125.

Auburn University, Graduate School, College of Business, Program in Business Administration, Auburn University, AL 36849. Offers MBA. *Accreditation:* AACSB. Part-time programs available. *Faculty:* 61 full-time (10 women), 11 part-time/adjunct (3 women). *Students:* 73 full-time (22 women), 340 part-time (89 women); includes 66 minority (30 African Americans, 3 American Indian/Alaska Native, 16 Asian Americans or Pacific Islanders, 17 Hispanic Americans), 18 international. Average age 34. 363 applicants, 51% accepted, 124 enrolled. In 2009, 158 master's awarded. *Entrance requirements:* For master's, GMAT. *Application deadline:* For fall admission, 7/7 for domestic students; for spring admission, 11/24 for domestic students. Applications are processed on a rolling basis. Application fee: $50 ($60 for international students). Electronic applications accepted. *Expenses:* Tuition, state resident: full-time $6240. Tuition, nonresident: full-time $18,720. International tuition: $18,938 full-time. Required fees: $492. Tuition and fees vary according to course load, program and reciprocity agreements. *Financial support:* Federal Work-Study available. Support available to part-time students. Financial award application deadline: 3/15; financial award applicants required to submit FAFSA. *Unit head:* Dr. Daniel M. Gropper, Director, 334-844-4060. *Application contact:* Dr. George Flowers, Dean of the Graduate School, 334-844-2125.

Business Administration and Management—General

Auburn University Montgomery, School of Business, Montgomery, AL 36124-4023. Offers MBA. *Accreditation:* AACSB. Part-time and evening/weekend programs available. *Faculty:* 21 full-time (5 women), 3 part-time/adjunct (1 woman). *Students:* 66 full-time (25 women), 90 part-time (48 women); includes 35 minority (25 African Americans, 8 Asian Americans or Pacific Islanders, 2 Hispanic Americans), 11 international. Average age 29. In 2009, 78 master's awarded. *Degree requirements:* For master's, comprehensive exam. *Entrance requirements:* For master's, GMAT. Additional exam requirements/recommendations for international students: Required—TOEFL. *Application deadline:* Applications are processed on a rolling basis. Electronic applications accepted. *Expenses:* Tuition, state resident: full-time $2841; part-time $225 per credit hour. Tuition, nonresident: full-time $8241; part-time $675 per credit hour. Required fees: $282; $8 per hour. $45 per term. *Financial support:* Research assistantships, career-related internships or fieldwork and scholarships/grants available. Support available to part-time students. Financial award application deadline: 3/1; financial award applicants required to submit FAFSA. *Unit head:* Dr. Jane Goodson, Dean, 334-244-3478, Fax: 334-244-3792, E-mail: jgoodson@aum.edu. *Application contact:* Joy Strong, Associate Director, Advising and Information, 334-244-3565, Fax: 334-244-3792, E-mail: jstrong@aum.edu.

Augsburg College, Program in Business Administration, Minneapolis, MN 55454-1351. Offers MBA. Evening/weekend programs available. Electronic applications accepted. *Expenses:* Tuition: Full-time $16,713; part-time $1857 per course. Required fees: $450; $50 per course. Tuition and fees vary according to course load and program.

Augusta State University, Graduate Studies, Hull College of Business, Augusta, GA 30904-2200. Offers MBA. *Accreditation:* AACSB. Part-time and evening/weekend programs available. *Entrance requirements:* For master's, GMAT.

Aurora University, College of Professional Studies, Dunham School of Business, Aurora, IL 60506-4892. Offers MBA. Part-time and evening/weekend programs available. *Entrance requirements:* For master's, minimum GPA of 2.75, 2 years of work experience. Additional exam requirements/recommendations for international students: Required—TOEFL (minimum score 550 paper-based; 213 computer-based). Electronic applications accepted. *Expenses:* Contact institution.

Austin Peay State University, College of Graduate Studies, College of Business, Clarksville, TN 37044. Offers management (MS). Part-time and evening/weekend programs available. Postbaccalaureate distance learning degree programs offered (no on-campus study). *Faculty:* 5 full-time (1 woman). *Students:* 4 full-time (1 woman), 98 part-time (61 women); includes 30 minority (22 African Americans, 1 American Indian/Alaska Native, 7 Hispanic Americans). Average age 34. 82 applicants, 96% accepted, 31 enrolled. In 2009, 48 master's awarded. *Degree requirements:* For master's, comprehensive exam. *Entrance requirements:* For master's, GMAT, 3 letters of recommendation. Additional exam requirements/recommendations for international students: Required—TOEFL (minimum score 500 paper-based; 173 computer-based). *Application deadline:* For fall admission, 7/27 priority date for domestic students; for spring admission, 12/17 priority date for domestic students. Applications are processed on a rolling basis. Application fee: $25. Electronic applications accepted. *Expenses:* Tuition, state resident: full-time $6160; part-time $608 per credit hour. Tuition, nonresident: full-time $17,080; part-time $854 per credit hour. Required fees: $1224; $61.20 per credit hour. *Financial support:* In 2009–10, 1 student received support, including 1 research assistantship with full tuition reimbursement available (averaging $5,184 per year); career-related internships or fieldwork, Federal Work-Study, institutionally sponsored loans, scholarships/grants, and unspecified assistantships also available. Support available to part-time students. Financial award application deadline: 3/1; financial award applicants required to submit FAFSA. *Unit head:* Dr. Carmen Reagan, Interim Director, 931-221-7674, Fax: 931-221-7355, E-mail: reaganc@apsu.edu. *Application contact:* Dr. Dixie Dennis, Dean, College of Graduate Studies, 931-221-7662, Fax: 931-221-7641, E-mail: dennisdi@apsu.edu.

Averett University, Program in Business Administration, Danville, VA 24541. Offers MBA. Part-time programs available. *Faculty:* 10 full-time (1 woman), 22 part-time/adjunct (3 women). *Students:* 86 full-time (58 women), 438 part-time (257 women); includes 254 minority (234 African Americans, 2 American Indian/Alaska Native, 7 Asian Americans or Pacific Islanders, 11 Hispanic Americans). Average age 37. 164 applicants, 99% accepted, 135 enrolled. In 2009, 159 master's awarded. *Entrance requirements:* For master's, minimum cumulative GPA of 3.0 for last 60 undergraduate credit hours, 3 letters of recommendation, resume, 3 years of work experience. Additional exam requirements/recommendations for international students: Required—TOEFL (minimum score 600 paper-based; 250 computer-based). *Application deadline:* Applications are processed on a rolling basis. Application fee: $50. *Financial support:* Institutionally sponsored loans available. Support available to part-time students. *Unit head:* Dr. Eugene Steadman, E-mail: eugene.steadman@averett.edu. *Application contact:* Dr. Eugene Steadman, E-mail: eugene.steadman@averett.edu.

Avila University, School of Business, Kansas City, MO 64145-1698. Offers accounting (MBA); finance (MBA); general management (MBA); health care administration (MBA); international business (MBA); management information systems (MBA); marketing (MBA). Part-time and evening/weekend programs available. *Faculty:* 9 full-time (3 women), 24 part-time/adjunct (5 women). *Students:* 148 full-time (71 women), 86 part-time (47 women); includes 56 minority (36 African Americans, 2 American Indian/Alaska Native, 13 Asian Americans or Pacific Islanders, 5 Hispanic Americans), 63 international. Average age 32. 53 applicants, 75% accepted, 40 enrolled. In 2009, 93 master's awarded. *Degree requirements:* For master's, comprehensive exam, capstone course. *Entrance requirements:* For master's, GMAT, minimum GPA of 3.0, interview. Additional exam requirements/recommendations for international students: Required—TOEFL (minimum score 550 paper-based). *Application deadline:* For fall admission, 7/30 priority date for domestic students, 7/30 for international students; for winter admission, 11/30 priority date for domestic students, 11/30 for international students; for spring admission, 2/28 priority date for domestic students, 2/28 for international students. Applications are processed on a rolling basis. Application fee: $0. Electronic applications accepted. *Expenses:* Contact institution. *Financial support:* In 2009–10, 102 students received support. Career-related internships or fieldwork available. Support available to part-time students. Financial award applicants required to submit FAFSA. *Faculty research:* Leadership characteristics, financial hedging, group dynamics. *Unit head:* Dr. Richard Woodall, Dean, 816-501-3720, Fax: 816-501-2463, E-mail: richard.woodall@avila.edu. *Application contact:* JoAnna Giffin, MBA Admissions Director, 816-501-3601, Fax: 816-501-2463, E-mail: joanna.giffin@avila.edu.

Azusa Pacific University, School of Business and Management, Program in Business Administration, Azusa, CA 91702-7000. Offers MBA.

Babson College, F. W. Olin Graduate School of Business, Wellesley, Babson Park, MA 02457-0310. Offers accounting (MSA); advanced management (Certificate); business administration (MBA); global entrepreneurship (MS); technological entrepreneurship (MS). *Accreditation:* AACSB. Part-time and evening/weekend programs available. Postbaccalaureate distance learning degree programs offered (minimal on-campus study). *Faculty:* 144 full-time (37 women), 46 part-time/adjunct (10 women). *Students:* 503 full-time (171 women), 1,019 part-time (276 women); includes 221 minority (28 African Americans, 152 Asian Americans or Pacific Islanders, 41 Hispanic Americans), 285 international. Average age 32. 1,102 applicants, 57% accepted, 407 enrolled. In 2009, 712 master's, 2 other advanced degrees awarded. *Entrance requirements:* For master's, GMAT, 2 years of work experience, resume, letters of recommendation. Additional exam requirements/recommendations for international students: Required—TOEFL (minimum score 600 paper-based; 250 computer-based; 100 iBT). *Application*

deadline: For fall admission, 4/15 priority date for domestic students, 1/15 priority date for international students. Application fee: $100. Electronic applications accepted. *Expenses:* Tuition: Full-time $40,600; part-time $1137 per credit. One-time fee: $1270. Full-time tuition and fees vary according to course load, program and student level. *Financial support:* In 2009–10, 317 students received support, including 43 fellowships (averaging $33,969 per year); career-related internships or fieldwork, Federal Work-Study, institutionally sponsored loans, scholarships/grants, and unspecified assistantships also available. Financial award application deadline: 4/15. *Faculty research:* Entrepreneurship, innovation and quality management, global management, e-commerce marketing, leadership and change management. Total annual research expenditures: $89,516. *Unit head:* Dr. Raghu Tadepalli, Dean, E-mail: rtadepalli@babson.edu. *Application contact:* Martha Snelling, Admission Services Team, 781-239-4317, Fax: 781-239-4194, E-mail: mbaadmission@babson.edu.

See Display on page 112 and Close-Up on page 235.

Baker College Center for Graduate Studies—Online, Graduate Programs—Online, Flint, MI 48507-9843. Offers accounting (MBA); business administration (DBA); finance (MBA); general business (MBA); health care management (MBA); human resources management (MBA); information management (MBA); leadership studies (MBA); management information systems (MSIS); marketing (MBA). Part-time and evening/weekend programs available. Postbaccalaureate distance learning degree programs offered. *Faculty:* 750. *Students:* 500 full-time, 500 part-time. Average age 37. *Degree requirements:* For master's, portfolio. *Entrance requirements:* For master's, 3 years of work experience, minimum undergraduate GPA of 2.5, writing sample, 3 letters of recommendation; for doctorate, MBA or acceptable related master's degree from accredited association, 5 years work experience, minimum graduate GPA of 3.25, writing sample, 3 professional references. Additional exam requirements/recommendations for international students: Required—TOEFL (minimum score 550 paper-based; 213 computer-based). *Application deadline:* For fall admission, 8/6 priority date for domestic students; for winter admission, 12/15 priority date for domestic students; for spring admission, 2/15 priority date for domestic students. Applications are processed on a rolling basis. Application fee: $25. Electronic applications accepted. *Expenses:* Tuition: Part-time $330 per credit hour. Tuition and fees vary according to degree level. *Financial support:* Scholarships/grants available. Support available to part-time students. Financial award applicants required to submit FAFSA. *Unit head:* Dr. Julia Teahen, President, 810-766-4023, Fax: 810-766-4399, E-mail: julia@baker.edu. *Application contact:* Chuck J. Gurden, Vice President for Graduate and Online Admissions, 800-469-3165, Fax: 810-766-4399, E-mail: adm-ol@baker.edu.

Baker University, School of Professional and Graduate Studies, Programs in Business, Baldwin City, KS 66006-0065. Offers MBA, MSM. Programs also offered in Lee's Summit, MO; Overland Park, KS; Topeka, KS; and Wichita, KS. *Accreditation:* ACBSP. Evening/weekend programs available. Postbaccalaureate distance learning degree programs offered (minimal on-campus study). *Degree requirements:* For master's, comprehensive exam. *Entrance requirements:* For master's, 2 years of full-time work experience. Additional exam requirements/recommendations for international students: Required—TOEFL (minimum score 600 paper-based; 250 computer-based).

Bakke Graduate University, Programs in Pastoral Ministry and Business, Seattle, WA 98104. Offers business (MBA); global urban ministry (MA); social and civic entrepreneurship (MA); transformational leadership for the global city (D Min). Part-time programs available. Postbaccalaureate distance learning degree programs offered (minimal on-campus study). *Faculty:* 7 full-time (2 women), 30 part-time/adjunct (4 women). *Students:* 84 full-time (24 women), 284 part-time (74 women); includes 199 minority (99 African Americans, 1 American Indian/Alaska Native, 90 Asian Americans or Pacific Islanders, 9 Hispanic Americans). Average age 38. 41 applicants, 98% accepted, 25 enrolled. In 2009, 11 master's, 37 doctorates awarded. *Degree requirements:* For master's, thesis; for doctorate, thesis/dissertation. *Entrance requirements:* For master's, 2 years of ministry experience, BA in Biblical studies or theology; for doctorate, 3 years of ministry experience, M Div. Additional exam requirements/recommendations for international students: Required—TOEFL (minimum score 60 computer-based). *Application deadline:* For fall admission, 7/1 priority date for domestic students; for winter admission, 12/1 for domestic students; for spring admission, 3/15 for domestic students. Applications are processed on a rolling basis. Application fee: $75 ($25 for international students). Electronic applications accepted. *Expenses:* Tuition: Full-time $8000; part-time $2000 per course. Required fees: $175; $50 per course. *Financial support:* In 2009–10, 140 students received support. Scholarships/grants and tuition waivers (partial) available. Financial award applicants required to submit FAFSA. *Faculty research:* Theological systems, church management, worship. *Unit head:* Dr. Gwen Dewey, Academic Dean, 206-264-9100 Ext. 119, Fax: 206-264-8828, E-mail: gwend@bgu.edu. *Application contact:* Lauren Geiser, Assistant Registrar, 206-246-9100 Ext. 110, Fax: 206-264-8828, E-mail: laureng@bgu.edu.

Baldwin-Wallace College, Graduate Programs, Division of Business, Program in Business Administration-Systems Management, Berea, OH 44017-2088. Offers MBA. Part-time and evening/weekend programs available. *Students:* 102 full-time (41 women), 112 part-time (55 women); includes 26 minority (15 African Americans, 7 Asian Americans or Pacific Islanders, 4 Hispanic Americans), 2 international. Average age 34. 75 applicants, 72% accepted, 39 enrolled. In 2009, 56 master's awarded. *Entrance requirements:* For master's, GMAT, bachelor's degree in field, work experience, minimum GPA of 3.0. Additional exam requirements/recommendations for international students: Required—TOEFL (minimum score 523 paper-based; 193 computer-based; 70 iBT). *Application deadline:* For fall admission, 7/25 priority date for domestic students, 4/30 priority date for international students; for spring admission, 12/15 priority date for domestic students, 9/30 priority date for international students. Applications are processed on a rolling basis. Application fee: $25. Electronic applications accepted. *Expenses:* Contact institution. *Financial support:* Career-related internships or fieldwork available. Support available to part-time students. Financial award application deadline: 5/1. *Unit head:* Dale Kramer, Director, 440-826-2392, Fax: 440-826-3868, E-mail: dkramer@bw.edu. *Application contact:* Peggy Shepard, Graduate Business Coordinator, 440-826-2196, Fax: 440-826-3868, E-mail: pshepard@bw.edu.

Baldwin-Wallace College, Graduate Programs, Division of Business, Program in Executive Management, Berea, OH 44017-2088. Offers MBA. Part-time and evening/weekend programs available. *Students:* 31 full-time (12 women); includes 4 minority (2 American Indian/Alaska Native, 1 Asian American or Pacific Islander, 1 Hispanic American). Average age 40. 14 applicants, 93% accepted, 11 enrolled. In 2009, 11 master's awarded. *Degree requirements:* For master's, project. *Entrance requirements:* For master's, interview, 10 years of work experience, current professional or managerial position, bachelor's degree in any field. Additional exam requirements/recommendations for international students: Required—TOEFL (minimum score 523 paper-based; 193 computer-based; 70 iBT). *Application deadline:* For fall admission, 7/25 priority date for domestic students, 4/30 priority date for international students; for spring admission, 12/15 priority date for domestic students, 9/30 priority date for international students. Applications are processed on a rolling basis. Application fee: $25. Electronic applications accepted. *Expenses:* Contact institution. *Financial support:* Career-related internships or fieldwork available. Support available to part-time students. Financial award application deadline: 5/1; financial award applicants required to submit FAFSA. *Unit head:* Dale Kramer, Director, 440-826-2392, Fax: 440-826-3868, E-mail: dkramer@bw.edu. *Application contact:* Barbara Peterson, Graduate Business Coordinator, 440-826-2064, Fax: 440-826-3868, E-mail: bpeterson@bw.edu.

Ball State University, Graduate School, Miller College of Business, Interdepartmental Program in Business Administration, Muncie, IN 47306-1099. Offers MBA. *Accreditation:* AACSB. *Entrance requirements:* For master's, GMAT, resume.

Barry University, Andreas School of Business, Graduate Certificate Programs, Miami Shores, FL 33161-6695. Offers finance (Certificate); health services administration (Certificate); international business (Certificate); management (Certificate); management information systems (Certificate); marketing (Certificate).

Barry University, Andreas School of Business, Program in Business Administration, Miami Shores, FL 33161-6695. Offers MBA, DPM/MBA, MBA/MS, MBA/MSN.

Barry University, School of Adult and Continuing Education, Program in Administrative Studies, Miami Shores, FL 33161-6695. Offers MA. Part-time and evening/weekend programs available. *Entrance requirements:* For master's, GMAT, GRE or MAT, recommendations. Electronic applications accepted.

Barry University, School of Graduate Medical Sciences, Podiatric Medicine and Surgery Program and Andreas School of Business, Podiatric Medicine/Business Administration Option, Miami Shores, FL 33161-6695. Offers DPM/MBA.

Barry University, School of Human Performance and Leisure Sciences and Andreas School of Business, Program in Sport Management and Business Administration, Miami Shores, FL 33161-6695. Offers MS/MBA. Part-time and evening/weekend programs available. Electronic applications accepted. *Faculty research:* Economic impact of professional sports, sport marketing.

Barry University, School of Nursing and Andreas School of Business, Program in Nursing Administration and Business Administration, Miami Shores, FL 33161-6695. Offers MSN/MBA. *Accreditation:* AACN. Part-time and evening/weekend programs available. Electronic applications accepted. *Faculty research:* Power/empowerment, health delivery systems, managed care, employee health well-being.

Bayamón Central University, Graduate Programs, Program in Business Administration, Bayamón, PR 00960-1725. Offers accounting (MBA); finance (MBA); general business (MBA); management (MBA); management of security and protection (MBA); marketing (MBA). Part-time and evening/weekend programs available. *Degree requirements:* For master's, comprehensive exam (for some programs). *Entrance requirements:* For master's, EXADEP, bachelor's degree in business or related field.

Baylor University, Graduate School, Hankamer School of Business, Program in Business Administration, Waco, TX 76798. Offers MBA, JD/MBA, MBA/MSIS. *Accreditation:* AACSB. Part-time programs available. *Students:* 219 full-time (51 women), 3 part-time (1 woman); includes 54 minority (16 African Americans, 1 American Indian/Alaska Native, 14 Asian Americans or Pacific Islanders, 23 Hispanic Americans), 19 international. In 2009, 101 master's awarded. *Entrance requirements:* For master's, GMAT, minimum AACSB index of 1050. *Application deadline:* For fall admission, 8/1 for domestic students; for spring admission, 12/1 for domestic students. Applications are processed on a rolling basis. Application fee: $25. *Expenses:* Contact institution. *Financial support:* Research assistantships, teaching assistantships, career-related internships or fieldwork, Federal Work-Study, and institutionally sponsored loans available. *Unit head:* Dr. Gary Carini, Graduate Program Director, 254-710-3718, Fax: 254-710-1092, E-mail: gary_carini@baylor.edu. *Application contact:* Laurie Wilson, Director, Graduate Business Degree Programs, 254-710-4163, Fax: 254-710-1066, E-mail: laurie_wilson@baylor.edu.

Belhaven University, School of Business, Jackson, MS 39202-1789. Offers business administration (MBA); leadership (MSL); public administration (MPA). MBA program also offered in Houston, TX, Memphis, TN and Orlando, FL. Evening/weekend programs available. *Faculty:* 13 full-time (3 women), 17 part-time/adjunct (2 women). *Students:* 246 full-time (165 women), 21 part-time (15 women); includes 185 minority (166 African Americans, 11 American Indian/Alaska Native, 2 Asian Americans or Pacific Islanders, 6 Hispanic Americans). Average age 36. 222 applicants, 70% accepted, 111 enrolled. In 2009, 60 master's awarded. *Degree requirements:* For master's, comprehensive exam (for some programs), thesis (for some programs). *Entrance requirements:* For master's, GMAT, GRE General Test or MAT, minimum GPA of 2.8. *Application deadline:* Applications are processed on a rolling basis. Application fee: $25. Electronic applications accepted. *Expenses:* Tuition: Full-time $8730; part-time $485 per credit hour. Required fees: $1260; $70 per credit hour. Tuition and fees vary according to campus/location. *Financial support:* Applicants required to submit FAFSA. *Unit head:* Dr. Ralph Mason, Dean, 601-968-8949, Fax: 601-968-8951, E-mail: cmason@belhaven.edu. *Application contact:* Dr. Audrey Kelleher, Vice President of Adult and Graduate Marketing and Development, 407-804-1424, Fax: 407-620-5210, E-mail: akelleher@belhaven.edu.

Bellarmine University, W. Fielding Rubel School of Business, Louisville, KY 40205-0671. Offers EMBA, MBA. *Accreditation:* AACSB. Part-time and evening/weekend programs available. *Faculty:* 17 full-time (5 women), 11 part-time/adjunct (3 women). *Students:* 87 full-time (39 women), 110 part-time (45 women); includes 17 minority (10 African Americans, 6 Asian Americans or Pacific Islanders, 1 Hispanic American), 2 international. Average age 30. 120 applicants, 92% accepted, 101 enrolled. In 2009, 89 master's awarded. *Degree requirements:* For master's, comprehensive exam. *Entrance requirements:* For master's, GMAT, baccalaureate degree from accredited institution. Additional exam requirements/recommendations for international students: Required—TOEFL (minimum score 550 paper-based; 213 computer-based; 80 iBT). *Application deadline:* Applications are processed on a rolling basis. Application fee: $25. Electronic applications accepted. *Expenses:* Contact institution. *Financial support:* Career-related internships or fieldwork, scholarships/grants, and unspecified assistantships available. Support available to part-time students. Financial award application deadline: 7/1. *Faculty research:* Marketing, management, small business and entrepreneurship, finance, economics. *Unit head:* Dr. Daniel L. Bauer, Dean, 800-274-4723 Ext. 8026, Fax: 502-452-8013, E-mail: dbauer@bellarmine.edu. *Application contact:* Dr. Sara Yount, Dean of Graduate Admission, 800-274-4723 Ext. 8258, Fax: 502-452-8002, E-mail: syount@bellarmine.edu.

Bellevue University, Graduate School, Bellevue, NE 68005-3098. Offers acquisition and contract management (MS); business administration (MBA); clinical counseling (MS); computer information systems (MS); healthcare administration (MA, MHA, MS), including healthcare administration (MHA), human services (MA, MS); human capital management (MS, PhD); instructional design and development (MS); leadership (MA); management (MA); management information systems (MS); organizational performance (MS); public administration (MPA); public health (MPH); security management (MS). Part-time and evening/weekend programs available. Postbaccalaureate distance learning degree programs offered (no on-campus study). *Degree requirements:* For master's, thesis or project. *Entrance requirements:* For master's, minimum GPA of 2.5 in last 60 hours. Additional exam requirements/recommendations for international students: Required—TOEFL (minimum score 538 paper-based; 200 computer-based).

Belmont University, Jack C. Massey Graduate School of Business, Nashville, TN 37212-3757. Offers M Acc, MBA. *Accreditation:* AACSB. Part-time and evening/weekend programs available. *Entrance requirements:* For master's, GMAT, 2 years of work experience (MBA). Additional exam requirements/recommendations for international students: Required—TOEFL (minimum score 550 paper-based; 213 computer-based). Electronic applications accepted. *Expenses:* Contact institution. *Faculty research:* Music business, strategy, ethics, finance, accounting systems.

Benedictine College, Executive Master of Business Administration Program, Atchison, KS 66002-1499. Offers EMBA. Evening/weekend programs available. *Faculty:* 2 full-time (0 women), 8 part-time/adjunct (1 woman). *Students:* 12 full-time (2 women); includes 3 African Americans, 1 Hispanic American. Average age 35. 13 applicants, 100% accepted, 12 enrolled. In 2009, 16 master's awarded. *Entrance requirements:* For master's, 5 years of management experience, interview. Additional exam requirements/recommendations for international students: Required—TOEFL (minimum score 533 paper-based). *Application deadline:* For fall admission, 7/15 priority date for domestic students, 7/1 for international students; for spring admission, 4/15 priority date for domestic students, 4/1 for international students. Applications are processed on a rolling basis. Application fee: $100. Electronic applications accepted. *Expenses:* Contact institution. *Financial support:* In 2009–10, 6 students received support. Scholarships/grants and tuition waivers (full and partial) available. Financial award application deadline: 4/15; financial award applicants required to submit FAFSA. *Faculty research:* Banking, strategic planning, ethics, leadership and entrepreneurship. *Unit head:* Dave Geenens, Executive Director, Graduate Business Programs, 913-367-5340 Ext. 7633, Fax: 913-360-7301, E-mail: emba@benedictine.edu. *Application contact:* Donna Bonnel, Administrative of Graduation Programs, 913-367-5340 Ext. 7589, Fax: 913-360-7301, E-mail: dbonnel@benedictine.edu.

Business Administration and Management—General

Benedictine College, Traditional Business Administration Program, Atchison, KS 66002. Offers MBA. Part-time and evening/weekend programs available. *Faculty:* 2 full-time (1 woman), 4 part-time/adjunct (0 women). *Students:* 18 full-time (5 women), 20 part-time (11 women); includes 2 minority (1 Asian American or Pacific Islander, 1 Hispanic American). Average age 22. 38 applicants, 100% accepted, 38 enrolled. In 2009, 14 master's awarded. *Degree requirements:* For master's, comprehensive exam. *Entrance requirements:* For master's, GMAT. Additional exam requirements/recommendations for international students: Required—TOEFL (minimum score 533 paper-based; 200 computer-based; 72 iBT). *Application deadline:* For fall admission, 8/1 priority date for domestic students, 7/1 priority date for international students; for winter admission, 1/7 priority date for domestic students, 12/1 priority date for international students; for spring admission, 5/1 priority date for domestic students, 4/1 priority date for international students. Applications are processed on a rolling basis. Application fee: $50. Electronic applications accepted. *Expenses:* Contact institution. *Financial support:* In 2009–10, 7 students received support. Scholarships/grants and unspecified assistantships available. Support available to part-time students. Financial award application deadline: 3/15; financial award applicants required to submit FAFSA. *Unit head:* Dave Geenens, Executive Director, Graduate Business Programs, 913-367-5340 Ext. 7633, Fax: 913-360-7301, E-mail: emba@benedictine.edu. *Application contact:* Donna Bonnel, Administrative Specialist, 913-360-7589, Fax: 913-360-7301, E-mail: dbonnel@benedictine.edu.

Benedictine University, Graduate Programs, Program in Business Administration, Lisle, IL 60532-0900. Offers accounting (MBA); entrepreneurship and managing innovation (MBA); financial management (MBA); health administration (MBA); human resource management (MBA); information systems security (MBA); international business (MBA); management consulting (MBA); management information systems (MBA); marketing management (MBA); operations management and logistics (MBA); organizational leadership (MBA); MBA/MPH; MBA/MS. Part-time and evening/weekend programs available. Postbaccalaureate distance learning degree programs offered (minimal on-campus study). *Faculty:* 4 full-time (2 women), 24 part-time/adjunct (3 women). *Students:* 247 full-time (141 women), 644 part-time (339 women); includes 223 minority (134 African Americans, 5 American Indian/Alaska Native, 44 Asian Americans or Pacific Islanders, 40 Hispanic Americans), 25 international. Average age 34. 287 applicants, 92% accepted, 229 enrolled. In 2009, 219 master's awarded. *Entrance requirements:* For master's, GMAT. Additional exam requirements/recommendations for international students: Required—TOEFL (minimum score 550 paper-based; 213 computer-based). *Application deadline:* For fall admission, 9/1 for domestic students; for winter admission, 12/1 for domestic students; for spring admission, 2/15 for domestic students. Applications are processed on a rolling basis. Application fee: $40. Electronic applications accepted. *Expenses:* Tuition: Part-time $750 per credit hour. Tuition and fees vary according to campus/location and program. *Financial support:* Career-related internships or fieldwork and health care benefits available. Support available to part-time students. *Faculty research:* Strategic leadership in professional organizations, sociology of professions, organizational change, social identity theory, applications to change management. *Unit head:* Dr. Sharon Borowicz, Director, 630-829-6219, E-mail: sborowicz@ben.edu. *Application contact:* Kari Gibbons, Director, Admissions, 630-829-6200, Fax: 630-829-6584, E-mail: kgibbons@ben.edu.

Benedictine University, Graduate Programs, Program in Management and Organizational Behavior, Lisle, IL 60532-0900. Offers MS, MBA/MS, MPH/MS. Part-time and evening/weekend programs available. *Faculty:* 1 full-time (0 women), 15 part-time/adjunct (7 women). *Students:* 67 full-time (34 women), 117 part-time (74 women); includes 36 minority (25 African Americans, 5 Asian Americans or Pacific Islanders, 6 Hispanic Americans), 2 international. Average age 40. 90 applicants, 96% accepted, 72 enrolled. In 2009, 47 master's awarded. *Entrance requirements:* For master's, GMAT. Additional exam requirements/recommendations for international students: Required—TOEFL (minimum score 550 paper-based; 213 computer-based). *Application deadline:* For fall admission, 9/1 for domestic students; for winter admission, 12/1 for domestic students; for spring admission, 2/15 for domestic students. Applications are processed on a rolling basis. Application fee: $40. Electronic applications accepted. *Expenses:* Tuition: Part-time $750 per credit hour. Tuition and fees vary according to campus/location and program. *Financial support:* Career-related internships or fieldwork and health care benefits available. Support available to part-time students. *Faculty research:* Organizational change, transformation, development, learning organizations, career transitions for academics. *Unit head:* Dr. Peter F. Sorensen, Director, 630-829-6220, Fax: 630-960-1126, E-mail: psorensen@ben.edu. *Application contact:* Kari Gibbons, Director, Admissions, 630-829-6200, Fax: 630-829-6584, E-mail: kgibbons@ben.edu.

Bentley University, McCallum Graduate School of Business, Business PhD Program, Waltham, MA 02452-4705. Offers PhD. Part-time programs available. *Faculty:* 65 full-time (24 women), 16 part-time/adjunct (6 women). *Students:* 20 full-time (10 women), 5 part-time (3 women); includes 4 minority (1 African American, 1 American Indian/Alaska Native, 1 Asian American or Pacific Islander, 1 Hispanic American), 10 international. Average age 37. 49 applicants, 16% accepted, 8 enrolled. *Degree requirements:* For doctorate, comprehensive exam, thesis/dissertation. *Entrance requirements:* For doctorate, GMAT or GRE General Test. Additional exam requirements/recommendations for international students: Required—TOEFL (minimum score 600 paper-based; 250 computer-based) or IELTS (minimum score 7). Application fee: $0. Electronic applications accepted. *Expenses:* Tuition: Full-time $26,208; part-time $1092 per credit. Required fees: $404. *Financial support:* Scholarships/grants available. *Faculty research:* Information systems, management (including organization behavior, strategy, entrepreneurship, business ethics), marketing, business analytics. *Unit head:* Dr. Sue Newell, PhD Program Director, 781-891-2399, Fax: 781-891-3121, E-mail: snewell@bentley.edu. *Application contact:* Dr. Sue Newell, PhD Program Director, 781-891-2399, Fax: 781-891-3121, E-mail: snewell@bentley.edu.

Bentley University, McCallum Graduate School of Business, Evening MBA Program, Waltham, MA 02452-4705. Offers MBA. *Accreditation:* AACSB. Part-time and evening/weekend programs available. *Faculty:* 65 full-time (24 women), 16 part-time/adjunct (6 women). *Students:* 471 part-time (175 women); includes 41 minority (4 African Americans, 1 American Indian/Alaska Native, 28 Asian Americans or Pacific Islanders, 8 Hispanic Americans), 25 international. Average age 29. 215 applicants, 84% accepted, 123 enrolled. *Entrance requirements:* For master's, GMAT. Additional exam requirements/recommendations for international students: Required—TOEFL (minimum score 600 paper-based; 250 computer-based; 100 iBT) or IELTS (minimum score 7). *Application deadline:* For fall admission, 6/1 for domestic students, 6/1 priority date for international students; for spring admission, 11/1 for domestic students, 10/1 for international students. Application fee: $50. Electronic applications accepted. *Expenses:* Tuition: Full-time $26,208; part-time $1092 per credit. Required fees: $404. *Financial support:* Application deadline: 6/1. *Unit head:* Dr. Alan Hoffman, Director, 781-891-3433, Fax: 781-891-2464, E-mail: ahoffman@bentley.edu. *Application contact:* Sharon Hill, Director of Graduate Admissions, 781-891-2108, Fax: 781-891-2464, E-mail: bentleygraduateadmissions@bentley.edu.

Bentley University, McCallum Graduate School of Business, Graduate Business Certificate Program, Waltham, MA 02452-4705. Offers accounting (GBC); accounting information systems (GBC); business (GSS); business ethics (GBC); data analysis (GBC); financial planning (GBC); fraud and forensic accounting (GBC); marketing analytics (GBC); taxation (GBC). Part-time and evening/weekend programs available. *Faculty:* 65 full-time (24 women), 16 part-time/adjunct (6 women). *Students:* 18 part-time (9 women); includes 2 minority (1 Asian American or Pacific Islander, 1 Hispanic American). Average age 40. 13 applicants, 100% accepted, 7 enrolled. *Entrance requirements:* Additional exam requirements/recommendations for international students: Required—TOEFL (minimum score 600 paper-based; 250 computer-based; 100 iBT) or IELTS (minimum score 7). *Application deadline:* For fall admission, 12/1 priority date for domestic and international students; for spring admission, 10/1 priority date for domestic and international students. Applications are processed on a rolling basis. Application fee: $50. Electronic applications accepted. *Expenses:* Tuition: Full-time $26,208; part-time $1092 per credit. Required fees: $404. *Financial support:* Application deadline: 6/1. *Unit head:* Dr. Michael J. Page, Dean. *Application contact:* Sharon Hill, Director of Graduate Admissions, 781-891-2108, Fax: 781-891-2464, E-mail: bentleygraduateadmissions@bentley.edu.

Bentley University, McCallum Graduate School of Business, MBA Program, Waltham, MA 02452-4705. Offers MBA. *Accreditation:* AACSB. *Faculty:* 65 full-time (24 women), 16 part-time/adjunct (6 women). *Students:* 72 full-time (30 women); includes 4 minority (2 Asian Americans or Pacific Islanders, 2 Hispanic Americans), 45 international. Average age 26. 231 applicants, 44% accepted, 41 enrolled. *Entrance requirements:* For master's, GMAT. Additional exam requirements/recommendations for international students: Required—TOEFL (minimum score 600 paper-based; 250 computer-based; 100 iBT) or IELTS (minimum score 7). *Application deadline:* For fall admission, 12/1 priority date for domestic and international students. Application fee: $50. Electronic applications accepted. *Expenses:* Tuition: Full-time $26,208; part-time $1092 per credit. Required fees: $404. *Financial support:* Research assistantships, scholarships/grants and unspecified assistantships available. Financial award application deadline: 6/1; financial award applicants required to submit CSS PROFILE or FAFSA. *Faculty research:* Information technology, team dynamics, strategy and innovation, business process management, corporate social responsibility, organizational change and knowledge management. *Unit head:* Dr. Alan Hoffman, Director, 781-891-2287, Fax: 781-891-2464, E-mail: ahoffman@bentley.edu. *Application contact:* Sharon Hill, Director of Graduate Admissions, 781-891-2108, Fax: 781-891-2464, E-mail: bentleygraduateadmissions@bentley.edu.

Bentley University, McCallum Graduate School of Business, MS and MBA Program, Waltham, MA 02452-4705. Offers MS/MBA. *Faculty:* 65 full-time (24 women), 16 part-time/adjunct (6 women). *Students:* 15 full-time (6 women); includes 1 minority (Asian American or Pacific Islander), 7 international. Average age 26. 17 applicants, 59% accepted, 7 enrolled. *Entrance requirements:* Additional exam requirements/recommendations for international students: Required—TOEFL (minimum score 600 paper-based; 250 computer-based; 100 iBT) or IELTS (minimum score 7). *Application deadline:* For fall admission, 12/1 priority date for domestic and international students; for spring admission, 10/1 priority date for domestic and international students. Application fee: $50. Electronic applications accepted. *Expenses:* Tuition: Full-time $26,208; part-time $1092 per credit. Required fees: $404. *Financial support:* Application deadline: 6/1. *Unit head:* Dr. Alan Hoffman, Director, 781-891-3433, Fax: 781-891-2464, E-mail: ahoffman@bentley.edu. *Application contact:* Sharon Hill, Director of Graduate Admissions, 781-891-2108, Fax: 781-891-2464, E-mail: bentleygraduateadmissions@bentley.edu.

Bernard M. Baruch College of the City University of New York, Zicklin School of Business, New York, NY 10010-5585. Offers MBA, MS, PhD, Certificate, JD/MBA. *Accreditation:* AACSB. Part-time and evening/weekend programs available. *Degree requirements:* For doctorate, comprehensive exam, thesis/dissertation. *Entrance requirements:* For master's, GMAT, 2 letters of recommendation, resume, 2 years of work experience; for doctorate, GMAT. Additional exam requirements/recommendations for international students: Required—TOEFL (minimum score 590 paper-based; 243 computer-based), TWE (minimum score 5). Electronic applications accepted.

Bernard M. Baruch College of the City University of New York, Zicklin School of Business, Zicklin Executive Programs, Executive MBA Program, New York, NY 10010-5585. Offers MBA. *Accreditation:* AACSB. *Entrance requirements:* For master's, 5 years of management-level work experience, personal interview. Additional exam requirements/recommendations for international students: Required—TOEFL. *Expenses:* Contact institution. *Faculty research:* Entrepreneurship, corporate governance, international finance, mergers and acquisitions.

Berry College, Graduate Programs, Campbell School of Business, Mount Berry, GA 30149-0159. Offers MBA. *Accreditation:* AACSB. Part-time and evening/weekend programs available. *Faculty:* 5 part-time/adjunct (2 women). *Students:* 4 full-time (0 women), 28 part-time (10 women); includes 2 minority (both African Americans), 2 international. Average age 30. In 2009, 8 master's awarded. *Entrance requirements:* For master's, GMAT, minimum GPA of 3.0. Additional exam requirements/recommendations for international students: Required—TOEFL (minimum score 550 paper-based; 213 computer-based). *Application deadline:* For fall admission, 7/23 for domestic students; for spring admission, 12/12 for domestic students. Applications are processed on a rolling basis. Application fee: $25 ($30 for international students). *Expenses:* Contact institution. *Financial support:* In 2009–10, 17 students received support, including 10 research assistantships with full tuition reimbursements available (averaging $4,926 per year); scholarships/grants, tuition waivers (partial), and unspecified assistantships also available. Support available to part-time students. Financial award application deadline: 4/1; financial award applicants required to submit FAFSA. *Faculty research:* Marketing, risk management, accounting strategies, business law, mistake proofing. *Unit head:* Dr. John Grout, Dean, 706-236-2233, Fax: 706-802-6728, E-mail: jgrout@berry.edu. *Application contact:* Brett Kennedy, Director of Admissions, 706-236-2215, Fax: 706-290-2178, E-mail: admissions@berry.edu.

Bethel College, Division of Graduate Studies, Program in Business Administration, Mishawaka, IN 46545-5591. Offers MBA. Part-time and evening/weekend programs available. *Faculty:* 4 part-time/adjunct (1 woman). *Students:* 4 full-time (2 women), 45 part-time (22 women); includes 10 minority (6 African Americans, 1 Asian American or Pacific Islander, 3 Hispanic Americans), 1 international. 39 applicants, 82% accepted, 23 enrolled. In 2009, 14 master's awarded. *Entrance requirements:* For master's, GMAT. Additional exam requirements/recommendations for international students: Required—TOEFL (minimum score 540 paper-based; 207 computer-based). *Application deadline:* For fall admission, 5/1 for international students; for spring admission, 10/1 for international students. Applications are processed on a rolling basis. Application fee: $25. Electronic applications accepted. *Financial support:* Career-related internships or fieldwork available. Financial award applicants required to submit FAFSA. *Faculty research:* Marketing. *Unit head:* Dr. Bradley D. Smith, Director, 574-257-3363, Fax: 574-257-7617, E-mail: smithb@bethelcollege.edu. *Application contact:* Dr. Bradley D. Smith, Director, 574-257-3363, Fax: 574-257-7617, E-mail: smithb@bethelcollege.edu.

Bethel University, Graduate School, The Bethel MBA, St. Paul, MN 55112-6999. Offers MBA. Part-time and evening/weekend programs available. Postbaccalaureate distance learning degree programs offered (minimal on-campus study). *Faculty:* 6 full-time (0 women), 34 part-time/adjunct (8 women). *Students:* 189 full-time (100 women), 51 part-time (26 women); includes 17 minority (11 African Americans, 5 Asian Americans or Pacific Islanders, 1 Hispanic American), 9 international. Average age 36. 176 applicants, 73% accepted, 115 enrolled. In 2009, 110 degrees awarded. *Degree requirements:* For master's, thesis or alternative, capstone. *Entrance requirements:* For master's, baccalaureate degree, letters of reference, accounting admission prerequisite, minimum GPA of 3.0, interview. Additional exam requirements/recommendations for international students: Required—TOEFL (minimum score 550 paper-based; 213 computer-based; 80 iBT). *Application deadline:* For fall admission, 5/1 priority date for domestic students; for winter admission, 11/1 priority date for domestic students. Applications are processed on a rolling basis. Application fee: $25. Electronic applications accepted. *Expenses:* Contact institution. *Financial support:* Applicants required to submit FAFSA. *Unit head:* Nikki Daniels, Assistant Dean, 651-635-8000, Fax: 651-635-8039, E-mail: n-daniels@bethel.edu. *Application contact:* Michael Price, Director of Admissions, 651-635-8000, Fax: 651-635-8004, E-mail: m-price@bethel.edu.

Biola University, Crowell School of Business, La Mirada, CA 90639-0001. Offers MBA. *Accreditation:* ACBSP. Part-time and evening/weekend programs available. *Entrance requirements:* For master's, GMAT, minimum GPA of 3.0. Additional exam requirements/recommendations for international students: Required—TOEFL (minimum score 550 paper-based; 213 computer-based). *Faculty research:* Integration of theology with business principles.

Birmingham-Southern College, Program in Public and Private Management, Birmingham, AL 35254. Offers MPPM. *Accreditation:* AACSB. Part-time and evening/weekend programs available. *Degree requirements:* For master's, thesis optional. *Entrance requirements:* For master's, GMAT, GRE, or MAT.

Black Hills State University, Graduate Studies, Program in Business Administration, Spearfish, SD 57799. Offers MBA. *Entrance requirements:* Additional exam requirements/recommendations for international students: Required—TOEFL (minimum score 500 paper-based; 171 computer-based; 60 iBT). *Application deadline:* Applications are processed on a rolling basis. Application fee: $35. *Expenses:* Tuition, state resident: full-time $4170; part-time $139 per credit hour.

Tuition, nonresident: full-time $8828; part-time $294 per credit. Required fees: $3476; $116 per credit hour. *Unit head:* Dr. Kristi Pearce, Associate Provost and Director of Graduate Studies, 605-642-6270, E-mail: kristi.pearce@bhsu.edu. *Application contact:* Dr. Kristi Pearce, Director of Graduate Studies, 605-642-6270, Fax: 605-642-6273, E-mail: kristi.pearce@bhsu.edu.

Bloomsburg University of Pennsylvania, School of Graduate Studies, College of Business, Program in Business Administration, Bloomsburg, PA 17815-1301. Offers MBA. *Accreditation:* AACSB. *Entrance requirements:* For master's, GMAT, minimum QPA of 3.0, resume, 3 letters of recommendation. Additional exam requirements/recommendations for international students: Required—TOEFL (minimum score 550 paper-based; 213 computer-based; 79 iBT). Electronic applications accepted.

Bluffton University, Programs in Business, Bluffton, OH 45817. Offers business administration (MBA); organizational management (MA). Evening/weekend programs available. *Entrance requirements:* Additional exam requirements/recommendations for international students: Required—TOEFL. Electronic applications accepted.

Bob Jones University, Graduate Programs, Greenville, SC 29614. Offers accountancy (MS); Bible (MA); Bible translation (MA); Biblical studies (Certificate); broadcast management (MS); business administration (MBA); church history (MA, PhD); church ministries (MA); church music (MM); cinema and video production (MA); counseling (MS); curriculum and instruction (Ed D); divinity (M Div); dramatic production (MA); educational leadership (MS, Ed D, Ed S); elementary education (M Ed, MAT); English (M Ed, MA, MAT); fine arts (MA); graphic design (MA); history (M Ed, MA); illustration (MA); interpretative speech (MA); mathematics (M Ed, MAT); medical missions (Certificate); ministry (MM, D Min); multi-categorical special education (M Ed, MAT); music (M Ed); New Testament interpretation (PhD); Old Testament interpretation (PhD); orchestral instrument performance (MM); organ performance (MM); pastoral studies (MA); personnel services (MS, Ed S); piano pedagogy (MM); piano performance (MM); platform arts (MA); radio and television broadcasting (MS); rhetoric and public address (MA); secondary education (M Ed); studio art (MA); teaching Bible (MA); theology (MA, PhD); voice performance (MM); youth ministries (MA); M Div/MM.

Boise State University, Graduate College, College of Business and Economics, Program in Business Administration, Boise, ID 83725-0399. Offers MBA. *Accreditation:* AACSB. Part-time programs available. *Entrance requirements:* For master's, GMAT, minimum GPA of 3.0. Additional exam requirements/recommendations for international students: Required—TOEFL. Electronic applications accepted. *Expenses:* Tuition, state resident: full-time $3106; part-time $209 per credit. Tuition, nonresident: part-time $284 per credit.

Boston College, Carroll School of Management, Business Administration Program, Chestnut Hill, MA 02467-3800. Offers MBA, JD/MBA, MBA/MA, MBA/MS, MBA/MSA, MBA/MSF, MBA/MSW, MBA/PhD. *Accreditation:* AACSB. Part-time and evening/weekend programs available. *Faculty:* 42 full-time (9 women), 22 part-time/adjunct (7 women). *Students:* 207 full-time (66 women), 491 part-time (156 women); includes 78 minority (3 African Americans, 1 American Indian/Alaska Native, 61 Asian Americans or Pacific Islanders, 13 Hispanic Americans), 66 international. Average age 27. 1,165 applicants, 35% accepted, 193 enrolled. In 2009, 273 master's awarded. *Entrance requirements:* For master's, GMAT, 2 letters of recommendation, resume. Additional exam requirements/recommendations for international students: Required—TOEFL (minimum score 600 paper-based; 250 computer-based; 100 iBT). *Application deadline:* For fall admission, 4/15 for domestic and international students; for spring admission, 10/15 for domestic students. Application fee: $100. Electronic applications accepted. *Financial support:* In 2009–10, 69 fellowships, 103 research assistantships with full and partial tuition reimbursements were awarded; career-related internships or fieldwork, Federal Work-Study, scholarships/grants, tuition waivers (full and partial), and unspecified assistantships also available. Support available to part-time students. Financial award application deadline: 3/1; financial award applicants required to submit FAFSA. *Faculty research:* Investments, e-commerce, corporate finance, management of financial services, strategic management. *Unit head:* Dr. Jeffrey L. Ringuest, Associate Dean for Graduate Programs, 617-552-9100, Fax: 617-552-0514, E-mail: jeffrey.ringuest@bc.edu. *Application contact:* Shelley A. Burt, Director of Graduate Enrollment, 617-552-3920, Fax: 617-552-8078, E-mail: bcmba@bc.edu.

Boston University, Metropolitan College, Department of Administrative Sciences, Boston, MA 02215. Offers banking and financial management (MSM); business continuity in emergency management (MSM); economics development and tourism management (MSAS); electronic commerce, systems, and technology (MSAS); financial economics (MSAS); human resource management (MSM); innovation and technology (MSAS); insurance management (MSM); international market management (MSM); multinational commerce (MSAS); project management (MSM). *Accreditation:* AACSB. Part-time and evening/weekend programs available. Postbaccalaureate distance learning degree programs offered (no on-campus study). *Students:* 123 full-time (48 women), 204 part-time (92 women); includes 31 minority (10 African Americans, 1 American Indian/Alaska Native, 11 Asian Americans or Pacific Islanders, 9 Hispanic Americans), 146 international. Average age 30. In 2009, 154 master's awarded. *Degree requirements:* For master's, thesis optional. *Entrance requirements:* For master's, 1 year of work experience, minimum GPA of 3.0. Additional exam requirements/recommendations for international students: Required—TOEFL (minimum score 560 paper-based; 220 computer-based; 84 iBT). *Application deadline:* Applications are processed on a rolling basis. Application fee: $70. Electronic applications accepted. *Expenses:* Tuition: Full-time $37,910; part-time $1184 per credit hour. Required fees: $386; $40 per semester. Part-time tuition and fees vary according to class time, course level, degree level and program. *Financial support:* In 2009–10, 15 students received support, including 8 research assistantships (averaging $10,000 per year); career-related internships or fieldwork and Federal Work-Study also available. *Faculty research:* International business, innovative process. *Unit head:* Dr. Kip Becker, Chairman, 617-353-3016, E-mail: adminsc@bu.edu. *Application contact:* Lucille Dicker, Administrative Sciences Department, 617-353-3016, E-mail: adminsc@bu.edu.

Boston University, School of Management, Doctorate in Business Administration Program, Boston, MA 02215. Offers accounting (PhD); information systems (PhD); marketing (PhD); operations and technology management (PhD); organizational behavior (PhD); strategy and innovation (PhD). *Students:* 31 full-time (18 women), 21 international. Average age 32. 158 applicants, 7% accepted, 6 enrolled. In 2009, 12 doctorates awarded. *Degree requirements:* For doctorate, comprehensive exam, thesis/dissertation, curriculum paper. *Entrance requirements:* For doctorate, GMAT or GRE General Test, resume, 3 letters of evaluation. Additional exam requirements/recommendations for international students: Required—TOEFL or IELTS. *Application deadline:* For fall admission, 1/5 for domestic and international students. Application fee: $125. *Expenses:* Tuition: Full-time $37,910; part-time $1184 per credit hour. Required fees: $386; $40 per semester. Part-time tuition and fees vary according to class time, course level, degree level and program. *Financial support:* Fellowships, research assistantships, teaching assistantships, career-related internships or fieldwork, Federal Work-Study, institutionally sponsored loans, scholarships/grants, and tuition waivers available. Support available to part-time students. Financial award applicants required to submit FAFSA. *Unit head:* Dr. Lloyd Baird, Director, 617-353-2670, E-mail: dba@bu.edu. *Application contact:* Hayden Estrada, Assistant Dean, Admissions, 617-353-2670, Fax: 617-353-7368, E-mail: dba@bu.edu.

Boston University, School of Management, Executive MBA Program, Boston, MA 02215. Offers EMBA. *Accreditation:* AACSB. *Faculty:* 15 full-time (1 woman), 5 part-time/adjunct (0 women). *Students:* 75 full-time (18 women); includes 2 Asian Americans or Pacific Islanders. Average age 38. 80 applicants, 58% accepted, 40 enrolled. In 2009, 29 master's awarded. *Entrance requirements:* For master's, at least 10 years of work experience, two recommendations, essay, resume. Additional exam requirements/recommendations for international students: Required—TOEFL or IELTS. *Application deadline:* For winter admission, 10/15 for domestic and international students. Application fee: $125. Electronic applications accepted. *Expenses:* Tuition: Full-time $37,910; part-time $1184 per credit hour. Required fees: $386; $40 per semester. Part-time tuition and fees vary according to class time, course level, degree level and program. *Faculty research:* Intersection of business, policy, and law; marketing; finance; information systems; strategy. *Unit head:* Janice Dolnick, Director, 617-353-8470, Fax: 617-353-3477, E-mail: emba@bu.edu. *Application contact:* Hayden Estrada, Assistant Dean, Admissions, 617-353-2670, Fax: 617-353-7368, E-mail: emba@bu.edu.

Boston University, School of Management, Master of Business Administration Program, Boston, MA 02215. Offers entrepreneurship (MBA); finance (MBA); health sector management (MBA); international management (MBA); marketing (MBA); operations and technology management (MBA); public and nonprofit management (MBA); strategy and business analysis (MBA); JD/MBA; MBA/MA; MBA/MPH; MBA/MS; MBA/MSIS; MS/MBA. Part-time and evening/weekend programs available. *Faculty:* 119 full-time (31 women), 99 part-time/adjunct (30 women). *Students:* 326 full-time (138 women), 677 part-time (257 women); includes 149 minority (13 African Americans, 119 Asian Americans or Pacific Islanders, 17 Hispanic Americans), 149 international. Average age 30. 1,617 applicants, 38% accepted, 317 enrolled. In 2009, 284 master's awarded. *Entrance requirements:* For master's, GMAT, resume, 2 letters of recommendation. Additional exam requirements/recommendations for international students: Required—TOEFL or IELTS. *Application deadline:* For fall admission, 3/15 for domestic and international students; for spring admission, 11/15 for domestic students. Application fee: $125. Electronic applications accepted. *Expenses:* Tuition: Full-time $37,910; part-time $1184 per credit hour. Required fees: $386; $40 per semester. Part-time tuition and fees vary according to class time, course level, degree level and program. *Financial support:* Career-related internships or fieldwork, Federal Work-Study, institutionally sponsored loans, and scholarships/grants available. Support available to part-time students. Financial award applicants required to submit FAFSA. *Unit head:* Katherine Nolan, Assistant Dean, Graduate Programs, 617-353-4157, Fax: 617-353-5003, E-mail: mba@bu.edu. *Application contact:* Hayden Estrada, Assistant Dean, Admissions, 617-353-2670, Fax: 617-353-7368, E-mail: mba@bu.edu.

Bowie State University, Graduate Programs, Program in Business Administration, Bowie, MD 20715-9465. Offers MBA. *Accreditation:* ACBSP. Part-time and evening/weekend programs available. *Degree requirements:* For master's, comprehensive exam. *Entrance requirements:* For master's, GMAT, minimum undergraduate GPA of 2.5. Electronic applications accepted.

Bowling Green State University, Graduate College, College of Business Administration, Graduate Studies in Business Program, Bowling Green, OH 43403. Offers MBA. *Accreditation:* AACSB. Part-time and evening/weekend programs available. *Degree requirements:* For master's, thesis or alternative, research project. *Entrance requirements:* For master's, GMAT. Additional exam requirements/recommendations for international students: Required—TOEFL. Electronic applications accepted. *Faculty research:* Management of change processes, supply chain management, impacts of money on society, corporate financing strategies, macro-marketing/management of sales staff and services.

Bradley University, Graduate School, Foster College of Business Administration, Executive MBA Program, Peoria, IL 61625-0002. Offers MBA. Evening/weekend programs available. *Entrance requirements:* For master's, company sponsorship, 7 years of managerial experience, letters of recommendation. Additional exam requirements/recommendations for international students: Required—TOEFL (minimum score 550 paper-based; 213 computer-based; 79 iBT). *Expenses:* Contact institution.

Bradley University, Graduate School, Foster College of Business Administration, Program in Business Administration, Peoria, IL 61625-0002. Offers MBA. *Accreditation:* AACSB. Part-time and evening/weekend programs available. *Degree requirements:* For master's, comprehensive exam. *Entrance requirements:* For master's, GMAT, minimum undergraduate GPA of 2.75 in major, 2 letters of recommendation. Additional exam requirements/recommendations for international students: Required—TOEFL (minimum score 550 paper-based; 213 computer-based; 79 iBT).

Brandeis University, The Heller School for Social Policy and Management, Program in Nonprofit Management, Waltham, MA 02454-9110. Offers aging services management (MBA); child, youth, and family management (MBA); health care management (MBA); social impact management (MBA); social policy and management (MBA); sustainable development (MBA); MBA/MA. *Accreditation:* AACSB. Part-time and evening/weekend programs available. *Degree requirements:* For master's, team consulting project. *Entrance requirements:* For master's, GMAT. Additional exam requirements/recommendations for international students: Required—TOEFL (minimum score 600 paper-based). Electronic applications accepted. *Expenses:* Contact institution. *Faculty research:* Health care, child and family, elder and disabled services, general human services.

Brenau University, Graduate Programs, School of Business and Mass Communication, Gainesville, GA 30501. Offers accounting (MBA); business administration (MBA); healthcare management (MBA); organizational leadership (MS); project management (MBA). Part-time and evening/weekend programs available. Postbaccalaureate distance learning degree programs offered (no on-campus study). *Faculty:* 11 full-time (6 women), 22 part-time/adjunct (6 women). *Students:* 116 full-time (74 women), 256 part-time (181 women); includes 113 minority (98 African Americans, 6 Asian Americans or Pacific Islanders, 9 Hispanic Americans), 20 international. Average age 35. 278 applicants, 90% accepted, 185 enrolled. In 2009, 125 master's awarded. *Entrance requirements:* For master's, resume, minimum undergraduate GPA of 3.5. Additional exam requirements/recommendations for international students: Required—TOEFL (minimum score 500 paper-based). *Application deadline:* Applications are processed on a rolling basis. Electronic applications accepted. *Expenses:* Contact institution. *Financial support:* In 2009–10, 1 student received support. Application deadline: 7/15. *Unit head:* Dr. William S. Lightfoot, Dean, 770-538-5330, Fax: 770-537-4701, E-mail: wlightfoot@brenau.edu. *Application contact:* Christina White, Graduate Admissions Specialist, 770-718-5320, Fax: 770-718-5338, E-mail: cwhite@brenau.edu.

Brescia University, Program in Business Administration, Owensboro, KY 42301-3023. Offers MBA. Part-time and evening/weekend programs available. *Faculty:* 3 full-time (1 woman). *Entrance requirements:* For master's, GMAT or GRE. *Application deadline:* Applications are processed on a rolling basis. Application fee: $50. *Expenses:* Tuition: Full-time $7200; part-time $400 per credit hour. *Financial support:* Institutionally sponsored loans available. Support available to part-time students. Financial award application deadline: 3/1; financial award applicants required to submit FAFSA. *Unit head:* Dr. Duane Smith, Director, 270-686-4331, Fax: 270-6864266, E-mail: duanes@brescia.edu. *Application contact:* Christopher Houk, Vice President for Enrollment, 270-686-4241, Fax: 270-686-4201, E-mail: admissions@brescia.edu.

Brescia University, Program in Management, Owensboro, KY 42301-3023. Offers MSM. Part-time and evening/weekend programs available. *Faculty:* 3 full-time (1 woman). *Students:* 1 part-time (0 women), all international. Average age 37. In 2009, 1 master's awarded. *Entrance requirements:* For master's, GMAT, minimum GPA of 2.5. *Application deadline:* Applications are processed on a rolling basis. Application fee: $50. *Expenses:* Tuition: Full-time $7200; part-time $400 per credit hour. *Financial support:* Institutionally sponsored loans available. Support available to part-time students. Financial award application deadline: 3/1; financial award applicants required to submit FAFSA. *Unit head:* Dr. Duane Smith, Director, 270-686-4331, Fax: 270-686-4266, E-mail: duanes@brescia.edu. *Application contact:* Christopher Houk, Director of Admissions, 270-686-4241, Fax: 270-686-4201, E-mail: admissions@brescia.edu.

Bridgewater State University, School of Graduate Studies, School of Business, Department of Management, Bridgewater, MA 02325-0001. Offers MSM. *Entrance requirements:* For master's, GMAT.

Briercrest Seminary, Graduate Programs, Program in Leadership and Management, Caronport, SK S0H 0S0, Canada. Offers organizational leadership (MA). Part-time programs available. *Degree requirements:* For master's, comprehensive exam, thesis optional. *Entrance requirements:* Additional exam requirements/recommendations for international students: Required—TOEFL (minimum score 550 paper-based; 213 computer-based).

Brigham Young University, Graduate Studies, Marriott School of Management, Executive Master of Business Administration Program, Provo, UT 84602. Offers MBA. *Accreditation:* AACSB. Part-time and evening/weekend programs available. *Faculty:* 13 full-time (0 women). *Students:* 132 part-time (6 women); includes 11 minority (9 Asian Americans or Pacific Islanders,

Business Administration and Management—General

Brigham Young University (continued)
2 Hispanic Americans). Average age 36. 172 applicants, 53% accepted, 65 enrolled. In 2009, 66 master's awarded. *Entrance requirements:* For master's, GMAT, 5 years of management experience, minimum GPA of 3.0 in last 60 undergraduate hours. Additional exam requirements/recommendations for international students: Required—TOEFL (minimum score 590 paper-based; 240 computer-based; 94 iBT). *Application deadline:* For fall admission, 5/1 for domestic and international students. Applications are processed on a rolling basis. Application fee: $50. Electronic applications accepted. *Expenses:* Contact institution. *Financial support:* Applicants required to submit FAFSA. *Unit head:* Tad Brinkerhoff, Director, 801-422-3721, Fax: 801-422-0513, E-mail: emba@byu.edu. *Application contact:* Yvette Anderson, MBA Program Admissions Director, 801-422-3500, Fax: 801-422-0513, E-mail: mba@byu.edu.

Brigham Young University, Graduate Studies, Marriott School of Management, Master of Business Administration Program, Provo, UT 84602. Offers MBA, JD/MBA, MBA/MS. *Accreditation:* AACSB. *Students:* 316 full-time (50 women); includes 29 minority (2 African Americans, 2 American Indian/Alaska Native, 16 Asian Americans or Pacific Islanders, 9 Hispanic Americans), 41 international. Average age 29. 478 applicants, 51% accepted, 166 enrolled. In 2009, 157 master's awarded. *Entrance requirements:* For master's, GMAT, minimum GPA of 3.0 in last 60 hours. Additional exam requirements/recommendations for international students: Required—TOEFL (minimum score 590 paper-based; 240 computer-based). *Application deadline:* For fall admission, 3/1 for domestic students, 1/15 for international students. Applications are processed on a rolling basis. Application fee: $50. Electronic applications accepted. *Expenses:* Contact institution. *Financial support:* In 2009–10, 291 students received support; teaching assistantships, career-related internships or fieldwork, institutionally sponsored loans, scholarships/grants, and unspecified assistantships available. Financial award application deadline: 4/15; financial award applicants required to submit FAFSA. *Faculty research:* Finance, organizational behavior/human relations, marketing, supply chain management, strategy. *Unit head:* Craig B. Merrill, Director, 801-422-3500, Fax: 801-422-0513, E-mail: mba@byu.edu. *Application contact:* Yvette Anderson, MBA Program Admissions Director, 801-422-3500, Fax: 801-422-0513, E-mail: mba@byu.edu.

Brock University, Faculty of Graduate Studies, Faculty of Business, Program in Business Administration, St. Catharines, ON L2S 3A1, Canada. Offers MBA. *Degree requirements:* For master's, thesis or alternative. *Entrance requirements:* For master's, honours degree. Additional exam requirements/recommendations for international students: Required—TOEFL (minimum score 575 paper-based; 230 computer-based; 89 iBT), IELTS (minimum score 7), TWE (minimum score 4.5). Electronic applications accepted.

Brock University, Faculty of Graduate Studies, Faculty of Business, Program in Management, St. Catharines, ON L2S 3A1, Canada. Offers M Sc. Part-time programs available. *Degree requirements:* For master's, thesis. *Entrance requirements:* For master's, GMAT, honors degree. Additional exam requirements/recommendations for international students: Required—TOEFL (minimum score 600 paper-based; 250 computer-based; 100 iBT), IELTS (minimum score 7), TWE (minimum score 4.5). Electronic applications accepted.

Bryan College, MBA Program, Dayton, TN 37321-7000. Offers MBA. *Entrance requirements:* For master's, resume, 2 letters of recommendation.

Bryant University, Graduate School of Business, Master of Business Administration Program, Smithfield, RI 02917. Offers general business (MBA). *Accreditation:* AACSB. Part-time and evening/weekend programs available. *Faculty:* 38 full-time (11 women), 2 part-time/adjunct (1 woman). *Students:* 41 full-time (16 women), 143 part-time (48 women); includes 9 minority (4 African Americans, 1 American Indian/Alaska Native, 2 Asian Americans or Pacific Islanders, 2 Hispanic Americans), 8 international. Average age 28. 161 applicants, 70% accepted, 80 enrolled. In 2009, 123 master's awarded. *Entrance requirements:* For master's, GMAT, transcripts, recommendation, resume, statement of objectives. Additional exam requirements/recommendations for international students: Required—TOEFL (minimum score 580 paper-based; 237 computer-based; 95 iBT). *Application deadline:* For fall admission, 7/15 for domestic and international students; for spring admission, 11/15 for domestic and international students. Applications are processed on a rolling basis. Application fee: $80. Electronic applications accepted. *Expenses:* Tuition: Full-time $29,880; part-time $2367 per course. One-time fee: $750. Tuition and fees vary according to program. *Financial support:* In 2009–10, 27 students received support, including 16 research assistantships (averaging $15,242 per year); unspecified assistantships also available. Financial award application deadline: 2/15; financial award applicants required to submit FAFSA. *Faculty research:* International business, information systems security, leadership, financial markets microstructure, commercial lending practice. *Unit head:* Kristopher T. Sullivan, Assistant Dean of the Graduate School, 401-232-6230, Fax: 401-232-6494, E-mail: gradprog@bryant.edu. *Application contact:* Jean Ginchereau, Assistant Director of Graduate Admission, 401-232-6230, Fax: 401-232-6494, E-mail: jgincher@bryant.edu.

Butler University, College of Business Administration, Indianapolis, IN 46208-3485. Offers MBA, MP Acc. *Accreditation:* AACSB. Part-time and evening/weekend programs available. *Faculty:* 14 full-time (4 women), 3 part-time/adjunct (0 women). *Students:* 25 full-time (10 women), 196 part-time (49 women); includes 10 minority (6 African Americans, 4 Asian Americans or Pacific Islanders), 11 international. Average age 32. 178 applicants, 36% accepted, 36 enrolled. In 2009, 65 master's awarded. *Entrance requirements:* For master's, GMAT, minimum AACSB index of 950. *Application deadline:* For fall admission, 8/15 priority date for domestic students. Applications are processed on a rolling basis. Application fee: $35. Electronic applications accepted. *Financial support:* Career-related internships or fieldwork and institutionally sponsored loans available. Support available to part-time students. Financial award application deadline: 7/15; financial award applicants required to submit FAFSA. *Faculty research:* Real estate law, international finance, total quality management, web-based commerce, pricing policies. *Unit head:* Dr. Chuck Williams, Dean, 317-940-8491, Fax: 317-940-9455, E-mail: crwillia@butler.edu. *Application contact:* Stephanie Judge, Director of Marketing, 317-940-9886, Fax: 317-940-9455, E-mail: sjudge@butler.edu.

Caldwell College, Graduate Studies, Program in Business Administration, Caldwell, NJ 07006-6195. Offers accounting (MBA); business administration (MBA). *Accreditation:* ACBSP. Part-time and evening/weekend programs available. *Degree requirements:* For master's, capstone course. *Entrance requirements:* For master's, GMAT, minimum GPA of 3.0. Additional exam requirements/recommendations for international students: Required—TOEFL (minimum score 580 paper-based; 237 computer-based). Electronic applications accepted.

California Baptist University, Program in Business Administration, Riverside, CA 92504-3206. Offers management (MBA). *Accreditation:* ACBSP. Part-time and evening/weekend programs available. *Faculty:* 6 full-time (2 women), 2 part-time/adjunct (both women). *Students:* 56 full-time (24 women), 18 part-time (10 women); includes 26 minority (9 African Americans, 2 Asian Americans or Pacific Islanders, 15 Hispanic Americans), 11 international. 87 applicants, 32% accepted, 23 enrolled. In 2009, 44 master's awarded. *Degree requirements:* For master's, thesis or alternative, capstone project. *Entrance requirements:* For master's, minimum undergraduate GPA of 3.25, course work in business. Additional exam requirements/recommendations for international students: Required—TOEFL (minimum score 575 paper-based; 230 computer-based; 89 iBT). *Application deadline:* For fall admission, 8/1 priority date for domestic students, 7/1 for international students; for spring admission, 12/1 priority date for domestic students, 10/15 for international students. Applications are processed on a rolling basis. Application fee: $45. Electronic applications accepted. *Expenses:* Contact institution. *Financial support:* In 2009–10, 73 students received support. Federal Work-Study and scholarships/grants available. Support available to part-time students. Financial award applicants required to submit FAFSA. *Unit head:* Dr. Andrew Herrity, Dean, School of Business, 951-343-4427, Fax: 951-343-4361, E-mail: aherrity@calbaptist.edu. *Application contact:* Gail Ronveaux, Dean of Graduate Enrollment, 951-343-5045, Fax: 951-343-5095, E-mail: graduateadmissions@calbaptist.edu.

California Coast University, Programs in Business Administration, Santa Ana, CA 92701. Offers human resources management (MBA); management (MBA); marketing (MBA). Part-time and evening/weekend programs available. Postbaccalaureate distance learning degree programs offered (no on-campus study). Application fee: $75. Electronic applications accepted. *Application contact:* Christi Okuma, 714-547-9625, Fax: 714-547-5777, E-mail: ccu@calcoast.edu.

California Intercontinental University, School of Business, Diamond Bar, CA 91765. Offers banking and finance (MBA); entrepreneurship and business management (DBA); global business leadership (DBA); international management and marketing (MBA); organizational management and human resource management (MBA).

California International Business University, Graduate Programs, San Diego, CA 92101. Offers MBA, MSIM, DBA.

California Lutheran University, Graduate Studies, School of Business, Thousand Oaks, CA 91360-2787. Offers business (IMBA); entrepreneurship (MBA, Certificate); finance (MBA, Certificate); financial planning (MBA, Certificate); information systems and technology (MS); information technology management (MBA, Certificate); international business (MBA, Certificate); management and organization behavior (MBA); management and organizational behavior (Certificate); marketing (MBA, Certificate). Evening/weekend programs available. Post-baccalaureate distance learning degree programs offered. *Entrance requirements:* For master's, GMAT, interview, minimum GPA of 3.0. *Expenses:* Contact institution.

California National University for Advanced Studies, College of Business Administration, Northridge, CA 91325. Offers MBA, MHRM. Part-time programs available. Postbaccalaureate distance learning degree programs offered (no on-campus study). *Entrance requirements:* For master's, minimum GPA of 3.0. Additional exam requirements/recommendations for international students: Required—TOEFL (minimum score 213 computer-based). Electronic applications accepted.

California Polytechnic State University, San Luis Obispo, Orfalea College of Business, Graduate Programs in Business, San Luis Obispo, CA 93407. Offers business (MBA); taxation (MSA). *Faculty:* 4 full-time (1 woman), 2 part-time/adjunct (1 woman). *Students:* 37 full-time (11 women), 22 part-time (12 women); includes 9 minority (4 Asian Americans or Pacific Islanders, 5 Hispanic Americans), 3 international. Average age 26. 132 applicants, 36% accepted, 36 enrolled. In 2009, 49 master's awarded. *Degree requirements:* For master's, comprehensive exam (for some programs), thesis or alternative. *Entrance requirements:* For master's, GMAT. Additional exam requirements/recommendations for international students: Required—TOEFL (minimum score 550 paper-based; 213 computer-based), or IELTS (minimum score 6). *Application deadline:* For fall admission, 7/1 for domestic students, 11/30 for international students. Applications are processed on a rolling basis. Application fee: $55. Electronic applications accepted. *Expenses:* Tuition; nonresident: full-time $11,160; part-time $248 per unit. Required fees: $7134; $1553 per quarter. *Financial support:* Career-related internships or fieldwork, Federal Work-Study, institutionally sponsored loans, scholarships/grants, and unspecified assistantships available. Support available to part-time students. Financial award application deadline: 3/2; financial award applicants required to submit FAFSA. *Faculty research:* International business, organizational behavior, graphic communication document systems management, commercial development of innovative technologies, effective communication skills for managers. *Unit head:* Dr. Brian Tietje, Associate Dean/Graduate Coordinator, 805-756-1757, Fax: 805-756-0110, E-mail: btietje@calpoly.edu. *Application contact:* Dr. Chris Carr, Associate Dean, 805-756-2637, Fax: 805-756-0110, E-mail: ccarr@calpoly.edu.

California State Polytechnic University, Pomona, Academic Affairs, College of Business Administration, Pomona, CA 91768-2557. Offers MBA, MS, PMBA. *Accreditation:* AACSB. Part-time programs available. Postbaccalaureate distance learning degree programs offered (minimal on-campus study). *Faculty:* 81 full-time (33 women), 51 part-time/adjunct (11 women). *Students:* 41 full-time (23 women), 143 part-time (58 women); includes 77 minority (3 African Americans, 54 Asian Americans or Pacific Islanders, 20 Hispanic Americans), 51 international. Average age 31. 254 applicants, 33% accepted, 46 enrolled. In 2009, 54 master's awarded. *Degree requirements:* For master's, thesis, project report. *Entrance requirements:* For master's, GMAT. *Application deadline:* For fall admission, 5/1 priority date for domestic students; for winter admission, 10/15 priority date for domestic students; for spring admission, 1/2 priority date for domestic students. Applications are processed on a rolling basis. Application fee: $55. Electronic applications accepted. *Expenses:* Tuition, nonresident: full-time $6696; part-time $248 per credit. Required fees: $5487; $3237 per term. Tuition and fees vary according to course load, degree level and program. *Financial support:* In 2009–10, 5 research assistantships, 3 teaching assistantships were awarded; career-related internships or fieldwork, Federal Work-Study, and institutionally sponsored loans also available. Support available to part-time students. Financial award application deadline: 3/2; financial award applicants required to submit FAFSA. *Faculty research:* Business strategy; investment, cash flow, and cost of capital; entrepreneurship; trade with China; creativity and innovation. *Unit head:* Dr. Richard S. Lapidus, Dean, 909-869-2400, E-mail: rslapidus@csupomona.edu. *Application contact:* Dr. Steven Curl, Associate Dean, 909-869-4244, E-mail: scurl@csupomona.edu.

California State University, Bakersfield, Division of Graduate Studies, Online Program in Administration, Bakersfield, CA 93311. Offers MS. *Accreditation:* AACSB. Postbaccalaureate distance learning degree programs offered. *Degree requirements:* For master's, capstone course. *Entrance requirements:* For master's, resume, 3 letters of reference. Additional exam requirements/recommendations for international students: Required—TOEFL (minimum score 550 paper-based; 213 computer-based).

California State University, Bakersfield, Division of Graduate Studies, School of Business and Public Administration, Program in Business Administration, Bakersfield, CA 93311. Offers MBA. *Accreditation:* AACSB. *Entrance requirements:* For master's, GMAT.

California State University Channel Islands, Extended Education, Program in Business Administration, Camarillo, CA 93012. Offers MBA. Part-time and evening/weekend programs available. *Entrance requirements:* For master's, GMAT, 2 years work experience. Additional exam requirements/recommendations for international students: Required—TOEFL (minimum score 550 paper-based).

California State University, Chico, Graduate School, College of Behavioral and Social Sciences, Department of Political Science, Program in Public Administration, Chico, CA 95929-0722. Offers health administration (MPA); local government management (MPA); public administration (MPA). *Accreditation:* NASPAA. Part-time programs available. *Students:* 21 full-time (7 women), 26 part-time (13 women); includes 18 minority (4 African Americans, 1 American Indian/Alaska Native, 5 Asian Americans or Pacific Islanders, 8 Hispanic Americans), 4 international. Average age 31. 44 applicants, 91% accepted, 19 enrolled. In 2009, 10 master's awarded. *Entrance requirements:* For master's, 2 letters of recommendation. Additional exam requirements/recommendations for international students: Required—TOEFL (minimum score 550 paper-based; 213 computer-based; 80 iBT), IELTS (minimum score 6.5). *Application deadline:* For fall admission, 3/1 priority date for domestic students, 3/1 for international students; for spring admission, 9/15 priority date for domestic students, 9/15 for international students. Applications are processed on a rolling basis. Application fee: $55. Electronic applications accepted. *Financial support:* Fellowships, career-related internships or fieldwork available. *Unit head:* Dr. Donna Kemp, Graduate Coordinator, 530-898-5734. *Application contact:* Dr. Donna Kemp, Graduate Coordinator, 530-898-5734.

California State University, Chico, Graduate School, College of Business, Program in Business Administration, Chico, CA 95929-0722. Offers MBA. *Accreditation:* AACSB. Part-time programs available. *Students:* 40 full-time (21 women), 34 part-time (13 women); includes 5 minority (1 African American, 3 Asian Americans or Pacific Islanders, 1 Hispanic American), 33 international. Average age 27. 137 applicants, 58% accepted, 32 enrolled. In 2009, 26 master's awarded. *Degree requirements:* For master's, thesis or alternative. *Entrance requirements:* For master's, GMAT, 3 letters of recommendation, resume. Additional exam requirements/recommendations for international students: Required—TOEFL (minimum score 550 paper-based; 213 computer-

based; 80 iBT), IELTS (minimum score 6.5). *Application deadline:* For fall admission, 3/1 for domestic and international students; for spring admission, 9/15 for domestic and international students. Applications are processed on a rolling basis. Application fee: $55. Electronic applications accepted. *Unit head:* Graduate Coordinator, 530-898-5895. *Application contact:* Dr. Ray Boykin, Head, 530-898-5895.

California State University, Dominguez Hills, College of Business Administration and Public Policy, Program in Business Administration, Carson, CA 90747-0001. Offers MBA. *Accreditation:* ACBSP. Part-time and evening/weekend programs available. Postbaccalaureate distance learning degree programs offered (no on-campus study). *Faculty:* 7 full-time (1 woman), 8 part-time/adjunct (1 woman). *Students:* 51 full-time (15 women), 85 part-time (31 women); includes 49 minority (6 African Americans, 25 Asian Americans or Pacific Islanders, 18 Hispanic Americans), 15 international. Average age 33. 265 applicants, 49% accepted, 42 enrolled. In 2009, 52 master's awarded. *Entrance requirements:* For master's, GMAT, minimum GPA of 2.75. Additional exam requirements/recommendations for international students: Required—TOEFL (minimum score 570 paper-based; 230 computer-based; 88 iBT). *Application deadline:* For fall admission, 4/1 for domestic and international students; for spring admission, 11/1 for domestic students, 10/1 for international students. Application fee: $55. *Expenses:* Tuition, nonresident: full-time $6696; part-time $372 per unit. Required fees: $5946; $1752 per semester. *Faculty research:* Management. *Unit head:* Kenneth Poertner, Program Director, 310-243-2714, Fax: 310-516-4178, E-mail: kpoertner@csudh.edu. *Application contact:* Eileen Hall, Graduate Advisor, 310-243-3465, E-mail: ehall@csudh.edu.

California State University, Fresno, Division of Graduate Studies, Craig School of Business, Program in Business Administration, Fresno, CA 93740-8027. Offers MBA. *Accreditation:* AACSB. Part-time programs available. *Degree requirements:* For master's, thesis or alternative. *Entrance requirements:* For master's, GMAT, minimum GPA of 2.53. Additional exam requirements/recommendations for international students: Required—TOEFL. Electronic applications accepted. *Faculty research:* International trade development, entrepreneurial outreach.

California State University, Fullerton, Graduate Studies, College of Business and Economics, Department of Information Systems and Decision Sciences, Fullerton, CA 92834-9480. Offers information systems (MS); information systems (decision sciences) (MS); information systems (e-commerce) (MS); information technology (MS); management science (MBA). Part-time programs available. *Students:* 9 full-time (3 women), 72 part-time (13 women); includes 32 minority (3 African Americans, 22 Asian Americans or Pacific Islanders, 7 Hispanic Americans), 16 international. Average age 33. 105 applicants, 50% accepted, 38 enrolled. In 2009, 29 master's awarded. *Degree requirements:* For master's, project or thesis. *Entrance requirements:* For master's, GMAT, minimum AACSB index of 950. Application fee: $55. *Expenses:* Tuition, nonresident: full-time $11,160; part-time $373 per credit. Required fees: $1440 per term. Tuition and fees vary according to course load, degree level and program. *Financial support:* Career-related internships or fieldwork, Federal Work-Study, institutionally sponsored loans, and scholarships/grants available. Support available to part-time students. Financial award application deadline: 3/1; financial award applicants required to submit FAFSA. *Unit head:* Dr. Bhushan Kapoor, Chair, 657-278-2221. *Application contact:* Admissions/Applications, 657-278-2371.

California State University, Fullerton, Graduate Studies, College of Business and Economics, Department of Management, Fullerton, CA 92834-9480. Offers entrepreneurship (MBA); management (MBA). *Accreditation:* AACSB. Part-time programs available. *Students:* 31 full-time (17 women), 42 part-time (13 women); includes 30 minority (2 African Americans, 1 American Indian/Alaska Native, 15 Asian Americans or Pacific Islanders, 12 Hispanic Americans), 12 international. Average age 29. 94 applicants, 36% accepted, 21 enrolled. In 2009, 23 master's awarded. *Degree requirements:* For master's, project or thesis. *Entrance requirements:* For master's, GMAT, minimum AACSB index of 950. Application fee: $55. *Expenses:* Tuition, nonresident: full-time $11,160; part-time $373 per credit. Required fees: $1440 per term. Tuition and fees vary according to course load, degree level and program. *Financial support:* Career-related internships or fieldwork, Federal Work-Study, institutionally sponsored loans, and scholarships/grants available. Support available to part-time students. Financial award application deadline: 3/1; financial award applicants required to submit FAFSA. *Unit head:* Dr. Ellen Dumond, Chair, 657-278-2251. *Application contact:* Admissions/Applications, 657-278-2371.

California State University, Fullerton, Graduate Studies, College of Business and Economics, Program in Business Administration, Fullerton, CA 92834-9480. Offers e-commerce (MBA); international business (MBA). *Accreditation:* AACSB. Part-time programs available. *Students:* 65 full-time (30 women), 68 part-time (31 women); includes 59 minority (3 African Americans, 1 American Indian/Alaska Native, 43 Asian Americans or Pacific Islanders, 12 Hispanic Americans), 32 international. Average age 28. 238 applicants, 42% accepted, 39 enrolled. In 2009, 33 master's awarded. *Degree requirements:* For master's, project or thesis. *Entrance requirements:* For master's, GMAT. *Expenses:* Tuition, nonresident: full-time $11,160; part-time $373 per credit. Required fees: $1440 per term. Tuition and fees vary according to course load, degree level and program. *Financial support:* Career-related internships or fieldwork, Federal Work-Study, institutionally sponsored loans, and scholarships/grants available. Support available to part-time students. Financial award application deadline: 3/1; financial award applicants required to submit FAFSA. *Unit head:* Dr. Anil Puri, Dean, 657-773-2592. *Application contact:* Admissions/Applications, 657-278-2371.

California State University, Long Beach, Graduate Studies, College of Business Administration, Long Beach, CA 90840. Offers MBA. *Accreditation:* AACSB. Part-time and evening/weekend programs available. *Faculty:* 23 full-time (7 women), 8 part-time/adjunct (1 woman). *Students:* 101 full-time (47 women), 178 part-time (73 women); includes 89 minority (5 African Americans, 1 American Indian/Alaska Native, 52 Asian Americans or Pacific Islanders, 31 Hispanic Americans), 46 international. Average age 30. 464 applicants, 44% accepted, 66 enrolled. *Entrance requirements:* For master's, GMAT. *Application deadline:* For fall admission, 3/30 for domestic students. Applications are processed on a rolling basis. Application fee: $55. Electronic applications accepted. *Expenses:* Required fees: $1802 per semester. Part-time tuition and fees vary according to course load. *Financial support:* Career-related internships or fieldwork and scholarships/grants available. Financial award application deadline: 3/2; financial award applicants required to submit FAFSA. *Faculty research:* Attitude formation theory, consumer motivation, gift giving, derivative and synthetic securities, financial applications of artificial intelligence. *Unit head:* Dr. Michael E. Solt, Dean, 562-985-5306, Fax: 562-985-5742, E-mail: msolt@csulb.edu. *Application contact:* Dr. H. Michael Chung, Director, Graduate Programs and Executive Education, 562-985-5565, Fax: 562-985-5742, E-mail: hmchung@csulb.edu.

California State University, Los Angeles, Graduate Studies, College of Business and Economics, Department of Information Systems, Los Angeles, CA 90032-8530. Offers business information systems (MBA); management (MS); management information systems (MS); office management (MBA). Part-time and evening/weekend programs available. *Faculty:* 3 full-time (0 women), 2 part-time/adjunct (0 women). *Students:* 12 full-time (3 women), 18 part-time (3 women); includes 5 minority (1 African American, 4 Asian Americans or Pacific Islanders), 18 international. Average age 28. 11 applicants, 91% accepted, 7 enrolled. In 2009, 18 master's awarded. *Degree requirements:* For master's, comprehensive exam (MBA), thesis (MS). *Entrance requirements:* For master's, GMAT, minimum GPA of 2.5 during previous 2 years of course work. Additional exam requirements/recommendations for international students: Required—TOEFL (minimum score 550 paper-based; 213 computer-based). *Application deadline:* For fall admission, 5/1 for domestic and international students. Applications are processed on a rolling basis. Application fee: $55. Electronic applications accepted. *Financial support:* Career-related internships or fieldwork and Federal Work-Study available. Support available to part-time students. Financial award application deadline: 3/1. *Unit head:* Dr. Adam Huarng, Chair, 323-343-2983, E-mail: ahuarng@calstatela.edu. *Application contact:* Dr. Cheryl L. Ney, Associate Vice President for Academic Affairs and Dean of Graduate Studies, 323-343-3820, Fax: 323-343-5653, E-mail: cney@cslanet.calstatela.edu.

California State University, Los Angeles, Graduate Studies, College of Business and Economics, Department of Management, Los Angeles, CA 90032-8530. Offers health care management (MS); management (MBA, MS). *Accreditation:* AACSB. Part-time and evening/weekend programs available. *Faculty:* 4 full-time (3 women), 2 part-time/adjunct (0 women). *Students:* 10 full-time (5 women), 47 part-time (28 women); includes 21 minority (4 African Americans, 9 Asian Americans or Pacific Islanders, 8 Hispanic Americans), 18 international. Average age 33. 29 applicants, 93% accepted, 8 enrolled. In 2009, 24 master's awarded. *Entrance requirements:* For master's, GMAT, minimum GPA of 2.5 during previous 2 years of course work. Additional exam requirements/recommendations for international students: Required—TOEFL (minimum score 550 paper-based; 213 computer-based). *Application deadline:* For fall admission, 5/1 for domestic and international students. Applications are processed on a rolling basis. Application fee: $55. Electronic applications accepted. *Financial support:* Application deadline: 3/1. *Unit head:* Dr. Paul Washburn, Chair, 323-343-2890, Fax: 323-343-6461, E-mail: pwashbu@calstatela.edu. *Application contact:* Dr. Cheryl L. Ney, Associate Vice President for Academic Affairs and Dean of Graduate Studies, 323-343-3820 Ext. 3827, Fax: 323-343-5653, E-mail: cney@cslanet.calstatela.edu.

California State University, Monterey Bay, College of Professional Studies, School of Business, Seaside, CA 93955-8001. Offers EMBA. Part-time and evening/weekend programs available. Postbaccalaureate distance learning degree programs offered (no on-campus study). *Entrance requirements:* For master's, recommendation, resume, work experience, bachelor's degree from accredited university. Additional exam requirements/recommendations for international students: Recommended—TOEFL (minimum score 550 paper-based; 213 computer-based; 79 iBT). Electronic applications accepted.

California State University, Northridge, Graduate Studies, College of Business and Economics, Northridge, CA 91330. Offers MBA. *Accreditation:* AACSB. Part-time programs available. *Faculty:* 84 full-time (22 women), 53 part-time/adjunct (10 women). *Students:* 55 full-time (33 women), 139 part-time (55 women); includes 49 minority (7 African Americans, 29 Asian Americans or Pacific Islanders, 13 Hispanic Americans), 26 international. Average age 31. 533 applicants, 28% accepted, 67 enrolled. In 2009, 103 master's awarded. *Degree requirements:* For master's, thesis or alternative. *Entrance requirements:* For master's, GMAT, minimum GPA of 3.0 in last 60 units. Additional exam requirements/recommendations for international students: Required—TOEFL. *Application deadline:* For fall admission, 11/30 for domestic students. Application fee: $55. *Financial support:* Teaching assistantships, Federal Work-Study available. Support available to part-time students. Financial award application deadline: 3/1. *Unit head:* Dr. William Jennings, Dean, 818-677-2455. *Application contact:* Dr. Deborah Cours, Director of Graduate Programs, 818-677-2466, E-mail: deborah.cours@csun.edu.

California State University, Sacramento, Graduate Studies, College of Business Administration, Sacramento, CA 95819. Offers accountancy (MS); business administration (MBA); human resources (MBA); management information science (MS); urban land development (MBA). *Accreditation:* AACSB. Part-time and evening/weekend programs available. *Degree requirements:* For master's, thesis or alternative, writing proficiency exam. *Entrance requirements:* For master's, GMAT. Additional exam requirements/recommendations for international students: Required—TOEFL. Electronic applications accepted.

California State University, San Bernardino, Graduate Studies, College of Business and Public Administration, Program in Business Administration, San Bernardino, CA 92407-2397. Offers business administration (MBA); for executives (MBA). *Accreditation:* AACSB. Part-time and evening/weekend programs available. *Faculty:* 16 full-time (5 women). *Students:* 290 full-time (133 women), 96 part-time (48 women); includes 138 minority (46 African Americans, 4 American Indian/Alaska Native, 35 Asian Americans or Pacific Islanders, 53 Hispanic Americans), 117 international. Average age 30. 477 applicants, 79% accepted, 178 enrolled. In 2009, 129 master's awarded. *Degree requirements:* For master's, comprehensive exam/comprehensive project. *Entrance requirements:* For master's, GMAT, minimum GPA of 2.5. Additional exam requirements/recommendations for international students: Required—TOEFL. *Application deadline:* For fall admission, 8/31 priority date for domestic students. Applications are processed on a rolling basis. Application fee: $55. *Financial support:* Career-related internships or fieldwork, Federal Work-Study, and institutionally sponsored loans available. Support available to part-time students. Financial award application deadline: 3/1. *Unit head:* Dr. Karen Dill Bowerman, Dean, 909-537-3703, Fax: 909-537-7026, E-mail: karenb@csusb.edu. *Application contact:* Olivia Rosas, Director of Admissions, 909-537-7577, Fax: 909-537-7034, E-mail: orosas@csusb.edu.

California State University, San Bernardino, Graduate Studies, College of Extended Learning, San Bernardino, CA 92407-2397. Offers executive business administration (MBA); TESOL (MA Ed). Part-time and evening/weekend programs available. *Students:* 356 full-time (268 women), 476 part-time (317 women); includes 353 minority (53 African Americans, 7 American Indian/Alaska Native, 38 Asian Americans or Pacific Islanders, 255 Hispanic Americans), 4 international. Average age 35. 745 applicants, 93% accepted, 356 enrolled. *Application deadline:* For fall admission, 8/31 for domestic students. Application fee: $55. *Financial support:* Application deadline: 3/1. *Unit head:* Dr. Tatiana Karmanova, Acting Dean, 909-537-3986, E-mail: tkarma@csusb.edu. *Application contact:* Olivia Rosas, Director of Admissions, 909-537-7577, Fax: 909-537-7034, E-mail: orosas@csusb.edu.

California State University, San Marcos, College of Business Administration, San Marcos, CA 92096-0001. Offers business management (MBA); government management (MBA). Evening/weekend programs available. *Degree requirements:* For master's, project. *Entrance requirements:* For master's, GMAT, minimum GPA of 3.0 in last 60 units, 3 years of full-time work experience. Additional exam requirements/recommendations for international students: Required—TOEFL (minimum score 550 paper-based; 213 computer-based). *Expenses:* Contact institution.

California State University, Stanislaus, College of Business Administration, Department of Business Administration, Turlock, CA 95382. Offers EMBA, MBA. Part-time and evening/weekend programs available. *Degree requirements:* For master's, comprehensive exam, thesis or alternative. *Entrance requirements:* For master's, GRE or GMAT, minimum GPA of 2.50, interview, 3 letters of reference. Additional exam requirements/recommendations for international students: Required—TOEFL (minimum score 550 paper-based; 213 computer-based). Electronic applications accepted. *Expenses:* Contact institution. *Faculty research:* Teaching creativity, graduate operations management, curricula data mining, foreign direct investment.

California University of Pennsylvania, School of Graduate Studies and Research, School of Science and Technology, Program in Business Administration, California, PA 15419-1394. Offers MSBA. Part-time and evening/weekend programs available. *Degree requirements:* For master's, comprehensive exam. *Entrance requirements:* For master's, minimum QPA of 3.0. Additional exam requirements/recommendations for international students: Required—TOEFL (minimum score 550 paper-based; 213 computer-based). Electronic applications accepted. *Faculty research:* Economics, applied economics, consumer behavior, technology and business, impact of technology.

Cambridge College, School of Management, Cambridge, MA 02138-5304. Offers business negotiation and conflict resolution (M Mgt); general business (M Mgt); health care informatics (M Mgt); health care management (M Mgt); leadership in human and organizational dynamics (M Mgt); non-profit and public organization management (M Mgt); small business development (M Mgt); technology management (M Mgt). Part-time and evening/weekend programs available. *Faculty:* 4 full-time (3 women), 65 part-time/adjunct (32 women). *Students:* 297 full-time (178 women), 234 part-time (155 women); includes 217 minority (122 African Americans, 53 Asian Americans or Pacific Islanders, 42 Hispanic Americans), 135 international. Average age 39. In 2009, 259 master's awarded. *Degree requirements:* For master's, thesis, seminars. *Entrance requirements:* For master's, resume, 2 professional references. Additional exam requirements/recommendations for international students: Required—TOEFL (minimum score 550 paper-based; 213 computer-based; 79 iBT); Recommended—IELTS (minimum score 6). *Application*

Business Administration and Management—General

Cambridge College (continued)

deadline: Applications are processed on a rolling basis. Application fee: $30. Electronic applications accepted. *Expenses:* Contact institution. *Financial support:* In 2009–10, 170 students received support. Career-related internships or fieldwork, Federal Work-Study, and scholarships/grants available. Financial award applicants required to submit FAFSA. *Faculty research:* Negotiation, mediation and conflict resolution; leadership; management of diverse organizations; case studies and simulation methodologies for management education, digital as a second language: social networking for digital immigrants. *Unit head:* Dr. Mary Ann Joseph, Acting Dean, 617-873-0227, E-mail: maryann.joseph@cambridgecollege.edu. *Application contact:* Stephen Lyons, Director of Enrollment, Graduate and N.I.T.E. Programs, 617-868-1000, Fax: 617-349-3561, E-mail: stephen.lyons@cambridgecollege.edu.

Cameron University, Office of Graduate Studies, Program in Business Administration, Lawton, OK 73505-6377. Offers MBA. *Accreditation:* ACBSP. Part-time and evening/weekend programs available. Postbaccalaureate distance learning degree programs offered (no on-campus study). *Degree requirements:* For master's, comprehensive exam. *Entrance requirements:* Additional exam requirements/recommendations for international students: Required—TOEFL (minimum score 550 paper-based; 213 computer-based). Electronic applications accepted. *Faculty research:* Financial liberalization, right to work, recession, teaching evaluations, database management.

Campbellsville University, School of Business and Economics, Campbellsville, KY 42718-2799. Offers business administration (MBA). Part-time and evening/weekend programs available. *Entrance requirements:* For master's, GRE or GMAT. Additional exam requirements/recommendations for international students: Required—TOEFL (minimum score 550 paper-based; 213 computer-based). Electronic applications accepted. *Expenses:* Contact institution.

Campbell University, Graduate and Professional Programs, Lundy-Fetterman School of Business, Buies Creek, NC 27506. Offers MBA, MTIM. Part-time and evening/weekend programs available. *Degree requirements:* For master's, comprehensive exam, thesis or alternative. *Entrance requirements:* For master's, GMAT, minimum GPA of 2.7, 3 letters of reference. Additional exam requirements/recommendations for international students: Required—TOEFL (minimum score 550 paper-based; 213 computer-based). *Faculty research:* Agricultural economics, investments, leadership, marketing, law and economics.

Canisius College, Graduate Division, Richard J. Wehle School of Business, Department of Management and Marketing, Buffalo, NY 14208-1098. Offers business administration (MBA). *Accreditation:* AACSB. Part-time and evening/weekend programs available. *Faculty:* 32 full-time (5 women), 3 part-time/adjunct (1 woman). *Students:* 89 full-time (37 women), 176 part-time (78 women); includes 22 minority (11 African Americans, 9 Asian Americans or Pacific Islanders, 2 Hispanic Americans), 8 international. Average age 28. 164 applicants, 73% accepted, 86 enrolled. In 2009, 96 master's awarded. *Entrance requirements:* For master's, GMAT. *Application deadline:* For fall admission, 7/1 priority date for domestic students; for spring admission, 11/1 priority date for domestic students. Applications are processed on a rolling basis. Application fee: $25. *Expenses:* Contact institution. *Financial support:* Research assistantships with partial tuition reimbursements, career-related internships or fieldwork, scholarships/grants, and unspecified assistantships available. Support available to part-time students. Financial award application deadline: 6/15; financial award applicants required to submit FAFSA. *Faculty research:* Risk aversion, information security, employee relations, urban finance, student expectations. *Unit head:* Dr. George Palumbo, Director, MBA Program, 716-888-2667, Fax: 716-888-3132, E-mail: palumbo@canisius.edu. *Application contact:* Laura McEwen, Director of Graduate Programs, 716-888-2140, Fax: 716-888-8211, E-mail: gradubus@canisius.edu.

Cape Breton University, Shannon School of Business, Sydney, NS B1P 6L2, Canada. Offers community economic development (MBA). *Faculty:* 12 full-time (2 women). *Students:* 162 full-time (90 women). 106 applicants, 81% accepted, 74 enrolled. In 2009, 1 master's awarded. *Degree requirements:* For master's, research project, research essay. *Entrance requirements:* For master's, interview, letters of reference. Additional exam requirements/recommendations for international students: Required—TOEFL. *Application deadline:* For spring admission, 5/31 for domestic students. Applications are processed on a rolling basis. *Expenses:* Contact institution. *Financial support:* Scholarships/grants and tuition waivers (full and partial) available. Financial award application deadline: 5/31. *Faculty research:* Community entrepreneurship, CED theory, transportation, governance, business and environmental issues in Canada. Total annual research expenditures: $20,000. *Unit head:* George Karaphillis, Director of the MBA Program, 902-563-1467, Fax: 902-563-1453, E-mail: george_karaphillis@cbu.ca. *Application contact:* Anne Michelle Chiasson, Program Coordinator, 902-563-1664, Fax: 902-563-1366, E-mail: anne_chiasson@cbu.ca.

Capella University, School of Business and Technology, Minneapolis, MN 55402. Offers accounting (MBA), including system design and programming; business (Certificate), including human resource management (MS, PhD, Certificate), information technology management (MS, PhD, Certificate), leadership (MBA, MS, PhD, Certificate); finance (MBA); general business (MBA); health care management (MBA); information technology (MS, Certificate), including general information technology (MS), information security, network architecture and design (MS), professional projects management (Certificate), project management and leadership (MS), system design and development (MS),); information technology management (MBA); marketing (MBA); organization and management (MBA, MS, PhD), including general business (PhD), general organization and management (MBA, MS), human resource management (MS, PhD, Certificate), information technology management (MS, PhD, Certificate), leadership (MBA, MS, PhD, Certificate); project management (MBA). Part-time and evening/weekend programs available. Postbaccalaureate distance learning degree programs offered (minimal on-campus study). Terminal master's awarded for partial completion of doctoral program. *Degree requirements:* For master's, thesis optional, integrative project; for doctorate, comprehensive exam, thesis/dissertation. *Entrance requirements:* Additional exam requirements/recommendations for international students: Required—TOEFL (minimum score 550 paper-based; 213 computer-based), TWE (minimum score 4). Electronic applications accepted. *Faculty research:* Business policies: strategic, corporate, and financial management; interplay of technological, organizational and social change.

Capital University, Law School, Program in Business Law and Taxation, Columbus, OH 43209-2394. Offers business (LL M); business and taxation (LL M); taxation (LL M); JD/LL M. Part-time and evening/weekend programs available. *Degree requirements:* For master's, thesis or alternative. *Entrance requirements:* For master's, previous course work in accounting, business law, and taxation. Additional exam requirements/recommendations for international students: Required—TOEFL (minimum score 600 paper-based; 250 computer-based). Electronic applications accepted.

Capital University, School of Management, Columbus, OH 43209-2394. Offers MBA, MBA/JD, MBA/LL M, MBA/MSN, MBA/MT. *Accreditation:* ACBSP. Part-time and evening/weekend programs available. *Degree requirements:* For master's, research project. *Entrance requirements:* For master's, GMAT, 2 years of work experience. Additional exam requirements/recommendations for international students: Required—TOEFL. Electronic applications accepted. *Faculty research:* Taxation, public policy, health care, management of non-profits.

Capitol College, Graduate Programs, Laurel, MD 20708-9759. Offers business administration (MBA); computer science (MS); electrical engineering (MS); information and telecommunications systems management (MS); information architecture (MS); network security (MS). Part-time and evening/weekend programs available. Postbaccalaureate distance learning degree programs offered (no on-campus study). *Entrance requirements:* For master's, minimum GPA of 3.0. Electronic applications accepted.

Cardinal Stritch University, College of Business and Management, Milwaukee, WI 53217-3985. Offers MBA, MSM. Programs also offered in Madison, WI and Minneapolis-St. Paul, MN. *Accreditation:* ACBSP. Part-time and evening/weekend programs available. *Degree requirements:* For master's, thesis (for some programs), case study, faculty recommendation. *Entrance requirements:* For master's, 3 years management or related experience, minimum GPA of 2.5. Additional exam requirements/recommendations for international students: Required—TOEFL. *Expenses:* Contact institution.

Carleton University, Faculty of Graduate Studies, Faculty of Business, Eric Sprott School of Business, Ottawa, ON K1S 5B6, Canada. Offers business administration (MBA); management (PhD). *Degree requirements:* For master's, thesis optional; for doctorate, comprehensive exam, thesis/dissertation. *Entrance requirements:* For master's, GMAT, honors degree; for doctorate, GMAT. Additional exam requirements/recommendations for international students: Required—TOEFL. *Faculty research:* Business information systems, finance, international business, marketing, production and operations.

Carlos Albizu University, Miami Campus, Graduate Programs, Miami, FL 33172-2209. Offers clinical psychology (Psy D); entrepreneurship (MBA); exceptional student education (MS); industrial/organizational psychology (MS); marriage and family therapy (MS); mental health counseling (MS); nonprofit management (MBA); organizational management (MBA); psychology (MS); school counseling (MS); teaching English as a second language (MS). *Accreditation:* APA. Part-time and evening/weekend programs available. *Faculty:* 23 full-time (13 women), 41 part-time/adjunct (21 women). *Students:* 529 full-time (420 women), 171 part-time (139 women); includes 551 minority (55 African Americans, 1 American Indian/Alaska Native, 5 Asian Americans or Pacific Islanders, 490 Hispanic Americans). Average age 37. 278 applicants, 57% accepted, 142 enrolled. In 2009, 139 master's, 26 doctorates awarded. Terminal master's awarded for partial completion of doctoral program. *Degree requirements:* For master's, one foreign language, comprehensive exam, integrative project (MBA), research project (exceptional student education, teaching English as a second language); for doctorate, one foreign language, comprehensive exam, internship, project. *Entrance requirements:* For master's, 3 letters of recommendation, interview, minimum GPA of 3.0, resume; for doctorate, 3 letters of recommendation, minimum GPA of 3.0, resume, interview. *Application deadline:* For fall admission, 8/1 priority date for domestic students; for spring admission, 11/30 priority date for domestic students. Applications are processed on a rolling basis. Application fee: $50. Electronic applications accepted. *Expenses:* Tuition: Full-time $9090; part-time $505 per credit hour. Required fees: $298 per term. Tuition and fees vary according to course load, degree level and program. *Financial support:* In 2009–10, 127 students received support. Federal Work-Study, scholarships/grants, and tuition discounts available. Financial award application deadline: 6/1; financial award applicants required to submit FAFSA. *Faculty research:* Psychotherapy, forensic psychology, neuropsychology, marketing strategy, entrepreneurship, special education. *Unit head:* Dr. Carmen S. Roca, Chancellor, 305-593-1223 Ext. 120, Fax: 305-629-8052, E-mail: croca@albizu.edu. *Application contact:* Annalye Alonso, Secretary, 305-593-1223 Ext. 137, Fax: 305-593-1854, E-mail: aalonso@albizu.edu.

Carlow University, School of Management, Pittsburgh, PA 15213-3165. Offers business administration (MBA). Part-time and evening/weekend programs available. Postbaccalaureate distance learning degree programs offered (minimal on-campus study). *Degree requirements:* For master's, strategic planning II, capstone experience. *Entrance requirements:* For master's, interview, minimum GPA of 3.0, resume, 2 letters of recommendation. Additional exam requirements/recommendations for international students: Required—TOEFL (minimum score 550 paper-based; 213 computer-based). Electronic applications accepted. *Expenses:* Tuition: Full-time $11,250; part-time $625 per credit. Tuition and fees vary according to course load, degree level and program. *Faculty research:* Learning styles and distance learning, women and distance learning, women and organizational behavior.

Carnegie Mellon University, H. John Heinz III College, Institute for the Management of Creative Enterprises, Program in Entertainment Industry Management, Pittsburgh, PA 15213-3891. Offers MEIM. *Accreditation:* AACSB.

Carnegie Mellon University, H. John Heinz III College, School of Public Policy and Management, Program in Biotechnology and Management, Pittsburgh, PA 15213-3891. Offers MS. *Accreditation:* AACSB.

Carnegie Mellon University, Tepper School of Business, Pittsburgh, PA 15213-3891. Offers accounting (PhD); algorithms, combinatorics, and optimization (MS, PhD); business management and software engineering (MBMSE); civil engineering and industrial management (MS); computational finance (MSCF); economics (MS, PhD); electronic commerce (MS); environmental engineering and management (MEEM); finance (PhD); financial economics (PhD); industrial administration (MBA), including administration and public management; information systems (PhD); management of manufacturing and automation (PhD); marketing (PhD); mathematical finance (PhD); operations research (PhD); organizational behavior and theory (PhD); political economy (PhD); production and operations management (PhD); public policy and management (MS, MSED); software engineering and business management (MS); JD/MS; JD/MSIA; M Div/MS; MOM/MSIA; MSCF/MSIA. Part-time programs available. Terminal master's awarded for partial completion of doctoral program. *Degree requirements:* For doctorate, thesis/dissertation. *Entrance requirements:* For master's, GMAT. Additional exam requirements/recommendations for international students: Required—TOEFL. *Expenses:* Contact institution.

Case Western Reserve University, Weatherhead School of Management, Department of Operations, Management Program, Cleveland, OH 44106. Offers operations research (MSM); supply chain (MSM); MBA/MSM. *Accreditation:* AACSB. Part-time and evening/weekend programs available. *Students:* Average age 28. *Entrance requirements:* For master's, GMAT or GRE, 3 letters of recommendation, resume. Additional exam requirements/recommendations for international students: Required—TOEFL (minimum score 600 paper-based; 250 computer-based). Application fee: $100. *Financial support:* Career-related internships or fieldwork, institutionally sponsored loans, scholarships/grants, tuition waivers (partial), and unspecified assistantships available. Financial award application deadline: 3/1. *Faculty research:* Supply chain management, operations management, operations/finance interface optimization, scheduling. *Unit head:* Kamlesh Mathur, Chairman, 216-368-3857, E-mail: kamlesh.mathur@case.edu. *Application contact:* Olivia Seifert, Program Manager, 216-368-2031, Fax: 216-368-5548, E-mail: deborah.bibb@case.edu.

Case Western Reserve University, Weatherhead School of Management, Executive Doctor of Management Program, Cleveland, OH 44106. Offers management (EDM). Part-time and evening/weekend programs available. *Students:* Average age 46. *Degree requirements:* For doctorate, thesis/dissertation. *Entrance requirements:* For doctorate, GMAT. *Application deadline:* Applications are processed on a rolling basis. Application fee: $100. Electronic applications accepted. *Expenses:* Contact institution. *Financial support:* Fellowships with partial tuition reimbursements, institutionally sponsored loans and scholarships/grants available. Financial award application deadline: 5/1. *Faculty research:* Information technology and design, emotional intelligence and leadership, entrepreneurship, governing of NP organizations, social ethics. *Unit head:* Bo Carlsson, Program Director, 216-368-1943, E-mail: bo.carlsson@case.edu. *Application contact:* Sue Nartker, Assistant Director, 216-368-1943, Fax: 216-368-6261, E-mail: sue.nartker@case.edu.

Case Western Reserve University, Weatherhead School of Management, Executive MBA Program, Cleveland, OH 44106. Offers EMBA. *Accreditation:* AACSB. *Students:* Average age 39. *Entrance requirements:* For master's, GMAT (if candidate does not have an undergraduate degree from an accredited institution), work experience, interview. *Application deadline:* For fall admission, 7/1 priority date for domestic and international students. Applications are processed on a rolling basis. Application fee: $100. Electronic applications accepted. *Expenses:* Contact institution. *Financial support:* In 2009–10, 11 students received support. Institutionally sponsored loans available. Financial award applicants required to submit FAFSA. *Unit head:* Carleen Bobrowski, Director, 216-368-2554, Fax: 216-368-0200, E-mail: carleen@case.edu. *Application contact:* Carleen Bobrowski, Director, 216-368-2554, Fax: 216-368-0200, E-mail: carleen@case.edu.

Case Western Reserve University, Weatherhead School of Management, Full Time MBA Program, Cleveland, OH 44106. Offers MBA, MBA/JD, MBA/M Acc, MBA/MD, MBA/MIM, MBA/MNO, MBA/MSM, MBA/MSN, MBA/MSSA. *Accreditation:* AACSB. *Students:* Average

age 27. *Entrance requirements:* For master's, GMAT, letters of recommendation, interview, work experience. Additional exam requirements/recommendations for international students: Required—TOEFL (minimum score 600 paper-based; 250 computer-based). *Application deadline:* Applications are processed on a rolling basis. Application fee: $75. Electronic applications accepted. *Financial support:* Career-related internships or fieldwork, Federal Work-Study, institutionally sponsored loans, scholarships/grants, and tuition waivers (full and partial) available. Financial award applicants required to submit FAFSA. *Unit head:* Deborah Bibb, Program Director, 216-368-6702, Fax: 216-368-5548, E-mail: dlb10@case.edu. *Application contact:* Monica Eastway, Admissions Counselor, 216-368-2030, Fax: 216-368-5548, E-mail: monica.eastway@case.edu.

Case Western Reserve University, Weatherhead School of Management, Part-time MBA Program, Cleveland, OH 44106. Offers MBA, MBA/M Acc, MBA/MSM, MBA/MSSA. *Accreditation:* AACSB. Part-time and evening/weekend programs available. *Students:* Average age 29. *Entrance requirements:* For master's, GMAT, interview, work experience. Additional exam requirements/recommendations for international students: Recommended—TOEFL (minimum score 600 paper-based; 250 computer-based). *Application deadline:* Applications are processed on a rolling basis. Application fee: $100. Electronic applications accepted. *Financial support:* Institutionally sponsored loans available. *Unit head:* Kevin Malecek, Program Director, 216-368-3315, Fax: 216-368-5548, E-mail: kevin.malecek@case.edu. *Application contact:* Collin Hanson, Graduate Admissions Advisor, 216-368-6208, Fax: 216-368-5548, E-mail: collin.hanson@case.edu.

The Catholic University of America, Metropolitan School of Professional Studies, Washington, DC 20064. Offers human resource management (MA); management (MSM). Part-time and evening/weekend programs available. *Faculty:* 75 part-time/adjunct (41 women). *Students:* 21 full-time, 152 part-time, 26 international. Average age 34. 198 applicants, 69% accepted, 106 enrolled. In 2009, 8 degrees awarded. *Degree requirements:* For master's, minimum GPA of 3.0, capstone course. *Entrance requirements:* For master's, statement of purpose, official copies of academic transcripts, three letters of recommendation, resume. Additional exam requirements/recommendations for international students: Required—TOEFL (minimum score 237 computer-based; 93 iBT). *Application deadline:* For fall admission, 8/1 priority date for domestic students, 7/15 for international students; for spring admission, 12/1 priority date for domestic students, 10/15 for international students. *Expenses:* Tuition: Full-time $31,740; part-time $1245 per credit hour. Required fees: $50; $25 per semester hour. One-time fee: $425. *Unit head:* Dr. Sara Thompson, Dean, 202-319-5256, Fax: 202-319-6032, E-mail: thompsons@cua.edu. *Application contact:* Julie Schwing, Director of Graduate Admissions, 202-319-5057, Fax: 202-319-6533, E-mail: cua-admissions@cua.edu.

See Close-Up on page 427.

The Catholic University of America, School of Arts and Sciences, Department of Business and Economics, Washington, DC 20064. Offers international political economics (MA). Part-time programs available. *Faculty:* 7 full-time (2 women), 10 part-time/adjunct (5 women). *Students:* 1 part-time (0 women); minority (African American). Average age 30. In 2009, 26 master's awarded. *Degree requirements:* For master's, comprehensive exam. *Entrance requirements:* For master's, GRE General Test, 3 letters of recommendation. Additional exam requirements/recommendations for international students: Required—TOEFL (minimum score 580 paper-based; 237 computer-based). *Application deadline:* For fall admission, 8/1 priority date for domestic students, 7/15 for international students; for spring admission, 12/1 priority date for domestic students, 10/15 for international students. Applications are processed on a rolling basis. Application fee: $55. Electronic applications accepted. *Expenses:* Tuition: Full-time $31,740; part-time $1245 per credit hour. Required fees: $50; $25 per semester hour. One-time fee: $425. *Financial support:* Fellowships, research assistantships, teaching assistantships, Federal Work-Study, scholarships/grants, tuition waivers (full and partial), and unspecified assistantships available. Financial award application deadline: 2/1; financial award applicants required to submit FAFSA. *Faculty research:* Integrity of the marketing process, economics of energy and the environment, emerging markets, social change, international finance and economic development. Total annual research expenditures: $6,459. *Unit head:* Dr. Andrew V. Abela, Chair, 202-319-5235, Fax: 202-319-4426, E-mail: abela@cua.edu. *Application contact:* Julie Schwing, Director of Graduate Admissions, 202-319-5057, Fax: 202-319-6533, E-mail: cua-admissions@cua.edu.

Centenary College, Program in Business Administration, Hackettstown, NJ 07840-2100. Offers MBA. Part-time and evening/weekend programs available. Postbaccalaureate distance learning degree programs offered (minimal on-campus study). *Entrance requirements:* For master's, GMAT.

Centenary College of Louisiana, Graduate Programs, Frost School of Business, Shreveport, LA 71104. Offers MBA. Part-time and evening/weekend programs available. *Degree requirements:* For master's, thesis. *Entrance requirements:* For master's, GMAT, minimum 5 years of professional/managerial experience. *Faculty research:* Leadership, organizational change strategy, market behavior, executive compensation.

Central Connecticut State University, School of Graduate Studies, School of Business, New Britain, CT 06050-4010. Offers MS, Certificate. Part-time and evening/weekend programs available. *Faculty:* 11 full-time (2 women), 7 part-time/adjunct (3 women). *Students:* 3 full-time (all women), 2 part-time (both women). Average age 38. In 2009, 3 master's awarded. *Degree requirements:* For master's, comprehensive exam, thesis or alternative; for Certificate, qualifying exam. *Entrance requirements:* For master's, minimum undergraduate GPA of 2.7. Additional exam requirements/recommendations for international students: Required—TOEFL. *Application deadline:* For fall admission, 7/1 for domestic students, 5/1 for international students; for spring admission, 12/1 for domestic students, 11/1 for international students. Applications are processed on a rolling basis. Application fee: $50. Electronic applications accepted. *Expenses:* Tuition, area resident: Full-time $4662; part-time $440 per credit. Tuition, state resident: full-time $6994; part-time $440 per credit. Tuition, nonresident: full-time $12,988; part-time $440 per credit. Required fees: $3606. One-time fee: $62 part-time. *Financial support:* Application deadline: 3/1. *Faculty research:* Business/marketing education, organizational management, international business. *Unit head:* Dr. Siamack Shojai, Dean, 860-832-3205. *Application contact:* Dr. Siamack Shojai, Dean, 860-832-3205.

Central European University, CEU Business School, Budapest, Hungary. Offers finance (MBA); general management (MBA); information technology (M Sc); information technology management (MBA); management (EMBA); marketing (MBA); real estate management (MBA). Part-time and evening/weekend programs available. *Entrance requirements:* For master's, GMAT. Additional exam requirements/recommendations for international students: Required—TOEFL (minimum score 570 paper-based; 230 computer-based). Electronic applications accepted. *Faculty research:* Social and ethical business, marketing.

Central Michigan University, Central Michigan University Off-Campus Programs, Program in Business Administration, Mount Pleasant, MI 48859. Offers logistics management (MBA, Certificate); SAP (MBA); value-driven organization (MBA). Part-time and evening/weekend programs available. *Entrance requirements:* For master's, GMAT. *Financial support:* Scholarships/grants available. Support available to part-time students. *Unit head:* Dr. Monica Holmes, Associate Dean, 989-774-3337, E-mail: holme1mc@cmich.edu. *Application contact:* Off-Campus Programs Call Center, 877-268-4636.

Central Michigan University, College of Graduate Studies, College of Business Administration, Mount Pleasant, MI 48859. Offers accounting (MBA); business economics (MBA); business information systems (MS, Graduate Certificate), including business computing (Graduate Certificate), information systems (MS); economics (MA); finance and law (MBA), including finance; management (MBA), including consulting, human resources management, international business; management information systems (MBA); management information systems/SAP (MBA); marketing and hospitality services administration (MBA), including marketing. *Accreditation:* AACSB. Part-time and evening/weekend programs available. *Degree requirements:* For master's, thesis or alternative. *Entrance requirements:* For master's, GMAT (MBA). Electronic applications accepted. *Faculty research:* Economics, enterprise software, business information systems, management, marketing.

Central Michigan University, College of Graduate Studies, Interdisciplinary Administration Programs, Mount Pleasant, MI 48859. Offers acquisitions administration (MSA, Graduate Certificate); general administration (MSA, Graduate Certificate); health services administration (MSA, Graduate Certificate); human resource administration (Graduate Certificate); human resources administration (MSA); information resource management (MSA, Graduate Certificate); international administration (MSA, Graduate Certificate); leadership (MSA); organizational communication (MSA, Graduate Certificate); public administration (MSA, Graduate Certificate); recreation and park administration (MSA); sport administration (MSA). *Accreditation:* AACSB. Part-time and evening/weekend programs available. Postbaccalaureate distance learning degree programs offered (no on-campus study). *Degree requirements:* For master's, thesis or alternative. *Entrance requirements:* For master's, bachelor's degree with minimum GPA of 2.7. Electronic applications accepted. *Faculty research:* Interdisciplinary studies in acquisitions administration, health services administration, sport administration, recreation and park administration, and international administration.

Chadron State College, School of Professional and Graduate Studies, Department of Business and Economics, Chadron, NE 69337. Offers MBA. *Accreditation:* ACBSP. Part-time and evening/weekend programs available. Postbaccalaureate distance learning degree programs offered (minimal on-campus study). *Degree requirements:* For master's, thesis optional. *Entrance requirements:* For master's, GMAT, minimum GPA of 2.75 or 12 graduate hours at CSC with minimum GPA of 3.25. Additional exam requirements/recommendations for international students: Required—TOEFL. Electronic applications accepted.

Chaminade University of Honolulu, Graduate Services, Program in Business Administration, Honolulu, HI 96816-1578. Offers MBA. Part-time and evening/weekend programs available. *Entrance requirements:* For master's, minimum GPA of 3.0, 2 letters of recommendation. Additional exam requirements/recommendations for international students: Required—TOEFL (minimum score 650 paper-based). *Faculty research:* Total quality management, international finance, not for profit accounting, service learning in business contexts.

Chancellor University, College of Business, Cleveland, OH 44114-4624. Offers MBA, MMG. Part-time and evening/weekend programs available. Postbaccalaureate distance learning degree programs offered (no on-campus study). *Entrance requirements:* For master's, references, interview.

Chapman University, Graduate Studies, The George L. Argyros School of Business and Economics, Orange, CA 92866. Offers business administration (Exec MBA, MBA); JD/MBA. *Accreditation:* AACSB. Part-time and evening/weekend programs available. *Faculty:* 52 full-time (11 women), 33 part-time/adjunct (6 women). *Students:* 160 full-time (57 women), 118 part-time (36 women); includes 59 minority (4 African Americans, 29 Asian Americans or Pacific Islanders, 26 Hispanic Americans), 34 international. Average age 29. 227 applicants, 66% accepted, 96 enrolled. In 2009, 95 master's awarded. *Entrance requirements:* For master's, GMAT, minimum undergraduate GPA of 2.5. Additional exam requirements/recommendations for international students: Required—TOEFL (minimum score 550 paper-based; 213 computer-based; 80 iBT). *Application deadline:* For fall admission, 2/1 priority date for domestic students; for spring admission, 10/15 priority date for domestic students. Application fee: $55. Electronic applications accepted. *Expenses:* Contact institution. *Financial support:* Fellowships, Federal Work-Study and scholarships/grants available. Financial award application deadline: 6/30; financial award applicants required to submit FAFSA. *Unit head:* Dr. Arthur Kraft, Dean, 714-997-6684. *Application contact:* Debra Gonda, Associate Dean, 714-997-6894, E-mail: gonda@chapman.edu.

Charleston Southern University, Program in Business, Charleston, SC 29423-8087. Offers accounting (MBA); finance (MBA); health care administration (MBA); information systems (MBA); organizational development (MBA). Part-time and evening/weekend programs available. *Faculty:* 14 full-time (1 woman), 6 part-time/adjunct (1 woman). *Students:* 316 part-time (157 women); includes 67 minority (53 African Americans, 1 American Indian/Alaska Native, 7 Asian Americans or Pacific Islanders, 6 Hispanic Americans), 7 international. Average age 32. 173 applicants, 85% accepted, 97 enrolled. In 2009, 69 master's awarded. *Degree requirements:* For master's, thesis optional. *Entrance requirements:* For master's, GMAT. Additional exam requirements/recommendations for international students: Required—TOEFL (minimum score 550 paper-based; 213 computer-based; 79 iBT). *Application deadline:* Applications are processed on a rolling basis. Application fee: $30. *Expenses:* Tuition: Part-time $350 per credit hour. Required fees: $40 per semester. Tuition and fees vary according to program. *Financial support:* Research assistantships with full tuition reimbursements available. Financial award application deadline: 4/15; financial award applicants required to submit FAFSA. *Unit head:* Dr. Scott Pearson, Director of the MBA Program, 843-863-7038, Fax: 843-863-7922, E-mail: spearson@csuniv.edu. *Application contact:* Alison Harrison, Graduate Enrollment Counselor, 843-863-7534, Fax: 843-863-7070, E-mail: aharrison@cusniv.edu.

Chatham University, Program in Business Administration, Pittsburgh, PA 15232-2826. Offers business administration (MBA); healthcare professionals (MBA). Part-time and evening/weekend programs available. *Students:* 29 full-time (22 women), 46 part-time (37 women). Average age 32. 56 applicants, 64% accepted, 23 enrolled. In 2009, 21 master's awarded. *Entrance requirements:* For master's, minimum GPA of 3.0, 2 years experience in healthcare (healthcare MBA only), letters of recommendation. Additional exam requirements/recommendations for international students: Required—TOEFL (minimum score 600 paper-based; 250 computer-based; 100 iBT), IELTS (minimum score 6.5), TWE. *Application deadline:* For fall admission, 7/1 for domestic students, 6/1 for international students; for spring admission, 12/1 for domestic students, 11/1 for international students. Applications are processed on a rolling basis. Application fee: $45. Electronic applications accepted. *Financial support:* Applicants required to submit FAFSA. *Unit head:* Dr. Bruce Rosenthal, Director of Business and Entrepreneurship Program, 412-365-2433. *Application contact:* Michael May, Director of Graduate Admissions, 412-365-1141, Fax: 412-365-1609, E-mail: gradadmissions@chatham.edu.

Christian Brothers University, School of Business, Memphis, TN 38104-5581. Offers business (MBA); financial planning (Certificate); project management (Certificate). Part-time and evening/weekend programs available. *Faculty:* 4 full-time (1 woman), 4 part-time/adjunct (1 woman). *Students:* 5 full-time (all women), 169 part-time (69 women); includes 64 minority (51 African Americans, 9 Asian Americans or Pacific Islanders, 4 Hispanic Americans), 3 international. Average age 35. In 2009, 59 master's awarded. *Entrance requirements:* For master's, GMAT, GRE. Additional exam requirements/recommendations for international students: Required—TOEFL. *Application deadline:* Applications are processed on a rolling basis. Application fee: $50. *Financial support:* Institutionally sponsored loans available. Support available to part-time students. *Unit head:* Dr. Scott Lawyer, Dean, 901-321-3104, Fax: 901-321-3566, E-mail: mlawyer@cbu.edu. *Application contact:* Dr. Scott Lawyer, Director, Graduate Business Programs, 901-321-3104, Fax: 901-321-3566, E-mail: mlawyer@cbu.edu.

The Citadel, The Military College of South Carolina, Citadel Graduate College, School of Business Administration, Charleston, SC 29409. Offers MBA. *Accreditation:* AACSB. Part-time and evening/weekend programs available. *Faculty:* 16 full-time (3 women), 6 part-time/adjunct (1 woman). *Students:* 62 full-time (23 women), 204 part-time (77 women); includes 20 minority (15 African Americans, 1 American Indian/Alaska Native, 2 Asian Americans or Pacific Islanders, 2 Hispanic Americans), 4 international. Average age 28. In 2009, 92 master's awarded. *Entrance requirements:* For master's, GMAT (minimum score 410), minimum undergraduate GPA of 3.0, 2 letters of reference, resume detailing previous work experience. Additional exam requirements/recommendations for international students: Required—TOEFL (minimum score 550 paper-based; 213 computer-based; 79 iBT). *Application deadline:* For fall admission, 7/20 for domestic students; for spring admission, 12/1 for domestic students. Application fee: $30. Electronic applications accepted. *Expenses:* Tuition, state resident: part-time $400 per credit hour. Tuition, nonresident: part-time $657 per credit hour. Required fees: $40 per term.

Business Administration and Management—General

The Citadel, The Military College of South Carolina (continued)
Financial support: Fellowships, career-related internships or fieldwork, health care benefits, and unspecified assistantships available. Support available to part-time students. Financial award application deadline: 7/1; financial award applicants required to submit FAFSA. *Faculty research:* Business statistics and regression analysis, mentoring university students, tax reform proposals, risk management data, teaching leadership, inventory costing methods, capitalism, ethics in behavioral accounting, ethics of neuro-marketing, European and Japanese business ethics, profit motives, team building, process costing, FIFO vs. weight average. *Unit head:* Dr. Ronald F. Green, Dean, 843-953-5056, Fax: 843-953-6764, E-mail: ron.green@citadel.edu. *Application contact:* Lt. Col. Kathy Jones, Director, MBA Program, 843-953-5257, Fax: 843-953-6764, E-mail: kathy.jones@citadel.edu.

City University of Seattle, Graduate Division, School of Management, Bellevue, WA 98005. Offers accounting (Certificate); change leadership (MBA, Certificate); financial management (MBA, Certificate); general management (MBA); general management-Europe (MBA); global leadership (Certificate); global marketing (MBA); individualized study (MBA); information security (MS); information systems (MBA); leadership (MA); marketing (MBA, Certificate); project management (MBA, MS, Certificate); sustainable business (Certificate); technology management (MBA, MS, Certificate). Part-time and evening/weekend programs available. Postbaccalaureate distance learning degree programs offered (no on-campus study). *Entrance requirements:* Additional exam requirements/recommendations for international students: Required—TOEFL (minimum score 540 paper-based; 207 computer-based); Recommended—IELTS. Electronic applications accepted. *Expenses:* Tuition: Full-time $14,760; part-time $615 per credit. Tuition and fees vary according to program.

Claflin University, Graduate Programs, Orangeburg, SC 29115. Offers biotechnology (MS); business administration (MBA); educational studies (M Ed). Part-time programs available. *Entrance requirements:* For master's, GRE, GMAT, baccalaureate degree, 3 letters of recommendation. Additional exam requirements/recommendations for international students: Recommended—TOEFL (minimum score 550 paper-based; 213 computer-based).

Claremont Graduate University, Graduate Programs, Peter F. Drucker and Masatoshi Ito Graduate School of Management, Claremont, CA 91711-6160. Offers EMBA, MA, MBA, MS, PhD, Certificate, MBA/MA, MBA/PhD. Part-time programs available. *Faculty:* 13 full-time (3 women). *Students:* 180 full-time (82 women), 100 part-time (43 women); includes 94 minority (15 African Americans, 42 Asian Americans or Pacific Islanders, 37 Hispanic Americans), 65 international. Average age 36. In 2009, 81 master's, 2 doctorates, 53 other advanced degrees awarded. *Entrance requirements:* For doctorate, GMAT or GRE General Test. Additional exam requirements/recommendations for international students: Required—TOEFL (minimum score 550 paper-based; 213 computer-based; 80 iBT). *Application deadline:* For fall admission, 2/15 priority date for domestic students. Applications are processed on a rolling basis. Application fee: $60. Electronic applications accepted. *Expenses:* Contact institution. *Financial support:* Fellowships, research assistantships, teaching assistantships, Federal Work-Study, institutionally sponsored loans, and scholarships/grants available. Support available to part-time students. Financial award application deadline: 2/15; financial award applicants required to submit FAFSA. *Faculty research:* Strategy and leadership, brand management, cost management and control, organizational transformation, general management. *Unit head:* Ira A. Jackson, Henry Y. Hwang Dean and Professor of Management, 909-607-9209, Fax: 909-621-8543, E-mail: ira.jackson@cgu.edu. *Application contact:* Albert Ramos, Program Coordinator, 909-621-8067, Fax: 909-621-8551, E-mail: albert.ramos@cgu.edu.

See Close-Up on page 237.

Clarion University of Pennsylvania, Office of Research and Graduate Studies, College of Business Administration, Clarion, PA 16214. Offers MBA. *Accreditation:* AACSB. Part-time and evening/weekend programs available. *Entrance requirements:* For master's, GMAT, minimum QPA of 2.75. Additional exam requirements/recommendations for international students: Required—TOEFL (minimum score 550 paper-based; 213 computer-based). Electronic applications accepted.

Clark Atlanta University, School of Business Administration, Department of Business Administration, Atlanta, GA 30314. Offers MBA. *Accreditation:* AACSB. Part-time programs available. *Faculty:* 17 full-time (4 women), 2 part-time/adjunct (0 women). *Students:* 48 full-time (25 women), 23 part-time (11 women); includes 59 minority (58 African Americans, 1 Hispanic American), 3 international. Average age 27. 67 applicants, 75% accepted, 30 enrolled. In 2009, 37 master's awarded. *Degree requirements:* For master's, thesis (for some programs). *Entrance requirements:* For master's, GMAT. Additional exam requirements/recommendations for international students: Required—TOEFL (minimum score 500 paper-based; 173 computer-based). *Application deadline:* For fall admission, 4/1 for domestic and international students; for spring admission, 11/1 for domestic and international students. Applications are processed on a rolling basis. Application fee: $40 ($55 for international students). Electronic applications accepted. *Expenses:* Tuition: Full-time $12,240; part-time $680 per credit hour. Required fees: $710; $355 per semester. *Financial support:* Career-related internships or fieldwork, Federal Work-Study, scholarships/grants, and unspecified assistantships available. Support available to part-time students. Financial award application deadline: 4/30; financial award applicants required to submit FAFSA. *Unit head:* Dr. Kasim Alli, Chairperson, 404-880-8740, E-mail: kalli@cau.edu. *Application contact:* Michelle Clark-Davis, Graduate Program Admissions, 404-880-6605, E-mail: cauadmissions@cau.edu.

Clarke College, Program in Business Administration, Dubuque, IA 52001-3198. Offers MBA. Part-time and evening/weekend programs available. *Faculty:* 5 full-time (1 woman), 2 part-time/adjunct (1 woman). *Students:* 24 full-time (7 women), 30 part-time (20 women); includes 1 minority (Asian American or Pacific Islander). Average age 38. 28 applicants, 79% accepted, 19 enrolled. In 2009, 28 master's awarded. *Entrance requirements:* For master's, GMAT, GRE General Test or MAT, minimum GPA of 3.0 in last 60 hours, previous undergraduate course work in business. *Application deadline:* Applications are processed on a rolling basis. Application fee: $25. Electronic applications accepted. *Expenses:* Tuition: Full-time $10,836; part-time $602 per credit hour. Required fees: $30 per credit hour. *Financial support:* Available to part-time students. Application deadline: 6/1. *Unit head:* Wanda Ryan, Coordinator, 563-588-8143, Fax: 563-588-6789, E-mail: wanda.ryan@clarke.edu. *Application contact:* Carrie Kirk, Information Contact, 563-588-6635, Fax: 563-588-6789, E-mail: graduate@clarke.edu.

Clarkson University, Graduate School, School of Business, One-Year MBA Program, Potsdam, NY 13699. Offers MBA. *Accreditation:* AACSB. *Faculty:* 34 full-time (9 women), 3 part-time/adjunct (0 women). *Students:* 31 full-time (10 women), 10 part-time (5 women); includes 2 minority (1 African American, 1 American Indian/Alaska Native), 7 international. Average age 26. 127 applicants, 45% accepted, 30 enrolled. In 2009, 56 master's awarded. *Entrance requirements:* For master's, GMAT or GRE, resume, 3 letters of recommendation. Additional exam requirements/recommendations for international students: Required—TOEFL (minimum score 550 paper-based; 213 computer-based; 80 iBT), IELTS (minimum score 6.5), TSE required unless TOEFL iBT score is 100 or better. *Application deadline:* For fall admission, 1/30 priority date for domestic and international students; for spring admission, 9/1 priority date for domestic and international students. Applications are processed on a rolling basis. Application fee: $25 ($35 for international students). Electronic applications accepted. *Expenses:* Tuition: Part-time $1074 per credit hour. *Financial support:* In 2009–10, 33 students received support. Scholarships/grants available. *Faculty research:* Industrial organization and regulated industries, end-user computing, systems analysis and design, technological marketing, leadership development. *Unit head:* Dr. Boris Jukic, Director, 315-268-3884, Fax: 315-268-3810, E-mail: bjukic@clarkson.edu. *Application contact:* Karen Fuhr, Assistant to the Graduate Director, 315-268-6613, Fax: 315-268-3810, E-mail: fuhrk@clarkson.edu.

Clark University, Graduate School, Graduate School of Management, Business Administration Program, Worcester, MA 01610-1477. Offers accounting (MBA); finance (MBA); global business (MBA); health care management (MBA); management (MBA); management of information technology (MBA); marketing (MBA). *Accreditation:* AACSB. Part-time and evening/weekend programs available. *Students:* 148 full-time (67 women), 120 part-time (52 women); includes 27 minority (12 African Americans, 2 American Indian/Alaska Native, 9 Asian Americans or Pacific Islanders, 4 Hispanic Americans), 108 international. Average age 29. 340 applicants, 57% accepted, 63 enrolled. In 2009, 118 master's awarded. *Degree requirements:* For master's, thesis optional. *Application deadline:* For fall admission, 6/1 priority date for domestic students; for spring admission, 12/1 priority date for domestic students. Applications are processed on a rolling basis. Application fee: $50. Electronic applications accepted. *Expenses:* Tuition: Full-time $34,900; part-time $4362.50 per course. *Financial support:* In 2009–10, research assistantships with partial tuition reimbursements (averaging $4,800 per year), teaching assistantships with partial tuition reimbursements (averaging $4,800 per year) were awarded; fellowships, career-related internships or fieldwork, Federal Work-Study, institutionally sponsored loans, and tuition waivers (partial) also available. Support available to part-time students. Financial award application deadline: 5/31. *Faculty research:* Organizational development, accounting, marketing, finance, human resource management. *Application contact:* Lynn Davis, Enrollment and Marketing Director, 508-793-7406, Fax: 508-793-8822, E-mail: clarkmba@clarku.edu.

Clayton State University, School of Graduate Studies, Program in Business Administration, Morrow, GA 30260-0285. Offers MBA. *Accreditation:* AACSB. Part-time and evening/weekend programs available. *Students:* 44 full-time (7 women), 32 part-time (11 women); includes 34 African Americans, 3 Asian Americans or Pacific Islanders, 3 Hispanic Americans, 2 international. Average age 34. 61 applicants, 87% accepted, 45 enrolled. In 2009, 31 master's awarded. *Degree requirements:* For master's, thesis. *Entrance requirements:* For master's, GMAT, 3 letters of recommendation. Additional exam requirements/recommendations for international students: Required—TOEFL (minimum score 550 paper-based; 213 computer-based; 80 iBT). *Application deadline:* For fall admission, 7/15 for domestic students, 5/1 for international students; for spring admission, 4/15 for domestic students, 2/1 for international students. Application fee: $50. Electronic applications accepted. *Expenses:* Contact institution. *Financial support:* Application deadline: 7/1. *Unit head:* Dr. Michael H. Deis, Director, 678-466-4500, Fax: 678-466-4599, E-mail: michaeldeis@clayton.edu. *Application contact:* Andrea Johnson, Administrative Assistant, 678-466-4500, Fax: 648-466-4599, E-mail: andreajohnson@clayton.edu.

Cleary University, Online Program in Business Administration, Ann Arbor, MI 48105-2659. Offers accounting (MBA); financial planning (MBA); financial planning (Graduate Certificate); green business strategy (MBA); management (MBA); nonprofit management (MBA); organizational leadership (MBA). Part-time and evening/weekend programs available. Postbaccalaureate distance learning degree programs offered (no on-campus study). *Degree requirements:* For master's, thesis. *Entrance requirements:* For master's, bachelor's degree; minimum GPA of 2.5; professional resume indicating minimum 2 years management or related experience; undergraduate degree from an accredited college or university with at least 18 quarter hours (or 12 semester hours) of accounting study (for MBA in accounting). Additional exam requirements/recommendations for international students: Required—TOEFL (minimum score 550 paper-based; 213 computer-based; 79 iBT), Michigan English Language Assessment Battery (minimum score: 75). Electronic applications accepted.

Clemson University, Graduate School, College of Architecture, Arts, and Humanities, Department of Planning and Landscape Architecture and College of Business and Behavioral Science, Program in Real Estate Development, Clemson, SC 29634. Offers MRED. *Students:* 40 full-time (7 women). Average age 26. 54 applicants, 43% accepted, 20 enrolled. In 2009, 19 master's awarded. *Entrance requirements:* For master's, GRE or GMAT, 3 letters of recommendation. Additional exam requirements/recommendations for international students: Required—TOEFL (minimum score 600 paper-based). *Application deadline:* For fall admission, 2/1 priority date for domestic and international students. Applications are processed on a rolling basis. Application fee: $70 ($80 for international students). Electronic applications accepted. *Expenses:* Tuition, state resident: full-time $8684; part-time $528 per credit hour. Tuition, nonresident: full-time $15,330; part-time $1078 per credit hour. Required fees: $736; $37 per semester. Part-time tuition and fees vary according to course load and program. *Financial support:* In 2009–10, 2 students received support, including 2 fellowships with full and partial tuition reimbursements available (averaging $5,000 per year); research assistantships with partial tuition reimbursements available, teaching assistantships with partial tuition reimbursements available, career-related internships or fieldwork, institutionally sponsored loans, scholarships/grants, health care benefits, and unspecified assistantships also available. Support available to part-time students. *Unit head:* Dr. Elaine M. Worzala, Director, Center for Real Estate Development, 864-656-3657, Fax: 864-656-7519, E-mail: eworzal@clemson.edu. *Application contact:* Dr. Terry Farris, Program Director, 864-656-3903, Fax: 864-656-7519.

Clemson University, Graduate School, College of Business and Behavioral Science, Program in Business Administration, Clemson, SC 29634. Offers MBA. *Accreditation:* AACSB. Part-time and evening/weekend programs available. *Faculty:* 25 full-time (0 women). *Students:* 90 full-time (27 women), 139 part-time (43 women); includes 18 minority (8 African Americans, 8 Asian Americans or Pacific Islanders, 2 Hispanic Americans), 28 international. Average age 30. 168 applicants, 64% accepted, 71 enrolled. In 2009, 71 master's awarded. *Entrance requirements:* For master's, GMAT or GRE. Additional exam requirements/recommendations for international students: Required—TOEFL. *Application deadline:* For fall admission, 5/1 priority date for domestic students, 4/15 for international students; for spring admission, 9/15 for international students. Applications are processed on a rolling basis. Application fee: $70 ($80 for international students). Electronic applications accepted. *Expenses:* Tuition, state resident: full-time $8684; part-time $528 per credit hour. Tuition, nonresident: full-time $15,330; part-time $1078 per credit hour. Required fees: $736; $37 per semester. Part-time tuition and fees vary according to course load and program. *Financial support:* In 2009–10, 40 students received support, including 1 fellowship with full and partial tuition reimbursement available (averaging $1,250 per year), 31 research assistantships with partial tuition reimbursements available (averaging $8,979 per year), 1 teaching assistantship with partial tuition reimbursement available (averaging $15,000 per year); career-related internships or fieldwork, institutionally sponsored loans, scholarships/grants, health care benefits, and unspecified assistantships also available. Support available to part-time students. Financial award application deadline: 5/1; financial award applicants required to submit FAFSA. *Unit head:* Gail DePriest, Director, 864-656-3975, Fax: 864-656-0947. *Application contact:* Gail DePriest, Director, 864-656-3975, Fax: 864-656-0947.

Cleveland State University, College of Graduate Studies, Nance College of Business Administration, Doctor of Business Administration (DBA) Program, Cleveland, OH 44115. Offers business administration (DBA); finance (DBA); information systems (DBA); marketing (DBA); operations management (DBA). *Accreditation:* AACSB. Part-time and evening/weekend programs available. *Degree requirements:* For doctorate, comprehensive exam, thesis/dissertation, oral dissertation defense. *Entrance requirements:* For doctorate, GMAT, MBA or equivalent. Additional exam requirements/recommendations for international students: Required—TOEFL (minimum score 550 paper-based; 213 computer-based; 79 iBT). Electronic applications accepted. *Faculty research:* Supply chain management, international business, strategic management, risk analysis.

Cleveland State University, College of Graduate Studies, Nance College of Business Administration, MBA Programs, Cleveland, OH 44115. Offers business administration (AMBA, MBA); executive business administration (EMBA); health care administration (MBA); off-campus programs (MBA); JD/MBA; MSN/MBA. *Accreditation:* AACSB. Part-time and evening/weekend programs available. *Entrance requirements:* For master's, GMAT or GRE. Additional exam requirements/recommendations for international students: Required—TOEFL (minimum score 550 paper-based; 213 computer-based; 79 iBT).

Coastal Carolina University, Wall College of Business Administration, Conway, SC 29528-6054. Offers accounting (MBA); business (MBA). *Accreditation:* AACSB. Part-time and evening/weekend programs available. *Faculty:* 9 full-time (4 women). *Students:* 35 full-time (15 women), 18 part-time (7 women); includes 2 minority (both African Americans), 3 international. Average age 27. 48 applicants, 69% accepted, 22 enrolled. In 2009, 28 master's awarded. *Entrance*

requirements: For master's, GMAT, 2 letters of recommendation, resume, completion of prerequisites with minimum B average grade. Additional exam requirements/recommendations for international students: Required—TOEFL (minimum score 575 paper-based). *Application deadline:* For fall admission, 3/15 priority date for domestic and international students; for spring admission, 10/15 priority date for domestic and international students. Applications are processed on a rolling basis. Application fee: $45. Electronic applications accepted. *Expenses:* Contact institution. *Financial support:* Application deadline: 3/1. *Unit head:* John O. Lox, MBA Director, 843-349-2469, Fax: 843-349-2455, E-mail: jlox@coastal.edu. *Application contact:* Dr. Richard L. Johnson, Director of Graduate Studies, 843-349-2192, Fax: 843-349-6444, E-mail: rjohnson@coastal.edu.

College of Charleston, Graduate School, School of Business and Economics, Charleston, SC 29424-0001. Offers MS. *Accreditation:* AACSB. *Faculty:* 10 full-time (3 women). *Students:* 28 full-time (17 women), 7 part-time (5 women); includes 1 minority (African American), 3 international. Average age 25. 53 applicants, 51% accepted, 17 enrolled. In 2009, 31 master's awarded. *Entrance requirements:* For master's, GMAT, minimum GPA of 3.0 in last 60 hours of undergraduate course work, 24 hours of course work in accounting. Additional exam requirements/recommendations for international students: Required—TOEFL. *Application deadline:* Applications are processed on a rolling basis. Application fee: $45. Electronic applications accepted. *Financial support:* In 2009–10, 2 research assistantships were awarded; scholarships/grants and unspecified assistantships also available. Support available to part-time students. Financial award applicants required to submit FAFSA. *Unit head:* Dr. Alan Shao, Dean, 843-953-6651, Fax: 843-953-5697, E-mail: shaoa@cofc.edu. *Application contact:* Susan Hallatt, Director of Graduate Admissions, 843-953-5614, Fax: 843-953-1434, E-mail: hallatts@cofc.edu.

College of Notre Dame of Maryland, Graduate Studies, Program in Management, Baltimore, MD 21210-2476. Offers MA. Part-time and evening/weekend programs available. *Degree requirements:* For master's, thesis optional. *Entrance requirements:* For master's, minimum GPA of 3.0. Additional exam requirements/recommendations for international students: Required—TOEFL (minimum score 500 paper-based; 173 computer-based; 61 iBT). Electronic applications accepted.

College of Saint Elizabeth, Department of Business Administration and Economics, Morristown, NJ 07960-6989. Offers management (MS). Part-time and evening/weekend programs available. *Faculty:* 3 full-time (1 woman), 9 part-time/adjunct (7 women). *Students:* 28 full-time (19 women), 53 part-time (41 women); includes 31 minority (18 African Americans, 5 Asian Americans or Pacific Islanders, 8 Hispanic Americans), 4 international. Average age 34. 21 applicants, 76% accepted, 14 enrolled. In 2009, 64 master's awarded. *Degree requirements:* For master's, capstone seminar. *Entrance requirements:* For master's, minimum GPA of 3.0, course work in principles of management. *Application deadline:* Applications are processed on a rolling basis. Application fee: $35. Electronic applications accepted. *Expenses:* Tuition: Part-time $797 per credit hour. Required fees: $65 per credit hour. *Financial support:* Career-related internships or fieldwork, tuition waivers (partial), and unspecified assistantships available. Support available to part-time students. Financial award application deadline: 3/15; financial award applicants required to submit FAFSA. *Faculty research:* American business history, business developments in Eastern Europe, MIS/programming languages, marketing strategy, strategic planning. *Unit head:* Dr. Kathleen Reddick, Director of the Graduate Program in Management, 973-290-4041, Fax: 973-290-4177, E-mail: kreddick@cse.edu. *Application contact:* Donna Tatarka, Dean of Admission, 973-290-4705, Fax: 973-290-4710, E-mail: dtatarka@cse.edu.

College of St. Joseph, Graduate Programs, Division of Business, Program in Business Administration, Rutland, VT 05701-3899. Offers MBA. Part-time and evening/weekend programs available. *Entrance requirements:* For master's, 2 letters of reference, interview. Electronic applications accepted. *Expenses:* Contact institution.

The College of Saint Rose, Graduate Studies, School of Business, Department of Business Administration, Albany, NY 12203-1419. Offers MBA, JD/MBA. *Accreditation:* ACBSP. Part-time and evening/weekend programs available. *Entrance requirements:* For master's, GMAT, graduate degree, or minimum undergraduate GPA of 3.0. Additional exam requirements/recommendations for international students: Required—TOEFL (minimum score 550 paper-based; 213 computer-based). Electronic applications accepted.

The College of St. Scholastica, Graduate Studies, Department of Management, Duluth, MN 55811-4199. Offers MA, Certificate. Part-time and evening/weekend programs available. Postbaccalaureate distance learning degree programs offered (minimal on-campus study). *Degree requirements:* For master's, thesis. *Entrance requirements:* For master's, minimum GPA of 2.8. Additional exam requirements/recommendations for international students: Required—TOEFL (minimum score 550 paper-based; 213 computer-based; 79 iBT). Electronic applications accepted. *Expenses:* Contact institution. *Faculty research:* Violence in higher education and workplace, screening and selection procedures in law enforcement, Internet use in criminal justice, stress management in law enforcement.

College of Santa Fe, Department of Business Administration, Santa Fe, NM 87505-7634. Offers finance (MBA); human resources (MBA). Program also available at Albuquerque campus. Part-time and evening/weekend programs available. *Entrance requirements:* For master's, minimum GPA of 3.0 in last 60 hours (preferred).

College of Staten Island of the City University of New York, Graduate Programs, Program in Business Management, Staten Island, NY 10314-6600. Offers MS. Evening/weekend programs available. *Faculty:* 5 full-time (3 women). *Students:* 2 full-time (0 women), 27 part-time (13 women); includes 25 minority (2 African Americans, 21 American Indian/Alaska Native, 2 Asian Americans or Pacific Islanders), 4 international. Average age 30. 37 applicants, 54% accepted, 11 enrolled. In 2009, 19 master's awarded. *Entrance requirements:* For master's, GMAT, minimum undergraduate GPA of 3.0. Additional exam requirements/recommendations for international students: Required—TOEFL (minimum score 600 paper-based; 250 computer-based; 100 iBT). *Application deadline:* Applications are processed on a rolling basis. Application fee: $125. Electronic applications accepted. *Expenses:* Tuition, state resident: full-time $7360; part-time $310 per credit. Tuition, nonresident: part-time $575 per credit. Required fees: $378; $113 per semester. *Financial support:* Career-related internships or fieldwork, Federal Work-Study, and scholarships/grants available. Support available to part-time students. Financial award applicants required to submit FAFSA. Total annual research expenditures: $1,000. *Unit head:* Dr. Gene Garaventa, Coordinator, 718-982-2963, E-mail: businessmaster@mail.csi.cuny.edu. *Application contact:* Sasha Spence, Assistant Director of Graduate Recruitment and Admissions, 718-982-2699, Fax: 718-982-2500, E-mail: sasha.spence@csi.cuny.edu.

The College of William and Mary, Mason School of Business, Williamsburg, VA 23185. Offers accounting (M Acc); business administration (EMBA, MBA); JD/MBA; MBA/MPP. *Accreditation:* AACSB. Part-time and evening/weekend programs available. *Faculty:* 52 full-time (13 women), 10 part-time/adjunct (0 women). *Students:* 308 full-time (127 women), 176 part-time (44 women); includes 49 minority (19 African Americans, 17 Asian Americans or Pacific Islanders, 13 Hispanic Americans), 99 international. Average age 29. 587 applicants, 62% accepted, 215 enrolled. In 2009, 220 master's awarded. *Degree requirements:* For master's, three domestic residencies and international trip (EMBA). *Entrance requirements:* For master's, GMAT. Additional exam requirements/recommendations for international students: Required—TOEFL (minimum score 600 paper-based; 250 computer-based; 100 iBT), IELTS (minimum score 6.5). *Application deadline:* For fall admission, 1/11 priority date for domestic students, 11/16 priority date for international students; for winter admission, 3/1 priority date for domestic students, 1/11 priority date for international students; for spring admission, 4/19 for domestic students, 3/1 for international students. Application fee: $100. *Expenses:* Contact institution. *Financial support:* In 2009–10, 179 students received support, including fellowships (averaging $7,250 per year), 30 research assistantships with partial tuition reimbursements available (averaging $9,715 per year); career-related internships or fieldwork, scholarships/grants, and unspecified assistantships also available. Financial award application deadline:

3/1; financial award applicants required to submit FAFSA. *Faculty research:* Saving and asset allocation decisions in retirement accounts, supply chain management, virtual and networked organizations, healthcare informatics, sustainable business ops. Total annual research expenditures: $106,167. *Unit head:* Dr. Lawrence Pulley, Dean, 757-221-2891, Fax: 757-221-2937, E-mail: larry.pulley@mason.wm.edu. *Application contact:* Amanda K. Barth, Interim Director, Full-time MBA Admissions, 757-221-2944, Fax: 757-221-2958, E-mail: amanda.barth@mason.wm.edu.

Colorado Christian University, Program in Business Administration, Lakewood, CO 80226. Offers MBA. Part-time and evening/weekend programs available. Postbaccalaureate distance learning degree programs offered (minimal on-campus study). *Degree requirements:* For master's, thesis optional. *Entrance requirements:* For master's, GMAT, 2 letters of recommendation, resume. Additional exam requirements/recommendations for international students: Required—TOEFL. Electronic applications accepted. *Expenses:* Contact institution.

Colorado State University, Graduate School, College of Business, MBA Program, Fort Collins, CO 80523-1201. Offers MBA, MBA/DVM. *Accreditation:* AACSB. Part-time and evening/weekend programs available. *Faculty:* 16 full-time (5 women). *Students:* 254 full-time (78 women), 734 part-time (188 women); includes 160 minority (34 African Americans, 8 American Indian/Alaska Native, 70 Asian Americans or Pacific Islanders, 48 Hispanic Americans), 60 international. Average age 36. 366 applicants, 97% accepted, 294 enrolled. In 2009, 232 master's awarded. *Entrance requirements:* For master's, GMAT, minimum undergraduate GPA of 3.0, 4 years post-undergraduate professional work experience. Additional exam requirements/recommendations for international students: Required—TOEFL (minimum score 565 paper-based; 227 computer-based; 86 iBT), IELTS (minimum score 6.5). *Application deadline:* For fall admission, 7/15 priority date for domestic students, 7/1 priority date for international students; for spring admission, 12/8 priority date for domestic students, 12/1 priority date for international students. Applications are processed on a rolling basis. Application fee: $50. Electronic applications accepted. *Expenses:* Contact institution. *Financial support:* Fellowships, teaching assistantships with partial tuition reimbursements, career-related internships or fieldwork and unspecified assistantships available. Support available to part-time students. Financial award application deadline: 6/1; financial award applicants required to submit FAFSA. *Faculty research:* E-commerce, entrepreneurship, global leadership, corporate citizenship, marketing management. Total annual research expenditures: $10,294. *Application contact:* Rachel Stoll, Admissions Coordinator, 970-491-3704, Fax: 970-491-3481, E-mail: rachel.stoll@colostate.edu.

Colorado State University–Pueblo, Malik and Seeme Hasan School of Business, Pueblo, CO 81001-4901. Offers MBA. *Accreditation:* AACSB. Part-time and evening/weekend programs available. *Degree requirements:* For master's, thesis optional. *Entrance requirements:* For master's, GMAT, minimum GPA of 3.0. Additional exam requirements/recommendations for international students: Required—TOEFL (minimum score 550 paper-based; 217 computer-based). *Faculty research:* Total quality management, leadership, small business studies, case research and writing.

Colorado Technical University Colorado Springs, Graduate Studies, Program in Management, Colorado Springs, CO 80907-3896. Offers accounting (MBA, MSA); business administration (MBA); finance (MBA); human resources management (MBA); logistics/supply chain management (MBA); management (DM); marketing (MBA); mediation and dispute resolution (MBA); operations management (MBA); project management (MBA); technology management (MBA). Part-time and evening/weekend programs available. Postbaccalaureate distance learning degree programs offered. *Degree requirements:* For master's, thesis or alternative; for doctorate, thesis/dissertation. *Entrance requirements:* For doctorate, minimum graduate GPA of 3.0, 5 years of related work experience. *Faculty research:* Sexual harassment, performance evaluation, critical thinking.

Colorado Technical University Denver, Programs in Business Administration and Management, Greenwood Village, CO 80111. Offers accounting (MBA); business administration (MBA); business administration and management (EMBA); finance (MBA); human resource management (MBA); marketing (MBA); mediation and dispute resolution (MBA); operations management (MBA); project management (MBA); technology management (MBA). Part-time and evening/weekend programs available. *Degree requirements:* For master's, thesis or alternative. *Entrance requirements:* For master's, minimum undergraduate GPA of 3.0, resume.

Colorado Technical University Sioux Falls, Programs in Business Administration and Management, Sioux Falls, SD 57108. Offers business administration (MBA); business management (MSM); health science management (MSM); human resources management (MSM); information technology (MSM); organizational leadership (MSM); project management (MBA); technology management (MBA). Evening/weekend programs available. *Degree requirements:* For master's, thesis optional. *Entrance requirements:* For master's, minimum 2 years work experience, resume.

Columbia College, Master of Business Administration Program, Columbia, MO 65216-0002. Offers MBA. Evening/weekend programs available. Postbaccalaureate distance learning degree programs offered (no on-campus study). *Faculty:* 4 full-time (2 women), 48 part-time/adjunct (18 women). *Students:* 503 full-time (297 women), 37 part-time (27 women); includes 115 minority (73 African Americans, 9 American Indian/Alaska Native, 11 Asian Americans or Pacific Islanders, 22 Hispanic Americans), 16 international. Average age 36. 184 applicants, 66% accepted, 67 enrolled. In 2009, 145 master's awarded. *Entrance requirements:* For master's, 3 letters of recommendation, minimum cumulative undergraduate GPA of 3.0, resume. Additional exam requirements/recommendations for international students: Required—TOEFL (minimum score 550 paper-based; 213 computer-based; 79 iBT). *Application deadline:* For fall admission, 8/9 priority date for domestic and international students; for spring admission, 12/27 priority date for domestic and international students. Applications are processed on a rolling basis. Application fee: $55. Electronic applications accepted. *Expenses:* Tuition: Full-time $3588; part-time $299 per credit hour. Tuition and fees vary according to course load. *Financial support:* In 2009–10, 22 students received support. Federal Work-Study and scholarships/grants available. Financial award applicants required to submit FAFSA. *Unit head:* Dr. Diane Suhler, Graduate Program Coordinator, 573-875-7640, Fax: 573-876-4493, E-mail: drsuhler@ccis.edu. *Application contact:* Samantha White, Director of Admissions, 573-875-7352, Fax: 573-875-7506, E-mail: sjwhite@ccis.edu.

Columbia Southern University, DBA Program, Orange Beach, AL 36561. Offers DBA. Part-time and evening/weekend programs available. Postbaccalaureate distance learning degree programs offered (minimal on-campus study). *Entrance requirements:* For doctorate, 2 years professional experience, relevant academic experience. Electronic applications accepted.

Columbia Southern University, MBA Program, Orange Beach, AL 36561. Offers electronic business and technology (MBA); finance (MBA); general (MBA); healthcare management (MBA); hospitality and tourism (MBA); human resources management (MBA); international management (MBA); marketing (MBA); project management (MBA); public administration (MBA); sport management (MBA). Part-time and evening/weekend programs available. Postbaccalaureate distance learning degree programs offered (no on-campus study). *Entrance requirements:* For master's, bachelor's degree from accredited/approved institution. Additional exam requirements/recommendations for international students: Required—TOEFL. Electronic applications accepted.

Columbia University, Graduate School of Business, Berkeley-Columbia Executive MBA Program, New York, NY 10027. Offers EMBA. Part-time programs available. *Students:* 135 part-time (29 women); includes 55 minority (2 African Americans, 1 American Indian/Alaska Native, 45 Asian Americans or Pacific Islanders, 7 Hispanic Americans), 5 international. Average age 37. In 2009, 60 master's awarded. *Entrance requirements:* For master's, GMAT, 2 letters of reference, interview, minimum 5 years of work experience, transcripts, resume, employee support, personal essays. Additional exam requirements/recommendations for international students: Required—TOEFL (minimum score 570 paper-based; 230 computer-based; 68 iBT). *Application deadline:* For winter admission, 1/4 priority date for domestic and inter-

Business Administration and Management—General

Columbia University (continued)
national students; for spring admission, 2/1 priority date for domestic and international students. Application fee: $200. Electronic applications accepted. *Expenses:* Contact institution. *Financial support:* Available to part-time students. Applicants required to submit FAFSA. *Unit head:* Ethan R. Hanabury, Senior Associate Dean, 212-854-6019, Fax: 212-932-0545, E-mail: embainfo@columbia.edu. *Application contact:* Marjorie DeGraca, Berkeley-Columbia Executive MBA Admissions Office, 510-643-1046, Fax: 510-642-5902, E-mail: emba@haas.berkeley.edu.

Columbia University, Graduate School of Business, Doctoral Program in Business, New York, NY 10027. Offers business (PhD), including accounting, decision, risk, and operations, finance and economics, management, marketing. *Accreditation:* AACSB. *Faculty:* 149 full-time (23 women), 134 part-time/adjunct (16 women). *Students:* 91 full-time (37 women); includes 10 minority (8 Asian Americans or Pacific Islanders, 2 Hispanic Americans), 64 international. Average age 27. 758 applicants, 6% accepted, 20 enrolled. In 2009, 15 doctorates awarded. *Degree requirements:* For doctorate, comprehensive exam, thesis/dissertation, major field exam, research paper, thesis proposal. *Entrance requirements:* For doctorate, GMAT or GRE (finance), 2 letters of reference, resume. Additional exam requirements/recommendations for international students: Required—TOEFL. *Application deadline:* For fall admission, 1/1 for domestic and international students. Application fee: $75. Electronic applications accepted. *Expenses:* Contact institution. *Financial support:* In 2009–10, 91 students received support, including fellowships with full tuition reimbursements available (averaging $22,000 per year), research assistantships (averaging $4,000 per year); teaching assistantships, career-related internships or fieldwork, health care benefits, and tuition waivers (full) also available. *Faculty research:* Human decision making and behavioral research; real estate market and mortgage defaults; financial crisis and corporate governance; international business; security analysis and accounting. *Unit head:* Elizabeth Elam Chang, Administrative Director, 212-854-2836, Fax: 212-932-2359, E-mail: phdinfo@gsb.columbia.edu. *Application contact:* Elizabeth Elam Chang, Administrative Director, 212-854-2836, Fax: 212-932-2359, E-mail: phdinfo@gsb.columbia.edu.

Columbia University, Graduate School of Business, Executive MBA Global Program, New York, NY 10027. Offers EMBA. Program offered jointly with London Business School. *Students:* 169 full-time (43 women); includes 12 minority (all Asian Americans or Pacific Islanders), 110 international. Average age 32. In 2009, 67 master's awarded. *Entrance requirements:* For master's, GMAT, 2 letters of reference, interview, minimum 5 years of work experience, curriculum vitae or resume, employer support. Additional exam requirements/recommendations for international students: Recommended—IELTS. *Application deadline:* For spring admission, 3/8 for domestic and international students. Applications are processed on a rolling basis. Application fee: $200. Electronic applications accepted. *Expenses:* Contact institution. *Unit head:* Kelley Martin Blanco, Assistant Dean, 212-854-2211, Fax: 212-854-8998, E-mail: embainfo@columbia.edu. *Application contact:* Mary J. Miller, Assistant Dean of Admissions, 212-854-1961, Fax: 212-662-6754, E-mail: apply@gsb.columbia.edu.

Columbia University, Graduate School of Business, Executive MBA Program, New York, NY 10027. Offers EMBA. *Faculty:* 149 full-time (23 women), 134 part-time/adjunct (16 women). *Students:* 368 full-time (99 women); includes 83 minority (6 African Americans, 69 Asian Americans or Pacific Islanders, 8 Hispanic Americans), 97 international. Average age 32. In 2009, 225 master's awarded. *Entrance requirements:* For master's, GMAT, minimum 5 years of work experience, 2 letters of reference, interview, company sponsorship. *Application deadline:* For fall admission, 6/1 for domestic and international students; for spring admission, 11/3 for domestic and international students. Applications are processed on a rolling basis. Application fee: $250. Electronic applications accepted. *Expenses:* Contact institution. *Faculty research:* Human decision making and behavioral research; real estate market and mortgage defaults; financial crisis and corporate governance; international business; and security analysis and accounting. *Unit head:* Kelley Martin Blanco, Assistant Dean, 212-854-2211, Fax: 212-854-8998, E-mail: embainfo@columbia.edu. *Application contact:* Mary J. Miller, Assistant Dean of Admissions, 212-854-1961, Fax: 212-662-6754, E-mail: apply@gsb.columbia.edu.

Columbia University, Graduate School of Business, MBA Program, New York, NY 10027. Offers accounting (MBA); decision, risk, and operations (MBA); entrepreneurship (MBA); finance and economics (MBA); healthcare and pharmaceutical management (MBA); human resource management (MBA); international business (MBA); leadership and ethics (MBA); management (MBA); marketing (MBA); media (MBA); private equity (MBA); real estate (MBA); social enterprise (MBA); value investing (MBA); DDS/MBA; JD/MBA; MBA/MIA; MBA/MPH; MBA/MS; MD/MBA. *Faculty:* 149 full-time (23 women), 134 part-time/adjunct (16 women). *Students:* 1,293 full-time (435 women); includes 235 minority (65 African Americans, 4 American Indian/Alaska Native, 135 Asian Americans or Pacific Islanders, 31 Hispanic Americans), 417 international. Average age 28. 6,885 applicants, 15% accepted, 737 enrolled. In 2009, 696 master's awarded. *Entrance requirements:* For master's, GMAT, 2 letters of recommendation. Additional exam requirements/recommendations for international students: Required—TOEFL. *Application deadline:* For fall admission, 4/14 for domestic students, 3/3 for international students; for spring admission, 10/7 for domestic and international students. Applications are processed on a rolling basis. Application fee: $250. Electronic applications accepted. *Expenses:* Contact institution. *Financial support:* In 2009–10, 358 students received support, including 101 fellowships (averaging $23,250 per year); research assistantships, teaching assistantships, career-related internships or fieldwork, institutionally sponsored loans, and scholarships/grants also available. Financial award application deadline: 3/1; financial award applicants required to submit CSS PROFILE or FAFSA. *Faculty research:* Human decision making and behavioral research; real estate market and mortgage defaults; financial crisis and corporate governance; international business; security analysis and accounting. *Unit head:* Prof. Amir Ziv, Vice Dean of Students and the MBA Program, 212-854-3485, Fax: 212-932-0545, E-mail: az50@columbia.edu. *Application contact:* Mary J. Miller, Assistant Dean of Admissions, 212-854-1961, Fax: 212-662-6754, E-mail: apply@gsb.columbia.edu.

Columbus State University, Graduate Studies, D. Abbott Turner College of Business and Computer Science, Columbus, GA 31907-5645. Offers applied computer science (MS); business administration (MBA). *Accreditation:* AACSB. *Faculty:* 12 full-time (2 women). *Students:* 43 full-time (11 women), 122 part-time (47 women); includes 39 minority (25 African Americans, 2 American Indian/Alaska Native, 8 Asian Americans or Pacific Islanders, 4 Hispanic Americans), 10 international. Average age 34. 118 applicants, 55% accepted, 48 enrolled. In 2009, 44 master's awarded. *Entrance requirements:* For master's, GMAT, GRE. Additional exam requirements/recommendations for international students: Required—TOEFL (minimum score 550 paper-based; 213 computer-based; 79 iBT). *Application deadline:* For fall admission, 5/1 priority date for domestic students, 5/1 for international students; for spring admission, 11/1 for domestic and international students. Applications are processed on a rolling basis. Application fee: $30. Electronic applications accepted. *Financial support:* In 2009–10, 55 students received support, including 11 research assistantships (averaging $3,000 per year). Financial award application deadline: 5/1. *Unit head:* Dr. Linda U. Hadley, Dean, 706-568-2044, Fax: 706-568-2184, E-mail: hadley_linda@colstate.edu. *Application contact:* Katie Thornton, Graduate Admissions Specialist, 706-568-2035, Fax: 706-568-2462, E-mail: thornton_katie@colstate.edu.

Concordia University, School of Business and Professional Studies, Irvine, CA 92612-3299. Offers business administration: business practice (MBA); international studies (MA). Part-time and evening/weekend programs available. Postbaccalaureate distance learning degree programs offered. *Faculty:* 4 full-time (0 women), 18 part-time/adjunct (3 women). *Students:* 84 full-time (32 women), 50 part-time (30 women); includes 38 minority (5 African Americans, 1 American Indian/Alaska Native, 21 Asian Americans or Pacific Islanders, 11 Hispanic Americans), 13 international. Average age 30. 36 applicants, 81% accepted, 22 enrolled. In 2009, 67 master's awarded. *Degree requirements:* For master's, capstone project or thesis. *Entrance requirements:* For master's, resume, 2 references, interview (MBA). Additional exam requirements/recommendations for international students: Required—TOEFL. *Application deadline:* For fall admission, 8/1 for domestic students, 6/1 for international students; for spring admission, 1/1 for domestic students, 11/1 for international students. Application fee: $50 ($125 for international students). Electronic applications accepted. *Expenses:* Contact institution. *Financial support:* In 2009–10, 95 students received support. Tuition waivers (full and partial) and unspecified assistantships available. Financial award applicants required to submit FAFSA. *Unit head:* Dr. Timothy Peters, Dean, 949-854-8002 Ext. 1333, E-mail: tim.peters@cui.edu. *Application contact:* Aaron Stewart, Assistant Director of Graduate and Adult Admissions, 949-854-8002 Ext. 1343, Fax: 949-854-6894, E-mail: aaron.stewart@cui.edu.

Concordia University, School of Graduate Studies, John Molson School of Business, Montréal, QC H3G 1M8, Canada. Offers administration (M Sc, Diploma); aviation management (Certificate, Diploma); business administration (MBA, UA Undergraduate Associate, PhD), including international aviation (UA Undergraduate Associate); chartered accountancy (Diploma); community organizational development (Certificate); event management and fundraising (Certificate); executive business administration (EMBA); investment management (Diploma); investment management option (MBA); management accounting (Certificate); management of healthcare organizations (Certificate); sport administration (Diploma). *Accreditation:* AACSB. Part-time and evening/weekend programs available. *Degree requirements:* For master's, one foreign language, thesis (for some programs), research project; for doctorate, one foreign language, thesis/dissertation; for other advanced degree, one foreign language. *Entrance requirements:* For master's and doctorate, GMAT. Additional exam requirements/recommendations for international students: Required—TOEFL. *Expenses:* Contact institution. *Faculty research:* General business, capital markets, international business.

Concordia University, School of Management, Portland, OR 97211-6099. Offers MBA. Evening/weekend programs available. *Degree requirements:* For master's, thesis optional. *Entrance requirements:* For master's, GMAT or professional portfolio, minimum GPA of 3.0, 2 letters of recommendation, 5 years of work experience, resume. Additional exam requirements/recommendations for international students: Required—TOEFL (minimum score 525 paper-based; 195 computer-based). *Faculty research:* Leadership characteristics in internships, marketing of MBA programs, entrepreneurship.

Concordia University Chicago, College of Graduate and Innovative Programs, Program in Business Administration, River Forest, IL 60305-1499. Offers MBA.

Concordia University, St. Paul, College of Business and Organizational Leadership, St. Paul, MN 55104-5494. Offers business and organizational leadership (MBA); criminal justice leadership (MA); health care management (MBA); human resources management (MA); leadership and management (MA). *Accreditation:* ACBSP. Evening/weekend programs available. Postbaccalaureate distance learning degree programs offered (minimal on-campus study). *Faculty:* 10 full-time (5 women), 19 part-time/adjunct (4 women). *Students:* 295 full-time (169 women), 3 part-time (2 women); includes 30 minority (19 African Americans, 2 American Indian/Alaska Native, 5 Asian Americans or Pacific Islanders, 4 Hispanic Americans), 3 international. Average age 32. In 2009, 114 master's awarded. *Application deadline:* Applications are processed on a rolling basis. Application fee: $50. Electronic applications accepted. *Financial support:* Applicants required to submit FAFSA. *Unit head:* Dr. Bruce Corrie, Dean, 651-641-8226, Fax: 651-641-8807, E-mail: corrie@csp.edu. *Application contact:* Kimberly Craig, Director of Graduate and Cohort Admission, 651-603-6223, Fax: 651-603-6320, E-mail: craig@csp.edu.

Concordia University Wisconsin, Graduate Programs, School of Business and Legal Studies, MBA Program, Mequon, WI 53097-2402. Offers finance (MBA); health care administration (MBA); human resource management (MBA); international business (MBA); international business-bilingual English/Chinese (MBA); management (MBA); management information systems (MBA); managerial communications (MBA); marketing (MBA); public administration (MBA); risk management (MBA). Postbaccalaureate distance learning degree programs offered (minimal on-campus study). *Degree requirements:* For master's, comprehensive exam, thesis or alternative. *Entrance requirements:* Additional exam requirements/recommendations for international students: Required—TOEFL. *Expenses:* Contact institution.

Corban University, Graduate School, The Corban MBA, Salem, OR 97301-9392. Offers management (MBA); non-profit management (MBA). Postbaccalaureate distance learning degree programs offered (no on-campus study).

Cornell University, Graduate School, Graduate Field of Management, Ithaca, NY 14853-0001. Offers accounting (PhD); behavioral decision theory (PhD); finance (PhD); marketing (PhD); organizational behavior (PhD); production and operations management (PhD). *Accreditation:* AACSB. *Faculty:* 72 full-time (15 women). *Students:* 39 full-time (15 women); includes 2 minority (both Asian Americans or Pacific Islanders), 23 international. Average age 31. 388 applicants, 2% accepted, 4 enrolled. In 2009, 4 doctorates awarded. *Degree requirements:* For doctorate, comprehensive exam, thesis/dissertation. *Entrance requirements:* For doctorate, GMAT or GRE General Test. Additional exam requirements/recommendations for international students: Required—TOEFL (minimum score 600 paper-based; 250 computer-based; 77 iBT). *Application deadline:* For fall admission, 1/3 for domestic students. Application fee: $70. Electronic applications accepted. *Expenses:* Contact institution. *Financial support:* In 2009–10, 38 students received support, including 1 fellowship with full tuition reimbursement available, 3 research assistantships with full tuition reimbursements available; teaching assistantships with full tuition reimbursements available, institutionally sponsored loans, scholarships/grants, health care benefits, tuition waivers (full and partial), and unspecified assistantships also available. Financial award applicants required to submit FAFSA. *Faculty research:* Operations and manufacturing. *Unit head:* Director of Graduate Studies, 607-255-3669. *Application contact:* Graduate Field Assistant, 607-255-9431, E-mail: js_phd@cornell.edu.

Cornell University, Johnson Graduate School of Management, Ithaca, NY 14853. Offers MBA, JD/MBA, M Eng/MBA, MBA/MILR. *Accreditation:* AACSB. *Faculty:* 52 full-time (11 women), 3 part-time/adjunct (0 women). *Students:* 957 full-time (280 women); includes 186 minority (27 African Americans, 128 Asian Americans or Pacific Islanders, 31 Hispanic Americans), 288 international. Average age 30. 3,242 applicants, 510 enrolled. In 2009, 468 master's awarded. *Entrance requirements:* For master's, GMAT. Additional exam requirements/recommendations for international students: Required—TOEFL (minimum score 250 computer-based; 100 iBT); Recommended—IELTS (minimum score 7), TWE. *Application deadline:* For fall admission, 3/15 for domestic students, 1/1 for international students. Application fee: $200. Electronic applications accepted. *Expenses:* Contact institution. *Financial support:* Fellowships, research assistantships, career-related internships or fieldwork, Federal Work-Study, institutionally sponsored loans, and tuition waivers (full and partial) available. Financial award application deadline: 2/15; financial award applicants required to submit FAFSA. Total annual research expenditures: $17,444. *Unit head:* Dr. L. Joseph Thomas, Dean, 607-255-4854, E-mail: ljt3@cornell.edu. *Application contact:* 800-847-2082, Fax: 607-255-0065, E-mail: mba@johnson.cornell.edu.

Cornerstone University, Graduate Programs, Grand Rapids, MI 49525-5897. Offers business administration (MBA); education (MA Ed); management (MSM); teaching English to speakers of other languages (MA, Graduate Certificate). Programs also offered at Holland, Kalamazoo, and Troy, MI campuses. Part-time programs available. Postbaccalaureate distance learning degree programs offered. *Degree requirements:* For master's, comprehensive exam (for some programs), thesis (for some programs). *Entrance requirements:* For master's, minimum GPA of 2.5, 2 letters of reference. Additional exam requirements/recommendations for international students: Required—TOEFL (minimum score 575 paper-based; 235 computer-based). Electronic applications accepted.

Creighton University, Graduate School, Eugene C. Eppley College of Business Administration, Omaha, NE 68178-0001. Offers business administration (MBA); information technology management (MS); securities and portfolio management (MSAPM); JD/MBA; MBA/INR; MBA/MS-ITM; MBA/MSAPM; MS ITM/JD; Pharm D/MBA. *Accreditation:* AACSB. Part-time and evening/weekend programs available. Postbaccalaureate distance learning degree programs offered (minimal on-campus study). *Faculty:* 38 full-time (5 women). *Students:* 46 full-time (12 women), 222 part-time (36 women); includes 30 minority (12 African Americans, 13 Asian Americans or Pacific Islanders, 5 Hispanic Americans), 18 international. Average age 30. 160

applicants, 79% accepted, 118 enrolled. In 2009, 78 master's awarded. *Degree requirements:* For master's, thesis optional. *Entrance requirements:* For master's, GMAT, resume, 2 letters of recommendation. Additional exam requirements/recommendations for international students: Required—TOEFL (minimum score 550 paper-based; 213 computer-based; 80 iBT). *Application deadline:* For fall admission, 7/1 priority date for domestic students, 3/1 for international students; for winter admission, 10/1 priority date for domestic students, 7/1 for international students; for spring admission, 4/1 priority date for domestic students, 10/1 for international students. Applications are processed on a rolling basis. Application fee: $50. Electronic applications accepted. *Expenses:* Tuition: Full-time $11,700; part-time $650 per credit hour. Required fees: $126 per semester. *Financial support:* In 2009–10, 8 research assistantships with full tuition reimbursements (averaging $8,650 per year) were awarded; career-related internships or fieldwork, tuition waivers (partial), and unspecified assistantships also available. Financial award application deadline: 3/1. *Faculty research:* Small business issues. *Unit head:* Dr. Deborah Wells, Associate Dean for Graduate Programs, 402-280-2841, E-mail: deborahwells@creighton.edu. *Application contact:* Gail Hafer, Assistant Dean, 402-280-2829, Fax: 402-280-2172, E-mail: ghafer@creighton.edu.

Cumberland University, Program in Business Administration, Lebanon, TN 37087. Offers MBA. *Accreditation:* ACBSP. Part-time and evening/weekend programs available. *Degree requirements:* For master's, comprehensive exam. *Entrance requirements:* For master's, GMAT or GRE General Test, 3 letters of recommendation. Additional exam requirements/recommendations for international students: Required—TOEFL (minimum score 500 paper-based; 173 computer-based). *Expenses:* Contact institution.

Curry College, Graduate Studies, Program in Business Administration, Milton, MA 02186-9984. Offers business administration (MBA); finance (Certificate). Part-time and evening/weekend programs available. *Faculty:* 5 full-time (1 woman), 2 part-time/adjunct (0 women). *Students:* 111 part-time (68 women). Average age 36. 44 applicants, 89% accepted, 39 enrolled. In 2009, 49 master's awarded. *Degree requirements:* For master's, capstone applied project. *Entrance requirements:* For master's, resume, recommendations, interview, written statement. Additional exam requirements/recommendations for international students: Required—TOEFL (minimum score 550 paper-based; 213 computer-based; 80 iBT). *Application deadline:* For fall admission, 8/1 priority date for domestic students, 6/1 for international students; for winter admission, 10/1 for international students; for spring admission, 12/15 priority date for domestic students, 1/28 for international students. Applications are processed on a rolling basis. Application fee: $50. *Expenses:* Contact institution. *Unit head:* Dr. Gail Arch, Director and Professor, 617-333-2197. *Application contact:* John Bresnahan, Director of Graduate Enrollment and Student Services, 617-333-2243, Fax: 617-979-3535, E-mail: jbresnah0104@curry.edu.

Daemen College, Program in Executive Leadership and Change, Amherst, NY 14226-3592. Offers MS. Part-time and evening/weekend programs available. *Faculty:* 1 full-time (0 women), 5 part-time/adjunct (2 women). *Students:* 9 full-time (5 women), 9 part-time (6 women); includes 4 minority (all African Americans). Average age 40. 14 applicants, 71% accepted, 4 enrolled. In 2009, 7 master's awarded. *Degree requirements:* For master's, thesis, cohort learning sequence. *Entrance requirements:* For master's, 2 letters of recommendation, interview. Additional exam requirements/recommendations for international students: Required—TOEFL (minimum score 500 paper-based; 173 computer-based; 61 iBT). *Application deadline:* For fall admission, 3/1 priority date for domestic and international students; for spring admission, 10/1 priority date for domestic and international students. Applications are processed on a rolling basis. Application fee: $25. Electronic applications accepted. *Expenses:* Tuition: Part-time $770 per credit hour. Tuition and fees vary according to course load, program and reciprocity agreements. *Financial support:* In 2009–10, 1 student received support. Institutionally sponsored loans and scholarships/grants available. Financial award application deadline: 2/15; financial award applicants required to submit FAFSA. *Unit head:* Dr. John S. Frederick, Executive Director, 716-839-8342, Fax: 716-839-8261, E-mail: jfrederi@daemen.edu. *Application contact:* Scott Rowe, Associate Director of Graduate Admissions, 716-839-8225, Fax: 716-839-8229, E-mail: srowe@daemen.edu.

Dalhousie University, Faculty of Management, Centre for Advanced Management Education, Halifax, NS B3H 3J5, Canada. Offers financial services (MBA); information management (MIM); management (MPA); natural resources (MBA). Part-time programs available. Postbaccalaureate distance learning degree programs offered. *Faculty:* 10 full-time (5 women). *Students:* 19 part-time (4 women). Average age 27. 50 applicants, 42% accepted. *Entrance requirements:* For master's, GMAT, minimum GPA of 3.0, resume. Additional exam requirements/recommendations for international students: Required—TOEFL, IELTS, CANTEST, CAEL, or Michigan English Language Assessment Battery. *Application deadline:* Applications are processed on a rolling basis. Application fee: $70. Electronic applications accepted. *Unit head:* Michelle Hunter, Associate Director (Administration), 902-494-1828, Fax: 902-494-7154, E-mail: mhunter@dal.ca. *Application contact:* Deborah McColl, Admissions and Registration Coordinator, 902-494-6391, E-mail: mbafs@dal.ca.

Dalhousie University, Faculty of Management, School of Business Administration, Halifax, NS B3H 3J5, Canada. Offers business administration (MBA); financial services (MBA); LL B/MBA; MBA/MLIS. Part-time programs available. *Students:* 156 full-time (56 women), 122 part-time (51 women). Average age 26. 504 applicants, 38% accepted. *Entrance requirements:* For master's, GMAT, letter of non-financial guarantee for non-Canadian students, resume, Corporate Residency Preference Form. Additional exam requirements/recommendations for international students: Required—TOEFL, IELTS, CANTEST, CAEL, or Michigan English Language Assessment Battery. *Application deadline:* For spring admission, 5/15 priority date for domestic students, 12/31 priority date for international students. Applications are processed on a rolling basis. Application fee: $70. Electronic applications accepted. *Financial support:* In 2009–10, 12 students received support; fellowships, teaching assistantships available. Financial award application deadline: 5/15. *Faculty research:* International business, quantitative methods, operations research, MIS, marketing, finance. *Unit head:* Marianne Hagen, Graduate Coordinator, 902-494-1814, Fax: 902-494-1107, E-mail: mba.admissions@dal.ca. *Application contact:* Heather Frausell, Administrative Secretary, 902-494-1814, Fax: 902-494-1107, E-mail: mba.admissions@dal.ca.

Dalhousie University, Faculty of Management, School of Public Administration, Halifax, NS B3H 3J5, Canada. Offers management (MPA); public administration (MPA, GDPA); LL B/MPA; MLIS/MPA. Part-time programs available. *Faculty:* 9 full-time (1 woman), 6 part-time/adjunct (1 woman). *Students:* 59 full-time (36 women), 25 part-time (13 women). 58 applicants, 79% accepted. *Entrance requirements:* For master's, GMAT. Additional exam requirements/recommendations for international students: Required—TOEFL, IELTS, CANTEST, CAEL, or Michigan English Language Assessment Battery. *Application deadline:* Applications are processed on a rolling basis. Application fee: $70. Electronic applications accepted. *Expenses:* Contact institution. *Financial support:* Fellowships, teaching assistantships, career-related internships or fieldwork available. *Faculty research:* Municipal management, policy and program management, environmental policy, economic and social policy, business and government. *Unit head:* Fazley Siddiq, Director, 902-494-8802, Fax: 902-494-7023, E-mail: dalmpa@dal.ca. *Application contact:* Cecilia MacDonald, Graduate Coordinator, 902-494-3743, Fax: 902-494-7023, E-mail: dalmpa@dal.ca.

Dallas Baptist University, College of Adult Education, Professional Development Program, Dallas, TX 75211-9299. Offers accounting (MA); church leadership (MA); counseling (MA); criminal justice (MA); English as a second language (MA); finance (MA); higher education (MA); leadership studies (MA); management (MA); management information systems (MA); marketing (MA); missions (MA). Part-time and evening/weekend programs available. *Entrance requirements:* For master's, minimum GPA of 3.0. Additional exam requirements/recommendations for international students: Required—TOEFL, IELTS. *Expenses:* Tuition: Full-time $10,674; part-time $593 per credit hour.

Dallas Baptist University, College of Business, Business Administration Program, Dallas, TX 75211-9299. Offers accounting (MBA); business communication (MBA); conflict resolution management (MBA); e-business (MBA); entrepreneurship (MBA); finance (MBA); health care management (MBA); international business (MBA); leading the non-profit organization (MBA); management (MBA); management information systems (MBA); marketing (MBA); project management (MBA); technology and engineering management (MBA). *Accreditation:* ACBSP. Part-time and evening/weekend programs available. *Entrance requirements:* For master's, GMAT, minimum GPA of 3.0. Additional exam requirements/recommendations for international students: Required—TOEFL, IELTS. Electronic applications accepted. *Expenses:* Tuition: Full-time $10,674; part-time $593 per credit hour. *Faculty research:* Sports management, services marketing, retailing, strategic management, financial planning/investments.

Dallas Baptist University, College of Business, Management Program, Dallas, TX 75211-9299. Offers business communication (MA); conflict resolution management (MA); general management (MA); health care management (MA); human resource management (MA); performance management (MA). Part-time and evening/weekend programs available. *Entrance requirements:* For master's, GRE General Test, minimum GPA of 3.0. Additional exam requirements/recommendations for international students: Required—TOEFL, IELTS. Electronic applications accepted. *Expenses:* Tuition: Full-time $10,674; part-time $593 per credit hour. *Faculty research:* Organizational behavior, conflict personalities.

Dallas Baptist University, Gary Cook School of Leadership, Program in Christian Education, Dallas, TX 75211-9299. Offers adult ministry (MA); business ministry (MA); childhood ministry (MA); collegiate ministry (MA); communication ministry (MA); counseling ministry (MA); education ministry (MA); general ministry (MA); missions ministry (MA); student ministry (MA); worship ministry (MA). Part-time and evening/weekend programs available. *Entrance requirements:* For master's, minimum GPA of 3.0. Additional exam requirements/recommendations for international students: Required—TOEFL. Electronic applications accepted. *Expenses:* Tuition: Full-time $10,674; part-time $593 per credit hour.

Dallas Baptist University, Gary Cook School of Leadership, Program in Christian Education and Business Administration, Dallas, TX 75211-9299. Offers MA, MBA. Part-time and evening/weekend programs available. *Entrance requirements:* For master's, GMAT, minimum GPA of 3.0. Additional exam requirements/recommendations for international students: Required—TOEFL, IELTS. *Expenses:* Tuition: Full-time $10,674; part-time $593 per credit hour.

Daniel Webster College, MBA Program, Nashua, NH 03063-1300. Offers applied management (MBA). Part-time and evening/weekend programs available. *Degree requirements:* For master's, capstone research project. *Entrance requirements:* Additional exam requirements/recommendations for international students: Required—TOEFL (minimum score 550 paper-based; 213 computer-based; 79 iBT). Electronic applications accepted.

Daniel Webster College–Portsmouth Campus, MBA Program, Portsmouth, NH 03801. Offers applied management (MBA). Part-time and evening/weekend programs available. *Degree requirements:* For master's, capstone research project. *Entrance requirements:* Additional exam requirements/recommendations for international students: Required—TOEFL (minimum score 550 paper-based; 213 computer-based; 79 iBT). Electronic applications accepted.

Dartmouth College, Tuck School of Business at Dartmouth, Hanover, NH 03755. Offers MBA, MBA/MPH, MD/MBA, PhD/MBA. *Accreditation:* AACSB. *Faculty:* 47 full-time (11 women). *Students:* 510 full-time (166 women); includes 84 minority (25 African Americans, 3 American Indian/Alaska Native, 38 Asian Americans or Pacific Islanders, 18 Hispanic Americans), 157 international. Average age 28. 2,804 applicants, 19% accepted, 258 enrolled. In 2009, 253 master's awarded. *Entrance requirements:* For master's, GMAT or GRE, 2 letters of recommendation, resume/curriculum vitae. Additional exam requirements/recommendations for international students: Required—TOEFL. *Application deadline:* For fall admission, 10/14 for domestic and international students; for winter admission, 1/6 for domestic and international students; for spring admission, 4/2 for domestic and international students. Application fee: $225. Electronic applications accepted. *Expenses:* Contact institution. *Financial support:* In 2009–10, 389 students received support. Institutionally sponsored loans and scholarships/grants available. Financial award application deadline: 4/15; financial award applicants required to submit FAFSA. *Faculty research:* Database marketing, mutual fund investment performance, dynamic capabilities of firms, return on marketing investment, tradeoff between risk and return in international financial markets, strategic innovation in established firms. *Unit head:* Paul Danos, Dean, 603-646-2460, Fax: 603-646-1308, E-mail: tuck.public.relations@dartmouth.edu. *Application contact:* Dawna Clarke, Director of Admissions, 603-646-3162, Fax: 603-646-1441, E-mail: tuck.admissions@dartmouth.edu.

Davenport University, Sneden Graduate School, Grand Rapids, MI 49503. Offers accounting (MBA); business administration (EMBA); finance (MBA); health care management (MBA); human resources (MBA); information assurance (MS); public health (MPH); strategic management (MBA). Evening/weekend programs available. *Entrance requirements:* For master's, GMAT, minimum undergraduate GPA of 2.75. Additional exam requirements/recommendations for international students: Required—TOEFL. Electronic applications accepted. *Faculty research:* Leadership, management, marketing, organizational culture.

Davenport University, Sneden Graduate School, Warren, MI 48092-5209. Offers accounting (MBA); business administration (EMBA); finance (MBA); health care management (MBA); human resources management (MBA); information assurance (MS); public health (MPH); strategic management (MBA). *Entrance requirements:* For master's, minimum undergraduate GPA of 2.7.

Davenport University, Sneden Graduate School, Dearborn, MI 48126-3799. Offers accounting (MBA); business administration (EMBA); finance (MBA); health care management (MBA); human resources management (MBA); information assurance (MS); marketing (MBA); public health (MPH); strategic management (MBA). Part-time and evening/weekend programs available. Postbaccalaureate distance learning degree programs offered (no on-campus study). *Entrance requirements:* For master's, minimum GPA of 2.7, previous course work in accounting and statistics. *Faculty research:* Accounting, international accounting, social and environmental accounting, finance.

Defiance College, Program in Business Administration, Defiance, OH 43512-1610. Offers criminal justice (MBA); health care (MBA); leadership (MBA). Part-time and evening/weekend programs available. *Degree requirements:* For master's, thesis. *Entrance requirements:* For master's, minimum GPA of 2.5.

Delaware State University, Graduate Programs, College of Business Administration, Program in Business Administration, Dover, DE 19901-2277. Offers MBA. *Accreditation:* AACSB. Part-time and evening/weekend programs available. *Degree requirements:* For master's, exit exam. *Entrance requirements:* For master's, GMAT (minimum score 400), minimum GPA of 3.0 in major, 2.75 overall. Additional exam requirements/recommendations for international students: Required—TOEFL (minimum score 550 paper-based). Electronic applications accepted. *Faculty research:* Managerial economics, strategic management, qualitative effort, finance.

Delaware Valley College, Program in Business Administration (MBA), Doylestown, PA 18901-2697. Offers accounting (MBA); food and agribusiness (MBA); general business (MBA); online global executive leadership (MBA). Part-time and evening/weekend programs available. Postbaccalaureate distance learning degree programs offered (no on-campus study). *Faculty:* 24 part-time/adjunct (10 women). *Students:* 25 full-time (16 women), 74 part-time (37 women); includes 7 minority (4 African Americans, 2 Asian Americans or Pacific Islanders, 1 Hispanic American). Average age 37. 18 applicants, 100% accepted, 18 enrolled. In 2009, 12 master's awarded. *Entrance requirements:* For master's, minimum undergraduate GPA of 3.0. *Application deadline:* Applications are processed on a rolling basis. Application fee: $50. *Expenses:* Contact institution. *Financial support:* Applicants required to submit FAFSA. *Unit head:* Thomas Kennedy, Director of MBA Program, 215-489-2322, E-mail: thomas.kennedy@delval.edu. *Application contact:* Pamela Heffner, Graduate and Continuing Studies Enrollment Manager, 215-489-4469, Fax: 215-489-4832, E-mail: pamela.heffner@deval.edu.

Business Administration and Management—General

Delta State University, Graduate Programs, College of Business, Cleveland, MS 38733-0001. Offers MBA, MCA, MPA. *Accreditation:* ACBSP. Part-time and evening/weekend programs available. Postbaccalaureate distance learning degree programs offered (minimal on-campus study). *Entrance requirements:* For master's, GMAT. *Expenses:* Tuition, state resident: full-time $4450; part-time $247 per credit hour. Tuition, nonresident: full-time $11,520; part-time $640 per credit hour.

DePaul University, Charles H. Kellstadt Graduate School of Business, Chicago, IL 60604. Offers M Acc, MA, MBA, MS, MSA, MSEPA, MSF, MSHR, MSMA, MSRE, MST, JD/MBA. *Accreditation:* AACSB. Part-time and evening/weekend programs available. *Faculty:* 148 full-time (68 women). *Students:* 1,376 full-time (519 women), 888 part-time (345 women); includes 326 minority (66 African Americans, 5 American Indian/Alaska Native, 178 Asian Americans or Pacific Islanders, 77 Hispanic Americans), 200 international. Average age 27. 1,276 applicants, 48% accepted, 408 enrolled. In 2009, 657 master's awarded. *Entrance requirements:* For master's, GMAT, 2 letters of recommendation, resume. Additional exam requirements/recommendations for international students: Required—TOEFL (minimum score 550 paper-based; 213 computer-based; 80 iBT). *Application deadline:* For fall admission, 7/1 for domestic students, 6/1 for international students; for winter admission, 10/1 for domestic students, 9/1 for international students; for spring admission, 2/1 for domestic students, 1/1 for international students. Applications are processed on a rolling basis. Application fee: $60. Electronic applications accepted. *Expenses:* Contact institution. *Financial support:* In 2009–10, 12 research assistantships (averaging $25,768 per year) were awarded; career-related internships or fieldwork, Federal Work-Study, institutionally sponsored loans, scholarships/grants, tuition waivers (full and partial), and unspecified assistantships also available. Support available to part-time students. Financial award application deadline: 4/1. *Unit head:* Robert T. Ryan, Assistant Dean and Director, 312-362-8810, Fax: 312-362-6677, E-mail: rryan1@depaul.edu. *Application contact:* Dustin Carnwell, Director of Recruiting and Admission, 312-362-8810, Fax: 312-362-6677, E-mail: kgsb@depaul.edu.

DeSales University, Graduate Division, Program in Business Administration, Center Valley, PA 18034-9568. Offers accounting (MBA); business administration (MBA); computer information systems (MBA); finance (MBA); health care systems management (MBA); management (MBA); marketing (MBA); project management (MBA); self-design (MBA); MSN/MBA. *Accreditation:* ACBSP. Part-time programs available. Postbaccalaureate distance learning degree programs offered (no on-campus study). *Students:* 433 part-time. In 2009, 218 master's awarded. *Entrance requirements:* For master's, minimum GPA of 3.0, 2 years of work experience. Additional exam requirements/recommendations for international students: Required—TOEFL. *Application deadline:* Applications are processed on a rolling basis. Application fee: $35. Electronic applications accepted. *Expenses:* Tuition: Full-time $17,500; part-time $665 per credit. Full-time tuition and fees vary according to program. Part-time tuition and fees vary according to course load. *Faculty research:* Quality improvement, executive development, productivity, cross-cultural managerial differences, leadership. *Unit head:* Dr. David Gilfoil, Director, 610-282-1100 Ext. 1828, Fax: 610-282-2869, E-mail: david.gilfoil@desales.edu. *Application contact:* Caryn Stopper, Director of Graduate Admissions, 610-282-1100 Ext. 1768, Fax: 610-282-0525, E-mail: caryn.stopper@desales.edu.

DeVry University, Keller Graduate School of Management, Phoenix, AZ 85021-2995. Offers MAFM, MBA, MHRM, MISM, MNCM, MPA, MPM. *Students:* 19 full-time (9 women), 195 part-time (101 women). In 2009, 78 master's awarded. *Application contact:* Student Application Contact, 602-870-9222.

DeVry University, Keller Graduate School of Management, Fremont, CA 94555. Offers MAFM, MBA, MHRM, MISM, MNCM, MPA, MPM. *Students:* 14 full-time (8 women), 198 part-time (92 women). In 2009, 64 master's awarded. *Application contact:* Student Application Contact, 510-574-1100.

DeVry University, Keller Graduate School of Management, Long Beach, CA 90806. Offers MAFM, MBA, MHRM, MISM, MNCM, MPA, MPM. *Students:* 5 full-time (3 women), 245 part-time (112 women). In 2009, 98 master's awarded. *Application contact:* Student Application Contact, 562-427-0861.

DeVry University, Keller Graduate School of Management, Pomona, CA 91768-2642. Offers MAFM, MBA, MHRM, MISM, MNCM, MPA, MPM. *Students:* 41 full-time (19 women), 262 part-time (109 women). In 2009, 96 master's awarded. *Application contact:* Student Application Contact, 909-622-8866.

DeVry University, Keller Graduate School of Management, Palmdale, CA 93551. Offers MAFM, MBA, MHRM, MPM, Graduate Certificate.

DeVry University, Keller Graduate School of Management, Colorado Springs, CO 80920. Offers MAFM, MBA, MHRM, MISM, MNCM, MPA, MPM, Graduate Certificate.

DeVry University, Keller Graduate School of Management, Miramar, FL 33027-4150. Offers MAFM, MBA, MHRM, MISM, MNCM, MPA, MPM. *Students:* 18 full-time (12 women), 142 part-time (81 women). In 2009, 54 master's awarded. *Application contact:* Student Application Contact, 954-499-9700.

DeVry University, Keller Graduate School of Management, Orlando, FL 32839. Offers MAFM, MBA, MHRM, MISM, MNCM, MPA, MPM. *Students:* 30 full-time (11 women), 170 part-time (94 women). In 2009, 63 master's awarded. *Application contact:* Student Application Contact, 407-345-2800.

DeVry University, Keller Graduate School of Management, Alpharetta, GA 30009. Offers MAFM, MBA, MHRM, MISM, MNCM, MPA, MPM. *Students:* 14 full-time (10 women), 166 part-time (94 women). In 2009, 52 master's awarded. *Application contact:* Student Application Contact, 770-619-3600.

DeVry University, Keller Graduate School of Management, Decatur, GA 30030-2556. Offers MAFM, MBA, MHRM, MISM, MNCM, MPA, MPM. *Students:* 53 full-time (36 women), 341 part-time (212 women). In 2009, 117 master's awarded. *Application contact:* Student Application Contact, 404-270-2700.

DeVry University, Keller Graduate School of Management, Tinley Park, IL 60477. Offers MAFM, MBA, MHRM, MISM, MNCM, MPA, MPM. *Students:* 42 full-time (27 women), 287 part-time (184 women). In 2009, 106 master's awarded. *Application contact:* Student Application Contact, 708-342-3300.

DeVry University, Keller Graduate School of Management, Columbus, OH 43209-2705. Offers MAFM, MBA, MHRM, MISM, MNCM, MPA, MPM. *Students:* 25 full-time (15 women), 281 part-time (152 women). In 2009, 87 master's awarded. *Application contact:* Student Application Contact, 614-253-7291.

DeVry University, Keller Graduate School of Management, Fort Washington, PA 19034. Offers MAFM, MBA, MHRM, MISM, MNCM, MPA, MPM. *Students:* 11 full-time (4 women), 146 part-time (81 women). In 2009, 44 master's awarded. *Application contact:* Student Application Contact, 215-591-5700.

DeVry University, Keller Graduate School of Management, Irving, TX 75063-2439. Offers MAFM, MBA, MHRM, MISM, MPM. *Students:* 26 full-time (10 women), 273 part-time (123 women). In 2009, 74 master's awarded. *Application contact:* Student Application Contact, 972-929-6777.

DeVry University, Keller Graduate School of Management, Arlington, VA 22202. Offers MAFM, MBA, MHRM, MISM, MNCM, MPA, MPM. *Students:* 13 full-time (5 women), 122 part-time (52 women). In 2009, 61 master's awarded. *Application contact:* Student Application Contact, 703-414-4000.

DeVry University, Keller Graduate School of Management, Federal Way, WA 98001. Offers MAFM, MBA, MHRM, MISM, MNCM, MPA, MPM. *Students:* 14 full-time (7 women), 139 part-time (62 women). In 2009, 31 master's awarded. *Application contact:* Student Application Contact, 253-943-2800.

DeVry University, Keller Graduate School of Management, Mesa, AZ 85210-2011. Offers MAFM, MBA, MHRM, MISM, MNCM, MPA, MPM, Graduate Certificate.

DeVry University, Keller Graduate School of Management, Phoenix, AZ 85054. Offers MAFM, MBA, MHRM, MISM, MNCM, MPA, MPM, Graduate Certificate.

DeVry University, Keller Graduate School of Management, Irvine, CA 92602-1303. Offers MAFM, MBA, MHRM, MISM, MNCM, MPA, MPM, Graduate Certificate.

DeVry University, Keller Graduate School of Management, Elk Grove, CA 95758. Offers MAFM, MBA, MHRM, MISM, MNCM, MPA, MPM, Graduate Certificate.

DeVry University, Keller Graduate School of Management, San Diego, CA 92108-1633. Offers MAFM, MBA, MHRM, MISM, MNCM, MPA, MPM, Graduate Certificate.

DeVry University, Keller Graduate School of Management, Miami, FL 33174-2535. Offers MAFM, MBA, MHRM, MISM, MNCM, MPA, MPM, Graduate Certificate.

DeVry University, Keller Graduate School of Management, Tampa, FL 33607-5901. Offers MAFM, MBA, MHRM, MISM, MNCM, MPA, MPM, Graduate Certificate.

DeVry University, Keller Graduate School of Management, Atlanta, GA 30305-1543. Offers MAFM, MBA, MHRM, MISM, MNCM, MPA, MPM, Graduate Certificate.

DeVry University, Keller Graduate School of Management, Duluth, GA 30096-7671. Offers MAFM, MBA, MHRM, MISM, MNCM, MPA, MPM, Graduate Certificate.

DeVry University, Keller Graduate School of Management, Elgin, IL 60123. Offers MAFM, MBA, MHRM, MISM, MNCM, MPA, MPM, Graduate Certificate.

DeVry University, Keller Graduate School of Management, Lincolnshire, IL 60069-4460. Offers MAFM, MBA, MHRM, MISM, MNCM, MPA, MPM, Graduate Certificate.

DeVry University, Keller Graduate School of Management, Schaumburg, IL 60173-5009. Offers MAFM, MBA, MHRM, MISM, MNCM, MPA, MPM, Graduate Certificate.

DeVry University, Keller Graduate School of Management, Gurnee, IL 60031-9126. Offers MAFM, MBA, MHRM, MISM, MNCM, MPA, MPM, Graduate Certificate.

DeVry University, Keller Graduate School of Management, Indianapolis, IN 46240-2158. Offers MAFM, MBA, MHRM, MISM, MNCM, MPA, MPM. *Students:* 15 full-time (8 women), 118 part-time (67 women). In 2009, 36 master's awarded. *Application contact:* Student Application Contact, 317-581-8854.

DeVry University, Keller Graduate School of Management, Merrillville, IN 46410-5673. Offers MAFM, MBA, MHRM, MISM, MNCM, MPA, MPM, Graduate Certificate.

DeVry University, Keller Graduate School of Management, Bethesda, MD 20814-3304. Offers MAFM, MBA, MHRM, MISM, MNCM, MPA, MPM. *Students:* 9 full-time (5 women), 65 part-time (34 women). In 2009, 24 master's awarded. *Application contact:* Student Application Contact, 301-652-8477.

DeVry University, Keller Graduate School of Management, Kansas City, MO 64105-2112. Offers MAFM, MBA, MHRM, MISM, MNCM, MPA, MPM, Graduate Certificate.

DeVry University, Keller Graduate School of Management, St. Louis, MO 63146-4020. Offers MAFM, MBA, MHRM, MISM, MNCM, MPA, MPM, Graduate Certificate.

DeVry University, Keller Graduate School of Management, Charlotte, NC 28273-4068. Offers MAFM, MBA, MHRM, MISM, MNCM, MPA, MPM. *Students:* 14 full-time (10 women), 129 part-time (80 women). In 2009, 41 master's awarded. *Application contact:* Student Application Contact, 704-362-2345.

DeVry University, Keller Graduate School of Management, Henderson, NV 89074-7120. Offers MAFM, MBA, MHRM, MISM, MNCM, MPA, MPM. *Students:* 11 full-time (8 women), 79 part-time (41 women). In 2009, 19 master's awarded. *Application contact:* Student Application Contact, 702-933-9700.

DeVry University, Keller Graduate School of Management, Seven Hills, OH 44131. Offers MAFM, MBA, MHRM, MISM, MNCM, MPA, MPM, Graduate Certificate.

DeVry University, Keller Graduate School of Management, Portland, OR 97225-6651. Offers MAFM, MBA, MHRM, MISM, MNCM, MPA, MPM. *Students:* 8 full-time (5 women), 78 part-time (39 women). In 2009, 24 master's awarded. *Application contact:* Student Application Contact, 503-296-7468.

DeVry University, Keller Graduate School of Management, Pittsburgh, PA 15222-2606. Offers MAFM, MBA, MHRM, MISM, MNCM, MPA, MPM, Graduate Certificate.

DeVry University, Keller Graduate School of Management, King of Prussia, PA 19406-2926. Offers MAFM, MBA, MHRM, MISM, MNCM, MPA, MPM, Graduate Certificate.

DeVry University, Keller Graduate School of Management, Richardson, TX 75080. Offers MBA, Graduate Certificate.

DeVry University, Keller Graduate School of Management, Houston, TX 77041. Offers MAFM, MBA, MISM, MPM. *Students:* 42 full-time (22 women), 207 part-time (114 women). In 2009, 76 master's awarded. *Application contact:* Student Application Contact, 713-973-3100.

DeVry University, Keller Graduate School of Management, Manassas, VA 20109-3173. Offers MAFM, MBA, MHRM, MISM, MNCM, MPA, MPM, Graduate Certificate.

DeVry University, Keller Graduate School of Management, Bellevue, WA 98004-5110. Offers MAFM, MBA, MHRM, MISM, MNCM, MPA, MPM, Graduate Certificate.

DeVry University, Keller Graduate School of Management, Milwaukee, WI 53202. Offers MAFM, MBA, MHRM, MISM, MNCM, MPA, MPM. *Students:* 5 full-time (3 women), 80 part-time (46 women). In 2009, 36 master's awarded. *Application contact:* Student Application Contact, 414-278-7677.

DeVry University, Keller Graduate School of Management, Waukesha, WI 53188-1157. Offers MAFM, MBA, MHRM, MISM, MNCM, MPA, MPM, Graduate Certificate.

DeVry University, Keller Graduate School of Management, Naperville, IL 60563-2361. Offers MAFM, MBA, MHRM, MISM, MNCM, MPA, MPM, Graduate Certificate.

DeVry University, Keller Graduate School of Management, Sandy, UT 84070. Offers MAFM, MBA, MHRM, MISM, MNCM, MPA, MPM.

DeVry University, Keller Graduate School of Management, Downers Grove, IL 60515. Offers accounting and financial management (MAFM); business administration (MBA); human resources management (MHRM); information systems management (MISM); network and communications management (MNCM); project management (MPM); public administration (MPA).

Doane College, Program in Management, Crete, NE 68333-2430. Offers MA. Part-time and evening/weekend programs available. *Faculty:* 2 full-time (1 woman), 21 part-time/adjunct (9 women). *Students:* 123 full-time (74 women), 11 part-time (6 women); includes 16 minority (6 African Americans, 1 American Indian/Alaska Native, 2 Asian Americans or Pacific Islanders, 7 Hispanic Americans). Average age 36. In 2009, 20 master's awarded. *Degree requirements:* For master's, thesis. *Entrance requirements:* For master's, minimum GPA of 3.0. *Application deadline:* Applications are processed on a rolling basis. Application fee: $25. *Expenses:* Contact institution. *Financial support:* Application deadline: 6/1. *Unit head:* Janice Hedfield, Dean, 880-333-6263, E-mail: janice.hedfield@doane.edu. *Application contact:* Janice Hedfield, Dean, 880-333-6263, E-mail: janice.hedfield@doane.edu.

Dominican College, MBA Program, Orangeburg, NY 10962-1210. Offers MBA. Evening/weekend programs available. *Entrance requirements:* For master's, GMAT, 2 letters of recommendation. Additional exam requirements/recommendations for international students: Required—TOEFL. Electronic applications accepted. *Expenses:* Contact institution.

Dominican University, Edward A. and Lois L. Brennan School of Business, River Forest, IL 60305-1099. Offers accounting (MSA); business administration (MBA); JD/MBA; MBA/MLIS. *Accreditation:* ACBSP. Part-time and evening/weekend programs available. *Faculty:* 18 full-time (6 women), 34 part-time/adjunct (9 women). *Students:* 159 full-time (64 women), 185 part-time (94 women); includes 35 minority (12 African Americans, 11 Asian Americans or Pacific Islanders, 12 Hispanic Americans), 90 international. Average age 31. In 2009, 96 master's awarded. *Entrance requirements:* For master's, GMAT. Additional exam requirements/recommendations for international students: Required—TOEFL (minimum score 550 paper-based; 213 computer-based; 79 iBT); Recommended—IELTS (minimum score 6). *Application deadline:* Applications are processed on a rolling basis. Application fee: $25. Electronic applications accepted. *Expenses:* Contact institution. *Financial support:* Career-related internships or fieldwork, tuition waivers (partial), and unspecified assistantships available. Support available to part-time students. Financial award applicants required to submit FAFSA. *Faculty research:* Entrepreneurship, small business finance, business ethics, marketing strategy. *Unit head:* Dr. Arvid Johnson, Dean, 708-524-6465, Fax: 708-524-6939, E-mail: ajohnson@dom.edu. *Application contact:* Linda Puvogel, Assistant Dean for Graduate Business Programs, 708-524-6507, Fax: 708-524-6939, E-mail: lpuvogel@dom.edu.

Dominican University of California, Graduate Programs, School of Business and Leadership, Green Business Administration Program, San Rafael, CA 94901-2298. Offers sustainable development (MBA). *Entrance requirements:* Additional exam requirements/recommendations for international students: Required—TOEFL (minimum score 550 paper-based; 213 computer-based).

Dominican University of California, Graduate Programs, School of Business and Leadership, Program in Management, San Rafael, CA 94901-2298. Offers MAM. Program offered through strategic alliance with the California Management Institute (CMI).

Dowling College, School of Business, Oakdale, NY 11769-1999. Offers aviation management (MBA, Certificate); banking and finance (MBA, Certificate); financial planning (Certificate); general management (MBA); health care management (MBA, Certificate); human resource management (Certificate); management and leadership (MBA); marketing (Certificate); project management (Certificate); public management (MBA, Certificate); total quality management (MBA, Certificate); JD/MBA. Part-time and evening/weekend programs available. *Faculty:* 14 full-time (5 women), 58 part-time/adjunct (5 women). *Students:* 324 full-time (142 women), 479 part-time (237 women); includes 238 minority (82 African Americans, 1 American Indian/Alaska Native, 117 Asian Americans or Pacific Islanders, 38 Hispanic Americans), 2 international. Average age 33. 457 applicants, 91% accepted, 153 enrolled. In 2009, 341 master's, 2 other advanced degrees awarded. *Degree requirements:* For master's, comprehensive exam, thesis optional. *Entrance requirements:* For master's, minimum GPA of 2.8, 2 letters of recommendation, courses in accounting and finance or seminar in accounting/finance, resume. Additional exam requirements/recommendations for international students: Required—TOEFL (minimum score 550 paper-based). *Application deadline:* For fall admission, 9/1 priority date for domestic students; for winter admission, 1/1 priority date for domestic students; for spring admission, 2/1 priority date for domestic students. Applications are processed on a rolling basis. Application fee: $50. Electronic applications accepted. *Expenses:* Tuition: Full-time $14,490; part-time $805 per credit. Required fees: $346 per term. *Financial support:* Career-related internships or fieldwork and Federal Work-Study available. Support available to part-time students. Financial award application deadline: 6/30; financial award applicants required to submit FAFSA. *Faculty research:* International finance, computer applications, labor relations, executive development. *Unit head:* Mathew Cordaro, Dean, 631-244-3162, Fax: 631-244-1018, E-mail: cordarom@dowling.edu. *Application contact:* Glenn M. Berman, Director of Admissions Operations, 631-244-3357, Fax: 631-244-1059, E-mail: glenn.berman@dowling.edu.

Drake University, College of Business and Public Administration, Des Moines, IA 50311-4516. Offers M Acc, MBA, MFM, MPA, JD/MBA, JD/MPA, Pharm D/MBA, Pharm D/MPA. *Accreditation:* AACSB. Part-time and evening/weekend programs available. *Faculty:* 18 full-time (4 women), 5 part-time/adjunct (0 women). *Students:* 59 full-time (22 women), 379 part-time (200 women); includes 16 African Americans, 14 Asian Americans or Pacific Islanders, 4 Hispanic Americans, 21 international. Average age 31. 269 applicants, 61% accepted, 116 enrolled. In 2009, 188 master's awarded. *Degree requirements:* For master's, comprehensive exam (for some programs), thesis (for some programs), internships. *Entrance requirements:* For master's, GMAT, letters of recommendation, resume. Additional exam requirements/recommendations for international students: Required—TOEFL (minimum score 550 paper-based; 213 computer-based). *Application deadline:* For fall admission, 8/15 priority date for domestic students; for winter admission, 12/20 priority date for domestic students; for spring admission, 12/1 priority date for domestic students. Applications are processed on a rolling basis. Application fee: $25. Electronic applications accepted. *Expenses:* Contact institution. *Financial support:* Fellowships with tuition reimbursements, teaching assistantships, career-related internships or fieldwork and institutionally sponsored loans available. Support available to part-time students. Financial award application deadline: 3/1; financial award applicants required to submit FAFSA. *Faculty research:* Venture capital, online commerce, professional ethics, process improvement, project management. *Unit head:* Dr. Charles Edwards, Dean, 515-271-2871, Fax: 515-271-4518, E-mail: charles.edwards@drake.edu. *Application contact:* Danette Kenne, Director of Graduate Programs, 515-271-2188, Fax: 515-271-4518, E-mail: cbpa.gradprograms@drake.edu.

Drexel University, LeBow College of Business, Program in Business Administration, Philadelphia, PA 19104-2875. Offers business administration (MBA, PhD, APC), including accounting (MBA, PhD), decision sciences (PhD), economics (MBA, PhD), finance (MBA, PhD), legal studies (MBA), management (MBA), marketing (MBA, PhD), organizational sciences (PhD), quantitative methods (MBA), strategic management (PhD). *Accreditation:* AACSB. Part-time and evening/weekend programs available. Postbaccalaureate distance learning degree programs offered (minimal on-campus study). Terminal master's awarded for partial completion of doctoral program. *Entrance requirements:* For master's, GMAT, minimum GPA of 2.75; for doctorate, GMAT. Additional exam requirements/recommendations for international students: Required—TOEFL. Electronic applications accepted. *Faculty research:* Decision support systems, individual and group behavior, operations research, techniques and strategy.

Drury University, Breech School of Business Administration, Springfield, MO 65802. Offers MBA. *Accreditation:* ACBSP. Part-time and evening/weekend programs available. *Entrance requirements:* For master's, GMAT. Additional exam requirements/recommendations for international students: Required—TOEFL. Electronic applications accepted. *Expenses:* Contact institution. *Faculty research:* Health care management, cross cultural management, philosophical orientation and decision making.

Duke University, The Fuqua School of Business, Cross Continent Executive MBA Program, Durham, NC 27708-0586. Offers EMBA. *Degree requirements:* For master's, one foreign language. *Entrance requirements:* For master's, GMAT. Electronic applications accepted.

Duke University, The Fuqua School of Business, Duke-Goethe Executive MBA Program, Durham, NC 27708-0586. Offers EMBA. EMBA held with Frankford University.

Duke University, The Fuqua School of Business, Global Executive MBA Program, Durham, NC 27708-0586. Offers GEMBA. Electronic applications accepted.

Duke University, The Fuqua School of Business, Weekend Executive MBA Program, Durham, NC 27708-0586. Offers WEMBA. Evening/weekend programs available. *Degree requirements:* For master's, one foreign language. *Entrance requirements:* For master's, GMAT. Electronic applications accepted.

Duke University, Graduate School, Department of Business Administration, Durham, NC 27708. Offers PhD. *Faculty:* 82 full-time. *Students:* 77 full-time (27 women); includes 8 minority (1 African American, 6 Asian Americans or Pacific Islanders, 1 Hispanic American), 44 international. 586 applicants, 6% accepted, 14 enrolled. In 2009, 15 doctorates awarded. *Degree requirements:* For doctorate, thesis/dissertation. *Entrance requirements:* For doctorate, GMAT or GRE General Test. Additional exam requirements/recommendations for international students: Required—TOEFL (minimum score 550 paper-based; 213 computer-based; 83 iBT), IELTS (minimum score 7). *Application deadline:* For fall admission, 12/8 for domestic and international students. Application fee: $75. Electronic applications accepted. *Financial support:* Fellowships with full tuition reimbursements, research assistantships, career-related internships or fieldwork, Federal Work-Study, and institutionally sponsored loans available. Financial award application deadline: 12/8; financial award applicants required to submit FAFSA. *Unit head:* James Bettman, Director of Graduate Studies, 919-660-7862, Fax: 919-681-6245, E-mail: bobbiec@mail.duke.edu. *Application contact:* Cynthia Robertson, Associate Dean for Enrollment Services.

Duquesne University, John F. Donahue Graduate School of Business, Pittsburgh, PA 15282-0001. Offers accountancy (MS); business administration (MBA); information systems management (MSISM); sustainability (MBA); JD/MBA; MBA/MA; MBA/MES; MBA/MHMS; MBA/MLLS; MBA/MS; MBA/MSN. *Accreditation:* AACSB. Part-time and evening/weekend programs available. *Faculty:* 52 full-time (12 women), 39 part-time/adjunct (7 women). *Students:* 122 full-time (56 women), 252 part-time (93 women); includes 14 minority (5 African Americans, 4 Asian Americans or Pacific Islanders, 5 Hispanic Americans), 30 international. Average age 31. 195 applicants, 95% accepted, 136 enrolled. In 2009, 97 master's awarded. *Entrance requirements:* For master's, GMAT, 2 letters of recommendation, current resume. Additional exam requirements/recommendations for international students: Required—TOEFL (minimum score 577 paper-based; 233 computer-based; 90 iBT); Recommended—TWE. *Application deadline:* For fall admission, 5/1 priority date for domestic students, 5/1 for international students; for spring admission, 10/1 for domestic and international students. Applications are processed on a rolling basis. Application fee: $0. Electronic applications accepted. *Expenses:* Tuition: Part-time $851 per credit. Required fees: $81 per credit. *Financial support:* In 2009–10, 46 students received support, including 14 fellowships with partial tuition reimbursements available, 32 research assistantships with partial tuition reimbursements available; career-related internships or fieldwork and unspecified assistantships also available. Support available to part-time students. Financial award application deadline: 7/1; financial award applicants required to submit FAFSA. *Faculty research:* International business, investment management, business ethics, technology management, supply chain management, business strategy, finance. *Unit head:* Alan R. Miciak, Dean, 412-396-5848, Fax: 412-396-5304, E-mail: miciaka@duq.edu. *Application contact:* Patricia Moore, Assistant Director, 412-396-6276, Fax: 412-396-1726, E-mail: moorep@duq.edu.

See Close-Up on page 239.

Duquesne University, School of Leadership and Professional Advancement, Pittsburgh, PA 15282-0001. Offers leadership (MS), including business ethics, community leadership, global leadership, information technology, leadership, liberal studies, professional administration, sports leadership. Part-time and evening/weekend programs available. Postbaccalaureate distance learning degree programs offered (no on-campus study). *Faculty:* 1 full-time (0 women), 70 part-time/adjunct (35 women). *Students:* 654 (307 women); includes 68 minority (57 African Americans, 1 American Indian/Alaska Native, 6 Asian Americans or Pacific Islanders, 4 Hispanic Americans). 161 applicants, 73% accepted, 103 enrolled. In 2009, 108 master's awarded. *Degree requirements:* For master's, capstone course. *Entrance requirements:* For master's, professional work experience, 500-word essay. Additional exam requirements/recommendations for international students: Required—TOEFL. *Application deadline:* Applications are processed on a rolling basis. Application fee: $0. Electronic applications accepted. *Expenses:* Tuition: Part-time $851 per credit. Required fees: $81 per credit. *Financial support:* Applicants required to submit FAFSA. *Unit head:* Dr. Dorothy Bassett, Dean, 412-396-2141, Fax: 412-396-4711, E-mail: bassettd@duq.edu. *Application contact:* Marianne Leister, Director of Student Services, 412-396-4933, Fax: 412-396-5072, E-mail: leister@duq.edu.

D'Youville College, Department of Business, Buffalo, NY 14201-1084. Offers business administration (MBA); international business (MS). Part-time and evening/weekend programs available. *Degree requirements:* For master's, one foreign language, project or thesis. *Entrance requirements:* For master's, minimum GPA of 3.0. Additional exam requirements/recommendations for international students: Required—TOEFL (minimum score 500 paper-based; 173 computer-based). Electronic applications accepted. *Faculty research:* Assessment, accreditation, supply chain, online learning, adult learning.

East Carolina University, Graduate School, College of Business, Greenville, NC 27858-4353. Offers MBA, MS, MSA. *Accreditation:* AACSB. Part-time and evening/weekend programs available. *Entrance requirements:* For master's, GMAT. Additional exam requirements/recommendations for international students: Required—TOEFL.

See Close-Up on page 241.

East Carolina University, Graduate School, College of Technology and Computer Science, Department of Technology Systems, Greenville, NC 27858-4353. Offers computer network professional (Certificate); industrial technology (MS), including computer networking management, digital communications, industrial distribution and logistics, information security, manufacturing, performance improvement, planning; information assurance (Certificate); occupational safety (MS); technology management (PhD); Website developer (Certificate). *Entrance requirements:* For master's and Certificate, GRE General Test or MAT, minimum GPA of 2.5; for doctorate, GRE General Test, related work experience.

Eastern Illinois University, Graduate School, Lumpkin College of Business and Applied Sciences, Program in Business Administration, Charleston, IL 61920-3099. Offers accountancy (MBA, Certificate); general management (MBA). *Accreditation:* AACSB. Part-time programs available. *Faculty:* 35 full-time (8 women). In 2009, 58 master's awarded. *Entrance requirements:* For master's, GMAT. *Application deadline:* For fall admission, 3/31 priority date for domestic students. Applications are processed on a rolling basis. Application fee: $30. *Expenses:* Tuition, state resident: full-time $9434; part-time $239 per credit hour. Tuition, nonresident: full-time $23,774; part-time $717 per credit hour. Required fees: $802.63. *Financial support:* In 2009–10, 4 research assistantships with tuition reimbursements (averaging $8,100 per year), 8 teaching assistantships with tuition reimbursements (averaging $8,100 per year) were awarded. *Unit head:* Dr. Cheryl Noll, Department Chair, 217-581-3028, E-mail: clnoll@eiu.edu. *Application contact:* Dr. John Willems, Coordinator, 217-581-3028, Fax: 217-581-6029, E-mail: jrwillems@eiu.edu.

Eastern Kentucky University, The Graduate School, College of Business and Technology, Program in Business Administration, Richmond, KY 40475-3102. Offers MBA. *Accreditation:* AACSB.

Eastern Mennonite University, Program in Business Administration, Harrisonburg, VA 22802-2462. Offers MBA. Part-time and evening/weekend programs available. *Faculty:* 9 full-time (0 women), 4 part-time/adjunct (0 women). *Students:* 2 full-time (1 woman), 37 part-time (17 women), 4 international. Average age 39. In 2009, 11 master's awarded. *Degree requirements:* For master's, final capstone course. *Entrance requirements:* For master's, GMAT, minimum GPA of 2.5, 2 years of work experience, 2 letters of reference. Additional exam requirements/recommendations for international students: Required—TOEFL (minimum score 500 paper-based). *Application deadline:* For fall admission, 3/1 priority date for domestic and international students. Applications are processed on a rolling basis. Application fee: $25. *Expenses:* Contact institution. *Financial support:* Application deadline: 6/30. *Faculty research:* Information security, Anabaptist/Mennonite experiences and perspectives, limits of multi-cultural education, international development performance criteria. *Unit head:* Dr. Ronald L. Stoltzfus, Co-Director, 540-432-4155, Fax: 540-432-4071, E-mail: stoltzfr@emu.edu. *Application contact:* Patricia S. Eckard, Office Coordinator, Business and Economics, 540-432-4150, Fax: 540-432-4071, E-mail: eckardp@emu.edu.

Business Administration and Management—General

Eastern Michigan University, Graduate School, College of Business, Department of Management, Ypsilanti, MI 48197. Offers human resources management and organizational development (MSHROD). Part-time and evening/weekend programs available. Postbaccalaureate distance learning degree programs offered (minimal on-campus study). *Faculty:* 20 full-time (9 women). *Students:* 28 full-time (12 women), 71 part-time (43 women); includes 16 minority (9 African Americans, 2 American Indian/Alaska Native, 1 Asian American or Pacific Islander, 4 Hispanic Americans), 44 international. Average age 31. 69 applicants, 83% accepted, 40 enrolled. In 2009, 54 master's awarded. *Degree requirements:* For master's, thesis optional. *Entrance requirements:* For master's, GMAT. Additional exam requirements/recommendations for international students: Required—TOEFL. *Application deadline:* For fall admission, 5/15 priority date for domestic and international students; for winter admission, 10/15 priority date for domestic and international students; for spring admission, 3/15 priority date for domestic and international students. Applications are processed on a rolling basis. Application fee: $35. Tuition and fees vary according to course level. *Financial support:* Fellowships, research assistantships with full tuition reimbursements, teaching assistantships with full tuition reimbursements, career-related internships or fieldwork, Federal Work-Study, institutionally sponsored loans, scholarships/grants, tuition waivers (partial), and unspecified assistantships available. Support available to part-time students. Financial award applicants required to submit FAFSA. *Unit head:* Dr. Fraya Wagner-Marsh, Department Head, 734-487-3240, Fax: 734-487-4100, E-mail: fraya.wagner@emich.edu. *Application contact:* Dr. Fraya Wagner-Marsh, Department Head, 734-487-3240, Fax: 734-487-4100, E-mail: fraya.wagner@emich.edu.

Eastern Michigan University, Graduate School, College of Business, Programs in Business Administration, Ypsilanti, MI 48197. Offers business administration (MBA, Graduate Certificate); computer information systems (Graduate Certificate); e-business (MBA, Graduate Certificate); enterprise business intelligence (MBA); entrepreneurship (MBA, Graduate Certificate); finance (MBA, Graduate Certificate); human resources (MBA); human resources management (Graduate Certificate); information systems (MBA); internal auditing (MBA); international business (MBA, Graduate Certificate); marketing management (Graduate Certificate); nonprofit management (MBA); organizational development (Graduate Certificate); supply chain management (MBA, Graduate Certificate). *Accreditation:* AACSB. Part-time programs available. Postbaccalaureate distance learning degree programs offered (no on-campus study). *Students:* 166 full-time (80 women), 439 part-time (231 women); includes 150 minority (103 African Americans, 7 American Indian/Alaska Native, 31 Asian Americans or Pacific Islanders, 9 Hispanic Americans), 97 international. Average age 34. In 2009, 3 other advanced degrees awarded. *Entrance requirements:* For master's, GMAT (minimum score 450), minimum cumulative undergraduate GPA of 2.75. Additional exam requirements/recommendations for international students: Required—TOEFL. *Application deadline:* For fall admission, 5/15 for domestic students, 5/1 for international students; for winter admission, 10/15 for domestic students, 10/1 for international students; for spring admission, 3/15 for domestic students, 3/1 for international students. Applications are processed on a rolling basis. Application fee: $35. Tuition and fees vary according to course level. *Financial support:* Fellowships, research assistantships with full tuition reimbursements, teaching assistantships with full tuition reimbursements, career-related internships or fieldwork, Federal Work-Study, institutionally sponsored loans, scholarships/grants, tuition waivers (partial), and unspecified assistantships available. Support available to part-time students. Financial award applicants required to submit FAFSA. *Unit head:* K. Michelle Henry, Director of Academic Services, 734-487-4444, Fax: 734-483-1316, E-mail: cob.grad@emich.edu. *Application contact:* Beste Windes, Advisor, 734-487-4444, Fax: 734-483-1316, E-mail: cob.grad@emich.edu.

Eastern New Mexico University, Graduate School, College of Business, Portales, NM 88130. Offers MBA. *Accreditation:* ACBSP. Part-time and evening/weekend programs available. Postbaccalaureate distance learning degree programs offered (minimal on-campus study). *Faculty:* 12 full-time (3 women). *Students:* 14 full-time (6 women), 77 part-time (48 women); includes 24 minority (5 African Americans, 2 American Indian/Alaska Native, 1 Asian American or Pacific Islander, 16 Hispanic Americans), 9 international. Average age 35. 59 applicants, 66% accepted, 29 enrolled. In 2009, 19 master's awarded. *Degree requirements:* For master's, comprehensive exam. *Entrance requirements:* For master's, GMAT (minimum score 450), minimum GPA of 3.0. Additional exam requirements/recommendations for international students: Required—TOEFL (minimum score 550 paper-based; 213 computer-based; 79 iBT), IELTS (minimum score 6). *Application deadline:* For fall admission, 7/20 priority date for domestic students, 6/20 priority date for international students. Applications are processed on a rolling basis. Application fee: $10. Electronic applications accepted. *Expenses:* Tuition, state resident: full-time $2922; part-time $121.75 per credit hour. Tuition, nonresident: full-time $8454; part-time $352.25 per credit hour. Required fees: $1038; $43.25 per credit hour. *Financial support:* In 2009–10, 9 research assistantships with partial tuition reimbursements (averaging $4,250 per year) were awarded; fellowships, teaching assistantships, tuition waivers (partial) and unspecified assistantships also available. Support available to part-time students. Financial award applicants required to submit FAFSA. *Unit head:* Dr. Sue Stockly, Graduate Coordinator, 575-562-2364, E-mail: sue.stockly@enmu.edu. *Application contact:* Dr. Sue Stockly, Graduate Coordinator, 575-562-2364, E-mail: sue.stockly@enmu.edu.

Eastern University, School of Leadership and Development, St. Davids, PA 19087-3696. Offers economic development (MBA), including international development, urban development (MA, MBA); international development (MA), including global development, urban development (MA, MBA); nonprofit management (MS); organizational leadership (MA); M Div/MBA. Part-time and evening/weekend programs available. *Degree requirements:* For master's, thesis (for some programs). *Entrance requirements:* For master's, GMAT (MBA), minimum GPA of 2.5. *Expenses:* Contact institution. *Faculty research:* Micro-level economic development, China welfare and economic development, macroethics, micro- and macro-level economic development in transitional economics, organizational effectiveness.

Eastern University, School of Management Studies, St. Davids, PA 19087-3696. Offers health administration (MBA); management (MBA).

Eastern Washington University, Graduate Studies, College of Business and Public Administration, Business Administration Program, Cheney, WA 99004-2431. Offers MBA, MBA/MPA. *Accreditation:* AACSB. *Degree requirements:* For master's, comprehensive exam, thesis optional. *Entrance requirements:* For master's, GMAT, minimum GPA of 3.0. *Expenses:* Tuition, state resident: full-time $7476; part-time $249 per quarter hour. Tuition, nonresident: full-time $18,030; part-time $601 per quarter hour. Required fees: $3.50 per quarter hour. $142 per quarter.

East Tennessee State University, School of Graduate Studies, College of Business and Technology, Johnson City, TN 37614. Offers M Acc, MBA, MCM, MPM, MS, Certificate. *Accreditation:* AACSB. Part-time and evening/weekend programs available. *Degree requirements:* For master's, comprehensive exam. *Entrance requirements:* For master's, GMAT, minimum GPA of 2.5. Additional exam requirements/recommendations for international students: Required—TOEFL (minimum score 550 paper-based; 213 computer-based). *Faculty research:* Artificial intelligence and accounting, profit vs. non-profit hospital comparisons, environmental compliance issues in manufacturing, international finance, case law on Americans with disabilities.

Edgewood College, Program in Business, Madison, WI 53711-1997. Offers accountancy (MS); business (MBA). *Accreditation:* ACBSP. Part-time and evening/weekend programs available. *Students:* 30 full-time (16 women), 118 part-time (50 women); includes 9 minority (2 African Americans, 1 American Indian/Alaska Native, 5 Asian Americans or Pacific Islanders, 1 Hispanic American), 3 international. Average age 34. In 2009, 39 master's awarded. *Entrance requirements:* For master's, GMAT (minimum score 425), minimum GPA of 2.75, 2 letters of recommendation. Additional exam requirements/recommendations for international students: Required—TOEFL (minimum score 213 computer-based). *Application deadline:* For fall admission, 8/26 for domestic students, 8/1 for international students; for spring admission, 1/10 for domestic students, 10/1 for international students. Applications are processed on a rolling basis. Application fee: $25. Electronic applications accepted. *Expenses:* Tuition: Part-time $688 per credit hour. *Financial support:* Career-related internships or fieldwork available. *Unit head:* Martin Preizler, Dean, 608-663-2898, Fax: 608-663-3291, E-mail: martinpreizler@edgewood.edu. *Application contact:* Joann Eastman, Admissions Counselor, 608-663-3250, Fax: 608-663-2214, E-mail: gps@edgewood.edu.

Elmhurst College, Graduate Programs, Program in Business Administration, Elmhurst, IL 60126-3296. Offers MBA. Part-time and evening/weekend programs available. *Faculty:* 1 full-time (0 women), 7 part-time/adjunct (0 women). *Students:* 74 part-time (26 women); includes 8 minority (3 African Americans, 4 Asian Americans or Pacific Islanders, 1 Hispanic American). Average age 31. 89 applicants, 58% accepted, 43 enrolled. In 2009, 41 master's awarded. *Entrance requirements:* For master's, 3 recommendations. Additional exam requirements/recommendations for international students: Required—TOEFL (minimum score 550 paper-based; 213 computer-based). *Application deadline:* Applications are processed on a rolling basis. Application fee: $25. Electronic applications accepted. *Expenses:* Contact institution. *Financial support:* In 2009–10, 5 students received support. Federal Work-Study and scholarships/grants available. Support available to part-time students. Financial award application deadline: 6/1; financial award applicants required to submit FAFSA. *Unit head:* Dr. Ted Lerud, Associate Dean of the Faculty, 630-617-3661, Fax: 630-617-6415, E-mail: gradadm@elmhurst.edu. *Application contact:* Elizabeth D. Kuebler, Director of Adult and Graduate Admission, 630-617-3069, Fax: 630-617-5501, E-mail: betsyk@elmhurst.edu.

Elon University, Program in Business Administration, Elon, NC 27244-2010. Offers MBA. *Accreditation:* AACSB. Part-time and evening/weekend programs available. *Faculty:* 20 full-time (7 women), 1 (woman) part-time/adjunct. *Students:* 141 part-time (54 women); includes 20 minority (11 African Americans, 1 American Indian/Alaska Native, 7 Asian Americans or Pacific Islanders, 1 Hispanic American), 5 international. Average age 31. 107 applicants, 63% accepted, 52 enrolled. In 2009, 46 master's awarded. *Entrance requirements:* For master's, GMAT. Additional exam requirements/recommendations for international students: Required—TOEFL (minimum score 550 paper-based; 213 computer-based; 79 iBT). *Application deadline:* For fall admission, 8/1 priority date for domestic students; for spring admission, 2/1 priority date for domestic students. Applications are processed on a rolling basis. Application fee: $50. Electronic applications accepted. *Financial support:* In 2009–10, 4 students received support. Federal Work-Study and scholarships/grants available. Support available to part-time students. Financial award application deadline: 3/15; financial award applicants required to submit FAFSA. *Faculty research:* Business ethics, international business and global economics, sales force management, sustainable business practices, consumer behavior. *Unit head:* Dr. William Burpit, Director, 336-278-5949, Fax: 336-278-5952, E-mail: wburpitt@elon.edu. *Application contact:* Art Fadde, Director of Graduate Admissions, 800-334-8448 Ext. 3, Fax: 336-278-7699, E-mail: afadde@elon.edu.

Embry-Riddle Aeronautical University, Daytona Beach Campus Graduate Program, Department of Business Administration, Daytona Beach, FL 32114-3900. Offers business administration in aviation (MBAA). *Accreditation:* ACBSP. Part-time and evening/weekend programs available. Postbaccalaureate distance learning degree programs offered (minimal on-campus study). *Faculty:* 1 part-time/adjunct (0 women). *Students:* 95 full-time (21 women), 71 part-time (26 women); includes 30 minority (16 African Americans, 7 Asian Americans or Pacific Islanders, 7 Hispanic Americans), 49 international. Average age 30. 96 applicants, 57% accepted, 42 enrolled. In 2009, 52 master's awarded. *Degree requirements:* For master's, thesis or alternative. *Entrance requirements:* For master's, minimum GPA of 2.5. Additional exam requirements/recommendations for international students: Required—TOEFL (minimum score 550 paper-based; 213 computer-based; 79 iBT). *Application deadline:* For fall admission, 8/1 priority date for domestic students; for spring admission, 12/1 priority date for domestic students. Applications are processed on a rolling basis. Application fee: $50. *Expenses:* Tuition: Full-time $13,740; part-time $1145 per credit hour. *Financial support:* In 2009–10, 39 students received support, including 21 research assistantships with partial tuition reimbursements available (averaging $4,492 per year), 3 teaching assistantships (averaging $4,492 per year); career-related internships or fieldwork, Federal Work-Study, and unspecified assistantships also available. Support available to part-time students. Financial award application deadline: 4/15; financial award applicants required to submit FAFSA. *Faculty research:* Aircraft safety operations analysis, energy consumption analysis, statistical analysis of general aviation accidents, airport funding strategies, industry assessment and marketing analysis for ENAER aerospace. Total annual research expenditures: $120,079. *Unit head:* Dr. Blaise Waguespack, Program Coordinator, 386-226-7235, Fax: 386-226-6696, E-mail: waguespb@erau.edu. *Application contact:* Keith Deaton, Director, International and Graduate Admissions, 800-388-3728, Fax: 386-226-7070, E-mail: graduate.admissions@erau.edu.

Embry-Riddle Aeronautical University Worldwide, Worldwide Headquarters, Program in Business Administration for Aviation, Daytona Beach, FL 32114-3900. Offers MBAA. *Faculty:* 16 full-time (2 women), 28 part-time/adjunct (9 women). *Students:* 137 full-time (22 women), 139 part-time (28 women); includes 83 minority (35 African Americans, 1 American Indian/Alaska Native, 18 Asian Americans or Pacific Islanders, 29 Hispanic Americans), 3 international. Average age 32. 181 applicants, 77% accepted, 104 enrolled. In 2009, 102 master's awarded. *Degree requirements:* For master's, thesis (for some programs). Application fee: $50. *Financial support:* In 2009–10, 22 students received support. *Unit head:* Dr. Martin A. Smith, Executive Vice President, 386-226-6961, Fax: 386-226-6984, E-mail: martin.smith@erau.edu. *Application contact:* Linda Dammer, Director of Admissions, 386-226-6910, Fax: 386-226-6984, E-mail: ecinfo@erau.edu.

Emmanuel College, Graduate Programs, Program in Management, Boston, MA 02115. Offers biopharmaceutical leadership (MSM); management (MSM); management and leadership (Certificate); research administration (MSM, Certificate). Part-time and evening/weekend programs available. Postbaccalaureate distance learning degree programs offered. *Faculty:* 1 (woman) full-time, 18 part-time/adjunct (4 women). *Students:* 7 full-time (6 women), 139 part-time (102 women); includes 30 minority (17 African Americans, 4 Asian Americans or Pacific Islanders, 9 Hispanic Americans). Average age 36. 66 applicants, 76% accepted, 50 enrolled. In 2009, 24 master's, 3 other advanced degrees awarded. *Degree requirements:* For master's, thesis or alternative. *Entrance requirements:* For master's, interview, essay, resume, 2 letters of recommendation, bachelor's degree. Additional exam requirements/recommendations for international students: Required—TOEFL (minimum score 600 paper-based; 250 computer-based). *Application deadline:* For fall admission, 8/15 priority date for domestic students; for spring admission, 12/8 priority date for domestic students. Applications are processed on a rolling basis. Application fee: $50. Electronic applications accepted. *Expenses:* Tuition: Part-time $665 per credit. *Unit head:* Dr. Judith Marley, Dean, Graduate and Professional Programs, 617-735-9700, Fax: 617-507-0434, E-mail: gpp@emmanuel.edu. *Application contact:* Enrollment Counselor, 617-735-9700, Fax: 617-507-0434, E-mail: gpp@emmanuel.edu.

Emory University, Goizueta Business School, Doctoral Program in Business, Atlanta, GA 30322-1100. Offers accounting (PhD); finance (PhD); information systems (PhD); marketing (PhD); organization and management (PhD). *Faculty:* 57 full-time (11 women). *Students:* 37 full-time (14 women); includes 8 minority (3 African Americans, 4 Asian Americans or Pacific Islanders, 1 Hispanic American), 19 international. Average age 30. 218 applicants, 9% accepted, 9 enrolled. In 2009, 11 doctorates awarded. *Degree requirements:* For doctorate, comprehensive exam, thesis/dissertation. *Entrance requirements:* For doctorate, GMAT (strongly preferred) or GRE. Additional exam requirements/recommendations for international students: Required—TOEFL (minimum score 250 computer-based). *Application deadline:* For fall admission, 1/3 priority date for domestic and international students. Application fee: $50. Electronic applications accepted. *Unit head:* Dr. Lawrence Benveniste, Dean, 404-727-6377, Fax: 404-727-0868, E-mail: larry_benveniste@bus.emory.edu. *Application contact:* Allison Gilmore, Director of Admissions and Student Services, 404-727-6353, Fax: 404-727-5337, E-mail: phd@bus.emory.edu.

Emory University, Goizueta Business School, Evening MBA Program, Atlanta, GA 30322-1100. Offers MBA. Part-time and evening/weekend programs available. *Faculty:* 83 full-time

(19 women), 17 part-time/adjunct (3 women). *Students:* 318 part-time (87 women); includes 84 minority (26 African Americans, 1 American Indian/Alaska Native, 45 Asian Americans or Pacific Islanders, 12 Hispanic Americans), 44 international. Average age 30. 221 applicants, 70% accepted, 106 enrolled. In 2009, 122 master's awarded. *Entrance requirements:* For master's, GMAT. Additional exam requirements/recommendations for international students: Required—TOEFL; Recommended—IELTS, TWE. *Application deadline:* For fall admission, 6/1 for domestic students. Applications are processed on a rolling basis. Application fee: $150. Electronic applications accepted. *Financial support:* In 2009–10, 188 students received support. Application deadline: 4/1. *Unit head:* Lawrence Benveniste, Dean, 404-727-6377, Fax: 404-727-0868, E-mail: larry_benveniste@bus.emory.edu. *Application contact:* Julie Barefoot, Associate Dean, 404-727-6311, Fax: 404-727-4612, E-mail: admissions@bus.emory.edu.

Emory University, Goizueta Business School, Executive MBA Program, Atlanta, GA 30322-1100. Offers EMBA, WEMBA. *Students:* 83 full-time (17 women); includes 19 minority (10 African Americans, 8 Asian Americans or Pacific Islanders, 1 Hispanic American), 11 international. *Unit head:* Lawrence Benveniste, Dean, 404-727-6377, Fax: 404-727-0868, E-mail: larry_benveniste@bus.emory.edu. *Application contact:* Julie Barefoot, Associate Dean, 404-727-6311, Fax: 404-727-4612, E-mail: admissions@bus.emory.edu.

Emory University, Goizueta Business School, Full Time MBA Program, Atlanta, GA 30322-1100. Offers MBA. *Faculty:* 83 full-time (19 women), 17 part-time/adjunct (3 women). *Students:* 375 full-time (119 women); includes 77 minority (37 African Americans, 1 American Indian/Alaska Native, 29 Asian Americans or Pacific Islanders, 10 Hispanic Americans), 118 international. Average age 28. 1,241 applicants, 32% accepted, 170 enrolled. In 2009, 222 master's awarded. *Entrance requirements:* For master's, GMAT. Additional exam requirements/recommendations for international students: Required—TOEFL (minimum score 600 paper-based; 100 iBT), IELTS, Pearson Test of English. *Application deadline:* For fall admission, 12/1 for domestic and international students; for winter admission, 2/1 priority date for domestic students, 2/1 for international students; for spring admission, 3/1 for domestic students. Applications are processed on a rolling basis. Application fee: $150. Electronic applications accepted. *Financial support:* In 2009–10, 236 students received support; fellowships, research assistantships, teaching assistantships, career-related internships or fieldwork, Federal Work-Study, institutionally sponsored loans, scholarships/grants, and unspecified assistantships available. Financial award application deadline: 2/1; financial award applicants required to submit FAFSA. *Unit head:* Lawrence Benveniste, Dean, 404-727-6377, Fax: 404-727-0868, E-mail: larry_benveniste@bus.emory.edu. *Application contact:* Julie Barefoot, Associate Dean, 404-727-6311, Fax: 404-727-4612, E-mail: admissions@bus.emory.edu.

Emporia State University, School of Graduate Studies, School of Business, Department of Business Administration and Education, Emporia, KS 66801-5087. Offers business administration (MBA); business education (MS). *Accreditation:* NCATE (one or more programs are accredited). Part-time programs available. Postbaccalaureate distance learning degree programs offered (minimal on-campus study). *Faculty:* 18 full-time (6 women). *Students:* 71 full-time (40 women), 40 part-time (24 women); includes 5 minority (1 African American, 3 Asian Americans or Pacific Islanders, 1 Hispanic American), 63 international. 32 applicants, 97% accepted, 30 enrolled. In 2009, 44 master's awarded. *Entrance requirements:* For master's, GMAT (MBA), appropriate bachelor's degree. Additional exam requirements/recommendations for international students: Required—TOEFL (minimum score 520 paper-based; 133 computer-based; 68 iBT). *Application deadline:* For fall admission, 8/15 priority date for domestic students. Applications are processed on a rolling basis. Application fee: $30 ($75 for international students). Electronic applications accepted. *Expenses:* Tuition, state resident: full-time $4154; part-time $173 per credit hour. Tuition, nonresident: full-time $12,864; part-time $536 per credit hour. Required fees: $948; $58 per credit hour. Tuition and fees vary according to campus/location. *Financial support:* In 2009–10, 3 research assistantships with full tuition reimbursements (averaging $4,706 per year) were awarded; career-related internships or fieldwork, Federal Work-Study, institutionally sponsored loans, health care benefits, and unspecified assistantships also available. Financial award application deadline: 3/15; financial award applicants required to submit FAFSA. *Unit head:* Dr. Jack Sterett, Chair, 620-341-5345, Fax: 620-341-6345, E-mail: jsteret@emporia.edu. *Application contact:* Dr. Donald Miller, Director, MBA Program, 620-341-5456, Fax: 620-341-6523, E-mail: dmiller1@emporia.edu.

Endicott College, Van Loan School of Graduate and Professional Studies, Program in Business Administration, Beverly, MA 01915-2096. Offers MBA. Part-time and evening/weekend programs available. *Faculty:* 3 full-time (1 woman), 22 part-time/adjunct (6 women). *Students:* 77 full-time (39 women), 79 part-time (42 women); includes 3 minority (1 African American, 1 Asian American or Pacific Islander, 1 Hispanic American), 4 international. Average age 32. 120 applicants, 96% accepted, 115 enrolled. In 2009, 57 master's awarded. *Degree requirements:* For master's, thesis, project. *Entrance requirements:* For master's, GMAT, letters of recommendation, resume. Additional exam requirements/recommendations for international students: Required—TOEFL. *Application deadline:* Applications are processed on a rolling basis. Application fee: $50. *Expenses:* Contact institution. *Financial support:* Tuition waivers (full) available. *Faculty research:* Adult learning and development, supply chain management, marketing, ethics. *Unit head:* Richard Benedetto, Associate Dean of Graduate School, 978-232-2744, Fax: 978-232-3000, E-mail: rbenedet@endicott.edu. *Application contact:* Richard Benedetto, Associate Dean of Graduate School, 978-232-2744, Fax: 978-232-3000, E-mail: rbenedet@endicott.edu.

Everest University, Department of Business Administration, Tampa, FL 33614-5899. Offers accounting (MBA); human resources (MBA); international business (MBA). Part-time and evening/weekend programs available. *Degree requirements:* For master's, thesis optional. *Entrance requirements:* For master's, GMAT or GRE General Test, minimum GPA of 3.0.

Everest University, Division of Business Administration, Orlando, FL 32810-5674. Offers MBA. Part-time and evening/weekend programs available. *Degree requirements:* For master's, thesis or alternative.

Everest University, Graduate Programs, Jacksonville, FL 32256. Offers business (MBA); criminal justice (MS).

Everest University, Graduate School of Business, Clearwater, FL 33759. Offers MBA. *Faculty research:* Management fads, learning styles, effective use of technology.

Everest University, Program in Business Administration, Melbourne, FL 32935-6657. Offers MBA.

Everest University, Program in Business Administration, Tampa, FL 33619. Offers MBA. Part-time and evening/weekend programs available. Postbaccalaureate distance learning degree programs offered (minimal on-campus study). *Faculty:* 2 part-time/adjunct (1 woman). *Students:* 4 full-time (3 women), 21 part-time (16 women); includes 8 African Americans, 5 Hispanic Americans. Average age 43. In 2009, 10 master's awarded. *Entrance requirements:* Additional exam requirements/recommendations for international students: Required—TOEFL (minimum score 550 paper-based; 213 computer-based). *Application deadline:* Applications are processed on a rolling basis. Application fee: $25. *Expenses:* Tuition: Full-time $12,120; part-time $505 per credit hour. Required fees: $60 per quarter. One-time fee: $245. *Financial support:* Institutionally sponsored loans and scholarships/grants available. *Unit head:* James Jehs, Chair, 813-621-0041 Ext. 140, Fax: 813-623-5769, E-mail: jjehs@cci.edu. *Application contact:* Shandretta Pointer, Admissions Office, 813-621-0041 Ext. 106, Fax: 813-628-0919, E-mail: spointer@cci.edu.

Everest University, Program in Business Administration, Orlando, FL 32819. Offers accounting (MBA); general management (MBA); human resources (MBA); international management (MBA).

Everest University, School of Business, Pompano Beach, FL 33062. Offers MBA. Part-time and evening/weekend programs available. *Entrance requirements:* For master's, minimum GPA of 3.0. *Faculty research:* E-learning.

Everglades University, Graduate Programs, Program in Business Administration, Boca Raton, FL 33431. Offers MBA. *Entrance requirements:* Additional exam requirements/recommendations for international students: Recommended—TOEFL (minimum score 500 paper-based; 173 computer-based). Electronic applications accepted.

Excelsior College, School of Business and Technology, Albany, NY 12203-5159. Offers MBA. Part-time and evening/weekend programs available. Postbaccalaureate distance learning degree programs offered (no on-campus study).

Fairfield University, Charles F. Dolan School of Business, Fairfield, CT 06824-5195. Offers accounting (MBA, MS, CAS); finance (MBA, MS, CAS); general management (MBA); human resource management (MBA, CAS); information systems and operations (MBA); information systems and operations management (CAS); international business (MBA, CAS); marketing (MBA, CAS); taxation (MBA, MS). *Accreditation:* AACSB. Part-time and evening/weekend programs available. *Degree requirements:* For master's, capstone course. *Entrance requirements:* For master's, GMAT (minimum score 500), 2 letters of reference, resume, minimum GPA of 3.0. Additional exam requirements/recommendations for international students: Required—TOEFL (minimum score 550 paper-based; 213 computer-based; 80 iBT). Electronic applications accepted. *Expenses:* Contact institution. *Faculty research:* Optimization strategies, international finance, consumer behavior, financial market volatility, Internet marketing, supply chain analysis, tax issues.

Fairleigh Dickinson University, College at Florham, Anthony J. Petrocelli College of Continuing Studies, School of Administrative Science, Program in Administrative Science, Madison, NJ 07940-1099. Offers MAS. Application fee: $40. *Application contact:* Susan Brooman, University Director, Graduate Admissions, 973-443-8905, Fax: 973-443-8088, E-mail: grad@fdu.edu.

Fairleigh Dickinson University, College at Florham, Silberman College of Business, Madison, NJ 07940-1099. Offers EMBA, MBA, MS, Certificate, MA/MBA, MBA/MA. *Accreditation:* AACSB. Part-time and evening/weekend programs available. *Students:* 118 full-time (51 women), 379 part-time (143 women), 32 international. Average age 33. 255 applicants, 67% accepted, 107 enrolled. In 2009, 142 master's awarded. *Application deadline:* Applications are processed on a rolling basis. Application fee: $40. *Unit head:* Dr. William Moore, Dean, 973-443-8500. *Application contact:* Susan Brooman, University Director of Graduate Admissions.

Fairleigh Dickinson University, College at Florham, Silberman College of Business, Departments of Management, Marketing, and Entrepreneurial Studies, Program in Management, Madison, NJ 07940-1099. Offers evolving technology (Certificate); management (MBA); MBA/MA. *Students:* 8 full-time (4 women), 32 part-time (15 women), 3 international. Average age 31. 25 applicants, 56% accepted, 8 enrolled. In 2009, 17 master's awarded. *Application deadline:* Applications are processed on a rolling basis. Application fee: $40.

Fairleigh Dickinson University, College at Florham, Silberman College of Business, Executive MBA Programs, Executive MBA Program in Management, Madison, NJ 07940-1099. Offers EMBA. *Students:* 2 full-time (0 women), 54 part-time (4 women), 3 international. Average age 38. 4 applicants, 75% accepted, 3 enrolled. *Application deadline:* Applications are processed on a rolling basis. Application fee: $40.

Fairleigh Dickinson University, Metropolitan Campus, Anthony J. Petrocelli College of Continuing Studies, School of Administrative Science, Program in Administrative Science, Teaneck, NJ 07666-1914. Offers MAS, Certificate. *Students:* 87 full-time (49 women), 447 part-time (197 women), 30 international. Average age 38. 220 applicants, 98% accepted, 161 enrolled. In 2009, 323 master's awarded. *Application deadline:* Applications are processed on a rolling basis. *Unit head:* Ronald Calissi, Director/Executive Associate Dean, 201-692-2000. *Application contact:* Susan Brooman, University Director of Graduate Admissions, 201-692-2554, Fax: 201-692-2560, E-mail: globaleducation@fdu.edu.

Fairleigh Dickinson University, Metropolitan Campus, Silberman College of Business, Teaneck, NJ 07666-1914. Offers EMBA, MBA, MS, Certificate, MBA/MA. *Accreditation:* AACSB. *Students:* 340 full-time (124 women), 134 part-time (58 women), 237 international. Average age 29. 623 applicants, 61% accepted, 121 enrolled. In 2009, 223 master's awarded. *Entrance requirements:* For master's, GMAT. *Application deadline:* Applications are processed on a rolling basis. Application fee: $40. *Unit head:* Dr. William Moore, Dean, 201-692-2000. *Application contact:* Susan Brooman, University Director of Graduate Admissions, 201-692-2554, Fax: 201-692-2560, E-mail: globaleducation@fdu.edu.

Fairleigh Dickinson University, Metropolitan Campus, Silberman College of Business, Departments of Management, Marketing, and Entrepreneurial Studies, Program in Management, Teaneck, NJ 07666-1914. Offers management (MBA); management information systems (Certificate). *Accreditation:* AACSB. *Students:* 34 full-time (12 women), 14 part-time (7 women), 29 international. Average age 27. 131 applicants, 43% accepted, 15 enrolled. In 2009, 19 master's awarded. *Application deadline:* Applications are processed on a rolling basis. Application fee: $40. *Application contact:* Susan Brooman, University Director of Graduate Admissions, 201-692-2554, Fax: 201-692-2560, E-mail: globaleducation@fdu.edu.

Fairmont State University, Graduate Studies, Program in Business Administration, Fairmont, WV 26554. Offers MBA. *Accreditation:* ACBSP. *Entrance requirements:* For master's, GRE, MAT, or GMAT, minimum overall undergraduate GPA of 2.75 or 3.0 on the last 60 hours.

Fashion Institute of Technology, School of Graduate Studies, Program in Global Fashion Management, New York, NY 10001-5992. Offers MPS. Offered in collaboration with Hong Kong Polytechnic University and Institut Francais de la Mode. *Entrance requirements:* Additional exam requirements/recommendations for international students: Required—TOEFL (minimum score 550 paper-based; 213 computer-based). Electronic applications accepted. *Expenses:* Tuition, state resident: full-time $8198; part-time $342 per credit. Tuition, nonresident: full-time $12,972; part-time $541 per credit. Required fees: $450.

Fayetteville State University, Graduate School, Program in Business Administration, Fayetteville, NC 28301-4298. Offers MBA. *Accreditation:* AACSB. *Faculty:* 16 full-time (6 women), 1 (woman) part-time/adjunct. *Students:* 11 full-time (5 women), 38 part-time (18 women); includes 21 minority (12 African Americans, 5 Asian Americans or Pacific Islanders, 4 Hispanic Americans), 2 international. Average age 32. 14 applicants, 100% accepted, 14 enrolled. In 2009, 28 master's awarded. *Entrance requirements:* For master's, GMAT. *Application deadline:* For fall admission, 4/15 for domestic students; for spring admission, 10/15 for domestic students. *Faculty research:* Business ethics, optimization and business simulation, consumer behavior, e-commerce and supply chain management, financial institutions. Total annual research expenditures: $15,000. *Unit head:* Dr. Assad Tavakoli, MBA Director/Assistant Dean, 910-672-1527, Fax: 910-672-1849, E-mail: atavakoli@uncfsu.edu. *Application contact:* Roxie Shabazz, Associate Vice-Chancellor for Enrollment Management, 910-672-1784, Fax: 910-672-2209, E-mail: rshabazz@uncfsu.edu.

Felician College, Program in Business, Lodi, NJ 07644-2117. Offers accounting (MBA); business administration (MBA); innovation and entrepreneurship (MBA); management (MBA). Part-time and evening/weekend programs available. *Students:* 3 full-time (2 women), 80 part-time (46 women); includes 16 minority (8 African Americans, 3 Asian Americans or Pacific Islanders, 5 Hispanic Americans), 5 international. 28 applicants, 89% accepted, 24 enrolled. *Entrance requirements:* For master's, GMAT. *Application deadline:* Applications are processed on a rolling basis. Application fee: $40. *Unit head:* Dr. Beth Castiglia, Dean, Division of Business and Management Services, 201-559-6140, E-mail: mctaggartp@felician.edu. *Application contact:* Tamara Vaughn, Senior Assistant Director, Graduate Admissions, 201-559-6097, Fax: 201-559-6138, E-mail: vaughant@felician.edu.

See Close-Up on page 243.

Ferris State University, College of Business, Big Rapids, MI 49307. Offers application development (MSISM); business intelligence and infomatics (MBA); database administration (MSISM); design and innovation management process (MBA); e-business (MSISM); networking (MSISM); quality management (MBA); security (MSISM). *Accreditation:* ACBSP. Part-time and

Business Administration and Management—General

Ferris State University (continued)
evening/weekend programs available. *Faculty:* 10 full-time (3 women), 2 part-time/adjunct (both women). *Students:* 33 full-time (6 women), 134 part-time (65 women); includes 13 minority (8 African Americans, 2 American Indian/Alaska Native, 2 Asian Americans or Pacific Islanders, 1 Hispanic American), 33 international. Average age 30. 120 applicants, 31% accepted, 26 enrolled. In 2009, 66 master's awarded. *Entrance requirements:* For master's, GRE or GMAT (waived if GPA is 3.5 or better), minimum GPA of 3.0 in CIS and business core, 2.75 overall; writing sample; 3 letters of reference; resume. Additional exam requirements/recommendations for international students: Required—TOEFL (minimum score 500 paper-based; 173 computer-based; 64 iBT). *Application deadline:* For fall admission, 7/1 priority date for domestic students, 6/15 for international students; for winter admission, 11/1 priority date for domestic students, 10/15 for international students; for spring admission, 3/1 priority date for domestic students, 2/15 for international students. Applications are processed on a rolling basis. Application fee: $30 for international students. Electronic applications accepted. *Financial support:* In 2009–10, 14 teaching assistantships were awarded; career-related internships or fieldwork, Federal Work-Study, and unspecified assistantships also available. Support available to part-time students. Financial award applicants required to submit FAFSA. *Faculty research:* Quality improvement, client/server end-user computing, information management and policy, security, digital forensics. *Unit head:* Dr. David Steenstra, Department Chair, 231-591-2168, Fax: 231-591-2973, E-mail: yosts@ferris.edu. *Application contact:* Shannon Yost, Department Secretary, 231-591-2168, Fax: 231-591-2973, E-mail: yosts@ferris.edu.

Fitchburg State University, Division of Graduate and Continuing Education, Program in Business Administration, Fitchburg, MA 01420-2697. Offers accounting (MBA); human resource management (MBA); management (MBA). Part-time and evening/weekend programs available. Postbaccalaureate distance learning degree programs offered (no on-campus study). *Students:* 24 full-time (9 women), 58 part-time (33 women); includes 10 minority (4 African Americans, 1 Asian American or Pacific Islander, 5 Hispanic Americans), 15 international. Average age 32. 64 applicants, 91% accepted, 27 enrolled. In 2009, 56 master's awarded. *Entrance requirements:* For master's, GMAT, minimum GPA of 2.8, letters of recommendation, resume. Additional exam requirements/recommendations for international students: Required—TOEFL (minimum score 550 paper-based; 213 computer-based; 79 iBT). *Application deadline:* Applications are processed on a rolling basis. Application fee: $25 ($50 for international students). *Expenses:* Tuition, area resident: Part-time $150 per credit. Tuition, state resident: part-time $150 per credit. Tuition, nonresident: part-time $150 per credit. Required fees: $120 per credit. *Financial support:* In 2009–10, research assistantships with partial tuition reimbursements (averaging $5,500 per year); Federal Work-Study, scholarships/grants, and unspecified assistantships also available. Support available to part-time students. Financial award application deadline: 3/1; financial award applicants required to submit FAFSA. *Unit head:* Joseph McAloon, Chair, 978-665-3745, Fax: 978-665-3658, E-mail: gce@fsc.edu. *Application contact:* Director of Admissions, 978-665-3144, Fax: 978-665-4540, E-mail: admissions@fsc.edu.

Florida Agricultural and Mechanical University, Division of Graduate Studies, Research, and Continuing Education, School of Business and Industry, Tallahassee, FL 32307-3200. Offers accounting (MBA); finance (MBA); management information systems (MBA); marketing (MBA). *Faculty:* 42 full-time (28 women). *Students:* 71 full-time (45 women), 15 part-time (9 women); includes 80 minority (all African Americans), 4 international. In 2009, 90 master's awarded. *Degree requirements:* For master's, residency. *Entrance requirements:* For master's, GMAT, minimum GPA of 3.0. *Application deadline:* For fall admission, 5/18 for domestic students, 12/18 for international students; for spring admission, 11/12 for domestic students, 5/12 for international students. Application fee: $30. *Financial support:* Fellowships, Federal Work-Study and scholarships/grants available. *Unit head:* Dr. Amos Bradford, Interim Dean, 850-599-3565. *Application contact:* Dr. Amos Bradford, Interim Dean, 850-599-3565.

Florida Atlantic University, College of Business, Boca Raton, FL 33431-0991. Offers Exec MBA, M Ac, M Tax, MBA, MHA, MS, PhD, Certificate. *Accreditation:* AACSB. Part-time and evening/weekend programs available. Postbaccalaureate distance learning degree programs offered (minimal on-campus study). *Faculty:* 124 full-time (42 women), 95 part-time/adjunct (23 women). *Students:* 415 full-time (177 women), 854 part-time (434 women); includes 389 minority (137 African Americans, 1 American Indian/Alaska Native, 80 Asian Americans or Pacific Islanders, 171 Hispanic Americans), 67 international. Average age 32. 1,225 applicants, 51% accepted, 197 enrolled. In 2009, 331 master's, 7 doctorates awarded. *Degree requirements:* For master's, thesis optional; for doctorate, comprehensive exam, thesis/dissertation. *Entrance requirements:* For master's, GMAT, minimum GPA of 3.0; for doctorate, GMAT, minimum graduate GPA of 3.5. Additional exam requirements/recommendations for international students: Required—TOEFL (minimum score 600 paper-based; 250 computer-based). *Application deadline:* For fall admission, 7/11 priority date for domestic students, 2/15 priority date for international students; for winter admission, 11/1 priority date for domestic students, 8/15 priority date for international students; for spring admission, 4/1 priority date for domestic students, 1/15 priority date for international students. Applications are processed on a rolling basis. Application fee: $30. *Expenses:* Tuition, state resident: full-time $7055; part-time $293.94 per credit hour. Tuition, nonresident: full-time $22,096; part-time $920.66 per credit hour. *Financial support:* Fellowships with partial tuition reimbursements, research assistantships with partial tuition reimbursements, teaching assistantships with full tuition reimbursements, career-related internships or fieldwork, Federal Work-Study, institutionally sponsored loans, tuition waivers (full and partial), and unspecified assistantships available. Support available to part-time students. Financial award application deadline: 3/1. *Faculty research:* International business, MIS, financial decision making, marketing policy, strategy. *Unit head:* Dr. Dennis Coates, Dean, 561-297-3635, Fax: 561-297-3686, E-mail: coates@fau.edu. *Application contact:* Fredrick G. Taylor, Graduate Adviser, 561-297-3196, Fax: 561-297-1315, E-mail: ftaylor@fau.edu.

Florida Gulf Coast University, Lutgert College of Business, Master of Business Administration Program, Fort Myers, FL 33965-6565. Offers MBA. *Accreditation:* AACSB. Part-time and evening/weekend programs available. *Faculty:* 63 full-time (20 women), 19 part-time/adjunct (2 women). *Students:* 120 full-time (56 women), 66 part-time (35 women); includes 24 minority (4 African Americans, 1 American Indian/Alaska Native, 4 Asian Americans or Pacific Islanders, 15 Hispanic Americans), 4 international. Average age 29. 94 applicants, 79% accepted, 55 enrolled. In 2009, 60 master's awarded. *Entrance requirements:* For master's, GMAT, minimum GPA of 3.0. Additional exam requirements/recommendations for international students: Required—TOEFL (minimum score 550 paper-based; 213 computer-based). *Application deadline:* For fall admission, 6/1 priority date for domestic students; for spring admission, 11/1 for domestic students. Applications are processed on a rolling basis. Application fee: $30. Electronic applications accepted. *Faculty research:* Fraud in audits, production planning in cell manufacturing systems, collaborative learning in distance courses, characteristics of minority and women-owned businesses. *Unit head:* Dr. Gerald Schoenfeld, Chair, 239-590-7300, Fax: 239-590-7330. *Application contact:* Carol Burnette, Associate Dean, 239-590-7350, Fax: 239-590-7330, E-mail: burnette@fgcu.edu.

Florida Institute of Technology, Graduate Programs, College of Business, Campus Programs, Melbourne, FL 32901-6975. Offers business administration (EMBA, MBA). Part-time and evening/weekend programs available. *Faculty:* 10 full-time (3 women), 3 part-time/adjunct (0 women). *Students:* 20 full-time (10 women), 24 part-time (12 women); includes 4 minority (1 African American, 1 American Indian/Alaska Native, 2 Hispanic Americans), 14 international. Average age 28. 107 applicants, 42% accepted, 17 enrolled. In 2009, 23 master's awarded. *Degree requirements:* For master's, thesis optional. *Entrance requirements:* For master's, GMAT or master's degree with minimum GPA of 3.25, minimum GPA of 3.25, 2 letters of recommendation, resume. Additional exam requirements/recommendations for international students: Required—TOEFL (minimum score 550 paper-based; 213 computer-based; 79 iBT). *Application deadline:* For fall admission, 4/1 for international students; for spring admission, 9/30 for international students. Applications are processed on a rolling basis. Application fee: $50. Electronic applications accepted. *Expenses:* Tuition: Part-time $1015 per credit. Tuition and fees vary according to campus/location and program. *Financial support:* Career-related internships or fieldwork, institutionally sponsored loans, unspecified assistantships, and tuition remissions available. Support available to part-time students. Financial award application deadline: 3/1; financial award applicants required to submit FAFSA. *Faculty research:* Investment analysis, marketing research, strategy analysis, ethics, small business. Total annual research expenditures: $731,951. *Unit head:* Dr. Robert E. Niebuhr, Dean, 321-674-7327, Fax: 321-674-8896, E-mail: rniebuhr@fit.edu. *Application contact:* Thomas M. Shea, Director of Graduate Admissions, 321-674-7577, Fax: 321-723-9468, E-mail: tshea@fit.edu.

See Close-Up on page 245.

Florida Institute of Technology, Graduate Programs, College of Business, Extended Studies Division, Melbourne, FL 32901-6975. Offers acquisition and contract management (PMBA); business administration (PMBA); computer information systems (MS); e-business (PMBA); human resource management (PMBA); human resources management (MS); logistics management (MS), including humanitarian and disaster relief logistics; management (MS), including acquisition and contract management, e-business, human resource management, information systems, logistics management, management, transportation management; material acquisition management (MS); project management (MS), including information systems, operations research; public administration (MPA); quality management (MS); space management (MS); space systems (MS); systems management (MS), including information systems, operations research, systems management. Part-time and evening/weekend programs available. Postbaccalaureate distance learning degree programs offered (no on-campus study). *Faculty:* 12 full-time (3 women), 117 part-time/adjunct (20 women). *Students:* 74 full-time (32 women), 1,041 part-time (484 women); includes 343 minority (240 African Americans, 12 American Indian/Alaska Native, 44 Asian Americans or Pacific Islanders, 47 Hispanic Americans), 22 international. Average age 35. 520 applicants, 72% accepted, 279 enrolled. In 2009, 509 master's awarded. *Degree requirements:* For master's, capstone course. *Entrance requirements:* For master's, GMAT or resume showing 8 years of supervised experience, minimum GPA of 3.0, 2 letters of recommendation, resume. Additional exam requirements/recommendations for international students: Required—TOEFL (minimum score 550 paper-based; 213 computer-based; 79 iBT). *Application deadline:* For fall admission, 4/1 for international students; for spring admission, 9/30 for international students. Applications are processed on a rolling basis. Application fee: $50. Electronic applications accepted. *Expenses:* Tuition: Part-time $1015 per credit. Tuition and fees vary according to campus/location and program. *Financial support:* Application deadline: 3/1. *Unit head:* Dr. Clifford Bragdon, Dean, 321-674-8821, Fax: 321-674-7597, E-mail: cbragdon@fit.edu. *Application contact:* Carolyn Farrior, Director of Graduate Admissions Online Learning and Off Campus Programs, 321-674-7118, Fax: 321-674-8216, E-mail: cfarrior@fit.edu.

Florida International University, Alvah H. Chapman, Jr. Graduate School of Business, Program in Business Administration, Miami, FL 33199. Offers EMBA, IMBA, MBA, PMBA, PhD. *Accreditation:* AACSB. Part-time and evening/weekend programs available. *Students:* 483 full-time (258 women), 348 part-time (171 women); includes 453 minority (59 African Americans, 26 Asian Americans or Pacific Islanders, 368 Hispanic Americans), 226 international. Average age 32. 791 applicants, 38% accepted, 285 enrolled. In 2009, 295 master's, 12 doctorates awarded. *Degree requirements:* For doctorate, comprehensive exam, thesis/dissertation. *Entrance requirements:* For master's, GMAT or GRE (depending on program), minimum GPA of 3.0 (upper-level coursework); for doctorate, GMAT or GRE, minimum GPA of 3.0 in post-secondary education; letter of intent; 3 letters of recommendation; resume. Additional exam requirements/recommendations for international students: Required—TOEFL (minimum score 550 paper-based; 213 computer-based; 80 iBT), or IELTS (minimum score 6.5). *Application deadline:* For fall admission, 6/1 for domestic students, 4/1 for international students; for spring admission, 10/1 for domestic students, 9/1 for international students. Applications are processed on a rolling basis. Application fee: $30. Electronic applications accepted. *Expenses:* Contact institution. *Financial support:* Institutionally sponsored loans, scholarships/grants, and unspecified assistantships available. Financial award application deadline: 3/1; financial award applicants required to submit FAFSA. *Faculty research:* Taxation, financial and managerial accounting, human resource management, multinational corps, strategy, international business, auditing, artificial intelligence, international banking, investments; entrepreneurship. *Unit head:* Dr. Christos Koulamas, Senior Associate Dean, 305-348-2830, Fax: 305-348-4126, E-mail: koulamas@fiu.edu. *Application contact:* Anna Pietraszek, Director, Chapman Graduate School Admissions and Recruiting, 305-348-7299, Fax: 305-348-2368, E-mail: pietrasa@fiu.edu.

Florida Memorial University, School of Business, Miami-Dade, FL 33054. Offers MBA. *Accreditation:* ACBSP. Part-time programs available. *Entrance requirements:* For master's, GMAT, 3 letters of recommendation.

Florida Southern College, Program in Business Administration, Lakeland, FL 33801-5698. Offers accounting (MBA); business administration (MBA); international business (MBA). Part-time and evening/weekend programs available. *Entrance requirements:* For master's, GMAT or GRE General Test, minimum GPA of 2.75. Additional exam requirements/recommendations for international students: Required—TOEFL (minimum score 550 paper-based). *Expenses:* Contact institution.

See Close-Up on page 247.

Florida State University, The Graduate School, College of Business, Tallahassee, FL 32306-1110. Offers accounting (M Acc), including accounting information services, assurance services, corporate accounting, taxation; business administration (MBA, PhD), including accounting (PhD), finance (PhD), management information systems (PhD), marketing (PhD), organizational behavior (PhD), risk management and insurance (PhD), strategic management (PhD); finance (MS); insurance (MSM); management information systems (MS); JD/MBA; MSW/MBA. *Accreditation:* AACSB. Part-time programs available. Postbaccalaureate distance learning degree programs offered (no on-campus study). *Faculty:* 107 full-time (31 women), 2 part-time/adjunct (0 women). *Students:* 212 full-time (73 women), 345 part-time (107 women); includes 123 minority (37 African Americans, 2 American Indian/Alaska Native, 48 Asian Americans or Pacific Islanders, 36 Hispanic Americans). Average age 30. 908 applicants, 43% accepted, 307 enrolled. In 2009, 257 master's, 18 doctorates awarded. Terminal master's awarded for partial completion of doctoral program. *Degree requirements:* For doctorate, comprehensive exam, thesis/dissertation. *Entrance requirements:* For master's, GMAT, work experience (MBA, MS), minimum GPA of 3.0, letters of recommendation; for doctorate, GMAT, minimum graduate GPA of 3.5, letters of recommendation. Additional exam requirements/recommendations for international students: Required—TOEFL (minimum score 600 paper-based; 80 computer-based); Recommended—IELTS (minimum score 6.5). *Application deadline:* For fall admission, 6/1 for domestic students, 5/1 for international students; for spring admission, 10/1 for domestic students, 9/1 for international students. Applications are processed on a rolling basis. Application fee: $30. Electronic applications accepted. *Expenses:* Tuition, state resident: full-time $7413. Tuition, nonresident: full-time $22,567. *Financial support:* In 2009–10, 102 students received support, including 32 fellowships with full tuition reimbursements available (averaging $6,900 per year), 30 research assistantships with full tuition reimbursements available (averaging $4,500 per year), 40 teaching assistantships with full tuition reimbursements available (averaging $11,500 per year); career-related internships or fieldwork, scholarships/grants, health care benefits, tuition waivers (full and partial), and unspecified assistantships also available. Support available to part-time students. Financial award application deadline: 1/1. *Unit head:* Dr. Caryn Beck-Dudley, Dean, 850-644-3090, Fax: 850-644-0915. *Application contact:* Lisa Beverly, Director, Graduate Programs Admissions, 850-644-6458, Fax: 850-644-0588, E-mail: lbeverly@cob.fsu.edu.

Fontbonne University, Graduate Programs, College of Global Business and Professional Studies, Options Program in Business Administration, St. Louis, MO 63105-3098. Offers MBA. *Accreditation:* ACBSP. Evening/weekend programs available. *Faculty:* 21 part-time/adjunct (6 women). *Students:* 119 full-time (84 women), 79 part-time (48 women); includes 110 minority (104 African Americans, 4 Asian Americans or Pacific Islanders, 2 Hispanic Americans). Average age 36. In 2009, 165 master's awarded. *Degree requirements:* For master's, applied management project. *Entrance requirements:* For master's, minimum GPA of 2.5. *Application deadline:* For fall admission, 8/1 priority date for domestic students. Applications are processed

on a rolling basis. Application fee: $25. *Expenses:* Contact institution. *Financial support:* Application deadline: 4/1. *Unit head:* Dean Linda Maurer, Executive Director, 314-889-1423, E-mail: lmaurer@fontbonne.edu. *Application contact:* Cindy Bluestone, Director of Marketing and Enrollment, 314-889-4576, Fax: 314-863-0917, E-mail: cbbushue@apollogrp.edu.

Fontbonne University, Graduate Programs, College of Global Business and Professional Studies, Options Program in Management, St. Louis, MO 63105-3098. Offers MM. *Accreditation:* ACBSP. Part-time and evening/weekend programs available. Postbaccalaureate distance learning degree programs offered. *Faculty:* 16 part-time/adjunct (4 women). *Students:* 88 full-time (71 women), 46 part-time (33 women); includes 72 minority (68 African Americans, 2 Asian Americans or Pacific Islanders, 2 Hispanic Americans), 1 international. Average age 41. In 2009, 62 master's awarded. *Application deadline:* For fall admission, 8/1 priority date for domestic students. Applications are processed on a rolling basis. Application fee: $25. *Expenses:* Contact institution. *Financial support:* Application deadline: 4/1. *Unit head:* Dean Linda Maurer, Dean of the College of Global Business and Professional Studies, 314-889-1423, Fax: 314-963-0327, E-mail: lmaurer@fontbonne.edu. *Application contact:* Fontbonne University OPTIONS, 314-863-2220, Fax: 314-963-0327, E-mail: cbbushue@apollogrp.edu.

Fontbonne University, Graduate Programs, College of Global Business and Professional Studies, Program in Business Administration, St. Louis, MO 63105-3098. Offers MBA. *Accreditation:* ACBSP. Part-time and evening/weekend programs available. *Faculty:* 1 (woman) full-time, 18 part-time/adjunct (6 women). *Students:* 39 full-time (19 women), 21 part-time (10 women); includes 12 minority (11 African Americans, 1 Asian American or Pacific Islander), 29 international. Average age 31. In 2009, 25 master's awarded. *Entrance requirements:* For master's, minimum GPA of 2.5. Additional exam requirements/recommendations for international students: Required—TOEFL (minimum score 450 paper-based; 133 computer-based; 45 iBT). *Application deadline:* For fall admission, 8/1 priority date for domestic and international students. Applications are processed on a rolling basis. Application fee: $25. *Expenses:* Tuition: Part-time $562 per credit hour. *Financial support:* Application deadline: 4/1. *Unit head:* Dr. Linda Maurer, Dean of College of Global Business and Professional Studies, 314-889-1423, E-mail: lmaurer@fontbonne.edu. *Application contact:* Fontbonne University OPTIONS, 314-863-2220, Fax: 314-963-0327, E-mail: options@fontbonne.edu.

Fordham University, Graduate School of Business Administration, New York, NY 10023. Offers accounting (MBA); communications and media management (MBA); executive business administration (EMBA); finance (MBA, MS); information systems (MBA, MS); management systems (MBA); marketing (MBA); media management (MS); taxation (MS); taxation and accounting (MTA);); JD/MBA; MBA/MIM; MS/MBA. *Accreditation:* AACSB. Part-time and evening/weekend programs available. *Entrance requirements:* For master's, GMAT, 2 letters of recommendation, resume. Additional exam requirements/recommendations for international students: Required—TOEFL (minimum score 600 paper-based; 250 computer-based; 100 iBT). Electronic applications accepted. *Expenses:* Contact institution.

Fort Hays State University, Graduate School, College of Business and Leadership, Department of Management and Marketing, Hays, KS 67601-4099. Offers management (MBA). *Degree requirements:* For master's, thesis optional. *Entrance requirements:* For master's, GMAT. Additional exam requirements/recommendations for international students: Required—TOEFL (minimum score 550 paper-based; 213 computer-based). Electronic applications accepted. *Faculty research:* Organizational behavior and performance appraisal, data processing, international marketing.

Framingham State University, Division of Graduate and Continuing Education, Program in Business Administration, Framingham, MA 01701-9101. Offers MBA. Part-time and evening/weekend programs available. *Entrance requirements:* For master's, GMAT, GRE, or MAT.

Franciscan University of Steubenville, Graduate Programs, Department of Business, Steubenville, OH 43952-1763. Offers MBA. Part-time and evening/weekend programs available. *Degree requirements:* For master's, research paper. *Entrance requirements:* For master's, GMAT, minimum undergraduate GPA of 2.5. *Expenses:* Contact institution.

Francis Marion University, Graduate Programs, School of Business, Florence, SC 29502-0547. Offers business (MBA); health management (MBA). *Accreditation:* AACSB. Part-time and evening/weekend programs available. *Faculty:* 16 full-time (2 women), 1 part-time/adjunct (0 women). *Students:* 7 full-time (3 women), 35 part-time (16 women); includes 12 minority (10 African Americans, 2 Asian Americans or Pacific Islanders), 2 international. Average age 38. 32 applicants, 28% accepted, 9 enrolled. In 2009, 10 degrees awarded. *Degree requirements:* For master's, comprehensive exam. *Entrance requirements:* For master's, GMAT. *Application deadline:* For fall admission, 3/15 priority date for domestic students; for spring admission, 10/15 priority date for domestic students. Applications are processed on a rolling basis. Application fee: $30. *Expenses:* Tuition, state resident: full-time $8345; part-time $417.25 per semester hour. Tuition, nonresident: full-time $16,690; part-time $814.50 per semester hour. Required fees: $335; $12.25 per semester hour. $30 per semester. *Financial support:* In 2009–10, 2 research assistantships (averaging $1,500 per year) were awarded; unspecified assistantships also available. Support available to part-time students. Financial award application deadline: 3/1; financial award applicants required to submit FAFSA. *Faculty research:* Ethics, directions of MBA, international business, regional economics, environmental issues. *Unit head:* Dr. M. Barry O'Brien, Dean, 843-661-1419, Fax: 843-661-1432, E-mail: mbobrien@fmarion.edu. *Application contact:* Dr. M. Barry O'Brien, Dean, 843-661-1419, Fax: 843-661-1432, E-mail: mbobrien@fmarion.edu.

Franklin Pierce University, Graduate Studies, Rindge, NH 03461-0060. Offers emerging network technology (Graduate Certificate); health practice management (MBA, Graduate Certificate); human resource management (MBA); human resources management (Graduate Certificate); information technology management (MS); leadership (MBA, DA), including transformational leadership (DA); nursing (MS); physical therapy (DPT); physician assistant (MPAS); sports facilities management (MS); teacher education (M Ed). *Accreditation:* APTA. Part-time programs available. Postbaccalaureate distance learning degree programs offered (no on-campus study). *Faculty:* 27 full-time (16 women), 18 part-time/adjunct (4 women). *Students:* 296 full-time (172 women), 249 part-time (165 women); includes 18 minority (5 African Americans, 7 Asian Americans or Pacific Islanders, 6 Hispanic Americans), 31 international. Average age 38. 227 applicants, 97% accepted, 185 enrolled. In 2009, 76 master's, 46 doctorates awarded. *Degree requirements:* For master's, concentrated original research projects; student teaching; fieldwork and/or internship; leadership project; for doctorate, concentrated original research projects, clinical fieldwork and/or internship, leadership project. *Entrance requirements:* For master's, minimum GPA of 2.5, 3 letters of recommendation; for doctorate, demonstrated success at previous academic institutions (minimum GPA of 2.5), 3 letters of recommendation, personal mission statement, interview; writing sample (for DA program). Additional exam requirements/recommendations for international students: Required—TOEFL (minimum score 550 paper-based; 195 computer-based). *Application deadline:* Applications are processed on a rolling basis. Application fee: $0. Electronic applications accepted. *Expenses:* Tuition: Part-time $1560 per course. Part-time tuition and fees vary according to degree level, campus/location and program. *Financial support:* In 2009–10, 36 students received support, including 22 teaching assistantships with full and partial tuition reimbursements available; career-related internships or fieldwork and unspecified assistantships also available. Support available to part-time students. Financial award applicants required to submit FAFSA. *Faculty research:* Evidence based practice in sports physical therapy, human resource management in economic crisis, leadership in nursing, innovation in sports facility management, differentiated learning and understanding by design. *Unit head:* Dr. Robert G. Goddard, Assistant Dean, 603-899-4361, Fax: 603-229-4580, E-mail: goddardr@franklinpierce.edu. *Application contact:* 800-325-1090, Fax: 603-898-0827, E-mail: gpsadmin@franklinpierce.edu.

Franklin University, Graduate School of Business, Columbus, OH 43215-5399. Offers MBA. Part-time and evening/weekend programs available. Postbaccalaureate distance learning degree programs offered (minimal on-campus study). *Faculty:* 3 full-time (1 woman), 83 part-time/adjunct (23 women). *Students:* 613 full-time (365 women), 125 part-time (68 women); includes 181 minority (142 African Americans, 26 Asian Americans or Pacific Islanders, 13 Hispanic Americans), 40 international. Average age 35. 405 applicants. In 2009, 358 master's awarded. *Degree requirements:* For master's, thesis. *Entrance requirements:* For master's, minimum undergraduate GPA of 2.75. Additional exam requirements/recommendations for international students: Required—TOEFL (minimum score 550 paper-based; 213 computer-based). *Application deadline:* For fall admission, 8/1 priority date for domestic students; for winter admission, 12/15 priority date for domestic students; for spring admission, 3/15 priority date for domestic students. Applications are processed on a rolling basis. Application fee: $30. Electronic applications accepted. *Expenses:* Tuition: Full-time $5880; part-time $490 per credit hour. *Financial support:* In 2009–10, 490 students received support. Institutionally sponsored loans available. Financial award application deadline: 6/15; financial award applicants required to submit FAFSA. *Unit head:* Dr. Doug Ross, Program Chair, 614-947-6149, Fax: 614-224-4025. *Application contact:* Graduate Services Office, 614-797-4700, Fax: 614-221-7723, E-mail: gradschl@franklin.edu.

Freed-Hardeman University, Program in Business Administration, Henderson, TN 38340-2399. Offers accounting (MBA); corporate responsibility (MBA); leadership (MBA). *Accreditation:* ACBSP. Part-time and evening/weekend programs available. Postbaccalaureate distance learning degree programs offered (no on-campus study). *Entrance requirements:* For master's, GMAT. Additional exam requirements/recommendations for international students: Required—TOEFL (minimum score 500 paper-based; 173 computer-based).

Fresno Pacific University, Graduate Programs, Program in Leadership and Organizational Studies, Fresno, CA 93702-4709. Offers MA. Part-time and evening/weekend programs available. *Degree requirements:* For master's, thesis. *Entrance requirements:* For master's, MAT, GRE or GMAT, interview, 2 writing samples. Additional exam requirements/recommendations for international students: Required—TOEFL (minimum score 550 paper-based; 213 computer-based). Electronic applications accepted. *Expenses:* Contact institution. *Faculty research:* Ethics, servant leadership, communication, creative problem solving.

Friends University, Graduate School, Division of Business, Technology, and Leadership, Program in Business Administration, Wichita, KS 67213. Offers MBA. Program also offered at Kansas City and Topeka campuses. Evening/weekend programs available. *Entrance requirements:* Additional exam requirements/recommendations for international students: Required—TOEFL (minimum score 560 paper-based; 220 computer-based). Electronic applications accepted.

Friends University, Graduate School, Division of Business, Technology, and Leadership, Program in Business Law, Wichita, KS 67213. Offers MBL. Evening/weekend programs available. *Entrance requirements:* Additional exam requirements/recommendations for international students: Required—TOEFL (minimum score 560 paper-based; 220 computer-based). Electronic applications accepted.

Friends University, Graduate School, Division of Business, Technology, and Leadership, Program in Management, Wichita, KS 67213. Offers MSM. Evening/weekend programs available. *Entrance requirements:* Additional exam requirements/recommendations for international students: Required—TOEFL (minimum score 560 paper-based; 220 computer-based). Electronic applications accepted.

Frostburg State University, Graduate School, College of Business, Frostburg, MD 21532-1099. Offers MBA. *Accreditation:* AACSB. Part-time and evening/weekend programs available. *Faculty:* 12 full-time (7 women). *Students:* 40 full-time (21 women), 75 part-time (31 women); includes 11 minority (9 African Americans, 2 Asian Americans or Pacific Islanders), 5 international. Average age 30. 79 applicants, 68% accepted, 44 enrolled. In 2009, 37 master's awarded. *Entrance requirements:* For master's, GMAT. Additional exam requirements/recommendations for international students: Required—TOEFL. *Application deadline:* For fall admission, 7/15 priority date for domestic students. Applications are processed on a rolling basis. Application fee: $30. Electronic applications accepted. *Expenses:* Tuition, state resident: full-time $5706; part-time $317 per credit hour. Tuition, nonresident: full-time $6948; part-time $386 per credit hour. Required fees: $1476; $82 per credit hour. $11 per term. One-time fee: $30 full-time. *Financial support:* In 2009–10, 8 research assistantships with full tuition reimbursements (averaging $5,000 per year) were awarded; career-related internships or fieldwork and Federal Work-Study also available. Financial award application deadline: 4/1; financial award applicants required to submit FAFSA. *Faculty research:* Cooperative teaching methods, strategic change processes, political marketing. *Unit head:* Dr. Ahmad Tootoonchi, Interim Dean, 301-687-4019, E-mail: tootoonchi@frostburg.edu. *Application contact:* Vickie Mazer, Director, Graduate Services, 301-687-7053, Fax: 301-687-4597, E-mail: vmmazer@frostburg.edu.

Full Sail University, Entertainment Business Master of Science Program—Online, Winter Park, FL 32792-7437. Offers MS. Postbaccalaureate distance learning degree programs offered. *Entrance requirements:* Additional exam requirements/recommendations for international students: Required—TOEFL (minimum score 550 paper-based; 213 computer-based; 79 iBT).

Gannon University, School of Graduate Studies, College of Engineering and Business, School of Business, Program in Business Administration, Erie, PA 16541-0001. Offers MBA. *Accreditation:* ACBSP. Part-time and evening/weekend programs available. Postbaccalaureate distance learning degree programs offered (no on-campus study). *Students:* 28 full-time (9 women), 54 part-time (28 women); includes 6 minority (4 African Americans, 2 Asian Americans or Pacific Islanders), 6 international. Average age 33. 130 applicants, 66% accepted, 4 enrolled. In 2009, 38 master's awarded. *Entrance requirements:* For master's, GMAT. Additional exam requirements/recommendations for international students: Required—TOEFL (minimum score 79 iBT). *Application deadline:* Applications are processed on a rolling basis. Application fee: $25. Electronic applications accepted. *Expenses:* Tuition: Full-time $13,590; part-time $755 per credit. Required fees: $524; $17 per credit. Tuition and fees vary according to course load, degree level, campus/location and program. *Financial support:* Career-related internships or fieldwork, scholarships/grants, and administrative assistantships available. Financial award application deadline: 7/1; financial award applicants required to submit FAFSA. *Unit head:* Scott Miller, Associate Director, 814-871-7397, E-mail: miller032@gannon.edu. *Application contact:* Kara Morgan, Assistant Director of Graduate Admissions, 814-871-5831, Fax: 814-871-5827, E-mail: graduate@gannon.edu.

Gannon University, School of Graduate Studies, College of Engineering and Business, School of Business, Program in Risk Management, Erie, PA 16541-0001. Offers Certificate. Part-time and evening/weekend programs available. *Entrance requirements:* For degree, GMAT. Additional exam requirements/recommendations for international students: Required—TOEFL (minimum score 79 iBT). *Application deadline:* Applications are processed on a rolling basis. Application fee: $25. Electronic applications accepted. *Expenses:* Tuition: Full-time $13,590; part-time $755 per credit. Required fees: $524; $17 per credit. Tuition and fees vary according to course load, degree level, campus/location and program. *Financial support:* Application deadline: 7/1. *Unit head:* Scott Miller, Associate Director, 814-871-7397, E-mail: miller032@gannon.edu. *Application contact:* Kara Morgan, Assistant Director of Graduate Admissions, 814-871-5831, Fax: 814-871-5827, E-mail: graduate@gannon.edu.

Gardner-Webb University, Graduate School of Business, Boiling Springs, NC 28017. Offers IMBA, M Acc, MBA. *Accreditation:* ACBSP. Part-time and evening/weekend programs available. Postbaccalaureate distance learning degree programs offered (no on-campus study). *Faculty:* 10 full-time (0 women), 5 part-time/adjunct (1 woman). *Students:* 37 full-time (20 women), 390 part-time (216 women); includes 103 minority (90 African Americans, 9 Asian Americans or Pacific Islanders, 4 Hispanic Americans), 4 international. Average age 35. 147 applicants, 80% accepted, 116 enrolled. In 2009, 122 master's awarded. *Entrance requirements:* For master's, GMAT, 2 semesters of course work each in economics, statistics, and accounting. *Application deadline:* For fall admission, 8/29 for domestic students; for spring admission, 1/13 for domestic students. Applications are processed on a rolling basis. Application fee: $25. Electronic applications accepted. *Expenses:* Contact institution. *Financial support:* In 2009–10, 23 students received support. Unspecified assistantships available. Support available to part-time students.

Business Administration and Management—General

Gardner-Webb University (continued)

Financial award applicants required to submit FAFSA. *Unit head:* Dr. Anthony Negbenebor, Director, 704-406-4622, Fax: 704-406-3895, E-mail: anegbenebor@gardner-webb.edu. *Application contact:* Kristen J. Setzer, Director of Admissions, 800-457-4622, Fax: 704-434-3895, E-mail: ksetzer@gardner-webb.edu.

Geneva College, Program in Business Administration, Beaver Falls, PA 15010-3599. Offers MBA. *Accreditation:* ACBSP. Part-time and evening/weekend programs available. *Faculty:* 6 full-time (1 woman), 1 part-time/adjunct (0 women). *Students:* 9 full-time (1 woman), 19 part-time (8 women); includes 4 minority (3 African Americans, 1 Asian American or Pacific Islander). 2 applicants, 100% accepted, 2 enrolled. In 2009, 5 master's awarded. *Entrance requirements:* For master's, GMAT (if college GPA less than 2.5), 2 letters of recommendation, resume. Additional exam requirements/recommendations for international students: Required—TOEFL. *Application deadline:* For fall admission, 3/1 priority date for domestic students; for spring admission, 11/1 priority date for domestic students. Applications are processed on a rolling basis. Electronic applications accepted. *Expenses:* Tuition: Full-time $11,250; part-time $625 per credit. Tuition and fees vary according to program. *Financial support:* Applicants required to submit FAFSA. *Unit head:* Dr. William Pearce, Chairperson, 724-847-6881, E-mail: bpearce@geneva.edu. *Application contact:* Lori Hartge, Graduate Student Support Specialist, 724-847-6571, E-mail: mba@geneva.edu.

George Fox University, School of Business, Newberg, OR 97132-2697. Offers finance (MBA); management (DBA); management/general (MBA); marketing (DBA); organizational strategy (MBA); strategic human resource management (MBA). MBA offered in part-time and full-time formats. Also offered in Portland, OR and Boise, ID. Part-time and evening/weekend programs available. Postbaccalaureate distance learning degree programs offered (minimal on-campus study). *Faculty:* 15 full-time (5 women), 7 part-time/adjunct (0 women). *Students:* 14 full-time (3 women), 223 part-time (77 women); includes 28 minority (7 African Americans, 3 American Indian/Alaska Native, 9 Asian Americans or Pacific Islanders, 9 Hispanic Americans), 2 international. Average age 38. 88 applicants, 86% accepted, 63 enrolled. In 2009, 66 master's, 2 doctorates awarded. *Degree requirements:* For master's, capstone project; for doctorate, credit-applied research project. *Entrance requirements:* For master's, resume (5 years professional experience required); 3 professional references; interview; financial e-learning course; for doctorate, GRE or GMAT, resume; personal mission statement; academic research writing sample; official transcript from each college/university attended; three professional references. Additional exam requirements/recommendations for international students: Required—TOEFL (minimum score 577 paper-based; 233 computer-based; 90 iBT), or IELTS (minimum score 7). *Application deadline:* For fall admission, 8/1 for domestic and international students; for spring admission, 12/1 for domestic and international students. Applications are processed on a rolling basis. Application fee: $40. Electronic applications accepted. *Expenses:* Contact institution. *Financial support:* In 2009–10, 2 students received support. Applicants required to submit FAFSA. *Unit head:* Dr. Ken Armstrong, Professor of Management and Dean, School of Management, 800-631-0921. *Application contact:* Robin Halverson, Admissions Counselor, 800-493-4937, Fax: 503-554-6111, E-mail: mba@georgefox.edu.

George Mason University, School of Management, Program in Business Administration, Fairfax, VA 22030. Offers MBA. *Accreditation:* AACSB. Part-time and evening/weekend programs available. *Faculty:* 80 full-time (26 women), 57 part-time/adjunct (13 women). *Students:* 57 full-time (31 women), 304 part-time (106 women); includes 40 minority (8 African Americans, 1 American Indian/Alaska Native, 22 Asian Americans or Pacific Islanders, 9 Hispanic Americans), 28 international. Average age 30. 270 applicants, 61% accepted, 93 enrolled. In 2009, 93 master's awarded. *Entrance requirements:* For master's, GMAT, college-level calculus course, 2 years of work experience, letters of recommendation, interview with director. Additional exam requirements/recommendations for international students: Required—TOEFL. *Application deadline:* For fall admission, 3/15 priority date for domestic students. Applications are processed on a rolling basis. Application fee: $75. Electronic applications accepted. *Expenses:* Tuition, state resident: full-time $7568; part-time $315.33 per credit hour. Tuition, nonresident: full-time $21,704; part-time $904.33 per credit hour. Required fees: $2184; $91 per credit hour. *Financial support:* In 2009–10, 9 students received support, including 7 research assistantships with full and partial tuition reimbursements available (averaging $2,676 per year), 3 teaching assistantships with full and partial tuition reimbursements available (averaging $3,001 per year); career-related internships or fieldwork, Federal Work-Study, unspecified assistantships, and health care benefits (full-time research or teaching assistantship recipients) also available. Support available to part-time students. Financial award application deadline: 3/1; financial award applicants required to submit FAFSA. *Faculty research:* Electronic commerce, marketing information systems, group decision making, corporate governance, risk management. *Unit head:* Angel Burgos, Director, 703-993-8949, Fax: 703-993-1778, E-mail: aburgos2@gmu.edu. *Application contact:* Lynda Carmichael, Program Manager, 703-993-4457, E-mail: lcarmic1@gmu.edu.

Georgetown University, Graduate School of Arts and Sciences, McDonough School of Business, Washington, DC 20057. Offers business administration (IEMBA, MBA). *Accreditation:* AACSB. *Entrance requirements:* For master's, GMAT. Additional exam requirements/recommendations for international students: Required—TOEFL. *Expenses:* Contact institution.

The George Washington University, School of Business, Washington, DC 20052. Offers M Accy, MBA, MS, MSF, MSIST, MTA, PMBA, PhD, Professional Certificate, JD/MBA, JD/MPA, MBA/MA. PMBA program also offered in Alexandria and Ashburn, VA. Part-time and evening/weekend programs available. *Faculty:* 120 full-time (35 women), 88 part-time/adjunct (16 women). *Students:* 878 full-time (415 women), 1,063 part-time (476 women); includes 449 minority (175 African Americans, 9 American Indian/Alaska Native, 187 Asian Americans or Pacific Islanders, 78 Hispanic Americans), 419 international. Average age 32. 1,982 applicants, 64% accepted, 646 enrolled. In 2009, 838 master's, 16 doctorates awarded. *Degree requirements:* For doctorate, thesis/dissertation. *Entrance requirements:* For doctorate, GMAT or GRE. Additional exam requirements/recommendations for international students: Required—TOEFL. *Application deadline:* For fall admission, 4/1 priority date for domestic students; for spring admission, 10/1 for domestic students. Applications are processed on a rolling basis. Application fee: $60. Electronic applications accepted. *Financial support:* In 2009–10, 194 students received support; fellowships with tuition reimbursements available, teaching assistantships with tuition reimbursements available, career-related internships or fieldwork, Federal Work-Study, institutionally sponsored loans, and tuition waivers (partial) available. Financial award application deadline: 4/1. *Unit head:* Dr. Susan M. Phillips, Dean, 202-994-6380, Fax: 202-994-6382. *Application contact:* Kristin Williams, Assistant Vice President for Graduate and Special Enrollment Management, 202-994-0467, Fax: 202-994-0371, E-mail: ksw@gwu.edu.

See Close-Up on page 249.

Georgia College & State University, Graduate School, The J. Whitney Bunting School of Business, Milledgeville, GA 31061. Offers accountancy (MACCT); accounting (MBA); business (MBA); health services administration (MBA); information systems (MIS); management information services (MBA). *Accreditation:* AACSB. Part-time and evening/weekend programs available. Postbaccalaureate distance learning degree programs offered (no on-campus study). *Faculty:* 43 full-time (17 women). *Students:* 70 full-time (32 women), 166 part-time (63 women); includes 29 minority (20 African Americans, 7 Asian Americans or Pacific Islanders, 2 Hispanic Americans), 23 international. Average age 29. 134 applicants, 84% accepted, 78 enrolled. In 2009, 75 master's awarded. *Entrance requirements:* For master's, GMAT. Additional exam requirements/recommendations for international students: Recommended—TOEFL (minimum score 550 paper-based; 213 computer-based; 79 iBT). *Application deadline:* For fall admission, 7/1 priority date for domestic students; for spring admission, 11/15 priority date for domestic students. Applications are processed on a rolling basis. Application fee: $40. Electronic applications accepted. *Expenses:* Tuition, area resident: Part-time $241 per credit hour. Tuition, state resident: full-time $4338. Tuition, nonresident: full-time $17,352; part-time $964 per credit hour. Required fees: $609 per semester. Tuition and fees vary according to course load and campus/location. *Financial support:* In 2009–10, 30 research assistantships with full tuition reimbursements were awarded; career-related internships or fieldwork and unspecified assistantships also available. Support available to part-time students. Financial award application deadline: 3/1; financial award applicants required to submit FAFSA. *Unit head:* Dr. Dale Young, Interim Dean, 478-445-5497, E-mail: dale.young@gcsu.edu. *Application contact:* Lynn Hanson, Director of Graduate Programs, 478-445-5115, E-mail: lynn.hanson@gcsu.edu.

Georgia Institute of Technology, Graduate Studies and Research, College of Management, Program in Business Administration, Atlanta, GA 30332-0001. Offers accounting (MBA); e-commerce (Certificate); engineering entrepreneurship (MBA); entrepreneurship (Certificate); finance (MBA); information technology management (MBA); international business (MBA, Certificate); management of technology (Certificate); marketing (MBA); operations management (MBA); organizational behavior (MBA); strategic management (MBA). *Accreditation:* AACSB.

Georgia Institute of Technology, Graduate Studies and Research, College of Management, Program in Management, Atlanta, GA 30332-0001. Offers accounting (PhD); finance (PhD); information technology management (PhD); marketing (PhD); operations management (PhD); organizational behavior (PhD); quantitative and computational finance (MS); strategic management (PhD). *Accreditation:* AACSB. *Degree requirements:* For doctorate, comprehensive exam, thesis/dissertation, oral exams. *Entrance requirements:* For master's and doctorate, GMAT. Additional exam requirements/recommendations for international students: Required—TOEFL. *Faculty research:* MIS, management of technology, international business, entrepreneurship, operations management.

Georgian Court University, School of Business, Lakewood, NJ 08701-2697. Offers accounting (Certificate); business administration (MBA). *Accreditation:* ACBSP. Part-time and evening/weekend programs available. *Faculty:* 10 full-time (6 women), 6 part-time/adjunct (1 woman). *Students:* 24 full-time (20 women), 110 part-time (74 women); includes 27 minority (12 African Americans, 5 Asian Americans or Pacific Islanders, 10 Hispanic Americans), 4 international. Average age 33. 60 applicants, 77% accepted, 28 enrolled. In 2009, 62 master's, 7 other advanced degrees awarded. *Entrance requirements:* For master's, GMAT or CPA exam, 3 letters of recommendation. Additional exam requirements/recommendations for international students: Required—TOEFL (minimum score 550 paper-based; 213 computer-based). *Application deadline:* For fall admission, 8/1 priority date for domestic students, 4/1 for international students; for spring admission, 1/1 priority date for domestic students, 7/1 for international students. Applications are processed on a rolling basis. Application fee: $40. Electronic applications accepted. *Expenses:* Tuition: Full-time $12,510; part-time $695 per credit. Required fees: $416 per year. Tuition and fees vary according to campus/location. *Financial support:* Scholarships/grants, health care benefits, and unspecified assistantships available. Financial award application deadline: 4/15; financial award applicants required to submit FAFSA. *Unit head:* Dr. Joseph Monahan, Dean, 732-987-2724, Fax: 732-987-2024, E-mail: monahanj@georgian.edu. *Application contact:* Eugene Soltys, Director of Graduate Admissions, 732-987-2770, Fax: 732-987-2084, E-mail: graduateadmissions@georgian.edu.

Georgia Southern University, Jack N. Averitt College of Graduate Studies, College of Business Administration, The Georgia WebMBA, Statesboro, GA 30460. Offers MBA. Part-time and evening/weekend programs available. Postbaccalaureate distance learning degree programs offered. *Students:* 71 part-time (25 women); includes 16 minority (12 African Americans, 2 Asian Americans or Pacific Islanders, 2 Hispanic Americans), 2 international. Average age 31. 62 applicants, 74% accepted, 23 enrolled. In 2009, 23 master's awarded. *Entrance requirements:* For master's, GMAT. Additional exam requirements/recommendations for international students: Required—TOEFL (minimum score 550 paper-based; 213 computer-based; 80 iBT). *Application deadline:* For fall admission, 3/1 priority date for domestic and international students. Applications are processed on a rolling basis. Application fee: $50. Electronic applications accepted. *Expenses:* Tuition, state resident: full-time $5040; part-time $210 per credit hour. Tuition, nonresident: full-time $20,136; part-time $839 per credit hour. Required fees: $1644. *Financial support:* In 2009–10, 42 students received support. Application deadline: 4/15. *Unit head:* Angela Leverett, Director, 912-478-0290, Fax: 912-478-0710, E-mail: aleveret@georgiasouthern.edu. *Application contact:* Dr. Charles Ziglar, Coordinator for Graduate Student Recruitment, 912-478-5384, Fax: 912-478-0740, E-mail: gradadmissions@georgiasouthern.edu.

Georgia Southern University, Jack N. Averitt College of Graduate Studies, College of Business Administration, Program in Business Administration, Statesboro, GA 30460. Offers MBA. *Accreditation:* AACSB. Part-time and evening/weekend programs available. Postbaccalaureate distance learning degree programs offered. *Students:* 94 full-time (34 women), 75 part-time (38 women); includes 23 minority (17 African Americans, 4 Asian Americans or Pacific Islanders, 2 Hispanic Americans), 15 international. Average age 27. 88 applicants, 82% accepted, 50 enrolled. In 2009, 61 master's awarded. *Entrance requirements:* For master's, GMAT. Additional exam requirements/recommendations for international students: Required—TOEFL (minimum score 550 paper-based; 213 computer-based; 80 iBT). *Application deadline:* For fall admission, 3/1 priority date for domestic students, 6/1 priority date for international students; for spring admission, 10/1 priority date for domestic students, 10/1 for international students. Applications are processed on a rolling basis. Application fee: $50. Electronic applications accepted. *Expenses:* Tuition, state resident: full-time $5040; part-time $210 per credit hour. Tuition, nonresident: full-time $20,136; part-time $839 per credit hour. Required fees: $1644. *Financial support:* In 2009–10, 106 students received support, including research assistantships with partial tuition reimbursements available (averaging $7,200 per year), teaching assistantships with partial tuition reimbursements available (averaging $7,200 per year); career-related internships or fieldwork, Federal Work-Study, scholarships/grants, tuition waivers (partial), and unspecified assistantships also available. Support available to part-time students. Financial award application deadline: 4/15; financial award applicants required to submit FAFSA. *Faculty research:* Applied, discipline, pedagogical theory-based, empirical-based. *Unit head:* Melissa Holland, Director, 912-478-2357, Fax: 912-478-7480, E-mail: mholland@georgiasouthern.edu. *Application contact:* Dr. Charles Ziglar, Coordinator for Graduate Student Recruitment, 912-478-5365, Fax: 912-478-0740, E-mail: gradadmissions@georgiasouthern.edu.

Georgia Southwestern State University, Graduate Studies, School of Business Administration, Americus, GA 31709-4693. Offers MBA. *Accreditation:* AACSB. *Entrance requirements:* For master's, GMAT or GRE General Test, minimum GPA of 2.5. Electronic applications accepted.

Georgia State University, J. Mack Robinson College of Business, Department of Managerial Sciences, Atlanta, GA 30302-3083. Offers business analysis (MBA, MS); decision sciences (PhD); entrepreneurship (MBA); human resources management (MBA, MS); management (MBA, PhD); operations management (MBA, MS); organization change (MS); personnel employee relations (PhD); strategic management (PhD). Part-time and evening/weekend programs available. *Degree requirements:* For doctorate, thesis/dissertation. *Entrance requirements:* For master's and doctorate, GMAT. Additional exam requirements/recommendations for international students: Required—TOEFL (minimum score 610 paper-based; 255 computer-based; 101 iBT). Electronic applications accepted. *Faculty research:* Abusive supervision, entrepreneurship, time series and neural networks, organizational controls, inventory control systems.

Georgia State University, J. Mack Robinson College of Business, Program in General Business Administration, Atlanta, GA 30302-3083. Offers accounting/information systems (MBA); economics (MBA, MS); enterprise risk management (MBA); general business (MBA); general business administration (EMBA, PMBA); information systems consulting (MBA); information systems risk management (MBA); international business and information technology (MBA); international entrepreneurship (MBA); MBA/JD. *Accreditation:* AACSB. Part-time and evening/weekend programs available. *Entrance requirements:* For master's, GMAT. Additional exam requirements/recommendations for international students: Required—TOEFL (minimum score 610 paper-based; 255 computer-based; 101 iBT). Electronic applications accepted.

Globe University, Minnesota School of Business, Woodbury, MN 55125. Offers business administration (MBA); health care management (MSM); information technology (MSM); managerial leadership (MSM).

Goddard College, Graduate Division, Master of Arts in Sustainable Business and Communities Program, Plainfield, VT 05667-9432. Offers MA. Postbaccalaureate distance learning degree programs offered (minimal on-campus study). *Faculty:* 7 part-time/adjunct (4 women). *Students:* 27 full-time. 21 applicants, 81% accepted, 14 enrolled. *Degree requirements:* For master's, thesis. *Entrance requirements:* For master's, 3 letters of recommendation, study plan and resource list, interview. Application fee: $40. *Expenses:* Tuition: Part-time $7223 per semester. Part-time tuition and fees vary according to program. *Financial support:* In 2009–10, 19 students received support. *Unit head:* Dr. Ann Driscoll, Director, 802-454-8311, Fax: 802-454-1029, E-mail: ann.driscoll@goddard.edu. *Application contact:* Jamie Kline, Admissions Counselor, 800-906-8312 Ext. 311, Fax: 802-454-1029, E-mail: jamie.kline@goddard.edu.

Golden Gate University, Ageno School of Business, San Francisco, CA 94105-2968. Offers accounting (MBA); business administration (EMBA, MBA, PMBA, DBA); finance (MBA, MS, Certificate); financial planning (MS, Certificate); human resource management (MBA, MS); human resources management (Certificate); information systems (MS); information technology (MBA); information technology management (Certificate); integrated marketing and communications (MS, Certificate); international business (MBA); management (MBA); marketing (MBA, MS, Certificate); operations management (Certificate); psychology (MA, Certificate); public relations (MS, Certificate); JD/MBA. Part-time and evening/weekend programs available. *Faculty:* 16 full-time (4 women), 241 part-time/adjunct (72 women). *Students:* 380 full-time (193 women), 750 part-time (414 women); includes 480 minority (98 African Americans, 2 American Indian/Alaska Native, 298 Asian Americans or Pacific Islanders, 82 Hispanic Americans), 166 international. Average age 33. 681 applicants, 78% accepted, 270 enrolled. In 2009, 550 master's, 13 doctorates awarded. *Degree requirements:* For doctorate, thesis/dissertation. *Entrance requirements:* For master's, GMAT (MBA), minimum GPA of 2.5 (MS). Additional exam requirements/recommendations for international students: Required—TOEFL. *Application deadline:* For fall admission, 5/15 for international students; for winter admission, 1/15 for international students; for spring admission, 9/15 for international students. Applications are processed on a rolling basis. Application fee: $70 ($110 for international students). Electronic applications accepted. *Expenses:* Contact institution. *Financial support:* Career-related internships or fieldwork, Federal Work-Study, institutionally sponsored loans, and scholarships/grants available. Support available to part-time students. Financial award applicants required to submit FAFSA. *Unit head:* Terry Connelly, Dean, 415-442-6519, Fax: 415-442-5369. *Application contact:* Angela Melero, Enrollment Services, 415-442-7800, Fax: 415-442-7807, E-mail: info@ggu.edu.

Goldey-Beacom College, Graduate Program, Wilmington, DE 19808-1999. Offers business administration (MBA); finance (MS); financial management (MBA); human resource management (MBA); information technology (MBA); international business management (MBA); management (MM); marketing management (MBA); taxation (MBA, MS). *Accreditation:* ACBSP. Part-time and evening/weekend programs available. *Faculty:* 20 full-time (8 women), 28 part-time/adjunct (10 women). *Students:* 38 full-time (18 women), 486 part-time (184 women); includes 350 minority (38 African Americans, 300 Asian Americans or Pacific Islanders, 12 Hispanic Americans). Average age 27. In 2009, 130 master's awarded. *Entrance requirements:* For master's, GMAT, MAT, GRE, minimum GPA of 3.0. Additional exam requirements/recommendations for international students: Required—TOEFL (minimum score 65 computer-based); Recommended—IELTS (minimum score 5). *Application deadline:* Applications are processed on a rolling basis. Electronic applications accepted. *Expenses:* Tuition: Full-time $14,166; part-time $787 per credit. Required fees: $180; $10 per credit. *Financial support:* In 2009–10, 486 students received support. Scholarships/grants available. Support available to part-time students. Financial award application deadline: 4/1; financial award applicants required to submit FAFSA. *Unit head:* Larry W. Eby, Director of Admissions, 302-225-6289, Fax: 302-996-5408, E-mail: ebylw@gbc.edu. *Application contact:* Ashley E. Mashington, Graduate Admissions Representative, 302-225-6259, Fax: 302-996-5408, E-mail: mashina@gbc.edu.

Gonzaga University, School of Business Administration, Spokane, WA 99258. Offers M Acc, MBA, JD/M Acc, JD/MBA. *Accreditation:* AACSB. Part-time and evening/weekend programs available. *Faculty:* 44 full-time (15 women). *Students:* 73 full-time (28 women), 121 part-time (47 women); includes 37 minority (2 African Americans, 19 American Indian/Alaska Native, 6 Asian Americans or Pacific Islanders, 10 Hispanic Americans), 9 international. Average age 29. In 2009, 89 master's awarded. *Entrance requirements:* For master's, GMAT. Additional exam requirements/recommendations for international students: Required—TOEFL. *Application deadline:* For fall admission, 7/20 priority date for domestic students; for spring admission, 11/1 for domestic students. Applications are processed on a rolling basis. Application fee: $50. Tuition and fees vary according to course level, course load, degree level, campus/location and program. *Financial support:* Teaching assistantships, Federal Work-Study available. Support available to part-time students. Financial award application deadline: 3/1. *Unit head:* Dr. Clarence H. Barnes, Dean, 509-328-4220 Ext. 5502. *Application contact:* Dr. Clarence H. Barnes, Dean, 509-328-4220 Ext. 5502.

Governors State University, College of Business and Public Administration, Program in Business Administration, University Park, IL 60466-0975. Offers MBA. *Accreditation:* ACBSP. Evening/weekend programs available. *Degree requirements:* For master's, thesis optional, competency exams in elementary and intermediate algebra. *Entrance requirements:* For master's, GMAT.

Graduate School and University Center of the City University of New York, Graduate Studies, Program in Business, New York, NY 10016-4039. Offers accounting (PhD); behavioral science (PhD); finance (PhD); management planning systems (PhD). *Faculty:* 66 full-time (5 women). *Students:* 64 full-time (37 women); includes 7 minority (3 African Americans, 1 American Indian/Alaska Native, 2 Asian Americans or Pacific Islanders, 1 Hispanic American), 34 international. Average age 33. 89 applicants, 28% accepted, 18 enrolled. In 2009, 7 doctorates awarded. *Degree requirements:* For doctorate, thesis/dissertation. *Entrance requirements:* For doctorate, GMAT, writing sample (15 pages). Additional exam requirements/recommendations for international students: Required—TOEFL. *Application deadline:* For fall admission, 1/15 for domestic students. Application fee: $125. Electronic applications accepted. *Financial support:* In 2009–10, 50 students received support, including 54 fellowships, 5 teaching assistantships; research assistantships, career-related internships or fieldwork, Federal Work-Study, institutionally sponsored loans, and tuition waivers (full and partial) also available. Financial award application deadline: 2/1; financial award applicants required to submit FAFSA. *Unit head:* Dr. Joseph Weintrop, Executive Officer, 646-312-3092, Fax: 646-312-3031. *Application contact:* Les Gribben, Director of Admissions, 212-817-7470, Fax: 212-817-1624, E-mail: lgribben@gc.cuny.edu.

Grand Canyon University, College of Business, Phoenix, AZ 85017-1097. Offers accounting (MBA); executive fire service leadership (MS); finance (MBA); general management (MBA); health systems management (MBA); leadership (MBA, MS); management of information system (MBA); marketing (MBA); six sigma (MBA). *Accreditation:* ACBSP. Part-time and evening/weekend programs available. Postbaccalaureate distance learning degree programs offered (no on-campus study). *Entrance requirements:* For master's, equivalent of two years full-time professional work experience. Additional exam requirements/recommendations for international students: Required—TOEFL (minimum score 575 paper-based; 233 computer-based; 90 iBT), IELTS (minimum score 7). Electronic applications accepted.

Grand Valley State University, Seidman College of Business, Program in Business Administration, Allendale, MI 49401-9403. Offers MBA, MSN/MBA. *Accreditation:* AACSB. Part-time and evening/weekend programs available. *Faculty:* 16 full-time (6 women), 10 part-time/adjunct (4 women). *Students:* 43 full-time (13 women), 212 part-time (59 women); includes 10 minority (7 Asian Americans or Pacific Islanders, 3 Hispanic Americans), 12 international. Average age 30. 84 applicants, 80% accepted, 51 enrolled. In 2009, 68 master's awarded. *Entrance requirements:* For master's, GMAT. Additional exam requirements/recommendations for international students: Required—TOEFL. *Application deadline:* For fall admission, 8/1 priority date for domestic students, 5/1 priority date for international students; for winter admission, 12/1 priority date for domestic students, 11/1 priority date for international students; for spring admission, 4/1 priority date for domestic students, 3/1 priority date for international students. Applications are processed on a rolling basis. Application fee: $30. Electronic applications accepted. *Expenses:* Tuition, state resident: part-time $471 per credit hour. Tuition, nonresident: part-time $646 per credit hour. Tuition and fees vary according to course level. *Financial support:* In 2009–10, 36 students received support, including 26 fellowships (averaging $2,823 per year), 14 research assistantships with full tuition reimbursements available (averaging $7,055 per year); institutionally sponsored loans and unspecified assistantships also available. Support available to part-time students. Financial award application deadline: 2/15. *Faculty research:* E-commerce, continuous improvement, currency futures, manufacturing flexibility. *Unit head:* Dr. Jaideep Motwani, Director, 616-331-7490, Fax: 616-331-7389, E-mail: bajemac@gvsu.edu. *Application contact:* Claudia J. Bajema, Director, Graduate Business Programs, 616-331-7387, Fax: 616-331-7389, E-mail: bajemac@gvsu.edu.

Grand View University, Program in Innovative Leadership, Des Moines, IA 50316-1599. Offers business (MS); education (MS); nursing (MS). *Entrance requirements:* For master's, GRE or GMAT, minimum undergraduate GPA of 3.0, professional resume, 3 letters of recommendation, interview. Additional exam requirements/recommendations for international students: Required—TOEFL (minimum score 550 paper-based; 210 computer-based). Electronic applications accepted.

Grantham University, Mark Skousen School of Business, Kansas City, MO 64153. Offers business administration (MBA); information management (MBA); information technology (MS); project management (MBA, MSIM). Part-time and evening/weekend programs available. Postbaccalaureate distance learning degree programs offered (no on-campus study). In 2009, 48 master's awarded. *Degree requirements:* For master's, capstone project. *Entrance requirements:* For master's, bachelor's degree from accredited degree-granting institution. Additional exam requirements/recommendations for international students: Required—TOEFL (minimum score 500 paper-based; 213 computer-based; 61 iBT). *Application deadline:* Applications are processed on a rolling basis. Application fee: $0. Electronic applications accepted. *Expenses:* Tuition: Part-time $265 per credit hour. One-time fee: $30 part-time. *Financial support:* Institutionally sponsored loans and scholarships/grants available. *Unit head:* Rhonda Corwin, Dean, 800-955-2527, Fax: 816-595-5757, E-mail: admissions@grantham.edu. *Application contact:* Matthew Hawes, Vice President of Enrollment Management, 800-955-2527, Fax: 816-595-5757, E-mail: admissions@grantham.edu.

Green Mountain College, Program in Business Administration, Poultney, VT 05764-1199. Offers MBA. Distance learning only. Postbaccalaureate distance learning degree programs offered (no on-campus study). *Entrance requirements:* For master's, GMAT or Quantitative Skills Assessment, 3 recommendations. Electronic applications accepted. *Faculty research:* Migrant farm workers and world systems theory ecosystem assessments.

Gwynedd-Mercy College, Center for Lifelong Learning, Gwynedd Valley, PA 19437-0901. Offers MSM. *Entrance requirements:* For master's, minimum GPA of 3.0.

Hamline University, School of Business, St. Paul, MN 55104-1284. Offers business (MBA); nonprofit management (MNM); public administration (MPA, DPA); JD/MANM; JD/MAPA; JD/MBA; LL M/MPA. Part-time and evening/weekend programs available. *Faculty:* 22 full-time (8 women), 39 part-time/adjunct (9 women). *Students:* 531 full-time (255 women), 154 part-time (87 women); includes 99 minority (55 African Americans, 6 American Indian/Alaska Native, 29 Asian Americans or Pacific Islanders, 9 Hispanic Americans), 76 international. Average age 33. 385 applicants, 72% accepted, 240 enrolled. In 2009, 228 master's, 1 doctorate awarded. *Degree requirements:* For master's, thesis (for some programs); for doctorate, comprehensive exam, thesis/dissertation. *Entrance requirements:* For master's, curriculum vitae, letters of recommendation, writing sample; for doctorate, personal statement, curriculum vitae, official transcripts, letters of recommendation, writing sample. Additional exam requirements/recommendations for international students: Required—TOEFL (minimum score 550 paper-based; 213 computer-based; 80 iBT). *Application deadline:* For fall admission, 8/15 priority date for domestic and international students; for spring admission, 1/15 for domestic students, 1/15 priority date for international students. Applications are processed on a rolling basis. Application fee: $0. Electronic applications accepted. *Expenses:* Tuition: Full-time $6816; part-time $426 per credit. Required fees: $6 per credit. One-time fee: $205. Tuition and fees vary according to degree level, campus/location and program. *Financial support:* In 2009–10, 14 students received support. Federal Work-Study and scholarships/grants available. Support available to part-time students. Financial award applicants required to submit FAFSA. *Faculty research:* Liberal arts based business programs, experiential learning, organizational process/politics, gender differences, social equity. *Unit head:* Dr. Julian Schuster, Dean, 651-523-2284, Fax: 651-523-3098, E-mail: jschuster01@hamline.edu. *Application contact:* Rae A. Lenway, Director, Graduate Recruitment and Admission, 651-523-2900, Fax: 651-523-3058, E-mail: rlenway@hamline.edu.

Hampton University, Graduate College, Program in Business, Hampton, VA 23668. Offers MBA. Part-time and evening/weekend programs available. *Entrance requirements:* For master's, GRE General Test.

Harding University, College of Business Administration, Searcy, AR 72149-0001. Offers accounting (MBA); health care management (MBA); information technology management (MBA); international business (MBA); leadership and organizational management (MBA). *Accreditation:* ACBSP. Part-time and evening/weekend programs available. Postbaccalaureate distance learning degree programs offered (no on-campus study). *Faculty:* 27 part-time/adjunct (6 women). *Students:* 105 full-time (46 women), 140 part-time (66 women); includes 31 minority (18 African Americans, 3 American Indian/Alaska Native, 6 Asian Americans or Pacific Islanders, 4 Hispanic Americans), 43 international. Average age 31. 82 applicants, 96% accepted, 66 enrolled. In 2009, 130 master's awarded. *Degree requirements:* For master's, portfolio. *Entrance requirements:* For master's, minimum GPA of 3.0, 2 letters of recommendation, resume. Additional exam requirements/recommendations for international students: Required—TOEFL (minimum score 550 paper-based; 213 computer-based; 80 iBT). *Application deadline:* For fall admission, 8/1 priority date for domestic and international students; for spring admission, 12/1 priority date for domestic and international students. Applications are processed on a rolling basis. Application fee: $35. *Expenses:* Tuition: Full-time $9720; part-time $540 per credit hour. Required fees: $22 per credit hour. Tuition and fees vary according to course load and program. *Financial support:* In 2009–10, 27 students received support. Unspecified assistantships available. Financial award application deadline: 7/30; financial award applicants required to submit FAFSA. *Unit head:* Glen Metheny, Director of Graduate Studies, 501-279-5851, Fax: 501-279-4805, E-mail: gmetheny@harding.edu. *Application contact:* Melanie Kiihnl, Recruiting Manager/Director of Marketing, 501-279-4523, Fax: 501-279-4805, E-mail: mba@harding.edu.

Hardin-Simmons University, The Acton MBA in Entrepreneurship, Austin, TX 78701. Offers MBA. *Entrance requirements:* For master's, GMAT, letters of recommendation. Additional exam requirements/recommendations for international students: Required—TOEFL. *Application deadline:* For fall admission, 5/1 for domestic students, 2/25 for international students. Application fee: $150. *Expenses:* Tuition: Full-time $11,430; part-time $635 per credit hour. Required fees: $650; $110 per semester. Tuition and fees vary according to degree level. *Application contact:* Jessica Blanchard, Director of Recruiting, 512-703-1231, E-mail: jblanchard@actonmba.org.

Hardin-Simmons University, Graduate School, Kelley College of Business, Abilene, TX 79698-0001. Offers MBA. *Accreditation:* ACBSP. Part-time and evening/weekend programs available. *Faculty:* 5 full-time (2 women), 2 part-time/adjunct (0 women). *Students:* 11 full-time (5 women), 19 part-time (8 women); includes 2 minority (both Hispanic Americans). Average age 27. 12 applicants, 100% accepted, 12 enrolled. In 2009, 15 master's awarded. *Degree requirements:* For master's, thesis or alternative. *Entrance requirements:* For master's, GMAT, minimum GPA of 3.0 in upper level course work, resume, interview. Additional exam requirements/recommendations for international students: Required—TOEFL (minimum score 600 paper-based; 232 computer-based; 75 iBT). *Application deadline:* For fall admission, 8/15 priority date for domestic students, 4/1 for international students; for spring admission, 1/5 priority date for domestic students, 9/1 for international students. Applications are processed

Business Administration and Management—General

Hardin-Simmons University (continued)

on a rolling basis. Application fee: $50. *Expenses:* Tuition: Full-time $11,430; part-time $635 per credit hour. Required fees: $650; $110 per semester. Tuition and fees vary according to degree level. *Financial support:* In 2009–10, 16 students received support; fellowships, scholarships/grants available. Support available to part-time students. Financial award application deadline: 6/30; financial award applicants required to submit FAFSA. *Unit head:* Dr. Nancy Kucinski, Director, 325-670-1503, Fax: 325-670-1523, E-mail: kucinski@hsutx.edu. *Application contact:* Dr. Gary Stanlake, Dean of Graduate Studies, 325-670-1298, Fax: 325-670-1564, E-mail: gradoff@hsutx.edu.

Harvard University, Extension School, Cambridge, MA 02138-3722. Offers applied sciences (CAS); biotechnology (ALM); educational technologies (ALM); educational technology (CET); English for graduate and professional studies (DGP); environmental management (ALM, CEM); information technology (ALM); journalism (ALM); liberal arts (ALM); management (ALM, CM); mathematics for teaching (ALM); museum studies (ALM); premedical studies (Diploma); publication and communication (CPC). Part-time and evening/weekend programs available. *Degree requirements:* For master's, thesis. *Entrance requirements:* For master's, 3 completed graduate courses with grade of B or higher. Additional exam requirements/recommendations for international students: Required—TOEFL (minimum score 600 paper-based; 250 computer-based), TWE (minimum score 5). *Expenses:* Contact institution.

Harvard University, Harvard Business School, Doctoral Programs in Management, Boston, MA 02163. Offers accounting and management (DBA); business economics (PhD); health policy management (PhD); management (DBA); marketing (DBA); organizational behavior (PhD); science, technology and management (PhD); strategy (DBA); technology and operations management (DBA). *Degree requirements:* For doctorate, comprehensive exam (for some programs), thesis/dissertation. *Entrance requirements:* For doctorate, GRE General Test or GMAT. Additional exam requirements/recommendations for international students: Required—TOEFL. *Expenses:* Tuition: Full-time $33,696. Required fees: $1126. Full-time tuition and fees vary according to program.

Harvard University, Harvard Business School, Master's Program in Business Administration, Boston, MA 02163. Offers MBA, JD/MBA. *Entrance requirements:* For master's, GMAT. Additional exam requirements/recommendations for international students: Required—TOEFL. *Expenses:* Tuition: Full-time $33,696. Required fees: $1126. Full-time tuition and fees vary according to program.

Hawai'i Pacific University, College of Business Administration, Honolulu, HI 96813. Offers accounting/CPA (MBA); e-business (MBA); economics (MBA); finance (MBA); human resource management (MA, MBA); information systems (MBA, MSIS), including knowledge management (MSIS), software engineering (MSIS), telecommunications security (MSIS); international business (MBA); management (MBA); marketing (MBA); organizational change (MA, MBA); travel industry management (MBA). Part-time and evening/weekend programs available. *Faculty:* 15 full-time (5 women), 11 part-time/adjunct (4 women). *Students:* 206 full-time (107 women), 197 part-time (105 women); includes 136 minority (18 African Americans, 3 American Indian/Alaska Native, 98 Asian Americans or Pacific Islanders, 17 Hispanic Americans), 151 international. Average age 30. 235 applicants, 90% accepted, 127 enrolled. In 2009, 141 master's awarded. *Degree requirements:* For master's, thesis. *Entrance requirements:* For master's, GMAT. Additional exam requirements/recommendations for international students: Recommended—TOEFL (minimum score 550 paper-based; 213 computer-based; 80 iBT), TWE (minimum score 5). *Application deadline:* For fall admission, 2/15 priority date for domestic students; for spring admission, 10/15 priority date for domestic students. Applications are processed on a rolling basis. Application fee: $50. Electronic applications accepted. *Expenses:* Tuition: Full-time $12,600; part-time $700 per credit hour. Tuition and fees vary according to program. *Financial support:* In 2009–10, 164 students received support; research assistantships, career-related internships or fieldwork, Federal Work-Study, scholarships/grants, and unspecified assistantships available. Support available to part-time students. Financial award application deadline: 3/1; financial award applicants required to submit FAFSA. *Faculty research:* Statistical control process as used by management, studies in comparative cross-cultural management styles, not-for-profit management. *Unit head:* Dr. Aytun Ozturk, Dean, 808-544-9301, Fax: 808-544-0283, E-mail: uozturk@hpu.edu. *Application contact:* Danny Lam, Assistant Director of Graduate Admissions, 808-544-1135, Fax: 808-544-0280, E-mail: graduate@hpu.edu.

See Close-Up on page 251.

HEC Montreal, School of Business Administration, Diploma Programs in Administration, Program in Management, Montréal, QC H3T 2A7, Canada. Offers Diploma. All courses are given in French. *Accreditation:* AACSB. Part-time programs available. *Students:* 73 full-time (41 women), 350 part-time (185 women). 254 applicants, 72% accepted, 127 enrolled. In 2009, 140 Diplomas awarded. *Degree requirements:* For Diploma, one foreign language. *Application deadline:* For fall admission, 4/15 for domestic and international students; for winter admission, 10/1 for domestic and international students; for spring admission, 2/15 for domestic and international students. Application fee: $77 Canadian dollars. Electronic applications accepted. Tuition and fees charges are reported in Canadian dollars. *Expenses:* Tuition, area resident: Part-time $65.60 Canadian dollars per credit. Tuition, state resident: full-time $2361.60 Canadian dollars; part-time $183.36 Canadian dollars per credit. Tuition, nonresident: full-time $6601 Canadian dollars; part-time $448.13 Canadian dollars per credit. International tuition: $16,132.68 Canadian dollars full-time. Required fees: $1254.15 Canadian dollars; $28.99 Canadian dollars per course. $91.68 Canadian dollars per term. Tuition and fees vary according to degree level and program. *Financial support:* Scholarships/grants available. *Unit head:* Louise Cote, Director, 514-340-6205, Fax: 514-340-5640, E-mail: louise.cote@hec.ca. *Application contact:* Marie Deshaies, Senior Student Advisor, 514-340-6135, Fax: 514-340-6411, E-mail: marie.deshaies@hec.ca.

HEC Montreal, School of Business Administration, Diploma Programs in Administration, Program in Management and Sustainable Development, Montréal, QC H3T 2A7, Canada. Offers Diploma. Part-time programs available. *Students:* 20 full-time (9 women), 66 part-time (35 women). 88 applicants, 72% accepted, 46 enrolled. In 2009, 13 Diplomas awarded. *Degree requirements:* For Diploma, one foreign language. *Application deadline:* For fall admission, 5/15 for domestic and international students. Application fee: $77. Tuition and fees charges are reported in Canadian dollars. *Expenses:* Tuition, area resident: Part-time $65.60 Canadian dollars per credit. Tuition, state resident: full-time $2361.60 Canadian dollars; part-time $183.36 Canadian dollars per credit. Tuition, nonresident: full-time $6601 Canadian dollars; part-time $448.13 Canadian dollars per credit. International tuition: $16,132.68 Canadian dollars full-time. Required fees: $1254.15 Canadian dollars; $28.99 Canadian dollars per course. $91.68 Canadian dollars per term. Tuition and fees vary according to degree level and program. *Financial support:* Research assistantships, teaching assistantships available. Financial award application deadline: 10/2. *Unit head:* Louise Cote, Director, 514-340-6205, Fax: 514-340-5640, E-mail: louise.cote@hec.ca. *Application contact:* Marie Deshaies, Senior Student Advisor, 514-340-6135, Fax: 514-340-6411, E-mail: marie.deshaies@hec.ca.

HEC Montreal, School of Business Administration, Doctoral Program in Administration, Montréal, QC H3T 2A7, Canada. Offers PhD. *Accreditation:* AACSB. *Students:* 142 full-time (61 women). 57 applicants, 54% accepted, 24 enrolled. In 2009, 21 doctorates awarded. *Degree requirements:* For doctorate, one foreign language, thesis/dissertation. *Entrance requirements:* For doctorate, GMAT, GRE, master's degree in administration or related field. *Application deadline:* For fall admission, 2/1 for domestic and international students; for winter admission, 9/15 for domestic and international students. Application fee: $77. Electronic applications accepted. Tuition and fees charges are reported in Canadian dollars. *Expenses:* Tuition, area resident: Part-time $65.60 Canadian dollars per credit. Tuition, state resident: full-time $2361.60 Canadian dollars; part-time $183.36 Canadian dollars per credit. Tuition, nonresident: full-time $6601 Canadian dollars; part-time $448.13 Canadian dollars per credit. International tuition: $16,132.68 Canadian dollars full-time. Required fees: $1254.15 Canadian dollars; $28.99 Canadian dollars per course. $91.68 Canadian dollars per term. Tuition and fees vary according to degree level and program. *Financial support:* Research assistantships, teaching assistantships available. Financial award application deadline: 10/2. *Unit head:* Dr. Francois Bellavance, Director, 514-340-6485, Fax: 514-340-5690, E-mail: francois.bellavance@hec.ca. *Application contact:* Francine Blais, Administrative Director, 514-340-6112, Fax: 514-340-6411, E-mail: francine.blais@hec.ca.

HEC Montreal, School of Business Administration, Master of Science Programs in Administration, Montréal, QC H3T 2A7, Canada. Offers applied economics (M Sc); applied financial economics (M Sc); business analytics (M Sc); business intelligence (M Sc); electronic commerce (M Sc); finance (M Sc); financial and strategic accounting (M Sc); financial engineering (M Sc); human resources management (M Sc); information systems (M Sc); international business (M Sc); international management (M Sc); logistics (M Sc); management (M Sc); management control (M Sc); marketing (M Sc); organizational development (M Sc); organizational studies (M Sc); production and operations management (M Sc); public accounting (M Sc). *Accreditation:* AACSB. Part-time programs available. *Students:* 582 full-time (278 women), 99 part-time (49 women). 669 applicants, 57% accepted, 196 enrolled. In 2009, 176 master's awarded. *Degree requirements:* For master's, one foreign language, thesis. *Entrance requirements:* For master's, bachelor's degree in business administration or equivalent. Additional exam requirements/recommendations for international students: Required—GMAT or TAGE-MAGE and TFI. *Application deadline:* For fall admission, 3/15 for domestic and international students; for winter admission, 9/15 for domestic and international students. Application fee: $77 Canadian dollars. Electronic applications accepted. Tuition and fees charges are reported in Canadian dollars. *Expenses:* Tuition, area resident: Part-time $65.60 Canadian dollars per credit. Tuition, state resident: full-time $2361.60 Canadian dollars; part-time $183.36 Canadian dollars per credit. Tuition, nonresident: full-time $6601 Canadian dollars; part-time $448.13 Canadian dollars per credit. International tuition: $16,132.68 Canadian dollars full-time. Required fees: $1254.15 Canadian dollars; $28.99 Canadian dollars per course. $91.68 Canadian dollars per term. Tuition and fees vary according to degree level and program. *Financial support:* Research assistantships, teaching assistantships, scholarships/grants available. Financial award application deadline: 10/2. *Unit head:* Dr. Claude Laurin, Director, 514-340-6536, Fax: 514-340-5690, E-mail: claude.laurin@hec.ca. *Application contact:* Francine Blais, Administrative Director, 514-340-6112, Fax: 514-340-6411, E-mail: francine.blais@hec.ca.

HEC Montreal, School of Business Administration, Master's Program in Business Administration and Management, Montréal, QC H3T 2A7, Canada. Offers MBA. Courses are given in French or English. *Accreditation:* AACSB. Part-time programs available. *Students:* 238 full-time (77 women), 332 part-time (88 women). 547 applicants, 55% accepted, 227 enrolled. In 2009, 250 master's awarded. *Degree requirements:* For master's, one foreign language. *Entrance requirements:* For master's, GMAT, 3 years of related work experience. Additional exam requirements/recommendations for international students: Required—TOEFL (minimum score 550 paper-based; 213 computer-based). *Application deadline:* For fall admission, 3/15 for domestic students, 2/1 for international students; for winter admission, 10/1 for domestic students. Application fee: $77 Canadian dollars. Electronic applications accepted. Tuition and fees charges are reported in Canadian dollars. *Expenses:* Tuition, area resident: Part-time $65.60 Canadian dollars per credit. Tuition, state resident: full-time $2361.60 Canadian dollars; part-time $183.36 Canadian dollars per credit. Tuition, nonresident: full-time $6601 Canadian dollars; part-time $448.13 Canadian dollars per credit. International tuition: $16,132.68 Canadian dollars full-time. Required fees: $1254.15 Canadian dollars; $28.99 Canadian dollars per course. $91.68 Canadian dollars per term. Tuition and fees vary according to degree level and program. *Financial support:* Scholarships/grants available. *Unit head:* Dr. Jacques Roy, Director, 514-340-6293, Fax: 514-340-6880, E-mail: jacques.roy@hec.ca. *Application contact:* Julie Benoit, Administrative Director, 514-340-6137, Fax: 514-340-5640, E-mail: julie.benoit@hec.ca.

Heidelberg University, Program in Business, Tiffin, OH 44883-2462. Offers MBA. Part-time and evening/weekend programs available. *Faculty:* 5 full-time (3 women), 4 part-time/adjunct (2 women). *Students:* 2 full-time (0 women), 43 part-time (23 women); includes 5 African Americans. Average age 30. 45 applicants, 42% accepted, 18 enrolled. In 2009, 15 master's awarded. *Degree requirements:* For master's, thesis or alternative, internship, practicum. *Entrance requirements:* For master's, previous undergraduate course work in business, minimum GPA of 2.7. Additional exam requirements/recommendations for international students: Required—TOEFL. *Application deadline:* Applications are processed on a rolling basis. Application fee: $25. *Expenses:* Contact institution. *Financial support:* In 2009–10, 17 students received support. Federal Work-Study available. Support available to part-time students. Financial award applicants required to submit FAFSA. *Unit head:* Dr. Andrew Weiss, Director of School of Business, 419-448-2036, Fax: 419-448-2072, E-mail: aweiss@heidelberg.edu. *Application contact:* Melissa Nye, Administrative Assistant for Graduate Studies, 419-448-2288, Fax: 419-448-2072, E-mail: mnye@heidelberg.edu.

Henderson State University, Graduate Studies, School of Business Administration, Arkadelphia, AR 71999-0001. Offers MBA. *Accreditation:* AACSB. Part-time programs available. *Faculty:* 14 full-time (5 women), 2 part-time/adjunct (0 women). *Students:* 25 full-time (9 women), 25 part-time (15 women); includes 7 minority (5 African Americans, 1 Asian American or Pacific Islander, 1 Hispanic American), 6 international. Average age 29. 36 applicants, 100% accepted, 36 enrolled. In 2009, 45 master's awarded. *Entrance requirements:* For master's, GMAT (minimum score 400), minimum AACSB index of 1000, minimum GPA of 2.7. Additional exam requirements/recommendations for international students: Required—TOEFL (minimum score 550 paper-based; 213 computer-based); Recommended—IELTS (minimum score 6). *Application deadline:* For fall admission, 8/1 priority date for domestic students, 6/30 priority date for international students; for spring admission, 1/1 priority date for domestic students, 11/30 priority date for international students. Application fee: $25 ($75 for international students). Electronic applications accepted. *Expenses:* Tuition, state resident: full-time $3798; part-time $211 per credit hour. Tuition, nonresident: full-time $7596; part-time $422 per credit hour. Required fees: $903. *Financial support:* Teaching assistantships with tuition reimbursements, Federal Work-Study and institutionally sponsored loans available. Support available to part-time students. *Unit head:* Dr. Jeffrey L. Hamm, Dean, 870-230-5377, Fax: 870-230-5286, E-mail: hammj@hsu.edu. *Application contact:* Dr. Marck L. Beggs, Graduate Dean, 870-230-5126, Fax: 870-230-5479, E-mail: beggsm@hsu.edu.

High Point University, Norcross Graduate School, High Point, NC 27262-3598. Offers business administration (MBA); educational leadership (M Ed); elementary education (M Ed); history (MA); nonprofit management (MA); special education (M Ed); sport studies (MS). *Accreditation:* ACBSP; NCATE. Part-time and evening/weekend programs available. *Degree requirements:* For master's, comprehensive exam (for some programs), thesis (for some programs). *Entrance requirements:* For master's, GMAT (MBA), GRE General Test, MAT, minimum GPA of 3.0. Additional exam requirements/recommendations for international students: Required—TOEFL (minimum score 550 paper-based). Electronic applications accepted.

Hodges University, Graduate Programs, Naples, FL 34119. Offers business administration (MBA); computer information technology (MS); criminal justice (MCJ); education (MPS); information systems management (MIS); interdisciplinary (MPS); law (MPS); management (MSM); professional studies (MPS); psychology (MPS); public administration (MPA). Part-time and evening/weekend programs available. Postbaccalaureate distance learning degree programs offered (no on-campus study). *Faculty:* 14 full-time (4 women), 4 part-time/adjunct (3 women). *Students:* 37 full-time (28 women), 217 part-time (142 women); includes 76 minority (35 African Americans, 5 Asian Americans or Pacific Islanders, 36 Hispanic Americans). Average age 36. 92 applicants, 91% accepted, 81 enrolled. In 2009, 92 master's awarded. *Degree requirements:* For master's, comprehensive exam (for some programs), thesis (for some programs). *Entrance requirements:* For master's, in-house entrance exam. *Application deadline:* Applications are processed on a rolling basis. Application fee: $50. Electronic applications accepted. *Expenses:* Tuition: Full-time $16,605; part-time $615 per credit hour. Required fees: $570. *Financial support:* In 2009–10, 200 students received support. Federal Work-Study and scholarships/grants available. Financial award application deadline: 7/9; financial award applicants required to submit FAFSA. *Unit head:* Terry McMahan, President, 239-513-1122, Fax: 239-598-6253, E-mail: tmcmahan@hodges.edu. *Application contact:* Rita Lampus, Vice

President of Student Enrollment Management, 239-513-1122, Fax: 239-598-6253, E-mail: rlampus@hodges.edu.

Hofstra University, Frank G. Zarb School of Business, Department of Accounting, Taxation and Legal Studies, Hempstead, NY 11549. Offers accounting (MS); business administration (MBA), including accounting, taxation; taxation (MS). Part-time and evening/weekend programs available. *Faculty:* 11 full-time (3 women), 3 part-time/adjunct (1 woman). *Students:* 58 full-time (20 women), 50 part-time (23 women); includes 10 minority (1 African American, 6 Asian Americans or Pacific Islanders, 3 Hispanic Americans), 22 international. Average age 28. 154 applicants, 63% accepted, 49 enrolled. In 2009, 20 master's awarded. *Degree requirements:* For master's, capstone course (MBA), thesis (MS). *Entrance requirements:* For master's, GMAT or GRE, 2 letters of recommendation, resume. Additional exam requirements/recommendations for international students: Required—TOEFL (minimum score 550 paper-based; 213 computer-based; 80 iBT); Recommended—IELTS (minimum score 6). *Application deadline:* Applications are processed on a rolling basis. Application fee: $60. Electronic applications accepted. *Expenses:* Contact institution. *Financial support:* In 2009–10, 24 students received support, including 21 fellowships with full and partial tuition reimbursements available (averaging $9,560 per year), 2 research assistantships with full and partial tuition reimbursements available (averaging $15,406 per year); Federal Work-Study, institutionally sponsored loans, scholarships/grants, health care benefits, tuition waivers (full and partial), and unspecified assistantships also available. Support available to part-time students. Financial award applicants required to submit FAFSA. *Faculty research:* Corporate governance and executive compensation, Sarbanes-Oxley and certification compliance for financial statement, student performance and evaluation models, decomposing the elements of nonprofit organizational performance, accounting for sustainability. *Unit head:* Dr. Nathan S. Slavin, Chairperson, 516-463-5690, Fax: 516-463-4834, E-mail: actnzs@hofstra.edu. *Application contact:* Carol Drummer, Dean of Graduate Admissions, 516-463-4876, Fax: 516-463-4664, E-mail: gradstudent@hofstra.edu.

Hofstra University, Frank G. Zarb School of Business, Department of Finance, Hempstead, NY 11549. Offers business administration (MBA), including finance, real estate; finance (MS); quantitative finance (MS). Part-time and evening/weekend programs available. *Faculty:* 10 full-time (2 women), 3 part-time/adjunct (0 women). *Students:* 122 full-time (36 women), 93 part-time (30 women); includes 24 minority (7 African Americans, 11 Asian Americans or Pacific Islanders, 6 Hispanic Americans), 73 international. Average age 27. 223 applicants, 76% accepted, 67 enrolled. In 2009, 70 master's awarded. *Degree requirements:* For master's, capstone course (MBA), thesis (MS). *Entrance requirements:* For master's, GMAT or GRE, 2 letters of recommendation, resume. Additional exam requirements/recommendations for international students: Required—TOEFL (minimum score 550 paper-based; 213 computer-based; 80 iBT); Recommended—IELTS (minimum score 6). *Application deadline:* Applications are processed on a rolling basis. Application fee: $60. Electronic applications accepted. *Expenses:* Contact institution. *Financial support:* In 2009–10, 44 students received support, including 38 fellowships with full and partial tuition reimbursements available (averaging $9,548 per year), 1 research assistantship with full and partial tuition reimbursement available (averaging $14,532 per year); Federal Work-Study, institutionally sponsored loans, scholarships/grants, and tuition waivers (full and partial) also available. Support available to part-time students. Financial award applicants required to submit FAFSA. *Faculty research:* Corporate finance, investments, banking, real estate, derivatives. *Unit head:* Dr. Nancy W. White, Chairperson, 516-463-5699, Fax: 516-463-4834, E-mail: finnwh@hofstra.edu. *Application contact:* Carol Drummer, Dean of Graduate Admissions, 516-463-4876, Fax: 516-463-4664, E-mail: gradstudent@hofstra.edu.

Hofstra University, Frank G. Zarb School of Business, Department of Information Technology and Quantitative Methods, Hempstead, NY 11549. Offers business administration (MBA), including information technology, quality management; information technology (MS). Part-time and evening/weekend programs available. *Faculty:* 10 full-time (2 women), 1 part-time/adjunct (0 women). *Students:* 8 full-time (2 women), 16 part-time (4 women); includes 5 minority (1 African American, 3 Asian Americans or Pacific Islanders, 1 Hispanic American), 2 international. Average age 30. 22 applicants, 64% accepted, 9 enrolled. In 2009, 9 master's awarded. *Degree requirements:* For master's, capstone course (MBA), thesis (MS). *Entrance requirements:* For master's, GMAT or GRE, 2 letters of recommendation, resume. Additional exam requirements/recommendations for international students: Required—TOEFL (minimum score 550 paper-based; 213 computer-based; 80 iBT); Recommended—IELTS (minimum score 6). *Application deadline:* Applications are processed on a rolling basis. Application fee: $60. Electronic applications accepted. *Expenses:* Contact institution. *Financial support:* In 2009–10, 3 students received support, including 3 fellowships with full and partial tuition reimbursements available (averaging $14,483 per year); research assistantships with full and partial tuition reimbursements available, career-related internships or fieldwork, Federal Work-Study, institutionally sponsored loans, scholarships/grants, tuition waivers (full and partial), and unspecified assistantships also available. Support available to part-time students. Financial award applicants required to submit FAFSA. *Faculty research:* IT outsourcing: IT strategy; SAP and enterprise systems; data mining/electronic medical records; IT and crisis management; inventory theory and modeling, forecasting. *Unit head:* Dr. Mohammed H. Tafti, Chairperson, 516-463-5720, E-mail: acsmht@hofstra.edu. *Application contact:* Carol Drummer, Dean of Graduate Admissions, 516-463-4876, Fax: 516-463-4664, E-mail: gradstudent@hofstra.edu.

Hofstra University, Frank G. Zarb School of Business, Department of Management, Entrepreneurship and General Management, Hempstead, NY 11549. Offers business administration (MBA), including health services management, management, sports and entertainment management; human resource management (MS). Part-time and evening/weekend programs available. *Faculty:* 6 full-time (2 women), 4 part-time/adjunct (0 women). *Students:* 75 full-time (35 women), 185 part-time (72 women); includes 55 minority (19 African Americans, 24 Asian Americans or Pacific Islanders, 12 Hispanic Americans), 26 international. Average age 33. 215 applicants, 61% accepted, 71 enrolled. In 2009, 53 master's awarded. *Degree requirements:* For master's, capstone course (MBA), thesis (MS). *Entrance requirements:* For master's, GMAT or GRE, 2 letters of recommendation, resume. Additional exam requirements/recommendations for international students: Required—TOEFL (minimum score 550 paper-based; 213 computer-based; 80 iBT); Recommended—IELTS (minimum score 6). *Application deadline:* Applications are processed on a rolling basis. Application fee: $60. Electronic applications accepted. *Expenses:* Contact institution. *Financial support:* In 2009–10, 23 students received support, including 20 fellowships with full and partial tuition reimbursements available (averaging $10,251 per year), 2 research assistantships with full and partial tuition reimbursements available (averaging $20,788 per year); career-related internships or fieldwork, Federal Work-Study, institutionally sponsored loans, scholarships/grants, tuition waivers (full and partial), and unspecified assistantships also available. Support available to part-time students. Financial award applicants required to submit FAFSA. *Faculty research:* Business/personal ethics; emotion in workplace; gender issues; learning and pedagogical issues; family business. *Unit head:* Dr. Mamdouh I. Farid, Chairperson, 516-463-5735, Fax: 516-463-4834, E-mail: mgbmif@hofstra.edu. *Application contact:* Carol Drummer, Dean of Graduate Admissions, 516-463-4876, Fax: 516-463-4664, E-mail: gradstudent@hofstra.edu.

Hofstra University, Frank G. Zarb School of Business, Department of Marketing and International Business, Hempstead, NY 11549. Offers business administration (MBA), including international business, marketing; marketing (MS); marketing research (MS). Part-time and evening/weekend programs available. *Faculty:* 9 full-time (0 women), 1 part-time/adjunct (0 women). *Students:* 52 full-time (28 women), 38 part-time (21 women); includes 9 minority (2 African Americans, 3 Asian Americans or Pacific Islanders, 4 Hispanic Americans), 40 international. Average age 27. 114 applicants, 71% accepted, 26 enrolled. In 2009, 29 master's awarded. *Degree requirements:* For master's, capstone course (MBA), thesis (MS). *Entrance requirements:* For master's, GMAT or GRE, 2 letters of recommendation, resume. Additional exam requirements/recommendations for international students: Required—TOEFL (minimum score 550 paper-based; 213 computer-based; 80 iBT); Recommended—IELTS (minimum score 6). *Application deadline:* Applications are processed on a rolling basis. Application fee: $60. Electronic applications accepted. *Expenses:* Contact institution. *Financial support:* In 2009–10, 24 students received support, including 21 fellowships with full and partial tuition reimbursements available (averaging $9,582 per year), 2 research assistantships with full and partial tuition reimbursements available (averaging $14,187 per year); career-related internships or fieldwork, Federal Work-Study, institutionally sponsored loans, scholarships/grants, tuition waivers (full and partial), and unspecified assistantships also available. Support available to part-time students. Financial award applicants required to submit FAFSA. *Faculty research:* Outsourcing, global alliances, retailing, web marketing, cross-cultural age research. *Unit head:* Dr. Benny Barak, Chairperson, 516-463-5707, Fax: 516-463-4834, E-mail: mktbzb@hofstra.edu. *Application contact:* Carol Drummer, Dean of Graduate Admissions, 516-463-4876, Fax: 516-463-4664, E-mail: gradstudent@hofstra.edu.

Hofstra University, Frank G. Zarb School of Business, Executive Master's Program in Business Administration, Hempstead, NY 11549. Offers executive program in management (EMBA). Evening/weekend programs available. *Students:* 12 full-time (6 women), 14 part-time (4 women); includes 10 minority (3 African Americans, 2 Asian Americans or Pacific Islanders, 5 Hispanic Americans). Average age 34. 32 applicants, 63% accepted, 13 enrolled. In 2009, 6 master's awarded. *Entrance requirements:* For master's, 2 letters of recommendation, minimum 7 years of management experience, resume, interview. Additional exam requirements/recommendations for international students: Required—TOEFL (minimum score 550 paper-based; 213 computer-based; 80 iBT); Recommended—IELTS (minimum score 6). *Application deadline:* Applications are processed on a rolling basis. Application fee: $60. Electronic applications accepted. *Expenses:* Contact institution. *Financial support:* In 2009–10, 6 students received support, including 6 fellowships with full and partial tuition reimbursements available (averaging $4,000 per year); research assistantships with full and partial tuition reimbursements available, Federal Work-Study, institutionally sponsored loans, scholarships/grants, and tuition waivers (full and partial) also available. Support available to part-time students. Financial award applicants required to submit FAFSA. *Faculty research:* Business strategy, international business, financial management, marketing management. *Unit head:* Dr. Barry Berman, Director, 516-463-5711, E-mail: mktbxb@hofstra.edu. *Application contact:* Carol Drummer, Dean of Graduate Admissions, 516-463-4876, Fax: 516-463-4664, E-mail: gradstudent@hofstra.edu.

Holy Family University, Division of Extended Learning, Philadelphia, PA 19114. Offers business administration (MBA); finance (MBA); health care administration (MBA). Part-time and evening/weekend programs available. *Faculty:* 78 part-time/adjunct (32 women). *Students:* 116 part-time (71 women); includes 18 minority (10 African Americans, 6 Asian Americans or Pacific Islanders, 2 Hispanic Americans). Average age 35. 46 applicants, 93% accepted, 41 enrolled. In 2009, 47 master's awarded. *Entrance requirements:* For master's, interview, essay. Additional exam requirements/recommendations for international students: Required—TOEFL. *Application deadline:* Applications are processed on a rolling basis. Application fee: $50. Electronic applications accepted. *Expenses:* Tuition: Part-time $600 per credit. Required fees: $58 per semester. *Financial support:* Applicants required to submit FAFSA. *Unit head:* Honour Moore, Associate Vice President, 267-341-5008, Fax: 215-633-0558, E-mail: hmoore@holyfamily.edu. *Application contact:* Don Reinmold, Director of Admissions, 267-341-5001 Ext. 3230, Fax: 215-633-0558, E-mail: dreinmold@holyfamily.edu.

Holy Family University, Graduate School, School of Business, Philadelphia, PA 19114. Offers human resources management (MS); information systems management (MS). Part-time and evening/weekend programs available. *Faculty:* 3 full-time (0 women), 3 part-time/adjunct (0 women). *Students:* 7 full-time (6 women), 49 part-time (32 women); includes 9 minority (4 African Americans, 3 Asian Americans or Pacific Islanders, 2 Hispanic Americans), 5 international. Average age 35. 18 applicants, 94% accepted, 15 enrolled. In 2009, 24 master's awarded. *Degree requirements:* For master's, comprehensive exam, thesis optional. *Entrance requirements:* For master's, GMAT, GRE, or MAT, minimum GPA of 3.0. *Application deadline:* For fall admission, 7/1 priority date for domestic students; for winter admission, 11/1 priority date for domestic students. Applications are processed on a rolling basis. Application fee: $25. *Expenses:* Tuition: Part-time $600 per credit. Required fees: $58 per semester. *Financial support:* Federal Work-Study available. Support available to part-time students. Financial award application deadline: 2/15; financial award applicants required to submit FAFSA. *Unit head:* Dr. Jan Duggar, Dean, 267-341-3373, Fax: 215-637-5937, E-mail: jduggar@holyfamily.edu. *Application contact:* Gidget Marie Montelibano, Graduate Admissions Counselor, 267-341-3558, Fax: 215-637-1478, E-mail: gmontelibano@holyfamily.edu.

Holy Names University, Graduate Division, Department of Business, Oakland, CA 94619-1699. Offers energy and environment management (MBA); finance (MBA); management and leadership (MBA); marketing (MBA); sports management (MBA). Part-time and evening/weekend programs available. *Entrance requirements:* For master's, minimum undergraduate GPA of 2.6 overall, 3.0 in major. Additional exam requirements/recommendations for international students: Required—TOEFL (minimum score 550 paper-based; 213 computer-based; 80 iBT). *Faculty research:* Business ethics, sustainable economics, accounting models, cross-cultural management, diversity in organizations.

Hood College, Graduate School, Department of Economics and Management, Frederick, MD 21701-8575. Offers accounting (MBA); administration and management (MBA); finance (MBA); human resource management (MBA); information systems (MBA); marketing (MBA); public management (MBA). Part-time and evening/weekend programs available. *Faculty:* 5 full-time (1 woman), 9 part-time/adjunct (1 woman). *Students:* 21 full-time (16 women), 166 part-time (85 women); includes 33 minority (18 African Americans, 8 Asian Americans or Pacific Islanders, 7 Hispanic Americans), 15 international. Average age 32. 47 applicants, 87% accepted, 32 enrolled. In 2009, 31 master's awarded. *Degree requirements:* For master's, capstone/final research project. *Entrance requirements:* For master's, minimum GPA of 2.75, resume, letters of recommendation. *Application deadline:* For fall admission, 7/15 for domestic and international students; for spring admission, 12/15 for domestic and international students. Applications are processed on a rolling basis. Application fee: $35. Electronic applications accepted. *Expenses:* Tuition: Full-time $6480; part-time $360 per credit. Required fees: $100; $50 per term. *Financial support:* Applicants required to submit FAFSA. *Faculty research:* Corporate strategy and sustainable competitive advantages, business ethics, entrepreneurship, investments management, economic development. *Unit head:* Dr. Anita Jose, Program Director, 301-696-3691, Fax: 301-696-3597, E-mail: jose@hood.edu. *Application contact:* Dr. Allen P. Flora, Dean of Graduate School, 301-696-3811, Fax: 301-696-3597, E-mail: gofurther@hood.edu.

Hope International University, School of Graduate and Professional Studies, Program in Business Administration, Fullerton, CA 92831-3138. Offers business administration (MBA); educational administration (MSM); international development (MBA, MSM); management (MBA); nonprofit management (MBA). Part-time programs available. Postbaccalaureate distance learning degree programs offered (no on-campus study). *Degree requirements:* For master's, comprehensive exam (for some programs), thesis (for some programs), project. *Entrance requirements:* For master's, minimum GPA of 3.0; 2 references. Additional exam requirements/recommendations for international students: Required—TOEFL (minimum score 550 paper-based; 213 computer-based; 86 iBT); Recommended—IELTS (minimum score 6.5). Electronic applications accepted. *Expenses:* Contact institution.

Houston Baptist University, College of Business and Economics, Program in Business Administration, Houston, TX 77074-3298. Offers MBA, MSM. *Accreditation:* ACBSP. Part-time and evening/weekend programs available. *Entrance requirements:* For master's, GMAT, minimum GPA of 2.5. Additional exam requirements/recommendations for international students: Required—TOEFL (minimum score 550 paper-based; 213 computer-based). *Expenses:* Contact institution.

Howard University, School of Business, Graduate Programs in Business, Washington, DC 20059-0002. Offers accounting (MBA); entrepreneurship (MBA); finance (MBA); general management (MBA); human resources management (MBA); information systems (MBA); international business (MBA); marketing (MBA); supply chain management (MBA); JD/MBA. *Accreditation:* AACSB. Part-time and evening/weekend programs available. Postbaccalaureate distance learning degree programs offered (no on-campus study). *Entrance requirements:* For

Business Administration and Management—General

Howard University (continued)
master's, GMAT, minimum 1 year post undergraduate work experience, resume, 3 letters of recommendation, advanced college algebra. Additional exam requirements/recommendations for international students: Required—TOEFL. *Faculty research:* Marketing research in multi-ethnic populations, U.S. trade policies and international relations, risk management (finance).

Hult International Business School, MBA Program, Cambridge, MA 02141. Offers MBA. *Entrance requirements:* For master's, GMAT, 3 years of management experience. Additional exam requirements/recommendations for international students: Required—TOEFL (minimum score 240 computer-based). Electronic applications accepted. *Faculty research:* Management for international development.

Hult International Business School, Program in Business Administration—Hult London Campus, London, MA WC 1B 4JP, United Kingdom. Offers entrepreneurship (MBA); international business (MBA); international finance (MBA); marketing (MBA). Part-time programs available. *Degree requirements:* For master's, comprehensive exam, thesis, internship. *Entrance requirements:* Additional exam requirements/recommendations for international students: Required—TOEFL (minimum score 580 paper-based; 237 computer-based), TWE (minimum score 5). Electronic applications accepted.

Humboldt State University, Graduate Studies, College of Professional Studies, School of Business, Arcata, CA 95521-8299. Offers MBA. Part-time and evening/weekend programs available. *Students:* 22 full-time (10 women), 3 part-time (1 woman); includes 3 minority (1 African American, 2 Hispanic Americans), 2 international. Average age 31. 44 applicants, 59% accepted, 16 enrolled. In 2009, 20 master's awarded. *Degree requirements:* For master's, thesis or alternative. *Entrance requirements:* For master's, GMAT or GRE, minimum GPA of 2.5. Additional exam requirements/recommendations for international students: Required—TOEFL (minimum score 500 paper-based; 173 computer-based). *Application deadline:* For fall admission, 6/30 for domestic and international students; for spring admission, 12/15 for domestic and international students. Applications are processed on a rolling basis. Application fee: $55. *Expenses:* Contact institution. *Financial support:* Fellowships, Federal Work-Study available. Support available to part-time students. Financial award application deadline: 3/1; financial award applicants required to submit FAFSA. *Faculty research:* International business development, small town entrepreneurship, international trade: Pacific Rim. *Unit head:* Dr. Saeed Mortazavi, Chair, 707-826-3846, Fax: 707-826-6666, E-mail: sm5@humboldt.edu. *Application contact:* Dr. Kien-Quoc Van Pham, MBA Graduate Coordinator, 707-826-5665, Fax: 707-826-6666, E-mail: kv7@humboldt.edu.

Husson University, School of Graduate and Professional Studies, Program in Business, Bangor, ME 04401-2999. Offers health care management (MSB); nonprofit management (MSB). Part-time and evening/weekend programs available. *Degree requirements:* For master's, thesis optional. *Entrance requirements:* For master's, GMAT, minimum GPA of 2.5.

Idaho State University, Office of Graduate Studies, College of Business, Pocatello, ID 83209-8020. Offers business administration (MBA, Postbaccalaureate Certificate); computer information systems (MS, Postbaccalaureate Certificate). *Accreditation:* AACSB. Part-time programs available. *Faculty:* 27 full-time (5 women). *Students:* 49 full-time (15 women), 73 part-time (17 women); includes 7 minority (1 African American, 2 American Indian/Alaska Native, 1 Asian American or Pacific Islander, 3 Hispanic Americans), 7 international. Average age 32. 38 applicants, 74% accepted, 5 enrolled. In 2009, 39 master's, 2 other advanced degrees awarded. *Degree requirements:* For master's, comprehensive exam, thesis (for some programs), oral exam; for Postbaccalaureate Certificate, comprehensive exam, thesis (for some programs), 6 hours of clerkship. *Entrance requirements:* For master's, GMAT, GRE General Test, minimum GPA of 3.0, resume outlining work experience, 2 letters of reference; for Postbaccalaureate Certificate, GMAT, GRE General Test, minimum upper-level GPA of 3.0, resume of work experience. Additional exam requirements/recommendations for international students: Required—TOEFL (minimum score 550 paper-based; 213 computer-based; 80 iBT). *Application deadline:* For fall admission, 7/1 for domestic students, 6/1 for international students; for spring admission, 12/1 for domestic students, 11/1 for international students. Applications are processed on a rolling basis. Application fee: $55. Electronic applications accepted. *Expenses:* Tuition, state resident: full-time $3318; part-time $297 per credit hour. Tuition, nonresident: full-time $13,120; part-time $437 per credit hour. Required fees: $2530. Tuition and fees vary according to program. *Financial support:* In 2009–10, 10 teaching assistantships with full and partial tuition reimbursements (averaging $10,841 per year) were awarded; career-related internships or fieldwork, Federal Work-Study, institutionally sponsored loans, scholarships/grants, health care benefits, tuition waivers (full and partial), and unspecified assistantships also available. Support available to part-time students. Financial award application deadline: 1/1; financial award applicants required to submit FAFSA. *Faculty research:* Information assurance, computer information technology, finance management, marketing. *Unit head:* Dr. Ken Smith, Dean, 208-282-3585, Fax: 208-282-4367, E-mail: smithken@isu.edu. *Application contact:* Tami Carson, Graduate School Technical Records Specialist, 208-282-2150, Fax: 208-282-4847, E-mail: carstami@isu.edu.

Illinois Institute of Technology, Stuart School of Business, Program in Business Administration, Chicago, IL 60616-3793. Offers financial management (MBA); innovation and emerging enterprises (MBA); management science (MBA); marketing (MBA); sustainability (MBA); JD/MBA; MBA/MS. *Accreditation:* AACSB. Part-time and evening/weekend programs available. *Faculty:* 14 full-time (2 women), 3 part-time/adjunct (all women). *Students:* 71 full-time (28 women), 45 part-time (18 women); includes 8 minority (4 African Americans, 4 Asian Americans or Pacific Islanders), 69 international. Average age 29. 274 applicants, 50% accepted, 33 enrolled. In 2009, 48 master's, 6 other advanced degrees awarded. *Entrance requirements:* For master's, GMAT. Additional exam requirements/recommendations for international students: Required—TOEFL (minimum score 600 paper-based; 250 computer-based; 90 iBT). *Application deadline:* For fall admission, 8/1 for domestic students, 5/1 for international students; for spring admission, 12/15 for domestic students, 10/15 for international students. Applications are processed on a rolling basis. Application fee: $75. Electronic applications accepted. *Expenses:* Contact institution. *Financial support:* Career-related internships or fieldwork, Federal Work-Study, institutionally sponsored loans, scholarships/grants, traineeships, health care benefits, and tuition waivers (partial) available. Support available to part-time students. Financial award applicants required to submit FAFSA. *Faculty research:* Global management and marketing strategy, technological innovation, management science, financial management, knowledge management. *Unit head:* M. Krishna Erramilli, Interim Director, 312-906-6573, Fax: 312-906-6549. *Application contact:* M. Krishna Erramilli, Interim Director, 312-906-6573, Fax: 312-906-6549.

Illinois Institute of Technology, Stuart School of Business, Program in Management Science, Chicago, IL 60616-3793. Offers PhD. *Accreditation:* AACSB. Part-time programs available. *Faculty:* 1 full-time (0 women). *Students:* 23 full-time (10 women), 20 part-time (1 woman), 28 international. Average age 36. 47 applicants, 43% accepted, 8 enrolled. In 2009, 1 doctorate awarded. *Degree requirements:* For doctorate, comprehensive exam, thesis/dissertation, qualifying exam. *Entrance requirements:* For doctorate, GMAT OR GRE. Additional exam requirements/recommendations for international students: Required—TOEFL (minimum score 575 paper-based; 90 iBT). *Application deadline:* For fall admission, 5/1 for domestic and international students; for spring admission, 10/15 for domestic and international students. Applications are processed on a rolling basis. Application fee: $75. Electronic applications accepted. *Expenses:* Contact institution. *Financial support:* Career-related internships or fieldwork, Federal Work-Study, institutionally sponsored loans, scholarships/grants, traineeships, health care benefits, and tuition waivers (partial) available. Support available to part-time students. Financial award applicants required to submit FAFSA. *Faculty research:* Scheduling systems, queuing systems, optimization, quality systems, foreign exchange, enterprise risk management, credit risk modeling. *Unit head:* Dr. John Bilson, Director, MS Finance Program/Associate Director, PhD in Management Science Program, 312-906-6538, Fax: 312-906-6549, E-mail: bilson@stuart.iit.edu. *Application contact:* Dr. John Bilson, Director, MS Finance Program/Associate Director, PhD in Management Science Program, 312-906-6538, Fax: 312-906-6549, E-mail: bilson@stuart.iit.edu.

Illinois State University, Graduate School, College of Business, Program in Business Administration, Normal, IL 61790-2200. Offers MBA. *Accreditation:* AACSB. Part-time programs available. *Degree requirements:* For master's, thesis optional. *Entrance requirements:* For master's, GMAT, minimum GPA of 2.75 during previous 2 years of course work. Additional exam requirements/recommendations for international students: Required—TOEFL. *Faculty research:* McLean County small business development center.

IMCA–International Management Centres Association, Programs in Business Administration, Buckingham, United Kingdom. Offers M Mgt, M Phil, MBA, MS. Postbaccalaureate distance learning degree programs offered (no on-campus study).

Independence University, Program in Business Administration, Salt Lake City, UT 84107. Offers MBA. *Expenses:* Required fees: $475 per credit. One-time fee: $100 part-time.

Indiana State University, School of Graduate Studies, College of Business, Terre Haute, IN 47809. Offers MBA. *Accreditation:* AACSB. Part-time and evening/weekend programs available. *Degree requirements:* For master's, thesis optional. *Entrance requirements:* For master's, GMAT. Electronic applications accepted. *Faculty research:* Small business and entrepreneurial sciences, production and operations management.

Indiana Tech, Program in Business Administration, Fort Wayne, IN 46803-1297. Offers accounting (MBA); health care administration (MBA); human resources (MBA); management (MBA); marketing (MBA). Part-time and evening/weekend programs available. Postbaccalaureate distance learning degree programs offered (no on-campus study). *Students:* 202 full-time (97 women), 37 part-time (18 women); includes 60 minority (45 African Americans, 2 American Indian/Alaska Native, 7 Asian Americans or Pacific Islanders, 6 Hispanic Americans), 5 international. Average age 38. *Entrance requirements:* For master's, GMAT, minimum undergraduate GPA of 2.5, 3 letters of recommendation. *Application deadline:* Applications are processed on a rolling basis. Application fee: $25. Electronic applications accepted. *Expenses:* Tuition: Full-time $5160; part-time $430 per credit hour. Tuition and fees vary according to degree level and program. *Financial support:* Applicants required to submit FAFSA. *Unit head:* Dr. Andrew Nwanne, Associate Dean of College of Professional Studies, 260-422-5561 Ext. 2214, E-mail: ainwanne@indianatech.edu. *Application contact:* Steve Herendeen, Manager of Campus Development and Support, 260-422-5561 Ext. 2121, E-mail: saherendeen@indianatech.edu.

Indiana Tech, Program in Management, Fort Wayne, IN 46803-1297. Offers MSM. Part-time and evening/weekend programs available. *Students:* 37 full-time (25 women), 1 part-time (0 women); includes 22 minority (20 African Americans, 1 American Indian/Alaska Native, 1 Asian American or Pacific Islander). Average age 37. *Entrance requirements:* For master's, GMAT. *Application deadline:* Applications are processed on a rolling basis. Application fee: $25. Electronic applications accepted. *Expenses:* Tuition: Full-time $5160; part-time $430 per credit hour. Tuition and fees vary according to degree level and program. *Financial support:* Applicants required to submit FAFSA. *Application contact:* Steve Herendeen, Associate Vice President of College of Professional Studies Admissions, 260-422-5561 Ext. 2121, E-mail: saherendeen@indianatech.edu.

Indiana University Bloomington, Kelley School of Business, Bloomington, IN 47405-7000. Offers MBA, MPA, MS, DBA, PhD, DBA/MIS, JD/MBA, JD/MPA, MBA/MA, PhD/MIS. PhD offered through University Graduate School. *Accreditation:* AACSB. *Faculty:* 71 full-time (10 women). *Students:* 1,351 full-time (364 women), 435 part-time (102 women); includes 225 minority (50 African Americans, 1 American Indian/Alaska Native, 145 Asian Americans or Pacific Islanders, 29 Hispanic Americans), 409 international. Average age 31. 2,661 applicants, 39% accepted, 684 enrolled. In 2009, 498 master's, 12 doctorates awarded. *Degree requirements:* For doctorate, thesis/dissertation. *Entrance requirements:* For master's, GMAT; for doctorate, GMAT, GRE General Test. Additional exam requirements/recommendations for international students: Required—TOEFL. *Application deadline:* For fall admission, 1/15 priority date for domestic students, 12/1 priority date for international students; for winter admission, 3/1 priority date for domestic students; for spring admission, 4/15 for domestic students, 9/1 for international students. Application fee: $55 ($65 for international students). Electronic applications accepted. *Expenses:* Contact institution. *Financial support:* Fellowships with full and partial tuition reimbursements, research assistantships, teaching assistantships, career-related internships or fieldwork, Federal Work-Study, institutionally sponsored loans, tuition waivers (full and partial), and unspecified assistantships available. Support available to part-time students. Financial award application deadline: 3/1; financial award applicants required to submit FAFSA. Total annual research expenditures: $1.1 million. *Unit head:* Daniel Smith, Dean, 812-855-8100, Fax: 812-855-8679, E-mail: business@indiana.edu. *Application contact:* Director of Admissions and Financial Aid, 812-855-8006, Fax: 812-855-9039.

Indiana University Kokomo, School of Business, Kokomo, IN 46904-9003. Offers business administration (MBA). *Accreditation:* AACSB. Part-time and evening/weekend programs available. *Faculty:* 14 full-time (6 women). *Students:* 14 full-time (8 women), 20 part-time (8 women); includes 2 minority (both Asian Americans or Pacific Islanders), 1 international. Average age 32. In 2009, 23 master's awarded. *Degree requirements:* For master's, thesis optional, research project. *Entrance requirements:* For master's, GMAT. Additional exam requirements/recommendations for international students: Required—TOEFL (minimum score 550 paper-based; 213 computer-based). *Application deadline:* For fall admission, 8/1 priority date for domestic and international students; for spring admission, 12/15 priority date for domestic and international students. Applications are processed on a rolling basis. Application fee: $40 ($50 for international students). *Expenses:* Contact institution. *Financial support:* In 2009–10, 2 students received support, including 2 fellowships (averaging $500 per year); research assistantships, teaching assistantships, career-related internships or fieldwork and tuition waivers (partial) also available. *Faculty research:* Investments, outsourcing, technology, adoption. *Unit head:* Dr. Niranjan Pati, Dean, 756-455-9275, Fax: 756-455-9348, E-mail: npati@iuk.edu. *Application contact:* Dr. Linda Ficht, Director of MBA Program, 765-455-9275, Fax: 765-455-9348, E-mail: lficht@iuk.edu.

Indiana University Northwest, School of Business and Economics, Gary, IN 46408-1197. Offers accountancy (M Acc); accounting (Certificate); business administration (MBA). *Accreditation:* AACSB. Part-time and evening/weekend programs available. *Faculty:* 5 full-time (0 women). *Students:* 53 full-time (19 women), 67 part-time (25 women); includes 44 minority (27 African Americans, 5 Asian Americans or Pacific Islanders, 12 Hispanic Americans), 2 international. Average age 33. In 2009, 43 master's awarded. *Entrance requirements:* For master's, GMAT, letter of recommendation. *Application deadline:* For fall admission, 7/15 priority date for domestic students; for spring admission, 11/15 for domestic students. Applications are processed on a rolling basis. Application fee: $25. *Expenses:* Contact institution. *Financial support:* In 2009–10, 9 students received support. Federal Work-Study, institutionally sponsored loans, and unspecified assistantships available. Support available to part-time students. Financial award application deadline: 7/15. *Faculty research:* International finance, wellness in the workplace, handicapped employment, MIS, regional economic forecasting. *Unit head:* Anna Rominger, Dean, 219-980-6636, Fax: 219-980-6916, E-mail: iunbiz@iun.edu. *Application contact:* John Gibson, Director of Graduate Program, 219-980-6635, Fax: 219-980-6916, E-mail: jagibson@iun.edu.

Indiana University of Pennsylvania, School of Graduate Studies and Research, Eberly College of Business and Information Technology, Program in Business Administration, Indiana, PA 15705-1087. Offers business administration (MBA); executive track (MBA). *Accreditation:* AACSB. Part-time programs available. *Faculty:* 35 full-time (7 women). *Students:* 280 full-time (90 women), 20 part-time (9 women); includes 5 minority (4 African Americans, 1 Asian American or Pacific Islander), 223 international. Average age 25. 305 applicants, 65% accepted, 163 enrolled. In 2009, 142 master's awarded. *Degree requirements:* For master's, thesis optional. *Entrance requirements:* For master's, GMAT, 2 letters of recommendation. Additional exam requirements/recommendations for international students: Required—TOEFL. *Application*

deadline: For fall admission, 7/1 priority date for domestic students; for spring admission, 11/1 for domestic students. Applications are processed on a rolling basis. Application fee: $40. *Expenses:* Tuition, state resident: full-time $6666; part-time $370 per credit hour. Tuition, nonresident: full-time $10,666; part-time $593 per credit hour. Required fees: $813 per semester. *Financial support:* In 2009–10, 1 fellowship (averaging $500 per year), 40 research assistantships with full and partial tuition reimbursements (averaging $2,005 per year) were awarded; career-related internships or fieldwork and Federal Work-Study also available. Support available to part-time students. Financial award application deadline: 3/15; financial award applicants required to submit FAFSA. *Unit head:* Dr. Krish Krishnan, Graduate Coordinator, 724-357-2522, E-mail: krishnan@iup.edu. *Application contact:* Donna Griffith, Assistant Dean, 724-357-2222, Fax: 724-357-4862, E-mail: graduate-admissions@iup.edu.

Indiana University–Purdue University Fort Wayne, School of Business and Management Sciences, Fort Wayne, IN 46805-1499. Offers business administration (MBA); business administration-accelerated (MBA). *Accreditation:* AACSB. Part-time programs available. *Faculty:* 31 full-time (11 women). *Students:* 50 full-time (20 women), 81 part-time (33 women); includes 14 minority (4 African Americans, 7 Asian Americans or Pacific Islanders, 3 Hispanic Americans), 7 international. Average age 33. 134 applicants, 47% accepted, 53 enrolled. In 2009, 57 master's awarded. *Entrance requirements:* For master's, GMAT, minimum GPA of 3.0, two letters of recommendation, essay. Additional exam requirements/recommendations for international students: Required—TOEFL (minimum score 600 paper-based; 250 computer-based; 100 iBT). *Application deadline:* For fall admission, 7/15 for domestic students, 5/1 for international students; for spring admission, 11/15 for domestic students, 10/1 for international students. Applications are processed on a rolling basis. Application fee: $55. *Expenses:* Tuition, state resident: full-time $4595; part-time $255 per credit. Tuition, nonresident: full-time $10,963; part-time $609 per credit. Required fees: $528; $29.35 per credit. Tuition and fees vary according to course load. *Financial support:* In 2009–10, 8 teaching assistantships with partial tuition reimbursements (averaging $12,740 per year) were awarded; scholarships/grants and unspecified assistantships also available. Support available to part-time students. Financial award application deadline: 3/1; financial award applicants required to submit FAFSA. *Faculty research:* Minimum wage regulations, U.S. Trade Deficit, supply chain management. Total annual research expenditures: $73,706. *Unit head:* Dr. Otto Chang, Dean, 260-481-0219, Fax: 260-481-6879, E-mail: chango@ipfw.edu. *Application contact:* Dr. Lyman Lewis, MBA Program Administrator, 260-481-6474, Fax: 260-481-6879, E-mail: lewisl@ipfw.edu.

Indiana University–Purdue University Indianapolis, Kelley School of Business, Indianapolis, IN 46202-2896. Offers accounting (MSA); business (MBA). *Accreditation:* AACSB. Part-time and evening/weekend programs available. Postbaccalaureate distance learning degree programs offered (minimal on-campus study). *Faculty:* 20 full-time (4 women), 1 part-time/adjunct (0 women). *Students:* 121 full-time (58 women), 469 part-time (163 women); includes 90 minority (33 African Americans, 45 Asian Americans or Pacific Islanders, 12 Hispanic Americans), 91 international. Average age 30. 592 applicants, 83% accepted, 198 enrolled. In 2009, 400 master's awarded. *Entrance requirements:* For master's, GMAT, previous course work in accounting, statistics. *Application deadline:* For fall admission, 4/15 priority date for domestic and international students; for spring admission, 11/1 priority date for domestic and international students. Application fee: $55 ($65 for international students). Electronic applications accepted. *Expenses:* Contact institution. *Financial support:* In 2009–10, 3 fellowships (averaging $16,193 per year), 1 teaching assistantship (averaging $9,000 per year) were awarded; Federal Work-Study, institutionally sponsored loans, and scholarships/grants also available. Support available to part-time students. Financial award application deadline: 3/1; financial award applicants required to submit FAFSA. *Unit head:* Phil Cochran, Associate Dean, Indianapolis Programs, 317-274-2481, Fax: 317-274-2483, E-mail: busugrad@iupui.edu. *Application contact:* Julie L. Moore, Recorder/Admission Coordinator, 317-274-4895, Fax: 317-274-2483, E-mail: mbaindy@iupui.edu.

Indiana University South Bend, School of Business and Economics, South Bend, IN 46634-7111. Offers accounting (MSA); business administration (MBA); management of information technologies (MS). Part-time and evening/weekend programs available. *Faculty:* 17 full-time (2 women), 3 part-time/adjunct (1 woman). *Students:* 67 full-time (34 women), 110 part-time (49 women); includes 12 minority (7 African Americans, 1 American Indian/Alaska Native, 1 Asian American or Pacific Islander, 3 Hispanic Americans), 56 international. Average age 32. In 2009, 58 master's awarded. *Entrance requirements:* For master's, GMAT. Additional exam requirements/recommendations for international students: Required—TOEFL (minimum score 550 paper-based; 213 computer-based). *Application deadline:* For fall admission, 7/1 priority date for domestic and international students; for spring admission, 11/1 priority date for domestic and international students. Applications are processed on a rolling basis. Application fee: $46 ($58 for international students). *Expenses:* Contact institution. *Financial support:* In 2009–10, 1 fellowship (averaging $3,846 per year) was awarded; Federal Work-Study and institutionally sponsored loans also available. Support available to part-time students. Financial award applicants required to submit FAFSA. *Faculty research:* Financial accounting, consumer research, capital budgeting research, business strategy research. *Unit head:* Robert H. Ducoffe, Dean, 574-520-4228, Fax: 574-520-4866. *Application contact:* Sharon Peterson, Secretary, Graduate Business, 574-520-4138, Fax: 574-520-4866, E-mail: speterso@iusb.edu.

Indiana University Southeast, School of Business, New Albany, IN 47150-6405. Offers business administration (MBA); strategic finance (MS). *Accreditation:* AACSB. *Faculty:* 11 full-time (2 women). *Students:* 17 full-time (7 women), 257 part-time (108 women); includes 26 minority (8 African Americans, 16 Asian Americans or Pacific Islanders, 2 Hispanic Americans), 7 international. Average age 31. In 2009, 57 master's awarded. *Degree requirements:* For master's, community service. *Entrance requirements:* For master's, GMAT, work experience. Additional exam requirements/recommendations for international students: Required—TOEFL. Application fee: $35. *Expenses:* Contact institution. *Financial support:* In 2009–10, 2 teaching assistantships (averaging $4,500 per year) were awarded. *Unit head:* Dr. Jay White, Dean, 812-941-2362, Fax: 812-941-2672. *Application contact:* Dr. Jay White, Dean, 812-941-2362, Fax: 812-941-2672.

Indiana Wesleyan University, College of Adult and Professional Studies, Department of Graduate Studies in Business, Marion, IN 46953. Offers accounting (MBA); applied management (MBA); business administration (MBA); health care (MBA); human resources (MBA); management (MS). Part-time and evening/weekend programs available. Postbaccalaureate distance learning degree programs offered (no on-campus study). *Degree requirements:* For master's, applied business or management project. *Entrance requirements:* For master's, minimum GPA of 2.5, 2 years of related work experience. Additional exam requirements/recommendations for international students: Required—TOEFL (minimum score 550 paper-based; 213 computer-based). Electronic applications accepted. *Expenses:* Tuition: Full-time $7380; part-time $410 per credit. One-time fee: $85. Tuition and fees vary according to campus/location.

Instituto Centroamericano de Administración de Empresas, Graduate Programs, La Garita, Costa Rica. Offers agribusiness (MIAM); business administration (EMBA); economics and finance (MBA); industry and technology (MBA); sustainable development (MBA). *Degree requirements:* For master's, comprehensive exam, essay. *Entrance requirements:* For master's, GMAT or GRE General Test, fluency in Spanish, interview, letters of recommendation, minimum 1 year of work experience. Electronic applications accepted. *Faculty research:* Competitiveness, production.

Instituto Tecnologico de Santo Domingo, Graduate School, Santo Domingo, Dominican Republic. Offers applied linguistics (MA); construction administration (M Mgmt); corporate finance (M Mgmt); education (M Ed); engineering (M Eng), including data telecommunications, industrial engineering, logistics and supply chain, maintenance engineering, sanitary and environmental engineering, structural engineering; environmental science (M En S), including environmental education, environmental management, marine and coastal ecosystems, natural resources management; family therapy (MA); food science and technology (MS); human development (MA); human resources administration (M Mgmt); international business (M Mgmt); labor risks (M Mgmt); management (M Mgmt); marketing (M Mgmt); mathematics (MS); organizational development (M Mgmt); planning and taxation (M Mgmt); psychology (MA); social science (M Ed); upper management (M Mgmt). *Entrance requirements:* For master's, birth certificate, minimum GPA of 2.0.

Instituto Tecnológico y de Estudios Superiores de Monterrey, Campus Central de Veracruz, Graduate Programs, Córdoba, Mexico. Offers administration (MA); administration of information technologies (MTI); computer sciences (MCC); education (MEE); educational institution administration (MAD); educational technology (MTE); electronic commerce (MCE); finance (MAF); humanistic studies (MEH); international business for Latin America (MNL); marketing (MMT); science (MCP); technology management (MTT). Part-time and evening/weekend programs available. Postbaccalaureate distance learning degree programs offered (minimal on-campus study). *Degree requirements:* For master's, thesis (for some programs). *Entrance requirements:* For master's, PAEP College Board. Electronic applications accepted.

Instituto Tecnológico y de Estudios Superiores de Monterrey, Campus Ciudad de México, Division of Business, Ciudad de Mexico, Mexico. Offers business administration (EMBA, MBA, PhD); economy (MBA); finance (MBA). Part-time and evening/weekend programs available. Postbaccalaureate distance learning degree programs offered (minimal on-campus study). *Entrance requirements:* For master's and doctorate, Instituto entrance exam. Additional exam requirements/recommendations for international students: Required—TOEFL.

Instituto Tecnológico y de Estudios Superiores de Monterrey, Campus Ciudad Juárez, Program in Business Administration, Ciudad Juárez, Mexico. Offers MBA. Part-time programs available. Postbaccalaureate distance learning degree programs offered. *Entrance requirements:* Additional exam requirements/recommendations for international students: Required—TOEFL (minimum score 500 paper-based).

Instituto Tecnológico y de Estudios Superiores de Monterrey, Campus Ciudad Obregón, Program in Administration, Ciudad Obregón, Mexico. Offers MA.

Instituto Tecnológico y de Estudios Superiores de Monterrey, Campus Cuernavaca, Programs in Business Administration, Temixco, Mexico. Offers finance (MA); human resources management (MA); international business (MA); marketing (MA).

Instituto Tecnológico y de Estudios Superiores de Monterrey, Campus Estado de México, Professional and Graduate Division, Estado de Mexico, Mexico. Offers administration of information technologies (MITA); architecture (M Arch); business administration (GMBA, MBA); computer sciences (MCS, PhD); education (M Ed); educational institution administration (MAD); educational technology and innovation (PhD); electronic commerce (MEC); environmental systems (MS); finance (MAF); humanistic studies (MHS); information sciences and knowledge management (MISKM); information systems (MS); manufacturing systems (MS); marketing (MEM); quality systems and productivity (MS); science and materials engineering (PhD); telecommunications management (MTM). Part-time programs available. Postbaccalaureate distance learning degree programs offered (minimal on-campus study). *Degree requirements:* For master's, one foreign language, thesis (for some programs); for doctorate, one foreign language, thesis/dissertation. *Entrance requirements:* For master's, E-PAEP 500, interview; for doctorate, E-PAEP 500, research proposal. Additional exam requirements/recommendations for international students: Required—TOEFL (minimum score 550 paper-based). *Faculty research:* Surface treatments by plasmas, mechanical properties, robotics, graphical computing, mechatronics security protocols.

Instituto Tecnológico y de Estudios Superiores de Monterrey, Campus Guadalajara, Program in Business Administration, Zapopan, Mexico. Offers IEMBA, M Ad. Part-time and evening/weekend programs available. Postbaccalaureate distance learning degree programs offered. *Degree requirements:* For master's, one foreign language. *Entrance requirements:* For master's, ITESM admission test. *Faculty research:* Strategic alliances in small business, family business practice in Mexico, competitiveness under NAFTA for Mexican firms.

Instituto Tecnológico y de Estudios Superiores de Monterrey, Campus Irapuato, Graduate Programs, Irapuato, Mexico. Offers administration (MBA); administration of information technology (MAIT); administration of telecommunications (MAT); architecture (M Arch); computer science (MCS); education (M Ed); educational administration (MEA); educational innovation and technology (DEIT); educational technology (MET); electronic commerce (MBA); environmental administration and planning (MEAP); environmental systems (MES); finances (MBA); humanistic studies (MHS); international management for Latin American executives (MIMLAE); library and information science (MLIS); manufacturing quality management (MMQM); marketing research (MBA).

Instituto Tecnológico y de Estudios Superiores de Monterrey, Campus Laguna, Graduate School, Torreón, Mexico. Offers business administration (MBA); industrial engineering (MIE); management information systems (MS). Part-time programs available. *Entrance requirements:* For master's, GMAT. *Faculty research:* Computer communications from home to the university.

Instituto Tecnológico y de Estudios Superiores de Monterrey, Campus León, Program in Business Administration, León, Mexico. Offers MBA. Part-time programs available.

Instituto Tecnológico y de Estudios Superiores de Monterrey, Campus Monterrey, Graduate School of Business Administration and Leadership, Program in Business Administration, Monterrey, Mexico. Offers business administration (MA, MBA); finance (M Sc); international business (M Sc); marketing (M Sc). *Accreditation:* AACSB. Part-time programs available. *Degree requirements:* For master's, one foreign language, thesis. *Entrance requirements:* For master's, GMAT. Additional exam requirements/recommendations for international students: Required—TOEFL. *Faculty research:* Technology management, quality management, organizational theory and behavior.

Instituto Tecnológico y de Estudios Superiores de Monterrey, Campus Monterrey, Graduate School of Business Administration and Leadership, Program in Management, Monterrey, Mexico. Offers PhD. Part-time programs available. *Degree requirements:* For doctorate, one foreign language, thesis/dissertation. *Entrance requirements:* For doctorate, GMAT. Additional exam requirements/recommendations for international students: Required—TOEFL. *Faculty research:* Quality management, manufacturing and technology management, information systems, managerial economics, business policy.

Instituto Tecnológico y de Estudios Superiores de Monterrey, Campus Querétaro, School of Business, Santiago de Querétaro, Mexico. Offers MBA. *Entrance requirements:* For master's, GRE General Test. *Faculty research:* Organizational analysis, industrial marketing, international trade.

Instituto Tecnológico y de Estudios Superiores de Monterrey, Campus Sonora Norte, Program in Business, Hermosillo, Mexico. Offers MA. *Entrance requirements:* For master's, GMAT.

Instituto Tecnológico y de Estudios Superiores de Monterrey, Campus Toluca, Graduate Programs, Toluca, Mexico. Offers MBA. Part-time and evening/weekend programs available. *Degree requirements:* For master's, one foreign language. *Faculty research:* Management in the industrial valley of Toluca.

Inter American University of Puerto Rico, Aguadilla Campus, Graduate School, Aguadilla, PR 00605. Offers accounting (MBA); business information systems (MBA); counseling psychology with an emphasis in family (MS); criminal justice (MA); educative management and leadership (MA); elementary education (MA); finance (MBA); human resources (MBA); industrial management (MBA); marketing (MBA). Part-time and evening/weekend programs available. *Degree requirements:* For master's, comprehensive exam. *Entrance requirements:* For master's, EXADEP, 2 letters of recommendation, minimum GPA of 2.5. Electronic applications accepted.

Inter American University of Puerto Rico, Arecibo Campus, Program in Business Administration, Arecibo, PR 00614-4050. Offers accounting (MBA); finance (MBA); human resources (MBA).

Business Administration and Management—General

Inter American University of Puerto Rico, Barranquitas Campus, Program in Business Administration, Barranquitas, PR 00794. Offers accounting (IMBA); finance (IMBA).

Inter American University of Puerto Rico, Metropolitan Campus, Graduate Programs, Program in General Business, San Juan, PR 00919-1293. Offers MBA.

Inter American University of Puerto Rico, San Germán Campus, Graduate Studies Center, Program in Business Administration, San Germán, PR 00683-5008. Offers accounting (MBA); finance (MBA); human resources (PhD); human resources management (MBA); industrial management (MBA); international business (PhD); management information systems (MBA); marketing management (MBA). Part-time and evening/weekend programs available. *Degree requirements:* For master's, comprehensive exam. *Entrance requirements;* For master's, GRE General Test or EXADEP, minimum GPA of 3.0.

Inter American University of Puerto Rico, San Germán Campus, Graduate Studies Center, Program in Entrepreneurial and Managerial Development, San Germán, PR 00683-5008. Offers interregional and international business (PhD). Part-time and evening/weekend programs available. *Degree requirements:* For doctorate, comprehensive exam, thesis/dissertation. *Entrance requirements:* For doctorate, EXADEP or GMAT, minimum graduate GPA of 3.25.

International College of the Cayman Islands, Graduate Program in Management, Newlands, Cayman Islands. Offers business administration (MBA); management (MS), including education, human resources. Part-time and evening/weekend programs available. *Degree requirements:* For master's, comprehensive exam. *Faculty research:* International human resources administration.

International Technological University, Program in Business Administration, Santa Clara, CA 95050. Offers MBA. Part-time and evening/weekend programs available. *Degree requirements:* For master's, thesis or alternative. *Entrance requirements:* For master's, 1 semester of calculus, minimum GPA of 2.5. Additional exam requirements/recommendations for international students: Required—TOEFL. *Faculty research:* High tech management, business management, international marketing.

International University in Geneva, Master of Business Administration Program, Geneva, Switzerland. Offers finance (MBA); international business (MIB); investment management (MBA); luxury management (MBA); marketing (MBA); wealth management (MBA). *Accreditation:* ACBSP. Part-time and evening/weekend programs available. *Degree requirements:* For master's, comprehensive exam. *Entrance requirements:* For master's, GMAT. Additional exam requirements/recommendations for international students: Required—TOEFL. Electronic applications accepted.

The International University of Monaco, Graduate Programs, Monte Carlo, Monaco. Offers entrepreneurship (EMBA, MBA); financial engineering (M Sc); hedge fund and private equity (M Sc); international marketing (EMBA, MBA); international wealth management (M Sc); luxury goods and services (EMBA, M Sc, MBA); wealth and asset management (EMBA, MBA). Part-time programs available. *Degree requirements:* For master's, comprehensive exam (for some programs), applied research project. *Entrance requirements:* Additional exam requirements/recommendations for international students: Required—TOEFL (minimum score 550 paper-based; 213 computer-based), IELTS. Electronic applications accepted. *Faculty research:* Gaming, leadership, disintermediation.

Iona College, Hagan School of Business, New Rochelle, NY 10801-1890. Offers MBA, PMC. *Accreditation:* AACSB. Part-time and evening/weekend programs available. *Faculty:* 30 full-time (8 women), 17 part-time/adjunct (2 women). *Students:* 84 full-time (42 women), 325 part-time (161 women); includes 45 minority (19 African Americans, 1 American Indian/Alaska Native, 9 Asian Americans or Pacific Islanders, 16 Hispanic Americans), 7 international. Average age 30. 169 applicants, 77% accepted, 83 enrolled. In 2009, 153 master's, 94 other advanced degrees awarded. *Entrance requirements:* For master's, GMAT, 2 letters of recommendation. Additional exam requirements/recommendations for international students: Required—TOEFL (minimum score 550 paper-based; 213 computer-based). *Application deadline:* For fall admission, 8/15 priority date for domestic students, 8/1 for international students; for winter admission, 11/15 priority date for domestic students, 11/1 for international students; for spring admission, 2/15 priority date for domestic students, 2/1 for international students. Applications are processed on a rolling basis. Application fee: $50. Electronic applications accepted. *Expenses:* Contact institution. *Financial support:* Fellowships with tuition reimbursements, Federal Work-Study, scholarships/grants, tuition waivers (partial), and unspecified assistantships available. Support available to part-time students. Financial award application deadline: 4/15; financial award applicants required to submit FAFSA. *Faculty research:* Artificial intelligence, financial services, value-based management, public policy, business ethics. *Unit head:* Dr. Vincent Calluzo, Dean, 914-633-2256, E-mail: vcalluzo@iona.edu. *Application contact:* Jude Fleurismond, Director of MBA Admissions, 914-633-2289, Fax: 914-637-2708, E-mail: jfleurismond@iona.edu.

See Close-Up on page 253.

Iowa State University of Science and Technology, Graduate College, College of Business, Ames, IA 50011. Offers M Acc, MBA, MS, PhD, M Arch/MBA, MBA/MCRP, MBA/MS. *Accreditation:* AACSB. *Faculty:* 71 full-time (17 women), 1 (woman) part-time/adjunct. *Students:* 176 full-time (66 women), 104 part-time (42 women); includes 21 minority (7 African Americans, 8 Asian Americans or Pacific Islanders, 6 Hispanic Americans), 66 international. 256 applicants, 49% accepted, 97 enrolled. In 2009, 116 master's awarded. *Entrance requirements:* For master's, GMAT, resume. Additional exam requirements/recommendations for international students: Required—TOEFL. Application fee: $40 ($90 for international students). Electronic applications accepted. *Expenses:* Contact institution. *Financial support:* In 2009–10, 51 research assistantships with full and partial tuition reimbursements (averaging $7,600 per year), 2 teaching assistantships with full and partial tuition reimbursements (averaging $7,600 per year) were awarded; scholarships/grants, health care benefits, and unspecified assistantships also available. *Unit head:* Dr. Labh S. Hira, Dean, 515-294-2422, E-mail: busgrad@iastate.edu. *Application contact:* Dr. Labh S. Hira, Dean, 515-294-2422, E-mail: busgrad@iastate.edu.

Ithaca College, Division of Graduate and Professional Studies, School of Business, Program in Business Administration, Ithaca, NY 14850. Offers MBA. *Accreditation:* AACSB. Part-time programs available. *Faculty:* 16 full-time (4 women). *Students:* 19 full-time (9 women), 5 part-time (2 women); includes 4 minority (2 African Americans, 1 Asian American or Pacific Islander, 1 Hispanic American), 2 international. Average age 28. 48 applicants, 69% accepted, 20 enrolled. In 2009, 28 master's awarded. *Degree requirements:* For master's, comprehensive exam (for some programs), thesis optional. *Entrance requirements:* For master's, GMAT, minimum GPA of 3.0. Additional exam requirements/recommendations for international students: Required—TOEFL (minimum score 550 paper-based; 213 computer-based; 80 iBT). *Application deadline:* For fall admission, 8/1 for domestic and international students; for spring admission, 12/1 for domestic and international students. Applications are processed on a rolling basis. Application fee: $40. Electronic applications accepted. *Expenses:* Contact institution. *Financial support:* In 2009–10, 20 students received support, including 5 fellowships (averaging $5,875 per year), 4 teaching assistantships (averaging $6,764 per year); career-related internships or fieldwork, Federal Work-Study, and scholarships/grants also available. Support available to part-time students. Financial award application deadline: 4/15; financial award applicants required to submit CSS PROFILE or FAFSA. *Unit head:* Dr. Donald Eckrich, MBA Program Director, 607-274-3527, Fax: 607-274-1263, E-mail: gps@ithaca.edu. *Application contact:* Rob Gearhart, Dean, Graduate and Professional Studies, 607-274-3527, Fax: 607-274-1263, E-mail: gps@ithaca.edu.

ITT Technical Institute, Online MBA Program, Indianapolis, IN 46268-1119. Offers MBA.

Jackson State University, Graduate School, School of Business, Department of Business Administration, Jackson, MS 39217. Offers PhD. *Accreditation:* AACSB. Part-time and evening/weekend programs available. *Degree requirements:* For doctorate, comprehensive exam, thesis/dissertation. *Entrance requirements:* For doctorate, MAT, GMAT.

Jackson State University, Graduate School, School of Business, Department of Economics, Finance and General Business, Jackson, MS 39217. Offers business administration (MBA).

Part-time and evening/weekend programs available. *Degree requirements:* For master's, comprehensive exam, thesis. *Entrance requirements:* For master's, GRE General Test, GMAT. Additional exam requirements/recommendations for international students: Required—TOEFL.

Jacksonville State University, College of Graduate Studies and Continuing Education, College of Commerce and Business Administration, Jacksonville, AL 36265-1602. Offers MBA. *Accreditation:* AACSB. Part-time and evening/weekend programs available. *Degree requirements:* For master's, comprehensive exam, thesis (for some programs). *Entrance requirements:* For master's, GMAT. Additional exam requirements/recommendations for international students: Required—TOEFL (minimum score 500 paper-based; 173 computer-based; 61 iBT). Electronic applications accepted.

Jacksonville University, Davis College of Business, Executive Master's in Business Administration Program, Jacksonville, FL 32211. Offers Exec MBA. Part-time and evening/weekend programs available. *Entrance requirements:* For master's, 5 years of managerial or professional experience. Additional exam requirements/recommendations for international students: Required—TOEFL. *Faculty research:* Economic impact, vicarious learning, psychology and advertising.

Jacksonville University, Davis College of Business, Master's in Business Administration Program, Jacksonville, FL 32211. Offers MBA. Part-time and evening/weekend programs available. *Entrance requirements:* For master's, GMAT. Additional exam requirements/recommendations for international students: Required—TOEFL.

James Madison University, The Graduate School, College of Business, Program in Business Administration, Harrisonburg, VA 22807. Offers MBA. *Accreditation:* AACSB. Part-time and evening/weekend programs available. Postbaccalaureate distance learning degree programs offered (no on-campus study). *Students:* 17 full-time (4 women), 50 part-time (14 women); includes 10 minority (2 African Americans, 7 Asian Americans or Pacific Islanders, 1 Hispanic American), 5 international. Average age 27. In 2009, 40 master's awarded. *Entrance requirements:* For master's, GMAT, resume, 2 letters of recommendation. Additional exam requirements/recommendations for international students: Required—TOEFL. *Application deadline:* For fall admission, 6/1 priority date for domestic students, 5/1 for international students; for spring admission, 6/1 for domestic students, 9/1 for international students. Applications are processed on a rolling basis. Application fee: $55. Electronic applications accepted. *Expenses:* Tuition, area resident: Part-time $305 per credit hour. Tuition, state resident: part-time $305 per credit hour. Tuition, nonresident: part-time $890 per credit hour. *Financial support:* Federal Work-Study available. Financial award application deadline: 3/1; financial award applicants required to submit FAFSA. *Unit head:* Dr. Paul E. Bierly, Director, 540-568-3009. *Application contact:* Lynette M. Bible, Director of Graduate Admissions, 540-568-6395, Fax: 540-568-7860, E-mail: biblelm@jmu.edu.

John Brown University, Graduate Business Division, Siloam Springs, AR 72761-2121. Offers business administration (MBA), including international business, leadership and ethics; leadership and ethics (MS), including higher education. Part-time and evening/weekend programs available. Postbaccalaureate distance learning degree programs offered (minimal on-campus study). *Faculty:* 2 full-time (0 women), 13 part-time/adjunct (6 women). *Students:* 13 full-time (6 women), 143 part-time (56 women); includes 19 minority (6 African Americans, 2 American Indian/Alaska Native, 6 Asian Americans or Pacific Islanders, 5 Hispanic Americans), 5 international. Average age 35. 94 applicants, 85% accepted, 71 enrolled. In 2009, 54 master's awarded. *Entrance requirements:* For master's, GRE General Test, MAT, minimum GPA of 3.0. Additional exam requirements/recommendations for international students: Required—TOEFL (minimum score 550 paper-based; 173 computer-based). *Application deadline:* For fall admission, 8/11 priority date for domestic students; for spring admission, 1/12 priority date for domestic students. Applications are processed on a rolling basis. Application fee: $35 ($100 for international students). Electronic applications accepted. *Expenses:* Tuition: Full-time $8100; part-time $450 per credit. *Financial support:* In 2009–10, 8 students received support, including 8 fellowships (averaging $5,500 per year); scholarships/grants, tuition waivers (full), and unspecified assistantships also available. Financial award application deadline: 3/1; financial award applicants required to submit FAFSA. *Unit head:* Dr. Joe Walenciak, Program Director, 479-524-7170, Fax: 479-524-9548. *Application contact:* Brent Young, Graduate Business Representative, 479-631-0496, E-mail: byoung@jbu.edu.

John Carroll University, Graduate School, John M. and Mary Jo Boler School of Business, University Heights, OH 44118-4581. Offers accountancy (MS); business (MBA). *Accreditation:* AACSB. Part-time and evening/weekend programs available. *Entrance requirements:* For master's, GMAT, minimum GPA of 2.5. Additional exam requirements/recommendations for international students: Required—TOEFL (minimum score 550 paper-based; 213 computer-based). Electronic applications accepted. *Expenses:* Contact institution. *Faculty research:* Accounting, economics and finance, management, marketing and logistics.

John F. Kennedy University, School of Management, Program in Business Administration, Pleasant Hill, CA 94523-4817. Offers business administration (MBA); organizational leadership (Certificate). Part-time and evening/weekend programs available. *Degree requirements:* For master's, thesis or alternative. *Entrance requirements:* For master's, interview. Additional exam requirements/recommendations for international students: Required—TOEFL.

The Johns Hopkins University, Carey Business School, Management Programs, Baltimore, MD 21218-2699. Offers leadership development (Certificate); organization development and human resources (MS); skilled facilitator (Certificate). Evening/weekend programs available. *Faculty:* 29 full-time (6 women), 135 part-time/adjunct (29 women). *Students:* 2 full-time (both women), 65 part-time (44 women); includes 40 minority (30 African Americans, 4 Asian Americans or Pacific Islanders, 6 Hispanic Americans), 4 international. Average age 35. 35 applicants, 94% accepted, 29 enrolled. In 2009, 93 master's, 37 other advanced degrees awarded. *Degree requirements:* For master's, 36 credits including final project. *Entrance requirements:* For master's and Certificate, minimum GPA of 3.0, resume, work experience, two letters of recommendation. Additional exam requirements/recommendations for international students: Required—TOEFL (minimum score 600 paper-based; 250 computer-based; 100 iBT). *Application deadline:* For fall admission, 5/1 for international students; for spring admission, 10/15 for international students. Applications are processed on a rolling basis. Application fee: $100. Electronic applications accepted. *Financial support:* Scholarships/grants available. Support available to part-time students. Financial award application deadline: 4/1; financial award applicants required to submit FAFSA. *Faculty research:* Agency theory and theory of the firm, technological entrepreneurship, technology policy and economic development, strategic human resources management, ethics and stakeholder theory. Total annual research expenditures: $57,832. *Unit head:* Dr. Dipankar Chakravarti, Vice Dean of Programs, 410-516-8561, E-mail: dipankar.chakravarti@jhu.edu. *Application contact:* Robin Greeberg, Admissions Coordinator, 410-516-4234, Fax: 410-516-0826, E-mail: carey.admissions@jhu.edu.

The Johns Hopkins University, Carey Business School, MBA Department, Baltimore, MD 21218-2699. Offers MBA, MBA/MA, MBA/MPH, MBA/MS, MBA/MSIS, MBA/MSN. Part-time and evening/weekend programs available. Postbaccalaureate distance learning degree programs offered (minimal on-campus study). *Faculty:* 29 full-time (6 women), 135 part-time/adjunct (29 women). *Students:* 128 full-time (58 women), 496 part-time (211 women); includes 201 minority (88 African Americans, 2 American Indian/Alaska Native, 84 Asian Americans or Pacific Islanders, 27 Hispanic Americans), 69 international. Average age 33. 267 applicants, 66% accepted, 136 enrolled. In 2009, 244 master's awarded. *Degree requirements:* For master's, capstone project (MBA). *Entrance requirements:* For master's, GMAT or GRE, minimum GPA of 3.0, resume, work experience, two letters of recommendation. Additional exam requirements/recommendations for international students: Required—TOEFL (minimum score 600 paper-based; 250 computer-based; 100 iBT). *Application deadline:* For fall admission, 5/1 for international students; for spring admission, 10/15 for international students. Applications are processed on a rolling basis. Application fee: $100. Electronic applications accepted. *Financial support:* Scholarships/grants available. Support available to part-time students. Financial award application deadline: 4/1; financial award applicants required to submit FAFSA. *Unit head:* Dr.

Dipankar Chakravarti, Vice Dean of Programs, 410-516-8561, Fax: 410-516-2033, E-mail: dipankar.chakravarti@jhu.edu. *Application contact:* Robin Greenberg, Admissions Coordinator, 410-516-4234, Fax: 410-516-0826, E-mail: carey.admissions@jhu.edu.

The Johns Hopkins University, School of Education, Division of Public Safety Leadership, Baltimore, MD 21218. Offers intelligence analysis (MS); management (MS). Part-time and evening/weekend programs available. *Faculty:* 10 full-time (3 women), 23 part-time/adjunct (7 women). *Students:* 159 full-time (47 women), 1 part-time (0 women); includes 55 minority (47 African Americans, 1 American Indian/Alaska Native, 3 Asian Americans or Pacific Islanders, 4 Hispanic Americans). Average age 39. 81 applicants, 75% accepted, 54 enrolled. In 2009, 110 master's awarded. *Entrance requirements:* For master's, minimum undergraduate GPA of 3.0, curriculum vitae/resume, interview, professional experience, endorsement letter (MS in management). Additional exam requirements/recommendations for international students: Required—TOEFL (minimum score 600 paper-based; 250 computer-based; 100 iBT). *Application deadline:* For fall admission, 5/1 for international students; for spring admission, 10/15 for international students. Applications are processed on a rolling basis. Application fee: $0. Electronic applications accepted. *Financial support:* Scholarships/grants available. Support available to part-time students. Financial award application deadline: 6/1; financial award applicants required to submit FAFSA. *Faculty research:* Campus and school safety, prevention and effective response to violence against women, counterterrorism training, leadership development for public safety and homeland security executives. *Unit head:* Dr. Sheldon Greenberg, Associate Dean, 410-516-9900, Fax: 410-290-1061, E-mail: psl@jhu.edu. *Application contact:* Jennifer Shaffer, Director of Admissions, 410-516-9797, Fax: 410-516-9799, E-mail: educationinfo@jhu.edu.

Jones International University, School of Business, Centennial, CO 80112. Offers accounting (MBA); business communication (MABC); entrepreneurship (MABC, MBA); finance (MBA); global enterprise management (MBA); health care management (MBA); information security management (MBA); information technology management (MBA); leadership and influence (MABC); leading the customer-driven organization (MABC); negotiation and conflict management (MBA); project management (MABC, MBA). Program only offered online. Part-time and evening/weekend programs available. Postbaccalaureate distance learning degree programs offered (no on-campus study). *Degree requirements:* For master's, capstone project. *Entrance requirements:* For master's, minimum cumulative GPA of 2.5. Additional exam requirements/recommendations for international students: Recommended—TOEFL (minimum score 550 paper-based; 213 computer-based). Electronic applications accepted.

Kansas State University, Graduate School, College of Business Administration, Program in Business Administration, Manhattan, KS 66506. Offers MBA. *Accreditation:* AACSB. Part-time programs available. *Faculty:* 1 full-time (0 women), 2 part-time/adjunct (0 women). *Students:* 51 full-time (22 women), 21 part-time (7 women); includes 7 minority (2 African Americans, 2 Asian Americans or Pacific Islanders, 3 Hispanic Americans), 8 international. Average age 27. 68 applicants, 59% accepted, 21 enrolled. In 2009, 33 master's awarded. *Degree requirements:* For master's, comprehensive exam. *Entrance requirements:* For master's, GMAT, minimum undergraduate GPA of 3.0. Additional exam requirements/recommendations for international students: Required—TOEFL (minimum score 550 paper-based; 213 computer-based). *Application deadline:* For fall admission, 2/1 priority date for domestic and international students; for spring admission, 8/1 priority date for domestic and international students. Applications are processed on a rolling basis. Application fee: $60. Electronic applications accepted. *Financial support:* In 2009–10, 16 research assistantships with partial tuition reimbursements (averaging $8,320 per year) were awarded; institutionally sponsored loans and scholarships/grants also available. Support available to part-time students. Financial award application deadline: 3/1; financial award applicants required to submit FAFSA. *Faculty research:* Organizational citizenship behavior, service marketing, impression management, human resources management, lean manufacturing and supply chain management, financial market behavior and investment management. Total annual research expenditures: $151,822. *Unit head:* Richard Ott, 785-532-6184, E-mail: rlo@ksu.edu. *Application contact:* Jeff Katz, Director, 785-532-7451, Fax: 785-532-5959, E-mail: jkatz@ksu.edu.

Kansas Wesleyan University, Program in Business Administration, Salina, KS 67401-6196. Offers business administration (MBA); sports management (MBA). Part-time and evening/weekend programs available. *Entrance requirements:* For master's, GMAT, minimum graduate GPA of 3.0 or undergraduate GPA of 3.25.

Kaplan University, Davenport Campus, School of Business, Davenport, IA 52807-2095. Offers business administration (MBA); change leadership (MS); entrepreneurship (MBA); finance (MBA); health care management (MBA, MS); human resource (MBA); international business (MBA); management (MS); marketing (MBA); project management (MBA, MS); supply chain management and logistics (MBA, MS). Part-time and evening/weekend programs available. Postbaccalaureate distance learning degree programs offered (no on-campus study). *Entrance requirements:* Additional exam requirements/recommendations for international students: Required—TOEFL (minimum score 550 paper-based; 218 computer-based; 80 iBT). Electronic applications accepted.

Kean University, Nathan Weiss Graduate College, Program in Educational Administration, Union, NJ 07083. Offers school business administration (MA); supervisors and principals (MA). *Accreditation:* NCATE. Part-time and evening/weekend programs available. *Faculty:* 7 full-time (2 women). *Students:* 16 full-time (10 women), 253 part-time (164 women); includes 74 minority (44 African Americans, 5 Asian Americans or Pacific Islanders, 25 Hispanic Americans). Average age 36. 118 applicants, 98% accepted, 79 enrolled. In 2009, 83 master's awarded. *Degree requirements:* For master's, comprehensive exam, portfolio, field experience, research component. *Entrance requirements:* For master's, GRE General Test or MAT, minimum GPA of 3.0, interview, 2 letters of recommendation, 1 year of teaching experience, teacher certification. *Application deadline:* For fall admission, 5/1 for domestic students; for spring admission, 11/1 for domestic students. Application fee: $60 ($150 for international students). Electronic applications accepted. *Expenses:* Tuition, state resident: full-time $10,440; part-time $435 per credit. Tuition, nonresident: full-time $14,160; part-time $590 per credit. Required fees: $2642; $110 per credit. Part-time tuition and fees vary according to course load and degree level. *Financial support:* In 2009–10, 1 research assistantship with full tuition reimbursement (averaging $3,263 per year) was awarded; unspecified assistantships also available. *Unit head:* Dr. Gerard Babo, Program Coordinator, 908-737-4270, E-mail: gbabo@kean.edu. *Application contact:* Ann-Marie Kay, Assistant Director of Graduate Admissions, 908-737-5922, Fax: 908-737-5965, E-mail: akay@kean.edu.

Keiser University, MBA, Master of Business Administration Program, Fort Lauderdale, FL 33309. Offers international business (MBA); leadership for managers (MBA); marketing (MBA). Part-time programs available. Postbaccalaureate distance learning degree programs offered (minimal on-campus study). *Faculty:* 8 full-time (3 women), 7 part-time/adjunct (2 women). *Students:* 18 full-time (14 women), 83 part-time (51 women); includes 51 minority (30 African Americans, 2 American Indian/Alaska Native, 2 Asian Americans or Pacific Islanders, 17 Hispanic Americans), 1 international. Average age 42. 30 applicants, 77% accepted, 18 enrolled. In 2009, 21 master's awarded. *Entrance requirements:* For master's, minimum GPA of 2.7 from an accredited institution. Additional exam requirements/recommendations for international students: Required—TOEFL. *Application deadline:* Applications are processed on a rolling basis. Application fee: $50. Electronic applications accepted. *Financial support:* In 2009–10, 95 students received support. Federal Work-Study available. Financial award applicants required to submit FAFSA. *Unit head:* Dr. Sara Malmstrom, Dean, 954-318-1620. *Application contact:* Manuel Christiansen, Associate Director of Admissions, 954-318-1620 Ext. 309, E-mail: mchristiansen@keiseruniversity.edu.

Keller Graduate School of Management, Keller Graduate School of Management, Long Island City, NY 11101-3051. Offers MAFM, MBA, MISM, Graduate Certificate.

Keller Graduate School of Management, Keller Graduate School of Management, New York, NY 10036-4041. Offers MBA, MISM.

Kennesaw State University, Michael J. Coles College of Business, Doctor of Business Administration Program, Kennesaw, GA 30144-5591. Offers DBA. Part-time programs available. *Students:* 17 part-time (6 women); includes 3 minority (2 African Americans, 1 Asian American or Pacific Islander). Average age 50. *Degree requirements:* For doctorate, thesis/dissertation. *Entrance requirements:* Additional exam requirements/recommendations for international students: Required—TOEFL (minimum score 550 paper-based; 213 computer-based; 80 iBT), IELTS (minimum score 6). *Application deadline:* For spring admission, 10/1 for domestic and international students. Applications are processed on a rolling basis. Application fee: $100. Electronic applications accepted. *Expenses:* Tuition, state resident: full-time $2341; part-time $196 per credit hour. Tuition, nonresident: full-time $9396; part-time $783 per credit hour. Required fees: $573 per semester. *Unit head:* Joe Hair, Director, 770-499-3280, E-mail: jhair3@kennesaw.edu. *Application contact:* Vilma Marquez, Admissions Counselor, 770-420-4377, Fax: 770-423-6885, E-mail: ksugrad@kennesaw.edu.

Kennesaw State University, Michael J. Coles College of Business, Program in Business Administration, Kennesaw, GA 30144-5591. Offers MBA. Part-time and evening/weekend programs available. Postbaccalaureate distance learning degree programs offered (no on-campus study). *Students:* 265 full-time (97 women), 355 part-time (128 women); includes 167 minority (121 African Americans, 36 Asian Americans or Pacific Islanders, 10 Hispanic Americans), 45 international. Average age 34. 475 applicants, 48% accepted, 187 enrolled. In 2009, 359 master's awarded. *Entrance requirements:* For master's, GMAT (minimum score: 500), minimum GPA of 2.8, 1 year of work experience. Additional exam requirements/recommendations for international students: Required—TOEFL (minimum score 550 paper-based; 213 computer-based; 80 iBT), IELTS (minimum score 6). *Application deadline:* For fall admission, 8/1 for domestic and international students; for spring admission, 12/1 for domestic and international students. Applications are processed on a rolling basis. Application fee: $60. Electronic applications accepted. *Expenses:* Tuition, state resident: full-time $2341; part-time $196 per credit hour. Tuition, nonresident: full-time $9396; part-time $783 per credit hour. Required fees: $573 per semester. *Financial support:* In 2009–10, 4 research assistantships with tuition reimbursements (averaging $4,000 per year) were awarded; unspecified assistantships also available. Financial award application deadline: 6/15; financial award applicants required to submit FAFSA. *Unit head:* Dr. Sheb True, Director, 770-423-6087, E-mail: strue@kennesaw.edu. *Application contact:* Vilma Marquez, Admissions Counselor, 770-420-4377, Fax: 770-423-6885, E-mail: ksugrad@kennesaw.edu.

Kent State University, Graduate School of Management, Master's Program in Business Administration, Kent, OH 44242-0001. Offers MBA. *Accreditation:* AACSB. Part-time and evening/weekend programs available. *Faculty:* 57 full-time (15 women), 8 part-time/adjunct (5 women). *Students:* 108 full-time (47 women), 162 part-time (72 women); includes 21 minority (10 African Americans, 7 Asian Americans or Pacific Islanders, 4 Hispanic Americans), 20 international. Average age 27. 159 applicants, 86% accepted, 100 enrolled. In 2009, 95 master's awarded. *Entrance requirements:* For master's, GMAT, minimum GPA of 2.75. Additional exam requirements/recommendations for international students: Required—TOEFL (minimum score 550 paper-based; 213 computer-based; 79 iBT). *Application deadline:* For fall admission, 7/1 for domestic students, 4/1 for international students; for spring admission, 12/15 for domestic students. Applications are processed on a rolling basis. Application fee: $30 ($60 for international students). Electronic applications accepted. *Financial support:* In 2009–10, 33 students received support, including 33 research assistantships with full tuition reimbursements available (averaging $6,700 per year); fellowships, career-related internships or fieldwork, Federal Work-Study, and institutionally sponsored loans also available. Financial award application deadline: 4/1; financial award applicants required to submit FAFSA. *Unit head:* Louise M. Ditchey, Director, 330-672-2282, Fax: 330-672-7303, E-mail: gradbus@kent.edu. *Application contact:* Felecia A. Urbanek, Coordinator, Graduate Programs, 330-672-2282, Fax: 330-672-7303, E-mail: gradbus@kent.edu.

See Display on page 138.

Kent State University at Stark, Professional MBA Program, Canton, OH 44720-7599. Offers MBA.

Kentucky State University, College of Professional Studies, Frankfort, KY 40601. Offers business administration (MBA), including accounting, finance, management, marketing; public administration (MPA), including human resource management, international administration and development, management information systems, nonprofit management; special education (MA). Part-time and evening/weekend programs available. Postbaccalaureate distance learning degree programs offered (minimal on-campus study). *Faculty:* 11 full-time (3 women), 2 part-time/adjunct (both women). *Students:* 79 full-time (51 women), 66 part-time (34 women); includes 88 minority (85 African Americans, 2 Asian Americans or Pacific Islanders, 1 Hispanic American), 4 international. Average age 34. 92 applicants, 75% accepted, 52 enrolled. In 2009, 32 master's awarded. *Degree requirements:* For master's, comprehensive exam, thesis optional. *Entrance requirements:* For master's, GMAT, GRE. Additional exam requirements/recommendations for international students: Required—TOEFL (minimum score 525 paper-based; 173 computer-based). *Application deadline:* For fall admission, 7/1 priority date for domestic students, 4/15 priority date for international students; for spring admission, 11/15 priority date for domestic students, 8/1 priority date for international students. Applications are processed on a rolling basis. Application fee: $30 ($100 for international students). Electronic applications accepted. *Expenses:* Tuition, state resident: full-time $5634; part-time $313 per credit hour. Tuition, nonresident: full-time $14,598; part-time $811 per credit hour. Required fees: $450; $25 per credit hour. *Financial support:* In 2009–10, 113 students received support, including 4 research assistantships (averaging $14,035 per year); career-related internships or fieldwork, scholarships/grants, tuition waivers (partial), and unspecified assistantships also available. Financial award application deadline: 4/15; financial award applicants required to submit FAFSA. *Unit head:* Dr. Gashaw Lake, Dean, College of Professional Studies, 502-597-6105, Fax: 502-597-6715, E-mail: gashaw.lake@kysu.edu. *Application contact:* Cedric Cunningham, Administrative Assistant, Office of Graduate Studies, 502-597-6536, E-mail: cedric.cunningham@kysu.edu.

Kettering University, Graduate School, Department of Business, Flint, MI 48504. Offers business administration (MBA); engineering management (MSEM); information technology (MSIT); manufacturing management (MSMM); manufacturing operations (MSMO); operations management (MSOM). *Accreditation:* ACBSP. Part-time and evening/weekend programs available. Postbaccalaureate distance learning degree programs offered (no on-campus study). *Faculty:* 9 full-time (3 women), 4 part-time/adjunct (0 women). *Students:* 12 full-time (5 women), 251 part-time (79 women); includes 42 minority (27 African Americans, 1 American Indian/Alaska Native, 9 Asian Americans or Pacific Islanders, 5 Hispanic Americans), 15 international. Average age 32. 74 applicants, 78% accepted, 31 enrolled. In 2009, 123 master's awarded. *Entrance requirements:* Additional exam requirements/recommendations for international students: Required—TOEFL (minimum score 550 paper-based; 213 computer-based; 79 iBT). *Application deadline:* For fall admission, 9/15 for domestic students, 6/15 for international students; for winter admission, 12/15 for domestic students, 9/15 for international students; for spring admission, 3/15 for domestic students, 12/15 for international students. Applications are processed on a rolling basis. Electronic applications accepted. *Expenses:* Tuition: Full-time $11,120; part-time $695 per credit hour. *Financial support:* In 2009–10, 101 students received support, including fellowships with full tuition reimbursements available (averaging $13,000 per year), research assistantships with full tuition reimbursements available (averaging $13,000 per year), teaching assistantships with full tuition reimbursements available (averaging $13,000 per year); Federal Work-Study, scholarships/grants, and tuition waivers (partial) also available. Support available to part-time students. Financial award application deadline: 7/15. *Unit head:* Dr. Tony Hain, Vice President of Graduate Studies and Corporate Connections, 810-762-9616, Fax: 810-762-9935, E-mail: thain@kettering.edu. *Application contact:* Bonnie Switzer, Admissions Representative, 810-762-7953, Fax: 810-762-9935, E-mail: bswitzer@kettering.edu.

Keuka College, Program in Management, Keuka Park, NY 14478-0098. Offers MS. Evening/weekend programs available. *Faculty:* 3 full-time (1 woman), 15 part-time/adjunct (5 women).

Business Administration and Management—General

Keuka College (continued)

Students: 108 full-time (76 women), 28 part-time (17 women); includes 13 minority (7 African Americans, 1 American Indian/Alaska Native, 1 Asian American or Pacific Islander, 4 Hispanic Americans). 31 applicants, 100% accepted, 31 enrolled. In 2009, 54 master's awarded. *Degree requirements:* For master's, thesis. *Entrance requirements:* For master's, 2 letters of reference, minimum GPA of 3.0. Additional exam requirements/recommendations for international students: Required—TOEFL (minimum score 550 paper-based; 213 computer-based). *Application deadline:* For fall admission, 8/15 priority date for domestic students; for winter admission, 12/15 priority date for domestic students; for spring admission, 4/15 priority date for domestic students. Applications are processed on a rolling basis. Application fee: $30. *Expenses:* Contact institution. *Faculty research:* Leadership, adult education, decision making, strategic planning, business ethics. *Unit head:* Gary M. Smith, Chair, Division of Business and Management, 315-279-5352, E-mail: gsmith@mail.keuka.edu. *Application contact:* Claudine Ninestine, Director of Admissions, 315-279-5413, Fax: 315-279-5386, E-mail: admissions@mail.keuka.edu.

King College, School of Business and Economics, Bristol, TN 37620-2699. Offers MBA. Part-time and evening/weekend programs available. Postbaccalaureate distance learning degree programs offered (no on-campus study). *Degree requirements:* For master's, comprehensive exam, thesis optional. *Entrance requirements:* For master's, GMAT, 2 years of work experience. Additional exam requirements/recommendations for international students: Required—TOEFL (minimum score 550 paper-based). Electronic applications accepted. *Faculty research:* Leadership, international monetary policy.

King's College, William G. McGowan School of Business, Wilkes-Barre, PA 18711-0801. Offers health care administration (MS). *Accreditation:* AACSB. Part-time programs available. *Entrance requirements:* Additional exam requirements/recommendations for international students: Required—TOEFL (minimum score 600 paper-based; 250 computer-based).

Kutztown University of Pennsylvania, College of Business, Program in Business Administration, Kutztown, PA 19530-0730. Offers MBA. Part-time and evening/weekend programs available. *Faculty:* 10 full-time (2 women), 2 part-time/adjunct (0 women). *Students:* 25 full-time (6 women), 39 part-time (21 women); includes 10 minority (4 African Americans, 1 Asian American or Pacific Islander, 5 Hispanic Americans), 8 international. Average age 31. 61 applicants, 74% accepted, 23 enrolled. In 2009, 26 master's awarded. *Degree requirements:* For master's, comprehensive exam, thesis (for some programs). *Entrance requirements:* For master's, GMAT. Additional exam requirements/recommendations for international students: Required—TOEFL. *Application deadline:* For fall admission, 8/15 for domestic students, 8/15 priority date for international students; for spring admission, 12/15 for domestic students, 12/15 priority date for international students. Applications are processed on a rolling basis. Application fee: $35. Electronic applications accepted. *Expenses:* Tuition, state resident: full-time $6666; part-time $370 per credit. Tuition, nonresident: full-time $10,666; part-time $593 per credit. Required fees: $62 per credit. $60 per semester. *Financial support:* Career-related internships or fieldwork, Federal Work-Study, scholarships/grants, tuition waivers (partial), and unspecified assistantships available. Financial award application deadline: 3/1; financial award applicants required to submit FAFSA. *Unit head:* Dr. William Dempsey, Interim Dean, 610-683-4575, Fax: 610-683-4573, E-mail: dempsey@kutztown.edu. *Application contact:* Kelly D. Burr, Associate Director, Graduate Admissions, 610-683-4200, Fax: 610-683-1393, E-mail: graduate@kutztown.edu.

Lake Erie College, Division of Management Studies, Painesville, OH 44077-3389. Offers general management (MBA); management healthcare administration (MBA). Part-time and evening/weekend programs available. *Entrance requirements:* For master's, GMAT or minimum GPA of 3.0, resume, references. Additional exam requirements/recommendations for international students: Required—TOEFL (minimum score 590 paper-based). Electronic applications accepted. *Faculty research:* Organizational effectiveness.

Lake Forest Graduate School of Management, MBA Program, Program at Chicago, Lake Forest, IL 60045. Offers MBA. Part-time and evening/weekend programs available. *Entrance requirements:* For master's, GMAT, 4 years business experience, interview, 2 letters of recommendation. Electronic applications accepted.

Lake Forest Graduate School of Management, MBA Program, Program at Lake Forest, Lake Forest, IL 60045. Offers MBA. Part-time and evening/weekend programs available. *Entrance requirements:* For master's, GMAT, 4 years of work experience, interview, 2 letters of recommendation. Electronic applications accepted.

Lake Forest Graduate School of Management, MBA Program, Program at Schaumburg, Lake Forest, IL 60045. Offers MBA. Part-time and evening/weekend programs available. *Entrance requirements:* For master's, GMAT, 4 years of work experience, interview, 2 letters of recommendation. Electronic applications accepted.

Lakeland College, Graduate Studies Division, Program in Business Administration, Sheboygan, WI 53082-0359. Offers accounting (MBA); finance (MBA); healthcare management (MBA); project management (MBA). *Entrance requirements:* For master's, GMAT. *Expenses:* Contact institution.

Lamar University, College of Graduate Studies, College of Business, Beaumont, TX 77710. Offers accounting (MBA); experiential business and entrepreneurship (MBA); financial management (MBA); healthcare administration (MBA); information systems (MBA); management (MBA). *Accreditation:* AACSB. Part-time and evening/weekend programs available. *Faculty:* 18 full-time (4 women), 4 part-time/adjunct (0 women). *Students:* 62 full-time (27 women), 59 part-time (16 women); includes 19 minority (8 African Americans, 6 Asian Americans or Pacific Islanders, 5 Hispanic Americans), 19 international. Average age 29. 210 applicants, 34% accepted, 33 enrolled. In 2009, 41 master's awarded. *Degree requirements:* For master's, comprehensive exam (for some programs), thesis optional. *Entrance requirements:* For master's, GMAT. Additional exam requirements/recommendations for international students: Required—TOEFL (minimum score 525 paper-based; 197 computer-based). *Application deadline:* For fall admission, 3/15 priority date for domestic students; for spring admission, 10/1 priority date for domestic students. Applications are processed on a rolling basis. Application fee: $25 ($50 for international students). *Financial support:* In 2009–10, 12 students received support, including 4 research assistantships with partial tuition reimbursements available; fellowships with tuition reimbursements available, career-related internships or fieldwork, Federal Work-Study, institutionally sponsored loans, scholarships/grants, and tuition waivers (partial) also available. Support available to part-time students. Financial award application deadline: 4/1; financial award applicants required to submit FAFSA. *Faculty research:* Marketing, finance, quantitative methods, management information systems, legal, environmental. *Unit head:* Dr. Enrique R. Venta, Dean, 409-880-8604, Fax: 409-880-8088, E-mail: henry.venta@lamar.edu. *Application contact:* Dr. Brad Mayer, Professor and Associate Dean, 409-880-2383, Fax: 409-880-8605, E-mail: bradley.mayer@lamar.edu.

La Salle University, School of Business, Philadelphia, PA 19141-1199. Offers MBA, MS, Certificate, MSN/MBA. *Accreditation:* AACSB. Part-time and evening/weekend programs available. *Entrance requirements:* For master's, GMAT; for Certificate, MBA. Additional exam requirements/recommendations for international students: Required—TOEFL. Electronic applications accepted. *Expenses:* Contact institution. *Faculty research:* Small business development, unemployment insurance costs, nonprofit business, transfer pricing, forecasting.

Lasell College, Graduate and Professional Studies in Management, Newton, MA 02466-2709. Offers elder care administration (MSM, Graduate Certificate); elder care marketing (MSM, Graduate Certificate); fundraising management (MSM, Graduate Certificate); human resource management (MSM, Graduate Certificate); management (MSM, Graduate Certificate); marketing (MSM, Graduate Certificate); non-profit management (MSM, Graduate Certificate);

project management (MSM, Graduate Certificate). Part-time and evening/weekend programs available. Postbaccalaureate distance learning degree programs offered (no on-campus study). *Faculty:* 2 full-time (both women), 8 part-time/adjunct (6 women). *Students:* 26 full-time (18 women), 85 part-time (60 women); includes 10 African Americans, 4 Asian Americans or Pacific Islanders, 9 Hispanic Americans, 17 international. Average age 31. 55 applicants, 80% accepted, 31 enrolled. In 2009, 31 master's awarded. *Entrance requirements:* For master's and Graduate Certificate, bachelor's degree from an accredited institution. Additional exam requirements/recommendations for international students: Required—TOEFL (minimum score 550 paper-based; 213 computer-based; 75 iBT) or IELTS. *Application deadline:* For fall admission, 8/31 priority date for domestic students, 6/30 priority date for international students; for spring admission, 12/31 priority date for domestic students, 10/31 priority date for international students. Applications are processed on a rolling basis. Application fee: $40. Electronic applications accepted. *Expenses:* Tuition: Full-time $4890; part-time $525 per credit hour. Required fees: $55 per term. *Financial support:* Available to part-time students. Application deadline: 8/31. *Unit head:* Dr. Joan Dolamore, Dean of Graduate and Professional Studies, 617-243-2485, Fax: 617-243-2450, E-mail: gradinfo@lasell.edu. *Application contact:* Adrienne Franciosi, Director of Graduate Admission, 617-243-2214, Fax: 617-243-2450, E-mail: gradinfo@lasell.edu.

La Sierra University, School of Business and Management, Riverside, CA 92515. Offers accounting (MBA); finance (MBA); general management (MBA); human resources management (MBA); leadership, values, and ethics for business and management (Certificate); marketing (MBA). *Degree requirements:* For master's, research project. *Entrance requirements:* For master's, GMAT, minimum GPA of 3.0. Additional exam requirements/recommendations for international students: Required—TOEFL. *Faculty research:* Financial econometrics, institutional assessment and strategic planning, legal issues in management, behavioral finance, content of financial reports.

Laurentian University, School of Graduate Studies and Research, School of Commerce and Administration, Sudbury, ON P3E 2C6, Canada. Offers MBA. Part-time and evening/weekend programs available. *Entrance requirements:* For master's, GMAT, 2 years of work experience. *Faculty research:* Small business and entrepreneurship development, mutual fund performance, donorship behavior, stress and organizations, quality programs.

Lawrence Technological University, College of Management, Southfield, MI 48075-1058. Offers business administration (MBA, DBA); information systems (MS); information technology (DM); operations management (MS). *Accreditation:* ACBSP. Part-time and evening/weekend programs available. *Faculty:* 14 full-time (6 women), 53 part-time/adjunct (14 women). *Students:* 17 full-time (6 women), 565 part-time (234 women); includes 149 minority (103 African Americans, 2 American Indian/Alaska Native, 37 Asian Americans or Pacific Islanders, 7 Hispanic Americans), 96 international. Average age 34. 353 applicants, 58% accepted, 125 enrolled. In 2009, 263 master's, 5 doctorates awarded. *Degree requirements:* For master's, thesis (for some programs). *Entrance requirements:* For master's, GMAT. Additional exam requirements/recommendations for international students: Required—TOEFL (minimum score 550 paper-based; 213 computer-based; 79 iBT). *Application deadline:* For fall admission, 8/1 priority date for domestic students, 6/1 for international students; for winter admission, 12/1 priority date for domestic students, 10/1 for international students; for spring admission, 5/1 priority date for domestic students, 3/1 for international students. Applications are processed on a rolling basis. Application fee: $50. Electronic applications accepted. *Expenses:* Tuition: Full-time $11,320; part-time $798 per credit hour. *Financial support:* Federal Work-Study and institutionally sponsored loans available. Support available to part-time students. Financial award application deadline: 4/1; financial award applicants required to submit FAFSA. *Unit head:* Dr. Lou DeGennaro, Dean, 248-204-3050, E-mail: degennaro@ltu.edu. *Application contact:* Jane Rohrback, Director of Admissions, 248-204-3160, Fax: 248-204-3188, E-mail: admissions@ltu.edu.

Lebanese American University, School of Business, Beirut, Lebanon. Offers MBA.

Lebanon Valley College, Graduate Studies and Continuing Education, Program in Business Administration, Annville, PA 17003-1400. Offers MBA. Part-time and evening/weekend programs available. *Faculty:* 1 full-time (0 women), 13 part-time/adjunct (3 women). *Students:* 144 part-time (59 women); includes 14 minority (4 African Americans, 8 Asian Americans or Pacific Islanders, 2 Hispanic Americans). Average age 35. In 2009, 31 master's awarded. *Entrance requirements:* For master's, 3 years of work experience. *Application deadline:* Applications are processed on a rolling basis. Application fee: $30. Electronic applications accepted. *Expenses:* Tuition: Full-time $32,740; part-time $410 per credit hour. Required fees: $610. *Financial support:* Application deadline: 5/1. *Unit head:* Jennifer Easter, Director of the MBA Program, 717-867-6335. *Application contact:* Elaine D. Feather, Director of Graduate Studies and Continuing Education, 717-867-6213, Fax: 717-867-6018, E-mail: feather@lvc.edu.

Lehigh University, College of Business and Economics, Bethlehem, PA 18015. Offers accounting (MS), including accounting and information analysis; business administration (MBA); economics (MS, PhD), including economics, health and bio-pharmaceutical economics (MS); entrepreneurship (Certificate); finance (MS), including analytical finance; project management (Certificate); supply chain management (Certificate); MBA/E; MBA/M Ed. *Accreditation:* AACSB. Part-time and evening/weekend programs available. Postbaccalaureate distance learning degree programs offered (minimal on-campus study). *Faculty:* 42 full-time (11 women), 12 part-time/adjunct (2 women). *Students:* 145 full-time (64 women), 264 part-time (82 women); includes 28 minority (6 African Americans, 19 Asian Americans or Pacific Islanders, 3 Hispanic Americans), 111 international. Average age 30. 624 applicants, 47% accepted, 114 enrolled. In 2009, 111 master's, 2 doctorates awarded. Terminal master's awarded for partial completion of doctoral program. *Degree requirements:* For master's, thesis optional; for doctorate, comprehensive exam, thesis/dissertation, proposal defense. *Entrance requirements:* For master's, GMAT, GRE General Test; MCAT, DAT (health and biopharmaceutical economics); for doctorate, GMAT or GRE General Test. Additional exam requirements/recommendations for international students: Required—TOEFL (minimum score 600 paper-based; 250 computer-based; 94 iBT). *Application deadline:* For fall admission, 7/15 for domestic students, 5/1 for international students; for spring admission, 12/1 for domestic and international students. Applications are processed on a rolling basis. Application fee: $100. Electronic applications accepted. *Expenses:* Contact institution. *Financial support:* In 2009–10, 2 fellowships with full tuition reimbursements (averaging $13,200 per year), 10 research assistantships with full and partial tuition reimbursements (averaging $2,800 per year), 17 teaching assistantships with full tuition reimbursements (averaging $13,840 per year) were awarded; career-related internships or fieldwork, scholarships/grants, health care benefits, tuition waivers (full and partial), and unspecified assistantships also available. Support available to part-time students. Financial award application deadline: 1/15. *Faculty research:* Public finance, energy, investments, activity-based costing, management information systems. *Unit head:* Martin K. Saffer, Graduate Business Programs, 610-758-4450, Fax: 610-758-5283, E-mail: mks207@lehigh.edu. *Application contact:* Corinn McBride, Director of Recruitment and Admissions, 610-758-3418, Fax: 610-758-5283, E-mail: com207@lehigh.edu.

Le Moyne College, Division of Management, Syracuse, NY 13214. Offers MBA. *Accreditation:* AACSB. Part-time and evening/weekend programs available. *Faculty:* 16 full-time (4 women), 6 part-time/adjunct (1 woman). *Students:* 14 full-time (6 women), 79 part-time (26 women); includes 3 minority (1 American Indian/Alaska Native, 2 Asian Americans or Pacific Islanders), 1 international. Average age 30. 54 applicants, 72% accepted, 35 enrolled. In 2009, 54 master's awarded. *Degree requirements:* For master's, capstone level course. *Entrance requirements:* For master's, GMAT, interview, minimum GPA of 3.0, resume, 2 letters of recommendation. Additional exam requirements/recommendations for international students: Required—TOEFL (minimum score 550 paper-based; 213 computer-based; 79 iBT). *Application deadline:* For fall admission, 7/1 priority date for domestic and international students; for spring admission, 11/1 priority date for domestic and international students. Applications are processed on a rolling basis. Application fee: $0. *Expenses:* Tuition: Full-time $11,232; part-time $624 per credit hour. Required fees: $25 per semester. *Financial support:* In 2009–10, 15 students received support. Career-related internships or fieldwork, scholarships/grants, health care benefits, and unspecified assistantships available. Support available to part-time students. Financial award applicants required to submit FAFSA. *Faculty research:* Performance evaluation outcomes assessment, technology outsourcing, international business, systems for web-based information seeking, non-profit business practices, business sustainability practices. *Unit head:* Dr. George Kulick, Associate Dean, 315-445-4786, Fax: 315-445-4787, E-mail: kulick@lemoyne.edu. *Application contact:* Kristen P. Trapasso, Director of Graduate Admission, 315-445-4265, Fax: 315-445-6027, E-mail: trapaskp@lemoyne.edu.

Lenoir-Rhyne University, Graduate Programs, Charles M. Snipes School of Business, Hickory, NC 28601. Offers accounting (MBA); entrepreneurship (MBA); global leadership (MBA); leadership development (MBA). *Accreditation:* ACBSP. Part-time and evening/weekend programs available. *Degree requirements:* For master's, capstone course. *Entrance requirements:* For master's, GMAT, minimum undergraduate GPA of 2.7, graduate 3.0. Additional exam requirements/recommendations for international students: Required—TOEFL (minimum score 600 paper-based). Electronic applications accepted. *Expenses:* Contact institution.

LeTourneau University, School of Graduate and Professional Studies, Longview, TX 75607-7001. Offers business administration (MBA); curriculum and instruction (M Ed); educational administration (M Ed); strategic leadership (MSL); teaching and learning (M Ed). Part-time and evening/weekend programs available. Postbaccalaureate distance learning degree programs offered (no on-campus study). *Faculty:* 8 full-time (1 woman), 19 part-time/adjunct (7 women). *Students:* 43 full-time (30 women), 245 part-time (164 women); includes 158 minority (130 African Americans, 2 American Indian/Alaska Native, 2 Asian Americans or Pacific Islanders, 24 Hispanic Americans). Average age 36. 1,717 applicants, 31% accepted, 288 enrolled. *Entrance requirements:* For master's, minimum GPA of 2.8. Additional exam requirements/recommendations for international students: Required—TOEFL. *Application deadline:* Applications are processed on a rolling basis. Electronic applications accepted. *Expenses:* Tuition: Full-time $10,710; part-time $595 per credit hour. *Financial support:* Applicants required to submit FAFSA. *Unit head:* Dr. Carol Green, Vice President, 903-233-3250, Fax: 903-233-3227, E-mail: carolgreen@letu.edu. *Application contact:* Chris Fontaine, Assistant Vice President for Enrollment Management and Market Research, 903-233-3250, Fax: 903-233-3227, E-mail: chrisfontaine@letu.edu.

Lewis University, College of Business, Graduate School of Management, Romeoville, IL 60446. Offers business administration (MBA), including accounting, custom elective option, e-business, finance, healthcare management, human resources management, information security, international business, management information systems, marketing, project management, technology and operations management; finance (MS); management (MS). *Expenses:* Tuition: Full-time $6480; part-time $720 per credit. One-time fee: $40. Tuition and fees vary according to course load, degree level and program. *Financial support:* Applicants required to submit FAFSA. *Application contact:* Michele King, Director of Admission, 815-836-5384, E-mail: gsm@lewisu.edu.

Lewis University, College of Nursing and Health Professions and College of Business, Program in Nursing/Business, Romeoville, IL 60446. Offers MSN/MBA. Part-time and evening/weekend programs available. *Students:* 12 full-time (11 women), 32 part-time (all women); includes 18 minority (12 African Americans, 3 Asian Americans or Pacific Islanders, 3 Hispanic Americans), 1 international. Average age 38. 13 applicants, 69% accepted, 8 enrolled. *Entrance requirements:* Additional exam requirements/recommendations for international students: Required—TOEFL (minimum score 550 paper-based; 213 computer-based). *Application deadline:* For fall admission, 5/1 priority date for international students; for spring admission, 11/15 priority date for international students. Applications are processed on a rolling basis. Electronic applications accepted. *Expenses:* Tuition: Full-time $6480; part-time $720 per credit. One-time fee: $40. Tuition and fees vary according to course load, degree level and program. *Financial support:* Scholarships/grants, tuition waivers (full and partial), and unspecified assistantships available. Financial award application deadline: 5/1; financial award applicants required to submit FAFSA. *Faculty research:* Cancer prevention, phenomenological methods, public policy analysis. Total annual research expenditures: $1,000. *Unit head:* Dr. Nan Yancey, Director, 815-838-0500 Ext. 5878, E-mail: yanceyna@lewisu.edu. *Application contact:* Kathy Lisak, Information Contact, 815-838-0500 Ext. 5355, E-mail: lisakka@lewisu.edu.

Liberty University, School of Business, Lynchburg, VA 24502. Offers MBA, MS. Part-time programs available. Postbaccalaureate distance learning degree programs offered (minimal on-campus study). *Entrance requirements:* For master's, minimum undergraduate GPA of 3.0. Additional exam requirements/recommendations for international students: Required—TOEFL (minimum score 600 paper-based; 250 computer-based). Electronic applications accepted. *Expenses:* Contact institution. *Faculty research:* International business, export management strategy, knowledge management, global industries and operations, tourism.

LIM College, MBA Program, New York, NY 10022-5268. Offers entrepreneurship (MBA); fashion management (MBA).

Lincoln Memorial University, School of Business, Harrogate, TN 37752-1901. Offers MBA. Part-time and evening/weekend programs available. *Faculty:* 6 full-time (0 women), 1 part-time/adjunct (0 women). *Students:* 7 full-time (1 woman), 99 part-time (43 women). Average age 27. 48 applicants, 94% accepted, 38 enrolled. In 2009, 23 master's awarded. *Degree requirements:* For master's, comprehensive exam, thesis. *Entrance requirements:* For master's, GMAT, resume, letters of recommendation, interview. Additional exam requirements/recommendations for international students: Required—TOEFL (minimum score 500 paper-based). *Application deadline:* For fall admission, 7/15 for domestic and international students; for spring admission, 12/1 for domestic and international students. Applications are processed on a rolling basis. Application fee: $25. *Expenses:* Tuition: Full-time $11,700; part-time $390 per hour. *Financial support:* Career-related internships or fieldwork, health care benefits, and unspecified assistantships available. Support available to part-time students. Financial award applicants required to submit FAFSA. *Unit head:* Dr. Jack McCann, Dean, 423-869-7085, Fax: 423-869-6298, E-mail: jack.mccann@lmunet.edu. *Application contact:* Dr. Michael E. Dillon, Director, MBA Program, 423-869-7141, E-mail: michael.dillon@lmunet.edu.

Lincoln University, Graduate Center, Lincoln University, PA 19352. Offers administration (MSA), including finance, human resources management; early childhood education (M Ed); elementary education (M Ed); human services (M Hum Svcs); reading (MSR). Evening/weekend programs available. *Degree requirements:* For master's, thesis. *Entrance requirements:* For master's, 5 years of work experience in human services. *Faculty research:* Gerontology/minority aging, computers in composition instruction.

Lincoln University, Graduate Degree Programs, Oakland, CA 94612. Offers finance and investments (DBA); finance management and investment banking (MBA); general business (MBA); human resource management (MBA); international business (MBA); management information systems (MBA). Part-time and evening/weekend programs available. *Faculty:* 7 full-time (2 women), 13 part-time/adjunct (1 woman). *Students:* 295 full-time (133 women), 3 part-time (0 women). 177 applicants, 100% accepted, 71 enrolled. In 2009, 98 master's awarded. *Degree requirements:* For master's, research project (thesis) or internship report, or comprehensive exam; for doctorate, comprehensive exam, thesis/dissertation. *Entrance requirements:* For master's, minimum GPA of 2.7; for doctorate, GMAT (minimum score: 550), GRE (minimum score: 1000), or equivalent test results (waived for master's degree with cumulative GPA of 3.3). Additional exam requirements/recommendations for international students: Required—TOEFL or IELTS. *Application deadline:* For fall admission, 7/3 priority date for domestic students; for spring admission, 11/27 priority date for domestic students. Applications are processed on a rolling basis. Application fee: $75. Electronic applications accepted. *Expenses:* Tuition: Full-time $6750. Required fees: $190 per term. *Financial support:* In 2009–10, 1 teaching assistantship was awarded; career-related internships or fieldwork and scholarships/grants also available. *Unit head:* Dr. Marshall Burak, Director of Graduate Programs, 510-628-8016, Fax: 510-628-8012, E-mail: mburak@lincolnuca.edu. *Application contact:* Peggy Au, Director of Admissions and Records, 510-628-8010, Fax: 510-628-8012, E-mail: admissions@lincolnuca.edu.

Business Administration and Management—General

Lincoln University, School of Graduate Studies and Continuing Education, Jefferson City, MO 65102. Offers business administration (MBA), including accounting, entrepreneurship, management, public administration and policy; educational leadership (Ed S), including elementary leadership, secondary leadership, superintendency; guidance and counseling (M Ed), including community/agency counseling, elementary school, secondary school; history (MA); school administration and supervision (M Ed), including elementary school administration, secondary school administration, special education administration; school teaching (M Ed), including elementary school teaching, secondary school teaching; social science (MA), including history, political science, sociology; sociology (MA); sociology/criminal justice (MA). Part-time and evening/weekend programs available. *Students:* 52 full-time (27 women), 146 part-time (107 women); includes 40 minority (39 African Americans, 1 Asian American or Pacific Islander), 15 international. Average age 35. 76 applicants, 95% accepted, 46 enrolled. In 2009, 60 master's, 6 other advanced degrees awarded. *Degree requirements:* For master's and Ed S, comprehensive exam, thesis optional. *Entrance requirements:* For master's and Ed S, GRE, MAT or GMAT, minimum GPA of 2.75 in major, 2.5 overall; 3 letters of recommendation; minimum C average in English composition; personal statement of purpose. Additional exam requirements/recommendations for international students: Required—TOEFL (minimum score 500 paper-based; 173 computer-based; 61 iBT). *Application deadline:* For fall admission, 7/1 priority date for domestic and international students; for spring admission, 12/1 priority date for domestic and international students. Applications are processed on a rolling basis. Application fee: $20. *Expenses:* Tuition, state resident: full-time $4185; part-time $232.50 per credit hour. Tuition, nonresident: full-time $7767; part-time $431.50 per credit hour. Required fees: $270; $15 per credit hour. $20 per term. *Financial support:* Federal Work-Study and scholarships/grants available. Financial award application deadline: 4/1; financial award applicants required to submit FAFSA. *Faculty research:* Suicide prevention. *Unit head:* Dr. Linda S. Bickel, Dean, 573-681-5247, Fax: 573-681-5106, E-mail: gradschool@lincolnu.edu. *Application contact:* Irasema Steck, Administrative Assistant, 573-681-5247, Fax: 573-681-5106, E-mail: gradschool@lincolnu.edu.

Lindenwood University, Graduate Programs, College of Individualized Education, St. Charles, MO 63301-1695. Offers administration (MSA); business administration (MBA); communications (MA); criminal justice and administration (MS); gerontology (MA); health management (MS); human resource management (MS); information technology (MBA, Certificate); management (MSA); managing information technology (MS); marketing (MSA); writing (MFA). Part-time and evening/weekend programs available. *Faculty:* 15 full-time (8 women), 128 part-time/adjunct (53 women). *Students:* 679 full-time (432 women), 90 part-time (57 women); includes 138 minority (121 African Americans, 2 American Indian/Alaska Native, 5 Asian Americans or Pacific Islanders, 10 Hispanic Americans), 18 international. Average age 34. 223 applicants, 44% accepted, 87 enrolled. In 2009, 478 master's awarded. *Degree requirements:* For master's, thesis (for some programs), 1 colloquium per term. *Entrance requirements:* For master's, interview, minimum GPA of 3.0. Additional exam requirements/recommendations for international students: Required—TOEFL (minimum score 550 paper-based; 213 computer-based; 80 iBT). *Application deadline:* For fall admission, 10/2 priority date for domestic and international students; for winter admission, 1/8 priority date for domestic and international students; for spring admission, 4/8 priority date for domestic and international students. Applications are processed on a rolling basis. Application fee: $30 ($100 for international students). *Expenses:* Tuition: Full-time $12,960; part-time $370 per credit hour. Required fees: $340. One-time fee: $30 full-time. Tuition and fees vary according to course level and course load. *Financial support:* In 2009–10, 631 students received support. Career-related internships or fieldwork, institutionally sponsored loans, tuition waivers (partial), and unspecified assistantships available. Financial award application deadline: 6/30; financial award applicants required to submit FAFSA. *Unit head:* Dan Kemper, Dean, 636-949-4501, Fax: 636-949-4505, E-mail: dkemper@lindenwood.edu. *Application contact:* Brett Barger, Dean of Evening Admissions and Extension Campuses, 636-949-4934, Fax: 636-949-4109, E-mail: adultadmissions@lindenwood.edu.

Lindenwood University, Graduate Programs, School of Business and Entrepreneurship, St. Charles, MO 63301-1695. Offers accounting (MBA, MS); business administration (MBA); entrepreneurial studies (MBA, MS); finance (MBA, MS); human resource management (MBA); human resources (MS); international business (MBA, MS); management (MBA, MS); management information systems (MBA, MS); marketing (MBA, MS); public management (MBA, MS); sport management (MA). *Accreditation:* ACBSP. Part-time and evening/weekend programs available. *Faculty:* 20 full-time (8 women), 17 part-time/adjunct (5 women). *Students:* 129 full-time (60 women), 138 part-time (61 women); includes 15 minority (11 African Americans, 2 Asian Americans or Pacific Islanders, 2 Hispanic Americans), 84 international. Average age 28. 149 applicants, 73 enrolled. In 2009, 142 master's awarded. *Degree requirements:* For master's, comprehensive exam (for some programs), thesis (for some programs). *Entrance requirements:* For master's, interview, minimum GPA of 3.0, letter of recommendation. Additional exam requirements/recommendations for international students: Required—TOEFL (minimum score 550 paper-based; 213 computer-based; 80 iBT). *Application deadline:* For fall admission, 7/30 priority date for domestic students, 9/16 priority date for international students; for winter admission, 12/19 priority date for domestic students, 12/17 priority date for international students; for spring admission, 2/25 priority date for domestic students, 2/11 priority date for international students. Applications are processed on a rolling basis. Application fee: $30 ($100 for international students). Electronic applications accepted. *Expenses:* Tuition: Full-time $12,960; part-time $370 per credit hour. Required fees: $340. One-time fee: $30 full-time. Tuition and fees vary according to course level and course load. *Financial support:* In 2009–10, 209 students received support. Career-related internships or fieldwork, Federal Work-Study, institutionally sponsored loans, and tuition waivers (partial) available. Financial award application deadline: 6/30; financial award applicants required to submit FAFSA. *Unit head:* Ed Morris, Dean of Management, 636-949-4832, E-mail: emorris@lindenwood.edu. *Application contact:* Brett Barger, Dean of Evening Admissions and Extension Campuses, 636-949-4934, Fax: 636-949-4109, E-mail: adultadmissions@lindenwood.edu.

Lipscomb University, MBA Program, Nashville, TN 37204-3951. Offers accounting (MBA); business administration (general) (MBA); conflict management (MBA); financial services (MBA); healthcare management (MBA); leadership (MBA); nonprofit management (MBA); sports administration (MBA); sustainable practice (MBA). *Accreditation:* ACBSP. Part-time and evening/weekend programs available. *Faculty:* 10 full-time (1 woman), 7 part-time/adjunct (2 women). *Students:* 43 full-time (23 women), 86 part-time (38 women); includes 23 minority (18 African Americans, 1 Asian American or Pacific Islander, 4 Hispanic Americans), 1 international. Average age 31. 95 applicants, 64% accepted, 35 enrolled. In 2009, 59 master's awarded. *Entrance requirements:* For master's, GMAT, interview, 2 references, resume. Additional exam requirements/recommendations for international students: Required—TOEFL (minimum score 570 paper-based; 230 computer-based). *Application deadline:* For fall admission, 2/1 for international students; for winter admission, 6/1 for international students. Applications are processed on a rolling basis. Application fee: $50 ($75 for international students). Electronic applications accepted. *Expenses:* Contact institution. *Financial support:* Career-related internships or fieldwork, Federal Work-Study, scholarships/grants, tuition waivers (partial), and unspecified assistantships available. Support available to part-time students. Financial award application deadline: 7/1; financial award applicants required to submit FAFSA. *Faculty research:* Impact of spirituality on organization commitment, leadership, psychological empowerment, training. *Unit head:* Dr. Mike Kendrick, Interim Chair of Graduate Business Studies, 615-966-1833, Fax: 615-966-1818, E-mail: mikekendrick@lipscomb.edu. *Application contact:* Emily Landsdell, 615-966-5284, E-mail: emily.lansdell@lipscomb.edu.

Long Island University, Brooklyn Campus, School of Business, Public Administration and Information Sciences, Program in Business Administration, Brooklyn, NY 11201-8423. Offers MBA. Part-time and evening/weekend programs available. *Entrance requirements:* For master's, GMAT or GRE General Test, 2 letters of recommendation. Additional exam requirements/recommendations for international students: Required—TOEFL (minimum score 500 paper-based; 173 computer-based). Electronic applications accepted.

Long Island University, C.W. Post Campus, College of Management, Department of Management, Brookville, NY 11548-1300. Offers MBA.

Long Island University, C.W. Post Campus, College of Management, School of Business, Brookville, NY 11548-1300. Offers accounting and taxation (Certificate); business administration (Certificate); finance (MBA, Certificate); general business administration (MBA); international business (MBA, Certificate); management (MBA, Certificate); management information systems (MBA, Certificate); marketing (MBA, Certificate). *Accreditation:* AACSB. Part-time and evening/weekend programs available. *Entrance requirements:* For master's, GMAT, resume, minimum GPA of 3.0, 2 letters of recommendation. Additional exam requirements/recommendations for international students: Required—TOEFL (minimum score 527 paper-based; 197 computer-based). Electronic applications accepted. *Faculty research:* Financial markets, consumer behavior.

Long Island University, Rockland Graduate Campus, Graduate School, Masters of Business Administration Program, Orangeburg, NY 10962. Offers business administration (Post Master's Certificate); entrepreneurship (MBA); finance (MBA); management (MBA). Part-time and evening/weekend programs available. *Faculty:* 12 part-time/adjunct (2 women). *Students:* 35 part-time (21 women). 51 applicants, 67% accepted, 22 enrolled. In 2009, 14 master's awarded. *Entrance requirements:* For master's, GMAT. Additional exam requirements/recommendations for international students: Required—TOEFL. *Application deadline:* Applications are processed on a rolling basis. Application fee: $30. *Expenses:* Tuition: Part-time $930 per credit. Required fees: $200 per semester. *Financial support:* In 2009–10, 34 students received support. Scholarships/grants available. Support available to part-time students. Financial award applicants required to submit FAFSA. *Unit head:* Dr. Lynn Johnson, Program Director, 845-359-7200 Ext. 5410, Fax: 845-359-7248, E-mail: ken.reilly@liu.edu. *Application contact:* Peter S. Reiner, Director of Admissions and Marketing, 845-359-7200, Fax: 845-359-7248, E-mail: peter.reiner@liu.edu.

Long Island University, Westchester Graduate Campus, Program in Business Administration, Purchase, NY 10577. Offers MBA. Part-time and evening/weekend programs available. *Entrance requirements:* For master's, GMAT. Additional exam requirements/recommendations for international students: Required—TOEFL (minimum score 500 paper-based; 173 computer-based).

Longwood University, Office of Graduate Studies, College of Business and Economics, Farmville, VA 23909. Offers retail management (MBA). *Accreditation:* AACSB. *Degree requirements:* For master's, internship. *Entrance requirements:* For master's, GMAT.

Louisiana State University and Agricultural and Mechanical College, Graduate School, E. J. Ourso College of Business, Department of Finance, Baton Rouge, LA 70803. Offers business administration (PhD), including finance; finance (MS). *Faculty:* 13 full-time (3 women), 1 (woman) part-time/adjunct. *Students:* 46 full-time (16 women), 2 part-time (0 women); includes 1 Asian American or Pacific Islander, 23 international. Average age 27. 126 applicants, 34% accepted, 12 enrolled. In 2009, 2 master's, 2 doctorates awarded. *Degree requirements:* For master's, thesis or alternative; for doctorate, thesis/dissertation. *Entrance requirements:* For master's and doctorate, GMAT. Additional exam requirements/recommendations for international students: Required—TOEFL (minimum score 550 paper-based; 213 computer-based; 79 iBT) or IELTS (minimum score 6.5). *Application deadline:* For fall admission, 1/25 priority date for domestic students, 5/15 for international students; for spring admission, 10/15 for international students. Applications are processed on a rolling basis. Application fee: $50 ($70 for international students). *Financial support:* In 2009–10, 33 students received support, including 11 research assistantships with full and partial tuition reimbursements available (averaging $16,272 per year), 5 teaching assistantships with full and partial tuition reimbursements available (averaging $15,760 per year); fellowships, career-related internships or fieldwork, Federal Work-Study, scholarships/grants, health care benefits, and unspecified assistantships also available. Support available to part-time students. Financial award application deadline: 4/1; financial award applicants required to submit FAFSA. *Faculty research:* Derivatives and risk management, capital structure, asset pricing, spatial statistics, financial institutions and underwriting. Total annual research expenditures: $14,214. *Unit head:* Dr. Vestor Carlos Slawson, Interim Chair, 225-578-6367, Fax: 225-578-6366, E-mail: cslawson@lsu.edu. *Application contact:* Dr. Vestor Carlos Slawson, Interim Chair, 225-578-6367, Fax: 225-578-6366, E-mail: cslawson@lsu.edu.

Louisiana State University and Agricultural and Mechanical College, Graduate School, E. J. Ourso College of Business, Department of Management, Baton Rouge, LA 70803. Offers business administration (PhD), including management. *Accreditation:* AACSB. *Faculty:* 10 full-time (2 women). *Students:* 10 full-time (3 women); includes 1 Asian American or Pacific Islander, 5 international. Average age 32. 23 applicants, 26% accepted, 2 enrolled. In 2009, 1 doctorate awarded. *Degree requirements:* For doctorate, thesis/dissertation. *Entrance requirements:* For doctorate, GMAT. Additional exam requirements/recommendations for international students: Required—TOEFL (minimum score 550 paper-based; 213 computer-based; 79 iBT) or IELTS (minimum score 6.5). *Application deadline:* For fall admission, 1/25 priority date for domestic students, 5/15 for international students; for spring admission, 10/15 for international students. Applications are processed on a rolling basis. Application fee: $50 ($70 for international students). Electronic applications accepted. *Financial support:* In 2009–10, 10 students received support, including 5 research assistantships with full and partial tuition reimbursements available (averaging $19,900 per year), 5 teaching assistantships with full and partial tuition reimbursements available (averaging $16,500 per year); fellowships, Federal Work-Study, institutionally sponsored loans, scholarships/grants, health care benefits, and unspecified assistantships also available. Support available to part-time students. Financial award applicants required to submit FAFSA. *Faculty research:* Human resource management, organizational behavior, strategy. Total annual research expenditures: $21,265. *Unit head:* Dr. Timothy Chandler, Chair, 225-578-6101, Fax: 225-578-6983, E-mail: mgchan@lsu.edu. *Application contact:* Hettie Richardson, Graduate Adviser, 225-578-6146, Fax: 225-578-6140, E-mail: hricha4@lsu.edu.

Louisiana State University and Agricultural and Mechanical College, Graduate School, E. J. Ourso College of Business, Department of Marketing, Baton Rouge, LA 70803. Offers business administration (PhD), including marketing. Part-time programs available. *Faculty:* 12 full-time (2 women). *Students:* 7 full-time (4 women), 4 part-time (2 women), 5 international. Average age 31. 14 applicants, 0% accepted, 0 enrolled. In 2009, 3 doctorates awarded. *Degree requirements:* For doctorate, thesis/dissertation. *Entrance requirements:* Additional exam requirements/recommendations for international students: Required—TOEFL (minimum score 550 paper-based; 213 computer-based; 79 iBT) or IELTS (minimum score 6.5). *Application deadline:* For fall admission, 1/25 priority date for domestic students, 5/15 for international students; for spring admission, 10/15 for international students. Applications are processed on a rolling basis. Application fee: $50 ($70 for international students). Electronic applications accepted. *Financial support:* In 2009–10, 10 students received support, including 7 teaching assistantships with full and partial tuition reimbursements available (averaging $16,328 per year); fellowships, research assistantships with partial tuition reimbursements available, career-related internships or fieldwork, Federal Work-Study, institutionally sponsored loans, scholarships/grants, health care benefits, and unspecified assistantships also available. Support available to part-time students. Financial award applicants required to submit FAFSA. *Faculty research:* Consumer behavior, marketing strategy, global marketing, e-commerce, branding/brand equity. Total annual research expenditures: $610. *Unit head:* Dr. Alvin C. Burns, Chair, 225-578-8786, Fax: 225-578-8616, E-mail: alburns@lsu.edu. *Application contact:* Dr. Ron Niedrich, Graduate Adviser, 225-578-9068, Fax: 225-578-8616, E-mail: niedrich@lsu.edu.

Louisiana State University and Agricultural and Mechanical College, Graduate School, E. J. Ourso College of Business, Flores MBA Program, Baton Rouge, LA 70803. Offers EMBA, MBA, PMBA. *Accreditation:* AACSB. *Students:* 256 full-time (92 women), 106 part-time (42 women); includes 46 minority (34 African Americans, 2 American Indian/Alaska Native, 4 Asian Americans or Pacific Islanders, 6 Hispanic Americans), 24 international. Average age 28. 350 applicants, 50% accepted, 143 enrolled. In 2009, 153 master's awarded. *Entrance requirements:*

Additional exam requirements/recommendations for international students: Required—TOEFL (minimum score 550 paper-based; 213 computer-based; 79 iBT) or IELTS (minimum score 6.5). *Application deadline:* For fall admission, 1/25 priority date for domestic students, 5/15 for international students; for spring admission, 10/15 for international students. Application fee: $50 ($70 for international students). Electronic applications accepted. *Financial support:* In 2009–10, 217 students received support, including 3 fellowships (averaging $25,565 per year), 26 research assistantships with partial tuition reimbursements available (averaging $10,000 per year), 39 teaching assistantships with full and partial tuition reimbursements available (averaging $9,680 per year); Federal Work-Study, institutionally sponsored loans, scholarships/grants, health care benefits, and unspecified assistantships also available. Support available to part-time students. Financial award applicants required to submit FAFSA. Total annual research expenditures: $4,876. *Unit head:* Dr. Ed Watson, Director, 225-578-8867, Fax: 225-578-2421. *Application contact:* Dana Hart, 225-578-8867, Fax: 225-578-2421, E-mail: dhart@lsu.edu.

Louisiana State University in Shreveport, College of Business Administration, Program in Business Administration, Shreveport, LA 71115-2399. Offers MBA. Part-time and evening/weekend programs available. *Students:* 14 full-time (4 women), 85 part-time (35 women); includes 17 minority (14 African Americans, 3 Hispanic Americans), 4 international. Average age 32. 105 applicants, 98% accepted, 55 enrolled. In 2009, 19 master's awarded. *Degree requirements:* For master's, comprehensive exam. *Entrance requirements:* For master's, GMAT, minimum undergraduate GPA of 2.5, 2.75 for last 60 credits. Additional exam requirements/recommendations for international students: Required—TOEFL (minimum score 500 paper-based; 173 computer-based; 61 iBT). *Application deadline:* For fall admission, 6/30 for domestic and international students; for spring admission, 11/30 for domestic and international students. Applications are processed on a rolling basis. Application fee: $10 ($20 for international students). *Financial support:* In 2009–10, 1 fellowship, 4 research assistantships with full and partial tuition reimbursements (averaging $10,000 per year) were awarded; scholarships/grants also available. *Unit head:* Dr. Bill Bigler, Program Director, Fax: 318-797-5176, E-mail: bbigler@lsus.edu. *Application contact:* Dr. Bill Bigler, Program Director, Fax: 318-797-5176, E-mail: bbigler@lsus.edu.

Louisiana Tech University, Graduate School, College of Business, Ruston, LA 71272. Offers MBA, MPA, DBA. *Accreditation:* AACSB. Part-time programs available. *Degree requirements:* For doctorate, thesis/dissertation. *Entrance requirements:* For master's and doctorate, GMAT.

Loyola Marymount University, College of Business Administration, Los Angeles, CA 90045-2659. Offers MBA, MBA/JD, MBA/MS. *Accreditation:* AACSB. *Expenses:* Contact institution. *Unit head:* Dr. Dennis Draper, Dean, 310-338-2848, Fax: 310-338-2899. *Application contact:* Dr. Dennis Draper, Dean, 310-338-2848, Fax: 310-338-2899.

Loyola University Chicago, Graduate School of Business, Chicago, IL 60660. Offers accountancy (MS, MSA); business administration (MBA); finance (MS); healthcare management (MBA); human resources and employee relations (MS, MSHR); information systems and operations management (MS), including information systems management; marketing (MS, MSIMC), including integrated marketing communications (MS), marketing (MSIMC); strategic financial services (MBA); JD/MBA; MBA/MSA; MSIMC/MBA; MSISM/MBA; MSN/MBA. *Accreditation:* AACSB. *Expenses:* Tuition: Full-time $14,220; part-time $790 per credit hour. Required fees: $60 per semester hour. Tuition and fees vary according to program.

Loyola University Maryland, Graduate Programs, Sellinger School of Business and Management, Program in Business Administration, Baltimore, MD 21210-2699. Offers accounting (MBA); finance (MBA); general business (MBA); international business (MBA); management (MBA); management information systems (MBA); marketing (MBA). *Accreditation:* AACSB. Part-time and evening/weekend programs available. *Entrance requirements:* For master's, GMAT. Additional exam requirements/recommendations for international students: Required—TOEFL (minimum score 550 paper-based; 213 computer-based).

Loyola University Maryland, Graduate Programs, Sellinger School of Business and Management, Program in Executive Business Administration, Baltimore, MD 21210-2699. Offers MBA. *Accreditation:* AACSB. Part-time and evening/weekend programs available. *Entrance requirements:* Additional exam requirements/recommendations for international students: Required—TOEFL (minimum score 550 paper-based; 213 computer-based).

Loyola University New Orleans, Joseph A. Butt, S.J., College of Business, Program in Business Administration, New Orleans, LA 70118-6195. Offers MBA, JD/MBA. *Accreditation:* AACSB. Part-time and evening/weekend programs available. Postbaccalaureate distance learning degree programs offered (minimal on-campus study). *Students:* 45 full-time (21 women), 37 part-time (19 women); includes 10 minority (3 African Americans, 1 American Indian/Alaska Native, 2 Asian Americans or Pacific Islanders, 4 Hispanic Americans), 2 international. Average age 27. 54 applicants, 94% accepted, 31 enrolled. In 2009, 26 master's awarded. *Entrance requirements:* For master's, GMAT, minimum GPA of 3.0, resume, 2 letters of recommendation, work experience in field. Additional exam requirements/recommendations for international students: Required—TOEFL (minimum score 550 paper-based; 213 computer-based). *Application deadline:* For fall admission, 6/15 priority date for domestic and international students; for spring admission, 11/15 priority date for domestic and international students. Applications are processed on a rolling basis. Application fee: $50. Electronic applications accepted. *Financial support:* In 2009–10, 15 research assistantships (averaging $2,200 per year) were awarded; scholarships/grants, tuition waivers (partial), and unspecified assistantships also available. Financial award application deadline: 5/1; financial award applicants required to submit FAFSA. *Faculty research:* Ethics, international business, entrepreneurship, quality management, risk management. *Unit head:* William B. Locander, Dean, 504-864-7979, Fax: 504-864-7970, E-mail: locander@loyno.edu. *Application contact:* Stephanie L. Mansfield, Assistant Director, Graduate Programs, 504-864-7965, Fax: 504-864-7970, E-mail: smans@loyno.edu.

Lynchburg College, Graduate Studies, School of Business and Economics, Lynchburg, VA 24501-3199. Offers business (MBA). *Accreditation:* ACBSP. Part-time and evening/weekend programs available. *Entrance requirements:* For master's, GMAT, GRE Subject Test. Additional exam requirements/recommendations for international students: Required—TOEFL. *Expenses:* Tuition: Full-time $7020; part-time $390 per credit hour.

Lynn University, College of Business and Management, Boca Raton, FL 33431-5598. Offers aviation management (MBA); financial valuation and investment management (MBA); hospitality management (MBA); international business (MBA); marketing (MBA); mass communication and media management (MBA); sports and athletics administration (MBA). Part-time and evening/weekend programs available. Postbaccalaureate distance learning degree programs offered. *Degree requirements:* For master's, project. *Entrance requirements:* For master's, GMAT or GRE, minimum undergraduate GPA of 3.0, resume, 2 letters of recommendation. Additional exam requirements/recommendations for international students: Required—TOEFL (minimum score 550 paper-based; 213 computer-based). *Application deadline:* Applications are processed on a rolling basis. Application fee: $50. Electronic applications accepted. *Expenses:* Tuition: Part-time $580 per credit. One-time fee: $200 part-time. Part-time tuition and fees vary according to degree level. *Financial support:* Career-related internships or fieldwork, Federal Work-Study, institutionally sponsored loans, scholarships/grants, tuition waivers (full and partial), and unspecified assistantships available. Support available to part-time students. Financial award application deadline: 8/1; financial award applicants required to submit FAFSA. *Faculty research:* Labor relations, dynamic balance in leisure-time skills, ethics in athletics, hotel development. *Unit head:* Dr. Ralph Norcio, Associate Dean, 561-237-7010, Fax: 561-237-7014, E-mail: rnorcio@lynn.edu. *Application contact:* Dr. Larissa Baia, Assistant Director of Graduate Admissions, 561-237-7916, Fax: 561-237-7100, E-mail: admissionpm@lynn.edu.

Madonna University, School of Business, Livonia, MI 48150-1173. Offers business administration (MBA); international business (MSBA); leadership studies (MSBA); leadership studies in criminal justice (MSBA); quality and operations management (MSBA). Part-time and evening/weekend programs available. Postbaccalaureate distance learning degree programs offered (minimal on-campus study). *Degree requirements:* For master's, thesis (for some programs), foreign language proficiency (international business). *Entrance requirements:* For master's, GMAT, GRE General Test, minimum GPA of 3.0. Electronic applications accepted. *Faculty research:* Management, women in management, future studies.

Maharishi University of Management, Graduate Studies, Program in Business Administration, Fairfield, IA 52557. Offers accounting (MBA); business administration (PhD); sustainability (MBA). Evening/weekend programs available. Postbaccalaureate distance learning degree programs offered (minimal on-campus study). *Degree requirements:* For doctorate, thesis/dissertation. *Entrance requirements:* For master's, GMAT, minimum GPA of 3.0; for doctorate, minimum GPA of 3.0. Additional exam requirements/recommendations for international students: Required—TOEFL. *Faculty research:* Leadership, effects of the group dynamics of consciousness on the economy, innovation, employee development, cooperative strategy.

Malone University, Graduate Program in Business, Canton, OH 44709. Offers MBA. *Accreditation:* ACBSP. Part-time and evening/weekend programs available. *Faculty:* 12 full-time (5 women), 9 part-time/adjunct (2 women). *Students:* 8 full-time (3 women), 125 part-time (47 women); includes 14 minority (12 African Americans, 1 Asian American or Pacific Islander, 1 Hispanic American), 2 international. Average age 35. In 2009, 30 master's awarded. *Entrance requirements:* For master's, institution's own math prerequisite diagnostic test, minimum GPA of 3.0. Additional exam requirements/recommendations for international students: Required—TOEFL (minimum score 550 paper-based; 213 computer-based; 79 iBT). *Application deadline:* Applications are processed on a rolling basis. Application fee: $25. *Expenses:* Contact institution. *Financial support:* Tuition waivers (partial) available. Support available to part-time students. Financial award application deadline: 6/30. *Faculty research:* Leadership, business ethics, sustainability, globalization, non-profit financial management. *Unit head:* Dr. Julia A. Frankland, Director, 330-471-8552, Fax: 330-471-8563, E-mail: jfrankland@malone.edu. *Application contact:* David L. Kleffman, Assistant Director of Enrollment, 330-471-8447, Fax: 330-471-8343, E-mail: dkleffman@malone.edu.

Marian University, Business Division, Fond du Lac, WI 54935-4699. Offers organizational leadership and quality (MS). Part-time and evening/weekend programs available. *Faculty:* 10 part-time/adjunct (2 women). *Students:* 7 full-time (5 women), 86 part-time (62 women); includes 10 minority (5 African Americans, 3 Asian Americans or Pacific Islanders, 2 Hispanic Americans). Average age 38. 48 applicants, 79% accepted, 38 enrolled. In 2009, 49 master's awarded. *Degree requirements:* For master's, comprehensive group project. *Entrance requirements:* For master's, 3 years of managerial experience, minimum GPA of 2.75, letters of professional reference. *Application deadline:* Applications are processed on a rolling basis. Application fee: $25. Electronic applications accepted. *Expenses:* Contact institution. *Financial support:* In 2009–10, 25 students received support. Institutionally sponsored loans available. Support available to part-time students. Financial award application deadline: 3/1; financial award applicants required to submit FAFSA. *Faculty research:* Organizational values, statistical decision making, learning organization, quality planning, customer research. *Unit head:* Donna Innes, Assistant Provost and Dean of PACE, 920-923-8760, Fax: 920-923-7167, E-mail: dinnes@marianuniversity.edu. *Application contact:* Tracy Qualman, Director of Marketing and Admission, 920-923-7159, Fax: 920-923-7167, E-mail: tqualmann@marianuniversity.edu.

Marist College, Graduate Programs, School of Management, Business Administration Program, Poughkeepsie, NY 12601-1387. Offers business administration (MBA); executive leadership (Adv C). *Accreditation:* AACSB. Part-time and evening/weekend programs available. Postbaccalaureate distance learning degree programs offered (no on-campus study). *Entrance requirements:* For master's, GMAT, resume, 2 letters of recommendation. Additional exam requirements/recommendations for international students: Required—TOEFL (minimum score 550 paper-based; 213 computer-based; 80 iBT); Recommended—IELTS (minimum score 6.5). Electronic applications accepted. *Expenses:* Tuition: Full-time $12,510; part-time $695 per credit hour. *Faculty research:* International trade law, process management, AIDS and the medical provider, mid-Hudson region economics, time quality management and organizational behavior.

Marlboro College, Graduate School, Program in Business Administration, Marlboro, VT 05344. Offers managing for sustainability (MBA). Part-time and evening/weekend programs available. Postbaccalaureate distance learning degree programs offered (minimal on-campus study). *Faculty:* 1 full-time (0 women), 15 part-time/adjunct (6 women). *Students:* 15 full-time (6 women), 6 part-time (3 women). Average age 41. *Degree requirements:* For master's, capstone project. *Entrance requirements:* For master's, 2 letters of recommendation. *Application deadline:* For winter admission, 10/30 priority date for domestic students. Application fee: $0. Electronic applications accepted. *Expenses:* Tuition: Full-time $9520; part-time $680 per credit. Tuition and fees vary according to course load and program. *Financial support:* Applicants required to submit FAFSA. *Unit head:* Ralph Meima, Program Director, 802-251-7690, Fax: 802-258-9201, E-mail: rmeima@marlboro.edu. *Application contact:* Joe Heslin, Associate Director of Admissions, 802-258-9209, Fax: 802-258-9201, E-mail: jheslin@gradcenter.marlboro.edu.

Marquette University, Graduate School of Management, Executive MBA Program, Milwaukee, WI 53201-1881. Offers MBA. *Accreditation:* AACSB. *Faculty:* 3 full-time (1 woman), 2 part-time/adjunct (0 women). *Students:* 26 full-time (7 women); includes 2 minority (both Asian Americans or Pacific Islanders), 2 international. Average age 38. 16 applicants, 81% accepted, 11 enrolled. In 2009, 15 master's awarded. *Entrance requirements:* For master's, GMAT. *Application deadline:* Applications are processed on a rolling basis. Electronic applications accepted. *Unit head:* Dr. Jeanne Simmons, Graduate Director, 414-288-7145, Fax: 414-288-1660, E-mail: jeanne.simmons@marquette.edu. *Application contact:* Erin Fox, Assistant Director for Recruitment, 414-288-5319, Fax: 414-288-1902, E-mail: erin.fox@marquette.edu.

Marquette University, Graduate School of Management, Program in Business Administration, Milwaukee, WI 53201-1881. Offers MBA, JD/MBA. *Accreditation:* AACSB. Part-time and evening/weekend programs available. *Faculty:* 38 full-time (9 women), 24 part-time/adjunct (8 women). *Students:* 55 full-time (21 women), 392 part-time (107 women); includes 40 minority (5 African Americans, 2 American Indian/Alaska Native, 25 Asian Americans or Pacific Islanders, 8 Hispanic Americans), 27 international. Average age 31. 153 applicants, 75% accepted, 79 enrolled. In 2009, 192 master's awarded. *Entrance requirements:* For master's, GMAT. Additional exam requirements/recommendations for international students: Required—TOEFL. Application fee: $40. *Financial support:* In 2009–10, 4 research assistantships, 13 teaching assistantships were awarded; Federal Work-Study, institutionally sponsored loans, scholarships/grants, and tuition waivers (full and partial) also available. Support available to part-time students. Financial award application deadline: 2/15. *Faculty research:* Ethics in the professions, services marketing, technology impact on decision making, mentoring. *Unit head:* Dr. Jeanne Simmons, Graduate Director, 414-288-7145, Fax: 414-288-1660, E-mail: jeanne.simmons@marquette.edu. *Application contact:* Erin Fox, Assistant Director for Recruitment, 414-288-5319, Fax: 414-288-1902, E-mail: erin.fox@marquette.edu.

Marshall University, Academic Affairs Division, Lewis College of Business, Graduate School of Management, Huntington, WV 25755. Offers IMBA, MBA, MS, DMPNA, Graduate Certificate. *Accreditation:* AACSB. Part-time and evening/weekend programs available. *Faculty:* 5 full-time (1 woman), 5 part-time/adjunct (1 woman). *Students:* 210 full-time (88 women), 132 part-time (73 women); includes 21 minority (10 African Americans, 10 Asian Americans or Pacific Islanders, 1 Hispanic American), 55 international. Average age 29. In 2009, 192 master's awarded. *Degree requirements:* For master's, comprehensive assessment. *Application deadline:* Applications are processed on a rolling basis. Application fee: $40. *Expenses:* Contact institution. *Financial support:* Career-related internships or fieldwork and tuition waivers (full) available. Support available to part-time students. Financial award applicants required to submit FAFSA. *Unit head:* Dr. Andrew Sikula, Associate Dean, 304-746-1956, E-mail: sikula@marshall.edu. *Application contact:* Steven Shumlas, Information Contact, 304-746-8964, Fax: 304-746-1902, E-mail: shumlas@marshall.edu.

Business Administration and Management—General

Marylhurst University, Department of Business Administration, Marylhurst, OR 97036-0261. Offers finance (MBA); general management (MBA); government policy and administration (MBA); green development (MBA); health care management (MBA); marketing (MBA); natural and organic resources (MBA); nonprofit management (MBA); organizational behavior (MBA); real estate (MBA); renewable energy (MBA); sustainable business (MBA). Part-time and evening/weekend programs available. Postbaccalaureate distance learning degree programs offered (no on-campus study). *Faculty:* 2 full-time (1 woman), 28 part-time/adjunct (5 women). *Students:* 30 full-time (12 women), 627 part-time (323 women); includes 79 minority (28 African Americans, 3 American Indian/Alaska Native, 17 Asian Americans or Pacific Islanders, 31 Hispanic Americans), 9 international. Average age 37. 299 applicants, 80% accepted, 209 enrolled. In 2009, 193 master's awarded. *Degree requirements:* For master's, comprehensive exam, capstone course. *Entrance requirements:* For master's, GMAT (if GPA less than 3.0 and fewer than 5 years of work experience), interview, resume, 2 letters of recommendation. Additional exam requirements/recommendations for international students: Recommended—TOEFL (minimum score 550 paper-based; 213 computer-based; 80 iBT). *Application deadline:* For fall admission, 9/11 priority date for domestic and international students; for winter admission, 12/15 priority date for domestic and international students; for spring admission, 3/17 priority date for domestic and international students. Applications are processed on a rolling basis. Application fee: $40 ($50 for international students). Electronic applications accepted. *Financial support:* Scholarships/grants available. Support available to part-time students. Financial award applicants required to submit FAFSA. *Unit head:* Bob Hanks, Director of Business and Real Estate Programs, 503-636-8141, Fax: 503-697-5597, E-mail: mba@marylhurst.edu. *Application contact:* Kathleen Schneff, Admissions Specialist, 800-634-9982 Ext. 3322, Fax: 503-635-6585, E-mail: admissions@marylhurst.edu.

Marymount University, Educational Partnerships Program, Arlington, VA 22207-4299. Offers business administration (MBA); health care management (MS); management studies (Certificate); organization development (Certificate). Part-time and evening/weekend programs available. *Students:* 25 part-time (17 women); includes 12 minority (11 African Americans, 1 Asian American or Pacific Islander), 1 international. Average age 43. *Entrance requirements:* For master's, GRE or GMAT, resume; for Certificate, resume. Additional exam requirements/recommendations for international students; Required—TOEFL (minimum score 600 paper-based; 250 computer-based; 96 iBT), IELTS (minimum score 6.5). *Application deadline:* For fall admission, 7/1 for international students; for spring admission, 10/15 for international students. Applications are processed on a rolling basis. Application fee: $40. Electronic applications accepted. *Expenses:* Tuition: Full-time $13,050; part-time $725 per credit hour. Required fees: $135; $7.50 per credit hour. *Financial support:* Career-related internships or fieldwork, Federal Work-Study, scholarships/grants, and unspecified assistantships available. Support available to part-time students. Financial award applicants required to submit FAFSA. *Unit head:* Dr. Sherri Hughes, Vice President for Academic Affairs and Provost, 703-284-1550, E-mail: sherri.hughes@marymount.edu. *Application contact:* Francesca Reed, Director, Graduate Admissions, 703-284-5901, Fax: 703-527-3815, E-mail: grad.admissions@marymount.edu.

Marymount University, School of Business Administration, Program in Business Administration, Arlington, VA 22207-4299. Offers MBA. *Accreditation:* ACBSP. Part-time and evening/weekend programs available. *Students:* 42 full-time (20 women), 130 part-time (82 women); includes 63 minority (29 African Americans, 17 Asian Americans or Pacific Islanders, 17 Hispanic Americans), 15 international. Average age 30. 83 applicants, 86% accepted, 42 enrolled. In 2009, 44 master's awarded. *Entrance requirements:* For master's, GMAT, resume. Additional exam requirements/recommendations for international students: Required—TOEFL (minimum score 600 paper-based; 250 computer-based; 96 iBT), IELTS (minimum score 6.5). *Application deadline:* For fall admission, 7/15 for domestic students, 7/1 for international students; for spring admission, 11/15 for domestic students, 10/15 for international students. Applications are processed on a rolling basis. Application fee: $40. Electronic applications accepted. *Expenses:* Tuition: Full-time $13,050; part-time $725 per credit hour. Required fees: $135; $7.50 per credit hour. *Financial support:* In 2009–10, 5 students received support; research assistantships with full and partial tuition reimbursements available, career-related internships or fieldwork, Federal Work-Study, scholarships/grants, and unspecified assistantships available. Support available to part-time students. Financial award applicants required to submit FAFSA. *Unit head:* Dr. Terri Long, Director, 703-284-5918, E-mail: terri.long@marymount.edu. *Application contact:* Francesca Reed, Director, Graduate Admissions, 703-284-5901, Fax: 703-527-3815, E-mail: grad.admissions@marymount.edu.

Marymount University, School of Business Administration, Program in Management, Arlington, VA 22207-4299. Offers leadership (Certificate); management (MS); project management (Certificate). Part-time and evening/weekend programs available. *Faculty:* 11 full-time (7 women), 11 part-time/adjunct (4 women). *Students:* 1 (woman) full-time, 25 part-time (17 women); includes 10 minority (7 African Americans, 1 Asian American or Pacific Islander, 2 Hispanic Americans), 1 international. Average age 40. 12 applicants, 83% accepted, 8 enrolled. In 2009, 11 master's, 2 other advanced degrees awarded. *Entrance requirements:* For master's, GMAT or GRE General Test, resume, at least 3 years of managerial experience, essay; for Certificate, resume, at least 3 years of managerial experience. Additional exam requirements/recommendations for international students: Required—TOEFL (minimum score 600 paper-based; 250 computer-based; 96 iBT), IELTS (minimum score 6.5). *Application deadline:* For fall admission, 7/15 for domestic students, 7/1 for international students; for spring admission, 11/15 for domestic students, 10/15 for international students. Applications are processed on a rolling basis. Application fee: $40. Electronic applications accepted. *Expenses:* Tuition: Full-time $13,050; part-time $725 per credit hour. Required fees: $135; $7.50 per credit hour. *Financial support:* In 2009–10, 4 students received support; research assistantships with full tuition reimbursements available, career-related internships or fieldwork, Federal Work-Study, scholarships/grants, and unspecified assistantships available. Support available to part-time students. Financial award applicants required to submit FAFSA. *Unit head:* Dr. Lorri Cooper, Director, Master's in Management, 703-284-5950, Fax: 703-527-3830, E-mail: lorri.cooper@marymount.edu. *Application contact:* Francesca Reed, Director, Graduate Admissions, 703-284-5901, Fax: 703-527-3815, E-mail: grad.admissions@marymount.edu.

Maryville University of Saint Louis, The John E. Simon School of Business, St. Louis, MO 63141-7299. Offers accounting (MBA, PGC); business studies (PGC); internet marketing (MBA, PGC); management (MBA, PGC); marketing (MBA, PGC). *Accreditation:* ACBSP. Part-time and evening/weekend programs available. *Students:* 17 full-time (9 women), 133 part-time (70 women); includes 14 minority (6 African Americans, 1 American Indian/Alaska Native, 3 Asian Americans or Pacific Islanders, 4 Hispanic Americans), 4 international. Average age 30. In 2009, 68 master's awarded. *Entrance requirements:* For master's, GMAT (unless applicant possesses undergraduate business degree with minimum cumulative GPA of 3.0, or has completed master's degree from accredited university, or has completed one early access course prior to undergraduate degree). Additional exam requirements/recommendations for international students: Required—TOEFL (minimum score 550 paper-based). *Application deadline:* Applications are processed on a rolling basis. Application fee: $40 ($60 for international students). Electronic applications accepted. *Expenses:* Tuition: Full-time $20,384; part-time $627.50 per credit hour. Required fees: $100 per semester. *Financial support:* Career-related internships or fieldwork, Federal Work-Study, tuition waivers (partial), and campus employment available. Financial award application deadline: 3/1; financial award applicants required to submit FAFSA. *Faculty research:* International business, e-marketing, strategic planning, interpersonal management skills, financial analysis. *Unit head:* Dr. Pamela Horwitz, Dean, 314-529-9418, Fax: 314-529-9975, E-mail: horwitz@maryville.edu. *Application contact:* Kathy Dougherty, Director of MBA Admissions and Enrollment, 314-529-9382, Fax: 314-529-9975, E-mail: business@maryville.edu.

Marywood University, Academic Affairs, College of Liberal Arts and Sciences, Department of Business and Managerial Science, Scranton, PA 18509-1598. Offers management information systems (MS); finance and investments (MBA); financial information systems (MS); general management (MBA); management information systems (MBA). *Accreditation:* ACBSP. *Students:* 14 full-time (9 women), 31 part-time (14 women); includes 2 minority (both African Americans),

2 international. Average age 32. In 2009, 11 master's awarded. *Entrance requirements:* Additional exam requirements/recommendations for international students: Required—TOEFL (minimum score 550 paper-based; 213 computer-based; 79 iBT). *Application deadline:* For fall admission, 4/1 priority date for domestic students, 3/31 priority date for international students; for spring admission, 11/1 priority date for domestic students, 8/31 priority date for international students. Applications are processed on a rolling basis. Application fee: $35. Electronic applications accepted. *Expenses:* Tuition: Part-time $715 per credit. Required fees: $270 per semester. Tuition and fees vary according to degree level, campus/location and program. *Financial support:* Research assistantships, career-related internships or fieldwork, scholarships/grants, and unspecified assistantships available. Support available to part-time students. Financial award application deadline: 6/30; financial award applicants required to submit FAFSA. *Faculty research:* Problem formulation in ill-structured situations, corporate tax structures. *Unit head:* Dr. Samir Dagher, Chair, 570-348-6274, E-mail: dagher@marywood.edu. *Application contact:* Tammy Manka, Assistant Director of Graduate Admissions, 866-279-9663, E-mail: tmanka@marywood.edu.

Massachusetts Institute of Technology, MIT Sloan School of Management, Cambridge, MA 02142. Offers M Fin, MBA, MS, SM, PhD. *Accreditation:* AACSB. *Faculty:* 106 full-time (23 women). *Students:* 938 full-time (331 women). Average age 28. 4,555 applicants, 542 enrolled. In 2009, 492 master's, 13 doctorates awarded. *Degree requirements:* For master's, thesis (for some programs); for doctorate, thesis/dissertation, exams. *Entrance requirements:* For master's, GMAT, previous course work in calculus and economics; for doctorate, GMAT, GRE, previous course work in calculus and economics. *Application deadline:* For fall admission, 1/12 for domestic and international students. Application fee: $250. Electronic applications accepted. *Expenses:* Contact institution. *Financial support:* Fellowships with tuition reimbursements, research assistantships with tuition reimbursements, teaching assistantships with tuition reimbursements, Federal Work-Study, institutionally sponsored loans, scholarships/grants, health care benefits, and unspecified assistantships available. Support available to part-time students. *Faculty research:* Financial engineering, entrepreneurship, e-business, work and employment, leaders for manufacturing. *Unit head:* David C. Schmittlein, Dean, 617-253-2804, Fax: 617-258-6617, E-mail: dschmitt@mit.edu. *Application contact:* Rod Garcia, Director of Admissions, 617-253-5434, Fax: 617-253-6405, E-mail: mbaadmissions@sloan.mit.edu.

McGill University, Faculty of Graduate and Postdoctoral Studies, Desautels Faculty of Management, Montréal, QC H3A 2T5, Canada. Offers administration (PhD); entrepreneurial studies (MBA); finance (MBA); general management (Post Master's Certificate); information systems (MBA); international business (exchange program) (MBA); international Master's program in practicing management (MM); management (MBA); management for development (MBA); manufacturing management (MMM); marketing (MBA); operations management (MBA); public accountancy (Diploma); strategic management (MBA); MBA/LL B; MD/MBA.

McKendree University, Graduate Programs, Master of Business Administration Program, Lebanon, IL 62254-1299. Offers business administration (MBA); human resource management (MBA); international business (MBA). Part-time and evening/weekend programs available. Postbaccalaureate distance learning degree programs offered (no on-campus study). *Faculty:* 8 full-time (1 woman), 18 part-time/adjunct (6 women). *Students:* 68 full-time (26 women), 122 part-time (63 women); includes 23 minority (17 African Americans, 1 Asian American or Pacific Islander, 5 Hispanic Americans), 1 international. Average age 34. 80 applicants, 68% accepted, 47 enrolled. In 2009, 37 master's awarded. *Entrance requirements:* For master's, official transcripts from all institutions attended, essay, minimum GPA of 3.0, three references, resume. Additional exam requirements/recommendations for international students: Required—TOEFL. *Application deadline:* Applications are processed on a rolling basis. Application fee: $0. Electronic applications accepted. *Expenses:* Tuition: Full-time $6300; part-time $350 per credit hour. One-time fee: $125. *Financial support:* Applicants required to submit FAFSA. *Unit head:* Dr. Frank Spreng, Director of MBA Program, 618-537-6902, E-mail: fspreng@mckendree.edu. *Application contact:* Patty Aubel, Graduate Admission Counselor, 618-537-6943, Fax: 618-537-6410, E-mail: plaubel@mckendree.edu.

McMaster University, School of Graduate Studies, Faculty of Business, Hamilton, ON L8S 4M2, Canada. Offers MBA, PhD. *Accreditation:* AACSB. Part-time programs available. *Degree requirements:* For doctorate, comprehensive exam, thesis/dissertation. *Entrance requirements:* For master's, GMAT; for doctorate, GMAT or GRE, master's degree. Additional exam requirements/recommendations for international students: Required—TOEFL (minimum score 580 paper-based; 237 computer-based). *Faculty research:* Mergers, acquisitions, and restructuring; business investment; capital structure and dividend policy; employee pay/reward systems; pay and employment equity.

McNeese State University, Doré School of Graduate Studies, College of Business, Master of Business Administration Program, Lake Charles, LA 70609. Offers accounting (MBA). *Accreditation:* AACSB. Evening/weekend programs available. *Faculty:* 15 full-time (1 woman). *Students:* 68 full-time (29 women), 37 part-time (18 women); includes 6 minority (3 African Americans, 2 Asian Americans or Pacific Islanders, 1 Hispanic American), 35 international. In 2009, 35 master's awarded. *Degree requirements:* For master's, written exam. *Entrance requirements:* For master's, GMAT. *Application deadline:* For fall admission, 5/15 priority date for domestic and international students; for spring admission, 10/15 priority date for domestic and international students. Applications are processed on a rolling basis. Application fee: $20 ($30 for international students). *Expenses:* Tuition, area resident: Full-time $2556. Tuition, state resident: full-time $2556. Required fees: $1031. Tuition and fees vary according to course load. *Financial support:* Research assistantships, teaching assistantships, Federal Work-Study available. Support available to part-time students. Financial award application deadline: 5/1. *Faculty research:* Management development, integrating technology into the work force, union/management relations, economic development. *Unit head:* Dr. Akm Rahman, MBA Director, 337-475-5573, Fax: 337-475-5010, E-mail: mrahman@mcneese.edu. *Application contact:* Dr. Akm Rahman, MBA Director, 337-475-5573, Fax: 337-475-5010, E-mail: mrahman@mcneese.edu.

Medaille College, Program in Business Administration—Amherst, Amherst, NY 14221. Offers business administration (MBA); organizational leadership (MA). Evening/weekend programs available. *Faculty:* 6 full-time (2 women), 23 part-time/adjunct (4 women). *Students:* 211 full-time (126 women); includes 34 minority (29 African Americans, 1 Asian American or Pacific Islander, 4 Hispanic Americans). Average age 31. 107 applicants, 62% accepted, 66 enrolled. In 2009, 89 master's awarded. *Degree requirements:* For master's, thesis or alternative. *Entrance requirements:* For master's, GMAT, minimum undergraduate GPA of 2.7, 3 years of work experience. Additional exam requirements/recommendations for international students: Required—TOEFL (minimum score 550 paper-based; 213 computer-based). *Application deadline:* Applications are processed on a rolling basis. Application fee: $100. *Expenses:* Contact institution. *Financial support:* In 2009–10, 180 students received support. Federal Work-Study available. Financial award applicants required to submit FAFSA. *Unit head:* Jennifer Bavifard, Associate Dean for Special Programs, 716-631-1061 Ext. 150, Fax: 716-631-1380, E-mail: jbavifar@medaille.edu. *Application contact:* Jacqueline Matheny, Executive Director of Marketing and Enrollment, 716-932-2541, Fax: 716-632-1811, E-mail: jmatheny@medaille.edu.

Medaille College, Program in Business Administration—Rochester, Rochester, NY 14623. Offers business administration (MBA); organizational leadership (MA). Evening/weekend programs available. *Degree requirements:* For master's, thesis or alternative. *Entrance requirements:* For master's, GMAT, 3 years of work experience, minimum undergraduate GPA of 2.7. Additional exam requirements/recommendations for international students: Required—TOEFL (minimum score 550 paper-based; 213 computer-based). *Expenses:* Contact institution.

Memorial University of Newfoundland, School of Graduate Studies, Faculty of Business Administration, St. John's, NL A1C 5S7, Canada. Offers EMBA, MBA. *Accreditation:* AACSB. Part-time programs available. *Degree requirements:* For master's, thesis (for some programs). *Entrance requirements:* For master's, GMAT. Additional exam requirements/recommendations for international students: Required—TOEFL (minimum score 580 paper-based; 237 computer-

based), TWE (minimum score 4). Electronic applications accepted. *Faculty research:* International business, marketing, organizational theory and behavior, management science and information systems, small business.

Mercer University, Graduate Studies, Cecil B. Day Campus, Eugene W. Stetson School of Business and Economics (Atlanta), Macon, GA 31207-0003. Offers business administration (MBA, XMBA); Pharm D/MBA. *Accreditation:* AACSB. Part-time and evening/weekend programs available. *Faculty:* 18 full-time (6 women), 4 part-time/adjunct (0 women). *Students:* 178 full-time (74 women), 99 part-time (55 women); includes 69 minority (49 African Americans, 15 Asian Americans or Pacific Islanders, 5 Hispanic Americans), 15 international. Average age 32. 169 applicants, 54% accepted, 64 enrolled. In 2009, 160 master's awarded. *Entrance requirements:* For master's, GMAT. Additional exam requirements/recommendations for international students: Required—TOEFL (minimum score 550 paper-based; 213 computer-based; 80 iBT). *Application deadline:* For fall admission, 7/1 priority date for domestic students, 7/1 for international students; for spring admission, 11/1 priority date for domestic students, 11/1 for international students. Applications are processed on a rolling basis. Application fee: $50 ($100 for international students). Electronic applications accepted. *Financial support:* Federal Work-Study available. Financial award application deadline: 5/1; financial award applicants required to submit FAFSA. *Faculty research:* Entrepreneurship, market studies, international business strategy, financial analysis. *Unit head:* Dr. Gina L. Miller, Associate Dean, 678-547-6177, Fax: 678-547-6337, E-mail: miller_gl@mercer.edu. *Application contact:* Jamie Thomas, Graduate Enrollment Associate, 678-547-6177, Fax: 678-547-6337, E-mail: atlbusadm@mercer.edu.

Mercer University, Graduate Studies, Macon Campus, Eugene W. Stetson School of Business and Economics (Macon), Macon, GA 31207-0003. Offers MBA. *Accreditation:* AACSB. Part-time and evening/weekend programs available. *Faculty:* 9 full-time (5 women), 1 (woman) part-time/adjunct. *Students:* 11 full-time (2 women), 29 part-time (12 women); includes 7 minority (4 African Americans, 1 Asian American or Pacific Islander, 2 Hispanic Americans), 2 international. Average age 26. In 2009, 18 master's awarded. *Entrance requirements:* For master's, GMAT. Additional exam requirements/recommendations for international students: Required—TOEFL (minimum score 550 paper-based; 213 computer-based). *Application deadline:* For fall admission, 8/1 for domestic students; for spring admission, 12/1 for domestic students. Applications are processed on a rolling basis. Application fee: $50 ($100 for international students). *Faculty research:* Federal Reserve System, management of nurses, sales promotion, systems for common stock selection, interest rate premiums. *Unit head:* Dr. Paul David Shields, Dean, 478-301-2990, Fax: 478-301-2635, E-mail: shields_pd@mercer.edu. *Application contact:* Robert Holland, Director, Academic Administrator, 478-301-2835, Fax: 478-301-2635, E-mail: holland_r@mercer.edu.

Mercy College, School of Business, Program in Business Administration, Dobbs Ferry, NY 10522-1189. Offers MBA. Part-time and evening/weekend programs available. Postbaccalaureate distance learning degree programs offered (minimal on-campus study). *Students:* 5 full-time (all women), 85 part-time (45 women); includes 19 African Americans, 6 Asian Americans or Pacific Islanders, 17 Hispanic Americans, 7 international. Average age 33. 115 applicants, 51% accepted, 25 enrolled. In 2009, 30 master's awarded. *Degree requirements:* For master's, thesis or alternative, capstone. *Entrance requirements:* For master's, GMAT, interview, two letters of recommendation, undergraduate transcripts. Additional exam requirements/recommendations for international students: Required—TOEFL (minimum score 600 paper-based; 250 computer-based; 100 iBT). *Application deadline:* For fall admission, 8/1 for international students. Applications are processed on a rolling basis. Application fee: $40. Electronic applications accepted. *Expenses:* Tuition: Full-time $13,158; part-time $731 per credit. Required fees: $500. Tuition and fees vary according to degree level and program. *Financial support:* In 2009–10, 1 student received support. Career-related internships or fieldwork, Federal Work-Study, scholarships/grants, and unspecified assistantships available. Support available to part-time students. Financial award applicants required to submit FAFSA. *Faculty research:* Marketing systems, international business, diverse management challenges, decision making. *Unit head:* Dr. Geoffrey Mills, Dean for the School of Business, 914-674-7481, E-mail: gmills@mercy.edu. *Application contact:* Saira Vargas, MBA Coordinator, 914-674-7481, E-mail: svargas@mercy.edu.

Meredith College, John E. Weems Graduate School, School of Business, Raleigh, NC 27607-5298. Offers business administration (MBA). Part-time and evening/weekend programs available. *Faculty:* 9 full-time (7 women), 2 part-time/adjunct (both women). *Students:* 1 full-time (0 women), 81 part-time (57 women); includes 20 minority (12 African Americans, 6 Asian Americans or Pacific Islanders, 2 Hispanic Americans). Average age 34. 45 applicants, 67% accepted, 23 enrolled. In 2009, 28 master's awarded. *Degree requirements:* For master's, thesis optional. *Entrance requirements:* For master's, GMAT, interview, minimum GPA of 2.5, letters of recommendation. Additional exam requirements/recommendations for international students: Required—TOEFL. *Application deadline:* For fall admission, 7/1 priority date for domestic and international students; for spring admission, 11/1 priority date for domestic and international students. Applications are processed on a rolling basis. Application fee: $50. Electronic applications accepted. *Financial support:* Career-related internships or fieldwork, institutionally sponsored loans, scholarships/grants, and tuition waivers (partial) available. Support available to part-time students. Financial award application deadline: 2/15; financial award applicants required to submit FAFSA. *Unit head:* Dr. Denise Rotundo, Dean, 919-760-8471, Fax: 919-760-8470. *Application contact:* Page Midyette, Coordinator, 919-760-2281, Fax: 919-760-2898, E-mail: midyette@meredith.edu.

Meritus University, School of Business, Fredericton, NB E3C 2R2, Canada. Offers global management (MBA); health care management (MBA); human resources management (MBA); information technology management (MBA); marketing (MBA); technology management (MBA). Evening/weekend programs available. Postbaccalaureate distance learning degree programs offered (no on-campus study). *Faculty:* 5 full-time (1 woman), 50 part-time/adjunct (15 women). *Students:* 77 full-time (29 women). Average age 35. *Entrance requirements:* For master's, undergraduate degree or comparable equivalent with minimum cumulative GPA of 2.5; minimum equivalent of two years of full-time, post high-school work experience; current employment. Additional exam requirements/recommendations for international students: Required—TOEFL (minimum score 213 computer-based; 79 iBT), IELTS (minimum score 6.5), or TOEIC (minimum score 750) or Berlitz (minimum score 550). *Application deadline:* Applications are processed on a rolling basis. Application fee: $45. Electronic applications accepted. Tuition and fees charges are reported in Canadian dollars. *Expenses:* Tuition: Full-time $14,400 Canadian dollars. Required fees: $720 Canadian dollars. *Unit head:* Dr. Albert K. S. Wong, Program Chair, Business Administration, 604-657-5465, Fax: 602-643-4624, E-mail: albert.wong@staff.meritusu.ca. *Application contact:* Jeremy S. DeMerchant, Enrolment Manager, 506-443-8413, Fax: 602-759-3688, E-mail: jeremy.demerchant@staff.meritusu.ca.

Mesa State College, Department of Business, Grand Junction, CO 81501-3122. Offers MBA. Part-time and evening/weekend programs available. *Faculty:* 12 full-time (1 woman), 1 part-time/adjunct (0 women). *Students:* 7 full-time (3 women), 24 part-time (13 women); includes 2 Hispanic Americans. Average age 36. 22 applicants, 82% accepted, 11 enrolled. In 2009, 10 master's awarded. *Degree requirements:* For master's, thesis or research practicum. *Entrance requirements:* For master's, GMAT, MAT, or GRE, minimum GPA of 3.0 for last 60 undergraduate hours, 2 letters of recommendation. Additional exam requirements/recommendations for international students: Required—TOEFL (minimum score 550 paper-based; 207 computer-based). *Application deadline:* For fall admission, 7/27 priority date for domestic students; for spring admission, 12/22 priority date for domestic students. Applications are processed on a rolling basis. Application fee: $50. Electronic applications accepted. *Expenses:* Tuition, state resident: full-time $5400; part-time $300 per credit hour. Tuition, nonresident: full-time $16,200; part-time $900 per credit hour. Required fees: $460; $25 per credit hour. Tuition and fees vary according to program. *Financial support:* In 2009–10, 11 students received support. Applicants required to submit FAFSA. *Unit head:* Dr. Morgan Bridge, Department Head, 970-248-1169, Fax: 970-248-1730, E-mail: mbridge@mesastate.edu. *Application contact:* Jane Sandoval, MBA Coordinator, 970-248-1778, Fax: 970-248-1730, E-mail: jsandova@mesastate.edu.

Methodist University, School of Graduate Studies, Program in Business Administration, Fayetteville, NC 28311-1498. Offers MBA. *Accreditation:* ACBSP. Part-time and evening/weekend programs available. *Faculty:* 7 full-time (2 women), 1 part-time/adjunct (0 women). *Students:* 28 full-time (14 women), 31 part-time (16 women); includes 4 African Americans, 2 Hispanic Americans, 4 international. Average age 31. 34 applicants, 76% accepted, 24 enrolled. In 2009, 32 master's awarded. *Entrance requirements:* For master's, GMAT or MAT. Additional exam requirements/recommendations for international students: Required—TOEFL (minimum score 500 paper-based; 173 computer-based; 60 iBT). *Application deadline:* For fall admission, 5/19 for domestic and international students; for spring admission, 10/19 for domestic and international students. Application fee: $100. *Expenses:* Tuition: Full-time $26,895; part-time $698 per course. Required fees: $110; $600 per year. One-time fee: $1125 full-time; $175 part-time. Full-time tuition and fees vary according to program. Part-time tuition and fees vary according to campus/location. *Financial support:* In 2009–10, 24 students received support. Scholarships/grants available. Support available to part-time students. Financial award application deadline: 8/10; financial award applicants required to submit FAFSA. *Unit head:* Dr. Warren G. McDonald, Professional MBA Director, 800-488-7110 Ext. 7116, E-mail: wmcdonald@methodist.edu. *Application contact:* Anne C. Way, Professional MBA Coordinator, 800-488-7110 Ext. 7493, E-mail: away@methodist.edu.

Metropolitan College of New York, Program in General Management, New York, NY 10013. Offers MBA. Evening/weekend programs available. *Degree requirements:* For master's, thesis, 10 day study abroad. *Entrance requirements:* For master's, GMAT. Additional exam requirements/recommendations for international students: Required—TOEFL (minimum score 600 paper-based; 220 computer-based). Electronic applications accepted. *Expenses:* Contact institution.

Metropolitan State University, College of Management, St. Paul, MN 55106-5000. Offers business administration (MBA); information assurance security (Graduate Certificate); information management (MMIS); MIS generalist (Graduate Certificate); MIS systems analysis and design (Graduate Certificate); nonprofit management (MPNA); project management (Graduate Certificate); public administration (MPNA); systems management (MMIS). Part-time and evening/weekend programs available. *Degree requirements:* For master's, thesis optional, computer language (MMIS). *Entrance requirements:* For master's, GMAT (MBA), resume. Additional exam requirements/recommendations for international students: Required—TOEFL (minimum score 550 paper-based; 213 computer-based). *Expenses:* Tuition, state resident: full-time $5520; part-time $276 per credit hour. Tuition, nonresident: full-time $11,040; part-time $552 per credit hour. Required fees: $209; $10 per credit hour. Tuition and fees vary according to degree level. *Faculty research:* Yugoslav economic system, workers' cooperatives, participative management and job enrichment, global business systems.

Miami University, Graduate School, Farmer School of Business, Oxford, OH 45056. Offers accountancy (M Acc); business administration (MBA); economics (MA). *Accreditation:* AACSB. Part-time and evening/weekend programs available. *Students:* 69 full-time (19 women), 32 part-time (10 women); includes 7 minority (1 African American, 1 American Indian/Alaska Native, 5 Asian Americans or Pacific Islanders), 14 international. *Entrance requirements:* For master's, GMAT, minimum undergraduate GPA of 3.0 during previous 2 years or 2.75 overall. Additional exam requirements/recommendations for international students: Required—TOEFL. Application fee: $50. *Expenses:* Tuition, state resident: full-time $11,280. Tuition, nonresident: full-time $24,912. Required fees: $516. *Financial support:* Fellowships with tuition reimbursements, research assistantships, Federal Work-Study, tuition waivers (full), and unspecified assistantships available. Financial award application deadline: 3/1; financial award applicants required to submit FAFSA. *Unit head:* Dr. Roger Jenkins, Dean, 513-529-3631, Fax: 513-529-6992, E-mail: deanofbusiness@muohio.edu. *Application contact:* Graduate Admission Coordinator, 513-529-3734, Fax: 513-529-3762, E-mail: gradschool@muohio.edu.

Michigan State University, The Graduate School, Eli Broad Graduate School of Management, Department of Management, East Lansing, MI 48824. Offers business administration (PhD). *Faculty:* 19 full-time (4 women), 1 (woman) part-time/adjunct. *Students:* 18 full-time (8 women); includes 2 minority (both Hispanic Americans), 10 international. Average age 31. 52 applicants, 10% accepted. In 2009, 6 doctorates awarded. *Entrance requirements:* Additional exam requirements/recommendations for international students: Required—TOEFL (minimum score 550 paper-based; 213 computer-based). Electronic applications accepted. *Expenses:* Tuition, state resident: part-time $478.25 per credit hour. Tuition, nonresident: part-time $966.50 per credit hour. Part-time tuition and fees vary according to program. *Financial support:* In 2009–10, 12 research assistantships with tuition reimbursements (averaging $6,554 per year), 3 teaching assistantships with tuition reimbursements (averaging $6,342 per year) were awarded. Total annual research expenditures: $262,478. *Unit head:* Dr. Donald E. Conlon, Chairperson, 517-355-1878, Fax: 517-432-1111, E-mail: conlon@bus.msu.edu. *Application contact:* Susan Polhamus, Program Information, 517-355-1878, Fax: 517-432-111, E-mail: mgt@msu.edu.

Michigan State University, The Graduate School, Eli Broad Graduate School of Management, Department of Supply Chain Management, East Lansing, MI 48824. Offers business administration (PhD); supply chain management (MS). Part-time programs available. *Faculty:* 17 full-time (3 women). *Students:* 22 full-time (7 women), 36 part-time (8 women); includes 11 minority (6 African Americans, 1 Asian American or Pacific Islander, 4 Hispanic Americans), 12 international. Average age 33. 51 applicants, 6% accepted. In 2009, 23 master's, 1 doctorate awarded. *Degree requirements:* For master's, field study, research project; for doctorate, comprehensive exam, thesis/dissertation, oral defense of dissertation proposal and dissertation. *Entrance requirements:* For master's, GMAT, bachelor's degree in related field, letters of recommendation, 2-3 years of work experience, minimum GPA of 3.0 in last 2 years of undergraduate course work; for doctorate, GMAT or GRE, letters of recommendation. Additional exam requirements/recommendations for international students: Required—TOEFL. Electronic applications accepted. *Expenses:* Contact institution. *Financial support:* In 2009–10, 8 research assistantships with tuition reimbursements (averaging $7,799 per year) were awarded. Total annual research expenditures: $244,341. *Unit head:* Dr. David J. Closs, Chairperson, 517-432-6406, Fax: 517-432-8048, E-mail: closs@msu.edu. *Application contact:* Cheryl Lundeen, Program Information, 517-432-6335, Fax: 517-432-8048, E-mail: lundeenc@bus.msu.edu.

Michigan State University, The Graduate School, Eli Broad Graduate School of Management, Program in Business Administration, East Lansing, MI 48824. Offers business administration (MBA, PhD); business research (MBA); corporate business administration (MBA); integrative management (MBA). Evening/weekend programs available. *Students:* 476 full-time (111 women); includes 91 minority (25 African Americans, 1 American Indian/Alaska Native, 54 Asian Americans or Pacific Islanders, 11 Hispanic Americans), 85 international. Average age 31. 203 applicants, 81% accepted. In 2009, 230 master's awarded. *Degree requirements:* For master's, enrichment experience. *Entrance requirements:* For master's, GMAT. Additional exam requirements/recommendations for international students: Required—TOEFL. *Application deadline:* Applications are processed on a rolling basis. Electronic applications accepted. *Expenses:* Contact institution. *Financial support:* In 2009–10, 63 research assistantships with tuition reimbursements (averaging $5,865 per year), 5 teaching assistantships with tuition reimbursements (averaging $5,949 per year) were awarded. *Unit head:* Dr. Karyll Shaw, Acting Associate Dean for MBA and MS Programs, 517-355-8377, Fax: 517-353-6395, E-mail: shawk@bus.msu.edu. *Application contact:* Program Information, 517-355-7604, E-mail: mba@msu.edu.

Michigan Technological University, Graduate School, School of Business and Economics, Program in Business Administration, Houghton, MI 49931. Offers MBA. Part-time programs available. *Degree requirements:* For master's, thesis or alternative. *Entrance requirements:* For master's, GMAT, minimum GPA of 2.9. Additional exam requirements/recommendations for international students: Required—TOEFL (minimum score 590 paper-based; 240 computer-based). Electronic applications accepted.

Mid-America Christian University, Program in Business Administration, Oklahoma City, OK 73170-4504. Offers MBA. *Entrance requirements:* For master's, bachelor's degree from a regionally accredited college or university, minimum overall cumulative GPA of 2.75 of bachelor

Business Administration and Management—General

Mid-America Christian University (continued)

course work. Additional exam requirements/recommendations for international students: Required—TOEFL (minimum score 550 paper-based; 213 computer-based).

MidAmerica Nazarene University, Graduate Studies in Management, Olathe, KS 66062-1899. Offers management (MBA); organizational administration (MA), including finance, international business, leadership, non-profit. Evening/weekend programs available. *Faculty:* 6 full-time (2 women), 18 part-time/adjunct (7 women). *Students:* 107 full-time (49 women), 7 part-time (3 women); includes 25 minority (18 African Americans, 1 Asian American or Pacific Islander, 6 Hispanic Americans). Average age 36. In 2009, 81 master's awarded. *Entrance requirements:* For master's, mathematical assessment, minimum undergraduate GPA of 3.0, letters of recommendation. Additional exam requirements/recommendations for international students: Required—TOEFL. *Application deadline:* For fall admission, 9/1 priority date for domestic students; for spring admission, 5/1 priority date for domestic students. Applications are processed on a rolling basis. Application fee: $100. Electronic applications accepted. *Financial support:* Application deadline: 5/1. *Faculty research:* Economic development, international finance, business development, employee evaluation. *Unit head:* Dr. Willadee Wehmeyer, Director, 913-971-3276, Fax: 913-791-3409, E-mail: wwehmeye@mnu.edu. *Application contact:* Melanie Sutherland, Administrative Assistant, 913-971-3276, Fax: 913-971-3409, E-mail: mba@mnu.edu.

Middle Tennessee State University, College of Graduate Studies, Jennings A. Jones College of Business, Department of Management and Marketing, Murfreesboro, TN 37132. Offers MBA. *Accreditation:* AACSB. Part-time and evening/weekend programs available. Postbaccalaureate distance learning degree programs offered. *Faculty:* 18 full-time (4 women). *Students:* 69 full-time (25 women), 278 part-time (123 women); includes 88 minority (54 African Americans, 2 American Indian/Alaska Native, 23 Asian Americans or Pacific Islanders, 9 Hispanic Americans). Average age 27. 213 applicants, 66% accepted, 140 enrolled. In 2009, 121 master's awarded. *Degree requirements:* For master's, comprehensive exam. *Entrance requirements:* Additional exam requirements/recommendations for international students: Required—TOEFL (minimum score 525 paper-based; 195 computer-based; 71 iBT) or IELTS (minimum score 6). *Application deadline:* For fall admission, 6/1 for domestic and international students. Applications are processed on a rolling basis. Application fee: $25 ($30 for international students). Electronic applications accepted. *Expenses:* Tuition, state resident: full-time $4404. Tuition, nonresident: full-time $10,956. *Financial support:* In 2009–10, 8 students received support. Institutionally sponsored loans available. Support available to part-time students. Financial award application deadline: 5/1; financial award applicants required to submit FAFSA. *Faculty research:* International business, business strategy, organizational culture/leadership, consumer behavior, services marketing. *Unit head:* Dr. Jill Austin, Chair, 615-898-2736, Fax: 615-898-5308, E-mail: jaustin@mtsu.edu. *Application contact:* Dr. Michael Allen, Dean and Vice Provost for Research, 615-898-2840, Fax: 615-904-8020, E-mail: mallen@mtsu.edu.

Midway College, Leadership MBA Program, Midway, KY 40347-1120. Offers MBA. *Degree requirements:* For master's, capstone course. *Entrance requirements:* For master's, GMAT, bachelor's degree, minimum GPA of 3.0, 3 years of professional work experience, interview. Additional exam requirements/recommendations for international students: Required—TOEFL (minimum score 550 paper-based; 213 computer-based; 80 iBT). *Expenses:* Tuition: Part-time $500 per credit hour. One-time fee: $100 part-time.

Midwestern State University, Graduate Studies, College of Business Administration, Wichita Falls, TX 76308. Offers business administration (MBA); health services administration (MBA). *Accreditation:* ACBSP. Part-time and evening/weekend programs available. *Degree requirements:* For master's, comprehensive exam, thesis optional. *Entrance requirements:* For master's, GMAT. Additional exam requirements/recommendations for international students: Required—TOEFL (minimum score 550 paper-based; 213 computer-based). Electronic applications accepted. *Expenses:* Tuition, state resident: full-time $1620; part-time $90 per credit hour. Tuition, nonresident: full-time $2160; part-time $120 per credit hour. International tuition: $7506 full-time. Required fees: $3068.80; $145.60 per credit hour. $179 per semester. *Faculty research:* Small business management, health care personnel administration, Pacific Rim trade, AIDS in the workplace, technology transfer.

Milligan College, Program in Business Administration, Milligan College, TN 37682. Offers MBA. Postbaccalaureate distance learning degree programs offered (minimal on-campus study). *Faculty:* 9 full-time (3 women), 1 part-time/adjunct (0 women). *Students:* 48 full-time (23 women), 2 part-time (1 woman); includes 1 African American, 1 Asian American or Pacific Islander. 41 applicants, 95% accepted, 33 enrolled. In 2009, 31 master's awarded. *Degree requirements:* For master's, comprehensive exam (for some programs), thesis or alternative. *Entrance requirements:* For master's, GMAT if undergraduate GPA less than 3.0, 2 professional recommendations, 3 years related work experience. Additional exam requirements/recommendations for international students: Required—TOEFL. *Application deadline:* For fall admission, 8/1 for domestic and international students; for spring admission, 1/15 for domestic and international students. Application fee: $30. Electronic applications accepted. *Expenses:* Tuition: Part-time $450 per credit hour. *Financial support:* Applicants required to submit FAFSA. *Unit head:* Bob Mahan, Director, 423-461-8673, Fax: 423-461-8677, E-mail: rlmahan@milligan.edu. *Application contact:* Courtney Kieslich, Admissions Specialist, 423-461-8482, Fax: 423-461-8789, E-mail: ckieslich@milligan.edu.

Millikin University, Tabor School of Business, Decatur, IL 62522-2084. Offers MBA. *Accreditation:* ACBSP. Evening/weekend programs available. *Faculty:* 7 full-time (2 women), 5 part-time/adjunct (0 women). *Students:* 22 full-time (7 women); includes 1 minority (African American). Average age 35. 40 applicants, 98% accepted. In 2009, 29 master's awarded. *Entrance requirements:* For master's, GMAT, resume, 3 reference letters, interview. Additional exam requirements/recommendations for international students: Required—TOEFL (minimum score 550 paper-based; 79 iBT). *Application deadline:* For spring admission, 11/1 priority date for domestic students, 8/1 priority date for international students. Applications are processed on a rolling basis. Application fee: $0. Electronic applications accepted. *Expenses:* Tuition: Full-time $24,890; part-time $655 per credit hour. *Financial support:* Applicants required to submit FAFSA. *Faculty research:* E-commerce, international marketing, pedagogy, total quality management, auditing. *Unit head:* Dr. James G. Dahl, Dean, 217-420-6634, Fax: 217-424-6286, E-mail: jdahl@millikin.edu. *Application contact:* Dr. Anthony Liberatore, Director of MBA Program, 217-424-6338, E-mail: aliberatore@millikin.edu.

Millsaps College, Else School of Management, Jackson, MS 39210-0001. Offers accounting (M Acc); business administration (MBA). *Accreditation:* AACSB. Part-time programs available. *Entrance requirements:* For master's, GMAT. Additional exam requirements/recommendations for international students: Required—TOEFL. Electronic applications accepted. *Faculty research:* Ethics, audit independence, satisfaction with assurance services, political business cycles.

Mills College, Graduate Studies, Lori I. Lokey Graduate School of Business, Oakland, CA 94613-1000. Offers management (MBA). *Faculty:* 5 full-time (2 women), 10 part-time/adjunct (6 women). *Students:* 81 full-time (78 women), 5 part-time (all women); includes 43 minority (20 African Americans, 11 Asian Americans or Pacific Islanders, 12 Hispanic Americans), 2 international. Average age 32. 64 applicants, 95% accepted, 43 enrolled. In 2009, 33 master's awarded. *Application deadline:* For fall admission, 2/1 for domestic and international students. Application fee: $50. *Expenses:* Tuition: Full-time $26,326; part-time $6584 per course. Required fees: $896. One-time fee: $896 part-time. Tuition and fees vary according to program. *Financial support:* In 2009–10, 96 fellowships (averaging $8,351 per year) were awarded; scholarships/grants also available. Support available to part-time students. Financial award applicants required to submit FAFSA. *Faculty research:* Information systems, corporate and financial planning, interest-based marketing, organizational behavior, international trade and finance. *Unit head:* Nancy Thornborrow, Dean, 510-430-2344, Fax: 510-430-3314, E-mail: nancy@mills.edu. *Application contact:* Jessica King, Graduate Admission Specialist, 510-430-3305, Fax: 510-430-2159, E-mail: grad-studies@mills.edu.

Milwaukee School of Engineering, Rader School of Business, Milwaukee, WI 53202-3109. Offers engineering management (MS); marketing and export management (MS); medical informatics (MS); new product management (MS). Part-time and evening/weekend programs available. *Faculty:* 6 full-time (1 woman), 16 part-time/adjunct (3 women). *Students:* 8 full-time (2 women), 116 part-time (32 women); includes 12 minority (3 African Americans, 1 American Indian/Alaska Native, 6 Asian Americans or Pacific Islanders, 2 Hispanic Americans), 1 international. Average age 26. 61 applicants, 69% accepted, 20 enrolled. In 2009, 32 master's awarded. *Degree requirements:* For master's, thesis (for some programs), thesis defense or capstone project. *Entrance requirements:* For master's, GMAT, GRE General Test, or MCAT, BS in engineering, science, business or related fields; 2 letters of recommendation. Additional exam requirements/recommendations for international students: Required—TOEFL (minimum score 79 iBT). *Application deadline:* Applications are processed on a rolling basis. Application fee: $30. Electronic applications accepted. *Expenses:* Tuition: Part-time $603 per credit. *Financial support:* In 2009–10, 36 students received support, including 2 research assistantships (averaging $15,000 per year); career-related internships or fieldwork also available. Support available to part-time students. Financial award applicants required to submit FAFSA. *Faculty research:* Operations, project management, quality marketing, information technology, data bases. *Unit head:* Dr. Steven Bialek, Chairman, 414-277-7364, Fax: 414-277-7479, E-mail: bialek@msoe.edu. *Application contact:* Dr. Steven Bialek, Chairman, 414-277-7364, Fax: 414-277-7479, E-mail: bialek@msoe.edu.

Minnesota State University Mankato, College of Graduate Studies, College of Business, Mankato, MN 56001. Offers MBA. *Accreditation:* AACSB. *Students:* 6 full-time (3 women), 52 part-time (16 women). *Entrance requirements:* For master's, GMAT, 2 letters of reference, resume. Additional exam requirements/recommendations for international students: Required—TOEFL. *Application deadline:* For fall admission, 7/1 for domestic students, 5/1 for international students; for spring admission, 11/1 for domestic students, 10/1 for international students. Electronic applications accepted. *Expenses:* Tuition, state resident: full-time $5364. Tuition, nonresident: full-time $8314. *Unit head:* Dr. Kevin Elliott, Graduate Coordinator, 507-389-5420. *Application contact:* Dr. Kevin Elliott, Graduate Coordinator, 507-389-5420.

Minot State University, Graduate School, Program in Management, Minot, ND 58707-0002. Offers MS. *Degree requirements:* For master's, comprehensive exam (for some programs), thesis (for some programs). *Entrance requirements:* For master's, minimum GPA of 2.75. Additional exam requirements/recommendations for international students: Required—TOEFL. *Expenses:* Tuition, state resident: full-time $5720; part-time $283 per credit hour. Tuition, nonresident: full-time $5720; part-time $283 per credit hour. Required fees: $1034; $1034 per year. Tuition and fees vary according to course load, degree level and program. *Faculty research:* Distance education.

Misericordia University, College of Professional Studies and Social Sciences, Masters of Business Administration Program, Dallas, PA 18612-1098. Offers MBA. Part-time and evening/weekend programs available. Postbaccalaureate distance learning degree programs offered. *Faculty:* 4 full-time (1 woman), 5 part-time/adjunct (2 women). *Students:* 77 part-time (37 women). Average age 32. *Entrance requirements:* For master's, GMAT, MAT or GRE (50th percentile or higher) or minimum undergraduate GPA of 2.79. *Financial support:* In 2009–10, 46 students received support. Scholarships/grants and tuition waivers available. Support available to part-time students. Financial award applicants required to submit FAFSA. *Unit head:* Dr. Corina Mihai, Director of Business Graduate Programs, 570-674-8022, E-mail: cmihai@misericordia.edu. *Application contact:* Larree Brown, Coordinator of Part-Time Undergraduate and Graduate Programs, 570-674-6451, Fax: 570-674-6232, E-mail: lbrown@misericordia.edu.

Mississippi College, Graduate School, School of Business, Clinton, MS 39058. Offers accounting (Certificate); business administration (MBA), including accounting; business education (M Ed); finance (MBA, Certificate); JD/MBA. *Accreditation:* ACBSP. Part-time and evening/weekend programs available. *Faculty:* 12 full-time (2 women), 5 part-time/adjunct (1 woman). *Students:* 101 full-time (41 women), 144 part-time (75 women); includes 41 minority (37 African Americans, 3 Asian Americans or Pacific Islanders, 1 Hispanic American), 78 international. Average age 28. In 2009, 90 master's awarded. *Degree requirements:* For master's, comprehensive exam, thesis optional. *Entrance requirements:* For master's, GMAT, minimum GPA of 2.5, 24 hours of undergraduate course work in business. Additional exam requirements/recommendations for international students: Recommended—IELTS. *Application deadline:* For fall admission, 8/15 priority date for domestic students. Applications are processed on a rolling basis. Application fee: $30. Electronic applications accepted. *Expenses:* Tuition: Part-time $452 per credit hour. Required fees: $101 per semester. Tuition and fees vary according to degree level, campus/location, program and student level. *Financial support:* Federal Work-Study and unspecified assistantships available. Support available to part-time students. Financial award application deadline: 4/1; financial award applicants required to submit FAFSA. *Unit head:* Dr. Marcelo Eduardo, Dean, 601-925-3420, E-mail: eduardo@mc.edu. *Application contact:* Elnora Lewis, Secretary, 601-925-3225, Fax: 601-925-3889, E-mail: lewis09@mc.edu.

Mississippi State University, College of Business, Department of Management and Information Systems, Mississippi State, MS 39762. Offers business administration (PhD), including business information systems, management; information systems (MSIS). Part-time programs available. *Faculty:* 16 full-time (4 women), 1 part-time/adjunct (0 women). *Students:* 20 full-time (6 women), 5 part-time (2 women); includes 4 minority (2 African Americans, 1 American Indian/Alaska Native, 1 Asian American or Pacific Islander), 7 international. Average age 31. 49 applicants, 33% accepted, 12 enrolled. In 2009, 9 master's, 5 doctorates awarded. *Degree requirements:* For master's, comprehensive exam; for doctorate, comprehensive exam, thesis/dissertation. *Entrance requirements:* For master's, GMAT, minimum GPA of 3.0 in last 60 hours of course work; for doctorate, GMAT, minimum graduate GPA of 3.25 in last 60 hours. Additional exam requirements/recommendations for international students: Required—TOEFL (minimum score 575 paper-based; 233 computer-based; 90 iBT); Recommended—IELTS (minimum score 7). *Application deadline:* For fall admission, 7/1 for domestic students, 5/1 for international students; for spring admission, 11/1 for domestic students, 9/1 for international students. Applications are processed on a rolling basis. Application fee: $40. Electronic applications accepted. *Expenses:* Tuition, state resident: full-time $2575.50; part-time $286.25 per credit hour. Tuition, nonresident: full-time $6510; part-time $723.50 per credit hour. Tuition and fees vary according to course load. *Financial support:* In 2009–10, 6 teaching assistantships (averaging $10,037 per year) were awarded; Federal Work-Study and institutionally sponsored loans also available. Financial award applicants required to submit FAFSA. *Faculty research:* Electronic commerce, management of information technology. *Unit head:* Dr. Rodney Pearson, Department Head and Professor of Information Systems, 662-325-3928, Fax: 662-325-8651, E-mail: rodney.pearson@msstate.edu. *Application contact:* Dr. Barbara Spencer, Associate Dean for Research and Outreach, 662-325-1891, Fax: 662-325-8161, E-mail: bspencer@cobian.msstate.edu.

Mississippi State University, College of Business, Department of Marketing, Quantitative Analysis and Business Law, Mississippi State, MS 39762. Offers business administration (MBA, PhD), including marketing. Part-time and evening/weekend programs available. *Faculty:* 11 full-time (3 women). *Students:* 12 full-time (7 women), 1 (woman) part-time; includes 1 minority (African American), 3 international. Average age 31. 29 applicants, 10% accepted, 2 enrolled. In 2009, 2 doctorates awarded. *Degree requirements:* For doctorate, comprehensive exam, thesis/dissertation. *Entrance requirements:* For doctorate, GMAT, minimum GPA of 2.75 in last 60 undergraduate hours. Additional exam requirements/recommendations for international students: Required—TOEFL (minimum score 575 paper-based; 233 computer-based; 90 iBT); Recommended—IELTS (minimum score 6.5). *Application deadline:* For fall admission, 7/1 for domestic students, 5/1 for international students; for spring admission, 11/1 for domestic students, 9/1 for international students. Applications are processed on a rolling basis. Application fee: $40. Electronic applications accepted. *Expenses:* Tuition, state resident: full-time $2575.50; part-time $286.25 per credit hour. Tuition, nonresident: full-time $6510; part-time $723.50 per credit hour. Tuition and fees vary according to course load. *Financial support:* In 2009–10, 3 teaching assistantships (averaging $10,037 per year) were awarded; Federal Work-Study,

institutionally sponsored loans, and scholarships/grants also available. Financial award application deadline: 4/1; financial award applicants required to submit FAFSA. *Unit head:* Dr. Brian Engelland, Professor and Department Head, 662-325-3163, Fax: 662-325-7012, E-mail: mqabl@cobilan.msstate.edu. *Application contact:* Dr. Barbara Spencer, Associate Dean for Research and Outreach, 662-325-1891, Fax: 662-325-8161, E-mail: gsbi@cobilan.msstate.edu.

Mississippi State University, College of Business, Graduate Studies in Business, MS State, MS 39762. Offers business administration (MBA); project management (MBA). *Accreditation:* AACSB. Part-time and evening/weekend programs available. Postbaccalaureate distance learning degree programs offered (no on-campus study). *Students:* 114 full-time (38 women), 207 part-time (54 women); includes 27 minority (12 African Americans, 9 Asian Americans or Pacific Islanders, 6 Hispanic Americans), 20 international. Average age 29. 215 applicants, 70% accepted, 113 enrolled. In 2009, 148 master's awarded. Terminal master's awarded for partial completion of doctoral program. *Degree requirements:* For master's, comprehensive exam (for some programs), thesis optional. *Entrance requirements:* For master's, GMAT, minimum GPA of 3.0 in last 60 hours of course work. Additional exam requirements/recommendations for international students: Required—TOEFL (minimum score 575 paper-based; 233 computer-based; 90 iBT); Recommended—IELTS (minimum score 6.5). *Application deadline:* For fall admission, 7/1 for domestic students, 5/1 for international students; for spring admission, 11/1 for domestic students, 9/1 for international students. Applications are processed on a rolling basis. Application fee: $40. Electronic applications accepted. *Expenses:* Tuition, state resident: full-time $2575.50; part-time $286.25 per credit hour. Tuition, nonresident: full-time $6510; part-time $723.50 per credit hour. Tuition and fees vary according to course load. *Financial support:* In 2009–10, 27 research assistantships with full tuition reimbursements (averaging $8,462 per year), 16 teaching assistantships with full tuition reimbursements (averaging $10,037 per year) were awarded; Federal Work-Study, institutionally sponsored loans, scholarships/grants, and unspecified assistantships also available. Financial award application deadline: 4/1; financial award applicants required to submit FAFSA. *Unit head:* Dr. Barbara Spencer, Director, 662-325-1891, Fax: 662-325-8161, E-mail: gsbi@cobilan.msstate.edu. *Application contact:* Dr. Barbara Spencer, Director, 662-325-1891, Fax: 662-325-8161, E-mail: gsbi@cobilan.msstate.edu.

Mississippi State University, College of Business, School of Accountancy, Mississippi State, MS 39762. Offers accounting (MPA), including accounting (MPA, PhD), systems; business administration (PhD), including accounting (MPA, PhD); taxation (MTX). *Accreditation:* AACSB. *Faculty:* 8 full-time (3 women). *Students:* 41 full-time (23 women), 10 part-time (8 women); includes 5 minority (all Asian Americans or Pacific Islanders), 3 international. Average age 26. 56 applicants, 45% accepted, 20 enrolled. In 2009, 41 master's awarded. *Degree requirements:* For master's, comprehensive exam. *Entrance requirements:* For master's, GMAT (minimum score of 510), minimum GPA of 2.75 overall and in upper-level accounting, 3.0 in last 60 hours of course work; for doctorate, GMAT, minimum undergraduate GPA of 3.0, both cumulative and over the last 60 hours of undergraduate work; 3.25 on all prior graduate work. Additional exam requirements/recommendations for international students: Required—TOEFL (minimum score 575 paper-based; 233 computer-based; 84 iBT); Recommended—IELTS (minimum score 7). *Application deadline:* For fall admission, 7/1 for domestic students, 5/1 for international students; for spring admission, 11/1 for domestic students, 9/1 for international students. Applications are processed on a rolling basis. Application fee: $40. Electronic applications accepted. *Expenses:* Tuition, state resident: full-time $2575.50; part-time $286.25 per credit hour. Tuition, nonresident: full-time $6510; part-time $723.50 per credit hour. Tuition and fees vary according to course load. *Financial support:* Career-related internships or fieldwork, Federal Work-Study, institutionally sponsored loans, scholarships/grants, and unspecified assistantships available. Support available to part-time students. Financial award applicants required to submit FAFSA. *Faculty research:* Income tax, financial accounting system, managerial accounting, auditing. *Unit head:* Dr. Louis Dawkins, Director, 662-325-1633, E-mail: ldawkins@cobilan.msstate.edu. *Application contact:* Dr. Barbara Spencer, Graduate Coordinator, 662-325-3710, Fax: 662-325-1646, E-mail: sac@cobilan.msstate.edu.

Missouri Baptist University, Graduate Programs, St. Louis, MO 63141-8660. Offers business administration (MBA); Christian ministries (MACM); counseling (MAC); education (MSE); education administration (MEA); educational leadership (MSE, Ed S); teaching (MAT).

Missouri Southern State University, Program in Business Administration, Joplin, MO 64801-1595. Offers MBA. *Accreditation:* ACBSP. Postbaccalaureate distance learning degree programs offered. *Degree requirements:* For master's, capstone seminar.

Missouri State University, Graduate College, College of Business Administration, Department of Computer Information Systems, Springfield, MO 65897. Offers computer information systems (MS); secondary education (MS Ed), including business. Part-time and evening/weekend programs available. Postbaccalaureate distance learning degree programs offered (no on-campus study). *Faculty:* 13 full-time (3 women), 1 part-time/adjunct (0 women). *Students:* 34 full-time (7 women), 4 part-time (all women); includes 1 minority (Asian American or Pacific Islander), 1 international. Average age 41. 15 applicants, 100% accepted, 13 enrolled. In 2009, 16 master's awarded. *Degree requirements:* For master's, thesis optional. *Entrance requirements:* For master's, GMAT, 3 years of work experience in computer information systems, minimum GPA of 2.75 (MS), 9-12 teaching certification (MS Ed). Additional exam requirements/recommendations for international students: Required—TOEFL (minimum score 550 paper-based; 213 computer-based; 79 iBT). *Application deadline:* For fall admission, 7/20 priority date for domestic students, 5/1 for international students; for spring admission, 12/20 priority date for domestic students, 9/1 for international students. Applications are processed on a rolling basis. Application fee: $35 ($50 for international students). Electronic applications accepted. *Expenses:* Contact institution. *Financial support:* Federal Work-Study, institutionally sponsored loans, scholarships/grants, and unspecified assistantships available. Support available to part-time students. Financial award application deadline: 3/31; financial award applicants required to submit FAFSA. *Faculty research:* Decision support systems, algorithms in Visual Basic, end-user satisfaction, information security. *Unit head:* Dr. Jerry Chin, Head, 417-836-4131, Fax: 417-836-6907, E-mail: jerrychin@missouristate.edu. *Application contact:* Dr. Jerry Chin, Head, 417-836-4131, Fax: 417-836-6907, E-mail: jerrychin@missouristate.edu.

Missouri State University, Graduate College, College of Business Administration, Program in Business Administration, Springfield, MO 65897. Offers MBA. *Accreditation:* AACSB. Part-time and evening/weekend programs available. *Students:* 343 full-time (151 women), 215 part-time (88 women); includes 23 minority (10 African Americans, 1 American Indian/Alaska Native, 9 Asian Americans or Pacific Islanders, 3 Hispanic Americans), 148 international. Average age 28. 270 applicants, 99% accepted, 188 enrolled. In 2009, 216 master's awarded. *Degree requirements:* For master's, thesis optional. *Entrance requirements:* For master's, GMAT, minimum GPA of 2.75. Additional exam requirements/recommendations for international students: Required—TOEFL (minimum score 550 paper-based; 213 computer-based; 79 iBT). *Application deadline:* For fall admission, 7/20 priority date for domestic students, 5/1 for international students; for spring admission, 12/20 priority date for domestic students, 9/1 for international students. Applications are processed on a rolling basis. Application fee: $35 ($50 for international students). Electronic applications accepted. *Expenses:* Tuition, state resident: full-time $3852; part-time $214 per credit hour. Tuition, nonresident: full-time $7524; part-time $418 per credit hour. Required fees: $696; $172 per semester. Tuition and fees vary according to course level, course load, degree level and program. *Financial support:* In 2009–10, 2 research assistantships with full tuition reimbursements (averaging $7,340 per year), 2 teaching assistantships with full tuition reimbursements (averaging $9,730 per year) were awarded; Federal Work-Study, institutionally sponsored loans, scholarships/grants, and unspecified assistantships also available. Support available to part-time students. Financial award application deadline: 3/31; financial award applicants required to submit FAFSA. *Unit head:* Dr. Elizabeth Rozell, MBA Program Director, 417-836-5616, Fax: 417-836-4407, E-mail: erozell@missouristate.edu. *Application contact:* Eric Eckert, Coordinator of Graduate Admissions and Recruitment, 417-836-5331, Fax: 417-836-6200, E-mail: ericeckert@missouristate.edu.

Molloy College, Graduate Business Program, Rockville Centre, NY 11571-5002. Offers accounting (MBA); accounting and management (MBA); management (MBA); personal financial planning and accounting (MBA); personal financial planning and management (MBA). Part-time programs available. *Faculty:* 5 full-time (0 women), 8 part-time/adjunct (2 women). *Students:* 26 full-time (12 women), 60 part-time (33 women); includes 30 minority (12 African Americans, 4 Asian Americans or Pacific Islanders, 14 Hispanic Americans), 2 international. Average age 33. In 2009, 21 master's awarded. *Application deadline:* Applications are processed on a rolling basis. *Expenses:* Tuition: Part-time $765 per credit. Required fees: $340 per semester. *Unit head:* Dr. Raymond Manganelli, Associate Dean and Director of Graduate Programs, 516-678-5000 Ext. 6905, E-mail: rmanganelli@molloy.edu. *Application contact:* Alina Haitz, Assistant Director of Graduate Admissions, 516-678-5000 Ext. 6399, Fax: 516-256-2247, E-mail: ahaitz@molloy.edu.

Monmouth University, Graduate School, Leon Hess Business School, West Long Branch, NJ 07764-1898. Offers accounting (Post-Master's Certificate); healthcare management (MBA, Post-Master's Certificate). *Accreditation:* AACSB. Part-time and evening/weekend programs available. *Faculty:* 31 full-time (10 women), 4 part-time/adjunct (0 women). *Students:* 81 full-time (24 women), 153 part-time (63 women); includes 19 minority (7 African Americans, 6 Asian Americans or Pacific Islanders, 6 Hispanic Americans), 18 international. Average age 29. 183 applicants, 76% accepted, 80 enrolled. In 2009, 70 master's awarded. *Degree requirements:* For master's, capstone course. *Entrance requirements:* For master's, GMAT, minimum GPA of 3.0 in major, 2.75 overall. Additional exam requirements/recommendations for international students: Required—TOEFL (minimum score 550 paper-based; 213 computer-based; 79 iBT), IELTS (minimum score 5), Michigan English Language Assessment Battery (minimum score 77), Cambridge A, B, C. *Application deadline:* For fall admission, 7/15 priority date for domestic students, 6/1 for international students; for spring admission, 11/15 priority date for domestic students, 11/1 for international students. Applications are processed on a rolling basis. Application fee: $50. Electronic applications accepted. *Expenses:* Tuition: Part-time $773 per credit. Required fees: $157 per semester. *Financial support:* In 2009–10, 154 students received support, including 128 fellowships (averaging $1,796 per year), 19 research assistantships (averaging $8,633 per year); career-related internships or fieldwork, scholarships/grants, and unspecified assistantships also available. Support available to part-time students. Financial award applicants required to submit FAFSA. *Faculty research:* Information technology and marketing, behavioral research in accounting, human resources, management of technology. *Unit head:* Donald Smith, Program Director, 732-571-7536, Fax: 732-263-5517, E-mail: dsmith@monmouth.edu. *Application contact:* Kevin Roane, Director, Office of Graduate Admission, 732-571-3452, Fax: 732-263-5123, E-mail: gradadm@monmouth.edu.

Monroe College, King School of Business, Bronx, NY 10468-5407. Offers business management (MBA). Program also offered in New Rochelle, NY. Postbaccalaureate distance learning degree programs offered.

Montclair State University, The Graduate School, School of Business, Montclair, NJ 07043-1624. Offers MBA, Certificate. *Accreditation:* AACSB. Part-time and evening/weekend programs available. *Faculty:* 79 full-time (25 women), 35 part-time/adjunct (7 women). *Students:* 106 full-time (53 women), 265 part-time (117 women). Average age 29. 199 applicants, 53% accepted, 69 enrolled. In 2009, 115 master's, 1 other advanced degree awarded. *Degree requirements:* For master's, comprehensive exam. *Entrance requirements:* For master's, GMAT, 2 letters of recommendation, resume. Additional exam requirements/recommendations for international students: Required—TOEFL (minimum score 83 computer-based), or IELTS. *Application deadline:* For fall admission, 6/1 for international students; for spring admission, 10/1 for international students. Applications are processed on a rolling basis. Application fee: $60. Electronic applications accepted. *Expenses:* Tuition, area resident: Part-time $486.74 per credit. Tuition, state resident: part-time $486.74 per credit. Tuition, nonresident: part-time $751.34 per credit. Tuition and fees vary according to degree level and program. *Financial support:* In 2009–10, 28 students received support, including 21 research assistantships with full tuition reimbursements available (averaging $7,000 per year); Federal Work-Study, scholarships/grants, and unspecified assistantships also available. Support available to part-time students. Financial award application deadline: 3/1; financial award applicants required to submit FAFSA. *Unit head:* Dr. E. LeBrent Chrite, Dean, 973-655-4304, E-mail: chritee@mail.montclair.edu. *Application contact:* Amy Aiello, Director of Graduate Admissions and Operations, 973-655-5147, Fax: 973-655-7869, E-mail: graduate.school@montclair.edu.

Monterey Institute of International Studies, Graduate School of International Policy and Management, Fisher International MBA Program, Monterey, CA 93940-2691. Offers MBA. *Accreditation:* AACSB. *Students:* 67 full-time (27 women), 4 part-time (1 woman); includes 13 minority (1 African American, 7 Asian Americans or Pacific Islanders, 5 Hispanic Americans), 15 international. Average age 28. In 2009, 66 master's awarded. *Degree requirements:* For master's, one foreign language, thesis. *Entrance requirements:* For master's, GMAT, minimum GPA of 3.0, proficiency in a foreign language. Additional exam requirements/recommendations for international students: Required—TOEFL (minimum score 550 paper-based; 213 computer-based; 80 iBT). *Application deadline:* For fall admission, 3/15 priority date for domestic students, 3/5 priority date for international students; for spring admission, 10/1 priority date for domestic and international students. Applications are processed on a rolling basis. Application fee: $50. Electronic applications accepted. *Expenses:* Tuition: Full-time $31,000; part-time $1500 per credit. Required fees: $56. *Financial support:* Career-related internships or fieldwork, Federal Work-Study, institutionally sponsored loans, scholarships/grants, tuition waivers (partial), and unspecified assistantships available. Support available to part-time students. Financial award application deadline: 3/15; financial award applicants required to submit FAFSA. *Faculty research:* Cross-cultural consumer behavior, foreign direct investment, marketing and entrepreneurial orientation, political risk analysis and area studies, managing international human resources. *Application contact:* 831-647-4123, Fax: 831-647-6405, E-mail: admit@miis.edu.

See Close-Up on page 465.

Montreat College, School of Professional and Adult Studies, Montreat, NC 28757-1267. Offers business administration (MBA); K-6 education (MA Ed). Evening/weekend programs available. Postbaccalaureate distance learning degree programs offered. *Entrance requirements:* Additional exam requirements/recommendations for international students: Required—TOEFL (minimum score 500 paper-based; 190 computer-based).

Moravian College, Moravian College Comenius Center, Business and Management Programs, Bethlehem, PA 18018-6650. Offers general management (MBA); health care management (MBA); leadership (MSHRM); learning and performance management (MSHRM); supply chain management (MBA). Part-time and evening/weekend programs available. *Faculty:* 6 full-time (2 women), 10 part-time/adjunct (3 women). *Students:* 59 part-time (30 women). Average age 29. 27 applicants, 74% accepted, 10 enrolled. In 2009, 20 master's awarded. *Entrance requirements:* For master's, GMAT. Additional exam requirements/recommendations for international students: Required—TOEFL (minimum score 550 paper-based; 260 computer-based; 90 iBT). *Application deadline:* Applications are processed on a rolling basis. Application fee: $40. *Expenses:* Contact institution. *Financial support:* In 2009–10, 1 fellowship with full tuition reimbursement was awarded. *Faculty research:* Leadership, change management, human resources. *Unit head:* Dr. William A. Kleintop, Associate Dean for Business and Management Programs, 610-507-1400, Fax: 610-861-1400, E-mail: comenius@moravian.edu. *Application contact:* Linda J. Doyle, Information Contact, 610-861-1400, Fax: 610-861-1466, E-mail: mba@moravian.edu.

Morehead State University, Graduate Programs, College of Business and Public Affairs, Morehead, KY 40351. Offers MA, MBA, MPA, MSIS. *Accreditation:* AACSB. Part-time and evening/weekend programs available. Postbaccalaureate distance learning degree programs offered (minimal on-campus study). *Faculty:* 26 full-time (9 women), 4 part-time/adjunct (1 woman). *Students:* 62 full-time (28 women), 204 part-time (103 women); includes 17 minority (10 African Americans, 5 Asian Americans or Pacific Islanders, 2 Hispanic Americans), 4 international. Average age 31. 135 applicants, 70% accepted, 64 enrolled. In 2009, 66 master's awarded. *Entrance requirements:* For master's, GMAT, GRE General Test, minimum GPA of 2.5 on undergraduate work. Additional exam requirements/recommendations for international

Business Administration and Management—General

Morehead State University (continued)
students: Required—TOEFL (minimum score 525 paper-based; 173 computer-based). *Application deadline:* For fall admission, 8/1 priority date for domestic and international students; for spring admission, 12/1 priority date for domestic and international students. Applications are processed on a rolling basis. Application fee: $30. Electronic applications accepted. *Expenses:* Tuition, state resident: full-time $6318; part-time $351 per credit hour. Tuition, nonresident: full-time $15,804; part-time $878 per credit hour. *Financial support:* In 2009–10, 11 research assistantships (averaging $10,000 per year), 10 teaching assistantships (averaging $10,000 per year) were awarded; career-related internships or fieldwork, Federal Work-Study, and unspecified assistantships also available. Financial award application deadline: 3/15; financial award applicants required to submit FAFSA. *Faculty research:* Regional economic development, accounting systems, banking market structures, macroeconomics, distance learning. *Unit head:* Dr. Robert L. Albert, Dean, 606-783-5158, Fax: 606-783-5025, E-mail: r.albert@moreheadstate.edu. *Application contact:* Michelle Barber, Graduate Recruitment and Retention Assistant Director, 606-783-5127, Fax: 606-783-5061, E-mail: m.barber@moreheadstate.edu.

Morgan State University, School of Graduate Studies, Earl G. Graves School of Business and Management, PhD Program in Business Administration, Baltimore, MD 21251. Offers PhD. *Degree requirements:* For doctorate, thesis/dissertation. *Entrance requirements:* For doctorate, GMAT. Additional exam requirements/recommendations for international students: Required—TOEFL (minimum score 550 paper-based; 213 computer-based).

Morrison University, Graduate School, Reno, NV 89521. Offers business administration (MBA). Part-time and evening/weekend programs available. *Degree requirements:* For master's, thesis. *Entrance requirements:* For master's, GMAT, minimum 3 years minimum work experience, interview, minimum GPA of 3.0. Electronic applications accepted.

Mount Aloysius College, Masters in Business Administration Program, Cresson, PA 16630. Offers MBA. Part-time and evening/weekend programs available. *Application deadline:* For fall admission, 8/1 for domestic students; for spring admission, 12/1 for domestic students. Applications are processed on a rolling basis. Electronic applications accepted. *Financial support:* Applicants required to submit FAFSA. *Application contact:* Andrew D. Clouse, Associate Director of Admissions and Coordinator of Graduate Admissions, 814-886-6480.

Mount Ida College, Program in Management, Newton, MA 02459-3310. Offers MSM. Part-time and evening/weekend programs available. Postbaccalaureate distance learning degree programs offered (minimal on-campus study). *Faculty:* 4 full-time (2 women), 2 part-time/adjunct (0 women). *Students:* 7 part-time (5 women); includes 1 African American. Average age 26. 10 applicants, 100% accepted, 7 enrolled. *Entrance requirements:* Additional exam requirements/recommendations for international students: Required—TOEFL (minimum score 550 paper-based; 220 computer-based; 79 iBT); Recommended—IELTS (minimum score 5.5). *Application deadline:* For fall admission, 8/15 for domestic and international students; for spring admission, 1/3 for domestic and international students. Applications are processed on a rolling basis. Application fee: $50. Electronic applications accepted. *Expenses:* Tuition: Part-time $650 per credit. *Financial support:* Teaching assistantships, Federal Work-Study available. Financial award applicants required to submit FAFSA. *Unit head:* Ronald Akie, Director, School of Business, 617-928-7336, E-mail: reakie@mountida.edu. *Application contact:* Jay Titus, Dean of Admissions, 617-928-4553, Fax: 617-928-4507, E-mail: jtitus@mountida.edu.

Mount Marty College, Graduate Studies Division, Yankton, SD 57078-3724. Offers business administration (MBA); nurse anesthesia (MS); pastoral ministries (MPM). *Accreditation:* AANA/CANAEP (one or more programs are accredited). *Degree requirements:* For master's, thesis or alternative. *Entrance requirements:* For master's, GRE General Test, minimum GPA of 3.0. Electronic applications accepted. *Faculty research:* Clinical anesthesia, professional characteristics, motivations of applicants.

Mount Mary College, Graduate Programs, Program in Business Administration, Milwaukee, WI 53222-4597. Offers MBA. *Faculty:* 1 full-time (0 women), 5 part-time/adjunct (2 women). *Students:* 40 full-time (39 women), 3 part-time (2 women); includes 13 minority (7 African Americans, 2 Asian Americans or Pacific Islanders, 4 Hispanic Americans). Average age 37. 23 applicants, 74% accepted, 13 enrolled. *Degree requirements:* For master's, terminal project. *Entrance requirements:* For master's, minimum GPA of 2.75. Additional exam requirements/recommendations for international students: Required—TOEFL (minimum score 500 paper-based; 173 computer-based). *Application deadline:* For fall admission, 8/1 priority date for domestic and international students; for spring admission, 12/1 priority date for domestic and international students. Application fee: $35 ($100 for international students). Electronic applications accepted. *Expenses:* Tuition: Part-time $595 per credit. Tuition and fees vary according to program. *Financial support:* In 2009–10, 2 students received support. Career-related internships or fieldwork and Federal Work-Study available. Support available to part-time students. Financial award application deadline: 5/1; financial award applicants required to submit FAFSA. *Unit head:* Robert Crombie, Director, 414-258-4810 Ext. 478, E-mail: crombier@mtmary.edu. *Application contact:* Robert Crombie, Director, 414-258-4810 Ext. 478, E-mail: crombier@mtmary.edu.

Mount Mercy College, Program in Business Administration, Cedar Rapids, IA 52402-4797. Offers MBA. Evening/weekend programs available. *Entrance requirements:* For master's, minimum cumulative GPA of 3.0, 2 letters of recommendation, resume. Additional exam requirements/recommendations for international students: Required—TOEFL (minimum score 570 paper-based; 88 iBT). Electronic applications accepted.

Mount Saint Mary College, Division of Business, Newburgh, NY 12550-3494. Offers business (MBA); financial planning (MBA). Part-time and evening/weekend programs available. *Faculty:* 5 full-time (1 woman), 5 part-time/adjunct (1 woman). *Students:* 28 full-time (16 women), 66 part-time (32 women); includes 15 minority (2 African Americans, 4 Asian Americans or Pacific Islanders, 9 Hispanic Americans), 31 international. Average age 30. 36 applicants, 100% accepted, 23 enrolled. In 2009, 70 master's awarded. *Degree requirements:* For master's, thesis or alternative. *Entrance requirements:* For master's, GMAT or minimum undergraduate GPA of 2.7. *Application deadline:* Applications are processed on a rolling basis. Application fee: $45. *Expenses:* Tuition: Full-time $13,356; part-time $742 per credit. Required fees: $50 per semester. *Financial support:* In 2009–10, 19 students received support. Unspecified assistantships available. Financial award application deadline: 4/15; financial award applicants required to submit FAFSA. *Faculty research:* Financial reform, entrepreneurship and small business development, global business relations, technology's impact on business decision-making, college-assisted business education. *Unit head:* Dr. Moira Tolan, Coordinator, 845-569-3288, Fax: 845-562-6762, E-mail: tolan@msmc.edu. *Application contact:* Janice Banker, Secretary, 845-569-3582, Fax: 845-569-3885, E-mail: banker@msmc.edu.

Mount St. Mary's College, Graduate Division, Program in Business Administration, Los Angeles, CA 90049-1599. Offers MBA. *Faculty:* 5 full-time (2 women), 12 part-time/adjunct (6 women). *Students:* 38 full-time (25 women); includes 20 minority (7 African Americans, 4 Asian Americans or Pacific Islanders, 9 Hispanic Americans). Average age 35. In 2009, 21 master's awarded. *Entrance requirements:* Additional exam requirements/recommendations for international students: Required—TOEFL. *Application deadline:* For fall admission, 4/15 for domestic students; for spring admission, 7/15 for domestic students. Electronic applications accepted. *Expenses:* Tuition: Part-time $730 per unit. Part-time tuition and fees vary according to degree level and program. *Financial support:* Application deadline: 3/15. *Unit head:* Janet Robinson, Director, 310-954-4151, E-mail: jrobinson@msmc.la.edu. *Application contact:* Director of Graduate Admission.

Mount St. Mary's University, Program in Business Administration, Emmitsburg, MD 21727-7799. Offers MBA. Part-time and evening/weekend programs available. *Faculty:* 11 full-time (3 women), 7 part-time/adjunct (2 women). *Students:* 44 full-time (15 women), 164 part-time (72 women); includes 28 minority (16 African Americans, 8 Asian Americans or Pacific Islanders, 4 Hispanic Americans), 9 international. Average age 31. 68 applicants, 84% accepted, 39 enrolled. In 2009, 75 master's awarded. *Degree requirements:* For master's, thesis. *Entrance requirements:* For master's, minimum undergraduate GPA of 2.75, 5 years' relevant professional business experience, or GMAT (minimum score of 500). Additional exam requirements/recommendations for international students: Required—TOEFL (minimum score 550 paper-based; 213 computer-based). *Application deadline:* Applications are processed on a rolling basis. Application fee: $35. *Expenses:* Tuition: Full-time $8280; part-time $460 per credit hour. Tuition and fees vary according to program. *Financial support:* In 2009–10, 78 students received support. Career-related internships or fieldwork and unspecified assistantships available. Financial award applicants required to submit FAFSA. *Faculty research:* Corporate social responsibility, socially responsible investing, leadership, Russian economics and law, knowledge management. *Unit head:* Dr. Carolyn Jacobson, Director, MBA Program, 301-447-5326, Fax: 301-447-5335, E-mail: jacobson@msmary.edu. *Application contact:* Dr. Carolyn Jacobson, Director, MBA Program, 301-447-5326, Fax: 301-447-5335, E-mail: jacobson@msmary.edu.

Mount Vernon Nazarene University, Program in Management, Mount Vernon, OH 43050-9500. Offers MSM. *Accreditation:* ACBSP. Part-time and evening/weekend programs available.

Murray State University, College of Business and Public Affairs, MBA Program, Murray, KY 42071. Offers MBA. *Accreditation:* AACSB. Part-time and evening/weekend programs available. *Entrance requirements:* For master's, GMAT. Additional exam requirements/recommendations for international students: Required—TOEFL.

National American University, Graduate Programs, Rapid City, SD 57701. Offers MBA, MM. Programs also offered in Wichita, KS; Albuquerque, NM; Bloomington, MN; Brooklyn Center, MN; Colorado Springs, CO; Denver, CO; Independence, MO; Overland Park, KS; Rio Rancho, NM; Roseville, MN; Zona Rosa, MO. Part-time and evening/weekend programs available. Postbaccalaureate distance learning degree programs offered. *Entrance requirements:* For master's, minimum undergraduate GPA of 2.75. Additional exam requirements/recommendations for international students: Required—TOEFL, TWE. Electronic applications accepted. *Faculty research:* Tourism, finance, marketing.

The National Graduate School of Quality Management, Program in Quality Systems Management, Falmouth, MA 02541. Offers e-commerce (MS); management (MS); six sigma (MS).

National-Louis University, College of Management and Business, Program in Business Administration, Chicago, IL 60603. Offers MBA. *Entrance requirements:* For master's, college-administered critical thinking and writing skills test, minimum GPA of 3.0, resume. *Expenses:* Tuition: Full-time $17,160; part-time $715 per semester hour. Tuition and fees vary according to course load, degree level, campus/location and program.

National-Louis University, College of Management and Business, Program in Management, Chicago, IL 60603. Offers MS. Evening/weekend programs available. *Entrance requirements:* For master's, college-administered critical thinking and writing skills test, minimum GPA of 3.0, resume. *Expenses:* Tuition: Full-time $17,160; part-time $715 per semester hour. Tuition and fees vary according to course load, degree level, campus/location and program.

National University, Academic Affairs, School of Business and Management, La Jolla, CA 92037-1011. Offers MA, MBA, MS. Part-time and evening/weekend programs available. Postbaccalaureate distance learning degree programs offered (no on-campus study). *Faculty:* 38 full-time (17 women), 146 part-time/adjunct (70 women). *Students:* 627 full-time (318 women), 998 part-time (475 women); includes 587 minority (192 African Americans, 5 American Indian/Alaska Native, 178 Asian Americans or Pacific Islanders, 212 Hispanic Americans), 307 international. Average age 35. 993 applicants, 100% accepted, 631 enrolled. In 2009, 385 master's awarded. *Degree requirements:* For master's, thesis. *Entrance requirements:* For master's, interview, minimum GPA of 2.5. Additional exam requirements/recommendations for international students: Required—TOEFL (minimum score 550 paper-based; 213 computer-based; 79 iBT), IELTS (minimum score 6). *Application deadline:* Applications are processed on a rolling basis. Application fee: $60 ($65 for international students). Electronic applications accepted. *Expenses:* Tuition: Part-time $338 per quarter hour. *Financial support:* Career-related internships or fieldwork, scholarships/grants, and tuition waivers (partial) available. Support available to part-time students. Financial award application deadline: 6/30; financial award applicants required to submit FAFSA. *Unit head:* Dr. Thomas M. Green, Interim Dean, 858-642-8401, Fax: 858-642-8406, E-mail: acooper@nu.edu. *Application contact:* Dominick Giovanniello, Associate Regional Dean—San Diego, 800-NAT-UNIV, Fax: 858-541-7792, E-mail: dgiovann@nu.edu.

Naval Postgraduate School, Graduate Programs, School of Business and Public Policy, Monterey, CA 93943. Offers contract management (MS); defense-focused business administration (MBA); executive business administration (MBA); leadership and human resource development (MS); management (MS); program management (MS); systems engineering management (MS). Program only open to commissioned officers of the United States and friendly nations and selected United States federal civilian employees. *Accreditation:* AACSB; NASPAA. Part-time programs available. Postbaccalaureate distance learning degree programs offered (minimal on-campus study). *Degree requirements:* For master's, thesis.

Nazareth College of Rochester, Graduate Studies, Department of Business, Program in Management, Rochester, NY 14618-3790. Offers MS. Part-time and evening/weekend programs available. *Entrance requirements:* For master's, minimum GPA of 3.0.

New England College, Program in Management, Henniker, NH 03242-3293. Offers accounting (MSA); healthcare administration (MS); international relations (MA); marketing management (MS); nonprofit leadership (MS); project management (MS); strategic leadership (MS). Part-time and evening/weekend programs available. *Degree requirements:* For master's, independent research project. Electronic applications accepted.

New Jersey City University, Graduate Studies and Continuing Education, College of Professional Studies, Department of Business Administration, Jersey City, NJ 07305-1597. Offers accounting (MS); finance (MBA, MS); marketing (MBA); organizational management and leadership (MBA). *Accreditation:* ACBSP. Part-time and evening/weekend programs available. *Faculty:* 8. *Students:* 3 full-time (1 woman), 4 part-time (1 woman); includes 3 minority (1 African American, 2 Hispanic Americans). Average age 34. *Application deadline:* For fall admission, 8/1 priority date for domestic students; for spring admission, 12/1 for domestic students. Applications are processed on a rolling basis. Application fee: $0. *Expenses:* Tuition, area resident: Part-time $456.75 per credit. Tuition, nonresident: part-time $842.55 per credit. Required fees: $65 per term. *Financial support:* Career-related internships or fieldwork and unspecified assistantships available. *Unit head:* Dr. Marilyn Ettinger, Head, 201-200-3353, E-mail: mettinger@njcu.edu. *Application contact:* Dr. Marilyn Ettinger, Head, 201-200-3353, E-mail: mettinger@njcu.edu.

New Jersey Institute of Technology, Office of Graduate Studies, School of Management, Program in Management of Business Administration, Newark, NJ 07102. Offers MBA. *Accreditation:* AACSB. Part-time and evening/weekend programs available. *Entrance requirements:* For master's, GMAT. Additional exam requirements/recommendations for international students: Required—TOEFL (minimum score 550 paper-based; 213 computer-based; 79 iBT). Electronic applications accepted.

Newman University, School of Business, Wichita, KS 67213-2097. Offers finance (MBA); international business (MBA); leadership (MBA); management (MBA); technology (MBA). Part-time programs available. *Faculty:* 5 full-time (1 woman), 8 part-time/adjunct (2 women). *Students:* 29 full-time (13 women), 105 part-time (52 women); includes 30 minority (9 African Americans, 1 American Indian/Alaska Native, 10 Asian Americans or Pacific Islanders, 10 Hispanic Americans), 23 international. Average age 32. 80 applicants, 76% accepted, 47 enrolled. In 2009, 76 master's awarded. *Degree requirements:* For master's, thesis optional. *Entrance requirements:* For master's, interview; minimum GPA of 3.0; 3 letters of recommendation; course work in algebra, statistics, macroeconomics, and financial accounting. Additional exam requirements/recommendations for international students: Required—TOEFL (minimum score 600 paper-based; 250 computer-based; 100 iBT). *Application deadline:* For

fall admission, 8/1 priority date for domestic students, 7/15 priority date for international students; for winter admission, 1/1 priority date for domestic students; for spring admission, 1/1 priority date for domestic students, 11/15 priority date for international students. Applications are processed on a rolling basis. Application fee: $25 ($40 for international students). Electronic applications accepted. *Expenses:* Contact institution. *Financial support:* In 2009–10, 3 students received support. Federal Work-Study available. Financial award application deadline: 8/15; financial award applicants required to submit FAFSA. *Unit head:* Dr. Joe Goetz, Dean of the College of Professional Studies/Director, 316-942-4291 Ext. 2111, Fax: 316-942-4486, E-mail: goetzj@newmanu.edu. *Application contact:* Linda Kay Sabala, Director of Graduate Admissions, 316-942-4291 Ext. 2230, Fax: 316-942-4483, E-mail: sabalal@newmanu.edu.

New Mexico Highlands University, Graduate Studies, School of Business, Las Vegas, NM 87701. Offers business administration (MBA), including government nonprofit management, human resource management, international business, management, management information systems. *Accreditation:* ACBSP. *Degree requirements:* For master's, comprehensive exam, thesis or alternative. *Entrance requirements:* For master's, minimum undergraduate GPA of 3.0. Additional exam requirements/recommendations for international students: Required—TOEFL (minimum score 540 paper-based; 207 computer-based). *Faculty research:* Real estate valuation, studying expert judgments in complex accounting, decision environments, green marketing, environmentalism, marketing research methodology.

New Mexico State University, Graduate School, College of Business, Department of Management, Las Cruces, NM 88003-8001. Offers business administration (PhD), including management. *Faculty:* 16 full-time (3 women). *Students:* 14 full-time (5 women), 3 part-time (0 women); includes 2 minority (1 American Indian/Alaska Native, 1 Hispanic American), 6 international. Average age 35. 31 applicants, 58% accepted, 6 enrolled. In 2009, 3 doctorates awarded. *Degree requirements:* For doctorate, comprehensive exam, thesis/dissertation. *Entrance requirements:* For doctorate, GMAT or GRE, references, writing sample. Additional exam requirements/recommendations for international students: Required—TOEFL (minimum score 530 paper-based; 197 computer-based). *Application deadline:* For fall admission, 2/15 priority date for domestic and international students. Application fee: $30 ($50 for international students). Electronic applications accepted. *Expenses:* Tuition, state resident: full-time $4080; part-time $223 per credit. Tuition, nonresident: full-time $14,256; part-time $647 per credit. Required fees: $1278; $639 per semester. *Financial support:* In 2009–10, 10 students received support, including 11 teaching assistantships (averaging $19,680 per year); health care benefits and unspecified assistantships also available. *Faculty research:* Cross-cultured leadership, deviant behavior in the work place, quality management, transaction cost analysis, issues in post-modernism. *Unit head:* Dr. Bonnie F. Daily, Head, 575-646-1201, Fax: 575-646-1372, E-mail: bdaily@nmsu.edu. *Application contact:* Dr. Steven Elias, Associate Professor, 575-646-7642, Fax: 575-646-1372, E-mail: phddirector@business.nmsu.edu.

New Mexico State University, Graduate School, College of Business, Program in Business Administration, Las Cruces, NM 88003-8001. Offers MBA, PhD. *Accreditation:* AACSB. Part-time and evening/weekend programs available. *Students:* 135 full-time (57 women), 212 part-time (94 women); includes 156 minority (12 African Americans, 3 American Indian/Alaska Native, 6 Asian Americans or Pacific Islanders, 135 Hispanic Americans), 42 international. Average age 31. 201 applicants, 96% accepted, 132 enrolled. In 2009, 91 master's awarded. *Degree requirements:* For master's, comprehensive exam, thesis optional; for doctorate, comprehensive exam, thesis/dissertation. *Entrance requirements:* For master's, GMAT; for doctorate, GMAT or GRE, MBA, writing samples, letters of reference. Additional exam requirements/recommendations for international students: Required—TOEFL (minimum score 530 paper-based; 197 computer-based). *Application deadline:* For fall admission, 7/1 priority date for domestic students, 3/1 priority date for international students; for spring admission, 11/1 priority date for domestic students, 10/1 priority date for international students. Applications are processed on a rolling basis. Application fee: $30 ($50 for international students). Electronic applications accepted. *Expenses:* Tuition, state resident: full-time $4080; part-time $223 per credit. Tuition, nonresident: full-time $14,256; part-time $647 per credit. Required fees: $1278; $639 per semester. *Financial support:* In 2009–10, 22 research assistantships with partial tuition reimbursements (averaging $13,655 per year), 27 teaching assistantships with partial tuition reimbursements (averaging $8,141 per year) were awarded; fellowships with partial tuition reimbursements, Federal Work-Study, institutionally sponsored loans, scholarships/grants, health care benefits, and unspecified assistantships also available. Financial award application deadline: 3/1. *Faculty research:* Small business/entrepreneurship, international business/global marketing, e-business, total quality management, supply chain management. *Unit head:* Dr. Bobbie Green, Director, 575-646-8003, Fax: 575-646-7977, E-mail: mba@nmsu.edu. *Application contact:* Dr. Bobbie Green, Director, 575-646-8003, Fax: 575-646-7977, E-mail: mba@nmsu.edu.

New York Institute of Technology, Graduate Division, School of Management, Program in Business Administration, Old Westbury, NY 11568-8000. Offers accounting (Advanced Certificate); business administration (MBA); finance (Advanced Certificate); international business (Advanced Certificate); management of information systems (Advanced Certificate); marketing (Advanced Certificate). Part-time and evening/weekend programs available. *Students:* 599 full-time (262 women), 528 part-time (200 women); includes 51 minority (17 African Americans, 24 Asian Americans or Pacific Islanders, 10 Hispanic Americans), 324 international. Average age 29. In 2009, 691 master's, 7 other advanced degrees awarded. *Degree requirements:* For master's, thesis (for some programs). *Entrance requirements:* For master's, minimum QPA of 2.85. Additional exam requirements/recommendations for international students: Required—TOEFL (minimum score 550 paper-based; 213 computer-based). *Application deadline:* For fall admission, 7/1 priority date for domestic students; for spring admission, 12/1 priority date for domestic students. Applications are processed on a rolling basis. Application fee: $50. Electronic applications accepted. *Expenses:* Tuition: Part-time $825 per credit. *Financial support:* Fellowships, research assistantships with partial tuition reimbursements, institutionally sponsored loans, tuition waivers (full and partial), and unspecified assistantships available. Support available to part-time students. Financial award applicants required to submit FAFSA. *Faculty research:* Instructor performance appraisal; relationship between TOEFL, GMAT, GRE, and performance in foreign students. *Unit head:* Dr. Diamando Afxentiou, Acting Associate Dean, 516-686-3937, Fax: 516-686-7430, E-mail: dafxenti@nyit.edu. *Application contact:* Dr. Jacquelyn Nealon, Vice President for Enrollment Services, 516-686-7925, Fax: 516-686-7597, E-mail: jnealon@nyit.edu.

New York University, Leonard N. Stern School of Business, Department of Marketing, New York, NY 10012-1019. Offers entertainment, media and technology (MBA); general marketing (MBA); marketing (PhD); product management (MBA). *Expenses:* Tuition: Full-time $30,528; part-time $1272 per credit. Required fees: $2177.

New York University, Robert F. Wagner Graduate School of Public Service, Program in Management, New York, NY 10012-1019. Offers EMPA, EMPA/MS, MSW/EMPA. *Accreditation:* AACSB. Part-time and evening/weekend programs available. *Faculty:* 10 full-time (3 women), 2 part-time/adjunct (both women). *Students:* 13 full-time (9 women), 72 part-time (43 women); includes 24 minority (10 African Americans, 10 Asian Americans or Pacific Islanders, 4 Hispanic Americans), 11 international. Average age 39. 65 applicants, 71% accepted, 37 enrolled. In 2009, 43 master's awarded. *Entrance requirements:* For master's, minimum undergraduate GPA of 3.0. Additional exam requirements/recommendations for international students: Required—TOEFL (minimum score 600 paper-based; 250 computer-based; 100 iBT), TWE (minimum score 4). *Application deadline:* For fall admission, 6/1 for domestic students; for spring admission, 11/15 for domestic students. Applications are processed on a rolling basis. Application fee: $80. Electronic applications accepted. *Expenses:* Contact institution. *Financial support:* In 2009–10, 8 students received support, including 8 fellowships (averaging $7,382 per year); research assistantships with full and partial tuition reimbursements available, institutionally sponsored loans, scholarships/grants, health care benefits, and unspecified assistantships also available. Support available to part-time students. Financial award application deadline: 1/15; financial award applicants required to submit FAFSA. *Unit head:* David Elcott, Director, 212-992-9894, Fax: 212-995-4164, E-mail: david.elcott@nyu.edu. *Application contact:* Christopher Alexander, Administrative Aide, Enrollment, 212-998-7414, Fax: 212-995-4611, E-mail: wagner.admissions@nyu.edu.

New York University, School of Law, New York, NY 10012-1019. Offers law (JD, LL M, JSD); law and business (Advanced Certificate); taxation (Advanced Certificate); JD/LL B; JD/LL M; JD/MA; JD/MBA; JD/MPA; JD/MPP; JD/MSW; JD/MUP; JD/PhD. *Accreditation:* ABA. Part-time programs available. *Faculty:* 125 full-time (36 women), 70 part-time/adjunct (23 women). *Students:* 1,427 full-time (628 women); includes 332 minority (88 African Americans, 3 American Indian/Alaska Native, 150 Asian Americans or Pacific Islanders, 91 Hispanic Americans), 44 international. 7,272 applicants, 450 enrolled. In 2009, 471 first professional degrees, 534 master's, 3 doctorates awarded. *Entrance requirements:* LSAT. *Application deadline:* For fall admission, 2/1 for domestic students. Application fee: $75. Electronic applications accepted. *Expenses:* Contact institution. *Financial support:* Fellowships, research assistantships, teaching assistantships, career-related internships or fieldwork, Federal Work-Study, institutionally sponsored loans, scholarships/grants, tuition waivers (partial), and loan repayment assistance available. Financial award application deadline: 4/15; financial award applicants required to submit FAFSA. *Faculty research:* International law, environmental law, corporate law, globalization of law, philosophy of law. *Unit head:* Richard L. Revesz, Dean, 212-998-6000, Fax: 212-995-3150. *Application contact:* Kenneth J. Kleinrock, Assistant Dean for Admissions, 212-998-6060, Fax: 212-995-4527.

Niagara University, Graduate Division of Business Administration, Niagara Falls, Niagara University, NY 14109. Offers business (MBA); commerce (MBA). *Accreditation:* AACSB. Part-time and evening/weekend programs available. *Entrance requirements:* For master's, GMAT. Additional exam requirements/recommendations for international students: Required—TOEFL. *Faculty research:* Capital flows, Federal Reserve policy, human resource management, public policy, issues in marketing.

Nicholls State University, Graduate Studies, College of Business Administration, Thibodaux, LA 70310. Offers MBA. *Accreditation:* AACSB. Part-time and evening/weekend programs available. *Degree requirements:* For master's, thesis optional. *Entrance requirements:* For master's, GMAT. Additional exam requirements/recommendations for international students: Required—TOEFL (minimum score 550 paper-based; 213 computer-based). Electronic applications accepted.

Nichols College, Graduate Program in Business Administration, Dudley, MA 01571-5000. Offers business administration (MBA, MOL); security management (MBA); sport management (MBA). Part-time and evening/weekend programs available. Postbaccalaureate distance learning degree programs offered (no on-campus study). *Entrance requirements:* For master's, 2 letters of recommendation. Additional exam requirements/recommendations for international students: Required—TOEFL (minimum score 500 paper-based; 213 computer-based). Electronic applications accepted.

North Carolina Agricultural and Technical State University, Graduate School, School of Education, Department of Human Development and Services, Greensboro, NC 27411. Offers adult education (MS); counselor education (MS); human resources-agency counseling (MS); human resources-rehabilitation counseling (MS); leadership studies (PhD); school administration (MS). *Accreditation:* ACA. Part-time and evening/weekend programs available. *Degree requirements:* For master's, comprehensive exam, thesis, qualifying exam. *Entrance requirements:* For master's, GRE General Test, minimum GPA of 3.0.

North Carolina Central University, Division of Academic Affairs, School of Business, Durham, NC 27707-3129. Offers MBA, JD/MBA. *Accreditation:* AACSB; ACBSP. Part-time and evening/weekend programs available. *Degree requirements:* For master's, thesis. *Entrance requirements:* For master's, GMAT. Additional exam requirements/recommendations for international students: Required—TOEFL. *Faculty research:* Small business issues, research of pedagogy, African business environment.

North Carolina State University, Graduate School, College of Management, Program in Business Administration, Raleigh, NC 27695. Offers biosciences management (MBA); entrepreneurship and technology commercialization (MBA); financial management (MBA); innovation management (MBA); marketing management (MBA); services management and consulting (MBA); supply chain management (MBA). *Accreditation:* AACSB. Part-time programs available. *Degree requirements:* For master's, thesis optional. *Entrance requirements:* For master's, GMAT, interview, 3 letters of recommendation. Additional exam requirements/recommendations for international students: Required—TOEFL (minimum score 600 paper-based; 250 computer-based; 100 iBT). Electronic applications accepted. *Faculty research:* Manufacturing strategy, information systems, technology commercialization, managing research and development, historical stock returns.

North Central College, Graduate Programs, Department of Business, Program in Business Administration, Naperville, IL 60566-7063. Offers MBA. *Degree requirements:* For master's, project. *Entrance requirements:* For master's, interview.

North Central College, Graduate Programs, Department of Leadership Studies, Naperville, IL 60566-7063. Offers MLD. Part-time and evening/weekend programs available. *Degree requirements:* For master's, project. *Entrance requirements:* For master's, interview. *Expenses:* Contact institution.

Northcentral University, Graduate Studies, Prescott Valley, AZ 86314. Offers business (MBA, DBA, PhD, CAGS); education (M Ed, Ed D, PhD, CAGS); marriage and family therapy (MA, PhD); psychology (MA, PhD, CAGS). Evening/weekend programs available. Postbaccalaureate distance learning degree programs offered (no on-campus study). *Students:* 8,148 full-time (4,063 women); includes 984 minority (646 African Americans, 54 American Indian/Alaska Native, 125 Asian Americans or Pacific Islanders, 159 Hispanic Americans). Average age 43. In 2009, 271 master's, 189 doctorates, 13 other advanced degrees awarded. *Entrance requirements:* For master's, bachelor's degree from regionally-accredited institution, current resume; for doctorate and CAGS, master's degree from regionally-accredited university. Additional exam requirements/recommendations for international students: Required—TOEFL (minimum score 95 computer-based), IELTS (minimum score 7), Pearson Test of English (minimum score 65). *Application deadline:* Applications are processed on a rolling basis. Application fee: $75. *Expenses:* Tuition: Part-time $560 per credit. Part-time tuition and fees vary according to degree level and program. *Financial support:* Scholarships/grants available. *Unit head:* Dr. Barnaby Barratt, Provost and Professor of Psychology, 888-327-2877, Fax: 928-759-6381, E-mail: bbarratt@ncu.edu. *Application contact:* Kevin Lustig, Director of Admissions, 480-478-7490, Fax: 928-759-6285, E-mail: klustig@ncu.edu.

North Dakota State University, College of Graduate and Interdisciplinary Studies, College of Business, Fargo, ND 58108. Offers MBA. *Accreditation:* AACSB. Part-time and evening/weekend programs available. *Faculty:* 25 full-time (5 women). *Students:* 52 full-time (26 women), 23 part-time (11 women); includes 4 minority (1 African American, 2 Asian Americans or Pacific Islanders, 1 Hispanic American), 18 international. Average age 29. 55 applicants, 76% accepted, 38 enrolled. In 2009, 26 master's awarded. *Entrance requirements:* For master's, GMAT. Additional exam requirements/recommendations for international students: Required—TOEFL (minimum score 550 paper-based; 213 computer-based; 79 iBT). *Application deadline:* For fall admission, 7/15 priority date for domestic students; for spring admission, 11/15 for domestic students. Applications are processed on a rolling basis. Application fee: $45 ($60 for international students). *Financial support:* In 2009–10, 14 students received support, including 13 research assistantships, 1 teaching assistantship; institutionally sponsored loans and tuition waivers (partial) also available. Support available to part-time students. Financial award application deadline: 5/15; financial award applicants required to submit FAFSA. *Faculty research:* Labor management, operations, international finance, agency, Internet marketing. *Unit head:* Dr. Ron Johnson, Dean, 701-231-8805. *Application contact:* Paul R. Brown, Director, 701-231-7681, Fax: 701-231-7508, E-mail: paul.brown@ndsu.edu.

Northeastern Illinois University, Graduate College, College of Business and Management, Chicago, IL 60625-4699. Offers accounting (MBA); finance (MBA); management (MBA);

Business Administration and Management—General

Northeastern Illinois University *(continued)*
marketing (MBA). Part-time and evening/weekend programs available. *Degree requirements:* For master's, thesis optional. *Entrance requirements:* For master's, GMAT, minimum GPA of 2.75. Additional exam requirements/recommendations for international students: Required—TOEFL (minimum score 550 paper-based; 213 computer-based; 80 iBT). Electronic applications accepted. *Faculty research:* Perception of accountants and non-accountants toward future of the accounting industry, asynchronous learning outcomes, cost and efficiency of financial markets, impact of deregulation on airline industry, analysis of derivational instruments.

Northeastern State University, Graduate College, College of Business and Technology, Program in Business Administration, Tahlequah, OK 74464-2399. Offers MBA. *Accreditation:* ACBSP. Part-time and evening/weekend programs available. *Degree requirements:* For master's, comprehensive exam, thesis, business plan, oral exam. *Entrance requirements:* For master's, GMAT, minimum GPA of 2.5. Additional exam requirements/recommendations for international students: Required—TOEFL (minimum score 213 computer-based). Electronic applications accepted.

Northeastern University, Graduate School of Business Administration, Boston, MA 02115-5096. Offers EMBA, MBA, MS, CAGS, JD/MBA, MBA/MSN, MS/MBA. *Accreditation:* AACSB. Part-time and evening/weekend programs available. Postbaccalaureate distance learning degree programs offered (no on-campus study). *Faculty:* 46 full-time (7 women), 5 part-time/adjunct (0 women). *Students:* 176 full-time (67 women), 466 part-time (178 women); includes 66 minority (14 African Americans, 1 American Indian/Alaska Native, 34 Asian Americans or Pacific Islanders, 17 Hispanic Americans), 81 international. 640 applicants, 54% accepted, 196 enrolled. In 2009, 255 master's awarded. *Entrance requirements:* For master's, GMAT, interview. Additional exam requirements/recommendations for international students: Required—TOEFL (minimum score 600 paper-based; 250 computer-based; 100 iBT). *Application deadline:* For fall admission, 11/30 for domestic and international students; for winter admission, 2/1 for domestic and international students; for spring admission, 4/15 for domestic students. Application fee: $100. Electronic applications accepted. *Expenses:* Contact institution. *Financial support:* Federal Work-Study, institutionally sponsored loans, and scholarships/grants available. Support available to part-time students. Financial award application deadline: 3/1; financial award applicants required to submit FAFSA. *Unit head:* Kate Klepper, Associate Dean, Graduate Business Programs, 617-373-5417, Fax: 617-373-8564, E-mail: k.klepper@neu.edu. *Application contact:* Evelyn Tate, Director, Graduate Admissions, 617-373-5992, Fax: 617-373-8564, E-mail: e.tate@neu.edu.

Northern Arizona University, Graduate College, NAU-Yuma, Master of Administration Program, Flagstaff, AZ 86011. Offers M Adm. Postbaccalaureate distance learning degree programs offered (no on-campus study). *Faculty:* 2 full-time (both women). *Students:* 69 full-time (40 women), 344 part-time (184 women); includes 142 minority (34 African Americans, 24 American Indian/Alaska Native, 11 Asian Americans or Pacific Islanders, 73 Hispanic Americans), 1 international. Average age 25. 154 applicants, 97% accepted, 109 enrolled. In 2009, 94 master's awarded. *Degree requirements:* For master's, projects. *Entrance requirements:* For master's, five years' related work experience, minimum GPA of 3.0. Additional exam requirements/recommendations for international students: Required—TOEFL (minimum score 550 paper-based; 213 computer-based; 80 iBT), IELTS (minimum score 7), or a bachelor's degree from an English-speaking university and demonstrated proficiency. *Application deadline:* For fall admission, 10/1 for domestic students, 9/1 for international students. Applications are processed on a rolling basis. Application fee: $65. Electronic applications accepted. *Financial support:* Federal Work-Study and scholarships/grants available. Support available to part-time students. Financial award application deadline: 3/30; financial award applicants required to submit FAFSA. *Unit head:* Dr. Alex Steenstra, Chair, 928-317-6083, E-mail: alex.steenstra@nau.edu. *Application contact:* Pam Torbico, Coordinator, 928-523-6694, E-mail: pamela.torbico@nau.edu.

Northern Arizona University, Graduate College, The W. A. Franke College of Business, Flagstaff, AZ 86011. Offers MBA. *Accreditation:* AACSB. Part-time programs available. *Faculty:* 76 full-time (24 women). *Students:* 25 full-time (7 women), 3 part-time (2 women); includes 3 minority (2 American Indian/Alaska Native, 1 Hispanic American), 2 international. Average age 32. 81 applicants, 36% accepted. In 2009, 57 master's awarded. *Entrance requirements:* For master's, GMAT. Additional exam requirements/recommendations for international students: Required—TOEFL (minimum score 550 paper-based; 213 computer-based; 80 iBT), IELTS (minimum score 7). *Application deadline:* For fall admission, 3/1 priority date for domestic students. Applications are processed on a rolling basis. Application fee: $65. Electronic applications accepted. *Expenses:* Contact institution. *Financial support:* In 2009–10, 10 research assistantships, 3 teaching assistantships were awarded; Federal Work-Study, institutionally sponsored loans, and tuition waivers (full and partial) also available. Financial award application deadline: 3/30. *Faculty research:* Data processing applications for business situations and problems, accounting fraud, effects of sales tactics, self-efficacy and performance. *Unit head:* Dr. Alex Steenstra, Chair, 928-317-6083, Fax: 928-523-7331, E-mail: alex.steenstra@nau.edu. *Application contact:* Jane Thompson, Coordinator, 928-523-7387, Fax: 928-523-6559, E-mail: jane.thompson@nau.edu.

Northern Illinois University, Graduate School, College of Business, MBA Program, De Kalb, IL 60115-2854. Offers MBA. *Accreditation:* AACSB. Part-time and evening/weekend programs available. *Faculty:* 53 full-time (17 women), 3 part-time/adjunct (0 women). *Students:* 105 full-time (25 women), 394 part-time (144 women); includes 105 minority (21 African Americans, 1 American Indian/Alaska Native, 60 Asian Americans or Pacific Islanders, 23 Hispanic Americans), 21 international. Average age 31. 210 applicants, 65% accepted, 103 enrolled. In 2009, 207 master's awarded. *Degree requirements:* For master's, thesis optional, seminar. *Entrance requirements:* For master's, GMAT, minimum GPA of 2.75. Additional exam requirements/recommendations for international students: Required—TOEFL (minimum score 550 paper-based; 213 computer-based). *Application deadline:* For fall admission, 6/1 for domestic students, 5/1 for international students; for spring admission, 11/1 for domestic students, 10/1 for international students. Applications are processed on a rolling basis. Application fee: $30. Electronic applications accepted. *Expenses:* Tuition, state resident: full-time $6576; part-time $274 per credit hour. Tuition, nonresident: full-time $13,152; part-time $548 per credit hour. Required fees: $1813; $75.53 per credit hour. Part-time tuition and fees vary according to course load. *Financial support:* In 2009–10, 20 research assistantships with full tuition reimbursements, 1 teaching assistantship with full tuition reimbursement were awarded; fellowships with full tuition reimbursements, career-related internships or fieldwork, Federal Work-Study, scholarships/grants, tuition waivers (full), and unspecified assistantships also available. Support available to part-time students. Financial award applicants required to submit FAFSA. *Unit head:* Jeff Probhaker, Associate Dean of Graduate Affairs, 815-753-6176, E-mail: hwright@niu.edu. *Application contact:* Office of Graduate Studies in Business, 815-753-6301.

Northern Kentucky University, Office of Graduate Programs, College of Business, Program in Business Administration, Highland Heights, KY 41099. Offers business administration (MBA); entrepreneurship (Certificate); finance (Certificate); international business (Certificate); marketing (Certificate); project management (Certificate); JD/MBA. *Accreditation:* AACSB. Part-time and evening/weekend programs available. *Students:* 33 full-time (16 women), 155 part-time (63 women); includes 16 minority (9 African Americans, 7 Asian Americans or Pacific Islanders), 7 international. Average age 30. 105 applicants, 65% accepted, 34 enrolled. In 2009, 42 master's, 31 other advanced degrees awarded. *Degree requirements:* For master's, thesis optional. *Entrance requirements:* For master's, GMAT (minimum score 450), minimum GPA of 2.5. Additional exam requirements/recommendations for international students: Required—TOEFL (minimum score 550 paper-based; 213 computer-based; 79 iBT); Recommended—IELTS (minimum score 6.5). *Application deadline:* For fall admission, 8/1 priority date for domestic students, 6/1 priority date for international students; for spring admission, 12/1 priority date for domestic students, 10/1 priority date for international students. Applications are processed on a rolling basis. Application fee: $40. Electronic applications accepted. *Expenses:* Tuition, state

resident: full-time $6912; part-time $384 per credit hour. Tuition, nonresident: full-time $12,150; part-time $675 per credit hour. Tuition and fees vary according to course load, program and reciprocity agreements. *Financial support:* Unspecified assistantships available. Financial award applicants required to submit FAFSA. *Unit head:* James Bast, Director of MBA Programs, 859-572-7695, Fax: 859-572-7694, E-mail: mbusiness@nku.edu. *Application contact:* Dr. Peg Griffin, Director of Graduate Programs, 859-572-6934, Fax: 859-572-6670, E-mail: griffinp@nku.edu.

Northern Kentucky University, Office of Graduate Programs, College of Business, Program in Executive Leadership and Organizational Change, Highland Heights, KY 41099. Offers MS. Part-time and evening/weekend programs available. *Students:* 44 part-time (21 women); includes 6 minority (4 African Americans, 1 Asian American or Pacific Islander, 1 Hispanic American). Average age 41. 51 applicants, 55% accepted, 24 enrolled. In 2009, 25 master's awarded. *Degree requirements:* For master's, field research project. *Entrance requirements:* For master's, minimum GPA of 2.5; essay on professional career objective; 3 letters of recommendation, 1 from a current organization; 3 years of professional or managerial work experience. Additional exam requirements/recommendations for international students: Required—TOEFL (minimum score 600 paper-based; 213 computer-based; 79 iBT); Recommended—IELTS (minimum score 6.5). *Application deadline:* For fall admission, 6/15 priority date for domestic students, 6/1 priority date for international students. Application fee: $40. Electronic applications accepted. *Expenses:* Tuition, state resident: full-time $6912; part-time $384 per credit hour. Tuition, nonresident: full-time $12,150; part-time $675 per credit hour. Tuition and fees vary according to course load, program and reciprocity agreements. *Financial support:* Unspecified assistantships available. Financial award applicants required to submit FAFSA. *Faculty research:* Leadership and development, organizational change, field research, team and conflict management, strategy development and systems thinking. *Unit head:* Dr. Kenneth Rhee, Program Director, 859-572-6310, Fax: 859-572-7694, E-mail: rhee@nku.edu. *Application contact:* Amberly Hurst-Nutini, Coordinator, 859-572-5947, Fax: 859-572-7694, E-mail: hurstam@nku.edu.

North Park University, School of Business and Nonprofit Management, Chicago, IL 60625-4895. Offers MBA, MHEA, MHRM, MM, MNA. Part-time and evening/weekend programs available. *Entrance requirements:* For master's, GMAT. *Expenses:* Contact institution.

Northwest Christian University, School of Business and Management, Eugene, OR 97401-3745. Offers MBA. Part-time and evening/weekend programs available. *Faculty:* 1 full-time (0 women). *Students:* 25 full-time, 5 part-time. 20 applicants, 80% accepted, 11 enrolled. *Degree requirements:* For master's, thesis. *Entrance requirements:* For master's, GMAT, GRE, MAT, interview, minimum undergraduate GPA of 3.0. *Application deadline:* For fall admission, 3/15 priority date for domestic students. Applications are processed on a rolling basis. Application fee: $50. Electronic applications accepted. *Expenses:* Tuition: Full-time $9900; part-time $550 per credit hour. Tuition and fees vary according to program. *Unit head:* Dr. Michael Kennedy, Professor, 541-684-7243, Fax: 541-684-7333, E-mail: mkennedy@northwestchristian.edu. *Application contact:* Kathy Wilson, Assistant Director of Admission, Graduate and Professional Studies, 541-684-7326, Fax: 541-684-7333, E-mail: kwilson@northwestchristian.edu.

Northwestern Polytechnic University, School of Business and Information Technology, Fremont, CA 94539-7482. Offers MBA. Part-time and evening/weekend programs available. *Degree requirements:* For master's, thesis optional. *Entrance requirements:* For master's, GMAT, minimum GPA of 3.0. Additional exam requirements/recommendations for international students: Required—TOEFL (minimum score 550 paper-based; 213 computer-based; 79 iBT). *Expenses:* Contact institution. *Faculty research:* Entrepreneurship, accounting, information technology.

Northwestern University, The Graduate School, Kellogg School of Management, MBA Programs, Evanston, IL 60208. Offers business administration (MBA); JD/MBA; MBA/MEM. *Accreditation:* CAHME (one or more programs are accredited). Part-time and evening/weekend programs available. *Faculty:* 181 full-time, 104 part-time/adjunct. *Students:* 1,094 full-time (379 women), 1,120 part-time (336 women). Average age 28. 5,251 applicants, 19% accepted, 554 enrolled. In 2009, 562 master's awarded. *Entrance requirements:* For master's, GMAT, interview, 2 letters of recommendation. Additional exam requirements/recommendations for international students: Required—TOEFL. *Application deadline:* For fall admission, 10/15 for domestic students; for winter admission, 1/14 for domestic students; for spring admission, 3/4 for domestic students. Application fee: $250. Electronic applications accepted. *Expenses:* Contact institution. *Financial support:* Fellowships, career-related internships or fieldwork, institutionally sponsored loans, and scholarships/grants available. Support available to part-time students. Financial award application deadline: 5/31; financial award applicants required to submit FAFSA. *Unit head:* Sunil Chopra, Interim Dean. *Application contact:* Beth Flye, Director of Admissions and Financial Aid, 847-491-3308, Fax: 847-491-4960, E-mail: mbaadmissions@kellogg.northwestern.edu.

Northwest Missouri State University, Graduate School, Melvin and Valorie Booth College of Business and Professional Studies, Program in Business Administration, Maryville, MO 64468-6001. Offers MBA. *Accreditation:* ACBSP. *Faculty:* 15 full-time (2 women). *Students:* 58 full-time (29 women), 82 part-time (44 women); includes 9 minority (2 African Americans, 3 Asian Americans or Pacific Islanders, 4 Hispanic Americans), 12 international. 117 applicants, 68% accepted, 60 enrolled. In 2009, 45 master's awarded. *Degree requirements:* For master's, comprehensive exam. *Entrance requirements:* For master's, GMAT, minimum GPA of 2.5. Additional exam requirements/recommendations for international students: Required—TOEFL (minimum score 550 paper-based; 213 computer-based). *Application deadline:* For fall admission, 7/1 for domestic and international students; for spring admission, 12/1 for domestic students, 11/15 for international students. Applications are processed on a rolling basis. Application fee: $0 ($50 for international students). Electronic applications accepted. *Expenses:* Tuition, state resident: part-time $296.34 per credit hour. Tuition, nonresident: part-time $510.43 per credit hour. *Financial support:* In 2009–10, 3 research assistantships with full tuition reimbursements (averaging $6,000 per year), 1 teaching assistantship with full tuition reimbursement (averaging $6,000 per year) were awarded; unspecified assistantships also available. Financial award application deadline: 4/1; financial award applicants required to submit FAFSA. *Unit head:* Dr. Mark Jelavich, Head, 660-562-1763. *Application contact:* Dr. Gregory Haddock, Dean of Graduate School, 660-562-1145, Fax: 660-562-1096, E-mail: gradsch@nwmissouri.edu.

Northwest Nazarene University, Graduate Studies, Program in Business Administration, Nampa, ID 83686-5897. Offers MBA. *Accreditation:* ACBSP. Part-time and evening/weekend programs available. *Entrance requirements:* For master's, GMAT, minimum GPA of 3.0. Electronic applications accepted. *Expenses:* Contact institution.

Northwest University, School of Business and Management, Kirkland, WA 98033. Offers business administration (MBA); social entrepreneurship (MA). Evening/weekend programs available. *Faculty:* 9 full-time (1 woman), 6 part-time/adjunct (4 women). *Students:* 25 full-time (9 women), 4 part-time (1 woman); includes 6 minority (4 African Americans, 2 Asian Americans or Pacific Islanders), 4 international. Average age 34. 31 applicants, 90% accepted, 16 enrolled. In 2009, 11 master's awarded. *Degree requirements:* For master's, formalized research. *Entrance requirements:* For master's, GMAT, 4 foundation courses. Additional exam requirements/recommendations for international students: Required—TOEFL (minimum score 550 paper-based). *Application deadline:* For fall admission, 8/1 for domestic and international students; for spring admission, 12/1 for domestic and international students. Applications are processed on a rolling basis. Application fee: $75. Electronic applications accepted. *Financial support:* Federal Work-Study, scholarships/grants, health care benefits, and tuition waivers (full) available. Financial award applicants required to submit FAFSA. *Unit head:* Dr. Teresa Gillespie, Dean, 425-889-5290, E-mail: teresa.gillespie@northwestu.edu. *Application contact:* Roy Rowland, Director of Graduate and Professional Studies Enrollment, 425-889-5213, Fax: 425-803-3059, E-mail: roy.rowland@northwestu.edu.

Northwood University, Richard DeVos Graduate School of Management, Midland, MI 48640-2398. Offers EMBA, MBA, MMBA. Part-time and evening/weekend programs available. *Degree*

requirements: For master's, capstone project. *Entrance requirements:* For master's, GMAT, interview, letters of recommendation, resume. Additional exam requirements/recommendations for international students: Required—TOEFL (minimum score 550 paper-based; 213 computer-based). Electronic applications accepted.

Norwich University, School of Graduate and Continuing Studies, Program in Business Administration, Northfield, VT 05663. Offers MBA. *Accreditation:* ACBSP. Evening/weekend programs available. *Faculty:* 26 part-time/adjunct (0 women). *Students:* 407 full-time (131 women); includes 31 minority (19 African Americans, 3 American Indian/Alaska Native, 2 Asian Americans or Pacific Islanders, 7 Hispanic Americans), 4 international. Average age 36. 609 applicants, 81% accepted, 407 enrolled. In 2009, 389 master's awarded. *Degree requirements:* For master's, comprehensive exam (for some programs), thesis optional. *Entrance requirements:* For master's, minimum undergraduate GPA of 2.75. Additional exam requirements/recommendations for international students: Required—TOEFL (minimum score 550 paper-based; 213 computer-based; 83 iBT). *Application deadline:* For fall admission, 8/10 for domestic and international students; for winter admission, 11/7 for domestic and international students; for spring admission, 2/6 for domestic and international students. Application fee: $50. Full-time tuition and fees vary according to course level and course load. *Financial support:* Scholarships/grants available. Financial award applicants required to submit FAFSA. *Unit head:* Dr. Jose Cordova, Faculty Director, 802-485-2567, Fax: 802-485-2533, E-mail: jcordova@norwich.edu. *Application contact:* Janet Mara, Administrative Director, 802-485-2567, Fax: 802-485-2533, E-mail: jmara@norwich.edu.

Notre Dame College, Graduate Studies, South Euclid, OH 44121-4293. Offers accounting (Certificate); creative critical thinking (M Ed); financial services management (Certificate); information systems (Certificate); learning disabilities (M Ed); management (Certificate); paralegal (Certificate); pastoral ministry (Certificate); reading (M Ed); teacher education (Certificate). Part-time and evening/weekend programs available. *Degree requirements:* For master's, thesis. *Entrance requirements:* For master's, GRE General Test, MAT, minimum GPA of 2.75, valid teaching certificate. *Faculty research:* Cognitive psychology, teaching critical thinking in the classroom.

Notre Dame de Namur University, Division of Academic Affairs, School of Business and Management, Department of Business Administration, Belmont, CA 94002-1908. Offers business administration (MBA); finance (MBA); human resource management (MBA); marketing (MBA). Part-time and evening/weekend programs available. *Faculty:* 7 full-time (1 woman), 6 part-time/adjunct (0 women). *Students:* 21 full-time (17 women), 87 part-time (49 women); includes 47 minority (3 African Americans, 4 American Indian/Alaska Native, 21 Asian Americans or Pacific Islanders, 19 Hispanic Americans), 9 international. Average age 34. 27 applicants, 100% accepted, 20 enrolled. In 2009, 43 master's awarded. *Entrance requirements:* For master's, minimum GPA of 2.5. Additional exam requirements/recommendations for international students: Required—TOEFL (minimum score 550 paper-based; 213 computer-based; 79 iBT). *Application deadline:* For fall admission, 8/1 priority date for domestic students; for spring admission, 12/1 priority date for domestic students. Applications are processed on a rolling basis. Application fee: $60. Electronic applications accepted. *Expenses:* Tuition: Part-time $720 per credit. Required fees: $35 per semester hour. *Financial support:* Career-related internships or fieldwork available. Support available to part-time students. Financial award applicants required to submit FAFSA. *Unit head:* Henry Roth, Director, 650-508-3721, E-mail: hroth@ndnu.edu. *Application contact:* Candace Hallmark, Associate Director of Admissions, 650-508-3592, Fax: 650-508-3426, E-mail: grad.admit@ndnu.edu.

Notre Dame de Namur University, Division of Academic Affairs, School of Business and Management, Department of Management, Belmont, CA 94002-1908. Offers MSM. Part-time and evening/weekend programs available. *Faculty:* 3 full-time (1 woman), 1 part-time/adjunct (0 women). *Students:* 2 full-time (both women), 30 part-time (25 women); includes 18 minority (2 African Americans, 1 Asian American or Pacific Islander, 15 Hispanic Americans), 1 international. Average age 31. 9 applicants, 100% accepted, 9 enrolled. In 2009, 10 master's awarded. *Entrance requirements:* For master's, minimum GPA of 2.5. Additional exam requirements/recommendations for international students: Required—TOEFL (minimum score 550 paper-based; 213 computer-based). *Application deadline:* For fall admission, 8/1 priority date for domestic students; for spring admission, 12/1 priority date for domestic students. Applications are processed on a rolling basis. Application fee: $60. Electronic applications accepted. *Expenses:* Tuition: Part-time $720 per credit. Required fees: $35 per semester hour. *Financial support:* Available to part-time students. Applicants required to submit FAFSA. *Unit head:* Henry Roth, Director, 650-508-3721, E-mail: hroth@ndnu.edu. *Application contact:* Candace Hallmark, Associate Director of Admissions, 650-508-3592, Fax: 650-508-3426, E-mail: grad.admit@ndnu.edu.

Nova Southeastern University, H. Wayne Huizenga School of Business and Entrepreneurship, Doctoral Program in Business Administration, Fort Lauderdale, FL 33314-7796. Offers accounting (DBA); decision sciences (DBA); finance (DBA); human resource management (DBA); international business (DBA); management (DBA); marketing (DBA). Part-time and evening/weekend programs available. *Faculty:* 34 full-time (11 women), 2 part-time/adjunct (1 woman). *Students:* 6 full-time (1 woman), 129 part-time (41 women); includes 33 minority (17 African Americans, 6 Asian Americans or Pacific Islanders, 10 Hispanic Americans), 12 international. Average age 47. 58 applicants, 14% accepted, 5 enrolled. In 2009, 32 doctorates awarded. *Degree requirements:* For doctorate, comprehensive exam, thesis/dissertation. *Entrance requirements:* For doctorate, GMAT. Additional exam requirements/recommendations for international students: Required—TOEFL (minimum score 600 paper-based; 250 computer-based; 100 iBT), IELTS (minimum score 7). *Application deadline:* Applications are processed on a rolling basis. Application fee: $50. Electronic applications accepted. *Financial support:* Available to part-time students. Applicants required to submit FAFSA. *Faculty research:* Reputation management, call centers, international social capital, corporate earnings guidance, corporate governance. *Unit head:* Kristie Tetrault, Director of Program Administration, 954-262-5120, Fax: 954-262-3849, E-mail: kristie@huizenga.nova.edu. *Application contact:* Karen Goldberg, Associate Director of Recruitment and Special Events, 954-262-5039, Fax: 954-262-3822, E-mail: karen@huizenga.nova.edu.

Nova Southeastern University, H. Wayne Huizenga School of Business and Entrepreneurship, Master's Program in Business Administration, Fort Lauderdale, FL 33314-7796. Offers business administration (MBA); JD/MBA; Pharm D/MBA. Part-time and evening/weekend programs available. Postbaccalaureate distance learning degree programs offered (minimal on-campus study). *Faculty:* 25 full-time (9 women), 78 part-time/adjunct (17 women). *Students:* 273 full-time (140 women), 1,992 part-time (1,145 women); includes 1,425 minority (695 African Americans, 4 American Indian/Alaska Native, 92 Asian Americans or Pacific Islanders, 634 Hispanic Americans), 131 international. Average age 33. 575 applicants, 57% accepted, 248 enrolled. In 2009, 730 master's awarded. *Degree requirements:* For master's, thesis optional. *Entrance requirements:* Additional exam requirements/recommendations for international students: Required—TOEFL (minimum score 550 paper-based; 213 computer-based; 79 iBT), IELTS (minimum score 6). *Application deadline:* For fall admission, 8/15 for domestic and international students; for winter admission, 12/10 for domestic and international students; for spring admission, 2/10 for domestic and international students. Applications are processed on a rolling basis. Application fee: $50. Electronic applications accepted. *Financial support:* Career-related internships or fieldwork, Federal Work-Study, and scholarships/grants available. Support available to part-time students. Financial award applicants required to submit FAFSA. *Unit head:* Steve Harvey, Assistant Dean of Program Administration, 954-262-5047, Fax: 954-262-3829, E-mail: harvey@nsu.nova.edu. *Application contact:* Karen Goldberg, Associate Director of Recruitment and Special Events, 954-262-5039, Fax: 954-262-3822, E-mail: karen@nova.edu.

Nova Southeastern University, H. Wayne Huizenga School of Business and Entrepreneurship, Program in Leadership, Fort Lauderdale, FL 33314-7796. Offers MS. Part-time and evening/weekend programs available. Postbaccalaureate distance learning degree programs offered (minimal on-campus study). *Faculty:* 2 full-time (both women), 5 part-time/adjunct (3 women). *Students:* 4 full-time (2 women), 197 part-time (119 women); includes 123 minority (68 African Americans, 1 American Indian/Alaska Native, 1 Asian American or Pacific Islander, 53 Hispanic Americans), 5 international. Average age 37. 69 applicants, 57% accepted, 25 enrolled. In 2009, 47 master's awarded. *Degree requirements:* For master's, situational leadership seminar. *Entrance requirements:* Additional exam requirements/recommendations for international students: Required—TOEFL (minimum score 550 paper-based; 213 computer-based; 79 iBT), IELTS (minimum score 6). *Application deadline:* For fall admission, 8/15 for domestic and international students; for winter admission, 12/10 for domestic and international students; for spring admission, 2/10 for domestic and international students. Applications are processed on a rolling basis. Application fee: $50. Electronic applications accepted. *Financial support:* Federal Work-Study and scholarships/grants available. Support available to part-time students. Financial award applicants required to submit FAFSA. *Unit head:* Steve Harvey, Assistant Dean of Program Administration, 954-262-5047, Fax: 954-262-3829, E-mail: harvey@nsu.nova.edu. *Application contact:* Karen Goldberg, Associate Director of Recruitment and Special Events, 954-262-5039, Fax: 954-262-3822, E-mail: karen@nova.edu.

Nyack College, School of Business, Nyack, NY 10960-3698. Offers accounting (MBA); business administration (MBA). Evening/weekend programs available. *Degree requirements:* For master's, thesis. *Entrance requirements:* For master's, GMAT (may be waived based on business experience), minimum GPA of 3.0. *Expenses:* Contact institution.

Oakland City University, School of Adult and Extended Learning, Oakland City, IN 47660-1099. Offers MS Mgt. Part-time and evening/weekend programs available. *Degree requirements:* For master's, thesis or alternative. *Entrance requirements:* For master's, GMAT, GRE, or MAT, appropriate bachelor's degree, computer literacy. Additional exam requirements/recommendations for international students: Required—TOEFL. *Faculty research:* Leadership and management styles, international business, new technologies.

Oakland University, Graduate Study and Lifelong Learning, School of Business Administration, Rochester, MI 48309-4401. Offers M Acc, MBA, MS, Certificate. *Accreditation:* AACSB. Part-time and evening/weekend programs available. *Entrance requirements:* For master's, GMAT, minimum GPA of 3.0 for unconditional admission. Additional exam requirements/recommendations for international students: Required—TOEFL (minimum score 550 paper-based; 213 computer-based). Electronic applications accepted. *Expenses:* Contact institution. *Faculty research:* Rotor manufacturing induced anomaly database, Globalization Challenges project.

OGI School of Science & Engineering at Oregon Health & Science University, Graduate Studies, Department of Management in Science and Technology, Beaverton, OR 97006-8921. Offers health care management (Certificate); management in science and technology (MS, Certificate). Part-time and evening/weekend programs available. *Degree requirements:* For master's, thesis. *Entrance requirements:* For master's, 2 years of work experience. Additional exam requirements/recommendations for international students: Recommended—TOEFL (minimum score 625 paper-based; 263 computer-based). Electronic applications accepted.

Oglala Lakota College, Graduate Studies, Program in Lakota Leadership and Management, Kyle, SD 57752-0490. Offers MA. Part-time and evening/weekend programs available. *Degree requirements:* For master's, thesis. *Entrance requirements:* For master's, minimum GPA of 2.5. *Faculty research:* Curriculum, values, retention of administrators, behavior, graduate follow-up.

Ohio Dominican University, Graduate Programs, Division of Business, Columbus, OH 43219-2099. Offers MBA. Program also offered in Dayton, OH. *Accreditation:* ACBSP. Part-time and evening/weekend programs available. *Students:* 343 full-time (165 women), 17 part-time (11 women); includes 111 minority (97 African Americans, 2 American Indian/Alaska Native, 6 Asian Americans or Pacific Islanders, 6 Hispanic Americans), 1 international. Average age 33. In 2009, 122 master's awarded. *Degree requirements:* For master's, thesis or alternative. *Entrance requirements:* For master's, minimum GPA of 3.0, 3 letters of recommendation. Additional exam requirements/recommendations for international students: Required—TOEFL (minimum score 550 paper-based; 213 computer-based). *Application deadline:* For fall admission, 7/15 priority date for domestic and international students; for spring admission, 12/15 priority date for domestic and international students. Applications are processed on a rolling basis. Application fee: $25. *Financial support:* Applicants required to submit FAFSA. *Unit head:* Dr. Kenneth C. Fah, Director of Graduate Business Programs, 614-251-4566, E-mail: fahk@ohiodominican.edu. *Application contact:* Jill M. Westerfeld, Graduate Admissions Recruiter, 614-251-4725, Fax: 614-251-4634, E-mail: westerfj@ohiodominican.edu.

The Ohio State University, Graduate School, Max M. Fisher College of Business, Program in Business Administration, Columbus, OH 43210. Offers MA, MBA, PhD. *Accreditation:* AACSB. *Faculty:* 75. *Students:* 441 full-time (122 women), 220 part-time (66 women); includes 84 minority (25 African Americans, 47 Asian Americans or Pacific Islanders, 12 Hispanic Americans), 135 international. Average age 30. In 2009, 338 master's, 10 doctorates awarded. *Degree requirements:* For doctorate, thesis/dissertation. *Entrance requirements:* For master's and doctorate, GMAT. Additional exam requirements/recommendations for international students: Required—TOEFL (minimum score 600 paper-based; 250 computer-based). *Application deadline:* For fall admission, 8/15 priority date for domestic students, 7/1 priority date for international students; for winter admission, 12/1 priority date for domestic students, 11/1 priority date for international students; for spring admission, 3/1 priority date for domestic students, 2/1 priority date for international students. Applications are processed on a rolling basis. Application fee: $40 ($50 for international students). Electronic applications accepted. *Expenses:* Tuition, state resident: full-time $10,683. Tuition, nonresident: full-time $25,923. Tuition and fees vary according to course load and program. *Financial support:* Fellowships, research assistantships, teaching assistantships, Federal Work-Study, institutionally sponsored loans, and unspecified assistantships available. Support available to part-time students. *Unit head:* Ingrid Werner, Head, 614-292-6040, Fax: 614-292-9006, E-mail: werner.47@osu.edu. *Application contact:* 614-292-9444, Fax: 614-292-3895, E-mail: domestic.grad@osu.edu.

The Ohio State University, Graduate School, Max M. Fisher College of Business, Program in Business Logistics Engineering, Columbus, OH 43210. Offers MBLE. *Students:* 32 full-time (15 women), 15 part-time (8 women); includes 1 minority (Asian American or Pacific Islander), 40 international. Average age 26. In 2009, 16 master's awarded. *Entrance requirements:* For master's, GRE or GMAT. Additional exam requirements/recommendations for international students: Required—TOEFL. *Application deadline:* Applications are processed on a rolling basis. Application fee: $40 ($50 for international students). Electronic applications accepted. *Expenses:* Tuition, state resident: full-time $10,683. Tuition, nonresident: full-time $25,923. Tuition and fees vary according to course load and program. *Unit head:* Walter Zinn, Graduate Studies Committee Chair, 416-292-0797, Fax: 416-292-9006, E-mail: zinn.13@osu.edu. *Application contact:* Graduate Admissions, 614-292-9444, Fax: 614-292-3895, E-mail: domestic.grad@osu.edu.

Ohio University, Graduate College, College of Business, Executive Business Administration Program, Athens, OH 45701-2979. Offers EMBA. *Accreditation:* AACSB. Part-time and evening/weekend programs available. *Faculty:* 44 full-time (15 women), 16 part-time/adjunct (7 women). *Students:* 56 full-time (11 women); includes 8 minority (4 African Americans, 4 Asian Americans or Pacific Islanders). Average age 34. 48 applicants, 79% accepted. In 2009, 28 master's awarded. *Entrance requirements:* For master's, work experience in management (7-10 years). *Application deadline:* For fall admission, 6/1 priority date for domestic students. Applications are processed on a rolling basis. Application fee: $50 ($55 for international students). *Expenses:* Contact institution. *Faculty research:* Business, strategy, issues. *Application contact:* Virginia Finsterwald, Assistant Director, 740-593-2028, Fax: 740-593-0319, E-mail: finsterw@ohio.edu.

Ohio University, Graduate College, College of Business, Program in Business Administration, Athens, OH 45701-2979. Offers MBA. *Accreditation:* AACSB. Part-time and evening/weekend programs available. *Faculty:* 44 full-time (15 women), 16 part-time/adjunct (7 women). *Students:* 60 full-time (27 women), 8 part-time (2 women); includes 6 minority (5 African Americans, 1 Hispanic American), 23 international. In 2009, 182 master's awarded. *Entrance requirements:* For master's, GMAT (minimum score 500), minimum GPA of 3.0. Additional exam requirements/

Business Administration and Management—General

Ohio University *(continued)*
recommendations for international students: Required—TOEFL (minimum score 600 paper-based; 250 computer-based). *Application deadline:* For fall admission, 2/1 priority date for domestic students, 1/15 priority date for international students. Applications are processed on a rolling basis. Application fee: $50 ($55 for international students). Electronic applications accepted. *Expenses:* Contact institution. *Financial support:* In 2009–10, 20 research assistantships with full and partial tuition reimbursements (averaging $8,000 per year) were awarded; career-related internships or fieldwork and institutionally sponsored loans also available. Financial award application deadline: 2/1. *Application contact:* Jan Ross, Assistant Dean, 740-593-2007, Fax: 740-593-1388, E-mail: rossj@ohio.edu.

Oklahoma City University, Meinders School of Business, Program in Business Administration, Oklahoma City, OK 73106-1402. Offers finance (MBA); health administration (MBA); information technology (MBA); integrated marketing communications (MBA); international business (MBA); marketing (MBA); JD/MBA. *Accreditation:* ACBSP. Part-time and evening/weekend programs available. *Faculty:* 24 full-time (7 women), 11 part-time/adjunct (1 woman). *Students:* 268 full-time (91 women), 180 part-time (62 women); includes 51 minority (20 African Americans, 7 American Indian/Alaska Native, 11 Asian Americans or Pacific Islanders, 13 Hispanic Americans), 257 international. Average age 30. 158 applicants, 90% accepted, 35 enrolled. In 2009, 236 master's awarded. *Degree requirements:* For master's, comprehensive exam. *Entrance requirements:* Additional exam requirements/recommendations for international students: Required—TOEFL (minimum score 560 paper-based; 220 computer-based; 83 iBT). *Application deadline:* For fall admission, 8/20 for domestic students; for spring admission, 1/6 for domestic students. Applications are processed on a rolling basis. Application fee: $70 ($70 for international students). *Expenses:* Tuition: Full-time $15,930; part-time $885 per hour. *Financial support:* Fellowships with partial tuition reimbursements, career-related internships or fieldwork, Federal Work-Study, institutionally sponsored loans, and tuition waivers (partial) available. Support available to part-time students. Financial award application deadline: 8/1. *Faculty research:* Management information systems, international business strategies. *Unit head:* Dr. Mahmood Shandiz, Senior Associate Dean, 405-208-5130, Fax: 405-208-5098, E-mail: mshandiz@okcu.edu. *Application contact:* Michelle Lockhart, Director, Graduate Admissions, 800-633-7242, Fax: 405-208-5916, E-mail: gadmissions@okcu.edu.

Oklahoma City University, Petree College of Arts and Sciences, Program in Liberal Arts, Oklahoma City, OK 73106-1402. Offers art (MLA); general studies (MLA); leadership/management (MLA); literature (MLA); mass communications (MLA); philosophy (MLA); writing (MLA). Part-time and evening/weekend programs available. *Faculty:* 23 full-time (6 women), 5 part-time/adjunct (3 women). *Students:* 50 full-time (24 women), 23 part-time (14 women); includes 6 minority (4 African Americans, 1 Asian American or Pacific Islander, 1 Hispanic American), 50 international. Average age 31. 31 applicants, 94% accepted, 15 enrolled. In 2009, 21 master's awarded. *Degree requirements:* For master's, comprehensive exam, thesis optional. *Entrance requirements:* Additional exam requirements/recommendations for international students: Required—TOEFL (minimum score 550 paper-based). *Application deadline:* For fall admission, 8/20 for domestic students; for spring admission, 1/6 for domestic students. Applications are processed on a rolling basis. Application fee: $50 ($70 for international students). *Expenses:* Tuition: Full-time $15,930; part-time $885 per hour. *Financial support:* Fellowships with partial tuition reimbursements, career-related internships or fieldwork, Federal Work-Study, and tuition waivers (partial) available. Support available to part-time students. Financial award application deadline: 8/1; financial award applicants required to submit FAFSA. *Unit head:* Dr. Regina Bennett, Director, 405-208-5207, Fax: 405-208-5451, E-mail: rbennett@okcu.edu. *Application contact:* Michelle Lockhart, Director, Admissions, 800-633-7242, Fax: 405-208-5916, E-mail: gadmissions@okcu.edu.

Oklahoma State University, William S. Spears School of Business, Department of Management, Stillwater, OK 74078. Offers MBA, MS, PhD. Part-time programs available. *Faculty:* 22 full-time (5 women), 8 part-time/adjunct (5 women). *Students:* 4 full-time (0 women), 5 part-time (0 women), 1 international. Average age 34. In 2009, 3 doctorates awarded. *Degree requirements:* For master's, thesis or alternative; for doctorate, comprehensive exam, thesis/dissertation. *Entrance requirements:* For master's and doctorate, GRE or GMAT. Additional exam requirements/recommendations for international students: Required—TOEFL (minimum score 550 paper-based; 79 iBT). *Application deadline:* For fall admission, 3/1 priority date for international students; for spring admission, 8/1 priority date for international students. Applications are processed on a rolling basis. Application fee: $40 ($75 for international students). Electronic applications accepted. *Expenses:* Tuition, state resident: full-time $3716; part-time $154.85 per credit hour. Tuition, nonresident: full-time $14,448; part-time $602 per credit hour. Required fees: $1772; $73.85 per credit hour. One-time fee: $50. Tuition and fees vary according to course load and campus/location. *Financial support:* In 2009–10, 5 research assistantships (averaging $18,984 per year), 2 teaching assistantships (averaging $18,984 per year) were awarded; career-related internships or fieldwork, Federal Work-Study, scholarships/grants, health care benefits, tuition waivers (partial), and unspecified assistantships also available. Support available to part-time students. Financial award application deadline: 3/1; financial award applicants required to submit FAFSA. *Faculty research:* Telecommunications management, innovative decision support techniques, knowledge networking, organizational research methods, strategic planning. *Unit head:* Dr. Kenneth Eastman, Head, 405-744-5201, Fax: 405-744-5180. *Application contact:* Dr. Gordon Emslie, Dean, 405-744-6368, Fax: 405-744-0355, E-mail: grad-i@okstate.edu.

Oklahoma State University, William S. Spears School of Business, Programs in Business Administration, Stillwater, OK 74078. Offers MBA, PhD. *Accreditation:* AACSB. Part-time programs available. Postbaccalaureate distance learning degree programs offered. *Faculty:* 3 full-time (1 woman). *Students:* 159 full-time (53 women), 281 part-time (92 women); includes 64 minority (12 African Americans, 29 American Indian/Alaska Native, 14 Asian Americans or Pacific Islanders, 9 Hispanic Americans), 28 international. Average age 29. 591 applicants, 30% accepted, 144 enrolled. In 2009, 151 master's awarded. *Degree requirements:* For master's, thesis or alternative; for doctorate, comprehensive exam, thesis/dissertation. *Entrance requirements:* For master's and doctorate, GMAT. Additional exam requirements/recommendations for international students: Required—TOEFL (minimum score 550 paper-based; 79 iBT). *Application deadline:* For fall admission, 3/1 priority date for international students; for spring admission, 8/1 priority date for international students. Applications are processed on a rolling basis. Application fee: $40 ($75 for international students). Electronic applications accepted. *Expenses:* Tuition, state resident: full-time $3716; part-time $154.85 per credit hour. Tuition, nonresident: full-time $14,448; part-time $602 per credit hour. Required fees: $1772; $73.85 per credit hour. One-time fee: $50. Tuition and fees vary according to course load and campus/location. *Financial support:* In 2009–10, 1 research assistantship (averaging $18,984 per year) was awarded; career-related internships or fieldwork, Federal Work-Study, scholarships/grants, health care benefits, tuition waivers, and unspecified assistantships also available. Support available to part-time students. Financial award application deadline: 3/1; financial award applicants required to submit FAFSA. *Unit head:* Dr. Sara Freedman, Dean, 405-744-5075. *Application contact:* Jan Analla, Assistant Director of Graduate Programs, 405-744-2951.

See Display below.

Old Dominion University, College of Business and Public Administration, Doctoral Program in Business Administration, Norfolk, VA 23529. Offers finance (PhD); information technology (PhD); marketing (PhD); strategic management (PhD). *Accreditation:* AACSB. *Faculty:* 21 full-time (2 women). *Students:* 28 full-time (12 women), 14 part-time (6 women); includes 5

minority (3 African Americans, 2 Asian Americans or Pacific Islanders), 25 international. Average age 35. 31 applicants, 65% accepted, 8 enrolled. In 2009, 6 doctorates awarded. *Degree requirements:* For doctorate, comprehensive exam, thesis/dissertation. *Entrance requirements:* For doctorate, GMAT. Additional exam requirements/recommendations for international students: Required—TOEFL (minimum score 550 paper-based; 213 computer-based; 79 iBT). *Application deadline:* For fall admission, 4/1 priority date for domestic and international students. Application fee: $50. Electronic applications accepted. *Expenses:* Tuition, state resident: full-time $8112; part-time $338 per credit. Tuition, nonresident: full-time $20,256; part-time $844 per credit. Required fees: $119 per semester. One-time fee: $50. *Financial support:* In 2009–10, 23 students received support, including 4 fellowships with full tuition reimbursements available (averaging $15,000 per year), 13 research assistantships with full tuition reimbursements available (averaging $15,000 per year), 6 teaching assistantships with full tuition reimbursements available (averaging $15,000 per year); career-related internships or fieldwork and scholarships/grants also available. Financial award application deadline: 4/1; financial award applicants required to submit FAFSA. *Faculty research:* International business, buyer behavior, financial markets, strategy, operations research. *Unit head:* Dr. Sylvia C. Hudgins, Graduate Program Director, 757-683-3551, Fax: 757-683-4076, E-mail: shudgins@odu.edu. *Application contact:* Dr. Sylvia C. Hudgins, Graduate Program Director, 757-683-3551, Fax: 757-683-4076, E-mail: shudgins@odu.edu.

Old Dominion University, College of Business and Public Administration, MBA Program, Norfolk, VA 23529. Offers business and economic forecasting (MBA); financial analysis and valuation (MBA); information technology and enterprise integration (MBA); international business (MBA); maritime and port management (MBA); public administration (MBA). *Accreditation:* AACSB. Part-time and evening/weekend programs available. *Faculty:* 66 full-time (15 women), 6 part-time/adjunct (1 woman). *Students:* 81 full-time (27 women), 198 part-time (92 women); includes 46 minority (25 African Americans, 1 American Indian/Alaska Native, 13 Asian Americans or Pacific Islanders, 7 Hispanic Americans), 31 international. Average age 30. 169 applicants, 52% accepted, 61 enrolled. In 2009, 81 master's awarded. *Entrance requirements:* For master's, GMAT, letters of reference, resume, coursework in calculus. Additional exam requirements/recommendations for international students: Required—TOEFL (minimum score 550 paper-based; 213 computer-based; 80 iBT). *Application deadline:* For fall admission, 6/1 priority date for domestic students, 4/15 priority date for international students; for spring admission, 11/1 priority date for domestic students, 10/1 priority date for international students. Applications are processed on a rolling basis. Application fee: $50. Electronic applications accepted. *Expenses:* Tuition, state resident: full-time $8112; part-time $338 per credit. Tuition, nonresident: full-time $20,256; part-time $844 per credit. Required fees: $119 per semester. One-time fee: $50. *Financial support:* In 2009–10, 46 students received support, including 31 research assistantships with partial tuition reimbursements available (averaging $7,000 per year), 3 teaching assistantships with partial tuition reimbursements available (averaging $6,300 per year); career-related internships or fieldwork, scholarships/grants, and unspecified assistantships also available. Support available to part-time students. Financial award application deadline: 2/15; financial award applicants required to submit FAFSA. *Faculty research:* International business, buyer behavior, financial markets, strategy, operations research. *Unit head:* Dr. Bruce Rubin, Graduate Program Director, 757-683-3585, E-mail: mbainfo@odu.edu. *Application contact:* Shanna Wood, MBA Program Manager, 757-683-3585, Fax: 757-683-5750, E-mail: mbainfo@odu.edu.

Olivet Nazarene University, Graduate School, Department of Business, Bourbonnais, IL 60914. Offers business administration (MBA). Evening/weekend programs available. *Degree requirements:* For master's, thesis or alternative. *Expenses:* Contact institution.

Oral Roberts University, School of Business, Tulsa, OK 74171. Offers accounting (MBA); entrepreneurship (MBA); finance (MBA); international business (MBA); management (MBA); marketing (MBA); non-profit management (MBA); not for profit management (MNM). *Accreditation:* ACBSP. Part-time programs available. Postbaccalaureate distance learning degree programs offered (minimal on-campus study). *Faculty:* 7 full-time (0 women), 5 part-time/adjunct (4 women). *Students:* 68 full-time (30 women), 55 part-time (27 women); includes 54 minority (32 African Americans, 5 American Indian/Alaska Native, 8 Asian Americans or Pacific Islanders, 9 Hispanic Americans), 3 international. Average age 28. 71 applicants, 94% accepted, 56 enrolled. In 2009, 36 master's awarded. *Degree requirements:* For master's, thesis optional. *Entrance requirements:* For master's, minimum cumulative GPA of 3.0. Additional exam requirements/recommendations for international students: Required—TOEFL (minimum score 550 paper-based; 213 computer-based; 79 iBT). *Application deadline:* For fall admission, 7/1 priority date for domestic and international students; for spring admission, 12/1 priority date for domestic students, 10/15 priority date for international students. Applications are processed on a rolling basis. Application fee: $35. Electronic applications accepted. *Financial support:* In 2009–10, 39 students received support. Federal Work-Study, scholarships/grants, and unspecified assistantships available. Financial award application deadline: 6/1; financial award applicants required to submit FAFSA. *Faculty research:* Social media, international business and marketing. *Unit head:* Dr. Steven Greene, Dean, 918-495-7040, Fax: 918-495-7876, E-mail: businessdean@oru.edu. *Application contact:* Rebecca Gunn, Representative/Recruiter, 918-495-6117, Fax: 918-495-6500, E-mail: gradbusiness@oru.edu.

Oregon State University, Graduate School, College of Business, Corvallis, OR 97331. Offers MAIS, MBA, Certificate. *Accreditation:* AACSB. Part-time programs available. *Faculty:* 35 full-time (8 women), 18 part-time/adjunct (5 women). *Students:* 63 full-time (22 women), 24 part-time (11 women); includes 10 minority (2 African Americans, 1 American Indian/Alaska Native, 5 Asian Americans or Pacific Islanders, 2 Hispanic Americans), 14 international. Average age 30. In 2009, 92 master's awarded. *Degree requirements:* For master's, portfolio. *Entrance requirements:* For master's, GMAT, minimum GPA of 3.0 in last 90 hours. Additional exam requirements/recommendations for international students: Required—TOEFL. *Application deadline:* For fall admission, 3/15 for domestic students. Applications are processed on a rolling basis. Application fee: $50. *Expenses:* Tuition, state resident: full-time $9774; part-time $362 per credit. Tuition, nonresident: full-time $15,849; part-time $587 per credit. Required fees: $1639. Full-time tuition and fees vary according to course load and program. *Financial support:* Fellowships, teaching assistantships, career-related internships or fieldwork, Federal Work-Study, and institutionally sponsored loans available. Financial award application deadline: 2/1. *Faculty research:* Financial and account services, market analysis and planning, innovation, family business, tourism. *Unit head:* Dr. Ilene K. Kleinsorge, Dean, 541-737-6024, Fax: 541-737-3033, E-mail: ilene@bus.oregonstate.edu. *Application contact:* Brenda R. Sallee, Head Advisor, 541-737-3716, Fax: 541-737-4890, E-mail: brenda.sallee@bus.oregonstate.edu.

Ottawa University, Graduate Studies-Arizona, Programs in Business, Ottawa, KS 66067-3399. Offers business administration (MBA); finance (MBA); human resources (MA, MBA); leadership (MBA); marketing (MBA). Programs offered in Mesa, Phoenix, Tempe and West Valley, AZ. Part-time and evening/weekend programs available. Postbaccalaureate distance learning degree programs offered. *Degree requirements:* For master's, thesis or alternative. *Entrance requirements:* For master's, minimum undergraduate GPA of 3.0. Additional exam requirements/recommendations for international students: Required—TOEFL (minimum score 550 paper-based; 213 computer-based). Electronic applications accepted.

Ottawa University, Graduate Studies-International, Ottawa, KS 66067-3399. Offers business administration (MBA). Postbaccalaureate distance learning degree programs offered (minimal on-campus study). *Degree requirements:* For master's, thesis or alternative. *Entrance requirements:* For master's, minimum undergraduate GPA of 3.0. Additional exam requirements/recommendations for international students: Required—TOEFL (minimum score 550 paper-based; 213 computer-based). Electronic applications accepted. *Expenses:* Contact institution.

Ottawa University, Graduate Studies-Kansas City, Overland Park, KS 66211. Offers business administration (MBA); human resources (MA). Part-time and evening/weekend programs available. Postbaccalaureate distance learning degree programs offered (minimal on-campus study). *Degree requirements:* For master's, thesis or alternative. *Entrance requirements:* For master's, resume, 3 letters of recommendation. Additional exam requirements/recommendations for international students: Required—TOEFL (minimum score 550 paper-based; 213 computer-based). Electronic applications accepted. *Expenses:* Contact institution.

Ottawa University, Graduate Studies-Wisconsin, Brookfield, WI 53005. Offers business administration (MBA). Part-time and evening/weekend programs available. Postbaccalaureate distance learning degree programs offered. *Degree requirements:* For master's, thesis or alternative. *Entrance requirements:* For master's, resume, 3 letters of recommendation. Additional exam requirements/recommendations for international students: Required—TOEFL (minimum score 550 paper-based; 213 computer-based). Electronic applications accepted.

Otterbein University, Department of Business, Accounting and Economics, Westerville, OH 43081. Offers MBA. Part-time and evening/weekend programs available. *Degree requirements:* For master's, consulting project team. *Entrance requirements:* For master's, GMAT, 2 reference forms, resume. Additional exam requirements/recommendations for international students: Required—TOEFL (minimum score 550 paper-based; 213 computer-based; 79 iBT). *Expenses:* Contact institution. *Faculty research:* Organizational design, dispute resolution international trade, developing economies, marketing consumer goods, human resources development.

Our Lady of the Lake University of San Antonio, School of Business and Leadership, Program in Management, San Antonio, TX 78207-4689. Offers MBA. *Students:* 13 full-time (10 women), 113 part-time (61 women); includes 79 minority (10 African Americans, 1 American Indian/Alaska Native, 3 Asian Americans or Pacific Islanders, 65 Hispanic Americans), 1 international. Average age 34. In 2009, 56 master's awarded. *Expenses:* Tuition: Full-time $12,330; part-time $685 per contact hour. Required fees: $139; $12 per contact hour. $57 per semester. Tuition and fees vary according to campus/location. *Unit head:* Dr. Robert Bisking, Dean, 210-434-6711, Fax: 210-434-0821, E-mail: rbisking@ollusa.edu. *Application contact:* Dr. Robert Bisking, Dean, 210-434-6711, Fax: 210-434-0821, E-mail: rbisking@ollusa.edu.

Pace University, Lubin School of Business, New York, NY 10038. Offers MBA, MS, DPS, APC. *Accreditation:* AACSB. Part-time and evening/weekend programs available. Postbaccalaureate distance learning degree programs offered (minimal on-campus study). *Students:* 231 full-time (104 women), 926 part-time (409 women); includes 190 minority (50 African Americans, 1 American Indian/Alaska Native, 109 Asian Americans or Pacific Islanders, 30 Hispanic Americans), 434 international. Average age 27. 1,559 applicants, 73% accepted, 335 enrolled. In 2009, 352 master's, 11 doctorates, 2 other advanced degrees awarded. *Degree requirements:* For doctorate, thesis/dissertation, oral and written exams. *Entrance requirements:* For master's, GMAT; for doctorate, GMAT, interview. Additional exam requirements/recommendations for international students: Required—TOEFL. *Application deadline:* For fall admission, 7/31 priority date for domestic students; for spring admission, 11/30 for domestic students. Applications are processed on a rolling basis. Application fee: $70. Electronic applications accepted. *Expenses:* Contact institution. *Financial support:* Research assistantships, career-related internships or fieldwork, Federal Work-Study, and tuition waivers (full and partial) available. Support available to part-time students. Financial award applicants required to submit FAFSA. *Unit head:* Joseph R. Baczko, Dean, 212-346-1963. *Application contact:* Susan Ford-Goldschein, Director of Admissions, 212-346-1652, Fax: 212-346-1585, E-mail: gradnyc@pace.edu.

Pacific Lutheran University, Division of Graduate Studies, School of Business, Tacoma, WA 98447. Offers business administration (MBA), including technology and innovation management. *Accreditation:* AACSB. Part-time and evening/weekend programs available. *Entrance requirements:* For master's, GMAT. Additional exam requirements/recommendations for international students: Required—TOEFL (minimum score 550 paper-based; 213 computer-based).

Pacific States University, College of Business, Los Angeles, CA 90006. Offers accounting (MBA); business administration (DBA); finance (MBA); international business (MBA); management of information technology (MBA); real estate management (MBA). Part-time and evening/weekend programs available. Postbaccalaureate distance learning degree programs offered (no on-campus study). *Entrance requirements:* For master's, minimum undergraduate GPA of 2.5 during last 90 hours of course work. Additional exam requirements/recommendations for international students: Required—TOEFL (minimum score 133 computer-based).

Palm Beach Atlantic University, Rinker School of Business, West Palm Beach, FL 33416-4708. Offers MBA. Part-time and evening/weekend programs available. *Faculty:* 8 part-time/adjunct (2 women). *Students:* 38 full-time (15 women), 81 part-time (43 women); includes 28 minority (16 African Americans, 1 American Indian/Alaska Native, 2 Asian Americans or Pacific Islanders, 9 Hispanic Americans), 23 international. Average age 32. 69 applicants, 62% accepted, 43 enrolled. In 2009, 57 master's awarded. *Entrance requirements:* For master's, GMAT, minimum GPA of 3.0. Additional exam requirements/recommendations for international students: Required—TOEFL (minimum score 550 paper-based; 213 computer-based). *Application deadline:* For fall admission, 7/15 priority date for domestic students; for spring admission, 11/15 priority date for domestic students. Applications are processed on a rolling basis. Application fee: $45. Electronic applications accepted. *Expenses:* Tuition: Full-time $8010; part-time $445 per credit hour. Required fees: $99 per semester. Tuition and fees vary according to course load and degree level. *Financial support:* Applicants required to submit FAFSA. *Unit head:* Dr. Edgar Langlois, MBA Program Director, 561-803-2462, E-mail: edgar_langlois@pba.edu. *Application contact:* Graduate Admissions, 888-468-6722, Fax: 561-803-2115, E-mail: grad@pba.edu.

Park University, College of Graduate and Professional Studies, Kansas City, MO 54105. Offers adult education (M Ed); at-risk students (M Ed); disaster and emergency management (MPA); educational administration (M Ed); entrepreneurship (MBA); general business (MBA); general education (M Ed); government/business relations (MPA); healthcare/services management (MBA, MPA); international business (MBA); K-12 certification (MAT); management information systems (MBA); management of information systems (MPA); middle school certification (MAT); multi-cultural education (M Ed); nonprofit management (MPA); public management (MPA); school law (M Ed); secondary school certification (MAT); special education (M Ed). Part-time and evening/weekend programs available. Postbaccalaureate distance learning degree programs offered (no on-campus study). *Degree requirements:* For master's, comprehensive exam, thesis (for some programs). *Entrance requirements:* For master's, GRE, GMAT, teacher certification (M Ed). Additional exam requirements/recommendations for international students: Required—TOEFL (minimum score 550 paper-based). Electronic applications accepted. *Faculty research:* Literacy, leadership, brain based research, multicultural education, diversity.

Penn State Great Valley, Graduate Studies, Management Division, Malvern, PA 19355-1488. Offers M Fin, MBA, MLD. *Unit head:* Dr. Daniel Indro, Division Head, 610-725-5283, Fax: 610-725-5224, E-mail: dci1@psu.edu. *Application contact:* Dr. Daniel Indro, Division Head, 610-725-5283, Fax: 610-725-5224, E-mail: dci1@psu.edu.

Penn State Harrisburg, Graduate School, School of Business Administration, Program in Business Administration, Middletown, PA 17057-4898. Offers MBA, MBA/JD, MBA/PhD. *Accreditation:* AACSB. *Entrance requirements:* For master's, GMAT.

Penn State University Park, Graduate School, Intercollege Graduate Programs, State College, University Park, PA 16802-1503. Offers acoustics (M Eng, MS, PhD); bioengineering (MS, PhD); biogeochemistry (dual) (PhD); business administration (MBA); cell and developmental biology (PhD); demography (dual) (MA); ecology (MS, PhD); environmental pollution control (MEPC, MS); genetics (MS, PhD); human dimensions of natural resources and the environment (dual) (MA, MS, PhD); immunology and infectious diseases (MS); integrative biosciences (MS, PhD), including integrative biosciences; materials science and engineering (PhD); operations research (dual) (M Eng, MA, MS, PhD); physiology (MS, PhD); plant physiology (MS, PhD); quality and manufacturing management (MMM). *Students:* 371 full-time (157 women), 22 part-time (7 women). Average age 27. 1,074 applicants, 18% accepted, 130 enrolled. *Entrance requirements:* Additional exam requirements/recommendations for international students: Required—TOEFL (minimum score 550 paper-based; 213 computer-based; 80 iBT). *Application deadline:* Applications are processed on a rolling basis. Application fee: $45. Electronic

Business Administration and Management—General

Penn State University Park (continued)
applications accepted. *Financial support:* Fellowships, research assistantships, teaching assistantships available. Financial award applicants required to submit FAFSA. *Unit head:* Dr. Regina Vasilatos-Younken, Senior Associate Dean, 814-865-2516, Fax: 814-863-4627, E-mail: rxv@psu.edu. *Application contact:* Cynthia E. Nicosia, Director, Graduate Enrollment Services, 814-865-1795, Fax: 814-865-4627, E-mail: cey1@psu.edu.

Pepperdine University, Graziadio School of Business and Management, Malibu, CA 90263. Offers applied finance (MS); business administration (MBA); fully-employed (MBA); international business administration (IMBA); management and leadership (MS); organizational development (MSOD); presidential and key executive business administration (Exec MBA). *Accreditation:* AACSB. Part-time and evening/weekend programs available. *Faculty:* 86 full-time (18 women), 49 part-time/adjunct (12 women). *Students:* 872 full-time (343 women), 804 part-time (357 women); includes 530 minority (76 African Americans, 7 American Indian/Alaska Native, 306 Asian Americans or Pacific Islanders, 141 Hispanic Americans), 162 international. *Entrance requirements:* For master's, GMAT or MAT. Additional exam requirements/recommendations for international students: Required—TOEFL (minimum score 550 paper-based). *Application deadline:* For fall admission, 6/28 for domestic students. Applications are processed on a rolling basis. Application fee: $45. *Expenses:* Contact institution. *Financial support:* Career-related internships or fieldwork, institutionally sponsored loans, scholarships/grants, and unspecified assistantships available. Support available to part-time students. Financial award applicants required to submit FAFSA. *Unit head:* Dr. Linda A. Livingstone, Dean, 310-568-5689, Fax: 310-568-5766, E-mail: linda.livingstone@pepperdine.edu. *Application contact:* Darrell Eriksen, Director of Admission and Student Accounts, 310-568-5525, E-mail: darrell.eriksen@pepperdine.edu.

Pfeiffer University, Program in Business Administration, Misenheimer, NC 28109-0960. Offers business administration (MBA); organizational management (MS); MBA/MHA; MBA/MS. Part-time and evening/weekend programs available. Postbaccalaureate distance learning degree programs offered (minimal on-campus study). *Entrance requirements:* For master's, GMAT, minimum GPA of 3.0.

Philadelphia University, School of Business Administration, Program in Business Administration, Philadelphia, PA 19144. Offers business administration (MBA); finance (MBA); health care management (MBA); international business (MBA); marketing (MBA); MBA/MS. Part-time and evening/weekend programs available. Postbaccalaureate distance learning degree programs offered (no on-campus study). *Entrance requirements:* For master's, GMAT. Additional exam requirements/recommendations for international students: Required—TOEFL (minimum score 550 paper-based; 213 computer-based; 79 iBT).

Phillips Theological Seminary, Programs in Theology, Tulsa, OK 74116. Offers administration of church agencies (M Div); campus ministry (M Div); church-related social work (M Div); college and seminary teaching (M Div); global mission work (M Div); institutional chaplaincy (M Div); ministerial vocations in Christian education (M Div); ministry (D Min), including parish ministry, pastoral counseling, practices of ministry; ministry and culture (MAMC), including Christian education, congregational leadership, history and practice of Christian spirituality, theology, ethics, and culture; ministry of music (M Div); pastoral care and counseling (M Div); pastoral ministry (M Div); theological studies (MTS). *Accreditation:* ATS. Part-time programs available. Postbaccalaureate distance learning degree programs offered (minimal on-campus study). *Degree requirements:* For master's, thesis (for some programs); for doctorate, thesis/dissertation. *Entrance requirements:* For master's, minimum GPA of 2.5; for doctorate, M Div, minimum GPA of 3.0. *Faculty research:* Biblical studies, historical studies, theology and culture, practical theology, theology and film.

Piedmont College, School of Business, Demorest, GA 30535-0010. Offers MBA. *Accreditation:* ACBSP. *Entrance requirements:* For master's, GMAT, GRE or MAT, minimum GPA of 2.5. Additional exam requirements/recommendations for international students: Required—TOEFL (minimum score 550 paper-based; 213 computer-based).

Pittsburg State University, Graduate School, Kelce College of Business, Department of Management and Marketing, Pittsburg, KS 66762. Offers general administration (MBA). *Accreditation:* AACSB. *Degree requirements:* For master's, thesis or alternative. *Entrance requirements:* For master's, GMAT. *Expenses:* Tuition, state resident: full-time $4212; part-time $176 per credit. Tuition, nonresident: full-time $11,530; part-time $480 per credit. Required fees: $940; $43 per credit. Tuition and fees vary according to course level, course load, degree level, campus/location, reciprocity agreements and student level. *Faculty research:* Consumer behavior, productions management, forecasting interest rate swaps, strategy management.

Plymouth State University, College of Graduate Studies, Department of Graduate Studies in Business, Plymouth, NH 03264-1595. Offers MBA. *Accreditation:* ACBSP. Part-time and evening/weekend programs available. *Entrance requirements:* For master's, minimum GPA of 2.5. Additional exam requirements/recommendations for international students: Required—TOEFL (minimum score 550 paper-based). *Expenses:* Contact institution.

Point Loma Nazarene University, Program in Business Administration, San Diego, CA 92106-2899. Offers MBA. *Accreditation:* ACBSP. Part-time and evening/weekend programs available. *Students:* 47 full-time (18 women), 33 part-time (16 women); includes 20 minority (2 African Americans, 1 American Indian/Alaska Native, 12 Asian Americans or Pacific Islanders, 5 Hispanic Americans). Average age 32. In 2009, 12 master's awarded. *Entrance requirements:* For master's, GMAT, letters of recommendation. Application fee: $35. *Unit head:* Dr. Bruce Schooling, Dean, 619-849-2667, E-mail: bruceschooling@pointloma.edu. *Application contact:* Dejon Davis, Director of Graduate Admission, 619-563-2846, E-mail: dejondavis@pointloma.edu.

Point Park University, School of Business, Pittsburgh, PA 15222-1984. Offers business (MBA); organizational leadership (MA). Part-time and evening/weekend programs available. *Faculty:* 13 full-time, 18 part-time/adjunct. *Students:* 151 full-time (84 women), 236 part-time (118 women); includes 102 minority (92 African Americans, 2 American Indian/Alaska Native, 6 Asian Americans or Pacific Islanders, 2 Hispanic Americans), 29 international. Average age 33. 416 applicants, 67% accepted, 194 enrolled. In 2009, 186 master's awarded. *Degree requirements:* For master's, comprehensive exam (for some programs), thesis or alternative. *Entrance requirements:* For master's, minimum QPA of 2.75; 2 letters of recommendation; resume (MA). Additional exam requirements/recommendations for international students: Required—TOEFL (minimum score 550 paper-based; 79 iBT). *Application deadline:* Applications are processed on a rolling basis. Application fee: $30. Electronic applications accepted. *Expenses:* Tuition: Full-time $11,880; part-time $660 per credit. Required fees: $486; $27 per credit. *Financial support:* In 2009–10, 122 students received support, including 6 research assistantships with full tuition reimbursements available (averaging $6,400 per year); scholarships/grants also available. Financial award application deadline: 4/15; financial award applicants required to submit FAFSA. *Faculty research:* Technology issues, foreign direct investment, multinational corporate issues, cross-cultural international organizations/administrations, regional integration issues. *Unit head:* Dr. Angela Isaac, Dean, 412-392-8011, Fax: 412-392-8048, E-mail: aisaac@pointpark.edu. *Application contact:* Marty M. Paonessa, Associate Director, Graduate and Adult Enrollment, 412-392-3915, Fax: 412-392-6164, E-mail: mpaonessa@pointpark.edu.

Polytechnic Institute of NYU, Department of Technology Management, Brooklyn, NY 11201-2990. Offers construction management (Advanced Certificate); electronic business management (Advanced Certificate); entrepreneurship (Advanced Certificate); human resources management (Advanced Certificate); information management (Advanced Certificate); management (MS); management of technology (MS); organizational behavior (MS, Advanced Certificate); project management (Advanced Certificate); technology management (MBA, PhD, Advanced Certificate); telecommunications and information management (MS); telecommunications management (Advanced Certificate). Part-time and evening/weekend programs available. *Faculty:* 5 full-time (1 woman), 26 part-time/adjunct (3 women). *Students:* 272 full-time (111 women), 103 part-time (41 women); includes 64 minority (20 African Americans, 1 American Indian/Alaska Native, 34 Asian Americans or Pacific Islanders, 9 Hispanic Americans), 193 international. Average age 30. 518 applicants, 57% accepted, 135 enrolled. In 2009, 148 master's awarded. *Degree requirements:* For master's, comprehensive exam (for some programs), thesis (for some programs); for doctorate, comprehensive exam, thesis/dissertation. *Entrance requirements:* For master's, GMAT, minimum B average in undergraduate course work. Additional exam requirements/recommendations for international students: Required—TOEFL (minimum score 550 paper-based; 213 computer-based; 80 iBT); Recommended—IELTS (minimum score 6.5). *Application deadline:* For fall admission, 7/31 priority date for domestic students, 4/30 priority date for international students; for spring admission, 12/31 priority date for domestic students, 11/30 priority date for international students. Applications are processed on a rolling basis. Application fee: $75. Electronic applications accepted. *Expenses:* Tuition: Full-time $21,492; part-time $1194 per credit hour. Required fees: $1160; $204 per course. *Financial support:* In 2009–10, 1 fellowship (averaging $26,400 per year) was awarded; research assistantships, teaching assistantships, institutionally sponsored loans, scholarships/grants, and unspecified assistantships also available. Support available to part-time students. *Unit head:* Prof. Bharadwaj Rao, Head, 718-260-3617, Fax: 718-260-3874, E-mail: brao@poly.edu. *Application contact:* JeanCarlo Bonilla, Director of Graduate Enrollment Management, 718-260-3182, Fax: 718-260-3624, E-mail: gradinfo@poly.edu.

Polytechnic Institute of NYU, Westchester Graduate Center, Graduate Programs, Department of Technology Management, Major in Management, Hawthorne, NY 10532-1507. Offers MS. Part-time and evening/weekend programs available. *Students:* 12 full-time (0 women), 10 part-time (2 women), 12 international. 3 applicants, 100% accepted, 3 enrolled. In 2009, 3 master's awarded. *Degree requirements:* For master's, comprehensive exam (for some programs), thesis (for some programs). *Entrance requirements:* Additional exam requirements/recommendations for international students: Required—TOEFL (minimum score 550 paper-based; 213 computer-based; 80 iBT); Recommended—IELTS (minimum score 6.5). *Application deadline:* For fall admission, 7/31 priority date for domestic students, 4/30 priority date for international students; for spring admission, 12/31 priority date for domestic students, 11/30 priority date for international students. Applications are processed on a rolling basis. Application fee: $75. Electronic applications accepted. *Financial support:* Institutionally sponsored loans, scholarships/grants, and unspecified assistantships available. Support available to part-time students. *Unit head:* Dr. Bharadwaj Rao, Department Head, 718-260-3617, E-mail: brao@poly.edu. *Application contact:* JeanCarlo Bonilla, Director of Graduate Enrollment Management, 718-260-3182, Fax: 718-260-3624, E-mail: gradinfo@poly.edu.

Polytechnic University of Puerto Rico, Graduate School, Hato Rey, PR 00919. Offers business administration (MBA), including general studies, management of information systems, management of international enterprises; civil engineering (ME, MS); computer engineering (ME, MS); computer science (MS); electrical engineering (ME, MS); engineering management (MEM); environmental management (MEPM); landscape architecture (M Land Arch); manufacturing competitiveness (MMC, MS); manufacturing engineering (ME, MS). Part-time and evening/weekend programs available. *Entrance requirements:* For master's, 3 letters of recommendation.

Polytechnic University of the Americas–Miami Campus, Graduate School, Miami, FL 33166. Offers business administration (MBA); engineering management (MEM). Part-time and evening/weekend programs available. Postbaccalaureate distance learning degree programs offered (no on-campus study). *Entrance requirements:* For master's, minimum GPA of 3.0. Electronic applications accepted.

Polytechnic University of the Americas–Orlando Campus, Graduate School, Winter Park, FL 32792. Offers business administration (MBA); civil engineering (MS); computer engineering (MS); electrical engineering (MS); engineering management (MEM). Part-time and evening/weekend programs available. Postbaccalaureate distance learning degree programs offered (no on-campus study). *Entrance requirements:* For master's, minimum GPA of 3.0. Electronic applications accepted.

Pontifical Catholic University of Puerto Rico, College of Business Administration, Ponce, PR 00717-0777. Offers MBA, PhD. Part-time and evening/weekend programs available. *Degree requirements:* For master's, thesis; for doctorate, comprehensive exam, thesis/dissertation. *Entrance requirements:* For master's, GRE, interview, minimum GPA of 2.75; for doctorate, 2 letters of recommendation, 2 years experience in a related field, interview.

Pontificia Universidad Catolica Madre y Maestra, Graduate School, Santiago, Dominican Republic. Offers administration (M Adm); architecture of interiors (M Arch); architecture of tourist lodgings (M Arch); banking and financial management (M Mgmt); civil law (LL M); construction administration (ME); corporate business law (LL M); criminal procedure law (LL M); environmental engineering (ME, MEE); finance (M Mgmt); history applied to education (M Ed); human resources (EMBA); insurance (M Mgmt); international business (M Mgmt); labor law and Social Security (LL M); logistics management (ME); marketing (M Mgmt); renewable energy (ME); strategic cost management (M Mgmt). *Entrance requirements:* For master's, curriculum vitae, interview.

Portland State University, Graduate Studies, School of Business Administration, Portland, OR 97207-0751. Offers MBA, MIM, MSFA, PhD. *Accreditation:* AACSB. Part-time and evening/weekend programs available. *Degree requirements:* For doctorate, thesis/dissertation. *Entrance requirements:* For master's, GMAT, minimum GPA of 2.75, 2 recommendations, resume, interview, BA/BS in business or economics. Additional exam requirements/recommendations for international students: Required—TOEFL (minimum score 550 paper-based; 213 computer-based).

Portland State University, Graduate Studies, Systems Science Program, Portland, OR 97207-0751. Offers computational intelligence (Certificate); computer modeling and simulation (Certificate); systems science (MS); systems science/anthropology (PhD); systems science/business administration (PhD); systems science/civil engineering (PhD); systems science/economics (PhD); systems science/engineering management (PhD); systems science/general (PhD); systems science/mathematical sciences (PhD); systems science/mechanical engineering (PhD); systems science/psychology (PhD); systems science/sociology (PhD). *Degree requirements:* For doctorate, variable foreign language requirement, thesis/dissertation. *Entrance requirements:* For master's, 2 letters of recommendation; for doctorate, GMAT, GRE General Test, minimum undergraduate GPA of 3.0. Additional exam requirements/recommendations for international students: Required—TOEFL. *Faculty research:* Systems theory and methodology, artificial intelligence neural networks, information theory, nonlinear dynamics/chaos, modeling and simulation.

Post University, Program in Business Administration, Waterbury, CT 06723-2540. Offers business administration (MBA); corporate innovation (MBA); entrepreneurship (MBA); finance (MBA); leadership (MBA); marketing (MBA). Postbaccalaureate distance learning degree programs offered.

Prairie View A&M University, College of Business, Prairie View, TX 77446-0519. Offers accounting (MS); general business administration (MBA). *Accreditation:* AACSB. Part-time and evening/weekend programs available. *Faculty:* 14 full-time (5 women). *Students:* 275 full-time (256 women), 429 part-time (126 women); includes 655 minority (622 African Americans, 1 American Indian/Alaska Native, 13 Asian Americans or Pacific Islanders, 19 Hispanic Americans), 25 international. Average age 23. In 2009, 38 master's awarded. *Entrance requirements:* For master's, GMAT, minimum GPA of 2.45. Additional exam requirements/recommendations for international students: Required—TOEFL. *Application deadline:* For fall admission, 7/1 for domestic students, 6/1 priority date for international students; for spring admission, 11/1 for domestic students, 10/1 priority date for international students. Applications are processed on a rolling basis. Application fee: $50. Electronic applications accepted. *Expenses:* Tuition, state resident: full-time $2200. Tuition, nonresident: full-time $5600. Required fees: $1720. Tuition and fees vary according to course load. *Financial support:* Research assistantships, career-related internships or fieldwork, Federal Work-Study, institutionally sponsored loans, and tuition waivers (partial) available. Support available to part-time students. Financial award application deadline: 4/1; financial award applicants required to submit FAFSA.

Faculty research: Operations, finance, marketing. Total annual research expenditures: $30,000. *Unit head:* Dr. Munir Quddus, Dean, 936-261-9217, Fax: 936-261-9241, E-mail: muquddus@pvamu.edu. *Application contact:* Dr. John Dyck, Director, Graduate Programs in Business, 936-261-9217, Fax: 936-261-9232, E-mail: jwdyck@pvamu.edu.

Providence College, Graduate Studies, School of Business, Providence, RI 02918. Offers accountancy (MBA); economics (MBA); entrepreneurship (MBA); finance (MBA); international business (MBA); management (MBA); marketing (MBA); not-for-profit (MBA); quantitative (MBA). Part-time and evening/weekend programs available. *Faculty:* 14 full-time (8 women), 7 part-time/adjunct (3 women). *Students:* 63 full-time (18 women), 46 part-time (19 women); includes 4 minority (2 African Americans, 2 Asian Americans or Pacific Islanders), 7 international. Average age 26. 43 applicants, 88% accepted. In 2009, 40 master's awarded. *Degree requirements:* For master's, thesis optional. *Entrance requirements:* For master's, GMAT. Additional exam requirements/recommendations for international students: Required—TOEFL (minimum score 550 paper-based; 213 computer-based; 80 iBT). *Application deadline:* For fall admission, 8/1 priority date for domestic and international students; for spring admission, 12/1 priority date for domestic and international students. Applications are processed on a rolling basis. Application fee: $55. *Expenses:* Contact institution. *Financial support:* In 2009–10, 34 research assistantships with full tuition reimbursements (averaging $8,400 per year) were awarded; Federal Work-Study, institutionally sponsored loans, and unspecified assistantships also available. Support available to part-time students. Financial award application deadline: 8/1; financial award applicants required to submit FAFSA. *Unit head:* Dr. MaryJane Lenon, Director, MBA Program, 401-865-2566, Fax: 401-865-2978, E-mail: mjlenon@providence.edu. *Application contact:* Katherine A. Follett, Administrative Coordinator, 401-865-2333, Fax: 401-865-2978, E-mail: kfollett@providence.edu.

Purdue University, Graduate School, Krannert School of Management, Doctoral Program in Management, West Lafayette, IN 47907-2056. Offers PhD. *Students:* 68 full-time (19 women); includes 6 minority (1 African American, 2 American Indian/Alaska Native, 2 Asian Americans or Pacific Islanders, 1 Hispanic American). Average age 34. 543 applicants, 3% accepted, 14 enrolled. In 2009, 10 doctorates awarded. *Degree requirements:* For doctorate, comprehensive exam, thesis/dissertation, dissertation proposal. *Entrance requirements:* For doctorate, GMAT or GRE. Additional exam requirements/recommendations for international students: Required—TOEFL (minimum score 575 paper-based; 233 computer-based); Recommended—TWE. *Application deadline:* For fall admission, 1/15 priority date for domestic and international students. Application fee: $55. Electronic applications accepted. *Financial support:* In 2009–10, fellowships with full tuition reimbursements (averaging $25,000 per year), research assistantships with partial tuition reimbursements (averaging $18,000 per year), teaching assistantships with full tuition reimbursements (averaging $10,000 per year) were awarded; institutionally sponsored loans, scholarships/grants, health care benefits, tuition waivers (full and partial), unspecified assistantships, and travel funds to present at a major conference also available. Financial award application deadline: 1/15. *Faculty research:* Accounting, finance, marketing, management information systems, operations management, organizational behavior and human resource management, quantitative methods/management science, strategic management. *Unit head:* Dr. R. A. Cosier, Dean, 765-494-4366. *Application contact:* Krannert PhD Admissions, 765-494-4375, Fax: 765-494-0136, E-mail: krannertphd@purdue.edu.

Purdue University, Graduate School, Krannert School of Management, Executive MBA Program, West Lafayette, IN 47907. Offers MBA. *Faculty:* 12 full-time (0 women), 3 part-time/adjunct (0 women). *Students:* 15 full-time (1 woman); includes 2 minority (both Asian Americans or Pacific Islanders). Average age 39. 45 applicants, 49% accepted. In 2009, 22 master's awarded. *Entrance requirements:* For master's, GMAT. Additional exam requirements/recommendations for international students: Required—TOEFL (minimum score 77 computer-based). *Application deadline:* For fall admission, 6/1 for domestic students. Application fee: $55. *Financial support:* Application deadline: 1/3. *Unit head:* Dr. R. A. Cosier, Dean, 765-494-4366. *Application contact:* Brenda Knebel, Director of Admissions, 765-494-0773, E-mail: krannertmasters@purdue.edu.

Purdue University, Graduate School, Krannert School of Management, GISMA Program, Hannover, IN 30625, Germany. Offers general business (MBA). *Faculty:* 25 full-time (3 women), 5 part-time/adjunct (0 women). *Students:* 54 full-time (17 women), 46 international. Average age 26. 114 applicants, 53% accepted, 54 enrolled. In 2009, 70 master's awarded. *Entrance requirements:* For master's, GMAT, letters of recommendation. Additional exam requirements/recommendations for international students: Required—TOEFL (minimum score 550 paper-based; 213 computer-based; 77 iBT). *Application deadline:* For fall admission, 7/31 for domestic students, 8/1 for international students. Applications are processed on a rolling basis. Application fee: $55 ($60 for international students). *Expenses:* Contact institution. *Unit head:* Dr. David Schoorman, Dean/Professor of Organizational Behavior and Human Resource Management, 765-494-4391, E-mail: schoor@purdue.edu. *Application contact:* Monika Baer, Director of Admissions, E-mail: mbaer@gisma.com.

Purdue University, Graduate School, Krannert School of Management, Master of Business Administration Program, West Lafayette, IN 47907. Offers MBA. *Faculty:* 102 full-time (29 women), 16 part-time/adjunct (1 woman). *Students:* 267 full-time (66 women); includes 45 minority (15 African Americans, 28 Asian Americans or Pacific Islanders, 2 Hispanic Americans), 113 international. Average age 28. 823 applicants, 36% accepted, 114 enrolled. In 2009, 137 master's awarded. *Entrance requirements:* For master's, GMAT, four-year baccalaureate degree, minimum GPA of 3.0, essays, recommendation letters, work/internship experience. Additional exam requirements/recommendations for international students: Required—TOEFL (minimum score 550 paper-based; 213 computer-based; 77 iBT). *Application deadline:* For fall admission, 1/10 priority date for domestic students, 2/1 for international students. Applications are processed on a rolling basis. Application fee: $55. Electronic applications accepted. *Financial support:* In 2009–10, 80 research assistantships, 20 teaching assistantships were awarded; scholarships/grants and unspecified assistantships also available. Financial award applicants required to submit FAFSA. *Unit head:* Dr. R. A. Cosier, Dean, 765-494-4366. *Application contact:* Brenda Knebel, Director, Master's and Executive Admissions, 765-494-0773, Fax: 765-494-9841, E-mail: krannertmasters@purdue.edu.

Purdue University, Graduate School, Krannert School of Management, Weekend Master of Business Administration Program, West Lafayette, IN 47907. Offers MBA. Part-time and evening/weekend programs available. *Faculty:* 8 full-time (1 woman), 1 (woman) part-time/adjunct. *Students:* 162 part-time (30 women); includes 47 minority (11 African Americans, 1 American Indian/Alaska Native, 28 Asian Americans or Pacific Islanders, 7 Hispanic Americans), 14 international. 90 applicants, 86% accepted, 59 enrolled. In 2009, 58 master's awarded. *Entrance requirements:* For master's, GMAT. Additional exam requirements/recommendations for international students: Required—or IELTS; Recommended—TOEFL (minimum score 77 iBT). *Application deadline:* For winter admission, 12/1 for domestic and international students. Applications are processed on a rolling basis. Electronic applications accepted. *Financial support:* Partial scholarships available. Financial award application deadline: 12/1; financial award applicants required to submit FAFSA. *Unit head:* Dr. R. A. Cosier, Dean, 765-494-4366. *Application contact:* JoAnn Whitford, Director of Admissions, 765-494-4580, E-mail: jwhitfor@purdue.edu.

Purdue University Calumet, Graduate School, School of Management, Hammond, IN 46323-2094. Offers accountancy (M Acc); business administration (MBA); business administration for executives (EMBA). Part-time and evening/weekend programs available. *Entrance requirements:* For master's, GMAT. Additional exam requirements/recommendations for international students: Required—TOEFL. Electronic applications accepted.

Queen's University at Kingston, Queens School of Business, Program in Business Administration, Kingston, ON K7L 3N6, Canada. Offers consulting and project management (MBA); finance (MBA); innovation and entrepreneurship (MBA); marketing (MBA). *Accreditation:* AACSB. *Degree requirements:* For master's, thesis optional, research project. *Entrance requirements:* For master's, GMAT, minimum B+ average. Additional exam requirements/recommendations for international students: Required—TOEFL. Electronic applications accepted. *Faculty research:* Management fundamentals, strategic thinking, global business, innovation and change, leadership.

Queens University of Charlotte, McColl School of Business, Charlotte, NC 28274-0002. Offers business administration (EMBA, MBA). *Accreditation:* AACSB; ACBSP. Part-time and evening/weekend programs available. *Degree requirements:* For master's, capstone course. *Entrance requirements:* For master's, GMAT, minimum GPA of 2.5. Additional exam requirements/recommendations for international students: Required—TOEFL. Electronic applications accepted. *Expenses:* Contact institution.

Quincy University, Program in Business Administration, Quincy, IL 62301-2699. Offers business administration (MBA); human resource management (MBA). Part-time and evening/weekend programs available. *Faculty:* 4 full-time (3 women). *Students:* 4 full-time (2 women), 26 part-time (7 women); includes 1 African American, 1 Hispanic American. In 2009, 24 master's awarded. *Entrance requirements:* For master's, GMAT, previous course work in accounting, economics, finance, management, marketing, and statistics. Additional exam requirements/recommendations for international students: Required—TOEFL. *Application deadline:* Applications are processed on a rolling basis. Application fee: $25. Electronic applications accepted. *Expenses:* Contact institution. *Financial support:* Available to part-time students. Applicants required to submit FAFSA. *Faculty research:* Macroeconomic forecasting, business ethics/social responsibility. *Unit head:* Dr. John Palmer, Director, 217-228-5432 Ext. 3070, E-mail: palmejo@quincy.edu. *Application contact:* Jennifer O'Donnell, Coordinator of Adult Studies, 217-228-5404, Fax: 217-228-5479, E-mail: admissions@quincy.edu.

Quinnipiac University, School of Business, Program in Business Administration, Hamden, CT 06518-1940. Offers chartered financial analyst (MBA); finance (MBA); healthcare management (MBA); information systems management (MBA); international business (MBA); management (MBA); marketing (MBA); JD/MBA. *Accreditation:* AACSB. Part-time and evening/weekend programs available. *Faculty:* 24 full-time (6 women), 12 part-time/adjunct (4 women). *Students:* 83 full-time (30 women), 106 part-time (36 women); includes 11 minority (2 African Americans, 1 American Indian/Alaska Native, 6 Asian Americans or Pacific Islanders, 2 Hispanic Americans), 13 international. Average age 29. 124 applicants, 79% accepted, 77 enrolled. In 2009, 63 master's awarded. *Entrance requirements:* For master's, GMAT, minimum GPA of 3.0. Additional exam requirements/recommendations for international students: Required—TOEFL (minimum score 575 paper-based; 233 computer-based; 90 iBT), IELTS (minimum score 6.5). *Application deadline:* For fall admission, 7/30 priority date for domestic students, 4/30 priority date for international students; for spring admission, 12/15 priority date for domestic students, 9/15 priority date for international students. Applications are processed on a rolling basis. Application fee: $45. Electronic applications accepted. *Expenses:* Tuition: Full-time $16,030; part-time $770 per credit. Required fees: $630; $35 per credit. *Financial support:* In 2009–10, 110 students received support. Federal Work-Study, tuition waivers (partial), and unspecified assistantships available. Support available to part-time students. Financial award application deadline: 4/15; financial award applicants required to submit FAFSA. *Faculty research:* Equity compensation, marketing relationships and public policy, corporate governance, international business, supply chain management. *Unit head:* Kimberly McKeage, MBA Program Director, 203-582-3676. *Application contact:* Jennifer Boutin, 800-462-1944, Fax: 203-582-3443, E-mail: jennifer.boutin@quinnipiac.edu.

Radford University, College of Graduate and Professional Studies, College of Business and Economics, Program in Business Administration, Radford, VA 24142. Offers MBA. *Accreditation:* AACSB. Part-time and evening/weekend programs available. *Faculty:* 33 full-time (4 women). *Students:* 33 full-time (15 women), 49 part-time (21 women); includes 6 minority (3 African Americans, 3 Hispanic Americans), 6 international. Average age 29. 71 applicants, 76% accepted, 35 enrolled. In 2009, 44 master's awarded. *Degree requirements:* For master's, comprehensive exam. *Entrance requirements:* For master's, GMAT, minimum GPA of 2.75, 2 letters of reference. Additional exam requirements/recommendations for international students: Required—TOEFL (minimum score 550 paper-based; 213 computer-based; 79 iBT). *Application deadline:* For fall admission, 12/1 for international students; for spring admission, 7/1 for international students. Applications are processed on a rolling basis. Application fee: $50. Electronic applications accepted. *Expenses:* Tuition, state resident: full-time $5086; part-time $211 per credit hour. Tuition, nonresident: full-time $12,608; part-time $525 per credit hour. Required fees: $2508; $105 per credit hour. *Financial support:* In 2009–10, 20 students received support, including 11 research assistantships with partial tuition reimbursements available (averaging $8,000 per year), 4 teaching assistantships with partial tuition reimbursements available (averaging $8,700 per year); career-related internships or fieldwork, Federal Work-Study, institutionally sponsored loans, scholarships/grants, and unspecified assistantships also available. Financial award application deadline: 3/1; financial award applicants required to submit FAFSA. *Unit head:* Elizabeth C. Jamison, Director of MBA, 540-831-6712, Fax: 540-831-6655, E-mail: rumba@radford.edu. *Application contact:* Graduate Admissions, 540-831-5431, Fax: 540-831-6061, E-mail: gradcollege@radford.edu.

Regent's American College London, Webster Graduate School, London, United Kingdom. Offers business (MBA); finance (MS); human resources (MA); information technology management (MA); international business (MA); international non-governmental organizations (MA); international relations (MA); management and leadership (MA); marketing (MA). Part-time programs available.

Regent University, Graduate School, School of Global Leadership and Entrepreneurship, Virginia Beach, VA 23464-9800. Offers business administration (MBA); management (MA); organizational leadership (MA, PhD, Certificate); strategic foresight (MA); strategic leadership (DSL). Part-time and evening/weekend programs available. Postbaccalaureate distance learning degree programs offered (minimal on-campus study). *Faculty:* 15 full-time (3 women), 10 part-time/adjunct (3 women). *Students:* 14 full-time (4 women), 407 part-time (156 women); includes 123 minority (97 African Americans, 3 American Indian/Alaska Native, 6 Asian Americans or Pacific Islanders, 17 Hispanic Americans), 59 international. Average age 41. 153 applicants, 55% accepted, 31 enrolled. In 2009, 110 master's, 52 doctorates awarded. *Degree requirements:* For master's, thesis or alternative, 3 credit hour culminating experience; for doctorate, thesis/dissertation. *Entrance requirements:* For master's, GRE, GMAT, minimum undergraduate GPA of 2.75, computer literacy survey, 2 recommendations, resume, transcripts, essay; for doctorate, GRE, GMAT, sample of writing, minimum 3 years of relevant experience, computer literacy survey, 2 recommendations, resume, essay, transcripts; for Certificate, writing sample, resume, transcripts. Additional exam requirements/recommendations for international students: Required—TOEFL (minimum score 577 paper-based; 233 computer-based). *Application deadline:* For fall admission, 5/1 priority date for domestic students; for spring admission, 10/1 priority date for domestic students. Applications are processed on a rolling basis. Application fee: $50. Electronic applications accepted. *Expenses:* Contact institution. *Financial support:* In 2009–10, 258 students received support. Career-related internships or fieldwork, scholarships/grants, and tuition waivers (full and partial) available. Support available to part-time students. Financial award application deadline: 9/1. *Faculty research:* Servant leadership, ethics and values, telecommuting and family values, organizational communications, distance education. *Unit head:* Dr. Bruce Winston, Dean, 757-352-4306, Fax: 757-352-4634, E-mail: brucwin@regent.edu. *Application contact:* Matthew Chadwick, Director of Admissions, 800-373-5504, Fax: 757-352-4381, E-mail: admissions@regent.edu.

Regis University, College for Professional Studies, MBA Program in Emerging Markets, Denver, CO 80221-1099. Offers MBA. Postbaccalaureate distance learning degree programs offered.

Regis University, College for Professional Studies, School of Management, Denver, CO 80221-1099. Offers accounting (MS); business administration (MBA); computer information technology (MSOL); executive internal management (Certificate); executive leadership (Certificate); finance (MBA); finance and accounting (MBA); human resource management (MSOL); international business (MBA); marketing (MBA); operations management (MBA); organization leadership (MS); organizational leadership (MSOL); project leadership and management (MSOL, Certificate); project management (Certificate); strategic business

Business Administration and Management—General

Regis University (continued)

(Certificate); strategic human resource (Certificate); technical management (Certificate). Offered at Colorado Springs Campus, Northwest Denver Campus, Southeast Denver Campus, Fort Collins Campus, Broomfield Campus, Henderson (Nevada) Campus, and Summerlin (Nevada) Campus and online. Part-time and evening/weekend programs available. Postbaccalaureate distance learning degree programs offered (no on-campus study). *Degree requirements:* For master's, thesis optional, capstone project. *Entrance requirements:* For master's, GMAT or essays, interview, 2 years of full-time business work experience, resume; for Certificate, GMAT. Additional exam requirements/recommendations for international students: Required—TOEFL, TOEFL or university-based test; Recommended—TWE (minimum score 5). Electronic applications accepted. *Faculty research:* Impact of Info Technology on Small Business Regulation of Accounting, International Project financing, Mineral Development, Delivery of Healthcare to rural indigenos communities.

Reinhardt University, Program in Business Administration (Alpharetta Campus), Alpharetta, GA 30005-4442. Offers MBA. Part-time and evening/weekend programs available. *Faculty:* 3 full-time (1 woman). *Students:* 22 full-time (11 women), 1 (woman) part-time; includes 3 minority (2 African Americans, 1 Asian American or Pacific Islander). Average age 35. 16 applicants, 100% accepted, 12 enrolled. In 2009, 9 master's awarded. *Degree requirements:* For master's, comprehensive exam. *Entrance requirements:* For master's, GRE (upper 50th percentile) or GMAT (minimum score 500), bachelor's degree with minimum GPA of 2.75, current resume, interview, 3 professional references. Additional exam requirements/recommendations for international students: Required—TOEFL. *Application deadline:* For fall admission, 5/7 for domestic and international students; for spring admission, 8/9 for domestic and international students. Applications are processed on a rolling basis. Application fee: $25. Electronic applications accepted. *Expenses:* Tuition: Full-time $16,500; part-time $325 per credit hour. One-time fee: $100. Tuition and fees vary according to course load and program. *Financial support:* Application deadline: 5/1. *Unit head:* Ray Schumacher, Admissions Counselor, 770-993-6971, Fax: 770-475-0263, E-mail: res@reinhardt.edu. *Application contact:* Ray Schumacher, Admissions Counselor, 770-993-6971, Fax: 770-475-0263, E-mail: res@reinhardt.edu.

Rensselaer at Hartford, Lally School of Management and Technology, Hartford, CT 06120-2991. Offers MBA, MS. Part-time and evening/weekend programs available. Postbaccalaureate distance learning degree programs offered (no on-campus study). *Faculty:* 11 full-time (2 women), 13 part-time/adjunct (2 women). *Students:* 38 full-time (10 women), 286 part-time (76 women); includes 97 minority (28 African Americans, 2 American Indian/Alaska Native, 46 Asian Americans or Pacific Islanders, 21 Hispanic Americans), 3 international. Average age 34. 67 applicants, 75% accepted, 50 enrolled. In 2009, 171 master's awarded. *Degree requirements:* For master's, capstone course. *Entrance requirements:* For master's, GMAT (MBA). Additional exam requirements/recommendations for international students: Required—TOEFL (minimum score 600 paper-based; 250 computer-based; 100 iBT). *Application deadline:* For fall admission, 8/30 priority date for domestic students, 8/1 priority date for international students. Applications are processed on a rolling basis. Application fee: $75. Electronic applications accepted. *Expenses:* Tuition: Full-time $31,800; part-time $1325 per credit hour. *Financial support:* Research assistantships, tuition waivers (full and partial) and unspecified assistantships available. Support available to part-time students. Financial award applicants required to submit FAFSA. *Unit head:* Dr. John Maleyeff, Area Coordinator, 860-548-7870, E-mail: maleyj@rpi.edu. *Application contact:* Kristin Galligan, Director, Enrollment Management and Marketing, 860-548-2480, Fax: 860-548-7823, E-mail: info@ewp.rpi.edu.

Rensselaer Polytechnic Institute, Graduate School, Lally School of Management and Technology, Troy, NY 12180-3590. Offers business (MBA); financial engineering and risk analysis (MS); management (MS, PhD); technology, commercialization, and entrepreneurship (MS). *Accreditation:* AACSB. Part-time and evening/weekend programs available. *Faculty:* 47 full-time (11 women), 18 part-time/adjunct (1 woman). *Students:* 145 full-time (46 women), 492 part-time (202 women); includes 152 minority (45 African Americans, 1 American Indian/Alaska Native, 79 Asian Americans or Pacific Islanders, 27 Hispanic Americans), 62 international. Average age 28. 437 applicants, 71% accepted, 196 enrolled. In 2009, 231 master's, 6 doctorates awarded. *Degree requirements:* For doctorate, thesis/dissertation. *Entrance requirements:* For master's, GMAT, 2 letters of recommendation, resume; for doctorate, GMAT or GRE General Test, 2 letters of recommendation. Additional exam requirements/recommendations for international students: Required—TOEFL (minimum score 600 paper-based; 250 computer-based; 100 iBT); Recommended—IELTS (minimum score 7). *Application deadline:* For fall admission, 3/15 priority date for domestic and international students. Applications are processed on a rolling basis. Application fee: $75. Electronic applications accepted. *Expenses:* Tuition: Full-time $38,100. *Financial support:* Fellowships with partial tuition reimbursements, career-related internships or fieldwork, institutionally sponsored loans, and scholarships/grants available. Financial award application deadline: 3/15; financial award applicants required to submit FAFSA. *Faculty research:* Technological entrepreneurship, operations management, new product development and marketing, finance and financial engineering and risk analytics, information systems. *Unit head:* Dr. Iftekhar Hasan, Acting Dean and Cary L. Wellington Professor, 518-276-6586, Fax: 518-276-2665, E-mail: lallymba@rpi.edu. *Application contact:* Michele M. Martens, Manager of Graduate Programs, 518-276-6586, Fax: 518-276-2665, E-mail: lallymba@rpi.edu.

Rice University, Graduate Programs, Jesse H. Jones Graduate School of Management, Houston, TX 77251-1892. Offers business administration (EMBA, MBA, PMBA); MBA/M Eng; MD/MBA. *Accreditation:* AACSB. Evening/weekend programs available. *Entrance requirements:* For master's, GMAT. Additional exam requirements/recommendations for international students: Required—TOEFL (minimum score 600 paper-based; 250 computer-based). Electronic applications accepted. *Expenses:* Contact institution. *Faculty research:* Marketing strategy, technology transfer initiatives, management accounting, leadership and change management, financial management.

The Richard Stockton College of New Jersey, School of Graduate and Continuing Education, Program in Business Administration, Pomona, NJ 08240-0195. Offers MBA. Part-time and evening/weekend programs available. *Degree requirements:* For master's, project. *Entrance requirements:* For master's, GMAT. Additional exam requirements/recommendations for international students: Required—TOEFL. *Expenses:* Tuition, state resident: part-time $497.36 per credit hour. Tuition, nonresident: part-time $765.61 per credit hour. Required fees: $129.12 per credit hour. Tuition and fees vary according to degree level. *Faculty research:* Business ethics, marketing channels development, event studies, total quality management.

Rider University, College of Business Administration, Lawrenceville, NJ 08648-3001. Offers M Acc, MBA. *Accreditation:* AACSB. Part-time and evening/weekend programs available. *Entrance requirements:* For master's, GMAT, minimum AACSB index of 1050, resume. Additional exam requirements/recommendations for international students: Required—TOEFL (minimum score 550 paper-based; 213 computer-based). Electronic applications accepted. *Expenses:* Contact institution.

Rivier College, School of Graduate Studies, Department of Business Administration, Nashua, NH 03060. Offers MBA. Part-time and evening/weekend programs available. *Faculty:* 4 full-time (2 women), 15 part-time/adjunct (4 women). *Students:* 30 full-time (16 women), 64 part-time (38 women); includes 11 minority (1 African American, 9 Asian Americans or Pacific Islanders, 1 Hispanic American). Average age 36. 38 applicants, 95% accepted, 13 enrolled. In 2009, 71 master's awarded. *Application deadline:* Applications are processed on a rolling basis. Application fee: $25. *Expenses:* Tuition: Part-time $447 per credit. *Financial support:* Available to part-time students. Application deadline: 2/1. *Unit head:* Maria Matarazzo, Division Chair, 603-897-8532, Fax: 603-897-8885, E-mail: mmatarazzo@rivier.edu. *Application contact:* Mathew Kittredge, Director of Graduate Admissions, 603-897-8129, Fax: 603-897-8810, E-mail: mkittredge@rivier.edu.

Robert Morris University, Graduate Studies, School of Business, Moon Township, PA 15108-1189. Offers business administration and management (MBA); human resource management (MS); nonprofit management (MS); taxation (MS). *Accreditation:* AACSB. Part-time and evening/weekend programs available. *Faculty:* 29 full-time (11 women), 3 part-time/adjunct (0 women). *Students:* 209 part-time (97 women); includes 11 minority (9 African Americans, 1 Asian American or Pacific Islander, 1 Hispanic American), 4 international. Average age 31. 126 applicants, 70% accepted, 54 enrolled. In 2009, 85 master's awarded. *Entrance requirements:* For master's, GMAT, letters of recommendation. Additional exam requirements/recommendations for international students: Required—TOEFL (minimum score 550 paper-based; 213 computer-based; 79 iBT). *Application deadline:* For fall admission, 7/1 priority date for domestic and international students; for spring admission, 11/1 priority date for domestic and international students. Applications are processed on a rolling basis. Application fee: $35. Electronic applications accepted. *Expenses:* Tuition: Part-time $765 per credit. Required fees: $15 per credit. Full-time tuition and fees vary according to degree level. Part-time tuition and fees vary according to program. *Financial support:* Research assistantships with partial tuition reimbursements, Federal Work-Study, institutionally sponsored loans, and unspecified assistantships available. Support available to part-time students. Financial award application deadline: 5/1; financial award applicants required to submit FAFSA. *Unit head:* Dr. Derya A. Jacobs, Dean, 412-397-2191, Fax: 412-397-2585, E-mail: jacobs@rmu.edu. *Application contact:* Deborah Roach, Assistant Dean, Graduate Admissions, 412-397-5200, Fax: 412-397-2425, E-mail: graduateadmissions@rmu.edu.

Robert Morris University Illinois, Morris Graduate School of Management, Chicago, IL 60605. Offers accounting (MBA); accounting/finance (MBA); human resource management (MBA); information technology (MIS); leadership (MBA); management/finance (MIS); management/human resource management (MBA). Part-time and evening/weekend programs available. *Faculty:* 16 full-time (6 women), 25 part-time/adjunct (9 women). *Students:* 275 full-time (169 women), 194 part-time (134 women); includes 267 minority (176 African Americans, 1 American Indian/Alaska Native, 26 Asian Americans or Pacific Islanders, 64 Hispanic Americans), 17 international. Average age 32. 202 applicants, 84% accepted, 135 enrolled. In 2009, 161 master's awarded. *Degree requirements:* For master's, 44 residency hours. *Entrance requirements:* Additional exam requirements/recommendations for international students: Required—TOEFL (minimum score 500 paper-based; 173 computer-based). *Application deadline:* Applications are processed on a rolling basis. Application fee: $30 ($100 for international students). Electronic applications accepted. *Expenses:* Tuition: Full-time $18,000; part-time $2000 per course. *Financial support:* In 2009–10, 420 students received support. Federal Work-Study, scholarships/grants, and tuition waivers available. Support available to part-time students. *Unit head:* Kayed Akkawi, Dean, 312-935-4244, Fax: 312-935-4248, E-mail: kakkawi@robertmorris.edu. *Application contact:* Courtney A. Kohn Sanders, Dean of Graduate Admissions, 312-935-4240, Fax: 312-935-4248, E-mail: ckohn@robertmorris.edu.

Roberts Wesleyan College, Division of Business, Rochester, NY 14624-1997. Offers nonprofit leadership (Certificate); strategic leadership (MS); strategic marketing (MS). Evening/weekend programs available. *Degree requirements:* For master's, thesis or alternative. *Entrance requirements:* For master's, GMAT, minimum GPA of 2.75, verifiable work experience. *Expenses:* Contact institution.

Rochester Institute of Technology, Graduate Enrollment Services, E. Philip Saunders College of Business, Graduate Business Programs, Executive MBA Program, Rochester, NY 14623-5603. Offers Exec MBA. *Accreditation:* AACSB. Part-time and evening/weekend programs available. Postbaccalaureate distance learning degree programs offered (minimal on-campus study). *Students:* 50 full-time (14 women), 1 (woman) part-time; includes 5 African Americans, 3 Asian Americans or Pacific Islanders, 3 international. Average age 39. 37 applicants, 92% accepted, 30 enrolled. In 2009, 23 master's awarded. *Degree requirements:* For master's, thesis. *Entrance requirements:* For master's, GMAT, minimum 6 years of work experience. Additional exam requirements/recommendations for international students: Required—TOEFL (minimum score 580 paper-based; 237 computer-based; 92 iBT), or IELTS (minimum score 7). *Application deadline:* For fall admission, 6/30 priority date for domestic students, 2/15 priority date for international students. Applications are processed on a rolling basis. Application fee: $50. *Expenses:* Contact institution. *Financial support:* In 2009–10, 41 students received support. Scholarships/grants available. Support available to part-time students. Financial award applicants required to submit FAFSA. *Faculty research:* Linking business strategies and requirements with the most appropriate selection and implementation of technology, impact of and barriers to preparation and implementation of strategic growth plans in small and medium size businesses. *Unit head:* Dr. Donald Wilson, Associate Dean/Director, 585-475-6798, Fax: 585-475-7450, E-mail: dwilson@saunders.rit.edu. *Application contact:* Diane Ellison, Assistant Vice President, Graduate Enrollment Services, 585-475-2229, Fax: 585-475-7164, E-mail: gradinfo@rit.edu.

Rochester Institute of Technology, Graduate Enrollment Services, E. Philip Saunders College of Business, Graduate Business Programs, Program in Business Administration, Rochester, NY 14623-5603. Offers MBA. *Accreditation:* AACSB. Part-time and evening/weekend programs available. *Students:* 107 full-time (38 women), 98 part-time (30 women); includes 15 minority (2 African Americans, 12 Asian Americans or Pacific Islanders, 1 Hispanic American), 60 international. Average age 27. 349 applicants, 58% accepted, 66 enrolled. In 2009, 110 master's awarded. *Degree requirements:* For master's, comprehensive exam (for some programs), thesis (for some programs). *Entrance requirements:* For master's, GMAT, minimum GPA of 2.5. Additional exam requirements/recommendations for international students: Required—TOEFL (minimum score 580 paper-based; 237 computer-based; 92 iBT), or IELTS (minimum score 7). *Application deadline:* For fall admission, 2/15 priority date for domestic and international students; for winter admission, 11/1 priority date for domestic students, 10/1 priority date for international students; for spring admission, 2/1 priority date for domestic students, 1/1 priority date for international students. Applications are processed on a rolling basis. Application fee: $50. *Expenses:* Tuition: Full-time $31,533; part-time $876 per credit hour. Required fees: $210. *Financial support:* In 2009–10, 111 students received support; research assistantships with partial tuition reimbursements available, teaching assistantships with partial tuition reimbursements available, career-related internships or fieldwork, scholarships/grants, and unspecified assistantships available. Support available to part-time students. Financial award applicants required to submit FAFSA. *Faculty research:* Strategic use of information technology to gain a competitive advantage, developing new statistical quality control techniques and revising the existing techniques to improve their performance corporate governance. *Unit head:* Peggy Tirrell, Associate Director of Graduate Business Programs, 585-475-2795, Fax: 585-475-7450, E-mail: ptirrell@saunders.rit.edu. *Application contact:* Diane Ellison, Assistant Vice President, Graduate Enrollment Services, 585-475-2229, Fax: 585-475-7164, E-mail: gradinfo@rit.edu.

Rockford College, Graduate Studies, Program in Business Administration, Rockford, IL 61108-2393. Offers MBA. Part-time and evening/weekend programs available. *Entrance requirements:* For master's, GMAT, 3 letters of recommendation. Additional exam requirements/recommendations for international students: Required—TOEFL (minimum score 550 paper-based; 213 computer-based; 79 iBT). Electronic applications accepted. *Faculty research:* Entrepreneurship, leadership, international business, services marketing, project management.

Rockhurst University, Helzberg School of Management, Kansas City, MO 64110-2561. Offers MBA. *Accreditation:* AACSB. Part-time and evening/weekend programs available. *Faculty:* 3 full-time (1 woman), 17 part-time/adjunct (3 women). *Students:* 167 full-time (65 women), 164 part-time (52 women); includes 25 minority (9 African Americans, 2 American Indian/Alaska Native, 6 Asian Americans or Pacific Islanders, 8 Hispanic Americans), 8 international. Average age 30. 171 applicants, 61% accepted, 98 enrolled. In 2009, 159 master's awarded. *Entrance requirements:* For master's, GMAT. Additional exam requirements/recommendations for international students: Required—TOEFL (minimum score 550 paper-based; 213 computer-based; 79 iBT). *Application deadline:* For fall admission, 7/25 priority date for domestic students; for spring admission, 12/15 for domestic students. Applications are processed on a rolling basis. Application fee: $0. Electronic applications accepted. *Financial support:* Career-

related internships or fieldwork available. Support available to part-time students. Financial award application deadline: 4/1; financial award applicants required to submit FAFSA. *Faculty research:* Offshoring/outsourcing, systems analysis/synthesis, work teams, multilateral trade, path dependencies/creation. *Unit head:* Dr. James Daley, Dean, 816-501-4201, Fax: 816-501-4650, E-mail: james.daley@rockhurst.edu. *Application contact:* Michele Haggerty, Director of MBA Admission, 816-501-4823, E-mail: michele.haggerty@rockhurst.edu.

Rollins College, Crummer Graduate School of Business, Winter Park, FL 32789-4499. Offers entrepreneurship (MBA); finance (MBA); international business (MBA); management (MBA); marketing (MBA); operations and technology management (MBA). *Accreditation:* AACSB. Part-time and evening/weekend programs available. Postbaccalaureate distance learning degree programs offered (minimal on-campus study). *Faculty:* 25 full-time (3 women), 8 part-time/adjunct (2 women). *Students:* 277 full-time (105 women), 192 part-time (79 women); includes 95 minority (26 African Americans, 31 Asian Americans or Pacific Islanders, 38 Hispanic Americans), 48 international. Average age 29. 373 applicants, 53% accepted, 140 enrolled. In 2009, 220 master's awarded. *Entrance requirements:* For master's, GMAT. Additional exam requirements/recommendations for international students: Required—TOEFL. *Application deadline:* For fall admission, 6/1 priority date for domestic students; for spring admission, 12/1 for domestic students. Applications are processed on a rolling basis. Application fee: $50. Electronic applications accepted. *Expenses:* Contact institution. *Financial support:* In 2009–10, 95 students received support, including 95 fellowships, 56 research assistantships (averaging $2,400 per year); career-related internships or fieldwork, scholarships/grants, tuition waivers (full), and unspecified assistantships also available. *Faculty research:* Sustainability, world financial markets, international business, market research, strategic marketing. *Unit head:* Dr. Craig M. McAllaster, Dean, 407-646-2249, Fax: 407-646-1550, E-mail: cmcallaster@rollins.edu. *Application contact:* Linda Puritz, Student Admissions Office, 407-646-2405, Fax: 407-646-1550, E-mail: mbaadmissions@rollins.edu.

Roosevelt University, Graduate Division, Walter E. Heller College of Business Administration, Program in Business Administration, Chicago, IL 60605. Offers MBA. *Accreditation:* ACBSP. Part-time and evening/weekend programs available. *Entrance requirements:* For master's, GMAT.

Rosemont College, Schools of Graduate and Professional Studies, Program in Business Administration and Management, Rosemont, PA 19010-1699. Offers business administration (MBA); management (MSM). Part-time and evening/weekend programs available. Postbaccalaureate distance learning degree programs offered. *Degree requirements:* For master's, thesis (unless seeking certificate). *Expenses:* Contact institution.

Rowan University, Graduate School, William G. Rohrer College of Business, Glassboro, NJ 08028-1701. Offers MBA. *Accreditation:* AACSB. Part-time and evening/weekend programs available. *Faculty:* 8 full-time (2 women), 3 part-time/adjunct (1 woman). *Students:* 52 full-time (24 women), 78 part-time (36 women); includes 36 minority (7 African Americans, 24 Asian Americans or Pacific Islanders, 5 Hispanic Americans). Average age 28. 63 applicants, 67% accepted, 33 enrolled. In 2009, 29 master's awarded. *Degree requirements:* For master's, thesis. *Entrance requirements:* For master's, GMAT, minimum GPA of 2.8. Additional exam requirements/recommendations for international students: Required—TOEFL. *Application deadline:* Applications are processed on a rolling basis. Application fee: $50. Electronic applications accepted. *Expenses:* Tuition, state resident: full-time $10,624; part-time $590 per semester hour. Tuition, nonresident: full-time $10,624; part-time $590 per semester hour. Required fees: $2320; $125 per semester hour. *Financial support:* Career-related internships or fieldwork, scholarships/grants, health care benefits, and unspecified assistantships available. *Unit head:* Dr. Mira Lalovic-Hand, Interim Associate Provost/Director of Graduate School, 856-256-5120, E-mail: lalovic-hand@rowan.edu. *Application contact:* Karen Haynes, Graduate Coordinator, 856-256-4052, E-mail: haynes@rowan.edu.

Royal Military College of Canada, Division of Graduate Studies and Research, Continuing Studies, Department of Business Administration, Kingston, ON K7K 7B4, Canada. Offers MBA. *Degree requirements:* For master's, thesis. *Entrance requirements:* For master's, GMAT, honours degree with second-class standing. Electronic applications accepted.

Royal Roads University, Graduate Studies, Applied Leadership and Management Program, Victoria, BC V9B 5Y2, Canada. Offers executive coaching (Graduate Certificate); health systems leadership (Graduate Certificate); project management (Graduate Certificate); public relations management (Graduate Certificate); strategic human resources management (Graduate Certificate).

Royal Roads University, Graduate Studies, Faculty of Management, Victoria, BC V9B 5Y2, Canada. Offers digital technologies management (MBA); executive management (MBA), including global aviation management, knowledge management, leadership; human resources management (MBA). Postbaccalaureate distance learning degree programs offered (minimal on-campus study). *Degree requirements:* For master's, thesis. *Entrance requirements:* For master's, 5-7 years of related work experience. Additional exam requirements/recommendations for international students: Required—TOEFL (paper-based 570; computer-based 233) or IELTS (paper-based 7) (recommended). Electronic applications accepted. *Expenses:* Contact institution. *Faculty research:* Global venture analysis standards; computer assisted venture opportunity screening; teaching philosophies, instructions and methods.

Rutgers, The State University of New Jersey, Camden, School of Business, Camden, NJ 08102-1401. Offers MBA, JD/MBA. *Accreditation:* AACSB. Part-time and evening/weekend programs available. *Entrance requirements:* For master's, GMAT, 2 letters of recommendation. Additional exam requirements/recommendations for international students: Required—TOEFL (minimum score 230 computer-based; 89 iBT). Electronic applications accepted. *Expenses:* Contact institution. *Faculty research:* Efficiency in utility industry, management information systems development, management/labor relations.

Rutgers, The State University of New Jersey, Newark, Graduate School, Program in Management, Newark, NJ 07102. Offers accounting (PhD); accounting information systems (PhD); computer information systems (PhD); finance (PhD); information technology (PhD); international business (PhD); management science (PhD); marketing (PhD); organization management (PhD). *Accreditation:* AACSB. *Degree requirements:* For doctorate, thesis/dissertation, cumulative exams. *Entrance requirements:* For doctorate, GMAT or GRE General Test, minimum undergraduate B average. Additional exam requirements/recommendations for international students: Required—TOEFL. Electronic applications accepted. *Faculty research:* Technology management, leadership and teams, consumer behavior, financial and markets, logistics.

Rutgers, The State University of New Jersey, Newark, Rutgers Business School–Newark and New Brunswick, Newark, NJ 07102. Offers M Accy, MBA, MQF, PhD, Certificate, JD/MBA, MBA/MS, MD/MBA, MPH/MBA, MS/MBA. *Accreditation:* AACSB. Part-time and evening/weekend programs available. Terminal master's awarded for partial completion of doctoral program. *Degree requirements:* For doctorate, thesis/dissertation. *Entrance requirements:* For doctorate, GMAT. Additional exam requirements/recommendations for international students: Required—TOEFL. Electronic applications accepted. *Expenses:* Contact institution. *Faculty research:* Finance/economics, accounting, international business, operations research, marketing, organizational behavior.

Sacred Heart University, Graduate Programs, John F. Welch College of Business, Fairfield, CT 06825-1000. Offers accounting (MBA); finance (MBA); management (MBA); marketing (MBA). *Accreditation:* AACSB. Part-time and evening/weekend programs available. Postbaccalaureate distance learning degree programs offered. *Faculty:* 33 full-time, 15 part-time/adjunct. *Students:* 36 full-time (12 women), 124 part-time (64 women); includes 28 minority (10 African Americans, 8 Asian Americans or Pacific Islanders, 10 Hispanic Americans), 6 international. Average age 32. 63 applicants, 71% accepted, 37 enrolled. In 2009, 41 master's awarded. *Degree requirements:* For master's, thesis or alternative. *Entrance requirements:* For master's, GMAT (preferred) or GRE General Test. Additional exam requirements/

recommendations for international students: Required—TOEFL (minimum score 550 paper-based; 213 computer-based; 75 iBT). *Application deadline:* Applications are processed on a rolling basis. Application fee: $50 ($100 for international students). Electronic applications accepted. *Expenses:* Contact institution. *Financial support:* Career-related internships or fieldwork, institutionally sponsored loans, and unspecified assistantships available. Support available to part-time students. Financial award applicants required to submit FAFSA. *Faculty research:* Management of organizations, international business management of technology. *Unit head:* Dr. John J. Petillo, Dean, 203-396-8084, E-mail: petilloj@sacredheart.edu. *Application contact:* Dean Alexis Haakonsen, Dean of Graduate Admissions, 203-365-7619, Fax: 203-365-4732, E-mail: gradstudies@sacredheart.edu.

Sage Graduate School, Graduate School, School of Management, Program in Business Administration, Troy, NY 12180-4115. Offers business strategy (MBA); finance (MBA); human resources (MBA); marketing (MBA); JD/MBA. Part-time and evening/weekend programs available. *Faculty:* 4 full-time (2 women), 6 part-time/adjunct (0 women). *Students:* 9 full-time (7 women), 68 part-time (44 women); includes 11 minority (5 African Americans, 2 Asian Americans or Pacific Islanders, 4 Hispanic Americans), 2 international. Average age 31. 50 applicants, 60% accepted, 17 enrolled. In 2009, 19 master's awarded. *Entrance requirements:* For master's, minimum GPA of 2.75, resume, 2 letters of recommendation. Additional exam requirements/recommendations for international students: Required—TOEFL (minimum score 550 paper-based; 213 computer-based). *Application deadline:* Applications are processed on a rolling basis. Application fee: $40. *Expenses:* Tuition: Full-time $10,620; part-time $590 per credit hour. *Financial support:* Fellowships, research assistantships, Federal Work-Study, scholarships/grants, and unspecified assistantships available. Support available to part-time students. Financial award application deadline: 3/1; financial award applicants required to submit FAFSA. *Unit head:* Daniel Robeson, Chair, Management Department, 518-292-1770, Fax: 518-292-5414, E-mail: robesd@sage.edu. *Application contact:* Wendy D. Diefendorf, Director of Graduate and Adult Admission, 518-244-2443, Fax: 518-244-6880, E-mail: diefew@sage.edu.

Saginaw Valley State University, College of Business and Management, Program in Business Administration, University Center, MI 48710. Offers MBA. *Accreditation:* AACSB. Part-time and evening/weekend programs available. *Faculty:* 23 full-time (4 women), 1 part-time/adjunct (0 women). *Students:* 76 full-time (24 women), 78 part-time (36 women); includes 5 minority (4 African Americans, 1 American Indian/Alaska Native), 87 international. Average age 28. 130 applicants, 85% accepted, 43 enrolled. In 2009, 28 master's awarded. *Entrance requirements:* Additional exam requirements/recommendations for international students: Required—TOEFL (minimum score 525 paper-based; 197 computer-based; 71 iBT). *Application deadline:* Applications are processed on a rolling basis. Application fee: $25. Electronic applications accepted. *Financial support:* Federal Work-Study and scholarships/grants available. Support available to part-time students. Financial award application deadline: 4/15; financial award applicants required to submit FAFSA. *Unit head:* Dr. Mark Potts, Assistant Dean of Graduate and Undergraduate Programs, 989-964-4064, E-mail: mdpotts@svsu.edu. *Application contact:* Dr. Mark Potts, Assistant Dean of Graduate and Undergraduate Programs, 989-964-4064, E-mail: mdpotts@svsu.edu.

St. Ambrose University, College of Business, Program in Business Administration, Davenport, IA 52803-2898. Offers business administration (DBA); health care (MBA); human resources (MBA). *Accreditation:* ACBSP. Part-time and evening/weekend programs available. *Faculty:* 19 full-time (4 women), 8 part-time/adjunct (3 women). *Students:* 29 full-time (11 women), 279 part-time (146 women); includes 16 minority (6 African Americans, 3 Asian Americans or Pacific Islanders, 7 Hispanic Americans). Average age 36. 95 applicants, 86% accepted, 82 enrolled. In 2009, 146 master's, 3 doctorates awarded. *Degree requirements:* For master's, comprehensive exam (for some programs), thesis or alternative, capstone seminar; for doctorate, comprehensive exam, thesis/dissertation, oral and written exams. *Entrance requirements:* For master's, GMAT; for doctorate, GMAT, master's degree. Additional exam requirements/recommendations for international students: Required—TOEFL. *Application deadline:* For fall admission, 8/15 priority date for domestic students; for winter admission, 12/15 for domestic students; for spring admission, 1/1 for domestic students. Applications are processed on a rolling basis. Application fee: $25. Electronic applications accepted. *Expenses:* Contact institution. *Financial support:* In 2009–10, 48 students received support, including 5 research assistantships with partial tuition reimbursements available (averaging $3,600 per year); career-related internships or fieldwork, scholarships/grants, tuition waivers (partial), and unspecified assistantships also available. Financial award application deadline: 3/15; financial award applicants required to submit FAFSA. *Unit head:* Joseph L. Kehoe, Director of MBA, 563-322-1142, Fax: 563-333-6268, E-mail: kehoejosephl@sau.edu. *Application contact:* Erin E. Leifker, Assistant MBA Director, 563-322-1165, Fax: 563-333-6268, E-mail: leifkererine@sau.edu.

St. Bonaventure University, School of Graduate Studies, School of Business, St. Bonaventure, NY 14778-2284. Offers general business (MBA); professional leadership (MS). *Accreditation:* AACSB. Part-time and evening/weekend programs available. *Faculty:* 22 full-time (5 women), 1 part-time/adjunct (0 women). *Students:* 74 full-time (24 women), 64 part-time (25 women); includes 6 minority (3 African Americans, 1 American Indian/Alaska Native, 1 Asian American or Pacific Islander, 1 Hispanic American), 5 international. Average age 30. 105 applicants, 60% accepted, 53 enrolled. In 2009, 123 master's awarded. *Entrance requirements:* For master's, GMAT. Additional exam requirements/recommendations for international students: Required—TOEFL (minimum score 550 paper-based; 225 computer-based; 85 iBT). *Application deadline:* For fall admission, 7/15 priority date for domestic students, 12/15 for international students; for spring admission, 12/1 priority date for domestic students, 3/15 for international students. Applications are processed on a rolling basis. Application fee: $30. *Expenses:* Tuition: Full-time $11,700; part-time $650 per credit. *Financial support:* In 2009–10, 11 research assistantships with full and partial tuition reimbursements were awarded; career-related internships or fieldwork and scholarships/grants also available. Support available to part-time students. Financial award application deadline: 4/15; financial award applicants required to submit FAFSA. *Faculty research:* Stock options, small business, market relationships, auditing, taxes, entrepreneurship family business. *Unit head:* Dr. John G. Watson, Dean, 716-375-2200, E-mail: jwatson@sbu.edu. *Application contact:* John B. Stevens, MBA Director, 716-375-7662, Fax: 716-375-2191, E-mail: jstevens@sbu.edu.

St. Cloud State University, School of Graduate Studies, G.R. Herberger College of Business, Program in Business Administration, St. Cloud, MN 56301-4498. Offers business administration (MBA); information assurance (MS). Part-time and evening/weekend programs available. *Faculty:* 62 full-time (17 women), 4 part-time/adjunct (1 woman). *Students:* 67 full-time (24 women), 151 part-time (62 women); includes 19 minority (2 African Americans, 3 American Indian/Alaska Native, 14 Asian Americans or Pacific Islanders), 32 international. 58 applicants, 90% accepted. In 2009, 63 master's awarded. *Degree requirements:* For master's, thesis or alternative. *Entrance requirements:* For master's, GMAT, minimum GPA of 2.75. Additional exam requirements/recommendations for international students: Required—Michigan English Language Assessment Battery; Recommended—TOEFL (minimum score 550 paper-based; 213 computer-based), IELTS (minimum score 6.5). *Application deadline:* For fall admission, 6/1 priority date for domestic students, 4/1 for international students; for spring admission, 10/1 priority date for domestic students, 8/1 for international students. *Financial support:* Federal Work-Study, scholarships/grants, and unspecified assistantships available. Financial award application deadline: 3/1. *Unit head:* Michele Mumm, Graduate Director, 320-308-3212, E-mail: michelem@stcloudstate.edu. *Application contact:* Linda Lou Krueger, School of Graduate Studies, 320-308-2113, Fax: 320-308-5371, E-mail: lekrueger@stcloudstate.edu.

St. Edward's University, School of Management and Business, Austin, TX 78704. Offers M Ac, MA, MBA, MS, Certificate. Part-time and evening/weekend programs available. *Faculty:* 28 full-time (12 women), 29 part-time/adjunct (6 women). *Students:* 73 full-time (35 women), 477 part-time (253 women); includes 198 minority (49 African Americans, 1 American Indian/Alaska Native, 24 Asian Americans or Pacific Islanders, 124 Hispanic Americans), 12 international. Average age 33. 274 applicants, 76% accepted, 161 enrolled. In 2009, 179 master's awarded. *Degree requirements:* For master's, minimum of 24 hours in residence.

Business Administration and Management—General

St. Edward's University (continued)
Entrance requirements: For master's, GMAT or GRE General Test, minimum GPA of 2.75 in last 60 hours of course work. Additional exam requirements/recommendations for international students: Required—TOEFL (minimum score 550 paper-based; 213 computer-based; 79 iBT) or IELTS (minimum score 6). *Application deadline:* For fall admission, 7/1 for domestic and international students; for spring admission, 11/1 for domestic and international students. Applications are processed on a rolling basis. Application fee: $45 ($50 for international students). Electronic applications accepted. *Expenses:* Tuition: Full-time $14,922; part-time $829 per credit hour. Required fees: $50 per trimester. Full-time tuition and fees vary according to course load and program. *Financial support:* In 2009–10, 17 students received support. Scholarships/grants available. *Faculty research:* Business ethics, organizational management, minority entrepreneurship, globalization, system design. *Unit head:* Marsha Kelliher, Dean, 512-448-8588, Fax: 512-448-8492, E-mail: marshak@stedwards.edu. *Application contact:* Kelly Luna, Graduate Admissions Coordinator, 512-233-1697, Fax: 512-428-1032, E-mail: kellyl@stedwards.edu.

Saint Francis University, Graduate School of Business and Human Resource Management, Loretto, PA 15940-0600. Offers business administration (MBA); human resource management (MHRM). Part-time and evening/weekend programs available. *Faculty:* 8 full-time (2 women), 25 part-time/adjunct (12 women). *Students:* 16 full-time (8 women), 141 part-time (66 women); includes 2 minority (both African Americans). Average age 32. 40 applicants, 88% accepted, 25 enrolled. In 2009, 67 master's awarded. *Entrance requirements:* For master's, 2 letters of recommendation, minimum GPA of 2.75. Additional exam requirements/recommendations for international students: Required—TOEFL (minimum score 550 paper-based; 213 computer-based; 57 iBT). *Application deadline:* For fall admission, 8/1 priority date for domestic and international students; for spring admission, 12/1 priority date for domestic students, 12/1 for international students. Applications are processed on a rolling basis. Application fee: $30. *Expenses:* Contact institution. *Financial support:* Fellowships with partial tuition reimbursements, career-related internships or fieldwork and unspecified assistantships available. *Unit head:* Dr. Randy Frye, Director, 814-472-3041, Fax: 814-472-3174, E-mail: rfrye@francis.edu. *Application contact:* Dr. Peter Raymond Skoner, Associate Vice President for Academic Affairs, 814-472-3085, Fax: 814-472-3365, E-mail: pskoner@francis.edu.

St. John Fisher College, Ronald L. Bittner School of Business, MBA Program, Rochester, NY 14618-3597. Offers MBA. *Accreditation:* AACSB. Part-time and evening/weekend programs available. *Faculty:* 13 full-time (3 women), 4 part-time/adjunct (1 woman). *Students:* 19 full-time (7 women), 72 part-time (36 women); includes 10 minority (3 African Americans, 5 Asian Americans or Pacific Islanders, 2 Hispanic Americans). Average age 29. 104 applicants, 54% accepted, 37 enrolled. In 2009, 25 master's awarded. *Degree requirements:* For master's, capstone project. *Entrance requirements:* For master's, GMAT, 2 letters of recommendation, personal statement, current resume, interview. Additional exam requirements/recommendations for international students: Required—TOEFL (minimum score 575 paper-based; 233 computer-based; 80 iBT). *Application deadline:* Applications are processed on a rolling basis. Application fee: $30. Electronic applications accepted. *Expenses:* Tuition: Part-time $680 per credit hour. Required fees: $25 per semester. Tuition and fees vary according to degree level and program. *Financial support:* In 2009–10, 66 students received support. Federal Work-Study and scholarships/grants available. Financial award applicants required to submit FAFSA. *Faculty research:* Business strategy, consumer behavior, cross-cultural management practices, international finance, organizational trust. *Unit head:* Edward Ciaschi, Program Director, 585-385-5266, E-mail: eciaschi@sjfc.edu. *Application contact:* Jose Perales, Director of Graduate Admissions, 585-385-8067, E-mail: jperales@sjfc.edu.

St. John's University, The Peter J. Tobin College of Business, Queens, NY 11439. Offers MBA, MS, Adv C, JD/MBA. *Accreditation:* AACSB. Part-time and evening/weekend programs available. *Faculty:* 97 full-time (22 women), 46 part-time/adjunct (7 women). *Students:* 518 full-time (277 women), 317 part-time (141 women); includes 177 minority (57 African Americans, 85 Asian Americans or Pacific Islanders, 35 Hispanic Americans), 324 international. Average age 26. 910 applicants, 69% accepted, 337 enrolled. In 2009, 323 master's, 1 other advanced degree awarded. *Degree requirements:* For master's, comprehensive exam (for some programs), thesis optional. *Entrance requirements:* For master's, GMAT, 2 letters of recommendation, resume; for Adv C, GMAT, 2 letters of recommendation, resume, undergraduate transcripts, essay. Additional exam requirements/recommendations for international students: Required—TOEFL (minimum score 500 paper-based; 173 computer-based; 61 iBT), IELTS (minimum score 5.5). *Application deadline:* For fall admission, 5/1 priority date for domestic and international students; for spring admission, 11/1 priority date for domestic and international students. Applications are processed on a rolling basis. Application fee: $70. Electronic applications accepted. *Expenses:* Contact institution. *Financial support:* In 2009–10, 355 students received support, including 47 research assistantships with full and partial tuition reimbursements available (averaging $17,490 per year); scholarships/grants also available. Support available to part-time students. Financial award application deadline: 3/1; financial award applicants required to submit FAFSA. *Unit head:* Dr. Victoria Shoaf, Interim Dean, 718-990-6458, E-mail: shoafv@stjohns.edu. *Application contact:* Nicole T. Bryan, Assistant Dean, 718-990-2599, Fax: 718-990-5242, E-mail: tcbgradadmissions@stjohns.edu.

Saint Joseph College, Department of Business, West Hartford, CT 06117-2700. Offers management (MS). Part-time and evening/weekend programs available. *Students:* 16 full-time (10 women), 38 part-time (26 women); includes 17 minority (8 African Americans, 5 Asian Americans or Pacific Islanders, 4 Hispanic Americans). *Entrance requirements:* For master's, 2 letters of recommendation. *Application deadline:* Applications are processed on a rolling basis. Application fee: $50. Electronic applications accepted. *Expenses:* Tuition: Part-time $595 per credit. Required fees: $30 per credit. Tuition and fees vary according to program. *Financial support:* Career-related internships or fieldwork and unspecified assistantships available. Support available to part-time students. Financial award applicants required to submit FAFSA. *Application contact:* Graduate Admissions Assistant, 860-231-5261, E-mail: graduate@sjc.edu.

St. Joseph's College, Long Island Campus, Executive MBA Program, Patchogue, NY 11772-2399. Offers EMBA.

St. Joseph's College, Long Island Campus, Program in Management, Patchogue, NY 11772-2399. Offers health care (AC); health care management (MS); human resource management (AC); human resources management (MS); organizational management (MS).

St. Joseph's College, New York, Graduate Programs, Program in Business, Field of Executive Business Administration, Brooklyn, NY 11205-3688. Offers EMBA.

See Close-Up on page 255.

Saint Joseph's College of Maine, Program in Business Administration, Standish, ME 04084. Offers quality leadership (MBA). Part-time programs available. *Entrance requirements:* For master's, 2 years work experience.

Saint Joseph's University, Erivan K. Haub School of Business, Philadelphia, PA 19131-1395. Offers MBA, MS, Post Master's Certificate, DO/MBA. *Accreditation:* AACSB. Part-time and evening/weekend programs available. Postbaccalaureate distance learning degree programs offered (minimal on-campus study). *Faculty:* 69 full-time (14 women), 31 part-time/adjunct (5 women). *Students:* 184 full-time (91 women), 819 part-time (317 women); includes 136 minority (69 African Americans, 1 American Indian/Alaska Native, 48 Asian Americans or Pacific Islanders, 18 Hispanic Americans), 90 international. Average age 32. In 2009, 331 master's awarded. *Entrance requirements:* For master's, GMAT, MAT, GRE, letters of recommendation, resume. Additional exam requirements/recommendations for international students: Required—TOEFL (minimum score: paper 550, computer 213, iBT 79) or IELTS (6.5). *Application deadline:* For fall admission, 7/15 priority date for domestic students, 4/15 priority date for international students; for spring admission, 11/15 priority date for domestic students, 10/15 priority date for international students. Applications are processed on a rolling basis. Application fee: $35. Electronic applications accepted. *Expenses:* Tuition: Part-time $729 per credit hour. Tuition and fees vary according to degree level and program. *Financial support:* In 2009–10, research assistantships with full and partial tuition reimbursements (averaging $4,000 per year), teaching assistantships with full and partial tuition reimbursements (averaging $4,000 per year) were awarded; fellowships, scholarships/grants and unspecified assistantships also available. Financial award application deadline: 5/1; financial award applicants required to submit FAFSA. *Faculty research:* Food marketing, agriculture, finance and accounting systems, advertising cues and effects. Total annual research expenditures: $2.1 million. *Unit head:* Dr. Joseph A. DiAngelo, Dean, 610-660-1645, Fax: 610-660-1649, E-mail: jodiange@sju.edu. *Application contact:* Janine N. Guerra, Esq., Assistant Director, MBA Program, 610-660-1695, Fax: 610-660-1599, E-mail: jguerra@sju.edu.

Saint Leo University, Graduate Business Studies, Saint Leo, FL 33574-6665. Offers accounting (MBA); business (MBA); criminal justice (MBA); health services management (MBA); human resource administration (MBA); information security management (MBA); marketing (MBA); sport business (MBA). Part-time and evening/weekend programs available. Postbaccalaureate distance learning degree programs offered (no on-campus study). *Faculty:* 31 full-time (5 women), 48 part-time/adjunct (17 women). *Students:* 1,433 full-time (856 women), 3 part-time (1 woman); includes 601 minority (429 African Americans, 8 American Indian/Alaska Native, 75 Asian Americans or Pacific Islanders, 89 Hispanic Americans), 11 international. Average age 37. In 2009, 405 master's awarded. *Entrance requirements:* For master's, GMAT (minimum score 500 if applicant does not have 5 years of professional work experience), bachelor's degree from regionally-accredited college or university with minimum GPA of 3.0 in the last 60 hours of coursework; 5 years of professional work experience; resume; 2 letters of recommendation. Additional exam requirements/recommendations for international students: Required—TOEFL (minimum score 550 paper-based; 213 computer-based; 80 iBT). *Application deadline:* For fall admission, 7/1 priority date for domestic students; for spring admission, 11/12 priority date for domestic students. Applications are processed on a rolling basis. Application fee: $75. Electronic applications accepted. *Expenses:* Contact institution. *Financial support:* In 2009–10, 1 student received support. Career-related internships or fieldwork, Federal Work-Study, and health care benefits available. Financial award application deadline: 3/1; financial award applicants required to submit FAFSA. *Unit head:* Dr. Robert Robertson, Director, 352-588-7390, Fax: 352-588-8585, E-mail: mba@saintleo.edu. *Application contact:* Jared Welling, Director, Graduate/Weekend and Evening Admission, 800-707-8846, Fax: 352-588-7873, E-mail: grad.admissions@saintleo.edu.

Saint Louis University, Graduate School, John Cook School of Business, Program in Business Administration, St. Louis, MO 63103-2097. Offers MBA. *Accreditation:* AACSB. Part-time and evening/weekend programs available. *Entrance requirements:* For master's, GMAT, letter of recommendation, resume. Additional exam requirements/recommendations for international students: Required—TOEFL (minimum score 570 paper-based; 230 computer-based; 88 iBT). Electronic applications accepted. *Expenses:* Contact institution.

Saint Martin's University, Graduate Programs, School of Business, Lacey, WA 98503. Offers MBA. Part-time and evening/weekend programs available. *Faculty:* 5 full-time (0 women), 5 part-time/adjunct (0 women). *Students:* 45 full-time (29 women), 29 part-time (18 women); includes 10 minority (3 African Americans, 6 Asian Americans or Pacific Islanders, 1 Hispanic American), 11 international. Average age 33. 34 applicants, 94% accepted, 28 enrolled. In 2009, 21 master's awarded. *Degree requirements:* For master's, thesis (for some programs). *Entrance requirements:* For master's, GMAT. Additional exam requirements/recommendations for international students: Required—TOEFL (minimum score 525 paper-based; 197 computer-based; 71 iBT). *Application deadline:* Applications are processed on a rolling basis. Application fee: $35. *Expenses:* Tuition: Full-time $12,440; part-time $827 per credit hour. *Financial support:* In 2009–10, 29 students received support. Career-related internships or fieldwork and scholarships/grants available. Support available to part-time students. Financial award application deadline: 3/1; financial award applicants required to submit FAFSA. *Unit head:* Dr. Haldon Wilson, Director, 360-438-4326, Fax: 360-438-4522, E-mail: hwilson@stmartin.edu. *Application contact:* Keri Olsen, Administrative Assistant, 360-438-4512, Fax: 360-438-4522, E-mail: kolsen@stmartin.edu.

Saint Mary's College of California, Graduate Business Programs, Evening MBA Program, Moraga, CA 94556. Offers MBA. Part-time and evening/weekend programs available. *Faculty:* 3 full-time (2 women), 6 part-time/adjunct (0 women). *Students:* 67 part-time (29 women); includes 15 minority (3 African Americans, 6 Asian Americans or Pacific Islanders, 6 Hispanic Americans), 2 international. Average age 28. 32 applicants, 78% accepted, 21 enrolled. In 2009, 33 master's awarded. *Degree requirements:* For master's, 4 half-day management practica. *Entrance requirements:* For master's, GMAT. Additional exam requirements/recommendations for international students: Required—TOEFL. *Application deadline:* Applications are processed on a rolling basis. Application fee: $50. *Expenses:* Contact institution. *Financial support:* Available to part-time students. Application deadline: 3/2. *Application contact:* Bob Peterson, Director of Admissions, 925-631-4505, Fax: 925-376-6521, E-mail: smcmba@stmarys-ca.edu.

Saint Mary's College of California, Graduate Business Programs, Executive MBA Program, Moraga, CA 94556. Offers MBA. Part-time and evening/weekend programs available. Postbaccalaureate distance learning degree programs offered (minimal on-campus study). *Faculty:* 25 full-time (8 women), 40 part-time/adjunct (10 women). *Students:* 59 applicants, 93% accepted, 46 enrolled. In 2009, 97 master's awarded. *Entrance requirements:* For master's, 5 years of management experience. Additional exam requirements/recommendations for international students: Required—TOEFL (minimum score 91 computer-based). *Application deadline:* Applications are processed on a rolling basis. Application fee: $50. *Expenses:* Contact institution. *Financial support:* Available to part-time students. Applicants required to submit FAFSA. *Unit head:* Dr. Guido Krickx, Program Director, 925-631-4514, Fax: 925-376-6521, E-mail: gak1@stmarys-ca.edu. *Application contact:* Bob Peterson, Director of Admissions, 925-631-4504, Fax: 925-376-6521, E-mail: bpeterso@stmarys-ca.edu.

Saint Mary's College of California, School of Liberal Arts, Leadership Studies Programs, MORAGA, CA 94556. Offers MA. Part-time and evening/weekend programs available. Postbaccalaureate distance learning degree programs offered (minimal on-campus study). *Faculty:* 5 full-time (2 women), 12 part-time/adjunct (9 women). *Students:* 1 full-time (0 women), 10 part-time (7 women); includes 1 minority (Hispanic American). Average age 42. In 2009, 55 master's awarded. *Degree requirements:* For master's, research project. *Entrance requirements:* For master's, letters of recommendation, interview. *Application deadline:* For fall admission, 8/1 priority date for domestic students; for winter admission, 12/1 priority date for domestic students; for spring admission, 3/31 priority date for domestic students. Applications are processed on a rolling basis. Application fee: $50. Electronic applications accepted. *Expenses:* Contact institution. *Financial support:* Available to part-time students. Applicants required to submit FAFSA. *Faculty research:* Leadership, organizational change, values, adult learning, transformative learning. *Unit head:* Kenneth Otter, Program Director, 925-631-8692, Fax: 925-631-9214, E-mail: kotter@stmarys-ca.edu. *Application contact:* Tammy Cabading, Manager, Marketing and Admissions, 925-631-4541, Fax: 925-631-9214, E-mail: tappling@stmarys-ca.edu.

Saint Mary's University, Faculty of Commerce, Halifax, NS B3H 3C3, Canada. Offers MBA, MF, PhD. *Accreditation:* AACSB. Part-time and evening/weekend programs available. *Degree requirements:* For master's, research project; for doctorate, thesis/dissertation. *Entrance requirements:* For master's, GMAT, minimum B average; for doctorate, GMAT or GRE, MBA or other master's-level degree, minimum B+ average. *Application deadline:* Applications are processed on a rolling basis. Application fee: $35. *Expenses:* Contact institution. *Financial support:* Research assistantships, scholarships/grants available. *Unit head:* Dr. David Wicks, Dean, 902-420-5422, Fax: 902-420-5892, E-mail: david.wicks@smu.ca. *Application contact:* Dr. David Wicks, Dean, 902-420-5422, Fax: 902-420-5892, E-mail: david.wicks@smu.ca.

St. Mary's University, Graduate School, Bill Greehey School of Business, San Antonio, TX 78228-8507. Offers business administration (MBA), including finance, international business, management; JD/MBA. *Accreditation:* AACSB. Part-time and evening/weekend programs available. Postbaccalaureate distance learning degree programs offered (minimal on-campus

study). *Degree requirements:* For master's, comprehensive exam. *Entrance requirements:* For master's, GMAT. Additional exam requirements/recommendations for international students: Required—TOEFL (minimum score 550 paper-based; 213 computer-based; 80 iBT). Electronic applications accepted. *Expenses:* Tuition: Full-time $8004. Required fees: $536. One-time fee: $5 full-time. Full-time tuition and fees vary according to program. *Faculty research:* International operations, job satisfaction, total quality management, taxation, stress management.

Saint Mary's University of Minnesota, Schools of Graduate and Professional Programs, Graduate School of Business and Technology, Business Administration Program, Winona, MN 55987-1399. Offers MBA. *Unit head:* Matthew Nowakowski, Director, 612-728-5142, Fax: 612-728-5121, E-mail: mjnowa05@smumn.edu. *Application contact:* Yasin Alsaidi, Director of Admissions for Graduate and Professional Programs, 612-728-5207, Fax: 612-728-5121, E-mail: yalsaidi@smumn.edu.

Saint Mary's University of Minnesota, Schools of Graduate and Professional Programs, Graduate School of Business and Technology, Management Program, Winona, MN 55987-1399. Offers MA. *Unit head:* Janet Dunn, Director, 612-238-4546, E-mail: jdunn@smumn.edu. *Application contact:* Yasin Alsaidi, Director of Admissions for Graduate and Professional Programs, 612-728-5207, Fax: 612-728-5121, E-mail: yalsaidi@smumn.edu.

Saint Michael's College, Graduate Programs, Program in Administration and Management, Colchester, VT 05439. Offers MSA, CAMS. Part-time and evening/weekend programs available. *Degree requirements:* For master's, portfolio. *Entrance requirements:* For master's, GMAT or GRE or 3 years of work experience, minimum undergraduate GPA of 2.8. Additional exam requirements/recommendations for international students: Required—TOEFL (minimum score 550 paper-based; 213 computer-based; 80 iBT), IELTS (minimum score 6). Electronic applications accepted. *Faculty research:* Learnership/leadership, international banking, top-quality management and organizational changes, national health care, management and ethics.

Saint Peter's College, Graduate Business Programs, MBA Program, Jersey City, NJ 07306-5997. Offers finance (MBA); health care administration (MBA); international business (MBA); management (MBA); management information systems (MBA); marketing (MBA); MBA/MS. Part-time and evening/weekend programs available. *Entrance requirements:* Additional exam requirements/recommendations for international students: Required—TOEFL. *Application deadline:* Applications are processed on a rolling basis. Electronic applications accepted. *Expenses:* Tuition: Part-time $971 per credit. *Financial support:* Career-related internships or fieldwork, Federal Work-Study, and institutionally sponsored loans available. *Faculty research:* Finance, health care management, human resource management, international business, management, management information systems, marketing, risk management.

St. Thomas Aquinas College, Division of Business Administration, Sparkill, NY 10976. Offers business administration (MBA); finance (MBA); management (MBA); marketing (MBA). Part-time and evening/weekend programs available. *Entrance requirements:* For master's, GMAT. Additional exam requirements/recommendations for international students: Required—TOEFL. Electronic applications accepted.

St. Thomas University, School of Business, Department of Business Administration, Miami Gardens, FL 33054-6459. Offers M Acc, MBA, Certificate. Part-time and evening/weekend programs available. *Degree requirements:* For master's, comprehensive exam. *Entrance requirements:* Additional exam requirements/recommendations for international students: Required—TOEFL (minimum score 550 paper-based; 213 computer-based; 79 iBT). Electronic applications accepted.

St. Thomas University, School of Business, Department of Management, Miami Gardens, FL 33054-6459. Offers accounting (MBA); general management (MSM, Certificate); health management (MBA, MSM, Certificate); human resource management (MBA, MSM, Certificate); international business (MBA, MIB, MSM, Certificate); justice administration (MSM, Certificate); management accounting (MSM, Certificate); public management (MSM, Certificate); sports administration (MS). Part-time and evening/weekend programs available. *Degree requirements:* For master's, comprehensive exam. *Entrance requirements:* For master's, interview, minimum GPA of 3.0 or GMAT. Additional exam requirements/recommendations for international students: Required—TOEFL (minimum score 550 paper-based; 213 computer-based; 79 iBT). Electronic applications accepted.

St. Thomas University, School of Leadership Studies, Program in Professional Studies, Miami Gardens, FL 33054-6459. Offers executive management (MPS). *Entrance requirements:* Additional exam requirements/recommendations for international students: Required—TOEFL (minimum score 550 paper-based; 213 computer-based; 79 iBT).

Saint Xavier University, Graduate Studies, Graham School of Management, Chicago, IL 60655-3105. Offers e-commerce (MBA); employee health benefits (Certificate); finance (MBA, MS); financial analysis and investments (MBA); financial planning (MBA, Certificate); financial trading and practice (MBA, Certificate); generalist/administration (MBA); health administration (MBA, MS); managed care (Certificate); management (MBA, MS); marketing (MBA); public and non-profit management (MBA); public health (MPH); service management (MBA); training and performance management (MBA); MBA/MS. *Accreditation:* ACBSP. Part-time and evening/weekend programs available. *Entrance requirements:* For master's, GMAT, minimum GPA of 3.0, 2 years of work experience. Electronic applications accepted. *Expenses:* Contact institution.

Salem International University, School of Business, Salem, WV 26426-0500. Offers information security (MBA); international business (MBA). Part-time programs available. Postbaccalaureate distance learning degree programs offered (no on-campus study). *Entrance requirements:* For master's, minimum undergraduate GPA of 2.5, course work in business, resume. Additional exam requirements/recommendations for international students: Recommended—TOEFL (minimum score 550 paper-based; 213 computer-based), IELTS (minimum score 6.5). Electronic applications accepted. *Expenses:* Contact institution. *Faculty research:* Organizational behavior strategy, marketing services.

Salem State College, School of Graduate Studies, Program in Business Administration, Salem, MA 01970-5353. Offers MBA. Part-time and evening/weekend programs available. *Students:* 22 full-time (12 women), 42 part-time (25 women); includes 5 minority (1 African American, 3 Asian Americans or Pacific Islanders, 1 Hispanic American), 11 international. Average age 32. 12 applicants, 92% accepted, 11 enrolled. In 2009, 19 master's awarded. *Entrance requirements:* For master's, GMAT. Additional exam requirements/recommendations for international students: Required—TOEFL (minimum score 550 paper-based; 80 iBT), or IELTS (minimum score 5.5). *Application deadline:* For fall admission, 5/1 for domestic students; for spring admission, 11/1 for domestic students. Applications are processed on a rolling basis. Application fee: $50. *Expenses:* Tuition, state resident: full-time $2520; part-time $275 per credit hour. Tuition, nonresident: full-time $4140; part-time $365 per credit hour. Required fees: $2430. *Financial support:* In 2009–10, 18 students received support. Career-related internships or fieldwork, Federal Work-Study, scholarships/grants, and unspecified assistantships available. Support available to part-time students. Financial award application deadline: 5/1; financial award applicants required to submit FAFSA. *Unit head:* Raminder Luther, Coordinator, 978-542-2229, E-mail: rluther@salemstate.edu. *Application contact:* Dr. Lee A. Brossoit, Assistant Dean of Graduate Admissions, 978-542-6673, Fax: 978-542-7215, E-mail: lbrossoit@salemstate.edu.

Salisbury University, Graduate Division, Department of Business Administration, Salisbury, MD 21801. Offers accounting track (MBA); general track (MBA). *Accreditation:* AACSB. Part-time and evening/weekend programs available. *Faculty:* 13 full-time (3 women), 1 part-time/adjunct (0 women). *Students:* 21 full-time (8 women), 43 part-time (20 women); includes 6 minority (2 African Americans, 1 Asian American or Pacific Islander, 3 Hispanic Americans), 9 international. Average age 31. 59 applicants, 46% accepted, 26 enrolled. In 2009, 41 master's awarded. *Entrance requirements:* For master's, GMAT, resume; 2 recommendations. Additional exam requirements/recommendations for international students: Required—TOEFL (minimum score 550 paper-based; 79 iBT). *Application deadline:* For fall admission, 3/1 priority date for domestic students; for spring admission, 10/15 priority date for domestic students. Applications are processed on a rolling basis. Application fee: $45. Electronic applications accepted. *Expenses:* Tuition, area resident: Part-time $278 per credit hour. Tuition, state resident: part-time $278 per credit hour. Tuition, nonresident: part-time $574 per credit hour. Required fees: $57 per credit hour. *Financial support:* In 2009–10, 13 students received support. Institutionally sponsored loans, scholarships/grants, and unspecified assistantships available. Support available to part-time students. Financial award applicants required to submit FAFSA. *Unit head:* Yvonne Downie, MBA Director, 410-548-3983, Fax: 410-546-6208, E-mail: yxdownie@salisbury.edu. *Application contact:* Yvonne Downie, MBA Director, 410-548-3983, Fax: 410-546-6208, E-mail: yxdownie@salisbury.edu.

Salve Regina University, Graduate Studies, Program in Business Administration, Newport, RI 02840-4192. Offers business administration (MBA); business studies (Certificate); human resources management (Certificate); management (Certificate); organizational development (Certificate). Part-time and evening/weekend programs available. Postbaccalaureate distance learning degree programs offered (minimal on-campus study). *Faculty:* 4 full-time (2 women), 13 part-time/adjunct (4 women). *Students:* 39 full-time (17 women), 89 part-time (39 women); includes 10 minority (5 African Americans, 3 Asian Americans or Pacific Islanders, 2 Hispanic Americans), 3 international. Average age 33. 62 applicants, 82% accepted, 45 enrolled. In 2009, 50 master's awarded. *Entrance requirements:* For master's, GMAT, GRE General Test, or MAT, 6 undergraduate credits each in accounting, economics, quantitative analysis and calculus or statistics. Additional exam requirements/recommendations for international students: Required—TOEFL (minimum score 600 paper-based; 250 computer-based; 100 iBT), or IELTS. *Application deadline:* For fall admission, 3/15 priority date for domestic and international students; for spring admission, 9/15 priority date for domestic and international students. Applications are processed on a rolling basis. Application fee: $60. Electronic applications accepted. *Expenses:* Tuition: Part-time $395 per credit. Part-time tuition and fees vary according to degree level. *Financial support:* Career-related internships or fieldwork and Federal Work-Study available. Support available to part-time students. Financial award application deadline: 3/1; financial award applicants required to submit FAFSA. *Unit head:* Dr. Myra Edelstein, Director, 401-341-3139, E-mail: edelstem@salve.edu. *Application contact:* Kelly Alverson, Graduate Admissions Counselor, 401-341-2153, Fax: 401-341-2973, E-mail: kelly.alverson@salve.edu.

Salve Regina University, Graduate Studies, Program in Management, Newport, RI 02840-4192. Offers MS, Certificate. Part-time and evening/weekend programs available. Postbaccalaureate distance learning degree programs offered (minimal on-campus study). *Faculty:* 4 full-time (2 women), 13 part-time/adjunct (4 women). *Students:* 10 full-time (7 women), 40 part-time (19 women); includes 2 minority (both African Americans). Average age 37. 26 applicants, 73% accepted, 18 enrolled. In 2009, 13 master's awarded. *Entrance requirements:* For master's, GMAT, GRE General Test, or MAT. Additional exam requirements/recommendations for international students: Required—TOEFL (minimum score 600 paper-based; 250 computer-based; 100 iBT). *Application deadline:* For fall admission, 3/15 priority date for domestic students, 3/5 priority date for international students; for spring admission, 3/15 priority date for domestic students, 9/15 priority date for international students. Applications are processed on a rolling basis. Application fee: $60. Electronic applications accepted. *Expenses:* Tuition: Part-time $395 per credit. Part-time tuition and fees vary according to degree level. *Financial support:* Career-related internships or fieldwork and Federal Work-Study available. Support available to part-time students. Financial award application deadline: 3/1; financial award applicants required to submit FAFSA. *Unit head:* Dr. Myra Edelstein, Director, 401-341-3139, E-mail: edelstem@salve.edu. *Application contact:* Kelly Alverson, Graduate Admissions Counselor, 401-341-2153, Fax: 401-341-2973, E-mail: kelly.alverson@salve.edu.

Samford University, Brock School of Business, Birmingham, AL 35229. Offers M Acc, MBA, JD/M Acc, JD/MBA, M Div/MBA, MBA/M Acc, MBA/MSN. *Accreditation:* AACSB. Part-time and evening/weekend programs available. *Faculty:* 11 full-time (3 women). *Students:* 87 full-time (37 women), 22 part-time (9 women); includes 12 minority (7 African Americans, 5 Asian Americans or Pacific Islanders), 1 international. Average age 26. 133 applicants, 81% accepted, 97 enrolled. In 2009, 43 master's awarded. *Entrance requirements:* For master's, GMAT. Additional exam requirements/recommendations for international students: Recommended—TOEFL (minimum score 550 paper-based; 213 computer-based). *Application deadline:* For fall admission, 7/31 priority date for domestic students, 6/1 for international students; for spring admission, 12/1 priority date for domestic students, 10/1 for international students. Applications are processed on a rolling basis. Application fee: $25. *Expenses:* Tuition: Full-time $26,660; part-time $595 per credit hour. Required fees: $110 per semester. *Financial support:* In 2009–10, 26 students received support. Career-related internships or fieldwork, institutionally sponsored loans, scholarships/grants, and tuition waivers (partial) available. Support available to part-time students. Financial award applicants required to submit FAFSA. *Faculty research:* Entrepreneurship, finance, organizational behavior, leadership, supply chain. *Unit head:* Dr. Beck Taylor, Dean, 205-726-2364, Fax: 205-726-2464, E-mail: btaylor@samford.edu. *Application contact:* Larron Harper, Director of Graduate Programs, 205-726-2931, Fax: 205-726-4555, E-mail: lcharper@samford.edu.

Sam Houston State University, College of Business Administration, Huntsville, TX 77341. Offers accounting (MS); business administration (MBA); general business and finance (MS), including finance. *Accreditation:* AACSB. Part-time and evening/weekend programs available. *Faculty:* 31 full-time (8 women). *Students:* 128 full-time (48 women), 101 part-time (44 women); includes 36 minority (11 African Americans, 1 American Indian/Alaska Native, 11 Asian Americans or Pacific Islanders, 13 Hispanic Americans), 31 international. Average age 29. 141 applicants, 83% accepted, 78 enrolled. In 2009, 97 master's awarded. *Entrance requirements:* For master's, GMAT. Additional exam requirements/recommendations for international students: Required—TOEFL (minimum score 550 paper-based; 213 computer-based; 79 iBT). *Application deadline:* For fall admission, 8/1 for domestic students; for spring admission, 12/1 for domestic students. Applications are processed on a rolling basis. Application fee: $20. *Expenses:* Tuition, state resident: full-time $3690; part-time $205 per credit hour. Tuition, nonresident: full-time $8676; part-time $482 per credit hour. Required fees: $1474. Tuition and fees vary according to course load and campus/location. *Financial support:* Research assistantships, Federal Work-Study, institutionally sponsored loans, and unspecified assistantships available. Financial award application deadline: 5/31; financial award applicants required to submit FAFSA. *Unit head:* Dr. Mitchell J. Muehsam, Dean, 936-294-1254, Fax: 936-294-3612, E-mail: mmuehsam@shsu.edu. *Application contact:* Dr. Leroy Ashorn, Advisor, 936-294-1246, Fax: 936-294-3612, E-mail: busgrad@shsu.edu.

San Diego State University, Graduate and Research Affairs, College of Business Administration, Department of Management, San Diego, CA 92182. Offers entrepreneurship (MS); human resources management (MS); management science (MS). Part-time and evening/weekend programs available. *Degree requirements:* For master's, thesis or alternative. *Entrance requirements:* For master's, GMAT, resume, letters of reference. Additional exam requirements/recommendations for international students: Required—TOEFL. Electronic applications accepted.

San Diego State University, Graduate and Research Affairs, College of Business Administration, Program in Business Administration, San Diego, CA 92182. Offers MBA. *Accreditation:* AACSB. Part-time programs available. *Degree requirements:* For master's, thesis or alternative. *Entrance requirements:* For master's, GMAT, resume, letters of reference. Additional exam requirements/recommendations for international students: Required—TOEFL. Electronic applications accepted.

San Francisco State University, Division of Graduate Studies, College of Business, San Francisco, CA 94132-1722. Offers MBA, MSBA.

San Jose State University, Graduate Studies and Research, Lucas Graduate School of Business, Programs in Business Administration, San Jose, CA 95192-0001. Offers MBA. *Accreditation:* AACSB. *Degree requirements:* For master's, comprehensive exam, thesis or alternative. *Entrance requirements:* For master's, GMAT, minimum GPA of 3.0. *Application deadline:* For fall admission, 6/29 for domestic students; for spring admission, 11/30 for domestic students. Applications are processed on a rolling basis. Application fee: $59. Electronic applications accepted. *Financial support:* Applicants required to submit FAFSA.

Business Administration and Management—General

Santa Clara University, Leavey School of Business, Program in Business Administration, Santa Clara, CA 95053. Offers accounting (MBA); entrepreneurship (MBA); executive MBA (EMBA); finance (MBA); food and agribusiness (MBA); international business (MBA); leading people and organizations (MBA); managing technology and innovation (MBA); marketing management (MBA); supply chain management (MBA). *Accreditation:* AACSB. Part-time and evening/weekend programs available. *Students:* 228 full-time (88 women), 838 part-time (265 women); includes 388 minority (17 African Americans, 2 American Indian/Alaska Native, 326 Asian Americans or Pacific Islanders, 43 Hispanic Americans), 218 international. Average age 31. 486 applicants, 77% accepted, 263 enrolled. In 2009, 317 master's awarded. *Degree requirements:* For master's, thesis or alternative. *Entrance requirements:* For master's, GMAT, GRE. Additional exam requirements/recommendations for international students: Required—TOEFL (minimum score 600 paper-based; 250 computer-based; 100 iBT). *Application deadline:* For fall admission, 6/1 for domestic and international students; for spring admission, 1/19 for domestic students, 1/17 for international students. Applications are processed on a rolling basis. Application fee: $75 ($100 for international students). Electronic applications accepted. *Expenses:* Contact institution. *Financial support:* Fellowships with partial tuition reimbursements, research assistantships with partial tuition reimbursements, career-related internships or fieldwork, Federal Work-Study, institutionally sponsored loans, scholarships/grants, health care benefits, and unspecified assistantships available. Support available to part-time students. Financial award applicants required to submit FAFSA. *Unit head:* Elizabeth B. Ford, Senior Assistant Dean, 408-554-2752, Fax: 408-554-4571, E-mail: eford@scu.edu. *Application contact:* Jennifer W. Taylor, Senior Director, 408-554-4539, Fax: 408-554-4571, E-mail: mbaadmissions@scu.edu.

Savannah State University, Master of Business Administration Program, Savannah, GA 31404. Offers MBA. *Accreditation:* AACSB. Part-time programs available. *Students:* 6 full-time (4 women), 12 part-time (9 women); includes 17 African Americans. In 2009, 10 master's awarded. *Entrance requirements:* For master's, GMAT or GRE. Additional exam requirements/recommendations for international students: Required—TOEFL (minimum score 550 paper-based; 240 computer-based; 96 iBT). *Application deadline:* For fall admission, 7/1 for domestic students, 5/15 for international students; for spring admission, 10/31 for domestic students, 10/1 for international students. Applications are processed on a rolling basis. Application fee: $20. Electronic applications accepted. *Expenses:* Tuition, state resident: full-time $3662; part-time $153 per credit hour. Tuition, nonresident: full-time $14,648. Required fees: $450 per term. *Financial support:* Career-related internships or fieldwork, Federal Work-Study, institutionally sponsored loans, scholarships/grants, and unspecified assistantships available. Financial award applicants required to submit FAFSA. *Unit head:* Dr. Mostafa Sarhan, Dean, College of Business Administration, 912-356-2335, E-mail: sarhanm@savannahstate.edu. *Application contact:* Emily Crawford, Interim Dean of Graduate Studies, 912-356-2244, E-mail: crawford@savannahstate.edu.

Schiller International University, MBA Program, Madrid, Spain, Madrid, Spain. Offers international business (MBA). Part-time programs available. *Degree requirements:* For master's, comprehensive exam, thesis optional. *Entrance requirements:* Additional exam requirements/recommendations for international students: Required—TOEFL (minimum score 550 paper-based; 213 computer-based).

Schiller International University, MBA Program Paris, France, Paris, France. Offers international business (MBA). Bilingual French/English MBA available for native French speakers. Part-time and evening/weekend programs available. Postbaccalaureate distance learning degree programs offered (no on-campus study). *Degree requirements:* For master's, comprehensive exam, thesis or alternative. *Entrance requirements:* Additional exam requirements/recommendations for international students: Required—TOEFL (minimum score 550 paper-based; 213 computer-based).

Schiller International University, MBA Programs, Florida, Largo, FL 33770. Offers financial planning (MBA); information technology (MBA); international business (MBA); international hotel and tourism management (MBA). Part-time and evening/weekend programs available. Postbaccalaureate distance learning degree programs offered (no on-campus study). *Degree requirements:* For master's, thesis optional. *Entrance requirements:* Additional exam requirements/recommendations for international students: Required—TOEFL (minimum score 550 paper-based; 213 computer-based).

Schiller International University, MBA Programs, Heidelberg, Germany, Heidelberg, Germany. Offers international business (MBA, MIM); management of information technology (MBA). Part-time and evening/weekend programs available. *Degree requirements:* For master's, thesis optional. *Entrance requirements:* Additional exam requirements/recommendations for international students: Required—TOEFL (minimum score 550 paper-based; 213 computer-based). *Faculty research:* Leadership, international economy, foreign direct investment.

Schiller International University, MBA Program, Strasbourg, France Campus, Strasbourg, France. Offers international business (MBA). Part-time and evening/weekend programs available. Postbaccalaureate distance learning degree programs offered (no on-campus study). *Degree requirements:* For master's, oral comprehensive exam or thesis. *Entrance requirements:* Additional exam requirements/recommendations for international students: Recommended—TOEFL (minimum score 550 paper-based; 213 computer-based).

Seattle Pacific University, Master's Degree in Business Administration (MBA) Program, Seattle, WA 98119-1997. Offers MBA. *Accreditation:* AACSB. Part-time programs available. *Faculty:* 11 full-time (3 women), 2 part-time/adjunct (1 woman). *Students:* 21 full-time (8 women), 87 part-time (30 women); includes 23 minority (4 African Americans, 19 Asian Americans or Pacific Islanders), 15 international. Average age 32. 56 applicants, 36% accepted, 20 enrolled. In 2009, 40 master's awarded. *Entrance requirements:* For master's, GMAT, minimum GPA of 3.0. Additional exam requirements/recommendations for international students: Required—TOEFL (minimum score 225 computer-based). *Application deadline:* For fall admission, 8/1 for domestic and international students; for winter admission, 11/1 for domestic and international students; for spring admission, 2/1 for domestic and international students. Applications are processed on a rolling basis. Application fee: $50. Electronic applications accepted. *Expenses:* Tuition: Part-time $485 per credit. Part-time tuition and fees vary according to course level, degree level and program. *Financial support:* In 2009–10, 28 students received support. Scholarships/grants available. Financial award applicants required to submit FAFSA. *Unit head:* Gary Karns, Graduate Director, 206-281-2948, Fax: 206-281-2733. *Application contact:* The Grad Center, 206-281-2091.

Seattle University, Albers School of Business and Economics, Program in Business Administration, Seattle, WA 98122-1090. Offers MBA, MIB, Certificate, JD/MBA, JD/MIB. *Accreditation:* AACSB. Part-time and evening/weekend programs available. *Entrance requirements:* For master's, GMAT, minimum GPA of 3.0, 1 year of related work experience. Additional exam requirements/recommendations for international students: Required—TOEFL.

Seton Hall University, Stillman School of Business, South Orange, NJ 07079-2697. Offers MBA, MS, Certificate. *Accreditation:* AACSB. Part-time and evening/weekend programs available. *Faculty:* 57 full-time (13 women), 33 part-time/adjunct (10 women). *Students:* 20 full-time (7 women), 23 part-time (7 women); includes 10 minority (2 African Americans, 7 Asian Americans or Pacific Islanders, 1 Hispanic American). Average age 28. 414 applicants, 71% accepted. In 2009, 162 master's awarded. *Entrance requirements:* For master's, GMAT or 10 years of managerial experience, minimum GPA of 3.0. Additional exam requirements/recommendations for international students: Required—TOEFL (minimum score 607 paper-based; 254 computer-based; 102 iBT), IELTS or PTE also accepted. *Application deadline:* For fall admission, 5/31 priority date for domestic students, 3/31 priority date for international students; for spring admission, 10/31 priority date for domestic students, 9/30 priority date for international students. Applications are processed on a rolling basis. Application fee: $75. Electronic applications accepted. *Expenses:* Contact institution. *Financial support:* In 2009–10, research assistantships with full tuition reimbursements (averaging $34,404 per year); career-related internships or fieldwork, Federal Work-Study, scholarships/grants, and unspecified assistantships also available. Support available to part-time students. Financial award application deadline: 6/30; financial award applicants required to submit FAFSA. *Faculty research:* Financial, hedge funds, international business, legal issues, disclosure and branding. Total annual research expenditures: $500,000. *Unit head:* Dr. Karen E. Boroff, Dean, 973-761-9013, Fax: 973-275-2465, E-mail: karen.boroff@shu.edu. *Application contact:* Catherine Bianchi, Director of Graduate Admissions, 973-761-9262, Fax: 973-761-9208, E-mail: catherine.bianchi@shu.edu.

Seton Hill University, Program in Business Administration, Greensburg, PA 15601. Offers entrepreneurship (MBA); management (MBA). Part-time and evening/weekend programs available. *Entrance requirements:* For master's, resume, minimum GPA of 3.0. Additional exam requirements/recommendations for international students: Required—TOEFL (minimum score 600 paper-based; 250 computer-based). *Application deadline:* For fall admission, 8/15 priority date for domestic students; for spring admission, 12/15 for domestic students. Applications are processed on a rolling basis. Application fee: $35. Electronic applications accepted. *Expenses:* Tuition: Full-time $12,780; part-time $710 per credit. Required fees: $300; $150 per semester. Tuition and fees vary according to course load and program. *Financial support:* Scholarships/grants, tuition waivers (partial), and unspecified assistantships available. Support available to part-time students. Financial award application deadline: 8/15; financial award applicants required to submit FAFSA. *Faculty research:* Women in business, entrepreneurship. *Unit head:* Dr. Lloyd Gibson, Director, 724-830-4738, E-mail: gibson@setonhill.edu. *Application contact:* Christine Schaeffer, Director of Graduate and Adult Studies, 724-838-4283, Fax: 724-830-1891, E-mail: schaeffer@setonhill.edu.

Shenandoah University, Byrd School of Business, Winchester, VA 22601-5195. Offers business administration (MBA). *Accreditation:* AACSB. Part-time and evening/weekend programs available. *Faculty:* 12 full-time (2 women), 1 part-time/adjunct (0 women). *Students:* 50 full-time (23 women), 13 part-time (7 women); includes 17 minority (9 African Americans, 1 American Indian/Alaska Native, 7 Asian Americans or Pacific Islanders), 8 international. Average age 35. 67 applicants, 87% accepted, 48 enrolled. In 2009, 29 master's awarded. *Entrance requirements:* For master's, GMAT or GRE General Test, 2 letters of recommendation, resume, interview. Additional exam requirements/recommendations for international students: Required—TOEFL (minimum score 550 paper-based; 213 computer-based; 79 iBT), IELTS (minimum score 6.5), Sakae Institute of Study Abroad (550). *Application deadline:* Applications are processed on a rolling basis. Application fee: $30. Electronic applications accepted. *Expenses:* Tuition: Full-time $11,925; part-time $695 per credit. Required fees: $400 per semester. *Financial support:* Career-related internships or fieldwork, institutionally sponsored loans, and unspecified assistantships available. Support available to part-time students. Financial award application deadline: 3/15; financial award applicants required to submit FAFSA. *Unit head:* Dr. Randy Boxx, Dean, 540-665-4572, Fax: 540-665-5437, E-mail: rboxx@su.edu. *Application contact:* David Anthony, Dean of Admissions, 540-665-4581, Fax: 540-665-4627, E-mail: admit@su.edu.

Shippensburg University of Pennsylvania, School of Graduate Studies, College of Arts and Sciences, Department of Sociology and Anthropology, Shippensburg, PA 17257-2299. Offers organizational development and leadership (MS), including business, communications, education, environmental management, higher education, historical administration, individual and organizational development, public organizations, social structures and organizations. Part-time and evening/weekend programs available. *Degree requirements:* For master's, capstone experience. *Entrance requirements:* For master's, interview (if GPA less than 2.75), resume. Additional exam requirements/recommendations for international students: Required—TOEFL (minimum score 560 paper-based; 220 computer-based); Recommended—IELTS (minimum score 6). Electronic applications accepted.

Shippensburg University of Pennsylvania, School of Graduate Studies, John L. Grove College of Business, Shippensburg, PA 17257-2299. Offers advanced studies in business (Certificate); business administration (MBA). *Accreditation:* AACSB. Part-time and evening/weekend programs available. Postbaccalaureate distance learning degree programs offered (minimal on-campus study). *Entrance requirements:* For master's, GMAT, resume, relevant work/classroom experience, computer literacy. Additional exam requirements/recommendations for international students: Required—TOEFL (minimum score 560 paper-based; 220 computer-based); Recommended—IELTS (minimum score 6). Electronic applications accepted.

Shorter University, Professional Studies, Rome, GA 30165. Offers business administration (MBA); curriculum and instruction (M Ed); leadership (MA). Evening/weekend programs available. *Degree requirements:* For master's, project. *Entrance requirements:* For master's, minimum undergraduate GPA of 2.75 in last 60 hours, 3 years of work experience. Additional exam requirements/recommendations for international students: Required—TOEFL (minimum score 550 paper-based; 213 computer-based; 79 iBT). *Faculty research:* Systems design, leadership, pedagogy using technology.

Silicon Valley University, Graduate Programs, San Jose, CA 95131. Offers business administration (MBA); computer engineering (MSCE); computer science (MSCS). *Degree requirements:* For master's, project (MSCS).

Silver Lake College, Division of Graduate Studies, Program in Management and Organizational Behavior, Manitowoc, WI 54220-9319. Offers MS. Part-time and evening/weekend programs available. Postbaccalaureate distance learning degree programs offered (minimal on-campus study). *Faculty:* 21 part-time/adjunct (9 women). *Students:* 11 full-time (9 women), 50 part-time (33 women); includes 8 minority (1 African American, 6 American Indian/Alaska Native, 1 Asian American or Pacific Islander). Average age 34. 29 applicants, 62% accepted, 13 enrolled. In 2009, 47 master's awarded. *Degree requirements:* For master's, thesis optional. *Entrance requirements:* For master's, interview, minimum undergraduate GPA of 3.0, writing sample, three letters of recommendation, professional resume. Additional exam requirements/recommendations for international students: Required—TOEFL. *Application deadline:* For fall admission, 8/1 priority date for domestic students; for spring admission, 12/1 priority date for domestic students. Applications are processed on a rolling basis. Application fee: $50. Electronic applications accepted. *Expenses:* Tuition: Full-time $7380; part-time $410 per credit. Required fees: $10 per term. Part-time tuition and fees vary according to course load. *Financial support:* In 2009–10, 10 students received support. Career-related internships or fieldwork, Federal Work-Study, and scholarships/grants available. Support available to part-time students. Financial award application deadline: 6/30; financial award applicants required to submit FAFSA. *Unit head:* Suzanne M. Lawrence, Director, 920-686-6198, Fax: 920-684-7082, E-mail: law@silver.sl.edu. *Application contact:* Cindy St. John, Associate Director of Admissions, 800-236-4752 Ext. 350, Fax: 920-686-6350, E-mail: cstjohn@silver.sl.edu.

Simmons College, School of Management, Boston, MA 02115. Offers health care administration (MHA); management (MBA). Part-time and evening/weekend programs available. *Faculty:* 27 full-time (22 women), 4 part-time/adjunct (2 women). *Students:* 57 full-time (all women), 111 part-time (all women); includes 17 minority (8 African Americans, 7 Asian Americans or Pacific Islanders, 2 Hispanic Americans), 10 international. Average age 31. 90 applicants, 93% accepted, 56 enrolled. In 2009, 65 master's, 12 other advanced degrees awarded. *Entrance requirements:* For master's, GMAT, 2 letters of recommendation, resume. Additional exam requirements/recommendations for international students: Required—TOEFL. *Application deadline:* For fall admission, 2/15 priority date for domestic and international students; for spring admission, 10/1 for domestic and international students. Applications are processed on a rolling basis. Application fee: $75. Electronic applications accepted. *Expenses:* Contact institution. *Financial support:* Institutionally sponsored loans and scholarships/grants available. Financial award application deadline: 3/1; financial award applicants required to submit FAFSA. *Faculty research:* Corporate social responsibility, corporate governance, women and leadership: cross-cultural analysis of women leaders, brand meaning and consumer brand leadership, quality and service innovations. *Unit head:* Deborah Marlino, Interim Dean. *Application contact:* Alicia Roberto, MBA Admissions Coordinator, 617-521-3840, Fax: 617-521-3880, E-mail: somadm@simmons.edu.

Simon Fraser University, Graduate Studies, Faculty of Business Administration, Burnaby, BC V5A 1S6, Canada. Offers business administration (EMBA, PhD); financial management (MA);

general business (MBA); global asset and wealth management (MBA); management of technology/biotechnology (MBA); MBA/MRM. *Accreditation:* AACSB. Postbaccalaureate distance learning degree programs offered. *Degree requirements:* For master's, thesis or written project. *Entrance requirements:* For master's, minimum GPA of 3.0. Additional exam requirements/recommendations for international students: Required—TOEFL. *Expenses:* Contact institution. *Faculty research:* Leadership, marketing and technology, wealth management.

SIT Graduate Institute, Graduate Programs, Master's Programs in Intercultural Service, Leadership, and Management, Brattleboro, VT 05302-0676. Offers conflict transformation (MA); intercultural service, leadership, and management (MA); international education (MA); management (MS); social justice in intercultural relations (MA); sustainable development (MA). Postbaccalaureate distance learning degree programs offered (minimal on-campus study). *Degree requirements:* For master's, one foreign language, thesis. *Entrance requirements:* For master's, 3 letters of reference. Additional exam requirements/recommendations for international students: Required—TOEFL. *Faculty research:* Intercultural communication, conflict resolution, advising and training, world issues, international business.

Sonoma State University, School of Business and Economics, Department of Business Administration, Rohnert Park, CA 94928-3609. Offers MBA. *Accreditation:* AACSB. Part-time and evening/weekend programs available. *Faculty:* 4 full-time (2 women), 1 part-time/adjunct (0 women). *Students:* 4 full-time (3 women), 47 part-time (15 women); includes 5 minority (2 Asian Americans or Pacific Islanders, 3 Hispanic Americans). Average age 30. 66 applicants, 55% accepted, 12 enrolled. In 2009, 51 master's awarded. *Degree requirements:* For master's, thesis or alternative. *Entrance requirements:* For master's, GMAT. Additional exam requirements/recommendations for international students: Required—TOEFL (minimum score 500 paper-based; 173 computer-based). *Application deadline:* For fall admission, 1/31 for domestic students; for spring admission, 8/31 for domestic students. Applications are processed on a rolling basis. Application fee: $55. *Expenses:* Tuition, nonresident: full-time $11,160. Required fees: $6226. Full-time tuition and fees vary according to course load. *Financial support:* Career-related internships or fieldwork, Federal Work-Study, institutionally sponsored loans, and scholarships/grants available. Support available to part-time students. Financial award application deadline: 3/2; financial award applicants required to submit FAFSA. *Unit head:* Dr. Terry Lease, Chair, 707-664-2377, E-mail: lease@sonoma.edu. *Application contact:* Dr. Terry Lease, Chair, 707-664-2377, E-mail: lease@sonoma.edu.

Southeastern Louisiana University, College of Business, Hammond, LA 70402. Offers business administration (MBA). *Accreditation:* AACSB. Part-time and evening/weekend programs available. *Faculty:* 15 full-time (3 women), 3 part-time/adjunct (0 women). *Students:* 101 full-time (58 women), 42 part-time (21 women); includes 10 minority (7 African Americans, 3 Asian Americans or Pacific Islanders), 16 international. Average age 27. 113 applicants, 34% accepted, 23 enrolled. In 2009, 99 master's awarded. *Entrance requirements:* For master's, GMAT (minimum score 450), minimum cumulative GPA of 2.75 for all undergraduate work attempted or 3.0 on all upper-division undergraduate coursework attempted. Additional exam requirements/recommendations for international students: Required—TOEFL (minimum score 525 paper-based; 195 computer-based; 61 iBT). *Application deadline:* For fall admission, 7/15 priority date for domestic students, 6/1 priority date for international students; for spring admission, 12/1 priority date for domestic students, 10/1 priority date for international students. Applications are processed on a rolling basis. Application fee: $20 ($30 for international students). Electronic applications accepted. *Expenses:* Tuition, state resident: full-time $3086; part-time $225 per credit hour. Tuition, nonresident: part-time $529 per credit hour. Required fees: $1195. Tuition and fees vary according to course level and course load. *Financial support:* In 2009–10, 19 students received support. Career-related internships or fieldwork, Federal Work-Study, institutionally sponsored loans, scholarships/grants, and administrative assistantships available. Support available to part-time students. Financial award application deadline: 5/1; financial award applicants required to submit FAFSA. *Faculty research:* Radio frequency identification, corporate and portfolio diversification, effect of inexperienced workers on organizational performance, improving information technology project management, pay-for-performance methods and their utility in the workplace. Total annual research expenditures: $27,595. *Unit head:* Dr. Randy Settoon, Dean, 985-549-2258, Fax: 985-549-5038, E-mail: rsettoon@selu.edu. *Application contact:* Sandra Meyers, Graduate Admissions Analyst, 985-549-5620, Fax: 985-549-5882, E-mail: admissions@selu.edu.

Southeastern Oklahoma State University, School of Business, Durant, OK 74701-0609. Offers MBA, MS. *Accreditation:* AACSB; ACBSP. Part-time and evening/weekend programs available. *Faculty:* 13 full-time (6 women), 5 part-time/adjunct (0 women). *Students:* 11 full-time (3 women), 37 part-time (25 women); includes 11 minority (1 African American, 9 American Indian/Alaska Native, 1 Asian American or Pacific Islander), 2 international. Average age 35. 232 applicants, 10% accepted, 23 enrolled. *Degree requirements:* For master's, thesis optional. *Entrance requirements:* For master's, GMAT, minimum GPA of 3.0 in last 60 hours or 2.75 overall. Additional exam requirements/recommendations for international students: Required—TOEFL (minimum score 550 paper-based; 213 computer-based). *Application deadline:* For fall admission, 8/1 for domestic students, 6/1 for international students; for spring admission, 1/5 for domestic students, 11/1 for international students. Application fee: $20 ($55 for international students). Electronic applications accepted. *Financial support:* In 2009–10, 30 students received support, including 3 teaching assistantships with full tuition reimbursements available (averaging $5,000 per year); Federal Work-Study, institutionally sponsored loans, and tuition waivers (partial) also available. Support available to part-time students. Financial award application deadline: 6/15; financial award applicants required to submit FAFSA. *Unit head:* Dr. Buddy Gaster, Dean, 580-745-2030, Fax: 580-970-7479, E-mail: bgaster@se.edu. *Application contact:* Carrie Williamson, Graduate Secretary, 580-745-2200, Fax: 580-745-7474, E-mail: cwilliamson@se.edu.

Southeastern University, College of Business and Legal Studies, Lakeland, FL 33801-6099. Offers business administration (MBA). Evening/weekend programs available. Postbaccalaureate distance learning degree programs offered. *Entrance requirements:* For master's, GMAT, minimum cumulative GPA of 3.0, writing sample. Electronic applications accepted.

Southeast Missouri State University, School of Graduate Studies, Harrison College of Business, Cape Girardeau, MO 63701-4799. Offers accounting (MBA); entrepreneurship (MBA); environmental management (MBA); financial management (MBA); general management (MBA); health administration (MBA); industrial management (MBA); international business (MBA); sport management (MBA). *Accreditation:* AACSB. Part-time and evening/weekend programs available. Postbaccalaureate distance learning degree programs offered (no on-campus study). *Degree requirements:* For master's, applied research project. *Entrance requirements:* For master's, GMAT, minimum undergraduate GPA of 2.5. Additional exam requirements/recommendations for international students: Required—TOEFL (minimum score 550 paper-based; 213 computer-based); Recommended—IELTS (minimum score 6). *Expenses:* Tuition, state resident: full-time $4266; part-time $237 per credit hour. Tuition, nonresident: full-time $7506; part-time $417 per credit hour. Required fees: $427; $427. *Faculty research:* Human resources, laws impacting accounting, advertising.

Southern Adventist University, School of Business and Management, Collegedale, TN 37315-0370. Offers accounting (MBA); church administration (MSA); church and nonprofit leadership (MBA); financial management (MFM); healthcare administration (MBA); management (MBA); marketing management (MBA); outdoor education (MSA); MFM. Part-time and evening/weekend programs available. Postbaccalaureate distance learning degree programs offered (no on-campus study). *Faculty:* 2 full-time (0 women), 8 part-time/adjunct (1 woman). *Students:* 55 full-time (32 women), 30 part-time (22 women); includes 23 minority (14 African Americans, 1 American Indian/Alaska Native, 1 Asian American or Pacific Islander, 7 Hispanic Americans). Average age 35. In 2009, 20 master's awarded. *Entrance requirements:* For master's, GMAT. Additional exam requirements/recommendations for international students: Required—TOEFL (minimum score 600 paper-based; 250 computer-based; 100 iBT). *Application deadline:* For fall admission, 8/1 priority date for domestic students, 7/1 for international students; for winter admission, 12/1 priority date for domestic students, 11/1 for international students; for spring admission, 4/1 priority date for domestic students, 3/1 for international students. Applications are processed on a rolling basis. Application fee: $25. Electronic applications accepted. *Expenses:* Tuition: Full-time $13,149; part-time $487 per credit hour. *Financial support:* In 2009–10, 32 students received support. Scholarships/grants and unspecified assistantships available. Financial award application deadline: 9/1; financial award applicants required to submit FAFSA. *Unit head:* Dr. Don Van Ornam, Dean, 423-236-2750, Fax: 423-236-1527, E-mail: dvanorna@southern.edu. *Application contact:* Linda Wilhelm, Admissions Coordinator, 423-236-2751, Fax: 423-236-1527, E-mail: sbm@southern.edu.

Southern Arkansas University–Magnolia, Graduate Programs, Magnolia, AR 71753. Offers agriculture (MS); business administration (MBA); computer and information sciences (MS); counseling (MS); education (M Ed), including counseling and development, curriculum and instruction emphasis, educational administration and supervision, elementary education, middle level emphasis, reading emphasis, secondary education, TESOL emphasis; kinesiology (MS); library media and information specialist (M Ed); mental health and clinical counseling (MS); public administration (EMPA); school counseling (M Ed); teaching (MAT). *Accreditation:* NCATE. Part-time and evening/weekend programs available. *Faculty:* 43 full-time (24 women), 12 part-time/adjunct (7 women). *Students:* 116 full-time (78 women), 333 part-time (255 women); includes 105 minority (98 African Americans, 3 American Indian/Alaska Native, 3 Asian Americans or Pacific Islanders, 1 Hispanic American), 11 international. Average age 33. In 2009, 88 master's awarded. *Degree requirements:* For master's, comprehensive exam, thesis optional. *Entrance requirements:* For master's, GRE, MAT or GMAT, minimum GPA of 2.75. *Application deadline:* For fall admission, 8/15 for domestic students; for winter admission, 1/8 for domestic students; for spring admission, 1/8 for domestic students. Applications are processed on a rolling basis. Application fee: $0. *Expenses:* Tuition, state resident: full-time $3798; part-time $211 per hour. Tuition, nonresident: full-time $5580; part-time $310 per hour. Required fees: $584. *Financial support:* Career-related internships or fieldwork, Federal Work-Study, scholarships/grants, tuition waivers (full), and unspecified assistantships available. Financial award applicants required to submit FAFSA. *Faculty research:* Alternative certification for teachers, supervision of instruction, instructional leadership, counseling. *Unit head:* Dr. Kim Bloss, Dean, Graduate Studies, 870-235-4150, Fax: 870-235-5227, E-mail: kkbloss@saumag.edu. *Application contact:* Dr. Kim Bloss, Dean, Graduate Studies, 870-235-4150, Fax: 870-235-5227, E-mail: kkbloss@saumag.edu.

Southern Connecticut State University, School of Graduate Studies, School of Business, Program in Business Administration, New Haven, CT 06515-1355. Offers MBA. Part-time and evening/weekend programs available. *Faculty:* 7 full-time, 2 part-time/adjunct. *Students:* 64 full-time (30 women), 109 part-time (46 women); includes 67 minority (34 African Americans, 20 Asian Americans or Pacific Islanders, 13 Hispanic Americans). In 2009, 62 master's awarded. *Entrance requirements:* For master's, GMAT, interview. *Application deadline:* For fall admission, 7/1 priority date for domestic students. Applications are processed on a rolling basis. Application fee: $50. Electronic applications accepted. Tuition and fees vary according to program. *Financial support:* Application deadline: 4/15. *Unit head:* Dr. Wafeek Abdelsayed, Director, 203-392-5873, Fax: 203-392-5988, E-mail: abdelsayedw1@southernct.edu. *Application contact:* Dr. Wafeek Abdelsayed, Director, 203-392-5873, Fax: 203-392-5988, E-mail: abdelsayedw1@southernct.edu.

Southern Illinois University Carbondale, Graduate School, College of Business and Administration, Department of Business Administration, Carbondale, IL 62901-4701. Offers MBA, PhD, JD/MBA, MBA/MA, MBA/MS. *Accreditation:* AACSB. *Degree requirements:* For doctorate, thesis/dissertation. *Entrance requirements:* For master's, GMAT, minimum GPA of 2.7; for doctorate, GMAT, minimum graduate GPA of 3.25. Additional exam requirements/recommendations for international students: Required—TOEFL. *Faculty research:* Marketing, corporate finance, organizational behavior, accounting, MIS, international business.

Southern Illinois University Edwardsville, Graduate Studies and Research, School of Business, Program in Business Administration, Edwardsville, IL 62026-0001. Offers management information systems (MBA); project management (MBA). *Accreditation:* AACSB. Part-time and evening/weekend programs available. *Students:* 27 full-time (16 women), 120 part-time (45 women); includes 7 minority (all African Americans), 7 international. Average age 26. 124 applicants, 43% accepted. In 2009, 95 master's awarded. *Degree requirements:* For master's, thesis or alternative, final exam. *Entrance requirements:* For master's, GMAT. Additional exam requirements/recommendations for international students: Required—TOEFL (minimum score 550 paper-based; 213 computer-based; 79 iBT), IELTS (minimum score 6.5). *Application deadline:* For fall admission, 7/23 for domestic students, 6/1 for international students; for spring admission, 12/11 for domestic students, 10/1 for international students. Applications are processed on a rolling basis. Application fee: $30. Electronic applications accepted. *Expenses:* Tuition, state resident: part-time $1252.50 per semester. Tuition, nonresident: part-time $3131.25 per semester. Required fees: $586.85 per semester. Tuition and fees vary according to course load. *Financial support:* In 2009–10, 15 teaching assistantships with full tuition reimbursements (averaging $8,064 per year) were awarded; fellowships with full tuition reimbursements, research assistantships with full tuition reimbursements, career-related internships or fieldwork, Federal Work-Study, institutionally sponsored loans, scholarships/grants, traineeships, and unspecified assistantships also available. Support available to part-time students. Financial award application deadline: 3/1; financial award applicants required to submit FAFSA. *Unit head:* Dr. Janice Joplin, Director, 618-650-2485, E-mail: jjoplin@siue.edu. *Application contact:* Dr. Janice Joplin, Director, 618-650-2485, E-mail: jjoplin@siue.edu.

Southern Methodist University, Cox School of Business, Dallas, TX 75275. Offers accounting (MSA); business (Exec MBA); business administration (MBA), including accounting, finance, information technology and operations management, management, marketing, strategy and entrepreneurship; entrepreneurship (MS); management (MSM); JD/MBA. *Accreditation:* AACSB. Part-time and evening/weekend programs available. *Faculty:* 39 full-time (7 women), 14 part-time/adjunct (2 women). *Students:* 471 full-time (133 women), 441 part-time (126 women); includes 209 minority (44 African Americans, 5 American Indian/Alaska Native, 111 Asian Americans or Pacific Islanders, 49 Hispanic Americans), 87 international. Average age 30. 1,164 applicants, 49% accepted, 421 enrolled. In 2009, 449 master's awarded. *Degree requirements:* For master's, community service project, presentation proficiency exams. *Entrance requirements:* For master's, GMAT. Additional exam requirements/recommendations for international students: Required—TOEFL, PTE. *Application deadline:* Applications are processed on a rolling basis. Application fee: $75. Electronic applications accepted. *Expenses:* Contact institution. *Financial support:* In 2009–10, 10 research assistantships (averaging $2,800 per year) were awarded; unspecified assistantships also available. Financial award application deadline: 3/1; financial award applicants required to submit FAFSA. *Faculty research:* Financial markets structure, international finance, accounting disclosure, corporate finance, leadership, change management, organizational behavior, entrepreneurship, strategic marketing, corporate strategy, product innovation, information systems, knowledge management, energy markets, customer relationship management. *Unit head:* Dr. Albert W. Niemi, Dean, 214-768-3012, Fax: 214-768-3713, E-mail: aniemi@mail.cox.smu.edu. *Application contact:* Patti Cudney, Director of MBA Admissions, 214-768-3001, Fax: 214-768-3956, E-mail: pcudney@cox.smu.edu.

Southern Nazarene University, Graduate College, School of Business, Bethany, OK 73008. Offers MBA, MS Mgt. *Accreditation:* ACBSP. Part-time and evening/weekend programs available. *Degree requirements:* For master's, thesis optional. *Entrance requirements:* For master's, GMAT, English proficiency exam, minimum GPA of 3.0 in last 60 hours/major, 2.7 overall. Electronic applications accepted.

Southern New Hampshire University, School of Business, Manchester, NH 03106-1045. Offers accounting (MS); business administration (MBA, Certificate), including accounting (Certificate), business administration (MBA), finance (Certificate), forensic accounting (Certificate), human resources management (Certificate), international business (Certificate), international sport management (Certificate), leadership of not for profit organizations (Certificate), marketing (Certificate), operations management (Certificate), sport management (Certificate), taxation (Certificate); finance (MS); hospitality and tourism leadership (Certificate);

Business Administration and Management—General

Southern New Hampshire University (continued)
information technology (MS, Certificate); information technology/international business (Certificate); integrated marketing communications (Certificate); international business (MS, DBA); marketing (MS); operations and project management (MS); organizational leadership (MS); project management (Certificate); sport management (MS); MBA/Certificate. *Accreditation:* ACBSP. Part-time and evening/weekend programs available. Postbaccalaureate distance learning degree programs offered (no on-campus study). Terminal master's awarded for partial completion of doctoral program. *Degree requirements:* For master's, one foreign language, comprehensive exam (for some programs), thesis or alternative; for doctorate, one foreign language, comprehensive exam, thesis/dissertation. *Entrance requirements:* For master's, minimum GPA of 2.5; for doctorate, GMAT. Additional exam requirements/recommendations for international students: Required—TOEFL (minimum score 500 paper-based). Electronic applications accepted.

Southern Oregon University, Graduate Studies, School of Business, Ashland, OR 97520. Offers MBA, MIM. *Degree requirements:* For master's, comprehensive exam. *Entrance requirements:* For master's, GMAT. Electronic applications accepted.

Southern Polytechnic State University, School of Engineering Technology and Management, Department of Business Administration, Marietta, GA 30060-2896. Offers accounting (MSA); business administration (MBA, Graduate Transition Certificate). *Accreditation:* ACBSP. Part-time and evening/weekend programs available. Postbaccalaureate distance learning degree programs offered (no on-campus study). *Faculty:* 10 full-time (4 women), 4 part-time/adjunct (1 woman). *Students:* 75 full-time (40 women), 83 part-time (34 women); includes 47 African Americans, 11 Asian Americans or Pacific Islanders, 6 Hispanic Americans, 57 international. Average age 31. 78 applicants, 92% accepted, 51 enrolled. In 2009, 40 master's awarded. *Degree requirements:* For master's, comprehensive exam, thesis or alternative. *Entrance requirements:* For master's, GMAT. Additional exam requirements/recommendations for international students: Required—TOEFL (minimum score 550 paper-based; 213 computer-based; 79 iBT), IELTS (minimum score 6.5). *Application deadline:* For fall admission, 7/1 priority date for domestic students, 5/1 priority date for international students; for spring admission, 11/1 priority date for domestic students, 9/1 priority date for international students. Applications are processed on a rolling basis. Application fee: $20. Electronic applications accepted. *Expenses:* Tuition, state resident: full-time $2896; part-time $181 per credit hour. Tuition, nonresident: full-time $11,552; part-time $722 per credit hour. Required fees: $1096. *Financial support:* In 2009–10, 37 students received support, including 4 research assistantships with tuition reimbursements available (averaging $4,500 per year); career-related internships or fieldwork, scholarships/grants, and unspecified assistantships also available. Support available to part-time students. Financial award application deadline: 5/1; financial award applicants required to submit FAFSA. *Faculty research:* Ethics, virtual reality, sustainability, management of technology, quality management, capacity planning, human-computer interaction/interface, enterprise integration planning, economic impact of educational institutions, behavioral accounting, accounting ethics, taxation, information security, visualizational simulation, human-computer interaction. *Unit head:* Dr. Ronny Richardson, Chair, 678-915-7440, Fax: 678-915-4967, E-mail: rrichard@spsu.edu. *Application contact:* Nikki Palamiotis, Director of Graduate Studies, 678-915-4276, Fax: 678-915-7292, E-mail: npalamio@spsu.edu.

Southern University and Agricultural and Mechanical College, College of Business, Baton Rouge, LA 70813. Offers MBA. *Accreditation:* AACSB. *Degree requirements:* For master's, comprehensive exam. *Entrance requirements:* For master's, GMAT. Additional exam requirements/recommendations for international students: Required—TOEFL (minimum score 525 paper-based; 193 computer-based). *Faculty research:* Accounting theory, auditing, governmental and non-profit accounting.

Southern Utah University, School of Business, Program in Business Administration, Cedar City, UT 84720-2498. Offers MBA. *Accreditation:* AACSB; ACBSP. Part-time programs available. *Faculty:* 7 full-time (2 women), 3 part-time/adjunct (0 women). *Students:* 25 full-time (8 women), 55 part-time (10 women); includes 3 minority (all Asian Americans or Pacific Islanders). 67 applicants, 79% accepted, 35 enrolled. In 2009, 33 master's awarded. *Degree requirements:* For master's, thesis or alternative. *Application deadline:* For fall admission, 8/1 priority date for domestic students. Applications are processed on a rolling basis. Application fee: $50 ($65 for international students). Electronic applications accepted. *Expenses:* Contact institution. *Financial support:* In 2009–10, 5 research assistantships with full tuition reimbursements (averaging $1,200 per year) were awarded; career-related internships or fieldwork, institutionally sponsored loans, tuition waivers (full and partial), and unspecified assistantships also available. *Unit head:* Dr. Alan Hamlin, Chair, Management and Marketing Department, 435-586-5147, Fax: 435-586-5493, E-mail: hamlin@suu.edu. *Application contact:* Chris Proctor, Associate Director of Admissions, 435-586-7742, Fax: 435-865-8223, E-mail: alger@suu.edu.

Southern Wesleyan University, Program in Business Administration, Central, SC 29630-1020. Offers MBA. Evening/weekend programs available. *Degree requirements:* For master's, comprehensive exam. *Entrance requirements:* For master's, GMAT, GRE, or MAT.

Southern Wesleyan University, Program in Management, Central, SC 29630-1020. Offers MSM. Evening/weekend programs available. *Degree requirements:* For master's, comprehensive exam. *Entrance requirements:* For master's, GMAT, GRE, or MAT. *Expenses:* Contact institution.

South University, Graduate Programs, College of Business, Savannah, GA 31406. Offers corrections (MBA); entrepreneurship and small business (MBA); hospitality management (MBA); sustainability (MBA).

South University, Program in Business Administration, Royal Palm Beach, FL 33411. Offers business administration (MBA); healthcare administration (MBA).

South University, Program in Business Administration, Montgomery, AL 36116-1120. Offers business administration (MBA); healthcare administration (MBA).

South University, Program in Business Administration, Columbia, SC 29203. Offers business administration (MBA); healthcare administration (MBA).

South University, Program in Business Administration, Glen Allen, VA 23060. Offers MBA.

South University, Program in Business Administration, Virginia Beach, VA 23452. Offers MBA.

Southwest Baptist University, Program in Business, Bolivar, MO 65613-2597. Offers business administration (MBA); health administration (MBA). *Accreditation:* ACBSP. Part-time programs available. Postbaccalaureate distance learning degree programs offered (no on-campus study). *Degree requirements:* For master's, comprehensive exam. *Entrance requirements:* For master's, interviews, minimum GPA of 2.75. Additional exam requirements/recommendations for international students: Required—TOEFL (minimum score 550 paper-based; 213 computer-based).

Southwestern Adventist University, Business Department, Graduate Program, Keene, TX 76059. Offers accounting (MBA); finance (MBA); management / leadership (MBA). Part-time and evening/weekend programs available. *Degree requirements:* For master's, capstone course. *Entrance requirements:* For master's, GMAT, GRE General Test.

Southwestern College, Fifth-Year Graduate Programs, Winfield, KS 67156-2499. Offers leadership (MS); management (MBA). Part-time programs available. *Faculty:* 4 full-time (2 women), 6 part-time/adjunct (3 women). *Students:* 21 full-time (9 women), 4 part-time (1 woman); includes 5 minority (3 African Americans, 1 American Indian/Alaska Native, 1 Hispanic American), 4 international. Average age 24. 22 applicants, 86% accepted, 16 enrolled. In 2009, 17 master's awarded. *Entrance requirements:* For master's, baccalaureate degree, minimum GPA of 3.0. Additional exam requirements/recommendations for international students: Required—TOEFL (minimum score 550 paper-based; 213 computer-based). *Application deadline:* For fall admission, 4/1 priority date for domestic students; for spring admission, 12/1 priority date for domestic students. Applications are processed on a rolling basis. Application fee: $25. Electronic applications accepted. *Financial support:* In 2009–10, 20 students received support. Federal Work-Study, tuition waivers (partial), and unspecified assistantships available. Financial award application deadline: 4/1; financial award applicants required to submit FAFSA. *Unit head:* Dr. James Sheppard, Vice President for Academic Affairs, 620-229-6227, Fax: 620-229-6224, E-mail: james.sheppard@sckans.edu. *Application contact:* Marla Sexson, Director of Admissions, 800-846-1543 Ext. 6364, Fax: 620-229-6344, E-mail: marla.sexson@sckans.edu.

Southwestern College, Professional Studies Programs, Wichita, KS 67207. Offers business administration (MBA); leadership (MS); management (MS); security administration (MS); specialized ministries (MA). Part-time and evening/weekend programs available. Postbaccalaureate distance learning degree programs offered (minimal on-campus study). *Faculty:* 1 full-time (0 women), 26 part-time/adjunct (10 women). *Students:* 143 part-time (59 women); includes 25 minority (17 African Americans, 2 Asian Americans or Pacific Islanders, 6 Hispanic Americans). Average age 36. 33 applicants, 100% accepted, 28 enrolled. In 2009, 62 master's awarded. *Degree requirements:* For master's, practicum/capstone project. *Entrance requirements:* For master's, baccalaureate degree; minimum GPA of 2.5, 3.0 for MBA. Additional exam requirements/recommendations for international students: Required—TOEFL (minimum score 550 paper-based; 213 computer-based). *Application deadline:* For fall admission, 8/1 for domestic students; for spring admission, 12/1 for domestic students. Applications are processed on a rolling basis. Application fee: $0. Electronic applications accepted. *Financial support:* In 2009–10, 85 students received support. Federal Work-Study, tuition waivers (partial), and unspecified assistantships available. Financial award application deadline: 4/1; financial award applicants required to submit FAFSA. *Unit head:* Gail Cullen, Director of Academic Affairs, 888-684-5335 Ext. 203, Fax: 316-688-5218, E-mail: gail.cullen@sckans.edu. *Application contact:* Gail Cullen, Director of Academic Affairs, 888-684-5335 Ext. 203, Fax: 316-688-5218, E-mail: gail.cullen@sckans.edu.

Southwestern Oklahoma State University, College of Professional and Graduate Studies, School of Business and Technology, Weatherford, OK 73096-3098. Offers MBA. MBA distance learning degree program offered to Oklahoma residents only. Part-time and evening/weekend programs available. Postbaccalaureate distance learning degree programs offered (minimal on-campus study). *Degree requirements:* For master's, comprehensive exam. *Entrance requirements:* For master's, GMAT, minimum GPA of 2.5. Additional exam requirements/recommendations for international students: Required—TOEFL.

Southwest Minnesota State University, Department of Business and Public Affairs, Marshall, MN 56258. Offers MBA. Part-time and evening/weekend programs available. Postbaccalaureate distance learning degree programs offered (no on-campus study). *Faculty:* 11 full-time (3 women), 1 (woman) part-time/adjunct. *Students:* 28 full-time (13 women), 79 part-time (35 women); includes 7 minority (2 African Americans, 2 American Indian/Alaska Native, 2 Asian Americans or Pacific Islanders, 1 Hispanic American), 17 international. Average age 30. 49 applicants, 55% accepted, 18 enrolled. In 2009, 20 master's awarded. *Degree requirements:* For master's, thesis. *Entrance requirements:* Additional exam requirements/recommendations for international students: Required—TOEFL. *Application deadline:* For fall admission, 8/28 for domestic students, 6/15 for international students; for spring admission, 1/15 for domestic students, 12/15 for international students. Applications are processed on a rolling basis. Application fee: $20. Electronic applications accepted. *Expenses:* Tuition, state resident: full-time $5487; part-time $304.85 per credit. Tuition, nonresident: full-time $5487; part-time $304.85 per credit. Required fees: $680; $37.76 per credit. Tuition and fees vary according to course load and reciprocity agreements. *Financial support:* Institutionally sponsored loans and unspecified assistantships available. Support available to part-time students. Financial award application deadline: 3/1; financial award applicants required to submit FAFSA. *Unit head:* Dr. William Thomas, Professor, 507-537-7392, E-mail: will.thomas@smsu.edu. *Application contact:* CoriAnn Dahlager, Graduate Office Coordinator, 507-537-6819, Fax: 507-537-6227, E-mail: coriann.dahlager@smsu.edu.

Spalding University, Graduate Studies, College of Business and Communication, Louisville, KY 40203-2188. Offers business communication (MS). Part-time and evening/weekend programs available. *Faculty:* 6 full-time (2 women), 3 part-time/adjunct (2 women). *Students:* 39 full-time (30 women), 29 part-time (22 women); includes 19 minority (17 African Americans, 1 Asian American or Pacific Islander, 1 Hispanic American). Average age 37. 33 applicants, 73% accepted, 24 enrolled. In 2009, 20 master's awarded. *Degree requirements:* For master's, project. *Entrance requirements:* For master's, GRE or GMAT, writing sample, interview, letters of recommendation. Additional exam requirements/recommendations for international students: Required—TOEFL (minimum score 535 paper-based; 203 computer-based). *Application deadline:* Applications are processed on a rolling basis. Application fee: $30. Electronic applications accepted. *Expenses:* Tuition: Full-time $11,340; part-time $630 per credit hour. Tuition and fees vary according to program. *Financial support:* In 2009–10, 17 students received support, including 1 research assistantship (averaging $4,815 per year). Financial award application deadline: 3/15; financial award applicants required to submit FAFSA. *Faculty research:* Curriculum development, consumer behavior, interdisciplinary pedagogy. *Unit head:* Dr. Diane Tobin, Dean, 502-585-9911 Ext. 2747, E-mail: dtobin@spalding.edu. *Application contact:* Claire Rayburn, Administrative Assistant, 502-585-9911 Ext. 2120, E-mail: cbc@spalding.edu.

Spring Arbor University, School of Business and Management, Spring Arbor, MI 49283-9799. Offers MBA. Part-time and evening/weekend programs available. Postbaccalaureate distance learning degree programs offered. *Faculty:* 7 full-time (1 woman), 5 part-time/adjunct (2 women). *Students:* 70 full-time (35 women), 12 part-time (5 women); includes 16 minority (11 African Americans, 1 American Indian/Alaska Native, 1 Asian American or Pacific Islander, 3 Hispanic Americans), 2 international. Average age 35. In 2009, 45 master's awarded. *Degree requirements:* For master's, thesis. *Entrance requirements:* For master's, minimum GPA of 3.0, current resume, 2 letters of recommendation. Additional exam requirements/recommendations for international students: Required—TOEFL (minimum score 550 paper-based; 220 computer-based). *Application deadline:* Applications are processed on a rolling basis. Application fee: $40. *Expenses:* Tuition: Full-time $5400; part-time $450 per credit hour. Required fees: $240; $150 per year. Tuition and fees vary according to course load and program. *Financial support:* Career-related internships or fieldwork, scholarships/grants, and tuition waivers (partial) available. Support available to part-time students. Financial award application deadline: 8/25; financial award applicants required to submit FAFSA. *Unit head:* Dr. James Coe, Dean, 517-750-1200 Ext. 1569, Fax: 517-750-6624, E-mail: jcoe@arbor.edu. *Application contact:* Greg Bentle, Coordinator of Graduate Recruitment, 517-750-6763, Fax: 517-750-6624, E-mail: gbentle@arbor.edu.

Spring Hill College, Graduate Programs, Program in Business Administration, Mobile, AL 36608-1791. Offers MBA. *Accreditation:* ACBSP. Part-time and evening/weekend programs available. *Faculty:* 3 full-time (0 women), 1 part-time/adjunct (0 women). *Students:* 7 full-time (3 women), 11 part-time (4 women); includes 2 minority (1 African American, 1 American Indian/Alaska Native), 3 international. Average age 28. 24 applicants, 50% accepted, 9 enrolled. In 2009, 13 master's awarded. *Degree requirements:* For master's, comprehensive exam, capstone course, completion of program within 6 calendar years. *Entrance requirements:* For master's, GMAT, bachelor's degree. Additional exam requirements/recommendations for international students: Required—TOEFL (minimum score 550 paper-based; 213 computer-based; 80 iBT), IELTS (minimum score 6.5). *Application deadline:* For fall admission, 8/1 priority date for domestic and international students; for spring admission, 12/1 priority date for domestic and international students. Applications are processed on a rolling basis. Application fee: $25 ($35 for international students). Electronic applications accepted. *Expenses:* Contact institution. *Financial support:* In 2009–10, 15 students received support. Career-related internships or fieldwork, institutionally sponsored loans, and scholarships/grants available. Support available to part-time students. Financial award applicants required to submit FAFSA. *Unit head:* Dr. Sergio Castello, Director, Graduate Business Program, 251-380-4123, Fax: 251-460-2178, E-mail: scastello@shc.edu. *Application contact:* Donna B. Tarasavage, Director of Marketing and Recruiting, Graduate and Continuing Studies, 251-380-3067, Fax: 251-460-2190, E-mail: dtarasavage@shc.edu.

Stanford University, Graduate School of Business, Stanford, CA 94305-9991. Offers MBA, PhD, JD/MBA, MBA/MS. *Accreditation:* AACSB. Terminal master's awarded for partial completion of doctoral program. *Degree requirements:* For doctorate, thesis/dissertation. *Entrance requirements:* For master's, GMAT; for doctorate, GMAT, GRE. Electronic applications accepted. *Expenses:* Contact institution.

State University of New York at Binghamton, Graduate School, School of Management, Program in Business Administration, Binghamton, NY 13902-6000. Offers business administration (MBA, PhD); health care professional executive (MBA). *Accreditation:* AACSB. *Students:* 170 full-time (60 women), 21 part-time (6 women); includes 28 minority (2 African Americans, 18 Asian Americans or Pacific Islanders, 8 Hispanic Americans), 73 international. Average age 28. 353 applicants, 47% accepted, 91 enrolled. In 2009, 115 master's, 2 doctorates awarded. *Degree requirements:* For doctorate, thesis/dissertation. *Entrance requirements:* For master's and doctorate, GMAT. Additional exam requirements/recommendations for international students: Required—TOEFL (minimum score 550 paper-based; 213 computer-based; 80 iBT). *Application deadline:* For fall admission, 3/1 priority date for domestic and international students; for spring admission, 10/15 priority date for domestic and international students. Applications are processed on a rolling basis. Application fee: $60. Electronic applications accepted. *Financial support:* Fellowships, research assistantships, teaching assistantships, career-related internships or fieldwork, Federal Work-Study, institutionally sponsored loans, scholarships/grants, health care benefits, and unspecified assistantships available. Financial award application deadline: 2/15; financial award applicants required to submit FAFSA. *Unit head:* Dr. George Bobinski, Associate Dean, 607-777-2315, E-mail: gbobins@binghamton.edu. *Application contact:* Victoria Williams, Recruiting and Admissions Coordinator, 607-777-2151, Fax: 607-777-2501, E-mail: vwilliam@binghamton.edu.

State University of New York at Fredonia, Graduate Studies, Department of Business Administration, Fredonia, NY 14063-1136. Offers accounting (MS). *Expenses:* Tuition, state resident: full-time $8370; part-time $349 per credit. Tuition, nonresident: full-time $13,250; part-time $552 per credit. Required fees: $1289; $53.55 per credit.

State University of New York at New Paltz, Graduate School, School of Business, New Paltz, NY 12561. Offers business administration (MBA); public accountancy (MBA). Part-time and evening/weekend programs available. *Faculty:* 15 full-time (3 women), 1 (woman) part-time/adjunct. *Students:* 42 full-time (20 women), 40 part-time (24 women); includes 12 minority (1 African American, 1 American Indian/Alaska Native, 6 Asian Americans or Pacific Islanders, 4 Hispanic Americans), 16 international. Average age 31. 50 applicants, 68% accepted, 21 enrolled. In 2009, 42 master's awarded. *Degree requirements:* For master's, internship. *Entrance requirements:* For master's, GMAT or GRE, minimum GPA of 3.0. Additional exam requirements/recommendations for international students: Required—TOEFL (minimum score 550 paper-based; 213 computer-based; 80 iBT), IELTS (minimum score 6.5). *Application deadline:* For fall admission, 5/15 priority date for domestic students, 5/15 for international students; for spring admission, 11/15 for domestic and international students. Applications are processed on a rolling basis. Application fee: $50. Electronic applications accepted. *Expenses:* Contact institution. *Financial support:* In 2009–10, 8 students received support, including 7 research assistantships with partial tuition reimbursements available (averaging $5,000 per year), 1 teaching assistantship with partial tuition reimbursement available (averaging $5,000 per year); fellowships, career-related internships or fieldwork, scholarships/grants, traineeships, and unspecified assistantships also available. Financial award application deadline: 8/1; financial award applicants required to submit FAFSA. *Faculty research:* Cognitive styles in management education, supporting SME e-commerce migration through e-learning, earnings management and board activity, trading future spread portfolio, global equity market correlation and volatility. *Unit head:* Dr. Hadi Salavitabar, Dean, 845-257-2930, E-mail: mba@newpaltz.edu. *Application contact:* Aaron Hines, Coordinator, 845-257-2968, E-mail: mba@newpaltz.edu.

State University of New York at Oswego, Graduate Studies, School of Business, Program in Business Administration, Oswego, NY 13126. Offers MBA. *Accreditation:* AACSB. Part-time and evening/weekend programs available. *Entrance requirements:* For master's, GMAT, minimum GPA of 2.6. Additional exam requirements/recommendations for international students: Required—TOEFL (minimum score 560 paper-based; 220 computer-based). *Faculty research:* Marketing, industrial finance, technology.

State University of New York College at Geneseo, Graduate Studies, School of Business, Geneseo, NY 14454-1401. Offers accounting (MS). *Accreditation:* AACSB. *Faculty:* 3 full-time (1 woman), 1 part-time/adjunct (0 women). *Students:* 9 full-time (3 women); includes 1 minority (Asian American or Pacific Islander). Average age 24. 20 applicants, 95% accepted, 9 enrolled. In 2009, 5 master's awarded. *Entrance requirements:* For master's, GMAT, bachelor's degree in accounting. *Application deadline:* For fall admission, 2/1 priority date for domestic students; for spring admission, 9/1 for domestic students. Application fee: $50. *Expenses:* Tuition, state resident: full-time $8370; part-time $349 per credit hour. Tuition, nonresident: full-time $13,250; part-time $552 per credit hour. Required fees: $700.52; $29 per credit hour. *Financial support:* Application deadline: 4/1. *Unit head:* Dr. Michael Schinski, Interim Dean, 585-245-5367, Fax: 585-245-5467, E-mail: schinski@geneseo.edu. *Application contact:* Dr. Harry Howe, Director, MS in Accounting, 585-245-5465, Fax: 585-245-5467, E-mail: howeh@geneseo.edu.

State University of New York Empire State College, Graduate Studies, Program in Business Administration, Saratoga Springs, NY 12866-4391. Offers MBA. Part-time programs available. Postbaccalaureate distance learning degree programs offered (minimal on-campus study). *Degree requirements:* For master's, thesis or alternative. *Entrance requirements:* For master's, previous course work in statistics, macroeconomics, microeconomics, and accounting. Additional exam requirements/recommendations for international students: Required—TOEFL (minimum score 600 paper-based; 250 computer-based). Electronic applications accepted. *Expenses:* Contact institution. *Faculty research:* Corporate strategy, managerial competencies, decision analysis, economics in transition, organizational communication.

State University of New York Empire State College, Graduate Studies, Program in Business and Policy Studies, Saratoga Springs, NY 12866-4391. Offers MA. Part-time and evening/weekend programs available. Postbaccalaureate distance learning degree programs offered (minimal on-campus study). *Degree requirements:* For master's, thesis, exam. *Entrance requirements:* For master's, proficiency in statistics. Additional exam requirements/recommendations for international students: Required—TOEFL (minimum score 600 paper-based; 280 computer-based). Electronic applications accepted. *Faculty research:* Business history, applied business statistics, labor/management relations, American social problems and business, effect of government economic policies on business.

State University of New York Institute of Technology, School of Business, Utica, NY 13504-3050. Offers accountancy (MS); business administration in technology management (MBA), including technology management; health services administration (MS). *Accreditation:* AACSB. Part-time and evening/weekend programs available. Postbaccalaureate distance learning degree programs offered (no on-campus study). *Entrance requirements:* For master's, GMAT, minimum GPA of 3.0. Additional exam requirements/recommendations for international students: Required—TOEFL (minimum score 550 paper-based; 213 computer-based). *Faculty research:* Bond performance, paying for college tuition, mergers with utilities companies.

Stephen F. Austin State University, Graduate School, College of Business, Program in Business Administration, Nacogdoches, TX 75962. Offers business (MBA); management and marketing (MBA). *Accreditation:* AACSB. Part-time and evening/weekend programs available. *Degree requirements:* For master's, comprehensive exam. *Entrance requirements:* For master's, GMAT, minimum AACSB index of 1000. Additional exam requirements/recommendations for international students: Required—TOEFL (minimum score 550 paper-based; 213 computer-based). *Faculty research:* Strategic implications, information search, multinational firms, philosophical guidance.

Stephens College, Division of Graduate and Continuing Studies, Graduate Business Programs, Columbia, MO 65215-0002. Offers MBA, MSL. Part-time programs available. Postbaccalaureate distance learning degree programs offered (minimal on-campus study). *Faculty:* 1 (woman) full-time, 9 part-time/adjunct (3 women). *Students:* 77 full-time (62 women), 20 part-time (16 women); includes 14 minority (7 African Americans, 2 Asian Americans or Pacific Islanders, 5 Hispanic Americans). Average age 36. 33 applicants, 67% accepted, 21 enrolled. In 2009, 16 master's awarded. *Entrance requirements:* For master's, minimum GPA of 3.0 in last 60 hours. Additional exam requirements/recommendations for international students: Required—TOEFL (minimum score 213 computer-based). *Application deadline:* For fall admission, 7/25 priority date for domestic and international students; for winter admission, 12/1 priority date for domestic and international students; for spring admission, 4/25 priority date for domestic and international students. Applications are processed on a rolling basis. Application fee: $40. Electronic applications accepted. *Expenses:* Tuition: Part-time $350 per credit. Required fees: $25 per credit. *Financial support:* In 2009–10, 78 students received support, including 6 fellowships with full tuition reimbursements available (averaging $6,805 per year); scholarships/grants and unspecified assistantships also available. Financial award applicants required to submit FAFSA. *Unit head:* Susan Bartel, Department Chair, 800-388-7579. *Application contact:* Jennifer Deaver, Director of Recruitment, 800-388-7579, E-mail: online@stephens.edu.

Stetson University, School of Business Administration, Program in Business Administration, DeLand, FL 32723. Offers MBA, JD/MBA. *Accreditation:* AACSB. Part-time and evening/weekend programs available. *Students:* 82 full-time (32 women), 151 part-time (68 women); includes 26 minority (9 African Americans, 1 American Indian/Alaska Native, 6 Asian Americans or Pacific Islanders, 10 Hispanic Americans), 17 international. Average age 29. In 2009, 108 master's awarded. *Entrance requirements:* For master's, GMAT. *Application deadline:* For fall admission, 7/1 for domestic students. Application fee: $25. Tuition and fees vary according to course load, campus/location and program. *Financial support:* Application deadline: 3/15. *Unit head:* Dr. Fred Augustine, Director, 386-822-7410. *Application contact:* Jeanne Bosco, Administrative Assistant, 386-822-7410, Fax: 386-822-7413, E-mail: jbosco@stetson.edu.

Stevens Institute of Technology, Graduate School, Wesley J. Howe School of Technology Management, Program in Business Administration, Hoboken, NJ 07030. Offers engineering management (MBA); financial engineering (MBA); information management (MBA); information technology in financial services (MBA); information technology in the pharmaceutical industry (MBA); information technology outsourcing (MBA); pharmaceutical management (MBA); project management (MBA); technology management (MBA); telecommunications management (MBA). *Expenses:* Tuition: Full-time $9900; part-time $1100 per credit. Required fees: $286 per semester.

Stevens Institute of Technology, Graduate School, Wesley J. Howe School of Technology Management, Program in Management, Hoboken, NJ 07030. Offers general management (MS); global innovation management (MS); human resource management (MS); information management (MS); project management (MS); technology commercialization (MS); technology management (MS). Part-time programs available. *Degree requirements:* For master's, thesis optional. *Entrance requirements:* For master's, GMAT, GRE General Test. Additional exam requirements/recommendations for international students: Required—TOEFL. Electronic applications accepted. *Expenses:* Tuition: Full-time $9900; part-time $1100 per credit. Required fees: $286 per semester. *Faculty research:* Industrial economics.

Stony Brook University, State University of New York, Graduate School, College of Business, Program in Business Administration, Stony Brook, NY 11794. Offers finance (MBA, Certificate); health care management (MBA, Certificate); human resource management (Certificate); human resources (MBA); information systems management (MBA, Certificate); management (MBA); marketing (MBA). *Faculty:* 17 full-time (2 women), 25 part-time/adjunct (5 women). *Students:* 134 full-time (64 women), 112 part-time (44 women); includes 54 minority (8 African Americans, 1 American Indian/Alaska Native, 35 Asian Americans or Pacific Islanders, 10 Hispanic Americans), 56 international. 222 applicants, 55% accepted. In 2009, 134 master's, 5 other advanced degrees awarded. Application fee: $60. *Expenses:* Tuition, state resident: full-time $8370; part-time $349 per credit. Tuition, nonresident: full-time $13,250; part-time $552 per credit. Required fees: $933. *Financial support:* In 2009–10, 2 teaching assistantships were awarded. *Unit head:* Joseph McDonnell, Interim Dean, 631-632-7180. *Application contact:* Dr. Aristotle Lekacos, Director, Graduate Program, 631-632-7171, E-mail: aristotle.lekacost@notes.cc.sunysb.edu.

Stratford University, School of Graduate Studies, Falls Church, VA 22043. Offers accounting (MS); business administration (IMBA, MBA); enterprise business management (MS); entrepreneurial management (MS); information assurance (MS); information systems (MS); software engineering (MS); telecommunications (MS). Part-time and evening/weekend programs available. Postbaccalaureate distance learning degree programs offered (no on-campus study). *Faculty:* 35 full-time (15 women), 115 part-time/adjunct (25 women). *Students:* 944 full-time (430 women), 15 part-time (5 women). Average age 26. 950 applicants, 45% accepted, 415 enrolled. In 2009, 412 master's awarded. *Degree requirements:* For master's, comprehensive exam, capstone project. *Entrance requirements:* For master's, baccalaureate degree. Additional exam requirements/recommendations for international students: Required—TOEFL (minimum score 500 paper-based; 173 computer-based; 61 iBT). *Application deadline:* Applications are processed on a rolling basis. Application fee: $50. Electronic applications accepted. *Expenses:* Tuition: Full-time $10,530; part-time $390 per credit. Tuition and fees vary according to course load. *Financial support:* Federal Work-Study available. Financial award applicants required to submit FAFSA. *Unit head:* Dr. Habib Khan, Chief Academic Officer, 703-821-8570 Ext. 3305, Fax: 703-734-5335, E-mail: hkhan@stratford.edu. *Application contact:* James Ray, Director of Admissions, 703-821-8570 Ext. 3021, Fax: 703-734-5339, E-mail: jray@stratford.edu.

Strayer University, Graduate Studies, Washington, DC 20005-2603. Offers accounting (MS); acquisition (MBA); business administration (MBA); communications technology (MS); educational management (M Ed); finance (MBA); health services administration (MHSA); hospitality and tourism management (MBA); human resource management (MBA); information systems (MS), including computer security management, decision support system management, enterprise resource management, network management, software engineering management, systems development management; management (MBA); management information systems (MS); marketing (MBA); professional accounting (MS), including accounting information systems, controllership, taxation; public administration (MPA); supply chain management (MBA); technology in education (M Ed). Programs also offered at campus locations in Birmingham, AL; Chamblee, GA; Cobb County, GA; Morrow, GA; White Marsh, MD; Charleston, SC; Columbia, SC; Greensboro, NC; Greenville, SC; Lexington, KY; Louisville, KY; Nashville, TN; North Raleigh, NC; Washington, DC. Part-time and evening/weekend programs available. Postbaccalaureate distance learning degree programs offered (minimal on-campus study). *Degree requirements:* For master's, thesis. *Entrance requirements:* For master's, GMAT, GRE General Test, bachelor's degree from an accredited college or university, minimum undergraduate GPA of 2.75. Electronic applications accepted.

Suffolk University, Sawyer Business School, Master of Business Administration Program, Boston, MA 02108-2770. Offers accounting (MBA); business administration (APC); corporate financial executive track (MBA); entrepreneurship (MBA); executive business administration (EMBA); finance (MBA); global business administration (GMBA); health administration (MBA); international business (MBA); marketing (MBA); organizational behavior (MBA); strategic management (MBA); taxation (MBA); JD/MBA; MBA/GDPA; MBA/MHA; MBA/MSA; MBA/MSF; MBA/MST. *Accreditation:* AACSB. Part-time and evening/weekend programs available. Postbaccalaureate distance learning degree programs offered (no on-campus study). *Faculty:* 103 full-time (30 women), 63 part-time/adjunct (19 women). *Students:* 173 full-time (68 women), 406 part-time (178 women); includes 51 minority (16 African Americans, 3 American Indian/Alaska Native, 22 Asian Americans or Pacific Islanders, 10 Hispanic Americans), 90 international. Average age 29. 460 applicants, 72% accepted, 157 enrolled. In 2009, 245 master's awarded. *Entrance requirements:* For master's, GMAT, minimum undergraduate GPA of 2.75 (MBA), 5 years of managerial experience (EMBA). Additional exam requirements/recommendations for international students: Required—TOEFL (minimum score 550 paper-based; 213 computer-based). *Application deadline:* For fall admission, 6/15 priority date for domestic students, 6/15 for international students; for spring admission, 11/1 priority date for domestic students, 11/1

Business Administration and Management—General

Suffolk University (continued)

for international students. Applications are processed on a rolling basis. Application fee: $50. Electronic applications accepted. *Expenses:* Tuition: Full-time $33,000; part-time $1100 per credit. Required fees: $20. Tuition and fees vary according to program. *Financial support:* In 2009–10, 284 students received support, including 99 fellowships with full and partial tuition reimbursements available (averaging $13,599 per year); career-related internships or fieldwork, Federal Work-Study, and institutionally sponsored loans also available. Support available to part-time students. Financial award application deadline: 4/1; financial award applicants required to submit FAFSA. *Faculty research:* Foreign investments; career strategies and boundaryless careers; corporate ethics codes; interest rates, inflation, and growth options; innovation and product development performance. *Unit head:* Lillian Hallberg, Assistant Dean of Graduate Programs/Director of MBA Programs, 617-573-8306, E-mail: lhallber@suffolk.edu. *Application contact:* Judith Reynolds, Director of Graduate Admissions, 617-573-8302, Fax: 617-305-1733, E-mail: grad.admission@suffolk.edu.

Sullivan University, School of Business, Louisville, KY 40205. Offers business administration (MBA); collaborative leadership (MSCL); conflict management (MSCM); dispute resolution (MSDR); executive business administration (EMBA); human resource leadership (MSHRL); information technology (MSMIT); management and information technology (MBIT); pharmacy (Pharm D). Part-time programs available. Postbaccalaureate distance learning degree programs offered (no on-campus study). *Entrance requirements:* Additional exam requirements/recommendations for international students: Required—TOEFL.

Sul Ross State University, Rio Grande College of Sul Ross State University, Alpine, TX 79832. Offers business administration (MBA); teacher education (M Ed), including bilingual education, counseling, educational diagnostics, elementary education, general education, reading, school administration, secondary education. Part-time and evening/weekend programs available. *Degree requirements:* For master's, thesis optional. *Entrance requirements:* For master's, GMAT or GRE General Test, minimum GPA of 2.5 in last 60 hours of undergraduate work. *Faculty research:* Drug and substance abuse counseling, U.S.-Mexico border economic development.

Sul Ross State University, School of Professional Studies, Department of Business Administration, Alpine, TX 79832. Offers MBA. Part-time and evening/weekend programs available. *Degree requirements:* For master's, thesis optional. *Entrance requirements:* For master's, GMAT or GRE General Test, minimum GPA of 2.5 in last 60 hours of undergraduate work. *Faculty research:* Cross-cultural comparisons, U.S.-Mexico management relations.

Syracuse University, Martin J. Whitman School of Management, Syracuse, NY 13244. Offers MBA, MS Acct, MSF, PhD, JD/MBA, JD/MS Acct, JD/MSF. *Accreditation:* AACSB. Part-time programs available. Postbaccalaureate distance learning degree programs offered (minimal on-campus study). *Degree requirements:* For doctorate, comprehensive exam, thesis/dissertation, summer research paper. *Entrance requirements:* For master's, GMAT, 2 letters of recommendation; for doctorate, GMAT or GRE, 3 letters of recommendation. Additional exam requirements/recommendations for international students: Required—TOEFL (minimum score 600 paper-based; 250 computer-based; 100 iBT). Electronic applications accepted. *Expenses:* Contact institution.

Tabor College, Graduate Program, Hillsboro, KS 67063. Offers accounting (MBA). Program offered at the Wichita campus only.

Tarleton State University, College of Graduate Studies, College of Business Administration, Stephenville, TX 76402. Offers MBA, MS. *Accreditation:* ACBSP. Part-time and evening/weekend programs available. Postbaccalaureate distance learning degree programs offered (minimal on-campus study). *Degree requirements:* For master's, comprehensive exam, thesis optional. *Entrance requirements:* For master's, GMAT or GRE General Test, minimum GPA of 3.0. Additional exam requirements/recommendations for international students: Required—TOEFL (minimum score 550 paper-based; 213 computer-based; 80 iBT). Electronic applications accepted.

Taylor University, Master of Business Administration Program, Upland, IN 46989-1001. Offers emerging business strategies (MBA); global leadership (MBA). Part-time programs available. *Faculty:* 1 full-time (0 women), 9 part-time/adjunct (0 women). *Students:* 57 full-time (21 women), 4 part-time (1 woman); includes 3 African Americans, 1 Asian American or Pacific Islander, 2 Hispanic Americans. Average age 36. 55 applicants, 100% accepted, 52 enrolled. In 2009, 27 master's awarded. *Application deadline:* Applications are processed on a rolling basis. Application fee: $100. *Expenses:* Tuition: Full-time $10,800. *Financial support:* In 2009–10, 2 students received support. Applicants required to submit FAFSA. *Unit head:* Dr. Larry Rottmeyer, Graduate Chair, 260-399-1622, E-mail: lrrottmeyer@taylor.edu. *Application contact:* Wendy Speakman, Program Director, 866-471-6062, Fax: 260-492-0452, E-mail: wnspeakman@taylor.edu.

See Display below and Close-Up on page 257.

Temple University, Graduate School, Fox School of Business, Doctoral Programs in Business, Philadelphia, PA 19122-6096. Offers accounting (PhD); entrepreneurship (PhD); finance (PhD); human resource administration (PhD); international business (PhD); management information systems (PhD); marketing (PhD); risk management and insurance (PhD); statistics (PhD); strategic management (PhD); tourism and sport (PhD). *Accreditation:* AACSB. *Degree requirements:* For doctorate, thesis/dissertation. *Entrance requirements:* For doctorate, GRE General Test, GMAT, minimum GPA of 3.0, master's degree. Additional exam requirements/recommendations for international students: Required—TOEFL (minimum score 600 paper-based; 250 computer-based; 100 iBT), IELTS (minimum score 7.5). Electronic applications accepted.

Temple University, Graduate School, Fox School of Business, MBA Programs, Philadelphia, PA 19122-6096. Offers accounting (MBA); business management (MBA); financial management (MBA); healthcare and life sciences innovation (MBA); human resource management (MBA); international business (IMBA); IT management (MBA); marketing management (MBA); pharmaceutical management (MBA); strategic management (EMBA, MBA). EMBA offered in Philadelphia, PA and Tokyo, Japan. *Accreditation:* AACSB. Part-time and evening/weekend programs available. Postbaccalaureate distance learning degree programs offered (minimal on-campus study). *Entrance requirements:* For master's, GMAT, minimum undergraduate GPA of 3.0. Additional exam requirements/recommendations for international students: Required—TOEFL (minimum score 600 paper-based; 250 computer-based; 100 iBT), IELTS (minimum score 7.5).

Temple University, Graduate School, Fox School of Business, Specialized Master's Programs, Philadelphia, PA 19122-6096. Offers accounting and financial management (MS); actuarial science (MS); finance (MS); financial engineering (MS); healthcare financial management (MS); healthcare management (MHM); human resource management (MS); management information systems (MS); marketing (MS); statistics (MS). *Accreditation:* AACSB. Part-time programs available. *Entrance requirements:* For master's, GRE General Test or GMAT, minimum

undergraduate GPA of 3.0. Additional exam requirements/recommendations for international students: Required—TOEFL (minimum score 600 paper-based; 250 computer-based; 100 iBT), IELTS (minimum score 7.5).

Tennessee State University, The School of Graduate Studies and Research, College of Business, Nashville, TN 37209-1561. Offers MBA. *Accreditation:* AACSB. Part-time and evening/weekend programs available. Postbaccalaureate distance learning degree programs offered. *Entrance requirements:* For master's, GMAT. Additional exam requirements/recommendations for international students: Required—TOEFL (minimum score 500 paper-based). Electronic applications accepted. *Faculty research:* Supply chain management, health economics, accounting, e-commerce, international business.

Tennessee Technological University, Graduate School, College of Business, Cookeville, TN 38505. Offers accounting (MBA); finance (MBA); human resource management (MBA); international business (MBA); management information systems (MBA); risk management & insurance (MBA). *Accreditation:* AACSB. Part-time and evening/weekend programs available. *Faculty:* 28 full-time (5 women). *Students:* 64 full-time (26 women), 163 part-time (70 women); includes 17 minority (6 African Americans, 8 Asian Americans or Pacific Islanders, 3 Hispanic Americans). Average age 25. 203 applicants, 52% accepted, 75 enrolled. In 2009, 105 master's awarded. *Entrance requirements:* For master's, GMAT. Additional exam requirements/recommendations for international students: Required—TOEFL (minimum score 550 paper-based; 79 iBT), IELTS (minimum score 5.5). *Application deadline:* For fall admission, 8/1 for domestic and international students; for spring admission, 12/1 for domestic students, 10/1 for international students. Application fee: $25 ($30 for international students). Electronic applications accepted. *Expenses:* Tuition, state resident: full-time $7034; part-time $368 per credit hour. *Financial support:* In 2009–10, 5 fellowships (averaging $10,000 per year), 18 research assistantships (averaging $4,000 per year), teaching assistantships (averaging $4,000 per year) were awarded. Support available to part-time students. Financial award application deadline: 4/1. *Unit head:* Dr. Bob G. Wood, Director, 931-372-3600, Fax: 931-372-6249. *Application contact:* Shelia K. Kendrick, Coordinator of Graduate Studies, 931-372-3808, Fax: 931-372-3497, E-mail: skendrick@tntech.edu.

Texas A&M International University, Office of Graduate Studies and Research, College of Business Administration, Laredo, TX 78041-1900. Offers MBA, MP Acc, MSIS. *Accreditation:* AACSB. Part-time and evening/weekend programs available. *Faculty:* 27 full-time (1 woman), 6 part-time/adjunct (0 women). *Students:* 105 full-time (34 women), 279 part-time (121 women); includes 200 minority (5 African Americans, 4 Asian Americans or Pacific Islanders, 191 Hispanic Americans), 165 international. Average age 29. 290 applicants, 51% accepted, 120 enrolled. In 2009, 150 master's awarded. *Degree requirements:* For master's, thesis (for some programs). *Entrance requirements:* For master's, GMAT or GRE General Test. Additional exam requirements/recommendations for international students: Required—TOEFL (minimum score 550 paper-based; 213 computer-based). *Application deadline:* For fall admission, 4/30 priority date for domestic students; for spring admission, 11/30 for domestic students. Applications are processed on a rolling basis. Application fee: $25. *Financial support:* In 2009–10, 27 students received support, including 10 teaching assistantships; fellowships, research assistantships, Federal Work-Study, institutionally sponsored loans, and scholarships/grants also available. Support available to part-time students. Financial award application deadline: 11/1; financial award applicants required to submit FAFSA. *Unit head:* Dr. Stephen R. Sears, Dean, 956-326-2480, E-mail: steve.sears@tamiu.edu. *Application contact:* Imelda Lopez, Graduate Admissions Counselor, 956-326-2485, Fax: 956-326-2459, E-mail: lopez@tamiu.edu.

Texas A&M University, Mays Business School, Department of Management, College Station, TX 77843. Offers human resource management (MS); management (PhD). Terminal master's awarded for partial completion of doctoral program. *Degree requirements:* For master's, comprehensive exam; for doctorate, thesis/dissertation. *Entrance requirements:* For master's, GMAT or GRE; for doctorate, GMAT or GRE General Test. Additional exam requirements/recommendations for international students: Required—TOEFL. *Expenses:* Tuition, state resident: full-time $3991; part-time $221.74 per credit hour. Tuition, nonresident: full-time $9049; part-time $502.74 per credit hour. *Faculty research:* Strategic and human resource management, business and public policy, organizational behavior, organizational theory.

Texas A&M University, Mays Business School, Executive MBA Program, College Station, TX 77843. Offers EMBA. *Accreditation:* AACSB. *Entrance requirements:* For master's, GMAT or GRE. Additional exam requirements/recommendations for international students: Required—TOEFL. Electronic applications accepted. *Expenses:* Contact institution.

Texas A&M University, Mays Business School, MBA Program, College Station, TX 77843. Offers MBA. *Accreditation:* AACSB. *Entrance requirements:* For master's, GMAT. Additional exam requirements/recommendations for international students: Required—TOEFL (minimum score 600 paper-based; 250 computer-based; 100 iBT), IELTS (minimum score 7). Electronic applications accepted. *Expenses:* Contact institution.

Texas A&M University–Commerce, Graduate School, College of Business and Technology, Department of General Business and Systems Management, Commerce, TX 75429-3011. Offers business administration (MBA). *Accreditation:* AACSB. Part-time programs available. *Degree requirements:* For master's, comprehensive exam, thesis (for some programs). *Entrance requirements:* For master's, GMAT.

Texas A&M University–Corpus Christi, Graduate Studies and Research, College of Business, Corpus Christi, TX 78412-5503. Offers accounting (M Acc); health care administration (MBA); international business (MBA). *Accreditation:* AACSB. Part-time and evening/weekend programs available. *Degree requirements:* For master's, comprehensive exam, thesis (for some programs). *Entrance requirements:* For master's, GMAT. Additional exam requirements/recommendations for international students: Required—TOEFL. Electronic applications accepted.

Texas A&M University–Kingsville, College of Graduate Studies, College of Business Administration, Kingsville, TX 78363. Offers MBA, MS. *Accreditation:* ACBSP. Part-time and evening/weekend programs available. *Degree requirements:* For master's, comprehensive exam, thesis or alternative. *Entrance requirements:* For master's, GMAT, minimum GPA of 2.5. Additional exam requirements/recommendations for international students: Required—TOEFL. *Faculty research:* Capital budgeting, international trade.

Texas A&M University–Texarkana, Graduate Studies and Research, College of Business, Texarkana, TX 75505-5518. Offers accounting (MSA); business administration (MBA, MS). Part-time and evening/weekend programs available. *Degree requirements:* For master's, thesis or alternative. *Entrance requirements:* For master's, minimum GPA of 2.5 in last 60 hours of bachelor's degree. Additional exam requirements/recommendations for international students: Required—TOEFL. Electronic applications accepted.

Texas Christian University, College of Science and Engineering, Department of Physics and Astronomy, Fort Worth, TX 76129-0002. Offers physics (MA, MS, PhD), including astrophysics (PhD), business (PhD), physics (PhD). Part-time and evening/weekend programs available. *Degree requirements:* For master's, comprehensive exam, thesis; for doctorate, comprehensive exam, thesis/dissertation, paper submitted to a scientific journal. *Entrance requirements:* For master's, GRE; for doctorate, GRE General Test. Additional exam requirements/recommendations for international students: Required—TOEFL (minimum score 600 paper-based). *Application deadline:* For fall admission, 3/1 for domestic students; for spring admission, 12/1 for domestic students. Applications are processed on a rolling basis. Application fee: $50. *Expenses:* Tuition: Full-time $17,640; part-time $980 per credit hour. Tuition and fees vary according to program. *Financial support:* In 2009–10, 10 teaching assistantships (averaging $18,000 per year) were awarded; tuition waivers also available. Financial award application deadline: 3/1. *Unit head:* Dr. T. W. Zerda, Chairperson, 817-257-7375 Ext. 7124, Fax: 817-257-7742, E-mail: t.zerda@tcu.edu. *Application contact:* Dr. William R. M. Graham, Professor, 817-257-7375 Ext. 6383', Fax: 817-257-7742, E-mail: w.graham@tcu.edu.

Texas Christian University, The Neeley School of Business at TCU, Program in Business Administration, Fort Worth, TX 76129-0002. Offers MBA. *Accreditation:* AACSB. Part-time and evening/weekend programs available. *Entrance requirements:* For master's, GMAT, 3 hours of course work in college algebra. Additional exam requirements/recommendations for international students: Required—TOEFL (minimum score 600 paper-based; 250 computer-based; 100 iBT). *Application deadline:* For fall admission, 4/15 priority date for domestic students, 3/1 priority date for international students. Applications are processed on a rolling basis. Application fee: $100. Electronic applications accepted. *Expenses:* Tuition: Full-time $17,640; part-time $980 per credit hour. Tuition and fees vary according to program. *Financial support:* Career-related internships or fieldwork, Federal Work-Study, institutionally sponsored loans, scholarships/grants, and unspecified assistantships available. Support available to part-time students. Financial award application deadline: 5/1; financial award applicants required to submit FAFSA. *Faculty research:* Emerging financial markets, derivative trading activity, salesforce deployment, examining sales activity, litigation against tax practitioners. Total annual research expenditures: $2.5 million. *Unit head:* Dr. Bill Cron, Associate Dean, Graduate Programs, 817-257-7531, Fax: 817-257-6431. *Application contact:* Peggy Conway, Director, MBA Admissions, 817-257-7531, Fax: 817-257-6431, E-mail: mbainfo@tcu.edu.

Texas Southern University, Jesse H. Jones School of Business, Program in Business Administration, Houston, TX 77004-4584. Offers MBA. *Accreditation:* AACSB. Part-time and evening/weekend programs available. *Faculty:* 10 full-time (1 woman), 1 (woman) part-time/adjunct. *Students:* 61 full-time (29 women), 37 part-time (20 women); includes 88 minority (82 African Americans, 4 Asian Americans or Pacific Islanders, 2 Hispanic Americans), 5 international. Average age 30. 143 applicants, 100% accepted, 41 enrolled. In 2009, 26 master's awarded. *Degree requirements:* For master's, comprehensive exam. *Entrance requirements:* For master's, GMAT, minimum GPA of 2.5. *Application deadline:* For fall admission, 7/1 for domestic and international students; for spring admission, 11/1 for domestic and international students. Applications are processed on a rolling basis. Application fee: $50 ($75 for international students). Electronic applications accepted. *Expenses:* Tuition, state resident: full-time $1805; part-time $100 per credit hour. Tuition, nonresident: full-time $6470; part-time $343 per credit hour. Tuition and fees vary according to course level, course load and degree level. *Financial support:* In 2009–10, 3 research assistantships (averaging $2,833 per year), 4 teaching assistantships (averaging $3,650 per year) were awarded; fellowships, career-related internships or fieldwork, scholarships/grants, and unspecified assistantships also available. Financial award application deadline: 5/1. *Unit head:* Dr. K. V. Ramaswamy, Chair, 713-313-7309, Fax: 713-313-7705, E-mail: ramaswamy_kv@tsu.edu. *Application contact:* Bobbie J. Richardson, Executive Secretary, 713-313-7309, Fax: 713-313-7705, E-mail: richardson_bj@tsu.edu.

Texas State University–San Marcos, Graduate School, Emmett and Miriam McCoy College of Business Administration, Program in Business Administration, San Marcos, TX 78666. Offers MBA. *Accreditation:* AACSB. Part-time programs available. *Faculty:* 24 full-time (8 women). *Students:* 105 full-time (45 women), 209 part-time (80 women); includes 70 minority (8 African Americans, 1 American Indian/Alaska Native, 22 Asian Americans or Pacific Islanders, 39 Hispanic Americans), 31 international. Average age 29. 148 applicants, 82% accepted, 98 enrolled. In 2009, 91 master's awarded. *Degree requirements:* For master's, comprehensive exam, thesis optional. *Entrance requirements:* For master's, GMAT (minimum preferred score of 450 prior to admission decision), minimum GPA of 2.0 in last 60 hours of undergraduate work. Additional exam requirements/recommendations for international students: Required—TOEFL (minimum score 550 paper-based; 213 computer-based). *Application deadline:* For fall admission, 6/1 for domestic and international students; for spring admission, 10/1 for domestic and international students. Applications are processed on a rolling basis. Application fee: $40 ($90 for international students). Electronic applications accepted. *Expenses:* Tuition, state resident: full-time $5784; part-time $241 per credit hour. Tuition, nonresident: full-time $13,224; part-time $551 per credit hour. Required fees: $1728; $48 per credit hour. $306. Tuition and fees vary according to course load. *Financial support:* In 2009–10, 158 students received support, including 4 research assistantships (averaging $5,190 per year), 10 teaching assistantships (averaging $5,121 per year); Federal Work-Study and institutionally sponsored loans also available. Support available to part-time students. Financial award application deadline: 4/1; financial award applicants required to submit FAFSA. *Faculty research:* Organizational change and communication, artificial intelligence systems. *Unit head:* Dr. Robert Davis, Associate Dean, 512-245-3591, Fax: 512-245-7973, E-mail: rd23@txstate.edu. *Application contact:* Dr. J. Michael Willoughby, Dean of Graduate School, 512-245-2581, Fax: 512-245-8365, E-mail: gradcollege@txstate.edu.

Texas Tech University, Jerry S. Rawls College of Business Administration, Area of Management, Lubbock, TX 79409. Offers PhD. *Accreditation:* AACSB. Part-time programs available. *Faculty:* 14 full-time (3 women), 1 part-time/adjunct (0 women). *Students:* 13 full-time (5 women), 5 international. Average age 30. 27 applicants, 37% accepted, 6 enrolled. In 2009, 2 doctorates awarded. *Degree requirements:* For doctorate, comprehensive exam, thesis/dissertation, qualifying exams. *Entrance requirements:* For doctorate, GMAT, holistic profile of academic credentials. Additional exam requirements/recommendations for international students: Required—TOEFL (minimum score 550 paper-based; 213 computer-based; 79 iBT). *Application deadline:* For fall admission, 4/1 priority date for domestic students, 1/15 priority date for international students; for spring admission, 9/1 priority date for domestic students, 7/15 priority date for international students. Applications are processed on a rolling basis. Application fee: $50 ($75 for international students). Electronic applications accepted. *Expenses:* Tuition, state resident: full-time $5100; part-time $213 per credit hour. Tuition, nonresident: full-time $11,748; part-time $490 per credit hour. Required fees: $2298; $50 per credit hour. $555 per semester. *Financial support:* In 2009–10, 10 research assistantships (averaging $8,000 per year), 10 teaching assistantships (averaging $17,000 per year) were awarded; career-related internships or fieldwork, Federal Work-Study, and scholarships/grants also available. Financial award applicants required to submit FAFSA. *Faculty research:* Entrepreneurship, leadership, health care, organization theory. *Unit head:* Dr. William Gardner, Area Coordinator, 806-742-1055, Fax: 806-742-2308, E-mail: william.gardner@ttu.edu. *Application contact:* Cynthia D. Barnes, Director, Graduate Services Center, 806-742-3184, Fax: 806-742-3958, E-mail: ba_grad@ttu.edu.

Texas Tech University, Jerry S. Rawls College of Business Administration, Programs in Business Administration, Lubbock, TX 79409. Offers agricultural business (MBA); business administration (IMBA); entrepreneurship (MBA); finance (MBA); general business (MBA); health organization management (MBA); international business (MBA); management and leadership skills (MBA); management information systems (MBA); marketing (MBA); statistics (MBA); JD/MBA; MBA/M Arch; MBA/MA; MBA/MD; MBA/MS; MBA/Pharm D. Part-time and evening/weekend programs available. *Faculty:* 54 full-time (9 women), 5 part-time/adjunct (0 women). *Students:* 59 full-time (15 women), 487 part-time (148 women); includes 107 minority (24 African Americans, 4 American Indian/Alaska Native, 30 Asian Americans or Pacific Islanders, 49 Hispanic Americans), 51 international. Average age 30. 477 applicants, 81% accepted, 302 enrolled. In 2009, 185 degrees awarded. *Degree requirements:* For master's, capstone course. *Entrance requirements:* For master's, GMAT, holistic review of academic credentials. Additional exam requirements/recommendations for international students: Required—TOEFL (minimum score 550 paper-based; 213 computer-based; 79 iBT). *Application deadline:* For fall admission, 4/1 priority date for domestic students, 1/15 priority date for international students; for spring admission, 9/1 priority date for domestic students, 7/15 priority date for international students. Applications are processed on a rolling basis. Application fee: $50 ($75 for international students). Electronic applications accepted. *Expenses:* Tuition, state resident: full-time $5100; part-time $213 per credit hour. Tuition, nonresident: full-time $11,748; part-time $490 per credit hour. Required fees: $2298; $50 per credit hour. $555 per semester. *Financial support:* In 2009–10, 13 research assistantships (averaging $8,000 per year) were awarded; teaching assistantships, career-related internships or fieldwork, Federal Work-Study, scholarships/grants, health care benefits, and unspecified assistantships also available. Support available to part-time students. Financial award applicants required to submit FAFSA. *Unit head:* Dr. W. Jay Conover, Director, 806-742-1546, Fax: 806-742-3958, E-mail: jay.conover@ttu.edu. *Application contact:* Cynthia D. Barnes, Director, Graduate Services Center, 806-742-3184, Fax: 806-742-3958, E-mail: ba_grad@ttu.edu.

Business Administration and Management—General

Texas Wesleyan University, Graduate Programs, Graduate Business Programs, Fort Worth, TX 76105-1536. Offers business administration (MBA); health services administration (MS); management (MiM). *Accreditation:* ACBSP. Part-time and evening/weekend programs available. *Faculty:* 16 full-time (6 women), 6 part-time/adjunct (4 women). *Students:* 16 full-time (4 women), 36 part-time (20 women); includes 15 minority (11 African Americans, 1 American Indian/Alaska Native, 3 Hispanic Americans), 8 international. Average age 32. 27 applicants, 74% accepted, 15 enrolled. In 2009, 18 master's awarded. *Degree requirements:* For master's, capstone course. *Entrance requirements:* For master's, GMAT, 3 letters of recommendation. *Application deadline:* For fall admission, 7/7 priority date for domestic students; for spring admission, 11/1 priority date for domestic students. Applications are processed on a rolling basis. Application fee: $50. *Expenses:* Contact institution. *Financial support:* Federal Work-Study, scholarships/grants, and tuition waivers (full and partial) available. Support available to part-time students. Financial award application deadline: 3/15; financial award applicants required to submit FAFSA. *Unit head:* Dr. Hector Quintanilla, Dean, 817-531-4840, Fax: 817-531-6585. *Application contact:* Dr. Hector Quintanilla, Dean, 817-531-4840, Fax: 817-531-6585.

Texas Woman's University, Graduate School, College of Arts and Sciences, School of Management, Denton, TX 76201. Offers business administration (EMBA, MBA); health systems management (MHSM). Part-time programs available. *Faculty:* 17 full-time (8 women), 3 part-time/adjunct (all women). *Students:* 543 full-time (444 women), 384 part-time (312 women); includes 547 minority (353 African Americans, 3 American Indian/Alaska Native, 98 Asian Americans or Pacific Islanders, 93 Hispanic Americans), 45 international. Average age 36. 471 applicants, 86% accepted, 326 enrolled. In 2009, 369 master's awarded. *Degree requirements:* For master's, thesis optional. *Entrance requirements:* For master's, 3 letters of reference, resume, minimum GPA of 3.0; 5 years relevant experience (EMBA). Additional exam requirements/recommendations for international students: Required—TOEFL (minimum score 550 paper-based; 213 computer-based; 79 iBT). *Application deadline:* For fall admission, 8/1 priority date for domestic students, 3/1 for international students; for spring admission, 12/1 priority date for domestic students, 7/1 for international students. Applications are processed on a rolling basis. Application fee: $50. Electronic applications accepted. *Expenses:* Tuition, state resident: full-time $3564; part-time $198 per credit hour. Tuition, nonresident: full-time $8550; part-time $475 per credit hour. Required fees: $69.26 per credit hour. Tuition and fees vary according to course load. *Financial support:* In 2009–10, 441 students received support, including 15 research assistantships (averaging $9,684 per year), teaching assistantships (averaging $9,684 per year), career-related internships or fieldwork, Federal Work-Study, institutionally sponsored loans, scholarships/grants, traineeships, health care benefits, and unspecified assistantships also available. Support available to part-time students. Financial award application deadline: 3/1; financial award applicants required to submit FAFSA. *Faculty research:* Leadership, tax, women in management, sales, job satisfaction. *Unit head:* Dr. P. Ann Hughes, Director, 940-898-2458, Fax: 940-898-2120, E-mail: som@twu.edu. *Application contact:* Samuel Wheeler, Assistant Director of Admissions, 940-898-3188, Fax: 940-898-3081, E-mail: wheelersr@twu.edu.

Thomas College, Graduate School, Programs in Business, Waterville, ME 04901-5097. Offers business (MBA); computer technology education (MS); education (MS); human resource management (MBA). Part-time and evening/weekend programs available. *Entrance requirements:* For master's, GMAT, GRE, MAT or minimum GPA of 3.3 in first 3 graduate-level courses.

Thomas Edison State College, School of Business and Management, Program in Management, Trenton, NJ 08608-1176. Offers MSM. Part-time programs available. Postbaccalaureate distance learning degree programs offered (minimal on-campus study). *Students:* 317 part-time (117 women); includes 106 minority (69 African Americans, 3 American Indian/Alaska Native, 9 Asian Americans or Pacific Islanders, 25 Hispanic Americans), 3 international. Average age 43. In 2009, 45 master's awarded. *Degree requirements:* For master's, final capstone project. *Entrance requirements:* For master's, bachelor's degree from a regionally-accredited college or university; minimum 2 letters of recommendation; 3-5 years of related working experience; current resume. Additional exam requirements/recommendations for international students: Required—TOEFL (minimum score 550 paper-based; 213 computer-based; 79 iBT). *Application deadline:* For fall admission, 8/15 priority date for domestic and international students; for winter admission, 11/15 priority date for domestic and international students; for spring admission, 2/15 priority date for domestic and international students. Applications are processed on a rolling basis. Application fee: $75. Electronic applications accepted. *Expenses:* Tuition, area resident: Part-time $479 per credit. Tuition, state resident: part-time $479 per credit. Tuition, nonresident: part-time $479 per credit. *Financial support:* Applicants required to submit FAFSA. *Unit head:* Dr. Joseph Santora, Dean, School of Business and Management, 609-984-1130, Fax: 609-984-3898, E-mail: info@tesc.edu. *Application contact:* David Hoftiezer, Director of Admissions, 888-442-8372, Fax: 609-984-8447, E-mail: admissions@tesc.edu.

Thomas More College, Program in Business Administration, Crestview Hills, KY 41017-3495. Offers MBA. *Faculty:* 12 full-time (3 women). *Students:* 116 full-time (54 women); includes 3 minority (2 African Americans, 1 Hispanic American). Average age 33. 76 applicants, 67% accepted, 40 enrolled. In 2009, 45 master's awarded. *Degree requirements:* For master's, comprehensive exam, final project. *Entrance requirements:* For master's, GMAT, minimum GPA of 2.7. Additional exam requirements/recommendations for international students: Required—TOEFL (minimum score 600 paper-based; 250 computer-based; 100 iBT). *Application deadline:* Applications are processed on a rolling basis. Application fee: $25. Electronic applications accepted. *Expenses:* Tuition: Full-time $11,242.50; part-time $527 per credit. Tuition and fees vary according to program. *Financial support:* In 2009–10, 9 students received support. Federal Work-Study, institutionally sponsored loans, and scholarships/grants available. Financial award application deadline: 3/15; financial award applicants required to submit FAFSA. *Faculty research:* Comparison level and consumer satisfaction, history of U.S. business development, share price reaction, quality and competition, personnel development. *Unit head:* Nathan Hartman, Director of Lifelong Learning, 859-344-3333, Fax: 859-344-3686, E-mail: nathan.hartman@thomasmore.edu. *Application contact:* Judy Bautista, Enrollment Manager, 859-341-4554, Fax: 859-578-3589, E-mail: judy.bautista@apollogrp.edu.

Thomas University, Department of Business Administration, Thomasville, GA 31792-7499. Offers MBA. Part-time programs available. *Entrance requirements:* For master's, resume, 3 professional or academic references. Additional exam requirements/recommendations for international students: Required—TOEFL (minimum score 600 paper-based; 250 computer-based). Electronic applications accepted.

Thompson Rivers University, Program in Business Administration, Kamloops, BC V2C 5N3, Canada. Offers MBA. Part-time programs available. *Entrance requirements:* For master's, GMAT, undergraduate degree with minimum B- average in last 60 credits, personal resume. Additional exam requirements/recommendations for international students: Required—TOEFL (570 paper-based, 230 computer-based, 88 iBT), IELTS (6.5), or CAEL (70).

Thunderbird School of Global Management, Master's Programs in Global Management, Glendale, AZ 85306-6000. Offers global affairs and management (MA); global management (MS). *Accreditation:* AACSB. *Faculty:* 47 full-time (13 women). *Students:* 109 full-time (60 women); includes 6 minority (3 Asian Americans or Pacific Islanders, 3 Hispanic Americans), 44 international. 153 applicants, 80% accepted, 69 enrolled. In 2009, 43 master's awarded. *Degree requirements:* For master's, one foreign language. *Entrance requirements:* For master's, GMAT/GRE. Additional exam requirements/recommendations for international students: Required—TOEFL. *Application deadline:* For fall admission, 6/10 for domestic students, 4/30 for international students. Application fee: $125. *Expenses:* Tuition: Full-time $38,970; part-time $1299 per credit. Required fees: $1330. One-time fee: $625 full-time. *Financial support:* Career-related internships or fieldwork, Federal Work-Study, scholarships/grants, and unspecified assistantships available. *Unit head:* Dr. Glenn Fong, Unit Head, 602-978-7156. *Application contact:* Jay Bryant, Director of Admissions, 602-978-7294, Fax: 602-439-5432, E-mail: jay.bryant@thunderbird.edu.

Tiffin University, Program in Business Administration, Tiffin, OH 44883-2161. Offers general management (MBA); leadership (MBA); safety and security management (MBA); sports management (MBA). *Accreditation:* ACBSP. Part-time and evening/weekend programs available. Postbaccalaureate distance learning degree programs offered (no on-campus study). *Entrance requirements:* For master's, minimum undergraduate GPA of 2.5, work experience. Additional exam requirements/recommendations for international students: Required—TOEFL (minimum score 550 paper-based; 213 computer-based). Electronic applications accepted. *Faculty research:* Small business, executive development operations, research and statistical analysis, market research, management information systems.

Towson University, Joint University of Baltimore/Towson University (UB/Towson) MBA Program, Baltimore, MD 21201. Offers MBA, MBA/JD, MBA/MSN, MBA/PhD, MBA/Pharm D. *Entrance requirements:* For master's, GMAT, 2 letters of recommendation, minimum GPA of 3.0, resume. Electronic applications accepted.

Trevecca Nazarene University, Graduate Division, Graduate Business Programs, Major in Business Administration, Nashville, TN 37210-2877. Offers MBA. Evening/weekend programs available. *Students:* 18 part-time (10 women); includes 6 minority (5 African Americans, 1 Hispanic American). In 2009, 27 master's awarded. *Entrance requirements:* For master's, GMAT, proficiency exam (quantitative skills), minimum GPA of 2.5, resume, employer letter of recommendation, 2 letters of recommendation, written business analysis. Additional exam requirements/recommendations for international students: Required—TOEFL (minimum score 550 paper-based; 213 computer-based). *Application deadline:* Applications are processed on a rolling basis. Application fee: $25. *Expenses:* Contact institution. *Financial support:* Applicants required to submit FAFSA. *Unit head:* Dr. Jon Burch, Director of Graduate Management Program, 615-248-1529, E-mail: management@trevecca.edu. *Application contact:* Marcus Lackey, Admissions Counselor, 615-248-1529, Fax: 615-248-1700, E-mail: management@trevecca.edu.

Trinity International University, Trinity Evangelical Divinity School, Deerfield, IL 60015-1284. Offers Biblical and Near Eastern archaeology and languages (MA); Christian studies (MA, Certificate); Christian thought (MA); church history (MA, Th M); congregational ministry: pastor-teacher (M Div); congregational ministry: team ministry (M Div); counseling ministries (MA); counseling psychology (MA); cross-cultural ministry (M Div); educational studies (PhD); evangelism (MA); history of Christianity in America (MA); intercultural studies (MA, PhD); leadership and ministry management (D Min); military chaplaincy (D Min); ministry (MA); mission and evangelism (Th M); missions and evangelism (D Min); New Testament (MA, Th M); Old Testament (Th M); Old Testament and Semitic languages (MA); pastoral care (M Div); pastoral care and counseling (D Min); pastoral counseling and psychology (Th M); pastoral theology (Th M); philosophy of religion (MA); preaching (D Min); religion (MA); research ministry (M Div); systematic theology (Th M); theological studies (PhD); urban ministry (MA). *Accreditation:* ATS (one or more programs are accredited). Part-time programs available. Postbaccalaureate distance learning degree programs offered (minimal on-campus study). *Degree requirements:* For master's, comprehensive exam, thesis, fieldwork; for doctorate, comprehensive exam (for some programs), thesis/dissertation; for M Div, 2 foreign languages, fieldwork; for Certificate, comprehensive exam, integrative papers. *Entrance requirements:* For M Div, GRE, MAT; for master's, GRE, MAT, minimum cumulative undergraduate GPA of 3.0; for doctorate, GRE, minimum cumulative graduate GPA of 3.2; for Certificate, GRE, MAT, minimum undergraduate GPA of 2.5. Additional exam requirements/recommendations for international students: Required—TOEFL (minimum score 580 paper-based; 237 computer-based), TWE (minimum score 4). Electronic applications accepted.

Trinity University, Department of Business Administration, San Antonio, TX 78212-7200. Offers accounting (MS). *Accreditation:* AACSB. Part-time programs available. *Entrance requirements:* For master's, GMAT, minimum GPA of 3.0, course work in accounting and business law.

Trinity (Washington) University, School of Professional Studies, Washington, DC 20017-1094. Offers business administration (MBA); communication (MA); international security studies (MA); organizational management (MSA), including federal program management, human resource management, nonprofit management, organizational development, public and community health. Part-time and evening/weekend programs available. *Degree requirements:* For master's, thesis (for some programs), capstone project (MSA). *Entrance requirements:* For master's, minimum GPA of 2.5. Additional exam requirements/recommendations for international students: Required—TOEFL (minimum score 550 paper-based; 213 computer-based).

Trinity Western University, School of Graduate Studies, Program in Business Administration, Langley, BC V2Y 1Y1, Canada. Offers international business (MBA); managing the growing enterprise (MBA); non-profit and charitable organization management (MBA). Part-time programs available. Postbaccalaureate distance learning degree programs offered (minimal on-campus study). *Degree requirements:* For master's, thesis or alternative, applied project. *Entrance requirements:* For master's, GMAT (minimum score of 550 recommended). Additional exam requirements/recommendations for international students: Required—TOEFL (minimum score 600 paper-based; 250 computer-based; 100 iBT), IELTS. Electronic applications accepted.

Troy University, Graduate School, College of Business, Program in Business Administration, Troy, AL 36082. Offers accounting (EMBA, MBA); criminal justice (EMBA); finance (MBA); general management (EMBA); healthcare management (EMBA); information systems (EMBA, MBA); international economic development (MBA). *Accreditation:* ACBSP. Part-time and evening/weekend programs available. *Students:* 382 full-time (196 women), 732 part-time (457 women); includes 616 minority (483 African Americans, 14 American Indian/Alaska Native, 96 Asian Americans or Pacific Islanders, 23 Hispanic Americans). Average age 29. 869 applicants, 61% accepted. In 2009, 296 master's awarded. *Degree requirements:* For master's, thesis or alternative. *Entrance requirements:* For master's, GMAT (minimum score 500) or GRE General Test (minimum score 900), minimum GPA of 2.5; letter of recommendation. Additional exam requirements/recommendations for international students: Required—TOEFL (minimum score 523 paper-based; 193 computer-based; 70 iBT), IELTS (minimum score 6), or ACT Compass ESL (minimum score 270 on Listening, Reading, and Grammar with no individual score below 85 and a minimum score of 8 out of 12 on writing test). *Application deadline:* Applications are processed on a rolling basis. Application fee: $50. *Unit head:* Dr. Henry M. Findley, Interim Chair/Professor, 334-670-3271, Fax: 334-670-3599, E-mail: hfindley@troy.edu. *Application contact:* Brenda K. Campbell, Director of Graduate Admissions, 334-670-3178, Fax: 334-670-3733, E-mail: bcamp@troy.edu.

Troy University, Graduate School, College of Business, Program in Management, Troy, AL 36082. Offers healthcare management (MSM); human resources management (MSM); information systems (MSM); international hospitality management (MSM); international management (MSM); leadership and organizational effectiveness (MSM); public management (MS, MSM). *Accreditation:* ACBSP. Evening/weekend programs available. *Students:* 193 full-time (130 women), 575 part-time (374 women); includes 473 minority (417 African Americans, 12 American Indian/Alaska Native, 20 Asian Americans or Pacific Islanders, 24 Hispanic Americans). Average age 35. 275 applicants, 91% accepted. In 2009, 332 master's awarded. *Degree requirements:* For master's, thesis or alternative. *Entrance requirements:* For master's, GMAT (minimum score 500) or GRE General Test (minimum score 900), minimum GPA of 2.5; letter of recommendation. Additional exam requirements/recommendations for international students: Required—TOEFL (minimum score 523 paper-based; 193 computer-based; 70 iBT), IELTS, or ACT Compass ESL (minimum score 270 on Listening, Reading, and Grammar with no individual score below 85 and a minimum score of 8 out of 12 on writing test). *Application deadline:* Applications are processed on a rolling basis. Application fee: $50. Electronic applications accepted. *Expenses:* Contact institution. *Unit head:* Dr. Henry M. Findley, Interim Chair/Professor, 334-670-3271, Fax: 334-670-3599, E-mail: hfindley@troy.edu. *Application contact:* Brenda K. Campbell, Director of Graduate Admissions, 334-670-3178, Fax: 334-670-3733, E-mail: bcamp@troy.edu.

TUI University, College of Business Administration, Program in Business Administration, Cypress, CA 90630. Offers business administration (PhD); conflict and negotiation management (MBA); criminal justice administration (MBA); entrepreneurship (MBA); finance (MBA); general management (MBA); government accounting (MBA); human resource management (MBA); information security and digital assurance management (MBA); information technology management (MBA); international business (MBA); logistics management (MBA); marketing (MBA); project management (MBA); public management (MBA); quality management (MBA); strategic leadership (MBA). Part-time and evening/weekend programs available. Postbaccalaureate distance learning degree programs offered (no on-campus study). *Degree requirements:* For doctorate, comprehensive exam, thesis/dissertation, defense of dissertation. *Entrance requirements:* For master's, minimum GPA of 2.5 (students with GPA 3.0 or greater may transfer up to 30% of graduate level credits); for doctorate, minimum GPA of 3.4, curriculum vitae, course work in research methods or statistics. Additional exam requirements/recommendations for international students: Required—TOEFL. Electronic applications accepted.

Tulane University, A. B. Freeman School of Business, New Orleans, LA 70118-5669. Offers EMBA, M Acct, M Fin, MBA, PMBA, PhD, JD/M Acct, JD/MBA, MBA/M Acc, MBA/MA, MBA/MD, MBA/ME, MBA/MPH. *Accreditation:* AACSB. Part-time and evening/weekend programs available. Terminal master's awarded for partial completion of doctoral program. *Entrance requirements:* For master's, GMAT, interview. Additional exam requirements/recommendations for international students: Required—TOEFL. Electronic applications accepted. *Expenses:* Contact institution.

Union Graduate College, School of Management, Schenectady, NY 12308-3107. Offers Business Administration (MBA); Financial Management (Certificate); General Management (Certificate); Health Systems Administration (MBA, Certificate); Human Resources (Certificate). *Accreditation:* AACSB. Part-time and evening/weekend programs available. *Faculty:* 9 full-time (1 woman), 25 part-time/adjunct (9 women). *Students:* 112 full-time (53 women), 86 part-time (38 women); includes 24 minority (4 African Americans, 16 Asian Americans or Pacific Islanders, 4 Hispanic Americans), 13 international. Average age 26. 173 applicants, 61% accepted, 93 enrolled. In 2009, 76 master's, 15 other advanced degrees awarded. *Degree requirements:* For master's, internship, capstone course. *Entrance requirements:* For master's, GMAT, minimum GPA of 3.0, 3 letters of recommendation. Additional exam requirements/recommendations for international students: Required—TOEFL (minimum score 550 paper-based; 213 computer-based). *Application deadline:* Applications are processed on a rolling basis. Application fee: $60. *Financial support:* Research assistantships, career-related internships or fieldwork, Federal Work-Study, scholarships/grants, health care benefits, and tuition waivers (partial) available. Support available to part-time students. Financial award applicants required to submit FAFSA. *Unit head:* Dr. Eric Lewis, Dean, 518-631-9890, Fax: 518-631-9902, E-mail: lewise@uniongraduatecollege.edu. *Application contact:* Diane Trzaskos, Admissions Coordinator, 518-631-9837, Fax: 518-631-9901, E-mail: trzaskod@uniongraduatecollege.edu.

Union University, McAfee School of Business Administration, Jackson, TN 38305-3697. Offers MBA. Also available at Germantown campus. Evening/weekend programs available. *Entrance requirements:* For master's, GMAT, minimum GPA of 2.5. Electronic applications accepted. *Expenses:* Contact institution. *Faculty research:* Personal financial management, strategy, accounting, marketing, economics.

United States International University, School of Business Administration, Nairobi, Kenya. Offers finance (MBA); information technology management (MBA); integrated studies (MBA); management and organizational development (MS); marketing (MBA); strategic management (MBA). Part-time and evening/weekend programs available. *Degree requirements:* For master's, thesis. *Entrance requirements:* For master's, GMAT, 2 letters of reference, resume. Additional exam requirements/recommendations for international students: Required—TOEFL (minimum score 550 paper-based; 213 computer-based). *Faculty research:* Marketing in small business enterprises, total quality management in Kenya.

Universidad Autonoma de Guadalajara, Graduate Programs, Guadalajara, Mexico. Offers administrative law and justice (LL M); advertising and corporate communications (MA); architecture (M Arch); business (MBA); computational science (MCC); education (Ed M, Ed D); English-Spanish translation (MA); fiscal law (MA); integrated management of digital animation (MA); international business (MIB); international corporate law (LL M); internet technologies (MS); labor health (MS); manufacturing systems (MMS); philosophy (MA, PhD); power electronics (MS); quality systems (MQS); renewable energy (MS); social evaluation of projects (MBA); strategic market research (MBA); teaching mathematics (MA).

Universidad Central del Este, Graduate School, San Pedro de Macoris, Dominican Republic. Offers administration (M Ad); dentistry (DMD); development of educational and social policies (PhD); environmental engineering (ME); financial management (M Ad); higher education (M Ed); human resources (M Ad); public health (MPH). *Entrance requirements:* For master's, letters of recommendation.

Universidad de las Americas, A.C., Program in Business Administration, Mexico City, Mexico. Offers finance (MBA); marketing research (MBA); production and quality (MBA).

Universidad de las Américas–Puebla, Division of Graduate Studies, School of Business and Economics, Puebla, Mexico. Offers business administration (MBA); finance (M Adm). Part-time and evening/weekend programs available. *Degree requirements:* For master's, one foreign language, thesis. *Entrance requirements:* Additional exam requirements/recommendations for international students: Required—TOEFL. *Faculty research:* System dynamics, information technology, marketing, international business, strategic planning, quality.

Universidad del Este, Graduate School, Carolina, PR 00984. Offers accounting (MBA); adult education (M Ed); agribusiness (MBA); bilingual education (M Ed); criminal justice and criminology (MA); early education (M Ed); elementary education (M Ed); human resources (MBA); information security management (MBA); information technology and Web business development (MBA); management (MBA); public policy (MPA); social work (MA), including clinical social work; special education (M Ed); strategic leadership (MBA); teaching English (M Ed); teaching Spanish (M Ed).

Universidad del Turabo, Graduate Programs, School in Business Administration, Online Business Administration Program, Gurabo, PR 00778-3030. Offers human resources (MBA); management (MBA); marketing (MBA); materials management (MBA).

Universidad del Turabo, Graduate Programs, School in Business Administration, Program in Management, Gurabo, PR 00778-3030. Offers MBA, DBA. Part-time and evening/weekend programs available. *Students:* 55 full-time (31 women), 106 part-time (45 women); includes 147 Hispanic Americans. Average age 37. 73 applicants, 89% accepted, 48 enrolled. In 2009, 37 master's, 11 doctorates awarded. *Entrance requirements:* For master's, GRE, EXADEP, interview. *Application deadline:* For fall admission, 8/5 for domestic students. Application fee: $25. *Unit head:* Marcelino Rivera, Dean, 787-743-7979 Ext. 4117. *Application contact:* Virginia Gonzalez, Admissions Officer, 787-746-3009.

Universidad Metropolitana, School of Business Administration, San Juan, PR 00928-1150. Offers accounting (MBA); finance (MBA); human resources management (MBA); international business (MBA); management (MBA); management information systems (MBA); marketing (MBA); public accounting (Certificate). Part-time and evening/weekend programs available. *Degree requirements:* For master's, thesis or alternative. Electronic applications accepted. *Faculty research:* Latin American trade, international investments, central city business development, Hispanic consumer research, Caribbean and Asian trade cooperation.

Universidad Nacional Pedro Henriquez Urena, Graduate School, Santo Domingo, Dominican Republic. Offers administrative sciences (PhD); business administration (MBA); environmental engineering (MEE); project management (M Man, MPM); sanitation engineering (ME); veterinary medicine (DVM).

Université de Moncton, Faculty of Administration, Moncton, NB E1A 3E9, Canada. Offers MBA, LL B/MBA. Part-time and evening/weekend programs available. Postbaccalaureate distance learning degree programs offered (no on-campus study). *Faculty:* 23 full-time (7 women), 21 part-time/adjunct (1 woman). *Students:* 35 full-time (11 women), 115 part-time (56 women), 18 international. Average age 28. 121 applicants, 51% accepted, 27 enrolled. In 2009, 23 master's awarded. *Degree requirements:* For master's, one foreign language, thesis. *Entrance requirements:* For master's, minimum undergraduate GPA of 3.0. *Application deadline:* For fall admission, 6/1 for domestic students, 2/1 for international students; for winter admission, 11/15 for domestic students, 9/1 for international students; for spring admission, 3/31 for domestic students, 1/1 for international students. Applications are processed on a rolling basis. Application fee: $39. Electronic applications accepted. *Financial support:* In 2009–10, 7 fellowships (averaging $2,500 per year) were awarded; teaching assistantships, institutionally sponsored loans also available. Support available to part-time students. Financial award application deadline: 5/30. *Faculty research:* Service management, corporate reputation, financial management, accounting, supply chain. Total annual research expenditures: $150,000. *Unit head:* Dr. Nha Nguyen, Director, 506-858-4231, Fax: 506-858-4093, E-mail: nha.nguyen@umoncton.ca. *Application contact:* Natalie Allain, Admission Counselor, 506-858-4273, Fax: 506-858-4093, E-mail: natalie.allain@umoncton.ca.

Université de Sherbrooke, Faculty of Administration, Doctoral Program in Business Administration, Sherbrooke, QC J1K 2R1, Canada. Offers DBA. Part-time programs available. *Degree requirements:* For doctorate, one foreign language, thesis/dissertation. *Entrance requirements:* For doctorate, MBA, 3 years of pertinent experience. Electronic applications accepted. *Faculty research:* Change management, international business and finance, work organization, information technology implementation and impact on organizations, strategic management.

Université de Sherbrooke, Faculty of Administration, Master of Business Administration Program, Sherbrooke, QC J1K2R1, Canada. Offers MBA.

Université de Sherbrooke, Faculty of Law, Sherbrooke, QC J1K 2R1, Canada. Offers alternative dispute resolution (LL M, Diploma); biotechnology (LL B); business administration (LL B); business law (Diploma); health law (LL M, Diploma); law (LL B, LL D); legal management (Diploma); notarial law (DDN); transnational law (Diploma). Part-time and evening/weekend programs available. *Degree requirements:* For master's, thesis; for other advanced degree, one foreign language. *Entrance requirements:* For master's and other advanced degree, LL B. Electronic applications accepted.

Université du Québec à Chicoutimi, Graduate Programs, Program in Small and Medium-Sized Organization Management, Chicoutimi, QC G7H 2B1, Canada. Offers M Sc. Part-time programs available. *Degree requirements:* For master's, thesis. *Entrance requirements:* For master's, appropriate bachelor's degree, proficiency in French.

Université du Québec à Montréal, Graduate Programs, PhD Program in Business Administration, Montréal, QC H3C 3P8, Canada. Offers PhD. Part-time programs available. *Degree requirements:* For doctorate, thesis/dissertation. *Entrance requirements:* For doctorate, appropriate master's degree or equivalent, proficiency in French.

Université du Québec à Montréal, Graduate Programs, Program in Business Administration (Professional), Montréal, QC H3C 3P8, Canada. Offers business administration (MBA); management consultant (Diploma). Part-time programs available. *Entrance requirements:* For master's and Diploma, appropriate bachelor's degree or equivalent, proficiency in French.

Université du Québec à Montréal, Graduate Programs, Program in Business Administration (Research), Montréal, QC H3C 3P8, Canada. Offers MBA. Part-time programs available. *Entrance requirements:* For master's, appropriate bachelor's degree or equivalent and proficiency in French.

Université du Québec à Rimouski, Graduate Programs, Program in Business Administration, Rimouski, QC G5L 3A1, Canada. Offers MBA.

Université du Québec à Rimouski, Graduate Programs, Program in Management of People in Working Situation, Rimouski, QC G5L 3A1, Canada. Offers M Sc, Diploma.

Université du Québec à Trois-Rivières, Graduate Programs, Program in Business Administration, Trois-Rivières, QC G9A 5H7, Canada. Offers MBA, DBA. *Degree requirements:* For doctorate, thesis/dissertation.

Université du Québec en Abitibi-Témiscamingue, Graduate Programs, Program in Business Administration, Rouyn-Noranda, QC J9X 5E4, Canada. Offers MBA.

Université du Québec en Abitibi-Témiscamingue, Graduate Programs, Program in Organization Management, Rouyn-Noranda, QC J9X 5E4, Canada. Offers M Sc. Part-time programs available. *Degree requirements:* For master's, thesis. *Entrance requirements:* For master's, appropriate bachelor's degree, proficiency in French.

Université Laval, Faculty of Administrative Sciences, Program in Organizations Management and Development, Québec, QC G1K 7P4, Canada. Offers Diploma. Part-time programs available. *Entrance requirements:* For degree, knowledge of French. Electronic applications accepted.

Université Laval, Faculty of Administrative Sciences, Programs in Administrative Studies, Québec, QC G1K 7P4, Canada. Offers administrative studies (M Sc, PhD); financial engineering (M Sc). *Accreditation:* AACSB. Terminal master's awarded for partial completion of doctoral program. *Degree requirements:* For master's, thesis (for some programs); for doctorate, comprehensive exam, thesis/dissertation. *Entrance requirements:* For master's and doctorate, knowledge of French and English. Electronic applications accepted.

Université Laval, Faculty of Administrative Sciences, Programs in Business Administration, Québec, QC G1K 7P4, Canada. Offers accounting (MBA); agri-food management (MBA); electronic business (MBA, Diploma); factory management and logistics (MBA); finance (MBA); firm management (MBA); geomatic management (MBA); information technology management (MBA); international management (MBA); management (MBA); management accounting (MBA, Diploma); marketing (MBA); modeling and organizational decision (MBA); occupational health and safety management (MBA); pharmacy management (MBA); social and environmental responsibility (MBA); technological entrepreneurship (Diploma). *Accreditation:* AACSB. Part-time and evening/weekend programs available. Postbaccalaureate distance learning degree programs offered (no on-campus study). *Entrance requirements:* For master's and Diploma, knowledge of French and English. Electronic applications accepted.

University at Albany, State University of New York, School of Business, Albany, NY 12222-0001. Offers MBA, MS. *Accreditation:* AACSB. Part-time and evening/weekend programs available. Terminal master's awarded for partial completion of doctoral program. *Degree requirements:* For master's, project. *Entrance requirements:* For master's, GMAT. Additional exam requirements/recommendations for international students: Required—TOEFL (minimum score 550 paper-based; 213 computer-based). Electronic applications accepted.

University at Buffalo, the State University of New York, Graduate School, School of Management, Buffalo, NY 14260. Offers accounting (MS); business administration (EMBA, MBA, PMBA); finance (MS), including financial engineering, financial management; information assurance (Certificate); management (PhD); management information systems (MS); supply chains and operations management (MS); Au D/MBA; JD/MBA; M Arch/MBA; MA/MBA; MD/MBA; MPH/MBA; MSW/MBA; Pharm D/MBA. *Accreditation:* AACSB. Part-time and evening/weekend programs available. *Faculty:* 66 full-time (19 women), 21 part-time/adjunct (4 women). *Students:* 502 full-time (176 women), 199 part-time (54 women); includes 29 minority (10 African Americans, 16 Asian Americans or Pacific Islanders, 3 Hispanic Americans), 306 international. Average age 27. 1,944 applicants, 31% accepted, 324 enrolled. In 2009, 363 master's, 7 doctorates, 3 other advanced degrees awarded. *Degree requirements:* For master's, thesis (for some programs); for doctorate, comprehensive exam, thesis/dissertation. *Entrance requirements:* For master's, GMAT (MBA, MS in accounting), GRE General Test (for all other MS concentrations); for doctorate, GMAT or GRE. Additional exam requirements/

Business Administration and Management—General

University at Buffalo, the State University of New York (continued)

recommendations for international students: Required—TOEFL (minimum score 230 computer-based; 95 iBT). *Application deadline:* For fall admission, 6/2 priority date for domestic students, 3/1 priority date for international students. Applications are processed on a rolling basis. Application fee: $100. Electronic applications accepted. *Expenses:* Contact institution. *Financial support:* In 2009–10, 91 students received support, including 5 fellowships with full and partial tuition reimbursements available (averaging $4,000 per year), 41 research assistantships with full and partial tuition reimbursements available (averaging $16,000 per year), 28 teaching assistantships with full and partial tuition reimbursements available (averaging $15,000 per year); career-related internships or fieldwork, Federal Work-Study, institutionally sponsored loans, scholarships/grants, health care benefits, and unspecified assistantships also available. Financial award application deadline: 2/15; financial award applicants required to submit FAFSA. *Faculty research:* Earnings management and electronic information assurance, supply chains and operations management, corporate financing and asset pricing, consumer behavior and quantitative modeling of marketing behavior, leadership and politics in organizations. Total annual research expenditures: $230,000. *Unit head:* David W. Frasier, Assistant Dean, 716-645-3204, Fax: 716-645-2341, E-mail: davidf@buffalo.edu. *Application contact:* David W. Frasier, Assistant Dean, 716-645-3204, Fax: 716-645-2341, E-mail: davidf@buffalo.edu.

The University of Akron, Graduate School, College of Business Administration, Department of Management, Akron, OH 44325. Offers electronic business (MBA); entrepreneurship (MBA); management (MBA); management of technology (MBA); management-health services administration (MSM); management-human resources (MSM); management-information systems (MSM); management-supply chain management (MSM); JD/MBA; JD/MSM. *Accreditation:* AACSB. Part-time and evening/weekend programs available. *Faculty:* 19 full-time (2 women), 5 part-time/adjunct (2 women). *Students:* 64 full-time (22 women), 140 part-time (53 women); includes 17 minority (10 African Americans, 5 Asian Americans or Pacific Islanders, 2 Hispanic Americans), 40 international. Average age 31. 50 applicants, 68% accepted, 23 enrolled. In 2009, 48 master's awarded. *Entrance requirements:* For master's, GMAT, minimum GPA of 2.75, letters of recommendation, resume. Additional exam requirements/recommendations for international students: Required—TOEFL (minimum score 550 paper-based; 213 computer-based; 79 iBT). *Application deadline:* For fall admission, 8/1 for domestic and international students; for spring admission, 12/1 for domestic and international students. Applications are processed on a rolling basis. Application fee: $30 ($40 for international students). Electronic applications accepted. *Expenses:* Tuition, state resident: full-time $6570; part-time $365 per credit hour. Tuition, nonresident: full-time $11,250; part-time $625 per credit hour. *Financial support:* In 2009–10, 27 research assistantships with full and partial tuition reimbursements were awarded; career-related internships or fieldwork and Federal Work-Study also available. *Faculty research:* Human resource management, innovation, entrepreneurship, technology management and technology transfer, artificial intelligence and belief functions. *Unit head:* Dr. Steve Ash, Interim Chair, 330-972-6086, Fax: 330-972-6588, E-mail: ash@uakron.edu. *Application contact:* Dr. Susan Hanlon, Director of Graduate Business Programs, 330-972-7043, Fax: 330-972-6588, E-mail: shanlon@uakron.edu.

The University of Alabama, Graduate School, Manderson Graduate School of Business, Department of Information Systems, Statistics, and Management Science, Program of Information Systems, Statistics, and Management Science—Operations Management, Tuscaloosa, AL 35487. Offers operations management (MS, PhD). Part-time programs available. Postbaccalaureate distance learning degree programs offered (no on-campus study). *Faculty:* 23 full-time (3 women). *Students:* 28 full-time (7 women), 21 part-time (3 women); includes 6 minority (2 African Americans, 1 American Indian/Alaska Native, 3 Asian Americans or Pacific Islanders), 12 international. Average age 32. 65 applicants, 26% accepted, 16 enrolled. In 2009, 16 master's, 2 doctorates awarded. Terminal master's awarded for partial completion of doctoral program. *Median time to degree:* Of those who began their doctoral program in fall 2001, 75% received their degree in 8 years or less. *Degree requirements:* For master's, comprehensive exam, business calculus; for doctorate, comprehensive exam, thesis/dissertation. *Entrance requirements:* For master's, GMAT or GRE; for doctorate, GRE or GMAT. Additional exam requirements/recommendations for international students: Required—TOEFL (minimum score 550 paper-based; 213 computer-based), IELTS (minimum score 6.5). *Application deadline:* For spring admission, 3/1 priority date for domestic and international students. Applications are processed on a rolling basis. Application fee: $50 ($60 for international students). Electronic applications accepted. *Expenses:* Tuition, state resident: full-time $7000. Tuition, nonresident: full-time $19,200. *Financial support:* In 2009–10, 11 students received support, including 7 teaching assistantships with full tuition reimbursements available (averaging $13,500 per year); scholarships/grants and health care benefits also available. Financial award application deadline: 3/1. *Faculty research:* Supply chain management, inventory, simulation, logistics. *Unit head:* Dr. Michael D. Conerly, Head, 205-348-8902, Fax: 205-348-0560, E-mail: mconerly@cba.ua.edu. *Application contact:* Dana Merchant, Administrative Secretary, 205-348-8904, E-mail: dmerchan@cba.ua.edu.

The University of Alabama, Graduate School, Manderson Graduate School of Business, Department of Management and Marketing, Program in Management, Tuscaloosa, AL 35487. Offers MA, MS, PhD. Part-time and evening/weekend programs available. Postbaccalaureate distance learning degree programs offered (no on-campus study). *Faculty:* 24 full-time (7 women). *Students:* 27 full-time (12 women), 19 part-time (8 women); includes 6 minority (5 African Americans, 1 Hispanic American), 18 international. Average age 28. 73 applicants, 38% accepted, 20 enrolled. In 2009, 1 degree awarded. Terminal master's awarded for partial completion of doctoral program. *Degree requirements:* For master's, comprehensive exam (for some programs), thesis (for some programs), formal project paper; for doctorate, comprehensive exam, thesis/dissertation. *Entrance requirements:* For master's and doctorate, GMAT or GRE, minimum GPA of 3.0. Additional exam requirements/recommendations for international students: Required—TOEFL (minimum score 600 paper-based) or IELTS (minimum score 6.5). *Application deadline:* For fall admission, 6/30 priority date for domestic students, 1/31 for international students; for spring admission, 10/30 for domestic students. Applications are processed on a rolling basis. Application fee: $50 ($60 for international students). *Expenses:* Tuition, state resident: full-time $7000. Tuition, nonresident: full-time $19,200. *Financial support:* In 2009–10, 5 fellowships with full and partial tuition reimbursements (averaging $15,000 per year), 2 research assistantships (averaging $18,444 per year), 2 teaching assistantships (averaging $16,200 per year) were awarded; scholarships/grants, health care benefits, and unspecified assistantships also available. *Faculty research:* Leadership, entrepreneurship, health care management, organizational behavior, strategy. *Unit head:* Dr. Robert M. Morgan, Department Head, 205-348-6183, Fax: 205-348-6695, E-mail: rmorgan@cba.ua.edu. *Application contact:* Courtney Cox, Office Associate II, 205-348-6183, Fax: 205-348-6695, E-mail: crhodes@cba.ua.edu.

The University of Alabama, Graduate School, Manderson Graduate School of Business, Program in General Commerce and Business, Tuscaloosa, AL 35487. Offers EMBA, MBA. Part-time programs available. *Students:* 208 full-time (52 women), 4 part-time (1 woman); includes 24 minority (13 African Americans, 6 Asian Americans or Pacific Islanders, 5 Hispanic Americans), 13 international. Average age 28. 303 applicants, 37% accepted, 83 enrolled. In 2009, 89 degrees awarded. *Entrance requirements:* For master's, GMAT or GRE. Additional exam requirements/recommendations for international students: Required—TOEFL (minimum score 550 paper-based). *Application deadline:* For winter admission, 1/2 priority date for domestic and international students; for spring admission, 4/15 for domestic and international students. Applications are processed on a rolling basis. Application fee: $50 ($60 for international students). Electronic applications accepted. *Expenses:* Tuition, state resident: full-time $7000. Tuition, nonresident: full-time $19,200. *Financial support:* In 2009–10, 26 students received support, including 22 research assistantships (averaging $5,400 per year), 4 teaching assistantships; health care benefits also available. Financial award application deadline: 4/15. *Unit head:* Susan C. West, Assistant Dean and Director of MBA Programs, 205-348-0954, Fax: 205-348-0479, E-mail: swest@cba.ua.edu. *Application contact:* Blake Bedsole, Coordinator of Graduate Recruiting/Admissions, 205-348-9122, Fax: 205-348-4504, E-mail: bbedsole@cba.ua.edu.

The University of Alabama at Birmingham, School of Business, Birmingham, AL 35294. Offers M Acct, MBA, PhD. *Accreditation:* AACSB. *Entrance requirements:* For master's, GMAT. Electronic applications accepted.

The University of Alabama in Huntsville, School of Graduate Studies, College of Business Administration, Department of Management and Marketing, Huntsville, AL 35899. Offers management (MBA), including acquisition management, finance, human resource management, logistics and supply chain management, marketing, project management. *Accreditation:* AACSB. Part-time and evening/weekend programs available. *Faculty:* 7 full-time (1 woman), 1 part-time/adjunct (0 women). *Students:* 41 full-time (19 women), 155 part-time (59 women); includes 30 minority (15 African Americans, 5 American Indian/Alaska Native, 7 Asian Americans or Pacific Islanders, 3 Hispanic Americans), 20 international. Average age 32. 138 applicants, 63% accepted, 68 enrolled. In 2009, 38 master's awarded. *Degree requirements:* For master's, comprehensive exam, thesis or alternative. *Entrance requirements:* For master's, GMAT (minimum score 500), minimum AACSB index of 1080. Additional exam requirements/recommendations for international students: Required—TOEFL (minimum score 550 paper-based; 213 computer-based; 62 iBT). *Application deadline:* For fall admission, 8/1 for domestic students, 4/1 for international students; for spring admission, 12/1 for domestic students, 9/1 for international students. Applications are processed on a rolling basis. Application fee: $40 ($50 for international students). Electronic applications accepted. *Expenses:* Tuition, state resident: part-time $355.75 per credit hour. Tuition, nonresident: part-time $847.10 per credit hour. Required fees: $210.80 per semester. Tuition and fees vary according to course load and program. *Financial support:* In 2009–10, 3 students received support, including 2 research assistantships with full tuition reimbursements available (averaging $14,400 per year), 1 teaching assistantship with full tuition reimbursement available (averaging $11,800 per year); career-related internships or fieldwork, Federal Work-Study, institutionally sponsored loans, scholarships/grants, health care benefits, and unspecified assistantships also available. Support available to part-time students. Financial award application deadline: 4/1; financial award applicants required to submit FAFSA. *Unit head:* Dr. Brent Wren, Chair, 256-824-6408, Fax: 256-824-6328, E-mail: wrenb@uah.edu. *Application contact:* Jennifer Pettitt, Director of Graduate Programs, 256-824-6681, Fax: 256-824-7571, E-mail: jennifer.pettitt@uah.edu.

University of Alaska Anchorage, College of Business and Public Policy, Program in Business Administration, Anchorage, AK 99508. Offers MBA. *Accreditation:* AACSB. Part-time programs available. *Degree requirements:* For master's, comprehensive exam, thesis (for some programs), capstone projects. *Entrance requirements:* Additional exam requirements/recommendations for international students: Required—TOEFL (minimum score 550 paper-based; 213 computer-based). *Faculty research:* Complex global environments.

University of Alaska Fairbanks, School of Management, Department of Business Administration, Fairbanks, AK 99775-6080. Offers capital markets (MBA); general management (MBA). *Accreditation:* AACSB. Part-time programs available. *Faculty:* 8 full-time (1 woman), 4 part-time/adjunct (1 woman). *Students:* 23 full-time (10 women), 35 part-time (25 women); includes 3 minority (all Hispanic Americans), 5 international. Average age 43. 36 applicants, 61% accepted, 18 enrolled. In 2009, 36 master's awarded. *Degree requirements:* For master's, comprehensive exam, thesis or alternative. *Entrance requirements:* For master's, GMAT. Additional exam requirements/recommendations for international students: Required—TOEFL (minimum score 550 paper-based; 213 computer-based; 80 iBT). *Application deadline:* For fall admission, 6/1 priority date for domestic students, 2/1 for international students; for spring admission, 10/15 priority date for domestic students, 9/1 for international students. Applications are processed on a rolling basis. Application fee: $60. Electronic applications accepted. *Expenses:* Tuition, state resident: full-time $7584; part-time $316 per credit. Tuition, nonresident: full-time $15,504; part-time $646 per credit. Required fees: $23 per credit. $135 per semester. Tuition and fees vary according to course level, course load and reciprocity agreements. *Financial support:* In 2009–10, 4 teaching assistantships (averaging $12,323 per year) were awarded; fellowships, research assistantships, career-related internships or fieldwork, Federal Work-Study, scholarships/grants, health care benefits, and unspecified assistantships also available. Support available to part-time students. Financial award application deadline: 2/15; financial award applicants required to submit FAFSA. *Faculty research:* Consumer behavior, marketing, international finance and business, strategic risk, organization theory. *Unit head:* Dr. Ping Lan, Director, MBA Program, 907-474-7688, Fax: 907-474-5219, E-mail: plan@alaska.edu. *Application contact:* Dr. Ping Lan, Director, MBA Program, 907-474-7688, Fax: 907-474-5219, E-mail: plan@alaska.edu.

University of Alaska Southeast, Graduate Programs, Program in Business Administration, Juneau, AK 99801. Offers MBA. Part-time and evening/weekend programs available. Postbaccalaureate distance learning degree programs offered (minimal on-campus study). *Degree requirements:* For master's, residential seminar. *Entrance requirements:* For master's, curriculum vitae, letters of reference, minimum GPA of 3.0. Electronic applications accepted. *Faculty research:* Services marketing; marketing and technology issues: social capital and entrepreneurship; motivation and managerial tactics.

University of Alberta, Faculty of Graduate Studies and Research, Doctoral Program in Business, Edmonton, AB T6G 2E1, Canada. Offers accounting (PhD); finance (PhD); human resources/industrial relations (PhD); management science (PhD); marketing (PhD); organizational analysis (PhD); MBA/PhD. *Accreditation:* AACSB. Part-time programs available. *Faculty:* 41 full-time (7 women), 1 part-time/adjunct (0 women). *Students:* 46 full-time (27 women), 5 part-time (3 women). Average age 34. 307 applicants, 7% accepted, 11 enrolled. In 2009, 2 doctorates awarded. *Degree requirements:* For doctorate, comprehensive exam, thesis/dissertation. *Entrance requirements:* For doctorate, GMAT. Additional exam requirements/recommendations for international students: Required—TOEFL (minimum score 550 paper-based; 213 computer-based). *Application deadline:* For fall admission, 6/1 priority date for domestic students; for winter admission, 5/1 for domestic students. Application fee: $0. Electronic applications accepted. Tuition and fees charges are reported in Canadian dollars. *Expenses:* Tuition, area resident: Full-time $4626 Canadian dollars; part-time $99.72 Canadian dollars per unit. International tuition: $8216 Canadian dollars full-time. Required fees: $3590 Canadian dollars; $99.72 Canadian dollars per unit. $215 Canadian dollars per term. *Financial support:* In 2009–10, 29 students received support, including 11 fellowships with full tuition reimbursements available (averaging $17,000 per year); scholarships/grants and tuition waivers (partial) also available. *Faculty research:* Accounting, capital markets and corporate finance, organizational change and human resource management, marketing, strategic management. Total annual research expenditures: $7.7 million. *Unit head:* Dr. Mike Percy, Director, 780-492-2361, Fax: 780-492-3325, E-mail: busphd@ualberta.ca. *Application contact:* Jeanette Gosine, Program Coordinator, 780-492-2361, Fax: 780-492-3325, E-mail: busphd@ualberta.ca.

University of Alberta, Faculty of Graduate Studies and Research, Executive MBA Program, Edmonton, AB T6G 2E1, Canada. Offers business administration (Exec MBA). *Accreditation:* AACSB. *Students:* 14 full-time (5 women). 18 applicants, 83% accepted. In 2009, 7 master's awarded. *Entrance requirements:* For master's, GMAT. Additional exam requirements/recommendations for international students: Required—TOEFL. *Application deadline:* For fall admission, 5/15 priority date for domestic students. Applications are processed on a rolling basis. Application fee: $0. Electronic applications accepted. *Expenses:* Contact institution. *Unit head:* Dr. Vern Jones, Director, 780-465-3946, Fax: 403-465-8760. *Application contact:* Marjorie McCullen, Information Contact, 780-492-4213, Fax: 780-492-7825, E-mail: mba@ualberta.ca.

University of Alberta, Faculty of Graduate Studies and Research, Program in Business Administration, Edmonton, AB T6G 2E1, Canada. Offers international business (MBA); leisure and sport management (MBA); natural resources and energy (MBA); technology commercialization (MBA); MBA/LL B; MBA/M Ag; MBA/M Eng; MBA/MF; MBA/PhD. *Accreditation:* AACSB. Part-time and evening/weekend programs available. *Faculty:* 77 full-time, 20 part-time/adjunct. *Students:* 131 full-time (56 women), 109 part-time (51 women). Average age 29. 525 applicants, 30% accepted, 90 enrolled. In 2009, 114 master's awarded. *Degree requirements:* For master's, thesis or alternative. *Entrance requirements:* For master's, GMAT. Additional exam requirements/recommendations for international students: Required—TOEFL

(minimum score 600 paper-based; 250 computer-based). *Application deadline:* For fall admission, 4/30 priority date for domestic students, 4/30 for international students. Applications are processed on a rolling basis. Application fee: $0. Electronic applications accepted. Tuition and fees charges are reported in Canadian dollars. *Expenses:* Tuition, area resident: Full-time $4626 Canadian dollars; part-time $99.72 Canadian dollars per unit. International tuition: $8216 Canadian dollars full-time. Required fees: $3590 Canadian dollars; $99.72 Canadian dollars per unit. $215 Canadian dollars per term. *Financial support:* Fellowships, research assistantships, teaching assistantships, career-related internships or fieldwork, scholarships/grants, health care benefits, and unspecified assistantships available. *Faculty research:* Natural resources and energy/management and policy/family enterprise/international business/healthcare research management. Total annual research expenditures: $1 million. *Unit head:* Dr. Douglas Olsen, Associate Dean, 780-492-5412, Fax: 780-492-7825. *Application contact:* Joan A. White, Secretary, 780-492-3679, Fax: 780-492-2024, E-mail: mba@ualberta.ca.

The University of Arizona, Graduate College, Eller College of Management, Tucson, AZ 85721. Offers M Ac, MA, MBA, MPA, MS, PhD, JD/MA, JD/MBA, JD/PhD. *Accreditation:* AACSB. Evening/weekend programs available. *Faculty:* 74. *Students:* 596 full-time (203 women), 94 part-time (33 women); includes 40 minority (8 African Americans, 2 American Indian/Alaska Native, 9 Asian Americans or Pacific Islanders, 21 Hispanic Americans), 222 international. Average age 30. 1,601 applicants, 40% accepted, 280 enrolled. In 2009, 361 master's, 15 doctorates awarded. *Degree requirements:* For doctorate, thesis/dissertation. *Entrance requirements:* Additional exam requirements/recommendations for international students: Required—TOEFL (minimum score 550 paper-based; 213 computer-based; 79 iBT). *Application deadline:* Applications are processed on a rolling basis. Application fee: $75. Electronic applications accepted. *Expenses:* Contact institution. *Financial support:* In 2009–10, 42 research assistantships with full tuition reimbursements (averaging $16,374 per year), 136 teaching assistantships with full tuition reimbursements (averaging $13,454 per year) were awarded; career-related internships or fieldwork, Federal Work-Study, scholarships/grants, health care benefits, tuition waivers (partial), and unspecified assistantships also available. Financial award application deadline: 3/15. Total annual research expenditures: $4.8 million. *Unit head:* Dr. Paul R. Portney, Dean, 520-621-2125, Fax: 520-621-8105, E-mail: pportney@email.arizona.edu. *Application contact:* Information Contact, 520-621-2165, Fax: 520-621-8105, E-mail: mbaadmissions@eller.arizona.edu.

University of Arkansas, Graduate School, Sam M. Walton College of Business Administration, Program in Business Administration, Fayetteville, AR 72701-1201. Offers MBA, PhD. *Accreditation:* AACSB. Part-time and evening/weekend programs available. Postbaccalaureate distance learning degree programs offered (minimal on-campus study). *Students:* 43 full-time (18 women), 106 part-time (26 women); includes 13 minority (2 African Americans, 2 American Indian/Alaska Native, 6 Asian Americans or Pacific Islanders, 3 Hispanic Americans), 19 international. In 2009, 81 master's awarded. *Degree requirements:* For doctorate, thesis/dissertation. *Entrance requirements:* For master's and doctorate, GMAT. Application fee: $40 ($50 for international students). *Expenses:* Tuition, state resident: full-time $7355; part-time $356.58 per hour. Tuition, nonresident: full-time $17,401; part-time $775.17 per hour. Required fees: $1203. *Financial support:* In 2009–10, 22 fellowships with tuition reimbursements, 37 research assistantships were awarded; teaching assistantships, career-related internships or fieldwork and Federal Work-Study also available. Support available to part-time students. Financial award application deadline: 4/1; financial award applicants required to submit FAFSA. *Unit head:* Dr. Alan Ellstrand, MBA Director, 479-575-2851, E-mail: aellstra@uark.edu. *Application contact:* Dr. Alan Ellstrand, MBA Director, 479-575-2851, E-mail: aellstra@uark.edu.

University of Arkansas at Little Rock, Graduate School, College of Business Administration, Little Rock, AR 72204-1099. Offers accountancy (M Acc, Graduate Certificate); business administration (MBA); construction management (Graduate Certificate); management (Graduate Certificate); management information system (MIS); management information systems (Graduate Certificate); management information systems leadership (Graduate Certificate); taxation (MS, Graduate Certificate). *Accreditation:* AACSB. Part-time and evening/weekend programs available. *Entrance requirements:* For master's, GMAT, minimum undergraduate GPA of 2.7. Additional exam requirements/recommendations for international students: Required—TOEFL (minimum score 525 paper-based; 195 computer-based).

University of Atlanta, Graduate Programs, Atlanta, GA 30360. Offers business (MS); business administration (Exec MBA, MBA); computer science (MS); educational leadership (MS, Ed D); healthcare administration (MS, D Sc, Graduate Certificate); information technology for management (Graduate Certificate); international project management (Graduate Certificate); law (JD); managerial science (DBA); project management (Graduate Certificate); social science (MS). Postbaccalaureate distance learning degree programs offered. *Faculty:* 54 part-time/adjunct (10 women). *Students:* 251 full-time. *Entrance requirements:* For master's, minimum cumulative GPA of 2.5. *Expenses:* Tuition: Part-time $1000 per course. Part-time tuition and fees vary according to course load and degree level.

University of Baltimore, Graduate School, Merrick School of Business, Baltimore, MD 21201-5779. Offers MBA, MS, Graduate Certificate, JD/MBA, MBA/MSN, MBA/Pharm D. Part-time and evening/weekend programs available. Postbaccalaureate distance learning degree programs offered (no on-campus study). *Entrance requirements:* For master's, GMAT. Additional exam requirements/recommendations for international students: Required—TOEFL (minimum score 550 paper-based; 213 computer-based). Electronic applications accepted. *Faculty research:* Finance, economics, accounting, health care, management information systems.

University of Baltimore, Joint University of Baltimore/Towson University (UB/Towson) MBA Program, Baltimore, MD 21201-5779. Offers MBA, JD/MBA, MBA/MSN, MBA/Pharm D. *Accreditation:* AACSB. Part-time and evening/weekend programs available. Postbaccalaureate distance learning degree programs offered (no on-campus study). *Entrance requirements:* For master's, GMAT. Additional exam requirements/recommendations for international students: Required—TOEFL (minimum score 550 paper-based; 213 computer-based).

University of Bridgeport, School of Business, Program in Business Administration, Bridgeport, CT 06604. Offers MBA. *Accreditation:* ACBSP. Part-time and evening/weekend programs available. *Degree requirements:* For master's, thesis optional. *Entrance requirements:* For master's, GMAT. Additional exam requirements/recommendations for international students: Recommended—TOEFL (minimum score 550 paper-based; 213 computer-based; 80 iBT), IELTS (minimum score 6.5). Electronic applications accepted.

The University of British Columbia, Sauder School of Business, Doctoral Program in Commerce and Business Administration, Vancouver, BC V6T 1Z1, Canada. Offers accounting (PhD); finance (PhD); international business (PhD); management information systems (PhD); management science (PhD); marketing (PhD); organizational behavior (PhD); strategy and business economics (PhD); transportation and logistics (PhD); urban land economics (PhD). *Degree requirements:* For doctorate, comprehensive exam, thesis/dissertation. *Entrance requirements:* For doctorate, GMAT or GRE. Additional exam requirements/recommendations for international students: Required—TOEFL (minimum score 600 paper-based; 250 computer-based; 100 iBT). Electronic applications accepted.

The University of British Columbia, Sauder School of Business, MBA Program, Vancouver, BC V6T 1Z1, Canada. Offers IMBA, MBA. *Accreditation:* AACSB. Part-time and evening/weekend programs available. Postbaccalaureate distance learning degree programs offered (minimal on-campus study). *Entrance requirements:* For master's, GMAT, minimum B average in undergraduate course work. Additional exam requirements/recommendations for international students: Required—TOEFL, IELTS or Michigan English Language Assessment Battery. Electronic applications accepted. *Expenses:* Contact institution. *Faculty research:* Financial economics and reporting, human resources, information systems, management science, marketing.

University of Calgary, Faculty of Graduate Studies, Haskayne School of Business, Alberta/Haskayne Executive MBA Program, Calgary, AB T2N 1N4, Canada. Offers EMBA. Program offered with School of Business at The University of Alberta. *Accreditation:* AACSB. Part-time programs available. *Entrance requirements:* For master's, GMAT, minimum GPA of 3.0, minimum 7 years of work experience, 3 letters of reference. Additional exam requirements/recommendations for international students: Required—TOEFL (minimum score 600 paper-based; 250 computer-based; 100 iBT). *Expenses:* Contact institution. *Faculty research:* Accounting, data analysis and modeling, strategy, entrepreneurship, negotiations.

University of Calgary, Faculty of Graduate Studies, Haskayne School of Business, Program in Business Administration, Calgary, AB T2N 1N4, Canada. Offers MBA, MBA/LL B, MBA/MBT, MBA/MD, MBA/MSW. *Accreditation:* AACSB. Part-time and evening/weekend programs available. *Degree requirements:* For master's, comprehensive exam, thesis optional. *Entrance requirements:* For master's, GMAT (minimum score 550), minimum GPA of 3.0, resume, 3 years of work experience, 3 letters of reference, 4 year bachelor degree. Additional exam requirements/recommendations for international students: Required—TOEFL (minimum score 600 paper-based; 250 computer-based). Electronic applications accepted. *Expenses:* Contact institution. *Faculty research:* Entrepreneurship, ethics, strategy, finance energy management and sustainability.

University of Calgary, Faculty of Graduate Studies, Haskayne School of Business, Program in Management, Calgary, AB T2N 1N4, Canada. Offers MBA, PhD. *Accreditation:* AACSB. Terminal master's awarded for partial completion of doctoral program. *Degree requirements:* For master's, one foreign language, comprehensive exam, thesis; for doctorate, one foreign language, comprehensive exam, thesis/dissertation, written and oral exams. *Entrance requirements:* For master's, GMAT, GRE, minimum GPA of 3.3 in last 2 years of course work, 2 letters of ref.; for doctorate, GMAT, GRE, minimum GPA of 3.5 in last 2 years of course work, 2 letters of reference. Additional exam requirements/recommendations for international students: Required—TOEFL (minimum score 600 paper-based; 250 computer-based; 100 iBT), IELTS (minimum score 7). Electronic applications accepted. *Faculty research:* Operations management, international business, management information systems, accounting, finance, sustainable development.

University of California, Berkeley, Graduate Division, Haas School of Business, Berkeley-Columbia Executive MBA Program, Berkeley, CA 94720-1500. Offers MBA. *Accreditation:* AACSB. Part-time programs available. *Students:* 135 part-time (29 women); includes 55 minority (2 African Americans, 1 American Indian/Alaska Native, 45 Asian Americans or Pacific Islanders, 7 Hispanic Americans), 5 international. Average age 37. In 2009, 60 master's awarded. *Entrance requirements:* For master's, GMAT. Additional exam requirements/recommendations for international students: Required—TOEFL (minimum score 570 paper-based; 230 computer-based; 68 iBT). *Application deadline:* For winter admission, 1/4 priority date for domestic and international students; for spring admission, 2/1 priority date for domestic and international students. Application fee: $200. Electronic applications accepted. *Expenses:* Contact institution. *Financial support:* Available to part-time students. Applicants required to submit FAFSA. *Unit head:* Katherine Lilygren, Executive Director, 510-642-0306, Fax: 510-642-0631, E-mail: lilygren@haas.berkeley.edu. *Application contact:* Marjorie DeGraca, Berkeley-Columbia Executive MBA Admissions Office, 510-643-1046, Fax: 510-642-5902, E-mail: emba@haas.berkeley.edu.

University of California, Berkeley, Graduate Division, Haas School of Business and School of Law, Concurrent JD/MBA Program, Berkeley, CA 94720-1500. Offers JD/MBA. *Accreditation:* AACSB; ABA. *Students:* 1 full-time (0 women). *Entrance requirements:* Additional exam requirements/recommendations for international students: Required—TOEFL. Application fee: $200. Electronic applications accepted. *Financial support:* Application deadline: 3/1. *Unit head:* Julia Hwang, Director, MBA Program, 510-642-1405, Fax: 510-643-6659, E-mail: julia_hwang@haas.berkeley.edu. *Application contact:* Office of Admissions, 510-642-1405, Fax: 510-643-6659, E-mail: admissions@boalt.berkeley.edu.

University of California, Berkeley, Graduate Division, Haas School of Business and School of Public Health, Concurrent MBA/MPH Program, Berkeley, CA 94720-1500. Offers MBA/MPH. *Accreditation:* AACSB; CEPH. *Students:* 39 full-time (23 women); includes 9 minority (all Asian Americans or Pacific Islanders), 6 international. Average age 28. *Entrance requirements:* Additional exam requirements/recommendations for international students: Required—TOEFL. Application fee: $200. Electronic applications accepted. *Financial support:* Fellowships with tuition reimbursements, teaching assistantships with tuition reimbursements, career-related internships or fieldwork, scholarships/grants, and unspecified assistantships available. Financial award applicants required to submit FAFSA. *Unit head:* Prof. Kristi Raube, Director, Health Services Management Program, 510-642-5023, Fax: 510-643-6659, E-mail: raube@haas.berkeley.edu. *Application contact:* Lee Forgue, Student Affairs Officer, 510-642-5023, Fax: 510-643-6659, E-mail: eilis@haas.berkeley.edu.

University of California, Berkeley, Graduate Division, Haas School of Business, Evening and Weekend MBA Program, Berkeley, CA 94720-1500. Offers MBA. *Accreditation:* AACSB. Part-time and evening/weekend programs available. *Faculty:* 80 full-time (20 women), 130 part-time/adjunct (22 women). *Students:* 776 part-time (186 women); includes 176 minority (4 African Americans, 154 Asian Americans or Pacific Islanders, 18 Hispanic Americans), 363 international. Average age 32. In 2009, 230 master's awarded. *Degree requirements:* For master's, academic retreat. *Entrance requirements:* For master's, GMAT. Additional exam requirements/recommendations for international students: Required—TOEFL (minimum score 570 paper-based; 230 computer-based; 68 iBT). *Application deadline:* For fall admission, 11/2 for domestic students, 3/1 for international students; for winter admission, 1/5 for domestic students; for spring admission, 3/1 for domestic students. Application fee: $200. Electronic applications accepted. *Expenses:* Contact institution. *Financial support:* Scholarships/grants and unspecified assistantships available. Support available to part-time students. Financial award application deadline: 3/1; financial award applicants required to submit FAFSA. *Faculty research:* Accounting, business and public policy, economic analysis and public policy, finance, management of organizations, marketing, operations and information technology management, real estate. *Unit head:* David Gent, Executive Director, 510-642-1406, Fax: 510-643-5902, E-mail: ewmbaadm@haas.berkeley.edu. *Application contact:* Evening and Weekend MBA Admissions Officer, 510-642-0292, Fax: 510-643-5902, E-mail: ewmbaadm@haas.berkeley.edu.

University of California, Berkeley, Graduate Division, Haas School of Business, Full-Time MBA Program, Berkeley, CA 94720-1500. Offers MBA. *Accreditation:* AACSB. *Faculty:* 80 full-time (20 women), 130 part-time/adjunct (22 women). *Students:* 494 full-time (143 women); includes 90 minority (4 African Americans, 80 Asian Americans or Pacific Islanders, 6 Hispanic Americans), 189 international. Average age 29. 4,064 applicants, 11% accepted, 239 enrolled. In 2009, 239 master's awarded. *Entrance requirements:* For master's, GMAT. Additional exam requirements/recommendations for international students: Required—TOEFL (minimum score 570 paper-based; 230 computer-based; 68 iBT), IELTS. *Application deadline:* For fall admission, 10/20 for domestic students, 3/10 for international students; for winter admission, 12/10 for domestic students; for spring admission, 3/10 for domestic students. Application fee: $200. Electronic applications accepted. *Expenses:* Contact institution. *Financial support:* Fellowships with full tuition reimbursements, research assistantships with tuition reimbursements, teaching assistantships with partial tuition reimbursements, career-related internships or fieldwork, scholarships/grants, and unspecified assistantships available. Financial award application deadline: 3/1; financial award applicants required to submit FAFSA. *Faculty research:* Accounting, business and public policy, finance, management of organizations, marketing, operations and information technology management, real estate. *Unit head:* Julia Hwang, Executive Director, 510-642-1405, Fax: 510-643-6659, E-mail: julia_hwang@haas.berkeley.edu. *Application contact:* Pete Johnson, Executive Director, Full-Time MBA Admissions, 510-642-1405, Fax: 510-643-6659.

University of California, Berkeley, Graduate Division, Haas School of Business and Group in International and Area Studies, MBA/MA Program in International and Area Studies, Berkeley, CA 94720-1500. Offers MBA/MA. *Accreditation:* AACSB. *Students:* 1 full-time (0 women). *Entrance requirements:* Additional exam requirements/recommendations for international students: Required—TOEFL. Application fee: $200. *Financial support:* Fellowships with full tuition reimbursements, research assistantships, teaching assistantships with partial tuition

Business Administration and Management—General

University of California, Berkeley (continued)
reimbursements, career-related internships or fieldwork, scholarships/grants, and unspecified assistantships available. Financial award application deadline: 3/1; financial award applicants required to submit FAFSA. *Unit head:* Julia Hwang, Director, MBA Program, 510-642-1405, Fax: 510-643-6659, E-mail: julia_hwang@haas.berkeley.edu. *Application contact:* 510-642-1405, Fax: 510-643-6659.

University of California, Berkeley, Graduate Division, Haas School of Business, PhD in Business Administration Program, Berkeley, CA 94720-1500. Offers accounting (PhD); business and public policy (PhD); finance (PhD); management of organizations (PhD); marketing (PhD); operations management (PhD); real estate (PhD). *Accreditation:* AACSB. *Faculty:* 80 full-time (20 women), 130 part-time/adjunct (22 women). *Students:* 82 full-time (23 women); includes 22 minority (18 Asian Americans or Pacific Islanders, 4 Hispanic Americans), 29 international. Average age 30. 511 applicants, 5% accepted, 16 enrolled. In 2009, 8 doctorates awarded. *Degree requirements:* For doctorate, comprehensive exam, thesis/dissertation, oral exam, written preliminary exams. *Entrance requirements:* For doctorate, GMAT or GRE, minimum GPA of 3.0 in undergraduate and graduate coursework. Additional exam requirements/recommendations for international students: Required—TOEFL (minimum score 570 paper-based; 230 computer-based; 68 iBT), IELTS (minimum score 7). *Application deadline:* For fall admission, 12/10 for domestic and international students. Application fee: $70 ($90 for international students). Electronic applications accepted. *Financial support:* Fellowships with full and partial tuition reimbursements, research assistantships with full and partial tuition reimbursements, teaching assistantships with full and partial tuition reimbursements, career-related internships or fieldwork, Federal Work-Study, scholarships/grants, health care benefits, tuition waivers (full), unspecified assistantships, and transit pass, travel grants available. Financial award application deadline: 12/10; financial award applicants required to submit FAFSA. *Faculty research:* Accounting, business and public policy, finance, management of organizations, marketing, operations and information technology management, real estate. *Unit head:* Sunil Dutta, Director, 510-642-1229, Fax: 510-643-4255, E-mail: kimg@haas.berkeley.edu. *Application contact:* Kim Guilfoyle, Director, Student Affairs, 510-642-3944, Fax: 510-643-4255, E-mail: kimg@haas.berkeley.edu.

University of California, Berkeley, UC Berkeley Extension, Certificate Programs in Business, Berkeley, CA 94720-1500. Offers accounting (Certificate); business administration (Certificate); finance (Certificate); human resource management (Certificate); management (Certificate); marketing (Certificate); project management (Certificate). Postbaccalaureate distance learning degree programs offered. *Unit head:* Diana Wu, Dean, 510-642-4181. *Application contact:* Business, 510-642-4231, E-mail: business@unex.berkeley.edu.

University of California, Berkeley, UC Berkeley Extension, International Diploma Programs, Berkeley, CA 94720-1500. Offers business administration (Certificate); finance (Certificate); global business management (Certificate); marketing (Certificate); project management (Certificate). *Unit head:* Diana Wu, Dean, 510-642-4181. *Application contact:* International Diploma Programs, 510-642-2564, E-mail: diploma@unex.berkeley.edu.

University of California, Davis, Graduate School of Management, Daytime MBA Program, Davis, CA 95616. Offers MBA, JD/MBA, M Engr/MBA, MBA/MPH, MBA/MS, MD/MBA. *Faculty:* 31 full-time (12 women), 32 part-time/adjunct (1 woman). *Students:* 118 full-time (42 women); includes 24 minority (2 African Americans, 19 Asian Americans or Pacific Islanders, 3 Hispanic Americans), 22 international. Average age 28. 575 applicants, 21% accepted, 60 enrolled. *Entrance requirements:* For master's, GMAT, letters of recommendation, resume, essays, equivalent of a 4-year U.S. undergraduate degree. Additional exam requirements/recommendations for international students: Required—TOEFL (minimum score 600 paper-based; 250 computer-based; 100 iBT), IELTS (minimum score 7). *Application deadline:* For fall admission, 3/6 priority date for domestic and international students. Applications are processed on a rolling basis. Application fee: $125. Electronic applications accepted. *Financial support:* In 2009–10, 105 students received support; research assistantships with partial tuition reimbursements available, teaching assistantships with partial tuition reimbursements available, career-related internships or fieldwork, Federal Work-Study, institutionally sponsored loans, scholarships/grants, tuition waivers (partial), and unspecified assistantships available. Financial award application deadline: 3/6; financial award applicants required to submit FAFSA. *Faculty research:* Technology management, finance, marketing, corporate governance and investor welfare, organizational behavior. *Unit head:* James Stevens, Assistant Dean of Student Affairs, 530-752-7658, Fax: 530-754-9355, E-mail: admissions@gsm.ucdavis.edu. *Application contact:* Heather O'Leary, Director, Admissions and Student Services, 530-754-4080, Fax: 530-754-9355, E-mail: admissions@gsm.ucdavis.edu.

University of California, Davis, Graduate School of Management, Working Professional MBA Program, Davis, CA 95616. Offers MBA. Part-time and evening/weekend programs available. *Faculty:* 31 full-time (12 women), 32 part-time/adjunct (1 woman). *Students:* 422 part-time (121 women); includes 177 minority (10 African Americans, 2 American Indian/Alaska Native, 141 Asian Americans or Pacific Islanders, 24 Hispanic Americans), 45 international. Average age 30. 267 applicants, 68% accepted, 141 enrolled. *Entrance requirements:* For master's, GMAT, letters of recommendation, resume, equivalent of a 4 year undergraduate degree. Additional exam requirements/recommendations for international students: Required—TOEFL (minimum score 600 paper-based; 250 computer-based; 100 iBT), IELTS (minimum score 7). *Application deadline:* For fall admission, 3/31 priority date for domestic and international students. Applications are processed on a rolling basis. Application fee: $125. Electronic applications accepted. *Expenses:* Contact institution. *Financial support:* In 2009–10, 173 students received support. Scholarships/grants available. Financial award application deadline: 3/31; financial award applicants required to submit FAFSA. *Faculty research:* Technology management, finance, marketing, corporate governance and investor welfare, organizational behavior. *Unit head:* James Stevens, Assistant Dean of Student Affairs, 530-752-7658, Fax: 530-754-9355, E-mail: admissions@gsm.ucdavis.edu. *Application contact:* Heather O'Leary, Director, Admissions and Student Services, 530-754-4080, Fax: 530-754-9355, E-mail: admissions@gsm.ucdavis.edu.

University of California, Irvine, Office of Graduate Studies, The Paul Merage School of Business, Irvine, CA 92697. Offers business administration (MBA); management (PhD). *Accreditation:* AACSB. Part-time and evening/weekend programs available. *Students:* 456 full-time (165 women), 377 part-time (110 women); includes 299 minority (12 African Americans, 3 American Indian/Alaska Native, 252 Asian Americans or Pacific Islanders, 32 Hispanic Americans), 132 international. Average age 31. 1,563 applicants, 33% accepted, 301 enrolled. In 2009, 375 master's, 10 doctorates awarded. Terminal master's awarded for partial completion of doctoral program. *Degree requirements:* For doctorate, thesis/dissertation. *Entrance requirements:* For master's, GMAT, minimum GPA of 3.0; for doctorate, GMAT or GRE, minimum GPA of 3.0. Additional exam requirements/recommendations for international students: Required—TOEFL (minimum score 570 paper-based; 230 computer-based). *Application deadline:* For fall admission, 1/4 priority date for domestic and international students. Applications are processed on a rolling basis. Electronic applications accepted. *Expenses:* Contact institution. *Financial support:* Career-related internships or fieldwork, Federal Work-Study, institutionally sponsored loans, scholarships/grants, traineeships, health care benefits, and unspecified assistantships available. Support available to part-time students. Financial award application deadline: 3/1; financial award applicants required to submit FAFSA. *Faculty research:* Organizational behavior, finance, informational technology, marketing, accounting. *Unit head:* Jone Pearce, Dean, 949-824-6505, Fax: 949-824-8469, E-mail: jlpearce@uci.edu. *Application contact:* Wendy Gillett, Admissions Coordinator, 949-824-8318, Fax: 949-824-2944, E-mail: wgillett@uci.edu.

University of California, Los Angeles, Graduate Division, UCLA Anderson School of Management, Los Angeles, CA 90095. Offers MBA, MFE, PhD, DDS/MBA, JD/MBA, MBA/MLIS, MBA/MPH, MBA/MPP, MBA/MSCS, MBA/MSN, MBA/MUP, MD/MBA. *Accreditation:* AACSB. Part-time programs available. *Faculty:* 98 full-time (16 women), 39 part-time/adjunct (9 women). *Students:* 730 full-time (251 women), 805 part-time (235 women); includes 489 minority (21 African Americans, 3 American Indian/Alaska Native, 400 Asian Americans or Pacific Islanders, 65 Hispanic Americans), 367 international. Average age 28. *Degree requirements:* For master's, thesis (MS); for doctorate, thesis/dissertation, oral and written qualifying exams. *Entrance requirements:* For master's, GMAT (MBA), GMAT or GRE General Test (MS), minimum GPA of 3.0; for doctorate, GMAT or GRE General Test, minimum undergraduate GPA of 3.0. Additional exam requirements/recommendations for international students: Required—TOEFL. *Application deadline:* For fall admission, 10/14 for domestic students; for winter admission, 1/6 for domestic students; for spring admission, 3/17 for domestic students. Applications are processed on a rolling basis. Application fee: $200. *Expenses:* Contact institution. *Financial support:* Fellowships, research assistantships, teaching assistantships, career-related internships or fieldwork, Federal Work-Study, institutionally sponsored loans, scholarships/grants, and tuition waivers (full and partial) available. Financial award application deadline: 3/2; financial award applicants required to submit FAFSA. *Unit head:* Judy D. Olian, Dean, 310-825-7982, Fax: 310-206-2073. *Application contact:* Mae Jennifer Shores, Assistant Dean and Director of MBA Admissions and Financial Aid, 310-825-6944, E-mail: mba.admissions@anderson.ucla.edu.

See Close-Up on page 259.

University of California, Riverside, Graduate Division, A. Gary Anderson Graduate School of Management, Riverside, CA 92521-0102. Offers MBA. *Accreditation:* AACSB. Part-time and evening/weekend programs available. *Faculty:* 29 full-time (3 women), 14 part-time/adjunct (2 women). *Students:* 166 full-time (80 women), 6 part-time (4 women); includes 40 minority (4 African Americans, 29 Asian Americans or Pacific Islanders, 7 Hispanic Americans), 94 international. Average age 28. 488 applicants, 39% accepted, 81 enrolled. In 2009, 61 master's awarded. *Degree requirements:* For master's, thesis optional. *Entrance requirements:* For master's, GMAT, minimum GPA of 3.2. Additional exam requirements/recommendations for international students: Required—TOEFL (minimum score 550 paper-based; 213 computer-based; 80 iBT). *Application deadline:* For fall admission, 9/1 for domestic students, 5/1 for international students; for winter admission, 12/1 for domestic students, 9/1 for international students; for spring admission, 3/1 for domestic students, 10/1 for international students. Applications are processed on a rolling basis. Application fee: $100 ($125 for international students). *Expenses:* Contact institution. *Financial support:* In 2009–10, 46 students received support, including 46 fellowships with partial tuition reimbursements available (averaging $18,306 per year), 47 teaching assistantships with partial tuition reimbursements available (averaging $16,500 per year); research assistantships, career-related internships or fieldwork, institutionally sponsored loans, scholarships/grants, and tuition waivers (full) also available. Financial award application deadline: 5/1; financial award applicants required to submit FAFSA. *Faculty research:* Option pricing, marketing, decision modeling, new technologies in cost accounting, supply chain management, operations, production and inventory systems, entrepreneurial finance, e-commerce. *Unit head:* Dr. David W. Stewart, Dean, 951-827-6329, Fax: 951-827-3970, E-mail: mba@ucr.edu. *Application contact:* Dr. Mohsen El Hafsi, Associate Dean and Graduate Adviser, 951-827-4557, Fax: 951-827-3970, E-mail: mba@ucr.edu.

University of California, San Diego, Office of Graduate Studies, Rady School of Management, La Jolla, CA 92093. Offers MBA.

University of Central Arkansas, Graduate School, College of Business Administration, Program in Business Administration, Conway, AR 72035-0001. Offers MBA. *Accreditation:* AACSB. Part-time and evening/weekend programs available. *Faculty:* 1 full-time (0 women). *Students:* 25 full-time (7 women), 15 part-time (4 women), 6 international. Average age 26. 56 applicants, 82% accepted. In 2009, 55 master's awarded. *Entrance requirements:* For master's, GMAT, minimum GPA of 2.7. Additional exam requirements/recommendations for international students: Required—TOEFL (minimum score 550 paper-based; 213 computer-based). *Application deadline:* For fall admission, 3/1 priority date for domestic and international students; for spring admission, 10/1 priority date for domestic and international students. Applications are processed on a rolling basis. Application fee: $25 ($50 for international students). *Expenses:* Tuition, state resident: full-time $5136; part-time $214 per credit hour. Required fees: $379.50; $127 per term. Tuition and fees vary according to course level, course load and campus/location. *Financial support:* In 2009–10, 4 research assistantships with partial tuition reimbursements (averaging $5,000 per year) were awarded; career-related internships or fieldwork, Federal Work-Study, scholarships/grants, tuition waivers (partial), and unspecified assistantships also available. Support available to part-time students. Financial award application deadline: 2/15. *Unit head:* Dr. David Kim, MBA Director, 501-450-5316, Fax: 501-450-5302, E-mail: davidk@uca.edu. *Application contact:* Brenda Herring, Admissions Assistant, 501-450-5065, Fax: 501-450-5678, E-mail: bherring@uca.edu.

University of Central Florida, College of Business Administration, Department of Management, Orlando, FL 32816. Offers entrepreneurship (Graduate Certificate); management (MSM); technology ventures (Graduate Certificate). *Accreditation:* AACSB. *Faculty:* 25 full-time (8 women), 2 part-time/adjunct (both women). *Students:* 3 full-time (2 women), 24 part-time (21 women); includes 5 minority (2 African Americans, 1 Asian American or Pacific Islander, 2 Hispanic Americans). Average age 34. 11 applicants, 82% accepted, 9 enrolled. In 2009, 2 master's, 4 other advanced degrees awarded. *Entrance requirements:* For master's, GMAT, minimum GPA of 3.0 in last 60 hours. *Application deadline:* For fall admission, 2/1 priority date for domestic students; for spring admission, 11/1 priority date for domestic students. Application fee: $30. Electronic applications accepted. *Expenses:* Tuition, state resident: part-time $306.31 per credit hour. Tuition, nonresident: part-time $1099.01 per credit hour. Part-time tuition and fees vary according to degree level and program. *Financial support:* Fellowships, research assistantships, teaching assistantships available. *Unit head:* Dr. Foard Jones, Chair, 407-823-2925, Fax: 407-823-3725, E-mail: foard.jones@bus.ucf.edu. *Application contact:* Dr. Foard Jones, Chair, 407-823-2925, Fax: 407-823-3725, E-mail: foard.jones@bus.ucf.edu.

University of Central Florida, College of Business Administration, Program in Business Administration, Orlando, FL 32816. Offers MBA, PhD. *Accreditation:* AACSB. Part-time and evening/weekend programs available. *Students:* 263 full-time (101 women), 281 part-time (116 women); includes 97 minority (21 African Americans, 32 Asian Americans or Pacific Islanders, 44 Hispanic Americans), 40 international. Average age 30. In 2009, 246 master's, 12 doctorates awarded. *Degree requirements:* For master's, exam; for doctorate, thesis/dissertation, departmental candidacy exam. *Entrance requirements:* For master's and doctorate, GMAT, minimum GPA of 3.0 in last 60 hours. Additional exam requirements/recommendations for international students: Required—TOEFL. *Application deadline:* For fall admission, 2/1 priority date for domestic students; for spring admission, 11/1 priority date for domestic students. Application fee: $30. Electronic applications accepted. *Expenses:* Tuition, state resident: part-time $306.31 per credit hour. Tuition, nonresident: part-time $1099.01 per credit hour. Part-time tuition and fees vary according to degree level and program. *Financial support:* In 2009–10, 50 students received support, including 13 fellowships with partial tuition reimbursements available (averaging $50 per year), 2 research assistantships with partial tuition reimbursements available (averaging $7,000 per year), 38 teaching assistantships with partial tuition reimbursements available (averaging $11,800 per year); career-related internships or fieldwork, Federal Work-Study, institutionally sponsored loans, tuition waivers (partial), and unspecified assistantships also available. Financial award application deadline: 3/1; financial award applicants required to submit FAFSA. *Unit head:* Dr. Foard L. Jones, Interim Associate Dean, 407-823-2925, E-mail: foard.jones@bus.ucf.edu. *Application contact:* Judy Ryder, Director, Graduate Admissions, 407-823-2364, Fax: 407-823-0219, E-mail: judy.ryder@bus.ucf.edu.

University of Central Missouri, The Graduate School, Harmon College of Business Administration, Warrensburg, MO 64093. Offers accountancy (MA); accounting (MBA); ethical strategic leadership (MBA); finance (MBA); general business (MBA); information systems (MBA); information technology (MS); marketing (MBA). Part-time programs available. Postbaccalaureate distance learning degree programs offered. *Faculty:* 31. *Students:* 87 full-time (34 women), 62 part-time (25 women); includes 10 minority (3 African Americans, 1 American Indian/Alaska Native, 5 Asian Americans or Pacific Islanders, 1 Hispanic American), 66 international. Average age 27. 55 applicants, 64% accepted, 27 enrolled. In 2009, 83 master's awarded. *Entrance requirements:* Additional exam requirements/recommendations for international students: Required—TOEFL (minimum score 550 paper-based; 79 computer-based).

Application deadline: For fall admission, 6/1 priority date for domestic students, 5/1 for international students; for spring admission, 10/1 priority date for domestic students, 10/1 for international students. Applications are processed on a rolling basis. Application fee: $30 ($75 for international students). Electronic applications accepted. *Expenses:* Tuition, area resident: Part-time $245.80 per credit hour. Tuition, nonresident: part-time $491.60 per credit hour. Required fees: $24.20 per credit hour. Full-time tuition and fees vary according to course load, degree level, campus/location and reciprocity agreements. *Financial support:* Research assistantships with full and partial tuition reimbursements, teaching assistantships with full and partial tuition reimbursements, career-related internships or fieldwork, Federal Work-Study, scholarships/grants, and administrative and laboratory assistantships available. Support available to part-time students. Financial award application deadline: 3/1; financial award applicants required to submit FAFSA. *Unit head:* Dr. Roger Best, Dean, 660-543-4560, Fax: 660-543-8350, E-mail: best@ucmo.edu. *Application contact:* Laurie Delap, Admissions Coordinator, 660-543-4621, Fax: 660-543-4778, E-mail: gradinfo@ucmo.edu.

University of Central Oklahoma, College of Graduate Studies and Research, College of Business Administration, Program in Business Administration, Edmond, OK 73034-5209. Offers MBA. *Accreditation:* ACBSP. *Faculty:* 15 full-time (2 women). *Students:* 141 full-time (66 women), 100 part-time (48 women); includes 33 minority (11 African Americans, 8 American Indian/Alaska Native, 8 Asian Americans or Pacific Islanders, 6 Hispanic Americans), 17 international. Average age 29. 163 applicants, 99% accepted. In 2009, 78 master's awarded. *Degree requirements:* For master's, thesis optional. *Entrance requirements:* For master's, GMAT. Additional exam requirements/recommendations for international students: Required—TOEFL (minimum score 550 paper-based; 213 computer-based). *Application deadline:* For fall admission, 7/1 for international students; for spring admission, 11/1 for international students. Applications are processed on a rolling basis. Application fee: $25. Electronic applications accepted. *Expenses:* Tuition, state resident: full-time $4128; part-time $172 per credit hour. Tuition, nonresident: full-time $10,373; part-time $432.20 per credit hour. Required fees: $433.20; $18.05 per credit hour. *Financial support:* Unspecified assistantships available. Financial award application deadline: 3/31; financial award applicants required to submit FAFSA. *Unit head:* Dr. Timothy Bridges, Dean, College of Business Administration, 405-9745330. *Application contact:* Dr. Richard Bernard, Dean, Graduate College, 405-974-3493, Fax: 405-974-3852, E-mail: gradcoll@uco.edu.

University of Charleston, Executive Master of Business Administration Program, Charleston, WV 25304-1099. Offers EMBA. Part-time and evening/weekend programs available. *Faculty:* 4 full-time (0 women), 1 part-time/adjunct (0 women). *Students:* 60 full-time (27 women). Average age 35. 25 applicants, 84% accepted, 21 enrolled. In 2009, 38 master's awarded. *Degree requirements:* For master's, successful completion of practicum paper. *Entrance requirements:* For master's, GMAT, undergraduate degree from regionally-accredited institution; minimum GPA of 3.0 in undergraduate work (recommended); three years of work experience since receiving the undergraduate degree (recommended); minimum of two professional recommendations, one from current employer, addressing career potential and ability to do graduate work. Additional exam requirements/recommendations for international students: Required—TOEFL, IELTS. *Application deadline:* Applications are processed on a rolling basis. Application fee: $40. Electronic applications accepted. *Expenses:* Tuition: Full-time $25,224; part-time $875 per credit hour. Full-time tuition and fees vary according to degree level. *Financial support:* In 2009–10, 3 students received support. Scholarships/grants available. Support available to part-time students. Financial award application deadline: 3/1; financial award applicants required to submit FAFSA. *Unit head:* Dr. Robert B. Bliss, Associate Dean, 304-357-4865, Fax: 304-357-4872, E-mail: robertbliss@ucwv.edu. *Application contact:* Dr. Robert B. Bliss, Associate Dean, 304-357-4865, Fax: 304-357-4872, E-mail: robertbliss@ucwv.edu.

University of Charleston, Master of Business Administration and Leadership Program, Charleston, WV 25304-1099. Offers MBA. *Faculty:* 3 full-time (1 woman). *Students:* 11 full-time (5 women); includes 1 minority (African American), 2 international. Average age 24. 20 applicants, 55% accepted, 7 enrolled. *Degree requirements:* For master's, thesis, successful completion of professional portfolio. *Entrance requirements:* Additional exam requirements/recommendations for international students: Required—TOEFL, IELTS. *Application deadline:* Applications are processed on a rolling basis. Application fee: $0. Electronic applications accepted. *Expenses:* Tuition: Full-time $25,224; part-time $875 per credit hour. Full-time tuition and fees vary according to degree level. *Financial support:* Scholarships/grants available. Financial award application deadline: 3/1; financial award applicants required to submit FAFSA. *Unit head:* Dr. J. Bart Morrison, Dean, 304-357-4373, E-mail: bartmorrison@ucwv.edu. *Application contact:* Cheryl Fout, Administrative Assistant to the Dean, 304-357-4373, E-mail: cherylfout@ucwv.edu.

University of Chicago, Booth School of Business, Doctoral Program in Business, Chicago, IL 60637-1513. Offers PhD. *Accreditation:* AACSB. *Faculty:* 144 full-time, 36 part-time/adjunct. *Students:* 115 full-time (38 women); includes 19 minority (1 African American, 1 American Indian/Alaska Native, 15 Asian Americans or Pacific Islanders, 2 Hispanic Americans), 62 international. Average age 26. In 2009, 17 doctorates awarded. *Degree requirements:* For doctorate, thesis/dissertation, workshops, curriculum paper. *Entrance requirements:* For doctorate, GMAT or GRE, resume, transcripts, letters of referral, essay, interview. Additional exam requirements/recommendations for international students: Required—TOEFL, IELTS. *Application deadline:* For fall admission, 1/1 for domestic and international students. Application fee: $65. Electronic applications accepted. *Financial support:* Fellowships with tuition reimbursements, research assistantships with tuition reimbursements, teaching assistantships with tuition reimbursements, tuition waivers (full) available. *Faculty research:* Accounting, finance, marketing, economics, econometrics and statistics. *Unit head:* Dr. Pradeep Chintagunta, Faculty Director, 773-702-7298, Fax: 773-702-5257. *Application contact:* Malaina Brown, Associate Director, 773-702-0093, Fax: 773-702-5257, E-mail: malaina.brown@chicagobooth.edu.

University of Chicago, Booth School of Business, Full-Time MBA Program, Chicago, IL 60637. Offers MBA. *Faculty:* 138 full-time, 47 part-time/adjunct. *Students:* 1,185 full-time (415 women); includes 277 minority (59 African Americans, 2 American Indian/Alaska Native, 177 Asian Americans or Pacific Islanders, 39 Hispanic Americans), 419 international. Average age 28. 3,843 applicants, 25% accepted, 592 enrolled. *Entrance requirements:* For master's, GMAT, 2 letters of recommendation, resume, interview. Additional exam requirements/recommendations for international students: Required—TOEFL (minimum score 600 paper-based; 250 computer-based), IELTS. *Application deadline:* For fall admission, 10/17 priority date for domestic and international students; for winter admission, 1/9 for domestic and international students; for spring admission, 3/12 for domestic and international students. Application fee: $200. Electronic applications accepted. *Expenses:* Contact institution. *Financial support:* In 2009–10, 300 fellowships were awarded. Financial award applicants required to submit FAFSA. *Faculty research:* Finance, marketing, international business, general management, strategy. *Unit head:* Stacey Kole, Deputy Dean, 773-702-7121. *Application contact:* Rosemaria Martinelli, Associate Dean of Admissions and Financial Aid, 773-702-7369, Fax: 773-702-9085, E-mail: admissions@chicagobooth.edu.

University of Chicago, Booth School of Business, Part-Time Evening MBA Program, Chicago, IL 60611. Offers MBA. *Accreditation:* AACSB. Part-time and evening/weekend programs available. *Faculty:* 144 full-time, 36 part-time/adjunct. *Students:* 1,275 part-time (291 women); includes 292 minority (22 African Americans, 246 Asian Americans or Pacific Islanders, 24 Hispanic Americans), 211 international. Average age 29. *Entrance requirements:* For master's, GMAT, 2 letters of recommendation, interview. Additional exam requirements/recommendations for international students: Required—TOEFL (minimum score 600 paper-based; 250 computer-based), IELTS. *Application deadline:* Applications are processed on a rolling basis. Application fee: $175. Electronic applications accepted. *Expenses:* Contact institution. *Financial support:* Applicants required to submit FAFSA. *Faculty research:* Finance, entrepreneurship, strategy, marketing, international business. *Unit head:* George Andrews, Associate Dean, 312-464-8660, Fax: 312-464-8778, E-mail: george.andrews@chicagobooth.edu. *Application contact:* Information Contact, 312-464-8700, Fax: 312-464-8778, E-mail: eveningweekend-admissions@chicagobooth.edu.

University of Chicago, Booth School of Business, Part-Time Weekend MBA Program, Chicago, IL 60611. Offers MBA. *Accreditation:* AACSB. Part-time and evening/weekend programs available. *Faculty:* 144 full-time, 36 part-time/adjunct. *Students:* 369 part-time (64 women); includes 141 minority (13 African Americans, 120 Asian Americans or Pacific Islanders, 8 Hispanic Americans), 108 international. Average age 31. *Entrance requirements:* For master's, GMAT, 2 letters of recommendation, interview, resume. Additional exam requirements/recommendations for international students: Required—TOEFL or IELTS. *Application deadline:* For fall admission, 5/1 for domestic students, 6/6 for international students. Application fee: $175. *Faculty research:* Finance, marketing, international business, strategy, entrepreneurship. *Unit head:* George Andrews, Associate Dean, 312-464-8660, Fax: 312-464-8778, E-mail: george.andrews@chicagobooth.edu. *Application contact:* Gretchen Cooper, Information Contact, 312-464-8703, E-mail: eveningweekend-admission@chicagobooth.edu.

University of Cincinnati, Graduate School, College of Business, MBA Program, Cincinnati, OH 45221. Offers MBA. Part-time and evening/weekend programs available. *Degree requirements:* For master's, capstone project. *Entrance requirements:* For master's, GMAT, resume, letters of recommendation, essays, official transcripts. Additional exam requirements/recommendations for international students: Required—TOEFL (minimum score 600 paper-based; 250 computer-based; 100 iBT). *Application deadline:* For fall admission, 7/1 for domestic students, 1/15 for international students. Electronic applications accepted. *Expenses:* Contact institution. *Financial support:* In 2009–10, 2 research assistantships with full tuition reimbursements (averaging $9,000 per year) were awarded; scholarships/grants, tuition waivers (full and partial), and unspecified assistantships also available. Financial award application deadline: 2/1; financial award applicants required to submit FAFSA. *Unit head:* Dr. Robert Dwyer, Academic Program Director, 513-556-7103, E-mail: robert.dwyer@uc.edu. *Application contact:* Dona Clary, Director, Graduate Programs Office, 513-556-3546, Fax: 513-558-7006, E-mail: dona.clary@uc.edu.

University of Cincinnati, Graduate School, College of Business, PhD Program, Cincinnati, OH 45221. Offers accounting (PhD); finance (PhD); information systems (PhD); management (PhD); marketing (PhD); quantitative analysis and operations management (PhD). *Degree requirements:* For doctorate, comprehensive exam, thesis/dissertation. *Entrance requirements:* For doctorate, GMAT, GRE, resume, letters of recommendation. Additional exam requirements/recommendations for international students: Required—TOEFL (minimum score 600 paper-based; 250 computer-based; 100 iBT). Electronic applications accepted. *Expenses:* Contact institution.

University of Colorado at Boulder, Leeds School of Business, Master of Business Administration Program, Boulder, CO 80309. Offers MBA. *Students:* 234 full-time (74 women), 119 part-time (38 women); includes 19 minority (2 American Indian/Alaska Native, 14 Asian Americans or Pacific Islanders, 3 Hispanic Americans), 24 international. Average age 30. 221 applicants, 97% accepted, 116 enrolled. In 2009, 110 master's awarded. *Entrance requirements:* For master's, GMAT, minimum undergraduate GPA of 2.75. *Application deadline:* Applications are processed on a rolling basis. Application fee: $50 ($60 for international students). *Financial support:* In 2009–10, 79 fellowships (averaging $5,842 per year), 1 research assistantship (averaging $2,016 per year) were awarded. Financial award applicants required to submit FAFSA.

See Display on page 170 and Close-Up on page 261.

University of Colorado at Colorado Springs, Graduate School, Graduate School of Business Administration, Colorado Springs, CO 80933-7150. Offers MBA. *Accreditation:* AACSB. Part-time and evening/weekend programs available. *Faculty:* 36 full-time (13 women), 4 part-time/adjunct (0 women). *Students:* 184 full-time (69 women), 264 part-time (101 women); includes 55 minority (12 African Americans, 1 American Indian/Alaska Native, 21 Asian Americans or Pacific Islanders, 21 Hispanic Americans), 3 international. Average age 32. 274 applicants, 72% accepted, 90 enrolled. In 2009, 106 master's awarded. *Entrance requirements:* For master's, GMAT. *Application deadline:* For fall admission, 6/1 for domestic students; for spring admission, 11/1 for domestic students. Application fee: $60 ($75 for international students). *Expenses:* Contact institution. *Financial support:* Career-related internships or fieldwork, Federal Work-Study, and scholarships/grants available. Support available to part-time students. Financial award application deadline: 3/1; financial award applicants required to submit FAFSA. *Faculty research:* Quality financial reporting, investments and corporate governance, group support systems, environmental and project management, customer relationship management. *Unit head:* Dr. Venkateshwar Reddy, Dean, 719-255-3113, Fax: 719-255-3100, E-mail: vreddy@uccs.edu. *Application contact:* Windy Haddad, MBA Program Director, 719-255-3401, Fax: 719-255-3100, E-mail: whaddad@uccs.edu.

University of Colorado Denver, Business School, Master of Business Administration Program, Denver, CO 80217-3364. Offers MBA. *Accreditation:* AACSB. Part-time and evening/weekend programs available. *Students:* 220 full-time (95 women), 548 part-time (201 women); includes 138 minority (13 African Americans, 35 American Indian/Alaska Native, 56 Asian Americans or Pacific Islanders, 34 Hispanic Americans), 41 international. 403 applicants, 77% accepted, 175 enrolled. In 2009, 347 master's awarded. *Entrance requirements:* For master's, GMAT. Additional exam requirements/recommendations for international students: Required—TOEFL (minimum score 525 paper-based; 197 computer-based). *Application deadline:* For fall admission, 6/1 for domestic students, 3/15 for international students; for spring admission, 11/1 for domestic students, 10/1 for international students. Applications are processed on a rolling basis. Application fee: $50 ($75 for international students). *Financial support:* Federal Work-Study, institutionally sponsored loans, and scholarships/grants available. Support available to part-time students. Financial award application deadline: 4/1; financial award applicants required to submit FAFSA. *Unit head:* Elizabeth Cooperman, Director, 303-556-5948, Fax: 303-556-5899, E-mail: elizabeth.cooperman@ucdenver.edu. *Application contact:* Shelly Townley, Admissions Coordinator, 303-556-5956, Fax: 303-556-5904, E-mail: shelly.townley@ucdenver.edu.

University of Colorado Denver, Business School, Program in Management and Organization, Denver, CO 80217-3364. Offers MS. *Accreditation:* AACSB. Part-time and evening/weekend programs available. *Students:* 8 full-time (2 women), 20 part-time (11 women); includes 3 minority (1 African American, 1 Asian American or Pacific Islander, 1 Hispanic American), 2 international. 32 applicants, 63% accepted, 11 enrolled. In 2009, 14 master's awarded. *Entrance requirements:* For master's, GMAT. Additional exam requirements/recommendations for international students: Required—TOEFL (minimum score 525 paper-based; 197 computer-based). *Application deadline:* For fall admission, 6/1 for domestic students, 3/15 for international students; for spring admission, 11/1 for domestic students, 10/1 for international students. Applications are processed on a rolling basis. Application fee: $50 ($75 for international students). Electronic applications accepted. *Financial support:* Federal Work-Study, institutionally sponsored loans, and scholarships/grants available. Support available to part-time students. Financial award application deadline: 4/1; financial award applicants required to submit FAFSA. *Faculty research:* Human resource management, management of catastrophe, turnaround strategies. *Unit head:* Dr. Kenneth Bettenhausen, Program Director, 303-556-5816, Fax: 303-556-6619, E-mail: kenneth.bettehausen@ucdenver.edu. *Application contact:* Shelly Townley, Admissions Coordinator, 303-556-5956, Fax: 303-556-5904, E-mail: shelly.townley@ucdenver.edu.

University of Connecticut, Graduate School, School of Business, Storrs, CT 06269. Offers accounting (MS, PhD); business administration (Exec MBA, MBA, PhD); finance (PhD); health care management and insurance studies (MBA); management (PhD); management consulting (MBA); marketing (PhD); marketing intelligence (MBA); MA/MBA; MBA/MSW. *Accreditation:* AACSB. *Faculty:* 75 full-time (14 women). *Students:* 405 full-time (134 women), 999 part-time (364 women); includes 198 minority (43 African Americans, 3 American Indian/Alaska Native, 102 Asian Americans or Pacific Islanders, 50 Hispanic Americans), 136 international. Average age 31. 956 applicants, 20% accepted, 187 enrolled. In 2009, 413 master's, 6 doctorates awarded. *Degree requirements:* For master's, comprehensive exam; for doctorate, thesis/

Business Administration and Management—General

University of Connecticut (continued)
dissertation. *Entrance requirements:* For master's and doctorate, GMAT. Additional exam requirements/recommendations for international students: Required—TOEFL (minimum score 550 paper-based; 213 computer-based). *Application deadline:* For fall admission, 2/1 priority date for domestic and international students; for spring admission, 11/1 for domestic students, 10/1 for international students. Applications are processed on a rolling basis. Electronic applications accepted. *Expenses:* Tuition, state resident: full-time $4725; part-time $525 per credit. Tuition, nonresident: full-time $12,267; part-time $1363 per credit. Required fees: $346 per semester. Tuition and fees vary according to course load. *Financial support:* In 2009–10, 76 research assistantships with full tuition reimbursements, 41 teaching assistantships with full tuition reimbursements were awarded; fellowships, career-related internships or fieldwork, Federal Work-Study, scholarships/grants, health care benefits, and unspecified assistantships also available. Financial award application deadline: 2/1; financial award applicants required to submit FAFSA. *Unit head:* P. Christopher Earley, Dean, 860-486-2317, Fax: 860-846-0889, E-mail: paul.earley@uconn.edu. *Application contact:* Richard Dino, Admissions Chairperson, 860-486-4483, E-mail: rich.dino@uconn.edu.

See Close-Up on page 263.

University of Dallas, Graduate School of Management, Irving, TX 75062-4736. Offers accounting (MBA, MM, MS); business management (MBA, MM); corporate finance (MBA, MM); financial services (MBA); global business (MBA, MM); health services management (MBA, MM); human resource management (MBA, MM); information assurance (MBA, MM, MS); information technology (MBA, MM, MS); information technology service management (MBA, MM, MS); marketing management (MBA, MM); organization development (MBA, MM); project management (MBA, MM); sports and entertainment management (MBA, MM); strategic leadership (MBA, MM); supply chain management (MBA); supply chain management and market logistics (MM). *Accreditation:* ACBSP. Part-time and evening/weekend programs available. Postbaccalaureate distance learning degree programs offered (no on-campus study). *Faculty:* 25 full-time (6 women), 31 part-time/adjunct (6 women). *Students:* 232 full-time (95 women), 923 part-time (365 women); includes 462 minority (184 African Americans, 14 American Indian/Alaska Native, 153 Asian Americans or Pacific Islanders, 111 Hispanic Americans), 184 international. Average age 34. 474 applicants, 85% accepted, 237 enrolled. In 2009, 399 master's awarded. *Entrance requirements:* Additional exam requirements/recommendations for international students: Required—TOEFL. *Application deadline:* Applications are processed on a rolling basis. Application fee: $50. Electronic applications accepted. *Expenses:* Contact institution. *Financial support:* In 2009–10, 399 students received support. Scholarships/grants and unspecified assistantships available. Financial award application deadline: 2/15; financial award applicants required to submit FAFSA. *Unit head:* Alounda Joseph, Director of Enrollment Processes, 972-721-5356, E-mail: admiss@gsm.udallas.edu. *Application contact:* Alounda Joseph, Director of Enrollment Processes, 972-721-5356, E-mail: admiss@gsm.udallas.edu.

University of Dayton, Graduate School, School of Business Administration, Dayton, OH 45469-1300. Offers accounting (MBA); business intelligence (MBA); entrepreneurship (MBA); finance (MBA); international business (MBA); marketing (MBA); MIS (MBA); operations management (MBA); technology-enhanced business/e-commerce (MBA); JD/MBA. *Accreditation:* AACSB. Part-time and evening/weekend programs available. *Faculty:* 29 full-time (8 women), 15 part-time/adjunct (2 women). *Students:* 134 full-time (48 women), 111 part-time (31 women); includes 14 minority (9 African Americans, 3 Asian Americans or Pacific Islanders, 2 Hispanic Americans), 29 international. Average age 29. 179 applicants, 63% accepted, 73

enrolled. In 2009, 102 master's awarded. *Entrance requirements:* For master's, GMAT. Additional exam requirements/recommendations for international students: Required—TOEFL (minimum score 550 paper-based; 213 computer-based; 79 iBT). *Application deadline:* For fall admission, 3/1 priority date for international students; for winter admission, 7/1 priority date for international students; for spring admission, 1/1 priority date for international students. Applications are processed on a rolling basis. Application fee: $0 ($50 for international students). Electronic applications accepted. *Expenses:* Contact institution. *Financial support:* In 2009–10, 13 fellowships with partial tuition reimbursements, 17 research assistantships with full and partial tuition reimbursements (averaging $7,020 per year) were awarded; career-related internships or fieldwork, institutionally sponsored loans, scholarships/grants, health care benefits, and unspecified assistantships also available. Support available to part-time students. Financial award application deadline: 3/15; financial award applicants required to submit FAFSA. *Faculty research:* Management information systems, economics, finance, entrepreneurship, marketing. *Unit head:* Janice M. Glynn, Director, MBA Program, 937-229-3733, Fax: 937-229-3882, E-mail: glynn@udayton.edu. *Application contact:* Jeffrey Carter, Assistant Director, MBA Program, 937-229-3733, Fax: 937-229-3882, E-mail: jeff.carter@notes.udayton.edu.

University of Delaware, Alfred Lerner College of Business and Economics, Program in Business Administration, Newark, DE 19716. Offers MBA, MA/MBA, MBA/MIB, MBA/MS. *Accreditation:* AACSB. Part-time and evening/weekend programs available. *Entrance requirements:* For master's, GMAT, 2 letters of recommendation, resume. Additional exam requirements/recommendations for international students: Required—TOEFL (minimum score 600 paper-based; 260 computer-based; 79 iBT). Electronic applications accepted. *Expenses:* Contact institution. *Faculty research:* Finance, corporate governance, information systems, leadership, marketing.

See Close-Up on page 265.

University of Delaware, College of Agriculture and Natural Resources, Department of Entomology and Wildlife Ecology, Newark, DE 19716. Offers entomology and applied ecology (MS, PhD), including avian ecology, evolution and taxonomy, insect biological control, insect ecology and behavior (MS), insect genetics, pest management, plant-insect interactions, wildlife ecology and management. Part-time programs available. *Degree requirements:* For master's, comprehensive exam, thesis, oral exam, seminar; for doctorate, comprehensive exam, thesis/dissertation, qualifying exam, seminar. *Entrance requirements:* For master's, GRE General Test, minimum GPA of 3.0 in field, 2.8 overall; for doctorate, GRE General Test, GRE Subject Test (biology), minimum GPA of 3.0 in field, 2.8 overall. Additional exam requirements/recommendations for international students: Required—TOEFL. Electronic applications accepted. *Faculty research:* Ecology and evolution of plant-insect interactions, ecology of wildlife conservation management, habitat restoration, biological control, applied ecosystem management.

University of Denver, Daniels College of Business, Denver, CO 80208. Offers IMBA, M Acc, MBA, MS. *Accreditation:* AACSB. Part-time and evening/weekend programs available. *Faculty:* 82 full-time (20 women), 13 part-time/adjunct (6 women). *Students:* 505 full-time (172 women), 490 part-time (187 women); includes 78 minority (13 African Americans, 6 American Indian/Alaska Native, 31 Asian Americans or Pacific Islanders, 28 Hispanic Americans), 212 international. Average age 29. 1,357 applicants, 71% accepted, 416 enrolled. In 2009, 565 master's awarded. *Entrance requirements:* For master's, GMAT. *Application deadline:* For fall admission, 1/15 priority date for domestic students. Applications are processed on a rolling basis. Application fee: $50. Electronic applications accepted. *Expenses:* Tuition: Full-time

$34,596; part-time $961 per quarter hour. Required fees: $4 per quarter hour. Tuition and fees vary according to course load, campus/location and program. *Financial support:* In 2009–10, 1 research assistantship (averaging $7,000 per year), 83 teaching assistantships with full and partial tuition reimbursements (averaging $4,100 per year) were awarded; career-related internships or fieldwork, Federal Work-Study, institutionally sponsored loans, and scholarships/grants also available. Support available to part-time students. Financial award application deadline: 2/15; financial award applicants required to submit FAFSA. *Unit head:* Dr. Chris Riordan, Dean, 303-871-4324. *Application contact:* Admissions, 303-871-3416, Fax: 303-571-4466, E-mail: daniels@du.edu.

University of Denver, University College, Denver, CO 80208. Offers applied communication (MAS, MPS, Certificate); computer information systems (MAS, Certificate); environmental policy and management (MAS, Certificate); geographic information systems (MAS, Certificate); human resource administration (MPS, Certificate); knowledge and information technologies (MAS); liberal studies (MLS, Certificate); modern languages (MLS, Certificate); organizational leadership (MPS, Certificate); security management (Certificate); technology management (MAS, Certificate), including 21st century strategic management (MAS), international markets (MAS), project management (MAS), research and development management (MAS); telecommunications (MAS, Certificate), including broadband (MAS), telecommunications management and policy (MAS), telecommunications technology (MAS), wireless networks (MAS). Part-time and evening/weekend programs available. Postbaccalaureate distance learning degree programs offered (no on-campus study). *Faculty:* 160 part-time/adjunct (64 women). *Students:* 53 full-time (25 women), 984 part-time (551 women); includes 171 minority (72 African Americans, 10 American Indian/Alaska Native, 33 Asian Americans or Pacific Islanders, 56 Hispanic Americans), 75 international. Average age 36. 537 applicants, 96% accepted, 494 enrolled. In 2009, 229 master's, 109 Certificates awarded. *Entrance requirements:* Additional exam requirements/recommendations for international students: Required—TOEFL (minimum score 550 paper-based; 213 computer-based). *Application deadline:* Applications are processed on a rolling basis. Application fee: $75. Electronic applications accepted. *Expenses:* Contact institution. *Financial support:* Applicants required to submit FAFSA. *Unit head:* Dr. James Davis, Dean, 303-871-2291, Fax: 303-871-4047, E-mail: jdavis@du.edu. *Application contact:* Information Contact, 303-871-3155.

University of Detroit Mercy, College of Business Administration, Program in Business Administration, Detroit, MI 48221. Offers MBA, JD/MBA. *Accreditation:* AACSB. Part-time and evening/weekend programs available. *Degree requirements:* For master's, thesis or alternative. *Entrance requirements:* For master's, GMAT, minimum GPA of 2.75.

University of Detroit Mercy, College of Business Administration, Program in Business Turnaround Management, Detroit, MI 48221. Offers MS, Certificate.

University of Detroit Mercy, College of Business Administration, Program in Executive MBA, Detroit, MI 48221. Offers EMBA.

University of Dubuque, Program in Business Administration, Dubuque, IA 52001-5099. Offers MBA. Part-time and evening/weekend programs available. *Entrance requirements:* For master's, 2 letters of recommendation. Electronic applications accepted.

University of Evansville, Schroeder Family School of Business Administration, Evansville, IN 47722. Offers executive business administration (MBA). *Accreditation:* AACSB. Part-time and evening/weekend programs available. *Faculty:* 3 full-time (0 women). *Students:* 7 full-time (0 women), 1 part-time (0 women). Average age 39. *Entrance requirements:* For master's, GMAT or GRE, minimum 5 years professional experience, 2 letters of recommendation. *Application deadline:* Applications are processed on a rolling basis. Application fee: $75. *Expenses:* Contact institution. *Financial support:* In 2009–10, 1 student received support. Application deadline: 6/1. *Unit head:* Christine McKeag, Interim Dean, 812-488-2851, Fax: 812-488-2872, E-mail: cm2@evansville.edu. *Application contact:* Dr. Gale Blalock, Chair, EMBA Admissions, 812-488-2455, Fax: 812-488-2872, E-mail: emba@evansville.edu.

The University of Findlay, Graduate and Professional Studies, College of Business, Findlay, OH 45840-3653. Offers financial management (MBA); human resource management (MBA); international management (MBA); management (MBA); marketing (MBA); public management (MBA). Part-time and evening/weekend programs available. Postbaccalaureate distance learning degree programs offered (no on-campus study). *Degree requirements:* For master's, thesis, cumulative project. *Entrance requirements:* For master's, GMAT, minimum undergraduate GPA of 3.0 in last 64 hours of course work. Additional exam requirements/recommendations for international students: Required—TOEFL (minimum score 550 paper-based; 213 computer-based; 80 iBT). Electronic applications accepted. *Expenses:* Contact institution. *Faculty research:* Health care management, operations and logistics management.

University of Florida, Graduate School, Warrington College of Business Administration, Hough Graduate School of Business, Department of Finance, Insurance and Real Estate, Gainesville, FL 32611. Offers business administration (MS), including entrepreneurship, insurance, real estate and urban analysis, retailing; finance (PhD); financial services (Certificate); insurance (PhD); real estate and urban analysis (PhD); JD/MS. Terminal master's awarded for partial completion of doctoral program. *Degree requirements:* For doctorate, thesis/dissertation. *Entrance requirements:* For master's, GMAT or GRE General Test, minimum GPA of 3.0 for last 60 hours of undergraduate degree, work experience (preferred); for doctorate, GMAT or GRE General Test, minimum GPA of 3.0. Additional exam requirements/recommendations for international students: Required—TOEFL (minimum score 550 paper-based; 213 computer-based). Electronic applications accepted. *Faculty research:* Financial management, financial markets and institutions, investments, risk and insurance, real estate development.

University of Florida, Graduate School, Warrington College of Business Administration, Hough Graduate School of Business, Department of Management, Gainesville, FL 32611. Offers international business (MAIB); management (MS, PhD). *Accreditation:* AACSB. Terminal master's awarded for partial completion of doctoral program. *Degree requirements:* For master's, thesis; for doctorate, thesis/dissertation. *Entrance requirements:* For master's and doctorate, GMAT or GRE General Test, minimum GPA of 3.0. Additional exam requirements/recommendations for international students: Required—TOEFL (minimum score 550 paper-based; 213 computer-based). Electronic applications accepted. *Faculty research:* Organizational behavior, organizational theory, strategy and business policy.

University of Florida, Graduate School, Warrington College of Business Administration, Hough Graduate School of Business, Programs in Business Administration, Gainesville, FL 32611. Offers accounting (MBA); arts administration (MBA); business strategy and public policy (MBA); competitive strategy (MBA); decision and information sciences (MBA); electronic commerce (MBA); finance (MBA); general business (MBA); global management (MBA); Graham-Buffett security analysis (MBA); health administration (MBA); human resources management (MBA); international studies (MBA); Latin American business (MBA); management (MBA); marketing (MBA); sports administration (MBA); JD/MBA; MBA/MS; MBA/PhD; MBA/Pharm D; MD/MBA. *Accreditation:* AACSB. Part-time and evening/weekend programs available. Postbaccalaureate distance learning degree programs offered. *Entrance requirements:* For master's, GMAT, minimum GPA of 3.0, interview. Additional exam requirements/recommendations for international students: Required—TOEFL (minimum score 550 paper-based; 213 computer-based). Electronic applications accepted. *Faculty research:* Accounting, finance, insurance, management, real estate and urban analysis marketing.

University of Georgia, Graduate School, Terry College of Business, Program in Business Administration, Athens, GA 30602. Offers MA, MBA, PhD, JD/MBA. *Accreditation:* AACSB. *Students:* 171 full-time (46 women), 2 part-time (0 women); includes 17 minority (9 African Americans, 5 Asian Americans or Pacific Islanders, 3 Hispanic Americans), 45 international. 632 applicants, 43% accepted. In 2009, 81 master's, 4 doctorates awarded. *Degree requirements:* For master's, thesis (MA); for doctorate, thesis/dissertation. *Entrance requirements:* For master's, GMAT (MBA), GRE General Test (MA); for doctorate, GMAT or GRE General Test. *Application deadline:* For fall admission, 7/1 priority date for domestic students; for spring admission, 11/15 for domestic students. Application fee: $50. Electronic applications accepted. *Expenses:* Tuition, state resident: full-time $6000; part-time $250 per credit hour. Tuition, nonresident: full-time $20,904; part-time $871 per credit hour. Required fees: $730 per semester. *Financial support:* Fellowships, research assistantships, teaching assistantships, unspecified assistantships available. *Unit head:* Dr. Richard L. Daniels, Director, 404-842-4862, Fax: 706-542-5351, E-mail: rdaniels@terry.uga.edu. *Application contact:* Interim Associate Dean, E-mail: rdaniels@terry.uga.edu.

University of Guam, Office of Graduate Studies, School of Business and Public Administration, Business Administration Program, Mangilao, GU 96923. Offers PMBA. *Entrance requirements:* For master's, GMAT. Additional exam requirements/recommendations for international students: Required—TOEFL.

University of Guelph, Graduate Program Services, College of Management and Economics, Guelph, ON N1G 2W1, Canada. Offers M Sc, MA, MBA, PhD.

University of Hartford, Barney School of Business, Program in Business Administration, West Hartford, CT 06117-1599. Offers MBA, MBA/M Eng. *Accreditation:* AACSB. Part-time and evening/weekend programs available. *Entrance requirements:* For master's, GMAT, 2 letters of recommendation, resume. Additional exam requirements/recommendations for international students: Required—TOEFL (minimum score 550 paper-based; 213 computer-based). Electronic applications accepted.

University of Hartford, College of Education, Nursing, and Health Professions, Program in Nursing, West Hartford, CT 06117-1599. Offers community/public health nursing (MSN); nursing education (MSN); nursing management (MSN). *Accreditation:* AACN. Part-time and evening/weekend programs available. *Degree requirements:* For master's, research project. *Entrance requirements:* For master's, BSN, Connecticut RN license. Additional exam requirements/recommendations for international students: Required—TOEFL (minimum score 550 paper-based; 213 computer-based). Electronic applications accepted. *Expenses:* Contact institution. *Faculty research:* Child development, women in doctoral study, applying feminist theory in teaching methods, near death experience, grandmothers as primary care providers.

University of Hawaii at Manoa, Graduate Division, Shidler College of Business, Executive MBA Programs, Honolulu, HI 96822. Offers executive business administration (EMBA); Vietnam focused business administration (EMBA). Part-time programs available. *Entrance requirements:* For master's, GMAT, minimum GPA of 3.0. *Expenses:* Tuition, state resident: full-time $8900; part-time $372 per credit. Tuition, nonresident: full-time $21,400; part-time $898 per credit. Required fees: $207 per semester.

University of Hawaii at Manoa, Graduate Division, Shidler College of Business, Program in Business Administration, Honolulu, HI 96822. Offers Asian business studies (MBA); Chinese business studies (MBA); decision sciences (MBA); entrepreneurship (MBA); finance (MBA); finance and banking (MBA); human resources management (MBA); information management (MBA); information technology (MBA); international business (MBA); Japanese business studies (MBA); marketing (MBA); organizational behavior (MBA); organizational management (MBA); real estate (MBA); student-designed track (MBA). *Accreditation:* AACSB. Part-time and evening/weekend programs available. *Faculty:* 46 full-time (8 women), 9 part-time/adjunct (4 women). *Students:* 259 full-time (90 women), 105 part-time (43 women); includes 123 minority (118 Asian Americans or Pacific Islanders, 5 Hispanic Americans), 119 international. Average age 32. 336 applicants, 52% accepted, 150 enrolled. In 2009, 113 master's awarded. *Degree requirements:* For master's, thesis optional. *Entrance requirements:* For master's, GMAT, minimum GPA of 3.0. Additional exam requirements/recommendations for international students: Required—TOEFL (minimum score 600 paper-based; 250 computer-based; 100 iBT), IELTS (minimum score 7). *Application deadline:* For fall admission, 5/1 for domestic students, 3/1 for international students. Application fee: $60. *Expenses:* Contact institution. *Financial support:* In 2009–10, 24 students received support, including 98 fellowships (averaging $3,481 per year), 3 research assistantships (averaging $16,626 per year). Total annual research expenditures: $427,000. *Application contact:* Tung Bui, Graduate Chair, 808-956-5565, Fax: 808-956-9889, E-mail: tung.bui@hawaii.edu.

University of Houston, Bauer College of Business, Houston, TX 77204. Offers MBA, MS, MS Accy, PhD. *Accreditation:* AACSB. Part-time and evening/weekend programs available. *Faculty:* 50 full-time (11 women), 45 part-time/adjunct (9 women). *Students:* 713 full-time (301 women), 684 part-time (226 women); includes 476 minority (104 African Americans, 2 American Indian/Alaska Native, 225 Asian Americans or Pacific Islanders, 145 Hispanic Americans), 235 international. Average age 29. 881 applicants, 66% accepted, 459 enrolled. In 2009, 464 master's, 11 doctorates awarded. *Degree requirements:* For master's, 30 hours completed in residence; for doctorate, comprehensive exam, thesis/dissertation, minimum GPA of 3.25, continuous full time enrollment, dissertation defense within 6 years of entering the program. *Entrance requirements:* For master's, GMAT, letters of recommendation, resume; for doctorate, GMAT or GRE, letter of financial backing, statement of understanding, reference letters, statement of academic and research interests. Additional exam requirements/recommendations for international students: Required—TOEFL (minimum score 603 paper-based; 250 computer-based; 100 iBT), IELTS (minimum score 6.5), Pearson Test of English (minimum 70). *Application deadline:* For fall admission, 6/1 for domestic students, 4/1 for international students; for spring admission, 11/1 for domestic students, 10/1 for international students. Applications are processed on a rolling basis. Application fee: $75. Electronic applications accepted. *Expenses:* Tuition, state resident: full-time $7676; part-time $320 per credit hour. Tuition, nonresident: full-time $14,324; part-time $597 per credit hour. Required fees: $3034. *Financial support:* In 2009–10, 9 fellowships with full tuition reimbursements (averaging $8,700 per year), 91 teaching assistantships with full tuition reimbursements (averaging $7,100 per year) were awarded; research assistantships with full tuition reimbursements, career-related internships or fieldwork, Federal Work-Study, institutionally sponsored loans, scholarships/grants, health care benefits, and unspecified assistantships also available. Support available to part-time students. Financial award application deadline: 2/1; financial award applicants required to submit FAFSA. *Faculty research:* Accountancy and taxation, finance, international business, management. *Unit head:* Dr. Arthur Warga, Dean, 713-743-4604, Fax: 713-743-4622, E-mail: warga@uh.edu. *Application contact:* Daniel Currie, Assistant Dean, 713-743-4806, Fax: 713-743-4706, E-mail: dcurrie@uh.edu.

University of Houston–Clear Lake, School of Business, Program in Business Administration, Houston, TX 77058-1098. Offers MBA. *Accreditation:* AACSB. Part-time and evening/weekend programs available. *Degree requirements:* For master's, thesis optional. *Entrance requirements:* For master's, GMAT. Additional exam requirements/recommendations for international students: Required—TOEFL (minimum score 550 paper-based; 213 computer-based). Electronic applications accepted.

University of Houston–Victoria, School of Business Administration, Victoria, TX 77901-4450. Offers accounting (MBA); economic development and entrepreneurship (MS); finance (GMBA, MBA); general business (MBA); international business (MBA); management (GMBA, MBA); marketing (MBA). *Accreditation:* AACSB. Part-time and evening/weekend programs available. Postbaccalaureate distance learning degree programs offered (no on-campus study). *Entrance requirements:* For master's, GMAT. Additional exam requirements/recommendations for international students: Required—TOEFL (minimum score 550 paper-based; 213 computer-based). Electronic applications accepted. *Faculty research:* Economic development, marketing, finance.

University of Idaho, College of Graduate Studies, College of Business and Economics, Moscow, ID 83844-2282. Offers EMBA, M Acct, MS. *Accreditation:* AACSB. *Faculty:* 12 full-time. *Students:* 39 full-time, 16 part-time. In 2009, 29 master's awarded. *Degree requirements:* For master's, comprehensive exam. *Application deadline:* For fall admission, 8/1 for domestic students; for spring admission, 12/15 for domestic students. Application fee: $55 ($60 for international students). *Expenses:* Tuition, state resident: full-time $6120. Tuition, nonresident: full-time $17,712. *Financial support:* Research assistantships, teaching assistantships, Federal Work-Study and scholarships/grants available. Support available to part-time students. Financial

Business Administration and Management—General

University of Idaho (continued)
award application deadline: 2/15. *Unit head:* Dr. John Morris, Dean, 208-885-6478. *Application contact:* Dr. John Morris, Dean, 208-885-6478.

University of Illinois at Chicago, Graduate College, Liautaud Graduate School of Business, Program in Business Administration, Chicago, IL 60607-7128. Offers MBA, PhD, MBA/MA, MBA/MD, MBA/MPH, MBA/MS. *Accreditation:* AACSB. Part-time programs available. *Entrance requirements:* For master's, GMAT, minimum GPA of 2.75; for doctorate, GMAT. Additional exam requirements/recommendations for international students: Required—TOEFL. Electronic applications accepted.

University of Illinois at Springfield, Graduate Programs, College of Business and Management, Program in Business Administration, Springfield, IL 62703-5407. Offers MBA. *Accreditation:* AACSB. Part-time and evening/weekend programs available. *Faculty:* 5 full-time (1 woman), 3 part-time/adjunct (0 women). *Students:* 82 full-time (44 women), 68 part-time (30 women); includes 15 minority (2 African Americans, 1 American Indian/Alaska Native, 7 Asian Americans or Pacific Islanders, 5 Hispanic Americans), 11 international. Average age 31. 127 applicants, 71% accepted, 61 enrolled. In 2009, 33 master's awarded. *Degree requirements:* For master's, closure course. *Entrance requirements:* For master's, GMAT, 3 letters of reference, resume. Additional exam requirements/recommendations for international students: Required—TOEFL (minimum score 550 paper-based; 176 computer-based; 61 iBT). *Application deadline:* Applications are processed on a rolling basis. Application fee: $50 ($60 for international students). Electronic applications accepted. *Expenses:* Tuition, state resident: full-time $6390; part-time $266.25 per credit hour. Tuition, nonresident: full-time $14,226; part-time $592.75 per credit hour. Required fees: $2044; $14.36 per credit hour. $722.50 per term. *Financial support:* In 2009–10, research assistantships with full tuition reimbursements (averaging $8,109 per year), teaching assistantships with full tuition reimbursements (averaging $8,109 per year) were awarded; career-related internships or fieldwork, Federal Work-Study, scholarships/grants, health care benefits, and unspecified assistantships also available. Support available to part-time students. Financial award application deadline: 11/15; financial award applicants required to submit FAFSA. *Unit head:* Dr. Mark Puclik, Program Administrator, 217-206-6781, Fax: 217-206-7543, E-mail: puclik.mark@uis.edu. *Application contact:* Dr. Lynn Pardie, Office of Graduate Studies, 800-252-8533, Fax: 217-206-7623, E-mail: pardie.lynn@uis.edu.

University of Illinois at Urbana–Champaign, Graduate College, College of Business, Department of Business Administration, Champaign, IL 61820. Offers business administration (MS, PhD); technology management (MS). *Accreditation:* AACSB. *Faculty:* 43 full-time (10 women), 8 part-time/adjunct (1 woman). *Students:* 91 full-time (29 women), 8 part-time (4 women); includes 5 minority (all Asian Americans or Pacific Islanders), 77 international. 275 applicants, 33% accepted, 54 enrolled. In 2009, 51 master's, 9 doctorates awarded. *Entrance requirements:* For master's, minimum GPA of 3.0; for doctorate, GMAT or GRE, minimum GPA of 3.0. Additional exam requirements/recommendations for international students: Required—TOEFL (minimum score 550 paper-based; 231 computer-based; 79 iBT) or IELTS (6.5). *Application deadline:* Applications are processed on a rolling basis. Application fee: $60 ($75 for international students). Electronic applications accepted. *Expenses:* Contact institution. *Financial support:* In 2009–10, 23 fellowships, 39 research assistantships, 14 teaching assistantships were awarded; tuition waivers (full and partial) also available. *Unit head:* William J. Qualls, Interim Head, 217-265-0794, Fax: 217-244-7969, E-mail: wqualls@illinois.edu. *Application contact:* J. E. Miller, Coordinator of Graduate Programs, 217-244-8002, Fax: 217-244-7969, E-mail: j-miller@illinois.edu.

University of Illinois at Urbana–Champaign, Graduate College, College of Business, Program in Business Administration, Champaign, IL 61820. Offers MBA, Ed M/MBA, JD/MBA, M Arch/MBA, MCS/MBA, MHRIR/MBA, MS/MBA, PhD/MBA. *Accreditation:* AACSB. Part-time programs available. *Students:* 394 full-time (108 women), 3 part-time (1 woman); includes 74 minority (20 African Americans, 44 Asian Americans or Pacific Islanders, 10 Hispanic Americans), 148 international. 779 applicants, 28% accepted, 152 enrolled. *Entrance requirements:* For master's, GMAT. Additional exam requirements/recommendations for international students: Required—TOEFL. Application fee: $60 ($75 for international students). Electronic applications accepted. *Financial support:* In 2009–10, 1 fellowship, 5 research assistantships, 3 teaching assistantships were awarded. *Unit head:* Stig Lanneskog, Interim Associate Dean, 217-244-8019, Fax: 217-333-1156, E-mail: slanessk@illinois.edu. *Application contact:* Courtney Joan Hainline, Assistant Director, 217-265-7155, Fax: 217-333-1156, E-mail: hainline@illinois.edu.

University of Indianapolis, Graduate Programs, School of Business, Indianapolis, IN 46227-3697. Offers EMBA, MBA, Graduate Certificate. *Accreditation:* ACBSP. Part-time and evening/weekend programs available. *Faculty:* 3 full-time (1 woman), 4 part-time/adjunct (1 woman). *Students:* 20 full-time (9 women), 194 part-time (70 women); includes 14 minority (6 African Americans, 5 Asian Americans or Pacific Islanders, 3 Hispanic Americans), 14 international. Average age 31. *Entrance requirements:* For master's, GMAT, interview, minimum GPA of 2.8, 2 letters of recommendation, resume. Additional exam requirements/recommendations for international students: Required—TOEFL (minimum score 550 paper-based; 213 computer-based). *Application deadline:* Applications are processed on a rolling basis. Application fee: $50. *Financial support:* Tuition waivers (full and partial) and unspecified assistantships available. Support available to part-time students. Financial award application deadline: 5/1; financial award applicants required to submit FAFSA. *Unit head:* Dr. Sheela Yadav, Dean, 317-788-3232, E-mail: syadav@uindy.edu. *Application contact:* Stephen A. Tokar, Director of Graduate Business Programs, 317-788-4905, E-mail: tokarsa@uindy.edu.

The University of Iowa, Henry B. Tippie College of Business, Department of Accounting, Program in Accounting, Iowa City, IA 52242-1316. Offers accountancy (M Ac); business administration (PhD), including accounting; JD/M Ac. *Faculty:* 18 full-time (3 women). *Students:* 11 full-time (5 women), 1 part-time (0 women); includes 2 minority (both Asian Americans or Pacific Islanders), 5 international. Average age 27. 46 applicants, 13% accepted, 3 enrolled. In 2009, 4 doctorates awarded. *Degree requirements:* For doctorate, comprehensive exam, thesis/dissertation, thesis defense. *Entrance requirements:* For doctorate, GMAT. Additional exam requirements/recommendations for international students: Required—TOEFL (minimum score 600 paper-based; 250 computer-based; 100 iBT). *Application deadline:* For fall admission, 1/31 priority date for domestic students, 1/15 priority date for international students. Applications are processed on a rolling basis. Application fee: $60 ($85 for international students). Electronic applications accepted. *Financial support:* In 2009–10, 12 students received support, including 9 fellowships with partial tuition reimbursements available (averaging $8,500 per year), 1 research assistantship with full tuition reimbursement available (averaging $16,575 per year), 8 teaching assistantships with full tuition reimbursements available (averaging $16,575 per year); institutionally sponsored loans, scholarships/grants, health care benefits, unspecified assistantships, and ALS students: 2 awarded ($30,000 each) also available. Financial award application deadline: 1/15. *Faculty research:* Corporate financial reporting issues; financial statement information and capital markets; cost structure: analysis, estimation, and management; experimental and prediction economics; income taxes and interaction of financial and tax reporting systems. *Unit head:* Prof. Douglas V. DeJong, Department Executive Officer, 319-355-0910, Fax: 319-335-1956, E-mail: bruce-johnson@uiowa.edu. *Application contact:* Renea L. Jay, PhD Program Coordinator, 319-335-0830, Fax: 319-335-1956, E-mail: renea-jay@uiowa.edu.

The University of Iowa, Henry B. Tippie College of Business, Department of Finance, Iowa City, IA 52242-1316. Offers business administration (PhD), including finance. *Faculty:* 19 full-time (1 woman), 1 part-time/adjunct (0 women). *Students:* 13 full-time (6 women), 10 international. Average age 29. 94 applicants, 3% accepted, 2 enrolled. *Degree requirements:* For doctorate, comprehensive exam, thesis/dissertation, thesis defense. *Entrance requirements:* For doctorate, GMAT or GRE. Additional exam requirements/recommendations for international students: Required—TOEFL (minimum score 600 paper-based; 250 computer-based; 100 iBT). *Application deadline:* For fall admission, 1/31 for domestic and international students. Applications are processed on a rolling basis. Application fee: $60 ($85 for international

students). Electronic applications accepted. *Financial support:* In 2009–10, 13 students received support, including 13 fellowships with partial tuition reimbursements available (averaging $6,000 per year), 12 teaching assistantships with full tuition reimbursements available (averaging $16,575 per year); institutionally sponsored loans, scholarships/grants, health care benefits, and unspecified assistantships also available. Financial award application deadline: 1/31. *Faculty research:* International finance, real estate finance, theoretical and empirical corporate finance, theoretical and empirical asset pricing bond pricing and derivatives. *Unit head:* Prof. Paul Weller, Department Executive Officer, 319-335-0929, Fax: 319-335-3690, E-mail: paul-weller@uiowa.edu. *Application contact:* Renea L. Jay, PhD Program Coordinator, 319-335-0830, Fax: 319-335-1956, E-mail: renea-jay@uiowa.edu.

The University of Iowa, Henry B. Tippie College of Business, Department of Management and Organizations, Iowa City, IA 52242-1316. Offers business administration (PhD), including management and organizations. *Accreditation:* AACSB. *Faculty:* 17 full-time (7 women), 4 part-time/adjunct (0 women). *Students:* 12 full-time (3 women), 1 (woman) part-time, 2 international. Average age 31. 58 applicants, 10% accepted, 3 enrolled. In 2009, 2 doctorates awarded. *Degree requirements:* For doctorate, comprehensive exam, thesis/dissertation, thesis defense. *Entrance requirements:* For doctorate, GMAT or GRE. Additional exam requirements/recommendations for international students: Required—TOEFL (minimum score 600 paper-based; 250 computer-based; 100 iBT). *Application deadline:* For fall admission, 1/15 for domestic and international students. Applications are processed on a rolling basis. Application fee: $60 ($85 for international students). Electronic applications accepted. *Financial support:* In 2009–10, 12 students received support, including 4 fellowships with full tuition reimbursements available (averaging $20,000 per year), 1 research assistantship with full tuition reimbursement available (averaging $16,575 per year), 7 teaching assistantships with full tuition reimbursements available (averaging $16,575 per year); institutionally sponsored loans, scholarships/grants, health care benefits, unspecified assistantships, and 12 partial fellowships ($6000 average) also available. Financial award application deadline: 2/1; financial award applicants required to submit FAFSA. *Faculty research:* Decision making, human resources, personal selection, organizational behavior, training. *Unit head:* Prof. Jay Christensen-Szalanski, Department Executive Officer, 319-335-0927, Fax: 319-335-1956, E-mail: jay-christensen-szalanski@uiowa.edu. *Application contact:* Renea L. Jay, PhD Program Coordinator, 319-335-0830, Fax: 319-335-1956, E-mail: renea-jay@uiowa.edu.

The University of Iowa, Henry B. Tippie College of Business, Department of Management Sciences, Iowa City, IA 52242-1316. Offers business administration (PhD), including management sciences. *Accreditation:* AACSB. *Faculty:* 15 full-time (2 women), 2 part-time/adjunct (0 women). *Students:* 12 full-time (3 women), 1 part-time (0 women), 8 international. Average age 29. 31 applicants, 19% accepted, 5 enrolled. *Degree requirements:* For doctorate, comprehensive exam, thesis/dissertation, thesis defense. *Entrance requirements:* For doctorate, GRE General Test or GMAT, minimum GPA of 3.0. Additional exam requirements/recommendations for international students: Required—TOEFL (minimum score 600 paper-based; 250 computer-based; 100 iBT). *Application deadline:* For fall admission, 2/15 for domestic and international students. Applications are processed on a rolling basis. Application fee: $60 ($85 for international students). Electronic applications accepted. *Financial support:* In 2009–10, 12 students received support, including 1 fellowship with full tuition reimbursement available (averaging $20,000 per year), 1 research assistantship with full tuition reimbursement available (averaging $16,575 per year), 8 teaching assistantships with full tuition reimbursements available (averaging $16,575 per year); institutionally sponsored loans, scholarships/grants, health care benefits, unspecified assistantships, and 12 partial fellowships ($2750 yearly average) also available. Financial award application deadline: 2/15. *Faculty research:* Optimization, supply chain management, data mining, logistics, database management. *Unit head:* Prof. Kurt Anstreicher, Department Executive Officer, 319-335-0858, Fax: 319-335-1956, E-mail: kurt-anstreicher@uiowa.edu. *Application contact:* Renea L. Jay, PhD Program Coordinator, 319-335-0830, Fax: 319-335-1956, E-mail: renea-jay@uiowa.edu.

The University of Iowa, Henry B. Tippie College of Business, Department of Marketing, Iowa City, IA 52242-1316. Offers business administration (PhD), including marketing. *Faculty:* 13 full-time (4 women), 5 part-time/adjunct (2 women). *Students:* 10 full-time (4 women); includes 2 minority (1 American Indian/Alaska Native, 1 Asian American or Pacific Islander), 8 international. Average age 30. 32 applicants, 13% accepted, 3 enrolled. In 2009, 2 doctorates awarded. *Degree requirements:* For doctorate, comprehensive exam, thesis/dissertation, thesis defense. *Entrance requirements:* For doctorate, GMAT or GRE, minimum undergraduate GPA of 2.7. Additional exam requirements/recommendations for international students: Required—TOEFL (minimum score 600 paper-based; 250 computer-based; 100 iBT). *Application deadline:* For fall admission, 1/15 for domestic and international students. Applications are processed on a rolling basis. Application fee: $60 ($85 for international students). Electronic applications accepted. *Financial support:* In 2009–10, 10 students received support, including 1 fellowship with full tuition reimbursement available (averaging $20,000 per year), 1 research assistantship with full tuition reimbursement available (averaging $16,575 per year), 8 teaching assistantships with full tuition reimbursements available (averaging $16,575 per year); institutionally sponsored loans, scholarships/grants, health care benefits, unspecified assistantships, and 10 partial fellowships ($1800 yearly average) also available. Financial award application deadline: 1/15. *Faculty research:* Judgments and decision making under certainty; consumer behavior: cognitive neuroscience, attitudes and evaluation; hierarchical bayesian estimation; marketing-finance interface; advertising effects. *Unit head:* Prof. Gary J. Russell, Department Executive Officer, 319-335-1013, Fax: 319-335-1956, E-mail: gary-j-russell@uiowa.edu. *Application contact:* Renea L. Jay, PhD Program Coordinator, 319-335-0830, Fax: 319-335-1956, E-mail: renea-jay@uiowa.edu.

The University of Iowa, Henry B. Tippie College of Business, Henry B. Tippie School of Management, Iowa City, IA 52242-1316. Offers corporate finance (MBA); investment management (MBA); marketing (MBA); process excellence (MBA); strategic innovation (MBA); JD/MBA; MBA/MA; MBA/MD; MBA/MHA; MBA/MSN. *Accreditation:* AACSB. Part-time and evening/weekend programs available. *Faculty:* 46 full-time (7 women), 12 part-time/adjunct (2 women). *Students:* 250 full-time (64 women), 794 part-time (277 women); includes 92 minority (17 African Americans, 2 American Indian/Alaska Native, 52 Asian Americans or Pacific Islanders, 21 Hispanic Americans), 146 international. Average age 32. 602 applicants, 60% accepted, 302 enrolled. In 2009, 348 master's awarded. *Entrance requirements:* For master's, GMAT, work experience, references. Additional exam requirements/recommendations for international students: Required—TOEFL (minimum score 600 paper-based; 250 computer-based; 100 iBT), IELTS (minimum score 7). *Application deadline:* For fall admission, 7/30 for domestic students, 4/15 for international students; for spring admission, 12/15 for domestic and international students. Applications are processed on a rolling basis. Application fee: $60 ($100 for international students). Electronic applications accepted. *Expenses:* Contact institution. *Financial support:* In 2009–10, 100 students received support, including 100 fellowships (averaging $6,819 per year), 92 research assistantships with partial tuition reimbursements available (averaging $10,388 per year); career-related internships or fieldwork, scholarships/grants, health care benefits, and unspecified assistantships also available. Financial award application deadline: 4/15; financial award applicants required to submit FAFSA. *Faculty research:* Capital markets, econometrics, optimization, investments and empirical corporate finance, Iowa electronic markets. *Unit head:* Prof. Jarjisu Sa-Aadu, Associate Dean, MBA Programs, 800-622-4692, Fax: 319-335-3604, E-mail: jsa-aadu@uiowa.edu. *Application contact:* Jodi Schafer, Director of Admissions and Financial Aid, 319-335-0864, Fax: 319-335-3604, E-mail: jodi-schafer@uiowa.edu.

The University of Kansas, Graduate Studies, School of Business, Program in Business, Lawrence, KS 66045. Offers PhD. *Accreditation:* AACSB. *Students:* 65 full-time (20 women), 2 part-time (1 woman); includes 8 minority (3 African Americans, 1 American Indian/Alaska Native, 2 Asian Americans or Pacific Islanders, 2 Hispanic Americans), 25 international. Average age 34. 188 applicants, 19% accepted, 29 enrolled. In 2009, 3 doctorates awarded. *Degree requirements:* For doctorate, comprehensive exam, thesis/dissertation, departmental qualifying exam. *Entrance requirements:* For doctorate, GMAT or GRE. Additional exam

requirements/recommendations for international students: Required—TOEFL (minimum score 600 paper-based; 250 computer-based; 100 iBT). *Application deadline:* For fall admission, 1/10 for domestic and international students. Applications are processed on a rolling basis. Application fee: $60. Electronic applications accepted. *Expenses:* Tuition, state resident: full-time $6492; part-time $270.50 per credit hour. Tuition, nonresident: full-time $15,510; part-time $646.25 per credit hour. Required fees: $847; $70.56 per credit hour. Tuition and fees vary according to course load and program. *Financial support:* Fellowships with full tuition reimbursements, research assistantships with full tuition reimbursements, teaching assistantships with full tuition reimbursements, scholarships/grants, health care benefits, tuition waivers (full), and unspecified assistantships available. *Faculty research:* Tax, mergers and acquisitions, risk analysis personality and work outcomes, services, marketing, business ethics, corporate turnarounds. *Unit head:* Charly Edmonds, Associate Director, 785-864-3841, Fax: 785-864-5376, E-mail: bschoolphd@ku.edu. *Application contact:* Charly Edmonds, Associate Director, 785-864-3841, E-mail: bschoolphd@ku.edu.

The University of Kansas, Graduate Studies, School of Business, Program in Business Administration and Management, Lawrence, KS 66045. Offers animal health (MBA); finance (MBA); human resources management (MBA); information systems (MBA); international business (MBA); management (MBA); marketing (MBA); strategic management (MBA); JD/MBA; MBA/MA; MBA/MM; MBA/MS; MBA/Pharm D. *Accreditation:* AACSB. Part-time and evening/weekend programs available. *Faculty:* 57 full-time (12 women), 20 part-time/adjunct (13 women). *Students:* 153 full-time (41 women), 235 part-time (68 women); includes 44 minority (8 African Americans, 1 American Indian/Alaska Native, 26 Asian Americans or Pacific Islanders, 9 Hispanic Americans), 34 international. Average age 30. 221 applicants, 72% accepted, 129 enrolled. In 2009, 108 master's awarded. *Degree requirements:* For master's, comprehensive exam (for some programs), thesis optional. *Entrance requirements:* For master's, GMAT, 2 years of professional work experience. Additional exam requirements/recommendations for international students: Required—TOEFL; Recommended—IELTS (minimum score 6). *Application deadline:* For fall admission, 6/1 priority date for domestic students, 5/1 priority date for international students; for spring admission, 11/1 priority date for domestic students, 10/1 for international students. Applications are processed on a rolling basis. Application fee: $60. Electronic applications accepted. *Expenses:* Tuition, state resident: full-time $6492; part-time $270.50 per credit hour. Tuition, nonresident: full-time $15,510; part-time $646.25 per credit hour. Required fees: $847; $70.56 per credit hour. Tuition and fees vary according to course load and program. *Financial support:* Research assistantships, teaching assistantships with full and partial tuition reimbursements, career-related internships or fieldwork, Federal Work-Study, institutionally sponsored loans, scholarships/grants, and unspecified assistantships available. Financial award application deadline: 6/1; financial award applicants required to submit FAFSA. *Faculty research:* Advanced audit technologies, real options and asset pricing, corporate governance, foreign direct investment, CEO characteristics and organizational innovation. *Unit head:* Dr. Charles Krider, Director of MBA Programs, 785-864-7543, E-mail: ckrider@ku.edu. *Application contact:* Dee Steinle, Administrative Director of Master's Programs, 785-864-7596, Fax: 785-864-5376, E-mail: dsteinle@ku.edu.

University of Kentucky, Graduate School, Gatton College of Business and Economics, Program in Business Administration, Lexington, KY 40506-0032. Offers MBA, PhD. *Accreditation:* AACSB. *Degree requirements:* For master's, comprehensive exam; for doctorate, comprehensive exam, thesis/dissertation. *Entrance requirements:* For master's, GMAT, minimum undergraduate GPA of 2.75; for doctorate, GMAT, minimum undergraduate GPA of 3.0. Additional exam requirements/recommendations for international students: Required—TOEFL (minimum score 550 paper-based; 213 computer-based). Electronic applications accepted. *Faculty research:* Expert systems in manufacturing, knowledge acquisition and management, financial institutions, market in service organizations, strategic planning.

University of La Verne, College of Business and Public Management, Graduate Programs in Business Administration, La Verne, CA 91750-4443. Offers accounting (MBA); executive management (MBA-EP); finance (MBA, MBA-EP); health services management (MBA); information technology (MBA, MBA-EP); international business (MBA, MBA-EP); leadership (MBA-EP); managed care (MBA); management (MBA, MBA-EP); marketing (MBA, MBA-EP). Part-time and evening/weekend programs available. *Faculty:* 22 full-time (11 women), 41 part-time/adjunct (8 women). *Students:* 409 full-time (213 women), 156 part-time (74 women); includes 371 minority (23 African Americans, 7 American Indian/Alaska Native, 259 Asian Americans or Pacific Islanders, 82 Hispanic Americans), 9 international. Average age 29. In 2009, 356 master's awarded. *Entrance requirements:* For master's, minimum undergraduate GPA of 3.0, 2 letters of recommendation, resume. Additional exam requirements/recommendations for international students: Required—TOEFL (minimum score 550 paper-based; 213 computer-based). *Application deadline:* Applications are processed on a rolling basis. Application fee: $50. *Expenses:* Contact institution. *Financial support:* Career-related internships or fieldwork, institutionally sponsored loans, and scholarships/grants available. Financial award application deadline: 3/2; financial award applicants required to submit FAFSA. *Unit head:* Dr. Abe Helou, Chairperson, 909-593-3511 Ext. 4211, Fax: 909-392-2704, E-mail: ihelou@laverne.edu. *Application contact:* Rina Lazarian, Program and Admission Specialist, 909-593-3511 Ext. 4819, Fax: 909-392-2704, E-mail: cbpm@ulv.edu.

University of La Verne, College of Business and Public Management, Program in Organizational Management and Leadership, La Verne, CA 91750-4443. Offers nonprofit management (Certificate); organizational leadership (Certificate); organizational management and leadership (MS). Part-time programs available. *Faculty:* 22 full-time (11 women), 41 part-time/adjunct (8 women). *Students:* 96 full-time (47 women), 60 part-time (34 women); includes 72 minority (17 African Americans, 24 Asian Americans or Pacific Islanders, 31 Hispanic Americans). Average age 33. In 2009, 68 master's awarded. *Degree requirements:* For master's, thesis or research project. *Entrance requirements:* For master's, minimum undergraduate GPA of 2.75, 2 letters of recommendation, interview, resume. Additional exam requirements/recommendations for international students: Required—TOEFL (minimum score 550 paper-based; 213 computer-based). *Application deadline:* Applications are processed on a rolling basis. Application fee: $50. *Expenses:* Contact institution. *Financial support:* Institutionally sponsored loans available. Financial award application deadline: 3/2; financial award applicants required to submit FAFSA. *Unit head:* Dr. Kathy Duncan, Chairperson, 909-593-3511 Ext. 4415, E-mail: kduncan2@laverne.edu. *Application contact:* Program and Admissions Specialist, 909-593-3511 Ext. 4819, E-mail: cbpm@laverne.edu.

University of La Verne, Regional Campus Administration, Graduate Programs, Central Coast/Vandenberg Air Force Base Campuses, La Verne, CA 91750-4443. Offers business (MBA-EP), including health services management, information technology; health administration (MHA); leadership and management (MS). *Faculty:* 18 part-time/adjunct (6 women). *Students:* 19 full-time (12 women), 35 part-time (14 women); includes 20 minority (7 African Americans, 2 American Indian/Alaska Native, 2 Asian Americans or Pacific Islanders, 9 Hispanic Americans). Average age 36. In 2009, 20 master's awarded. *Entrance requirements:* For master's, 2 letters of recommendation, resume. *Application deadline:* Applications are processed on a rolling basis. Application fee: $50. *Expenses:* Contact institution. *Financial support:* Institutionally sponsored loans available. Financial award application deadline: 3/2; financial award applicants required to submit FAFSA. *Unit head:* Kitt Vincent, Director, Central Coast Campus, 805-542-9690 Ext. 6043, Fax: 805-542-9735, E-mail: kvincent@laverne.edu. *Application contact:* Kitt Vincent, Director, Central Coast Campus, 805-542-9690 Ext. 6043, Fax: 805-542-9735, E-mail: kvincent@laverne.edu.

University of La Verne, Regional Campus Administration, Graduate Programs, High Desert Campus, Victorville, CA 92392. Offers business (MBA). *Faculty:* 5 part-time/adjunct (1 woman). *Students:* 9 full-time (7 women), 1 (woman) part-time; includes 8 minority (6 African Americans, 2 Hispanic Americans). Average age 36. In 2009, 7 master's awarded. *Entrance requirements:* For master's, 2 letters of recommendation, resume. *Application deadline:* Applications are processed on a rolling basis. Application fee: $50. *Expenses:* Contact institution. *Financial support:* Application deadline: 3/2. *Unit head:* Juli Roberts, Director, 760-843-0086 Ext. 222, Fax: 760-843-9505, E-mail: jroberts@laverne.edu. *Application contact:* Juli Roberts, Director, 760-843-0086 Ext. 222, Fax: 760-843-9505, E-mail: jroberts@laverne.edu.

University of La Verne, Regional Campus Administration, Graduate Programs, Inland Empire Campus, Rancho Cucamonga, CA 91730. Offers business (MBA-EP), including health services management, information technology, management, marketing; leadership and management (MS). *Faculty:* 2 full-time (both women), 12 part-time/adjunct (2 women). *Students:* 20 full-time (13 women), 61 part-time (41 women); includes 50 minority (10 African Americans, 11 Asian Americans or Pacific Islanders, 29 Hispanic Americans). Average age 37. In 2009, 24 master's awarded. *Entrance requirements:* For master's, 2 letters of recommendation, resume. *Application deadline:* Applications are processed on a rolling basis. Application fee: $50. *Expenses:* Contact institution. *Financial support:* Institutionally sponsored loans available. Financial award application deadline: 3/2; financial award applicants required to submit FAFSA. *Unit head:* Allan Stout, Director, 909-484-3858 Ext. 6002, Fax: 909-484-9469, E-mail: astout@laverne.edu. *Application contact:* Allan Stout, Director, 909-484-3858 Ext. 6002, Fax: 909-484-9469, E-mail: astout@laverne.edu.

University of La Verne, Regional Campus Administration, Graduate Programs, Kern County Campus, Bakersfield, CA 93301. Offers business (MBA-EP); health administration (MHA); leadership and management (MS). *Faculty:* 1 part-time/adjunct (0 women). *Students:* 10 part-time (5 women); includes 5 minority (2 Asian Americans or Pacific Islanders, 3 Hispanic Americans). Average age 32. In 2009, 2 master's awarded. *Entrance requirements:* For master's, 2 letters of recommendation, resume. *Application deadline:* Applications are processed on a rolling basis. Application fee: $50. *Expenses:* Contact institution. *Financial support:* Institutionally sponsored loans available. Financial award application deadline: 3/2; financial award applicants required to submit FAFSA. *Unit head:* Nora Dominguez, Interim Director, 661-328-1430 Ext. 6024, E-mail: ndominguez@laverne.edu. *Application contact:* Nora Dominguez, Interim Director, 661-328-1430 Ext. 6024, E-mail: ndominguez@laverne.edu.

University of La Verne, Regional Campus Administration, Graduate Programs, Orange County Campus, Garden Grove, CA 92840. Offers business (MBA); health administration (MHA); leadership and management (MS). *Faculty:* 3 full-time (1 woman), 11 part-time/adjunct (2 women). *Students:* 11 full-time (6 women), 64 part-time (30 women); includes 41 minority (3 African Americans, 4 American Indian/Alaska Native, 18 Asian Americans or Pacific Islanders, 16 Hispanic Americans). Average age 40. In 2009, 35 master's awarded. *Entrance requirements:* For master's, 2 letters of recommendation, resume. *Application deadline:* Applications are processed on a rolling basis. Application fee: $50. *Expenses:* Contact institution. *Financial support:* Institutionally sponsored loans available. Financial award application deadline: 3/2; financial award applicants required to submit FAFSA. *Unit head:* Pamela Bergovoy, Director, 714-505-1682 Ext. 6900, E-mail: pbergovoy@laverne.edu. *Application contact:* Pamela Bergovoy, Director, 714-505-1682 Ext. 6900, E-mail: pbergovoy@laverne.edu.

University of La Verne, Regional Campus Administration, Graduate Programs, San Fernando Valley Campus, Burbank, CA 91505. Offers business (MBA-EP); leadership and management (MS). *Faculty:* 2 full-time (1 woman), 11 part-time/adjunct (4 women). *Students:* 35 full-time (18 women), 80 part-time (44 women); includes 64 minority (20 African Americans, 10 Asian Americans or Pacific Islanders, 34 Hispanic Americans). Average age 38. In 2009, 29 master's awarded. *Entrance requirements:* For master's, 2 letters of recommendation, resume. *Application deadline:* Applications are processed on a rolling basis. Application fee: $50. *Expenses:* Contact institution. *Financial support:* Institutionally sponsored loans available. Financial award application deadline: 3/2; financial award applicants required to submit FAFSA. *Unit head:* Nelly Kazman, Director, 818-846-4008 Ext. 6088, Fax: 818-566-1047, E-mail: nkazman@laverne.edu. *Application contact:* Nelly Kazman, Director, 818-846-4008 Ext. 6088, Fax: 818-566-1047, E-mail: nkazman@laverne.edu.

University of La Verne, Regional Campus Administration, Graduate Programs, Ventura County/Point Mugu Naval Air Station Campuses, La Verne, CA 91750-4443. Offers leadership and management (MS). *Faculty:* 12 part-time/adjunct (1 woman). *Students:* 14 full-time (5 women), 25 part-time (10 women); includes 22 minority (2 African Americans, 8 Asian Americans or Pacific Islanders, 12 Hispanic Americans). Average age 39. In 2009, 22 master's awarded. *Entrance requirements:* For master's, 2 letters of recommendation, resume. Application fee: $50. *Expenses:* Contact institution. *Financial support:* Institutionally sponsored loans available. Financial award application deadline: 3/2; financial award applicants required to submit FAFSA. *Unit head:* Jamie Dempsey, Director, Point Mugu, 805-986-1783 Ext. 6955, Fax: 805-981-8033, E-mail: jdempsey@laverne.edu. *Application contact:* Jamie Dempsey, Director, Point Mugu, 805-986-1783 Ext. 6955, Fax: 805-981-8033, E-mail: jdempsey@laverne.edu.

University of La Verne, Regional Campus Administration, Graduate Program, ULV Online, La Verne, CA 91750-4443. Offers business administration (MBA). *Faculty:* 4 full-time (2 women), 4 part-time/adjunct (1 woman). *Students:* 33 full-time (18 women), 69 part-time (38 women); includes 45 minority (16 African Americans, 7 Asian Americans or Pacific Islanders, 22 Hispanic Americans). Average age 36. In 2009, 25 master's awarded. *Entrance requirements:* For master's, resume, 2 letters of recommendation. *Application deadline:* Applications are processed on a rolling basis. Application fee: $50. *Expenses:* Tuition: Part-time $575 per credit hour. Required fees: $575 per contact hour. Tuition and fees vary according to degree level, program and student level. *Financial support:* Application deadline: 3/2. *Unit head:* Barbara Colley, La Verne Online Coordinator, 800-695-4858 Ext. 5322, E-mail: bcolley@ulv.edu. *Application contact:* Barbara Colley, La Verne Online Coordinator, 800-695-4858 Ext. 5322, E-mail: bcolley@ulv.edu.

University of Lethbridge, School of Graduate Studies, Lethbridge, AB T1K 3M4, Canada. Offers accounting (MScM); addictions counseling (M Sc); agricultural biotechnology (M Sc); agricultural studies (M Sc, MA); anthropology (MA); archaeology (MA); art (MA, MFA); biochemistry (M Sc); biological sciences (M Sc); biomolecular science (PhD); biosystems and biodiversity (PhD); Canadian studies (MA); chemistry (M Sc); computer science (M Sc); computer science and geographical information science (M Sc); counseling psychology (M Ed); dramatic arts (MA); earth, space, and physical science (PhD); economics (MA); educational leadership (M Ed); English (MA); environmental science (M Sc); evolution and behavior (PhD); exercise science (M Sc); finance (MScM); French (MA); French/German (MA); French/Spanish (MA); general education (M Ed); general management (MScM); geography (M Sc, MA); German (MA); health science (M Sc); health sciences (MA); history (MA); human resource management and labour relations (MScM); individualized multidisciplinary (M Sc, MA); information systems (MScM); international management (MScM); kinesiology (M Sc, MA); management (M Sc, MA); marketing (MScM); mathematics (M Sc); music (M Mus, MA); Native American studies (MA); neuroscience (M Sc, PhD); new media (MA); nursing (M Sc); philosophy (MA); physics (M Sc); policy and strategy (MScM); political science (MA); psychology (M Sc, MA); religious studies (MA); social sciences (MA); sociology (MA); theatre and dramatic arts (MFA); theoretical and computational science (PhD); urban and regional studies (MA); women's studies (MA). Part-time and evening/weekend programs available. *Degree requirements:* For doctorate, comprehensive exam, thesis/dissertation. *Entrance requirements:* For master's, GMAT (M Sc in management), bachelor's degree in related field, minimum GPA of 3.0 during previous 20 graded semester courses, 2 years teaching or related experience (M Ed); for doctorate, master's degree, minimum graduate GPA of 3.5. Additional exam requirements/recommendations for international students: Required—TOEFL. *Faculty research:* Movement and brain plasticity, gibberellin physiology, photosynthesis, carbon cycling, molecular properties of main-group ring components.

University of Louisiana at Lafayette, BI Moody III College of Business Administration MBA Program, Lafayette, LA 70504. Offers MBA. *Accreditation:* AACSB. Part-time and evening/weekend programs available. *Entrance requirements:* For master's, GRE General Test. Additional exam requirements/recommendations for international students: Required—TOEFL (minimum score 550 paper-based; 213 computer-based).

University of Louisiana at Monroe, Graduate School, College of Business Administration, Monroe, LA 71209-0001. Offers MBA. *Accreditation:* AACSB. Part-time and evening/weekend

Business Administration and Management—General

University of Louisiana at Monroe (continued)
programs available. *Faculty:* 26 full-time (9 women). *Students:* 47 full-time (13 women), 36 part-time (16 women); includes 10 minority (8 African Americans, 1 American Indian/Alaska Native, 1 Hispanic American), 20 international. Average age 28. In 2009, 27 master's awarded. *Degree requirements:* For master's, comprehensive exam. *Entrance requirements:* For master's, GMAT, minimum GPA of 2.5, minimum AACSB index of 950. Additional exam requirements/recommendations for international students: Required—TOEFL (minimum score 500 paper-based; 61 computer-based). *Application deadline:* For fall admission, 8/24 for domestic students, 7/1 for international students; for winter admission, 12/14 for domestic students; for spring admission, 1/19 for domestic students, 11/1 for international students. Applications are processed on a rolling basis. Application fee: $20 ($30 for international students). Electronic applications accepted. *Expenses:* Tuition, state resident: part-time $159 per credit hour. Tuition, nonresident: part-time $159 per credit hour. Required fees: $1300 per year. Tuition and fees vary according to course load. *Financial support:* In 2009–10, 19 research assistantships with full tuition reimbursements (averaging $2,500 per year) were awarded; career-related internships or fieldwork, Federal Work-Study, and unspecified assistantships also available. Financial award application deadline: 4/1; financial award applicants required to submit FAFSA. *Faculty research:* Information assurance framework, TPB in e-learning, bias in balanced scorecard. *Unit head:* Dr. Ronald Berry, Dean, 318-342-1100, Fax: 318-342-1101, E-mail: rberry@ulm.edu. *Application contact:* Dr. Donna Walton Luse, Program Chair, 318-342-1106, Fax: 318-342-1101, E-mail: luse@ulm.edu.

University of Louisville, Graduate School, College of Business, MBA Programs, Louisville, KY 40292-0001. Offers business administration (MBA); entrepreneurship (MBA). *Accreditation:* AACSB. Part-time and evening/weekend programs available. *Faculty:* 25 full-time (4 women), 1 (woman) part-time/adjunct. *Students:* 211 part-time (54 women); includes 29 minority (10 African Americans, 2 American Indian/Alaska Native, 11 Asian Americans or Pacific Islanders, 6 Hispanic Americans), 8 international. Average age 30. 90 applicants, 67% accepted, 48 enrolled. In 2009, 156 master's awarded. *Entrance requirements:* For master's, GMAT, 2 letters of reference, personal interview, resume. Additional exam requirements/recommendations for international students: Required—TOEFL (minimum score 557 paper-based; 213 computer-based; 79 iBT). *Application deadline:* For fall admission, 7/31 for domestic students; for spring admission, 12/1 for domestic students. Applications are processed on a rolling basis. Application fee: $50. *Financial support:* In 2009–10, 10 research assistantships with full tuition reimbursements (averaging $12,000 per year) were awarded; health care benefits and unspecified assistantships also available. Financial award application deadline: 3/31; financial award applicants required to submit FAFSA. *Faculty research:* Entrepreneurship, supply chain management, venture capital, retailing/franchising, corporate governance. Total annual research expenditures: $297,040. *Unit head:* Dr. Charles Moyer, Dean, 502-852-6443, Fax: 502-852-7557, E-mail: charlie.moyer@louisville.edu. *Application contact:* Joshua M. Philpot, Graduate Programs Manager, 502-852-7257, Fax: 502-852-4901, E-mail: josh.philpot@louisville.edu.

University of Maine, Graduate School, College of Business, Public Policy and Health, The Maine Business School, Orono, ME 04469. Offers accounting (MS); business administration (MBA); business and sustainability (MBA). *Accreditation:* AACSB. Part-time and evening/weekend programs available. *Faculty:* 25 full-time (10 women), 1 (woman) part-time/adjunct. *Students:* 47 full-time (19 women), 14 part-time (6 women); includes 3 minority (2 American Indian/Alaska Native, 1 Hispanic American), 4 international. Average age 28. 56 applicants, 63% accepted, 25 enrolled. In 2009, 21 master's awarded. *Entrance requirements:* For master's, GMAT. Additional exam requirements/recommendations for international students: Required—TOEFL (minimum score 550 paper-based; 213 computer-based). *Application deadline:* For fall admission, 6/1 priority date for domestic and international students; for spring admission, 11/1 priority date for domestic and international students. Applications are processed on a rolling basis. Application fee: $65. Electronic applications accepted. *Expenses:* Contact institution. *Financial support:* In 2009–10, 16 students received support, including 4 teaching assistantships with tuition reimbursements available (averaging $12,790 per year); career-related internships or fieldwork, Federal Work-Study, institutionally sponsored loans, scholarships/grants, tuition waivers (full and partial), and unspecified assistantships also available. Financial award application deadline: 3/1. *Faculty research:* Entrepreneurship, investment management, international markets, decision support systems, strategic planning. *Unit head:* Dr. Nory Jones, Director of Graduate Programs, 207-581-1971, Fax: 207-581-1930, E-mail: mba@maine.edu. *Application contact:* Scott G. Delcourt, Associate Dean of the Graduate School, 207-581-3291, Fax: 207-581-3232, E-mail: graduate@maine.edu.

University of Management and Technology, Program in Business Administration, Arlington, VA 22209. Offers acquisition management (DBA); general management (MBA, DBA); project management (MBA, DBA). Part-time and evening/weekend programs available. Postbaccalaureate distance learning degree programs offered (no on-campus study). *Degree requirements:* For master's, comprehensive exam. *Entrance requirements:* For master's, 3 recommendations, resume. Additional exam requirements/recommendations for international students: Required—TOEFL (minimum score 550 paper-based; 213 computer-based). Electronic applications accepted.

University of Management and Technology, Program in Management, Arlington, VA 22209. Offers acquisition management (MS, AC); general management (MS); project management (MS, AC); public administration (MPA, MS, AC). Part-time and evening/weekend programs available. Postbaccalaureate distance learning degree programs offered (no on-campus study). *Entrance requirements:* For master's, 3 recommendations, resume. Additional exam requirements/recommendations for international students: Required—TOEFL (minimum score 550 paper-based; 213 computer-based). Electronic applications accepted.

University of Manitoba, Faculty of Graduate Studies, Asper School of Business, Winnipeg, MB R3T 2N2, Canada. Offers M Sc, MBA, PhD. *Accreditation:* AACSB.

University of Mary, Gary Tharaldson School of Business, Bismarck, ND 58504-9652. Offers health care (MBA); human resource management (MBA); management (MBA); project management (MPM); strategic leadership (MSSL). Part-time and evening/weekend programs available. *Degree requirements:* For master's, strategic planning seminar. *Entrance requirements:* For master's, minimum GPA of 2.5. Additional exam requirements/recommendations for international students: Required—TOEFL. *Expenses:* Tuition: Full-time $10,062; part-time $430 per credit. Tuition and fees vary according to course load, degree level, program and student level.

University of Mary Hardin-Baylor, Graduate Studies in Business Administration, Belton, TX 76513. Offers accounting (MBA); management (MBA). Part-time and evening/weekend programs available. *Degree requirements:* For master's, comprehensive exam. *Entrance requirements:* For master's, GMAT, minimum GPA of 3.0, work experience, interview. Electronic applications accepted.

University of Maryland, College Park, Academic Affairs, Joint Program in Business and Management/Public Policy, College Park, MD 20742. Offers MBA/MPM. *Accreditation:* AACSB. *Students:* 10 full-time (2 women), 2 part-time (1 woman); includes 2 minority (both Asian Americans or Pacific Islanders), 1 international. 26 applicants, 31% accepted, 8 enrolled. *Application deadline:* For fall admission, 12/15 for domestic students, 2/1 for international students; for spring admission, 10/15 for domestic students, 6/1 for international students. Applications are processed on a rolling basis. Application fee: $60. Electronic applications accepted. *Expenses:* Tuition, area resident: Part-time $471 per credit hour. Tuition, state resident: part-time $471 per credit hour. Tuition, nonresident: part-time $1016 per credit hour. Required fees: $337.04 per term. *Financial support:* In 2009–10, 6 teaching assistantships (averaging $15,006 per year) were awarded; fellowships, research assistantships also available. Financial award applicants required to submit FAFSA. *Unit head:* Dr. Charles Caramello, Dean of the Graduate School, 301-405-0358, Fax: 301-314-9305, E-mail: ccaramel@umd.edu. *Application contact:* Dean of Graduate School, 301-405-0376, Fax: 301-314-9305.

University of Maryland, College Park, Academic Affairs, Robert H. Smith School of Business, Combined MSW/MBA Program, College Park, MD 20742. Offers MSW/MBA. *Accreditation:* AACSB. *Students:* 1 part-time (0 women). 4 applicants, 50% accepted, 0 enrolled. *Entrance requirements:* Additional exam requirements/recommendations for international students: Required—TOEFL. *Application deadline:* For fall admission, 12/15 priority date for domestic students, 12/15 for international students; for spring admission, 11/30 for domestic students, 6/1 for international students. Application fee: $60. *Expenses:* Tuition, area resident: Part-time $471 per credit hour. Tuition, state resident: part-time $471 per credit hour. Tuition, nonresident: part-time $1016 per credit hour. Required fees: $337.04 per term. *Financial support:* Fellowships available. *Unit head:* Dr. Robert Krapfel, Associate Dean, 301-405-2198, E-mail: bkrapfel@umd.edu. *Application contact:* Dean of Graduate School, 301-405-0358.

University of Maryland, College Park, Academic Affairs, Robert H. Smith School of Business, Executive MBA Program, College Park, MD 20742. Offers EMBA. *Students:* 77 full-time (24 women), 22 part-time (7 women); includes 16 minority (7 African Americans, 9 Asian Americans or Pacific Islanders), 22 international. 24 applicants, 88% accepted, 21 enrolled. In 2009, 154 master's awarded. *Entrance requirements:* For master's, minimum GPA of 3.0, 7-12 years professional experience. Additional exam requirements/recommendations for international students: Required—TOEFL. *Application deadline:* For fall admission, 12/15 priority date for domestic and international students; for spring admission, 11/30 for domestic students, 6/1 for international students. Application fee: $60. *Expenses:* Tuition, area resident: Part-time $471 per credit hour. Tuition, state resident: part-time $471 per credit hour. Tuition, nonresident: part-time $1016 per credit hour. Required fees: $337.04 per term. *Financial support:* In 2009–10, 13 fellowships with full and partial tuition reimbursements (averaging $20,061 per year) were awarded. *Unit head:* Dr. Robert Krapfel, Associate Dean, 301-405-2198, E-mail: bkrapfel@umd.edu. *Application contact:* Dean of Graduate School, 301-405-0358.

University of Maryland, College Park, Academic Affairs, Robert H. Smith School of Business, Joint Program in Business and Management, College Park, MD 20742. Offers MBA/MS. *Students:* 21 full-time (3 women), 8 part-time (2 women); includes 8 minority (1 African American, 1 American Indian/Alaska Native, 6 Asian Americans or Pacific Islanders), 5 international. 28 applicants, 18% accepted, 3 enrolled. *Entrance requirements:* Additional exam requirements/recommendations for international students: Required—TOEFL. *Application deadline:* For fall admission, 12/15 for domestic and international students; for spring admission, 11/30 for domestic students, 6/1 for international students. Applications are processed on a rolling basis. Application fee: $60. Electronic applications accepted. *Expenses:* Tuition, area resident: Part-time $471 per credit hour. Tuition, state resident: part-time $471 per credit hour. Tuition, nonresident: part-time $1016 per credit hour. Required fees: $337.04 per term. *Financial support:* In 2009–10, 2 teaching assistantships (averaging $16,953 per year) were awarded; fellowships also available. *Unit head:* Dr. Anand Anandalingam, Dean, 301-405-0582, E-mail: ganand@umd.edu. *Application contact:* Dean of Graduate School, 301-405-0358.

University of Maryland, College Park, Academic Affairs, Robert H. Smith School of Business, Program in Business Administration, College Park, MD 20742. Offers MBA. *Accreditation:* AACSB. Part-time and evening/weekend programs available. Postbaccalaureate distance learning degree programs offered. *Students:* 561 full-time (189 women), 738 part-time (239 women); includes 392 minority (100 African Americans, 3 American Indian/Alaska Native, 248 Asian Americans or Pacific Islanders, 41 Hispanic Americans), 160 international. 1,547 applicants, 50% accepted, 497 enrolled. In 2009, 448 master's awarded. *Entrance requirements:* For master's, GMAT, minimum GPA of 3.0, resume, 3 letters of recommendation. Additional exam requirements/recommendations for international students: Required—TOEFL. *Application deadline:* For fall admission, 5/1 for domestic students, 2/1 for international students. Applications are processed on a rolling basis. Application fee: $60. Electronic applications accepted. *Expenses:* Tuition, area resident: Part-time $471 per credit hour. Tuition, state resident: part-time $471 per credit hour. Tuition, nonresident: part-time $1016 per credit hour. Required fees: $337.04 per term. *Financial support:* In 2009–10, 24 fellowships with full and partial tuition reimbursements (averaging $28,372 per year), 82 teaching assistantships (averaging $14,916 per year) were awarded. Financial award applicants required to submit FAFSA. *Faculty research:* Accounting, entrepreneurship, finance management and organization, management server and statistical information systems. *Unit head:* Robert Krapfel, Associate Dean, 301-405-2198, E-mail: bkrapfel@umd.edu. *Application contact:* Dean of Graduate School, 301-405-0376.

University of Maryland, College Park, Academic Affairs, Robert H. Smith School of Business, Program in Business and Management, College Park, MD 20742. Offers MS, PhD. *Accreditation:* AACSB. Part-time programs available. *Students:* 188 full-time (94 women), 33 part-time (14 women); includes 67 minority (28 African Americans, 34 Asian Americans or Pacific Islanders, 5 Hispanic Americans), 97 international. 838 applicants, 17% accepted, 97 enrolled. In 2009, 20 master's, 9 doctorates awarded. *Degree requirements:* For master's, thesis optional; for doctorate, comprehensive exam, thesis/dissertation. *Entrance requirements:* For master's, GMAT, minimum GPA of 3.0, resume, 2 letters of recommendation; for doctorate, GMAT or GRE General Test, minimum GPA of 3.0, resume, 2 letters of recommendation. Additional exam requirements/recommendations for international students: Required—TOEFL. *Application deadline:* For fall admission, 12/15 for domestic and international students; for spring admission, 11/30 for domestic students, 6/1 for international students. Applications are processed on a rolling basis. Application fee: $60. Electronic applications accepted. *Expenses:* Tuition, area resident: Part-time $471 per credit hour. Tuition, state resident: part-time $471 per credit hour. Tuition, nonresident: part-time $1016 per credit hour. Required fees: $337.04 per term. *Financial support:* In 2009–10, 1 fellowship with partial tuition reimbursement (averaging $10,800 per year), 90 teaching assistantships with tuition reimbursements (averaging $19,895 per year) were awarded; research assistantships with tuition reimbursements. Financial award applicants required to submit FAFSA. *Application contact:* Dean of Graduate School, 301-405-0358.

University of Maryland, College Park, Academic Affairs, Robert H. Smith School of Business, Program in Business Management/Law, College Park, MD 20742. Offers JD/MBA. *Accreditation:* AACSB. *Students:* 5 full-time (0 women), 3 part-time (0 women); includes 2 minority (1 Asian American or Pacific Islander, 1 Hispanic American). 13 applicants, 38% accepted, 5 enrolled. *Entrance requirements:* Additional exam requirements/recommendations for international students: Required—TOEFL. *Application deadline:* For fall admission, 12/15 for domestic and international students; for spring admission, 11/30 for domestic students, 6/1 for international students. Applications are processed on a rolling basis. Application fee: $60. *Expenses:* Tuition, area resident: Part-time $471 per credit hour. Tuition, state resident: part-time $471 per credit hour. Tuition, nonresident: part-time $1016 per credit hour. Required fees: $337.04 per term. *Financial support:* In 2009–10, 1 fellowship with full tuition reimbursement (averaging $15,000 per year) was awarded; teaching assistantships. Financial award applicants required to submit FAFSA. *Unit head:* Dr. Anand Anandalingam, Dean, 301-405-0582, E-mail: ganand@umd.edu. *Application contact:* Dean of Graduate School, 301-405-0358.

University of Maryland University College, Graduate School of Management and Technology, Doctoral Program in Management, Adelphi, MD 20783. Offers DM. Part-time programs available. *Students:* 246 part-time (99 women); includes 98 minority (78 African Americans, 14 Asian Americans or Pacific Islanders, 6 Hispanic Americans), 10 international. Average age 45. 287 applicants, 100% accepted, 18 enrolled. In 2009, 30 doctorates awarded. *Degree requirements:* For doctorate, comprehensive exam, thesis/dissertation. *Application deadline:* Applications are processed on a rolling basis. Application fee: $100. Electronic applications accepted. *Expenses:* Tuition, state resident: full-time $7704; part-time $428 per credit hour. Tuition, nonresident: full-time $11,862; part-time $659 per credit hour. *Financial support:* Federal Work-Study and scholarships/grants available. Support available to part-time students. Financial award application deadline: 6/1; financial award applicants required to submit FAFSA. *Unit head:* Dr. Bryan Booth, Executive Director, 240-684-2400, Fax: 240-684-2401, E-mail: bbooth@umuc.edu. *Application contact:* Admissions Coordinator, 800-888-UMUC, Fax: 240-684-2151, E-mail: newgrad@umuc.edu.

University of Maryland University College, Graduate School of Management and Technology, Executive Programs, Adelphi, MD 20783. Offers EMBA. *Students:* 81 part-time (29 women);

includes 33 minority (28 African Americans, 1 American Indian/Alaska Native, 1 Asian American or Pacific Islander, 3 Hispanic Americans), 1 international. Average age 43. 49 applicants, 100% accepted, 27 enrolled. In 2009, 33 master's awarded. *Degree requirements:* For master's, thesis or alternative. *Application deadline:* Applications are processed on a rolling basis. Application fee: $50. Electronic applications accepted. *Expenses:* Tuition, state resident: full-time $7704; part-time $428 per credit hour. Tuition, nonresident: full-time $11,862; part-time $659 per credit hour. *Financial support:* Application deadline: 6/1. *Unit head:* Dr. Mary Ann Spilman, Director, 240-684-2400, Fax: 240-684-2401, E-mail: mspilman@umuc.edu. *Application contact:* Coordinator, Graduate Admissions, 800-888-UMUC, Fax: 240-684-2151, E-mail: newgrad@umuc.edu.

University of Maryland University College, Graduate School of Management and Technology, Program in Business Administration, Adelphi, MD 20783. Offers MBA, Certificate. Part-time and evening/weekend programs available. Postbaccalaureate distance learning degree programs offered (no on-campus study). *Students:* 14 full-time (5 women), 3,006 part-time (1,690 women); includes 1,529 minority (1,192 African Americans, 12 American Indian/Alaska Native, 204 Asian Americans or Pacific Islanders, 121 Hispanic Americans), 85 international. Average age 33. 1,856 applicants, 100% accepted, 677 enrolled. In 2009, 727 master's awarded. *Degree requirements:* For master's, thesis or alternative. *Application deadline:* Applications are processed on a rolling basis. Application fee: $50. Electronic applications accepted. *Expenses:* Tuition, state resident; full-time $7704; part-time $428 per credit hour. Tuition, nonresident: full-time $11,862; part-time $659 per credit hour. *Financial support:* Federal Work-Study and scholarships/grants available. Support available to part-time students. Financial award application deadline: 6/1; financial award applicants required to submit FAFSA. *Unit head:* Dr. Robert Goodwin, Chair, Business and Executive Programs, 240-684-2400, Fax: 240-684-2401, E-mail: rgoodwin@umuc.edu. *Application contact:* Coordinator, Graduate Admissions, 800-888-UMUC, Fax: 240-684-2151, E-mail: newgrad@umuc.edu.

University of Maryland University College, Graduate School of Management and Technology, Program in Management, Adelphi, MD 20783. Offers MS, Certificate. Offered evenings and weekends only. Part-time and evening/weekend programs available. Postbaccalaureate distance learning degree programs offered (no on-campus study). *Students:* 111 full-time (71 women), 3,096 part-time (2,135 women); includes 1,711 minority (1,425 African Americans, 11 American Indian/Alaska Native, 143 Asian Americans or Pacific Islanders, 132 Hispanic Americans), 60 international. Average age 36. 802 applicants, 100% accepted, 563 enrolled. In 2009, 519 master's, 99 other advanced degrees awarded. *Degree requirements:* For master's, thesis or alternative. *Application deadline:* Applications are processed on a rolling basis. Application fee: $50. Electronic applications accepted. *Expenses:* Tuition, state resident: full-time $7704; part-time $428 per credit hour. Tuition, nonresident; full-time $11,862; part-time $659 per credit hour. *Financial support:* Federal Work-Study and scholarships/grants available. Support available to part-time students. Financial award application deadline: 6/1; financial award applicants required to submit FAFSA. *Unit head:* Dr. Alan Sutherland, Director, 240-684-2400, Fax: 240-684-2401, E-mail: asutherland@umuc.edu. *Application contact:* Coordinator, Graduate Admissions, 888-888-UMUC, Fax: 240-684-2151, E-mail: newgrad@umuc.edu.

University of Mary Washington, College of Graduate and Professional Studies, Fredericksburg, VA 22406-7239. Offers business administration (MBA); education (M Ed); management information systems (MSMIS). Part-time and evening/weekend programs available. *Entrance requirements:* For master's, GMAT (MBA), PRAXIS I (M Ed), minimum GPA of 3.0. Additional exam requirements/recommendations for international students: Required—TOEFL (minimum score 600 paper-based; 250 computer-based; 100 iBT).

University of Massachusetts Amherst, Graduate School, Interdisciplinary Programs, Program in Public Policy and Business Administration, Amherst, MA 01003. Offers MPPA/MBA. Part-time programs available. *Students:* 4 full-time (3 women). Average age 27. 12 applicants, 42% accepted, 2 enrolled. *Entrance requirements:* Additional exam requirements/recommendations for international students: Required—TOEFL (minimum score 600 paper-based; 250 computer-based; 100 iBT), IELTS (minimum score 7). *Application deadline:* For fall admission, 2/1 for domestic and international students. Applications are processed on a rolling basis. Application fee: $50 ($65 for international students). Electronic applications accepted. *Expenses:* Tuition, state resident: full-time $2640; part-time $110 per credit. Tuition, nonresident: full-time $9936; part-time $414 per credit. Tuition and fees vary according to course load. *Financial support:* Career-related internships or fieldwork, Federal Work-Study, scholarships/grants, traineeships, health care benefits, tuition waivers (full), and unspecified assistantships available. Support available to part-time students. Financial award application deadline: 2/1. *Unit head:* Dr. M. V. Lee Badgett, Graduate Program Director, 413-545-3956, Fax: 413-545-1108. *Application contact:* Jean M. Ames, Supervisor of Admissions, 413-545-0722, Fax: 413-577-0010, E-mail: gradadm@grad.umass.edu.

University of Massachusetts Amherst, Graduate School, Isenberg School of Management, Part-time Master of Business Administration Program, Amherst, MA 01003. Offers MBA. *Accreditation:* AACSB. Part-time and evening/weekend programs available. Postbaccalaureate distance learning degree programs offered (no on-campus study). *Students:* 34 full-time (8 women), 983 part-time (287 women); includes 179 minority (38 African Americans, 4 American Indian/Alaska Native, 113 Asian Americans or Pacific Islanders, 24 Hispanic Americans), 52 international. Average age 35. 392 applicants, 94% accepted, 289 enrolled. In 2009, 249 master's awarded. *Entrance requirements:* For master's, GMAT. Additional exam requirements/recommendations for international students: Required—TOEFL (minimum score 600 paper-based; 250 computer-based; 100 iBT), IELTS (minimum score 7). *Application deadline:* For fall admission, 7/1 for domestic and international students; for spring admission, 12/1 for domestic and international students. Applications are processed on a rolling basis. Application fee: $50 ($65 for international students). Electronic applications accepted. *Expenses:* Tuition, state resident: full-time $2640; part-time $110 per credit. Tuition, nonresident: full-time $9936; part-time $414 per credit. Tuition and fees vary according to course load. *Unit head:* Dr. Eric N. Berkowitz, Graduate Program Director, 413-545-5608, Fax: 413-577-2234, E-mail: gradprog@som.umass.edu. *Application contact:* Jean M. Ames, Supervisor of Admissions, 415-545-0722, Fax: 413-577-0010, E-mail: gradadm@grad.umass.edu.

University of Massachusetts Amherst, Graduate School, Isenberg School of Management, Program in Management, Amherst, MA 01003. Offers MBA, MS, PhD. *Accreditation:* AACSB. Part-time programs available. *Faculty:* 55 full-time (11 women). *Students:* 99 full-time (40 women), 10 part-time (3 women); includes 8 minority (3 African Americans, 2 Asian Americans or Pacific Islanders, 3 Hispanic Americans), 46 international. Average age 31. 328 applicants, 23% accepted, 36 enrolled. In 2009, 34 master's, 9 doctorates awarded. Terminal master's awarded for partial completion of doctoral program. *Degree requirements:* For master's, thesis or alternative; for doctorate, comprehensive exam, thesis/dissertation. *Entrance requirements:* For master's and doctorate, GMAT. Additional exam requirements/recommendations for international students: Required—TOEFL (minimum score 550 paper-based; 213 computer-based; 80 iBT), IELTS (minimum score 6.5). *Application deadline:* For fall admission, 2/1 for domestic and international students. Applications are processed on a rolling basis. Application fee: $50 ($65 for international students). Electronic applications accepted. *Expenses:* Tuition, state resident: full-time $2640; part-time $110 per credit. Tuition, nonresident: full-time $9936; part-time $414 per credit. Tuition and fees vary according to course load. *Financial support:* In 2009–10, 7 fellowships with full tuition reimbursements (averaging $16,857 per year), 71 research assistantships with full tuition reimbursements (averaging $11,108 per year), 54 teaching assistantships with full tuition reimbursements (averaging $9,690 per year) were awarded; career-related internships or fieldwork, Federal Work-Study, scholarships/grants, traineeships, health care benefits, tuition waivers (full), and unspecified assistantships also available. Support available to part-time students. Financial award application deadline: 2/1. *Unit head:* Dr. Lawrence Zacharias, Chair, 413-545-5583, Fax: 413-577-2234. *Application contact:* Jean M. Ames, Supervisor of Admissions, 413-545-0722, Fax: 413-577-0010, E-mail: gradadm@grad.umass.edu.

University of Massachusetts Boston, Office of Graduate Studies, College of Management, Program in Business Administration, Boston, MA 02125-3393. Offers MBA, MS/MBA.

Accreditation: AACSB. Part-time and evening/weekend programs available. *Degree requirements:* For master's, capstone project. *Entrance requirements:* For master's, GMAT, minimum GPA of 3.0. *Faculty research:* International finance, human resource management, management information systems, investment and corporate finance, international marketing.

University of Massachusetts Dartmouth, Graduate School, Charlton College of Business, Program in Business Administration, North Dartmouth, MA 02747-2300. Offers accounting (Postbaccalaureate Certificate); business administration (MBA); e-commerce (PMC); finance (PMC); general management (PMC); leadership (PMC); management (Postbaccalaureate Certificate); marketing (PMC); supply chain management (PMC). *Accreditation:* AACSB. Part-time programs available. *Faculty:* 42 full-time (13 women), 26 part-time/adjunct (6 women). *Students:* 93 full-time (41 women), 132 part-time (64 women); includes 22 minority (5 African Americans, 2 American Indian/Alaska Native, 6 Asian Americans or Pacific Islanders, 9 Hispanic Americans), 42 international. Average age 30. 186 applicants, 82% accepted, 94 enrolled. In 2009, 55 master's, 19 other advanced degrees awarded. *Entrance requirements:* For master's, GMAT, resume, letters of recommendation. Additional exam requirements/recommendations for international students: Required—TOEFL (minimum score 500 paper-based; 200 computer-based; 72 iBT). *Application deadline:* For fall admission, 6/1 for domestic students, 5/1 for international students; for spring admission,. 10/1 for domestic students, 8/1 for international students. Application fee: $40 ($60 for international students). Electronic applications accepted. *Expenses:* Tuition, state resident: full-time $2071; part-time $86.29 per credit. Tuition, nonresident: full-time $8099; part-time $337.46 per credit. Required fees: $9446. Tuition and fees vary according to class time, course load and reciprocity agreements. *Financial support:* In 2009–10, 1 research assistantship with full tuition reimbursement (averaging $6,000 per year) was awarded; teaching assistantships, Federal Work-Study and unspecified assistantships also available. Support available to part-time students. Financial award application deadline: 3/1; financial award applicants required to submit FAFSA. *Faculty research:* Competitiveness of south coast enterprises, global sales, key performance indicators, agile manufacturing, green business. Total annual research expenditures: $19,000. *Unit head:* Dr. Norm Barber, Assistant Dean, 508-999-8543, E-mail: nbarber@umassd.edu. *Application contact:* Elan Turcotte-Shamski, Graduate Admissions Officer, 508-999-8604, Fax: 508-999-8183, E-mail: graduate@umassd.edu.

University of Massachusetts Lowell, College of Management, Lowell, MA 01854-2881. Offers business administration (MBA); foundations of business (Graduate Certificate); new venture creation (Graduate Certificate). *Accreditation:* AACSB. Part-time and evening/weekend programs available. *Entrance requirements:* For master's, GMAT.

University of Memphis, Graduate School, Fogelman College of Business and Economics, Program in Business Administration, Memphis, TN 38152. Offers accounting (MBA, PhD); economics (MBA, PhD); executive business administration (MBA); finance (PhD); finance, insurance, and real estate (MBA, MS); international business administration (IMBA); management (MBA, MS, PhD); management information systems (MBA, MS, PhD); management science (MBA); marketing (MBA, MS); marketing and supply chain management (PhD); real estate development (MS); JD/MBA. *Accreditation:* AACSB. *Faculty:* 44 full-time (9 women), 5 part-time/adjunct (0 women). *Students:* 263 full-time (106 women), 181 part-time (66 women); includes 70 minority (46 African Americans, 3 American Indian/Alaska Native, 16 Asian Americans or Pacific Islanders, 5 Hispanic Americans), 109 international. Average age 31. 374 applicants, 73% accepted, 119 enrolled. In 2009, 140 master's, 17 doctorates awarded. *Degree requirements:* For master's, comprehensive exam; for doctorate, comprehensive exam, thesis/dissertation. *Entrance requirements:* For master's, GMAT, resume; for doctorate, GMAT, interview, minimum GPA of 3.4, resume, letter of recommendation. Additional exam requirements/recommendations for international students: Required—TOEFL (minimum score 550 paper-based; 220 computer-based). *Application deadline:* For fall admission, 8/1 for domestic students; for spring admission, 12/1 for domestic students. Application fee: $35 ($60 for international students). *Expenses:* Tuition, state resident: full-time $6246; part-time $347 per credit hour. Tuition, nonresident: full-time $15,894; part-time $883 per credit hour. Required fees: $1160. Full-time tuition and fees vary according to course load, degree level and program. *Financial support:* In 2009–10, 164 students received support; research assistantships with full tuition reimbursements available, teaching assistantships with full tuition reimbursements available, career-related internships or fieldwork, Federal Work-Study, scholarships/grants, and unspecified assistantships available. Financial award application deadline: 2/15; financial award applicants required to submit FAFSA. *Faculty research:* Competitive business strategy, finance microstructures, supply chain management innovations, health care economics, litigation risks and corporate audits. *Unit head:* Rajiv Grover, Dean, 901-678-3759, E-mail: rgrover@memphis.edu. *Application contact:* Dr. Carol V. Danehower, Associate Dean for Programs, 901-678-5402, Fax: 901-678-3579, E-mail: fcbegp@memphis.edu.

University of Miami, Graduate School, School of Business Administration, Program in Business Administration, Coral Gables, FL 33124. Offers accounting (MBA); computer information systems (MBA); executive and professional (MBA), including international business, management; finance (MBA); international business (MBA); management (MBA); management science (MBA); marketing (MBA); professional management (MSPM); JD/MBA; MBA/MSIE. *Accreditation:* AACSB. Evening/weekend programs available. *Degree requirements:* For master's, comprehensive exam. *Entrance requirements:* For master's, GMAT. Additional exam requirements/recommendations for international students: Required—TOEFL (minimum score 550 paper-based; 213 computer-based; 59 iBT). Electronic applications accepted. *Faculty research:* Leadership, e-commerce, supply chain management.

University of Michigan, Ross School of Business at the University of Michigan, Doctoral Program in Business Administration, Ann Arbor, MI 48109-1234. Offers PhD. Offered through the Horace H. Rackham School of Graduate Studies. *Accreditation:* AACSB. *Degree requirements:* For doctorate, comprehensive exam, thesis/dissertation, oral defense of dissertation, preliminary exam. *Entrance requirements:* For doctorate, GMAT or GRE. Additional exam requirements/recommendations for international students: Required—TOEFL (paper-based 600, computer-based 250, iBT 106) or IELTS (7). Electronic applications accepted. *Expenses:* Tuition, state resident: full-time $17,286; part-time $1099 per credit hour. Tuition, nonresident: full-time $34,944; part-time $2080 per credit hour. Required fees: $95 per semester. Tuition and fees vary according to course load, degree level and program. *Faculty research:* Accounting; business information technology; finance; international business/business economics; management and organizations; marketing; operations and management science; strategy.

University of Michigan–Dearborn, School of Management, Dearborn, MI 48128-1491. Offers accounting (MBA, MS); finance (MBA, MS); information systems (MS); international business (MBA); management (MBA); management information systems (MBA); marketing (MBA); supply chain management (MBA); MBA/MHSA; MBA/MSE; MBA/MSF. *Accreditation:* AACSB. Part-time and evening/weekend programs available. Postbaccalaureate distance learning degree programs offered (no on-campus study). *Faculty:* 26 full-time (6 women), 8 part-time/adjunct (4 women). *Students:* 73 full-time (30 women), 412 part-time (134 women); includes 65 minority (20 African Americans, 1 American Indian/Alaska Native, 38 Asian Americans or Pacific Islanders, 6 Hispanic Americans), 76 international. Average age 30. 185 applicants, 56% accepted, 78 enrolled. In 2009, 151 master's awarded. *Entrance requirements:* For master's, GMAT, 2 years of work experience (MBA); course work in computer applications, statistics, and pre-calculus or finite mathematics; 18 credits of accounting course work beyond introductory courses (MS in accounting). Additional exam requirements/recommendations for international students: Required—TOEFL (minimum score 560 paper-based; 220 computer-based; 84 iBT). *Application deadline:* For fall admission, 8/1 priority date for domestic students, 6/1 for international students; for winter admission, 12/1 priority date for domestic students, 10/1 for international students; for spring admission, 4/1 priority date for domestic students, 2/1 for international students. Applications are processed on a rolling basis. Application fee: $60. Electronic applications accepted. *Expenses:* Contact institution. *Financial support:* Career-related internships or fieldwork, Federal Work-Study, and scholarships/grants available. Support available to part-time students. Financial award application deadline: 9/1; financial award

Business Administration and Management—General

University of Michigan–Dearborn *(continued)*
applicants required to submit FAFSA. *Faculty research:* Cultural diversity, buyer-supplier relations, error detection in data, economic evolution. *Unit head:* Dr. Kim Schatzel, Dean, 313-593-5248, Fax: 313-271-9835, E-mail: schatzel@umd.umich.edu. *Application contact:* Joan Doherty, Academic Advisor/Counselor, 313-593-5460, Fax: 313-271-9838, E-mail: gradbusiness@umd.umich.edu.

University of Michigan–Flint, School of Management, Flint, MI 48502-1950. Offers MBA. *Accreditation:* AACSB. Part-time programs available. Postbaccalaureate distance learning degree programs offered (minimal on-campus study). *Faculty:* 10 full-time (1 woman), 3 part-time/adjunct (0 women). *Students:* 26 full-time (10 women), 166 part-time (68 women); includes 22 minority (12 African Americans, 2 American-Indian/Alaska Native, 7 Asian Americans or Pacific Islanders, 1 Hispanic American), 26 international. Average age 33. 120 applicants, 53% accepted, 49 enrolled. In 2009, 91 master's awarded. *Degree requirements:* For master's, thesis or alternative. *Entrance requirements:* For master's, GMAT, 2 years of work experience, minimum GPA of 3.0, 1 year college course work in mathematics. Additional exam requirements/recommendations for international students: Required—TOEFL (minimum score 560 paper-based; 220 computer-based; 84 iBT), IELTS (minimum score 6.5). *Application deadline:* For fall admission, 8/1 priority date for domestic students, 5/1 priority date for international students; for winter admission, 12/1 priority date for domestic students, 9/1 priority date for international students; for spring admission, 2/15 priority date for domestic students, 1/15 priority date for international students. Applications are processed on a rolling basis. Application fee: $55. Electronic applications accepted. *Expenses:* Tuition, state resident: full-time $10,470; part-time $436.25 per credit hour. Tuition, nonresident: full-time $15,704; part-time $654.40 per credit hour. Required fees: $380; $144.50 per term. Tuition and fees vary according to course level, course load, degree level and student level. *Financial support:* Federal Work-Study, scholarships/grants, and unspecified assistantships available. Support available to part-time students. Financial award application deadline: 6/1; financial award applicants required to submit FAFSA. *Faculty research:* Business performance evaluations, consumer satisfaction, mergers and acquisitions success. *Unit head:* Dr. Jack A. Helmuth, Dean, 810-237-6589, Fax: 810-237-6685, E-mail: jhelmuth@umflint.edu. *Application contact:* D. Nicol Taylor-Vargo, MBA Program Coordinator, 810-237-6591, Fax: 810-237-6685, E-mail: dntaylor@umflint.edu.

University of Minnesota, Duluth, Graduate School, Labovitz School of Business and Economics, Program in Business Administration, Duluth, MN 55812-2496. Offers MBA. *Accreditation:* AACSB. Part-time and evening/weekend programs available. *Faculty:* 35 full-time (9 women). *Students:* 68 part-time (30 women); includes 5 minority (all Asian Americans or Pacific Islanders), 7 international. Average age 32. 24 applicants, 83% accepted, 18 enrolled. In 2009, 25 master's awarded. *Entrance requirements:* For master's, GMAT, minimum GPA of 3.0; course work in accounting, business administration, and economics. Additional exam requirements/recommendations for international students: Required—TOEFL (minimum score 550 paper-based; 213 computer-based; 79 iBT). *Application deadline:* For fall admission, 7/15 for domestic and international students; for spring admission, 11/1 for domestic and international students. Applications are processed on a rolling basis. Application fee: $75 ($95 for international students). *Expenses:* Contact institution. *Financial support:* In 2009–10, 5 students received support, including 5 research assistantships with full and partial tuition reimbursements available (averaging $13,000 per year); institutionally sponsored loans also available. Financial award application deadline: 5/1; financial award applicants required to submit FAFSA. *Faculty research:* Regional economic analysis, marketing, management, human resources, organizational behavior. *Unit head:* Dr. Rajiv Vaidyanathan, Director of Graduate Studies, 218-726-6817, Fax: 218-726-7578, E-mail: rvaidyan@d.umn.edu. *Application contact:* Candy Furo, Associate Administrator, 218-726-8986, Fax: 218-726-6789, E-mail: cfuro@d.umn.edu.

University of Minnesota, Twin Cities Campus, Carlson School of Management, Minneapolis, MN 55455. Offers EMBA, M Acc, MA, MBA, MBT, PhD, JD/MBA, MBA/MPP, MD/MBA, MHA/MBA, Pharm D/MBA. *Accreditation:* AACSB. Part-time and evening/weekend programs available. *Faculty:* 137 full-time (38 women), 86 part-time/adjunct (35 women). *Students:* 578 full-time (301 women), 2,053 part-time (729 women); includes 265 minority (46 African Americans, 2 American Indian/Alaska Native, 181 Asian Americans or Pacific Islanders, 36 Hispanic Americans), 309 international. Average age 28. In 2009, 633 master's, 16 doctorates awarded. Terminal master's awarded for partial completion of doctoral program. *Degree requirements:* For doctorate, comprehensive exam, thesis/dissertation. Electronic applications accepted. *Expenses:* Contact institution. *Financial support:* Fellowships with full and partial tuition reimbursements, research assistantships with full tuition reimbursements, teaching assistantships with full and partial tuition reimbursements, career-related internships or fieldwork, Federal Work-Study, institutionally sponsored loans, scholarships/grants, health care benefits, tuition waivers (full and partial), and unspecified assistantships available. Support available to part-time students. Financial award application deadline: 4/1; financial award applicants required to submit FAFSA. *Unit head:* Dr. Alison Davis-Blake, Dean, 612-626-9636, Fax: 612-624-6374, E-mail: csdean@umn.edu. *Application contact:* Dr. Alison Davis-Blake, Dean, 612-626-9636, Fax: 612-624-6374, E-mail: csdean@umn.edu.

See Display below.

University of Mississippi, Graduate School, School of Business Administration, Oxford, University, MS 38677. Offers business administration (MBA, PhD); systems management (MS); JD/MBA. *Accreditation:* AACSB. *Faculty:* 58 full-time (14 women), 7 part-time/adjunct (2 women). *Students:* 77 full-time (28 women), 54 part-time (5 women); includes 14 minority (8 African Americans, 1 American Indian/Alaska Native, 4 Asian Americans or Pacific Islanders, 1 Hispanic American), 13 international. In 2009, 47 master's, 4 doctorates awarded. *Degree requirements:* For doctorate, thesis/dissertation. *Entrance requirements:* For master's, GMAT, minimum GPA of 3.0; for doctorate, GMAT. Additional exam requirements/recommendations for international students: Required—TOEFL. *Application deadline:* For fall admission, 2/1 for domestic students; for spring admission, 10/1 for domestic students. Applications are processed on a rolling basis. Application fee: $25. Electronic applications accepted. *Financial support:* Fellowships, career-related internships or fieldwork, scholarships/grants, tuition waivers (full), and unspecified assistantships available. Financial award application deadline: 3/1; financial award applicants required to submit FAFSA. *Unit head:* Dr. Brian Reithel, Dean, 662-915-5820, Fax: 662-915-5821, E-mail: breithel@bus.olemiss.edu. *Application contact:* Dr. Christy M. Wyandt, Associate Dean, 662-915-7474, Fax: 662-915-7577, E-mail: cwyandt@olemiss.edu.

University of Missouri, Graduate School, Robert J. Trulaske, Sr. College of Business, Program in Business Administration, Columbia, MO 65211. Offers MBA, PhD. *Accreditation:* AACSB. *Degree requirements:* For doctorate, thesis/dissertation. *Entrance requirements:* For master's and doctorate, GMAT, minimum GPA of 3.0. Additional exam requirements/recommendations for international students: Required—TOEFL (minimum score 500 paper-based; 173 computer-based; 61 iBT).

University of Missouri–Kansas City, Henry W. Bloch School of Business and Public Administration, Kansas City, MO 64110-2499. Offers accounting (MS); business administration (MBA); entrepreneurship and innovation (PhD); public affairs (MPA, PhD); JD/MBA; LL M/MPA. PhD (interdisciplinary) offered through the School of Graduate Studies. *Accreditation:* AACSB; NASPAA. Part-time and evening/weekend programs available. *Faculty:* 43 full-time (14 women), 22 part-time/adjunct (7 women). *Students:* 234 full-time (108 women), 437 part-time (193 women); includes 79 minority (33 African Americans, 27 Asian Americans or Pacific Islanders, 19 Hispanic Americans), 51 international. Average age 30. 387 applicants, 65% accepted, 222 enrolled. In 2009, 240 master's awarded. Terminal master's awarded for partial completion of

doctoral program. *Entrance requirements:* For master's, GMAT, GRE, 2 writing essays, 2 references and support of employer; for doctorate, GRE, minimum GPA of 3.0. Additional exam requirements/recommendations for international students: Required—TOEFL (minimum score 550 paper-based; 213 computer-based; 80 iBT). *Application deadline:* For fall admission, 5/1 priority date for domestic and international students; for spring admission, 10/1 priority date for domestic and international students. Applications are processed on a rolling basis. Application fee: $45 ($50 for international students). Electronic applications accepted. *Expenses:* Tuition, state resident: full-time $5378; part-time $299 per credit hour. Tuition, nonresident: full-time $13,881; part-time $771 per credit hour. Required fees: $641; $71 per credit hour. Tuition and fees vary according to course load and program. *Financial support:* In 2009–10, 18 research assistantships with partial tuition reimbursements (averaging $8,766 per year), 5 teaching assistantships with partial tuition reimbursements (averaging $8,430 per year) were awarded; career-related internships or fieldwork, Federal Work-Study, institutionally sponsored loans, scholarships/grants, tuition waivers (full and partial), and unspecified assistantships also available. Support available to part-time students. Financial award application deadline: 3/1; financial award applicants required to submit FAFSA. *Faculty research:* Entrepreneurship, finance, non-profit, risk management. Total annual research expenditures: $751,788. *Unit head:* Dr. Teng-Kee Tan, Dean, 816-235-2215, Fax: 816-235-2206. *Application contact:* 816-235-1111, E-mail: admit@umkc.edu.

University of Missouri–St. Louis, College of Business Administration, Program in Business Administration, St. Louis, MO 63121. Offers accounting (MBA); business administration (Certificate); finance (MBA); human resource management (Certificate); logistics and supply chain management (MBA, Certificate); management (MBA); marketing (MBA); marketing management (Certificate); operations (MBA); quantitative management science (MBA). *Accreditation:* AACSB. Part-time and evening/weekend programs available. *Faculty:* 30 full-time (5 women), 11 part-time/adjunct (2 women). *Students:* 107 full-time (47 women), 310 part-time (120 women); includes 32 minority (17 African Americans, 6 Asian Americans or Pacific Islanders, 9 Hispanic Americans), 66 international. Average age 31. 285 applicants, 58% accepted, 130 enrolled. In 2009, 149 master's, 13 other advanced degrees awarded. *Entrance requirements:* For master's, GMAT, 2 letters of recommendation. Additional exam requirements/recommendations for international students: Required—TOEFL (minimum score 550 paper-based; 213 computer-based). *Application deadline:* For fall admission, 7/1 for domestic students; for spring admission, 11/1 for domestic students. Applications are processed on a rolling basis. Application fee: $35 ($40 for international students). Electronic applications accepted. *Expenses:* Tuition, state resident: full-time $5377; part-time $297.70 per credit hour. Tuition, nonresident: full-time $13,882; part-time $771.20 per credit hour. Required fees: $220; $12.20 per credit hour. One-time fee: $12. Tuition and fees vary according to course level, campus/location and program. *Financial support:* In 2009–10, 27 research assistantships with full and partial tuition reimbursements (averaging $8,525 per year), 6 teaching assistantships with full and partial tuition reimbursements (averaging $13,950 per year) were awarded; career-related internships or fieldwork, Federal Work-Study, and institutionally sponsored loans also available. Support available to part-time students. Financial award application deadline: 4/1; financial award applicants required to submit FAFSA. *Faculty research:* Human resources, strategic management, marketing strategy, consumer behavior product development, advertising. *Unit head:* Karl Kottemann, Assistant Director, 314-516-5885, Fax: 314-516-6420, E-mail: mba@umsl.edu. *Application contact:* 314-516-5458, Fax: 314-516-6996, E-mail: gradadm@umsl.edu.

University of Missouri–St. Louis, Graduate School, Program in Public Policy Administration, St. Louis, MO 63121. Offers health policy (MPPA); local government management (MPPA); managing human resources and organization (MPPA); nonprofit organization management (MPPA); nonprofit organization management and leadership (Certificate); policy research and analysis (MPPA). *Accreditation:* NASPAA. Part-time and evening/weekend programs available. *Faculty:* 7 full-time (4 women), 6 part-time/adjunct (1 woman). *Students:* 20 full-time (8 women), 69 part-time (45 women); includes 13 minority (11 African Americans, 2 Hispanic Americans), 8 international. Average age 31. 85 applicants, 58% accepted, 28 enrolled. In 2009, 12 master's, 34 Certificates awarded. *Degree requirements:* For master's, exit project. *Entrance requirements:* For master's, 3 letters of recommendation. Additional exam requirements/recommendations for international students: Required—TOEFL (minimum score 550 paper-based; 213 computer-based). *Application deadline:* For fall admission, 7/1 priority date for domestic and international students; for spring admission, 12/1 priority date for domestic and international students. Applications are processed on a rolling basis. Application fee: $35 ($40 for international students). Electronic applications accepted. *Expenses:* Tuition, state resident: full-time $5377; part-time $297.70 per credit hour. Tuition, nonresident: full-time $13,882; part-time $771.20 per credit hour. Required fees: $220; $12.20 per credit hour. One-time fee: $12. Tuition and fees vary according to course level, campus/location and program. *Financial support:* In 2009–10, 2 research assistantships with full and partial tuition reimbursements (averaging $12,000 per year) were awarded; career-related internships or fieldwork also available. Financial award application deadline: 4/1; financial award applicants required to submit FAFSA. *Faculty research:* Urban policy, public finance, evaluation. *Unit head:* Dr. Brady Baybeck, Director, 314-516-5145, Fax: 314-516-5210, E-mail: baybeck@umsl.edu. *Application contact:* 314-516-5458, Fax: 314-516-6996, E-mail: gradadm@umsl.edu.

University of Mobile, Graduate Programs, Program in Business Administration, Mobile, AL 36613. Offers MBA. *Accreditation:* ACBSP. Part-time and evening/weekend programs available. *Faculty:* 3 full-time (all women), 2 part-time/adjunct (0 women). *Students:* 9 full-time (2 women), 28 part-time (15 women); includes 14 minority (all African Americans), 4 international. Average age 32. 18 applicants, 100% accepted, 13 enrolled. In 2009, 6 master's awarded. *Degree requirements:* For master's, comprehensive exam. *Entrance requirements:* For master's, GMAT. Additional exam requirements/recommendations for international students: Required—TOEFL (minimum score 550 paper-based; 213 computer-based; 80 iBT). *Application deadline:* For fall admission, 8/3 priority date for domestic students; for spring admission, 12/23 for domestic students. Applications are processed on a rolling basis. Application fee: $40 ($50 for international students). *Financial support:* Application deadline: 8/1. *Faculty research:* Management, personnel management, small business, diversity. *Unit head:* Dr. Jane Finley, Dean, School of Business, 251-442-2219, Fax: 251-442-2523, E-mail: jfinley@umobile.edu. *Application contact:* Tammy C. Eubanks, Administrative Assistant to Dean of Graduate Programs, 251-442-2270, Fax: 251-442-2523, E-mail: teubanks@umobile.edu.

The University of Montana, Graduate School, School of Business Administration, MBA Professional Program, Missoula, MT 59812-0002. Offers MBA, JD/MBA, MBA/Pharm D. *Accreditation:* AACSB. Part-time and evening/weekend programs available. Postbaccalaureate distance learning degree programs offered (minimal on-campus study). *Degree requirements:* For master's, thesis optional. *Entrance requirements:* For master's, GMAT. Additional exam requirements/recommendations for international students: Required—TOEFL. *Faculty research:* Information systems, research methods, international business, human resource management, marketing.

University of Nebraska at Kearney, College of Graduate Study, College of Business and Technology, Department of Business, Kearney, NE 68849-0001. Offers business administration (MBA). *Accreditation:* AACSB. Part-time and evening/weekend programs available. *Degree requirements:* For master's, thesis optional. *Entrance requirements:* For master's, GMAT. Additional exam requirements/recommendations for international students: Required—TOEFL (minimum score 550 paper-based; 213 computer-based). Electronic applications accepted. *Faculty research:* Small business financial management, employment law, expert systems, international trade and marketing, environmental economics.

University of Nebraska at Omaha, Graduate Studies, College of Business Administration, Program in Business Administration, Omaha, NE 68182. Offers EMBA, MBA. *Accreditation:* AACSB. Part-time and evening/weekend programs available. *Faculty:* 26 full-time (8 women). *Students:* 90 full-time (26 women), 277 part-time (94 women); includes 36 minority (10 African Americans, 1 American Indian/Alaska Native, 18 Asian Americans or Pacific Islanders, 7 Hispanic Americans), 21 international. Average age 33. 197 applicants, 59% accepted, 95 enrolled. In 2009, 87 master's awarded. *Degree requirements:* For master's, thesis (for some programs), capstone course. *Entrance requirements:* For master's, GMAT, minimum AACSB index of 1040, minimum GPA of 3.0, resume. Additional exam requirements/recommendations for international students: Required—TOEFL (minimum score 550 paper-based; 213 computer-based; 80 iBT). *Application deadline:* For fall admission, 7/1 for domestic students; for spring admission, 11/15 for domestic students. Applications are processed on a rolling basis. Application fee: $45. Electronic applications accepted. *Financial support:* In 2009–10, 109 students received support; research assistantships with tuition reimbursements available, Federal Work-Study, institutionally sponsored loans, scholarships/grants, tuition waivers (partial), and unspecified assistantships available. Support available to part-time students. Financial award application deadline: 3/1; financial award applicants required to submit FAFSA. *Unit head:* Dr. Lynn Harland, Associate Dean, 402-554-2303. *Application contact:* Lex Kaczmarek, Director, 402-554-2303.

University of Nebraska–Lincoln, Graduate College, College of Business Administration, Interdepartmental Area of Business, Lincoln, NE 68588. Offers accountancy (PhD); business (MBA); finance (MA, PhD), including business; management (MA, PhD), including business; marketing (MA, PhD), including business; JD/MBA; M Arch/MBA. *Accreditation:* AACSB. Part-time programs available. Postbaccalaureate distance learning degree programs offered. *Degree requirements:* For doctorate, comprehensive exam, thesis/dissertation. *Entrance requirements:* For master's and doctorate, GMAT. Additional exam requirements/recommendations for international students: Required—TOEFL (minimum score 550 paper-based; 213 computer-based). Electronic applications accepted.

University of Nevada, Las Vegas, Graduate College, College of Business, Program in Business Administration, Las Vegas, NV 89154-6031. Offers EMBA, MBA, DMD/MBA, MBA/JD, MBA/MS. *Accreditation:* AACSB. Part-time and evening/weekend programs available. *Faculty:* 21 full-time (1 woman), 1 (woman) part-time/adjunct. *Students:* 184 full-time (69 women), 96 part-time (38 women); includes 33 minority (6 African Americans, 18 Asian Americans or Pacific Islanders, 9 Hispanic Americans), 22 international. Average age 31. 271 applicants, 50% accepted, 92 enrolled. In 2009, 97 master's awarded. *Entrance requirements:* For master's, GMAT. Additional exam requirements/recommendations for international students: Required—TOEFL (minimum score 550 paper-based; 213 computer-based; 80 iBT), IELTS (minimum score 7). *Application deadline:* For fall admission, 4/1 priority date for domestic and international students; for spring admission, 10/1 priority date for domestic and international students. Applications are processed on a rolling basis. Application fee: $60 ($95 for international students). Electronic applications accepted. *Financial support:* In 2009–10, 18 students received support, including 17 research assistantships with partial tuition reimbursements available (averaging $10,000 per year), 1 teaching assistantship with partial tuition reimbursement available (averaging $10,000 per year); institutionally sponsored loans, scholarships/grants, health care benefits, and unspecified assistantships also available. Financial award application deadline: 3/1. *Faculty research:* Executive compensation and performance, impact of advertising, supply chain management practices, determinants of housing price differentials, knowledge transfer in multinationals. *Unit head:* Dr. Reza Torkzadeh, Department Chair/ Professor/ Associate Dean, 702-895-1832, Fax: 702-895-3655, E-mail: reza.torkzadeh@unlv.edu. *Application contact:* Graduate College Admissions Evaluator, 702-895-3320, Fax: 702-895-4180, E-mail: gradcollege@unlv.edu.

University of Nevada, Reno, Graduate School, College of Business Administration, Department of Business Administration, Reno, NV 89557. Offers MBA. *Accreditation:* AACSB. Part-time and evening/weekend programs available. Postbaccalaureate distance learning degree programs offered. *Entrance requirements:* For master's, GMAT, minimum GPA of 2.75. Additional exam requirements/recommendations for international students: Required—TOEFL (minimum score 500 paper-based; 173 computer-based; 61 iBT), IELTS (minimum score 6). Electronic applications accepted.

University of New Brunswick Fredericton, School of Graduate Studies, Faculty of Business Administration, Fredericton, NB E3B 5A3, Canada. Offers business administration (MBA); engineering management (MBA); entrepreneurship (MBA); sports and recreation management (MBA); MBA/LL B. Part-time programs available. *Faculty:* 37 full-time (13 women). *Students:* 27 full-time (10 women), 51 part-time (25 women). In 2009, 72 master's awarded. *Degree requirements:* For master's, thesis optional. *Entrance requirements:* For master's, GMAT (550 minimum score), minimum GPA of 3.0; 3-5 years work experience. Additional exam requirements/recommendations for international students: Required—TOEFL (minimum score 580 paper-based; 92 iBT), IELTS (minimum score 7), TOEFL or IELTS. *Application deadline:* For fall admission, 3/1 priority date for domestic students. Applications are processed on a rolling basis. Application fee: $50 Canadian dollars. Tuition and fees charges are reported in Canadian dollars. *Expenses:* Tuition, area resident: Full-time $5562 Canadian dollars; part-time $2781 Canadian dollars per year. Required fees: $49.75 Canadian dollars per term. *Financial support:* In 2009–10, 4 research assistantships (averaging $4,500 per year), 11 teaching assistantships (averaging $2,250 per year) were awarded. *Faculty research:* Strategic management, entrepreneurship, investment practices, marketing and supply chain management, operations management. *Unit head:* Judy Roy, Director of Graduate Studies, 506-458-7307, Fax: 506-453-3561, E-mail: jroy@unb.ca. *Application contact:* Marilyn Davis, Acting Graduate Secretary, 506-453-4766, Fax: 506-453-3561, E-mail: mbacontact@unb.ca.

University of New Brunswick Saint John, Faculty of Business, Saint John, NB E2L 4L5, Canada. Offers administration (MBA); electronic commerce (MBA); international business (MBA); natural resource management (MBA). Part-time programs available. *Faculty:* 19 full-time (4 women), 14 part-time/adjunct (8 women). *Students:* 45 full-time (14 women), 18 part-time (8 women). 93 applicants, 78% accepted, 25 enrolled. In 2009, 45 master's awarded. *Entrance requirements:* For master's, GMAT, minimum GPA of 3.0. Additional exam requirements/recommendations for international students: Required—TOEFL (minimum score 580 paper-based; 237 computer-based), IELTS (minimum score 7), TWE (minimum score 4.5). *Application deadline:* For fall admission, 5/15 for domestic and international students. Applications are processed on a rolling basis. Application fee: $100. Electronic applications accepted. *Expenses:* Contact institution. *Financial support:* In 2009–10, 4 students received support. Career-related internships or fieldwork and scholarships/grants available. *Faculty research:* Business use of weblogs and podcasts to communicate, corporate governance, high-involvement work systems, international competitiveness, supply chain management and logistics. *Unit head:* Henryk Sterniczuk, Director of Graduate Studies, 506-648-5573, Fax: 506-648-5574, E-mail: sterniczt@unbsj.ca. *Application contact:* Tammy Morin, Secretary, 506-648-5746, Fax: 506-648-5574, E-mail: tmorin@unbsj.ca.

University of New Hampshire, Center for Graduate and Professional Studies, Manchester, NH 03101. Offers business administration (MBA); counseling (M Ed); education (M Ed, MAT); educational administration and supervision (M Ed, CAGS); industrial statistics (Certificate); public administration (MPA); public health (MPH, Certificate); social work (MSW). Part-time and evening/weekend programs available. *Students:* 86 full-time (57 women), 150 part-time (87 women); includes 13 minority (3 African Americans, 6 Asian Americans or Pacific Islanders, 4 Hispanic Americans), 7 international. 127 applicants, 73% accepted, 60 enrolled. In 2009, 81 master's, 5 other advanced degrees awarded. *Degree requirements:* For master's, thesis or alternative. *Entrance requirements:* Additional exam requirements/recommendations for international students: Required—TOEFL (minimum score 550 paper-based; 213 computer-based; 80 iBT), TOEIC, TSE. *Application deadline:* For fall admission, 6/1 for domestic students, 4/1 for international students; for spring admission, 12/1 for domestic students. Applications are processed on a rolling basis. Application fee: $65. Electronic applications accepted. *Expenses:* Tuition, state resident: full-time $10,380; part-time $577 per credit hour. Tuition, nonresident: full-time $24,350; part-time $1002 per credit hour. Required fees: $1550; $387.50 per semester. Tuition and fees vary according to course load and program. *Financial support:* In 2009–10, 20 students received support, including 1 fellowship, 1 teaching assistantship; research assistantships, Federal Work-Study, scholarships/grants, health care benefits, and unspecified assistantships also available. Support available to part-time students. Financial award application deadline: 3/1; financial award applicants required to submit FAFSA. *Unit head:* Kate Ferreira,

Business Administration and Management—General

University of New Hampshire (continued)
Director, 603-641-4313, E-mail: unhm.gradcenter@unh.edu. *Application contact:* Graduate Admissions Office, 603-862-3000, Fax: 603-862-0275, E-mail: grad.school@unh.edu.

University of New Hampshire, Graduate School, Whittemore School of Business and Economics, Department of Business Administration, Durham, NH 03824. Offers business administration (MBA); executive business administration (MBA); health management (MBA); management of technology (MS, Postbaccalaureate Certificate). *Accreditation:* AACSB. Part-time and evening/weekend programs available. *Faculty:* 24 full-time (4 women). *Students:* 113 full-time (33 women), 100 part-time (27 women); includes 10 minority (1 African American, 6 Asian Americans or Pacific Islanders, 3 Hispanic Americans), 13 international. Average age 36. 185 applicants, 60% accepted, 85 enrolled. In 2009, 145 master's awarded. *Entrance requirements:* For master's, GMAT. Additional exam requirements/recommendations for international students: Required—TOEFL (minimum score 550 paper-based; 213 computer-based; 80 iBT). *Application deadline:* For fall admission, 7/1 priority date for domestic students, 4/1 for international students; for spring admission, 11/1 for domestic students. Applications are processed on a rolling basis. Application fee: $65. *Expenses:* Contact institution. *Financial support:* In 2009–10, 35 students received support, including 1 research assistantship; fellowships, teaching assistantships, career-related internships or fieldwork, Federal Work-Study, scholarships/grants, and tuition waivers (full and partial) also available. Financial award application deadline: 2/15. *Unit head:* Christine Shea, Chairperson, 603-862-3316. *Application contact:* Rachel Hopkins, Administrative Assistant, 603-862-3316, E-mail: wsbe.grad@unh.edu.

University of New Haven, Graduate School, School of Business, Executive Program in Business Administration, West Haven, CT 06516-1916. Offers EMBA. Part-time and evening/weekend programs available. *Faculty:* 10 full-time (2 women), 3 part-time/adjunct (0 women). *Students:* 5 full-time (0 women), 2 part-time (both women); includes 1 minority (African American), 1 international. Average age 45. In 2009, 33 master's awarded. *Entrance requirements:* Additional exam requirements/recommendations for international students: Required—TOEFL (minimum score 520 paper-based; 190 computer-based; 70 iBT), IELTS (minimum score 5.5). *Application deadline:* For fall admission, 5/31 for international students; for winter admission, 10/15 for international students; for spring admission, 1/15 for international students. Applications are processed on a rolling basis. Application fee: $50. Electronic applications accepted. *Expenses:* Contact institution. *Financial support:* Application deadline: 5/1. *Unit head:* Linda Carlone, Coordinator, 203-932-7433. *Application contact:* Eloise Gormley, Director of Graduate Admissions, 203-932-7449, Fax: 203-932-7137, E-mail: gradinfo@newhaven.edu.

University of New Haven, Graduate School, School of Business, Program in Business Administration, West Haven, CT 06516-1916. Offers accounting (MBA, Certificate), including CPA (MBA); business management (Certificate); business policy and strategy (MBA); finance (MBA), including CFA; global marketing (MBA); human resource management (Certificate); human resources management (MBA); international business (Certificate); marketing (Certificate); sports management (MBA); telcommunications management (Certificate); MBA/MPA. Part-time and evening/weekend programs available. *Faculty:* 26 full-time (3 women), 23 part-time/adjunct (5 women). *Students:* 302 full-time (120 women), 194 part-time (101 women); includes 109 minority (56 African Americans, 3 American Indian/Alaska Native, 28 Asian Americans or Pacific Islanders, 22 Hispanic Americans), 110 international. Average age 31. 372 applicants, 83% accepted, 172 enrolled. In 2009, 194 master's, 31 other advanced degrees awarded. *Degree requirements:* For master's, thesis or alternative. *Entrance requirements:* For master's, GMAT. Additional exam requirements/recommendations for international students: Required—TOEFL (minimum score 520 paper-based; 190 computer-based; 70 iBT), IELTS (minimum score 5.5). *Application deadline:* For fall admission, 5/31 for international students; for winter admission, 10/15 for international students; for spring admission, 1/15 for international students. Applications are processed on a rolling basis. Application fee: $50. Electronic applications accepted. *Expenses:* Contact institution. *Financial support:* Research assistantships with partial tuition reimbursements, teaching assistantships with partial tuition reimbursements, Federal Work-Study, scholarships/grants, health care benefits, tuition waivers, and unspecified assistantships available. Support available to part-time students. Financial award applicants required to submit FAFSA. *Unit head:* Charles Coleman, Chairman, 203-932-7375. *Application contact:* Eloise Gormley, Director of Graduate Admissions, 203-932-7449, Fax: 203-932-7137, E-mail: gradinfo@newhaven.edu.

University of New Mexico, Robert O. Anderson Graduate School of Management, Albuquerque, NM 87131. Offers EMBA, M Acct, MBA, JD/M Acct, JD/MBA, MBA/MA, MBA/MEME. *Accreditation:* AACSB. Part-time and evening/weekend programs available. *Faculty:* 52 full-time (18 women), 18 part-time/adjunct (4 women). *Students:* 240 full-time (122 women), 270 part-time (137 women); includes 188 minority (10 African Americans, 10 American Indian/Alaska Native, 29 Asian Americans or Pacific Islanders, 139 Hispanic Americans), 33 international. Average age 31. 311 applicants, 61% accepted, 180 enrolled. In 2009, 188 master's awarded. *Entrance requirements:* For master's, GMAT or GRE (can be waived in some instances). Additional exam requirements/recommendations for international students: Required—TOEFL (minimum score 550 paper-based; 213 computer-based; 79 iBT). *Application deadline:* For fall admission, 4/1 priority date for domestic students, 5/1 for international students; for spring admission, 10/1 priority date for domestic students, 10/1 for international students. Applications are processed on a rolling basis. Application fee: $50. Electronic applications accepted. *Expenses:* Tuition, state resident: full-time $2099; part-time $233.20 per credit hour. Tuition, nonresident: full-time $6650. Required fees: $25 per semester. Tuition and fees vary according to course load, program and reciprocity agreements. *Financial support:* In 2009–10, 62 students received support, including 62 fellowships (averaging $3,400 per year), 50 research assistantships with partial tuition reimbursements available (averaging $6,000 per year), 1 teaching assistantship with partial tuition reimbursement available (averaging $7,500 per year); career-related internships or fieldwork, Federal Work-Study, scholarships/grants, and unspecified assistantships also available. Support available to part-time students. Financial award application deadline: 6/1. *Faculty research:* Organizational and social aspects of accounting, international management of technology and entrepreneurship, business ethics and corporate social responsibility, marketing, information assurance and fraud. *Unit head:* Douglas M. Brown, Dean, 505-277-6471, Fax: 505-277-0344, E-mail: browndm@mgt.unm.edu. *Application contact:* Megan Conner, Academic Advisement Manager, 505-277-3290, Fax: 505-277-8436, E-mail: mconner@mgt.unm.edu.

University of New Orleans, Graduate School, College of Business Administration, Program in Business Administration, New Orleans, LA 70148. Offers MBA. *Accreditation:* AACSB. *Degree requirements:* For master's, thesis optional. *Entrance requirements:* For master's, GMAT. Additional exam requirements/recommendations for international students: Required—TOEFL (minimum score 550 paper-based; 213 computer-based; 79 iBT). Electronic applications accepted.

University of North Alabama, College of Business, Florence, AL 35632-0001. Offers MBA. *Accreditation:* ACBSP. Part-time and evening/weekend programs available. *Faculty:* 3 full-time (0 women), 17 part-time/adjunct (4 women). *Students:* 146 full-time (55 women), 409 part-time (180 women); includes 109 minority (46 African Americans, 7 American Indian/Alaska Native, 45 Asian Americans or Pacific Islanders, 11 Hispanic Americans), 184 international. Average age 33. In 2009, 367 master's awarded. *Entrance requirements:* For master's, GMAT, minimum GPA of 2.75 in last 60 hours, 2.5 overall on a 3.0 scale; 27 hours of course work in business and economics. *Application deadline:* For fall admission, 7/1 priority date for domestic students; for spring admission, 12/1 for domestic students. Applications are processed on a rolling basis. Application fee: $25. Electronic applications accepted. *Expenses:* Tuition, state resident: full-time $5040; part-time $210 per credit hour. Tuition, nonresident: full-time $10,080; part-time $420 per credit hour. Required fees: $906. *Financial support:* Federal Work-Study available. Support available to part-time students. Financial award application deadline: 4/1. *Unit head:* Dr. Kerry Gatlin, Dean, 256-765-4261, Fax: 256-765-4170, E-mail: kpgatlin@una.edu. *Application contact:* Kim Mauldin, Director of Admissions, 256-765-4608, Fax: 256-765-4960, E-mail: komauldin@una.edu.

The University of North Carolina at Chapel Hill, Kenan-Flagler Business School, Doctoral Program in Business Administration, Chapel Hill, NC 27599. Offers accounting (PhD); finance (PhD); marketing (PhD); operations management (PhD); organizational behavior (PhD); strategy (PhD). *Accreditation:* AACSB. *Degree requirements:* For doctorate, thesis/dissertation. *Entrance requirements:* For doctorate, GMAT or GRE General Test. Electronic applications accepted. *Expenses:* Contact institution.

The University of North Carolina at Chapel Hill, Kenan-Flagler Business School, Executive MBA Programs, Chapel Hill, NC 27599. Offers MBA. *Accreditation:* AACSB. Evening/weekend programs available. Postbaccalaureate distance learning degree programs offered (minimal on-campus study). *Degree requirements:* For master's, exams, project. *Entrance requirements:* For master's, GMAT, 5 years of full-time work experience, interview. Electronic applications accepted. *Expenses:* Contact institution.

The University of North Carolina at Chapel Hill, Kenan-Flagler Business School, MBA Program, Chapel Hill, NC 27599. Offers MBA, MBA/JD, MBA/MHA, MBA/MRP, MBA/MSIS. *Accreditation:* AACSB. *Degree requirements:* For master's, exams, practicum. *Entrance requirements:* For master's, GMAT, interview, minimum 2 years of work experience. Additional exam requirements/recommendations for international students: Required—TOEFL. Electronic applications accepted.

The University of North Carolina at Charlotte, Graduate School, Belk College of Business, Program in Business Administration, Charlotte, NC 28223-0001. Offers MBA, PhD. *Accreditation:* AACSB. Part-time and evening/weekend programs available. *Faculty:* 77 full-time (18 women), 1 part-time/adjunct (0 women). *Students:* 166 full-time (63 women), 339 part-time (131 women); includes 61 minority (26 African Americans, 1 American Indian/Alaska Native, 23 Asian Americans or Pacific Islanders, 11 Hispanic Americans), 170 international. Average age 30. 362 applicants, 63% accepted, 178 enrolled. In 2009, 202 master's awarded. *Entrance requirements:* For master's, GMAT, minimum GPA of 3.0 in undergraduate major, 2.8 overall. Additional exam requirements/recommendations for international students: Required—TOEFL (minimum score 557 paper-based; 220 computer-based; 83 iBT). *Application deadline:* For fall admission, 7/15 for domestic students, 5/1 for international students; for spring admission, 11/15 for domestic students, 10/1 for international students. Applications are processed on a rolling basis. Application fee: $55. Electronic applications accepted. *Financial support:* In 2009–10, 48 students received support, including 8 research assistantships (averaging $5,891 per year), 40 teaching assistantships (averaging $12,202 per year); career-related internships or fieldwork, Federal Work-Study, institutionally sponsored loans, scholarships/grants, and administrative assistantship also available. Support available to part-time students. Financial award application deadline: 4/1; financial award applicants required to submit FAFSA. Total annual research expenditures: $32,908. *Unit head:* Jeremiah Nelson, Interim Director, MBA Program, 704-687-6058, Fax: 704-687-4014, E-mail: jeremiah.nelson@uncc.edu. *Application contact:* Kathy B. Giddings, Director of Graduate Admissions, 704-687-5503, Fax: 704-687-3279, E-mail: gradadm@uncc.edu.

The University of North Carolina at Greensboro, Graduate School, Bryan School of Business and Economics, Department of Business Administration, Greensboro, NC 27412-5001. Offers MBA, PMC, Postbaccalaureate Certificate, MS/MBA, MSN/MBA. *Accreditation:* AACSB. *Entrance requirements:* For master's, GMAT, GRE General Test, managerial experience. Additional exam requirements/recommendations for international students: Required—TOEFL. Electronic applications accepted.

The University of North Carolina at Pembroke, Graduate Studies, School of Business, Program in Business Administration, Pembroke, NC 28372-1510. Offers MBA. Part-time and evening/weekend programs available. *Degree requirements:* For master's, thesis optional. *Entrance requirements:* For master's, GMAT, minimum GPA of 3.0 in major or 2.5 overall. Additional exam requirements/recommendations for international students: Required—TOEFL.

The University of North Carolina Wilmington, School of Business, Program in Business Administration, Wilmington, NC 28403-3297. Offers MBA. *Accreditation:* AACSB. Part-time and evening/weekend programs available. *Degree requirements:* For master's, comprehensive exam, thesis (for some programs), final project. *Entrance requirements:* For master's, GMAT, 1 year of appropriate work experience. Additional exam requirements/recommendations for international students: Required—TOEFL (minimum score 550 paper-based; 217 computer-based; 79 iBT), IELTS (minimum score 6.5).

University of North Dakota, Graduate School, College of Business and Public Administration, Business Administration Program, Grand Forks, ND 58202. Offers MBA. *Accreditation:* AACSB. Part-time and evening/weekend programs available. Postbaccalaureate distance learning degree programs offered (minimal on-campus study). *Degree requirements:* For master's, comprehensive exam, thesis or alternative, project. *Entrance requirements:* For master's, GMAT, minimum GPA of 3.25. Additional exam requirements/recommendations for international students: Required—TOEFL (minimum score 550 paper-based; 213 computer-based; 79 iBT), IELTS (minimum score 6.5). Electronic applications accepted.

University of Northern Iowa, Graduate College, College of Business Administration, Program in Business Administration, Cedar Falls, IA 50614. Offers MBA. *Accreditation:* AACSB. Part-time and evening/weekend programs available. *Students:* 31 full-time (10 women), 21 part-time (3 women); includes 2 minority (1 Asian American or Pacific Islander, 1 Hispanic American), 28 international. 56 applicants, 39% accepted, 16 enrolled. In 2009, 42 master's awarded. *Entrance requirements:* For master's, GMAT (minimum score 500), minimum GPA of 3.0. Additional exam requirements/recommendations for international students: Required—TOEFL (minimum score 500 paper-based; 180 computer-based; 61 iBT). *Application deadline:* For fall admission, 8/1 priority date for domestic students. Applications are processed on a rolling basis. Application fee: $30 ($50 for international students). Electronic applications accepted. *Financial support:* Career-related internships or fieldwork, Federal Work-Study, scholarships/grants, and tuition waivers (full and partial) available. Support available to part-time students. Financial award application deadline: 2/1. *Unit head:* Dr. Leslie K. Wilson, Acting Associate Dean, 319-273-6240, Fax: 319-273-6230, E-mail: leslie.wilson@uni.edu. *Application contact:* Laurie S. Russell, Record Analyst, 319-273-2623, Fax: 319-273-6792, E-mail: laurie.russell@uni.edu.

University of North Florida, Coggin College of Business, Department of Management, Marketing, and Logistics, Jacksonville, FL 32224. Offers business administration (MBA). *Accreditation:* AACSB. Part-time and evening/weekend programs available. *Faculty:* 25 full-time (7 women). *Students:* 153 full-time (60 women), 273 part-time (108 women); includes 75 minority (23 African Americans, 30 Asian Americans or Pacific Islanders, 22 Hispanic Americans), 17 international. Average age 30. 230 applicants, 40% accepted, 58 enrolled. In 2009, 183 master's awarded. *Entrance requirements:* For master's, GMAT, minimum GPA of 3.0 in last 60 hours. Additional exam requirements/recommendations for international students: Required—TOEFL (minimum score 550 paper-based; 213 computer-based; 79 iBT). *Application deadline:* For fall admission, 7/6 priority date for domestic students, 5/1 for international students; for spring admission, 11/1 priority date for domestic students, 10/1 for international students. Applications are processed on a rolling basis. Application fee: $30. *Expenses:* Tuition, state resident: full-time $6649.20; part-time $277.05 per credit hour. Tuition, nonresident: full-time $22,970; part-time $957.08 per credit hour. Required fees: $985; $41.03 per credit hour. *Financial support:* In 2009–10, 158 students received support; research assistantships, teaching assistantships, Federal Work-Study and tuition waivers (partial) available. Support available to part-time students. Financial award application deadline: 4/1; financial award applicants required to submit FAFSA. *Faculty research:* Performance measures, costing, and inventory issues in logistics and supply chain management; inter-organizational systems; international management and marketing practices; e-commerce; organizational learning and socialization processes. Total annual research expenditures: $19,255. *Unit head:* Dr. C. Bryce Kavan, Chair, 904-620-2780, Fax: 904-620-2832. *Application contact:* Cheryl Campbell, Graduate Advisor, 904-620-2575, Fax: 904-620-2832, E-mail: ccampbell@unf.edu.

University of North Texas, Robert B. Toulouse School of Graduate Studies, College of Business Administration, Denton, TX 76203. Offers MBA, MS, PhD. *Accreditation:* AACSB. Part-time and evening/weekend programs available. *Degree requirements:* For master's, thesis or alternative; for doctorate, thesis/dissertation. *Entrance requirements:* For master's, GMAT or GRE General Test, resume, 3 letters of recommendation; for doctorate, GMAT or GRE General Test, statement of purpose, resume, 3 letters of recommendation. Additional exam requirements/recommendations for international students: Required—proof of English language proficiency required for non-native English speakers; Recommended—TOEFL (minimum score 550 paper-based; 213 computer-based; 79 iBT). *Application deadline:* Applications are processed on a rolling basis. Application fee: $75 for international students. Electronic applications accepted. *Expenses:* Tuition, state resident: full-time $4298; part-time $239 per contact hour. Tuition, nonresident: full-time $9878; part-time $549 per contact hour. Required fees: $265 per contact hour. *Financial support:* Fellowships, research assistantships, teaching assistantships, career-related internships or fieldwork, Federal Work-Study, and institutionally sponsored loans available. Financial award applicants required to submit FAFSA. *Faculty research:* Oil and gas accounting, expert systems, stock returns, occupational safety, service marketing. *Application contact:* Associate Dean for Graduate Programs, 940-565-8977, Fax: 940-369-8978, E-mail: mbacoba@unt.edu.

University of Notre Dame, Mendoza College of Business, Executive Master of Business Administration Program, Notre Dame, IN 46556. Offers MBA. *Faculty:* 27 full-time (3 women), 7 part-time/adjunct (0 women). *Students:* 240 full-time (69 women); includes 36 minority (10 African Americans, 3 American Indian/Alaska Native, 10 Asian Americans or Pacific Islanders, 13 Hispanic Americans), 4 international. Average age 36. 279 applicants, 54% accepted, 124 enrolled. In 2009, 115 master's awarded. *Entrance requirements:* For master's, 5 years of work experience in management. *Application deadline:* For fall admission, 6/1 for domestic students; for winter admission, 11/1 for domestic students. Applications are processed on a rolling basis. Application fee: $100. Electronic applications accepted. *Expenses:* Contact institution. *Financial support:* In 2009–10, 100 students received support, including 8 fellowships (averaging $10,000 per year); institutionally sponsored loans also available. Financial award application deadline: 4/1; financial award applicants required to submit FAFSA. *Faculty research:* Exchange rates, compensation, market microstructure or volatility in foreign currency, ethical negotiation/decision making. *Unit head:* Paul C. Velasco, Director of Degree Programs, 574-631-8876, Fax: 574-631-6783, E-mail: pcvelasco@nd.edu. *Application contact:* Dr. Barry J. VanDyck, Director of Admissions and Recruiting, Executive MBA, 574-631-8351, Fax: 574-631-6783, E-mail: bvandyck@nd.edu.

University of Notre Dame, Mendoza College of Business, Master of Business Administration Program, Notre Dame, IN 46556. Offers MBA, MBA/JD. *Accreditation:* AACSB. *Faculty:* 68 full-time (9 women), 21 part-time/adjunct (5 women). *Students:* 342 full-time (80 women); includes 48 minority (13 African Americans, 5 American Indian/Alaska Native, 19 Asian Americans or Pacific Islanders, 11 Hispanic Americans), 48 international. Average age 27. 912 applicants, 37% accepted, 137 enrolled. In 2009, 178 master's awarded. *Degree requirements:* For master's, Requirements vary depending on concentration: http://business.nd.edu/MBA/Two-Year_MBA/Curriculum_Overview. *Entrance requirements:* For master's, GMAT, GRE, work experience. Additional exam requirements/recommendations for international students: Required—TOEFL (minimum score 600 paper-based; 250 computer-based). *Application deadline:* For fall admission, 11/16 priority date for domestic and international students; for winter admission, 1/18 priority date for domestic and international students; for spring admission, 3/15 for domestic students, 5/17 for international students. Applications are processed on a rolling basis. Application fee: $100. Electronic applications accepted. *Financial support:* In 2009–10, 206 students received support, including fellowships with full and partial tuition reimbursements available (averaging $18,550 per year), research assistantships (averaging $3,000 per year), teaching assistantships (averaging $3,000 per year); career-related internships or fieldwork, Federal Work-Study, institutionally sponsored loans, scholarships/grants, and unspecified assistantships also available. Financial award application deadline: 2/15; financial award applicants required to submit FAFSA. *Faculty research:* Market microstructure, marketing and public policy, corporate finance and accounting, corporate governance and ethical behavior, high performing organizations. *Unit head:* Dr. Edward J. Conlon, Associate Dean, Graduate Programs, 574-631-9295, Fax: 574-631-4825, E-mail: econlon@nd.edu. *Application contact:* Brian T. Lohr, Director of MBA Admissions, 574-631-8488, Fax: 574-631-8800, E-mail: blohr@nd.edu.

University of Oklahoma, Graduate College, Michael F. Price College of Business, Division of Management Information Systems, Norman, OK 73019. Offers management (MS). Part-time programs available. *Faculty:* 9 full-time (3 women). *Students:* 6 full-time (2 women), 5 part-time (1 woman); includes 4 minority (3 Asian Americans or Pacific Islanders, 1 Hispanic American), 1 international. 14 applicants, 36% accepted, 4 enrolled. In 2009, 4 master's awarded. *Entrance requirements:* Additional exam requirements/recommendations for international students: Required—TOEFL (minimum score 550 paper-based; 213 computer-based). *Application deadline:* For fall admission, 2/1 for domestic students, 4/1 for international students; for spring admission, 11/1 for domestic students, 9/1 for international students. Applications are processed on a rolling basis. Application fee: $40 ($90 for international students). Electronic applications accepted. *Expenses:* Tuition, state resident: full-time $3744; part-time $156 per credit hour. Tuition, nonresident: full-time $13,577; part-time $565.70 per credit hour. Required fees: $2415; $90.10 per credit hour. *Financial support:* In 2009–10, 9 students received support, including 9 research assistantships with full tuition reimbursements available (averaging $12,042 per year), 3 teaching assistantships with full tuition reimbursements available (averaging $13,278 per year); scholarships/grants and unspecified assistantships also available. Financial award applicants required to submit FAFSA. *Faculty research:* IT enabled teams, business value of IT, knowledge management, technology adoption. Total annual research expenditures: $25,679. *Unit head:* Laku Chidambaram, Director, 405-325-5721, Fax: 405-325-2096, E-mail: laku@ou.edu. *Application contact:* Jim Smith, Senior Academic Counselor, 405-325-3744, Fax: 405-325-7753, E-mail: jlsmith@ou.edu.

University of Oklahoma, Graduate College, Michael F. Price College of Business, Program in Business Administration, Norman, OK 73019. Offers MBA, PhD, JD/MBA, MBA/MA, MBA/MPH, MBA/MS. *Accreditation:* AACSB. Part-time and evening/weekend programs available. *Students:* 128 full-time (37 women), 119 part-time (26 women); includes 28 minority (1 African American, 4 American Indian/Alaska Native, 15 Asian Americans or Pacific Islanders, 8 Hispanic Americans), 45 international. 250 applicants, 52% accepted, 108 enrolled. In 2009, 89 master's, 6 doctorates awarded. Terminal master's awarded for partial completion of doctoral program. *Degree requirements:* For master's, comprehensive exam (for some programs); for doctorate, thesis/dissertation. *Entrance requirements:* For master's, GMAT, minimum GPA of 3.2; for doctorate, GMAT. Additional exam requirements/recommendations for international students: Required—TOEFL (minimum score 550 paper-based; 213 computer-based). *Application deadline:* For fall admission, 6/1 for domestic students, 4/1 for international students; for spring admission, 11/1 for domestic students, 9/1 for international students. Applications are processed on a rolling basis. Application fee: $40 ($90 for international students). Electronic applications accepted. *Expenses:* Tuition, state resident: full-time $3744; part-time $156 per credit hour. Tuition, nonresident: full-time $13,577; part-time $565.70 per credit hour. Required fees: $2415; $90.10 per credit hour. *Financial support:* In 2009–10, 126 students received support, including 17 fellowships (averaging $5,300 per year); career-related internships or fieldwork, scholarships/grants, health care benefits, and unspecified assistantships also available. Financial award applicants required to submit FAFSA. *Faculty research:* Corporate finance issues (capital structure, dividend policy), IT and organizational behavior, entrepreneurship and venture capital, corporate and risk management, global logistics systems. *Unit head:* Dr. Kenneth Evans, Dean, 405-325-0100, Fax: 405-325-3421, E-mail: evansk@ou.edu. *Application contact:* Jim Smith, Academic Counselor, 405-325-4107, Fax: 405-325-7753, E-mail: jlsmith@ou.edu.

See Close-Up on page 267.

University of Oklahoma, Graduate College, School of International and Area Studies, Norman, OK 73019-0390. Offers international studies (MA), including global affairs, global management. *Faculty:* 17 full-time (5 women), 1 part-time/adjunct (0 women). *Students:* 15 full-time (10 women), 4 part-time (2 women); includes 3 minority (1 Asian American or Pacific Islander, 2 Hispanic Americans). 13 applicants, 69% accepted, 5 enrolled. In 2009, 2 master's awarded. *Degree requirements:* For master's, one foreign language, thesis optional. *Entrance requirements:* For master's, GMAT or GRE. Additional exam requirements/recommendations for international students: Required—TOEFL (minimum score 550 paper-based; 213 computer-based). *Application deadline:* For fall admission, 2/15 for domestic students, 4/1 for international students; for spring admission, 10/15 for domestic students, 9/1 for international students. Applications are processed on a rolling basis. Application fee: $40 ($90 for international students). Electronic applications accepted. *Expenses:* Tuition, state resident: full-time $3744; part-time $156 per credit hour. Tuition, nonresident: full-time $13,577; part-time $565.70 per credit hour. Required fees: $2415; $90.10 per credit hour. *Financial support:* In 2009–10, 19 students received support, including 7 research assistantships (averaging $11,302 per year), 6 teaching assistantships with partial tuition reimbursements available (averaging $13,590 per year); tuition waivers (full) and unspecified assistantships also available. Financial award applicants required to submit FAFSA. *Faculty research:* Political economy, foreign policy, linguistics, environmental affairs, international law. Total annual research expenditures: $379,964. *Unit head:* Mark Fraizer, Director, 405-325-1584, Fax: 405-325-7738, E-mail: markfrazier@ou.edu. *Application contact:* Mitchell Smith, Associate Professor, 405-325-8893, Fax: 405-325-0718, E-mail: mps@ou.edu.

University of Oregon, Graduate School, Charles H. Lundquist College of Business, Department of Management, Eugene, OR 97403. Offers PhD. *Accreditation:* AACSB. Part-time programs available. Terminal master's awarded for partial completion of doctoral program. *Degree requirements:* For doctorate, thesis/dissertation, 2 comprehensive exams. *Entrance requirements:* For doctorate, GMAT. Additional exam requirements/recommendations for international students: Required—TOEFL.

University of Oregon, Graduate School, Charles H. Lundquist College of Business, Department of Management: General Business, Eugene, OR 97403. Offers MBA. *Accreditation:* AACSB. *Entrance requirements:* For master's, GMAT. Additional exam requirements/recommendations for international students: Required—TOEFL.

University of Ottawa, Faculty of Graduate and Postdoctoral Studies, Telfer School of Management, Business Administration Program, Ottawa, ON K1N 6N5, Canada. Offers MBA. *Accreditation:* AACSB. Part-time and evening/weekend programs available. *Degree requirements:* For master's, thesis optional. *Entrance requirements:* For master's, GMAT, bachelor's degree or equivalent, minimum B average, minimum 2 years of work experience. Additional exam requirements/recommendations for international students: Recommended—TOEFL (minimum score 237 computer-based). Electronic applications accepted.

See Close-Up on page 269.

University of Ottawa, Faculty of Graduate and Postdoctoral Studies, Telfer School of Management, Executive Business Administration Program, Ottawa, ON K1N 6N5, Canada. Offers EMBA. *Accreditation:* AACSB. Evening/weekend programs available. *Entrance requirements:* For master's, bachelor's degree or equivalent, minimum B average, business experience. Additional exam requirements/recommendations for international students: Recommended—TOEFL (minimum score 237 computer-based). Electronic applications accepted. *Expenses:* Contact institution.

University of Pennsylvania, Wharton School, Management Department, Philadelphia, PA 19104. Offers MBA, PhD. *Accreditation:* AACSB. *Entrance requirements:* For master's, GMAT; for doctorate, GMAT or GRE. *Expenses:* Tuition: Full-time $25,660; part-time $4758 per course. Required fees: $2152; $270 per course. Tuition and fees vary according to course load, degree level and program. *Faculty research:* Cross-cultural leadership, international technology transfers, human resource management, financial services.

University of Pennsylvania, Wharton School, Wharton Doctoral Programs, Philadelphia, PA 19104. Offers accounting (PhD); applied economics (PhD); ethics and legal studies (PhD); finance (PhD); health care management and economics (PhD); management (PhD); marketing (PhD); operations and information management (PhD); statistics (PhD). *Accreditation:* AACSB. *Degree requirements:* For doctorate, thesis/dissertation. *Entrance requirements:* For doctorate, GMAT or GRE, letters of recommendation. Additional exam requirements/recommendations for international students: Required—TOEFL, TWE. Electronic applications accepted. *Expenses:* Tuition: Full-time $25,660; part-time $4758 per course. Required fees: $2152; $270 per course. Tuition and fees vary according to course load, degree level and program.

University of Pennsylvania, Wharton School, The Wharton MBA Program, Philadelphia, PA 19104. Offers MBA, DMD/MBA, JD/MBA, MBA/MA, MBA/MS, MBA/MSN, MBA/MSW, MBA/PhD, MD/MBA, VMD/MBA. *Accreditation:* AACSB. *Entrance requirements:* For master's, GMAT, interview, 2 letters of recommendation, resume/curriculum vitae. Additional exam requirements/recommendations for international students: Required—TOEFL. Electronic applications accepted. *Expenses:* Tuition: Full-time $25,660; part-time $4758 per course. Required fees: $2152; $270 per course. Tuition and fees vary according to course load, degree level and program. *Faculty research:* Entrepreneurial studies, finance, management of technology.

University of Pennsylvania, Wharton School, The Wharton MBA Program for Executives, Wharton Executive MBA East, Philadelphia, PA 19104. Offers MBA. *Accreditation:* AACSB. Evening/weekend programs available. *Entrance requirements:* For master's, GMAT. *Expenses:* Tuition: Full-time $25,660; part-time $4758 per course. Required fees: $2152; $270 per course. Tuition and fees vary according to course load, degree level and program.

University of Pennsylvania, Wharton School, The Wharton MBA Program for Executives, Wharton Executive MBA West, Philadelphia, PA 19104. Offers MBA. *Accreditation:* AACSB. Evening/weekend programs available. *Entrance requirements:* For master's, GMAT. *Expenses:* Tuition: Full-time $25,660; part-time $4758 per course. Required fees: $2152; $270 per course. Tuition and fees vary according to course load, degree level and program.

University of Phoenix, School of Advanced Studies, Phoenix, AZ 85034-7209. Offers business administration (DBA); education (Ed D); educational leadership (Ed D), including curriculum and instruction, educational leadership, educational technology; health administration (DHA); higher education administration (PhD); industrial/organizational psychology (PhD); nursing (PhD); organizational leadership (DM), including information systems and technology, organizational leadership. Evening/weekend programs available. *Faculty:* 83 full-time (47 women), 540 part-time/adjunct (264 women). *Students:* 7,749 full-time (5,032 women); includes 3,180 minority (2,473 African Americans, 61 American Indian/Alaska Native, 221 Asian Americans or Pacific Islanders, 425 Hispanic Americans), 490 international. Average age 44. In 2009, 467 doctorates awarded. *Degree requirements:* For doctorate, thesis/dissertation. *Entrance requirements:* For doctorate, 3 letters of recommendation, minimum master's GPA of 3.0, 3 years professional work experience. Additional exam requirements/recommendations for international students: Required—TOEFL (minimum score 550 paper-based; 213 computer-based; 79 iBT). *Application deadline:* Applications are processed on a rolling basis. Application fee: $45. Electronic applications accepted. *Expenses:* Tuition: Full-time $13,272. Required fees: $660. Full-time tuition and fees vary according to course level, degree level and program. *Financial support:* Institutionally sponsored loans and scholarships/grants available. Financial award applicants required to submit FAFSA. *Unit head:* Dr. Jeremy Moreland, Dean/Executive Director, 480-557-3231, E-mail: jeremy.moreland@phoenix.edu. *Application contact:* Information Contact, 800-697-8223.

University of Phoenix, School of Business, College of Graduate Business and Management, Phoenix, AZ 85034-7209. Offers accountancy (MSA); accounting (MBA); business administration (MBA); global management (MBA); human resources management (MBA, MM); management (MM); marketing (MBA); public administration (MBA, MM). *Accreditation:* ACBSP. Evening/weekend programs available. Postbaccalaureate distance learning degree programs offered. *Faculty:* 25 full-time (15 women), 4,861 part-time/adjunct (1,504 women). *Students:* 6,681 full-time (5,284 women); includes 2,558 minority (1,955 African Americans, 69 American

Business Administration and Management—General

University of Phoenix (continued)
Indian/Alaska Native, 90 Asian Americans or Pacific Islanders, 444 Hispanic Americans), 137 international. Average age 35. In 2009, 1,740 master's awarded. *Degree requirements:* For master's, thesis (for some programs). *Entrance requirements:* For master's, 3 years of work experience, minimum undergraduate GPA of 3.0. Additional exam requirements/recommendations for international students: Required—TOEFL (minimum score 550 paper-based; 213 computer-based; 79 iBT). *Application deadline:* Applications are processed on a rolling basis. Application fee: $45. Electronic applications accepted. *Expenses:* Tuition: Full-time $13,272. Required fees: $660. Full-time tuition and fees vary according to course level, degree level and program. *Financial support:* Institutionally sponsored loans and scholarships/grants available. Financial award applicants required to submit FAFSA. *Unit head:* Brian Lindquist, Dean/Executive Director and Associate Vice President, 480-557-1221, E-mail: brian.lindquist@phoenix.edu. *Application contact:* Chair, 602-387-7000, Fax: 602-387-6020.

University of Phoenix, School of Business, College of Information Systems and Technology, Phoenix, AZ 85034-7209. Offers management (MIS). Evening/weekend programs available. *Faculty:* 8 full-time (4 women), 124 part-time/adjunct (38 women). *Students:* 2,693 full-time (937 women); includes 853 minority (539 African Americans, 16 American Indian/Alaska Native, 136 Asian Americans or Pacific Islanders, 162 Hispanic Americans), 187 international. Average age 38. In 2009, 1,104 master's awarded. *Degree requirements:* For master's, thesis (for some programs). *Entrance requirements:* For master's, 3 years of work experience, minimum undergraduate GPA of 3.0. Additional exam requirements/recommendations for international students: Required—TOEFL (minimum score 550 paper-based; 213 computer-based; 79 iBT). *Application deadline:* Applications are processed on a rolling basis. Application fee: $45. Electronic applications accepted. *Expenses:* Tuition: Full-time $13,272. Required fees: $660. Full-time tuition and fees vary according to course level, degree level and program. *Financial support:* Institutionally sponsored loans and scholarships/grants available. Financial award applicants required to submit FAFSA. *Unit head:* Dr. Blair Sith, Dean/Executive Director, 480-557-1241, Fax: 480-929-7164, E-mail: blair.smitha@phoenix.edu. *Application contact:* Chair, 680-766-0766.

University of Phoenix–Atlanta Campus, John Sperling School of Business, College of Graduate Business and Management, Sandy Springs, GA 30350-4153. Offers accounting (MBA); business administration (MBA); global management (MBA); human resources management (MBA, MM); management (MM); marketing (MBA); public administration (MM). Evening/weekend programs available. Postbaccalaureate distance learning degree programs offered. *Degree requirements:* For master's, thesis (for some programs). *Entrance requirements:* For master's, minimum undergraduate GPA of 3.0, 3 years of work experience. Additional exam requirements/recommendations for international students: Required—TOEFL (minimum score 550 paper-based; 213 computer-based; 79 iBT).

University of Phoenix–Augusta Campus, College of Graduate Business and Management, Augusta, GA 30909-4583. Offers accounting (MBA); business administration (MBA); business and management (MBA, MM); global management (MBA); human resources management (MBA, MM); management (MM); marketing (MBA); public administration (MBA, MM). Postbaccalaureate distance learning degree programs offered.

University of Phoenix–Austin Campus, College of Graduate Business and Management, Austin, TX 78759. Offers accounting (MBA); business administration (MBA); business and management (MBA); e-business (MBA); global management (MBA); human resources management (MBA, MM); management (MM); marketing (MBA); public administration (MBA). Postbaccalaureate distance learning degree programs offered.

University of Phoenix–Bay Area Campus, John Sperling School of Business, College of Graduate Business and Management, Pleasanton, CA 94588-3677. Offers accounting (MBA); business administration (MBA); global management (MBA); human resources management (MBA, MM); marketing (MBA); public administration (MBA, MM). Evening/weekend programs available. Postbaccalaureate distance learning degree programs offered (no on-campus study). *Degree requirements:* For master's, thesis (for some programs). *Entrance requirements:* For master's, minimum undergraduate GPA of 3.0, 3 years of work experience. Additional exam requirements/recommendations for international students: Required—TOEFL (minimum score 550 paper-based; 213 computer-based; 79 iBT). Electronic applications accepted.

University of Phoenix–Birmingham Campus, College of Graduate Business and Management, Birmingham, AL 35244. Offers accounting (MBA); business administration (MBA); global management (MBA); human resources management (MBA, MM); management (MM); marketing (MBA); public administration (MM).

University of Phoenix–Boston Campus, John Sperling School of Business, College of Graduate Business and Management, Braintree, MA 02184-4949. Offers administration (MBA); global management (MBA). Evening/weekend programs available. *Degree requirements:* For master's, thesis (for some programs). *Entrance requirements:* For master's, 3 years of work experience, minimum undergraduate GPA of 3.0. Additional exam requirements/recommendations for international students: Required—TOEFL (minimum score 550 paper-based; 213 computer-based; 79 iBT).

University of Phoenix–Central Florida Campus, John Sperling School of Business, College of Graduate Business and Management, Maitland, FL 32751-7057. Offers accounting (MBA); business administration (MBA); business and management (MM); global management (MBA); human resources management (MBA, MM); management (MM); marketing (MBA); public administration (MBA, MM). Evening/weekend programs available. *Degree requirements:* For master's, thesis (for some programs). *Entrance requirements:* For master's, minimum undergraduate GPA of 3.0, 3 years work experience. Additional exam requirements/recommendations for international students: Required—TOEFL (minimum score 550 paper-based; 213 computer-based; 79 iBT). Electronic applications accepted.

University of Phoenix–Central Florida Campus, John Sperling School of Business, College of Information Systems and Technology, Maitland, FL 32751-7057. Offers management (MIS); technology management (MBA). Evening/weekend programs available. *Degree requirements:* For master's, thesis (for some programs). *Entrance requirements:* For master's, minimum undergraduate GPA of 3.0, 3 years work experience. Additional exam requirements/recommendations for international students: Required—TOEFL (minimum score 550 paper-based; 213 computer-based; 79 iBT). Electronic applications accepted.

University of Phoenix–Central Massachusetts Campus, John Sperling School of Business, College of Graduate Business and Management, Westborough, MA 01581-3906. Offers business administration (MBA); global management (MBA). Evening/weekend programs available. *Degree requirements:* For master's, thesis (for some programs). *Entrance requirements:* For master's, minimum undergraduate GPA of 3.0, 3 years of work experience. Additional exam requirements/recommendations for international students: Required—TOEFL (minimum score 550 paper-based; 213 computer-based; 79 iBT). Electronic applications accepted.

University of Phoenix–Central Valley Campus, College of Graduate Business and Management, Fresno, CA 93720-1562. Offers accounting (MBA); business administration (MBA); global management (MBA); human resources management (MBA, MM); management (MM); marketing (MBA); public administration (MBA, MM).

University of Phoenix–Charlotte Campus, John Sperling School of Business, College of Graduate Business and Management, Charlotte, NC 28273-3409. Offers accounting (MBA); business administration (MBA); global management (MBA). Evening/weekend programs available. *Degree requirements:* For master's, thesis (for some programs). *Entrance requirements:* For master's, minimum undergraduate GPA of 3.0, 3 years work experience. Additional exam requirements/recommendations for international students: Required—TOEFL (minimum score 550 paper-based; 213 computer-based; 79 iBT). Electronic applications accepted.

University of Phoenix–Chattanooga Campus, College of Graduate Business and Management, Chattanooga, TN 37421-3707. Offers accounting (MBA); business administration (MBA); business and management (MBA); global management (MBA); human resources management (MBA, MM); management (MM); marketing (MBA); public administration (MBA, MM). Postbaccalaureate distance learning degree programs offered.

University of Phoenix–Cheyenne Campus, College of Graduate Business and Management, Cheyenne, WY 82009. Offers global management (MBA); human resources management (MBA, MM); management (MM); marketing (MBA); public administration (MBA, MM). Postbaccalaureate distance learning degree programs offered.

University of Phoenix–Chicago Campus, John Sperling School of Business, College of Graduate Business and Management, Schaumburg, IL 60173-4399. Offers business administration (MBA); global management (MBA); human resources management (MBA); information systems (MIS); management (MM). Evening/weekend programs available. *Degree requirements:* For master's, thesis (for some programs). *Entrance requirements:* For master's, minimum undergraduate GPA of 3.0, 3 years of work experience. Additional exam requirements/recommendations for international students: Required—TOEFL (minimum score 550 paper-based; 213 computer-based; 79 iBT). Electronic applications accepted.

University of Phoenix–Cincinnati Campus, John Sperling School of Business, College of Graduate Business and Management, West Chester, OH 45069-4875. Offers accounting (MBA); business administration (MBA); global management (MBA); human resources management (MBA, MM); management (MM); marketing (MBA); public administration (MM). Evening/weekend programs available. *Degree requirements:* For master's, thesis (for some programs). *Entrance requirements:* For master's, minimum undergraduate GPA of 3.0, 3 years of work experience. Additional exam requirements/recommendations for international students: Required—TOEFL (minimum score 550 paper-based; 213 computer-based; 79 iBT). Electronic applications accepted.

University of Phoenix–Cleveland Campus, John Sperling School of Business, College of Graduate Business and Management, Independence, OH 44131-2194. Offers accounting (MBA); business administration (MBA); global management (MBA); human resources management (MBA, MM); management (MM); marketing (MBA); public administration (MBA, MM). Evening/weekend programs available. Postbaccalaureate distance learning degree programs offered (no on-campus study). *Degree requirements:* For master's, thesis (for some programs). *Entrance requirements:* For master's, minimum undergraduate GPA of 3.0, 3 years of work experience. Additional exam requirements/recommendations for international students: Required—TOEFL (minimum score 550 paper-based; 213 computer-based; 79 iBT). Electronic applications accepted.

University of Phoenix–Columbia Campus, College of Graduate Business and Management, Columbia, SC 29223. Offers business administration (MBA). Postbaccalaureate distance learning degree programs offered.

University of Phoenix–Columbus Georgia Campus, John Sperling School of Business, College of Graduate Business and Management, Columbus, GA 31904-6321. Offers accounting (MBA); business administration (MBA); global management (MBA); human resources management (MBA, MM); management (MM); marketing (MBA); public administration (MBA). Evening/weekend programs available. *Degree requirements:* For master's, thesis (for some programs). *Entrance requirements:* For master's, minimum undergraduate GPA of 3.0, 3 years of work experience. Additional exam requirements/recommendations for international students: Required—TOEFL (minimum score 550 paper-based; 213 computer-based; 79 iBT). Electronic applications accepted.

University of Phoenix–Columbus Ohio Campus, John Sperling School of Business, College of Graduate Business and Management, Columbus, OH 43240-4032. Offers accounting (MBA); business administration (MBA); global management (MBA); human resources management (MBA, MM); management (MM); marketing (MBA); public administration (MM). Evening/weekend programs available. Postbaccalaureate distance learning degree programs offered. *Degree requirements:* For master's, thesis (for some programs). *Entrance requirements:* For master's, minimum undergraduate GPA of 3.0, 3 years of work experience. Additional exam requirements/recommendations for international students: Required—TOEFL (minimum score 550 paper-based; 213 computer-based; 79 iBT). Electronic applications accepted.

University of Phoenix–Dallas Campus, John Sperling School of Business, College of Graduate Business and Management, Dallas, TX 75251-2009. Offers accounting (MBA); business administration (MBA); global management (MBA); human resources management (MBA, MM); management (MM); marketing (MBA); public administration (MBA, MM). Evening/weekend programs available. Postbaccalaureate distance learning degree programs offered. *Degree requirements:* For master's, thesis (for some programs). *Entrance requirements:* For master's, 3 years of work experience, minimum undergraduate GPA of 3.0. Additional exam requirements/recommendations for international students: Required—TOEFL (minimum score 550 paper-based; 213 computer-based; 79 iBT). Electronic applications accepted.

University of Phoenix–Denver Campus, John Sperling School of Business, College of Graduate Business and Management, Lone Tree, CO 80124-5453. Offers accountancy (MSA); accounting (MBA); business administration (MBA); e-business (MBA); global management (MBA); human resources management (MBA, MM); management (MM); marketing (MBA); public administration (MBA, MM). Evening/weekend programs available. Postbaccalaureate distance learning degree programs offered. *Degree requirements:* For master's, thesis (for some programs). *Entrance requirements:* For master's, minimum undergraduate GPA of 3.0, 3 years work experience. Additional exam requirements/recommendations for international students: Required—TOEFL (minimum score 550 paper-based; 213 computer-based; 79 iBT). Electronic applications accepted.

University of Phoenix–Denver Campus, John Sperling School of Business, College of Information Systems and Technology, Lone Tree, CO 80124-5453. Offers e-business (MBA); management (MIS); technology management (MBA). Evening/weekend programs available. Postbaccalaureate distance learning degree programs offered. *Degree requirements:* For master's, thesis (for some programs). *Entrance requirements:* For master's, minimum undergraduate GPA of 3.0, 3 years of work experience. Additional exam requirements/recommendations for international students: Required—TOEFL (minimum score 550 paper-based; 213 computer-based; 79 iBT). Electronic applications accepted.

University of Phoenix–Des Moines Campus, College of Graduate Business and Management, Des Moines, IA 50266. Offers accounting (MBA); business administration (MBA); global management (MBA); human resources management (MBA, MM); management (MM); marketing (MBA); public administration (MBA, MM). Postbaccalaureate distance learning degree programs offered.

University of Phoenix–Eastern Washington Campus, John Sperling School of Business, College of Graduate Business and Management, Spokane Valley, WA 99212-2531. Offers accounting (MBA); business administration (MBA); human resources management (MBA); marketing (MBA); public administration (MBA). Evening/weekend programs available. *Degree requirements:* For master's, thesis (for some programs). *Entrance requirements:* For master's, minimum undergraduate GPA of 3.0, 3 years of work experience. Additional exam requirements/recommendations for international students: Required—TOEFL (minimum score 550 paper-based; 213 computer-based; 79 iBT). Electronic applications accepted.

University of Phoenix–Fairfield County Campus, College of Graduate Business and Management, Norwalk, CT 06854-1799. Offers MBA.

University of Phoenix–Harrisburg Campus, College of Graduate Business and Management, Harrisburg, PA 17112. Offers accounting (MBA); business administration (MBA); business and management (MBA); global management (MBA); human resources management (MBA, MM); management (MM); marketing (MBA); public administration (MBA, MM). Postbaccalaureate distance learning degree programs offered.

University of Phoenix–Hawaii Campus, John Sperling School of Business, College of Graduate Business and Management, Honolulu, HI 96813-4317. Offers accounting (MBA); business administration (MBA); global management (MBA); human resources management (MBA, MM); management (MM); marketing (MBA); public administration (MBA, MM). Evening/weekend programs available. *Degree requirements:* For master's, thesis (for some programs). *Entrance requirements:* For master's, minimum undergraduate GPA of 3.0, 3 years of work experience. Additional exam requirements/recommendations for international students: Required—TOEFL (minimum score 550 paper-based; 213 computer-based; 79 iBT). Electronic applications accepted.

University of Phoenix–Houston Campus, John Sperling School of Business, College of Graduate Business and Management, Houston, TX 77079-2004. Offers accounting (MBA); business administration (MBA); global management (MBA); human resources management (MBA, MM); management (MM); marketing (MBA); public administration (MBA, MM). Evening/weekend programs available. Postbaccalaureate distance learning degree programs offered. *Degree requirements:* For master's, thesis (for some programs). *Entrance requirements:* For master's, 3 years of work experience, minimum undergraduate GPA of 3.0. Additional exam requirements/recommendations for international students: Required—TOEFL (minimum score 550 paper-based; 213 computer-based; 79 iBT). Electronic applications accepted.

University of Phoenix–Idaho Campus, John Sperling School of Business, College of Graduate Business and Management, Meridian, ID 83642-3014. Offers accounting (MBA); administration (MBA); global management (MBA); human resources management (MBA, MM); management (MM); marketing (MBA); public administration (MM). Evening/weekend programs available. Postbaccalaureate distance learning degree programs offered. *Degree requirements:* For master's, thesis (for some programs). *Entrance requirements:* For master's, 3 years of work experience, minimum undergraduate GPA of 3.0. Additional exam requirements/recommendations for international students: Required—TOEFL (minimum score 550 paper-based; 213 computer-based). Electronic applications accepted.

University of Phoenix–Indianapolis Campus, John Sperling School of Business, College of Graduate Business and Management, Indianapolis, IN 46250-932. Offers accounting (MBA); business administration (MBA); global management (MBA); human resources management (MBA, MM); management (MM); marketing (MBA); public administration (MM). Evening/weekend programs available. *Degree requirements:* For master's, thesis (for some programs). *Entrance requirements:* For master's, minimum undergraduate GPA of 3.0, 3 years of work experience. Additional exam requirements/recommendations for international students: Required—TOEFL (minimum score 550 paper-based; 213 computer-based). Electronic applications accepted.

University of Phoenix–Jersey City Campus, College of Graduate Business and Management, Jersey City, NJ 07310. Offers accounting (MBA); business administration (MBA); global management (MBA); human resources management (MBA, MM); management (MM); marketing (MBA); public administration (MBA, MM).

University of Phoenix–Kansas City Campus, John Sperling School of Business, College of Graduate Business and Management, Kansas City, MO 64131-4517. Offers accounting (MBA); business administration (MBA); global management (MBA); human resources management (MBA, MM); management (MM); marketing (MBA); public administration (MBA). Evening/weekend programs available. *Degree requirements:* For master's, thesis (for some programs). *Entrance requirements:* For master's, minimum undergraduate GPA of 3.0, 3 years of work experience. Additional exam requirements/recommendations for international students: Required—TOEFL (minimum score 550 paper-based; 213 computer-based). Electronic applications accepted.

University of Phoenix–Las Vegas Campus, John Sperling School of Business, College of Graduate Business and Management, Las Vegas, NV 89128. Offers accounting (MBA); business administration (MBA); global management (MBA); human resources management (MBA, MM); management (MM); marketing (MBA); public administration (MM). Evening/weekend programs available. Postbaccalaureate distance learning degree programs offered (no on-campus study). *Degree requirements:* For master's, thesis (for some programs). *Entrance requirements:* For master's, minimum undergraduate GPA of 3.0, 3 years of work experience. Additional exam requirements/recommendations for international students: Required—TOEFL (minimum score 550 paper-based; 213 computer-based; 79 iBT). Electronic applications accepted.

University of Phoenix–Little Rock Campus, John Sperling School of Business, College of Graduate Business and Management, Little Rock, AR 72211-3500. Offers MBA, MM. Evening/weekend programs available. *Degree requirements:* For master's, thesis (for some programs). *Entrance requirements:* For master's, minimum undergraduate GPA of 3.0, 3 years of work experience. Additional exam requirements/recommendations for international students: Required—TOEFL (minimum score 550 paper-based; 213 computer-based). Electronic applications accepted.

University of Phoenix–Louisiana Campus, John Sperling School of Business, College of Graduate Business and Management, Metairie, LA 70001-2082. Offers accounting (MBA); business administration (MBA); global management (MBA); human resources management (MBA, MM); management (MM); marketing (MBA); public administration (MBA). Evening/weekend programs available. *Degree requirements:* For master's, thesis (for some programs). *Entrance requirements:* For master's, minimum undergraduate GPA of 3.0, 3 years work experience. Additional exam requirements/recommendations for international students: Required—TOEFL (minimum score 550 paper-based; 213 computer-based; 79 iBT). Electronic applications accepted.

University of Phoenix–Louisville Campus, College of Graduate Business and Management, Louisville, KY 40223-3839. Offers business administration (MBA); e-business (MBA); management (MM). Postbaccalaureate distance learning degree programs offered.

University of Phoenix–Madison Campus, College of Graduate Business and Management, Madison, WI 53718-2416. Offers accounting (MBA); business and management (MBA); e-business (MBA); global management (MBA); human resources management (MBA, MM); management (MM); marketing (MBA); public administration (MBA).

University of Phoenix–Madison Campus, John Sperling School of Business, College of Graduate Business and Management, Madison, WI 53718-2416. Offers accounting (MBA); administration (MBA); global management (MBA); human resources management (MM); marketing (MBA); public administration (MBA). Evening/weekend programs available. *Degree requirements:* For master's, thesis (for some programs). *Entrance requirements:* For master's, 3 years of work experience, minimum undergraduate GPA of 3.0. Additional exam requirements/recommendations for international students: Required—TOEFL (minimum score 550 paper-based; 213 computer-based; 79 iBT). Electronic applications accepted.

University of Phoenix–Maryland Campus, John Sperling School of Business, College of Graduate Business and Management, Columbia, MD 21045-5424. Offers accounting (MBA); business administration (MBA); e-business (MBA); global management (MBA); human resources management (MBA, MM); management (MM); marketing (MBA); public administration (MBA, MM). Evening/weekend programs available. *Degree requirements:* For master's, thesis (for some programs). *Entrance requirements:* For master's, minimum undergraduate GPA of 3.0, 3 years of work experience. Additional exam requirements/recommendations for international students: Required—TOEFL (minimum score 550 paper-based; 213 computer-based; 79 iBT). Electronic applications accepted.

University of Phoenix–Memphis Campus, College of Graduate Business and Management, Cordova, TN 38018. Offers accounting (MBA); business and management (MBA); e-business (MBA); global management (MBA); human resources management (MBA, MM); management (MM); marketing (MBA); public administration (MBA, MM).

University of Phoenix–Metro Detroit Campus, School of Business, College of Graduate Business and Management, Troy, MI 48098-2623. Offers accountancy (MS); accounting (MBA); business administration (MBA); global management (MBA); human resources management (MBA, MM); management (MM); marketing (MBA). Evening/weekend programs available. *Degree requirements:* For master's, thesis (for some programs). *Entrance requirements:* For master's, minimum undergraduate GPA of 3.0, 3 years work experience. Additional exam requirements/recommendations for international students: Required—TOEFL (minimum score 550 paper-based; 213 computer-based; 79 iBT). Electronic applications accepted. *Expenses:* Tuition: Full-time $14,136. Required fees: $660.

University of Phoenix–Minneapolis/St. Louis Park Campus, College of Graduate Business and Management, St. Louis Park, MN 55426. Offers accounting (MBA); business administration (MBA); global management (MBA); human resources management (MBA); management (MM); marketing (MBA); public administration (MBA).

University of Phoenix–Nashville Campus, John Sperling School of Business, College of Graduate Business and Management, Nashville, TN 37214-5048. Offers business administration (MBA); human resources management (MBA); management (MM). Evening/weekend programs available. *Degree requirements:* For master's, thesis (for some programs). *Entrance requirements:* For master's, minimum undergraduate GPA of 3.0, 3 years of work experience. Additional exam requirements/recommendations for international students: Required—TOEFL (minimum score 550 paper-based; 213 computer-based; 79 iBT). Electronic applications accepted.

University of Phoenix–New Mexico Campus, John Sperling School of Business, College of Graduate Business and Management, Albuquerque, NM 87113-1570. Offers accounting (MBA); business administration (MBA); global management (MBA); human resource management (MBA); human resources management (MM); management (MM); marketing (MBA). Evening/weekend programs available. *Degree requirements:* For master's, thesis (for some programs). *Entrance requirements:* For master's, 3 years of work experience, minimum undergraduate GPA of 3.0. Additional exam requirements/recommendations for international students: Required—TOEFL (minimum score 550 paper-based; 213 computer-based; 79 iBT). Electronic applications accepted.

University of Phoenix–Northern Nevada Campus, College of Graduate Business and Management, Reno, NV 89521-5862. Offers accounting (MBA); business administration (MBA); global management (MBA); human resources management (MBA, MM); management (MM); marketing (MBA); public administration (MBA, MM).

University of Phoenix–Northern Virginia Campus, College of Graduate Business and Management, Reston, VA 20190. Offers accounting (MBA); business administration (MBA); e-business (MBA); global management (MBA); human resources management (MBA, MM); management (MM); marketing (MBA); public administration (MBA).

University of Phoenix–Northern Virginia Campus, College of Information Systems and Technology, Reston, VA 20190. Offers information systems and technology (MIS); management (MIS); technology management (MBA).

University of Phoenix–North Florida Campus, John Sperling School of Business, College of Graduate Business and Management, Jacksonville, FL 32216-0959. Offers accounting (MBA); business administration (MBA); global management (MBA); human resources management (MBA, MM); management (MM); marketing (MBA); public administration (MBA, MM). Evening/weekend programs available. *Degree requirements:* For master's, thesis (for some programs). *Entrance requirements:* For master's, minimum undergraduate GPA of 3.0, 3 years work experience. Additional exam requirements/recommendations for international students: Required—TOEFL (minimum score 550 paper-based; 213 computer-based; 79 iBT). Electronic applications accepted.

University of Phoenix–North Florida Campus, John Sperling School of Business, College of Information Systems and Technology, Jacksonville, FL 32216-0959. Offers information systems (MIS); management (MIS). Evening/weekend programs available. *Degree requirements:* For master's, thesis (for some programs). *Entrance requirements:* For master's, minimum undergraduate GPA of 3.0, 3 years work experience. Additional exam requirements/recommendations for international students: Required—TOEFL (minimum score 550 paper-based; 213 computer-based; 79 iBT). Electronic applications accepted.

University of Phoenix–Northwest Arkansas Campus, College of Graduate Business and Management, Rogers, AR 72756-9615. Offers accounting (MBA); business and management (MBA); global management (MBA); human resources management (MBA, MM); management (MM); marketing (MBA); public administration (MBA, MM).

University of Phoenix–Oklahoma City Campus, John Sperling School of Business, College of Graduate Business and Management, Oklahoma City, OK 73116-8244. Offers accounting (MBA); business administration (MBA); global management (MBA); human resource management (MBA); management (MM); marketing (MBA). Evening/weekend programs available. *Degree requirements:* For master's, thesis (for some programs). *Entrance requirements:* For master's, minimum undergraduate GPA of 3.0, 3 years of work experience. Additional exam requirements/recommendations for international students: Required—TOEFL (minimum score 550 paper-based; 213 computer-based; 79 iBT). Electronic applications accepted.

University of Phoenix–Omaha Campus, College of Graduate Business and Management, Omaha, NE 68154-5240. Offers accounting (MBA); business and management (MBA); global management (MBA); human resources management (MBA, MM); management (MM); marketing (MBA); public administration (MBA, MM).

University of Phoenix–Oregon Campus, The John Sperling School of Business, College of Graduate Business and Management, Tigard, OR 97223. Offers accounting (MBA); business administration (MBA); global management (MBA); human resource management (MM); human resources management (MBA); management (MM); marketing (MBA); public administration (MM). Evening/weekend programs available. *Degree requirements:* For master's, thesis (for some programs). *Entrance requirements:* For master's, minimum undergraduate GPA of 3.0, 3 years of work experience. Additional exam requirements/recommendations for international students: Required—TOEFL (minimum score 550 paper-based; 213 computer-based; 79 iBT). Electronic applications accepted.

University of Phoenix–Philadelphia Campus, The John Sperling School of Business, College of Graduate Business and Management, Wayne, PA 19087-2121. Offers accounting (MBA); business administration (MBA); global management (MBA); human resources management (MBA, MM); management (MM); marketing (MBA); public administration (MM). Evening/weekend programs available. *Degree requirements:* For master's, thesis (for some programs). *Entrance requirements:* For master's, minimum undergraduate GPA of 3.0, 3 years work experience. Additional exam requirements/recommendations for international students: Required—TOEFL (minimum score 550 paper-based; 213 computer-based; 79 iBT). Electronic applications accepted.

University of Phoenix–Pittsburgh Campus, John Sperling School of Business, College of Graduate Business and Management, Pittsburgh, PA 15276. Offers accounting (MBA); business administration (MBA); global management (MBA); human resources management (MBA, MM); management (MM); marketing (MBA); public administration (MBA, MM). Evening/weekend programs available. *Degree requirements:* For master's, thesis (for some programs). *Entrance requirements:* For master's, minimum undergraduate GPA of 3.0, 3 years work experience. Additional exam requirements/recommendations for international students: Required—TOEFL (minimum score 550 paper-based; 213 computer-based; 79 iBT). Electronic applications accepted.

University of Phoenix–Puerto Rico Campus, John Sperling School of Business, College of Graduate Business and Management, Guaynabo, PR 00968. Offers accounting (MBA); business administration (MBA); global management (MBA); human resource management (MBA);

Business Administration and Management—General

University of Phoenix–Puerto Rico Campus (continued)
marketing (MBA). Evening/weekend programs available. *Degree requirements:* For master's, thesis (for some programs). *Entrance requirements:* For master's, minimum undergraduate GPA of 3.0, 3 years work experience. Additional exam requirements/recommendations for international students: Required—TOEFL (minimum score 550 paper-based; 213 computer-based; 79 iBT). Electronic applications accepted.

University of Phoenix–Raleigh Campus, College of Graduate Business and Management, Raleigh, NC 27606. Offers accounting (MBA); business administration (MBA); e-business (MBA); global management (MBA); human resources management (MBA); marketing (MBA).

University of Phoenix–Raleigh Campus, College of Information Systems and Technology, Raleigh, NC 27606. Offers information systems and technology (MIS); management (MIS); technology management (MBA).

University of Phoenix–Richmond Campus, John Sperling School of Business, College of Graduate Business and Management, Richmond, VA 23230. Offers accounting (MBA); business administration (MBA); global management (MBA); human resources management (MBA, MM); management (MM); marketing (MBA); public administration (MBA, MM). Evening/weekend programs available. *Degree requirements:* For master's, thesis (for some programs). *Entrance requirements:* For master's, minimum undergraduate GPA of 3.0, 3 years work experience. Additional exam requirements/recommendations for international students: Required—TOEFL (minimum score 550 paper-based; 213 computer-based; 79 iBT). Electronic applications accepted.

University of Phoenix–Sacramento Valley Campus, John Sperling School of Business, College of Graduate Business and Management, Sacramento, CA 95833-3632. Offers accounting (MBA); business administration (MBA); global management (MBA); human resources management (MBA, MM); management (MM); marketing (MBA); public administration (MBA, MM). Evening/weekend programs available. *Degree requirements:* For master's, thesis (for some programs). *Entrance requirements:* For master's, minimum undergraduate GPA of 3.0, 3 years work experience. Additional exam requirements/recommendations for international students: Required—TOEFL (minimum score 550 paper-based; 213 computer-based; 79 iBT). Electronic applications accepted.

University of Phoenix–Sacramento Valley Campus, John Sperling School of Business, College of Information Systems and Technology, Sacramento, CA 95833-3632. Offers management (MIS); technology management (MBA). Evening/weekend programs available. *Degree requirements:* For master's, thesis (for some programs). *Entrance requirements:* For master's, minimum undergraduate GPA of 3.0, 3 years work experience. Additional exam requirements/recommendations for international students: Required—TOEFL (minimum score 550 paper-based; 213 computer-based; 79 iBT). Electronic applications accepted.

University of Phoenix–St. Louis Campus, John Sperling School of Business, College of Graduate Business and Management, St. Louis, MO 63043-4828. Offers accounting (MBA); business administration (MBA); global management (MBA); human resources management (MBA, MM); management (MM); marketing (MBA); public administration (MM). Evening/weekend programs available. *Degree requirements:* For master's, thesis (for some programs). *Entrance requirements:* For master's, 3 years of work experience, minimum undergraduate GPA of 3.0. Additional exam requirements/recommendations for international students: Required—TOEFL (minimum score 550 paper-based; 213 computer-based; 79 iBT). Electronic applications accepted.

University of Phoenix–San Antonio Campus, College of Graduate Business and Management, San Antonio, TX 78230. Offers accounting (MBA); business administration (MBA); e-business (MBA); global management (MBA); human resources management (MBA, MM); management (MM); marketing (MBA); public administration (MBA, MM).

University of Phoenix–San Diego Campus, John Sperling School of Business, College of Graduate Business and Management, San Diego, CA 92123. Offers accounting (MBA); business administration (MBA); global management (MBA); human resources management (MBA, MM); management (MM); marketing (MBA); public administration (MBA). Evening/weekend programs available. *Degree requirements:* For master's, thesis (for some programs). *Entrance requirements:* For master's, 3 years of work experience, minimum undergraduate GPA of 3.0. Additional exam requirements/recommendations for international students: Required—TOEFL (minimum score 550 paper-based; 213 computer-based; 79 iBT). Electronic applications accepted.

University of Phoenix–San Diego Campus, John Sperling School of Business, College of Information Systems and Technology, San Diego, CA 92123. Offers management (MIS); technology management (MBA). Evening/weekend programs available. *Degree requirements:* For master's, thesis (for some programs). *Entrance requirements:* For master's, minimum undergraduate GPA of 3.0, 3 years work experience. Additional exam requirements/recommendations for international students: Required—TOEFL (minimum score 550 paper-based; 213 computer-based; 79 iBT). Electronic applications accepted.

University of Phoenix–Savannah Campus, College of Graduate Business and Management, Savannah, GA 31405-7400. Offers accounting (MBA); business administration (MBA); global management (MBA); human resources management (MBA, MM); management (MM); marketing (MBA); public administration (MBA, MM).

University of Phoenix–Southern Arizona Campus, John Sperling School of Business, College of Graduate Business and Management, Tucson, AZ 85711. Offers accountancy (MS); accounting (MBA); business administration (MBA); global management (MBA); human resources management (MBA); management (MM); marketing (MBA). Evening/weekend programs available. *Degree requirements:* For master's, thesis (for some programs). *Entrance requirements:* For master's, minimum undergraduate GPA of 3.0, 3 years of work experience. Additional exam requirements/recommendations for international students: Required—TOEFL (minimum score 550 paper-based; 213 computer-based; 79 iBT). Electronic applications accepted.

University of Phoenix–Southern Colorado Campus, John Sperling School of Business, College of Graduate Business and Management, Colorado Springs, CO 80919-2335. Offers accounting (MBA); business administration (MBA); global management (MBA); human resources management (MBA, MM); management (MM); marketing (MBA); public administration (MM). Evening/weekend programs available. *Degree requirements:* For master's, thesis (for some programs). *Entrance requirements:* For master's, minimum undergraduate GPA of 3.0, 3 years of work experience. Additional exam requirements/recommendations for international students: Required—TOEFL (minimum score 550 paper-based; 213 computer-based; 79 iBT). Electronic applications accepted.

University of Phoenix–South Florida Campus, John Sperling School of Business, College of Graduate Business and Management, Fort Lauderdale, FL 33309. Offers accounting (MBA); business administration (MBA); global management (MBA); human resource management (MBA); human resources management (MM); management (MM); marketing (MBA); public administration (MBA, MM). Evening/weekend programs available. *Degree requirements:* For master's, thesis (for some programs). *Entrance requirements:* For master's, minimum undergraduate GPA of 3.0, 3 years work experience. Additional exam requirements/recommendations for international students: Required—TOEFL (minimum score 550 paper-based; 213 computer-based; 79 iBT). Electronic applications accepted.

University of Phoenix–South Florida Campus, John Sperling School of Business, College of Information Systems and Technology, Fort Lauderdale, FL 33309. Offers management (MIS); technology management (MBA). Evening/weekend programs available. *Degree requirements:* For master's, thesis (for some programs). *Entrance requirements:* For master's, minimum undergraduate GPA of 3.0, 3 years of work experience. Additional exam requirements/recommendations for international students: Required—TOEFL (minimum score 550 paper-based; 213 computer-based; 79 iBT). Electronic applications accepted.

University of Phoenix–Springfield Campus, College of Graduate Business and Management, Springfield, MO 65804-7211. Offers accounting (MBA); business administration (MBA); global management (MBA); human resources management (MBA, MM); management (MM); marketing (MBA); public administration (MBA, MM).

University of Phoenix–Tulsa Campus, John Sperling School of Business, College of Graduate Business and Management, Tulsa, OK 74134-1412. Offers accounting (MBA); business (MM); business administration (MBA); global management (MBA); human resources management (MBA); marketing (MBA). Evening/weekend programs available. *Degree requirements:* For master's, thesis (for some programs). *Entrance requirements:* For master's, minimum undergraduate GPA of 3.0, 3 years work experience. Additional exam requirements/recommendations for international students: Required—TOEFL (minimum score 550 paper-based; 213 computer-based; 79 iBT).

University of Phoenix–Utah Campus, John Sperling School of Business, College of Graduate Business and Management, Salt Lake City, UT 84123-4617. Offers accounting (MBA); business administration (MBA); global management (MBA); human resource management (MBA, MM); management (MM); marketing (MBA); technology management (MBA). Evening/weekend programs available. *Degree requirements:* For master's, thesis (for some programs). *Entrance requirements:* For master's, minimum undergraduate GPA of 3.0, 3 years of work experience. Additional exam requirements/recommendations for international students: Required—TOEFL (minimum score 550 paper-based; 213 computer-based; 79 iBT). Electronic applications accepted.

University of Phoenix–Vancouver Campus, John Sperling School of Business, College of Graduate Business and Management, Burnaby, BC V5C 6G9, Canada. Offers accounting (MBA); business administration (MBA); global management (MBA); human resources management (MBA, MM); marketing (MBA). Evening/weekend programs available. *Degree requirements:* For master's, thesis (for some programs). *Entrance requirements:* For master's, minimum undergraduate GPA of 3.0, 3 years of work experience. Additional exam requirements/recommendations for international students: Required—TOEFL (minimum score 550 paper-based; 213 computer-based; 79 iBT). Electronic applications accepted.

University of Phoenix–Western Washington Campus, College of Graduate Business and Management, Tukwila, WA 98188. Offers accounting (MBA); business and management (MBA, MM); global management (MBA); human resources management (MBA, MM); marketing (MBA); public administration (MBA, MM). Evening/weekend programs available. *Degree requirements:* For master's, thesis (for some programs). *Entrance requirements:* For master's, minimum undergraduate GPA of 3.0, 3 years of work experience. Additional exam requirements/recommendations for international students: Required—TOEFL (minimum score 550 paper-based; 213 computer-based; 79 iBT). Electronic applications accepted.

University of Phoenix–West Florida Campus, The John Sperling School of Business, College of Graduate Business and Management, Temple Terrace, FL 33637. Offers accounting (MBA); business administration (MBA); global management (MBA); human resources management (MBA, MM); management (MM); marketing (MBA); public administration (MBA, MM). Evening/weekend programs available. *Degree requirements:* For master's, thesis (for some programs). *Entrance requirements:* For master's, 3 years of work experience, minimum undergraduate GPA of 3.0. Additional exam requirements/recommendations for international students: Required—TOEFL (minimum score 550 paper-based; 213 computer-based; 79 iBT). Electronic applications accepted.

University of Phoenix–Wichita Campus, John Sperling School of Business, College of Graduate Business and Management, Wichita, KS 67226-4011. Offers MBA. Evening/weekend programs available. *Degree requirements:* For master's, thesis (for some programs). *Entrance requirements:* For master's, minimum undergraduate GPA of 3.0, 3 years of work experience. Additional exam requirements/recommendations for international students: Required—TOEFL (minimum score 550 paper-based; 213 computer-based; 79 iBT). Electronic applications accepted.

University of Pittsburgh, Graduate School of Public and International Affairs, Public Policy and Management Program for Mid-Career Professionals, Pittsburgh, PA 15260. Offers development planning (MPPM); international development (MPPM); international political economy (MPPM); international security studies (MPPM); management of non profit organizations (MPPM); metropolitan management and regional development (MPPM); policy analysis and evaluation (MPPM). Part-time programs available. *Faculty:* 28 full-time (8 women), 56 part-time/adjunct (20 women). *Students:* 3 full-time (0 women), 39 part-time (21 women); includes 2 minority (both African Americans), 1 international. Average age 38. 48 applicants, 75% accepted, 19 enrolled. In 2009, 17 master's awarded. *Degree requirements:* For master's, thesis optional, capstone seminar. *Entrance requirements:* For master's, 2 letters of recommendation, resume, 5 years of supervisory or budgetary experience. Additional exam requirements/recommendations for international students: Required—TOEFL (minimum score 600 paper-based; 250 computer-based; 100 iBT), TWE (minimum score 4); Recommended—IELTS (minimum score 7). *Application deadline:* For fall admission, 6/1 priority date for domestic students, 2/15 for international students; for spring admission, 1/1 priority date for domestic students, 8/1 for international students. Applications are processed on a rolling basis. Application fee: $50. Electronic applications accepted. *Expenses:* Tuition, state resident: full-time $16,402; part-time $665 per credit. Tuition, nonresident: full-time $28,694; part-time $1175 per credit. Required fees: $690; $175 per term. Tuition and fees vary according to program. *Financial support:* In 2009–10, 10 students received support. Institutionally sponsored loans, scholarships/grants, and tuition waivers (partial) available. Support available to part-time students. Financial award application deadline: 2/1. *Faculty research:* Nonprofit management, urban and regional affairs, policy analysis and evaluation, security and intelligence studies, global political economy, nongovernmental organizations, civil society, development planning and environmental sustainability, human security. Total annual research expenditures: $357,117. *Unit head:* Dr. George Dougherty, Director, Executive Education, 412-648-7603, Fax: 412-648-2605, E-mail: gwdjr@pitt.edu. *Application contact:* Michael T. Rizzi, Associate Director of Student Services, 412-648-7640, Fax: 412-648-7641, E-mail: rizzim@pitt.edu.

University of Pittsburgh, Katz Graduate School of Business, Doctoral Program in Business Administration, Pittsburgh, PA 15260. Offers accounting (PhD); finance (PhD); information systems (PhD); marketing (PhD); operations/decision sciences/artificial intelligence (PhD); organizational behavior and human resource management (PhD); strategic planning (PhD). *Accreditation:* AACSB. *Faculty:* 50 full-time (15 women). *Students:* 53 full-time (21 women); includes 8 minority (4 African Americans, 2 Asian Americans or Pacific Islanders, 2 Hispanic Americans), 22 international. 324 applicants, 4% accepted, 12 enrolled. In 2009, 11 doctorates awarded. *Degree requirements:* For doctorate, comprehensive exam, thesis/dissertation. *Entrance requirements:* For doctorate, GMAT or GRE, references, work experience relevant for individual program. Additional exam requirements/recommendations for international students: Required—TOEFL or IELTS. *Application deadline:* For fall admission, 2/1 priority date for domestic and international students. Applications are processed on a rolling basis. Application fee: $50. Electronic applications accepted. *Expenses:* Tuition, state resident: full-time $16,402; part-time $665 per credit. Tuition, nonresident: full-time $28,694; part-time $1175 per credit. Required fees: $690; $175 per term. Tuition and fees vary according to program. *Financial support:* In 2009–10, 36 students received support, including 31 research assistantships with full tuition reimbursements available (averaging $18,450 per year), 5 teaching assistantships with full tuition reimbursements available (averaging $23,511 per year); fellowships, Federal Work-Study, scholarships/grants, health care benefits, and unspecified assistantships also available. Financial award application deadline: 2/1. *Faculty research:* Accounting statements and reporting, incentives and governance; corporate finance, mergers and acquisitions; information systems processes, structures, OR, supply chain, and decision-making; organizational structure, knowledge management, and corporate strategy; consumer behavior and

marketing models. Total annual research expenditures: $362,777. *Unit head:* Dr. John E. Hulland, Director, 412-648-1534, Fax: 412-624-3633, E-mail: jhulland@katz.pitt.edu. *Application contact:* Carrie Woods, Assistant Director, 412-648-1525, Fax: 412-624-3633, E-mail: cawoods@katz.pitt.edu.

University of Pittsburgh, Katz Graduate School of Business, Executive MBA Program, Pittsburgh, PA 15260. Offers MBA. *Accreditation:* AACSB. Evening/weekend programs available. *Faculty:* 58 full-time (12 women), 23 part-time/adjunct (7 women). *Students:* 66 full-time (14 women); includes 3 minority (1 African American, 2 Asian Americans or Pacific Islanders), 39 international. Average age 36. 115 applicants, 66% accepted, 66 enrolled. In 2009, 87 master's awarded. *Entrance requirements:* For master's, GMAT (candidates with less than 10 years experience, GPA less than 3.0, or limited quantitative background), 3 credits of course work in college-level calculus, minimum 5 years management experience. Additional exam requirements/recommendations for international students: Required—TOEFL or IELTS. *Application deadline:* For winter admission, 12/1 priority date for domestic students, 3/1 priority date for international students. Applications are processed on a rolling basis. Application fee: $0. Electronic applications accepted. *Expenses:* Contact institution. *Financial support:* In 2009–10, 20 students received support, including 2 fellowships (averaging $1,000 per year); scholarships/grants, tuition waivers (partial), and unspecified assistantships also available. Financial award application deadline: 12/1. *Faculty research:* Transitional economies, incentives and governance; corporate finance, mergers and acquisitions; global information systems and structures; consumer behavior and marketing models; entrepreneurship and globalization. *Unit head:* Anne M. Nemer, Executive Director for EMBA Worldwide, 412-648-1694, Fax: 412-648-1787, E-mail: annemer@katz.pitt.edu. *Application contact:* Kristen Carothers, Director, Executive MBA, 866-623-3622, Fax: 412-648-1787, E-mail: embaprogram@katz.pitt.edu.

University of Pittsburgh, Katz Graduate School of Business, Masters of Business Administration Programs, Pittsburgh, PA 15260. Offers accounting (MS); finance (MBA); general management (MBA); information systems (MBA, MSIS); marketing (MBA); organizational behavior and human resource management (MBA); organizational leadership (Certificate); six sigma (Certificate); strategy (MBA); technology, innovation and entrepreneurship (Certificate); MBA/JD; MBA/MIB; MBA/MPIA; MBA/MSE; MBA/MSIS. *Accreditation:* AACSB. Part-time and evening/weekend programs available. *Faculty:* 58 full-time (12 women), 23 part-time/adjunct (7 women). *Students:* 192 full-time (62 women), 506 part-time (179 women); includes 58 minority (29 African Americans, 1 American Indian/Alaska Native, 24 Asian Americans or Pacific Islanders, 4 Hispanic Americans), 101 international. Average age 29. 674 applicants, 52% accepted, 204 enrolled. In 2009, 263 master's awarded. *Entrance requirements:* For master's, GMAT, references, work experience relevant for individual programs. Additional exam requirements/recommendations for international students: Required—TOEFL (minimum score 600 paper-based; 250 computer-based; 100 iBT), or IELTS. *Application deadline:* For fall admission, 7/1 for domestic and international students; for winter admission, 11/1 for domestic and international students; for spring admission, 3/1 for domestic and international students. Applications are processed on a rolling basis. Application fee: $50. Electronic applications accepted. *Expenses:* Tuition, state resident: full-time $16,402; part-time $665 per credit. Tuition, nonresident: full-time $28,694; part-time $1175 per credit. Required fees: $690; $175 per term. Tuition and fees vary according to program. *Financial support:* In 2009–10, 75 students received support. Career-related internships or fieldwork and scholarships/grants available. Financial award application deadline: 6/1; financial award applicants required to submit FAFSA. *Faculty research:* Accounting statements and reporting, incentives and governance; corporate finance, mergers and acquisitions; information systems processes, structures, and decision-making; organizational structure, knowledge management, and corporate strategy; consumer behavior and marketing models. *Unit head:* William T. Valenta, Assistant Dean/MBA Program Director, 412-648-1610, Fax: 412-648-1659, E-mail: wtvalenta@katz.pitt.edu. *Application contact:* Cliff McCormick, Director of MBA Admissions, 412-648-1700, Fax: 412-648-1659, E-mail: mba@katz.pitt.edu.

University of Pittsburgh, Katz Graduate School of Business, MBA/Juris Doctor Dual Degree Program, Pittsburgh, PA 15260. Offers MBA/JD. *Students:* 22 full-time (4 women); includes 4 minority (1 African American, 2 Asian Americans or Pacific Islanders, 1 Hispanic American). Average age 26. 16 applicants, 100% accepted, 13 enrolled. *Entrance requirements:* Additional exam requirements/recommendations for international students: Required—TOEFL (minimum score 600 paper-based; 250 computer-based; 100 iBT), or IELTS. *Application deadline:* For fall admission, 2/1 for international students; for spring admission, 4/1 for domestic students. Application fee: $50. Electronic applications accepted. *Expenses:* Tuition, state resident: full-time $16,402; part-time $665 per credit. Tuition, nonresident: full-time $28,694; part-time $1175 per credit. Required fees: $690; $175 per term. Tuition and fees vary according to program. *Financial support:* In 2009–10, 8 students received support. Scholarships/grants available. Financial award application deadline: 6/1; financial award applicants required to submit FAFSA. *Faculty research:* Accounting statements and reporting, incentives and governance; corporate finance, mergers and acquisitions; information systems processes, structures, and decision-making; organizational structure, knowledge management, and corporate strategy; consumer behavior and marketing models. *Unit head:* William T. Valenta, Assistant Dean/Director of MBA Programs, 412-648-1610, Fax: 412-648-1659, E-mail: wtvalenta@katz.pitt.edu. *Application contact:* Cliff McCormick, Director of MBA Admissions, 412-648-1700, Fax: 412-648-1659, E-mail: mba@katz.pitt.edu.

University of Pittsburgh, Katz Graduate School of Business, MBA/Master of Public and International Affairs Dual-Degree Program, Pittsburgh, PA 15260. Offers MBA/MPIA. Part-time and evening/weekend programs available. *Students:* 22 applicants, 59% accepted, 7 enrolled. *Entrance requirements:* Additional exam requirements/recommendations for international students: Required—TOEFL (minimum score 600 paper-based; 250 computer-based; 100 iBT), or IELTS. *Application deadline:* For fall admission, 7/1 for domestic and international students; for winter admission, 11/1 for domestic and international students; for spring admission, 3/1 for domestic and international students. Applications are processed on a rolling basis. Application fee: $50. Electronic applications accepted. *Expenses:* Tuition, state resident: full-time $16,402; part-time $665 per credit. Tuition, nonresident: full-time $28,694; part-time $1175 per credit. Required fees: $690; $175 per term. Tuition and fees vary according to program. *Financial support:* In 2009–10, 3 students received support. Career-related internships or fieldwork, institutionally sponsored loans, and scholarships/grants available. Financial award application deadline: 6/1; financial award applicants required to submit FAFSA. *Unit head:* William T. Valenta, Assistant Dean/Director of MBA Programs, 412-648-1610, Fax: 412-648-1659, E-mail: wtvalenta@katz.pitt.edu. *Application contact:* Cliff McCormick, Director of MBA Admissions, 412-648-1700, Fax: 412-648-1659, E-mail: mba@katz.pitt.edu.

University of Pittsburgh, Katz Graduate School of Business, MBA/Master of Science in Engineering Dual-Degree Program, Pittsburgh, PA 15260. Offers MBA/MSE. Part-time and evening/weekend programs available. *Students:* 9 full-time (2 women), 20 part-time (2 women); includes 4 minority (all Hispanic Americans). Average age 26. 26 applicants, 81% accepted, 13 enrolled. *Entrance requirements:* Additional exam requirements/recommendations for international students: Required—TOEFL (minimum score 600 paper-based; 250 computer-based; 100 iBT), or IELTS. *Application deadline:* For fall admission, 7/1 for domestic and international students; for winter admission, 11/1 for domestic and international students; for spring admission, 3/1 for domestic and international students. Applications are processed on a rolling basis. Application fee: $50. Electronic applications accepted. *Expenses:* Tuition, state resident: full-time $16,402; part-time $665 per credit. Tuition, nonresident: full-time $28,694; part-time $1175 per credit. Required fees: $690; $175 per term. Tuition and fees vary according to program. *Financial support:* In 2009–10, 4 students received support. Career-related internships or fieldwork and scholarships/grants available. Financial award application deadline: 6/1; financial award applicants required to submit FAFSA. *Faculty research:* Diffusion of technology-driven innovation, customer-focused development of engineered and high-tech products and services, logistics and operations research, global supply chains, value innovation and sustainable innovation—green products for the planet's population. *Unit head:* William T. Valenta, Assistant Dean/Director of MBA Programs, 412-648-1610, Fax: 412-648-1659, E-mail: wtvalenta@katz.pitt.edu. *Application contact:* Cliff McCormick, Director of MBA Admissions, 412-648-1700, Fax: 412-648-1659, E-mail: mba@katz.pitt.edu.

University of Portland, Dr. Robert B. Pamplin, Jr. School of Business, Portland, OR 97203-5798. Offers MBA. *Accreditation:* AACSB. Part-time and evening/weekend programs available. *Faculty:* 24 full-time (5 women). *Students:* 60 full-time (29 women), 68 part-time (26 women); includes 18 minority (2 African Americans, 11 Asian Americans or Pacific Islanders, 5 Hispanic Americans), 26 international. Average age 30. In 2009, 59 master's awarded. *Entrance requirements:* For master's, GMAT, minimum GPA of 3.0, resume, 2 letters of recommendation. Additional exam requirements/recommendations for international students: Required—TOEFL (minimum score 570 paper-based; 89 iBT), IELTS (minimum score 7). *Application deadline:* For fall admission, 7/15 priority date for domestic and international students; for spring admission, 12/15 priority date for domestic and international students. Applications are processed on a rolling basis. Application fee: $50. *Expenses:* Contact institution. *Financial support:* Federal Work-Study, scholarships/grants, and tuition waivers (partial) available. Support available to part-time students. Financial award application deadline: 3/1; financial award applicants required to submit FAFSA. *Unit head:* Dr. Howard Feldman, Associate Dean, 503-943-7224, E-mail: feldman@up.edu. *Application contact:* Melissa McCarthy, Academic Specialist, 503-943-7225, E-mail: mccarthy@up.edu.

University of Puerto Rico, Mayagüez Campus, Graduate Studies, College of Business Administration, Mayagüez, PR 00681-9000. Offers business administration (MBA); finance (MBA); human resources (MBA); industrial management (MBA). Part-time and evening/weekend programs available. *Degree requirements:* For master's, comprehensive exam. *Entrance requirements:* For master's, GMAT or EXADEP, bachelor's degree with courses in calculus, microeconomics, accounting and statistics. Additional exam requirements/recommendations for international students: Required—TOEFL (minimum score 500 paper-based; 173 computer-based). *Faculty research:* Organizational studies, management, accounting.

University of Puerto Rico, Río Piedras, College of Business Administration, San Juan, PR 00931-3300. Offers accounting (MBA); finance (MBA, PhD); general business (MBA); human resources management (MBA); international trade and business (MBA, PhD); marketing (MBA); operations management (MBA); quantitative methods (MBA). *Accreditation:* ACBSP. Part-time programs available. *Degree requirements:* For master's, comprehensive exam, thesis or alternative, research project. *Entrance requirements:* For master's, GMAT or PAEG, minimum GPA of 3.0, letter of recommendation; for doctorate, GMAT, PAEG, minimum GPA of 3.0, master degree. *Faculty research:* Management.

University of Redlands, School of Business, Redlands, CA 92373-0999. Offers business (MBA); information technology (MS); management (MA). Evening/weekend programs available. *Entrance requirements:* For master's, minimum GPA of 3.0, 2 letters of recommendation. *Expenses:* Tuition: Part-time $766 per unit. Required fees: $74 per semester. Part-time tuition and fees vary according to program. *Faculty research:* Human resources management, educational leadership, humanities, teacher education.

University of Regina, Faculty of Graduate Studies and Research, Kenneth Levene Graduate School of Business, Regina, SK S4S 0A2, Canada. Offers MBA, MHRM, Master's Certificate. Part-time and evening/weekend programs available. *Faculty:* 25 full-time (5 women), 3 part-time/adjunct (0 women). *Students:* 77 full-time (25 women), 56 part-time (35 women). 145 applicants, 86% accepted. In 2009, 49 master's awarded. *Entrance requirements:* Additional exam requirements/recommendations for international students: Required—TOEFL (minimum score 580 paper-based; 287 computer-based; 80 iBT). *Application deadline:* Applications are processed on a rolling basis. Application fee: $90 ($100 for international students). Electronic applications accepted. *Expenses:* Contact institution. *Financial support:* In 2009–10, 9 fellowships (averaging $19,000 per year), 2 research assistantships (averaging $16,910 per year), 6 teaching assistantships (averaging $6,650 per year) were awarded; scholarships/grants also available. Financial award application deadline: 6/15. *Faculty research:* Management of public and private sector organizations. *Unit head:* Dr. Ann Lavack, Associate Dean, 306-585-4716, Fax: 306-585-4805, E-mail: ann.lavack@uregina.ca. *Application contact:* Information Contact.

University of Rhode Island, Graduate School, College of Business Administration, Kingston, RI 02881. Offers accounting (MS); business administration (MBA, PhD), including finance and insurance (PhD), management (PhD), marketing (PhD), operations and supply chain management (MBA); finance (MBA); general business (MBA); management (MBA); marketing (MBA); supply chain management (MBA). *Accreditation:* AACSB. Part-time and evening/weekend programs available. *Faculty:* 54 full-time (15 women), 2 part-time/adjunct (1 woman). *Students:* 71 full-time (27 women), 157 part-time (56 women); includes 24 minority (6 African Americans, 10 Asian Americans or Pacific Islanders, 8 Hispanic Americans), 23 international. In 2009, 86 master's, 3 doctorates awarded. *Degree requirements:* For master's, comprehensive exam (for some programs), thesis optional; for doctorate, comprehensive exam, thesis/dissertation. *Entrance requirements:* For master's, GMAT or GRE, 2 letters of recommendation, resume; for doctorate, GMAT or GRE, 3 letters of recommendation, resume. Additional exam requirements/recommendations for international students: Required—TOEFL (minimum score 575 paper-based; 233 computer-based; 91 iBT). Application fee: $65. Electronic applications accepted. *Expenses:* Tuition, state resident: full-time $8828; part-time $490 per credit hour. Tuition, nonresident: full-time $22,100; part-time $1228 per credit hour. Required fees: $1118; $57 per semester. Tuition and fees vary according to program. *Financial support:* In 2009–10, 13 teaching assistantships with full and partial tuition reimbursements (averaging $13,095 per year) were awarded. Financial award applicants required to submit FAFSA. Total annual research expenditures: $245,746. *Unit head:* Dr. Mark Higgins, Dean, 401-874-4244, Fax: 401-874-4312, E-mail: markhiggins@uri.edu. *Application contact:* Lisa Lancellotta, Coordinator, MBA Programs, 401-874-4241, Fax: 401-874-4312, E-mail: mba@uri.edu.

University of Richmond, Robins School of Business, Richmond, University of Richmond, VA 23173. Offers MBA, JD/MBA. *Accreditation:* AACSB. Part-time and evening/weekend programs available. *Faculty:* 28 full-time (7 women), 5 part-time/adjunct (1 woman). *Students:* 21 full-time (5 women), 89 part-time (27 women); includes 13 minority (5 African Americans, 6 Asian Americans or Pacific Islanders, 2 Hispanic Americans), 6 international. Average age 28. 79 applicants, 73% accepted, 42 enrolled. In 2009, 52 master's awarded. *Degree requirements:* For master's, capstone project. *Entrance requirements:* For master's, GMAT, 2 years of work experience. Additional exam requirements/recommendations for international students: Required—TOEFL (minimum score 600 paper-based; 250 computer-based; 100 iBT). *Application deadline:* For fall admission, 5/1 for domestic and international students. Application fee: $50. Electronic applications accepted. *Financial support:* In 2009–10, 75 students received support, including 8 research assistantships with full tuition reimbursements available (averaging $35,000 per year); unspecified assistantships also available. Support available to part-time students. Financial award applicants required to submit FAFSA. *Faculty research:* Entrepreneurship, investments, auditing, consumer behavior, strategic management. *Unit head:* Dr. Nancy Bagranoff, Dean, 804-289-8550, Fax: 804-287-6544. *Application contact:* Dr. Richard S. Coughlan, Senior Associate Dean, 804-289-8553, Fax: 804-287-1228, E-mail: rcoughla@richmond.edu.

University of Rochester, William E. Simon Graduate School of Business Administration, Doctoral Program in Business Administration, Rochester, NY 14627. Offers PhD. *Accreditation:* AACSB. *Degree requirements:* For doctorate, comprehensive exam, thesis/dissertation, qualifying exam. *Entrance requirements:* For doctorate, GMAT or GRE, previous course work in calculus. Additional exam requirements/recommendations for international students: Required—TOEFL. *Expenses:* Contact institution.

University of Rochester, William E. Simon Graduate School of Business Administration, Master's Program in Business Administration, Rochester, NY 14627. Offers MBA, MS. *Accreditation:* AACSB. Part-time and evening/weekend programs available. *Entrance requirements:* For master's, GMAT, previous course work in calculus. Additional exam requirements/recommendations for international students: Required—TOEFL.

Business Administration and Management—General

University of St. Francis, College of Business and Health Administration, School of Business, Joliet, IL 60435-6169. Offers MBA, MSM. Part-time and evening/weekend programs available. Postbaccalaureate distance learning degree programs offered (no on-campus study). *Faculty:* 8 full-time (3 women), 9 part-time/adjunct (3 women). *Students:* 38 full-time (20 women), 124 part-time (76 women); includes 27 minority (16 African Americans, 3 Asian Americans or Pacific Islanders, 8 Hispanic Americans). Average age 37. 110 applicants, 76% accepted, 53 enrolled. In 2009, 54 master's awarded. *Entrance requirements:* Additional exam requirements/recommendations for international students: Required—TOEFL (minimum score 213 computer-based). *Application deadline:* Applications are processed on a rolling basis. Application fee: $30. Electronic applications accepted. *Expenses:* Tuition: Part-time $589 per credit hour. Tuition and fees vary according to degree level, campus/location and program. *Financial support:* In 2009–10, 113 students received support. Scholarships/grants, tuition waivers (partial), and unspecified assistantships available. Support available to part-time students. Financial award applicants required to submit FAFSA. *Unit head:* Dr. Michael LaRocco. *Application contact:* Sandra Sloka, Director of Admissions for Graduate and Degree Completion Programs, 800-735-7500, Fax: 815-740-5032, E-mail: ssloka@stfrancis.edu.

University of Saint Francis, Graduate School, Department of Business Administration, Fort Wayne, IN 46808-3994. Offers MBA. Part-time and evening/weekend programs available. *Entrance requirements:* For master's, GMAT, minimum AACSB index of 900, minimum GPA of 2.5.

University of Saint Mary, Graduate Programs, Program in Business Administration, Leavenworth, KS 66048-5082. Offers MBA. Part-time and evening/weekend programs available. *Degree requirements:* For master's, thesis. *Entrance requirements:* For master's, minimum undergraduate GPA of 2.75.

University of Saint Mary, Graduate Programs, Program in Management, Leavenworth, KS 66048-5082. Offers MS. Part-time and evening/weekend programs available. *Degree requirements:* For master's, thesis, oral or written exam. *Entrance requirements:* For master's, minimum undergraduate GPA of 2.75.

University of St. Thomas, Cameron School of Business, Houston, TX 77006-4696. Offers MBA, MSA. *Accreditation:* ACBSP. Part-time and evening/weekend programs available. *Faculty:* 22 full-time (7 women), 5 part-time/adjunct (1 woman). *Students:* 128 full-time (52 women), 263 part-time (133 women); includes 143 minority (41 African Americans, 1 American Indian/Alaska Native, 30 Asian Americans or Pacific Islanders, 71 Hispanic Americans), 77 international. Average age 31. 146 applicants, 97% accepted, 100 enrolled. In 2009, 229 master's awarded. *Entrance requirements:* For master's, GMAT, minimum GPA of 2.5. Additional exam requirements/recommendations for international students: Required—TOEFL (minimum score 550 paper-based; 213 computer-based). *Application deadline:* Applications are processed on a rolling basis. Application fee: $35. Electronic applications accepted. *Expenses:* Tuition: Full-time $14,436; part-time $802 per credit hour. Required fees: $224. *Financial support:* In 2009–10, 23 students received support. Federal Work-Study, scholarships/grants, and unspecified assistantships available. Support available to part-time students. Financial award application deadline: 3/1; financial award applicants required to submit FAFSA. *Faculty research:* Monetary and accounting theory, portfolio diversification and international finance, leadership and teamwork, business ethics and corporate governance, consumer behavior. *Unit head:* Dr. Bahman Mirshab, Dean, 713-525-2100, Fax: 713-525-2110, E-mail: mirshab@stthom.edu. *Application contact:* Sandra Flanagan, Enrollment Coordinator, 713-525-2115, Fax: 713-525-2110, E-mail: flanags@stthom.edu.

University of St. Thomas, Graduate Studies, Opus College of Business, Evening UST MBA Program, Minneapolis, MN 55403. Offers MBA. Part-time and evening/weekend programs available. *Students:* 1,139 part-time (454 women); includes 93 minority (21 African Americans, 3 American Indian/Alaska Native, 52 Asian Americans or Pacific Islanders, 17 Hispanic Americans), 28 international. Average age 32. 222 applicants, 95% accepted, 156 enrolled. In 2009, 358 master's awarded. *Entrance requirements:* For master's, GMAT. Additional exam requirements/recommendations for international students: Required—TOEFL, IELTS or Michigan English Language Assessment Battery. *Application deadline:* For fall admission, 6/1 priority date for domestic students; for spring admission, 11/1 priority date for domestic students. Applications are processed on a rolling basis. Application fee: $60. Electronic applications accepted. *Financial support:* In 2009–10, 12 students received support. Institutionally sponsored loans and scholarships/grants available. Financial award application deadline: 6/1; financial award applicants required to submit FAFSA. *Unit head:* Corey Eakins, Program Director, 651-962-4200, Fax: 651-962-4129, E-mail: eveningmba@stthomas.edu. *Application contact:* Corey Eakins, Program Director, 651-962-4200, Fax: 651-962-4129, E-mail: eveningmba@stthomas.edu.

University of St. Thomas, Graduate Studies, Opus College of Business, Executive UST MBA Program, Minneapolis, MN 55403. Offers MBA. Part-time and evening/weekend programs available. *Students:* 56 part-time (25 women); includes 5 minority (3 African Americans, 1 American Indian/Alaska Native, 1 Hispanic American). Average age 41. 33 applicants, 91% accepted, 24 enrolled. In 2009, 30 master's awarded. *Entrance requirements:* For master's, five years of significant management or leadership experience. *Application deadline:* For fall admission, 10/8 for domestic students, 4/15 for international students. Applications are processed on a rolling basis. Application fee: $100. Electronic applications accepted. *Expenses:* Contact institution. *Financial support:* Institutionally sponsored loans and scholarships/grants available. Financial award application deadline: 7/1; financial award applicants required to submit FAFSA. *Unit head:* Dr. Jack Militello, Director, 651-962-4230, Fax: 651-962-4235, E-mail: execmba@stthomas.edu. *Application contact:* Jean Trudeau, Manager, 651-962-4230, Fax: 651-962-4235, E-mail: execmba@stthomas.edu.

See Close-Up on page 271.

University of St. Thomas, Graduate Studies, Opus College of Business, Full-time UST MBA Program, Minneapolis, MN 55403. Offers MBA. *Students:* 147 full-time (54 women); includes 16 minority (5 African Americans, 4 Asian Americans or Pacific Islanders, 7 Hispanic Americans), 29 international. Average age 26. 144 applicants, 90% accepted, 77 enrolled. In 2009, 55 master's awarded. *Entrance requirements:* For master's, GMAT. Additional exam requirements/recommendations for international students: Required—TOEFL, IELTS or Michigan English Language Assessment Battery. *Application deadline:* For fall admission, 6/15 for domestic students, 4/15 for international students. Applications are processed on a rolling basis. Application fee: $60. Electronic applications accepted. *Financial support:* In 2009–10, 107 students received support. Scholarships/grants, tuition waivers (full and partial), and unspecified assistantships available. Financial award application deadline: 4/15. *Unit head:* William Woodson, Assistant Dean and Director, 651-962-8800, Fax: 651-962-4129, E-mail: ustmba@stthomas.edu. *Application contact:* Dustin Cornwell, Director of Admissions, 651-962-8800, Fax: 651-962-4129, E-mail: dcornwell@stthomas.edu.

See Close-Up on page 271.

University of San Diego, School of Business Administration, San Diego, CA 92110-2492. Offers accountancy (MS); business administration (MBA); executive leadership (MSEL); global leadership (MSGL); international business administration (IMBA); real estate (MSRE); supply chain management (MS, Certificate); taxation (MS); JD/IMBA; JD/MBA. *Accreditation:* AACSB. Part-time and evening/weekend programs available. *Faculty:* 36 full-time (11 women), 18 part-time/adjunct (4 women). *Students:* 173 full-time (53 women), 259 part-time (91 women); includes 61 minority (9 African Americans, 4 American Indian/Alaska Native, 29 Asian Americans or Pacific Islanders, 19 Hispanic Americans), 32 international. Average age 31. 555 applicants, 61% accepted, 191 enrolled. In 2009, 248 master's awarded. *Degree requirements:* For master's, variable foreign language requirement, community service, capstone project. *Entrance requirements:* For master's, GMAT (MBA, IMBA, MSRE), minimum GPA of 3.0, minimum 2 years of full-time work experience. Additional exam requirements/recommendations for international students: Required—TOEFL (minimum score 580 paper-based; 237 computer-based; 92 iBT), TWE. Application fee: $80. Electronic applications accepted. *Expenses:* Tuition: Full-time $21,042; part-time $1169 per unit. Required fees: $224. Full-time tuition and fees vary according to course load and degree level. *Financial support:* In 2009–10, 312 students received support. Career-related internships or fieldwork, Federal Work-Study, institutionally sponsored loans, scholarships/grants, and unspecified assistantships available. Support available to part-time students. Financial award application deadline: 4/1; financial award applicants required to submit FAFSA. *Faculty research:* Exchange rate forecasting, corporate governance, performance of private equity funds, economic geography, food banking. *Unit head:* Dr. David Pyke, Interim Dean, 619-260-4886, E-mail: sbadean@sandiego.edu. *Application contact:* Dr. John Mosby, Associate Director of Graduate Admissions, 619-260-4524, Fax: 619-260-4158, E-mail: grads@sandiego.edu.

University of San Francisco, School of Business and Professional Studies, Masagung Graduate School of Management, MBA for Executives Program, San Francisco, CA 94117-1080. Offers MBA. *Accreditation:* AACSB. *Faculty:* 10 full-time (3 women), 4 part-time/adjunct (2 women). *Students:* 66 full-time (20 women); includes 21 minority (2 African Americans, 3 American Indian/Alaska Native, 11 Asian Americans or Pacific Islanders, 5 Hispanic Americans), 1 international. Average age 38. 29 applicants, 90% accepted, 20 enrolled. In 2009, 29 master's awarded. Application fee: $50. *Expenses:* Contact institution. *Financial support:* In 2009–10, 38 students received support. Applicants required to submit FAFSA. *Unit head:* Dr. Karl Boedecker, Director, 415-422-2511, Fax: 415-422-6315. *Application contact:* Kelly Tarry, Secretary, 415-422-2525, E-mail: mbae@usfca.edu.

University of San Francisco, School of Business and Professional Studies, Masagung Graduate School of Management, Program in Business Administration, San Francisco, CA 94117-1080. Offers business economics (MBA); e-business (MBA); entrepreneurship (MBA); finance (MBA); international business (MBA); management (MBA); marketing (MBA); telecommunications management and policy (MBA); JD/MBA; MSN/MBA. *Accreditation:* AACSB. *Faculty:* 17 full-time (4 women), 16 part-time/adjunct (7 women). *Students:* 278 full-time (140 women), 18 part-time (10 women); includes 94 minority (5 African Americans, 1 American Indian/Alaska Native, 69 Asian Americans or Pacific Islanders, 19 Hispanic Americans), 53 international. Average age 30. 410 applicants, 70% accepted, 133 enrolled. In 2009, 137 master's awarded. *Entrance requirements:* For master's, GMAT, minimum undergraduate GPA of 3.2. Additional exam requirements/recommendations for international students: Required—TOEFL. *Application deadline:* For fall admission, 7/1 priority date for domestic students; for spring admission, 11/30 for domestic students. Applications are processed on a rolling basis. Application fee: $55 ($65 for international students). *Expenses:* Tuition: Full-time $19,710; part-time $1095 per unit. Part-time tuition and fees vary according to degree level, campus/location and program. *Financial support:* In 2009–10, 155 students received support; fellowships available. Financial award application deadline: 3/2; financial award applicants required to submit FAFSA. *Faculty research:* International financial markets, technology transfer licensing, international marketing, strategic planning. Total annual research expenditures: $50,000. *Unit head:* Kelly Brookes, Director, 415-422-2221, Fax: 415-422-6315. *Application contact:* Director, MBA Program, 415-422-2221, Fax: 415-422-6315, E-mail: mba@usfca.edu.

University of Saskatchewan, College of Graduate Studies and Research, Edwards School of Business, Saskatoon, SK S7N 5A2, Canada. Offers M Sc, MBA, MP Acc. Part-time programs available. *Degree requirements:* For master's, thesis (for some programs). *Entrance requirements:* For master's, GMAT. Additional exam requirements/recommendations for international students: Required—TOEFL. Tuition and fees charges are reported in Canadian dollars. *Expenses:* Tuition, area resident: Full-time $3000 Canadian dollars; part-time $500 Canadian dollars per term. Required fees: $700 Canadian dollars; $100 Canadian dollars per term.

The University of Scranton, College of Graduate and Continuing Education, Program in Business Administration, Scranton, PA 18510. Offers accounting (MBA); finance (MBA); general business administration (MBA); health care management (MBA); international business (MBA); management information systems (MBA); marketing (MBA); operations management (MBA). *Accreditation:* AACSB. Part-time and evening/weekend programs available. Postbaccalaureate distance learning degree programs offered (no on-campus study). *Faculty:* 34 full-time (8 women). *Students:* 92 full-time (38 women), 137 part-time (58 women); includes 27 minority (15 African Americans, 5 Asian Americans or Pacific Islanders, 7 Hispanic Americans), 21 international. Average age 31. 255 applicants, 79% accepted. In 2009, 33 master's awarded. *Degree requirements:* For master's, capstone experience. *Entrance requirements:* For master's, GMAT, minimum GPA of 2.75. Additional exam requirements/recommendations for international students: Required—TOEFL (minimum score 500 paper-based; 173 computer-based), IELTS (minimum score 5.5). *Application deadline:* Applications are processed on a rolling basis. Application fee: $0. *Financial support:* In 2009–10, 10 students received support, including 10 teaching assistantships with full and partial tuition reimbursements available (averaging $6,600 per year); fellowships, career-related internships or fieldwork, Federal Work-Study, and unspecified assistantships also available. Support available to part-time students. Financial award application deadline: 3/1. *Faculty research:* Financial markets, strategic impact of total quality management, internal accounting controls, consumer preference, information systems and the Internet. *Unit head:* Dr. Murli Rajan, Director, 570-941-4043, Fax: 570-941-4342. *Application contact:* Joseph M. Roback, Director of Admissions, 570-941-4385, Fax: 570-941-5928, E-mail: robackj2@scranton.edu.

University of Sioux Falls, John T. Vucurevich School of Business, Sioux Falls, SD 57105-1699. Offers MBA. Part-time and evening/weekend programs available. *Degree requirements:* For master's, project. *Entrance requirements:* For master's, minimum GPA of 3.0. Additional exam requirements/recommendations for international students: Required—TOEFL. *Expenses:* Contact institution.

University of South Africa, College of Economic and Management Sciences, Pretoria, South Africa. Offers accounting (D Admin, D Com); accounting science (DA); auditing (D Admin, D Com); business administration (M Tech); business economics (D Admin); business leadership (DBL); business management (D Admin, D Com); economic management analysis (M Tech); economics (D Admin, D Com, PhD); human resource development (M Tech); industrial psychology (D Admin, D Com, PhD); logistics (D Com); marketing (M Tech); public administration (D Admin, D Com, DPA, PhD); public management (M Tech); quantitative management (D Admin, D Com); real estate (M Tech); statistics (D Admin, PhD); tourism management (D Admin, D Com); transport economics (D Admin, D Com).

University of South Africa, Graduate School of Business Leadership, Pretoria, South Africa. Offers MBA, MBL, DBL.

University of South Alabama, Graduate School, Mitchell College of Business, Program in Business Management, Mobile, AL 36688-0002. Offers general management (MBA). *Accreditation:* AACSB. Part-time and evening/weekend programs available. *Degree requirements:* For master's, comprehensive exam. *Entrance requirements:* For master's, GMAT, minimum undergraduate GPA of 3.0. *Expenses:* Tuition, state resident: part-time $218 per contact hour. Required fees: $1102 per year.

University of South Carolina, The Graduate School, Moore School of Business, Columbia, SC 29208. Offers accountancy (M Acc), including business measurement and assurance; business administration (MBA, PhD); economics (MA, PhD); human resources (MHR); international business administration (IMBA); JD/IMBA; JD/M Acc; JD/MA; JD/MHR. *Accreditation:* AACSB. Part-time and evening/weekend programs available. Postbaccalaureate distance learning degree programs offered (minimal on-campus study). *Degree requirements:* For doctorate, one foreign language, thesis/dissertation. *Entrance requirements:* For master's, GMAT, GRE, minimum GPA of 3.0; for doctorate, GMAT or GRE. Additional exam requirements/recommendations for international students: Required—TOEFL (minimum score 600 paper-based; 250 computer-based). Electronic applications accepted. *Expenses:* Contact institution. *Faculty research:* Finance, marketing, strategic management, international management, operations.

The University of South Dakota, Graduate School, Program in Administrative Studies, Vermillion, SD 57069-2390. Offers MS. Part-time and evening/weekend programs available.

Postbaccalaureate distance learning degree programs offered (no on-campus study). *Degree requirements:* For master's, thesis or alternative. *Entrance requirements:* For master's, 3 years of work or experience, minimum GPA of 2.7, resume. Additional exam requirements/recommendations for international students: Required—TOEFL (minimum score 550 paper-based; 213 computer-based; 79 iBT). Electronic applications accepted.

The University of South Dakota, Graduate School, School of Business, Department of Business Administration, Vermillion, SD 57069-2390. Offers MBA, JD/MBA. *Accreditation:* AACSB. Part-time and evening/weekend programs available. Postbaccalaureate distance learning degree programs offered (no on-campus study). *Degree requirements:* For master's, thesis or alternative. *Entrance requirements:* For master's, GMAT, minimum GPA of 2.7, resume. Additional exam requirements/recommendations for international students: Required—TOEFL (minimum score 550 paper-based; 213 computer-based; 79 iBT). Electronic applications accepted. *Expenses:* Contact institution.

University of Southern California, Graduate School, Marshall School of Business, Los Angeles, CA 90089. Offers M Acc, MBA, MBT, MMM, MS, PhD, DDS/MBA, JD/MBT, MBA/Ed D, MBA/M Pl, MBA/MD, MBA/MRED, MBA/MS, MBA/MSW, MBA/Pharm D. *Accreditation:* AACSB. *Faculty:* 214 full-time (57 women), 14 part-time/adjunct (0 women). *Students:* 1,405 full-time (413 women), 568 part-time (174 women); includes 785 minority (39 African Americans, 4 American Indian/Alaska Native, 637 Asian Americans or Pacific Islanders, 105 Hispanic Americans), 349 international. 3,631 applicants, 42% accepted, 947 enrolled. In 2009, 911 master's, 11 doctorates awarded. *Degree requirements:* For doctorate, thesis/dissertation. *Entrance requirements:* For master's, GMAT and/or CPA Exam; for doctorate, GMAT or GRE. Additional exam requirements/recommendations for international students: Required—TOEFL. Electronic applications accepted. *Expenses:* Tuition: Full-time $25,980; part-time $1315 per unit. Required fees: $554. One-time fee: $35 full-time. Full-time tuition and fees vary according to degree level and program. *Financial support:* Fellowships, research assistantships, teaching assistantships, institutionally sponsored loans and scholarships/grants available. *Unit head:* James Ellis, Dean, 213-740-6422, E-mail: dean@marshall.usc.edu. *Application contact:* James Ellis, Dean, 213-740-6422, E-mail: dean@marshall.usc.edu.

University of Southern Indiana, Graduate Studies, College of Business, Program in Business Administration, Evansville, IN 47712-3590. Offers MBA. *Accreditation:* AACSB. Part-time and evening/weekend programs available. *Faculty:* 16 full-time (3 women), 1 part-time/adjunct (0 women). *Students:* 12 full-time (3 women), 89 part-time (31 women); includes 1 minority (African American), 11 international. Average age 31. 33 applicants, 91% accepted, 25 enrolled. In 2009, 38 master's awarded. *Entrance requirements:* For master's, GMAT, minimum GPA of 2.5, resume. Additional exam requirements/recommendations for international students: Required—TOEFL (minimum score 550 paper-based; 213 computer-based; 79 iBT), IELTS (minimum score 6). *Application deadline:* For fall admission, 8/15 for domestic students, 3/1 priority date for international students. Applications are processed on a rolling basis. Application fee: $25. Electronic applications accepted. *Expenses:* Tuition, state resident: full-time $4592; part-time $255 per credit hour. Tuition, nonresident: full-time $9060; part-time $503 per credit hour. Required fees: $220; $22.75 per term. Tuition and fees vary according to course load and reciprocity agreements. *Financial support:* In 2009–10, 23 students received support. Federal Work-Study, scholarships/grants, tuition waivers (full and partial), and unspecified assistantships available. Financial award application deadline: 3/1; financial award applicants required to submit FAFSA. *Unit head:* Dr. Brian L. McGuire, Program Director, 812-465-7031, E-mail: bmcguire@usi.edu. *Application contact:* Information Contact, 812-464-1803.

University of Southern Maine, Lewiston-Auburn College, Program in Leadership Studies, Portland, ME 04104-9300. Offers MLS. Part-time programs available. Postbaccalaureate distance learning degree programs offered (minimal on-campus study). *Faculty:* 5 full-time (4 women), 7 part-time/adjunct (4 women). *Students:* 6 applicants, 83% accepted, 5 enrolled. In 2009, 6 master's awarded. *Application deadline:* Applications are processed on a rolling basis. Application fee: $65. *Financial support:* Federal Work-Study available. *Unit head:* Dr. Tara C. Coste, Director, 207-753-6596, Fax: 207-753-6555, E-mail: tcoste@usm.maine.edu. *Application contact:* Luisa Scott, Assistant Director, Office of Graduate Studies, 207-753-6523, Fax: 207-753-6555, E-mail: gradprograms@usm.maine.edu.

University of Southern Maine, School of Business, Portland, ME 04104-9300. Offers business administration (MBA); finance (MBA); taxation (MBA); JD/MBA; MBA/MSA; MBA/MSN; MS/MBA. *Accreditation:* AACSB. Part-time and evening/weekend programs available. *Faculty:* 20 full-time (5 women), 2 part-time/adjunct (1 woman). *Students:* 33 full-time (19 women), 102 part-time (42 women); includes 6 minority (2 African Americans, 1 American Indian/Alaska Native, 2 Asian Americans or Pacific Islanders, 1 Hispanic American), 4 international. Average age 32. 53 applicants, 55% accepted, 23 enrolled. In 2009, 45 master's awarded. *Entrance requirements:* For master's, GMAT, minimum AACSB index of 1100. Additional exam requirements/recommendations for international students: Required—TOEFL (minimum score 550 paper-based; 213 computer-based; 79 iBT). *Application deadline:* For fall admission, 8/1 priority date for domestic students, 5/1 priority date for international students; for spring admission, 12/1 priority date for domestic students, 9/1 priority date for international students. Applications are processed on a rolling basis. Application fee: $65. Electronic applications accepted. *Financial support:* In 2009–10, 3 research assistantships with partial tuition reimbursements (averaging $9,000 per year), 3 teaching assistantships with partial tuition reimbursements (averaging $9,000 per year) were awarded; career-related internships or fieldwork, Federal Work-Study, scholarships/grants, tuition waivers (full and partial), and unspecified assistantships also available. Support available to part-time students. Financial award application deadline: 2/15; financial award applicants required to submit FAFSA. *Faculty research:* Economic development, MIS, real options, system dynamics, simulation. *Unit head:* James B. Shaffer, Dean, 207-780-4020, Fax: 207-780-4662, E-mail: jshaffer@usm.maine.edu. *Application contact:* Alice B. Cash, Assistant Dean for Student Affairs, 207-780-4184, Fax: 207-780-4662, E-mail: acash@usm.maine.edu.

University of Southern Mississippi, Graduate School, College of Business, Department of Management and Marketing, Hattiesburg, MS 39406-0001. Offers business administration (MBA). *Accreditation:* AACSB. Part-time and evening/weekend programs available. *Faculty:* 61 full-time (27 women). *Students:* 37 full-time (18 women), 45 part-time (18 women); includes 15 minority (12 African Americans, 2 Asian Americans or Pacific Islanders, 1 Hispanic American), 7 international. Average age 29. 61 applicants, 46% accepted, 23 enrolled. In 2009, 39 master's awarded. *Degree requirements:* For master's, comprehensive exam. *Entrance requirements:* For master's, GMAT. Additional exam requirements/recommendations for international students: Required—TOEFL. *Application deadline:* For fall admission, 7/15 priority date for domestic students, 7/15 for international students; for spring admission, 11/15 priority date for domestic students, 11/15 for international students. Application fee: $35. Electronic applications accepted. *Expenses:* Tuition, state resident: full-time $5096; part-time $284 per hour. Tuition, nonresident: full-time $13,052; part-time $726 per hour. Required fees: $402. Tuition and fees vary according to course level and course load. *Financial support:* In 2009–10, 14 research assistantships with full and partial tuition reimbursements (averaging $6,000 per year), 1 teaching assistantship with full tuition reimbursement (averaging $6,000 per year) were awarded; Federal Work-Study and institutionally sponsored loans also available. Support available to part-time students. Financial award application deadline: 3/15; financial award applicants required to submit FAFSA. *Faculty research:* Inflation accounting, self-esteem training, international trade policy, health care marketing, ethics in strategic planning. *Unit head:* Dr. Barry Babin, Chair, 601-266-4627. *Application contact:* Dr. Francis Daniel, Graduate Coordinator, 601-266-4664, Fax: 601-266-5814.

University of Southern Nevada, MBA Program, Henderson, NV 89014. Offers MBA. Evening/weekend programs available. *Faculty:* 2 full-time (0 women), 16 part-time/adjunct (5 women). *Students:* 6 full-time (2 women), all minorities (3 African Americans, 3 Asian Americans or Pacific Islanders). Average age 33. 6 applicants, 50% accepted, 3 enrolled. In 2009, 3 master's awarded. *Degree requirements:* For master's, comprehensive exam, entrepreneurial project. *Entrance requirements:* Additional exam requirements/recommendations for inter-

national students: Required—TOEFL (minimum score 550 paper-based; 213 computer-based; 79 iBT). *Application deadline:* Applications are processed on a rolling basis. Application fee: $100. *Expenses:* Tuition: Full-time $37,900. Full-time tuition and fees vary according to program. *Financial support:* Scholarships/grants available. Financial award application deadline: 3/2; financial award applicants required to submit FAFSA. *Unit head:* Dr. Okeleke Nzeogwu, Program Director, 702-968-1659, Fax: 702-968-1685, E-mail: onzeogwu@usn.edu. *Application contact:* Dr. Okeleke Nzeogwu, Program Director, 702-968-1659, Fax: 702-968-1685, E-mail: onzeogwu@usn.edu.

University of South Florida, Graduate School, College of Business, Department of Business Administration, Tampa, FL 33620-9951. Offers accounting (PhD); entrepreneurship (MBA); finance (PhD); information systems (PhD); leadership and organizational effectiveness (MSM); management and organization (MBA); marketing (PhD). *Accreditation:* AACSB. Part-time and evening/weekend programs available. *Faculty:* 12 full-time (2 women). *Students:* 152 full-time (51 women), 201 part-time (65 women); includes 70 minority (14 African Americans, 30 Asian Americans or Pacific Islanders, 26 Hispanic Americans), 54 international. Average age 32. 460 applicants, 35% accepted, 93 enrolled. In 2009, 161 master's, 11 doctorates awarded. *Degree requirements:* For master's, comprehensive exam, thesis (for some programs); for doctorate, comprehensive exam, thesis/dissertation, 90 credit hours, minimum GPA of 3.0. *Entrance requirements:* For master's, GMAT, minimum GPA of 3.0 in last 60 hours of course work, 2 years of work experience, resume; for doctorate, GMAT, letters of recommendation, personal statement. Additional exam requirements/recommendations for international students: Required—TOEFL (minimum score 550 paper-based; 213 computer-based; 79 iBT). *Application deadline:* For fall admission, 6/1 for domestic students, 1/2 for international students; for spring admission, 10/15 for domestic students, 6/1 for international students. Application fee: $30. *Financial support:* Fellowships, research assistantships, teaching assistantships, scholarships/grants, health care benefits, and unspecified assistantships available. Financial award applicants required to submit FAFSA. *Unit head:* Irene Hurst, Program Director, 813-974-3335, Fax: 813-974-4518, E-mail: hurst@coba.usf.edu. *Application contact:* Wendy Baker, Assistant Director, Graduate Studies, 813-974-3335, Fax: 813-974-4518, E-mail: wbaker@usf.edu.

University of South Florida, Graduate School, College of Business, Department of Management and Organization, Tampa, FL 33620-9951. Offers management (MS). Part-time programs available. Postbaccalaureate distance learning degree programs offered (minimal on-campus study). *Faculty:* 9 full-time (4 women), 2 part-time/adjunct (1 woman). *Students:* 4 full-time (2 women), 22 part-time (15 women); includes 4 minority (1 African American, 2 Asian Americans or Pacific Islanders, 1 Hispanic American), 4 international. 10 applicants, 10% accepted, 0 enrolled. Terminal master's awarded for partial completion of doctoral program. *Degree requirements:* For master's, comprehensive exam. *Entrance requirements:* For master's, GRE General Test, minimum GPA of 3.0 in last 60 hours of coursework. Additional exam requirements/recommendations for international students: Required—TOEFL (minimum score 550 paper-based; 213 computer-based; 80 iBT). *Application deadline:* For fall admission, 6/1 for domestic students, 1/2 for international students. Application fee: $30. Electronic applications accepted. *Financial support:* Tuition waivers available. Financial award applicants required to submit FAFSA. *Unit head:* Alan Balfour, Program Director, 813-974-1785, E-mail: abalfour@coba.usf.edu. *Application contact:* Alan Balfour, Program Director, 813-974-1785, E-mail: abalfour@coba.usf.edu.

University of South Florida, Graduate School, College of Business, Executive Program in Business Administration, Tampa, FL 33620-9951. Offers MBA. *Accreditation:* AACSB. Evening/weekend programs available. *Students:* 52 full-time (14 women), 21 part-time (12 women); includes 21 minority (5 African Americans, 11 Asian Americans or Pacific Islanders, 5 Hispanic Americans), 8 international. Average age 32. 30 applicants, 90% accepted, 21 enrolled. In 2009, 35 master's awarded. *Degree requirements:* For master's, thesis or alternative. *Entrance requirements:* For master's, minimum 5 years of management/professional experience, minimum GPA of 3.0, interview, letters of recommendation. Additional exam requirements/recommendations for international students: Required—TOEFL (minimum score 550 paper-based; 213 computer-based). *Application deadline:* For fall admission, 5/31 for domestic students, 1/2 for international students. Applications are processed on a rolling basis. Application fee: $30. *Expenses:* Contact institution. *Financial support:* Applicants required to submit FAFSA. *Unit head:* Irene Hurst, Program Director, 813-974-3335, Fax: 813-974-4518, E-mail: ihurst@usf.edu. *Application contact:* Chris Williams, Program Administrator, 813-974-4876, Fax: 813-974-4518, E-mail: cmwilliams@usf.edu.

The University of Tampa, John H. Sykes College of Business, Tampa, FL 33606-1490. Offers accounting (MBA, MS); economics (MBA); entrepreneurship and innovation (MBA); finance (MBA, MS); information systems management (MBA); international business (MBA); management (MBA); marketing (MBA, MS); nonprofit management (MBA). *Accreditation:* AACSB. Part-time and evening/weekend programs available. *Faculty:* 62 full-time (22 women), 11 part-time/adjunct (4 women). *Students:* 240 full-time (101 women), 338 part-time (133 women); includes 95 minority (16 African Americans, 4 American Indian/Alaska Native, 24 Asian Americans or Pacific Islanders, 51 Hispanic Americans), 122 international. Average age 29. 564 applicants, 51% accepted, 186 enrolled. In 2009, 234 master's awarded. *Entrance requirements:* For master's, GMAT. Additional exam requirements/recommendations for international students: Required—TOEFL (minimum score 577 paper-based; 230 computer-based; 90 iBT), IELTS. *Application deadline:* For fall admission, 7/15 for domestic students, 6/1 for international students; for spring admission, 12/15 for domestic students, 11/1 for international students. Applications are processed on a rolling basis. Application fee: $40. Electronic applications accepted. *Expenses:* Tuition: Part-time $488 per credit hour. *Financial support:* In 2009–10, 332 students received support, including 71 research assistantships with full tuition reimbursements available (averaging $6,757 per year); career-related internships or fieldwork, scholarships/grants, and unspecified assistantships also available. Support available to part-time students. Financial award applicants required to submit FAFSA. *Faculty research:* Information systems, leadership, corporate governance, entrepreneurship, hedonic price estimation. *Unit head:* Dr. Don Morrill, Associate Dean, Graduate and Continuing Studies, 813-257-3557, E-mail: dmorrill@ut.edu. *Application contact:* Karen Full, Director of Admissions, Graduate and Continuing Studies, 813-257-3642, E-mail: kfull@ut.edu.

The University of Tennessee, Graduate School, College of Business Administration, Program in Business Administration, Knoxville, TN 37996. Offers accounting (PhD); finance (MBA, PhD); logistics and transportation (MBA, PhD); management (PhD); marketing (MBA, PhD); operations management (MBA); professional business administration (MBA); statistics (PhD); JD/MBA; MS/MBA. *Accreditation:* AACSB. Postbaccalaureate distance learning degree programs offered. *Degree requirements:* For master's, thesis or alternative; for doctorate, thesis/dissertation. *Entrance requirements:* For master's and doctorate, GMAT, minimum GPA of 2.7. Additional exam requirements/recommendations for international students: Required—TOEFL. Electronic applications accepted. *Expenses:* Tuition, state resident: full-time $6826; part-time $380 per semester hour. Tuition, nonresident: full-time $21,844; part-time $1147 per semester hour. Tuition and fees vary according to program.

The University of Tennessee, Graduate School, College of Business Administration, Program in Management Science, Knoxville, TN 37996. Offers MS, PhD. *Accreditation:* AACSB. *Degree requirements:* For master's, thesis or alternative; for doctorate, thesis/dissertation. *Entrance requirements:* For master's and doctorate, GMAT or GRE General Test, minimum GPA of 2.7. Additional exam requirements/recommendations for international students: Required—TOEFL. Electronic applications accepted. *Expenses:* Tuition, state resident: full-time $6826; part-time $380 per semester hour. Tuition, nonresident: full-time $21,844; part-time $1147 per semester hour. Tuition and fees vary according to program.

The University of Tennessee at Chattanooga, Graduate School, College of Business, Program in Business Administration, Chattanooga, TN 37403. Offers EMBA, MBA. *Accreditation:* AACSB. Part-time and evening/weekend programs available. *Faculty:* 9 full-time (3 women), 1 part-time/adjunct (0 women). *Students:* 103 full-time (36 women), 141 part-time (61 women); includes 32 minority (18 African Americans, 5 American Indian/Alaska Native, 5 Asian Americans

Business Administration and Management—General

The University of Tennessee at Chattanooga (continued)

or Pacific Islanders, 4 Hispanic Americans), 6 international. Average age 31. 112 applicants, 85% accepted, 63 enrolled. In 2009, 80 master's awarded. *Entrance requirements:* For master's, GMAT (minimum score 450) or GRE General Test (minimum score 1000). Additional exam requirements/recommendations for international students: Required—TOEFL (minimum score 550 paper-based; 213 computer-based; 79 iBT), IELTS (minimum score 6). *Application deadline:* For fall admission, 8/1 priority date for domestic students, 6/1 for international students; for spring admission, 12/1 priority date for domestic students, 10/1 for international students. Applications are processed on a rolling basis. Application fee: $35. Electronic applications accepted. *Expenses:* Tuition, state resident: full-time $5404; part-time $300 per credit hour. Tuition, nonresident: full-time $16,702; part-time $928 per credit hour. Required fees: $1150; $130 per credit hour. *Financial support:* In 2009–10, 8 research assistantships with full and partial tuition reimbursements (averaging $5,500 per year) were awarded; career-related internships or fieldwork, scholarships/grants, tuition waivers (partial), and unspecified assistantships also available. Support available to part-time students. *Faculty research:* Diversity, operations/production management, entrepreneurial processes, customer satisfaction and retention, branding. *Unit head:* Lawrence Ettkin, Department Head, 423-425-4403, Fax: 423-425-5255, E-mail: lawrence-ettkin@utc.edu. *Application contact:* Dr. Stephanie Bellar, Dean of Graduate Studies, 423-425-4666, Fax: 423-425-5223, E-mail: stephanie-bellar@utc.edu.

The University of Tennessee at Martin, Graduate Programs, College of Business and Global Affairs, Program in Business, Martin, TN 38238-1000. Offers MBA. *Accreditation:* AACSB. Part-time programs available. Postbaccalaureate distance learning degree programs offered (no on-campus study). *Faculty:* 28. *Students:* 52 (20 women). 161,513 applicants, 0% accepted, 15 enrolled. In 2009, 26 master's awarded. *Degree requirements:* For master's, comprehensive exam. *Entrance requirements:* For master's, GMAT, minimum GPA of 2.5, resume. Additional exam requirements/recommendations for international students: Required—TOEFL (minimum score 525 paper-based; 197 computer-based; 71 iBT). *Application deadline:* For fall admission, 8/1 priority date for domestic students, 8/1 for international students; for spring admission, 1/1 priority date for domestic students, 1/1 for international students. Applications are processed on a rolling basis. Application fee: $30 ($50 for international students). Electronic applications accepted. *Expenses:* Tuition, state resident: full-time $6660; part-time $372 per hour. Tuition, nonresident: full-time $18,000; part-time $1005 per hour. *Financial support:* In 2009–10, 11 students received support, including 11 research assistantships with full tuition reimbursements available (averaging $5,674 per year); career-related internships or fieldwork, scholarships/grants, and unspecified assistantships also available. Support available to part-time students. Financial award application deadline: 3/1. *Unit head:* Dr. Kevin Hammond, Coordinator, 731-881-7236, Fax: 731-881-7241, E-mail: bagrad@utm.edu. *Application contact:* Linda Arant, Student Services Specialist, 731-881-7012, Fax: 731-881-7499, E-mail: larant@utm.edu.

The University of Texas at Arlington, Graduate School, College of Business, Program in Business Administration, Arlington, TX 76019. Offers accounting (PhD); business statistics (PhD); finance (MBA, PhD); information systems (MBA, PhD); management (MBA, PhD); management sciences (MBA); marketing (MBA, PhD); operations management (PhD); real estate (MBA). *Accreditation:* AACSB. Part-time and evening/weekend programs available. Postbaccalaureate distance learning degree programs offered (no on-campus study). *Students:* 587 full-time (188 women), 349 part-time (140 women); includes 188 minority (66 African Americans, 62 Asian Americans or Pacific Islanders, 60 Hispanic Americans), 371 international. 282 applicants, 96% accepted, 145 enrolled. In 2009, 431 master's awarded. Terminal master's awarded for partial completion of doctoral program. *Degree requirements:* For master's, thesis optional; for doctorate, comprehensive exam, thesis/dissertation. *Entrance requirements:* For master's, GMAT; for doctorate, GMAT, minimum GPA of 3.0 (undergraduate), 3.4 (graduate); 30 hours of graduate course work. Additional exam requirements/recommendations for international students: Required—TOEFL (minimum score 550 paper-based; 213 computer-based; 79 iBT). *Application deadline:* For fall admission, 6/5 for domestic students, 4/1 for international students; for spring admission, 10/15 for domestic students, 9/1 for international students. Applications are processed on a rolling basis. Application fee: $35 ($50 for international students). Electronic applications accepted. *Financial support:* In 2009–10, 1 fellowship (averaging $1,000 per year), 30 research assistantships (averaging $6,000 per year), 45 teaching assistantships (averaging $13,000 per year) were awarded; career-related internships or fieldwork, scholarships/grants, and unspecified assistantships also available. Financial award application deadline: 6/1; financial award applicants required to submit FAFSA. *Unit head:* Greg Frazier, Director PhD Programs, 817-272-3559, Fax: 817-272-5799, E-mail: frazier@exchange.uta.edu. *Application contact:* Melanie McGee, Director of MBA Program, 817-272-0658, Fax: 817-272-5799, E-mail: mwmcgee@uta.edu.

See Close-Up on page 273.

The University of Texas at Austin, Graduate School, McCombs School of Business, Department of Management, Austin, TX 78712-1111. Offers PhD. *Accreditation:* AACSB. *Degree requirements:* For doctorate, thesis/dissertation. *Entrance requirements:* For doctorate, GMAT or GRE. Electronic applications accepted.

The University of Texas at Austin, Graduate School, McCombs School of Business, Executive MBA Program at Mexico City, Austin, TX 78712-1111. Offers MBA. *Accreditation:* AACSB. *Entrance requirements:* For master's, GMAT, 5 years of work experience. Additional exam requirements/recommendations for international students: Required—TOEFL.

The University of Texas at Austin, Graduate School, McCombs School of Business, Programs in MBA, Austin, TX 78712-1111. Offers MBA, JD/MBA, MBA/MA, MBA/MP Aff, MBA/MSN. *Accreditation:* AACSB. Part-time programs available. *Entrance requirements:* For master's, GMAT, minimum 2 years of full-time work experience. Additional exam requirements/recommendations for international students: Required—TOEFL. Electronic applications accepted.

The University of Texas at Brownsville, Graduate Studies, School of Business, Brownsville, TX 78520-4991. Offers MBA. Part-time and evening/weekend programs available. Postbaccalaureate distance learning degree programs offered (minimal on-campus study). *Degree requirements:* For master's, capstone courses. *Entrance requirements:* For master's, GRE General Test. Additional exam requirements/recommendations for international students: Required—TOEFL. *Faculty research:* Binational and international business.

The University of Texas at Dallas, School of Management, Richardson, TX 75080. Offers EMBA, MA, MBA, MS, PhD. Part-time and evening/weekend programs available. Postbaccalaureate distance learning degree programs offered. *Faculty:* 79 full-time (13 women), 29 part-time/adjunct (9 women). *Students:* 1,001 full-time (432 women), 1,431 part-time (525 women); includes 681 minority (102 African Americans, 8 American Indian/Alaska Native, 433 Asian Americans or Pacific Islanders, 138 Hispanic Americans), 787 international. Average age 30. 2,005 applicants, 57% accepted, 773 enrolled. In 2009, 833 master's, 11 doctorates awarded. *Degree requirements:* For doctorate, thesis/dissertation. *Entrance requirements:* For master's and doctorate, GMAT. Additional exam requirements/recommendations for international students: Required—TOEFL (minimum score 550 paper-based; 213 computer-based). *Application deadline:* For fall admission, 7/15 for domestic students, 5/1 priority date for international students; for spring admission, 11/15 for domestic students, 9/1 priority date for international students. Applications are processed on a rolling basis. Application fee: $50 ($100 for international students). Electronic applications accepted. *Expenses:* Tuition, state resident: full-time $11,068; part-time $461 per credit hour. Tuition, nonresident: full-time $21,178; part-time $882 per credit hour. Tuition and fees vary according to course load. *Financial support:* In 2009–10, 18 research assistantships with full tuition reimbursements (averaging $11,126 per year), 113 teaching assistantships with full tuition reimbursements (averaging $13,210 per year) were awarded; fellowships, career-related internships or fieldwork, Federal Work-Study, institutionally sponsored loans, scholarships/grants, and unspecified assistantships also available. Support available to part-time students. Financial award application deadline: 4/30; financial award applicants required to submit FAFSA. *Faculty research:* Finance, marketing and organization, strategy, management education for physicians. Total annual research expenditures: $633,017. *Unit head:* Dr. Hasan Pirkul, Dean, 972-883-2705, Fax: 972-883-2799, E-mail: hpirkul@utdallas.edu. *Application contact:* David B. Ritchey, Director of Advising, 972-883-2750, Fax: 972-883-6425, E-mail: davidr@utdallas.edu.

See Close-Up on page 275.

The University of Texas at El Paso, Graduate School, College of Business Administration, Programs in Business Administration, El Paso, TX 79968-0001. Offers international business (PhD). *Accreditation:* AACSB. Part-time and evening/weekend programs available. Postbaccalaureate distance learning degree programs offered (no on-campus study). *Entrance requirements:* For master's, GMAT, minimum GPA of 2.7. Additional exam requirements/recommendations for international students: Required—TOEFL. Electronic applications accepted.

The University of Texas at San Antonio, College of Business, Department of Management, San Antonio, TX 78249-0617. Offers business administration-organizational management (PhD); international business (MBA); management science (MBA). *Accreditation:* AACSB. Part-time and evening/weekend programs available. *Faculty:* 12 full-time (4 women), 4 part-time/adjunct (2 women). *Students:* 3 full-time (1 woman), 6 part-time (2 women); includes 3 minority (1 African American, 1 Asian American or Pacific Islander, 1 Hispanic American). Average age 34. 29 applicants, 59% accepted. In 2009, 1 master's awarded. *Degree requirements:* For master's, comprehensive exam (for some programs), thesis (for some programs). *Entrance requirements:* For master's, GMAT, minimum GPA of 3.0. Additional exam requirements/recommendations for international students: Required—TOEFL (minimum score 500 paper-based; 173 computer-based; 61 iBT), IELTS (minimum score 5). *Application deadline:* For fall admission, 7/1 for domestic students, 4/1 for international students; for spring admission, 11/1 for domestic students, 9/1 for international students. Applications are processed on a rolling basis. Application fee: $45 ($80 for international students). Electronic applications accepted. *Expenses:* Tuition, state resident: full-time $3975; part-time $221 per contact hour. Tuition, nonresident: full-time $13,947; part-time $775 per contact hour. Required fees: $1853. *Financial support:* In 2009–10, 2 research assistantships (averaging $15,600 per year), 8 teaching assistantships (averaging $7,800 per year) were awarded; career-related internships or fieldwork, Federal Work-Study, scholarships/grants, and unspecified assistantships also available. Support available to part-time students. *Faculty research:* Business ethics, entrepreneurship, human resource management, knowledge management, international management. *Unit head:* Dr. Robert L. Cardy, Chair, 210-458-7480, Fax: 210-458-6335, E-mail: robert.cardy@utsa.edu. *Application contact:* Cynthia Lengnick-Hall, Graduate Advisor, 210-458-5387, E-mail: cynthia.lengnickhall@utsa.edu.

The University of Texas at San Antonio, College of Business, Department of Management Science and Statistics, San Antonio, TX 78249-0617. Offers applied statistics (PhD); management science (MBA); statistics (MS). *Accreditation:* AACSB. Part-time and evening/weekend programs available. *Faculty:* 14 full-time (4 women), 1 part-time/adjunct (0 women). *Students:* 16 full-time (5 women), 88 part-time (22 women); includes 33 minority (4 African Americans, 1 American Indian/Alaska Native, 6 Asian Americans or Pacific Islanders, 22 Hispanic Americans), 8 international. Average age 34. 29 applicants, 59% accepted, 14 enrolled. In 2009, 14 master's awarded. *Degree requirements:* For master's, comprehensive exam (for some programs), thesis (for some programs). *Entrance requirements:* For master's, GMAT, minimum GPA of 3.0. Additional exam requirements/recommendations for international students: Required—TOEFL (minimum score 500 paper-based; 173 computer-based; 61 iBT). *Application deadline:* For fall admission, 7/1 for domestic students, 4/1 for international students; for spring admission, 11/1 for domestic students, 9/1 for international students. Applications are processed on a rolling basis. Application fee: $45 ($80 for international students). Electronic applications accepted. *Expenses:* Tuition, state resident: full-time $3975; part-time $221 per contact hour. Tuition, nonresident: full-time $13,947; part-time $775 per contact hour. Required fees: $1853. *Financial support:* In 2009–10, 13 students received support, including 16 research assistantships (averaging $12,703 per year), 15 teaching assistantships (averaging $8,400 per year). *Faculty research:* Applied statistics, biostatistics, supply chain management. Total annual research expenditures: $23,518. *Unit head:* Dr. Nandini Kannan, Head, 210-458-5691, Fax: 210-458-6350, E-mail: nandini.kannan@utsa.edu. *Application contact:* Dr. Dorothy A. Flannagan, Dean of the Graduate School, 210-458-4330, Fax: 210-458-4332, E-mail: dorothy.flannagan@utsa.edu.

The University of Texas at Tyler, College of Business and Technology, School of Business Administration, Tyler, TX 75799-0001. Offers business administration (MBA); general management (MBA); health care (MBA). Part-time programs available. Postbaccalaureate distance learning degree programs offered (no on-campus study). *Faculty:* 14 full-time (8 women). *Students:* 33 full-time (13 women), 116 part-time (44 women); includes 25 minority (12 African Americans, 2 American Indian/Alaska Native, 3 Asian Americans or Pacific Islanders, 8 Hispanic Americans), 7 international. Average age 29. 73 applicants, 96% accepted, 35 enrolled. In 2009, 37 master's awarded. *Entrance requirements:* Additional exam requirements/recommendations for international students: Required—TOEFL (minimum score 550 paper-based; 79 computer-based). *Application deadline:* For fall admission, 8/17 priority date for domestic students, 7/1 priority date for international students; for spring admission, 12/21 priority date for domestic students, 11/1 priority date for international students. Application fee: $25 ($50 for international students). *Expenses:* Tuition, state resident: part-time $665 per semester hour. Tuition, nonresident: part-time $942 per semester hour. Part-time tuition and fees vary according to degree level and program. *Faculty research:* General business, inventory control, institutional markets, service marketing, product distribution, accounting fraud, financial reporting and recognition. *Unit head:* Dr. Mary Fischer, Associate Dean/Interim Chair/Professor of Accounting, 903-566-7433, Fax: 903-566-7372. *Application contact:* Dr. Mary Fischer.

The University of Texas of the Permian Basin, Office of Graduate Studies, School of Business, Program in Management, Odessa, TX 79762-0001. Offers MBA. *Accreditation:* AACSB. *Entrance requirements:* For master's, GMAT. Additional exam requirements/recommendations for international students: Required—TOEFL (minimum score 550 paper-based; 213 computer-based).

The University of Texas–Pan American, College of Business Administration, Edinburg, TX 78539. Offers M Acc, MBA, MS, PhD. *Accreditation:* AACSB. Part-time and evening/weekend programs available. *Degree requirements:* For master's, thesis optional; for doctorate, one foreign language, thesis/dissertation, internship. *Entrance requirements:* For master's, GMAT, minimum AACSB index of 1000 (based on last 60 semester hours); for doctorate, GMAT. Additional exam requirements/recommendations for international students: Required—TOEFL. *Expenses:* Tuition, state resident: full-time $3630.60; part-time $201.70 per credit hour. Tuition, nonresident: full-time $8617; part-time $478.70 per credit hour. Required fees: $806.50.

University of the District of Columbia, School of Business and Public Administration, Program in Business Administration, Washington, DC 20008-1175. Offers MBA. *Accreditation:* ACBSP. *Students:* 20 full-time (10 women), 19 part-time (9 women); includes 22 minority (19 African Americans, 3 Asian Americans or Pacific Islanders). Average age 30. 50 applicants, 60% accepted. In 2009, 10 master's awarded. *Degree requirements:* For master's, comprehensive exam, thesis optional. *Entrance requirements:* For master's, GMAT, writing proficiency exam. *Application deadline:* For fall admission, 6/15 priority date for domestic students; for spring admission, 11/1 for domestic students. Applications are processed on a rolling basis. Application fee: $20. *Expenses:* Tuition, state resident: full-time $7580. Tuition, nonresident: full-time $14,580. Required fees: $620. *Financial support:* Career-related internships or fieldwork and Federal Work-Study available. *Unit head:* Dr. Hany Makhlouf, Chairperson, 202-274-7037. *Application contact:* Ann Marie Waterman, Associate Vice President of Admission, Recruitment and Financial Aid, 202-274-6069.

University of the Incarnate Word, School of Graduate Studies and Research, H-E-B School of Business and Administration, Programs in Administration, San Antonio, TX 78209-6397. Offers adult education (MAA); applied administration (MAA); communication arts (MAA); healthcare administration (MAA); instructional technology (MAA); international business (Certificate); nutrition (MAA); organizational development (MAA, Certificate); project management (Certificate); sports management (MAA). Part-time and evening/weekend programs available. Postbaccalaureate distance learning degree programs offered (no on-campus study). *Students:*

30 full-time (17 women), 163 part-time (114 women); includes 128 minority (18 African Americans, 3 Asian Americans or Pacific Islanders, 107 Hispanic Americans), 8 international. Average age 35. In 2009, 68 master's awarded. *Degree requirements:* For master's, capstone. *Entrance requirements:* For master's, GRE, GMAT, undergraduate degree, minimum GPA of 2.5. Additional exam requirements/recommendations for international students: Required—TOEFL (minimum score 560 paper-based; 220 computer-based; 83 iBT). *Application deadline:* Applications are processed on a rolling basis. Application fee: $20. Electronic applications accepted. *Expenses:* Tuition: Full-time $12,150; part-time $675 per credit hour. Required fees: $83 per credit hour. *Financial support:* Federal Work-Study and scholarships/grants available. Financial award applicants required to submit FAFSA. *Unit head:* Dr. Daniel Dominguez, MAA Director, 210-829-3180, Fax: 210-805-3564, E-mail: domingue@uiwtx.edu. *Application contact:* Andrea Cyterski-Acosta, Dean of Enrollment, 210-829-6005, Fax: 210-829-3921, E-mail: admis@uiwtx.edu.

University of the Incarnate Word, School of Graduate Studies and Research, H-E-B School of Business and Administration, Programs in Business Administration, San Antonio, TX 78209-6397. Offers general business (MBA); international business (MBA); international business strategy (MBA); sports management (MBA). *Accreditation:* ACBSP. Part-time and evening/weekend programs available. Postbaccalaureate distance learning degree programs offered. *Students:* 100 full-time (55 women), 255 part-time (155 women); includes 196 minority (19 African Americans, 1 American Indian/Alaska Native, 14 Asian Americans or Pacific Islanders, 162 Hispanic Americans), 41 international. Average age 32. In 2009, 111 master's awarded. *Degree requirements:* For master's, capstone. *Entrance requirements:* For master's, GMAT (minimum score 450), undergraduate degree with minimum overall GPA of 2.5. Additional exam requirements/recommendations for international students: Required—TOEFL (minimum score 560 paper-based; 220 computer-based; 83 iBT). *Application deadline:* Applications are processed on a rolling basis. Application fee: $20. Electronic applications accepted. *Expenses:* Tuition: Full-time $12,150; part-time $675 per credit hour. Required fees: $83 per credit hour. *Financial support:* Federal Work-Study and scholarships/grants available. Financial award applicants required to submit FAFSA. *Unit head:* Dr. Jeannie Scott, MBA Director, 210-283-5002, Fax: 210-805-3564, E-mail: scott@uiwtx.edu. *Application contact:* Andrea Cyterski-Acosta, Dean of Enrollment, 210-829-6005, Fax: 210-829-3921, E-mail: admis@uiwtx.edu.

University of the Pacific, Eberhardt School of Business, Stockton, CA 95211-0197. Offers MBA, JD/MBA. *Accreditation:* AACSB. Part-time programs available. *Faculty:* 25 full-time (8 women), 1 part-time/adjunct (0 women). *Students:* 44 full-time (15 women), 1 part-time (0 women); includes 17 minority (1 African American, 14 Asian Americans or Pacific Islanders, 2 Hispanic Americans), 9 international. Average age 25. 63 applicants, 62% accepted, 19 enrolled. In 2009, 19 master's awarded. *Entrance requirements:* For master's, GMAT. Additional exam requirements/recommendations for international students: Required—TOEFL (minimum score 475 paper-based; 150 computer-based). *Application deadline:* For fall admission, 7/31 priority date for domestic students; for spring admission, 11/30 for domestic students. Applications are processed on a rolling basis. Application fee: $75. *Financial support:* Fellowships, research assistantships, Federal Work-Study and institutionally sponsored loans available. Support available to part-time students. Financial award application deadline: 3/1; financial award applicants required to submit FAFSA. *Unit head:* Dr. Richard Flaherty, Dean, 209-946-2466, Fax: 209-946-2586. *Application contact:* Dr. Chris Lozano, MBA Recruiting Director, 209-946-2597, Fax: 209-946-2586, E-mail: clozano@pacific.edu.

University of the Sacred Heart, Graduate Programs, Department of Business Administration, San Juan, PR 00914-0383. Offers human resource management (MBA); information systems auditing (MS); information technology (Certificate); international marketing (MBA); management information systems (MBA); taxation (MBA). Part-time and evening/weekend programs available. *Degree requirements:* For master's, thesis. *Entrance requirements:* For master's, EXADEP, minimum undergraduate GPA of 2.75, interview.

University of the Southwest, Graduate Programs, Hobbs, NM 88240-9129. Offers business administration (MBA); curriculum and instruction (MSE); curriculum and instruction: bilingual (MSE); curriculum and instruction: reading (MSE); curriculum and instruction: TESOL (MSE); early childhood education (MSE); educational diagnostician (MSE); mental health counseling (MSE); school business administration (MSE); school counseling (MSE); special education (MSE). Part-time and evening/weekend programs available. Postbaccalaureate distance learning degree programs offered (no on-campus study). *Faculty:* 10 full-time (6 women), 10 part-time/adjunct (4 women). *Students:* 112 full-time (93 women), 99 part-time (72 women). Average age 35. 94 applicants, 47% accepted, 39 enrolled. In 2009, 32 master's awarded. *Degree requirements:* For master's, comprehensive exam. *Application deadline:* For fall admission, 3/1 priority date for domestic students; for spring admission, 10/1 for domestic students. Applications are processed on a rolling basis. Application fee: $25. Electronic applications accepted. *Expenses:* Tuition: Part-time $512 per hour. Tuition and fees vary according to course load. *Financial support:* In 2009–10, 196 students received support; research assistantships with partial tuition reimbursements available, Federal Work-Study, scholarships/grants, and tuition waivers (partial) available. Support available to part-time students. Financial award application deadline: 4/1; financial award applicants required to submit FAFSA. *Unit head:* Dr. Mary Harris, Dean of Education, 575-392-6561 Ext. 1056, Fax: 575-392-6006, E-mail: mharris@usw.edu. *Application contact:* Ryanne Evans, Assistant Registrar, 575-392-6561 Ext. 1031, Fax: 575-392-6006, E-mail: revans@usw.edu.

University of the Virgin Islands, Graduate Programs, Division of Business Administration, Saint Thomas, VI 00802-9990. Offers MBA. Part-time and evening/weekend programs available. *Degree requirements:* For master's, comprehensive exam or thesis. *Entrance requirements:* For master's, GMAT, minimum GPA of 2.5. Additional exam requirements/recommendations for international students: Required—TOEFL (minimum score 550 paper-based; 213 computer-based). *Faculty research:* Management information systems.

University of the West, Department of Business Administration, Rosemead, CA 91770. Offers business administration (EMBA); finance (MBA); information technology and management (MBA); international business (MBA); nonprofit organization management (MBA). Part-time and evening/weekend programs available. *Entrance requirements:* Additional exam requirements/recommendations for international students: Required—TOEFL.

The University of Toledo, College of Graduate Studies, College of Business Administration, Toledo, OH 43606-3390. Offers EMBA, MBA, MSA, DME. *Accreditation:* AACSB. Part-time and evening/weekend programs available. *Degree requirements:* For doctorate, thesis/dissertation. *Entrance requirements:* For master's and doctorate, GMAT. Additional exam requirements/recommendations for international students: Required—TOEFL. Electronic applications accepted.

The University of Toledo, College of Graduate Studies, College of Business Administration, Department of Management, Program in Management, Toledo, OH 43606-3390. Offers MBA. *Entrance requirements:* For master's, GMAT.

University of Toronto, School of Graduate Studies, Social Sciences Division, Faculty of Management, Toronto, ON M5S 1A1, Canada. Offers MBA, MMPA, PhD, MBA/MA, MBA/MN. *Accreditation:* AACSB. Part-time and evening/weekend programs available. *Degree requirements:* For doctorate, thesis/dissertation. *Entrance requirements:* For master's, GMAT (MBA, MMPA), minimum mid-B average in final undergraduate year (MMPA, MBA), 2 years of full-time work experiences (MBA), 8 years work experience preferred (EMBA), 2-3 letters of reference; for doctorate, GMAT, minimum B+ average, master's degree in business administration, 2-3 letters of reference. *Expenses:* Contact institution. *Faculty research:* Natural resources, organizational behavior, finance.

University of Tulsa, Graduate School, Collins College of Business, Business Administration/Computer Science Program, Tulsa, OK 74104-3189. Offers MBA/MS. Part-time programs available. *Students:* 2 full-time (0 women). Average age 27. 2 applicants, 100% accepted, 2 enrolled. *Entrance requirements:* Additional exam requirements/recommendations for international students: Required—TOEFL (minimum score 575 paper-based; 231 computer-based; 79 iBT), IELTS (minimum score 6.5). *Application deadline:* Applications are processed on a rolling basis. Application fee: $40. Electronic applications accepted. *Expenses:* Tuition: Full-time $16,182; part-time $899 per credit hour. Required fees: $4 per credit hour. Tuition and fees vary according to course load. *Financial support:* In 2009–10, 2 students received support, including 1 fellowship with full and partial tuition reimbursement available (averaging $2,175 per year), 1 teaching assistantship with full and partial tuition reimbursement available (averaging $11,594 per year); research assistantships with full and partial tuition reimbursements available, career-related internships or fieldwork, Federal Work-Study, institutionally sponsored loans, scholarships/grants, health care benefits, tuition waivers, and unspecified assistantships also available. Support available to part-time students. Financial award application deadline: 2/1; financial award applicants required to submit FAFSA. *Unit head:* Dr. Markham Collins, Associate Dean, 918-631-2783, Fax: 918-631-2142, E-mail: mark-collins@utulsa.edu. *Application contact:* Information Contact, E-mail: graduate-business@utulsa.edu.

University of Tulsa, Graduate School, Collins College of Business, Master of Business Administration Program, Tulsa, OK 74104-3189. Offers accounting (MBA); business administration (MBA); energy management (MBA); finance (MBA); international business (MBA); management information systems (MBA); taxation (MBA); JD/MBA; MBA/MSCS; MBA/MSF. *Accreditation:* AACSB. Part-time and evening/weekend programs available. *Faculty:* 32 full-time (6 women). *Students:* 59 full-time (26 women), 45 part-time (18 women); includes 13 minority (4 African Americans, 4 American Indian/Alaska Native, 1 Asian American or Pacific Islander, 4 Hispanic Americans), 9 international. Average age 25. 78 applicants, 53% accepted, 30 enrolled. In 2009, 36 master's awarded. *Entrance requirements:* For master's, GMAT. Additional exam requirements/recommendations for international students: Required—TOEFL (minimum score 575 paper-based; 232 computer-based; 90 iBT), IELTS (minimum score 6.5). *Application deadline:* Applications are processed on a rolling basis. Application fee: $40. Electronic applications accepted. *Expenses:* Tuition: Full-time $16,182; part-time $899 per credit hour. Required fees: $4 per credit hour. Tuition and fees vary according to course load. *Financial support:* In 2009–10, 42 students received support, including 5 fellowships (averaging $11,894 per year), 2 research assistantships (averaging $9,322 per year), 35 teaching assistantships (averaging $8,112 per year); institutionally sponsored loans, scholarships/grants, health care benefits, tuition waivers (full and partial), and unspecified assistantships also available. Support available to part-time students. Financial award application deadline: 2/1; financial award applicants required to submit FAFSA. *Faculty research:* Accounting, energy management, finance, international business, management information systems, taxation. *Unit head:* Dr. Markham Collins, Associate Dean of the Collins College of Business, 918-631-2783, Fax: 918-631-2142, E-mail: markham-collins@utulsa.edu. *Application contact:* Dr. Markham Collins, Associate Dean of the Collins College of Business, 918-631-2783, Fax: 918-631-2142, E-mail: markham-collins@utulsa.edu.

University of Utah, Graduate School, David Eccles School of Business, Salt Lake City, UT 84112. Offers EMBA, M Acc, M Stat, MBA, MRED, MS, PMBA, PhD. *Accreditation:* AACSB. Part-time and evening/weekend programs available. *Faculty:* 69 full-time (22 women), 3 part-time/adjunct (0 women). *Students:* 720 full-time (165 women), 136 part-time (31 women); includes 62 minority (4 African Americans, 3 American Indian/Alaska Native, 38 Asian Americans or Pacific Islanders, 17 Hispanic Americans), 90 international. Average age 31. 1,345 applicants, 51% accepted, 535 enrolled. In 2009, 375 master's, 6 doctorates awarded. *Degree requirements:* For doctorate, comprehensive exam, thesis/dissertation, oral and written qualifying exams. *Entrance requirements:* For master's, GMAT, GRE (for some programs), minimum undergraduate GPA of 3.0; for doctorate, GMAT, GRE. Additional exam requirements/recommendations for international students: Required—TOEFL (minimum score 600 paper-based; 250 computer-based; 100 iBT), IELTS (minimum score 7). Application fee: $55 ($65 for international students). Electronic applications accepted. *Expenses:* Contact institution. *Financial support:* In 2009–10, 50 students received support, including 8 fellowships with partial tuition reimbursements available, 13 teaching assistantships with partial tuition reimbursements available; career-related internships or fieldwork and health care benefits also available. Financial award applicants required to submit FAFSA. *Faculty research:* Information systems, investment, financial accounting, international strategy. Total annual research expenditures: $637,487. *Unit head:* Dr. Taylor Randall, Dean, 801-587-3860, Fax: 801-581-3074, E-mail: dean@business.utah.edu. *Application contact:* Andrea Chmelik, Program Coordinator, 801-581-7785, Fax: 801-581-3666, E-mail: andrea.chmelik@business.utah.edu.

University of Vermont, Graduate College, School of Business Administration, Burlington, VT 05405. Offers M Acc, MBA. *Accreditation:* AACSB. Part-time programs available. *Faculty:* 25. *Students:* 45 (15 women); includes 4 minority (2 African Americans, 1 Asian American or Pacific Islander, 1 Hispanic American), 6 international. 51 applicants, 65% accepted, 11 enrolled. In 2009, 23 master's awarded. *Entrance requirements:* For master's, GMAT. Additional exam requirements/recommendations for international students: Required—TOEFL (minimum score 550 paper-based; 213 computer-based; 80 iBT). *Application deadline:* For fall admission, 4/1 priority date for domestic students. Applications are processed on a rolling basis. Application fee: $40. Electronic applications accepted. *Expenses:* Tuition, state resident: part-time $508 per credit hour. Tuition, nonresident: part-time $1281 per credit hour. *Financial support:* Fellowships, teaching assistantships, Federal Work-Study available. Financial award application deadline: 3/1. *Unit head:* Dr. R. DeWitt, Dean, 802-656-0513. *Application contact:* Dr. Michael Gurdon, Coordinator, 802-656-4015.

University of Victoria, Faculty of Graduate Studies, Faculty of Business, Victoria, BC V8W 2Y2, Canada. Offers MBA, MBA/LL B. Part-time programs available. *Entrance requirements:* For master's, GMAT, minimum B average. Additional exam requirements/recommendations for international students: Required—TOEFL (minimum score 575 paper-based; 233 computer-based), IELTS (minimum score 7). Electronic applications accepted. *Expenses:* Contact institution. *Faculty research:* Organizational design and analysis, negotiation and conflict management, human resources management, entrepreneurship, international marketing and tourism.

University of Virginia, Darden Graduate School of Business Administration, Charlottesville, VA 22903. Offers MBA, PhD, MBA/JD, MBA/MA, MBA/MD, MBA/ME, MBA/MSN. *Accreditation:* AACSB. *Faculty:* 62 full-time (14 women), 8 part-time/adjunct (3 women). *Students:* 769 full-time (208 women), 4 part-time (1 woman); includes 125 minority (36 African Americans, 2 American Indian/Alaska Native, 54 Asian Americans or Pacific Islanders, 33 Hispanic Americans), 166 international. Average age 29. 2,618 applicants, 33% accepted, 314 enrolled. In 2009, 380 master's, 3 doctorates awarded. *Degree requirements:* For doctorate, thesis/dissertation. *Entrance requirements:* For master's, GMAT, resume; 2 letters of recommendation; interview; for doctorate, GMAT, resume; essay; 2 letters of recommendation; interview. Additional exam requirements/recommendations for international students: Required—TOEFL. *Application deadline:* For fall admission, 3/4 for domestic and international students. Applications are processed on a rolling basis. Application fee: $200. Electronic applications accepted. *Expenses:* Contact institution. *Financial support:* Career-related internships or fieldwork available. Financial award applicants required to submit FAFSA. *Unit head:* Robert F. Bruner, Dean, 434-924-3900, E-mail: darden@virginia.edu. *Application contact:* Sara Neher, Director of Admissions, 434-924-3900, E-mail: darden@virginia.edu.

University of Virginia, McIntire School of Commerce, Charlottesville, VA 22903. Offers accounting (MS); commerce (MSC), including financial services, marketing and management; management of information technology (MS). *Accreditation:* AACSB. *Faculty:* 63 full-time (20 women), 4 part-time/adjunct (1 woman). *Students:* 220 full-time (92 women), 38 part-time (7 women); includes 54 minority (9 African Americans, 2 American Indian/Alaska Native, 29 Asian Americans or Pacific Islanders, 14 Hispanic Americans), 36 international. Average age 27. 276 applicants, 73% accepted, 128 enrolled. In 2009, 173 master's awarded. *Entrance requirements:* For master's, GMAT, 2 letters of recommendation. Additional exam requirements/recommendations for international students: Required—TOEFL (minimum score 600 paper-based; 250 computer-based; 100 iBT), IELTS (minimum score 7). *Application deadline:* Applications are processed on a rolling basis. Application fee: $75. Electronic applications accepted. *Expenses:* Contact institution. *Financial support:* Fellowships, research assistant-

Business Administration and Management—General

University of Virginia *(continued)*
ships, teaching assistantships, career-related internships or fieldwork and Federal Work-Study available. Financial award applicants required to submit FAFSA. *Unit head:* Carl Zeithaml, Dean, 434-924-3110, Fax: 434-924-7074, E-mail: mcs@virginia.edu. *Application contact:* Carl Zeithaml, Dean, 434-924-3110, Fax: 434-924-7074, E-mail: mcs@virginia.edu.

University of Washington, Graduate School, Michael G. Foster School of Business, Seattle, WA 98195-3200. Offers auditing and assurance (MP Acc); business (PhD); business administration (evening) (MBA); business administration (full-time) (MBA); executive business administration (MBA); global business administration (MBA); global executive business administration (MBA); taxation (MP Acc); technology management (MBA); JD/MBA; MBA/MAIS; MBA/MHA. *Accreditation:* AACSB. Part-time and evening/weekend programs available. Terminal master's awarded for partial completion of doctoral program. *Degree requirements:* For doctorate, comprehensive exam, thesis/dissertation. *Entrance requirements:* For master's, GMAT; for doctorate, GMAT, GRE. Additional exam requirements/recommendations for international students: Required—TOEFL (minimum score 600 paper-based; 250 computer-based). Electronic applications accepted. *Expenses:* Contact institution. *Faculty research:* Finance, marketing, organizational behavior, information technology, strategy.

University of Washington, Bothell, Business Program, Bothell, WA 98011-8246. Offers leadership (MBA); technology (MA). Part-time programs available. *Faculty:* 18 full-time (2 women), 4 part-time/adjunct (2 women). *Students:* 105 full-time (25 women); includes 29 minority (3 African Americans, 23 Asian Americans or Pacific Islanders, 3 Hispanic Americans), 5 international. Average age 31. 133 applicants, 68% accepted, 70 enrolled. In 2009, 38 master's awarded. *Entrance requirements:* For master's, GMAT or GRE General Test. Additional exam requirements/recommendations for international students: Required—TOEFL (minimum score 580 paper-based; 237 computer-based; 92 iBT), IELTS (minimum score 7), TOEFL or IELTS unless a bachelor's degree is earned from a regionally accredited institution in the U. S., Australia, Bahamas, Canada, Ireland, New Zealand, Singapore, Trinidad and Tobago, or the U. K., or documentation that undergraduate instruction was all in English. *Application deadline:* For fall admission, 4/16 priority date for domestic and international students. Application fee: $50. Electronic applications accepted. *Expenses:* Contact institution. *Financial support:* In 2009–10, 67 students received support. Federal Work-Study and scholarships/grants available. Financial award application deadline: 2/28; financial award applicants required to submit FAFSA. *Faculty research:* New product marketing, supply chain management, entrepreneurship, financial accounting, interactive marketing, corporate finance. *Unit head:* Prof. Sandeep Krishnamurthy, Director, 425-352-5229, Fax: 425-352-5277, E-mail: sandeep@uw.edu. *Application contact:* Kathryn Chester, MBA Admissions Coordinator, 425-352-3275, Fax: 425-352-5277, E-mail: kchester@uwb.edu.

University of Washington, Tacoma, Graduate Programs, MBA Programs, Tacoma, WA 98402-3100. Offers accounting (MBA); certified financial analyst (MBA). Part-time and evening/weekend programs available. *Faculty:* 24 full-time (8 women), 3 part-time/adjunct (0 women). *Students:* 39 full-time (9 women), 10 part-time (2 women); includes 1 African American, 5 Asian Americans or Pacific Islanders, 1 Hispanic American, 1 international. Average age 33. 31 applicants, 68% accepted, 18 enrolled. In 2009, 18 master's awarded. *Entrance requirements:* For master's, GMAT, current resume, management and professional work summary, essay, 2 professional letters of recommendation. *Application deadline:* For fall admission, 4/15 priority date for domestic students. Applications are processed on a rolling basis. Application fee: $65. Electronic applications accepted. *Expenses:* Tuition, state resident: full-time $10,660; part-time $484 per credit. Tuition, nonresident: full-time $24,000; part-time $1119 per credit. Required fees: $150 per term. Tuition and fees vary according to course load and program. *Faculty research:* Leadership, bankruptcy, strategic marketing, customer Satisfaction, corporate social responsibility. *Unit head:* Dr. Shahrokh Saudagaran, Dean, 253-692-5630, Fax: 253-692-4523, E-mail: uwtmba@u.washington.edu. *Application contact:* Aubree Robinson, Academic Adviser, MBA and Undergraduate Programs, 253-692-5630, Fax: 253-692-4523, E-mail: uwtmba@u.washington.edu.

University of Waterloo, Graduate Studies, Centre for Business, Entrepreneurship and Technology, Waterloo, ON N2L 3G1, Canada. Offers MBET. *Entrance requirements:* For master's, honors degree. Additional exam requirements/recommendations for international students: Required—TOEFL (minimum score 550 paper-based; 213 computer-based), TWE. Electronic applications accepted.

The University of Western Ontario, Richard Ivey School of Business, London, ON N6A 3K7, Canada. Offers business (EMBA, PhD); corporate strategy and leadership elective (MBA); entrepreneurship elective (MBA); finance elective (MBA); health sector stream (MBA); international management elective (MBA); marketing elective (MBA); JD/MBA. *Faculty:* 61 full-time (13 women). *Students:* 164 full-time (50 women). Average age 29. In 2009, 167 master's awarded. *Degree requirements:* For master's, thesis (for some programs); for doctorate, thesis/dissertation. *Entrance requirements:* For master's, GMAT, 2 years of full-time work experience, interview. Additional exam requirements/recommendations for international students: Required—TOEFL (minimum score 100 computer-based; 100 iBT), IELTS (minimum score 6), IELTS or TOEFL. *Application deadline:* For fall admission, 10/12 for domestic students, 8/16 for international students; for winter admission, 12/16 for domestic students, 10/12 for international students; for spring admission, 1/10 priority date for domestic students, 12/16 for international students. Applications are processed on a rolling basis. Application fee: $150 Canadian dollars. Electronic applications accepted. *Financial support:* Scholarships/grants and health care benefits available. Financial award application deadline: 1/10. *Faculty research:* Strategy, organizational behavior, international business, finance, operations management. *Unit head:* Carol Stephenson, Dean, 519-661-3285, Fax: 519-661-4126, E-mail: cstephenson@ivey.ca. *Application contact:* Niki da Silva, Director, MBA Program Services, 519-661-3419, Fax: 519-661-3431, E-mail: ndasilva@ivey.ca.

University of West Florida, College of Business, Program in Business Administration, Pensacola, FL 32514-5750. Offers MBA. *Accreditation:* AACSB. Part-time and evening/weekend programs available. *Faculty:* 7 full-time (3 women), 4 part-time/adjunct (3 women). *Students:* 26 full-time (15 women), 76 part-time (41 women); includes 14 minority (5 African Americans, 1 American Indian/Alaska Native, 3 Asian Americans or Pacific Islanders, 5 Hispanic Americans), 10 international. Average age 28. 57 applicants, 74% accepted, 32 enrolled. In 2009, 55 master's awarded. *Degree requirements:* For master's, industry portfolio project based on information from five of the core MBA courses. *Entrance requirements:* For master's, GMAT (minimum score 450) or equivalent GRE score, bachelor's degree, two letters of recommendation, resume. Additional exam requirements/recommendations for international students: Required—TOEFL (minimum score 550 paper-based; 213 computer-based). *Application deadline:* For fall admission, 6/30 for domestic students, 5/15 for international students; for spring admission, 11/1 for domestic students, 10/1 for international students. Applications are processed on a rolling basis. Application fee: $30. *Expenses:* Tuition, state resident: full-time $4982; part-time $260 per credit hour. Tuition, nonresident: full-time $20,059; part-time $919 per credit hour. Required fees: $1247; $52 per credit hour. *Financial support:* In 2009–10, 32 fellowships (averaging $567 per year), 41 research assistantships with partial tuition reimbursements (averaging $3,473 per year) were awarded; unspecified assistantships also available. Financial award application deadline: 4/15; financial award applicants required to submit FAFSA. *Faculty research:* Robotics, corporate behavior, international trade, franchising, counterfeiting. *Unit head:* Dr. W. Timothy O'Keefe, Associate Dean and Director, 850-474-2348. *Application contact:* Cheryl Powell, Academic Advisor, 850-474-2348.

University of West Florida, College of Professional Studies, Department of Professional and Community Leadership, Program in Administration, Pensacola, FL 32514-5750. Offers acquisition and contract administration (MSA); biomedical/pharmaceutical (MSA); criminal justice administration (MSA); database administration (MSA); education leadership (MSA); healthcare administration (MSA); human performance technology (MSA); leadership (MSA); nursing administration (MSA); public administration (MSA); software engineering administration (MSA). Part-time and evening/weekend programs available. Postbaccalaureate distance learning degree

programs offered (no on-campus study). *Students:* 33 full-time (21 women), 168 part-time (97 women); includes 53 minority (32 African Americans, 2 American Indian/Alaska Native, 5 Asian Americans or Pacific Islanders, 14 Hispanic Americans), 1 international. Average age 34. 103 applicants, 74% accepted, 64 enrolled. In 2009, 47 master's awarded. *Entrance requirements:* For master's, GRE General Test, letter of intent, names of references. Additional exam requirements/recommendations for international students: Required—TOEFL (minimum score 550 paper-based; 213 computer-based). *Application deadline:* For fall admission, 6/1 for domestic students, 5/15 for international students; for spring admission, 11/1 for domestic students, 10/1 for international students. Applications are processed on a rolling basis. Application fee: $30. *Expenses:* Tuition, state resident: full-time $4982; part-time $260 per credit hour. Tuition, nonresident: full-time $20,059; part-time $919 per credit hour. Required fees: $1247; $52 per credit hour. *Financial support:* Unspecified assistantships available. Financial award application deadline: 4/15; financial award applicants required to submit FAFSA. *Unit head:* Dr. Karen Rasmussen, Chairperson, 850-474-2301, Fax: 850-474-2804. *Application contact:* Terry McCray, Assistant Director of Graduate Admissions, 850-473-7718, Fax: 850-473-7714, E-mail: gradadmissions@uwf.edu.

University of West Georgia, Graduate School, Richards College of Business, Program of Business Administration, Carrollton, GA 30118. Offers MBA. *Accreditation:* AACSB. Part-time and evening/weekend programs available. Postbaccalaureate distance learning degree programs offered (no on-campus study). *Faculty:* 10 full-time (3 women), 2 part-time/adjunct (0 women). *Students:* 43 full-time (19 women), 113 part-time (54 women); includes 42 minority (33 African Americans, 6 Asian Americans or Pacific Islanders, 3 Hispanic Americans), 9 international. Average age 30. 98 applicants, 50% accepted, 35 enrolled. In 2009, 49 master's awarded. *Degree requirements:* For master's, comprehensive exam. *Entrance requirements:* For master's, GMAT, minimum GPA of 2.5. Additional exam requirements/recommendations for international students: Required—TOEFL. *Application deadline:* For fall admission, 7/17 for domestic students; for spring admission, 11/20 for domestic students. Applications are processed on a rolling basis. Application fee: $30. Electronic applications accepted. *Expenses:* Tuition, state resident: full-time $2952; part-time $164 per semester hour. Tuition, nonresident: full-time $11,808; part-time $656 per semester hour. Required fees: $42.90 per semester hour. $307 per semester. Tuition and fees vary according to course load. *Financial support:* In 2009–10, 8 research assistantships with full tuition reimbursements (averaging $8,000 per year) were awarded; career-related internships or fieldwork, tuition waivers (partial), and unspecified assistantships also available. Support available to part-time students. Financial award application deadline: 7/1; financial award applicants required to submit FAFSA. *Faculty research:* Distance learning, small business development, e-commerce, computer self-efficacy. *Unit head:* Dr. Mary M. Kassis, Associate Dean/Interim MBA Director, 678-839-4777, E-mail: mkassis@westga.edu. *Application contact:* Dr. Charles W. Clark, Dean, 678-839-6508, E-mail: cclark@westga.edu.

University of Windsor, Faculty of Graduate Studies, Odette School of Business, Windsor, ON N9B 3P4, Canada. Offers MBA, MM, MBA/LL B. Evening/weekend programs available. *Degree requirements:* For master's, thesis or alternative. *Entrance requirements:* For master's, GMAT, minimum B average. Additional exam requirements/recommendations for international students: Required—TOEFL (minimum score 600 paper-based; 250 computer-based). Electronic applications accepted. *Faculty research:* Accounting, administrative studies, finance, marketing, business policy and strategy.

University of Wisconsin–Eau Claire, College of Business, Program in Business Administration, Eau Claire, WI 54702-4004. Offers MBA. *Accreditation:* AACSB. Part-time and evening/weekend programs available. Postbaccalaureate distance learning degree programs offered (no on-campus study). *Faculty:* 35 full-time (10 women). *Students:* 12 full-time (5 women), 228 part-time (108 women); includes 27 minority (8 African Americans, 3 American Indian/Alaska Native, 15 Asian Americans or Pacific Islanders, 1 Hispanic American), 3 international. Average age 32. 165 applicants, 63% accepted, 72 enrolled. In 2009, 65 master's awarded. Terminal master's awarded for partial completion of doctoral program. *Degree requirements:* For master's, thesis optional, applied field project. *Entrance requirements:* For master's, GMAT or GRE, minimum GPA of 2.75 overall or 2.9 in final 10 credit hours. Additional exam requirements/recommendations for international students: Required—TOEFL (minimum score 550 paper-based; 213 computer-based; 79 iBT). *Application deadline:* For fall admission, 7/1 priority date for domestic students, 6/1 priority date for international students; for spring admission, 12/1 priority date for domestic students, 11/1 priority date for international students. Applications are processed on a rolling basis. Application fee: $56. Electronic applications accepted. *Expenses:* Tuition, state resident: full-time $6705.90; part-time $372.55 per credit. Tuition, nonresident: full-time $16,771; part-time $931.74 per credit. Required fees: $925.50; $51.19 per credit. One-time fee: $56. *Financial support:* In 2009–10, 39 students received support, including 4 fellowships (averaging $1,750 per year); Federal Work-Study and unspecified assistantships also available. Financial award application deadline: 3/1; financial award applicants required to submit FAFSA. *Unit head:* Dr. Robert Erffmeyer, Director, 715-836-5509, Fax: 715-836-4014, E-mail: erffmerc@uwec.edu. *Application contact:* Kristina Anderson, Director of Admissions, 715-836-5415, Fax: 715-836-2409, E-mail: admissions@uwec.edu.

See Close-Up on page 277.

University of Wisconsin–Green Bay, Graduate Studies, Program in Management, Green Bay, WI 54311-7001. Offers MS. Part-time programs available. *Faculty:* 6 full-time (1 woman), 1 part-time/adjunct (0 women). *Students:* 4 full-time (3 women), 33 part-time (21 women); includes 5 minority (1 African American, 2 American Indian/Alaska Native, 1 Asian American or Pacific Islander, 1 Hispanic American), 4 international. Average age 31. 21 applicants, 29% accepted, 6 enrolled. In 2009, 15 master's awarded. *Degree requirements:* For master's, thesis or alternative. *Entrance requirements:* For master's, GMAT or GRE General Test, minimum GPA of 3.0. *Application deadline:* For fall admission, 8/1 for domestic students; for spring admission, 11/1 for domestic students. Applications are processed on a rolling basis. Application fee: $56. Electronic applications accepted. *Expenses:* Tuition, state resident: full-time $6706; part-time $373 per credit. Tuition, nonresident: full-time $16,722; part-time $932 per credit. Required fees: $1250; $52 per credit. Tuition and fees vary according to degree level and reciprocity agreements. *Financial support:* Career-related internships or fieldwork, Federal Work-Study, and institutionally sponsored loans available. Financial award application deadline: 7/15; financial award applicants required to submit FAFSA. *Faculty research:* Planning methods, budgeting, decision making, organizational behavior and theory, management. *Unit head:* Dr. Meir Russ, Chair, 920-465-2757, E-mail: russm@uwgb.edu. *Application contact:* Don McCartney, Adviser, 920-465-2520, E-mail: mccartnd@uwgb.edu.

University of Wisconsin–La Crosse, Office of University Graduate Studies, College of Business Administration, La Crosse, WI 54601-3742. Offers MBA. *Accreditation:* AACSB. Part-time and evening/weekend programs available. *Faculty:* 37 full-time (10 women). *Students:* 34 full-time (7 women), 35 part-time (15 women); includes 2 minority (1 Asian American or Pacific Islander, 1 Hispanic American), 31 international. Average age 29. 100 applicants, 53% accepted, 27 enrolled. In 2009, 27 master's awarded. *Degree requirements:* For master's, thesis optional. *Entrance requirements:* For master's, GMAT. Additional exam requirements/recommendations for international students: Required—TOEFL (minimum score 550 paper-based; 213 computer-based; 79 iBT). *Application deadline:* For fall admission, 6/15 priority date for domestic students; for spring admission, 11/15 priority date for domestic students. Applications are processed on a rolling basis. Application fee: $56. Electronic applications accepted. *Expenses:* Contact institution. *Financial support:* In 2009–10, 5 research assistantships with partial tuition reimbursements (averaging $6,648 per year) were awarded; Federal Work-Study, health care benefits, tuition waivers (partial), and unspecified assistantships also available. Support available to part-time students. Financial award application deadline: 3/15; financial award applicants required to submit FAFSA. *Faculty research:* Economics of sports, tax preparer regulation, stock performance indicators, public sector information technology, corporate social responsibility. *Unit head:* Dr. Bruce May, Associate Dean, 608-785-8095, Fax: 608-785-6700, E-mail: may.bruce@uwlax.edu. *Application contact:* Amelia Dittman, Assistant to the Dean, 608-785-8092, Fax: 608-785-6700, E-mail: dittman.amel@uwlax.edu.

See Close-Up on page 277.

University of Wisconsin–Madison, Graduate School, Wisconsin School of Business, Wisconsin Evening MBA Program, Madison, WI 53706-1380. Offers MBA. Part-time and evening/weekend programs available. *Faculty:* 16 full-time (4 women), 1 part-time/adjunct (0 women). *Students:* 180 part-time (52 women); includes 25 minority (5 African Americans, 1 American Indian/Alaska Native, 19 Asian Americans or Pacific Islanders), 9 international. Average age 31. 77 applicants, 87% accepted, 65 enrolled. In 2009, 43 master's awarded. *Entrance requirements:* For master's, GMAT, bachelor's degree, 2 years work experience. Additional exam requirements/recommendations for international students: Required—TOEFL (minimum score 600 paper-based; 250 computer-based; 100 iBT). *Application deadline:* For fall admission, 5/1 priority date for domestic and international students. Applications are processed on a rolling basis. Application fee: $56. Electronic applications accepted. *Expenses:* Contact institution. *Financial support:* Career-related internships or fieldwork and scholarships/grants available. Support available to part-time students. Financial award application deadline: 5/1; financial award applicants required to submit FAFSA. *Faculty research:* Regulation, housing economy, environmental issues on supply chain management, marketing strategy, cost management. *Unit head:* Jim Woodrum, Associate Dean for Wisconsin MBA Programs, 608-263-1169, E-mail: mbaenterprise@bus.wisc.edu. *Application contact:* Linda Uitvlugt, Executive Director, 608-263-1169, Fax: 608-262-3607, E-mail: mbaenterprise@bus.wisc.edu.

University of Wisconsin–Madison, Graduate School, Wisconsin School of Business, Wisconsin Executive MBA Program, Madison, WI 53706-1380. Offers MBA. Part-time and evening/weekend programs available. *Faculty:* 15 full-time (4 women), 3 part-time/adjunct (0 women). *Students:* 60 part-time (18 women); includes 9 minority (all Asian Americans or Pacific Islanders), 3 international. Average age 38. 32 applicants, 100% accepted, 27 enrolled. In 2009, 47 master's awarded. *Entrance requirements:* For master's, 8 years professional work experience, 5 years leadership experience, minimum GPA of 3.0. *Application deadline:* For fall admission, 5/1 for domestic and international students. Applications are processed on a rolling basis. Application fee: $56. Electronic applications accepted. *Expenses:* Tuition, state resident: part-time $594 per credit. Tuition, nonresident: part-time $1504 per credit. Required fees: $65 per credit. Tuition and fees vary according to course load, program and reciprocity agreements. *Financial support:* Scholarships/grants available. Support available to part-time students. Financial award application deadline: 5/1; financial award applicants required to submit FAFSA. *Faculty research:* Marketing strategy, housing markets, corporate governance, healthcare fiscal management, management in cross cultural boundaries. *Unit head:* Jim Woodrum, Associate Dean for Enterprise MBA Programs, 608-263-1169, E-mail: mbaenterprise@bus.wisc.edu. *Application contact:* Linda Uitvlugt, Executive Director, 608-263-1169, Fax: 608-262-3607, E-mail: mabenterprise@bus.wisc.edu.

University of Wisconsin–Madison, Graduate School, Wisconsin School of Business, Wisconsin Full-Time MBA Program, Madison, WI 53706-1380. Offers applied corporate finance (MBA); applied security analysis (MBA); arts administration (MBA); brand and product management (MBA); entrepreneurial management (MBA); marketing research (MBA); operations and technology management (MBA); real estate (MBA); risk management and insurance (MBA); strategic human resource management (MBA); strategic management in the life and engineering sciences (MBA); supply chain management (MBA). *Faculty:* 32 full-time (5 women). *Students:* 242 full-time (74 women); includes 47 minority (16 African Americans, 3 American Indian/Alaska Native, 16 Asian Americans or Pacific Islanders, 12 Hispanic Americans), 29 international. Average age 28. 526 applicants, 32% accepted, 117 enrolled. In 2009, 106 master's awarded. *Entrance requirements:* For master's, GMAT, bachelor's or equivalent degree, 2 years of work experience, letters of recommendation. Additional exam requirements/recommendations for international students: Required—TOEFL (minimum score 600 paper-based; 250 computer-based; 100 iBT), IELTS. *Application deadline:* For fall admission, 11/4 for domestic and international students; for winter admission, 2/5 for domestic and international students; for spring admission, 5/26 for domestic students, 4/5 for international students. Applications are processed on a rolling basis. Application fee: $56. Electronic applications accepted. *Expenses:* Tuition, state resident: part-time $594 per credit. Tuition, nonresident: part-time $1504 per credit. Required fees: $65 per credit. Tuition and fees vary according to course load, program and reciprocity agreements. *Financial support:* In 2009–10, 103 students received support, including 13 fellowships with full and partial tuition reimbursements available (averaging $15,000 per year), 53 research assistantships with full tuition reimbursements available (averaging $8,000 per year), 35 teaching assistantships with full tuition reimbursements available (averaging $11,000 per year); scholarships/grants, health care benefits, and unspecified assistantships also available. Financial award application deadline: 4/5; financial award applicants required to submit FAFSA. *Unit head:* Prof. Kenneth A. Kavajecz, Associate Dean, 608-265-3494, Fax: 608-265-4192, E-mail: kkavajecz@bus.wisc.edu. *Application contact:* Maria Reis, Assistant Director of MBA Marketing and Recruiting, 608-262-4000, Fax: 608-265-4192, E-mail: mreis@bus.wisc.edu.

University of Wisconsin–Milwaukee, Graduate School, Sheldon B. Lubar School of Business, Milwaukee, WI 53201. Offers business administration (MBA); enterprise resource planning (Certificate); investment management (Certificate); management science (MS, PhD); nonprofit management and leadership (MS, Certificate); state and local taxation (Certificate); MS/MBA. *Accreditation:* AACSB. Part-time and evening/weekend programs available. *Faculty:* 55 full-time (14 women). *Students:* 317 full-time (108 women), 420 part-time (179 women); includes 70 minority (20 African Americans, 5 American Indian/Alaska Native, 33 Asian Americans or Pacific Islanders, 12 Hispanic Americans), 73 international. Average age 31. 499 applicants, 59% accepted, 132 enrolled. In 2009, 286 master's, 10 doctorates awarded. *Degree requirements:* For master's, comprehensive exam (for some programs); for doctorate, comprehensive exam, thesis/dissertation. *Entrance requirements:* For master's and doctorate, GMAT or GRE General Test. Additional exam requirements/recommendations for international students: Required—TOEFL (minimum score 550 paper-based; 79 iBT), IELTS (minimum score 6.5). *Application deadline:* For fall admission, 1/1 priority date for domestic students; for spring admission, 9/1 for domestic students. Applications are processed on a rolling basis. Application fee: $45 ($75 for international students). *Expenses:* Contact institution. *Financial support:* In 2009–10, 5 fellowships, 41 teaching assistantships were awarded; career-related internships or fieldwork, Federal Work-Study, and unspecified assistantships also available. Support available to part-time students. Financial award application deadline: 4/15. *Faculty research:* Applied management research in finance, MIS, marketing, operations research, organizational sciences. Total annual research expenditures: $204,295. *Unit head:* Timothy L. Smunt, Dean, 414-229-6256, Fax: 414-229-2372, E-mail: tsmunt@uwm.edu. *Application contact:* Sara Sandin, 414-229-5403, E-mail: mba-ms@uwm.edu.

University of Wisconsin–Oshkosh, The Office of Graduate Studies, College of Business, Program in Business Administration, Oshkosh, WI 54901. Offers MBA. *Accreditation:* AACSB. Part-time programs available. *Degree requirements:* For master's, integrative seminar. *Entrance requirements:* For master's, GMAT, GRE, minimum undergraduate GPA of 2.75. Additional exam requirements/recommendations for international students: Required—TOEFL (minimum score 550 paper-based; 213 computer-based; 79 iBT). Electronic applications accepted.

See Close-Up on page 277.

University of Wisconsin–Parkside, School of Business and Technology, Kenosha, WI 53141-2000. Offers MBA, MSCIS. *Accreditation:* AACSB. Part-time and evening/weekend programs available. *Entrance requirements:* For master's, GMAT. Additional exam requirements/recommendations for international students: Required—TOEFL (minimum score 550 paper-based; 216 computer-based; 79 iBT). Electronic applications accepted. *Expenses:* Contact institution. *Faculty research:* Business strategy, ethics in accounting and finance, mutual funds, decision analysis and neural networks, management skills.

See Close-Up on page 277.

University of Wisconsin–River Falls, Outreach and Graduate Studies, College of Business and Economics, River Falls, WI 54022. Offers MBA, MM. *Accreditation:* AACSB. *Degree requirements:* For master's, thesis or alternative. *Entrance requirements:* Additional exam requirements/recommendations for international students: Required—TOEFL (minimum score 550 paper-based; 79 iBT). Electronic applications accepted.

University of Wisconsin–Stevens Point, College of Letters and Science, Division of Business and Economics, Stevens Point, WI 54481-3897. Offers MBA. *Application deadline:* Applications are processed on a rolling basis. Application fee: $45. *Expenses:* Tuition, state resident: full-time $7740; part-time $430 per credit hour. Tuition, nonresident: full-time $17,804; part-time $989 per credit hour. Tuition and fees vary according to course load and reciprocity agreements. *Financial support:* Application deadline: 5/1. *Unit head:* Dr. C. R. Marshall, Chair, 715-346-2728. *Application contact:* Catherine Glennon, Director of Admissions, 715-346-2441, E-mail: admiss@uwsp.edu.

University of Wisconsin–Whitewater, School of Graduate Studies, College of Business and Economics, Program in Business Administration, Whitewater, WI 53190-1790. Offers finance (MBA); human resource management (MBA); information technology management (MBA); international business (MBA); management (MBA); marketing (MBA); operations and supply chain management (MBA); technology and training (MBA). *Accreditation:* AACSB. Part-time and evening/weekend programs available. Postbaccalaureate distance learning degree programs offered (no on-campus study). *Degree requirements:* For master's, thesis or alternative. *Entrance requirements:* For master's, GMAT, minimum AACSB index of 1000, minimum GPA of 2.75. Additional exam requirements/recommendations for international students: Required—TOEFL (minimum score 550 paper-based; 213 computer-based). Electronic applications accepted. *Faculty research:* Interface between social institutions and individual behavior, technology and innovation management, occupational mental health, workplace deviance and workplace romance.

See Display on page 190.

University of Wyoming, College of Business, Program in Business Administration, Laramie, WY 82070. Offers MBA. *Accreditation:* AACSB. Part-time and evening/weekend programs available. Postbaccalaureate distance learning degree programs offered (minimal on-campus study). *Degree requirements:* For master's, comprehensive exam, thesis or alternative. *Entrance requirements:* For master's, GMAT, GRE General Test, minimum GPA of 3.0. Additional exam requirements/recommendations for international students: Required—TOEFL (minimum score 550 paper-based; 210 computer-based; 80 iBT). Electronic applications accepted. *Faculty research:* Natural resource marketing and product development, work place violence.

Upper Iowa University, Online Master's Programs, Fayette, IA 52142-1857. Offers accounting (MBA); corporate financial management (MBA); global business (MBA); health and human services (MPA); higher education administration (MHEA); homeland security (MPA); human resources management (MBA); justice administration (MPA); organizational development (MBA); public personnel management (MPA); quality management (MBA). MBA also available at Madison, WI campus. Part-time programs available. Postbaccalaureate distance learning degree programs offered (no on-campus study). *Faculty:* 3 full-time (0 women), 66 part-time/adjunct (27 women). *Students:* 723 full-time (442 women). *Degree requirements:* For master's, research project. *Entrance requirements:* For master's, GMAT, GRE, or minimum GPA of 2.7 during last 60 hours. Additional exam requirements/recommendations for international students: Required—TOEFL (minimum score 570 paper-based; 230 computer-based). *Application deadline:* Applications are processed on a rolling basis. Application fee: $50. Electronic applications accepted. *Expenses:* Tuition: Full-time $6948; part-time $386 per credit hour. *Financial support:* Available to part-time students. Applicants required to submit FAFSA. *Faculty research:* Total quality management, CQI, teams, organization culture and climate, management. *Application contact:* David Hannum, Admissions Advisor, 800-603-3756, E-mail: hannumd@uiu.edu.

Urbana University, Division of Business Administration, Urbana, OH 43078-2091. Offers MBA. Part-time and evening/weekend programs available. *Faculty:* 5 full-time (0 women). *Students:* 28 full-time (11 women), 28 part-time (16 women); includes 2 minority (both African Americans), 28 international. Average age 34. In 2009, 28 master's awarded. *Degree requirements:* For master's, comprehensive exam, thesis or alternative. *Entrance requirements:* For master's, GMAT, minimum GPA of 2.7, BS in business, 3 letters of recommendation, work experience. Additional exam requirements/recommendations for international students: Required—TOEFL (minimum score 550 paper-based; 213 computer-based). *Application deadline:* For fall admission, 7/30 priority date for domestic students, 7/15 priority date for international students; for winter admission, 12/15 priority date for domestic students, 12/1 priority date for international students; for spring admission, 9/15 priority date for domestic students, 4/1 priority date for international students. Applications are processed on a rolling basis. Application fee: $25. *Expenses:* Tuition: Full-time $8550; part-time $475 per semester hour. Required fees: $950; $475 per semester. One-time fee: $25. *Financial support:* Tuition waivers (partial) and unspecified assistantships available. Financial award applicants required to submit FAFSA. *Faculty research:* Organizational behavior, taxation, segmentation, information systems, retail gravitation. *Unit head:* Dr. John P. Thomas, Director, 937-484-1376, Fax: 937-484-1343, E-mail: mba@urbana.edu. *Application contact:* Brian Kesse, Director of Admissions, 937-484-1370, Fax: 937-484-1389, E-mail: bkesse@urbana.edu.

Ursuline College, School of Graduate Studies, Program in Management, Pepper Pike, OH 44124-4398. Offers MMT. Part-time programs available. *Faculty:* 1 (woman) full-time. *Students:* 18 full-time (15 women), 4 part-time (all women); includes 12 minority (all African Americans). Average age 38. 11 applicants, 100% accepted, 11 enrolled. In 2009, 8 master's awarded. *Degree requirements:* For master's, project. *Entrance requirements:* For master's, minimum undergraduate GPA of 3.0. Additional exam requirements/recommendations for international students: Required—TOEFL (minimum score 500 paper-based; 173 computer-based). *Application deadline:* For fall admission, 8/1 priority date for domestic students. Applications are processed on a rolling basis. Application fee: $25. *Expenses:* Tuition: Full-time $14,544; part-time $808 per credit hour. Required fees: $230; $75 per semester. *Financial support:* Federal Work-Study available. Financial award application deadline: 3/1; financial award applicants required to submit FAFSA. *Unit head:* Dr. Debra Fleming, Director, 440-646-8119, Fax: 440-684-6088, E-mail: dfleming@ursuline.edu. *Application contact:* Melanie Steele, Secretary, 440-646-8199, Fax: 440-684-6138, E-mail: gradsch@ursuline.edu.

Utah State University, School of Graduate Studies, College of Business, Program in Business Administration, Logan, UT 84322. Offers MBA. *Accreditation:* AACSB. Part-time and evening/weekend programs available. Postbaccalaureate distance learning degree programs offered (minimal on-campus study). *Degree requirements:* For master's, comprehensive exam. *Entrance requirements:* For master's, GMAT or GRE, minimum GPA of 3.0. Additional exam requirements/recommendations for international students: Required—TOEFL. Electronic applications accepted. *Faculty research:* Marketing strategy, technology and innovation, public utility finance, international competitiveness.

Valdosta State University, Graduate School, Program in Business Administration, Valdosta, GA 31698. Offers MBA. *Accreditation:* AACSB. Part-time programs available. *Degree requirements:* For master's, comprehensive written and/or oral exams. *Entrance requirements:* For master's, GMAT, minimum GPA of 2.75. Additional exam requirements/recommendations for international students: Required—TOEFL (minimum score 523 paper-based; 193 computer-based). Electronic applications accepted.

Valparaiso University, Graduate School, College of Business Administration, Valparaiso, IN 46383. Offers business administration (MBA); engineering management (MEM); management (Certificate); JD/MBA; MSN/MBA. *Accreditation:* AACSB. Part-time and evening/weekend programs available. *Faculty:* 15 part-time/adjunct (5 women). *Students:* 21 full-time (6 women), 46 part-time (15 women); includes 7 minority (3 African Americans, 1 Asian American or Pacific Islander, 3 Hispanic Americans), 9 international. Average age 28. In 2009, 29 master's, 6 other advanced degrees awarded. *Entrance requirements:* For master's, GMAT, GRE, minimum GPA of 3.0. Additional exam requirements/recommendations for international students: Required—TOEFL (minimum score 550 paper-based; 213 computer-based; 80 iBT). *Application deadline:* Applications are processed on a rolling basis. Application fee: $30 ($50 for international students). Electronic applications accepted. *Expenses:* Contact institution. *Financial support:* Available to part-time students. Applicants required to submit FAFSA. *Unit head:* Bruce MacLean, Director of Graduate Programs in Management, 219-464-6600, Fax: 219-

Business Administration and Management—General

Valparaiso University *(continued)*
464-5789, E-mail: bruce.maclean@valpo.edu. *Application contact:* Cindy Scanlan, Assistant Director of Graduate Programs in Management, 219-465-7965, Fax: 219-464-5789, E-mail: cindy.scanlan@valpo.edu.

Vancouver Island University, Program in Business Administration, Nanaimo, BC V9R 5S5, Canada. Offers EMBA, IMBA, MBA. Program offered jointly with University of Hertfordshire. *Accreditation:* ACBSP. Part-time and evening/weekend programs available. *Degree requirements:* For master's, thesis. *Entrance requirements:* Additional exam requirements/recommendations for international students: Required—TOEFL (minimum score 550 paper-based; 213 computer-based). Electronic applications accepted. *Faculty research:* Tourism development, entrepreneurship, organizational development, strategic planning, international business strategy.

Vanderbilt University, Owen Graduate School of Management, Executive MBA Program, Nashville, TN 37240-1001. Offers MBA. Evening/weekend programs available. *Faculty:* 16 full-time (2 women), 6 part-time/adjunct (2 women). *Students:* 97 full-time (12 women); includes 20 minority (8 African Americans, 11 Asian Americans or Pacific Islanders, 1 Hispanic American), 1 international. Average age 36. 77 applicants, 86% accepted, 52 enrolled. In 2009, 38 master's awarded. *Entrance requirements:* For master's, GMAT, minimum of 5 years of work experience. Additional exam requirements/recommendations for international students: Required—TOEFL. *Application deadline:* For fall admission, 6/1 for domestic students. Applications are processed on a rolling basis. Application fee: $150. Electronic applications accepted. *Expenses:* Contact institution. *Financial support:* In 2009–10, 1 student received support. Scholarships/grants available. *Faculty research:* Management, business policy, finance, marketing, operations management, health care. *Unit head:* Tami Fassinger, Associate Dean of Executive Education, 615-322-3120, Fax: 615-343-2293. *Application contact:* Juli Bennett, Coordinator, 615-322-9865, Fax: 615-343-2293, E-mail: juli.bennett@owen.vanderbilt.edu.

Vanderbilt University, Owen Graduate School of Management, Full Time MBA Program, Nashville, TN 37203. Offers MBA, JD/MBA, MBA/M Div, MBA/MA, MBA/MD, MBA/MSN. Students in the 5-year MBA program enter as undergraduates. *Accreditation:* AACSB. *Faculty:* 37 full-time (5 women), 25 part-time/adjunct (0 women). *Students:* 358 full-time (91 women); includes 28 minority (15 African Americans, 2 American Indian/Alaska Native, 10 Asian Americans or Pacific Islanders, 1 Hispanic American), 108 international. Average age 28. 915 applicants, 37% accepted, 186 enrolled. In 2009, 176 master's awarded. *Entrance requirements:* For master's, GMAT, minimum 2 years of work experience (strongly recommended). Additional exam requirements/recommendations for international students: Required—TOEFL; Recommended—TWE. *Application deadline:* For fall admission, 11/15 priority date for domestic students, 11/30 priority date for international students; for winter admission, 1/15 priority date for domestic and international students; for spring admission, 3/1 priority date for domestic students, 3/15 priority date for international students. Applications are processed on a rolling basis. Application fee: $125. Electronic applications accepted. *Financial support:* In 2009–10, 184 students received support. Scholarships/grants and tuition waivers (full and partial) available. Financial award application deadline: 5/1; financial award applicants required to submit FAFSA. *Faculty research:* Financial markets, services marketing, operations, organization studies, health care. Total annual research expenditures: $201,000. *Unit head:* John Roeder, Director of Admissions, 615-322-6469, Fax: 615-343-1175, E-mail: admissions@owen.vanderbilt.edu. *Application contact:* Sue Miller, Operations Manager, 615-322-4269, Fax: 615-343-1175, E-mail: admissions@owen.vanderbilt.edu.

Vanderbilt University, Owen Graduate School of Management and Graduate School, Master of Accountancy Program, Nashville, TN 37240-1001. Offers M Acc. *Accreditation:* AACSB. *Faculty:* 37 full-time (5 women), 25 part-time/adjunct (0 women). *Students:* 29 full-time (12

women); includes 3 minority (all Hispanic Americans). Average age 23. 130 applicants, 29% accepted, 29 enrolled. In 2009, 23 master's awarded. *Entrance requirements:* For master's, GMAT or GRE. Additional exam requirements/recommendations for international students: Required—TOEFL. *Application deadline:* For fall admission, 10/12 priority date for domestic students, 10/12 for international students; for winter admission, 1/11 for domestic and international students; for spring admission, 3/3 for domestic students. Electronic applications accepted. *Expenses:* Contact institution. *Financial support:* Scholarships/grants and tuition waivers available. Financial award application deadline: 5/1; financial award applicants required to submit FAFSA. *Faculty research:* Financial marketing, operations, human resources. *Unit head:* Dr. Karl Hackbrack, Faculty, 615-322-3641, E-mail: karl.hackenbrack@owen.vanderbilt.edu. *Application contact:* Amy Johnson, Program Director, 615-322-6506, E-mail: ajohnson@owen.vanderbilt.edu.

Vanguard University of Southern California, Graduate Program in Business, Costa Mesa, CA 92626-9601. Offers MBA. Part-time and evening/weekend programs available. *Students:* 11 full-time (6 women), 5 part-time (2 women). *Entrance requirements:* For master's, MAT or GMAT, minimum GPA of 3.0. Additional exam requirements/recommendations for international students: Required—TOEFL (minimum score 550 paper-based; 213 computer-based; 79 iBT). *Application deadline:* For fall admission, 4/1 priority date for domestic and international students; for spring admission, 10/1 priority date for domestic and international students. Applications are processed on a rolling basis. Application fee: $45. Electronic applications accepted. *Expenses:* Contact institution. *Financial support:* Scholarships/grants available. Financial award applicants required to submit FAFSA. *Unit head:* Dr. David Alford, Director, 714-556-3610 Ext. 3701, Fax: 714-662-5228, E-mail: dalford@vanguard.edu. *Application contact:* Graduate Coordinator, 714-556-3610 Ext. 3704, Fax: 714-662-5228.

Villanova University, Villanova School of Business, Executive MBA Program, Radnor, PA 19087. Offers EMBA. *Accreditation:* AACSB. Evening/weekend programs available. *Entrance requirements:* For master's, 8 years work experience. Additional exam requirements/recommendations for international students: Required—TOEFL (minimum score 550 paper-based; 213 computer-based; 80 iBT). Electronic applications accepted. *Expenses:* Contact institution. *Faculty research:* Leadership, management, corporate valuation, systems thinking, strategy.

Villanova University, Villanova School of Business, MBA—Fast Track Program, Villanova, PA 19085. Offers finance (MBA); international business (MBA); management information systems (MBA); marketing (MBA). *Accreditation:* AACSB. Part-time and evening/weekend programs available. *Entrance requirements:* For master's, GMAT, minimum 4.5 years of professional work experience. Additional exam requirements/recommendations for international students: Required—TOEFL (minimum score 550 paper-based; 213 computer-based; 80 iBT). Electronic applications accepted. *Expenses:* Tuition: Part-time $630 per credit. Required fees: $60 per credit. Part-time tuition and fees vary according to degree level and program. *Faculty research:* Developing and leveraging technology, ethical business practices, managing for innovation and creativity, the global political economy, strategic marketing management.

Villanova University, Villanova School of Business, MBA—Flex Track Program, Villanova, PA 19085. Offers corporate management (general) (MBA); finance (MBA); international business (MBA); management information systems (MBA); marketing (MBA); JD/MBA. *Accreditation:* AACSB. Part-time and evening/weekend programs available. Postbaccalaureate distance learning degree programs offered (minimal on-campus study). *Entrance requirements:* For master's, GMAT, minimum 4.5 years work experience. Additional exam requirements/recommendations for international students: Required—TOEFL (minimum score 550 paper-based; 213 computer-based; 80 iBT). Electronic applications accepted. *Expenses:* Tuition: Part-time $630 per credit. Required fees: $60 per credit. Part-time tuition and fees vary

according to degree level and program. *Faculty research:* Developing and leveraging technology, ethical business practices, managing for innovation and creativity, the global political economy, strategic marketing management.

Virginia College at Birmingham, Program in Business Administration, Birmingham, AL 35209. Offers MBA. Part-time and evening/weekend programs available. Postbaccalaureate distance learning degree programs offered (no on-campus study). In 2009, 3 master's awarded. *Financial support:* Career-related internships or fieldwork, Federal Work-Study, institutionally sponsored loans, scholarships/grants, and military educational benefits available. Support available to part-time students. Financial award applicants required to submit FAFSA. *Unit head:* Lisa Bacon, Unit Head, 877-812-8428, E-mail: admissions@vc.edu. *Application contact:* Angela Beck, Director of Admissions, 205-802-1200, E-mail: admissions@vc.edu.

Virginia College at Birmingham, Virginia College Online, Birmingham, AL 35209. Offers business administration (MBA); criminal justice (MCJ); cybersecurity (MC). Part-time and evening/weekend programs available. Postbaccalaureate distance learning degree programs offered (no on-campus study). *Financial support:* Military educational benefits available. Financial award applicants required to submit FAFSA. *Unit head:* Stan Banks, President, 877-207-1933, E-mail: vcoadm@vc.edu. *Application contact:* Christina Eschelman, Director of Admissions, 877-207-1933, E-mail: vcoadm@vc.edu.

Virginia Commonwealth University, Graduate School, School of Business, Program in Business Administration, Richmond, VA 23284-9005. Offers MBA, Postbaccalaureate Certificate. *Entrance requirements:* For master's, GMAT.

Virginia Commonwealth University, Graduate School, School of Business, Program in Management, Richmond, VA 23284-9005. Offers Certificate.

Virginia International University, Business Programs Department, Fairfax, VA 22030. Offers accounting (MBA); executive management (Graduate Certificate); global logistics (MBA); health care management (MBA); human resources management (MBA); international business management (MBA); international finance (MBA); marketing management (MBA). Part-time programs available. *Faculty:* 12 part-time/adjunct (1 woman). *Students:* 138 full-time (63 women), 7 part-time (5 women); includes 7 minority (1 African American, 5 Asian Americans or Pacific Islanders, 1 Hispanic American), 136 international. Average age 27. 331 applicants, 31% accepted, 40 enrolled. In 2009, 42 master's awarded. *Entrance requirements:* For master's and Graduate Certificate, bachelor's degree. Additional exam requirements/recommendations for international students: Required—TOEFL (minimum score 550 paper-based; 213 computer-based; 80 iBT), IELTS (minimum score 6). *Application deadline:* For fall admission, 7/31 for domestic students, 7/3 for international students; for spring admission, 12/18 for domestic students, 11/20 for international students. Applications are processed on a rolling basis. Application fee: $100. Electronic applications accepted. *Expenses:* Tuition: Full-time $10,044; part-time $569 per credit. One-time fee: $75. Tuition and fees vary according to degree level. *Financial support:* In 2009–10, 10 students received support. Scholarships/grants available. Financial award application deadline: 7/1. *Unit head:* Dr. Gail Whitaker, Chair, 703-591-7042 Ext. 346, Fax: 703-591-7046, E-mail: gwhitaker@viu.edu. *Application contact:* Emily L. Kraus, Director of Admissions, 703-591-7042 Ext. 309, Fax: 703-591-7048, E-mail: admissions@viu.edu.

Virginia Polytechnic Institute and State University, Graduate School, College of Science, Program in Biomedical Technology Development and Management, Blacksburg, VA 24061. Offers MS. *Expenses:* Tuition, area resident: Full-time $10,228; part-time $459 per credit hour. Tuition, nonresident: full-time $17,892; part-time $865 per credit hour. Required fees: $1966; $451 per semester.

Virginia Polytechnic Institute and State University, Graduate School, Pamplin College of Business, Department of Business Information Technology, Blacksburg, VA 24061. Offers business administration (PhD); business information technology (PhD). *Faculty:* 22 full-time (6 women). *Students:* 4 full-time (0 women), 3 part-time (0 women); includes 3 minority (2 American Indian/Alaska Native, 1 Asian American or Pacific Islander). Average age 36. 8 applicants, 13% accepted. *Entrance requirements:* For doctorate, GRE, GMAT. Additional exam requirements/recommendations for international students: Required—TOEFL (minimum score 550 paper-based; 213 computer-based). *Application deadline:* For fall admission, 5/15 for international students; for spring admission, 10/15 for international students. Applications are processed on a rolling basis. Application fee: $65. Electronic applications accepted. *Expenses:* Tuition, area resident: Full-time $10,228; part-time $459 per credit hour. Tuition, nonresident: full-time $17,892; part-time $865 per credit hour. Required fees: $1966; $451 per semester. *Financial support:* In 2009–10, 17 teaching assistantships with full tuition reimbursements (averaging $8,858 per year) were awarded; research assistantships, career-related internships or fieldwork, Federal Work-Study, scholarships/grants, and unspecified assistantships also available. Financial award application deadline: 1/15. *Faculty research:* Mathematical programming, computer simulation, decision support systems, production/operations research, information technology. Total annual research expenditures: $122,247. *Unit head:* Dr. Bernard W. Taylor, Dean, 540-231-6596, Fax: 540-231-7916, E-mail: betaylo3@vt.edu. *Application contact:* Cliff Ragsdale, Information Contact, 540-231-4697, Fax: 540-231-7916, E-mail: cragsdal@vt.edu.

Virginia Polytechnic Institute and State University, Graduate School, Pamplin College of Business, Department of Management, Blacksburg, VA 24061. Offers PhD. *Accreditation:* AACSB. *Faculty:* 19 full-time (6 women), 1 (woman) part-time/adjunct. *Students:* 9 full-time (2 women), 2 part-time (1 woman); includes 7 minority (all American Indian/Alaska Native). Average age 33. 27 applicants, 11% accepted, 2 enrolled. In 2009, 1 doctorate awarded. *Entrance requirements:* For doctorate, GRE, GMAT. Additional exam requirements/recommendations for international students: Required—TOEFL (minimum score 550 paper-based; 213 computer-based). *Application deadline:* For fall admission, 5/15 for international students; for spring admission, 10/15 for international students. Applications are processed on a rolling basis. Application fee: $65. Electronic applications accepted. *Expenses:* Tuition, area resident: Full-time $10,228; part-time $459 per credit hour. Tuition, nonresident: full-time $17,892; part-time $865 per credit hour. Required fees: $1966; $451 per semester. *Financial support:* In 2009–10, 11 teaching assistantships with full tuition reimbursements (averaging $12,057 per year) were awarded; career-related internships or fieldwork, Federal Work-Study, scholarships/grants, and unspecified assistantships also available. Financial award application deadline: 1/15. *Faculty research:* Compensation, organization effectiveness, selection, strategic planning, labor/management relations. Total annual research expenditures: $33,431. *Unit head:* Dr. Anju Seth, Head, 540-231-6353, Fax: 540-231-4487, E-mail: aseth@vt.edu. *Application contact:* Kevin Carlson, Information Contact, 540-231-4990, Fax: 540-231-4487, E-mail: kevinc@vt.edu.

Virginia Polytechnic Institute and State University, Graduate School, Pamplin College of Business, Program in Business Administration, Blacksburg, VA 24061. Offers MBA. *Accreditation:* AACSB. *Students:* 261 full-time (78 women), 95 part-time (33 women); includes 109 minority (2 African Americans, 70 American Indian/Alaska Native, 11 Asian Americans or Pacific Islanders, 26 Hispanic Americans), 26 international. Average age 32. 345 applicants, 41% accepted, 110 enrolled. In 2009, 124 master's awarded. *Entrance requirements:* For master's, GRE, GMAT. Additional exam requirements/recommendations for international students: Required—TOEFL (minimum score 550 paper-based; 213 computer-based). *Application deadline:* For fall admission, 5/15 for international students; for spring admission, 10/15 for international students. Applications are processed on a rolling basis. Application fee: $65. Electronic applications accepted. *Expenses:* Tuition, area resident: Full-time $10,228; part-time $459 per credit hour. Tuition, nonresident: full-time $17,892; part-time $865 per credit hour. Required fees: $1966; $451 per semester. *Financial support:* Career-related internships or fieldwork, Federal Work-Study, scholarships/grants, and unspecified assistantships available. Financial award application deadline: 1/15. Total annual research expenditures: $2.5 million. *Unit head:* Dr. Stephen J. Skripak, Dean, 540-231-6152, Fax: 540-231-4487, E-mail: sskripak@vt.edu. *Application contact:* Melanie Johnston, Information Contact, 540-231-6904, Fax: 540-231-4487, E-mail: mjohnston@vt.edu.

Viterbo University, Graduate Program in Business, La Crosse, WI 54601-4797. Offers MBA. *Accreditation:* ACBSP.

Wagner College, Division of Graduate Studies, Department of Business Administration, Staten Island, NY 10301-4495. Offers accelerated business administration (MBA); accounting (MS); finance (MBA); health care administration (MBA); international business (MBA); management (Exec MBA, MBA); marketing (MBA). *Accreditation:* ACBSP. Part-time and evening/weekend programs available. *Degree requirements:* For master's, thesis optional. *Entrance requirements:* For master's, GMAT, minimum GPA of 2.75, proficiency in computers and math. Additional exam requirements/recommendations for international students: Required—TOEFL (minimum score 550 paper-based; 217 computer-based). *Expenses:* Tuition: Full-time $15,570; part-time $865 per credit. Required fees: $2.

Wake Forest University, Babcock Graduate School of Management, Evening MBA Program–Charlotte, Charlotte, NC 28211. Offers MBA. *Accreditation:* AACSB. Evening/weekend programs available. *Faculty:* 62 full-time (13 women), 36 part-time/adjunct (14 women). *Students:* 98 full-time (17 women); includes 13 minority (8 African Americans, 1 American Indian/Alaska Native, 3 Asian Americans or Pacific Islanders, 1 Hispanic American), 1 international. Average age 30. In 2009, 42 master's awarded. *Entrance requirements:* For master's, GMAT or GRE, letters of recommendation, official transcripts, current resume or curriculum vitae, three years of work experience. Additional exam requirements/recommendations for international students: Required—TOEFL (minimum score 600 paper-based; 250 computer-based; 100 iBT), Pearson Test of English (PTE). *Application deadline:* For fall admission, 6/1 for domestic and international students. Applications are processed on a rolling basis. Application fee: $75. Electronic applications accepted. *Expenses:* Contact institution. *Financial support:* In 2009–10, 19 students received support. Scholarships/grants available. Financial award application deadline: 4/1; financial award applicants required to submit FAFSA. *Faculty research:* The influence of personal relationships on business decision making and management of change; drivers of perceived value and consumer behavior; impact of accounting on auditing, financial, managerial, systems and taxation stakeholders; corporate governance and executive compensation; impact of operations strategies on competitiveness. *Unit head:* Bill Davis, Associate Dean, Working Professional Programs, 704-365-1717, Fax: 704-365-3511, E-mail: clt.mba@mba.wfu.edu. *Application contact:* Judith Wright, Administrative Assistant, 704-365-1717, Fax: 704-365-3511, E-mail: clt.mba@mba.wfu.edu.

Wake Forest University, Babcock Graduate School of Management, Evening MBA Program–Winston-Salem, Winston-Salem, NC 27106. Offers MBA, PhD/MBA. *Accreditation:* AACSB. Evening/weekend programs available. *Faculty:* 62 full-time (13 women), 36 part-time/adjunct (14 women). *Students:* 81 full-time (29 women); includes 16 minority (11 African Americans, 1 Asian American or Pacific Islander, 4 Hispanic Americans), 1 international. Average age 33. In 2009, 43 master's awarded. *Entrance requirements:* For master's, GMAT or GRE, letters of recommendation, official transcripts, current resume or curriculum vitae, three years of work experience. Additional exam requirements/recommendations for international students: Required—TOEFL (minimum score 600 paper-based; 250 computer-based; 100 iBT), Pearson Test of English (PTE). *Application deadline:* For fall admission, 6/1 for domestic and international students. Applications are processed on a rolling basis. Application fee: $75. Electronic applications accepted. *Expenses:* Contact institution. *Financial support:* In 2009–10, 23 students received support. Scholarships/grants available. Financial award application deadline: 4/1; financial award applicants required to submit FAFSA. *Faculty research:* The influence of personal relationships on business decision making and management of change; drivers of perceived value and consumer behavior; impact of accounting on auditing, financial, managerial, systems and taxation stakeholders; corporate governance and executive compensation; impact of operations strategies on competitiveness. *Unit head:* Bill Davis, Associate Dean, Working Professional Programs, 336-758-5422, Fax: 336-758-5830, E-mail: admissions@mba.wfu.edu. *Application contact:* LaKesha Alston, Administrative Assistant, 336-758-5422, Fax: 336-758-5830, E-mail: admissions@mba.wfu.edu.

Wake Forest University, Babcock Graduate School of Management, Full-time MBA Program, Winston-Salem, NC 27106. Offers consulting/general management (MBA); entrepreneurship (MBA); finance (MBA); health (MBA); marketing (MBA); operations management (MBA); JD/MBA; MBA/MSA; MD/MBA. *Accreditation:* AACSB. *Faculty:* 62 full-time (13 women), 36 part-time/adjunct (14 women). *Students:* 144 full-time (36 women); includes 17 minority (8 African Americans, 9 Asian Americans or Pacific Islanders), 22 international. Average age 28. In 2009, 81 master's awarded. *Entrance requirements:* For master's, GMAT or GRE, letters of recommendation, official transcripts, current resume or curriculum vitae, 2 years of work experience with the exception of joint-degree candidates. Additional exam requirements/recommendations for international students: Required—TOEFL (minimum score 600 paper-based; 250 computer-based; 100 iBT), Pearson Test of English (PTE). *Application deadline:* For fall admission, 6/1 for domestic and international students. Applications are processed on a rolling basis. Application fee: $75. Electronic applications accepted. *Expenses:* Contact institution. *Financial support:* In 2009–10, 95 students received support. Career-related internships or fieldwork, scholarships/grants, and unspecified assistantships available. Financial award application deadline: 3/1; financial award applicants required to submit FAFSA. *Faculty research:* The influence of personal relationships on business decision making and management of change; drivers of perceived value and consumer behavior; impact of accounting on auditing, financial, managerial, systems and taxation stakeholders; corporate governance and executive compensation; impact of operations strategies on competitiveness. *Unit head:* Sherry Moss, Director, Full-time MBA Program, 336-758-5422, Fax: 336-758-5830, E-mail: admissions@mba.wfu.edu. *Application contact:* LaKesha Alston, Administrative Assistant, 336-758-5422, Fax: 336-758-5830, E-mail: admissions@mba.wfu.edu.

Wake Forest University, Babcock Graduate School of Management, MA in Management Program, Winston-Salem, NC 27106. Offers MA. *Faculty:* 62 full-time (13 women), 36 part-time/adjunct (14 women). *Students:* 91 full-time (38 women); includes 44 minority (37 African Americans, 4 Asian Americans or Pacific Islanders, 3 Hispanic Americans). Average age 22. In 2009, 27 master's awarded. *Entrance requirements:* For master's, GMAT or GRE, letters of recommendation, official transcripts, current resume or curriculum vitae. Additional exam requirements/recommendations for international students: Required—TOEFL (minimum score 600 paper-based; 250 computer-based; 100 iBT), Pearson Test of English (PTE). *Application deadline:* For fall admission, 6/1 for domestic and international students. Applications are processed on a rolling basis. Application fee: $75. Electronic applications accepted. *Financial support:* In 2009–10, 42 students received support. Scholarships/grants available. Financial award application deadline: 3/1; financial award applicants required to submit FAFSA. *Faculty research:* The influence of personal relationships on business decision making and management of change; drivers of perceived value and consumer behavior; impact of accounting on auditing, financial, managerial, systems and taxation stakeholders; corporate governance and executive compensation; impact of operations strategies on competitiveness. *Unit head:* Derrick Boone, Director, MA Program, 336-758-5422, Fax: 336-758-5830, E-mail: admissions@mba.wfu.edu. *Application contact:* LaKesha Alston, Administrative Assistant, 336-758-5422, Fax: 336-758-5830, E-mail: admissions@mba.wfu.edu.

Wake Forest University, Babcock Graduate School of Management, Saturday MBA Program–Charlotte, Charlotte, NC 28211. Offers MBA. *Accreditation:* AACSB. Evening/weekend programs available. *Faculty:* 62 full-time (13 women), 36 part-time/adjunct (14 women). *Students:* 79 full-time (19 women); includes 15 minority (4 African Americans, 10 Asian Americans or Pacific Islanders, 1 Hispanic American), 2 international. Average age 29. In 2009, 28 master's awarded. *Entrance requirements:* For master's, GMAT or GRE, letters of recommendation, official transcripts, current resume or curriculum vitae, three years of work experience. Additional exam requirements/recommendations for international students: Required—TOEFL (minimum score 600 paper-based; 250 computer-based; 100 iBT), Pearson Test of English (PTE).

Business Administration and Management—General

Wake Forest University (continued)
Application deadline: For spring admission, 11/1 for domestic and international students. Applications are processed on a rolling basis. Application fee: $75. Electronic applications accepted. *Expenses:* Contact institution. *Financial support:* Scholarships/grants available. Financial award application deadline: 9/1; financial award applicants required to submit FAFSA. *Faculty research:* The influence of personal relationships on business decision making and management of change; drivers of perceived value and consumer behavior; impact of accounting on auditing, financial, managerial, systems and taxation stakeholders; corporate governance and executive compensation; impact of operations strategies on competitiveness. *Unit head:* Bill Davis, Associate Dean, Working Professional Programs, 704-365-1717, Fax: 704-365-3511, E-mail: clt.mba@mba.wfu.edu. *Application contact:* Judith Wright, Administrative Assistant, 704-365-1717, Fax: 704-365-3511, E-mail: clt.mba@mba.wfu.edu.

Walden University, Graduate Programs, School of Management, Minneapolis, MN 55401. Offers applied management and decision sciences (PhD), including accounting, engineering management, finance, general applied management and decision sciences, information systems management, knowledge management, leadership and organizational change, learning management, operations research, self-designed program in applied management and design sciences; business information management (MISM); enterprise information security (MISM); entrepreneurship (MBA, DBA); finance (MBA, DBA); global supply chain management (DBA); healthcare management (MBA); healthcare system improvement (MBA); human resource management (MBA); information systems management (DBA); international business (MBA, DBA); IT strategy and governance (MISM); leadership (MBA, MS, DBA), including entrepreneurship (MS), general management (MS), human resources leadership (MS), innovation and technology (MS), leader development (MS), project management (MS), self-designed (MS), sustainable futures (MS); managing global software and service supply chains (MISM); marketing (MBA, DBA); project management (MBA, MS); risk management (MBA); self-designed (MBA, DBA); social impact management (DBA); sustainable futures (MBA); technology (MBA); technology entrepreneurship (DBA). Part-time and evening/weekend programs available. Postbaccalaureate distance learning degree programs offered (minimal on-campus study). *Faculty:* 17 full-time, 211 part-time/adjunct. *Students:* 3,389 full-time (1,774 women), 815 part-time (482 women); includes 1,969 minority (1,640 African Americans, 36 American Indian/Alaska Native, 123 Asian Americans or Pacific Islanders, 170 Hispanic Americans), 95 international. Average age 41. In 2009, 699 master's, 42 doctorates awarded. *Degree requirements:* For doctorate, thesis/dissertation (for some programs), residency. *Entrance requirements:* For master's, bachelor's degree or equivalent in related field; minimum GPA of 2.5; official transcripts; goal statement; access to computer and Internet; for doctorate, master's degree or equivalent in related field; minimum GPA of 3.0; 3 years of related professional/academic experience (preferred). Additional exam requirements/recommendations for international students: Required—TOEFL (minimum score 550 paper-based; 213 computer-based), IELTS (minimum score 6.5), TOEFL, IELTS, or Michigan English Language Assessment Battery (minimum score 82). *Application deadline:* Applications are processed on a rolling basis. Application fee: $50. Electronic applications accepted. *Expenses:* Tuition: Full-time $13,665; part-time $560 per credit. Required fees: $1375. Tuition and fees vary according to course load, degree level and program. *Financial support:* In 2009–10, 466 students received support: fellowships, Federal Work-Study, scholarships/grants, unspecified assistantships, and family tuition reduction, active duty/veteran tuition reduction, group tuition reduction, interest-free payment plans available. Support available to part-time students. Financial award applicants required to submit FAFSA. *Unit head:* William Schulz, Interim Associate Dean, 800-925-3368. *Application contact:* Jennifer Hall, Director of Enrollment, 866-4-WALDEN, E-mail: info@waldenu.edu.

Walsh College of Accountancy and Business Administration, Graduate Programs, Program in Business Administration, Troy, MI 48007-7006. Offers MBA. *Accreditation:* ACBSP. *Faculty:* 3 full-time (1 woman), 22 part-time/adjunct (6 women). *Students:* 61 full-time (29 women), 987 part-time (494 women); includes 171 minority (121 African Americans, 1 American Indian/Alaska Native, 34 Asian Americans or Pacific Islanders, 15 Hispanic Americans), 18 international. Average age 32. *Entrance requirements:* For master's, GMAT, minimum GPA of 2.75, previous course work in business. Additional exam requirements/recommendations for international students: Required—TOEFL. *Application deadline:* For fall admission, 8/24 priority date for domestic students; for winter admission, 1/1 priority date for domestic students; for spring admission, 4/1 priority date for domestic students. Applications are processed on a rolling basis. Application fee: $25. Electronic applications accepted. *Expenses:* Tuition: Part-time $525 per credit. Required fees: $125 per semester. *Financial support:* Application deadline: 6/30. *Unit head:* Dr. Sheila Ronis. *Application contact:* Jeremy Guc, Director of Admissions and Academic Advising, 248-823-1610, Fax: 248-689-0938, E-mail: jguc@walshcollege.edu.

Walsh College of Accountancy and Business Administration, Graduate Programs, Program in Management, Troy, MI 48007-7006. Offers MSIB, MSSL. Part-time and evening/weekend programs available. *Faculty:* 3 full-time (1 woman), 22 part-time/adjunct (6 women). *Students:* 6 full-time (2 women), 107 part-time (58 women); includes 19 minority (15 African Americans, 2 Asian Americans or Pacific Islanders, 2 Hispanic Americans). Average age 34. 26 applicants, 81% accepted, 15 enrolled. *Entrance requirements:* For master's, minimum GPA of 2.75, previous course work in business. Additional exam requirements/recommendations for international students: Required—TOEFL. *Application deadline:* For fall admission, 8/24 priority date for domestic students; for winter admission, 1/1 priority date for domestic students; for spring admission, 4/1 priority date for domestic students. Applications are processed on a rolling basis. Application fee: $25. Electronic applications accepted. *Expenses:* Tuition: Part-time $525 per credit. Required fees: $125 per semester. *Financial support:* Available to part-time students. Application deadline: 6/30. *Unit head:* Dr. Sheila Ronis, Director, 248-823-1261, Fax: 248-689-0920. *Application contact:* Jeremy Guc, Director of Admissions and Academic Advising, 248-823-1610, Fax: 248-689-0938, E-mail: jguc@walshcollege.edu.

Walsh University, Graduate Studies, MBA Program, North Canton, OH 44720-3396. Offers MBA. Part-time and evening/weekend programs available. *Faculty:* 6 full-time (2 women), 21 part-time/adjunct (4 women). *Students:* 16 full-time (12 women), 143 part-time (69 women); includes 11 minority (8 African Americans, 1 Asian American or Pacific Islander, 2 Hispanic Americans), 2 international. Average age 34. 60 applicants, 98% accepted, 49 enrolled. In 2009, 44 master's awarded. *Entrance requirements:* For master's, GMAT, minimum GPA of 3.0. Additional exam requirements/recommendations for international students: Required—TOEFL (minimum score 500 paper-based; 173 computer-based; 61 iBT). *Application deadline:* For fall admission, 7/15 priority date for domestic students. Applications are processed on a rolling basis. Application fee: $25. Electronic applications accepted. *Expenses:* Tuition: Full-time $9630; part-time $535 per credit hour. Tuition and fees vary according to course load and program. *Financial support:* In 2009–10, 98 students received support, including 9 research assistantships with partial tuition reimbursements available (averaging $5,518 per year); tuition waivers (partial), unspecified assistantships, and tuition discounts also available. Financial award application deadline: 12/31. *Faculty research:* Patient and physician satisfaction, advancing and improving learning with information technology, consumer-driven healthcare, branding and the service industry, service provider training and customer satisfaction. *Unit head:* Dr. Michael A. Petrochuk, Director of the MBA Program and Assistant Professor, 330-244-4764, Fax: 330-490-7359, E-mail: mpetrochuk@walsh.edu. *Application contact:* Stephanie Wheeler, Director of Graduate and Transfer Admissions, 330-490-7181, Fax: 330-490-7182, E-mail: swheeler@walsh.edu.

Warner Pacific College, Graduate Programs, Portland, OR 97215-4099. Offers biblical and theological studies (MA); biblical studies (M Rel); education (M Ed); management/organizational leadership (MS); pastoral ministries (M Rel); religion and ethics (M Rel); teaching (MA); theology (M Rel). Part-time programs available. *Degree requirements:* For master's, thesis or alternative, presentation of defense. *Entrance requirements:* For master's, interview, minimum GPA of 2.5, letters of recommendations. *Faculty research:* New Testament studies, nineteenth-century Wesleyan theology, preaching and church growth, Christian ethics.

Warner University, School of Business, Lake Wales, FL 33859. Offers MBA. Part-time and evening/weekend programs available. *Degree requirements:* For master's, comprehensive exam. *Entrance requirements:* For master's, GMAT, minimum GPA of 3.0, letters of recommendation (2). Additional exam requirements/recommendations for international students: Required—TOEFL. Electronic applications accepted.

Warner University, School of Professional Studies, Lake Wales, FL 33859. Offers management (MSM). Part-time and evening/weekend programs available. Postbaccalaureate distance learning degree programs offered. *Entrance requirements:* For master's, MAT, minimum GPA of 3.0; letters of recommendation (2). Additional exam requirements/recommendations for international students: Required—TOEFL (minimum score 550 paper-based). Electronic applications accepted.

Washburn University, School of Business, Topeka, KS 66621. Offers MBA. *Accreditation:* AACSB. Part-time and evening/weekend programs available. *Faculty:* 17 full-time (4 women), 4 part-time/adjunct (1 woman). *Students:* 19 full-time (8 women), 49 part-time (25 women). Average age 27. 48 applicants, 100% accepted, 47 enrolled. In 2009, 29 master's awarded. *Entrance requirements:* For master's, GMAT, minimum GPA of 2.75. Additional exam requirements/recommendations for international students: Required—TOEFL (minimum score 550 paper-based; 213 computer-based; 80 iBT); Recommended—IELTS (minimum score 6.5). *Application deadline:* For fall admission, 7/1 priority date for domestic and international students; for spring admission, 11/15 priority date for domestic and international students. Applications are processed on a rolling basis. Application fee: $40 ($70 for international students). Electronic applications accepted. *Financial support:* In 2009–10, 21 students received support. Available to part-time students. Application deadline: 2/15. *Faculty research:* Ethics in information technology, forecasting for shareholder value creation, model for measuring expected losses from litigation contingencies, business vs. family commitment in family businesses, calculated intangible value and brand recognition. Total annual research expenditures: $40,000. *Unit head:* Dr. David L. Sollars, Dean, 785-670-1308, Fax: 785-670-1063, E-mail: david.sollars@washburn.edu. *Application contact:* Dr. Robert J. Boncella, MBA Program Director, 785-670-2047, Fax: 785-670-1063, E-mail: mba.advisor@washburn.edu.

Washington Adventist University, MBA Program, Takoma Park, MD 20912. Offers MBA. Part-time programs available. *Faculty:* 15 part-time/adjunct. *Students:* 2 full-time (1 woman), 47 part-time (24 women); includes 21 African Americans, 3 Asian Americans or Pacific Islanders, 2 Hispanic Americans. Average age 36. In 2009, 22 master's awarded. *Entrance requirements:* For master's, minimum undergraduate GPA of 2.75, curriculum vitae, interview, essay, personal statement. Additional exam requirements/recommendations for international students: Required—TOEFL (minimum score 550 paper-based; 213 computer-based), IELTS (minimum score 5). *Application deadline:* Applications are processed on a rolling basis. Application fee: $50. *Financial support:* Institutionally sponsored loans available. Support available to part-time students. Financial award applicants required to submit FAFSA. *Unit head:* Dr. Davenia Lea, 301-891-4092. *Application contact:* Rahneeka Hazelton, 301-891-4092, Fax: 301-891-4023, E-mail: rhazelto@wau.edu.

Washington State University, Graduate School, College of Business, Graduate Programs in Business, Pullman, WA 99164. Offers accounting and business law (M Acc); business administration (MBA, PhD), including accounting (PhD), finance (PhD), management and operations (PhD), management information systems (PhD), marketing (PhD). *Accreditation:* AACSB. *Degree requirements:* For master's, comprehensive exam (for some programs), thesis (for some programs), final presentation; for doctorate, comprehensive exam, thesis/dissertation, oral and written exams. *Entrance requirements:* For master's and doctorate, GMAT, minimum GPA of 3.0, 3 letters of recommendation. Additional exam requirements/recommendations for international students: Required—TOEFL. Electronic applications accepted.

See Display on page 193.

Washington State University Tri-Cities, Graduate Programs, College of Business, Richland, WA 99354. Offers business management (MBA). Part-time and evening/weekend programs available. *Faculty:* 56. *Students:* 11 full-time (5 women), 37 part-time (5 women); includes 6 minority (1 American Indian/Alaska Native, 3 Asian Americans or Pacific Islanders, 2 Hispanic Americans), 1 international. Average age 35. In 2009, 16 master's awarded. *Degree requirements:* For master's, thesis (for some programs), oral presentation exam. *Entrance requirements:* For master's, GMAT, minimum GPA of 3.0, 3 letters of recommendation. Additional exam requirements/recommendations for international students: Required—TOEFL (minimum score 550 paper-based; 213 computer-based). *Application deadline:* For fall admission, 1/10 priority date for domestic students, 1/10 for international students; for spring admission, 7/1 priority date for domestic students, 7/1 for international students. Application fee: $50. *Expenses:* Tuition, state resident: part-time $423 per credit. Tuition, nonresident: part-time $1032 per credit. *Financial support:* In 2009–10, 17 students received support. *Faculty research:* Strategy, organizational transformation, technology and instructional effectiveness, market research effects of type (fonts), optimization of price structure, accounting ethic. *Unit head:* Dr. John Thornton, Director, 509-372-7246, Fax: 509-372-7354, E-mail: jthornt@tricity.wsu.edu. *Application contact:* Graduate School Admissions, 800-GRADWSU, Fax: 509-335-1949, E-mail: gradsch@wsu.edu.

Washington State University Vancouver, Graduate Programs, Program in Business Administration, Vancouver, WA 98686. Offers MBA. *Faculty:* 14. *Students:* 4 full-time (0 women), 46 part-time (14 women); includes 7 minority (1 African American, 5 Asian Americans or Pacific Islanders, 1 Hispanic American). *Degree requirements:* For master's, comprehensive exam (for some programs), thesis (for some programs), final presentation, portfolio. *Entrance requirements:* For master's, GMAT, minimum GPA of 3.0, 3 letters of recommendation, resume. Additional exam requirements/recommendations for international students: Required—TOEFL. *Application deadline:* For fall admission, 1/10 priority date for domestic students; for spring admission, 7/1 priority date for domestic students, 7/1 for international students. Application fee: $50. *Expenses:* Tuition, state resident: full-time $4228; part-time $423 per credit. Tuition, nonresident: full-time $10,322; part-time $1032 per credit. *Financial support:* In 2009–10, research assistantships (averaging $14,634 per year), teaching assistantships with full tuition reimbursements (averaging $13,383 per year) were awarded. Financial award application deadline: 2/15. *Faculty research:* Liquidity, cost of capital and firm value, business ethics, corporate governance, finance and nonfinancial performance measurement, negotiations, project management. *Unit head:* Dr. Jane Cote, Academic Director, 360-546-9756, E-mail: cotej@vancouver.wsu.edu. *Application contact:* Graduate School Admissions, 800-GRADWSU, Fax: 509-335-1949, E-mail: gradsch@wsu.edu.

Washington University in St. Louis, Olin Business School, St. Louis, MO 63130-4899. Offers EMBA, M Acc, MBA, MS, PhD, JD/MBA, M Arch/MBA, M Eng/MBA, MBA/MA, MBA/MSW. *Accreditation:* AACSB. *Faculty:* 73 full-time (14 women), 45 part-time/adjunct (7 women). *Students:* 439 full-time (156 women), 595 part-time (150 women); includes 219 minority (43 African Americans, 2 American Indian/Alaska Native, 163 Asian Americans or Pacific Islanders, 11 Hispanic Americans), 208 international. *Entrance requirements:* Additional exam requirements/recommendations for international students: Required—TOEFL. Electronic applications accepted.

Wayland Baptist University, Graduate Programs, Programs in Business Administration/Management, Plainview, TX 79072-6998. Offers general business (MBA); health care administration (MBA); human resource management (MBA); international management (MBA); management (MA, MBA), including health care administration (MA), human resource management (MA), organization management (MA); management information systems (MBA). Part-time and evening/weekend programs available. Postbaccalaureate distance learning degree programs offered (no on-campus study). *Faculty:* 10 full-time (3 women). *Students:* 6 full-time (1 woman), 55 part-time (31 women); includes 24 minority (9 African Americans, 1 American Indian/Alaska Native, 14 Hispanic Americans). Average age 34. 25 applicants, 76% accepted, 10 enrolled. In 2009, 8 master's awarded. *Degree requirements:* For master's, capstone course. *Entrance requirements:* For master's, GMAT, GRE or MAT. Additional exam requirements/recommendations for international students: Required—TOEFL (minimum score 500 paper-based; 173 computer-based; 61 iBT). *Application deadline:* Applications are processed on a rolling basis. Application fee: $50. Electronic applications accepted. *Expenses:* Tuition: Full-time $5796; part-time $322 per credit hour. Required fees: $782; $9 per credit hour. $60 per

Business Administration and Management—General

semester. Tuition and fees vary according to course load and campus/location. *Financial support:* Federal Work-Study, institutionally sponsored loans, and scholarships/grants available. Support available to part-time students. Financial award application deadline: 5/1; financial award applicants required to submit FAFSA. *Unit head:* Dr. Otto Schacht, Chairman, 806-291-1020, Fax: 806-291-1957. *Application contact:* Amanda Stanton, Graduate Studies, 806-291-3423, Fax: 806-291-1950, E-mail: stanton@wbu.edu.

Waynesburg University, Graduate and Professional Studies, Waynesburg, PA 15370-1222. Offers business (MBA), including finance, health systems, human resources, leadership, market development; counseling (MA), including addictions counseling, clinical mental health; education (MAT); nursing (MSN), including administration, education, informatics, palliative care; nursing practice (DNP); special education (M Ed); technology (M Ed); MSN/MBA. *Accreditation:* AACN. Part-time and evening/weekend programs available. *Faculty:* 11 full-time (5 women), 136 part-time/adjunct (80 women). *Students:* 116 full-time (85 women), 984 part-time (682 women). 711 applicants, 80% accepted, 485 enrolled. In 2009, 320 master's, 41 doctorates awarded. *Degree requirements:* For doctorate, thesis/dissertation. *Entrance requirements:* Additional exam requirements/recommendations for international students: Required—TOEFL. *Application deadline:* For fall admission, 8/1 priority date for domestic students. Applications are processed on a rolling basis. Electronic applications accepted. *Expenses:* Tuition: Part-time $520 per credit. *Financial support:* Available to part-time students. Application deadline: 5/1. *Unit head:* David Mariner, Dean, 724-743-4420, Fax: 724-743-4425, E-mail: dmariner@waynesburg.edu. *Application contact:* Michael Bednarski, Director of Admissions, 724-743-4420, Fax: 724-743-4425, E-mail: mbednars@waynesburg.edu.

Wayne State College, School of Business and Technology, Wayne, NE 68787. Offers MBA. Part-time and evening/weekend programs available. Postbaccalaureate distance learning degree programs offered (minimal on-campus study). *Entrance requirements:* For master's, GMAT, minimum overall GPA of 3.0. Additional exam requirements/recommendations for international students: Required—TOEFL (minimum score 550 paper-based; 213 computer-based).

Wayne State University, School of Business Administration, Detroit, MI 48202. Offers accounting (MS); business administration (MBA, PhD); interdisciplinary studies (PhD); taxation (MS); JD/MBA. *Accreditation:* AACSB. Part-time and evening/weekend programs available. *Degree requirements:* For master's, thesis optional. *Entrance requirements:* For master's, GMAT, minimum undergraduate GPA of 2.50. Additional exam requirements/recommendations for international students: Required—TOEFL (minimum score 550 paper-based; 213 computer-based); Recommended—TWE (minimum score 6). Electronic applications accepted. *Faculty research:* Corporate financial valuation, strategic advertising, information technology effectiveness, financial accounting and taxation, organizational performance and effectiveness.

See Close-Up on page 279.

Webber International University, Graduate School of Business, Babson Park, FL 33827-0096. Offers accounting (MBA); management (MBA); security management (MBA); sports management (MBA). Part-time and evening/weekend programs available. *Degree requirements:* For master's, thesis or alternative. *Entrance requirements:* For master's, previous course work in financial and managerial accounting. Additional exam requirements/recommendations for international students: Required—TOEFL. *Faculty research:* Finance strategy, market research, investments, intranet.

See Close-Up on page 281.

Weber State University, John B. Goddard School of Business and Economics, Program in Business Administration, Ogden, UT 84408-1001. Offers MBA. *Accreditation:* AACSB. Part-time and evening/weekend programs available. *Entrance requirements:* For master's, GMAT, resume, letters of recommendation. Additional exam requirements/recommendations for international students: Required—TOEFL (minimum score 550 paper-based; 213 computer-based). Electronic applications accepted.

Webster University, George Herbert Walker School of Business and Technology, Department of Business, St. Louis, MO 63119-3194. Offers business (MA); business and organizational security management (MBA); computer resources and information management (MBA); environmental management (MBA); finance (MA, MBA); health services management (MBA); human resources development (MBA); human resources management (MBA); international business (MA, MBA); management and leadership (MBA); marketing (MBA); procurement and acquisitions management (MBA); telecommunications management (MBA). *Accreditation:* ACBSP. Part-time and evening/weekend programs available. Postbaccalaureate distance learning degree programs offered (no on-campus study). *Faculty:* 9 full-time, 430 part-time/adjunct. *Students:* 1,190 full-time (543 women), 4,226 part-time (2,159 women). Average age 34. In 2009, 2,021 master's awarded. *Degree requirements:* For master's, comprehensive exam (for some programs), thesis (for some programs). *Entrance requirements:* Additional exam requirements/recommendations for international students: Required—TOEFL. *Application deadline:* Applications are processed on a rolling basis. Application fee: $35 ($50 for international students). *Expenses:* Tuition: Part-time $565 per credit hour. Tuition and fees vary according to degree level, campus/location and program. *Financial support:* Federal Work-Study available. Support available to part-time students. Financial award application deadline: 4/1; financial award applicants required to submit FAFSA. *Unit head:* Dr. Debbie Psihountas, Chair, 314-246-7553 Ext. 7017, Fax: 314-968-7077, E-mail: buschair@webster.edu. *Application contact:* Matt Nolan, Associate Vice President for Enrollment Management/Dean of Admissions, Fax: 314-968-7116, E-mail: gadmit@webster.edu.

Webster University, George Herbert Walker School of Business and Technology, Department of Management, St. Louis, MO 63119-3194. Offers business and organizational security management (MA); computer resources and information management (MA); environmental management (MS); government contracting (Certificate); health care management (MA); health services management (MA); human resources development (MA); human resources management (MA); management (DM); management and leadership (MA); marketing (MA); nonprofit management (Certificate); procurement and acquisitions management (MA); public administration (MA); quality management (MA); space systems operations management (MS); telecommunications management (MA). *Accreditation:* ACBSP. Part-time and evening/weekend programs available. Postbaccalaureate distance learning degree programs offered (no on-campus study). *Faculty:* 16 full-time, 781 part-time/adjunct. *Students:* 1,369 full-time (610 women), 5,182 part-time (3,047 women); includes 3,460 minority (2,835 African Americans, 38 American Indian/Alaska Native, 169 Asian Americans or Pacific Islanders, 418 Hispanic Americans), 80 international. Average age 37. In 2009, 2,491 master's, 13 doctorates, 68 other advanced degrees awarded. *Degree requirements:* For master's, thesis (for some programs); for doctorate, thesis/dissertation, written exam. *Entrance requirements:* For doctorate, GMAT, 3 years of work experience, MBA. Additional exam requirements/recommendations for international students: Required—TOEFL. *Application deadline:* Applications are processed on a rolling basis. Application fee: $25 ($50 for international students). *Expenses:* Tuition: Part-time $565 per credit hour. Tuition and fees vary according to degree level, campus/location and program. *Financial support:* Federal Work-Study available. Support available to part-time students. Financial award application deadline: 4/1; financial award applicants required to submit FAFSA. *Unit head:* Jim Brasfield, Chair, 314-961-2660 Ext. 7063, Fax: 314-968-7077, E-mail: mgtchair@webster.edu. *Application contact:* Matt Nolan, Associate Vice President for Enrollment Management/Dean of Admissions, Fax: 314-968-7116, E-mail: gadmit@webster.edu.

Wesleyan College, Department of Business and Economics, EMBA Program, Macon, GA 31210-4462. Offers EMBA. Evening/weekend programs available. *Entrance requirements:* For master's, GMAT, LSAT, GRE or MAT, 5 years of work experience, 5 years of management experience. Additional exam requirements/recommendations for international students: Required—TOEFL (minimum score 550 paper-based). Electronic applications accepted.

Wesley College, Business Program, Dover, DE 19901-3875. Offers environmental management (MBA); executive leadership (MBA); management (MBA). Executive leadership concentration also offered at New Castle, DE location. Part-time and evening/weekend programs available. *Entrance requirements:* For master's, GMAT or GRE, minimum undergraduate GPA of 2.75.

Business Administration and Management—General

West Chester University of Pennsylvania, Office of Graduate Studies, College of Business and Public Affairs, Department of Economics and Finance, West Chester, PA 19383. Offers business administration: economics-finance (MBA). Part-time and evening/weekend programs available. *Students:* 3 part-time (1 woman); includes 1 minority (Asian American or Pacific Islander). Average age 26. 1 applicant, 100% accepted, 1 enrolled. In 2009, 6 master's awarded. *Entrance requirements:* For master's, GMAT, statement of professional goals, resume, three letters of recommendation, interview . Additional exam requirements/recommendations for international students: Required—TOEFL (minimum score 550 paper-based; 213 computer-based; 80 iBT). *Application deadline:* For fall admission, 4/15 for domestic students, 3/15 for international students; for spring admission, 10/15 for domestic students, 9/1 for international students. Applications are processed on a rolling basis. Application fee: $35. Electronic applications accepted. *Expenses:* Tuition, state resident: full-time $6666; part-time $370 per credit. Tuition, nonresident: full-time $10,666; part-time $593 per credit. Required fees: $122.56 per credit. *Financial support:* In 2009–10, research assistantships with full and partial tuition reimbursements (averaging $5,000 per year); unspecified assistantships also available. Support available to part-time students. Financial award application deadline: 2/15; financial award applicants required to submit FAFSA. *Unit head:* Dr. Paul Christ, MBA Director and Graduate Coordinator, 610-425-5000, E-mail: pchrist@wcupa.edu. *Application contact:* Office of Graduate Studies, 610-436-2943, Fax: 610-436-2763, E-mail: gradstudy@wcupa.edu.

West Chester University of Pennsylvania, Office of Graduate Studies, College of Business and Public Affairs, Department of Management, West Chester, PA 19383. Offers business (Certificate); executive (MBA); general business (MBA); management (MBA). *Accreditation:* AACSB. Part-time and evening/weekend programs available. *Students:* 77 part-time (27 women); includes 10 minority (4 African Americans, 4 Asian Americans or Pacific Islanders, 2 Hispanic Americans), 1 international. Average age 31. 62 applicants, 94% accepted, 23 enrolled. In 2009, 23 master's, 11 other advanced degrees awarded. *Entrance requirements:* For master's, GMAT, statement of professional goals, resume, three letters of recommendation, interview. Additional exam requirements/recommendations for international students: Required—TOEFL (minimum score 550 paper-based; 213 computer-based; 80 iBT). *Application deadline:* For fall admission, 4/15 priority date for domestic students, 3/15 for international students; for spring admission, 10/15 for domestic students, 9/1 for international students. Applications are processed on a rolling basis. Application fee: $35. Electronic applications accepted. *Expenses:* Tuition, state resident: full-time $6666; part-time $370 per credit. Tuition, nonresident: full-time $10,666; part-time $593 per credit. Required fees: $122.56 per credit. *Financial support:* In 2009–10, 3 research assistantships with full and partial tuition reimbursements (averaging $5,000 per year) were awarded; unspecified assistantships also available. Support available to part-time students. Financial award application deadline: 2/15; financial award applicants required to submit FAFSA. *Unit head:* Dr. Paul Christ, MBA Director and Graduate Coordinator, 610-425-5000 Ext. 3232, E-mail: pchrist@wcupa.edu. *Application contact:* Dr. Paul Christ, MBA Director and Graduate Coordinator, 610-425-5000 Ext. 3232, E-mail: pchrist@wcupa.edu.

West Chester University of Pennsylvania, Office of Graduate Studies, College of Business and Public Affairs, Department of Marketing, West Chester, PA 19383. Offers business administration: tech-electronic (MBA). Part-time and evening/weekend programs available. *Students:* 2 part-time (1 woman). Average age 44. 1 applicant, 100% accepted, 0 enrolled. In 2009, 2 master's awarded. *Entrance requirements:* For master's, GMAT, statement of professional goals, resume, two letters of reference. Additional exam requirements/recommendations for international students: Required—TOEFL (minimum score 550 paper-based; 213 computer-based; 80 iBT). *Application deadline:* For fall admission, 4/15 for domestic students, 3/15 for international students; for spring admission, 10/15 for domestic students, 9/1 for international students. Applications are processed on a rolling basis. Application fee: $35. Electronic applications accepted. *Expenses:* Tuition, state resident: full-time $6666; part-time $370 per credit. Tuition, nonresident: full-time $10,666; part-time $593 per credit. Required fees: $122.56 per credit. *Financial support:* In 2009–10, research assistantships with full and partial tuition reimbursements (averaging $5,000 per year); unspecified assistantships also available. Support available to part-time students. Financial award application deadline: 2/15; financial award applicants required to submit FAFSA. *Unit head:* Dr. Paul Christ, MBA Director and Graduate Coordinator, 610-425-5000, E-mail: pchrist@wcupa.edu. *Application contact:* Office of Graduate Studies, 610-436-2943, Fax: 610-436-2763, E-mail: gradstudy@wcupa.edu.

Western Carolina University, Graduate School, College of Business, Program in Business Administration, Cullowhee, NC 28723. Offers MBA. *Accreditation:* AACSB. Part-time and evening/weekend programs available. *Students:* 34 full-time (17 women), 70 part-time (26 women). Average age 31. 73 applicants, 77% accepted, 42 enrolled. In 2009, 46 master's awarded. *Entrance requirements:* For master's, GMAT, appropriate undergraduate degree, 3 letters of recommendation. Additional exam requirements/recommendations for international students: Required—TOEFL (minimum score 550 paper-based; 270 computer-based; 79 iBT). *Application deadline:* For fall admission, 5/1 priority date for domestic students; for spring admission, 9/1 priority date for domestic students. Applications are processed on a rolling basis. Application fee: $45. *Financial support:* In 2009–10, 15 students received support, including 15 research assistantships with full and partial tuition reimbursements available (averaging $6,200 per year); fellowships, teaching assistantships with full and partial tuition reimbursements available, career-related internships or fieldwork, institutionally sponsored loans, traineeships, and unspecified assistantships also available. Financial award application deadline: 3/31; financial award applicants required to submit FAFSA. *Faculty research:* Marketing strategy, biotechnology, executive education, business statistics, supply chain management, innovation. *Unit head:* Kenneth Place, Director, 828-227-3588, Fax: 828-227-7414, E-mail: kplace@email.wcu.edu. *Application contact:* Admissions Specialist for Business Administration, 828-227-7398, Fax: 828-227-7480, E-mail: gradsch@email.wcu.edu.

Western Connecticut State University, Division of Graduate Studies, Ancell School of Business, Program in Business Administration, Danbury, CT 06810-6885. Offers accounting (MBA); business administration (MBA). Part-time programs available. *Faculty:* 7 full-time (1 woman). *Students:* 1 (woman) full-time, 53 part-time (30 women); includes 1 minority (Asian American or Pacific Islander), 1 international. Average age 32. 39 applicants, 69% accepted, 21 enrolled. In 2009, 15 master's awarded. *Degree requirements:* For master's, comprehensive exam, completion of program within 8 years. *Entrance requirements:* For master's, GMAT. Additional exam requirements/recommendations for international students: Recommended—TOEFL (minimum score 550 paper-based; 213 computer-based; 79 iBT), IELTS (minimum score 6). *Application deadline:* For fall admission, 8/5 priority date for domestic students; for spring admission, 1/5 priority date for domestic students. Applications are processed on a rolling basis. Application fee: $50. *Expenses:* Tuition, state resident: full-time $5012; part-time $278 per credit hour. Tuition, nonresident: full-time $13,962; part-time $284 per credit hour. Required fees: $3886; $139 per credit hour. Full-time tuition and fees vary according to course load and program. Part-time tuition and fees vary according to course level, degree level and program. *Financial support:* In 2009–10, 1 student received support. Application deadline: 5/1. *Unit head:* Dr. Fred Tesch, MBA Coordinator, 203-837-8654, Fax: 203-837-8527. *Application contact:* Chris Shankle, Associate Director of Graduate Studies, 203-837-9005, Fax: 203-837-8326, E-mail: shanklec@wcsu.edu.

Western Governors University, Programs in Business, Salt Lake City, UT 84107. Offers information technology management (MBA); management and strategy (MBA); strategic leadership (MBA). Postbaccalaureate distance learning degree programs offered. Electronic applications accepted.

Western Illinois University, School of Graduate Studies, College of Business and Technology, Program in Business Administration, Macomb, IL 61455-1390. Offers MBA. *Accreditation:* AACSB. Part-time programs available. *Students:* 56 full-time (22 women), 53 part-time (26 women); includes 4 minority (3 African Americans, 1 Asian American or Pacific Islander), 11 international. Average age 31. 55 applicants, 64% accepted. In 2009, 53 master's awarded. *Degree requirements:* For master's, thesis or alternative. *Entrance requirements:* For master's, GMAT. Additional exam requirements/recommendations for international students: Required—TOEFL (minimum score 550 paper-based; 213 computer-based; 80 iBT). *Application deadline:*

Applications are processed on a rolling basis. Application fee: $30. Electronic applications accepted. *Expenses:* Tuition, state resident: full-time $4486; part-time $249.21 per credit hour. Tuition, nonresident: full-time $8972; part-time $498.42 per credit hour. Required fees: $72.62 per credit hour. *Financial support:* In 2009–10, 27 students received support, including 27 research assistantships with full tuition reimbursements available (averaging $7,280 per year). Financial award applicants required to submit FAFSA. *Unit head:* Dr. John Elfrink, Associate Dean, 309-298-2442. *Application contact:* Evelyn Hoing, Assistant Director of Graduate Studies, 309-298-1806, Fax: 309-298-2345, E-mail: grad-office@wiu.edu.

Western International University, Graduate Programs in Business, Master of Business Administration Program, Phoenix, AZ 85021-2718. Offers MBA. Part-time and evening/weekend programs available. Postbaccalaureate distance learning degree programs offered (no on-campus study). *Faculty:* 60 part-time/adjunct (15 women). *Students:* 145 full-time (75 women); includes 37 minority (16 African Americans, 3 American Indian/Alaska Native, 7 Asian Americans or Pacific Islanders, 11 Hispanic Americans), 8 international. Average age 38. In 2009, 47 master's awarded. *Entrance requirements:* For master's, minimum GPA of 2.75. Additional exam requirements/recommendations for international students: Required—TOEFL (minimum score 550 paper-based; 213 computer-based; 79 iBT), TWE (minimum score 5), or IELTS (minimum score 6.5). *Application deadline:* Applications are processed on a rolling basis. Application fee: $25. Electronic applications accepted. *Expenses:* Tuition: Full-time $12,600. One-time fee: $25 full-time. *Financial support:* Applicants required to submit FAFSA. *Unit head:* Dr. Deborah DeSimone, Chief Academic Officer, 602-429-1135, Fax: 602-749-0752, E-mail: deborah.desimone@wintu.edu. *Application contact:* Melissa Machuca, Director of Enrollment, 602-943-2311, Fax: 602-371-8637.

Western International University, Graduate Programs in Business, Master of Business Administration Program in Management, Phoenix, AZ 85021-2718. Offers MBA. Part-time and evening/weekend programs available. Postbaccalaureate distance learning degree programs offered (no on-campus study). *Faculty:* 24 part-time/adjunct (5 women). *Students:* 125 full-time (63 women); includes 39 minority (9 African Americans, 3 American Indian/Alaska Native, 16 Asian Americans or Pacific Islanders, 11 Hispanic Americans), 6 international. Average age 37. In 2009, 47 master's awarded. *Entrance requirements:* For master's, minimum GPA of 2.75. Additional exam requirements/recommendations for international students: Required—TOEFL (minimum score 550 paper-based; 213 computer-based; 79 iBT), TWE (minimum score 5), or IELTS (minimum score 6.5). *Application deadline:* Applications are processed on a rolling basis. Application fee: $25. Electronic applications accepted. *Expenses:* Tuition: Full-time $12,600. One-time fee: $25 full-time. *Financial support:* Applicants required to submit FAFSA. *Unit head:* Dr. Deborah DeSiimone, Chief Academic Officer, 602-429-1135, E-mail: deborah.desimone@west.edu. *Application contact:* Melissa Machuca, Director of Enrollment, 602-943-2311, Fax: 602-371-8637.

Western Kentucky University, Graduate Studies, Gordon Ford College of Business, College of Business Administration, Bowling Green, KY 42101. Offers MBA. *Accreditation:* AACSB. Part-time and evening/weekend programs available. *Degree requirements:* For master's, comprehensive exam, thesis optional. *Entrance requirements:* For master's, GMAT, minimum GPA of 2.5. Additional exam requirements/recommendations for international students: Required—TOEFL (minimum score 555 paper-based; 213 computer-based; 79 iBT). *Expenses:* Tuition, state resident: full-time $4160; part-time $416 per credit hour. Tuition, nonresident: full-time $9550; part-time $506 per credit hour. Tuition and fees vary according to campus/location and reciprocity agreements. *Faculty research:* Business and international education, web page development, management training, international studies, globalization.

Western Michigan University, Graduate College, Haworth College of Business, Department of Finance and Commercial Law, Kalamazoo, MI 49008. Offers finance (MBA). *Accreditation:* AACSB. *Faculty:* 58 full-time (9 women). *Students:* 367 full-time (141 women), 238 part-time (74 women); includes 32 minority (11 African Americans, 1 American Indian/Alaska Native, 15 Asian Americans or Pacific Islanders, 5 Hispanic Americans), 188 international. 254 applicants, 89% accepted, 144 enrolled. In 2009, 146 master's awarded. *Entrance requirements:* For master's, GMAT. *Application deadline:* For fall admission, 2/15 priority date for domestic students. Applications are processed on a rolling basis. Application fee: $25. *Financial support:* Fellowships, research assistantships, teaching assistantships, Federal Work-Study available. Financial award application deadline: 2/15; financial award applicants required to submit FAFSA. *Application contact:* Admissions and Orientation, 269-387-2000, Fax: 269-387-2355.

Western New England College, School of Business, Program in Business Administration (General), Springfield, MA 01119. Offers general business (MBA); sport management (MBA). *Accreditation:* AACSB. Part-time and evening/weekend programs available. *Students:* 103 part-time (43 women); includes 5 African Americans, 2 Asian Americans or Pacific Islanders, 2 Hispanic Americans. In 2009, 22 master's awarded. *Entrance requirements:* For master's, GMAT, 2 letters of reference, resume. *Application deadline:* Applications are processed on a rolling basis. Application fee: $30. *Expenses:* Tuition: Part-time $552 per credit hour. Part-time tuition and fees vary according to program. *Financial support:* Available to part-time students. Applicants required to submit FAFSA. *Unit head:* Dr. Julie Siciliano, Dean, 413-782-1231. *Application contact:* Matt Fox, Director of Recruiting and Marketing for Adult Learners, 413-782-1249, Fax: 413-782-1779, E-mail: ce@wnec.edu.

Western New Mexico University, Graduate Division, Department of Business Administration and Criminal Justice, Silver City, NM 88062-0680. Offers business administration (MBA). *Accreditation:* ACBSP. Part-time and evening/weekend programs available. *Entrance requirements:* For master's, GMAT. Additional exam requirements/recommendations for international students: Required—TOEFL (minimum score 550 paper-based; 213 computer-based). Electronic applications accepted.

Western Washington University, Graduate School, College of Business and Economics, Bellingham, WA 98225-5996. Offers MBA, MP Acc. *Accreditation:* AACSB. Part-time and evening/weekend programs available. *Degree requirements:* For master's, comprehensive exam. *Entrance requirements:* For master's, GMAT, minimum GPA of 3.0 in last 60 semester hours or last 90 quarter hours. Additional exam requirements/recommendations for international students: Required—TOEFL (minimum score 567 paper-based; 227 computer-based). Electronic applications accepted. *Faculty research:* Enterprise strategy/corporate social performance, sustainability/environmental management/nonprofit marketing, managerial/environmental accounting, organizational applications of collaborative technology, environmental and resource economics.

Westminster College, The Bill and Vieve Gore School of Business, Salt Lake City, UT 84105-3697. Offers accountancy (M Acc); business administration (MBA, Certificate); technology management (MBATM). *Accreditation:* ACBSP. Part-time and evening/weekend programs available. *Faculty:* 27 full-time (7 women), 28 part-time/adjunct (5 women). *Students:* 189 full-time (36 women), 286 part-time (71 women); includes 32 minority (3 African Americans, 17 Asian Americans or Pacific Islanders, 12 Hispanic Americans), 5 international. Average age 32. 410 applicants, 48% accepted, 167 enrolled. In 2009, 141 master's, 44 other advanced degrees awarded. *Degree requirements:* For master's, international trip, minimum grade of C in all classes. *Entrance requirements:* For master's, GMAT, 2 professional recommendations, employer letter of support, personal resume. Additional exam requirements/recommendations for international students: Required—TOEFL (minimum score 600 paper-based; 214 computer-based; 100 iBT), IELTS (minimum score 7). *Application deadline:* Applications are processed on a rolling basis. Application fee: $40. Electronic applications accepted. *Expenses:* Contact institution. *Financial support:* In 2009–10, 205 students received support. Career-related internships or fieldwork and tuition reimbursement, tuition remission available. Support available to part-time students. Financial award applicants required to submit FAFSA. *Faculty research:* Innovation and entrepreneurship, business strategy and change, financial analysis and capital budgeting, leadership development. Total annual research expenditures: $100,000. *Unit head:* John Groesbeck, Dean, 801-832-2600, Fax: 801-832-3106, E-mail: jgroesbeck@westminstercollege.edu. *Application contact:* Joel Bauman, Vice President of Enrollment Services, 801-832-2200, Fax: 801-832-3101, E-mail: admission@westminstercollege.edu.

West Texas A&M University, College of Business, Department of Management, Marketing, and General Business, Canyon, TX 79016-0001. Offers business administration (MBA). Part-time and evening/weekend programs available. Postbaccalaureate distance learning degree programs offered (minimal on-campus study). *Entrance requirements:* For master's, GMAT. Additional exam requirements/recommendations for international students: Required—TOEFL (minimum score 550 paper-based). Electronic applications accepted. *Faculty research:* Human resources, international business, southern Asian markets, global strategies, international trade composition.

West Virginia University, College of Business and Economics, Program in Business Administration, Morgantown, WV 26506. Offers MBA, JD/MBA. *Accreditation:* AACSB. Part-time and evening/weekend programs available. *Entrance requirements:* For master's, GMAT. Additional exam requirements/recommendations for international students: Required—TOEFL. Electronic applications accepted. *Faculty research:* Financial management, managerial accounting, marketing, planning, corporate finance.

West Virginia Wesleyan College, Department of Business and Economics, Buckhannon, WV 26201. Offers MBA. Part-time and evening/weekend programs available. *Faculty:* 8 part-time/adjunct (3 women). *Students:* 23 full-time (8 women), 2 part-time (1 woman); includes 1 minority (Hispanic American), 3 international. Average age 28. 20 applicants, 75% accepted, 13 enrolled. In 2009, 20 master's awarded. *Degree requirements:* For master's, exit evaluation. *Entrance requirements:* For master's, GMAT. Additional exam requirements/recommendations for international students: Required—TOEFL. Application fee: $30. *Expenses:* Tuition: Part-time $360 per credit hour. *Financial support:* Federal Work-Study available. Support available to part-time students. *Unit head:* Kristina Smith, Director, MBA Program, 304-473-8MBA, Fax: 304-473-8479, E-mail: smith_k@wvwc.edu. *Application contact:* Kristina Smith, Director, MBA Program, 304-473-8MBA, Fax: 304-473-8479, E-mail: smith_k@wvwc.edu.

Wheeling Jesuit University, Department of Business, Wheeling, WV 26003-6295. Offers accounting (MS); business administration (MBA). *Accreditation:* ACBSP. Part-time and evening/weekend programs available. *Faculty:* 6 full-time (0 women), 3 part-time/adjunct (0 women). *Students:* 33 full-time (14 women), 30 part-time (14 women); includes 3 minority (2 African Americans, 1 Asian American or Pacific Islander), 7 international. Average age 28. 27 applicants, 96% accepted, 19 enrolled. In 2009, 20 master's awarded. *Entrance requirements:* For master's, GMAT, minimum undergraduate GPA of 2.8. Additional exam requirements/recommendations for international students: Required—TOEFL (minimum score 600 paper-based; 250 computer-based; 80 iBT). *Application deadline:* For fall admission, 8/1 priority date for domestic students, 8/1 for international students; for spring admission, 12/15 priority date for domestic students, 12/1 for international students. Applications are processed on a rolling basis. Application fee: $25. Electronic applications accepted. *Expenses:* Tuition: Full-time $9000; part-time $500 per credit hour. Required fees: $195 per semester. One-time fee: $375. Tuition and fees vary according to program. *Financial support:* In 2009–10, 47 students received support. Career-related internships or fieldwork and unspecified assistantships available. Financial award application deadline: 8/1; financial award applicants required to submit FAFSA. *Faculty research:* Forensic economics, philosophic economics, consumer behavior, international business, economic development. *Unit head:* Dr. Edward W. Younkins, Director, 304-243-2255, Fax: 304-243-8703, E-mail: younkins@wju.edu. *Application contact:* Melissa Rataiczak, Director of Admissions, Professional and Graduate Studies, 304-243-2250, Fax: 304-243-4441, E-mail: mrataiczak@wju.edu.

Wichita State University, Graduate School, W. Frank Barton School of Business, Department of Business, Wichita, KS 67260. Offers EMBA, MBA, MSN/MBA. *Accreditation:* AACSB. Part-time and evening/weekend programs available. *Expenses:* Tuition, state resident: full-time $4247; part-time $235.95 per credit hour. Tuition, nonresident: full-time $11,171; part-time $620.60 per credit hour. Required fees: $34; $3.60 per credit hour. $17 per term. Tuition and fees vary according to campus/location and program. *Unit head:* Angela Jones, Director, 316-978-3230, E-mail: angela.jones@wichita.edu. *Application contact:* Angela Jones, Director, 316-978-3230, E-mail: angela.jones@wichita.edu.

Widener University, School of Business Administration, Chester, PA 19013-5792. Offers MBA, MHA, MHR, MS, JD/MBA, MD/MBA, MD/MHA, ME/MBA, Psy D/MBA, Psy D/MHA, Psy D/MHR. *Accreditation:* AACSB. Part-time and evening/weekend programs available. *Faculty:* 14 full-time (6 women), 6 part-time/adjunct (2 women). *Students:* 29 full-time (14 women), 176 part-time (69 women); includes 20 minority (9 African Americans, 1 American Indian/Alaska Native, 9 Asian Americans or Pacific Islanders, 1 Hispanic American), 13 international. Average age 34. 254 applicants, 91% accepted. In 2009, 85 master's awarded. *Entrance requirements:* For master's, minimum GPA of 2.5. *Application deadline:* For fall admission, 8/1 priority date for domestic students; for spring admission, 12/1 for domestic students. Applications are processed on a rolling basis. Application fee: $25 ($300 for international students). Electronic applications accepted. *Expenses:* Contact institution. *Financial support:* In 2009–10, 11 research assistantships with full tuition reimbursements were awarded; career-related internships or fieldwork, Federal Work-Study, and traineeships also available. Support available to part-time students. Financial award application deadline: 5/1. *Faculty research:* Cost containment in health care, human resource management, productivity, globalization. *Unit head:* Dr. Savas Ozatalay, Dean, 610-499-4300, Fax: 610-499-4615. *Application contact:* Ann Seltzer, Graduate Enrollment Administrator, 610-499-4305, E-mail: apseltzer@widener.edu.

Wilfrid Laurier University, Faculty of Graduate Studies, School of Business and Economics, Department of Business, Waterloo, ON N2L 3C5, Canada. Offers M Fin, M Sc, PhD. *Degree requirements:* For master's, thesis optional; for doctorate, thesis/dissertation. *Entrance requirements:* For master's, GMAT, 4 year honors degree with minimum B+ average; for doctorate, GMAT, master's degree, minimum B+ average. Additional exam requirements/recommendations for international students: Required—TOEFL (minimum score 230 computer-based; 89 iBT). Electronic applications accepted. *Faculty research:* Financial economics, management and organizational behavior, operations and supply chain management.

Wilfrid Laurier University, Faculty of Graduate Studies, School of Business and Economics, Program in Business Administration, Waterloo, ON N2L 3C5, Canada. Offers MBA. *Accreditation:* AACSB. Part-time and evening/weekend programs available. *Entrance requirements:* For master's, GMAT, minimum 2 years of business experience, minimum B average in a 4 yr. BA program. Additional exam requirements/recommendations for international students: Required—TOEFL (minimum score 230 computer-based; 89 iBT). Electronic applications accepted. *Faculty research:* MBA, MBA with CMA option, MBA with CFA option, MBA with FCIP option, MBA co-op option.

Wilkes University, College of Graduate and Professional Studies, Jay S. Sidhu School of Business and Leadership, Wilkes-Barre, PA 18766-0002. Offers accounting (MBA); entrepreneurship (MBA); finance (MBA); human resource management (MBA); international business (MBA); management (MBA); marketing (MBA). *Accreditation:* ACBSP. Part-time and evening/weekend programs available. *Students:* 86 full-time (41 women), 118 part-time (59 women); includes 7 minority (4 African Americans, 1 Asian American or Pacific Islander, 2 Hispanic Americans), 48 international. Average age 29. In 2009, 59 master's awarded. *Entrance requirements:* For master's, GMAT. Additional exam requirements/recommendations for international students: Required—TOEFL (minimum score 500 paper-based; 173 computer-based; 79 iBT). *Application deadline:* Applications are processed on a rolling basis. Application fee: $45. *Expenses:* Contact institution. *Financial support:* Federal Work-Study and unspecified assistantships available. Financial award application deadline: 3/1; financial award applicants required to submit FAFSA. *Unit head:* Dr. Paul Browne, Dean, 570-408-4701, Fax: 570-408-7846, E-mail: paul.browne@wilkes.edu. *Application contact:* Kathleen Houlihan, Director of Graduate Studies, 570-408-3235, Fax: 570-408-7846, E-mail: kathleen.houlihan@wilkes.edu.

Willamette University, George H. Atkinson Graduate School of Management, Salem, OR 97301-3931. Offers early career MBA (full-time) (MBA); MBA for career change (full-time) (MBA); MBA for professionals (part-time) (MBA); JD/MBA. *Accreditation:* AACSB; NASPAA. Part-time and evening/weekend programs available. *Faculty:* 17 full-time (4 women), 27 part-time/adjunct (9 women). *Students:* 185 full-time (71 women), 106 part-time (42 women); includes 29 minority (2 African Americans, 2 American Indian/Alaska Native, 12 Asian Americans or Pacific Islanders, 13 Hispanic Americans), 63 international. Average age 25. 319 applicants, 72% accepted, 136 enrolled. In 2009, 174 master's awarded. *Entrance requirements:* For master's, GMAT or GRE. Additional exam requirements/recommendations for international students: Required—TOEFL (minimum score 570 paper-based; 230 computer-based; 88 iBT), IELTS (minimum score 6.5). *Application deadline:* For fall admission, 1/9 priority date for domestic and international students; for winter admission, 3/1 priority date for domestic and international students; for spring admission, 5/1 priority date for domestic and international students. Applications are processed on a rolling basis. Application fee: $0. Electronic applications accepted. *Expenses:* Contact institution. *Financial support:* In 2009–10, 240 students received support, including 12 research assistantships (averaging $1,500 per year); career-related internships or fieldwork, Federal Work-Study, scholarships/grants, and unspecified assistantships also available. Financial award application deadline: 5/1; financial award applicants required to submit FAFSA. *Faculty research:* Entrepreneurship, organizational behavior, general management, finance, marketing, public management, human resources, social networks, angel investing. *Unit head:* Debra J. Ringold, Dean, 503-370-6440, Fax: 503-370-3011, E-mail: dringold@willamette.edu. *Application contact:* Aimee Akimoff, Director of Recruitment, 503-370-6167, Fax: 503-370-3011, E-mail: aakimoff@willamette.edu.

William Carey University, School of Business, Hattiesburg, MS 39401-5499. Offers MBA. Part-time programs available. *Entrance requirements:* For master's, GMAT. Additional exam requirements/recommendations for international students: Required—TOEFL (minimum score 500 paper-based; 213 computer-based).

William Paterson University of New Jersey, Christos M. Cotsakos College of Business, Wayne, NJ 07470-8420. Offers MBA. *Accreditation:* AACSB. Part-time and evening/weekend programs available. *Students:* 42 full-time (25 women), 74 part-time (38 women); includes 23 minority (3 African Americans, 8 Asian Americans or Pacific Islanders, 12 Hispanic Americans), 13 international. *Entrance requirements:* For master's, GMAT, minimum AACSB index of 1000. *Application deadline:* Applications are processed on a rolling basis. Application fee: $50. Electronic applications accepted. *Financial support:* Research assistantships with full tuition reimbursements, unspecified assistantships available. Support available to part-time students. Financial award application deadline: 4/1; financial award applicants required to submit FAFSA. *Faculty research:* Appropriate marketing variables for international food retail chains, racial attitudes among corporate managers in northern New Jersey. *Unit head:* Sam Basu, Dean, 973-720-2964. *Application contact:* Tinu Adeniran, Assistant Director, Graduate Admissions, 973-720-2764, Fax: 973-720-2035, E-mail: adenirant@wpunj.edu.

Wilmington University, College of Business, New Castle, DE 19720-6491. Offers business administration (MBA); finance (MBA); health care administration (MBA, MS); homeland security (MBA, MS); human resource management (MS); management (MS); management information systems (MBA); organizational leadership (MS); public administration (MS); transportation and logistics (MBA, MS). Part-time and evening/weekend programs available. *Entrance requirements:* Additional exam requirements/recommendations for international students: Required—TOEFL (minimum score 500 paper-based; 173 computer-based). Electronic applications accepted.

Wingate University, Program in Business Administration, Wingate, NC 28174-0159. Offers MBA. *Accreditation:* ACBSP. Part-time and evening/weekend programs available. *Entrance requirements:* For master's, GMAT, work experience, 2 letters of recommendation. Electronic applications accepted. *Expenses:* Contact institution. *Faculty research:* Stochastic processes, business ethics, regional economic development, municipal finance, consumer behavior.

Winston-Salem State University, Program in Business Administration, Winston-Salem, NC 27110-0003. Offers MBA. *Accreditation:* AACSB. Part-time and evening/weekend programs available. Postbaccalaureate distance learning degree programs offered (minimal on-campus study). *Entrance requirements:* For master's, GMAT, resume, 3 letters of recommendation. Electronic applications accepted. *Faculty research:* Innovative entrepreneurship and customer service, econometrics and operations research.

Winthrop University, College of Business Administration, Program in Business Administration, Rock Hill, SC 29733. Offers MBA. *Accreditation:* AACSB. *Entrance requirements:* For master's, GMAT.

Woodbury University, School of Business and Management, Burbank, CA 91504-1099. Offers business administration (MBA); organizational leadership (MA). *Accreditation:* ACBSP. Part-time and evening/weekend programs available. *Faculty:* 11 full-time (5 women), 11 part-time/adjunct (3 women). *Students:* 184 full-time (114 women), 35 part-time (23 women); includes 55 minority (11 African Americans, 1 American Indian/Alaska Native, 12 Asian Americans or Pacific Islanders, 31 Hispanic Americans), 61 international. Average age 30. In 2009, 95 master's awarded. *Entrance requirements:* Additional exam requirements/recommendations for international students: Required—TOEFL (minimum score 550 paper-based; 213 computer-based; 80 iBT), IELTS (minimum score 5.5). *Application deadline:* For fall admission, 8/1 priority date for domestic students; for spring admission, 12/1 for domestic and international students. Applications are processed on a rolling basis. Application fee: $35 ($50 for international students). *Expenses:* Tuition: Full-time $9576; part-time $798 per unit. Required fees: $100; $8 per unit. $50 per year. *Financial support:* In 2009–10, 2 fellowships with tuition reimbursements (averaging $12,000 per year) were awarded. Financial award application deadline: 7/15; financial award applicants required to submit FAFSA. *Faculty research:* Total quality management, leadership. *Unit head:* Dr. Andre Van Niekerk, Dean, 818-767-0888 Ext. 264, Fax: 818-767-0032. *Application contact:* Frank Frias, MBA Recruitment, 818-767-0888 Ext. 224, Fax: 818-767-7520, E-mail: frank.frias@woodbury.edu.

Worcester Polytechnic Institute, Graduate Studies and Research, School of Business, Worcester, MA 01609-2280. Offers information technology (MS), including information security management; management (Graduate Certificate); marketing and technological innovation (MS); operations design and leadership (MS); technology (MBA). *Accreditation:* AACSB. Part-time and evening/weekend programs available. Postbaccalaureate distance learning degree programs offered (no on-campus study). *Faculty:* 25 full-time (12 women), 6 part-time/adjunct (2 women). *Students:* 89 full-time (44 women), 198 part-time (47 women). Average age 32. 229 applicants, 70% accepted, 71 enrolled. In 2009, 69 master's awarded. *Degree requirements:* For master's, thesis optional. *Entrance requirements:* For master's, GMAT (MBA), GMAT or GRE General Test (MS), resume; for Graduate Certificate, GMAT or GRE General Test, statement of purpose, 3 letters of recommendation. Additional exam requirements/recommendations for international students: Required—TOEFL (minimum score 550 paper-based; 213 computer-based; 79 iBT), IELTS (minimum score 6.5). *Application deadline:* For fall admission, 7/1 priority date for domestic students, 6/1 priority date for international students; for spring admission, 11/1 priority date for domestic students, 10/1 priority date for international students. Applications are processed on a rolling basis. Application fee: $70. Electronic applications accepted. *Financial support:* Career-related internships or fieldwork, institutionally sponsored loans, scholarships/grants, and unspecified assistantships available. Financial award application deadline: 6/1. *Faculty research:* Organizational aesthetics, resistance in organizations, dynamics of product innovation, economic approaches to productivity, corporate earnings forecasts and value relevance, ERP implementation, improving Web accessibility, information quality assessment, measuring strategic and transactional IT, website quality, service operations modeling, health care operations and performance analysis, loan process design. *Unit head:* Dr. Mark Rice, Dean, 508-831-5218, Fax: 508-831-5720, E-mail: rice@wpi.edu. *Application contact:* Norm Wilkinson, Director, Graduate Management Programs, 508-831-5957, Fax: 508-831-5720, E-mail: nwilkins@wpi.edu.

Worcester State College, Graduate Studies, Program in Management, Worcester, MA 01602-2597. Offers accounting (MS); organizational leadership (MS). *Faculty:* 4 full-time (3 women), 1 part-time/adjunct (0 women). *Students:* 2 full-time (0 women), 12 part-time (5 women); includes 1 minority (African American), 2 international. Average age 28. 17 applicants, 59% accepted, 1 enrolled. In 2009, 7 master's awarded. *Degree requirements:* For master's, comprehensive exam (for some programs), thesis optional. *Entrance requirements:* Additional

Business Administration and Management—General

Worcester State College (continued)
exam requirements/recommendations for international students: Required—TOEFL (minimum score 550 paper-based; 213 computer-based; 79 iBT). *Application deadline:* Applications are processed on a rolling basis. Application fee: $30. *Expenses:* Tuition, area resident: Part-time $150 per credit. Tuition, state resident: part-time $150 per credit. Tuition, nonresident: part-time $150 per credit. Required fees: $85. *Financial support:* In 2009–10, 3 students received support, including 3 research assistantships with full tuition reimbursements available (averaging $4,800 per year); career-related internships or fieldwork, scholarships/grants, and unspecified assistantships also available. Financial award application deadline: 3/1; financial award applicants required to submit FAFSA. *Unit head:* Dr. Elizabeth Wark, Coordinator, 508-929-8743, Fax: 508-929-8048, E-mail: ewark@worcester.edu. *Application contact:* Nicole Brown, Assistant Dean of Continuing Education, 508-929-8787, Fax: 508-929-8100, E-mail: nbrown@worcester.edu.

Wright State University, School of Graduate Studies, Raj Soin College of Business, Program in Business Administration, Dayton, OH 45435. Offers MBA.

Xavier University, Williams College of Business, Master of Business Administration Program, Cincinnati, OH 45207-3221. Offers business administration (Exec MBA, MBA); business intelligence (MBA); finance (MBA); international business (MBA); management information systems (MBA); marketing (MBA); MBA/MHSA; MSN/MBA. *Accreditation:* AACSB. Part-time and evening/weekend programs available. *Faculty:* 44 full-time (17 women), 9 part-time/adjunct (2 women). *Students:* 167 full-time (51 women), 862 part-time (283 women); includes 149 minority (60 African Americans, 62 Asian Americans or Pacific Islanders, 27 Hispanic Americans), 17 international. Average age 30. 355 applicants, 63% accepted, 187 enrolled. In 2009, 369 master's awarded. *Degree requirements:* For master's, capstone course. *Entrance requirements:* For master's, GMAT. Additional exam requirements/recommendations for international students: Required—TOEFL (minimum score 550 paper-based; 213 computer-based; 80 iBT). *Application deadline:* For fall admission, 8/1 priority date for domestic students, 5/1 for international students; for spring admission, 12/1 priority date for domestic students, 9/1 for international students. Applications are processed on a rolling basis. Application fee: $0. Electronic applications accepted. *Expenses:* Contact institution. *Financial support:* In 2009–10, 183 students received support. Scholarships/grants, tuition waivers (partial), and unspecified assistantships available. Financial award application deadline: 3/1; financial award applicants required to submit FAFSA. *Unit head:* Dr. Hema Krishnan, Associate Dean, 513-745-3206, Fax: 513-745-3455, E-mail: krishnan@xavier.edu. *Application contact:* Anna Marie Whelan, Assistant Director, MBA Programs, 513-745-3525, Fax: 513-745-2929, E-mail: whelana@xavier.edu.

Yale University, Yale School of Management and Graduate School of Arts and Sciences, Doctoral Program in Management, New Haven, CT 06520. Offers accounting (PhD); financial economics (PhD); marketing (PhD). *Accreditation:* AACSB. *Faculty:* 68 full-time (12 women). *Students:* 30 full-time (9 women), 13 international. Average age 28. 372 applicants, 7% accepted, 13 enrolled. In 2009, 5 doctorates awarded. *Degree requirements:* For doctorate, comprehensive exam, thesis/dissertation. *Entrance requirements:* For doctorate, GMAT or GRE General Test. Additional exam requirements/recommendations for international students: Required—TOEFL, IELTS. *Application deadline:* For fall admission, 1/2 for domestic and international students. Application fee: $85. Electronic applications accepted. *Expenses:* Contact institution. *Financial support:* In 2009–10, 29 students received support, including 29 fellowships with full tuition reimbursements available, 29 research assistantships with full tuition reimbursements available, 29 teaching assistantships with full tuition reimbursements available; institutionally sponsored loans, scholarships/grants, and health care benefits also available. Financial award application deadline: 1/2. *Faculty research:* Pricing of options and futures, term structure of interest rates, use of accounting numbers in debt contracts, product differentiation, e-commerce and marketing, behavioral finance. *Unit head:* Carla Mills, Registrar,

203-432-3955, Fax: 203-432-0342, E-mail: carla.mills@yale.edu. *Application contact:* Carla Mills, Registrar, 203-432-3955, Fax: 203-432-0342, E-mail: carla.mills@yale.edu.

See Close-Up on page 283.

Yale University, Yale School of Management, Program in Business Administration, New Haven, CT 06520. Offers MBA, PhD, JD/MBA, M Arch/MBA, M Div/MBA, MBA/MA, MBA/MF, MBA/MFA, MBA/MPH, MD/MBA. *Accreditation:* AACSB. *Faculty:* 65 full-time (3 women), 32 part-time/adjunct (14 women). *Students:* 429 full-time (148 women); includes 86 minority (20 African Americans, 2 American Indian/Alaska Native, 52 Asian Americans or Pacific Islanders, 12 Hispanic Americans), 116 international. Average age 28. 2,790 applicants, 18% accepted, 223 enrolled. In 2009, 187 master's, 5 doctorates awarded. Terminal master's awarded for partial completion of doctoral program. *Degree requirements:* For master's, international experience; for doctorate, comprehensive exam, thesis/dissertation. *Entrance requirements:* For master's, GMAT or GRE; for doctorate, GMAT or GRE General Test (preferred). Additional exam requirements/recommendations for international students: Required—TOEFL (minimum score 600 paper-based; 250 computer-based). *Application deadline:* For fall admission, 10/8 priority date for domestic and international students; for winter admission, 1/7 priority date for domestic and international students; for spring admission, 3/10 priority date for domestic and international students. Application fee: $220. Electronic applications accepted. *Expenses:* Contact institution. *Financial support:* Career-related internships or fieldwork, Federal Work-Study, institutionally sponsored loans, and scholarships/grants available. Financial award application deadline: 3/1; financial award applicants required to submit FAFSA. *Faculty research:* Finance, strategy, marketing, leadership, operations. *Application contact:* Bruce DelMonico, Director of Admissions, 203-432-5635, Fax: 203-432-7004, E-mail: mba.admissions@yale.edu.

York College of Pennsylvania, Department of Business Administration, York, PA 17405-7199. Offers MBA. *Accreditation:* ACBSP. Part-time and evening/weekend programs available. *Faculty:* 14 full-time (3 women), 2 part-time/adjunct (1 woman). *Students:* 20 full-time (8 women), 116 part-time (40 women); includes 7 minority (5 African Americans, 1 Asian American or Pacific Islander, 1 Hispanic American), 3 international. Average age 30. 53 applicants, 91% accepted, 40 enrolled. In 2009, 45 master's awarded. *Entrance requirements:* For master's, GMAT. Additional exam requirements/recommendations for international students: Required—TOEFL (minimum score 530 paper-based; 200 computer-based; 72 iBT). *Application deadline:* For fall admission, 7/15 priority date for domestic students; for spring admission, 12/15 priority date for domestic students. Applications are processed on a rolling basis. Application fee: $60. Electronic applications accepted. *Expenses:* Tuition: Full-time $10,980; part-time $610 per credit hour. Required fees: $320 per semester. *Financial support:* Federal Work-Study and scholarships/grants available. Financial award application deadline: 4/15; financial award applicants required to submit FAFSA. *Unit head:* Eric Hostler, MBA Director, 717-815-1947, E-mail: ehostler@ycp.edu. *Application contact:* Brenda Adams, 717-815-1491, Fax: 717-600-3999, E-mail: badams@ycp.edu.

York University, Faculty of Graduate Studies, Schulich School of Business, Toronto, ON M3J 1P3, Canada. Offers administration (PhD); business (MBA); finance (MF); international business (IMBA); public administration (MPA); MBA/JD; MBA/MA; MBA/MFA. Part-time and evening/weekend programs available. *Degree requirements:* For master's, advanced proficiency in a second language, work term (IMBA); for doctorate, comprehensive exam, thesis/dissertation. *Entrance requirements:* For master's, GMAT, minimum GPA of 3.0; for doctorate, GMAT, minimum GPA of 3.3. Electronic applications accepted.

See Close-Up on page 285.

Youngstown State University, Graduate School, Williamson College of Business Administration, Youngstown, OH 44555-0001. Offers MBA, Certificate. *Accreditation:* AACSB. Part-time and evening/weekend programs available. *Degree requirements:* For master's, thesis optional. *Entrance requirements:* For master's, GMAT, minimum GPA of 2.7. Additional exam requirements/recommendations for international students: Required—TOEFL. *Faculty research:* Taxation and compliance, business ethics, operations management, organizational behavior, gender issues.

ARGOSY UNIVERSITY, ATLANTA

College of Business

ARGOSY UNIVERSITY.

Programs of Study

Argosy University, Atlanta, offers the Master of Business Administration (M.B.A.), the Master of Science in Management (M.S.M.), and the Doctor of Business Administration (D.B.A.) degrees. The business programs are designed to serve the needs of talented students, regardless of their undergraduate degrees. The College of Business welcomes and encourages students from diverse academic backgrounds.

The Master of Business Administration program is designed to develop action-oriented managers and leaders who focus on leading themselves and others to solutions that serve their organizations. Students acquire skills to identify challenges and opportunities, draw on the latest technology and information, use advanced analytical and planning approaches, and execute plans for leading positive change. Competencies are developed through focusing on critical thinking, persuasive communications, technical knowledge, and a deep understanding of the human side of business. By focusing on competencies in this manner, the program builds upon the talents of students, independent of their undergraduate field of study. Students from diverse academic and professional backgrounds are welcomed and encouraged. In addition to completing the core course requirements, students develop expertise and specific insights in one of the following concentrations: corporate compliance, finance, fraud examination, health-care administration, information systems management (availability of this concentration is limited; program chair approval is necessary to enter), international business, management, marketing, public administration, or sustainable management. In addition, with approval of the student's program chair, a student may select four courses (12 credit hours) to create a customized concentration that better fits their specific career goals. For all students, the M.B.A. program culminates in an applied capstone project in which they integrate the core business competencies with their concentration specialty.

The Master of Science in Management program is designed to improve and extend the interpersonal and problem-solving skills necessary for successful leaders in the private, non-profit, and public sectors. The program focuses on situation diagnostics, opportunity and problem evaluation, and implementation of an action plan.

The Doctor of Business Administration program enables industry and academic professionals to build upon master's-level competencies, skills, and knowledge, preparing themselves to perform more effectively in existing professional roles, to qualify for roles with increasing responsibility, and/or develop capabilities for a second career in teaching at the college level. The program requires students to develop applied research inquiry and analytical skills. The D.B.A. program is designed to help students develop competencies in understanding and performing applied research, which can then be used to foster innovation and lead organizational change. Students must choose a concentration in accounting, global business sustainability, information systems (availability of this concentration is limited; program chair approval is necessary to enter), international business, management, or marketing. In addition, with approval of the student's program chair, a student may select four courses (12 credit hours) to create a customized concentration that better fits their specific career goals.

Research Facilities

Argosy University libraries provide curriculum support and educational resources, including current text materials, diagnostic training documents, reference materials and databases, journals and dissertations, and major and current titles in program areas. There is an online public-access catalog of library resources available throughout the Argosy University system. Students have remote access to the campus library database, enabling them to study and conduct research at home. Academic databases offer dissertation abstracts, academic journals, and professional periodicals. All library computers are Internet accessible. Software applications include Word, Excel, PowerPoint, SPSS, and various test-scoring programs.

Financial Aid

Financial aid is available to those who qualify. Argosy University, Atlanta, offers access to federal and state aid programs, merit-based awards, grants, loans, and a work-study program. As a first step, students should complete the Free Application for Federal Student Aid (FAFSA). Prospective students can apply electronically at http://www.fafsa.ed.gov or at the campus.

Cost of Study

Tuition varies by program. Students should contact Argosy University, Atlanta, for tuition information.

Living and Housing Costs

Students typically live in apartments in the metropolitan Atlanta area. Living expenses vary according to each student's preferred standard of living, housing, and transportation. The University does not offer or operate student housing. Most students are full-time working professionals who live within driving distance of the campus. Several nearby hotels offer special rates for those who commute from long distances. The Admissions Department also maintains a list of housing options, including contact information, for University students who wish to share housing. For more information, students should contact the Admissions Department.

Student Group

Admission to Argosy University, Atlanta, is selective to ensure a dynamic and engaged student body. It encourages diversity in academic and employment backgrounds and promotes integration of the student body into professional life through established connections with local and national professional associations. Argosy University offers a professionally oriented education with rich opportunities to gain practical experience in class, field placements, and internships. Full-time students and working professionals gain the extensive knowledge and range of skills necessary for effective performance in their chosen fields.

Student Outcomes

Students can register with the University's online career-services system and use select services from a distance, such as degree-specific career e-mail lists, national job posts, and virtual job fairs. Students should contact the University for more information.

Location

Argosy University, Atlanta, is housed in a modern building in Sandy Springs, a northern suburb of Atlanta. The campus features a café and an outdoor lakeside terrace. Beyond the University, students find a wide selection of affordable housing options. This major metropolitan area offers many social and recreational opportunities, from clubs and concerts to galleries and museums, from a growing restaurant scene to Braves baseball games and in-line skating in Piedmont Park.

Many businesses in the area provide varied opportunities for student training. Atlanta's business environment includes technology companies such as EarthLink and Macquarium as well as corporate giants such as the Coca-Cola Company, CNN, Delta Air Lines, AT&T, and Georgia Pacific.

The University

Argosy University is a private institution with nineteen locations across the nation. Argosy University, Atlanta, provides students with a career resources office, an academic resources center, and extensive information access for research. It offers the resources of a large university, plus the friendliness and personal attention of a small campus.

The innovative programs feature dynamic, relevant, and practical curricula delivered in flexible class formats. Students enjoy scheduling options that make it easier to fit school into their busy lives, choosing from day and evening courses, on campus or online. Many students find a combination of class formats to be an ideal way of continuing their education while meeting family and professional demands.

Argosy University is accredited by the Higher Learning Commission and a member of the North Central Association (30 North LaSalle Street, Suite 2400, Chicago, Illinois 60602; 800-621-7440 (toll-free); http://www.ncahlc.org).

Applying

Argosy University, Atlanta, accepts students year-round on a rolling admissions basis, depending on availability of required courses. Applications for admission are available online or by contacting the campus.

Correspondence and Information

Argosy University, Atlanta
980 Hammond Drive, Suite 100
Atlanta, Georgia 30328
Phone: 770-671-1200
　　　888-671-4777 (toll-free)
Fax: 770-671-0476
E-mail: auadmissions@argosy.edu
Web site: http://www.argosy.edu/atlanta

Argosy University, Atlanta

THE FACULTY

The Argosy University faculty comprises working professionals who are eager to help students succeed. Members bring real-world experience and the latest practice innovations to the academic setting. The diverse faculty members of the College of Business are widely recognized for contributions to the field. Many are published scholars, and most hold doctoral degrees. They are committed to providing a substantive education that combines comprehensive knowledge with critical skills and practical workplace relevance. Above all, faculty members are committed to their students' personal and professional growth.

ARGOSY UNIVERSITY

ARGOSY UNIVERSITY, CHICAGO

College of Business

Programs of Study
Argosy University, Chicago, offers the Master of Business Administration (M.B.A.), the Master of Science in Management (M.S.M.), the Doctor of Education (Ed.D.) in organizational leadership, and the Doctor of Business Administration (D.B.A.) degrees. The business programs are designed to serve the needs of talented students, regardless of their undergraduate degrees. The College of Business welcomes and encourages students from diverse academic backgrounds.

The Master of Business Administration program is designed to develop action-oriented managers and leaders who focus on leading themselves and others to solutions that serve their organizations. Students acquire skills to identify challenges and opportunities, draw on the latest technology and information, use advanced analytical and planning approaches, and execute plans for leading positive change. Competencies are developed through focusing on critical thinking, persuasive communications, technical knowledge, and a deep understanding of the human side of business. By focusing on competencies in this manner, the program builds upon the talents of students, independent of their undergraduate field of study. Students from diverse academic and professional backgrounds are welcomed and encouraged. In addition to completing the core course requirements, students develop expertise and specific insights in one of the following concentrations: corporate compliance, finance, fraud examination, health-care administration, information systems management (availability of this concentration is limited; program chair approval is necessary to enter), international business, management, marketing, public administration, or sustainable management. In addition, with approval of the student's program chair, a student may select four courses (12 credit hours) to create a customized concentration that better fits their specific career goals. For all students, the M.B.A. program culminates in an applied capstone project in which they integrate the core business competencies with their concentration specialty.

The Master of Science in Management program is designed to improve and extend the interpersonal and problem-solving skills necessary for successful leaders in the private, non-profit, and public sectors. The program focuses on situation diagnostics, opportunity and problem evaluation, and implementation of an action plan.

The Doctor of Education in organizational leadership program is designed for working professionals who wish to develop the knowledge and skills required to hold leadership positions in complex organizations. The program focuses on transformational leadership skills in addition to managerial attributes. This approach prepares students for such strategic challenges as increasing globalization, changing economies, societal shifts, and individual-organizational relationships.

The Doctor of Business Administration program enables industry and academic professionals to build upon master's-level competencies, skills, and knowledge, preparing themselves to perform more effectively in existing professional roles, to qualify for roles with increasing responsibility, and/or develop capabilities for a second career in teaching at the college level. The program requires students to develop applied research inquiry and analytical skills. The D.B.A. program is designed to help students develop competencies in understanding and performing applied research, which can then be used to foster innovation and lead organizational change. Students must choose a concentration in accounting, global business sustainability, information systems (availability of this concentration is limited; program chair approval is necessary to enter), international business, management, or marketing. In addition, with approval of the student's program chair, a student may select four courses (12 credit hours) to create a customized concentration that better fits their specific career goals.

Research Facilities
Argosy University libraries provide curriculum support and educational resources, including current text materials, diagnostic training documents, reference materials and databases, journals and dissertations, and major and current titles in program areas. There is an online public-access catalog of library resources available throughout the Argosy University system. Students have remote access to the campus library database, enabling them to study and conduct research at home. Academic databases offer dissertation abstracts, academic journals, and professional periodicals. All library computers are Internet accessible. Software applications include Word, Excel, PowerPoint, SPSS, and various test-scoring programs.

Financial Aid
Financial aid is available to those who qualify. Argosy University, Chicago, offers access to federal and state aid programs, merit-based awards, grants, loans, and a work-study program. As a first step, students should complete the Free Application for Federal Student Aid (FAFSA). Prospective students can apply electronically at http://www.fafsa.ed.gov or at the campus.

Cost of Study
Tuition varies by program. Students should contact Argosy University, Chicago, for tuition information.

Living and Housing Costs
Students typically live in apartments in the metropolitan Chicago area. Living expenses vary according to each student's preferred standard of living, housing, and transportation. The University does not offer or operate student housing. Most of the students are full-time working professionals who live within driving distance of the campus. Several nearby hotels offer special rates for those who commute from long distances. The Admissions Department also maintains a list of housing options, including contact information for university students who wish to share housing. For more information, students should contact the Admissions Department.

Student Group
Admission to Argosy University, Chicago, is selective to ensure a dynamic and engaged student body. It encourages diversity in academic and employment backgrounds and promotes integration of the student body into professional life through established connections with local and national professional associations. Argosy University offers a professionally oriented education with rich opportunities to gain practical experience in class, field placements, and internships. Full-time students and working professionals gain the extensive knowledge and range of skills necessary for effective performance in their chosen fields.

Student Outcomes
Students can register with the University's online career-services system and use select services from a distance, such as degree-specific career e-mail lists, national job posts, and virtual job fairs. Students should contact the University for more information.

Location
Chicago is a city of world-class status and beauty, drawing visitors from around the globe. Argosy University, Chicago, sits in the heart of The Loop, the city's business and entertainment center. Located on the shores of Lake Michigan, Chicago is home to world-champion sports teams, an internationally acclaimed symphony orchestra, renowned architecture, and a variety of history and art museums. Recreational opportunities include hiking and cycling on miles of lakefront trails, golfing, and shopping. Many businesses in the area provide excellent opportunities for student training. Chicago's business environment includes a broad array of companies including Boeing and Pepsi America. The commercial banking headquarters of JP Morgan Chase is also located in Chicago.

The University
Argosy University is a private institution with nineteen locations across the nation. Argosy University, Chicago, provides students with an academic resources center and extensive information access for research. It offers the resources of a large university plus the friendliness and personal attention of a small campus. Argosy University, Chicago, is closely associated with Argosy University, Schaumburg, located 45 minutes from downtown Chicago.

The innovative programs feature dynamic, relevant, and practical curricula delivered in flexible class formats. Students enjoy scheduling options that make it easier to fit school into their busy lives, choosing from day and evening courses, on campus or online. Many students find a combination of class formats to be an ideal way of continuing their education while meeting family and professional demands.

Argosy University is accredited by the Higher Learning Commission and a member of the North Central Association (30 North LaSalle Street, Suite 2400, Chicago, Illinois 60602; 800-621-7440 (toll-free); http://www.ncahlc.org).

Applying
Argosy University, Chicago, accepts students year-round on a rolling admissions basis, depending on availability of required courses. Applications for admission are available online or by contacting the campus.

Correspondence and Information
Argosy University, Chicago
225 North Michigan Avenue, Suite 1300
Chicago, Illinois 60601
Phone: 312-777-7600
          800-626-4123 (toll-free)
Fax: 312-777-7748
E-mail: auadmissions@argosy.edu
Web site: http://www.argosy.edu/chicago

Argosy University, Chicago

THE FACULTY

The Argosy University faculty comprises working professionals who are eager to help students succeed. Members bring real-world experience and the latest practice innovations to the academic setting. The diverse faculty members of the College of Business are widely recognized for contributions to their fields. Many are published scholars, and most hold doctoral degrees. They are committed to providing a substantive education that combines comprehensive knowledge with critical skills and practical workplace relevance. Above all, faculty members are committed to their students' personal and professional development.

ARGOSY UNIVERSITY

ARGOSY UNIVERSITY, DALLAS

College of Business

Programs of Study

Argosy University, Dallas, offers the Master of Business Administration (M.B.A.) and the Doctor of Business Administration (D.B.A.) degrees. The programs are designed to serve the needs of talented students, regardless of their undergraduate degrees. The College of Business welcomes and encourages students from diverse academic backgrounds.

The Master of Business Administration program is designed to develop action-oriented managers and leaders who focus on leading themselves and others to solutions that serve their organizations. Students acquire skills to identify challenges and opportunities, draw on the latest technology and information, use advanced analytical and planning approaches, and execute plans for leading positive change. Competencies are developed through focusing on critical thinking, persuasive communications, technical knowledge, and a deep understanding of the human side of business. By focusing on competencies in this manner, the program builds upon the talents of students, independent of their undergraduate field of study. Students from diverse academic and professional backgrounds are welcomed and encouraged. In addition to completing the core course requirements, students develop expertise and specific insights in one of the following concentrations: corporate compliance, finance, fraud examination, health-care administration, information systems management (availability of this concentration is limited; program chair approval is necessary to enter), international business, management, marketing, public administration, or sustainable management. In addition, with approval of the student's program chair, a student may select four courses (12 credit hours) to create a customized concentration that better fits their specific career goals. For all students, the M.B.A. program culminates in an applied capstone project in which they integrate the core business competencies with their concentration specialty.

The Doctor of Business Administration program enables industry and academic professionals to build upon master's-level competencies, skills, and knowledge, preparing themselves to perform more effectively in existing professional roles, to qualify for roles with increasing responsibility, and/or develop capabilities for a second career in teaching at the college level. The program requires students to develop applied research inquiry and analytical skills. The D.B.A. program is designed to help students develop competencies in understanding and performing applied research, which can then be used to foster innovation and lead organizational change. Students must choose a concentration in accounting, global business sustainability, information systems (availability of this concentration is limited; program chair approval is necessary to enter), international business, management, or marketing. In addition, with approval of the student's program chair, a student may select four courses (12 credit hours) to create a customized concentration that better fits their specific career goals.

Research Facilities

Argosy University libraries provide curriculum support and educational resources, including current text materials, diagnostic training documents, reference materials and databases, journals and dissertations, and major and current titles in program areas. There is an online public-access catalog of library resources available throughout the Argosy University system. Students have remote access to the campus library database, enabling them to study and conduct research at home. Academic databases offer dissertation abstracts, academic journals, and professional periodicals. All library computers are Internet accessible. Software applications include Word, Excel, PowerPoint, SPSS, and various test-scoring programs.

Financial Aid

Financial aid is available to those who qualify. Argosy University, Dallas, offers access to federal and state aid programs, merit-based awards, grants, loans, and a work-study program. As a first step, students should complete the Free Application for Federal Student Aid (FAFSA). Prospective students can apply electronically at http://www.fafsa.ed.gov or at the campus.

Cost of Study

Tuition varies by program. Students should contact Argosy University, Dallas, for tuition information.

Living and Housing Costs

Students typically live in apartments in the metropolitan Dallas area. Living expenses vary according to each student's preferred standard of living, housing, and transportation. The University does not offer or operate student housing. Most of the students are full-time working professionals who live within driving distance of the campus. Several nearby hotels offer special rates for those who commute from long distances. The Admissions Department also maintains a list of housing options, including contact information, for University students who wish to share housing. For more information, students should contact the Admissions Department.

Student Group

Admission to Argosy University, Dallas, is selective to ensure a dynamic and engaged student body. It encourages diversity in academic and employment backgrounds and promotes integration of the student body into professional life through established connections with local and national professional associations. Argosy University offers a professionally oriented education with rich opportunities to gain practical experience in class, field placements, and internships. Full-time students and working professionals gain the extensive knowledge and range of skills necessary for effective performance in their chosen fields.

Student Outcomes

Students can register with the University's online career-services system and use select services from a distance, such as degree-specific career e-mail lists, national job posts, and virtual job fairs. Students should contact the University for more information.

Location

Argosy University, Dallas, offers a north-central location in Dallas, with easy access to freeways, neighboring colleges and universities, libraries, shops, restaurants, theaters, art museums, and other tourist attractions. Many businesses in the metropolitan area offer excellent training facilities for students. The city is home to a broad array of companies, including Lockheed Martin Corporation, Baylor University Medical System, and Southwest Airlines.

The University

Argosy University is a private institution with nineteen locations across the nation. Argosy University, Dallas, provides students with a career resources office, an academic resources center, and extensive information access for research. It offers the resources of a large university, plus the friendliness and personal attention of a small campus.

Argosy University, Dallas, offers the opportunity to take one class at a time, with each class lasting for one month. Students are never required to study for multiple exams at the same time. New classes start each month. This flexible format lets students begin working on a graduate degree without waiting for the traditional semester to start.

Argosy University is accredited by the Higher Learning Commission and a member of the North Central Association (30 North LaSalle Street, Suite 2400, Chicago, Illinois 60602; 800-621-7440 (toll-free); http://www.ncahlc.org).

Applying

Argosy University, Dallas, accepts students year-round on a rolling admissions basis, depending on availability of required courses. Applications for admission are available online or by contacting the campus.

Correspondence and Information

Argosy University, Dallas
5001 Lyndon B. Johnson Freeway
Heritage Square
Farmers Branch, Texas 75244
Phone: 214-890-9900
     866-954-9900 (toll-free)
Fax: 214-378-8555
E-mail: auadmissions@argosy.edu
Web site: http://www.argosy.edu/dallas

Argosy University, Dallas

THE FACULTY

The Argosy University faculty comprises working professionals who are eager to help students succeed. Members bring real-world experience and the latest practice innovations to the academic setting. The diverse faculty members of the College of Business are widely recognized for contributions to the field. Many are published scholars, and most hold doctoral degrees. They are committed to providing a substantive education that combines comprehensive knowledge with critical skills and practical workplace relevance. Above all, faculty members are committed to their students' personal and professional development.

ARGOSY UNIVERSITY.

ARGOSY UNIVERSITY, DENVER

College of Business

Programs of Study
Argosy University, Denver, offers the Master of Business Administration (M.B.A.), the Master of Science in Management (M.S.M.), the Doctor of Business Administration (D.B.A.), and the Doctor of Education (Ed.D.) in organizational leadership degrees. The business programs are designed to serve the needs of talented students, regardless of their undergraduate degrees. The College of Business welcomes and encourages students from diverse academic backgrounds.

The Master of Business Administration program is designed to develop action-oriented managers and leaders who focus on leading themselves and others to solutions that serve their organizations. Students acquire skills to identify challenges and opportunities, draw on the latest technology and information, use advanced analytical and planning approaches, and execute plans for leading positive change. Competencies are developed through focusing on critical thinking, persuasive communications, technical knowledge, and a deep understanding of the human side of business. By focusing on competencies in this manner, the program builds upon the talents of students, independent of their undergraduate field of study. Students from diverse academic and professional backgrounds are welcomed and encouraged. In addition to completing the core course requirements, students develop expertise and specific insights in one of the following concentrations: corporate compliance, finance, fraud examination, health-care administration, information systems management (availability of this concentration is limited; program chair approval is necessary to enter), international business, management, marketing, public administration, or sustainable management. In addition, with approval of the student's program chair, a student may select four courses (12 credit hours) to create a customized concentration that better fits their specific career goals. For all students, the M.B.A. program culminates in an applied capstone project in which they integrate the core business competencies with their concentration specialty.

The Master of Science in Management program is designed to improve and extend the interpersonal and problem-solving skills necessary for successful leaders in the private, non-profit, and public sectors. The program focuses on situation diagnostics, opportunity and problem evaluation, and implementation of an action plan.

The Doctor of Business Administration program enables industry and academic professionals to build upon master's-level competencies, skills, and knowledge, preparing themselves to perform more effectively in existing professional roles, to qualify for roles with increasing responsibility, and/or develop capabilities for a second career in teaching at the college level. The program requires students to develop applied research inquiry and analytical skills. The D.B.A. program is designed to help students develop competencies in understanding and performing applied research, which can then be used to foster innovation and lead organizational change. Students must choose a concentration in accounting, global business sustainability, information systems (availability of this concentration is limited; program chair approval is necessary to enter), international business, management, or marketing. In addition, with approval of the student's program chair, a student may select four courses (12 credit hours) to create a customized concentration that better fits their specific career goals.

The Doctor of Education in organizational leadership program is designed for working professionals who wish to develop the knowledge and skills required to hold leadership positions in complex organizations. The program focuses on transformational leadership skills in addition to managerial attributes. This approach prepares students for such strategic challenges as increasing globalization, changing economies, societal shifts, and individual-organizational relationships.

Research Facilities
Argosy University libraries provide curriculum support and educational resources, including current text materials, diagnostic training documents, reference materials and databases, journals and dissertations, and major and current titles in program areas. There is an online public-access catalog of library resources available throughout the Argosy University system. Students have remote access to the campus library database, enabling them to study and conduct research at home. Academic databases offer dissertation abstracts, academic journals, and professional periodicals. All library computers are Internet accessible. Software applications include Word, Excel, PowerPoint, SPSS, and various test-scoring programs.

Financial Aid
Financial aid is available to those who qualify. Argosy University, Denver, offers access to federal and state aid programs, merit-based awards, grants, loans, and a work-study program. As a first step, students should complete the Free Application for Federal Student Aid (FAFSA). Prospective students can apply electronically at http://www.fafsa.ed.gov or at the campus.

Cost of Study
Tuition varies by program. Students should contact Argosy University, Denver, for tuition information.

Living and Housing Costs
Students typically live in apartments in the metropolitan Denver area. Living expenses vary according to each student's preferred standard of living, housing, and transportation. The University does not offer or operate student housing. Most of the students are full-time working professionals who live within driving distance of the campus. Several nearby hotels offer special rates for those who commute from long distances. The Admissions Department also maintains a list of housing options, including contact information for University students who wish to share housing. For more information, students should contact the Admissions Department.

Student Group
Admission to Argosy University, Denver, is selective to ensure a dynamic and engaged student body. It encourages diversity in academic and employment backgrounds and promotes integration of the student body into professional life through established connections with local and national professional associations. Argosy University offers a professionally oriented education with rich opportunities to gain practical experience in class, field placements, and internships. Full-time students and working professionals gain the extensive knowledge and range of skills necessary for effective performance in their chosen fields.

Student Outcomes
Students can register with the University's online career-services system and use select services from a distance, such as degree-specific career e-mail lists, national job posts, and virtual job fairs. Students should contact the University for more information.

Location
Argosy University, Denver, is conveniently located at 7600 East Eastman Avenue in Denver, Colorado. The campus is close to a variety of local libraries, shops, restaurants, theaters, and art museums. Denver's thriving professional organizations, major corporations, high-tech companies, hospitals, schools, clinics, and social service agencies can also provide varied training opportunities for students.

The University
Argosy University is a private institution with nineteen locations across the nation. Argosy University, Denver, provides students with a career resources office, an academic resources center, and extensive information access for research. It offers the resources of a large university, plus the friendliness and personal attention of a small campus.

The innovative programs feature dynamic, relevant, and practical curricula delivered in flexible class formats. Students enjoy scheduling options that make it easier to fit school into their busy lives, choosing from day and evening courses, on campus or online. Many students find a combination of class formats to be an ideal way of continuing their education while meeting family and professional demands.

Argosy University is accredited by the Higher Learning Commission and a member of the North Central Association (30 North LaSalle Street, Suite 2400, Chicago, Illinois 60602; 800-621-7440 (toll-free); http://www.ncahlc.org).

Applying
Argosy University, Denver, accepts students year-round on a rolling admissions basis, depending on availability of required courses. Applications for admission are available online or by contacting the campus.

Correspondence and Information
Argosy University, Denver
7600 East Eastman Avenue
Denver, Colorado 80231

Phone: 303-248-2700
　　　 866-431-5981 (toll-free)
Fax: 303-248-2800
E-mail: auadmissions@argosy.edu
Web site: http://www.argosy.edu/denver

Argosy University, Denver

THE FACULTY

The Argosy University faculty comprises working professionals who are eager to help students succeed. Members bring real-world experience and the latest practice innovations to the academic setting. The diverse faculty members of the College of Business are widely recognized for contributions to the field. Many are published scholars, and most hold doctoral degrees. They are committed to providing a substantive education that combines comprehensive knowledge with critical skills and practical workplace relevance. Above all, faculty members are committed to their students' personal and professional development.

ARGOSY UNIVERSITY

ARGOSY UNIVERSITY, HAWAI'I

College of Business

Programs of Study
Argosy University, Hawai'i, offers the Master of Business Administration (M.B.A.), the Master of Science in Management (M.S.M.), the Master of Public Administration (M.P.A.), the Doctor of Business Administration (D.B.A.), and the Doctor of Education (Ed.D.) in organizational leadership degrees. The business programs are designed to serve the needs of talented students, regardless of their undergraduate degrees. The College of Business welcomes and encourages students from diverse academic backgrounds.

The Master of Business Administration program is designed to develop action-oriented managers and leaders who focus on leading themselves and others to solutions that serve their organizations. Students acquire skills to identify challenges and opportunities, draw on the latest technology and information, use advanced analytical and planning approaches, and execute plans for leading positive change. Competencies are developed through focusing on critical thinking, persuasive communications, technical knowledge, and a deep understanding of the human side of business. By focusing on competencies in this manner, the program builds upon the talents of students, independent of their undergraduate field of study. Students from diverse academic and professional backgrounds are welcomed and encouraged. In addition to completing the core course requirements, students develop expertise and specific insights in one of the following concentrations: corporate compliance, finance, fraud examination, health-care administration, information systems management (availability of this concentration is limited; program chair approval is necessary to enter), international business, management, marketing, public administration, or sustainable management. In addition, with approval of the student's program chair, a student may select four courses (12 credit hours) to create a customized concentration that better fits their specific career goals. For all students, the M.B.A. program culminates in an applied capstone project in which they integrate the core business competencies with their concentration specialty.

The Master of Science in Management program is designed to improve and extend the interpersonal and problem-solving skills necessary for successful leaders in the private, non-profit, and public sectors. The program focuses on situation diagnostics, opportunity and problem evaluation, and implementation of an action plan.

The Master of Public Administration program is designed to develop action-oriented, problem-solving managers for the public sector, especially at the state and local levels of government. Students have the opportunity to develop the competencies required to execute the duties and responsibilities of public sector managers, including evaluation and supervision of employees, reinforcement of the organizational mission, and the effective management of organizational resources.

The Doctor of Business Administration program enables industry and academic professionals to build upon master's-level competencies, skills, and knowledge, preparing themselves to perform more effectively in existing professional roles, to qualify for roles with increasing responsibility, and/or develop capabilities for a second career in teaching at the college level. The program requires students to develop applied research inquiry and analytical skills. The D.B.A. program is designed to help students develop competencies in understanding and performing applied research, which can then be used to foster innovation and lead organizational change. Students must choose a concentration in accounting, global business sustainability, information systems (availability of this concentration is limited; program chair approval is necessary to enter), international business, management, or marketing. In addition, with approval of the student's program chair, a student may select four courses (12 credit hours) to create a customized concentration that better fits their specific career goals.

The Doctor of Education in organizational leadership program is designed for working professionals who wish to develop the knowledge and skills required to hold leadership positions in complex organizations. The program focuses on transformational leadership skills in addition to managerial attributes. This approach prepares students for such strategic challenges as increasing globalization, changing economies, societal shifts, and individual-organizational relationships.

Research Facilities
Argosy University libraries provide curriculum support and educational resources, including current text materials, diagnostic training documents, reference materials and databases, journals and dissertations, and major and current titles in program areas. There is an online public-access catalog of library resources available throughout the Argosy University system. Students have remote access to the campus library database, enabling them to study and conduct research at home. Academic databases offer dissertation abstracts, academic journals, and professional periodicals. All library computers are Internet accessible. Software applications include Word, Excel, PowerPoint, SPSS, and various test-scoring programs.

Financial Aid
Financial aid is available to those who qualify. Argosy University, Hawai'i, offers access to federal and state aid programs, merit-based awards, grants, loans, and a work-study program. As a first step, students should complete the Free Application for Federal Student Aid (FAFSA). Prospective students can apply electronically at http://www.fafsa.ed.gov or at the campus.

Cost of Study
Tuition varies by program. Students should contact Argosy University, Hawai'i, for tuition information.

Living and Housing Costs
Students typically live in apartments in the metropolitan Honolulu area. Living expenses vary according to each student's preferred standard of living, housing, and transportation. The University does not offer or operate student housing. Most of the students are full-time working professionals who live within driving distance of the campus. Several nearby hotels offer special rates for those who commute from long distances. The Admissions Department also maintains a list of housing options, including contact information for University students who wish to share housing. For more information, students should contact the Admissions Department.

Student Group
Admission to Argosy University, Hawai'i, is selective to ensure a dynamic and engaged student body. The University encourages diversity in academic and employment backgrounds and promotes integration of the student body into professional life through established connections with local and national professional associations. Argosy University offers a professionally oriented education with rich opportunities to gain practical experience in class, field placements, and internships. Full-time students and working professionals gain the extensive knowledge and range of skills necessary for effective performance in their chosen fields.

Student Outcomes
Students can register with the University's online career-services system and use select services from a distance, such as degree-specific career e-mail lists, national job posts, and virtual job fairs. Students should contact the University for more information.

Location
Argosy University, Hawai'i, is located in downtown Honolulu on Oahu. Additional satellite locations on Maui and in Hilo on the Island of Hawaii offer programs to communities on the neighboring islands. These locations connect the campus to Hawaii and to the local and native communities of the Pacific Islands and the Pacific Rim. Students enjoy the cultural and recreational opportunities that these locations provide. University faculty and staff members often work in cooperation with the Hawaii community to create an educational focus on social issues, human diversity, and programs that make a difference to underserved populations.

Honolulu's business environment includes a broad array of companies. The area's largest employers include Bank of Hawaii, Queens Medical Center, and the U.S. government. Many businesses in the metropolitan area provide varied opportunities for student training.

The University
Argosy University is a private institution with nineteen locations across the nation. Argosy University, Hawai'i, provides students with a career resources office, an academic resources center, and extensive information access for research. It offers the resources of a large university, plus the friendliness and personal attention of a small campus. The innovative programs feature dynamic, relevant, and practical curricula delivered in flexible class formats. Students enjoy scheduling options that make it easier to fit school into their busy lives, choosing from day and evening courses, on campus or online. Many students find a combination of class formats to be an ideal way of continuing their education while meeting family and professional demands.

Argosy University is accredited by the Higher Learning Commission and a member of the North Central Association (30 North LaSalle Street, Suite 2400, Chicago, Illinois 60602; 800-621-7440 (toll-free); http://www.ncahlc.org).

Applying
Argosy University, Hawai'i, accepts students year-round on a rolling admissions basis, depending on availability of required courses. Applications for admission are available online or by contacting the campus.

Correspondence and Information
Argosy University, Hawai'i
400 ASB Tower
1001 Bishop Street
Honolulu, Hawaii 96813

Phone: 808-536-5555
        888-323-2777 (toll-free)
Fax: 808-536-5505
E-mail: auadmissions@argosy.edu
Web site: http://www.argosy.edu/hawaii

Argosy University, Hawai'i

THE FACULTY

The Argosy University faculty comprises working professionals who are eager to help students succeed. Members bring real-world experience and the latest practice innovations to the academic setting. The diverse faculty members of the College of Business are widely recognized for contributions to the field. Many are published scholars, and most hold doctoral degrees. They are committed to providing a substantive education that combines comprehensive knowledge with critical skills and practical workplace relevance. Above all, faculty members are committed to their students' personal and professional development.

ARGOSY UNIVERSITY

ARGOSY UNIVERSITY, INLAND EMPIRE

College of Business

Programs of Study
Argosy University, Inland Empire, offers the Master of Business Administration (M.B.A.) the Master of Science in Management (M.S.M.), the Master of Public Administration (M.P.A.), the Doctor of Education (Ed.D.) in organizational leadership, and the Doctor of Business Administration (D.B.A.) degrees. The business programs are designed to serve the needs of talented students, regardless of their undergraduate degrees. The College of Business welcomes and encourages students from diverse academic backgrounds.

The Master of Business Administration program is designed to develop action-oriented managers and leaders who focus on leading themselves and others to solutions that serve their organizations. Students acquire skills to identify challenges and opportunities, draw on the latest technology and information, use advanced analytical and planning approaches, and execute plans for leading positive change. Competencies are developed through focusing on critical thinking, persuasive communications, technical knowledge, and a deep understanding of the human side of business. By focusing on competencies in this manner, the program builds upon the talents of students, independent of their undergraduate field of study. Students from diverse academic and professional backgrounds are welcomed and encouraged. In addition to completing the core course requirements, students develop expertise and specific insights in one of the following concentrations: corporate compliance, finance, fraud examination, health-care administration, information systems management (availability of this concentration is limited; program chair approval is necessary to enter), international business, management, marketing, public administration, or sustainable management. In addition, with approval of the student's program chair, a student may select four courses (12 credit hours) to create a customized concentration that better fits their specific career goals. For all students, the M.B.A. program culminates in an applied capstone project in which they integrate the core business competencies with their concentration specialty.

The Master of Science in Management program was designed to develop leadership and operational skills in those who wish to hold managerial or supervisory positions in public, private, and not-for-profit industries. Students learn the multifaceted process of business administration. The program enables students to diagnose multiple organizational circumstances, determine and evaluate options, then implement and evaluate a plan of action.

The Master of Public Administration program is designed to develop action-oriented, problem-solving managers for the public sector, especially at the state and local levels of government. Students have the opportunity to develop the competencies required to execute the duties and responsibilities of public sector managers, including evaluation and supervision of employees, reinforcement of the organizational mission, and the effective management of organizational resources.

The Doctor of Education in organizational leadership program is designed for working professionals who wish to develop the knowledge and skills required to hold leadership positions in complex organizations. The program focuses on transformational leadership skills in addition to managerial attributes. This approach prepares students for such strategic challenges as increasing globalization, changing economies, societal shifts, and individual-organizational relationships.

The Doctor of Business Administration program enables industry and academic professionals to build upon master's-level competencies, skills, and knowledge, preparing themselves to perform more effectively in existing professional roles, to qualify for roles with increasing responsibility, and/or develop capabilities for a second career in teaching at the college level. The program requires students to develop applied research inquiry and analytical skills. The D.B.A. program is designed to help students develop competencies in understanding and performing applied research, which can then be used to foster innovation and lead organizational change. Students must choose a concentration in accounting, global business sustainability, information systems (availability of this concentration is limited; program chair approval is necessary to enter), international business, management, or marketing. In addition, with approval of the student's program chair, a student may select four courses (12 credit hours) to create a customized concentration that better fits their specific career goals.

Research Facilities
Argosy University libraries provide curriculum support and educational resources, including current text materials, diagnostic training documents, reference materials and databases, journals and dissertations, and major and current titles in program areas. There is an online public-access catalog of library resources available throughout the Argosy University system. Students have remote access to the campus library database, enabling them to study and conduct research at home. Academic databases offer dissertation abstracts, academic journals, and professional periodicals. All library computers are Internet accessible. Software applications include Word, Excel, PowerPoint, SPSS, and various test-scoring programs.

Financial Aid
Financial aid is available to those who qualify. Argosy University, Inland Empire, offers access to federal and state aid programs, merit-based awards, grants, loans, and a work-study program. As a first step, students should complete the Free Application for Federal Student Aid (FAFSA). Prospective students can apply electronically at http://www.fafsa.ed.gov or at the campus.

Cost of Study
Tuition varies by program. Students should contact Argosy University, Inland Empire, for tuition information.

Living and Housing Costs
Students typically live in apartments in the metropolitan San Bernardino area. Living expenses vary according to each student's preferred standard of living, housing, and transportation. The University does not offer or operate student housing. Most of the students are full-time working professionals who live within driving distance of the campus. Several nearby hotels offer special rates for those who commute from long distances. The Admissions Department also maintains a list of housing options, including contact information for university students who wish to share housing. For more information, students should contact the Admissions Department.

Student Group
Admission to Argosy University, Inland Empire, is selective to ensure a dynamic and engaged student body. The University encourages diversity in academic and employment backgrounds and promotes integration of the student body into professional life through established connections with local and national professional associations. Argosy University offers a professionally oriented education with rich opportunities to gain practical experience in class, field placements, and internships. Full-time students and working professionals gain the extensive knowledge and range of skills necessary for effective performance in their chosen fields.

Student Outcomes
Students can register with the University's online career-services system and use select services from a distance, such as degree-specific career e-mail lists, national job posts, and virtual job fairs. Students should contact the University for more information.

Location
Argosy University, Inland Empire, is conveniently located in the Hospitality Lane section of San Bernardino, California. The facility features classrooms, computer labs, a resource center with Internet access, student lounge, staff and faculty offices, and proximity to the region's many cultural and recreational attractions. The University provides a supportive educational environment with convenient class options that enable students to earn a degree while fulfilling other life responsibilities. All of the programs are thoroughly oriented to the real working world with a focus on developing technical proficiency in each student's field as well as an overall professional career approach. Many businesses in the area provide varied opportunities for student training.

The University
Argosy University is a private institution with nineteen locations across the nation. Argosy University, Inland Empire, provides students with a career resources office, an academic resources center, and extensive information access for research. It offers the resources of a large university plus the friendliness and personal attention of a small campus.

The innovative programs feature dynamic, relevant, and practical curricula delivered in flexible class formats. Students enjoy scheduling options that make it easier to fit school into their busy lives, choosing from day and evening courses, on campus or online. Many students find a combination of class formats to be an ideal way of continuing their education while meeting family and professional demands.

Argosy University is accredited by the Higher Learning Commission and a member of the North Central Association (30 North LaSalle Street, Suite 2400, Chicago, Illinois 60602; 800-621-7440 (toll-free); http://www.ncahlc.org).

Applying
Argosy University, Inland Empire, accepts students year-round on a rolling admissions basis, depending on availability of required courses. Applications for admission are available online or by contacting the campus.

Correspondence and Information
Argosy University, Inland Empire
636 East Brier Drive, Suite 120
San Bernardino, California 92408
Phone: 909-915-3800
866-217-9075 (toll-free)
Fax: 909-915-3810
E-mail: auadmissions@argosy.edu
Web site: http://www.argosy.edu/inlandempire

Argosy University, Inland Empire

THE FACULTY

The Argosy University faculty comprises working professionals who are eager to help students succeed. Members bring real-world experience and the latest practice innovations to the academic setting. The diverse faculty members of the College of Business are widely recognized for contributions to the field. Many are published scholars, and most hold doctoral degrees. They are committed to providing a substantive education that combines comprehensive knowledge with critical skills and practical workplace relevance. Above all, faculty members are committed to their students' personal and professional development.

ARGOSY UNIVERSITY.

ARGOSY UNIVERSITY, LOS ANGELES

College of Business

Programs of Study
Argosy University, Los Angeles, offers the Master of Business Administration (M.B.A.), the Master of Science in Management (M.S.M.), the Master of Public Administration (M.P.A), the Doctor of Business Administration (D.B.A.), and the Doctor of Education (Ed.D.) in organizational leadership degrees. The business programs are designed to serve the needs of talented students, regardless of their undergraduate degrees. The College of Business welcomes and encourages students from diverse academic backgrounds.

The Master of Business Administration program is designed to develop action-oriented managers and leaders who focus on leading themselves and others to solutions that serve their organizations. Students acquire skills to identify challenges and opportunities, draw on the latest technology and information, use advanced analytical and planning approaches, and execute plans for leading positive change. Competencies are developed through focusing on critical thinking, persuasive communications, technical knowledge, and a deep understanding of the human side of business. By focusing on competencies in this manner, the program builds upon the talents of students, independent of their undergraduate field of study. Students from diverse academic and professional backgrounds are welcomed and encouraged. In addition to completing the core course requirements, students develop expertise and specific insights in one of the following concentrations: corporate compliance, finance, fraud examination, health-care administration, information systems management (availability of this concentration is limited; program chair approval is necessary to enter), international business, management, marketing, public administration, or sustainable management. In addition, with approval of the student's program chair, a student may select four courses (12 credit hours) to create a customized concentration that better fits their specific career goals. For all students, the M.B.A. program culminates in an applied capstone project in which they integrate the core business competencies with their concentration specialty.

The Master of Science in Management program is designed to improve and extend the interpersonal and problem-solving skills necessary for successful leaders in the private, non-profit, and public sectors. The program focuses on situation diagnostics, opportunity and problem evaluation, and implementation of an action plan.

The Master of Public Administration program is designed to develop action-oriented, problem-solving managers for the public sector, especially at the state and local levels of government. Students have the opportunity to develop the competencies required to execute the duties and responsibilities of public sector managers, including evaluation and supervision of employees, reinforcement of the organizational mission, and the effective management of organizational resources.

The Doctor of Business Administration program enables industry and academic professionals to build upon master's-level competencies, skills, and knowledge, preparing themselves to perform more effectively in existing professional roles, to qualify for roles with increasing responsibility, and/or develop capabilities for a second career in teaching at the college level. The program requires students to develop applied research inquiry and analytical skills. The D.B.A. program is designed to help students develop competencies in understanding and performing applied research, which can then be used to foster innovation and lead organizational change. Students must choose a concentration in accounting, global business sustainability, information systems (availability of this concentration is limited; program chair approval is necessary to enter), international business, management, or marketing. In addition, with approval of the student's program chair, a student may select four courses (12 credit hours) to create a customized concentration that better fits their specific career goals.

The Doctor of Education in organizational leadership program is designed for working professionals who wish to develop the knowledge and skills required to hold leadership positions in complex organizations. The program focuses on transformational leadership skills in addition to managerial attributes. This approach prepares students for such strategic challenges as increasing globalization, changing economies, societal shifts, and individual-organizational relationships.

Research Facilities
Argosy University libraries provide curriculum support and educational resources, including current text materials, diagnostic training documents, reference materials and databases, journals and dissertations, and major and current titles in program areas. There is an online public-access catalog of library resources available throughout the Argosy University system. Students have remote access to the campus library database, enabling them to study and conduct research at home. Academic databases offer dissertation abstracts, academic journals, and professional periodicals. All library computers are Internet accessible. Software applications include Word, Excel, PowerPoint, SPSS, and various test-scoring programs.

Financial Aid
Financial aid is available to those who qualify. Argosy University, Los Angeles, offers access to federal and state aid programs, merit-based awards, grants, loans, and a work-study program. As a first step, students should complete the Free Application for Federal Student Aid (FAFSA). Prospective students can apply electronically at http://www.fafsa.ed.gov or at the campus.

Cost of Study
Tuition varies by program. Students should contact Argosy University, Los Angeles, for tuition information.

Living and Housing Costs
Students typically live in apartments in the metropolitan Santa Monica area. Living expenses vary according to each student's preferred standard of living, housing, and transportation. The University does not offer or operate student housing. Most of the students are full-time working professionals who live within driving distance of the campus. Several nearby hotels offer special rates for those who commute from long distances. The Admissions Department also maintains a list of housing options, including contact information for university students who wish to share housing. For more information, students should contact the Admissions Department.

Student Group
Admission to Argosy University, Los Angeles, is selective to ensure a dynamic and engaged student body. The University encourages diversity in academic and employment backgrounds and promotes integration of the student body into professional life through established connections with local and national professional associations. Argosy University offers a professionally oriented education with rich opportunities to gain practical experience in class, field placements, and internships. Full-time students and working professionals gain the extensive knowledge and range of skills necessary for effective performance in their chosen fields.

Student Outcomes
Students can register with the University's online career-services system and use select services from a distance, such as degree-specific career e-mail lists, national job posts, and virtual job fairs. Students should contact the University for more information.

Location
Argosy University, Los Angeles, is only minutes away from Los Angeles International Airport and the Pacific coast, and is conveniently located near the interchange between I-405 and I-105.

The business environment in the Los Angeles metropolitan area includes a broad array of companies, including a proliferation of entertainment, technology, and software firms. Among the principal employers in the area are Yahoo!, MTV Networks, RAND Corporation, and Symantec Corporation. The many businesses in the area provide varied opportunities for student training.

The University
Argosy University is a private institution with nineteen locations across the nation. Argosy University, Los Angeles, provides students with a career resources office, an academic resources center, and extensive information access for research. It offers the resources of a large university plus the friendliness and personal attention of a small campus.

The innovative programs feature dynamic, relevant, and practical curricula delivered in flexible class formats. Students enjoy scheduling options that make it easier to fit school into their busy lives, choosing from day and evening courses, on campus or online. Many students find a combination of class formats to be an ideal way of continuing their education while meeting family and professional demands.

Argosy University is accredited by the Higher Learning Commission and a member of the North Central Association (30 North LaSalle Street, Suite 2400, Chicago, Illinois 60602; 800-621-7440 (toll-free); http://www.ncahlc.org).

Applying
Argosy University, Los Angeles, accepts students year-round on a rolling admissions basis, depending on availability of required courses. Applications for admission are available online or by contacting the campus.

Correspondence and Information
Argosy University, Los Angeles
5230 Pacific Concourse
Los Angeles, California 90045

Phone: 310-866-4000
866-505-0332 (toll-free)
Fax: 310-399-1804
E-mail: auadmissions@argosy.edu
Web site: http://www.argosy.edu/losangeles

Argosy University, Los Angeles

THE FACULTY

The Argosy University faculty comprises working professionals who are eager to help students succeed. Members bring real-world experience and the latest practice innovations to the academic setting. The diverse faculty members of the College of Business are widely recognized for contributions to the field. Many are published scholars, and most hold doctoral degrees. They are committed to providing a substantive education that combines comprehensive knowledge with critical skills and practical workplace relevance. Above all, faculty members are committed to their students' personal and professional development.

ARGOSY UNIVERSITY.

ARGOSY UNIVERSITY, NASHVILLE

College of Business

Program of Study

Argosy University, Nashville, offers the Master of Business Administration (M.B.A.), the Master of Science in Management (M.S.M.), and the Doctor of Business Administration (D.B.A.) degrees. The business programs are designed to serve the needs of talented students, regardless of their undergraduate degrees. The College of Business welcomes and encourages students from diverse academic backgrounds.

The Master of Business Administration program is designed to develop action-oriented managers and leaders who focus on leading themselves and others to solutions that serve their organizations. Students acquire skills to identify challenges and opportunities, draw on the latest technology and information, use advanced analytical and planning approaches, and execute plans for leading positive change. Competencies are developed through focusing on critical thinking, persuasive communications, technical knowledge, and a deep understanding of the human side of business. By focusing on competencies in this manner, the program builds upon the talents of students, independent of their undergraduate field of study. Students from diverse academic and professional backgrounds are welcomed and encouraged. In addition to completing the core course requirements, students develop expertise and specific insights in one of the following concentrations: corporate compliance, finance, fraud examination, health-care administration, information systems management (availability of this concentration is limited; program chair approval is necessary to enter), international business, management, marketing, public administration, or sustainable management. In addition, with approval of the student's program chair, a student may select four courses (12 credit hours) to create a customized concentration that better fits their specific career goals. For all students, the M.B.A. program culminates in an applied capstone project in which they integrate the core business competencies with their concentration specialty.

The Master of Science in Management program is designed to improve and extend the interpersonal and problem-solving skills necessary for successful leaders in the private, non-profit, and public sectors. The program focuses on situation diagnostics, opportunity and problem evaluation, and implementation of an action plan.

The Doctor of Business Administration program enables industry and academic professionals to build upon master's-level competencies, skills, and knowledge, preparing themselves to perform more effectively in existing professional roles, to qualify for roles with increasing responsibility, and/or develop capabilities for a second career in teaching at the college level. The program requires students to develop applied research inquiry and analytical skills. The D.B.A. program is designed to help students develop competencies in understanding and performing applied research, which can then be used to foster innovation and lead organizational change. Students must choose a concentration in accounting, global business sustainability, information systems (availability of this concentration is limited; program chair approval is necessary to enter), international business, management, or marketing. In addition, with approval of the student's program chair, a student may select four courses (12 credit hours) to create a customized concentration that better fits their specific career goals.

Research Facilities

Argosy University libraries provide curriculum support and educational resources, including current text materials, diagnostic training documents, reference materials and databases, journals and dissertations, and major and current titles in program areas. There is an online public-access catalog of library resources available throughout the Argosy University system. Students have remote access to the campus library database, enabling them to study and conduct research at home. Academic databases offer dissertation abstracts, academic journals, and professional periodicals. All library computers are Internet accessible. Software applications include Word, Excel, PowerPoint, SPSS, and various test-scoring programs.

Financial Aid

Financial aid is available to those who qualify. Argosy University, Nashville, offers access to federal and state aid programs, merit-based awards, grants, loans, and a work-study program. As a first step, students should complete the Free Application for Federal Student Aid (FAFSA). Prospective students can apply electronically at http://www.fafsa.ed.gov or at the campus.

Cost of Study

Tuition varies by program. Students should contact Argosy University, Nashville, for tuition information.

Living and Housing Costs

Students typically live in apartments in the metropolitan Nashville area. Living expenses vary according to each student's preferred standard of living, housing, and transportation. The University does not offer or operate student housing. Most of the students are full-time working professionals who live within driving distance of the campus. Several nearby hotels offer special rates for those who commute from long distances. The Admissions Department also maintains a list of housing options, including contact information, for University students who wish to share housing. For more information, students should contact the Admissions Department.

Student Group

Admission to Argosy University, Nashville, is selective to ensure a dynamic and engaged student body. It encourages diversity in academic and employment backgrounds and promotes integration of the student body into professional life through established connections with local and national professional associations. Argosy University offers a professionally oriented education with rich opportunities to gain practical experience in class, field placements, and internships. Full-time students and working professionals gain the extensive knowledge and range of skills necessary for effective performance in their chosen fields.

Student Outcomes

Students can register with the University's online career-services system and use select services from a distance, such as degree-specific career e-mail lists, national job posts, and virtual job fairs. Students should contact the University for more information.

Location

Argosy University, Nashville, is located at 100 Centerview Drive in Nashville, Tennessee. This growing city offers a variety of recreational activities, including the ballet and symphony, the newly established Frist Museum of Art, and professional sports. Nashville is known as Music City, USA, and is home to the Country Music Hall of Fame. The business environment includes companies such as Moses Cone Health Systems, Inc., and Novant Health, Inc.

The University

Argosy University is a private institution with nineteen locations across the nation. Argosy University, Nashville, provides students with a career resources office, an academic resources center, and extensive information access for research. It offers the resources of a large university, plus the friendliness and personal attention of a small campus.

The innovative programs feature dynamic, relevant, and practical curricula delivered in flexible class formats. Students enjoy scheduling options that make it easier to fit school into their busy lives, choosing from day and evening courses, on campus or online. Many students find a combination of class formats to be an ideal way of continuing their education while meeting family and professional demands.

Argosy University is accredited by the Higher Learning Commission and a member of the North Central Association (30 North LaSalle Street, Suite 2400, Chicago, Illinois 60602; 800-621-7440 (toll-free); http://www.ncahlc.org).

Applying

Argosy University, Nashville, accepts students year-round on a rolling admissions basis, depending on availability of required courses. Applications for admission are available online or by contacting the campus.

Correspondence and Information

Argosy University, Nashville
100 Centerview Drive, Suite 225
Nashville, Tennessee 37214
Phone: 615-525-2800
    866-833-6598 (toll-free)
Fax: 615-525-2900
E-mail: auadmissions@argosy.edu
Web site: http://www.argosy.edu/nashville

Argosy University, Nashville

THE FACULTY

The Argosy University faculty comprises working professionals who are eager to help students succeed. Members bring real-world experience and the latest practice innovations to the academic setting. The diverse faculty members of the College of Business are widely recognized for contributions to the field. Most hold doctoral degrees. They are committed to providing a substantive education that combines comprehensive knowledge with critical skills and practical workplace relevance. Above all, faculty members are committed to their students' personal and professional development.

ARGOSY UNIVERSITY

ARGOSY UNIVERSITY, ORANGE COUNTY

College of Business

Programs of Study

Argosy University, Orange County, offers the Master of Business Administration (M.B.A.), the Master of Science in Management (M.S.M.), the Master of Public Administration (M.P.A.), the Doctor of Education (Ed.D.) in organizational leadership, and the Doctor of Business Administration (D.B.A.) degrees. The business programs are designed to serve the needs of talented students, regardless of their undergraduate degrees. The College of Business welcomes and encourages students from diverse academic backgrounds.

The Master of Business Administration program offers a solutions-based, action-oriented approach to organizational change and human dynamics. It is designed to develop a new breed of leader—one who can identify challenges and opportunities, draw on the latest technology and information, use advanced analytical and planning approaches, and execute plans for positive change. Core courses include a broad array of foundation subjects, all relevant to meeting challenges and problems encountered in modern organizations. Students are required to choose from a variety of concentrations: customized professional concentration, finance, fraud examination, health-care administration, information systems management, international business, management, marketing, public administration, or sustainable management. This program can enhance future career potential and prepare students for postgraduate work in business.

The Master of Science in management program was designed to develop leadership and operational skills in those who wish to hold managerial or supervisory positions in public, private, and not-for-profit industries. Students learn the multifaceted process of business administration. The program enables students to diagnose multiple organizational circumstances, determine and evaluate options, and then implement and evaluate a plan of action.

The Master of Public Administration program is designed to develop action-oriented, problem-solving managers for the public sector, especially at the state and local levels of government. Students have the opportunity to develop the competencies required to execute the duties and responsibilities of public sector managers, including evaluation and supervision of employees, reinforcement of the organizational mission, and the effective management of organizational resources.

The Doctor of Education in organizational leadership program is designed for working professionals who wish to develop the knowledge and skills required to hold leadership positions in complex organizations. The program focuses on transformational leadership skills in addition to managerial attributes. This approach prepares students for such strategic challenges as increasing globalization, changing economies, societal shifts, and individual-organizational relationships.

The Doctor of Business Administration program provides industry and academic professionals the opportunity to build upon core skills and knowledge gained through the master's program. Students develop advanced comprehension of theoretical and applied literature in a chosen discipline and a higher level of competence in conducting action research. The program is designed to develop critical knowledge and skills for success in service to the profession and the community and in attaining credentials essential to leading, consulting, and teaching. Students must choose a concentration in accounting, customized professional concentration, information systems, global business sustainability, international business, management, or marketing.

Research Facilities

Argosy University libraries provide curriculum support and educational resources, including current text materials, diagnostic training documents, reference materials and databases, journals and dissertations, and major and current titles in program areas. There is an online public-access catalog of library resources available throughout the Argosy University system. Students have remote access to the campus library database, enabling them to study and conduct research at home. Academic databases offer dissertation abstracts, academic journals, and professional periodicals. All library computers are Internet accessible. Software applications include Word, Excel, PowerPoint, SPSS, and various test-scoring programs.

Financial Aid

Financial aid is available to those who qualify. Argosy University, Orange County, offers access to federal and state aid programs, merit-based awards, grants, loans, and a work-study program. As a first step, students should complete the Free Application for Federal Student Aid (FAFSA). Prospective students can apply electronically at http://www.fafsa.ed.gov or at the campus.

Cost of Study

Tuition varies by program. Students should contact Argosy University, Orange County, for tuition information.

Living and Housing Costs

Students typically live in apartments in the Santa Ana metropolitan area. Living expenses vary according to each student's preferred standard of living, housing, and transportation. The University does not offer or operate student housing. Most of the students are full-time working professionals who live within driving distance of the campus. Several nearby hotels offer special rates for those who commute from long distances. The Admissions Department also maintains a list of housing options, including contact information, for University students who wish to share housing. For more information, students should contact the Admissions Department.

Student Group

Admission to Argosy University, Orange County, is selective to ensure a dynamic and engaged student body. It encourages diversity in academic and employment backgrounds and promotes integration of the student body into professional life through established connections with local and national professional associations. Argosy University offers a professionally oriented education with rich opportunities to gain practical experience in class, field placements, and internships. Full-time students and working professionals gain the extensive knowledge and range of skills necessary for effective performance in their chosen fields.

Student Outcomes

Students can register with the University's online career-services system and use select services from a distance, such as degree-specific career e-mail lists, national job posts, and virtual job fairs. Students should contact the University for more information.

Location

Argosy University, Orange County, attracts students from Southern California as well as around the country and the world. Orange County features a temperate climate, sunny beaches, and a host of cultural and entertainment options. The campus is located approximately 30 miles south of downtown Los Angeles, 90 miles north of San Diego, and just minutes from one of the many freeways that connect the Southern California basin. Regional parks and preserved lands provide opportunities for hiking, biking, riding, and other recreational activities. Whether it is ultrachic Newport Beach, artsy Laguna Beach, or unspoiled Catalina Island, Orange County's oceanside personalities are as varied as the people who visit the area.

Many businesses in the area provide excellent opportunities for student training. Orange County's business environment includes a broad array of companies. The area's largest employers include Ingram Micro Inc., the *Orange County Register,* ITT Industries, and OneSource.

The University

Argosy University is a private institution with nineteen locations across the nation. Argosy University, Orange County, provides students with a career resources office, an academic resources center, and extensive information access for research. It offers the resources of a large university plus the friendliness and personal attention of a small campus.

The innovative programs feature dynamic, relevant, and practical curricula delivered in flexible class formats. Students enjoy scheduling options that make it easier to fit school into their busy lives, choosing from day and evening courses, on campus or online. Many students find a combination of class formats to be an ideal way of continuing their education while meeting family and professional demands.

Argosy University is accredited by the Higher Learning Commission and a member of the North Central Association (30 North LaSalle Street, Suite 2400, Chicago, Illinois 60602; 800-621-7440 (toll-free); http://www.ncahlc.org).

Applying

Argosy University, Orange County, accepts students year-round on a rolling admissions basis, depending on availability of required courses. Applications for admission are available online or by contacting the campus.

Correspondence and Information

Argosy University, Orange County
601 South Lewis Street
Orange, California 92868

Phone: 714-620-3700
        800-716-9598 (toll-free)
Fax: 714-620-3800
E-mail: auadmissions@argosy.edu
Web site: http://www.argosy.edu/orangecounty/

Argosy University, Orange County

THE FACULTY

The Argosy University faculty comprises working professionals who are eager to help students succeed. Members bring real-world experience and the latest practice innovations to the academic setting. The diverse faculty members of the College of Business are widely recognized for contributions to the field. Many are published scholars, and most hold doctoral degrees. They are committed to providing a substantive education that combines comprehensive knowledge with critical skills and practical workplace relevance. Above all, faculty members are committed to their students' personal and professional development.

ARGOSY UNIVERSITY

ARGOSY UNIVERSITY, PHOENIX

College of Business

Programs of Study
Argosy University, Phoenix, offers the Master of Business Administration (M.B.A.), the Master of Public Administration (M.P.A.), and the Doctor of Business Administration (D.B.A.) degrees. The business programs are designed to serve the needs of talented students, regardless of their undergraduate degrees. The College of Business welcomes and encourages students from diverse academic backgrounds.

The Master of Business Administration program offers a solutions-based, action-oriented approach to organizational change and human dynamics. It is designed to develop a new breed of leader—one who can identify challenges and opportunities, draw on the latest technology and information, use advanced analytical and planning approaches, and execute plans for positive change. Core courses include a broad array of foundation subjects, all relevant to meeting challenges and problems encountered in modern organizations. Students are required to choose from a variety of concentrations: customized professional concentration, finance, health-care administration, information systems management, international business, management, or marketing. This program can enhance future career potential and prepare students for postgraduate work in business.

The Master of Public Administration program is designed to develop action-oriented, problem-solving managers for the public sector, especially at the state and local levels of government. Students have the opportunity to develop the competencies required to execute the duties and responsibilities of public sector managers, including evaluation and supervision of employees, reinforcement of the organizational mission, and the effective management of organizational resources.

The Doctor of Business Administration program provides industry and academic professionals the opportunity to build upon core skills and knowledge gained through the master's program. Students develop advanced comprehension of theoretical and applied literature in a chosen discipline and a higher level of competence in conducting action research. The program is designed to develop critical knowledge and skills for success in service to the profession and the community and in attaining credentials essential to leading, consulting, and teaching. Students must choose a concentration in accounting, customized professional concentration, information systems, international business, management, or marketing.

Research Facilities
Argosy University libraries provide curriculum support and educational resources, including current text materials, diagnostic training documents, reference materials and databases, journals and dissertations, and major and current titles in program areas. There is an online public-access catalog of library resources available throughout the Argosy University system. Students have remote access to the campus library database, enabling them to study and conduct research at home. Academic databases offer dissertation abstracts, academic journals, and professional periodicals. All library computers are Internet accessible. Software applications include Word, Excel, PowerPoint, SPSS, and various test-scoring programs.

Financial Aid
Financial aid is available to those who qualify. Argosy University, Phoenix, offers access to federal and state aid programs, merit-based awards, grants, loans, and a work-study program. As a first step, students should complete the Free Application for Federal Student Aid (FAFSA). Prospective students can apply electronically at http://www.fafsa.ed.gov or at the campus.

Cost of Study
Tuition varies by program. Students should contact Argosy University, Phoenix, for tuition information.

Living and Housing Costs
Students typically live in apartments in the metropolitan Phoenix area. Living expenses vary according to each student's preferred standard of living, housing, and transportation. The University does not offer or operate student housing. Most of the students are full-time working professionals who live within driving distance of the campus. Several nearby hotels offer special rates for those who commute from long distances. The Admissions Department also maintains a list of housing options, including contact information for University students who wish to share housing. For more information, students should contact the Admissions Department.

Student Group
Admission to Argosy University, Phoenix, is selective to ensure a dynamic and engaged student body. It encourages diversity in academic and employment backgrounds and promotes integration of the student body into professional life through established connections with local and national professional associations. Argosy University offers a professionally oriented education with rich opportunities to gain practical experience in class, field placements, and internships. Full-time students and working professionals gain the extensive knowledge and range of skills necessary for effective performance in their chosen fields.

Student Outcomes
Students can register with the University's online career-services system and use select services from a distance, such as degree-specific career e-mail lists, national job posts, and virtual job fairs. Students should contact the University for more information.

Location
Argosy University, Phoenix offers classes in an intimate, small-group setting. The campus is conveniently located near I-17, close to shops, restaurants, and recreational areas. Phoenix is home to several major league sports teams, and the city offers an array of cultural activities ranging from opera and theater to science museums. The multicultural environment of Arizona, coupled with Argosy University's professional training affiliations throughout the state, creates an exciting opportunity for students to work with urban, rural, and culturally diverse populations.

Many businesses in the area provide varied opportunities for student training. The business environment in Phoenix includes a wide variety of companies such as Intel and Go Daddy Group, an Internet company. Wells Fargo, Home Depot, Lowe's, and Wal-Mart also represent some of the area's largest employers.

The University
Argosy University is a private institution with nineteen locations across the nation. Argosy University, Phoenix, provides students with a career resources office, an academic resources center, and extensive information access for research. It offers the resources of a large university, plus the friendliness and personal attention of a small campus. The innovative programs feature dynamic, relevant, and practical curricula delivered in flexible class formats. Students enjoy scheduling options that make it easier to fit school into their busy lives, choosing from day and evening courses, on campus or online. Many students find a combination of class formats to be an ideal way of continuing their education while meeting family and professional demands.

Argosy University is accredited by the Higher Learning Commission and a member of the North Central Association (30 North LaSalle Street, Suite 2400, Chicago, Illinois 60602; 800-621-7440 (toll-free); http://www.ncahlc.org).

Applying
Argosy University, Phoenix, accepts students year-round on a rolling admissions basis, depending on availability of required courses. Applications for admission are available online or by contacting the campus.

Correspondence and Information
Argosy University, Phoenix
2233 West Dunlap Avenue
Phoenix, Arizona 85021
Phone: 602-216-2600
        866-216-2777 (toll-free)
Fax: 602-216-2601
E-mail: auadmissions@argosy.edu
Web site: http://www.argosy.edu/phoenix/

Argosy University, Phoenix

THE FACULTY

The Argosy University faculty comprises working professionals who are eager to help students succeed. Members bring real-world experience and the latest practice innovations to the academic setting. The diverse faculty members of the College of Business are widely recognized for contributions to the field. Many are published scholars, and most hold doctoral degrees. They are committed to providing a substantive education that combines comprehensive knowledge with critical skills and practical workplace relevance. Above all, faculty members are committed to their students' personal and professional development.

ARGOSY UNIVERSITY.

ARGOSY UNIVERSITY, SALT LAKE CITY

College of Business

Programs of Study

Argosy University, Salt Lake City, offers the Master of Business Administration (M.B.A.) degree and the Doctor of Business Administration (D.B.A.) degrees. The business programs are designed to serve the needs of talented students, regardless of their undergraduate degrees. The College of Business welcomes and encourages students from diverse academic backgrounds.

The Master of Business Administration program is designed to develop action-oriented managers and leaders who focus on leading themselves and others to solutions that serve their organizations. Students acquire skills to identify challenges and opportunities, draw on the latest technology and information, use advanced analytical and planning approaches, and execute plans for leading positive change. Competencies are developed through focusing on critical thinking, persuasive communications, technical knowledge, and a deep understanding of the human side of business. By focusing on competencies in this manner, the program builds upon the talents of students, independent of their undergraduate field of study. Students from diverse academic and professional backgrounds are welcomed and encouraged. In addition to completing the core course requirements, students develop expertise and specific insights in one of the following concentrations: corporate compliance, finance, fraud examination, health-care administration, information systems management (availability of this concentration is limited; program chair approval is necessary to enter), international business, management, marketing, public administration, or sustainable management. In addition, with approval of the student's program chair, a student may select four courses (12 credit hours) to create a customized concentration that better fits their specific career goals. For all students, the M.B.A. program culminates in an applied capstone project in which they integrate the core business competencies with their concentration specialty.

The Doctor of Business Administration program enables industry and academic professionals to build upon master's-level competencies, skills, and knowledge, preparing themselves to perform more effectively in existing professional roles, to qualify for roles with increasing responsibility, and/or develop capabilities for a second career in teaching at the college level. The program requires students to develop applied research inquiry and analytical skills. The D.B.A. program is designed to help students develop competencies in understanding and performing applied research, which can then be used to foster innovation and lead organizational change. Students must choose a concentration in accounting, global business sustainability, information systems (availability of this concentration is limited; program chair approval is necessary to enter), international business, management, or marketing. In addition, with approval of the student's program chair, a student may select four courses (12 credit hours) to create a customized concentration that better fits their specific career goals.

Research Facilities

Argosy University libraries provide curriculum support and educational resources, including current text materials, diagnostic training documents, reference materials and databases, journals and dissertations, and major and current titles in program areas. There is an online public-access catalog of library resources available throughout the Argosy University system. Students have remote access to the campus library database, enabling them to study and conduct research at home. Academic databases offer dissertation abstracts, academic journals, and professional periodicals. All library computers are Internet accessible. Software applications include Word, Excel, PowerPoint, SPSS, and various test-scoring programs.

Financial Aid

Financial aid is available to those who qualify. Argosy University, Salt Lake City, offers access to federal and state aid programs, merit-based awards, grants, loans, and a work-study program. As a first step, students should complete the Free Application for Federal Student Aid (FAFSA). Prospective students can apply electronically at http://www.fafsa.ed.gov or at the campus.

Cost of Study

Tuition varies by program. Students should contact Argosy University, Salt Lake City, for tuition information.

Living and Housing Costs

Students typically live in apartments in the metropolitan Salt Lake City area. Living expenses vary according to each student's preferred standard of living, housing, and transportation. The University does not offer or operate student housing. Most of the students are full-time working professionals who live within driving distance of the campus. Several nearby hotels offer special rates for those who commute from long distances. The Admissions Department also maintains a list of housing options, including contact information for University students who wish to share housing. For more information, students should contact the Admissions Department.

Student Group

Admission to Argosy University, Salt Lake City, is selective to ensure a dynamic and engaged student body. It encourages diversity in academic and employment backgrounds and promotes integration of the student body into professional life through established connections with local and national professional associations. Argosy University offers a professionally oriented education with rich opportunities to gain practical experience in class, field placements, and internships. Full-time students and working professionals gain the extensive knowledge and range of skills necessary for effective performance in their chosen fields.

Student Outcomes

Students can register with the University's online career-services system and use select services from a distance, such as degree-specific career e-mail lists, national job posts, and virtual job fairs. Students should contact the University for more information.

Location

Argosy University, Salt Lake City, offers a supportive, engaging learning environment in an intimate, small-group setting. Argosy University, Salt Lake City, is conveniently located in Draper, Utah, nestled in the Wasatch Mountains about 20 miles south of Salt Lake City. The area's business climate and numerous hospitals, schools, clinics, and social service agencies can provide many training opportunities for students.

The University

Argosy University is a private institution with nineteen locations across the nation. Argosy University, Salt Lake City, provides students with a career resources office, an academic resources center, and extensive information access for research. It offers the resources of a large university, plus the friendliness and personal attention of a small campus. The innovative programs feature dynamic, relevant, and practical curricula delivered in flexible class formats. Students enjoy scheduling options that make it easier to fit school into their busy lives, choosing from day and evening courses, on campus or online. Many students find a combination of class formats to be an ideal way of continuing their education while meeting family and professional demands.

Argosy University is accredited by the Higher Learning Commission and a member of the North Central Association (30 North LaSalle Street, Suite 2400, Chicago, Illinois 60602; 800-621-7440 (toll-free); http://www.ncahlc.org).

Applying

Argosy University, Salt Lake City, accepts students year-round on a rolling admissions basis, depending on availability of required courses. Applications for admission are available online or by contacting the campus.

Correspondence and Information

Argosy University, Salt Lake City
121 Election Road, Suite 300
Draper, Utah 84020
Phone: 801-601-5000
    888-639-4756 (toll-free)
Fax: 801-601-4990
E-mail: auadmissions@argosy.edu
Web site: http://www.argosy.edu/saltlakecity

Argosy University, Salt Lake City

THE FACULTY

The Argosy University faculty comprises working professionals who are eager to help students succeed. Members bring real-world experience and the latest practice innovations to the academic setting. The diverse faculty members of the College of Business are widely recognized for contributions to the field. Many are published scholars, and most hold doctoral degrees. They are committed to providing a substantive education that combines comprehensive knowledge with critical skills and practical workplace relevance. Above all, faculty members are committed to their students' personal and professional development.

ARGOSY UNIVERSITY

ARGOSY UNIVERSITY, SAN DIEGO

College of Business

Programs of Study

Argosy University, San Diego, offers the Master of Business Administration (M.B.A.), the Master of Science in Management (M.S.M), the Master of Public Administration (M.P.A), the Doctor of Business Administration (D.B.A.), and the Doctor of Education (Ed.D.) in organizational leadership degrees. The business programs are designed to serve the needs of talented students, regardless of their undergraduate degrees. The College of Business welcomes and encourages students from diverse academic backgrounds.

The Master of Business Administration program is designed to develop action-oriented managers and leaders who focus on leading themselves and others to solutions that serve their organizations. Students acquire skills to identify challenges and opportunities, draw on the latest technology and information, use advanced analytical and planning approaches, and execute plans for leading positive change. Competencies are developed through focusing on critical thinking, persuasive communications, technical knowledge, and a deep understanding of the human side of business. By focusing on competencies in this manner, the program builds upon the talents of students, independent of their undergraduate field of study. Students from diverse academic and professional backgrounds are welcomed and encouraged. In addition to completing the core course requirements, students develop expertise and specific insights in one of the following concentrations: corporate compliance, finance, fraud examination, health-care administration, information systems management (availability of this concentration is limited; program chair approval is necessary to enter), international business, management, marketing, public administration, or sustainable management. In addition, with approval of the student's program chair, a student may select four courses (12 credit hours) to create a customized concentration that better fits their specific career goals. For all students, the M.B.A. program culminates in an applied capstone project in which they integrate the core business competencies with their concentration specialty.

The Master of Science in Management program is designed to improve and extend the interpersonal and problem-solving skills necessary for successful leaders in the private, non-profit, and public sectors. The program focuses on situation diagnostics, opportunity and problem evaluation, and implementation of an action plan.

The Master of Public Administration program is designed to develop action-oriented, problem-solving managers for the public sector, especially at the state and local levels of government. Students have the opportunity to develop the competencies required to execute the duties and responsibilities of public sector managers, including evaluation and supervision of employees, reinforcement of the organizational mission, and the effective management of organizational resources.

The Doctor of Business Administration program enables industry and academic professionals to build upon master's-level competencies, skills, and knowledge, preparing themselves to perform more effectively in existing professional roles, to qualify for roles with increasing responsibility, and/or develop capabilities for a second career in teaching at the college level. The program requires students to develop applied research inquiry and analytical skills. The D.B.A. program is designed to help students develop competencies in understanding and performing applied research, which can then be used to foster innovation and lead organizational change. Students must choose a concentration in accounting, global business sustainability, information systems (availability of this concentration is limited; program chair approval is necessary to enter), international business, management, or marketing. In addition, with approval of the student's program chair, a student may select four courses (12 credit hours) to create a customized concentration that better fits their specific career goals.

The Doctor of Education in organizational leadership program is designed for working professionals who wish to develop the knowledge and skills required to hold leadership positions in complex organizations. The program focuses on transformational leadership skills in addition to managerial attributes. This approach prepares students for such strategic challenges as increasing globalization, changing economies, societal shifts, and individual-organizational relationships.

Research Facilities

Argosy University libraries provide curriculum support and educational resources, including current text materials, diagnostic training documents, reference materials and databases, journals and dissertations, and major and current titles in program areas. There is an online public-access catalog of library resources available throughout the Argosy University system. Students have remote access to the campus library database, enabling them to study and conduct research at home. Academic databases offer dissertation abstracts, academic journals, and professional periodicals. All library computers are Internet accessible. Software applications include Word, Excel, PowerPoint, SPSS, and various test-scoring programs.

Financial Aid

Financial aid is available to those who qualify. Argosy University, San Diego, offers access to federal and state aid programs, merit-based awards, grants, loans, and a work-study program. As a first step, students should complete the Free Application for Federal Student Aid (FAFSA). Prospective students can apply electronically at http://www.fafsa.ed.gov or at the campus.

Cost of Study

Tuition varies by program. Students should contact Argosy University, San Diego, for tuition information.

Living and Housing Costs

Students typically live in apartments in the metropolitan San Diego area. Living expenses vary according to each student's preferred standard of living, housing, and transportation. The University does not offer or operate student housing. Most of the students are full-time working professionals who live within driving distance of the campus. Several nearby hotels offer special rates for those who commute from long distances. The Admissions Department also maintains a list of housing options, including contact information, for University students who wish to share housing. For more information, students should contact the Admissions Department.

Student Group

Admission to Argosy University, San Diego, is selective to ensure a dynamic and engaged student body. It encourages diversity in academic and employment backgrounds and promotes integration of the student body into professional life through established connections with local and national professional associations. Argosy University offers a professionally oriented education with rich opportunities to gain practical experience in class, field placements, and internships. Full-time students and working professionals gain the extensive knowledge and range of skills necessary for effective performance in their chosen fields.

Student Outcomes

Students can register with the University's online career-services system and use select services from a distance, such as degree-specific career e-mail lists, national job posts, and virtual job fairs. Students should contact the University for more information.

Location

San Diego, southern California's second-largest city, offers an ideal climate year-round, 70 miles of beautiful beaches, colorful neighborhoods, and a dynamic downtown district. Argosy University, San Diego, offers classrooms, a library resource center, a student lounge, staff and faculty offices, and other amenities. The area offers numerous attractions, including the famous San Diego Zoo and Wild Animal Park and Sea World.

Many businesses in the area provide varied opportunities for student training. San Diego's business environment includes several Fortune 500 companies such as QUALCOMM and Pfizer, Inc., and a concentration of technology companies.

The University

Argosy University is a private institution with nineteen locations across the nation. Argosy University, San Diego, provides students with a career resources office, an academic resources center, and extensive information access for research. It offers the resources of a large university, plus the friendliness and personal attention of a small campus.

The innovative programs feature dynamic, relevant, and practical curricula delivered in flexible class formats. Students enjoy scheduling options that make it easier to fit school into their busy lives, choosing from day and evening courses, on campus or online. Many students find a combination of class formats to be an ideal way of continuing their education while meeting family and professional demands.

Argosy University is accredited by the Higher Learning Commission and a member of the North Central Association (30 North LaSalle Street, Suite 2400, Chicago, Illinois 60602; 800-621-7440 (toll-free); http://www.ncahlc.org).

Applying

Argosy University, San Diego, accepts students year-round on a rolling admissions basis, depending on availability of required courses. Applications for admission are available online or by contacting the campus.

Correspondence and Information

Argosy University, San Diego
1615 Murray Canyon Road
San Diego, California 92108

Phone: 619-321-3000
          866-505-0333 (toll-free)
Fax: 619-321-3005
E-mail: auadmissions@argosy.edu
Web site: http://www.argosy.edu/sandiego/

Argosy University, San Diego

THE FACULTY

The Argosy University faculty comprises working professionals who are eager to help students succeed. Members bring real-world experience and the latest practice innovations to the academic setting. The diverse faculty members of the College of Business are widely recognized for contributions to the field. Many are published scholars, and most hold doctoral degrees. They are committed to providing a substantive education that combines comprehensive knowledge with critical skills and practical workplace relevance. Above all, faculty members are committed to their students' personal and professional development.

ARGOSY UNIVERSITY

ARGOSY UNIVERSITY, SAN FRANCISCO BAY AREA

College of Business

Programs of Study

Argosy University, San Francisco Bay Area, offers the Master of Business Administration (M.B.A.), the Master of Science in Management (M.S.M.), the Master of Public Administration (M.P.A), the Doctor of Business Administration (D.B.A.), and the Doctor of Education (Ed.D.) in organizational leadership degrees. The business programs are designed to serve the needs of talented students, regardless of their undergraduate degrees. The College of Business welcomes and encourages students from diverse academic backgrounds.

The Master of Business Administration program is designed to develop action-oriented managers and leaders who focus on leading themselves and others to solutions that serve their organizations. Students acquire skills to identify challenges and opportunities, draw on the latest technology and information, use advanced analytical and planning approaches, and execute plans for leading positive change. Competencies are developed through focusing on critical thinking, persuasive communications, technical knowledge, and a deep understanding of the human side of business. By focusing on competencies in this manner, the program builds upon the talents of students, independent of their undergraduate field of study. Students from diverse academic and professional backgrounds are welcomed and encouraged. In addition to completing the core course requirements, students develop expertise and specific insights in one of the following concentrations: corporate compliance, finance, fraud examination, health-care administration, information systems management (availability of this concentration is limited; program chair approval is necessary to enter), international business, management, marketing, public administration, or sustainable management. In addition, with approval of the student's program chair, a student may select four courses (12 credit hours) to create a customized concentration that better fits their specific career goals. For all students, the M.B.A. program culminates in an applied capstone project in which they integrate the core business competencies with their concentration specialty.

The Master of Science in Management program is designed to improve and extend the interpersonal and problem-solving skills necessary for successful leaders in the private, non-profit, and public sectors. The program focuses on situation diagnostics, opportunity and problem evaluation, and implementation of an action plan.

The Master of Public Administration program is designed to develop action-oriented, problem-solving managers for the public sector, especially at the state and local levels of government. Students have the opportunity to develop the competencies required to execute the duties and responsibilities of public sector managers, including evaluation and supervision of employees, reinforcement of the organizational mission, and the effective management of organizational resources.

The Doctor of Business Administration program enables industry and academic professionals to build upon master's-level competencies, skills, and knowledge, preparing themselves to perform more effectively in existing professional roles, to qualify for roles with increasing responsibility, and/or develop capabilities for a second career in teaching at the college level. The program requires students to develop applied research inquiry and analytical skills. The D.B.A. program is designed to help students develop competencies in understanding and performing applied research, which can then be used to foster innovation and lead organizational change. Students must choose a concentration in accounting, global business sustainability, information systems (availability of this concentration is limited; program chair approval is necessary to enter), international business, management, or marketing. In addition, with approval of the student's program chair, a student may select four courses (12 credit hours) to create a customized concentration that better fits their specific career goals.

The Doctor of Education in organizational leadership program is designed for working professionals who wish to develop the knowledge and skills required to hold leadership positions in complex organizations. The program focuses on transformational leadership skills in addition to managerial attributes. This approach prepares students for such strategic challenges as increasing globalization, changing economies, societal shifts, and individual-organizational relationships.

Research Facilities

Argosy University libraries provide curriculum support and educational resources, including current text materials, diagnostic training documents, reference materials and databases, journals and dissertations, and major and current titles in program areas. There is an online public-access catalog of library resources available throughout the Argosy University system. Students have remote access to the campus library database, enabling them to study and conduct research at home. Academic databases offer dissertation abstracts, academic journals, and professional periodicals. All library computers are Internet accessible. Software applications include Word, Excel, PowerPoint, SPSS, and various test-scoring programs.

Financial Aid

Financial aid is available to those who qualify. Argosy University, San Francisco Bay Area, offers access to federal and state aid programs, merit-based awards, grants, loans, and a work-study program. As a first step, students should complete the Free Application for Federal Student Aid (FAFSA). Prospective students can apply electronically at http://www.fafsa.ed.gov or at the campus.

Cost of Study

Tuition varies by program. Students should contact Argosy University, San Francisco Bay Area, for tuition information.

Living and Housing Costs

Students typically live in apartments in the metropolitan San Francisco area. Living expenses vary according to each student's preferred standard of living, housing, and transportation. The University does not offer or operate student housing. Most of the students are full-time working professionals who live within driving distance of the campus. Several nearby hotels offer special rates for those who commute from long distances. The Admissions Department also maintains a list of housing options, including contact information for University students who wish to share housing. For more information, students should contact the Admissions Department.

Student Group

Admission to Argosy University, San Francisco Bay Area, is selective to ensure a dynamic and engaged student body. The University encourages diversity in academic and employment backgrounds and promotes integration of the student body into professional life through established connections with local and national professional associations. Argosy University offers a professionally oriented education with rich opportunities to gain practical experience in class, field placements, and internships. Full-time students and working professionals gain the extensive knowledge and range of skills necessary for effective performance in their chosen fields.

Student Outcomes

Students can register with the University's online career-services system and use select services from a distance, such as degree-specific career e-mail lists, national job posts, and virtual job fairs. Students should contact the University for more information.

Location

Located in northern California, Argosy University, San Francisco Bay Area, attracts students from the immediate area as well as from around the country and the world. In July 2007, the San Francisco Bay Area campus moved to its new location at 1005 Atlantic Avenue in Alameda. The energy in San Francisco is contagious. Numerous surveys rank San Francisco as the most wired city in the world, thanks to its high concentration of computer-savvy citizens and businesses.

Many businesses in the area provide varied opportunities for student training. The Bay Area and nearby Silicon Valley are home to leading new media companies such as Pixar, ILM, and Sega. A who's who of technology companies call the Bay Area home, including Apple, Cisco, Hewlett-Packard, Intel, Oracle, and Sun Microsystems. San Francisco also is the home of traditional companies such as BankAmerica, Chevron, Levi-Strauss, Safeway, and Wells Fargo.

The University

Argosy University is a private institution with nineteen locations across the nation. Argosy University, San Francisco Bay Area, provides students with a career resources office, an academic resources center, and extensive information access for research. It offers the resources of a large university plus the friendliness and personal attention of a small campus.

The innovative programs feature dynamic, relevant, and practical curricula delivered in flexible class formats. Students enjoy scheduling options that make it easier to fit school into their busy lives, choosing from day and evening courses, on campus or online. Many students find a combination of class formats to be an ideal way of continuing their education while meeting family and professional demands.

Argosy University is accredited by the Higher Learning Commission and a member of the North Central Association (30 North LaSalle Street, Suite 2400, Chicago, Illinois 60602; 800-621-7440 (toll-free); http://www.ncahlc.org).

Applying

Argosy University, San Francisco Bay Area, accepts students year-round on a rolling admissions basis, depending on availability of required courses. Applications for admission are available online or by contacting the campus.

Correspondence and Information

Argosy University, San Francisco Bay Area
1005 Atlantic Avenue
Alameda, California 94501

Phone: 510-215-0277
866-215-2777 (toll-free)
Fax: 510-215-0299
E-mail: auadmissions@argosy.edu
Web site: http://www.argosy.edu/sanfrancisco

Argosy University, San Francisco Bay Area

THE FACULTY

The Argosy University faculty comprises working professionals who are eager to help students succeed. Members bring real-world experience and the latest practice innovations to the academic setting. The diverse faculty members of the College of Business are widely recognized for contributions to the field. Many are published scholars, and most hold doctoral degrees. They committed to providing a substantive education that combines comprehensive knowledge with critical skills and practical workplace relevance. Above all, faculty members are committed to their students' personal and professional development.

ARGOSY UNIVERSITY.

ARGOSY UNIVERSITY, SARASOTA

College of Business

Programs of Study
Argosy University, Sarasota, offers the Master of Business Administration (M.B.A.), the Master of Science in Management (M.S.M.), the Doctor of Business Administration (D.B.A.), and the Doctor of Education (Ed.D.) in organizational leadership degrees. The business programs are designed to serve the needs of talented students, regardless of their undergraduate degrees. The College of Business welcomes and encourages students from diverse academic backgrounds.

The Master of Business Administration program is designed to develop action-oriented managers and leaders who focus on leading themselves and others to solutions that serve their organizations. Students acquire skills to identify challenges and opportunities, draw on the latest technology and information, use advanced analytical and planning approaches, and execute plans for leading positive change. Competencies are developed through focusing on critical thinking, persuasive communications, technical knowledge, and a deep understanding of the human side of business. By focusing on competencies in this manner, the program builds upon the talents of students, independent of their undergraduate field of study. Students from diverse academic and professional backgrounds are welcomed and encouraged. In addition to completing the core course requirements, students develop expertise and specific insights in one of the following concentrations: corporate compliance, finance, fraud examination, health-care administration, information systems management (availability of this concentration is limited; program chair approval is necessary to enter), international business, management, marketing, public administration, or sustainable management. In addition, with approval of the student's program chair, a student may select four courses (12 credit hours) to create a customized concentration that better fits their specific career goals. For all students, the M.B.A. program culminates in an applied capstone project in which they integrate the core business competencies with their concentration specialty.

The Master of Science in Management program is designed to improve and extend the interpersonal and problem-solving skills necessary for successful leaders in the private, non-profit, and public sectors. The program focuses on situation diagnostics, opportunity and problem evaluation, and implementation of an action plan.

The Doctor of Business Administration program enables industry and academic professionals to build upon master's-level competencies, skills, and knowledge, preparing themselves to perform more effectively in existing professional roles, to qualify for roles with increasing responsibility, and/or develop capabilities for a second career in teaching at the college level. The program requires students to develop applied research inquiry and analytical skills. The D.B.A. program is designed to help students develop competencies in understanding and performing applied research, which can then be used to foster innovation and lead organizational change. Students must choose a concentration in accounting, global business sustainability, information systems (availability of this concentration is limited; program chair approval is necessary to enter), international business, management, or marketing. In addition, with approval of the student's program chair, a student may select four courses (12 credit hours) to create a customized concentration that better fits their specific career goals.

The Doctor of Education in organizational leadership program is designed for working professionals who wish to develop the knowledge and skills required to hold leadership positions in complex organizations. The program focuses on transformational leadership skills in addition to managerial attributes. This approach prepares students for such strategic challenges as increasing globalization, changing economies, societal shifts, and individual-organizational relationships.

Research Facilities
Argosy University libraries provide curriculum support and educational resources, including current text materials, diagnostic training documents, reference materials and databases, journals and dissertations, and major and current titles in program areas. There is an online public-access catalog of library resources available throughout the Argosy University system. Students have remote access to the campus library database, enabling them to study and conduct research at home. Academic databases offer dissertation abstracts, academic journals, and professional periodicals. All library computers are Internet accessible. Software applications include Word, Excel, PowerPoint, SPSS, and various test-scoring programs.

Financial Aid
Financial aid is available to those who qualify. Argosy University, Sarasota, offers access to federal and state aid programs, merit-based awards, grants, loans, and a work-study program. As a first step, students should complete the Free Application for Federal Student Aid (FAFSA). Prospective students can apply electronically at http://www.fafsa.ed.gov or at the campus.

Cost of Study
Tuition varies by program. Students should contact Argosy University, Sarasota, for tuition information.

Living and Housing Costs
Students typically live in apartments in the metropolitan Sarasota area. Living expenses vary according to each student's preferred standard of living, housing, and transportation. The University does not offer or operate student housing. Most of the students are full-time working professionals who live within driving distance of the campus. Several nearby hotels offer special rates for those who commute from long distances. The Admissions Department also maintains a list of housing options, including contact information for University students who wish to share housing. For more information, students should contact the Admissions Department.

Student Group
Admission to Argosy University, Sarasota, is selective to ensure a dynamic and engaged student body. It encourages diversity in academic and employment backgrounds and promotes integration of the student body into professional life through established connections with local and national professional associations. Argosy University offers a professionally oriented education with rich opportunities to gain practical experience in class, field placements, and internships. Full-time students and working professionals gain the extensive knowledge and range of skills necessary for effective performance in their chosen fields.

Student Outcomes
Students can register with the University's online career-services system and use select services from a distance, such as degree-specific career e-mail lists, national job posts, and virtual job fairs. Students should contact the University for more information.

Location
Located in northeast Sarasota, the campus is specifically designed for postsecondary and graduate-level instruction through a unique combination of in-residence course work, tutorials, and online study courses. Several of the programs are off-site tutorials and intensive one-week classroom sessions. Students may also complete up to 49 percent of the work of some degree programs via online courses that allow interaction with faculty members and classmates from any Internet connection.

Sarasota is recognized as Florida's cultural center and is home to a professional symphony, ballet, and opera as well as dozens of theaters and art galleries. Well-known vacation attractions such as Disney World, Busch Gardens–Tampa, and the city of Miami are within a few hours' drive. The area enjoys mild winters and endless summer beauty.

The growing business sector in the Gulf Coast community helps make it one of the top 20 places to live and work. ASO Corporation, Nelson Publishing, and Select Technology Group are among the numerous companies headquartered in Sarasota County. The area's top employers include Sarasota Memorial Hospital and Publix Supermarkets. Many businesses in the area provide varied opportunities for student training.

The University
Argosy University is a private institution with nineteen locations across the nation. Argosy University, Sarasota, provides students with a career resources office, an academic resources center, and extensive information access for research. It offers the resources of a large university plus the friendliness and personal attention of a small campus. The innovative programs feature dynamic, relevant, and practical curricula delivered in flexible class formats.

Students enjoy scheduling options that make it easier to fit school into their busy lives, choosing from day and evening courses, on campus or online. Many students find a combination of class formats to be an ideal way of continuing their education while meeting family and professional demands.

Argosy University is accredited by the Higher Learning Commission and a member of the North Central Association (30 North LaSalle Street, Suite 2400, Chicago, Illinois 60602; 800-621-7440 (toll-free); http://www.ncahlc.org).

Applying
Argosy University, Sarasota, accepts students year-round on a rolling admissions basis, depending on availability of required courses. Applications for admission are available online or by contacting the campus.

Correspondence and Information
Argosy University, Sarasota
5250 17th Street
Sarasota, Florida 34235

Phone: 941-379-0404
          800-331-5995 (toll-free)
Fax: 941-371-8910
E-mail: auadmissions@argosy.edu
Web site: http://www.argosy.edu/sarasota

Argosy University, Sarasota

THE FACULTY

The Argosy University faculty comprises working professionals who are eager to help students succeed. Members bring real-world experience and the latest practice innovations to the academic setting. The diverse faculty members of the College of Business are widely recognized for contributions to the field. Many are published scholars, and most hold doctoral degrees. They are committed to providing a substantive education that combines comprehensive knowledge with critical skills and practical workplace relevance. Above all, faculty members are committed to their students' personal and professional development.

ARGOSY UNIVERSITY.

ARGOSY UNIVERSITY, SCHAUMBURG

College of Business

Programs of Study
Argosy University, Schaumburg, offers the Master of Business Administration (M.B.A.), the Master of Science in Management (M.S.M.), the Doctor of Education (Ed.D.) in organizational leadership, and the Doctor of Business Administration (D.B.A.) degrees. The business programs are designed to serve the needs of talented students, regardless of their undergraduate degrees. The College of Business welcomes and encourages students from diverse academic backgrounds.

The Master of Business Administration program is designed to develop action-oriented managers and leaders who focus on leading themselves and others to solutions that serve their organizations. Students acquire skills to identify challenges and opportunities, draw on the latest technology and information, use advanced analytical and planning approaches, and execute plans for leading positive change. Competencies are developed through focusing on critical thinking, persuasive communications, technical knowledge, and a deep understanding of the human side of business. By focusing on competencies in this manner, the program builds upon the talents of students, independent of their undergraduate field of study. Students from diverse academic and professional backgrounds are welcomed and encouraged. In addition to completing the core course requirements, students develop expertise and specific insights in one of the following concentrations: corporate compliance, finance, fraud examination, health-care administration, information systems management (availability of this concentration is limited; program chair approval is necessary to enter), international business, management, marketing, public administration, or sustainable management. In addition, with approval of the student's program chair, a student may select four courses (12 credit hours) to create a customized concentration that better fits their specific career goals. For all students, the M.B.A. program culminates in an applied capstone project in which they integrate the core business competencies with their concentration specialty.

The Master of Science in Management program is designed to improve and extend the interpersonal and problem-solving skills necessary for successful leaders in the private, non-profit, and public sectors. The program focuses on situation diagnostics, opportunity and problem evaluation, and implementation of an action plan.

The Doctor of Education in organizational leadership program is designed for working professionals who wish to develop the knowledge and skills required to hold leadership positions in complex organizations. The program focuses on transformational leadership skills in addition to managerial attributes. This approach prepares students for such strategic challenges as increasing globalization, changing economies, societal shifts, and individual-organizational relationships.

The Doctor of Business Administration program enables industry and academic professionals to build upon master's-level competencies, skills, and knowledge, preparing themselves to perform more effectively in existing professional roles, to qualify for roles with increasing responsibility, and/or develop capabilities for a second career in teaching at the college level. The program requires students to develop applied research inquiry and analytical skills. The D.B.A. program is designed to help students develop competencies in understanding and performing applied research, which can then be used to foster innovation and lead organizational change. Students must choose a concentration in accounting, global business sustainability, information systems (availability of this concentration is limited; program chair approval is necessary to enter), international business, management, or marketing. In addition, with approval of the student's program chair, a student may select four courses (12 credit hours) to create a customized concentration that better fits their specific career goals.

Research Facilities
Argosy University libraries provide curriculum support and educational resources, including current text materials, diagnostic training documents, reference materials and databases, journals and dissertations, and major and current titles in program areas. There is an online public-access catalog of library resources available throughout the Argosy University system. Students have remote access to the campus library database, enabling them to study and conduct research at home. Academic databases offer dissertation abstracts, academic journals, and professional periodicals. All library computers are Internet accessible. Software applications include Word, Excel, PowerPoint, SPSS, and various test-scoring programs.

Financial Aid
Financial aid is available to those who qualify. Argosy University, Schaumburg, offers access to federal and state aid programs, merit-based awards, grants, loans, and a work-study program. As a first step, students should complete the Free Application for Federal Student Aid (FAFSA). Prospective students can apply electronically at http://www.fafsa.ed.gov or at the campus.

Cost of Study
Tuition varies by program. Students should contact Argosy University, Schaumburg, for tuition information.

Living and Housing Costs
Students typically live in apartments in the metropolitan Schaumburg area. Living expenses vary according to each student's preferred standard of living, housing, and transportation. The University does not offer or operate student housing. Most of the students are full-time working professionals who live within driving distance of the campus. Several nearby hotels offer special rates for those who commute from long distances. The Admissions Department also maintains a list of housing options, including contact information for University students who wish to share housing. For more information, students should contact the Admissions Department.

Student Group
Admission to Argosy University, Schaumburg, is selective to ensure a dynamic and engaged student body. The University encourages diversity in academic and employment backgrounds and promotes integration of the student body into professional life through established connections with local and national professional associations. Argosy University offers a professionally oriented education with rich opportunities to gain practical experience in class, field placements, and internships. Full-time students and working professionals gain the extensive knowledge and range of skills necessary for effective performance in their chosen fields.

Student Outcomes
Students can register with the University's online career-services system and use select services from a distance, such as degree-specific career e-mail lists, national job posts, and virtual job fairs. Students should contact the University for more information.

Location
Argosy University, Schaumburg, is located in the northwest suburban area, approximately 45 minutes from downtown Chicago. The campus's small size allows it to offer a highly personal atmosphere and flexible programs tailored to students' needs. Visitors to Chicago experience a range of attractions to stimulate both intellectual and recreational pursuits. Located on the shores of Lake Michigan in the Midwest, Chicago is home to world-champion sports teams, an internationally acclaimed symphony orchestra, renowned architecture, and nearly 3 million residents. Among the variety of history and art museums in the city, the Chicago Cultural Center offers more than 600 art programs and exhibits each year. Recreational opportunities include hiking and cycling on miles of lakefront trails, golfing, and shopping. Many businesses in the area provide varied opportunities for student training. Schaumburg's thriving business environment includes 5,000 businesses that employ 80,000 people. The area's largest employers are Motorola, Experian, Cingular, and IBM.

The University
Argosy University is a private institution with nineteen locations across the nation. Argosy University, Schaumburg, provides students with a career resources office, an academic resources center, and extensive information access for research. It offers the resources of a large university plus the friendliness and personal attention of a small campus. Argosy University, Schaumburg, is closely associated with Argosy University's Chicago campus.

The innovative programs feature dynamic, relevant, and practical curricula delivered in flexible class formats. Students enjoy scheduling options that make it easier to fit school into their busy lives, choosing from day and evening courses, on campus or online. Many students find a combination of class formats to be an ideal way of continuing their education while meeting family and professional demands.

Argosy University is accredited by the Higher Learning Commission and a member of the North Central Association (30 North LaSalle Street, Suite 2400, Chicago, Illinois 60602; 800-621-7440 (toll-free); http://www.ncahlc.org).

Applying
Argosy University, Schaumburg, accepts students year-round on a rolling admissions basis, depending on availability of required courses. Applications for admission are available online or by contacting the campus.

Correspondence and Information
Argosy University, Schaumburg
999 North Plaza Drive, Suite 111
Schaumburg, Illinois 60173-5403
Phone: 847-969-4900
866-290-2777 (toll-free)
Fax: 847-969-4998
E-mail: auadmissions@argosy.edu
Web site: http://www.argosy.edu/schaumburg

Argosy University, Schaumburg

THE FACULTY

The Argosy University faculty comprises working professionals who are eager to help students succeed. Members bring real-world experience and the latest practice innovations to the academic setting. The diverse faculty members of the College of Business are widely recognized for contributions to their fields. Many are published scholars, and most hold doctoral degrees. They are committed to providing a substantive education that combines comprehensive knowledge with critical skills and practical workplace relevance. Above all, faculty members are committed to their students' personal and professional development.

ARGOSY UNIVERSITY

ARGOSY UNIVERSITY, SEATTLE

College of Business

Programs of Study

Argosy University, Seattle, offers the Master of Business Administration (M.B.A.), the Master of Science in Management (M.S.M.), the Doctor of Business Administration (D.B.A.), and the Doctor of Education (Ed.D.) in organizational leadership degrees. The business programs are designed to serve the needs of talented students, regardless of their undergraduate degrees. The College of Business welcomes and encourages students from diverse academic backgrounds.

The Master of Business Administration program is designed to develop action-oriented managers and leaders who focus on leading themselves and others to solutions that serve their organizations. Students acquire skills to identify challenges and opportunities, draw on the latest technology and information, use advanced analytical and planning approaches, and execute plans for leading positive change. Competencies are developed through focusing on critical thinking, persuasive communications, technical knowledge, and a deep understanding of the human side of business. By focusing on competencies in this manner, the program builds upon the talents of students, independent of their undergraduate field of study. Students from diverse academic and professional backgrounds are welcomed and encouraged. In addition to completing the core course requirements, students develop expertise and specific insights in one of the following concentrations: corporate compliance, finance, fraud examination, health-care administration, information systems management (availability of this concentration is limited; program chair approval is necessary to enter), international business, management, marketing, public administration, or sustainable management. In addition, with approval of the student's program chair, a student may select four courses (12 credit hours) to create a customized concentration that better fits their specific career goals. For all students, the M.B.A. program culminates in an applied capstone project in which they integrate the core business competencies with their concentration specialty.

The Master of Science in Management program is designed to improve and extend the interpersonal and problem-solving skills necessary for successful leaders in the private, non-profit, and public sectors. The program focuses on situation diagnostics, opportunity and problem evaluation, and implementation of an action plan.

The Doctor of Business Administration program enables industry and academic professionals to build upon master's-level competencies, skills, and knowledge, preparing themselves to perform more effectively in existing professional roles, to qualify for roles with increasing responsibility, and/or develop capabilities for a second career in teaching at the college level. The program requires students to develop applied research inquiry and analytical skills. The D.B.A. program is designed to help students develop competencies in understanding and performing applied research, which can then be used to foster innovation and lead organizational change. Students must choose a concentration in accounting, global business sustainability, information systems (availability of this concentration is limited; program chair approval is necessary to enter), international business, management, or marketing. In addition, with approval of the student's program chair, a student may select four courses (12 credit hours) to create a customized concentration that better fits their specific career goals.

The Doctor of Education in organizational leadership program is designed for working professionals who wish to develop the knowledge and skills required to hold leadership positions in complex organizations. The program focuses on transformational leadership skills in addition to managerial attributes. This approach prepares students for such strategic challenges as increasing globalization, changing economies, societal shifts, and individual-organizational relationships.

Research Facilities

Argosy University libraries provide curriculum support and educational resources, including current text materials, diagnostic training documents, reference materials and databases, journals and dissertations, and major and current titles in program areas. There is an online public-access catalog of library resources available throughout the Argosy University system. Students have remote access to the campus library database, enabling them to study and conduct research at home. Academic databases offer dissertation abstracts, academic journals, and professional periodicals. All library computers are Internet accessible. Software applications include Word, Excel, PowerPoint, SPSS, and various test-scoring programs.

Financial Aid

Financial aid is available to those who qualify. Argosy University, Seattle, offers access to federal and state aid programs, merit-based awards, grants, loans, and a work-study program. As a first step, students should complete the Free Application for Federal Student Aid (FAFSA). Prospective students can apply electronically at http://www.fafsa.ed.gov or at the campus.

Cost of Study

Tuition varies by program. Students should contact Argosy University, Seattle, for tuition information.

Living and Housing Costs

Students typically live in apartments in the metropolitan Seattle area. Living expenses vary according to each student's preferred standard of living, housing, and transportation. The University does not offer or operate student housing. Most of the students are full-time working professionals who live within driving distance of the campus. Several nearby hotels offer special rates for those who commute from long distances. The Admissions Department also maintains a list of housing options, including contact information for university students who wish to share housing. For more information, students should contact the Admissions Department.

Student Group

Admission to Argosy University, Seattle, is selective to ensure a dynamic and engaged student body. It encourages diversity in academic and employment backgrounds and promotes integration of the student body into professional life through established connections with local and national professional associations. Argosy University offers a professionally oriented education with rich opportunities to gain practical experience in class, field placements, and internships. Full-time students and working professionals gain the extensive knowledge and range of skills necessary for effective performance in their chosen fields.

Student Outcomes

Students can register with the University's online career-services system and use select services from a distance, such as degree-specific career e-mail lists, national job posts, and virtual job fairs. Students should contact the University for more information.

Location

The faculty and staff members at Argosy University, Seattle, aspire to provide a supportive, collaborative, engaging, yet challenging learning environment. Easily reached through the King County Public Transportation System, the campus offers convenient access to local libraries, shops, and restaurants. Seattle offers numerous historical and multicultural museums, a symphony, ballet, and many theater companies. Seattle is home to several major league sports teams, and offers a myriad of outdoor recreational opportunities, such as camping, hiking, fishing, skiing, and rock-climbing.

Many businesses in the area provide varied opportunities for student training. Seattle's business environment encompasses a wide range of industries and features such giants as Microsoft, Boeing, and Alaska Air Group. The Port of Seattle and University of Washington are also among the area's largest employers.

The University

Argosy University is a private institution with nineteen locations across the nation. Argosy University, Seattle, provides students with a career resources office, an academic resources center, and extensive information access for research. It offers the resources of a large university plus the friendliness and personal attention of a small campus.

The innovative programs feature dynamic, relevant, and practical curricula delivered in flexible class formats. Students enjoy scheduling options that make it easier to fit school into their busy lives, choosing from day and evening courses, on campus or online. Many students find a combination of class formats to be an ideal way of continuing their education while meeting family and professional demands.

Argosy University is accredited by the Higher Learning Commission and a member of the North Central Association (30 North LaSalle Street, Suite 2400, Chicago, Illinois 60602; 800-621-7440 (toll-free); http://www.ncahlc.org).

Applying

Argosy University, Seattle, accepts students year-round on a rolling admissions basis, depending on availability of required courses. Applications for admission are available online or by contacting the campus.

Correspondence and Information

Argosy University, Seattle
2601-A Elliott Avenue
Seattle, Washington 98121
Phone: 206-283-4500
    866-283-2777 (toll-free)
Fax: 206-283-5777
E-mail: auadmissions@argosy.edu
Web site: http://www.argosy.edu/seattle

Argosy University, Seattle

THE FACULTY

The Argosy University faculty comprises working professionals who are eager to help students succeed. Members bring real-world experience and the latest practice innovations to the academic setting. The diverse faculty members of the College of Business are widely recognized for contributions to their field. Many are published scholars, and most hold doctoral degrees. They are committed to providing a substantive education that combines comprehensive knowledge with critical skills and practical workplace relevance. Above all, faculty members are committed to their students' personal and professional development.

ARGOSY UNIVERSITY

ARGOSY UNIVERSITY, TAMPA

College of Business

Programs of Study

Argosy University, Tampa, offers the Master of Business Administration (M.B.A.), the Master of Science in Management (M.S.M.), the Doctor of Business Administration (D.B.A.), and the Doctor of Education (Ed.D.) in organizational leadership degrees. The business programs are designed to serve the needs of talented students, regardless of their undergraduate degrees. The College of Business welcomes and encourages students from diverse academic backgrounds.

The Master of Business Administration program is designed to develop action-oriented managers and leaders who focus on leading themselves and others to solutions that serve their organizations. Students acquire skills to identify challenges and opportunities, draw on the latest technology and information, use advanced analytical and planning approaches, and execute plans for leading positive change. Competencies are developed through focusing on critical thinking, persuasive communications, technical knowledge, and a deep understanding of the human side of business. By focusing on competencies in this manner, the program builds upon the talents of students, independent of their undergraduate field of study. Students from diverse academic and professional backgrounds are welcomed and encouraged. In addition to completing the core course requirements, students develop expertise and specific insights in one of the following concentrations: corporate compliance, finance, fraud examination, health-care administration, information systems management (availability of this concentration is limited; program chair approval is necessary to enter), international business, management, marketing, public administration, or sustainable management. In addition, with approval of the student's program chair, a student may select four courses (12 credit hours) to create a customized concentration that better fits their specific career goals. For all students, the M.B.A. program culminates in an applied capstone project in which they integrate the core business competencies with their concentration specialty.

The Master of Science in Management program is designed to improve and extend the interpersonal and problem-solving skills necessary for successful leaders in the private, non-profit, and public sectors. The program focuses on situation diagnostics, opportunity and problem evaluation, and implementation of an action plan.

The Doctor of Business Administration program enables industry and academic professionals to build upon master's-level competencies, skills, and knowledge, preparing themselves to perform more effectively in existing professional roles, to qualify for roles with increasing responsibility, and/or develop capabilities for a second career in teaching at the college level. The program requires students to develop applied research inquiry and analytical skills. The D.B.A. program is designed to help students develop competencies in understanding and performing applied research, which can then be used to foster innovation and lead organizational change. Students must choose a concentration in accounting, global business sustainability, information systems (availability of this concentration is limited; program chair approval is necessary to enter), international business, management, or marketing. In addition, with approval of the student's program chair, a student may select four courses (12 credit hours) to create a customized concentration that better fits their specific career goals.

The Doctor of Education in organizational leadership program is designed for working professionals who wish to develop the knowledge and skills required to hold leadership positions in complex organizations. The program focuses on transformational leadership skills in addition to managerial attributes. This approach prepares students for such strategic challenges as increasing globalization, changing economies, societal shifts, and individual-organizational relationships.

Research Facilities

Argosy University libraries provide curriculum support and educational resources, including current text materials, diagnostic training documents, reference materials and databases, journals and dissertations, and major and current titles in program areas. There is an online public-access catalog of library resources available throughout the Argosy University system. Students have remote access to the campus library database, enabling them to study and conduct research at home. Academic databases offer dissertation abstracts, academic journals, and professional periodicals. All library computers are Internet accessible. Software applications include Word, Excel, PowerPoint, SPSS, and various test-scoring programs.

Financial Aid

Financial aid is available to those who qualify. Argosy University, Tampa, offers access to federal and state aid programs, merit-based awards, grants, loans, and a work-study program. As a first step, students should complete the Free Application for Federal Student Aid (FAFSA). Prospective students can apply electronically at http://www.fafsa.ed.gov or on the campus.

Cost of Study

Tuition varies by program. Students should contact Argosy University, Tampa, for tuition information.

Living and Housing Costs

Students typically live in apartments in the metropolitan Tampa area. Living expenses vary according to each student's preferred standard of living, housing, and transportation. The University does not offer or operate student housing. Most of the students are full-time working professionals who live within driving distance of the campus. Several nearby hotels offer special rates for those who commute from long distances. The Admissions Department also maintains a list of housing options, including contact information for University students who wish to share housing. For more information, students should contact the Admissions Department.

Student Group

Admission to Argosy University, Tampa, is selective to ensure a dynamic and engaged student body. It encourages diversity in academic and employment backgrounds and promotes integration of the student body into professional life through established connections with local and national professional associations. Argosy University offers a professionally oriented education with rich opportunities to gain practical experience in class, field placements, and internships. Full-time students and working professionals gain the extensive knowledge and range of skills necessary for effective performance in their chosen fields.

Student Outcomes

Students can register with the University's online career-services system and use select services from a distance, such as degree-specific career e-mail lists, national job posts, and virtual job fairs. Students should contact the University for more information.

Location

Located in sunny Florida, Argosy University, Tampa, attracts a diverse student population from throughout the United States, the Caribbean, Europe, Africa, and Asia. Tampa's central location affords students the opportunity to work for major corporations and hear speakers of international acclaim. The school offers rigorous programs of study in a supportive, collaborative environment. The campus sits within an hour's drive of some of the most popular tourist destinations in the world, including the Disney theme parks, Busch Gardens, and the Florida Gulf Coast beaches. Major-league sporting events, concerts, theaters, world-renowned restaurants, recreational facilities, and a cosmopolitan social scene are all within easy reach. Tampa combines the opportunities of a large city with the friendliness of a small town with a strong sense of community.

The Tampa-St. Petersburg-Clearwater metropolitan area offers a diversified economic base fueled by a broad array of companies, including Verizon Communications and JP Morgan Chase. In addition, Tampa serves as headquarters for three Fortune 100 companies—OSI Restaurant Partners; TECO, an energy provider; and Raymond Jones Financial. Many businesses in the area provide varied opportunities for student training.

The University

Argosy University is a private institution with nineteen locations across the nation. Argosy University, Tampa, provides students with a career resources office, an academic resources center, and extensive information access for research. It offers the resources of a large university plus the friendliness and personal attention of a small campus.

The innovative programs feature dynamic, relevant, and practical curricula delivered in flexible class formats. Students enjoy scheduling options that make it easier to fit school into their busy lives, choosing from day and evening courses, on campus or online. Many students find a combination to be an ideal way of continuing their education while meeting family and professional demands.

Argosy University is accredited by the Higher Learning Commission and a member of the North Central Association (30 North LaSalle Street, Suite 2400, Chicago, Illinois 60602; 800-621-7440 (toll-free); http://www.ncahlc.org).

Applying

Argosy University, Tampa, accepts students on a rolling admissions basis year-round, depending on availability of required courses. Applications for admission are available online or by contacting the campus.

Correspondence and Information

Argosy University, Tampa
1403 North Howard Avenue
Tampa, Florida 33607
Phone: 813-393-5290
        800-850-6488 (toll-free)
Fax: 813-874-1989
E-mail: auadmissions@argosy.edu
Web site: http://www.argosy.edu/tampa

Argosy University, Tampa

THE FACULTY

The Argosy University faculty comprises working professionals who are eager to help students succeed. Members bring real-world experience and the latest practice innovations to the academic setting. The diverse faculty members of the College of Business are widely recognized for contributions to the field. Many are published scholars, and most hold doctoral degrees. They are committed to providing a substantive education that combines comprehensive knowledge with critical skills and practical workplace relevance. Above all, faculty members are committed to their students' personal and professional development.

ARGOSY UNIVERSITY, TWIN CITIES

College of Business

ARGOSY UNIVERSITY

Programs of Study
Argosy University, Twin Cities, offers the Master of Business Administration (M.B.A.), the Master of Science in Management (M.S.M.), the Master of Public Administration (M.P.A.), the Doctor of Education (Ed.D.) in organizational leadership, and the Doctor of Business Administration (D.B.A.) degrees. The business programs are designed to serve the needs of talented students, regardless of their undergraduate degrees. The College of Business welcomes and encourages students from diverse academic backgrounds.

The Master of Business Administration program is designed to develop action-oriented managers and leaders who focus on leading themselves and others to solutions that serve their organizations. Students acquire skills to identify challenges and opportunities, draw on the latest technology and information, use advanced analytical and planning approaches, and execute plans for leading positive change. Competencies are developed through focusing on critical thinking, persuasive communications, technical knowledge, and a deep understanding of the human side of business. By focusing on competencies in this manner, the program builds upon the talents of students, independent of their undergraduate field of study. Students from diverse academic and professional backgrounds are welcomed and encouraged. In addition to completing the core course requirements, students develop expertise and specific insights in one of the following concentrations: corporate compliance, finance, fraud examination, health-care administration, information systems management (availability of this concentration is limited; program chair approval is necessary to enter), international business, management, marketing, public administration, or sustainable management. In addition, with approval of the student's program chair, a student may select four courses (12 credit hours) to create a customized concentration that better fits their specific career goals. For all students, the M.B.A. program culminates in an applied capstone project in which they integrate the core business competencies with their concentration specialty.

The Master of Science in Management program is designed to improve and extend the interpersonal and problem-solving skills necessary for successful leaders in the private, non-profit, and public sectors. The program focuses on situation diagnostics, opportunity and problem evaluation, and implementation of an action plan.

The Master of Public Administration program is designed to develop action-oriented, problem-solving managers for the public sector, especially at the state and local levels of government. Students have the opportunity to develop the competencies required to execute the duties and responsibilities of public sector managers, including evaluation and supervision of employees, reinforcement of the organizational mission, and the effective management of organizational resources.

The Doctor of Education in organizational leadership program is designed for working professionals who wish to develop the knowledge and skills required to hold leadership positions in complex organizations. The program focuses on transformational leadership skills in addition to managerial attributes. This approach prepares students for such strategic challenges as increasing globalization, changing economies, societal shifts, and individual-organizational relationships.

The Doctor of Business Administration program enables industry and academic professionals to build upon master's-level competencies, skills, and knowledge, preparing themselves to perform more effectively in existing professional roles, to qualify for roles with increasing responsibility, and/or develop capabilities for a second career in teaching at the college level. The program requires students to develop applied research inquiry and analytical skills. The D.B.A. program is designed to help students develop competencies in understanding and performing applied research, which can then be used to foster innovation and lead organizational change. Students must choose a concentration in accounting, global business sustainability, information systems (availability of this concentration is limited; program chair approval is necessary to enter), international business, management, or marketing. In addition, with approval of the student's program chair, a student may select four courses (12 credit hours) to create a customized concentration that better fits their specific career goals.

Research Facilities
Argosy University libraries provide curriculum support and educational resources, including current text materials, diagnostic training documents, reference materials and databases, journals and dissertations, and major and current titles in program areas. There is an online public-access catalog of library resources available throughout the Argosy University system. Students have remote access to the campus library database, enabling them to study and conduct research at home. Academic databases offer dissertation abstracts, academic journals, and professional periodicals. All library computers are Internet accessible. Software applications include Word, Excel, PowerPoint, SPSS, and various test-scoring programs.

Financial Aid
Financial aid is available to those who qualify. Argosy University, Twin Cities, offers access to federal and state aid programs, merit-based awards, grants, loans, and a work-study program. As a first step, students should complete the Free Application for Federal Student Aid (FAFSA). Prospective students can apply electronically at http://www.fafsa.ed.gov or at the campus.

Cost of Study
Tuition varies by program. Students should contact Argosy University, Twin Cities, for tuition information.

Living and Housing Costs
Students typically live in apartments in the metropolitan Eagan area. Living expenses vary according to each student's preferred standard of living, housing, and transportation. The University does not offer or operate student housing. Most of the students are full-time working professionals who live within driving distance of the campus. Several nearby hotels offer special rates for those who commute from long distances. The Admissions Department also maintains a list of housing options, including contact information for university students who wish to share housing. For more information, students should contact the Admissions Department.

Student Group
Admission to Argosy University, Twin Cities, is selective to ensure a dynamic and engaged student body. The University encourages diversity in academic and employment backgrounds and promotes integration of the student body into professional life through established connections with local and national professional associations. Argosy University offers a professionally oriented education with rich opportunities to gain practical experience in class, field placements, and internships. Full-time students and working professionals gain the extensive knowledge and range of skills necessary for effective performance in their chosen fields.

Student Outcomes
Students can register with the University's online career-services system and use select services from a distance, such as degree-specific career e-mail lists, national job posts, and virtual job fairs. Students should contact the University for more information.

Location
Argosy University, Twin Cities, offers challenging academics in a supportive environment. The campus is nestled in a parklike suburban setting within 10 miles of the airport and the Mall of America. Students enjoy the convenience of nearby shops, restaurants, and housing and easy freeway access. The neighboring Eagan Community Center offers many amenities, including walking paths, a fitness center, meeting rooms, and an outdoor amphitheater. The Twin Cities of Minneapolis and St. Paul have been rated by popular magazines as one of the most livable metropolitan areas in the country. With a population of 2.5 million, the area offers an abundance of recreational activities. Year-round outdoor activities, nationally acclaimed venues for theater art and music, and professional sports teams attract residents and visitors alike.

Many businesses in the area provide varied opportunities for student training. The Minneapolis-St. Paul metropolitan area offers a diversified economic base fueled by a broad array of companies. Among the numerous publicly traded companies headquartered in the area are Target, UnitedHealth Group, 3M, General Mills, and U.S. Bancorp.

The University
Argosy University is a private institution with nineteen locations across the nation. Argosy University, Twin Cities, provides students with a career resources office, an academic resources center, and extensive information access for research. It offers the resources of a large university plus the friendliness and personal attention of a small campus.

The innovative programs feature dynamic, relevant, and practical curricula delivered in flexible class formats. Students enjoy scheduling options that make it easier to fit school into their busy lives, choosing from day and evening courses, on campus or online. Many students find a combination of class formats to be an ideal way of continuing their education while meeting family and professional demands.

Argosy University is accredited by the Higher Learning Commission and a member of the North Central Association (30 North LaSalle Street, Suite 2400, Chicago, Illinois 60602; 800-621-7440 (toll-free); http://www.ncahlc.org).

Applying
Argosy University, Twin Cities, accepts students year-round on a rolling admissions basis, depending on availability of required courses. Applications for admission are available online or by contacting the campus.

Correspondence and Information
Argosy University, Twin Cities
1515 Central Parkway
Eagan, Minnesota 55121
Phone: 651-846-2882
  888-844-2004 (toll-free)
Fax: 651-994-7956
E-mail: auadmissions@argosy.edu
Web site: http://www.argosy.edu/twincities

Argosy University, Twin Cities

THE FACULTY

The Argosy University faculty comprises working professionals who are eager to help students succeed. Members bring real-world experience and the latest practice innovations to the academic setting. The diverse faculty members of the College of Business are widely recognized for contributions to the field. Many are published scholars, and most hold doctoral degrees. They are committed to providing a substantive education that combines comprehensive knowledge with critical skills and practical workplace relevance. Above all, faculty members are committed to their students' personal and professional development.

ARGOSY UNIVERSITY

ARGOSY UNIVERSITY, WASHINGTON DC

College of Business

Programs of Study

Argosy University, Washington DC, offers the Master of Business Administration (M.B.A.), the Master of Science in Management (M.S.M.), the Doctor of Business Administration (D.B.A.), and the Doctor of Education (Ed.D.) in organizational leadership degrees. The business programs are designed to serve the needs of talented students, regardless of their undergraduate degrees. The College of Business welcomes and encourages students from diverse academic backgrounds.

The Master of Business Administration program is designed to develop action-oriented managers and leaders who focus on leading themselves and others to solutions that serve their organizations. Students acquire skills to identify challenges and opportunities, draw on the latest technology and information, use advanced analytical and planning approaches, and execute plans for leading positive change. Competencies are developed through focusing on critical thinking, persuasive communications, technical knowledge, and a deep understanding of the human side of business. By focusing on competencies in this manner, the program builds upon the talents of students, independent of their undergraduate field of study. Students from diverse academic and professional backgrounds are welcomed and encouraged. In addition to completing the core course requirements, students develop expertise and specific insights in one of the following concentrations: corporate compliance, finance, fraud examination, health-care administration, information systems management (availability of this concentration is limited; program chair approval is necessary to enter), international business, management, marketing, public administration, or sustainable management. In addition, with approval of the student's program chair, a student may select four courses (12 credit hours) to create a customized concentration that better fits their specific career goals. For all students, the M.B.A. program culminates in an applied capstone project in which they integrate the core business competencies with their concentration specialty.

The Master of Science in Management program is designed to improve and extend the interpersonal and problem-solving skills necessary for successful leaders in the private, non-profit, and public sectors. The program focuses on situation diagnostics, opportunity and problem evaluation, and implementation of an action plan.

The Doctor of Business Administration program enables industry and academic professionals to build upon master's-level competencies, skills, and knowledge, preparing themselves to perform more effectively in existing professional roles, to qualify for roles with increasing responsibility, and/or develop capabilities for a second career in teaching at the college level. The program requires students to develop applied research inquiry and analytical skills. The D.B.A. program is designed to help students develop competencies in understanding and performing applied research, which can then be used to foster innovation and lead organizational change. Students must choose a concentration in accounting, global business sustainability, information systems (availability of this concentration is limited; program chair approval is necessary to enter), international business, management, or marketing. In addition, with approval of the student's program chair, a student may select four courses (12 credit hours) to create a customized concentration that better fits their specific career goals.

The Doctor of Education in organizational leadership program is designed for working professionals who wish to develop the knowledge and skills required to hold leadership positions in complex organizations. The program focuses on transformational leadership skills in addition to managerial attributes. This approach prepares students for such strategic challenges as increasing globalization, changing economies, societal shifts, and individual-organizational relationships.

Research Facilities

Argosy University libraries provide curriculum support and educational resources, including current text materials, diagnostic training documents, reference materials and databases, journals and dissertations, and major and current titles in program areas. There is an online public-access catalog of library resources available throughout the Argosy University system. Students have remote access to the campus library database, enabling them to study and conduct research at home. Academic databases offer dissertation abstracts, academic journals, and professional periodicals. All library computers are Internet accessible. Software applications include Word, Excel, PowerPoint, SPSS, and various test-scoring programs.

Financial Aid

Financial aid is available to those who qualify. Argosy University, Washington DC, offers access to federal and state aid programs, merit-based awards, grants, loans, and a work-study program. As a first step, students should complete the Free Application for Federal Student Aid (FAFSA). Prospective students can apply electronically at http://www.fafsa.ed.gov or at the campus.

Cost of Study

Tuition varies by program. Students should contact Argosy University, Washington DC, for tuition information.

Living and Housing Costs

Students typically live in apartments in the metropolitan Arlington, Virginia, area. Living expenses vary according to each student's preferred standard of living, housing, and transportation. The University does not offer or operate student housing. Most of the students are full-time working professionals who live within driving distance of the campus. Several nearby hotels offer special rates for those who commute from long distances. The Admissions Department also maintains a list of housing options, including contact information for University students who wish to share housing. For more information, students should contact the Admissions Department.

Student Group

Admission to Argosy University, Washington DC, is selective to ensure a dynamic and engaged student body. It encourages diversity in academic and employment backgrounds and promotes integration of the student body into professional life through established connections with local and national professional associations. Argosy University offers a professionally oriented education with rich opportunities to gain practical experience in class, field placements, and internships. Full-time students and working professionals gain the extensive knowledge and range of skills necessary for effective performance in their chosen fields.

Student Outcomes

Students can register with the University's online career-services system and use select services from a distance, such as degree-specific career e-mail lists, national job posts, and virtual job fairs. Students should contact the University for more information.

Location

Argosy University, Washington DC, is located in suburban Arlington, Virginia. The University is conveniently situated to provide access to most major highways in the area and is easily accessible by public transportation. In proximity to Georgetown, students enjoy access to the many diverse attractions of the D.C. area. Additional campus space is located at The Art Institute of Washington Building (1820 Fort Myer Drive). The University houses administrative offices and seven classrooms at this location. Perhaps best known as the home of the Pentagon and Arlington National Cemetery, Arlington, Virginia, is one of the most highly educated areas in the nation. It is also one of the most diverse. Many businesses in the area provide varied opportunities for student training. Major employers in the region include MCI Telecommunications Corporation; Bell Atlantic Network Services, Inc.; and Gannett/USA Today Company, Inc.

Argosy University, Washington DC, is certified to operate by the State Council of Higher Education for Virginia (James Monroe Building, 101 North 14th Street, Richmond, Virginia 23219; 804-225-2600).

The University

Argosy University is a private institution with nineteen locations across the nation. Argosy University, Washington DC, provides students with a career resources office, an academic resources center, and extensive information access for research. It offers the resources of a large university, plus the friendliness and personal attention of a small campus. The innovative programs feature dynamic, relevant, and practical curricula delivered in flexible class formats. Students enjoy scheduling options that make it easier to fit school into their busy lives, choosing from day and evening courses, on campus or online. Many students find a combination of class formats to be an ideal way of continuing their education while meeting family and professional demands.

Argosy University is accredited by the Higher Learning Commission and a member of the North Central Association (30 North LaSalle Street, Suite 2400, Chicago, Illinois 60602; 800-621-7440 (toll-free); http://www.ncahlc.org).

Applying

Argosy University, Washington DC, accepts students year-round on a rolling admissions basis, depending on availability of required courses. Applications for admission are available online or by contacting the campus.

Correspondence and Information

Argosy University, Washington DC
1550 Wilson Boulevard, Suite 600
Arlington, Virginia 22209
Phone: 703-526-5800
        866-703-2777 (toll-free)
Fax: 703-243-8973
E-mail: auadmissions@argosy.edu
Web site: http://www.argosy.edu/washingtondc

Argosy University, Washington DC

THE FACULTY

The Argosy University faculty comprises working professionals who are eager to help students succeed. Members bring real-world experience and the latest practice innovations to the academic setting. The diverse faculty members of the College of Business are widely recognized for contributions to the field. Many are published scholars, and most hold doctoral degrees. They are committed to providing a substantive education that combines comprehensive knowledge with critical skills and practical workplace relevance. Above all, faculty members are committed to their students' personal and professional development.

BABSON COLLEGE

F. W. Olin Graduate School of Business

BABSON
F.W. OLIN GRADUATE SCHOOL
OF BUSINESS

Program of Study

Babson's F.W. Olin Graduate School of Business develops global leaders with a strong business foundation as well as an entrepreneurial mindset. Students learn how to recognize opportunities and create value in a competitive, global marketplace. Graduates often launch startups or lead global enterprises, and drive the inspiration to develop new products, processes, and markets.

Entrepreneurship is a unique way of thinking and acting that permeates every aspect of the School's approach to management education, from finance and accounting to marketing and strategic planning. It's about using proven creative techniques to unearth new business opportunities. It's about analyzing the costs, risks, and benefits of promising ideas. And it's about realization—how to marshal resources to grow ideas from infancy to maturity, in a start-up or a global corporation.

Babson's M.B.A. programs feature an integrated, cross-disciplinary approach to business education in a team-based learning environment, preparing graduates to address real business problems. Babson students benefit from experiential learning opportunities, where students can work as consultants or complete internships in the U.S. or abroad. There are four innovative M.B.A. programs to meet the needs of a broad range of students.

Babson's Two-Year M.B.A. program features a real-world consulting project as well as international experience. The One-Year M.B.A. program offers the opportunity to earn an M.B.A. in twelve months to those students with an academic background in business. The part-time Evening M.B.A. program allows students to earn an M.B.A. at their own pace, varying their course load as needed. The innovative Fast Track M.B.A., offered on the East and West coasts, combines periodic classroom sessions with distance learning, allowing busy professionals the ability to earn an M.B.A. in two years without leaving the workplace.

Babson offers a Global Management Concentration which includes international course work or internships, as well as courses that emphasize a global perspective. The Global Management program places students in structured field-consulting projects with corporations around the world. International electives combine intensive classroom experience with industry-based projects in international settings. International internships, electives, and study-abroad opportunities are open to students in all Babson M.B.A. programs.

Successful business partnerships have always been a major component of Babson's programs. First-year student teams consult with Boston-area organizations through the yearlong Babson Consulting Alliance Program. The Management Consulting Field Experience offers a variety of second-year consulting projects, which can range from Fortune 500 companies to small, privately held firms, and from entrepreneurial ventures to nonprofits.

Research Facilities

Babson students have access to an extensive business collection of print, media, and electronic resources. The library subscribes to a browsing collection of 700 periodicals and newspapers; thousands more are available from any computer on campus through Internet subscriptions with Dow Jones Interactive, InfoTrac Web, Lexis/Nexis Universe, ProQuest Direct, FirstSearch, and Primark's Global Access.

Within Horn Library, students may access a variety of electronic resources, such as Bloomberg, Reuters, Bridge, Compustat, and Morningstar, for economics, financial information, marketing, accounting, and entrepreneurship. Group study rooms linked to Babson's computer network provide space for team meetings and individual study.

The Stephen D. Cutler Center for Investments and Finance, a joint venture between the Finance Division and Horn Library, exemplifies Babson College's innovative, real-world approach to business education and applied research. It serves as the hub for investment education programs and finance-related student organizations, and as a forum for thought leadership where industry practitioners, faculty, and students collaborate, exchange ideas, and learn from each other. The Center's programs and resources enhance understanding of the importance of investments and finance in funding the growth engines of the global economy.

The Horn Computer Center is equipped with computer workstations that run a diversified library of business-oriented programs in a Windows environment. The Horn Center operates a 24-hour computer lab.

Financial Aid

Babson is committed to educating students from diverse backgrounds and distributes grants, loans, and merit-based scholarships. Merit awards include Olin Fellowships and Scholarships, Babson Fellowships and Scholarships, Forté Foundation Fellowships, Women's Leadership Awards, and several awards based on entrepreneurial accomplishments.

Cost of Study

Nine-month academic-year cost estimates for 2010–11 for the first year of the Two-Year M.B.A. program are $46,000 for tuition, $1200 for books and supplies, and approximately $20,228 for living expenses.

Twelve-month cost estimates for 2010–11 for the One-Year M.B.A. program are $59,140 for tuition and fees, $2220 for books and supplies, and approximately $26,680 for living expenses. Fast Track tuition estimate for students enrolling in spring 2011 is $71,900. Per-credit tuition for the Evening M.B.A. program is $1220.

Living and Housing Costs

Graduate students at Babson may live on or off campus. On campus accommodations include studios and one-bedroom apartments.

Student Group

Students in the incoming 2009 Two-Year M.B.A. class were, on average, 28 years old with five years of work experience. Eighty percent of the newly enrolled students had GMAT scores between 570 and 680. Women made up 32 percent of the class. Students come from such diverse industries as banking and investment institutions to biotechnology, high technology, nonprofit businesses, and consulting. International students made up 35 percent of the Two-Year M.B.A. enrollment and represented twenty-four countries.

Student Outcomes

The Center for Career Development's Relationship Management team works with students in planning a career strategy, including developing a personal marketing communication plan and preparing for networking activities and interviews.

Location

Babson College, founded in 1919 by financier and entrepreneur Roger W. Babson, is located on 370 acres of woods, rolling hills, and carefully landscaped grounds in Wellesley, Massachusetts, just 14 miles from Boston. Nearby Boston, renowned for its history and cultural and intellectual life, is an exciting and lively setting for the student experience.

The College

Babson College is recognized internationally for its entrepreneurial leadership in a changing global environment. Its business programs are accredited by AACSB International—The Association to Advance Collegiate Schools of Business, and the New England Association of Schools and Colleges. In addition, Babson offers distinct executive education programs to help companies reach their strategic goals: Custom Degree and Credit Programs, Consortium Programs, and Open-Enrollment Programs. By infusing the spirit of innovation into its academic programs, Babson educates leaders capable of anticipating, initiating, and managing change.

Applying

Students are admitted to the program based on a careful evaluation of academic records, professional qualifications, GMAT scores, and personal attributes. Interviews are required for admission to full-time M.B.A. programs. The current class's GMAT scores are in the 510–760 range, and the average undergraduate GPA is 3.2. International students must submit TOEFL results and official English translations of all academic documents. A minimum score of 100 (Internet-based version), 250 (computer-based version), or 600 (paper-based version) on the TOEFL is required. All candidates should have strong mathematics, computer, economics, and business writing skills.

Application deadlines for the Two-Year M.B.A. program are November 1, January 15, and March 1. International applications should be submitted by January 15. Application deadlines and decision dates for all programs may be found at http://mba.babson.edu/admissions/applynow_timetable.aspx.

Correspondence and Information

Office of Graduate Admission
F. W. Olin Graduate School of Business
Babson College
231 Forest Street
Babson Park, Massachusetts 02457-0310
Phone: 781-239-4317
    800-488-4512 (toll-free)
Fax: 781-239-4194
E-mail: mbaadmission@babson.edu
Web site: http://www.babson.edu/mba

Babson College

THE FACULTY

Babson's faculty is an internationally and professionally diverse group, representing nations in Asia, Australia, Europe, and North and South America and with backgrounds in pharmaceuticals, banking, high technology, retailing, and other industries. They are practitioners and scholars, executives and teachers, and researchers and consultants who have lived and worked in international settings.

More information about the faculty is available at http://mba.babson.edu/babsonexperience/faculty.aspx.

Building on the strength of more than seventy-five years of excellence in management education, Babson College embraces new challenges and opportunities and furthers successes.

CLAREMONT GRADUATE UNIVERSITY

Peter F. Drucker and Masatoshi Ito Graduate School of Management

Program of Study

The Drucker M.B.A. embodies the philosophies of management pioneer Peter F. Drucker, a longtime faculty member and prolific writer and lecturer on management. The program is based on the belief that management is not only about tasks, but it is also about people—motivating them and leading them. The curriculum provides students with substantial value to complement their unique talents, undergraduate course work, and work experience. The classroom experience is enriched through student participation and faculty blending of theory and practice.

The Drucker M.B.A. is made up of 60 academic units (with 4 units allotted to a typical course). The program takes between eighteen and thirty-six months to complete, depending on whether a student attends full- or part-time. The curriculum instills a powerful knowledge base from the required core courses, yet provides the opportunity to concentrate elective courses in one of seven areas: leadership, strategy, finance, marketing, global management, entrepreneurship, or nonprofit management.

As part of the Claremont College consortium, a Drucker student may earn a dual degree with any of the other schools of Claremont Graduate University (CGU). Some of the most popular dual-degree programs include the M.B.A./Ph.D. in economics; the M.B.A./M.A. in human resources design, and the M.B.A./M.P.H. in Public Health. In addition, the Drucker School offers joint degrees with the School of Mathematics (M.S. in Financial Engineering) and the School of Arts and Humanities (M.A. in Arts Management). The M.S. in Financial Engineering program at Claremont Graduate University is ranked among the top financial engineering programs in the United States.

Drucker students are able to study at Oxford University (England), University of St. Gallen (Switzerland), Rotterdam School of Management (the Netherlands), Hitotsubashi Business School (Japan), Inha University (South Korea), and the Chinese University of Hong Kong. Full-time students may pursue internships between the spring term of their first year and the fall term of their second year with assistance from the Drucker Career Management Office.

In addition to the M.B.A., the Drucker School offers an Executive M.B.A., a Master of Arts in Management (M.A.M.), and a Master of Science in Advanced Management (M.S.A.M.). These programs are designed for experienced managers who are looking for a classroom experience that updates their leadership and strategy skills to match their changing responsibilities.

Research Facilities

Claremont Graduate University has an academic computing center reserved for student use where IBM, Apple, and Digital Equipment computers are provided. Most software packages utilized in instruction are Microsoft products, but many other software packages are available. The Claremont Colleges' Honnold-Mudd Library is advanced in electronic access and CD-ROM capability. CGU also has wireless laptop capabilities in some buildings and courtyards.

Financial Aid

Approximately 57 percent of Drucker M.B.A. students receive fellowships, assistantships, or other grants, with the average award amounting to about $12,000 a year. Institutional aid programs based on both academic merit and financial need are available, as are loans and work-study programs.

Cost of Study

Tuition and fees for the 2010–11 academic year are $1554 per unit in the M.B.A. program and $1785 per unit in the Executive Management Program.

Living and Housing Costs

Living expenses are about $12,360 for on-campus residents and $16,000 for off-campus residents.

Student Group

The Drucker M.B.A. program enrolls approximately 200 students with a variety of educational and work experiences. Approximately 25 percent of the students are fully employed and enrolled as part-time students. These students bring their daily work experience into the classroom and, together with the faculty, relate business theory to practice. A number of the Drucker full-time students are sponsored by their overseas employers and bring global realities to the Drucker experience. The average Drucker M.B.A. student is 26 years old with five years of work experience. Women make up approximately 41 percent of the student body.

Students receive an intimate educational experience through the small-class format (average class size is 25 students), while enjoying the benefits provided by the facilities of Claremont Graduate University and the Claremont Colleges Consortium.

Student Outcomes

The Drucker Career Management Office helps students and alumni effectively manage their career paths to ensure long-term success in their chosen fields. Beginning with their first day on campus, Drucker students meet individually with a Career Management staff member. Ongoing workshops with alumni and local employers help prepare the students for a successful career.

Drucker Career Management and leaders within the Drucker School conduct a consistent marketing and corporate communications program to solicit additional placement opportunities in areas of interest to CGU students and alumni. Career Management maintains an aggressive program of flexible and tailored response to potential employers based on a state-of-the-art resume database. Career Management also offers a variety of services, including one-on-one counseling, resume and cover letter critiquing, networking opportunities, individual job listings, on- and off-campus recruiting, a career resources library, and career skills workshops.

Location

Claremont is a beautiful residential community of 34,000 located 35 miles east of Los Angeles, close to skiing, the beach, the desert, and other recreational areas. This pleasant college town with an Ivy League atmosphere is situated in the foothills of the San Gabriel Mountains.

The University

The Claremont Colleges are a group of small and distinguished liberal arts colleges. Claremont Graduate University, founded in 1925, was the second member of The Claremont Colleges. CGU enrolls approximately 2,200 students in seven schools or centers. The mission of Claremont Graduate University is to prepare a diverse group of outstanding individuals to assume leadership roles in the worldwide community through research, teaching, and practice in selected fields.

Applying

Applicants to the Drucker M.B.A. program must submit a completed application, a GMAT score, undergraduate and graduate school transcripts, three letters of reference, a resume, a personal statement, and the application fee to the Admissions Office of Claremont Graduate University. Interviews are held by invitation only. Prospective students may apply online at the School's Web site.

The Drucker School utilizes a rolling admissions process for fall, spring, and summer admissions. Applicants generally are notified of the decision within four weeks of submitting a complete application file. Prospective students should visit the School's Web site for priority application deadlines.

Correspondence and Information

Peter F. Drucker and Masatoshi Ito Graduate School of Management
Claremont Graduate University
1021 North Dartmouth Avenue
Claremont, California 91711-6184
Phone: 909-607-7811
          800-944-4312 (toll-free)
Fax: 909-607-9104
E-mail: drucker@cgu.edu
Web site: http://www.drucker.cgu.edu

Claremont Graduate University

THE FACULTY

Drucker alumni reflecting on their M.B.A experience generally mention outstanding teaching and courses as some of the unique characteristics of the Drucker experience. World-renowned authors, such as Jean Lipman-Blumen *(Toxic Leadership* and *Connective Leadership)* teach inimitable courses based on their cutting-edge research. The Drucker School's faculty members are selected for the high quality of their academic training and research, their knowledge of management and leadership practice, and their superior teaching skills. Most of the full-time faculty members are experienced consultants or have significant managerial experience.

Core Faculty Members

Murat Binay, Assistant Professor of Financial Management. Corporate finance, investments, institutional investors, initial public offerings payout policy, performance evaluation, corporate governance.

Jenny Darroch, Associate Professor of Marketing and M.B.A. Academic Director. Marketing strategy, brand management, entrepreneurship innovation, marketing research.

Richard R. Ellsworth, Professor of Management, Emeritus. Leadership, strategy implementation, ethics, and management.

Donald Griesinger, Professor of Management, Emeritus.

Ira Jackson, Henry Y. Hwang Dean and Professor of Management.

Jean Lipman-Blumen, Thornton F. Bradshaw Professor of Public Policy and Professor of Organizational Behavior. Leadership, achieving styles, crisis management, female leadership, and other gender issues.

Joseph A. Maciariello, Horton Professor of Management. Management control systems, cost management systems, Drucker on Management.

James Mills, Visiting Professor of Finance and Co-Academic Director of the Financial Engineering Program. Financial derivatives, risk management.

Katharina Pick, Visiting Assistant Professor. Organizational behavior, leadership, boards of directors/corporate governance.

Jay Prag, Clinical Associate Professor and EMP Academic Director. Corporate finance, investments, economics of strategy, macroeconomics.

Vijay Sathe, Professor of Management. Strategy, corporate entrepreneurship, corporate revitalization, cultural change, building winning executive teams, building a global organization.

James Wallace, Associate Professor of Accounting. Financial accounting, managerial accounting, performance measurement, corporate governance, earnings management, corporate social responsibility.

Hideki Yamawaki, Professor of Management and Academic Dean. International business strategy, multinational corporate management.

Distinguished Visiting Faculty

John Bachmann, Chairman, Board of Visitors of The Drucker School; M.B.A., Northwestern. Senior Partner, Edward Jones.

The Peter F. Drucker and Masatoshi Ito Graduate School of Management at Claremont.

DUQUESNE UNIVERSITY

John F. Donahue Graduate School of Business
Master of Business Administration

Programs of Study

The Donahue Graduate School of Business at Duquesne University in Pittsburgh, Pennsylvania, prepares responsible leaders who are capable of transforming organizations, communities, and the world. The School challenges its students to reach their full potential, reflecting the University's century-long commitment to ethics and service, excellence, and innovation.

The Donahue School is among the elite 5 percent of graduate business schools accredited by AACSB International. It is ranked among the Global Top 20 by Beyond Grey Pinstripes for integrating social and environmental stewardship (Aspen Institute, 2009). The Princeton Review includes Duquesne among the most connected campuses in terms of its use of technology (2010), and in a recent survey by the Academy of Management Learning and Education, Duquesne was named one of the top three universities in the nation for infusing ethics content into the graduate business curriculum.

The Donahue School offers a portfolio of current and managerially relevant M.B.A. curricula for full-time students and working professionals.

The **Evening M.B.A.** program offers a traditional approach to M.B.A. course work and convenient evening and weekend classes for busy professionals. Duquesne's M.B.A. program has been providing professional business career preparation for over fifty years and enjoys a productive, ongoing relationship with high-profile employers in Western Pennsylvania.

Classes are offered at Duquesne's campus in the heart of Pittsburgh's downtown business district, as well as at the Regional Learning Alliance in Cranberry Township, a northern suburb and emergent office park community. Students may begin their studies in August or January, and classes are offered year-round. Students can complete the program in approximately two years if taking a full-time course load or three years if studying on a part-time basis. More details can be found at http://www.duq.edu/business/grad.

An accelerated, one-year daytime cohort program, the **M.B.A. Sustainability** explicitly focuses on managing social, environmental, and financial capital for prosperity today without compromising resources for tomorrow. This internationally recognized, 45-credit program integrates rigorous course work in all business disciplines with practical application of global best practices in sustainability through an innovative delivery model that features live consulting projects, team teaching, cross-functional integration, professional skill development, and international travel. Students begin their studies in August and complete the program requirements at the end of the following July.

Two faculty-supervised consulting engagements anchor the M.B.A. Sustainability program and provide an unmatched proving ground for managing social, environmental, and financial resources. Through these contemporary problem-solving experiences, small teams of students make an immediate bottom line impact for multinational corporations, regional businesses, government, and not-for-profit organizations.

M.B.A. Sustainability students investigate international best practices firsthand, expand their perspectives by studying global economics at a partnering university abroad, and collaborate on field projects with students at a host university. They interface regularly with international thought leaders, corporate executives, and alumni advisers through their study trips, an annual sustainability symposium, ethics luncheons, Idea Cafes and Net Impact activities. Sustainability fellows, chosen on merit, support faculty research and coauthor papers for publication. More information can be found at http://mba.sustainability.duq.edu.

The newly launched, full-time **Master of Accountancy (M.Acc.)** is a unique program of study that responds to three emerging areas of critical importance to the accounting profession: forensic accounting, ethics, and regulation and reporting. Students enrolled in the program will complete in-depth course work in these areas by taking classes such as Fraud Examination, SEC Reporting, Accounting Ethics, Advanced Forensic Techniques, and International Financial Reporting. Students will benefit significantly from face-to-face classroom interaction with award-winning, knowledgeable, and experienced accounting faculty members.

The **Master of Science in Information Systems Management (M.S.I.S.M.)** program prepares students for IS management and analytical positions involving the strategic role of information technology in modern business. Students graduating with an M.S.I.S.M. degree pursue careers as business/systems analysts, information systems managers, and IT auditors, among many others.

Research Facilities

The Gumberg Library's primary mission is to support the teaching, learning, and research of Duquesne students, faculty, and staff. The library's Web site (http://www.duq.edu/library) provides a convenient gateway to research databases, electronic journals and books, library services, and DuCat, the library's catalog. Reference librarians are available to provide assistance 24 hours a day, 365 days a year through Duquesne's online chat service, Ask A Librarian.

Duquesnes Investment Center offers students instant access to information and sophisticated analytical techniques in a classroom setting that mimics worldwide trading operations. The center provides data feeds that supply real-time news and market data on stocks, bonds, international markets, futures, and options and other securities. Also, a state-of-the-art technology center features three technology-rich classroom learning centers that provide access to enterprise resource planning (ERP) software applications, and a general computer laboratory available for use by students and faculty members in courses throughout the graduate curriculum.

Financial Aid

A limited number of graduate assistantships, which provide up to 9 credits of tuition remission each semester and a monthly cash stipend, are available to evening students who take a full-time course load.

The M.B.A. Sustainability program considers all applicants for merit scholarships and research fellowships. A few graduate assistantships are available each year.

Cost of Study

Evening M.B.A. and M.Acc. programs are billed on a per-credit basis. Tuition for the 2010–11 academic year is $884 per credit. An $84 University fee is added per credit.

The M.B.A. Sustainability program is billed in three equal installments. For the 2010–11 academic year, tuition and fees are $14,338 per semester, totaling $43,014 for the three-semester program. Tuition and fees do not include airfare, incidentals, or some meals for the mandatory international study trip.

Living and Housing Costs

On campus housing is available to graduate students. The cost of room and board may vary depending on the student's living arrangements. Details are available at the Office of Residence Life Web site at http://www.duq.edu/residence-life.

Student Group

The student body of approximately 350 students is diverse. In the evening program, full-time students, who make up approximately 25 percent of the enrollment, are enriched by sharing classes with full-time business professionals who are attending on a part-time basis. Part-time students bring an average of five years of professional work experience to the classroom, providing a rich source of real-world issues that add value to the educational experience. M.B.A. Sustainability students, 60 percent of whom hail from outside the region, take their core courses as a cohort, but have an opportunity to take electives with the evening M.B.A. students.

Location

Long noted as one of the world's great business centers, Pittsburgh combines the features of big-city living with many of the charms and personal characteristics of a much smaller town. Pittsburgh has one of the largest concentrations of corporate headquarters in the United States and has developed a strong civic identity and sense of pride in its rebirth as a modern urban community. Students from Duquesne and other colleges and universities in the city can choose from a wide variety of cultural, social, and sporting events and programs.

The University

Nestled in a private 49-acre campus in the heart of Pittsburgh, Duquesne University provides a unique world-renowned education that continues to be grounded in the values of the Holy Spirit Fathers who founded it in 1878. Faculty members are recognized time and again both nationally and internationally for their instruction and research, and their support and encouragement provide an energetic and productive environment in which students thrive.

Applying

Required application materials for all programs include an online application form, official transcripts and GMAT scores, two professional references/ratings, personal essays (questions vary by program), and a resume or vitae. The Test of English as a Foreign Language (TOEFL) is required for international students. Additional information can be found at http://www.duq.edu/business/grad.

The Evening M.B.A. program accepts new students in fall and spring. Application deadlines are May 1 for fall enrollment and October 1 for spring admissions. A separate application is required for candidates interested in graduate assistantships.

The M.B.A. Sustainability program admits one cohort per academic year. Early decision applications are accepted from September through December, and the regular decision deadline is March 31 for enrollment in August. Scholarships, fellowships, and graduate assistantships are granted on a merit basis, and all applicants are considered based on the strength of application materials. Propspective students should go to http://mba.sustainability.duq.edu for more details.

The M.Acc. program is accepting applications for fall 2012 in January 2011.

Correspondence and Information

John F. Donahue Graduate School of Business
704 Rockwell Hall
Duquesne University
600 Forbes Avenue
Pittsburgh, Pennsylvania 15282

Phone: 412-396-6276
E-mail: grad-bus@duq.edu (Evening M.B.A. or joint degree programs)
            sustainablemba@duq.edu (M.B.A. Sustainability program)
            kollar@duq.edu (M.Acc.)
Web site: http://www.duq.edu/business/grad
            http://mba.sustainability.duq.edu

Duquesne University

THE FACULTY AND THEIR RESEARCH

The faculty members of the Donahue Graduate School of Business are committed to teaching excellence, scholarship that focuses on real business problems, and developing creative academic-business partnerships. The academic and professional experiences of the faculty members are complemented by the executive adjunct faculty members who teach classes in their areas of expertise, directly relating their daily experiences to the material covered in the courses. Graduate students benefit from exposure to a roster of executives who share their knowledge and experience. Please refer to the Donahue Graduate School of Business Web site for additional information: http://www.business.duq.edu/faculty/AllFaculty.asp.

EAST CAROLINA UNIVERSITY
College of Business

EAST CAROLINA UNIVERSITY
COLLEGE of
BUSINESS

Program of Study

The M.B.A. program at East Carolina University (ECU) is one of approximately 454 graduate business programs accredited by AACSB International–The Association to Advance Collegiate Schools of Business. It was the second program to be accredited by the AACSB in North Carolina and is one of approximately 174 M.B.A. programs that belong to the Graduate Management Admissions Council.

The goal of the ECU M.B.A. is to prepare men and women for managerial leadership in both profit and nonprofit organizations. Required and elective courses are taught from a managerial perspective with a blend of teaching methods, including lectures, discussions, computer simulations, team projects, cases, and independent study, to develop critical-thinking and human relations skills. The average class size is 27 students.

The ECU M.B.A. program is for both business and non-business undergraduates. The program is customized to fit each student based on past academic experience and performance. The degree is completely self-contained, requiring no prerequisite business experience or course work. The program is a maximum of twenty classes, or 60 semester hours, divided into the core level and breadth level at ten classes each.

Students may begin the M.B.A. program in any term—fall, spring, or summer. All M.B.A. core and breadth courses are offered every fall and spring semester. The availability of two terms each summer allows students to accelerate the completion of their program.

Students can pursue the M.B.A. program completely on campus, completely online, or as a mixture of the two delivery methods. These methods can mix, match, and change each semester. The requirements and structure of the program are the same regardless of face-to-face or online delivery.

Students set their own pace throughout the program, taking from one to five classes each semester. The number of classes each semester can change to suit a student's schedule; a student can even take a semester or more off if needed. Courses can be taken in any order, provided the prerequisites are met. Full-time students may finish the program in as little as one year, while most part-time students finish in two to five years.

The ECU Brody School of Medicine and the College of Business offer a joint M.D./M.B.A. dual-degree program. The M.D./M.B.A. is also available to students who are accepted to or enrolled in other accredited medical schools and medical residents whose training program allows one year away from clinical responsibilities. Students enter in late June and complete the M.B.A. twelve months later. A part-time schedule is also available. The GMAT requirement is waived for applicants with M.D. degrees or students from accredited medical schools.

The College of Business offers a Master of Science in Accounting (M.S.A.) program to prepare students for the CPA exam and careers in public and management accounting. The M.S.A. for students with an undergraduate degree in accounting is typically 30–45 semester hours, depending on undergraduate courses and grades. For students with degrees in fields other than accounting, the M.S.A. is generally 45 semester hours. Current enrollment in the M.S.A. program is approximately 100 students. A focus in auditing or taxation is also available.

In addition to elective courses in the traditional business subjects, East Carolina's M.B.A. program offers twelve optional certificates. Optional certificates can be earned in the following areas: development and environmental planning, finance, health-care management, hospitality management, international management, management information systems, professional investment management and operations, school business management, security studies (homeland security), sport management, tax, and supply chain management. M.S.A. candidates may choose to focus on a track in taxation or auditing, in addition to those listed above.

Research Facilities

The M.B.A. program is housed in a modern facility, which includes group and individual study areas and a dedicated graduate computer lab. M.B.A. students also have access to other College of Business computer labs. ECU's College of Business is equipped with multiple "smart classrooms" and free WiFi.

Financial Aid

The College of Business offers approximately 90 graduate assistantships. Students may earn between $3750 and $7500 per year working 10 to 20 hours each week assisting professors in research or working with undergraduates in computer labs. In addition, the College offers a variety of other scholarships with awards ranging from $1000 to $3500 per semester. Last year the College of Business awarded approximately $300,000 in graduate student scholarships.

Cost of Study

Value is a function of quality and cost. East Carolina provides a substantial accredited M.B.A. program at a reasonable cost. Tuition and fees for on-campus full-time students (at least 9 hours) are $3423 per semester for North Carolina residents and $8766.50 per semester for nonresidents, with additional charges for optional summer sessions. Distance Education courses are charged per semester hour ($269/hour for North Carolina residents) regardless of how many courses are taken. One 3-hour course through Distance Education (for North Carolina residents) is $807; each subsequent course is charged the same amount. Tuition and fees for part-time students are lower.

Living and Housing Costs

Off-campus housing, which is estimated at $6000 per calendar year, is readily available and is used by most graduate students. University housing is also available.

Student Group

East Carolina's M.B.A. students are drawn from a wide variety of educational and business backgrounds. Approximately 230 attend full-time, while 540 work full-time and attend part-time. In addition, 574 students attend entirely online. The typical student is 31 years old. The 2009–10 student body included 40 percent women and 16 percent members of minority groups. Approximately 50 percent have undergraduate degrees in disciplines other than business, with 20 percent in engineering, science, social science, and health professions, including 8 to 10 students with M.D. degrees.

Many M.B.A. students work full-time for major organizations and attend graduate school part-time. Full- and part-time students are in class together and work on projects that enhance learning and networking opportunities.

Student Outcomes

Eastern North Carolina is home to scores of major corporations, including Abbott Laboratories, Black & Decker, Bosch, DuPont, Firestone, Frigidaire, NACCO, Sara Lee, TRW, and Weyerhaeuser. Students are also able to get hands-on experience consulting with local businesses through the Small Business Institute, the Small Business Technology and Development Center, and other not-for-profit entities.

The College of Business Career Services Office provides career and placement services to M.B.A. students and recent alumni. Resume preparation, interviewing skills workshops, internship placement, and computerized databases are all part of the services offered, while career fairs and on-campus recruiting are augmented by business contacts through the College of Business.

The office also assists M.B.A. students in preparing for and securing career-related temporary employment, usually of a semester's duration. This is particularly valuable for students who do not have extensive full-time work experience. With ECU's flexible M.B.A. program, co-op jobs do not create scheduling problems because students can easily suspend and resume their programs or enroll in online courses.

Location

Quality of life during the M.B.A. experience is an important consideration. Greenville is a comfortable city of 84,986 with a reasonable cost of living, a temperate climate, and a relaxed outdoor lifestyle. It is an educational, commercial, industrial, medical, and cultural center for eastern North Carolina, with the beaches 90 minutes away and the mountains and skiing just a half-day's drive. Greenville is 45 miles from I-95 and is served by regional airports.

The University

East Carolina University, which was founded in 1907, is the third-largest campus of the University of North Carolina System. Current enrollment is more than 27,000 students, including 5,892 graduate students and 286 medical students. The ECU Brody School of Medicine is one of the top producers of primary-care physicians in the nation.

Applying

The ECU M.B.A. program is open to applicants with baccalaureate degrees from accredited institutions in business and non-business fields. Work experience is recommended but not required. Ability is evaluated based on the applicant's prior undergraduate record and performance on the Graduate Management Admission Test (GMAT). The average GMAT score is approximately 525 in any given semester.

Applicants from non-English-speaking countries must submit results of the Test of English as a Foreign Language (TOEFL). The minimum acceptable TOEFL score is 550 for the paper-based test or 213 for the computer-based test. For the TOEFL iBT (Internet based exam), the minimum score is 20 for each of the four sections with a total score of 80.

Applications are accepted for any term. Admission requirements and application deadlines are available on the Web site. Early applications are strongly encouraged because of the rolling admission process.

Correspondence and Information

Tina Williams, Director of Graduate Programs
College of Business
3203 Bate Building
East Carolina University
Greenville, North Carolina 27858-4353
Phone: 252-328-6970
     866-592-0835 (toll-free)
Fax: 252-328-2106
E-mail: gradbus@ecu.edu
Web site: http://www.business.ecu.edu/grad/

East Carolina University

THE FACULTY

ECU is committed to high-quality teaching. Faculty members' backgrounds are diverse and cosmopolitan and include extensive business, consulting, teaching, and research experience. The business faculty members hold graduate degrees from institutions such as Arizona State, Chicago, Duke, Florida, Georgetown, Georgia, Harvard, Illinois, Indiana, Michigan State, North Carolina, Tennessee, Texas, Texas A&M, Virginia, and Wisconsin. Professors are dedicated to providing meaningful, challenging experiences for ECU's M.B.A. students and are readily available for discussion and assistance outside the classroom.

In addition, the College of Business is served by a distinguished Business Advisory Council of 35 senior executives who advise the dean on a broad range of issues. These executives participate as guest lecturers in many courses each year.

Administration

Frederick D. Niswander, Dean and Professor, Department of Accounting; Ph.D., Texas A&M; CPA. Public accounting, real estate, and small business management. Eighteen years' experience in public accounting, financial management, distribution and real estate, and small business.
Stanley G. Eakins, Associate Dean and Professor, Department of Finance; M.B.A., Alaska Fairbanks; Ph.D., Arizona State. Corporate control, institutional investment decisions, institutional control, neural networks, and multimedia instruction methods. Ten years' experience in banking.
Margaret T. O'Hara, Assistant Dean for Online Programs and Associate Professor, Department of Management Information Systems; Ph.D., Georgia. Management information systems.
Paul Schwager, Assistant Dean for Assessment, Accreditation, and Curriculum and Associate Professor, Department of Management Information Systems; M.B.A., Florida Atlantic; Ph.D., Auburn. Management information systems.

Department of Accounting

Dan L. Schisler, Professor and Chair, Department of Accounting. M.B.A., Auburn; Ph.D., Memphis State; CPA. Individual and corporate tax issues.

Department of Finance

Scott D. Below, Associate Professor and Chair, Department of Finance; Ph.D., Kentucky. Investments, portfolio management, and securitized real estate. Consultant for mutual funds and investment advisory firms; experience in retail brokerage industry.

Department of Management

Joseph M. Tomkiewicz, Professor and Chair, Department of Management; M.B.A., Ph.D., Temple. Human resource management, labor issues, gender and racial/ethnic workplace issues.

Department of Management Information Systems

Richard D. Hauser, Jr. Associate Professor and Chair, Department of Management Information Systems; M.B.A., East Carolina; Ph.D., Florida State. Interaction of IS with organizational culture, technology diffusion, requirements analysis, total quality management (TQM) and organizational culture.

Department of Marketing and Supply Chain Management

Kenneth Anselmi, Associate Professor and Chair, Department of Marketing and Supply Chain Management; M.B.A., Arizona State; Ph.D., Nebraska–Lincoln. Supply-chain governance, relationships-marketing, general management.

A student studying outside of ECU's College of Business.

FELICIAN COLLEGE

Division of Business and Management Sciences

Programs of Study

The Division of Business and Management Science is a shining example of Felician College's high-quality programs and academic excellence. The Division of Business has a unique and entrepreneurial spirit—it is innovative, dynamic, visionary, on the cutting edge and highly responsive to the needs of students, corporations, and the workforce. This spirit is quickly earning Felician a reputation as a leader in business education in New Jersey.

Felician College offers an M.B.A. that focuses on innovation and entrepreneurship. This program has an approach unlike other M.B.A. programs—it focuses on the development of competencies through the delivery of academic content, allowing students to become competent, ethical, articulate, and creative leaders. Students can earn their degrees in one of four tracks—innovation and entrepreneurship, management, marketing, or accounting. The program uses a unique combination of classroom and online learning intertwined with hands-on practical application. The goal of the program is to create visionary thinking and innovative leadership for individuals who wish to start their own businesses or be agents of change within their corporations.

Specially tailored to meet the needs of working adults, the program meets only one night a week, from 6 to 10 p.m., and allows students to complete the 36-credit degree in just two years. The program is conveniently located at the Felician College campuses in Lodi and Rutherford and several branch campuses across the state.

The cohort-based program allows students to progress with a cohesive learning team so they can grow and benefit from teamwork and the support and guidance of an academic learning community. The curriculum prepares students with both the technical knowledge they need for solving complex problems and the core competencies that will equip them with the survival skills necessary for the competitive business world. The Felician M.B.A. core competencies, which are intertwined with content in every course, include critical reasoning, effective communication, emotional intelligence, teamwork, ethical decision making, and creativity.

Research Facilities

The College Library is a two-story building that serves the needs of students, faculty and staff members, and alumni with more than 110,000 books and over 800 periodical subscriptions. This collection is enhanced by large holdings of materials in microform, which can be used on the library's reader/printer equipment. With its computers linked to information services such as Dialog and OCLC, and as a member of the New Jersey Library Network and VALE, the library locates and obtains information, journal articles, and books not available in its collection from sources all over the country. Computerized databases can also be accessed directly by users through the online FirstSearch workstation, where up-to-date information on 40 million books and an index of 15,000 periodicals is available. The library is also connected to the Internet and has several CD-ROM workstations. Through EBSCOhost, Bell & Howell's ProQuest, CINAHL, and other services, students and faculty and staff members have access to numerous online journal indexes—as well as articles from thousands of periodicals—from anywhere on the campus computer network or from their home computers. An experienced staff of professional librarians is available to assist users.

The College's computer facilities include an academic and administrative network, four computerized labs, a computerized learning center, and two computer centers that are available for students, with a total of about 200 computers available for student/faculty member use. All classrooms, offices, and facilities are wired for Internet and e-mail.

Financial Aid

To qualify for financial aid, a student must complete the Free Application for Federal Student Aid (FAFSA).

Cost of Study

In 2010–11, graduate tuition is $825 per credit. Fees are additional. Scholarships, fellowships, work-study programs, and loans are available.

Living and Housing Costs

Students are housed in two dormitories on the Rutherford campus, Milton and Elliott Halls. Both buildings have housing organized around student suites containing semiprivate baths. On-campus room and board is approximately $10,150 per year. On-campus housing is not available to married students.

Student Group

Felician College enrolls approximately 2,300 students. In fall 2009, there were approximately 350 students enrolled in graduate programs. A close-knit community, business students participate in clubs and activities that build relationships and networks for the future. For example, Students in Free Enterprise (SIFE) is an innovative group that helps students develop skills by learning and putting into proactive practice the principles of free enterprise. Working in teams, students undertake projects that use free market economic principles, entrepreneurial strategies and management skills to achieve stated objectives and goals. Felician's SIFE group recently placed second in competition with other such groups from colleges and universities around the country.

Location

Felician College's Lodi campus is located on the banks of the Saddle River on a beautifully landscaped campus of 27 acres and offers a collegiate setting in suburban Bergen County, within easy driving distance of New York City. The Felician College Rutherford Campus is set on 10.5 beautifully landscaped acres in the heart of the historic community of Rutherford, New Jersey. Only 15 minutes from the Lodi campus, the Rutherford complex contains student residences, classroom buildings, a student center, and a gymnasium. The campus is a short distance from downtown Rutherford, where there are many shops and businesses of interest to students. Regular shuttle bus service between the two campuses is a quick 10-minute ride that turns two campuses into a one-campus home for the students.

The College

Felician College, a coeducational liberal arts college, is a Catholic, private, independent institution for students representing diverse religious, racial, and ethnic backgrounds. The College operates on two campuses in Lodi and Rutherford, New Jersey. The College is one of the institutions of higher learning conducted by the Felician Sisters in the United States. Its mission is to provide a values-oriented education based in the liberal arts while it prepares students for meaningful lives and careers in contemporary society. To meet the needs of students and to provide personal enrichment courses to matriculated and nonmatriculated students, Felician College offers day, evening, and weekend programs. The College is accredited by the Middle States Association of Colleges and Schools and carries program accreditation from the Commission on Collegiate Nursing Education, the International Assembly for Collegiate Business Education, and the Teacher Education Accreditation Council.

Applying

Admission to Felician College is as personalized as the College's educational programs. Each application is holistically reviewed, including careful consideration of the applicant's academic achievement, work history, motivation, and suitability. Students must submit the completed application, the $40 nonrefundable application fee, official transcripts, GMAT scores, a resume, and a personal statement. Upon the discretion of the division admission committee, the GMAT requirement may be waived for those students with significant and progressive postgraduate professional experience. Applications are processed on a rolling basis.

Correspondence and Information

Department of Admissions
Felician College
262 South Main Street
Lodi, New Jersey 07644-2117
Phone: 201-559-6077 (Admissions)
       201-559-6092 (Business Division)
Fax: 201-559-6120
E-mail: adultandgraduate@felician.edu
Web site: http://www.felician.edu/business/index.asp

Felician College

THE FACULTY

All courses are taught by fully qualified faculty members with advanced degrees, who are dedicated to teaching, advising, and continued involvement in their disciplines. The student-faculty ratio of 12:1 facilitates close working relationships and the development of individualized programs of instruction. The faculty is composed of both lay and religious men and women who are committed to the intellectual and spiritual growth of every student.

Beth Castiglia, Dean of the Division of Business and Management Sciences; Ph.D. (Applied Management and Decision Sciences), Walden.
Ossa Elhardary, Assistant Professor; D.B.A., Maastricht School of Management (Netherlands).
Martha Geaney, Assistant Professor and Director of the M.B.A. Program; Ph.D., Union (Ohio).
Michael Omansky, Associate Professor; M.B.A., Columbia.
Irene Parietti, Assistant Professor and Chair of Economics and Finance; M.B.A., Pennsylvania (Wharton).

FLORIDA INSTITUTE OF TECHNOLOGY

The Nathan M. Bisk College of Business
Graduate Business Programs

Programs of Study

Graduate business students at Florida Institute of Technology have the options to complete their degree in traditional on-campus residence programs or through online delivery methods. The online programs of study are the same curriculum for the comparable on-campus degree program. The choice of delivery makes the programs both very accessible as well as portable in case students relocate during their program.

Florida Tech's three academic divisions for graduate business degrees include the following:

Residential M.B.A. Program: A residential M.B.A. program is available at Florida Tech's main campus in Melbourne, Florida. As part of the M.B.A. program studies, students may emphasize accounting for CPA certification, entrepreneurship, or health-care management. For additional details, prospective students should visit the Web site at http://cob.fit.edu/.

Extended Studies Division: M.B.A. and specialized M.S. programs are available in a variety of fields including logistics, project management, and contract management. Offered at ten sites in five states, courses are provided both on-site and online. For further details, prospective students are encouraged to visit the Web site at http://es.fit.edu/.

Online: An online M.B.A. degree is available with specializations in accounting and finance, health-care management, information technology, Internet marketing, management, marketing, and project management. For more information, visit the Web site at http://www.floridatechonline.com.

Research Facilities

The Center for Applied Business Research (CABR) serves to consolidate the College of Business programs that interact directly with local business, to provide focus and establish responsibility and accountability for activities and relationships with local businesses, to establish a forum for local businesses to interact with the College of Business, to establish and maintain a database of activities involving local businesses for tracking and research purposes, and to support faculty research activities. Working in close cooperation with the College of Business faculty, the center oversees the: Local Business Assistance Program, which offers research assistance to businesses (both for-profit and not-for-profit) in marketing, finance, organizational behavior and general management; Internship Practicum Program; Mentor Program; Classroom Guest Speaker Program; Industry Visitation Program; and Faculty Externship Program. The center also maintains a repository of longitudinal data for business research and analysis.

Cost of Study

Tuition for the academic degree program is based on both the program selected and the delivery method used. A review of the rates can be found at the specific program Web site.

Living and Housing Costs

For residential M.B.A. students, the room and board on-campus costs are approximately $4500 per semester in 2010–11. On-campus housing (dormitories and apartments) is available for full-time single and married graduate students; however priority for dormitory rooms is given to undergraduate students. Many apartment complexes and rental houses are available near the Melbourne Campus.

Location

The main campus is in Melbourne, Florida, and is located about 30 miles south of Cape Canaveral. Melbourne is a medium-sized community with a subtropical climate. The Melbourne and Orlando Airports serve the community and campus with flights from all major cities. There are beaches approximately 3 miles from the campus for surfing, sailing, swimming, and water-skiing.

The Extended Studies Division has locations in Alabama, Florida, Maryland, New Jersey, and Virginia, often close to a military base or a major government operation.

The Institute

First established in the mid-1960's as a response to the request from NASA for engineers who needed better management skills, Florida Tech's business school has remained committed to educating both full-time resident students and working professionals. Today, the total graduate business student population at Florida Tech includes more than 2,000 students.

Florida Tech ranks among the best major research universities in the nation, being listed in the top National Universities category as noted in the most recent *U.S. News & World Report* rankings. The university's focus on "High Tech with a Human Touch" is reinforced by the business school policy of fostering a personalized education for every student by having no class larger than 30 students.

Applying

The applicant to the Master of Business Administration program must have a bachelor's degree; however, the degree need not be in business administration. Applicants who are graduates of non-business programs are encouraged to apply. Applications are processed on a rolling basis.

The admissions decision is based on a review of the application documentation including work experience, academic performance, references and written statement of purpose. The GMAT is not required; however it is optional.

Correspondence and Information

Nathan M. Bisk College of Business
Florida Institute of Technology
150 W. University Boulevard
Melbourne, Florida 32901-6975
Phone: 321-674-7392 (Residential M.B.A.)
     321-674-8806 (Extended Studies M.B.A.)
     813-621-6200 (Online M.B.A.)
     888-352-8324 (toll-free in United States)
E-mail: BUS-Info@fit.edu (Residential M.B.A.)
     ES@fit.edu (Extended Studies M.B.A.)
     information@FloridaTechOnline.com (Online M.B.A.)
Web site: http://cob.fit.edu (Residential M.B.A.)
     http://es.fit.edu (Extended Studies M.B.A.)
     http://floridatechonline.com (Online M.B.A.)

Office of Graduate Admissions
Florida Institute of Technology
150 W. University Boulevard
Melbourne, Florida 32901-6975
Phone: 321-674-8027
Fax: 321-723-9468
E-mail: grad-admissions@fit.edu
Web site: http://www.fit.edu

Florida Institute of Technology

THE FACULTY

Florida Institute of Technology, an organization that values and encourages intellectual curiosity, is committed to the pursuit of excellence in teaching and research. In support of this commitment, the faculty, internationally recognized as educators, scholars and researchers, employ innovative technologies and research facilities to serve the diverse needs of local, state, national, and international communities.

Widely known for its strong philosophy of hands-on study and its passionate support of relevant research, Florida Tech attracts world-class faculty members who are devoted to building relationships with the students to motivate them to reach their full academic and professional potential.

To learn more about the Bisk College of Business faculty members, search the online database of profiles at http://www.fit.edu/faculty/profiles/.

Florida Institute of Technology

FLORIDA SOUTHERN COLLEGE

Master of Business Administration

Programs of Study

The Master of Business Administration (M.B.A.) at Florida Southern College (FSC) is a full-time, innovative, accelerated sixteen-month M.B.A. program open to graduates with a degree in any major. Prior work experience is not required but may enhance a student's application credentials.

M.B.A. students at Florida Southern develop the skills necessary to lead an organization, a small business, or a large company. Students also understand the complexities and challenges of today's global business environment because of the intensive global focus of the program, the College's connections with international companies and organizations, and the optional international summer study program.

The M.B.A. program integrates functional skills in accounting, finance, economics, marketing, statistics, and database analysis with the managerial and communication skills necessary to lead organizations. Emphasis is placed on real-world learning—both inside and outside the classroom—through a guaranteed internship, an assigned executive mentor, the CEO Lecture Series and Executives-in-Residence program, and the integration of case studies and other experiences.

All students begin their journey with two 2-credit-hour foundations (Flying Start) courses, held prior to beginning the core course sequence. The program also includes six 4-credit-hour courses and 8 elective credits for a total of 36 credit hours.

Classes meet in late afternoon and early evening to allow for work experience and internships earlier in the day. M.B.A. students are offered dynamic internships, case studies, and practica through FSC's established partnerships with nationally and internationally recognized companies. The M.B.A. placement director assists students directly with internship placements and job opportunities.

The Mentor Program, a critical part of the Florida Southern M.B.A., delivers insight into the day-to-day challenges of specific fields. Students explore career paths, build relationships with nurturing professionals, and see firsthand what opportunities are available to them after graduation.

FSC's dynamic classroom approach helps M.B.A. students master the team-building and communication skills necessary to manage teams and lead organizations through in-depth group projects and case studies. Professional networking and peer experience sharing are also benefits of the program.

As citizens of a global community and one of the world's most vibrant nations of commerce, it is essential that business professionals understand the dynamics of the international business environment. The M.B.A. at Florida Southern is designed to provide a solid background in the nature and foundations of international business. Armed with analytical, logical, and communication skills, as well as insight into the global marketplace, graduates are prepared to manage an organization's multifaceted business environment and excel in leadership.

The M.B.A. program's optional international summer study experience—studying manufacturing in China, trade in Brazil, or marketing in Europe, for example—is a great opportunity for students to gain a better sense of issues affecting the global business environment through hands-on experience.

Research Facilities

A computer lab in the School of Business and Economics offers software tailored to the needs of graduate business students. In addition, M.B.A. students have access to the College's new state-of-the-art Rinker Technology Center, as well as the extensive resources of the Roux Library and the McKay Archives Center.

Financial Aid

A limited number of graduate assistantships are offered. For more information, prospective students should contact Dr. Larry Ross, program director. In addition, students may apply for financial aid by completing the Free Application for Federal Student Aid (FAFSA). Students should contact the M.B.A. Admissions Office at 863-680-4205 or the Financial Aid Office at 800-205-1600 (toll-free) for more information.

Cost of Study

Earning an M.B.A. is an investment of both time and money, and Florida Southern's M.B.A. program is an incredible value. The tuition cost for the entire 16-month program is $23,975. Additional costs include books and supplies, personal expenses, and travel for the optional international study program. M.B.A. students who wish to live on campus (depending on space availability) also should plan for room and board expenses.

Living and Housing Costs

Any student living in a College (double occupancy) residence hall room could expect to pay $8310 in room and board for the academic year. All students, living on campus or off, have access to amenities such as the modern Hollis Wellness Center and competition pool, high-tech computer labs, libraries and archives, and free, on-campus entertainment programming.

Location

Florida Southern College is situated on a picturesque 100-acre campus in Lakeland, Florida, 30 minutes from Tampa and 45 minutes from Orlando and world-class beaches. The campus is home to the world's largest single-site collection of Frank Lloyd Wright architecture. With beautiful Lake Hollingsworth just across the street, water-skiing, sailing, and kayaking are popular pastimes. A 3-mile walking and biking path around the lake stays busy day and night, year-round, as students and community members take advantage of the weather and spectacular scenery to make their workouts more fun. Lakeland's vibrant downtown—brimming with museums, sidewalk cafés, and charming retail shops—is within walking or biking distance. The city also has an active arts community, with year-round live performances planned in local venues.

The College

Founded in 1885, Florida Southern is a private, comprehensive college that offers fifty undergraduate programs and distinctive graduate programs in business, nursing, and education. Florida Southern College is a rapidly rising star among the nation's best private colleges. The College enrolls 2,427 students from forty-four states and thirty-one countries. A national leader in engaged learning, FSC provides students with numerous opportunities for internships, study abroad, collaborative research, performance, and service learning. The College is committed to the development of the whole student through vibrant student life programs that prepare graduates to make a positive, consequential impact on society.

Applying

Compelling candidates for Florida Southern's M.B.A. program possess strong academic ability, excellent interpersonal skills, and a desire to succeed. Florida Southern's M.B.A. program considers a combination of the undergraduate GPA, GRE or GMAT scores, and previous work experience to determine acceptance to the program. M.B.A. candidates may hold a bachelor's degree in any major.

International students are encouraged to apply. The M.B.A. program has a significant global component at its core, and the College's philosophy is that the enrollment of international students provides for lively interaction, discussion, and peer learning.

The priority application date is April 15, and the application deadline is June 1 for the August program start date.

Correspondence and Information

M.B.A. Admissions Office
Florida Southern College
111 Lake Hollingsworth Drive
Lakeland, Florida 33801-5698

Phone: 863-680-4205
E-mail: fscmba@flsouthern.edu
Web site: http://www.flsouthern.edu/mba

Florida Southern College

THE FACULTY AND THEIR RESEARCH

Peter Bias, Ph.D.; Professor of Business Administration and Economics. E-mail: pbias@flsouthern.edu.

Carl C. Brown, Ph.D., Professor of Economics. E-mail: cbrown@flsouthern.edu.

Craig Bythewood, Ph.D., Assistant Professor of Business. E-mail: cbythewood@flsouthern.edu.

Lynn H. Clements, D.B.A., Professor of Accounting. E-mail: lclements@flsouthern.edu.

H. Bernard Davis, Executive in Residence. E-mail: hdavis@flsouthern.edu.

Paul B. Eberle, Ph.D., Professor of Finance and Economics. E-mail: peberle@flsouthern.edu.

James Farrell, Ph.D., Visiting Assistant Professor, Finance and Economics. E-mail: jfarrell@flsouthern.edu.

David Grossman, D.B.A., Assistant Professor of Business Administration. E-mail: dgrossman@flsouthern.edu.

Cindy Hardin, J.D., Professor of Business Administration. E-mail: chardin@flsouthern.edu.

Michael Knudstrup, Ph.D., Assistant Professor of Business Administration. E-mail: mknudstrup@flsouthern.edu.

Nicholas Nugent, Ph.D., Assistant Professor of Business and Economics. E-mail: nnugent@flsouthern.edu.

William Quilliam, Ph.D., Associate Professor of Accounting. E-mail: wquilliam@flsouthern.edu.

William Rhey, Ph.D., Dean of the School of Business and Economics. E-mail: wrhey@flsouthern.edu.

Lawrence E. Ross, Ph.D., Professor of Business Administration. E-mail: lross@flsouthern.edu.

John Stancil, D.B.A., Professor of Accounting. E-mail: jstancil@flsouthern.edu.

Mike Tracy, Executive in Residence. E-mail: mtracy@flsouthern.edu.

Full-time M.B.A. students at Florida Southern develop the skills necessary to lead an organization, a small business, or a large company through a guaranteed internship, FSC's CEO Lecture Series and Executive Mentor program, and an optional international field experience. Graduates of the Florida Southern M.B.A. program understand the challenges and complexities of today's global business environment and are well-prepared for a successful career.

THE GEORGE WASHINGTON UNIVERSITY

School of Business

THE GEORGE
WASHINGTON
UNIVERSITY
WASHINGTON DC

Programs of Study

In 2008, The George Washington University School of Business (GWSB) launched a unique and innovative M.B.A. curriculum developed around core values of ethics, corporate responsibility, sustainability, globalization, and entrepreneurial leadership. GWSB's commitment and mission is to educate and prepare global leaders with integrity. Innovation, integration, team teaching, elective opportunities, project-based residencies, and international partnerships provide for an inspirational and engaging educational experience.

The full-time Global M.B.A. program (57 credit hours) is designed with a first-year cohort experience structured to promote teamwork; it provides opportunities to approach problems and issues across the curriculum and is enhanced by a series of curricular activities that are designed to support and expand upon classroom concepts. An international practicum and a capstone course, designed to integrate the M.B.A. courses, are also required. Students may pursue any of sixteen areas of interest (accounting; finance and investments; health services administration; environmental policy and management; human resources management; decision sciences and operations management; information systems management; international business; management of science, technology, and innovation; marketing; organizational behavior and development; real estate and urban development; small business and entrepreneurship; strategic management and public policy; sport management; and tourism and hospitality management). Electives provide flexibility and opportunities for additional depth and breadth.

There are a number of options for students whose lives do not permit full-time study. The Professional Accelerated M.B.A. program provides a fast-paced cohort option for employed students. Students attend this program (52.5 credits) on a year-round basis, and this option includes an opening residency as well as applied and integrated projects. The Professional Flex M.B.A. program (also 52.5 credits) permits enrollment in any combination of semesters and at any credit load as long as the program is completed in five years. Electives, which constitute a third of the program, help students position themselves for immediate and long-range opportunities. The Executive M.B.A. program, a 56-hour, twenty-one month cohort program, is designed for middle- and senior-level managers who seek an intensive program to enhance their career development. The program consists of courses taught on alternating Fridays and Saturdays, plus three residencies, including a multicity international experience. The curriculum emphasis is on strategic leadership in a complex world. The Healthcare M.B.A. is an interactive online program. The program is structured for students to complete 52.5 credits hours within two years. Students complete twenty-three core courses and have the freedom to choose from electives that meet their professional and personal goals. Students in the program include a wide variety of professionals with health-care backgrounds, as well as those with diverse undergraduate and graduate educational backgrounds. Over 60 percent of the students in the program are board-certified health-care professionals.

Through a special credit-hour transfer arrangement between the School of Business and GW's School of Law, students can complete both the M.B.A. and J.D. degrees within four years. Also, students may pursue degrees in the School of Business and GW's Elliott School of International Affairs simultaneously, receiving the M.B.A. and M.A. in two to three years. In addition, the School of Business offers a joint M.B.A./M.S.F. in Finance.

In addition to the M.B.A., the GW School of Business offers a Master of Accountancy, Master of Science in Finance (M.S.F.), Master of Science in Information Systems Technology (M.S.I.S.T.), Master of Science in Project Management (M.S.P.M.), and Master of Tourism Administration (M.T.A.). The Ph.D. is offered in accountancy, decision sciences, finance, information systems and technology management, international business, management, marketing, strategic management and public policy, and tourism and hospitality.

With students from all continents except Antarctica, GW offers a culturally diverse environment for learning about life and business around the world. Core courses in the M.B.A. programs include Global Perspectives and International Management, but the concept of international business is interwoven throughout the curriculum. For students who choose to study abroad or participate in exchanges, programs have been established in Europe, Asia, and Latin America.

Research Facilities

GW offers many opportunities for students to participate in research topics that interest them. Some of these include the Institute for Corporate Responsibility (ICR), the Center for International Business Education and Research (GW-CIBER), the Center for Latin American Issues (CLAI), the Institute of Brazilian Issues (IBI), the Center for Real Estate and Urban Analysis, the Financial Services Research Program (FSRP), the European Union Research Center (EURC), the Global and Entrepreneurial Finance Research Institute (GEFRI), the GW Women's Leadership Institute (WLI), the International Institute of Tourism Studies (IITS); and the Institute for Integrating Statistics in Decision Sciences (ISDS).

Financial Aid

A number of graduate fellowships and scholarships are available and are awarded based on academic merit. To be considered for University fellowships, applicants must complete the admissions application process no later than January 14. The School of Business also has scholarships to offer; applicants should apply early to enhance their chances. Additional aid sources are available at http://business.gwu.edu/.

Cost of Study

Tuition for academic year 2010–11 is $1250 per credit hour, including University fees. The application fee was $60. Full-time students normally take 15–18 credits per semester during the first year and 12–15 during the second year. Part-time students generally register for 6–9 credit hours per semester. Books, supplies, and health insurance cost approximately $2500 per year. Estimated costs for room, board, and miscellaneous personal expenses total about $18,000 per academic year.

Living and Housing Costs

University housing is not generally available to graduate students. Information on off-campus housing is available through the Office of Campus Life. The cost of living in the Washington area is comparable to that of other major metropolitan areas.

Student Group

GW M.B.A. students are intellectually mature people who have exhibited a strong potential for management and leadership. The average student is 27 years old. Of the M.B.A. students, 44 percent are women, 9 percent are members of U.S. minority groups, and 27 percent are international students. More than 90 percent of GW M.B.A. students possess substantial business experience before beginning their graduate work. They come from domestic and foreign corporations, family-owned companies, nonprofit organizations, private practices, and the arts.

Student Outcomes

Students of the School of Business develop an extraordinary loyalty to their alma mater, as evidenced by more than 30,000 alumni in the fifty states and seventy countries. This extensive network is the key to helping graduating students establish contacts in the area in which they plan to settle. Through the mentor program, alumni offer guidance in their various areas of expertise, serve on panels to help students make intelligent career decisions, and evaluate students' performance in workshops and case studies.

Location

Located five blocks from the White House, bordering the World Bank and U.S. State Department in the historic Foggy Bottom area of northwest Washington, The George Washington University is an integral part of the city. Modern and efficient public transportation makes it easy to participate in the exciting life of the capital city.

One of the most exciting cities in the world, Washington, D.C., is a global center of power and influence. Courses and faculty members provide opportunities for access to, and the development of, insider perspectives. Living in Washington means enjoying the beauty of four seasons and being in the midst of a region filled with historic sites and natural beauty. Attracting interesting people from all over the world, Washington boasts the highest percentage of college graduates of any metropolitan area in the country. In addition to a wide array of Fortune 500 companies and technology-based industries, the area provides a wealth of cultural and recreational attractions that few cities can match.

The School

The George Washington University, chartered by Congress in 1821, is private and nonsectarian. It holds regional accreditation from the Middle States Association of Colleges and Schools and has received professional recognition for specific programs. Diversified offerings at all levels of the University associate it with the people and activities of many organizations that are exclusive to the Washington area.

Applying

The School of Business seeks candidates who have demonstrated potential for management and who have the intellectual ability, maturity, initiative, and creativity to fully participate in the challenging interdisciplinary environment. Applicants must have a bachelor's degree from a regionally accredited college or university. Selection is based upon the applicant's academic record, work experience, statement of purpose, recommendations, and scores on the required Graduate Management Admission Test (GMAT).

Applications from international students are welcome. Proficiency in reading, writing, and speaking English must be demonstrated by all students from countries where English is not an official language. International students must also submit certified English translations of all academic records of course work corresponding to a bachelor's degree in the United States; scores for the Test of English as a Foreign Language (TOEFL), with a total score of 100 or higher (Internet-based) or a score of 7.0 or higher on the International English Language Testing System (IELTS); and a financial certificate, which is required of any applicant who plans to enter or remain in the United States to study and whose immigration status will be either F-1 (student) or J-1 (exchange visitor).

The full-time Global M.B.A. program accepts applications only for fall of each year and the final deadline to submit the application is April 30. The part-time Professional M.B.A. program admits students in both the fall and spring semesters (Accelerated is fall only). The deadlines are June 1 for fall and November 15 for spring.

Correspondence and Information

Judith Stockmon, Executive Director of Admissions
M.B.A. Programs
School of Business
The George Washington University
2201 G Street NW, Suite 550
Washington, D.C. 20052
Phone: 202-994-1212
Fax: 202-994-3571
E-mail: gwmba@gwu.edu
Web site: http://business.gwu.edu/grad/

The George Washington University

THE FACULTY

The GW School of Business has world-class faculty (over 125 strong) who are leaders in their fields, innovators in emerging professions, and pioneers in scholarship. A commitment to excellence in learning is further strengthened by the Business School's location in Washington, D.C., where it draws on the knowledge of skilled practitioners in finance, business-government relations, and international business. These professionals share their experiences with students in the classroom as guest speakers and adjunct faculty members.

Hossein G. Askari, Aryamehr Professor of International Business; Ph.D., MIT.
Philippe Delquie, Associate Professor of Decision Sciences; Ph.D., MIT.
Robert F. Dyer, Professor of Marketing; D.B.A., Maryland.
Ernie Englander, Associate Professor of Strategic Management and Public Policy; Ph.D., Washington (Seattle).
Timothy Fort, Lindner-Gambal Professor of Business Ethics; Ph.D., Northwestern.
Jennifer Griffin, Associate Professor of Strategic Management and Public Policy; D.B.A., Boston University.
William C. Handorf, Professor of Finance; Ph.D., Michigan State.
Stephen Hansen, Assistant Professor of Accountancy; Ph.D., Carnegie Mellon.
Susan L. Kulp, Assistant Professor of Accountancy; Ph.D., Stanford.
Tjai M. Nielsen, Assistant Professor of Management; Ph.D., Tennessee.
Srinivas Y. Prasad, Associate Professor of Decision Sciences; Ph.D., SUNY at Buffalo.
Liesl Anna Riddle, Associate Professor of International Business and International Affairs; Ph.D., Texas at Austin.
Larry G. Singleton, Associate Dean of Undergraduate Programs and Associate Professor of Accountancy; Ph.D., LSU.
Murat Tarimcilar, Associate Dean of Graduate Programs and Professor of Decision Sciences; Ph.D., LSU.
Robert Weiner, Professor of International Business and International Affairs; Ph.D., Harvard.
Erik K. Winslow, Professor of Management; Ph.D., Case Western Reserve.

HAWAI'I PACIFIC UNIVERSITY

College of Business Administration

Programs of Study

Hawai'i Pacific University (HPU), an established institution with leading programs in business administration, information systems, and management, offers a comprehensive Master of Business Administration (M.B.A.) degree program. This program is noted for several distinctive features. First, it is pragmatic, emphasizing real-world applications, case studies, and specific skills and competencies needed in contemporary business. Second, most courses include both an entrepreneurial and an international perspective. Third, computer applications are integrated into many of the M.B.A. courses. Fourth, interpersonal and communication skills are stressed throughout the curriculum. Fifth, as a major partner in the downtown business community, Hawai'i Pacific University coordinates a large internship program that provides part-time and full-time managerial, technical, and professional positions in leading business firms. Through this internship program, M.B.A. candidates have the opportunity to supplement their income while earning academic credit.

The M.B.A. program at Hawai'i Pacific University requires 42 semester hours of graduate work. Prerequisite courses in business subjects may be required. The curriculum is organized into eight core courses (24 semester hours), three College of Business seminars (3 semester hours), three elective courses (9 semester hours), and two capstone courses (6 semester hours). Students may concentrate in any one of twelve business areas, including accounting, e-business, economics, finance, health-care management, human resource management, information systems, international business, management, marketing, organizational change, and travel industry management. The M.B.A. program is also available completely online, with the same high quality curriculum as the classroom format. There is a complete set of online courses for five of the twelve M.B.A. concentrations. For more information, prospective students may visit http://online.hpu.edu.

The University also offers an M.A. in global leadership and sustainable development, which is designed for the exceptional student whose background, education, and worldview have inspired an interest in assuming leadership positions in the global community. In addition, the M.A. in organizational change examines the models and strategies for leading change, continuous improvement, and performance management. Courses include organizational change and development, national and community change and development, culture and human organization, and organizational behavior.

Research Facilities

To support graduate studies, HPU's Meader and Atherton libraries offer over 110,000 bound volumes, 350,000 microfiche items, and periodical subscriptions to 1,500 print titles and 30,000 electronic journals. Databases of public and state university libraries, legislative information, and business-oriented statistical data are also available in the library or online. Students can access HPU's library databases, course information, their academic information, and an e-mail account through Pipeline, the University's internal Web site for students. The University's accessible on-campus computer center houses more than 100 computers with specialized software to support graduate academic programs. HPU also provides free Wi-Fi so students have wireless access to Pipeline resources anywhere on campus. A significant number of online courses are available as well.

Financial Aid

The University participates in all federal financial aid programs designated for graduate students. These programs provide aid in the form of subsidized (need-based) and unsubsidized (non-need-based) Federal Stafford Student Loans. Through these loans, funds may be available to cover a student's entire cost of education. To apply for aid, students must submit the Free Application for Federal Student Aid (FAFSA) beginning January 1. Mailing of student award letters usually begins by the end of March. The University also offers several types of institutional graduate scholarships to new full-time, degree-seeking students. The Graduate Trustee Scholarship provides $6000 for two semesters, the Graduate Dean Scholarship provides $4000 for two semesters, and the Graduate Kokua Scholarship provides $2000 for two semesters. Priority consideration is given to those students who apply by the deadline.

Cost of Study

Tuition for graduate students enrolled in fall and spring semesters is determined on a per-credit basis; full-time status for a graduate student is 9 credits. Tuition for the optional winter and summer sessions is also determined on a per-credit basis. The estimated minimum funds needed for a nine-month academic year (September to May), based on 2010–11 school year expenses is $26,639. For the 2010–11 academic year, full-time tuition is $12,780 for the M.B.A. program while books, supplies, and transportation cost $1885, and health insurance costs $880.

Living and Housing Costs

Most graduate students live in off-campus housing. The cost of living in off-campus apartments is approximately $11,094 for a double-occupancy room.

Student Group

University enrollment currently stands at more than 8,000, including more than 1,200 graduate students. All fifty states and more than 100 countries are represented.

Location

Hawai'i Pacific combines the excitement of an urban, downtown campus with the serenity of a residential campus. The main campus is ideally located in downtown Honolulu, the business and financial center of the Pacific. The downtown campus comprises six buildings in the center of Honolulu's business district and is home to the College of Business Administration and the College of Humanities and Social Sciences. Eight miles away, situated on 135 acres in Kaneohe, the windward Hawai'i Loa campus is the site of the College of Nursing and Health Sciences and the College of Natural and Computational Sciences. HPU is affiliated with the Oceanic Institute, an applied aquaculture research facility located on a 56-acre site at Makapu'u Point on the windward coast of Oahu, Hawaii. Students can conveniently travel between the three sites using the HPU shuttle service. There are also eight military campus programs located at Pearl Harbor, Barbers Point, Hickam Air Force Base, Schofield Barracks, Fort Shafter, Tripler Army Medical Center, Kaneohe Marine Corps Air Station, and Camp Smith.

The University

Hawai'i Pacific University is a private, nonprofit university with approximately 8,200 students. Founded in 1965, HPU prides itself on maintaining strong academic programs, small class sizes, individual attention to students, and a diverse faculty and student population. HPU is recognized as a "Best in the West" college by Princeton Review and a "Best Buy" by *Barron's* business magazine. HPU offers more than fifty acclaimed undergraduate programs and thirteen distinguished graduate programs. The University has a faculty of more than 500, a student-faculty ratio of 15:1, and an average class size of fewer than 20 students. A wide range of counseling and other student support services are available. There are more than seventy student organizations on campus, including the Graduate Student Organization.

Applying

Hawai'i Pacific University seeks students with academic promise, outstanding career potential, and high motivation. Applicants should complete and forward a graduate admissions application form, have official transcripts sent from all colleges or universities previously attended, have two letters of recommendation forwarded, and submit GMAT results (M.B.A. applicants). International applicants should submit scores from a recognized English proficiency test such as TOEFL. Admissions decisions are made on a rolling basis, and applicants are notified between one and two weeks after all documents have been submitted. Applicants to Hawai'i Pacific University's graduate program are encouraged to submit applications online at http://www.hpu.edu/mba.

Correspondence and Information

Graduate Admissions
Hawai'i Pacific University
1164 Bishop Street, #911
Honolulu, Hawaii 96813

Phone: 808-544-1135
     866-GRAD-HPU (toll-free)
Fax: 808-544-0280
E-mail: graduate@hpu.edu
Web site: http://www.hpu.edu/hawaiimba

Hawai'i Pacific University

THE FACULTY AND THEIR RESEARCH

Leinaala Ahu-Isa, Assistant Professor of Management; Ed.D., Hawai'i at Manoa.
Michelle Alarcon-Catt, Assistant Professor of Management; M.B.A., Pepperdine.
Randall Chang, Assistant Professor of Economics; Ph.D., Claremont.
Justin Gukhyun Cho, Associate Professor of Management; Ph.D., MIT.
Bee-Leng Chua, Associate Professor of Management; Ph.D., Ohio.
Eric Drabkin, Affiliate Associate Professor of Economics; Ph.D., UCLA.
Susan Fox-Wolfgramm, Professor of Management; Ph.D., Texas Tech.
Joseph Ha, Associate Professor of Marketing; Ph.D., Rutgers.
Mark Lane, Associate Professor of Finance; Ph.D., Missouri–Columbia.
Leroy Laney, Professor of Finance and Economics; Ph.D., Colorado at Boulder.
Aytun Ozturk, Associate Professor of Quantitative Methods; Ph.D., Pittsburgh.
Joseph D. Patoskie, Associate Professor of Travel Industry Management; Ph.D., Texas Tech.
Lawrence Rowland, Assistant Professor of Information Systems; Ed.D., USC.
Min Min Thaw, Assistant Professor of Economics; M.A., Hawaii at Manoa.
Niti Villinger, Associate Professor of Management; Ph.D., Cambridge.
Warren Wee, Associate Professor of Accounting; Ph.D., Hawai'i at Manoa.

IONA COLLEGE

Hagan School of Business

Programs of Study

The Hagan School of Business offers classes leading to the Master of Business Administration (M.B.A.) degree as well as advanced certificates and the Post-Master's Certificate (PMC) in business administration.

The programs are designed to meet the needs of both full-time and part-time students and are organized on a trimester basis during the academic year, September to May. Two summer sessions are also available in June and July.

The goal of the M.B.A. program is to prepare students for management careers in business and other organizations. Effective managers must know themselves, work in teams, lead organizational change, and understand the macro factors affecting the future. They must also appreciate the role of information technology, ethically and socially responsible decision making, and the globalization of business. The School's concentrations in accounting, financial management, health-care management, human resource management, information systems management, management, and marketing provide solid knowledge in a specific functional area of business. Required course work consists of 27 credits in the core curriculum and 30 credits in the major and related fields. Waivers are possible out of the core curriculum if certain criteria are met. Students must complete at least 33 credits of graduate work at Iona. The M.B.A. program is offered at the main campus at New Rochelle and the Rockland Graduate Center in Pearl River, New York.

The program also offers certificate options in business continuity and risk management, e-commerce, general accounting, health-care management, infrastructure management, international business, long-term care services management, public accounting, and sports and entertainment studies, which can be completed concurrently with the M.B.A. curriculum. A minimum of 15 credits is required to earn the New York State–approved certificate.

Research Facilities

The newly expanded and renovated main campus library opened in fall 2009. This transformed facility provides traditional library space, a multimedia seminar room, group study rooms, and a digital archive room. The library is also equipped with fifty-two dual-boot iMacs that can run both Microsoft Windows and the latest Mac OS, making Iona one of a handful of colleges to invest in the cutting-edge technology. Iona College features fully wireless facilities offering students high-speed access to the Internet and possesses more than 700 networked computers and two fully networked computer labs located at Iona's Graduate Center in Rockland County. Computer lab assistants are available to help students with their questions, and one lab stays open 24 hours a day, seven days a week.

Financial Aid

Tuition scholarships based on exceptional GMAT scores are available. Loans are provided through the Federal Stafford Student Loan program. Employment opportunities are also available on campus and at local corporate businesses.

Cost of Study

Tuition for 2010–11 is $830 per credit. The initial application fee is $50. An $80 registration fee is charged for the summer sessions. Other charges depend on the course of study.

Living and Housing Costs

While Iona does not offer on-campus graduate housing, the Office of Off-Campus Housing provides information about living off campus, estimated apartment costs, and contact information for student-friendly real estate agents.

Student Group

There are approximately 350 students enrolled in the M.B.A. program; 85 percent are part-time students.

Location

The main campus is located in New Rochelle, a suburban community in Westchester County, 20 minutes north of Manhattan. All degree programs are offered on this site. A branch campus is located in Rockland County. Major highways and public transportation connect both campuses with the cultural and business centers of the Greater New York metropolitan area.

The College

Founded in 1940, Iona is a private coeducational institution with a total enrollment of 3,200 students, of whom 900 study at the graduate level. The Hagan School of Business was instituted in 1965.

Applying

Candidates may enter the graduate program in the fall (September), winter (November), or spring (March) trimester and summer sessions. The completed application, with fee, must be supported by official transcripts from each institution of higher education attended, a resume, two letters of recommendation, and Graduate Management Admission Test (GMAT) scores. All required documents should be received no later than two weeks prior to the start of the trimester or summer session for which the candidate is applying.

Correspondence and Information

Director of Admissions
Hagan School of Business
Iona College
New Rochelle, New York 10801
Phone: 914-633-2288
Fax: 914-633-2012
Web site: http://www.iona.edu/hagan

Iona College

DEPARTMENT AND PROGRAM HEADS

Accounting: Robert Strittmatter, Associate Professor and Chair; M.B.A., NYU; CPA.
Finance, Business Economics and Legal Studies: Anand Shetty, Professor and Chair; Ph.D., Pittsburgh.
Health-Care Management: Mary Helen McSweeney-Feld, Associate Professor and Chair; Ph.D., CUNY Graduate Center.
Information Systems: Robert Richardson, Associate Professor and Chair; Ph.D., Pittsburgh.
Management/Business Administration: Fredrica Rudell, Associate Professor and Acting Chair; Ph.D., Columbia.
Marketing/International Business: Fredrica Rudell, Associate Professor and Chair; Ph.D., Columbia.

ST. JOSEPH'S COLLEGE, NEW YORK

Programs in Business

Programs of Study

The Graduate Management Programs at St. Joseph's College (SJC) were designed around two interrelated concepts—developing specific abilities needed for success in the workplace and relating theoretical knowledge to the real world. Consonant with the values espoused in the mission and goals of the College, the programs support ethical behavior and social responsibility as a foundation of managerial practice. The curricula encourage a proactive perspective relative to the challenges and opportunities inherent in promoting diversity in the workplace.

Designed for working adults holding leadership positions in the public service, private, and nonprofit sectors, the graduate management programs promote managerial effectiveness and the enhancement of human performance in organizations. Students select from degree options and specialties that bolster their marketability in their chosen field. Choices include an Executive Master of Business Administration (E.M.B.A.), which is also available online; an M.B.A. in accounting; an M.B.A. in health-care management; or a Master of Science in Management with a specialization in organizational management, health-care management, or human resources management. Each program is solidly rooted in groundbreaking research—that is, innovative scholarly investigation into the key distinctions between superior leaders and average performers in the workplace. Based on this research, the programs help students strengthen a variety of abilities, including goal and action management, people management, and analytic reasoning. Students create an individualized plan to target those abilities they wish to develop.

The Self-Directed Managerial Applications Component of each course addresses an appropriate issue, problem, or task within an actual organizational environment. Students learn to apply classroom knowledge and develop one or more managerial-effectiveness abilities. Students are also required to complete a minimum of two projects as participants in management teams.

Certificates in health-care management and human resources management are also offered. These 15-credit programs are designed to provide practitioners with advanced study of current health-care or human resources trends and practices and the latest leadership and management tools necessary to advance their careers.

Research Facilities

The Callahan Library at the Long Island Campus is a modern, 25,000-square-foot, freestanding facility with seating for more than 300 readers. A curriculum library, seminar rooms, administrative offices, and two classrooms are housed in this building. Holdings include more than 105,000 volumes and 307 periodical titles, and they are supplemented by videos and other instructional aids. Patrons have access to the Internet and to several online academic databases. A fully automated library system, Endeavor, ensures the efficient retrieval and management of all library resources. Other resources include the library at St. Joseph's Brooklyn Campus, with more than 109,000 volumes, and membership in the Long Island Library Resources Council, which facilitates cooperative associations with the academic and special libraries on Long Island. Internet access, subscriptions to several online full-text databases, and membership in the international bibliographic utility, OCLC, allow almost limitless access to available information.

McEntegart Hall is a fully air-conditioned five-level structure. Three spacious reading areas with a capacity for 300 readers, including individual study carrels and shelf space for 200,000 volumes, provide an excellent environment for research. In addition, McEntegart Hall houses the college archives, a curriculum library, three computer laboratories, a nursing education laboratory, and a videoconference room. There are eight classrooms, a chapel, cafeteria, and faculty and student lounges.

A high-speed fiber-optic intracampus network connects all offices, instructional facilities, computer laboratories, and libraries on both the Brooklyn and Long Island campuses. The network provides Internet access to all students and faculty and staff members. An integrated online library system enables students to search for and check out books at either campus. Online databases and other electronic resources are available to students from either campus or from their home computers. Two wireless laptop classrooms with "smart classroom" features provide flexible instruction spaces with the latest technologies. Videoconferencing facilities connect the two campuses, allowing for real-time distance learning in a small-group setting.

Financial Aid

Financial aid is available in the form of federal and private loans and scholarships. Students should contact the Financial Aid Office for more information (Brooklyn Campus, telephone: 718-940-5700; Long Island Campus, telephone: 631-687-2600).

Cost of Study

In 2010–11, tuition is $650 per credit. Per semester, the college and technology fees for 12 or more credits totaled $200.

Living and Housing Costs

On-campus housing is not available. The St. George Hotel, New York's number-one resource for student housing, and St. Joseph's College have partnered to offer off-campus housing. Accommodations include cable TV, high-speed access, a completely furnished bedroom, a full bath, a closet, a kitchen on each floor, and 24-hour security. Housing applications are available online.

Student Group

The total enrollment for all graduate programs on both campuses is 678.

Location

St. Joseph's College has two campuses—the main campus in the residential Clinton Hill section of Brooklyn and the campus in Patchogue, New York. The main campus offers easy access to all transit lines; to the Long Island Expressway; to all bridges in Brooklyn, Manhattan, and Queens; and to the Verrazano-Narrows Bridge to Staten Island. Within the space of half an hour, students leaving St. Joseph's College may find themselves in the Metropolitan Museum of Art, the 42nd Street Library, Carnegie Hall and Lincoln Center, the Broadway theater district, Madison Square Garden, or Shea Stadium. The College itself stands in the center of one of the nation's most diversified academic communities, consisting of six colleges and universities within a 2-mile radius of each other. The 27-acre Long Island campus, adjacent to Great Patchogue Lake, is an ideal setting for studying, socializing, and partaking in extracurricular activities. Just off Sunrise Highway, the College is easily accessible from all parts of Long Island.

The College

St. Joseph's College is a fully accredited institution that has been dedicated to providing a diverse population of students in the New York metropolitan area with an affordable education rooted in the liberal arts tradition since 1916. Independent and coeducational, the College provides a strong academic and value-oriented education at the undergraduate and graduate levels. For the eighth year in a row, the 2010 ranking of America's Best Colleges by *U.S. News & World Report* placed St. Joseph's College in the top tier of the Northern Comprehensive Colleges–Bachelor's category.

Applying

All applicants must have a baccalaureate degree from an accredited institution of higher education with an undergraduate grade point average of at least 3.0. In addition, applicants typically are required to be employed in a full-time position and to have substantial work experience involving supervision, program development, specialized training, considerable responsibility, and/or independent judgment. When an applicant's experiential qualifications fall short of the aforementioned criteria, the GMAT is required. Students must submit the completed application; the application fee; official transcripts; a current chronological resume; a completed verification of employment form, with a verification letter outlining designated duties from the current (or previous) employer; and two letters of recommendation. An interview is required.

Correspondence and Information

Brooklyn Campus
St. Joseph's College
245 Clinton Avenue
Brooklyn, New York 11205
Phone: 718-940-5800
E-mail: brooklynap@sjcny.edu
Web site: http://www.sjcny.edu/Academics/Graduate-Programs/
260

Long Island Campus
St. Joseph's College
155 West Roe Boulevard
Patchogue, New York 11772
Phone: 631-687-4501
E-mail: suffolkap@sjcny.edu

St. Joseph's College, New York

THE FACULTY

FULL-TIME FACULTY

James J. Barkocy, Assistant Professor of Business; M.B.A., NYU.
Mary Chance, Assistant Professor of Business and Director of Graduate Management Studies; M.S.T., Long Island; CPA.
Stanley Chu, Accounting; M.B.A., St. John's (New York).
Stanley F. Fox, Associate Professor of Business; Ph.D., Walden.
Eileen White Jahn, Associate Professor of Business; Ph.D., CUNY, Baruch.
William Cotesworth Keller, Associate Professor of Business; Ph.D., Walden.
Robert A. Marose, Associate Professor of Business; Ph.D., Polytechnic.
Robert J. Nobile, Assistant Professor of Business; J.D., St. John's (New York).
Charles J. Pendola, Assistant Professor of Business; J.D., Touro; CPA.
Lauren Grace Pete, Associate Professor of Health Administration; J.D., Yeshiva; Ph.D., CUNY Graduate Center.
Diane Pfadenhauer, Assistant Professor of Business; J.D., St. John's (New York).
John Sardelis, Assistant Professor of Health Administration; Dr.P.H., Columbia.
Robert Seperson, Assistant Professor of Business; M.B.A., Dowling.
John J. Skinnon, Assistant Professor of Accounting; M.S.T., Long Island; CPA.
Richard Torz, Associate Professor of Economics; Ph.D., CUNY Graduate Center.

PRECEPTORS

Sharon Didier, Business; Ph.D., Capella.
Charles Dyon, Business; M.B.A., NYU.
Thomas Horan, Business; M.S., Long Island; CPA.
Marie Losquadro, Associate Dean of the Suffolk Campus, Business; M.S., NYIT.
Jay Zuckerman, Health Administration; M.P.A., SUNY at Albany; M.S., SUNY at Stony Brook.

LECTURERS

Ivo Antoniazzi, Business; Ed.D., Columbia.
Hsien-hung Chiu, Economics; M.A., Fu-Jen Catholic; M.A., SUNY at Stony Brook.
John Furnari, Business; M.A., CUNY, Queens.
Brenda Gill, Business; J.D., Fordham.
Heidi Hayden, Business; M.S., St. Joseph's (New York).
Steven Jarmon, Business; M.A., Denver.
Linda Lombardi, Health Administration; Ph.D., CUNY Graduate Center.
Verina Mathis-Crawford, Business; M.B.A., Pace.
Arthur Rescigno, Business; M.S., Columbia.
M. Par Rostom, Business; M.A, Temple.
Alan Vitters, Business; Ph.D., Utah.
Gail Whelan, Business; M.S., NYIT.

TAYLOR UNIVERSITY

Master of Business Administration Program

Program of Study

Founded in 2003, Taylor University's Master of Business Administration (M.B.A.) program combines online learning with a residential environment. Two convenient locations in Fort Wayne and Indianapolis offer professionals the flexibility to complete the sixteen-month, 36-credit-hour program while maintaining their career. Approximately every other month, students complete M.B.A. residencies where they attend class sessions, business seminars, and discussions from Thursday evening through Saturday afternoon. Course work and Internet-based communication are completed between residencies and include both individual and group projects. Courses emphasize faith-based leadership, global business practices, business development and creativity, and management strategy. Many courses offer learning labs with corporations and nonprofit organizations.

Taylor University has a long history and national reputation for quality Christian liberal arts education. The M.B.A. program is accredited by the Higher Learning Commission, and is a member of the North Central Association of Colleges and Schools (NCA). Experienced graduate business faculty serve as facilitators, resources, coaches, and mentors. The M.B.A. program draws on the rich heritage of Taylor tradition, and emphasizes values and developing relationships. Students receive personalized attention and service, including small cohort sizes, contact with faculty and staff members, professional networking opportunities, and numerous opportunities to create meaningful and enduring relationships with likeminded peers and mentors.

Faith-based leadership is a key component of the Taylor M.B.A. program. This intentional integration of faith and graduate business education transcends class discussions, readings, assignments, and projects. The Taylor M.B.A. is relevant, as students complete projects and assignments related to their career and employment interests.

M.B.A. students also have the opportunity to take a ten-day Global Business Tour in which they visit local businesses and experience another country's culture.

Research Facilities

The Zondervan Library at Taylor University offers students unprecedented tools for discovering information. From the library's online catalog to WorldCat, there is a vast range of resources available online with thousands of journals, magazines, newspapers, books, and recordings available through the library.

Financial Aid

Taylor University graduate students are eligible for the Federal Stafford Loan program. Graduate students can borrow up to the full cost of attendance (tuition and fees, international travel expense, books and materials, and other related expenses) through this program up to the maximum allowed amount of $20,500 per year.

Cost of Study

For the 2010–11 academic year, full-time tuition is $415 per credit hour with a course fee of $170 per course/per term (fixed). Estimated cost of the Global Business Study Tour is $3950 (cost is estimated until arrangements are finalized).

Living and Housing Costs

Due to the nature of the Taylor M.B.A. program, graduate students are responsible for their own housing accommodations.

Student Group

In the 2009–10 academic year, Taylor's overall enrollment was more than 2,500. There were 61 students in the M.B.A. program.

Location

Taylor University M.B.A. classes are offered in Fort Wayne and Indianapolis. The Indianapolis office is located near the Castleton area on the north side of Indianapolis. The M.B.A. office shares space with several other businesses—these partnerships offer a unique opportunity for projects and coaching, creating a dynamic and fast-paced work environment. The Fort Wayne office is located in the Northeast Indiana Innovation Center, which is dedicated to developing ideas and growing businesses in northeast Indiana. The Innovation Center nurtures technology businesses by developing the venture during start-up, early development, and growth stages. Great opportunities are available for M.B.A. student projects, graduate internships, and full-time employment.

The University

Founded in 1846, Taylor University is an interdenominational liberal arts university of evangelical faith located in Upland, Indiana. In 2010 *U.S. News and World Report's* America's Best Colleges ranked Taylor the number one baccalaureate college in the Midwest. This was Taylor's third straight top ranking following ten straight years of being ranked in the region's top three.

Applying

Applicants should submit the following materials: Application, application fee (personal check made payable to Taylor University), three letters of recommendation from appropriate people sent directly from them to the M.B.A. office, and official transcript(s) from an accredited university or college sent directly from the university or college.

Correspondence and Information

Taylor University
8604 Allisonville Road
Suite 300
Indianapolis, Indiana 46250

Phone: 866-471-6062
E-mail: mba@taylor.edu
Web site: http://www.taylor.edu/mba

Taylor University

THE FACULTY

The Taylor M.B.A. faculty participates in research surrounding the areas of international business, business education, innovation and creativity, management strategy, and organization sustainability. The Taylor M.B.A. faculty engages graduate students in applied research projects that both directly benefit their employers and the broader business community.

School of Management

UNIVERSITY OF CALIFORNIA, LOS ANGELES

UCLA Anderson School of Management
Master of Business Administration Program

Programs of Study

Professional management education at UCLA Anderson School of Management requires rigorous study, creativity and imagination, analytical thinking, problem diagnosis and solution, and teamwork. The UCLA Anderson M.B.A. program is designed for highly motivated, exceptional students and is structured to ensure that each graduate leaves with a leadership-level knowledge of all key management disciplines, as well as the conceptual and analytical frameworks underlying those disciplines. Consisting of three components—the management core, advanced electives, and the applied management research project (formerly management field study)—the curriculum is regularly updated to address the evolving challenges today's business managers must meet.

The management core is a set of ten courses that provides the fundamental knowledge of the major functional fields of management and builds a foundation for advanced study in a variety of areas. The integrated and sequential nature of the management core courses ensures that each successive course builds upon the knowledge gained in prior courses.

Chosen from course offerings in ten curriculum areas and several interdisciplinary areas, advanced electives compose about half of the M.B.A. curriculum. The large number of advanced electives lends great flexibility and diversity to each student's program of study. Because of the program's general management focus, M.B.A. students are not required to declare a major or concentration. Traditional areas of study offered at UCLA Anderson are discipline-based. Students may tailor an individual M.B.A. program that reflects several interdisciplinary areas of study. These include entrepreneurial studies, finance, international business and comparative management, and real estate.

The applied management research project is the capstone requirement of the M.B.A. program and is conducted during the second year of the program. In this project, students integrate and apply their knowledge and skills in a professional setting outside the classroom.

Research Facilities

The UCLA Library System is ranked in the top five among the nation's college and university libraries. While the resources of all UCLA libraries are available to UCLA Anderson students, the collections, online systems, and services available in the School's Rosenfeld Library are of particular value. Holdings include 147,000 volumes; subscriptions to nearly 3,000 journals, periodicals, and newspapers; 445,000 items on microfilm and microfiche; and 85,000 pamphlets including annual reports and working papers from other schools. Research programs and study centers associated with the School and its faculty include the Harold and Pauline Price Center for Entrepreneurial Studies, the Center for International Business Education and Research, the Richard S. Ziman Center for Real Estate, the UCLA Anderson Forecast, the Laurence D. and Lori W. Fink Center for Finance & Investments, and the Center for Management of Enterprise in Media, Entertainment, and Sports.

Financial Aid

All applicants to UCLA Anderson interested in obtaining financial assistance must complete a Free Application for Federal Student Aid (FAFSA) by March 2, regardless of when they are admitted. The FAFSA may be accessed on the Web at http://www.ed.gov/. All admitted full-time students who are U.S. citizens or permanent residents may apply for need-based financial aid. A limited number of research and teaching assistantship positions are also available. Merit-based fellowships for entering students attending UCLA Anderson are awarded by the Anderson Admissions Office based on academic performance and leadership activities as seen in the application for admission. Private student loans are available for all students, including international students.

Cost of Study

For 2010–11, tuition and fees per academic year total $40,985 for California residents and $48,931 for nonresidents. These costs are subject to change.

Living and Housing Costs

Room and board for the 2010–11 academic year are estimated to be $14,040. Books and supplies will be $4900 (including a $2500 laptop computer). These costs are for students living off campus in shared housing. Additional costs may include support of dependents and medical expenses. Married students should expect to budget about $4000 in additional costs from personal resources as financial aid only covers the student's costs.

Student Group

UCLA Anderson has a vibrant student body whose extraordinary intellectual, cultural, social, and athletic energies spill out of the classroom into a plethora of nonacademic activities. The average student is 28 years old, with more than five years of full-time work experience. Women compose 31 percent of the student population, members of minority groups make up 32 percent, and international students make up 31 percent.

Location

Los Angeles is among the world's most vibrant and exciting cities. In addition to being the entertainment capital of the world, businesses in Los Angeles create four times the gross domestic product and diversity of the Silicon Valley. The city is home to Fortune 500 companies and major industries ranging from financial services and health care to manufacturing and aerospace. The city hosts even more small businesses, which are a significant source of U.S. economic growth. Located in Southern California, Los Angeles serves as a gateway to both South America and the Pacific Rim.

UCLA Anderson students enjoy access to extensive cultural and recreational opportunities with museums, sporting events, theaters, and countless other activities offered both on campus and throughout the city. Because the location is such a cultural crossroads, there are always opportunities to engage with people from various backgrounds and points of view. Students benefit from this interaction both professionally and personally, learning as they share cultural traditions with each other.

The School

UCLA Anderson's management education complex is a testament to the School's vision of the growing importance of superior management education. Continuing the School's reputation as a national leader in the use of computing in M.B.A. instruction, the eleven specially designed case study rooms have data ports at each seating station to integrate the instructional program of each faculty member with the School's central computing facility in the Rosenfeld Library.

Applying

Applicants may apply for fall 2011 admission from July 14, 2010 through April 13, 2011. The Admissions Committee begins considering applications in November of each year.

Correspondence and Information

Ms. Mae Jennifer Shores
Assistant Dean and Director of M.B.A. Admissions and Financial Aid
UCLA Anderson School of Management
110 Westwood Plaza, Suite B201
Box 951481
Los Angeles, California 90095-1481
Phone: 310-825-6944
Fax: 310-825-8582
E-mail: mba.admissions@anderson.ucla.edu
Web site: http://www.anderson.ucla.edu/programs/mba/

University of California, Los Angeles

THE FACULTY

Judy D. Olian, Dean and John E. Anderson Chair in Management, UCLA Anderson School of Management; Ph.D. (industrial relations), Wisconsin–Madison.

Accounting

David Aboody, Professor; Ph.D., Berkeley. Shlomo Benartzi, Professor; Ph.D., Cornell. Judson Caskey, Assistant Professor; Ph.D., Michigan. Jane Guerin, Lecturer; J.D., Denver. Gonzalo Freixes, Lecturer; J.D., Loyola Marymount. Carla Hayn, Professor; Ph.D., Michigan. John S. Hughes, Professor and Ernst and Young Chair in Accounting; Ph.D., Purdue. Gordon Klein, J.D., Lecturer. Danny Litt, Lecturer; M.B.A., UCLA. Jing Liu, Associate Professor; Ph.D., Columbia. Bruce L. Miller, Professor; Ph.D., Stanford, Richard Saouma, Assistant Professor; Ph.D., Stanford. Eric Sussman, Lecturer; M.B.A., Stanford. Brett Trueman, Professor and Area Chair; Ph.D., Columbia.

Decisions, Operations, and Technology Management

Reza Ahmadi, Professor; Ph.D., Texas at Austin. Sushil Bikhchandani, Professor and Associate Dean; Ph.D., Stanford. Scott Carr, Assistant Professor; Ph.D., Michigan. Charles Corbett, Associate Professor and Associate Dean; Ph.D., INSEAD. Robert Foster, Adjunct Associate Professor; M.B.A., UCLA. Arthur Geoffrion, Professor; Ph.D., Stanford. Ariella Herman, Senior Lecturer; Ph.D., Paris. Uday S. Karmarkar, Professor and Times Mirror Chair in Management Strategy and Policy; Ph.D., MIT. John Mamer, Professor; Ph.D., Berkeley. Kevin McCardle, Professor; Ph.D., UCLA. Donald Morrison, William E. Leonhard Professor of Management; Ph.D., Stanford. Kumar Rajaram, Professor; Ph.D., Pennsylvania. Guillaume Roels, Assistant Professor; Ph.D., MIT. Rakesh K. Sarin, Professor; Paine Chair in Management, and Faculty Chair; Ph.D., UCLA. Richard Stern, Lecturer; Ph.D., Chicago. Christopher S. Tang, Professor and Edward W. Carter Chair in Business Administration; Ph.D., Yale.

Finance

Theodore Andersen, Associate Professor Emeritus; Ph.D., Wisconsin. Antonio E. Bernardo, Professor; Ph.D., Stanford. Michael J. Brennan, Professor Emeritus; Ph.D., MIT. Bruce Carlin, Assistant Professor; Ph.D., Duke. Stephen Cauley, Lecturer; Ph.D., UCLA. Bhagwan Chowdhry, Professor; Ph.D., Chicago. William Cockrum, Adjunct Professor; M.B.A., Harvard. Stuart Gabriel, Professor; Ph.D., Berkeley. Mark Garmaise, Assistant Professor; Ph.D., Stanford. Robert L. Geske, Associate Professor; Ph.D., Berkeley. Mark S. Grinblatt, Professor; Ph.D., Yale. Jason Hsu, Adjunct Assistant Professor; Ph.D., UCLA. Francis Longstaff, Professor and Allstate Chair of Insurance and Finance; Ph.D., Chicago. Hanno Lustig, Assistant Professor; Ph.D., Stanford. Marc Martos-Vila, Assistant Professor; Ph.D., Princeton. Richard W. Roll, Professor and Japan Alumni Chair in International Finance; Ph.D., Chicago. Pedro Santa-Clara, Professor; Ph.D., INSEAD. Jan Schneider, Assistant Professor; Ph.D., British Columbia. Eduardo S. Schwartz, Professor and California Chair in Real Estate and Land Economics; Ph.D., British Columbia. Avanidhar Subrahmanyam, Professor; Ph.D., UCLA. Geoff Tate, Assistant Professor; Ph.D., Harvard. Walt Torous, Professor; Ph.D., Pennsylvania, J. Fred Weston, Professor Emeritus; Ph.D., Chicago. Bruce Willison, Professor; M.B.A., USC. Liu Yang, Assistant Professor; Ph.D., Maryland.

Global Economics and Management

Antonio Bernardo, Professor; Ph.D., Stanford. Bhagwan Chowdhry, Professor; Ph.D., Chicago. Jeffrey Dubin, Adjunct Professor; Ph.D., MIT. Sebastian Edwards, Professor and Henry Ford II Chair in International Management; Ph.D., Stanford. Mark Garmaise, Assistant Professor; Ph.D., Stanford. Paola Giuliano, Assistant Professor; Ph.D., Berkeley. Jonathan Greenblatt, Lecturer; M.B.A., Northwestern. Edward E. Leamer, Professor and Chauncey J. Medberry Chair in Management; Ph.D., Michigan. Alfred E. Osborne Jr., Professor and Senior Associate Dean; Ph.D., Stanford. Richard W. Roll, Professor and Japan Alumni Chair in International Finance; Ph.D., Chicago. Hans Schollhammer, Professor; D.B.A., Indiana. Robert Spich, Lecturer; Ph.D., Washington (Seattle). Victor Tabbush, Adjunct Professor; Ph.D., UCLA. Nico Voigtlander, Assistant Professor; Ph.D., Universitat Pompea Fabra. Roman Wacziarg, Associate Professor; Ph.D., Harvard.

Human Resources and Organizational Behavior

Corinne Bendersky, Assistant Professor; Ph.D., MIT. Samuel A. Culbert, Professor; Ph.D., UCLA. Christopher L. Erickson, Professor; Ph.D., MIT. Iris Firstenberg, Adjunct Associate Professor; Ph.D., UCLA. Eric G. Flamholtz, Professor; Ph.D., Michigan. Noah Goldstein, Assistant Professor; Ph.D., Arizona State. Sanford M. Jacoby, Professor and Howard Noble Chair in Management; Ph.D., Berkeley. Barbara S. Lawrence, Professor; Ph.D., MIT. David Lewin, Professor; Neil Jacoby Chair in Management, and Senior Associate Dean; Ph.D., UCLA. Fred Massarik, Professor Emeritus; Ph.D., UCLA. Daniel J. B. Mitchell, Professor and Ho-Su Wu Chair in Management; Ph.D., MIT. Judy D. Olian, Dean and John E. Anderson Chair in Management; Ph.D., Wisconsin–Madison. William G. Ouchi, Professor and Sanford and Betty Sigoloff Chair in Corporate Renewal; M.B.A., Stanford; Ph.D., Chicago. Anthony Raia, Professor Emeritus; Ph.D., UCLA. Margaret Shih, Associate Professor; Ph.D., Harvard. John Ullmen, Lecturer; Ph.D., UCLA. Miguel Unzueta, Assistant Professor; Ph.D., Stanford. Maia Young, Assistant Professor; Ph.D., Stanford.

Information Systems

Jason Frand, Adjunct Assistant Professor; Assistant Dean, and Director; Ph.D., UCLA. George Geis, Adjunct Professor; Ph.D., USC. Martin Greenberger, Professor and IBM Chair in Computers and Information Systems; Ph.D., Harvard. Bennet P. Lientz, Professor; Ph.D., Washington (Seattle). R. Clay Sprowls, Professor Emeritus; Ph.D. Chicago. E. Burton Swanson, Professor; Ph.D., Berkeley.

Marketing

Andrew Ainslie, Associate Professor; Ph.D., Chicago. Anand Bodapati, Associate Professor; Ph.D., Stanford. Bart Bronnenberg, Professor; Ph.D., INSEAD. Randolph E. Bucklin, Professor; Ph.D., Stanford. Lee G. Cooper, Professor Emeritus; Ph.D., Illinois. Ely Dahan, Assistant Professor; Ph.D., Stanford. Jeremy Dann, Lecturer; M.B.A., Harvard. Scott Davis, Assistant Professor; Ph.D., Stanford. Aimee Drolet, Associate Professor; Ph.D., Stanford. Dominique M. Hanssens, Professor and Bud Knapp Chair in Management; Ph.D., Purdue. Harold Kassarjian, Professor Emeritus; Ph.D., UCLA. Wendy Liu, Assistant Professor; Ph.D., Stanford. Donald G. Morrison, Professor and William E. Leonhard Chair in Management; Ph.D., Stanford. Carol A. Scott, Professor; Ph.D., Northwestern. Suzanne Shu, Assistant Professor; Ph.D., Chicago. Sanjay Sood, Associate Professor; Ph.D., Stanford. Raphael Thomadsen, Assistant Professor; Ph.D., Stanford. Robert Zeithammer, Assistant Professor; Ph.D., MIT. Shi Zhang, Associate Professor; Ph.D., Columbia and Arizona.

Policy

Sushil Bikhchandani, Professor and Area Chair; Ph.D., Stanford. Michael R. Darby, Professor and Warren C. Cordner Chair in Money and Financial Markets; Ph.D., Chicago. John de Figueiredo, Associate Professor; Ph.D., Berkeley. Craig Fox, Professor; Ph.D., Stanford. Marvin B. Lieberman, Professor; Ph.D., Harvard. Steven A. Lippman, Professor and George W. Robbins Chair in Management; Ph.D., Stanford. John Mamer, Professor; Ph.D., Berkeley. John McDonough, Professor; D.B.A., Harvard. Subramaniam Ramanarayanan, Assistant Professor; Ph.D., Northwestern. Richard P. Rumelt, Professor and Harry and Elsa Kunin Chair in Business and Society; D.B.A., Harvard. Mariko Sakakibara, Associate Professor; Ph.D., Harvard. Jason Snyder, Assistant Professor; Ph.D., Berkeley.

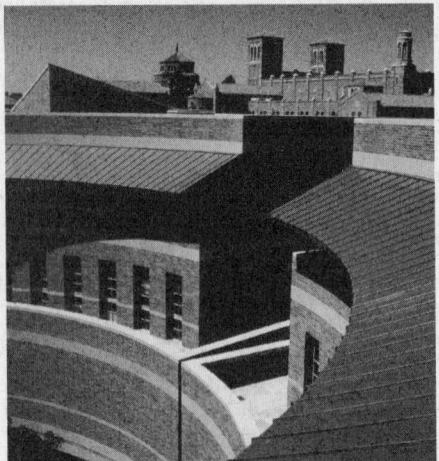

A view of the campus at UCLA.

College of Business
& Administration

UNIVERSITY OF COLORADO AT BOULDER

Master of Business Administration Program

Program of Study

Always be entrepreneurial: Challenge. Create. Act. That's the guiding principle of the Leeds School of Business, at the University of Colorado at Boulder (CU–Boulder). At Leeds, being entrepreneurial is more than a course of study—it's a way to approach business challenges, find solutions, and foster growth. Whatever the student's goal in pursing an M.B.A.—career advancement, a broader skill set, or a career change—Leeds serves as a foundation for professional and personal development. The supportive Leeds community encourages students to embrace an entrepreneurial spirit, create change, and act on new ideas.

The Leeds M.B.A. program is an immersive experience. Two years of rigorous study help develop each student's leadership and management potential and provides the grounding for entrepreneurial ideas. The education, professional network, and career direction established at Leeds can last a lifetime. The flexible curriculum allows students to build a strong portfolio of course work and the M.B.A. can be customized to suit career goals. Opportunities for personal interaction with faculty members, business professionals, successful entrepreneurs, and alumni enable students to expand their professional horizons and put their new knowledge into practice.

The M.B.A. requires 55 credits with a minimum GPA of 3.0 for graduation. The required core courses create a strong foundation in business theory and application (28 credits). In addition to the robust offerings in the functional areas of business—finance, management, marketing, and operations and information management—Leeds also offers niche specializations in entrepreneurship, real estate, or sustainability. The curriculum provides industry expertise and networking opportunities that places students at the leading edge of the area of emphasis.

Dual-degree agreements between the Leeds School of Business and other highly renowned schools and colleges on the CU–Boulder campus offer the opportunity to combine the requirements of two disciplines. With these combined degree programs, both degrees can be earned together in less time than earning them sequentially. Candidates must apply to and meet the application and admissions standards of each program separately. All the dual-degree options offered at the Leeds School require 43 credit hours in the M.B.A. program. When pursuing a dual-degree program the requirements for both degrees must be completed in order to receive either one of them. Leeds' dual-degree options include the J.D./M.B.A. with the School of Law; M.B.A./M.S. degrees in conjunction with computer science, environmental studies, or telecommunications; and M.B.A./M.A. degrees in conjunction with anthropology, fine arts, theater and dance, or Germanic languages.

The Leeds faculty is at the forefront of knowledge creation. With outstanding research records and extensive private sector experience, members of the faculty bring the latest thinking into their classes, along with practical applications of business knowledge. Class projects offer hands-on experience with real companies and enable students to connect with and learn from successful professionals.

Research Facilities

The William M. White Business Library includes research materials for management and administration as well as corporate annual shareholder reports, SEC 10-K reports for Colorado and Fortune 500 companies, and proxy statements for all companies on primary U.S. exchanges. The Douglas H. Buck Electronic Media Center provides access to more than 50 online databases. The Business Research Division conducts research that assists companies, educational institutions, and governmental agencies in making sound business and policy decisions. Its primary competencies are in the areas of manufacturing issues and trends, the impact of government policy, and the impact of technology. The Richard M. Burridge Center for Securities Analysis and Valuation supports the creation and dissemination of new knowledge about the world financial markets, with an emphasis on the U.S. financial markets.

Financial Aid

University of Colorado Foundation fellowships are awarded to incoming M.B.A. students each year. The Robert H. and Beverly A. Deming Center for Entrepreneurship offers fellowships to students who plan to pursue the study of entrepreneurship. The CU Real Estate Center offers fellowships to students who plan to pursue the study of real estate. The Barney Ford Fellowship creates additional support for students of diverse backgrounds. The Leeds School of Business M.B.A. program has also partnered with the National Society of Hispanic M.B.A.s to offer an M.B.A. fellowship for students who meet the necessary requirements. Students may apply for Federal Work-Study, federal grants, and loans. Second-year students who have established high levels of achievement in core courses may qualify for paid teaching assistantships or work in research positions.

Cost of Study

Full-time tuition per year (9 or more credits) for 2010–11 is $14,760 for residents and $27,432 for nonresidents. Students also pay approximately $1500 in required fees each year.

Living and Housing Costs

Most M.B.A. students choose to live off campus. The University estimates ten months of living expenses (rent, utilities, and food) in Boulder totals $8478.

Student Group

In 2010–11, 104 students enrolled in the program (out of 356 applicants). Of these, 32 percent are women and 15 percent come from other countries. They entered the program with an average GMAT score of 631 and an average undergraduate GPA of 3.35. On average, they are 28 years old with 4.4 years of work experience in industries ranging from consulting and engineering to tourism, marketing, and technology.

Student Outcomes

Graduates of the program have found employment in some of the world's largest companies across a wide range of industries; examples include McKinsey & Co, Ernst & Young LLP, IBM, Hitachi Consulting, Horizon Organic Dairy, Celestial Seasonings, MillerCoors, Level 3 Communications, Navigant Consulting, Rally Software, Oracle, NREL, Vestas, Ball Aerospace, CH2M Hill, and Xcel Energy. Leeds' M.B.A. graduates work in all functional areas, across all disciplines.

Location

Boulder is regarded as one of the most desirable places to live in the country, with a mild, dry climate and 300 days of sunshine per year. Denver, Colorado is 25 miles from Boulder. Rocky Mountain National Park is located only 45 miles away, and Eldora Mountain is approximately 20 miles away. Other popular attractions include the Rocky Mountains, the Colorado Shakespeare Festival, and Chautauqua Park Historic District.

The University

Founded in 1876 at the base of the Rocky Mountains, the University of Colorado at Boulder is now one of the most prestigious universities in the nation. More than 29,000 students are enrolled in 165 degree programs and participate in research at ninety research centers, institutes, and laboratories. *U.S. News & World Report* ranked the Deming Center for Entrepreneurship in the top 20, and the school is one of thirty-four U.S. public research universities invited to join the prestigious Association of American Universities.

Applying

Prospective students should submit an online application for admission, official college transcripts, responses to specific essay questions, official GMAT scores, three letters of recommendation, and a $70 application fee. Deadlines for applying to the M.B.A. program are November 15 (for candidates requesting an early decision), January 15 (encouraged for international candidates and applicants requesting fellowship consideration), and April 1 (final application deadline).

Correspondence and Information

Leeds School of Business
UCB 419
University of Colorado at Boulder
Boulder, Colorado 80302
Phone: 303-492-8397
Fax: 303-492-1727
E-mail: LeedsMBA@Colorado.edu
Web site: http://leeds.colorado.edu/mba/

University of Colorado at Boulder

THE FACULTY AND THEIR RESEARCH

David Balkin, Professor of Strategy and Organization Management and Chair, Management Division; Ph.D., Minnesota, 1981. Relationship between pay policies and firm strategy, strategic human resource management, corporate governance.

Sanjai Bhagat, Professor of Finance; Ph.D., Washington (Seattle), 1982. Corporate lawsuits, business valuation, corporate finance, corporate governance, entrepreneurial finance.

R. Wayne Boss, Professor of Strategy and Organizational Management; D.P.A., Georgia, 1973. Organization effectiveness, organization development, consultation skills, organization behavior.

Thomas Buchman, Associate Professor of Accounting; Ph.D., Illinois at Urbana-Champaign, 1976. Financial reporting, financial accounting.

Margaret C. Campbell, Assistant Professor of Marketing; Ph.D., Stanford, 1992. Consumer understanding of persuasion, perceptions of unfairness in prices and marketing, branding, advertising effects.

Calvin Duncan, Associate Professor of Marketing and Chair, Marketing Division; D.B.A., Indiana, 1977. Effects of message structure and content on advertising effectiveness, influence of consumer heuristics on information search and brand/store choice behaviors.

Maw der Foo, Associate Professor of Management; Ph.D., MIT, 1999. Emotion management in organizations, entrepreneurship, opportunity recognition.

Bret Fund, Assistant Professor of Management and Entrepreneurship; Ph.D., Penn State, 2008. Network perspective in the examination of the social capital of founders and venture capitalist in start-up environments.

Susan Jung Grant, Assistant Professor of Marketing; Ph.D., Northwestern, 2002. Effects of contextual factors on consumer information processing, persuasion, judgment and decision making, temporal framing, goal states and motivation, psychology of financial decision making, advertising effects.

Mathew L. A. Hayward, Assistant Professor of Management; Ph.D., Columbia, 1998. Confidence in decision making, media accounts of and effects on organizations, power and learning in organizations.

Alan Jagolinzer, Associate Professor of Accounting; Ph.D., Penn State, 2004. Corporate governance, executive compensation, international accounting standards.

Bjorn Jorgensen, Associate Professor of Accounting; Ph.D., Northwestern, 1999. Risk, measurement, management, control.

Matthias Kahl, Assistant Professor of Finance; Ph.D., Pennsylvania, 1997. Theoretical and empirical corporate finance, mergers and acquisitions, financial distress and bankruptcy, capital structure, financial flexibility.

Laura J. Kornish, Assistant Professor; Ph.D., Stanford, 1998. Sequential decision problems related to innovation and technological change, search for the best alternative, product development, issues at the intersection of operations and marketing, incentives in information revelation.

Manuel Laguna, Interim Dean, Professor of Operations Management Systems, and Chair, Systems Doctoral Programs; Ph.D., Texas at Austin, 1990. Developing models and solution methods for combinatorial optimization problems, interface between operations research and artificial intelligence as applied to heuristic search, model formulation and solution methods for decision problems under uncertainty.

Stephen Lawrence, Associate Professor of Operations Management; Ph.D., Carnegie Mellon, 1988. Technology management, technology adoption, operations scheduling, operations strategy, entrepreneurship.

J. Chris Leach, Associate Professor of Finance; Ph.D., Cornell, 1988. Corporate and venture financing, mergers and acquisitions, structure of securities markets, real options, information economics and game theory.

John Lynch, Professor of Marketing; Ph.D., Illinois, 1979. Consumers' financial decision making, intertemporal choice and saving for retirement, mortgage decisions, propensity to plan, assistive technologies on Internet mediation tests.

Sharon Matusik, Assistant Professor of Management; Ph.D., Washington (Seattle), 1998. Strategic management, firm knowledge and innovation, entrepreneurship innovation, entrepreneurship.

Ronald Melicher, Professor of Finance and Chair, Finance Division; D.B.A., Washington (St. Louis), 1968. Corporate mergers, bankruptcy, and other restructuring; asymmetric information and financial signaling topics; entrepreneurial finance issues.

Ramiro Montealegre, Associate Professor of Information Systems and Chair, Systems Division; D.B.A., Harvard, 1994. Assimilation of information technology, organizational transformation through implementation of information technology, transfer of technology to less developed countries.

Page Moreau, Assistant Professor of Marketing; Ph.D., Columbia, 1998. Consumer learning and knowledge transfer, new-product development and acceptance, creativity, product design.

Nathalie Moyen, Assistant Professor of Finance; Ph.D., British Columbia, 1999. Corporate finance, derivative securities.

Mattias Nilsson, Assistant Professor of Finance; Ph.D., Stockholm School of Economics, 2002. Corporate governance, economics of organizations, international corporate finance.

Liang Peng, Assistant Professor of Finance; Ph.D., Yale, 2002. Real estate economics and finance, venture capital.

Philip Shane, Associate Professor of Accounting; Ph.D., Oregon, 1982. Valuation implications of financial accounting information, stock market efficiency with respect to financial accounting information and the intermediary role of financial analysts, financial reporting quality, corporate social responsibility.

Atanu Sinha, Assistant Professor of Marketing; Ph.D., NYU, 1992. Pricing, auctions, and bundling; loyalty rewards; theoretical and empirical marketing strategy.

Naomi Soderstrom, Associate Professor of Accounting; Ph.D., Northwestern, 1990. Empirical managerial accounting, accounting for environmental costs and health care.

Michael Stutzer, Professor of Finance; Ph.D., Minnesota, 1981. Continuing development of a unified approach to investment, securities valuation, valuation model parameter estimation based on the statistical theory of large deviations.

Thomas Thibodeau, Professor of Finance; Ph.D., SUNY at Stony Brook, 1980. Measuring and modeling spatial and temporal variation in real estate prices, identifying real estate submarket boundaries, real estate investment.

Tony Tong, Assistant Professor of Management; Ph.D., Ohio State, 2004. Alliances, mergers and acquisitions, venture capital, market entry, application of real options theory in strategy, international strategy, strategic entrepreneurship.

Thomas Vossen, Associate Professor of Operations Management and Information Systems; Ph.D., Maryland, 2002. Modeling and analysis of real-time transportation and logistics operations, collaborative decision making in air traffic flow management, hybrid artificial intelligence/integer programming techniques applied to planning and scheduling.

Richard Wobbekind, Associate Professor of Business Economics and Director, Business Research Division. Ph.D., Colorado at Boulder, 1984. Public policy, macroeconomic forecasting, regional economic development, economics of salary arbitration.

Jaime Zender, Associate Professor of Finance; Ph.D., Yale, 1988. Corporate control, corporate finance, financial contracting, auction theory.

School of Business

UNIVERSITY OF CONNECTICUT

School of Business
M.B.A. Program

Program of Study	Educating leaders for over 125 years, the University of Connecticut (UConn) is ranked among the top 5 percent of business schools worldwide, according to *Business Week, Forbes,* and *U.S. News & World Report.*
	UConn's flagship full-time M.B.A. program offers students a practical, comprehensive, and individualized business education that integrates basic business fundamentals, innovative experiential learning, and personal interests. This carefully blended curriculum differentiates UConn M.B.A. graduates and uniquely positions them for career success.
	Essential to UConn's M.B.A. curriculum is the incorporation of innovative experiential learning accelerators, such as the GE/UConn *edgelab,* SS&C Technologies Financial Accelerator, Innovation Accelerator, Student Managed Fund, and Sustainable Community Outreach and Public Engagement (SCOPE) program. These unique practice-based initiatives integrate traditional teaching and classroom experience with high-profile business partnering to close the gap between theory and practice.
	The UConn M.B.A. program also offers a number of international learning opportunities that allow students to participate in a variety of international electives abroad. These one- to two-week courses are typically held in January, May, and during other break periods to minimize conflict with regular semester course work.
	Year One of the program follows a lockstep format in which all students go through the core curriculum together—no exceptions. This ensures the same foundation of knowledge for every UConn M.B.A. student. The first-year core curriculum covers fundamentals across all business disciplines including preterm work on business law and ethics; a multisemester project, the Application of Core Teaching (ACT), the first formal exposure to experiential and integrated learning; and a non-credit seminar series focused on enhancing personal, team, and communication skills for the workplace.
	In the spring of Year One, M.B.A. students develop an Individualized plan of study in consultation with an advisory committee comprised of business school faculty, career counselors, and alumni/experts in the field. A student's individualized plan of study consists of eight courses (24 credits) including a primary area of emphasis, one to two courses (3–6 credits) of experiential learning, and carefully selected electives. Ultimately, the approved plan is a coherent bundle of courses and experiences that best aligns with each student's personal career goals and objectives.
	After fulfilling the summer internship milestone, M.B.A. students continue with Year Two, pursuing the customized plan of study developed and approved in Year One. Most, if not all, second-year course offerings will be delivered in Hartford, Stamford, and/or Waterbury to best coordinate with the experiential learning centers where students will be participating.
	The integration of business fundamentals and experiential learning helps provide the real-world experience that today's global businesses demand.
Research Facilities	UConn M.B.A. students study in state-of-the-art research and learning facilities. Classrooms and meeting spaces are outfitted with broad multimedia capability reflecting the School's commitment to meet the demands of the information era.
	The GE/UConn *edgelab,* a nationally recognized multimillion-dollar, 10,000-square-foot e-lab, offers a superb research facility providing an exceptional learning and applied research experience for M.B.A. students. The SS&C Technologies Financial Accelerator and the Innovation Accelerator also serve as advanced business solution centers in which M.B.A. students, research faculty, and corporate managers jointly investigate and develop solutions to real-world, real-time, complex challenges facing business today.
	The School of Business, the Connecticut Center for Entrepreneurship and Innovation, the Center for Real Estate and Urban Economic Studies, and the Center for Health Care and Insurance Studies provide specialized resources for students at the University of Connecticut.
	The University of Connecticut libraries form the largest public research collection in the state. The collection contains some 3.6 million volumes; 51,000 currently received print and electronic periodicals; 4.3 million units of microform; 15,000 reference sources; 232,000 maps; sound and video recordings; musical scores; and a growing array of electronic resources, including e-books, e-sound recordings, and image databases.
Financial Aid	Although the cost of a UConn M.B.A. is reasonable, candidates often need financial assistance. Financial aid is available in the form of loans and scholarships. Most financial aid is awarded on the basis of established need, primarily determined through an analysis of an applicant's Free Application for Federal Student Aid (FAFSA). The School of Business also offers a limited number of merit-based graduate teaching assistantships. Out-of-state candidates who have demonstrated a high likelihood of success can also benefit from the Tuition Assistance Program. In this program, out-of-state students receive the benefit of paying in-state tuition fees. There are a limited number of these awards, so work experience and GMAT scores are important determinants. For more information, contact the University of Connecticut financial aid office at 860-486-2819 or visit the Web site at http://www.financialaid.uconn.edu.
Cost of Study	Tuition and fees for the 2010–11 academic year (two semesters) for the full-time M.B.A. program at UConn are $11,828 for Connecticut residents and $27,740 for nonresidents. Additional costs, including required health insurance, textbooks, mobile computer, laundry, and incidentals, can add up to an estimated $7500. Fees are subject to change without notice.
Living and Housing Costs	For a nine-month academic year, the approximate cost of living, in addition to tuition and fees, is estimated to be $11,800. Many unmarried students reside in the Graduate Residence in single dormitory rooms. Specific information is available by contacting the Department of Residential Life at http://www.reslife.uconn.edu. A wide variety of off-campus housing is available to students. A visit to the area is recommended for all students interested in finding off-campus housing.
Student Group	UConn M.B.A. students come from a wide variety of undergraduate institutions, both domestic and international. Their undergraduate degrees represent majors in many diverse areas—from engineering and English, sciences and fine arts, to business to economics. In a typical class of students, 40 percent are women, the average age is 28, and approximately 30 percent are international students. Friendliness and informality characterize student life at the main campus. Social and professional organizations, including the Graduate Business Association (GBA), offer a variety of activities to satisfy the needs of students.
Student Outcomes	UConn's career-planning activities begin during orientation and continue throughout the M.B.A. Primary recruiters include General Electric, CIGNA, Aetna, IBM, United Technologies Corp., Wachovia, Hartford Financial Services, PricewaterhouseCoopers, Gerber Technologies, ESPN, and UBS. For the class of 2009, the median salary was $94,000 with a median sign-on bonus of $14,740.
Location	The University's span of more than 4,300 acres includes ten schools and colleges at its main campus in Storrs, separate schools of law and social work in Hartford, five regional campuses throughout the state, and schools of medicine and dental medicine at the UConn Health Center in Farmington. Right in the middle of Fortune 500 territory, the state capital and metropolitan area of Hartford is 30 minutes away, Boston is a 90-minute drive, and New York City is a 3-hour drive.
The University and The School	UConn has grown in recent years from a strong regional school to a prominent national academic institution with over 29,000 students and 190,000 alumni. The UConn School of Business is nationally accredited by AACSB International and is a member of the Graduate Management Admissions Council (GMAC) and the European Foundation for Management Development (EFMD). UConn is also accredited by the New England Association of Schools and Colleges (NEASC).
Applying	Admission to UConn's M.B.A. program is very competitive. The minimum requirements for admission include two years of postgraduate professional work experience; a minimum 3.0 GPA on a 4.0 scale, or the equivalent, from a four-year accredited institution; and a total GMAT score of at least 560. For international students whose native language is not English, a TOEFL score of at least 233 (computer-based) is required. The application deadline for international applicants is February 1. For domestic applicants the deadline is March 1.
Correspondence and Information	For the master's program: Full-Time M.B.A. Director, Storrs School of Business University of Connecticut 2100 Hillside Road, Unit 1041 Storrs, Connecticut 06269-1041 Phone: 860-486-2872 Fax: 860-486-5222 E-mail: UConnMBA@business.uconn.edu Web site: http://mba.uconn.edu	For the Ph.D. program: Ph.D. Director School of Business University of Connecticut 2100 Hillside Road, Unit 1041 Storrs, Connecticut 06269-1041 Phone: 860-486-5822 Fax: 860-486-0270 E-mail: phdmail@business.uconn.edu Web site: http://www.business.uconn.edu

University of Connecticut

THE FACULTY

Accounting
Stanley Biggs, Ph.D., Minnesota.
Joseph Bittner, M.B.A., Connecticut.
Wayne Bragg, M.B.A., Connecticut.
Amy Dunbar, Ph.D., Texas at Austin.
Larry Gramling, Ph.D., Maryland.
Robert Hoskin, Ph.D., Cornell.
Richard Hurley, Ph.D., Connecticut.
Mohamed E. Hussein, Ph.D., Pittsburgh.
Alfred Zhu Liu, Ph.D., California, Irvine.
Brent McCallum, M.S., American.
Cliff Nelson, D.B.A., Illinois.
Jose Oaks, M.B.A., NYU.
David Papandria, B.S., Marian (Indianapolis); CPA.
John Phillips, Ph.D., Iowa.
George Plesko, Ph.D., Wisconsin–Madison.
Paul A. Ramunni, M.S.A., LIU.
Michael Redemske, M.S., DePaul.
Sarah Rice, Ph.D., Ohio State.
Andrew Rosman, Ph.D., North Carolina at Chapel Hill.
Gim Seow, Ph.D., Oregon.
David Weber, Ph.D., Colorado at Boulder.
Michael Willenborg, Ph.D., Penn State.

Finance
Kathleen Bailey, J.D., Connecticut.
Walter Dolde, Ph.D., Yale.
Assaf Eisdorfer, Ph.D., Rochester.
Chinmoy Ghosh, Ph.D., Penn State.
Carmelo Giaccotto, Ph.D., Kentucky.
Paul Gilson, Ph.D., Georgia Tech.
Joseph Golec, Ph.D., Washington (St. Louis).
Shantaram P. Hegde, Ph.D., Massachusetts.
Paul Hsu, Ph.D., Columbia.
Linda S. Klein, Ph.D., Florida State.
John Knopf, Ph.D., NYU.
Jeffrey Kramer, Ph.D., Connecticut.
Norman Moore, Ph.D., Florida State.
Thomas O'Brien, Ph.D., Florida.
James Sfiridis, Ph.D., Connecticut.
Rexford Santerre, Ph.D., Connecticut.

Management
T. Lane Barrow, M.A., Harvard.
Qing Cao, Ph.D., Maryland.
Kathleen Dechant, Ed.D., Columbia.
Dimo Dimov, Ph.D., London.
Richard Dino, Ph.D., SUNY at Buffalo.
P. Christopher Earley, Ph.D., Illinois at Urbana-Champaign
Lucy Gilson, Ph.D., Georgia Tech.
Jodi Goodman, Ph.D., Georgia Tech.
David Lavoie, Ph.D., Wisconsin.
Michael Lubatkin, D.B.A., Tennessee.
Nora Madjar-Nanovska, Ph.D., Illinois.
John Mathieu, Ph.D., Old Dominion.
Elaine Mosakowski, Ph.D., Berkeley.
Gary Powell, Ph.D., Massachusetts.
Gregory Reilly, Ph.D., Wisconsin.

Jeffrey Roberts, Ph.D., Connecticut.
Eugene Salorio, D.B.A., Harvard.
Zeki Simsek, Ph.D., Connecticut.
David Souder, Ph.D., Minnesota.
Henry Ulrich, Ph.D., Rhode Island.
John F. Veiga, D.B.A., Kent State.
Luke Weinstein, Ph.D., Connecticut.

Marketing and Business Law
Robert Bird, J.D., Boston University.
Mary Caravella, D.B.A., Harvard.
Vincent Carrafiello, J.D., Connecticut.
Robin Coulter, Ph.D., Pittsburgh.
Mark DeAngelis, J.D., Suffolk.
Karla Fox, J.D., Duke.
Wynd Harris, Ph.D., Oklahoma.
Subhash C. Jain, Ph.D., Oregon.
Hongju Liu, Ph.D., Chicago.
Kevin McEvoy, M.B.A., Boston College.
Joseph Pancras, Ph.D., NYU.
Charles Peterson, M.B.A., NYU.
Girish Punj, Ph.D., Carnegie Mellon.
Samuel Schrager, J.D., Miami.
Murphy Sewall, Ph.D., Washington (St. Louis).
Susan Spiggle, Ph.D., Connecticut.
Mark Spurling, J.D., Western New England.
Narasimhan Srinivasan, Ph.D., SUNY at Buffalo.

Operations and Information Management
Sulin Ba, Ph.D., Texas at Austin.
Xue Bai, Ph.D., Carnegie Mellon.
S. Bhattacharjee, Ph.D., SUNY at Buffalo.
Fidan Boylu, Ph.D., Florida.
Hsuan-Wei Michelle Chen, Ph.D., Texas at Austin.
John Clapp, Ph.D., Columbia.
Jose Cruz, Ph.D., Massachusetts Amherst.
Robert Day, Ph.D., Maryland, College Park.
Moustapha Diaby, Ph.D., SUNY at Buffalo.
Timothy Dowding, Ph.D., Connecticut.
Robert Garfinkel, Ph.D., Johns Hopkins.
Ram Gopal, Ph.D., SUNY at Buffalo.
John Harding, Ph.D., Berkeley.
Wei-Kuang Huang, Ph.D., Rutgers.
Robert Johnson, Ph.D., Rochester.
Ray Kehrahn, M.B.A., Connecticut.
Cuihong Li, Ph.D., Carnegie Mellon.
Xinxin Li, Ph.D., Pennsylvania.
James Marsden, Ph.D., Purdue.
Suresh Nair, Ph.D., Northwestern.
Manuel Nunez, Ph.D., MIT.
Katherine Pancak, J.D., Boston College.
Ramesh Sankaranarayanan, Ph.D., NYU.
Jan Stallaert, Ph.D., UCLA.
Lakshman Thakur, Eng.Sc.D., Columbia.
Yung-Chin (Alex) Tung, Ph.D., Kentucky.
Zhongju Zhang, Ph.D., Washington (Seattle).
Dmitry Zhdanov, Ph.D., Minnesota, Twin Cities.

UConn provides state-of-the-art experiential learning opportunities through such collaborative initiatives as the SS&C Technologies Financial Accelerator (above).

The University of Connecticut's $27-million School of Business facility opened its doors in 2001.

UNIVERSITY OF DELAWARE

Alfred Lerner College of Business and Economics
Master of Business Administration Programs

Programs of Study

The Alfred Lerner College of Business and Economics offers rigorous programs for superior students leading to the M.B.A. and several dual M.B.A./M.S. degrees. The combination of academically accomplished faculty members, highly qualified students, and ideal location—a small university town in the midst of a large eastern megalopolis—provides the necessary environment for an outstanding experience in graduate business education.

The Delaware M.B.A. program's curriculum includes courses that focus on experiential learning, data-based management, global perspective, and ethical leadership. The College of Business and Economics offers M.B.A. programs that are designed to serve different groups of students. The Professional M.B.A. program is highly flexible and offers students the option to pursue full- or part-time study. Students who attend full-time are exposed to a combination of course work and opportunities to apply their skills in business settings, work with faculty members on research, attend presentations by business leaders, and become involved in volunteer projects to develop the skills required for successful employment after graduation. Full-time students complete the program in twenty-one months. The part-time study option is designed for the adult who is working full-time and needs the flexibility to complete the M.B.A. in three years through a series of courses offered in the evening. All Professional M.B.A. students have the opportunity to select concentrations from a diverse set of alternatives and to participate in special programs such as a condensed study-abroad experience or a dual-degree program. Dual-degree programs include M.B.A./M.S. Information Systems Technology Management, M.B.A./M.S. Organizational Effectiveness Development and Change, M.B.A./ M.A. Economics, M.B.A./M.S. Finance, M.B.A./M.S. Accounting , M.S. Engineering/M.B.A., and Ph.D. Biological Sciences/M.B.A.

The Executive M.B.A. program, designed for senior-level managers with extensive work experience, is offered in lock-step format on Friday evenings and all day Saturdays for nineteen months.

The Lerner M.B.A. programs are highly selective and comparatively small, allowing for a high level of student involvement. The combination of small classroom size, classroom theory, and students' practical experiences creates a stimulating environment for the analysis of today's business world. All programs are accredited by AACSB International–The Association to Advance Collegiate Schools of Business. The University of Delaware is also a long-standing member of the Graduate Management Admissions Council.

Research Facilities

The University library, a modern research facility with more than 2.5 million volumes and 3.3 million microforms, is a member of the Association of Research Libraries and is a depository for U.S. government documents and patents.

All computing at the University is conducted over a high-speed, fiber-optic network connecting all buildings, laboratories, offices, and student housing on campus. Also connected to the network is an array of computing resources ranging from NT servers to supercomputing clusters. The College offers a high-speed network, computing labs, computer classrooms, a variety of NT servers, an SAP environment, multimedia conferencing, and a behavioral research facility.

Financial Aid

Some financial aid packages are available to superior full-time Professional M.B.A. students. These include corporate assistantships, graduate assistantships, and tuition grants, which are awarded on a competitive basis. Awards to first-year students are based on prior academic performance, work experience, and test scores. Awards to second-year students are based on academic performance in the program.

A typical aid package may include a stipend of $7600 per year and/or a 50 percent waiver of tuition. A corporate assistant position provides full tuition remission and a $15,200 stipend per academic year. This requires that the student interns with the corporate partner.

Cost of Study

The 2009–10 yearly tuition for full-time M.B.A. students was $10,462 for Delaware residents and $22,240 for nonresidents. Part-time study was $582 per credit hour for Delaware residents and $1236 per credit hour for nonresident students. Tuition for the Executive M.B.A. program was $65,000.

Living and Housing Costs

Rental costs for shared occupancy in a graduate student complex were $450 per month in 2009–10. University and privately owned apartments, furnished and unfurnished, were available at costs ranging from $500 to $1200 per month.

Student Group

While a minimum GMAT score is not strictly enforced, a score of 550 or above is preferred, and most entering classes typically average 590. The College also prefers to admit students who hold undergraduate GPAs of not less than 2.8. Entering classes for the past several years have an average minimum GPA of 3.0.

Location

The University of Delaware is located in Newark, a suburban community of approximately 30,000. Newark is situated in the northwest corner of Delaware within 3 miles of the Pennsylvania and Maryland borders. It is located within easy driving distance of Philadelphia (45 miles), Baltimore (50 miles), Washington, D.C. (100 miles), and New York City (130 miles). Nearby Wilmington is a major center for credit banking and the chemical industry. More than 50 percent of all Fortune 500 companies are incorporated in Delaware. The College maintains strong ties with the corporate sector. The Wilmington campus is ideal for part-time M.B.A. students whose jobs are located nearby. The Executive M.B.A. program is offered exclusively on the Wilmington campus.

The University and The College

The University of Delaware, founded in 1743 as a small liberal arts school, was moved to Newark, where it became both a land-grant and a sea-grant college. It now ranks among the finest of the nation's medium-sized universities, with approximately 16,000 undergraduate and 4,000 graduate students. Included in the College of Business and Economics are the five Departments of Accounting; Business Administration; Economics; Finance; and Hotel, Restaurant, and Institutional Management. All accounting and business programs are accredited by AACSB International–The Association to Advance Collegiate Schools of Business.

Applying

Students must have two years of full-time professional work experience prior to entering the program and need to submit a resume, official copies of all undergraduate and graduate transcripts, GMAT scores, answers to essay questions, and two letters of recommendation. A personal interview may be scheduled for qualified applicants. All students whose native language is not English must have a minimum score of 100 on the TOEFL or 7.5 on the IELTS. International students may apply to enter the program through conditional admission which would require studying English at the University's English Language Institute (ELI) prior to entering the M.B.A. program. Students would not be required to submit TOEFL or IELTS scores if applying through this program.

Although there are no prerequisite courses, applicants are expected to possess basic skills in written and oral communication, mathematics, and computer usage.

Correspondence and Information

M.B.A. Program Admissions
Alfred Lerner College of Business and Economics
103 Alfred Lerner Hall
University of Delaware
Newark, Delaware 19716
Phone: 302-831-2221
Fax: 302-831-3329
E-mail: mbaprogram@udel.edu
Web site: http://www.mba.udel.edu

University of Delaware

THE FACULTY AND ADMINISTRATION

ADMINISTRATION

Conrado (Bobby) Gempesaw, Dean, Alfred Lerner College of Business and Economics; Ph.D., Penn State.

Rick Andrews, Deputy Dean and Chairperson, Alfred Lerner College of Business and Economics; Ph.D., Virginia Tech.

Ajay Manrai, Faculty Director, Graduate and Executive Programs; Ph.D., Northwestern.

John H. Wragge, Faculty Director of Executive Education and Associate Professor of Accounting and MIS; Ph.D., Houston; CPA.

Denise Waters, Director, Recruitment and Admissions; M.S.Ed., Johns Hopkins.

Paul Rollison, Program Manager, Executive Programs, and Manager, Career Services; M.Ed., New Hampshire.

Amy Estey, Manager, M.B.A. Program; B.S., Ohio State.

FACULTY

Burton A. Abrams, Professor of Economics; Ph.D., Ohio State.

Richard J. Agnello, Associate Professor of Economics; Ph.D., Johns Hopkins.

Rick Andrews, Deputy Dean and Chairperson, Alfred Lerner College of Business and Economics; Ph.D., Virginia Tech.

John H. Antil, Associate Professor of Marketing; Ph.D., Penn State.

Michael A. Arnold, Associate Professor of Economics; Ph.D., UCLA.

Naveed Baqir, Assistant Professor of Hotel, Restaurant, and Institutional Management; Ph.D., North Carolina at Greensboro.

Jack Baroudi, Professor of MIS; Ph.D., NYU.

Julia Bayuk, Assistant Professor of Marketing; Ph.D., Florida.

Stacie Beck, Associate Professor of Economics; Ph.D., Pennsylvania.

Thomas E. Becker, Associate Professor of Management; Ph.D., Ohio State.

Srikanth Beldona, Assistant Professor of Hospitality Management; Ph.D., Purdue.

Kenneth R. Biederman, Professor of Finance; Ph.D., Purdue.

David E. Black, Associate Professor of Economics; Ph.D., MIT.

John Blue, Assistant Professor of MIS; Ph.D., Virginia Commonwealth.

Helen M. Bowers, Associate Professor of Finance; Ph.D., South Carolina.

James L. Butkiewicz, Professor of Economics; Ph.D., Virginia.

Terry L. Campbell, Assistant Professor of Finance; Ph.D., Penn State.

Jin Wei Cao, Assistant Professor of MIS; Ph.D., Arizona.

David Cicero, Assistant Professor of Finance; Ph.D., Georgia.

Cihan Cobanoglu, Associate Professor of Hospitality Information Technology; Ph.D., Oklahoma State.

Roger Coffin, Associate Professor of the Practice; J.D., St. John's.

Jay F. Coughenour, Assistant Professor of Finance; Ph.D., Pittsburgh.

Eleanor D. Craig, Associate Professor of Economics; M.A., Pennsylvania.

Pamela Cummings, Associate Professor of Hospitality Management; Ph.D., Oklahoma State.

Joseph I. Daniel, Associate Professor of Economics; Ph.D., Minnesota.

Darwin J. Davis, Assistant Professor of Operations Management; Ph.D., Indiana.

Araya Debessay, Professor of Accounting; Ph.D., Penn State; CPA.

Fred De Micco, Professor of International Strategic Management; Ph.D., Virginia Tech.

Bernadine Dykes, Assistant Professor of Management; Ph.D., Michigan State.

Charles Elson, Edgar S. Woolard Jr. Professor of Corporate Governance, Professor of Finance, and Director of the Center for Corporate Governance; J.D., Virginia.

Andrea Everard, Associate Professor of MIS; Ph.D., Pittsburgh.

Evangelos Falaris, Associate Professor of Economics; Ph.D., Minnesota.

Diane L. Ferry, Associate Professor of Management; Ph.D., Pennsylvania.

M. Andrew Fields, Associate Professor of Finance and Chair of Finance; Ph.D., Virginia Tech.

Adam Fleischhacker, Assistant Professor of Operations Management; Ph.D., Rutgers.

Daniel Freeman, Assistant Professor; Ph.D., Arizona.

Meryl P. Gardner, Associate Professor of Marketing; Ph.D., Carnegie Mellon.

Howard Garland, Chaplin Tyler Professor of Business; Ph.D., Cornell.

Guido L. Geerts, Assistant Professor; Ph.D., Free University of Brussels.

William V. Gehrlein, Professor of Operations Management; Ph.D., Penn State.

Jackson E. Gillespie, Associate Professor of Accounting; Ph.D., Virginia Tech; CMA.

Brian Greenstein, Associate Professor of Accounting; Ph.D., Houston.

Farley Grubb, Professor of Economics; Ph.D., Chicago.

Jeffrey Harris, Assistant Professor of Finance; Ph.D., Ohio State.

William Harris, Associate Professor of Economics; Ph.D., Virginia Tech.

Kolve Hernandez-Arreortua, Associate Professor of Economics; Ph.D., Boston College.

Michal Herzenstein, Assistant Professor of Marketing; Ph.D., Rochester.

Saul D. Hoffman, Professor of Economics and Chair of Economics; Ph.D., Michigan.

David Jenkins, Associate Professor of Accounting; Ph.D., Maryland.

Scott K. Jones, Professor of Accounting; Ph.D., Drexel.

Gregory D. Kane, Associate Professor of Accounting; Ph.D., Virginia Tech; CPA.

Robert J. Kent, Associate Professor of Marketing and Head of Marketing; Ph.D., Cincinnati.

Mary C. Kernan, Associate Professor of Management; Ph.D., Akron.

Hemant V. Kher, Assistant Professor of Operations Management; Ph.D., South Carolina.

John L. Kmetz, Associate Professor of Management; D.B.A., Maryland.

Francis A. Kwansa, Associate Professor of Hospitality Financial Management; Ph.D., Virginia Tech.

Christine T. Kydd, Associate Professor of Operations Management; Ph.D., Pennsylvania.

William R. Latham III, Associate Professor of Economics and Associate Professor of Urban Affairs; Ph.D., Illinois.

Paul Laux, Professor of Finance; Ph.D., Vanderbilt.

Kenneth A. Lewis, Chaplin Tyler Professor of Business and Associate Chair of Economics; Ph.D., Princeton.

Charles R. Link, Professor of Economics; Ph.D., Wisconsin.

Xiaoxia Lou, Assistant Professor of Finance; Ph.D., Washington.

Ajay K. Manrai, Professor of Marketing and Faculty Director of M.B.A. Programs; Ph.D., Northwestern.

Patrick McClelland, Assistant Professor of Management; Ph.D., Kansas.

Brian Miller, Associate Professor of Hospitality Finance; Ph.D., Massachusetts.

Jeffrey B. Miller, Professor of Economics; Ph.D., Pennsylvania.

James G. Mulligan, Professor of Economics; Ph.D., Minnesota.

Robert Nelson, Associate Professor of Hotel, Restaurant, and Institutional Management; M.B.A., Drexel.

James B. O'Neill, Professor of Economics; Ph.D., Purdue.

Robert L. Paretta, Associate Professor of Accounting; Ph.D., Syracuse; CPA.

Sheldon D. Pollack, Associate Professor of Business Law; J.D., Ph.D., Cornell.

Ali A. Poorani, Associate Professor of Hospitality Human Resource Management; Ph.D., U.S. International.

John F. Preble, Associate Professor of Management; Ph.D., Massachusetts.

Erwin M. Saniga, Professor of Operations Management and Head of Operations Management Faculty; Ph.D., Penn State.

John E. Sawyer, Associate Professor of Management; Ph.D., Illinois.

Peter Schnabl, Assistant Professor of Economics; Ph.D., MIT

Robert L. Schweitzer, Professor of Finance; Ph.D., Duke.

Laurence S. Seidman, Professor of Economics and Chaplin Tyler Professor of Business; Ph.D., Berkeley.

Mark Serva, Assistant Professor of Accounting; Ph.D., Texas at Austin.

Paul Sestak, Associate Professor of Hotel, Restaurant, and Institutional Management; B.S., Drexel.

Stewart A. Shapiro, Assistant Professor of Marketing; Ph.D., Arizona.

Anu Sivaraman, Assistant Professor of Marketing; Ph.D., Houston.

Wendy Smith, Assistant Professor of Management; Ph.D., Harvard.

Jorges Soares, Associate Professor of Economics; Ph.D., Rochester.

E. Kent St. Pierre, Professor of Accounting and Director of M.S. Program; Ph.D., Washington (St. Louis); CPA.

John Stocker, Instructor of Finance; Ph.D., Kent State.

David R. Stockman, Assistant Professor of Economics; Ph.D., Chicago.

Daniel P. Sullivan, Associate Professor of Management; Ph.D., South Carolina.

Suresh Sundaram, Assistant Professor of Marketing; Ph.D., Houston.

Peggy Tseng, Assistant Professor of Marketing; Ph.D., Maryland.

Raj S. Varma, Associate Professor of Finance; Ph.D., Penn State.

Uma Velury, Assistant Professor of Accounting; Ph.D., South Carolina.

Thomas Vermeer, Associate Professor of MIS; Ph.D., North Texas.

Jiannan Wang, Assistant Professor of MIS; Ph.D., Arizona.

Siyan Wang, Assistant Professor of Economics; Ph.D., USC.

Sharon Watson, Assistant Professor of Management; Ph.D., South Carolina.

Gary R. Weaver, Associate Professor of Management; Ph.D., Iowa; Ph.D., Penn State.

Richard M. Weiss, Associate Professor of Management; Ph.D., Cornell.

Clinton E. White, Associate Professor of Accounting and Head of MIS Faculty; D.B.A., Indiana.

John H. Wragge, Associate Professor of Accounting and Faculty Director of Executive Education; Ph.D., Houston; CPA.

Scott Wycoff, Instructor of Management; Ph.D., Delaware.

John S. Ying, Associate Professor of Economics; Ph.D., Berkeley.

UNIVERSITY OF OKLAHOMA

Price College of Business

Programs of Study	The Price College of Business at the University of Oklahoma (OU) offers the following graduate programs: the Master of Business Administration (M.B.A.), the Master of Accountancy (M.Acc.), the Master of Science in Management Information Systems (M.S. in MIS), and the Doctor of Philosophy (Ph.D.). Dual-degree programs offered include the M.B.A./M.S. in MIS, M.B.A./J.D., and generic dual degrees, which combine any other graduate program available at OU with the M.B.A. For the dual-degree programs, applicants must apply and be admitted to each program separately. Programs in the Price College of Business are fully accredited by AACSB International–The Association to Advance Collegiate Schools of Business.

The full-time M.B.A. is a 47-credit hour, sixteen-month program, with all courses taken at the graduate level. The full-time program facilitates the development of professional skills and broad business perspectives through opportunities such as unique summer internships in New York (Price Scholars), London (Dunham Scholars), and Dallas (Corporate Scholars) along with other domestic and international internships, case competitions, and working in teams on real-life cases. Interacting with excellent faculty members keeps OU M.B.A. students on the cutting edge of knowledge. A customized program in one of six specializations—finance, risk management, energy, marketing/supply chain management, entrepreneurship, or MIS—allows personal attention for each student. Low tuition costs plus significant scholarship and assistantship opportunities make the OU M.B.A. an outstanding program for those looking to improve their professional opportunities and create a pathway to business leadership.

The professional part-time M.B.A. requires 47 credit hours, with all courses taken at the graduate level. Designed for the working professional, all courses are offered in the evening and are based in downtown Oklahoma City.

Both M.B.A. programs require that the student become familiar with the functional areas of business, the necessary tools for management decision making, and the environment in which business firms operate. Students from all undergraduate majors are encouraged to apply.

The M.Acc. is a 33-hour program for students with an undergraduate degree in accounting from a program accredited by AACSB International. Other students may enter this program, but they must take a minimum of 24 hours of undergraduate accounting courses as well as other core business courses. The core business courses are all graduate courses. The M.Acc. is a terminal professional degree.

The M.S. in MIS is a 33-hour program designed for people with an undergraduate degree in a discipline other than MIS who wish to embark on a career as an information system analyst or designer. The program combines a solid base of business and organizational knowledge with in-depth exposure to information systems technologies. The curriculum contains 17 hours of graduate business courses and 16 hours of graduate MIS courses. In addition, candidates must demonstrate competency in two programming languages. The M.S. in MIS program admits a small number of highly qualified students.

The full-time Ph.D. program is small and research-oriented. The program requires a minimum of 90 graduate hours past a bachelor's degree. Eighteen hours of course work are stipulated; most degree requirements and major, in addition to supporting fields, are determined on an individual basis. Close association with faculty members, as well as early research involvement, is standard. Doctoral students normally receive financial aid. Doctoral majors are available in accounting, finance, management, management information systems, and marketing/supply chain management. A master's degree is not required to enter the doctoral program.

Research Facilities	Research facilities that are available to graduate students include an extensive university library, the Amoco Business Resource Information Center, a graduate computer lab, the Bass Business History Collection, the Oklahoma University Research Institute, the Center for Economic and Management Research, and extensive computer facilities including a new trading floor lab.
Financial Aid	Graduate assistantships of up to $15,300 a year, special instructorships, fellowships and scholarships, and tuition-waiver scholarships are available for qualified graduate students. Graduate assistantships may include a full waiver of resident and nonresident tuition.
Cost of Study	Tuition in 2009–10 for full-time state residents was $279 per credit hour; nonresident students paid $689 per credit hour. Books and supplies are estimated at $1250 per academic year; other fees vary by program.
Living and Housing Costs	Many graduate students live on campus in one of the university's three apartment complexes or in the residence halls. Prices for apartments vary from $475 to $1000 per month. Room and board rates for the residence halls are approximately $3500 for one semester. For more information, students should call 405-325-2511 or visit the Web site at http://www.housing.ou.edu.
Student Group	Typically, 45 percent of an M.B.A. class consists of business majors, 24 percent engineering majors, and the remainder science and humanities majors. More than 40 percent have two years or more of work experience. The average age is 27 and approximately 30 percent are women. There are generally 300 to 350 graduate students in the College.
Location	Although part of the Oklahoma City metropolitan area, Norman began and continues as an independent community with a permanent population of nearly 105,000. It has extensive parks and recreation programs, a 10,000-acre lake and park area, a community theater, an art center and art league, and other amenities of a university town. Norman is minutes from downtown Oklahoma City and 3 hours from Dallas. Summers are hot with high humidity, and winters are mild to cold.
The University	The University of Oklahoma, which was founded in 1890, is a doctoral degree-granting research university. The Norman campus serves as home to all of the university's academic programs, except health-related fields. Both the Norman and Health Sciences Center colleges offer programs at the Schusterman Center, the site of OU-Tulsa. OU enrolls more than 31,000 students, has more than 2,400 full-time faculty members, and has twenty colleges offering 163 majors at the baccalaureate level, 166 majors at the master's level, eighty-one majors at the doctoral level, twenty-seven majors at the first-professional level, and twenty-six graduate certificates.
Applying	There is a nonrefundable application processing fee of $40 for U.S. citizens and permanent residents and $90 for international applicants. Admission is open to qualified individuals holding a bachelor's degree from an accredited college or university who show high promise of success in graduate study. Applicants need not have undergraduate backgrounds in business. All applicants must submit satisfactory scores on the Graduate Management Admission Test (GMAT). International applicants must submit satisfactory scores on the Test of English as a Foreign Language (TOEFL) or the Cambridge IELTS. In addition, the Test of Spoken English (TSE) is required of international applicants to the Ph.D. program. Letters of recommendation are required for all applicants.

Students may enter the M.Acc. program in the fall semester beginning in late August, the spring semester beginning in early January, or the eight-week summer session beginning in early June. Students may enter the M.B.A. program, M.S. in MIS program, and doctoral program in the fall semester only.

Correspondence and Information	Graduate Programs Office Price College of Business 1003 Asp Avenue, Suite 1040 University of Oklahoma Norman, Oklahoma 73019-4302 Phone: 405-325-4107 Fax: 405-325-7753 E-mail: oklahomamba@ou.edu Web site: http://price.ou.edu/mba/

University of Oklahoma

THE FACULTY AND THEIR RESEARCH

Frances L. Ayres, John W. Jr. and Barbara J. Branch Professor of Accounting and Director, Steed School of Accounting; Ph.D., Iowa. Financial accounting, financial accounting theory, economics of accounting choice, interaction between tax and financial reporting.

Samir Barman, Professor of Marketing and Supply Chain Management; Ph.D., Clemson. Aggregate production planning, job scheduling, inventory modeling.

Mark Bolino, McCasland Foundation Professor of American Free Enterprise and Associate Professor Of Management; Ph.D., South Carolina. Organizational behavior, international business, human resources management.

Michael R. Buckley, JCPenney Company Leadership Chair, Professor of Management and Professor of Psychology; Ph.D., Auburn. Human resource management, performance appraisal, interviewing, management principles.

Lowell A. Busenitz, Puterbaugh Chair in American Enterprise, Center for Entrepreneurship; Academic Director and Professor of Entrepreneurship and Management; Ph.D., Texas A&M. Strategic management, entrepreneurship.

Traci A. Carte, Associate Professor of Management Information Systems; Ph.D., Georgia. Database management, accounting information systems, leveraging technology to support diverse teams.

Laku Chidambaram, W. P. Wood Professor of Management Information Systems and Director of the Division of Management Information Systems; Ph.D., Indiana. Application of information technology.

Terry L. Crain, Dale Looper Chair in Accounting and Associate Professor of Accounting; Ph.D., Texas Tech. Oil and gas accounting; estate and gift; corporate, partnership, and individual taxation.

Andrew D. Cuccia, Grant Thorton Faculty Fellow and Associate Professor of Accounting; Ph.D., Florida. Judgment and decision making in tax professional judgment and taxpayer compliance.

Rajiv P. Dant, Helen Robson Walton Centennial Chair in Marketing Strategy and Professor of Marketing and Supply Chain Management; Ph.D., Virginia Tech. Channels of distribution, research methodology, supply chain management and franchising.

Robert C. Dauffenbach, Professor of Management Information Systems, Associate Dean for Research and Graduate Programs, and Director, Center for Economic and Management Research; Ph.D., Illinois at Urbana-Champaign. Quantitative analysis, business economics, operations management, information systems.

Patricia J. Daugherty, Robin Siegfried Centennial Chair of Marketing and Director, Division of Marketing and Supply Chain Management; Ph.D., Michigan State. Reverse logistics, outsourcing and supply chain relationships.

Louis H. Ederington, Michael F. Price Chair in Finance and Professor of Finance; Ph.D., Washington (St. Louis). Fixed-income securities, futures and options, financial markets and institutions, interest rate structure.

Gary W. Emery, Oklahoma Bankers' Chair in Finance and Professor of Finance; Ph.D., Kansas. Corporate finance and investments.

Chitru S. Fernando, Michael F. Price Professor of Finance, Director of the Center for Energy Solutions and the Center for Financial Studies; Ph.D., Pennsylvania. Corporate finance, corporate risk management, liquidity risk in financial marketing, commodity and energy markets.

Dipankar Ghosh, John T. Steed Professor of Accounting, John Mertes Jr. Presidential Professor, and Executive Director, M.B.A. Program; Ph.D., Penn State. Managerial accounting, accounting information for judgment and decision-making, transfer pricing and negotiation.

Evgenia Golubeva, Assistant Professor of Finance; Ph.D., Utah. Asset pricing and market microstructure.

Kevan L. Jensen, Associate Professor of Accounting; Ph.D., Florida. Market for audit services both as a control mechanism and as a provider of assurance.

Carol A. Knapp, John Mertes Jr. Presidential Professor and Assistant Professor of Accounting; Ph.D., Oklahoma. Judgment and decision making in the context of auditing, fraud detection by auditors.

M. Chris Knapp, McLaughlin Chair in Business Ethics and Professor of Accounting; Ph.D., Oklahoma. Policy issues related to the professional practice of public accounting and behavioral issues concerning the author-client dyad.

Scott Linn, R. W. "Dick" Moore Chair in Finance and Economic Development; Ph.D., Purdue. Corporate finance; corporate governance; corporate control; capital markets and security pricing and behavior; risk management, including investment and portfolio management; behavior of intermediaries in real markets.

Marlys Gascho Lipe, Rath Chair in Accounting and Professor of Accounting; Ph.D., Chicago. Judgment and decision making.

Robert C. Lipe, KPMG Centennial Professor of Accounting and Professor of Accounting; Ph.D., Chicago. Corporate financial reports.

William L. Megginson, Rainbolt Chair in Finance and Professor of Finance; Ph.D., Florida State. International finance and corporate finance issues.

Shaila Miranda, Associate Professor of Management Information Systems; Ph.D., Georgia. Outsourcing, electronic collaboration, knowledge management, sociological and organizational theory.

Ning Nan, Associate Professor of Management Information Systems; Ph.D., Michigan. Behavioral and economic factors in management information systems.

Daniel T. Ostas, James G. Harlow Jr. Chair in Business Ethics and Community Service and Professor of Legal Studies; Ph.D., J.D., Indiana. Economic analysis of marketplace ethics, institutional economic analysis of law and corporate social responsibility.

David A. Ralston, Price Chair in International Business; D.B.A., Florida State. Cross-cultural management.

Nim Razook Jr., Associate Dean of Undergraduate Programs, David Ross Boyd Professor of Legal Studies and Robert Zinke Chair in Energy Management; J.D., Oklahoma. The legal environment, ethics, commercial law.

Anthony S. Roath, Associate Professor of Marketing and Supply Chain Management; Ph.D., Michigan State. Efficiency of global logistics systems and relationship management of cross-border alliances.

Craig J. Russell, Professor Of Management; Ph.D., Iowa. Advancing theory and practice in the selection and development of organizational leaders.

Jeffrey B. Schmidt, Associate Professor of Marketing; Ph.D., Michigan. Managerial decision making during new product development, new product performance, adaptation of products for international markets, and marketing strategy.

A. B. Schwarzkopf, Associate Professor of Management Information Systems; Ph.D., Virginia. Database and end-user computing applications.

Teresa Shaft, Associate Professor of Management Information Systems; Ph.D., Penn State. Cognitive processes used by IS professionals during system development and maintenance, role of IS in environmental management.

Mark Sharfman, Professor of Strategic Management and Director, Division of Management; Ph.D., Arizona. How the business environment affects the firm, how the firm affects the natural environment, and how firms manage the social issues they face in the business environment.

Bryan E. Stanhouse, Associate Professor of Finance; Ph.D., Illinois at Urbana-Champaign. Application of time to first passage mathematics for pricing bank credit lines or revolver loans.

Duane R. Stock, Michael F. Price Student Investment Fund Professor and Professor of Finance; Ph.D., Illinois at Urbana-Champaign. Corporate bonds, municipal bonds, options, interest rate risk and banking.

Wayne B. Thomas, John Mertes Jr. Presidential Professor and Professor of Accounting; Ph.D., Oklahoma State. Market-based accounting research, earnings management, time-series properties of earnings and earnings components, segment disclosures, financial statement analysis and international accounting issues.

Vahap B. Uysal, Assistant Professor of Finance; Ph.D., Texas. Corporate finance, capital structure, mergers and acquisitions.

Jeffrey P. Wallman, Assistant Professor of Marketing; Ph.D., Wisconsin–Madison. Entrepreneurship, marketing management and marketing strategy.

G. Lee Willinger, John F. Y. Stambaugh Centennial Professor of Accounting and Professor of Accounting; D.B.A., Florida State. Pension accounting, contingent claims modeling in accounting, the economic impact of accounting information and the information content of accounting numbers as reflected in the capital markets.

Pradeep K. Yadav, W. Ross Johnston Chair in Finance and Director, Division of Finance; Ph.D., Texas. Market microstructure; derivatives, including risk management, index futures pricing, early exercise premiums, and implied distributions; ownership structure and corporate governance; mergers and acquisitions; performance of managed funds.

Han Yi, Assistant Professor of Accounting; Ph.D., Michigan State. Financial reporting—causes and consequences of accounting choices, earnings management and benchmarks, and financial reporting regulations.

Robert W. Zmud, Michael F. Price Chair in Management Information Systems and Professor of Management Information Systems; Ph.D., Arizona. Impact of IT in facilitating organizational behaviors and organizational efforts involved with planning, managing, and diffusing information technology.

UNIVERSITY OF OTTAWA

Telfer School of Management
Master of Business Administration

Programs of Study

Ideally located in Canada's capital, at the crossroads of business, trade, policy, and government, the Telfer School of Management at the University of Ottawa offers a Master of Business Administration (M.B.A.) that distinguishes itself by preparing the future leaders of high performance organizations. During the program, students become confidentially familiar with the framework for organizational performance management, which leading-edge organizations use to ensure their strategies remain relevant, their operations integrated and balanced, and their resources (financial, human, etc.) efficiently used.

Telfer MBA courses, which cover fundamental business disciplines such as strategy, marketing, finance, accounting, human resources, and information systems, are integrated within this unifying framework. Moreover, the School takes great pride in ensuring that students gain hands-on, practical, and transferable skills through the use and support of specific tools and applications such as leading-edge business intelligence software that is used to maximize organizational performance.

Telfer MBA graduates are prepared to manage and lead by focusing on results, value, and outcomes with discipline and adaptability. The training provided during the program is applicable to all sectors and industries, and is instrumental in advancing the careers of the School's graduates. Using the extensive network within the local business community and the public sector, students must complete a major project under the supervision of a faculty member, the mentorship of a Certified Management Consultant from the Canadian Association of Management (CAMC) and the direction of an executive from the host organization. While completing the project, students apply their newly acquired knowledge and skills, balance theory and practice, and gain valuable management experience. Students have recently completed projects for Adobe, Alcatel Lucent, Bank of Canada, Canada Post, Cirque du Soleil, ClimateCheck, Foreign Affairs Canada, International Trade Canada, Live Work Learn Play LLP, Lumenera Corporation, March Networks, National Research Council (NRC), PAI Medical Group, RBC, SNC-Lavalin, SuzukiMusic, the *Ottawa Citizen*, Volvo Cars of Canada, and Yellow Pages/Pages Jaunes.

Program delivery is flexible. Full- and part-time study options allow students to complete the degree requirements in as little as twelve months or as long as sixty months. Courses are offered in a variety of formats ranging from day or evening classes spread over twelve weeks, to half courses delivered intensively over a weekend. There are also opportunities to undertake directed readings.

Work groups are carefully created to ensure an effective mix of students with different academic and professional environments. As they progress through the core modules of the program within their work group, students are exposed to all the basic management disciplines and develop the skills to think strategically.

The Telfer M.B.A. draws students from around the world, from a variety of educational backgrounds and diverse professional experiences. The program is designed to build on the diversity and wealth of its students' profiles. A cohort environment allows students to work and learn together, benefiting from each other's strengths, capabilities, and experiences. Students participate in national and international case competitions annually. The strong performance of the Telfer School's M.B.A. teams over the years is a clear reflection of its talented students and the high quality of the Telfer M.B.A. program.

Other graduate management programs offered at the Telfer School include the Executive M.B.A. (EMBA), a twenty-one-month program with classes one day a week; the Master of Health Administration (M.H.A.), a sixteen-month program that includes a four-month administrative residency; the Master of Science in management (M.Sc.); the Master of Science in Health Systems (M.Sc.); and e-commerce and e-business graduate certificates.

Research Facilities

Recently, the Telfer School moved into the new Desmarais Building. This twelve-storey structure offers management students an unparalleled learning environment.

The Telfer School fosters the development of the students' high-tech skills by providing them with state-of-the-art computing and teaching facilities. From private rooms to multimedia labs and teaching rooms, students can prepare their assignments using common and specialized software, advanced financial and accounting databases, the Internet, electronic mail, and the computerized libraries of the University.

A dedicated Management Library ensures that students can access—directly and easily—indispensable learning materials, such as the latest academic journals and trade publications and the increasing number of online databases and electronic resources applied to management

The Telfer School of Management proudly promotes its Career Centre, which is dedicated exclusively to management students. The purpose of the Career Centre is to partner with students, alumni, and employers to create employment opportunities, enhance student value, and facilitate the employers' recruitment process. The center organizes and assists with career fairs, company information sessions, workshops, and networking events. Employers post jobs on the Career Centre's Web site in order to offer employment opportunities for full-time, part-time, and summer job positions. Interested students should visit the Web site http://www.telfer.uOttawa.ca/careercentre for more information.

The University also offers a variety of services and resources that contribute to the student's professional development and success in achieving career goals.

Financial Aid

The Telfer School of Management's goal is to attract top quality candidates to its M.B.A. program. Numerous scholarships are awarded, which reflects the Telfer School's ongoing commitment to reward exceptional students for their academic successes and achievements. Students should visit the Web site at http://www.telfer.uOttawa.ca/mba to learn more about scholarships and awards.

Canadian citizens and permanent residents in need of financial aid can apply for government assistance. The Telfer School of Management provides funds for teaching assistants and research assistants. The University also offers various awards primarily for Canadian citizens or permanent residents who intend to pursue or are pursuing full-time graduate studies.

Cost of Study

Tuition for a full-time M.B.A. program (three semesters) is Can$19,800 for Canadian students and Can$31,710 for international students. For part-time students, tuition is Can$341 per credit, with 54 credits needed.

Living and Housing Costs

Other estimated costs for the academic year include housing (off campus), Can$7500; food, Can$4800; books, Can$1500; and for non-Canadians, health insurance, Can$750.

Location

Located in the heart of the nation's capital, the Telfer School of Management at the University of Ottawa is at the center of an extensive group of government and private organizations that drive most of Canada's business and trade nationally and internationally. The main campus is located in the downtown core and is within walking distance of shopping malls, restaurants, cinemas, and museums.

The University and The Telfer School

The University of Ottawa is a cosmopolitan campus where more than 36,000 students live and learn in a variety of cultural heritages live and learn in an atmosphere of tolerance and understanding. International students benefit from the University's long tradition of excellence in teaching and research while learning about the multicultural Canadian social mosaic. The Telfer School of Management provides a rich educational experience, both inside and outside the classroom, that prepares students to be leaders in the new global, knowledge-based economy. The Telfer School's graduates are in demand by high-technology companies, leading consulting firms, financial institutions, and public-sector organizations in Canada and abroad. The Telfer School of Management at the University of Ottawa received accreditation from AACSB International in 2003, AMBA in 2005, and EQUIS in 2009. It is the only Ottawa-based business school to be recognized by these prestigious international organizations.

Applying

Admission to the Telfer M.B.A. program is competitive and granted to candidates who clearly demonstrate high promise of success. The admission requirements are: a baccalaureate degree with at least a B or a 70 percent overall standing, at least two years of full-time work experience, and at least a 50th percentile score on the GMAT. The most recent average score was 615 and the range was 550–780. Application deadlines are February 1 for international students and April 1 for students from the United States and Canada. Students should allow four to six weeks for notification. Preference is given to candidates who have greater work experience, particularly where there is evidence of career progression.

Correspondence and Information

M.B.A. Program
University of Ottawa Telfer School of Management
55 Laurier Avenue East, Room 4160
Ottawa, Ontario K1N 6N5
Canada

Phone: 613-562-5884
          800-965-5512 (toll-free)
Fax: 613-562-5912
E-mail: mba@telfer.uottawa.ca
Web site: http://www.telfer.uOttawa.ca/mba

University of Ottawa

THE FACULTY

Many of the Telfer School's faculty members serve as consultants to major corporations and government organizations around the world. Holders of numerous teaching and research awards, the professors combine excellence in teaching with outstanding scholarship.

Administration

Acting Dean: François Julien, Associate Professor; Ph.D., Waterloo.
Associate Dean (Academic) and Secretary: Joanne Leck, Associate Professor; M.B.A., Ph.D., McGill.
Associate Dean (Strategy, Planning and Management Systems): Michel Nedzela, Associate Professor; M.S., Stanford.
Director of the Master of Business Administration (M.B.A.) Program: Michael Miles, Assistant Professor; Ph.D., Fielding Institute.
Associate Director of the Master of Business Administration (M.B.A.) Program: Laurent Lapierre, Associate Professor; Ph.D., McMaster.
Director of the Executive M.B.A. (EMBA) Program: Terrence Kulka, Ph.D., McGill.
Acting Director of the Master of Health Administration (M.H.A.) Program: François Julien, Associate Professor; Ph.D., Waterloo.
Director of the Master of Science in Health Systems (M.Sc.): Craig Kuziemsky, Assistant Professor; Ph.D., Victoria.
Director of the Master of Science in Management (M.Sc.): Mark Freel, Associate Professor; Ph.D., Aberdeen.
Director, Undergraduate Program (B.Com.) and Assistant Dean, Student Services: Peter Koppel; M.B.A., York; CLU.

Section Coordinators

Merridee Bujaki, Associate Professor; M.B.A., Ph.D., Queen's at Kingston; CA.
Swee Goh, Professor; M.B.A., Ph.D., Toronto.
Patrick Woodcock, Assistant Professor; M.B.A., Ph.D., Western Ontario.

Professors

Fodil Adjaoud, Professor; M.B.A., Ph.D., Laval.
Douglas Angus, Professor; M.A., Ottawa.
Jacques Barrette, Associate Professor; Ph.D., Montréal.
Julie Beauchamp, Assistant Professor; Ph.D., McGill.
Walid Ben Amar, Assistant Professor; Ph.D., HEC-Montréal.
Sarah Ben Amor, Assistant Professor; Ph.D., Laval.
Morad Benyoucef, Assistant Professor; Ph.D., Montréal.
Silvia Bonaccio, Assistant Professor; Ph.D., Purdue.
Ameur Boujenoui, Assistant Professor; Lic. en sc. econ., Rabat; Ph.D., HEC-Montréal.
James E. Bowen, Adjunct Professor; Ph.D., Carleton.
Richard Bozec, Associate Professor; Ph.D., Montréal.
Kevin Brand, Assistant Professor; S.M., Sc.D., Harvard.
Tom Brzustowski, Visiting Professor; Ph.D., Princeton.
Jonathan Calof, Associate Professor; M.B.A., Ph.D., Western Ontario.
A. Louis Calvet, Professor; M.B.A., Queen's at Kingston; Ph.D., MIT.
Denis H. J. Caro, Professor; M.B.A., Ph.D., Minnesota.
Jules Carrière, Associate Professor; Ph.D., Montréal.
Tyler Chamberlin, Assistant Professor; Ph.D., Manchester.
Imed Eddine Chkir, Associate Professor; Ph.D., Laval.
Samia Chreim, Associate Professor; Ph.D., HEC-Montréal.
Robert Collier, Teaching Associate; B.A., Carleton; CMA.
Brian Conheady, Teaching Associate, M.B.A., McGill; CMA.
Jean Couillard, Associate Professor; M.B.A., Ph.D., Laval.
Margaret Dalziel, Assistant Professor; M.B.A., McGill; Ph.D., Montréal.
David H. J. Delcorde, Visiting Professor; M.B.A., Heriot-Watt (Edinburgh); Ph.D., London South Bank (UK).
Anna Dodonova, Assistant Professor; Ph.D., Michigan.
David Doloreux, Associate Professor; Ph.D., Waterloo.
Sylvain Durocher, Associate Professor; Ph.D., Quebec (Montréal).
Ronald Eden, Associate Professor; M.B.A., Dalhousie; Ph.D., NYU; CA.
Prescott Ensign, Assistant Professor; M.B.A., Clemson; Ph.D., HEC-Montréal.
Leila Hamzaoui Essoussi, Assistant Professor; D.E.A., Doctorat en Gestion, Aix en Provence.
Dominique J. Ferrand, Associate Professor; D.E.S.C., Paris; M.S.G., Paris IX; Ph.D., Laval.
Bruce M. Firestone, Entrepreneur-in-Residence; Ph.D., Australian National.
Devinder Gandhi, Visiting Professor; Ph.D., Pennsylvania.

Chen Guo, Associate Professor; M.B.A., Ph.D., Queen's at Kingston.
Michael Guolla, Teaching Associate; Ph.D., Michigan.
Leila Hamzaoui Essoussi, Assistant Professor; Ph.D., Aix-Marseilles III.
Mirou Jaana, Assistant Professor; Ph.D., Iowa.
Pavlo Kalyta, Assistant Professor; Ph.D., Concordia.
Yuri Khoroshilov, Assistant Professor; Ph.D., Michigan.
Gurprit S. Kindra, Professor; M.B.A., Northwest Missouri State; Ph.D., Iowa.
Kaouthar Lajili-Kobeissi, Associate Professor; Ph.D., Illinois.
Daniel E. Lane, Professor; Ph.D., British Columbia.
David Large, Assistant Professor; M.B.A., Ph.D., Western Ontario.
Sharon Leiba-O'Sullivan, Associate Professor; M.B.A., McGill; Ph.D., Toronto.
Brigitte Levy, Associate Professor; D.E.A., Doct.S.Écon., Paris X.
Jonathan Linton, Associate Professor; Ph.D., York.
Judith Madill, Full Professor; Ph.D., Western Ontario.
Michael Maingot, Full Professor; Ph.D., Queen's (Belfast).
Pranlal Manga, Professor; Ph.D., Toronto.
Philip McIlkenny, Associate Professor; Ph.D., Essex.
Wojtek Michalowski, Professor; M.Econ., Ph.D., Warsaw.
Muriel Mignerat, Assistant Professor; Ph.D., HEC-Montréal.
Michael Mulvey, Assistant Professor; Ph.D., Penn State.
John Nash, Professor; D.Phil., Oxford.
Christian Navarre, Professor; M.Sc., Agrégé de l'Université; D.Ét., Lille.
Barbara Orser, Associate Professor; Ph.D., Bradford.
Alan O'Sullivan, Assistant Professor; M.B.A., Dublin; Ph.D., McGill.
Jonathan Patrick, Assistant Professor; Ph.D., British Columbia.
Ajax Persaud, Associate Professor; Ph.D., Carleton.
Kathryn Pedwell, Assistant Professor; M.B.A., Ph.D., Calgary.
Rhonda Pyper, Lecturer; M.B.A., Laurentian; CMA.
Tony Quon, Associate Professor; Ph.D., Princeton.
Bijan Raajemi, Assistant Professor; Ph.D., Waterloo.
Abdul Rahman, Associate Professor; Ph.D., Concordia.
William Rentz, Associate Professor; Ph.D., Rochester.
Greg Richards, Visiting Professor; Cognos Professorship, Carleton.
Allan Riding, Professor; Ph.D., McGill.
Martine Spence, Associate Professor; M.B.A., Concordia; Ph.D., Middlesex.
David J. Wright, Professor; Ph.D., Cambridge.
Daniel Zeghal, Professor; M.B.A., Ph.D., Laval; CGA.
David Zussman, Jarislowsky Chair; Ph.D., McGill.

UNIVERSITY OF ST. THOMAS

Opus College of Business

Programs of Study

The Opus College of Business at the University of St. Thomas (UST) offers four distinct M.B.A. programs to meet the needs of a diverse community interested in excelling in business: the Full-time UST M.B.A. (twenty-one months), the Evening UST M.B.A. for working professionals, the weekend Executive UST M.B.A. for established leaders and the Health Care UST M.B.A. for physicians and health-care professionals. In addition, the College offers the Master of Business Communication, the Master of Science degree in accountancy for CPA seekers, and the Master of Science degree in real estate. The goal of the Opus College of Business is to be recognized nationally and internationally for its overall excellence in educating highly principled global business leaders prepared to impact their careers, their communities, and their organizations. Faculty members are leading scholars in their fields who also understand the value of practical experience. This recognized combination of theory and practice gives students the relevance necessary for rapid advancement in their careers.

The Full-time UST M.B.A. offers a traditional business core curriculum augmented by unique learning laboratories that prepare students with advanced analytical, communications, and problem-solving skills. A distinct feature of the program is applied business research, an opportunity for UST M.B.A. students to consult with external organizations on research projects critical to organizational viability and growth. Special attention is given to understanding the process of ethical decision making in today's complicated global environment. Elective options cover a variety of career tracks, and students have access to extensive career counseling and a network of successful alumni.

The Evening UST M.B.A. offers flexible class schedules to accommodate working professionals. Classes meet one night per week, with selected courses available on Saturdays. A similar variety of elective tracks enables students to tailor the program to support their career interests. The typical time to complete the degree is approximately four years. Industrious part-time students can finish in three years.

The weekend Executive UST M.B.A. is designed for leaders and managers seeking the opportunity to enhance their leadership skills and gain a comprehensive understanding of the challenges facing businesses today. With classes held on a Friday and Saturday one weekend per month, the accelerated M.B.A. program features a curriculum that emphasizes strategic and conceptual managerial competencies across industries, organizations, and functions.

The Health Care UST M.B.A. offers course delivery through a combination of distance learning and intensive residencies to accommodate working health-care professionals from throughout the continental United States and Canada.

The Master of Business Communication is a part-time evening program designed for communicators who want to expand their communication expertise while building core business knowledge. The program includes specialties such as public relations, advertising, and marketing communication.

The Master of Science degree in accountancy program is designed for students with an undergraduate accounting major and prepares them for a fast track in the accounting profession while meeting the 150-hour education requirement for CPA licensure.

The Master of Science degree in real estate program provides the opportunity for real estate professionals to enhance their business and real estate acumen to advance in the field of commercial real estate.

All programs feature smaller class sizes that enable each student to have regular interactions with members of the highly talented faculty. The Full-time UST M.B.A., the Executive UST M.B.A., and the Health Care UST M.B.A. are all cohort-based programs. Cocurricular activities include an investment management course in which students actively manage $2 million and a venture capital fund that invests in technology-based start-up businesses. Other activities include clubs and organizations such as the Accounting and Finance Club; Marketing, Consulting, New Impact, and New Venture Clubs; and the UST MBA Student Association.

Research Facilities

The majority of graduate programs at the UST Opus College of Business are delivered at the College's downtown Minneapolis campus. This state-of-the-art facility offers comprehensive services and a dynamic educational environment. An 86,000-square-foot technology-laden School of Entrepreneurship opened in fall 2005. The College of Business also conducts classes and programs in St. Paul on the beautiful 78-acre original campus. In addition, graduate courses are offered in the surrounding Minnesota communities of Maple Grove and Bloomington. Students have access to state-of-the-art computing facilities and leading-edge software. Comprehensive library resources, with more than 300,000 volumes, are located on both the Minneapolis and St. Paul campuses. All students in the Full-time UST M.B.A. participate in an applied business research course designed to give them extensive practical experience in collecting relevant information for business decisions.

Financial Aid

Financial aid is available through a variety of private, institutional, and federal programs on both a need and merit basis. For information on these programs, students should contact Student Financial Services at 651-962-6550 or send an e-mail to financialaid@stthomas.edu. In addition, many employers pay or subsidize their employees' tuition expenses.

Cost of Study

Tuition for 2010–11 is between $819 and $1399 per credit hour, depending on the program. Expenses for course materials vary by program and course. Nondegree professional development courses are also available for both companies and individuals through the UST Center for Business Excellence.

Living and Housing Costs

Most graduate students live off campus. Both Minneapolis and St. Paul offer a variety of reasonably priced housing options. Students who elect to live in St. Paul can take advantage of a free shuttle service that runs throughout the day between the campuses. A number of services and publications in the Twin Cities area provide off-campus residential listings. The Student Life Office in the Full-time UST M.B.A. program maintains a roommate referral listing service.

Student Group

Students in the part-time graduate business programs include a variety of working professionals, and students in the Full-time UST M.B.A. include individuals who have left the workforce to pursue full-time study. The student body has broad ethnic diversity and maintains close connections with the National Black MBA Association (NBMBAA) and the National Society for Hispanic MBAs (NSHMBA).

Location

The Twin Cities of Minneapolis and St. Paul are among the country's most vibrant cultural centers. The business community features nineteen Fortune 500 corporations. The Twin Cities are also home to two world-class symphonies and internationally acclaimed theaters and art museums. In addition, Minneapolis features many professional sports teams and provides a wide range of opportunities for recreational athletes. The Mall of America in Bloomington is within minutes of the St. Paul and Minneapolis campuses.

The University

The University of St. Thomas is a comprehensive, coeducational, Catholic university. Founded in 1885, St. Thomas is now the largest private university in Minnesota. It is dedicated to providing career-oriented, value-centered education in a dynamic, stimulating environment. St. Thomas does not discriminate on the basis of race, color, creed, religion, national origin, sex, age, marital status, sexual orientation, or disability in its programs and activities.

Applying

Admission requirements vary by degree program, especially with regard to previous work or managerial experience; however, most programs require official scores from the GMAT, transcripts from all undergraduate institutions attended, and TOEFL scores for those students whose native language is not English and who did not graduate from a North American undergraduate institution. Personal interviews are required for certain programs.

Students can apply online at the Web site (http://www.stthomas.edu/business) or through the traditional application forms available on the Internet or from the program office. Applications are considered on a rolling basis for most programs. The Full-time UST M.B.A. offers fall admission only, but applications are considered in five rounds, beginning in November. The other programs offer fall and spring admission. For specific information and application materials, students should contact the Opus College of Business.

Correspondence and Information

Opus College of Business
TMH 100
University of St. Thomas
1000 LaSalle Avenue
Minneapolis, Minnesota 55403-2025
Phone: 651-962-4200
          800-328-6819 Ext. 2-4200 (toll-free)
E-mail: cob@stthomas.edu
Web site: http://www.stthomas.edu/business

University of St. Thomas

THE FACULTY

The St. Thomas full-time and adjunct faculty members, many of whom are leaders in their industries, bring a wealth of business and academic experience to the classroom. This unique mixture of expertise results in leading-edge curricula and the real-world applied approach that makes a University of St. Thomas degree so valued in the business community. Students benefit from this expertise through the accessibility resulting from small class sizes and the advisory or mentoring roles assumed by many faculty members.

Deans and Directors of the Master's Programs
Christopher P. Puto, Dean.
Bill Woodson, Assistant Dean, UST M.B.A. programs.

Dustin Cornwell, Director of the Full-time UST M.B.A.
Corey Eakins, Director of the Evening UST M.B.A.
John Militello, Interim Director of the Executive UST M.B.A.
John Militello, Director of the Health Care UST M.B.A.
Mike Porter, Director of the Master of Business Communication program.
Herb Tousley, Director of the Master of Science degree in real estate program.
Kristine Sharockman, Director of the Master of Science degree in accountancy program.

THE UNIVERSITY OF TEXAS AT ARLINGTON

College of Business

Programs of Study

The College of Business at The University of Texas at Arlington (UT Arlington), accredited by AACSB International–The Association to Advance Collegiate Schools of Business, offers four versions of the M.B.A. and ten specialized master's degrees. Students may begin their studies in any semester and complete those studies on either a part-time or full-time basis. Programs may require up to 30 hours of foundation work for students with nonbusiness backgrounds.

The Master of Professional Accounting (42 semester hours in accounting) is appropriate for students without prior study in business or accounting. The M.S. in Accounting (36 semester hours) allows specialization in accounting information systems, auditing, financial accounting, and managerial accounting. The M.S. in Taxation (36 semester hours) is open to students with undergraduate degrees in accounting and includes course work in the following areas of taxation: corporations, partnerships, estates, gifts, trusts, state and local, practice and procedure, international, and research. The M.S. in Information Systems (30 to 33 semester hours) offers management and technology courses to prepare students for careers in software and systems development, security and CSI, and systems management. The M.S. in Marketing Research (37 semester hours) prepares students for careers in marketing research, product/service management, and marketing planning. The M.S. in Human Resource Management (30 to 36 semester hours) has courses in compensation administration, employee relations law, diversity, planning and policy, industrial and labor relations, staffing, and performance management. The M.S. in Real Estate (36 semester hours) is a specialized degree in real estate decision making and focuses on appraisal, architecture, investment analysis, land utilization, mortgage-backed securities, primary and secondary mortgage markets, real asset management, real property law, and urban and regional planning. The M.A. in Economics (30 to 36 semester hours) prepares students for jobs in government, business, research, and teaching. The program can be tailored to fit the student's interests, with special emphases in forecasting, international business, and quantitative analysis. The M.S. in Health Care Administration (36 semester hours) is a twenty-four-month, cohort-based program that integrates business topics with the delivery of health care services to prepare students for various positions in the health care industry. The M.B.A. program includes a 36-hour advanced program with areas of study in accounting, economics, finance, information systems, management, operations management, marketing, or real estate. The Professional Cohort M.B.A. program (45 semester hours) allows working professionals with no business background to complete their degrees in twenty-four months. The Monday evening and Saturday morning schedule enables students to focus on one course at a time. The Online M.B.A. program is a general management (36–45 semester hours) degree offered exclusively online. The Executive M.B.A. program targets mid-level executives/managers with at least seven to eight years of work experience. The program, offered in Fort Worth, features sixty-two class meetings, a four-day orientation, and a thirteen-day China International Residency experience. Classes are held alternating Friday and Saturday weekends. The Ph.D. in Business Administration (67 semester hours) is a research-oriented program. Major fields of study are accounting, finance, management, information systems, operations management, marketing, and statistics.

Research Facilities

Teaching and research activities take place in a modern building with 149,000 square feet of space. The building has six computer lab facilities with more than 211 desktop systems, one specialty lab with ten desktop systems, and one mobile "lab" with twenty-four laptops. In addition, there are twenty-four classrooms, each with a multimedia teaching station that is connected to the campus network and the Internet, and a distance learning classroom operated by UT Arlington's Distance Education. The Goolsby Leadership Academy, the Center for Research on Organizational and Managerial Excellence, the Center for Research in Information Technology Management, the Center for Marketing Research, and the Ryan-Reilly Center for Urban Land Utilization provide research assistance to faculty members and graduate students.

Financial Aid

Approximately eighty-five assistantships are available to students on a competitive basis. For 2010–11, master's stipends are $6000 and doctoral stipends $13,000 to $15,000 for a nine-month period. Individuals desiring part-time work off campus are served by one of the nation's best student employment service centers. Students with excellent academic credentials may apply for scholarships and fellowships.

Cost of Study

In 2010–11, tuition and fees for Texas residents were $5500 for 12 semester hours, while nonresidents paid $9305 for the same course work. Students with assistantships, fellowships, or scholarships may qualify for resident tuition rates.

Living and Housing Costs

Information about University and off-campus housing can be obtained by contacting the housing office at 817-272-2827. An ample supply of moderately priced apartments is available for both single and married students.

Student Group

The College enrolls approximately 1,500 master's students and 80 doctoral students. These students come from a variety of academic backgrounds in more than 200 universities in the United States and seventy-two other countries. Nearly 80 percent of the students have significant professional and technical work experience.

Location

Arlington, with a population of more than 369,000, is one of the fastest-growing cities in north Texas. It is located in the center of the vast Dallas–Fort Worth metroplex, which is a regional market and distribution center, a major convention site, a growing financial and cultural center, the tenth-largest market in the United States, and the home of the largest industrial district in the Southwest.

The University

The University of Texas at Arlington was founded in 1895 as a private liberal arts college called Arlington College. In recent years, it has grown significantly and is one of the largest institutions in the University of Texas System with nearly 29,000 enrolled. The University is composed of nine academic units, of which the College of Business is one of the largest (approximately 5,500 students).

Applying

Application may be made for fall, spring, or summer semesters. U.S. students are encouraged to submit their applications and all related material prior to May 15 for the fall semester, September 15 for the spring semester, and February 15 for the summer semester. International students are encouraged to submit their applications by April 1, September 1, and January 1, respectively. Applications, official transcripts, scores on the GMAT, and three letters of recommendation are required. International students are required to provide a TOEFL score or IELTS, financial statements, and statements of educational background.

Correspondence and Information

Director of Graduate Business Services
College of Business
UTA Box 19376
University of Texas at Arlington
Arlington, Texas 76019

Phone: 817-272-3005
E-mail: admit@uta.edu
Web site: http://www.uta.edu/gradbiz

University of Texas at Arlington

THE FACULTY AND THEIR RESEARCH

John Adams, Ph.D., Texas Tech, 2005. Finance.
Ryan C. Amacher, Ph.D., Virginia, 1971. International economics, microeconomics, public finance.
R. C. Baker, Ph.D., Texas A&M, 1971. Production, quality, and operations management.
Myrtle Bell, Ph.D., Texas at Arlington, 1996. Human resource management and diversity.
George Benson, Ph.D., USC, 2002. Human resource management.
Elten Briggs, Ph.D., Oklahoma, 2006. Services marketing.
Marcus Butts, Ph.D., Georgia, 2007. Organizational behavior and research methods.
Alan Cannon, Ph.D., Clemson, 1999. Operations management.
Wendy J. Casper, Ph.D., George Mason, 2000. Industrial/organizational psychology.
C. Y. Choi, Ph.D., Ohio State, 2000. International macroeconomics and finance, time-series econometrics, money and macroeconomics.
Larry Chonko, Ph.D., Houston, 1978. Sales management and marketing research.
William J. Crowder, Ph.D., Arizona State, 1992. International money and finance.
Deepak Datta, Ph.D., Pittsburgh, 1986. Strategic planning and policy, industrial economics.
Jeffery DeSimone, Ph.D., Yale, 1998. Education and health economics.
J. David Diltz, Ph.D., Illinois, 1980. Corporate finance, capital budgeting.
Mark Eakin, Ph.D., Texas A&M, 1980. Management science, statistics.
Jap Efendi, Ph.D., Texas A&M, 2004. Financial accounting.
Gregory Frazier, Ph.D., Texas A&M, 1989. Operations management.
Traci Freling, Ph.D., Texas A&M, 2007. Sales and marketing.
John Gallo, Ph.D., Texas at Arlington, 1992. Finance.
David Gray, Ph.D., Massachusetts, 1974. Management, industrial relations.
Douglas Grisaffe, Ph.D., Vanderbilt, 1989. Consumer research, decision making.
Bethane Jo Pierce Hall, Ph.D., North Texas State, 1987. Accounting, taxation.
Thomas W. Hall, Ph.D., Oklahoma State, 1980. Financial accounting, auditing.
Darren K. Hayunga, Ph.D., LSU, 2006. Real estate investments.
Daniel Himarios, Ph.D., Virginia Tech, 1984. Macroeconomics.
Li Chin Ho, Ph.D., Texas at Austin, 1990. Managerial and financial accounting.
Jorge Fernando Jaramillo, Ph.D., South Florida, 2004. Sales-force performance and marketing strategy.
Susanna Khavul, Ph.D., Boston, 2001. Entrepreneurship and strategic management.
Cagatay Koc, Ph.D., Texas at Austin, 2000. Applied econometrics, health economics, industrial organization, applied microeconomics.
Adwait Khare, Ph.D., Pittsburg, 2003, Business administration.
James Lavelle, Ph.D., Utah, 1999. Organizational behavior.
Pie Lung, Ph.D., Texas Tech, 2001. Finance and real estate.
Yongmei Liu, Ph.D., Florida State, 2006. Organizational behavior.
Xueming Luo, D.B.A., Louisiana Tech, 2003. Strategic marketing, modeling, international business/marketing.
Radha Mahapatra, Ph.D., Texas A&M, 1994. Information systems.
Sudha Mani, Ph.D., Western Ontario, 2007. Marketing and product development.
Richard Mark, LL.M., Denver, 1977. Accounting, taxation.
Donald McConnell, Ph.D., North Texas State, 1981. Financial accounting and auditing.
Ann McFadyen, Ph.D., Texas A&M, 2001. Strategic management.
Jeff McGee, Ph.D., Georgia, 1992. Venture development, small business management.
Gary McMahan, Ph.D., Texas A&M, 1993. Human resource management.
Roger Meiners, Ph.D., Virginia Tech, 1978. Law and economics.
Sridhar Nerur, Ph.D., Texas at Arlington, 1994. Information systems.
Liliana Nordtvedt, Ph.D., Memphis, 2005. Strategic and international management.
Edmund Prater, Ph.D., Georgia Tech, 1999. Operations management, supply chain management.
Joshua Price, Ph.D., Cornell, 2010, Economics of education and health.
James C. Quick, Ph.D., Houston, 1977. Management, organizational behavior.
M. K. Raja, Ph.D., Texas Tech, 1971. Management information systems.
Abdul Rasheed, Ph.D., Pittsburgh, 1988. Management, business policy.
Sanjiv Sabherwal, Ph.D., Georgia Tech, 2000. International finance and investments.
Ritesh Saini, Ph.D., Pennsylvania, 2008. Marketing.
Salil K. Sarkar, Ph.D., LSU, 1991. Corporate finance and investments.
Jian Shi, Ph.D., Syracuse, 2004. Corporate finance.
Riyaz Sikora, Ph.D., Illinois, 1994. Information systems.
Terrence Skantz, Ph.D., Oklahoma State, 1979. Accounting.
Craig Slinkman, Ph.D., Minnesota, 1982. Statistics, information systems.
Aaron D. Smallwood, Ph.D., Florida State, 2001. Time-series econometrics, international finance and international trade.
Chandra Subramaniam, Ph.D., Minnesota, 1993. Accounting and executive compensation.
Peggy Swanson, Ph.D., SMU, 1978. Corporate and international finance.
Martin E. Taylor, Ph.D., Texas at Austin, 1974. Auditing.
James T. C. Teng, Ph.D., Minnesota, 1980. E-commerce, information management.
Jeffrey Tsay, Ph.D., Missouri, 1973. Managerial accounting, information systems.
Jingguo Wang, Ph.D., SUNY at Buffalo, 2007. Network communications.
Michael Ward, Ph.D., Chicago, 1993. Applied price theory, industrial organization.
Kenneth Wheeler, Ph.D., Minnesota, 1978. Personnel and human resource management.
Mary Whiteside, Ph.D., Texas Tech, 1974. Statistics, management science.
Glyn Winterbotham, Ph.D., Oklahoma, 2008. Financial accounting.
Zhiyong Yang, Ph.D., Concordia, 2007. Consumer behavior and marketing.
Mahmut Yasar, Ph.D., Illinois, 2002. Trade and investments.
Li Yong, Ph.D., Texas at Austin, 2005. Investments and corporate finance.
Jennifer Zhang, Ph.D., Rochester, 2003. E-commerce and Web programming.

THE UNIVERSITY OF TEXAS AT DALLAS

School of Management

Programs of Study

The School of Management's ten dynamic master's programs answer the challenges facing today's business leaders. The curriculum for each of these degree programs is built around a strong core of classes with detailed study to address specific industry issues. These master's programs—accounting, finance, health-care management, information technology management, innovation and entrepreneurship, international management sciences, management and administrative services, project management, supply chain management, and systems engineering and management—also prepare students to take national certification exams, including CPA, CFA, CFP, Certified Internal Auditor, Project Management Professional, and others.

Master's degree programs require 36 credit hours for completion. School of Management classes are offered year-round, with a full schedule of course offerings in the evening to accommodate working professionals. The University of Texas at Dallas (UT Dallas) campus is centrally located in the Dallas metropolitan area, making it convenient to U.S. Highway 75 (Central Expressway), the Dallas North Tollway, and the George Bush Turnpike.

The School of Management also offers eight different M.B.A. programs, providing opportunities for students to match their particular career goals with specific programs. These programs are nationally recognized and offer a terrific tuition value for in-state students. Several of these 53-hour programs include an international study trip, many offer opportunities to take classes online, and all develop skills sought by the most competitive employers in the nation and around the world. Past graduates have gone on to positions at the World Bank, as leaders in health care and transportation, and at both mature and start-up IT companies.

Representatives from many corporations—ranging from retail to transportation to banking, finance, healthcare and communications—serve in various partnering capacities with the School of Management. These industry executives sit on various School of Management advisory panels, provide financial and research support, and serve as mentors to undergraduate and graduate students. Because of these strong ties, faculty members seek these outside professionals as classroom speakers, adding real-life perspective to textbook learning.

Graduate students may join one or several of about twenty preprofessional student clubs and organizations that have chapters at the School of Management. These organizations provide networking and leadership opportunities, a chance to meet other students with similar career interests, and specific ways to volunteer with UT Dallas or the community at large. Some organizations send teams to local, regional, and national competitions. Many offer access to internships and scholarships. These groups include AITP (Association of Information Technology Professionals), Beta Alpha Psi (accounting honors fraternity), Dean's Council, Graduate Business Society, Institute of Internal Auditors, SAP Users Group, SIFE (Students in Free Enterprise), Healthcare Management Club, and WIB (Women In Business), among others.

The School of Management is a Project Management Institute Registered Education Provider, one of the few universities nationwide to hold this distinction. The School's internal audit program has been endorsed by the Institute of Internal Auditing (IIA) as a Center for Internal Auditing Excellence, the highest designation of the IIA. UT Dallas is one of only two schools in the nation and five worldwide at this level. The School's executive M.B.A. has been ranked first among public university executive M.B.A. programs in Texas for three consecutive years by *Financial Times*. The full-time M.B.A. program has been ranked among the top 50 nationwide for two consecutive years by *U.S. News & World Report* and the professional part-time M.B.A. was ranked twenty-second in the nation this year by *U.S. News & World Report*.

Research Facilities

School of Management faculty has been recognized globally for its research productivity. The faculty ranks sixteenth in North America and seventeeth globally, according to the UTD Top 100 Business School Research Rankings, and ranks twentieth worldwide according to *Financial Times*. Research by the information systems faculty and operations management faculty ranks in the top 5 nationally in those respective fields. The School of Management also hosts twelve Centers of Excellence where faculty and students join to tackle real-world issues faced by local businesses. Students also have the opportunity to apply for internships with these centers and participate in the meetings and lectures they sponsor for industry professionals.

Financial Aid

The UT Dallas School of Management Scholarship Committee makes awards each fall based on merit, need, or a combination of the two. The annual Scholarship Breakfast most recently generated more than $100,000 in scholarships specifically for School of Management students at all levels. Students may also apply for the Dean's Excellence Scholarships, several of which are awarded each year. Full-time M.B.A. students with strong academic potential are eligible for significant scholarship and grant assistance. Applications are available from the UT Dallas Office of Financial Aid. The University participates in most federal and state aid programs. Short-term loans are also available. Prospective students should visit the School of Management's Web site at http://som.utdallas.edu for more information.

Cost of Study

Tuition for in-state full-time graduate students (9 hours) for fall 2010 is $4288. For graduate students attending school part-time, tuition is $1962 for 3 hours and $3187 for 6 hours. These prices exclude fees and other charges. The cost of obtaining a master's degree depends upon how many hours a student completes each semester. The full-time M.B.A. costs about $26,000 for students entering in fall 2010.

Living and Housing Costs

UT Dallas offers on-campus apartments, Waterview Park, which are operated by a private company. These apartments offer a variety of floorplans and are competitively priced. Interested students should visit http://www.utdallas.edu for information about on-campus housing. In addition, many off-campus housing options in the surrounding metropolitan area are available. An array of shopping and dining establishments, representing everything from large chains to small, single proprietor–run shops, are within bicycling distance of campus.

Student Group

About 60 percent of School of Management graduate students are working professionals seeking an advanced degree; they often take classes online, in the evening, and during the summer semester. The School's environment is both challenging and naturally diverse. About a third of the graduate students take 9 or more hours a semester. The School of Management, with about 5,000 students, is the largest of the seven schools of UT Dallas. School of Management students are equally split between undergraduate and graduate studies.

Most graduate students have at least five years of managerial experience. Women make up about 40 percent of master's students, and minorities represent almost 30 percent of the student population. About 30 percent of the students are from another country. Students range in age from 20 to more than 70; the average age is 30.

Location

The University of Texas at Dallas campus, in Richardson, is convenient to the George Bush Turnpike, U.S. Highway 75 (Central Expressway) and the Dallas North Tollway. It is within a 20-minute drive of most of Dallas' northern suburbs and businesses along Interstate 635 (LBJ Freeway) in Dallas. In addition to on-campus dining options, there are several restaurants and fast-food spots representing a cross-section of food options within about a mile of campus.

The University and The School

The University of Texas at Dallas was established in 1969 by the Texas Legislature. The School of Management, the largest college on the UT Dallas campus, enrolls about 5,000 students a year, almost evenly split between its undergraduate and graduate programs. The School of Management is fully accredited by AACSB International–The Association to Advance Collegiate Schools of Business.

The School of Management occupies a 204,000 square-foot building that opened in 2003. Each classroom is fully wired and the building has Wi-Fi access throughout. Computer labs offer a broad range of software. Various research centers operating from the School of Management seek graduate students to run studies and conduct research for corporate clients, offering students a high level of interaction with real-life business issues during their time in school.

Applying

Prerequisites for all graduate admissions include completion of an undergraduate calculus class and personal computer proficiency; spreadsheet proficiency is also a must. Completion of a baccalaureate degree from an accredited institution is required; previous undergraduate work in business courses is not a requirement. Additional requirements include GMAT or GRE scores, a complete application, and three recent letters of reference. A TOEFL score is required from those for whom English is not the native language. Applicants are evaluated on personal qualities and academic backgrounds, following admission formula guidelines of the International Association for Management Education. Personal interviews are not required. Admission deadlines vary by program and according to the applicant's citizenship status. Application requirements and deadlines are available on the School's Web site at http://som.utdallas.edu. To receive an application, students should send an e-mail to grad-admission@utdallas.edu.

Most programs will allow students to begin their coursework in the fall, spring, or summer semester. Certain programs, including the full-time M.B.A. and executive M.B.A., admit students only once each year.

Correspondence and Information

James Parker, Assistant Director of Graduate Recruiting
School of Management, SM40
The University of Texas at Dallas
Richardson, Texas 75080

Phone: 972-883-5842
Fax: 972-883-4095
E-mail: jparker@utdallas.edu
Web site: http://som.utdallas.edu

The University of Texas at Dallas

THE FACULTY AND THEIR RESEARCH

Hans-Joachim Adler, Senior Lecturer of Information Systems and Operations Management; Ph.D., Lyon (France).

Arthur Agulnek, Senior Lecturer of Accounting; B.S., Brooklyn State.

Shawn Alborz, Senior Lecturer of Information Systems and Operations Management; Ph.D., Melbourne (Australia).

Ashiq Ali, Davidson Distinguished Professor of Accounting; Ph.D., Columbia.

Frank Anderson, Senior Lecturer of Finance and Managerial Economics; M.B.A., SMU.

Mark Anderson, Associate Professor of Accounting; Ph.D., Florida.

Nina Baranchuk, Assistant Professor of Finance and Managerial Economics; Ph.D., Washington (St. Louis).

John Barden, Senior Lecturer of Accounting; M.B.A., Manhattan.

Indranil Bardhan, Associate Professor of Accounting and Management Information Systems; Ph.D., Texas at Austin.

George Barnes, Senior Lecturer of Organizations, Strategy, and International Management; M.A., Tufts.

Alain Bensoussan, Distinguished Research Professor of Risk Management, Operations Management; Ph.D., Paris.

Abhijit Biswas, Senior Lecturer of Marketing; Ph.D. candidate, Purdue.

Ron Blair, Senior Lecturer of Accounting; M.B.A., Oklahoma.

Daniel Bochsler, Senior Lecturer of Organizations, Strategy, and International Management; M.B.A., Houston.

Tiffany Bortz, Senior Lecturer of Accounting; M.S., Texas A&M.

Judd Bradbury, Senior Lecturer of Information Systems and Operations Management; M.S., Purdue.

Norris Bruce, Associate Professor of Marketing; Ph.D., Duke.

Metin Cakanyildirim, Associate Professor of Information Management and Operations Management; Ph.D., Cornell.

Huseyin Cavusoglu, Associate Professor in Information Systems and Operations Management; Ph.D., Texas at Dallas.

Ramaswamy Chandrasekaran, Professor of Information Systems and Operations Management; Ph.D., Berkeley.

Bobby Chang, Senior Lecturer and Director of Global Leadership Executive M.B.A.; M.B.A., USC.

Daniel Cohen, Associate Professor Accounting; Ph.D., Northwestern.

David Cordell, Clinical Professor of Finance and Managerial Economics; Ph.D., Texas at Austin.

William Cready, Ashbel Smith Professor of Accounting; Ph.D., Ohio State.

Rachel Croson, Professor of Organizations, Strategy, and International Management and Professor of Economics; Ph.D., Harvard.

Zhonglan (Di) Dai, Assistant Professor of Accounting; Ph.D., North Carolina at Chapel Hill.

Tevfik Dalgic, Clinical Professor of Organizations, Strategy, and International Management; Ph.D., Gazi (Turkey).

Milind Dawande, Professor of Information Systems and Operations Management; Ph.D., Carnegie Mellon.

Ted Day, Professor of Finance and Managerial Economics; Ph.D., Stanford.

Gene Deluke, Senior Lecturer of Information Systems and Operations Management; M.S., SMU.

Greg Dess, Andrew R. Cecil Endowed Chair in Applied Ethics; Ph.D., Washington (Seattle).

Alexander Edsel, Senior Lecturer of Marketing; J.D., Buenos Aires (Argentina).

Amal El-Ashmawi, Senior Lecturer of Finance and Managerial Economics; M.S., Texas at Dallas.

Adolf Enthoven, Professor of Accounting; Ph.D., Rotterdam.

Rebecca Files, Assistant Professor of Accounting; Ph.D., Texas A&M.

Forney Fleming, Clinical Professor of Healthcare Management; M.D., Texas Medical Branch.

David Ford, Jr., Professor of Organizations, Strategy, and International Management; Ph.D., Wisconsin–Madison.

Bernhard Ganglmair, Assistant Professor of Finance and Managerial Economics; Ph.D., Zurich (Switzerland).

Xianjun Geng, Assistant Professor of Information Systems and Operations Management; Ph.D., Texas at Austin.

Mary Beth Goodrich, Senior Lecturer of Accounting; M.B.A., LSU.

Umit Gurun, Assistant Professor of Accounting; Ph.D., Michigan State.

Richard Harrison, Associate Professor of International Management Studies; Ph.D., Stanford.

Ernan Haruvy, Associate Professor of Marketing; Ph.D., Texas at Austin.

Maria Hasenhuttl, Senior Lecturer of Organizations, Strategy, and International Management; Ph.D., Texas at Dallas.

Julie Haworth, Senior Lecturer of Marketing; M.B.A.; Texas at Austin.

Charlie Hazzard, Clinical Professor of Organizations, Strategy, and International Management; M.B.A. Pennsylvania.

Robert Hicks, Clinical Professor in Organizational Behavior; Ph.D., USC.

Gerald Hoag, Clinical Professor and Associate Dean for Executive Education and Director of Leadership Center at UT Dallas; M.B.A., Stanford.

Jonathan Hochberg, Senior Lecturer; Ed.D., Nova Southeastern.

Varghese Jacob, Ashbel Smith Professor of Information Systems and Operations Management and Senior Associate Dean; Ph.D., Purdue.

Ganesh Janakiraman, Associate Professor of Information Systems and Operations Management; Ph.D., Cornell.

Surya Janakiraman, Associate Professor of Accounting; Ph.D., Pennsylvania.

Jennifer Johnson, Senior Lecturer of Accounting; M.S., Texas A&M.

Marilyn Kaplan, Senior Lecturer of Organizations, Strategy, and International Management; Ph.D., Texas at Dallas.

Robert Kieschnick, Associate Professor of Finance and Managerial Economics; Ph.D., Texas at Austin.

Jackie Kimzey, Senior Lecturer of Organizations, Strategy, and International Management; M.B.A., Dallas.

Constantine Konstans, Professor of Accounting; Ph.D., Michigan State.

Todd Kravet, Assistant Professor of Accounting; Ph.D., Washington (Seattle).

Nanda Kumar, Associate Professor of Marketing; Ph.D., Chicago.

Seung-Hyun Lee, Associate Professor of Organizations, Strategy, and International Management; Ph.D., Ohio State.

Peter Lewin, Clinical Professor of Finance and Managerial Economics; Ph.D., Chicago.

Stan Liebowitz, Ashbel Smith Professor of Finance and Managerial Economics; Ph.D., UCLA.

Elizabeth Lim, Assistant Professor of Organizations, Strategy, and International Management; Ph.D., Connecticut.

Zhiang (John) Lin, Professor of Organizations, Strategy, and International Management; Ph.D., Carnegie Mellon.

Chris Linsteadt, Senior Lecturer of Accounting; M.S., M.B.A., Texas at Dallas.

Xiaohui (Gloria) Liu, Assistant Professor of Accounting; Ph.D., Northwestern.

Holly Lutze, Assistant Professor of Information Systems and Operations Management; Ph.D., Stanford.

Sumit Majumdar, Professor of Information Systems and Operations Management; Ph.D., Minnesota.

Livia Markoczy, Associate Professor of Organizations, Strategy, and International Management; Ph.D., Cambridge.

Stanimir Markov, Associate Professor of Accounting; Ph.D., Rochester.

David Mauer, Ashbel Smith Professor of Finance and Managerial Economics; Ph.D., Purdue.

John McCracken, Clinical Professor of Medical Management; Ph.D., Pennsylvania (Wharton).

Dennis McCuistion, Clinical Professor of Corporate Governance; M.L.A., SMU.

Diane McNulty, Associate Dean for External Affairs and Senior Lecturer of Business Policy; Ph.D., Texas at Dallas.

Syam Menon, Associate Professor of Information Systems and Operations Management; Ph.D., Chicago.

Radha Mookerjee, Senior Lecturer of Information Systems and Operations Management; Ph.D., Purdue.

Vijay Mookerjee, Professor of Information Systems and Operations Management; Ph.D., Purdue.

B. P. S. Murthi, Associate Professor of Marketing; Ph.D., Carnegie Mellon.

Volkan Muslu, Assistant Professor of Accounting; Ph.D., MIT.

Kumar Nair, Senior Lecturer of Strategy, Organizational Performance, and Leadership; Ph.D., Twente (Netherlands).

Ramachandran Natarajan, Associate Professor of Accounting; Ph.D., Pennsylvania (Wharton).

Shun-Chen Niu, Professor of Information Systems and Operations Management; Ph.D., Berkeley.

Ozalp Ozer, Associate Professor of Information Systems and Operations Management; Ph.D. Columbia.

Arzu Ozoguz, Assistant Professor of Finance and Managerial Economics; Ph.D., INSEAD.

Madison Pedigo, Senior Lecturer of Organizations, Strategy, and International Management; M.B.A., Ohio State.

Mike Peng, Provost's Distinguished Professor of Global Strategy, Organizations, Strategy, and International Management; Ph.D., Washington (Seattle).

Joseph Picken, Clinical Professor of Organizations, Strategy, and International Management; Ph.D., Texas at Arlington.

Hasan Pirkul, Dean and Caruth Chair Professor of Decision Sciences; Ph.D., Rochester.

Nataliya Polkovnichenko, Senior Lecturer of Finance and Managerial Economics; M.S., Minnesota.

Valery Polkovnichenko, Assistant Professor of Finance and Managerial Economics; Ph.D., Northwestern.

Matt Polze, Senior Lecturer of Accounting; J.D., M.P.A., Texas.

Ashutosh Prasad, Associate Professor of Marketing; Ph.D., Texas at Austin.

Suresh Radhakrishnan, Professor of Accounting; Ph.D., NYU.

Srinivasan Raghunathan, Professor of Information Systems and Operations Management; Ph.D., Pittsburgh.

Roberto Ragozzino, Assistant Professor of Organizations, Strategy, and International Management; Ph.D., Ohio State.

Divakar Rajamani, Clinical Professor of Information Systems and Operations Management; Ph.D., Windsor.

Kannan Ramanathan, Senior Lecturer of Information Systems and Operations Management; Ph.D., Illinois at Urbana-Champaign.

Ram Rao, Founders Professor of Marketing; Ph.D., Carnegie Mellon.

Brian Ratchford, Davidson Distinguished Professor of Marketing; Ph.D., Rochester.

Michael Rebello, Professor of Finance and Managerial Economics; Ph.D., Texas at Austin.

Carolyn Reichert, Senior Lecturer of Finance and Managerial Economics; Ph.D., Penn State.

Orlando Richard, Associate Professor of Organizations, Strategy, and International Management; Ph.D., Kentucky.

Robert Robb, Senior Lecturer of Organizations, Strategy, and International Management; M.S., Utah.

Tracey Rockett, Senior Lecturer of Organizations, Strategy, and International Management; Ph.D., Texas at Dallas.

Young Ryu, Associate Professor of Information Systems and Operations Management; Ph.D., Texas at Dallas.

Mark Salamasick, Senior Lecturer of Accounting; M.B.A., Central Michigan.

Jane Salk, Associate Professor of Organizations, Strategy, and International Management; Ph.D., MIT.

Phil Sanchez III, Senior Lecturer and Director of Executive M.B.A. Program; M.B.A., Tarleton State.

Sumit Sarkar, Ashbel Smith Professor of Information Systems and Operations Management; Ph.D., Rochester.

Michael Savoie, Director of Center for Information Technology and Management and Senior Lecturer of Information Systems and Operations Management; Ph.D., North Texas.

Avanti Sethi, Senior Lecturer of Information Systems and Operations Management; Ph.D., Carnegie Mellon.

Suresh Sethi, Ashbel Smith Professor of Operations Management and Fellow of the Royal Society of Canada and the New York Academy; Ph.D., Carnegie Mellon.

Rajiv Shah, Clinical Professor of Organizations, Strategy, and International Management; Ph.D., Rice.

Harpreet Singh, Assistant Professor of Information Systems and Operations Management; Ph.D., Connecticut.

Jeanne Sluder, Senior Lecturer of Organizations, Strategy, and International Management; Ph.D., Texas Woman's.

Charles Solcher, Senior Lecturer of Accounting; J.D., South Texas Law.

Gonca Soysal, Assistant Professor of Marketing; Ph.D., Northwestern.

David Springate, Associate Professor of Finance and Managerial Economics; D.B.A., Harvard.

Chelliah Sriskandarajah, Ashbel Smith Professor of Information Systems and Operations Management; Ph.D., National Polytechnic Institute of Grenoble (France).

Kathryn Stecke, Ashbel Smith Professor of Information Systems and Operations Management; Ph.D., Purdue.

Andrei Strijnev, Assistant Professor of Marketing; Ph.D., Washington (St. Louis).

Upender Subramanian, Assistant Professor Marketing; Ph.D., Pennsylvania.

Francisco Szekely, Visiting Professor of Business and Sustainability; Ph.D., Washington (Seattle).

Jim Szot, Senior Lecturer and Interim Director, Executive Education Project Management Program; M.B.A., Dallas.

Lou Thompson, Senior Lecturer of Information Systems and Operations Management; M.S., DePaul.

Mark Thouin, Senior Lecturer of Information Systems and Operations Management; Ph.D., Texas Tech.

Amy Troutman, Assistant Director of Accounting Programs and Senior Lecturer; M.P.A., Texas at Austin.

Eric Tsang, Associate Professor of Organizations, Strategy, and International Management; Ph.D., Cambridge.

Yu Wang, Assistant Professor of Marketing; Ph.D., Michigan.

McClain (John) Watson, Senior Lecturer of Organizations, Strategy, and International Management; Ph.D., Iowa.

Kelsey Wei, Assistant Professor of Finance and Managerial Economics; Ph.D., Texas.

Joe Wells, Clinical Professor of Finance and Managerial Economics; Ph.D., Cornell.

John Wiorkowski, Professor of Information Systems and Operations Management; Ph.D., Chicago.

Habte Woldu, Senior Lecturer of Organizations, Strategy, and International Management; Ph.D., Poznan (Poland).

Fang Wu, Clinical Professor of Marketing; Ph.D., Texas at Austin.

Yexiao Xu, Associate Professor of Finance and Managerial Economics; Ph.D., Princeton.

Yuanping Ying, Assistant Professor of Marketing; Ph.D., Michigan.

Alejandro Zentner, Assistant Professor of Finance and Managerial Economics; Ph.D., Chicago.

Harold Zhang, Professor of Finance and Managerial Economics; Ph.D., Duke.

Jun Zhang, Assistant Professor of Information Systems and Operations Management; Ph.D., Carnegie Mellon.

Feng Zhao, Assistant Professor of Finance and Managerial Economics; Ph.D., Cornell.

Zhiqiang (Eric) Zheng; Associate Professor of Information Systems and Operations Management; Ph.D., Pennsylvania.

Yibin Zhou, Assistant Professor of Accounting; Ph.D., Toronto.

Laurie Ziegler, Senior Lecturer of Organizations, Strategy, and International Management; Ph.D., Texas at Arlington.

UNIVERSITY OF WISCONSIN

M.B.A. Consortium

Program of Study	Students in the UW MBA Consortium program gain a broad, practical understanding of business and the dynamic global environment in which it operates. Students develop the skills and entrepreneurial spirit needed to manage change and recognize the opportunities it creates, and they learn guidelines for confronting situations in an ethical and socially responsible manner. The M.B.A. curriculum balances theory with application, number crunching with interpersonal skill development, and team projects with individual assignments.

The 30-credit online program consists of a required core of 16 credits of interdisciplinary modules and 1 credit of leadership/teamwork, with the remaining 13 credits chosen from elective offerings. Individuals without baccalaureate business degrees must complete preliminary M.B.A. foundation courses. M.B.A. students enroll in 4 to 6 credits per semester and 1 to 3 credits in the summer session. All M.B.A. modules and electives are offered online. Using the latest in Web-based course work, faculty members teach each course and conduct virtual office hours. Grades are based on class participation, projects, written case studies and reports, quizzes, and examinations. The consortium's M.B.A. program enables students with multiple commitments to make reasonably paced progress toward their degree. The degree can be completed within two years after M.B.A. foundation requirements have been met.

The 16 interdisciplinary credits are divided into four 4-credit courses composed of themes and skill development activities. This required core of study consists of integrated team-taught modules to give today's business leader a comprehensive perspective of the big picture. Successful leaders must be able to think outside their areas of expertise, synthesize ideas and concepts from other disciplines, and understand how decisions made in one functional area impact the entire firm.

The four M.B.A. modules reflect the situations managers face as their organizations move through the business cycle. Each module is taught by a team of 2 to 3 graduate faculty members from the four University of Wisconsin–M.B.A. Consortium schools.

The first module, Strategies for Managing Ongoing Operations, focuses on the strategies needed to manage the day-to-day operations of an organization and the interplay among the various functional areas of business.

The second module, Developing New Products and Services, introduces students to the complexities involved in launching new products/services, business ventures, subsidiaries, or divisions within existing businesses. Two themes predominate in this module: a marketing theme focusing on the identification and fulfillment of customer needs and a financial theme exploring capital budgeting and long-term financial issues.

The required 1-credit minimodule is taken concurrently with Module 2 and focuses on leadership and teamwork, leading students to examine the challenges and responsibilities inherent in the role of leadership.

Managing Strategically in a Global Environment is the third module. In this course, students develop the critical skills and integrated knowledge necessary to function effectively in today's global environment. Course work involves analyzing the impact of multinational corporate lobbying on geopolitical issues and discussing how global agreements, changing technologies, global institutions, and evolving political patterns affect the conduct of global business.

The fourth module, Focusing on the Future, builds on the previous modules by preparing students to consider present conditions and analyze possible future events during their careers. Participants identify and analyze trends in business and project their potential impact on managerial practice.

Electives are 1- to 2-credit courses in which students participate in brief explorations into topics relevant to their particular needs and interests. Upcoming electives include such topics as business process simulation, decision analysis, project management, strategy and tactics of pricing, international marketing research, introduction to assurance services, regional marketing agreements and emerging markets, selling ideas at work, reengineering financial performance measures, and enterprise resource planning. Elective offerings vary from semester to semester, and new electives are added each term.

Students requiring preliminary foundation courses work with the M.B.A. Director to determine the appropriate foundation courses needed.

Research Facilities	The Consortium has its own design team dedicated to working with faculty members on course development. Students have access to advising, library services, career services, online textbook ordering, and both phone and e-mail technology support through the Consortium's managing partner, UW–Eau Claire.
Financial Aid	There are several forms of financial aid assistance available to graduate students.
Cost of Study	Tuition for the online M.B.A. for 2010–11 is $650 per credit.
Student Group	The University of Wisconsin MBA Consortium program is designed to meet the needs of graduates in the workforce as well as students seeking direct admission from their undergraduate degree programs. The program also welcomes applications from international students.
The University	The University of Wisconsin–M.B.A. Consortium is an association of four business schools accredited by AACSB International–The Association to Advance Collegiate Schools of Business: the University of Wisconsin–Eau Claire, the University of Wisconsin–La Crosse, the University of Wisconsin–Oshkosh, and the University of Wisconsin–Parkside. Located in America's heartland, the universities are part of the University of Wisconsin (UW) system, one of the largest and most prestigious higher education systems in the United States. The on-campus M.B.A. programs of the four schools are among the finest graduate programs in the region. Using the knowledge gained from managing the on-campus M.B.A. programs, the four schools have come together to develop the only collaborative online M.B.A. program offered by the UW system.
Applying	Requirements for admission to the M.B.A. program include a baccalaureate degree from an accredited college or university, a cumulative GPA of at least 2.75, completion of the M.B.A. foundation courses if necessary, a Graduate Management Admission Test (GMAT) score of at least 475 or a comparable score on the Graduate Record Examinations (GRE), and, for students whose native language is not English, a score on the Test of English as a Foreign Language (TOEFL) of at least 550 on the paper-based test or 213 on the computer-based test. Applications from international students are welcomed.

In addition, the online courses require home high-speed access to the Internet, a computer capable of playing and saving multimedia files, and Microsoft Office. More in-depth information about technology requirements and skills needed for the online program is provided on the consortium's Web site.

Students can officially begin the M.B.A. program in either the fall or the spring semester by enrolling in Module 1. Students who wish to start prior to Module 1 may take elective courses during the summer session. Applications are submitted through UW–Eau Claire and can be found online at http://apply.wisconsin.edu/graduate/eau. There is a $56 application fee.

Correspondence and Information	UW–M.B.A. Consortium Program c/o UW–Eau Claire Schneider Hall, Room 215 P.O. Box 4004 Eau Claire, Wisconsin 54702-4004 Phone: 715-836-6019 888-832-7090 (toll-free) Fax: 715-836-3923 E-mail: uwcmba@uwec.edu Web site: http://www.wisconsinonlinemba.org/

University of Wisconsin

THE FACULTY

Faculty members have Ph.D.'s and strong academic credentials. They are professionally active in consulting and applied research and serve on boards of corporate and nonprofit organizations. Most are also teaching in the face-to-face environment on their own campuses as well as participating in the online program. Any faculty member teaching in the University of Wisconsin Consortium MBA Program must pass the program-specific four-week preparation course prior to teaching online.

WAYNE STATE UNIVERSITY
SCHOOL OF BUSINESS ADMINISTRATION

WAYNE STATE UNIVERSITY

School of Business Administration

Programs of Study

Wayne State University (WSU) offers several graduate programs in business: the Master of Business Administration (M.B.A.), Master of Science in Accounting (M.S.A.), Master of Science in Taxation (M.S.T.), Doctor of Philosophy (Ph.D.) in business administration, and the joint J.D./M.B.A. degree. One of the nation's most diverse campuses with students representing more than seventy countries, WSU offers many perspectives in the study of global business. Wayne State's graduate business programs are accredited by AACSB International—The Association to Advance Collegiate Schools of Business. This organization holds the highest standards of achievement for business schools worldwide. Member institutions confirm their commitment to quality and continuous improvement through a rigorous and comprehensive peer review.

The **Master of Business Administration (M.B.A.)** program at WSU emphasizes practical and conceptual knowledge to prepare individuals for successful careers in business, government, nonprofit, and other organizations. The program is designed to meet the demands of the ever-changing workplace. The flexible, generalized program includes accelerated, Saturday, and online options. A basic foundation in accounting, computing, economics, finance, management, marketing, production management, and business writing is essential for starting the M.B.A. program. Applicants who do not have a prior background in business must enroll in accelerated foundation courses to meet these requirements. Often, applicants with prior business education are able to waive all or some of these foundation courses. Once foundation requirements are fulfilled, students take six core courses in general business and six course electives based on their personal interests. M.B.A. students can choose from a wide range of elective courses, allowing them to design a program that is most relevant to their needs and interests. Elective options cover a wide range of disciplines including accounting, finance, marketing, management, information systems management, global supply chain management, entrepreneurship, human resource management, labor relations, international business, leadership, organizational behavior, quality management, and taxation.

The **Master of Science in Accounting (M.S.A.)** program prepares individuals for professional careers in public accounting. The primary objective of the program is to prepare students for public accounting careers rather than entry-level jobs, while meeting the 150-hour education requirement for licensure as a certified public accountant (CPA) in the state of Michigan. A secondary objective is to better prepare students for professional examinations, especially the CPA exam. Students with undergraduate degrees in accounting who are pursuing careers in private industry, financial institutions, government, and nonprofit organizations will benefit from the expanded study in accounting and business.

The **Master of Science in Taxation (M.S.T.)** program trains students for entry into professional tax practice in both the public and private sectors. Through the interdisciplinary nature of the program, students learn the accounting, legal, and public policy aspects of taxation. Students with a bachelor's degree in accounting usually meet all of the program's foundation requirements. Applicants with a bachelor's degree in a field other than accounting may have to complete foundation courses in the areas of accounting, business law, information systems management, and statistics.

The **Doctor of Philosophy (Ph.D.)** in business administration prepares students to become faculty members at major research universities. The program places a heavy emphasis on global perspectives and focuses on quantitative skills, which enables students to engage in research projects with faculty members. Currently, tracks are available in finance, marketing, and management. Assistantships, scholarships, and fellowships are available to doctoral students on a competitive basis.

Through WSU's **J.D./M.B.A. program,** qualified applicants may elect to complete both a law degree and the M.B.A. degree. The program allows students to fulfill the requirements of both programs concurrently. Students will need to complete all the requirements for both degrees, but Wayne State University Law School courses may count for up to 6 elective credits toward the M.B.A. degree. Students are granted five or six years to complete the requirements for both degrees, depending on whether the student entered as a part- or full-time student. The first year of the program is spent in the Law School. Students must be admitted to the Law School and to the M.B.A. program in the School of Business Administration and must obtain the separate approval of both units in order to participate. Students must take both the GMAT and the LSAT and meet all other admission requirements for both programs. For more information about the WSU Law School, visit http://www.law.wayne.edu.

Semesters begin in September, January, and May. The academic year has two 15-week semesters in fall and winter. For those interested in taking classes year round, Wayne State schedules some spring and summer courses in separate eight-week sessions and others in a thirteen-week combined spring/summer semester. A full schedule of graduate courses is offered each term.

Research Facilities

Wayne State University School of Business Administration offers a wide range of computing resources to students. The School has a dedicated computer laboratory exclusively for business school students. It is equipped with the latest PC workstations, network printers, and business software. Distance learning classrooms link WSU's main campus in Detroit with its suburban satellite campuses. Software products allow faculty members to record lectures that students can view from any computer with Internet access. Many M.B.A. courses are available online. High-speed wireless Internet is accessible is accessible to registered students in all campus buildings.

The University Library System provides access to many business resources, including electronic indexes with abstracts and full text, and subject guides that focus on specific areas of research. Many of these resources are accessible online. The library system provides open-access computer labs for the campus community; there are more than 800 computers with a variety of applications in support of student learning. A 24-hour Extended Study Center is open in the Undergraduate Library during the fall and winter semesters.

Financial Aid

The Office of Scholarships and Financial Aid provides students with information regarding sources of funds. The University awards graduate and professional scholarships to both full- and part-time graduate students. The School of Business also grants private scholarships to business students. The School's academic departments provide graduate teaching and research assistantships. Stipends for assistantships average $14,000 plus tuition and benefits for nine-month appointments.

Cost of Study

In 2009–10, tuition was $530 per credit hour for Michigan residents and $1082 per credit hour for non-residents. For current tuition and fee information, visit http://reg.wayne.edu/.

Living and Housing Costs

WSU Housing offers a number of options for students including residence halls, modern apartment buildings with views of the city, and historic apartments on campus. The University's residence halls, located in the heart of the campus, are just steps from the 24-hour Undergraduate Library, the Recreation and Fitness Center, the Student Center, and classes. The Towers Residential Suites provide housing for sophomores, juniors, seniors, graduate, and professional students. Apartment costs range from $419 per month for an efficiency apartment to $1244 per month for a three-bedroom apartment. Residence halls (including a meal plan) range from $4972 to $7716 for the academic year. For more specific information, visit http://www.housing.wayne.edu.

Student Group

The School of Business Administration enrolls approximately 250 full-time and 900 part-time graduate students. Women form 44 percent of current graduate enrollment and more than 7 percent is international students. The average age of an M.B.A. student is 30 years, although the age range is 17 to 58. A typical class size is about 35 students. Typically, M.B.A. students have five years of work experience, and approximately 93 percent are employed either full- or part-time, with more than half holding supervisory positions.

Student Outcomes

Most students pursuing a master's degree in business administration, accounting, or taxation have already made impressive starts to their careers. An advanced degree can be a vehicle to broaden expertise, enhance opportunities for advancement, and increase earning potential. The School of Business Administration has a Career Planning and Placement Office dedicated only to business students and regularly assists students in finding permanent positions locally, nationally, and internationally.

Location

Located in Detroit, an international gateway connecting the United States and Canada, Wayne State University provides a unique setting for learning business. The main campus is located in the heart of Detroit's University Cultural Center, which is home to renowned museums, galleries, and theaters, most within walking distance. It encompasses 203 acres of landscaped walkways and gathering spots, linking 100 buildings. Downtown Detroit is just a few miles away, with restaurants, professional sports venues, and many other entertainment and business activities.

In addition, Wayne State operates a number of extension centers in metropolitan Detroit. Business courses are offered at WSU's Oakland Center in Farmington Hills and the Advanced Technology Education Center in Warren.

The University

Wayne State University is Michigan's only urban research university, filling a unique niche by providing access to a world-class education at a great value. Wayne State's thirteen schools and colleges offer more than 350 academic programs to nearly 33,000 graduate and undergraduate students.

Applying

The M.B.A., M.S.A., and M.S.T. programs are open to students who hold a bachelor's degree from a regionally accredited institution and who demonstrate promise of success in pursuing graduate study. The online application for graduate admission (http://www.gradapply.wayne.edu), an application fee, official transcripts from all collegiate institutions attended, and GMAT results are required. Admission is granted each semester. The application and other required documents are due by July 1 for fall semester admission, November 1 for winter semester admission, and March 15 for spring-summer semester admission. International students must provide required materials four months prior to the beginning of the term in which they want to begin their studies.

Applicants to the Ph.D. program may be admitted with a bachelor's or a master's degree and are expected to have sufficient competence in math, computing, and statistics to satisfy prerequisites for the quantitative courses in the Ph.D. curriculum. Students who have not completed macroeconomics, microeconomics, and calculus prerequisites prior to admission must enroll in these courses during the first year of the doctoral program. Minimum requirements include a 3.0 undergraduate GPA (or 3.0 upper-division GPA), 3.5 graduate GPA, and a minimum 600 GMAT score. International applicants must meet the University requirements for TOEFL scores. Three letters of recommendation and an essay on career objectives must be included with applications for admission to the Ph.D. program.

Correspondence and Information

Office of Student Services
School of Business Administration
Wayne State University
Detroit, Michigan 48202

Phone: 313-577-4510
800-910-3276 (toll-free)
Fax: 313-577-5299
Web site: http://www.business.wayne.edu

Wayne State University

THE FACULTY

Angela Andrews, Assistant Professor of Accounting; Ph.D., Michigan State.
Mark E. Bayless, Associate Professor of Finance; Ph.D., Washington (St. Louis).
Richard F. Beltramini, Professor of Marketing; Ph.D., Texas at Austin.
B. Anthony Billings, Professor of Tax; Ph.D., Texas A&M.
Abhijit Biswas, Professor of Marketing and Kmart Endowed Chair; Ph.D., Houston.
William Burrell, Lecturer in Global Supply Chain Management; M.B.A., Wayne State.
Timothy W. Butler, Associate Professor of Global Supply Chain Management; Ph.D., South Carolina.
Hugh M. Cannon, Adcraft/Simons-Michelson Professor of Advertising; Ph.D., NYU.
Sudip Datta, Professor of Finance and T. Norris Hitchman Chair; Ph.D., SUNY.
Ranjan D'Mello, Associate Professor of Finance; Ph.D., Ohio State.
Sujay Dutta, Assistant Professor of Marketing; Ph.D., LSU.
Abhijit Guha, Assistant Professor of Marketing; Ph.D., Duke.
Jia Hao, Assistant Professor of Finance; Ph.D., Utah.
David Huff, Senior Lecturer in Information Systems Management; Ph.D., Wayne State.
Mai Iskandar-Datta, Professor of Finance; Ph.D., Missouri–Columbia.
Bill Jones, Senior Lecturer in Marketing; Ph.D., Kentucky.
Deborah Jones, Senior Lecturer of Accounting and Taxation; Ph.D., Kent State.
Scott Julian, Associate Professor of Management; Ph.D., LSU.
Kevin Ketels, Lecturer in Marketing; M.S., Boston University.
K. S. Krishnan, Associate Professor of Global Supply Chain Management; Ph.D., Pennsylvania.
Frank LaMarra, Lecturer in Accounting; M.B.A., Wayne State; CPA.
Cheol Lee, Assistant Professor of Accounting; Ph.D., SUNY at Buffalo.
Jaegul Lee, Assistant Professor of Management; Ph.D., Carnegie Mellon.
Ariel Levi, Senior Lecturer in Management; Ph.D., Yale.
Kun Liu, Assistant Professor in Management; Ph.D., Washington State.
David Lucas, Senior Lecturer in Management; Ph.D., Wayne State.
James E. Martin, Professor of Management and Industrial Relations; Ph.D., Washington (St. Louis).
Cathleen Miller, Associate Professor of Accounting; Ph.D., Kentucky.
Santanu Mitra, Associate Professor of Accounting; Ph.D., LSU.
Fred Morgan, Professor of Marketing and Chair of the Marketing Department; Ph.D., Michigan State.
Mbodja Mougoué, Associate Professor of Finance; Ph.D., New Orleans.
Thomas J. Naughton, Associate Professor of Management; Ph.D., SUNY at Buffalo.
Randolph Paschke, Chair of the Accounting Department and Interim Chair of the Finance Department; B.B.A., Michigan; CPA.
Sheri Perelli, Senior Lecturer in Management; Ph.D., Case Western Reserve.
Kelly R. Price, Associate Professor of Finance; Ph.D., Michigan.
Arik Ragowsky, Associate Professor of Information Systems Management and Director, Manufacturing Information Systems Center; Ph.D., Tel Aviv.
Paul Reagan, Senior Lecturer in Management; Ph.D., Michigan State.
Irvin D. Reid, Professor of Management; Ph.D., Pennsylvania.
Alan Reinstein, George Husband Endowed Professor of Accounting; D.B.A., Kentucky; CPA.
Celia Livermore Romm, Professor of Information Systems Management; Ph.D., Toronto.
Mark Savitskie, Lecturer in Accounting; M.B.A., Wayne State.
Pamela Schmidt, Instructor in Accounting; M.B.A., Northwestern.
Margaret Smoller, Associate Professor of Finance and Associate Dean for Undergraduate Programs; Ph.D., Florida.
Toni M. Somers, Professor of Information Systems Management; Ph.D., Toledo.
Albert D. Spalding Jr., Associate Professor of Business Law and Taxation; J.D., M.B.A., George Washington; CPA.
William Spaulding, Lecturer in Management; M.B.A., Wayne State.
Myles S. Stern, Associate Professor of Accounting; Ph.D., Michigan State; CMA.
Jeffrey J. Stoltman, Associate Professor of Marketing and Associate Dean for Graduate Programs; Ph.D., Syracuse.
Joseph Tan, Professor of Information Systems Management; Ph.D., British Columbia.
Andrea Tangari, Instructor in Marketing; M.B.A., Arkansas.
John Taylor, Associate Professor of Global Supply Chain Management; Ph.D., Michigan State.
Amanuel G. Tekleab, Associate Professor of Management; Ph.D., Maryland.
Frank Vandervegt, Senior Lecturer in Information Systems Management; Ph.D., Michigan.
Harish L. Verma, Associate Professor of Global Supply Chain Management; Ph.D., Michigan State.
William H. Volz, Professor of Business Law; J.D., Wayne State; M.B.A., Harvard.
John D. Wagster, Associate Professor of Finance; Ph.D., Texas A&M.
Tina Walsh, Senior Lecturer in Accounting; LL.M., Florida.
Daniel Weimer, Lecturer in Accounting; M.A., Michigan; CPA.
Mary Ann Welden, Lecturer in Accounting; M.B.A., Notre Dame; CPA.
David L. Williams, Associate Professor of Marketing and Dean; Ph.D., Wayne State.
Larry Williams, Professor of Management; Ph.D., Indiana.
Margaret Williams, Professor of Management and Chair of the Management Department; Ph.D., Indiana.
Sandra Williams, Senior Lecturer in Management; Ph.D., Wayne State.
Susan Williams, Lecturer in Marketing; M.B.A., Oakland.
Maef Woods, Assistant Professor of Accounting; Ph.D., Cincinnati.
Victor Wooddell, Senior Lecturer in Management; Ph.D., Wayne State.
Attila Yaprak, Professor of Marketing; Ph.D., Georgia State.

WEBBER INTERNATIONAL UNIVERSITY

Graduate School of Business

Program of Study

The Webber International University Graduate School of Business offers a unique eighteen-month, full-time program leading to a Master of Business Administration (M.B.A.), with options in accounting, international business (online), management, security management, or sport management. The degree consists of twelve courses (36 credit hours); students take two courses a term over six 10-week terms. Courses are offered two nights a week and online. The University is accredited by the Southern Association of Colleges and Schools and the International Assembly for Collegiate Business Education.

The Webber M.B.A. aims to assist students in enhancing managerial skills through the delivery of techniques and best practices that integrate academic theory with contemporary applications. The program places a premium level of concentration on developing students' critical-thinking skills, so that they may more easily adapt to paradigm shifts within business.

The Webber International University Graduate School of Business offers an M.B.A. program that focuses on the interdisciplinary nature of business practices. The program capitalizes on the faculty's ability to focus on proven traditional methods of teaching that integrate the various facets of effective business administration, while utilizing information technology to enhance problem-solving skills.

Through the practicum course(s), students undertake group-based consulting projects. Through these projects, students have the opportunity to test theoretical concepts in an applied setting. In Webber's new international business concentration, students will have the opportunity to gain hands-on field experience abroad.

Research Facilities

The Roger Babson Learning Center, located in the central part of the campus, is a modern and comprehensive library facility that contains extensive collections of reference, research, and reserve materials keyed to business research. The center also offers access to several external data sources, such as EbscoHost, LexisNexis Academic Universe, LIRN-Library, as well as others.

The computer resource center is a data processing center and teaching facility with microcomputers offering the latest modern technology for developing student excellence in business, communication, and creativity.

Financial Aid

Financial aid is available in the form of student loans for eligible students. For more information, prospective students should contact the Financial Aid Office (telephone: 863-638-2929). In addition, many employers provide for or subsidize their employees' tuition expenses. Webber also offers veterans' education benefits for those who qualify.

Cost of Study

Tuition for the 2010–11 academic year is $562 per credit hour. Book expenses vary by course.

Living and Housing Costs

On-campus housing is available to graduate students. Housing costs range from $1670 to $2290 per ten-week term. A meal plan is available for $825 per ten-week term. Additional fees include a cable and MicroFridge fee per term.

Student Group

The Graduate School of Business is small in size, with approximately 60 graduate students. With small class sizes, there is opportunity for students to exchange ideas with other students and interact closely with the faculty.

The students are distinguished by the diversity of their professional and ethnic backgrounds. The average age of the students in the M.B.A. program is 30, and approximately 55 percent of the class has had one year or more of professional, full-time employment experience. Students come from several states as well as several different countries. Approximately half are women and approximately 60 percent are employed full- or part-time.

Student Outcomes

Approximately 68 percent of Webber graduates live and work in Florida. Thirty-two percent are located throughout the United States and the world. A sample of position titles of recent graduates includes partner, manager, human resource manager, and assistant controller.

Location

Webber International University is located on a beautiful 110-acre campus along the shoreline of Crooked Lake, approximately 45 minutes south of Orlando. The town of Babson Park, a small rural residential community, is located in the heart of Florida's citrus country near a chain of freshwater lakes. Babson Park is conveniently located near many major recreational facilities and national tourist attractions in central Florida.

The University and The School

Webber International University was founded in 1927 by Grace Knight and Roger W. Babson as a women's college, with the exclusive purpose of teaching women about business. It was the first school chartered under the educational and charitable laws of the state of Florida as a nonprofit organization. In September 1971, the college began admitting men.

Webber is a small, private, nonprofit university with a total student body of approximately 650.

The Graduate School of Business was established in September 1997. The Graduate School of Business granted its first degrees in February 1999.

Applying

Men and women with baccalaureate degrees from regionally accredited colleges or universities or the international equivalent are eligible for consideration for admission. Admission to the Graduate School is based on both quantitative and qualitative criteria. In addition to the application, the applicant must submit a resume, an essay, and three letters of recommendation, and some may need to submit results from the GMAT. Academic qualifications are determined by evaluation of student performance at previous higher education institutions. In addition, international applicants are required to submit results from the TOEFL unless they have obtained a degree from a college or university where English is the language of instruction.

Students may take a full-time load of two courses per term or a part-time load of one class per term. The M.B.A. program admits students in the fall (August), winter (November), spring (February), and summer (May). Applications are accepted on a first-come, first-served basis. Applications may be submitted online, downloaded from the University's Web site, or requested and sent through conventional mail.

Correspondence and Information

M.B.A. Coordinator
Graduate School of Business
Webber International University
1201 North Scenic Highway
P.O. Box 96
Babson Park, Florida 33827-0096
Phone: 863-638-2927
Fax: 863-638-1591
E-mail: mba@webber.edu
Web site: http://www.webber.edu

Webber International University

THE FACULTY

The Webber International University Graduate School of Business faculty members bring both professional and academic expertise to the classroom. The faculty members are distinguished in their fields and are dedicated to teaching. The Webber International University Graduate School of Business emphasizes strong faculty-student interaction, as indicated by the small class size and the nature of the course work.

The Conference Center.

The campus of Webber International University.

YALE UNIVERSITY

Schools of Arts and Sciences and of Management
Ph.D. Program in Management

Program of Study	The Ph.D. Program in Management prepares students with strong quantitative backgrounds for careers in research and teaching in management. Students first acquire a strong methodological foundation in areas such as economics, statistics, and operations research. They then apply this knowledge to the study of a specific field of management. Currently specialization is offered in the management fields of accounting, financial economics, and marketing.
	Students take two years of course work. A set of core courses (designed to provide a broad basis that is common across the three specializations) is followed by courses in the social sciences (e.g., economics, psychology), empirical methods (e.g., statistics, econometrics), and a depth area designed to focus the students on a particular research paradigm. Each student has to pass a qualifying examination in his or her chosen field of specialization at the end of the second year. In addition, students have to write a research paper in the first summer of the program and another paper in their second year of residence. Students who have passed the qualifying examination, satisfied the two paper requirements, met all of the program's course requirements, and have been judged by the faculty to be able to satisfactorily complete a dissertation are admitted to Ph.D. candidacy. Students normally complete all requirements for the Ph.D. degree in four years. Students are eligible for an M.A. degree after satisfactory completion of two years of course work, for an M.Phil. degree upon admission to Ph.D. candidacy, and for the Ph.D. degree upon the submission and defense of an acceptable dissertation.
Research Facilities	Students can take advantage of the outstanding Yale University Library, including special collections in the mathematics and statistics departments; the Social Science Library; the Medical School; the Seeley G. Mudd Library for Government Documents; and the Cowles Foundation for Research in Economics. Students have access to a wide range of computing resources. They may use the School of Management's Sun minicomputer or one of its many IBM personal computers, which are linked by a network. The larger mainframe computers of the Yale University Computer Center are also accessible to students.
Financial Aid	All students admitted to the program receive a tuition waiver and a stipend (which consists of a combination of fellowship, research assistantship, and teaching assistantship) for five years as long as they are making suitable progress. The amount of the stipend is comparable to the stipends provided by other major schools of management.
Cost of Study	The tuition for full-time graduate study during the academic year 2010–11 is $33,500.
Living and Housing Costs	The 2010–11 estimated expense for housing, food, and moderate entertainment is $18,920 for a single student and $29,183 for a married student. The Housing Office provides information and help to students seeking off-campus housing.
Student Group	Approximately 5 students enter the program each fall. For the academic year 2010–11, 31 students are in residence, including 9 women.
Student Outcomes	Graduates have usually taken academic positions, many having been placed at the best universities in the United States and abroad. A few have taken research positions in government, business, or nonprofit organizations.
Location	Yale University is located in downtown New Haven, Connecticut, a small New England city of 126,000 situated on Long Island Sound. New Haven is a harbor city with a proud history, an energetic civil life, and challenging urban plans. It is a short walk from the campus to the historic New Haven Green. The city is a major center for theater and music, including the nationally acclaimed Long Wharf and Yale Repertory theaters. The Connecticut countryside is easily accessible, and there are delightful opportunities for bicycling, hiking, sailing, and swimming.
The University and The Program	Yale began to offer graduate education in 1847 and in 1861 conferred the first Ph.D. degree awarded in North America. With the appointment of a dean in 1892, the Graduate School was formally established. The School of Management is Yale's newest professional school; it granted its first degrees in 1978.
	The opportunities presented by the Ph.D. Program in Management reflect its organization within the University. While it is a program of Yale's Graduate School of Arts and Science, its faculty members hold primary appointments in the Yale School of Management, many with joint appointments in various departments of the Graduate School. Students also take courses offered by other educational units at Yale, such as the departments of the Graduate School (e.g., Computer Science, Economics, Mathematics, Statistics) and the other professional schools (e.g., Law, Forestry and Environmental Studies). Other distinguishing features in the program are an excellent research faculty, small classes, and an extensive amount of faculty-student interaction.
Applying	Applications should be initiated in the fall of the academic year preceding the one in which the individual proposes to register. Application materials may be secured by writing to Graduate School Admissions, Yale University, P.O. Box 1504A Yale Station, New Haven, Connecticut 06520-7368 (phone: 203-432-2770). When writing, students must state their interest in the Ph.D. Program in Management. Application files should be complete by January 2. Applicants are notified of action concerning admission by March 15.
	Applicants are judged on the basis of scholastic record, letters of recommendation, and scores on the Graduate Record Examinations (GRE) or the Graduate Management Admission Test (GMAT).
Correspondence and Information	Director of Graduate Studies Ph.D. Program in Management Yale School of Management 135 Prospect Street New Haven, Connecticut 06511 Phone: 203-432-3955 Fax: 203-432-0342 Web site: http://www.yale.edu

Yale University

THE FACULTY

Rick Antle, William S. Beinecke Professor of Accounting; Ph.D., Stanford.

Nicholas Barberis, Stephen and Camille Schramm Professor of Finance; Ph.D., Harvard.

James Baron, William S. Beinecke Professor of Management; Ph.D., California, Santa Barbara.

Paul Bracken, Professor of International Business and of Political Science; Ph.D., Yale.

Victoria Brescoll, Assistant Professor of Organizational Behavior; Ph.D., Yale.

Garry Brewer, Frederick K. Weyerhaeuser Professor of Resource Policy and Management; Ph.D., Yale.

Daylian Cain, Assistant Professor of Organizational Behavior; Ph.D., Carnegie Mellon.

Arthur Campbell, Assistant Professor of Economincs; Ph.D., MIT.

Rodrigo Canales, Assistant Professor of Organizational Behavior; Ph.D., MIT.

Constança Esteves-Sorenson, Assistant Professor of Management; Ph.D., Berkeley.

Keith Chen, Associate Professor of Economics; Ph.D., Harvard.

Zhiwu Chen, Professor of Finance; Ph.D., Yale.

Judith Chevalier, William S. Beinecke Professor of Economics and Finance; Ph.D., MIT.

James Choi, Associate Professor of Finance; Ph.D., Harvard.

Martijn Cremers, Associate Professor of Finance; Ph.D., NYU.

Ravi Dhar, George Rogers Clark Professor of Management and Marketing and Director of the Center for Customer Insights; Ph.D., Berkeley.

Frank Fabozzi, Professor in the Practice of Finance and Becton Fellow; Ph.D., CUNY.

Jonathan S. Feinstein, John G. Searle Professor of Economics and Management; Ph.D., MIT.

Shane Frederick, Associate Professor of Marketing; Ph.D., Carnegie Mellon.

Stanley J. Garstka, Professor in the Practice of Management; Ph.D., Carnegie Mellon.

Jeffrey E. Garten, Juan Trippe Professor in the Practice of International Trade, Finance, and Business; Ph.D., Johns Hopkins.

William Goetzmann, Edwin J. Beinecke Professor of Finance and Management Studies; Ph.D., Yale.

Gary B. Gorton, Frederick Frank Class of 1954 Professor of Management and Finance; Ph.D., Rochester.

Roger G. Ibbotson, Professor in the Practice of Finance; Ph.D., Chicago.

Jonathan E. Ingersoll Jr., Adrian C. Israel Professor of International Trade and Finance; Ph.D., MIT.

Lisa B. Kahn, Assistant Professor of Economics; Ph.D., Harvard.

Edward H. Kaplan, William N. and Marie A. Beach Professor of Management Sciences and Professor of Engineering and of Public Health; Ph.D., MIT.

Ahmed Khwaja, Assistant Professor of Marketing; Ph.D., Minnesota.

Sang-Hyun Kim, Assistant Professor of Operations Management; Ph.D., Pennsylvania.

Marissa D. King, Assistant Professor of Organizational Behavior; Ph.D., Columbia.

Kalin Kolev, Assistant Professor of Accounting; Ph.D., NYU.

Donald Lee, Assistant Professor of Operations Management; Ph.D., Stanford.

Alina Lerman, Assistant Professor of Accounting; Ph.D. candidate, NYU.

James A. Levinsohn, Charles W. Goodyear Professor in Global Affairs, Professor of Economics and Management, and Director of the Jackson Institute; Ph.D., Princeton.

Lode Li, Professor of Production Management; Ph.D., Northwestern.

Elisa F. Long, Assistant Professor of Operations Management; Ph.D., Stanford.

Theodore R. Marmor, Professor Emeritus of Public Policy and Management and of Political Science; Ph.D., Harvard.

B. Cade Massey, Assistant Professor of Organizational Behavior; Ph.D., Chicago.

Dina Mayzlin, Associate Professor of Marketing; Ph.D., MIT.

Andrew Metrick, Deputy Dean for Faculty Development, Theodore Nierenberg Professor of Corporate Governance, Professor of Finance, and Faculty Director of the Millstein Center for Corporate Governance; Ph.D., Harvard.

Ahmed Mushfiq Mobarak, Assistant Professor of Economics; Ph.D., Maryland, College Park.

Rakesh Mohan, Professor in the Practice of International Economics and Finance and Senior Fellow of the Jackson Institute; Ph.D., Princeton.

Susana Mondschein, Lecturer in Operations Management; Ph.D., MIT.

Justin Murfin, Assistant Professor of Finance; M.A., Southern Methodist; Ph.D. candidate, Duke.

Barry Nalebuff, Milton Steinbach Professor of Management; D.Phil., Oxford.

Nathan Novemsky, Professor of Marketing; Ph.D., Princeton.

Sharon M. Oster, Dean and Frederic D. Wolfe Professor of Management and Entrepreneurship; Ph.D., Harvard.

Benjamin Polak, Professor of Economics and Management; Ph.D., Harvard.

Douglas W. Rae, Richard S. Ely Professor of Organization and Management and Professor of Political Science; Ph.D., Wisconsin.

K. Geert Rouwenhorst, Deputy Dean for Curriculum Development, Professor of Finance, and Deputy Director of the International Center for Finance; Ph.D., Rochester.

Oliver Rutz, Assistant Professor of Marketing; Ph.D., UCLA.

Peter Schott, Professor of Economics; Ph.D., UCLA.

Fiona Scott-Morton, Professor of Economics; Ph.D., MIT.

Subrata K. Sen, Joseph F. Cullman 3rd Professor of Organization, Management and Marketing; Ph.D., Carnegie Mellon.

Robert Shiller, Stanley B. Resor Professor of Economics and Professor of Finance; PH.D., MIT.

Jiwoong Shin, Associate Professor of Marketing; Ph.D., MIT.

Martin S. Shubik, Seymour H. Knox Professor Emeritus of Mathematical Institutional Economics; Ph.D., Princeton.

Joseph Simmons, Assistant Professor of Marketing; Ph.D., Princeton.

Jeffrey A. Sonnenfeld, Lester Crown Professor in the Practice of Management; D.B.A., Harvard.

Olav Sorenson, Professor of Organizational Behavior; Ph.D., Stanford.

Matthew Spiegel, Professor of Finance; Ph.D., Princeton.

K. Sudhir, Professor of Marketing; Ph.D., Cornell.

Shyam Sunder, James L. Frank Professor of Accounting, Economics, and Finance; Ph.D., Carnegie-Mellon.

Arthur J. Swersey, Professor of Operations Research; D.Eng.Sci., Columbia.

Jacob Thomas, Williams Brothers Professor of Accounting and Finance; Ph.D., Michigan.

Heather Tookes, Associate Professor of Finance; Ph.D., Cornell.

Victor H. Vroom, BreakingPoint Professor of Management and Professor of Psychology; Ph.D., Michigan.

Amy Wrzesniewski, Associate Professor of Organizational Behavior; Ph.D., Michigan.

Hongjun Yan, Associate Professor of Finance; Ph.D., London Business School.

Frank Zhang, Associate Professor of Accounting; Ph.D., Chicago.

Recent Ph.D. Dissertations
Student's affiliation upon leaving the program is in parentheses.

"Individual Investor Trading Behavior: Three Empirical Studies," Bjorn Johnson, 2010. (DePaul University).

"Two Essays on Thinking Big versus Thinking Small in Consumer Decision Making," Eunice Kim, 2010. (University of Toronto).

"Breaking New Grounds in Capital Markets Research: Do We Know What We Think We Know?" Panos Patatoukas, 2010. (University of California, Berkeley).

"Three Essays in Finance," Roy Zuckerman, 2010. (Rutgers University).

"Information Flow, Predictability, and Disagreement," Foong Soon Cheong, 2009. (Rutgers University).

"Essays on Asset Classes, Traders, and Stock Prices," Darwin Choi, 2009. (Hong Kong University of Science and Technology).

"Retail, Entry and Location Choice: Retail Zoning, Unobserved Location Characteristics and the Agglomeration-Differentiation Trade-off," Sumon Datta, 2009. (Purdue University).

"Two Essays on Consumer Goals and Motivation," Kelly Ann Goldsmith, 2009. (Northwestern University).

"Essays on the Causes and Implication of Market Inefficiencies," Dong Lou, 2009. (London School of Economics).

"Essays on the Trading Behavior of Institutional Investors and Stock Return Anomalies," Ankur Pareek, 2009. (Rutgers University).

"Essays on Combining Individual and Aggregate Data and Marketing in Emerging Economics," Sachin Sancheti, 2009. (Cornerstone Research Boston).

"Essays on the Role of Social Interactions and Networks in Marketing," Hema Yoganarasimhan, 2009. (University of California, Davis).

"Labor Unions and Management's Incentive to Signal Declining Profitability," Francesco Bova, 2008. (Rotman School of Management).

"Accounting Disclosures in Capital Market," Pingyang Gao, 2008. (University of Chicago).

"Context Effects in Consumer Choice," Anastasiya Pocheptsova, 2008. (University of Maryland).

"Value Creation Through Corporate Finance Decisions," Vicente Pons-Sanz , 2008. (Citigroup, London).

"Information Processing and Investment Choice," Denis Sosyura, 2008. (University of Michigan).

"Lay Theories and Consumer Decision-Making," Jing Wang, 2008. (Singapore Management University).

"Strategic Decentralization, Bargaining, and Transfer Pricing in Supply Chair Efficiency," Dae-Hee Yoon 2008. (Baruch College, City University of New York).

"Essays on New Product Release Strategy: Advertising and Release Timing," Ye Luan, 2007. (Tuck School of Business at Dartmouth).

YORK UNIVERSITY

Schulich School of Business

Programs of Study

The Schulich School of Business at York University is known as Canada's Global Business School™. Since its inception in 1966, Schulich has built a strong reputation worldwide due to its global reach, innovative programs, and diverse perspectives on management and leadership. Through the graduate management programs offered by Schulich, students examine business issues in a global environment and learn how to manage complexity, ambiguity, and change.

Schulich's innovative master's level programs emphasize relevance to real world contexts. The School's broad range of degrees lets students choose the program of study that fits their needs and career direction. Programs include the Master of Business Administration (M.B.A.), International M.B.A. (I.M.B.A.), Executive M.B.A., Master of Finance (M.F.), Master of Public Administration (M.P.A.), and the M.B.A./J.D., M.B.A./M.F.A. or M.B.A./M.A. joint programs which combine business with law, fine arts, or arts respectively. For those considering a career in academia, the Ph.D. in administration is offered.

The Schulich M.B.A. offers an integrated approach to general management fundamentals. It balances qualitative and quantitative skills and combines classroom learning with hands-on experience through a six-month strategic consulting project. The sixteen-month program offers multiple start dates, the ability to switch between full- and part-time study, and the option to specialize in one or more areas.

Schulich's I.M.B.A. is an ideal choice for those interested in launching a global career or growing an existing one. Building upon the M.B.A. curriculum, students master a second language, gain specialized knowledge of two global trading regions, and complete an internationally focused strategic consulting project.

The Kellogg-Schulich Executive M.B.A., in conjunction with Northwestern University, is an eighteen-month program that emphasizes U.S., Canadian, and international perspectives on global leadership and strategic management. The E.M.B.A. includes three residence weeks, alternating study weekends, and international study seminars abroad.

The Ph.D. in administration prepares students for a stimulating career in academic teaching and research. Graduates from this rigorous program of study contribute to the global practice and knowledge of business. Students are exposed to quantitative and qualitative research methods and techniques through core and elective courses. Students can tailor specializations to their individual needs in either management functions or thematic issues such as international business and change management.

Schulich's practical management education is complemented by over 100 electives and 18 specializations. Students can choose to focus on a management function (accounting, economics, finance, marketing, strategic management, operations management, or organizational behavior), an industry sector (arts and media, health industry management, not-for-profit management), or special business topics (business and sustainability, entrepreneurship, international business). Depending on the program of study, there may be additional opportunities to deepen and broaden specialized knowledge using diploma and professional designation programs.

Research Facilities

York University houses five libraries with considerable resources, including a book collection of more than 2.5 million volumes and more than 205,000 serials (periodicals, magazines, reports and digests, collections of microfiche, maps, videos, films, sound recordings, compact discs, and databases). In addition, the Peter Bronfman Business Library at Schulich houses one of the best business reference collections in metropolitan Toronto.

Financial Aid

A range of financial support is available to students of the Schulich School of Business. Scholarships, awards, and bursaries are awarded based on achievement or financial need. Full-time applicants are automatically considered for entrance scholarships based on admissions information. The School's entrance scholarships and awards are among the highest value offered to M.B.A. students in Canada and recognize excellence in academics and community involvement.

In addition to these funding opportunities, Schulich students may apply for support through private and government student loan programs. On-campus jobs, research, and teaching assistantships are also available.

Cost of Study

Students pay fees each semester according to whether they are enrolled on a full- or part-time basis. The 2010–11 full-time tuition is approximately $13,000 per term for Canadian residents and $15,000 per term for non-residents. Tuition for the entire two-year Executive M.B.A. is $110,000 for both Canadian and international students. All costs are in Canadian dollars.

Living and Housing Costs

On-campus housing is available at reasonable rates. Housing, travel, course materials, and personal expenses vary with each student but range from $6500 to $8000 per term. All costs are in Canadian dollars.

Student Group

Schulich attracts a diverse student population. Approximately 46 percent of the student body is international, 32 percent are women, and almost 70 percent come from an undergraduate program other than business. The average age of an incoming M.B.A. is 28 years old and students possess an average of five years of work experience.

For many students, involvement in the Schulich community is critical to their experience. Student groups, clubs, social functions, and recruiting events provide countless opportunities to enrich formal in-class learning with extracurricular activities. Schulich alumni often say their involvement outside of the classroom helped to build lifelong friendships and create treasured memories that enhanced the value of their Schulich experience.

Student Outcomes

At Schulich, career management is a lifetime investment and helping students to transition into a new post-M.B.A. career is a top priority. Whether moving into a new function or switching industries, the Career Development Centre (CDC) works closely with students to identify career choices and objectives, develop a proactive career plan, and hone skill sets. Students can take advantage of training, counseling expertise, and networking opportunities. This support has helped over 90 percent of Schulich graduates land their first job offer within three months of graduation.

Graduates join Schulich's network of more than 22,000 alumni living in over ninety countries around the world. Schulich alumni are among award recipients in the Caldwell Partner's national program that honours Canadians under the age of 40 who have reached a significant level of success. Graduates are recruited by leading companies such as Bombardier, CIBC, Deloitte, Ernst & Young, Canadian government agencies, Kraft, Labatt/AB InBev, Procter and Gamble, RBC, Starbucks, Sick Kids Hospital, Telus, and Walmart Canada.

Location

Located in Toronto, the financial and cultural centre of Canada and one of the world's greatest multicultural cities, Schulich has built strong ties to the corporate community. The School has access to the head offices of many organizations. Close to 200 distinguished CEOs, leading academics, and senior government representatives act as advisors on Schulich's boards, teach in its classrooms, and provide guidance and counsel to students through the Schulich mentorship program.

The University and The School

Founded in 1959, York University has earned an international reputation for excellence in teaching, research, and scholarship in both undergraduate and graduate studies. Today, York is the third largest university in Canada and home to the Schulich School of Business.

The Schulich M.B.A. is ranked in the world's top tier of business schools by the Economist Intelligence Unit (first in Canada, twelfth in the world); *Forbes* (first in Canada, sixth best non-U.S. school); the Aspen Institute, a U.S. think tank (first in the world in social and environmental stewardship); and *Expansión* (first in Canada, eighteenth in the world) in their most recent global surveys.

The School's continued success can be attributed its cutting-edge programs; challenging classes; and focus on teaching students to examine business from multiple perspectives, implement effective strategies, and excel in team environments.

Applying

In order to be considered for admission, students must have an honours undergraduate degree from a recognized university, with a minimum B average in the last two years of full-time study; acceptable scores on all GMAT measures (not required for the E.M.B.A.); and at least two years of full-time work (post-undergraduate degree). Schulich also looks for leadership qualities, communication skills, creativity, and innovation in supplemental essays. Interviews may be required on a select basis.

In some instances, non-baccalaureate candidates may be considered for admission. These candidates must have at least eight years of high-quality management experience and must have demonstrated a strong upward progression in their careers in addition to the other admission requirements.

Application deadlines for the M.B.A., I.M.B.A. and M.P.A. programs are May 1 for the fall term, October 1 for the winter term, and February 1 for the summer term (part-time studies only). For scholarship consideration, application deadlines are February 1 and September 1 for the fall and winter terms respectively. International student applications are due February 1 and September 1 for the fall and winter terms respectively. The application deadline for the Ph.D. program is January 15.

Correspondence and Information

Division of Student Services and International Relations
Schulich School of Business
York University
4700 Keele Street
Toronto, Ontario M3J 1P3
Canada

Phone: 416-736-5060
Fax: 416-650-8174
E-mail: admissions@schulich.yorku.ca
Web site: http://www.schulich.yorku.ca

York University

THE FACULTY

Schulich faculty members are leading scholars from the world's top universities, passionate about their chosen fields, dedicated to their students, and committed to award-winning research. As pioneers in areas such as risk management, business and sustainability, global marketing, and entrepreneurism, they draw on their research findings to enrich every class. Many professors are also working practitioners and believe that a combination of active and interactive learning leads to the most effective teaching process. Schulich faculty members draw on a range of pedagogical approaches, including lectures, group work, case studies, simulations, and real-world projects.

Dezsö J. Horváth, Professor of Policy, Dean, and Tanna H. Schulich Chair in Strategic Management; Ph.D., Umeå (Sweden).

Accounting

Marcia Annisette, Associate Professor; Ph.D., Manchester (England).
Thomas H. Beechy, Professor Emeritus; D.B.A., Washington (St. Louis); CPA.
Kathryn Bewley, Associate Professor; Ph.D., Waterloo; CA.
Janne Chung, Associate Professor; Ph.D., Edith Cowan (Australia).
Cameron Graham, Associate Professor; Ph.D., Calgary.
Sylvia Hsingwen Hsu, Assistant Professor; Ph.D., Wisconsin–Madison.
Amin Mawani, Associate Professor; Ph.D., Waterloo.
Dean Neu, Professor; Ph.D., Queens; CA.
Sandy Qian Qu, Assistant Professor; Ph.D., Alberta.
Alan J. Richardson, Professor; Ph.D., Queen's at Kingston; CGA, FCGA.
Linda Thorne, Associate Professor; Ph.D., McGill; CA.
Viswanath Umashanker Trivedi, Associate Professor; Ph.D., Arizona.

Economics

A. Bhanich Supapol, Associate Professor; Ph.D., Carleton (Ottawa).
Irene Henriques, Associate Professor; Ph.D., Queen's at Kingston.
Fred Lazar, Associate Professor; Ph.D., Harvard.
Perry A. Sadorsky, Associate Professor; Ph.D., Queen's at Kingston.
John N. Smithin, Professor; Ph.D., McMaster.
Bernard M. Wolf, Professor Emeritus; Ph.D., Yale.

Finance

Kee-Hong Bae, Professor; Ph.D., Ohio State.
Melanie Cao, Associate Professor; Ph.D., Toronto.
Archishman Chakraborty, Associate Professor; Ph.D., Princeton.
Ming Dong, Associate Professor; Ph.D., Ohio.
Mark Kamstra, Associate Professor; Ph.D., California, San Diego.
Nadia Massoud, Associate Professor; Ph.D., Queen's at Kingston.
Elizabeth M. Maynes, Associate Professor; Ph.D., Queen's at Kingston.
Moshe Arye Milevsky, Associate Professor; Ph.D., York.
Debarshi Nandy, Assistant Professor; Ph.D., Boston College.
Eliezer Prisman, Professor and Nigel Martin Chair in Finance; D.Sc., Technion (Israel).
Gordon S. Roberts, Professor and CIBC Professor of Financial Services; Ph.D., Boston College.

Pauline M. Shum, Associate Professor; Ph.D., Toronto.
Yisong Sam Tian, Associate Professor; Ph.D., York.

Marketing

Russell Belk, Professor and Kraft Foods Canada Chair in Marketing; Ph.D., Minnesota.
Samuel K. Bonsu, Associate Professor; Ph.D., Rhode Island.
Alexandra Campbell, Associate Professor; Ph.D., Toronto.
Peter Darke, Associate Professor; Ph.D., Toronto.
Eileen Fischer, Professor and Anne and Max Tanenbaum Chair in Entrepreneurship and Family Enterprise; Ph.D., Queen's at Kingston.
Brenda Gainer, Associate Professor and Royal Bank Professor of Nonprofit Management; Ph.D., York.
Markus Giesler, Assistant Professor; Ph.D., Witten/Herdecke (Germany).
Ashwin Joshi, Associate Professor; Ph.D., Queen's at Kingston.
Robert Kozinets, Associate Professor; Ph.D., Queen's at Kingston.
Alan Middleton, Assistant Professor; Ph.D., York.
Yigang Pan, Professor; Ph.D., Columbia.
Marshall D. Rice, Associate Professor; Ph.D., Illinois.
Ajay K. Sirsi, Associate Professor; Ph.D., Arizona.
Donald N. Thompson, Professor Emeritus; Ph.D., Berkeley.
Detlev Zwick, Associate Professor; Ph.D., Rhode Island.

Operations Management and Information Systems

Markus Biehl, Associate Professor; Ph.D., Georgia Tech.
John Buzacott, Professor Emeritus; Ph.D., Birmingham (England).
Wade D. Cook, Professor and Gordon Charlton Shaw Professor of Management Science; Ph.D., Dalhousie.
Richard H. Irving, Associate Professor; Ph.D., Waterloo.
David Johnston, Associate Professor; Ph.D., Western Ontario.
Henry Kim, Associate Professor; Ph.D., Toronto.
Mehmet Murat Kristal, Assistant Professor; Ph.D., North Carolina.
Moran Levesque, Associate Professor, Ph.D., British Columbia.
Ronald J. McClean, Assistant Professor; Ph.D., Waterloo.
Dorit Nevo, Associate Professor; Ph.D., British Columbia.
Mark Pagell, Associate Professor; Ph.D., Michigan.
Danièle Thomassin-Singh, Assistant Professor; Ph.D., Case Western Reserve.
Peter Tryfos, Professor Emeritus; Ph.D., Berkeley.
Michael Wade, Associate Professor; Ph.D., Western Ontario.
J. Scott Yeomans, Associate Professor; Ph.D., McMaster.

Organizational Behavior and Industrial Relations

Chris Bell, Associate Professor; Ph.D., Duke.
Patricia Bradshaw, Associate Professor; Ph.D., York.
Ronald J. Burke, Professor Emeritus; Ph.D., Michigan.

André deCarufel, Associate Professor; Ph.D., North Carolina.
David E. Dimick, Associate Professor and Associate Dean, Academic; Ph.D., Minnesota.
Ingo Holzinger, Assistant Professor; Ph.D., Wisconsin–Madison.
Rekha Karambayya, Associate Professor; Ph.D., Northwestern.
Gareth Morgan, Distinguished Research Professor; Ph.D., Lancaster (England).
Christine Oliver, Professor and Henry J. Knowles Chair in Organizational Strategy; Ph.D., Toronto.
Hazel Rosin, Associate Professor; Ph.D., Yale.
Mary Waller, Associate Professor; Ph.D., Texas at Austin.
Eleanor Westney, Professor and Scotiabank Professor in International Business; Ph.D., Princeton.
Lorna Wright, Associate Professor; Ph.D., Western Ontario.

Policy/Strategic Management

Jean Adams, Assistant Professor; Ph.D., York.
Preet Aulakh, Professor and Pierre Lassonde Chair in International Business; Ph.D., Texas at Austin.
Ellen Auster, Professor; Ph.D., Cornell.
Wesley Cragg, Professor Emeritus; D.Phil., Oxford.
Andrew Crane, Professor and George R. Gardiner Professor of Business Ethics; Ph.D., Nottingham (England).
James L. Darroch, Associate Professor; Ph.D., York.
Yuval Deutsch, Associate Professor; Ph.D., British Columbia.
Burkard Eberlein, Assistant Professor; Ph.D., Konstanz (Germany).
Moshe Farjoun, Associate Professor; Ph.D., Northwestern.
James M. Gillies, Professor Emeritus; Ph.D., Indiana.
Dezsö J. Horváth, Dean and Tanna H. Schulich Chair in Strategic Management; Ph.D., Umeå (Sweden).
Bryan Husted, Professor and Erivan K. Haub Chair in Business and Sustainability; Ph.D., Berkeley.
Matthias Kipping; D.Phil., München (Germany).
Stan Li, Associate Professor; Ph.D., Toronto.
H. Ian Macdonald, Professor Emeritus and President Emeritus; B.Phil., Oxford.
Anoop Madhok, Professor; Ph.D., McGill.
Dirk Matten, Professor and Hewlett-Packard Chair in Corporate Social Responsibility; Dr.rer.pol., Dr.habil., Düsseldorf (Germany).
Charles J. McMillan, Professor; Ph.D., Bradford (England).
Theodore Peridis, Associate Professor; Ph.D., NYU.
Willow Sheremata, Associate Professor; Ph.D., NYU.
Justin Tan, Professor and Newmont Mining Chair in Business Strategy; Ph.D., Virginia Tech.
Stephen Weiss, Associate Professor; Ph.D., Pennsylvania.
Tom Wesson, Associate Professor; Ph.D., Harvard.
Brenda J. Zimmerman, Associate Professor; Ph.D., York; CA, Ontario.

The Schulich School of Business and Executive Learning Centre.

Section 2
Accounting and Finance

This section contains a directory of institutions offering graduate work in accounting and finance, followed by an in-depth entry submitted by an institution that chose to prepare a detailed program description. Additional information about programs listed in the directory but not augmented by an in-depth entry may be obtained by writing directly to the dean of a graduate school or chair of a department at the address given in the directory.

For programs offering related work, see also in this book *Business Administration and Management, International Business,* and *Nonprofit Management.* In the other guides in this series:

Graduate Programs in the Humanities, Arts & Social Sciences
See *Economics* and *Family and Consumer Sciences (Consumer Economics)*

Graduate Programs in the Physical Sciences, Mathematics, Agricultural Sciences, the Environment & Natural Resources
See *Mathematical Sciences*

Graduate Programs in Engineering & Applied Sciences
See *Computer Science and Information Technology*

CONTENTS

Program Directories

Close-Up

See also:

Accounting

Abilene Christian University, Graduate School, College of Business Administration, Abilene, TX 79699-9100. Offers M Acc. *Accreditation:* AACSB. Part-time programs available. *Faculty:* 7 part-time/adjunct (0 women). *Students:* 47 full-time (16 women), 7 part-time (5 women); includes 2 minority (1 African American, 1 Hispanic American), 10 international. 42 applicants, 93% accepted, 31 enrolled. In 2009, 31 master's awarded. *Entrance requirements:* For master's, GMAT. Additional exam requirements/recommendations for international students: Required—TOEFL (minimum score 525 paper-based; 197 computer-based). *Application deadline:* For fall admission, 4/1 priority date for domestic students; for spring admission, 11/1 for domestic students. Applications are processed on a rolling basis. Application fee: $40. Electronic applications accepted. *Expenses:* Tuition: Full-time $11,520; part-time $640 per hour. Required fees: $1090; $53.50 per hour. $10 per term. Tuition and fees vary according to program. *Financial support:* In 2009–10, 39 students received support; teaching assistantships, Federal Work-Study available. Support available to part-time students. Financial award application deadline: 4/1; financial award applicants required to submit FAFSA. *Faculty research:* Organizational structure, financial management, cost accounting, unit analysis management. *Unit head:* Bill Fowler, Department Chair, 325-674-2080, Fax: 325-674-2564, E-mail: bill.fowler@coba.acu.edu. *Application contact:* William Horn, Graduate Admissions Counselor, 325-674-2656, Fax: 325-674-6717, E-mail: gradinfo@acu.edu.

Adelphi University, School of Business, Graduate Opportunity for Accelerated Learning MBA Program, Garden City, NY 11530-0701. Offers accounting (MBA); finance (MBA). *Accreditation:* AACSB. Part-time and evening/weekend programs available. *Students:* 4 full-time (3 women), 25 part-time (13 women); includes 11 minority (8 African Americans, 1 Asian American or Pacific Islander, 2 Hispanic Americans), 1 international. Average age 35. In 2009, 14 master's awarded. *Entrance requirements:* For master's, GMAT, 2 letters of recommendation. Additional exam requirements/recommendations for international students: Required—TOEFL (minimum score 550 paper-based; 213 computer-based; 80 iBT). *Application deadline:* For fall admission, 4/1 for international students; for spring admission, 11/1 for international students. Applications are processed on a rolling basis. Application fee: $50. Electronic applications accepted. *Expenses:* Tuition: Full-time $28,340; part-time $830 per credit. Required fees: $600; $250 per credit. Full-time tuition and fees vary according to course load and program. *Financial support:* Research assistantships with full and partial tuition reimbursements, career-related internships or fieldwork, Federal Work-Study, institutionally sponsored loans, scholarships/grants, and unspecified assistantships available. Financial award application deadline: 3/1; financial award applicants required to submit FAFSA. *Faculty research:* Capital market, executive compensation, business ethics, classical value theory, labor economics. *Unit head:* Rakesh Gupta, Chairperson, 516-877-4670, Fax: 516-877-4607, E-mail: gradbusinquiries@adelphi.edu. *Application contact:* Christine Murphy, Director of Admissions, 516-877-3050, Fax: 516-877-3039, E-mail: graduateadmissions@adelphi.edu.

Alabama State University, School of Graduate Studies, College of Business Administration, Department of Accounting and Finance, Montgomery, AL 36101-0271. Offers accountancy (M Acc). *Entrance requirements:* For master's, GMAT, graduate writing competency test. Additional exam requirements/recommendations for international students: Required—TOEFL (minimum score 500 paper-based; 173 computer-based).

Albany State University, College of Business, Albany, GA 31705-2717. Offers accounting (MBA); business administration (MBA). *Accreditation:* ACBSP. Part-time and evening/weekend programs available. Postbaccalaureate distance learning degree programs offered (no on-campus study). *Students:* 2 full-time (1 woman), 24 part-time (18 women); includes 21 minority (20 African Americans, 1 Asian American or Pacific Islander). Average age 34. 13 applicants, 85% accepted, 9 enrolled. In 2009, 15 master's awarded. *Degree requirements:* For master's, comprehensive exam. *Entrance requirements:* For master's, GMAT, minimum GPA of 2.5, 2 letters of reference. *Application deadline:* For fall admission, 11/16 for domestic students, 9/16 for international students; for spring admission, 4/19 for domestic students, 2/19 for international students. Applications are processed on a rolling basis. Application fee: $20. Electronic applications accepted. *Expenses:* Tuition, state resident: full-time $2970; part-time $162 per credit hour. Tuition, nonresident: full-time $12,168; part-time $676 per credit hour. Required fees: $962; $75 per credit hour. *Financial support:* Application deadline: 6/30. *Unit head:* Dr. Jonathon Jefferson, Dean, 229-430-2749, Fax: 229-430-5119, E-mail: jonathon.jefferson@asurams.edu. *Application contact:* Nicole Lane, Interim Graduate School Admissions Officer, 229-430-4862, Fax: 229-430-6398, E-mail: nicole.lane@asurams.edu.

American InterContinental University Buckhead Campus, Program in Business Administration, Atlanta, GA 30326-1016. Offers accounting and finance (MBA); management (MBA); marketing (MBA). Evening/weekend programs available. Postbaccalaureate distance learning degree programs offered. *Entrance requirements:* For master's, minimum cumulative undergraduate GPA of 2.0. Additional exam requirements/recommendations for international students: Required—TOEFL (minimum score 530 paper-based; 230 computer-based). Electronic applications accepted. *Faculty research:* Leadership management, international advertising.

American InterContinental University Online, Program in Business Administration, Hoffman Estates, IL 60192. Offers accounting and finance (MBA); finance (MBA); healthcare management (MBA); human resource management (MBA); international business (MBA); management (MBA); marketing (MBA); operations management (MBA); organizational psychology and development (MBA); project management (MBA). Evening/weekend programs available. Postbaccalaureate distance learning degree programs offered (no on-campus study). *Entrance requirements:* Additional exam requirements/recommendations for international students: Required—TOEFL (minimum score 550 paper-based; 213 computer-based). Electronic applications accepted.

American InterContinental University South Florida, Program in International Business, Weston, FL 33326. Offers accounting and finance (MBA); human resource management (MBA); management (MBA); marketing (MBA). Part-time and evening/weekend programs available. Postbaccalaureate distance learning degree programs offered. Electronic applications accepted.

American International College, School of Business Administration, MBA Program, Springfield, MA 01109-3189. Offers accounting (MBA); corporate/public communication (MBA); finance (MBA); general business (MBA); hospitality, hotel and service management (MBA); international business (MBA); international business practice (MBA); management (MBA); management information systems (MBA); marketing (MBA). International business practice program developed in cooperation with the Mountbatten Institute. *Expenses:* Tuition: Full-time $12,510; part-time $695 per credit hour. Required fees: $35 per term.

American International College, School of Business Administration, Program in Accounting and Taxation, Springfield, MA 01109-3189. Offers MSAT. *Expenses:* Tuition: Full-time $12,510; part-time $695 per credit hour. Required fees: $35 per term.

American University, Kogod School of Business, Department of Accounting, Program in Accounting, Washington, DC 20016-8044. Offers MS. Part-time and evening/weekend programs available. *Students:* 30 full-time (18 women), 33 part-time (23 women); includes 13 minority (9 African Americans, 3 Asian Americans or Pacific Islanders, 1 Hispanic American), 23 international. Average age 27. In 2009, 26 master's awarded. *Entrance requirements:* For master's, GMAT. Additional exam requirements/recommendations for international students: Required—TOEFL. *Application deadline:* For fall admission, 2/1 priority date for domestic students; for spring admission, 10/1 priority date for domestic students. Applications are processed on a rolling basis. Application fee: $100. *Expenses:* Contact institution. *Financial support:* Fellowships, research assistantships, career-related internships or fieldwork, Federal Work-Study, and institutionally sponsored loans available. Support available to part-time students. Financial award application deadline: 2/1. *Unit head:* Dr. Donald Williamson, Chair, 202-885-1942. *Application contact:* Shannon Demko, Associate Director of Graduate Admissions, 202-885-1994, Fax: 202-885-1108, E-mail: demko@american.edu.

American University, Kogod School of Business, Master of Business Administration Program, Washington, DC 20016-8044. Offers accounting (MBA); consulting (MBA), including information technology, international business, management; corporate finance: commercial banking (MBA); corporate finance: corporate financial management (MBA); corporate finance: investment banking (MBA), including corporate finance and private equity, trading and selling; entrepreneurship (MBA); global emerging markets (MBA), including business, finance, information technology; international trade and global supply chain management (MBA); leadership (MBA); marketing management (MBA); marketing research (MBA); real estate (MBA); MBA/JD; MBA/LL M. Part-time and evening/weekend programs available. *Faculty:* 14 full-time (6 women). *Students:* 133 full-time (56 women), 121 part-time (48 women); includes 54 minority (23 African Americans, 1 American Indian/Alaska Native, 16 Asian Americans or Pacific Islanders, 14 Hispanic Americans), 43 international. Average age 29. 539 applicants, 51% accepted, 86 enrolled. In 2009, 114 master's awarded. *Entrance requirements:* For master's, GMAT. Additional exam requirements/recommendations for international students: Required—TOEFL. *Application deadline:* For fall admission, 2/1 priority date for domestic students; for spring admission, 10/1 priority date for domestic students. Applications are processed on a rolling basis. Application fee: $100. *Expenses:* Contact institution. *Financial support:* In 2009–10, 19 students received support; fellowships, research assistantships with partial tuition reimbursements available, career-related internships or fieldwork, Federal Work-Study, and institutionally sponsored loans available. Support available to part-time students. Financial award application deadline: 2/1. *Faculty research:* Information technology, decision-aiding methodology, negotiation. *Unit head:* Dr. Stevan Holmberg, Chair, 202-885-6193, E-mail: sholmbe@american.edu. *Application contact:* Shannon Demko, Associate Director of Graduate Admissions, 202-885-1994, Fax: 202-885-1108, E-mail: demko@american.edu.

Anderson University, Falls School of Business, Anderson, IN 46012-3495. Offers accountancy (MA); business administration (MBA, DBA). *Accreditation:* ACBSP.

Andrews University, School of Graduate Studies, School of Business, Graduate Programs in Business, Berrien Springs, MI 49104. Offers MBA, MSA. *Students:* 7 full-time (6 women), 12 part-time (6 women); includes 6 minority (4 African Americans, 1 Asian American or Pacific Islander, 1 Hispanic American), 5 international. Average age 27. 35 applicants, 46% accepted, 10 enrolled. In 2009, 7 master's awarded. *Entrance requirements:* For master's, GMAT. Additional exam requirements/recommendations for international students: Required—TOEFL (minimum score 550 paper-based). Application fee: $40. *Unit head:* Dr. Leonard K. Gashugi, Chair, 769-471-3429, E-mail: gashugi@andrews.edu. *Application contact:* Carolyn Hurst, Supervisor of Graduate Admission, 800-253-2874, Fax: 269-471-6321, E-mail: graduate@andrews.edu.

Angelo State University, College of Graduate Studies, College of Business, Department of Accounting, Economics, and Finance, San Angelo, TX 76909. Offers accounting (MBA); professional accountancy (MPAC). Part-time and evening/weekend programs available. *Faculty:* 4 full-time (0 women), 1 part-time/adjunct (0 women). *Students:* 18 full-time (11 women), 1 (woman) part-time; includes 2 minority (both Hispanic Americans). Average age 24. 5 applicants, 80% accepted, 3 enrolled. In 2009, 7 master's awarded. *Entrance requirements:* For master's, GMAT. Additional exam requirements/recommendations for international students: Required—TOEFL or IELTS. *Application deadline:* For fall admission, 7/15 priority date for domestic students, 6/10 for international students; for spring admission, 12/1 priority date for domestic students, 11/1 for international students. Applications are processed on a rolling basis. Application fee: $40 ($50 for international students). Electronic applications accepted. *Expenses:* Tuition, state resident: full-time $3396; part-time $142 per credit hour. Tuition, nonresident: full-time $10,152; part-time $423 per credit hour. Required fees: $1786; $36.25 per credit hour. $494 per semester. Full-time tuition and fees vary according to course load, degree level and program. *Financial support:* In 2009–10, 15 students received support. Career-related internships or fieldwork, Federal Work-Study, and scholarships/grants available. Support available to part-time students. Financial award application deadline: 3/1; financial award applicants required to submit FAFSA. *Unit head:* Dr. Thomas A. Bankston, Department Head, 325-942-2046 Ext. 248, Fax: 325-942-2285, E-mail: thomas.bankston@angelo.edu. *Application contact:* Dr. Norman A. Sunderman, Graduate Advisor, 325-942-2046 Ext. 245, E-mail: norman.sunderman@angelo.edu.

Appalachian State University, Cratis D. Williams Graduate School, Department of Accounting, Boone, NC 28608. Offers MS. Part-time programs available. *Faculty:* 14 full-time (5 women). *Students:* 61 full-time (24 women); includes 4 minority (2 African Americans, 2 Asian Americans or Pacific Islanders), 1 international. 78 applicants, 82% accepted, 49 enrolled. In 2009, 32 master's awarded. *Degree requirements:* For master's, comprehensive exam, thesis optional. *Entrance requirements:* For master's, GMAT, 3 letters of recommendation. Additional exam requirements/recommendations for international students: Required—TOEFL (minimum score 550 paper-based; 230 computer-based; 79 iBT), IELTS (minimum score 6.5). *Application deadline:* For fall admission, 6/1 for domestic students, 2/1 for international students; for spring admission, 11/1 for domestic students, 7/1 for international students. Applications are processed on a rolling basis. Application fee: $50. Electronic applications accepted. *Expenses:* Tuition, state resident: full-time $2960. Tuition, nonresident: full-time $14,051. Required fees: $2320. *Financial support:* In 2009–10, 17 research assistantships (averaging $7,000 per year) were awarded; fellowships, teaching assistantships, Federal Work-Study, scholarships/grants, and unspecified assistantships also available. Financial award application deadline: 4/1; financial award applicants required to submit FAFSA. *Faculty research:* Audit assurance risk, state taxation, financial accounting inconsistencies, management information systems, charitable contribution taxation. *Unit head:* Dr. Timothy Forsyth, Chairman, 828-262-2036, Fax: 828-262-6640. *Application contact:* Dr. William Pollard, Director, 828-262-6232, Fax: 828-262-6640, E-mail: pollardwb@appstate.edu.

Argosy University, Atlanta, College of Business, Atlanta, GA 30328. Offers accounting (DBA); corporate compliance (MBA); customized professional concentration (MBA, DBA); finance (MBA); healthcare administration (MBA); information systems (DBA); information systems management (MBA); international business (MBA, DBA); management (MBA, MSM, DBA); marketing (MBA, DBA).

See Close-Up on page 197.

Argosy University, Chicago, College of Business, Chicago, IL 60601. Offers accounting (DBA); customized professional concentration (MBA, DBA); finance (MBA); fraud examination (MBA); global business sustainability (DBA); healthcare administration (MBA); information systems (DBA); information systems management (MBA); international business (MBA, DBA); management (MBA, MSM, DBA); marketing (MBA, DBA); organizational leadership (Ed D); public administration (MBA); sustainable management (MBA). Postbaccalaureate distance learning degree programs offered (minimal on-campus study).

See Close-Up on page 199.

Argosy University, Dallas, College of Business, Farmers Branch, TX 75244. Offers accounting (DBA, AGC); corporate compliance (MBA, Graduate Certificate); customized professional concentration (MBA); finance (MBA, Graduate Certificate); fraud examination (MBA, Graduate Certificate); global business sustainability (DBA, AGC); healthcare administration (Graduate Certificate); healthcare management (MBA); information systems (MBA, DBA, AGC); information systems management (Graduate Certificate); international business (MBA, DBA, AGC, Graduate Certificate); management (MBA, DBA, AGC, Graduate Certificate); marketing (MBA, DBA, AGC, Graduate Certificate); public administration (MBA, Graduate Certificate); sustainable management (MBA, Graduate Certificate).

See Close-Up on page 201.

Argosy University, Denver, College of Business, Denver, CO 80231. Offers accounting (DBA); corporate compliance (MBA); customized professional concentration (MBA, DBA); finance (MBA); fraud examination (MBA); global business sustainability (DBA); healthcare administration (MBA); information systems (DBA); information systems management (MBA); international business (MBA, DBA); management (MBA, MSM, DBA); marketing (MBA, DBA); organizational leadership (Ed D); public administration (MBA); sustainable management (MBA).
See Close-Up on page 203.

Argosy University, Hawai'i, College of Business, Honolulu, HI 96813. Offers accounting (DBA); corporate compliance (MBA); customized professional concentration (MBA, DBA); finance (MBA, Certificate); fraud examination (MBA); global business sustainability (DBA); healthcare administration (MBA, Certificate); information systems (DBA); information systems management (MBA, Certificate); international business (MBA, DBA, Certificate); management (MBA, MSM, DBA); marketing (MBA, DBA, Certificate); organizational leadership (Ed D); public administration (MBA); sustainable management (MBA).
See Close-Up on page 205.

Argosy University, Inland Empire, College of Business, San Bernardino, CA 92408. Offers accounting (DBA); corporate compliance (MBA); customized professional concentration (MBA, DBA); finance (MBA); fraud examination (MBA); global business sustainability (DBA); healthcare administration (MBA); information systems (DBA); information systems management (MBA); international business (MBA, DBA); management (MBA, MSM, DBA); marketing (MBA, DBA); organizational leadership (Ed D); public administration (MBA); sustainable management (MBA).
See Close-Up on page 207.

Argosy University, Los Angeles, College of Business, Santa Monica, CA 90045. Offers accounting (DBA); corporate compliance (MBA); customized professional concentration (MBA, DBA); finance (MBA); fraud examination (MBA); global business sustainability (DBA); healthcare administration (MBA); information systems (DBA); information systems management (MBA); international business (MBA, DBA); management (MBA, MSM, DBA); marketing (MBA, DBA); organizational leadership (Ed D); public administration (MBA); sustainable management (MBA).
See Close-Up on page 209.

Argosy University, Nashville, College of Business, Nashville, TN 37214. Offers accounting (DBA); customized professional concentration (MBA, DBA); finance (MBA); healthcare administration (MBA); information systems (MBA, DBA); international business (MBA, DBA); management (MBA, MSM, DBA); marketing (MBA, DBA).
See Close-Up on page 211.

Argosy University, Orange County, College of Business, Orange, CA 92868. Offers accounting (DBA, Adv C); corporate compliance (MBA); customized professional concentration (MBA, DBA); finance (MBA, Certificate); fraud examination (MBA); global business sustainability (DBA); healthcare administration (MBA, Certificate); information systems (DBA, Adv C, Certificate); information systems management (MBA); international business (MBA, DBA, Adv C, Certificate); management (MBA, MSM, DBA, Adv C); marketing (MBA, DBA, Adv C, Certificate); organizational leadership (Ed D); public administration (MBA, Certificate); sustainable management (MBA).
See Close-Up on page 213.

Argosy University, Phoenix, College of Business, Phoenix, AZ 85021. Offers accounting (DBA); corporate compliance (MBA); customized professional concentration (MBA, DBA); finance (MBA); fraud examination (MBA); global business sustainability (DBA); healthcare administration (MBA); information systems (DBA); information systems management (MBA); international business (MBA, DBA); management (MBA, DBA); marketing (MBA, DBA); public administration (MBA); sustainable management (MBA).
See Close-Up on page 215.

Argosy University, Salt Lake City, College of Business, Draper, UT 84020. Offers accounting (DBA); corporate compliance (MBA); customized professional concentration (MBA, DBA); finance (MBA); fraud examination (MBA); global business sustainability (DBA); healthcare administration (MBA); information systems (DBA); information systems management (MBA); international business (MBA, DBA); management (MBA, DBA); marketing (MBA, DBA); public administration (MBA); sustainable management (MBA).
See Close-Up on page 217.

Argosy University, San Diego, College of Business, San Diego, CA 92108. Offers accounting (DBA); corporate compliance (MBA); customized professional concentration (MBA, DBA); finance (MBA); fraud examination (MBA); global business sustainability (DBA); information systems (DBA); information systems management (MBA); international business (MBA, DBA); management (MBA, MSM, DBA); marketing (MBA, DBA); organizational leadership (Ed D); public administration (MBA).
See Close-Up on page 219.

Argosy University, San Francisco Bay Area, College of Business, Alameda, CA 94501. Offers accounting (DBA); corporate compliance (MBA); customized professional concentration (MBA, DBA); finance (MBA); fraud examination (MBA); global business sustainability (DBA); healthcare administration (MBA); information systems (DBA); information systems management (MBA); international business (MBA, DBA); management (MBA, MSM, DBA); marketing (MBA, DBA); organizational leadership (Ed D); public administration (MBA); sustainable management (MBA).
See Close-Up on page 221.

Argosy University, Sarasota, College of Business, Sarasota, FL 34235. Offers accounting (DBA, Adv C); corporate compliance (MBA, DBA, Certificate); customized professional concentration (MBA, DBA); finance (MBA, Certificate); fraud examination (MBA, Certificate); global business sustainability (DBA, Adv C); healthcare administration (MBA, Certificate); information systems (DBA, Adv C, Certificate); information systems management (MBA); international business (MBA, DBA, Adv C, Certificate); management (MBA, MSM, DBA, Adv C, Certificate); marketing (MBA, DBA, Adv C, Certificate); organizational leadership (Ed D); public administration (MBA, Certificate); sustainable management (MBA, Certificate).
See Close-Up on page 223.

Argosy University, Schaumburg, College of Business, Schaumburg, IL 60173-5403. Offers accounting (DBA, Adv C); customized professional concentration (MBA, DBA); finance (MBA, Certificate); fraud examination (MBA); global business sustainability (DBA); healthcare administration (MBA, Certificate); information systems (DBA, Adv C, Certificate); information systems management (MBA); international business (MBA, DBA, Adv C, Certificate); management (MBA, MSM, DBA, Adv C, Certificate); marketing (MBA, DBA, Adv C, Certificate); organizational leadership (Ed D); public administration (MBA); sustainable management (MBA).
See Close-Up on page 225.

Argosy University, Seattle, College of Business, Seattle, WA 98121. Offers accounting (DBA); corporate compliance (MBA); customized professional concentration (MBA, DBA); finance (MBA); fraud examination (MBA); global business sustainability (DBA); healthcare administration (MBA); information systems (DBA); information systems management (MBA); international business (MBA, DBA); management (MBA, MSM, DBA); marketing (MBA, DBA); organizational leadership (Ed D); public administration (MBA); sustainable management (MBA).
See Close-Up on page 227.

Argosy University, Tampa, College of Business, Tampa, FL 33607. Offers accounting (DBA); corporate compliance (MBA); customized professional concentration (MBA, DBA); finance (MBA); fraud examination (MBA); global business sustainability (DBA); healthcare administration (MBA); information systems (DBA); information systems management (MBA); international business (MBA, DBA); management (MBA, MSM, DBA); marketing (MBA, DBA); organizational leadership (Ed D); public administration (MBA); sustainable management (MBA).
See Close-Up on page 229.

Argosy University, Twin Cities, College of Business, Eagan, MN 55121. Offers accounting (DBA); customized professional concentration (MBA, DBA); finance (MBA); fraud examination (MBA); global business sustainability (DBA); healthcare administration (MBA); information systems (DBA); information systems management (MBA); international business (MBA, DBA); management (MBA, MSM, DBA); marketing (MBA, DBA); organizational leadership (Ed D); public administration (MBA); sustainable management (MBA).
See Close-Up on page 231.

Argosy University, Washington DC, College of Business, Arlington, VA 22209. Offers accounting (DBA); customized professional concentration (MBA, DBA); finance (MBA); fraud examination (MBA); global business sustainability (DBA); healthcare administration (MBA); information systems (DBA); information systems management (MBA); international business (MBA, DBA, Certificate); management (MBA, MSM, DBA); marketing (MBA, DBA, Certificate); organizational leadership (Ed D); public administration (MBA); sustainable management (MBA).
See Close-Up on page 233.

Arizona State University, Graduate College, W.P. Carey School of Business, School of Accountancy, Tempe, AZ 85287. Offers M Acc, M Tax, PhD, MBA/M Tax. *Accreditation:* AACSB. *Degree requirements:* For master's, thesis optional. *Entrance requirements:* For master's, GMAT.

Arkansas State University—Jonesboro, Graduate School, College of Business, Department of Accounting, Jonesboro, State University, AR 72467. Offers accountancy (M Acc). Part-time programs available. *Faculty:* 5 full-time (2 women), 2 part-time/adjunct (1 woman). *Students:* 15 full-time (11 women), 12 part-time (7 women); includes 4 minority (2 African Americans, 1 American Indian/Alaska Native, 1 Asian American or Pacific Islander), 6 international. Average age 27. 28 applicants, 82% accepted, 12 enrolled. In 2009, 8 master's awarded. *Degree requirements:* For master's, comprehensive exam, thesis or alternative. *Entrance requirements:* For master's, GMAT, appropriate bachelor's degree, letters of reference, official transcript, immunization records. Additional exam requirements/recommendations for international students: Required—TOEFL (minimum score 550 paper-based; 213 computer-based; 79 iBT), IELTS (minimum score 6). *Application deadline:* For fall admission, 7/15 for domestic students, 7/1 for international students; for spring admission, 12/1 for domestic students, 11/13 for international students. Applications are processed on a rolling basis. Application fee: $30 ($40 for international students). Electronic applications accepted. *Expenses:* Contact institution. *Financial support:* In 2009–10, 2 students received support. Career-related internships or fieldwork, scholarships/grants, and unspecified assistantships available. Financial award application deadline: 7/1; financial award applicants required to submit FAFSA. *Unit head:* Dr. John Robertson, Chair, 870-972-3038, Fax: 870-972-3868, E-mail: jfrobert@astate.edu. *Application contact:* Dr. Andrew Sustich, Dean of the Graduate School, 870-972-3029, Fax: 870-972-3857, E-mail: sustich@astate.edu.

Assumption College, Graduate School, Department of Business Studies, Worcester, MA 01609-1296. Offers accounting (MBA); business administration (CAGS); finance/economics (MBA); general business (MBA); human resources (MBA); international business (MBA); management (MBA); marketing (MBA); nonprofit leadership (MBA). Part-time and evening/weekend programs available. *Faculty:* 6 full-time (1 woman), 14 part-time/adjunct (2 women). *Students:* 19 full-time (11 women), 127 part-time (68 women); includes 22 minority (13 African Americans, 3 Asian Americans or Pacific Islanders, 6 Hispanic Americans). Average age 27. 88 applicants, 99% accepted. In 2009, 40 master's, 2 other advanced degrees awarded. *Entrance requirements:* For master's, 3 letters of recommendation, resume; for CAGS, 3 letters of recommendation, resume, essay. Additional exam requirements/recommendations for international students: Required—TOEFL (minimum score 540 paper-based; 200 computer-based; 76 iBT), IELTS (minimum score 6). *Application deadline:* For fall admission, 6/1 priority date for domestic students, 5/1 priority date for international students; for spring admission, 11/1 priority date for domestic students, 9/1 priority date for international students. Applications are processed on a rolling basis. Application fee: $30. Electronic applications accepted. *Expenses:* Tuition: Part-time $503 per credit. Required fees: $20 per semester. One-time fee: $100 part-time. Part-time tuition and fees vary according to campus/location. *Financial support:* In 2009–10, 47 students received support. Application deadline: 6/1. *Faculty research:* Workplace diversity, dynamics of team interaction, utilization of leased employees. *Unit head:* Michael Lewis, Director, 508-767-7372, Fax: 508-767-7252, E-mail: jhunter@assumption.edu. *Application contact:* Adrian O. Dumas, Director of Graduate Enrollment Management and Services, 508-767-7365, Fax: 508-767-7030, E-mail: adumas@assumption.edu.

Auburn University, Graduate School, College of Business, School of Accountancy, Auburn University, AL 36849. Offers M Acc. *Accreditation:* AACSB. Part-time programs available. *Faculty:* 15 full-time (5 women), 3 part-time/adjunct (2 women). *Students:* 51 full-time (36 women), 44 part-time (25 women); includes 6 minority (2 African Americans, 3 Asian Americans or Pacific Islanders, 1 Hispanic American). Average age 28. 170 applicants, 47% accepted, 62 enrolled. In 2009, 48 master's awarded. *Entrance requirements:* For master's, GMAT, GRE General Test. Additional exam requirements/recommendations for international students: Required—TOEFL. *Application deadline:* For fall admission, 7/7 for domestic students; for spring admission, 11/24 for domestic students. Applications are processed on a rolling basis. Application fee: $50 ($60 for international students). Electronic applications accepted. *Expenses:* Tuition, state resident: full-time $6240. Tuition, nonresident: full-time $18,720. International tuition: $18,938 full-time. Required fees: $492. Tuition and fees vary according to course load, program and reciprocity agreements. *Financial support:* Teaching assistantships, Federal Work-Study available. Support available to part-time students. Financial award application deadline: 3/15; financial award applicants required to submit FAFSA. *Unit head:* Norman H. Godwin, Director, 334-844-5340. *Application contact:* Dr. George Flowers, Dean of the Graduate School, 334-844-2125.

Avila University, School of Business, Kansas City, MO 64145-1698. Offers accounting (MBA); finance (MBA); general management (MBA); health care administration (MBA); international business (MBA); management information systems (MBA); marketing (MBA). Part-time and evening/weekend programs available. *Faculty:* 9 full-time (3 women), 24 part-time/adjunct (5 women). *Students:* 148 full-time (71 women), 86 part-time (47 women); includes 56 minority (36 African Americans, 2 American Indian/Alaska Native, 13 Asian Americans or Pacific Islanders, 5 Hispanic Americans), 63 international. Average age 32. 53 applicants, 75% accepted, 40 enrolled. In 2009, 93 master's awarded. *Degree requirements:* For master's, comprehensive exam, capstone course. *Entrance requirements:* For master's, GMAT, minimum GPA of 3.0, interview. Additional exam requirements/recommendations for international students: Required—TOEFL (minimum score 550 paper-based). *Application deadline:* For fall admission, 7/30 priority date for domestic students, 7/30 for international students; for winter admission, 11/30 priority date for domestic students, 11/30 for international students; for spring admission, 2/28 priority date for domestic students, 2/28 for international students. Applications are processed on a rolling basis. Application fee: $0. Electronic applications accepted. *Expenses:* Contact institution. *Financial support:* In 2009–10, 102 students received support. Career-related internships or fieldwork available. Support available to part-time students. Financial award applicants required to submit FAFSA. *Faculty research:* Leadership characteristics, financial hedging, group dynamics. *Unit head:* Dr. Richard Woodall, Dean, 816-501-3720, Fax: 816-501-2463, E-mail: richard.woodall@avila.edu. *Application contact:* JoAnna Giffin, MBA Admissions Director, 816-501-3601, Fax: 816-501-2463, E-mail: joanna.giffin@avila.edu.

Babson College, F. W. Olin Graduate School of Business, Wellesley, Babson Park, MA 02457-0310. Offers accounting (MSA); advanced management (Certificate); business administration (MBA); global entrepreneurship (MS); technological entrepreneurship (MS). *Accreditation:* AACSB. Part-time and evening/weekend programs available. Postbaccalaureate distance learning degree programs offered (minimal on-campus study). *Faculty:* 144 full-time

Accounting

Babson College (continued)

(37 women), 46 part-time/adjunct (10 women). *Students:* 503 full-time (171 women), 1,019 part-time (276 women); includes 221 minority (28 African Americans, 152 Asian Americans or Pacific Islanders, 41 Hispanic Americans), 285 international. Average age 32. 1,102 applicants, 57% accepted, 407 enrolled. In 2009, 712 master's, 2 other advanced degrees awarded. *Entrance requirements:* For master's, GMAT, 2 years of work experience, resume, letters of recommendation. Additional exam requirements/recommendations for international students: Required—TOEFL (minimum score 600 paper-based; 250 computer-based; 100 iBT). *Application deadline:* For fall admission, 4/15 priority date for domestic students, 1/15 priority date for international students. Application fee: $100. Electronic applications accepted. *Expenses:* Tuition: Full-time $40,600; part-time $1137 per credit. One-time fee: $1270. Full-time tuition and fees vary according to course load, program and student level. *Financial support:* In 2009–10, 317 students received support, including 43 fellowships (averaging $33,969 per year); career-related internships or fieldwork, Federal Work-Study, institutionally sponsored loans, scholarships/grants, and unspecified assistantships also available. Financial award application deadline: 4/15. *Faculty research:* Entrepreneurship, innovation and quality management, global management, e-commerce marketing, leadership and change management. Total annual research expenditures: $89,516. *Unit head:* Dr. Raghu Tadepalli, Dean, E-mail: rtadepalli@babson.edu. *Application contact:* Martha Snelling, Admission Services Team, 781-239-4317, Fax: 781-239-4194, E-mail: mbaadmission@babson.edu.

Baker College Center for Graduate Studies—Online, Graduate Programs—Online, Flint, MI 48507-9843. Offers accounting (MBA); business administration (DBA); finance (MBA); general business (MBA); health care management (MBA); human resources management (MBA); information management (MBA); leadership studies (MBA); management information systems (MSIS); marketing (MBA). Part-time and evening/weekend programs available. Post-baccalaureate distance learning degree programs offered. *Faculty:* 750. *Students:* 500 full-time, 500 part-time. Average age 37. *Degree requirements:* For master's, portfolio. *Entrance requirements:* For master's, 3 years of work experience, minimum undergraduate GPA of 2.5, writing sample, 3 letters of recommendation; for doctorate, MBA or acceptable related master's degree from accredited association, 5 years work experience, minimum graduate GPA of 3.25, writing sample, 3 professional references. Additional exam requirements/recommendations for international students: Required—TOEFL (minimum score 550 paper-based; 213 computer-based). *Application deadline:* For fall admission, 8/6 priority date for domestic students; for winter admission, 12/15 priority date for domestic students; for spring admission, 2/15 priority date for domestic students. Applications are processed on a rolling basis. Application fee: $25. Electronic applications accepted. *Expenses:* Tuition: Part-time $330 per credit hour. Tuition and fees vary according to degree level. *Financial support:* Scholarships/grants available. Support available to part-time students. Financial award applicants required to submit FAFSA. *Unit head:* Dr. Julia Teahen, President, 810-766-4023, Fax: 810-766-4399, E-mail: julia@baker.edu. *Application contact:* Chuck J. Gurden, Vice President for Graduate and Online Admissions, 800-469-3165, Fax: 810-766-4399, E-mail: adm-ol@baker.edu.

Baldwin-Wallace College, Graduate Programs, Division of Business, Program in Accounting, Berea, OH 44017-2088. Offers MBA. Part-time and evening/weekend programs available. *Students:* 28 full-time (19 women), 17 part-time (9 women); includes 7 minority (all African Americans), 1 international. Average age 33. 18 applicants, 61% accepted, 7 enrolled. In 2009, 40 master's awarded. *Entrance requirements:* For master's, GMAT, minimum GPA of 3.0, work experience, bachelor's degree in field, undergraduate accounting coursework. Additional exam requirements/recommendations for international students: Required—TOEFL (minimum score 523 paper-based; 193 computer-based; 70 iBT). *Application deadline:* For fall admission, 7/25 priority date for domestic students, 4/30 priority date for international students; for spring admission, 12/15 priority date for domestic students, 9/30 priority date for international students. Applications are processed on a rolling basis. Application fee: $25. Electronic applications accepted. *Expenses:* Contact institution. *Financial support:* Career-related internships or fieldwork available. Support available to part-time students. Financial award application deadline: 5/1. *Unit head:* Dale Kramer, Director, 440-826-3331, Fax: 440-826-3868, E-mail: dkramer@bw.edu. *Application contact:* Peggy Shepard, Graduate Business Coordinator, 440-826-2196, Fax: 440-826-3868, E-mail: pshepard@bw.edu.

Ball State University, Graduate School, Miller College of Business, Department of Accounting, Muncie, IN 47306-1099. Offers MS. *Accreditation:* AACSB.

Barry University, Andreas School of Business, Program in Accounting, Miami Shores, FL 33161-6695. Offers MSA.

Bayamón Central University, Graduate Programs, Program in Business Administration, Bayamón, PR 00960-1725. Offers accounting (MBA); finance (MBA); general business (MBA); management (MBA); management of security and protection (MBA); marketing (MBA). Part-time and evening/weekend programs available. *Degree requirements:* For master's, comprehensive exam (for some programs). *Entrance requirements:* For master's, EXADEP, bachelor's degree in business or related field.

Baylor University, Graduate School, Hankamer School of Business, Department of Accounting and Business Law, Waco, TX 76798. Offers M Acc, MT, JD/M Acc, JD/MT. *Accreditation:* AACSB. Part-time programs available. *Faculty:* 11 full-time (2 women). *Students:* 43 full-time (24 women), 6 part-time (4 women); includes 8 minority (3 African Americans, 1 American Indian/Alaska Native, 3 Asian Americans or Pacific Islanders, 1 Hispanic American), 1 international. In 2009, 46 master's awarded. *Entrance requirements:* For master's, GMAT. *Application deadline:* For fall admission, 8/1 for domestic students; for spring admission, 12/1 for domestic students. Applications are processed on a rolling basis. Application fee: $25. *Financial support:* Research assistantships, career-related internships or fieldwork, Federal Work-Study, and institutionally sponsored loans available. *Faculty research:* Continuing professional education (CPE), accounting education, retirement plans. *Unit head:* Dr. Jane Baldwin, Adviser, 254-710-3536, Fax: 254-710-2421, E-mail: jane_baldwin@baylor.edu. *Application contact:* Vicky Todd, Administrative Assistant, 254-710-3718, Fax: 254-710-1066, E-mail: mba@hsb.baylor.edu.

Benedictine University, Graduate Programs, Program in Accountancy, Lisle, IL 60532-0900. Offers MS. Evening/weekend programs available. *Students:* 7 full-time (3 women), 25 part-time (11 women); includes 7 minority (3 African Americans, 4 Asian Americans or Pacific Islanders), 8 international. 21 applicants, 90% accepted, 15 enrolled. In 2009, 5 master's awarded. *Entrance requirements:* For master's, official transcripts, 2 letters of reference, resume. Additional exam requirements/recommendations for international students: Required—TOEFL. *Application deadline:* Applications are processed on a rolling basis. Electronic applications accepted. *Expenses:* Tuition: Part-time $750 per credit hour. Tuition and fees vary according to campus/location and program. *Unit head:* Dr. Sharon Borowicz, Director, 630-829-6219, E-mail: sborowicz@ben.edu. *Application contact:* Kari Gibbons, Director, Admissions, 630-829-6200, Fax: 630-829-6584, E-mail: kgibbons@ben.edu.

Benedictine University, Graduate Programs, Program in Business Administration, Lisle, IL 60532-0900. Offers accounting (MBA); entrepreneurship and managing innovation (MBA); financial management (MBA); health administration (MBA); human resource management (MBA); information systems security (MBA); international business (MBA); management consulting (MBA); management information systems (MBA); marketing management (MBA); operations management and logistics (MBA); organizational leadership (MBA); MBA/MPH; MBA/MS. Part-time and evening/weekend programs available. Postbaccalaureate distance learning degree programs offered (minimal on-campus study). *Faculty:* 4 full-time (2 women), 24 part-time/adjunct (3 women). *Students:* 247 full-time (141 women), 644 part-time (339 women); includes 223 minority (134 African Americans, 5 American Indian/Alaska Native, 44 Asian Americans or Pacific Islanders, 40 Hispanic Americans), 25 international. Average age 34. 287 applicants, 92% accepted, 229 enrolled. In 2009, 219 master's awarded. *Entrance requirements:* For master's, GMAT. Additional exam requirements/recommendations for international students: Required—TOEFL (minimum score 550 paper-based; 213 computer-

based). *Application deadline:* For fall admission, 9/1 for domestic students; for winter admission, 12/1 for domestic students; for spring admission, 2/15 for domestic students. Applications are processed on a rolling basis. Application fee: $40. Electronic applications accepted. *Expenses:* Tuition: Part-time $750 per credit hour. Tuition and fees vary according to campus/location and program. *Financial support:* Career-related internships or fieldwork and health care benefits available. Support available to part-time students. *Faculty research:* Strategic leadership in professional organizations, sociology of professions, organizational change, social identity theory, applications to change management. *Unit head:* Dr. Sharon Borowicz, Director, 630-829-6219, E-mail: sborowicz@ben.edu. *Application contact:* Kari Gibbons, Director, Admissions, 630-829-6200, Fax: 630-829-6584, E-mail: kgibbons@ben.edu.

Bentley University, McCallum Graduate School of Business, Accountancy PhD Program, Waltham, MA 02452-4705. Offers PhD. Part-time programs available. *Faculty:* 65 full-time (24 women), 16 part-time/adjunct (6 women). *Students:* 8 full-time (4 women), 3 part-time (2 women), 2 international. Average age 35. 20 applicants, 20% accepted, 4 enrolled. In 2009, 1 doctorate awarded. *Degree requirements:* For doctorate, comprehensive exam, thesis/dissertation. *Entrance requirements:* For doctorate, GMAT or GRE General Test. Additional exam requirements/recommendations for international students: Required—TOEFL (minimum score 650 paper-based; 250 computer-based) or IELTS (minimum score 7). Application fee: $0. Electronic applications accepted. *Expenses:* Tuition: Full-time $26,208; part-time $1092 per credit. Required fees: $404. *Financial support:* Scholarships/grants available. *Faculty research:* Accounting information systems, financial fraud, forensic accounting, enterprise risks and controls, managerial incentive systems, earnings management, auditor ethos and independence, audit team brainstorming, auditor-client negotiations, information technology auditing, corporate ethics and internal controls; corporate governance. *Unit head:* Dr. Sue Newell, PhD Program Director, 781-891-2399, Fax: 781-891-3121, E-mail: snewell@bentley.edu. *Application contact:* Dr. Sue Newell, PhD Program Director, 781-891-2399, Fax: 781-891-3121, E-mail: snewell@bentley.edu.

Bentley University, McCallum Graduate School of Business, Master's Program in Accounting, Waltham, MA 02452-4705. Offers MSA. *Accreditation:* AACSB. Part-time and evening/weekend programs available. *Faculty:* 65 full-time (24 women), 16 part-time/adjunct (6 women). *Students:* 112 full-time (65 women), 122 part-time (65 women); includes 35 minority (4 African Americans, 1 American Indian/Alaska Native, 26 Asian Americans or Pacific Islanders, 4 Hispanic Americans), 55 international. Average age 26. 535 applicants, 64% accepted, 140 enrolled. *Entrance requirements:* For master's, GMAT. Additional exam requirements/recommendations for international students: Required—TOEFL (minimum score 600 paper-based; 250 computer-based; 100 iBT) or IELTS (minimum score 7). *Application deadline:* For fall admission, 6/1 priority date for domestic students, 12/1 priority date for international students. Application fee: $50. Electronic applications accepted. *Expenses:* Tuition: Full-time $26,208; part-time $1092 per credit. Required fees: $404. *Financial support:* Scholarships/grants and unspecified assistantships available. Financial award application deadline: 6/1; financial award applicants required to submit CSS PROFILE or FAFSA. *Faculty research:* Audit risk assessment, ethics in accounting, corporate governance, accounting information systems and management control, tax policy, forensic accounting. *Unit head:* Martha Howe, Director, 781-891-2573, E-mail: mhowe@bentley.edu. *Application contact:* Sharon Hill, Director of Graduate Admissions, 781-891-2108, Fax: 781-891-2464, E-mail: bentleygraduateadmissions@bentley.edu.

Bernard M. Baruch College of the City University of New York, Zicklin School of Business, Department of Accounting, Program in Accounting, New York, NY 10010-5585. Offers MBA, MS, PhD. *Accreditation:* AACSB. Part-time and evening/weekend programs available. *Degree requirements:* For doctorate, comprehensive exam, thesis/dissertation. *Entrance requirements:* For master's, GMAT, 2 letters of recommendation, resume, 2 years of work experience; for doctorate, GMAT. Additional exam requirements/recommendations for international students: Required—TOEFL (minimum score 590 paper-based; 243 computer-based), TWE (minimum score 5).

Bob Jones University, Graduate Programs, Greenville, SC 29614. Offers accountancy (MS); Bible (MA); Bible translation (MA); Biblical studies (Certificate); broadcast management (MS); business administration (MBA); church history (MA, PhD); church ministries (MA); church music (MM); cinema and video production (MA); counseling (MS); curriculum and instruction (Ed D); divinity (M Div); dramatic production (MA); educational leadership (MS, Ed D, Ed S); elementary education (M Ed, MAT); English (M Ed, MA, MAT); fine arts (MA); graphic design (MA); history (M Ed, MA); illustration (MA); interpretative speech (MA); mathematics (M Ed, MAT); medical missions (Certificate); ministry (MM, D Min); multi-categorical special education (M Ed, MAT); music (M Ed); New Testament interpretation (PhD); Old Testament interpretation (PhD); orchestral instrument performance (MM); organ performance (MM); pastoral studies (MA); personnel services (MS, Ed S); piano pedagogy (MM); piano performance (MM); platform arts (MA); radio and television broadcasting (MS); rhetoric and public address (MA); secondary education (M Ed); studio art (MA); teaching Bible (MA); theology (MA, PhD); voice performance (MM); youth ministries (MA); M Div/MM.

Boise State University, Graduate College, College of Business and Economics, Program in Accountancy, Boise, ID 83725-0399. Offers accountancy (MSA); taxation (MSA). *Accreditation:* AACSB. Part-time programs available. *Entrance requirements:* For master's, GMAT, minimum GPA of 3.0. Additional exam requirements/recommendations for international students: Required—TOEFL. Electronic applications accepted. *Expenses:* Tuition, state resident: full-time $3106; part-time $209 per credit. Tuition, nonresident: part-time $284 per credit.

Boston College, Carroll School of Management, Programs in Accounting, Chestnut Hill, MA 02467-3800. Offers MSA. *Faculty:* 14 full-time (6 women), 5 part-time/adjunct (1 woman). *Students:* 40 full-time (25 women); includes 4 minority (all Asian Americans or Pacific Islanders), 17 international. Average age 26. 381 applicants, 40% accepted. In 2009, 74 master's awarded. *Entrance requirements:* For master's, GMAT, recommendations, resume. Additional exam requirements/recommendations for international students: Required—TOEFL (minimum score 600 paper-based; 250 computer-based; 100 iBT). *Application deadline:* For fall admission, 3/15 for domestic and international students; for spring admission, 2/15 for domestic and international students. Application fee: $100. Electronic applications accepted. *Financial support:* In 2009–10, 151 fellowships, 158 research assistantships were awarded; tuition waivers (partial) also available. *Faculty research:* Financial reporting, auditing, tax planning, financial statement analysis. *Unit head:* Dr. Jeffrey L. Ringuest, Associate Dean, Graduate Programs, 617-552-9100, Fax: 617-552-0514, E-mail: gsomdean@bc.edu. *Application contact:* Shelley A. Burt, Director of Graduate Enrollment, 617-552-3920, Fax: 617-552-8078, E-mail: bcmba@bc.edu.

Boston University, School of Management, Doctorate in Business Administration Program, Boston, MA 02215. Offers accounting (PhD); information systems (PhD); marketing (PhD); operations and technology management (PhD); organizational behavior (PhD); strategy and innovation (PhD). *Students:* 31 full-time (18 women), 21 international. Average age 32. 158 applicants, 7% accepted, 6 enrolled. In 2009, 12 doctorates awarded. *Degree requirements:* For doctorate, comprehensive exam, thesis/dissertation, curriculum paper. *Entrance requirements:* For doctorate, GMAT or GRE General Test, resume, 3 letters of evaluation. Additional exam requirements/recommendations for international students: Required—TOEFL or IELTS. *Application deadline:* For fall admission, 1/5 for domestic and international students. Application fee: $125. *Expenses:* Tuition: Full-time $37,910; part-time $1184 per credit hour. Required fees: $386; $40 per semester. Part-time tuition and fees vary according to class time, course level, degree level and program. *Financial support:* Fellowships, research assistantships, teaching assistantships, career-related internships or fieldwork, Federal Work-Study, institutionally sponsored loans, scholarships/grants, and tuition waivers available. Support available to part-time students. Financial award applicants required to submit FAFSA. *Unit head:* Dr. Lloyd Baird, Director, 617-353-2670, E-mail: dba@bu.edu. *Application contact:* Hayden Estrada, Assistant Dean, Admissions, 617-353-2670, Fax: 617-353-7368, E-mail: dba@bu.edu.

Bowling Green State University, Graduate College, College of Business Administration, Program in Accountancy, Bowling Green, OH 43403. Offers M Acc. *Accreditation:* AACSB. Part-time programs available. *Degree requirements:* For master's, thesis or alternative. *Entrance requirements:* For master's, GMAT. Additional exam requirements/recommendations for international students: Required—TOEFL. Electronic applications accepted. *Faculty research:* Financial reporting and auditing, accounting information systems, taxation.

Bradley University, Graduate School, Foster College of Business Administration, Program in Accounting, Peoria, IL 61625-0002. Offers MSA. *Accreditation:* AACSB. Part-time and evening/weekend programs available. *Degree requirements:* For master's, comprehensive exam. *Entrance requirements:* For master's, GMAT, minimum undergraduate GPA of 2.75 in major, 2 letters of recommendation. Additional exam requirements/recommendations for international students: Required—TOEFL (minimum score 550 paper-based; 213 computer-based; 79 iBT).

Brenau University, Graduate Programs, School of Business and Mass Communication, Gainesville, GA 30501. Offers accounting (MBA); business administration (MBA); healthcare management (MBA); organizational leadership (MS); project management (MBA). Part-time and evening/weekend programs available. Postbaccalaureate distance learning degree programs offered (no on-campus study). *Faculty:* 11 full-time (6 women), 22 part-time/adjunct (6 women). *Students:* 116 full-time (74 women), 256 part-time (181 women); includes 113 minority (98 African Americans, 6 Asian Americans or Pacific Islanders, 9 Hispanic Americans), 20 international. Average age 35. 278 applicants, 90% accepted, 185 enrolled. In 2009, 125 master's awarded. *Entrance requirements:* For master's, resume, minimum undergraduate GPA of 3.5. Additional exam requirements/recommendations for international students: Required—TOEFL (minimum score 500 paper-based). *Application deadline:* Applications are processed on a rolling basis. Electronic applications accepted. *Expenses:* Contact institution. *Financial support:* In 2009–10, 1 student received support. Application deadline: 7/15. *Unit head:* Dr. William S. Lightfoot, Dean, 770-538-5330, Fax: 770-537-4701, E-mail: wlightfoot@brenau.edu. *Application contact:* Christina White, Graduate Admissions Specialist, 770-718-5320, Fax: 770-718-5338, E-mail: cwhite@brenau.edu.

Bridgewater State University, School of Graduate Studies, School of Business, Department of Accounting and Finance, Bridgewater, MA 02325-0001. Offers MSM. Part-time and evening/weekend programs available. *Entrance requirements:* For master's, GMAT.

Brigham Young University, Graduate Studies, Marriott School of Management, Master of Accountancy Program, Provo, UT 84602. Offers M Acc, JD/M Acc. *Accreditation:* AACSB. *Faculty:* 15 full-time (1 woman), 1 part-time/adjunct (0 women). *Students:* 175 full-time (31 women); includes 10 minority (1 American Indian/Alaska Native, 4 Asian Americans or Pacific Islanders, 5 Hispanic Americans), 6 international. Average age 24. 296 applicants, 57% accepted, 161 enrolled. In 2009, 161 master's awarded. *Entrance requirements:* For master's, GMAT, minimum GPA of 3.0 in last 60 hours. Additional exam requirements/recommendations for international students: Required—TOEFL (minimum score 580 paper-based; 230 computer-based). *Application deadline:* For fall admission, 3/1 for domestic and international students. Application fee: $50. Electronic applications accepted. *Expenses:* Contact institution. *Financial support:* In 2009–10, 175 students received support. Application deadline: 4/15. *Unit head:* Dr. Kevin D. Stocks, Director, 801-422-4613, Fax: 801-422-0621, E-mail: kevin_stocks@byu.edu. *Application contact:* Julie Averett, Academic Advisor, 801-422-3951, Fax: 801-422-0621, E-mail: soa@byu.edu.

Brock University, Faculty of Graduate Studies, Faculty of Business, Program in Accountancy, St. Catharines, ON L2S 3A1, Canada. Offers M Acc. *Degree requirements:* For master's, thesis or alternative. *Entrance requirements:* For master's, honours degree. Additional exam requirements/recommendations for international students: Required—TOEFL (minimum score 550 paper-based; 213 computer-based; 80 iBT), IELTS (minimum score 6.5), TWE (minimum score 4.5). Electronic applications accepted.

Brooklyn College of the City University of New York, Division of Graduate Studies, Department of Economics, Brooklyn, NY 11210-2889. Offers accounting (MS); economics (MA). Part-time and evening/weekend programs available. *Students:* 30 full-time (16 women), 161 part-time (85 women); includes 76 minority (56 African Americans, 15 Asian Americans or Pacific Islanders, 5 Hispanic Americans), 55 international. Average age 32. 109 applicants, 73% accepted, 61 enrolled. In 2009, 33 master's awarded. *Degree requirements:* For master's, comprehensive exam, thesis or alternative. *Entrance requirements:* For master's, GMAT (for MS), 2 letters of recommendation. Additional exam requirements/recommendations for international students: Required—TOEFL (minimum score 550 paper-based; 213 computer-based; 79 iBT). *Application deadline:* For fall admission, 3/1 priority date for domestic students, 2/1 priority date for international students; for spring admission, 11/1 priority date for domestic students, 10/1 priority date for international students. Applications are processed on a rolling basis. Application fee: $125. Electronic applications accepted. *Expenses:* Tuition, state resident: full-time $7360; part-time $310 per credit hour. Tuition, nonresident: full-time $13,800; part-time $575 per credit hour. Required fees: $140.10 per semester. *Financial support:* Career-related internships or fieldwork, Federal Work-Study, institutionally sponsored loans, and scholarships/grants available. Support available to part-time students. Financial award application deadline: 5/1; financial award applicants required to submit FAFSA. *Faculty research:* Econometrics, environmental economics, microeconomics, macroeconomics, taxation. *Unit head:* Dr. Robert Bell, Chairperson, 718-951-5317, E-mail: rbell brooklyn.cuny.edu. *Application contact:* Hernan Sierra, Graduate Admissions Coordinator, 718-951-4536, Fax: 718-951-4506, E-mail: grads@brooklyn.cuny.edu.

Bryant University, Graduate School of Business, Master of Professional Accountancy Program, Smithfield, RI 02917. Offers MPAC. Part-time programs available. *Faculty:* 10 full-time (3 women). *Students:* 35 full-time (17 women); includes 4 minority (3 African Americans, 1 Hispanic American), 2 international. Average age 23. 14 applicants, 86% accepted, 6 enrolled. In 2009, 33 master's awarded. *Entrance requirements:* For master's, GMAT, transcripts, resume, recommendation, personal statement. Additional exam requirements/recommendations for international students: Required—TOEFL (minimum score 580 paper-based; 237 computer-based; 95 iBT). *Application deadline:* For fall admission, 7/15 for domestic and international students; for spring admission, 11/15 for domestic students, 7/15 for international students. Applications are processed on a rolling basis. Application fee: $80. Electronic applications accepted. *Expenses:* Tuition: Full-time $29,880; part-time $2367 per course. One-time fee: $750. Tuition and fees vary according to program. *Financial support:* In 2009–10, 9 students received support, including 4 research assistantships (averaging $11,411 per year). Financial award application deadline: 2/15; financial award applicants required to submit FAFSA. *Faculty research:* Director compensation, public sector auditing, employee stock options, financial disclosure, XBRL. *Unit head:* Kristopher T. Sullivan, Assistant Dean of the Graduate School, 401-232-6320, Fax: 401-232-6494, E-mail: sullivan@bryant.edu. *Application contact:* Ellen Hudon, Assistant Director of Graduate Admission, 401-232-6529, Fax: 401-232-6494, E-mail: ehudon@bryant.edu.

Caldwell College, Graduate Studies, Program in Business Administration, Caldwell, NJ 07006-6195. Offers accounting (MBA); business administration (MBA). *Accreditation:* ACBSP. Part-time and evening/weekend programs available. *Degree requirements:* For master's, capstone course. *Entrance requirements:* For master's, GMAT, minimum GPA of 3.0. Additional exam requirements/recommendations for international students: Required—TOEFL (minimum score 580 paper-based; 237 computer-based). Electronic applications accepted.

California State University, East Bay, Graduate Programs, College of Business and Economics, Department of Accounting and Finance, Option in Accounting/Finance, Hayward, CA 94542-3000. Offers MBA. *Degree requirements:* For master's, comprehensive exam or thesis. *Entrance requirements:* For master's, GMAT, minimum GPA of 2.75. Additional exam requirements/recommendations for international students: Required—TOEFL (minimum score 550 paper-based; 213 computer-based). *Application deadline:* For fall admission, 6/30 for domestic and international students. Applications are processed on a rolling basis. Application fee: $55. Electronic applications accepted. *Financial support:* Career-related internships or fieldwork, Federal Work-Study, and institutionally sponsored loans available. Support available to part-time students. Financial award application deadline: 3/1; financial award applicants required to submit FAFSA. *Unit head:* Prof. Micah Frankel, Graduate Adviser, 510-885-3397, Fax: 510-885-4796, E-mail: micah.frankel@csueastbay.edu. *Application contact:* Donna Wiley, Interim Associate Director, 510-885-2928, Fax: 510-885-4777, E-mail: donna.wiley@csueastbay.edu.

California State University, Fresno, Division of Graduate Studies, Craig School of Business, Department of Accountancy, Fresno, CA 93740-8027. Offers MS. Part-time programs available. *Degree requirements:* For master's, comprehensive exam. *Entrance requirements:* For master's, GMAT, minimum GPA of 2.75. Additional exam requirements/recommendations for international students: Required—TOEFL. Electronic applications accepted.

California State University, Fullerton, Graduate Studies, College of Business and Economics, Department of Accounting, Fullerton, CA 92834-9480. Offers accounting (MBA, MS); taxation (MS). *Accreditation:* AACSB. Part-time programs available. *Students:* 115 full-time (71 women), 84 part-time (50 women); includes 84 minority (1 African American, 75 Asian Americans or Pacific Islanders, 8 Hispanic Americans), 60 international. Average age 29. 233 applicants, 55% accepted, 59 enrolled. In 2009, 62 master's awarded. *Degree requirements:* For master's, thesis or alternative, project. *Entrance requirements:* For master's, GMAT, minimum AACSB index of 950. *Application deadline:* Applications are processed on a rolling basis. Application fee: $55. Electronic applications accepted. *Expenses:* Tuition, nonresident: full-time $11,160; part-time $373 per credit. Required fees: $1440 per term. Tuition and fees vary according to course load, degree level and program. *Financial support:* Career-related internships or fieldwork, Federal Work-Study, institutionally sponsored loans, and scholarships/grants available. Support available to part-time students. Financial award application deadline: 3/1; financial award applicants required to submit FAFSA. *Unit head:* Dr. Betty Chavis, Chair, 657-278-2225. *Application contact:* Admissions/Applications, 657-278-2371.

California State University, Los Angeles, Graduate Studies, College of Business and Economics, Department of Accounting, Los Angeles, CA 90032-8530. Offers accountancy (MS), including business taxation, financial accounting, information systems, management accounting; accounting (MBA). Part-time and evening/weekend programs available. *Faculty:* 4 full-time (1 woman), 4 part-time/adjunct (0 women). *Students:* 47 full-time (31 women), 54 part-time (33 women); includes 32 minority (1 African American, 25 Asian Americans or Pacific Islanders, 6 Hispanic Americans), 51 international. Average age 30. 34 applicants, 97% accepted, 16 enrolled. In 2009, 37 master's awarded. *Degree requirements:* For master's, comprehensive exam (MBA), thesis (MS). *Entrance requirements:* For master's, GMAT, minimum GPA of 2.5 during previous 2 years of course work. Additional exam requirements/recommendations for international students: Required—TOEFL (minimum score 550 paper-based; 213 computer-based). *Application deadline:* For fall admission, 5/1 for domestic and international students. Applications are processed on a rolling basis. Application fee: $55. Electronic applications accepted. *Financial support:* Career-related internships or fieldwork and Federal Work-Study available. Support available to part-time students. Financial award application deadline: 3/1. *Unit head:* Dr. Greg Kunkel, Chair, 323-343-2830, Fax: 323-343-6439, E-mail: gkunkel@calstatela.edu. *Application contact:* Dr. Cheryl L. Ney, Associate Vice President for Academic Affairs and Dean of Graduate Studies, 323-343-3820, Fax: 323-343-5653, E-mail: cney@cslanet.calstatela.edu.

California State University, Sacramento, Graduate Studies, College of Business Administration, Sacramento, CA 95819. Offers accountancy (MS); business administration (MBA); human resources (MBA); management information science (MS); urban land development (MBA). *Accreditation:* AACSB. Part-time and evening/weekend programs available. *Degree requirements:* For master's, thesis or alternative, writing proficiency exam. *Entrance requirements:* For master's, GMAT. Additional exam requirements/recommendations for international students: Required—TOEFL. Electronic applications accepted.

California Western School of Law, Graduate and Professional Programs, San Diego, CA 92101-3090. Offers law (JD, LL M); JD/MBA; JD/MSW; JD/PhD; MCL/LL M. *Accreditation:* ABA. Part-time programs available. *Entrance requirements:* LSAT. Additional exam requirements/recommendations for international students: Required—TOEFL. Electronic applications accepted. *Faculty research:* Biotechnology, child and family law, international law, labor and employment law, sports law.

Canisius College, Graduate Division, Richard J. Wehle School of Business, Department of Accounting, Buffalo, NY 14208-1098. Offers accounting (MBA); professional accounting (MBAPA). Part-time and evening/weekend programs available. *Faculty:* 9 full-time (1 woman), 1 part-time/adjunct (0 women). *Students:* 24 full-time (13 women), 19 part-time (10 women); includes 3 minority (all Hispanic Americans), 4 international. Average age 30. 22 applicants, 86% accepted, 15 enrolled. In 2009, 22 master's awarded. *Entrance requirements:* For master's, GMAT. *Application deadline:* For fall admission, 7/1 priority date for domestic students; for spring admission, 11/1 priority date for domestic students. Applications are processed on a rolling basis. *Financial support:* Research assistantships, career-related internships or fieldwork, scholarships/grants, health care benefits, tuition waivers (partial), and unspecified assistantships available. Support available to part-time students. Financial award application deadline: 6/15; financial award applicants required to submit FAFSA. *Unit head:* Dr. Joseph B. O'Donnell, Chair, 716-888-2868, E-mail: odonnelj@canisius.edu. *Application contact:* Laura McEwen, Director, 716-888-2140, Fax: 716-888-3211, E-mail: gradubus@canisius.edu.

Capella University, School of Business and Technology, Minneapolis, MN 55402. Offers accounting (MBA), including system design and programming; business (Certificate), including human resource management (MS, PhD, Certificate), information technology management (MS, PhD, Certificate), leadership (MBA, MS, PhD, Certificate); finance (MBA); general business (MBA); health care management (MBA); information technology (MS, Certificate), including general information technology (MS), information security, network architecture and design (MS), professional projects management (Certificate), project management and leadership (MS), system design and development (MS),); information technology management (MBA); marketing (MBA); organization and management (MBA, MS, PhD), including general business (PhD), general organization and management (MBA, MS), human resource management (MS, PhD, Certificate), information technology management (MS, PhD, Certificate), leadership (MBA, MS, PhD, Certificate); project management (MBA). Part-time and evening/weekend programs available. Postbaccalaureate distance learning degree programs offered (minimal on-campus study). Terminal master's awarded for partial completion of doctoral program. *Degree requirements:* For master's, thesis optional, integrative project; for doctorate, comprehensive exam, thesis/dissertation. *Entrance requirements:* Additional exam requirements/recommendations for international students: Required—TOEFL (minimum score 550 paper-based; 213 computer-based), TWE (minimum score 4). Electronic applications accepted. *Faculty research:* Business policies: strategic, corporate, and financial management; interplay of technological, organizational and social change.

Carnegie Mellon University, Tepper School of Business, Program in Accounting, Pittsburgh, PA 15213-3891. Offers PhD. *Accreditation:* AACSB. *Degree requirements:* For doctorate, thesis/dissertation. *Entrance requirements:* For doctorate, GRE.

Case Western Reserve University, Weatherhead School of Management, Department of Accountancy, Cleveland, OH 44106. Offers M Acc, PhD, MBA/M Acc. *Accreditation:* AACSB. Evening/weekend programs available. *Degree requirements:* For doctorate, thesis/dissertation. *Entrance requirements:* For master's and doctorate, GMAT. *Application deadline:* For fall admission, 4/15 priority date for domestic students. Applications are processed on a rolling basis. Application fee: $100. *Financial support:* Career-related internships or fieldwork, Federal Work-Study, institutionally sponsored loans, scholarships/grants, and tuition waivers (full and partial) available. Support available to part-time students. Financial award application deadline: 5/1; financial award applicants required to submit FAFSA. *Faculty research:* Auditing, regulation, financial reporting, public interest, efficient markets. *Unit head:* Larry Parker, Chairman, 216-

Accounting

Case Western Reserve University (continued)

368-2065, E-mail: larry.parker@case.edu. *Application contact:* Tiffany Welch, Director of Marketing and Admissions, 216-368-2058, Fax: 216-368-4776, E-mail: clg3@po.cwru.edu.

Centenary College, Program in Professional Accounting, Hackettstown, NJ 07840-2100. Offers MS. Part-time and evening/weekend programs available. Postbaccalaureate distance learning degree programs offered (minimal on-campus study).

Central Michigan University, College of Graduate Studies, College of Business Administration, School of Accounting, Mount Pleasant, MI 48859. Offers MBA. *Accreditation:* AACSB. Part-time and evening/weekend programs available. *Degree requirements:* For master's, comprehensive exam (for some programs), thesis (for some programs). *Entrance requirements:* For master's, GMAT. Electronic applications accepted. *Faculty research:* Accounting and financial reporting for local government, tax accounting for partnerships and small corporations, accounting for employee stock ownership plans.

Central Washington University, Graduate Studies and Research, College of Business, Department of Accounting, Ellensburg, WA 98926. Offers MPA. Part-time programs available. *Faculty:* 8 full-time (4 women). *Students:* 28 full-time (16 women), 2 part-time (both women); includes 1 minority (American Indian/Alaska Native), 4 international. 66 applicants, 67% accepted, 30 enrolled. In 2009, 21 master's awarded. *Degree requirements:* For master's, comprehensive exam. *Entrance requirements:* For master's, GMAT, minimum GPA of 3.0. Additional exam requirements/recommendations for international students: Required—TOEFL (minimum score 550 paper-based; 213 computer-based; 79 iBT). *Application deadline:* For fall admission, 2/1 priority date for domestic students; for winter admission, 10/1 for domestic students; for spring admission, 1/1 for domestic students. Applications are processed on a rolling basis. Application fee: $50. Electronic applications accepted. *Expenses:* Tuition, state resident: full-time $7353; part-time $245 per credit. Tuition, nonresident: full-time $16,383; part-time $546 per credit. Required fees: $882. Tuition and fees vary according to degree level. *Financial support:* In 2009–10, 1 research assistantship with full and partial tuition reimbursement (averaging $9,145 per year), 1 teaching assistantship with full and partial tuition reimbursement (averaging $9,145 per year) were awarded; Federal Work-Study, health care benefits, and unspecified assistantships also available. *Unit head:* Dr. Ronald Tidd, Program Director, 509-963-3340, Fax: 509-963-2875, E-mail: tiddr@cwu.edu. *Application contact:* Justine Eason, Admissions Program Coordinator, 509-963-3103, Fax: 509-963-1799, E-mail: masters@cwu.edu.

Charleston Southern University, Program in Business, Charleston, SC 29423-8087. Offers accounting (MBA); finance (MBA); health care administration (MBA); information systems (MBA); organizational development (MBA). Part-time and evening/weekend programs available. *Faculty:* 14 full-time (1 woman), 6 part-time/adjunct (1 woman). *Students:* 316 part-time (157 women); includes 67 minority (53 African Americans, 1 American Indian/Alaska Native, 7 Asian Americans or Pacific Islanders, 6 Hispanic Americans), 7 international. Average age 32. 173 applicants, 85% accepted, 97 enrolled. In 2009, 69 master's awarded. *Degree requirements:* For master's, thesis optional. *Entrance requirements:* For master's, GMAT. Additional exam requirements/recommendations for international students: Required—TOEFL (minimum score 550 paper-based; 213 computer-based; 79 iBT). *Application deadline:* Applications are processed on a rolling basis. Application fee: $30. *Expenses:* Tuition: Part-time $350 per credit hour. Required fees: $40 per semester. Tuition and fees vary according to program. *Financial support:* Research assistantships with full tuition reimbursements available. Financial award application deadline: 4/15; financial award applicants required to submit FAFSA. *Unit head:* Dr. Scott Pearson, Director of the MBA Program, 843-863-7038, Fax: 843-863-7922, E-mail: spearson@csuniv.edu. *Application contact:* Alison Harrison, Graduate Enrollment Counselor, 843-863-7534, Fax: 843-863-7070, E-mail: aharrison@cusniv.edu.

Chatham University, Program in Accounting, Pittsburgh, PA 15232-2826. Offers M Acc, MAC. Part-time and evening/weekend programs available. *Students:* 10 full-time (4 women), 10 part-time (8 women). Average age 28. 24 applicants, 50% accepted, 8 enrolled. *Entrance requirements:* Additional exam requirements/recommendations for international students: Required—TOEFL (minimum score 600 paper-based; 250 computer-based; 100 iBT), IELTS (minimum score 6.5), TWE. *Application deadline:* For fall admission, 7/1 for domestic students, 6/1 for international students; for spring admission, 12/1 for domestic students, 11/1 for international students. Applications are processed on a rolling basis. Application fee: $45. Electronic applications accepted. *Financial support:* Applicants required to submit FAFSA. *Unit head:* Dr. Bruce Rosenthal, Director of Business and Entrepreneurship Program, 412-365-2433. *Application contact:* Michael May, Director of Graduate Admissions, 412-365-1141, Fax: 412-365-1609, E-mail: gradadmissions@chatham.edu.

City University of Seattle, Graduate Division, School of Management, Bellevue, WA 98005. Offers accounting (Certificate); change leadership (MBA, Certificate); financial management (MBA, Certificate); general management (MBA); general management-Europe (MBA); global leadership (Certificate); global marketing (MBA); individualized study (MBA); information security (MS); information systems (MBA); leadership (MA); marketing (MBA, Certificate); project management (MBA, MS, Certificate); sustainable business (Certificate); technology management (MBA, MS, Certificate). Part-time and evening/weekend programs available. Postbaccalaureate distance learning degree programs offered (no on-campus study). *Entrance requirements:* Additional exam requirements/recommendations for international students: Required—TOEFL (minimum score 540 paper-based; 207 computer-based); Recommended—IELTS. Electronic applications accepted. *Expenses:* Tuition: Full-time $14,760; part-time $615 per credit. Tuition and fees vary according to program.

Clark Atlanta University, School of Business Administration, Department of Accounting, Atlanta, GA 30314. Offers MA. Part-time programs available. *Faculty:* 2 full-time (both women). *Students:* 12 full-time (10 women); includes 11 minority (all African Americans), 1 international. Average age 25. 15 applicants, 73% accepted, 7 enrolled. In 2009, 11 master's awarded. *Entrance requirements:* For master's, GMAT, minimum undergraduate GPA of 2.5. Additional exam requirements/recommendations for international students: Required—TOEFL (minimum score 500 paper-based; 173 computer-based). *Application deadline:* For fall admission, 4/1 for domestic and international students; for spring admission, 11/1 for domestic and international students. Applications are processed on a rolling basis. Application fee: $40 ($55 for international students). Electronic applications accepted. *Expenses:* Tuition: Full-time $12,240; part-time $680 per credit hour. Required fees: $710; $355 per semester. *Financial support:* Career-related internships or fieldwork, Federal Work-Study, scholarships/grants, and unspecified assistantships available. Support available to part-time students. Financial award application deadline: 4/30; financial award applicants required to submit FAFSA. *Unit head:* Dr. Kasim Alli, Chairperson, 404-880-8740, E-mail: kalli@cau.edu. *Application contact:* Michelle Clark-Davis, Graduate Program Admissions, 404-880-6605, E-mail: cauadmissions@cau.edu.

Clark University, Graduate School, Graduate School of Management, Business Administration Program, Worcester, MA 01610-1477. Offers accounting (MBA); finance (MBA); global business (MBA); health care management (MBA); management (MBA); management of information technology (MBA); marketing (MBA). *Accreditation:* AACSB. Part-time and evening/weekend programs available. *Students:* 148 full-time (67 women), 120 part-time (52 women); includes 27 minority (12 African Americans, 2 American Indian/Alaska Native, 9 Asian Americans or Pacific Islanders, 4 Hispanic Americans), 108 international. Average age 29. 340 applicants, 57% accepted, 63 enrolled. In 2009, 118 master's awarded. *Degree requirements:* For master's, thesis optional. *Application deadline:* For fall admission, 6/1 priority date for domestic students; for spring admission, 12/1 priority date for domestic students. Applications are processed on a rolling basis. Application fee: $50. Electronic applications accepted. *Expenses:* Tuition: Full-time $34,900; part-time $4362.50 per course. *Financial support:* In 2009–10, research assistantships with partial tuition reimbursements (averaging $4,800 per year), teaching assistantships with partial tuition reimbursements (averaging $4,800 per year) were awarded; fellowships, career-related internships or fieldwork, Federal Work-Study, institutionally sponsored loans, and tuition waivers (partial) also available. Support available to part-time students. Financial award application deadline: 5/31. *Faculty research:* Organizational development, accounting, marketing, finance, human resource management. *Application contact:* Lynn Davis, Enrollment and Marketing Director, 508-793-7406, Fax: 508-793-8822, E-mail: clarkmba@clarku.edu.

Cleary University, Online Program in Business Administration, Ann Arbor, MI 48105-2659. Offers accounting (MBA); financial planning (MBA); financial planning (Graduate Certificate); green business strategy (MBA); management (MBA); nonprofit management (MBA); organizational leadership (MBA). Part-time and evening/weekend programs available. Postbaccalaureate distance learning degree programs offered (no on-campus study). *Degree requirements:* For master's, thesis. *Entrance requirements:* For master's, bachelor's degree; minimum GPA of 2.5; professional resume indicating minimum 2 years management or related experience; undergraduate degree from an accredited college or university with at least 18 quarter hours (or 12 semester hours) of accounting study (for MBA in accounting). Additional exam requirements/recommendations for international students: Required—TOEFL (minimum score 550 paper-based; 213 computer-based; 79 iBT), Michigan English Language Assessment Battery (minimum score: 75). Electronic applications accepted.

Clemson University, Graduate School, College of Business and Behavioral Science, School of Accountancy and Finance, Clemson, SC 29634. Offers MP Acc. *Accreditation:* AACSB. Part-time programs available. *Faculty:* 25 full-time (6 women), 1 part-time/adjunct (0 women). *Students:* 45 full-time (32 women), 6 part-time (3 women), 5 international. Average age 23. 101 applicants, 58% accepted, 39 enrolled. In 2009, 22 master's awarded. *Degree requirements:* For master's, oral final exam. *Entrance requirements:* For master's, GMAT, BS in accounting or equivalent, minimum GPA of 3.0. Additional exam requirements/recommendations for international students: Required—TOEFL. *Application deadline:* For fall admission, 5/1 priority date for domestic students, 4/15 for international students; for spring admission, 10/1 for domestic students, 9/15 for international students. Applications are processed on a rolling basis. Application fee: $70 ($80 for international students). Electronic applications accepted. *Expenses:* Tuition, state resident: full-time $8684; part-time $528 per credit hour. Tuition, nonresident: full-time $15,330; part-time $1078 per credit hour. Required fees: $736; $37 per semester. Part-time tuition and fees vary according to course load and program. *Financial support:* In 2009–10, 25 students received support, including 1 research assistantship with partial tuition reimbursement available (averaging $14,354 per year); fellowships with full and partial tuition reimbursements available, teaching assistantships with partial tuition reimbursements available, career-related internships or fieldwork, institutionally sponsored loans, scholarships/grants, health care benefits, and unspecified assistantships also available. Support available to part-time students. Financial award applicants required to submit FAFSA. *Unit head:* Dr. Ralph E. Welton, Director, 864-656-4881, Fax: 864-656-4892, E-mail: edwlsur@clemson.edu. *Application contact:* Dr. Thomas L. Dickens, Program Coordinator, 864-656-4890, Fax: 864-656-4892, E-mail: dickent@clemson.edu.

Cleveland State University, College of Graduate Studies, Nance College of Business Administration, Department of Accounting, Cleveland, OH 44115. Offers financial accounting/audit (M Acc); taxation (M Acc). *Accreditation:* AACSB. Part-time and evening/weekend programs available. *Entrance requirements:* For master's, GMAT, minimum GPA of 2.75. Additional exam requirements/recommendations for international students: Required—TOEFL (minimum score 525 paper-based; 197 computer-based). *Faculty research:* Internal auditing, computer auditing, accounting education, managerial accounting.

Coastal Carolina University, Wall College of Business Administration, Conway, SC 29528-6054. Offers accounting (MBA); business (MBA). *Accreditation:* AACSB. Part-time and evening/weekend programs available. *Faculty:* 9 full-time (4 women). *Students:* 35 full-time (15 women), 18 part-time (7 women); includes 2 minority (both African Americans), 3 international. Average age 27. 48 applicants, 69% accepted, 22 enrolled. In 2009, 28 master's awarded. *Entrance requirements:* For master's, GMAT, 2 letters of recommendation, resume, completion of prerequisites with minimum B average grade. Additional exam requirements/recommendations for international students: Required—TOEFL (minimum score 575 paper-based). *Application deadline:* For fall admission, 3/15 priority date for domestic and international students; for spring admission, 10/15 priority date for domestic and international students. Applications are processed on a rolling basis. Application fee: $45. Electronic applications accepted. *Expenses:* Contact institution. *Financial support:* Application deadline: 3/1. *Unit head:* John O. Lox, MBA Director, 843-349-2469, Fax: 843-349-2455, E-mail: jlox@coastal.edu. *Application contact:* Dr. Richard L. Johnson, Director of Graduate Studies, 843-349-2192, Fax: 843-349-6444, E-mail: rjohnson@coastal.edu.

The College at Brockport, State University of New York, Office of the Vice Provost, Department of Business Administration and Economics, Brockport, NY 14420-2997. Offers accounting (MS); forensic accounting (MS). Part-time programs available. *Students:* 8 full-time (6 women), 4 part-time (all women). 16 applicants, 88% accepted. *Entrance requirements:* For master's, GMAT or GRE General Test, minimum GPA of 3.0, letters of recommendation, statement of objectives. Additional exam requirements/recommendations for international students: Required—TOEFL (minimum score 550 paper-based; 213 computer-based; 79 iBT). *Application deadline:* For fall admission, 7/15 priority date for domestic and international students; for spring admission, 11/15 priority date for domestic and international students. Application fee: $50. Electronic applications accepted. *Expenses:* Tuition, state resident: full-time $8370; part-time $349 per credit. Tuition, nonresident: full-time $13,250; part-time $522 per credit. *Financial support:* Federal Work-Study, scholarships/grants, and unspecified assistantships available. Support available to part-time students. Financial award application deadline: 3/15; financial award applicants required to submit FAFSA. *Unit head:* Dr. John Keiser, Chairperson and Associate Professor, 585-395-2623, Fax: 585-395-2542, E-mail: jkeiser@brockport.edu. *Application contact:* Dr. D. Donald Kent, Graduate Director, 585-395-2623, Fax: 585-395-2542, E-mail: dkent@brockport.edu.

College of Charleston, Graduate School, School of Business and Economics, Program in Accountancy, Charleston, SC 29424-0001. Offers MS. *Accreditation:* AACSB. Part-time and evening/weekend programs available. *Faculty:* 10 full-time (3 women). *Students:* 28 full-time (17 women), 7 part-time (5 women); includes 1 minority (African American), 3 international. Average age 25. 53 applicants, 51% accepted, 17 enrolled. In 2009, 31 master's awarded. *Entrance requirements:* For master's, GMAT, minimum GPA of 3.0 in last 60 hours of undergraduate course work, 24 hours of course work in accounting, 2 letters of reference. Additional exam requirements/recommendations for international students: Required—TOEFL or IELTS. *Application deadline:* For fall admission, 7/1 for domestic students. Applications are processed on a rolling basis. Application fee: $45. Electronic applications accepted. *Financial support:* In 2009–10, research assistantships (averaging $6,200 per year); institutionally sponsored loans and unspecified assistantships also available. Support available to part-time students. Financial award application deadline: 3/1; financial award applicants required to submit FAFSA. *Unit head:* Dr. Michael C. Cipriano, Director, 843-953-7166, Fax: 843-953-5697, E-mail: ciprianom@cofc.edu. *Application contact:* Susan Hallatt, Director of Admissions, 843-953-5614, Fax: 843-953-1434, E-mail: hallatts@cofc.edu.

The College of Saint Rose, Graduate Studies, School of Business, Department of Accounting, Albany, NY 12203-1419. Offers MS. Part-time and evening/weekend programs available. *Entrance requirements:* For master's, GMAT, graduate degree, or minimum undergraduate GPA of 3.0. Additional exam requirements/recommendations for international students: Required—TOEFL (minimum score 550 paper-based; 213 computer-based). Electronic applications accepted.

The College of William and Mary, Mason School of Business, Master of Accounting Program, Williamsburg, VA 23185. Offers M Acc. *Accreditation:* AACSB. *Faculty:* 15 full-time (6 women), 2 part-time/adjunct (0 women). *Students:* 64 full-time (41 women); includes 12 minority (4 African Americans, 6 Asian Americans or Pacific Islanders, 2 Hispanic Americans), 14 international. Average age 24. 151 applicants, 66% accepted, 61 enrolled. In 2009, 50 master's awarded. *Entrance requirements:* For master's, GMAT, 2 written recommendations, interview. Additional exam requirements/recommendations for international students: Required—TOEFL (minimum score 620 paper-based; 260 computer-based; 104 IBT) or IELTS (minimum score

7). *Application deadline:* Applications are processed on a rolling basis. Application fee: $80. Electronic applications accepted. *Expenses:* Contact institution. *Financial support:* In 2009–10, 59 students received support, including fellowships with partial tuition reimbursements available (averaging $7,250 per year), 12 research assistantships (averaging $4,000 per year); scholarships/grants and unspecified assistantships also available. Financial award application deadline: 3/15; financial award applicants required to submit FAFSA. *Faculty research:* Valuation, voluntary disclosure, auditing, taxation, executive compensation. *Unit head:* Linda Espahbodi, Director, 757-221-2953, Fax: 757-221-7862, E-mail: linda.espahbodi@mason.wm.edu. *Application contact:* Martha Howard, Associate Director, 757-221-2875, Fax: 757-221-7862, E-mail: martha.howard@mason.wm.edu.

Colorado State University, Graduate School, College of Business, Department of Accounting, Fort Collins, CO 80523-1271. Offers M Acc. Part-time programs available. *Faculty:* 11 full-time (3 women). *Students:* 45 full-time (29 women), 14 part-time (11 women); includes 8 minority (1 Asian American or Pacific Islander, 7 Hispanic Americans), 11 international. Average age 33. 65 applicants, 80% accepted, 33 enrolled. In 2009, 26 master's awarded. *Degree requirements:* For master's, thesis or alternative. *Entrance requirements:* For master's, GMAT, minimum GPA of 3.0; BA/BS. Additional exam requirements/recommendations for international students: Required—TOEFL (minimum score 565 paper-based; 227 computer-based; 86 iBT). *Application deadline:* For fall admission, 7/15 for domestic students, 4/1 for international students; for spring admission, 11/15 for domestic students, 10/1 for international students. Applications are processed on a rolling basis. Application fee: $50. Electronic applications accepted. *Expenses:* Tuition, state resident: full-time $6434; part-time $359.10 per credit. Tuition, nonresident: full-time $18,116; part-time $1006.45 per credit. Required fees: $1496; $83 per credit. *Financial support:* Fellowships, research assistantships, teaching assistantships with full and partial tuition reimbursements, career-related internships or fieldwork, Federal Work-Study, and traineeships available. Financial award application deadline: 3/1; financial award applicants required to submit FAFSA. *Faculty research:* Financial accounting and reporting, managerial accounting, earnings management, stock options, corporate social responsibility. *Unit head:* Dr. Barry L. Lewis, Chair, 970-491-2977, Fax: 970-491-2676, E-mail: barry.lewis@business.colostate.edu. *Application contact:* Sharon K. Wilson, Administrative Assistant III, 970-491-5102, Fax: 970-491-2676, E-mail: sharon.wilson@colostate.edu.

Colorado Technical University Colorado Springs, Graduate Studies, Program in Management, Colorado Springs, CO 80907-3896. Offers accounting (MBA, MSA); business administration (MBA); finance (MBA); human resources management (MBA); logistics/supply chain management (MBA); management (DM); marketing (MBA); mediation and dispute resolution (MBA); operations management (MBA); project management (MBA); technology management (MBA). Part-time and evening/weekend programs available. Postbaccalaureate distance learning degree programs offered. *Degree requirements:* For master's, thesis or alternative; for doctorate, thesis/dissertation. *Entrance requirements:* For doctorate, minimum graduate GPA of 3.0, 5 years of related work experience. *Faculty research:* Sexual harassment, performance evaluation, critical thinking.

Colorado Technical University Denver, Programs in Business Administration and Management, Greenwood Village, CO 80111. Offers accounting (MBA); business administration (MBA); business administration and management (EMBA); finance (MBA); human resource management (MBA); marketing (MBA); mediation and dispute resolution (MBA); operations management (MBA); project management (MBA); technology management (MBA). Part-time and evening/weekend programs available. *Degree requirements:* For master's, thesis or alternative. *Entrance requirements:* For master's, minimum undergraduate GPA of 3.0, resume.

Columbia University, Graduate School of Business, Doctoral Program in Business, New York, NY 10027. Offers business (PhD), including accounting, decision, risk, and operations, finance and economics, management, marketing. *Accreditation:* AACSB. *Faculty:* 149 full-time (23 women), 134 part-time/adjunct (16 women). *Students:* 91 full-time (37 women); includes 10 minority (8 Asian Americans or Pacific Islanders, 2 Hispanic Americans), 64 international. Average age 27. 758 applicants, 6% accepted, 20 enrolled. In 2009, 15 doctorates awarded. *Degree requirements:* For doctorate, comprehensive exam, thesis/dissertation, major field exam, research paper, thesis proposal. *Entrance requirements:* For doctorate, GMAT or GRE (finance), 2 letters of reference, resume. Additional exam requirements/recommendations for international students: Required—TOEFL. *Application deadline:* For fall admission, 1/1 for domestic and international students. Application fee: $75. Electronic applications accepted. *Expenses:* Contact institution. *Financial support:* In 2009–10, 91 students received support, including fellowships with full tuition reimbursements available (averaging $22,000 per year), research assistantships (averaging $4,000 per year); teaching assistantships, career-related internships or fieldwork, health care benefits, and tuition waivers (full) also available. *Faculty research:* Human decision making and behavioral research; real estate market and mortgage defaults; financial crisis and corporate governance; international business; security analysis and accounting. *Unit head:* Elizabeth Elam Chang, Administrative Director, 212-854-2836, Fax: 212-932-2359, E-mail: phdinfo@gsb.columbia.edu. *Application contact:* Elizabeth Elam Chang, Administrative Director, 212-854-2836, Fax: 212-932-2359, E-mail: phdinfo@gsb.columbia.edu.

Columbia University, Graduate School of Business, MBA Program, New York, NY 10027. Offers accounting (MBA); decision, risk, and operations (MBA); entrepreneurship (MBA); finance and economics (MBA); healthcare and pharmaceutical management (MBA); human resource management (MBA); international business (MBA); leadership and ethics (MBA); management (MBA); marketing (MBA); media (MBA); private equity (MBA); real estate (MBA); social enterprise (MBA); value investing (MBA); DDS/MBA; JD/MBA; MBA/MIA; MBA/MPH; MBA/MS; MD/MBA. *Faculty:* 149 full-time (23 women), 134 part-time/adjunct (16 women). *Students:* 1,293 full-time (435 women); includes 235 minority (65 African Americans, 4 American Indian/Alaska Native, 135 Asian Americans or Pacific Islanders, 31 Hispanic Americans), 417 international. Average age 28. 6,885 applicants, 15% accepted, 737 enrolled. In 2009, 696 master's awarded. *Entrance requirements:* For master's, GMAT, 2 letters of recommendation. Additional exam requirements/recommendations for international students: Required—TOEFL. *Application deadline:* For fall admission, 4/14 for domestic students, 3/3 for international students; for spring admission, 10/7 for domestic and international students. Applications are processed on a rolling basis. Application fee: $250. Electronic applications accepted. *Expenses:* Contact institution. *Financial support:* In 2009–10, 358 students received support, including 101 fellowships (averaging $23,250 per year); research assistantships, teaching assistantships, career-related internships or fieldwork, institutionally sponsored loans, and scholarships/grants also available. Financial award application deadline: 3/1; financial award applicants required to submit CSS PROFILE or FAFSA. *Faculty research:* Human decision making and behavioral research; real estate market and mortgage defaults; financial crisis and corporate governance; international business; security analysis and accounting. *Unit head:* Prof. Amir Ziv, Vice Dean of Students and the MBA Program, 212-854-3485, Fax: 212-932-0545, E-mail: az50@columbia.edu. *Application contact:* Mary J. Miller, Assistant Dean of Admissions, 212-854-1961, Fax: 212-662-6754, E-mail: apply@gsb.columbia.edu.

Concordia University, School of Graduate Studies, John Molson School of Business, Montréal, QC H3G 1M8, Canada. Offers administration (M Sc, Diploma); aviation management (Certificate, Diploma); business administration (MBA, UA Undergraduate Associate, PhD), including international aviation (UA Undergraduate Associate); chartered accountancy (Diploma); community organizational development (Certificate); event management and fundraising (Certificate); executive business administration (EMBA); investment management (Diploma); investment management option (MBA); management accounting (Certificate); management of healthcare organizations (Certificate); sport administration (Diploma). *Accreditation:* AACSB. Part-time and evening/weekend programs available. *Degree requirements:* For master's, one foreign language, thesis (for some programs), research project; for doctorate, one foreign language, thesis/dissertation; for other advanced degree, one foreign language. *Entrance requirements:* For master's and doctorate, GMAT. Additional exam requirements/recommendations for international students: Required—TOEFL. *Expenses:* Contact institution. *Faculty research:* General business, capital markets, international business.

Cornell University, Graduate School, Graduate Field of Management, Ithaca, NY 14853-0001. Offers accounting (PhD); behavioral decision theory (PhD); finance (PhD); marketing (PhD); organizational behavior (PhD); production and operations management (PhD). *Accreditation:* AACSB. *Faculty:* 72 full-time (15 women). *Students:* 39 full-time (15 women); includes 2 minority (both Asian Americans or Pacific Islanders), 23 international. Average age 31. 388 applicants, 2% accepted, 4 enrolled. In 2009, 4 doctorates awarded. *Degree requirements:* For doctorate, comprehensive exam, thesis/dissertation. *Entrance requirements:* For doctorate, GMAT or GRE General Test. Additional exam requirements/recommendations for international students: Required—TOEFL (minimum score 600 paper-based; 250 computer-based; 77 iBT). *Application deadline:* For fall admission, 1/3 for domestic students. Application fee: $70. Electronic applications accepted. *Expenses:* Contact institution. *Financial support:* In 2009–10, 38 students received support, including 1 fellowship with full tuition reimbursement available, 3 research assistantships with full tuition reimbursements available; teaching assistantships with full tuition reimbursements available, institutionally sponsored loans, scholarships/grants, health care benefits, tuition waivers (full and partial), and unspecified assistantships also available. Financial award applicants required to submit FAFSA. *Faculty research:* Operations and manufacturing. *Unit head:* Director of Graduate Studies, 607-255-3669. *Application contact:* Graduate Field Assistant, 607-255-9431, E-mail: js_phd@cornell.edu.

Dallas Baptist University, College of Adult Education, Professional Development Program, Dallas, TX 75211-9299. Offers accounting (MA); church leadership (MA); counseling (MA); criminal justice (MA); English as a second language (MA); finance (MA); higher education (MA); leadership studies (MA); management (MA); management information systems (MA); marketing (MA); missions (MA). Part-time and evening/weekend programs available. *Entrance requirements:* For master's, minimum GPA of 3.0. Additional exam requirements/recommendations for international students: Required—TOEFL, IELTS. *Expenses:* Tuition: Full-time $10,674; part-time $593 per credit hour.

Dallas Baptist University, College of Business, Business Administration Program, Dallas, TX 75211-9299. Offers accounting (MBA); business communication (MBA); conflict resolution management (MBA); e-business (MBA); entrepreneurship (MBA); finance (MBA); health care management (MBA); international business (MBA); leading the non-profit organization (MBA); management (MBA); management information systems (MBA); marketing (MBA); project management (MBA); technology and engineering management (MBA). *Accreditation:* ACBSP. Part-time and evening/weekend programs available. *Entrance requirements:* For master's, GMAT, minimum GPA of 3.0. Additional exam requirements/recommendations for international students: Required—TOEFL, IELTS. Electronic applications accepted. *Expenses:* Tuition: Full-time $10,674; part-time $593 per credit hour. *Faculty research:* Sports management, services marketing, retailing, strategic management, financial planning/investments.

Davenport University, Sneden Graduate School, Grand Rapids, MI 49503. Offers accounting (MBA); business administration (EMBA); finance (MBA); health care management (MBA); human resources (MBA); information assurance (MS); public health (MPH); strategic management (MBA). Evening/weekend programs available. *Entrance requirements:* For master's, GMAT, minimum undergraduate GPA of 2.75. Additional exam requirements/recommendations for international students: Required—TOEFL. Electronic applications accepted. *Faculty research:* Leadership, management, marketing, organizational culture.

Davenport University, Sneden Graduate School, Warren, MI 48092-5209. Offers accounting (MBA); business administration (EMBA); finance (MBA); health care management (MBA); human resources management (MBA); information assurance (MS); public health (MPH); strategic management (MBA). *Entrance requirements:* For master's, minimum undergraduate GPA of 2.7.

Davenport University, Sneden Graduate School, Dearborn, MI 48126-3799. Offers accounting (MBA); business administration (EMBA); finance (MBA); health care management (MBA); human resources management (MBA); information assurance (MS); marketing (MBA); public health (MPH); strategic management (MBA). Part-time and evening/weekend programs available. Postbaccalaureate distance learning degree programs offered (no on-campus study). *Entrance requirements:* For master's, minimum GPA of 2.7, previous course work in accounting and statistics. *Faculty research:* Accounting, international accounting, social and environmental accounting, finance.

Delaware Valley College, Program in Business Administration (MBA), Doylestown, PA 18901-2697. Offers accounting (MBA); food and agribusiness (MBA); general business (MBA); online global executive leadership (MBA). Part-time and evening/weekend programs available. Postbaccalaureate distance learning degree programs offered (no on-campus study). *Faculty:* 24 part-time/adjunct (10 women). *Students:* 25 full-time (16 women), 74 part-time (37 women); includes 7 minority (4 African Americans, 2 Asian Americans or Pacific Islanders, 1 Hispanic American). Average age 37. 18 applicants, 100% accepted, 18 enrolled. In 2009, 12 master's awarded. *Entrance requirements:* For master's, minimum undergraduate GPA of 3.0. *Application deadline:* Applications are processed on a rolling basis. Application fee: $50. *Expenses:* Contact institution. *Financial support:* Applicants required to submit FAFSA. *Unit head:* Thomas Kennedy, Director of MBA Program, 215-489-2322, E-mail: thomas.kennedy@delval.edu. *Application contact:* Pamela Heffner, Graduate and Continuing Studies Enrollment Manager, 215-489-4469, Fax: 215-489-4832, E-mail: pamela.heffner@deval.edu.

Delta State University, Graduate Programs, College of Business, Division of Accounting, Computer Information Systems, and Finance, Cleveland, MS 38733-0001. Offers accountancy (MPAC). *Expenses:* Tuition, state resident: full-time $4450; part-time $247 per credit hour. Tuition, nonresident: full-time $11,520; part-time $640 per credit hour.

DePaul University, Charles H. Kellstadt Graduate School of Business, School of Accountancy and Management Information Systems, Chicago, IL 60604-2287. Offers accountancy (M Acc, MSA); business information technology (MS); e-business (MBA, MS); financial management and control (MBA); management accounting (MBA); management information systems (MBA); taxation (MST). Part-time and evening/weekend programs available. *Faculty:* 30 full-time (9 women), 54 part-time/adjunct (7 women). *Students:* 167 full-time (82 women), 237 part-time (106 women); includes 52 minority (8 African Americans, 1 American Indian/Alaska Native, 30 Asian Americans or Pacific Islanders, 13 Hispanic Americans), 49 international. In 2009, 141 master's awarded. *Entrance requirements:* For master's, GMAT, 2 letters of recommendation, resume. Additional exam requirements/recommendations for international students: Required—TOEFL (minimum score 550 paper-based; 213 computer-based). *Application deadline:* For fall admission, 7/1 for domestic students; for winter admission, 10/1 for domestic students; for spring admission, 2/1 for domestic students. Applications are processed on a rolling basis. Application fee: $60. *Expenses:* Tuition: Full-time $37,525; part-time $620 per credit hour. *Financial support:* In 2009–10, 7 research assistantships with full tuition reimbursements (averaging $4,100 per year) were awarded; institutionally sponsored loans also available. Financial award application deadline: 4/2. *Faculty research:* Tax policy, property transactions, stock options as compensation, standards setting, activity-based costing in health care. *Unit head:* Kevin Stevens, Director, 312-362-6989, E-mail: kstevens@depaul.edu. *Application contact:* Christopher E. Kinsella, Director of Cohort MBA Programs, 312-362-8810, Fax: 312-362-6677, E-mail: kgsb@depaul.edu.

DeSales University, Graduate Division, Program in Business Administration, Center Valley, PA 18034-9568. Offers accounting (MBA); business administration (MBA); computer information systems (MBA); finance (MBA); health care systems management (MBA); management (MBA); marketing (MBA); project management (MBA); self-design (MBA); MSN/MBA. *Accreditation:* ACBSP. Part-time programs available. Postbaccalaureate distance learning degree programs offered (no on-campus study). *Students:* 433 part-time. In 2009, 218 master's awarded. *Entrance requirements:* For master's, minimum GPA of 3.0, 2 years of work experience. Additional exam requirements/recommendations for international students: Required—TOEFL. *Application deadline:* Applications are processed on a rolling basis. Application fee: $35. Electronic applications accepted. *Expenses:* Tuition: Full-time $17,500; part-time $665 per credit. Full-time tuition and fees vary according to program. Part-time tuition and fees vary

Accounting

DeSales University (continued)
according to course load. *Faculty research:* Quality improvement, executive development, productivity, cross-cultural managerial differences, leadership. *Unit head:* Dr. David Gilfoil, Director, 610-282-1100 Ext. 1828, Fax: 610-282-2869, E-mail: david.gilfoil@desales.edu. *Application contact:* Caryn Stopper, Director of Graduate Admissions, 610-282-1100 Ext. 1768, Fax: 610-282-0525, E-mail: caryn.stopper@desales.edu.

DeVry University, Keller Graduate School of Management, Downers Grove, IL 60515. Offers accounting and financial management (MAFM); business administration (MBA); human resources management (MHRM); information systems management (MISM); network and communications management (MNCM); project management (MPM); public administration (MPA).

Dominican University, Edward A. and Lois L. Brennan School of Business, River Forest, IL 60305-1099. Offers accounting (MSA); business administration (MBA); JD/MBA; MBA/MLIS. *Accreditation:* ACBSP. Part-time and evening/weekend programs available. *Faculty:* 18 full-time (6 women), 34 part-time/adjunct (9 women). *Students:* 159 full-time (64 women), 185 part-time (94 women); includes 35 minority (12 African Americans, 11 Asian Americans or Pacific Islanders, 12 Hispanic Americans), 90 international. Average age 31. In 2009, 96 master's awarded. *Entrance requirements:* For master's, GMAT. Additional exam requirements/recommendations for international students: Required—TOEFL (minimum score 550 paper-based; 213 computer-based; 79 iBT); Recommended—IELTS (minimum score 6). *Application deadline:* Applications are processed on a rolling basis. Application fee: $25. Electronic applications accepted. *Expenses:* Contact institution. *Financial support:* Career-related internships or fieldwork, tuition waivers (partial), and unspecified assistantships available. Support available to part-time students. Financial award applicants required to submit FAFSA. *Faculty research:* Entrepreneurship, small business finance, business ethics, marketing strategy. *Unit head:* Dr. Arvid Johnson, Dean, 708-524-6465, Fax: 708-524-6939, E-mail: ajohnson@dom.edu. *Application contact:* Linda Puvogel, Assistant Dean for Graduate Business Programs, 708-524-6507, Fax: 708-524-6939, E-mail: lpuvogel@dom.edu.

Drexel University, LeBow College of Business, Department of Accounting, Program in Accounting, Philadelphia, PA 19104-2875. Offers MS. *Entrance requirements:* For master's, GMAT, minimum GPA of 2.75. Additional exam requirements/recommendations for international students: Required—TOEFL. Electronic applications accepted.

Drexel University, LeBow College of Business, Program in Business Administration, Philadelphia, PA 19104-2875. Offers business administration (MBA, PhD, APC), including accounting (MBA, PhD), decision sciences (PhD), economics (MBA, PhD), finance (MBA, PhD), legal studies (MBA), management (MBA), marketing (MBA, PhD), organizational sciences (PhD), quantitative methods (MBA), strategic management (PhD). *Accreditation:* AACSB. Part-time and evening/weekend programs available. Postbaccalaureate distance learning degree programs offered (minimal on-campus study). Terminal master's awarded for partial completion of doctoral program. *Entrance requirements:* For master's, GMAT, minimum GPA of 2.75; for doctorate, GMAT. Additional exam requirements/recommendations for international students: Required—TOEFL. Electronic applications accepted. *Faculty research:* Decision support systems, individual and group behavior, operations research, techniques and strategy.

Duquesne University, John F. Donahue Graduate School of Business, Pittsburgh, PA 15282-0001. Offers accountancy (MS); business administration (MBA); information systems management (MSISM); sustainability (MBA); JD/MBA; MBA/MA; MBA/MES; MBA/MHMS; MBA/MLLS; MBA/MS; MBA/MSN. *Accreditation:* AACSB. Part-time and evening/weekend programs available. *Faculty:* 52 full-time (12 women), 39 part-time/adjunct (7 women). *Students:* 122 full-time (56 women), 252 part-time (93 women); includes 14 minority (5 African Americans, 4 Asian Americans or Pacific Islanders, 5 Hispanic Americans), 30 international. Average age 31. 195 applicants, 95% accepted, 136 enrolled. In 2009, 97 master's awarded. *Entrance requirements:* For master's, GMAT, 2 letters of recommendation, current resume. Additional exam requirements/recommendations for international students: Required—TOEFL (minimum score 577 paper-based; 233 computer-based; 90 iBT); Recommended—TWE. *Application deadline:* For fall admission, 5/1 priority date for domestic students, 5/1 for international students; for spring admission, 10/1 for domestic and international students. Applications are processed on a rolling basis. Application fee: $0. Electronic applications accepted. *Expenses:* Tuition: Part-time $851 per credit. Required fees: $81 per credit. *Financial support:* In 2009–10, 46 students received support, including 14 fellowships with partial tuition reimbursements available, 32 research assistantships with partial tuition reimbursements available; career-related internships or fieldwork and unspecified assistantships also available. Support available to part-time students. Financial award application deadline: 7/1; financial award applicants required to submit FAFSA. *Faculty research:* International business, investment management, business ethics, technology management, supply chain management, business strategy, finance. *Unit head:* Alan R. Miciak, Dean, 412-396-5848, Fax: 412-396-5304, E-mail: miciaka@duq.edu. *Application contact:* Patricia Moore, Assistant Director, 412-396-6276, Fax: 412-396-1726, E-mail: moorep@duq.edu.

See Close-Up on page 239.

East Carolina University, Graduate School, College of Business, Department of Accounting, Greenville, NC 27858-4353. Offers MS.

Eastern Illinois University, Graduate School, Lumpkin College of Business and Applied Sciences, Program in Business Administration, Charleston, IL 61920-3099. Offers accountancy (MBA, Certificate); general management (MBA). *Accreditation:* AACSB. Part-time programs available. *Faculty:* 35 full-time (8 women). In 2009, 58 master's awarded. *Entrance requirements:* For master's, GMAT. *Application deadline:* For fall admission, 3/31 priority date for domestic students. Applications are processed on a rolling basis. Application fee: $30. *Expenses:* Tuition, state resident: full-time $9434; part-time $239 per credit hour. Tuition, nonresident: full-time $23,774; part-time $717 per credit hour. Required fees: $802.63. *Financial support:* In 2009–10, 4 research assistantships with tuition reimbursements (averaging $8,100 per year), 8 teaching assistantships with tuition reimbursements (averaging $8,100 per year) were awarded. *Unit head:* Dr. Cheryl Noll, Department Chair, 217-581-3028, E-mail: clnoll@eiu.edu. *Application contact:* Dr. John Willems, Coordinator, 217-581-3028, Fax: 217-581-6029, E-mail: jrwillems@eiu.edu.

Eastern Michigan University, Graduate School, College of Business, Department of Accounting and Finance, Ypsilanti, MI 48197. Offers accounting (MS); accounting information systems (MS). Part-time and evening/weekend programs available. Postbaccalaureate distance learning degree programs offered (minimal on-campus study). *Faculty:* 20 full-time (6 women). *Students:* 52 full-time (25 women), 53 part-time (35 women); includes 15 minority (5 African Americans, 10 Asian Americans or Pacific Islanders), 15 international. Average age 30. 73 applicants, 55% accepted, 31 enrolled. In 2009, 45 master's awarded. *Entrance requirements:* For master's, GMAT. Additional exam requirements/recommendations for international students: Required—TOEFL. *Application deadline:* Applications are processed on a rolling basis. Application fee: $35. Tuition and fees vary according to course level. *Financial support:* In 2009–10, 6 research assistantships with full tuition reimbursements (averaging $8,736 per year) were awarded; fellowships, teaching assistantships with full tuition reimbursements, career-related internships or fieldwork, Federal Work-Study, institutionally sponsored loans, scholarships/grants, tuition waivers (partial), and unspecified assistantships also available. Support available to part-time students. Financial award applicants required to submit FAFSA. *Unit head:* Dr. Jens Stephan, Department Head, 734-487-3320, Fax: 734-482-0806, E-mail: jens.stephan@emich.edu. *Application contact:* Dr. Phil Lewis, Advisor, 734-487-6817, Fax: 734-482-0806, E-mail: cob.grad@emich.edu.

East Tennessee State University, School of Graduate Studies, College of Business and Technology, Department of Accountancy, Johnson City, TN 37614. Offers M Acc. *Accreditation:* AACSB. Part-time and evening/weekend programs available. *Degree requirements:* For master's, comprehensive exam. *Entrance requirements:* For master's, GMAT, minimum GPA of 2.5. Additional exam requirements/recommendations for international students: Required—TOEFL

(minimum score 550 paper-based; 213 computer-based). *Faculty research:* Financial accounting, taxation, auditing, management accounting.

Edgewood College, Program in Business, Madison, WI 53711-1997. Offers accountancy (MS); business (MBA). *Accreditation:* ACBSP. Part-time and evening/weekend programs available. *Students:* 30 full-time (16 women), 118 part-time (50 women); includes 9 minority (2 African Americans, 1 American Indian/Alaska Native, 5 Asian Americans or Pacific Islanders, 1 Hispanic American), 3 international. Average age 34. In 2009, 39 master's awarded. *Entrance requirements:* For master's, GMAT (minimum score 425), minimum GPA of 2.75, 2 letters of recommendation. Additional exam requirements/recommendations for international students: Required—TOEFL (minimum score 213 computer-based). *Application deadline:* For fall admission, 8/26 for domestic students, 8/1 for international students; for spring admission, 1/10 for domestic students, 10/1 for international students. Applications are processed on a rolling basis. Application fee: $25. Electronic applications accepted. *Expenses:* Tuition: Part-time $688 per credit hour. *Financial support:* Career-related internships or fieldwork available. *Unit head:* Martin Preizler, Dean, 608-663-2898, Fax: 608-663-3291, E-mail: martinpreizler@edgewood.edu. *Application contact:* Joann Eastman, Admissions Counselor, 608-663-3250, Fax: 608-663-2214, E-mail: gps@edgewood.edu.

Elmhurst College, Graduate Programs, Program in Professional Accountancy, Elmhurst, IL 60126-3296. Offers MPA. Part-time and evening/weekend programs available. *Faculty:* 1 full-time (0 women), 3 part-time/adjunct (0 women). *Students:* 3 full-time (2 women), 17 part-time (8 women); includes 1 minority (African American). Average age 23. 13 applicants, 62% accepted, 5 enrolled. In 2009, 6 master's awarded. *Entrance requirements:* For master's, 3 recommendations. Additional exam requirements/recommendations for international students: Required—TOEFL (minimum score 550 paper-based; 213 computer-based). *Application deadline:* Applications are processed on a rolling basis. Application fee: $25. Electronic applications accepted. *Expenses:* Contact institution. *Financial support:* In 2009–10, 5 students received support. Federal Work-Study and scholarships/grants available. Support available to part-time students. Financial award application deadline: 6/1; financial award applicants required to submit FAFSA. *Unit head:* Dr. Ted Lerud, Associate Dean of the Faculty, 630-617-3661, Fax: 630-617-6415, E-mail: gradadm@elmhurst.edu. *Application contact:* Elizabeth D. Kuebler, Director of Adult and Graduate Admission, 630-617-3069, Fax: 630-617-5501, E-mail: betsyk@elmhurst.edu.

Emory University, Goizueta Business School, Doctoral Program in Business, Atlanta, GA 30322-1100. Offers accounting (PhD); finance (PhD); information systems (PhD); marketing (PhD); organization and management (PhD). *Faculty:* 57 full-time (11 women). *Students:* 37 full-time (14 women); includes 8 minority (3 African Americans, 4 Asian Americans or Pacific Islanders, 1 Hispanic American), 19 international. Average age 30. 218 applicants, 9% accepted, 9 enrolled. In 2009, 11 doctorates awarded. *Degree requirements:* For doctorate, comprehensive exam, thesis/dissertation. *Entrance requirements:* For doctorate, GMAT (strongly preferred) or GRE. Additional exam requirements/recommendations for international students: Required—TOEFL (minimum score 250 computer-based). *Application deadline:* For fall admission, 1/3 priority date for domestic and international students. Application fee: $50. Electronic applications accepted. *Unit head:* Dr. Lawrence Benveniste, Dean, 404-727-6377, Fax: 404-727-0868, E-mail: larry_benveniste@bus.emory.edu. *Application contact:* Allison Gilmore, Director of Admissions and Student Services, 404-727-6353, Fax: 404-727-5337, E-mail: phd@bus.emory.edu.

Everest University, Department of Business Administration, Tampa, FL 33614-5899. Offers accounting (MBA); human resources (MBA); international business (MBA). Part-time and evening/weekend programs available. *Degree requirements:* For master's, thesis optional. *Entrance requirements:* For master's, GMAT or GRE General Test, minimum GPA of 3.0.

Everest University, Program in Business Administration, Orlando, FL 32819. Offers accounting (MBA); general management (MBA); human resources (MBA); international management (MBA).

Fairfield University, Charles F. Dolan School of Business, Fairfield, CT 06824-5195. Offers accounting (MBA, MS, CAS); finance (MBA, MS, CAS); general management (MBA); human resource management (MBA, CAS); information systems and operations (MBA); information systems and operations management (CAS); international business (MBA, CAS); marketing (MBA, CAS); taxation (MBA, MS). *Accreditation:* AACSB. Part-time and evening/weekend programs available. *Degree requirements:* For master's, capstone course. *Entrance requirements:* For master's, GMAT (minimum score 500), 2 letters of reference, resume, minimum GPA of 3.0. Additional exam requirements/recommendations for international students: Required—TOEFL (minimum score 550 paper-based; 213 computer-based; 80 iBT). Electronic applications accepted. *Expenses:* Contact institution. *Faculty research:* Optimization strategies, international finance, consumer behavior, financial market volatility, Internet marketing, supply chain analysis, tax issues.

Fairleigh Dickinson University, College at Florham, Silberman College of Business, Department of Accounting, Law, and Tax, Program in Accounting, Madison, NJ 07940-1099. Offers MS. *Students:* 19 full-time (8 women), 35 part-time (15 women), 2 international. Average age 29. 28 applicants, 64% accepted, 18 enrolled. In 2009, 34 master's awarded. *Entrance requirements:* For master's, GMAT. *Application deadline:* Applications are processed on a rolling basis. Application fee: $40.

Fairleigh Dickinson University, Metropolitan Campus, Silberman College of Business, Department of Accounting, Law, and Tax, Program in Accounting, Teaneck, NJ 07666-1914. Offers MS, Certificate. *Students:* 83 full-time (21 women), 32 part-time (12 women), 25 international. Average age 30. 66 applicants, 76% accepted, 20 enrolled. In 2009, 90 master's awarded. *Application deadline:* Applications are processed on a rolling basis. Application fee: $40. *Faculty research:* Corporate accounting, legal issues. *Application contact:* Susan Brooman, University Director of Graduate Admissions, 201-692-2554, Fax: 201-692-2560, E-mail: globaleducation@fdu.edu.

Felician College, Program in Business, Lodi, NJ 07644-2117. Offers accounting (MBA); business administration (MBA); innovation and entrepreneurship (MBA); management (MBA). Part-time and evening/weekend programs available. *Students:* 3 full-time (2 women), 80 part-time (46 women); includes 16 minority (8 African Americans, 3 Asian Americans or Pacific Islanders, 5 Hispanic Americans), 5 international. 28 applicants, 89% accepted, 24 enrolled. *Entrance requirements:* For master's, GMAT. *Application deadline:* Applications are processed on a rolling basis. Application fee: $40. *Unit head:* Dr. Beth Castiglia, Dean, Division of Business and Management Services, 201-559-6140, E-mail: mctaggartp@felician.edu. *Application contact:* Tamara Vaughn, Senior Assistant Director, Graduate Admissions, 201-559-6097, Fax: 201-559-6138, E-mail: vaughant@felician.edu.

See Close-Up on page 243.

Fitchburg State University, Division of Graduate and Continuing Education, Program in Business Administration, Fitchburg, MA 01420-2697. Offers accounting (MBA); human resource management (MBA); management (MBA). Part-time and evening/weekend programs available. Postbaccalaureate distance learning degree programs offered (no on-campus study). *Students:* 24 full-time (9 women), 58 part-time (33 women); includes 10 minority (4 African Americans, 1 Asian American or Pacific Islander, 5 Hispanic Americans), 15 international. Average age 32. 64 applicants, 91% accepted, 27 enrolled. In 2009, 56 master's awarded. *Entrance requirements:* For master's, GMAT, minimum GPA of 2.8, letters of recommendation, resume. Additional exam requirements/recommendations for international students: Required—TOEFL (minimum score 550 paper-based; 213 computer-based; 79 iBT). *Application deadline:* Applications are processed on a rolling basis. Application fee: $25 ($50 for international students). *Expenses:* Tuition, area resident: Part-time $150 per credit. Tuition, state resident: part-time $150 per credit. Tuition, nonresident: part-time $150 per credit. Required fees: $120 per credit. *Financial support:* In 2009–10, research assistantships with partial tuition reimbursements (averaging $5,500 per year); Federal Work-Study, scholarships/grants, and unspecified assistantships also available. Support available to part-time students. Financial award application deadline:

3/1; financial award applicants required to submit FAFSA. *Unit head:* Joseph McAloon, Chair, 978-665-3745, Fax: 978-665-3658, E-mail: gce@fsc.edu. *Application contact:* Director of Admissions, 978-665-3144, Fax: 978-665-4540, E-mail: admissions@fsc.edu.

Florida Agricultural and Mechanical University, Division of Graduate Studies, Research, and Continuing Education, School of Business and Industry, Tallahassee, FL 32307-3200. Offers accounting (MBA); finance (MBA); management information systems (MBA); marketing (MBA). *Faculty:* 42 full-time (28 women). *Students:* 71 full-time (45 women), 15 part-time (9 women); includes 80 minority (all African Americans), 4 international. In 2009, 90 master's awarded. *Degree requirements:* For master's, residency. *Entrance requirements:* For master's, GMAT, minimum GPA of 3.0. *Application deadline:* For fall admission, 5/18 for domestic students, 12/18 for international students; for spring admission, 11/12 for domestic students, 5/12 for international students. Application fee: $30. *Financial support:* Fellowships, Federal Work-Study and scholarships/grants available. *Unit head:* Dr. Amos Bradford, Interim Dean, 850-599-3565. *Application contact:* Dr. Amos Bradford, Interim Dean, 850-599-3565.

Florida Atlantic University, College of Business, School of Accounting, Boca Raton, FL 33431-0991. Offers M Ac, M Tax, PhD. *Accreditation:* AACSB. Part-time and evening/weekend programs available. Postbaccalaureate distance learning degree programs offered (minimal on-campus study). *Faculty:* 22 full-time (10 women), 12 part-time/adjunct (1 woman). *Students:* 94 full-time (36 women), 361 part-time (209 women); includes 127 minority (47 African Americans, 24 Asian Americans or Pacific Islanders, 56 Hispanic Americans), 7 international. Average age 32. 438 applicants, 56% accepted, 78 enrolled. In 2009, 78 master's awarded. *Degree requirements:* For master's, comprehensive exam, thesis optional. *Entrance requirements:* For master's, GMAT, BS in accounting or equivalent, minimum GPA of 3.0 in accounting. Additional exam requirements/recommendations for international students: Required—TOEFL (minimum score 600 paper-based; 250 computer-based). *Application deadline:* For fall admission, 7/1 priority date for domestic students, 2/15 priority date for international students; for spring admission, 11/1 priority date for domestic students, 7/15 priority date for international students. Applications are processed on a rolling basis. Application fee: $30. *Expenses:* Tuition, state resident: full-time $7055; part-time $293.94 per credit hour. Tuition, nonresident: full-time $22,096; part-time $920.66 per credit hour. *Financial support:* Fellowships, research assistantships with partial tuition reimbursements, teaching assistantships, career-related internships or fieldwork, Federal Work-Study, institutionally sponsored loans, scholarships/grants, and tuition waivers (partial) available. Support available to part-time students. Financial award application deadline: 3/1. *Faculty research:* Systems and computer applications, accounting theory, information systems. *Unit head:* Dr. Somnath Bhattacharya, Director, 561-297-3638, Fax: 561-297-7023, E-mail: sbhatt@fau.edu. *Application contact:* Dr. Kim Dunn, Graduate Adviser, 561-297-3643, Fax: 561-297-1315, E-mail: kdunn@fau.edu.

Florida Gulf Coast University, Lutgert College of Business, Program in Accounting and Taxation, Fort Myers, FL 33965-6565. Offers MS. Part-time and evening/weekend programs available. *Faculty:* 63 full-time (20 women), 19 part-time/adjunct (2 women). *Students:* 44 full-time (28 women), 11 part-time (10 women); includes 10 minority (2 African Americans, 1 Asian American or Pacific Islander, 7 Hispanic Americans), 2 international. Average age 32. 34 applicants, 74% accepted, 19 enrolled. In 2009, 16 master's awarded. *Degree requirements:* For master's, thesis or alternative. *Entrance requirements:* For master's, GMAT, minimum GPA of 3.0. Additional exam requirements/recommendations for international students: Required—TOEFL (minimum score 550 paper-based; 213 computer-based). *Application deadline:* For fall admission, 6/1 priority date for domestic students; for spring admission, 11/1 for domestic students. Applications are processed on a rolling basis. Application fee: $30. Electronic applications accepted. *Faculty research:* Stock petitions, mergers and acquisitions, deferred taxes, fraud and accounting regulations, graphical reporting practices. *Unit head:* Dr. Ara Volkan, Chair, 239-590-7380, Fax: 239-590-7330, E-mail: avolkan@fgcu.edu. *Application contact:* Carol Burnette, Associate Dean, 239-590-7350, Fax: 239-590-7330, E-mail: burnette@fgcu.edu.

Florida Institute of Technology, Graduate Programs, College of Business, Online Programs, Melbourne, FL 32901-6975. Offers accounting and finance (MBA); healthcare management (MBA); information technology (MS); information technology management (MBA); management (MBA); marketing (MBA); project management (MBA). Part-time and evening/weekend programs available. Postbaccalaureate distance learning degree programs offered (no on-campus study). *Faculty:* 30 part-time/adjunct (6 women). *Students:* 6 full-time (2 women), 875 part-time (387 women); includes 290 minority (194 African Americans, 6 American Indian/Alaska Native, 44 Asian Americans or Pacific Islanders, 46 Hispanic Americans), 32 international. Average age 37. 329 applicants, 64% accepted, 177 enrolled. In 2009, 33 master's awarded. *Entrance requirements:* For master's, GMAT or resume showing 8 years of supervised experience, 2 letters of recommendation, resume, competency in math past college algebra. Additional exam requirements/recommendations for international students: Required—TOEFL (minimum score 550 paper-based; 213 computer-based; 79 iBT). *Application deadline:* For fall admission, 4/1 for international students; for spring admission, 9/30 for international students. Applications are processed on a rolling basis. Application fee: $50. Electronic applications accepted. *Expenses:* Tuition: Part-time $1015 per credit. Tuition and fees vary according to campus/location and program. *Financial support:* Available to part-time students. Application deadline: 3/1. *Unit head:* Dr. Mary S. Bonhomme, Dean, Florida Tech Online/Associate Provost for Online Learning, 321-674-8883, Fax: 321-674-8216, E-mail: bonhomme@fit.edu. *Application contact:* Carolyn Farrior, Director of Graduate Admissions Online Learning and Off Campus Programs, 321-674-7118, Fax: 321-674-8216, E-mail: cfarrior@fit.edu.

Florida International University, Alvah H. Chapman, Jr. Graduate School of Business, School of Accounting, Program in Accounting, Miami, FL 33199. Offers M Acc. *Accreditation:* AACSB. Part-time and evening/weekend programs available. *Students:* 52 full-time (18 women), 52 part-time (27 women); includes 73 minority (8 African Americans, 5 Asian Americans or Pacific Islanders, 60 Hispanic Americans), 10 international. Average age 32. 104 applicants, 58% accepted, 55 enrolled. In 2009, 64 master's awarded. *Entrance requirements:* For master's, GMAT or GRE, minimum GPA of 3.0 (upper-level coursework); resume. Additional exam requirements/recommendations for international students: Required—TOEFL (minimum score 550 paper-based; 213 computer-based; 80 iBT), or IELTS (minimum score 6.5). *Application deadline:* For fall admission, 6/1 for domestic and international students; for spring admission, 10/1 for domestic students, 9/1 for international students. Applications are processed on a rolling basis. Application fee: $30. Electronic applications accepted. *Expenses:* Contact institution. *Financial support:* Institutionally sponsored loans and scholarships/grants available. Financial award application deadline: 3/1; financial award applicants required to submit FAFSA. *Faculty research:* Financial and managerial accounting. *Unit head:* Dr. Sharon Lassar, Director, School of Accounting, 305-348-3501, Fax: 305-348-2914, E-mail: sharon.lassar@fiu.edu. *Application contact:* Teresita Brunken, 305-348-4224, Fax: 305-348-2914, E-mail: brunkent@fiu.edu.

Florida Southern College, Program in Business Administration, Lakeland, FL 33801-5698. Offers accounting (MBA); business administration (MBA); international business (MBA). Part-time and evening/weekend programs available. *Entrance requirements:* For master's, GMAT or GRE General Test, minimum GPA of 2.75. Additional exam requirements/recommendations for international students: Required—TOEFL (minimum score 550 paper-based). *Expenses:* Contact institution.

See Close-Up on page 247.

Florida State University, The Graduate School, College of Business, Tallahassee, FL 32306-1110. Offers accounting (M Acc), including accounting information services, assurance services, corporate accounting, taxation; business administration (MBA, PhD), including accounting (PhD), finance (PhD), management information systems (PhD), marketing (PhD), organizational behavior (PhD), risk management and insurance (PhD), strategic management (PhD); finance (MS); insurance (MSM); management information systems (MS); JD/MBA; MSW/MBA. *Accreditation:* AACSB. Part-time programs available. Postbaccalaureate distance learning degree programs offered (no on-campus study). *Faculty:* 107 full-time (31 women), 2 part-time/adjunct (0 women). *Students:* 212 full-time (73 women), 345 part-time (107 women); includes 123 minority (37 African Americans, 2 American Indian/Alaska Native, 48 Asian Americans or Pacific Islanders, 36 Hispanic Americans). Average age 30. 908 applicants, 43% accepted, 307 enrolled. In 2009, 257 master's, 18 doctorates awarded. Terminal master's awarded for partial completion of doctoral program. *Degree requirements:* For doctorate, comprehensive exam, thesis/dissertation. *Entrance requirements:* For master's, GMAT, work experience (MBA, MS), minimum GPA of 3.0, letters of recommendation; for doctorate, GMAT, minimum graduate GPA of 3.5, letters of recommendation. Additional exam requirements/recommendations for international students: Required—TOEFL (minimum score 600 paper-based; 80 computer-based); Recommended—IELTS (minimum score 6.5). *Application deadline:* For fall admission, 6/1 for domestic students, 5/1 for international students; for spring admission, 10/1 for domestic students, 9/1 for international students. Applications are processed on a rolling basis. Application fee: $30. Electronic applications accepted. *Expenses:* Tuition, state resident: full-time $7413. Tuition, nonresident: full-time $22,567. *Financial support:* In 2009–10, 102 students received support, including 32 fellowships with full tuition reimbursements available (averaging $6,900 per year), 30 research assistantships with full tuition reimbursements available (averaging $4,500 per year), 40 teaching assistantships with full tuition reimbursements available (averaging $11,500 per year); career-related internships or fieldwork, scholarships/grants, health care benefits, tuition waivers (full and partial), and unspecified assistantships also available. Support available to part-time students. Financial award application deadline: 1/1. *Unit head:* Dr. Caryn Beck-Dudley, Dean, 850-644-3090, Fax: 850-644-0915. *Application contact:* Lisa Beverly, Director, Graduate Programs Admissions, 850-644-6458, Fax: 850-644-0588, E-mail: lbeverly@cob.fsu.edu.

Fontbonne University, Graduate Programs, College of Global Business and Professional Studies, Program in Accounting, St. Louis, MO 63105-3098. Offers MS. Part-time programs available. *Faculty:* 4 part-time/adjunct (3 women). *Students:* 8 full-time (5 women), 34 part-time (23 women); includes 4 minority (all African Americans), 4 international. Average age 35. In 2009, 21 master's awarded. *Entrance requirements:* For master's, GMAT. Additional exam requirements/recommendations for international students: Required—TOEFL (minimum score 197 computer-based; 71 iBT). *Expenses:* Tuition: Part-time $562 per credit hour. *Financial support:* Federal Work-Study and scholarships/grants available. Financial award application deadline: 4/1; financial award applicants required to submit FAFSA. *Unit head:* Dr. Linda Maurer, Dean of the College of Business and Professional Studies, 314-889-1423, E-mail: lmaurer@fontbonne.edu. *Application contact:* Fontbonne University OPTIONS, 314-863-2220, Fax: 314-963-0327, E-mail: options@fontbonne.edu.

Fordham University, Graduate School of Business Administration, New York, NY 10023. Offers accounting (MBA); communications and media management (MBA); executive business administration (EMBA); finance (MBA, MS); information systems (MBA, MS); management systems (MBA); marketing (MBA); media management (MS); taxation (MS); taxation and accounting (MTA);); JD/MBA; MBA/MIM; MS/MBA. *Accreditation:* AACSB. Part-time and evening/weekend programs available. *Entrance requirements:* For master's, GMAT, 2 letters of recommendation, resume. Additional exam requirements/recommendations for international students: Required—TOEFL (minimum score 600 paper-based; 250 computer-based; 100 iBT). Electronic applications accepted. *Expenses:* Contact institution.

Freed-Hardeman University, Program in Business Administration, Henderson, TN 38340-2399. Offers accounting (MBA); corporate responsibility (MBA); leadership (MBA). *Accreditation:* ACBSP. Part-time and evening/weekend programs available. Postbaccalaureate distance learning degree programs offered (no on-campus study). *Entrance requirements:* For master's, GMAT. Additional exam requirements/recommendations for international students: Required—TOEFL (minimum score 500 paper-based; 173 computer-based).

Gannon University, School of Graduate Studies, College of Engineering and Business, School of Business, Program in Accounting, Erie, PA 16541-0001. Offers Certificate. Part-time and evening/weekend programs available. *Students:* 1 part-time (0 women). Average age 28. *Entrance requirements:* For degree, GMAT. Additional exam requirements/recommendations for international students: Required—TOEFL (minimum score 79 iBT). *Application deadline:* Applications are processed on a rolling basis. Application fee: $25. Electronic applications accepted. *Expenses:* Tuition: Full-time $13,590; part-time $755 per credit. Required fees: $524; $17 per credit. Tuition and fees vary according to course load, degree level, campus/location and program. *Financial support:* Application deadline: 7/1. *Unit head:* Scott Miller, Associate Director, 814-871-7397, E-mail: miller032@gannon.edu. *Application contact:* Kara Morgan, Assistant Director of Graduate Admissions, 814-871-5831, Fax: 814-871-5827, E-mail: graduate@gannon.edu.

George Mason University, School of Management, Program in Accounting, Fairfax, VA 22030. Offers MS. *Accreditation:* AACSB. *Students:* 21 full-time (14 women), 30 part-time (14 women); includes 6 minority (5 Asian Americans or Pacific Islanders, 1 Hispanic American), 5 international. Average age 25. 62 applicants, 58% accepted, 26 enrolled. In 2009, 7 master's awarded. *Entrance requirements:* For master's, GMAT, 2 letters of recommendation, resume. Additional exam requirements/recommendations for international students: Required—TOEFL, IELTS. *Application deadline:* For fall admission, 3/15 priority date for domestic students; for spring admission, 10/15 for domestic students. Applications are processed on a rolling basis. Application fee: $75. Electronic applications accepted. *Expenses:* Tuition, state resident: full-time $7568; part-time $315.33 per credit hour. Tuition, nonresident: full-time $21,704; part-time $904.33 per credit hour. Required fees: $2184; $91 per credit hour. *Financial support:* In 2009–10, 4 students received support, including 3 research assistantships with tuition reimbursements available (averaging $4,998 per year), 1 teaching assistantship with tuition reimbursement available (averaging $5,040 per year); Federal Work-Study, scholarships/grants, unspecified assistantships, and health care benefits (full-time research or teaching assistantship recipients) also available. Support available to part-time students. Financial award application deadline: 3/1. *Faculty research:* Current leading global business issues, including offshore outsourcing, international financial risk, and comparative systems of innovation; business management/practices; emerging technology and generating new business. *Unit head:* Sarah Nutter, Chair, 703-993-1860, E-mail: snutter@gmu.edu. *Application contact:* Michelle Hanson, Program Coordinator, 703-993-1974, E-mail: mhanson1@gmu.edu.

The George Washington University, School of Business, Department of Accountancy, Washington, DC 20052. Offers M Accy, MBA, PhD. *Accreditation:* AACSB. Part-time and evening/weekend programs available. *Faculty:* 15 full-time (7 women), 20 part-time/adjunct (0 women). *Students:* 131 full-time (87 women), 46 part-time (23 women); includes 14 minority (11 Asian Americans or Pacific Islanders, 3 Hispanic Americans), 108 international. Average age 28. 236 applicants, 75% accepted, 78 enrolled. In 2009, 76 master's awarded. *Degree requirements:* For doctorate, thesis/dissertation. *Entrance requirements:* For master's, GMAT; for doctorate, GMAT or GRE. Additional exam requirements/recommendations for international students: Required—TOEFL. *Application deadline:* For fall admission, 4/1 priority date for domestic students; for spring admission, 10/1 for domestic students. Applications are processed on a rolling basis. Application fee: $60. *Financial support:* In 2009–10, 50 students received support; fellowships, teaching assistantships, career-related internships or fieldwork, Federal Work-Study, and institutionally sponsored loans available. Financial award application deadline: 4/1. *Faculty research:* Management accounting and capital markets, financial accounting and the analytic hierarchy process, ethics and accounting, accounting information systems. *Unit head:* Dr. Keith Smith, Chair, 202-994-7461, E-mail: kes@gwu.edu. *Application contact:* Louba Hatoum, Program Director, 202-994-4450, E-mail: lhatoum@gwu.edu.

Georgia College & State University, Graduate School, The J. Whitney Bunting School of Business, Milledgeville, GA 31061. Offers accountancy (MACCT); accounting (MBA); business (MBA); health services administration (MBA); information systems (MIS); management information services (MBA). *Accreditation:* AACSB. Part-time and evening/weekend programs available. Postbaccalaureate distance learning degree programs offered (no on-campus study). *Faculty:* 43 full-time (17 women). *Students:* 70 full-time (32 women), 166 part-time (63 women); includes 29 minority (20 African Americans, 7 Asian Americans or Pacific Islanders, 2 Hispanic Americans), 23 international. Average age 29. 134 applicants, 84% accepted, 78 enrolled. In

Accounting

Georgia College & State University (continued)
2009, 75 master's awarded. *Entrance requirements:* For master's, GMAT. Additional exam requirements/recommendations for international students: Recommended—TOEFL (minimum score 550 paper-based; 213 computer-based; 79 iBT). *Application deadline:* For fall admission, 7/1 priority date for domestic students; for spring admission, 11/15 priority date for domestic students. Applications are processed on a rolling basis. Application fee: $40. Electronic applications accepted. *Expenses:* Tuition, area resident: Part-time $241 per credit hour. Tuition, state resident: full-time $4338. Tuition, nonresident: full-time $17,352; part-time $964 per credit hour. Required fees: $609 per semester. Tuition and fees vary according to course load and campus/location. *Financial support:* In 2009–10, 30 research assistantships with full tuition reimbursements were awarded; career-related internships or fieldwork and unspecified assistantships also available. Support available to part-time students. Financial award application deadline: 3/1; financial award applicants required to submit FAFSA. *Unit head:* Dr. Dale Young, Interim Dean, 478-445-5497, E-mail: dale.young@gcsu.edu. *Application contact:* Lynn Hanson, Director of Graduate Programs, 478-445-5115, E-mail: lynn.hanson@gcsu.edu.

Georgia Institute of Technology, Graduate Studies and Research, College of Management, Program in Business Administration, Atlanta, GA 30332-0001. Offers accounting (MBA); e-commerce (Certificate); engineering entrepreneurship (MBA); entrepreneurship (Certificate); finance (MBA); information technology management (MBA); international business (MBA, Certificate); management of technology (Certificate); marketing (MBA); operations management (MBA); organizational behavior (MBA); strategic management (MBA). *Accreditation:* AACSB.

Georgia Institute of Technology, Graduate Studies and Research, College of Management, Program in Management, Atlanta, GA 30332-0001. Offers accounting (PhD); finance (PhD); information technology management (PhD); marketing (PhD); operations management (PhD); organizational behavior (PhD); quantitative and computational finance (MS); strategic management (PhD). *Accreditation:* AACSB. *Degree requirements:* For doctorate, comprehensive exam, thesis/dissertation, oral exams. *Entrance requirements:* For master's and doctorate, GMAT. Additional exam requirements/recommendations for international students: Required—TOEFL. *Faculty research:* MIS, management of technology, international business, entrepreneurship, operations management.

Georgian Court University, School of Business, Lakewood, NJ 08701-2697. Offers accounting (Certificate); business administration (MBA). *Accreditation:* ACBSP. Part-time and evening/weekend programs available. *Faculty:* 10 full-time (6 women), 6 part-time/adjunct (1 woman). *Students:* 24 full-time (20 women), 110 part-time (74 women); includes 27 minority (12 African Americans, 5 Asian Americans or Pacific Islanders, 10 Hispanic Americans), 4 international. Average age 33. 60 applicants, 77% accepted, 28 enrolled. In 2009, 62 master's, 7 other advanced degrees awarded. *Entrance requirements:* For master's, GMAT or CPA exam, 3 letters of recommendation. Additional exam requirements/recommendations for international students: Required—TOEFL (minimum score 550 paper-based; 213 computer-based). *Application deadline:* For fall admission, 8/1 priority date for domestic students, 4/1 for international students; for spring admission, 1/1 priority date for domestic students, 7/1 for international students. Applications are processed on a rolling basis. Application fee: $40. Electronic applications accepted. *Expenses:* Tuition: Full-time $12,510; part-time $695 per credit. Required fees: $416 per year. Tuition and fees vary according to campus/location. *Financial support:* Scholarships/grants, health care benefits, and unspecified assistantships available. Financial award application deadline: 4/15; financial award applicants required to submit FAFSA. *Unit head:* Dr. Joseph Monahan, Dean, 732-987-2724, Fax: 732-987-2024, E-mail: monahanj@georgian.edu. *Application contact:* Eugene Soltys, Director of Graduate Admissions, 732-987-2770, Fax: 732-987-2084, E-mail: graduateadmissions@georgian.edu.

Georgia Southern University, Jack N. Averitt College of Graduate Studies, College of Business Administration, School of Accountancy, Statesboro, GA 30460. Offers accounting (M Acc). *Accreditation:* AACSB. Part-time and evening/weekend programs available. *Students:* 77 full-time (33 women), 23 part-time (14 women); includes 12 minority (11 African Americans, 1 Hispanic American), 17 international. Average age 25. 45 applicants, 87% accepted, 30 enrolled. In 2009, 45 master's awarded. *Entrance requirements:* For master's, GMAT. Additional exam requirements/recommendations for international students: Required—TOEFL (minimum score 550 paper-based; 213 computer-based; 80 iBT). *Application deadline:* For fall admission, 3/1 priority date for domestic and international students; for spring admission, 10/1 priority date for domestic students, 10/1 for international students. Applications are processed on a rolling basis. Application fee: $50. Electronic applications accepted. *Expenses:* Contact institution. *Financial support:* In 2009–10, 75 students received support, including research assistantships with partial tuition reimbursements available (averaging $7,200 per year), teaching assistantships with partial tuition reimbursements available (averaging $7,200 per year); career-related internships or fieldwork, Federal Work-Study, scholarships/grants, tuition waivers (partial), and unspecified assistantships also available. Support available to part-time students. Financial award application deadline: 4/15; financial award applicants required to submit FAFSA. *Faculty research:* Consolidation of fraud in the financial statement, reasons why firms switch auditions for the financial audit, internalization of accounting standards, pedagogy issues in accounting and law courses. *Unit head:* Dr. Mary Jill Lockwood, Director, 912-478-2228, Fax: 912-478-0105, E-mail: mjl@georgiasouthern.edu. *Application contact:* Dr. Charles Ziglar, Coordinator for Graduate Student Recruitment, 912-478-5365, Fax: 912-478-0740, E-mail: gradadmissions@georgiasouthern.edu.

Georgia State University, J. Mack Robinson College of Business, Program in General Business Administration, Atlanta, GA 30302-3083. Offers accounting/information systems (MBA); economics (MBA, MS); enterprise risk management (MBA); general business (MBA); general business administration (EMBA, PMBA); information systems consulting (MBA); information systems risk management (MBA); international business and information technology (MBA); international entrepreneurship (MBA); MBA/JD. *Accreditation:* AACSB. Part-time and evening/weekend programs available. *Entrance requirements:* For master's, GMAT. Additional exam requirements/recommendations for international students: Required—TOEFL (minimum score 610 paper-based; 255 computer-based; 101 iBT). Electronic applications accepted.

Georgia State University, J. Mack Robinson College of Business, School of Accountancy, School of Accountancy, Atlanta, GA 30303. Offers MBA, MPA, PhD, Certificate. *Accreditation:* AACSB. Part-time programs available. *Degree requirements:* For doctorate, thesis/dissertation. *Entrance requirements:* For master's and doctorate, GMAT. Additional exam requirements/recommendations for international students: Required—TOEFL (minimum score 610 paper-based; 255 computer-based; 101 iBT). Electronic applications accepted.

Golden Gate University, Ageno School of Business, San Francisco, CA 94105-2968. Offers accounting (MBA); business administration (EMBA, MBA, PMBA, DBA); finance (MBA, MS, Certificate); financial planning (MS, Certificate); human resource management (MBA, MS); human resources management (Certificate); information systems (MS); information technology (MBA); information technology management (Certificate); integrated marketing and communications (MS, Certificate); international business (MBA); management (MBA); marketing (MBA, MS, Certificate); operations management (Certificate); psychology (MA, Certificate); public relations (MS, Certificate); JD/MBA. Part-time and evening/weekend programs available. *Faculty:* 16 full-time (4 women), 241 part-time/adjunct (72 women). *Students:* 380 full-time (193 women), 750 part-time (414 women); includes 480 minority (98 African Americans, 2 American Indian/Alaska Native, 298 Asian Americans or Pacific Islanders, 82 Hispanic Americans), 166 international. Average age 33. 681 applicants, 78% accepted, 270 enrolled. In 2009, 550 master's, 13 doctorates awarded. *Degree requirements:* For doctorate, thesis/dissertation. *Entrance requirements:* For master's, GMAT (MBA), minimum GPA of 2.5 (MS). Additional exam requirements/recommendations for international students: Required—TOEFL. *Application deadline:* For fall admission, 5/15 for international students; for winter admission, 1/15 for international students; for spring admission, 9/15 for international students. Applications are processed on a rolling basis. Application fee: $70 ($110 for international students). Electronic applications accepted. *Expenses:* Contact institution. *Financial support:* Career-related internships or fieldwork, Federal Work-Study, institutionally sponsored loans, and scholarships/grants available. Support available to part-time students. Financial award applicants required to submit FAFSA. *Unit head:* Terry Connelly, Dean, 415-442-6519, Fax: 415-442-5369. *Application contact:* Angela Melero, Enrollment Services, 415-442-7800, Fax: 415-442-7807, E-mail: info@ggu.edu.

Golden Gate University, School of Accounting, San Francisco, CA 94105-2968. Offers accounting (M Ac, Graduate Certificate); forensic accounting (Graduate Certificate). Part-time and evening/weekend programs available. *Faculty:* 5 full-time (2 women), 35 part-time/adjunct (12 women). *Students:* 92 full-time (61 women), 154 part-time (99 women); includes 99 minority (6 African Americans, 82 Asian Americans or Pacific Islanders, 11 Hispanic Americans), 47 international. Average age 33. 132 applicants, 80% accepted, 52 enrolled. In 2009, 61 master's awarded. *Entrance requirements:* For master's, minimum GPA of 3.0. Additional exam requirements/recommendations for international students: Required—TOEFL. *Application deadline:* For fall admission, 5/15 for international students; for winter admission, 1/15 for international students; for spring admission, 9/15 for international students. Applications are processed on a rolling basis. Application fee: $70 ($110 for international students). Electronic applications accepted. *Financial support:* Career-related internships or fieldwork, Federal Work-Study, institutionally sponsored loans, and scholarships/grants available. Support available to part-time students. Financial award applicants required to submit FAFSA. *Faculty research:* Forensic accounting, audit, tax, CPA exam. *Unit head:* Mary Canning, 415-442-6559, Fax: 415-442-7807. *Application contact:* Angela Melero, Enrollment Services, 415-442-7800, Fax: 415-442-7807, E-mail: info@ggu.edu.

Gonzaga University, School of Business Administration, Spokane, WA 99258. Offers M Acc, MBA, JD/M Acc, JD/MBA. *Accreditation:* AACSB. Part-time and evening/weekend programs available. *Faculty:* 44 full-time (15 women). *Students:* 73 full-time (28 women), 121 part-time (47 women); includes 37 minority (2 African Americans, 19 American Indian/Alaska Native, 6 Asian Americans or Pacific Islanders, 10 Hispanic Americans), 9 international. Average age 29. In 2009, 89 master's awarded. *Entrance requirements:* For master's, GMAT. Additional exam requirements/recommendations for international students: Required—TOEFL. *Application deadline:* For fall admission, 7/20 priority date for domestic students; for spring admission, 11/1 for domestic students. Applications are processed on a rolling basis. Application fee: $50. Tuition and fees vary according to course level, course load, degree level, campus/location and program. *Financial support:* Teaching assistantships, Federal Work-Study available. Support available to part-time students. Financial award application deadline: 3/1. *Unit head:* Dr. Clarence H. Barnes, Dean, 509-328-4220 Ext. 5502. *Application contact:* Dr. Clarence H. Barnes, Dean, 509-328-4220 Ext. 5502.

Governors State University, College of Business and Public Administration, Program in Accounting, University Park, IL 60466-0975. Offers MS. *Entrance requirements:* For master's, GMAT.

Graduate School and University Center of the City University of New York, Graduate Studies, Program in Business, New York, NY 10016-4039. Offers accounting (PhD); behavioral science (PhD); finance (PhD); management planning systems (PhD). *Faculty:* 66 full-time (5 women). *Students:* 64 full-time (37 women); includes 7 minority (3 African Americans, 1 American Indian/Alaska Native, 2 Asian Americans or Pacific Islanders, 1 Hispanic American), 34 international. Average age 33. 89 applicants, 28% accepted, 18 enrolled. In 2009, 7 doctorates awarded. *Degree requirements:* For doctorate, thesis/dissertation. *Entrance requirements:* For doctorate, GMAT, writing sample (15 pages). Additional exam requirements/recommendations for international students: Required—TOEFL. *Application deadline:* For fall admission, 1/15 for domestic students. Application fee: $125. Electronic applications accepted. *Financial support:* In 2009–10, 50 students received support, including 54 fellowships, 5 teaching assistantships; research assistantships, career-related internships or fieldwork, Federal Work-Study, institutionally sponsored loans, and tuition waivers (full and partial) also available. Financial award application deadline: 2/1; financial award applicants required to submit FAFSA. *Unit head:* Dr. Joseph Weintrop, Executive Officer, 646-312-3092, Fax: 646-312-3031. *Application contact:* Les Gribben, Director of Admissions, 212-817-7470, Fax: 212-817-1624, E-mail: lgribben@gc.cuny.edu.

Grand Canyon University, College of Business, Phoenix, AZ 85017-1097. Offers accounting (MBA); executive fire service leadership (MS); finance (MBA); general management (MBA); health systems management (MBA); leadership (MBA, MS); management of information system (MBA); marketing (MBA); six sigma (MBA). *Accreditation:* ACBSP. Part-time and evening/weekend programs available. Postbaccalaureate distance learning degree programs offered (no on-campus study). *Entrance requirements:* For master's, equivalent of two years full-time professional work experience. Additional exam requirements/recommendations for international students: Required—TOEFL (minimum score 575 paper-based; 233 computer-based; 90 iBT), IELTS (minimum score 7). Electronic applications accepted.

Grand Valley State University, Seidman College of Business, Program in Accounting, Allendale, MI 49401-9403. Offers MSA. *Accreditation:* AACSB. Part-time and evening/weekend programs available. *Faculty:* 11 full-time (4 women), 4 part-time/adjunct (0 women). *Students:* 48 full-time (23 women), 60 part-time (29 women); includes 6 minority (3 African Americans, 2 Asian Americans or Pacific Islanders, 1 Hispanic American), 6 international. Average age 28. 49 applicants, 80% accepted, 21 enrolled. In 2009, 60 master's awarded. *Degree requirements:* For master's, comprehensive exam. *Entrance requirements:* For master's, GMAT. Additional exam requirements/recommendations for international students: Required—TOEFL. *Application deadline:* For fall admission, 8/1 priority date for domestic students, 5/1 priority date for international students; for winter admission, 11/1 priority date for domestic and international students; for spring admission, 4/1 priority date for domestic students, 3/1 priority date for international students. Applications are processed on a rolling basis. Application fee: $30. *Expenses:* Tuition, state resident: part-time $471 per credit hour. Tuition, nonresident: part-time $646 per credit hour. Tuition and fees vary according to course level. *Financial support:* In 2009–10, 18 students received support, including 10 fellowships (averaging $2,650 per year), 13 research assistantships with full and partial tuition reimbursements available (averaging $5,226 per year); Federal Work-Study, scholarships/grants, and unspecified assistantships also available. Support available to part-time students. Financial award application deadline: 2/15; financial award applicants required to submit FAFSA. *Faculty research:* Public trust, capacity measurement, theoretical capacity, economic order quantity. *Unit head:* Dr. Steve Goldberg, Director, 616-331-7190, Fax: 616-331-7389, E-mail: goldbers@gvsu.edu. *Application contact:* Claudia J. Bajema, Director, Graduate Business Programs, 616-331-7387, Fax: 616-331-7389, E-mail: bajemac@gvsu.edu.

Harding University, College of Business Administration, Searcy, AR 72149-0001. Offers accounting (MBA); health care management (MBA); information technology management (MBA); international business (MBA); leadership and organizational management (MBA). *Accreditation:* ACBSP. Part-time and evening/weekend programs available. Postbaccalaureate distance learning degree programs offered (no on-campus study). *Faculty:* 27 part-time/adjunct (6 women). *Students:* 105 full-time (46 women), 140 part-time (66 women); includes 31 minority (18 African Americans, 3 American Indian/Alaska Native, 6 Asian Americans or Pacific Islanders, 4 Hispanic Americans), 43 international. Average age 31. 82 applicants, 96% accepted, 66 enrolled. In 2009, 130 master's awarded. *Degree requirements:* For master's, portfolio. *Entrance requirements:* For master's, minimum GPA of 3.0, 2 letters of recommendation, resume. Additional exam requirements/recommendations for international students: Required—TOEFL (minimum score 550 paper-based; 213 computer-based; 80 iBT). *Application deadline:* For fall admission, 8/1 priority date for domestic and international students; for spring admission, 12/1 priority date for domestic and international students. Applications are processed on a rolling basis. Application fee: $35. *Expenses:* Tuition: Full-time $9720; part-time $540 per credit hour. Required fees: $22 per credit hour. Tuition and fees vary according to course load and program. *Financial support:* In 2009–10, 27 students received support. Unspecified assistantships available. Financial award application deadline: 7/30; financial award applicants required to submit FAFSA. *Unit head:* Glen Metheny, Director of Graduate Studies, 501-279-5851, Fax:

501-279-4805, E-mail: gmetheny@harding.edu. *Application contact:* Melanie Kiihnl, Recruiting Manager/Director of Marketing, 501-279-4523, Fax: 501-279-4805, E-mail: mba@harding.edu.

Harvard University, Harvard Business School, Doctoral Programs in Management, Boston, MA 02163. Offers accounting and management (DBA); business economics (PhD); health policy management (PhD); management (DBA); marketing (DBA); organizational behavior (PhD); science, technology and management (PhD); strategy (DBA); technology and operations management (DBA). *Degree requirements:* For doctorate, comprehensive exam (for some programs), thesis/dissertation. *Entrance requirements:* For doctorate, GRE General Test or GMAT. Additional exam requirements/recommendations for international students: Required—TOEFL. *Expenses:* Tuition: Full-time $33,696. Required fees: $1126. Full-time tuition and fees vary according to program.

Hawai'i Pacific University, College of Business Administration, Honolulu, HI 96813. Offers accounting/CPA (MBA); e-business (MBA); economics (MBA); finance (MBA); human resource management (MA, MBA); information systems (MBA, MSIS), including knowledge management (MSIS), software engineering (MSIS), telecommunications security (MSIS); international business (MBA); management (MBA); marketing (MBA); organizational change (MA, MBA); travel industry management (MBA). Part-time and evening/weekend programs available. *Faculty:* 15 full-time (5 women), 11 part-time/adjunct (4 women). *Students:* 206 full-time (107 women), 197 part-time (105 women); includes 136 minority (18 African Americans, 3 American Indian/Alaska Native, 98 Asian Americans or Pacific Islanders, 17 Hispanic Americans), 151 international. Average age 30. 235 applicants, 90% accepted, 127 enrolled. In 2009, 141 master's awarded. *Degree requirements:* For master's, thesis. *Entrance requirements:* For master's, GMAT. Additional exam requirements/recommendations for international students: Recommended—TOEFL (minimum score 550 paper-based; 213 computer-based; 80 iBT), TWE (minimum score 5). *Application deadline:* For fall admission, 2/15 priority date for domestic students; for spring admission, 10/15 priority date for domestic students. Applications are processed on a rolling basis. Application fee: $50. Electronic applications accepted. *Expenses:* Tuition: Full-time $12,600; part-time $700 per credit hour. Tuition and fees vary according to program. *Financial support:* In 2009–10, 164 students received support; research assistantships, career-related internships or fieldwork, Federal Work-Study, scholarships/grants, and unspecified assistantships available. Support available to part-time students. Financial award application deadline: 3/1; financial award applicants required to submit FAFSA. *Faculty research:* Statistical control process as used by management, studies in comparative cross-cultural management styles, not-for-profit management. *Unit head:* Dr. Aytun Ozturk, Dean, 808-544-9301, Fax: 808-544-0283, E-mail: uozturk@hpu.edu. *Application contact:* Danny Lam, Assistant Director of Graduate Admissions, 808-544-1135, Fax: 808-544-0280, E-mail: graduate@hpu.edu.

See Close-Up on page 251.

HEC Montreal, School of Business Administration, Diploma Programs in Administration, Program in Public Accountancy, Montréal, QC H3T 2A7, Canada. Offers Diploma. All courses are given in French. Part-time programs available. *Students:* 195 full-time (104 women), 43 part-time (30 women). 257 applicants, 85% accepted, 206 enrolled. In 2009, 176 Diplomas awarded. *Degree requirements:* For Diploma, one foreign language. *Entrance requirements:* For degree, bachelor's degree in accounting. *Application deadline:* For spring admission, 2/15 for domestic and international students. Application fee: $77 Canadian dollars. Electronic applications accepted. Tuition and fees charges are reported in Canadian dollars. *Expenses:* Tuition, area resident: Part-time $65.60 Canadian dollars per credit. Tuition, state resident: full-time $2361.60 Canadian dollars; part-time $183.36 Canadian dollars per credit. Tuition, nonresident: full-time $6601 Canadian dollars; part-time $448.13 Canadian dollars per credit. International tuition: $16,132.68 Canadian dollars full-time. Required fees: $1254.15 Canadian dollars; $28.99 Canadian dollars per course. $91.68 Canadian dollars per term. Tuition and fees vary according to degree level and program. *Financial support:* Research assistantships, teaching assistantships, scholarships/grants available. Financial award application deadline: 10/2. *Unit head:* Louise Cote, Director, 514-340-6205, Fax: 514-340-5640, E-mail: louise.cote@hec.ca. *Application contact:* Marie Deshaies, Senior Student Advisor, 514-340-6135, Fax: 514-340-6411, E-mail: marie.deshaies@hec.ca.

HEC Montreal, School of Business Administration, Master of Science Programs in Administration, Program in Financial and Strategic Accounting, Montréal, QC H3T 2A7, Canada. Offers M Sc. Part-time programs available. *Students:* 1 applicant, 0% accepted, 0 enrolled. *Degree requirements:* For master's, one foreign language, thesis. *Application deadline:* For fall admission, 3/15 for domestic and international students; for winter admission, 8/15 for domestic students, 9/15 for international students. Application fee: $77. Tuition and fees charges are reported in Canadian dollars. *Expenses:* Tuition, area resident: Part-time $65.60 Canadian dollars per credit. Tuition, state resident: full-time $2361.60 Canadian dollars; part-time $183.36 Canadian dollars per credit. Tuition, nonresident: full-time $6601 Canadian dollars; part-time $448.13 Canadian dollars per credit. International tuition: $16,132.68 Canadian dollars full-time. Required fees: $1254.15 Canadian dollars; $28.99 Canadian dollars per course. $91.68 Canadian dollars per term. Tuition and fees vary according to degree level and program. *Financial support:* Research assistantships, teaching assistantships, scholarships/grants available. Financial award application deadline: 10/2. *Unit head:* Claude Laurin, Director, 514-340-6847, Fax: 514-340-5633, E-mail: claude.laurin@hec.ca. *Application contact:* Francine Blais, Administrative Director, 514-340-6112, Fax: 514-340-6411, E-mail: francine.blais@hec.ca.

HEC Montreal, School of Business Administration, Master of Science Programs in Administration, Program in Management Control, Montréal, QC H3T 2A7, Canada. Offers M Sc. All courses are given in French. Part-time programs available. *Students:* 16 full-time (14 women), 6 part-time (3 women). 25 applicants, 64% accepted, 11 enrolled. In 2009, 1 degree awarded. *Degree requirements:* For master's, one foreign language, thesis. *Application deadline:* For fall admission, 3/15 for domestic and international students; for winter admission, 9/15 for domestic and international students. Application fee: $77 Canadian dollars. Electronic applications accepted. Tuition and fees charges are reported in Canadian dollars. *Expenses:* Tuition, area resident: Part-time $65.60 Canadian dollars per credit. Tuition, state resident: full-time $2361.60 Canadian dollars; part-time $183.36 Canadian dollars per credit. Tuition, nonresident: full-time $6601 Canadian dollars; part-time $448.13 Canadian dollars per credit. International tuition: $16,132.68 Canadian dollars full-time. Required fees: $1254.15 Canadian dollars; $28.99 Canadian dollars per course. $91.68 Canadian dollars per term. Tuition and fees vary according to degree level and program. *Financial support:* Fellowships, research assistantships, teaching assistantships, scholarships/grants available. Financial award application deadline: 10/2. *Unit head:* Dr. Claude Laurin, Director, 514-340-6485, Fax: 514-340-5690, E-mail: claude.laurin@hec.ca. *Application contact:* Francine Blais, Administrative Director, 514-340-6112, Fax: 514-340-6411, E-mail: francine.blais@hec.ca.

HEC Montreal, School of Business Administration, Master of Science Programs in Administration, Program in Public Accounting, Montréal, QC H3T 2A7, Canada. Offers M Sc. Part-time programs available. *Students:* 5 full-time (3 women), 5 part-time (3 women). 3 applicants, 33% accepted, 0 enrolled. *Degree requirements:* For master's, one foreign language, thesis. *Application deadline:* For fall admission, 3/15 for domestic and international students; for winter admission, 9/15 for domestic and international students. Application fee: $77. Tuition and fees charges are reported in Canadian dollars. *Expenses:* Tuition, area resident: Part-time $65.60 Canadian dollars per credit. Tuition, state resident: full-time $2361.60 Canadian dollars; part-time $183.36 Canadian dollars per credit. Tuition, nonresident: full-time $6601 Canadian dollars; part-time $448.13 Canadian dollars per credit. International tuition: $16,132.68 Canadian dollars full-time. Required fees: $1254.15 Canadian dollars; $28.99 Canadian dollars per course. $91.68 Canadian dollars per term. Tuition and fees vary according to degree level and program. *Financial support:* Research assistantships, teaching assistantships, scholarships/grants available. Financial award application deadline: 10/2. *Unit head:* Claude Laurin, Director, 514-340-6485, Fax: 514-340-5690, E-mail: claude.laurin@hec.ca. *Application contact:* Francine Blais, Administrative Director, 514-340-6112, Fax: 514-340-6411, E-mail: francine.blais@hec.ca.

Hendrix College, Program in Accounting, Conway, AR 72032-3080. Offers MA. Part-time programs available. *Entrance requirements:* For master's, GMAT. Additional exam requirements/recommendations for international students: Required—TOEFL. *Faculty research:* Meta-analysis, utility regulatory entities.

Hofstra University, Frank G. Zarb School of Business, Department of Accounting, Taxation and Legal Studies, Hempstead, NY 11549. Offers accounting (MS); business administration (MBA), including accounting, taxation; taxation (MS). Part-time and evening/weekend programs available. *Faculty:* 11 full-time (3 women), 3 part-time/adjunct (1 woman). *Students:* 58 full-time (20 women), 50 part-time (23 women); includes 10 minority (1 African American, 6 Asian Americans or Pacific Islanders, 3 Hispanic Americans), 22 international. Average age 28. 154 applicants, 63% accepted, 49 enrolled. In 2009, 20 master's awarded. *Degree requirements:* For master's, capstone course (MBA), thesis (MS). *Entrance requirements:* For master's, GMAT or GRE, 2 letters of recommendation, resume. Additional exam requirements/recommendations for international students: Required—TOEFL (minimum score 550 paper-based; 213 computer-based; 80 iBT); Recommended—IELTS (minimum score 6). *Application deadline:* Applications are processed on a rolling basis. Application fee: $60. Electronic applications accepted. *Expenses:* Contact institution. *Financial support:* In 2009–10, 24 students received support, including 21 fellowships with full and partial tuition reimbursements available (averaging $9,560 per year), 2 research assistantships with full and partial tuition reimbursements available (averaging $15,406 per year); Federal Work-Study, institutionally sponsored loans, scholarships/grants, health care benefits, tuition waivers (full and partial), and unspecified assistantships also available. Support available to part-time students. Financial award applicants required to submit FAFSA. *Faculty research:* Corporate governance and executive compensation, Sarbanes-Oxley and certification compliance for financial statement, student performance and evaluation models, decomposing the elements of nonprofit organizational performance, accounting for sustainability. *Unit head:* Dr. Nathan S. Slavin, Chairperson, 516-463-5690, Fax: 516-463-4834, E-mail: actnzs@hofstra.edu. *Application contact:* Carol Drummer, Dean of Graduate Admissions, 516-463-4876, Fax: 516-463-4664, E-mail: gradstudent@hofstra.edu.

Hood College, Graduate School, Department of Economics and Management, Frederick, MD 21701-8575. Offers accounting (MBA); administration and management (MBA); finance (MBA); human resource management (MBA); information systems (MBA); marketing (MBA); public management (MBA). Part-time and evening/weekend programs available. *Faculty:* 5 full-time (1 woman), 9 part-time/adjunct (1 woman). *Students:* 21 full-time (16 women), 166 part-time (85 women); includes 33 minority (18 African Americans, 8 Asian Americans or Pacific Islanders, 7 Hispanic Americans), 15 international. Average age 32. 47 applicants, 87% accepted, 32 enrolled. In 2009, 31 master's awarded. *Degree requirements:* For master's, capstone/final research project. *Entrance requirements:* For master's, minimum GPA of 2.75, resume, letters of recommendation. *Application deadline:* For fall admission, 7/15 for domestic and international students; for spring admission, 12/15 for domestic and international students. Applications are processed on a rolling basis. Application fee: $35. Electronic applications accepted. *Expenses:* Tuition: Full-time $6480; part-time $360 per credit. Required fees: $100; $50 per term. *Financial support:* Applicants required to submit FAFSA. *Faculty research:* Corporate strategy and sustainable competitive advantages, business ethics, entrepreneurship, investments management, economic development. *Unit head:* Dr. Anita Jose, Program Director, 301-696-3691, Fax: 301-696-3597, E-mail: jose@hood.edu. *Application contact:* Dr. Allen P. Flora, Dean of Graduate School, 301-696-3811, Fax: 301-696-3597, E-mail: gofurther@hood.edu.

Houston Baptist University, College of Business and Economics, Program in Accounting, Houston, TX 77074-3298. Offers MACCT. *Entrance requirements:* For master's, GMAT. Additional exam requirements/recommendations for international students: Required—TOEFL (minimum score 550 paper-based; 213 computer-based).

Howard University, School of Business, Graduate Programs in Business, Washington, DC 20059-0002. Offers accounting (MBA); entrepreneurship (MBA); finance (MBA); general management (MBA); human resources management (MBA); information systems (MBA); international business (MBA); marketing (MBA); supply chain management (MBA); JD/MBA. *Accreditation:* AACSB. Part-time and evening/weekend programs available. Postbaccalaureate distance learning degree programs offered (no on-campus study). *Entrance requirements:* For master's, GMAT, minimum 1 year post undergraduate work experience, resume, 3 letters of recommendation, advanced college algebra. Additional exam requirements/recommendations for international students: Required—TOEFL. *Faculty research:* Marketing research in multi-ethnic populations, U.S. trade policies and international relations, risk management (finance).

Hunter College of the City University of New York, Graduate School, School of Arts and Sciences, Department of Economics, Program in Accounting, New York, NY 10021-5085. Offers MS. *Faculty:* 7 full-time (0 women), 6 part-time/adjunct (0 women). *Students:* 5 full-time (3 women), 21 part-time (15 women); includes 13 minority (4 African Americans, 7 Asian Americans or Pacific Islanders, 2 Hispanic Americans). Average age 30. 38 applicants, 29% accepted, 10 enrolled. In 2009, 10 master's awarded. *Application deadline:* For fall admission, 4/1 for domestic students, 2/1 for international students; for spring admission, 11/1 for domestic students, 9/1 for international students. Application fee: $125. *Expenses:* Tuition, state resident: full-time $7360; part-time $310 per credit. Required fees: $250 per semester. *Unit head:* Dr. Marjorie P. Honig, Chairperson, 212-772-5400, Fax: 212-772-5398, E-mail: mhonig@hunter.cuny.edu. *Application contact:* Dr. Tashiaki Mitsudome, Graduate Advisor, 212-772-5430, E-mail: tashiaki.mitsudome@hunter.cuny.edu.

Illinois State University, Graduate School, College of Business, Department of Accounting, Normal, IL 61790-2200. Offers MPA, MS. *Accreditation:* AACSB. *Degree requirements:* For master's, comprehensive exam. *Entrance requirements:* For master's, GMAT, minimum GPA of 2.75 in last 60 hours of course work. Additional exam requirements/recommendations for international students: Required—TOEFL.

Indiana Tech, Program in Business Administration, Fort Wayne, IN 46803-1297. Offers accounting (MBA); health care administration (MBA); human resources (MBA); management (MBA); marketing (MBA). Part-time and evening/weekend programs available. Postbaccalaureate distance learning degree programs offered (no on-campus study). *Students:* 202 full-time (97 women), 37 part-time (18 women); includes 60 minority (45 African Americans, 2 American Indian/Alaska Native, 7 Asian Americans or Pacific Islanders, 6 Hispanic Americans), 5 international. Average age 38. *Entrance requirements:* For master's, GMAT, minimum undergraduate GPA of 2.5, 3 letters of recommendation. *Application deadline:* Applications are processed on a rolling basis. Application fee: $25. Electronic applications accepted. *Expenses:* Tuition: Full-time $5160; part-time $430 per credit hour. Tuition and fees vary according to degree level and program. *Financial support:* Applicants required to submit FAFSA. *Unit head:* Dr. Andrew Nwanne, Associate Dean of College of Professional Studies, 260-422-5561 Ext. 2214, E-mail: ainwanne@indianatech.edu. *Application contact:* Steve Herendeen, Manager of Campus Development and Support, 260-422-5561 Ext. 2121, E-mail: saherendeen@indianatech.edu.

Indiana University Northwest, School of Business and Economics, Gary, IN 46408-1197. Offers accountancy (M Acc); accounting (Certificate); business administration (MBA). *Accreditation:* AACSB. Part-time and evening/weekend programs available. *Faculty:* 5 full-time (0 women). *Students:* 53 full-time (19 women), 67 part-time (25 women); includes 44 minority (27 African Americans, 5 Asian Americans or Pacific Islanders, 12 Hispanic Americans), 2 international. Average age 33. In 2009, 43 master's awarded. *Entrance requirements:* For master's, GMAT, letter of recommendation. *Application deadline:* For fall admission, 7/15 priority date for domestic students; for spring admission, 11/15 for domestic students. Applications are processed on a rolling basis. Application fee: $25. *Expenses:* Contact institution. *Financial support:* In 2009–10, 9 students received support. Federal Work-Study, institutionally sponsored loans, and unspecified assistantships available. Support available to part-time students. Financial award application deadline: 7/15. *Faculty research:* International finance, wellness in the workplace, handicapped employment, MIS, regional economic forecasting. *Unit head:* Anna Rominger, Dean, 219-980-6636, Fax: 219-980-6916, E-mail: iunbiz@iun.edu. *Application contact:* John Gibson, Director of Graduate Program, 219-980-6635, Fax: 219-980-6916, E-mail: jagibson@iun.edu.

Accounting

Indiana University–Purdue University Indianapolis, Kelley School of Business, Indianapolis, IN 46202-2896. Offers accounting (MSA); business (MBA). *Accreditation:* AACSB. Part-time and evening/weekend programs available. Postbaccalaureate distance learning degree programs offered (minimal on-campus study). *Faculty:* 20 full-time (4 women), 1 part-time/adjunct (0 women). *Students:* 121 full-time (58 women), 469 part-time (163 women); includes 90 minority (33 African Americans, 45 Asian Americans or Pacific Islanders, 12 Hispanic Americans), 91 international. Average age 30. 592 applicants, 83% accepted, 198 enrolled. In 2009, 400 master's awarded. *Entrance requirements:* For master's, GMAT, previous course work in accounting, statistics. *Application deadline:* For fall admission, 4/15 priority date for domestic and international students; for spring admission, 11/1 priority date for domestic and international students. Application fee: $55 ($65 for international students). Electronic applications accepted. *Expenses:* Contact institution. *Financial support:* In 2009–10, 3 fellowships (averaging $16,193 per year), 1 teaching assistantship (averaging $9,000 per year) were awarded; Federal Work-Study, institutionally sponsored loans, and scholarships/grants also available. Support available to part-time students. Financial award application deadline: 3/1; financial award applicants required to submit FAFSA. *Unit head:* Phil Cochran, Associate Dean, Indianapolis Programs, 317-274-2481, Fax: 317-274-2483, E-mail: busugrad@iupui.edu. *Application contact:* Julie L. Moore, Recorder/Admission Coordinator, 317-274-4895, Fax: 317-274-2483, E-mail: mbaindy@iupui.edu.

Indiana University South Bend, School of Business and Economics, South Bend, IN 46634-7111. Offers accounting (MSA); business administration (MBA); management of information technologies (MS). Part-time and evening/weekend programs available. *Faculty:* 17 full-time (2 women), 3 part-time/adjunct (1 woman). *Students:* 67 full-time (34 women), 110 part-time (49 women); includes 12 minority (7 African Americans, 1 American Indian/Alaska Native, 1 Asian American or Pacific Islander, 3 Hispanic Americans), 56 international. Average age 32. In 2009, 58 master's awarded. *Entrance requirements:* For master's, GMAT. Additional exam requirements/recommendations for international students: Required—TOEFL (minimum score 550 paper-based; 213 computer-based). *Application deadline:* For fall admission, 7/1 priority date for domestic and international students; for spring admission, 11/1 priority date for domestic and international students. Applications are processed on a rolling basis. Application fee: $46 ($58 for international students). *Expenses:* Contact institution. *Financial support:* In 2009–10, 1 fellowship (averaging $3,846 per year) was awarded; Federal Work-Study and institutionally sponsored loans also available. Support available to part-time students. Financial award applicants required to submit FAFSA. *Faculty research:* Financial accounting, consumer research, capital budgeting research, business strategy research. *Unit head:* Robert H. Ducoffe, Dean, 574-520-4228, Fax: 574-520-4866. *Application contact:* Sharon Peterson, Secretary, Graduate Business, 574-520-4138, Fax: 574-520-4866, E-mail: speterso@iusb.edu.

Indiana Wesleyan University, College of Adult and Professional Studies, Department of Graduate Studies in Business, Marion, IN 46953. Offers accounting (MBA); applied management (MBA); business administration (MBA); health care (MBA); human resources (MBA); management (MS). Part-time and evening/weekend programs available. Postbaccalaureate distance learning degree programs offered (no on-campus study). *Degree requirements:* For master's, applied business or management project. *Entrance requirements:* For master's, minimum GPA of 2.5, 2 years of related work experience. Additional exam requirements/recommendations for international students: Required—TOEFL (minimum score 550 paper-based; 213 computer-based). Electronic applications accepted. *Expenses:* Tuition: Full-time $7380; part-time $410 per credit. One-time fee: $85. Tuition and fees vary according to campus/location.

Inter American University of Puerto Rico, Aguadilla Campus, Graduate School, Aguadilla, PR 00605. Offers accounting (MBA); business information systems (MBA); counseling psychology with an emphasis in family (MS); criminal justice (MA); educative management and leadership (MA); elementary education (MA); finance (MBA); human resources (MBA); industrial management (MBA); marketing (MBA). Part-time and evening/weekend programs available. *Degree requirements:* For master's, comprehensive exam. *Entrance requirements:* For master's, EXADEP, 2 letters of recommendation, minimum GPA of 2.5. Electronic applications accepted.

Inter American University of Puerto Rico, Arecibo Campus, Program in Business Administration, Arecibo, PR 00614-4050. Offers accounting (MBA); finance (MBA); human resources (MBA).

Inter American University of Puerto Rico, Barranquitas Campus, Program in Business Administration, Barranquitas, PR 00794. Offers accounting (IMBA); finance (IMBA).

Inter American University of Puerto Rico, Metropolitan Campus, Graduate Programs, Program in Accounting, San Juan, PR 00919-1293. Offers MBA. *Degree requirements:* For master's, comprehensive exam. *Entrance requirements:* For master's, GRE or EXADEP, interview. Electronic applications accepted.

Inter American University of Puerto Rico, Ponce Campus, Graduate School, Mercedita, PR 00715-1602. Offers accounting (MBA); biology (M Ed); chemistry (M Ed); criminal justice (MA); elementary education (M Ed); English as a Second Language (M Ed); finance (MBA); history (M Ed); human resources (MBA); marketing (MBA); mathematics (M Ed); Spanish (M Ed). *Entrance requirements:* For master's, minimum GPA of 2.5.

Inter American University of Puerto Rico, San Germán Campus, Graduate Studies Center, Program in Accounting, San Germán, PR 00683-5008. Offers financial accounting (M Acc); managerial accounting (M Acc).

Inter American University of Puerto Rico, San Germán Campus, Graduate Studies Center, Program in Business Administration, San Germán, PR 00683-5008. Offers accounting (MBA); finance (MBA); human resources (PhD); human resources management (MBA); industrial management (MBA); international business (PhD); management information systems (MBA); marketing management (MBA). Part-time and evening/weekend programs available. *Degree requirements:* For master's, comprehensive exam. *Entrance requirements:* For master's, GRE General Test or EXADEP, minimum GPA of 3.0.

Iona College, Hagan School of Business, Department of Accounting, New Rochelle, NY 10801-1890. Offers MBA, PMC. *Accreditation:* ASHA. Part-time and evening/weekend programs available. *Faculty:* 6 full-time (1 woman), 2 part-time/adjunct (0 women). *Students:* 4 full-time (3 women), 9 part-time (3 women). Average age 28. 13 applicants, 69% accepted, 7 enrolled. In 2009, 1 master's, 1 other advanced degree awarded. *Entrance requirements:* For master's, GMAT, two letters of recommendation; for PMC, GMAT. Additional exam requirements/recommendations for international students: Required—TOEFL (minimum score 550 paper-based; 213 computer-based). *Application deadline:* Applications are processed on a rolling basis. Application fee: $50. Electronic applications accepted. *Expenses:* Tuition: Part-time $830 per credit. *Financial support:* Scholarships/grants, tuition waivers (partial), and unspecified assistantships available. Support available to part-time students. Financial award application deadline: 4/15; financial award applicants required to submit FAFSA. *Unit head:* Dr. Jeffry Haber, Chair, 914-633-2244, E-mail: jhaber@iona.edu. *Application contact:* Jude Fleurismond, Director of MBA Admissions, 914-633-2289, Fax: 914-637-2708, E-mail: jfleurismond@iona.edu.

Iowa State University of Science and Technology, Graduate College, College of Business, Department of Accounting, Ames, IA 50011. Offers M Acc. *Accreditation:* AACSB. *Faculty:* 12 full-time (5 women), 1 (woman) part-time/adjunct. *Students:* 41 full-time (21 women), 13 part-time (12 women); includes 2 minority (1 African American, 1 Asian American or Pacific Islander), 19 international. 53 applicants, 55% accepted, 25 enrolled. In 2009, 32 master's awarded. *Degree requirements:* For master's, thesis or alternative. *Entrance requirements:* For master's, GMAT, resume. Additional exam requirements/recommendations for international students: Required—TOEFL (minimum score 600 paper-based; 250 computer-based; 100 iBT) or IELTS (minimum score 7). *Application deadline:* For fall admission, 4/1 priority date for domestic and international students; for spring admission, 11/1 priority date for domestic and international students. Application fee: $40 ($90 for international students). Electronic applications accepted. *Expenses:* Tuition, state resident: full-time $6716. Tuition, nonresident: full-time $8908. Tuition and fees vary according to course level, course load, program and student level. *Financial support:* In 2009–10, 3 research assistantships with full and partial tuition reimbursements (averaging $7,600 per year) were awarded; teaching assistantships, career-related internships or fieldwork, scholarships/grants, health care benefits, and unspecified assistantships also available. *Unit head:* Dr. Frederick H. Dark, Interim Chair, 515-294-8118, E-mail: busgrad@iastate.edu. *Application contact:* Dr. Frederick H. Dark, Interim Chair, 515-294-8118, E-mail: busgrad@iastate.edu.

Ithaca College, Division of Graduate and Professional Studies, School of Business, Program in Professional Accountancy, Ithaca, NY 14850. Offers MBA. Part-time programs available. *Faculty:* 3 full-time (2 women). *Students:* 8 full-time (3 women), 1 part-time (0 women), 2 international. Average age 22. 10 applicants, 80% accepted, 8 enrolled. In 2009, 14 master's awarded. *Entrance requirements:* For master's, GMAT, minimum GPA of 3.0. Additional exam requirements/recommendations for international students: Required—TOEFL (minimum score 550 paper-based; 213 computer-based; 80 iBT). *Application deadline:* For fall admission, 8/1 for domestic and international students; for spring admission, 12/1 for domestic and international students. Applications are processed on a rolling basis. Application fee: $40. Electronic applications accepted. *Expenses:* Contact institution. *Financial support:* In 2009–10, 8 students received support, including 2 fellowships (averaging $5,332 per year); career-related internships or fieldwork, Federal Work-Study, and scholarships/grants also available. Support available to part-time students. Financial award application deadline: 4/15; financial award applicants required to submit CSS PROFILE or FAFSA. *Unit head:* Dr. Joanne Burress, Chairperson, 607-274-3527, Fax: 607-274-1263, E-mail: gps@ithaca.edu. *Application contact:* Rob Gearhart, Dean, Graduate and Professional Studies, 607-274-3527, Fax: 607-274-1263, E-mail: gps@ithaca.edu.

Jackson State University, Graduate School, School of Business, Department of Accounting, Jackson, MS 39217. Offers MPA. Part-time and evening/weekend programs available. *Degree requirements:* For master's, comprehensive exam. *Entrance requirements:* For master's, GRE General Test, GMAT. Additional exam requirements/recommendations for international students: Required—TOEFL.

James Madison University, The Graduate School, College of Business, Program in Accounting, Harrisonburg, VA 22807. Offers MS. *Accreditation:* AACSB. Part-time and evening/weekend programs available. *Students:* 59 full-time (26 women), 5 part-time (2 women); includes 6 minority (2 African Americans, 2 Asian Americans or Pacific Islanders, 2 Hispanic Americans). Average age 27. In 2009, 63 master's awarded. *Entrance requirements:* For master's, GMAT or CPA exam. Additional exam requirements/recommendations for international students: Required—TOEFL. *Application deadline:* For fall admission, 5/1 priority date for domestic students, 5/1 for international students; for spring admission, 9/1 priority date for domestic students, 9/1 for international students. Applications are processed on a rolling basis. Application fee: $55. Electronic applications accepted. *Expenses:* Tuition, area resident: Part-time $305 per credit hour. Tuition, state resident: part-time $305 per credit hour. Tuition, nonresident: part-time $890 per credit hour. *Financial support:* In 2009–10, 19 students received support. Federal Work-Study available. Financial award application deadline: 3/1; financial award applicants required to submit FAFSA. *Faculty research:* Controllership, government accounting. *Unit head:* Dr. Paul A. Copley, Academic Unit Head, 540-568-3081. *Application contact:* Dr. Nancy Nichols, Program Director, 540-568-3081.

John Carroll University, Graduate School, John M. and Mary Jo Boler School of Business, University Heights, OH 44118-4581. Offers accountancy (MS); business (MBA). *Accreditation:* AACSB. Part-time and evening/weekend programs available. *Entrance requirements:* For master's, GMAT, minimum GPA of 2.5. Additional exam requirements/recommendations for international students: Required—TOEFL (minimum score 550 paper-based; 213 computer-based). Electronic applications accepted. *Expenses:* Contact institution. *Faculty research:* Accounting, economics and finance, management, marketing and logistics.

Johnson & Wales University, The Alan Shawn Feinstein Graduate School, MBA Program in Global Business Leadership, Providence, RI 02903-3703. Offers accounting (MBA); enhanced accounting (MBA); financial management (MBA); international trade (MBA); marketing (MBA); organizational leadership (MBA). Part-time programs available. *Faculty:* 13 full-time (3 women), 17 part-time/adjunct (4 women). *Students:* 523 full-time (272 women), 162 part-time (85 women); includes 29 minority (18 African Americans, 4 Asian Americans or Pacific Islanders, 7 Hispanic Americans), 385 international. Average age 27. 330 applicants, 82% accepted, 151 enrolled. In 2009, 274 master's awarded. *Entrance requirements:* For master's, minimum GPA of 2.75. Additional exam requirements/recommendations for international students: Required—TOEFL, TOEFL (minimum score 550 paper-based; 210 computer-based) or IELTS recommended; Recommended—TWE. *Application deadline:* For fall admission, 8/15 priority date for domestic students, 6/28 priority date for international students; for winter admission, 11/10 priority date for domestic students, 9/20 priority date for international students; for spring admission, 2/5 priority date for domestic students, 12/20 priority date for international students. Applications are processed on a rolling basis. *Expenses:* Required fees: $340 per quarter hour. *Financial support:* Tuition waivers (partial) and unspecified assistantships available. Support available to part-time students. Financial award application deadline: 5/1. *Faculty research:* International banking, global economy, international trade, cultural differences. *Unit head:* Dr. Frank Pontarelli, Dean, 401-598-1333, Fax: 401-598-1125. *Application contact:* Dr. Allan G. Freedman, Director of Graduate Admissions, 401-598-1015, Fax: 401-598-1286, E-mail: gradadm@jwu.edu.

Jones International University, School of Business, Centennial, CO 80112. Offers accounting (MBA); business communication (MABC); entrepreneurship (MABC, MBA); finance (MBA); global enterprise management (MBA); health care management (MBA); information security management (MBA); information technology management (MBA); leadership and influence (MABC); leading the customer-driven organization (MABC); negotiation and conflict management (MBA); project management (MABC, MBA). Program only offered online. Part-time and evening/weekend programs available. Postbaccalaureate distance learning degree programs offered (no on-campus study). *Degree requirements:* For master's, capstone project. *Entrance requirements:* For master's, minimum cumulative GPA of 2.5. Additional exam requirements/recommendations for international students: Recommended—TOEFL (minimum score 550 paper-based; 213 computer-based). Electronic applications accepted.

Kansas State University, Graduate School, College of Business Administration, Department of Accounting, Manhattan, KS 66506. Offers M Acc. *Accreditation:* AACSB. *Faculty:* 7 full-time (1 woman). *Students:* 42 full-time (18 women), 5 international. Average age 23. 75 applicants, 67% accepted, 32 enrolled. In 2009, 37 master's awarded. *Degree requirements:* For master's, comprehensive exam. *Entrance requirements:* For master's, GMAT, minimum undergraduate GPA of 3.0. Additional exam requirements/recommendations for international students: Required—TOEFL (minimum score 550 paper-based; 213 computer-based). *Application deadline:* For fall admission, 2/1 priority date for domestic and international students; for spring admission, 8/1 priority date for domestic and international students. Applications are processed on a rolling basis. Application fee: $60. Electronic applications accepted. *Financial support:* In 2009–10, 1 research assistantship with partial tuition reimbursement (averaging $9,220 per year), 4 teaching assistantships with full and partial tuition reimbursements (averaging $9,240 per year) were awarded; institutionally sponsored loans and scholarships/grants also available. Support available to part-time students. Financial award application deadline: 3/1; financial award applicants required to submit FAFSA. *Faculty research:* Accounting education, accounting ethics, capital markets (empirical/archival), research in tax and financial reporting, behavioral research in accounting. Total annual research expenditures: $70,692. *Unit head:* Richard Ott, Head, 785-532-6184, Fax: 785-532-5959, E-mail: rlo@ksu.edu. *Application contact:* Jeff Katz, Director, 785-532-7451, Fax: 785-532-5959, E-mail: jkatz@ksu.edu.

Kean University, College of Business and Public Administration, Program in Accounting, Union, NJ 07083. Offers MS. Part-time and evening/weekend programs available. *Faculty:* 10 full-time (2 women). *Students:* 22 full-time (10 women), 50 part-time (33 women); includes 31

minority (8 African Americans, 11 Asian Americans or Pacific Islanders, 12 Hispanic Americans), 7 international. Average age 32. 51 applicants, 73% accepted, 27 enrolled. In 2009, 38 master's awarded. *Entrance requirements:* For master's, GMAT, 2 letters of recommendation, interview, minimum GPA of 3.0. *Application deadline:* For fall admission, 5/1 for domestic students; for spring admission, 11/1 for domestic students. Application fee: $60 ($150 for international students). Electronic applications accepted. *Expenses:* Tuition, state resident: full-time $10,440; part-time $435 per credit. Tuition, nonresident: full-time $14,160; part-time $590 per credit. Required fees: $2642; $110 per credit. Part-time tuition and fees vary according to course load and degree level. *Financial support:* In 2009–10, 3 research assistantships with full tuition reimbursements (averaging $3,263 per year) were awarded; unspecified assistantships also available. *Unit head:* Dr. James Capone, Program Coordinator, 908-737-4110, E-mail: jcapone@kean.edu. *Application contact:* Reenat Hasan, Pre-Admissions Coordinator, 908-737-5923, Fax: 908-737-5965, E-mail: rhasan@exchange.kean.edu.

Kennesaw State University, Michael J. Coles College of Business, Program in Accounting, Kennesaw, GA 30144-5591. Offers M Acc. *Accreditation:* AACSB. Part-time and evening/weekend programs available. *Students:* 85 full-time (43 women), 86 part-time (48 women); includes 47 minority (29 African Americans, 16 Asian Americans or Pacific Islanders, 2 Hispanic Americans), 27 international. Average age 31. 96 applicants, 51% accepted, 33 enrolled. In 2009, 65 master's awarded. *Entrance requirements:* For master's, GMAT (minimum score 500), minimum GPA of 2.8. Additional exam requirements/recommendations for international students: Required—TOEFL (minimum score 550 paper-based; 213 computer-based; 80 iBT), IELTS (minimum score 6). *Application deadline:* For fall admission, 4/1 for domestic and international students. Applications are processed on a rolling basis. Application fee: $60. Electronic applications accepted. *Expenses:* Tuition, state resident: full-time $2341; part-time $196 per credit hour. Tuition, nonresident: full-time $9396; part-time $783 per credit hour. Required fees: $573 per semester. *Financial support:* In 2009–10, 4 research assistantships with tuition reimbursements (averaging $4,000 per year) were awarded; unspecified assistantships also available. *Unit head:* Dr. Kathyrn Epps, Director, 770-423-6085, E-mail: kepps@kennesaw.edu. *Application contact:* Vilma Marquez, Admissions Counselor, 770-420-4377, Fax: 770-423-6885, E-mail: vmarquez@kennesaw.edu.

Kent State University, Graduate School of Management, Doctoral Program in Accounting, Kent, OH 44242-0001. Offers PhD. *Faculty:* 8 full-time (3 women). *Students:* 7 full-time (1 woman), 2 international. Average age 30. In 2009, 1 doctorate awarded. *Degree requirements:* For doctorate, comprehensive exam, thesis/dissertation, oral defense. *Entrance requirements:* For doctorate, GMAT. Additional exam requirements/recommendations for international students: Required—TOEFL (minimum score 600 paper-based; 250 computer-based; 100 iBT). *Application deadline:* For fall admission, 2/1 for domestic students, 1/1 for international students. Application fee: $30 ($60 for international students). Electronic applications accepted. *Financial support:* In 2009–10, 4 students received support, including fellowships with full tuition reimbursements available (averaging $15,000 per year), 4 teaching assistantships with full tuition reimbursements available (averaging $15,000 per year); Federal Work-Study and tuition waivers (full) also available. Financial award application deadline: 2/1; financial award applicants required to submit FAFSA. *Faculty research:* Information economics, capital management, use of accounting information, curriculum design. *Unit head:* Dr. Linda Zucca, Chair and Associate Professor, 330-672-2545, Fax: 330-672-2548, E-mail: lzucca@kent.edu. *Application contact:* Felecia A. Urbanek, Coordinator, Graduate Programs, 330-672-2282, Fax: 330-672-7303, E-mail: gradbus@kent.edu.

Kent State University, Graduate School of Management, Master's Program in Accounting, Kent, OH 44242-0001. Offers MS. Part-time programs available. *Faculty:* 8 full-time (3 women), 1 part-time/adjunct (0 women). *Students:* 44 full-time (14 women), 14 part-time (12 women); includes 3 minority (2 African Americans, 1 Asian American or Pacific Islander), 12 international. Average age 23. 44 applicants, 89% accepted, 21 enrolled. In 2009, 24 master's awarded. *Degree requirements:* For master's, internship. *Entrance requirements:* For master's, GMAT, minimum GPA of 2.75. Additional exam requirements/recommendations for international students: Required—TOEFL (minimum score 550 paper-based; 213 computer-based; 79 iBT). *Application deadline:* For fall admission, 4/1 priority date for domestic students, 4/1 for international students; for spring admission, 12/1 for domestic students. Applications are processed on a rolling basis. Application fee: $30 ($60 for international students). Electronic applications accepted. *Financial support:* In 2009–10, 9 students received support, including 9 research assistantships with full tuition reimbursements available (averaging $3,350 per year); Federal Work-Study and tuition waivers (full) also available. Financial award application deadline: 4/1; financial award applicants required to submit FAFSA. *Faculty research:* Financial accounting, managerial accounting, auditing, systems, nonprofit. *Unit head:* Dr. Linda Zucca, Chair and Associate Professor, 330-672-2545, Fax: 330-672-2548, E-mail: lzucca@kent.edu. *Application contact:* Louise M. Ditchey, Director, 330-672-2282, Fax: 330-672-7303, E-mail: gradbus@kent.edu.

Kentucky State University, College of Professional Studies, Frankfort, KY 40601. Offers business administration (MBA), including accounting, finance, management, marketing; public administration (MPA), including human resource management, international administration and development, management information systems, nonprofit management; special education (MA). Part-time and evening/weekend programs available. Postbaccalaureate distance learning degree programs offered (minimal on-campus study). *Faculty:* 11 full-time (3 women), 2 part-time/adjunct (both women). *Students:* 79 full-time (51 women), 66 part-time (34 women); includes 88 minority (85 African Americans, 2 Asian Americans or Pacific Islanders, 1 Hispanic American), 4 international. Average age 34. 92 applicants, 75% accepted, 52 enrolled. In 2009, 32 master's awarded. *Degree requirements:* For master's, comprehensive exam, thesis optional. *Entrance requirements:* For master's, GMAT, GRE. Additional exam requirements/recommendations for international students: Required—TOEFL (minimum score 525 paper-based; 173 computer-based). *Application deadline:* For fall admission, 7/1 priority date for domestic students, 4/15 priority date for international students; for spring admission, 11/15 priority date for domestic students, 8/1 priority date for international students. Applications are processed on a rolling basis. Application fee: $30 ($100 for international students). Electronic applications accepted. *Expenses:* Tuition, state resident: full-time $5634; part-time $313 per credit hour. Tuition, nonresident: full-time $14,598; part-time $811 per credit hour. Required fees: $450; $25 per credit hour. *Financial support:* In 2009–10, 113 students received support, including 4 research assistantships (averaging $14,035 per year); career-related internships or fieldwork, scholarships/grants, tuition waivers (partial), and unspecified assistantships also available. Financial award application deadline: 4/15; financial award applicants required to submit FAFSA. *Unit head:* Dr. Gashaw Lake, Dean, College of Professional Studies, 502-597-6105, Fax: 502-597-6715, E-mail: gashaw.lake@kysu.edu. *Application contact:* Cedric Cunningham, Administrative Assistant, Office of Graduate Studies, 502-597-6536, E-mail: cedric.cunningham@kysu.edu.

Lakeland College, Graduate Studies Division, Program in Business Administration, Sheboygan, WI 53082-0359. Offers accounting (MBA); finance (MBA); healthcare management (MBA); project management (MBA). *Entrance requirements:* For master's, GMAT. *Expenses:* Contact institution.

Lamar University, College of Graduate Studies, College of Business, Beaumont, TX 77710. Offers accounting (MBA); experiential business and entrepreneurship (MBA); financial management (MBA); healthcare administration (MBA); information systems (MBA); management (MBA). *Accreditation:* AACSB. Part-time and evening/weekend programs available. *Faculty:* 18 full-time (4 women), 4 part-time/adjunct (0 women). *Students:* 62 full-time (27 women), 59 part-time (16 women); includes 19 minority (8 African Americans, 6 Asian Americans or Pacific Islanders, 5 Hispanic Americans), 19 international. Average age 29. 210 applicants, 34% accepted, 33 enrolled. In 2009, 41 master's awarded. *Degree requirements:* For master's, comprehensive exam (for some programs), thesis optional. *Entrance requirements:* For master's, GMAT. Additional exam requirements/recommendations for international students: Required—TOEFL (minimum score 525 paper-based; 197 computer-based). *Application deadline:* For fall admission, 3/15 priority date for domestic students; for spring admission, 10/1 priority date for domestic students. Applications are processed on a rolling basis. Application fee: $25 ($50 for international students). *Financial support:* In 2009–10, 12 students received support, including 4 research assistantships with partial tuition reimbursements available; fellowships with tuition reimbursements available, career-related internships or fieldwork, Federal Work-Study, institutionally sponsored loans, scholarships/grants, and tuition waivers (partial) also available. Support available to part-time students. Financial award application deadline: 4/1; financial award applicants required to submit FAFSA. *Faculty research:* Marketing, finance, quantitative methods, management information systems, legal, environmental. *Unit head:* Dr. Enrique R. Venta, Dean, 409-880-8604, Fax: 409-880-8088, E-mail: henry.venta@lamar.edu. *Application contact:* Dr. Brad Mayer, Professor and Associate Dean, 409-880-2383, Fax: 409-880-8605, E-mail: bradley.mayer@lamar.edu.

La Sierra University, School of Business and Management, Riverside, CA 92515. Offers accounting (MBA); finance (MBA); general management (MBA); human resources management (MBA); leadership, values, and ethics for business and management (Certificate); marketing (MBA). *Degree requirements:* For master's, research project. *Entrance requirements:* For master's, GMAT, minimum GPA of 3.0. Additional exam requirements/recommendations for international students: Required—TOEFL. *Faculty research:* Financial econometrics, institutional assessment and strategic planning, legal issues in management, behavioral finance, content of financial reports.

Lehigh University, College of Business and Economics, Department of Accounting, Bethlehem, PA 18015. Offers accounting and information analysis (MS). *Accreditation:* AACSB. *Faculty:* 7 full-time (0 women), 2 part-time/adjunct (0 women). *Students:* 28 full-time (11 women), 5 part-time (4 women), 6 international. Average age 26. 157 applicants, 33% accepted, 14 enrolled. In 2009, 22 master's awarded. *Entrance requirements:* For master's, GMAT. Additional exam requirements/recommendations for international students: Required—TOEFL (minimum score 105 iBT). *Application deadline:* For fall admission, 5/1 for domestic and international students. Applications are processed on a rolling basis. Application fee: $100. Electronic applications accepted. *Expenses:* Contact institution. *Financial support:* In 2009–10, 6 research assistantships with partial tuition reimbursements (averaging $1,000 per year) were awarded; scholarships/grants and tuition waivers (partial) also available. Financial award application deadline: 1/15. *Faculty research:* Behavioral accounting, internal control, information systems, supply chain management, financial accounting. *Unit head:* Dr. James A. Largay, Director, 610-758-3409, Fax: 610-758-6429, E-mail: jal3@lehigh.edu. *Application contact:* Corinn McBride, Director of Recruitment and Admissions, 610-758-3418, Fax: 610-758-5283, E-mail: com207@lehigh.edu.

Lehman College of the City University of New York, Division of Natural and Social Sciences, Department of Economics and Accounting, Bronx, NY 10468-1589. Offers accounting (MS). *Entrance requirements:* For master's, GMAT.

Lenoir-Rhyne University, Graduate Programs, Charles M. Snipes School of Business, Hickory, NC 28601. Offers accounting (MBA); entrepreneurship (MBA); global leadership (MBA); leadership development (MBA). *Accreditation:* ACBSP. Part-time and evening/weekend programs available. *Degree requirements:* For master's, capstone course. *Entrance requirements:* For master's, GMAT, minimum undergraduate GPA of 2.7, graduate 3.0. Additional exam requirements/recommendations for international students: Required—TOEFL (minimum score 600 paper-based). Electronic applications accepted. *Expenses:* Contact institution.

Lewis University, College of Business, Graduate School of Management, Program in Business Administration, Romeoville, IL 60446. Offers accounting (MBA); custom elective option (MBA); e-business (MBA); finance (MBA); healthcare management (MBA); human resources management (MBA); information security (MBA); international business (MBA); management information systems (MBA); marketing (MBA); project management (MBA); technology and operations management (MBA). Part-time and evening/weekend programs available. *Faculty:* 15 full-time (2 women), 18 part-time/adjunct (4 women). *Students:* 120 full-time (64 women), 222 part-time (103 women); includes 97 minority (62 African Americans, 4 Asian Americans or Pacific Islanders, 31 Hispanic Americans), 9 international. Average age 31. In 2009, 84 master's awarded. *Entrance requirements:* For master's, interview, bachelor's degree, resume, 2 recommendations. Additional exam requirements/recommendations for international students: Required—TOEFL (minimum score 550 paper-based; 213 computer-based). *Application deadline:* For fall admission, 8/15 priority date for domestic students, 5/1 priority date for international students; for spring admission, 11/15 priority date for international students. Applications are processed on a rolling basis. Application fee: $40. Electronic applications accepted. *Expenses:* Tuition: Full-time $6480; part-time $720 per credit. One-time fee: $40. Tuition and fees vary according to course load, degree level and program. *Financial support:* Career-related internships or fieldwork, Federal Work-Study, scholarships/grants, and unspecified assistantships available. Financial award application deadline: 5/1; financial award applicants required to submit FAFSA. *Unit head:* Dr. Maureen Culleeney, Academic Program Director, 815-838-0500 Ext. 5631, E-mail: culleema@lewisu.edu. *Application contact:* Michele King, Director of Admission, 815-838-0500 Ext. 5384, E-mail: gsm@lewisu.edu.

Lincoln University, School of Graduate Studies and Continuing Education, Jefferson City, MO 65102. Offers business administration (MBA), including accounting, entrepreneurship, management, public administration and policy; educational leadership (Ed S), including elementary leadership, secondary leadership, superintendency; guidance and counseling (M Ed), including community/agency counseling, elementary school, secondary school; history (MA); school administration and supervision (M Ed), including elementary school administration, secondary school administration, special education administration; school teaching (M Ed), including elementary school teaching, secondary school teaching; social science (MA), including history, political science, sociology; sociology (MA); sociology/criminal justice (MA). Part-time and evening/weekend programs available. *Students:* 52 full-time (27 women), 146 part-time (107 women); includes 40 minority (39 African Americans, 1 Asian American or Pacific Islander), 15 international. Average age 35. 76 applicants, 95% accepted, 46 enrolled. In 2009, 60 master's, 6 other advanced degrees awarded. *Degree requirements:* For master's and Ed S, comprehensive exam, thesis optional. *Entrance requirements:* For master's and Ed S, GRE, MAT or GMAT, minimum GPA of 2.75 in major, 2.5 overall; 3 letters of recommendation; minimum C average in English composition; personal statement of purpose. Additional exam requirements/recommendations for international students: Required—TOEFL (minimum score 500 paper-based; 173 computer-based; 61 iBT). *Application deadline:* For fall admission, 7/1 priority date for domestic and international students; for spring admission, 12/1 priority date for domestic and international students. Applications are processed on a rolling basis. Application fee: $20. *Expenses:* Tuition, state resident: full-time $4185; part-time $232.50 per credit hour. Tuition, nonresident: full-time $7767; part-time $431.50 per credit hour. Required fees: $270; $15 per credit hour. $20 per term. *Financial support:* Federal Work-Study and scholarships/grants available. Financial award application deadline: 4/1; financial award applicants required to submit FAFSA. *Faculty research:* Suicide prevention. *Unit head:* Dr. Linda S. Bickel, Dean, 573-681-5247, Fax: 573-681-5106, E-mail: gradschool@lincolnu.edu. *Application contact:* Irasema Steck, Administrative Assistant, 573-681-5247, Fax: 573-681-5106, E-mail: gradschool@lincolnu.edu.

Lindenwood University, Graduate Programs, School of Business and Entrepreneurship, St. Charles, MO 63301-1695. Offers accounting (MBA, MS); business administration (MBA); entrepreneurial studies (MBA, MS); finance (MBA, MS); human resource management (MBA); human resources (MS); international business (MBA, MS); management (MBA, MS); management information systems (MBA, MS); marketing (MBA, MS); public management (MBA, MS); sport management (MA). *Accreditation:* ACBSP. Part-time and evening/weekend programs available. *Faculty:* 20 full-time (8 women), 17 part-time/adjunct (5 women). *Students:* 129 full-time (60 women), 138 part-time (61 women); includes 15 minority (11 African Americans, 2 Asian Americans or Pacific Islanders, 2 Hispanic Americans), 84 international. Average age 28. 149 applicants, 73 enrolled. In 2009, 142 master's awarded. *Degree requirements:* For master's, comprehensive exam (for some programs), thesis (for some programs). *Entrance requirements:* For master's, interview, minimum GPA of 3.0, letter of recommendation. Additional

Accounting

Lindenwood University (continued)

exam requirements/recommendations for international students: Required—TOEFL (minimum score 550 paper-based; 213 computer-based; 80 iBT). *Application deadline:* For fall admission, 7/30 priority date for domestic students, 9/16 priority date for international students; for winter admission, 12/19 priority date for domestic students, 12/17 priority date for international students; for spring admission, 2/25 priority date for domestic students, 2/11 priority date for international students. Applications are processed on a rolling basis. Application fee: $30 ($100 for international students). Electronic applications accepted. *Expenses:* Tuition: Full-time $12,960; part-time $370 per credit hour. Required fees: $340. One-time fee: $30 full-time. Tuition and fees vary according to course level and course load. *Financial support:* In 2009–10, 209 students received support. Career-related internships or fieldwork, Federal Work-Study, institutionally sponsored loans, and tuition waivers (partial) available. Financial award application deadline: 6/30; financial award applicants required to submit FAFSA. *Unit head:* Ed Morris, Dean of Management, 636-949-4832, E-mail: emorris@lindenwood.edu. *Application contact:* Brett Barger, Dean of Evening Admissions and Extension Campuses, 636-949-4934, Fax: 636-949-4109, E-mail: adultadmissions@lindenwood.edu.

Lipscomb University, MBA Program, Nashville, TN 37204-3951. Offers accounting (MBA); business administration (general) (MBA); conflict management (MBA); financial services (MBA); healthcare management (MBA); leadership (MBA); nonprofit management (MBA); sports administration (MBA); sustainable practice (MBA). *Accreditation:* ACBSP. Part-time and evening/weekend programs available. *Faculty:* 10 full-time (1 woman), 7 part-time/adjunct (2 women). *Students:* 43 full-time (23 women), 86 part-time (38 women); includes 23 minority (18 African Americans, 1 Asian American or Pacific Islander, 4 Hispanic Americans), 1 international. Average age 31. 95 applicants, 64% accepted, 35 enrolled. In 2009, 59 master's awarded. *Entrance requirements:* For master's, GMAT, interview, 2 references, resume. Additional exam requirements/recommendations for international students: Required—TOEFL (minimum score 570 paper-based; 230 computer-based). *Application deadline:* For fall admission, 2/1 for international students; for winter admission, 6/1 for international students. Applications are processed on a rolling basis. Application fee: $50 ($75 for international students). Electronic applications accepted. *Expenses:* Contact institution. *Financial support:* Career-related internships or fieldwork, Federal Work-Study, scholarships/grants, tuition waivers (partial), and unspecified assistantships available. Support available to part-time students. Financial award application deadline: 7/1; financial award applicants required to submit FAFSA. *Faculty research:* Impact of spirituality on organization commitment, leadership, psychological empowerment, training. *Unit head:* Dr. Mike Kendrick, Interim Chair of Graduate Business Studies, 615-966-1833, Fax: 615-966-1818, E-mail: mikekendrick@lipscomb.edu. *Application contact:* Emily Landsdell, 615-966-5284, E-mail: emily.lansdell@lipscomb.edu.

Lipscomb University, Program in Accountancy, Nashville, TN 37204-3951. Offers M Acc. Part-time and evening/weekend programs available. *Degree requirements:* For master's, internship. *Entrance requirements:* For master's, GMAT, 2 references, interview. Application fee: $50 ($75 for international students). *Expenses:* Contact institution. *Financial support:* Career-related internships or fieldwork, Federal Work-Study, scholarships/grants, and tuition waivers available. Support available to part-time students. Financial award application deadline: 7/1. *Faculty research:* Internal auditing, ethics and fraud. *Unit head:* Dr. Perry Moore, Director, 615-966-5795, Fax: 615-966-1818, E-mail: perry.moore@lipscomb.edu. *Application contact:* Emily B. Lansdell, Graduate Business Program Assistant, 615-966-5284, Fax: 615-966-1818, E-mail: emily.lansdell@lipscomb.edu.

Long Island University, Brooklyn Campus, School of Business, Public Administration and Information Sciences, Program in Accountancy, Taxation and Law, Brooklyn, NY 11201-8423. Offers accounting (MS); taxation (MS). Part-time and evening/weekend programs available. *Entrance requirements:* For master's, GMAT or GRE General Test, 2 letters of recommendation. Additional exam requirements/recommendations for international students: Required—TOEFL (minimum score 500 paper-based; 173 computer-based). Electronic applications accepted.

Long Island University, C.W. Post Campus, College of Management, School of Business, Brookville, NY 11548-1300. Offers accounting and taxation (Certificate); business administration (Certificate); finance (MBA, Certificate); general business administration (MBA); international business (MBA, Certificate); management (MBA, Certificate); management information systems (MBA, Certificate); marketing (MBA, Certificate). *Accreditation:* AACSB. Part-time and evening/weekend programs available. *Entrance requirements:* For master's, GMAT, resume, minimum GPA of 3.0, 2 letters of recommendation. Additional exam requirements/recommendations for international students: Required—TOEFL (minimum score 527 paper-based; 197 computer-based). Electronic applications accepted. *Faculty research:* Financial markets, consumer behavior.

Long Island University, C.W. Post Campus, College of Management, School of Professional Accountancy, Brookville, NY 11548-1300. Offers accounting (MS); taxation (MS). Part-time and evening/weekend programs available. *Entrance requirements:* For master's, GMAT, minimum GPA of 2.5, BS in accounting from accredited college or university. Electronic applications accepted. *Faculty research:* International taxation.

Louisiana State University and Agricultural and Mechanical College, Graduate School, E. J. Ourso College of Business, Department of Accounting, Baton Rouge, LA 70803. Offers MS, PhD. *Faculty:* 11 full-time (4 women). *Students:* 60 full-time (30 women), 9 part-time (6 women); includes 4 minority (1 African American, 2 Asian Americans or Pacific Islanders, 1 Hispanic American), 13 international. Average age 26. 91 applicants, 54% accepted, 31 enrolled. In 2009, 52 master's, 1 doctorate awarded. *Degree requirements:* For doctorate, thesis/dissertation. *Entrance requirements:* For master's, GMAT, minimum GPA of 3.2; for doctorate, GMAT, minimum GPA of 3.4. Additional exam requirements/recommendations for international students: Required—TOEFL (minimum score 550 paper-based; 213 computer-based; 79 iBT) or IELTS (minimum score 6.5). *Application deadline:* For fall admission, 1/25 priority date for domestic students, 5/15 for international students; for spring admission, 10/15 for international students. Applications are processed on a rolling basis. Application fee: $50 ($70 for international students). Electronic applications accepted. *Financial support:* In 2009–10, 39 students received support, including 4 research assistantships with full and partial tuition reimbursements available (averaging $17,000 per year), 20 teaching assistantships with full and partial tuition reimbursements available (averaging $9,249 per year); fellowships, Federal Work-Study, scholarships/grants, health care benefits, tuition waivers (full and partial), and unspecified assistantships also available. Support available to part-time students. Financial award application deadline: 4/15; financial award applicants required to submit FAFSA. *Faculty research:* Financial accounting, auditing fraud. Total annual research expenditures: $19,042. *Unit head:* Dr. Sam Tiras, Chair, 225-578-6202, Fax: 225-578-6201, E-mail: tiras@lsu.edu. *Application contact:* Dr. Jacquelyn Moffit, MS Program Advisor, 225-578-6211, Fax: 225-578-6201, E-mail: jsmoff22@lsu.edu.

Louisiana Tech University, Graduate School, College of Business, School of Professional Accountancy, Ruston, LA 71272. Offers MBA, MPA, DBA. *Accreditation:* AACSB. Part-time programs available. *Degree requirements:* For doctorate, thesis/dissertation. *Entrance requirements:* For master's and doctorate, GMAT.

Loyola University Chicago, Graduate School of Business, Accountancy Department, Chicago, IL 60660. Offers MS, MSA. *Accreditation:* AACSB. Part-time and evening/weekend programs available. *Entrance requirements:* For master's, GMAT, letters of recommendation. Additional exam requirements/recommendations for international students: Required—TOEFL (minimum score 550 paper-based; 213 computer-based; 80 iBT). Electronic applications accepted. *Expenses:* Tuition: Full-time $14,220; part-time $790 per credit hour. Required fees: $60 per semester hour. Tuition and fees vary according to program. *Faculty research:* Financial disclosure, web-based accounting issues, activities-based costing.

Loyola University Maryland, Graduate Programs, Sellinger School of Business and Management, Program in Business Administration, Baltimore, MD 21210-2699. Offers accounting (MBA); finance (MBA); general business (MBA); international business (MBA); management (MBA); management information systems (MBA); marketing (MBA). *Accreditation:* AACSB. Part-time and evening/weekend programs available. *Entrance requirements:* For master's, GMAT. Additional exam requirements/recommendations for international students: Required—TOEFL (minimum score 550 paper-based; 213 computer-based).

Maharishi University of Management, Graduate Studies, Program in Business Administration, Fairfield, IA 52557. Offers accounting (MBA); business administration (PhD); sustainability (MBA). Evening/weekend programs available. Postbaccalaureate distance learning degree programs offered (minimal on-campus study). *Degree requirements:* For doctorate, thesis/dissertation. *Entrance requirements:* For master's, GMAT, minimum GPA of 3.0; for doctorate, minimum GPA of 3.0. Additional exam requirements/recommendations for international students: Required—TOEFL. *Faculty research:* Leadership, effects of the group dynamics of consciousness on the economy, innovation, employee development, cooperative strategy.

Marquette University, Graduate School of Management, Program in Accounting, Milwaukee, WI 53201-1881. Offers MSA. *Accreditation:* AACSB. *Faculty:* 10 full-time (3 women), 5 part-time/adjunct (0 women). *Students:* 21 full-time (12 women), 5 part-time (3 women); includes 1 minority (Asian American or Pacific Islander), 14 international. Average age 25. 49 applicants, 84% accepted, 17 enrolled. In 2009, 20 master's awarded. *Entrance requirements:* For master's, GMAT. Application fee: $40. *Unit head:* Dr. Michael Akers, Chair, 414-288-1453. *Application contact:* James Trebby, Information Contact, 414-288-7344.

Maryville University of Saint Louis, The John E. Simon School of Business, St. Louis, MO 63141-7299. Offers accounting (MBA, PGC); business studies (PGC); internet marketing (MBA, PGC); management (MBA, PGC); marketing (MBA, PGC). *Accreditation:* ACBSP. Part-time and evening/weekend programs available. *Students:* 17 full-time (9 women), 133 part-time (70 women); includes 14 minority (6 African Americans, 1 American Indian/Alaska Native, 3 Asian Americans or Pacific Islanders, 4 Hispanic Americans), 4 international. Average age 30. In 2009, 68 master's awarded. *Entrance requirements:* For master's, GMAT (unless applicant possesses undergraduate business degree with minimum cumulative GPA of 3.0, or has completed master's degree from accredited university, or has completed one early access course prior to undergraduate degree). Additional exam requirements/recommendations for international students: Required—TOEFL (minimum score 550 paper-based). *Application deadline:* Applications are processed on a rolling basis. Application fee: $40 ($60 for international students). Electronic applications accepted. *Expenses:* Tuition: Full-time $20,384; part-time $627.50 per credit hour. Required fees: $100 per semester. *Financial support:* Career-related internships or fieldwork, Federal Work-Study, tuition waivers (partial), and campus employment available. Financial award application deadline: 3/1; financial award applicants required to submit FAFSA. *Faculty research:* International business, e-marketing, strategic planning, interpersonal management skills, financial analysis. *Unit head:* Dr. Pamela Horwitz, Dean, 314-529-9418, Fax: 314-529-9975, E-mail: horwitz@maryville.edu. *Application contact:* Kathy Dougherty, Director of MBA Admissions and Enrollment, 314-529-9382, Fax: 314-529-9975, E-mail: business@maryville.edu.

McGill University, Faculty of Graduate and Postdoctoral Studies, Desautels Faculty of Management, Montréal, QC H3A 2T5, Canada. Offers administration (PhD); entrepreneurial studies (MBA); finance (MBA); general management (Post Master's Certificate); information systems (MBA); international business (exchange program) (MBA); international Master's program in practicing management (MM); management (MBA); management for development (MBA); manufacturing management (MMM); marketing (MBA); operations management (MBA); public accountancy (Diploma); strategic management (MBA); MBA/LL B; MD/MBA.

McNeese State University, Doré School of Graduate Studies, College of Business, Master of Business Administration Program, Lake Charles, LA 70609. Offers accounting (MBA). *Accreditation:* AACSB. Evening/weekend programs available. *Faculty:* 15 full-time (1 woman). *Students:* 68 full-time (29 women), 37 part-time (18 women); includes 6 minority (3 African Americans, 2 Asian Americans or Pacific Islanders, 1 Hispanic American), 35 international. In 2009, 35 master's awarded. *Degree requirements:* For master's, written exam. *Entrance requirements:* For master's, GMAT. *Application deadline:* For fall admission, 5/15 priority date for domestic and international students; for spring admission, 10/15 priority date for domestic and international students. Applications are processed on a rolling basis. Application fee: $20 ($30 for international students). *Expenses:* Tuition, area resident: Full-time $2556. Tuition, state resident: full-time $2556. Required fees: $1031. Tuition and fees vary according to course load. *Financial support:* Research assistantships, teaching assistantships, Federal Work-Study available. Support available to part-time students. Financial award application deadline: 5/1. *Faculty research:* Management development, integrating technology into the work force, union/management relations, economic development. *Unit head:* Dr. Akm Rahman, MBA Director, 337-475-5573, Fax: 337-475-5010, E-mail: mrahman@mcneese.edu. *Application contact:* Dr. Akm Rahman, MBA Director, 337-475-5573, Fax: 337-475-5010, E-mail: mrahman@mcneese.edu.

Mercy College, School of Business, Program in Public Accounting, Dobbs Ferry, NY 10522-1189. Offers MS. Part-time and evening/weekend programs available. *Students:* 15 part-time (10 women); includes 4 African Americans, 1 Asian American or Pacific Islander, 3 Hispanic Americans. Average age 34. 22 applicants, 32% accepted, 6 enrolled. In 2009, 12 master's awarded. *Entrance requirements:* For master's, GMAT, two page written professional goals statement, resume, two letters of reference, interview, undergraduate transcripts. Additional exam requirements/recommendations for international students: Required—TOEFL (minimum score 600 paper-based; 250 computer-based; 100 iBT). *Application deadline:* For fall admission, 8/1 for international students. Applications are processed on a rolling basis. Application fee: $40. Electronic applications accepted. *Expenses:* Contact institution. *Financial support:* Career-related internships or fieldwork, Federal Work-Study, scholarships/grants, and unspecified assistantships available. Support available to part-time students. Financial award applicants required to submit FAFSA. *Faculty research:* Auditing, taxation, financial statements. *Unit head:* Lucretia Mann, Director, Accounting Program, 914-674-7492, E-mail: accountinginfo@mercy.edu. *Application contact:* Valerie Peattie, Administrative Assistant, 914-674-7492, E-mail: vpeattie@mercy.edu.

Miami University, Graduate School, Farmer School of Business, Department of Accountancy, Oxford, OH 45056. Offers M Acc. *Accreditation:* AACSB. *Students:* 34 full-time (13 women); includes 1 minority (Asian American or Pacific Islander), 7 international. *Entrance requirements:* For master's, GMAT, minimum cumulative undergraduate GPA of 3.0. Additional exam requirements/recommendations for international students: Required—TOEFL. *Application deadline:* For fall admission, 1/1 for domestic students, 11/1 for international students. Application fee: $50. *Expenses:* Tuition, state resident: full-time $11,280. Tuition, nonresident: full-time $24,912. Required fees: $516. *Financial support:* Fellowships with full tuition reimbursements, research assistantships, Federal Work-Study, health care benefits, tuition waivers (full), and unspecified assistantships available. Financial award application deadline: 3/1; financial award applicants required to submit FAFSA. *Unit head:* Marc Rubin, Chair, 513-529-6200, Fax: 513-529-4740, E-mail: rubinma@muohio.edu. *Application contact:* Gretchen Radler, Academic Program Director, 513-529-3372, E-mail: miamiacc@muohio.edu.

Michigan State University, The Graduate School, Eli Broad Graduate School of Management, Department of Accounting and Information Systems, East Lansing, MI 48824. Offers accounting (MS); business administration (PhD). *Accreditation:* AACSB. *Faculty:* 27 full-time (10 women). *Students:* 175 full-time (69 women), 12 part-time (7 women); includes 16 minority (4 African Americans, 1 American Indian/Alaska Native, 8 Asian Americans or Pacific Islanders, 3 Hispanic Americans), 39 international. Average age 24. 472 applicants, 26% accepted. In 2009, 143 master's, 2 doctorates awarded. *Entrance requirements:* Additional exam requirements/recommendations for international students: Required—TOEFL. *Application deadline:* Applications are processed on a rolling basis. Electronic applications accepted. *Expenses:* Tuition, state resident: part-time $478.25 per credit hour. Tuition, nonresident: part-time $966.50 per credit hour. Part-time tuition and fees vary according to program. *Financial support:* In 2009–10, 11 research assistantships with tuition reimbursements (averaging $6,274 per year), 20 teaching assistantships with tuition reimbursements (averaging $5,920

per year) were awarded. Total annual research expenditures: $414,022. *Unit head:* Dr. Sanjay Gupta, Chairperson, 517-355-3388, Fax: 517-432-1101, E-mail: gupta@bus.msu.edu. *Application contact:* Program Information, 517-355-7486, Fax: 517-432-1101, E-mail: acct@bus.msu.edu.

Middle Tennessee State University, College of Graduate Studies, Jennings A. Jones College of Business, Department of Accounting, Murfreesboro, TN 37132. Offers MS. *Accreditation:* AACSB. Part-time and evening/weekend programs available. Postbaccalaureate distance learning degree programs offered. *Faculty:* 11 full-time (4 women). *Students:* 20 full-time (9 women), 87 part-time (42 women); includes 28 minority (6 African Americans, 19 Asian Americans or Pacific Islanders, 3 Hispanic Americans). Average age 27. 41 applicants, 78% accepted, 32 enrolled. In 2009, 25 master's awarded. *Entrance requirements:* Additional exam requirements/recommendations for international students: Required—TOEFL (minimum score 525 paper-based; 195 computer-based; 71 iBT) or IELTS (minimum score 6). *Application deadline:* For fall admission, 6/1 for domestic and international students. Applications are processed on a rolling basis. Application fee: $25 ($30 for international students). Electronic applications accepted. *Expenses:* Tuition, state resident: full-time $4404. Tuition, nonresident: full-time $10,956. *Financial support:* In 2009–10, 10 students received support. Institutionally sponsored loans available. Support available to part-time students. Financial award application deadline: 5/1; financial award applicants required to submit FAFSA. *Unit head:* G. Robert Smith, Interim Chair, 615-898-2558, Fax: 615-898-5045, E-mail: smitty@mtsu.edu. *Application contact:* Dr. Michael Allen, Dean and Vice Provost for Research, 615-898-2840, Fax: 615-904-8020, E-mail: mallen@mtsu.edu.

Millsaps College, Else School of Management, Jackson, MS 39210-0001. Offers accounting (M Acc); business administration (MBA). *Accreditation:* AACSB. Part-time programs available. *Entrance requirements:* For master's, GMAT. Additional exam requirements/recommendations for international students: Required—TOEFL. Electronic applications accepted. *Faculty research:* Ethics, audit independence, satisfaction with assurance services, political business cycles.

Mississippi College, Graduate School, School of Business, Clinton, MS 39058. Offers accounting (Certificate); business administration (MBA), including accounting; business education (M Ed); finance (MBA, Certificate); JD/MBA. *Accreditation:* ACBSP. Part-time and evening/weekend programs available. *Faculty:* 12 full-time (2 women), 5 part-time/adjunct (1 woman). *Students:* 101 full-time (41 women), 144 part-time (75 women); includes 41 minority (37 African Americans, 3 Asian Americans or Pacific Islanders, 1 Hispanic American), 78 international. Average age 28. In 2009, 90 master's awarded. *Degree requirements:* For master's, comprehensive exam, thesis optional. *Entrance requirements:* For master's, GMAT, minimum GPA of 2.5, 24 hours of undergraduate course work in business. Additional exam requirements/recommendations for international students: Recommended—IELTS. *Application deadline:* For fall admission, 8/15 priority date for domestic students. Applications are processed on a rolling basis. Application fee: $30. Electronic applications accepted. *Expenses:* Tuition: Part-time $452 per credit hour. Required fees: $101 per semester. Tuition and fees vary according to degree level, campus/location, program and student level. *Financial support:* Federal Work-Study and unspecified assistantships available. Support available to part-time students. Financial award application deadline: 4/1; financial award applicants required to submit FAFSA. *Unit head:* Dr. Marcelo Eduardo, Dean, 601-925-3420, E-mail: eduardo@mc.edu. *Application contact:* Elnora Lewis, Secretary, 601-925-3225, Fax: 601-925-3889, E-mail: lewis09@mc.edu.

Mississippi State University, College of Business, School of Accountancy, Mississippi State, MS 39762. Offers accounting (MPA), including accounting (MPA, PhD); systems; business administration (PhD), including accounting (MPA, PhD); taxation (MTX). *Accreditation:* AACSB. *Faculty:* 8 full-time (3 women). *Students:* 41 full-time (23 women), 10 part-time (8 women); includes 5 minority (all Asian Americans or Pacific Islanders), 3 international. Average age 26. 56 applicants, 45% accepted, 20 enrolled. In 2009, 41 master's awarded. *Degree requirements:* For master's, comprehensive exam. *Entrance requirements:* For master's, GMAT (minimum score of 510), minimum GPA of 2.75 overall and in upper-level accounting, 3.0 in last 60 hours of course work; for doctorate, GMAT, minimum undergraduate GPA of 3.0, both cumulative and over the last 60 hours of undergraduate work; 3.25 on all prior graduate work. Additional exam requirements/recommendations for international students: Required—TOEFL (minimum score 575 paper-based; 233 computer-based; 84 iBT); Recommended—IELTS (minimum score 7). *Application deadline:* For fall admission, 7/1 for domestic students, 5/1 for international students; for spring admission, 11/1 for domestic students, 9/1 for international students. Applications are processed on a rolling basis. Application fee: $40. Electronic applications accepted. *Expenses:* Tuition, state resident: full-time $2575.50; part-time $286.25 per credit hour. Tuition, nonresident: full-time $6510; part-time $723.50 per credit hour. Tuition and fees vary according to course load. *Financial support:* Career-related internships or fieldwork, Federal Work-Study, institutionally sponsored loans, scholarships/grants, and unspecified assistantships available. Support available to part-time students. Financial award applicants required to submit FAFSA. *Faculty research:* Income tax, financial accounting system, managerial accounting, auditing. *Unit head:* Dr. Louis Dawkins, Director, 662-325-1633, E-mail: ldawkins@cobilan.msstate.edu. *Application contact:* Dr. Barbara Spencer, Graduate Coordinator, 662-325-3710, Fax: 662-325-1646, E-mail: sac@cobilan.msstate.edu.

Missouri State University, Graduate College, College of Business Administration, School of Accountancy, Springfield, MO 65897. Offers M Acc. *Accreditation:* AACSB. Part-time and evening/weekend programs available. *Faculty:* 18 full-time (3 women). *Students:* 78 full-time (42 women), 34 part-time (23 women); includes 7 minority (1 African American, 1 American Indian/Alaska Native, 4 Asian Americans or Pacific Islanders, 1 Hispanic American), 23 international. Average age 28. 51 applicants, 76% accepted, 31 enrolled. In 2009, 53 master's awarded. *Entrance requirements:* For master's, GMAT, minimum GPA of 2.75. Additional exam requirements/recommendations for international students: Required—TOEFL (minimum score 550 paper-based; 213 computer-based; 79 iBT). *Application deadline:* For fall admission, 7/20 priority date for domestic students, 5/1 for international students; for spring admission, 12/20 priority date for domestic students, 9/1 for international students. Applications are processed on a rolling basis. Application fee: $35 ($50 for international students). Electronic applications accepted. *Expenses:* Tuition, state resident: full-time $3852; part-time $214 per credit hour. Tuition, nonresident: full-time $7524; part-time $418 per credit hour. Required fees: $696; $172 per semester. Tuition and fees vary according to course level, course load, degree level and program. *Financial support:* Career-related internships or fieldwork, Federal Work-Study, institutionally sponsored loans, scholarships/grants, tuition waivers (partial), and unspecified assistantships available. Support available to part-time students. Financial award application deadline: 3/31; financial award applicants required to submit FAFSA. *Faculty research:* Forensic accounting, international accounting standards, accounting education, tax compliance. *Unit head:* Dr. John R. Williams, Director, 417-836-5414, Fax: 417-836-6337, E-mail: accountancy@missouristate.edu. *Application contact:* Eric Eckert, Coordinator for Graduate Admissions and Recruitment, 417-836-5331, Fax: 417-836-6200, E-mail: ericeckert@missouristate.edu.

Molloy College, Graduate Business Program, Rockville Centre, NY 11571-5002. Offers accounting (MBA); accounting and management (MBA); management (MBA); personal financial planning and accounting (MBA); personal financial planning and management (MBA). Part-time programs available. *Faculty:* 5 full-time (0 women), 8 part-time/adjunct (2 women). *Students:* 26 full-time (12 women), 60 part-time (33 women); includes 30 minority (12 African Americans, 4 Asian Americans or Pacific Islanders, 14 Hispanic Americans), 2 international. Average age 33. In 2009, 21 master's awarded. *Application deadline:* Applications are processed on a rolling basis. *Expenses:* Tuition: Part-time $765 per credit. Required fees: $340 per semester. *Unit head:* Dr. Raymond Manganelli, Associate Dean and Director of Graduate Programs, 516-678-5000 Ext. 6905, E-mail: rmanganelli@molloy.edu. *Application contact:* Alina Haitz, Assistant Director of Graduate Admissions, 516-678-5000 Ext. 6399, Fax: 516-256-2247, E-mail: ahaitz@molloy.edu.

Monmouth University, Graduate School, Leon Hess Business School, West Long Branch, NJ 07764-1898. Offers accounting (Post-Master's Certificate); healthcare management (MBA, Post-Master's Certificate). *Accreditation:* AACSB. Part-time and evening/weekend programs available. *Faculty:* 31 full-time (10 women), 4 part-time/adjunct (0 women). *Students:* 81 full-time (24 women), 153 part-time (63 women); includes 19 minority (7 African Americans, 6 Asian Americans or Pacific Islanders, 6 Hispanic Americans), 18 international. Average age 29. 183 applicants, 76% accepted, 80 enrolled. In 2009, 70 master's awarded. *Degree requirements:* For master's, capstone course. *Entrance requirements:* For master's, GMAT, minimum GPA of 3.0 in major, 2.75 overall. Additional exam requirements/recommendations for international students: Required—TOEFL (minimum score 550 paper-based; 213 computer-based; 79 iBT), IELTS (minimum score 5), Michigan English Language Assessment Battery (minimum score 77), Cambridge A, B, C. *Application deadline:* For fall admission, 7/15 priority date for domestic students, 6/1 for international students; for spring admission, 11/15 priority date for domestic students, 11/1 for international students. Applications are processed on a rolling basis. Application fee: $50. Electronic applications accepted. *Expenses:* Tuition: Part-time $773 per credit. Required fees: $157 per semester. *Financial support:* In 2009–10, 154 students received support, including 128 fellowships (averaging $1,796 per year), 19 research assistantships (averaging $8,633 per year); career-related internships or fieldwork, scholarships/grants, and unspecified assistantships also available. Support available to part-time students. Financial award applicants required to submit FAFSA. *Faculty research:* Information technology and marketing, behavioral research in accounting, human resources, management of technology. *Unit head:* Donald Smith, Program Director, 732-571-7536, Fax: 732-263-5517, E-mail: dsmith@monmouth.edu. *Application contact:* Kevin Roane, Director, Office of Graduate Admission, 732-571-3452, Fax: 732-263-5123, E-mail: gradadm@monmouth.edu.

Montana State University, College of Graduate Studies, College of Business, Bozeman, MT 59717. Offers professional accountancy (MP Ac). *Accreditation:* AACSB. Part-time programs available. *Faculty:* 28 full-time (11 women), 25 part-time/adjunct (10 women). *Students:* 42 full-time (26 women), 6 part-time (3 women), 1 international. Average age 24. 21 applicants. In 2009, 43 master's awarded. *Degree requirements:* For master's, comprehensive exam. *Entrance requirements:* For master's, GRE General Test, GMAT. Additional exam requirements/recommendations for international students: Required—TOEFL (minimum score 550 paper-based; 213 computer-based). *Application deadline:* For fall admission, 7/15 priority date for domestic students, 5/15 priority date for international students; for spring admission, 12/1 priority date for domestic students, 10/1 priority date for international students. Applications are processed on a rolling basis. Application fee: $30. Electronic applications accepted. *Expenses:* Tuition, state resident: full-time $5635; part-time $3492 per year. Tuition, nonresident: full-time $17,212; part-time $7865.10 per year. Required fees: $1441; $153.15 per credit. Tuition and fees vary according to course load and program. *Financial support:* In 2009–10, 6 students received support, including 6 teaching assistantships with partial tuition reimbursements available (averaging $1,900 per year). Financial award application deadline: 3/1; financial award applicants required to submit FAFSA. *Faculty research:* Tax research, accounting education, fraud issues, CPA exams. Total annual research expenditures: $74,599. *Unit head:* Dr. Dan Moshavi, Dean, 406-994-4423, Fax: 406-994-6206, E-mail: dmoshavi@montana.edu. *Application contact:* Dr. Carl A. Fox, Vice Provost for Graduate Education, 406-994-4145, Fax: 406-994-7433, E-mail: gradstudy@montana.edu.

Montclair State University, The Graduate School, School of Business, Department of Accounting, Law and Taxation, Montclair, NJ 07043-1624. Offers accounting (MBA, Certificate); finance (Certificate); management information systems (Certificate); marketing (Certificate). Part-time and evening/weekend programs available. *Faculty:* 15 full-time (5 women), 11 part-time/adjunct (9 women). *Students:* 44 full-time (23 women), 94 part-time (40 women). Average age 30. 81 applicants, 56% accepted, 29 enrolled. In 2009, 31 master's, 1 other advanced degree awarded. *Entrance requirements:* For master's, GMAT, 2 letters of recommendation, resume. Additional exam requirements/recommendations for international students: Required—TOEFL (minimum score 83 computer-based), or IELTS. *Application deadline:* For fall admission, 6/1 for international students; for spring admission, 10/1 for international students. Applications are processed on a rolling basis. Application fee: $60. Electronic applications accepted. *Expenses:* Tuition, area resident: Part-time $486.74 per credit. Tuition, state resident: part-time $486.74 per credit. Tuition, nonresident: part-time $751.34 per credit. Tuition and fees vary according to degree level and program. *Financial support:* In 2009–10, 2 research assistantships with full tuition reimbursements (averaging $7,000 per year) were awarded; Federal Work-Study and scholarships/grants also available. Support available to part-time students. Financial award application deadline: 3/1; financial award applicants required to submit FAFSA. *Unit head:* Prof. Frank Aquilino, Head, 973-655-4174. *Application contact:* Amy Aiello, Director of Graduate Admissions and Operations, 973-655-5147; Fax: 973-655-7869, E-mail: graduate.school@montclair.edu.

Murray State University, College of Business and Public Affairs, Master of Professional Accountancy (MPAC) Program, Murray, KY 42071. Offers MPAC. Part-time programs available. *Degree requirements:* For master's, thesis. *Entrance requirements:* For master's, GMAT or GRE. Additional exam requirements/recommendations for international students: Required—TOEFL (minimum score 525 paper-based; 197 computer-based). *Faculty research:* Corporate governance, information systems innovations, public finances, accounting education.

National University, Academic Affairs, School of Business and Management, Department of Accounting and Finance, La Jolla, CA 92037-1011. Offers accountancy (MS); corporate and international finance (MS). Part-time and evening/weekend programs available. Postbaccalaureate distance learning degree programs offered (no on-campus study). *Faculty:* 8 full-time (1 woman), 37 part-time/adjunct (10 women). *Students:* 67 full-time (32 women), 68 part-time (27 women); includes 41 minority (10 African Americans, 2 American Indian/Alaska Native, 13 Asian Americans or Pacific Islanders, 16 Hispanic Americans), 23 international. Average age 33. 145 applicants, 100% accepted, 75 enrolled. In 2009, 14 master's awarded. *Degree requirements:* For master's, thesis. *Entrance requirements:* For master's, interview, minimum GPA of 2.5. Additional exam requirements/recommendations for international students: Required—TOEFL (minimum score 550 paper-based; 213 computer-based; 79 iBT), IELTS (minimum score 6). *Application deadline:* Applications are processed on a rolling basis. Application fee: $60 ($65 for international students). Electronic applications accepted. *Expenses:* Tuition: Part-time $338 per quarter hour. *Financial support:* Career-related internships or fieldwork, institutionally sponsored loans, scholarships/grants, and tuition waivers (partial) available. Support available to part-time students. Financial award application deadline: 6/30; financial award applicants required to submit FAFSA. *Unit head:* Prof. Donald A. Schwartz, Chair and Associate Professor, 858-642-8420, Fax: 858-642-8740, E-mail: dschwartz@nu.edu. *Application contact:* Dominick Giovanniello, Associate Regional Dean—San Diego, 800-NAT-UNIV, Fax: 858-541-7792, E-mail: dgiovann@nu.edu.

New England College, Program in Management, Henniker, NH 03242-3293. Offers accounting (MSA); healthcare administration (MS); international relations (MA); marketing management (MS); nonprofit leadership (MS); project management (MS); strategic leadership (MS). Part-time and evening/weekend programs available. *Degree requirements:* For master's, independent research project. Electronic applications accepted.

New Jersey City University, Graduate Studies and Continuing Education, College of Professional Studies, Department of Business Administration, Program in Accounting, Jersey City, NJ 07305-1597. Offers MS. Part-time and evening/weekend programs available. *Students:* 15 full-time (11 women), 20 part-time (11 women); includes 13 minority (3 African Americans, 9 Asian Americans or Pacific Islanders, 1 Hispanic American), 5 international. In 2009, 10 master's awarded. *Entrance requirements:* Additional exam requirements/recommendations for international students: Required—TOEFL. *Expenses:* Tuition, area resident: Part-time $456.75 per credit. Tuition, nonresident: part-time $842.55 per credit. Required fees: $65 per term. *Unit head:* Robert J. Matthews, Graduate Coordinator, 201-200-3353, E-mail: rmatthews@njcu.edu. *Application contact:* Robert J. Matthews, Graduate Coordinator, 201-200-3353, E-mail: rmatthews@njcu.edu.

New Mexico State University, Graduate School, College of Business, Department of Accounting and Information Systems, Las Cruces, NM 88003-8001. Offers M Acct. *Accreditation:* AACSB. Part-time programs available. *Faculty:* 9 full-time (2 women). *Students:* 28 full-time (20 women), 12 part-time (10 women); includes 15 minority (1 Asian American or Pacific Islander, 14

Accounting

New Mexico State University (continued)

Hispanic Americans), 8 international. Average age 30. 44 applicants, 93% accepted, 27 enrolled. In 2009, 28 master's awarded. *Degree requirements:* For master's, comprehensive exam, thesis optional. *Entrance requirements:* For master's, GMAT, minimum undergraduate accounting GPA of 2.85 (upper division). Additional exam requirements/recommendations for international students: Required—TOEFL (minimum score 530 paper-based; 197 computer-based). *Application deadline:* For fall admission, 7/1 priority date for domestic students; for spring admission, 11/1 priority date for domestic students. Applications are processed on a rolling basis. Application fee: $30 ($50 for international students). Electronic applications accepted. *Expenses:* Tuition, state resident: full-time $4080; part-time $223 per credit. Tuition, nonresident: full-time $14,256; part-time $647 per credit. Required fees: $1278; $639 per semester. *Financial support:* In 2009–10, 4 research assistantships (averaging $6,912 per year), 14 teaching assistantships (averaging $5,078 per year) were awarded; career-related internships or fieldwork, Federal Work-Study, and health care benefits also available. Support available to part-time students. Financial award application deadline: 3/1. *Faculty research:* Taxation, financial accounting, managerial accounting, accounting systems, accounting education. *Unit head:* Dr. Ed Scribner, Department Head, 575-646-4901, Fax: 575-646-1552, E-mail: escribne@nmsu.edu. *Application contact:* Dr. Cindy L. Seipel, Director, 575-646-5206, Fax: 575-646-1552, E-mail: cseipel@nmsu.edu.

New York Institute of Technology, Graduate Division, School of Management, Program in Business Administration, Old Westbury, NY 11568-8000. Offers accounting (Advanced Certificate); business administration (MBA); finance (Advanced Certificate); international business (Advanced Certificate); management of information systems (Advanced Certificate); marketing (Advanced Certificate). Part-time and evening/weekend programs available. *Students:* 599 full-time (262 women), 528 part-time (200 women); includes 51 minority (17 African Americans, 24 Asian Americans or Pacific Islanders, 10 Hispanic Americans), 324 international. Average age 29. In 2009, 691 master's, 7 other advanced degrees awarded. *Degree requirements:* For master's, thesis (for some programs). *Entrance requirements:* For master's, minimum QPA of 2.85. Additional exam requirements/recommendations for international students: Required—TOEFL (minimum score 550 paper-based; 213 computer-based). *Application deadline:* For fall admission, 7/1 priority date for domestic students; for spring admission, 12/1 priority date for domestic students. Applications are processed on a rolling basis. Application fee: $50. Electronic applications accepted. *Expenses:* Tuition: Part-time $825 per credit. *Financial support:* Fellowships, research assistantships with partial tuition reimbursements, institutionally sponsored loans, tuition waivers (full and partial), and unspecified assistantships available. Support available to part-time students. Financial award applicants required to submit FAFSA. *Faculty research:* Instructor performance appraisal; relationship between TOEFL, GMAT, GRE, and performance in foreign students. *Unit head:* Dr. Diamando Afxentiou, Acting Associate Dean, 516-686-3937, Fax: 516-686-7430, E-mail: dafxenti@nyit.edu. *Application contact:* Dr. Jacquelyn Nealon, Vice President for Enrollment Services, 516-686-7925, Fax: 516-686-7597, E-mail: jnealon@nyit.edu.

New York University, Leonard N. Stern School of Business, Department of Accounting, New York, NY 10012-1019. Offers MBA, PhD. *Expenses:* Tuition: Full-time $30,528; part-time $1272 per credit. Required fees: $2177. *Faculty research:* Earnings management and financial analysis effectiveness and accounting policy, value-relevance of financial reporting, intangibles-related reporting and analysis, equity.

North Carolina State University, Graduate School, College of Management, Program in Accounting, Raleigh, NC 27695. Offers MAC. Part-time programs available. *Degree requirements:* For master's, thesis optional. *Entrance requirements:* For master's, GMAT, interview. Additional exam requirements/recommendations for international students: Required—TOEFL. Electronic applications accepted. *Faculty research:* Financial reporting issues using positive economic models and empirical studies of human behavior related to accounting decisions.

Northeastern Illinois University, Graduate College, College of Business and Management, Chicago, IL 60625-4699. Offers accounting (MBA); finance (MBA); management (MBA); marketing (MBA). Part-time and evening/weekend programs available. *Degree requirements:* For master's, thesis optional. *Entrance requirements:* For master's, GMAT, minimum GPA of 2.75. Additional exam requirements/recommendations for international students: Required—TOEFL (minimum score 550 paper-based; 213 computer-based; 80 iBT). Electronic applications accepted. *Faculty research:* Perception of accountants and non-accountants toward future of the accounting industry, asynchronous learning outcomes, cost and efficiency of financial markets, impact of deregulation on airline industry, analysis of derivational instruments.

Northeastern State University, Graduate College, College of Business and Technology, Program in Accounting and Financial Analysis, Tahlequah, OK 74464-2399. Offers MS. Part-time and evening/weekend programs available. *Entrance requirements:* For master's, GMAT. Additional exam requirements/recommendations for international students: Required—TOEFL (minimum score 213 computer-based). Electronic applications accepted.

Northeastern University, Graduate School of Professional Accounting, Boston, MA 02115-5096. Offers MS, MST, MS/MBA. Postbaccalaureate distance learning degree programs offered (no on-campus study). *Faculty:* 8 full-time (2 women), 6 part-time/adjunct (0 women). *Students:* 63 full-time (35 women), 104 part-time (51 women); includes 5 African Americans, 11 Asian Americans or Pacific Islanders, 6 Hispanic Americans, 2 international. 221 applicants, 88% accepted, 167 enrolled. In 2009, 126 master's awarded. *Entrance requirements:* For master's, GMAT, interview. Additional exam requirements/recommendations for international students: Required—TOEFL (minimum score 600 paper-based; 250 computer-based; 100 iBT). *Application deadline:* For fall admission, 11/15 for domestic and international students; for winter admission, 1/15 for domestic and international students; for spring admission, 4/1 for domestic students. Application fee: $100. Electronic applications accepted. *Expenses:* Contact institution. *Financial support:* Career-related internships or fieldwork, Federal Work-Study, institutionally sponsored loans, and scholarships/grants available. Support available to part-time students. Financial award application deadline: 3/1; financial award applicants required to submit FAFSA. *Unit head:* Kate Klepper, Associate Dean, Graduate Business Programs, 617-373-5417, Fax: 617-373-8564, E-mail: k.klepper@neu.edu. *Application contact:* Annarita Meeker, Director, Graduate Accounting and Tax Programs, 617-373-4621, Fax: 617-373-8564, E-mail: a.meeker@neu.edu.

Northern Illinois University, Graduate School, College of Business, Department of Accountancy, De Kalb, IL 60115-2854. Offers MAS, MST. *Accreditation:* AACSB. Part-time and evening/weekend programs available. *Faculty:* 14 full-time (4 women). *Students:* 165 full-time (65 women), 85 part-time (51 women); includes 31 minority (4 African Americans, 25 Asian Americans or Pacific Islanders, 2 Hispanic Americans), 40 international. Average age 28. 161 applicants, 58% accepted, 48 enrolled. In 2009, 149 master's awarded. *Degree requirements:* For master's, thesis optional. *Entrance requirements:* For master's, GMAT, minimum GPA of 2.75. Additional exam requirements/recommendations for international students: Required—TOEFL (minimum score 550 paper-based; 213 computer-based). *Application deadline:* For fall admission, 4/1 priority date for domestic students, 5/1 for international students; for spring admission, 9/15 priority date for domestic students, 10/1 for international students. Applications are processed on a rolling basis. Application fee: $30. Electronic applications accepted. *Expenses:* Tuition, state resident: full-time $6576; part-time $274 per credit hour. Tuition, nonresident: full-time $13,152; part-time $548 per credit hour. Required fees: $1813; $75.53 per credit hour. Part-time tuition and fees vary according to course load. *Financial support:* In 2009–10, 25 research assistantships with full tuition reimbursements, 11 teaching assistantships with full tuition reimbursements were awarded; fellowships with full tuition reimbursements, career-related internships or fieldwork, Federal Work-Study, scholarships/grants, tuition waivers (full), and unspecified assistantships also available. Support available to part-time students. Financial award applicants required to submit FAFSA. *Faculty research:* Accounting fraud, governmental accounting, corporate income tax planning, auditing, ethics. *Unit head:* Dr. James C. Young, Chair, 815-753-1250, Fax: 815-753-8515. *Application contact:* Dr. Rowene Linden, Graduate Adviser, 815-753-6200.

Northern Kentucky University, Office of Graduate Programs, College of Business, Program in Accountancy, Highland Heights, KY 41099. Offers accountancy (M Acc); advanced taxation (Certificate). Part-time and evening/weekend programs available. *Students:* 13 full-time (3 women), 59 part-time (31 women); includes 3 minority (1 African American, 1 American Indian/Alaska Native, 1 Asian American or Pacific Islander), 2 international. Average age 32. 59 applicants, 71% accepted, 34 enrolled. In 2009, 17 master's awarded. *Entrance requirements:* For master's, GMAT (minimum score 450), minimum GPA of 2.5. Additional exam requirements/recommendations for international students: Required—TOEFL (minimum score 550 paper-based; 213 computer-based; 79 iBT); Recommended—IELTS (minimum score 6.5). *Application deadline:* For fall admission, 8/1 priority date for domestic students, 6/1 for international students; for spring admission, 12/1 priority date for domestic students, 10/1 for international students. Applications are processed on a rolling basis. Application fee: $40. Electronic applications accepted. *Expenses:* Tuition, state resident: full-time $6912; part-time $384 per credit hour. Tuition, nonresident: full-time $12,150; part-time $675 per credit hour. Tuition and fees vary according to course load, program and reciprocity agreements. *Financial support:* Unspecified assistantships available. Financial award applicants required to submit FAFSA. *Unit head:* Robert Salyer, Director, 859-572-5164, Fax: 859-572-6177, E-mail: salyerb@nku.edu. *Application contact:* Dr. Peg Griffin, Director of Graduate Programs, 859-572-6934, Fax: 859-572-6670, E-mail: griffinp@nku.edu.

Northwestern University, The Graduate School, Kellogg School of Management, Department of Accounting Information and Management, Evanston, IL 60208. Offers accounting (PhD). Admissions and degree offered through The Graduate School. *Degree requirements:* For doctorate, comprehensive exam, thesis/dissertation. *Entrance requirements:* For doctorate, GMAT or GRE General Test. Additional exam requirements/recommendations for international students: Required—TOEFL. Electronic applications accepted. *Faculty research:* Managerial and financial accounting theory, financial accounting/theory, managerial accounting and performance measurement, international accounting, joint cost allocation.

Northwest Missouri State University, Graduate School, Melvin and Valorie Booth College of Business and Professional Studies, Program in Accounting, Maryville, MO 64468-6001. Offers MBA. *Faculty:* 8 full-time (0 women). *Students:* 2 full-time (both women), 1 (woman) part-time, 2 international. 11 applicants, 18% accepted, 0 enrolled. In 2009, 4 master's awarded. *Degree requirements:* For master's, comprehensive exam. *Entrance requirements:* For master's, GMAT, minimum GPA of 2.5. Additional exam requirements/recommendations for international students: Required—TOEFL (minimum score 550 paper-based; 213 computer-based). *Application deadline:* For fall admission, 7/1 for domestic and international students; for spring admission, 12/1 for domestic students, 11/15 for international students. Applications are processed on a rolling basis. Application fee: $0 ($50 for international students). Electronic applications accepted. *Expenses:* Tuition, state resident: part-time $296.34 per credit hour. Tuition, nonresident: part-time $510.43 per credit hour. *Financial support:* In 2009–10, 3 research assistantships with full tuition reimbursements (averaging $6,000 per year) were awarded. Financial award application deadline: 4/1; financial award applicants required to submit FAFSA. *Unit head:* Dr. Rahnl Wood, Advisor, 660-562-1759. *Application contact:* Dr. Gregory Haddock, Dean of Graduate School, 660-562-1145, Fax: 660-562-1096, E-mail: gradsch@nwmissouri.edu.

Notre Dame College, Graduate Studies, South Euclid, OH 44121-4293. Offers accounting (Certificate); creative critical thinking (M Ed); financial services management (Certificate); information systems (Certificate); learning disabilities (M Ed); management (Certificate); paralegal (Certificate); pastoral ministry (Certificate); reading (M Ed); teacher education (Certificate). Part-time and evening/weekend programs available. *Degree requirements:* For master's, thesis. *Entrance requirements:* For master's, GRE General Test, MAT, minimum GPA of 2.75, valid teaching certificate. *Faculty research:* Cognitive psychology, teaching critical thinking in the classroom.

Nova Southeastern University, H. Wayne Huizenga School of Business and Entrepreneurship, Doctoral Program in Business Administration, Fort Lauderdale, FL 33314-7796. Offers accounting (DBA); decision sciences (DBA); finance (DBA); human resource management (DBA); international business (DBA); management (DBA); marketing (DBA). Part-time and evening/weekend programs available. *Faculty:* 34 full-time (11 women), 2 part-time/adjunct (1 woman). *Students:* 6 full-time (1 woman), 129 part-time (41 women); includes 33 minority (17 African Americans, 6 Asian Americans or Pacific Islanders, 10 Hispanic Americans), 12 international. Average age 47. 58 applicants, 14% accepted, 5 enrolled. In 2009, 32 doctorates awarded. *Degree requirements:* For doctorate, comprehensive exam, thesis/dissertation. *Entrance requirements:* For doctorate, GMAT. Additional exam requirements/recommendations for international students: Required—TOEFL (minimum score 600 paper-based; 250 computer-based; 100 iBT), IELTS (minimum score 7). *Application deadline:* Applications are processed on a rolling basis. Application fee: $50. Electronic applications accepted. *Financial support:* Available to part-time students. Applicants required to submit FAFSA. *Faculty research:* Reputation management, call centers, international social capital, corporate earnings guidance, corporate governance. *Unit head:* Kristie Tetrault, Director of Program Administration, 954-262-5120, Fax: 954-262-3849, E-mail: kristie@huizenga.nova.edu. *Application contact:* Karen Goldberg, Associate Director of Recruitment and Special Events, 954-262-5039, Fax: 954-262-3822, E-mail: karen@huizenga.nova.edu.

Nova Southeastern University, H. Wayne Huizenga School of Business and Entrepreneurship, Master's Program in Accounting, Fort Lauderdale, FL 33314-7796. Offers M Acc. Part-time and evening/weekend programs available. Postbaccalaureate distance learning degree programs offered (no on-campus study). *Faculty:* 4 full-time (0 women), 8 part-time/adjunct (4 women). *Students:* 26 full-time (13 women), 543 part-time (335 women); includes 351 minority (153 African Americans, 2 American Indian/Alaska Native, 29 Asian Americans or Pacific Islanders, 167 Hispanic Americans), 19 international. Average age 34. 218 applicants, 65% accepted, 89 enrolled. In 2009, 114 master's awarded. *Entrance requirements:* For master's, undergraduate degree in accounting, work experience. Additional exam requirements/recommendations for international students: Required—TOEFL (minimum score 550 paper-based; 213 computer-based; 79 iBT), IELTS (minimum score 6). *Application deadline:* For fall admission, 8/15 for domestic and international students; for winter admission, 12/10 for domestic and international students; for spring admission, 2/10 for domestic and international students. Applications are processed on a rolling basis. Application fee: $50. Electronic applications accepted. *Financial support:* Federal Work-Study and scholarships/grants available. Support available to part-time students. Financial award applicants required to submit FAFSA. *Unit head:* Dr. Walter Moore, Chair and Professor for Accounting Programs, 954-262-5101, Fax: 954-262-3822, E-mail: moore@huizenga.nova.edu. *Application contact:* Aimee Fernandez, Assistant Director, 954-262-5091, Fax: 954-262-3822, E-mail: aimeefernandez@huizenga.nova.edu.

Nyack College, School of Business, Nyack, NY 10960-3698. Offers accounting (MBA); business administration (MBA). Evening/weekend programs available. *Degree requirements:* For master's, thesis. *Entrance requirements:* For master's, GMAT (may be waived based on business experience), minimum GPA of 3.0. *Expenses:* Contact institution.

Oakland University, Graduate Study and Lifelong Learning, School of Business Administration, Department of Accounting and Finance, Rochester, MI 48309-4401. Offers accounting (M Acc, Certificate); finance (Certificate).

The Ohio State University, Graduate School, Max M. Fisher College of Business, Department of Accounting and Management Information Systems, Program in Accounting, Columbus, OH 43210. Offers M Acc, MA, MS. *Students:* 88 full-time (40 women), 2 part-time (both women); includes 8 minority (3 African Americans, 4 Asian Americans or Pacific Islanders, 1 Hispanic American), 25 international. Average age 24. In 2009, 84 master's awarded. *Application deadline:* Applications are processed on a rolling basis. Application fee: $40 ($50 for international students). Electronic applications accepted. *Expenses:* Tuition, state resident: full-time $10,683. Tuition, nonresident: full-time $25,923. Tuition and fees vary according to course load

and program. *Unit head:* Annette Beatty, Graduate Studies Committee Chair, 614-292-2081, Fax: 614-292-2118, E-mail: beatty.86@osu.edu. *Application contact:* Graduate Admissions, 614-292-9444, Fax: 614-292-3895, E-mail: domestic.grad@osu.edu.

Oklahoma City University, Meinders School of Business, Program in Accounting, Oklahoma City, OK 73106-1402. Offers MSA. Part-time and evening/weekend programs available. *Faculty:* 5 full-time (2 women). *Students:* 20 full-time (7 women), 12 part-time (8 women); includes 1 minority (African American), 18 international. Average age 30. 13 applicants, 85% accepted, 6 enrolled. In 2009, 23 master's awarded. *Entrance requirements:* Additional exam requirements/recommendations for international students: Required—TOEFL (minimum score 570 paper-based; 230 computer-based; 88 iBT). *Application deadline:* For fall admission, 8/20 for domestic students; for spring admission, 1/6 for domestic students. Applications are processed on a rolling basis. Application fee: $50 ($70 for international students). *Expenses:* Tuition: Full-time $15,930; part-time $885 per hour. *Financial support:* Fellowships with partial tuition reimbursements, career-related internships or fieldwork, Federal Work-Study, institutionally sponsored loans, and tuition waivers (partial) available. Support available to part-time students. Financial award application deadline: 8/1; financial award applicants required to submit FAFSA. *Faculty research:* Financial accounting, auditing, tax. *Unit head:* Dr. Jacci Rodgers, Chair, Accounting and Information Technology, 405-208-5824, Fax: 405-208-5356, E-mail: jrodgers@okcu.edu. *Application contact:* Michelle Lockhart, Director, Admissions, 800-633-7242, Fax: 405-208-5916, E-mail: gadmissions@okcu.edu.

Oklahoma State University, William S. Spears School of Business, School of Accounting, Stillwater, OK 74078. Offers MS, PhD. *Accreditation:* AACSB. Part-time programs available. *Faculty:* 18 full-time (6 women), 1 part-time/adjunct (0 women). *Students:* 67 full-time (27 women), 22 part-time (14 women); includes 4 minority (all American Indian/Alaska Native), 15 international. Average age 27. 108 applicants, 31% accepted, 24 enrolled. In 2009, 35 master's, 3 doctorates awarded. *Degree requirements:* For master's, thesis or alternative; for doctorate, comprehensive exam, thesis/dissertation. *Entrance requirements:* For master's and doctorate, GRE or GMAT. Additional exam requirements/recommendations for international students: Required—TOEFL (minimum score 550 paper-based; 79 iBT). *Application deadline:* For fall admission, 3/1 priority date for international students; for spring admission, 8/1 priority date for international students. Applications are processed on a rolling basis. Application fee: $40 ($75 for international students). Electronic applications accepted. *Expenses:* Tuition, state resident: full-time $3716; part-time $154.85 per credit hour. Tuition, nonresident: full-time $14,448; part-time $602 per credit hour. Required fees: $1772; $73.85 per credit hour. One-time fee: $50. Tuition and fees vary according to course load and campus/location. *Financial support:* In 2009–10, 10 research assistantships (averaging $12,597 per year), 30 teaching assistantships (averaging $7,359 per year) were awarded; career-related internships or fieldwork, Federal Work-Study, scholarships/grants, health care benefits, tuition waivers (partial), and unspecified assistantships also available. Support available to part-time students. Financial award application deadline: 3/1; financial award applicants required to submit FAFSA. *Faculty research:* International accounting, accounting education, cost-management, taxation, oil and gas. *Unit head:* Dr. Don Hansen, Head, 405-744-5123, Fax: 405-744-1680. *Application contact:* Dr. Gordon Emslie, Dean, 405-744-6368, Fax: 405-744-0355, E-mail: grad-i@okstate.edu.

Old Dominion University, College of Business and Public Administration, Program in Accounting, Norfolk, VA 23529. Offers MS. *Accreditation:* AACSB. Part-time and evening/weekend programs available. *Faculty:* 12 full-time (4 women), 4 part-time/adjunct (2 women). *Students:* 9 full-time (6 women), 33 part-time (19 women); includes 5 minority (3 African Americans, 2 Asian Americans or Pacific Islanders), 8 international. Average age 30. 37 applicants, 68% accepted, 22 enrolled. In 2009, 21 master's awarded. *Degree requirements:* For master's, comprehensive exam. *Entrance requirements:* For master's, GMAT, minimum GPA of 3.0. Additional exam requirements/recommendations for international students: Required—TOEFL (minimum score 550 paper-based). *Application deadline:* For fall admission, 7/1 priority date for domestic students, 4/15 priority date for international students; for spring admission, 11/1 priority date for domestic students, 10/1 priority date for international students. Applications are processed on a rolling basis. Application fee: $50. *Expenses:* Tuition, state resident: full-time $8112; part-time $338 per credit. Tuition, nonresident: full-time $20,256; part-time $844 per credit. Required fees: $119 per semester. One-time fee: $50. *Financial support:* In 2009–10, 10 students received support, including 5 research assistantships with partial tuition reimbursements available (averaging $7,500 per year); career-related internships or fieldwork, tuition waivers (partial), and unspecified assistantships also available. Support available to part-time students. Financial award application deadline: 2/15; financial award applicants required to submit FAFSA. *Faculty research:* Assurance services, international accounting, strategic costing, business valuation. *Unit head:* Dr. Yin Xu, Graduate Program Director, 757-683-3554, Fax: 757-683-5639, E-mail: acctgpd@odu.edu. *Application contact:* Dr. Yin Xu, Graduate Program Director, 757-683-3554, Fax: 757-683-5639, E-mail: acctgpd@odu.edu.

Oral Roberts University, School of Business, Tulsa, OK 74171. Offers accounting (MBA); entrepreneurship (MBA); finance (MBA); international business (MBA); management (MBA); marketing (MBA); non-profit management (MBA); not for profit management (MNM). *Accreditation:* ACBSP. Part-time programs available. Postbaccalaureate distance learning degree programs offered (minimal on-campus study). *Faculty:* 7 full-time (0 women), 5 part-time/adjunct (4 women). *Students:* 68 full-time (30 women), 55 part-time (27 women); includes 54 minority (32 African Americans, 5 American Indian/Alaska Native, 8 Asian Americans or Pacific Islanders, 9 Hispanic Americans), 3 international. Average age 28. 71 applicants, 94% accepted, 56 enrolled. In 2009, 36 master's awarded. *Degree requirements:* For master's, thesis optional. *Entrance requirements:* For master's, minimum cumulative GPA of 3.0. Additional exam requirements/recommendations for international students: Required—TOEFL (minimum score 550 paper-based; 213 computer-based; 79 iBT). *Application deadline:* For fall admission, 7/1 priority date for domestic and international students; for spring admission, 12/1 priority date for domestic students, 10/15 priority date for international students. Applications are processed on a rolling basis. Application fee: $35. Electronic applications accepted. *Financial support:* In 2009–10, 39 students received support. Federal Work-Study, scholarships/grants, and unspecified assistantships available. Financial award application deadline: 6/1; financial award applicants required to submit FAFSA. *Faculty research:* Social media, international business and marketing. *Unit head:* Dr. Steven Greene, Dean, 918-495-7040, Fax: 918-495-7876, E-mail: businessdean@oru.edu. *Application contact:* Rebecca Gunn, Representative/Recruiter, 918-495-6117, Fax: 918-495-6500, E-mail: gradbusiness@oru.edu.

Our Lady of the Lake University of San Antonio, School of Business and Leadership, Program in Accounting/Finance, San Antonio, TX 78207-4689. Offers MBA. Part-time and evening/weekend programs available. *Students:* 5 full-time (4 women), 63 part-time (29 women); includes 57 minority (10 Asian Americans or Pacific Islanders, 47 Hispanic Americans), 1 international. Average age 34. In 2009, 36 master's awarded. *Expenses:* Tuition: Full-time $12,330; part-time $685 per contact hour. Required fees: $139; $12 per contact hour. $57 per semester. Tuition and fees vary according to campus/location. *Unit head:* Dr. Robert Bisking, Dean, 210-434-6711, Fax: 210-434-0821. *Application contact:* Dr. Robert Bisking, Dean, 210-434-6711, Fax: 210-434-0821.

Pace University, Lubin School of Business, Accounting Program, New York, NY 10038. Offers managerial accounting (MBA); public accounting (MBA, MS). *Accreditation:* AACSB. Part-time and evening/weekend programs available. *Students:* 48 full-time (26 women), 156 part-time (93 women); includes 45 minority (5 African Americans, 35 Asian Americans or Pacific Islanders, 5 Hispanic Americans), 81 international. Average age 27. 315 applicants, 80% accepted, 75 enrolled. In 2009, 86 master's awarded. *Entrance requirements:* For master's, GMAT. Additional exam requirements/recommendations for international students: Required—TOEFL. *Application deadline:* For fall admission, 7/31 priority date for domestic students; for spring admission, 11/30 for domestic students. Applications are processed on a rolling basis. Application fee: $70. Electronic applications accepted. *Expenses:* Tuition: Part-time $954 per credit. Tuition and fees vary according to course load, degree level and program. *Financial support:* Research assistantships, career-related internships or fieldwork and Federal Work-Study available. Support

available to part-time students. Financial award applicants required to submit FAFSA. *Unit head:* Dr. Rudolph Jacob, Chairperson, 212-346-1960. *Application contact:* Susan Ford-Goldschein, Director of Admissions, 212-346-1652, Fax: 212-346-1585, E-mail: gradnyc@pace.edu.

Pacific States University, College of Business, Los Angeles, CA 90006. Offers accounting (MBA); business administration (DBA); finance (MBA); international business (MBA); management of information technology (MBA); real estate management (MBA). Part-time and evening/weekend programs available. Postbaccalaureate distance learning degree programs offered (no on-campus study). *Entrance requirements:* For master's, minimum undergraduate GPA of 2.5 during last 90 hours of course work. Additional exam requirements/recommendations for international students: Required—TOEFL (minimum score 133 computer-based).

Pittsburg State University, Graduate School, Kelce College of Business, Department of Accounting, Pittsburg, KS 66762. Offers MBA. *Degree requirements:* For master's, thesis or alternative. *Entrance requirements:* For master's, GMAT. *Expenses:* Tuition, state resident: full-time $4212; part-time $176 per credit. Tuition, nonresident: full-time $11,530; part-time $480 per credit. Required fees: $940; $43 per credit. Tuition and fees vary according to course level, course load, degree level, campus/location, reciprocity agreements and student level. *Faculty research:* Accountant's legal liability, computer audit.

Pontifical Catholic University of Puerto Rico, College of Business Administration, Program in Accounting, Ponce, PR 00717-0777. Offers MBA. Part-time and evening/weekend programs available. *Degree requirements:* For master's, thesis. *Entrance requirements:* For master's, GRE, interview, minimum GPA of 2.75.

Prairie View A&M University, College of Business, Prairie View, TX 77446-0519. Offers accounting (MS); general business administration (MBA). *Accreditation:* AACSB. Part-time and evening/weekend programs available. *Faculty:* 14 full-time (5 women). *Students:* 275 full-time (256 women), 429 part-time (126 women); includes 655 minority (622 African Americans, 1 American Indian/Alaska Native, 13 Asian Americans or Pacific Islanders, 19 Hispanic Americans), 25 international. Average age 23. In 2009, 38 master's awarded. *Entrance requirements:* For master's, GMAT, minimum GPA of 2.45. Additional exam requirements/recommendations for international students: Required—TOEFL. *Application deadline:* For fall admission, 7/1 for domestic students, 6/1 priority date for international students; for spring admission, 11/1 for domestic students, 10/1 priority date for international students. Applications are processed on a rolling basis. Application fee: $50. Electronic applications accepted. *Expenses:* Tuition, state resident: full-time $2200. Tuition, nonresident: full-time $5600. Required fees: $1720. Tuition and fees vary according to course load. *Financial support:* Research assistantships, career-related internships or fieldwork, Federal Work-Study, institutionally sponsored loans, and tuition waivers (partial) available. Support available to part-time students. Financial award application deadline: 4/1; financial award applicants required to submit FAFSA. *Faculty research:* Operations, finance, marketing. Total annual research expenditures: $30,000. *Unit head:* Dr. Munir Quddus, Dean, 936-261-9217, Fax: 936-261-9241, E-mail: muquddus@pvamu.edu. *Application contact:* Dr. John Dyck, Director, Graduate Programs in Business, 936-261-9217, Fax: 936-261-9232, E-mail: jwdyck@pvamu.edu.

Providence College, Graduate Studies, School of Business, Providence, RI 02918. Offers accountancy (MBA); economics (MBA); entrepreneurship (MBA); finance (MBA); international business (MBA); management (MBA); marketing (MBA); not-for-profit (MBA); quantitative (MBA). Part-time and evening/weekend programs available. *Faculty:* 14 full-time (8 women), 7 part-time/adjunct (3 women). *Students:* 63 full-time (18 women), 46 part-time (19 women); includes 4 minority (2 African Americans, 2 Asian Americans or Pacific Islanders), 7 international. Average age 26. 43 applicants, 88% accepted. In 2009, 40 master's awarded. *Degree requirements:* For master's, thesis optional. *Entrance requirements:* For master's, GMAT. Additional exam requirements/recommendations for international students: Required—TOEFL (minimum score 550 paper-based; 213 computer-based; 80 iBT). *Application deadline:* For fall admission, 8/1 priority date for domestic and international students; for spring admission, 12/1 priority date for domestic and international students. Applications are processed on a rolling basis. Application fee: $55. *Expenses:* Contact institution. *Financial support:* In 2009–10, 34 research assistantships with full tuition reimbursements (averaging $8,400 per year) were awarded; Federal Work-Study, institutionally sponsored loans, and unspecified assistantships also available. Support available to part-time students. Financial award application deadline: 8/1; financial award applicants required to submit FAFSA. *Unit head:* Dr. MaryJane Lenon, Director, MBA Program, 401-865-2566, Fax: 401-865-2978, E-mail: mjlenon@providence.edu. *Application contact:* Katherine A. Follett, Administrative Coordinator, 401-865-2333, Fax: 401-865-2978, E-mail: kfollett@providence.edu.

Purdue University Calumet, Graduate School, School of Management, Hammond, IN 46323-2094. Offers accountancy (M Acc); business administration (MBA); business administration for executives (EMBA). Part-time and evening/weekend programs available. *Entrance requirements:* For master's, GMAT. Additional exam requirements/recommendations for international students: Required—TOEFL. Electronic applications accepted.

Queens College of the City University of New York, Division of Graduate Studies, Social Science Division, Department of Accounting, Flushing, NY 11367-1597. Offers MS. *Faculty:* 19 full-time (1 woman). *Students:* 20 full-time (8 women), 146 part-time (85 women). 215 applicants, 57% accepted, 80 enrolled. In 2009, 23 master's awarded. Application fee: $125. *Expenses:* Tuition, state resident: full-time $7360; part-time $310 per credit. Tuition, nonresident: part-time $575 per credit. One-time fee: $195 full-time; $145.25 part-time. *Unit head:* Dr. Israel Blumenfrucht, Chairperson, 718-997-5070, E-mail: israel_blumenfrucht@qc.edu. *Application contact:* Mario Caruso, Director of Graduate Admissions, 718-997-5200, Fax: 718-997-5193, E-mail: graduate_admissions@qc.edu.

Regis University, College for Professional Studies, School of Management, Denver, CO 80221-1099. Offers accounting (MS); business administration (MBA); computer information technology (MSOL); executive internal management (Certificate); executive leadership (Certificate); finance (MBA); finance and accounting (MBA); human resource management (MSOL); international business (MBA); marketing (MBA); operations management (MBA); organization leadership (MS); organizational leadership (MSOL); project leadership and management (MSOL, Certificate); project management (Certificate); strategic business (Certificate); strategic human resource (Certificate); technical management (Certificate). Offered at Colorado Springs Campus, Northwest Denver Campus, Southeast Denver Campus, Fort Collins Campus, Broomfield Campus, Henderson (Nevada) Campus, and Summerlin (Nevada) Campus and online. Part-time and evening/weekend programs available. Postbaccalaureate distance learning degree programs offered (no on-campus study). *Degree requirements:* For master's, thesis optional, capstone project. *Entrance requirements:* For master's, GMAT or essays, interview, 2 years of full-time business work experience, resume; for Certificate, GMAT. Additional exam requirements/recommendations for international students: Required—TOEFL, TOEFL or university-based test; Recommended—TWE (minimum score 5). Electronic applications accepted. *Faculty research:* Impact of Info Technology on Small Business Regulation of Accounting, International Project financing, Mineral Development, Delivery of Healthcare to rural indigenos communities.

Rhode Island College, School of Graduate Studies, School of Management, Department of Accounting and Computer Information Systems, Providence, RI 02908-1991. Offers accounting (MP Ac); financial planning (CGS). Part-time and evening/weekend programs available. *Faculty:* 2 full-time (1 woman). *Students:* 1 full-time (0 women), 9 part-time (6 women), 1 international. Average age 32. In 2009, 7 master's awarded. *Entrance requirements:* For master's, GMAT (unless applicant is a CPA or has passed a state bar exam); for CGS, GMAT, bachelor's degree from an accredited college or university, official transcripts of all undergraduate and graduate records. Additional exam requirements/recommendations for international students: Recommended—TOEFL (minimum score 550 paper-based; 213 computer-based; 79 iBT). *Application deadline:* For fall admission, 4/1 for domestic students; for spring admission, 11/1 for domestic students. Applications are processed on a rolling basis. Application fee: $50.

Accounting

Rhode Island College *(continued)*

Expenses: Tuition, state resident: full-time $7440; part-time $310 per credit hour. Tuition, nonresident: full-time $14,784; part-time $616 per credit hour. Required fees: $552; $20 per credit. $70 per term. *Financial support:* Federal Work-Study, scholarships/grants, and health care benefits available. Support available to part-time students. Financial award application deadline: 5/15; financial award applicants required to submit FAFSA. *Unit head:* Prof. David Filipek, Chair, 401-456-8009. *Application contact:* Graduate Studies, 401-456-8700.

Rhodes College, Department of Economics and Business Administration, Memphis, TN 38112-1690. Offers accounting (MS). Part-time programs available. *Faculty:* 5 full-time (3 women), 2 part-time/adjunct (0 women). *Students:* 10 full-time (6 women). Average age 22. In 2009, 9 master's awarded. *Entrance requirements:* For master's, GMAT. Additional exam requirements/recommendations for international students: Required—TOEFL (minimum score 550 paper-based). *Application deadline:* For fall admission, 3/1 for domestic students. Application fee: $25. *Expenses:* Tuition: Full-time $33,400; part-time $1400 per credit. Required fees: $310. *Financial support:* Career-related internships or fieldwork and scholarships/grants available. Financial award application deadline: 3/1; financial award applicants required to submit FAFSA. *Unit head:* Dr. Pamela H. Church, Program Director, 901-843-3863, Fax: 901-843-3798, E-mail: church@rhodes.edu. *Application contact:* Dr. Pamela H. Church, Program Director, 901-843-3863, Fax: 901-843-3798, E-mail: church@rhodes.edu.

Rider University, College of Business Administration, Program in Accountancy, Lawrenceville, NJ 08648-3001. Offers M Acc. *Accreditation:* AACSB. *Entrance requirements:* For master's, GMAT, resume. Additional exam requirements/recommendations for international students: Required—TOEFL (minimum score 550 paper-based; 213 computer-based). Electronic applications accepted. *Faculty research:* Financial reporting, corporate governance, information technology, ethics, pedagogy.

Robert Morris University Illinois, Morris Graduate School of Management, Chicago, IL 60605. Offers accounting (MBA); accounting/finance (MBA); human resource management (MBA); information technology (MIS); leadership (MBA); management/finance (MIS); management/human resource management (MBA). Part-time and evening/weekend programs available. *Faculty:* 16 full-time (6 women), 25 part-time/adjunct (9 women). *Students:* 275 full-time (169 women), 194 part-time (134 women); includes 267 minority (176 African Americans, 1 American Indian/Alaska Native, 26 Asian Americans or Pacific Islanders, 64 Hispanic Americans), 17 international. Average age 32. 202 applicants, 84% accepted, 135 enrolled. In 2009, 161 master's awarded. *Degree requirements:* For master's, 44 residency hours. *Entrance requirements:* Additional exam requirements/recommendations for international students: Required—TOEFL (minimum score 500 paper-based; 173 computer-based). *Application deadline:* Applications are processed on a rolling basis. Application fee: $30 ($100 for international students). Electronic applications accepted. *Expenses:* Tuition: Full-time $18,000; part-time $2000 per course. *Financial support:* In 2009–10, 420 students received support. Federal Work-Study, scholarships/grants, and tuition waivers available. Support available to part-time students. *Unit head:* Kayed Akkawi, Dean, 312-935-4244, Fax: 312-935-4248, E-mail: kakkawi@robertmorris.edu. *Application contact:* Courtney A. Kohn Sanders, Dean of Graduate Admissions, 312-935-4240, Fax: 312-935-4248, E-mail: ckohn@robertmorris.edu.

Rochester Institute of Technology, Graduate Enrollment Services, E. Philip Saunders College of Business, Graduate Business Programs, Program in Accounting, Rochester, NY 14623-5603. Offers MBA. Part-time and evening/weekend programs available. *Students:* 16 full-time (6 women), 8 part-time (6 women); includes 2 African Americans, 2 Asian Americans or Pacific Islanders, 8 international. Average age 29. 60 applicants, 45% accepted, 13 enrolled. In 2009, 6 master's awarded. *Entrance requirements:* For master's, GMAT, minimum GPA of 2.5. Additional exam requirements/recommendations for international students: Required—TOEFL (minimum score 580 paper-based; 237 computer-based; 92 iBT), or IELTS (minimum score 7). *Application deadline:* For fall admission, 2/15 priority date for domestic and international students; for winter admission, 11/1 priority date for domestic students; for spring admission, 2/1 priority date for domestic students. Applications are processed on a rolling basis. Application fee: $50. *Expenses:* Tuition: Full-time $31,533; part-time $876 per credit hour. Required fees: $210. *Financial support:* In 2009–10, 21 students received support; research assistantships with partial tuition reimbursements available, teaching assistantships with partial tuition reimbursements available, career-related internships or fieldwork, scholarships/grants, and unspecified assistantships available. Support available to part-time students. Financial award applicants required to submit FAFSA. *Faculty research:* Formation and taxation of business entities, auditor independence: the conundrum of tax services, ethics in accounting and business or the lack thereof, accounting crisis: a curricular response. *Unit head:* Kathy Ozminkowski, Assistant Dean for Student Services, 585-475-6985, Fax: 585-475-7450, E-mail: kozminkowski@saunders.rit.edu. *Application contact:* Diane Ellison, Assistant Vice President, Graduate Enrollment Services, 585-475-2229, Fax: 585-475-7164, E-mail: gradinfo@rit.edu.

Rocky Mountain College, Graduate Programs, Billings, MT 59102-1796. Offers accounting (M Acc); educational leadership (M Ed); physician assistant studies (MPAS). Part-time programs available. *Faculty:* 10 full-time (3 women), 12 part-time/adjunct (4 women). *Students:* 65 full-time (34 women), 1 part-time (0 women). Average age 28. In 2009, 55 master's awarded. *Entrance requirements:* Additional exam requirements/recommendations for international students: Required—TOEFL (minimum score 570 paper-based; 230 computer-based; 88 iBT), IELTS (minimum score 6.5). *Application deadline:* Applications are processed on a rolling basis. Application fee: $35 ($40 for international students). Electronic applications accepted. *Expenses:* Tuition: Full-time $25,070. Required fees: $450. Full-time tuition and fees vary according to program. *Financial support:* In 2009–10, 65 students received support. Federal Work-Study and scholarships/grants available. Financial award applicants required to submit FAFSA. *Unit head:* Anthony Piltz, Academic Vice President, 406-657-1020, Fax: 406-259-9751, E-mail: piltza@rocky.edu. *Application contact:* Kelly Edwards, Director of Admissions, 406-657-1026, Fax: 406-657-1189, E-mail: admissions@rocky.edu.

Roosevelt University, Graduate Division, Walter E. Heller College of Business Administration, Program in Accounting, Chicago, IL 60605. Offers MSA. Part-time and evening/weekend programs available. *Entrance requirements:* For master's, GMAT.

Rowan University, Graduate School, William G. Rohrer College of Business, Department of Accounting and Finance, Program in Accounting, Glassboro, NJ 08028-1701. Offers MBA. Part-time and evening/weekend programs available. *Students:* 14 full-time (5 women), 7 part-time (3 women); includes 11 minority (4 African Americans, 6 Asian Americans or Pacific Islanders, 1 Hispanic American). Average age 26. 9 applicants, 78% accepted, 6 enrolled. In 2009, 4 master's awarded. *Degree requirements:* For master's, comprehensive exam, thesis. *Entrance requirements:* For master's, GRE General Test. Additional exam requirements/recommendations for international students: Required—TOEFL. *Application deadline:* Applications are processed on a rolling basis. Application fee: $50. Electronic applications accepted. *Expenses:* Tuition, state resident: full-time $10,624; part-time $590 per semester hour. Tuition, nonresident: full-time $10,624; part-time $590 per semester hour. Required fees: $2320; $125 per semester hour. *Financial support:* Career-related internships or fieldwork, Federal Work-Study, and unspecified assistantships available. Support available to part-time students. *Unit head:* Dr. Mira Lalovic-Hand, Interim Associate Provost/Director of Graduate School, 856-256-5120, E-mail: lalovic-hand@rowan.edu. *Application contact:* Karen Haynes, Graduate Coordinator, 856-256-4052, E-mail: haynes@rowan.edu.

Rutgers, The State University of New Jersey, Newark, Graduate School, Program in Management, Newark, NJ 07102. Offers accounting (PhD); accounting information systems (PhD); computer information systems (PhD); finance (PhD); information technology (PhD); international business (PhD); management science (PhD); marketing (PhD); organization management (PhD). *Accreditation:* AACSB. *Degree requirements:* For doctorate, thesis/dissertation, cumulative exams. *Entrance requirements:* For doctorate, GMAT or GRE General Test, minimum undergraduate B average. Additional exam requirements/recommendations for

international students: Required—TOEFL. Electronic applications accepted. *Faculty research:* Technology management, leadership and teams, consumer behavior, financial and markets, logistics.

Rutgers, The State University of New Jersey, Newark, Rutgers Business School–Newark and New Brunswick, Department of Accounting and Information Systems, Newark, NJ 07102. Offers professional accounting (MBA). *Accreditation:* AACSB. *Entrance requirements:* For master's, GMAT. Additional exam requirements/recommendations for international students: Required—TOEFL. Electronic applications accepted.

Rutgers, The State University of New Jersey, Newark, Rutgers Business School–Newark and New Brunswick, Doctoral Programs in Business, Newark, NJ 07102. Offers accounting (PhD); accounting information systems (PhD); finance (PhD); individualized study (PhD); information technology (PhD); international business (PhD); management science (PhD); organizational management (PhD); supply chain management (PhD).

Rutgers, The State University of New Jersey, Newark, Rutgers Business School–Newark and New Brunswick, Master of Accountancy in Governmental Accounting Program, Newark, NJ 07102. Offers government financial management (Certificate); governmental accounting (M Accy). *Accreditation:* AACSB. Postbaccalaureate distance learning degree programs offered.

Sacred Heart University, Graduate Programs, John F. Welch College of Business, Fairfield, CT 06825-1000. Offers accounting (MBA); finance (MBA); management (MBA); marketing (MBA). *Accreditation:* AACSB. Part-time and evening/weekend programs available. Postbaccalaureate distance learning degree programs offered. *Faculty:* 33 full-time, 15 part-time/adjunct. *Students:* 36 full-time (12 women), 124 part-time (64 women); includes 28 minority (10 African Americans, 8 Asian Americans or Pacific Islanders, 10 Hispanic Americans), 6 international. Average age 32. 63 applicants, 71% accepted, 37 enrolled. In 2009, 41 master's awarded. *Degree requirements:* For master's, thesis or alternative. *Entrance requirements:* For master's, GMAT (preferred) or GRE General Test. Additional exam requirements/recommendations for international students: Required—TOEFL (minimum score 550 paper-based; 213 computer-based; 75 iBT). *Application deadline:* Applications are processed on a rolling basis. Application fee: $50 ($100 for international students). Electronic applications accepted. *Expenses:* Contact institution. *Financial support:* Career-related internships or fieldwork, institutionally sponsored loans, and unspecified assistantships available. Support available to part-time students. Financial award applicants required to submit FAFSA. *Faculty research:* Management of organizations, international business management of technology. *Unit head:* Dr. John J. Petillo, Dean, 203-396-8084, E-mail: petilloj@sacredheart.edu. *Application contact:* Dean Alexis Haakonsen, Dean of Graduate Admissions, 203-365-7619, Fax: 203-365-4732, E-mail: gradstudies@sacredheart.edu.

St. Ambrose University, College of Business, Program in Accounting, Davenport, IA 52803-2898. Offers MAC. Part-time and evening/weekend programs available. *Faculty:* 3 full-time (2 women), 2 part-time/adjunct (1 woman). *Students:* 15 full-time (7 women), 11 part-time (4 women); includes 2 minority (1 African American, 1 Asian American or Pacific Islander), 2 international. Average age 29. 15 applicants, 100% accepted, 15 enrolled. In 2009, 18 master's awarded. *Degree requirements:* For master's, comprehensive exam (for some programs), thesis or alternative, capstone seminar. *Entrance requirements:* For master's, GMAT. *Application deadline:* For fall admission, 8/15 priority date for domestic students; for winter admission, 12/15 priority date for domestic students; for spring admission, 1/1 priority date for domestic students. Applications are processed on a rolling basis. Application fee: $25. Electronic applications accepted. *Expenses:* Tuition: Part-time $702 per credit hour. Tuition and fees vary according to degree level, program and reciprocity agreements. *Financial support:* In 2009–10, 17 students received support, including 1 research assistantship with partial tuition reimbursement available (averaging $3,600 per year); career-related internships or fieldwork, scholarships/grants, tuition waivers (partial), and unspecified assistantships also available. Financial award application deadline: 3/15; financial award applicants required to submit FAFSA. *Unit head:* Lewis Marx, Director, 563-333-6186, Fax: 563-333-6243, E-mail: marxlewisd@sau.edu. *Application contact:* Deborah K. Bennett, Administrative Assistant, 563-333-6266, Fax: 563-333-6268, E-mail: bennettdeborahk@sau.edu.

St. Edward's University, School of Management and Business, Area of Business Administration, Austin, TX 78704. Offers accounting (MBA); business management (MBA); corporate finance (MBA, Certificate); global entrepreneurship (MBA); human resource management (MBA, Certificate); management information systems (MBA, Certificate); marketing (MBA, Certificate); operations management (MBA, Certificate). Part-time and evening/weekend programs available. *Faculty:* 20 full-time (9 women), 13 part-time/adjunct (4 women). *Students:* 29 full-time (16 women), 307 part-time (152 women); includes 116 minority (27 African Americans, 1 American Indian/Alaska Native, 16 Asian Americans or Pacific Islanders, 72 Hispanic Americans), 9 international. Average age 33. 129 applicants, 75% accepted, 74 enrolled. In 2009, 108 master's awarded. *Degree requirements:* For master's, minimum of 24 resident hours. *Entrance requirements:* For master's, GMAT or GRE General Test, minimum GPA of 2.75 in last 60 hours of course work. Additional exam requirements/recommendations for international students: Required—TOEFL (minimum score 550 paper-based; 213 computer-based; 79 iBT) or IELTS (minimum score 6). *Application deadline:* For fall admission, 7/1 for domestic and international students; for spring admission, 11/1 for domestic and international students. Applications are processed on a rolling basis. Application fee: $45 ($50 for international students). Electronic applications accepted. *Expenses:* Tuition: Full-time $14,922; part-time $829 per credit hour. Required fees: $50 per trimester. Full-time tuition and fees vary according to course load and program. *Financial support:* In 2009–10, 14 students received support. Scholarships/grants available. *Faculty research:* Operations management, minority entrepreneurship, globalization, professional services marketing. *Unit head:* Dr. Dianne Hill, Director, 512-428-1295, Fax: 512-448-8492, E-mail: dianneh@stedwards.edu. *Application contact:* Kelly Luna, Graduate Admissions Coordinator, 512-233-1697, Fax: 512-428-1032, E-mail: kellyl@stedwards.edu.

St. Edward's University, School of Management and Business, Program in Accounting, Austin, TX 78704. Offers M Ac. Part-time and evening/weekend programs available. *Students:* 4 full-time (1 woman), 14 part-time (7 women); includes 4 minority (all Hispanic Americans), 1 international. Average age 29. 29 applicants, 79% accepted, 12 enrolled. *Degree requirements:* For master's, minimum of 24 resident hours. *Entrance requirements:* For master's, GMAT or GRE General Test, minimum GPA of 2.75 in last 60 hours of course work and in accounting. Additional exam requirements/recommendations for international students: Required—TOEFL (minimum score 550 paper-based; 213 computer-based; 79 iBT) or IELTS (minimum score 6). *Application deadline:* For fall admission, 7/1 for domestic and international students; for spring admission, 11/1 for domestic and international students. Applications are processed on a rolling basis. Application fee: $45 ($50 for international students). Electronic applications accepted. *Expenses:* Tuition: Full-time $14,922; part-time $829 per credit hour. Required fees: $50 per trimester. Full-time tuition and fees vary according to course load and program. *Financial support:* Scholarships/grants available. *Unit head:* Dr. Kay Guess, Director, 512-448-8562, Fax: 512-448-8492, E-mail: aundreag@stedwards.edu. *Application contact:* Kelly Luna, Graduate Admissions Coordinator, 512-233-1697, Fax: 512-428-1032, E-mail: kellyl@stedwards.edu.

St. John's University, The Peter J. Tobin College of Business, Department of Accounting and Taxation, Program in Accounting, Queens, NY 11439. Offers MBA, MS, Adv C. *Accreditation:* AACSB. Part-time and evening/weekend programs available. *Students:* 219 full-time (137 women), 64 part-time (28 women); includes 53 minority (10 African Americans, 35 Asian Americans or Pacific Islanders, 8 Hispanic Americans), 141 international. Average age 25. 419 applicants, 69% accepted, 156 enrolled. In 2009, 109 master's, 1 other advanced degree awarded. *Degree requirements:* For master's, comprehensive exam (for some programs), thesis optional. *Entrance requirements:* For master's, GMAT, 2 letters of recommendation, resume; for Adv C, GMAT, 2 letters of recommendation, resume, undergraduate transcripts, essay. Additional exam requirements/recommendations for international students: Required—TOEFL (minimum score 500 paper-based; 173 computer-based; 61 iBT), IELTS (minimum score 5.5). *Application deadline:* For fall admission, 5/1 priority date for domestic and inter-

national students; for spring admission, 11/1 priority date for domestic and international students. Applications are processed on a rolling basis. Application fee: $70. Electronic applications accepted. *Expenses:* Contact institution. *Financial support:* Research assistantships available. Support available to part-time students. Financial award application deadline: 3/1; financial award applicants required to submit FAFSA. *Unit head:* Dr. James Thompson, Chair, 718-990-6460, Fax: 718-380-3803, E-mail: thompsoj@stjohns.edu. *Application contact:* Nicole T. Bryan, Assistant Dean, 718-990-2599, Fax: 718-990-5242, E-mail: tcbgradadmissions@stjohns.edu.

St. Joseph's College, Long Island Campus, Program in Accounting, Patchogue, NY 11772-2399. Offers MBA.

St. Joseph's College, New York, Graduate Programs, Program in Business, Field of Accounting, Brooklyn, NY 11205-3688. Offers MBA.

Saint Joseph's University, Erivan K. Haub School of Business, Professional MBA Program, Philadelphia, PA 19131-1395. Offers accounting (MBA); finance (MBA), including finance; general business (MBA); health and medical services administration (MBA); human resource management (MBA); international business (MBA); international marketing (MBA); management (MBA); marketing (MBA); DO/MBA. Part-time and evening/weekend programs available. *Students:* 51 full-time (24 women), 480 part-time (184 women); includes 71 minority (32 African Americans, 1 American Indian/Alaska Native, 30 Asian Americans or Pacific Islanders, 8 Hispanic Americans), 38 international. Average age 30. In 2009, 190 master's awarded. *Entrance requirements:* For master's, GMAT or GRE, 2 letters of recommendation, resume. Additional exam requirements/recommendations for international students: Required—TOEFL (minimum score 550 paper-based; 213 computer-based; 79 iBT) or IELTS (minimum score 6.5). *Application deadline:* For fall admission, 7/15 priority date for domestic students, 4/15 priority date for international students; for spring admission, 11/15 priority date for domestic students, 10/15 priority date for international students. Applications are processed on a rolling basis. Application fee: $35. Electronic applications accepted. *Expenses:* Tuition: Part-time $729 per credit hour. Tuition and fees vary according to degree level and program. *Financial support:* Scholarships/grants and unspecified assistantships available. Financial award application deadline: 5/1. *Unit head:* Adele C. Foley, Associate Dean/Director, Graduate Business Programs, 610-660-1691, Fax: 610-660-1599, E-mail: afoley@sju.edu. *Application contact:* Janine N. Guerra, Esq., Assistant Director, MBA Program, 610-660-1695, Fax: 610-660-1599, E-mail: jguerra@sju.edu.

Saint Leo University, Graduate Business Studies, Saint Leo, FL 33574-6665. Offers accounting (MBA); business (MBA); criminal justice (MBA); health services management (MBA); human resource administration (MBA); information security management (MBA); marketing (MBA); sport business (MBA). Part-time and evening/weekend programs available. Postbaccalaureate distance learning degree programs offered (no on-campus study). *Faculty:* 31 full-time (5 women), 48 part-time/adjunct (17 women). *Students:* 1,433 full-time (856 women), 3 part-time (1 woman); includes 601 minority (429 African Americans, 8 American Indian/Alaska Native, 75 Asian Americans or Pacific Islanders, 89 Hispanic Americans), 11 international. Average age 37. In 2009, 405 master's awarded. *Entrance requirements:* For master's, GMAT (minimum score 500 if applicant does not have 5 years of professional work experience), bachelor's degree from regionally-accredited college or university with minimum GPA of 3.0 in the last 60 hours of coursework; 5 years of professional work experience; resume; 2 letters of recommendation. Additional exam requirements/recommendations for international students: Required—TOEFL (minimum score 550 paper-based; 213 computer-based; 80 iBT). *Application deadline:* For fall admission, 7/1 priority date for domestic students; for spring admission, 11/12 priority date for domestic students. Applications are processed on a rolling basis. Application fee: $75. Electronic applications accepted. *Expenses:* Contact institution. *Financial support:* In 2009–10, 1 student received support. Career-related internships or fieldwork, Federal Work-Study, and health care benefits available. Financial award application deadline: 3/1; financial award applicants required to submit FAFSA. *Unit head:* Dr. Robert Robertson, Director, 352-588-7390, Fax: 352-588-8585, E-mail: mba@saintleo.edu. *Application contact:* Jared Welling, Director, Graduate/Weekend and Evening Admission, 800-707-8846, Fax: 352-588-7873, E-mail: grad.admissions@saintleo.edu.

Saint Louis University, Graduate School, John Cook School of Business, Department of Accounting, St. Louis, MO 63103-2097. Offers M Acct, MBA. Part-time and evening/weekend programs available. *Entrance requirements:* For master's, GMAT. Additional exam requirements/recommendations for international students: Required—TOEFL (minimum score 570 paper-based; 230 computer-based; 88 iBT). Electronic applications accepted. *Expenses:* Contact institution. *Faculty research:* Tax policy, market valuation/corporate governance, foreign currency translation, accounting for income taxes, earnings quality.

St. Mary's University, Graduate School, Bill Greehey School of Business, Program in Accounting, San Antonio, TX 78228-8507. Part-time programs available. Postbaccalaureate distance learning degree programs offered (minimal on-campus study). *Entrance requirements:* Additional exam requirements/recommendations for international students: Required—TOEFL (minimum score 550 paper-based; 213 computer-based; 80 iBT). Electronic applications accepted. *Expenses:* Tuition: Full-time $8004. Required fees: $536. One-time fee: $5 full-time. Full-time tuition and fees vary according to program.

Saint Peter's College, Graduate Business Programs, Program in Accountancy, Jersey City, NJ 07306-5997. Offers MS, MBA/MS. Part-time and evening/weekend programs available. *Entrance requirements:* Additional exam requirements/recommendations for international students: Required—TOEFL. *Application deadline:* Applications are processed on a rolling basis. Electronic applications accepted. *Expenses:* Tuition: Part-time $971 per credit. *Financial support:* Career-related internships or fieldwork, Federal Work-Study, and institutionally sponsored loans available.

St. Thomas University, School of Business, Department of Management, Miami Gardens, FL 33054-6459. Offers accounting (MBA); general management (MSM, Certificate); health management (MBA, MSM, Certificate); human resource management (MBA, MSM, Certificate); international business (MBA, MIB, MSM, Certificate); justice administration (MSM, Certificate); management accounting (MSM, Certificate); public management (MSM, Certificate); sports administration (MS). Part-time and evening/weekend programs available. *Degree requirements:* For master's, comprehensive exam. *Entrance requirements:* For master's, interview, minimum GPA of 3.0 or GMAT. Additional exam requirements/recommendations for international students: Required—TOEFL (minimum score 550 paper-based; 213 computer-based; 79 iBT). Electronic applications accepted.

Salisbury University, Graduate Division, Department of Business Administration, Salisbury, MD 21801. Offers accounting track (MBA); general track (MBA). *Accreditation:* AACSB. Part-time and evening/weekend programs available. *Faculty:* 13 full-time (3 women), 1 part-time/adjunct (0 women). *Students:* 21 full-time (8 women), 43 part-time (20 women); includes 6 minority (2 African Americans, 1 Asian American or Pacific Islander, 3 Hispanic Americans), 9 international. Average age 31. 59 applicants, 46% accepted, 26 enrolled. In 2009, 41 master's awarded. *Entrance requirements:* For master's, GMAT, resume; 2 recommendations. Additional exam requirements/recommendations for international students: Required—TOEFL (minimum score 550 paper-based; 79 iBT). *Application deadline:* For fall admission, 3/1 priority date for domestic students; for spring admission, 10/15 priority date for domestic students. Applications are processed on a rolling basis. Application fee: $45. Electronic applications accepted. *Expenses:* Tuition, area resident: Part-time $278 per credit hour. Tuition, state resident: part-time $278 per credit hour. Tuition, nonresident: part-time $574 per credit hour. Required fees: $57 per credit hour. *Financial support:* In 2009–10, 13 students received support. Institutionally sponsored loans, scholarships/grants, and unspecified assistantships available. Support available to part-time students. Financial award applicants required to submit FAFSA. *Unit head:* Yvonne Downie, MBA Director, 410-548-3983, Fax: 410-546-6208, E-mail: yxdownie@salisbury.edu. *Application contact:* Yvonne Downie, MBA Director, 410-548-3983, Fax: 410-546-6208, E-mail: yxdownie@salisbury.edu.

Sam Houston State University, College of Business Administration, Huntsville, TX 77341. Offers accounting (MS); business administration (MBA); general business and finance (MS), including finance. *Accreditation:* AACSB. Part-time and evening/weekend programs available. *Faculty:* 31 full-time (8 women). *Students:* 128 full-time (48 women), 101 part-time (44 women); includes 36 minority (11 African Americans, 1 American Indian/Alaska Native, 11 Asian Americans or Pacific Islanders, 13 Hispanic Americans), 31 international. Average age 29. 141 applicants, 83% accepted, 78 enrolled. In 2009, 97 master's awarded. *Entrance requirements:* For master's, GMAT. Additional exam requirements/recommendations for international students: Required—TOEFL (minimum score 550 paper-based; 213 computer-based; 79 iBT). *Application deadline:* For fall admission, 8/1 for domestic students; for spring admission, 12/1 for domestic students. Applications are processed on a rolling basis. Application fee: $20. *Expenses:* Tuition, state resident: full-time $3690; part-time $205 per credit hour. Tuition, nonresident: full-time $8676; part-time $482 per credit hour. Required fees: $1474. Tuition and fees vary according to course load and campus/location. *Financial support:* Research assistantships, Federal Work-Study, institutionally sponsored loans, and unspecified assistantships available. Financial award application deadline: 5/31; financial award applicants required to submit FAFSA. *Unit head:* Dr. Mitchell J. Muehsam, Dean, 936-294-1254, Fax: 936-294-3612, E-mail: mmuehsam@shsu.edu. *Application contact:* Dr. Leroy Ashorn, Advisor, 936-294-1246, Fax: 936-294-3612, E-mail: busgrad@shsu.edu.

San Diego State University, Graduate and Research Affairs, College of Business Administration, School of Accountancy, San Diego, CA 92182. Offers MS. *Accreditation:* AACSB. *Degree requirements:* For master's, thesis or alternative. *Entrance requirements:* For master's, GMAT, resume, letters of reference. Additional exam requirements/recommendations for international students: Required—TOEFL. Electronic applications accepted.

San Jose State University, Graduate Studies and Research, Lucas Graduate School of Business, Program in Accounting, San Jose, CA 95192-0001. Offers MS. *Degree requirements:* For master's, comprehensive exam, thesis or alternative. *Entrance requirements:* For master's, GMAT, minimum GPA of 3.0. *Application deadline:* For fall admission, 6/29 for domestic students; for spring admission, 11/30 for domestic students. Applications are processed on a rolling basis. Application fee: $59. Electronic applications accepted. *Financial support:* Applicants required to submit FAFSA. *Unit head:* Lori Wilkin, Coordinator, 408-924-3460, Fax: 408-924-3463, E-mail: wilkin_l@cob.sjsu.edu. *Application contact:* Lori Wilkin, Coordinator, 408-924-3460, Fax: 408-924-3463, E-mail: wilkin_l@cob.sjsu.edu.

Santa Clara University, Leavey School of Business, Program in Business Administration, Santa Clara, CA 95053. Offers accounting (MBA); entrepreneurship (MBA); executive MBA (EMBA); finance (MBA); food and agribusiness (MBA); international business (MBA); leading people and organizations (MBA); managing technology and innovation (MBA); marketing management (MBA); supply chain management (MBA). *Accreditation:* AACSB. Part-time and evening/weekend programs available. *Students:* 228 full-time (88 women), 838 part-time (265 women); includes 388 minority (17 African Americans, 2 American Indian/Alaska Native, 326 Asian Americans or Pacific Islanders, 43 Hispanic Americans), 218 international. Average age 31. 486 applicants, 77% accepted, 263 enrolled. In 2009, 317 master's awarded. *Degree requirements:* For master's, thesis or alternative. *Entrance requirements:* For master's, GMAT, GRE. Additional exam requirements/recommendations for international students: Required—TOEFL (minimum score 600 paper-based; 250 computer-based; 100 iBT). *Application deadline:* For fall admission, 6/1 for domestic and international students; for spring admission, 1/19 for domestic students, 1/17 for international students. Applications are processed on a rolling basis. Application fee: $75 ($100 for international students). Electronic applications accepted. *Expenses:* Contact institution. *Financial support:* Fellowships with partial tuition reimbursements, research assistantships with partial tuition reimbursements, career-related internships or fieldwork, Federal Work-Study, institutionally sponsored loans, scholarships/grants, health care benefits, and unspecified assistantships available. Support available to part-time students. Financial award applicants required to submit FAFSA. *Unit head:* Elizabeth B. Ford, Senior Assistant Dean, 408-554-2752, Fax: 408-554-4571, E-mail: eford@scu.edu. *Application contact:* Jennifer W. Taylor, Senior Director, 408-554-4539, Fax: 408-554-4571, E-mail: mbaadmissions@scu.edu.

Seattle University, Albers School of Business and Economics, Program in Professional Accounting, Seattle, WA 98122-1090. Offers MPAC. *Entrance requirements:* For master's, GMAT, minimum GPA of 3.0, 1 year related experience. Additional exam requirements/recommendations for international students: Required—TOEFL.

Seton Hall University, Stillman School of Business, Department of Accounting, South Orange, NJ 07079-2697. Offers accounting (MS); professional accounting (MS); taxation (Certificate). Part-time and evening/weekend programs available. *Faculty:* 10 full-time (2 women), 5 part-time/adjunct (2 women). *Students:* 20 full-time (7 women), 23 part-time (7 women); includes 10 minority (2 African Americans, 7 Asian Americans or Pacific Islanders, 1 Hispanic American). Average age 28. 85 applicants, 80% accepted, 43 enrolled. In 2009, 23 master's awarded. *Entrance requirements:* For master's, GMAT, minimum GPA of 3.0. Additional exam requirements/recommendations for international students: Required—TOEFL (minimum score 607 paper-based; 254 computer-based; 102 iBT), or IELTS, or Pearson Test of English (PTE). *Application deadline:* For fall admission, 5/31 priority date for domestic students, 3/31 for international students; for spring admission, 10/31 for domestic students, 9/30 for international students. Applications are processed on a rolling basis. Application fee: $75. Electronic applications accepted. *Financial support:* In 2009–10, 2 students received support, including research assistantships with full tuition reimbursements available (averaging $34,404 per year); career-related internships or fieldwork, scholarships/grants, and unspecified assistantships also available. Support available to part-time students. Financial award application deadline: 6/30; financial award applicants required to submit FAFSA. *Faculty research:* Voluntary disclosure, international accounting, pension and retirement accounting, ethics in financial reporting. *Unit head:* Dr. Mark Holtzman, Chair, 973-261-4133, Fax: 973-761-9207, E-mail: mark.holtzman@shu.edu. *Application contact:* Catherine Bianchi, Director of Graduate Admissions, 973-761-9262, Fax: 973-761-9208, E-mail: catherine.bianchi@shu.edu.

Seton Hall University, Stillman School of Business, Programs in Business Administration, South Orange, NJ 07079-2697. Offers accounting (MBA); finance (MBA); information technology management (MBA); international business (MBA); management (MBA); marketing (MBA); sport management (MBA). Part-time and evening/weekend programs available. *Faculty:* 57 full-time (13 women), 30 part-time/adjunct (3 women). *Students:* 69 full-time (26 women), 217 part-time (91 women); includes 53 minority (11 African Americans, 35 Asian Americans or Pacific Islanders, 7 Hispanic Americans), 38 international. Average age 29. 286 applicants, 70% accepted, 130 enrolled. In 2009, 110 master's awarded. *Degree requirements:* For master's, 20 hours of community service (Social Responsibility Project). *Entrance requirements:* For master's, GMAT, minimum GPA of 3.0. Additional exam requirements/recommendations for international students: Required—TOEFL (minimum score 607 paper-based; 254 computer-based; 102 iBT), or IELTS, or Pearson Test of English (PTE). *Application deadline:* For fall admission, 5/31 priority date for domestic students, 3/31 priority date for international students; for spring admission, 10/31 priority date for domestic students, 4/30 priority date for international students. Applications are processed on a rolling basis. Application fee: $75. Electronic applications accepted. *Financial support:* In 2009–10, research assistantships with full tuition reimbursements (averaging $34,404 per year); career-related internships or fieldwork, Federal Work-Study, scholarships/grants, and unspecified assistantships also available. Support available to part-time students. Financial award application deadline: 6/30; financial award applicants required to submit FAFSA. *Faculty research:* Financial, hedge funds, international business, legal issues, disclosure and branding. *Unit head:* Dr. Joyce A. Strawser, Associate Dean for Undergraduate and MBA Curricula, 973-761-9225, Fax: 973-761-9217, E-mail: strawsjo@shu.edu. *Application contact:* Catherine Bianchi, Director of Graduate Admissions, 973-761-9262, Fax: 973-761-9208, E-mail: catherine.bianchi@shu.edu.

Southeast Missouri State University, School of Graduate Studies, Harrison College of Business, Cape Girardeau, MO 63701-4799. Offers accounting (MBA); entrepreneurship (MBA);

Accounting

Southeast Missouri State University (continued)
environmental management (MBA); financial management (MBA); general management (MBA); health administration (MBA); industrial management (MBA); international business (MBA); sport management (MBA). *Accreditation:* AACSB. Part-time and evening/weekend programs available. Postbaccalaureate distance learning degree programs offered (no on-campus study). *Degree requirements:* For master's, applied research project. *Entrance requirements:* For master's, GMAT, minimum undergraduate GPA of 2.5. Additional exam requirements/recommendations for international students: Required—TOEFL (minimum score 550 paper-based; 213 computer-based); Recommended—IELTS (minimum score 6). *Expenses:* Tuition, state resident: full-time $4266; part-time $237 per credit hour. Tuition, nonresident: full-time $7506; part-time $417 per credit hour. Required fees: $427; $427. *Faculty research:* Human resources, laws impacting accounting, advertising.

Southern Adventist University, School of Business and Management, Collegedale, TN 37315-0370. Offers accounting (MBA); church administration (MSA); church and nonprofit leadership (MBA); financial management (MFM); healthcare administration (MBA); management (MBA); marketing management (MBA); outdoor education (MSA); MFM. Part-time and evening/weekend programs available. Postbaccalaureate distance learning degree programs offered (no on-campus study). *Faculty:* 2 full-time (0 women), 8 part-time/adjunct (1 woman). *Students:* 55 full-time (32 women), 30 part-time (22 women); includes 23 minority (14 African Americans, 1 American Indian/Alaska Native, 1 Asian American or Pacific Islander, 7 Hispanic Americans). Average age 35. In 2009, 20 master's awarded. *Entrance requirements:* For master's, GMAT. Additional exam requirements/recommendations for international students: Required—TOEFL (minimum score 600 paper-based; 250 computer-based; 100 iBT). *Application deadline:* For fall admission, 8/1 priority date for domestic students, 7/1 for international students; for winter admission, 12/1 priority date for domestic students, 11/1 for international students; for spring admission, 4/1 priority date for domestic students, 3/1 for international students. Applications are processed on a rolling basis. Application fee: $25. Electronic applications accepted. *Expenses:* Tuition: Full-time $13,149; part-time $487 per credit hour. *Financial support:* In 2009–10, 32 students received support. Scholarships/grants and unspecified assistantships available. Financial award application deadline: 9/1; financial award applicants required to submit FAFSA. *Unit head:* Dr. Don Van Ornam, Dean, 423-236-2750, Fax: 423-236-1527, E-mail: dvanorna@southern.edu. *Application contact:* Linda Wilhelm, Admissions Coordinator, 423-236-2751, Fax: 423-236-1527, E-mail: sbm@southern.edu.

Southern Illinois University Carbondale, Graduate School, College of Business and Administration, School of Accountancy, Carbondale, IL 62901-4701. Offers M Acc, PhD, JD/M Acc. *Accreditation:* AACSB. Part-time programs available. *Degree requirements:* For doctorate, thesis/dissertation. *Entrance requirements:* For master's, GMAT, minimum GPA of 2.7; for doctorate, GMAT, minimum graduate GPA of 3.25. Additional exam requirements/recommendations for international students: Required—TOEFL. *Faculty research:* Not-for-profit accounting, SEC regulations, computers and accounting education, taxation.

Southern Illinois University Edwardsville, Graduate Studies and Research, School of Business, Department of Accounting, Edwardsville, IL 62026-0001. Offers accountancy (MSA); taxation (MSA). *Accreditation:* AACSB. Part-time and evening/weekend programs available. *Faculty:* 5 full-time (1 woman). *Students:* 16 full-time (6 women), 19 part-time (13 women); includes 1 minority (African American), 2 international. Average age 26. 38 applicants, 50% accepted. In 2009, 23 master's awarded. *Degree requirements:* For master's, thesis or alternative, final exam. *Entrance requirements:* For master's, GMAT. Additional exam requirements/recommendations for international students: Required—TOEFL (minimum score 550 paper-based; 213 computer-based; 79 iBT), IELTS (minimum score 6.5). *Application deadline:* For fall admission, 7/23 for domestic students, 6/1 for international students; for spring admission, 12/11 for domestic students, 10/1 for international students. Applications are processed on a rolling basis. Application fee: $30. Electronic applications accepted. *Expenses:* Tuition, state resident: part-time $1252.50 per semester. Tuition, nonresident: part-time $3131.25 per semester. Required fees: $586.85 per semester. Tuition and fees vary according to course load. *Financial support:* In 2009–10, 1 fellowship with full tuition reimbursement (averaging $8,370 per year), 10 teaching assistantships with full tuition reimbursements (averaging $8,064 per year) were awarded; research assistantships with full tuition reimbursements, career-related internships or fieldwork, Federal Work-Study, institutionally sponsored loans, scholarships/grants, traineeships, and unspecified assistantships also available. Support available to part-time students. Financial award application deadline: 3/1; financial award applicants required to submit FAFSA. *Unit head:* Dr. Michael Costigan, Chair, 618-650-2633, E-mail: mcostig@siue.edu. *Application contact:* Dr. Michael Costigan, Chair, 618-650-2633, E-mail: mcostig@siue.edu.

Southern Methodist University, Cox School of Business, MBA Program, Dallas, TX 75275. Offers accounting (MBA); finance (MBA); information technology and operations management (MBA); management (MBA); marketing (MBA); strategy and entrepreneurship (MBA). *Students:* 396 full-time (91 women), 401 part-time (109 women); includes 185 minority (34 African Americans, 5 American Indian/Alaska Native, 102 Asian Americans or Pacific Islanders, 44 Hispanic Americans), 76 international. Average age 31. In 2009, 363 master's awarded. *Unit head:* Dr. Albert W. Niemi, Dean, 214-768-3012, Fax: 214-768-3713, E-mail: aniemi@mail.cox.smu.edu. *Application contact:* Path Cudney, Director of MBA Admissions, 214-768-3001, Fax: 214-768-3956, E-mail: pcudney@mail.cox.smu.edu.

Southern Methodist University, Cox School of Business, Program in Accounting, Dallas, TX 75275. Offers MSA. Part-time programs available. *Faculty:* 14 full-time (4 women), 10 part-time/adjunct (4 women). *Students:* 75 full-time (42 women), 12 part-time (6 women); includes 14 minority (4 African Americans, 7 Asian Americans or Pacific Islanders, 3 Hispanic Americans), 11 international. Average age 24. 65 applicants, 57% accepted. In 2009, 58 master's awarded. *Entrance requirements:* For master's, GMAT. Additional exam requirements/recommendations for international students: Required—TOEFL. *Application deadline:* For fall admission, 5/15 priority date for domestic students; for winter admission, 11/30 for domestic students. Application fee: $75. *Expenses:* Contact institution. *Financial support:* In 2009–10, 17 students received support, including 17 fellowships (averaging $3,800 per year); scholarships/grants and tuition waivers (partial) also available. Financial award application deadline: 5/15. *Faculty research:* Capital markets, taxation, business combinations, intangibles accounting, accounting history. *Unit head:* Joseph Magliolo, Head, 214-768-1678, Fax: 214-768-4099, E-mail: jmagliol@mail.cox.smu.edu. *Application contact:* Jeffrey R. Austin, Coordinator, 214-768-3630, Fax: 214-768-4099, E-mail: jraustin@mail.cox.smu.edu.

Southern New Hampshire University, School of Business, Manchester, NH 03106-1045. Offers accounting (MS); business administration (MBA, Certificate), including accounting (Certificate), business administration (MBA), finance (Certificate), forensic accounting (Certificate), human resources management (Certificate), international business (Certificate), international sport management (Certificate), leadership of not for profit organizations (Certificate), marketing (Certificate), operations management (Certificate), sport management (Certificate), taxation (Certificate); finance (MS); hospitality and tourism leadership (Certificate); information technology (MS, Certificate); information technology/international business (Certificate); integrated marketing communications (Certificate); international business (MS, DBA); marketing (MS); operations and project management (MS); organizational leadership (MS); project management (Certificate); sport management (MS); MBA/Certificate. *Accreditation:* ACBSP. Part-time and evening/weekend programs available. Postbaccalaureate distance learning degree programs offered (no on-campus study). Terminal master's awarded for partial completion of doctoral program. *Degree requirements:* For master's, one foreign language, comprehensive exam (for some programs), thesis or alternative; for doctorate, one foreign language, comprehensive exam, thesis/dissertation. *Entrance requirements:* For master's, minimum GPA of 2.5; for doctorate, GMAT. Additional exam requirements/recommendations for international students: Required—TOEFL (minimum score 500 paper-based). Electronic applications accepted.

Southern Polytechnic State University, School of Engineering Technology and Management, Department of Business Administration, Marietta, GA 30060-2896. Offers accounting (MSA); business administration (MBA, Graduate Transition Certificate). *Accreditation:* ACBSP. Part-time and evening/weekend programs available. Postbaccalaureate distance learning degree programs offered (no on-campus study). *Faculty:* 10 full-time (4 women), 4 part-time/adjunct (1 woman). *Students:* 75 full-time (40 women), 83 part-time (34 women); includes 47 African Americans, 11 Asian Americans or Pacific Islanders, 6 Hispanic Americans, 57 international. Average age 31. 78 applicants, 92% accepted, 51 enrolled. In 2009, 40 master's awarded. *Degree requirements:* For master's, comprehensive exam, thesis or alternative. *Entrance requirements:* For master's, GMAT. Additional exam requirements/recommendations for international students: Required—TOEFL (minimum score 550 paper-based; 213 computer-based; 79 iBT), IELTS (minimum score 6.5). *Application deadline:* For fall admission, 7/1 priority date for domestic students, 5/1 priority date for international students; for spring admission, 11/1 priority date for domestic students, 9/1 priority date for international students. Applications are processed on a rolling basis. Application fee: $20. Electronic applications accepted. *Expenses:* Tuition, state resident: full-time $2896; part-time $181 per credit hour. Tuition, nonresident: full-time $11,552; part-time $722 per credit hour. Required fees: $1096. *Financial support:* In 2009–10, 37 students received support, including 4 research assistantships with tuition reimbursements available (averaging $4,500 per year); career-related internships or fieldwork, scholarships/grants, and unspecified assistantships also available. Support available to part-time students. Financial award application deadline: 5/1; financial award applicants required to submit FAFSA. *Faculty research:* Ethics, virtual reality, sustainability, management of technology, quality management, capacity planning, human-computer interaction/interface, enterprise integration planning, economic impact of educational institutions, behavioral accounting, accounting ethics, taxation, information security, visualizational simulation, human-computer interaction. *Unit head:* Dr. Ronny Richardson, Chair, 678-915-7440, Fax: 678-915-4967, E-mail: rrichard@spsu.edu. *Application contact:* Nikki Palamiotis, Director of Graduate Studies, 678-915-4276, Fax: 678-915-7292, E-mail: npalamio@spsu.edu.

Southern Utah University, School of Business, Program in Accounting, Cedar City, UT 84720-2498. Offers M Acc. Part-time programs available. *Faculty:* 6 full-time (1 woman), 2 part-time/adjunct (0 women). *Students:* 39 full-time (15 women), 18 part-time (7 women); includes 2 minority (both Asian Americans or Pacific Islanders). 35 applicants, 49% accepted, 17 enrolled. In 2009, 33 master's awarded. *Application deadline:* For fall admission, 8/1 priority date for domestic students. Applications are processed on a rolling basis. Application fee: $50 ($65 for international students). Electronic applications accepted. *Expenses:* Contact institution. *Financial support:* In 2009–10, 5 research assistantships with full tuition reimbursements (averaging $1,200 per year) were awarded; career-related internships or fieldwork, institutionally sponsored loans, tuition waivers (full and partial), and unspecified assistantships also available. *Faculty research:* Cost accounting, intermediate accounting text, GAAP policy, statements on Standards for Accounting and Review Services (SSARS). *Unit head:* Dr. David Christensen, Chair, Accounting Department, 435-865-8058, Fax: 435-586-5493, E-mail: christensen@suu.edu. *Application contact:* Chris Proctor, Associate Director of Admissions, 435-586-7742, Fax: 435-865-8223, E-mail: alger@suu.edu.

Southwestern Adventist University, Business Department, Graduate Program, Keene, TX 76059. Offers accounting (MBA); finance (MBA); management / leadership (MBA). Part-time and evening/weekend programs available. *Degree requirements:* For master's, capstone course. *Entrance requirements:* For master's, GMAT, GRE General Test.

State University of New York at Binghamton, Graduate School, School of Management, Program in Accounting, Binghamton, NY 13902-6000. Offers MS, PhD. Evening/weekend programs available. *Students:* 110 full-time (64 women), 16 part-time (10 women); includes 20 minority (4 African Americans, 12 Asian Americans or Pacific Islanders, 4 Hispanic Americans), 77 international. Average age 25. 296 applicants, 34% accepted, 62 enrolled. In 2009, 59 master's awarded. *Degree requirements:* For doctorate, thesis/dissertation. *Entrance requirements:* For master's and doctorate, GMAT. Additional exam requirements/recommendations for international students: Required—TOEFL (minimum score 550 paper-based; 213 computer-based; 80 iBT). *Application deadline:* For fall admission, 3/1 priority date for domestic and international students; for spring admission, 10/15 priority date for domestic and international students. Applications are processed on a rolling basis. Application fee: $60. Electronic applications accepted. *Financial support:* Fellowships, research assistantships, teaching assistantships, career-related internships or fieldwork, Federal Work-Study, institutionally sponsored loans, scholarships/grants, health care benefits, and unspecified assistantships available. Financial award application deadline: 2/15; financial award applicants required to submit FAFSA. *Unit head:* Dr. Upinder Dhillon, Dean of School of Management, 607-777-2314, E-mail: dhillon@binghamton.edu. *Application contact:* Victoria Williams, Recruiting and Admissions Coordinator, 607-777-2151, Fax: 607-777-2501, E-mail: vwilliam@binghamton.edu.

State University of New York at Fredonia, Graduate Studies, Department of Business Administration, Fredonia, NY 14063-1136. Offers accounting (MS). *Expenses:* Tuition, state resident: full-time $8370; part-time $349 per credit. Tuition, nonresident: full-time $13,250; part-time $552 per credit. Required fees: $1289; $53.55 per credit.

State University of New York at New Paltz, Graduate School, School of Business, New Paltz, NY 12561. Offers business administration (MBA); public accountancy (MBA). Part-time and evening/weekend programs available. *Faculty:* 15 full-time (3 women), 1 (woman) part-time/adjunct. *Students:* 42 full-time (20 women), 40 part-time (24 women); includes 12 minority (1 African American, 1 American Indian/Alaska Native, 6 Asian Americans or Pacific Islanders, 4 Hispanic Americans), 16 international. Average age 31. 50 applicants, 68% accepted, 21 enrolled. In 2009, 42 master's awarded. *Degree requirements:* For master's, internship. *Entrance requirements:* For master's, GMAT or GRE, minimum GPA of 3.0. Additional exam requirements/recommendations for international students: Required—TOEFL (minimum score 550 paper-based; 213 computer-based; 80 iBT), IELTS (minimum score 6.5). *Application deadline:* For fall admission, 5/15 priority date for domestic students, 5/15 for international students; for spring admission, 11/15 for domestic and international students. Applications are processed on a rolling basis. Application fee: $50. Electronic applications accepted. *Expenses:* Contact institution. *Financial support:* In 2009–10, 8 students received support, including 7 research assistantships with partial tuition reimbursements available (averaging $5,000 per year), 1 teaching assistantship with partial tuition reimbursement available (averaging $5,000 per year); fellowships, career-related internships or fieldwork, scholarships/grants, traineeships, and unspecified assistantships also available. Financial award application deadline: 8/1; financial award applicants required to submit FAFSA. *Faculty research:* Cognitive styles in management education, supporting SME e-commerce migration through e-learning, earnings management and board activity, trading future spread portfolio, global equity market correlation and volatility. *Unit head:* Dr. Hadi Salavitabar, Dean, 845-257-2930, E-mail: mba@newpaltz.edu. *Application contact:* Aaron Hines, Coordinator, 845-257-2968, E-mail: mba@newpaltz.edu.

State University of New York College at Geneseo, Graduate Studies, School of Business, Geneseo, NY 14454-1401. Offers accounting (MS). *Accreditation:* AACSB. *Faculty:* 3 full-time (1 woman), 1 part-time/adjunct (0 women). *Students:* 9 full-time (3 women); includes 1 minority (Asian American or Pacific Islander). Average age 24. 20 applicants, 95% accepted, 9 enrolled. In 2009, 5 master's awarded. *Entrance requirements:* For master's, GMAT, bachelor's degree in accounting. *Application deadline:* For fall admission, 2/1 priority date for domestic students; for spring admission, 9/1 for domestic students. Application fee: $50. *Expenses:* Tuition, state resident: full-time $8370; part-time $349 per credit hour. Tuition, nonresident: full-time $13,250; part-time $552 per credit hour. Required fees: $700.52; $29 per credit hour. *Financial support:* Application deadline: 4/1. *Unit head:* Dr. Michael Schinski, Interim Dean, 585-245-5367, Fax: 585-245-5467, E-mail: schinski@geneseo.edu. *Application contact:* Dr. Harry Howe, Director, MS in Accounting, 585-245-5465, Fax: 585-245-5467, E-mail: howeh@geneseo.edu.

State University of New York College at Old Westbury, Program in Accounting, Old Westbury, NY 11568-0210. Offers MS. Part-time and evening/weekend programs available. *Faculty:* 9 full-time (2 women), 2 part-time/adjunct (0 women). *Students:* 30 full-time (15

women), 27 part-time (11 women); includes 12 minority (2 African Americans, 1 American Indian/Alaska Native, 5 Asian Americans or Pacific Islanders, 4 Hispanic Americans), 3 international. Average age 33. *Entrance requirements:* For master's, GMAT, 2 letters of recommendation. Additional exam requirements/recommendations for international students: Required—TOEFL (minimum score 550 paper-based; 213 computer-based). *Application deadline:* For fall admission, 6/15 priority date for domestic students; for spring admission, 11/15 priority date for domestic students. Applications are processed on a rolling basis. Application fee: $50. Electronic applications accepted. *Expenses:* Tuition, state resident: full-time $8400; part-time $349 per credit. Tuition, nonresident: full-time $13,200; part-time $552 per credit. Required fees: $600; $60 per credit. *Faculty research:* Corporate governance, asset pricing, corporate finance, hedge funds, taxation. *Unit head:* Dr. James M. Fornaro, Director of Graduate Business Programs, 516-876-2883, E-mail: fornaroj@oldwestbury.edu. *Application contact:* Philip D'Angelo, Graduate Admissions Office, 516-876-3073, E-mail: enroll@oldwestbury.edu.

State University of New York Institute of Technology, School of Business, Program in Accountancy, Utica, NY 13504-3050. Offers MS. *Accreditation:* AACSB. Part-time and evening/weekend programs available. Postbaccalaureate distance learning degree programs offered (no on-campus study). *Degree requirements:* For master's, capstone courses. *Entrance requirements:* For master's, GMAT, minimum GPA of 3.0, letters of recommendation. Additional exam requirements/recommendations for international students: Required—TOEFL (minimum score 550 paper-based; 213 computer-based). *Faculty research:* Cash flows, accounting earnings, stock price analysis.

Stephen F. Austin State University, Graduate School, College of Business, Program in Professional Accountancy, Nacogdoches, TX 75962. Offers MPAC. Students admitted at the undergraduate level. *Degree requirements:* For master's, comprehensive exam. *Entrance requirements:* For master's, GMAT. Additional exam requirements/recommendations for international students: Required—TOEFL.

Stetson University, School of Business Administration, Program in Accounting, DeLand, FL 32723. Offers M Acc. *Accreditation:* AACSB. Part-time programs available. *Students:* 35 full-time (26 women), 6 part-time (3 women); includes 6 minority (3 African Americans, 3 Asian Americans or Pacific Islanders). Average age 30. In 2009, 17 master's awarded. *Entrance requirements:* For master's, GMAT. *Application deadline:* For fall admission, 7/1 for domestic students. Application fee: $25. Tuition and fees vary according to course load, campus/location and program. *Financial support:* In 2009–10, 3 research assistantships were awarded; Federal Work-Study and institutionally sponsored loans also available. Support available to part-time students. Financial award application deadline: 3/15. *Unit head:* Dr. Judson P. Stryker, Director, 386-822-7410. *Application contact:* Jeanne Bosco, Administrative Assistant, 386-822-7410, Fax: 386-822-7413, E-mail: jbosco@stetson.edu.

Stratford University, School of Graduate Studies, Falls Church, VA 22043. Offers accounting (MS); business administration (IMBA, MBA); enterprise business management (MS); entrepreneurial management (MS); information assurance (MS); information systems (MS); software engineering (MS); telecommunications (MS). Part-time and evening/weekend programs available. Postbaccalaureate distance learning degree programs offered (no on-campus study). *Faculty:* 35 full-time (15 women), 115 part-time/adjunct (25 women). *Students:* 944 full-time (430 women), 15 part-time (5 women). Average age 26. 950 applicants, 45% accepted, 415 enrolled. In 2009, 412 master's awarded. *Degree requirements:* For master's, comprehensive exam, capstone project. *Entrance requirements:* For master's, baccalaureate degree. Additional exam requirements/recommendations for international students: Required—TOEFL (minimum score 500 paper-based; 173 computer-based; 61 iBT). *Application deadline:* Applications are processed on a rolling basis. Application fee: $50. Electronic applications accepted. *Expenses:* Tuition: Full-time $10,530; part-time $390 per credit. Tuition and fees vary according to course load. *Financial support:* Federal Work-Study available. Financial award applicants required to submit FAFSA. *Unit head:* Dr. Habib Khan, Chief Academic Officer, 703-821-8570 Ext. 3305, Fax: 703-734-5335, E-mail: hkhan@stratford.edu. *Application contact:* James Ray, Director of Admissions, 703-821-8570 Ext. 3021, Fax: 703-734-5339, E-mail: jray@stratford.edu.

Strayer University, Graduate Studies, Washington, DC 20005-2603. Offers accounting (MS); acquisition (MBA); business administration (MBA); communications technology (MS); educational management (M Ed); finance (MBA); health services administration (MHSA); hospitality and tourism management (MBA); human resource management (MBA); information systems (MS), including computer security management, decision support system management, enterprise resource management, network management, software engineering management, systems development management; management (MBA); management information systems (MS); marketing (MBA); professional accounting (MS), including accounting information systems, controllership, taxation; public administration (MPA); supply chain management (MBA); technology in education (M Ed). Programs also offered at campus locations in Birmingham, AL; Chamblee, GA; Cobb County, GA; Morrow, GA; White Marsh, MD; Charleston, SC; Columbia, SC; Greensboro, NC; Greenville, SC; Lexington, KY; Louisville, KY; Nashville, TN; North Raleigh, NC; Washington, DC. Part-time and evening/weekend programs available. Postbaccalaureate distance learning degree programs offered (minimal on-campus study). *Degree requirements:* For master's, thesis. *Entrance requirements:* For master's, GMAT, GRE General Test, bachelor's degree from an accredited college or university, minimum undergraduate GPA of 2.75. Electronic applications accepted.

Suffolk University, Sawyer Business School, Department of Accounting, Boston, MA 02108-2770. Offers accounting (MSA, GDPA); taxation (MST); GDPA/MST; MBA/GDPA; MBA/MSA; MBA/MST. *Accreditation:* AACSB. Part-time and evening/weekend programs available. *Faculty:* 17 full-time (5 women), 7 part-time/adjunct (2 women). *Students:* 81 full-time (63 women), 149 part-time (81 women); includes 24 minority (5 African Americans, 17 Asian Americans or Pacific Islanders, 2 Hispanic Americans), 84 international. Average age 29. 457 applicants, 68% accepted, 85 enrolled. In 2009, 78 master's, 3 GDPAs awarded. *Entrance requirements:* For master's, GMAT. Additional exam requirements/recommendations for international students: Required—TOEFL (minimum score 550 paper-based; 213 computer-based; 80 iBT). *Application deadline:* For fall admission, 6/15 priority date for domestic students, 6/15 for international students; for spring admission, 11/1 priority date for domestic students, 11/1 for international students. Applications are processed on a rolling basis. Application fee: $50. Electronic applications accepted. *Expenses:* Tuition: Full-time $33,000; part-time $1100 per credit. Required fees: $20. Tuition and fees vary according to program. *Financial support:* In 2009–10, 105 students received support, including 74 fellowships with full and partial tuition reimbursements available (averaging $18,915 per year); career-related internships or fieldwork, Federal Work-Study, and institutionally sponsored loans also available. Support available to part-time students. Financial award application deadline: 4/1; financial award applicants required to submit CSS PROFILE. *Faculty research:* Tax policy, tax research, decision making in accounting, accounting information systems, capital markets and strategic planning. *Unit head:* Lewis Shaw, Chair, 617-573-8615, Fax: 617-994-4260, E-mail: lshaw@suffolk.edu. *Application contact:* Judith Reynolds, Director of Graduate Admissions, 617-573-8302, Fax: 617-305-1733, E-mail: grad.admission@suffolk.edu.

Suffolk University, Sawyer Business School, Master of Business Administration Program, Boston, MA 02108-2770. Offers accounting (MBA); business administration (APC); corporate financial executive track (MBA); entrepreneurship (MBA); executive business administration (EMBA); finance (MBA); global business administration (GMBA); health administration (MBA); international business (MBA); marketing (MBA); organizational behavior (MBA); strategic management (MBA); taxation (MBA); JD/MBA; MBA/GDPA; MBA/MHA; MBA/MSA; MBA/MSF; MBA/MST. *Accreditation:* AACSB. Part-time and evening/weekend programs available. Postbaccalaureate distance learning degree programs offered (no on-campus study). *Faculty:* 103 full-time (30 women), 63 part-time/adjunct (19 women). *Students:* 173 full-time (68 women), 406 part-time (178 women); includes 51 minority (16 African Americans, 3 American Indian/Alaska Native, 22 Asian Americans or Pacific Islanders, 10 Hispanic Americans), 90 international. Average age 29. 460 applicants, 72% accepted, 157 enrolled. In 2009, 245 master's awarded.

Entrance requirements: For master's, GMAT, minimum undergraduate GPA of 2.75 (MBA), 5 years of managerial experience (EMBA). Additional exam requirements/recommendations for international students: Required—TOEFL (minimum score 550 paper-based; 213 computer-based). *Application deadline:* For fall admission, 6/15 priority date for domestic students, 6/15 for international students; for spring admission, 11/1 priority date for domestic students, 11/1 for international students. Applications are processed on a rolling basis. Application fee: $50. Electronic applications accepted. *Expenses:* Tuition: Full-time $33,000; part-time $1100 per credit. Required fees: $20. Tuition and fees vary according to program. *Financial support:* In 2009–10, 284 students received support, including 99 fellowships with full and partial tuition reimbursements available (averaging $13,599 per year); career-related internships or fieldwork, Federal Work-Study, and institutionally sponsored loans also available. Support available to part-time students. Financial award application deadline: 4/1; financial award applicants required to submit FAFSA. *Faculty research:* Foreign investments; career strategies and boundaryless careers; corporate ethics codes; interest rates, inflation, and growth options; innovation and product development performance. *Unit head:* Lillian Hallberg, Assistant Dean of Graduate Programs/Director of MBA Programs, 617-573-8306, E-mail: lhallber@suffolk.edu. *Application contact:* Judith Reynolds, Director of Graduate Admissions, 617-573-8302, Fax: 617-305-1733, E-mail: grad.admission@suffolk.edu.

Syracuse University, Martin J. Whitman School of Management, PhD Program in Business Administration, Syracuse, NY 13244. Offers accounting (PhD); finance (PhD); management information systems (PhD); managerial statistics (PhD); marketing (PhD); operations management (PhD); organizational behavior (PhD); strategy and human resources (PhD); supply chain management (PhD). *Degree requirements:* For doctorate, comprehensive exam, thesis/dissertation, summer research paper. *Entrance requirements:* For doctorate, GMAT or GRE General Test, 3 recommendations. Additional exam requirements/recommendations for international students: Required—TOEFL (minimum score 600 paper-based; 250 computer-based; 100 iBT). Electronic applications accepted. *Expenses:* Tuition: Full-time $26,808; part-time $1117 per credit. Required fees: $1024. *Faculty research:* Marketing models, market microstructure, supply chain, auditing, corporate governance.

Syracuse University, Martin J. Whitman School of Management, Program in Accounting, Syracuse, NY 13244. Offers MS Acct, JD/MS Acct. Postbaccalaureate distance learning degree programs offered (minimal on-campus study). *Entrance requirements:* For master's, GMAT, 2 letters of recommendation, bachelor's degree in accounting. Additional exam requirements/recommendations for international students: Required—TOEFL (minimum score 600 paper-based; 250 computer-based; 100 iBT). Electronic applications accepted. *Expenses:* Tuition: Full-time $26,808; part-time $1117 per credit. Required fees: $1024.

Syracuse University, Martin J. Whitman School of Management, Program in Business Administration, Syracuse, NY 13244. Offers accounting (MBA); entrepreneurship (MBA); finance (MBA); marketing (MBA); supply chain management (MBA). Postbaccalaureate distance learning degree programs offered (minimal on-campus study). *Entrance requirements:* For master's, GMAT, 2 letters of recommendation. Additional exam requirements/recommendations for international students: Required—TOEFL (minimum score 600 paper-based; 250 computer-based; 100 iBT). Electronic applications accepted. *Expenses:* Tuition: Full-time $26,808; part-time $1117 per credit. Required fees: $1024.

Syracuse University, Martin J. Whitman School of Management, Program in Professional Accounting, Syracuse, NY 13244. Offers MS. *Expenses:* Tuition: Full-time $26,808; part-time $1117 per credit. Required fees: $1024.

Tabor College, Graduate Program, Hillsboro, KS 67063. Offers accounting (MBA). Program offered at the Wichita campus only.

Tarleton State University, College of Graduate Studies, College of Business Administration, Department of Accounting, Finance and Economics, Stephenville, TX 76402. Offers business administration (MBA). Part-time and evening/weekend programs available. *Degree requirements:* For master's, comprehensive exam. *Entrance requirements:* For master's, GRE or GMAT, minimum GPA of 3.0. Additional exam requirements/recommendations for international students: Required—TOEFL (minimum score 550 paper-based; 213 computer-based; 80 iBT). Electronic applications accepted.

Temple University, Graduate School, Fox School of Business, Doctoral Programs in Business, Philadelphia, PA 19122-6096. Offers accounting (PhD); entrepreneurship (PhD); finance (PhD); human resource administration (PhD); international business (PhD); management information systems (PhD); marketing (PhD); risk management and insurance (PhD); statistics (PhD); strategic management (PhD); tourism and sport (PhD). *Accreditation:* AACSB. *Degree requirements:* For doctorate, thesis/dissertation. *Entrance requirements:* For doctorate, GRE General Test, GMAT, minimum GPA of 3.0, master's degree. Additional exam requirements/recommendations for international students: Required—TOEFL (minimum score 600 paper-based; 250 computer-based; 100 iBT), IELTS (minimum score 7.5). Electronic applications accepted.

Temple University, Graduate School, Fox School of Business, MBA Programs, Philadelphia, PA 19122-6096. Offers accounting (MBA); business management (MBA); financial management (MBA); healthcare and life sciences innovation (MBA); human resource management (MBA); international business (IMBA); IT management (MBA); marketing management (MBA); pharmaceutical management (MBA); strategic management (EMBA, MBA). EMBA offered in Philadelphia, PA and Tokyo, Japan. *Accreditation:* AACSB. Part-time and evening/weekend programs available. Postbaccalaureate distance learning degree programs offered (minimal on-campus study). *Entrance requirements:* For master's, GMAT, minimum undergraduate GPA of 3.0. Additional exam requirements/recommendations for international students: Required—TOEFL (minimum score 600 paper-based; 250 computer-based; 100 iBT), IELTS (minimum score 7.5).

Temple University, Graduate School, Fox School of Business, Specialized Master's Programs, Philadelphia, PA 19122-6096. Offers accounting and financial management (MS); actuarial science (MS); finance (MS); financial engineering (MS); healthcare financial management (MS); healthcare management (MHM); human resource management (MS); management information systems (MS); marketing (MS); statistics (MS). *Accreditation:* AACSB. Part-time programs available. *Entrance requirements:* For master's, GRE General Test or GMAT, minimum undergraduate GPA of 3.0. Additional exam requirements/recommendations for international students: Required—TOEFL (minimum score 600 paper-based; 250 computer-based; 100 iBT), IELTS (minimum score 7.5).

Tennessee Technological University, Graduate School, College of Business, Cookeville, TN 38505. Offers accounting (MBA); finance (MBA); human resource management (MBA); international business (MBA); management information systems (MBA); risk management & insurance (MBA). *Accreditation:* AACSB. Part-time and evening/weekend programs available. *Faculty:* 28 full-time (5 women). *Students:* 64 full-time (26 women), 163 part-time (70 women); includes 17 minority (6 African Americans, 8 Asian Americans or Pacific Islanders, 3 Hispanic Americans). Average age 25. 203 applicants, 52% accepted, 75 enrolled. In 2009, 105 master's awarded. *Entrance requirements:* For master's, GMAT. Additional exam requirements/recommendations for international students: Required—TOEFL (minimum score 550 paper-based; 79 iBT), IELTS (minimum score 5.5). *Application deadline:* For fall admission, 8/1 for domestic and international students; for spring admission, 12/1 for domestic students, 10/1 for international students. Application fee: $25 ($30 for international students). Electronic applications accepted. *Expenses:* Tuition, state resident: full-time $7034; part-time $368 per credit hour. *Financial support:* In 2009–10, 5 fellowships (averaging $10,000 per year), 18 research assistantships (averaging $4,000 per year), teaching assistantships (averaging $4,000 per year) were awarded. Support available to part-time students. Financial award application deadline: 4/1. *Unit head:* Dr. Bob G. Wood, Director, 931-372-3600, Fax: 931-372-6249. *Application contact:* Shelia K. Kendrick, Coordinator of Graduate Studies, 931-372-3808, Fax: 931-372-3497, E-mail: skendrick@tntech.edu.

Accounting

Texas A&M International University, Office of Graduate Studies and Research, College of Business Administration, Division of International Banking and Finance Studies, Laredo, TX 78041-1900. Offers accounting (MP Acc); international banking (MBA). *Faculty:* 15 full-time (1 woman), 6 part-time/adjunct (0 women). *Students:* 51 full-time (23 women), 224 part-time (106 women); includes 171 minority (2 African Americans, 2 Asian Americans or Pacific Islanders, 167 Hispanic Americans), 92 international. Average age 29. 145 applicants, 63% accepted, 86 enrolled. In 2009, 108 master's awarded. *Entrance requirements:* For master's, GMAT or GRE General Test. Additional exam requirements/recommendations for international students: Required—TOEFL (minimum score 550 paper-based; 213 computer-based). *Application deadline:* For fall admission, 4/30 priority date for domestic students; for spring admission, 11/30 for domestic students. Applications are processed on a rolling basis. Application fee: $25. *Financial support:* In 2009–10, 21 students received support. *Unit head:* Dr. Ken Hung, Chair, 956-326-2541, Fax: 956-326-2481, E-mail: ken.hung@tamiu.edu. *Application contact:* Imelda Lopez, Graduate Admissions Counselor, 956-326-2485, Fax: 956-326-2459, E-mail: lopez@tamiu.edu.

Texas A&M University, Mays Business School, Department of Accounting, College Station, TX 77843. Offers MS, PhD. *Accreditation:* AACSB. Terminal master's awarded for partial completion of doctoral program. *Degree requirements:* For master's, comprehensive exam; for doctorate, thesis/dissertation. *Entrance requirements:* For master's, GMAT; for doctorate, GMAT or GRE General Test. Additional exam requirements/recommendations for international students: Required—TOEFL. *Expenses:* Tuition, state resident: full-time $3991; part-time $221.74 per credit hour. Tuition, nonresident: full-time $9049; part-time $502.74 per credit hour. *Faculty research:* Financial reporting, taxation management, decision making, accounting information systems, government accounting.

Texas A&M University–Corpus Christi, Graduate Studies and Research, College of Business, Corpus Christi, TX 78412-5503. Offers accounting (M Acc); health care administration (MBA); international business (MBA). *Accreditation:* AACSB. Part-time and evening/weekend programs available. *Degree requirements:* For master's, comprehensive exam, thesis (for some programs). *Entrance requirements:* For master's, GMAT. Additional exam requirements/recommendations for international students: Required—TOEFL. Electronic applications accepted.

Texas A&M University–Texarkana, Graduate Studies and Research, College of Business, Texarkana, TX 75505-5518. Offers accounting (MSA); business administration (MBA, MS). Part-time and evening/weekend programs available. *Degree requirements:* For master's, thesis or alternative. *Entrance requirements:* For master's, minimum GPA of 2.5 in last 60 hours of bachelor's degree. Additional exam requirements/recommendations for international students: Required—TOEFL. Electronic applications accepted.

Texas Christian University, The Neeley School of Business at TCU, Program in Accounting, Fort Worth, TX 76129-0002. Offers M Ac. *Accreditation:* AACSB. *Entrance requirements:* For master's, GMAT, undergraduate degree in accounting. Additional exam requirements/recommendations for international students: Required—TOEFL. *Application deadline:* For fall admission, 3/15 priority date for domestic students. Application fee: $50. *Expenses:* Tuition: Full-time $17,640; part-time $980 per credit hour. Tuition and fees vary according to program. *Financial support:* Tuition waivers available. Financial award application deadline: 3/15; financial award applicants required to submit FAFSA. *Unit head:* Dr. Ray Pfeiffer, Chairperson, 817-257-7223, E-mail: r.pfeiffer@tcu.edu. *Application contact:* Dr. Jerry Turner, Director, 817-257-7223, Fax: 817-257-7227.

Texas State University–San Marcos, Graduate School, Emmett and Miriam McCoy College of Business Administration, Program in Accounting, San Marcos, TX 78666. Offers M Acy. Part-time programs available. *Faculty:* 9 full-time (6 women), 1 part-time/adjunct (0 women). *Students:* 76 full-time (44 women), 41 part-time (24 women); includes 28 minority (2 African Americans, 1 American Indian/Alaska Native, 11 Asian Americans or Pacific Islanders, 14 Hispanic Americans), 14 international. Average age 28. 54 applicants, 83% accepted, 22 enrolled. In 2009, 67 master's awarded. *Degree requirements:* For master's, comprehensive exam. *Entrance requirements:* For master's, GMAT (minimum preferred score of 450 prior to admission decision), minimum GPA of 2.0 in last 60 hours of undergraduate work. Additional exam requirements/recommendations for international students: Required—TOEFL (minimum score 550 paper-based; 213 computer-based). *Application deadline:* For fall admission, 6/1 for domestic and international students; for spring admission, 10/1 for domestic and international students. Applications are processed on a rolling basis. Application fee: $40 ($90 for international students). Electronic applications accepted. *Expenses:* Tuition, state resident: full-time $5784; part-time $241 per credit hour. Tuition, nonresident: full-time $13,224; part-time $551 per credit hour. Required fees: $1728; $48 per credit hour. $306. Tuition and fees vary according to course load. *Financial support:* In 2009–10, 70 students received support, including 1 research assistantship (averaging $4,927 per year), 6 teaching assistantships (averaging $5,119 per year); Federal Work-Study and institutionally sponsored loans also available. Support available to part-time students. Financial award application deadline: 4/1; financial award applicants required to submit FAFSA. *Faculty research:* Tax and estate planning, foreign exchange risk. *Unit head:* Dr. Robert Davis, Associate Dean, 512-245-3591, Fax: 512-245-7973, E-mail: rd23@txstate.edu. *Application contact:* Dr. Robert Davis, Associate Dean, 512-245-3591, Fax: 512-245-7973, E-mail: rd23@txstate.edu.

Texas State University–San Marcos, Graduate School, Emmett and Miriam McCoy College of Business Administration, Program in Accounting and Information Technology, San Marcos, TX 78666. Offers MS. *Faculty:* 7 full-time (2 women). *Students:* 15 full-time (5 women), 10 part-time (5 women); includes 9 minority (3 African Americans, 5 Asian Americans or Pacific Islanders, 1 Hispanic American), 2 international. Average age 29. 7 applicants, 100% accepted, 5 enrolled. In 2009, 2 master's awarded. *Degree requirements:* For master's, comprehensive exam. *Entrance requirements:* For master's, GMAT, official transcript from each college or university attended, 2 letters of recommendation, resume. Additional exam requirements/recommendations for international students: Required—TOEFL (minimum score 550 paper-based; 213 computer-based). *Application deadline:* For fall admission, 6/1 for domestic and international students; for spring admission, 10/1 for domestic and international students. Application fee: $40 ($90 for international students). *Expenses:* Tuition, state resident: full-time $5784; part-time $241 per credit hour. Tuition, nonresident: full-time $13,224; part-time $551 per credit hour. Required fees: $1728; $48 per credit hour. $306. Tuition and fees vary according to course load. *Financial support:* In 2009–10, 12 students received support, including 1 research assistantship (averaging $5,076 per year), 6 teaching assistantships (averaging $5,145 per year). *Unit head:* Dr. Robert Davis, Associate Dean, 512-245-3591, Fax: 512-245-7973, E-mail: rd23@txstate.edu. *Application contact:* Dr. J. Michael Willoughby, Dean of Graduate School, 512-245-2581, Fax: 512-245-8365, E-mail: gradcollege@txstate.edu.

Texas Tech University, Jerry S. Rawls College of Business Administration, Area of Accounting, Lubbock, TX 79409. Offers accounting (PhD); audit/financial reporting (MSA); taxation (MSA); JD/MSA. *Accreditation:* AACSB. Part-time programs available. *Faculty:* 15 full-time (4 women). *Students:* 97 full-time (52 women), 6 part-time (1 woman); includes 13 minority (3 American Indian/Alaska Native, 3 Asian Americans or Pacific Islanders, 7 Hispanic Americans), 4 international. Average age 24. 111 applicants, 50% accepted, 49 enrolled. In 2009, 57 master's, 3 doctorates awarded. Terminal master's awarded for partial completion of doctoral program. *Degree requirements:* For master's, capstone course; for doctorate, comprehensive exam, thesis/dissertation, qualifying exams. *Entrance requirements:* For master's and doctorate, GMAT, holistic profile of academic credentials. Additional exam requirements/recommendations for international students: Required—TOEFL (minimum score 550 paper-based; 213 computer-based; 79 iBT). *Application deadline:* For fall admission, 2/1 priority date for domestic students, 1/15 priority date for international students. Applications are processed on a rolling basis. Application fee: $50 ($75 for international students). Electronic applications accepted. *Expenses:* Tuition, state resident: full-time $5100; part-time $213 per credit hour. Tuition, nonresident: full-time $11,748; part-time $490 per credit hour. Required fees: $2298; $50 per credit hour. $555 per semester. *Financial support:* In 2009–10, 6 research assistantships (averaging $8,000 per year), 8 teaching assistantships (averaging $17,000 per year) were awarded; fellowships, career-related internships or fieldwork, Federal Work-Study, scholarships/grants, health care benefits, and unspecified assistantships also available. Financial award applicants required to submit FAFSA. *Faculty research:* Governmental and nonprofit accounting, managerial and financial accounting. *Unit head:* Dr. Linda Nichols, Area Coordinator, 806-742-1541, Fax: 806-742-3182, E-mail: linda.nichols@ttu.edu. *Application contact:* Cynthia D. Barnes, 806-742-3184, Fax: 806-742-3958, E-mail: ba_grad@ttu.edu.

Towson University, College of Graduate Studies and Research, Joint Program in Accounting and Business Advisory Services, Towson, MD 21252-0001. Offers MS. *Accreditation:* AACSB. Part-time and evening/weekend programs available. *Entrance requirements:* For master's, GMAT, GRE General Test, minimum GPA of 3.0. Electronic applications accepted.

Trinity University, Department of Business Administration, San Antonio, TX 78212-7200. Offers accounting (MS). *Accreditation:* AACSB. Part-time programs available. *Entrance requirements:* For master's, GMAT, minimum GPA of 3.0, course work in accounting and business law.

Troy University, Graduate School, College of Business, Program in Business Administration, Troy, AL 36082. Offers accounting (EMBA, MBA); criminal justice (EMBA); finance (MBA); general management (EMBA); healthcare management (EMBA); information systems (EMBA, MBA); international economic development (MBA). *Accreditation:* ACBSP. Part-time and evening/weekend programs available. *Students:* 382 full-time (196 women), 732 part-time (457 women); includes 616 minority (483 African Americans, 14 American Indian/Alaska Native, 96 Asian Americans or Pacific Islanders, 23 Hispanic Americans). Average age 29. 869 applicants, 61% accepted. In 2009, 296 master's awarded. *Degree requirements:* For master's, thesis or alternative. *Entrance requirements:* For master's, GMAT (minimum score 500) or GRE General Test (minimum score 900), minimum GPA of 2.5; letter of recommendation. Additional exam requirements/recommendations for international students: Required—TOEFL (minimum score 523 paper-based; 193 computer-based; 70 iBT), IELTS (minimum score 6), or ACT Compass ESL (minimum score 270 on Listening, Reading, and Grammar with no individual score below 85 and a minimum score of 8 out of 12 on writing test). *Application deadline:* Applications are processed on a rolling basis. Application fee: $50. *Unit head:* Dr. Henry M. Findley, Interim Chair/Professor, 334-670-3271, Fax: 334-670-3599, E-mail: hfindley@troy.edu. *Application contact:* Brenda K. Campbell, Director of Graduate Admissions, 334-670-3178, Fax: 334-670-3733, E-mail: bcamp@troy.edu.

Truman State University, Graduate School, School of Business, Program in Accounting, Kirksville, MO 63501-4221. Offers M Ac. *Accreditation:* AACSB. *Degree requirements:* For master's, comprehensive exam. *Entrance requirements:* For master's, GMAT, minimum GPA of 3.0. Additional exam requirements/recommendations for international students: Required—TOEFL (minimum score 550 paper-based; 213 computer-based). Electronic applications accepted. *Expenses:* Tuition, state resident: part-time $291 per credit. Tuition, nonresident: part-time $499 per credit hour. Tuition and fees vary according to course load.

Universidad del Este, Graduate School, Carolina, PR 00984. Offers accounting (MBA); adult education (M Ed); agribusiness (MBA); bilingual education (M Ed); criminal justice and criminology (MA); early education (M Ed); elementary education (M Ed); human resources (MBA); information security management (MBA); information technology and Web business development (MBA); management (MBA); public policy (MPA); social work (MA), including clinical social work; special education (M Ed); strategic leadership (MBA); teaching English (M Ed); teaching Spanish (M Ed).

Universidad del Turabo, Graduate Programs, School in Business Administration, Program in Accounting, Gurabo, PR 00778-3030. Offers MBA. Part-time and evening/weekend programs available. *Students:* 18 full-time (12 women), 32 part-time (22 women); includes 47 Hispanic Americans. Average age 33. 25 applicants, 84% accepted, 15 enrolled. In 2009, 43 master's awarded. *Entrance requirements:* For master's, GRE, EXADEP, interview. *Application deadline:* For fall admission, 8/5 for domestic students. Application fee: $25. *Unit head:* Marcelino Rivera, Dean, 787-743-7979 Ext. 4117. *Application contact:* Virginia Gonzalez, Admissions Officer, 787-746-3009.

Universidad Metropolitana, School of Business Administration, Program in Accounting, San Juan, PR 00928-1150. Offers MBA. Part-time programs available. *Degree requirements:* For master's, thesis or alternative. *Entrance requirements:* For master's, GMAT, PAEG, interview. Electronic applications accepted.

Universidad Metropolitana, School of Business Administration, Program in Public Accounting, San Juan, PR 00928-1150. Offers Certificate. Part-time programs available.

Université de Sherbrooke, Faculty of Administration, Program in Accounting, Sherbrooke, QC J1K 2R1, Canada. Offers M Sc. *Entrance requirements:* For master's, bachelor's degree. Electronic applications accepted.

Université du Québec à Montréal, Graduate Programs, Program in Accounting, Montréal, QC H3C 3P8, Canada. Offers M Sc, MPA, Diploma. Part-time programs available. *Degree requirements:* For master's, thesis (for some programs). *Entrance requirements:* For master's, appropriate bachelor's degree or equivalent and proficiency in French.

Université du Québec à Trois-Rivières, Graduate Programs, Program in Accounting Science, Trois-Rivières, QC G9A 5H7, Canada. Offers MBA.

Université du Québec en Outaouais, Graduate Programs, Program in Accounting, Gatineau, QC J8X 3X7, Canada. Offers DESS.

Université du Québec en Outaouais, Graduate Programs, Program in Executive Certified Management Accounting, Gatineau, QC J8X 3X7, Canada. Offers MBA, DESS.

Université Laval, Faculty of Administrative Sciences, Programs in Business Administration, Québec, QC G1K 7P4, Canada. Offers accounting (MBA); agri-food management (MBA); electronic business (MBA, Diploma); factory management and logistics (MBA); finance (MBA); firm management (MBA); geomatic management (MBA); information technology management (MBA); international management (MBA); management (MBA); management accounting (MBA, Diploma); marketing (MBA); modeling and organizational decision (MBA); occupational health and safety management (MBA); pharmacy management (MBA); social and environmental responsibility (MBA); technological entrepreneurship (Diploma). *Accreditation:* AACSB. Part-time and evening/weekend programs available. Postbaccalaureate distance learning degree programs offered (no on-campus study). *Entrance requirements:* For master's and Diploma, knowledge of French and English. Electronic applications accepted.

Université Laval, Faculty of Administrative Sciences, Programs in Public Accountancy, Québec, QC G1K 7P4, Canada. Offers MBA, Diploma. Part-time programs available. *Entrance requirements:* For master's and Diploma, knowledge of French and English. Electronic applications accepted.

University at Albany, State University of New York, School of Business, Department of Accounting, Albany, NY 12222-0001. Offers accounting (MS); taxation (MS). *Accreditation:* AACSB. *Degree requirements:* For master's, research project. *Entrance requirements:* For master's, GMAT. Additional exam requirements/recommendations for international students: Required—TOEFL (minimum score 550 paper-based; 213 computer-based). Electronic applications accepted. *Faculty research:* Professional ethics, statistical analysis, cost management systems, accounting theory.

University at Buffalo, the State University of New York, Graduate School, School of Management, Buffalo, NY 14260. Offers accounting (MS); business administration (EMBA, MBA, PMBA); finance (MS), including financial engineering, financial management; information assurance (Certificate); management (PhD); management information systems (MS); supply chains and operations management (MS); Au D/MBA; JD/MBA; M Arch/MBA; MA/MBA; MD/MBA; MPH/MBA; MSW/MBA; Pharm D/MBA. *Accreditation:* AACSB. Part-time and evening/weekend programs available. *Faculty:* 66 full-time (19 women), 21 part-time/adjunct (4 women).

Students: 502 full-time (176 women), 199 part-time (54 women); includes 29 minority (10 African Americans, 16 Asian Americans or Pacific Islanders, 3 Hispanic Americans), 306 international. Average age 27. 1,944 applicants, 31% accepted, 324 enrolled. In 2009, 363 master's, 7 doctorates, 3 other advanced degrees awarded. *Degree requirements:* For master's, thesis (for some programs); for doctorate, comprehensive exam, thesis/dissertation. *Entrance requirements:* For master's, GMAT (MBA, MS in accounting), GRE General Test (for all other MS concentrations); for doctorate, GMAT or GRE. Additional exam requirements/recommendations for international students: Required—TOEFL (minimum score 230 computer-based; 95 iBT). *Application deadline:* For fall admission, 6/2 priority date for domestic students, 3/1 priority date for international students. Applications are processed on a rolling basis. Application fee: $100. Electronic applications accepted. *Expenses:* Contact institution. *Financial support:* In 2009–10, 91 students received support, including 5 fellowships with full and partial tuition reimbursements available (averaging $4,000 per year), 41 research assistantships with full and partial tuition reimbursements available (averaging $16,000 per year), 28 teaching assistantships with full and partial tuition reimbursements available (averaging $15,000 per year); career-related internships or fieldwork, Federal Work-Study, institutionally sponsored loans, scholarships/grants, health care benefits, and unspecified assistantships also available. Financial award application deadline: 2/15; financial award applicants required to submit FAFSA. *Faculty research:* Earnings management and electronic information assurance, supply chains and operations management, corporate financing and asset pricing, consumer behavior and quantitative modeling of marketing behavior, leadership and politics in organizations. Total annual research expenditures: $230,000. *Unit head:* David W. Frasier, Assistant Dean, 716-645-3204, Fax: 716-645-2341, E-mail: davidf@buffalo.edu. *Application contact:* David W. Frasier, Assistant Dean, 716-645-3204, Fax: 716-645-2341, E-mail: davidf@buffalo.edu.

The University of Akron, Graduate School, College of Business Administration, School of Accountancy, Akron, OH 44325. Offers accountancy (MS); accounting-information systems (MS); taxation (MT); JD/MT. *Accreditation:* AACSB. Part-time and evening/weekend programs available. *Faculty:* 10 full-time (2 women), 14 part-time/adjunct (3 women). *Students:* 73 full-time (46 women), 79 part-time (35 women); includes 12 minority (8 African Americans, 4 Asian Americans or Pacific Islanders), 21 international. Average age 28. 72 applicants, 82% accepted, 47 enrolled. In 2009, 54 master's awarded. *Entrance requirements:* For master's, GMAT, minimum GPA of 2.75, letters of recommendation, resume. Additional exam requirements/recommendations for international students: Required—TOEFL (minimum score 550 paper-based; 213 computer-based; 79 iBT). *Application deadline:* For fall admission, 8/1 for domestic and international students; for spring admission, 12/1 for domestic and international students. Applications are processed on a rolling basis. Application fee: $30 ($40 for international students). Electronic applications accepted. *Expenses:* Tuition, state resident: full-time $6570; part-time $365 per credit hour. Tuition, nonresident: full-time $11,250; part-time $625 per credit hour. *Financial support:* In 2009–10, 25 research assistantships with full and partial tuition reimbursements were awarded. *Faculty research:* Financial reporting and management accounting auditing and assurance of financial information, business and information systems risk and security management, corporate governance and ethics, accounting education. Total annual research expenditures: $121,911. *Unit head:* Dr. Thomas Calderon, Chair, 330-972-6099, E-mail: tcalderon@uakron.edu. *Application contact:* Dr. Susan Hanlon, Director of Graduate Business Programs, 330-972-7043, Fax: 330-972-6588, E-mail: shanlon@uakron.edu.

The University of Alabama, Graduate School, Manderson Graduate School of Business, Culverhouse School of Accountancy, Tuscaloosa, AL 35487. Offers accounting (M Acc, PhD); tax accounting (MTA). *Accreditation:* AACSB. *Faculty:* 15 full-time (3 women). *Students:* 105 full-time (48 women), 3 part-time (2 women); includes 2 minority (both African Americans), 3 international. Average age 24. 218 applicants, 41% accepted, 77 enrolled. In 2009, 95 master's, 3 doctorates awarded. *Degree requirements:* For doctorate, thesis/dissertation. *Entrance requirements:* For master's and doctorate, GMAT, minimum GPA of 3.0. Additional exam requirements/recommendations for international students: Required—TOEFL. *Application deadline:* For fall admission, 7/1 priority date for domestic students, 6/1 priority date for international students; for spring admission, 11/1 priority date for domestic students, 10/1 priority date for international students. Applications are processed on a rolling basis. Application fee: $50 ($60 for international students). Electronic applications accepted. *Expenses:* Tuition, state resident: full-time $7000. Tuition, nonresident: full-time $19,200. *Financial support:* In 2009–10, 99 students received support, including 6 fellowships with full tuition reimbursements available (averaging $15,000 per year), 19 research assistantships with full and partial tuition reimbursements available (averaging $5,454 per year), 18 teaching assistantships with full and partial tuition reimbursements available (averaging $5,454 per year); career-related internships or fieldwork, Federal Work-Study, institutionally sponsored loans, scholarships/grants, health care benefits, and unspecified assistantships also available. Financial award application deadline: 3/31. *Faculty research:* Corporate governance, audit decision making, earning management, valuation, executive compensation, not-for-profit. *Unit head:* Dr. Mary S. Stone, Director, 205-348-2915, Fax: 205-348-8453, E-mail: mstone@cba.ua.edu. *Application contact:* Sandy D. Davidson, Advisor, 205-348-8997, Fax: 205-348-8453, E-mail: sdavidso@cba.ua.edu.

The University of Alabama at Birmingham, School of Business, Program in Accounting, Birmingham, AL 35294. Offers M Acct.

The University of Alabama in Huntsville, School of Graduate Studies, College of Business Administration, Department of Accounting and Finance, Huntsville, AL 35899. Offers accounting (M Acc, Certificate), including CPA preparatory with an emphasis in taxation (M Acc), CPA preparatory with emphasis in assurance and financial reporting (M Acc), general accounting (M Acc), information systems audit and control (ISAC) (M Acc). Part-time and evening/weekend programs available. *Faculty:* 5 full-time (3 women), 3 part-time/adjunct (0 women). *Students:* 16 full-time (10 women), 31 part-time (15 women); includes 5 minority (4 African Americans, 1 Asian American or Pacific Islander), 3 international. Average age 30. 42 applicants, 69% accepted, 21 enrolled. In 2009, 13 master's awarded. *Degree requirements:* For master's, comprehensive exam, thesis or alternative. *Entrance requirements:* For master's and Certificate, GMAT (minimum score 500), minimum AACSB index of 1080. Additional exam requirements/recommendations for international students: Required—TOEFL (minimum score 550 paper-based; 213 computer-based; 62 iBT). *Application deadline:* For fall admission, 8/1 for domestic students, 4/1 for international students; for spring admission, 12/1 for domestic students, 9/1 for international students. Applications are processed on a rolling basis. Application fee: $40 ($50 for international students). Electronic applications accepted. *Expenses:* Tuition, state resident: part-time $355.75 per credit hour. Tuition, nonresident: part-time $847.10 per credit hour. Required fees: $210.80 per semester. Tuition and fees vary according to course load and program. *Financial support:* Career-related internships or fieldwork, Federal Work-Study, institutionally sponsored loans, scholarships/grants, health care benefits, and unspecified assistantships available. Support available to part-time students. Financial award application deadline: 4/1; financial award applicants required to submit FAFSA. *Faculty research:* Accounting information systems, emerging technologies in accounting, behavioral accounting, state and local taxation, financial accounting. Total annual research expenditures: $67,010. *Unit head:* Dr. John Burnett, Interim Chair, 256-824-2923, Fax: 256-824-2929, E-mail: burnettj@uah.edu. *Application contact:* Jennifer Pettitt, Director of Graduate Programs, 256-824-6681, Fax: 256-824-7571, E-mail: jennifer.pettitt@uah.edu.

University of Alberta, Faculty of Graduate Studies and Research, Doctoral Program in Business, Edmonton, AB T6G 2E1, Canada. Offers accounting (PhD); finance (PhD); human resources/industrial relations (PhD); management science (PhD); marketing (PhD); organizational analysis (PhD); MBA/PhD. *Accreditation:* AACSB. Part-time programs available. *Faculty:* 41 full-time (7 women), 1 part-time/adjunct (0 women). *Students:* 46 full-time (27 women), 5 part-time (3 women). Average age 34. 307 applicants, 7% accepted, 11 enrolled. In 2009, 2 doctorates awarded. *Degree requirements:* For doctorate, comprehensive exam, thesis/dissertation. *Entrance requirements:* For doctorate, GMAT. Additional exam requirements/recommendations for international students: Required—TOEFL (minimum score 550 paper-based; 213 computer-based). *Application deadline:* For fall admission, 6/1 priority date for domestic students; for winter admission, 5/1 for domestic students. Application fee: $0. Electronic applications accepted. Tuition and fees charges are reported in Canadian dollars. *Expenses:* Tuition, area resident: Full-time $4626 Canadian dollars; part-time $99.72 Canadian dollars per unit. International tuition: $8216 Canadian dollars full-time. Required fees: $3590 Canadian dollars; $99.72 Canadian dollars per unit. $215 Canadian dollars per term. *Financial support:* In 2009–10, 29 students received support, including 11 fellowships with full tuition reimbursements available (averaging $17,000 per year); scholarships/grants and tuition waivers (partial) also available. *Faculty research:* Accounting, capital markets and corporate finance, organizational change and human resource management, marketing, strategic management. Total annual research expenditures: $7.7 million. *Unit head:* Dr. Mike Percy, Director, 780-492-2361, Fax: 780-492-3325, E-mail: busphd@ualberta.ca. *Application contact:* Jeanette Gosine, Program Coordinator, 780-492-2361, Fax: 780-492-3325, E-mail: busphd@ualberta.ca.

The University of Arizona, Graduate College, Eller College of Management, Department of Accounting, Tucson, AZ 85721. Offers M Ac. *Accreditation:* AACSB. Part-time programs available. *Faculty:* 9. *Students:* 51 full-time (23 women), 4 part-time (0 women); includes 4 minority (1 African American, 1 American Indian/Alaska Native, 2 Hispanic Americans), 12 international. Average age 26. 168 applicants, 39% accepted, 36 enrolled. In 2009, 41 master's awarded. *Degree requirements:* For master's, comprehensive exam, 1-year residency. *Entrance requirements:* For master's, GMAT (minimum score 550), 2 letters of recommendation, 3 writing samples, resume. Additional exam requirements/recommendations for international students: Required—TOEFL (minimum score 600 paper-based; 250 computer-based; 100 iBT). *Application deadline:* For fall admission, 3/1 priority date for domestic and international students; for spring admission, 10/1 priority date for domestic and international students. Applications are processed on a rolling basis. Application fee: $75. Electronic applications accepted. *Expenses:* Contact institution. *Financial support:* In 2009–10, 30 teaching assistantships with full tuition reimbursements (averaging $15,154 per year) were awarded; career-related internships or fieldwork, Federal Work-Study, scholarships/grants, health care benefits, tuition waivers (partial), and unspecified assistantships also available. Financial award application deadline: 3/15. *Faculty research:* Auditing, financial reporting and financial markets, taxation policy and markets, behavioral research in accounting. Total annual research expenditures: $35,764. *Unit head:* Dr. Dan S. Dhaliwal, Head, 520-621-2146, Fax: 520-621-3742, E-mail: dhaliwal@eller.arizona.edu. *Application contact:* Carol Plagman, Programs Coordinator, 520-621-3712, Fax: 520-621-3742, E-mail: accounting@eller.arizona.edu.

University of Arkansas, Graduate School, Sam M. Walton College of Business Administration, Department of Accounting, Fayetteville, AR 72701-1201. Offers M Acc. *Accreditation:* AACSB. *Students:* 45 full-time (23 women), 7 part-time (3 women); includes 4 minority (2 American Indian/Alaska Native, 1 Asian American or Pacific Islander, 1 Hispanic American), 9 international. In 2009, 23 master's awarded. *Entrance requirements:* For master's, GMAT. Application fee: $40 ($50 for international students). *Expenses:* Tuition, state resident: full-time $7355; part-time $356.58 per hour. Tuition, nonresident: full-time $17,401; part-time $775.17 per hour. Required fees: $1203. *Financial support:* In 2009–10, 8 fellowships with tuition reimbursements, 15 research assistantships, 4 teaching assistantships were awarded; career-related internships or fieldwork and Federal Work-Study also available. Support available to part-time students. Financial award application deadline: 4/1; financial award applicants required to submit FAFSA. *Unit head:* Dr. Vernon Richardson, Chair, 479-575-4051, Fax: 479-575-2863, E-mail: vrichardson@walton.uark.edu. *Application contact:* Dr. Gary Peters, Graduate Coordinator, 479-575-4117, Fax: 479-575-2863, E-mail: peters@uark.edu.

University of Arkansas at Little Rock, Graduate School, College of Business Administration, Little Rock, AR 72204-1099. Offers accountancy (M Acc, Graduate Certificate); business administration (MBA); construction management (Graduate Certificate); management (Graduate Certificate); management information system (MIS); management information systems (Graduate Certificate); management information systems leadership (Graduate Certificate); taxation (MS, Graduate Certificate). *Accreditation:* AACSB. Part-time and evening/weekend programs available. *Entrance requirements:* For master's, GMAT, minimum undergraduate GPA of 2.7. Additional exam requirements/recommendations for international students: Required—TOEFL (minimum score 525 paper-based; 195 computer-based).

University of Baltimore, Graduate School, Merrick School of Business, Department of Accounting and Management Information Systems, Baltimore, MD 21201-5779. Offers accounting and business advisory services (MS); accounting fundamentals (Graduate Certificate); forensic accounting (Graduate Certificate). Part-time and evening/weekend programs available. *Entrance requirements:* For master's, GMAT. Additional exam requirements/recommendations for international students: Required—TOEFL (minimum score 550 paper-based; 213 computer-based). Electronic applications accepted. *Faculty research:* Health care, accounting and administration, managerial accounting, financial accounting theory, accounting information.

The University of British Columbia, Sauder School of Business, Doctoral Program in Commerce and Business Administration, Vancouver, BC V6T 1Z1, Canada. Offers accounting (PhD); finance (PhD); international business (PhD); management information systems (PhD); management science (PhD); marketing (PhD); organizational behavior (PhD); strategy and business economics (PhD); transportation and logistics (PhD); urban land economics (PhD). *Degree requirements:* For doctorate, comprehensive exam, thesis/dissertation. *Entrance requirements:* For doctorate, GMAT or GRE. Additional exam requirements/recommendations for international students: Required—TOEFL (minimum score 600 paper-based; 250 computer-based; 100 iBT). Electronic applications accepted.

University of California, Berkeley, Graduate Division, Haas School of Business, PhD in Business Administration Program, Berkeley, CA 94720-1500. Offers accounting (PhD); business and public policy (PhD); finance (PhD); management of organizations (PhD); marketing (PhD); operations management (PhD); real estate (PhD). *Accreditation:* AACSB. *Faculty:* 80 full-time (20 women), 130 part-time/adjunct (22 women). *Students:* 82 full-time (23 women); includes 22 minority (18 Asian Americans or Pacific Islanders, 4 Hispanic Americans), 29 international. Average age 30. 511 applicants, 5% accepted, 16 enrolled. In 2009, 8 doctorates awarded. *Degree requirements:* For doctorate, comprehensive exam, thesis/dissertation, oral exam, written preliminary exams. *Entrance requirements:* For doctorate, GMAT or GRE, minimum GPA of 3.0 in undergraduate and graduate coursework. Additional exam requirements/recommendations for international students: Required—TOEFL (minimum score 570 paper-based; 230 computer-based; 68 iBT), IELTS (minimum score 7). *Application deadline:* For fall admission, 12/10 for domestic and international students. Application fee: $70 ($90 for international students). Electronic applications accepted. *Financial support:* Fellowships with full and partial tuition reimbursements, research assistantships with full and partial tuition reimbursements, teaching assistantships with full and partial tuition reimbursements, career-related internships or fieldwork, Federal Work-Study, scholarships/grants, health care benefits, tuition waivers (full), unspecified assistantships, and transit pass, travel grants available. Financial award application deadline: 12/10; financial award applicants required to submit FAFSA. *Faculty research:* Accounting, business and public policy, finance, management of organizations, marketing, operations and information technology management, real estate. *Unit head:* Sunil Dutta, Director, 510-642-1229, Fax: 510-643-4255, E-mail: kimg@haas.berkeley.edu. *Application contact:* Kim Guilfoyle, Director, Student Affairs, 510-642-3944, Fax: 510-643-4255, E-mail: kimg@haas.berkeley.edu.

University of California, Berkeley, UC Berkeley Extension, Certificate Programs in Business, Berkeley, CA 94720-1500. Offers accounting (Certificate); business administration (Certificate); finance (Certificate); human resource management (Certificate); management (Certificate); marketing (Certificate); project management (Certificate). Postbaccalaureate distance learning degree programs offered. *Unit head:* Diana Wu, Dean, 510-642-4181. *Application contact:* Business, 510-642-4231, E-mail: business@unex.berkeley.edu.

University of Central Arkansas, Graduate School, College of Business Administration, Program in Accounting, Conway, AR 72035-0001. Offers M Acc. *Faculty:* 8 full-time (3 women). *Students:* 24 full-time (15 women), 8 part-time (7 women); includes 2 minority (1 African American, 1

Accounting

University of Central Arkansas (continued)
Asian American or Pacific Islander), 2 international. Average age 24. 23 applicants, 96% accepted, 22 enrolled. In 2009, 9 master's awarded. *Degree requirements:* For master's, capstone course. *Entrance requirements:* For master's, GMAT, minimum GPA of 2.7. Additional exam requirements/recommendations for international students: Required—TOEFL (minimum score 550 paper-based; 213 computer-based). *Application deadline:* For fall admission, 3/1 for domestic and international students; for spring admission, 10/1 for domestic and international students. Applications are processed on a rolling basis. Application fee: $25 ($50 for international students). *Expenses:* Tuition, state resident: full-time $5136; part-time $214 per credit hour. Required fees: $379.50; $127 per term. Tuition and fees vary according to course level, course load and campus/location. *Financial support:* In 2009–10, 4 research assistantships with partial tuition reimbursements (averaging $5,000 per year) were awarded; career-related internships or fieldwork, Federal Work-Study, scholarships/grants, tuition waivers (partial), and unspecified assistantships also available. Support available to part-time students. Financial award application deadline: 2/15. *Unit head:* Dr. Patricia Mounce, Interim Chair, 501-450-5333, Fax: 501-450-5302. *Application contact:* Brenda Herring, Admissions Assistant, 501-450-5065, Fax: 501-450-5678, E-mail: bherring@uca.edu.

University of Central Florida, College of Business Administration, Kenneth G. Dixon School of Accounting, Orlando, FL 32816. Offers MSA, MST. *Accreditation:* AACSB. Part-time and evening/weekend programs available. *Faculty:* 22 full-time (10 women), 2 part-time/adjunct (both women). *Students:* 101 full-time (47 women), 103 part-time (57 women); includes 48 minority (9 African Americans, 19 Asian Americans or Pacific Islanders, 20 Hispanic Americans), 15 international. Average age 27. 142 applicants, 63% accepted, 64 enrolled. In 2009, 108 master's awarded. *Degree requirements:* For master's, comprehensive exam. *Entrance requirements:* For master's, GMAT, minimum GPA of 3.0 in last 60 hours. Additional exam requirements/recommendations for international students: Required—TOEFL. *Application deadline:* For fall admission, 6/15 priority date for domestic students; for spring admission, 11/1 priority date for domestic students. Electronic applications accepted. *Expenses:* Tuition, state resident: part-time $306.31 per credit hour. Tuition, nonresident: part-time $1099.01 per credit hour. Part-time tuition and fees vary according to degree level and program. *Financial support:* In 2009–10, 8 students received support, including 3 fellowships with partial tuition reimbursements available (averaging $10,000 per year), 5 teaching assistantships with partial tuition reimbursements available (averaging $7,000 per year); career-related internships or fieldwork, Federal Work-Study, institutionally sponsored loans, tuition waivers (partial), and unspecified assistantships also available. Financial award application deadline: 3/1; financial award applicants required to submit FAFSA. *Unit head:* Dr. Robin W. Roberts, Director, 407-823-2876, E-mail: robin.roberts@bus.ucf.edu. *Application contact:* Dr. Robin W. Roberts, Director, 407-823-2876, E-mail: robin.roberts@bus.ucf.edu.

University of Central Missouri, The Graduate School, Harmon College of Business Administration, Warrensburg, MO 64093. Offers accountancy (MA); accounting (MBA); ethical strategic leadership (MBA); finance (MBA); general business (MBA); information systems (MBA); information technology (MS); marketing (MBA). Part-time programs available. Postbaccalaureate distance learning degree programs offered. *Faculty:* 31. *Students:* 87 full-time (34 women), 62 part-time (25 women); includes 10 minority (3 African Americans, 1 American Indian/Alaska Native, 5 Asian Americans or Pacific Islanders, 1 Hispanic American), 66 international. Average age 27. 55 applicants, 64% accepted, 27 enrolled. In 2009, 83 master's awarded. *Entrance requirements:* Additional exam requirements/recommendations for international students: Required—TOEFL (minimum score 550 paper-based; 79 computer-based). *Application deadline:* For fall admission, 6/1 priority date for domestic students, 5/1 for international students; for spring admission, 10/1 priority date for domestic students, 10/1 for international students. Applications are processed on a rolling basis. Application fee: $30 ($75 for international students). Electronic applications accepted. *Expenses:* Tuition, area resident: Part-time $245.80 per credit hour. Tuition, nonresident: part-time $491.60 per credit hour. Required fees: $24.20 per credit hour. Full-time tuition and fees vary according to course load, degree level, campus/location and reciprocity agreements. *Financial support:* Research assistantships with full and partial tuition reimbursements, teaching assistantships with full and partial tuition reimbursements, career-related internships or fieldwork, Federal Work-Study, scholarships/grants, and administrative and laboratory assistantships available. Support available to part-time students. Financial award application deadline: 3/1; financial award applicants required to submit FAFSA. *Unit head:* Dr. Roger Best, Dean, 660-543-4560, Fax: 660-543-8350, E-mail: best@ucmo.edu. *Application contact:* Laurie Delap, Admissions Coordinator, 660-543-4621, Fax: 660-543-4778, E-mail: gradinfo@ucmo.edu.

University of Charleston, Executive Master of Forensic Accounting Program, Charleston, WV 25304-1099. Offers EMFA. Part-time and evening/weekend programs available. *Faculty:* 6 part-time/adjunct (1 woman). *Students:* 10 full-time (7 women). Average age 38. 14 applicants, 64% accepted, 9 enrolled. *Entrance requirements:* For master's, undergraduate degree from regionally-accredited institution; minimum GPA of 3.0 in undergraduate work (recommended); three years of work experience since receiving undergraduate degree (recommended); minimum of two professional recommendations, one from current employer, addressing career potential and ability to do graduate work. Additional exam requirements/recommendations for international students: Required—TOEFL. *Application deadline:* Applications are processed on a rolling basis. Application fee: $50. Electronic applications accepted. *Expenses:* Tuition: Full-time $25,224; part-time $875 per credit hour. Full-time tuition and fees vary according to degree level. *Financial support:* In 2009–10, 1 student received support. Applicants required to submit FAFSA. *Unit head:* Dr. Robert B. Bliss, Associate Dean, 304-357-4865, Fax: 304-357-4872, E-mail: robertbliss@ucwv.edu. *Application contact:* Dr. Robert B. Bliss, Associate Dean, 304-357-4865, Fax: 304-357-4872, E-mail: robertbliss@ucwv.edu.

University of Cincinnati, Graduate School, College of Business, MS Program, Cincinnati, OH 45221. Offers accounting (MS); information systems (MS); marketing (MS); quantitative analysis (MS). Part-time and evening/weekend programs available. *Degree requirements:* For master's, thesis (for some programs). *Entrance requirements:* For master's, GMAT, GRE, resume, letters of recommendation. Additional exam requirements/recommendations for international students: Required—TOEFL (minimum score 600 paper-based; 250 computer-based; 100 iBT). Electronic applications accepted. *Expenses:* Contact institution.

University of Cincinnati, Graduate School, College of Business, PhD Program, Cincinnati, OH 45221. Offers accounting (PhD); finance (PhD); information systems (PhD); management (PhD); marketing (PhD); quantitative analysis and operations management (PhD). *Degree requirements:* For doctorate, comprehensive exam, thesis/dissertation. *Entrance requirements:* For doctorate, GMAT, GRE, resume, letters of recommendation. Additional exam requirements/recommendations for international students: Required—TOEFL (minimum score 600 paper-based; 250 computer-based; 100 iBT). Electronic applications accepted. *Expenses:* Contact institution.

University of Colorado at Boulder, Leeds School of Business, Division of Business Administration, Boulder, CO 80309. Offers accounting (MS, PhD); finance (PhD); information systems (PhD); marketing (PhD); operations (PhD); strategic, organizational, and entrepreneurial studies (PhD). Part-time and evening/weekend programs available. *Students:* 74 full-time (27 women), 15 part-time (8 women); includes 6 minority (1 African American, 3 Asian Americans or Pacific Islanders, 2 Hispanic Americans), 21 international. Average age 28. 271 applicants, 8% accepted, 19 enrolled. In 2009, 40 master's, 6 doctorates awarded. *Entrance requirements:* For master's, GMAT, minimum undergraduate GPA of 3.0. *Application deadline:* For fall admission, 3/31 for domestic and international students; for spring admission, 10/31 for domestic and international students. Application fee: $50 ($60 for international students). Electronic applications accepted. *Financial support:* In 2009–10, 16 fellowships (averaging $1,038 per year), 26 research assistantships (averaging $17,558 per year), 11 teaching assistantships (averaging $12,576 per year) were awarded; career-related internships or fieldwork, Federal Work-Study, scholarships/grants, and unspecified assistantships also available. Financial award applicants required to submit FAFSA.

University of Colorado Denver, Business School, Program in Accounting, Denver, CO 80217-3364. Offers MS. *Accreditation:* AACSB. Part-time and evening/weekend programs available. *Students:* 54 full-time (32 women), 101 part-time (55 women); includes 40 minority (5 African Americans, 1 American Indian/Alaska Native, 23 Asian Americans or Pacific Islanders, 11 Hispanic Americans), 15 international. 81 applicants, 70% accepted, 46 enrolled. In 2009, 52 master's awarded. *Entrance requirements:* For master's, GMAT. Additional exam requirements/recommendations for international students: Required—TOEFL (minimum score 525 paper-based; 197 computer-based). *Application deadline:* For fall admission, 6/1 for domestic students, 3/15 for international students; for spring admission, 11/1 priority date for domestic students, 10/1 for international students. Applications are processed on a rolling basis. Application fee: $50 ($75 for international students). Electronic applications accepted. *Financial support:* Federal Work-Study, institutionally sponsored loans, and scholarships/grants available. Support available to part-time students. Financial award application deadline: 4/1; financial award applicants required to submit FAFSA. *Faculty research:* Transfer pricing, behavioral accounting, environmental accounting, health services, international auditing. *Unit head:* Bruce Neumann, Director, 303-556-5884, Fax: 303-556-5899, E-mail: bruce.neumann@ucdenver.edu. *Application contact:* Shelly Townley, Admissions Coordinator, 303-556-5956, Fax: 303-556-5904, E-mail: shelly.townley@ucdenver.edu.

University of Connecticut, Graduate School, School of Business, Field of Accounting, Storrs, CT 06269. Offers MS, PhD. *Accreditation:* AACSB. *Faculty:* 11 full-time (2 women). *Students:* 30 full-time (12 women), 185 part-time (80 women); includes 14 minority (4 African Americans, 9 Asian Americans or Pacific Islanders, 1 Hispanic American), 3 international. Average age 27. 217 applicants, 4% accepted, 7 enrolled. In 2009, 87 master's, 1 doctorate awarded. *Entrance requirements:* Additional exam requirements/recommendations for international students: Required—TOEFL (minimum score 550 paper-based; 213 computer-based). *Application deadline:* For fall admission, 2/1 priority date for domestic and international students; for spring admission, 11/1 for domestic students, 10/1 for international students. Applications are processed on a rolling basis. Electronic applications accepted. *Expenses:* Tuition, state resident: full-time $4725; part-time $525 per credit. Tuition, nonresident: full-time $12,267; part-time $1363 per credit. Required fees: $346 per semester. Tuition and fees vary according to course load. *Financial support:* In 2009–10, 6 research assistantships were awarded; Federal Work-Study, scholarships/grants, health care benefits, and unspecified assistantships also available. Financial award application deadline: 2/1. *Unit head:* Andrew Rosman, Admissions Chairperson, 860-486-5891, Fax: 860-486-4838, E-mail: andrew.rosman@uconn.edu. *Application contact:* Margaret Sweeney, Administrative Assistant, 860-486-3860, Fax: 860-846-4838, E-mail: msacct@sba.uconn.edu.

University of Dallas, Graduate School of Management, Irving, TX 75062-4736. Offers accounting (MBA, MM, MS); business management (MBA, MM); corporate finance (MBA, MM); financial services (MBA); global business (MBA, MM); health services management (MBA, MM); human resource management (MBA, MM); information assurance (MBA, MM, MS); information technology (MBA, MM, MS); information technology service management (MBA, MM, MS); marketing management (MBA, MM); organization development (MBA, MM); project management (MBA, MM); sports and entertainment management (MBA, MM); strategic leadership (MBA, MM); supply chain management (MBA); supply chain management and market logistics (MM). *Accreditation:* ACBSP. Part-time and evening/weekend programs available. Postbaccalaureate distance learning degree programs offered (no on-campus study). *Faculty:* 25 full-time (6 women), 31 part-time/adjunct (6 women). *Students:* 232 full-time (95 women), 923 part-time (365 women); includes 462 minority (184 African Americans, 14 American Indian/Alaska Native, 153 Asian Americans or Pacific Islanders, 111 Hispanic Americans), 184 international. Average age 34. 474 applicants, 85% accepted, 237 enrolled. In 2009, 399 master's awarded. *Entrance requirements:* Additional exam requirements/recommendations for international students: Required—TOEFL. *Application deadline:* Applications are processed on a rolling basis. Application fee: $50. Electronic applications accepted. *Expenses:* Contact institution. *Financial support:* In 2009–10, 399 students received support. Scholarships/grants and unspecified assistantships available. Financial award application deadline: 2/15; financial award applicants required to submit FAFSA. *Unit head:* Alounda Joseph, Director of Enrollment Processes, 972-721-5356, E-mail: admiss@gsm.udallas.edu. *Application contact:* Alounda Joseph, Director of Enrollment Processes, 972-721-5356, E-mail: admiss@gsm.udallas.edu.

University of Dayton, Graduate School, School of Business Administration, Dayton, OH 45469-1300. Offers accounting (MBA); business intelligence (MBA); entrepreneurship (MBA); finance (MBA); international business (MBA); marketing (MBA); MIS (MBA); operations management (MBA); technology-enhanced business/e-commerce (MBA); JD/MBA. *Accreditation:* AACSB. Part-time and evening/weekend programs available. *Faculty:* 29 full-time (8 women), 15 part-time/adjunct (2 women). *Students:* 134 full-time (48 women), 111 part-time (31 women); includes 14 minority (9 African Americans, 3 Asian Americans or Pacific Islanders, 2 Hispanic Americans), 29 international. Average age 29. 179 applicants, 63% accepted, 73 enrolled. In 2009, 102 master's awarded. *Entrance requirements:* For master's, GMAT. Additional exam requirements/recommendations for international students: Required—TOEFL (minimum score 550 paper-based; 213 computer-based; 79 iBT). *Application deadline:* For fall admission, 3/1 priority date for international students; for winter admission, 7/1 priority date for international students; for spring admission, 1/1 priority date for international students. Applications are processed on a rolling basis. Application fee: $0 ($50 for international students). Electronic applications accepted. *Expenses:* Contact institution. *Financial support:* In 2009–10, 13 fellowships with partial tuition reimbursements, 17 research assistantships with full and partial tuition reimbursements (averaging $7,020 per year) were awarded; career-related internships or fieldwork, institutionally sponsored loans, scholarships/grants, health care benefits, and unspecified assistantships also available. Support available to part-time students. Financial award application deadline: 3/15; financial award applicants required to submit FAFSA. *Faculty research:* Management information systems, economics, finance, entrepreneurship, marketing. *Unit head:* Janice M. Glynn, Director, MBA Program, 937-229-3733, Fax: 937-229-3882, E-mail: glynn@udayton.edu. *Application contact:* Jeffrey Carter, Assistant Director, MBA Program, 937-229-3733, Fax: 937-229-3882, E-mail: jeff.carter@notes.udayton.edu.

University of Delaware, Alfred Lerner College of Business and Economics, Department of Accounting and Management Information Systems, Newark, DE 19716. Offers accounting (MS); information systems and technology management (MS). *Accreditation:* AACSB. Part-time and evening/weekend programs available. *Degree requirements:* For master's, thesis optional. *Entrance requirements:* For master's, GMAT. Additional exam requirements/recommendations for international students: Required—TOEFL (minimum score 550 paper-based; 213 computer-based). Electronic applications accepted. *Faculty research:* External reporting, managerial accounting, auditing information systems, taxation.

University of Denver, Daniels College of Business, School of Accountancy, Denver, CO 80208. Offers accountancy (M Acc); accounting (MBA). *Accreditation:* AACSB. Part-time and evening/weekend programs available. *Faculty:* 13 full-time (4 women), 3 part-time/adjunct (1 woman). *Students:* 23 full-time (14 women), 51 part-time (37 women); includes 4 minority (1 American Indian/Alaska Native, 1 Asian American or Pacific Islander, 2 Hispanic Americans), 42 international. Average age 27. 164 applicants, 72% accepted, 51 enrolled. In 2009, 55 master's awarded. *Entrance requirements:* For master's, GMAT. *Application deadline:* For fall admission, 1/15 priority date for domestic students. Applications are processed on a rolling basis. Application fee: $50. Electronic applications accepted. *Expenses:* Tuition: Full-time $34,596; part-time $961 per quarter hour. Required fees: $4 per quarter hour. Tuition and fees vary according to course load, campus/location and program. *Financial support:* Career-related internships or fieldwork, Federal Work-Study, institutionally sponsored loans, and scholarships/grants available. Support available to part-time students. Financial award application deadline: 2/15; financial award applicants required to submit FAFSA. *Faculty research:* Management accounting, activity-based management, benchmarking, financial management and human services, derivatives. *Unit head:* Dr. Ronald Kucic, Director, 303-871-2017. *Application contact:* Information Contact, 303-871-3416, Fax: 303-871-4466, E-mail: daniels@du.edu.

University of Florida, Graduate School, Warrington College of Business Administration, Fisher School of Accounting, Gainesville, FL 32611. Offers M Acc, PhD, JD/M Acc. *Accreditation:*

AACSB. Part-time programs available. *Entrance requirements:* For master's, GMAT or GRE General Test, minimum GPA of 3.0. Additional exam requirements/recommendations for international students: Required—TOEFL (minimum score 550 paper-based; 213 computer-based). Electronic applications accepted. *Faculty research:* Auditing/financial accounting, accounting systems, taxation.

University of Florida, Graduate School, Warrington College of Business Administration, Hough Graduate School of Business, Programs in Business Administration, Gainesville, FL 32611. Offers accounting (MBA); arts administration (MBA); business strategy and public policy (MBA); competitive strategy (MBA); decision and information sciences (MBA); electronic commerce (MBA); finance (MBA); general business (MBA); global management (MBA); Graham-Buffett security analysis (MBA); health administration (MBA); human resources management (MBA); international studies (MBA); Latin American business (MBA); management (MBA); marketing (MBA); sports administration (MBA); JD/MBA; MBA/MS; MBA/PhD; MBA/Pharm D; MD/MBA. *Accreditation:* AACSB. Part-time and evening/weekend programs available. Postbaccalaureate distance learning degree programs offered. *Entrance requirements:* For master's, GMAT, minimum GPA of 3.0, interview. Additional exam requirements/recommendations for international students: Required—TOEFL (minimum score 550 paper-based; 213 computer-based). Electronic applications accepted. *Faculty research:* Accounting, finance, insurance, management, real estate and urban analysis marketing.

University of Georgia, Graduate School, Terry College of Business, J. M. Tull School of Accounting, Athens, GA 30602. Offers M Acc, JD/M Acc. *Accreditation:* AACSB. *Faculty:* 15 full-time (7 women). *Students:* 116 full-time (56 women), 7 part-time (4 women); includes 13 minority (5 African Americans, 7 Asian Americans or Pacific Islanders, 1 Hispanic American), 7 international. 131 applicants, 54% accepted, 30 enrolled. In 2009, 102 master's awarded. *Entrance requirements:* For master's, GMAT. *Application deadline:* For fall admission, 7/1 priority date for domestic students; for spring admission, 11/15 for domestic students. Application fee: $50. Electronic applications accepted. *Expenses:* Tuition, state resident: full-time $6000; part-time $250 per credit hour. Tuition, nonresident: full-time $20,904; part-time $871 per credit hour. Required fees: $730 per semester. *Financial support:* Fellowships, research assistantships, teaching assistantships, unspecified assistantships available. *Unit head:* Dr. Benjamin C. Ayers, Director, 706-542-1616, Fax: 706-542-3630, E-mail: bayers@terry.uga.edu. *Application contact:* Jennifer J. Gaver, Graduate Coordinator, 706-542-3699, E-mail: jgaver@terry.uga.edu.

University of Hartford, Barney School of Business, Department of Accounting and Taxation, West Hartford, CT 06117-1599. Offers professional accounting (Certificate); taxation (MSAT). Part-time and evening/weekend programs available. *Entrance requirements:* For master's, GMAT, 2 letters of recommendation, resume. Additional exam requirements/recommendations for international students: Required—TOEFL (minimum score 550 paper-based; 213 computer-based). Electronic applications accepted.

University of Hawaii at Manoa, Graduate Division, Shidler College of Business, Program in Accounting, Honolulu, HI 96822. Offers accounting (M Acc); accounting law (M Acc); information systems (M Acc); taxation (M Acc). Part-time programs available. *Faculty:* 8 full-time (2 women), 1 part-time/adjunct (0 women). *Students:* 63 full-time (31 women), 30 part-time (18 women); includes 57 minority (1 African American, 53 Asian Americans or Pacific Islanders, 3 Hispanic Americans), 17 international. Average age 28. 83 applicants, 80% accepted, 42 enrolled. In 2009, 37 master's awarded. *Entrance requirements:* For master's, GMAT, bachelor's degree in accounting, minimum GPA of 3.0. Additional exam requirements/recommendations for international students: Required—TOEFL (minimum score 550 paper-based; 213 computer-based; 79 iBT), IELTS (minimum score 5). *Application deadline:* For fall admission, 5/1 for domestic students, 3/1 for international students; for spring admission, 11/1 for domestic students, 10/1 for international students. Application fee: $60. *Expenses:* Tuition, state resident: full-time $8900; part-time $372 per credit. Tuition, nonresident: full-time $21,400; part-time $898 per credit. Required fees: $207 per semester. *Financial support:* In 2009–10, 5 students received support, including 17 fellowships (averaging $3,470 per year), 5 research assistantships (averaging $16,592 per year); career-related internships or fieldwork, Federal Work-Study, and tuition waivers (full) also available. *Faculty research:* International accounting, current tax topics, insurance industry financial reporting, behavioral accounting, auditing. *Application contact:* Liming Guan, Graduate Chair, 808-956-7332, Fax: 808-956-9888, E-mail: lguan@hawaii.edu.

University of Hawaii at Manoa, Graduate Division, Shidler College of Business, Program in International Management, Honolulu, HI 96822. Offers Asian finance (PhD); global information technology management (PhD); international accounting (PhD); international marketing (PhD); international organization and strategy (PhD). Part-time programs available. *Students:* 28 full-time (12 women), 5 part-time (0 women); includes 7 minority (all Asian Americans or Pacific Islanders), 17 international. Average age 33. 65 applicants, 18% accepted, 5 enrolled. In 2009, 1 doctorate awarded. *Degree requirements:* For doctorate, comprehensive exam, thesis/dissertation. *Entrance requirements:* For doctorate, GMAT or GRE General Test, minimum GPA of 3.0. Additional exam requirements/recommendations for international students: Required—TOEFL (minimum score 600 paper-based; 250 computer-based; 100 iBT), IELTS (minimum score 7). *Application deadline:* For fall admission, 3/1 for domestic and international students. Application fee: $60. *Expenses:* Contact institution. *Financial support:* In 2009–10, 2 fellowships (averaging $6,945 per year), 21 research assistantships (averaging $17,766 per year) were awarded. *Application contact:* Erica Okada, Graduate Chair, 808-956-6723, Fax: 808-956-6889, E-mail: emokada@hawaii.edu.

University of Houston, Bauer College of Business, Accountancy and Taxation Program, Houston, TX 77204. Offers accountancy (MS Accy); accounting (PhD). *Accreditation:* AACSB. Part-time and evening/weekend programs available. *Faculty:* 13 full-time (4 women), 17 part-time/adjunct (3 women). *Students:* 205 full-time (110 women), 81 part-time (39 women); includes 124 minority (17 African Americans, 1 American Indian/Alaska Native, 80 Asian Americans or Pacific Islanders, 26 Hispanic Americans), 53 international. Average age 26. 174 applicants, 70% accepted, 102 enrolled. In 2009, 161 master's awarded. *Degree requirements:* For master's, minimum GPA of 3.0, 30 hours completed in residence; for doctorate, continuous full time enrollment, dissertation defense within 6 years of entering the program. *Entrance requirements:* For master's, GMAT, letters of recommendation, resume; for doctorate, GMAT or GRE, letter of financial backing, statement of understanding, reference letters, statement of academic and research interests. Additional exam requirements/recommendations for international students: Required—TOEFL (minimum score 603 paper-based; 250 computer-based; 100 iBT), IELTS (minimum score 6.5), Pearson Test of English (minimum score 70). *Application deadline:* For fall admission, 6/1 for domestic students, 4/1 for international students; for spring admission, 11/1 for domestic students, 10/1 for international students. Applications are processed on a rolling basis. Application fee: $75. Electronic applications accepted. *Expenses:* Tuition, state resident: full-time $7676; part-time $320 per credit hour. Tuition, nonresident: full-time $14,324; part-time $597 per credit hour. Required fees: $3034. *Financial support:* In 2009–10, 6 fellowships with full tuition reimbursements (averaging $8,700 per year), 34 teaching assistantships with full tuition reimbursements (averaging $7,100 per year) were awarded; research assistantships with full tuition reimbursements, career-related internships or fieldwork, Federal Work-Study, institutionally sponsored loans, scholarships/grants, and unspecified assistantships also available. Support available to part-time students. Financial award application deadline: 2/1; financial award applicants required to submit FAFSA. *Faculty research:* Accountancy and taxation, finance, international business, management. *Unit head:* Dr. Gerald Lobo, Chairperson, 713-743-4821, Fax: 713-743-4828, E-mail: gjlobo@uh.edu.

University of Houston–Clear Lake, School of Business, Program in Accounting, Houston, TX 77058-1098. Offers accounting (MS); professional accounting (MS). *Accreditation:* AACSB. Part-time and evening/weekend programs available. *Degree requirements:* For master's, thesis optional. *Entrance requirements:* For master's, GMAT. Additional exam requirements/recommendations for international students: Required—TOEFL (minimum score 550 paper-based; 213 computer-based). Electronic applications accepted.

University of Houston–Victoria, School of Business Administration, Victoria, TX 77901-4450. Offers accounting (MBA); economic development and entrepreneurship (MS); finance (GMBA, MBA); general business (MBA); international business (MBA); management (GMBA, MBA); marketing (MBA). *Accreditation:* AACSB. Part-time and evening/weekend programs available. Postbaccalaureate distance learning degree programs offered (no on-campus study). *Entrance requirements:* For master's, GMAT. Additional exam requirements/recommendations for international students: Required—TOEFL (minimum score 550 paper-based; 213 computer-based). Electronic applications accepted. *Faculty research:* Economic development, marketing, finance.

University of Idaho, College of Graduate Studies, College of Business and Economics, Department of Accounting, Moscow, ID 83844-2282. Offers M Acct. *Accreditation:* AACSB. *Faculty:* 5 full-time. *Students:* 30 full-time, 3 part-time. In 2009, 15 master's awarded. *Degree requirements:* For master's, comprehensive exam. *Entrance requirements:* For master's, minimum GPA of 3.0. *Application deadline:* For fall admission, 8/1 for domestic students; for spring admission, 12/15 for domestic students. Application fee: $55 ($60 for international students). *Expenses:* Tuition, state resident: full-time $6120. Tuition, nonresident: full-time $17,712. *Financial support:* Research assistantships, teaching assistantships available. Financial award application deadline: 2/15. *Unit head:* Dr. Marla Kraut, Head, 208-885-7116, Fax: 208-885-2939. *Application contact:* Dr. Marla Kraut, Head, 208-885-7116, Fax: 208-885-2939.

University of Illinois at Chicago, Graduate College, Liautaud Graduate School of Business, Department of Accounting, Chicago, IL 60607-7128. Offers MS, MBA/MS. *Accreditation:* AACSB. Part-time programs available. *Entrance requirements:* For master's, GMAT, minimum GPA of 2.75. Additional exam requirements/recommendations for international students: Required—TOEFL. Electronic applications accepted. *Faculty research:* Governmental accounting, managerial accounting, auditing.

University of Illinois at Springfield, Graduate Programs, College of Business and Management, Program in Accountancy, Springfield, IL 62703-5407. Offers MA. Part-time and evening/weekend programs available. *Faculty:* 4 full-time (0 women), 7 part-time/adjunct (6 women). *Students:* 50 full-time (27 women), 60 part-time (37 women); includes 15 minority (3 African Americans, 2 American Indian/Alaska Native, 7 Asian Americans or Pacific Islanders, 3 Hispanic Americans), 7 international. Average age 29. 73 applicants, 70% accepted, 43 enrolled. In 2009, 25 master's awarded. *Degree requirements:* For master's, capstone course. *Entrance requirements:* For master's, minimum undergraduate GPA of 2.7 in prerequisite coursework. Additional exam requirements/recommendations for international students: Required—TOEFL (minimum score 550 paper-based). *Application deadline:* Applications are processed on a rolling basis. Application fee: $50 ($60 for international students). Electronic applications accepted. *Expenses:* Tuition, state resident: full-time $6390; part-time $266.25 per credit hour. Tuition, nonresident: full-time $14,226; part-time $592.75 per credit hour. Required fees: $2044; $14.36 per credit hour. $722.50 per term. *Financial support:* In 2009–10, research assistantships with full tuition reimbursements (averaging $8,109 per year), teaching assistantships with full tuition reimbursements (averaging $8,109 per year) were awarded; career-related internships or fieldwork, Federal Work-Study, scholarships/grants, health care benefits, and unspecified assistantships also available. Support available to part-time students. Financial award application deadline: 11/15; financial award applicants required to submit FAFSA. *Unit head:* Dr. Leonard Branson, Program Administrator, 217-206-6299, Fax: 217-206-7543, E-mail: branson.leonard@uis.edu. *Application contact:* Dr. Lynn Pardie, Office of Graduate Studies, 800-252-8533, Fax: 217-206-7623, E-mail: pardie.lynn@uis.edu.

University of Illinois at Urbana–Champaign, Graduate College, College of Business, Department of Accountancy, Champaign, IL 61820. Offers accountancy (MAS, MS, PhD); taxation (MS); MAS/JD. *Accreditation:* AACSB. *Faculty:* 30 full-time (8 women), 4 part-time/adjunct (1 woman). *Students:* 406 full-time (208 women), 7 part-time (3 women); includes 64 minority (8 African Americans, 42 Asian Americans or Pacific Islanders, 14 Hispanic Americans), 155 international. 858 applicants, 54% accepted, 364 enrolled. In 2009, 330 master's, 2 doctorates awarded. *Entrance requirements:* For master's, GMAT (for MAS program), minimum GPA of 3.0; for doctorate, GMAT, minimum GPA of 3.0. Additional exam requirements/recommendations for international students: Required—TOEFL. *Application deadline:* Applications are processed on a rolling basis. Application fee: $60 ($75 for international students). Electronic applications accepted. *Financial support:* In 2009–10, 13 fellowships, 23 research assistantships, 78 teaching assistantships were awarded; tuition waivers (full and partial) also available. *Unit head:* Ira Soloman, Head, 217-333-3808, Fax: 217-244-0902, E-mail: isolomon@illinois.edu. *Application contact:* Yvonne Harden, Assistant Director, 217-333-4572, Fax: 217-244-0902, E-mail: yaharden@illinois.edu.

The University of Iowa, Henry B. Tippie College of Business, Department of Accounting, Program in Accounting, Iowa City, IA 52242-1316. Offers accountancy (M Ac); business administration (PhD), including accounting; JD/M Ac. *Faculty:* 18 full-time (3 women). *Students:* 11 full-time (5 women), 1 part-time (0 women); includes 2 minority (both Asian Americans or Pacific Islanders), 5 international. Average age 27. 46 applicants, 13% accepted, 3 enrolled. In 2009, 4 doctorates awarded. *Degree requirements:* For doctorate, comprehensive exam, thesis/dissertation, thesis defense. *Entrance requirements:* For doctorate, GMAT. Additional exam requirements/recommendations for international students: Required—TOEFL (minimum score 600 paper-based; 250 computer-based; 100 iBT). *Application deadline:* For fall admission, 1/31 priority date for domestic students, 1/15 priority date for international students. Applications are processed on a rolling basis. Application fee: $60 ($85 for international students). Electronic applications accepted. *Financial support:* In 2009–10, 12 students received support, including 9 fellowships with partial tuition reimbursements available (averaging $8,500 per year), 1 research assistantship with full tuition reimbursement available (averaging $16,575 per year), 8 teaching assistantships with full tuition reimbursements available (averaging $16,575 per year); institutionally sponsored loans, scholarships/grants, health care benefits, unspecified assistantships, and ALS students: 2 awarded ($30,000 each) also available. Financial award application deadline: 1/15. *Faculty research:* Corporate financial reporting issues; financial statement information and capital markets; cost structure: analysis, estimation, and management; experimental and prediction economics; income taxes and interaction of financial and tax reporting systems. *Unit head:* Prof. Douglas V. DeJong, Department Executive Officer, 319-355-0910, Fax: 319-335-1956, E-mail: bruce-johnson@uiowa.edu. *Application contact:* Renea L. Jay, PhD Program Coordinator, 319-335-0830, Fax: 319-335-1956, E-mail: renea-jay@uiowa.edu.

The University of Kansas, Graduate Studies, School of Business, Program in Accounting, Lawrence, KS 66045. Offers M Acc. *Accreditation:* AACSB. *Students:* 143 full-time (68 women), 15 part-time (6 women); includes 10 minority (5 Asian Americans or Pacific Islanders, 5 Hispanic Americans), 9 international. Average age 24. 132 applicants, 72% accepted, 86 enrolled. In 2009, 95 master's awarded. *Degree requirements:* For master's, 52 credits. *Entrance requirements:* For master's, GMAT. Additional exam requirements/recommendations for international students: Required—TOEFL; Recommended—IELTS (minimum score 6). *Application deadline:* For fall admission, 3/13 priority date for domestic students, 2/27 priority date for international students; for spring admission, 11/1 for domestic students, 10/1 for international students. Applications are processed on a rolling basis. Application fee: $60. Electronic applications accepted. *Expenses:* Tuition, state resident: full-time $6492; part-time $270.50 per credit hour. Tuition, nonresident: full-time $15,510; part-time $646.25 per credit hour. Required fees: $847; $70.56 per credit hour. Tuition and fees vary according to course load and program. *Financial support:* Fellowships, research assistantships with partial tuition reimbursements, teaching assistantships with full and partial tuition reimbursements available. Financial award application deadline: 6/1; financial award applicants required to submit FAFSA. *Faculty research:* Audit; artificial intelligence; agency theory; compensation; production, regulation, and use of accounting information. *Unit head:* Dr. James A. Heintz, Director, 785-864-4500, Fax: 785-864-5328, E-mail: jheintz@ku.edu. *Application contact:* Dee Steinle, Administrative Director of Master's Programs, 785-864-7596, Fax: 785-864-5376, E-mail: dsteinle@ku.edu.

Accounting

University of Kentucky, Graduate School, Gatton College of Business and Economics, Program in Accounting, Lexington, KY 40506-0032. Offers MSACC. *Accreditation:* AACSB. *Degree requirements:* For master's, comprehensive exam. *Entrance requirements:* For master's, GRE General Test, minimum undergraduate GPA of 2.75. Additional exam requirements/recommendations for international students: Required—TOEFL (minimum score 550 paper-based; 213 computer-based). Electronic applications accepted. *Faculty research:* Taxation, financial accounting and auditing, managerial accounting, not-for-profit accounting.

University of La Verne, College of Business and Public Management, Graduate Programs in Business Administration, La Verne, CA 91750-4443. Offers accounting (MBA); executive management (MBA-EP); finance (MBA, MBA-EP); health services management (MBA); information technology (MBA, MBA-EP); international business (MBA, MBA-EP); leadership (MBA-EP); managed care (MBA); management (MBA, MBA-EP); marketing (MBA, MBA-EP). Part-time and evening/weekend programs available. *Faculty:* 22 full-time (11 women), 41 part-time/adjunct (8 women). *Students:* 409 full-time (213 women), 156 part-time (74 women); includes 371 minority (23 African Americans, 7 American Indian/Alaska Native, 259 Asian Americans or Pacific Islanders, 82 Hispanic Americans), 9 international. Average age 29. In 2009, 356 master's awarded. *Entrance requirements:* For master's, minimum undergraduate GPA of 3.0, 2 letters of recommendation, resume. Additional exam requirements/recommendations for international students: Required—TOEFL (minimum score 550 paper-based; 213 computer-based). *Application deadline:* Applications are processed on a rolling basis. Application fee: $50. *Expenses:* Contact institution. *Financial support:* Career-related internships or fieldwork, institutionally sponsored loans, and scholarships/grants available. Financial award application deadline: 3/2; financial award applicants required to submit FAFSA. *Unit head:* Dr. Abe Helou, Chairperson, 909-593-3511 Ext. 4211, Fax: 909-392-2704, E-mail: ihelou@laverne.edu. *Application contact:* Rina Lazarian, Program and Admission Specialist, 909-593-3511 Ext. 4819, Fax: 909-392-2704, E-mail: cbpm@ulv.edu.

University of Lethbridge, School of Graduate Studies, Lethbridge, AB T1K 3M4, Canada. Offers accounting (MScM); addictions counseling (M Sc); agricultural biotechnology (M Sc); agricultural studies (M Sc, MA); anthropology (MA); archaeology (MA); art (MA, MFA); biochemistry (M Sc); biological sciences (M Sc); biomolecular science (PhD); biosystems and biodiversity (PhD); Canadian studies (MA); chemistry (M Sc); computer science (M Sc); computer science and geographical information science (M Sc); counseling psychology (M Ed); dramatic arts (MA); earth, space, and physical science (PhD); economics (MA); educational leadership (M Ed); English (MA); environmental science (M Sc); evolution and behavior (PhD); exercise science (M Sc); finance (MScM); French (MA); French/German (MA); French/Spanish (MA); general education (M Ed); general management (MScM); geography (M Sc, MA); German (MA); health science (M Sc); health sciences (MA); history (MA); human resource management and labour relations (MScM); individualized multidisciplinary (M Sc, MA); information systems (MScM); international management (MScM); kinesiology (M Sc, MA); management (M Sc, MA); marketing (MScM); mathematics (M Sc); music (M Mus, MA); Native American studies (MA); neuroscience (M Sc, PhD); new media (MA); nursing (M Sc); philosophy (MA); physics (M Sc); policy and strategy (MScM); political science (MA); psychology (M Sc, MA); religious studies (MA); social sciences (MA); sociology (MA); theatre and dramatic arts (MFA); theoretical and computational science (PhD); urban and regional studies (MA); women's studies (MA). Part-time and evening/weekend programs available. *Degree requirements:* For doctorate, comprehensive exam, thesis/dissertation. *Entrance requirements:* For master's, GMAT (M Sc in management), bachelor's degree in related field, minimum GPA of 3.0 during previous 20 graded semester courses, 2 years teaching or related experience (M Ed); for doctorate, master's degree, minimum graduate GPA of 3.5. Additional exam requirements/recommendations for international students: Required—TOEFL. *Faculty research:* Movement and brain plasticity, gibberellin physiology, photosynthesis, carbon cycling, molecular properties of main-group ring components.

University of Louisville, Graduate School, College of Business, School of Accountancy, Louisville, KY 40292-0001. Offers MAC. *Accreditation:* AACSB. Part-time and evening/weekend programs available. *Faculty:* 7 full-time (1 woman). *Students:* 14 full-time (8 women), 12 part-time (4 women); includes 1 minority (African American), 6 international. Average age 29. 20 applicants, 55% accepted, 7 enrolled. In 2009, 16 master's awarded. *Entrance requirements:* For master's, GMAT, 2 letters of reference, resume. Additional exam requirements/recommendations for international students: Required—TOEFL (minimum score 550 paper-based; 213 computer-based; 79 iBT). *Application deadline:* For fall admission, 7/15 priority date for domestic students; for winter admission, 11/15 priority date for domestic students; for spring admission, 4/15 priority date for domestic students. Applications are processed on a rolling basis. Application fee: $50. *Financial support:* In 2009–10, 2 research assistantships with full tuition reimbursements (averaging $11,000 per year) were awarded; health care benefits and unspecified assistantships also available. Financial award application deadline: 3/15; financial award applicants required to submit FAFSA. *Faculty research:* Audit judgment and decision-making, information systems, taxation, cost and managerial accounting. *Unit head:* Dr. Charles Moyer, Dean, 502-852-6443, Fax: 502-852-7557, E-mail: charlie.moyer@louisville.edu. *Application contact:* Kevin J. Kane, Director, Master's Program, 502-852-3969, Fax: 502-852-4901, E-mail: kevin.kane@louisville.edu.

University of Maine, Graduate School, College of Business, Public Policy and Health, The Maine Business School, Orono, ME 04469. Offers accounting (MS); business administration (MBA); business and sustainability (MBA). *Accreditation:* AACSB. Part-time and evening/weekend programs available. *Faculty:* 25 full-time (10 women), 1 (woman) part-time/adjunct. *Students:* 47 full-time (19 women), 14 part-time (6 women); includes 3 minority (2 American Indian/Alaska Native, 1 Hispanic American), 4 international. Average age 28. 56 applicants, 63% accepted, 25 enrolled. In 2009, 21 master's awarded. *Entrance requirements:* For master's, GMAT. Additional exam requirements/recommendations for international students: Required—TOEFL (minimum score 550 paper-based; 213 computer-based). *Application deadline:* For fall admission, 6/1 priority date for domestic and international students; for spring admission, 11/1 priority date for domestic and international students. Applications are processed on a rolling basis. Application fee: $65. Electronic applications accepted. *Expenses:* Contact institution. *Financial support:* In 2009–10, 16 students received support, including 4 teaching assistantships with tuition reimbursements available (averaging $12,790 per year); career-related internships or fieldwork, Federal Work-Study, institutionally sponsored loans, scholarships/grants, tuition waivers (full and partial), and unspecified assistantships also available. Financial award application deadline: 3/1. *Faculty research:* Entrepreneurship, investment management, international markets, decision support systems, strategic planning. *Unit head:* Dr. Nory Jones, Director of Graduate Programs, 207-581-1971, Fax: 207-581-1930, E-mail: mba@maine.edu. *Application contact:* Scott G. Delcourt, Associate Dean of the Graduate School, 207-581-3291, Fax: 207-581-3232, E-mail: graduate@maine.edu.

University of Mary Hardin-Baylor, Graduate Studies in Business Administration, Belton, TX 76513. Offers accounting (MBA); management (MBA). Part-time and evening/weekend programs available. *Degree requirements:* For master's, comprehensive exam. *Entrance requirements:* For master's, GMAT, minimum GPA of 3.0, work experience, interview. Electronic applications accepted.

University of Maryland University College, Graduate School of Management and Technology, Program in Accounting and Financial Management, Adelphi, MD 20783. Offers MS, Certificate. Part-time and evening/weekend programs available. Postbaccalaureate distance learning degree programs offered (no on-campus study). *Students:* 17 full-time (11 women), 585 part-time (387 women); includes 281 minority (198 African Americans, 2 American Indian/Alaska Native, 48 Asian Americans or Pacific Islanders, 33 Hispanic Americans), 21 international. Average age 36. 142 applicants, 100% accepted, 100 enrolled. In 2009, 83 master's awarded. *Degree requirements:* For master's, thesis or alternative. *Application deadline:* Applications are processed on a rolling basis. Application fee: $50. Electronic applications accepted. *Expenses:* Tuition, state resident: full-time $7704; part-time $428 per credit hour. Tuition, nonresident: full-time $11,862; part-time $659 per credit hour. *Financial support:* Federal Work-Study and scholarships/grants available. Support available to part-time students. Financial award application deadline: 6/1; financial award applicants required to submit FAFSA. *Unit head:* Dr. James Howard, Program Director, Finance, 240-684-2400, Fax: 240-684-2401, E-mail: jhoward@umuc.edu. *Application contact:* Coordinator, Graduate Admissions, 800-888-UMUC, Fax: 240-684-2151, E-mail: newgrad@umuc.edu.

University of Maryland University College, Graduate School of Management and Technology, Program in Accounting and Information Technology, Adelphi, MD 20783. Offers MS, Certificate. Part-time and evening/weekend programs available. Postbaccalaureate distance learning degree programs offered (no on-campus study). *Students:* 3 full-time (1 woman), 204 part-time (117 women); includes 113 minority (88 African Americans, 18 Asian Americans or Pacific Islanders, 7 Hispanic Americans), 2 international. Average age 37. 92 applicants, 100% accepted, 40 enrolled. In 2009, 35 master's, 2 other advanced degrees awarded. *Degree requirements:* For master's, thesis or alternative. *Application deadline:* Applications are processed on a rolling basis. Application fee: $50. Electronic applications accepted. *Expenses:* Tuition, state resident: full-time $7704; part-time $428 per credit hour. Tuition, nonresident: full-time $11,862; part-time $659 per credit hour. *Financial support:* Federal Work-Study and scholarships/grants available. Support available to part-time students. Financial award application deadline: 6/1; financial award applicants required to submit FAFSA. *Unit head:* Dr. Kathryn Klose, Program Director, Financial Management and Accounting, 240-684-2400, Fax: 301-684-2401, E-mail: kklose@umuc.edu. *Application contact:* Coordinator, Graduate Admissions, 800-888-UMUC, Fax: 240-684-2151, E-mail: newgrad@umuc.edu.

University of Massachusetts Amherst, Graduate School, Isenberg School of Management, Program in Accounting, Amherst, MA 01003. Offers MS. *Accreditation:* AACSB. Part-time programs available. *Students:* 34 full-time (15 women), 32 part-time (9 women); includes 7 minority (1 African American, 5 Asian Americans or Pacific Islanders, 1 Hispanic American), 1 international. Average age 23. 92 applicants, 83% accepted, 62 enrolled. In 2009, 59 master's awarded. *Entrance requirements:* For master's, GMAT. Additional exam requirements/recommendations for international students: Required—TOEFL (minimum score 550 paper-based; 213 computer-based; 80 iBT), IELTS (minimum score 6.5). *Application deadline:* For fall admission, 2/1 for domestic and international students. Applications are processed on a rolling basis. Application fee: $50 ($65 for international students). Electronic applications accepted. *Expenses:* Tuition, state resident: full-time $2640; part-time $110 per credit. Tuition, nonresident: full-time $9936; part-time $414 per credit. Tuition and fees vary according to course load. *Unit head:* Dr. James F. Smith, Graduate Program Director, 413-545-5645, Fax: 413-545-3858. *Application contact:* Jean M. Ames, Supervisor of Admissions, 413-545-0722, Fax: 413-577-0010, E-mail: gradadm@grad.umass.edu.

University of Massachusetts Dartmouth, Graduate School, Charlton College of Business, Program in Business Administration, North Dartmouth, MA 02747-2300. Offers accounting (Postbaccalaureate Certificate); business administration (MBA); e-commerce (PMC); finance (PMC); general management (PMC); leadership (PMC); management (Postbaccalaureate Certificate); marketing (PMC); supply chain management (PMC). *Accreditation:* AACSB. Part-time programs available. *Faculty:* 42 full-time (13 women), 26 part-time/adjunct (6 women). *Students:* 93 full-time (41 women), 132 part-time (64 women); includes 22 minority (5 African Americans, 2 American Indian/Alaska Native, 6 Asian Americans or Pacific Islanders, 9 Hispanic Americans), 42 international. Average age 30. 186 applicants, 82% accepted, 94 enrolled. In 2009, 55 master's, 19 other advanced degrees awarded. *Entrance requirements:* For master's, GMAT, resume, letters of recommendation. Additional exam requirements/recommendations for international students: Required—TOEFL (minimum score 500 paper-based; 200 computer-based; 72 iBT). *Application deadline:* For fall admission, 6/1 for domestic students, 5/1 for international students; for spring admission, 10/1 for domestic students, 8/1 for international students. Application fee: $40 ($60 for international students). Electronic applications accepted. *Expenses:* Tuition, state resident: full-time $2071; part-time $86.29 per credit. Tuition, nonresident: full-time $8099; part-time $337.46 per credit. Required fees: $9446. Tuition and fees vary according to class time, course load and reciprocity agreements. *Financial support:* In 2009–10, 1 research assistantship with full tuition reimbursement (averaging $6,000 per year) was awarded; teaching assistantships, Federal Work-Study and unspecified assistantships also available. Support available to part-time students. Financial award application deadline: 3/1; financial award applicants required to submit FAFSA. *Faculty research:* Competitiveness of south coast enterprises, global sales, key performance indicators, agile manufacturing, green business. Total annual research expenditures: $19,000. *Unit head:* Dr. Norm Barber, Assistant Dean, 508-999-8543, E-mail: nbarber@umassd.edu. *Application contact:* Elan Turcotte-Shamski, Graduate Admissions Officer, 508-999-8604, Fax: 508-999-8183, E-mail: graduate@umassd.edu.

University of Memphis, Graduate School, Fogelman College of Business and Economics, Program in Business Administration, Memphis, TN 38152. Offers accounting (MBA, PhD); economics (MBA, PhD); executive business administration (MBA); finance (PhD); finance, insurance, and real estate (MBA, MS); international business administration (IMBA); management (MBA, MS, PhD); management information systems (MBA, MS, PhD); management science (MBA); marketing (MBA, MS); marketing and supply chain management (PhD); real estate development (MS); JD/MBA. *Accreditation:* AACSB. *Faculty:* 44 full-time (9 women), 5 part-time/adjunct (0 women). *Students:* 263 full-time (106 women), 181 part-time (66 women); includes 70 minority (46 African Americans, 3 American Indian/Alaska Native, 16 Asian Americans or Pacific Islanders, 5 Hispanic Americans), 109 international. Average age 31. 374 applicants, 73% accepted, 119 enrolled. In 2009, 140 master's, 17 doctorates awarded. *Degree requirements:* For master's, comprehensive exam; for doctorate, comprehensive exam, thesis/dissertation. *Entrance requirements:* For master's, GMAT, resume; for doctorate, GMAT, interview, minimum GPA of 3.4, resume, letter of recommendation. Additional exam requirements/recommendations for international students: Required—TOEFL (minimum score 550 paper-based; 220 computer-based). *Application deadline:* For fall admission, 8/1 for domestic students; for spring admission, 12/1 for domestic students. Application fee: $35 ($60 for international students). *Expenses:* Tuition, state resident: full-time $6246; part-time $347 per credit hour. Tuition, nonresident: full-time $15,894; part-time $883 per credit hour. Required fees: $1160. Full-time tuition and fees vary according to course load, degree level and program. *Financial support:* In 2009–10, 164 students received support; research assistantships with full tuition reimbursements available, teaching assistantships with full tuition reimbursements available, career-related internships or fieldwork, Federal Work-Study, scholarships/grants, and unspecified assistantships available. Financial award application deadline: 2/15; financial award applicants required to submit FAFSA. *Faculty research:* Competitive business strategy, finance microstructures, supply chain management innovations, health care economics, litigation risks and corporate audits. *Unit head:* Rajiv Grover, Dean, 901-678-3759, E-mail: rgrover@memphis.edu. *Application contact:* Dr. Carol V. Danehower, Associate Dean for Programs, 901-678-5402, Fax: 901-678-3579, E-mail: fcbegp@memphis.edu.

University of Memphis, Graduate School, Fogelman College of Business and Economics, School of Accountancy, Memphis, TN 38152. Offers accounting (MS); accounting systems (MS); taxation (MS). *Accreditation:* AACSB. *Faculty:* 10 full-time (2 women), 1 part-time/adjunct (0 women). *Students:* 25 full-time (10 women), 21 part-time (14 women); includes 10 minority (7 African Americans, 2 Asian Americans or Pacific Islanders, 1 Hispanic American), 10 international. Average age 29. 33 applicants, 76% accepted, 9 enrolled. In 2009, 27 master's awarded. *Degree requirements:* For master's, comprehensive exam. *Entrance requirements:* For master's, GMAT. *Application deadline:* For fall admission, 8/1 for domestic students; for spring admission, 12/1 for domestic students. Application fee: $35 ($60 for international students). *Expenses:* Tuition, state resident: full-time $6246; part-time $347 per credit hour. Tuition, nonresident: full-time $15,894; part-time $883 per credit hour. Required fees: $1160. Full-time tuition and fees vary according to course load, degree level and program. *Financial support:* In 2009–10, 32 students received support; research assistantships with full tuition reimbursements available, teaching assistantships with full tuition reimbursements available, Federal Work-Study, scholarships/grants, and unspecified assistantships available. Financial award application deadline: 2/15; financial award applicants required to submit FAFSA. *Faculty research:* Financial accounting, corporate governance, EDP auditing,

evolution of system analysis, investor behavior and investment decisions. *Unit head:* Dr. Carolyn Callahan, Director, 901-678-4022, E-mail: cmcllhan@memphis.edu. *Application contact:* Dr. Craig Langstraat, Program Coordinator, 901-678-4577, E-mail: cjlngstr@memphis.edu.

University of Miami, Graduate School, School of Business Administration, Department of Accounting, Coral Gables, FL 33124. Offers professional accounting (MP Acc); taxation (MS Tax). *Accreditation:* AACSB. Part-time and evening/weekend programs available. *Entrance requirements:* For master's, GMAT or CPA exam. Additional exam requirements/recommendations for international students: Required—TOEFL. Electronic applications accepted. *Faculty research:* Financial reporting, audit risk, public policy and taxation issues, government accounting and public choice, corporate governance.

University of Miami, Graduate School, School of Business Administration, Program in Business Administration, Coral Gables, FL 33124. Offers accounting (MBA); computer information systems (MBA); executive and professional (MBA), including international business, management; finance (MBA); international business (MBA); management (MBA); management science (MBA); marketing (MBA); professional management (MSPM); JD/MBA; MBA/MSIE. *Accreditation:* AACSB. Evening/weekend programs available. *Degree requirements:* For master's, comprehensive exam. *Entrance requirements:* For master's, GMAT. Additional exam requirements/recommendations for international students: Required—TOEFL (minimum score 550 paper-based; 213 computer-based; 59 iBT). Electronic applications accepted. *Faculty research:* Leadership, e-commerce, supply chain management.

University of Michigan–Dearborn, School of Management, Dearborn, MI 48128-1491. Offers accounting (MBA, MS); finance (MBA, MS); information systems (MS); international business (MBA); management (MBA); management information systems (MBA); marketing (MBA); supply chain management (MBA); MBA/MHSA; MBA/MSE; MBA/MSF. *Accreditation:* AACSB. Part-time and evening/weekend programs available. Postbaccalaureate distance learning degree programs offered (no on-campus study). *Faculty:* 26 full-time (6 women), 8 part-time/adjunct (4 women). *Students:* 73 full-time (30 women), 412 part-time (134 women); includes 65 minority (20 African Americans, 1 American Indian/Alaska Native, 38 Asian Americans or Pacific Islanders, 6 Hispanic Americans), 76 international. Average age 30. 185 applicants, 56% accepted, 78 enrolled. In 2009, 151 master's awarded. *Entrance requirements:* For master's, GMAT, 2 years of work experience (MBA); course work in computer applications, statistics, and pre-calculus or finite mathematics; 18 credits of accounting course work beyond introductory courses (MS in accounting). Additional exam requirements/recommendations for international students: Required—TOEFL (minimum score 560 paper-based; 220 computer-based; 84 iBT). *Application deadline:* For fall admission, 8/1 priority date for domestic students, 6/1 for international students; for winter admission, 12/1 priority date for domestic students, 10/1 for international students; for spring admission, 4/1 priority date for domestic students, 2/1 for international students. Applications are processed on a rolling basis. Application fee: $60. Electronic applications accepted. *Expenses:* Contact institution. *Financial support:* Career-related internships or fieldwork, Federal Work-Study, and scholarships/grants available. Support available to part-time students. Financial award application deadline: 9/1; financial award applicants required to submit FAFSA. *Faculty research:* Cultural diversity, buyer-supplier relations, error detection in data, economic evolution. *Unit head:* Dr. Kim Schatzel, Dean, 313-593-5248, Fax: 313-271-9835, E-mail: schatzel@umd.umich.edu. *Application contact:* Joan Doherty, Academic Advisor/Counselor, 313-593-5460, Fax: 313-271-9838, E-mail: gradbusiness@umd.umich.edu.

University of Minnesota, Twin Cities Campus, Carlson School of Management, Doctoral Program in Business Administration, Minneapolis, MN 55455-0213. Offers accounting (PhD); finance (PhD); information and decision sciences (PhD); marketing and logistics management (PhD); operations and management science (PhD); strategic management and organization (PhD). *Faculty:* 74 full-time (19 women). *Students:* 68 full-time (28 women); includes 7 minority (1 African American, 3 Asian Americans or Pacific Islanders, 3 Hispanic Americans), 46 international. Average age 29. 250 applicants, 5% accepted, 9 enrolled. In 2009, 11 doctorates awarded. *Degree requirements:* For doctorate, comprehensive exam, thesis/dissertation, written and oral preliminary exams, proposal defense. *Entrance requirements:* For doctorate, GMAT, GRE General Test. Additional exam requirements/recommendations for international students: Required—TOEFL (minimum score 600 paper-based; 250 computer-based; 100 iBT), IELTS (minimum score 7.5). *Application deadline:* For fall admission, 12/31 for domestic students, 12/31 priority date for international students. Applications are processed on a rolling basis. Application fee: $55 ($75 for international students). Electronic applications accepted. *Financial support:* In 2009–10, 68 fellowships with full tuition reimbursements (averaging $11,500 per year), 63 research assistantships with full tuition reimbursements (averaging $6,750 per year), 53 teaching assistantships with full tuition reimbursements (averaging $6,750 per year) were awarded; institutionally sponsored loans, scholarships/grants, health care benefits, and unspecified assistantships also available. Financial award application deadline: 12/31. *Faculty research:* Corporate strategy, finance, entrepreneurship, marketing, information and decision science, operations, accounting. Total annual research expenditures: $300,000. *Unit head:* Dr. Shawn P. Curley, Director of Graduate Studies/Program Director, 612-624-6546, Fax: 612-624-8221, E-mail: curley@umn.edu. *Application contact:* Earlene K. Bronson, Assistant Director, 612-624-0875, Fax: 612-624-8221, E-mail: brons003@umn.edu.

University of Minnesota, Twin Cities Campus, Carlson School of Management, Master's Program in Accountancy, Minneapolis, MN 55455-0213. Offers M Acc. *Accreditation:* AACSB. Part-time and evening/weekend programs available. *Faculty:* 1 full-time (0 women). *Students:* 54 full-time (30 women); includes 4 minority (all Asian Americans or Pacific Islanders), 20 international. Average age 23. 154 applicants, 35% accepted, 40 enrolled. In 2009, 19 master's awarded. *Entrance requirements:* For master's, GMAT, letters of recommendation. Additional exam requirements/recommendations for international students: Required—TOEFL (minimum score 550 paper-based; 213 computer-based; 79 iBT), IELTS (minimum score 6.5). *Application deadline:* For fall admission, 4/30 priority date for domestic and international students; for spring admission, 10/15 priority date for domestic and international students. Applications are processed on a rolling basis. Application fee: $75 ($95 for international students). Electronic applications accepted. *Expenses:* Contact institution. *Financial support:* In 2009–10, 13 fellowships (averaging $1,500 per year), 5 teaching assistantships with partial tuition reimbursements (averaging $5,900 per year) were awarded; institutionally sponsored loans also available. Financial award applicants required to submit FAFSA. *Faculty research:* Capitol market-based accounting, cognitive skill acquisition in auditing, incentives and control in organizations, economic consequences of securities regulation, earnings management. *Unit head:* Larry Kallio, Director of Graduate Studies, 612-624-9818, Fax: 612-626-7795, E-mail: kalli008@umn.edu. *Application contact:* JoAnn Ash, Administrator, 612-624-3320, Fax: 612-626-7795, E-mail: jash@umn.edu.

University of Mississippi, Graduate School, School of Accountancy, Oxford, University, MS 38677. Offers accountancy (M Acc, PhD); taxation accounting (M Tax). *Accreditation:* AACSB. *Faculty:* 13 full-time (4 women), 3 part-time/adjunct (2 women). *Students:* 108 full-time (31 women), 16 part-time (10 women); includes 7 minority (4 African Americans, 1 Asian American or Pacific Islander, 2 Hispanic Americans), 4 international. In 2009, 56 master's, 2 doctorates awarded. *Degree requirements:* For doctorate, thesis/dissertation. *Entrance requirements:* For master's, GMAT, minimum GPA of 3.0; for doctorate, GMAT. Additional exam requirements/recommendations for international students: Required—TOEFL. *Application deadline:* For fall admission, 4/1 for domestic students; for spring admission, 10/1 for domestic students. Applications are processed on a rolling basis. Application fee: $25. *Financial support:* Scholarships/grants available. Financial award application deadline: 3/1; financial award applicants required to submit FAFSA. *Unit head:* Dr. Mark Wilder, Interim Dean, 662-915-7468, Fax: 662-915-7483, E-mail: umaccy@olemiss.edu. *Application contact:* Dr. Christy M. Wyandt, Associate Dean, 662-915-7474, Fax: 662-915-7577, E-mail: cwyandt@olemiss.edu.

University of Missouri, Graduate School, Robert J. Trulaske, Sr. College of Business, School of Accountancy, Columbia, MO 65211. Offers M Acc, PhD. *Accreditation:* AACSB. Part-time programs available. *Degree requirements:* For master's, thesis or alternative; for doctorate, thesis/dissertation. *Entrance requirements/recommendations:* For master's and doctorate, GMAT, minimum GPA of 3.0. Additional exam requirements/recommendations for international students: Required—TOEFL (minimum score 600 paper-based; 250 computer-based; 100 iBT).

University of Missouri–Kansas City, Henry W. Bloch School of Business and Public Administration, Kansas City, MO 64110-2499. Offers accounting (MS); business administration (MBA); entrepreneurship and innovation (PhD); public affairs (MPA, PhD); JD/MBA; LL M/MPA. PhD (interdisciplinary) offered through the School of Graduate Studies. *Accreditation:* AACSB; NASPAA. Part-time and evening/weekend programs available. *Faculty:* 43 full-time (14 women), 22 part-time/adjunct (7 women). *Students:* 234 full-time (108 women), 437 part-time (193 women); includes 79 minority (33 African Americans, 27 Asian Americans or Pacific Islanders, 19 Hispanic Americans), 51 international. Average age 30. 387 applicants, 65% accepted, 222 enrolled. In 2009, 240 master's awarded. Terminal master's awarded for partial completion of doctoral program. *Entrance requirements:* For master's, GMAT, GRE, 2 writing essays, 2 references and support of employer; for doctorate, GRE, minimum GPA of 3.0. Additional exam requirements/recommendations for international students: Required—TOEFL (minimum score 550 paper-based; 213 computer-based; 80 iBT). *Application deadline:* For fall admission, 5/1 priority date for domestic and international students; for spring admission, 10/1 priority date for domestic and international students. Applications are processed on a rolling basis. Application fee: $45 ($50 for international students). Electronic applications accepted. *Expenses:* Tuition, state resident: full-time $5378; part-time $299 per credit hour. Tuition, nonresident: full-time $13,881; part-time $771 per credit hour. Required fees: $641; $71 per credit hour. Tuition and fees vary according to course load and program. *Financial support:* In 2009–10, 18 research assistantships with partial tuition reimbursements (averaging $8,766 per year), 5 teaching assistantships with partial tuition reimbursements (averaging $8,430 per year) were awarded; career-related internships or fieldwork, Federal Work-Study, institutionally sponsored loans, scholarships/grants, tuition waivers (full and partial), and unspecified assistantships also available. Support available to part-time students. Financial award application deadline: 3/1; financial award applicants required to submit FAFSA. *Faculty research:* Entrepreneurship, finance, non-profit, risk management. Total annual research expenditures: $751,788. *Unit head:* Dr. Teng-Kee Tan, Dean, 816-235-2215, Fax: 816-235-2206. *Application contact:* 816-235-1111, E-mail: admit@umkc.edu.

University of Missouri–St. Louis, College of Business Administration, Program in Accounting, St. Louis, MO 63121. Offers M Acc. *Accreditation:* AACSB. Part-time and evening/weekend programs available. *Faculty:* 9 full-time (5 women). *Students:* 40 full-time (15 women), 41 part-time (24 women); includes 8 minority (1 African American, 6 Asian Americans or Pacific Islanders, 1 Hispanic American), 8 international. Average age 27. 52 applicants, 54% accepted, 28 enrolled. In 2009, 29 master's awarded. *Entrance requirements:* For master's, GMAT, 2 letters of recommendation. Additional exam requirements/recommendations for international students: Required—TOEFL (minimum score 550 paper-based; 213 computer-based). *Application deadline:* For fall admission, 3/15 for domestic and international students; for spring admission, 10/15 for domestic and international students. Application fee: $35 ($40 for international students). Electronic applications accepted. *Expenses:* Tuition, state resident: full-time $5377; part-time $297.70 per credit hour. Tuition, nonresident: full-time $13,882; part-time $771.20 per credit hour. Required fees: $220; $12.20 per credit hour. One-time fee: $12. Tuition and fees vary according to course level, campus/location and program. *Financial support:* Career-related internships or fieldwork, Federal Work-Study, and institutionally sponsored loans available. Support available to part-time students. Financial award application deadline: 4/1; financial award applicants required to submit FAFSA. *Faculty research:* Accounting information in contracts, financial reporting issues, empirical valuation issues. *Unit head:* Karl Kottemann, Assistant Director, 314-516-5885, Fax: 314-516-6420, E-mail: mba@umsl.edu. *Application contact:* 314-516-5458, Fax: 314-516-6996, E-mail: gradadm@umsl.edu.

University of Missouri–St. Louis, College of Business Administration, Program in Business Administration, St. Louis, MO 63121. Offers accounting (MBA); business administration (Certificate); finance (MBA); human resource management (Certificate); logistics and supply chain management (MBA, Certificate); management (MBA); marketing (MBA); marketing management (Certificate); operations (MBA); quantitative management science (MBA). *Accreditation:* AACSB. Part-time and evening/weekend programs available. *Faculty:* 30 full-time (5 women), 11 part-time/adjunct (2 women). *Students:* 107 full-time (47 women), 310 part-time (120 women); includes 32 minority (17 African Americans, 6 Asian Americans or Pacific Islanders, 9 Hispanic Americans), 66 international. Average age 31. 285 applicants, 58% accepted, 130 enrolled. In 2009, 149 master's, 13 other advanced degrees awarded. *Entrance requirements:* For master's, GMAT, 2 letters of recommendation. Additional exam requirements/recommendations for international students: Required—TOEFL (minimum score 550 paper-based; 213 computer-based). *Application deadline:* For fall admission, 7/1 for domestic students; for spring admission, 11/1 for domestic students. Applications are processed on a rolling basis. Application fee: $35 ($40 for international students). Electronic applications accepted. *Expenses:* Tuition, state resident: full-time $5377; part-time $297.70 per credit hour. Tuition, nonresident: full-time $13,882; part-time $771.20 per credit hour. Required fees: $220; $12.20 per credit hour. One-time fee: $12. Tuition and fees vary according to course level, campus/location and program. *Financial support:* In 2009–10, 27 research assistantships with full and partial tuition reimbursements (averaging $8,525 per year), 6 teaching assistantships with full and partial tuition reimbursements (averaging $13,950 per year) were awarded; career-related internships or fieldwork, Federal Work-Study, and institutionally sponsored loans also available. Support available to part-time students. Financial award application deadline: 4/1; financial award applicants required to submit FAFSA. *Faculty research:* Human resources, strategic management, marketing strategy, consumer behavior product development, advertising. *Unit head:* Karl Kottemann, Assistant Director, 314-516-5885, Fax: 314-516-6420, E-mail: mba@umsl.edu. *Application contact:* 314-516-5458, Fax: 314-516-6996, E-mail: gradadm@umsl.edu.

The University of Montana, Graduate School, School of Business Administration, Department of Accounting and Finance, Missoula, MT 59812-0002. Offers accounting (M Acct). *Accreditation:* AACSB. *Degree requirements:* For master's, thesis optional. *Entrance requirements:* For master's, GMAT. Additional exam requirements/recommendations for international students: Required—TOEFL (minimum score 580 paper-based; 237 computer-based). *Faculty research:* Income tax, financial markets, nonprofit accounting, accounting information systems, auditing.

University of Nebraska at Omaha, Graduate Studies, College of Business Administration, Department of Accounting, Omaha, NE 68182. Offers M Acc. Part-time and evening/weekend programs available. *Faculty:* 9 full-time (3 women). *Students:* 12 full-time (6 women), 19 part-time (11 women); includes 1 minority (Asian American or Pacific Islander), 5 international. Average age 28. 26 applicants, 46% accepted, 3 enrolled. In 2009, 6 master's awarded. *Entrance requirements:* For master's, GMAT, minimum GPA of 3.0, resume. Additional exam requirements/recommendations for international students: Required—TOEFL (minimum score 600 paper-based; 213 computer-based; 100 iBT). *Application deadline:* For fall admission, 5/1 priority date for domestic students; for spring admission, 12/1 priority date for domestic students. Applications are processed on a rolling basis. Application fee: $45. Electronic applications accepted. *Financial support:* In 2009–10, 15 students received support; research assistantships with tuition reimbursements available, Federal Work-Study, institutionally sponsored loans, scholarships/grants, tuition waivers (partial), and unspecified assistantships available. Support available to part-time students. Financial award application deadline: 3/1; financial award applicants required to submit FAFSA. *Unit head:* Dr. Jack Armitage, Chairperson, 402-554-3650. *Application contact:* Dr. Jack Armitage, Chairperson, 402-554-3650.

University of Nebraska–Lincoln, Graduate College, College of Business Administration, Interdepartmental Area of Business, Lincoln, NE 68588. Offers accountancy (PhD); business (MBA); finance (MA, PhD), including business; management (MA, PhD), including business; marketing (MA, PhD), including business; JD/MBA; M Arch/MBA. *Accreditation:* AACSB. Part-time programs available. Postbaccalaureate distance learning degree programs offered. *Degree requirements:* For doctorate, comprehensive exam, thesis/dissertation. *Entrance requirements:* For master's and doctorate, GMAT. Additional exam requirements/

Accounting

University of Nebraska–Lincoln *(continued)*
recommendations for international students: Required—TOEFL (minimum score 550 paper-based; 213 computer-based). Electronic applications accepted.

University of Nebraska–Lincoln, Graduate College, College of Business Administration, School of Accountancy, Lincoln, NE 68588. Offers MPA, PhD, JD/MPA. *Accreditation:* AACSB. *Entrance requirements:* For master's, GMAT. Additional exam requirements/recommendations for international students: Required—TOEFL (minimum score 550 paper-based; 213 computer-based). Electronic applications accepted. *Faculty research:* Auditing, financial accounting, managerial accounting, capital markets, tax accounting.

University of Nevada, Las Vegas, Graduate College, College of Business, Department of Accounting, Las Vegas, NV 89154-6003. Offers MS. *Accreditation:* AACSB. Part-time and evening/weekend programs available. *Faculty:* 11 full-time (3 women), 4 part-time/adjunct (1 woman). *Students:* 50 full-time (29 women), 56 part-time (31 women); includes 15 minority (1 African American, 12 Asian Americans or Pacific Islanders, 2 Hispanic Americans), 11 international. Average age 33. 66 applicants, 74% accepted, 33 enrolled. In 2009, 53 master's awarded. *Entrance requirements:* For master's, GMAT. Additional exam requirements/recommendations for international students: Required—TOEFL (minimum score 550 paper-based; 213 computer-based; 80 iBT), IELTS (minimum score 7). *Application deadline:* For fall admission, 6/1 priority date for domestic students, 5/1 for international students; for spring admission, 11/15 priority date for domestic students, 10/1 for international students. Applications are processed on a rolling basis. Application fee: $60 ($95 for international students). Electronic applications accepted. *Financial support:* In 2009–10, 6 students received support, including 6 research assistantships with partial tuition reimbursements available (averaging $10,000 per year); institutionally sponsored loans, scholarships/grants, health care benefits, and unspecified assistantships also available. Financial award application deadline: 3/1. *Faculty research:* Audit efficiency, incidence of earnings management, audit practice and fraud detection, knowledge-based systems, optimal tax management. *Unit head:* Dr. Paulette Tandy, Chair/Associate Professor, 702-895-1559, Fax: 702-895-4306, E-mail: paulette.tandy@unlv.edu. *Application contact:* Graduate College Admissions Evaluator, 702-895-3320, Fax: 702-895-4180, E-mail: gradcollege@unlv.edu.

University of Nevada, Reno, Graduate School, College of Business Administration, Department of Accounting and Information Systems, Reno, NV 89557. Offers M Acc. *Accreditation:* AACSB. *Entrance requirements:* For master's, GMAT or GRE (if undergraduate degree is not from an AACSB-accredited business school with minimum GPA of 3.5), minimum GPA of 2.75. Additional exam requirements/recommendations for international students: Required—TOEFL (minimum score 500 paper-based; 173 computer-based; 61 iBT), IELTS (minimum score 6). Electronic applications accepted. *Faculty research:* Financial reporting/auditing, taxation.

University of New Hampshire, Graduate School, Whittemore School of Business and Economics, Department of Accounting and Finance, Durham, NH 03824. Offers accounting (MS). Part-time programs available. *Faculty:* 8 full-time (2 women). *Students:* 28 full-time (14 women); includes 1 minority (Asian American or Pacific Islander), 5 international. Average age 27. 50 applicants, 62% accepted, 25 enrolled. In 2009, 17 master's awarded. *Entrance requirements:* For master's, GMAT. Additional exam requirements/recommendations for international students: Required—TOEFL (minimum score 550 paper-based; 213 computer-based; 80 iBT). *Application deadline:* For fall admission, 5/1 priority date for domestic students, 4/1 for international students; for spring admission, 12/1 for domestic students. Applications are processed on a rolling basis. Application fee: $65. *Expenses:* Tuition, state resident: full-time $10,380; part-time $577 per credit hour. Tuition, nonresident: full-time $24,350; part-time $1002 per credit hour. Required fees: $1550; $387.50 per semester. Tuition and fees vary according to course load and program. *Financial support:* In 2009–10, 7 students received support; fellowships, research assistantships, teaching assistantships available. Financial award application deadline: 2/15. *Unit head:* Dr. Ahmad Etebari, Chairperson, 603-862-3359, E-mail: ahmad.etebari@unh.edu. *Application contact:* Lindsey Terestre, Administrative Assistant, 603-862-3326, E-mail: wsbe.grad@unh.edu.

University of New Haven, Graduate School, School of Business, Program in Accounting, West Haven, CT 06516-1916. Offers financial accounting (MS); managerial accounting (MS). In 2009, 5 master's awarded. *Degree requirements:* For master's, thesis. *Application deadline:* Applications are processed on a rolling basis. Application fee: $50. *Expenses:* Tuition: Part-time $700 per credit. Required fees: $45 per term. One-time fee: $390 part-time. *Financial support:* Federal Work-Study available. Support available to part-time students. Financial award application deadline: 5/1; financial award applicants required to submit FAFSA. *Unit head:* Robert Wnek, Coordinator, 203-932-7111. *Application contact:* Eloise Gormley, Director of Graduate Admissions, 203-932-7449, Fax: 203-932-7137, E-mail: gradinfo@newhaven.edu.

University of New Haven, Graduate School, School of Business, Program in Business Administration, West Haven, CT 06516-1916. Offers accounting (MBA, Certificate), including CPA (MBA); business management (Certificate); business policy and strategy (MBA); finance (MBA), including CFA; global marketing (MBA); human resource management (Certificate); human resources management (MBA); international business (Certificate); marketing (Certificate); sports management (MBA); telecommunications management (Certificate); MBA/MPA. Part-time and evening/weekend programs available. *Faculty:* 26 full-time (3 women), 23 part-time/adjunct (5 women). *Students:* 302 full-time (120 women), 194 part-time (101 women); includes 109 minority (56 African Americans, 3 American Indian/Alaska Native, 28 Asian Americans or Pacific Islanders, 22 Hispanic Americans), 110 international. Average age 31. 372 applicants, 83% accepted, 172 enrolled. In 2009, 194 master's, 31 other advanced degrees awarded. *Degree requirements:* For master's, thesis or alternative. *Entrance requirements:* For master's, GMAT. Additional exam requirements/recommendations for international students: Required—TOEFL (minimum score 520 paper-based; 190 computer-based; 70 iBT), IELTS (minimum score 5.5). *Application deadline:* For fall admission, 5/31 for international students; for winter admission, 10/15 for international students; for spring admission, 1/15 for international students. Applications are processed on a rolling basis. Application fee: $50. Electronic applications accepted. *Expenses:* Contact institution. *Financial support:* Research assistantships with partial tuition reimbursements, teaching assistantships with partial tuition reimbursements, Federal Work-Study, scholarships/grants, health care benefits, tuition waivers, and unspecified assistantships available. Support available to part-time students. Financial award applicants required to submit FAFSA. *Unit head:* Charles Coleman, Chairman, 203-932-7375. *Application contact:* Eloise Gormley, Director of Graduate Admissions, 203-932-7449, Fax: 203-932-7137, E-mail: gradinfo@newhaven.edu.

University of New Mexico, Robert O. Anderson Graduate School of Management, Department of Accounting, Albuquerque, NM 87131. Offers accounting (MBA); advanced accounting (M Acct); professional accounting (M Acct); tax accounting (M Acct); JD/M Acct. *Accreditation:* AACSB. Part-time and evening/weekend programs available. *Faculty:* 12 full-time (4 women), 2 part-time/adjunct (1 woman). *Students:* 57 full-time (32 women), 60 part-time (39 women); includes 42 minority (1 African American, 5 Asian Americans or Pacific Islanders, 36 Hispanic Americans), 8 international. Average age 32. 77 applicants, 66% accepted, 46 enrolled. In 2009, 64 master's awarded. *Entrance requirements:* For master's, GMAT or GRE (can be waived in some instances). Additional exam requirements/recommendations for international students: Required—TOEFL (minimum score 550 paper-based; 213 computer-based; 79 iBT). *Application deadline:* For fall admission, 4/1 priority date for domestic students, 5/1 for international students; for spring admission, 10/1 priority date for domestic students, 10/1 for international students. Applications are processed on a rolling basis. Application fee: $50. Electronic applications accepted. *Expenses:* Tuition, state resident: full-time $2099; part-time $233.20 per credit hour. Tuition, nonresident: full-time $6650. Required fees: $25 per semester. Tuition and fees vary according to course load, program and reciprocity agreements. *Financial support:* Fellowships, research assistantships, teaching assistantships, career-related internships or fieldwork, Federal Work-Study, scholarships/grants, and unspecified assistantships available. Support available to part-time students. *Faculty research:* Critical accounting, accounting pedagogy, theory, taxation, information fraud. *Unit head:* Dr. Craig White, Chair, 505-277-6471, Fax:

505-277-7108, E-mail: white@mgt.unm.edu. *Application contact:* Tina Armijo, Office Administrator, 505-277-6471, Fax: 505-277-7108, E-mail: profmacct@mgt.unm.edu.

University of New Orleans, Graduate School, College of Business Administration, Department of Accounting, Program in Accounting, New Orleans, LA 70148. Offers MS. *Accreditation:* AACSB. Part-time and evening/weekend programs available. *Degree requirements:* For master's, thesis optional. *Entrance requirements:* For master's, GMAT. Additional exam requirements/recommendations for international students: Required—TOEFL (minimum score 550 paper-based; 213 computer-based; 79 iBT). Electronic applications accepted.

The University of North Carolina at Chapel Hill, Kenan-Flagler Business School, Accounting Program, Chapel Hill, NC 27599. Offers MAC. *Entrance requirements:* For master's, GMAT. Additional exam requirements/recommendations for international students: Required—TOEFL. *Expenses:* Contact institution. *Faculty research:* Corporate taxation, international taxation, financial accounting, corporate governance, strategy.

The University of North Carolina at Chapel Hill, Kenan-Flagler Business School, Doctoral Program in Business Administration, Chapel Hill, NC 27599. Offers accounting (PhD); finance (PhD); marketing (PhD); operations management (PhD); organizational behavior (PhD); strategy (PhD). *Accreditation:* AACSB. *Degree requirements:* For doctorate, thesis/dissertation. *Entrance requirements:* For doctorate, GMAT or GRE General Test. Electronic applications accepted. *Expenses:* Contact institution.

The University of North Carolina at Charlotte, Graduate School, Belk College of Business, Department of Accounting, Charlotte, NC 28223-0001. Offers MACC. *Accreditation:* AACSB. Part-time and evening/weekend programs available. *Faculty:* 11 full-time (2 women). *Students:* 73 full-time (46 women), 72 part-time (32 women); includes 20 minority (8 African Americans, 9 Asian Americans or Pacific Islanders, 3 Hispanic Americans), 12 international. Average age 28. 157 applicants, 70% accepted, 82 enrolled. In 2009, 51 master's awarded. *Entrance requirements:* For master's, GMAT, minimum GPA of 3.0 in undergraduate major, 2.8 overall. Additional exam requirements/recommendations for international students: Required—TOEFL (minimum score 557 paper-based; 220 computer-based; 83 iBT). *Application deadline:* For fall admission, 7/15 for domestic students, 5/1 for international students; for spring admission, 11/15 for domestic students, 10/1 for international students. Applications are processed on a rolling basis. Application fee: $55. Electronic applications accepted. *Financial support:* Research assistantships, career-related internships or fieldwork, institutionally sponsored loans, scholarships/grants, and unspecified assistantships available. Support available to part-time students. Financial award application deadline: 4/1; financial award applicants required to submit FAFSA. *Faculty research:* Corporate financial reporting trends, use of latest software for accounting and business applications, latest developments in federal and international taxation. *Unit head:* Dr. Jack Cathey, Interim Department Chair, 704-687-7690, Fax: 704-687-6938, E-mail: jmcathey@uncc.edu. *Application contact:* Kathy B. Giddings, Director of Graduate Admissions, 704-687-5503, Fax: 704-687-3279, E-mail: gradadm@uncc.edu.

The University of North Carolina at Greensboro, Graduate School, Bryan School of Business and Economics, Department of Accounting, Greensboro, NC 27412-5001. Offers accounting (MS); accounting systems (MS); financial accounting and reporting (MS); financial analysis (PMC); tax concentration (MS). *Accreditation:* AACSB. *Entrance requirements:* For master's, GMAT, GRE General Test, previous course work in accounting and business. Additional exam requirements/recommendations for international students: Required—TOEFL. Electronic applications accepted.

The University of North Carolina Wilmington, School of Business, Program in Accountancy, Wilmington, NC 28403-3297. Offers MSA. *Degree requirements:* For master's, thesis or alternative, portfolio project. *Entrance requirements:* For master's, GMAT. Additional exam requirements/recommendations for international students: Required—TOEFL (minimum score 550 paper-based; 217 computer-based; 79 iBT), IELTS (minimum score 6.5).

University of North Dakota, Graduate School, College of Business and Public Administration, Department of Accountancy, Grand Forks, ND 58202. Offers M Acc.

University of Northern Iowa, Graduate College, College of Business Administration, Program in Accounting, Cedar Falls, IA 50614. Offers M Acc. *Students:* 31 full-time (11 women), 2 part-time (1 woman); includes 1 minority (African American), 3 international. 35 applicants, 43% accepted, 13 enrolled. In 2009, 36 master's awarded. *Degree requirements:* For master's, thesis or alternative. *Entrance requirements:* For master's, GMAT. Additional exam requirements/recommendations for international students: Required—TOEFL (minimum score 575 paper-based; 230 computer-based; 89 iBT). *Application deadline:* For fall admission, 8/1 priority date for domestic students. Applications are processed on a rolling basis. Application fee: $30 ($50 for international students). *Financial support:* Application deadline: 2/1. *Unit head:* Dr. Martha Wartick, Head, 319-273-7754, Fax: 319-273-2922, E-mail: marty.wartick@uni.edu. *Application contact:* Laurie S. Russell, Record Analyst, 319-273-2623, Fax: 319-273-6792, E-mail: laurie.russell@uni.edu.

University of North Florida, Coggin College of Business, Department of Accounting and Finance, Jacksonville, FL 32224. Offers accounting (M Acct). *Accreditation:* AACSB. Part-time and evening/weekend programs available. *Faculty:* 18 full-time (3 women). *Students:* 32 full-time (17 women), 50 part-time (27 women); includes 8 minority (2 African Americans, 4 Asian Americans or Pacific Islanders, 2 Hispanic Americans), 3 international. Average age 29. 36 applicants, 53% accepted, 11 enrolled. In 2009, 51 master's awarded. *Entrance requirements:* For master's, GMAT, minimum GPA of 3.0 in last 60 hours. Additional exam requirements/recommendations for international students: Required—TOEFL (minimum score 550 paper-based; 213 computer-based; 79 iBT). *Application deadline:* For fall admission, 7/6 priority date for domestic students, 5/1 for international students; for spring admission, 11/1 priority date for domestic students, 10/1 for international students. Applications are processed on a rolling basis. Application fee: $30. Electronic applications accepted. *Expenses:* Tuition, state resident: full-time $6649.20; part-time $277.05 per credit hour. Tuition, nonresident: full-time $22,970; part-time $957.08 per credit hour. Required fees: $985; $41.03 per credit hour. *Financial support:* In 2009–10, 45 students received support; teaching assistantships, career-related internships or fieldwork, Federal Work-Study, and tuition waivers (partial) available. Support available to part-time students. Financial award application deadline: 4/1; financial award applicants required to submit FAFSA. *Faculty research:* Enterprise-wide risk management, accounting input in the strategic planning process, accounting information systems, taxation issues in lawsuits and damage awards, database design. *Unit head:* Dr. Charles Calhoun, Chair, 904-620-2630, Fax: 904-620-3861, E-mail: ccalhoun@unf.edu. *Application contact:* Dr. Charles Calhoun, Chair, 904-620-2630, Fax: 904-620-3861, E-mail: ccalhoun@unf.edu.

University of North Texas, Robert B. Toulouse School of Graduate Studies, College of Business Administration, Department of Accounting, Denton, TX 76203-5017. Offers accounting (MS, PhD); taxation (MS). *Accreditation:* AACSB. Part-time programs available. *Degree requirements:* For master's, comprehensive exam; for doctorate, thesis/dissertation. *Entrance requirements:* For master's, GMAT or GRE General Test, essay, 3 letters of recommendation, resume; for doctorate, GMAT or GRE General Test, statement of purpose, resume, 3 letters of recommendation. Additional exam requirements/recommendations for international students: Recommended—TOEFL (minimum score 550 paper-based; 213 computer-based). *Application deadline:* Applications are processed on a rolling basis. Application fee: $50 ($75 for international students). Electronic applications accepted. *Expenses:* Tuition, state resident: full-time $4298; part-time $239 per contact hour. Tuition, nonresident: full-time $9878; part-time $549 per contact hour. Required fees: $265 per contact hour. *Financial support:* In 2009–10, 34 students received support; fellowships, career-related internships or fieldwork, Federal Work-Study, and institutionally sponsored loans available. Financial award applicants required to submit FAFSA. *Faculty research:* Empirical tax research issues, empirical financial accounting issues, problems and issues in public interest areas, historical perspective for accounting issues, behavioral issues in auditing and accounting systems. *Application contact:* Graduate Programs Office, 940-369-8977, Fax: 940-369-8978, E-mail: mbacob@unt.edu.

University of Notre Dame, Mendoza College of Business, Program in Accountancy, Notre Dame, IN 46556. Offers financial reporting and assurance services (MS); tax services (MS). *Accreditation:* AACSB. *Faculty:* 37 full-time (3 women), 14 part-time/adjunct (0 women). *Students:* 85 full-time (39 women); includes 12 minority (1 African American, 5 Asian Americans or Pacific Islanders, 6 Hispanic Americans), 10 international. Average age 22. 302 applicants, 39% accepted, 85 enrolled. In 2009, 95 master's awarded. *Entrance requirements:* For master's, GMAT. Additional exam requirements/recommendations for international students: Required—TOEFL (minimum score 630 paper-based; 267 computer-based; 109 iBT). *Application deadline:* For fall admission, 11/1 for domestic and international students; for spring admission, 5/12 for domestic and international students. Applications are processed on a rolling basis. Application fee: $50 ($100 for international students). Electronic applications accepted. *Financial support:* In 2009–10, 83 students received support, including 82 fellowships (averaging $12,200 per year); scholarships/grants and unspecified assistantships also available. Financial award application deadline: 2/28; financial award applicants required to submit FAFSA. *Faculty research:* Stock valuation, accounting information in decision-making, choice of accounting method, taxes cost on capital. *Unit head:* Dr. Michael H. Morris, Director, 574-631-9732, Fax: 574-631-5300, E-mail: msacct.1@nd.edu. *Application contact:* Helen High, Program Manager, 574-631-6499, Fax: 574-631-5300, E-mail: msacct.1@nd.edu.

University of Oklahoma, Graduate College, Michael F. Price College of Business, School of Accounting, Norman, OK 73019. Offers M Acc. *Accreditation:* AACSB. *Faculty:* 13 full-time (4 women). *Students:* 63 full-time (35 women), 13 part-time (7 women); includes 7 minority (2 African Americans, 4 American Indian/Alaska Native, 1 Hispanic American), 13 international. 27 applicants, 56% accepted, 9 enrolled. In 2009, 40 master's awarded. *Degree requirements:* For master's, comprehensive exam. *Entrance requirements:* For master's, GMAT, minimum GPA of 3.0 in last 60 hours. Additional exam requirements/recommendations for international students: Required—TOEFL (minimum score 550 paper-based; 213 computer-based). *Application deadline:* For fall admission, 6/15 for domestic students, 4/1 for international students; for spring admission, 11/15 for domestic students, 9/1 for international students. Applications are processed on a rolling basis. Application fee: $40 ($90 for international students). Electronic applications accepted. *Expenses:* Tuition, state resident: full-time $3744; part-time $156 per credit hour. Tuition, nonresident: full-time $13,577; part-time $565.70 per credit hour. Required fees: $2415; $90.10 per credit hour. *Financial support:* In 2009–10, 48 students received support, including 8 research assistantships with partial tuition reimbursements available (averaging $17,684 per year), 11 teaching assistantships with partial tuition reimbursements available (averaging $12,634 per year); career-related internships or fieldwork and scholarships/grants also available. Financial award application deadline: 4/1; financial award applicants required to submit FAFSA. *Faculty research:* Information content of financial disclosures, professional judgment, audit markets, capital markets. *Unit head:* Dr. Frances L. Ayres, Director, 405-325-4221, Fax: 405-325-2096, E-mail: fayres@ou.edu. *Application contact:* Jim Smith, Academic Advisor, 405-325-3744, Fax: 405-325-7753, E-mail: jlsmith@ou.edu.

University of Oregon, Graduate School, Charles H. Lundquist College of Business, Department of Accounting, Eugene, OR 97403. Offers M Actg, PhD. *Accreditation:* AACSB. Part-time programs available. *Degree requirements:* For doctorate, thesis/dissertation, 2 comprehensive exams. *Entrance requirements:* For master's, GMAT, minimum GPA of 3.0, bachelor's degree in accounting or equivalent; for doctorate, GMAT. Additional exam requirements/recommendations for international students: Required—TOEFL. *Faculty research:* Empirical financial accounting, effects of regulation on accounting standards, use of protocol analysis as a research methodology in accounting.

University of Pennsylvania, Wharton School, Accounting Department, Philadelphia, PA 19104. Offers MBA, PhD. Terminal master's awarded for partial completion of doctoral program. *Degree requirements:* For doctorate, thesis/dissertation. *Entrance requirements:* For master's, GMAT; for doctorate, GMAT or GRE. *Expenses:* Tuition: Full-time $25,660; part-time $4758 per course. Required fees: $2152; $270 per course. Tuition and fees vary according to course load, degree level and program. *Faculty research:* Financial reporting, information disclosure, performance measurement, executive compensation, corporate governance.

University of Phoenix, School of Business, College of Graduate Business and Management, Phoenix, AZ 85034-7209. Offers accountancy (MSA); accounting (MBA); business administration (MBA); global management (MBA); human resources management (MBA, MM); management (MM); marketing (MBA); public administration (MBA, MM). *Accreditation:* ACBSP. Evening/weekend programs available. Postbaccalaureate distance learning degree programs offered. *Faculty:* 25 full-time (15 women), 4,861 part-time/adjunct (1,504 women). *Students:* 6,681 full-time (5,284 women); includes 2,558 minority (1,955 African Americans, 69 American Indian/Alaska Native, 90 Asian Americans or Pacific Islanders, 444 Hispanic Americans), 137 international. Average age 35. In 2009, 1,740 master's awarded. *Degree requirements:* For master's, thesis (for some programs). *Entrance requirements:* For master's, 3 years of work experience, minimum undergraduate GPA of 3.0. Additional exam requirements/recommendations for international students: Required—TOEFL (minimum score 550 paper-based; 213 computer-based; 79 iBT). *Application deadline:* Applications are processed on a rolling basis. Application fee: $45. Electronic applications accepted. *Expenses:* Tuition: Full-time $13,272. Required fees: $660. Full-time tuition and fees vary according to course level, degree level and program. *Financial support:* Institutionally sponsored loans and scholarships/grants available. Financial award applicants required to submit FAFSA. *Unit head:* Brian Lindquist, Dean/Executive Director and Associate Vice President, 480-557-1221, E-mail: brian.lindquist@phoenix.edu. *Application contact:* Chair, 602-387-7000, Fax: 602-387-6020.

University of Phoenix–Atlanta Campus, John Sperling School of Business, College of Graduate Business and Management, Sandy Springs, GA 30350-4153. Offers accounting (MBA); business administration (MBA); global management (MBA); human resources management (MBA, MM); management (MM); marketing (MBA); public administration (MM). Evening/weekend programs available. Postbaccalaureate distance learning degree programs offered. *Degree requirements:* For master's, thesis (for some programs). *Entrance requirements:* For master's, minimum undergraduate GPA of 3.0, 3 years of work experience. Additional exam requirements/recommendations for international students: Required—TOEFL (minimum score 550 paper-based; 213 computer-based; 79 iBT).

University of Phoenix–Augusta Campus, College of Graduate Business and Management, Augusta, GA 30909-4583. Offers accounting (MBA); business administration (MBA); business and management (MBA, MM); global management (MBA); human resources management (MBA, MM); management (MM); marketing (MBA); public administration (MBA, MM). Postbaccalaureate distance learning degree programs offered.

University of Phoenix–Austin Campus, College of Graduate Business and Management, Austin, TX 78759. Offers accounting (MBA); business administration (MBA); business and management (MBA); e-business (MBA); global management (MBA); human resources management (MBA, MM); management (MM); marketing (MBA); public administration (MBA). Postbaccalaureate distance learning degree programs offered.

University of Phoenix–Bay Area Campus, John Sperling School of Business, College of Graduate Business and Management, Pleasanton, CA 94588-3677. Offers accounting (MBA); business administration (MBA); global management (MBA); human resources management (MBA, MM); marketing (MBA); public administration (MBA, MM). Evening/weekend programs available. Postbaccalaureate distance learning degree programs offered (no on-campus study). *Degree requirements:* For master's, thesis (for some programs). *Entrance requirements:* For master's, minimum undergraduate GPA of 3.0, 3 years of work experience. Additional exam requirements/recommendations for international students: Required—TOEFL (minimum score 550 paper-based; 213 computer-based; 79 iBT). Electronic applications accepted.

University of Phoenix–Birmingham Campus, College of Graduate Business and Management, Birmingham, AL 35244. Offers accounting (MBA); business administration (MBA); global management (MBA); human resources management (MBA, MM); management (MM); marketing (MBA); public administration (MM).

University of Phoenix–Central Florida Campus, John Sperling School of Business, College of Graduate Business and Management, Maitland, FL 32751-7057. Offers accounting (MBA); business administration (MBA); business and management (MM); global management (MBA); human resources management (MBA, MM); management (MM); marketing (MBA); public administration (MBA, MM). Evening/weekend programs available. *Degree requirements:* For master's, thesis (for some programs). *Entrance requirements:* For master's, minimum undergraduate GPA of 3.0, 3 years work experience. Additional exam requirements/recommendations for international students: Required—TOEFL (minimum score 550 paper-based; 213 computer-based; 79 iBT). Electronic applications accepted.

University of Phoenix–Central Valley Campus, College of Graduate Business and Management, Fresno, CA 93720-1562. Offers accounting (MBA); business administration (MBA); global management (MBA); human resources management (MBA, MM); management (MM); marketing (MBA); public administration (MBA, MM).

University of Phoenix–Charlotte Campus, John Sperling School of Business, College of Graduate Business and Management, Charlotte, NC 28273-3409. Offers accounting (MBA); business administration (MBA); global management (MBA). Evening/weekend programs available. *Degree requirements:* For master's, thesis (for some programs). *Entrance requirements:* For master's, minimum undergraduate GPA of 3.0, 3 years work experience. Additional exam requirements/recommendations for international students: Required—TOEFL (minimum score 550 paper-based; 213 computer-based; 79 iBT). Electronic applications accepted.

University of Phoenix–Chattanooga Campus, College of Graduate Business and Management, Chattanooga, TN 37421-3707. Offers accounting (MBA); business administration (MBA); business and management (MBA); global management (MBA); human resources management (MBA, MM); management (MM); marketing (MBA); public administration (MBA, MM). Postbaccalaureate distance learning degree programs offered.

University of Phoenix–Cincinnati Campus, John Sperling School of Business, College of Graduate Business and Management, West Chester, OH 45069-4875. Offers accounting (MBA); business administration (MBA); global management (MBA); human resources management (MBA, MM); management (MM); marketing (MBA); public administration (MM). Evening/weekend programs available. *Degree requirements:* For master's, thesis (for some programs). *Entrance requirements:* For master's, minimum undergraduate GPA of 3.0, 3 years of work experience. Additional exam requirements/recommendations for international students: Required—TOEFL (minimum score 550 paper-based; 213 computer-based; 79 iBT). Electronic applications accepted.

University of Phoenix–Cleveland Campus, John Sperling School of Business, College of Graduate Business and Management, Independence, OH 44131-2194. Offers accounting (MBA); business administration (MBA); global management (MBA); human resources management (MBA, MM); management (MM); marketing (MBA); public administration (MBA, MM). Evening/weekend programs available. Postbaccalaureate distance learning degree programs offered (no on-campus study). *Degree requirements:* For master's, thesis (for some programs). *Entrance requirements:* For master's, minimum undergraduate GPA of 3.0, 3 years of work experience. Additional exam requirements/recommendations for international students: Required—TOEFL (minimum score 550 paper-based; 213 computer-based; 79 iBT). Electronic applications accepted.

University of Phoenix–Columbus Georgia Campus, John Sperling School of Business, College of Graduate Business and Management, Columbus, GA 31904-6321. Offers accounting (MBA); business administration (MBA); global management (MBA); human resources management (MBA, MM); management (MM); marketing (MBA); public administration (MBA). Evening/weekend programs available. *Degree requirements:* For master's, thesis (for some programs). *Entrance requirements:* For master's, minimum undergraduate GPA of 3.0, 3 years of work experience. Additional exam requirements/recommendations for international students: Required—TOEFL (minimum score 550 paper-based; 213 computer-based; 79 iBT). Electronic applications accepted.

University of Phoenix–Columbus Ohio Campus, John Sperling School of Business, College of Graduate Business and Management, Columbus, OH 43240-4032. Offers accounting (MBA); business administration (MBA); global management (MBA); human resources management (MBA, MM); management (MM); marketing (MBA); public administration (MM). Evening/weekend programs available. Postbaccalaureate distance learning degree programs offered. *Degree requirements:* For master's, thesis (for some programs). *Entrance requirements:* For master's, minimum undergraduate GPA of 3.0, 3 years of work experience. Additional exam requirements/recommendations for international students: Required—TOEFL (minimum score 550 paper-based; 213 computer-based; 79 iBT). Electronic applications accepted.

University of Phoenix–Dallas Campus, John Sperling School of Business, College of Graduate Business and Management, Dallas, TX 75251-2009. Offers accounting (MBA); business administration (MBA); global management (MBA); human resources management (MBA, MM); management (MM); marketing (MBA); public administration (MBA, MM). Evening/weekend programs available. Postbaccalaureate distance learning degree programs offered. *Degree requirements:* For master's, thesis (for some programs). *Entrance requirements:* For master's, 3 years of work experience, minimum undergraduate GPA of 3.0. Additional exam requirements/recommendations for international students: Required—TOEFL (minimum score 550 paper-based; 213 computer-based; 79 iBT). Electronic applications accepted.

University of Phoenix–Denver Campus, John Sperling School of Business, College of Graduate Business and Management, Lone Tree, CO 80124-5453. Offers accountancy (MSA); accounting (MBA); business administration (MBA); e-business (MBA); global management (MBA); human resources management (MBA, MM); management (MM); marketing (MBA); public administration (MBA, MM). Evening/weekend programs available. Postbaccalaureate distance learning degree programs offered. *Degree requirements:* For master's, thesis (for some programs). *Entrance requirements:* For master's, minimum undergraduate GPA of 3.0, 3 years work experience. Additional exam requirements/recommendations for international students: Required—TOEFL (minimum score 550 paper-based; 213 computer-based; 79 iBT). Electronic applications accepted.

University of Phoenix–Des Moines Campus, College of Graduate Business and Management, Des Moines, IA 50266. Offers accounting (MBA); business administration (MBA); global management (MBA); human resources management (MBA, MM); management (MM); marketing (MBA); public administration (MBA, MM). Postbaccalaureate distance learning degree programs offered.

University of Phoenix–Eastern Washington Campus, John Sperling School of Business, College of Graduate Business and Management, Spokane Valley, WA 99212-2531. Offers accounting (MBA); business administration (MBA); human resources management (MBA); marketing (MBA); public administration (MBA). Evening/weekend programs available. *Degree requirements:* For master's, thesis (for some programs). *Entrance requirements:* For master's, minimum undergraduate GPA of 3.0, 3 years of work experience. Additional exam requirements/recommendations for international students: Required—TOEFL (minimum score 550 paper-based; 213 computer-based; 79 iBT). Electronic applications accepted.

University of Phoenix–Harrisburg Campus, College of Graduate Business and Management, Harrisburg, PA 17112. Offers accounting (MBA); business administration (MBA); business and management (MBA); global management (MBA); human resources management (MBA, MM); management (MM); marketing (MBA); public administration (MBA, MM). Postbaccalaureate distance learning degree programs offered.

University of Phoenix–Hawaii Campus, John Sperling School of Business, College of Graduate Business and Management, Honolulu, HI 96813-4317. Offers accounting (MBA); business administration (MBA); global management (MBA); human resources management (MBA, MM); management (MM); marketing (MBA); public administration (MBA, MM). Evening/

Accounting

University of Phoenix–Hawaii Campus (continued)
weekend programs available. *Degree requirements:* For master's, thesis (for some programs). *Entrance requirements:* For master's, minimum undergraduate GPA of 3.0, 3 years of work experience. Additional exam requirements/recommendations for international students: Required—TOEFL (minimum score 550 paper-based; 213 computer-based; 79 iBT). Electronic applications accepted.

University of Phoenix–Houston Campus, John Sperling School of Business, College of Graduate Business and Management, Houston, TX 77079-2004. Offers accounting (MBA); business administration (MBA); global management (MBA); human resources management (MBA, MM); management (MM); marketing (MBA); public administration (MBA, MM). Evening/weekend programs available. Postbaccalaureate distance learning degree programs offered. *Degree requirements:* For master's, thesis (for some programs). *Entrance requirements:* For master's, 3 years of work experience, minimum undergraduate GPA of 3.0. Additional exam requirements/recommendations for international students: Required—TOEFL (minimum score 550 paper-based; 213 computer-based; 79 iBT). Electronic applications accepted.

University of Phoenix–Idaho Campus, John Sperling School of Business, College of Graduate Business and Management, Meridian, ID 83642-3014. Offers accounting (MBA); administration (MBA); global management (MBA); human resources management (MBA, MM); management (MM); marketing (MBA); public administration (MM). Evening/weekend programs available. Postbaccalaureate distance learning degree programs offered. *Degree requirements:* For master's, thesis (for some programs). *Entrance requirements:* For master's, 3 years of work experience, minimum undergraduate GPA of 3.0. Additional exam requirements/recommendations for international students: Required—TOEFL (minimum score 550 paper-based; 213 computer-based). Electronic applications accepted.

University of Phoenix–Indianapolis Campus, John Sperling School of Business, College of Graduate Business and Management, Indianapolis, IN 46250-932. Offers accounting (MBA); business administration (MBA); global management (MBA); human resources management (MBA, MM); management (MM); marketing (MBA); public administration (MM). Evening/weekend programs available. *Degree requirements:* For master's, thesis (for some programs). *Entrance requirements:* For master's, minimum undergraduate GPA of 3.0, 3 years of work experience. Additional exam requirements/recommendations for international students: Required—TOEFL (minimum score 550 paper-based; 213 computer-based). Electronic applications accepted.

University of Phoenix–Jersey City Campus, College of Graduate Business and Management, Jersey City, NJ 07310. Offers accounting (MBA); business administration (MBA); global management (MBA); human resources management (MBA, MM); management (MM); marketing (MBA); public administration (MBA, MM).

University of Phoenix–Kansas City Campus, John Sperling School of Business, College of Graduate Business and Management, Kansas City, MO 64131-4517. Offers accounting (MBA); business administration (MBA); global management (MBA); human resources management (MBA, MM); management (MM); marketing (MBA); public administration (MBA). Evening/weekend programs available. *Degree requirements:* For master's, thesis (for some programs). *Entrance requirements:* For master's, minimum undergraduate GPA of 3.0, 3 years of work experience. Additional exam requirements/recommendations for international students: Required—TOEFL (minimum score 550 paper-based; 213 computer-based). Electronic applications accepted.

University of Phoenix–Las Vegas Campus, John Sperling School of Business, College of Graduate Business and Management, Las Vegas, NV 89128. Offers accounting (MBA); business administration (MBA); global management (MBA); human resources management (MBA, MM); management (MM); marketing (MBA); public administration (MM). Evening/weekend programs available. Postbaccalaureate distance learning degree programs offered (no on-campus study). *Degree requirements:* For master's, thesis (for some programs). *Entrance requirements:* For master's, minimum undergraduate GPA of 3.0, 3 years of work experience. Additional exam requirements/recommendations for international students: Required—TOEFL (minimum score 550 paper-based; 213 computer-based; 79 iBT). Electronic applications accepted.

University of Phoenix–Louisiana Campus, John Sperling School of Business, College of Graduate Business and Management, Metairie, LA 70001-2082. Offers accounting (MBA); business administration (MBA); global management (MBA); human resources management (MBA, MM); management (MM); marketing (MBA); public administration (MBA). Evening/weekend programs available. *Degree requirements:* For master's, thesis (for some programs). *Entrance requirements:* For master's, minimum undergraduate GPA of 3.0, 3 years work experience. Additional exam requirements/recommendations for international students: Required—TOEFL (minimum score 550 paper-based; 213 computer-based; 79 iBT). Electronic applications accepted.

University of Phoenix–Madison Campus, College of Graduate Business and Management, Madison, WI 53718-2416. Offers accounting (MBA); business and management (MBA); e-business (MBA); global management (MBA); human resources management (MBA, MM); management (MM); marketing (MBA); public administration (MBA).

University of Phoenix–Madison Campus, John Sperling School of Business, College of Graduate Business and Management, Madison, WI 53718-2416. Offers accounting (MBA); administration (MBA); global management (MBA); human resources management (MBA); management (MM); marketing (MBA); public administration (MBA). Evening/weekend programs available. *Degree requirements:* For master's, thesis (for some programs). *Entrance requirements:* For master's, 3 years of work experience, minimum undergraduate GPA of 3.0. Additional exam requirements/recommendations for international students: Required—TOEFL (minimum score 550 paper-based; 213 computer-based; 79 iBT). Electronic applications accepted.

University of Phoenix–Maryland Campus, John Sperling School of Business, College of Graduate Business and Management, Columbia, MD 21045-5424. Offers accounting (MBA); business administration (MBA); e-business (MBA); global management (MBA); human resources management (MBA, MM); management (MM); marketing (MBA); public administration (MBA, MM). Evening/weekend programs available. *Degree requirements:* For master's, thesis (for some programs). *Entrance requirements:* For master's, minimum undergraduate GPA of 3.0, 3 years of work experience. Additional exam requirements/recommendations for international students: Required—TOEFL (minimum score 550 paper-based; 213 computer-based; 79 iBT). Electronic applications accepted.

University of Phoenix–Memphis Campus, College of Graduate Business and Management, Cordova, TN 38018. Offers accounting (MBA); business and management (MBA); e-business (MBA); global management (MBA); human resources management (MBA, MM); management (MM); marketing (MBA); public administration (MBA, MM).

University of Phoenix–Metro Detroit Campus, School of Business, College of Graduate Business and Management, Troy, MI 48098-2623. Offers accountancy (MS); accounting (MBA); business administration (MBA); global management (MBA); human resources management (MBA, MM); management (MM); marketing (MBA). Evening/weekend programs available. *Degree requirements:* For master's, thesis (for some programs). *Entrance requirements:* For master's, minimum undergraduate GPA of 3.0, 3 years work experience. Additional exam requirements/recommendations for international students: Required—TOEFL (minimum score 550 paper-based; 213 computer-based; 79 iBT). Electronic applications accepted. *Expenses:* Tuition: Full-time $14,136. Required fees: $660.

University of Phoenix–Minneapolis/St. Louis Park Campus, College of Graduate Business and Management, St. Louis Park, MN 55426. Offers accounting (MBA); business administration (MBA); global management (MBA); human resources management (MBA); management (MM); marketing (MBA); public administration (MBA).

University of Phoenix–New Mexico Campus, John Sperling School of Business, College of Graduate Business and Management, Albuquerque, NM 87113-1570. Offers accounting (MBA); business administration (MBA); global management (MBA); human resource management (MBA); human resources management (MM); management (MM); marketing (MBA). Evening/weekend programs available. *Degree requirements:* For master's, thesis (for some programs). *Entrance requirements:* For master's, 3 years of work experience, minimum undergraduate GPA of 3.0. Additional exam requirements/recommendations for international students: Required—TOEFL (minimum score 550 paper-based; 213 computer-based; 79 iBT). Electronic applications accepted.

University of Phoenix–Northern Nevada Campus, College of Graduate Business and Management, Reno, NV 89521-5862. Offers accounting (MBA); business administration (MBA); global management (MBA); human resources management (MBA, MM); management (MM); marketing (MBA); public administration (MBA, MM).

University of Phoenix–Northern Virginia Campus, College of Graduate Business and Management, Reston, VA 20190. Offers accounting (MBA); business administration (MBA); e-business (MBA); global management (MBA); human resources management (MBA, MM); management (MM); marketing (MBA); public administration (MBA).

University of Phoenix–North Florida Campus, John Sperling School of Business, College of Graduate Business and Management, Jacksonville, FL 32216-0959. Offers accounting (MBA); business administration (MBA); global management (MBA); human resources management (MBA, MM); management (MM); marketing (MBA); public administration (MBA, MM). Evening/weekend programs available. *Degree requirements:* For master's, thesis (for some programs). *Entrance requirements:* For master's, minimum undergraduate GPA of 3.0, 3 years work experience. Additional exam requirements/recommendations for international students: Required—TOEFL (minimum score 550 paper-based; 213 computer-based; 79 iBT). Electronic applications accepted.

University of Phoenix–Northwest Arkansas Campus, College of Graduate Business and Management, Rogers, AR 72756-9615. Offers accounting (MBA); business and management (MBA); global management (MBA); human resources management (MBA, MM); management (MM); marketing (MBA); public administration (MBA, MM).

University of Phoenix–Oklahoma City Campus, John Sperling School of Business, College of Graduate Business and Management, Oklahoma City, OK 73116-8244. Offers accounting (MBA); business administration (MBA); global management (MBA); human resource management (MBA); management (MM); marketing (MBA). Evening/weekend programs available. *Degree requirements:* For master's, thesis (for some programs). *Entrance requirements:* For master's, minimum undergraduate GPA of 3.0, 3 years of work experience. Additional exam requirements/recommendations for international students: Required—TOEFL (minimum score 550 paper-based; 213 computer-based; 79 iBT). Electronic applications accepted.

University of Phoenix–Omaha Campus, College of Graduate Business and Management, Omaha, NE 68154-5240. Offers accounting (MBA); business and management (MBA); global management (MBA); human resources management (MBA, MM); management (MM); marketing (MBA); public administration (MBA, MM).

University of Phoenix–Oregon Campus, The John Sperling School of Business, College of Graduate Business and Management, Tigard, OR 97223. Offers accounting (MBA); business administration (MBA); global management (MBA); human resource management (MM); human resources management (MBA); management (MM); marketing (MBA); public administration (MM). Evening/weekend programs available. *Degree requirements:* For master's, thesis (for some programs). *Entrance requirements:* For master's, minimum undergraduate GPA of 3.0, 3 years of work experience. Additional exam requirements/recommendations for international students: Required—TOEFL (minimum score 550 paper-based; 213 computer-based; 79 iBT). Electronic applications accepted.

University of Phoenix–Philadelphia Campus, The John Sperling School of Business, College of Graduate Business and Management, Wayne, PA 19087-2121. Offers accounting (MBA); business administration (MBA); global management (MBA); human resources management (MBA, MM); management (MM); marketing (MBA); public administration (MM). Evening/weekend programs available. *Degree requirements:* For master's, thesis (for some programs). *Entrance requirements:* For master's, minimum undergraduate GPA of 3.0, 3 years work experience. Additional exam requirements/recommendations for international students: Required—TOEFL (minimum score 550 paper-based; 213 computer-based; 79 iBT). Electronic applications accepted.

University of Phoenix–Pittsburgh Campus, John Sperling School of Business, College of Graduate Business and Management, Pittsburgh, PA 15276. Offers accounting (MBA); business administration (MBA); global management (MBA); human resources management (MBA, MM); management (MM); marketing (MBA); public administration (MBA, MM). Evening/weekend programs available. *Degree requirements:* For master's, thesis (for some programs). *Entrance requirements:* For master's, minimum undergraduate GPA of 3.0, 3 years work experience. Additional exam requirements/recommendations for international students: Required—TOEFL (minimum score 550 paper-based; 213 computer-based; 79 iBT). Electronic applications accepted.

University of Phoenix–Puerto Rico Campus, John Sperling School of Business, College of Graduate Business and Management, Guaynabo, PR 00968. Offers accounting (MBA); business administration (MBA); global management (MBA); human resource management (MBA); marketing (MBA). Evening/weekend programs available. *Degree requirements:* For master's, thesis (for some programs). *Entrance requirements:* For master's, minimum undergraduate GPA of 3.0, 3 years work experience. Additional exam requirements/recommendations for international students: Required—TOEFL (minimum score 550 paper-based; 213 computer-based; 79 iBT). Electronic applications accepted.

University of Phoenix–Raleigh Campus, College of Graduate Business and Management, Raleigh, NC 27606. Offers accounting (MBA); business administration (MBA); e-business (MBA); global management (MBA); human resources management (MBA); marketing (MBA).

University of Phoenix–Richmond Campus, John Sperling School of Business, College of Graduate Business and Management, Richmond, VA 23230. Offers accounting (MBA); business administration (MBA); global management (MBA); human resources management (MBA, MM); management (MM); marketing (MBA); public administration (MBA, MM). Evening/weekend programs available. *Degree requirements:* For master's, thesis (for some programs). *Entrance requirements:* For master's, minimum undergraduate GPA of 3.0, 3 years work experience. Additional exam requirements/recommendations for international students: Required—TOEFL (minimum score 550 paper-based; 213 computer-based; 79 iBT). Electronic applications accepted.

University of Phoenix–Sacramento Valley Campus, John Sperling School of Business, College of Graduate Business and Management, Sacramento, CA 95833-3632. Offers accounting (MBA); business administration (MBA); global management (MBA); human resources management (MBA, MM); management (MM); marketing (MBA); public administration (MBA, MM). Evening/weekend programs available. *Degree requirements:* For master's, thesis (for some programs). *Entrance requirements:* For master's, minimum undergraduate GPA of 3.0, 3 years work experience. Additional exam requirements/recommendations for international students: Required—TOEFL (minimum score 550 paper-based; 213 computer-based; 79 iBT). Electronic applications accepted.

University of Phoenix–St. Louis Campus, John Sperling School of Business, College of Graduate Business and Management, St. Louis, MO 63043-4828. Offers accounting (MBA); business administration (MBA); global management (MBA); human resources management (MBA, MM); management (MM); marketing (MBA); public administration (MM). Evening/weekend programs available. *Degree requirements:* For master's, thesis (for some programs). *Entrance requirements:* For master's, 3 years of work experience, minimum undergraduate

GPA of 3.0. Additional exam requirements/recommendations for international students: Required—TOEFL (minimum score 550 paper-based; 213 computer-based; 79 iBT). Electronic applications accepted.

University of Phoenix–San Antonio Campus, College of Graduate Business and Management, San Antonio, TX 78230. Offers accounting (MBA); business administration (MBA); e-business (MBA); global management (MBA); human resources management (MBA, MM); management (MM); marketing (MBA); public administration (MBA, MM).

University of Phoenix–San Diego Campus, John Sperling School of Business, College of Graduate Business and Management, San Diego, CA 92123. Offers accounting (MBA); business administration (MBA); global management (MBA); human resources management (MBA, MM); management (MM); marketing (MBA); public administration (MBA). Evening/weekend programs available. *Degree requirements:* For master's, thesis (for some programs). *Entrance requirements:* For master's, 3 years of work experience, minimum undergraduate GPA of 3.0. Additional exam requirements/recommendations for international students: Required—TOEFL (minimum score 550 paper-based; 213 computer-based; 79 iBT). Electronic applications accepted.

University of Phoenix–Savannah Campus, College of Graduate Business and Management, Savannah, GA 31405-7400. Offers accounting (MBA); business administration (MBA); global management (MBA); human resources management (MBA, MM); management (MM); marketing (MBA); public administration (MBA, MM).

University of Phoenix–Southern Arizona Campus, John Sperling School of Business, College of Graduate Business and Management, Tucson, AZ 85711. Offers accountancy (MS); accounting (MBA); business administration (MBA); global management (MBA); human resources management (MBA); management (MM); marketing (MBA). Evening/weekend programs available. *Degree requirements:* For master's, thesis (for some programs). *Entrance requirements:* For master's, minimum undergraduate GPA of 3.0, 3 years of work experience. Additional exam requirements/recommendations for international students: Required—TOEFL (minimum score 550 paper-based; 213 computer-based; 79 iBT). Electronic applications accepted.

University of Phoenix–Southern Colorado Campus, John Sperling School of Business, College of Graduate Business and Management, Colorado Springs, CO 80919-2335. Offers accounting (MBA); business administration (MBA); global management (MBA); human resources management (MBA, MM); management (MM); marketing (MBA); public administration (MM). Evening/weekend programs available. *Degree requirements:* For master's, thesis (for some programs). *Entrance requirements:* For master's, minimum undergraduate GPA of 3.0, 3 years of work experience. Additional exam requirements/recommendations for international students: Required—TOEFL (minimum score 550 paper-based; 213 computer-based; 79 iBT). Electronic applications accepted.

University of Phoenix–South Florida Campus, John Sperling School of Business, College of Graduate Business and Management, Fort Lauderdale, FL 33309. Offers accounting (MBA); business administration (MBA); global management (MBA); human resource management (MBA); human resources management (MM); management (MM); marketing (MBA); public administration (MBA, MM). Evening/weekend programs available. *Degree requirements:* For master's, thesis (for some programs). *Entrance requirements:* For master's, minimum undergraduate GPA of 3.0, 3 years work experience. Additional exam requirements/recommendations for international students: Required—TOEFL (minimum score 550 paper-based; 213 computer-based; 79 iBT). Electronic applications accepted.

University of Phoenix–Springfield Campus, College of Graduate Business and Management, Springfield, MO 65804-7211. Offers accounting (MBA); business administration (MBA); global management (MBA); human resources management (MBA, MM); management (MM); marketing (MBA); public administration (MBA, MM).

University of Phoenix–Tulsa Campus, John Sperling School of Business, College of Graduate Business and Management, Tulsa, OK 74134-1412. Offers accounting (MBA); business (MM); business administration (MBA); global management (MBA); human resources management (MBA); marketing (MBA). Evening/weekend programs available. *Degree requirements:* For master's, thesis (for some programs). *Entrance requirements:* For master's, minimum undergraduate GPA of 3.0, 3 years work experience. Additional exam requirements/recommendations for international students: Required—TOEFL (minimum score 550 paper-based; 213 computer-based; 79 iBT).

University of Phoenix–Utah Campus, John Sperling School of Business, College of Graduate Business and Management, Salt Lake City, UT 84123-4617. Offers accounting (MBA); business administration (MBA); global management (MBA); human resource management (MBA, MM); management (MM); marketing (MBA); technology management (MBA). Evening/weekend programs available. *Degree requirements:* For master's, thesis (for some programs). *Entrance requirements:* For master's, minimum undergraduate GPA of 3.0, 3 years of work experience. Additional exam requirements/recommendations for international students: Required—TOEFL (minimum score 550 paper-based; 213 computer-based; 79 iBT). Electronic applications accepted.

University of Phoenix–Vancouver Campus, John Sperling School of Business, College of Graduate Business and Management, Burnaby, BC V5C 6G9, Canada. Offers accounting (MBA); business administration (MBA); global management (MBA); human resources management (MBA, MM); marketing (MBA). Evening/weekend programs available. *Degree requirements:* For master's, thesis (for some programs). *Entrance requirements:* For master's, minimum undergraduate GPA of 3.0, 3 years of work experience. Additional exam requirements/recommendations for international students: Required—TOEFL (minimum score 550 paper-based; 213 computer-based; 79 iBT). Electronic applications accepted.

University of Phoenix–Western Washington Campus, College of Graduate Business and Management, Tukwila, WA 98188. Offers accounting (MBA); business and management (MBA, MM); global management (MBA); human resources management (MBA, MM); marketing (MBA); public administration (MBA, MM). Evening/weekend programs available. *Degree requirements:* For master's, thesis (for some programs). *Entrance requirements:* For master's, minimum undergraduate GPA of 3.0, 3 years of work experience. Additional exam requirements/recommendations for international students: Required—TOEFL (minimum score 550 paper-based; 213 computer-based; 79 iBT). Electronic applications accepted.

University of Phoenix–West Florida Campus, The John Sperling School of Business, College of Graduate Business and Management, Temple Terrace, FL 33637. Offers accounting (MBA); business administration (MBA); global management (MBA); human resources management (MBA, MM); management (MM); marketing (MBA); public administration (MBA, MM). Evening/weekend programs available. *Degree requirements:* For master's, thesis (for some programs). *Entrance requirements:* For master's, 3 years of work experience, minimum undergraduate GPA of 3.0. Additional exam requirements/recommendations for international students: Required—TOEFL (minimum score 550 paper-based; 213 computer-based; 79 iBT). Electronic applications accepted.

University of Pittsburgh, Katz Graduate School of Business, Doctoral Program in Business Administration, Pittsburgh, PA 15260. Offers accounting (PhD); finance (PhD); information systems (PhD); marketing (PhD); operations/decision sciences/artificial intelligence (PhD); organizational behavior and human resource management (PhD); strategic planning (PhD). *Accreditation:* AACSB. *Faculty:* 50 full-time (15 women). *Students:* 53 full-time (21 women); includes 8 minority (4 African Americans, 2 Asian Americans or Pacific Islanders, 2 Hispanic Americans), 22 international. 324 applicants, 4% accepted, 12 enrolled. In 2009, 11 doctorates awarded. *Degree requirements:* For doctorate, comprehensive exam, thesis/dissertation. *Entrance requirements:* For doctorate, GMAT or GRE, references, work experience relevant for individual program. Additional exam requirements/recommendations for international students: Required—TOEFL or IELTS. *Application deadline:* For fall admission, 2/1 priority date for domestic and international students. Applications are processed on a rolling basis. Application fee: $50. Electronic applications accepted. *Expenses:* Tuition, state resident: full-time $16,402; part-time $665 per credit. Tuition, nonresident: full-time $28,694; part-time $1175 per credit. Required fees: $690; $175 per term. Tuition and fees vary according to program. *Financial support:* In 2009–10, 36 students received support, including 31 research assistantships with full tuition reimbursements available (averaging $18,450 per year), 5 teaching assistantships with full tuition reimbursements available (averaging $23,511 per year); fellowships, Federal Work-Study, scholarships/grants, health care benefits, and unspecified assistantships also available. Financial award application deadline: 2/1. *Faculty research:* Accounting statements and reporting, incentives and governance; corporate finance, mergers and acquisitions; information systems processes, structures, OR, supply chain, and decision-making; organizational structure, knowledge management, and corporate strategy; consumer behavior and marketing models. Total annual research expenditures: $362,777. *Unit head:* Dr. John E. Hulland, Director, 412-648-1534, Fax: 412-624-3633, E-mail: jhulland@katz.pitt.edu. *Application contact:* Carrie Woods, Assistant Director, 412-648-1525, Fax: 412-624-3633, E-mail: cawoods@katz.pitt.edu.

University of Pittsburgh, Katz Graduate School of Business, Masters of Business Administration Programs, Master of Science in Accounting Program, Pittsburgh, PA 15260. Offers MS. Part-time and evening/weekend programs available. *Students:* 26 full-time (12 women), 1 (woman) part-time; includes 2 minority (1 African American, 1 Asian American or Pacific Islander), 13 international. Average age 25. 43 applicants, 84% accepted, 27 enrolled. *Entrance requirements:* For master's, GMAT or GRE, references, work experience relevant for program, interview. Additional exam requirements/recommendations for international students: Required—TOEFL (minimum score 600 paper-based; 250 computer-based; 100 iBT), or IELTS. *Application deadline:* For fall admission, 10/15 for domestic and international students; for winter admission, 12/1 for domestic and international students; for spring admission, 4/1 for domestic students, 2/1 for international students. Applications are processed on a rolling basis. Application fee: $50. Electronic applications accepted. *Expenses:* Contact institution. *Financial support:* In 2009–10, 24 students received support. Scholarships/grants available. Financial award application deadline: 2/1; financial award applicants required to submit FAFSA. *Faculty research:* Auditing and fraudulent reporting, management reporting, financial analysts, forecasts and investors, reactions, labor markets and employment contracts, agency, performance measurement and incentive compensation, corporate governance, restructuring and organizational design. *Unit head:* Dr. Donald Moser, Dean, 412-648-1726, Fax: 412-624-5198, E-mail: dmoser@katz.pitt.edu. *Application contact:* Jessica Fick, Administrative Assistant, 412-624-0147, Fax: 412-624-5198, E-mail: macc@katz.pitt.edu.

University of Puerto Rico, Río Piedras, College of Business Administration, San Juan, PR 00931-3300. Offers accounting (MBA); finance (MBA, PhD); general business (MBA); human resources management (MBA); international trade and business (MBA, PhD); marketing (MBA); operations management (MBA); quantitative methods (MBA). *Accreditation:* ACBSP. Part-time programs available. *Degree requirements:* For master's, comprehensive exam, thesis or alternative, research project. *Entrance requirements:* For master's, GMAT or PAEG, minimum GPA of 3.0, letter of recommendation; for doctorate, GMAT, PAEG, minimum GPA of 3.0, master degree. *Faculty research:* Management.

University of Rhode Island, Graduate School, College of Business Administration, Kingston, RI 02881. Offers accounting (MS); business administration (MBA, PhD), including finance and insurance (PhD), management (PhD), marketing (PhD), operations and supply chain management (MBA); finance (MBA); general business (MBA); management (MBA); marketing (MBA); supply chain management (MBA). *Accreditation:* AACSB. Part-time and evening/weekend programs available. *Faculty:* 54 full-time (15 women), 2 part-time/adjunct (1 woman). *Students:* 71 full-time (27 women), 157 part-time (56 women); includes 24 minority (6 African Americans, 10 Asian Americans or Pacific Islanders, 8 Hispanic Americans), 23 international. In 2009, 86 master's, 3 doctorates awarded. *Degree requirements:* For master's, comprehensive exam (for some programs), thesis optional; for doctorate, comprehensive exam, thesis/dissertation. *Entrance requirements:* For master's, GMAT or GRE, 2 letters of recommendation, resume; for doctorate, GMAT or GRE, 3 letters of recommendation, resume. Additional exam requirements/recommendations for international students: Required—TOEFL (minimum score 575 paper-based; 233 computer-based; 91 iBT). Application fee: $65. Electronic applications accepted. *Expenses:* Tuition, state resident: full-time $8828; part-time $490 per credit hour. Tuition, nonresident: full-time $22,100; part-time $1228 per credit hour. Required fees: $1118; $57 per semester. Tuition and fees vary according to program. *Financial support:* In 2009–10, 13 teaching assistantships with full and partial tuition reimbursements (averaging $13,095 per year) were awarded. Financial award applicants required to submit FAFSA. Total annual research expenditures: $245,746. *Unit head:* Dr. Mark Higgins, Dean, 401-874-4244, Fax: 401-874-4312, E-mail: markhiggins@uri.edu. *Application contact:* Lisa Lancellotta, Coordinator, MBA Programs, 401-874-4241, Fax: 401-874-4312, E-mail: mba@uri.edu.

University of St. Thomas, Graduate Studies, Opus College of Business, Master of Science in Accountancy Program, Minneapolis, MN 55403. Offers MS. *Students:* 21 full-time (8 women); includes 1 minority (Asian American or Pacific Islander), 2 international. Average age 22. 41 applicants, 71% accepted. In 2009, 27 master's awarded. *Entrance requirements:* For master's, GMAT. Additional exam requirements/recommendations for international students: Required—TOEFL (minimum score 94 iBT), IELTS (minimum score 7). *Application deadline:* Applications are processed on a rolling basis. Application fee: $30 ($90 for international students). *Financial support:* Career-related internships or fieldwork, institutionally sponsored loans, and scholarships/grants available. Financial award applicants required to submit FAFSA. *Unit head:* Kristine Sharockman, Director, 651-962-4110, Fax: 651-962-4141, E-mail: msacct@stthomas.edu. *Application contact:* Cathy Davis, Program Coordinator, 651-962-4110, Fax: 651-962-4141, E-mail: msacct@stthomas.edu.

University of San Diego, School of Business Administration, San Diego, CA 92110-2492. Offers accountancy (MS); business administration (MBA); executive leadership (MSEL); global leadership (MSGL); international business administration (IMBA); real estate (MSRE); supply chain management (MS, Certificate); taxation (MS); JD/IMBA; JD/MBA. *Accreditation:* AACSB. Part-time and evening/weekend programs available. *Faculty:* 36 full-time (11 women), 18 part-time/adjunct (4 women). *Students:* 173 full-time (53 women), 259 part-time (91 women); includes 61 minority (9 African Americans, 4 American Indian/Alaska Native, 29 Asian Americans or Pacific Islanders, 19 Hispanic Americans), 32 international. Average age 31. 555 applicants, 61% accepted, 191 enrolled. In 2009, 248 master's awarded. *Degree requirements:* For master's, variable foreign language requirement, community service, capstone project. *Entrance requirements:* For master's, GMAT (MBA, IMBA, MSRE), minimum GPA of 3.0, minimum 2 years of full-time work experience. Additional exam requirements/recommendations for international students: Required—TOEFL (minimum score 580 paper-based; 237 computer-based; 92 iBT), TWE. Application fee: $80. Electronic applications accepted. *Expenses:* Tuition: Full-time $21,042; part-time $1169 per unit. Required fees: $224. Full-time tuition and fees vary according to course load and degree level. *Financial support:* In 2009–10, 312 students received support. Career-related internships or fieldwork, Federal Work-Study, institutionally sponsored loans, scholarships/grants, and unspecified assistantships available. Support available to part-time students. Financial award application deadline: 4/1; financial award applicants required to submit FAFSA. *Faculty research:* Exchange rate forecasting, corporate governance, performance of private equity funds, economic geography, food banking. *Unit head:* Dr. David Pyke, Interim Dean, 619-260-4886, E-mail: sbadean@sandiego.edu. *Application contact:* Dr. John Mosby, Associate Director of Graduate Admissions, 619-260-4524, Fax: 619-260-4158, E-mail: grads@sandiego.edu.

University of Saskatchewan, College of Graduate Studies and Research, Edwards School of Business, Department of Accounting, Saskatoon, SK S7N 5A2, Canada. Offers M Sc, MP Acc. Part-time programs available. *Degree requirements:* For master's, thesis (for some programs). *Entrance requirements:* For master's, GMAT. Additional exam requirements/recommendations for international students: Required—TOEFL. Tuition and fees charges are reported in Canadian

Accounting

University of Saskatchewan (continued)

dollars. *Expenses:* Tuition, area resident: Full-time $3000 Canadian dollars; part-time $500 Canadian dollars per term. Required fees: $700 Canadian dollars; $100 Canadian dollars per term.

The University of Scranton, College of Graduate and Continuing Education, Program in Business Administration, Scranton, PA 18510. Offers accounting (MBA); finance (MBA); general business administration (MBA); health care management (MBA); international business (MBA); management information systems (MBA); marketing (MBA); operations management (MBA). *Accreditation:* AACSB. Part-time and evening/weekend programs available. Postbaccalaureate distance learning degree programs offered (no on-campus study). *Faculty:* 34 full-time (8 women). *Students:* 92 full-time (38 women), 137 part-time (58 women); includes 27 minority (15 African Americans, 5 Asian Americans or Pacific Islanders, 7 Hispanic Americans), 21 international. Average age 31. 255 applicants, 79% accepted. In 2009, 33 master's awarded. *Degree requirements:* For master's, capstone experience. *Entrance requirements:* For master's, GMAT, minimum GPA of 2.75. Additional exam requirements/recommendations for international students: Required—TOEFL (minimum score 500 paper-based; 173 computer-based), IELTS (minimum score 5.5). *Application deadline:* Applications are processed on a rolling basis. Application fee: $0. *Financial support:* In 2009–10, 10 students received support, including 10 teaching assistantships with full and partial tuition reimbursements available (averaging $6,600 per year); fellowships, career-related internships or fieldwork, Federal Work-Study, and unspecified assistantships also available. Support available to part-time students. Financial award application deadline: 3/1. *Faculty research:* Financial markets, strategic impact of total quality management, internal accounting controls, consumer preference, information systems and the Internet. *Unit head:* Dr. Murli Rajan, Director, 570-941-4043, Fax: 570-941-4342. *Application contact:* Joseph M. Roback, Director of Admissions, 570-941-4385, Fax: 570-941-5928, E-mail: robackj2@scranton.edu.

University of South Africa, College of Economic and Management Sciences, Pretoria, South Africa. Offers accounting (D Admin, D Com); accounting science (DA); auditing (D Admin, D Com); business administration (M Tech); business economics (D Admin); business leadership (DBL); business management (D Admin, D Com); economic management analysis (M Tech); economics (D Admin, D Com, PhD); human resource development (M Tech); industrial psychology (D Admin, D Com, PhD); logistics (D Com); marketing (M Tech); public administration (D Admin, D Com, DPA, PhD); public management (M Tech); quantitative management (D Admin, D Com); real estate (M Tech); statistics (D Admin, PhD); tourism management (D Admin, D Com); transport economics (D Admin, D Com).

University of South Alabama, Graduate School, Mitchell College of Business, Program in Accounting, Mobile, AL 36688-0002. Offers M Acct. Part-time and evening/weekend programs available. *Degree requirements:* For master's, comprehensive exam. *Entrance requirements:* For master's, GMAT, minimum undergraduate GPA of 3.0. *Expenses:* Tuition, state resident: part-time $218 per contact hour. Required fees: $1102 per year.

University of South Carolina, The Graduate School, Moore School of Business, Accountancy Program, Columbia, SC 29208. Offers business measurement and assurance (M Acc); JD/M Acc. *Accreditation:* AACSB. Part-time programs available. *Degree requirements:* For master's, comprehensive exam. *Entrance requirements:* For master's, GMAT. Additional exam requirements/recommendations for international students: Required—TOEFL (minimum score 600 paper-based; 250 computer-based). Electronic applications accepted. *Faculty research:* Judgment modeling, international accounting, accounting information systems, behavioral accounting, cost/management accounting.

The University of South Dakota, Graduate School, School of Business, Department of Accounting, Vermillion, SD 57069-2390. Offers professional accountancy (MP Acc); JD/MP Acc. Part-time programs available. Postbaccalaureate distance learning degree programs offered. *Degree requirements:* For master's, comprehensive exam. *Entrance requirements:* For master's, GMAT, minimum GPA of 2.7, resume. Additional exam requirements/recommendations for international students: Required—TOEFL (minimum score 550 paper-based; 213 computer-based; 79 iBT). Electronic applications accepted.

University of Southern California, Graduate School, Marshall School of Business, Leventhal School of Accounting, Los Angeles, CA 90089. Offers accounting (M Acc); business taxation (MBT); JD/MBT. Part-time programs available. *Students:* 149 full-time (81 women), 130 part-time (61 women); includes 124 minority (8 African Americans, 99 Asian Americans or Pacific Islanders, 17 Hispanic Americans), 49 international. 776 applicants, 35% accepted, 201 enrolled. In 2009, 152 master's awarded. *Entrance requirements:* For master's, GMAT, undergraduate degree, communication skills. Additional exam requirements/recommendations for international students: Required—TOEFL (minimum score 100 computer-based). *Application deadline:* For fall admission, 3/31 for domestic students, 1/10 for international students; for spring admission, 11/1 for domestic students. Applications are processed on a rolling basis. Application fee: $85. Electronic applications accepted. *Expenses:* Tuition: Full-time $25,980; part-time $1315 per unit. Required fees: $554. One-time fee: $35 full-time. Full-time tuition and fees vary according to degree level and program. *Financial support:* In 2009–10, 62 students received support. Institutionally sponsored loans and scholarships/grants available. Financial award application deadline: 1/10. *Faculty research:* State and local taxation, Securities and Exchange Commission, governance, auditing fees, financial accounting, enterprise zones, women in business. *Unit head:* Shirley Maxey, Associate Dean, 213-740-4838, E-mail: smaxey@marshall.usc.edu. *Application contact:* Jenna Belknap, Associate Program Director, 213-740-4838, E-mail: belknap@marshall.usc.edu.

University of Southern Mississippi, Graduate School, College of Business, School of Accountancy and Information Systems, Hattiesburg, MS 39406-0001. Offers accountancy (MPA). *Accreditation:* AACSB. Part-time and evening/weekend programs available. *Faculty:* 7 full-time (4 women), 2 part-time/adjunct (both women). *Students:* 15 full-time (10 women), 3 part-time (all women); includes 1 minority (African American). Average age 26. 15 applicants, 73% accepted, 11 enrolled. In 2009, 10 master's awarded. *Degree requirements:* For master's, comprehensive exam. *Entrance requirements:* For master's, GMAT. Additional exam requirements/recommendations for international students: Required—TOEFL. *Application deadline:* For fall admission, 7/15 priority date for domestic students, 7/15 for international students; for spring admission, 11/15 priority date for domestic students, 11/15 for international students. Applications are processed on a rolling basis. Application fee: $35. Electronic applications accepted. *Expenses:* Tuition, state resident: full-time $5096; part-time $284 per hour. Tuition, nonresident: full-time $13,052; part-time $726 per hour. Required fees: $402. Tuition and fees vary according to course level and course load. *Financial support:* In 2009–10, 7 research assistantships with full tuition reimbursements (averaging $6,000 per year) were awarded; Federal Work-Study and institutionally sponsored loans also available. Support available to part-time students. Financial award application deadline: 3/15; financial award applicants required to submit FAFSA. *Faculty research:* Bank liquidity, subchapter S corporations, internal auditing, governmental accounting, inflation accounting. *Unit head:* Dr. Stan Lewis, Director, 601-266-4322, Fax: 601-266-4639. *Application contact:* Dr. Francis Daniel, Graduate Coordinator, 601-266-4664, Fax: 601-266-5814.

University of South Florida, Graduate School, College of Business, Department of Business Administration, Tampa, FL 33620-9951. Offers accounting (PhD); entrepreneurship (MBA); finance (PhD); information systems (PhD); leadership and organizational effectiveness (MSM); management and organization (MBA); marketing (PhD). *Accreditation:* AACSB. Part-time and evening/weekend programs available. *Faculty:* 12 full-time (2 women). *Students:* 152 full-time (51 women), 201 part-time (65 women); includes 70 minority (14 African Americans, 30 Asian Americans or Pacific Islanders, 26 Hispanic Americans), 54 international. Average age 32. 460 applicants, 35% accepted, 93 enrolled. In 2009, 161 master's, 11 doctorates awarded. *Degree requirements:* For master's, comprehensive exam, thesis (for some programs); for doctorate, comprehensive exam, thesis/dissertation, 90 credit hours, minimum GPA of 3.0. *Entrance requirements:* For master's, GMAT, minimum GPA of 3.0 in last 60 hours of course work, 2 years of work experience, resume; for doctorate, GMAT, letters of recommendation, personal statement. Additional exam requirements/recommendations for international students: Required—TOEFL (minimum score 550 paper-based; 213 computer-based; 79 iBT). *Application deadline:* For fall admission, 6/1 for domestic students, 1/2 for international students; for spring admission, 10/15 for domestic students, 6/1 for international students. Application fee: $30. *Financial support:* Fellowships, research assistantships, teaching assistantships, scholarships/grants, health care benefits, and unspecified assistantships available. Financial award applicants required to submit FAFSA. *Unit head:* Irene Hurst, Program Director, 813-974-3335, Fax: 813-974-4518, E-mail: hurst@coba.usf.edu. *Application contact:* Wendy Baker, Assistant Director, Graduate Studies, 813-974-3335, Fax: 813-974-4518, E-mail: wbaker@usf.edu.

University of South Florida, Graduate School, College of Business, School of Accounting, Tampa, FL 33620-9951. Offers accounting (M Acc); business administration (PhD), including accounting. *Accreditation:* AACSB. Part-time and evening/weekend programs available. *Faculty:* 13 full-time (7 women). *Students:* 45 full-time (25 women), 35 part-time (24 women); includes 17 minority (1 African American, 1 American Indian/Alaska Native, 7 Asian Americans or Pacific Islanders, 8 Hispanic Americans), 3 international. Average age 32. 105 applicants, 33% accepted, 22 enrolled. In 2009, 45 master's awarded. Terminal master's awarded for partial completion of doctoral program. *Degree requirements:* For master's, thesis or alternative, 30 credits, minimum GPA of 3.0; for doctorate, comprehensive exam, thesis/dissertation. *Entrance requirements:* For master's, GMAT, minimum GPA of 3.0 in upper-level accounting course work in last 5 years; for doctorate, GMAT, letters of recommendation, personal statement. Additional exam requirements/recommendations for international students: Required—TOEFL (minimum score 550 paper-based; 213 computer-based; 79 iBT). *Application deadline:* For fall admission, 6/1 for domestic students, 1/2 for international students; for spring admission, 10/15 for domestic students, 6/1 for international students. Application fee: $30. Electronic applications accepted. *Financial support:* In 2009–10, teaching assistantships with tuition reimbursements (averaging $21,828 per year); scholarships/grants, health care benefits, and unspecified assistantships also available. Financial award applicants required to submit FAFSA. *Faculty research:* Auditor independence, audit committee decisions, fraud detection and reporting, disclosure effects, effects of information technology on accounting, governmental accounting/auditing, accounting information systems, the reporting and use of financial information, fair value accounting issues, corporate governance and financial reporting quality. Total annual research expenditures: $283,982. *Unit head:* Dr. Stephanie Bryant, Chairperson, 813-974-4186, Fax: 813-974-6528, E-mail: sbryant2@usf.edu. *Application contact:* Christy Ward, Advisor, 813-974-4290, Fax: 813-974-2797, E-mail: cward@coba.usf.edu.

The University of Tampa, John H. Sykes College of Business, Tampa, FL 33606-1490. Offers accounting (MBA, MS); economics (MBA); entrepreneurship and innovation (MBA); finance (MBA, MS); information systems management (MBA); international business (MBA); management (MBA); marketing (MBA, MS); nonprofit management (MBA). *Accreditation:* AACSB. Part-time and evening/weekend programs available. *Faculty:* 62 full-time (22 women), 11 part-time/adjunct (4 women). *Students:* 240 full-time (101 women), 338 part-time (133 women); includes 95 minority (16 African Americans, 4 American Indian/Alaska Native, 24 Asian Americans or Pacific Islanders, 51 Hispanic Americans), 122 international. Average age 29. 564 applicants, 51% accepted, 186 enrolled. In 2009, 234 master's awarded. *Entrance requirements:* For master's, GMAT. Additional exam requirements/recommendations for international students: Required—TOEFL (minimum score 577 paper-based; 230 computer-based; 90 iBT), IELTS. *Application deadline:* For fall admission, 7/15 for domestic students, 6/1 for international students; for spring admission, 12/15 for domestic students, 11/1 for international students. Applications are processed on a rolling basis. Application fee: $40. Electronic applications accepted. *Expenses:* Tuition: Part-time $488 per credit hour. *Financial support:* In 2009–10, 332 students received support, including 71 research assistantships with full tuition reimbursements available (averaging $6,757 per year); career-related internships or fieldwork, scholarships/grants, and unspecified assistantships also available. Support available to part-time students. Financial award applicants required to submit FAFSA. *Faculty research:* Information systems, leadership, corporate governance, entrepreneurship, hedonic price estimation. *Unit head:* Dr. Don Morrill, Associate Dean, Graduate and Continuing Studies, 813-257-3557, E-mail: dmorrill@ut.edu. *Application contact:* Karen Full, Director of Admissions, Graduate and Continuing Studies, 813-257-3642, E-mail: kfull@ut.edu.

The University of Tennessee, Graduate School, College of Business Administration, Department of Accounting, Knoxville, TN 37996. Offers accounting (M Acc), including assurance; systems (M Acc); taxation (M Acc). *Accreditation:* AACSB. *Degree requirements:* For master's, thesis or alternative. *Entrance requirements:* For master's, GMAT, minimum GPA of 2.7. Additional exam requirements/recommendations for international students: Required—TOEFL. Electronic applications accepted. *Expenses:* Tuition, state resident: full-time $6826; part-time $380 per semester hour. Tuition, nonresident: full-time $21,844; part-time $1147 per semester hour. Tuition and fees vary according to program.

The University of Tennessee, Graduate School, College of Business Administration, Program in Business Administration, Knoxville, TN 37996. Offers accounting (PhD); finance (MBA, PhD); logistics and transportation (MBA, PhD); management (PhD); marketing (MBA, PhD); operations management (MBA); professional business administration (MBA); statistics (PhD); JD/MBA; MS/MBA. *Accreditation:* AACSB. Postbaccalaureate distance learning degree programs offered. *Degree requirements:* For master's, thesis or alternative; for doctorate, thesis/dissertation. *Entrance requirements:* For master's and doctorate, GMAT, minimum GPA of 2.7. Additional exam requirements/recommendations for international students: Required—TOEFL. Electronic applications accepted. *Expenses:* Tuition, state resident: full-time $6826; part-time $380 per semester hour. Tuition, nonresident: full-time $21,844; part-time $1147 per semester hour. Tuition and fees vary according to program.

The University of Tennessee at Chattanooga, Graduate School, College of Business, Program in Accountancy, Chattanooga, TN 37403. Offers M Acc. *Accreditation:* AACSB. Part-time and evening/weekend programs available. *Faculty:* 5 full-time (1 woman), 2 part-time/adjunct (1 woman). *Students:* 14 full-time (9 women), 18 part-time (10 women); includes 2 minority (1 African American, 1 Asian American or Pacific Islander), 4 international. Average age 29. 16 applicants, 63% accepted, 8 enrolled. In 2009, 12 master's awarded. *Entrance requirements:* For master's, GMAT (minimum score 450). Additional exam requirements/recommendations for international students: Required—TOEFL (minimum score 550 paper-based; 213 computer-based; 79 iBT), IELTS (minimum score 6). *Application deadline:* For fall admission, 8/1 priority date for domestic students, 6/1 for international students; for spring admission, 12/1 priority date for domestic students, 10/1 for international students. Applications are processed on a rolling basis. Application fee: $35. Electronic applications accepted. *Expenses:* Tuition, state resident: full-time $5404; part-time $300 per credit hour. Tuition, nonresident: full-time $16,702; part-time $928 per credit hour. Required fees: $1150; $130 per credit hour. *Financial support:* In 2009–10, 1 research assistantship with full and partial tuition reimbursement (averaging $5,500 per year) was awarded; career-related internships or fieldwork, scholarships/grants, and unspecified assistantships also available. Support available to part-time students. *Faculty research:* Performance measurement, auditing, income taxation, corporate efficiency, portfolio management and performance. *Unit head:* Dr. Stan Davis, Head, 423-425-4152, Fax: 423-425-5255, E-mail: stan-davis@utc.edu. *Application contact:* Dr. Stephanie Bellar, Dean of Graduate Studies, 423-425-4666, Fax: 423-425-5223, E-mail: stephanie-bellar@utc.edu.

The University of Texas at Arlington, Graduate School, College of Business, Accounting Department, Arlington, TX 76019. Offers accounting (MP Acc, MS); taxation (MS). Part-time and evening/weekend programs available. *Faculty:* 9 full-time (4 women), 3 part-time/adjunct (0 women). *Students:* 119 full-time (61 women), 161 part-time (76 women); includes 57 minority (10 African Americans, 2 American Indian/Alaska Native, 22 Asian Americans or Pacific Islanders, 23 Hispanic Americans), 40 international. 208 applicants, 75% accepted, 81 enrolled. In 2009, 67 master's awarded. *Degree requirements:* For master's, thesis optional. *Entrance requirements:* For master's, GMAT. Additional exam requirements/recommendations for international students: Required—TOEFL (minimum score 550 paper-based; 213 computer-

based; 79 iBT). *Application deadline:* For fall admission, 6/15 for domestic students. Applications are processed on a rolling basis. Application fee: $35 ($50 for international students). *Financial support:* In 2009–10, 2 fellowships (averaging $1,000 per year), 2 research assistantships (averaging $6,000 per year), 10 teaching assistantships (averaging $13,000 per year) were awarded; career-related internships or fieldwork, scholarships/grants, and unspecified assistantships also available. Financial award application deadline: 6/1; financial award applicants required to submit FAFSA. *Unit head:* Dr. Larry Walther, Chair, 817-272-3481, Fax: 817-282-5793, E-mail: walther@uta.edu. *Application contact:* Carly S. Andrews, Graduate Advisor, 817-272-3047, Fax: 817-272-5793, E-mail: graduate.accounting.advisor@uta.edu.

The University of Texas at Arlington, Graduate School, College of Business, Program in Business Administration, Arlington, TX 76019. Offers accounting (PhD); business statistics (PhD); finance (MBA, PhD); information systems (MBA, PhD); management (MBA, PhD); management sciences (MBA); marketing (MBA, PhD); operations management (PhD); real estate (MBA). *Accreditation:* AACSB. Part-time and evening/weekend programs available. Postbaccalaureate distance learning degree programs offered (no on-campus study). *Students:* 587 full-time (188 women), 349 part-time (140 women); includes 188 minority (66 African Americans, 62 Asian Americans or Pacific Islanders, 60 Hispanic Americans), 371 international. 282 applicants, 96% accepted, 145 enrolled. In 2009, 431 master's awarded. Terminal master's awarded for partial completion of doctoral program. *Degree requirements:* For master's, thesis optional; for doctorate, comprehensive exam, thesis/dissertation. *Entrance requirements:* For master's, GMAT; for doctorate, GMAT, minimum GPA of 3.0 (undergraduate), 3.4 (graduate); 30 hours of graduate course work. Additional exam requirements/recommendations for international students: Required—TOEFL (minimum score 550 paper-based; 213 computer-based; 79 iBT). *Application deadline:* For fall admission, 6/5 for domestic students, 4/1 for international students; for spring admission, 10/15 for domestic students, 9/1 for international students. Applications are processed on a rolling basis. Application fee: $35 ($50 for international students). Electronic applications accepted. *Financial support:* In 2009–10, 1 fellowship (averaging $1,000 per year), 30 research assistantships (averaging $6,000 per year), 45 teaching assistantships (averaging $13,000 per year) were awarded; career-related internships or fieldwork, scholarships/grants, and unspecified assistantships also available. Financial award application deadline: 6/1; financial award applicants required to submit FAFSA. *Unit head:* Greg Frazier, Director PhD Programs, 817-272-3559, Fax: 817-272-5799, E-mail: frazier@exchange.uta.edu. *Application contact:* Melanie McGee, Director of MBA Program, 817-272-0658, Fax: 817-272-5799, E-mail: mwmcgee@uta.edu.

See Close-Up on page 273.

The University of Texas at Austin, Graduate School, McCombs School of Business, Department of Accounting, Austin, TX 78712-1111. Offers MPA, PhD. *Accreditation:* AACSB. *Degree requirements:* For doctorate, comprehensive exam, thesis/dissertation. *Entrance requirements:* For master's and doctorate, GMAT. Additional exam requirements/recommendations for international students: Required—TOEFL. Electronic applications accepted.

The University of Texas at Dallas, School of Management, Program in Accounting and Information Management, Richardson, TX 75080. Offers assurance services (MS); financial planning and analysis (MS); information management (MS); international services (MS); management consulting (MS); software management (MS); taxation services (MS). *Accreditation:* AACSB. *Faculty:* 19 full-time (4 women), 10 part-time/adjunct (3 women). *Students:* 295 full-time (173 women), 275 part-time (156 women); includes 172 minority (29 African Americans, 3 American Indian/Alaska Native, 108 Asian Americans or Pacific Islanders, 32 Hispanic Americans), 171 international. Average age 29. 356 applicants, 74% accepted, 203 enrolled. In 2009, 254 master's awarded. *Entrance requirements:* For master's, GMAT. Additional exam requirements/recommendations for international students: Required—TOEFL (minimum score 550 paper-based; 213 computer-based). *Application deadline:* For fall admission, 7/15 for domestic students, 5/1 priority date for international students; for spring admission, 11/15 for domestic students, 9/1 priority date for international students. Applications are processed on a rolling basis. Application fee: $50 ($100 for international students). Electronic applications accepted. *Expenses:* Tuition, state resident: full-time $11,068; part-time $461 per credit hour. Tuition, nonresident: full-time $21,178; part-time $882 per credit hour. Tuition and fees vary according to course load. *Financial support:* In 2009–10, 3 research assistantships with full tuition reimbursements (averaging $10,072 per year), 4 teaching assistantships with full tuition reimbursements (averaging $10,050 per year) were awarded; fellowships, career-related internships or fieldwork, Federal Work-Study, institutionally sponsored loans, scholarships/grants, and unspecified assistantships also available. Support available to part-time students. Financial award application deadline: 4/30; financial award applicants required to submit FAFSA. *Faculty research:* Privatization and accounting/auditing, corporate performance and executive compensation, risk management, information technology in accounting. *Unit head:* Amy Troutman, Assistant Director, 972-883-6719, Fax: 972-883-6823, E-mail: amybass@utdallas.edu. *Application contact:* James Parker, Assistant Director of Graduate Recruitment, 972-883-5842, E-mail: jparker@utdallas.edu.

The University of Texas at Dallas, School of Management, Programs in Management Science, Richardson, TX 75080. Offers accounting (PhD); decision sciences (PhD); finance (PhD); management strategy and public policy (PhD); marketing (PhD); organizational behavior (PhD). *Accreditation:* AACSB. Part-time and evening/weekend programs available. *Faculty:* 12 full-time (3 women). *Students:* 72 full-time (23 women), 12 part-time (6 women); includes 10 minority (all Asian Americans or Pacific Islanders), 63 international. Average age 34. 173 applicants, 12% accepted, 7 enrolled. In 2009, 8 doctorates awarded. *Degree requirements:* For doctorate, thesis/dissertation. *Entrance requirements:* For doctorate, GMAT, minimum GPA of 3.0. Additional exam requirements/recommendations for international students: Required—TOEFL (minimum score 550 paper-based; 213 computer-based). *Application deadline:* For fall admission, 7/15 for domestic students, 5/1 priority date for international students; for spring admission, 11/15 for domestic students, 9/1 priority date for international students. Applications are processed on a rolling basis. Application fee: $50 ($100 for international students). Electronic applications accepted. *Expenses:* Tuition, state resident: full-time $11,068; part-time $461 per credit hour. Tuition, nonresident: full-time $21,178; part-time $882 per credit hour. Tuition and fees vary according to course load. *Financial support:* In 2009–10, 1 research assistantship with full tuition reimbursement (averaging $13,050 per year), 43 teaching assistantships with full tuition reimbursements (averaging $14,795 per year) were awarded; fellowships, career-related internships or fieldwork, Federal Work-Study, institutionally sponsored loans, scholarships/grants, and unspecified assistantships also available. Support available to part-time students. Financial award application deadline: 4/30; financial award applicants required to submit FAFSA. *Faculty research:* Empirical generalizations in marketing, diffusion of generations of technology, stochastic brand-choice theory, acceptance of trade deals by supermarkets, nonparametric estimations of market share response. *Unit head:* Dr. Sumit Sarkar, Program Director, 972-883-2745, Fax: 972-883-5977, E-mail: som-phd.@utdallas.edu. *Application contact:* James Parker, Assistant Director, 972-883-5842, E-mail: jparker@utdallas.edu.

The University of Texas at El Paso, Graduate School, College of Business Administration, Department of Accounting, El Paso, TX 79968-0001. Offers M Acc. *Accreditation:* AACSB. Part-time and evening/weekend programs available. *Students:* 39 (20 women); includes 22 minority (1 African American, 1 Asian American or Pacific Islander, 20 Hispanic Americans), 6 international. Average age 34. In 2009, 18 master's awarded. *Entrance requirements:* For master's, GMAT, minimum GPA of 3.0. Additional exam requirements/recommendations for international students: Required—TOEFL; Recommended—IELTS. *Application deadline:* For fall admission, 8/1 priority date for domestic students, 3/1 for international students; for spring admission, 11/1 priority date for domestic students, 9/1 for international students. Applications are processed on a rolling basis. Application fee: $45 ($80 for international students). Electronic applications accepted. *Financial support:* In 2009–10, research assistantships with partial tuition reimbursements (averaging $18,750 per year), teaching assistantships with partial tuition reimbursements (averaging $15,000 per year) were awarded; fellowships with partial tuition reimbursements, institutionally sponsored loans, scholarships/grants, health care benefits, tuition waivers (partial), and unspecified assistantships also available. Support available to part-time students. Financial award application deadline: 3/15; financial award applicants required to submit FAFSA. *Faculty research:* International accounting, tax, not-for-profit accounting. *Unit head:* Dr. Ray Zimmerman, Chair, 915-747-5192, Fax: 915-747-8618, E-mail: rzimmer@utep.edu. *Application contact:* Dr. Patricia D. Witherspoon, Dean of the Graduate School, 915-747-5491, Fax: 915-747-5788, E-mail: withersp@utep.edu.

The University of Texas at San Antonio, College of Business, Department of Accounting, San Antonio, TX 78249-0617. Offers accountancy (M Accy); business administration-accounting (PhD); management accounting (MBA); taxation (MBA). *Accreditation:* AACSB. Part-time and evening/weekend programs available. *Faculty:* 11 full-time (3 women), 4 part-time/adjunct (2 women). *Students:* 44 full-time (22 women), 35 part-time (16 women); includes 29 minority (1 African American, 4 Asian Americans or Pacific Islanders, 24 Hispanic Americans), 9 international. Average age 29. 68 applicants, 57% accepted, 32 enrolled. In 2009, 32 master's awarded. *Degree requirements:* For master's, comprehensive exam (for some programs), thesis (for some programs). *Entrance requirements:* For master's, GMAT. Additional exam requirements/recommendations for international students: Required—TOEFL (minimum score 500 paper-based; 173 computer-based; 61 iBT), IELTS (minimum score 5). *Application deadline:* For fall admission, 7/1 for domestic students, 4/1 for international students; for spring admission, 11/1 for domestic students, 9/1 for international students. Application fee: $45 ($80 for international students). *Expenses:* Tuition, state resident: full-time $3975; part-time $221 per contact hour. Tuition, nonresident: full-time $13,947; part-time $775 per contact hour. Required fees: $1853. *Financial support:* In 2009–10, 17 students received support, including 10 research assistantships (averaging $8,580 per year), 6 teaching assistantships (averaging $7,800 per year); scholarships/grants, tuition waivers, and unspecified assistantships also available. Support available to part-time students. *Faculty research:* Financial reporting, auditing, tax, health care accounting. *Unit head:* Dr. James E. Groff, Interim Chair, 210-458-5239, Fax: 210-458-4322, E-mail: james.groff@utsa.edu. *Application contact:* Jeff Boone, Graduate Advisor, 210-458-7091, E-mail: jeff.boone@utsa.edu.

The University of Texas of the Permian Basin, Office of Graduate Studies, School of Business, Program in Accountancy, Odessa, TX 79762-0001. Offers MPA. *Entrance requirements:* For master's, GMAT. Additional exam requirements/recommendations for international students: Required—TOEFL (minimum score 550 paper-based; 213 computer-based).

The University of Texas–Pan American, College of Business Administration, Program in Accounting, Edinburg, TX 78539. Offers M Acc, MS. Part-time and evening/weekend programs available. *Entrance requirements:* For master's, GMAT. Additional exam requirements/recommendations for international students: Required—TOEFL (minimum score 500 paper-based). Electronic applications accepted. *Expenses:* Tuition, state resident: full-time $3630.60; part-time $201.70 per credit hour. Tuition, nonresident: full-time $8617; part-time $478.70 per credit hour. Required fees: $806.50. *Faculty research:* Financial and managerial accounting, international accounting; taxation, ethics.

University of the Incarnate Word, School of Graduate Studies and Research, H-E-B School of Business and Administration, Programs in Accounting, San Antonio, TX 78209-6397. Offers MS. Part-time and evening/weekend programs available. *Students:* 21 full-time (11 women), 36 part-time (21 women); includes 30 minority (2 African Americans, 2 Asian Americans or Pacific Islanders, 26 Hispanic Americans), 5 international. Average age 30. In 2009, 25 master's awarded. *Entrance requirements:* For master's, GMAT. Additional exam requirements/recommendations for international students: Required—TOEFL (minimum score 560 paper-based; 220 computer-based; 83 iBT). *Application deadline:* Applications are processed on a rolling basis. Application fee: $20. Electronic applications accepted. *Expenses:* Tuition: Full-time $12,150; part-time $675 per credit hour. Required fees: $83 per credit hour. *Financial support:* Federal Work-Study and scholarships/grants available. Financial award applicants required to submit FAFSA. *Unit head:* Henry Elrod, 210-829-3184, Fax: 210-805-3564, E-mail: elrod@uiwtx.edu. *Application contact:* Andrea Cyterski-Acosta, Dean of Enrollment, 210-829-6005, Fax: 210-829-3921, E-mail: admis@uiwtx.edu.

University of the Sacred Heart, Graduate Programs, Department of Business Administration, San Juan, PR 00914-0383. Offers human resource management (MBA); information systems auditing (MS); information technology (Certificate); international marketing (MBA); management information systems (MBA); taxation (MBA). Part-time and evening/weekend programs available. *Degree requirements:* For master's, thesis. *Entrance requirements:* For master's, EXADEP, minimum undergraduate GPA of 2.75, interview.

The University of Toledo, College of Graduate Studies, College of Business Administration, Department of Accounting, Toledo, OH 43606-3390. Offers accounting (MBA, MSA). Part-time and evening/weekend programs available. *Entrance requirements:* For master's, GMAT. Additional exam requirements/recommendations for international students: Required—TOEFL. *Faculty research:* Estate gift tax, audit and legal liability, corporate tax, accounting information systems.

University of Toronto, School of Graduate Studies, Social Sciences Division, Faculty of Management, Toronto, ON M5S 1A1, Canada. Offers MBA, MMPA, PhD, MBA/MA, MBA/MN. *Accreditation:* AACSB. Part-time and evening/weekend programs available. *Degree requirements:* For doctorate, thesis/dissertation. *Entrance requirements:* For master's, GMAT (MBA, MMPA), minimum mid-B average in final undergraduate year (MMPA, MBA), 2 years of full-time work experiences (MBA), 8 years work experience preferred (EMBA), 2-3 letters of reference; for doctorate, GMAT, minimum B+ average, master's degree in business administration, 2-3 letters of reference. *Expenses:* Contact institution. *Faculty research:* Natural resources, organizational behavior, finance.

University of Tulsa, Graduate School, Collins College of Business, Master of Business Administration Program, Tulsa, OK 74104-3189. Offers accounting (MBA); business administration (MBA); energy management (MBA); finance (MBA); international business (MBA); management information systems (MBA); taxation (MBA); JD/MBA; MBA/MSCS; MBA/MSF. *Accreditation:* AACSB. Part-time and evening/weekend programs available. *Faculty:* 32 full-time (6 women). *Students:* 59 full-time (26 women), 45 part-time (18 women); includes 13 minority (4 African Americans, 4 American Indian/Alaska Native, 1 Asian American or Pacific Islander, 4 Hispanic Americans), 9 international. Average age 25. 78 applicants, 53% accepted, 30 enrolled. In 2009, 36 master's awarded. *Entrance requirements:* For master's, GMAT. Additional exam requirements/recommendations for international students: Required—TOEFL (minimum score 575 paper-based; 232 computer-based; 90 iBT), IELTS (minimum score 6.5). *Application deadline:* Applications are processed on a rolling basis. Application fee: $40. Electronic applications accepted. *Expenses:* Tuition: Full-time $16,182; part-time $899 per credit hour. Required fees: $4 per credit hour. Tuition and fees vary according to course load. *Financial support:* In 2009–10, 42 students received support, including 5 fellowships (averaging $11,894 per year), 2 research assistantships (averaging $9,322 per year), 35 teaching assistantships (averaging $8,112 per year); institutionally sponsored loans, scholarships/grants, health care benefits, tuition waivers (full and partial), and unspecified assistantships also available. Support available to part-time students. Financial award application deadline: 2/1; financial award applicants required to submit FAFSA. *Faculty research:* Accounting, energy management, finance, international business, management information systems, taxation. *Unit head:* Dr. Markham Collins, Associate Dean of the Collins College of Business, 918-631-2783, Fax: 918-631-2142, E-mail: markham-collins@utulsa.edu. *Application contact:* Dr. Markham Collins, Associate Dean of the Collins College of Business, 918-631-2783, Fax: 918-631-2142, E-mail: markham-collins@utulsa.edu.

University of Utah, Graduate School, David Eccles School of Business, Business Administration Program, Salt Lake City, UT 84112. Offers accounting (PhD); business administration (EMBA, MBA, PMBA); statistics (M Stat). Part-time and evening/weekend programs available. *Faculty:* 18 full-time (8 women). *Students:* 525 full-time (97 women), 91 part-time (18 women); includes 44 minority (3 African Americans, 1 American Indian/Alaska Native, 27 Asian Americans or

Accounting

University of Utah (continued)

Pacific Islanders, 13 Hispanic Americans), 47 international. Average age 32. 936 applicants, 47% accepted, 337 enrolled. In 2009, 258 master's, 6 doctorates awarded. Terminal master's awarded for partial completion of doctoral program. *Degree requirements:* For doctorate, thesis/dissertation, oral qualifying exams, written qualifying exams. *Entrance requirements:* For master's, GMAT, statistics course with minimum B grade, minimum undergraduate GPA of 3.0; for doctorate, GMAT or GRE General Test. Additional exam requirements/recommendations for international students: Required—TOEFL (minimum score 600 paper-based; 250 computer-based; 100 iBT), IELTS (minimum score 7). *Application deadline:* For fall admission, 2/15 priority date for domestic and international students. Applications are processed on a rolling basis. Application fee: $55 ($65 for international students). Electronic applications accepted. *Expenses:* Contact institution. *Financial support:* In 2009–10, 20 students received support, including 1 fellowship with partial tuition reimbursement available (averaging $9,000 per year), 58 teaching assistantships with partial tuition reimbursements available (averaging $6,350 per year); scholarships/grants and unspecified assistantships also available. Financial award application deadline: 2/15; financial award applicants required to submit FAFSA. *Faculty research:* Corporate finance, strategy services, consumer behavior, financial disclosures, operations. Total annual research expenditures: $60,805. *Unit head:* Don Wardell, 801-581-8774, Fax: 801-581-3666, E-mail: don.wardell@utah.edu. *Application contact:* Andrea Chmelik, Coordinator, 801-581-1719, Fax: 801-581-3666, E-mail: andrea.chmelik@business.utah.edu.

University of Utah, Graduate School, David Eccles School of Business, School of Accounting, Salt Lake City, UT 84112. Offers M Acc, PhD. *Accreditation:* AACSB. Part-time and evening/weekend programs available. *Faculty:* 14 full-time (6 women), 1 part-time/adjunct (0 women). *Students:* 91 full-time (38 women), 19 part-time (7 women); includes 8 minority (1 American Indian/Alaska Native, 7 Asian Americans or Pacific Islanders), 5 international. Average age 28. 160 applicants, 62% accepted, 80 enrolled. In 2009, 70 master's awarded. *Degree requirements:* For doctorate, thesis/dissertation, oral qualifying exams, written qualifying exams. *Entrance requirements:* For master's, GMAT, minimum undergraduate GPA of 3.0; 7 prerequisite courses; for doctorate, GMAT. Additional exam requirements/recommendations for international students: Required—TOEFL (minimum score 600 paper-based; 250 computer-based; 100 iBT), IELTS (minimum score 7). *Application deadline:* For fall admission, 3/1 priority date for domestic and international students; for spring admission, 11/1 for domestic and international students. Applications are processed on a rolling basis. Application fee: $55 ($65 for international students). Electronic applications accepted. *Expenses:* Contact institution. *Financial support:* In 2009–10, 15 students received support, including 8 fellowships with partial tuition reimbursements available (averaging $5,500 per year), 6 teaching assistantships with partial tuition reimbursements available (averaging $1,100 per year); research assistantships, Federal Work-Study, tuition waivers (full), and unspecified assistantships also available. Financial award application deadline: 4/1; financial award applicants required to submit FAFSA. *Faculty research:* Auditing, taxation, information systems, financial accounting, accounting theory, international accounting. Total annual research expenditures: $82,791. *Unit head:* Dr. Martha Eining, Chair, 801-581-7673, Fax: 801-581-3581, E-mail: martha.eining@utah.edu. *Application contact:* Andrea Chmelik, Admissions Coordinator, 801-585-1719, Fax: 801-581-3666, E-mail: andrea.chmelik@business.utah.edu.

University of Vermont, Graduate College, School of Business Administration, Program in Accounting, Burlington, VT 05405. Offers M Acc. *Students:* 7 (2 women); includes 2 Asian Americans or Pacific Islanders. 25 applicants, 44% accepted, 6 enrolled. *Entrance requirements:* For master's, GMAT, GRE. Additional exam requirements/recommendations for international students: Required—TOEFL (minimum score 550 paper-based; 213 computer-based; 80 iBT). *Application deadline:* For fall admission, 4/1 for domestic and international students; for spring admission, 12/1 for domestic and international students. Applications are processed on a rolling basis. Application fee: $40. Electronic applications accepted. *Expenses:* Tuition, state resident: part-time $508 per credit hour. Tuition, nonresident: part-time $1281 per credit hour. *Unit head:* Dr. Michael Gurdon, Coordinator, 802-656-3177. *Application contact:* Dr. M. Gurdon, Coordinator, 802-656-0513.

University of Virginia, McIntire School of Commerce, Program in Accounting, Charlottesville, VA 22903. Offers MS. *Accreditation:* AACSB. *Students:* 112 full-time (62 women); includes 27 minority (6 African Americans, 2 American Indian/Alaska Native, 11 Asian Americans or Pacific Islanders, 8 Hispanic Americans), 21 international. Average age 23. 132 applicants, 76% accepted, 54 enrolled. In 2009, 103 master's awarded. *Entrance requirements:* For master's, GMAT, 2 letters of recommendation, 12 hours of accounting courses. Additional exam requirements/recommendations for international students: Required—TOEFL (minimum score 600 paper-based; 250 computer-based; 100 iBT), IELTS (minimum score 7). *Application deadline:* For fall admission, 9/1 priority date for domestic students, 12/1 for international students. Applications are processed on a rolling basis. Application fee: $75. Electronic applications accepted. *Expenses:* Contact institution. *Financial support:* Fellowships, Federal Work-Study available. Financial award applicants required to submit FAFSA. *Unit head:* Carl P. Zeithaml, Dean, 434-924-3110. *Application contact:* Cathy Fox, Manager, Graduate Admissions and Marketing, 434-924-3571, E-mail: msaccounting@virginia.edu.

University of Washington, Graduate School, Michael G. Foster School of Business, Seattle, WA 98195-3200. Offers auditing and assurance (MP Acc); business (PhD); business administration (evening) (MBA); business administration (full-time) (MBA); executive business administration (MBA); global business administration (MBA); global executive business administration (MBA); taxation (MP Acc); technology management (MBA); JD/MBA; MBA/MAIS; MBA/MHA. *Accreditation:* AACSB. Part-time and evening/weekend programs available. Terminal master's awarded for partial completion of doctoral program. *Degree requirements:* For doctorate, comprehensive exam, thesis/dissertation. *Entrance requirements:* For master's, GMAT; for doctorate, GMAT, GRE. Additional exam requirements/recommendations for international students: Required—TOEFL (minimum score 600 paper-based; 250 computer-based). Electronic applications accepted. *Expenses:* Contact institution. *Faculty research:* Finance, marketing, organizational behavior, information technology, strategy.

University of Washington, Tacoma, Graduate Programs, MBA Programs, Tacoma, WA 98402-3100. Offers accounting (MBA); certified financial analyst (MBA). Part-time and evening/weekend programs available. *Faculty:* 24 full-time (8 women), 3 part-time/adjunct (0 women). *Students:* 39 full-time (9 women), 10 part-time (2 women); includes 1 African American, 5 Asian Americans or Pacific Islanders, 1 Hispanic American, 1 international. Average age 33. 31 applicants, 68% accepted, 18 enrolled. In 2009, 18 master's awarded. *Entrance requirements:* For master's, GMAT, current resume, management and professional work summary, essay, 2 professional letters of recommendation. *Application deadline:* For fall admission, 4/15 priority date for domestic students. Applications are processed on a rolling basis. Application fee: $65. Electronic applications accepted. *Expenses:* Tuition, state resident: full-time $10,660; part-time $484 per credit. Tuition, nonresident: full-time $24,000; part-time $1119 per credit. Required fees: $150 per term. Tuition and fees vary according to course load and program. *Faculty research:* Leadership, bankruptcy, strategic marketing, customer Satisfaction, corporate social responsibility. *Unit head:* Dr. Shahrokh Saudagaran, Dean, 253-692-5630, Fax: 253-692-4523, E-mail: uwtmba@u.washington.edu. *Application contact:* Aubree Robinson, Academic Adviser, MBA and Undergraduate Programs, 253-692-5630, Fax: 253-692-4523, E-mail: uwtmba@u.washington.edu.

University of Waterloo, Graduate Studies, Faculty of Arts, School of Accounting and Finance, Waterloo, ON N2L 3G1, Canada. Offers accounting (M Acc, PhD); finance (M Acc); taxation (M Tax). *Degree requirements:* For master's, thesis or alternative; for doctorate, thesis/dissertation. *Entrance requirements:* For master's, honors degree, minimum B average, resumé; for doctorate, GMAT, master's degree, minimum A- average, resume. Additional exam requirements/recommendations for international students: Required—TOEFL, TWE. Electronic applications accepted. *Expenses:* Contact institution. *Faculty research:* Auditing, management accounting.

University of West Florida, College of Business, Department of Accounting, Pensacola, FL 32514-5750. Offers M Acc, MA. Part-time and evening/weekend programs available. *Faculty:* 10 full-time (1 woman). *Students:* 15 full-time (13 women), 23 part-time (15 women); includes 6 minority (1 African American, 3 Asian Americans or Pacific Islanders, 2 Hispanic Americans), 2 international. Average age 31. 24 applicants, 79% accepted, 11 enrolled. In 2009, 11 master's awarded. *Entrance requirements:* For master's, GMAT (minimum score 450) or equivalent GRE score, bachelor's degree, two letters of recommendation, resume. Additional exam requirements/recommendations for international students: Required—TOEFL (minimum score 550 paper-based; 213 computer-based). *Application deadline:* For fall admission, 6/30 priority date for domestic students, 5/15 for international students; for spring admission, 11/1 for domestic students, 10/1 for international students. Application fee: $30. *Expenses:* Tuition, state resident: full-time $4982; part-time $260 per credit hour. Tuition, nonresident: full-time $20,059; part-time $919 per credit hour. Required fees: $1247; $52 per credit hour. *Financial support:* In 2009–10, 7 fellowships (averaging $557 per year), 6 research assistantships with partial tuition reimbursements (averaging $2,136 per year) were awarded; unspecified assistantships also available. Financial award application deadline: 4/15; financial award applicants required to submit FAFSA. *Faculty research:* Audit risk, tax legislation, product costing, bank core deposit intangibles, financial reporting. *Unit head:* Dr. Robert Fahnestock, Chairperson, 850-474-2738. *Application contact:* Terry McCray, Assistant Director of Graduate Admissions, 850-473-7718, Fax: 850-473-7714, E-mail: gradadmissions@uwf.edu.

University of West Georgia, Graduate School, Richards College of Business, Department of Accounting and Finance, Carrollton, GA 30118. Offers MP Acc. *Accreditation:* AACSB. Part-time and evening/weekend programs available. *Faculty:* 8 full-time (2 women). *Students:* 14 full-time (8 women), 21 part-time (12 women); includes 8 minority (6 African Americans, 1 Asian American or Pacific Islander, 1 Hispanic American), 3 international. Average age 33. 18 applicants, 44% accepted, 4 enrolled. In 2009, 10 master's awarded. *Degree requirements:* For master's, comprehensive exam. *Entrance requirements:* For master's, GMAT, minimum GPA of 2.5. Additional exam requirements/recommendations for international students: Required—TOEFL (minimum score 550 paper-based; 213 computer-based). *Application deadline:* For fall admission, 7/17 for domestic students; for spring admission, 11/20 for domestic students. Applications are processed on a rolling basis. Application fee: $30. Electronic applications accepted. *Expenses:* Tuition, state resident: full-time $2952; part-time $164 per semester hour. Tuition, nonresident: full-time $11,808; part-time $656 per semester hour. Required fees: $42.90 per semester hour. $307 per semester. Tuition and fees vary according to course load. *Financial support:* In 2009–10, 1 student received support, including 1 research assistantship with full tuition reimbursement available (averaging $4,500 per year); tuition waivers (partial) also available. Financial award application deadline: 7/1; financial award applicants required to submit FAFSA. *Faculty research:* Taxpayer insolvency, non-gap financial measures, deferred taxes, financial accounting issues. Total annual research expenditures: $40,000. *Unit head:* Dr. James R. Colley, Chair, 678-839-6469, Fax: 678-839-5041, E-mail: jcolley@westga.edu. *Application contact:* Dr. Charles W. Clark, Dean, 678-839-6508, E-mail: cclark@westga.edu.

University of Wisconsin–Madison, Graduate School, Wisconsin School of Business, Doctoral Program in Accounting and Information Systems, Madison, WI 53706-1380. Offers PhD. *Accreditation:* AACSB. *Faculty:* 15 full-time (5 women), 1 part-time/adjunct (0 women). *Students:* 11 full-time (6 women), 2 international. Average age 33. 59 applicants, 15% accepted, 2 enrolled. *Degree requirements:* For doctorate, comprehensive exam, thesis/dissertation. *Entrance requirements:* For doctorate, GMAT or GRE. Additional exam requirements/recommendations for international students: Required—Pearson Test of English (minimum score 73, written 80); Recommended—TOEFL (minimum score 623 paper-based; 263 computer-based; 106 iBT), IELTS (minimum score 7.5). *Application deadline:* For fall admission, 12/15 priority date for domestic and international students. Application fee: $56. Electronic applications accepted. *Expenses:* Tuition, state resident: part-time $594 per credit. Tuition, nonresident: part-time $1504 per credit. Required fees: $65 per credit. Tuition and fees vary according to course load, program and reciprocity agreements. *Financial support:* In 2009–10, 11 students received support, including fellowships with full tuition reimbursements available (averaging $18,567 per year), research assistantships with full tuition reimbursements available (averaging $16,506 per year), 11 teaching assistantships with full tuition reimbursements available (averaging $14,088 per year); Federal Work-Study, institutionally sponsored loans, scholarships/grants, health care benefits, and unspecified assistantships also available. Financial award application deadline: 2/1. *Faculty research:* Auditing, financial reporting, economic theory, strategy, computer models. *Unit head:* Prof. Jon Davis, Chair, 608-263-4264. *Application contact:* Belle Heberling, Assistant Director for Research Programs, 608-262-3749, Fax: 608-890-0180, E-mail: phd@bus.wisc.edu.

University of Wisconsin–Madison, Graduate School, Wisconsin School of Business, Master of Accountancy Program, Madison, WI 53706-1380. Offers audit (IM Acc); tax (GM Acc). *Faculty:* 13 full-time (5 women). *Students:* 98 full-time (54 women); includes 10 minority (9 Asian Americans or Pacific Islanders, 1 Hispanic American), 13 international. Average age 22. 129 applicants, 22% accepted, 13 enrolled. In 2009, 85 master's awarded. *Entrance requirements:* For master's, GMAT, essays. Additional exam requirements/recommendations for international students: Required—TOEFL (minimum score 100 computer-based), IELTS, Pearson Test of English (PTE). *Application deadline:* For fall admission, 9/12 for domestic and international students. Application fee: $56. Electronic applications accepted. *Expenses:* Tuition, state resident: part-time $594 per credit. Tuition, nonresident: part-time $1504 per credit. Required fees: $65 per credit. Tuition and fees vary according to course load, program and reciprocity agreements. *Financial support:* In 2009–10, 82 students received support, including 6 research assistantships with partial tuition reimbursements available (averaging $8,100 per year), 54 teaching assistantships with full tuition reimbursements available (averaging $28,175 per year); career-related internships or fieldwork also available. Financial award application deadline: 5/1; financial award applicants required to submit FAFSA. *Faculty research:* Internal control deficiencies, impairment recognition, accounting misstatements, earnings restatements, voluntary disclosure. *Unit head:* Dr. Jon Davis, Professor/Chair of Accounting and Information Systems, 608-263-4264, E-mail: jdavis@bus.wisc.edu. *Application contact:* Kristen Ann Fuhremann, Director, 608-262-0316, Fax: 608-263-0477, E-mail: kfuhremann@bus.wisc.edu.

University of Wisconsin–Whitewater, School of Graduate Studies, College of Business and Economics, Department of Accounting, Whitewater, WI 53190-1790. Offers MPA. Part-time and evening/weekend programs available. Postbaccalaureate distance learning degree programs offered (no on-campus study). *Degree requirements:* For master's, thesis or alternative. *Entrance requirements:* For master's, GMAT, minimum AACSB index of 1000, minimum GPA of 2.75. Additional exam requirements/recommendations for international students: Required—TOEFL (minimum score 550 paper-based; 213 computer-based). Electronic applications accepted. *Faculty research:* Laws/economy/quality of life; tax, accounting and public policy.

University of Wyoming, College of Business, Program in Accounting, Laramie, WY 82070. Offers MS. *Degree requirements:* For master's, thesis optional. *Entrance requirements:* For master's, GMAT or GRE, minimum GPA of 3.0. Additional exam requirements/recommendations for international students: Required—TOEFL (minimum score 540 paper-based; 207 computer-based; 76 iBT). Electronic applications accepted. *Faculty research:* Taxation, accounting education, assessment, not-for-profit accounting, fraud examination, ethics, management accounting.

Upper Iowa University, Online Master's Programs, Fayette, IA 52142-1857. Offers accounting (MBA); corporate financial management (MBA); global business (MBA); health and human services (MPA); higher education administration (MHEA); homeland security (MPA); human resources management (MBA); justice administration (MPA); organizational development (MBA); public personnel management (MPA); quality management (MBA). MBA also available at Madison, WI campus. Part-time programs available. Postbaccalaureate distance learning degree programs offered (no on-campus study). *Faculty:* 3 full-time (0 women), 66 part-time/adjunct (27 women). *Students:* 723 full-time (442 women). *Degree requirements:* For master's,

research project. *Entrance requirements:* For master's, GMAT, GRE, or minimum GPA of 2.7 during last 60 hours. Additional exam requirements/recommendations for international students: Required—TOEFL (minimum score 570 paper-based; 230 computer-based). *Application deadline:* Applications are processed on a rolling basis. Application fee: $50. Electronic applications accepted. *Expenses:* Tuition: Full-time $6948; part-time $386 per credit hour. *Financial support:* Available to part-time students. Applicants required to submit FAFSA. *Faculty research:* Total quality management, CQI, teams, organization culture and climate, management. *Application contact:* David Hannum, Admissions Advisor, 800-603-3756, E-mail: hannumd@uiu.edu.

Utah State University, School of Graduate Studies, College of Business, School of Accountancy, Logan, UT 84322. Offers M Acc. *Accreditation:* AACSB. Part-time programs available. *Entrance requirements:* For master's, GMAT, minimum GPA of 3.0, 3 recommendation letters. Additional exam requirements/recommendations for international students: Required—TOEFL. *Faculty research:* Relationship theory, enterprise systems, just in time/loan, reported earnings measures, accounting education.

Utica College, Program in Accountancy, Utica, NY 13502-4892. Offers MBA. Part-time and evening/weekend programs available. Postbaccalaureate distance learning degree programs offered. *Faculty:* 7 full-time (0 women). *Students:* 18 part-time (13 women); includes 3 minority (2 African Americans, 1 Hispanic American). Average age 37. In 2009, 11 master's awarded. *Entrance requirements:* For master's, BS, minimum GPA of 3.0. Additional exam requirements/recommendations for international students: Required—TOEFL (minimum score 525 paper-based; 195 computer-based). *Application deadline:* Applications are processed on a rolling basis. Application fee: $50. Electronic applications accepted. *Expenses:* Contact institution. *Financial support:* Career-related internships or fieldwork, scholarships/grants, tuition waivers (partial), and unspecified assistantships available. Support available to part-time students. Financial award application deadline: 3/15; financial award applicants required to submit FAFSA. *Unit head:* Dr. Hartwell Herring, MBA Director, 315-792-3335, E-mail: hherring@utica.edu. *Application contact:* John D. Rowe, Director of Graduate Admissions, 315-792-3824, Fax: 315-792-3003, E-mail: jrowe@utica.edu.

Villanova University, Villanova School of Business, Master of Accountancy Program, Villanova, PA 19085. Offers MAC. *Accreditation:* AACSB. *Entrance requirements:* For master's, accounting major or the following pre-requisite courses: intermediate accounting I and II, federal income tax and auditing. Additional exam requirements/recommendations for international students: Required—TOEFL (minimum score 550 paper-based; 213 computer-based; 80 iBT). Electronic applications accepted. *Expenses:* Tuition: Part-time $630 per credit. Required fees: $60 per credit. Part-time tuition and fees vary according to degree level and program. *Faculty research:* Global accounting standards, strategic planning and cost measurement, performance evaluation, the impact of e-business on the business value chain.

Virginia Commonwealth University, Graduate School, School of Business, Program in Accounting, Richmond, VA 23284-9005. Offers M Acc, MBA, PhD. *Accreditation:* AACSB. *Degree requirements:* For doctorate, thesis/dissertation. *Entrance requirements:* For master's, GMAT; for doctorate, GMAT, relevant work experience.

Virginia International University, Business Programs Department, Fairfax, VA 22030. Offers accounting (MBA); executive management (Graduate Certificate); global logistics (MBA); health care management (MBA); human resources management (MBA); international business management (MBA); international finance (MBA); marketing management (MBA). Part-time programs available. *Faculty:* 12 part-time/adjunct (1 woman). *Students:* 138 full-time (63 women), 7 part-time (5 women); includes 7 minority (1 African American, 5 Asian Americans or Pacific Islanders, 1 Hispanic American), 136 international. Average age 27. 331 applicants, 31% accepted, 40 enrolled. In 2009, 42 master's awarded. *Entrance requirements:* For master's and Graduate Certificate, bachelor's degree. Additional exam requirements/recommendations for international students: Required—TOEFL (minimum score 550 paper-based; 213 computer-based; 80 iBT), IELTS (minimum score 6). *Application deadline:* For fall admission, 7/31 for domestic students, 7/3 for international students; for spring admission, 12/18 for domestic students, 11/20 for international students. Applications are processed on a rolling basis. Application fee: $100. Electronic applications accepted. *Expenses:* Tuition: Full-time $10,044; part-time $569 per credit. One-time fee: $75. Tuition and fees vary according to degree level. *Financial support:* In 2009–10, 10 students received support. Scholarships/grants available. Financial award application deadline: 7/1. *Unit head:* Dr. Gail Whitaker, Chair, 703-591-7042 Ext. 346, Fax: 703-591-7046, E-mail: gwhitaker@viu.edu. *Application contact:* Emily L. Kraus, Director of Admissions, 703-591-7042 Ext. 309, Fax: 703-591-7048, E-mail: admissions@viu.edu.

Virginia Polytechnic Institute and State University, Graduate School, Pamplin College of Business, Department of Accounting and Information Systems, Blacksburg, VA 24061. Offers MACIS, PhD. *Accreditation:* AACSB. *Faculty:* 26 full-time (9 women). *Students:* 112 full-time (57 women), 11 part-time (9 women); includes 39 minority (32 American Indian/Alaska Native, 1 Asian American or Pacific Islander, 6 Hispanic Americans), 3 international. Average age 26. 179 applicants, 57% accepted, 76 enrolled. In 2009, 61 master's, 4 doctorates awarded. *Entrance requirements:* For master's and doctorate, GRE, GMAT. Additional exam requirements/recommendations for international students: Required—TOEFL (minimum score 550 paper-based; 213 computer-based). *Application deadline:* For fall admission, 5/15 for international students; for spring admission, 10/15 for international students. Applications are processed on a rolling basis. Application fee: $65. Electronic applications accepted. *Expenses:* Tuition, area resident: Full-time $10,228; part-time $459 per credit hour. Tuition, nonresident: full-time $17,892; part-time $865 per credit hour. Required fees: $1966; $451 per semester. *Financial support:* In 2009–10, 2 research assistantships with full tuition reimbursements (averaging $19,312 per year), 41 teaching assistantships with full tuition reimbursements (averaging $7,804 per year) were awarded; career-related internships or fieldwork, Federal Work-Study, scholarships/grants, and unspecified assistantships also available. Financial award application deadline: 1/15. *Faculty research:* Financial accounting, international accounting, management accounting. Total annual research expenditures: $277,677. *Unit head:* Dr. Robert M. Brown, Dean, 540-231-6591, Fax: 540-231-2511, E-mail: acis@vt.edu. *Application contact:* Arnita Perfater, Information Contact, 540-231-6592, Fax: 540-231-2511, E-mail: arnita@vt.edu.

Wagner College, Division of Graduate Studies, Department of Business Administration, Program in Accounting, Staten Island, NY 10301-4495. Offers MS. Part-time programs available. *Degree requirements:* For master's, thesis. *Entrance requirements:* For master's, bachelor's degree in accounting or business with a concentration in accounting. Additional exam requirements/recommendations for international students: Required—TOEFL (minimum score 550 paper-based; 217 computer-based). *Expenses:* Tuition: Full-time $15,570; part-time $865 per credit. Required fees: $2.

Wake Forest University, Babcock Graduate School of Management, MSA Program in Accountancy, Winston-Salem, NC 27106. Offers assurance services (MSA); tax consulting (MSA); transaction services (MSA). *Faculty:* 62 full-time (13 women), 36 part-time/adjunct (14 women). *Students:* 113 full-time (57 women); includes 24 minority (13 African Americans, 1 American Indian/Alaska Native, 8 Asian Americans or Pacific Islanders, 2 Hispanic Americans), 10 international. Average age 23. In 2009, 68 master's awarded. *Entrance requirements:* For master's, GMAT, letters of recommendation, official transcripts, current resume or curriculum vitae. Additional exam requirements/recommendations for international students: Required—TOEFL (minimum score 600 paper-based; 250 computer-based; 100 iBT), Pearson Test of English (PTE). *Application deadline:* For fall admission, 6/1 for domestic and international students. Applications are processed on a rolling basis. Application fee: $75. Electronic applications accepted. *Financial support:* In 2009–10, 100 students received support. Career-related internships or fieldwork and scholarships/grants available. Financial award application deadline: 3/1; financial award applicants required to submit FAFSA. *Faculty research:* The influence of personal relationships on business decision making and management of change; drivers of perceived value and consumer behavior; impact of accounting on auditing, financial, managerial, systems and taxation stakeholders; corporate governance and executive compensation; impact of operations strategies on competitiveness. *Unit head:* Yvonne Hinson, Director of Accountancy, 336-758-5422, Fax: 336-758-5830, E-mail: admissions@mba.wfu.edu. *Application contact:* LaKesha Alston, Administrative Assistant, 336-758-5422, Fax: 336-758-5830, E-mail: admissions@mba.wfu.edu.

Wake Forest University, Graduate School of Arts and Sciences, Department of Accountancy, Winston-Salem, NC 27109. Offers MSA. *Accreditation:* AACSB. *Entrance requirements:* For master's, GMAT. Additional exam requirements/recommendations for international students: Required—TOEFL (minimum score 213 computer-based). Electronic applications accepted.

Walden University, Graduate Programs, School of Management, Minneapolis, MN 55401. Offers applied management and decision sciences (PhD), including accounting, engineering management, finance, general applied management and decision sciences, information systems management, knowledge management, leadership and organizational change, learning management, operations research, self-designed program in applied management and design sciences; business information management (MISM); enterprise information security (MISM); entrepreneurship (MBA, DBA); finance (MBA, DBA); global supply chain management (DBA); healthcare management (MBA); healthcare system improvement (MBA); human resource management (MBA); information systems management (DBA); international business (MBA, DBA); IT strategy and governance (MISM); leadership (MBA, MS, DBA), including entrepreneurship (MS), general management (MS), human resources leadership (MS), innovation and technology (MS), leader development (MS), project management (MS), self-designed (MS), sustainable futures (MS); managing global software and service supply chains (MISM); marketing (MBA, DBA); project management (MBA, MS); risk management (MBA); self-designed (MBA, DBA); social impact management (DBA); sustainable futures (MBA); technology (MBA); technology entrepreneurship (DBA). Part-time and evening/weekend programs available. Postbaccalaureate distance learning degree programs offered (minimal on-campus study). *Faculty:* 17 full-time, 211 part-time/adjunct. *Students:* 3,389 full-time (1,774 women), 815 part-time (482 women); includes 1,969 minority (1,640 African Americans, 36 American Indian/Alaska Native, 123 Asian Americans or Pacific Islanders, 170 Hispanic Americans), 95 international. Average age 41. In 2009, 699 master's, 42 doctorates awarded. *Degree requirements:* For doctorate, thesis/dissertation (for some programs), residency. *Entrance requirements:* For master's, bachelor's degree or equivalent in related field; minimum GPA of 2.5; official transcripts; goal statement; access to computer and Internet; for doctorate, master's degree or equivalent in related field; minimum GPA of 3.0; 3 years of related professional/academic experience (preferred). Additional exam requirements/recommendations for international students: Required—TOEFL (minimum score 550 paper-based; 213 computer-based), IELTS (minimum score 6.5), TOEFL, IELTS, or Michigan English Language Assessment Battery (minimum score 82). *Application deadline:* Applications are processed on a rolling basis. Application fee: $50. Electronic applications accepted. *Expenses:* Tuition: Full-time $13,665; part-time $560 per credit. Required fees: $1375. Tuition and fees vary according to course load, degree level and program. *Financial support:* In 2009–10, 466 students received support; fellowships, Federal Work-Study, scholarships/grants, unspecified assistantships, and family tuition reduction, active duty/veteran tuition reduction, group tuition reduction, interest-free payment plans available. Support available to part-time students. Financial award applicants required to submit FAFSA. *Unit head:* William Schulz, Interim Associate Dean, 800-925-3368. *Application contact:* Jennifer Hall, Director of Enrollment, 866-4-WALDEN, E-mail: info@waldenu.edu.

Walsh College of Accountancy and Business Administration, Graduate Programs, Program in Accountancy, Troy, MI 48007-7006. Offers MSPA. Part-time and evening/weekend programs available. *Faculty:* 3 full-time (1 woman), 6 part-time/adjunct (2 women). *Students:* 26 full-time (11 women), 276 part-time (165 women); includes 60 minority (34 African Americans, 24 Asian Americans or Pacific Islanders, 2 Hispanic Americans), 15 international. Average age 32. *Degree requirements:* For master's, thesis optional. *Entrance requirements:* For master's, minimum GPA of 2.75, previous course work in business. Additional exam requirements/recommendations for international students: Required—TOEFL. *Application deadline:* For fall admission, 8/24 priority date for domestic students; for winter admission, 1/1 priority date for domestic students; for spring admission, 4/1 priority date for domestic students. Applications are processed on a rolling basis. Application fee: $25. Electronic applications accepted. *Expenses:* Tuition: Part-time $525 per credit. Required fees: $125 per semester. *Financial support:* Available to part-time students. Application deadline: 6/30. *Unit head:* Rick Bershbeck, Director, 248-823-1345, Fax: 248-689-0920. *Application contact:* Karen Mahaffy, Director of Admissions and Academic Advising, 248-823-1610, Fax: 248-689-0938, E-mail: kmahaffy@walshcollege.edu.

Washington State University, Graduate School, College of Business, Department of Accounting and Business Law, Pullman, WA 99164. Offers accounting and information systems (M Acc); accounting and taxation (M Acc). *Accreditation:* AACSB. *Faculty:* 9. *Students:* 36 full-time (16 women), 6 part-time (5 women); includes 5 minority (3 Asian Americans or Pacific Islanders, 2 Hispanic Americans), 11 international. Average age 27. 114 applicants, 42% accepted, 30 enrolled. In 2009, 25 master's awarded. *Degree requirements:* For master's, comprehensive exam (for some programs), thesis (for some programs), oral exam, research paper. *Entrance requirements:* For master's, GMAT (minimum score of 600), resume; statement of purpose identifying area of interest, experiences, and intended research focus; minimum GPA of 3.25. Additional exam requirements/recommendations for international students: Required—TOEFL (minimum score 580 paper-based; 237 computer-based), IELTS. *Application deadline:* For fall admission, 1/10 priority date for domestic students, 1/10 for international students. Applications are processed on a rolling basis. Application fee: $50. Electronic applications accepted. *Financial support:* In 2009–10, 19 students received support, including 1 fellowship (averaging $5,500 per year), research assistantships (averaging $13,917 per year), 8 teaching assistantships with tuition reimbursements available (averaging $13,056 per year); Federal Work-Study, institutionally sponsored loans, tuition waivers (partial), and teaching associateships also available. Financial award application deadline: 3/1. *Faculty research:* Ethics, taxation, auditing. *Unit head:* Dr. John Sweeney, Chair, 509-335-8541, Fax: 509-335-4275, E-mail: jtsweeney@wsu.edu. *Application contact:* Graduate School Admissions, 800-GRADWSU, Fax: 509-335-1949, E-mail: gradsch@wsu.edu.

Washington State University, Graduate School, College of Business, Graduate Programs in Business, Pullman, WA 99164. Offers accounting and business law (M Acc); business administration (MBA, PhD), including accounting (PhD), finance (PhD), management and operations (PhD), management information systems (PhD), marketing (PhD). *Accreditation:* AACSB. *Degree requirements:* For master's, comprehensive exam (for some programs), thesis (for some programs), final presentation; for doctorate, comprehensive exam, thesis/dissertation, oral and written exams. *Entrance requirements:* For master's and doctorate, GMAT, minimum GPA of 3.0, 3 letters of recommendation. Additional exam requirements/recommendations for international students: Required—TOEFL. Electronic applications accepted.

See Display on page 193.

Washington University in St. Louis, Olin Business School, Program in Accounting, St. Louis, MO 63130-4899. Offers MS. Part-time programs available. *Faculty:* 73 full-time (14 women), 45 part-time/adjunct (7 women). *Students:* 34 full-time (25 women); includes 2 Asian Americans or Pacific Islanders, 1 Hispanic American, 18 international. 180 applicants, 28% accepted, 33 enrolled. In 2009, 16 master's awarded. *Entrance requirements:* For master's, GMAT or GRE. Additional exam requirements/recommendations for international students: Required—TOEFL. *Application deadline:* For fall admission, 11/9 for domestic and international students; for winter admission, 2/8 for domestic and international students; for spring admission, 3/8 for domestic students. Application fee: $100. Electronic applications accepted. *Financial support:* Applicants required to submit FAFSA. *Unit head:* Joseph Peter Fox, Associate Dean and Director of MBA Programs, 314-935-6322, Fax: 314-935-4464, E-mail: fox@wustl.edu. *Application contact:* Dr. Gary Hochberg, Director, Specialized Master's Programs, 314-935-6380, Fax: 314-935-4464, E-mail: hochberg@wustl.edu.

Wayne State University, School of Business Administration, Detroit, MI 48202. Offers accounting (MS); business administration (MBA, PhD); interdisciplinary studies (PhD); taxation

Accounting

Wayne State University (continued)
(MS); JD/MBA. *Accreditation:* AACSB. Part-time and evening/weekend programs available. *Degree requirements:* For master's, thesis optional. *Entrance requirements:* For master's, GMAT, minimum undergraduate GPA of 2.50. Additional exam requirements/recommendations for international students: Required—TOEFL (minimum score 550 paper-based; 213 computer-based); Recommended—TWE (minimum score 6). Electronic applications accepted. *Faculty research:* Corporate financial valuation, strategic advertising, information technology effectiveness, financial accounting and taxation, organizational performance and effectiveness.

See Close-Up on page 279.

Webber International University, Graduate School of Business, Babson Park, FL 33827-0096. Offers accounting (MBA); management (MBA); security management (MBA); sports management (MBA). Part-time and evening/weekend programs available. *Degree requirements:* For master's, thesis or alternative. *Entrance requirements:* For master's, previous course work in financial and managerial accounting. Additional exam requirements/recommendations for international students: Required—TOEFL. *Faculty research:* Finance strategy, market research, investments, intranet.

See Close-Up on page 281.

Weber State University, John B. Goddard School of Business and Economics, School of Accountancy, Ogden, UT 84408-1001. Offers M Acc. *Accreditation:* AACSB. Part-time programs available. *Entrance requirements:* For master's, GMAT. *Faculty research:* Taxation, financial accounting, auditing, managerial accounting, accounting education.

Western Carolina University, Graduate School, College of Business, Program in Accountancy, Cullowhee, NC 28723. Offers M Ac. Part-time and evening/weekend programs available. *Students:* 18 full-time (5 women), 29 part-time (21 women). Average age 33. 37 applicants, 76% accepted, 23 enrolled. In 2009, 24 master's awarded. *Entrance requirements:* For master's, GMAT, appropriate undergraduate degree, 3 letters of recommendation. Additional exam requirements/recommendations for international students: Required—TOEFL (minimum score 550 paper-based; 270 computer-based; 79 iBT). *Application deadline:* For fall admission, 5/1 priority date for domestic students; for spring admission, 9/1 priority date for domestic students. Applications are processed on a rolling basis. Application fee: $45. *Financial support:* In 2009–10, 6 students received support, including 5 research assistantships with full and partial tuition reimbursements available (averaging $6,750 per year); fellowships, teaching assistantships with full and partial tuition reimbursements available, career-related internships or fieldwork, institutionally sponsored loans, scholarships/grants, and unspecified assistantships also available. Financial award application deadline: 3/31; financial award applicants required to submit FAFSA. *Unit head:* Dr. Susan Swanger, Director, 828-227-3525, Fax: 828-227-7414, E-mail: swanger@email.wcu.edu. *Application contact:* Admissions Specialist for Accountancy, 828-227-7398, Fax: 828-227-7480, E-mail: gradsch@email.wcu.edu.

Western Connecticut State University, Division of Graduate Studies, Ancell School of Business, Program in Business Administration, Danbury, CT 06810-6885. Offers accounting (MBA); business administration (MBA). Part-time programs available. *Faculty:* 7 full-time (1 woman). *Students:* 1 (woman) full-time, 53 part-time (30 women); includes 1 minority (Asian American or Pacific Islander), 1 international. Average age 32. 39 applicants, 69% accepted, 21 enrolled. In 2009, 15 master's awarded. *Degree requirements:* For master's, comprehensive exam, completion of program within 8 years. *Entrance requirements:* For master's, GMAT. Additional exam requirements/recommendations for international students: Recommended—TOEFL (minimum score 550 paper-based; 213 computer-based; 79 iBT), IELTS (minimum score 6). *Application deadline:* For fall admission, 8/5 priority date for domestic students; for spring admission, 1/5 priority date for domestic students. Applications are processed on a rolling basis. Application fee: $50. *Expenses:* Tuition, state resident: full-time $5012; part-time $278 per credit hour. Tuition, nonresident: full-time $13,962; part-time $284 per credit hour. Required fees: $3886; $139 per credit hour. Full-time tuition and fees vary according to course load and program. Part-time tuition and fees vary according to course level, degree level and program. *Financial support:* In 2009–10, 1 student received support. Application deadline: 5/1. *Unit head:* Dr. Fred Tesch, MBA Coordinator, 203-837-8654, Fax: 203-837-8527. *Application contact:* Chris Shankle, Associate Director of Graduate Studies, 203-837-9005, Fax: 203-837-8326, E-mail: shanklec@wcsu.edu.

Western Illinois University, School of Graduate Studies, College of Business and Technology, Department of Accountancy, Macomb, IL 61455-1390. Offers M Acct. *Accreditation:* AACSB. Part-time programs available. *Students:* 12 full-time (5 women), 2 part-time (1 woman), 3 international. Average age 24. 15 applicants, 40% accepted. In 2009, 4 master's awarded. *Degree requirements:* For master's, thesis or alternative. *Entrance requirements:* For master's, GMAT. Additional exam requirements/recommendations for international students: Required—TOEFL (minimum score 550 paper-based; 213 computer-based; 80 iBT). *Application deadline:* Applications are processed on a rolling basis. Application fee: $30. Electronic applications accepted. *Expenses:* Tuition, state resident: full-time $4486; part-time $249.21 per credit hour. Tuition, nonresident: full-time $8972; part-time $498.42 per credit hour. Required fees: $72.62 per credit hour. *Financial support:* In 2009–10, 10 students received support, including 10 research assistantships with full tuition reimbursements available (averaging $7,280 per year). Financial award applicants required to submit FAFSA. *Unit head:* Dr. Hassanali Espahbodi, Chairperson, 309-298-1152. *Application contact:* Evelyn Hoing, Assistant Director of Graduate Studies, 309-298-1806, Fax: 309-298-2345, E-mail: grad-office@wiu.edu.

Western Michigan University, Graduate College, Haworth College of Business, Department of Accountancy, Kalamazoo, MI 49008. Offers MSA. *Accreditation:* AACSB. *Faculty:* 15 full-time (4 women). *Students:* 7 full-time (4 women), 2 part-time (both women), 2 international. 9 applicants, 67% accepted, 0 enrolled. In 2009, 7 master's awarded. *Entrance requirements:* For master's, GMAT. *Application deadline:* For fall admission, 2/15 priority date for domestic students. Applications are processed on a rolling basis. Application fee: $25. *Financial support:* Fellowships, research assistantships, teaching assistantships, Federal Work-Study available. Financial award application deadline: 2/15; financial award applicants required to submit FAFSA. *Unit head:* Dr. Don Gribbin, Chairperson, 269-387-5209. *Application contact:* Admissions and Orientation, 269-387-2000, Fax: 269-387-2355.

Western New England College, School of Business, Program in Accounting, Springfield, MA 01119. Offers MSA. Part-time and evening/weekend programs available. *Students:* 47 part-time (25 women); includes 3 African Americans. In 2009, 18 master's awarded. *Entrance requirements:* For master's, GMAT, 2 letters of reference, resume. *Application deadline:* Applications are processed on a rolling basis. Application fee: $30. *Expenses:* Tuition: Part-time $552 per credit hour. Part-time tuition and fees vary according to program. *Financial support:* Available to part-time students. Applicants required to submit FAFSA. *Unit head:* Dr. William Bosworth, Chair, Accounting and Finance, 413-782-1231, E-mail: wboswort@wnec.edu. *Application contact:* Matt Fox, Director of Recruiting and Marketing for Adult Learners, 413-782-1249, Fax: 413-782-1779, E-mail: ce@wnec.edu.

Westminster College, The Bill and Vieve Gore School of Business, Salt Lake City, UT 84105-3697. Offers accountancy (M Acc); business administration (MBA, Certificate); technology management (MBATM). *Accreditation:* ACBSP. Part-time and evening/weekend programs available. *Faculty:* 27 full-time (7 women), 28 part-time/adjunct (5 women). *Students:* 189 full-time (36 women), 286 part-time (71 women); includes 32 minority (3 African Americans, 17 Asian Americans or Pacific Islanders, 12 Hispanic Americans), 5 international. Average age 32. 410 applicants, 48% accepted, 167 enrolled. In 2009, 141 master's, 44 other advanced degrees awarded. *Degree requirements:* For master's, international trip, minimum grade of C in all classes. *Entrance requirements:* For master's, GMAT, 2 professional recommendations, employer letter of support, personal resume. Additional exam requirements/recommendations for international students: Required—TOEFL (minimum score 600 paper-based; 214 computer-based; 100 iBT), IELTS (minimum score 7). *Application deadline:* Applications are processed on a rolling basis. Application fee: $40. Electronic applications accepted. *Expenses:* Contact institution. *Financial support:* In 2009–10, 205 students received support. Career-related internships or fieldwork and tuition reimbursement, tuition remission available. Support available to part-time students. Financial award applicants required to submit FAFSA. *Faculty research:* Innovation and entrepreneurship, business strategy and change, financial analysis and capital budgeting, leadership development. Total annual research expenditures: $100,000. *Unit head:* John Groesbeck, Dean, 801-832-2600, Fax: 801-832-3106, E-mail: jgroesbeck@westminstercollege.edu. *Application contact:* Joel Bauman, Vice President of Enrollment Services, 801-832-2200, Fax: 801-832-3101, E-mail: admission@westminstercollege.edu.

West Texas A&M University, College of Business, Department of Accounting, Economics, and Finance, Program in Accounting, Canyon, TX 79016-0001. Offers MP Acc. Part-time and evening/weekend programs available. Postbaccalaureate distance learning degree programs offered (minimal on-campus study). *Degree requirements:* For master's, comprehensive exam, thesis optional. *Entrance requirements:* For master's, GMAT. Additional exam requirements/recommendations for international students: Required—TOEFL (minimum score 550 paper-based). Electronic applications accepted. *Faculty research:* Texas economy, service learnings, small business, entrepreneurship, corporation conversion.

West Texas A&M University, College of Business, Department of Accounting, Economics, and Finance, Program in Accounting/Business Administration, Canyon, TX 79016-0001. Offers professional accounting (MPA). Integrated program that allows students to enter program as undergraduates; after bachelor's degree in business administration is earned they progress into graduate accounting phase. Part-time programs available. Postbaccalaureate distance learning degree programs offered (minimal on-campus study). *Entrance requirements:* For master's, GMAT. Additional exam requirements/recommendations for international students: Required—TOEFL (minimum score 550 paper-based). Electronic applications accepted.

West Virginia University, College of Business and Economics, Division of Accounting, Morgantown, WV 26506. Offers MPA. *Accreditation:* AACSB. Part-time and evening/weekend programs available. *Entrance requirements:* For master's, GMAT (minimum 50th percentile), BS in accounting or equivalent, minimum GPA of 3.0. Additional exam requirements/recommendations for international students: Required—TOEFL. Electronic applications accepted. *Faculty research:* Financial reporting, government/not-for-profit accounting, information systems/technology, forensic accounting, internal control.

Wheeling Jesuit University, Department of Business, Wheeling, WV 26003-6295. Offers accounting (MS); business administration (MBA). *Accreditation:* ACBSP. Part-time and evening/weekend programs available. *Faculty:* 6 full-time (0 women), 3 part-time/adjunct (0 women). *Students:* 33 full-time (14 women), 30 part-time (14 women); includes 3 minority (2 African Americans, 1 Asian American or Pacific Islander), 7 international. Average age 28. 27 applicants, 96% accepted, 19 enrolled. In 2009, 20 master's awarded. *Entrance requirements:* For master's, GMAT, minimum undergraduate GPA of 2.8. Additional exam requirements/recommendations for international students: Required—TOEFL (minimum score 600 paper-based; 250 computer-based; 80 iBT). *Application deadline:* For fall admission, 8/1 priority date for domestic students, 8/1 for international students; for spring admission, 12/15 priority date for domestic students, 12/1 for international students. Applications are processed on a rolling basis. Application fee: $25. Electronic applications accepted. *Expenses:* Tuition: Full-time $9000; part-time $500 per credit hour. Required fees: $195 per semester. One-time fee: $375. Tuition and fees vary according to program. *Financial support:* In 2009–10, 47 students received support. Career-related internships or fieldwork and unspecified assistantships available. Financial award application deadline: 8/1; financial award applicants required to submit FAFSA. *Faculty research:* Forensic economics, philosophic economics, consumer behavior, international business, economic development. *Unit head:* Dr. Edward W. Younkins, Director, 304-243-2255, Fax: 304-243-8703, E-mail: younkins@wju.edu. *Application contact:* Melissa Rataiczak, Director of Admissions, Professional and Graduate Studies, 304-243-2250, Fax: 304-243-4441, E-mail: mrataiczak@wju.edu.

Wichita State University, Graduate School, W. Frank Barton School of Business, School of Accountancy, Wichita, KS 67260. Offers M Acc. *Accreditation:* AACSB. Part-time and evening/weekend programs available. *Expenses:* Tuition, state resident: full-time $4247; part-time $235.95 per credit hour. Tuition, nonresident: full-time $11,171; part-time $620.60 per credit hour. Required fees: $34; $3.60 per credit hour. $17 per term. Tuition and fees vary according to campus/location and program. *Unit head:* Dr. Paul D. Harrison, Director, 316-978-3215, Fax: 316-978-3660, E-mail: paul.harrison@wichita.edu. *Application contact:* Michael B. Flores, Assistant Director and Graduate Advisor, 316-978-3724, E-mail: michael.flores@wichita.edu.

Widener University, School of Business Administration, Program in Accounting Information Systems, Chester, PA 19013-5792. Offers MS. Part-time and evening/weekend programs available. *Faculty:* 6 full-time (2 women), 3 part-time/adjunct (0 women). *Students:* 1 full-time (0 women), 4 part-time (2 women), 1 international. Average age 36. 9 applicants, 100% accepted. In 2009, 5 master's awarded. *Entrance requirements:* For master's, Certified Management Accountant Exam, Certified Public Accountant Exam, or GMAT, minimum GPA of 2.5. *Application deadline:* For fall admission, 8/1 priority date for domestic students; for spring admission, 12/1 for domestic students. Applications are processed on a rolling basis. Application fee: $25 ($300 for international students). Electronic applications accepted. *Financial support:* Application deadline: 5/1. *Unit head:* Frank C. Lordi, Head, 610-499-4308, E-mail: frank.c.lordi@widener.edu. *Application contact:* Ann Seltzer, Graduate Enrollment Administrator, 610-499-4305, E-mail: apseltzer@widener.edu.

Wilkes University, College of Graduate and Professional Studies, Jay S. Sidhu School of Business and Leadership, Wilkes-Barre, PA 18766-0002. Offers accounting (MBA); entrepreneurship (MBA); finance (MBA); human resource management (MBA); international business (MBA); management (MBA); marketing (MBA). *Accreditation:* ACBSP. Part-time and evening/weekend programs available. *Students:* 86 full-time (41 women), 118 part-time (59 women); includes 7 minority (4 African Americans, 1 Asian American or Pacific Islander, 2 Hispanic Americans), 48 international. Average age 29. In 2009, 59 master's awarded. *Entrance requirements:* For master's, GMAT. Additional exam requirements/recommendations for international students: Required—TOEFL (minimum score 500 paper-based; 173 computer-based; 79 iBT). *Application deadline:* Applications are processed on a rolling basis. Application fee: $45. *Expenses:* Contact institution. *Financial support:* Federal Work-Study and unspecified assistantships available. Financial award application deadline: 3/1; financial award applicants required to submit FAFSA. *Unit head:* Dr. Paul Browne, Dean, 570-408-4701, Fax: 570-408-7846, E-mail: paul.browne@wilkes.edu. *Application contact:* Kathleen Houlihan, Director of Graduate Studies, 570-408-3235, Fax: 570-408-7846, E-mail: kathleen.houlihan@wilkes.edu.

Worcester State College, Graduate Studies, Program in Management, Worcester, MA 01602-2597. Offers accounting (MS); organizational leadership (MS). *Faculty:* 4 full-time (3 women), 1 part-time/adjunct (0 women). *Students:* 2 full-time (0 women), 12 part-time (5 women); includes 1 minority (African American), 2 international. Average age 28. 17 applicants, 59% accepted, 1 enrolled. In 2009, 7 master's awarded. *Degree requirements:* For master's, comprehensive exam (for some programs), thesis optional. *Entrance requirements:* Additional exam requirements/recommendations for international students: Required—TOEFL (minimum score 550 paper-based; 213 computer-based; 79 iBT). *Application deadline:* Applications are processed on a rolling basis. Application fee: $30. *Expenses:* Tuition, area resident: Part-time $150 per credit. Tuition, state resident: part-time $150 per credit. Tuition, nonresident: part-time $150 per credit. Required fees: $85. *Financial support:* In 2009–10, 3 students received support, including 3 research assistantships with full tuition reimbursements available (averaging $4,800 per year); career-related internships or fieldwork, scholarships/grants, and unspecified assistantships also available. Financial award application deadline: 3/1; financial award applicants required to submit FAFSA. *Unit head:* Dr. Elizabeth Wark, Coordinator, 508-929-8743, Fax: 508-929-8048, E-mail: ewark@worcester.edu. *Application contact:* Nicole Brown, Assistant Dean of Continuing Education, 508-929-8787, Fax: 508-929-8100, E-mail: nbrown@worcester.edu.

Wright State University, School of Graduate Studies, Raj Soin College of Business, Department of Accountancy, Accountancy Program, Dayton, OH 45435. Offers M Acc.

Yale University, Yale School of Management and Graduate School of Arts and Sciences, Doctoral Program in Management, New Haven, CT 06520. Offers accounting (PhD); financial economics (PhD); marketing (PhD). *Accreditation:* AACSB. *Faculty:* 68 full-time (12 women). *Students:* 30 full-time (9 women), 13 international. Average age 28. 372 applicants, 7% accepted, 13 enrolled. In 2009, 5 doctorates awarded. *Degree requirements:* For doctorate, comprehensive exam, thesis/dissertation. *Entrance requirements:* For doctorate, GMAT or GRE General Test. Additional exam requirements/recommendations for international students: Required—TOEFL, IELTS. *Application deadline:* For fall admission, 1/2 for domestic and international students. Application fee: $85. Electronic applications accepted. *Expenses:* Contact institution. *Financial support:* In 2009–10, 29 students received support, including 29 fellowships with full tuition reimbursements available, 29 research assistantships with full tuition reimbursements available, 29 teaching assistantships with full tuition reimbursements available; institutionally sponsored loans, scholarships/grants, and health care benefits also available. Financial award application deadline: 1/2. *Faculty research:* Pricing of options and futures, term structure of interest rates, use of accounting numbers in debt contracts, product differentiation, e-commerce and marketing, behavioral finance. *Unit head:* Carla Mills, Registrar, 203-432-3955, Fax: 203-432-0342, E-mail: carla.mills@yale.edu. *Application contact:* Carla Mills, Registrar, 203-432-3955, Fax: 203-432-0342, E-mail: carla.mills@yale.edu.

See Close-Up on page 283.

Yeshiva University, Sy Syms School of Business, New York, NY 10016. Offers accounting (MS). Part-time programs available. *Faculty:* 6 full-time (0 women). *Students:* 9 full-time (2 women), 4 part-time (1 woman). Average age 22. *Entrance requirements:* For master's, minimum GPA of 3.5 or GMAT. *Application deadline:* For fall admission, 6/15 priority date for domestic students; for spring admission, 12/1 priority date for domestic students. Applications are processed on a rolling basis. Application fee: $50. *Expenses:* Tuition: Full-time $24,918; part-time $1022 per credit. Required fees: $175. *Financial support:* Scholarships/grants available. *Unit head:* Margie Martin, Associate Director of Program Recruitment, 917-326-4852, E-mail: mmartin4@yu.edu. *Application contact:* Michael Kranzler, Associate Director of Admissions, 212-960-5277, Fax: 212-960-0086.

Youngstown State University, Graduate School, Williamson College of Business Administration, Department of Accounting and Finance, Youngstown, OH 44555-0001. Offers accounting (MBA). *Accreditation:* AACSB. Part-time and evening/weekend programs available. *Degree requirements:* For master's, thesis optional. *Entrance requirements:* For master's, GMAT, minimum GPA of 2.7. Additional exam requirements/recommendations for international students: Required—TOEFL. *Faculty research:* Taxation and compliance, capital markets, accounting information systems, accounting theory, tax and government accounting.

Finance and Banking

Adelphi University, School of Business, Graduate Opportunity for Accelerated Learning MBA Program, Garden City, NY 11530-0701. Offers accounting (MBA); finance (MBA). *Accreditation:* AACSB. Part-time and evening/weekend programs available. *Students:* 4 full-time (3 women), 25 part-time (13 women); includes 11 minority (8 African Americans, 1 Asian American or Pacific Islander, 2 Hispanic Americans), 1 international. Average age 35. In 2009, 14 master's awarded. *Entrance requirements:* For master's, GMAT, 2 letters of recommendation. Additional exam requirements/recommendations for international students: Required—TOEFL (minimum score 550 paper-based; 213 computer-based; 80 iBT). *Application deadline:* For fall admission, 4/1 for international students; for spring admission, 11/1 for international students. Applications are processed on a rolling basis. Application fee: $50. Electronic applications accepted. *Expenses:* Tuition: Full-time $28,340; part-time $830 per credit. Required fees: $600; $250 per credit. Full-time tuition and fees vary according to course load and program. *Financial support:* Research assistantships with full and partial tuition reimbursements, career-related internships or fieldwork, Federal Work-Study, institutionally sponsored loans, scholarships/grants, and unspecified assistantships available. Financial award application deadline: 3/1; financial award applicants required to submit FAFSA. *Faculty research:* Capital market, executive compensation, business ethics, classical value theory, labor economics. *Unit head:* Rakesh Gupta, Chairperson, 516-877-4670, Fax: 516-877-4607, E-mail: gradbusinquiries@adelphi.edu. *Application contact:* Christine Murphy, Director of Admissions, 516-877-3050, Fax: 516-877-3039, E-mail: graduateadmissions@adelphi.edu.

Adelphi University, School of Business, MBA Program, Garden City, NY 11530-0701. Offers finance (MBA); management information systems (MBA); management/human resource management (MBA); marketing/e-commerce (MBA). *Accreditation:* AACSB. Part-time and evening/weekend programs available. *Students:* 77 full-time (30 women), 183 part-time (91 women); includes 56 minority (29 African Americans, 17 Asian Americans or Pacific Islanders, 10 Hispanic Americans), 81 international. Average age 30. In 2009, 64 master's awarded. *Degree requirements:* For master's, capstone course. *Entrance requirements:* For master's, GMAT, 2 letters of recommendation. Additional exam requirements/recommendations for international students: Required—TOEFL (minimum score 550 paper-based; 213 computer-based; 80 iBT). *Application deadline:* For fall admission, 4/1 for international students; for spring admission, 11/1 for international students. Applications are processed on a rolling basis. Application fee: $50. Electronic applications accepted. *Expenses:* Tuition: Full-time $28,340; part-time $830 per credit. Required fees: $600; $250 per credit. Full-time tuition and fees vary according to course load and program. *Financial support:* Research assistantships with full and partial tuition reimbursements, career-related internships or fieldwork, Federal Work-Study, institutionally sponsored loans, scholarships/grants, and unspecified assistantships available. Financial award application deadline: 3/1; financial award applicants required to submit FAFSA. *Faculty research:* Supply chain management, distribution channels, productivity benchmark analysis, data envelopment analysis, financial portfolio analysis. *Unit head:* Rakesh Gupta, 516-877-4670, Fax: 516-877-4607, E-mail: gradbusinquiries@adelphi.edu. *Application contact:* Christine Murphy, Director of Admissions, 516-877-3050, Fax: 516-877-3039, E-mail: graduateadmissions@adelphi.edu.

Alliant International University–San Diego, Marshall Goldsmith School of Management, Business and Management Division, San Diego, CA 92131-1799. Offers business administration (MBA); information and technology management (DBA); international business (MIBA, DBA), including finance (DBA), marketing (DBA); strategic business (DBA); sustainable management (MBA); MBA/MA; MBA/PhD. Part-time and evening/weekend programs available. *Degree requirements:* For doctorate, thesis/dissertation. *Entrance requirements:* For master's, GMAT, minimum GPA of 3.0; for doctorate, GMAT, minimum GPA of 3.3. Additional exam requirements/recommendations for international students: Required—TOEFL (minimum score 550 paper-based; 213 computer-based), TWE (minimum score 5). Electronic applications accepted. *Faculty research:* Consumer behavior, international business, strategic management, information systems.

The American College, Richard D. Irwin Graduate School, Bryn Mawr, PA 19010-2105. Offers financial services (MSFS); leadership (MSM). Part-time and evening/weekend programs available. Postbaccalaureate distance learning degree programs offered (minimal on-campus study). Electronic applications accepted. *Faculty research:* Retirement counseling, social security, aging, family composition, inflation.

American College of Thessaloniki, Department of Business Administration, Pylea, Greece. Offers banking and finance (MBA); entrepreneurship (MBA, Certificate); finance (Certificate); management (MBA, Certificate); marketing (MBA, Certificate). Part-time and evening/weekend programs available. *Faculty:* 6 full-time (1 woman), 10 part-time/adjunct (2 women). *Students:* 6 full-time (3 women), 44 part-time (30 women), 17 international. 25 applicants, 96% accepted, 24 enrolled. *Degree requirements:* For master's, thesis. *Entrance requirements:* For master's, bachelor's degree. *Application deadline:* For fall admission, 9/30 priority date for domestic students; for spring admission, 2/18 priority date for domestic students. Applications are processed on a rolling basis. Application fee: $70. Electronic applications accepted. *Unit head:* Dr. Nikolaos Kourkoumelis, Chair, Business Division, 30-310-398386, E-mail: nikolaos@act.edu. *Application contact:* Elli Konstantinou, Director of Student Recruitment, 30-310-398238, E-mail: elli@act.edu.

American InterContinental University Buckhead Campus, Program in Business Administration, Atlanta, GA 30326-1016. Offers accounting and finance (MBA); management (MBA); marketing (MBA). Evening/weekend programs available. Postbaccalaureate distance learning degree programs offered. *Entrance requirements:* For master's, minimum cumulative undergraduate GPA of 2.0. Additional exam requirements/recommendations for international students: Required—TOEFL (minimum score 530 paper-based; 230 computer-based). Electronic applications accepted. *Faculty research:* Leadership management, international advertising.

American InterContinental University Online, Program in Business Administration, Hoffman Estates, IL 60192. Offers accounting and finance (MBA); finance (MBA); healthcare management (MBA); human resource management (MBA); international business (MBA); management (MBA); marketing (MBA); operations management (MBA); organizational psychology and development (MBA); project management (MBA). Evening/weekend programs available. Postbaccalaureate distance learning degree programs offered (no on-campus study). *Entrance requirements:* Additional exam requirements/recommendations for international students: Required—TOEFL (minimum score 550 paper-based; 213 computer-based). Electronic applications accepted.

American InterContinental University South Florida, Program in International Business, Weston, FL 33326. Offers accounting and finance (MBA); human resource management (MBA); management (MBA); marketing (MBA). Part-time and evening/weekend programs available. Postbaccalaureate distance learning degree programs offered. Electronic applications accepted.

American International College, School of Business Administration, MBA Program, Springfield, MA 01109-3189. Offers accounting (MBA); corporate/public communication (MBA); finance (MBA); general business (MBA); hospitality, hotel and service management (MBA); international business (MBA); international business practice (MBA); management (MBA); management information systems (MBA); marketing (MBA). International business practice program developed in cooperation with the Mountbatten Institute. *Expenses:* Tuition: Full-time $12,510; part-time $695 per credit hour. Required fees: $35 per term.

American University, Kogod School of Business, Department of Finance, Program in Finance, Washington, DC 20016-8044. Offers MS. Part-time and evening/weekend programs available. *Students:* 19 full-time (5 women), 11 part-time (1 woman); includes 7 minority (3 African Americans, 3 Asian Americans or Pacific Islanders, 1 Hispanic American), 8 international. Average age 26. In 2009, 1 master's awarded. *Entrance requirements:* For master's, GMAT. Additional exam requirements/recommendations for international students: Required—TOEFL. *Application deadline:* For fall admission, 2/1 priority date for domestic students; for spring admission, 10/1 priority date for domestic students. Applications are processed on a rolling basis. Application fee: $100. *Expenses:* Tuition: Full-time $22,266; part-time $1237 per credit hour. Required fees: $430. Tuition and fees vary according to program. *Financial support:* In 2009–10, 15 students received support; fellowships, research assistantships with partial tuition reimbursements available, career-related internships or fieldwork, Federal Work-Study, institutionally sponsored loans, and tuition waivers (partial) available. Support available to part-time students. Financial award application deadline: 2/1. *Faculty research:* Development finance, market microstructure, international investment, real estate finance, quantitative modeling.

American University, Kogod School of Business, Master of Business Administration Program, Washington, DC 20016-8044. Offers accounting (MBA); consulting (MBA), including information technology, international business, management; corporate finance: commercial banking (MBA); corporate finance: corporate financial management (MBA); corporate finance: investment banking (MBA), including corporate finance and private equity, trading and selling; entrepreneurship (MBA); global emerging markets (MBA), including business, finance, information technology; international trade and global supply chain management (MBA); leadership (MBA); marketing management (MBA); marketing research (MBA); real estate (MBA); MBA/JD; MBA/LL M. Part-time and evening/weekend programs available. *Faculty:* 14 full-time (6 women). *Students:* 133 full-time (56 women), 121 part-time (48 women); includes 54 minority (23 African Americans, 1 American Indian/Alaska Native, 16 Asian Americans or Pacific Islanders, 14 Hispanic Americans), 43 international. Average age 29. 539 applicants, 51% accepted, 86 enrolled. In 2009, 114 master's awarded. *Entrance requirements:* For master's, GMAT. Additional exam requirements/recommendations for international students: Required—TOEFL. *Application deadline:* For fall admission, 2/1 priority date for domestic students; for spring admission, 10/1 priority date for domestic students. Applications are processed on a rolling basis. Application fee: $100. *Expenses:* Contact institution. *Financial support:* In 2009–10, 19 students received support; fellowships, research assistantships with partial tuition reimbursements available, career-related internships or fieldwork, Federal Work-Study, and institutionally sponsored loans available. Support available to part-time students. Financial award application deadline: 2/1. *Faculty research:* Information technology, decision-aiding methodology, negotiation. *Unit head:* Dr. Stevan Holmberg, Chair, 202-885-6193, E-mail: sholmbe@american.edu. *Application contact:* Shannon Demko, Associate Director of Graduate Admissions, 202-885-1994, Fax: 202-885-1108, E-mail: demko@american.edu.

American University, School of Public Affairs, Department of Public Administration, Washington, DC 20016-8070. Offers advanced organization development (Certificate); fundamentals of organization development (Certificate); key executive leadership (MPA); leadership for organizational change (Certificate); non-profit management (Certificate); organization development (MSOD); organizational change (Certificate); public administration (MPA, PhD); public financial management (Certificate); public management (Certificate); public policy (MPP); public policy analysis (Certificate); LL M/MPA; MPA/JD; MPP/JD; MPP/LLM. Part-time and evening/weekend programs available. *Faculty:* 23 full-time (9 women), 13 part-time/adjunct (4 women). *Students:* 184 full-time (117 women), 252 part-time (165 women); includes 109 minority (68 African Americans, 3 American Indian/Alaska Native, 25 Asian Americans or Pacific Islanders, 13 Hispanic Americans), 23 international. Average age 31. 843 applicants, 71% accepted, 156 enrolled. In 2009, 172 master's, 4 doctorates awarded. *Degree requirements:* For master's, comprehensive exam; for doctorate, comprehensive exam, thesis/dissertation. *Entrance requirements:* For master's, GRE, statement of purpose; 2 recommendations; for doctorate, GRE, 3 recommendations; for Certificate, bachelor's degree. Additional exam requirements/recommendations for international students: Required—TOEFL. *Application deadline:* For fall admission, 2/1 for domestic students; for spring admission, 11/1 for domestic students.

Finance and Banking

American University (continued)

Application fee: $55. *Expenses:* Tuition: Full-time $22,266; part-time $1237 per credit hour. Required fees: $430. Tuition and fees vary according to program. *Financial support:* Fellowships, research assistantships, teaching assistantships, career-related internships or fieldwork, Federal Work-Study, and institutionally sponsored loans available. Financial award application deadline: 2/1. *Faculty research:* Urban management, conservation politics, state and local budgeting, tax policy. *Unit head:* Dr. Howard McCurdy, Chair, 202-885-6236, E-mail: mccurdy@american.edu. *Application contact:* Dr. Howard McCurdy, Chair, 202-885-6236, E-mail: mccurdy@american.edu.

The American University in Dubai, Master in Business Administration Program, Dubai, United Arab Emirates. Offers general (MBA); healthcare management (MBA); international finance (MBA); international marketing (MBA); management of construction enterprises (MBA). Part-time and evening/weekend programs available. *Degree requirements:* For master's, thesis optional. *Entrance requirements:* For master's, GMAT, Interview. Additional exam requirements/recommendations for international students: Required—TOEFL (minimum score 550 paper-based; 213 computer-based; 79 iBT). Electronic applications accepted.

Andrew Jackson University, Brian Tracy College of Business and Entrepreneurship, Birmingham, AL 35244. Offers entrepreneurship (MBA); finance (MBA); health services management (MBA); hospitality and tourism management (MBA); human resource management (MBA); international business (MBA); management (MBA); marketing (MBA). Part-time and evening/weekend programs available. Postbaccalaureate distance learning degree programs offered (no on-campus study). *Entrance requirements:* For master's, course work in calculus, statistics, macroeconomics. Additional exam requirements/recommendations for international students: Required—TOEFL (minimum score 550 paper-based; 213 computer-based). Electronic applications accepted.

Andrews University, School of Graduate Studies, School of Business, Graduate Programs in Business, Berrien Springs, MI 49104. Offers MBA, MSA. *Students:* 7 full-time (6 women), 12 part-time (6 women); includes 6 minority (4 African Americans, 1 Asian American or Pacific Islander, 1 Hispanic American), 5 international. Average age 27. 35 applicants, 46% accepted, 10 enrolled. In 2009, 7 master's awarded. *Entrance requirements:* For master's, GMAT. Additional exam requirements/recommendations for international students: Required—TOEFL (minimum score 550 paper-based). Application fee: $40. *Unit head:* Dr. Leonard K. Gashugi, Chair, 769-471-3429, E-mail: gashugi@andrews.edu. *Application contact:* Carolyn Hurst, Supervisor of Graduate Admission, 800-253-2874, Fax: 269-471-6321, E-mail: graduate@andrews.edu.

Argosy University, Atlanta, College of Business, Atlanta, GA 30328. Offers accounting (DBA); corporate compliance (MBA); customized professional concentration (MBA, DBA); finance (MBA); healthcare administration (MBA); information systems (DBA); information systems management (MBA); international business (MBA, DBA); management (MBA, MSM, DBA); marketing (MBA, DBA).

See Close-Up on page 197.

Argosy University, Chicago, College of Business, Chicago, IL 60601. Offers accounting (DBA); customized professional concentration (MBA, DBA); finance (MBA); fraud examination (MBA); global business sustainability (DBA); healthcare administration (MBA); information systems (DBA); information systems management (MBA); international business (MBA, DBA); management (MBA, MSM, DBA); marketing (MBA, DBA); organizational leadership (Ed D); public administration (MBA); sustainable management (MBA). Postbaccalaureate distance learning degree programs offered (minimal on-campus study).

See Close-Up on page 199.

Argosy University, Dallas, College of Business, Farmers Branch, TX 75244. Offers accounting (DBA, AGC); corporate compliance (MBA, Graduate Certificate); customized professional concentration (MBA); finance (MBA, Graduate Certificate); fraud examination (MBA, Graduate Certificate); global business sustainability (DBA, AGC); healthcare administration (Graduate Certificate); healthcare management (MBA); information systems (MBA, DBA, AGC); information systems management (Graduate Certificate); international business (MBA, DBA, AGC, Graduate Certificate); management (MBA, DBA, AGC, Graduate Certificate); marketing (MBA, DBA, AGC, Graduate Certificate); public administration (MBA, Graduate Certificate); sustainable management (MBA, Graduate Certificate).

See Close-Up on page 201.

Argosy University, Denver, College of Business, Denver, CO 80231. Offers accounting (DBA); corporate compliance (MBA); customized professional concentration (MBA, DBA); finance (MBA); fraud examination (MBA); global business sustainability (DBA); healthcare administration (MBA); information systems (DBA); information systems management (MBA); international business (MBA, DBA); management (MBA, MSM, DBA); marketing (MBA, DBA); organizational leadership (Ed D); public administration (MBA); sustainable management (MBA).

See Close-Up on page 203.

Argosy University, Hawai'i, College of Business, Honolulu, HI 96813. Offers accounting (DBA); corporate compliance (MBA); customized professional concentration (MBA, DBA); finance (MBA, Certificate); fraud examination (MBA); global business sustainability (DBA); healthcare administration (MBA, Certificate); information systems (DBA); information systems management (MBA, Certificate); international business (MBA, DBA, Certificate); management (MBA, MSM, DBA); marketing (MBA, DBA, Certificate); organizational leadership (Ed D); public administration (MBA); sustainable management (MBA).

See Close-Up on page 205.

Argosy University, Inland Empire, College of Business, San Bernardino, CA 92408. Offers accounting (DBA); corporate compliance (MBA); customized professional concentration (MBA, DBA); finance (MBA); fraud examination (MBA); global business sustainability (DBA); healthcare administration (MBA); information systems (DBA); information systems management (MBA); international business (MBA, DBA); management (MBA, MSM, DBA); marketing (MBA, DBA); organizational leadership (Ed D); public administration (MBA); sustainable management (MBA).

See Close-Up on page 207.

Argosy University, Los Angeles, College of Business, Santa Monica, CA 90045. Offers accounting (DBA); corporate compliance (MBA); customized professional concentration (MBA, DBA); finance (MBA); fraud examination (MBA); global business sustainability (DBA); healthcare administration (MBA); information systems (DBA); information systems management (MBA); international business (MBA, DBA); management (MBA, MSM, DBA); marketing (MBA, DBA); organizational leadership (Ed D); public administration (MBA); sustainable management (MBA).

See Close-Up on page 209.

Argosy University, Nashville, College of Business, Nashville, TN 37214. Offers accounting (DBA); customized professional concentration (MBA, DBA); finance (MBA); healthcare administration (MBA); information systems (MBA, DBA); international business (MBA, DBA); management (MBA, MSM, DBA); marketing (MBA, DBA).

See Close-Up on page 211.

Argosy University, Orange County, College of Business, Orange, CA 92868. Offers accounting (DBA, Adv C); corporate compliance (MBA); customized professional concentration (MBA, DBA); finance (MBA, Certificate); fraud examination (MBA); global business sustainability (DBA); healthcare administration (MBA, Certificate); information systems (DBA, Adv C, Certificate); information systems management (MBA); international business (MBA, DBA, Adv C, Certificate); management (MBA, MSM, DBA, Adv C); marketing (MBA, DBA, Adv C, Certificate); organizational leadership (Ed D); public administration (MBA, Certificate); sustainable management (MBA).

See Close-Up on page 213.

Argosy University, Phoenix, College of Business, Phoenix, AZ 85021. Offers accounting (DBA); corporate compliance (MBA); customized professional concentration (MBA, DBA); finance (MBA); fraud examination (MBA); global business sustainability (DBA); healthcare administration (MBA); information systems (DBA); information systems management (MBA); international business (MBA, DBA); management (MBA, DBA); marketing (MBA, DBA); public administration (MBA); sustainable management (MBA).

See Close-Up on page 215.

Argosy University, Salt Lake City, College of Business, Draper, UT 84020. Offers accounting (DBA); corporate compliance (MBA); customized professional concentration (MBA, DBA); finance (MBA); fraud examination (MBA); global business sustainability (DBA); healthcare administration (MBA); information systems (DBA); information systems management (MBA); international business (MBA, DBA); management (MBA, DBA); marketing (MBA, DBA); public administration (MBA); sustainable management (MBA).

See Close-Up on page 217.

Argosy University, San Diego, College of Business, San Diego, CA 92108. Offers accounting (DBA); corporate compliance (MBA); customized professional concentration (MBA, DBA); finance (MBA); fraud examination (MBA); global business sustainability (DBA); information systems (DBA); information systems management (MBA); international business (MBA, DBA); management (MBA, MSM, DBA); marketing (MBA, DBA); organizational leadership (Ed D); public administration (MBA).

See Close-Up on page 219.

Argosy University, San Francisco Bay Area, College of Business, Alameda, CA 94501. Offers accounting (DBA); corporate compliance (MBA); customized professional concentration (MBA, DBA); finance (MBA); fraud examination (MBA); global business sustainability (DBA); healthcare administration (MBA); information systems (DBA); information systems management (MBA); international business (MBA, DBA); management (MBA, MSM, DBA); marketing (MBA, DBA); organizational leadership (Ed D); public administration (MBA); sustainable management (MBA).

See Close-Up on page 221.

Argosy University, Sarasota, College of Business, Sarasota, FL 34235. Offers accounting (DBA, Adv C); corporate compliance (MBA, DBA, Certificate); customized professional concentration (MBA, DBA); finance (MBA, Certificate); fraud examination (MBA, Certificate); global business sustainability (DBA, Adv C); healthcare administration (MBA, Certificate); information systems (DBA, Adv C, Certificate); information systems management (MBA); international business (MBA, DBA, Adv C, Certificate); management (MBA, MSM, DBA, Adv C, Certificate); marketing (MBA, DBA, Adv C, Certificate); organizational leadership (Ed D); public administration (MBA, Certificate); sustainable management (MBA, Certificate).

See Close-Up on page 223.

Argosy University, Schaumburg, College of Business, Schaumburg, IL 60173-5403. Offers accounting (DBA, Adv C); customized professional concentration (MBA, DBA); finance (MBA, Certificate); fraud examination (MBA); global business sustainability (DBA); healthcare administration (MBA, Certificate); information systems (DBA, Adv C, Certificate); information systems management (MBA); international business (MBA, DBA, Adv C, Certificate); management (MBA, MSM, DBA, Adv C, Certificate); marketing (MBA, DBA, Adv C, Certificate); organizational leadership (Ed D); public administration (MBA); sustainable management (MBA).

See Close-Up on page 225.

Argosy University, Seattle, College of Business, Seattle, WA 98121. Offers accounting (DBA); corporate compliance (MBA); customized professional concentration (MBA, DBA); finance (MBA); fraud examination (MBA); global business sustainability (DBA); healthcare administration (MBA); information systems (DBA); information systems management (MBA); international business (MBA, DBA); management (MBA, MSM, DBA); marketing (MBA, DBA); organizational leadership (Ed D); public administration (MBA); sustainable management (MBA).

See Close-Up on page 227.

Argosy University, Tampa, College of Business, Tampa, FL 33607. Offers accounting (DBA); corporate compliance (MBA); customized professional concentration (MBA, DBA); finance (MBA); fraud examination (MBA); global business sustainability (DBA); healthcare administration (MBA); information systems (DBA); information systems management (MBA); international business (MBA, DBA); management (MBA, MSM, DBA); marketing (MBA, DBA); organizational leadership (Ed D); public administration (MBA); sustainable management (MBA).

See Close-Up on page 229.

Argosy University, Twin Cities, College of Business, Eagan, MN 55121. Offers accounting (DBA); customized professional concentration (MBA, DBA); finance (MBA); fraud examination (MBA); global business sustainability (DBA); healthcare administration (MBA); information systems (DBA); information systems management (MBA); international business (MBA, DBA); management (MBA, MSM, DBA); marketing (MBA, DBA); organizational leadership (Ed D); public administration (MBA); sustainable management (MBA).

See Close-Up on page 231.

Argosy University, Washington DC, College of Business, Arlington, VA 22209. Offers accounting (DBA); customized professional concentration (MBA, DBA); finance (MBA); fraud examination (MBA); global business sustainability (DBA); healthcare administration (MBA); information systems (DBA); information systems management (MBA); international business (MBA, DBA, Certificate); management (MBA, MSM, DBA); marketing (MBA, DBA, Certificate); organizational leadership (Ed D); public administration (MBA); sustainable management (MBA).

See Close-Up on page 233.

Arizona State University, Graduate College, W.P. Carey School of Business, Program in Business Administration, Tempe, AZ 85287. Offers agribusiness (PhD); business administration (MBA); finance (MBA, PhD); health sector management (MBA); information systems (PhD); management (MBA, PhD); marketing (MBA, PhD); supply chain management (MBA, PhD); JD/MBA; MBA/M Arch; MBA/MHSM. *Accreditation:* AACSB. *Degree requirements:* For master's, thesis optional; for doctorate, thesis/dissertation. *Entrance requirements:* For master's, GMAT.

Aspen University, Program in Business Administration, Denver, CO 80246. Offers business administration (MBA); finance (MBA); information management (MBA); project management (MBA, Certificate). Part-time and evening/weekend programs available. Postbaccalaureate distance learning degree programs offered (no on-campus study). *Entrance requirements:* Additional exam requirements/recommendations for international students: Required—TOEFL (minimum score 530 paper-based; 71 computer-based). Electronic applications accepted.

Assumption College, Graduate School, Department of Business Studies, Worcester, MA 01609-1296. Offers accounting (MBA); business administration (CAGS); finance/economics (MBA); general business (MBA); human resources (MBA); international business (MBA); management (MBA); marketing (MBA); nonprofit leadership (MBA). Part-time and evening/weekend programs available. *Faculty:* 6 full-time (1 woman), 14 part-time/adjunct (2 women). *Students:* 19 full-time (11 women), 127 part-time (68 women); includes 22 minority (13 African Americans, 3 Asian Americans or Pacific Islanders, 6 Hispanic Americans). Average age 27. 88 applicants, 99% accepted. In 2009, 40 master's, 2 other advanced degrees awarded. *Entrance requirements:* For master's, 3 letters of recommendation, resume; for CAGS, 3 letters of recommendation, resume, essay. Additional exam requirements/recommendations for international students: Required—TOEFL (minimum score 540 paper-based; 200 computer-based; 76 iBT), IELTS (minimum score 6). *Application deadline:* For fall admission, 6/1 priority date for domestic students, 5/1 priority date for international students; for spring admission, 11/1 priority date for domestic students, 9/1 priority date for international students. Applications are processed on a rolling basis. Application fee: $30. Electronic applications accepted. *Expenses:* Tuition: Part-time $503 per credit. Required fees: $20 per semester. One-time fee: $100 part-time. Part-time tuition and fees vary according to campus/location. *Financial support:*

In 2009–10, 47 students received support. Application deadline: 6/1. *Faculty research:* Workplace diversity, dynamics of team interaction, utilization of leased employees. *Unit head:* Michael Lewis, Director, 508-767-7372, Fax: 508-767-7252, E-mail: jhunter@assumption.edu. *Application contact:* Adrian O. Dumas, Director of Graduate Enrollment Management and Services, 508-767-7365, Fax: 508-767-7030, E-mail: adumas@assumption.edu.

Auburn University, Graduate School, College of Business, Department of Finance, Auburn University, AL 36849. Offers MS. *Faculty:* 15 full-time (2 women), 4 part-time/adjunct (3 women). *Students:* 23 full-time (12 women), 5 part-time (3 women); includes 3 minority (all African Americans), 10 international. Average age 25. 72 applicants, 71% accepted, 19 enrolled. In 2009, 9 master's awarded. Application fee: $50 ($60 for international students). *Expenses:* Tuition, state resident: full-time $6240. Tuition, nonresident: full-time $18,720. International tuition: $18,938 full-time. Required fees: $492. Tuition and fees vary according to course load, program and reciprocity agreements. *Financial support:* Applicants required to submit FAFSA. *Unit head:* Dr. John S. Janera, Head, 334-844-5344. *Application contact:* Dr. George Flowers, Dean of the Graduate School, 334-844-2125.

Avila University, School of Business, Kansas City, MO 64145-1698. Offers accounting (MBA); finance (MBA); general management (MBA); health care administration (MBA); international business (MBA); management information systems (MBA); marketing (MBA). Part-time and evening/weekend programs available. *Faculty:* 9 full-time (3 women), 24 part-time/adjunct (5 women). *Students:* 148 full-time (71 women), 86 part-time (47 women); includes 56 minority (36 African Americans, 2 American Indian/Alaska Native, 13 Asian Americans or Pacific Islanders, 5 Hispanic Americans), 63 international. Average age 32. 53 applicants, 75% accepted, 40 enrolled. In 2009, 93 master's awarded. *Degree requirements:* For master's, comprehensive exam, capstone course. *Entrance requirements:* For master's, GMAT, minimum GPA of 3.0, interview. Additional exam requirements/recommendations for international students: Required—TOEFL (minimum score 550 paper-based). *Application deadline:* For fall admission, 7/30 priority date for domestic students, 7/30 for international students; for winter admission, 11/30 priority date for domestic students, 11/30 for international students; for spring admission, 2/28 priority date for domestic students, 2/28 for international students. Applications are processed on a rolling basis. Application fee: $0. Electronic applications accepted. *Expenses:* Contact institution. *Financial support:* In 2009–10, 102 students received support. Career-related internships or fieldwork available. Support available to part-time students. Financial award applicants required to submit FAFSA. *Faculty research:* Leadership characteristics, financial hedging, group dynamics. *Unit head:* Dr. Richard Woodall, Dean, 816-501-3720, Fax: 816-501-2463, E-mail: richard.woodall@avila.edu. *Application contact:* JoAnna Giffin, MBA Admissions Director, 816-501-3601, Fax: 816-501-2463, E-mail: joanna.giffin@avila.edu.

Baker College Center for Graduate Studies—Online, Graduate Programs—Online, Flint, MI 48507-9843. Offers accounting (MBA); business administration (DBA); finance (MBA); general business (MBA); health care management (MBA); human resources management (MBA); information management (MBA); leadership studies (MBA); management information systems (MSIS); marketing (MBA). Part-time and evening/weekend programs available. Post-baccalaureate distance learning degree programs offered. *Faculty:* 750. *Students:* 500 full-time, 500 part-time. Average age 37. *Degree requirements:* For master's, portfolio. *Entrance requirements:* For master's, 3 years of work experience, minimum undergraduate GPA of 2.5, writing sample, 3 letters of recommendation; for doctorate, MBA or acceptable related master's degree from accredited association, 5 years work experience, minimum graduate GPA of 3.25, writing sample, 3 professional references. Additional exam requirements/recommendations for international students: Required—TOEFL (minimum score 550 paper-based; 213 computer-based). *Application deadline:* For fall admission, 8/6 priority date for domestic students; for winter admission, 12/15 priority date for domestic students; for spring admission, 2/15 priority date for domestic students. Applications are processed on a rolling basis. Application fee: $25. Electronic applications accepted. *Expenses:* Tuition: Part-time $330 per credit hour. Tuition and fees vary according to degree level. *Financial support:* Scholarships/grants available. Support available to part-time students. Financial award applicants required to submit FAFSA. *Unit head:* Dr. Julia Teahen, President, 810-766-4023, Fax: 810-766-4399, E-mail: julia@baker.edu. *Application contact:* Chuck J. Gurden, Vice President for Graduate and Online Admissions, 800-469-3165, Fax: 810-766-4399, E-mail: adm-ol@baker.edu.

Barry University, Andreas School of Business, Graduate Certificate Programs, Miami Shores, FL 33161-6695. Offers finance (Certificate); health services administration (Certificate); international business (Certificate); management (Certificate); management information systems (Certificate); marketing (Certificate).

Bayamón Central University, Graduate Programs, Program in Business Administration, Bayamón, PR 00960-1725. Offers accounting (MBA); finance (MBA); general business (MBA); management (MBA); management of security and protection (MBA); marketing (MBA). Part-time and evening/weekend programs available. *Degree requirements:* For master's, comprehensive exam (for some programs). *Entrance requirements:* For master's, EXADEP, bachelor's degree in business or related field.

Benedictine University, Graduate Programs, Program in Business Administration, Lisle, IL 60532-0900. Offers accounting (MBA); entrepreneurship and managing innovation (MBA); financial management (MBA); health administration (MBA); human resource management (MBA); information systems security (MBA); international business (MBA); management consulting (MBA); management information systems (MBA); marketing management (MBA); operations management and logistics (MBA); organizational leadership (MBA); MBA/MPH; MBA/MS. Part-time and evening/weekend programs available. Postbaccalaureate distance learning degree programs offered (minimal on-campus study). *Faculty:* 4 full-time (2 women), 24 part-time/adjunct (3 women). *Students:* 247 full-time (141 women), 644 part-time (339 women); includes 223 minority (134 African Americans, 5 American Indian/Alaska Native, 44 Asian Americans or Pacific Islanders, 40 Hispanic Americans), 25 international. Average age 34. 287 applicants, 92% accepted, 229 enrolled. In 2009, 219 master's awarded. *Entrance requirements:* For master's, GMAT. Additional exam requirements/recommendations for international students: Required—TOEFL (minimum score 550 paper-based; 213 computer-based). *Application deadline:* For fall admission, 9/1 for domestic students; for winter admission, 12/1 for domestic students; for spring admission, 2/15 for domestic students. Applications are processed on a rolling basis. Application fee: $40. Electronic applications accepted. *Expenses:* Tuition: Part-time $750 per credit hour. Tuition and fees vary according to campus/location and program. *Financial support:* Career-related internships or fieldwork and health care benefits available. Support available to part-time students. *Faculty research:* Strategic leadership in professional organizations, sociology of professions, organizational change, social identity theory, applications to change management. *Unit head:* Dr. Sharon Borowicz, Director, 630-829-6219, E-mail: sborowicz@ben.edu. *Application contact:* Kari Gibbons, Director, Admissions, 630-829-6200, Fax: 630-829-6584, E-mail: kgibbons@ben.edu.

Bentley University, McCallum Graduate School of Business, Program in Finance, Waltham, MA 02452-4705. Offers MSF. Part-time and evening/weekend programs available. *Faculty:* 65 full-time (24 women), 16 part-time/adjunct (6 women). *Students:* 61 full-time (25 women), 49 part-time (19 women); includes 14 minority (1 African American, 1 American Indian/Alaska Native, 9 Asian Americans or Pacific Islanders, 3 Hispanic Americans), 51 international. Average age 26. 339 applicants, 61% accepted, 52 enrolled. *Entrance requirements:* For master's, GMAT or GRE General Test. Additional exam requirements/recommendations for international students: Required—TOEFL (minimum score 600 paper-based; 250 computer-based; 100 iBT) or IELTS (minimum score 7). *Application deadline:* For fall admission, 12/1 priority date for domestic students, 10/1 priority date for international students; for spring admission, 10/1 priority date for domestic students, 10/1 for international students. Application fee: $50. Electronic applications accepted. *Expenses:* Tuition: Full-time $26,208; part-time $1092 per credit. Required fees: $404. *Financial support:* Scholarships/grants and unspecified assistantships available. Financial award application deadline: 6/1; financial award applicants required to submit CSS PROFILE or FAFSA. *Faculty research:* Large investments and project finance, quantitative finance and market risk, emerging market financial systems, credit risk in financial markets, risk management. *Unit head:* Philipp Uhlmann, MSF Director, 781-891-3175, E-mail: puhlmann@bentley.edu. *Application contact:* Sharon Hill, Director of Graduate Admissions, 781-891-2108, Fax: 781-891-2464, E-mail: bentleygraduateadmissions@bentley.edu.

Bentley University, McCallum Graduate School of Business, Program in Financial Planning, Waltham, MA 02452-4705. Offers MSFP. Part-time and evening/weekend programs available. Postbaccalaureate distance learning degree programs offered (no on-campus study). *Faculty:* 65 full-time (24 women), 16 part-time/adjunct (6 women). *Students:* 5 full-time (2 women), 38 part-time (11 women); includes 4 minority (1 African American, 2 Asian Americans or Pacific Islanders, 1 Hispanic American), 1 international. Average age 35. 29 applicants, 86% accepted, 17 enrolled. *Entrance requirements:* For master's, GMAT. Additional exam requirements/recommendations for international students: Required—TOEFL (minimum score 600 paper-based; 250 computer-based; 100 iBT) or IELTS (minimum score 7). *Application deadline:* For fall admission, 12/1 priority date for domestic and international students; for spring admission, 10/1 priority date for domestic and international students. Application fee: $50. Electronic applications accepted. *Expenses:* Tuition: Full-time $26,208; part-time $1092 per credit. Required fees: $404. *Financial support:* Tuition waivers available. Financial award application deadline: 6/1; financial award applicants required to submit CSS PROFILE or FAFSA. *Faculty research:* International financial planning, compensation and benefits, retirement planning. *Unit head:* Jack Lynch, MSFP Director, 781-891-2624, E-mail: jlynch@bentley.edu. *Application contact:* Sharon Hill, Director of Graduate Admissions, 781-891-2108, Fax: 781-891-2464, E-mail: bentleygraduateadmissions@bentley.edu.

Bernard M. Baruch College of the City University of New York, Zicklin School of Business, Department of Economics and Finance, Program in Finance, New York, NY 10010-5585. Offers MBA, MS, PhD. Part-time and evening/weekend programs available. *Degree requirements:* For doctorate, comprehensive exam, thesis/dissertation. *Entrance requirements:* For master's, GMAT, 2 letters of recommendation, resume, 2 years of work experience; for doctorate, GMAT. Additional exam requirements/recommendations for international students: Required—TOEFL (minimum score 590 paper-based; 243 computer-based), TWE (minimum score 5).

Bernard M. Baruch College of the City University of New York, Zicklin School of Business, Zicklin Executive Programs, Executive Program in Finance, New York, NY 10010-5585. Offers MS. Evening/weekend programs available. *Entrance requirements:* For master's, personal interview, work experience. *Expenses:* Contact institution. *Faculty research:* Corporate finance, investments, options, securities, system risk.

Boston College, Carroll School of Management, Graduate Finance Programs, Chestnut Hill, MA 02467-3800. Offers MSF, PhD, MBA/MSF. Part-time programs available. *Faculty:* 10 full-time (1 woman), 6 part-time/adjunct (0 women). *Students:* 26 full-time (9 women), 60 part-time (17 women). Average age 26. 645 applicants, 15% accepted, 62 enrolled. In 2009, 79 master's, 6 doctorates awarded. *Degree requirements:* For doctorate, thesis/dissertation. *Entrance requirements:* For master's, GMAT, resume, recommendations; for doctorate, GMAT or GRE, curriculum vitae, recommendations. Additional exam requirements/recommendations for international students: Required—TOEFL (minimum score 600 paper-based; 250 computer-based; 100 iBT). *Application deadline:* For fall admission, 3/15 for domestic and international students; for spring admission, 10/15 for domestic and international students. Application fee: $100. Electronic applications accepted. *Financial support:* In 2009–10, 35 fellowships with partial tuition reimbursements, 38 research assistantships with tuition reimbursements were awarded; teaching assistantships with tuition reimbursements, Federal Work-Study, scholarships/grants, and unspecified assistantships also available. Financial award application deadline: 3/1; financial award applicants required to submit FAFSA. *Faculty research:* Security and derivative markets, financial institutions, corporate finance and capital markets, market macrostructure, investments, portfolio analysis. *Unit head:* Dr. Jeffrey L. Ringuest, Associate Dean for Graduate Programs, 617-552-9100, Fax: 617-552-0541, E-mail: gsomdean@bc.edu. *Application contact:* Shelley A. Burt, Director of Graduate Enrollment, 617-552-3920, Fax: 617-552-8078, E-mail: bcmba@bc.edu.

Boston University, Graduate School of Arts and Sciences, Department of Mathematics and Statistics, Boston, MA 02215. Offers mathematical finance (MA); mathematics (MA, PhD). *Students:* 41 full-time (11 women), 2 part-time (0 women); includes 2 minority (1 African American, 1 Hispanic American), 20 international. Average age 27. 198 applicants, 17% accepted, 12 enrolled. In 2009, 9 master's, 7 doctorates awarded. Terminal master's awarded for partial completion of doctoral program. *Degree requirements:* For master's, one foreign language, comprehensive exam; for doctorate, one foreign language, comprehensive exam, thesis/dissertation. *Entrance requirements:* For master's and doctorate, GRE General Test, GRE Subject Test, 3 letters of recommendation. Additional exam requirements/recommendations for international students: Required—TOEFL (minimum score 600 paper-based; 250 computer-based). *Application deadline:* For fall admission, 1/15 for domestic and international students; for spring admission, 10/15 for domestic and international students. Application fee: $70. Electronic applications accepted. *Expenses:* Tuition: Full-time $37,910; part-time $1184 per credit hour. Required fees: $386; $40 per semester. Part-time tuition and fees vary according to class time, course level, degree level and program. *Financial support:* In 2009–10, 3 fellowships with full tuition reimbursements (averaging $18,900 per year), 17 research assistantships with full tuition reimbursements (averaging $18,400 per year), 28 teaching assistantships with full tuition reimbursements (averaging $18,400 per year) were awarded; Federal Work-Study and scholarships/grants also available. Support available to part-time students. Financial award application deadline: 1/15; financial award applicants required to submit FAFSA. *Unit head:* Ralph D'Agostino, Chairman, 617-353-2767, Fax: 617-353-8100, E-mail: ralph@bu.edu. *Application contact:* Kathleen Heavey, Staff Coordinator, 617-353-2560, Fax: 617-353-8100, E-mail: kheavey@bu.edu.

Boston University, Metropolitan College, Department of Administrative Sciences, Boston, MA 02215. Offers banking and financial management (MSM); business continuity in emergency management (MSM); economics development and tourism management (MSAS); electronic commerce, systems, and technology (MSAS); financial economics (MSAS); human resource management (MSM); innovation and technology (MSAS); insurance management (MSM); international market management (MSM); multinational commerce (MSAS); project management (MSM). *Accreditation:* AACSB. Part-time and evening/weekend programs available. Post-baccalaureate distance learning degree programs offered (no on-campus study). *Students:* 123 full-time (48 women), 204 part-time (92 women); includes 31 minority (10 African Americans, 1 American Indian/Alaska Native, 11 Asian Americans or Pacific Islanders, 9 Hispanic Americans), 146 international. Average age 30. In 2009, 154 master's awarded. *Degree requirements:* For master's, thesis optional. *Entrance requirements:* For master's, 1 year of work experience, minimum GPA of 3.0. Additional exam requirements/recommendations for international students: Required—TOEFL (minimum score 560 paper-based; 220 computer-based; 84 iBT). *Application deadline:* Applications are processed on a rolling basis. Application fee: $70. Electronic applications accepted. *Expenses:* Tuition: Full-time $37,910; part-time $1184 per credit hour. Required fees: $386; $40 per semester. Part-time tuition and fees vary according to class time, course level, degree level and program. *Financial support:* In 2009–10, 15 students received support, including 8 research assistantships (averaging $10,000 per year); career-related internships or fieldwork and Federal Work-Study also available. *Faculty research:* International business, innovative process. *Unit head:* Dr. Kip Becker, Chairman, 617-353-3016, E-mail: adminsc@bu.edu. *Application contact:* Lucille Dicker, Administrative Sciences Department, 617-353-3016, E-mail: adminsc@bu.edu.

Boston University, School of Law, Boston, MA 02215. Offers American law (LL M); banking (LL M); intellectual property law (LL M); law (JD); taxation (LL M); JD/LL M; JD/MA; JD/MBA; JD/MPH; JD/MS. *Accreditation:* ABA. *Faculty:* 65 full-time (26 women), 88 part-time/adjunct (32 women). *Students:* 1,014 full-time (507 women), 83 part-time (45 women); includes 211 minority (50 African Americans, 2 American Indian/Alaska Native, 104 Asian Americans or Pacific Islanders, 55 Hispanic Americans), 164 international. Average age 27. 7,660 applicants, 23% accepted, 271 enrolled. In 2009, 269 JDs, 213 master's awarded. *Degree requirements:*

Finance and Banking

Boston University (continued)
For master's, thesis (for some programs); for JD, thesis/dissertation, research project resulting in a paper. *Entrance requirements:* For JD, LSAT; for master's, JD. Additional exam requirements/recommendations for international students: Required—TOEFL (minimum score 600 paper-based; 250 computer-based; 100 iBT). *Application deadline:* For fall admission, 3/1 for domestic and international students. Applications are processed on a rolling basis. Application fee: $75. Electronic applications accepted. *Expenses:* Tuition: Full-time $37,910; part-time $1184 per credit hour. Required fees: $386; $40 per semester. Part-time tuition and fees vary according to class time, course level, degree level and program. *Financial support:* In 2009–10, 533 students received support. Career-related internships or fieldwork, Federal Work-Study, institutionally sponsored loans, and scholarships/grants available. Financial award application deadline: 3/1; financial award applicants required to submit FAFSA. *Faculty research:* Litigation and dispute resolution, intellectual property law, business organizations and finance law, international law, health law. *Unit head:* Maureen A. O'Rourke, Dean, 617-353-3112, Fax: 617-353-7400, E-mail: lawdean@bu.edu. *Application contact:* Alissa Leonard, Director of Admissions and Financial Aid, 617-353-3100, Fax: 617-353-0578, E-mail: bulawadm@bu.edu.

Boston University, School of Management, Master of Business Administration Program, Boston, MA 02215. Offers entrepreneurship (MBA); finance (MBA); health sector management (MBA); international management (MBA); marketing (MBA); operations and technology management (MBA); public and nonprofit management (MBA); strategy and business analysis (MBA); JD/MBA; MBA/MA; MBA/MPH; MBA/MS; MBA/MSIS; MS/MBA. Part-time and evening/weekend programs available. *Faculty:* 119 full-time (31 women), 99 part-time/adjunct (30 women). *Students:* 326 full-time (138 women), 677 part-time (257 women); includes 149 minority (13 African Americans, 119 Asian Americans or Pacific Islanders, 17 Hispanic Americans), 149 international. Average age 30. 1,617 applicants, 38% accepted, 317 enrolled. In 2009, 284 master's awarded. *Entrance requirements:* For master's, GMAT, resume, 2 letters of recommendation. Additional exam requirements/recommendations for international students: Required—TOEFL or IELTS. *Application deadline:* For fall admission, 3/15 for domestic and international students; for spring admission, 11/15 for domestic students. Application fee: $125. Electronic applications accepted. *Expenses:* Tuition: Full-time $37,910; part-time $1184 per credit hour. Required fees: $386; $40 per semester. Part-time tuition and fees vary according to class time, course level, degree level and program. *Financial support:* Career-related internships or fieldwork, Federal Work-Study, institutionally sponsored loans, and scholarships/grants available. Support available to part-time students. Financial award applicants required to submit FAFSA. *Unit head:* Katherine Nolan, Assistant Dean, Graduate Programs, 617-353-4157, Fax: 617-353-5003, E-mail: mba@bu.edu. *Application contact:* Hayden Estrada, Assistant Dean, Admissions, 617-353-2670, Fax: 617-353-7368, E-mail: mba@bu.edu.

Boston University, School of Management, Program in Investment Management, Boston, MA 02215. Offers MSIM. Part-time and evening/weekend programs available. *Faculty:* 8 full-time (0 women), 4 part-time/adjunct (0 women). *Students:* 66 part-time (11 women); includes 6 Asian Americans or Pacific Islanders, 2 Hispanic Americans. Average age 29. 60 applicants, 58% accepted, 32 enrolled. In 2009, 32 master's awarded. *Entrance requirements:* For master's, GMAT, resume, 2 letters of recommendation. Additional exam requirements/recommendations for international students: Required—TOEFL or IELTS. *Application deadline:* For spring admission, 11/15 for domestic and international students. Applications are processed on a rolling basis. Application fee: $125. Electronic applications accepted. *Expenses:* Tuition: Full-time $37,910; part-time $1184 per credit hour. Required fees: $386; $40 per semester. Part-time tuition and fees vary according to class time, course level, degree level and program. *Financial support:* Career-related internships or fieldwork, Federal Work-Study, and institutionally sponsored loans available. Support available to part-time students. Financial award applicants required to submit FAFSA. *Faculty research:* Behavioral finance, computational finance, risk management, portfolio management, derivatives. *Unit head:* Scott Stewart, Faculty Director, 617-353-2353, Fax: 617-353-6667, E-mail: msim@bu.edu. *Application contact:* Hayden Estrada, Assistant Dean, Admissions, 617-353-2670, Fax: 617-353-7368, E-mail: msim@bu.edu.

Brandeis University, International Business School, Waltham, MA 02454-9110. Offers finance (MSF); international business (MBAi); international economics and finance (MA, PhD); international finance/international economics (MBAi). Part-time and evening/weekend programs available. Terminal master's awarded for partial completion of doctoral program. *Degree requirements:* For master's, one foreign language, semester abroad; for doctorate, thesis/dissertation. *Entrance requirements:* For master's, GMAT or GRE General Test (MA), GMAT (MBAi, MSF); for doctorate, GRE General Test. Additional exam requirements/recommendations for international students: Required—TOEFL (minimum score 600 paper-based; 250 computer-based), IELTS (minimum score 7). Electronic applications accepted. *Faculty research:* International finance and business, trade policy, macroeconomics, Asian economic issues, developmental economics.

Bridgewater State University, School of Graduate Studies, School of Business, Department of Accounting and Finance, Bridgewater, MA 02325-0001. Offers MSM. Part-time and evening/weekend programs available. *Entrance requirements:* For master's, GMAT.

Brigham Young University, Graduate Studies, Marriott School of Management, Master of Public Administration Program, Provo, UT 84602. Offers finance (MPA); human resources (MPA); local government (MPA); nonprofit management (MPA); JD/MPA. *Faculty:* 10 full-time (4 women), 18 part-time/adjunct (1 woman). *Students:* 128 full-time (54 women); includes 26 minority (3 African Americans, 13 Asian Americans or Pacific Islanders, 10 Hispanic Americans). Average age 27. 136 applicants, 66% accepted, 62 enrolled. In 2009, 53 master's awarded. *Entrance requirements:* For master's, GRE, GMAT, minimum GPA of 3.0. Additional exam requirements/recommendations for international students: Required—TOEFL (minimum score 580 paper-based; 85 iBT), IELTS (minimum score 7). *Application deadline:* For fall admission, 2/1 for domestic and international students. Application fee: $50. Electronic applications accepted. *Expenses:* Tuition: Full-time $5580; part-time $301 per credit hour. Tuition and fees vary according to student's religious affiliation. *Financial support:* In 2009–10, 96 students received support. Career-related internships or fieldwork and scholarships/grants available. Financial award application deadline: 4/15; financial award applicants required to submit FAFSA. *Faculty research:* Taxes, budgeting, nonprofit, ethics, decision modeling, work balance, organizational behavior. *Unit head:* Dr. David W. Hart, Director, 801-422-4221, Fax: 801-422-0311, E-mail: mpa@byu.edu. *Application contact:* Catherine Cooper, Director of Student Services, E-mail: mpa@byu.edu.

California College of the Arts, Graduate Programs, Program in Design Strategy, San Francisco, CA 94107. Offers MBA.

California Intercontinental University, School of Business, Diamond Bar, CA 91765. Offers banking and finance (MBA); entrepreneurship and business management (DBA); global business leadership (DBA); international management and marketing (MBA); organizational management and human resource management (MBA).

California Lutheran University, Graduate Studies, School of Business, Thousand Oaks, CA 91360-2787. Offers business (IMBA); entrepreneurship (MBA, Certificate); finance (MBA, Certificate); financial planning (MBA, Certificate); information systems and technology (MS); information technology management (MBA, Certificate); international business (MBA, Certificate); management and organization behavior (MBA); management and organizational behavior (Certificate); marketing (MBA, Certificate). Evening/weekend programs available. Post-baccalaureate distance learning degree programs offered. *Entrance requirements:* For master's, GMAT, interview, minimum GPA of 3.0. *Expenses:* Contact institution.

California State University, East Bay, Graduate Programs, College of Business and Economics, Department of Accounting and Finance, Option in Accounting/Finance, Hayward, CA 94542-3000. Offers MBA. *Degree requirements:* For master's, comprehensive exam or thesis. *Entrance requirements:* For master's, GMAT, minimum GPA of 2.75. Additional exam requirements/recommendations for international students: Required—TOEFL (minimum score 550 paper-based; 213 computer-based). *Application deadline:* For fall admission, 6/30 for domestic and international students. Applications are processed on a rolling basis. Application fee: $55. Electronic applications accepted. *Financial support:* Career-related internships or fieldwork, Federal Work-Study, and institutionally sponsored loans available. Support available to part-time students. Financial award application deadline: 3/1; financial award applicants required to submit FAFSA. *Unit head:* Prof. Micah Frankel, Graduate Adviser, 510-885-3397, Fax: 510-885-4796, E-mail: micah.frankel@csueastbay.edu. *Application contact:* Donna Wiley, Interim Associate Director, 510-885-2928, Fax: 510-885-4777, E-mail: donna.wiley@csueastbay.edu.

California State University, Fullerton, Graduate Studies, College of Business and Economics, Department of Finance, Fullerton, CA 92834-9480. Offers MBA. Part-time programs available. *Students:* 58 full-time (31 women), 77 part-time (22 women); includes 48 minority (5 African Americans, 35 Asian Americans or Pacific Islanders, 8 Hispanic Americans), 45 international. Average age 29. 112 applicants, 46% accepted, 32 enrolled. In 2009, 61 master's awarded. *Degree requirements:* For master's, project or thesis. *Entrance requirements:* For master's, GMAT, minimum AACSB index of 950. Application fee: $55. *Expenses:* Tuition, nonresident: full-time $11,160; part-time $373 per credit. Required fees: $1440 per term. Tuition and fees vary according to course load, degree level and program. *Financial support:* Career-related internships or fieldwork, Federal Work-Study, institutionally sponsored loans, and scholarships/grants available. Support available to part-time students. Financial award application deadline: 3/1; financial award applicants required to submit FAFSA. *Unit head:* Dr. John Erickson, Chair, 657-278-2217. *Application contact:* Admissions/Applications, 657-278-2371.

California State University, Los Angeles, Graduate Studies, College of Business and Economics, Department of Finance and Law, Los Angeles, CA 90032-8530. Offers finance and banking (MBA, MS). Part-time and evening/weekend programs available. *Faculty:* 2 full-time (0 women). *Students:* 6 full-time (2 women), 14 part-time (6 women); includes 4 minority (3 Asian Americans or Pacific Islanders, 1 Hispanic American), 9 international. Average age 29. 16 applicants, 100% accepted, 5 enrolled. In 2009, 28 master's awarded. *Degree requirements:* For master's, comprehensive exam (MBA), thesis (MS). *Entrance requirements:* For master's, GMAT, minimum GPA of 2.5 during previous 2 years of course work. Additional exam requirements/recommendations for international students: Required—TOEFL (minimum score 550 paper-based; 213 computer-based). *Application deadline:* For fall admission, 5/1 for domestic and international students. Applications are processed on a rolling basis. Application fee: $55. Electronic applications accepted. *Financial support:* Career-related internships or fieldwork and Federal Work-Study available. Support available to part-time students. Financial award application deadline: 3/1. *Unit head:* Dr. Hsing Fang, Chair, 323-343-2870, Fax: 323-343-2885, E-mail: hfang@calstatela.edu. *Application contact:* Dr. Cheryl L. Ney, Associate Vice President for Academic Affairs and Dean of Graduate Studies, 323-343-3820, Fax: 323-343-5653, E-mail: cney@cslanet.calstatela.edu.

California State University, Stanislaus, College of Business Administration, Department of Accounting and Finance, Turlock, CA 95382. Offers finance and international finance (MSBA). *Degree requirements:* For master's, comprehensive exam. *Entrance requirements:* For master's, GMAT, minimum GPA 2.50, 3 letters of reference. Additional exam requirements/recommendations for international students: Required—TOEFL (minimum score 550 paper-based; 213 computer-based). Electronic applications accepted. *Expenses:* Contact institution. *Faculty research:* Marketing valuation and corporate investment, investment and cash-flow from Asian countries.

Capella University, School of Business and Technology, Minneapolis, MN 55402. Offers accounting (MBA), including system design and programming; business (Certificate), including human resource management (MS, PhD, Certificate), information technology management (MS, PhD, Certificate), leadership (MBA, MS, PhD, Certificate); finance (MBA); general business (MBA); health care management (MBA); information technology (MS, Certificate), including general information technology (MS), information security, network architecture and design (MS), professional projects management (Certificate), project management and leadership (MS), system design and development (MS),); information technology management (MBA); marketing (MBA); organization and management (MBA, MS, PhD), including general business (PhD), general organization and management (MBA, MS), human resource management (MS, PhD, Certificate), information technology management (MS, PhD, Certificate), leadership (MBA, MS, PhD, Certificate); project management (MBA). Part-time and evening/weekend programs available. Postbaccalaureate distance learning degree programs offered (minimal on-campus study). Terminal master's awarded for partial completion of doctoral program. *Degree requirements:* For master's, thesis optional, integrative project; for doctorate, comprehensive exam, thesis/dissertation. *Entrance requirements:* Additional exam requirements/recommendations for international students: Required—TOEFL (minimum score 550 paper-based; 213 computer-based), TWE (minimum score 4). Electronic applications accepted. *Faculty research:* Business policies: strategic, corporate, and financial management; interplay of technological, organizational and social change.

Carnegie Mellon University, Tepper School of Business, Program in Financial Economics, Pittsburgh, PA 15213-3891. Offers PhD. *Degree requirements:* For doctorate, thesis/dissertation. *Entrance requirements:* For doctorate, GRE General Test.

Case Western Reserve University, Weatherhead School of Management, Department of Banking and Finance, Cleveland, OH 44106. Offers MBA. *Entrance requirements:* For master's, GMAT. *Application deadline:* For fall admission, 4/15 priority date for domestic students. Application fee: $100. *Faculty research:* Monetary and fiscal policy, corporate finance, future markets, derivative pricing, capital market efficiency. *Unit head:* Peter Ritchken, Chair, 216-368-2040, Fax: 216-368-5548, E-mail: peter.ritchken@case.edu. *Application contact:* Olivia Seifert, Program Director, 216-368-2031, Fax: 216-368-5548, E-mail: olivia.seifert@case.edu.

Case Western Reserve University, Weatherhead School of Management, Department of Operations, Cleveland, OH 44106. Offers management (MS, MSM), including finance (MS), information systems (MS), marketing (MS), operations research, quality management (MS), supply chain (MSM); management for liberal arts graduates (MSM); operations research (PhD); MBA/MSM. Part-time programs available. *Degree requirements:* For doctorate, thesis/dissertation. *Entrance requirements:* For master's, GRE General Test; for doctorate, GMAT, GRE General Test. *Application deadline:* Applications are processed on a rolling basis. Application fee: $100. *Financial support:* Tuition waivers (full and partial) available. Financial award application deadline: 5/1. *Faculty research:* Mathematical finance, mathematical programming, scheduling, stochastic optimization, environmental/energy models. *Unit head:* Kamlesh Mathur, Chairman, 216-368-3857, E-mail: kamlesh.mathur@case.edu. *Application contact:* Kamlesh Mathur, Chairman, 216-368-3857, E-mail: kamlesh.mathur@case.edu.

Central European University, CEU Business School, Budapest, Hungary. Offers finance (MBA); general management (MBA); information technology (M Sc); information technology management (MBA); management (EMBA); marketing (MBA); real estate management (MBA). Part-time and evening/weekend programs available. *Entrance requirements:* For master's, GMAT. Additional exam requirements/recommendations for international students: Required—TOEFL (minimum score 570 paper-based; 230 computer-based). Electronic applications accepted. *Faculty research:* Social and ethical business, marketing.

Central Michigan University, College of Graduate Studies, College of Business Administration, Department of Finance and Law, Mount Pleasant, MI 48859. Offers finance (MBA). Part-time and evening/weekend programs available. *Degree requirements:* For master's, thesis or alternative. *Entrance requirements:* For master's, GMAT. Electronic applications accepted. *Faculty research:* Investments, commercial banking, financial management.

Charleston Southern University, Program in Business, Charleston, SC 29423-8087. Offers accounting (MBA); finance (MBA); health care administration (MBA); information systems (MBA); organizational development (MBA). Part-time and evening/weekend programs available. *Faculty:* 14 full-time (1 woman), 6 part-time/adjunct (1 woman). *Students:* 316 part-time (157 women); includes 67 minority (53 African Americans, 1 American Indian/Alaska Native, 7 Asian Americans or Pacific Islanders, 6 Hispanic Americans), 7 international. Average age 32. 173

Finance and Banking

applicants, 85% accepted, 97 enrolled. In 2009, 69 master's awarded. *Degree requirements:* For master's, thesis optional. *Entrance requirements:* For master's, GMAT. Additional exam requirements/recommendations for international students: Required—TOEFL (minimum score 550 paper-based; 213 computer-based; 79 iBT). *Application deadline:* Applications are processed on a rolling basis. Application fee: $30. *Expenses:* Tuition: Part-time $350 per credit hour. Required fees: $40 per semester. Tuition and fees vary according to program. *Financial support:* Research assistantships with full tuition reimbursements available. Financial award application deadline: 4/15; financial award applicants required to submit FAFSA. *Unit head:* Dr. Scott Pearson, Director of the MBA Program, 843-863-7038, Fax: 843-863-7922, E-mail: spearson@csuniv.edu. *Application contact:* Alison Harrison, Graduate Enrollment Counselor, 843-863-7534, Fax: 843-863-7070, E-mail: aharrison@cusniv.edu.

Christian Brothers University, School of Business, Memphis, TN 38104-5581. Offers business (MBA); financial planning (Certificate); project management (Certificate). Part-time and evening/weekend programs available. *Faculty:* 4 full-time (1 woman), 4 part-time/adjunct (1 woman). *Students:* 5 full-time (all women), 169 part-time (69 women); includes 64 minority (51 African Americans, 9 Asian Americans or Pacific Islanders, 4 Hispanic Americans), 3 international. Average age 35. In 2009, 59 master's awarded. *Entrance requirements:* For master's, GMAT, GRE. Additional exam requirements/recommendations for international students: Required—TOEFL. *Application deadline:* Applications are processed on a rolling basis. Application fee: $50. *Financial support:* Institutionally sponsored loans available. Support available to part-time students. *Unit head:* Dr. Scott Lawyer, Dean, 901-321-3104, Fax: 901-321-3566, E-mail: mlawyer@cbu.edu. *Application contact:* Dr. Scott Lawyer, Director, Graduate Business Programs, 901-321-3104, Fax: 901-321-3566, E-mail: mlawyer@cbu.edu.

City University of Seattle, Graduate Division, School of Management, Bellevue, WA 98005. Offers accounting (Certificate); change leadership (MBA, Certificate); financial management (MBA, Certificate); general management (MBA); general management-Europe (MBA); global leadership (Certificate); global marketing (MBA); individualized study (MBA); information security (MS); information systems (MBA); leadership (MA); marketing (MBA, Certificate); project management (MBA, MS, Certificate); sustainable business (Certificate); technology management (MBA, MS, Certificate). Part-time and evening/weekend programs available. Postbaccalaureate distance learning degree programs offered (no on-campus study). *Entrance requirements:* Additional exam requirements/recommendations for international students: Required—TOEFL (minimum score 540 paper-based; 207 computer-based); Recommended—IELTS. Electronic applications accepted. *Expenses:* Tuition: Full-time $14,760; part-time $615 per credit. Tuition and fees vary according to program.

Claremont McKenna College, Robert Day School of Economics and Finance, Claremont, CA 91711. Offers finance (MAF). *Faculty:* 9 full-time (2 women), 2 part-time/adjunct (0 women). *Students:* 20 (3 women); includes 2 minority (both Asian Americans or Pacific Islanders), 3 international. Average age 23. 82 applicants, 35% accepted, 20 enrolled. *Entrance requirements:* For master's, GMAT or GRE, interview, 2 letters of recommendation. Additional exam requirements/recommendations for international students: Required—TOEFL or IELTS. *Application deadline:* For fall admission, 10/3 priority date for domestic students; for winter admission, 1/7 for domestic students; for spring admission, 3/10 for domestic students. Applications are processed on a rolling basis. Application fee: $70. Electronic applications accepted. *Financial support:* In 2009–10, 20 students received support, including 20 fellowships with full and partial tuition reimbursements available. Financial award applicants required to submit FAFSA. *Unit head:* Janet Kiholm Smith, Dean, 909-607-9597, E-mail: jsmith@cmc.edu. *Application contact:* Darren Filson, Director of Graduate Programs, 909-607-6796, E-mail: dfilson@cmc.edu.

See Display below and Close-Up on page 363.

Clark University, Graduate School, Graduate School of Management, Business Administration Program, Worcester, MA 01610-1477. Offers accounting (MBA); finance (MBA); global business (MBA); health care management (MBA); management (MBA); management of information technology (MBA); marketing (MBA). *Accreditation:* AACSB. Part-time and evening/weekend programs available. *Students:* 148 full-time (67 women), 120 part-time (52 women); includes 27 minority (12 African Americans, 2 American Indian/Alaska Native, 9 Asian Americans or Pacific Islanders, 4 Hispanic Americans), 108 international. Average age 29. 340 applicants, 57% accepted, 63 enrolled. In 2009, 118 master's awarded. *Degree requirements:* For master's, thesis optional. *Application deadline:* For fall admission, 6/1 priority date for domestic students; for spring admission, 12/1 priority date for domestic students. Applications are processed on a rolling basis. Application fee: $50. Electronic applications accepted. *Expenses:* Tuition: Full-time $34,900; part-time $4362.50 per course. *Financial support:* In 2009–10, research assistantships with partial tuition reimbursements (averaging $4,800 per year), teaching assistantships with partial tuition reimbursements (averaging $4,800 per year) were awarded; fellowships, career-related internships or fieldwork, Federal Work-Study, institutionally sponsored loans, and tuition waivers (partial) also available. Support available to part-time students. Financial award application deadline: 5/31. *Faculty research:* Organizational development, accounting, marketing, finance, human resource management. *Application contact:* Lynn Davis, Enrollment and Marketing Director, 508-793-7406, Fax: 508-793-8822, E-mail: clarkmba@clarku.edu.

Clark University, Graduate School, Graduate School of Management, Program in Finance, Worcester, MA 01610-1477. Offers MSF. *Students:* 141 full-time (81 women), 39 part-time (24 women), 175 international. Average age 24. 607 applicants, 73% accepted, 101 enrolled. In 2009, 27 master's awarded. *Degree requirements:* For master's, thesis optional. *Application deadline:* For fall admission, 6/1 priority date for domestic students; for spring admission, 12/1 priority date for domestic students. Applications are processed on a rolling basis. Application fee: $50. Electronic applications accepted. *Expenses:* Tuition: Full-time $34,900; part-time $4362.50 per course. *Financial support:* In 2009–10, research assistantships with partial tuition reimbursements (averaging $4,800 per year), teaching assistantships with partial tuition reimbursements (averaging $4,800 per year) were awarded; fellowships, tuition waivers (partial) also available. Financial award application deadline: 5/31. *Application contact:* Lynn Davis, Enrollment and Marketing Director, 508-793-7406, Fax: 508-793-8822, E-mail: clarkmba@clarku.edu.

Cleary University, Online Program in Business Administration, Ann Arbor, MI 48105-2659. Offers accounting (MBA); financial planning (MBA); financial planning (Graduate Certificate); green business strategy (MBA); management (MBA); nonprofit management (MBA); organizational leadership (MBA). Part-time and evening/weekend programs available. Postbaccalaureate distance learning degree programs offered (no on-campus study). *Degree requirements:* For master's, thesis. *Entrance requirements:* For master's, bachelor's degree; minimum GPA of 2.5; professional resume indicating minimum 2 years management or related experience; undergraduate degree from an accredited college or university with at least 18 quarter hours (or 12 semester hours) of accounting study (for MBA in accounting). Additional exam requirements/recommendations for international students: Required—TOEFL (minimum score 550 paper-based; 213 computer-based; 79 iBT), Michigan English Language Assessment Battery (minimum score: 75). Electronic applications accepted.

Cleveland State University, College of Graduate Studies, Maxine Goodman Levin College of Urban Affairs, Program in Environmental Studies, Cleveland, OH 44115. Offers environmental studies (MAES); geographic information systems (Certificate); urban real estate development and finance (Certificate); JD/MAES. Part-time and evening/weekend programs available. *Degree requirements:* For master's, thesis or alternative, exit project. *Entrance requirements:* For master's, GRE General Test (minimum score: verbal and quantitative 40th percentile, analytical writing 4.0), minimum GPA of 3.0. Additional exam requirements/recommendations for international students: Required—TOEFL (minimum score 525 paper-based; 197 computer-based;

Finance and Banking

Cleveland State University *(continued)*
65 iBT). Electronic applications accepted. *Faculty research:* Environmental policy and administration, environmental planning, geographic information systems (GIS), nonprofit management.

Cleveland State University, College of Graduate Studies, Maxine Goodman Levin College of Urban Affairs, Program in Urban Planning, Design, and Development, Cleveland, OH 44115. Offers geographic information systems (Certificate); local and urban management (Certificate); urban economic development (Certificate); urban planning, design, and development (MUPDD); urban real estate development and finance (Certificate); JD/MUPDD. *Accreditation:* ACSP. Part-time and evening/weekend programs available. *Degree requirements:* For master's, project or thesis. *Entrance requirements:* For master's, GRE General Test (minimum 50th percentile verbal and quantitative, 4.0 analytical writing), minimum GPA of 3.0. Additional exam requirements/recommendations for international students: Required—TOEFL (minimum score 525 paper-based; 197 computer-based; 65 iBT). Electronic applications accepted. *Faculty research:* Housing and neighborhood development, urban housing policy, environmental sustainability, economic development.

Cleveland State University, College of Graduate Studies, Maxine Goodman Levin College of Urban Affairs, Program in Urban Studies, Cleveland, OH 44115. Offers geographic information systems (Certificate); local and urban management (Certificate); nonprofit management (Certificate); urban economic development (Certificate); urban real estate development and finance (Certificate); urban studies (MS); urban studies and public affairs (PhD). Part-time and evening/weekend programs available. *Degree requirements:* For master's, thesis or alternative, exit project, capstone course; for doctorate, comprehensive exam, thesis/dissertation. *Entrance requirements:* For master's, GRE General Test, minimum GPA of 3.0; for doctorate, GRE General Test, minimum GPA of 3.5. Additional exam requirements/recommendations for international students: Required—TOEFL (minimum score 525 paper-based; 197 computer-based; 65 iBT). Electronic applications accepted. *Faculty research:* Environmental issues, economic development, urban and public policy, public management.

Cleveland State University, College of Graduate Studies, Nance College of Business Administration, Doctor of Business Administration (DBA) Program, Cleveland, OH 44115. Offers business administration (DBA); finance (DBA); information systems (DBA); marketing (DBA); operations management (DBA). *Accreditation:* AACSB. Part-time and evening/weekend programs available. *Degree requirements:* For doctorate, comprehensive exam, thesis/dissertation, oral dissertation defense. *Entrance requirements:* For doctorate, GMAT, MBA or equivalent. Additional exam requirements/recommendations for international students: Required—TOEFL (minimum score 550 paper-based; 213 computer-based; 79 iBT). Electronic applications accepted. *Faculty research:* Supply chain management, international business, strategic management, risk analysis.

College for Financial Planning, Graduate Programs, Greenwood Village, CO 80111. Offers finance (MS); financial analysis (MS); personal financial planning (MS). Part-time and evening/weekend programs available. Postbaccalaureate distance learning degree programs offered (no on-campus study). *Faculty:* 4 full-time (0 women), 8 part-time/adjunct (2 women). *Students:* 850 part-time. *Degree requirements:* For master's, thesis. *Entrance requirements:* Additional exam requirements/recommendations for international students: Required—TOEFL (minimum score 550 paper-based; 213 computer-based). *Application deadline:* Applications are processed on a rolling basis. Application fee: $75. Electronic applications accepted. *Expenses:* Tuition: Part-time $975 per course. *Unit head:* Dr. Jesse B. Arman, Vice President, Academic Affairs, 303-220-4823, Fax: 303-220-4811, E-mail: jesse.arman@cffp.edu. *Application contact:* Brett Sanborn, Director of Enrollment, 303-220-4951, Fax: 303-220-1810, E-mail: brett.sanborn@cffp.edu.

College of Santa Fe, Department of Business Administration, Santa Fe, NM 87505-7634. Offers finance (MBA); human resources (MBA). Program also available at Albuquerque campus. Part-time and evening/weekend programs available. *Entrance requirements:* For master's, minimum GPA of 3.0 in last 60 hours (preferred).

Colorado State University, Graduate School, College of Business, Program in Financial Risk Management, Fort Collins, CO 80523-0015. Offers MSBA. *Entrance requirements:* For master's, GMAT or GRE, undergraduate degree with minimum GPA of 3.0; coursework in business finance, probability and statistics, and differential equations; academic experience with computer programming; current resume; 3 letters of recommendation. Additional exam requirements/recommendations for international students: Required—TOEFL (minimum score 565 paper-based; 227 computer-based; 86 iBT) or IELTS (minimum score 6.5). *Application deadline:* For fall admission, 7/1 for domestic students, 6/1 for international students. Application fee: $50. Electronic applications accepted. *Expenses:* Tuition, state resident: full-time $6434; part-time $359.10 per credit. Tuition, nonresident: full-time $18,116; part-time $1006.45 per credit. Required fees: $1496; $83 per credit. *Unit head:* Dr. John Hoxmeier, Associate Dean, 970-491-2142, Fax: 970-491-0596, E-mail: john.hoxmeier@colostate.edu. *Application contact:* Rachel Stoll, Admissions Coordinator, 970-491-3704, Fax: 970-491-3481, E-mail: rachel.stoll@colostate.edu.

Colorado Technical University Colorado Springs, Graduate Studies, Program in Management, Colorado Springs, CO 80907-3896. Offers accounting (MBA, MSA); business administration (MBA); finance (MBA); human resources management (MBA); logistics/supply chain management (MBA); management (DM); marketing (MBA); mediation and dispute resolution (MBA); operations management (MBA); project management (MBA); technology management (MBA). Part-time and evening/weekend programs available. Postbaccalaureate distance learning degree programs offered. *Degree requirements:* For master's, thesis or alternative; for doctorate, thesis/dissertation. *Entrance requirements:* For doctorate, minimum graduate GPA of 3.0, 5 years of related work experience. *Faculty research:* Sexual harassment, performance evaluation, critical thinking.

Colorado Technical University Denver, Programs in Business Administration and Management, Greenwood Village, CO 80111. Offers accounting (MBA); business administration (MBA); business administration and management (EMBA); finance (MBA); human resource management (MBA); marketing (MBA); mediation and dispute resolution (MBA); operations management (MBA); project management (MBA); technology management (MBA). Part-time and evening/weekend programs available. *Degree requirements:* For master's, thesis or alternative. *Entrance requirements:* For master's, minimum undergraduate GPA of 3.0, resume.

Columbia Southern University, MBA Program, Orange Beach, AL 36561. Offers electronic business and technology (MBA); finance (MBA); general (MBA); healthcare management (MBA); hospitality and tourism (MBA); human resources management (MBA); international management (MBA); marketing (MBA); project management (MBA); public administration (MBA); sport management (MBA). Part-time and evening/weekend programs available. Postbaccalaureate distance learning degree programs offered (no on-campus study). *Entrance requirements:* For master's, bachelor's degree from accredited/approved institution. Additional exam requirements/recommendations for international students: Required—TOEFL. Electronic applications accepted.

Columbia University, Graduate School of Business, Doctoral Program in Business, New York, NY 10027. Offers business (PhD), including accounting, decision, risk, and operations, finance and economics, management, marketing. *Accreditation:* AACSB. *Faculty:* 149 full-time (23 women), 134 part-time/adjunct (16 women). *Students:* 91 full-time (37 women); includes 10 minority (8 Asian Americans or Pacific Islanders, 2 Hispanic Americans), 64 international. Average age 27. 758 applicants, 6% accepted, 20 enrolled. In 2009, 15 doctorates awarded. *Degree requirements:* For doctorate, comprehensive exam, thesis/dissertation, major field exam, research paper, thesis proposal. *Entrance requirements:* For doctorate, GMAT or GRE (finance), 2 letters of reference, resume. Additional exam requirements/recommendations for international students: Required—TOEFL. *Application deadline:* For fall admission, 1/1 for domestic and international students. Application fee: $75. Electronic applications accepted.

Expenses: Contact institution. *Financial support:* In 2009–10, 91 students received support, including fellowships with full tuition reimbursements available (averaging $22,000 per year), research assistantships (averaging $4,000 per year); teaching assistantships; career-related internships or fieldwork, health care benefits, and tuition waivers (full) also available. *Faculty research:* Human decision making and behavioral research; real estate market and mortgage defaults; financial crisis and corporate governance; international business; security analysis and accounting. *Unit head:* Elizabeth Elam Chang, Administrative Director, 212-854-2836, Fax: 212-932-2359, E-mail: phdinfo@gsb.columbia.edu. *Application contact:* Elizabeth Elam Chang, Administrative Director, 212-854-2836, Fax: 212-932-2359, E-mail: phdinfo@gsb.columbia.edu.

Columbia University, Graduate School of Business, MBA Program, New York, NY 10027. Offers accounting (MBA); decision, risk, and operations (MBA); entrepreneurship (MBA); finance and economics (MBA); healthcare and pharmaceutical management (MBA); human resource management (MBA); international business (MBA); leadership and ethics (MBA); management (MBA); marketing (MBA); media (MBA); private equity (MBA); real estate (MBA); social enterprise (MBA); value investing (MBA); DDS/MBA; JD/MBA; MBA/MIA; MBA/MPH; MBA/MS; MD/MBA. *Faculty:* 149 full-time (23 women), 134 part-time/adjunct (16 women). *Students:* 1,293 full-time (435 women); includes 235 minority (65 African Americans, 4 American Indian/Alaska Native, 135 Asian Americans or Pacific Islanders, 31 Hispanic Americans), 417 international. Average age 28. 6,885 applicants, 15% accepted, 737 enrolled. In 2009, 696 master's awarded. *Entrance requirements:* For master's, GMAT, 2 letters of recommendation. Additional exam requirements/recommendations for international students: Required—TOEFL. *Application deadline:* For fall admission, 4/14 for domestic students, 3/3 for international students; for spring admission, 10/7 for domestic and international students. Applications are processed on a rolling basis. Application fee: $250. Electronic applications accepted. *Expenses:* Contact institution. *Financial support:* In 2009–10, 358 students received support, including 101 fellowships (averaging $23,250 per year); research assistantships, teaching assistantships, career-related internships or fieldwork, institutionally sponsored loans, and scholarships/grants also available. Financial award application deadline: 3/1; financial award applicants required to submit CSS PROFILE or FAFSA. *Faculty research:* Human decision making and behavioral research; real estate market and mortgage defaults; financial crisis and corporate governance; international business; security analysis and accounting. *Unit head:* Prof. Amir Ziv, Vice Dean of Students and the MBA Program, 212-854-3485, Fax: 212-932-0545, E-mail: az50@columbia.edu. *Application contact:* Mary J. Miller, Assistant Dean of Admissions, 212-854-1961, Fax: 212-662-6754, E-mail: apply@gsb.columbia.edu.

Concordia University Wisconsin, Graduate Programs, School of Business and Legal Studies, MBA Program, Mequon, WI 53097-2402. Offers finance (MBA); health care administration (MBA); human resource management (MBA); international business (MBA); international business-bilingual English/Chinese (MBA); management (MBA); management information systems (MBA); managerial communications (MBA); marketing (MBA); public administration (MBA); risk management (MBA). Postbaccalaureate distance learning degree programs offered (minimal on-campus study). *Degree requirements:* For master's, comprehensive exam, thesis or alternative. *Entrance requirements:* Additional exam requirements/recommendations for international students: Required—TOEFL. *Expenses:* Contact institution.

Cornell University, Graduate School, Graduate Field of Management, Ithaca, NY 14853-0001. Offers accounting (PhD); behavioral decision theory (PhD); finance (PhD); marketing (PhD); organizational behavior (PhD); production and operations management (PhD). *Accreditation:* AACSB. *Faculty:* 72 full-time (15 women). *Students:* 39 full-time (15 women); includes 2 minority (both Asian Americans or Pacific Islanders), 23 international. Average age 31. 388 applicants, 2% accepted, 4 enrolled. In 2009, 4 doctorates awarded. *Degree requirements:* For doctorate, comprehensive exam, thesis/dissertation. *Entrance requirements:* For doctorate, GMAT or GRE General Test. Additional exam requirements/recommendations for international students: Required—TOEFL (minimum score 600 paper-based; 250 computer-based; 77 iBT). *Application deadline:* For fall admission, 1/3 for domestic students. Application fee: $70. Electronic applications accepted. *Expenses:* Contact institution. *Financial support:* In 2009–10, 38 students received support, including 1 fellowship with full tuition reimbursement available, 3 research assistantships with full tuition reimbursements available; teaching assistantships with full tuition reimbursements available, institutionally sponsored loans, scholarships/grants, health care benefits, tuition waivers (full and partial), and unspecified assistantships also available. Financial award applicants required to submit FAFSA. *Faculty research:* Operations and manufacturing. *Unit head:* Director of Graduate Studies, 607-255-3669. *Application contact:* Graduate Field Assistant, 607-255-9431, E-mail: js_phd@cornell.edu.

Cornell University, Graduate School, Graduate Fields of Arts and Sciences, Field of Economics, Ithaca, NY 14853-0001. Offers applied economics (PhD); basic analytical economics (PhD); econometrics and economic statistics (PhD); economic development and planning (PhD); economic theory (PhD); industrial organization and control (PhD); international economics (PhD); labor economics (PhD); monetary and macroeconomics (PhD); public finance (PhD). *Faculty:* 89 full-time (13 women). *Students:* 93 full-time (34 women); includes 6 minority (2 African Americans, 3 Asian Americans or Pacific Islanders, 1 Hispanic American), 51 international. Average age 28. 625 applicants, 11% accepted, 21 enrolled. In 2009, 21 doctorates awarded. *Degree requirements:* For doctorate, comprehensive exam, thesis/dissertation. *Entrance requirements:* For doctorate, GRE General Test, 3 letters of recommendation. Additional exam requirements/recommendations for international students: Required—TOEFL (minimum score 550 paper-based; 213 computer-based; 77 iBT). *Application deadline:* For fall admission, 1/15 priority date for domestic students. Application fee: $70. Electronic applications accepted. *Expenses:* Tuition: Full-time $29,500. Required fees: $70. Full-time tuition and fees vary according to degree level, program and student level. *Financial support:* In 2009–10, 81 students received support, including 12 fellowships with full tuition reimbursements available, 2 teaching assistantships with full tuition reimbursements available; research assistantships with full tuition reimbursements available, institutionally sponsored loans, scholarships/grants, health care benefits, tuition waivers (full and partial), and unspecified assistantships also available. Financial award applicants required to submit FAFSA. *Faculty research:* Learning and games, economics of education, political economy, transfer payments, time series and nonparametrics. *Unit head:* Director of Graduate Studies, 607-255-4893, Fax: 607-255-2818. *Application contact:* Graduate Field Assistant, 607-255-4893, Fax: 607-255-2818, E-mail: econ_phd@cornell.edu.

Curry College, Graduate Studies, Program in Business Administration, Milton, MA 02186-9984. Offers business administration (MBA); finance (Certificate). Part-time and evening/weekend programs available. *Faculty:* 5 full-time (1 woman), 2 part-time/adjunct (0 women). *Students:* 111 part-time (68 women). Average age 36. 44 applicants, 89% accepted, 39 enrolled. In 2009, 49 master's awarded. *Degree requirements:* For master's, capstone applied project. *Entrance requirements:* For master's, resume, recommendations, interview, written statement. Additional exam requirements/recommendations for international students: Required—TOEFL (minimum score 550 paper-based; 213 computer-based; 80 iBT). *Application deadline:* For fall admission, 8/1 priority date for domestic students, 6/1 for international students; for winter admission, 10/1 for international students; for spring admission, 12/15 priority date for domestic students, 1/28 for international students. Applications are processed on a rolling basis. Application fee: $50. *Expenses:* Contact institution. *Unit head:* Dr. Gail Arch, Director and Professor, 617-333-2197. *Application contact:* John Bresnahan, Director of Graduate Enrollment and Student Services, 617-333-2243, Fax: 617-979-3535, E-mail: jbresnah0104@curry.edu.

Dalhousie University, Faculty of Management, Centre for Advanced Management Education, Halifax, NS B3H 3J5, Canada. Offers financial services (MBA); information management (MIM); management (MPA); natural resources (MBA). Part-time programs available. Postbaccalaureate distance learning degree programs offered. *Faculty:* 10 full-time (5 women). *Students:* 19 part-time (4 women). Average age 27. 50 applicants, 42% accepted. *Entrance requirements:* For master's, GMAT, minimum GPA of 3.0, resume. Additional exam requirements/recommendations for international students: Required—TOEFL, IELTS, CANTEST, CAEL, or

Michigan English Language Assessment Battery. *Application deadline:* Applications are processed on a rolling basis. Application fee: $70. Electronic applications accepted. *Unit head:* Michelle Hunter, Associate Director (Administration), 902-494-1828, Fax: 902-494-7154, E-mail: mhunter@dal.ca. *Application contact:* Deborah McColl, Admissions and Registration Coordinator, 902-494-6391, E-mail: mbafs@dal.ca.

Dalhousie University, Faculty of Management, School of Business Administration, Halifax, NS B3H 3J5, Canada. Offers business administration (MBA); financial services (MBA); LL B/MBA; MBA/MLIS. Part-time programs available. *Students:* 156 full-time (56 women), 122 part-time (51 women). Average age 26. 504 applicants, 38% accepted. *Entrance requirements:* For master's, GMAT, letter of non-financial guarantee for non-Canadian students, resume, Corporate Residency Preference Form. Additional exam requirements/recommendations for international students: Required—TOEFL, IELTS, CANTEST, CAEL, or Michigan English Language Assessment Battery. *Application deadline:* For spring admission, 5/15 priority date for domestic students, 12/31 priority date for international students. Applications are processed on a rolling basis. Application fee: $70. Electronic applications accepted. *Financial support:* In 2009–10, 12 students received support; fellowships, teaching assistantships available. Financial award application deadline: 5/15. *Faculty research:* International business, quantitative methods, operations research, MIS, marketing, finance. *Unit head:* Marianne Hagen, Graduate Coordinator, 902-494-1814, Fax: 902-494-1107, E-mail: mba.admissions@dal.ca. *Application contact:* Heather Frausell, Administrative Secretary, 902-494-1814, Fax: 902-494-1107, E-mail: mba.admissions@dal.ca.

Dallas Baptist University, College of Adult Education, Professional Development Program, Dallas, TX 75211-9299. Offers accounting (MA); church leadership (MA); counseling (MA); criminal justice (MA); English as a second language (MA); finance (MA); higher education (MA); leadership studies (MA); management (MA); management information systems (MA); marketing (MA); missions (MA). Part-time and evening/weekend programs available. *Entrance requirements:* For master's, minimum GPA of 3.0. Additional exam requirements/recommendations for international students: Required—TOEFL, IELTS. *Expenses:* Tuition: Full-time $10,674; part-time $593 per credit hour.

Dallas Baptist University, College of Business, Business Administration Program, Dallas, TX 75211-9299. Offers accounting (MBA); business communication (MBA); conflict resolution management (MBA); e-business (MBA); entrepreneurship (MBA); finance (MBA); health care management (MBA); international business (MBA); leading the non-profit organization (MBA); management (MBA); management information systems (MBA); marketing (MBA); project management (MBA); technology and engineering management (MBA). *Accreditation:* ACBSP. Part-time and evening/weekend programs available. *Entrance requirements:* For master's, GMAT, minimum GPA of 3.0. Additional exam requirements/recommendations for international students: Required—TOEFL, IELTS. Electronic applications accepted. *Expenses:* Tuition: Full-time $10,674; part-time $593 per credit hour. *Faculty research:* Sports management, services marketing, retailing, strategic management, financial planning/investments.

Davenport University, Sneden Graduate School, Grand Rapids, MI 49503. Offers accounting (MBA); business administration (EMBA); finance (MBA); health care management (MBA); human resources (MBA); information assurance (MS); public health (MPH); strategic management (MBA). Evening/weekend programs available. *Entrance requirements:* For master's, GMAT, minimum undergraduate GPA of 2.75. Additional exam requirements/recommendations for international students: Required—TOEFL. Electronic applications accepted. *Faculty research:* Leadership, management, marketing, organizational culture.

Davenport University, Sneden Graduate School, Warren, MI 48092-5209. Offers accounting (MBA); business administration (EMBA); finance (MBA); health care management (MBA); human resources management (MBA); information assurance (MS); public health (MPH); strategic management (MBA). *Entrance requirements:* For master's, minimum undergraduate GPA of 2.7.

Davenport University, Sneden Graduate School, Dearborn, MI 48126-3799. Offers accounting (MBA); business administration (EMBA); finance (MBA); health care management (MBA); human resources management (MBA); information assurance (MS); marketing (MBA); public health (MPH); strategic management (MBA). Part-time and evening/weekend programs available. Postbaccalaureate distance learning degree programs offered (no on-campus study). *Entrance requirements:* For master's, minimum GPA of 2.7, previous course work in accounting and statistics. *Faculty research:* Accounting, international accounting, social and environmental accounting, finance.

DePaul University, Charles H. Kellstadt Graduate School of Business, Department of Finance, Chicago, IL 60604-2287. Offers behavioral finance (MBA); computational finance (MS); finance (MBA, MSF); financial analysis (MBA); financial management and control (MBA); international marketing and finance (MBA); managerial finance (MBA); real estate (MS); real estate finance and investment (MBA); strategy, execution and valuation (MBA). Part-time and evening/weekend programs available. *Faculty:* 26 full-time (5 women), 23 part-time/adjunct (2 women). *Students:* 432 full-time (120 women), 197 part-time (47 women); includes 94 minority (13 African Americans, 1 American Indian/Alaska Native, 55 Asian Americans or Pacific Islanders, 25 Hispanic Americans), 82 international. In 2009, 239 master's awarded. *Entrance requirements:* For master's, GMAT, 2 letters of recommendation, resume. Additional exam requirements/recommendations for international students: Required—TOEFL (minimum score 550 paper-based; 213 computer-based; 80 iBT). *Application deadline:* For fall admission, 7/1 for domestic students, 6/1 for international students; for winter admission, 10/1 for domestic students, 9/1 for international students; for spring admission, 2/1 for domestic students, 1/1 for international students. Applications are processed on a rolling basis. Application fee: $60. Electronic applications accepted. *Expenses:* Tuition: Full-time $37,525; part-time $620 per credit hour. *Financial support:* In 2009–10, 8 students received support, including 6 research assistantships with partial tuition reimbursements available (averaging $4,340 per year); scholarships/grants and unspecified assistantships also available. Financial award application deadline: 4/1; financial award applicants required to submit FAFSA. *Faculty research:* Derivatives, valuation, international finance, real estate, corporate finance. *Unit head:* Ali M. Fatemi, Professor and Chair, 312-362-8826, Fax: 312-362-6566, E-mail: afatemi@depaul.edu. *Application contact:* Christopher E. Kinsella, Director of Cohort MBA Programs, 312-362-8810, Fax: 312-362-6677, E-mail: kgsb@depaul.edu.

DePaul University, Charles H. Kellstadt Graduate School of Business, School of Accountancy and Management Information Systems, Chicago, IL 60604-2287. Offers accountancy (M Acc, MSA); business information technology (MS); e-business (MBA, MS); financial management and control (MBA); management accounting (MBA); management information systems (MBA); taxation (MST). Part-time and evening/weekend programs available. *Faculty:* 30 full-time (9 women), 54 part-time/adjunct (7 women). *Students:* 167 full-time (82 women), 237 part-time (106 women); includes 52 minority (8 African Americans, 1 American Indian/Alaska Native, 30 Asian Americans or Pacific Islanders, 13 Hispanic Americans), 49 international. In 2009, 141 master's awarded. *Entrance requirements:* For master's, GMAT, 2 letters of recommendation, resume. Additional exam requirements/recommendations for international students: Required—TOEFL (minimum score 550 paper-based; 213 computer-based). *Application deadline:* For fall admission, 7/1 for domestic students; for winter admission, 10/1 for domestic students; for spring admission, 2/1 for domestic students. Applications are processed on a rolling basis. Application fee: $60. *Expenses:* Tuition: Full-time $37,525; part-time $620 per credit hour. *Financial support:* In 2009–10, 7 research assistantships with full tuition reimbursements (averaging $4,100 per year) were awarded; institutionally sponsored loans also available. Financial award application deadline: 4/2. *Faculty research:* Tax policy, property transactions, stock options as compensation, standards setting, activity-based costing in health care. *Unit head:* Kevin Stevens, Director, 312-362-6989, E-mail: kstevens@depaul.edu. *Application contact:* Christopher E. Kinsella, Director of Cohort MBA Programs, 312-362-8810, Fax: 312-362-6677, E-mail: kgsb@depaul.edu.

DePaul University, School of Public Service, Chicago, IL 60604. Offers financial administration management (Certificate); health administration (Certificate); health law and policy (MS); international public services (MS); leadership and policy studies (MS); metropolitan planning (Certificate); public administration (MPA); public service management (MS), including association management, fundraising and philanthropy, healthcare administration, higher education administration, metropolitan planning; public services (Certificate); JD/MS. Part-time and evening/weekend programs available. Postbaccalaureate distance learning degree programs offered (minimal on-campus study). *Faculty:* 14 full-time (3 women), 43 part-time/adjunct (24 women). *Students:* 283 full-time (206 women), 298 part-time (208 women); includes 196 minority (112 African Americans, 1 American Indian/Alaska Native, 30 Asian Americans or Pacific Islanders, 53 Hispanic Americans), 18 international. Average age 26. 162 applicants, 100% accepted, 94 enrolled. In 2009, 108 master's awarded. *Degree requirements:* For master's, thesis or integrative seminar. *Entrance requirements:* For master's, minimum GPA of 2.7. Additional exam requirements/recommendations for international students: Required—TOEFL (minimum score 550 paper-based; 213 computer-based; 80 iBT), IELTS (minimum score 6.5). *Application deadline:* Applications are processed on a rolling basis. Application fee: $40. Electronic applications accepted. *Expenses:* Tuition: Full-time $37,525; part-time $620 per credit hour. *Financial support:* In 2009–10, 60 students received support, including 3 research assistantships with full tuition reimbursements available (averaging $7,000 per year); career-related internships or fieldwork, Federal Work-Study, institutionally sponsored loans, scholarships/grants, tuition waivers (partial), and unspecified assistantships also available. Support available to part-time students. Financial award application deadline: 7/1; financial award applicants required to submit FAFSA. *Faculty research:* Government financing, transportation, leadership, health care, volunteerism and organizational behavior, non-profit organizations. Total annual research expenditures: $20,000. *Unit head:* Dr. J. Patrick Murphy, Director, 312-362-5608, Fax: 312-362-5506, E-mail: jpmurphy@depaul.edu. *Application contact:* Megan B. Balderston, Director of Admissions and Marketing, 312-362-5565, Fax: 312-362-5506, E-mail: pubserv@depaul.edu.

DeSales University, Graduate Division, Program in Business Administration, Center Valley, PA 18034-9568. Offers accounting (MBA); business administration (MBA); computer information systems (MBA); finance (MBA); health care systems management (MBA); management (MBA); marketing (MBA); project management (MBA); self-design (MBA); MSN/MBA. *Accreditation:* ACBSP. Part-time programs available. Postbaccalaureate distance learning degree programs offered (no on-campus study). *Students:* 433 part-time. In 2009, 218 master's awarded. *Entrance requirements:* For master's, minimum GPA of 3.0, 2 years of work experience. Additional exam requirements/recommendations for international students: Required—TOEFL. *Application deadline:* Applications are processed on a rolling basis. Application fee: $35. Electronic applications accepted. *Expenses:* Tuition: Full-time $17,500; part-time $665 per credit. Full-time tuition and fees vary according to program. Part-time tuition and fees vary according to course load. *Faculty research:* Quality improvement, executive development, productivity, cross-cultural managerial differences, leadership. *Unit head:* Dr. David Gilfoil, Director, 610-282-1100 Ext. 1828, Fax: 610-282-2869, E-mail: david.gilfoil@desales.edu. *Application contact:* Caryn Stopper, Director of Graduate Admissions, 610-282-1100 Ext. 1768, Fax: 610-282-0525, E-mail: caryn.stopper@desales.edu.

DeVry University, Keller Graduate School of Management, Downers Grove, IL 60515. Offers accounting and financial management (MAFM); business administration (MBA); human resources management (MHRM); information systems management (MISM); network and communications management (MNCM); project management (MPM); public administration (MPA).

Dowling College, School of Business, Oakdale, NY 11769-1999. Offers aviation management (MBA, Certificate); banking and finance (MBA, Certificate); financial planning (Certificate); general management (MBA); health care management (MBA, Certificate); human resource management (Certificate); management and leadership (MBA); marketing (Certificate); project management (Certificate); public management (MBA, Certificate); total quality management (MBA, Certificate); JD/MBA. Part-time and evening/weekend programs available. *Faculty:* 14 full-time (5 women), 58 part-time/adjunct (5 women). *Students:* 324 full-time (142 women), 479 part-time (237 women); includes 238 minority (82 African Americans, 1 American Indian/Alaska Native, 117 Asian Americans or Pacific Islanders, 38 Hispanic Americans), 2 international. Average age 33. 457 applicants, 91% accepted, 153 enrolled. In 2009, 341 master's, 2 other advanced degrees awarded. *Degree requirements:* For master's, comprehensive exam, thesis optional. *Entrance requirements:* For master's, minimum GPA of 2.8, 2 letters of recommendation, courses in accounting and finance or seminar in accounting/finance, resume. Additional exam requirements/recommendations for international students: Required—TOEFL (minimum score 550 paper-based). *Application deadline:* For fall admission, 9/1 priority date for domestic students; for winter admission, 1/1 priority date for domestic students; for spring admission, 2/1 priority date for domestic students. Applications are processed on a rolling basis. Application fee: $50. Electronic applications accepted. *Expenses:* Tuition: Full-time $14,490; part-time $805 per credit. Required fees: $346 per term. *Financial support:* Career-related internships or fieldwork and Federal Work-Study available. Support available to part-time students. Financial award application deadline: 6/30; financial award applicants required to submit FAFSA. *Faculty research:* International finance, computer applications, labor relations, executive development. *Unit head:* Mathew Cordaro, Dean, 631-244-3162, Fax: 631-244-1018, E-mail: cordarom@dowling.edu. *Application contact:* Glenn M. Berman, Director of Admissions Operations, 631-244-3357, Fax: 631-244-1059, E-mail: glenn.berman@dowling.edu.

Drexel University, LeBow College of Business, Department of Finance, Philadelphia, PA 19104-2875. Offers MS. *Degree requirements:* For master's, seminar paper. *Entrance requirements:* For master's, GMAT, minimum GPA of 2.75. Additional exam requirements/recommendations for international students: Required—TOEFL. Electronic applications accepted. *Faculty research:* Investment analysis, portfolio mix, capital budgeting, banking and financial institutions, international finance.

Drexel University, LeBow College of Business, Program in Business Administration, Philadelphia, PA 19104-2875. Offers business administration (MBA, PhD, APC), including accounting (MBA, PhD), decision sciences (PhD), economics (MBA, PhD), finance (MBA, PhD), legal studies (MBA), management (MBA), marketing (MBA, PhD), organizational sciences (PhD), quantitative methods (MBA), strategic management (PhD). *Accreditation:* AACSB. Part-time and evening/weekend programs available. Postbaccalaureate distance learning degree programs offered (minimal on-campus study). Terminal master's awarded for partial completion of doctoral program. *Entrance requirements:* For master's, GMAT, minimum GPA of 2.75; for doctorate, GMAT. Additional exam requirements/recommendations for international students: Required—TOEFL. Electronic applications accepted. *Faculty research:* Decision support systems, individual and group behavior, operations research, techniques and strategy.

Eastern Michigan University, Graduate School, College of Business, Programs in Business Administration, Ypsilanti, MI 48197. Offers business administration (MBA, Graduate Certificate); computer information systems (Graduate Certificate); e-business (MBA, Graduate Certificate); enterprise business intelligence (MBA); entrepreneurship (MBA, Graduate Certificate); finance (MBA, Graduate Certificate); human resources (MBA); human resources management (Graduate Certificate); information systems (MBA); internal auditing (MBA); international business (MBA, Graduate Certificate); marketing management (Graduate Certificate); nonprofit management (MBA); organizational development (Graduate Certificate); supply chain management (MBA, Graduate Certificate). *Accreditation:* AACSB. Part-time programs available. Postbaccalaureate distance learning degree programs offered (no on-campus study). *Students:* 166 full-time (80 women), 439 part-time (231 women); includes 150 minority (103 African Americans, 7 American Indian/Alaska Native, 31 Asian Americans or Pacific Islanders, 9 Hispanic Americans), 97 international. Average age 34. In 2009, 3 other advanced degrees awarded. *Entrance requirements:* For master's, GMAT (minimum score 450), minimum cumulative undergraduate GPA of 2.75. Additional exam requirements/recommendations for international students: Required—TOEFL. *Application deadline:* For fall admission, 5/15 for domestic students, 5/1 for international students; for winter admission, 10/15 for domestic students, 10/1 for inter-

Finance and Banking

Eastern Michigan University (continued)

national students; for spring admission, 3/15 for domestic students, 3/1 for international students. Applications are processed on a rolling basis. Application fee: $35. Tuition and fees vary according to course level. *Financial support:* Fellowships, research assistantships with full tuition reimbursements, teaching assistantships with full tuition reimbursements, career-related internships or fieldwork, Federal Work-Study, institutionally sponsored loans, scholarships/grants, tuition waivers (partial), and unspecified assistantships available. Support available to part-time students. Financial award applicants required to submit FAFSA. *Unit head:* K. Michelle Henry, Director of Academic Services, 734-487-4444, Fax: 734-483-1316, E-mail: cob.grad@emich.edu. *Application contact:* Beste Windes, Advisor, 734-487-4444, Fax: 734-483-1316, E-mail: cob.grad@emich.edu.

East Tennessee State University, School of Graduate Studies, College of Business and Technology, Department of Economics, Finance, and Urban Studies, Johnson City, TN 37614. Offers city management (MCM); community development (MPM); general administration (MPM); municipal service management (MPM); urban and regional economic development (MPM); urban and regional planning (MPM). *Degree requirements:* For master's, internship, oral defense of thesis, research report. *Entrance requirements:* For master's, GRE General Test, minimum GPA of 3.0. Additional exam requirements/recommendations for international students: Required—TOEFL (minimum score 550 paper-based; 213 computer-based).

Emory University, Goizueta Business School, Doctoral Program in Business, Atlanta, GA 30322-1100. Offers accounting (PhD); finance (PhD); information systems (PhD); marketing (PhD); organization and management (PhD). *Faculty:* 57 full-time (11 women). *Students:* 37 full-time (14 women); includes 8 minority (3 African Americans, 4 Asian Americans or Pacific Islanders, 1 Hispanic American), 19 international. Average age 30. 218 applicants, 9% accepted, 9 enrolled. In 2009, 11 doctorates awarded. *Degree requirements:* For doctorate, comprehensive exam, thesis/dissertation. *Entrance requirements:* For doctorate, GMAT (strongly preferred) or GRE. Additional exam requirements/recommendations for international students: Required—TOEFL (minimum score 250 computer-based). *Application deadline:* For fall admission, 1/3 priority date for domestic and international students. Application fee: $50. Electronic applications accepted. *Unit head:* Dr. Lawrence Benveniste, Dean, 404-727-6377, Fax: 404-727-0868, E-mail: larry_benveniste@bus.emory.edu. *Application contact:* Allison Gilmore, Director of Admissions and Student Services, 404-727-6353, Fax: 404-727-5337, E-mail: phd@bus.emory.edu.

Fairfield University, Charles F. Dolan School of Business, Fairfield, CT 06824-5195. Offers accounting (MBA, MS, CAS); finance (MBA, MS, CAS); general management (MBA); human resource management (MBA, CAS); information systems and operations (MBA); information systems and operations management (CAS); international business (MBA, CAS); marketing (MBA, CAS); taxation (MBA, MS). *Accreditation:* AACSB. Part-time and evening/weekend programs available. *Degree requirements:* For master's, capstone course. *Entrance requirements:* For master's, GMAT (minimum score 500), 2 letters of reference, resume, minimum GPA of 3.0. Additional exam requirements/recommendations for international students: Required—TOEFL (minimum score 550 paper-based; 213 computer-based; 80 iBT). Electronic applications accepted. *Expenses:* Contact institution. *Faculty research:* Optimization strategies, international finance, consumer behavior, financial market volatility, Internet marketing, supply chain analysis, tax issues.

Fairleigh Dickinson University, College at Florham, Silberman College of Business, Department of Economics, Finance, and International Business, Program in Finance, Madison, NJ 07940-1099. Offers MBA, Certificate. *Students:* 25 full-time (8 women), 80 part-time (27 women), 5 international. Average age 29. 39 applicants, 62% accepted, 17 enrolled. In 2009, 19 master's awarded. *Application deadline:* Applications are processed on a rolling basis. Application fee: $40.

Fairleigh Dickinson University, Metropolitan Campus, Silberman College of Business, Department of Economics, Finance and International Business, Program in Finance, Teaneck, NJ 07666-1914. Offers MBA, Certificate. *Students:* 59 full-time (24 women), 31 part-time (11 women), 69 international. Average age 26. 91 applicants, 55% accepted, 12 enrolled. In 2009, 54 master's awarded. *Application deadline:* Applications are processed on a rolling basis. Application fee: $40. *Application contact:* Susan Brooman, University Director of Graduate Admissions, 201-692-2554, Fax: 201-692-2560, E-mail: globaleducation@fdu.edu.

Florida Agricultural and Mechanical University, Division of Graduate Studies, Research, and Continuing Education, School of Business and Industry, Tallahassee, FL 32307-3200. Offers accounting (MBA); finance (MBA); management information systems (MBA); marketing (MBA). *Faculty:* 42 full-time (28 women). *Students:* 71 full-time (45 women), 15 part-time (9 women); includes 80 minority (all African Americans), 4 international. In 2009, 90 master's awarded. *Degree requirements:* For master's, residency. *Entrance requirements:* For master's, GMAT, minimum GPA of 3.0. *Application deadline:* For fall admission, 5/18 for domestic students, 12/18 for international students; for spring admission, 11/12 for domestic students, 5/12 for international students. Application fee: $30. *Financial support:* Fellowships, Federal Work-Study and scholarships/grants available. *Unit head:* Dr. Amos Bradford, Interim Dean, 850-599-3565. *Application contact:* Dr. Amos Bradford, Interim Dean, 850-599-3565.

Florida Atlantic University, College of Business, Department of Finance, Boca Raton, FL 33431-0991. Offers MS, PhD. *Faculty:* 15 full-time (4 women), 2 part-time/adjunct (0 women). In 2009, 2 master's awarded. *Degree requirements:* For master's, comprehensive exam, thesis optional. *Entrance requirements:* For master's, GMAT or GRE General Test, minimum GPA of 3.0. Additional exam requirements/recommendations for international students: Required—TOEFL (minimum score 600 paper-based; 250 computer-based). *Application deadline:* For fall admission, 7/1 priority date for domestic students, 2/15 priority date for international students; for winter admission, 11/1 priority date for domestic students, 8/15 priority date for international students; for spring admission, 4/1 priority date for domestic students, 1/15 priority date for international students. Applications are processed on a rolling basis. Application fee: $30. *Expenses:* Tuition, state resident: full-time $7055; part-time $293.94 per credit hour. Tuition, nonresident: full-time $22,096; part-time $920.66 per credit hour. *Unit head:* Dr. Emilio R. Zarruk, Chair, 561-297-3995. *Application contact:* Fredrick G. Taylor, Graduate Adviser, 561-297-3196, Fax: 561-297-1315, E-mail: ftaylor@fau.edu.

Florida Institute of Technology, Graduate Programs, College of Business, Online Programs, Melbourne, FL 32901-6975. Offers accounting and finance (MBA); healthcare management (MBA); information technology (MS); information technology management (MBA); management (MBA); marketing (MBA); project management (MBA). Part-time and evening/weekend programs available. Postbaccalaureate distance learning degree programs offered (no on-campus study). *Faculty:* 30 part-time/adjunct (6 women). *Students:* 6 full-time (2 women), 875 part-time (387 women); includes 290 minority (194 African Americans, 6 American Indian/Alaska Native, 44 Asian Americans or Pacific Islanders, 46 Hispanic Americans), 32 international. Average age 37. 329 applicants, 64% accepted, 177 enrolled. In 2009, 33 master's awarded. *Entrance requirements:* For master's, GMAT or resume showing 8 years of supervised experience, 2 letters of recommendation, resume, competency in math past college algebra. Additional exam requirements/recommendations for international students: Required—TOEFL (minimum score 550 paper-based; 213 computer-based; 79 iBT). *Application deadline:* For fall admission, 4/1 for international students; for spring admission, 9/30 for international students. Applications are processed on a rolling basis. Application fee: $50. Electronic applications accepted. *Expenses:* Tuition: Part-time $1015 per credit. Tuition and fees vary according to campus/location and program. *Financial support:* Available to part-time students. Application deadline: 3/1. *Unit head:* Dr. Mary S. Bonhomme, Dean, Florida Tech Online/Associate Provost for Online Learning, 321-674-8883, Fax: 321-674-8216, E-mail: bonhomme@fit.edu. *Application contact:* Carolyn Farrior, Director of Graduate Admissions Online Learning and Off Campus Programs, 321-674-7118, Fax: 321-674-8216, E-mail: cfarrior@fit.edu.

Florida International University, Alvah H. Chapman, Jr. Graduate School of Business, Department of Finance and Real Estate, Miami, FL 33199. Offers finance (MSF); international real estate (MS); real estate (MS). Part-time and evening/weekend programs available. *Faculty:* 17 full-time (3 women). *Students:* 94 full-time (24 women), 12 part-time (5 women); includes 55 minority (15 African Americans, 5 Asian Americans or Pacific Islanders, 35 Hispanic Americans), 28 international. Average age 30. 184 applicants, 32% accepted, 51 enrolled. In 2009, 109 master's awarded. *Entrance requirements:* For master's, GMAT or GRE, minimum GPA of 3.0 (upper-level coursework); letter of intent; resume. Additional exam requirements/recommendations for international students: Required—TOEFL (minimum score 550 paper-based; 213 computer-based; 80 iBT), or IELTS (minimum score 6.5). *Application deadline:* For fall admission, 6/1 for domestic students, 4/1 for international students; for spring admission, 10/1 for domestic students, 9/1 for international students. Applications are processed on a rolling basis. Application fee: $30. Electronic applications accepted. *Expenses:* Contact institution. *Financial support:* Institutionally sponsored loans and scholarships/grants available. Financial award application deadline: 3/1; financial award applicants required to submit FAFSA. *Faculty research:* Investment; corporate and international finance; commercial real estate. *Unit head:* Dr. Chun-Hao Chang, Chair, 305-348-2680, Fax: 305-348-4245, E-mail: chun-hao.chang@fiu.edu. *Application contact:* Isabel Lopez, Assistant Director, Finance and Real Estate Graduate Programs, 305-348-4198, E-mail: lopezi@fiu.edu.

Florida State University, The Graduate School, College of Business, Tallahassee, FL 32306-1110. Offers accounting (M Acc), including accounting information services, assurance services, corporate accounting, taxation; business administration (MBA, PhD), including accounting (PhD), finance (PhD), management information systems (PhD), marketing (PhD), organizational behavior (PhD), risk management and insurance (PhD), strategic management (PhD); finance (MS); insurance (MSM); management information systems (MS); JD/MBA; MSW/MBA. *Accreditation:* AACSB. Part-time programs available. Postbaccalaureate distance learning degree programs offered (no on-campus study). *Faculty:* 107 full-time (31 women), 2 part-time/adjunct (0 women). *Students:* 212 full-time (73 women), 345 part-time (107 women); includes 123 minority (37 African Americans, 2 American Indian/Alaska Native, 48 Asian Americans or Pacific Islanders, 36 Hispanic Americans). Average age 30. 908 applicants, 43% accepted, 307 enrolled. In 2009, 257 master's, 18 doctorates awarded. Terminal master's awarded for partial completion of doctoral program. *Degree requirements:* For doctorate, comprehensive exam, thesis/dissertation. *Entrance requirements:* For master's, GMAT, work experience (MBA, MS), minimum GPA of 3.0, letters of recommendation; for doctorate, GMAT, minimum graduate GPA of 3.5, letters of recommendation. Additional exam requirements/recommendations for international students: Required—TOEFL (minimum score 600 paper-based; 80 computer-based); Recommended—IELTS (minimum score 6.5). *Application deadline:* For fall admission, 6/1 for domestic students, 5/1 for international students; for spring admission, 10/1 for domestic students, 9/1 for international students. Applications are processed on a rolling basis. Application fee: $30. Electronic applications accepted. *Expenses:* Tuition, state resident: full-time $7413. Tuition, nonresident: full-time $22,567. *Financial support:* In 2009–10, 102 students received support, including 32 fellowships with full tuition reimbursements available (averaging $6,900 per year), 30 research assistantships with full tuition reimbursements available (averaging $4,500 per year), 40 teaching assistantships with full tuition reimbursements available (averaging $11,500 per year); career-related internships or fieldwork, scholarships/grants, health care benefits, tuition waivers (full and partial), and unspecified assistantships also available. Support available to part-time students. Financial award application deadline: 1/1. *Unit head:* Dr. Caryn Beck-Dudley, Dean, 850-644-3090, Fax: 850-644-0915. *Application contact:* Lisa Beverly, Director, Graduate Programs Admissions, 850-644-6458, Fax: 850-644-0588, E-mail: lbeverly@cob.fsu.edu.

Fordham University, Graduate School of Business Administration, New York, NY 10023. Offers accounting (MBA); communications and media management (MBA); executive business administration (EMBA); finance (MBA, MS); information systems (MBA, MS); management systems (MBA); marketing (MBA); media management (MS); taxation (MS); taxation and accounting (MTA);); JD/MBA; MBA/MIM; MS/MBA. *Accreditation:* AACSB. Part-time and evening/weekend programs available. *Entrance requirements:* For master's, GMAT, 2 letters of recommendation, resume. Additional exam requirements/recommendations for international students: Required—TOEFL (minimum score 600 paper-based; 250 computer-based; 100 iBT). Electronic applications accepted. *Expenses:* Contact institution.

Gannon University, School of Graduate Studies, College of Engineering and Business, School of Business, Program in Finance, Erie, PA 16541-0001. Offers Certificate. Part-time and evening/weekend programs available. *Entrance requirements:* For degree, GMAT. Additional exam requirements/recommendations for international students: Required—TOEFL (minimum score 79 iBT). *Application deadline:* Applications are processed on a rolling basis. Application fee: $25. Electronic applications accepted. *Expenses:* Tuition: Full-time $13,590; part-time $755 per credit. Required fees: $524; $17 per credit. Tuition and fees vary according to course load, degree level, campus/location and program. *Financial support:* Application deadline: 7/1. *Unit head:* Scott Miller, Associate Director, 814-871-7397, E-mail: miller032@gannon.edu. *Application contact:* Kara Morgan, Assistant Director of Graduate Admissions, 814-871-5831, Fax: 814-871-5827, E-mail: graduate@gannon.edu.

George Fox University, School of Business, Newberg, OR 97132-2697. Offers finance (MBA); management (DBA); management/general (MBA); marketing (DBA); organizational strategy (MBA); strategic human resource management (MBA). MBA offered in part-time and full-time formats. Also offered in Portland, OR and Boise, ID. Part-time and evening/weekend programs available. Postbaccalaureate distance learning degree programs offered (minimal on-campus study). *Faculty:* 15 full-time (5 women), 7 part-time/adjunct (0 women). *Students:* 14 full-time (3 women), 223 part-time (77 women); includes 28 minority (7 African Americans, 3 American Indian/Alaska Native, 9 Asian Americans or Pacific Islanders, 9 Hispanic Americans), 2 international. Average age 38. 88 applicants, 86% accepted, 63 enrolled. In 2009, 66 master's, 2 doctorates awarded. *Degree requirements:* For master's, capstone project; for doctorate, credit-applied research project. *Entrance requirements:* For master's, resume (5 years professional experience required); 3 professional references; interview; financial e-learning course; for doctorate, GRE or GMAT, resume; personal mission statement; academic research writing sample; official transcript from each college/university attended; three professional references. Additional exam requirements/recommendations for international students: Required—TOEFL (minimum score 577 paper-based; 233 computer-based; 90 iBT), or IELTS (minimum score 7). *Application deadline:* For fall admission, 8/1 for domestic and international students; for spring admission, 12/1 for domestic and international students. Applications are processed on a rolling basis. Application fee: $40. Electronic applications accepted. *Expenses:* Contact institution. *Financial support:* In 2009–10, 2 students received support. Applicants required to submit FAFSA. *Unit head:* Dr. Ken Armstrong, Professor of Management and Dean, School of Management, 800-631-0921. *Application contact:* Robin Halverson, Admissions Counselor, 800-493-4937, Fax: 503-554-6111, E-mail: mba@georgefox.edu.

Georgetown University, Graduate School of Arts and Sciences, Department of Economics, Washington, DC 20057. Offers econometrics (PhD); economic development (PhD); economic theory (PhD); industrial organization (PhD); international macro and finance (PhD); international trade (PhD); labor economics (PhD); macroeconomics (PhD); public economics and political economics (PhD); MA/PhD; MS/MA. *Degree requirements:* For doctorate, comprehensive exam, thesis/dissertation. *Entrance requirements:* For doctorate, GRE General Test. Additional exam requirements/recommendations for international students: Required—TOEFL. *Faculty research:* International economics, economic development.

The George Washington University, Columbian College of Arts and Sciences, Trachtenberg School of Public Policy and Public Administration, Washington, DC 20052. Offers public administration (MPA), including budget and public finance, federal policy, politics, and management, international development management, managing public organizations, managing state and local governments, nonprofit management, policy analysis and evaluation, public administration, public-private policy and management; public policy (MA, MPP), including environmental and resource policy (MA), philosophy and social policy (MA), women's studies (MA); public policy and administration (PhD); JD/MPP; MPA/JD; PhD/MPP. Part-time and evening/weekend programs available. *Faculty:* 35 full-time (12 women), 19 part-time/adjunct

(10 women). *Students:* 187 full-time (114 women), 232 part-time (151 women); includes 62 minority (15 African Americans, 3 American Indian/Alaska Native, 29 Asian Americans or Pacific Islanders, 15 Hispanic Americans), 23 international. Average age 26. 913 applicants, 56% accepted, 186 enrolled. In 2009, 106 master's, 9 doctorates awarded. *Degree requirements:* For doctorate, thesis/dissertation, general exam. *Entrance requirements:* For master's, GRE General Test, minimum GPA of 3.0; for doctorate, GRE General Test, interview, minimum GPA of 3.0. Additional exam requirements/recommendations for international students: Required—TOEFL (minimum score 600 paper-based; 250 computer-based; 100 iBT). *Application deadline:* For fall admission, 1/15 priority date for domestic and international students; for spring admission, 10/1 priority date for domestic students, 9/1 priority date for international students. Applications are processed on a rolling basis. Application fee: $60. Electronic applications accepted. *Financial support:* In 2009–10, 87 students received support; fellowships, research assistantships, teaching assistantships, institutionally sponsored loans available. Financial award application deadline: 1/15. *Unit head:* Dr. Kathyrn E. Newcomer, Director, 202-994-3959, Fax: 202-994-3959, E-mail: newcomer@gwu.edu. *Application contact:* Information Contact, 202-994-6295, Fax: 202-994-6295, E-mail: tspppa@gwu.edu.

The George Washington University, Columbian College of Arts and Sciences, Trachtenberg School of Public Policy and Public Administration, Programs in Public Administration, Program in Budget and Public Finance, Washington, DC 20052. Offers MPA. Part-time and evening/weekend programs available. *Students:* 1 (woman) full-time, 1 part-time (0 women), 1 international. Average age 28. *Entrance requirements:* For master's, GRE General Test. Additional exam requirements/recommendations for international students: Required—TOEFL (minimum score 600 paper-based; 250 computer-based; 100 iBT). *Application deadline:* For fall admission, 4/1 priority date for domestic students; for spring admission, 10/1 for domestic students. Applications are processed on a rolling basis. Application fee: $60. *Financial support:* Fellowships, teaching assistantships, career-related internships or fieldwork, Federal Work-Study, and institutionally sponsored loans available. Financial award application deadline: 1/15. *Unit head:* Philip Joyce, Lead Professor, 202-994-4071, Fax: 202-994-6792, E-mail: pgjoyce@gwu.edu. *Application contact:* David Toomer, Director of Enrollment Management, 202-994-6584, Fax: 202-994-6382.

The George Washington University, School of Business, Department of Finance, Washington, DC 20052. Offers finance (MSF, PhD); finance and investments (MBA); real estate and urban development (MBA). Part-time and evening/weekend programs available. *Faculty:* 17 full-time (3 women), 10 part-time/adjunct (2 women). *Students:* 74 full-time (26 women), 40 part-time (13 women); includes 15 minority (4 African Americans, 8 Asian Americans or Pacific Islanders, 3 Hispanic Americans), 74 international. Average age 30. 211 applicants, 58% accepted, 59 enrolled. In 2009, 61 master's awarded. *Degree requirements:* For doctorate, thesis/dissertation. *Entrance requirements:* For master's, GMAT; for doctorate, GMAT or GRE. Additional exam requirements/recommendations for international students: Required—TOEFL. *Application deadline:* For fall admission, 4/1 priority date for domestic students; for spring admission, 10/1 for domestic students. Applications are processed on a rolling basis. Application fee: $60. *Financial support:* In 2009–10, 38 students received support; fellowships, teaching assistantships, career-related internships or fieldwork, Federal Work-Study, and institutionally sponsored loans available. Financial award application deadline: 4/1. *Unit head:* Mark S. Klock, Chair, 202-994-5996, E-mail: klock@gwu.edu. *Application contact:* Kristin Williams, Assistant Vice President for Graduate and Special Enrollment Management, 202-994-0467, Fax: 202-994-0371, E-mail: ksw@gwu.edu.

Georgia Institute of Technology, Graduate Studies and Research, College of Management, Program in Business Administration, Atlanta, GA 30332-0001. Offers accounting (MBA); e-commerce (Certificate); engineering entrepreneurship (MBA); entrepreneurship (Certificate); finance (MBA); information technology management (MBA); international business (MBA, Certificate); management of technology (Certificate); marketing (MBA); operations management (MBA); organizational behavior (MBA); strategic management (MBA). *Accreditation:* AACSB.

Georgia Institute of Technology, Graduate Studies and Research, College of Management, Program in Management, Atlanta, GA 30332-0001. Offers accounting (PhD); finance (PhD); information technology management (PhD); marketing (PhD); operations management (PhD); organizational behavior (PhD); quantitative and computational finance (MS); strategic management (PhD). *Accreditation:* AACSB. *Degree requirements:* For doctorate, comprehensive exam, thesis/dissertation, oral exams. *Entrance requirements:* For master's and doctorate, GMAT. Additional exam requirements/recommendations for international students: Required—TOEFL. *Faculty research:* MIS, management of technology, international business, entrepreneurship, operations management.

Georgia State University, Andrew Young School of Policy Studies, Department of Public Management and Policy, Atlanta, GA 30303. Offers disaster management (Certificate); nonprofit management (Certificate); planning and economic development (Certificate); public administration (MPA), including criminal justice, management and finance, nonprofit management, planning and economic development, policy analysis and evaluation, public health; public policy (MPP, PhD), including disaster policy (MPP), nonprofit policy (MPP), planning and economic development policy (MPP), public finance policy (MPP), social policy (MPP); JD/MPA. *Accreditation:* NASPAA (one or more programs are accredited). Part-time and evening/weekend programs available. Terminal master's awarded for partial completion of doctoral program. *Degree requirements:* For master's, thesis optional; for doctorate, comprehensive exam, thesis/dissertation. *Entrance requirements:* For master's and doctorate, GRE General Test. Additional exam requirements/recommendations for international students: Required—TOEFL. Electronic applications accepted. *Faculty research:* Public management, policy analysis, public finance, planning and economic development, nonprofit leadership and policy.

Georgia State University, J. Mack Robinson College of Business, Department of Finance, Atlanta, GA 30302-3083. Offers MBA, MS, PhD. Part-time and evening/weekend programs available. Terminal master's awarded for partial completion of doctoral program. *Degree requirements:* For doctorate, comprehensive exam, thesis/dissertation. *Entrance requirements:* For master's and doctorate, GMAT. Additional exam requirements/recommendations for international students: Required—TOEFL (minimum score 610 paper-based; 253 computer-based; 101 iBT). Electronic applications accepted.

Georgia State University, J. Mack Robinson College of Business, Department of Risk Management and Insurance, Program in Personal Financial Planning, Atlanta, GA 30302-3083. Offers MBA, MS, Certificate. Part-time and evening/weekend programs available. *Entrance requirements:* For master's, GMAT, GRE. Additional exam requirements/recommendations for international students: Required—TOEFL (minimum score 610 paper-based; 255 computer-based; 101 iBT). Electronic applications accepted.

Golden Gate University, Ageno School of Business, San Francisco, CA 94105-2968. Offers accounting (MBA); business administration (EMBA, MBA, PMBA, DBA); finance (MBA, MS, Certificate); financial planning (MS, Certificate); human resource management (MBA, MS); human resources management (Certificate); information systems (MS); information technology (MBA); information technology management (Certificate); integrated marketing and communications (MS, Certificate); international business (MBA); management (MBA); marketing (MBA, MS, Certificate); operations management (Certificate); psychology (MA, Certificate); public relations (MS, Certificate); JD/MBA. Part-time and evening/weekend programs available. *Faculty:* 16 full-time (4 women), 241 part-time/adjunct (72 women). *Students:* 380 full-time (193 women), 750 part-time (414 women); includes 480 minority (98 African Americans, 2 American Indian/Alaska Native, 298 Asian Americans or Pacific Islanders, 82 Hispanic Americans), 166 international. Average age 33. 681 applicants, 78% accepted, 270 enrolled. In 2009, 550 master's, 13 doctorates awarded. *Degree requirements:* For doctorate, thesis/dissertation. *Entrance requirements:* For master's, GMAT (MBA), minimum GPA of 2.5 (MS). Additional exam requirements/recommendations for international students: Required—TOEFL. *Application deadline:* For fall admission, 5/15 for international students; for winter admission, 1/15 for international students; for spring admission, 9/15 for international students. Applications are processed on a rolling basis. Application fee: $70 ($110 for international students). Electronic applications accepted. *Expenses:* Contact institution. *Financial support:* Career-related internships or fieldwork, Federal Work-Study, institutionally sponsored loans, and scholarships/grants available. Support available to part-time students. Financial award applicants required to submit FAFSA. *Unit head:* Terry Connelly, Dean, 415-442-6519, Fax: 415-442-5369. *Application contact:* Angela Melero, Enrollment Services, 415-442-7800, Fax: 415-442-7807, E-mail: info@ggu.edu.

Goldey-Beacom College, Graduate Program, Wilmington, DE 19808-1999. Offers business administration (MBA); finance (MS); financial management (MBA); human resource management (MBA); information technology (MBA); international business management (MBA); management (MM); marketing management (MBA); taxation (MBA, MS). *Accreditation:* ACBSP. Part-time and evening/weekend programs available. *Faculty:* 20 full-time (8 women), 28 part-time/adjunct (10 women). *Students:* 38 full-time (18 women), 486 part-time (184 women); includes 350 minority (38 African Americans, 300 Asian Americans or Pacific Islanders, 12 Hispanic Americans). Average age 27. In 2009, 130 master's awarded. *Entrance requirements:* For master's, GMAT, MAT, GRE, minimum GPA of 3.0. Additional exam requirements/recommendations for international students: Required—TOEFL (minimum score 65 computer-based); Recommended—IELTS (minimum score 5). *Application deadline:* Applications are processed on a rolling basis. Electronic applications accepted. *Expenses:* Tuition: Full-time $14,166; part-time $787 per credit. Required fees: $180; $10 per credit. *Financial support:* In 2009–10, 486 students received support. Scholarships/grants available. Support available to part-time students. Financial award application deadline: 4/1; financial award applicants required to submit FAFSA. *Unit head:* Larry W. Eby, Director of Admissions, 302-225-6289, Fax: 302-996-5408, E-mail: ebylw@gbc.edu. *Application contact:* Ashley E. Mashington, Graduate Admissions Representative, 302-225-6259, Fax: 302-996-5408, E-mail: mashina@gbc.edu.

Graduate School and University Center of the City University of New York, Graduate Studies, Program in Business, New York, NY 10016-4039. Offers accounting (PhD); behavioral science (PhD); finance (PhD); management planning systems (PhD). *Faculty:* 66 full-time (5 women). *Students:* 64 full-time (37 women); includes 7 minority (3 African Americans, 1 American Indian/Alaska Native, 2 Asian Americans or Pacific Islanders, 1 Hispanic American), 34 international. Average age 33. 89 applicants, 28% accepted, 18 enrolled. In 2009, 7 doctorates awarded. *Degree requirements:* For doctorate, thesis/dissertation. *Entrance requirements:* For doctorate, GMAT, writing sample (15 pages). Additional exam requirements/recommendations for international students: Required—TOEFL. *Application deadline:* For fall admission, 1/15 for domestic students. Application fee: $125. Electronic applications accepted. *Financial support:* In 2009–10, 50 students received support, including 54 fellowships, 5 teaching assistantships; research assistantships, career-related internships or fieldwork, Federal Work-Study, institutionally sponsored loans, and tuition waivers (full and partial) also available. Financial award application deadline: 2/1; financial award applicants required to submit FAFSA. *Unit head:* Dr. Joseph Weintrop, Executive Officer, 646-312-3092, Fax: 646-312-3031. *Application contact:* Les Gribben, Director of Admissions, 212-817-7470, Fax: 212-817-1624, E-mail: lgribben@gc.cuny.edu.

Grand Canyon University, College of Business, Phoenix, AZ 85017-1097. Offers accounting (MBA); executive fire service leadership (MS); finance (MBA); general management (MBA); health systems management (MBA); leadership (MBA, MS); management of information system (MBA); marketing (MBA); six sigma (MBA). *Accreditation:* ACBSP. Part-time and evening/weekend programs available. Postbaccalaureate distance learning degree programs offered (no on-campus study). *Entrance requirements:* For master's, equivalent of two years full-time professional work experience. Additional exam requirements/recommendations for international students: Required—TOEFL (minimum score 575 paper-based; 233 computer-based; 90 iBT), IELTS (minimum score 7). Electronic applications accepted.

Hawai'i Pacific University, College of Business Administration, Honolulu, HI 96813. Offers accounting/CPA (MBA); e-business (MBA); economics (MBA); finance (MBA); human resource management (MA, MBA); information systems (MBA, MSIS), including knowledge management (MSIS), software engineering (MSIS), telecommunications security (MSIS); international business (MBA); management (MBA); marketing (MBA); organizational change (MA, MBA); travel industry management (MBA). Part-time and evening/weekend programs available. *Faculty:* 15 full-time (5 women), 11 part-time/adjunct (4 women). *Students:* 206 full-time (107 women), 197 part-time (105 women); includes 136 minority (18 African Americans, 3 American Indian/Alaska Native, 98 Asian Americans or Pacific Islanders, 17 Hispanic Americans), 151 international. Average age 30. 235 applicants, 90% accepted, 127 enrolled. In 2009, 141 master's awarded. *Degree requirements:* For master's, thesis. *Entrance requirements:* For master's, GMAT. Additional exam requirements/recommendations for international students: Recommended—TOEFL (minimum score 550 paper-based; 213 computer-based; 80 iBT), TWE (minimum score 5). *Application deadline:* For fall admission, 2/15 priority date for domestic students; for spring admission, 10/15 priority date for domestic students. Applications are processed on a rolling basis. Application fee: $50. Electronic applications accepted. *Expenses:* Tuition: Full-time $12,600; part-time $700 per credit hour. Tuition and fees vary according to program. *Financial support:* In 2009–10, 164 students received support; research assistantships, career-related internships or fieldwork, Federal Work-Study, scholarships/grants, and unspecified assistantships available. Support available to part-time students. Financial award application deadline: 3/1; financial award applicants required to submit FAFSA. *Faculty research:* Statistical control process as used by management, studies in comparative cross-cultural management styles, not-for-profit management. *Unit head:* Dr. Aytun Ozturk, Dean, 808-544-9301, Fax: 808-544-0283, E-mail: uozturk@hpu.edu. *Application contact:* Danny Lam, Assistant Director of Graduate Admissions, 808-544-1135, Fax: 808-544-0280, E-mail: graduate@hpu.edu.

See Close-Up on page 251.

HEC Montreal, School of Business Administration, Diploma Programs in Administration, Program in Private Wealth Management, Montréal, QC H3T 2A7, Canada. Offers Diploma. Part-time programs available. *Students:* 14 part-time (4 women). 19 applicants, 0% accepted. In 2009, 1 Diploma awarded. *Application deadline:* For fall admission, 4/15 for domestic and international students. Application fee: $76. Electronic applications accepted. Tuition and fees charges are reported in Canadian dollars. *Expenses:* Tuition, area resident: Part-time $65.60 Canadian dollars per credit. Tuition, state resident: full-time $2361.60 Canadian dollars; part-time $183.36 Canadian dollars per credit. Tuition, nonresident: full-time $6601 Canadian dollars; part-time $448.13 Canadian dollars per credit. International tuition: $16,132.68 Canadian dollars full-time. Required fees: $1254.15 Canadian dollars; $28.99 Canadian dollars per course. $91.68 Canadian dollars per term. Tuition and fees vary according to degree level and program. *Unit head:* Louise Cote, Director, 514-340-6205, Fax: 514-340-5640, E-mail: louise.cote@hec.ca. *Application contact:* Francine Blais, Administrative Director, 514-340-6112, Fax: 514-340-6411, E-mail: francine.blais@hec.ca.

HEC Montreal, School of Business Administration, Diploma Programs in Administration, Program in Professional Finance, Montréal, QC H3T 2A7, Canada. Offers Diploma. Part-time programs available. *Students:* 21 full-time (6 women). 85 applicants, 54% accepted. *Application deadline:* For fall admission, 4/1 for domestic and international students; for winter admission, 10/1 for domestic and international students. Application fee: $77. Electronic applications accepted. Tuition and fees charges are reported in Canadian dollars. *Expenses:* Tuition, area resident: Part-time $65.60 Canadian dollars per credit. Tuition, state resident: full-time $2361.60 Canadian dollars; part-time $183.36 Canadian dollars per credit. Tuition, nonresident: full-time $6601 Canadian dollars; part-time $448.13 Canadian dollars per credit. International tuition: $16,132.68 Canadian dollars full-time. Required fees: $1254.15 Canadian dollars; $28.99 Canadian dollars per course. $91.68 Canadian dollars per term. Tuition and fees vary according to degree level and program. *Financial support:* Research assistantships, teaching assistantships, scholarships/grants available. Financial award application deadline: 10/2. *Unit head:* Louise Cote, Academic Supervisor, 514-340-6205, Fax: 514-340-5640, E-mail: louise.cote@hec.ca. *Application contact:* Marie Deshaies, Senior Student Advisor, 514-340-6135, Fax: 514-340-6411, E-mail: marie.deshaies@hec.ca.

HEC Montreal, School of Business Administration, Master of Science Programs in Administration, Program in Applied Financial Economics, Montréal, QC H3T 2A7, Canada. Offers M Sc.

Finance and Banking

HEC Montreal (continued)

Part-time programs available. *Students:* 26 full-time (10 women), 1 (woman) part-time. 24 applicants, 38% accepted, 5 enrolled. In 2009, 8 master's awarded. *Degree requirements:* For master's, one foreign language, thesis. *Application deadline:* For fall admission, 3/15 for domestic and international students; for winter admission, 9/15 for domestic and international students. Application fee: $77 Canadian dollars. Electronic applications accepted. Tuition and fees charges are reported in Canadian dollars. *Expenses:* Tuition, area resident: Part-time $65.60 Canadian dollars per credit. Tuition, state resident: full-time $2361.60 Canadian dollars; part-time $183.36 Canadian dollars per credit. Tuition, nonresident: full-time $6601 Canadian dollars; part-time $448.13 Canadian dollars per credit. International tuition: $16,132.68 Canadian dollars full-time. Required fees: $1254.15 Canadian dollars; $28.99 Canadian dollars per course. $91.68 Canadian dollars per term. Tuition and fees vary according to degree level and program. *Financial support:* Fellowships, research assistantships, teaching assistantships, scholarships/grants available. Financial award application deadline: 10/2. *Unit head:* Dr. Claude Laurin, Director, 514-340-6485, Fax: 514-340-5690, E-mail: claude.laurin@hec.ca. *Application contact:* Francine Blais, Administrative Director, 514-340-6112, Fax: 514-340-6411, E-mail: francine.blais@hec.ca.

HEC Montreal, School of Business Administration, Master of Science Programs in Administration, Program in Finance, Montréal, QC H3T 2A7, Canada. Offers M Sc. All courses are given in French. Part-time programs available. *Students:* 73 full-time (11 women), 9 part-time (0 women). 109 applicants, 47% accepted, 26 enrolled. In 2009, 18 master's awarded. *Degree requirements:* For master's, one foreign language. *Application deadline:* For fall admission, 3/15 for domestic and international students; for winter admission, 9/15 for domestic and international students. Application fee: $77 Canadian dollars. Electronic applications accepted. Tuition and fees charges are reported in Canadian dollars. *Expenses:* Tuition, area resident: Part-time $65.60 Canadian dollars per credit. Tuition, state resident: full-time $2361.60 Canadian dollars; part-time $183.36 Canadian dollars per credit. Tuition, nonresident: full-time $6601 Canadian dollars; part-time $448.13 Canadian dollars per credit. International tuition: $16,132.68 Canadian dollars full-time. Required fees: $1254.15 Canadian dollars; $28.99 Canadian dollars per course. $91.68 Canadian dollars per term. Tuition and fees vary according to degree level and program. *Financial support:* Fellowships, research assistantships, teaching assistantships, scholarships/grants available. Financial award application deadline: 10/2. *Unit head:* Dr. Claude Laurin, Director, 514-340-6485, Fax: 514-340-5690, E-mail: claude.laurin@hec.ca. *Application contact:* Francine Blais, Administrative Director, 514-340-6112, Fax: 514-340-6411, E-mail: francine.blais@hec.ca.

Hofstra University, Frank G. Zarb School of Business, Department of Finance, Hempstead, NY 11549. Offers business administration (MBA), including finance, real estate; finance (MS); quantitative finance (MS). Part-time and evening/weekend programs available. *Faculty:* 10 full-time (2 women), 3 part-time/adjunct (0 women). *Students:* 122 full-time (36 women), 93 part-time (30 women); includes 24 minority (7 African Americans, 11 Asian Americans or Pacific Islanders, 6 Hispanic Americans), 73 international. Average age 27. 223 applicants, 76% accepted, 67 enrolled. In 2009, 70 master's awarded. *Degree requirements:* For master's, capstone course (MBA), thesis (MS). *Entrance requirements:* For master's, GMAT or GRE, 2 letters of recommendation, resume. Additional exam requirements/recommendations for international students: Required—TOEFL (minimum score 550 paper-based; 213 computer-based; 80 iBT); Recommended—IELTS (minimum score 6). *Application deadline:* Applications are processed on a rolling basis. Application fee: $60. Electronic applications accepted. *Expenses:* Contact institution. *Financial support:* In 2009–10, 44 students received support, including 38 fellowships with full and partial tuition reimbursements available (averaging $9,548 per year), 1 research assistantship with full and partial tuition reimbursement available (averaging $14,532 per year); Federal Work-Study, institutionally sponsored loans, scholarships/grants, and tuition waivers (full and partial) also available. Support available to part-time students. Financial award applicants required to submit FAFSA. *Faculty research:* Corporate finance, investments, banking, real estate, derivatives. *Unit head:* Dr. Nancy W. White, Chairperson, 516-463-5699, Fax: 516-463-4834, E-mail: finnwh@hofstra.edu. *Application contact:* Carol Drummer, Dean of Graduate Admissions, 516-463-4876, Fax: 516-463-4664, E-mail: gradstudent@hofstra.edu.

Holy Family University, Division of Extended Learning, Philadelphia, PA 19114. Offers business administration (MBA); finance (MBA); health care administration (MBA). Part-time and evening/weekend programs available. *Faculty:* 78 part-time/adjunct (32 women). *Students:* 116 part-time (71 women); includes 18 minority (10 African Americans, 6 Asian Americans or Pacific Islanders, 2 Hispanic Americans). Average age 35. 46 applicants, 93% accepted, 41 enrolled. In 2009, 47 master's awarded. *Entrance requirements:* For master's, interview, essay. Additional exam requirements/recommendations for international students: Required—TOEFL. *Application deadline:* Applications are processed on a rolling basis. Application fee: $50. Electronic applications accepted. *Expenses:* Tuition: Part-time $600 per credit. Required fees: $58 per semester. *Financial support:* Applicants required to submit FAFSA. *Unit head:* Honour Moore, Associate Vice President, 267-341-5008, Fax: 215-633-0558, E-mail: hmoore@holyfamily.edu. *Application contact:* Don Reinmold, Director of Admissions, 267-341-5001 Ext. 3230, Fax: 215-633-0558, E-mail: dreinmold@holyfamily.edu.

Holy Names University, Graduate Division, Department of Business, Oakland, CA 94619-1699. Offers energy and environment management (MBA); finance (MBA); management and leadership (MBA); marketing (MBA); sports management (MBA). Part-time and evening/weekend programs available. *Entrance requirements:* For master's, minimum undergraduate GPA of 2.6 overall, 3.0 in major. Additional exam requirements/recommendations for international students: Required—TOEFL (minimum score 550 paper-based; 213 computer-based; 80 iBT). *Faculty research:* Business ethics, sustainable economics, accounting models, cross-cultural management, diversity in organizations.

Hood College, Graduate School, Department of Economics and Management, Frederick, MD 21701-8575. Offers accounting (MBA); administration and management (MBA); finance (MBA); human resource management (MBA); information systems (MBA); marketing (MBA); public management (MBA). Part-time and evening/weekend programs available. *Faculty:* 5 full-time (1 woman), 9 part-time/adjunct (1 woman). *Students:* 21 full-time (16 women), 166 part-time (85 women); includes 33 minority (18 African Americans, 8 Asian Americans or Pacific Islanders, 7 Hispanic Americans), 15 international. Average age 32. 47 applicants, 87% accepted, 32 enrolled. In 2009, 31 master's awarded. *Degree requirements:* For master's, capstone/final research project. *Entrance requirements:* For master's, minimum GPA of 2.75, resume, letters of recommendation. *Application deadline:* For fall admission, 7/15 for domestic and international students; for spring admission, 12/15 for domestic and international students. Applications are processed on a rolling basis. Application fee: $35. Electronic applications accepted. *Expenses:* Tuition: Full-time $6480; part-time $360 per credit. Required fees: $100; $50 per term. *Financial support:* Applicants required to submit FAFSA. *Faculty research:* Corporate strategy and sustainable competitive advantages, business ethics, entrepreneurship, investments management, economic development. *Unit head:* Dr. Anita Jose, Program Director, 301-696-3691, Fax: 301-696-3597, E-mail: jose@hood.edu. *Application contact:* Dr. Allen P. Flora, Dean of Graduate School, 301-696-3811, Fax: 301-696-3597, E-mail: gofurther@hood.edu.

Howard University, School of Business, Graduate Programs in Business, Washington, DC 20059-0002. Offers accounting (MBA); entrepreneurship (MBA); finance (MBA); general management (MBA); human resources management (MBA); information systems (MBA); international business (MBA); marketing (MBA); supply chain management (MBA); JD/MBA. *Accreditation:* AACSB. Part-time and evening/weekend programs available. Postbaccalaureate distance learning degree programs offered (no on-campus study). *Entrance requirements:* For master's, GMAT, minimum 1 year post undergraduate work experience, resume, 3 letters of recommendation, advanced college algebra. Additional exam requirements/recommendations for international students: Required—TOEFL. *Faculty research:* Marketing research in multi-ethnic populations, U.S. trade policies and international relations, risk management (finance).

Hult International Business School, Program in Business Administration—Hult London Campus, London, MA WC 1B 4JP, United Kingdom. Offers entrepreneurship (MBA); international business (MBA); international finance (MBA); marketing (MBA). Part-time programs available. *Degree requirements:* For master's, comprehensive exam, thesis, internship. *Entrance requirements:* Additional exam requirements/recommendations for international students: Required—TOEFL (minimum score 580 paper-based; 237 computer-based), TWE (minimum score 5). Electronic applications accepted.

Hult International Business School, Program in Finance, Cambridge, MA 02141. Offers MF.

Hult International Business School, Program in Finance—Hult Dubai Campus, Dubai, MA 02141, United Arab Emirates. Offers MF.

Hult International Business School, Program in Finance—Hult London Campus, London, MA WC 1B 4JP, United Kingdom. Offers MF. *Entrance requirements:* Additional exam requirements/recommendations for international students: Required—TOEFL (minimum score 580 paper-based; 237 computer-based), TWE (minimum score 5). Electronic applications accepted.

Illinois Institute of Technology, Chicago-Kent College of Law, Chicago, IL 60661-3691. Offers family law (LL M); financial services (LL M); international intellectual property (LL M); international law (LL M); law (JD); taxation (LL M); JD/LL M; JD/MBA; JD/MPA; JD/MPH; JD/MS. *Accreditation:* ABA. Part-time and evening/weekend programs available. *Faculty:* 70 full-time (26 women), 153 part-time/adjunct (29 women). *Students:* 879 full-time (428 women), 222 part-time (98 women); includes 192 minority (52 African Americans, 4 American Indian/Alaska Native, 91 Asian Americans or Pacific Islanders, 45 Hispanic Americans), 127 international. Average age 27. 3,652 applicants, 45% accepted, 388 enrolled. In 2009, 315 JDs, 140 master's awarded. *Entrance requirements:* LSAT, LSDAS. Additional exam requirements/recommendations for international students: Required—TOEFL (minimum score 600 paper-based; 250 computer-based; 100 iBT); Recommended—IELTS (minimum score 7). *Application deadline:* For fall admission, 3/1 priority date for domestic students, 2/1 priority date for international students. Applications are processed on a rolling basis. Application fee: $60 ($75 for international students). Electronic applications accepted. *Expenses:* Contact institution. *Financial support:* In 2009–10, 605 students received support. Career-related internships or fieldwork, Federal Work-Study, institutionally sponsored loans, scholarships/grants, and tuition waivers (full) available. Support available to part-time students. Financial award application deadline: 3/15; financial award applicants required to submit FAFSA. *Faculty research:* Constitutional law, bioethics, environmental law. Total annual research expenditures: $747,995. *Unit head:* Harold J. Krent, Dean, 312-906-5010, Fax: 312-906-5335, E-mail: hkrent@kentlaw.edu. *Application contact:* Nicole Vilches, Assistant Dean, 312-906-5020, Fax: 312-906-5274, E-mail: admissions@kentlaw.edu.

Illinois Institute of Technology, Stuart School of Business, Program in Business Administration, Chicago, IL 60616-3793. Offers financial management (MBA); innovation and emerging enterprises (MBA); management science (MBA); marketing (MBA); sustainability (MBA); JD/MBA; MBA/MS. *Accreditation:* AACSB. Part-time and evening/weekend programs available. *Faculty:* 14 full-time (2 women), 3 part-time/adjunct (all women). *Students:* 71 full-time (28 women), 45 part-time (18 women); includes 8 minority (4 African Americans, 4 Asian Americans or Pacific Islanders), 69 international. Average age 29. 274 applicants, 50% accepted, 33 enrolled. In 2009, 48 master's, 6 other advanced degrees awarded. *Entrance requirements:* For master's, GMAT. Additional exam requirements/recommendations for international students: Required—TOEFL (minimum score 600 paper-based; 250 computer-based; 90 iBT). *Application deadline:* For fall admission, 8/1 for domestic students, 5/1 for international students; for spring admission, 12/15 for domestic students, 10/15 for international students. Applications are processed on a rolling basis. Application fee: $75. Electronic applications accepted. *Expenses:* Contact institution. *Financial support:* Career-related internships or fieldwork, Federal Work-Study, institutionally sponsored loans, scholarships/grants, traineeships, health care benefits, and tuition waivers (partial) available. Support available to part-time students. Financial award applicants required to submit FAFSA. *Faculty research:* Global management and marketing strategy, technological innovation, management science, financial management, knowledge management. *Unit head:* M. Krishna Erramilli, Interim Director, 312-906-6573, Fax: 312-906-6549. *Application contact:* M. Krishna Erramilli, Interim Director, 312-906-6573, Fax: 312-906-6549.

Illinois Institute of Technology, Stuart School of Business, Program in Finance, Chicago, IL 60616-3793. Offers MS, MSF, JD/MS, MBA/MS, MBA/MSF. Part-time and evening/weekend programs available. *Faculty:* 10 full-time (0 women), 7 part-time/adjunct (1 woman). *Students:* 312 full-time (139 women), 64 part-time (16 women); includes 10 minority (8 Asian Americans or Pacific Islanders, 2 Hispanic Americans), 327 international. Average age 25. 641 applicants, 70% accepted, 130 enrolled. In 2009, 109 master's awarded. *Entrance requirements:* For master's, GMAT or GRE General Test. Additional exam requirements/recommendations for international students: Required—TOEFL (minimum score 575 paper-based; 90 iBT). *Application deadline:* For fall admission, 8/1 for domestic students, 5/1 for international students; for spring admission, 12/15 for domestic students, 10/15 for international students. Applications are processed on a rolling basis. Application fee: $75. Electronic applications accepted. *Expenses:* Contact institution. *Financial support:* Career-related internships or fieldwork, Federal Work-Study, institutionally sponsored loans, scholarships/grants, traineeships, health care benefits, and tuition waivers (partial) available. Support available to part-time students. Financial award applicants required to submit FAFSA. *Faculty research:* Factor models for investment management, credit rating and credit risk management, hedge fund performance analysis, option trading and risk management, global asset allocation strategies. *Unit head:* John Bilson, Director, MS Finance Program/Associate Director, PhD in Management Science Program, 312-906-6538, Fax: 312-906-6549, E-mail: bilson@stuart.iit.edu. *Application contact:* John Bilson, Director, MS Finance Program/Associate Director, PhD in Management Science Program, 312-906-6538, Fax: 312-906-6549, E-mail: bilson@stuart.iit.edu.

Indiana University Bloomington, School of Public and Environmental Affairs, Public Affairs Programs, Bloomington, IN 47405-7000. Offers comparative and international affairs (MPA); economic development (MPA); environmental policy and natural resource management (MPA); information systems (MPA); local government management (MPA); nonprofit management (MPA); policy analysis (MPA); public affairs (PhD, Certificate); public financial administration (MPA); public management (MPA); sustainability and sustainable development (MPA); JD/MPA; MPA/MIS; MPA/MLS; MSES/MPA. *Accreditation:* NASPAA (one or more programs are accredited). Part-time programs available. *Faculty:* 75 full-time (22 women), 91 part-time/adjunct (24 women). *Students:* 389 full-time (222 women), 45 part-time (24 women); includes 38 minority (18 African Americans, 1 American Indian/Alaska Native, 12 Asian Americans or Pacific Islanders, 7 Hispanic Americans), 72 international. Average age 26. 474 applicants, 206 enrolled. In 2009, 190 master's, 11 doctorates, 3 other advanced degrees awarded. Terminal master's awarded for partial completion of doctoral program. *Degree requirements:* For master's, thesis optional; for doctorate, comprehensive exam, thesis/dissertation or alternative, A thesis is required for the Public Affairs and Public Policy degree. *Entrance requirements:* For master's, GRE, LSAT (if also applying for the Law School), 3 letters of recommendation, resume or curriculum vitae; for doctorate, GRE General Test. Additional exam requirements/recommendations for international students: Required—TOEFL (minimum score 590 paper-based; 243 computer-based; 96 iBT). *Application deadline:* For fall admission, 2/1 priority date for domestic students, 12/1 priority date for international students; for spring admission, 9/1 for international students. Application fee: $55 ($65 for international students). Electronic applications accepted. *Financial support:* Fellowships with full tuition reimbursements, research assistantships with partial tuition reimbursements, teaching assistantships with partial tuition reimbursements, career-related internships or fieldwork, Federal Work-Study, institutionally sponsored loans, unspecified assistantships, and Service Corps programs available. Financial award application deadline: 2/1; financial award applicants required to submit FAFSA. *Faculty research:* Comparative and international affairs, environmental policy and resource management, policy analysis, public finance, public management, urban

management, nonprofit management. *Unit head:* Dean John Graham, Dean, School of Public and Environmental Affairs, 812-855-1432, E-mail: grahamjd@indiana.edu. *Application contact:* Jennifer Medlin, Assistant Director of Admissions and Financial Aid, 812-855-3784, Fax: 812-856-3665, E-mail: jlmedlin@indiana.edu.

Indiana University Southeast, School of Business, New Albany, IN 47150-6405. Offers business administration (MBA); strategic finance (MS). *Accreditation:* AACSB. *Faculty:* 11 full-time (2 women). *Students:* 17 full-time (7 women), 257 part-time (108 women); includes 26 minority (8 African Americans, 16 Asian Americans or Pacific Islanders, 2 Hispanic Americans), 7 international. Average age 31. In 2009, 57 master's awarded. *Degree requirements:* For master's, community service. *Entrance requirements:* For master's, GMAT, work experience. Additional exam requirements/recommendations for international students: Required—TOEFL. Application fee: $35. *Expenses:* Contact institution. *Financial support:* In 2009–10, 2 teaching assistantships (averaging $4,500 per year) were awarded. *Unit head:* Dr. Jay White, Dean, 812-941-2362, Fax: 812-941-2672. *Application contact:* Dr. Jay White, Dean, 812-941-2362, Fax: 812-941-2672.

Instituto Centroamericano de Administración de Empresas, Graduate Programs, La Garita, Costa Rica. Offers agribusiness (MIAM); business administration (EMBA); economics and finance (MBA); industry and technology (MBA); sustainable development (MBA). *Degree requirements:* For master's, comprehensive exam, essay. *Entrance requirements:* For master's, GMAT or GRE General Test, fluency in Spanish, interview, letters of recommendation, minimum 1 year of work experience. Electronic applications accepted. *Faculty research:* Competitiveness, production.

Instituto Tecnologico de Santo Domingo, Graduate School, Santo Domingo, Dominican Republic. Offers applied linguistics (MA); construction administration (M Mgmt); corporate finance (M Mgmt); education (M Ed); engineering (M Eng), including data telecommunications, industrial engineering, logistics and supply chain, maintenance engineering, sanitary and environmental engineering, structural engineering; environmental science (M En S), including environmental education, environmental management, marine and coastal ecosystems, natural resources management; family therapy (MA); food science and technology (MS); human development (MA); human resources administration (M Mgmt); international business (M Mgmt); labor risks (M Mgmt); management (M Mgmt); marketing (M Mgmt); mathematics (MS); organizational development (M Mgmt); planning and taxation (M Mgmt); psychology (MA); social science (M Ed); upper management (M Mgmt). *Entrance requirements:* For master's, birth certificate, minimum GPA of 2.0.

Instituto Tecnológico y de Estudios Superiores de Monterrey, Campus Central de Veracruz, Graduate Programs, Córdoba, Mexico. Offers administration (MA); administration of information technologies (MTI); computer sciences (MCC); education (MEE); educational institution administration (MAD); educational technology (MTE); electronic commerce (MCE); finance (MAF); humanistic studies (MEH); international business for Latin America (MNL); marketing (MMT); science (MCP); technology management (MTT). Part-time and evening/weekend programs available. Postbaccalaureate distance learning degree programs offered (minimal on-campus study). *Degree requirements:* For master's, thesis (for some programs). *Entrance requirements:* For master's, PAEP College Board. Electronic applications accepted.

Instituto Tecnológico y de Estudios Superiores de Monterrey, Campus Ciudad de México, Division of Business, Ciudad de Mexico, Mexico. Offers business administration (EMBA, MBA, PhD); economy (MBA); finance (MBA). Part-time and evening/weekend programs available. Postbaccalaureate distance learning degree programs offered (minimal on-campus study). *Entrance requirements:* For master's and doctorate, Instituto entrance exam. Additional exam requirements/recommendations for international students: Required—TOEFL.

Instituto Tecnológico y de Estudios Superiores de Monterrey, Campus Ciudad Obregón, Program in Finance, Ciudad Obregón, Mexico. Offers MF.

Instituto Tecnológico y de Estudios Superiores de Monterrey, Campus Cuernavaca, Programs in Business Administration, Temixco, Mexico. Offers finance (MA); human resources management (MA); international business (MA); marketing (MA).

Instituto Tecnológico y de Estudios Superiores de Monterrey, Campus Estado de México, Professional and Graduate Division, Estado de Mexico, Mexico. Offers administration of information technologies (MITA); architecture (M Arch); business administration (GMBA, MBA); computer sciences (MCS, PhD); education (M Ed); educational institution administration (MAD); educational technology and innovation (PhD); electronic commerce (MEC); environmental systems (MS); finance (MAF); humanistic studies (MHS); information sciences and knowledge management (MISKM); information systems (MS); manufacturing systems (MS); marketing (MEM); quality systems and productivity (MS); science and materials engineering (PhD); telecommunications management (MTM). Part-time programs available. Postbaccalaureate distance learning degree programs offered (minimal on-campus study). *Degree requirements:* For master's, one foreign language, thesis (for some programs); for doctorate, one foreign language, thesis/dissertation. *Entrance requirements:* For master's, E-PAEP 500, interview; for doctorate, E-PAEP 500, research proposal. Additional exam requirements/recommendations for international students: Required—TOEFL (minimum score 550 paper-based). *Faculty research:* Surface treatments by plasmas, mechanical properties, robotics, graphical computing, mechatronics security protocols.

Instituto Tecnológico y de Estudios Superiores de Monterrey, Campus Guadalajara, Program in Finance, Zapopan, Mexico. Offers MF. *Degree requirements:* For master's, one foreign language, thesis. *Entrance requirements:* For master's, ITESM admission test.

Instituto Tecnológico y de Estudios Superiores de Monterrey, Campus Irapuato, Graduate Programs, Irapuato, Mexico. Offers administration (MBA); administration of information technology (MAIT); administration of telecommunications (MAT); architecture (M Arch); computer science (MCS); education (M Ed); educational administration (MEA); educational innovation and technology (DEIT); educational technology (MET); electronic commerce (MBA); environmental administration and planning (MEAP); environmental systems (MES); finances (MBA); humanistic studies (MHS); international management for Latin American executives (MIMLAE); library and information science (MLIS); manufacturing quality management (MMQM); marketing research (MBA).

Instituto Tecnológico y de Estudios Superiores de Monterrey, Campus Monterrey, Graduate School of Business Administration and Leadership, Program in Business Administration, Monterrey, Mexico. Offers business administration (MA, MBA); finance (M Sc); international business (M Sc); marketing (M Sc). *Accreditation:* AACSB. Part-time programs available. *Degree requirements:* For master's, one foreign language, thesis. *Entrance requirements:* For master's, GMAT. Additional exam requirements/recommendations for international students: Required—TOEFL. *Faculty research:* Technology management, quality management, organizational theory and behavior.

Inter American University of Puerto Rico, Aguadilla Campus, Graduate School, Aguadilla, PR 00605. Offers accounting (MBA); business information systems (MBA); counseling psychology with an emphasis in family (MS); criminal justice (MA); educative management and leadership (MA); elementary education (MA); finance (MBA); human resources (MBA); industrial management (MBA); marketing (MBA). Part-time and evening/weekend programs available. *Degree requirements:* For master's, comprehensive exam. *Entrance requirements:* For master's, EXADEP, 2 letters of recommendation, minimum GPA of 2.5. Electronic applications accepted.

Inter American University of Puerto Rico, Arecibo Campus, Program in Business Administration, Arecibo, PR 00614-4050. Offers accounting (MBA); finance (MBA); human resources (MBA).

Inter American University of Puerto Rico, Barranquitas Campus, Program in Business Administration, Barranquitas, PR 00794. Offers accounting (IMBA); finance (IMBA).

Inter American University of Puerto Rico, Metropolitan Campus, Graduate Programs, Program in Finance, San Juan, PR 00919-1293. Offers MBA. *Degree requirements:* For master's, comprehensive exam. *Entrance requirements:* For master's, GRE or EXADEP, interview. Electronic applications accepted.

Inter American University of Puerto Rico, Ponce Campus, Graduate School, Mercedita, PR 00715-1602. Offers accounting (MBA); biology (M Ed); chemistry (M Ed); criminal justice (MA); elementary education (M Ed); English as a Second Language (M Ed); finance (MBA); history (M Ed); human resources (MBA); marketing (MBA); mathematics (M Ed); Spanish (M Ed). *Entrance requirements:* For master's, minimum GPA of 2.5.

Inter American University of Puerto Rico, San Germán Campus, Graduate Studies Center, Program in Business Administration, San Germán, PR 00683-5008. Offers accounting (MBA); finance (MBA); human resources (PhD); human resources management (MBA); industrial management (MBA); international business (PhD); management information systems (MBA); marketing management (MBA). Part-time and evening/weekend programs available. *Degree requirements:* For master's, comprehensive exam. *Entrance requirements:* For master's, GRE General Test or EXADEP, minimum GPA of 3.0.

International University in Geneva, Master of Business Administration Program, Geneva, Switzerland. Offers finance (MBA); international business (MIB); investment management (MBA); luxury management (MBA); marketing (MBA); wealth management (MBA). *Accreditation:* ACBSP. Part-time and evening/weekend programs available. *Degree requirements:* For master's, comprehensive exam. *Entrance requirements:* For master's, GMAT. Additional exam requirements/recommendations for international students: Required—TOEFL. Electronic applications accepted.

The International University of Monaco, Graduate Programs, Monte Carlo, Monaco. Offers entrepreneurship (EMBA, MBA); financial engineering (M Sc); hedge fund and private equity (M Sc); international marketing (EMBA, MBA); international wealth management (M Sc); luxury goods and services (EMBA, M Sc, MBA); wealth and asset management (EMBA, MBA). Part-time programs available. *Degree requirements:* For master's, comprehensive exam (for some programs), applied research project. *Entrance requirements:* Additional exam requirements/recommendations for international students: Required—TOEFL (minimum score 550 paper-based; 213 computer-based), IELTS. Electronic applications accepted. *Faculty research:* Gaming, leadership, disintermediation.

Iona College, Hagan School of Business, Department of Finance, Business Economics and Legal Studies, New Rochelle, NY 10801-1890. Offers financial management (MBA, PMC). Part-time and evening/weekend programs available. *Faculty:* 11 full-time (3 women), 6 part-time/adjunct (0 women). *Students:* 33 full-time (16 women), 101 part-time (35 women); includes 11 minority (3 African Americans, 4 Asian Americans or Pacific Islanders, 4 Hispanic Americans), 2 international. Average age 29. 33 applicants, 82% accepted, 17 enrolled. In 2009, 62 master's awarded. *Entrance requirements:* For master's, GMAT, 2 letters of recommendation. Additional exam requirements/recommendations for international students: Required—TOEFL (minimum score 550 paper-based; 213 computer-based). *Application deadline:* Applications are processed on a rolling basis. Application fee: $50. Electronic applications accepted. *Expenses:* Contact institution. *Financial support:* Scholarships/grants, tuition waivers (partial), and unspecified assistantships available. Support available to part-time students. Financial award application deadline: 4/15; financial award applicants required to submit FAFSA. *Faculty research:* Options, insurance financing, asset depreciation ranges, international finance, emerging markets. *Unit head:* Dr. Anand Shetty, Chairman, 914-633-2284, E-mail: ashetty@iona.edu. *Application contact:* Jude Fleurismond, Director of MBA Admissions, 914-633-2289, Fax: 914-637-2708, E-mail: jfleurismond@iona.edu.

The Johns Hopkins University, Carey Business School, Finance Programs, Baltimore, MD 21218-2699. Offers finance (MS); financial management (Certificate); investments (Certificate). Part-time and evening/weekend programs available. *Faculty:* 29 full-time (6 women), 135 part-time/adjunct (29 women). *Students:* 75 full-time (33 women), 95 part-time (33 women); includes 39 minority (9 African Americans, 1 American Indian/Alaska Native, 21 Asian Americans or Pacific Islanders, 8 Hispanic Americans), 69 international. Average age 29. 287 applicants, 40% accepted, 71 enrolled. In 2009, 61 master's, 14 other advanced degrees awarded. *Degree requirements:* For master's, 36 credits including final project. *Entrance requirements:* For master's, GMAT or GRE (recommended), minimum GPA of 3.0, resume, work experience, two letters of recommendation; for Certificate, minimum GPA of 3.0, resume, work experience, two letters of recommendation. Additional exam requirements/recommendations for international students: Required—TOEFL (minimum score 600 paper-based; 250 computer-based; 100 iBT). *Application deadline:* For fall admission, 5/1 for international students; for spring admission, 10/15 for international students. Applications are processed on a rolling basis. Application fee: $100. Electronic applications accepted. *Financial support:* Scholarships/grants available. Support available to part-time students. Financial award application deadline: 4/1; financial award applicants required to submit FAFSA. *Faculty research:* Financial econometrics, high frequency data modeling, corporate finance. *Unit head:* Dr. Dipankar Chakravarti, Vice Dean of Programs, 410-516-8561, E-mail: dipankar.chakravarti@jhu.edu. *Application contact:* Robin Greenberg, Admissions Coordinator, 410-516-4234, Fax: 410-516-0826, E-mail: carey.admissions@jhu.edu.

Johnson & Wales University, The Alan Shawn Feinstein Graduate School, MBA Program in Global Business Leadership, Providence, RI 02903-3703. Offers accounting (MBA); enhanced accounting (MBA); financial management (MBA); international trade (MBA); marketing (MBA); organizational leadership (MBA). Part-time programs available. *Faculty:* 13 full-time (3 women), 17 part-time/adjunct (4 women). *Students:* 523 full-time (272 women), 162 part-time (85 women); includes 29 minority (18 African Americans, 4 Asian Americans or Pacific Islanders, 7 Hispanic Americans), 385 international. Average age 27. 330 applicants, 82% accepted, 151 enrolled. In 2009, 274 master's awarded. *Entrance requirements:* For master's, minimum GPA of 2.75. Additional exam requirements/recommendations for international students: Required—TOEFL, TOEFL (minimum score 550 paper-based; 210 computer-based) or IELTS recommended; Recommended—TWE. *Application deadline:* For fall admission, 8/15 priority date for domestic students, 6/28 priority date for international students; for winter admission, 11/10 priority date for domestic students, 9/20 priority date for international students; for spring admission, 2/5 priority date for domestic students, 12/20 priority date for international students. Applications are processed on a rolling basis. *Expenses:* Required fees: $340 per quarter hour. *Financial support:* Tuition waivers (partial) and unspecified assistantships available. Support available to part-time students. Financial award application deadline: 5/1. *Faculty research:* International banking, global economy, international trade, cultural differences. *Unit head:* Dr. Frank Pontarelli, Dean, 401-598-1333, Fax: 401-598-1125. *Application contact:* Dr. Allan G. Freedman, Director of Graduate Admissions, 401-598-1015, Fax: 401-598-1286, E-mail: gradadm@jwu.edu.

Jones International University, School of Business, Centennial, CO 80112. Offers accounting (MBA); business communication (MABC); entrepreneurship (MABC, MBA); finance (MBA); global enterprise management (MBA); health care management (MBA); information security management (MBA); information technology management (MBA); leadership and influence (MABC); leading the customer-driven organization (MABC); negotiation and conflict management (MBA); project management (MABC, MBA). Program only offered online. Part-time and evening/weekend programs available. Postbaccalaureate distance learning degree programs offered (no on-campus study). *Degree requirements:* For master's, capstone project. *Entrance requirements:* For master's, minimum cumulative GPA of 2.5. Additional exam requirements/recommendations for international students: Recommended—TOEFL (minimum score 550 paper-based; 213 computer-based). Electronic applications accepted.

Kaplan University, Davenport Campus, School of Business, Davenport, IA 52807-2095. Offers business administration (MBA); change leadership (MS); entrepreneurship (MBA); finance (MBA); health care management (MBA, MS); human resource (MBA); international business (MBA); management (MS); marketing (MBA); project management (MBA, MS); supply chain management and logistics (MBA, MS). Part-time and evening/weekend programs

Finance and Banking

Kaplan University, Davenport Campus (continued)
available. Postbaccalaureate distance learning degree programs offered (no on-campus study). *Entrance requirements:* Additional exam requirements/recommendations for international students: Required—TOEFL (minimum score 550 paper-based; 218 computer-based; 80 iBT). Electronic applications accepted.

Kent State University, Graduate School of Management, Doctoral Program in Finance, Kent, OH 44242-0001. Offers PhD. *Faculty:* 9 full-time (2 women). *Students:* 17 full-time (6 women); includes 1 minority (African American), 6 international. Average age 34. 23 applicants, 26% accepted, 3 enrolled. In 2009, 1 doctorate awarded. *Degree requirements:* For doctorate, comprehensive exam, thesis/dissertation, oral defense. *Entrance requirements:* For doctorate, GMAT. Additional exam requirements/recommendations for international students: Required—TOEFL (minimum score 600 paper-based; 250 computer-based; 100 iBT). *Application deadline:* For fall admission, 2/1 for domestic students, 1/1 for international students. Application fee: $30 ($60 for international students). Electronic applications accepted. *Financial support:* In 2009–10, 11 students received support, including fellowships with full tuition reimbursements available (averaging $15,000 per year), 11 teaching assistantships with full tuition reimbursements available (averaging $15,000 per year); Federal Work-Study also available. Financial award application deadline: 2/1; financial award applicants required to submit FAFSA. *Faculty research:* Corporate finance, investments, international finance, futures and options, risk and insurance. *Unit head:* Dr. John Thornton, Interim Chair and Associate Professor, 330-672-2426, Fax: 330-672-9806, E-mail: jthornt5@kent.edu. *Application contact:* Felecia A. Urbanek, Coordinator, Graduate Programs, 330-672-2282, Fax: 330-672-7303, E-mail: gradbus@kent.edu.

Kentucky State University, College of Professional Studies, Frankfort, KY 40601. Offers business administration (MBA), including accounting, finance, management, marketing; public administration (MPA), including human resource management, international administration and development, management information systems, nonprofit management; special education (MA). Part-time and evening/weekend programs available. Postbaccalaureate distance learning degree programs offered (minimal on-campus study). *Faculty:* 11 full-time (3 women), 2 part-time/adjunct (both women). *Students:* 79 full-time (51 women), 66 part-time (34 women); includes 88 minority (85 African Americans, 2 Asian Americans or Pacific Islanders, 1 Hispanic American), 4 international. Average age 34. 92 applicants, 75% accepted, 52 enrolled. In 2009, 32 master's awarded. *Degree requirements:* For master's, comprehensive exam, thesis optional. *Entrance requirements:* For master's, GMAT, GRE. Additional exam requirements/recommendations for international students: Required—TOEFL (minimum score 525 paper-based; 173 computer-based). *Application deadline:* For fall admission, 7/1 priority date for domestic students, 4/15 priority date for international students; for spring admission, 11/15 priority date for domestic students, 8/1 priority date for international students. Applications are processed on a rolling basis. Application fee: $30 ($100 for international students). Electronic applications accepted. *Expenses:* Tuition, state resident: full-time $5634; part-time $313 per credit hour. Tuition, nonresident: full-time $14,598; part-time $811 per credit hour. Required fees: $450; $25 per credit hour. *Financial support:* In 2009–10, 113 students received support, including 4 research assistantships (averaging $14,035 per year); career-related internships or fieldwork, scholarships/grants, tuition waivers (partial), and unspecified assistantships also available. Financial award application deadline: 4/15; financial award applicants required to submit FAFSA. *Unit head:* Dr. Gashaw Lake, Dean, College of Professional Studies, 502-597-6105, Fax: 502-597-6715, E-mail: gashaw.lake@kysu.edu. *Application contact:* Cedric Cunningham, Administrative Assistant, Office of Graduate Studies, 502-597-6536, E-mail: cedric.cunningham@kysu.edu.

Lakeland College, Graduate Studies Division, Program in Business Administration, Sheboygan, WI 53082-0359. Offers accounting (MBA); finance (MBA); healthcare management (MBA); project management (MBA). *Entrance requirements:* For master's, GMAT. *Expenses:* Contact institution.

Lamar University, College of Graduate Studies, College of Business, Beaumont, TX 77710. Offers accounting (MBA); experiential business and entrepreneurship (MBA); financial management (MBA); healthcare administration (MBA); information systems (MBA); management (MBA). *Accreditation:* AACSB. Part-time and evening/weekend programs available. *Faculty:* 18 full-time (4 women), 4 part-time/adjunct (0 women). *Students:* 62 full-time (27 women), 59 part-time (16 women); includes 19 minority (8 African Americans, 6 Asian Americans or Pacific Islanders, 5 Hispanic Americans), 19 international. Average age 29. 210 applicants, 34% accepted, 33 enrolled. In 2009, 41 master's awarded. *Degree requirements:* For master's, comprehensive exam (for some programs), thesis optional. *Entrance requirements:* For master's, GMAT. Additional exam requirements/recommendations for international students: Required—TOEFL (minimum score 525 paper-based; 197 computer-based). *Application deadline:* For fall admission, 3/15 priority date for domestic students; for spring admission, 10/1 priority date for domestic students. Applications are processed on a rolling basis. Application fee: $25 ($50 for international students). *Financial support:* In 2009–10, 12 students received support, including 4 research assistantships with partial tuition reimbursements available; fellowships with tuition reimbursements available, career-related internships or fieldwork, Federal Work-Study, institutionally sponsored loans, scholarships/grants, and tuition waivers (partial) also available. Support available to part-time students. Financial award application deadline: 4/1; financial award applicants required to submit FAFSA. *Faculty research:* Marketing, finance, quantitative methods, management information systems, legal, environmental. *Unit head:* Dr. Enrique R. Venta, Dean, 409-880-8604, Fax: 409-880-8088, E-mail: henry.venta@lamar.edu. *Application contact:* Dr. Brad Mayer, Professor and Associate Dean, 409-880-2383, Fax: 409-880-8605, E-mail: bradley.mayer@lamar.edu.

La Sierra University, School of Business and Management, Riverside, CA 92515. Offers accounting (MBA); finance (MBA); general management (MBA); human resources management (MBA); leadership, values, and ethics for business and management (Certificate); marketing (MBA). *Degree requirements:* For master's, research project. *Entrance requirements:* For master's, GMAT, minimum GPA of 3.0. Additional exam requirements/recommendations for international students: Required—TOEFL. *Faculty research:* Financial econometrics, institutional assessment and strategic planning, legal issues in management, behavioral finance, content of financial reports.

Lehigh University, College of Business and Economics, Department of Finance, Bethlehem, PA 18015. Offers analytical finance (MS). *Faculty:* 8 full-time (2 women). *Students:* 42 full-time (25 women), 29 part-time (11 women); includes 3 minority (2 African Americans, 1 Asian American or Pacific Islander), 42 international. Average age 27. 162 applicants, 38% accepted, 30 enrolled. In 2009, 27 master's awarded. *Degree requirements:* For master's, capstone project. *Entrance requirements:* For master's, GMAT or GRE, bachelor's degree from a mathematically rigorous program, minimum GPA of 3.0. Additional exam requirements/recommendations for international students: Required—TOEFL (minimum score 600 paper-based; 250 computer-based; 94 iBT). *Application deadline:* For fall admission, 7/15 for domestic students, 5/1 for international students. Applications are processed on a rolling basis. Application fee: $100. Electronic applications accepted. *Expenses:* Contact institution. Total annual research expenditures: $169,555. *Unit head:* Richard Kish, Co-Director, 610-758-4205, E-mail: rjk7@lehigh.edu. *Application contact:* Corinn McBride, Director of Recruitment and Admissions, 610-758-3418, Fax: 610-758-5283, E-mail: com207@lehigh.edu.

Lewis University, College of Business, Graduate School of Management, Program in Business Administration, Romeoville, IL 60446. Offers accounting (MBA); custom elective option (MBA); e-business (MBA); finance (MBA); healthcare management (MBA); human resources management (MBA); information security (MBA); international business (MBA); management information systems (MBA); marketing (MBA); project management (MBA); technology and operations management (MBA). Part-time and evening/weekend programs available. *Faculty:* 15 full-time (2 women), 18 part-time/adjunct (4 women). *Students:* 120 full-time (64 women), 222 part-time (103 women); includes 97 minority (62 African Americans, 4 Asian Americans or Pacific Islanders, 31 Hispanic Americans), 9 international. Average age 31. In 2009, 84 master's awarded. *Entrance requirements:* For master's, interview, bachelor's degree, resume, 2 recommendations. Additional exam requirements/recommendations for international students: Required—TOEFL (minimum score 550 paper-based; 213 computer-based). *Application deadline:* For fall admission, 8/15 priority date for domestic students, 5/1 priority date for international students; for spring admission, 11/15 priority date for international students. Applications are processed on a rolling basis. Application fee: $40. Electronic applications accepted. *Expenses:* Tuition: Full-time $6480; part-time $720 per credit. One-time fee: $40. Tuition and fees vary according to course load, degree level and program. *Financial support:* Career-related internships or fieldwork, Federal Work-Study, scholarships/grants, and unspecified assistantships available. Financial award application deadline: 5/1; financial award applicants required to submit FAFSA. *Unit head:* Dr. Maureen Culleeney, Academic Program Director, 815-838-0500 Ext. 5631, E-mail: culleema@lewisu.edu. *Application contact:* Michele King, Director of Admission, 815-838-0500 Ext. 5384, E-mail: gsm@lewisu.edu.

Lewis University, College of Business, Graduate School of Management, Program in Finance, Romeoville, IL 60446. Offers MS. Part-time and evening/weekend programs available. *Faculty:* 4 full-time (0 women), 4 part-time/adjunct (1 woman). *Students:* 9 full-time (0 women), 12 part-time (5 women); includes 4 minority (2 African Americans, 1 Asian American or Pacific Islander, 1 Hispanic American), 2 international. Average age 29. In 2009, 7 master's awarded. *Entrance requirements:* For master's, bachelor's degree, interview, resume, 2 recommendations, minimum GPA of 2.75. Additional exam requirements/recommendations for international students: Required—TOEFL (minimum score 550 paper-based; 213 computer-based). *Application deadline:* For fall admission, 5/1 priority date for international students; for spring admission, 11/15 priority date for international students. Applications are processed on a rolling basis. Application fee: $40. Electronic applications accepted. *Expenses:* Tuition: Full-time $6480; part-time $720 per credit. One-time fee: $40. Tuition and fees vary according to course load, degree level and program. *Financial support:* Career-related internships or fieldwork, Federal Work-Study, scholarships/grants, and unspecified assistantships available. Support available to part-time students. Financial award application deadline: 5/1; financial award applicants required to submit FAFSA. *Unit head:* Dr. Robert Atra, Academic Program Director, 815-838-0500 Ext. 5804, E-mail: atraro@lewisu.edu. *Application contact:* Michele King, Director of Admission, 815-838-0500 Ext. 5384, E-mail: gsm@lewisu.edu.

Lincoln University, Graduate Center, Lincoln University, PA 19352. Offers administration (MSA), including finance, human resources management; early childhood education (M Ed); elementary education (M Ed); human services (M Hum Svcs); reading (MSR). Evening/weekend programs available. *Degree requirements:* For master's, thesis. *Entrance requirements:* For master's, 5 years of work experience in human services. *Faculty research:* Gerontology/minority aging, computers in composition instruction.

Lincoln University, Graduate Degree Programs, Oakland, CA 94612. Offers finance and investments (DBA); finance management and investment banking (MBA); general business (MBA); human resource management (MBA); international business (MBA); management information systems (MBA). Part-time and evening/weekend programs available. *Faculty:* 7 full-time (2 women), 13 part-time/adjunct (1 woman). *Students:* 295 full-time (133 women), 3 part-time (0 women). 177 applicants, 100% accepted, 71 enrolled. In 2009, 98 master's awarded. *Degree requirements:* For master's, research project (thesis) or internship report, or comprehensive exam; for doctorate, comprehensive exam, thesis/dissertation. *Entrance requirements:* For master's, minimum GPA of 2.7; for doctorate, GMAT (minimum score: 550), GRE (minimum score: 1000), or equivalent test results (waived for master's degree with cumulative GPA of 3.3). Additional exam requirements/recommendations for international students: Required—TOEFL or IELTS. *Application deadline:* For fall admission, 7/3 priority date for domestic students; for spring admission, 11/27 priority date for domestic students. Applications are processed on a rolling basis. Application fee: $75. Electronic applications accepted. *Expenses:* Tuition: Full-time $6750. Required fees: $190 per term. *Financial support:* In 2009–10, 1 teaching assistantship was awarded; career-related internships or fieldwork and scholarships/grants also available. *Unit head:* Dr. Marshall Burak, Director of Graduate Programs, 510-628-8016, Fax: 510-628-8012, E-mail: mburak@lincolnuca.edu. *Application contact:* Peggy Au, Director of Admissions and Records, 510-628-8010, Fax: 510-628-8012, E-mail: admissions@lincolnuca.edu.

Lindenwood University, Graduate Programs, School of Business and Entrepreneurship, St. Charles, MO 63301-1695. Offers accounting (MBA, MS); business administration (MBA); entrepreneurial studies (MBA, MS); finance (MBA, MS); human resource management (MBA); human resources (MS); international business (MBA, MS); management (MBA, MS); management information systems (MBA, MS); marketing (MBA, MS); public management (MBA, MS); sport management (MA). *Accreditation:* ACBSP. Part-time and evening/weekend programs available. *Faculty:* 20 full-time (8 women), 17 part-time/adjunct (5 women). *Students:* 129 full-time (60 women), 138 part-time (61 women); includes 15 minority (11 African Americans, 2 Asian Americans or Pacific Islanders, 2 Hispanic Americans), 84 international. Average age 28. 149 applicants, 73 enrolled. In 2009, 142 master's awarded. *Degree requirements:* For master's, comprehensive exam (for some programs), thesis (for some programs). *Entrance requirements:* For master's, interview, minimum GPA of 3.0, letter of recommendation. Additional exam requirements/recommendations for international students: Required—TOEFL (minimum score 550 paper-based; 213 computer-based; 80 iBT). *Application deadline:* For fall admission, 7/30 priority date for domestic students, 9/16 priority date for international students; for winter admission, 12/19 priority date for domestic students, 12/17 priority date for international students; for spring admission, 2/25 priority date for domestic students, 2/11 priority date for international students. Applications are processed on a rolling basis. Application fee: $30 ($100 for international students). Electronic applications accepted. *Expenses:* Tuition: Full-time $12,960; part-time $370 per credit hour. Required fees: $340. One-time fee: $30 full-time. Tuition and fees vary according to course level and course load. *Financial support:* In 2009–10, 209 students received support. Career-related internships or fieldwork, Federal Work-Study, institutionally sponsored loans, and tuition waivers (partial) available. Financial award application deadline: 6/30; financial award applicants required to submit FAFSA. *Unit head:* Ed Morris, Dean of Management, 636-949-4832, E-mail: emorris@lindenwood.edu. *Application contact:* Brett Barger, Dean of Evening Admissions and Extension Campuses, 636-949-4934, Fax: 636-949-4109, E-mail: adultadmissions@lindenwood.edu.

Lipscomb University, MBA Program, Nashville, TN 37204-3951. Offers accounting (MBA); business administration (general) (MBA); conflict management (MBA); financial services (MBA); healthcare management (MBA); leadership (MBA); nonprofit management (MBA); sports administration (MBA); sustainable practice (MBA). *Accreditation:* ACBSP. Part-time and evening/weekend programs available. *Faculty:* 10 full-time (1 woman), 7 part-time/adjunct (2 women). *Students:* 43 full-time (23 women), 86 part-time (38 women); includes 23 minority (18 African Americans, 1 Asian American or Pacific Islander, 4 Hispanic Americans), 1 international. Average age 31. 95 applicants, 64% accepted, 35 enrolled. In 2009, 59 master's awarded. *Entrance requirements:* For master's, GMAT, interview, 2 references, resume. Additional exam requirements/recommendations for international students: Required—TOEFL (minimum score 570 paper-based; 230 computer-based). *Application deadline:* For fall admission, 2/1 for international students; for winter admission, 6/1 for international students. Applications are processed on a rolling basis. Application fee: $50 ($75 for international students). Electronic applications accepted. *Expenses:* Contact institution. *Financial support:* Career-related internships or fieldwork, Federal Work-Study, scholarships/grants, tuition waivers (partial), and unspecified assistantships available. Support available to part-time students. Financial award application deadline: 7/1; financial award applicants required to submit FAFSA. *Faculty research:* Impact of spirituality on organization commitment, leadership, psychological empowerment, training. *Unit head:* Dr. Mike Kendrick, Interim Chair of Graduate Business Studies, 615-966-1833, Fax: 615-966-1818, E-mail: mikekendrick@lipscomb.edu. *Application contact:* Emily Landsdell, 615-966-5284, E-mail: emily.lansdell@lipscomb.edu.

Long Island University, C.W. Post Campus, College of Management, School of Business, Brookville, NY 11548-1300. Offers accounting and taxation (Certificate); business administration (Certificate); finance (MBA, Certificate); general business administration (MBA); international

business (MBA, Certificate); management (MBA, Certificate); management information systems (MBA, Certificate); marketing (MBA, Certificate). *Accreditation:* AACSB. Part-time and evening/weekend programs available. *Entrance requirements:* For master's, GMAT, resume, minimum GPA of 3.0, 2 letters of recommendation. Additional exam requirements/recommendations for international students: Required—TOEFL (minimum score 527 paper-based; 197 computer-based). Electronic applications accepted. *Faculty research:* Financial markets, consumer behavior.

Long Island University, Rockland Graduate Campus, Graduate School, Masters of Business Administration Program, Orangeburg, NY 10962. Offers business administration (Post Master's Certificate); entrepreneurship (MBA); finance (MBA); management (MBA). Part-time and evening/weekend programs available. *Faculty:* 12 part-time/adjunct (2 women). *Students:* 35 part-time (21 women). 51 applicants, 67% accepted, 22 enrolled. In 2009, 14 master's awarded. *Entrance requirements:* For master's, GMAT. Additional exam requirements/recommendations for international students: Required—TOEFL. *Application deadline:* Applications are processed on a rolling basis. Application fee: $30. *Expenses:* Tuition: Part-time $930 per credit. Required fees: $200 per semester. *Financial support:* In 2009–10, 34 students received support. Scholarships/grants available. Support available to part-time students. Financial award applicants required to submit FAFSA. *Unit head:* Dr. Lynn Johnson, Program Director, 845-359-7200 Ext. 5410, Fax: 845-359-7248, E-mail: ken.reilly@liu.edu. *Application contact:* Peter S. Reiner, Director of Admissions and Marketing, 845-359-7200, Fax: 845-359-7248, E-mail: peter.reiner@liu.edu.

Louisiana State University and Agricultural and Mechanical College, Graduate School, E. J. Ourso College of Business, Department of Finance, Baton Rouge, LA 70803. Offers business administration (PhD), including finance; finance (MS). *Faculty:* 13 full-time (3 women), 1 (woman) part-time/adjunct. *Students:* 46 full-time (16 women), 2 part-time (0 women); includes 1 Asian American or Pacific Islander, 23 international. Average age 27. 126 applicants, 34% accepted, 12 enrolled. In 2009, 2 master's, 2 doctorates awarded. *Degree requirements:* For master's, thesis or alternative; for doctorate, thesis/dissertation. *Entrance requirements:* For master's and doctorate, GMAT. Additional exam requirements/recommendations for international students: Required—TOEFL (minimum score 550 paper-based; 213 computer-based; 79 iBT) or IELTS (minimum score 6.5). *Application deadline:* For fall admission, 1/25 priority date for domestic students, 5/15 for international students; for spring admission, 10/15 for international students. Applications are processed on a rolling basis. Application fee: $50 ($70 for international students). *Financial support:* In 2009–10, 33 students received support, including 11 research assistantships with full and partial tuition reimbursements available (averaging $16,272 per year), 5 teaching assistantships with full and partial tuition reimbursements available (averaging $15,760 per year); fellowships, career-related internships or fieldwork, Federal Work-Study, scholarships/grants, health care benefits, and unspecified assistantships also available. Support available to part-time students. Financial award application deadline: 4/1; financial award applicants required to submit FAFSA. *Faculty research:* Derivatives and risk management, capital structure, asset pricing, spatial statistics, financial institutions and underwriting. Total annual research expenditures: $14,214. *Unit head:* Dr. Vestor Carlos Slawson, Interim Chair, 225-578-6367, Fax: 225-578-6366, E-mail: cslawson@lsu.edu. *Application contact:* Dr. Vestor Carlos Slawson, Interim Chair, 225-578-6367, Fax: 225-578-6366, E-mail: cslawson@lsu.edu.

Louisiana Tech University, Graduate School, College of Business, Department of Finance and Economics, Ruston, LA 71272. Offers business economics (MBA, DBA); finance (MBA, DBA). Part-time programs available. *Degree requirements:* For doctorate, thesis/dissertation. *Entrance requirements:* For master's and doctorate, GMAT.

Loyola University Chicago, Graduate School of Business, Chicago, IL 60660. Offers accountancy (MS, MSA); business administration (MBA); finance (MS); healthcare management (MBA); human resources and employee relations (MS, MSHR); information systems and operations management (MS), including information systems management; marketing (MS, MSIMC), including integrated marketing communications (MS), marketing (MSIMC); strategic financial services (MBA); JD/MBA; MBA/MSA; MSIMC/MBA; MSISM/MBA; MSN/MBA. *Accreditation:* AACSB. *Expenses:* Tuition: Full-time $14,220; part-time $790 per credit hour. Required fees: $60 per semester hour. Tuition and fees vary according to program.

Loyola University Maryland, Graduate Programs, Sellinger School of Business and Management, Program in Business Administration, Baltimore, MD 21210-2699. Offers accounting (MBA); finance (MBA); general business (MBA); international business (MBA); management (MBA); management information systems (MBA); marketing (MBA). *Accreditation:* AACSB. Part-time and evening/weekend programs available. *Entrance requirements:* For master's, GMAT. Additional exam requirements/recommendations for international students: Required—TOEFL (minimum score 550 paper-based; 213 computer-based).

Loyola University Maryland, Graduate Programs, Sellinger School of Business and Management, Program in Finance, Baltimore, MD 21210-2699. Offers MSF. Part-time and evening/weekend programs available. *Entrance requirements:* For master's, GMAT. Additional exam requirements/recommendations for international students: Required—TOEFL (minimum score 550 paper-based; 213 computer-based).

Manhattanville College, Graduate Programs, Humanities and Social Sciences Programs, Program in Finance, Purchase, NY 10577-2132. Offers MS. Part-time and evening/weekend programs available. *Students:* 8 part-time (4 women); includes 1 minority (African American). *Entrance requirements:* Additional exam requirements/recommendations for international students: Required—TOEFL. *Application deadline:* Applications are processed on a rolling basis. Application fee: $70. Electronic applications accepted. *Financial support:* Career-related internships or fieldwork, Federal Work-Study, scholarships/grants, and unspecified assistantships available. Financial award application deadline: 3/1; financial award applicants required to submit FAFSA. *Unit head:* Donald Richards, Interim Dean, School of Graduate and Professional Studies, 914-323-5469, Fax: 914-694-3488, E-mail: gps@mville.edu. *Application contact:* Office of Admissions for Graduate and Professional Studies, 914-323-5418, E-mail: gps@mville.edu.

Marylhurst University, Department of Business Administration, Marylhurst, OR 97036-0261. Offers finance (MBA); general management (MBA); government policy and administration (MBA); green development (MBA); health care management (MBA); marketing (MBA); natural and organic resources (MBA); nonprofit management (MBA); organizational behavior (MBA); real estate (MBA); renewable energy (MBA); sustainable business (MBA). Part-time and evening/weekend programs available. Postbaccalaureate distance learning degree programs offered (no on-campus study). *Faculty:* 2 full-time (1 woman), 28 part-time/adjunct (5 women). *Students:* 30 full-time (12 women), 627 part-time (323 women); includes 79 minority (28 African Americans, 3 American Indian/Alaska Native, 17 Asian Americans or Pacific Islanders, 31 Hispanic Americans), 9 international. Average age 37. 299 applicants, 80% accepted, 209 enrolled. In 2009, 193 master's awarded. *Degree requirements:* For master's, comprehensive exam, capstone course. *Entrance requirements:* For master's, GMAT (if GPA less than 3.0 and fewer than 5 years of work experience), interview, resume, 2 letters of recommendation. Additional exam requirements/recommendations for international students: Recommended—TOEFL (minimum score 550 paper-based; 213 computer-based; 80 iBT). *Application deadline:* For fall admission, 9/11 priority date for domestic and international students; for winter admission, 12/15 priority date for domestic and international students; for spring admission, 3/17 priority date for domestic and international students. Applications are processed on a rolling basis. Application fee: $40 ($50 for international students). Electronic applications accepted. *Financial support:* Scholarships/grants available. Support available to part-time students. Financial award applicants required to submit FAFSA. *Unit head:* Bob Hanks, Director of Business and Real Estate Programs, 503-636-8141, Fax: 503-697-5597, E-mail: mba@marylhurst.edu. *Application contact:* Kathleen Schneff, Admissions Specialist, 800-634-9982 Ext. 3322, Fax: 503-635-6585, E-mail: admissions@marylhurst.edu.

Marywood University, Academic Affairs, College of Liberal Arts and Sciences, Department of Business and Managerial Science, Emphasis in Finance and Investments, Scranton, PA 18509-1598. Offers MBA. *Students:* 4 full-time (2 women), 6 part-time (3 women). Average age 31. 6 applicants, 83% accepted. In 2009, 10 master's awarded. *Entrance requirements:* For master's, GMAT. Additional exam requirements/recommendations for international students: Required—TOEFL (minimum score 550 paper-based; 213 computer-based; 79 iBT). *Application deadline:* For fall admission, 4/1 priority date for domestic students, 3/31 priority date for international students; for spring admission, 11/1 priority date for domestic students, 8/31 priority date for international students. Applications are processed on a rolling basis. Application fee: $35. Electronic applications accepted. *Expenses:* Tuition: Part-time $715 per credit. Required fees: $270 per semester. Tuition and fees vary according to degree level, campus/location and program. *Financial support:* Career-related internships or fieldwork, scholarships/grants, and unspecified assistantships available. Support available to part-time students. Financial award application deadline: 6/30; financial award applicants required to submit FAFSA. *Faculty research:* Accountant/auditor liability, corporate finance acquisitions and mergers, corporate bankruptcy. *Application contact:* Tammy Manka, Assistant Director of Graduate Admissions, 866-279-9663, E-mail: tmanka@marywood.edu.

McGill University, Faculty of Graduate and Postdoctoral Studies, Desautels Faculty of Management, Montréal, QC H3A 2T5, Canada. Offers administration (PhD); entrepreneurial studies (MBA); finance (MBA); general management (Post Master's Certificate); information systems (MBA); international business (exchange program) (MBA); international Master's program in practicing management (MM); management (MBA); management for development (MBA); manufacturing management (MMM); marketing (MBA); operations management (MBA); public accountancy (Diploma); strategic management (MBA); MBA/LL B; MD/MBA.

Michigan State University, The Graduate School, Eli Broad Graduate School of Management, Department of Finance, East Lansing, MI 48824. Offers business administration (PhD); finance (MS). *Faculty:* 18 full-time (2 women). *Students:* 24 full-time (2 women); includes 1 minority (Asian American or Pacific Islander), 23 international. Average age 36. 116 applicants, 5% accepted. In 2009, 18 master's, 6 doctorates awarded. *Entrance requirements:* Additional exam requirements/recommendations for international students: Required—TOEFL. Electronic applications accepted. *Expenses:* Tuition, state resident: part-time $478.25 per credit hour. Tuition, nonresident: part-time $966.50 per credit hour. Part-time tuition and fees vary according to program. *Financial support:* In 2009–10, 5 research assistantships with tuition reimbursements (averaging $7,092 per year) were awarded. Total annual research expenditures: $39,688. *Unit head:* Dr. G. Geoffrey Booth, Chairperson, 517-355-8377, Fax: 517-432-1080, E-mail: boothg@bus.msu.edu. *Application contact:* Celeste Shoulders, Program Information, 517-353-1745, Fax: 517-432-1080, E-mail: fin@bus.msu.edu.

MidAmerica Nazarene University, Graduate Studies in Management, Olathe, KS 66062-1899. Offers management (MBA); organizational administration (MA), including finance, international business, leadership, non-profit. Evening/weekend programs available. *Faculty:* 6 full-time (2 women), 18 part-time/adjunct (7 women). *Students:* 107 full-time (49 women), 7 part-time (3 women); includes 25 minority (18 African Americans, 1 Asian American or Pacific Islander, 6 Hispanic Americans). Average age 36. In 2009, 81 master's awarded. *Entrance requirements:* For master's, mathematical assessment, minimum undergraduate GPA of 3.0, letters of recommendation. Additional exam requirements/recommendations for international students: Required—TOEFL. *Application deadline:* For fall admission, 9/1 priority date for domestic students; for spring admission, 5/1 priority date for domestic students. Applications are processed on a rolling basis. Application fee: $100. Electronic applications accepted. *Financial support:* Application deadline: 5/1. *Faculty research:* Economic development, international finance, business development, employee evaluation. *Unit head:* Dr. Willadee Wehmeyer, Director, 913-971-3276, Fax: 913-791-3409, E-mail: wwehmeye@mnu.edu. *Application contact:* Melanie Sutherland, Administrative Assistant, 913-971-3276, Fax: 913-971-3409, E-mail: mba@mnu.edu.

Mississippi College, Graduate School, School of Business, Clinton, MS 39058. Offers accounting (Certificate); business administration (MBA), including accounting; business education (M Ed); finance (MBA, Certificate); JD/MBA. *Accreditation:* ACBSP. Part-time and evening/weekend programs available. *Faculty:* 12 full-time (2 women), 5 part-time/adjunct (1 woman). *Students:* 101 full-time (41 women), 144 part-time (75 women); includes 41 minority (37 African Americans, 3 Asian Americans or Pacific Islanders, 1 Hispanic American), 78 international. Average age 28. In 2009, 90 master's awarded. *Degree requirements:* For master's, comprehensive exam, thesis optional. *Entrance requirements:* For master's, GMAT, minimum GPA of 2.5, 24 hours of undergraduate course work in business. Additional exam requirements/recommendations for international students: Recommended—IELTS. *Application deadline:* For fall admission, 8/15 priority date for domestic students. Applications are processed on a rolling basis. Application fee: $30. Electronic applications accepted. *Expenses:* Tuition: Part-time $452 per credit hour. Required fees: $101 per semester. Tuition and fees vary according to degree level, campus/location, program and student level. *Financial support:* Federal Work-Study and unspecified assistantships available. Support available to part-time students. Financial award application deadline: 4/1; financial award applicants required to submit FAFSA. *Unit head:* Dr. Marcelo Eduardo, Dean, 601-925-3420, E-mail: eduardo@mc.edu. *Application contact:* Elnora Lewis, Secretary, 601-925-3225, Fax: 601-925-3889, E-mail: lewis09@mc.edu.

Mississippi State University, College of Business, Department of Finance and Economics, Mississippi State, MS 39762. Offers applied economics (PhD); business administration (PhD), including finance; economics (MA); finance (MSBA). Part-time programs available. *Faculty:* 13 full-time (2 women). *Students:* 15 full-time (4 women), 4 part-time (1 woman); includes 1 minority (African American), 11 international. Average age 31. 31 applicants, 23% accepted, 3 enrolled. In 2009, 2 master's, 3 doctorates awarded. Terminal master's awarded for partial completion of doctoral program. *Degree requirements:* For master's, comprehensive exam, thesis optional; for doctorate, comprehensive exam, thesis/dissertation. *Entrance requirements:* For master's and doctorate, GMAT, GRE General Test. Additional exam requirements/recommendations for international students: Required—TOEFL (minimum score 575 paper-based; 233 computer-based; 90 iBT); Recommended—IELTS (minimum score 6.5). *Application deadline:* For fall admission, 7/1 for domestic students, 5/1 for international students; for spring admission, 11/1 for domestic students, 10/1 for international students. Applications are processed on a rolling basis. Application fee: $40. Electronic applications accepted. *Expenses:* Tuition, state resident: full-time $2575.50; part-time $286.25 per credit hour. Tuition, nonresident: full-time $6510; part-time $723.50 per credit hour. Tuition and fees vary according to course load. *Financial support:* In 2009–10, 5 teaching assistantships with tuition reimbursements (averaging $10,698 per year) were awarded; Federal Work-Study, scholarships/grants, health care benefits, and unspecified assistantships also available. Financial award application deadline: 4/1; financial award applicants required to submit FAFSA. *Faculty research:* Economics development, mergers, event studies, economic education, bank performance. Total annual research expenditures: $491,000. *Unit head:* Dr. Mike Highfield, Department Head, 662-325-3928, Fax: 662-325-1977, E-mail: mhighfield@cobilan.msstate.edu. *Application contact:* Dr. Benjamin F. Blair, Associate Professor/Graduate Coordinator, 662-325-1980, Fax: 662-325-1977, E-mail: bblair@cobilan.msstate.edu.

Molloy College, Graduate Business Program, Rockville Centre, NY 11571-5002. Offers accounting (MBA); accounting and management (MBA); management (MBA); personal financial planning and accounting (MBA); personal financial planning and management (MBA). Part-time programs available. *Faculty:* 5 full-time (0 women), 8 part-time/adjunct (2 women). *Students:* 26 full-time (12 women), 60 part-time (33 women); includes 30 minority (12 African Americans, 4 Asian Americans or Pacific Islanders, 14 Hispanic Americans), 2 international. Average age 33. In 2009, 21 master's awarded. *Application deadline:* Applications are processed on a rolling basis. *Expenses:* Tuition: Part-time $765 per credit. Required fees: $340 per semester. *Unit head:* Dr. Raymond Manganelli, Associate Dean and Director of Graduate Programs, 516-678-5000 Ext. 6905, E-mail: rmanganelli@molloy.edu. *Application contact:* Alina Haitz, Assistant Director of Graduate Admissions, 516-678-5000 Ext. 6399, Fax: 516-256-2247, E-mail: ahaitz@molloy.edu.

Finance and Banking

Montclair State University, The Graduate School, School of Business, Department of Accounting, Law and Taxation, Montclair, NJ 07043-1624. Offers accounting (MBA, Certificate); finance (Certificate); management information systems (Certificate); marketing (Certificate). Part-time and evening/weekend programs available. *Faculty:* 15 full-time (5 women), 11 part-time/adjunct (9 women). *Students:* 44 full-time (23 women), 94 part-time (40 women). Average age 30. 81 applicants, 56% accepted, 29 enrolled. In 2009, 31 master's, 1 other advanced degree awarded. *Entrance requirements:* For master's, GMAT, 2 letters of recommendation, resume. Additional exam requirements/recommendations for international students: Required—TOEFL (minimum score 83 computer-based), or IELTS. *Application deadline:* For fall admission, 6/1 for international students; for spring admission, 10/1 for international students. Applications are processed on a rolling basis. Application fee: $60. Electronic applications accepted. *Expenses:* Tuition, area resident: Part-time $486.74 per credit. Tuition, state resident: part-time $486.74 per credit. Tuition, nonresident: part-time $751.34 per credit. Tuition and fees vary according to degree level and program. *Financial support:* In 2009–10, 2 research assistantships with full tuition reimbursements (averaging $7,000 per year) were awarded; Federal Work-Study and scholarships/grants also available. Support available to part-time students. Financial award application deadline: 3/1; financial award applicants required to submit FAFSA. *Unit head:* Prof. Frank Aquilino, Head, 973-655-4174. *Application contact:* Amy Aiello, Director of Graduate Admissions and Operations, 973-655-5147, Fax: 973-655-7869, E-mail: graduate.school@montclair.edu.

Montclair State University, The Graduate School, School of Business, Department of Economics and Finance, Montclair, NJ 07043-1624. Offers business economics (MBA); finance (MBA). Part-time and evening/weekend programs available. *Faculty:* 16 full-time (4 women), 3 part-time/adjunct (1 woman). *Students:* 24 full-time (9 women), 62 part-time (21 women). Average age 30. 44 applicants, 48% accepted, 16 enrolled. In 2009, 42 master's awarded. *Entrance requirements:* For master's, GRE General Test, 2 letters of recommendation, resume. Additional exam requirements/recommendations for international students: Required—TOEFL (minimum score 83 computer-based), or IELTS. *Application deadline:* For fall admission, 6/1 for international students; for spring admission, 10/1 for international students. Applications are processed on a rolling basis. Application fee: $60. Electronic applications accepted. *Expenses:* Tuition, area resident: Part-time $486.74 per credit. Tuition, state resident: part-time $486.74 per credit. Tuition, nonresident: part-time $751.34 per credit. Tuition and fees vary according to degree level and program. *Financial support:* In 2009–10, 4 research assistantships with full tuition reimbursements (averaging $7,000 per year) were awarded; Federal Work-Study, scholarships/grants, and unspecified assistantships also available. Support available to part-time students. Financial award application deadline: 3/1; financial award applicants required to submit FAFSA. *Unit head:* Dr. Richard Lord, Chair, 973-655-5255. *Application contact:* Amy Aiello, Director of Graduate Admissions and Operations, 973-655-5147, Fax: 973-655-7869, E-mail: graduate.school@montclair.edu.

Mount Saint Mary College, Division of Business, Newburgh, NY 12550-3494. Offers business (MBA); financial planning (MBA). Part-time and evening/weekend programs available. *Faculty:* 5 full-time (1 woman), 5 part-time/adjunct (1 woman). *Students:* 28 full-time (16 women), 66 part-time (32 women); includes 15 minority (2 African Americans, 4 Asian Americans or Pacific Islanders, 9 Hispanic Americans), 31 international. Average age 30. 36 applicants, 100% accepted, 23 enrolled. In 2009, 70 master's awarded. *Degree requirements:* For master's, thesis or alternative. *Entrance requirements:* For master's, GMAT or minimum undergraduate GPA of 2.7. *Application deadline:* Applications are processed on a rolling basis. Application fee: $45. *Expenses:* Tuition: Full-time $13,356; part-time $742 per credit. Required fees: $50 per semester. *Financial support:* In 2009–10, 19 students received support. Unspecified assistantships available. Financial award application deadline: 4/15; financial award applicants required to submit FAFSA. *Faculty research:* Financial reform, entrepreneurship and small business development, global business relations, technology's impact on business decision-making, college-assisted business education. *Unit head:* Dr. Moira Tolan, Coordinator, 845-569-3288, Fax: 845-562-6762, E-mail: tolan@msmc.edu. *Application contact:* Janice Banker, Secretary, 845-569-3582, Fax: 845-569-3885, E-mail: banker@msmc.edu.

National University, Academic Affairs, College of Letters and Sciences, Department of Professional Studies, La Jolla, CA 92037-1011. Offers forensic science (MFS), including criminalistics and investigation; public administration (MPA), including alternative dispute resolution, human resource management, organizational leadership, public finance. Part-time and evening/weekend programs available. Postbaccalaureate distance learning degree programs offered (no on-campus study). *Faculty:* 5 full-time (3 women), 27 part-time/adjunct (7 women). *Students:* 167 full-time (95 women), 246 part-time (133 women); includes 188 minority (71 African Americans, 2 American Indian/Alaska Native, 41 Asian Americans or Pacific Islanders, 74 Hispanic Americans). Average age 38. 284 applicants, 100% accepted, 206 enrolled. In 2009, 104 master's awarded. *Degree requirements:* For master's, thesis. *Entrance requirements:* For master's, interview, minimum GPA of 2.5. Additional exam requirements/recommendations for international students: Required—TOEFL (minimum score 550 paper-based; 213 computer-based; 79 iBT), IELTS (minimum score 6). *Application deadline:* Applications are processed on a rolling basis. Application fee: $60 ($65 for international students). Electronic applications accepted. *Expenses:* Tuition: Part-time $338 per quarter hour. *Financial support:* Career-related internships or fieldwork, institutionally sponsored loans, scholarships/grants, and tuition waivers (partial) available. Support available to part-time students. Financial award application deadline: 6/30; financial award applicants required to submit FAFSA. *Unit head:* Chandrika M. Kelso, Associate Professor and Chair, 858-642-8433, Fax: 858-642-8715, E-mail: ckelso@nu.edu. *Application contact:* Dominick Giovanniello, Associate Regional Dean—San Diego, 800-NAT-UNIV, Fax: 858-541-7792, E-mail: dgiovann@nu.edu.

National University, Academic Affairs, School of Business and Management, Department of Accounting and Finance, La Jolla, CA 92037-1011. Offers accountancy (MS); corporate and international finance (MS). Part-time and evening/weekend programs available. Postbaccalaureate distance learning degree programs offered (no on-campus study). *Faculty:* 8 full-time (1 woman), 37 part-time/adjunct (10 women). *Students:* 67 full-time (32 women), 68 part-time (27 women); includes 41 minority (10 African Americans, 2 American Indian/Alaska Native, 13 Asian Americans or Pacific Islanders, 16 Hispanic Americans), 23 international. Average age 33. 145 applicants, 100% accepted, 75 enrolled. In 2009, 14 master's awarded. *Degree requirements:* For master's, thesis. *Entrance requirements:* For master's, interview, minimum GPA of 2.5. Additional exam requirements/recommendations for international students: Required—TOEFL (minimum score 550 paper-based; 213 computer-based; 79 iBT), IELTS (minimum score 6). *Application deadline:* Applications are processed on a rolling basis. Application fee: $60 ($65 for international students). Electronic applications accepted. *Expenses:* Tuition: Part-time $338 per quarter hour. *Financial support:* Career-related internships or fieldwork, institutionally sponsored loans, scholarships/grants, and tuition waivers (partial) available. Support available to part-time students. Financial award application deadline: 6/30; financial award applicants required to submit FAFSA. *Unit head:* Prof. Donald A. Schwartz, Chair and Associate Professor, 858-642-8420, Fax: 858-642-8740, E-mail: dschwartz@nu.edu. *Application contact:* Dominick Giovanniello, Associate Regional Dean—San Diego, 800-NAT-UNIV, Fax: 858-541-7792, E-mail: dgiovann@nu.edu.

National University, Academic Affairs, School of Business and Management, Department of Leadership and Business Administration, La Jolla, CA 92037-1011. Offers alternative dispute resolution (MBA); e-business (MBA); financial management (MBA); human resource management (MBA); human resources management (MA); international business (MBA); knowledge management (MS); marketing (MBA); organizational leadership (MBA, MS); technology management (MBA). Part-time and evening/weekend programs available. Postbaccalaureate distance learning degree programs offered (no on-campus study). *Faculty:* 4 full-time (2 women), 22 part-time/adjunct (9 women). *Students:* 95 full-time (56 women), 228 part-time (129 women); includes 63 African Americans, 24 Asian Americans or Pacific Islanders, 61 Hispanic Americans, 6 international. Average age 38. 191 applicants, 100% accepted, 131 enrolled. In 2009, 62 master's awarded. *Degree requirements:* For master's, thesis. *Entrance requirements:* For master's, interview, minimum GPA of 2.5. Additional exam requirements/

recommendations for international students: Required—TOEFL (minimum score 550 paper-based; 213 computer-based; 79 iBT), IELTS (minimum score 6). *Application deadline:* Applications are processed on a rolling basis. Application fee: $60 ($65 for international students). Electronic applications accepted. *Expenses:* Tuition: Part-time $338 per quarter hour. *Financial support:* Career-related internships or fieldwork, institutionally sponsored loans, scholarships/grants, and tuition waivers (partial) available. Support available to part-time students. Financial award application deadline: 6/30; financial award applicants required to submit FAFSA. *Unit head:* Dr. George Drops, Chair and Professor, 858-642-8438, Fax: 858-642-8406, E-mail: gdrops@nu.edu. *Application contact:* Dominick Giovanniello, Associate Regional Dean—San Diego, 800-NAT-UNIV, Fax: 858-541-7792, E-mail: dgiovann@nu.edu.

New Jersey City University, Graduate Studies and Continuing Education, College of Professional Studies, Department of Business Administration, Program in Finance, Jersey City, NJ 07305-1597. Offers MS. Part-time and evening/weekend programs available. *Students:* 11 full-time (4 women), 11 part-time (7 women); includes 8 minority (1 African American, 6 Asian Americans or Pacific Islanders, 1 Hispanic American), 5 international. *Degree requirements:* For master's, thesis. *Entrance requirements:* Additional exam requirements/recommendations for international students: Required—TOEFL. *Expenses:* Tuition, area resident: Part-time $456.75 per credit. Tuition, nonresident: part-time $842.55 per credit. Required fees: $65 per term. *Unit head:* Rosilyn Overton, Graduate Coordinator, 201-200-3353, E-mail: roverton@njcu.edu. *Application contact:* Rosilyn Overton, Graduate Coordinator, 201-200-3353, E-mail: roverton@njcu.edu.

Newman University, School of Business, Wichita, KS 67213-2097. Offers finance (MBA); international business (MBA); leadership (MBA); management (MBA); technology (MBA). Part-time programs available. *Faculty:* 5 full-time (1 woman), 8 part-time/adjunct (2 women). *Students:* 29 full-time (13 women), 105 part-time (52 women); includes 30 minority (9 African Americans, 1 American Indian/Alaska Native, 10 Asian Americans or Pacific Islanders, 10 Hispanic Americans), 23 international. Average age 32. 80 applicants, 76% accepted, 47 enrolled. In 2009, 76 master's awarded. *Degree requirements:* For master's, thesis optional. *Entrance requirements:* For master's, interview; minimum GPA of 3.0; 3 letters of recommendation; course work in algebra, statistics, macroeconomics, and financial accounting. Additional exam requirements/recommendations for international students: Required—TOEFL (minimum score 600 paper-based; 250 computer-based; 100 iBT). *Application deadline:* For fall admission, 8/1 priority date for domestic students, 7/15 priority date for international students; for winter admission, 1/1 priority date for domestic students; for spring admission, 1/1 priority date for domestic students, 11/15 priority date for international students. Applications are processed on a rolling basis. Application fee: $25 ($40 for international students). Electronic applications accepted. *Expenses:* Contact institution. *Financial support:* In 2009–10, 3 students received support. Federal Work-Study available. Financial award application deadline: 8/15; financial award applicants required to submit FAFSA. *Unit head:* Dr. Joe Goetz, Dean of the College of Professional Studies/Director, 316-942-4291 Ext. 2111, Fax: 316-942-4486, E-mail: goetzj@newmanu.edu. *Application contact:* Linda Kay Sabala, Director of Graduate Admissions, 316-942-4291 Ext. 2230, Fax: 316-942-4483, E-mail: sabalal@newmanu.edu.

The New School: A University, The New School for Social Research, Department of Economics, New York, NY 10003. Offers economics (M Phil, MA, MS, DS Sc, PhD); global finance (MS); global political economy and finance (MA). Part-time and evening/weekend programs available. *Faculty:* 9 full-time (2 women). *Students:* 103 full-time (32 women), 55 part-time (12 women); includes 28 minority (9 African Americans, 12 Asian Americans or Pacific Islanders, 7 Hispanic Americans), 64 international. Average age 32. 138 applicants, 84% accepted, 41 enrolled. In 2009, 46 master's, 8 doctorates awarded. Terminal master's awarded for partial completion of doctoral program. *Degree requirements:* For master's, exam; for doctorate, one foreign language, thesis/dissertation, qualifying exam. *Entrance requirements:* For master's, GRE General Test; for doctorate, GRE General Test, MA. Additional exam requirements/recommendations for international students: Required—TOEFL (minimum score 600 paper-based; 250 computer-based; 100 iBT). *Application deadline:* For fall admission, 1/17 priority date for domestic students, 1/17 for international students; for spring admission, 10/15 priority date for domestic students, 10/15 for international students. Applications are processed on a rolling basis. Application fee: $50. Electronic applications accepted. *Financial support:* Fellowships, research assistantships, teaching assistantships, Federal Work-Study, scholarships/grants, tuition waivers (full and partial), and unspecified assistantships available. Support available to part-time students. Financial award application deadline: 3/1; financial award applicants required to submit FAFSA. *Faculty research:* Heterodox, history of economic thought, post-Keynesian, global political economy and finance. *Unit head:* Dr. Will Milberg, Chair, 212-229-5717 Ext. 3045, E-mail: milbergw@newschool.edu. *Application contact:* Robert MacDonald, Director of Admissions, 212-229-5710 Ext. 3007, Fax: 212-989-7102, E-mail: macdonar@newschool.edu.

The New School: A University, The New School for Social Research, Global Finance Program, New York, NY 10003. Offers MS. Part-time and evening/weekend programs available. *Faculty:* 4 full-time (0 women). *Students:* 22 full-time (5 women), 11 part-time (3 women); includes 6 minority (2 African Americans, 1 American Indian/Alaska Native, 3 Asian Americans or Pacific Islanders), 11 international. Average age 30. *Entrance requirements:* For master's, GRE General Test or GMAT. Additional exam requirements/recommendations for international students: Required—TOEFL (minimum score 600 paper-based; 250 computer-based; 100 iBT). *Application deadline:* For fall admission, 8/1 priority date for domestic students, 5/15 for international students; for spring admission, 1/15 priority date for domestic students, 12/15 for international students. Applications are processed on a rolling basis. Application fee: $50. *Financial support:* Fellowships, research assistantships, teaching assistantships, career-related internships or fieldwork, Federal Work-Study, and scholarships/grants available. Financial award application deadline: 3/1; financial award applicants required to submit FAFSA. *Unit head:* Dr. Salih Neftei, Head, 212-229-5717 Ext. 3046, Fax: 212-229-5724, E-mail: sneftei@wwc.com. *Application contact:* Robert MacDonald, Director of Admissions, 212-229-5710 Ext. 3007, Fax: 212-989-7102, E-mail: macdonar@newschool.edu.

New York Institute of Technology, Graduate Division, School of Management, Program in Business Administration, Old Westbury, NY 11568-8000. Offers accounting (Advanced Certificate); business administration (MBA); finance (Advanced Certificate); international business (Advanced Certificate); management of information systems (Advanced Certificate); marketing (Advanced Certificate). Part-time and evening/weekend programs available. *Students:* 599 full-time (262 women), 528 part-time (200 women); includes 51 minority (17 African Americans, 24 Asian Americans or Pacific Islanders, 10 Hispanic Americans), 324 international. Average age 29. In 2009, 691 master's, 7 other advanced degrees awarded. *Degree requirements:* For master's, thesis (for some programs). *Entrance requirements:* For master's, minimum QPA of 2.85. Additional exam requirements/recommendations for international students: Required—TOEFL (minimum score 550 paper-based; 213 computer-based). *Application deadline:* For fall admission, 7/1 priority date for domestic students; for spring admission, 12/1 priority date for domestic students. Applications are processed on a rolling basis. Application fee: $50. Electronic applications accepted. *Expenses:* Tuition: Part-time $825 per credit. *Financial support:* Fellowships, research assistantships with partial tuition reimbursements, institutionally sponsored loans, tuition waivers (full and partial), and unspecified assistantships available. Support available to part-time students. Financial award applicants required to submit FAFSA. *Faculty research:* Instructor performance appraisal; relationship between TOEFL, GMAT, GRE, and performance in foreign students. *Unit head:* Dr. Diamando Afxentiou, Acting Associate Dean, 516-686-3937, Fax: 516-686-7430, E-mail: dafxenti@nyit.edu. *Application contact:* Dr. Jacquelyn Nealon, Vice President for Enrollment Services, 516-686-7925, Fax: 516-686-7597, E-mail: jnealon@nyit.edu.

New York University, Leonard N. Stern School of Business, Department of Finance, New York, NY 10012-1019. Offers MBA, PhD. *Expenses:* Tuition: Full-time $30,528; part-time $1272 per credit. Required fees: $2177. *Faculty research:* Derivative securities, pricing of assets, credit risk, portfolio management, international finance.

New York University, Robert F. Wagner Graduate School of Public Service, Program in Public Administration, New York, NY 10012-1019. Offers public administration (PhD); public and nonprofit management and policy (MPA, Advanced Certificate), including developmental administration (Advanced Certificate), financial management and public finance, human resources management (Advanced Certificate), international administration (Advanced Certificate), management (MPA), management for public and nonprofit organizations (Advanced Certificate), public policy analysis, quantitative analysis and computer applications (Advanced Certificate), urban public policy (Advanced Certificate); JD/MPA; MBA/MPA; MPA/MA. *Accreditation:* NASPAA (one or more programs are accredited). Part-time and evening/weekend programs available. *Faculty:* 31 full-time (13 women), 33 part-time/adjunct (16 women). *Students:* 363 full-time (270 women), 228 part-time (171 women); includes 146 minority (46 African Americans, 64 Asian Americans or Pacific Islanders, 36 Hispanic Americans), 76 international. Average age 28. 1,117 applicants, 57% accepted, 225 enrolled. In 2009, 236 master's, 3 doctorates awarded. *Degree requirements:* For master's, thesis or alternative, capstone end event; for doctorate, one foreign language, thesis/dissertation. *Entrance requirements:* For master's, minimum undergraduate GPA of 3.0; for doctorate, GMAT or GRE General Test, minimum GPA of 3.5. Additional exam requirements/recommendations for international students: Required—TOEFL (minimum score 600 paper-based; 250 computer-based; 100 iBT), TWE (minimum score 4). *Application deadline:* For fall admission, 6/1 for domestic students, 1/15 for international students; for spring admission, 11/15 for domestic students, 10/1 for international students. Applications are processed on a rolling basis. Application fee: $80. Electronic applications accepted. *Expenses:* Contact institution. *Financial support:* In 2009–10, 155 students received support, including 150 fellowships (averaging $11,335 per year), 5 research assistantships with full tuition reimbursements available (averaging $22,440 per year); career-related internships or fieldwork, Federal Work-Study, institutionally sponsored loans, scholarships/grants, health care benefits, and unspecified assistantships also available. Support available to part-time students. Financial award application deadline: 12/1; financial award applicants required to submit FAFSA. *Unit head:* Katty Jones, Director, Program Services, 212-998-7411, Fax: 212-995-4164, E-mail: katty.jones@nyu.edu. *Application contact:* Christopher Alexander, Administrative Aide, Enrollment, 212-998-7414, Fax: 212-995-4611, E-mail: wagner.admissions@nyu.edu.

New York University, School of Continuing and Professional Studies, The Preston Robert Tisch Center for Hospitality, Tourism, and Sports Management, Program in Sports Business, New York, NY 10012-1019. Offers finance and development (MS); marketing and media (MS); sports business (Advanced Certificate). Part-time and evening/weekend programs available. *Faculty:* 13 full-time (5 women), 11 part-time/adjunct (2 women). *Students:* 43 full-time (10 women), 65 part-time (21 women); includes 10 minority (5 African Americans, 2 Asian Americans or Pacific Islanders, 3 Hispanic Americans). Average age 28. 140 applicants, 49% accepted, 42 enrolled. In 2009, 45 master's, 6 other advanced degrees awarded. *Degree requirements:* For master's, comprehensive exam (for some programs), thesis. *Entrance requirements:* For master's, GMAT or GRE General Test (for recent graduates), resume, 2 letters of recommendation, essay. Additional exam requirements/recommendations for international students: Required—TOEFL (minimum score 600 paper-based; 250 computer-based; 100 iBT), TWE. *Application deadline:* For fall admission, 2/1 priority date for domestic and international students; for spring admission, 10/15 priority date for domestic students, 8/15 priority date for international students. Applications are processed on a rolling basis. Application fee: $75. Electronic applications accepted. *Expenses:* Tuition: Full-time $30,528; part-time $1272 per credit. Required fees: $2177. *Financial support:* In 2009–10, 39 students received support, including 39 fellowships (averaging $3,408 per year); career-related internships or fieldwork, Federal Work-Study, institutionally sponsored loans, and scholarships/grants also available. Support available to part-time students. Financial award application deadline: 3/1; financial award applicants required to submit FAFSA. *Faculty research:* Implications of college football's bowl coalition series from a legal, economic, and academic perspective; social history of sports. *Unit head:* Lalia Rach, Divisional Dean, 212-998-9100, Fax: 212-995-4676, E-mail: lalia.rach@nyu.edu. *Application contact:* Sandra Dove-Lowther, Academic Services Director, 212-998-9106, Fax: 212-995-4676, E-mail: sd2@nyu.edu.

New York University, School of Continuing and Professional Studies, Schack Institute of Real Estate, Program in Real Estate, New York, NY 10012-1019. Offers development (MS); finance and investment (MS); real estate (Advanced Certificate); strategic real estate management (MS). Part-time and evening/weekend programs available. *Faculty:* 12 full-time (2 women), 69 part-time/adjunct (8 women). *Students:* 120 full-time (16 women), 403 part-time (98 women); includes 87 minority (19 African Americans, 54 Asian Americans or Pacific Islanders, 14 Hispanic Americans). Average age 30. 292 applicants, 70% accepted, 118 enrolled. In 2009, 278 master's, 104 other advanced degrees awarded. *Degree requirements:* For master's, thesis, capstone. *Entrance requirements:* For master's, GRE General Test or GMAT (for recent graduates), resume, 2 letters of recommendation, essay. Additional exam requirements/recommendations for international students: Required—TOEFL (minimum score 600 paper-based; 250 computer-based; 100 iBT), TWE. *Application deadline:* For fall admission, 2/1 priority date for domestic and international students; for spring admission, 10/15 priority date for domestic students, 8/15 priority date for international students. Applications are processed on a rolling basis. Application fee: $75. Electronic applications accepted. *Expenses:* Tuition: Full-time $30,528; part-time $1272 per credit. Required fees: $2177. *Financial support:* In 2009–10, 138 students received support, including 138 fellowships (averaging $2,478 per year); scholarships/grants also available. Support available to part-time students. Financial award application deadline: 3/1; financial award applicants required to submit FAFSA. *Faculty research:* Economics and market cycles, international property rights, comparative metropolitan economies, current market trends. *Unit head:* James Stuckey, Divisional Dean, 212-992-3335, Fax: 212-992-3686, E-mail: james.stuckey@nyu.edu. *Application contact:* Jennifer Monahan, Director of Administration and Student Services, 212-992-3335, Fax: 212-992-3686, E-mail: jm189@nyu.edu.

Northeastern Illinois University, Graduate College, College of Business and Management, Chicago, IL 60625-4699. Offers accounting (MBA); finance (MBA); management (MBA); marketing (MBA). Part-time and evening/weekend programs available. *Degree requirements:* For master's, thesis optional. *Entrance requirements:* For master's, GMAT, minimum GPA of 2.75. Additional exam requirements/recommendations for international students: Required—TOEFL (minimum score 550 paper-based; 213 computer-based; 80 iBT). Electronic applications accepted. *Faculty research:* Perception of accountants and non-accountants toward future of the accounting industry, asynchronous learning outcomes, cost and efficiency of financial markets, impact of deregulation on airline industry, analysis of derivational instruments.

Northeastern State University, Graduate College, College of Business and Technology, Program in Accounting and Financial Analysis, Tahlequah, OK 74464-2399. Offers MS. Part-time and evening/weekend programs available. *Entrance requirements:* For master's, GMAT. Additional exam requirements/recommendations for international students: Required—TOEFL (minimum score 213 computer-based). Electronic applications accepted.

Northern Kentucky University, Office of Graduate Programs, College of Business, Program in Business Administration, Highland Heights, KY 41099. Offers business administration (MBA); entrepreneurship (Certificate); finance (Certificate); international business (Certificate); marketing (Certificate); project management (Certificate); JD/MBA. *Accreditation:* AACSB. Part-time and evening/weekend programs available. *Students:* 33 full-time (16 women), 155 part-time (63 women); includes 16 minority (9 African Americans, 7 Asian Americans or Pacific Islanders), 7 international. Average age 30. 105 applicants, 65% accepted, 34 enrolled. In 2009, 42 master's, 31 other advanced degrees awarded. *Degree requirements:* For master's, thesis optional. *Entrance requirements:* For master's, GMAT (minimum score 450), minimum GPA of 2.5. Additional exam requirements/recommendations for international students: Required—TOEFL (minimum score 550 paper-based; 213 computer-based; 79 iBT); Recommended—IELTS (minimum score 6.5). *Application deadline:* For fall admission, 8/1 priority date for domestic students, 6/1 priority date for international students; for spring admission, 12/1 priority date for domestic students, 10/1 priority date for international students. Applications are processed on

a rolling basis. Application fee: $40. Electronic applications accepted. *Expenses:* Tuition, state resident: full-time $6912; part-time $384 per credit hour. Tuition, nonresident: full-time $12,150; part-time $675 per credit hour. Tuition and fees vary according to course load, program and reciprocity agreements. *Financial support:* Unspecified assistantships available. Financial award applicants required to submit FAFSA. *Unit head:* James Bast, Director of MBA Programs, 859-572-7695, Fax: 859-572-7694, E-mail: mbusiness@nku.edu. *Application contact:* Dr. Peg Griffin, Director of Graduate Programs, 859-572-6934, Fax: 859-572-6670, E-mail: griffinp@nku.edu.

Northwestern University, The Graduate School, Kellogg School of Management, Department of Finance, Evanston, IL 60208. Offers PhD. Admissions and degree offered through The Graduate School. *Degree requirements:* For doctorate, comprehensive exam, thesis/dissertation. *Entrance requirements:* For doctorate, GMAT or GRE General Test, 2 years of undergraduate course work in mathematics. Additional exam requirements/recommendations for international students: Required—TOEFL. Electronic applications accepted. *Faculty research:* Corporate finance, asset pricing, international finance, micro-structure, empirical finance.

Notre Dame College, Graduate Studies, South Euclid, OH 44121-4293. Offers accounting (Certificate); creative critical thinking (M Ed); financial services management (Certificate); information systems (Certificate); learning disabilities (M Ed); management (Certificate); paralegal (Certificate); pastoral ministry (Certificate); reading (M Ed); teacher education (Certificate). Part-time and evening/weekend programs available. *Degree requirements:* For master's, thesis. *Entrance requirements:* For master's, GRE General Test, MAT, minimum GPA of 2.75, valid teaching certificate. *Faculty research:* Cognitive psychology, teaching critical thinking in the classroom.

Notre Dame de Namur University, Division of Academic Affairs, School of Business and Management, Department of Business Administration, Belmont, CA 94002-1908. Offers business administration (MBA); finance (MBA); human resource management (MBA); marketing (MBA). Part-time and evening/weekend programs available. *Faculty:* 7 full-time (1 woman), 6 part-time/adjunct (0 women). *Students:* 21 full-time (17 women), 87 part-time (49 women); includes 47 minority (3 African Americans, 4 American Indian/Alaska Native, 21 Asian Americans or Pacific Islanders, 19 Hispanic Americans), 9 international. Average age 34. 27 applicants, 100% accepted, 20 enrolled. In 2009, 43 master's awarded. *Entrance requirements:* For master's, minimum GPA of 2.5. Additional exam requirements/recommendations for international students: Required—TOEFL (minimum score 550 paper-based; 213 computer-based; 79 iBT). *Application deadline:* For fall admission, 8/1 priority date for domestic students; for spring admission, 12/1 priority date for domestic students. Applications are processed on a rolling basis. Application fee: $60. Electronic applications accepted. *Expenses:* Tuition: Part-time $720 per credit. Required fees: $35 per semester hour. *Financial support:* Career-related internships or fieldwork available. Support available to part-time students. Financial award applicants required to submit FAFSA. *Unit head:* Henry Roth, Director, 650-508-3721, E-mail: hroth@ndnu.edu. *Application contact:* Candace Hallmark, Associate Director of Admissions, 650-508-3592, Fax: 650-508-3426, E-mail: grad.admit@ndnu.edu.

Nova Southeastern University, H. Wayne Huizenga School of Business and Entrepreneurship, Doctoral Program in Business Administration, Fort Lauderdale, FL 33314-7796. Offers accounting (DBA); decision sciences (DBA); finance (DBA); human resource management (DBA); international business (DBA); management (DBA); marketing (DBA). Part-time and evening/weekend programs available. *Faculty:* 34 full-time (11 women), 2 part-time/adjunct (1 woman). *Students:* 6 full-time (1 woman), 129 part-time (41 women); includes 33 minority (17 African Americans, 6 Asian Americans or Pacific Islanders, 10 Hispanic Americans), 12 international. Average age 47. 58 applicants, 14% accepted, 5 enrolled. In 2009, 32 doctorates awarded. *Degree requirements:* For doctorate, comprehensive exam, thesis/dissertation. *Entrance requirements:* For doctorate, GMAT. Additional exam requirements/recommendations for international students: Required—TOEFL (minimum score 600 paper-based; 250 computer-based; 100 iBT), IELTS (minimum score 7). *Application deadline:* Applications are processed on a rolling basis. Application fee: $50. Electronic applications accepted. *Financial support:* Available to part-time students. Applicants required to submit FAFSA. *Faculty research:* Reputation management, call centers, international social capital, corporate earnings guidance, corporate governance. *Unit head:* Kristie Tetrault, Director of Program Administration, 954-262-5120, Fax: 954-262-3849, E-mail: kristie@huizenga.nova.edu. *Application contact:* Karen Goldberg, Associate Director of Recruitment and Special Events, 954-262-5039, Fax: 954-262-3822, E-mail: karen@huizenga.nova.edu.

Nova Southeastern University, H. Wayne Huizenga School of Business and Entrepreneurship, Program in Finance, Fort Lauderdale, FL 33314-7796. Offers MBA. Part-time and evening/weekend programs available. Postbaccalaureate distance learning degree programs offered (minimal on-campus study). *Students:* 3 part-time (1 woman); includes 2 minority (1 African American, 1 Asian American or Pacific Islander). Average age 32. 178 applicants, 62% accepted. *Degree requirements:* For master's, thesis optional. *Entrance requirements:* Additional exam requirements/recommendations for international students: Required—TOEFL (minimum score 550 paper-based; 213 computer-based; 79 iBT), IELTS (minimum score 6). *Application deadline:* For fall admission, 8/15 for domestic and international students; for winter admission, 12/10 for domestic and international students; for spring admission, 2/10 for domestic and international students. Applications are processed on a rolling basis. Application fee: $50. Electronic applications accepted. *Financial support:* Federal Work-Study and scholarships/grants available. Support available to part-time students. Financial award applicants required to submit FAFSA. *Unit head:* Steve Harvey, Assistant Dean of Program Administration, 954-262-5047, Fax: 954-262-3829, E-mail: harvey@nsu.nova.edu. *Application contact:* Karen Goldberg, Associate Director of Recruitment and Special Events, 954-262-5039, Fax: 954-262-3822, E-mail: karen@nova.edu.

Oakland University, Graduate Study and Lifelong Learning, School of Business Administration, Department of Accounting and Finance, Rochester, MI 48309-4401. Offers accounting (M Acc, Certificate); finance (Certificate).

The Ohio State University, Graduate School, Max M. Fisher College of Business, Program in Finance, Columbus, OH 43210. Offers MA, PhD. Electronic applications accepted. *Expenses:* Tuition, state resident: full-time $10,683. Tuition, nonresident: full-time $25,923. Tuition and fees vary according to course load and program.

Ohio University, Graduate College, College of Arts and Sciences, Department of Economics, Athens, OH 45701-2979. Offers applied economics (MA); financial economics (MFE). Part-time and evening/weekend programs available. *Faculty:* 15 full-time (3 women). *Students:* 56 full-time (20 women), 17 part-time (8 women); includes 10 minority (7 African Americans, 3 Asian Americans or Pacific Islanders), 33 international. 53 applicants, 57% accepted, 6 enrolled. In 2009, 49 master's awarded. *Degree requirements:* For master's, thesis or alternative. *Entrance requirements:* For master's, GRE or GMAT (recommended), minimum GPA of 3.0. Additional exam requirements/recommendations for international students: Required—TOEFL (minimum score 550 paper-based; 80 iBT) or IELTS Academic (minimum score 6.5). *Application deadline:* For fall admission, 2/15 priority date for domestic and international students; for winter admission, 12/1 for domestic students, 10/1 priority date for international students. Application fee: $50 ($55 for international students). Electronic applications accepted. *Expenses:* Tuition, state resident: full-time $7839; part-time $323 per quarter hour. Tuition, nonresident: full-time $15,831; part-time $654 per quarter hour. Required fees: $2931. *Financial support:* Research assistantships with full and partial tuition reimbursements, Federal Work-Study, tuition waivers (partial), and unspecified assistantships available. Financial award application deadline: 2/15. *Faculty research:* Macroeconomics, public finance, international economics and finance, monetary theory, healthcare economics. *Unit head:* Dr. Rosmary Rossiter, Chair, 740-593-2040, E-mail: rossiter@ohio.edu. *Application contact:* Dr. K. Doroodian, Graduate Chair, 740-593-2046, E-mail: doroodia@ohio.edu.

Oklahoma City University, Meinders School of Business, Program in Business Administration, Oklahoma City, OK 73106-1402. Offers finance (MBA); health administration (MBA); information

Finance and Banking

Oklahoma City University (continued)

technology (MBA); integrated marketing communications (MBA); international business (MBA); marketing (MBA); JD/MBA. *Accreditation:* ACBSP. Part-time and evening/weekend programs available. *Faculty:* 24 full-time (7 women), 11 part-time/adjunct (1 woman). *Students:* 268 full-time (91 women), 180 part-time (62 women); includes 51 minority (20 African Americans, 7 American Indian/Alaska Native, 11 Asian Americans or Pacific Islanders, 13 Hispanic Americans), 257 international. Average age 30. 158 applicants, 90% accepted, 35 enrolled. In 2009, 236 master's awarded. *Degree requirements:* For master's, comprehensive exam. *Entrance requirements:* Additional exam requirements/recommendations for international students: Required—TOEFL (minimum score 560 paper-based; 220 computer-based; 83 iBT). *Application deadline:* For fall admission, 8/20 for domestic students; for spring admission, 1/6 for domestic students. Applications are processed on a rolling basis. Application fee: $50 ($70 for international students). *Expenses:* Tuition: Full-time $15,930; part-time $885 per hour. *Financial support:* Fellowships with partial tuition reimbursements, career-related internships or fieldwork, Federal Work-Study, institutionally sponsored loans, and tuition waivers (partial) available. Support available to part-time students. Financial award application deadline: 8/1. *Faculty research:* Management information systems, international business strategies. *Unit head:* Dr. Mahmood Shandiz, Senior Associate Dean, 405-208-5130, Fax: 405-208-5098, E-mail: mshandiz@okcu.edu. *Application contact:* Michelle Lockhart, Director, Graduate Admissions, 800-633-7242, Fax: 405-208-5916, E-mail: gadmissions@okcu.edu.

Oklahoma State University, William S. Spears School of Business, Department of Finance, Stillwater, OK 74078. Offers finance (PhD); quantitative financial economics (MS). Part-time programs available. *Faculty:* 14 full-time (2 women), 5 part-time/adjunct (0 women). *Students:* 21 full-time (9 women), 8 part-time (1 woman), 12 international. Average age 30. 60 applicants, 35% accepted, 6 enrolled. In 2009, 9 master's, 1 doctorate awarded. *Degree requirements:* For master's, thesis or alternative; for doctorate, comprehensive exam, thesis/dissertation. *Entrance requirements:* For master's and doctorate, GRE or GMAT. Additional exam requirements/recommendations for international students: Required—TOEFL (minimum score 550 paper-based; 79 iBT). *Application deadline:* For fall admission, 3/1 priority date for international students; for spring admission, 8/1 priority date for international students. Applications are processed on a rolling basis. Application fee: $40 ($75 for international students). Electronic applications accepted. *Expenses:* Tuition, state resident: full-time $3716; part-time $154.85 per credit hour. Tuition, nonresident: full-time $14,448; part-time $602 per credit hour. Required fees: $1772; $73.85 per credit hour. One-time fee: $50. Tuition and fees vary according to course load and campus/location. *Financial support:* In 2009–10, 14 research assistantships (averaging $9,552 per year), 3 teaching assistantships (averaging $32,656 per year) were awarded; career-related internships or fieldwork, Federal Work-Study, scholarships/grants, health care benefits, tuition waivers (partial), and unspecified assistantships also available. Support available to part-time students. Financial award application deadline: 3/1; financial award applicants required to submit FAFSA. *Faculty research:* Corporate risk management, derivatives banking, investments and securities issuance, corporate governance, banking. *Unit head:* Dr. John Polonchek, Head, 405-744-5199, Fax: 405-744-5180. *Application contact:* Dr. Gordon Emslie, Dean, 405-744-6368, Fax: 405-744-0355, E-mail: grad-i@okstate.edu.

Old Dominion University, College of Business and Public Administration, Doctoral Program in Business Administration, Norfolk, VA 23529. Offers finance (PhD); information technology (PhD); marketing (PhD); strategic management (PhD). *Accreditation:* AACSB. *Faculty:* 21 full-time (2 women). *Students:* 28 full-time (12 women), 14 part-time (6 women); includes 5 minority (3 African Americans, 2 Asian Americans or Pacific Islanders), 25 international. Average age 35. 31 applicants, 65% accepted, 8 enrolled. In 2009, 6 doctorates awarded. *Degree requirements:* For doctorate, comprehensive exam, thesis/dissertation. *Entrance requirements:* For doctorate, GMAT. Additional exam requirements/recommendations for international students: Required—TOEFL (minimum score 550 paper-based; 213 computer-based; 79 iBT). *Application deadline:* For fall admission, 4/1 priority date for domestic and international students. Application fee: $50. Electronic applications accepted. *Expenses:* Tuition, state resident: full-time $8112; part-time $338 per credit. Tuition, nonresident: full-time $20,256; part-time $844 per credit. Required fees: $119 per semester. One-time fee: $50. *Financial support:* In 2009–10, 23 students received support, including 4 fellowships with full tuition reimbursements available (averaging $15,000 per year), 13 research assistantships with full tuition reimbursements available (averaging $15,000 per year), 6 teaching assistantships with full tuition reimbursements available (averaging $15,000 per year); career-related internships or fieldwork and scholarships/grants also available. Financial award application deadline: 4/1; financial award applicants required to submit FAFSA. *Faculty research:* International business, buyer behavior, financial markets, strategy, operations research. *Unit head:* Dr. Sylvia C. Hudgins, Graduate Program Director, 757-683-3551, Fax: 757-683-4076, E-mail: shudgins@odu.edu. *Application contact:* Dr. Sylvia C. Hudgins, Graduate Program Director, 757-683-3551, Fax: 757-683-4076, E-mail: shudgins@odu.edu.

Old Dominion University, College of Business and Public Administration, MBA Program, Norfolk, VA 23529. Offers business and economic forecasting (MBA); financial analysis and valuation (MBA); information technology and enterprise integration (MBA); international business (MBA); maritime and port management (MBA); public administration (MBA). *Accreditation:* AACSB. Part-time and evening/weekend programs available. *Faculty:* 66 full-time (15 women), 6 part-time/adjunct (1 woman). *Students:* 81 full-time (27 women), 198 part-time (92 women); includes 46 minority (25 African Americans, 1 American Indian/Alaska Native, 13 Asian Americans or Pacific Islanders, 7 Hispanic Americans), 31 international. Average age 30. 169 applicants, 52% accepted, 61 enrolled. In 2009, 81 master's awarded. *Entrance requirements:* For master's, GMAT, letters of reference, resume, coursework in calculus. Additional exam requirements/recommendations for international students: Required—TOEFL (minimum score 550 paper-based; 213 computer-based; 80 iBT). *Application deadline:* For fall admission, 6/1 priority date for domestic students, 4/15 priority date for international students; for spring admission, 11/1 priority date for domestic students, 10/1 priority date for international students. Applications are processed on a rolling basis. Application fee: $50. Electronic applications accepted. *Expenses:* Tuition, state resident: full-time $8112; part-time $338 per credit. Tuition, nonresident: full-time $20,256; part-time $844 per credit. Required fees: $119 per semester. One-time fee: $50. *Financial support:* In 2009–10, 46 students received support, including 31 research assistantships with partial tuition reimbursements available (averaging $7,000 per year), 3 teaching assistantships with partial tuition reimbursements available (averaging $6,300 per year); career-related internships or fieldwork, scholarships/grants, and unspecified assistantships also available. Support available to part-time students. Financial award application deadline: 2/15; financial award applicants required to submit FAFSA. *Faculty research:* International business, buyer behavior, financial markets, strategy, operations research. *Unit head:* Dr. Bruce Rubin, Graduate Program Director, 757-683-3585, E-mail: mbainfo@odu.edu. *Application contact:* Shanna Wood, MBA Program Manager, 757-683-3585, Fax: 757-683-5750, E-mail: mbainfo@odu.edu.

Oral Roberts University, School of Business, Tulsa, OK 74171. Offers accounting (MBA); entrepreneurship (MBA); finance (MBA); international business (MBA); management (MBA); marketing (MBA); non-profit management (MBA); not for profit management (MNM). *Accreditation:* ACBSP. Part-time programs available. Postbaccalaureate distance learning degree programs offered (minimal on-campus study). *Faculty:* 7 full-time (0 women), 5 part-time/adjunct (4 women). *Students:* 68 full-time (30 women), 55 part-time (27 women); includes 54 minority (32 African Americans, 5 American Indian/Alaska Native, 8 Asian Americans or Pacific Islanders, 9 Hispanic Americans), 3 international. Average age 28. 71 applicants, 94% accepted, 56 enrolled. In 2009, 36 master's awarded. *Degree requirements:* For master's, thesis optional. *Entrance requirements:* For master's, minimum cumulative GPA of 3.0. Additional exam requirements/recommendations for international students: Required—TOEFL (minimum score 550 paper-based; 213 computer-based; 79 iBT). *Application deadline:* For fall admission, 7/1 priority date for domestic and international students; for spring admission, 12/1 priority date for domestic students, 10/15 priority date for international students. Applications are processed on a rolling basis. Application fee: $35. Electronic applications accepted. *Financial support:* In 2009–10, 39 students received support. Federal Work-Study, scholarships/grants, and unspecified assistantships available. Financial award application deadline: 6/1; financial award applicants required to submit FAFSA. *Faculty research:* Social media, international business and marketing. *Unit head:* Dr. Steven Greene, Dean, 918-495-7040, Fax: 918-495-7876, E-mail: businessdean@oru.edu. *Application contact:* Rebecca Gunn, Representative/Recruiter, 918-495-6117, Fax: 918-495-6500, E-mail: gradbusiness@oru.edu.

Ottawa University, Graduate Studies-Arizona, Programs in Business, Ottawa, KS 66067-3399. Offers business administration (MBA); finance (MBA); human resources (MA, MBA); leadership (MBA); marketing (MBA). Programs offered in Mesa, Phoenix, Tempe and West Valley, AZ. Part-time and evening/weekend programs available. Postbaccalaureate distance learning degree programs offered. *Degree requirements:* For master's, thesis or alternative. *Entrance requirements:* For master's, minimum undergraduate GPA of 3.0. Additional exam requirements/recommendations for international students: Required—TOEFL (minimum score 550 paper-based; 213 computer-based). Electronic applications accepted.

Our Lady of the Lake University of San Antonio, School of Business and Leadership, Program in Accounting/Finance, San Antonio, TX 78207-4689. Offers MBA. Part-time and evening/weekend programs available. *Students:* 5 full-time (4 women), 63 part-time (29 women); includes 57 minority (10 Asian Americans or Pacific Islanders, 47 Hispanic Americans), 1 international. Average age 34. In 2009, 36 master's awarded. *Expenses:* Tuition: Full-time $12,330; part-time $685 per contact hour. Required fees: $139; $12 per contact hour. $57 per semester. Tuition and fees vary according to campus/location. *Unit head:* Dr. Robert Bisking, Dean, 210-434-6711, Fax: 210-434-0821. *Application contact:* Dr. Robert Bisking, Dean, 210-434-6711, Fax: 210-434-0821.

Pace University, Lubin School of Business, Financial Management Program, New York, NY 10038. Offers banking and finance (MBA); corporate financial management (MBA); financial management (MBA); investment management (MBA, MS). Part-time and evening/weekend programs available. *Students:* 95 full-time (36 women), 346 part-time (140 women); includes 57 minority (16 African Americans, 31 Asian Americans or Pacific Islanders, 10 Hispanic Americans), 235 international. Average age 27. 568 applicants, 73% accepted, 109 enrolled. In 2009, 133 master's awarded. *Entrance requirements:* For master's, GMAT. Additional exam requirements/recommendations for international students: Required—TOEFL. *Application deadline:* For fall admission, 7/31 priority date for domestic students; for spring admission, 11/30 for domestic students. Applications are processed on a rolling basis. Application fee: $70. Electronic applications accepted. *Expenses:* Tuition: Part-time $954 per credit. Tuition and fees vary according to course load, degree level and program. *Financial support:* Research assistantships, career-related internships or fieldwork, Federal Work-Study, and tuition waivers (full and partial) available. Support available to part-time students. Financial award application deadline: 8/15; financial award applicants required to submit FAFSA. *Unit head:* Dr. Edmund Mantell, Chairperson, 914-422-4165. *Application contact:* Susan Ford-Goldschein, Director of Admissions, 212-346-1652, Fax: 212-346-1585, E-mail: gradnyc@pace.edu.

Pacific States University, College of Business, Los Angeles, CA 90006. Offers accounting (MBA); business administration (DBA); finance (MBA); international business (MBA); management of information technology (MBA); real estate management (MBA). Part-time and evening/weekend programs available. Postbaccalaureate distance learning degree programs offered (no on-campus study). *Entrance requirements:* For master's, minimum undergraduate GPA of 2.5 during last 90 hours of course work. Additional exam requirements/recommendations for international students: Required—TOEFL (minimum score 133 computer-based).

Pepperdine University, Graziadio School of Business and Management, Malibu, CA 90263. Offers applied finance (MS); business administration (MBA); fully-employed (MBA); international business administration (IMBA); management and leadership (MS); organizational development (MSOD); presidential and key executive business administration (Exec MBA). *Accreditation:* AACSB. Part-time and evening/weekend programs available. *Faculty:* 86 full-time (18 women), 49 part-time/adjunct (12 women). *Students:* 872 full-time (343 women), 804 part-time (357 women); includes 530 minority (76 African Americans, 7 American Indian/Alaska Native, 306 Asian Americans or Pacific Islanders, 141 Hispanic Americans), 162 international. *Entrance requirements:* For master's, GMAT or MAT. Additional exam requirements/recommendations for international students: Required—TOEFL (minimum score 550 paper-based). *Application deadline:* For fall admission, 6/28 for domestic students. Applications are processed on a rolling basis. Application fee: $45. *Expenses:* Contact institution. *Financial support:* Career-related internships or fieldwork, institutionally sponsored loans, scholarships/grants, and unspecified assistantships available. Support available to part-time students. Financial award applicants required to submit FAFSA. *Unit head:* Dr. Linda A. Livingstone, Dean, 310-568-5689, Fax: 310-568-5766, E-mail: linda.livingstone@pepperdine.edu. *Application contact:* Darrell Eriksen, Director of Admission and Student Accounts, 310-568-5525, E-mail: darrell.eriksen@pepperdine.edu.

Philadelphia University, School of Business Administration, Program in Business Administration, Philadelphia, PA 19144. Offers business administration (MBA); finance (MBA); health care management (MBA); international business (MBA); marketing (MBA); MBA/MS. Part-time and evening/weekend programs available. Postbaccalaureate distance learning degree programs offered (no on-campus study). *Entrance requirements:* For master's, GMAT. Additional exam requirements/recommendations for international students: Required—TOEFL (minimum score 550 paper-based; 213 computer-based; 79 iBT).

Polytechnic Institute of NYU, Department of Finance and Risk Engineering, Brooklyn, NY 11201-2990. Offers financial engineering (MS, Advanced Certificate), including capital markets (MS), computational finance (MS), financial technology (MS); financial technology management (Advanced Certificate); organizational behavior (Advanced Certificate); risk management (Advanced Certificate); technology management (Advanced Certificate). Part-time and evening/weekend programs available. *Faculty:* 6 full-time (1 woman), 20 part-time/adjunct (4 women). *Students:* 196 full-time (71 women), 79 part-time (15 women); includes 28 minority (5 African Americans, 23 Asian Americans or Pacific Islanders), 202 international. Average age 26. 497 applicants, 45% accepted, 85 enrolled. In 2009, 102 master's awarded. *Degree requirements:* For master's, comprehensive exam (for some programs), thesis (for some programs). *Entrance requirements:* For master's, GMAT, minimum B average in undergraduate course work. Additional exam requirements/recommendations for international students: Required—TOEFL (minimum score 550 paper-based; 213 computer-based; 80 iBT); Recommended—IELTS (minimum score 6.5). *Application deadline:* For fall admission, 7/31 priority date for domestic students, 4/30 priority date for international students; for spring admission, 12/31 priority date for domestic students, 11/30 priority date for international students. Applications are processed on a rolling basis. Application fee: $75. Electronic applications accepted. *Expenses:* Tuition: Full-time $21,492; part-time $1194 per credit hour. Required fees: $1160; $204 per course. *Financial support:* Institutionally sponsored loans, scholarships/grants, and unspecified assistantships available. Support available to part-time students. Financial award applicants required to submit FAFSA. *Unit head:* Prof. Charles S. Tapiero, Academic Director, 718-260-3653, Fax: 718-260-3874, E-mail: ctapiero@poly.edu. *Application contact:* JeanCarlo Bonilla, Director of Graduate Enrollment Management, 718-260-3182, Fax: 718-260-3624.

Polytechnic Institute of NYU, Westchester Graduate Center, Graduate Programs, Department of Finance and Risk Engineering, Major in Financial Engineering, Hawthorne, NY 10532-1507. Offers capital markets (MS); computational finance (MS); financial engineering (AC); financial technology (MS); financial technology management (AC); information management (AC). *Students:* 9 full-time (6 women), 8 international. *Degree requirements:* For master's, comprehensive exam (for some programs), thesis (for some programs). *Entrance requirements:* Additional exam requirements/recommendations for international students: Required—TOEFL (minimum score 550 paper-based; 213 computer-based; 80 iBT); Recommended—IELTS (minimum score 6.5). *Application deadline:* For fall admission, 7/31 priority date for domestic students, 4/30 priority date for international students; for spring admission, 12/31 priority date for domestic students, 11/30 priority date for international students. Applications are processed

on a rolling basis. Application fee: $75. Electronic applications accepted. *Financial support:* Institutionally sponsored loans, scholarships/grants, and unspecified assistantships available. Support available to part-time students. *Unit head:* Dr. Charles S. Tapiero, Department Head, 718-260-3653, E-mail: ctapiero@poly.edu. *Application contact:* JeanCarlo Bonilla, Director of Graduate Enrollment Management, 718-260-3182, Fax: 718-260-3624, E-mail: gradinfo@poly.edu.

Pontifical Catholic University of Puerto Rico, College of Business Administration, Program in Finance, Ponce, PR 00717-0777. Offers MBA. Part-time and evening/weekend programs available. *Degree requirements:* For master's, thesis. *Entrance requirements:* For master's, GRE, interview, minimum GPA of 2.75.

Pontificia Universidad Catolica Madre y Maestra, Graduate School, Santiago, Dominican Republic. Offers administration (M Adm); architecture of interiors (M Arch); architecture of tourist lodgings (M Arch); banking and financial management (M Mgmt); civil law (LL M); construction administration (ME); corporate business law (LL M); criminal procedure law (LL M); environmental engineering (ME, MEE); finance (M Mgmt); history applied to education (M Ed); human resources (EMBA); insurance (M Mgmt); international business (M Mgmt); labor law and Social Security (LL M); logistics management (ME); marketing (M Mgmt); renewable energy (ME); strategic cost management (M Mgmt). *Entrance requirements:* For master's, curriculum vitae, interview.

Portland State University, Graduate Studies, School of Business Administration, Master of Science in Financial Analysis Program, Portland, OR 97207-0751. Offers MSFA. Part-time and evening/weekend programs available. *Entrance requirements:* For master's, GMAT, minimum GPA of 2.75, 2 recommendations, resume, interview. Additional exam requirements/recommendations for international students: Required—TOEFL (minimum score 550 paper-based; 213 computer-based).

Post University, Program in Business Administration, Waterbury, CT 06723-2540. Offers business administration (MBA); corporate innovation (MBA); entrepreneurship (MBA); finance (MBA); leadership (MBA); marketing (MBA). Postbaccalaureate distance learning degree programs offered.

Princeton University, Graduate School, Bendheim Center for Finance, Princeton, NJ 08544-1019. Offers M Fin. *Entrance requirements:* For master's, GRE General Test. Additional exam requirements/recommendations for international students: Required—TOEFL (minimum score 600 paper-based; 250 computer-based). Electronic applications accepted.

Providence College, Graduate Studies, School of Business, Providence, RI 02918. Offers accountancy (MBA); economics (MBA); entrepreneurship (MBA); finance (MBA); international business (MBA); management (MBA); marketing (MBA); not-for-profit (MBA); quantitative (MBA). Part-time and evening/weekend programs available. *Faculty:* 14 full-time (8 women), 7 part-time/adjunct (3 women). *Students:* 63 full-time (18 women), 46 part-time (19 women); includes 4 minority (2 African Americans, 2 Asian Americans or Pacific Islanders), 7 international. Average age 26. 43 applicants, 88% accepted. In 2009, 40 master's awarded. *Degree requirements:* For master's, thesis optional. *Entrance requirements:* For master's, GMAT. Additional exam requirements/recommendations for international students: Required—TOEFL (minimum score 550 paper-based; 213 computer-based; 80 iBT). *Application deadline:* For fall admission, 8/1 priority date for domestic and international students; for spring admission, 12/1 priority date for domestic and international students. Applications are processed on a rolling basis. Application fee: $55. *Expenses:* Contact institution. *Financial support:* In 2009–10, 34 research assistantships with full tuition reimbursements (averaging $8,400 per year) were awarded; Federal Work-Study, institutionally sponsored loans, and unspecified assistantships also available. Support available to part-time students. Financial award application deadline: 8/1; financial award applicants required to submit FAFSA. *Unit head:* Dr. MaryJane Lenon, Director, MBA Program, 401-865-2566, Fax: 401-865-2978, E-mail: mjlenon@providence.edu. *Application contact:* Katherine A. Follett, Administrative Coordinator, 401-865-2333, Fax: 401-865-2978, E-mail: kfollett@providence.edu.

Purdue University, Graduate School, Krannert School of Management, Master of Science in Finance Program, West Lafayette, IN 47907. Offers MSF. *Faculty:* 102 full-time (29 women), 16 part-time/adjunct (1 woman). *Students:* 22 full-time (12 women); includes 2 minority (both Asian Americans or Pacific Islanders), 16 international. Average age 26. 494 applicants, 8% accepted, 22 enrolled. In 2009, 25 master's awarded. *Entrance requirements:* For master's, GMAT or GRE, minimum GPA of 3.0, four-year baccalaureate degree, essays, letters of recommendation. Additional exam requirements/recommendations for international students: Required—TOEFL (minimum score 550 paper-based; 213 computer-based; 77 iBT). *Application deadline:* For fall admission, 1/10 priority date for domestic students, 2/1 for international students. Applications are processed on a rolling basis. Application fee: $55. Electronic applications accepted. *Expenses:* Contact institution. *Financial support:* Application deadline: 3/1. *Unit head:* Dr. R. A. Cosier, Dean, 765-494-4366. *Application contact:* Brenda Knebel, Director, Master's and Executive Admissions, 765-494-0773, Fax: 765-494-9841, E-mail: krannertmasters@purdue.edu.

Queen's University at Kingston, Queens School of Business, Program in Business Administration, Kingston, ON K7L 3N6, Canada. Offers consulting and project management (MBA); finance (MBA); innovation and entrepreneurship (MBA); marketing (MBA). *Accreditation:* AACSB. *Degree requirements:* For master's, thesis optional, research project. *Entrance requirements:* For master's, GMAT, minimum B+ average. Additional exam requirements/recommendations for international students: Required—TOEFL. Electronic applications accepted. *Faculty research:* Management fundamentals, strategic thinking, global business, innovation and change, leadership.

Quinnipiac University, School of Business, Program in Business Administration, Hamden, CT 06518-1940. Offers chartered financial analyst (MBA); finance (MBA); healthcare management (MBA); information systems management (MBA); international business (MBA); management (MBA); marketing (MBA); JD/MBA. *Accreditation:* AACSB. Part-time and evening/weekend programs available. *Faculty:* 24 full-time (6 women), 12 part-time/adjunct (4 women). *Students:* 83 full-time (30 women), 106 part-time (36 women); includes 11 minority (2 African Americans, 1 American Indian/Alaska Native, 6 Asian Americans or Pacific Islanders, 2 Hispanic Americans), 13 international. Average age 29. 124 applicants, 79% accepted, 77 enrolled. In 2009, 63 master's awarded. *Entrance requirements:* For master's, GMAT, minimum GPA of 3.0. Additional exam requirements/recommendations for international students: Required—TOEFL (minimum score 575 paper-based; 233 computer-based; 90 iBT), IELTS (minimum score 6.5). *Application deadline:* For fall admission, 7/30 priority date for domestic students, 4/30 priority date for international students; for spring admission, 12/15 priority date for domestic students, 9/15 priority date for international students. Applications are processed on a rolling basis. Application fee: $45. Electronic applications accepted. *Expenses:* Tuition: Full-time $16,030; part-time $770 per credit. Required fees: $630; $35 per credit. *Financial support:* In 2009–10, 110 students received support. Federal Work-Study, tuition waivers (partial), and unspecified assistantships available. Support available to part-time students. Financial award application deadline: 4/15; financial award applicants required to submit FAFSA. *Faculty research:* Equity compensation, marketing relationships and public policy, corporate governance, international business, supply chain management. *Unit head:* Kimberly McKeage, MBA Program Director, 203-582-3676. *Application contact:* Jennifer Boutin, 800-462-1944, Fax: 203-582-3443, E-mail: jennifer.boutin@quinnipiac.edu.

Regent's American College London, Webster Graduate School, London, United Kingdom. Offers business (MBA); finance (MS); human resources (MA); information technology management (MA); international business (MA); international non-governmental organizations (MA); international relations (MA); management and leadership (MA); marketing (MA). Part-time programs available.

Regis University, College for Professional Studies, School of Management, Denver, CO 80221-1099. Offers accounting (MS); business administration (MBA); computer information technology (MSOL); executive internal management (Certificate); executive leadership (Certificate); finance (MBA); finance and accounting (MBA); human resource management (MSOL); international business (MBA); marketing (MBA); operations management (MBA); organization leadership (MS); organizational leadership (MSOL); project leadership and management (MSOL, Certificate); project management (Certificate); strategic business (Certificate); strategic human resource (Certificate); technical management (Certificate). Offered at Colorado Springs Campus, Northwest Denver Campus, Southeast Denver Campus, Fort Collins Campus, Broomfield Campus, Henderson (Nevada) Campus, and Summerlin (Nevada) Campus and online. Part-time and evening/weekend programs available. Postbaccalaureate distance learning degree programs offered (no on-campus study). *Degree requirements:* For master's, thesis optional, capstone project. *Entrance requirements:* For master's, GMAT or essays, interview, 2 years of full-time business work experience, resume; for Certificate, GMAT. Additional exam requirements/recommendations for international students: Required—TOEFL, TOEFL or university-based test; Recommended—TWE (minimum score 5). Electronic applications accepted. *Faculty research:* Impact of Info Technology on Small Business Regulation of Accounting, International Project financing, Mineral Development, Delivery of Healthcare to rural indigenos communities.

Rhode Island College, School of Graduate Studies, School of Management, Department of Accounting and Computer Information Systems, Providence, RI 02908-1991. Offers accounting (MP Ac); financial planning (CGS). Part-time and evening/weekend programs available. *Faculty:* 2 full-time (1 woman). *Students:* 1 full-time (0 women), 9 part-time (6 women), 1 international. Average age 32. In 2009, 7 master's awarded. *Entrance requirements:* For master's, GMAT (unless applicant is a CPA or has passed a state bar exam); for CGS, GMAT, bachelor's degree from an accredited college or university, official transcripts of all undergraduate and graduate records. Additional exam requirements/recommendations for international students: Recommended—TOEFL (minimum score 550 paper-based; 213 computer-based; 79 iBT). *Application deadline:* For fall admission, 4/1 for domestic students; for spring admission, 11/1 for domestic students. Applications are processed on a rolling basis. Application fee: $50. *Expenses:* Tuition, state resident: full-time $7440; part-time $310 per credit hour. Tuition, nonresident: full-time $14,784; part-time $616 per credit hour. Required fees: $552; $20 per credit. $70 per term. *Financial support:* Federal Work-Study, scholarships/grants, and health care benefits available. Support available to part-time students. Financial award application deadline: 5/15; financial award applicants required to submit FAFSA. *Unit head:* Prof. David Filipek, Chair, 401-456-8009. *Application contact:* Graduate Studies, 401-456-8700.

Robert Morris University Illinois, Morris Graduate School of Management, Chicago, IL 60605. Offers accounting (MBA); accounting/finance (MBA); human resource management (MBA); information technology (MIS); leadership (MBA); management/finance (MIS); management/human resource management (MBA). Part-time and evening/weekend programs available. *Faculty:* 16 full-time (6 women), 25 part-time/adjunct (9 women). *Students:* 275 full-time (169 women), 194 part-time (134 women); includes 267 minority (176 African Americans, 1 American Indian/Alaska Native, 26 Asian Americans or Pacific Islanders, 64 Hispanic Americans), 17 international. Average age 32. 202 applicants, 84% accepted, 135 enrolled. In 2009, 161 master's awarded. *Degree requirements:* For master's, 44 residency hours. *Entrance requirements:* Additional exam requirements/recommendations for international students: Required—TOEFL (minimum score 500 paper-based; 173 computer-based). *Application deadline:* Applications are processed on a rolling basis. Application fee: $30 ($100 for international students). Electronic applications accepted. *Expenses:* Tuition: Full-time $18,000; part-time $2000 per course. *Financial support:* In 2009–10, 420 students received support. Federal Work-Study, scholarships/grants, and tuition waivers available. Support available to part-time students. *Unit head:* Kayed Akkawi, Dean, 312-935-4244, Fax: 312-935-4248, E-mail: kakkawi@robertmorris.edu. *Application contact:* Courtney A. Kohn Sanders, Dean of Graduate Admissions, 312-935-4240, Fax: 312-935-4248, E-mail: ckohn@robertmorris.edu.

Rochester Institute of Technology, Graduate Enrollment Services, E. Philip Saunders College of Business, Graduate Business Programs, Program in Finance, Rochester, NY 14623-5603. Offers MS. Part-time and evening/weekend programs available. *Students:* 25 full-time (11 women), 12 part-time (5 women); includes 1 American Indian/Alaska Native, 2 Asian Americans or Pacific Islanders, 25 international. Average age 28. 170 applicants, 47% accepted, 23 enrolled. In 2009, 14 master's awarded. *Degree requirements:* For master's, comprehensive exam (for some programs), thesis (for some programs). *Entrance requirements:* For master's, GMAT, minimum GPA of 2.5. Additional exam requirements/recommendations for international students: Required—TOEFL (minimum score 580 paper-based; 237 computer-based; 92 iBT), or IELTS (minimum score 7). *Application deadline:* For fall admission, 2/15 priority date for domestic and international students; for winter admission, 11/1 priority date for domestic students; for spring admission, 2/1 priority date for domestic students. Applications are processed on a rolling basis. Application fee: $50. *Expenses:* Tuition: Full-time $31,533; part-time $876 per credit hour. Required fees: $210. *Financial support:* In 2009–10, 20 students received support; research assistantships with partial tuition reimbursements available, teaching assistantships with partial tuition reimbursements available, career-related internships or fieldwork, scholarships/grants, and unspecified assistantships available. Support available to part-time students. Financial award applicants required to submit FAFSA. *Faculty research:* Formation and taxation of business entities, modeling demand, production and cost functions in computerized business and economic simulations, economic games and educational software. *Unit head:* Kathy Ozminkowski, Assistant Dean for Student Services, 585-475-6985, Fax: 585-475-7450, E-mail: kozminkowski@saunders.rit.edu. *Application contact:* Diane Ellison, Assistant Vice President, Graduate Enrollment Services, 585-475-2229, Fax: 585-475-7164, E-mail: gradinfo@rit.edu.

Rollins College, Crummer Graduate School of Business, Winter Park, FL 32789-4499. Offers entrepreneurship (MBA); finance (MBA); international business (MBA); management (MBA); marketing (MBA); operations and technology management (MBA). *Accreditation:* AACSB. Part-time and evening/weekend programs available. Postbaccalaureate distance learning degree programs offered (minimal on-campus study). *Faculty:* 25 full-time (3 women), 8 part-time/adjunct (2 women). *Students:* 277 full-time (105 women), 192 part-time (79 women); includes 95 minority (26 African Americans, 31 Asian Americans or Pacific Islanders, 38 Hispanic Americans), 48 international. Average age 29. 373 applicants, 53% accepted, 140 enrolled. In 2009, 220 master's awarded. *Entrance requirements:* For master's, GMAT. Additional exam requirements/recommendations for international students: Required—TOEFL. *Application deadline:* For fall admission, 6/1 priority date for domestic students; for spring admission, 12/1 for domestic students. Applications are processed on a rolling basis. Application fee: $50. Electronic applications accepted. *Expenses:* Contact institution. *Financial support:* In 2009–10, 95 students received support, including 95 fellowships, 56 research assistantships (averaging $2,400 per year); career-related internships or fieldwork, scholarships/grants, tuition waivers (full), and unspecified assistantships also available. *Faculty research:* Sustainability, world financial markets, international business, market research, strategic marketing. *Unit head:* Dr. Craig M. McAllaster, Dean, 407-646-2249, Fax: 407-646-1550, E-mail: cmcallaster@rollins.edu. *Application contact:* Linda Puritz, Student Admissions Office, 407-646-2405, Fax: 407-646-1550, E-mail: mbaadmissions@rollins.edu.

Rowan University, Graduate School, William G. Rohrer College of Business, Department of Accounting and Finance, Program in Finance, Glassboro, NJ 08028-1701. Offers MBA. Part-time and evening/weekend programs available. *Students:* 9 full-time (4 women), 7 part-time (2 women); includes 10 minority (4 African Americans, 1 Asian American or Pacific Islander, 5 Hispanic Americans). Average age 30. 4 applicants, 50% accepted, 1 enrolled. *Degree requirements:* For master's, comprehensive exam, thesis. *Entrance requirements:* For master's, GRE General Test. Additional exam requirements/recommendations for international students: Required—TOEFL. *Application deadline:* Applications are processed on a rolling basis. Application fee: $50. Electronic applications accepted. *Expenses:* Tuition, state resident: full-time $10,624; part-time $590 per semester hour. Tuition, nonresident: full-time $10,624; part-time $590 per semester hour. Required fees: $2320; $125 per semester hour. *Financial support:* Career-related internships or fieldwork, Federal Work-Study, and unspecified assistant-

Finance and Banking

Rowan University (continued)

ships available. Support available to part-time students. *Unit head:* Dr. Mira Lalovic-Hand, Interim Associate Provost/Director of Graduate School, 856-256-5120, E-mail: lalovic-hand@rowan.edu. *Application contact:* Karen Haynes, Graduate Coordinator, 856-256-4052, E-mail: haynes@rowan.edu.

Rutgers, The State University of New Jersey, Newark, Graduate School, Program in Management, Newark, NJ 07102. Offers accounting (PhD); accounting information systems (PhD); computer information systems (PhD); finance (PhD); information technology (PhD); international business (PhD); management science (PhD); marketing (PhD); organization management (PhD). *Accreditation:* AACSB. *Degree requirements:* For doctorate, thesis/dissertation, cumulative exams. *Entrance requirements:* For doctorate, GMAT or GRE General Test, minimum undergraduate B average. Additional exam requirements/recommendations for international students: Required—TOEFL. Electronic applications accepted. *Faculty research:* Technology management, leadership and teams, consumer behavior, financial and markets, logistics.

Rutgers, The State University of New Jersey, Newark, Rutgers Business School–Newark and New Brunswick, Department of Finance and Economics, Newark, NJ 07102. Offers MBA, MQF. *Entrance requirements:* For master's, GMAT (MBA), GRE General Test (MQF). Additional exam requirements/recommendations for international students: Required—TOEFL.

Rutgers, The State University of New Jersey, Newark, Rutgers Business School–Newark and New Brunswick, Doctoral Programs in Business, Newark, NJ 07102. Offers accounting (PhD); accounting information systems (PhD); finance (PhD); individualized study (PhD); information technology (PhD); international business (PhD); management science (PhD); organizational management (PhD); supply chain management (PhD).

Rutgers, The State University of New Jersey, Newark, Rutgers Business School–Newark and New Brunswick, Master of Accountancy in Governmental Accounting Program, Newark, NJ 07102. Offers government financial management (Certificate); governmental accounting (M Accy). *Accreditation:* AACSB. Postbaccalaureate distance learning degree programs offered.

Sacred Heart University, Graduate Programs, John F. Welch College of Business, Fairfield, CT 06825-1000. Offers accounting (MBA); finance (MBA); management (MBA); marketing (MBA). *Accreditation:* AACSB. Part-time and evening/weekend programs available. Postbaccalaureate distance learning degree programs offered. *Faculty:* 33 full-time, 15 part-time/adjunct. *Students:* 36 full-time (12 women), 124 part-time (64 women); includes 28 minority (10 African Americans, 8 Asian Americans or Pacific Islanders, 10 Hispanic Americans), 6 international. Average age 32. 63 applicants, 71% accepted, 37 enrolled. In 2009, 41 master's awarded. *Degree requirements:* For master's, thesis or alternative. *Entrance requirements:* For master's, GMAT (preferred) or GRE General Test. Additional exam requirements/recommendations for international students: Required—TOEFL (minimum score 550 paper-based; 213 computer-based; 75 iBT). *Application deadline:* Applications are processed on a rolling basis. Application fee: $50 ($100 for international students). Electronic applications accepted. *Expenses:* Contact institution. *Financial support:* Career-related internships or fieldwork, institutionally sponsored loans, and unspecified assistantships available. Support available to part-time students. Financial award applicants required to submit FAFSA. *Faculty research:* Management of organizations, international business management of technology. *Unit head:* Dr. John J. Petillo, Dean, 203-396-8084, E-mail: petilloj@sacredheart.edu. *Application contact:* Dean Alexis Haakonsen, Dean of Graduate Admissions, 203-365-7619, Fax: 203-365-4732, E-mail: gradstudies@sacredheart.edu.

Sage Graduate School, Graduate School, School of Management, Program in Business Administration, Troy, NY 12180-4115. Offers business strategy (MBA); finance (MBA); human resources (MBA); marketing (MBA); JD/MBA. Part-time and evening/weekend programs available. *Faculty:* 4 full-time (2 women), 6 part-time/adjunct (0 women). *Students:* 9 full-time (7 women), 68 part-time (44 women); includes 11 minority (5 African Americans, 2 Asian Americans or Pacific Islanders, 4 Hispanic Americans), 2 international. Average age 31. 50 applicants, 60% accepted, 17 enrolled. In 2009, 19 master's awarded. *Entrance requirements:* For master's, minimum GPA of 2.75, resume, 2 letters of recommendation. Additional exam requirements/recommendations for international students: Required—TOEFL (minimum score 550 paper-based; 213 computer-based). *Application deadline:* Applications are processed on a rolling basis. Application fee: $40. *Expenses:* Tuition: Full-time $10,620; part-time $590 per credit hour. *Financial support:* Fellowships, research assistantships, Federal Work-Study, scholarships/grants, and unspecified assistantships available. Support available to part-time students. Financial award application deadline: 3/1; financial award applicants required to submit FAFSA. *Unit head:* Daniel Robeson, Chair, Management Department, 518-292-1770, Fax: 518-292-5414, E-mail: robesd@sage.edu. *Application contact:* Wendy D. Diefendorf, Director of Graduate and Adult Admission, 518-244-2443, Fax: 518-244-6880, E-mail: diefew@sage.edu.

St. Edward's University, School of Management and Business, Area of Business Administration, Austin, TX 78704. Offers accounting (MBA); business management (MBA); corporate finance (MBA, Certificate); global entrepreneurship (MBA); human resource management (MBA, Certificate); management information systems (MBA, Certificate); marketing (MBA, Certificate); operations management (MBA, Certificate). Part-time and evening/weekend programs available. *Faculty:* 20 full-time (9 women), 13 part-time/adjunct (4 women). *Students:* 29 full-time (16 women), 307 part-time (152 women); includes 116 minority (27 African Americans, 1 American Indian/Alaska Native, 16 Asian Americans or Pacific Islanders, 72 Hispanic Americans), 9 international. Average age 33. 129 applicants, 75% accepted, 74 enrolled. In 2009, 108 master's awarded. *Degree requirements:* For master's, minimum of 24 resident hours. *Entrance requirements:* For master's, GMAT or GRE General Test, minimum GPA of 2.75 in last 60 hours of course work. Additional exam requirements/recommendations for international students: Required—TOEFL (minimum score 550 paper-based; 213 computer-based; 79 iBT) or IELTS (minimum score 6). *Application deadline:* For fall admission, 7/1 for domestic and international students; for spring admission, 11/1 for domestic and international students. Applications are processed on a rolling basis. Application fee: $45 ($50 for international students). Electronic applications accepted. *Expenses:* Tuition: Full-time $14,922; part-time $829 per credit hour. Required fees: $50 per trimester. Full-time tuition and fees vary according to course load and program. *Financial support:* In 2009–10, 14 students received support. Scholarships/grants available. *Faculty research:* Operations management, minority entrepreneurship, globalization, professional services marketing. *Unit head:* Dr. Dianne Hill, Director, 512-428-1295, Fax: 512-448-8492, E-mail: dianneh@stedwards.edu. *Application contact:* Kelly Luna, Graduate Admissions Coordinator, 512-233-1697, Fax: 512-428-1032, E-mail: kellyl@stedwards.edu.

St. John's University, The Peter J. Tobin College of Business, Department of Economics and Finance, Program in Finance, Queens, NY 11439. Offers MBA, MS, Adv C. Part-time and evening/weekend programs available. *Students:* 95 full-time (37 women), 104 part-time (43 women); includes 40 minority (12 African Americans, 16 Asian Americans or Pacific Islanders, 12 Hispanic Americans), 73 international. Average age 27. 119 applicants, 68% accepted, 44 enrolled. In 2009, 68 master's awarded. *Degree requirements:* For master's, comprehensive exam (for some programs), thesis optional. *Entrance requirements:* For master's, GMAT, 2 letters of recommendation, resume; for Adv C, GMAT, 2 letters of recommendation, resume, undergraduate transcripts, essay. Additional exam requirements/recommendations for international students: Required—TOEFL (minimum score 500 paper-based; 173 computer-based; 61 iBT), IELTS (minimum score 5.5). *Application deadline:* For fall admission, 5/1 priority date for domestic and international students; for spring admission, 11/1 priority date for domestic and international students. Applications are processed on a rolling basis. Application fee: $70. Electronic applications accepted. *Expenses:* Contact institution. *Financial support:* Research assistantships, scholarships/grants available. Support available to part-time students. Financial award application deadline: 3/1; financial award applicants required to submit FAFSA. *Unit head:* Dr. Vipul K. Bansal, Chair, 718-990-2113, E-mail: bansalv@stjohns.edu. *Application*

contact: Nicole T. Bryan, Assistant Dean, 718-990-2599, Fax: 718-990-5242, E-mail: tcbgradadmissions@stjohns.edu.

Saint Joseph's University, Erivan K. Haub School of Business, MS in Financial Services Program, Philadelphia, PA 19131-1395. Offers MS. Part-time and evening/weekend programs available. *Students:* 18 full-time (11 women), 59 part-time (18 women); includes 7 minority (5 African Americans, 2 Asian Americans or Pacific Islanders), 18 international. Average age 30. In 2009, 22 master's awarded. *Entrance requirements:* For master's, GMAT, 2 letters of recommendation, resume, personal statement. Additional exam requirements/recommendations for international students: Required—TOEFL (minimum score 550 paper-based; 213 computer-based; 79 iBT) or IELTS (minimum score 6.5). *Application deadline:* For fall admission, 7/15 priority date for domestic students, 5/15 priority date for international students; for spring admission, 11/15 priority date for domestic students, 10/15 priority date for international students. Applications are processed on a rolling basis. Application fee: $35. Electronic applications accepted. *Expenses:* Tuition: Part-time $729 per credit hour. Tuition and fees vary according to degree level and program. *Financial support:* Research assistantships, scholarships/grants and unspecified assistantships available. *Unit head:* David Benglian, Director, 610-660-1626, Fax: 610-660-1599, E-mail: david.benglian@sju.edu. *Application contact:* David Benglian, Director, 610-660-1626, Fax: 610-660-1599, E-mail: david.benglian@sju.edu.

Saint Joseph's University, Erivan K. Haub School of Business, Professional MBA Program, Philadelphia, PA 19131-1395. Offers accounting (MBA); finance (MBA), including finance; general business (MBA); health and medical services administration (MBA); human resource management (MBA); international business (MBA); international marketing (MBA); management (MBA); marketing (MBA); DO/MBA. Part-time and evening/weekend programs available. *Students:* 51 full-time (24 women), 480 part-time (184 women); includes 71 minority (32 African Americans, 1 American Indian/Alaska Native, 30 Asian Americans or Pacific Islanders, 8 Hispanic Americans), 38 international. Average age 30. In 2009, 190 master's awarded. *Entrance requirements:* For master's, GMAT or GRE, 2 letters of recommendation, resume. Additional exam requirements/recommendations for international students: Required—TOEFL (minimum score 550 paper-based; 213 computer-based; 79 iBT) or IELTS (minimum score 6.5). *Application deadline:* For fall admission, 7/15 priority date for domestic students, 4/15 priority date for international students; for spring admission, 11/15 priority date for domestic students, 10/15 priority date for international students. Applications are processed on a rolling basis. Application fee: $35. Electronic applications accepted. *Expenses:* Tuition: Part-time $729 per credit hour. Tuition and fees vary according to degree level and program. *Financial support:* Scholarships/grants and unspecified assistantships available. Financial award application deadline: 5/1. *Unit head:* Adele C. Foley, Associate Dean/Director, Graduate Business Programs, 610-660-1691, Fax: 610-660-1599, E-mail: afoley@sju.edu. *Application contact:* Janine N. Guerra, Esq., Assistant Director, MBA Program, 610-660-1695, Fax: 610-660-1599, E-mail: jguerra@sju.edu.

Saint Louis University, Graduate School, John Cook School of Business, Department of Finance, St. Louis, MO 63103-2097. Offers MBA, MSF. Part-time and evening/weekend programs available. *Degree requirements:* For master's, thesis. *Entrance requirements:* For master's, GMAT or GRE General Test, letters of recommendation, resume. Additional exam requirements/recommendations for international students: Required—TOEFL (minimum score 570 paper-based; 230 computer-based; 88 iBT). Electronic applications accepted. *Expenses:* Contact institution. *Faculty research:* Market microstructure, corporate governance, banking, portfolio performance and asset allocation.

St. Mary's University, Graduate School, Bill Greehey School of Business, MBA Program, San Antonio, TX 78228-8507. Offers finance (MBA); international business (MBA); management (MBA). Part-time and evening/weekend programs available. Postbaccalaureate distance learning degree programs offered (minimal on-campus study). *Degree requirements:* For master's, comprehensive exam. *Entrance requirements:* For master's, GMAT. Additional exam requirements/recommendations for international students: Required—TOEFL (minimum score 570 paper-based; 230 computer-based; 80 iBT). *Expenses:* Tuition: Full-time $8004. Required fees: $536. One-time fee: $5 full-time. Full-time tuition and fees vary according to program.

Saint Peter's College, Graduate Business Programs, MBA Program, Jersey City, NJ 07306-5997. Offers finance (MBA); health care administration (MBA); international business (MBA); management (MBA); management information systems (MBA); marketing (MBA); MBA/MS. Part-time and evening/weekend programs available. *Entrance requirements:* Additional exam requirements/recommendations for international students: Required—TOEFL. *Application deadline:* Applications are processed on a rolling basis. Electronic applications accepted. *Expenses:* Tuition: Part-time $971 per credit. *Financial support:* Career-related internships or fieldwork, Federal Work-Study, and institutionally sponsored loans available. *Faculty research:* Finance, health care management, human resource management, international business, management, management information systems, marketing, risk management.

St. Thomas Aquinas College, Division of Business Administration, Sparkill, NY 10976. Offers business administration (MBA); finance (MBA); management (MBA); marketing (MBA). Part-time and evening/weekend programs available. *Entrance requirements:* For master's, GMAT. Additional exam requirements/recommendations for international students: Required—TOEFL. Electronic applications accepted.

Saint Xavier University, Graduate Studies, Graham School of Management, Chicago, IL 60655-3105. Offers e-commerce (MBA); employee health benefits (Certificate); finance (MBA, MS); financial analysis and investments (MBA); financial planning (MBA, Certificate); financial trading and practice (MBA, Certificate); generalist/administration (MBA); health administration (MBA, MS); managed care (Certificate); management (MBA, MS); marketing (MBA); public and non-profit management (MBA); public health (MPH); service management (MBA); training and performance management (MBA); MBA/MS. *Accreditation:* ACBSP. Part-time and evening/weekend programs available. *Entrance requirements:* For master's, GMAT, minimum GPA of 3.0, 2 years of work experience. Electronic applications accepted. *Expenses:* Contact institution.

Sam Houston State University, College of Business Administration, Department of General Business and Finance, Huntsville, TX 77341. Offers finance (MS). *Faculty:* 11 full-time (4 women). *Students:* 101 full-time (37 women), 97 part-time (41 women); includes 31 minority (9 African Americans, 1 American Indian/Alaska Native, 10 Asian Americans or Pacific Islanders, 11 Hispanic Americans), 30 international. Average age 29. 124 applicants, 81% accepted, 65 enrolled. In 2009, 73 master's awarded. *Entrance requirements:* For master's, GMAT. Additional exam requirements/recommendations for international students: Required—TOEFL (minimum score 550 paper-based; 213 computer-based; 79 iBT). *Application deadline:* For fall admission, 8/1 for domestic students; for spring admission, 12/1 for domestic students. Application fee: $20. *Expenses:* Tuition, state resident: full-time $3690; part-time $205 per credit hour. Tuition, nonresident: full-time $8676; part-time $482 per credit hour. Required fees: $1474. Tuition and fees vary according to course load and campus/location. *Financial support:* Application deadline: 5/31. *Unit head:* Dr. Bala Maniam, Chair, 936-294-1290, E-mail: maniam@shsu.edu. *Application contact:* Dr. Leroy Ashorn, Advisor, 936-294-4040, Fax: 936-294-3612, E-mail: busgrad@shsu.edu.

San Diego State University, Graduate and Research Affairs, College of Business Administration, Department of Finance, San Diego, CA 92182. Offers MS. Part-time and evening/weekend programs available. *Degree requirements:* For master's, thesis or alternative. *Entrance requirements:* For master's, GMAT, resume, letters of reference. Additional exam requirements/recommendations for international students: Required—TOEFL. Electronic applications accepted.

Santa Clara University, Leavey School of Business, Program in Business Administration, Santa Clara, CA 95053. Offers accounting (MBA); entrepreneurship (MBA); executive MBA (EMBA); finance (MBA); food and agribusiness (MBA); international business (MBA); leading people and organizations (MBA); managing technology and innovation (MBA); marketing management (MBA); supply chain management (MBA). *Accreditation:* AACSB. Part-time and evening/weekend programs available. *Students:* 228 full-time (88 women), 838 part-time (265 women); includes 388 minority (17 African Americans, 2 American Indian/Alaska Native, 326

Asian Americans or Pacific Islanders, 43 Hispanic Americans), 218 international. Average age 31. 486 applicants, 77% accepted, 263 enrolled. In 2009, 317 master's awarded. *Degree requirements:* For master's, thesis or alternative. *Entrance requirements:* For master's, GMAT, GRE. Additional exam requirements/recommendations for international students: Required—TOEFL (minimum score 600 paper-based; 250 computer-based; 100 iBT). *Application deadline:* For fall admission, 6/1 for domestic and international students; for spring admission, 1/19 for domestic students, 1/17 for international students. Applications are processed on a rolling basis. Application fee: $75 ($100 for international students). Electronic applications accepted. *Expenses:* Contact institution. *Financial support:* Fellowships with partial tuition reimbursements, research assistantships with partial tuition reimbursements, career-related internships or fieldwork, Federal Work-Study, institutionally sponsored loans, scholarships/grants, health care benefits, and unspecified assistantships available. Support available to part-time students. Financial award applicants required to submit FAFSA. *Unit head:* Elizabeth B. Ford, Senior Assistant Dean, 408-554-2752, Fax: 408-554-4571, E-mail: eford@scu.edu. *Application contact:* Jennifer W. Taylor, Senior Director, 408-554-4539, Fax: 408-554-4571, E-mail: mbaadmissions@scu.edu.

Schiller International University, MBA Programs, Florida, Largo, FL 33770. Offers financial planning (MBA); information technology (MBA); international business (MBA); international hotel and tourism management (MBA). Part-time and evening/weekend programs available. Postbaccalaureate distance learning degree programs offered (no on-campus study). *Degree requirements:* For master's, thesis optional. *Entrance requirements:* Additional exam requirements/recommendations for international students: Required—TOEFL (minimum score 550 paper-based; 213 computer-based).

Seattle University, Albers School of Business and Economics, Program in Finance, Seattle, WA 98122-1090. Offers MSF, Certificate, JD/MSF. Part-time and evening/weekend programs available. *Entrance requirements:* For master's, GMAT, minimum GPA of 3.0, 1 year of related work experience. Additional exam requirements/recommendations for international students: Required—TOEFL.

Seton Hall University, Stillman School of Business, Programs in Business Administration, South Orange, NJ 07079-2697. Offers accounting (MBA); finance (MBA); information technology management (MBA); international business (MBA); management (MBA); marketing (MBA); sport management (MBA). Part-time and evening/weekend programs available. *Faculty:* 57 full-time (13 women), 30 part-time/adjunct (3 women). *Students:* 69 full-time (26 women), 217 part-time (91 women); includes 53 minority (11 African Americans, 35 Asian Americans or Pacific Islanders, 7 Hispanic Americans), 38 international. Average age 29. 286 applicants, 70% accepted, 130 enrolled. In 2009, 110 master's awarded. *Degree requirements:* For master's, 20 hours of community service (Social Responsibility Project). *Entrance requirements:* For master's, GMAT, minimum GPA of 3.0. Additional exam requirements/recommendations for international students: Required—TOEFL (minimum score 607 paper-based; 254 computer-based; 102 iBT), or IELTS, or Pearson Test of English (PTE). *Application deadline:* For fall admission, 5/31 priority date for domestic students, 3/31 priority date for international students; for spring admission, 10/31 priority date for domestic students, 4/30 priority date for international students. Applications are processed on a rolling basis. Application fee: $75. Electronic applications accepted. *Financial support:* In 2009–10, research assistantships with full tuition reimbursements (averaging $34,404 per year); career-related internships or fieldwork, Federal Work-Study, scholarships/grants, and unspecified assistantships also available. Support available to part-time students. Financial award application deadline: 6/30; financial award applicants required to submit FAFSA. *Faculty research:* Financial, hedge funds, international business, legal issues, disclosure and branding. *Unit head:* Dr. Joyce A. Strawser, Associate Dean for Undergraduate and MBA Curricula, 973-761-9225, Fax: 973-761-9217, E-mail: strawsjo@shu.edu. *Application contact:* Catherine Bianchi, Director of Graduate Admissions, 973-761-9262, Fax: 973-761-9208, E-mail: catherine.bianchi@shu.edu.

Simon Fraser University, Graduate Studies, Faculty of Business Administration, Burnaby, BC V5A 1S6, Canada. Offers business administration (EMBA, PhD); financial management (MA); general business (MBA); global asset and wealth management (MBA); management of technology/biotechnology (MBA); MBA/MRM. *Accreditation:* AACSB. Postbaccalaureate distance learning degree programs offered. *Degree requirements:* For master's, thesis or written project. *Entrance requirements:* For master's, minimum GPA of 3.0. Additional exam requirements/recommendations for international students: Required—TOEFL. *Expenses:* Contact institution. *Faculty research:* Leadership, marketing and technology, wealth management.

Southeast Missouri State University, School of Graduate Studies, Harrison College of Business, Cape Girardeau, MO 63701-4799. Offers accounting (MBA); entrepreneurship (MBA); environmental management (MBA); financial management (MBA); general management (MBA); health administration (MBA); industrial management (MBA); international business (MBA); sport management (MBA). *Accreditation:* AACSB. Part-time and evening/weekend programs available. Postbaccalaureate distance learning degree programs offered (no on-campus study). *Degree requirements:* For master's, applied research project. *Entrance requirements:* For master's, GMAT, minimum undergraduate GPA of 2.5. Additional exam requirements/recommendations for international students: Required—TOEFL (minimum score 550 paper-based; 213 computer-based); Recommended—IELTS (minimum score 6). *Expenses:* Tuition, state resident: full-time $4266; part-time $237 per credit hour. Tuition, nonresident: full-time $7506; part-time $417 per credit hour. Required fees: $427; $427. *Faculty research:* Human resources, laws impacting accounting, advertising.

Southern Adventist University, School of Business and Management, Collegedale, TN 37315-0370. Offers accounting (MBA); church administration (MSA); church and nonprofit leadership (MBA); financial management (MFM); healthcare administration (MBA); management (MBA); marketing management (MBA); outdoor education (MSA); MFM. Part-time and evening/weekend programs available. Postbaccalaureate distance learning degree programs offered (no on-campus study). *Faculty:* 2 full-time (0 women), 8 part-time/adjunct (1 woman). *Students:* 55 full-time (32 women), 30 part-time (22 women); includes 23 minority (14 African Americans, 1 American Indian/Alaska Native, 1 Asian American or Pacific Islander, 7 Hispanic Americans). Average age 35. In 2009, 20 master's awarded. *Entrance requirements:* For master's, GMAT. Additional exam requirements/recommendations for international students: Required—TOEFL (minimum score 600 paper-based; 250 computer-based; 100 iBT). *Application deadline:* For fall admission, 8/1 priority date for domestic students, 7/1 for international students; for winter admission, 12/1 priority date for domestic students, 11/1 for international students; for spring admission, 4/1 priority date for domestic students, 3/1 for international students. Applications are processed on a rolling basis. Application fee: $25. Electronic applications accepted. *Expenses:* Tuition: Full-time $13,149; part-time $487 per credit hour. *Financial support:* In 2009–10, 32 students received support. Scholarships/grants and unspecified assistantships available. Financial award application deadline: 9/1; financial award applicants required to submit FAFSA. *Unit head:* Dr. Don Van Ornam, Dean, 423-236-2750, Fax: 423-236-1527, E-mail: dvanorna@southern.edu. *Application contact:* Linda Wilhelm, Admissions Coordinator, 423-236-2751, Fax: 423-236-1527, E-mail: sbm@southern.edu.

Southern Illinois University Edwardsville, Graduate Studies and Research, School of Business, Department of Economics and Finance, Edwardsville, IL 62026-0001. Offers MA, MS. Part-time and evening/weekend programs available. *Faculty:* 12 full-time (3 women). *Students:* 17 full-time (3 women), 10 part-time (3 women), 11 international. Average age 26. 61 applicants, 44% accepted. In 2009, 16 master's awarded. *Degree requirements:* For master's, thesis or alternative, final exam, portfolio. *Entrance requirements:* For master's, GMAT or GRE. Additional exam requirements/recommendations for international students: Required—TOEFL (minimum score 550 paper-based; 213 computer-based; 79 iBT), IELTS (minimum score 6.5). *Application deadline:* For fall admission, 7/23 for domestic students, 6/1 for international students; for spring admission, 12/11 for domestic students, 10/1 for international students. Applications are processed on a rolling basis. Application fee: $30. Electronic applications accepted. *Expenses:* Tuition, state resident: part-time $1252.50 per semester. Tuition, nonresident: part-time $3131.25 per semester. Required fees: $586.85 per semester. Tuition and fees vary according to course load. *Financial support:* In 2009–10, 1 fellowship with full tuition reimbursement (averaging $8,370 per year), 13 teaching assistantships with full tuition reimbursements (averaging $8,064 per year) were awarded; research assistantships with full tuition reimbursements, career-related internships or fieldwork, Federal Work-Study, institutionally sponsored loans, scholarships/grants, traineeships, and unspecified assistantships also available. Support available to part-time students. Financial award application deadline: 3/1; financial award applicants required to submit FAFSA. *Unit head:* Dr. Rik Hafer, Chair, 618-650-2542, E-mail: rhafer@siue.edu. *Application contact:* Dr. Ali Kutan, Director, 618-650-3473, E-mail: akutan@siue.edu.

Southern Methodist University, Cox School of Business, MBA Program, Dallas, TX 75275. Offers accounting (MBA); finance (MBA); information technology and operations management (MBA); management (MBA); marketing (MBA); strategy and entrepreneurship (MBA). *Students:* 396 full-time (91 women), 401 part-time (109 women); includes 185 minority (34 African Americans, 5 American Indian/Alaska Native, 102 Asian Americans or Pacific Islanders, 44 Hispanic Americans), 76 international. Average age 31. In 2009, 363 master's awarded. *Unit head:* Dr. Albert W. Niemi, Dean, 214-768-3012, Fax: 214-768-3713, E-mail: aniemi@mail.cox.smu.edu. *Application contact:* Path Cudney, Director of MBA Admissions, 214-768-3001, Fax: 214-768-3956, E-mail: pcudney@mail.cox.smu.edu.

Southern New Hampshire University, School of Business, Manchester, NH 03106-1045. Offers accounting (MS); business administration (MBA, Certificate), including accounting (Certificate), business administration (MBA), finance (Certificate), forensic accounting (Certificate), human resources management (Certificate), international business (Certificate), international sport management (Certificate), leadership of not for profit organizations (Certificate), marketing (Certificate), operations management (Certificate), sport management (Certificate), taxation (Certificate); finance (MS); hospitality and tourism leadership (Certificate); information technology (MS, Certificate); information technology/international business (Certificate); integrated marketing communications (Certificate); international business (MS, DBA); marketing (MS); operations and project management (MS); organizational leadership (MS); project management (Certificate); sport management (MS); MBA/Certificate. *Accreditation:* ACBSP. Part-time and evening/weekend programs available. Postbaccalaureate distance learning degree programs offered (no on-campus study). Terminal master's awarded for partial completion of doctoral program. *Degree requirements:* For master's, one foreign language, comprehensive exam (for some programs), thesis or alternative; for doctorate, one foreign language, comprehensive exam, thesis/dissertation. *Entrance requirements:* For master's, minimum GPA of 2.5; for doctorate, GMAT. Additional exam requirements/recommendations for international students: Required—TOEFL (minimum score 500 paper-based). Electronic applications accepted.

Southwestern Adventist University, Business Department, Graduate Program, Keene, TX 76059. Offers accounting (MBA); finance (MBA); management / leadership (MBA). Part-time and evening/weekend programs available. *Degree requirements:* For master's, capstone course. *Entrance requirements:* For master's, GMAT, GRE General Test.

State University of New York at Binghamton, Graduate School, School of Arts and Sciences, Department of Economics, Binghamton, NY 13902-6000. Offers economics (MA, PhD); economics and finance (MA, PhD). *Faculty:* 23 full-time (4 women), 4 part-time/adjunct (0 women). *Students:* 43 full-time (16 women), 29 part-time (14 women); includes 7 minority (1 African American, 5 Asian Americans or Pacific Islanders, 1 Hispanic American), 52 international. Average age 29. 147 applicants, 67% accepted, 20 enrolled. In 2009, 16 master's, 7 doctorates awarded. Terminal master's awarded for partial completion of doctoral program. *Degree requirements:* For doctorate, thesis/dissertation. *Entrance requirements:* For master's and doctorate, GRE General Test. Additional exam requirements/recommendations for international students: Required—TOEFL (minimum score 550 paper-based; 213 computer-based; 80 iBT). *Application deadline:* For fall admission, 8/1 priority date for domestic and international students. Applications are processed on a rolling basis. Application fee: $60. Electronic applications accepted. *Financial support:* In 2009–10, 31 students received support, including 2 fellowships with full tuition reimbursements available (averaging $14,500 per year), 27 teaching assistantships with full tuition reimbursements available (averaging $14,500 per year); research assistantships, career-related internships or fieldwork, Federal Work-Study, institutionally sponsored loans, scholarships/grants, health care benefits, and unspecified assistantships also available. Financial award application deadline: 2/15; financial award applicants required to submit FAFSA. *Unit head:* Dr. Susan Wolcott, Chairperson, 607-777-2339, E-mail: swolcott@binghamton.edu. *Application contact:* Victoria Williams, Recruiting and Admissions Coordinator, 607-777-2151, Fax: 607-777-2501, E-mail: vwilliam@binghamton.edu.

Stevens Institute of Technology, Graduate School, Wesley J. Howe School of Technology Management, Program in Business Administration, Hoboken, NJ 07030. Offers engineering management (MBA); financial engineering (MBA); information management (MBA); information technology in financial services (MBA); information technology in the pharmaceutical industry (MBA); information technology outsourcing (MBA); pharmaceutical management (MBA); project management (MBA); technology management (MBA); telecommunications management (MBA). *Expenses:* Tuition: Full-time $9900; part-time $1100 per credit. Required fees: $286 per semester.

Stony Brook University, State University of New York, Graduate School, College of Business, Program in Business Administration, Stony Brook, NY 11794. Offers finance (MBA, Certificate); health care management (MBA, Certificate); human resource management (Certificate); human resources (MBA); information systems management (MBA, Certificate); management (MBA); marketing (MBA). *Faculty:* 17 full-time (2 women), 25 part-time/adjunct (5 women). *Students:* 134 full-time (64 women), 112 part-time (44 women); includes 54 minority (8 African Americans, 1 American Indian/Alaska Native, 35 Asian Americans or Pacific Islanders, 10 Hispanic Americans), 56 international. 222 applicants, 55% accepted. In 2009, 134 master's, 5 other advanced degrees awarded. Application fee: $60. *Expenses:* Tuition, state resident: full-time $8370; part-time $349 per credit. Tuition, nonresident: full-time $13,250; part-time $552 per credit. Required fees: $933. *Financial support:* In 2009–10, 2 teaching assistantships were awarded. *Unit head:* Joseph McDonnell, Interim Dean, 631-632-7180. *Application contact:* Dr. Aristotle Lekacos, Director, Graduate Program, 631-632-7171, E-mail: aristotle.lekacost@notes.cc.sunysb.edu.

Strayer University, Graduate Studies, Washington, DC 20005-2603. Offers accounting (MS); acquisition (MBA); business administration (MBA); communications technology (MS); educational management (M Ed); finance (MBA); health services administration (MHSA); hospitality and tourism management (MBA); human resource management (MBA); information systems (MS), including computer security management, decision support system management, enterprise resource management, network management, software engineering management, systems development management; management (MBA); management information systems (MS); marketing (MBA); professional accounting (MS), including accounting information systems, controllership, taxation; public administration (MPA); supply chain management (MBA); technology in education (M Ed). Programs also offered at campus locations in Birmingham, AL; Chamblee, GA; Cobb County, GA; Morrow, GA; White Marsh, MD; Charleston, SC; Columbia, SC; Greensboro, NC; Greenville, SC; Lexington, KY; Louisville, KY; Nashville, TN; North Raleigh, NC; Washington, DC. Part-time and evening/weekend programs available. Postbaccalaureate distance learning degree programs offered (minimal on-campus study). *Degree requirements:* For master's, thesis. *Entrance requirements:* For master's, GMAT, GRE General Test, bachelor's degree from an accredited college or university, minimum undergraduate GPA of 2.75. Electronic applications accepted.

Suffolk University, Sawyer Business School, Master of Business Administration Program, Boston, MA 02108-2770. Offers accounting (MBA); business administration (APC); corporate financial executive track (MBA); entrepreneurship (MBA); executive business administration (EMBA); finance (MBA); global business administration (GMBA); health administration (MBA); international business (MBA); marketing (MBA); organizational behavior (MBA); strategic

Finance and Banking

Suffolk University (continued)
management (MBA); taxation (MBA); JD/MBA; MBA/GDPA; MBA/MHA; MBA/MSA; MBA/MSF; MBA/MST. *Accreditation:* AACSB. Part-time and evening/weekend programs available. Postbaccalaureate distance learning degree programs offered (no on-campus study). *Faculty:* 103 full-time (30 women), 63 part-time/adjunct (19 women). *Students:* 173 full-time (68 women), 406 part-time (178 women); includes 51 minority (16 African Americans, 3 American Indian/Alaska Native, 22 Asian Americans or Pacific Islanders, 10 Hispanic Americans), 90 international. Average age 29. 460 applicants, 72% accepted, 157 enrolled. In 2009, 245 master's awarded. *Entrance requirements:* For master's, GMAT, minimum undergraduate GPA of 2.75 (MBA), 5 years of managerial experience (EMBA). Additional exam requirements/recommendations for international students: Required—TOEFL (minimum score 550 paper-based; 213 computer-based). *Application deadline:* For fall admission, 6/15 priority date for domestic students, 6/15 for international students; for spring admission, 11/1 priority date for domestic students, 11/1 for international students. Applications are processed on a rolling basis. Application fee: $50. Electronic applications accepted. *Expenses:* Tuition: Full-time $33,000; part-time $1100 per credit. Required fees: $20. Tuition and fees vary according to program. *Financial support:* In 2009–10, 284 students received support, including 99 fellowships with full and partial tuition reimbursements available (averaging $13,599 per year); career-related internships or fieldwork, Federal Work-Study, and institutionally sponsored loans also available. Support available to part-time students. Financial award application deadline: 4/1; financial award applicants required to submit FAFSA. *Faculty research:* Foreign investments; career strategies and boundaryless careers; corporate ethics codes; interest rates, inflation, and growth options; innovation and product development performance. *Unit head:* Lillian Hallberg, Assistant Dean of Graduate Programs/Director of MBA Programs, 617-573-8306, E-mail: lhallber@suffolk.edu. *Application contact:* Judith Reynolds, Director of Graduate Admissions, 617-573-8302, Fax: 617-305-1733, E-mail: grad.admission@suffolk.edu.

Suffolk University, Sawyer Business School, Program in Finance, Boston, MA 02108-2770. Offers MSF, MSFSB, CPASF, JD/MSF. *Accreditation:* AACSB. Part-time and evening/weekend programs available. *Faculty:* 16 full-time (2 women), 6 part-time/adjunct (0 women). *Students:* 54 part-time (17 women). Average age 28. 150 applicants, 38% accepted, 26 enrolled. In 2009, 37 master's awarded. *Entrance requirements:* For master's, GMAT, interview. Additional exam requirements/recommendations for international students: Required—TOEFL (minimum score 550 paper-based; 213 computer-based; 80 iBT). *Application deadline:* For fall admission, 6/15 priority date for domestic students, 6/15 for international students; for spring admission, 11/1 priority date for domestic students, 11/1 for international students. Applications are processed on a rolling basis. Application fee: $50. Electronic applications accepted. *Expenses:* Contact institution. *Financial support:* In 2009–10, 32 students received support, including 10 fellowships (averaging $10,463 per year); career-related internships or fieldwork, Federal Work-Study, and institutionally sponsored loans also available. Support available to part-time students. Financial award application deadline: 4/1; financial award applicants required to submit FAFSA. *Faculty research:* Financial institutions, corporate finance, ownership structure, dividend policy, corporate restructuring. *Unit head:* Dr. Ki Han, Director of Graduate Programs in Finance, 617-573-8641, E-mail: msf@suffolk.edu. *Application contact:* Judith Reynolds, Director of Graduate Admissions, 617-573-8302, Fax: 617-305-1733, E-mail: grad.admission@suffolk.edu.

Syracuse University, Martin J. Whitman School of Management, PhD Program in Business Administration, Syracuse, NY 13244. Offers accounting (PhD); finance (PhD); management information systems (PhD); managerial statistics (PhD); marketing (PhD); operations management (PhD); organizational behavior (PhD); strategy and human resources (PhD); supply chain management (PhD). *Degree requirements:* For doctorate, comprehensive exam, thesis/dissertation, summer research paper. *Entrance requirements:* For doctorate, GMAT or GRE General Test, 3 recommendations. Additional exam requirements/recommendations for international students: Required—TOEFL (minimum score 600 paper-based; 250 computer-based; 100 iBT). Electronic applications accepted. *Expenses:* Tuition: Full-time $26,808; part-time $1117 per credit. Required fees: $1024. *Faculty research:* Marketing models, market microstructure, supply chain, auditing, corporate governance.

Syracuse University, Martin J. Whitman School of Management, Program in Business Administration, Syracuse, NY 13244. Offers accounting (MBA); entrepreneurship (MBA); finance (MBA); marketing (MBA); supply chain management (MBA). Postbaccalaureate distance learning degree programs offered (minimal on-campus study). *Entrance requirements:* For master's, GMAT, 2 letters of recommendation. Additional exam requirements/recommendations for international students: Required—TOEFL (minimum score 600 paper-based; 250 computer-based; 100 iBT). Electronic applications accepted. *Expenses:* Tuition: Full-time $26,808; part-time $1117 per credit. Required fees: $1024.

Syracuse University, Martin J. Whitman School of Management, Program in Finance, Syracuse, NY 13244. Offers MSF, JD/MSF. *Entrance requirements:* For master's, GMAT, 2 letters of recommendation, bachelor's degree in finance or economics. Additional exam requirements/recommendations for international students: Required—TOEFL (minimum score 600 paper-based; 250 computer-based; 100 iBT). Electronic applications accepted. *Expenses:* Tuition: Full-time $26,808; part-time $1117 per credit. Required fees: $1024.

Tarleton State University, College of Graduate Studies, College of Business Administration, Department of Accounting, Finance and Economics, Stephenville, TX 76402. Offers business administration (MBA). Part-time and evening/weekend programs available. *Degree requirements:* For master's, comprehensive exam. *Entrance requirements:* For master's, GRE or GMAT, minimum GPA of 3.0. Additional exam requirements/recommendations for international students: Required—TOEFL (minimum score 550 paper-based; 213 computer-based; 80 iBT). Electronic applications accepted.

Télé-université, Graduate Programs, Québec, QC G1K 9H5, Canada. Offers computer science (PhD); corporate finance (MS); distance learning (MS). Part-time programs available.

Temple University, Graduate School, Fox School of Business, Doctoral Programs in Business, Philadelphia, PA 19122-6096. Offers accounting (PhD); entrepreneurship (PhD); finance (PhD); human resource administration (PhD); international business (PhD); management information systems (PhD); marketing (PhD); risk management and insurance (PhD); statistics (PhD); strategic management (PhD); tourism and sport (PhD). *Accreditation:* AACSB. *Degree requirements:* For doctorate, thesis/dissertation. *Entrance requirements:* For doctorate, GRE General Test, GMAT, minimum GPA of 3.0, master's degree. Additional exam requirements/recommendations for international students: Required—TOEFL (minimum score 600 paper-based; 250 computer-based; 100 iBT), IELTS (minimum score 7.5). Electronic applications accepted.

Temple University, Graduate School, Fox School of Business, Specialized Master's Programs, Philadelphia, PA 19122-6096. Offers accounting and financial management (MS); actuarial science (MS); finance (MS); financial engineering (MS); healthcare financial management (MS); healthcare management (MHM); human resource management (MS); management information systems (MS); marketing (MS); statistics (MS). *Accreditation:* AACSB. Part-time programs available. *Entrance requirements:* For master's, GRE General Test or GMAT, minimum undergraduate GPA of 3.0. Additional exam requirements/recommendations for international students: Required—TOEFL (minimum score 600 paper-based; 250 computer-based; 100 iBT), IELTS (minimum score 7.5).

Tennessee Technological University, Graduate School, College of Business, Cookeville, TN 38505. Offers accounting (MBA); finance (MBA); human resource management (MBA); international business (MBA); management information systems (MBA); risk management & insurance (MBA). *Accreditation:* AACSB. Part-time and evening/weekend programs available. *Faculty:* 28 full-time (5 women). *Students:* 64 full-time (26 women), 163 part-time (70 women); includes 17 minority (6 African Americans, 8 Asian Americans or Pacific Islanders, 3 Hispanic Americans). Average age 25. 203 applicants, 52% accepted, 75 enrolled. In 2009, 105 master's awarded. *Entrance requirements:* For master's, GMAT. Additional exam requirements/recommendations for international students: Required—TOEFL (minimum score 550 paper-based; 79 iBT), IELTS (minimum score 5.5). *Application deadline:* For fall admission, 8/1 for domestic and international students; for spring admission, 12/1 for domestic students, 10/1 for international students. Application fee: $25 ($30 for international students). Electronic applications accepted. *Expenses:* Tuition, state resident: full-time $7034; part-time $368 per credit hour. *Financial support:* In 2009–10, 5 fellowships (averaging $10,000 per year), 18 research assistantships (averaging $4,000 per year), teaching assistantships (averaging $4,000 per year) were awarded. Support available to part-time students. Financial award application deadline: 4/1. *Unit head:* Dr. Bob G. Wood, Director, 931-372-3600, Fax: 931-372-6249. *Application contact:* Shelia K. Kendrick, Coordinator of Graduate Studies, 931-372-3808, Fax: 931-372-3497, E-mail: skendrick@tntech.edu.

Texas A&M International University, Office of Graduate Studies and Research, College of Business Administration, Division of International Banking and Finance Studies, Laredo, TX 78041-1900. Offers accounting (MP Acc); international banking (MBA). *Faculty:* 15 full-time (1 woman), 6 part-time/adjunct (0 women). *Students:* 51 full-time (23 women), 224 part-time (106 women); includes 171 minority (2 African Americans, 2 Asian Americans or Pacific Islanders, 167 Hispanic Americans), 92 international. Average age 29. 145 applicants, 63% accepted, 86 enrolled. In 2009, 108 master's awarded. *Entrance requirements:* For master's, GMAT or GRE General Test. Additional exam requirements/recommendations for international students: Required—TOEFL (minimum score 550 paper-based; 213 computer-based). *Application deadline:* For fall admission, 4/30 priority date for domestic students; for spring admission, 11/30 for domestic students. Applications are processed on a rolling basis. Application fee: $25. *Financial support:* In 2009–10, 21 students received support. *Unit head:* Dr. Ken Hung, Chair, 956-326-2541, Fax: 956-326-2481, E-mail: ken.hung@tamiu.edu. *Application contact:* Imelda Lopez, Graduate Admissions Counselor, 956-326-2485, Fax: 956-326-2459, E-mail: lopez@tamiu.edu.

Texas A&M University, Mays Business School, Department of Finance, College Station, TX 77843. Offers MS, PhD. Terminal master's awarded for partial completion of doctoral program. *Degree requirements:* For master's, comprehensive exam; for doctorate, thesis/dissertation. *Entrance requirements:* For master's, GMAT; for doctorate, GMAT or GRE General Test. Additional exam requirements/recommendations for international students: Required—TOEFL. *Expenses:* Tuition, state resident: full-time $3991; part-time $221.74 per credit hour. Tuition, nonresident: full-time $9049; part-time $502.74 per credit hour.

Texas Tech University, Jerry S. Rawls College of Business Administration, Area of Finance, Lubbock, TX 79409. Offers MS, PhD. Part-time programs available. *Faculty:* 14 full-time (2 women). *Students:* 35 full-time (5 women), 3 part-time (1 woman); includes 2 minority (1 African American, 1 Asian American or Pacific Islander), 23 international. Average age 29. 41 applicants, 51% accepted, 16 enrolled. In 2009, 10 master's, 3 doctorates awarded. Terminal master's awarded for partial completion of doctoral program. *Degree requirements:* For master's, capstone course; for doctorate, comprehensive exam, thesis/dissertation, qualifying exams. *Entrance requirements:* For master's and doctorate, GMAT, holistic review of academic credentials. Additional exam requirements/recommendations for international students: Required—TOEFL (minimum score 550 paper-based; 213 computer-based; 79 iBT). *Application deadline:* For fall admission, 4/1 priority date for domestic students, 1/15 priority date for international students; for spring admission, 9/1 priority date for domestic students, 7/15 priority date for international students. Applications are processed on a rolling basis. Application fee: $50 ($75 for international students). Electronic applications accepted. *Expenses:* Tuition, state resident: full-time $5100; part-time $213 per credit hour. Tuition, nonresident: full-time $11,748; part-time $490 per credit hour. Required fees: $2298; $50 per credit hour. $555 per semester. *Financial support:* In 2009–10, 6 research assistantships (averaging $8,000 per year), 10 teaching assistantships (averaging $17,000 per year) were awarded; Federal Work-Study and scholarships/grants also available. Support available to part-time students. Financial award applicants required to submit FAFSA. *Faculty research:* Portfolio theory, banking and financial institutions, corporate finance, securities and options futures. *Unit head:* Dr. Drew Winters, Area Coordinator, 806-742-3350, Fax: 806-742-2099, E-mail: drew.winters@ttu.edu. *Application contact:* Cynthia D. Barnes, Director, Graduate Services Center, 806-742-3184, Fax: 806-742-3958, E-mail: ba_grad@ttu.edu.

Texas Tech University, Jerry S. Rawls College of Business Administration, Programs in Business Administration, Lubbock, TX 79409. Offers agricultural business (MBA); business administration (IMBA); entrepreneurship (MBA); finance (MBA); general business (MBA); health organization management (MBA); international business (MBA); management and leadership skills (MBA); management information systems (MBA); marketing (MBA); statistics (MBA); JD/MBA; MBA/M Arch; MBA/MA; MBA/MD; MBA/MS; MBA/Pharm D. Part-time and evening/weekend programs available. *Faculty:* 54 full-time (9 women), 5 part-time/adjunct (0 women). *Students:* 59 full-time (15 women), 487 part-time (148 women); includes 107 minority (24 African Americans, 4 American Indian/Alaska Native, 30 Asian Americans or Pacific Islanders, 49 Hispanic Americans), 51 international. Average age 30. 477 applicants, 81% accepted, 302 enrolled. In 2009, 185 degrees awarded. *Degree requirements:* For master's, capstone course. *Entrance requirements:* For master's, GMAT, holistic review of academic credentials. Additional exam requirements/recommendations for international students: Required—TOEFL (minimum score 550 paper-based; 213 computer-based; 79 iBT). *Application deadline:* For fall admission, 4/1 priority date for domestic students, 1/15 priority date for international students; for spring admission, 9/1 priority date for domestic students, 7/15 priority date for international students. Applications are processed on a rolling basis. Application fee: $50 ($75 for international students). Electronic applications accepted. *Expenses:* Tuition, state resident: full-time $5100; part-time $213 per credit hour. Tuition, nonresident: full-time $11,748; part-time $490 per credit hour. Required fees: $2298; $50 per credit hour. $555 per semester. *Financial support:* In 2009–10, 13 research assistantships (averaging $8,000 per year) were awarded; teaching assistantships, career-related internships or fieldwork, Federal Work-Study, scholarships/grants, health care benefits, and unspecified assistantships also available. Support available to part-time students. Financial award applicants required to submit FAFSA. *Unit head:* Dr. W. Jay Conover, Director, 806-742-1546, Fax: 806-742-3958, E-mail: jay.conover@ttu.edu. *Application contact:* Cynthia D. Barnes, Director, Graduate Services Center, 806-742-3184, Fax: 806-742-3958, E-mail: ba_grad@ttu.edu.

Troy University, Graduate School, College of Business, Program in Business Administration, Troy, AL 36082. Offers accounting (EMBA, MBA); criminal justice (EMBA); finance (MBA); general management (EMBA); healthcare management (EMBA); information systems (EMBA, MBA); international economic development (MBA). *Accreditation:* ACBSP. Part-time and evening/weekend programs available. *Students:* 382 full-time (196 women), 732 part-time (457 women); includes 616 minority (483 African Americans, 14 American Indian/Alaska Native, 96 Asian Americans or Pacific Islanders, 23 Hispanic Americans). Average age 29. 869 applicants, 61% accepted. In 2009, 296 master's awarded. *Degree requirements:* For master's, thesis or alternative. *Entrance requirements:* For master's, GMAT (minimum score 500) or GRE General Test (minimum score 900), minimum GPA of 2.5; letter of recommendation. Additional exam requirements/recommendations for international students: Required—TOEFL (minimum score 523 paper-based; 193 computer-based; 70 iBT), IELTS (minimum score 6), or ACT Compass ESL (minimum score 270 on Listening, Reading, and Grammar with no individual score below 85 and a minimum score of 8 out of 12 on writing test). *Application deadline:* Applications are processed on a rolling basis. Application fee: $50. *Unit head:* Dr. Henry M. Findley, Interim Chair/Professor, 334-670-3271, Fax: 334-670-3599, E-mail: hfindley@troy.edu. *Application contact:* Brenda K. Campbell, Director of Graduate Admissions, 334-670-3178, Fax: 334-670-3733, E-mail: bcamp@troy.edu.

TUI University, College of Business Administration, Program in Business Administration, Cypress, CA 90630. Offers business administration (PhD); conflict and negotiation management (MBA); criminal justice administration (MBA); entrepreneurship (MBA); finance (MBA); general management (MBA); government accounting (MBA); human resource management (MBA); information security and digital assurance management (MBA); information technology management (MBA); international business (MBA); logistics management (MBA); marketing

(MBA); project management (MBA); public management (MBA); quality management (MBA); strategic leadership (MBA). Part-time and evening/weekend programs available. Postbaccalaureate distance learning degree programs offered (no on-campus study). *Degree requirements:* For doctorate, comprehensive exam, thesis/dissertation, defense of dissertation. *Entrance requirements:* For master's, minimum GPA of 2.5 (students with GPA 3.0 or greater may transfer up to 30% of graduate level credits); for doctorate, minimum GPA of 3.4, curriculum vitae, course work in research methods or statistics. Additional exam requirements/recommendations for international students: Required—TOEFL. Electronic applications accepted.

Union Graduate College, School of Management, Schenectady, NY 12308-3107. Offers Business Administration (MBA); Financial Management (Certificate); General Management (Certificate); Health Systems Administration (MBA, Certificate); Human Resources (Certificate). *Accreditation:* AACSB. Part-time and evening/weekend programs available. *Faculty:* 9 full-time (1 woman), 25 part-time/adjunct (9 women). *Students:* 112 full-time (53 women), 86 part-time (38 women); includes 24 minority (4 African Americans, 16 Asian Americans or Pacific Islanders, 4 Hispanic Americans), 13 international. Average age 26. 173 applicants, 61% accepted, 93 enrolled. In 2009, 76 master's, 15 other advanced degrees awarded. *Degree requirements:* For master's, internship, capstone course. *Entrance requirements:* For master's, GMAT, minimum GPA of 3.0, 3 letters of recommendation. Additional exam requirements/recommendations for international students: Required—TOEFL (minimum score 550 paper-based; 213 computer-based). *Application deadline:* Applications are processed on a rolling basis. Application fee: $60. *Financial support:* Research assistantships, career-related internships or fieldwork, Federal Work-Study, scholarships/grants, health care benefits, and tuition waivers (partial) available. Support available to part-time students. Financial award applicants required to submit FAFSA. *Unit head:* Dr. Eric Lewis, Dean, 518-631-9890, Fax: 518-631-9902, E-mail: lewise@uniongraduatecollege.edu. *Application contact:* Diane Trzaskos, Admissions Coordinator, 518-631-9837, Fax: 518-631-9901, E-mail: trzaskod@uniongraduatecollege.edu.

United States International University, School of Business Administration, Nairobi, Kenya. Offers finance (MBA); information technology management (MBA); integrated studies (MBA); management and organizational development (MS); marketing (MBA); strategic management (MBA). Part-time and evening/weekend programs available. *Degree requirements:* For master's, thesis. *Entrance requirements:* For master's, GMAT, 2 letters of reference, resume. Additional exam requirements/recommendations for international students: Required—TOEFL (minimum score 550 paper-based; 213 computer-based). *Faculty research:* Marketing in small business enterprises, total quality management in Kenya.

Universidad Central del Este, Graduate School, San Pedro de Macoris, Dominican Republic. Offers administration (M Ad); dentistry (DMD); development of educational and social policies (PhD); environmental engineering (ME); financial management (M Ad); higher education (M Ed); human resources (M Ad); public health (MPH). *Entrance requirements:* For master's, letters of recommendation.

Universidad de las Americas, A.C., Program in Business Administration, Mexico City, Mexico. Offers finance (MBA); marketing research (MBA); production and quality (MBA).

Universidad de las Américas–Puebla, Division of Graduate Studies, School of Business and Economics, Puebla, Mexico. Offers business administration (MBA); finance (M Adm). Part-time and evening/weekend programs available. *Degree requirements:* For master's, one foreign language, thesis. *Entrance requirements:* Additional exam requirements/recommendations for international students: Required—TOEFL. *Faculty research:* System dynamics, information technology, marketing, international business, strategic planning, quality.

Universidad de las Américas–Puebla, Division of Graduate Studies, School of Social Sciences, Program in Economics, Puebla, Mexico. Offers economics (MA); finance (M Adm). Part-time and evening/weekend programs available. *Degree requirements:* For master's, one foreign language, thesis. *Faculty research:* Economic models (mathematics), industrial organization, assets and values market.

Universidad Metropolitana, School of Business Administration, Program in Finance, San Juan, PR 00928-1150. Offers MBA.

Université de Sherbrooke, Faculty of Administration, Program in Finance, Sherbrooke, QC J1K 2R1, Canada. Offers M Sc. *Entrance requirements:* For master's, bachelor's degree.

Université du Québec à Montréal, Graduate Programs, Program in Finance, Montréal, QC H3C 3P8, Canada. Offers Diploma. Part-time programs available. *Entrance requirements:* For degree, appropriate bachelor's degree or equivalent, proficiency in French.

Université du Québec à Trois-Rivières, Graduate Programs, Program in Finance, Trois-Rivières, QC G9A 5H7, Canada. Offers DESS.

Université du Québec en Outaouais, Graduate Programs, Program in Financial Services, Gatineau, QC J8X 3X7, Canada. Offers MBA, Diploma.

Université Laval, Faculty of Administrative Sciences, Programs in Business Administration, Québec, QC G1K 7P4, Canada. Offers accounting (MBA); agri-food management (MBA); electronic business (MBA, Diploma); factory management and logistics (MBA); finance (MBA); firm management (MBA); geomatic management (MBA); information technology management (MBA); international management (MBA); management (MBA); management accounting (MBA, Diploma); marketing (MBA); modeling and organizational decision (MBA); occupational health and safety management (MBA); pharmacy management (MBA); social and environmental responsibility (MBA); technological entrepreneurship (Diploma). *Accreditation:* AACSB. Part-time and evening/weekend programs available. Postbaccalaureate distance learning degree programs offered (no on-campus study). *Entrance requirements:* For master's and Diploma, knowledge of French and English. Electronic applications accepted.

University at Albany, State University of New York, School of Business, Department of Finance, Albany, NY 12222-0001. Offers MBA. *Degree requirements:* For master's, field study project. *Entrance requirements:* For master's, GMAT. Additional exam requirements/recommendations for international students: Required—TOEFL (minimum score 550 paper-based; 213 computer-based). Electronic applications accepted. *Faculty research:* Tax-exempt securities, public finance, financial engineering, international finance, investments management.

University at Buffalo, the State University of New York, Graduate School, School of Management, Buffalo, NY 14260. Offers accounting (MS); business administration (EMBA, MBA, PMBA); finance (MS), including financial engineering, financial management; information assurance (Certificate); management (PhD); management information systems (MS); supply chains and operations management (MS); Au D/MBA; JD/MBA; M Arch/MBA; MA/MBA; MD/MBA; MPH/MBA; MSW/MBA; Pharm D/MBA. *Accreditation:* AACSB. Part-time and evening/weekend programs available. *Faculty:* 66 full-time (19 women), 21 part-time/adjunct (4 women). *Students:* 502 full-time (176 women), 199 part-time (54 women); includes 29 minority (10 African Americans, 16 Asian Americans or Pacific Islanders, 3 Hispanic Americans), 306 international. Average age 27. 1,944 applicants, 31% accepted, 324 enrolled. In 2009, 363 master's, 7 doctorates, 3 other advanced degrees awarded. *Degree requirements:* For master's, thesis (for some programs); for doctorate, comprehensive exam, thesis/dissertation. *Entrance requirements:* For master's, GMAT (MBA, MS in accounting), GRE General Test (for all other MS concentrations); for doctorate, GMAT or GRE. Additional exam requirements/recommendations for international students: Required—TOEFL (minimum score 230 computer-based; 95 iBT). *Application deadline:* For fall admission, 6/2 priority date for domestic students, 3/1 priority date for international students. Applications are processed on a rolling basis. Application fee: $100. Electronic applications accepted. *Expenses:* Contact institution. *Financial support:* In 2009–10, 91 students received support, including 5 fellowships with full and partial tuition reimbursements available (averaging $4,000 per year), 41 research assistantships with full and partial tuition reimbursements available (averaging $16,000 per year), 28 teaching assistantships with full and partial tuition reimbursements available (averaging $15,000 per year); career-related internships or fieldwork, Federal Work-Study, institutionally sponsored loans, scholarships/grants, health care benefits, and unspecified assistantships also available. Financial award application deadline: 2/15; financial award applicants required to submit FAFSA. *Faculty research:* Earnings management and electronic information assurance, supply chains and operations management, corporate financing and asset pricing, consumer behavior and quantitative modeling of marketing behavior, leadership and politics in organizations. Total annual research expenditures: $230,000. *Unit head:* David W. Frasier, Assistant Dean, 716-645-3204, Fax: 716-645-2341, E-mail: davidf@buffalo.edu. *Application contact:* David W. Frasier, Assistant Dean, 716-645-3204, Fax: 716-645-2341, E-mail: davidf@buffalo.edu.

The University of Akron, Graduate School, College of Business Administration, Department of Finance, Akron, OH 44325. Offers MBA, JD/MBA. Part-time and evening/weekend programs available. *Faculty:* 9 full-time (3 women), 1 part-time/adjunct (0 women). *Students:* 41 full-time (11 women), 50 part-time (16 women); includes 5 minority (1 African American, 1 American Indian/Alaska Native, 3 Asian Americans or Pacific Islanders), 24 international. Average age 28. 47 applicants, 68% accepted, 16 enrolled. In 2009, 35 master's awarded. *Entrance requirements:* For master's, GMAT, minimum GPA of 2.75, letters of recommendation, resume. Additional exam requirements/recommendations for international students: Required—TOEFL (minimum score 550 paper-based; 213 computer-based; 79 iBT). *Application deadline:* For fall admission, 8/1 for domestic and international students; for spring admission, 12/1 for domestic students, 11/1 for international students. Application fee: $30 ($40 for international students). Electronic applications accepted. *Expenses:* Tuition, state resident: full-time $6570; part-time $365 per credit hour. Tuition, nonresident: full-time $11,250; part-time $625 per credit hour. *Financial support:* In 2009–10, 9 research assistantships with full and partial tuition reimbursements, 2 teaching assistantships with full tuition reimbursements were awarded. *Faculty research:* Corporate finance, financial markets and institutions, investment and equity market analysis, personal financial planning, real estate. *Unit head:* David A. Redle, Chair, 330-972-6329, E-mail: dredle@uakron.edu. *Application contact:* Dr. Susan Hanlon, Director of Graduate Business Programs, 330-972-7043, Fax: 330-972-6588, E-mail: shanlon@uakron.edu.

The University of Alabama, Graduate School, College of Human Environmental Sciences, Program in Human Environmental Science, Tuscaloosa, AL 35487. Offers family financial planning and counseling (MS); interactive technology (MS); quality management (MS); restaurant and meeting management (MS); rural community health (MS); sport management (MS). *Students:* 70 full-time (40 women), 99 part-time (45 women); includes 44 minority (42 African Americans, 2 Hispanic Americans), 1 international. Average age 33. 124 applicants, 71% accepted, 71 enrolled. In 2009, 70 degrees awarded. *Degree requirements:* For master's, comprehensive exam. *Entrance requirements:* For master's, GRE (for some specializations), minimum GPA of 3.0. Additional exam requirements/recommendations for international students: Required—TOEFL. *Application deadline:* Applications are processed on a rolling basis. Application fee: $50 ($60 for international students). Electronic applications accepted. *Expenses:* Tuition, state resident: full-time $7000. Tuition, nonresident: full-time $19,200. *Faculty research:* Hospitality management, sports medicine education, technology and education. *Unit head:* Dr. Milla D. Boschung, Dean, 205-348-6250, Fax: 205-348-1786, E-mail: mboschun@ches.ua.edu. *Application contact:* Dr. Stuart Usdan, Associate Dean, 205-348-6150, Fax: 205-348-3789, E-mail: susdan@ches.ua.edu.

The University of Alabama, Graduate School, Manderson Graduate School of Business, Economics, Finance and Legal Studies Department, Tuscaloosa, AL 35487. Offers economics (MA, PhD); finance (MS, PhD). *Faculty:* 25 full-time (1 woman). *Students:* 75 full-time (20 women); includes 8 minority (5 African Americans, 3 Asian Americans or Pacific Islanders), 12 international. Average age 26. 224 applicants, 20% accepted, 34 enrolled. In 2009, 24 master's, 2 doctorates awarded. Terminal master's awarded for partial completion of doctoral program. *Median time to degree:* Of those who began their doctoral program in fall 2001, 99% received their degree in 8 years or less. *Degree requirements:* For master's, comprehensive exam (MA), thesis (MS); for doctorate, comprehensive exam, thesis/dissertation. *Entrance requirements:* For master's, GMAT, GRE; for doctorate, GRE or GMAT. Additional exam requirements/recommendations for international students: Required—TOEFL (minimum score 550 paper-based; 213 computer-based). *Application deadline:* For fall admission, 7/1 priority date for domestic students, 1/15 for international students; for spring admission, 11/1 priority date for domestic students, 6/1 for international students. Applications are processed on a rolling basis. Application fee: $50 ($60 for international students). Electronic applications accepted. *Expenses:* Tuition, state resident: full-time $7000. Tuition, nonresident: full-time $19,200. *Financial support:* In 2009–10, 10 fellowships (averaging $10,000 per year), 21 research assistantships with full and partial tuition reimbursements (averaging $12,000 per year), 15 teaching assistantships with full and partial tuition reimbursements (averaging $12,000 per year) were awarded; Federal Work-Study, institutionally sponsored loans, and unspecified assistantships also available. *Faculty research:* Taxation, futures market, monetary theory and policy, income distribution. *Unit head:* Prof. Billy P. Helms, Head, 205-348-8067, E-mail: bhelms@cba.ua.edu. *Application contact:* Debra F. Wheatley, 205-348-6683, Fax: 205-348-0590, E-mail: dwheatle@cba.ua.edu.

The University of Alabama in Huntsville, School of Graduate Studies, College of Business Administration, Department of Accounting and Finance, Huntsville, AL 35899. Offers accounting (M Acc, Certificate), including CPA preparatory with an emphasis in taxation (M Acc), CPA preparatory with emphasis in assurance and financial reporting (M Acc), general accounting (M Acc), information systems audit and control (ISAC) (M Acc). Part-time and evening/weekend programs available. *Faculty:* 5 full-time (3 women), 3 part-time/adjunct (0 women). *Students:* 16 full-time (10 women), 31 part-time (15 women); includes 5 minority (4 African Americans, 1 Asian American or Pacific Islander), 3 international. Average age 30. 42 applicants, 69% accepted, 21 enrolled. In 2009, 13 master's awarded. *Degree requirements:* For master's, comprehensive exam, thesis or alternative. *Entrance requirements:* For master's and Certificate, GMAT (minimum score 500), minimum AACSB index of 1080. Additional exam requirements/recommendations for international students: Required—TOEFL (minimum score 550 paper-based; 213 computer-based; 62 iBT). *Application deadline:* For fall admission, 8/1 for domestic students, 4/1 for international students; for spring admission, 12/1 for domestic students, 9/1 for international students. Applications are processed on a rolling basis. Application fee: $40 ($50 for international students). Electronic applications accepted. *Expenses:* Tuition, state resident: part-time $355.75 per credit hour. Tuition, nonresident: part-time $847.10 per credit hour. Required fees: $210.80 per semester. Tuition and fees vary according to course load and program. *Financial support:* Career-related internships or fieldwork, Federal Work-Study, institutionally sponsored loans, scholarships/grants, health care benefits, and unspecified assistantships available. Support available to part-time students. Financial award application deadline: 4/1; financial award applicants required to submit FAFSA. *Faculty research:* Accounting information systems, emerging technologies in accounting, behavioral accounting, state and local taxation, financial accounting. Total annual research expenditures: $67,010. *Unit head:* Dr. John Burnett, Interim Chair, 256-824-2923, Fax: 256-824-2929, E-mail: burnettj@uah.edu. *Application contact:* Jennifer Pettitt, Director of Graduate Programs, 256-824-6681, Fax: 256-824-7571, E-mail: jennifer.pettitt@uah.edu.

The University of Alabama in Huntsville, School of Graduate Studies, College of Business Administration, Department of Management and Marketing, Huntsville, AL 35899. Offers management (MBA), including acquisition management, finance, human resource management, logistics and supply chain management, marketing, project management. *Accreditation:* AACSB. Part-time and evening/weekend programs available. *Faculty:* 7 full-time (1 woman), 1 part-time/adjunct (0 women). *Students:* 41 full-time (19 women), 155 part-time (59 women); includes 30 minority (15 African Americans, 5 American Indian/Alaska Native, 7 Asian Americans or Pacific Islanders, 3 Hispanic Americans), 20 international. Average age 32. 138 applicants, 63% accepted, 68 enrolled. In 2009, 38 master's awarded. *Degree requirements:* For master's, comprehensive exam, thesis or alternative. *Entrance requirements:* For master's, GMAT (minimum score 500), minimum AACSB index of 1080. Additional exam requirements/recommendations for international students: Required—TOEFL (minimum score 550 paper-based; 213 computer-based; 62 iBT). *Application deadline:* For fall admission, 8/1 for domestic students, 4/1 for international students; for spring admission, 12/1 for domestic students, 9/1 for international students. Applications are processed on a rolling basis. Application fee: $40

Finance and Banking

The University of Alabama in Huntsville (continued)

($50 for international students). Electronic applications accepted. *Expenses:* Tuition, state resident: part-time $355.75 per credit hour. Tuition, nonresident: part-time $847.10 per credit hour. Required fees: $210.80 per semester. Tuition and fees vary according to course load and program. *Financial support:* In 2009–10, 3 students received support, including 2 research assistantships with full tuition reimbursements available (averaging $14,400 per year), 1 teaching assistantship with full tuition reimbursement available (averaging $11,800 per year); career-related internships or fieldwork, Federal Work-Study, institutionally sponsored loans, scholarships/grants, health care benefits, and unspecified assistantships also available. Support available to part-time students. Financial award application deadline: 4/1; financial award applicants required to submit FAFSA. *Unit head:* Dr. Brent Wren, Chair, 256-824-6408, Fax: 256-824-6328, E-mail: wrenb@uah.edu. *Application contact:* Jennifer Pettitt, Director of Graduate Programs, 256-824-6681, Fax: 256-824-7571, E-mail: jennifer.pettitt@uah.edu.

University of Alaska Fairbanks, School of Management, Department of Business Administration, Fairbanks, AK 99775-6080. Offers capital markets (MBA); general management (MBA). *Accreditation:* AACSB. Part-time programs available. *Faculty:* 8 full-time (1 woman), 4 part-time/adjunct (1 woman). *Students:* 23 full-time (10 women), 35 part-time (25 women); includes 3 minority (all Hispanic Americans), 5 international. Average age 43. 36 applicants, 61% accepted, 18 enrolled. In 2009, 36 master's awarded. *Degree requirements:* For master's, comprehensive exam, thesis or alternative. *Entrance requirements:* For master's, GMAT. Additional exam requirements/recommendations for international students: Required—TOEFL (minimum score 550 paper-based; 213 computer-based; 80 iBT). *Application deadline:* For fall admission, 6/1 priority date for domestic students, 2/1 for international students; for spring admission, 10/15 priority date for domestic students, 9/1 for international students. Applications are processed on a rolling basis. Application fee: $60. Electronic applications accepted. *Expenses:* Tuition, state resident: full-time $7584; part-time $316 per credit. Tuition, nonresident: full-time $15,504; part-time $646 per credit. Required fees: $23 per credit. $135 per semester. Tuition and fees vary according to course level, course load and reciprocity agreements. *Financial support:* In 2009–10, 4 teaching assistantships (averaging $12,323 per year) were awarded; fellowships, research assistantships, career-related internships or fieldwork, Federal Work-Study, scholarships/grants, health care benefits, and unspecified assistantships also available. Support available to part-time students. Financial award application deadline: 2/15; financial award applicants required to submit FAFSA. *Faculty research:* Consumer behavior, marketing, international finance and business, strategic risk, organization theory. *Unit head:* Dr. Ping Lan, Director, MBA Program, 907-474-7688, Fax: 907-474-5219, E-mail: plan@alaska.edu. *Application contact:* Dr. Ping Lan, Director, MBA Program, 907-474-7688, Fax: 907-474-5219, E-mail: plan@alaska.edu.

University of Alberta, Faculty of Graduate Studies and Research, Department of Economics, Edmonton, AB T6G 2E1, Canada. Offers economics (MA, PhD); economics and finance (MA); environmental and natural resource economics (PhD). Part-time programs available. *Faculty:* 25 full-time (5 women), 3 part-time/adjunct (0 women). *Students:* 33 full-time (7 women), 7 part-time (3 women). Average age 26. 112 applicants, 58% accepted, 22 enrolled. In 2009, 8 master's, 1 doctorate awarded. *Degree requirements:* For doctorate, thesis/dissertation. *Entrance requirements:* For master's and doctorate, GRE. Additional exam requirements/recommendations for international students: Required—TOEFL. *Application deadline:* For fall admission, 6/15 for domestic students. Applications are processed on a rolling basis. Tuition and fees charges are reported in Canadian dollars. *Expenses:* Tuition, area resident: Full-time $4626 Canadian dollars; part-time $99.72 Canadian dollars per unit. International tuition: $8216 Canadian dollars full-time. Required fees: $3590 Canadian dollars; $99.72 Canadian dollars per unit. $215 Canadian dollars per term. *Financial support:* In 2009–10, 19 students received support, including 6 research assistantships with partial tuition reimbursements available (averaging $14,300 per year), 5 teaching assistantships with partial tuition reimbursements available (averaging $11,200 per year); career-related internships or fieldwork and scholarships/grants also available. Financial award application deadline: 3/1. *Faculty research:* Public finance, international trade, industrial organization, Pacific Rim economics, monetary economics. *Unit head:* Henry van Egteren, Graduate Coordinator, 780-492-7634, Fax: 780-492-3300. *Application contact:* Audrey Jackson, Graduate Program Administrator, 780-492-7634, Fax: 780-492-3300, E-mail: econapps@ualberta.ca.

University of Alberta, Faculty of Graduate Studies and Research, Doctoral Program in Business, Edmonton, AB T6G 2E1, Canada. Offers accounting (PhD); finance (PhD); human resources/industrial relations (PhD); management science (PhD); marketing (PhD); organizational analysis (PhD); MBA/PhD. *Accreditation:* AACSB. Part-time programs available. *Faculty:* 41 full-time (7 women), 1 part-time/adjunct (0 women). *Students:* 46 full-time (27 women), 5 part-time (3 women). Average age 34. 307 applicants, 7% accepted, 11 enrolled. In 2009, 2 doctorates awarded. *Degree requirements:* For doctorate, comprehensive exam, thesis/dissertation. *Entrance requirements:* For doctorate, GMAT. Additional exam requirements/recommendations for international students: Required—TOEFL (minimum score 550 paper-based; 213 computer-based). *Application deadline:* For fall admission, 6/1 priority date for domestic students; for winter admission, 5/1 for domestic students. Application fee: $0. Electronic applications accepted. Tuition and fees charges are reported in Canadian dollars. *Expenses:* Tuition, area resident: Full-time $4626 Canadian dollars; part-time $99.72 Canadian dollars per unit. International tuition: $8216 Canadian dollars full-time. Required fees: $3590 Canadian dollars; $99.72 Canadian dollars per unit. $215 Canadian dollars per term. *Financial support:* In 2009–10, 29 students received support, including 11 fellowships with full tuition reimbursements available (averaging $17,000 per year); scholarships/grants and tuition waivers (partial) also available. *Faculty research:* Accounting, capital markets and corporate finance, organizational change and human resource management, marketing, strategic management. Total annual research expenditures: $7.7 million. *Unit head:* Dr. Mike Percy, Director, 780-492-2361, Fax: 780-492-3325, E-mail: busphd@ualberta.ca. *Application contact:* Jeanette Gosine, Program Coordinator, 780-492-2361, Fax: 780-492-3325, E-mail: busphd@ualberta.ca.

The University of Arizona, Graduate College, Eller College of Management, Department of Finance, Tucson, AZ 85721. Offers MS, PhD. Part-time programs available. *Faculty:* 6. Terminal master's awarded for partial completion of doctoral program. *Degree requirements:* For master's, project; for doctorate, comprehensive exam, thesis/dissertation. *Entrance requirements:* Additional exam requirements/recommendations for international students: Required—TOEFL (minimum score 550 paper-based; 213 computer-based; 79 iBT). *Application deadline:* For fall admission, 2/15 for domestic and international students. Applications are processed on a rolling basis. Application fee: $75. Electronic applications accepted. *Expenses:* Contact institution. *Financial support:* In 2009–10, 5 research assistantships with full tuition reimbursements (averaging $16,746 per year), 4 teaching assistantships with full tuition reimbursements (averaging $17,101 per year) were awarded; health care benefits, tuition waivers (partial), and unspecified assistantships also available. Financial award application deadline: 3/15. *Faculty research:* Corporate finance, banking, investments, stock market. *Unit head:* Dr. Chris Lamoureux, Head, 520-621-7488, Fax: 520-621-1261, E-mail: lamoureu@lamfin.eller.arizona.edu. *Application contact:* Kay Ross, Program Coordinator, 520-621-1520, Fax: 520-621-1261, E-mail: kross@eller.arizona.edu.

University of Baltimore, Graduate School, Merrick School of Business, Department of Economics, Finance, and Management Science, Baltimore, MD 21201-5779. Offers business/finance (MS). Part-time and evening/weekend programs available. *Entrance requirements:* For master's, GMAT. Additional exam requirements/recommendations for international students: Required—TOEFL (minimum score 550 paper-based; 213 computer-based). Electronic applications accepted. *Faculty research:* International finance, corporate finance, health care, regional economics, small business.

The University of British Columbia, Sauder School of Business, Doctoral Program in Commerce and Business Administration, Vancouver, BC V6T 1Z1, Canada. Offers accounting (PhD); finance (PhD); international business (PhD); management information systems (PhD); management science (PhD); marketing (PhD); organizational behavior (PhD); strategy and business economics (PhD); transportation and logistics (PhD); urban land economics (PhD). *Degree requirements:* For doctorate, comprehensive exam, thesis/dissertation. *Entrance requirements:* For doctorate, GMAT or GRE. Additional exam requirements/recommendations for international students: Required—TOEFL (minimum score 600 paper-based; 250 computer-based; 100 iBT). Electronic applications accepted.

University of California, Berkeley, Graduate Division, Haas School of Business, PhD in Business Administration Program, Berkeley, CA 94720-1500. Offers accounting (PhD); business and public policy (PhD); finance (PhD); management of organizations (PhD); marketing (PhD); operations management (PhD); real estate (PhD). *Accreditation:* AACSB. *Faculty:* 80 full-time (20 women), 130 part-time/adjunct (22 women). *Students:* 82 full-time (23 women); includes 22 minority (18 Asian Americans or Pacific Islanders, 4 Hispanic Americans), 29 international. Average age 30. 511 applicants, 5% accepted, 16 enrolled. In 2009, 8 doctorates awarded. *Degree requirements:* For doctorate, comprehensive exam, thesis/dissertation, oral exam, written preliminary exams. *Entrance requirements:* For doctorate, GMAT or GRE, minimum GPA of 3.0 in undergraduate and graduate coursework. Additional exam requirements/recommendations for international students: Required—TOEFL (minimum score 570 paper-based; 230 computer-based; 68 iBT), IELTS (minimum score 7). *Application deadline:* For fall admission, 12/10 for domestic and international students. Application fee: $70 ($90 for international students). Electronic applications accepted. *Financial support:* Fellowships with full and partial tuition reimbursements, research assistantships with full and partial tuition reimbursements, teaching assistantships with full and partial tuition reimbursements, career-related internships or fieldwork, Federal Work-Study, scholarships/grants, health care benefits, tuition waivers (full), unspecified assistantships, and transit pass, travel grants available. Financial award application deadline: 12/10; financial award applicants required to submit FAFSA. *Faculty research:* Accounting, business and public policy, finance, management of organizations, marketing, operations and information technology management, real estate. *Unit head:* Sunil Dutta, Director, 510-642-1229, Fax: 510-643-4255, E-mail: kimg@haas.berkeley.edu. *Application contact:* Kim Guilfoyle, Director, Student Affairs, 510-642-3944, Fax: 510-643-4255, E-mail: kimg@haas.berkeley.edu.

University of California, Berkeley, UC Berkeley Extension, Certificate Programs in Business, Berkeley, CA 94720-1500. Offers accounting (Certificate); business administration (Certificate); finance (Certificate); human resource management (Certificate); management (Certificate); marketing (Certificate); project management (Certificate). Postbaccalaureate distance learning degree programs offered. *Unit head:* Diana Wu, Dean, 510-642-4181. *Application contact:* Business, 510-642-4231, E-mail: business@unex.berkeley.edu.

University of California, Berkeley, UC Berkeley Extension, International Diploma Programs, Berkeley, CA 94720-1500. Offers business administration (Certificate); finance (Certificate); global business management (Certificate); marketing (Certificate); project management (Certificate). *Unit head:* Diana Wu, Dean, 510-642-4181. *Application contact:* International Diploma Programs, 510-642-2564, E-mail: diploma@unex.berkeley.edu.

University of California, Santa Cruz, Division of Graduate Studies, Division of Social Sciences, Program in Applied Economics and Finance, Santa Cruz, CA 95064. Offers MS. *Degree requirements:* For master's, thesis or alternative, project. *Entrance requirements:* For master's, GRE General Test, GRE Subject Test. *Faculty research:* Economic decision-making skills for the design and operation of complex institutional systems.

University of Central Missouri, The Graduate School, Harmon College of Business Administration, Warrensburg, MO 64093. Offers accountancy (MA); accounting (MBA); ethical strategic leadership (MBA); finance (MBA); general business (MBA); information systems (MBA); information technology (MS); marketing (MBA). Part-time programs available. Postbaccalaureate distance learning degree programs offered. *Faculty:* 31. *Students:* 87 full-time (34 women), 62 part-time (25 women); includes 10 minority (3 African Americans, 1 American Indian/Alaska Native, 5 Asian Americans or Pacific Islanders, 1 Hispanic American), 66 international. Average age 27. 55 applicants, 64% accepted, 27 enrolled. In 2009, 83 master's awarded. *Entrance requirements:* Additional exam requirements/recommendations for international students: Required—TOEFL (minimum score 550 paper-based; 79 computer-based). *Application deadline:* For fall admission, 6/1 priority date for domestic students, 5/1 for international students; for spring admission, 10/1 priority date for domestic students, 10/1 for international students. Applications are processed on a rolling basis. Application fee: $30 ($75 for international students). Electronic applications accepted. *Expenses:* Tuition, area resident: Part-time $245.80 per credit hour. Tuition, nonresident: part-time $491.60 per credit hour. Required fees: $24.20 per credit hour. Full-time tuition and fees vary according to course load, degree level, campus/location and reciprocity agreements. *Financial support:* Research assistantships with full and partial tuition reimbursements, teaching assistantships with full and partial tuition reimbursements, career-related internships or fieldwork, Federal Work-Study, scholarships/grants, and administrative and laboratory assistantships available. Support available to part-time students. Financial award application deadline: 3/1; financial award applicants required to submit FAFSA. *Unit head:* Dr. Roger Best, Dean, 660-543-4560, Fax: 660-543-8350, E-mail: best@ucmo.edu. *Application contact:* Laurie Delap, Admissions Coordinator, 660-543-4621, Fax: 660-543-4778, E-mail: gradinfo@ucmo.edu.

University of Cincinnati, Graduate School, College of Business, PhD Program, Cincinnati, OH 45221. Offers accounting (PhD); finance (PhD); information systems (PhD); management (PhD); marketing (PhD); quantitative analysis and operations management (PhD). *Degree requirements:* For doctorate, comprehensive exam, thesis/dissertation. *Entrance requirements:* For doctorate, GMAT, GRE, resume, letters of recommendation. Additional exam requirements/recommendations for international students: Required—TOEFL (minimum score 600 paper-based; 250 computer-based; 100 iBT). Electronic applications accepted. *Expenses:* Contact institution.

University of Colorado at Boulder, Leeds School of Business, Division of Business Administration, Boulder, CO 80309. Offers accounting (MS, PhD); finance (PhD); information systems (PhD); marketing (PhD); operations (PhD); strategic, organizational, and entrepreneurial studies (PhD). Part-time and evening/weekend programs available. *Students:* 74 full-time (27 women), 15 part-time (8 women); includes 6 minority (1 African American, 3 Asian Americans or Pacific Islanders, 2 Hispanic Americans), 21 international. Average age 28. 271 applicants, 8% accepted, 19 enrolled. In 2009, 40 master's, 6 doctorates awarded. *Entrance requirements:* For master's, GMAT, minimum undergraduate GPA of 3.0. *Application deadline:* For fall admission, 3/31 for domestic and international students; for spring admission, 10/31 for domestic and international students. Application fee: $50 ($60 for international students). Electronic applications accepted. *Financial support:* In 2009–10, 16 fellowships (averaging $1,038 per year), 26 research assistantships (averaging $17,558 per year), 11 teaching assistantships (averaging $12,576 per year) were awarded; career-related internships or fieldwork, Federal Work-Study, scholarships/grants, and unspecified assistantships also available. Financial award applicants required to submit FAFSA.

University of Colorado Denver, Business School, Program in Finance, Denver, CO 80217-3364. Offers MS. Part-time and evening/weekend programs available. *Students:* 27 full-time (6 women), 69 part-time (20 women); includes 6 minority (1 African American, 1 American Indian/Alaska Native, 2 Asian Americans or Pacific Islanders, 2 Hispanic Americans), 20 international. 67 applicants, 61% accepted, 21 enrolled. In 2009, 43 master's awarded. *Entrance requirements:* For master's, GMAT. Additional exam requirements/recommendations for international students: Required—TOEFL (minimum score 525 paper-based; 197 computer-based). *Application deadline:* For fall admission, 6/1 for domestic students, 3/15 for international students; for spring admission, 11/1 priority date for domestic students, 10/1 for international students. Applications are processed on a rolling basis. Application fee: $50 ($75 for international students). *Financial support:* Federal Work-Study, institutionally sponsored loans, and scholarships/grants available. Support available to part-time students. Financial award application deadline: 4/1; financial award applicants required to submit FAFSA. *Faculty research:* Corporate governance, debt maturity policies, regulation and financial markets, option management strategies. *Unit head:* Dr. James Morris, Director, 303-556-4370, Fax: 303-556-5899, E-mail:

james.morris@ucdenver.edu. *Application contact:* Shelly Townley, Admissions Coordinator, 303-556-5956, Fax: 303-556-5904, E-mail: shelly.townley@ucdenver.edu.

University of Connecticut, Graduate School, College of Liberal Arts and Sciences, Department of Public Policy, Field of Public Administration, Storrs, CT 06269. Offers nonprofit management (Graduate Certificate); public administration (MPA); public financial management (Graduate Certificate); JD/MPA; MPA/MSW. *Accreditation:* NASPAA. *Faculty:* 10 full-time (4 women). *Students:* 45 full-time (29 women), 37 part-time (11 women); includes 12 minority (4 African Americans, 1 Asian American or Pacific Islander, 7 Hispanic Americans), 5 international. Average age 31. 79 applicants, 38% accepted, 29 enrolled. In 2009, 31 master's, 21 other advanced degrees awarded. *Degree requirements:* For master's, comprehensive exam, internship. *Entrance requirements:* For master's, GRE General Test. Additional exam requirements/recommendations for international students: Required—TOEFL (minimum score 550 paper-based; 213 computer-based). *Application deadline:* For fall admission, 2/1 priority date for domestic and international students; for spring admission, 11/1 for domestic students, 10/1 for international students. Applications are processed on a rolling basis. Application fee: $55. Electronic applications accepted. *Expenses:* Tuition, state resident: full-time $4725; part-time $525 per credit. Tuition, nonresident: full-time $12,267; part-time $1363 per credit. Required fees: $346 per semester. Tuition and fees vary according to course load. *Financial support:* In 2009–10, 23 research assistantships with full tuition reimbursements, 1 teaching assistantship with full tuition reimbursement were awarded; career-related internships or fieldwork, Federal Work-Study, scholarships/grants, health care benefits, and unspecified assistantships also available. Financial award application deadline: 2/1; financial award applicants required to submit FAFSA. *Unit head:* William Simonsen, Chairperson, 860-570-9045, E-mail: william.simonsen@uconn.edu. *Application contact:* Valerie Rogers, Program Director, 860-570-9047, Fax: 860-570-9114, E-mail: valerie.rogers@uconn.edu.

University of Connecticut, Graduate School, School of Business, Storrs, CT 06269. Offers accounting (MS, PhD); business administration (Exec MBA, MBA, PhD); finance (PhD); health care management and insurance studies (MBA); management (PhD); management consulting (MBA); marketing (PhD); marketing intelligence (MBA); MA/MBA; MBA/MSW. *Accreditation:* AACSB. *Faculty:* 75 full-time (14 women). *Students:* 405 full-time (134 women), 999 part-time (364 women); includes 198 minority (43 African Americans, 3 American Indian/Alaska Native, 102 Asian Americans or Pacific Islanders, 50 Hispanic Americans), 136 international. Average age 31. 956 applicants, 20% accepted, 187 enrolled. In 2009, 413 master's, 6 doctorates awarded. *Degree requirements:* For master's, comprehensive exam; for doctorate, thesis/dissertation. *Entrance requirements:* For master's and doctorate, GMAT. Additional exam requirements/recommendations for international students: Required—TOEFL (minimum score 550 paper-based; 213 computer-based). *Application deadline:* For fall admission, 2/1 priority date for domestic and international students; for spring admission, 11/1 for domestic students, 10/1 for international students. Applications are processed on a rolling basis. Electronic applications accepted. *Expenses:* Tuition, state resident: full-time $4725; part-time $525 per credit. Tuition, nonresident: full-time $12,267; part-time $1363 per credit. Required fees: $346 per semester. Tuition and fees vary according to course load. *Financial support:* In 2009–10, 76 research assistantships with full tuition reimbursements, 41 teaching assistantships with full tuition reimbursements were awarded; fellowships, career-related internships or fieldwork, Federal Work-Study, scholarships/grants, health care benefits, and unspecified assistantships also available. Financial award application deadline: 2/1; financial award applicants required to submit FAFSA. *Unit head:* P. Christopher Earley, Dean, 860-486-2317, Fax: 860-846-0889, E-mail: paul.earley@uconn.edu. *Application contact:* Richard Dino, Admissions Chairperson, 860-486-4483, E-mail: rich.dino@uconn.edu.

See Close-Up on page 263.

University of Dallas, Graduate School of Management, Irving, TX 75062-4736. Offers accounting (MBA, MM, MS); business management (MBA, MM); corporate finance (MBA, MM); financial services (MBA); global business (MBA, MM); health services management (MBA, MM); human resource management (MBA, MM); information assurance (MBA, MM, MS); information technology (MBA, MM, MS); information technology service management (MBA, MM, MS); marketing management (MBA, MM); organization development (MBA, MM); project management (MBA, MM); sports and entertainment management (MBA, MM); strategic leadership (MBA, MM); supply chain management (MBA); supply chain management and market logistics (MM). *Accreditation:* ACBSP. Part-time and evening/weekend programs available. Postbaccalaureate distance learning degree programs offered (no on-campus study). *Faculty:* 25 full-time (6 women), 31 part-time/adjunct (6 women). *Students:* 232 full-time (95 women), 923 part-time (365 women); includes 462 minority (184 African Americans, 14 American Indian/Alaska Native, 153 Asian Americans or Pacific Islanders, 111 Hispanic Americans), 184 international. Average age 34. 474 applicants, 85% accepted, 237 enrolled. In 2009, 399 master's awarded. *Entrance requirements:* Additional exam requirements/recommendations for international students: Required—TOEFL. *Application deadline:* Applications are processed on a rolling basis. Application fee: $50. Electronic applications accepted. *Expenses:* Contact institution. *Financial support:* In 2009–10, 399 students received support. Scholarships/grants and unspecified assistantships available. Financial award application deadline: 2/15; financial award applicants required to submit FAFSA. *Unit head:* Alounda Joseph, Director of Enrollment Processes, 972-721-5356, E-mail: admiss@gsm.udallas.edu. *Application contact:* Alounda Joseph, Director of Enrollment Processes, 972-721-5356, E-mail: admiss@gsm.udallas.edu.

University of Dayton, Graduate School, School of Business Administration, Dayton, OH 45469-1300. Offers accounting (MBA); business intelligence (MBA); entrepreneurship (MBA); finance (MBA); international business (MBA); marketing (MBA); MIS (MBA); operations management (MBA); technology-enhanced business/e-commerce (MBA); JD/MBA. *Accreditation:* AACSB. Part-time and evening/weekend programs available. *Faculty:* 29 full-time (8 women), 15 part-time/adjunct (2 women). *Students:* 134 full-time (48 women), 111 part-time (31 women); includes 14 minority (9 African Americans, 3 Asian Americans or Pacific Islanders, 2 Hispanic Americans), 29 international. Average age 29. 179 applicants, 63% accepted, 73 enrolled. In 2009, 102 master's awarded. *Entrance requirements:* For master's, GMAT. Additional exam requirements/recommendations for international students: Required—TOEFL (minimum score 550 paper-based; 213 computer-based; 79 iBT). *Application deadline:* For fall admission, 3/1 priority date for international students; for winter admission, 7/1 priority date for international students; for spring admission, 1/1 priority date for international students. Applications are processed on a rolling basis. Application fee: $0 ($50 for international students). Electronic applications accepted. *Expenses:* Contact institution. *Financial support:* In 2009–10, 13 fellowships with partial tuition reimbursements, 17 research assistantships with full and partial tuition reimbursements (averaging $7,020 per year) were awarded; career-related internships or fieldwork, institutionally sponsored loans, scholarships/grants, health care benefits, and unspecified assistantships also available. Support available to part-time students. Financial award application deadline: 3/15; financial award applicants required to submit FAFSA. *Faculty research:* Management information systems, economics, finance, entrepreneurship, marketing. *Unit head:* Janice M. Glynn, Director, MBA Program, 937-229-3733, Fax: 937-229-3882, E-mail: glynn@udayton.edu. *Application contact:* Jeffrey Carter, Assistant Director, MBA Program, 937-229-3733, Fax: 937-229-3882, E-mail: jeff.carter@notes.udayton.edu.

University of Delaware, Alfred Lerner College of Business and Economics, Department of Finance, Newark, DE 19716. Offers MS.

University of Denver, Daniels College of Business, Department of Finance, Denver, CO 80208. Offers IMBA, MBA, MS. Part-time and evening/weekend programs available. *Faculty:* 14 full-time (4 women). *Students:* 63 full-time (27 women), 83 part-time (36 women); includes 7 minority (2 African Americans, 3 Asian Americans or Pacific Islanders, 2 Hispanic Americans), 92 international. Average age 26. 306 applicants, 64% accepted, 55 enrolled. In 2009, 107 master's awarded. *Entrance requirements:* For master's, GMAT. *Application deadline:* For fall admission, 1/15 priority date for domestic students. Applications are processed on a rolling basis. Application fee: $50. Electronic applications accepted. *Expenses:* Tuition: Full-time $34,596; part-time $961 per quarter hour. Required fees: $4 per quarter hour. Tuition and fees vary according to course load, campus/location and program. *Financial support:* Career-related internships or fieldwork, Federal Work-Study, institutionally sponsored loans, and scholarships/grants available. Support available to part-time students. Financial award application deadline: 2/15; financial award applicants required to submit FAFSA. *Unit head:* Dr. Ron Rizzuto, Co-Director, 303-871-2010. *Application contact:* Information Contact, 303-871-3416, Fax: 303-871-4466, E-mail: daniels@du.edu.

The University of Findlay, Graduate and Professional Studies, College of Business, Findlay, OH 45840-3653. Offers financial management (MBA); human resource management (MBA); international management (MBA); management (MBA); marketing (MBA); public management (MBA). Part-time and evening/weekend programs available. Postbaccalaureate distance learning degree programs offered (no on-campus study). *Degree requirements:* For master's, thesis, cumulative project. *Entrance requirements:* For master's, GMAT, minimum undergraduate GPA of 3.0 in last 64 hours of course work. Additional exam requirements/recommendations for international students: Required—TOEFL (minimum score 550 paper-based; 213 computer-based; 80 iBT). Electronic applications accepted. *Expenses:* Contact institution. *Faculty research:* Health care management, operations and logistics management.

University of Florida, Graduate School, Warrington College of Business Administration, Hough Graduate School of Business, Department of Finance, Insurance and Real Estate, Gainesville, FL 32611. Offers business administration (MS), including entrepreneurship, insurance, real estate and urban analysis, retailing; finance (PhD); financial services (Certificate); insurance (PhD); real estate and urban analysis (PhD); JD/MS. Terminal master's awarded for partial completion of doctoral program. *Degree requirements:* For doctorate, thesis/dissertation. *Entrance requirements:* For master's, GMAT or GRE General Test, minimum GPA of 3.0 for last 60 hours of undergraduate degree, work experience (preferred); for doctorate, GMAT or GRE General Test, minimum GPA of 3.0. Additional exam requirements/recommendations for international students: Required—TOEFL (minimum score 550 paper-based; 213 computer-based). Electronic applications accepted. *Faculty research:* Financial management, financial markets and institutions, investments, risk and insurance, real estate development.

University of Florida, Graduate School, Warrington College of Business Administration, Hough Graduate School of Business, Programs in Business Administration, Gainesville, FL 32611. Offers accounting (MBA); arts administration (MBA); business strategy and public policy (MBA); competitive strategy (MBA); decision and information sciences (MBA); electronic commerce (MBA); finance (MBA); general business (MBA); global management (MBA); Graham-Buffett security analysis (MBA); health administration (MBA); human resources management (MBA); international studies (MBA); Latin American business (MBA); management (MBA); marketing (MBA); sports administration (MBA); JD/MBA; MBA/MS; MBA/PhD; MBA/Pharm D; MD/MBA. *Accreditation:* AACSB. Part-time and evening/weekend programs available. Postbaccalaureate distance learning degree programs offered. *Entrance requirements:* For master's, GMAT, minimum GPA of 3.0, interview. Additional exam requirements/recommendations for international students: Required—TOEFL (minimum score 550 paper-based; 213 computer-based). Electronic applications accepted. *Faculty research:* Accounting, finance, insurance, management, real estate and urban analysis marketing.

University of Hawaii at Manoa, Graduate Division, Shidler College of Business, Program in Business Administration, Honolulu, HI 96822. Offers Asian business studies (MBA); Chinese business studies (MBA); decision sciences (MBA); entrepreneurship (MBA); finance (MBA); finance and banking (MBA); human resources management (MBA); information management (MBA); information technology (MBA); international business (MBA); Japanese business studies (MBA); marketing (MBA); organizational behavior (MBA); organizational management (MBA); real estate (MBA); student-designed track (MBA). *Accreditation:* AACSB. Part-time and evening/weekend programs available. *Faculty:* 46 full-time (8 women), 9 part-time/adjunct (4 women). *Students:* 259 full-time (90 women), 105 part-time (43 women); includes 123 minority (118 Asian Americans or Pacific Islanders, 5 Hispanic Americans), 119 international. Average age 32. 336 applicants, 52% accepted, 150 enrolled. In 2009, 113 master's awarded. *Degree requirements:* For master's, thesis optional. *Entrance requirements:* For master's, GMAT, minimum GPA of 3.0. Additional exam requirements/recommendations for international students: Required—TOEFL (minimum score 600 paper-based; 250 computer-based; 100 iBT), IELTS (minimum score 7). *Application deadline:* For fall admission, 5/1 for domestic students, 3/1 for international students. Application fee: $60. *Expenses:* Contact institution. *Financial support:* In 2009–10, 24 students received support, including 98 fellowships (averaging $3,481 per year), 3 research assistantships (averaging $16,626 per year). Total annual research expenditures: $427,000. *Application contact:* Tung Bui, Graduate Chair, 808-956-5565, Fax: 808-956-9889, E-mail: tung.bui@hawaii.edu.

University of Hawaii at Manoa, Graduate Division, Shidler College of Business, Program in International Management, Honolulu, HI 96822. Offers Asian finance (PhD); global information technology management (PhD); international accounting (PhD); international marketing (PhD); international organization and strategy (PhD). Part-time programs available. *Students:* 28 full-time (12 women), 5 part-time (0 women); includes 7 minority (all Asian Americans or Pacific Islanders), 17 international. Average age 33. 65 applicants, 18% accepted, 5 enrolled. In 2009, 1 doctorate awarded. *Degree requirements:* For doctorate, comprehensive exam, thesis/dissertation. *Entrance requirements:* For doctorate, GMAT or GRE General Test, minimum GPA of 3.0. Additional exam requirements/recommendations for international students: Required—TOEFL (minimum score 600 paper-based; 250 computer-based; 100 iBT), IELTS (minimum score 7). *Application deadline:* For fall admission, 3/1 for domestic and international students. Application fee: $60. *Expenses:* Contact institution. *Financial support:* In 2009–10, 2 fellowships (averaging $6,945 per year), 21 research assistantships (averaging $17,766 per year) were awarded. *Application contact:* Erica Okada, Graduate Chair, 808-956-6723, Fax: 808-956-6889, E-mail: emokada@hawaii.edu.

University of Houston, Bauer College of Business, Finance Program, Houston, TX 77204. Offers MS, PhD. Part-time and evening/weekend programs available. *Faculty:* 8 full-time (1 woman), 8 part-time/adjunct (4 women). *Students:* 25 full-time (7 women), 29 part-time (3 women); includes 11 minority (2 African Americans, 5 Asian Americans or Pacific Islanders, 4 Hispanic Americans), 21 international. Average age 29. 44 applicants, 75% accepted, 21 enrolled. In 2009, 29 master's awarded. *Degree requirements:* For master's, 30 hours completed in residence; for doctorate, minimum GPA of 3.25, continuous full time enrollment, dissertation defense within 6 years of entering the program. *Entrance requirements:* For master's, GMAT, letters of recommendation, resume; for doctorate, GMAT or GRE, letter of financial backing, statement of understanding, reference letters, statement of academic and research interests. Additional exam requirements/recommendations for international students: Required—TOEFL (minimum score 603 paper-based; 250 computer-based; 100 iBT). *Application deadline:* For fall admission, 6/1 for domestic students, 4/1 for international students; for spring admission, 11/1 for domestic students, 10/1 for international students. Applications are processed on a rolling basis. Application fee: $75. Electronic applications accepted. *Expenses:* Tuition, state resident: full-time $7676; part-time $320 per credit hour. Tuition, nonresident: full-time $14,324; part-time $597 per credit hour. Required fees: $3034. *Financial support:* In 2009–10, 3 fellowships with full tuition reimbursements (averaging $8,700 per year), 23 teaching assistantships with full tuition reimbursements (averaging $7,100 per year) were awarded; research assistantships with full tuition reimbursements, career-related internships or fieldwork, Federal Work-Study, institutionally sponsored loans, scholarships/grants, health care benefits, and unspecified assistantships also available. Support available to part-time students. Financial award application deadline: 2/1; financial award applicants required to submit FAFSA. *Faculty research:* Accountancy and taxation, finance, international business, management. *Unit head:* Dr. Praveen Kumar, Chairperson, 713-743-4755, E-mail: pkumar@uh.edu.

University of Houston–Clear Lake, School of Business, Program in Finance, Houston, TX 77058-1098. Offers MS. Part-time and evening/weekend programs available. *Degree requirements:* For master's, thesis optional. *Entrance requirements:* For master's, GMAT. Additional exam requirements/recommendations for international students: Required—TOEFL (minimum score 550 paper-based; 213 computer-based). Electronic applications accepted.

Finance and Banking

University of Houston–Victoria, School of Business Administration, Victoria, TX 77901-4450. Offers accounting (MBA); economic development and entrepreneurship (MS); finance (GMBA, MBA); general business (MBA); international business (MBA); management (GMBA, MBA); marketing (MBA). *Accreditation:* AACSB. Part-time and evening/weekend programs available. Postbaccalaureate distance learning degree programs offered (no on-campus study). *Entrance requirements:* For master's, GMAT. Additional exam requirements/recommendations for international students: Required—TOEFL (minimum score 550 paper-based; 213 computer-based). Electronic applications accepted. *Faculty research:* Economic development, marketing, finance.

University of Illinois at Urbana–Champaign, Graduate College, College of Business, Department of Finance, Champaign, IL 61820. Offers MS, PhD. *Faculty:* 19 full-time (1 woman), 4 part-time/adjunct (1 woman). *Students:* 148 full-time (64 women), 5 part-time (3 women); includes 13 minority (3 African Americans, 10 Asian Americans or Pacific Islanders), 120 international. 826 applicants, 24% accepted, 115 enrolled. In 2009, 111 master's awarded. *Entrance requirements:* For master's and doctorate, GMAT or GRE, minimum GPA of 3.0. Additional exam requirements/recommendations for international students: Required—TOEFL. *Application deadline:* Applications are processed on a rolling basis. Application fee: $60 ($75 for international students). Electronic applications accepted. *Financial support:* In 2009–10, 6 fellowships, 15 research assistantships, 3 teaching assistantships were awarded; tuition waivers (full and partial) also available. *Unit head:* Charles M. Kahn, Chair, 217-333-2813, Fax: 217-244-3102, E-mail: c-kahn@illinois.edu. *Application contact:* H. Catherine Tyler, Office Manager, 217-244-9203, Fax: 217-244-9867, E-mail: tylerc@illinois.edu.

The University of Iowa, Henry B. Tippie College of Business, Department of Finance, Iowa City, IA 52242-1316. Offers business administration (PhD), including finance. *Faculty:* 19 full-time (1 woman), 1 part-time/adjunct (0 women). *Students:* 13 full-time (6 women), 10 international. Average age 29. 94 applicants, 3% accepted, 2 enrolled. *Degree requirements:* For doctorate, comprehensive exam, thesis/dissertation, thesis defense. *Entrance requirements:* For doctorate, GMAT or GRE. Additional exam requirements/recommendations for international students: Required—TOEFL (minimum score 600 paper-based; 250 computer-based; 100 iBT). *Application deadline:* For fall admission, 1/31 for domestic and international students. Applications are processed on a rolling basis. Application fee: $60 ($85 for international students). Electronic applications accepted. *Financial support:* In 2009–10, 13 students received support, including 13 fellowships with partial tuition reimbursements available (averaging $6,000 per year), 12 teaching assistantships with full tuition reimbursements available (averaging $16,575 per year); institutionally sponsored loans, scholarships/grants, health care benefits, and unspecified assistantships also available. Financial award application deadline: 1/31. *Faculty research:* International finance, real estate finance, theoretical and empirical corporate finance, theoretical and empirical asset pricing bond pricing and derivatives. *Unit head:* Prof. Paul Weller, Department Executive Officer, 319-335-0929, Fax: 319-335-3690, E-mail: paul-weller@uiowa.edu. *Application contact:* Renea L. Jay, PhD Program Coordinator, 319-335-0830, Fax: 319-335-1956, E-mail: renea-jay@uiowa.edu.

The University of Iowa, Henry B. Tippie College of Business, Henry B. Tippie School of Management, Iowa City, IA 52242-1316. Offers corporate finance (MBA); investment management (MBA); marketing (MBA); process excellence (MBA); strategic innovation (MBA); JD/MBA; MBA/MA; MBA/MD; MBA/MHA; MBA/MSN. *Accreditation:* AACSB. Part-time and evening/weekend programs available. *Faculty:* 46 full-time (7 women), 12 part-time/adjunct (2 women). *Students:* 250 full-time (64 women), 794 part-time (277 women); includes 92 minority (17 African Americans, 2 American Indian/Alaska Native, 52 Asian Americans or Pacific Islanders, 21 Hispanic Americans), 146 international. Average age 32. 602 applicants, 60% accepted, 302 enrolled. In 2009, 348 master's awarded. *Entrance requirements:* For master's, GMAT, work experience, references. Additional exam requirements/recommendations for international students: Required—TOEFL (minimum score 600 paper-based; 250 computer-based; 100 iBT), IELTS (minimum score 7). *Application deadline:* For fall admission, 7/30 for domestic students, 4/15 for international students; for spring admission, 12/15 for domestic and international students. Applications are processed on a rolling basis. Application fee: $60 ($100 for international students). Electronic applications accepted. *Expenses:* Contact institution. *Financial support:* In 2009–10, 100 students received support, including 100 fellowships (averaging $6,819 per year), 92 research assistantships with partial tuition reimbursements available (averaging $10,388 per year); career-related internships or fieldwork, scholarships/grants, health care benefits, and unspecified assistantships also available. Financial award application deadline: 4/15; financial award applicants required to submit FAFSA. *Faculty research:* Capital markets, econometrics, optimization, investments and empirical corporate finance, Iowa electronic markets. *Unit head:* Prof. Jarjisu Sa-Aadu, Associate Dean, MBA Programs, 800-622-4692, Fax: 319-335-3604, E-mail: jsa-aadu@uiowa.edu. *Application contact:* Jodi Schafer, Director of Admissions and Financial Aid, 319-335-0864, Fax: 319-335-3604, E-mail: jodi-schafer@uiowa.edu.

University of La Verne, College of Business and Public Management, Graduate Programs in Business Administration, La Verne, CA 91750-4443. Offers accounting (MBA); executive management (MBA-EP); finance (MBA, MBA-EP); health services management (MBA); information technology (MBA, MBA-EP); international business (MBA, MBA-EP); leadership (MBA-EP); managed care (MBA); management (MBA, MBA-EP); marketing (MBA, MBA-EP). Part-time and evening/weekend programs available. *Faculty:* 22 full-time (11 women), 41 part-time/adjunct (8 women). *Students:* 409 full-time (213 women), 156 part-time (74 women); includes 371 minority (23 African Americans, 7 American Indian/Alaska Native, 259 Asian Americans or Pacific Islanders, 82 Hispanic Americans), 9 international. Average age 29. In 2009, 356 master's awarded. *Entrance requirements:* For master's, minimum undergraduate GPA of 3.0, 2 letters of recommendation, resume. Additional exam requirements/recommendations for international students: Required—TOEFL (minimum score 550 paper-based; 213 computer-based). *Application deadline:* Applications are processed on a rolling basis. Application fee: $50. *Expenses:* Contact institution. *Financial support:* Career-related internships or fieldwork, institutionally sponsored loans, and scholarships/grants available. Financial award application deadline: 3/2; financial award applicants required to submit FAFSA. *Unit head:* Dr. Abe Helou, Chairperson, 909-593-3511 Ext. 4211, Fax: 909-392-2704, E-mail: ihelou@laverne.edu. *Application contact:* Rina Lazarian, Program and Admission Specialist, 909-593-3511 Ext. 4819, Fax: 909-392-2704, E-mail: cbpm@ulv.edu.

University of Lethbridge, School of Graduate Studies, Lethbridge, AB T1K 3M4, Canada. Offers accounting (MScM); addictions counseling (M Sc); agricultural biotechnology (M Sc); agricultural studies (M Sc, MA); anthropology (MA); archaeology (MA); art (MA, MFA); biochemistry (M Sc); biological sciences (M Sc); biomolecular science (PhD); biosystems and biodiversity (PhD); Canadian studies (MA); chemistry (M Sc); computer science (M Sc); computer science and geographical information science (M Sc); counseling psychology (M Ed); dramatic arts (MA); earth, space, and physical science (PhD); economics (MA); educational leadership (M Ed); English (MA); environmental science (M Sc); evolution and behavior (PhD); exercise science (M Sc); finance (MScM); French (MA); French/German (MA); French/Spanish (MA); general education (M Ed); general management (MScM); geography (M Sc, MA); German (MA); health science (M Sc); health sciences (MA); history (MA); human resource management and labour relations (MScM); individualized multidisciplinary (M Sc, MA); information systems (MScM); international management (MScM); kinesiology (M Sc, MA); management (M Sc, MA); marketing (MScM); mathematics (M Sc); music (M Mus, MA); Native American studies (MA); neuroscience (M Sc, PhD); new media (MA); nursing (M Sc); philosophy (MA); physics (M Sc); policy and strategy (MScM); political science (MA); psychology (M Sc, MA); religious studies (MA); social sciences (MA); sociology (MA); theatre and dramatic arts (MFA); theoretical and computational science (PhD); urban and regional studies (MA); women's studies (MA). Part-time and evening/weekend programs available. *Degree requirements:* For doctorate, comprehensive exam, thesis/dissertation. *Entrance requirements:* For master's, GMAT (M Sc in management), bachelor's degree in related field, minimum GPA of 3.0 during previous 20 graded semester courses, 2 years teaching or related experience (M Ed); for doctorate, master's degree, minimum graduate GPA of 3.5. Additional exam requirements/recommendations for international students: Required—TOEFL. *Faculty research:* Movement and brain plasticity, gibberellin physiology, photosynthesis, carbon cycling, molecular properties of main-group ring components.

University of Maryland University College, Graduate School of Management and Technology, Program in Accounting and Financial Management, Adelphi, MD 20783. Offers MS, Certificate. Part-time and evening/weekend programs available. Postbaccalaureate distance learning degree programs offered (no on-campus study). *Students:* 17 full-time (11 women), 585 part-time (387 women); includes 281 minority (198 African Americans, 2 American Indian/Alaska Native, 48 Asian Americans or Pacific Islanders, 33 Hispanic Americans), 21 international. Average age 36. 142 applicants, 100% accepted, 100 enrolled. In 2009, 83 master's awarded. *Degree requirements:* For master's, thesis or alternative. *Application deadline:* Applications are processed on a rolling basis. Application fee: $50. Electronic applications accepted. *Expenses:* Tuition, state resident: full-time $7704; part-time $428 per credit hour. Tuition, nonresident: full-time $11,862; part-time $659 per credit hour. *Financial support:* Federal Work-Study and scholarships/grants available. Support available to part-time students. Financial award application deadline: 6/1; financial award applicants required to submit FAFSA. *Unit head:* Dr. James Howard, Program Director, Finance, 240-684-2400, Fax: 240-684-2401, E-mail: jhoward@umuc.edu. *Application contact:* Coordinator, Graduate Admissions, 800-888-UMUC, Fax: 240-684-2151, E-mail: newgrad@umuc.edu.

University of Maryland University College, Graduate School of Management and Technology, Program in Financial Management and Information Systems, Adelphi, MD 20783. Offers MS, Certificate. Part-time and evening/weekend programs available. Postbaccalaureate distance learning degree programs offered (no on-campus study). *Students:* 7 full-time (2 women), 177 part-time (88 women); includes 105 minority (87 African Americans, 11 Asian Americans or Pacific Islanders, 7 Hispanic Americans), 4 international. Average age 34. In 2009, 13 master's, 1 other advanced degree awarded. *Degree requirements:* For master's, thesis or alternative. *Application deadline:* Applications are processed on a rolling basis. Application fee: $50. Electronic applications accepted. *Expenses:* Tuition, state resident: full-time $7704; part-time $428 per credit hour. Tuition, nonresident: full-time $11,862; part-time $659 per credit hour. *Financial support:* Federal Work-Study and scholarships/grants available. Support available to part-time students. Financial award application deadline: 6/1; financial award applicants required to submit FAFSA. *Unit head:* Dr. Jayanta Sen, Program Director, Finance and Management, 240-684-2400, Fax: 240-684-2401, E-mail: jsen@umuc.edu. *Application contact:* Coordinator, Graduate Admissions, 800-888-UMUC, Fax: 240-684-2151, E-mail: newgrad@umuc.edu.

University of Massachusetts Dartmouth, Graduate School, Charlton College of Business, Program in Business Administration, North Dartmouth, MA 02747-2300. Offers accounting (Postbaccalaureate Certificate); business administration (MBA); e-commerce (PMC); finance (PMC); general management (PMC); leadership (PMC); management (Postbaccalaureate Certificate); marketing (PMC); supply chain management (PMC). *Accreditation:* AACSB. Part-time programs available. *Faculty:* 42 full-time (13 women), 26 part-time/adjunct (6 women). *Students:* 93 full-time (41 women), 132 part-time (64 women); includes 22 minority (5 African Americans, 2 American Indian/Alaska Native, 6 Asian Americans or Pacific Islanders, 9 Hispanic Americans), 42 international. Average age 30. 186 applicants, 82% accepted, 94 enrolled. In 2009, 55 master's, 19 other advanced degrees awarded. *Entrance requirements:* For master's, GMAT, resume, letters of recommendation. Additional exam requirements/recommendations for international students: Required—TOEFL (minimum score 500 paper-based; 200 computer-based; 72 iBT). *Application deadline:* For fall admission, 6/1 for domestic students, 5/1 for international students; for spring admission, 10/1 for domestic students, 8/1 for international students. Application fee: $40 ($60 for international students). Electronic applications accepted. *Expenses:* Tuition, state resident: full-time $2071; part-time $86.29 per credit. Tuition, nonresident: full-time $8099; part-time $337.46 per credit. Required fees: $9446. Tuition and fees vary according to class time, course load and reciprocity agreements. *Financial support:* In 2009–10, 1 research assistantship with full tuition reimbursement (averaging $6,000 per year) was awarded; teaching assistantships, Federal Work-Study and unspecified assistantships also available. Support available to part-time students. Financial award application deadline: 3/1; financial award applicants required to submit FAFSA. *Faculty research:* Competitiveness of south coast enterprises, global sales, key performance indicators, agile manufacturing, green business. Total annual research expenditures: $19,000. *Unit head:* Dr. Norm Barber, Assistant Dean, 508-999-8543, E-mail: nbarber@umassd.edu. *Application contact:* Elan Turcotte-Shamski, Graduate Admissions Officer, 508-999-8604, Fax: 508-999-8183, E-mail: graduate@umassd.edu.

University of Memphis, Graduate School, Fogelman College of Business and Economics, Program in Business Administration, Memphis, TN 38152. Offers accounting (MBA, PhD); economics (MBA, PhD); executive business administration (MBA); finance (PhD); finance, insurance, and real estate (MBA, MS); international business administration (IMBA); management (MBA, MS, PhD); management information systems (MBA, MS, PhD); management science (MBA); marketing (MBA, MS); marketing and supply chain management (PhD); real estate development (MS); JD/MBA. *Accreditation:* AACSB. *Faculty:* 44 full-time (9 women), 5 part-time/adjunct (0 women). *Students:* 263 full-time (106 women), 181 part-time (66 women); includes 70 minority (46 African Americans, 3 American Indian/Alaska Native, 16 Asian Americans or Pacific Islanders, 5 Hispanic Americans), 109 international. Average age 31. 374 applicants, 73% accepted, 119 enrolled. In 2009, 140 master's, 17 doctorates awarded. *Degree requirements:* For master's, comprehensive exam; for doctorate, comprehensive exam, thesis/dissertation. *Entrance requirements:* For master's, GMAT, resume; for doctorate, GMAT, interview, minimum GPA of 3.4, resume, letter of recommendation. Additional exam requirements/recommendations for international students: Required—TOEFL (minimum score 550 paper-based; 220 computer-based). *Application deadline:* For fall admission, 8/1 for domestic students; for spring admission, 12/1 for domestic students. Application fee: $35 ($60 for international students). *Expenses:* Tuition, state resident: full-time $6246; part-time $347 per credit hour. Tuition, nonresident: full-time $15,894; part-time $883 per credit hour. Required fees: $1160. Full-time tuition and fees vary according to course load, degree level and program. *Financial support:* In 2009–10, 164 students received support; research assistantships with full tuition reimbursements available, teaching assistantships with full tuition reimbursements available, career-related internships or fieldwork, Federal Work-Study, scholarships/grants, and unspecified assistantships available. Financial award application deadline: 2/15; financial award applicants required to submit FAFSA. *Faculty research:* Competitive business strategy, finance microstructures, supply chain management innovations, health care economics, litigation risks and corporate audits. *Unit head:* Rajiv Grover, Dean, 901-678-3759, E-mail: rgrover@memphis.edu. *Application contact:* Dr. Carol V. Danehower, Associate Dean for Programs, 901-678-5402, Fax: 901-678-3579, E-mail: fcbegp@memphis.edu.

University of Miami, Graduate School, School of Business Administration, Program in Business Administration, Coral Gables, FL 33124. Offers accounting (MBA); computer information systems (MBA); executive and professional (MBA), including international business, management; finance (MBA); international business (MBA); management (MBA); management science (MBA); marketing (MBA); professional management (MSPM); JD/MBA; MBA/MSIE. *Accreditation:* AACSB. Evening/weekend programs available. *Degree requirements:* For master's, comprehensive exam. *Entrance requirements:* For master's, GMAT. Additional exam requirements/recommendations for international students: Required—TOEFL (minimum score 550 paper-based; 213 computer-based; 59 iBT). Electronic applications accepted. *Faculty research:* Leadership, e-commerce, supply chain management.

University of Michigan–Dearborn, School of Management, Dearborn, MI 48128-1491. Offers accounting (MBA, MS); finance (MBA, MS); information systems (MS); international business (MBA); management (MBA); management information systems (MBA); marketing (MBA); supply chain management (MBA); MBA/MHSA; MBA/MSE; MBA/MSF. *Accreditation:* AACSB. Part-time and evening/weekend programs available. Postbaccalaureate distance learning degree programs offered (no on-campus study). *Faculty:* 26 full-time (6 women), 8 part-time/adjunct (4 women). *Students:* 73 full-time (30 women), 412 part-time (134 women); includes 65 minority (20 African Americans, 1 American Indian/Alaska Native, 38 Asian Americans or Pacific

Islanders, 6 Hispanic Americans), 76 international. Average age 30. 185 applicants, 56% accepted, 78 enrolled. In 2009, 151 master's awarded. *Entrance requirements:* For master's, GMAT, 2 years of work experience (MBA); course work in computer applications, statistics, and pre-calculus or finite mathematics; 18 credits of accounting course work beyond introductory courses (MS in accounting). Additional exam requirements/recommendations for international students: Required—TOEFL (minimum score 560 paper-based; 220 computer-based; 84 iBT). *Application deadline:* For fall admission, 8/1 priority date for domestic students, 6/1 for international students; for winter admission, 12/1 priority date for domestic students, 10/1 for international students; for spring admission, 4/1 priority date for domestic students, 2/1 for international students. Applications are processed on a rolling basis. Application fee: $60. Electronic applications accepted. *Expenses:* Contact institution. *Financial support:* Career-related internships or fieldwork, Federal Work-Study, and scholarships/grants available. Support available to part-time students. Financial award application deadline: 9/1; financial award applicants required to submit FAFSA. *Faculty research:* Cultural diversity, buyer-supplier relations, error detection in data, economic evolution. *Unit head:* Dr. Kim Schatzel, Dean, 313-593-5248, Fax: 313-271-9835, E-mail: schatzel@umd.umich.edu. *Application contact:* Joan Doherty, Academic Advisor/Counselor, 313-593-5460, Fax: 313-271-9838, E-mail: gradbusiness@umd.umich.edu.

University of Minnesota, Twin Cities Campus, Carlson School of Management, Carlson Full-Time MBA Program, Minneapolis, MN 55455. Offers finance (MBA); information technology (MBA); management (MBA); marketing (MBA); medical industry orientation (MBA); supply chain and operations (MBA); JD/MBA; MBA/MPP; MD/MBA; MHA/MBA; Pharm D/MBA. *Accreditation:* AACSB. *Faculty:* 60 full-time (11 women), 15 part-time/adjunct (7 women). *Students:* 217 full-time (78 women); includes 23 minority (6 African Americans, 1 American Indian/Alaska Native, 14 Asian Americans or Pacific Islanders, 2 Hispanic Americans), 41 international. Average age 28. 548 applicants, 41% accepted, 104 enrolled. In 2009, 91 master's awarded. *Entrance requirements:* For master's, GMAT. Additional exam requirements/recommendations for international students: Required—TOEFL (minimum score 580 paper-based; 240 computer-based; 82 iBT), or IELTS (minimum score 7), or Pearson Test of English (PTE). *Application deadline:* For fall admission, 4/1 for domestic students, 2/1 for international students. Application fee: $60 ($90 for international students). Electronic applications accepted. *Expenses:* Contact institution. *Financial support:* In 2009–10, 107 students received support, including 107 fellowships with full and partial tuition reimbursements available (averaging $22,174 per year); research assistantships with partial tuition reimbursements available, teaching assistantships with partial tuition reimbursements available, career-related internships or fieldwork, Federal Work-Study, institutionally sponsored loans, scholarships/grants, health care benefits, and unspecified assistantships also available. Financial award application deadline: 2/1; financial award applicants required to submit FAFSA. *Unit head:* Kathryn J. Carlson, Assistant Dean, MBA Programs and Graduate Business Career Center, 612-625-5555, Fax: 612-625-1012, E-mail: mba@umn.edu. *Application contact:* Tracy J. Keeling, Associate Director of Admissions, Full-Time and Part-Time MBA Programs, 612-625-5555, Fax: 612-625-1012, E-mail: mba@umn.edu.

University of Minnesota, Twin Cities Campus, Carlson School of Management, Carlson Part-Time MBA Program, Minneapolis, MN 55455. Offers finance (MBA); information technology (MBA); management (MBA); marketing (MBA); supply chain and operations (MBA); JD/MBA; MBA/MPP; MD/MBA; MHA/MBA; Pharm D/MBA. Part-time and evening/weekend programs available. *Faculty:* 72 full-time (15 women), 26 part-time/adjunct (5 women). *Students:* 1,861 part-time (606 women); includes 188 minority (31 African Americans, 1 American Indian/Alaska Native, 132 Asian Americans or Pacific Islanders, 24 Hispanic Americans), 121 international. Average age 29. 387 applicants, 67% accepted, 238 enrolled. In 2009, 393 master's awarded. *Entrance requirements:* For master's, GMAT. Additional exam requirements/recommendations for international students: Required—TOEFL (minimum score 580 paper-based; 240 computer-based; 82 iBT), IELTS (minimum score 7) or Pearson Test of English (PTE) Academic. *Application deadline:* For fall admission, 5/1 priority date for domestic and international students; for spring admission, 10/1 priority date for domestic and international students. Application fee: $60 ($90 for international students). Electronic applications accepted. *Expenses:* Contact institution. *Financial support:* Applicants required to submit FAFSA. *Faculty research:* Strategy, IT, finance, marketing, operations, supply chain, entrepreneurship, quality management, accounting. *Unit head:* Kathryn J. Carlson, Assistant Dean, MBA Programs and Graduate Business Career Center, 612-624-2039, Fax: 612-625-1012, E-mail: mba@umn.edu. *Application contact:* Tracy J. Keeling, Associate Director of Admissions, Full-Time and Part-Time MBA Programs, 612-625-5555, Fax: 612-625-1012, E-mail: mba@umn.edu.

University of Minnesota, Twin Cities Campus, Carlson School of Management, Doctoral Program in Business Administration, Minneapolis, MN 55455-0213. Offers accounting (PhD); finance (PhD); information and decision sciences (PhD); marketing and logistics management (PhD); operations and management science (PhD); strategic management and organization (PhD). *Faculty:* 74 full-time (19 women). *Students:* 68 full-time (28 women); includes 7 minority (1 African American, 3 Asian Americans or Pacific Islanders, 3 Hispanic Americans), 46 international. Average age 29. 250 applicants, 5% accepted, 9 enrolled. In 2009, 11 doctorates awarded. *Degree requirements:* For doctorate, comprehensive exam, thesis/dissertation, written and oral preliminary exams, proposal defense. *Entrance requirements:* For doctorate, GMAT, GRE General Test. Additional exam requirements/recommendations for international students: Required—TOEFL (minimum score 600 paper-based; 250 computer-based; 100 iBT), IELTS (minimum score 7.5). *Application deadline:* For fall admission, 12/31 for domestic students, 12/31 priority date for international students. Applications are processed on a rolling basis. Application fee: $55 ($75 for international students). Electronic applications accepted. *Financial support:* In 2009–10, 68 fellowships with full tuition reimbursements (averaging $11,500 per year), 63 research assistantships with full tuition reimbursements (averaging $6,750 per year), 53 teaching assistantships with full tuition reimbursements (averaging $6,750 per year) were awarded; institutionally sponsored loans, scholarships/grants, health care benefits, and unspecified assistantships also available. Financial award application deadline: 12/31. *Faculty research:* Corporate strategy, finance, entrepreneurship, marketing, information and decision science, operations, accounting. Total annual research expenditures: $300,000. *Unit head:* Dr. Shawn P. Curley, Director of Graduate Studies/Program Director, 612-624-6546, Fax: 612-624-8221, E-mail: curley@umn.edu. *Application contact:* Earlene K. Bronson, Assistant Director, 612-624-0875, Fax: 612-624-8221, E-mail: brons003@umn.edu.

University of Missouri–St. Louis, College of Business Administration, Program in Business Administration, St. Louis, MO 63121. Offers accounting (MBA); business administration (Certificate); finance (MBA); human resource management (Certificate); logistics and supply chain management (MBA, Certificate); management (MBA); marketing (MBA); marketing management (Certificate); operations (MBA); quantitative management science (MBA). *Accreditation:* AACSB. Part-time and evening/weekend programs available. *Faculty:* 30 full-time (5 women), 11 part-time/adjunct (2 women). *Students:* 107 full-time (47 women), 310 part-time (120 women); includes 32 minority (17 African Americans, 6 Asian Americans or Pacific Islanders, 9 Hispanic Americans), 66 international. Average age 31. 285 applicants, 58% accepted, 130 enrolled. In 2009, 149 master's, 13 other advanced degrees awarded. *Entrance requirements:* For master's, GMAT, 2 letters of recommendation. Additional exam requirements/recommendations for international students: Required—TOEFL (minimum score 550 paper-based; 213 computer-based). *Application deadline:* For fall admission, 7/1 for domestic students; for spring admission, 11/1 for domestic students. Applications are processed on a rolling basis. Application fee: $35 ($40 for international students). Electronic applications accepted. *Expenses:* Tuition, state resident: full-time $5377; part-time $297.70 per credit hour. Tuition, nonresident: full-time $13,882; part-time $771.20 per credit hour. Required fees: $220; $12.20 per credit hour. One-time fee: $12. Tuition and fees vary according to course level, campus/location and program. *Financial support:* In 2009–10, 27 research assistantships with full and partial tuition reimbursements (averaging $8,525 per year), 6 teaching assistantships with full and partial tuition reimbursements (averaging $13,950 per year) were awarded; career-related internships or fieldwork, Federal Work-Study, and institutionally sponsored loans also available. Support available to part-time students. Financial award application deadline: 4/1; financial award

applicants required to submit FAFSA. *Faculty research:* Human resources, strategic management, marketing strategy, consumer behavior product development, advertising. *Unit head:* Karl Kottemann, Assistant Director, 314-516-5885, Fax: 314-516-6420, E-mail: mba@umsl.edu. *Application contact:* 314-516-5458, Fax: 314-516-6996, E-mail: gradadm@umsl.edu.

University of Nebraska–Lincoln, Graduate College, College of Business Administration, Interdepartmental Area of Business, Department of Finance, Lincoln, NE 68588. Offers business (MA, PhD). *Degree requirements:* For doctorate, comprehensive exam, thesis/dissertation. *Entrance requirements:* For master's and doctorate, GMAT. Additional exam requirements/recommendations for international students: Required—TOEFL (minimum score 100 iBT). Electronic applications accepted. *Faculty research:* Banking, investments, international finance, insurance, corporate finance.

University of Nevada, Reno, Graduate School, College of Business Administration, Department of Finance, Reno, NV 89557. Offers MS. Part-time programs available. *Degree requirements:* For master's, thesis optional. *Entrance requirements:* For master's, GMAT or GRE, minimum GPA of 2.75. Additional exam requirements/recommendations for international students: Required—TOEFL (minimum score 500 paper-based; 173 computer-based; 61 iBT), IELTS (minimum score 6). Electronic applications accepted. *Faculty research:* Financial business problems, economic theory, financial concepts theory.

University of New Haven, Graduate School, School of Business, Program in Business Administration, West Haven, CT 06516-1916. Offers accounting (MBA, Certificate), including CPA (MBA); business management (Certificate); business policy and strategy (MBA); finance (MBA), including CFA; global marketing (MBA); human resource management (Certificate); human resources management (MBA); international business (Certificate); marketing (Certificate); sports management (MBA); telcommunications management (Certificate); MBA/MPA. Part-time and evening/weekend programs available. *Faculty:* 26 full-time (3 women), 23 part-time/adjunct (5 women). *Students:* 302 full-time (120 women), 194 part-time (101 women); includes 109 minority (56 African Americans, 3 American Indian/Alaska Native, 28 Asian Americans or Pacific Islanders, 22 Hispanic Americans), 110 international. Average age 31. 372 applicants, 83% accepted, 172 enrolled. In 2009, 194 master's, 31 other advanced degrees awarded. *Degree requirements:* For master's, thesis or alternative. *Entrance requirements:* For master's, GMAT. Additional exam requirements/recommendations for international students: Required—TOEFL (minimum score 520 paper-based; 190 computer-based; 70 iBT), IELTS (minimum score 5.5). *Application deadline:* For fall admission, 5/31 for international students; for winter admission, 10/15 for international students; for spring admission, 1/15 for international students. Applications are processed on a rolling basis. Application fee: $50. Electronic applications accepted. *Expenses:* Contact institution. *Financial support:* Research assistantships with partial tuition reimbursements, teaching assistantships with partial tuition reimbursements, Federal Work-Study, scholarships/grants, health care benefits, tuition waivers, and unspecified assistantships available. Support available to part-time students. Financial award applicants required to submit FAFSA. *Unit head:* Charles Coleman, Chairman, 203-932-7375. *Application contact:* Eloise Gormley, Director of Graduate Admissions, 203-932-7449, Fax: 203-932-7137, E-mail: gradinfo@newhaven.edu.

University of New Haven, Graduate School, School of Business, Program in Finance and Financial Services, West Haven, CT 06516-1916. Offers finance (Certificate); finance and financial services (MS). In 2009, 1 master's, 3 other advanced degrees awarded. *Application deadline:* Applications are processed on a rolling basis. Application fee: $50. *Expenses:* Tuition: Part-time $700 per credit. Required fees: $45 per term. One-time fee: $390 part-time. *Financial support:* Career-related internships or fieldwork and Federal Work-Study available. Financial award application deadline: 5/1; financial award applicants required to submit FAFSA. *Unit head:* Dr. S. Shapiro, Coordinator, 203-932-7496. *Application contact:* Eloise Gormley, Director of Graduate Admissions, 203-932-7449, Fax: 203-932-7137, E-mail: gradinfo@newhaven.edu.

University of New Mexico, Robert O. Anderson Graduate School of Management, Department of Finance, International, Technology and Entrepreneurship, Albuquerque, NM 87131-1221. Offers finance (MBA); international management (MBA); international management in Latin America (MBA); management of technology (MBA). Part-time and evening/weekend programs available. *Faculty:* 12 full-time (0 women), 5 part-time/adjunct (1 woman). *Students:* 46 full-time (18 women), 28 part-time (9 women); includes 31 minority (1 African American, 2 American Indian/Alaska Native, 10 Asian Americans or Pacific Islanders, 18 Hispanic Americans), 7 international. Average age 30. 30 applicants, 97% accepted, 27 enrolled. In 2009, 43 master's awarded. *Entrance requirements:* For master's, GMAT or GRE (can be waived in some instances). Additional exam requirements/recommendations for international students: Required—TOEFL (minimum score 550 paper-based; 213 computer-based; 79 iBT). *Application deadline:* For fall admission, 4/1 priority date for domestic students, 5/1 for international students; for spring admission, 10/1 priority date for domestic students, 10/1 for international students. Applications are processed on a rolling basis. Application fee: $50. Electronic applications accepted. *Expenses:* Tuition, state resident: full-time $2099; part-time $233.20 per credit hour. Tuition, nonresident: full-time $6650. Required fees: $25 per semester. Tuition and fees vary according to course load, program and reciprocity agreements. *Financial support:* Fellowships, research assistantships, teaching assistantships, career-related internships or fieldwork, Federal Work-Study, scholarships/grants, and unspecified assistantships available. Support available to part-time students. Financial award application deadline: 6/1. *Faculty research:* Corporate finance, investments, management in Latin America, management of technology, entrepreneurship. *Unit head:* Dr. Raul de Gouvea, Chair, 505-277-6471, Fax: 505-277-7108. *Application contact:* Megan Conner, Academic Advisement Manager, 505-277-3290, Fax: 505-277-8436, E-mail: mconner@mgt.unm.edu.

University of New Orleans, Graduate School, College of Business Administration, Department of Economics and Finance, New Orleans, LA 70148. Offers economics and finance (MS); financial economics (PhD). *Accreditation:* AACSB. Terminal master's awarded for partial completion of doctoral program. *Degree requirements:* For master's, thesis optional; for doctorate, one foreign language, comprehensive exam, thesis/dissertation, general exams. *Entrance requirements:* For doctorate, GRE General Test, minimum GPA of 3.0. Additional exam requirements/recommendations for international students: Required—TOEFL (minimum score 550 paper-based; 213 computer-based; 79 iBT). *Faculty research:* Monetary economics, international economics, urban economics, real estate.

The University of North Carolina at Chapel Hill, Kenan-Flagler Business School, Doctoral Program in Business Administration, Chapel Hill, NC 27599. Offers accounting (PhD); finance (PhD); marketing (PhD); operations management (PhD); organizational behavior (PhD); strategy (PhD). *Accreditation:* AACSB. *Degree requirements:* For doctorate, thesis/dissertation. *Entrance requirements:* For doctorate, GMAT or GRE General Test. Electronic applications accepted. *Expenses:* Contact institution.

The University of North Carolina at Greensboro, Graduate School, Bryan School of Business and Economics, Department of Accounting, Greensboro, NC 27412-5001. Offers accounting (MS); accounting systems (MS); financial accounting and reporting (MS); financial analysis (PMC); tax concentration (MS). *Accreditation:* AACSB. *Entrance requirements:* For master's, GMAT, GRE General Test, previous course work in accounting and business. Additional exam requirements/recommendations for international students: Required—TOEFL. Electronic applications accepted.

University of North Texas, Robert B. Toulouse School of Graduate Studies, College of Business Administration, Department of Finance, Insurance, Real Estate, and Law, Denton, TX 76203. Offers finance (PhD); finance, insurance, real estate, and law (MS); real estate (MS). Part-time programs available. *Degree requirements:* For master's, thesis optional; for doctorate, comprehensive exam, thesis/dissertation. *Entrance requirements:* For master's, GMAT; for doctorate, GMAT or GRE General Test. Additional exam requirements/recommendations for international students: Recommended—TOEFL (minimum score 550 paper-based; 213 computer-based; 79 iBT). Application fee: $50 ($75 for international students).

Finance and Banking

University of North Texas (continued)

Expenses: Tuition, state resident: full-time $4298; part-time $239 per contact hour. Tuition, nonresident: full-time $9878; part-time $549 per contact hour. Required fees: $265 per contact hour. *Financial support:* Fellowships, research assistantships, teaching assistantships, career-related internships or fieldwork and tuition waivers (partial) available. Financial award application deadline: 4/1; financial award applicants required to submit FAFSA. *Faculty research:* Financial impact of regulation, risk management, taxes and valuation, bankruptcy, real financial options. *Application contact:* PhD Advisor, 940-565-2511, Fax: 940-565-4234, E-mail: john.kensinger@unt.edu.

University of Oregon, Graduate School, Charles H. Lundquist College of Business, Department of Finance, Eugene, OR 97403. Offers PhD. Part-time programs available. Terminal master's awarded for partial completion of doctoral program. *Degree requirements:* For doctorate, thesis/dissertation, 2 comprehensive exams. *Entrance requirements:* For doctorate, GMAT. Additional exam requirements/recommendations for international students: Required—TOEFL. *Faculty research:* Changes in firm value in response to corporate takeovers and defenses, capital structure, regulatory changes, financial intermediaries.

University of Ottawa, Faculty of Graduate and Postdoctoral Studies, Interdisciplinary Programs, Ottawa, ON K1N 6N5, Canada. Offers e-business (Certificate); e-commerce (Certificate); finance (Certificate); health services and policies research (Diploma); population health (PhD); population health risk assessment and management (Certificate); public management and governance (Certificate); systems science (Certificate).

University of Pennsylvania, Wharton School, Finance Department, Philadelphia, PA 19104. Offers MBA, PhD. *Degree requirements:* For doctorate, thesis/dissertation. *Entrance requirements:* For doctorate, GMAT or GRE. *Expenses:* Tuition: Full-time $25,660; part-time $4758 per course. Required fees: $2152; $270 per course. Tuition and fees vary according to course load, degree level and program. *Faculty research:* Corporate finance, investments, macroeconomics, international finance.

University of Pittsburgh, Katz Graduate School of Business, Doctoral Program in Business Administration, Pittsburgh, PA 15260. Offers accounting (PhD); finance (PhD); information systems (PhD); marketing (PhD); operations/decision sciences/artificial intelligence (PhD); organizational behavior and human resource management (PhD); strategic planning (PhD). *Accreditation:* AACSB. *Faculty:* 50 full-time (15 women). *Students:* 53 full-time (21 women); includes 8 minority (4 African Americans, 2 Asian Americans or Pacific Islanders, 2 Hispanic Americans), 22 international. 324 applicants, 4% accepted, 12 enrolled. In 2009, 11 doctorates awarded. *Degree requirements:* For doctorate, comprehensive exam, thesis/dissertation. *Entrance requirements:* For doctorate, GMAT or GRE, references, work experience relevant for individual program. Additional exam requirements/recommendations for international students: Required—TOEFL or IELTS. *Application deadline:* For fall admission, 2/1 priority date for domestic and international students. Applications are processed on a rolling basis. Application fee: $50. Electronic applications accepted. *Expenses:* Tuition, state resident: full-time $16,402; part-time $665 per credit. Tuition, nonresident: full-time $28,694; part-time $1175 per credit. Required fees: $690; $175 per term. Tuition and fees vary according to program. *Financial support:* In 2009–10, 36 students received support, including 31 research assistantships with full tuition reimbursements available (averaging $18,450 per year), 5 teaching assistantships with full tuition reimbursements available (averaging $23,511 per year); fellowships, Federal Work-Study, scholarships/grants, health care benefits, and unspecified assistantships also available. Financial award application deadline: 2/1. *Faculty research:* Accounting statements and reporting, incentives and governance; corporate finance, mergers and acquisitions; information systems processes, structures, OR, supply chain, and decision-making; organizational structure, knowledge management, and corporate strategy; consumer behavior and marketing models. Total annual research expenditures: $362,777. *Unit head:* Dr. John E. Hulland, Director, 412-648-1534, Fax: 412-624-3633, E-mail: jhulland@katz.pitt.edu. *Application contact:* Carrie Woods, Assistant Director, 412-648-1525, Fax: 412-624-3633, E-mail: cawoods@katz.pitt.edu.

University of Pittsburgh, Katz Graduate School of Business, Masters of Business Administration Programs, Pittsburgh, PA 15260. Offers accounting (MS); finance (MBA); general management (MBA); information systems (MBA, MSIS); marketing (MBA); organizational behavior and human resource management (MBA); organizational leadership (Certificate); six sigma (Certificate); strategy (MBA); technology, innovation and entrepreneurship (Certificate); MBA/JD; MBA/MIB; MBA/MPIA; MBA/MSE; MBA/MSIS. *Accreditation:* AACSB. Part-time and evening/weekend programs available. *Faculty:* 58 full-time (12 women), 23 part-time/adjunct (7 women). *Students:* 192 full-time (62 women), 506 part-time (179 women); includes 58 minority (29 African Americans, 1 American Indian/Alaska Native, 24 Asian Americans or Pacific Islanders, 4 Hispanic Americans), 101 international. Average age 29. 674 applicants, 52% accepted, 204 enrolled. In 2009, 263 master's awarded. *Entrance requirements:* For master's, GMAT, references, work experience relevant for individual programs. Additional exam requirements/recommendations for international students: Required—TOEFL (minimum score 600 paper-based; 250 computer-based; 100 iBT), or IELTS. *Application deadline:* For fall admission, 7/1 for domestic and international students; for winter admission, 11/1 for domestic and international students; for spring admission, 3/1 for domestic and international students. Applications are processed on a rolling basis. Application fee: $50. Electronic applications accepted. *Expenses:* Tuition, state resident: full-time $16,402; part-time $665 per credit. Tuition, nonresident: full-time $28,694; part-time $1175 per credit. Required fees: $690; $175 per term. Tuition and fees vary according to program. *Financial support:* In 2009–10, 75 students received support. Career-related internships or fieldwork and scholarships/grants available. Financial award application deadline: 6/1; financial award applicants required to submit FAFSA. *Faculty research:* Accounting statements and reporting, incentives and governance; corporate finance, mergers and acquisitions; information systems processes, structures, and decision-making; organizational structure, knowledge management, and corporate strategy; consumer behavior and marketing models. *Unit head:* William T. Valenta, Assistant Dean/MBA Program Director, 412-648-1610, Fax: 412-648-1659, E-mail: wtvalenta@katz.pitt.edu. *Application contact:* Cliff McCormick, Director of MBA Admissions, 412-648-1700, Fax: 412-648-1659, E-mail: mba@katz.pitt.edu.

University of Puerto Rico, Mayagüez Campus, Graduate Studies, College of Business Administration, Mayagüez, PR 00681-9000. Offers business administration (MBA); finance (MBA); human resources (MBA); industrial management (MBA). Part-time and evening/weekend programs available. *Degree requirements:* For master's, comprehensive exam. *Entrance requirements:* For master's, GMAT or EXADEP, bachelor's degree with courses in calculus, microeconomics, accounting and statistics. Additional exam requirements/recommendations for international students: Required—TOEFL (minimum score 500 paper-based; 173 computer-based). *Faculty research:* Organizational studies, management, accounting.

University of Puerto Rico, Río Piedras, College of Business Administration, San Juan, PR 00931-3300. Offers accounting (MBA); finance (MBA, PhD); general business (MBA); human resources management (MBA); international trade and business (MBA, PhD); marketing (MBA); operations management (MBA); quantitative methods (MBA). *Accreditation:* ACBSP. Part-time programs available. *Degree requirements:* For master's, comprehensive exam, thesis or alternative, research project. *Entrance requirements:* For master's, GMAT or PAEG, minimum GPA of 3.0, letter of recommendation; for doctorate, GMAT, PAEG, minimum GPA of 3.0, master degree. *Faculty research:* Management.

University of Rhode Island, Graduate School, College of Business Administration, Kingston, RI 02881. Offers accounting (MS); business administration (MBA, PhD), including finance and insurance (PhD), management (PhD), marketing (PhD), operations and supply chain management (MBA); finance (MBA); general business (MBA); management (MBA); marketing (MBA); supply chain management (MBA). *Accreditation:* AACSB. Part-time and evening/weekend programs available. *Faculty:* 54 full-time (15 women), 2 part-time/adjunct (1 woman). *Students:* 71 full-time (27 women), 157 part-time (56 women); includes 24 minority (6 African Americans, 10 Asian Americans or Pacific Islanders, 8 Hispanic Americans), 23 international. In 2009, 86 master's, 3 doctorates awarded. *Degree requirements:* For master's, comprehensive exam (for some programs), thesis optional; for doctorate, comprehensive exam, thesis/dissertation. *Entrance requirements:* For master's, GMAT or GRE, 2 letters of recommendation, resume; for doctorate, GMAT or GRE, 3 letters of recommendation, resume. Additional exam requirements/recommendations for international students: Required—TOEFL (minimum score 575 paper-based; 233 computer-based; 91 iBT). Application fee: $65. Electronic applications accepted. *Expenses:* Tuition, state resident: full-time $8828; part-time $490 per credit hour. Tuition, nonresident: full-time $22,100; part-time $1228 per credit hour. Required fees: $1118; $57 per semester. Tuition and fees vary according to program. *Financial support:* In 2009–10, 13 teaching assistantships with full and partial tuition reimbursements (averaging $13,095 per year) were awarded. Financial award applicants required to submit FAFSA. Total annual research expenditures: $245,746. *Unit head:* Dr. Mark Higgins, Dean, 401-874-4244, Fax: 401-874-4312, E-mail: markhiggins@uri.edu. *Application contact:* Lisa Lancellotta, Coordinator, MBA Programs, 401-874-4241, Fax: 401-874-4312, E-mail: mba@uri.edu.

University of San Francisco, College of Arts and Sciences, Department of Economics, Program in Financial Analysis, San Francisco, CA 94117-1080. Offers MS, MS/MBA. *Faculty:* 8 full-time (2 women), 9 part-time/adjunct (3 women). *Students:* 93 full-time (36 women), 2 part-time (1 woman); includes 26 minority (3 African Americans, 17 Asian Americans or Pacific Islanders, 6 Hispanic Americans), 46 international. Average age 29. 375 applicants, 48% accepted, 64 enrolled. In 2009, 60 master's awarded. *Expenses:* Tuition: Full-time $19,710; part-time $1095 per unit. Part-time tuition and fees vary according to degree level, campus/location and program. *Financial support:* In 2009–10, 53 students received support. *Unit head:* Dr. John Veitch. *Application contact:* Information Contact, 415-422-5135, Fax: 415-422-6983, E-mail: asgraduate@usfca.edu.

University of San Francisco, College of Arts and Sciences, Investor Relations Program, San Francisco, CA 94117-1080. Offers MA. *Faculty:* 9 full-time (2 women), 11 part-time/adjunct (3 women). *Students:* 7 full-time (5 women), all international. Average age 28. 15 applicants, 67% accepted, 7 enrolled. *Expenses:* Tuition: Full-time $19,710; part-time $1095 per unit. Part-time tuition and fees vary according to degree level, campus/location and program. *Financial support:* In 2009–10, 7 students received support. *Unit head:* John Veitch, Chair, 415-422-6784, Fax: 415-422-5784. *Application contact:* Information Contact, 415-422-5135, Fax: 415-422-2217, E-mail: asgraduate@usfca.edu.

University of San Francisco, School of Business and Professional Studies, Masagung Graduate School of Management, Program in Business Administration, San Francisco, CA 94117-1080. Offers business economics (MBA); e-business (MBA); entrepreneurship (MBA); finance (MBA); international business (MBA); management (MBA); marketing (MBA); telecommunications management and policy (MBA); JD/MBA; MSN/MBA. *Accreditation:* AACSB. *Faculty:* 17 full-time (4 women), 16 part-time/adjunct (7 women). *Students:* 278 full-time (140 women), 18 part-time (10 women); includes 94 minority (5 African Americans, 1 American Indian/Alaska Native, 69 Asian Americans or Pacific Islanders, 19 Hispanic Americans), 53 international. Average age 30. 410 applicants, 70% accepted, 133 enrolled. In 2009, 137 master's awarded. *Entrance requirements:* For master's, GMAT, minimum undergraduate GPA of 3.2. Additional exam requirements/recommendations for international students: Required—TOEFL. *Application deadline:* For fall admission, 7/1 priority date for domestic students; for spring admission, 11/30 for domestic students. Applications are processed on a rolling basis. Application fee: $55 ($65 for international students). *Expenses:* Tuition: Full-time $19,710; part-time $1095 per unit. Part-time tuition and fees vary according to degree level, campus/location and program. *Financial support:* In 2009–10, 155 students received support; fellowships available. Financial award application deadline: 3/2; financial award applicants required to submit FAFSA. *Faculty research:* International financial markets, technology transfer licensing, international marketing, strategic planning. Total annual research expenditures: $50,000. *Unit head:* Kelly Brookes, Director, 415-422-2221, Fax: 415-422-6315. *Application contact:* Director, MBA Program, 415-422-2221, Fax: 415-422-6315, E-mail: mba@usfca.edu.

University of Saskatchewan, College of Graduate Studies and Research, Edwards School of Business, Department of Finance and Management Science, Saskatoon, SK S7N 5A2, Canada. Offers finance (M Sc). Part-time programs available. *Degree requirements:* For master's, thesis. *Entrance requirements:* For master's, GMAT. Additional exam requirements/recommendations for international students: Required—TOEFL. Tuition and fees charges are reported in Canadian dollars. *Expenses:* Tuition, area resident: Full-time $3000 Canadian dollars; part-time $500 Canadian dollars per term. Required fees: $700 Canadian dollars; $100 Canadian dollars per term.

The University of Scranton, College of Graduate and Continuing Education, Program in Business Administration, Scranton, PA 18510. Offers accounting (MBA); finance (MBA); general business administration (MBA); health care management (MBA); international business (MBA); management information systems (MBA); marketing (MBA); operations management (MBA). *Accreditation:* AACSB. Part-time and evening/weekend programs available. Postbaccalaureate distance learning degree programs offered (no on-campus study). *Faculty:* 34 full-time (8 women). *Students:* 92 full-time (38 women), 137 part-time (58 women); includes 27 minority (15 African Americans, 5 Asian Americans or Pacific Islanders, 7 Hispanic Americans), 21 international. Average age 31. 255 applicants, 79% accepted. In 2009, 33 master's awarded. *Degree requirements:* For master's, capstone experience. *Entrance requirements:* For master's, GMAT, minimum GPA of 2.75. Additional exam requirements/recommendations for international students: Required—TOEFL (minimum score 500 paper-based; 173 computer-based), IELTS (minimum score 5.5). *Application deadline:* Applications are processed on a rolling basis. Application fee: $0. *Financial support:* In 2009–10, 10 students received support, including 10 teaching assistantships with full and partial tuition reimbursements available (averaging $6,600 per year); fellowships, career-related internships or fieldwork, Federal Work-Study, and unspecified assistantships also available. Support available to part-time students. Financial award application deadline: 3/1. *Faculty research:* Financial markets, strategic impact of total quality management, internal accounting controls, consumer preference, information systems and the Internet. *Unit head:* Dr. Murli Rajan, Director, 570-941-4043, Fax: 570-941-4342. *Application contact:* Joseph M. Roback, Director of Admissions, 570-941-4385, Fax: 570-941-5928, E-mail: robackj2@scranton.edu.

University of Southern Maine, School of Business, Portland, ME 04104-9300. Offers business administration (MBA); finance (MBA); taxation (MBA); JD/MBA; MBA/MSA; MBA/MSN; MS/MBA. *Accreditation:* AACSB. Part-time and evening/weekend programs available. *Faculty:* 20 full-time (5 women), 2 part-time/adjunct (1 woman). *Students:* 33 full-time (19 women), 102 part-time (42 women); includes 6 minority (2 African Americans, 1 American Indian/Alaska Native, 2 Asian Americans or Pacific Islanders, 1 Hispanic American), 4 international. Average age 32. 53 applicants, 55% accepted, 23 enrolled. In 2009, 45 master's awarded. *Entrance requirements:* For master's, GMAT, minimum AACSB index of 1100. Additional exam requirements/recommendations for international students: Required—TOEFL (minimum score 550 paper-based; 213 computer-based; 79 iBT). *Application deadline:* For fall admission, 8/1 priority date for domestic students, 5/1 priority date for international students; for spring admission, 12/1 priority date for domestic students, 9/1 priority date for international students. Applications are processed on a rolling basis. Application fee: $65. Electronic applications accepted. *Financial support:* In 2009–10, 3 research assistantships with partial tuition reimbursements (averaging $9,000 per year), 3 teaching assistantships with partial tuition reimbursements (averaging $9,000 per year) were awarded; career-related internships or fieldwork, Federal Work-Study, scholarships/grants, tuition waivers (full and partial), and unspecified assistantships also available. Support available to part-time students. Financial award application deadline: 2/15; financial award applicants required to submit FAFSA. *Faculty research:* Economic development, MIS, real options, system dynamics, simulation. *Unit head:* James B. Shaffer, Dean, 207-780-4020, Fax: 207-780-4662, E-mail: jshaffer@usm.maine.edu. *Application contact:* Alice B. Cash, Assistant Dean for Student Affairs, 207-780-4184, Fax: 207-780-4662, E-mail: acash@usm.maine.edu.

University of South Florida, Graduate School, College of Business, Department of Business Administration, Tampa, FL 33620-9951. Offers accounting (PhD); entrepreneurship (MBA); finance (PhD); information systems (PhD); leadership and organizational effectiveness (MSM); management and organization (MBA); marketing (PhD). *Accreditation:* AACSB. Part-time and evening/weekend programs available. *Faculty:* 12 full-time (2 women). *Students:* 152 full-time (51 women), 201 part-time (65 women); includes 70 minority (14 African Americans, 30 Asian Americans or Pacific Islanders, 26 Hispanic Americans), 54 international. Average age 32. 460 applicants, 35% accepted, 93 enrolled. In 2009, 161 master's, 11 doctorates awarded. *Degree requirements:* For master's, comprehensive exam, thesis (for some programs); for doctorate, comprehensive exam, thesis/dissertation, 90 credit hours, minimum GPA of 3.0. *Entrance requirements:* For master's, GMAT, minimum GPA of 3.0 in last 60 hours of course work, 2 years of work experience, resume; for doctorate, GMAT, letters of recommendation, personal statement. Additional exam requirements/recommendations for international students: Required—TOEFL (minimum score 550 paper-based; 213 computer-based; 79 iBT). *Application deadline:* For fall admission, 6/1 for domestic students, 1/2 for international students; for spring admission, 10/15 for domestic students, 6/1 for international students. Application fee: $30. *Financial support:* Fellowships, research assistantships, teaching assistantships, scholarships/grants, health care benefits, and unspecified assistantships available. Financial award applicants required to submit FAFSA. *Unit head:* Irene Hurst, Program Director, 813-974-3335, Fax: 813-974-4518, E-mail: hurst@coba.usf.edu. *Application contact:* Wendy Baker, Assistant Director, Graduate Studies, 813-974-3335, Fax: 813-974-4518, E-mail: wbaker@usf.edu.

University of South Florida, Graduate School, College of Business, Department of Finance, Tampa, FL 33620-9951. Offers business (PhD), including finance; finance (MS); real estate (MS). Part-time and evening/weekend programs available. *Faculty:* 12 full-time (2 women). *Students:* 10 full-time (3 women), 12 part-time (3 women); includes 6 minority (4 African Americans, 2 Hispanic Americans), 4 international. Average age 32. 86 applicants, 38% accepted, 7 enrolled. In 2009, 8 master's awarded. Terminal master's awarded for partial completion of doctoral program. *Degree requirements:* For master's, thesis or alternative, 30 credits, minimum GPA of 3.0; for doctorate, comprehensive exam, thesis/dissertation. *Entrance requirements:* For master's, GMAT, minimum GPA of 3.0; for doctorate, GMAT, letters of recommendation, personal statement. Additional exam requirements/recommendations for international students: Required—TOEFL (minimum score 550 paper-based; 213 computer-based; 79 iBT). *Application deadline:* For fall admission, 6/1 for domestic students, 1/2 for international students; for spring admission, 10/15 for domestic students, 6/1 for international students. Application fee: $30. Electronic applications accepted. *Financial support:* In 2009–10, teaching assistantships with tuition reimbursements (averaging $22,083 per year); scholarships/grants, health care benefits, and unspecified assistantships also available. Financial award application deadline: 6/30. *Faculty research:* Corporate governance, international finance, asset pricing models, risk management, market efficiency. Total annual research expenditures: $75,865. *Unit head:* Dr. Scott Besley, Chairperson, 813-974-2081, Fax: 813-974-3084, E-mail: sbesley@coba.usf.edu. *Application contact:* Dr. Scott Besley, Chairperson, 813-974-2081, Fax: 813-974-3084, E-mail: sbesley@coba.usf.edu.

The University of Tampa, John H. Sykes College of Business, Tampa, FL 33606-1490. Offers accounting (MBA, MS); economics (MBA); entrepreneurship and innovation (MBA); finance (MBA, MS); information systems management (MBA); international business (MBA); management (MBA); marketing (MBA, MS); nonprofit management (MBA). *Accreditation:* AACSB. Part-time and evening/weekend programs available. *Faculty:* 62 full-time (22 women), 11 part-time/adjunct (4 women). *Students:* 240 full-time (101 women), 338 part-time (133 women); includes 95 minority (16 African Americans, 4 American Indian/Alaska Native, 24 Asian Americans or Pacific Islanders, 51 Hispanic Americans), 122 international. Average age 29. 564 applicants, 51% accepted, 186 enrolled. In 2009, 234 master's awarded. *Entrance requirements:* For master's, GMAT. Additional exam requirements/recommendations for international students: Required—TOEFL (minimum score 577 paper-based; 230 computer-based; 90 iBT), IELTS. *Application deadline:* For fall admission, 7/15 for domestic students, 6/1 for international students; for spring admission, 12/15 for domestic students, 11/1 for international students. Applications are processed on a rolling basis. Application fee: $40. Electronic applications accepted. *Expenses:* Tuition: Part-time $488 per credit hour. *Financial support:* In 2009–10, 332 students received support, including 71 research assistantships with full tuition reimbursements available (averaging $6,757 per year); career-related internships or fieldwork, scholarships/grants, and unspecified assistantships also available. Support available to part-time students. Financial award applicants required to submit FAFSA. *Faculty research:* Information systems, leadership, corporate governance, entrepreneurship, hedonic price estimation. *Unit head:* Dr. Don Morrill, Associate Dean, Graduate and Continuing Studies, 813-257-3557, E-mail: dmorrill@ut.edu. *Application contact:* Karen Full, Director of Admissions, Graduate and Continuing Studies, 813-257-3642, E-mail: kfull@ut.edu.

The University of Tennessee, Graduate School, College of Business Administration, Program in Business Administration, Knoxville, TN 37996. Offers accounting (PhD); finance (MBA, PhD); logistics and transportation (MBA, PhD); management (PhD); marketing (MBA, PhD); operations management (MBA); professional business administration (MBA); statistics (PhD); JD/MBA; MS/MBA. *Accreditation:* AACSB. Postbaccalaureate distance learning degree programs offered. *Degree requirements:* For master's, thesis or alternative; for doctorate, thesis/dissertation. *Entrance requirements:* For master's and doctorate, GMAT, minimum GPA of 2.7. Additional exam requirements/recommendations for international students: Required—TOEFL. Electronic applications accepted. *Expenses:* Tuition, state resident: full-time $6826; part-time $380 per semester hour. Tuition, nonresident: full-time $21,844; part-time $1147 per semester hour. Tuition and fees vary according to program.

The University of Texas at Arlington, Graduate School, College of Business, Program in Business Administration, Arlington, TX 76019. Offers accounting (PhD); business statistics (PhD); finance (MBA, PhD); information systems (MBA, PhD); management (MBA, PhD); management sciences (MBA); marketing (MBA, PhD); operations management (PhD); real estate (MBA). *Accreditation:* AACSB. Part-time and evening/weekend programs available. Postbaccalaureate distance learning degree programs offered (no on-campus study). *Students:* 587 full-time (188 women), 349 part-time (140 women); includes 188 minority (66 African Americans, 62 Asian Americans or Pacific Islanders, 60 Hispanic Americans), 371 international. 282 applicants, 96% accepted, 145 enrolled. In 2009, 431 master's awarded. Terminal master's awarded for partial completion of doctoral program. *Degree requirements:* For master's, thesis optional; for doctorate, comprehensive exam, thesis/dissertation. *Entrance requirements:* For master's, GMAT; for doctorate, GMAT, minimum GPA of 3.0 (undergraduate), 3.4 (graduate); 30 hours of graduate course work. Additional exam requirements/recommendations for international students: Required—TOEFL (minimum score 550 paper-based; 213 computer-based; 79 iBT). *Application deadline:* For fall admission, 6/5 for domestic students, 4/1 for international students; for spring admission, 10/15 for domestic students, 9/1 for international students. Applications are processed on a rolling basis. Application fee: $35 ($50 for international students). Electronic applications accepted. *Financial support:* In 2009–10, 1 fellowship (averaging $1,000 per year), 30 research assistantships (averaging $6,000 per year), 45 teaching assistantships (averaging $13,000 per year) were awarded; career-related internships or fieldwork, scholarships/grants, and unspecified assistantships also available. Financial award application deadline: 6/1; financial award applicants required to submit FAFSA. *Unit head:* Greg Frazier, Director PhD Programs, 817-272-3559, Fax: 817-272-5799, E-mail: frazier@exchange.uta.edu. *Application contact:* Melanie McGee, Director of MBA Program, 817-272-0658, Fax: 817-272-5799, E-mail: mwmcgee@uta.edu.

See Close-Up on page 273.

The University of Texas at Austin, Graduate School, McCombs School of Business, Department of Finance, Austin, TX 78712-1111. Offers PhD. *Entrance requirements:* For doctorate, GMAT or GRE. Electronic applications accepted.

The University of Texas at Dallas, School of Management, Program in Accounting and Information Management, Richardson, TX 75080. Offers assurance services (MS); financial planning and analysis (MS); information management (MS); international services (MS); management consulting (MS); software management (MS); taxation services (MS). *Accreditation:* AACSB. *Faculty:* 19 full-time (4 women), 10 part-time/adjunct (3 women). *Students:* 295 full-time (173 women), 275 part-time (156 women); includes 172 minority (29 African Americans, 3 American Indian/Alaska Native, 108 Asian Americans or Pacific Islanders, 32 Hispanic Americans), 171 international. Average age 29. 356 applicants, 74% accepted, 203 enrolled. In 2009, 254 master's awarded. *Entrance requirements:* For master's, GMAT. Additional exam requirements/recommendations for international students: Required—TOEFL (minimum score 550 paper-based; 213 computer-based). *Application deadline:* For fall admission, 7/15 for domestic students, 5/1 priority date for international students; for spring admission, 11/15 for domestic students, 9/1 priority date for international students. Applications are processed on a rolling basis. Application fee: $50 ($100 for international students). Electronic applications accepted. *Expenses:* Tuition, state resident: full-time $11,068; part-time $461 per credit hour. Tuition, nonresident: full-time $21,178; part-time $882 per credit hour. Tuition and fees vary according to course load. *Financial support:* In 2009–10, 3 research assistantships with full tuition reimbursements (averaging $10,072 per year), 4 teaching assistantships with full tuition reimbursements (averaging $10,050 per year) were awarded; fellowships, career-related internships or fieldwork, Federal Work-Study, institutionally sponsored loans, scholarships/grants, and unspecified assistantships also available. Support available to part-time students. Financial award application deadline: 4/30; financial award applicants required to submit FAFSA. *Faculty research:* Privatization and accounting/auditing, corporate performance and executive compensation, risk management, information technology in accounting. *Unit head:* Amy Troutman, Assistant Director, 972-883-6719, Fax: 972-883-6823, E-mail: amybass@utdallas.edu. *Application contact:* James Parker, Assistant Director of Graduate Recruitment, 972-883-5842, E-mail: jparker@utdallas.edu.

The University of Texas at Dallas, School of Management, Program in Finance, Richardson, TX 75080. Offers MS. Part-time and evening/weekend programs available. *Faculty:* 14 full-time (2 women), 3 part-time/adjunct (2 women). *Students:* 103 full-time (41 women), 43 part-time (14 women); includes 28 minority (5 African Americans, 18 Asian Americans or Pacific Islanders, 5 Hispanic Americans), 83 international. Average age 27. 195 applicants, 65% accepted, 85 enrolled. In 2009, 9 master's awarded. *Entrance requirements:* For master's, GMAT. Additional exam requirements/recommendations for international students: Required—TOEFL (minimum score 550 paper-based; 213 computer-based). *Application deadline:* For fall admission, 7/15 for domestic students, 5/1 priority date for international students; for spring admission, 11/15 for domestic students, 9/1 priority date for international students. Applications are processed on a rolling basis. Application fee: $50 ($100 for international students). Electronic applications accepted. *Expenses:* Tuition, state resident: full-time $11,068; part-time $461 per credit hour. Tuition, nonresident: full-time $21,178; part-time $882 per credit hour. Tuition and fees vary according to course load. *Financial support:* In 2009–10, 2 research assistantships with full tuition reimbursements (averaging $13,509 per year), 4 teaching assistantships with full tuition reimbursements (averaging $11,137 per year) were awarded; career-related internships or fieldwork, Federal Work-Study, institutionally sponsored loans, scholarships/grants, and unspecified assistantships also available. Support available to part-time students. Financial award application deadline: 4/30; financial award applicants required to submit FAFSA. *Faculty research:* Econometrics, industrial organization, auction theory, file-sharing copyrights and bundling, international financial management, entrepreneurial finance. *Unit head:* Robert Kieschnick, Area Coordinator, 972-883-2718. *Application contact:* James Parker, Assistant Director, 972-883-5842, E-mail: jparker@utdallas.edu.

The University of Texas at Dallas, School of Management, Programs in Management Science, Richardson, TX 75080. Offers accounting (PhD); decision sciences (PhD); finance (PhD); management strategy and public policy (PhD); marketing (PhD); organizational behavior (PhD). *Accreditation:* AACSB. Part-time and evening/weekend programs available. *Faculty:* 12 full-time (3 women). *Students:* 72 full-time (23 women), 12 part-time (6 women); includes 10 minority (all Asian Americans or Pacific Islanders), 63 international. Average age 34. 173 applicants, 12% accepted, 7 enrolled. In 2009, 8 doctorates awarded. *Degree requirements:* For doctorate, thesis/dissertation. *Entrance requirements:* For doctorate, GMAT, minimum GPA of 3.0. Additional exam requirements/recommendations for international students: Required—TOEFL (minimum score 550 paper-based; 213 computer-based). *Application deadline:* For fall admission, 7/15 for domestic students, 5/1 priority date for international students; for spring admission, 11/15 for domestic students, 9/1 priority date for international students. Applications are processed on a rolling basis. Application fee: $50 ($100 for international students). Electronic applications accepted. *Expenses:* Tuition, state resident: full-time $11,068; part-time $461 per credit hour. Tuition, nonresident: full-time $21,178; part-time $882 per credit hour. Tuition and fees vary according to course load. *Financial support:* In 2009–10, 1 research assistantship with full tuition reimbursement (averaging $13,050 per year), 43 teaching assistantships with full tuition reimbursements (averaging $14,795 per year) were awarded; fellowships, career-related internships or fieldwork, Federal Work-Study, institutionally sponsored loans, scholarships/grants, and unspecified assistantships also available. Support available to part-time students. Financial award application deadline: 4/30; financial award applicants required to submit FAFSA. *Faculty research:* Empirical generalizations in marketing, diffusion of generations of technology, stochastic brand-choice theory, acceptance of trade deals by supermarkets, nonparametric estimations of market share response. *Unit head:* Dr. Sumit Sarkar, Program Director, 972-883-2745, Fax: 972-883-5977, E-mail: som-phd.@utdallas.edu. *Application contact:* James Parker, Assistant Director, 972-883-5842, E-mail: jparker@utdallas.edu.

The University of Texas at San Antonio, College of Business, Department of Finance, San Antonio, TX 78249-0617. Offers business administration-finance (PhD); business finance (MBA); finance (MS). Part-time and evening/weekend programs available. *Faculty:* 11 full-time (0 women). *Students:* 31 full-time (8 women), 57 part-time (10 women); includes 40 minority (2 African Americans, 10 Asian Americans or Pacific Islanders, 28 Hispanic Americans), 27 international. Average age 29. 61 applicants, 49% accepted, 22 enrolled. In 2009, 29 master's awarded. *Degree requirements:* For master's, comprehensive exam (for some programs), thesis (for some programs). *Entrance requirements:* For master's, GMAT, minimum GPA of 3.0. Additional exam requirements/recommendations for international students: Required—TOEFL (minimum score 500 paper-based; 173 computer-based; 61 iBT), IELTS (minimum score 5). *Application deadline:* For fall admission, 7/1 for domestic students, 4/1 for international students; for spring admission, 11/1 for domestic students, 9/1 for international students. Applications are processed on a rolling basis. Application fee: $45 ($85 for international students). Electronic applications accepted. *Expenses:* Tuition, state resident: full-time $3975; part-time $221 per contact hour. Tuition, nonresident: full-time $13,947; part-time $775 per contact hour. Required fees: $1853. *Financial support:* In 2009–10, 6 students received support, including 1 research assistantship (averaging $10,400 per year), 11 teaching assistantships (averaging $8,564 per year); career-related internships or fieldwork, scholarships/grants, tuition waivers, and unspecified assistantships also available. Support available to part-time students. *Faculty research:* Capital markets, corporate finance, asset pricing and investments, international finance, real estate, finance. *Unit head:* Dr. Keith Fairchild, Chair, 210-458-5307, Fax: 210-458-5320, E-mail: kfairchild@utsa.edu. *Application contact:* John Wald, Graduate Advisor, 210-458-6324, E-mail: john.wald@utsa.edu.

The University of Texas–Pan American, College of Business Administration, Program in International Business, Edinburg, TX 78539. Offers computer information systems (PhD); economics (PhD); finance (PhD); management (PhD); marketing (PhD). *Degree requirements:* For doctorate, comprehensive exam, thesis/dissertation. *Entrance requirements:* For doctorate, GMAT or GRE. Additional exam requirements/recommendations for international students: Required—TOEFL, IELTS. Electronic applications accepted. *Expenses:* Contact institution.

University of the West, Department of Business Administration, Rosemead, CA 91770. Offers business administration (EMBA); finance (MBA); information technology and management (MBA); international business (MBA); nonprofit organization management (MBA). Part-time and evening/weekend programs available. *Entrance requirements:* Additional exam requirements/recommendations for international students: Required—TOEFL.

Finance and Banking

The University of Toledo, College of Graduate Studies, College of Business Administration, Department of Finance and Business Economics, Toledo, OH 43606-3390. Offers MBA. Evening/weekend programs available. *Degree requirements:* For master's, thesis or alternative. *Entrance requirements:* For master's, GMAT. Additional exam requirements/recommendations for international students: Required—TOEFL. *Faculty research:* Financial management, banking, international finance, investments.

University of Tulsa, Graduate School, Collins College of Business, Master of Business Administration Program, Tulsa, OK 74104-3189. Offers accounting (MBA); business administration (MBA); energy management (MBA); finance (MBA); international business (MBA); management information systems (MBA); taxation (MBA); JD/MBA; MBA/MSCS; MBA/MSF. *Accreditation:* AACSB. Part-time and evening/weekend programs available. *Faculty:* 32 full-time (6 women). *Students:* 59 full-time (26 women), 45 part-time (18 women); includes 13 minority (4 African Americans, 4 American Indian/Alaska Native, 1 Asian American or Pacific Islander, 4 Hispanic Americans), 9 international. Average age 25. 78 applicants, 53% accepted, 30 enrolled. In 2009, 36 master's awarded. *Entrance requirements:* For master's, GMAT. Additional exam requirements/recommendations for international students: Required—TOEFL (minimum score 575 paper-based; 232 computer-based; 90 iBT), IELTS (minimum score 6.5). *Application deadline:* Applications are processed on a rolling basis. Application fee: $40. Electronic applications accepted. *Expenses:* Tuition: Full-time $16,182; part-time $899 per credit hour. Required fees: $4 per credit hour. Tuition and fees vary according to course load. *Financial support:* In 2009–10, 42 students received support, including 5 fellowships (averaging $11,894 per year), 2 research assistantships (averaging $9,322 per year), 35 teaching assistantships (averaging $8,112 per year); institutionally sponsored loans, scholarships/grants, health care benefits, tuition waivers (full and partial), and unspecified assistantships also available. Support available to part-time students. Financial award application deadline: 2/1; financial award applicants required to submit FAFSA. *Faculty research:* Accounting, energy management, finance, international business, management information systems, taxation. *Unit head:* Dr. Markham Collins, Associate Dean of the Collins College of Business, 918-631-2783, Fax: 918-631-2142, E-mail: markham-collins@utulsa.edu. *Application contact:* Dr. Markham Collins, Associate Dean of the Collins College of Business, 918-631-2783, Fax: 918-631-2142, E-mail: markham-collins@utulsa.edu.

University of Tulsa, Graduate School, Collins College of Business, Program in Finance, Tulsa, OK 74104-3189. Offers corporate finance (MS); investments and portfolio management (MS); risk management (MS); JD/MSF; MBA/MSF; MSF/MSAM. Part-time and evening/weekend programs available. *Faculty:* 10 full-time (1 woman). *Students:* 21 full-time (10 women), 7 part-time (5 women); includes 1 minority (Hispanic American), 10 international. Average age 25. 62 applicants, 52% accepted, 8 enrolled. In 2009, 11 master's awarded. *Degree requirements:* For master's, thesis optional. *Entrance requirements:* For master's, GMAT or GRE. Additional exam requirements/recommendations for international students: Required—TOEFL (minimum score 575 paper-based; 231 computer-based), IELTS (minimum score 6.5). *Application deadline:* Applications are processed on a rolling basis. Application fee: $40. Electronic applications accepted. *Expenses:* Tuition: Full-time $16,182; part-time $899 per credit hour. Required fees: $4 per credit hour. Tuition and fees vary according to course load. *Financial support:* In 2009–10, 8 students received support, including 1 research assistantship with full and partial tuition reimbursement available (averaging $12,088 per year), 7 teaching assistantships with full and partial tuition reimbursements available (averaging $9,506 per year); fellowships with full and partial tuition reimbursements available, career-related internships or fieldwork, Federal Work-Study, institutionally sponsored loans, scholarships/grants, health care benefits, tuition waivers (full and partial), and unspecified assistantships also available. Support available to part-time students. Financial award application deadline: 2/1; financial award applicants required to submit FAFSA. *Unit head:* Dr. Markham Collins, Associate Dean of the Collins College of Business, 918-631-2783, Fax: 918-631-2142, E-mail: markham-collins@utulsa.edu. *Application contact:* Dr. Markham Collins, Associate Dean of the Collins College of Business, 918-631-2783, Fax: 918-631-2142, E-mail: markham-collins@utulsa.edu.

University of Utah, Graduate School, David Eccles School of Business, Department of Finance, Salt Lake City, UT 84112. Offers MS, PhD. *Faculty:* 14 full-time (2 women), 2 part-time/adjunct (0 women). *Students:* 75 full-time (24 women), 24 part-time (6 women); includes 6 minority (1 African American, 2 Asian Americans or Pacific Islanders, 3 Hispanic Americans), 35 international. Average age 28. 162 applicants, 64% accepted, 78 enrolled. In 2009, 31 master's awarded. Terminal master's awarded for partial completion of doctoral program. *Degree requirements:* For master's, comprehensive exam; for doctorate, thesis/dissertation, oral qualifying exams, written qualifying exams, research paper. *Entrance requirements:* For master's, GMAT, minimum undergraduate GPA of 3.0; 2 prerequisite courses; for doctorate, GMAT/GRE. Additional exam requirements/recommendations for international students: Required—TOEFL (minimum score 600 paper-based; 250 computer-based; 100 iBT), IELTS (minimum score 7). *Application deadline:* For fall admission, 3/1 priority date for domestic and international students. Applications are processed on a rolling basis. Application fee: $55 ($65 for international students). Electronic applications accepted. *Expenses:* Tuition, state resident: full-time $4004; part-time $1674 per semester. Tuition, nonresident: full-time $14,134; part-time $5915 per semester. Required fees: $324 per semester. Tuition and fees vary according to course load, degree level and program. *Financial support:* In 2009–10, 11 students received support, including 7 teaching assistantships (averaging $7,950 per year); fellowships, research assistantships, tuition waivers (full and partial) and unspecified assistantships also available. Financial award application deadline: 4/1; financial award applicants required to submit FAFSA. *Faculty research:* Investment, managerial finance, corporate finance, capital budgeting, risk management. Total annual research expenditures: $116,540. *Unit head:* Dr. Uri Loewenstein, Chair, 801-581-4419, Fax: 801-581-3956, E-mail: uri.lowenstein@business.utah.edu. *Application contact:* Andrea Chmelik, Admissions and Program Coordinator, 801-585-1719, Fax: 801-581-3666, E-mail: andrea.chmelik@business.utah.edu.

University of Virginia, McIntire School of Commerce, Program in Commerce, Charlottesville, VA 22903. Offers financial services (MSC); marketing and management (MSC). *Students:* 72 full-time (25 women); includes 9 minority (1 African American, 5 Asian Americans or Pacific Islanders, 3 Hispanic Americans), 14 international. Average age 22. 144 applicants, 70% accepted. *Entrance requirements:* For master's, GMAT, 2 letters of recommendation; prerequisite course work in financial accounting, microeconomics, and introduction to business. Additional exam requirements/recommendations for international students: Required—TOEFL (minimum score 600 paper-based; 250 computer-based; 100 iBT), IELTS (minimum score 7). *Application deadline:* For fall admission, 9/15 priority date for domestic students, 1/15 priority date for international students. Applications are processed on a rolling basis. Application fee: $75. Electronic applications accepted. *Expenses:* Contact institution. *Financial support:* Scholarships/grants available. Financial award application deadline: 3/1; financial award applicants required to submit CSS PROFILE or FAFSA. *Unit head:* Ira C. Harris, Head, 434-924-8816, Fax: 434-924-7074, E-mail: ich3x@comm.virginia.edu. *Application contact:* Emma Jean Candelier, Assistant Director, Commerce Graduate Marketing and Admissions, 434-243-4992, Fax: 434-924-7074, E-mail: mscommerce@virginia.edu.

University of Washington, Graduate School, School of Public Health, Department of Health Services, Seattle, WA 98195. Offers bioinformatics (PhD); cancer prevention and control (PhD); clinical research (MS); community oriented public health practice (MPH); economics or finance (PhD); evaluation sciences (PhD); executive program (MHA); health behavior and health promotion (PhD); health care and population health research (MPH); health policy analysis and process (PhD); health policy and analysis and process (MPH); health services (MS, PhD); health services administration (EMHA, MHA); in residence program (MHA); occupational health (PhD); population health and social determinants (PhD); social and behavioral sciences (MPH); sociology and demography (PhD); JD/MHA; MHA/MBA; MHA/MD; MHA/MPA; MPH/JD; MPH/MD; MPH/MN; MPH/MPA; MPH/MSD; MPH/MSW; MPH/PhD. Part-time and evening/weekend programs available. Postbaccalaureate distance learning degree programs offered (minimal on-campus study). *Faculty:* 52 full-time (24 women), 60 part-time/adjunct (28 women). *Students:* 104 full-time (83 women), 100 part-time (76 women); includes 21 minority (6 African Americans, 1 American Indian/Alaska Native, 11 Asian Americans or Pacific Islanders, 3 Hispanic Americans), 6 international. Average age 34. 375 applicants, 17% accepted, 24 enrolled. In 2009, 33 master's awarded. Terminal master's awarded for partial completion of doctoral program. *Degree requirements:* For master's, thesis (for some programs), practicum (MPH); for doctorate, comprehensive exam, thesis/dissertation. *Entrance requirements:* For master's and doctorate, GRE General Test, minimum GPA of 3.0. Additional exam requirements/recommendations for international students: Required—TOEFL. *Application deadline:* For fall admission, 1/15 for domestic students, 11/1 for international students. Application fee: 50 Albanian leks. Electronic applications accepted. *Financial support:* In 2009–10, 64 students received support, including 10 fellowships with full and partial tuition reimbursements available (averaging $21,000 per year), 10 research assistantships with full and partial tuition reimbursements available (averaging $18,000 per year), 3 teaching assistantships with full and partial tuition reimbursements available (averaging $18,000 per year); career-related internships or fieldwork, Federal Work-Study, institutionally sponsored loans, and traineeships also available. Financial award application deadline: 2/28; financial award applicants required to submit FAFSA. *Faculty research:* Health promotion and disease prevention, maternal and child health, health services research design, program evaluation, health policy. Total annual research expenditures: $10.5 million. *Unit head:* Dr. Larry Kessler, Chair, 206-543-616-2930. *Application contact:* Kitty A. Andert, Program Manager, 206-616-2926, Fax: 206-543-3964, E-mail: kitander@u.washington.edu.

University of Washington, Tacoma, Graduate Programs, MBA Programs, Tacoma, WA 98402-3100. Offers accounting (MBA); certified financial analyst (MBA). Part-time and evening/weekend programs available. *Faculty:* 24 full-time (8 women), 3 part-time/adjunct (0 women). *Students:* 39 full-time (9 women), 10 part-time (2 women); includes 1 African American, 5 Asian Americans or Pacific Islanders, 1 Hispanic American, 1 international. Average age 33. 31 applicants, 68% accepted, 18 enrolled. In 2009, 18 master's awarded. *Entrance requirements:* For master's, GMAT, current resume, management and professional work summary, essay, 2 professional letters of recommendation. *Application deadline:* For fall admission, 4/15 priority date for domestic students. Applications are processed on a rolling basis. Application fee: $65. Electronic applications accepted. *Expenses:* Tuition, state resident: full-time $10,660; part-time $484 per credit. Tuition, nonresident: full-time $24,000; part-time $1119 per credit. Required fees: $150 per term. Tuition and fees vary according to course load and program. *Faculty research:* Leadership, bankruptcy, strategic marketing, customer Satisfaction, corporate social responsibility. *Unit head:* Dr. Shahrokh Saudagaran, Dean, 253-692-5630, Fax: 253-692-4523, E-mail: uwtmba@u.washington.edu. *Application contact:* Aubree Robinson, Academic Adviser, MBA and Undergraduate Programs, 253-692-5630, Fax: 253-692-4523, E-mail: uwtmba@u.washington.edu.

University of Waterloo, Graduate Studies, Faculty of Arts, School of Accounting and Finance, Waterloo, ON N2L 3G1, Canada. Offers accounting (M Acc, PhD); finance (M Acc); taxation (M Tax). *Degree requirements:* For master's, thesis or alternative; for doctorate, thesis/dissertation. *Entrance requirements:* For master's, honors degree, minimum B average, resumé; for doctorate, GMAT, master's degree, minimum A- average, resume. Additional exam requirements/recommendations for international students: Required—TOEFL, TWE. Electronic applications accepted. *Expenses:* Contact institution. *Faculty research:* Auditing, management accounting.

The University of Western Ontario, Richard Ivey School of Business, London, ON N6A 3K7, Canada. Offers business (EMBA, PhD); corporate strategy and leadership elective (MBA); entrepreneurship elective (MBA); finance elective (MBA); health sector stream (MBA); international management elective (MBA); marketing elective (MBA); JD/MBA. *Faculty:* 61 full-time (13 women). *Students:* 164 full-time (50 women). Average age 29. In 2009, 167 master's awarded. *Degree requirements:* For master's, thesis (for some programs); for doctorate, thesis/dissertation. *Entrance requirements:* For master's, GMAT, 2 years of full-time work experience, interview. Additional exam requirements/recommendations for international students: Required—TOEFL (minimum score 100 computer-based; 100 iBT), IELTS (minimum score 6), IELTS or TOEFL. *Application deadline:* For fall admission, 10/12 for domestic students, 8/16 for international students; for winter admission, 12/16 for domestic students, 10/12 for international students; for spring admission, 1/10 priority date for domestic students, 12/16 for international students. Applications are processed on a rolling basis. Application fee: $150 Canadian dollars. Electronic applications accepted. *Financial support:* Scholarships/grants and health care benefits available. Financial award application deadline: 1/10. *Faculty research:* Strategy, organizational behavior, international business, finance, operations management. *Unit head:* Carol Stephenson, Dean, 519-661-3285, Fax: 519-661-4126, E-mail: cstephenson@ivey.ca. *Application contact:* Niki da Silva, Director, MBA Program Services, 519-661-3419, Fax: 519-661-3431, E-mail: ndasilva@ivey.ca.

University of Wisconsin–Madison, Graduate School, Wisconsin School of Business, Doctoral Program in Finance, Investment and Banking, Madison, WI 53706-1380. Offers PhD. *Faculty:* 16 full-time (3 women), 4 part-time/adjunct (1 woman). *Students:* 10 full-time (3 women), 9 international. Average age 28. 104 applicants, 5% accepted, 3 enrolled. In 2009, 1 doctorate awarded. *Degree requirements:* For doctorate, comprehensive exam, thesis/dissertation. *Entrance requirements:* For doctorate, GMAT or GRE. Additional exam requirements/recommendations for international students: Required—Pearson Test of English (minimum score 73, written 80); Recommended—TOEFL (minimum score 623 paper-based; 263 computer-based; 106 iBT), IELTS (minimum score 7.5). *Application deadline:* For fall admission, 12/15 priority date for domestic and international students. Application fee: $56. Electronic applications accepted. *Expenses:* Tuition, state resident: part-time $594 per credit. Tuition, nonresident: part-time $1504 per credit. Required fees: $65 per credit. Tuition and fees vary according to course load, program and reciprocity agreements. *Financial support:* In 2009–10, 10 students received support, including fellowships with full tuition reimbursements available (averaging $18,567 per year), research assistantships with full tuition reimbursements available (averaging $16,506 per year), 10 teaching assistantships with full tuition reimbursements available (averaging $14,088 per year); Federal Work-Study, institutionally sponsored loans, scholarships/grants, health care benefits, and unspecified assistantships also available. Financial award application deadline: 2/1; financial award applicants required to submit FAFSA. *Faculty research:* Banking and financial institutions, business cycles, investments, derivatives, corporate finance. *Unit head:* Prof. Robert Krainer, Chair, 608-263-1253, Fax: 608-265-4195, E-mail: rkrainer@bus.wisc.edu. *Application contact:* Belle Heberling, Assistant Director for Research Programs, 608-262-3749, Fax: 608-890-0180, E-mail: phd@bus.wisc.edu.

University of Wisconsin–Madison, Graduate School, Wisconsin School of Business, MS Program in Quantitative Finance, Madison, WI 53706-1380. Offers MS. *Faculty:* 1 full-time (0 women). *Students:* 4 full-time (2 women), all international. Average age 25. 139 applicants, 3% accepted, 1 enrolled. In 2009, 3 master's awarded. *Entrance requirements:* For master's, GMAT or GRE. Additional exam requirements/recommendations for international students: Required—Pearson Test of English (minimum score 73, written 80); Recommended—TOEFL (minimum score 623 paper-based; 263 computer-based; 106 iBT), IELTS. *Application deadline:* For fall admission, 3/15 for domestic and international students. Application fee: $56. Electronic applications accepted. *Expenses:* Contact institution. *Financial support:* In 2009–10, 3 students received support, including 3 teaching assistantships with full tuition reimbursements available (averaging $9,392 per year); career-related internships or fieldwork, Federal Work-Study, institutionally sponsored loans, scholarships/grants, health care benefits, and unspecified assistantships also available. Financial award application deadline: 3/15; financial award applicants required to submit FAFSA. *Faculty research:* Capital markets, derivatives, financial markets, liquidity constraints. *Unit head:* Prof. David Brown, Director, 608-265-5281, Fax: 608-265-4195, E-mail: dbrownr@bus.wisc.edu. *Application contact:* Belle Heberling, Assistant Director for Research Programs, 608-262-3749, Fax: 608-890-0180, E-mail: ms@bus.wisc.edu.

University of Wisconsin–Madison, Graduate School, Wisconsin School of Business, Wisconsin Full-Time MBA Program, Madison, WI 53706-1380. Offers applied corporate finance (MBA);

applied security analysis (MBA); arts administration (MBA); brand and product management (MBA); entrepreneurial management (MBA); marketing research (MBA); operations and technology management (MBA); real estate (MBA); risk management and insurance (MBA); strategic human resource management (MBA); strategic management in the life and engineering sciences (MBA); supply chain management (MBA). *Faculty:* 32 full-time (5 women). *Students:* 242 full-time (74 women); includes 47 minority (16 African Americans, 3 American Indian/Alaska Native, 16 Asian Americans or Pacific Islanders, 12 Hispanic Americans), 29 international. Average age 28. 526 applicants, 32% accepted, 117 enrolled. In 2009, 106 master's awarded. *Entrance requirements:* For master's, GMAT, bachelor's or equivalent degree, 2 years of work experience, letters of recommendation. Additional exam requirements/recommendations for international students: Required—TOEFL (minimum score 600 paper-based; 250 computer-based; 100 iBT), IELTS. *Application deadline:* For fall admission, 11/4 for domestic and international students; for winter admission, 2/5 for domestic and international students; for spring admission, 5/26 for domestic students, 4/5 for international students. Applications are processed on a rolling basis. Application fee: $56. Electronic applications accepted. *Expenses:* Tuition, state resident: part-time $594 per credit. Tuition, nonresident: part-time $1504 per credit. Required fees: $65 per credit. Tuition and fees vary according to course load, program and reciprocity agreements. *Financial support:* In 2009–10, 103 students received support, including 13 fellowships with full and partial tuition reimbursements available (averaging $15,000 per year), 53 research assistantships with full tuition reimbursements available (averaging $8,000 per year), 35 teaching assistantships with full tuition reimbursements available (averaging $11,000 per year); scholarships/grants, health care benefits, and unspecified assistantships also available. Financial award application deadline: 4/5; financial award applicants required to submit FAFSA. *Unit head:* Prof. Kenneth A. Kavajecz, Associate Dean, 608-265-3494, Fax: 608-265-4192, E-mail: kkavajecz@bus.wisc.edu. *Application contact:* Maria Reis, Assistant Director of MBA Marketing and Recruiting, 608-262-4000, Fax: 608-265-4192, E-mail: mreis@bus.wisc.edu.

University of Wisconsin–Whitewater, School of Graduate Studies, College of Business and Economics, Program in Business Administration, Whitewater, WI 53190-1790. Offers finance (MBA); human resource management (MBA); information technology management (MBA); international business (MBA); management (MBA); marketing (MBA); operations and supply chain management (MBA); technology and training (MBA). *Accreditation:* AACSB. Part-time and evening/weekend programs available. Postbaccalaureate distance learning degree programs offered (no on-campus study). *Degree requirements:* For master's, thesis or alternative. *Entrance requirements:* For master's, GMAT, minimum AACSB index of 1000, minimum GPA of 2.75. Additional exam requirements/recommendations for international students: Required—TOEFL (minimum score 550 paper-based; 213 computer-based). Electronic applications accepted. *Faculty research:* Interface between social institutions and individual behavior, technology and innovation management, occupational mental health, workplace deviance and workplace romance.

See Display on page 190.

University of Wyoming, College of Business, Department of Economics and Finance, Program in Economics and Finance, Laramie, WY 82070. Offers MS. *Degree requirements:* For master's, thesis. *Entrance requirements:* For master's, GRE, minimum GPA of 3.0. Additional exam requirements/recommendations for international students: Required—TOEFL (minimum score 540 paper-based; 207 computer-based; 76 iBT). *Faculty research:* Financial economics.

University of Wyoming, College of Business, Department of Economics and Finance, Program in Finance, Laramie, WY 82070. Offers MS. Part-time programs available. *Degree requirements:* For master's, thesis. *Entrance requirements:* For master's, GMAT, GRE, minimum GPA of 3.0. Additional exam requirements/recommendations for international students: Required—TOEFL (minimum score 540 paper-based; 207 computer-based; 76 iBT). *Faculty research:* Banking.

Upper Iowa University, Online Master's Programs, Fayette, IA 52142-1857. Offers accounting (MBA); corporate financial management (MBA); global business (MBA); health and human services (MPA); higher education administration (MHEA); homeland security (MPA); human resources management (MBA); justice administration (MPA); organizational development (MBA); public personnel management (MPA); quality management (MBA). MBA also available at Madison, WI campus. Part-time programs available. Postbaccalaureate distance learning degree programs offered (no on-campus study). *Faculty:* 3 full-time (0 women), 66 part-time/adjunct (27 women). *Students:* 723 full-time (442 women). *Degree requirements:* For master's, research project. *Entrance requirements:* For master's, GMAT, GRE, or minimum GPA of 2.7 during last 60 hours. Additional exam requirements/recommendations for international students: Required—TOEFL (minimum score 570 paper-based; 230 computer-based). *Application deadline:* Applications are processed on a rolling basis. Application fee: $50. Electronic applications accepted. *Expenses:* Tuition: Full-time $6948; part-time $386 per credit hour. *Financial support:* Available to part-time students. Applicants required to submit FAFSA. *Faculty research:* Total quality management, CQI, teams, organization culture and climate, management. *Application contact:* David Hannum, Admissions Advisor, 800-603-3756, E-mail: hannumd@uiu.edu.

Valparaiso University, Graduate School, Program in International Economics and Finance, Valparaiso, IN 46383. Offers MS. Part-time and evening/weekend programs available. *Students:* 18 full-time (9 women), 4 part-time (2 women); includes 1 minority (Asian American or Pacific Islander), 17 international. Average age 23. *Entrance requirements:* For master's, 1 semester of college level calculus; 1 statistics or quantitative methods class; 2 semesters of introductory economics; 1 introductory accounting course; minimum undergraduate GPA of 3.0; 2 letters of recommendation. Additional exam requirements/recommendations for international students: Required—TOEFL (minimum score 550 paper-based; 213 computer-based; 80 iBT). Application fee: $30 ($50 for international students). *Financial support:* Available to part-time students. Applicants required to submit FAFSA. *Unit head:* Dr. David L. Rowland, Dean, Graduate Studies and Continuing Education/Associate Provost, 219-464-5313, Fax: 219-464-5381, E-mail: david.rowland@valpo.edu. *Application contact:* Jamie Haney, Coordinator of Graduate Admission, 219-464-5313, Fax: 219-464-5381, E-mail: jamie.haney@valpo.edu.

Vanderbilt University, Owen Graduate School of Management, MS in Finance Program, Nashville, TN 37240-1001. Offers MSF. *Faculty:* 34. *Students:* 34 full-time (6 women); includes 9 minority (2 African Americans, 7 Asian Americans or Pacific Islanders). Average age 26. 430 applicants, 19% accepted, 34 enrolled. *Entrance requirements:* For master's, GMAT and/or GRE. Additional exam requirements/recommendations for international students: Required—TOEFL (minimum score 640 paper-based; 105 computer-based). *Application deadline:* For fall admission, 11/2 priority date for domestic and international students; for winter admission, 1/6 priority date for domestic and international students; for spring admission, 3/1 priority date for domestic students. Application fee: $55. Electronic applications accepted. *Financial support:* Scholarships/grants available. Financial award applicants required to submit FAFSA. *Unit head:* Dr. Nick Bollen, Director, 615-322-2909, E-mail: cliff.ball@owen.vanderbilt.edu. *Application contact:* John Roeder, Program Director, 615-343-6109, Fax: 615-343-1175, E-mail: john.roeder@owen.vanderbilt.edu.

Villanova University, Villanova School of Business, Master of Science in Finance Program, Villanova, PA 19085-1699. Offers MSF. *Entrance requirements:* For master's, GMAT, prerequisite course in principles of finance. Additional exam requirements/recommendations for international students: Required—TOEFL (minimum score 550 paper-based; 213 computer-based; 80 iBT). Electronic applications accepted. *Expenses:* Tuition: Part-time $630 per credit. Required fees: $60 per credit. Part-time tuition and fees vary according to degree level and program. *Faculty research:* Derivatives, applied corporate finance, financial modeling, corporate risk management.

Villanova University, Villanova School of Business, MBA—Fast Track Program, Villanova, PA 19085. Offers finance (MBA); international business (MBA); management information systems (MBA); marketing (MBA). *Accreditation:* AACSB. Part-time and evening/weekend programs available. *Entrance requirements:* For master's, GMAT, minimum 4.5 years of professional work experience. Additional exam requirements/recommendations for international students: Required—TOEFL (minimum score 550 paper-based; 213 computer-based; 80 iBT). Electronic applications accepted. *Expenses:* Tuition: Part-time $630 per credit. Required fees: $60 per credit. Part-time tuition and fees vary according to degree level and program. *Faculty research:* Developing and leveraging technology, ethical business practices, managing for innovation and creativity, the global political economy, strategic marketing management.

Villanova University, Villanova School of Business, MBA—Flex Track Program, Villanova, PA 19085. Offers corporate management (general) (MBA); finance (MBA); international business (MBA); management information systems (MBA); marketing (MBA); JD/MBA. *Accreditation:* AACSB. Part-time and evening/weekend programs available. Postbaccalaureate distance learning degree programs offered (minimal on-campus study). *Entrance requirements:* For master's, GMAT, minimum 4.5 years work experience. Additional exam requirements/recommendations for international students: Required—TOEFL (minimum score 550 paper-based; 213 computer-based; 80 iBT). Electronic applications accepted. *Expenses:* Tuition: Part-time $630 per credit. Required fees: $60 per credit. Part-time tuition and fees vary according to degree level and program. *Faculty research:* Developing and leveraging technology, ethical business practices, managing for innovation and creativity, the global political economy, strategic marketing management.

Virginia Commonwealth University, Graduate School, School of Business, Program in Finance, Insurance, and Real Estate, Richmond, VA 23284-9005. Offers MS. *Entrance requirements:* For master's, GMAT.

Virginia International University, Business Programs Department, Fairfax, VA 22030. Offers accounting (MBA); executive management (Graduate Certificate); global logistics (MBA); health care management (MBA); human resources management (MBA); international business management (MBA); international finance (MBA); marketing management (MBA). Part-time programs available. *Faculty:* 12 part-time/adjunct (1 woman). *Students:* 138 full-time (63 women), 7 part-time (5 women); includes 7 minority (1 African American, 5 Asian Americans or Pacific Islanders, 1 Hispanic American), 136 international. Average age 27. 331 applicants, 31% accepted, 40 enrolled. In 2009, 42 master's awarded. *Entrance requirements:* For master's and Graduate Certificate, bachelor's degree. Additional exam requirements/recommendations for international students: Required—TOEFL (minimum score 550 paper-based; 213 computer-based; 80 iBT), IELTS (minimum score 6). *Application deadline:* For fall admission, 7/31 for domestic students, 7/3 for international students; for spring admission, 12/18 for domestic students, 11/20 for international students. Applications are processed on a rolling basis. Application fee: $100. Electronic applications accepted. *Expenses:* Tuition: Full-time $10,044; part-time $569 per credit. One-time fee: $75. Tuition and fees vary according to degree level. *Financial support:* In 2009–10, 10 students received support. Scholarships/grants available. Financial award application deadline: 7/1. *Unit head:* Dr. Gail Whitaker, Chair, 703-591-7042 Ext. 346, Fax: 703-591-7046, E-mail: gwhitaker@viu.edu. *Application contact:* Emily L. Kraus, Director of Admissions, 703-591-7042 Ext. 309, Fax: 703-591-7048, E-mail: admissions@viu.edu.

Virginia Polytechnic Institute and State University, Graduate School, Pamplin College of Business, Department of Finance, Blacksburg, VA 24061. Offers business administration (MS), including finance; finance (PhD). *Faculty:* 23 full-time (1 woman), 1 part-time/adjunct (0 women). *Students:* 9 full-time (2 women); all minorities (all American Indian/Alaska Native). Average age 30. 56 applicants, 7% accepted, 2 enrolled. *Entrance requirements:* For master's and doctorate, GRE, GMAT. Additional exam requirements/recommendations for international students: Required—TOEFL (minimum score 550 paper-based; 213 computer-based). *Application deadline:* For fall admission, 5/15 for international students; for spring admission, 10/15 for international students. Applications are processed on a rolling basis. Application fee: $65. Electronic applications accepted. *Expenses:* Tuition, area resident: Full-time $10,228; part-time $459 per credit hour. Tuition, nonresident: full-time $17,892; part-time $865 per credit hour. Required fees: $1966; $451 per semester. *Financial support:* In 2009–10, 145 teaching assistantships with full tuition reimbursements (averaging $9,918 per year) were awarded; career-related internships or fieldwork, Federal Work-Study, scholarships/grants, and unspecified assistantships also available. Financial award application deadline: 1/15. *Faculty research:* Capital markets, corporate finance, investment banking, derivatives, international finance. Total annual research expenditures: $13,527. *Unit head:* Dr. Vijay Singal, Dean, 540-231-7750, Fax: 540-231-4487, E-mail: singal@vt.edu. *Application contact:* Leanne Brownlee, Information Contact, 540-231-5886, Fax: 540-231-4487, E-mail: lbrownle@vt.edu.

Wagner College, Division of Graduate Studies, Department of Business Administration, Program in Finance, Staten Island, NY 10301-4495. Offers MBA. Part-time and evening/weekend programs available. *Degree requirements:* For master's, thesis optional. *Entrance requirements:* For master's, GMAT, minimum GPA of 2.6, computer and math proficiency. *Expenses:* Tuition: Full-time $15,570; part-time $865 per credit. Required fees: $2.

Wake Forest University, Babcock Graduate School of Management, Full-time MBA Program, Winston-Salem, NC 27106. Offers consulting/general management (MBA); entrepreneurship (MBA); finance (MBA); health (MBA); marketing (MBA); operations management (MBA); JD/MBA; MBA/MSA; MD/MBA. *Accreditation:* AACSB. *Faculty:* 62 full-time (13 women), 36 part-time/adjunct (14 women). *Students:* 144 full-time (36 women); includes 17 minority (8 African Americans, 9 Asian Americans or Pacific Islanders), 22 international. Average age 28. In 2009, 81 master's awarded. *Entrance requirements:* For master's, GMAT or GRE, letters of recommendation, official transcripts, current resume or curriculum vitae, 2 years of work experience with the exception of joint-degree candidates. Additional exam requirements/recommendations for international students: Required—TOEFL (minimum score 600 paper-based; 250 computer-based; 100 iBT), Pearson Test of English (PTE). *Application deadline:* For fall admission, 6/1 for domestic and international students. Applications are processed on a rolling basis. Application fee: $75. Electronic applications accepted. *Expenses:* Contact institution. *Financial support:* In 2009–10, 95 students received support. Career-related internships or fieldwork, scholarships/grants, and unspecified assistantships available. Financial award application deadline: 3/1; financial award applicants required to submit FAFSA. *Faculty research:* The influence of personal relationships on business decision making and management of change; drivers of perceived value and consumer behavior; impact of accounting on auditing, financial, managerial, systems and taxation stakeholders; corporate governance and executive compensation; impact of operations strategies on competitiveness. *Unit head:* Sherry Moss, Director, Full-time MBA Program, 336-758-5422, Fax: 336-758-5830, E-mail: admissions@mba.wfu.edu. *Application contact:* LaKesha Alston, Administrative Assistant, 336-758-5422, Fax: 336-758-5830, E-mail: admissions@mba.wfu.edu.

Walden University, Graduate Programs, School of Management, Minneapolis, MN 55401. Offers applied management and decision sciences (PhD), including accounting, engineering management, finance, general applied management and decision sciences, information systems management, knowledge management, leadership and organizational change, learning management, operations research, self-designed program in applied management and design sciences; business information management (MISM); enterprise information security (MISM); entrepreneurship (MBA, DBA); finance (MBA, DBA); global supply chain management (DBA); healthcare management (MBA); healthcare system improvement (MBA); human resource management (MBA); information systems management (DBA); international business (MBA, DBA); IT strategy and governance (MISM); leadership (MBA, MS, DBA), including entrepreneurship (MS), general management (MS), human resources leadership (MS), innovation and technology (MS), leader development (MS), project management (MS), self-designed (MS), sustainable futures (MS); managing global software and service supply chains (MISM); marketing (MBA, DBA); project management (MBA, MS); risk management (MBA); self-designed (MBA, DBA); social impact management (DBA); sustainable futures (MBA); technology (MBA); technology entrepreneurship (DBA). Part-time and evening/weekend programs available. Postbaccalaureate distance learning degree programs offered (minimal on-campus study). *Faculty:* 17 full-time, 211 part-time/adjunct. *Students:* 3,389 full-time (1,774 women), 815 part-time (482 women); includes 1,969 minority (1,640 African Americans, 36 American Indian/Alaska Native, 123 Asian Americans or Pacific Islanders, 170 Hispanic Americans), 95 international. Average age

Finance and Banking

Walden University (continued)

41. In 2009, 699 master's, 42 doctorates awarded. *Degree requirements:* For doctorate, thesis/dissertation (for some programs), residency. *Entrance requirements:* For master's, bachelor's degree or equivalent in related field; minimum GPA of 2.5; official transcripts; goal statement; access to computer and Internet; for doctorate, master's degree or equivalent in related field; minimum GPA of 3.0; 3 years of related professional/academic experience (preferred). Additional exam requirements/recommendations for international students: Required—TOEFL (minimum score 550 paper-based; 213 computer-based), IELTS (minimum score 6.5), TOEFL, IELTS, or Michigan English Language Assessment Battery (minimum score 82). *Application deadline:* Applications are processed on a rolling basis. Application fee: $50. Electronic applications accepted. *Expenses:* Tuition: Full-time $13,665; part-time $560 per credit. Required fees: $1375. Tuition and fees vary according to course load, degree level and program. *Financial support:* In 2009–10, 466 students received support; fellowships, Federal Work-Study, scholarships/grants, unspecified assistantships, and family tuition reduction, active duty/veteran tuition reduction, group tuition reduction, interest-free payment plans available. Support available to part-time students. Financial award applicants required to submit FAFSA. *Unit head:* William Schulz, Interim Associate Dean, 800-925-3368. *Application contact:* Jennifer Hall, Director of Enrollment, 866-4-WALDEN, E-mail: info@waldenu.edu.

Walsh College of Accountancy and Business Administration, Graduate Programs, Program in Finance, Troy, MI 48007-7006. Offers MSF. Part-time and evening/weekend programs available. *Faculty:* 4 full-time (2 women), 18 part-time/adjunct (1 woman). *Students:* 14 full-time (1 woman), 211 part-time (102 women); includes 45 minority (36 African Americans, 4 Asian Americans or Pacific Islanders, 5 Hispanic Americans), 7 international. Average age 34. 59 applicants, 97% accepted, 48 enrolled. *Entrance requirements:* For master's, minimum GPA of 2.75, previous course work in business. Additional exam requirements/recommendations for international students: Required—TOEFL. *Application deadline:* For fall admission, 8/24 priority date for domestic students; for winter admission, 1/1 priority date for domestic students; for spring admission, 4/1 priority date for domestic students. Applications are processed on a rolling basis. Application fee: $25. Electronic applications accepted. *Expenses:* Tuition: Part-time $525 per credit. Required fees: $125 per semester. *Financial support:* Available to part-time students. Application deadline: 6/30. *Unit head:* Dr. Linda Wiechowski, Chair, 248-823-1265, Fax: 248-689-0920. *Application contact:* Jeremy Guc, Director of Admissions and Academic Advising, 248-823-1610, Fax: 248-689-0938, E-mail: jguc@walshcollege.edu.

Washington State University, Graduate School, College of Business, Department of Finance, Insurance and Real Estate, Pullman, WA 99164. Offers PhD.

Washington State University, Graduate School, College of Business, Graduate Programs in Business, Pullman, WA 99164. Offers accounting and business law (M Acc); business administration (MBA, PhD), including accounting (PhD), finance (PhD), management and operations (PhD), management information systems (PhD), marketing (PhD). *Accreditation:* AACSB. *Degree requirements:* For master's, comprehensive exam (for some programs), thesis (for some programs), final presentation; for doctorate, comprehensive exam, thesis/dissertation, oral and written exams. *Entrance requirements:* For master's and doctorate, GMAT, minimum GPA of 3.0, 3 letters of recommendation. Additional exam requirements/recommendations for international students: Required—TOEFL. Electronic applications accepted.

See Display on page 193.

Washington University in St. Louis, Olin Business School, Program in Accounting and Finance, St. Louis, MO 63130-4899. Offers finance (MS). Part-time programs available. *Faculty:* 73 full-time (14 women), 45 part-time/adjunct (7 women). *Students:* 59 full-time (26 women), 9 part-time (1 woman); includes 9 Asian Americans or Pacific Islanders, 42 international. 480 applicants, 19% accepted, 44 enrolled. In 2009, 42 master's awarded. *Entrance requirements:* For master's, GMAT or GRE. Additional exam requirements/recommendations for international students: Required—TOEFL. *Application deadline:* For fall admission, 11/16 for domestic and international students; for winter admission, 2/15 for domestic and international students; for spring admission, 3/22 for domestic students. Application fee: $100. Electronic applications accepted. *Expenses:* Contact institution. *Financial support:* Applicants required to submit FAFSA. *Unit head:* Joseph Peter Fox, Associate Dean and Director of MBA Programs, 314-935-6322, Fax: 314-935-4464, E-mail: fox@wustl.edu. *Application contact:* Dr. Gary Hochberg, Director, Specialized Master's Programs, 314-935-6380, Fax: 314-935-4464, E-mail: hochberg@wustl.edu.

Waynesburg University, Graduate and Professional Studies, Waynesburg, PA 15370-1222. Offers business (MBA), including finance, health systems, human resources, leadership, market development; counseling (MA), including addictions counseling, clinical mental health; education (MAT); nursing (MSN), including administration, education, informatics, palliative care; nursing practice (DNP); special education (M Ed); technology (M Ed); MSN/MBA. *Accreditation:* AACN. Part-time and evening/weekend programs available. *Faculty:* 11 full-time (5 women), 136 part-time/adjunct (80 women). *Students:* 116 full-time (85 women), 984 part-time (682 women). 711 applicants, 80% accepted, 485 enrolled. In 2009, 320 master's, 41 doctorates awarded. *Degree requirements:* For doctorate, thesis/dissertation. *Entrance requirements:* Additional exam requirements/recommendations for international students: Required—TOEFL. *Application deadline:* For fall admission, 8/1 priority date for domestic students. Applications are processed on a rolling basis. Electronic applications accepted. *Expenses:* Tuition: Part-time $520 per credit. *Financial support:* Available to part-time students. Application deadline: 5/1. *Unit head:* David Mariner, Dean, 724-743-4420, Fax: 724-743-4425, E-mail: dmariner@waynesburg.edu. *Application contact:* Michael Bednarski, Director of Admissions, 724-743-4420, Fax: 724-743-4425, E-mail: mbednars@waynesburg.edu.

Webster University, George Herbert Walker School of Business and Technology, Department of Business, St. Louis, MO 63119-3194. Offers business (MA); business and organizational security management (MBA); computer resources and information management (MBA); environmental management (MBA); finance (MA, MBA); health services management (MBA); human resources development (MBA); human resources management (MBA); international business (MA, MBA); management and leadership (MBA); marketing (MBA); procurement and acquisitions management (MBA); telecommunications management (MBA). *Accreditation:* ACBSP. Part-time and evening/weekend programs available. Postbaccalaureate distance learning degree programs offered (no on-campus study). *Faculty:* 9 full-time, 430 part-time/adjunct. *Students:* 1,190 full-time (543 women), 4,226 part-time (2,159 women). Average age 34. In 2009, 2,021 master's awarded. *Degree requirements:* For master's, comprehensive exam (for some programs), thesis (for some programs). *Entrance requirements:* Additional exam requirements/recommendations for international students: Required—TOEFL. *Application deadline:* Applications are processed on a rolling basis. Application fee: $35 ($50 for international students). *Expenses:* Tuition: Part-time $565 per credit hour. Tuition and fees vary according to degree level, campus/location and program. *Financial support:* Federal Work-Study available. Support available to part-time students. Financial award application deadline: 4/1; financial award applicants required to submit FAFSA. *Unit head:* Dr. Debbie Psihountas, Chair, 314-246-7553 Ext. 7017, Fax: 314-968-7077, E-mail: buschair@webster.edu. *Application contact:* Matt Nolan, Associate Vice President for Enrollment Management/Dean of Admissions, Fax: 314-968-7116, E-mail: gadmit@webster.edu.

Western International University, Graduate Programs in Business, Master of Business Administration Program in Finance, Phoenix, AZ 85021-2718. Offers MBA. Part-time and evening/weekend programs available. Postbaccalaureate distance learning degree programs offered (no on-campus study). *Faculty:* 9 part-time/adjunct (0 women). *Students:* 105 full-time (50 women); includes 29 minority (6 African Americans, 2 American Indian/Alaska Native, 10 Asian Americans or Pacific Islanders, 11 Hispanic Americans), 8 international. Average age 33. In 2009, 25 master's awarded. *Entrance requirements:* For master's, minimum GPA of 2.75. Additional exam requirements/recommendations for international students: Required—TOEFL (minimum score 550 paper-based; 213 computer-based; 79 iBT), TWE (minimum score 5), or IELTS (minimum score 6.5). *Application deadline:* Applications are processed on a rolling basis. Application fee: $25. Electronic applications accepted. *Expenses:* Tuition: Full-time $12,600. One-time fee: $25 full-time. *Financial support:* Applicants required to submit FAFSA. *Unit head:* Dr. Deborah DeSimone, Chief Academic Officer, 602-429-1135, E-mail: deborah.desimone@west.edu. *Application contact:* Melissa Machuca, Director of Enrollment, 602-943-2311, Fax: 602-371-8637.

Western Michigan University, Graduate College, Haworth College of Business, Department of Finance and Commercial Law, Kalamazoo, MI 49008. Offers finance (MBA). *Accreditation:* AACSB. *Faculty:* 58 full-time (9 women). *Students:* 367 full-time (141 women), 238 part-time (74 women); includes 32 minority (11 African Americans, 1 American Indian/Alaska Native, 15 Asian Americans or Pacific Islanders, 5 Hispanic Americans), 188 international. 254 applicants, 89% accepted, 144 enrolled. In 2009, 146 master's awarded. *Entrance requirements:* For master's, GMAT. *Application deadline:* For fall admission, 2/15 priority date for domestic students. Applications are processed on a rolling basis. Application fee: $25. *Financial support:* Fellowships, research assistantships, teaching assistantships, Federal Work-Study available. Financial award application deadline: 2/15; financial award applicants required to submit FAFSA. *Application contact:* Admissions and Orientation, 269-387-2000, Fax: 269-387-2355.

West Texas A&M University, College of Business, Department of Accounting, Economics, and Finance, Program in Finance and Economics, Canyon, TX 79016-0001. Offers MS. Part-time and evening/weekend programs available. Postbaccalaureate distance learning degree programs offered (minimal on-campus study). *Degree requirements:* For master's, comprehensive exam, thesis optional. *Entrance requirements:* For master's, GMAT. Additional exam requirements/recommendations for international students: Required—TOEFL (minimum score 550 paper-based). Electronic applications accepted. *Faculty research:* International trade composition, cycle of poverty, trade effects in Asian countries, structural problems in Japanese economy, reform and the US sugar program-Nebraska.

Wilkes University, College of Graduate and Professional Studies, Jay S. Sidhu School of Business and Leadership, Wilkes-Barre, PA 18766-0002. Offers accounting (MBA); entrepreneurship (MBA); finance (MBA); human resource management (MBA); international business (MBA); management (MBA); marketing (MBA). *Accreditation:* ACBSP. Part-time and evening/weekend programs available. *Students:* 86 full-time (41 women), 118 part-time (59 women); includes 7 minority (4 African Americans, 1 Asian American or Pacific Islander, 2 Hispanic Americans), 48 international. Average age 29. In 2009, 59 master's awarded. *Entrance requirements:* For master's, GMAT. Additional exam requirements/recommendations for international students: Required—TOEFL (minimum score 500 paper-based; 173 computer-based; 79 iBT). *Application deadline:* Applications are processed on a rolling basis. Application fee: $45. *Expenses:* Contact institution. *Financial support:* Federal Work-Study and unspecified assistantships available. Financial award application deadline: 3/1; financial award applicants required to submit FAFSA. *Unit head:* Dr. Paul Browne, Dean, 570-408-4701, Fax: 570-408-7846, E-mail: paul.browne@wilkes.edu. *Application contact:* Kathleen Houlihan, Director of Graduate Studies, 570-408-3235, Fax: 570-408-7846, E-mail: kathleen.houlihan@wilkes.edu.

Wilmington University, College of Business, New Castle, DE 19720-6491. Offers business administration (MBA); finance (MBA); health care administration (MBA, MS); homeland security (MBA, MS); human resource management (MS); management (MS); management information systems (MBA); organizational leadership (MS); public administration (MS); transportation and logistics (MBA, MS). Part-time and evening/weekend programs available. *Entrance requirements:* Additional exam requirements/recommendations for international students: Required—TOEFL (minimum score 500 paper-based; 173 computer-based). Electronic applications accepted.

Wright State University, School of Graduate Studies, Raj Soin College of Business, Department of Finance and Financial Services, Dayton, OH 45435. Offers finance (MBA); MBA/MS. *Entrance requirements:* For master's, GMAT, minimum AACSB index of 1000. Additional exam requirements/recommendations for international students: Required—TOEFL.

Xavier University, Williams College of Business, Master of Business Administration Program, Cincinnati, OH 45207-3221. Offers business administration (Exec MBA, MBA); business intelligence (MBA); finance (MBA); international business (MBA); management information systems (MBA); marketing (MBA); MBA/MHSA; MSN/MBA. *Accreditation:* AACSB. Part-time and evening/weekend programs available. *Faculty:* 44 full-time (17 women), 9 part-time/adjunct (2 women). *Students:* 167 full-time (51 women), 862 part-time (283 women); includes 149 minority (60 African Americans, 62 Asian Americans or Pacific Islanders, 27 Hispanic Americans), 17 international. Average age 30. 355 applicants, 63% accepted, 187 enrolled. In 2009, 369 master's awarded. *Degree requirements:* For master's, capstone course. *Entrance requirements:* For master's, GMAT. Additional exam requirements/recommendations for international students: Required—TOEFL (minimum score 550 paper-based; 213 computer-based; 80 iBT). *Application deadline:* For fall admission, 8/1 priority date for domestic students, 5/1 for international students; for spring admission, 12/1 priority date for domestic students, 9/1 for international students. Applications are processed on a rolling basis. Application fee: $0. Electronic applications accepted. *Expenses:* Contact institution. *Financial support:* In 2009–10, 183 students received support. Scholarships/grants, tuition waivers (partial), and unspecified assistantships available. Financial award application deadline: 3/1; financial award applicants required to submit FAFSA. *Unit head:* Dr. Hema Krishnan, Associate Dean, 513-745-3206, Fax: 513-745-3455, E-mail: krishnan@xavier.edu. *Application contact:* Anna Marie Whelan, Assistant Director, MBA Programs, 513-745-3525, Fax: 513-745-2929, E-mail: whelana@xavier.edu.

Yale University, Yale School of Management and Graduate School of Arts and Sciences, Doctoral Program in Management, New Haven, CT 06520. Offers accounting (PhD); financial economics (PhD); marketing (PhD). *Accreditation:* AACSB. *Faculty:* 68 full-time (12 women). *Students:* 30 full-time (9 women), 13 international. Average age 28. 372 applicants, 7% accepted, 13 enrolled. In 2009, 5 doctorates awarded. *Degree requirements:* For doctorate, comprehensive exam, thesis/dissertation. *Entrance requirements:* For doctorate, GMAT or GRE General Test. Additional exam requirements/recommendations for international students: Required—TOEFL, IELTS. *Application deadline:* For fall admission, 1/2 for domestic and international students. Application fee: $85. Electronic applications accepted. *Expenses:* Contact institution. *Financial support:* In 2009–10, 29 students received support, including 29 fellowships with full tuition reimbursements available, 29 research assistantships with full tuition reimbursements available, 29 teaching assistantships with full tuition reimbursements available; institutionally sponsored loans, scholarships/grants, and health care benefits also available. Financial award application deadline: 1/2. *Faculty research:* Pricing of options and futures, term structure of interest rates, use of accounting numbers in debt contracts, product differentiation, e-commerce and marketing, behavioral finance. *Unit head:* Carla Mills, Registrar, 203-432-3955, Fax: 203-432-0342, E-mail: carla.mills@yale.edu. *Application contact:* Carla Mills, Registrar, 203-432-3955, Fax: 203-432-0342, E-mail: carla.mills@yale.edu.

See Close-Up on page 283.

York University, Faculty of Graduate Studies, Schulich School of Business, Toronto, ON M3J 1P3, Canada. Offers administration (PhD); business (MBA); finance (MF); international business (IMBA); public administration (MPA); MBA/JD; MBA/MA; MBA/MFA. Part-time and evening/weekend programs available. *Degree requirements:* For master's, advanced proficiency in a second language, work term (IMBA); for doctorate, comprehensive exam, thesis/dissertation. *Entrance requirements:* For master's, GMAT, minimum GPA of 3.0; for doctorate, GMAT, minimum GPA of 3.3. Electronic applications accepted.

See Close-Up on page 285.

Youngstown State University, Graduate School, College of Liberal Arts and Social Sciences, Department of Economics, Youngstown, OH 44555-0001. Offers economics (MA); financial economics (MA). Part-time programs available. *Degree requirements:* For master's, comprehensive exam, thesis optional. *Entrance requirements:* For master's, minimum GPA of 2.7, 21 hours in economics. Additional exam requirements/recommendations for international students: Required—TOEFL. *Faculty research:* Forecasting, applied econometrics, labor economics, applied macroeconomics, industrial organization.

Youngstown State University, Graduate School, Williamson College of Business Administration, Department of Accounting and Finance, Youngstown, OH 44555-0001. Offers accounting

(MBA). *Accreditation:* AACSB. Part-time and evening/weekend programs available. *Degree requirements:* For master's, thesis optional. *Entrance requirements:* For master's, GMAT, minimum GPA of 2.7. Additional exam requirements/recommendations for international students: Required—TOEFL. *Faculty research:* Taxation and compliance, capital markets, accounting information systems, accounting theory, tax and government accounting.

Investment Management

Alaska Pacific University, Graduate Programs, Business Administration Department, Anchorage, AK 99508-4672. Offers business administration (MBA), including business administration, health services administration; information and communication technology (MBAICT); investment (CGS). Part-time and evening/weekend programs available. *Degree requirements:* For master's, capstone course. *Entrance requirements:* For master's, GMAT or GRE General Test, minimum GPA of 3.0. Additional exam requirements/recommendations for international students: Required—TOEFL (minimum score 550 paper-based; 79 computer-based).

Boston University, School of Management, Program in Investment Management, Boston, MA 02215. Offers MSIM. Part-time and evening/weekend programs available. *Faculty:* 8 full-time (0 women), 4 part-time/adjunct (0 women). *Students:* 66 part-time (11 women); includes 6 Asian Americans or Pacific Islanders, 2 Hispanic Americans. Average age 29. 60 applicants, 58% accepted, 32 enrolled. In 2009, 32 master's awarded. *Entrance requirements:* For master's, GMAT, resume, 2 letters of recommendation. Additional exam requirements/recommendations for international students: Required—TOEFL or IELTS. *Application deadline:* For spring admission, 11/15 for domestic and international students. Applications are processed on a rolling basis. Application fee: $125. Electronic applications accepted. *Expenses:* Tuition: Full-time $37,910; part-time $1184 per credit hour. Required fees: $386; $40 per semester. Part-time tuition and fees vary according to class time, course level, degree level and program. *Financial support:* Career-related internships or fieldwork, Federal Work-Study, and institutionally sponsored loans available. Support available to part-time students. Financial award applicants required to submit FAFSA. *Faculty research:* Behavioral finance, computational finance, risk management, portfolio management, derivatives. *Unit head:* Scott Stewart, Faculty Director, 617-353-2353, Fax: 617-353-6667, E-mail: msim@bu.edu. *Application contact:* Hayden Estrada, Assistant Dean, Admissions, 617-353-2670, Fax: 617-353-7368, E-mail: msim@bu.edu.

Concordia University, School of Graduate Studies, John Molson School of Business, Montréal, QC H3G 1M8, Canada. Offers administration (M Sc, Diploma); aviation management (Certificate, Diploma); business administration (MBA, UA Undergraduate Associate, PhD), including international aviation (UA Undergraduate Associate); chartered accountancy (Diploma); community organizational development (Certificate); event management and fundraising (Certificate); executive business administration (EMBA); investment management (Diploma); investment management option (MBA); management accounting (Certificate); management of healthcare organizations (Certificate); sport administration (Diploma). *Accreditation:* AACSB. Part-time and evening/weekend programs available. *Degree requirements:* For master's, one foreign language, thesis (for some programs), research project; for doctorate, one foreign language, thesis/dissertation; for other advanced degree, one foreign language. *Entrance requirements:* For master's and doctorate, GMAT. Additional exam requirements/recommendations for international students: Required—TOEFL. *Expenses:* Contact institution. *Faculty research:* General business, capital markets, international business.

Gannon University, School of Graduate Studies, College of Engineering and Business, School of Business, Program in Investments, Erie, PA 16541-0001. Offers Certificate. Part-time and evening/weekend programs available. In 2009, 2 Certificates awarded. *Entrance requirements:* For degree, GMAT. Additional exam requirements/recommendations for international students: Required—TOEFL (minimum score 79 iBT). *Application deadline:* Applications are processed on a rolling basis. Application fee: $25. Electronic applications accepted. *Expenses:* Tuition: Full-time $13,590; part-time $755 per credit. Required fees: $524; $17 per credit. Tuition and fees vary according to course load, degree level, campus/location and program. *Financial support:* Application deadline: 7/1. *Unit head:* Scott Miller, Associate Director, 814-871-7397, E-mail: miller032@gannon.edu. *Application contact:* Kara Morgan, Assistant Director of Graduate Admissions, 814-871-5831, Fax: 814-871-5827, E-mail: graduate@gannon.edu.

The George Washington University, School of Business, Department of Finance, Washington, DC 20052. Offers finance (MSF, PhD); finance and investments (MBA); real estate and urban development (MBA). Part-time and evening/weekend programs available. *Faculty:* 17 full-time (3 women), 10 part-time/adjunct (2 women). *Students:* 74 full-time (26 women), 40 part-time (13 women); includes 15 minority (4 African Americans, 8 Asian Americans or Pacific Islanders, 3 Hispanic Americans), 74 international. Average age 30. 211 applicants, 58% accepted, 59 enrolled. In 2009, 61 master's awarded. *Degree requirements:* For doctorate, thesis/dissertation. *Entrance requirements:* For master's, GMAT; for doctorate, GMAT or GRE. Additional exam requirements/recommendations for international students: Required—TOEFL. *Application deadline:* For fall admission, 4/1 priority date for domestic students; for spring admission, 10/1 for domestic students. Applications are processed on a rolling basis. Application fee: $60. *Financial support:* In 2009–10, 38 students received support; fellowships, teaching assistantships, career-related internships or fieldwork, Federal Work-Study, and institutionally sponsored loans available. Financial award application deadline: 4/1. *Unit head:* Mark S. Klock, Chair, 202-994-5996, E-mail: klock@gwu.edu. *Application contact:* Kristin Williams, Assistant Vice President for Graduate and Special Enrollment Management, 202-994-0467, Fax: 202-994-0371, E-mail: ksw@gwu.edu.

International University in Geneva, Master of Business Administration Program, Geneva, Switzerland. Offers finance (MBA); international business (MIB); investment management (MBA); luxury management (MBA); marketing (MBA); wealth management (MBA). *Accreditation:* ACBSP. Part-time and evening/weekend programs available. *Degree requirements:* For master's, comprehensive exam. *Entrance requirements:* For master's, GMAT. Additional exam requirements/recommendations for international students: Required—TOEFL. Electronic applications accepted.

The Johns Hopkins University, Carey Business School, Finance Programs, Baltimore, MD 21218-2699. Offers finance (MS); financial management (Certificate); investments (Certificate). Part-time and evening/weekend programs available. *Faculty:* 29 full-time (6 women), 135 part-time/adjunct (29 women). *Students:* 75 full-time (33 women), 95 part-time (33 women); includes 39 minority (9 African Americans, 1 American Indian/Alaska Native, 21 Asian Americans or Pacific Islanders, 8 Hispanic Americans), 69 international. Average age 29. 287 applicants, 40% accepted, 71 enrolled. In 2009, 61 master's, 14 other advanced degrees awarded. *Degree requirements:* For master's, 36 credits including final project. *Entrance requirements:* For master's, GMAT or GRE (recommended), minimum GPA of 3.0, resume, work experience, two letters of recommendation; for Certificate, minimum GPA of 3.0, resume, work experience, two letters of recommendation. Additional exam requirements/recommendations for international students: Required—TOEFL (minimum score 600 paper-based; 250 computer-based; 100 iBT). *Application deadline:* For fall admission, 5/1 for international students; for spring admission, 10/15 for international students. Applications are processed on a rolling basis. Application fee: $100. Electronic applications accepted. *Financial support:* Scholarships/grants available. Support available to part-time students. Financial award application deadline: 4/1; financial award applicants required to submit FAFSA. *Faculty research:* Financial econometrics, high frequency data modeling, corporate finance. *Unit head:* Dr. Dipankar Chakravarti, Vice Dean of Programs, 410-516-8561, E-mail: dipankar.chakravarti@jhu.edu. *Application contact:* Robin Greenberg, Admissions Coordinator, 410-516-4234, Fax: 410-516-0826, E-mail: carey.admissions@jhu.edu.

Lincoln University, Graduate Degree Programs, Oakland, CA 94612. Offers finance and investments (DBA); finance management and investment banking (MBA); general business (MBA); human resource management (MBA); international business (MBA); management information systems (MBA). Part-time and evening/weekend programs available. *Faculty:* 7 full-time (2 women), 13 part-time/adjunct (1 woman). *Students:* 295 full-time (133 women), 3 part-time (0 women). 177 applicants, 100% accepted, 71 enrolled. In 2009, 98 master's awarded. *Degree requirements:* For master's, research project (thesis) or internship report, or comprehensive exam; for doctorate, comprehensive exam, thesis/dissertation. *Entrance requirements:* For master's, minimum GPA of 2.7; for doctorate, GMAT (minimum score: 550), GRE (minimum score: 1000), or equivalent test results (waived for master's degree with cumulative GPA of 3.3). Additional exam requirements/recommendations for international students: Required—TOEFL or IELTS. *Application deadline:* For fall admission, 7/3 priority date for domestic students; for spring admission, 11/27 priority date for domestic students. Applications are processed on a rolling basis. Application fee: $75. Electronic applications accepted. *Expenses:* Tuition: Full-time $6750. Required fees: $190 per term. *Financial support:* In 2009–10, 1 teaching assistantship was awarded; career-related internships or fieldwork and scholarships/grants also available. *Unit head:* Dr. Marshall Burak, Director of Graduate Programs, 510-628-8016, Fax: 510-628-8012, E-mail: mburak@lincolnuca.edu. *Application contact:* Peggy Au, Director of Admissions and Records, 510-628-8010, Fax: 510-628-8012, E-mail: admissions@lincolnuca.edu.

Lynn University, College of Business and Management, Boca Raton, FL 33431-5598. Offers aviation management (MBA); financial valuation and investment management (MBA); hospitality management (MBA); international business (MBA); marketing (MBA); mass communication and media management (MBA); sports and athletics administration (MBA). Part-time and evening/weekend programs available. Postbaccalaureate distance learning degree programs offered. *Degree requirements:* For master's, project. *Entrance requirements:* For master's, GMAT or GRE, minimum undergraduate GPA of 3.0, resume, 2 letters of recommendation. Additional exam requirements/recommendations for international students: Required—TOEFL (minimum score 550 paper-based; 213 computer-based). *Application deadline:* Applications are processed on a rolling basis. Application fee: $50. Electronic applications accepted. *Expenses:* Tuition: Part-time $580 per credit. One-time fee: $200 part-time. Part-time tuition and fees vary according to degree level. *Financial support:* Career-related internships or fieldwork, Federal Work-Study, institutionally sponsored loans, scholarships/grants, tuition waivers (full and partial), and unspecified assistantships available. Support available to part-time students. Financial award application deadline: 8/1; financial award applicants required to submit FAFSA. *Faculty research:* Labor relations, dynamic balance in leisure-time skills, ethics in athletics, hotel development. *Unit head:* Dr. Ralph Norcio, Associate Dean, 561-237-7010, Fax: 561-237-7014, E-mail: rnorcio@lynn.edu. *Application contact:* Dr. Larissa Baia, Assistant Director of Graduate Admissions, 561-237-7916, Fax: 561-237-7100, E-mail: admissionpm@lynn.edu.

Marywood University, Academic Affairs, College of Liberal Arts and Sciences, Department of Business and Managerial Science, Emphasis in Finance and Investments, Scranton, PA 18509-1598. Offers MBA. *Students:* 4 full-time (2 women), 6 part-time (3 women). Average age 31. 6 applicants, 83% accepted. In 2009, 10 master's awarded. *Entrance requirements:* For master's, GMAT. Additional exam requirements/recommendations for international students: Required—TOEFL (minimum score 550 paper-based; 213 computer-based; 79 iBT). *Application deadline:* For fall admission, 4/1 priority date for domestic students, 3/31 priority date for international students; for spring admission, 11/1 priority date for domestic students, 8/31 priority date for international students. Applications are processed on a rolling basis. Application fee: $35. Electronic applications accepted. *Expenses:* Tuition: Part-time $715 per credit. Required fees: $270 per semester. Tuition and fees vary according to degree level, campus/location and program. *Financial support:* Career-related internships or fieldwork, scholarships/grants, and unspecified assistantships available. Support available to part-time students. Financial award application deadline: 6/30; financial award applicants required to submit FAFSA. *Faculty research:* Accountant/auditor liability, corporate finance acquisitions and mergers, corporate bankruptcy. *Application contact:* Tammy Manka, Assistant Director of Graduate Admissions, 866-279-9663, E-mail: tmanka@marywood.edu.

Pace University, Lubin School of Business, Financial Management Program, New York, NY 10038. Offers banking and finance (MBA); corporate financial management (MBA); financial management (MBA); investment management (MBA, MS). Part-time and evening/weekend programs available. *Students:* 95 full-time (36 women), 346 part-time (140 women); includes 57 minority (16 African Americans, 31 Asian Americans or Pacific Islanders, 10 Hispanic Americans), 235 international. Average age 27. 568 applicants, 73% accepted, 109 enrolled. In 2009, 133 master's awarded. *Entrance requirements:* For master's, GMAT. Additional exam requirements/recommendations for international students: Required—TOEFL. *Application deadline:* For fall admission, 7/31 priority date for domestic students; for spring admission, 11/30 for domestic students. Applications are processed on a rolling basis. Application fee: $70. Electronic applications accepted. *Expenses:* Tuition: Part-time $954 per credit. Tuition and fees vary according to course load, degree level and program. *Financial support:* Research assistantships, career-related internships or fieldwork, Federal Work-Study, and tuition waivers (full and partial) available. Support available to part-time students. Financial award application deadline: 8/15; financial award applicants required to submit FAFSA. *Unit head:* Dr. Edmund Mantell, Chairperson, 914-422-4165. *Application contact:* Susan Ford-Goldschein, Director of Admissions, 212-346-1652, Fax: 212-346-1585, E-mail: gradnyc@pace.edu.

Quinnipiac University, School of Business, Program in Business Administration, Chartered Financial Analyst Track, Hamden, CT 06518-1940. Offers MBA. *Faculty:* 24 full-time (6 women), 12 part-time/adjunct (4 women). *Entrance requirements:* For master's, GMAT, minimum GPA of 3.0. Additional exam requirements/recommendations for international students: Required—TOEFL (minimum score 575 paper-based; 233 computer-based; 90 iBT). *Application deadline:* For fall admission, 7/30 priority date for domestic students; for spring admission, 12/15 for domestic students. Applications are processed on a rolling basis. Application fee: $45. Electronic applications accepted. *Expenses:* Tuition: Full-time $16,030; part-time $770 per credit. Required fees: $630; $35 per credit. *Unit head:* Dr. Kimberly McKeage, MBA Director, 203-582-3676, Fax: 203-582-8664, E-mail: kim.mckeage@quinnipiac.edu. *Application contact:* Jennifer Boutin, Associate Director of Graduate Admissions, 800-462-1944, Fax: 203-582-3443, E-mail: jennifer.boutin@quinnipiac.edu.

The University of Iowa, Henry B. Tippie College of Business, Henry B. Tippie School of Management, Iowa City, IA 52242-1316. Offers corporate finance (MBA); investment management (MBA); marketing (MBA); process excellence (MBA); strategic innovation (MBA); JD/MBA; MBA/MA; MBA/MD; MBA/MHA; MBA/MSN. *Accreditation:* AACSB. Part-time and evening/weekend programs available. *Faculty:* 46 full-time (7 women), 12 part-time/adjunct (2 women). *Students:* 250 full-time (64 women), 794 part-time (277 women); includes 92 minority

Investment Management

The University of Iowa (continued)
(17 African Americans, 2 American Indian/Alaska Native, 52 Asian Americans or Pacific Islanders, 21 Hispanic Americans), 146 international. Average age 32. 602 applicants, 60% accepted, 302 enrolled. In 2009, 348 master's awarded. *Entrance requirements:* For master's, GMAT, work experience, references. Additional exam requirements/recommendations for international students: Required—TOEFL (minimum score 600 paper-based; 250 computer-based; 100 iBT), IELTS (minimum score 7). *Application deadline:* For fall admission, 7/30 for domestic students, 4/15 for international students; for spring admission, 12/15 for domestic and international students. Applications are processed on a rolling basis. Application fee: $60 ($100 for international students). Electronic applications accepted. *Expenses:* Contact institution. *Financial support:* In 2009–10, 100 students received support, including 100 fellowships (averaging $6,819 per year), 92 research assistantships with partial tuition reimbursements available (averaging $10,388 per year); career-related internships or fieldwork, scholarships/grants, health care benefits, and unspecified assistantships also available. Financial award application deadline: 4/15; financial award applicants required to submit FAFSA. *Faculty research:* Capital markets, econometrics, optimization, investments and empirical corporate finance, Iowa electronic markets. *Unit head:* Prof. Jarjisu Sa-Aadu, Associate Dean, MBA Programs, 800-622-4692, Fax: 319-335-3604, E-mail: jsa-aadu@uiowa.edu. *Application contact:* Jodi Schafer, Director of Admissions and Financial Aid, 319-335-0864, Fax: 319-335-3604, E-mail: jodi-schafer@uiowa.edu.

University of San Francisco, College of Arts and Sciences, Risk Management Graduate Program, San Francisco, CA 94117-1080. Offers MS. *Expenses:* Tuition: Full-time $19,710; part-time $1095 per unit. Part-time tuition and fees vary according to degree level, campus/location and program. *Unit head:* John Veitch, Chair, 415-422-6784, Fax: 415-422-5784. *Application contact:* Information Contact, 415-422-5135, Fax: 415-422-2217, E-mail: asgraduate@usfca.edu.

University of Tulsa, Graduate School, Collins College of Business, Program in Finance, Tulsa, OK 74104-3189. Offers corporate finance (MS); investments and portfolio management (MS); risk management (MS); JD/MSF; MBA/MSF; MSF/MSAM. Part-time and evening/weekend programs available. *Faculty:* 10 full-time (1 woman). *Students:* 21 full-time (10 women), 7 part-time (5 women); includes 1 minority (Hispanic American), 10 international. Average age 25. 62 applicants, 52% accepted, 8 enrolled. In 2009, 11 master's awarded. *Degree requirements:* For master's, thesis optional. *Entrance requirements:* For master's, GMAT or GRE. Additional exam requirements/recommendations for international students: Required—TOEFL (minimum score 575 paper-based; 231 computer-based), IELTS (minimum score 6.5). *Application deadline:* Applications are processed on a rolling basis. Application fee: $40. Electronic applications accepted. *Expenses:* Tuition: Full-time $16,182; part-time $899 per credit hour. Required fees: $4 per credit hour. Tuition and fees vary according to course load. *Financial support:* In 2009–10, 8 students received support, including 1 research assistantship with full and partial tuition reimbursement available (averaging $12,088 per year), 7 teaching assistantships with full and partial tuition reimbursements available (averaging $9,506 per year); fellowships with full and partial tuition reimbursements available, career-related internships or fieldwork, Federal Work-Study, institutionally sponsored loans, scholarships/grants, health care benefits, tuition waivers (full and partial), and unspecified assistantships also available. Support available to part-time students. Financial award application deadline: 2/1; financial award applicants required to submit FAFSA. *Unit head:* Dr. Markham Collins, Associate Dean of the Collins College of Business, 918-631-2783, Fax: 918-631-2142, E-mail: markham-collins@utulsa.edu. *Application contact:* Dr. Markham Collins, Associate Dean of the Collins College of Business, 918-631-2783, Fax: 918-631-2142, E-mail: markham-collins@utulsa.edu.

University of Wisconsin–Madison, Graduate School, Wisconsin School of Business, Doctoral Program in Finance, Investment and Banking, Madison, WI 53706-1380. Offers PhD. *Faculty:* 16 full-time (3 women), 4 part-time/adjunct (1 woman). *Students:* 10 full-time (3 women), 9 international. Average age 28. 104 applicants, 5% accepted, 3 enrolled. In 2009, 1 doctorate awarded. *Degree requirements:* For doctorate, comprehensive exam, thesis/dissertation. *Entrance requirements:* For doctorate, GMAT or GRE. Additional exam requirements/recommendations for international students: Required—Pearson Test of English (minimum score 73, written 80); Recommended—TOEFL (minimum score 623 paper-based; 263 computer-based; 106 iBT), IELTS (minimum score 7.5). *Application deadline:* For fall admission, 12/15 priority date for domestic and international students. Application fee: $56. Electronic applications accepted. *Expenses:* Tuition, state resident: part-time $594 per credit. Tuition, nonresident: part-time $1504 per credit. Required fees: $65 per credit. Tuition and fees vary according to course load, program and reciprocity agreements. *Financial support:* In 2009–10, 10 students received support, including fellowships with full tuition reimbursements available (averaging $18,567 per year), research assistantships with full tuition reimbursements available (averaging $16,506 per year), 10 teaching assistantships with full tuition reimbursements available (averaging $14,088 per year); Federal Work-Study, institutionally sponsored loans, scholarships/grants, health care benefits, and unspecified assistantships also available. Financial award application deadline: 2/1; financial award applicants required to submit FAFSA. *Faculty research:* Banking and financial institutions, business cycles, investments, derivatives, corporate finance. *Unit head:* Prof. Robert Krainer, Chair, 608-263-1253, Fax: 608-265-4195, E-mail: rkrainer@bus.wisc.edu. *Application contact:* Belle Heberling, Assistant Director for Research Programs, 608-262-3749, Fax: 608-890-0180, E-mail: phd@bus.wisc.edu.

University of Wisconsin–Milwaukee, Graduate School, Sheldon B. Lubar School of Business, Milwaukee, WI 53201. Offers business administration (MBA); enterprise resource planning (Certificate); investment management (Certificate); management science (MS, PhD); nonprofit management and leadership (MS, Certificate); state and local taxation (Certificate); MS/MBA. *Accreditation:* AACSB. Part-time and evening/weekend programs available. *Faculty:* 55 full-time (14 women). *Students:* 317 full-time (108 women), 420 part-time (179 women); includes 70 minority (20 African Americans, 5 American Indian/Alaska Native, 33 Asian Americans or Pacific Islanders, 12 Hispanic Americans), 73 international. Average age 31. 499 applicants, 59% accepted, 132 enrolled. In 2009, 286 master's, 10 doctorates awarded. *Degree requirements:* For master's, comprehensive exam (for some programs); for doctorate, comprehensive exam, thesis/dissertation. *Entrance requirements:* For master's and doctorate, GMAT or GRE General Test. Additional exam requirements/recommendations for international students: Required—TOEFL (minimum score 550 paper-based; 79 iBT), IELTS (minimum score 6.5). *Application deadline:* For fall admission, 1/1 priority date for domestic students; for spring admission, 9/1 for domestic students. Applications are processed on a rolling basis. Application fee: $45 ($75 for international students). *Expenses:* Contact institution. *Financial support:* In 2009–10, 5 fellowships, 41 teaching assistantships were awarded; career-related internships or fieldwork, Federal Work-Study, and unspecified assistantships also available. Support available to part-time students. Financial award application deadline: 4/15. *Faculty research:* Applied management research in finance, MIS, marketing, operations research, organizational sciences. Total annual research expenditures: $204,295. *Unit head:* Timothy L. Smunt, Dean, 414-229-6256, Fax: 414-229-2372, E-mail: tsmunt@uwm.edu. *Application contact:* Sara Sandin, 414-229-5403, E-mail: mba-ms@uwm.edu.

Taxation

American International College, School of Business Administration, Program in Accounting and Taxation, Springfield, MA 01109-3189. Offers MSAT. *Expenses:* Tuition: Full-time $12,510; part-time $695 per credit hour. Required fees: $35 per term.

American University, Kogod School of Business, Department of Accounting, Program in Taxation, Washington, DC 20016-8044. Offers MS, Certificate. Part-time and evening/weekend programs available. *Students:* 14 full-time (8 women), 95 part-time (52 women); includes 28 minority (11 African Americans, 14 Asian Americans or Pacific Islanders, 3 Hispanic Americans), 9 international. Average age 33. In 2009, 24 master's, 1 other advanced degree awarded. *Entrance requirements:* For master's, GMAT or CPA exam; for Certificate, bachelor's degree. Additional exam requirements/recommendations for international students: Required—TOEFL. *Application deadline:* For fall admission, 2/1 priority date for domestic students; for spring admission, 10/1 priority date for domestic students. Applications are processed on a rolling basis. Application fee: $100. *Expenses:* Contact institution. *Financial support:* Fellowships, career-related internships or fieldwork, Federal Work-Study, and institutionally sponsored loans available. Support available to part-time students. Financial award application deadline: 2/1. *Faculty research:* International transactions, corporate partnership, taxation, real estate, estate gift planning. *Unit head:* Dr. Donald Williamson, Chair, 202-885-1942. *Application contact:* Shannon Demko, Associate Director of Graduate Admissions, 202-885-1994, Fax: 202-885-1108, E-mail: demko@american.edu.

Bentley University, McCallum Graduate School of Business, Program in Taxation, Waltham, MA 02452-4705. Offers MST. Part-time and evening/weekend programs available. Postbaccalaureate distance learning degree programs offered (no on-campus study). *Faculty:* 65 full-time (24 women), 16 part-time/adjunct (6 women). *Students:* 28 full-time (16 women), 163 part-time (72 women); includes 34 minority (5 African Americans, 3 American Indian/Alaska Native, 21 Asian Americans or Pacific Islanders, 5 Hispanic Americans), 7 international. Average age 32. 105 applicants, 92% accepted, 72 enrolled. *Entrance requirements:* For master's, GMAT. Additional exam requirements/recommendations for international students: Required—TOEFL (minimum score 600 paper-based; 250 computer-based; 100 iBT), or IELTS (minimum score 7). *Application deadline:* For fall admission, 12/1 priority date for domestic and international students; for spring admission, 10/1 priority date for domestic and international students. Application fee: $50. Electronic applications accepted. *Expenses:* Tuition: Full-time $26,208; part-time $1092 per credit. Required fees: $404. *Financial support:* Application deadline: 6/1. *Faculty research:* Taxation of intellectual property, tax dispute resolution, corporate tax planning and advocacy, estate and financial planning. *Unit head:* Jack Lynch, Director, 781-891-2624, E-mail: jlynch@bentley.edu. *Application contact:* Sharon Hill, Director of Graduate Admissions, 781-891-2108, Fax: 781-891-2464, E-mail: bentleygraduateadmissions@bentley.edu.

Bernard M. Baruch College of the City University of New York, Zicklin School of Business, Department of Accounting, Program in Taxation, New York, NY 10010-5585. Offers MBA, MS. Part-time and evening/weekend programs available. *Entrance requirements:* For master's, GMAT, 2 letters of recommendation, resume, 2 years of work experience. Additional exam requirements/recommendations for international students: Required—TOEFL (minimum score 590 paper-based; 243 computer-based), TWE.

Boise State University, Graduate College, College of Business and Economics, Program in Accountancy, Boise, ID 83725-0399. Offers accountancy (MSA); taxation (MSA). *Accreditation:* AACSB. Part-time programs available. *Entrance requirements:* For master's, GMAT, minimum GPA of 3.0. Additional exam requirements/recommendations for international students: Required—TOEFL. Electronic applications accepted. *Expenses:* Tuition, state resident: full-time $3106; part-time $209 per credit. Tuition, nonresident: part-time $284 per credit.

Boston University, School of Law, Boston, MA 02215. Offers American law (LL M); banking (LL M); intellectual property law (LL M); law (JD); taxation (LL M); JD/LL M; JD/MA; JD/MBA; JD/MPH; JD/MS. *Accreditation:* ABA. *Faculty:* 65 full-time (26 women), 88 part-time/adjunct (32 women). *Students:* 1,014 full-time (507 women), 83 part-time (45 women); includes 211 minority (50 African Americans, 2 American Indian/Alaska Native, 104 Asian Americans or Pacific Islanders, 55 Hispanic Americans), 164 international. Average age 27. 7,660 applicants, 23% accepted, 271 enrolled. In 2009, 269 JDs, 213 master's awarded. *Degree requirements:* For master's, thesis (for some programs); for JD, thesis/dissertation, research project resulting in a paper. *Entrance requirements:* For JD, LSAT; for master's, JD. Additional exam requirements/recommendations for international students: Required—TOEFL (minimum score 600 paper-based; 250 computer-based; 100 iBT). *Application deadline:* For fall admission, 3/1 for domestic and international students. Applications are processed on a rolling basis. Application fee: $75. Electronic applications accepted. *Expenses:* Tuition: Full-time $37,910; part-time $1184 per credit hour. Required fees: $386; $40 per semester. Part-time tuition and fees vary according to class time, course level, degree level and program. *Financial support:* In 2009–10, 533 students received support. Career-related internships or fieldwork, Federal Work-Study, institutionally sponsored loans, and scholarships/grants available. Financial award application deadline: 3/1; financial award applicants required to submit FAFSA. *Faculty research:* Litigation and dispute resolution, intellectual property law, business organizations and finance law, international law, health law. *Unit head:* Maureen A. O'Rourke, Dean, 617-353-3112, Fax: 617-353-7400, E-mail: lawdean@bu.edu. *Application contact:* Alissa Leonard, Director of Admissions and Financial Aid, 617-353-3100, Fax: 617-353-0578, E-mail: bulawadm@bu.edu.

Bryant University, Graduate School of Business, Master of Science in Taxation Program, Smithfield, RI 02917. Offers MST. Part-time and evening/weekend programs available. *Faculty:* 3 full-time (0 women), 9 part-time/adjunct (0 women). *Students:* 51 part-time (19 women); includes 3 minority (1 Asian American or Pacific Islander, 2 Hispanic Americans). Average age 33. 15 applicants, 80% accepted, 8 enrolled. In 2009, 12 master's awarded. *Entrance requirements:* For master's, GMAT, recommendation, resume. Additional exam requirements/recommendations for international students: Required—TOEFL (minimum score 580 paper-based; 237 computer-based; 95 iBT). *Application deadline:* For fall admission, 7/15 for domestic and international students; for spring admission, 11/15 for domestic and international students. Applications are processed on a rolling basis. Application fee: $80. Electronic applications accepted. *Expenses:* Contact institution. *Financial support:* In 2009–10, 1 student received support. Application deadline: 2/15. *Faculty research:* Tax efficiencies of mutual funds, cost segregation studies, taxation of partnerships, property transactions. *Unit head:* Kristopher T. Sullivan, Assistant Dean of the Graduate School, 401-232-6230, Fax: 401-232-6494, E-mail: sullivan@bryant.edu. *Application contact:* Ellen Hudon, Assistant Director of Graduate Admission, 401-232-6230, Fax: 401-232-6494, E-mail: ehudon@bryant.edu.

California Polytechnic State University, San Luis Obispo, Orfalea College of Business, Graduate Programs in Business, San Luis Obispo, CA 93407. Offers business (MBA); taxation (MSA). *Faculty:* 4 full-time (1 woman), 2 part-time/adjunct (1 woman). *Students:* 37 full-time (11 women), 22 part-time (12 women); includes 9 minority (4 Asian Americans or Pacific Islanders, 5 Hispanic Americans), 3 international. Average age 26. 132 applicants, 36% accepted, 36 enrolled. In 2009, 49 master's awarded. *Degree requirements:* For master's, comprehensive exam (for some programs), thesis or alternative. *Entrance requirements:* For master's, GMAT. Additional exam requirements/recommendations for international students: Required—TOEFL (minimum score 550 paper-based; 213 computer-based), or IELTS (minimum score 6). *Application deadline:* For fall admission, 7/1 for domestic students, 11/30 for international students. Applications are processed on a rolling basis. Application fee: $55. Electronic applications accepted. *Expenses:* Tuition, nonresident: full-time $11,160; part-time $248 per

unit. Required fees: $7134; $1553 per quarter. *Financial support:* Career-related internships or fieldwork, Federal Work-Study, institutionally sponsored loans, scholarships/grants, and unspecified assistantships available. Support available to part-time students. Financial award application deadline: 3/2; financial award applicants required to submit FAFSA. *Faculty research:* International business, organizational behavior, graphic communication document systems management, commercial development of innovative technologies, effective communication skills for managers. *Unit head:* Dr. Brian Tietje, Associate Dean/Graduate Coordinator, 805-756-1757, Fax: 805-756-0110, E-mail: btietje@calpoly.edu. *Application contact:* Dr. Chris Carr, Associate Dean, 805-756-2637, Fax: 805-756-0110, E-mail: ccarr@calpoly.edu.

California State University, East Bay, Graduate Programs, College of Business and Economics, Department of Accounting and Finance, Program in Taxation, Hayward, CA 94542-3000. Offers MS. Part-time and evening/weekend programs available. Postbaccalaureate distance learning degree programs offered. *Faculty:* 2 full-time (0 women), 1 (woman) part-time/adjunct. *Students:* 14 full-time (8 women), 18 part-time (14 women); includes 15 minority (1 African American, 14 Asian Americans or Pacific Islanders), 5 international. Average age 35. 25 applicants, 60% accepted, 12 enrolled. In 2009, 10 master's awarded. *Degree requirements:* For master's, final project. *Entrance requirements:* For master's, GMAT, U. S. CPA exam or Enrolled Agents Exam, minimum GPA of 2.75. Additional exam requirements/recommendations for international students: Required—TOEFL (minimum score 550 paper-based; 213 computer-based). *Application deadline:* For fall admission, 6/30 for domestic and international students. Application fee: $55. Electronic applications accepted. *Financial support:* Career-related internships or fieldwork, Federal Work-Study, and institutionally sponsored loans available. Support available to part-time students. Financial award application deadline: 3/1; financial award applicants required to submit FAFSA. *Unit head:* Prof. Gary McBride, Graduate Advisor, 510-885-3307, Fax: 510-885-4796, E-mail: gary.mcbride@csueastbay.edu. *Application contact:* Donna Wiley, Interim Associate Director, 510-885-2928, Fax: 510-885-4777, E-mail: donna.wiley@csueastbay.edu.

California State University, Fullerton, Graduate Studies, College of Business and Economics, Department of Accounting, Fullerton, CA 92834-9480. Offers accounting (MBA, MS); taxation (MS). *Accreditation:* AACSB. Part-time programs available. *Students:* 115 full-time (71 women), 84 part-time (50 women); includes 84 minority (1 African American, 75 Asian Americans or Pacific Islanders, 8 Hispanic Americans), 60 international. Average age 29. 233 applicants, 55% accepted, 59 enrolled. In 2009, 62 master's awarded. *Degree requirements:* For master's, thesis or alternative, project. *Entrance requirements:* For master's, GMAT, minimum AACSB index of 950. *Application deadline:* Applications are processed on a rolling basis. Application fee: $55. Electronic applications accepted. *Expenses:* Tuition, nonresident: full-time $11,160; part-time $373 per credit. Required fees: $1440 per term. Tuition and fees vary according to course load, degree level and program. *Financial support:* Career-related internships or fieldwork, Federal Work-Study, institutionally sponsored loans, and scholarships/grants available. Support available to part-time students. Financial award application deadline: 3/1; financial award applicants required to submit FAFSA. *Unit head:* Dr. Betty Chavis, Chair, 657-278-2225. *Application contact:* Admissions/Applications, 657-278-2371.

California State University, Los Angeles, Graduate Studies, College of Business and Economics, Department of Accounting, Los Angeles, CA 90032-8530. Offers accountancy (MS), including business taxation, financial accounting, information systems, management accounting; accounting (MBA). Part-time and evening/weekend programs available. *Faculty:* 4 full-time (1 woman), 4 part-time/adjunct (0 women). *Students:* 47 full-time (31 women), 54 part-time (33 women); includes 32 minority (1 African American, 25 Asian Americans or Pacific Islanders, 6 Hispanic Americans), 51 international. Average age 30. 34 applicants, 97% accepted, 16 enrolled. In 2009, 37 master's awarded. *Degree requirements:* For master's, comprehensive exam (MBA), thesis (MS). *Entrance requirements:* For master's, GMAT, minimum GPA of 2.5 during previous 2 years of course work. Additional exam requirements/recommendations for international students: Required—TOEFL (minimum score 550 paper-based; 213 computer-based). *Application deadline:* For fall admission, 5/1 for domestic and international students. Applications are processed on a rolling basis. Application fee: $55. Electronic applications accepted. *Financial support:* Career-related internships or fieldwork and Federal Work-Study available. Support available to part-time students. Financial award application deadline: 3/1. *Unit head:* Dr. Greg Kunkel, Chair, 323-343-2830, Fax: 323-343-6439, E-mail: gkunkel@calstatela.edu. *Application contact:* Dr. Cheryl L. Ney, Associate Vice President for Academic Affairs and Dean of Graduate Studies, 323-343-3820, Fax: 323-343-5653, E-mail: cney@cslanet.calstatela.edu.

California State University, Northridge, Graduate Studies, The Tseng College of Extended Learning, Northridge, CA 91330. Offers knowledge management (MKM); public administration (MPA); taxation (MS). *Entrance requirements:* For master's, GRE (if cumulative undergraduate GPA less than 3.0). *Unit head:* Joyce Feucht-Haviar, Dean, 866-873-6439. *Application contact:* Joyce Feucht-Haviar, Dean, 866-873-6439.

Capital University, Law School, Program in Business Law and Taxation, Columbus, OH 43209-2394. Offers business (LL M); business and taxation (LL M); taxation (LL M); JD/LL M. Part-time and evening/weekend programs available. *Degree requirements:* For master's, thesis or alternative. *Entrance requirements:* For master's, previous course work in accounting, business law, and taxation. Additional exam requirements/recommendations for international students: Required—TOEFL (minimum score 600 paper-based; 250 computer-based). Electronic applications accepted.

Capital University, Law School, Program in Taxation, Columbus, OH 43209-2394. Offers taxation (MT). Part-time and evening/weekend programs available. *Degree requirements:* For master's, thesis or alternative. *Entrance requirements:* For master's, previous course work in accounting, business law, and taxation. Additional exam requirements/recommendations for international students: Required—TOEFL (minimum score 600 paper-based; 250 computer-based). Electronic applications accepted. *Expenses:* Contact institution.

Chapman University, Graduate Studies, School of Law, Orange, CA 92866. Offers advocacy and dispute resolution (JD); entertainment law (JD); environmental, land use, and real estate (JD); international law (JD); law (LL M), including business law and economics, entertainment and media law, international and comparative law; prosecutorial science (LL M); tax law (JD); taxation (LL M); JD/MBA; JD/MFA. *Accreditation:* ABA. Part-time and evening/weekend programs available. *Faculty:* 56 full-time (21 women), 24 part-time/adjunct (4 women). *Students:* 535 full-time (260 women), 87 part-time (37 women); includes 126 minority (6 African Americans, 2 American Indian/Alaska Native, 79 Asian Americans or Pacific Islanders, 39 Hispanic Americans), 6 international. Average age 27. 2,996 applicants, 32% accepted, 226 enrolled. In 2009, 158 JDs, 7 master's awarded. *Entrance requirements:* LSAT, minimum undergraduate GPA of 2.75. Additional exam requirements/recommendations for international students: Required—TOEFL (minimum score 600 paper-based; 213 computer-based; 80 iBT). *Application deadline:* For fall admission, 4/1 priority date for domestic students. Applications are processed on a rolling basis. Application fee: $65. Electronic applications accepted. *Expenses:* Contact institution. *Financial support:* Fellowships, Federal Work-Study and scholarships/grants available. Financial award application deadline: 6/30; financial award applicants required to submit FAFSA. *Unit head:* Dr. John Eastman, Dean, 714-628-2500. *Application contact:* Marissa Vargas, Admissions Recruiter/Financial Aid Counselor, 877-CHAPLAW, E-mail: mvargas@chapman.edu.

Cleveland State University, College of Graduate Studies, Nance College of Business Administration, Department of Accounting, Cleveland, OH 44115. Offers financial accounting/audit (M Acc); taxation (M Acc). *Accreditation:* AACSB. Part-time and evening/weekend programs available. *Entrance requirements:* For master's, GMAT, minimum GPA of 2.75. Additional exam requirements/recommendations for international students: Required—TOEFL (minimum score 525 paper-based; 197 computer-based). *Faculty research:* Internal auditing, computer auditing, accounting education, managerial accounting.

DePaul University, Charles H. Kellstadt Graduate School of Business, School of Accountancy and Management Information Systems, Chicago, IL 60604-2287. Offers accountancy (M Acc, MSA); business information technology (MS); e-business (MBA, MS); financial management and control (MBA); management accounting (MBA); management information systems (MBA); taxation (MST). Part-time and evening/weekend programs available. *Faculty:* 30 full-time (9 women), 54 part-time/adjunct (7 women). *Students:* 167 full-time (82 women), 237 part-time (106 women); includes 52 minority (8 African Americans, 1 American Indian/Alaska Native, 30 Asian Americans or Pacific Islanders, 13 Hispanic Americans), 49 international. In 2009, 141 master's awarded. *Entrance requirements:* For master's, GMAT, 2 letters of recommendation, resume. Additional exam requirements/recommendations for international students: Required—TOEFL (minimum score 550 paper-based; 213 computer-based). *Application deadline:* For fall admission, 7/1 for domestic students; for winter admission, 10/1 for domestic students; for spring admission, 2/1 for domestic students. Applications are processed on a rolling basis. Application fee: $60. *Expenses:* Tuition: Full-time $37,525; part-time $620 per credit hour. *Financial support:* In 2009–10, 7 research assistantships with full tuition reimbursements (averaging $4,100 per year) were awarded; institutionally sponsored loans also available. Financial award application deadline: 4/2. *Faculty research:* Tax policy, property transactions, stock options as compensation, standards setting, activity-based costing in health care. *Unit head:* Kevin Stevens, Director, 312-362-6989, E-mail: kstevens@depaul.edu. *Application contact:* Christopher E. Kinsella, Director of Cohort MBA Programs, 312-362-8810, Fax: 312-362-6677, E-mail: kgsb@depaul.edu.

Fairfield University, Charles F. Dolan School of Business, Fairfield, CT 06824-5195. Offers accounting (MBA, MS, CAS); finance (MBA, MS, CAS); general management (MBA); human resource management (MBA, CAS); information systems and operations (MBA); information systems and operations management (CAS); international business (MBA, CAS); marketing (MBA, CAS); taxation (MBA, MS). *Accreditation:* AACSB. Part-time and evening/weekend programs available. *Degree requirements:* For master's, capstone course. *Entrance requirements:* For master's, GMAT (minimum score 500), 2 letters of reference, resume, minimum GPA of 3.0. Additional exam requirements/recommendations for international students: Required—TOEFL (minimum score 550 paper-based; 213 computer-based; 80 iBT). Electronic applications accepted. *Expenses:* Contact institution. *Faculty research:* Optimization strategies, international finance, consumer behavior, financial market volatility, Internet marketing, supply chain analysis, tax issues.

Fairleigh Dickinson University, College at Florham, Silberman College of Business, Department of Accounting, Law, and Tax, Program in Taxation, Madison, NJ 07940-1099. Offers MS, Certificate. *Students:* 4 full-time (3 women), 97 part-time (41 women), 5 international. Average age 37. 47 applicants, 91% accepted, 32 enrolled. In 2009, 24 master's awarded. *Application deadline:* Applications are processed on a rolling basis. Application fee: $40.

Fairleigh Dickinson University, Metropolitan Campus, Silberman College of Business, Department of Accounting, Law, and Tax, Program in Taxation, Teaneck, NJ 07666-1914. Offers MS. *Application deadline:* Applications are processed on a rolling basis. Application fee: $40. *Application contact:* Susan Brooman, University Director of Graduate Admissions, 201-692-2554, Fax: 201-692-2560, E-mail: globaleducation@fdu.edu.

Florida Atlantic University, College of Business, School of Accounting, Program in Taxation, Boca Raton, FL 33431-0991. Offers M Tax. Part-time and evening/weekend programs available. Postbaccalaureate distance learning degree programs offered (minimal on-campus study). *Faculty:* 22 full-time (10 women), 12 part-time/adjunct (1 woman). *Students:* 15 full-time (8 women), 17 part-time (6 women); includes 6 minority (2 African Americans, 4 Hispanic Americans). Average age 31. 33 applicants, 52% accepted, 3 enrolled. In 2009, 9 master's awarded. *Degree requirements:* For master's, comprehensive exam, thesis optional. *Entrance requirements:* For master's, GMAT, minimum GPA of 3.0. Additional exam requirements/recommendations for international students: Required—TOEFL (minimum score 600 paper-based; 250 computer-based). *Application deadline:* For fall admission, 7/1 priority date for domestic students, 2/15 priority date for international students; for spring admission, 11/1 priority date for domestic students, 7/15 priority date for international students. Applications are processed on a rolling basis. Application fee: $30. *Expenses:* Tuition, state resident: full-time $7055; part-time $293.94 per credit hour. Tuition, nonresident: full-time $22,096; part-time $920.66 per credit hour. *Financial support:* Career-related internships or fieldwork, Federal Work-Study, institutionally sponsored loans, scholarships/grants, tuition waivers (full and partial), and unspecified assistantships available. Support available to part-time students. Financial award application deadline: 3/1. *Application contact:* Fredrick G. Taylor, Graduate Adviser, 561-297-3196, Fax: 561-297-1315, E-mail: ftaylor@fau.edu.

Florida Gulf Coast University, Lutgert College of Business, Program in Accounting and Taxation, Fort Myers, FL 33965-6565. Offers MS. Part-time and evening/weekend programs available. *Faculty:* 63 full-time (20 women), 19 part-time/adjunct (2 women). *Students:* 44 full-time (28 women), 11 part-time (10 women); includes 10 minority (2 African Americans, 1 Asian American or Pacific Islander, 7 Hispanic Americans), 2 international. Average age 32. 34 applicants, 74% accepted, 19 enrolled. In 2009, 16 master's awarded. *Degree requirements:* For master's, thesis or alternative. *Entrance requirements:* For master's, GMAT, minimum GPA of 3.0. Additional exam requirements/recommendations for international students: Required—TOEFL (minimum score 550 paper-based; 213 computer-based). *Application deadline:* For fall admission, 6/1 priority date for domestic students; for spring admission, 11/1 for domestic students. Applications are processed on a rolling basis. Application fee: $30. Electronic applications accepted. *Faculty research:* Stock petitions, mergers and acquisitions, deferred taxes, fraud and accounting regulations, graphical reporting practices. *Unit head:* Dr. Ara Volkan, Chair, 239-590-7380, Fax: 239-590-7330, E-mail: avolkan@fgcu.edu. *Application contact:* Carol Burnette, Associate Dean, 239-590-7350, Fax: 239-590-7330, E-mail: burnette@fgcu.edu.

Florida International University, Alvah H. Chapman, Jr. Graduate School of Business, School of Accounting, Program in Taxation, Miami, FL 33199. Offers MST. Part-time and evening/weekend programs available. *Students:* 52 full-time (24 women), 3 part-time (2 women); includes 50 minority (5 African Americans, 1 Asian American or Pacific Islander, 44 Hispanic Americans), 2 international. Average age 31. 38 applicants, 89% accepted, 32 enrolled. In 2009, 43 master's awarded. *Entrance requirements:* For master's, GMAT or GRE, minimum GPA of 3.0; resume. Additional exam requirements/recommendations for international students: Required—TOEFL (minimum score 550 paper-based; 213 computer-based; 80 iBT), or IELTS (minimum score 6.5). *Application deadline:* For fall admission, 4/1 for domestic and international students; for spring admission, 10/1 for domestic students, 9/1 for international students. Applications are processed on a rolling basis. Application fee: $30. Electronic applications accepted. *Expenses:* Contact institution. *Financial support:* Institutionally sponsored loans, scholarships/grants, and traineeships available. Financial award application deadline: 3/1; financial award applicants required to submit FAFSA. *Faculty research:* Corporate taxation; small business taxation. *Unit head:* Dr. Sharon Lassar, Director, School of Accounting, 305-348-3501, Fax: 305-348-2914, E-mail: sharon.lassar@fiu.edu. *Application contact:* Teresita Brunken, 305-348-4224, Fax: 305-348-2914, E-mail: brunken@fiu.edu.

Florida State University, The Graduate School, College of Business, Tallahassee, FL 32306-1110. Offers accounting (M Acc), including accounting information services, assurance services, corporate accounting, taxation; business administration (MBA, PhD), including accounting (PhD), finance (PhD), management information systems (PhD), marketing (PhD), organizational behavior (PhD), risk management and insurance (PhD), strategic management (PhD); finance (MS); insurance (MSM); management information systems (MS); JD/MBA; MSW/MBA. *Accreditation:* AACSB. Part-time programs available. Postbaccalaureate distance learning degree programs offered (no on-campus study). *Faculty:* 107 full-time (31 women), 2 part-time/adjunct (0 women). *Students:* 212 full-time (73 women), 345 part-time (107 women); includes 123 minority (37 African Americans, 2 American Indian/Alaska Native, 48 Asian Americans or Pacific Islanders, 36 Hispanic Americans). Average age 30. 908 applicants, 43% accepted, 307 enrolled. In 2009, 257 master's, 18 doctorates awarded. Terminal master's awarded for partial completion of doctoral program. *Degree requirements:* For doctorate, comprehensive exam, thesis/dissertation. *Entrance requirements:* For master's, GMAT, work experience (MBA,

Taxation

Florida State University (continued)

MS), minimum GPA of 3.0, letters of recommendation; for doctorate, GMAT, minimum graduate GPA of 3.5, letters of recommendation. Additional exam requirements/recommendations for international students: Required—TOEFL (minimum score 600 paper-based; 80 computer-based); Recommended—IELTS (minimum score 6.5). *Application deadline:* For fall admission, 6/1 for domestic students, 5/1 for international students; for spring admission, 10/1 for domestic students, 9/1 for international students. Applications are processed on a rolling basis. Application fee: $30. Electronic applications accepted. *Expenses:* Tuition, state resident: full-time $7413. Tuition, nonresident: full-time $22,567. *Financial support:* In 2009–10, 102 students received support, including 32 fellowships with full tuition reimbursements available (averaging $6,900 per year), 30 research assistantships with full tuition reimbursements available (averaging $4,500 per year), 40 teaching assistantships with full tuition reimbursements available (averaging $11,500 per year); career-related internships or fieldwork, scholarships/grants, health care benefits, tuition waivers (full and partial), and unspecified assistantships also available. Support available to part-time students. Financial award application deadline: 1/1. *Unit head:* Dr. Caryn Beck-Dudley, Dean, 850-644-3090, Fax: 850-644-0915. *Application contact:* Lisa Beverly, Director, Graduate Programs Admissions, 850-644-6458, Fax: 850-644-0588, E-mail: lbeverly@cob.fsu.edu.

Fontbonne University, Graduate Programs, College of Global Business and Professional Studies, Program in Taxation, St. Louis, MO 63105-3098. Offers MST. Part-time and evening/weekend programs available. *Faculty:* 4 part-time/adjunct (3 women). *Students:* 8 part-time (7 women). Average age 37. In 2009, 3 master's awarded. *Entrance requirements:* For master's, minimum GPA of 2.5. Additional exam requirements/recommendations for international students: Required—TOEFL (minimum score 197 computer-based; 71 iBT). *Application deadline:* For fall admission, 9/1 priority date for domestic students; for spring admission, 4/15 priority date for domestic students. Applications are processed on a rolling basis. Application fee: $25. *Expenses:* Tuition: Part-time $562 per credit hour. *Financial support:* Application deadline: 4/1. *Unit head:* Dr. Linda Maurer, Dean of College of Business and Professional Studies, 314-889-1423, E-mail: lmaurer@fontbonne.edu. *Application contact:* Fontbonne University OPTIONS, 314-863-2220, Fax: 314-963-0327, E-mail: options@fontbonne.edu.

Fordham University, Graduate School of Business Administration, New York, NY 10023. Offers accounting (MBA); communications and media management (MBA); executive business administration (EMBA); finance (MBA, MS); information systems (MBA, MS); management systems (MBA); marketing (MBA); media management (MS); taxation (MS); taxation and accounting (MTA);); JD/MBA; MBA/MIM; MS/MBA. *Accreditation:* AACSB. Part-time and evening/weekend programs available. *Entrance requirements:* For master's, GMAT, 2 letters of recommendation, resume. Additional exam requirements/recommendations for international students: Required—TOEFL (minimum score 600 paper-based; 250 computer-based; 100 iBT). Electronic applications accepted. *Expenses:* Contact institution.

George Mason University, School of Management, Fairfax, VA 22030. Offers accounting (MS); business administration (MBA); executive business administration (EMBA); real estate development (MS); taxation (MS); technology management (MS). Part-time and evening/weekend programs available. *Faculty:* 80 full-time (26 women), 57 part-time/adjunct (13 women). *Students:* 162 full-time (72 women), 336 part-time (120 women); includes 55 minority (12 African Americans, 1 American Indian/Alaska Native, 29 Asian Americans or Pacific Islanders, 13 Hispanic Americans), 39 international. Average age 31. 371 applicants, 61% accepted, 145 enrolled. In 2009, 168 master's awarded. *Entrance requirements:* For master's, GMAT. Additional exam requirements/recommendations for international students: Required—TOEFL. *Application deadline:* Applications are processed on a rolling basis. Application fee: $75. Electronic applications accepted. *Expenses:* Tuition, state resident: full-time $7568; part-time $315.33 per credit hour. Tuition, nonresident: full-time $21,704; part-time $904.33 per credit hour. Required fees: $2184; $91 per credit hour. *Financial support:* In 2009–10, 13 students received support, including 10 research assistantships with full and partial tuition reimbursements available (averaging $3,372 per year), 4 teaching assistantships with full and partial tuition reimbursements available (averaging $3,511 per year); fellowships, career-related internships or fieldwork, Federal Work-Study, unspecified assistantships, and health care benefits (full-time research or teaching assistantship recipients) also available. Support available to part-time students. Financial award application deadline: 3/1; financial award applicants required to submit FAFSA. *Faculty research:* Current leading global issues: offshore outsourcing, international financial risk, comparative systems of innovation. Total annual research expenditures: $346,607. *Unit head:* Jorge Haddock, Dean, 703-993-1875, E-mail: jhaddock@gmu.edu. *Application contact:* Melanie Pflugshaupt, Administrative Coordinator to Dean's Office, 703-993-3638, E-mail: mpflugsh@gmu.edu.

Georgetown University, Law Center, Washington, DC 20001. Offers general (LL M); global health law (LL M); international and comparative law (LL M); international business and economic law (LL M); international legal studies (LL M); law (JD, SJD); securities and financial regulation (LL M); taxation (LL M); JD/LL M; JD/MA; JD/MBA; JD/MPH; JD/PhD. *Accreditation:* ABA. Part-time and evening/weekend programs available. *Degree requirements:* For master's, thesis; for doctorate, thesis/dissertation. *Entrance requirements:* For JD, LSAT; for master's and doctorate, JD, LL B, or first law degree earned in country of origin. Additional exam requirements/recommendations for international students: Required—TOEFL. *Expenses:* Contact institution. *Faculty research:* Constitutional law, legal history, jurisprudence.

Georgia State University, J. Mack Robinson College of Business, School of Accountancy, Program in Taxation, Atlanta, GA 30303. Offers MTX. Part-time and evening/weekend programs available. *Entrance requirements:* For master's, GMAT, GRE General Test or LSAT. Additional exam requirements/recommendations for international students: Required—TOEFL (minimum score 610 paper-based; 255 computer-based; 101 iBT). Electronic applications accepted.

Golden Gate University, School of Law, San Francisco, CA 94105-2968. Offers environmental law (LL M); intellectual property law (LL M); international legal studies (LL M, SJD); law (JD); taxation (LL M); U.S. legal studies (LL M); JD/MBA; JD/PhD. *Accreditation:* ABA. Part-time and evening/weekend programs available. *Degree requirements:* For doctorate, thesis/dissertation. *Entrance requirements:* LSAT. Additional exam requirements/recommendations for international students: Required—TOEFL (minimum score 600 paper-based; 250 computer-based). Electronic applications accepted. *Expenses:* Contact institution. *Faculty research:* International law, intellectual property law, environmental law, real estate, civil rights.

Golden Gate University, School of Taxation, San Francisco, CA 94105-2968. Offers advanced studies in taxation (Certificate); estate planning (Certificate); international tax (Certificate); tax (Certificate); taxation (MS). Part-time and evening/weekend programs available. *Faculty:* 6 full-time (1 woman), 65 part-time/adjunct (15 women). *Students:* 66 full-time (37 women), 653 part-time (346 women); includes 248 minority (28 African Americans, 2 American Indian/Alaska Native, 184 Asian Americans or Pacific Islanders, 34 Hispanic Americans), 22 international. Average age 36. 337 applicants, 87% accepted, 148 enrolled. In 2009, 242 master's awarded. *Entrance requirements:* For master's, minimum GPA of 3.0. Additional exam requirements/recommendations for international students: Required—TOEFL. *Application deadline:* For fall admission, 5/15 for international students; for winter admission, 1/15 for international students; for spring admission, 9/15 for international students. Applications are processed on a rolling basis. Application fee: $70 ($110 for international students). Electronic applications accepted. *Expenses:* Contact institution. *Financial support:* Career-related internships or fieldwork, Federal Work-Study, institutionally sponsored loans, and scholarships/grants available. Support available to part-time students. Financial award applicants required to submit FAFSA. *Unit head:* Mary Canning, Dean, 415-442-7885, Fax: 415-442-7807. *Application contact:* Angela Melero, Enrollment Services, 415-442-7800, Fax: 415-442-7807, E-mail: info@ggu.edu.

Goldey-Beacom College, Graduate Program, Wilmington, DE 19808-1999. Offers business administration (MBA); finance (MS); financial management (MBA); human resource management (MBA); information technology (MBA); international business management (MBA); management (MM); marketing management (MBA); taxation (MBA, MS). *Accreditation:* ACBSP. Part-time and evening/weekend programs available. *Faculty:* 20 full-time (8 women), 28 part-time/adjunct (10 women). *Students:* 38 full-time (18 women), 486 part-time (184 women); includes 350 minority (38 African Americans, 300 Asian Americans or Pacific Islanders, 12 Hispanic Americans). Average age 27. In 2009, 130 master's awarded. *Entrance requirements:* For master's, GMAT, MAT, GRE, minimum GPA of 3.0. Additional exam requirements/recommendations for international students: Required—TOEFL (minimum score 65 computer-based); Recommended—IELTS (minimum score 5). *Application deadline:* Applications are processed on a rolling basis. Electronic applications accepted. *Expenses:* Tuition: Full-time $14,166; part-time $787 per credit. Required fees: $180; $10 per credit. *Financial support:* In 2009–10, 486 students received support. Scholarships/grants available. Support available to part-time students. Financial award application deadline: 4/1; financial award applicants required to submit FAFSA. *Unit head:* Larry W. Eby, Director of Admissions, 302-225-6289, Fax: 302-996-5408, E-mail: ebylw@gbc.edu. *Application contact:* Ashley E. Mashington, Graduate Admissions Representative, 302-225-6259, Fax: 302-996-5408, E-mail: mashina@gbc.edu.

Grand Valley State University, Seidman College of Business, Program in Taxation, Allendale, MI 49401-9403. Offers MST. Part-time and evening/weekend programs available. *Faculty:* 2 full-time (0 women), 3 part-time/adjunct (0 women). *Students:* 7 full-time (4 women), 36 part-time (23 women); includes 2 minority (1 African American, 1 Asian American or Pacific Islander), 1 international. Average age 28. 15 applicants, 100% accepted, 11 enrolled. In 2009, 15 master's awarded. *Entrance requirements:* For master's, GMAT. Additional exam requirements/recommendations for international students: Required—TOEFL. *Application deadline:* For fall admission, 8/1 priority date for domestic students, 5/1 priority date for international students; for winter admission, 12/1 priority date for domestic students, 11/1 priority date for international students; for spring admission, 4/1 priority date for domestic students, 3/1 priority date for international students. Applications are processed on a rolling basis. Application fee: $30. Electronic applications accepted. *Expenses:* Tuition, state resident: part-time $471 per credit hour. Tuition, nonresident: part-time $646 per credit hour. Tuition and fees vary according to course level. *Financial support:* In 2009–10, 2 students received support, including 1 fellowship (averaging $344 per year), 1 research assistantship (averaging $2,826 per year); Federal Work-Study, institutionally sponsored loans, and unspecified assistantships also available. Financial award application deadline: 2/15. *Faculty research:* Individual income taxation, state taxation, pass-through entities, estate and gift taxation, sale-leasebacks. *Unit head:* Dr. Steve Goldberg, Director, 616-331-7190, Fax: 616-331-7389, E-mail: goldbers@gvsu.edu. *Application contact:* Claudia J. Bajema, Director, Graduate Business Programs, 616-331-7387, Fax: 616-331-7389, E-mail: bajemac@gvsu.edu.

HEC Montreal, School of Business Administration, Diploma Programs in Administration, Program in Taxation, Montréal, QC H3T 2A7, Canada. Offers LL M, Diploma. All courses are given in French. Part-time programs available. *Students:* 32 full-time (13 women), 85 part-time (42 women). 85 applicants, 65% accepted, 39 enrolled. In 2009, 13 Diplomas awarded. *Degree requirements:* For master's, one foreign language, thesis; for Diploma, one foreign language. *Entrance requirements:* For master's, diploma in taxation from HEC Montreal; for Diploma, work experience in Canadian taxation system. *Application deadline:* For fall admission, 4/1 for domestic and international students; for winter admission, 10/1 for domestic and international students. Application fee: $77 Canadian dollars. Electronic applications accepted. Tuition and fees charges are reported in Canadian dollars. *Expenses:* Tuition, area resident: Part-time $65.60 Canadian dollars per credit. Tuition, state resident: full-time $2361.60 Canadian dollars; part-time $183.36 Canadian dollars per credit. Tuition, nonresident: full-time $6601 Canadian dollars; part-time $448.13 Canadian dollars per credit. International tuition: $16,132.68 Canadian dollars full-time. Required fees: $1254.15 Canadian dollars; $28.99 Canadian dollars per course. $91.68 Canadian dollars per term. Tuition and fees vary according to degree level and program. *Financial support:* Research assistantships, teaching assistantships, scholarships/grants available. Financial award application deadline: 10/2. *Unit head:* Louise Cote, Director, 514-340-6205, Fax: 514-340-5640, E-mail: louise.cote@hec.ca. *Application contact:* Marie Deshaies, Senior Student Advisor, 514-340-6135, Fax: 514-340-6411, E-mail: marie.deshaies@hec.ca.

Hofstra University, Frank G. Zarb School of Business, Department of Accounting, Taxation and Legal Studies, Hempstead, NY 11549. Offers accounting (MS); business administration (MBA), including accounting, taxation; taxation (MS). Part-time and evening/weekend programs available. *Faculty:* 11 full-time (3 women), 3 part-time/adjunct (1 woman). *Students:* 58 full-time (20 women), 50 part-time (23 women); includes 10 minority (1 African American, 6 Asian Americans or Pacific Islanders, 3 Hispanic Americans), 22 international. Average age 28. 154 applicants, 63% accepted, 49 enrolled. In 2009, 20 master's awarded. *Degree requirements:* For master's, capstone course (MBA), thesis (MS). *Entrance requirements:* For master's, GMAT or GRE, 2 letters of recommendation, resume. Additional exam requirements/recommendations for international students: Required—TOEFL (minimum score 550 paper-based; 213 computer-based; 80 iBT); Recommended—IELTS (minimum score 6). *Application deadline:* Applications are processed on a rolling basis. Application fee: $60. Electronic applications accepted. *Expenses:* Contact institution. *Financial support:* In 2009–10, 24 students received support, including 21 fellowships with full and partial tuition reimbursements available (averaging $9,560 per year), 2 research assistantships with full and partial tuition reimbursements available (averaging $15,406 per year); Federal Work-Study, institutionally sponsored loans, scholarships/grants, health care benefits, tuition waivers (full and partial), and unspecified assistantships also available. Support available to part-time students. Financial award applicants required to submit FAFSA. *Faculty research:* Corporate governance and executive compensation, Sarbanes-Oxley and certification compliance for financial statement, student performance and evaluation models, decomposing the elements of nonprofit organizational performance, accounting for sustainability. *Unit head:* Dr. Nathan S. Slavin, Chairperson, 516-463-5690, Fax: 516-463-4834, E-mail: actnzs@hofstra.edu. *Application contact:* Carol Drummer, Dean of Graduate Admissions, 516-463-4876, Fax: 516-463-4664, E-mail: gradstudent@hofstra.edu.

Illinois Institute of Technology, Chicago-Kent College of Law, Chicago, IL 60661-3691. Offers family law (LL M); financial services (LL M); international intellectual property (LL M); international law (LL M); law (JD); taxation (LL M); JD/LL M; JD/MBA; JD/MPA; JD/MPH; JD/MS. *Accreditation:* ABA. Part-time and evening/weekend programs available. *Faculty:* 70 full-time (26 women), 153 part-time/adjunct (29 women). *Students:* 879 full-time (428 women), 222 part-time (98 women); includes 192 minority (52 African Americans, 4 American Indian/Alaska Native, 91 Asian Americans or Pacific Islanders, 45 Hispanic Americans), 127 international. Average age 27. 3,652 applicants, 45% accepted, 388 enrolled. In 2009, 315 JDs, 140 master's awarded. *Entrance requirements:* LSAT, LSDAS. Additional exam requirements/recommendations for international students: Required—TOEFL (minimum score 600 paper-based; 250 computer-based; 100 iBT); Recommended—IELTS (minimum score 7). *Application deadline:* For fall admission, 3/1 priority date for domestic students, 2/1 priority date for international students. Applications are processed on a rolling basis. Application fee: $60 ($75 for international students). Electronic applications accepted. *Expenses:* Contact institution. *Financial support:* In 2009–10, 605 students received support. Career-related internships or fieldwork, Federal Work-Study, institutionally sponsored loans, scholarships/grants, and tuition waivers (full) available. Support available to part-time students. Financial award application deadline: 3/15; financial award applicants required to submit FAFSA. *Faculty research:* Constitutional law, bioethics, environmental law. Total annual research expenditures: $747,995. *Unit head:* Harold J. Krent, Dean, 312-906-5010, Fax: 312-906-5335, E-mail: hkrent@kentlaw.edu. *Application contact:* Nicole Vilches, Assistant Dean, 312-906-5020, Fax: 312-906-5274, E-mail: admissions@kentlaw.edu.

Instituto Tecnologico de Santo Domingo, Graduate School, Santo Domingo, Dominican Republic. Offers applied linguistics (MA); construction administration (M Mgmt); corporate finance (M Mgmt); education (M Ed); engineering (M Eng), including data telecommunications, industrial engineering, logistics and supply chain, maintenance engineering, sanitary and environmental engineering, structural engineering; environmental science (M En S), including environmental education, environmental management, marine and coastal ecosystems, natural

resources management; family therapy (MA); food science and technology (MS); human development (MA); human resources administration (M Mgmt); international business (M Mgmt); labor risks (M Mgmt); management (M Mgmt); marketing (M Mgmt); mathematics (MS); organizational development (M Mgmt); planning and taxation (M Mgmt); psychology (MA); social science (M Ed); upper management (M Mgmt). *Entrance requirements:* For master's, birth certificate, minimum GPA of 2.0.

John Marshall Law School, Graduate and Professional Programs, Chicago, IL 60604-3968. Offers comparative legal studies (LL M); employee benefits (LL M, MS); information technology (LL M, MS); intellectual property (LL M); international business and trade (LL M); law (JD); real estate (LL M, MS); taxation (LL M, MS); JD/LL M; JD/MA; JD/MBA; JD/MPA. *Accreditation:* ABA. Part-time and evening/weekend programs available. *Faculty:* 73 full-time (26 women), 110 part-time/adjunct (33 women). *Students:* 1,139 full-time (505 women), 407 part-time (204 women); includes 353 minority (130 African Americans, 15 American Indian/Alaska Native, 91 Asian Americans or Pacific Islanders, 117 Hispanic Americans), 43 international. Average age 27. 3,027 applicants, 44% accepted, 385 enrolled. In 2009, 401 first professional degrees, 16 master's awarded. *Degree requirements:* For JD, 90 credits. *Entrance requirements:* For JD, LSAT; for master's, JD. Additional exam requirements/recommendations for international students: Required—TOEFL. *Application deadline:* For fall admission, 3/1 priority date for domestic and international students; for spring admission, 10/15 priority date for domestic and international students. Applications are processed on a rolling basis. Application fee: $60. Electronic applications accepted. *Expenses:* Contact institution. *Financial support:* In 2009–10, 1,350 students received support. Scholarships/grants and tuition waivers (full and partial) available. Support available to part-time students. Financial award application deadline: 6/1; financial award applicants required to submit FAFSA. *Unit head:* John Corkery, Dean, 312-427-2737. *Application contact:* William B. Powers, Associate Dean of Admission and Student Affairs, 800-537-4280, Fax: 312-427-5136, E-mail: admission@jmls.edu.

Long Island University, Brooklyn Campus, School of Business, Public Administration and Information Sciences, Program in Accountancy, Taxation and Law, Brooklyn, NY 11201-8423. Offers accounting (MS); taxation (MS). Part-time and evening/weekend programs available. *Entrance requirements:* For master's, GMAT or GRE General Test, 2 letters of recommendation. Additional exam requirements/recommendations for international students: Required—TOEFL (minimum score 500 paper-based; 173 computer-based). Electronic applications accepted.

Long Island University, C.W. Post Campus, College of Management, School of Business, Brookville, NY 11548-1300. Offers accounting and taxation (Certificate); business administration (Certificate); finance (MBA, Certificate); general business administration (MBA); international business (MBA, Certificate); management (MBA, Certificate); management information systems (MBA, Certificate); marketing (MBA, Certificate). *Accreditation:* AACSB. Part-time and evening/weekend programs available. *Entrance requirements:* For master's, GMAT, resume, minimum GPA of 3.0, 2 letters of recommendation. Additional exam requirements/recommendations for international students: Required—TOEFL (minimum score 527 paper-based; 197 computer-based). Electronic applications accepted. *Faculty research:* Financial markets, consumer behavior.

Long Island University, C.W. Post Campus, College of Management, School of Professional Accountancy, Brookville, NY 11548-1300. Offers accounting (MS); taxation (MS). Part-time and evening/weekend programs available. *Entrance requirements:* For master's, GMAT, minimum GPA of 2.5, BS in accounting from accredited college or university. Electronic applications accepted. *Faculty research:* International taxation.

Loyola Marymount University, Loyola Law School Los Angeles, Los Angeles, CA 90015. Offers law (JD); taxation (LL M); JD/MBA. *Accreditation:* ABA. Part-time and evening/weekend programs available. *Entrance requirements:* For JD, LSAT; for master's, JD (LLM). Additional exam requirements/recommendations for international students: Required—TOEFL. Electronic applications accepted.

Mississippi State University, College of Business, School of Accountancy, Mississippi State, MS 39762. Offers accounting (MPA), including accounting (MPA, PhD), systems; business administration (PhD), including accounting (MPA, PhD); taxation (MTX). *Accreditation:* AACSB. *Faculty:* 8 full-time (3 women). *Students:* 41 full-time (23 women), 10 part-time (8 women); includes 5 minority (all Asian Americans or Pacific Islanders), 3 international. Average age 26. 56 applicants, 45% accepted, 20 enrolled. In 2009, 41 master's awarded. *Degree requirements:* For master's, comprehensive exam. *Entrance requirements:* For master's, GMAT (minimum score of 510), minimum GPA of 2.75 overall and in upper-level accounting, 3.0 in last 60 hours of course work; for doctorate, GMAT, minimum undergraduate GPA of 3.0, both cumulative and over the last 60 hours of undergraduate work; 3.25 on all prior graduate work. Additional exam requirements/recommendations for international students: Required—TOEFL (minimum score 575 paper-based; 233 computer-based; 84 iBT); Recommended—IELTS (minimum score 7). *Application deadline:* For fall admission, 7/1 for domestic students, 5/1 for international students; for spring admission, 11/1 for domestic students, 9/1 for international students. Applications are processed on a rolling basis. Application fee: $40. Electronic applications accepted. *Expenses:* Tuition, state resident: full-time $2575.50; part-time $286.25 per credit hour. Tuition, nonresident: full-time $6510; part-time $723.50 per credit hour. Tuition and fees vary according to course load. *Financial support:* Career-related internships or fieldwork, Federal Work-Study, institutionally sponsored loans, scholarships/grants, and unspecified assistantships available. Support available to part-time students. Financial award applicants required to submit FAFSA. *Faculty research:* Income tax, financial accounting system, managerial accounting, auditing. *Unit head:* Dr. Louis Dawkins, Director, 662-325-1633, E-mail: ldawkins@cobilan.msstate.edu. *Application contact:* Dr. Barbara Spencer, Graduate Coordinator, 662-325-3710, Fax: 662-325-1646, E-mail: sac@cobilan.msstate.edu.

New York Law School, Graduate Programs, New York, NY 10013. Offers law (JD); mental disability law (MA); real estate (LL M); taxation (LL M); JD/MBA. *Accreditation:* ABA. Part-time and evening/weekend programs available. Postbaccalaureate distance learning degree programs offered. *Entrance requirements:* LSAT, letters of recommendation, resume. Additional exam requirements/recommendations for international students: Recommended—TOEFL (minimum score 600 paper-based; 250 computer-based; 100 iBT). Electronic applications accepted.

See Close-Up on page 1699.

New York University, School of Law, New York, NY 10012-1019. Offers law (JD, LL M, JSD); law and business (Advanced Certificate); taxation (Advanced Certificate); JD/LL B; JD/LL M; JD/MA; JD/MBA; JD/MPA; JD/MPP; JD/MSW; JD/MUP; JD/PhD. *Accreditation:* ABA. Part-time programs available. *Faculty:* 125 full-time (36 women), 70 part-time/adjunct (23 women). *Students:* 1,427 full-time (628 women); includes 332 minority (88 African Americans, 3 American Indian/Alaska Native, 150 Asian Americans or Pacific Islanders, 91 Hispanic Americans), 44 international. 7,272 applicants, 450 enrolled. In 2009, 471 first professional degrees, 534 master's, 3 doctorates awarded. *Entrance requirements:* LSAT. *Application deadline:* For fall admission, 2/1 for domestic students. Application fee: $75. Electronic applications accepted. *Expenses:* Contact institution. *Financial support:* Fellowships, research assistantships, teaching assistantships, career-related internships or fieldwork, Federal Work-Study, institutionally sponsored loans, scholarships/grants, tuition waivers (partial), and loan repayment assistance available. Financial award application deadline: 4/15; financial award applicants required to submit FAFSA. *Faculty research:* International law, environmental law, corporate law, globalization of law, philosophy of law. *Unit head:* Richard L. Revesz, Dean, 212-998-6000, Fax: 212-995-3150. *Application contact:* Kenneth J. Kleinrock, Assistant Dean for Admissions, 212-998-6060, Fax: 212-995-4527.

Northern Illinois University, Graduate School, College of Business, Department of Accountancy, De Kalb, IL 60115-2854. Offers MAS, MST. *Accreditation:* AACSB. Part-time and evening/weekend programs available. *Faculty:* 14 full-time (4 women). *Students:* 165 full-time (65 women), 85 part-time (51 women); includes 31 minority (4 African Americans, 25 Asian Americans or Pacific Islanders, 2 Hispanic Americans), 40 international. Average age 28. 161 applicants, 58% accepted, 48 enrolled. In 2009, 149 master's awarded. *Degree requirements:* For master's, thesis optional. *Entrance requirements:* For master's, GMAT, minimum GPA of 2.75. Additional exam requirements/recommendations for international students: Required—TOEFL (minimum score 550 paper-based; 213 computer-based). *Application deadline:* For fall admission, 4/1 priority date for domestic students, 5/1 for international students; for spring admission, 9/15 priority date for domestic students, 10/1 for international students. Applications are processed on a rolling basis. Application fee: $30. Electronic applications accepted. *Expenses:* Tuition, state resident: full-time $6576; part-time $274 per credit hour. Tuition, nonresident: full-time $13,152; part-time $548 per credit hour. Required fees: $1813; $75.53 per credit hour. Part-time tuition and fees vary according to course load. *Financial support:* In 2009–10, 25 research assistantships with full tuition reimbursements, 11 teaching assistantships with full tuition reimbursements were awarded; fellowships with full tuition reimbursements, career-related internships or fieldwork, Federal Work-Study, scholarships/grants, tuition waivers (full), and unspecified assistantships also available. Support available to part-time students. Financial award applicants required to submit FAFSA. *Faculty research:* Accounting fraud, governmental accounting, corporate income tax planning, auditing, ethics. *Unit head:* Dr. James C. Young, Chair, 815-753-1250, Fax: 815-753-8515. *Application contact:* Dr. Rowene Linden, Graduate Adviser, 815-753-6200.

Northern Kentucky University, Office of Graduate Programs, College of Business, Program in Accountancy, Highland Heights, KY 41099. Offers accountancy (M Acc); advanced taxation (Certificate). Part-time and evening/weekend programs available. *Students:* 13 full-time (3 women), 59 part-time (31 women); includes 3 minority (1 African American, 1 American Indian/Alaska Native, 1 Asian American or Pacific Islander), 2 international. Average age 32. 59 applicants, 71% accepted, 34 enrolled. In 2009, 17 master's awarded. *Entrance requirements:* For master's, GMAT (minimum score 450), minimum GPA of 2.5. Additional exam requirements/recommendations for international students: Required—TOEFL (minimum score 550 paper-based; 213 computer-based; 79 iBT); Recommended—IELTS (minimum score 6.5). *Application deadline:* For fall admission, 8/1 priority date for domestic students, 6/1 for international students; for spring admission, 12/1 priority date for domestic students, 10/1 for international students. Applications are processed on a rolling basis. Application fee: $40. Electronic applications accepted. *Expenses:* Tuition, state resident: full-time $6912; part-time $384 per credit hour. Tuition, nonresident: full-time $12,150; part-time $675 per credit hour. Tuition and fees vary according to course load, program and reciprocity agreements. *Financial support:* Unspecified assistantships available. Financial award applicants required to submit FAFSA. *Unit head:* Robert Salyer, Director, 859-572-5164, Fax: 859-572-6177, E-mail: salyerb@nku.edu. *Application contact:* Dr. Peg Griffin, Director of Graduate Programs, 859-572-6934, Fax: 859-572-6670, E-mail: griffinp@nku.edu.

Northwestern University, Law School, Chicago, IL 60611-3069. Offers executive (LL M); international human rights (LL M); law (JD, LL M); tax (LL M in Tax); two-year accelerated (JD); JD/LL M; JD/MBA; JD/PhD; LL M/Certificate. *Accreditation:* ABA. *Entrance requirements:* For JD, LSAT, 1 letter of recommendation, resume; for master's, law degree or equivalent, letter of recommendation, resume. Additional exam requirements/recommendations for international students: Required—TOEFL. Electronic applications accepted. *Expenses:* Contact institution. *Faculty research:* Constitutional law, corporate law, international law, law and social policy, ethical studies.

Nova Southeastern University, H. Wayne Huizenga School of Business and Entrepreneurship, Program in Taxation, Fort Lauderdale, FL 33314-7796. Offers M Tax. Part-time and evening/weekend programs available. Postbaccalaureate distance learning degree programs offered. *Faculty:* 2 full-time (1 woman), 5 part-time/adjunct (0 women). *Students:* 6 full-time (3 women), 139 part-time (73 women); includes 86 minority (49 African Americans, 1 Asian American or Pacific Islander, 36 Hispanic Americans), 4 international. Average age 36. 72 applicants, 78% accepted, 32 enrolled. In 2009, 44 master's awarded. *Entrance requirements:* Additional exam requirements/recommendations for international students: Required—TOEFL (minimum score 550 paper-based; 213 computer-based; 79 iBT), IELTS (minimum score 6). *Application deadline:* For fall admission, 8/15 for domestic and international students; for winter admission, 12/10 for domestic and international students; for spring admission, 2/10 for domestic and international students. Applications are processed on a rolling basis. Application fee: $50. Electronic applications accepted. *Financial support:* Federal Work-Study and scholarships/grants available. Support available to part-time students. Financial award applicants required to submit FAFSA. *Unit head:* Dr. Walter Moore, Chair and Professor for Accounting Programs, 954-262-5101, Fax: 954-262-3822, E-mail: moore@huizenga.nova.edu. *Application contact:* Aimee Fernandez, Assistant Director, 954-262-5091, Fax: 954-262-3822, E-mail: aimeefernandez@huizenga.nova.edu.

Pace University, Lubin School of Business, Taxation Program, New York, NY 10038. Offers MBA, MS. Part-time and evening/weekend programs available. *Students:* 77 part-time (34 women); includes 21 minority (3 African Americans, 15 Asian Americans or Pacific Islanders, 3 Hispanic Americans), 16 international. Average age 32. 54 applicants, 100% accepted, 14 enrolled. In 2009, 22 master's awarded. *Entrance requirements:* For master's, GMAT. Additional exam requirements/recommendations for international students: Required—TOEFL. *Application deadline:* For fall admission, 7/31 priority date for domestic students; for spring admission, 11/30 for domestic students. Applications are processed on a rolling basis. Application fee: $70. Electronic applications accepted. *Expenses:* Tuition: Part-time $954 per credit. Tuition and fees vary according to course load, degree level and program. *Financial support:* Research assistantships, career-related internships or fieldwork and Federal Work-Study available. Support available to part-time students. Financial award applicants required to submit FAFSA. *Unit head:* Dr. Arthur Magaldi, Chairperson, 212-346-1294. *Application contact:* Susan Ford-Goldschein, Director of Admissions, 212-346-1652, Fax: 212-346-1585, E-mail: gradnyc@pace.edu.

Philadelphia University, School of Business Administration, Program in Taxation, Philadelphia, PA 19144. Offers MS. Part-time and evening/weekend programs available. *Entrance requirements:* For master's, GMAT. Additional exam requirements/recommendations for international students: Required—TOEFL (minimum score 550 paper-based; 213 computer-based; 79 iBT). Electronic applications accepted.

Robert Morris University, Graduate Studies, School of Business, Moon Township, PA 15108-1189. Offers business administration and management (MBA); human resource management (MS); nonprofit management (MS); taxation (MS). *Accreditation:* AACSB. Part-time and evening/weekend programs available. *Faculty:* 29 full-time (11 women), 3 part-time/adjunct (0 women). *Students:* 209 part-time (97 women); includes 11 minority (9 African Americans, 1 Asian American or Pacific Islander, 1 Hispanic American), 4 international. Average age 31. 126 applicants, 70% accepted, 54 enrolled. In 2009, 85 master's awarded. *Entrance requirements:* For master's, GMAT, letters of recommendation. Additional exam requirements/recommendations for international students: Required—TOEFL (minimum score 550 paper-based; 213 computer-based; 79 iBT). *Application deadline:* For fall admission, 7/1 priority date for domestic and international students; for spring admission, 11/1 priority date for domestic and international students. Applications are processed on a rolling basis. Application fee: $35. Electronic applications accepted. *Expenses:* Tuition: Part-time $765 per credit. Required fees: $15 per credit. Full-time tuition and fees vary according to degree level. Part-time tuition and fees vary according to program. *Financial support:* Research assistantships with partial tuition reimbursements, Federal Work-Study, institutionally sponsored loans, and unspecified assistantships available. Support available to part-time students. Financial award application deadline: 5/1; financial award applicants required to submit FAFSA. *Unit head:* Dr. Derya A. Jacobs, Dean, 412-397-2191, Fax: 412-397-2585, E-mail: jacobs@rmu.edu. *Application contact:* Deborah Roach, Assistant Dean, Graduate Admissions, 412-397-5200, Fax: 412-397-2425, E-mail: graduateadmissions@rmu.edu.

Rutgers, The State University of New Jersey, Newark, Rutgers Business School–Newark and New Brunswick, Master of Accountancy in Taxation Program, Newark, NJ 07102. Offers M Accy.

Taxation

St. John's University, The Peter J. Tobin College of Business, Department of Accounting and Taxation, Program in Taxation, Queens, NY 11439. Offers MBA, MS, Adv C. Part-time and evening/weekend programs available. *Students:* 38 full-time (22 women), 31 part-time (12 women); includes 26 minority (9 African Americans, 15 Asian Americans or Pacific Islanders, 2 Hispanic Americans), 5 international. Average age 28. 105 applicants, 69% accepted, 38 enrolled. In 2009, 40 master's awarded. *Degree requirements:* For master's, comprehensive exam (for some programs), thesis optional. *Entrance requirements:* For master's, GMAT (waived for MS applicants who have successfully completed the CPA exam), 2 letters of recommendation, resume; for Adv C, 2 letters of recommendation, resume, undergraduate transcripts, essay. Additional exam requirements/recommendations for international students: Required—TOEFL (minimum score 500 paper-based; 173 computer-based; 61 iBT), IELTS (minimum score 5.5). *Application deadline:* For fall admission, 5/1 priority date for domestic and international students; for spring admission, 11/1 priority date for domestic and international students. Applications are processed on a rolling basis. Application fee: $70. Electronic applications accepted. *Expenses:* Contact institution. *Financial support:* Research assistantships available. Support available to part-time students. Financial award application deadline: 3/1; financial award applicants required to submit FAFSA. *Unit head:* Dr. James Thompson, Chair, 718-990-6460, Fax: 718-380-3803, E-mail: thompsoj@stjohns.edu. *Application contact:* Nicole T. Bryan, Assistant Dean, 718-990-2599, Fax: 718-990-5242, E-mail: tcbgradadmissions@stjohns.edu.

St. Thomas University, School of Law, Miami Gardens, FL 33054-6459. Offers international human rights (LL M); international taxation (LL M); law (JD); JD/MBA; JD/MS. *Accreditation:* ABA. Postbaccalaureate distance learning degree programs offered (no on-campus study). *Degree requirements:* For master's, thesis (international taxation). *Entrance requirements:* LSAT. Electronic applications accepted. *Expenses:* Contact institution.

San Jose State University, Graduate Studies and Research, Lucas Graduate School of Business, Program in Taxation, San Jose, CA 95192-0001. Offers MS. *Degree requirements:* For master's, comprehensive exam, thesis or alternative. *Entrance requirements:* For master's, GMAT, minimum GPA of 3.0. *Application deadline:* For fall admission, 6/29 for domestic students; for spring admission, 11/30 for domestic students. Applications are processed on a rolling basis. Application fee: $59. Electronic applications accepted. *Financial support:* Applicants required to submit FAFSA.

Seton Hall University, Stillman School of Business, Department of Accounting, South Orange, NJ 07079-2697. Offers accounting (MS); professional accounting (MS); taxation (Certificate). Part-time and evening/weekend programs available. *Faculty:* 10 full-time (2 women), 5 part-time/adjunct (2 women). *Students:* 20 full-time (7 women), 23 part-time (7 women); includes 10 minority (2 African Americans, 7 Asian Americans or Pacific Islanders, 1 Hispanic American). Average age 28. 85 applicants, 80% accepted, 43 enrolled. In 2009, 23 master's awarded. *Entrance requirements:* For master's, GMAT, minimum GPA of 3.0. Additional exam requirements/recommendations for international students: Required—TOEFL (minimum score 607 paper-based; 254 computer-based; 102 iBT), or IELTS, or Pearson Test of English (PTE). *Application deadline:* For fall admission, 5/31 priority date for domestic students, 3/31 for international students; for spring admission, 10/31 for domestic students, 9/30 for international students. Applications are processed on a rolling basis. Application fee: $75. Electronic applications accepted. *Financial support:* In 2009–10, 2 students received support, including research assistantships with full tuition reimbursements available (averaging $34,404 per year); career-related internships or fieldwork, scholarships/grants, and unspecified assistantships also available. Support available to part-time students. Financial award application deadline: 6/30; financial award applicants required to submit FAFSA. *Faculty research:* Voluntary disclosure, international accounting, pension and retirement accounting, ethics in financial reporting. *Unit head:* Dr. Mark Holtzman, Chair, 973-261-4133, Fax: 973-761-9207, E-mail: mark.holtzman@shu.edu. *Application contact:* Catherine Bianchi, Director of Graduate Admissions, 973-761-9262, Fax: 973-761-9208, E-mail: catherine.bianchi@shu.edu.

Seton Hall University, Stillman School of Business, Department of Taxation, South Orange, NJ 07079-2697. Offers MS. Part-time and evening/weekend programs available. *Faculty:* 3 full-time (0 women). *Students:* 34 part-time (11 women); includes 4 minority (1 African American, 2 Asian Americans or Pacific Islanders, 1 Hispanic American). Average age 30. 25 applicants, 84% accepted, 13 enrolled. In 2009, 18 master's awarded. *Entrance requirements:* For master's, GMAT or CPA license, minimum GPA of 2.75. Additional exam requirements/recommendations for international students: Required—TOEFL (minimum score 550 paper-based; 213 computer-based). *Application deadline:* For fall admission, 6/1 priority date for domestic students, 5/1 for international students; for spring admission, 11/1 priority date for domestic students, 10/1 for international students. Application fee: $75 ($100 for international students). Electronic applications accepted. *Expenses:* Contact institution. *Financial support:* In 2009–10, 3 students received support, including research assistantships with full tuition reimbursements available (averaging $5,400 per year); career-related internships or fieldwork, Federal Work-Study, scholarships/grants, health care benefits, and unspecified assistantships also available. Support available to part-time students. Financial award application deadline: 6/1; financial award applicants required to submit FAFSA. *Faculty research:* Issues affecting cost capitalization, estate valuation discounts, qualified terminable interest property elections, eastern European tax initiatives, realigning the capital structure of closely-held business enterprises. *Unit head:* Dr. Reed Easton, Chairperson, 973-761-9249, Fax: 973-761-9217, E-mail: eastonre@shu.edu. *Application contact:* Catherine Bianchi, Director of Graduate Admissions, 973-761-9220, Fax: 973-761-9208, E-mail: biancha@shu.edu.

Southern Illinois University Edwardsville, Graduate Studies and Research, School of Business, Department of Accounting, Edwardsville, IL 62026-0001. Offers accountancy (MSA); taxation (MSA). *Accreditation:* AACSB. Part-time and evening/weekend programs available. *Faculty:* 5 full-time (1 woman). *Students:* 16 full-time (6 women), 19 part-time (13 women); includes 1 minority (African American), 2 international. Average age 26. 38 applicants, 50% accepted. In 2009, 23 master's awarded. *Degree requirements:* For master's, thesis or alternative, final exam. *Entrance requirements:* For master's, GMAT. Additional exam requirements/recommendations for international students: Required—TOEFL (minimum score 550 paper-based; 213 computer-based; 79 iBT), IELTS (minimum score 6.5). *Application deadline:* For fall admission, 7/23 for domestic students, 6/1 for international students; for spring admission, 12/11 for domestic students, 10/1 for international students. Applications are processed on a rolling basis. Application fee: $30. Electronic applications accepted. *Expenses:* Tuition, state resident: part-time $1252.50 per semester. Tuition, nonresident: part-time $3131.25 per semester. Required fees: $586.85 per semester. Tuition and fees vary according to course load. *Financial support:* In 2009–10, 1 fellowship with full tuition reimbursement (averaging $8,370 per year), 10 teaching assistantships with full tuition reimbursements (averaging $8,064 per year) were awarded; research assistantships with full tuition reimbursements, career-related internships or fieldwork, Federal Work-Study, institutionally sponsored loans, scholarships/grants, traineeships, and unspecified assistantships also available. Support available to part-time students. Financial award application deadline: 3/1; financial award applicants required to submit FAFSA. *Unit head:* Dr. Michael Costigan, Chair, 618-650-2633, E-mail: mcostig@siue.edu. *Application contact:* Dr. Michael Costigan, Chair, 618-650-2633, E-mail: mcostig@siue.edu.

Southern Methodist University, Dedman School of Law, Dallas, TX 75275-0110. Offers foreign law school graduates (LL M); law (JD, SJD); law-general (LL M); taxation (LL M); JD/MA; JD/MBA. *Accreditation:* ABA. Part-time and evening/weekend programs available. *Faculty:* 44 full-time (17 women), 45 part-time/adjunct (9 women). *Students:* 534 full-time (254 women), 320 part-time (143 women); includes 189 minority (43 African Americans, 10 American Indian/Alaska Native, 60 Asian Americans or Pacific Islanders, 76 Hispanic Americans). Average age 27. 3,015 applicants, 26% accepted, 309 enrolled. In 2009, 282 JDs, 77 master's, 2 doctorates awarded. *Degree requirements:* For master's, thesis optional; for doctorate, thesis/dissertation; for JD, 30 hours of public service. *Entrance requirements:* For JD, LSAT, 2 letters of recommendation, resume, personal statement; for master's, JD; for doctorate, LL M. Additional exam requirements/recommendations for international students: Required—TOEFL (minimum score 575 paper-based; 233 computer-based; 91 iBT). *Application deadline:* For fall admission, 2/15 priority date for domestic students. Applications are processed on a rolling basis. Application fee: $75. Electronic applications accepted. *Expenses:* Contact institution. *Financial support:* Career-related internships or fieldwork, Federal Work-Study, and scholarships/grants available. Financial award application deadline: 2/15; financial award applicants required to submit FAFSA. *Faculty research:* Corporate law, intellectual property, international law, commercial law, dispute resolution. *Unit head:* John B. Attanasio, Dean, 214-768-8999, Fax: 214-768-2182, E-mail: jba@mail.smu.edu. *Application contact:* Virginia Keehan, Assistant Dean for Admissions, 214-768-2550, Fax: 214-768-2549, E-mail: lawadmit@smu.edu.

Southern New Hampshire University, School of Business, Manchester, NH 03106-1045. Offers accounting (MS); business administration (MBA, Certificate), including accounting (Certificate), business administration (MBA), finance (Certificate), forensic accounting (Certificate), human resources management (Certificate), international business (Certificate), international sport management (Certificate), leadership of not for profit organizations (Certificate), marketing (Certificate), operations management (Certificate), sport management (Certificate), taxation (Certificate); finance (MS); hospitality and tourism leadership (Certificate); information technology (MS, Certificate); information technology/international business (Certificate); integrated marketing communications (Certificate); international business (MS, DBA); marketing (MS); operations and project management (MS); organizational leadership (MS); project management (Certificate); sport management (MS); MBA/Certificate. *Accreditation:* ACBSP. Part-time and evening/weekend programs available. Postbaccalaureate distance learning degree programs offered (no on-campus study). Terminal master's awarded for partial completion of doctoral program. *Degree requirements:* For master's, one foreign language, comprehensive exam (for some programs), thesis or alternative; for doctorate, one foreign language, comprehensive exam, thesis/dissertation. *Entrance requirements:* For master's, minimum GPA of 2.5; for doctorate, GMAT. Additional exam requirements/recommendations for international students: Required—TOEFL (minimum score 500 paper-based). Electronic applications accepted.

Strayer University, Graduate Studies, Washington, DC 20005-2603. Offers accounting (MS); acquisition (MBA); business administration (MBA); communications technology (MS); educational management (M Ed); finance (MBA); health services administration (MHSA); hospitality and tourism management (MBA); human resource management (MBA); information systems (MS), including computer security management, decision support system management, enterprise resource management, network management, software engineering management, systems development management; management (MBA); management information systems (MS); marketing (MBA); professional accounting (MS), including accounting information systems, controllership, taxation; public administration (MPA); supply chain management (MBA); technology in education (M Ed). Programs also offered at campus locations in Birmingham, AL; Chamblee, GA; Cobb County, GA; Morrow, GA; White Marsh, MD; Charleston, SC; Columbia, SC; Greensboro, NC; Greenville, SC; Lexington, KY; Louisville, KY; Nashville, TN; North Raleigh, NC; Washington, DC. Part-time and evening/weekend programs available. Postbaccalaureate distance learning degree programs offered (minimal on-campus study). *Degree requirements:* For master's, thesis. *Entrance requirements:* For master's, GMAT, GRE General Test, bachelor's degree from an accredited college or university, minimum undergraduate GPA of 2.75. Electronic applications accepted.

Suffolk University, Sawyer Business School, Department of Accounting, Boston, MA 02108-2770. Offers accounting (MSA, GDPA); taxation (MST); GDPA/MST; MBA/GDPA; MBA/MSA; MBA/MST. *Accreditation:* AACSB. Part-time and evening/weekend programs available. *Faculty:* 17 full-time (5 women), 7 part-time/adjunct (2 women). *Students:* 81 full-time (63 women), 149 part-time (81 women); includes 24 minority (5 African Americans, 17 Asian Americans or Pacific Islanders, 2 Hispanic Americans), 84 international. Average age 29. 457 applicants, 68% accepted, 85 enrolled. In 2009, 78 master's, 3 GDPAs awarded. *Entrance requirements:* For master's, GMAT. Additional exam requirements/recommendations for international students: Required—TOEFL (minimum score 550 paper-based; 213 computer-based; 80 iBT). *Application deadline:* For fall admission, 6/15 priority date for domestic students, 6/15 for international students; for spring admission, 11/1 priority date for domestic students, 11/1 for international students. Applications are processed on a rolling basis. Application fee: $50. Electronic applications accepted. *Expenses:* Tuition: Full-time $33,000; part-time $1100 per credit. Required fees: $20. Tuition and fees vary according to program. *Financial support:* In 2009–10, 105 students received support, including 74 fellowships with full and partial tuition reimbursements available (averaging $18,915 per year); career-related internships or fieldwork, Federal Work-Study, and institutionally sponsored loans also available. Support available to part-time students. Financial award application deadline: 4/1; financial award applicants required to submit CSS PROFILE. *Faculty research:* Tax policy, tax research, decision making in accounting, accounting information systems, capital markets and strategic planning. *Unit head:* Lewis Shaw, Chair, 617-573-8615, Fax: 617-994-4260, E-mail: lshaw@suffolk.edu. *Application contact:* Judith Reynolds, Director of Graduate Admissions, 617-573-8302, Fax: 617-305-1733, E-mail: grad.admission@suffolk.edu.

Suffolk University, Sawyer Business School, Master of Business Administration Program, Boston, MA 02108-2770. Offers accounting (MBA); business administration (APC); corporate financial executive track (MBA); entrepreneurship (MBA); executive business administration (EMBA); finance (MBA); global business administration (GMBA); health administration (MBA); international business (MBA); marketing (MBA); organizational behavior (MBA); strategic management (MBA); taxation (MBA); JD/MBA; MBA/GDPA; MBA/MHA; MBA/MSA; MBA/MSF; MBA/MST. *Accreditation:* AACSB. Part-time and evening/weekend programs available. Postbaccalaureate distance learning degree programs offered (no on-campus study). *Faculty:* 103 full-time (30 women), 63 part-time/adjunct (19 women). *Students:* 173 full-time (68 women), 406 part-time (178 women); includes 51 minority (16 African Americans, 3 American Indian/Alaska Native, 22 Asian Americans or Pacific Islanders, 10 Hispanic Americans), 90 international. Average age 29. 460 applicants, 72% accepted, 157 enrolled. In 2009, 245 master's awarded. *Entrance requirements:* For master's, GMAT, minimum undergraduate GPA of 2.75 (MBA), 5 years of managerial experience (EMBA). Additional exam requirements/recommendations for international students: Required—TOEFL (minimum score 550 paper-based; 213 computer-based). *Application deadline:* For fall admission, 6/15 priority date for domestic students, 6/15 for international students; for spring admission, 11/1 priority date for domestic students, 11/1 for international students. Applications are processed on a rolling basis. Application fee: $50. Electronic applications accepted. *Expenses:* Tuition: Full-time $33,000; part-time $1100 per credit. Required fees: $20. Tuition and fees vary according to program. *Financial support:* In 2009–10, 284 students received support, including 99 fellowships with full and partial tuition reimbursements available (averaging $13,599 per year); career-related internships or fieldwork, Federal Work-Study, and institutionally sponsored loans also available. Support available to part-time students. Financial award application deadline: 4/1; financial award applicants required to submit FAFSA. *Faculty research:* Foreign investments; career strategies and boundaryless careers; corporate ethics codes; interest rates, inflation, and growth options; innovation and product development performance. *Unit head:* Lillian Hallberg, Assistant Dean of Graduate Programs/Director of MBA Programs, 617-573-8306, E-mail: lhallber@suffolk.edu. *Application contact:* Judith Reynolds, Director of Graduate Admissions, 617-573-8302, Fax: 617-305-1733, E-mail: grad.admission@suffolk.edu.

Temple University, James E. Beasley School of Law, Philadelphia, PA 19122. Offers law (JD); legal education (SJD); taxation (LL M); transnational law (LL M); trial advocacy (LL M); JD/LL M; JD/MBA. *Accreditation:* ABA. Part-time and evening/weekend programs available. *Entrance requirements:* LSAT, LSDAS. Electronic applications accepted. *Expenses:* Contact institution. *Faculty research:* Comparative constitutional law, gender issues, immigration law, international intellectual property law and popular culture.

Texas Tech University, Jerry S. Rawls College of Business Administration, Area of Accounting, Lubbock, TX 79409. Offers accounting (PhD); audit/financial reporting (MSA); taxation (MSA); JD/MSA. *Accreditation:* AACSB. Part-time programs available. *Faculty:* 15 full-time (4 women). *Students:* 97 full-time (52 women), 6 part-time (1 woman); includes 13 minority (3 American

Indian/Alaska Native, 3 Asian Americans or Pacific Islanders, 7 Hispanic Americans), 4 international. Average age 24. 111 applicants, 50% accepted, 49 enrolled. In 2009, 57 master's, 3 doctorates awarded. Terminal master's awarded for partial completion of doctoral program. *Degree requirements:* For master's, capstone course; for doctorate, comprehensive exam, thesis/dissertation, qualifying exams. *Entrance requirements:* For master's and doctorate, GMAT, holistic profile of academic credentials. Additional exam requirements/recommendations for international students: Required—TOEFL (minimum score 550 paper-based; 213 computer-based; 79 iBT). *Application deadline:* For fall admission, 2/1 priority date for domestic students, 1/15 priority date for international students. Applications are processed on a rolling basis. Application fee: $50 ($75 for international students). Electronic applications accepted. *Expenses:* Tuition, state resident: full-time $5100; part-time $213 per credit hour. Tuition, nonresident: full-time $11,748; part-time $490 per credit hour. Required fees: $2298; $50 per credit hour. $555 per semester. *Financial support:* In 2009–10, 6 research assistantships (averaging $8,000 per year), 8 teaching assistantships (averaging $17,000 per year) were awarded; fellowships, career-related internships or fieldwork, Federal Work-Study, scholarships/grants, health care benefits, and unspecified assistantships also available. Financial award applicants required to submit FAFSA. *Faculty research:* Governmental and nonprofit accounting, managerial and financial accounting. *Unit head:* Dr. Linda Nichols, Area Coordinator, 806-742-1541, Fax: 806-742-3182, E-mail: linda.nichols@ttu.edu. *Application contact:* Cynthia D. Barnes, 806-742-3184, Fax: 806-742-3958, E-mail: ba_grad@ttu.edu.

Thomas M. Cooley Law School, Graduate Programs, Lansing, MI 48901-3038. Offers corporate law and finance (LL M); intellectual property (LL M); law (JD); taxation (LL M). *Accreditation:* ABA. Part-time and evening/weekend programs available. *Degree requirements:* For JD, clinical experience. *Entrance requirements:* LSAT, LSDAS. Electronic applications accepted. *Faculty research:* Wrongful convictions, civil rights, environmental law, litigation techniques, death penalty.

Université de Montréal, Faculty of Law, Montréal, QC H3C 3J7, Canada. Offers business law (DESS); common law (North America) (JD); international law (DESS); law (LL B, LL M, LL D, DDN, DESS); tax law (LL M). Part-time programs available. *Faculty:* 63 full-time (24 women), 6 part-time/adjunct (4 women). *Students:* 441 full-time (267 women), 85 part-time (53 women). 794 applicants, 41% accepted, 225 enrolled. In 2009, 40 master's, 7 doctorates, 105 DDNs awarded. *Degree requirements:* For master's, thesis; for doctorate, thesis/dissertation, project; for other advanced degree, thesis (for some programs). *Application deadline:* For fall admission, 2/1 priority date for domestic students; for winter admission, 11/1 priority date for domestic students; for spring admission, 2/1 priority date for domestic students. Application fee: $100. Electronic applications accepted. *Financial support:* Fellowships, research assistantships, teaching assistantships available. *Faculty research:* Legal theory; constitutional, private, and public law. *Unit head:* Gilles Trudeau, Dean, 514-343-6469, Fax: 514-343-2199, E-mail: gilles.trudeau@umontreal.ca. *Application contact:* Guy Lefebvre, Associate Dean Graduate Studies, 514-343-7202, Fax: 514-343-2199, E-mail: guy.lefebvre@umontreal.ca.

Université de Sherbrooke, Faculty of Administration, Program in Taxation, Sherbrooke, QC J1K 2R1, Canada. Offers M Tax, Diploma.

University at Albany, State University of New York, School of Business, Department of Accounting, Albany, NY 12222-0001. Offers accounting (MS); taxation (MS). *Accreditation:* AACSB. *Degree requirements:* For master's, research project. *Entrance requirements:* For master's, GMAT. Additional exam requirements/recommendations for international students: Required—TOEFL (minimum score 550 paper-based; 213 computer-based). Electronic applications accepted. *Faculty research:* Professional ethics, statistical analysis, cost management systems, accounting theory.

The University of Akron, Graduate School, College of Business Administration, School of Accountancy, Program in Taxation, Akron, OH 44325. Offers MT. *Students:* 17 full-time (10 women), 44 part-time (16 women); includes 3 minority (1 African American, 2 Asian Americans or Pacific Islanders), 1 international. Average age 30. 35 applicants, 91% accepted, 29 enrolled. In 2009, 24 master's awarded. *Entrance requirements:* For master's, GMAT, minimum GPA of 2.75, letters of recommendation, resume. Additional exam requirements/recommendations for international students: Required—TOEFL (minimum score 550 paper-based; 213 computer-based; 79 iBT). *Application deadline:* For fall admission, 8/1 for domestic and international students; for spring admission, 12/1 for domestic and international students. Application fee: $30 ($40 for international students). Electronic applications accepted. *Expenses:* Tuition, state resident: full-time $6570; part-time $365 per credit hour. Tuition, nonresident: full-time $11,250; part-time $625 per credit hour. *Unit head:* Alvin Lieberman, Coordinator, 330-972-6229, E-mail: lieberm@uakron.edu. *Application contact:* Dr. Susan Hanlon, Director of Graduate Business Programs, 330-972-7043, Fax: 330-972-6588, E-mail: shanlon@uakron.edu.

The University of Alabama, Graduate School, Manderson Graduate School of Business, Culverhouse School of Accountancy, Tuscaloosa, AL 35487. Offers accounting (M Acc, PhD); tax accounting (MTA). *Accreditation:* AACSB. *Faculty:* 15 full-time (3 women). *Students:* 105 full-time (48 women), 3 part-time (2 women); includes 2 minority (both African Americans), 3 international. Average age 24. 218 applicants, 41% accepted, 77 enrolled. In 2009, 95 master's, 3 doctorates awarded. *Degree requirements:* For doctorate, thesis/dissertation. *Entrance requirements:* For master's and doctorate, GMAT, minimum GPA of 3.0. Additional exam requirements/recommendations for international students: Required—TOEFL. *Application deadline:* For fall admission, 7/1 priority date for domestic students, 6/1 priority date for international students; for spring admission, 11/1 priority date for domestic students, 10/1 priority date for international students. Applications are processed on a rolling basis. Application fee: $50 ($60 for international students). Electronic applications accepted. *Expenses:* Tuition, state resident: full-time $7000. Tuition, nonresident: full-time $19,200. *Financial support:* In 2009–10, 99 students received support, including 6 fellowships with full tuition reimbursements available (averaging $15,000 per year), 19 research assistantships with full and partial tuition reimbursements available (averaging $5,454 per year), 18 teaching assistantships with full and partial tuition reimbursements available (averaging $5,454 per year); career-related internships or fieldwork, Federal Work-Study, institutionally sponsored loans, scholarships/grants, health care benefits, and unspecified assistantships also available. Financial award application deadline: 3/31. *Faculty research:* Corporate governance, audit decision making, earning management, valuation, executive compensation, not-for-profit. *Unit head:* Dr. Mary S. Stone, Director, 205-348-2915, Fax: 205-348-8453, E-mail: mstone@cba.ua.edu. *Application contact:* Sandy D. Davidson, Advisor, 205-348-8997, Fax: 205-348-8453, E-mail: sdavidso@cba.ua.edu.

The University of Alabama in Huntsville, School of Graduate Studies, College of Business Administration, Department of Accounting and Finance, Huntsville, AL 35899. Offers accounting (M Acc, Certificate), including CPA preparatory with an emphasis in taxation (M Acc), CPA preparatory with emphasis in assurance and financial reporting (M Acc), general accounting (M Acc), information systems audit and control (ISAC) (M Acc). Part-time and evening/weekend programs available. *Faculty:* 5 full-time (3 women), 3 part-time/adjunct (0 women). *Students:* 16 full-time (10 women), 31 part-time (15 women); includes 5 minority (4 African Americans, 1 Asian American or Pacific Islander), 3 international. Average age 30. 42 applicants, 69% accepted, 21 enrolled. In 2009, 13 master's awarded. *Degree requirements:* For master's, comprehensive exam, thesis or alternative. *Entrance requirements:* For master's and Certificate, GMAT (minimum score 500), minimum AACSB index of 1080. Additional exam requirements/recommendations for international students: Required—TOEFL (minimum score 550 paper-based; 213 computer-based; 62 iBT). *Application deadline:* For fall admission, 8/1 for domestic students, 4/1 for international students; for spring admission, 12/1 for domestic students, 9/1 for international students. Applications are processed on a rolling basis. Application fee: $40 ($50 for international students). Electronic applications accepted. *Expenses:* Tuition, state resident: part-time $355.75 per credit hour. Tuition, nonresident: part-time $847.10 per credit hour. Required fees: $210.80 per semester. Tuition and fees vary according to course load and program. *Financial support:* Career-related internships or fieldwork, Federal Work-Study, institutionally sponsored loans, scholarships/grants, health care benefits, and unspecified assistantships available. Support available to part-time students. Financial award application deadline: 4/1; financial award applicants required to submit FAFSA. *Faculty research:* Accounting information systems, emerging technologies in accounting, behavioral accounting, state and local taxation, financial accounting. Total annual research expenditures: $67,010. *Unit head:* Dr. John Burnett, Interim Chair, 256-824-2923, Fax: 256-824-2929, E-mail: burnettj@uah.edu. *Application contact:* Jennifer Pettitt, Director of Graduate Programs, 256-824-6681, Fax: 256-824-7571, E-mail: jennifer.pettitt@uah.edu.

University of Arkansas at Little Rock, Graduate School, College of Business Administration, Little Rock, AR 72204-1099. Offers accountancy (M Acc, Graduate Certificate); business administration (MBA); construction management (Graduate Certificate); management (Graduate Certificate); management information system (MIS); management information systems (Graduate Certificate); management information systems leadership (Graduate Certificate); taxation (MS, Graduate Certificate). *Accreditation:* AACSB. Part-time and evening/weekend programs available. *Entrance requirements:* For master's, GMAT, minimum undergraduate GPA of 2.7. Additional exam requirements/recommendations for international students: Required—TOEFL (minimum score 525 paper-based; 195 computer-based).

University of Baltimore, Graduate School, Merrick School of Business, Program in Taxation, Baltimore, MD 21201-5779. Offers MS. Part-time and evening/weekend programs available. *Entrance requirements:* For master's, GMAT, minimum GPA of 3.0. Additional exam requirements/recommendations for international students: Required—TOEFL (minimum score 550 paper-based; 213 computer-based). *Expenses:* Contact institution. *Faculty research:* Taxation of not-for-profit entities.

University of Baltimore, School of Law, Baltimore, MD 21201. Offers law (JD); law of the United States (LL M); taxation (LL M); JD/LL M; JD/MBA; JD/MPA; JD/MS; JD/PhD. *Accreditation:* ABA. Part-time and evening/weekend programs available. *Entrance requirements:* LSAT. Electronic applications accepted. *Expenses:* Contact institution. *Faculty research:* Plain view doctrine, statute of limitations, bankruptcy, family law, international and comparative law, constitutional law.

University of Central Florida, College of Business Administration, Kenneth G. Dixon School of Accounting, Program in Taxation, Orlando, FL 32816. Offers MST. Part-time and evening/weekend programs available. *Students:* 21 full-time (11 women), 18 part-time (12 women); includes 8 minority (3 African Americans, 3 Asian Americans or Pacific Islanders, 2 Hispanic Americans), 2 international. Average age 28. 25 applicants, 72% accepted, 14 enrolled. In 2009, 20 master's awarded. *Degree requirements:* For master's, comprehensive exam. *Entrance requirements:* For master's, GMAT, minimum GPA of 3.0 in last 60 hours of course work. Additional exam requirements/recommendations for international students: Required—TOEFL. *Application deadline:* For fall admission, 2/1 priority date for domestic students; for spring admission, 11/1 priority date for domestic students. Application fee: $30. Electronic applications accepted. *Expenses:* Tuition, state resident: part-time $306.31 per credit hour. Tuition, nonresident: part-time $1099.01 per credit hour. Part-time tuition and fees vary according to degree level and program. *Financial support:* In 2009–10, 3 students received support, including 2 fellowships with partial tuition reimbursements available (averaging $10,000 per year), 1 teaching assistantship with partial tuition reimbursement available (averaging $7,100 per year); career-related internships or fieldwork, Federal Work-Study, institutionally sponsored loans, tuition waivers (partial), and unspecified assistantships also available. Financial award application deadline: 3/1; financial award applicants required to submit FAFSA.

University of Denver, College of Law, Taxation Program, Denver, CO 80208. Offers LL M, MT. Part-time and evening/weekend programs available. *Faculty:* 4 full-time (1 woman), 1 part-time/adjunct (0 women). *Students:* 76 full-time (31 women), 91 part-time (38 women); includes 19 minority (8 African Americans, 9 Asian Americans or Pacific Islanders, 2 Hispanic Americans), 10 international. Average age 32. 193 applicants, 100% accepted, 113 enrolled. In 2009, 84 master's awarded. *Entrance requirements:* For master's, LSAT, JD from an ABA approved institution. *Application deadline:* Applications are processed on a rolling basis. Application fee: $30. *Expenses:* Contact institution. *Financial support:* Federal Work-Study, institutionally sponsored loans, scholarships/grants, and tuition waivers (full and partial) available. Support available to part-time students. Financial award application deadline: 6/1; financial award applicants required to submit FAFSA. *Unit head:* Dr. Mark Vogel, Director, 303-871-6239. *Application contact:* Information Contact, 303-871-6239, Fax: 303-571-6358, E-mail: gtp@du.edu.

University of Florida, Levin College of Law, Gainesville, FL 32611. Offers comparative law (LL M); environmental law (LL M); international taxation (LL M); law (JD); taxation (LL M, SJD). *Accreditation:* ABA. *Faculty:* 77 full-time (37 women), 36 part-time/adjunct (10 women). *Students:* 1,369 full-time (620 women); includes 279 minority (69 African Americans, 8 American Indian/Alaska Native, 77 Asian Americans or Pacific Islanders, 125 Hispanic Americans), 71 international. Average age 24. 3,170 applicants, 25% accepted, 307 enrolled. In 2009, 497 JDs, 1 doctorate awarded. *Degree requirements:* For JD, thesis/dissertation or alternative. *Entrance requirements:* LSAT. Additional exam requirements/recommendations for international students: Required—TOEFL (minimum score 250 computer-based; 100 iBT). *Application deadline:* For fall admission, 1/15 for domestic and international students. Applications are processed on a rolling basis. Application fee: $30. Electronic applications accepted. *Expenses:* Contact institution. *Financial support:* In 2009–10, 299 students received support, including 25 fellowships (averaging $2,400 per year), 30 research assistantships with partial tuition reimbursements available (averaging $4,125 per year); career-related internships or fieldwork, Federal Work-Study, institutionally sponsored loans, scholarships/grants, traineeships, health care benefits, and unspecified assistantships also available. Financial award application deadline: 4/7; financial award applicants required to submit FAFSA. *Faculty research:* Environmental and land use law, taxation, family law, international law, constitutional law. *Unit head:* Robert Jerry, Dean, 352-273-0600, Fax: 352-392-8727, E-mail: jerryr@law.ufl.edu. *Application contact:* Michelle Adorno, Assistant Dean for Admissions, 352-273-0890, Fax: 352-392-4087, E-mail: madorno@law.ufl.edu.

University of Hartford, Barney School of Business, Department of Accounting and Taxation, West Hartford, CT 06117-1599. Offers professional accounting (Certificate); taxation (MSAT). Part-time and evening/weekend programs available. *Entrance requirements:* For master's, GMAT, 2 letters of recommendation, resume. Additional exam requirements/recommendations for international students: Required—TOEFL (minimum score 550 paper-based; 213 computer-based). Electronic applications accepted.

University of Hawaii at Manoa, Graduate Division, Shidler College of Business, Program in Accounting, Honolulu, HI 96822. Offers accounting (M Acc); accounting law (M Acc); information systems (M Acc); taxation (M Acc). Part-time programs available. *Faculty:* 8 full-time (2 women), 1 part-time/adjunct (0 women). *Students:* 63 full-time (31 women), 30 part-time (18 women); includes 57 minority (1 African American, 53 Asian Americans or Pacific Islanders, 3 Hispanic Americans), 17 international. Average age 28. 83 applicants, 80% accepted, 42 enrolled. In 2009, 37 master's awarded. *Entrance requirements:* For master's, GMAT, bachelor's degree in accounting, minimum GPA of 3.0. Additional exam requirements/recommendations for international students: Required—TOEFL (minimum score 550 paper-based; 213 computer-based; 79 iBT), IELTS (minimum score 5). *Application deadline:* For fall admission, 5/1 for domestic students, 3/1 for international students; for spring admission, 11/1 for domestic students, 10/1 for international students. Application fee: $60. *Expenses:* Tuition, state resident: full-time $8900; part-time $372 per credit. Tuition, nonresident: full-time $21,400; part-time $898 per credit. Required fees: $207 per semester. *Financial support:* In 2009–10, 5 students received support, including 17 fellowships (averaging $3,470 per year), 5 research assistantships (averaging $16,592 per year); career-related internships or fieldwork, Federal Work-Study, and tuition waivers (full) also available. *Faculty research:* International accounting, current tax topics, insurance industry financial reporting, behavioral accounting, auditing. *Application contact:* Liming Guan, Graduate Chair, 808-956-7332, Fax: 808-956-9888, E-mail: lguan@hawaii.edu.

Taxation

University of Illinois at Urbana–Champaign, Graduate College, College of Business, Department of Accountancy, Champaign, IL 61820. Offers accountancy (MAS, MS, PhD); taxation (MS); MAS/JD. *Accreditation:* AACSB. *Faculty:* 30 full-time (8 women), 4 part-time/adjunct (1 woman). *Students:* 406 full-time (208 women), 7 part-time (3 women); includes 64 minority (8 African Americans, 42 Asian Americans or Pacific Islanders, 14 Hispanic Americans), 155 international. 858 applicants, 54% accepted, 364 enrolled. In 2009, 330 master's, 2 doctorates awarded. *Entrance requirements:* For master's, GMAT (for MAS program), minimum GPA of 3.0; for doctorate, GMAT, minimum GPA of 3.0. Additional exam requirements/recommendations for international students: Required—TOEFL. *Application deadline:* Applications are processed on a rolling basis. Application fee: $60 ($75 for international students). Electronic applications accepted. *Financial support:* In 2009–10, 13 fellowships, 23 research assistantships, 78 teaching assistantships were awarded; tuition waivers (full and partial) also available. *Unit head:* Ira Soloman, Head, 217-333-3808, Fax: 217-244-0902, E-mail: isolomon@illinois.edu. *Application contact:* Yvonne Harden, Assistant Director, 217-333-4572, Fax: 217-244-0902, E-mail: yaharden@illinois.edu.

University of Memphis, Graduate School, Fogelman College of Business and Economics, School of Accountancy, Memphis, TN 38152. Offers accounting (MS); accounting systems (MS); taxation (MS). *Accreditation:* AACSB. *Faculty:* 10 full-time (2 women), 1 part-time/adjunct (0 women). *Students:* 25 full-time (10 women), 21 part-time (14 women); includes 10 minority (7 African Americans, 2 Asian Americans or Pacific Islanders, 1 Hispanic American), 10 international. Average age 29. 33 applicants, 76% accepted, 9 enrolled. In 2009, 27 master's awarded. *Degree requirements:* For master's, comprehensive exam. *Entrance requirements:* For master's, GMAT. *Application deadline:* For fall admission, 8/1 for domestic students; for spring admission, 12/1 for domestic students. Application fee: $35 ($60 for international students). *Expenses:* Tuition, state resident: full-time $6246; part-time $347 per credit hour. Tuition, nonresident: full-time $15,894; part-time $883 per credit hour. Required fees: $1160. Full-time tuition and fees vary according to course load, degree level and program. *Financial support:* In 2009–10, 32 students received support; research assistantships with full tuition reimbursements available, teaching assistantships with full tuition reimbursements available, Federal Work-Study, scholarships/grants, and unspecified assistantships available. Financial award application deadline: 2/15; financial award applicants required to submit FAFSA. *Faculty research:* Financial accounting, corporate governance, EDP auditing, evolution of system analysis, investor behavior and investment decisions. *Unit head:* Dr. Carolyn Callahan, Director, 901-678-4022, E-mail: cmcllhan@memphis.edu. *Application contact:* Dr. Craig Langstraat, Program Coordinator, 901-678-4577, E-mail: cjlngstr@memphis.edu.

University of Miami, Graduate School, School of Business Administration, Department of Accounting, Coral Gables, FL 33124. Offers professional accounting (MP Acc); taxation (MS Tax). *Accreditation:* AACSB. Part-time and evening/weekend programs available. *Entrance requirements:* For master's, GMAT or CPA exam. Additional exam requirements/recommendations for international students: Required—TOEFL. Electronic applications accepted. *Faculty research:* Financial reporting, audit risk, public policy and taxation issues, government accounting and public choice, corporate governance.

University of Michigan, Law School, Ann Arbor, MI 48109-1215. Offers comparative law (MCL); international tax (LL M); law (JD, LL M, SJD); JD/MA; JD/MBA; JD/MHSA; JD/MPH; JD/MPP; JD/MS; JD/MSI; JD/MSW; JD/MUP; JD/PhD. *Accreditation:* ABA. *Faculty:* 87 full-time (27 women), 33 part-time/adjunct (11 women). *Students:* 1,117 full-time (486 women); includes 256 minority (57 African Americans, 17 American Indian/Alaska Native, 135 Asian Americans or Pacific Islanders, 47 Hispanic Americans), 38 international. 5,414 applicants, 22% accepted, 371 enrolled. In 2009, 410 first professional degrees, 44 master's, 4 doctorates awarded. *Entrance requirements:* For JD, master's, and doctorate, LSAT. Additional exam requirements/recommendations for international students: Required—TOEFL. *Application deadline:* For fall admission, 2/15 for domestic students. Applications are processed on a rolling basis. Application fee: $75. Electronic applications accepted. *Expenses:* Contact institution. *Financial support:* In 2009–10, 1,035 students received support. Career-related internships or fieldwork, Federal Work-Study, institutionally sponsored loans, and scholarships/grants available. Financial award applicants required to submit FAFSA. *Unit head:* Evan H. Caminker, Dean, 734-764-1358. *Application contact:* Sarah C. Zearfoss, Assistant Dean and Director of Admissions, 734-764-0537, Fax: 734-647-3218, E-mail: law.jd.admissions@umich.edu.

University of Minnesota, Twin Cities Campus, Carlson School of Management, Master's Program in Business Taxation, Minneapolis, MN 55455-0213. Offers MBT. Part-time and evening/weekend programs available. *Faculty:* 3 full-time (0 women), 20 part-time/adjunct (2 women). *Students:* 43 full-time (27 women), 100 part-time (55 women); includes 14 minority (2 African Americans, 10 Asian Americans or Pacific Islanders, 2 Hispanic Americans), 19 international. Average age 32. 82 applicants, 80% accepted, 50 enrolled. In 2009, 34 master's awarded. *Entrance requirements:* For master's, GMAT or LSAT. Additional exam requirements/recommendations for international students: Required—TOEFL (minimum score 550 paper-based; 213 computer-based; 79 iBT), IELTS (minimum score 6.5). *Application deadline:* For fall admission, 6/15 priority date for domestic and international students; for spring admission, 10/15 priority date for domestic and international students. Applications are processed on a rolling basis. Application fee: $75 ($95 for international students). Electronic applications accepted. *Expenses:* Contact institution. *Financial support:* In 2009–10, 3 fellowships (averaging $4,000 per year), 2 teaching assistantships with partial tuition reimbursements (averaging $5,000 per year) were awarded; career-related internships or fieldwork and institutionally sponsored loans also available. Financial award application deadline: 4/1; financial award applicants required to submit FAFSA. *Faculty research:* Partnership taxation, tax theory, corporate taxation. *Unit head:* Mark Sellner, Director of Graduate Studies, 612-624-1050, Fax: 612-626-7795, E-mail: selln001@umn.edu. *Application contact:* JoAnn Ash, Administrator, 612-624-3320, Fax: 612-626-7795, E-mail: jash@umn.edu.

University of Mississippi, Graduate School, School of Accountancy, Oxford, University, MS 38677. Offers accountancy (M Acc, PhD); taxation accounting (M Tax). *Accreditation:* AACSB. *Faculty:* 13 full-time (4 women), 3 part-time/adjunct (2 women). *Students:* 108 full-time (31 women), 16 part-time (10 women); includes 7 minority (4 African Americans, 1 Asian American or Pacific Islander, 2 Hispanic Americans), 4 international. In 2009, 56 master's, 2 doctorates awarded. *Degree requirements:* For doctorate, thesis/dissertation. *Entrance requirements:* For master's, GMAT, minimum GPA of 3.0; for doctorate, GMAT. Additional exam requirements/recommendations for international students: Required—TOEFL. *Application deadline:* For fall admission, 4/1 for domestic students; for spring admission, 10/1 for domestic students. Applications are processed on a rolling basis. Application fee: $25. *Financial support:* Scholarships/grants available. Financial award application deadline: 3/1; financial award applicants required to submit FAFSA. *Unit head:* Dr. Mark Wilder, Interim Dean, 662-915-7468, Fax: 662-915-7483, E-mail: umaccy@olemiss.edu. *Application contact:* Dr. Christy M. Wyandt, Associate Dean, 662-915-7474, Fax: 662-915-7577, E-mail: cwyandt@olemiss.edu.

University of Missouri–Kansas City, School of Law, Kansas City, MO 64110-2499. Offers law (JD, LL M), including general (LL M), taxation (LL M); JD/LL M; JD/MBA; LL M/MPA. *Accreditation:* ABA. Part-time programs available. *Faculty:* 32 full-time (14 women), 1 part-time/adjunct (0 women). *Students:* 483 full-time (191 women), 59 part-time (28 women); includes 70 minority (35 African Americans, 4 American Indian/Alaska Native, 14 Asian Americans or Pacific Islanders, 17 Hispanic Americans), 27 international. Average age 27. 984 applicants, 50% accepted, 215 enrolled. In 2009, 153 JDs, 32 master's awarded. *Degree requirements:* For master's, thesis (general). *Entrance requirements:* For JD, LSAT; for master's, LSAT, minimum GPA of 3.0 (general), 2.7 (taxation). Additional exam requirements/recommendations for international students: Required—TOEFL (minimum score 550 paper-based; 213 computer-based; 80 iBT). *Application deadline:* For fall admission, 3/1 priority date for domestic and international students. Applications are processed on a rolling basis. Application fee: $50. Electronic applications accepted. *Expenses:* Contact institution. *Financial support:* In 2009–10, 27 teaching assistantships with partial tuition reimbursements (averaging $1,944 per year) were awarded; career-related internships or fieldwork, Federal Work-Study, institutionally sponsored loans, scholarships/grants, and tuition waivers (full and partial) also available. Support available to part-time students. Financial award application deadline: 3/1; financial award applicants required to submit FAFSA. *Faculty research:* Family and children's issues, litigation, estate planning, urban law, business, tax entrepreneurial law. *Unit head:* Ellen Y. Suni, Dean, 816-235-1677, Fax: 816-235-5276, E-mail: sunie@umkc.edu. *Application contact:* Debbie Brooks, Director of Admissions, 816-325-1644, Fax: 816-235-5276, E-mail: brooksdv@umkc.edu.

University of New Haven, Graduate School, School of Business, Program in Taxation, West Haven, CT 06516-1916. Offers MS. Part-time and evening/weekend programs available. *Faculty:* 5 full-time (0 women), 6 part-time/adjunct (0 women). *Students:* 1 (woman) full-time, 43 part-time (13 women); includes 16 minority (11 African Americans, 3 Asian Americans or Pacific Islanders, 2 Hispanic Americans). Average age 36. 16 applicants, 100% accepted, 10 enrolled. In 2009, 7 master's awarded. *Degree requirements:* For master's, thesis or alternative. *Entrance requirements:* For master's, GMAT. Additional exam requirements/recommendations for international students: Required—TOEFL (minimum score 520 paper-based; 190 computer-based; 70 iBT); Recommended—IELTS (minimum score 5.5). *Application deadline:* For fall admission, 5/31 for international students; for winter admission, 10/15 for international students; for spring admission, 1/15 for international students. Applications are processed on a rolling basis. Application fee: $50. Electronic applications accepted. *Expenses:* Contact institution. *Financial support:* Research assistantships with partial tuition reimbursements, teaching assistantships with partial tuition reimbursements, career-related internships or fieldwork, Federal Work-Study, scholarships/grants, tuition waivers, and unspecified assistantships available. Support available to part-time students. Financial award application deadline: 5/1; financial award applicants required to submit FAFSA. *Unit head:* Prof. Robert E. Wnek, Coordinator, 203-932-7111. *Application contact:* Eloise Gormley, Director of Graduate Admissions, 203-932-7449, Fax: 203-932-7137, E-mail: gradinfo@newhaven.edu.

University of New Mexico, Robert O. Anderson Graduate School of Management, Department of Accounting, Albuquerque, NM 87131. Offers accounting (MBA); advanced accounting (M Acct); professional accounting (M Acct); tax accounting (M Acct); JD/M Acct. *Accreditation:* AACSB. Part-time and evening/weekend programs available. *Faculty:* 12 full-time (4 women), 2 part-time/adjunct (1 woman). *Students:* 57 full-time (32 women), 60 part-time (39 women); includes 42 minority (1 African American, 5 Asian Americans or Pacific Islanders, 36 Hispanic Americans), 8 international. Average age 32. 77 applicants, 66% accepted, 46 enrolled. In 2009, 64 master's awarded. *Entrance requirements:* For master's, GMAT or GRE (can be waived in some instances). Additional exam requirements/recommendations for international students: Required—TOEFL (minimum score 550 paper-based; 213 computer-based; 79 iBT). *Application deadline:* For fall admission, 4/1 priority date for domestic students, 5/1 for international students; for spring admission, 10/1 priority date for domestic students, 10/1 for international students. Applications are processed on a rolling basis. Application fee: $50. Electronic applications accepted. *Expenses:* Tuition, state resident: full-time $2099; part-time $233.20 per credit hour. Tuition, nonresident: full-time $6650. Required fees: $25 per semester. Tuition and fees vary according to course load, program and reciprocity agreements. *Financial support:* Fellowships, research assistantships, teaching assistantships, career-related internships or fieldwork, Federal Work-Study, scholarships/grants, and unspecified assistantships available. Support available to part-time students. *Faculty research:* Critical accounting, accounting pedagogy, theory, taxation, information fraud. *Unit head:* Dr. Craig White, Chair, 505-277-6471, Fax: 505-277-7108, E-mail: white@mgt.unm.edu. *Application contact:* Tina Armijo, Office Administrator, 505-277-6471, Fax: 505-277-7108, E-mail: profmacct@mgt.unm.edu.

University of New Orleans, Graduate School, College of Business Administration, Department of Accounting, Program in Taxation, New Orleans, LA 70148. Offers MS. Part-time and evening/weekend programs available. *Degree requirements:* For master's, thesis optional. *Entrance requirements:* For master's, GMAT. Additional exam requirements/recommendations for international students: Required—TOEFL (minimum score 550 paper-based; 213 computer-based; 79 iBT). Electronic applications accepted.

The University of North Carolina at Greensboro, Graduate School, Bryan School of Business and Economics, Department of Accounting, Greensboro, NC 27412-5001. Offers accounting (MS); accounting systems (MS); financial accounting and reporting (MS); financial analysis (PMC); tax concentration (MS). *Accreditation:* AACSB. *Entrance requirements:* For master's, GMAT, GRE General Test, previous course work in accounting and business. Additional exam requirements/recommendations for international students: Required—TOEFL. Electronic applications accepted.

University of North Texas, Robert B. Toulouse School of Graduate Studies, College of Business Administration, Department of Accounting, Denton, TX 76203-5017. Offers accounting (MS, PhD); taxation (MS). *Accreditation:* AACSB. Part-time programs available. *Degree requirements:* For master's, comprehensive exam; for doctorate, thesis/dissertation. *Entrance requirements:* For master's, GMAT or GRE General Test, essay, 3 letters of recommendation, resume; for doctorate, GMAT or GRE General Test, statement of purpose, resume, 3 letters of recommendation. Additional exam requirements/recommendations for international students: Recommended—TOEFL (minimum score 550 paper-based; 213 computer-based). *Application deadline:* Applications are processed on a rolling basis. Application fee: $50 ($75 for international students). Electronic applications accepted. *Expenses:* Tuition, state resident: full-time $4298; part-time $239 per contact hour. Tuition, nonresident: full-time $9878; part-time $549 per contact hour. Required fees: $265 per contact hour. *Financial support:* In 2009–10, 34 students received support; fellowships, career-related internships or fieldwork, Federal Work-Study, and institutionally sponsored loans available. Financial award applicants required to submit FAFSA. *Faculty research:* Empirical tax research issues, empirical financial accounting issues, problems and issues in public interest areas, historical perspective for accounting issues, behavioral issues in auditing and accounting systems. *Application contact:* Graduate Programs Office, 940-369-8977, Fax: 940-369-8978, E-mail: mbacob@unt.edu.

University of Notre Dame, Mendoza College of Business, Program in Accountancy, Notre Dame, IN 46556. Offers financial reporting and assurance services (MS); tax services (MS). *Accreditation:* AACSB. *Faculty:* 37 full-time (3 women), 14 part-time/adjunct (0 women). *Students:* 85 full-time (39 women); includes 12 minority (1 African American, 5 Asian Americans or Pacific Islanders, 6 Hispanic Americans), 10 international. Average age 22. 302 applicants, 39% accepted, 85 enrolled. In 2009, 95 master's awarded. *Entrance requirements:* For master's, GMAT. Additional exam requirements/recommendations for international students: Required—TOEFL (minimum score 630 paper-based; 267 computer-based; 109 iBT). *Application deadline:* For fall admission, 11/1 for domestic and international students; for spring admission, 5/12 for domestic and international students. Applications are processed on a rolling basis. Application fee: $50 ($100 for international students). Electronic applications accepted. *Financial support:* In 2009–10, 83 students received support, including 82 fellowships (averaging $12,200 per year); scholarships/grants and unspecified assistantships also available. Financial award application deadline: 2/28; financial award applicants required to submit FAFSA. *Faculty research:* Stock valuation, accounting information in decision-making, choice of accounting method, taxes cost on capital. *Unit head:* Dr. Michael H. Morris, Director, 574-631-9732, Fax: 574-631-5300, E-mail: msacct.1@nd.edu. *Application contact:* Helen High, Program Manager, 574-631-6499, Fax: 574-631-5300, E-mail: msacct.1@nd.edu.

University of San Diego, School of Business Administration, San Diego, CA 92110-2492. Offers accountancy (MS); business administration (MBA); executive leadership (MSEL); global leadership (MSGL); international business administration (IMBA); real estate (MSRE); supply chain management (MS, Certificate); taxation (MS); JD/IMBA; JD/MBA. *Accreditation:* AACSB. Part-time and evening/weekend programs available. *Faculty:* 36 full-time (11 women), 18 part-time/adjunct (4 women). *Students:* 173 full-time (53 women), 259 part-time (91 women); includes 61 minority (9 African Americans, 4 American Indian/Alaska Native, 29 Asian Americans or Pacific Islanders, 19 Hispanic Americans), 32 international. Average age 31. 555 applicants, 61% accepted, 191 enrolled. In 2009, 248 master's awarded. *Degree requirements:* For master's, variable foreign language requirement, community service, capstone project. *Entrance requirements:* For master's, GMAT (MBA, IMBA, MSRE), minimum GPA of 3.0, minimum 2

years of full-time work experience. Additional exam requirements/recommendations for international students: Required—TOEFL (minimum score 580 paper-based; 237 computer-based; 92 iBT), TWE. Application fee: $80. Electronic applications accepted. *Expenses:* Tuition: Full-time $21,042; part-time $1169 per unit. Required fees: $224. Full-time tuition and fees vary according to course load and degree level. *Financial support:* In 2009–10, 312 students received support. Career-related internships or fieldwork, Federal Work-Study, institutionally sponsored loans, scholarships/grants, and unspecified assistantships available. Support available to part-time students. Financial award application deadline: 4/1; financial award applicants required to submit FAFSA. *Faculty research:* Exchange rate forecasting, corporate governance, performance of private equity funds, economic geography, food banking. *Unit head:* Dr. David Pyke, Interim Dean, 619-260-4886, E-mail: sbadean@sandiego.edu. *Application contact:* Dr. John Mosby, Associate Director of Graduate Admissions, 619-260-4524, Fax: 619-260-4158, E-mail: grads@sandiego.edu.

University of San Diego, School of Law, San Diego, CA 92110. Offers business and corporate law (LL M); comparative law (LL M); general studies (LL M); international law (LL M); law (JD); taxation (LL M, Diploma); JD/IMBA; JD/MA; JD/MBA. *Accreditation:* ABA. Part-time and evening/weekend programs available. *Faculty:* 43 full-time (17 women), 57 part-time/adjunct (18 women). *Students:* 882 full-time (412 women), 222 part-time (96 women); includes 297 minority (15 African Americans, 12 American Indian/Alaska Native, 177 Asian Americans or Pacific Islanders, 93 Hispanic Americans), 21 international. Average age 26. 4,424 applicants, 34% accepted, 324 enrolled. In 2009, 327 first professional degrees, 59 master's awarded. *Entrance requirements:* For JD, LSAT, bachelor's degree; for master's, JD, LLB or equivalent from an ABA-accredited law school. Additional exam requirements/recommendations for international students: Required—TOEFL (minimum score 600 paper-based; 250 computer-based; 98 iBT). *Application deadline:* For fall admission, 2/1 priority date for domestic students. Applications are processed on a rolling basis. Application fee: $50. Electronic applications accepted. *Expenses:* Contact institution. *Financial support:* In 2009–10, 973 students received support. Career-related internships or fieldwork, Federal Work-Study, institutionally sponsored loans, and scholarships/grants available. Support available to part-time students. Financial award application deadline: 3/1; financial award applicants required to submit FAFSA. *Unit head:* Kevin Cole, Dean, 619-260-2330, Fax: 619-260-2218. *Application contact:* Carl J. Eging, Director of Admissions and Financial Aid, 619-260-4528, Fax: 619-260-2218, E-mail: eging@sandiego.edu.

University of Southern California, Graduate School, Marshall School of Business, Leventhal School of Accounting, Los Angeles, CA 90089. Offers accounting (M Acc); business taxation (MBT); JD/MBT. Part-time programs available. *Students:* 149 full-time (81 women), 130 part-time (61 women); includes 124 minority (8 African Americans, 99 Asian Americans or Pacific Islanders, 17 Hispanic Americans), 49 international. 776 applicants, 35% accepted, 201 enrolled. In 2009, 152 master's awarded. *Entrance requirements:* For master's, GMAT, undergraduate degree, communication skills. Additional exam requirements/recommendations for international students: Required—TOEFL (minimum score 100 computer-based). *Application deadline:* For fall admission, 3/31 for domestic students, 1/10 for international students; for spring admission, 11/1 for domestic students. Applications are processed on a rolling basis. Application fee: $85. Electronic applications accepted. *Expenses:* Tuition: Full-time $25,980; part-time $1315 per unit. Required fees: $554. One-time fee: $35 full-time. Full-time tuition and fees vary according to degree level and program. *Financial support:* In 2009–10, 62 students received support. Institutionally sponsored loans and scholarships/grants available. Financial award application deadline: 1/10. *Faculty research:* State and local taxation, Securities and Exchange Commission, governance, auditing fees, financial accounting, enterprise zones, women in business. *Unit head:* Shirley Maxey, Associate Dean, 213-740-4838, E-mail: smaxey@marshall.usc.edu. *Application contact:* Jenna Belknap, Associate Program Director, 213-740-4838, E-mail: belknap@marshall.usc.edu.

University of Southern Maine, School of Business, Portland, ME 04104-9300. Offers business administration (MBA); finance (MBA); taxation (MBA); JD/MBA; MBA/MSA; MBA/MSN; MS/MBA. *Accreditation:* AACSB. Part-time and evening/weekend programs available. *Faculty:* 20 full-time (5 women), 2 part-time/adjunct (1 woman). *Students:* 33 full-time (19 women), 102 part-time (42 women); includes 6 minority (2 African Americans, 1 American Indian/Alaska Native, 2 Asian Americans or Pacific Islanders, 1 Hispanic American), 4 international. Average age 32. 53 applicants, 55% accepted, 23 enrolled. In 2009, 45 master's awarded. *Entrance requirements:* For master's, GMAT, minimum AACSB index of 1100. Additional exam requirements/recommendations for international students: Required—TOEFL (minimum score 550 paper-based; 213 computer-based; 79 iBT). *Application deadline:* For fall admission, 8/1 priority date for domestic students, 5/1 priority date for international students; for spring admission, 12/1 priority date for domestic students, 9/1 priority date for international students. Applications are processed on a rolling basis. Application fee: $65. Electronic applications accepted. *Financial support:* In 2009–10, 3 research assistantships with partial tuition reimbursements (averaging $9,000 per year), 3 teaching assistantships with partial tuition reimbursements (averaging $9,000 per year) were awarded; career-related internships or fieldwork, Federal Work-Study, scholarships/grants, tuition waivers (full and partial), and unspecified assistantships also available. Support available to part-time students. Financial award application deadline: 2/15; financial award applicants required to submit FAFSA. *Faculty research:* Economic development, MIS, real options, system dynamics, simulation. *Unit head:* James B. Shaffer, Dean, 207-780-4020, Fax: 207-780-4662, E-mail: jshaffer@usm.maine.edu. *Application contact:* Alice B. Cash, Assistant Dean for Student Affairs, 207-780-4184, Fax: 207-780-4662, E-mail: acash@usm.maine.edu.

The University of Texas at Arlington, Graduate School, College of Business, Accounting Department, Arlington, TX 76019. Offers accounting (MP Acc, MS); taxation (MS). Part-time and evening/weekend programs available. *Faculty:* 9 full-time (4 women), 3 part-time/adjunct (0 women). *Students:* 119 full-time (61 women), 161 part-time (76 women); includes 57 minority (10 African Americans, 2 American Indian/Alaska Native, 22 Asian Americans or Pacific Islanders, 23 Hispanic Americans), 40 international. 208 applicants, 75% accepted, 81 enrolled. In 2009, 67 master's awarded. *Degree requirements:* For master's, thesis optional. *Entrance requirements:* For master's, GMAT. Additional exam requirements/recommendations for international students: Required—TOEFL (minimum score 550 paper-based; 213 computer-based; 79 iBT). *Application deadline:* For fall admission, 6/15 for domestic students. Applications are processed on a rolling basis. Application fee: $35 ($50 for international students). *Financial support:* In 2009–10, 2 fellowships (averaging $1,000 per year), 2 research assistantships (averaging $6,000 per year), 10 teaching assistantships (averaging $13,000 per year) were awarded; career-related internships or fieldwork, scholarships/grants, and unspecified assistantships also available. Financial award application deadline: 6/1; financial award applicants required to submit FAFSA. *Unit head:* Dr. Larry Walther, Chair, 817-272-3481, Fax: 817-282-5793, E-mail: walther@uta.edu. *Application contact:* Carly S. Andrews, Graduate Advisor, 817-272-3047, Fax: 817-272-5793, E-mail: graduate.accounting.advisor@uta.edu.

The University of Texas at Dallas, School of Management, Program in Accounting and Information Management, Richardson, TX 75080. Offers assurance services (MS); financial planning and analysis (MS); information management (MS); international services (MS); management consulting (MS); software management (MS); taxation services (MS). *Accreditation:* AACSB. *Faculty:* 19 full-time (4 women), 10 part-time/adjunct (3 women). *Students:* 295 full-time (173 women), 275 part-time (156 women); includes 172 minority (29 African Americans, 3 American Indian/Alaska Native, 108 Asian Americans or Pacific Islanders, 32 Hispanic Americans), 171 international. Average age 29. 356 applicants, 74% accepted, 203 enrolled. In 2009, 254 master's awarded. *Entrance requirements:* For master's, GMAT. Additional exam requirements/recommendations for international students: Required—TOEFL (minimum score 550 paper-based; 213 computer-based). *Application deadline:* For fall admission, 7/15 for domestic students, 5/1 priority date for international students; for spring admission, 11/15 for domestic students, 9/1 priority date for international students. Applications are processed on a rolling basis. Application fee: $50 ($100 for international students). Electronic applications accepted. *Expenses:* Tuition, state resident: full-time $11,068; part-time $461 per credit hour.

Tuition, nonresident: full-time $21,178; part-time $882 per credit hour. Tuition and fees vary according to course load. *Financial support:* In 2009–10, 3 research assistantships with full tuition reimbursements (averaging $10,072 per year), 4 teaching assistantships with full tuition reimbursements (averaging $10,050 per year) were awarded; fellowships, career-related internships or fieldwork, Federal Work-Study, institutionally sponsored loans, scholarships/grants, and unspecified assistantships also available. Support available to part-time students. Financial award application deadline: 4/30; financial award applicants required to submit FAFSA. *Faculty research:* Privatization and accounting/auditing, corporate performance and executive compensation, risk management, information technology in accounting. *Unit head:* Amy Troutman, Assistant Director, 972-883-6719, Fax: 972-883-6823, E-mail: amybass@utdallas.edu. *Application contact:* James Parker, Assistant Director of Graduate Recruitment, 972-883-5842, E-mail: jparker@utdallas.edu.

The University of Texas at San Antonio, College of Business, Department of Accounting, San Antonio, TX 78249-0617. Offers accountancy (M Accy); business administration-accounting (PhD); management accounting (MBA); taxation (MBA). *Accreditation:* AACSB. Part-time and evening/weekend programs available. *Faculty:* 11 full-time (3 women), 4 part-time/adjunct (2 women). *Students:* 44 full-time (22 women), 35 part-time (16 women); includes 29 minority (1 African American, 4 Asian Americans or Pacific Islanders, 24 Hispanic Americans), 9 international. Average age 29. 68 applicants, 57% accepted, 32 enrolled. In 2009, 32 master's awarded. *Degree requirements:* For master's, comprehensive exam (for some programs), thesis (for some programs). *Entrance requirements:* For master's, GMAT. Additional exam requirements/recommendations for international students: Required—TOEFL (minimum score 500 paper-based; 173 computer-based; 61 iBT), IELTS (minimum score 5). *Application deadline:* For fall admission, 7/1 for domestic students, 4/1 for international students; for spring admission, 11/1 for domestic students, 9/1 for international students. Application fee: $45 ($80 for international students). *Expenses:* Tuition, state resident: full-time $3975; part-time $221 per contact hour. Tuition, nonresident: full-time $13,947; part-time $775 per contact hour. Required fees: $1853. *Financial support:* In 2009–10, 17 students received support, including 10 research assistantships (averaging $8,580 per year), 6 teaching assistantships (averaging $7,800 per year); scholarships/grants, tuition waivers, and unspecified assistantships also available. Support available to part-time students. *Faculty research:* Financial reporting, auditing, tax, health care accounting. *Unit head:* Dr. James E. Groff, Interim Chair, 210-458-5239, Fax: 210-458-4322, E-mail: james.groff@utsa.edu. *Application contact:* Jeff Boone, Graduate Advisor, 210-458-7091, E-mail: jeff.boone@utsa.edu.

University of the Pacific, McGeorge School of Law, Sacramento, CA 95817. Offers advocacy (JD); criminal justice (JD); experiential law teaching (LL M); intellectual property (JD); international legal studies (JD); international water resources law (LL M, JSD); law (JD); public law and policy (JD); public policy and law (LL M); tax (JD); transnational business practice (LL M); JD/MBA; JD/MPPA. *Accreditation:* ABA. Part-time and evening/weekend programs available. *Faculty:* 55 full-time (24 women), 57 part-time/adjunct (18 women). *Students:* 697 full-time (343 women), 377 part-time (197 women); includes 301 minority (33 African Americans, 11 American Indian/Alaska Native, 163 Asian Americans or Pacific Islanders, 94 Hispanic Americans). Average age 24. 2,659 applicants, 43% accepted, 236 enrolled. In 2009, 254 JDs, 51 master's awarded. *Degree requirements:* For master's, thesis (for some programs); for doctorate, thesis/dissertation. *Entrance requirements:* For JD, LSAT; for master's, JD; for doctorate, LL M. Additional exam requirements/recommendations for international students: Required—TOEFL (minimum score 600 paper-based; 250 computer-based; 100 iBT). *Application deadline:* For fall admission, 3/15 priority date for domestic students. Applications are processed on a rolling basis. Application fee: $50. Electronic applications accepted. *Expenses:* Contact institution. *Financial support:* In 2009–10, 887 students received support, including 1 fellowship, 114 research assistantships (averaging $1,839 per year), 12 teaching assistantships (averaging $953 per year); career-related internships or fieldwork, Federal Work-Study, institutionally sponsored loans, and scholarships/grants also available. Support available to part-time students. Financial award applicants required to submit FAFSA. *Faculty research:* International legal studies, public policy and law, advocacy, intellectual property law, taxation, criminal law. *Unit head:* Elizabeth Rindskopf Parker, Dean, 916-739-7151, E-mail: elizabeth@pacific.edu. *Application contact:* 916-739-7105, Fax: 916-739-7301, E-mail: mcgeorge@pacific.edu.

University of the Sacred Heart, Graduate Programs, Department of Business Administration, Program in Taxation, San Juan, PR 00914-0383. Offers MBA. Part-time and evening/weekend programs available. *Degree requirements:* For master's, thesis. *Entrance requirements:* For master's, EXADEP, minimum undergraduate GPA of 2.75, interview.

University of Tulsa, Graduate School, Collins College of Business, Master of Business Administration Program, Tulsa, OK 74104-3189. Offers accounting (MBA); business administration (MBA); energy management (MBA); finance (MBA); international business (MBA); management information systems (MBA); taxation (MBA); JD/MBA; MBA/MSCS; MBA/MSF. *Accreditation:* AACSB. Part-time and evening/weekend programs available. *Faculty:* 32 full-time (6 women). *Students:* 59 full-time (26 women), 45 part-time (18 women); includes 13 minority (4 African Americans, 4 American Indian/Alaska Native, 1 Asian American or Pacific Islander, 4 Hispanic Americans), 9 international. Average age 25. 78 applicants, 53% accepted, 30 enrolled. In 2009, 36 master's awarded. *Entrance requirements:* For master's, GMAT. Additional exam requirements/recommendations for international students: Required—TOEFL (minimum score 575 paper-based; 232 computer-based; 90 iBT), IELTS (minimum score 6.5). *Application deadline:* Applications are processed on a rolling basis. Application fee: $40. Electronic applications accepted. *Expenses:* Tuition: Full-time $16,182; part-time $899 per credit hour. Required fees: $4 per credit hour. Tuition and fees vary according to course load. *Financial support:* In 2009–10, 42 students received support, including 5 fellowships (averaging $11,894 per year), 2 research assistantships (averaging $9,322 per year), 35 teaching assistantships (averaging $8,112 per year); institutionally sponsored loans, scholarships/grants, health care benefits, tuition waivers (full and partial), and unspecified assistantships also available. Support available to part-time students. Financial award application deadline: 2/1; financial award applicants required to submit FAFSA. *Faculty research:* Accounting, energy management, finance, international business, management information systems, taxation. *Unit head:* Dr. Markham Collins, Associate Dean of the Collins College of Business, 918-631-2783, Fax: 918-631-2142, E-mail: markham-collins@utulsa.edu. *Application contact:* Dr. Markham Collins, Associate Dean of the Collins College of Business, 918-631-2783, Fax: 918-631-2142, E-mail: markham-collins@utulsa.edu.

University of Tulsa, Graduate School, Collins College of Business, Online Program in Taxation, Tulsa, OK 74104-3189. Offers M Tax, JD/M Tax. Part-time and evening/weekend programs available. Postbaccalaureate distance learning degree programs offered (no on-campus study). *Faculty:* 4 full-time (2 women), 1 part-time/adjunct (0 women). *Students:* 3 full-time (1 woman), 34 part-time (20 women); includes 1 minority (Asian American or Pacific Islander), 1 international. Average age 36. 24 applicants, 54% accepted, 8 enrolled. In 2009, 13 master's awarded. *Entrance requirements:* For master's, GMAT or LSAT. Additional exam requirements/recommendations for international students: Required—TOEFL (minimum score 575 paper-based; 231 computer-based; 91 iBT), IELTS (minimum score 6.5). *Application deadline:* Applications are processed on a rolling basis. Application fee: $40. Electronic applications accepted. *Expenses:* Tuition: Full-time $16,182; part-time $899 per credit hour. Required fees: $4 per credit hour. Tuition and fees vary according to course load. *Financial support:* Research assistantships, teaching assistantships with partial tuition reimbursements, career-related internships or fieldwork, Federal Work-Study, institutionally sponsored loans, scholarships/grants, health care benefits, tuition waivers (full and partial), and unspecified assistantships available. Support available to part-time students. Financial award application deadline: 2/1; financial award applicants required to submit FAFSA. *Unit head:* Dr. Markham Collins, Associate Dean of the Collins College of Business, 918-631-2783, Fax: 918-631-2142, E-mail: markham-collins@utulsa.edu. *Application contact:* Dr. Markham Collins, Associate Dean of the Collins College of Business, 918-631-2783, Fax: 918-631-2142, E-mail: markham-collins@utulsa.edu.

University of Washington, Graduate School, Michael G. Foster School of Business, Seattle, WA 98195-3200. Offers auditing and assurance (MP Acc); business (PhD); business

Taxation

University of Washington (continued)

administration (evening) (MBA); business administration (full-time) (MBA); executive business administration (MBA); global business administration (MBA); global executive business administration (MBA); taxation (MP Acc); technology management (MBA); JD/MBA; MBA/MAIS; MBA/MHA. *Accreditation:* AACSB. Part-time and evening/weekend programs available. Terminal master's awarded for partial completion of doctoral program. *Degree requirements:* For doctorate, comprehensive exam, thesis/dissertation. *Entrance requirements:* For master's, GMAT; for doctorate, GMAT, GRE. Additional exam requirements/recommendations for international students: Required—TOEFL (minimum score 600 paper-based; 250 computer-based). Electronic applications accepted. *Expenses:* Contact institution. *Faculty research:* Finance, marketing, organizational behavior, information technology, strategy.

University of Washington, Graduate School, School of Law, Seattle, WA 98195-3020. Offers Asian law (LL M, PhD); intellectual property law and policy (LL M); law (JD); law of sustainable international development (LL M); taxation (LL M); JD/LL M; JD/MA; JD/MAIS; JD/MBA; JD/MPA; JD/MS; JD/PhD. *Accreditation:* ABA. *Degree requirements:* For master's, thesis; for doctorate, thesis/dissertation. *Entrance requirements:* For JD, LSAT; for master's, language proficiency (LL M in Asian law). Additional exam requirements/recommendations for international students: Required—TOEFL. *Expenses:* Contact institution. *Faculty research:* Asian, international and comparative law, intellectual property law, health law, environmental law, taxation.

University of Waterloo, Graduate Studies, Faculty of Arts, School of Accounting and Finance, Waterloo, ON N2L 3G1, Canada. Offers accounting (M Acc, PhD); finance (M Acc); taxation (M Tax). *Degree requirements:* For master's, thesis or alternative; for doctorate, thesis/dissertation. *Entrance requirements:* For master's, honors degree, minimum B average, resumé; for doctorate, GMAT, master's degree, minimum A- average, resume. Additional exam requirements/recommendations for international students: Required—TOEFL, TWE. Electronic applications accepted. *Expenses:* Contact institution. *Faculty research:* Auditing, management accounting.

University of Wisconsin–Madison, Graduate School, Wisconsin School of Business, Master of Accountancy Program, Madison, WI 53706-1380. Offers audit (IM Acc); tax (GM Acc). *Faculty:* 13 full-time (5 women). *Students:* 98 full-time (54 women); includes 10 minority (9 Asian Americans or Pacific Islanders, 1 Hispanic American), 13 international. Average age 22. 129 applicants, 22% accepted, 13 enrolled. In 2009, 85 master's awarded. *Entrance requirements:* For master's, GMAT, essays. Additional exam requirements/recommendations for international students: Required—TOEFL (minimum score 100 computer-based), IELTS, Pearson Test of English (PTE). *Application deadline:* For fall admission, 9/12 for domestic and international students. Application fee: $56. Electronic applications accepted. *Expenses:* Tuition, state resident: part-time $594 per credit. Tuition, nonresident: part-time $1504 per credit. Required fees: $65 per credit. Tuition and fees vary according to course load, program and reciprocity agreements. *Financial support:* In 2009–10, 82 students received support, including 6 research assistantships with partial tuition reimbursements available (averaging $8,100 per year), 54 teaching assistantships with full tuition reimbursements available (averaging $28,175 per year); career-related internships or fieldwork also available. Financial award application deadline: 5/1; financial award applicants required to submit FAFSA. *Faculty research:* Internal control deficiencies, impairment recognition, accounting misstatements, earnings restatements, voluntary disclosure. *Unit head:* Dr. Jon Davis, Professor/Chair of Accounting and Information Systems, 608-263-4264, E-mail: jdavis@bus.wisc.edu. *Application contact:* Kristen Ann Fuhremann, Director, 608-262-0316, Fax: 608-263-0477, E-mail: kfuhremann@bus.wisc.edu.

University of Wisconsin–Milwaukee, Graduate School, Sheldon B. Lubar School of Business, Milwaukee, WI 53201. Offers business administration (MBA); enterprise resource planning (Certificate); investment management (Certificate); management science (MS, PhD); nonprofit management and leadership (MS, Certificate); state and local taxation (Certificate); MS/MBA. *Accreditation:* AACSB. Part-time and evening/weekend programs available. *Faculty:* 55 full-time (14 women). *Students:* 317 full-time (108 women), 420 part-time (179 women); includes 70 minority (20 African Americans, 5 American Indian/Alaska Native, 33 Asian Americans or Pacific Islanders, 12 Hispanic Americans), 73 international. Average age 31. 499 applicants, 59% accepted, 132 enrolled. In 2009, 286 master's, 10 doctorates awarded. *Degree requirements:* For master's, comprehensive exam (for some programs); for doctorate, comprehensive exam, thesis/dissertation. *Entrance requirements:* For master's and doctorate, GMAT or GRE General Test. Additional exam requirements/recommendations for international students: Required—TOEFL (minimum score 550 paper-based; 79 iBT), IELTS (minimum score 6.5). *Application deadline:* For fall admission, 1/1 priority date for domestic students; for spring admission, 9/1 for domestic students. Applications are processed on a rolling basis. Application fee: $45 ($75 for international students). *Expenses:* Contact institution. *Financial support:* In 2009–10, 5 fellowships, 41 teaching assistantships were awarded; career-related internships or fieldwork, Federal Work-Study, and unspecified assistantships also available. Support available to part-time students. Financial award application deadline: 4/15. *Faculty research:* Applied management research in finance, MIS, marketing, operations research, organizational sciences. Total annual research expenditures: $204,295. *Unit head:* Timothy L. Smunt, Dean, 414-229-6256, Fax: 414-229-2372, E-mail: tsmunt@uwm.edu. *Application contact:* Sara Sandin, 414-229-5403, E-mail: mba-ms@uwm.edu.

Villanova University, School of Law and Villanova School of Business, Tax Program, Villanova, PA 19085-1699. Offers LL M, JD/LL M. Part-time and evening/weekend programs available. *Faculty:* 5 full-time (2 women), 39 part-time/adjunct (4 women). *Students:* 22 full-time (8 women), 56 part-time (23 women); includes 14 minority (4 African Americans, 6 Asian Americans or Pacific Islanders, 4 Hispanic Americans), 3 international. Average age 33. 62 applicants, 77% accepted, 25 enrolled. In 2009, 40 master's awarded. *Entrance requirements:* For master's, LSAT, JD (LL M). Additional exam requirements/recommendations for international students: Required—TOEFL (minimum score 600 paper-based; 250 computer-based). *Application deadline:* For fall admission, 8/1 for domestic and international students; for spring admission, 12/1 for domestic and international students. Applications are processed on a rolling basis. Application fee: $50. *Expenses:* Contact institution. *Financial support:* Research assistantships, career-related internships or fieldwork, Federal Work-Study, and unspecified assistantships available. Support available to part-time students. Financial award application deadline: 3/15; financial award applicants required to submit FAFSA. *Faculty research:* Taxation and estate planning, corporate tax planning, international taxation, state taxation. *Unit head:* Prof. Leslie M. Book, Director, 610-519-6416, Fax: 610-519-8018, E-mail: book@law.villanova.edu. *Application contact:* Linda Love Vines, Assistant Director, 610-519-4533, Fax: 610-519-8018, E-mail: vines@law.villanova.edu.

Virginia Commonwealth University, Graduate School, School of Business, Program in Taxation, Richmond, VA 23284-9005. Offers M Tax. *Entrance requirements:* For master's, GMAT.

Wake Forest University, Babcock Graduate School of Management, MSA Program in Accountancy, Winston-Salem, NC 27106. Offers assurance services (MSA); tax consulting (MSA); transaction services (MSA). *Faculty:* 62 full-time (13 women), 36 part-time/adjunct (14 women). *Students:* 113 full-time (57 women); includes 24 minority (13 African Americans, 1 American Indian/Alaska Native, 8 Asian Americans or Pacific Islanders, 2 Hispanic Americans), 10 international. Average age 23. In 2009, 68 master's awarded. *Entrance requirements:* For master's, GMAT, letters of recommendation, official transcripts, current resume or curriculum vitae. Additional exam requirements/recommendations for international students: Required—TOEFL (minimum score 600 paper-based; 250 computer-based; 100 iBT), Pearson Test of English (PTE). *Application deadline:* For fall admission, 6/1 for domestic and international students. Applications are processed on a rolling basis. Application fee: $75. Electronic applications accepted. *Financial support:* In 2009–10, 100 students received support. Career-related internships or fieldwork and scholarships/grants available. Financial award application deadline: 3/1; financial award applicants required to submit FAFSA. *Faculty research:* The influence of personal relationships on business decision making and management of change; drivers of perceived value and consumer behavior; impact of accounting on auditing, financial, managerial, systems and taxation stakeholders; corporate governance and executive compensation; impact of operations strategies on competitiveness. *Unit head:* Yvonne Hinson, Director of Accountancy, 336-758-5422, Fax: 336-758-5830, E-mail: admissions@mba.wfu.edu. *Application contact:* LaKesha Alston, Administrative Assistant, 336-758-5422, Fax: 336-758-5830, E-mail: admissions@mba.wfu.edu.

Walsh College of Accountancy and Business Administration, Graduate Programs, Program in Taxation, Troy, MI 48007-7006. Offers MST. Part-time and evening/weekend programs available. *Faculty:* 2 full-time (0 women), 19 part-time/adjunct (0 women). *Students:* 3 full-time (1 woman), 96 part-time (45 women); includes 24 minority (10 African Americans, 3 Asian Americans or Pacific Islanders, 1 Hispanic American), 3 international. Average age 35. 25 applicants, 88% accepted, 21 enrolled. *Entrance requirements:* For master's, minimum GPA of 2.75, previous course work in individual income taxation and business. Additional exam requirements/recommendations for international students: Required—TOEFL. *Application deadline:* For fall admission, 8/24 priority date for domestic students; for winter admission, 1/1 priority date for domestic students; for spring admission, 4/1 priority date for domestic students. Applications are processed on a rolling basis. Application fee: $25. Electronic applications accepted. *Expenses:* Tuition: Part-time $525 per credit. Required fees: $125 per semester. *Financial support:* Available to part-time students. Application deadline: 6/30. *Unit head:* Mark R. Solomon, Director, 248-823-1277, Fax: 248-689-0920, E-mail: msolomon@walshcollege.edu. *Application contact:* Jeremy Guc, Director of Admissions and Academic Advising, 248-823-1610, Fax: 248-689-0938, E-mail: jguc@walshcollege.edu.

Washington State University, Graduate School, College of Business, Department of Accounting and Business Law, Pullman, WA 99164. Offers accounting and information systems (M Acc); accounting and taxation (M Acc). *Accreditation:* AACSB. *Faculty:* 9. *Students:* 36 full-time (16 women), 6 part-time (5 women); includes 5 minority (3 Asian Americans or Pacific Islanders, 2 Hispanic Americans), 11 international. Average age 27. 114 applicants, 42% accepted, 30 enrolled. In 2009, 25 master's awarded. *Degree requirements:* For master's, comprehensive exam (for some programs), thesis (for some programs), oral exam, research paper. *Entrance requirements:* For master's, GMAT (minimum score of 600), resume; statement of purpose identifying area of interest, experiences, and intended research focus; minimum GPA of 3.25. Additional exam requirements/recommendations for international students: Required—TOEFL (minimum score 580 paper-based; 237 computer-based), IELTS. *Application deadline:* For fall admission, 1/10 priority date for domestic students, 1/10 for international students. Applications are processed on a rolling basis. Application fee: $50. Electronic applications accepted. *Financial support:* In 2009–10, 19 students received support, including 1 fellowship (averaging $5,500 per year), research assistantships (averaging $13,917 per year), 8 teaching assistantships with tuition reimbursements available (averaging $13,056 per year); Federal Work-Study, institutionally sponsored loans, tuition waivers (partial), and teaching associateships also available. Financial award application deadline: 3/1. *Faculty research:* Ethics, taxation, auditing. *Unit head:* Dr. John Sweeney, Chair, 509-335-8541, Fax: 509-335-4275, E-mail: jtsweeney@wsu.edu. *Application contact:* Graduate School Admissions, 800-GRADWSU, Fax: 509-335-1949, E-mail: gradsch@wsu.edu.

Wayne State University, School of Business Administration, Detroit, MI 48202. Offers accounting (MS); business administration (MBA, PhD); interdisciplinary studies (PhD); taxation (MS); JD/MBA. *Accreditation:* AACSB. Part-time and evening/weekend programs available. *Degree requirements:* For master's, thesis optional. *Entrance requirements:* For master's, GMAT, minimum undergraduate GPA of 2.50. Additional exam requirements/recommendations for international students: Required—TOEFL (minimum score 550 paper-based; 213 computer-based); Recommended—TWE (minimum score 6). Electronic applications accepted. *Faculty research:* Corporate financial valuation, strategic advertising, information technology effectiveness, financial accounting and taxation, organizational performance and effectiveness.

See Close-Up on page 279.

Widener University, School of Business Administration, Program in Taxation, Chester, PA 19013-5792. Offers MS. Part-time and evening/weekend programs available. *Faculty:* 2 full-time (1 woman), 2 part-time/adjunct (1 woman). *Students:* 2 full-time (1 woman), 33 part-time (12 women); includes 6 minority (all African Americans), 3 international. Average age 35. 34 applicants, 94% accepted. In 2009, 11 master's awarded. *Entrance requirements:* For master's, Certified Public Accountant Exam or GMAT. *Application deadline:* For fall admission, 8/1 priority date for domestic students; for spring admission, 12/1 for domestic students. Applications are processed on a rolling basis. Application fee: $25 ($300 for international students). Electronic applications accepted. *Financial support:* Available to part-time students. Application deadline: 5/1. *Faculty research:* Financial planning, taxation fraud. *Unit head:* Frank C. Lordi, Head, 610-499-4308, E-mail: frank.c.lordi@widener.edu. *Application contact:* Ann Seltzer, Graduate Enrollment Administrator, 610-499-4305, E-mail: apseltzer@widener.edu.

William Howard Taft University, Graduate Programs, Bernard E. Witkin School of Law, Santa Ana, CA 92704. Offers American jurisprudence (LL M); law (JD); taxation (LL M).

William Howard Taft University, Graduate Programs, W. Edwards Deming School of Business, Santa Ana, CA 92704. Offers taxation (MS).

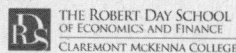
THE ROBERT DAY SCHOOL
OF ECONOMICS AND FINANCE
CLAREMONT MCKENNA COLLEGE

CLAREMONT MCKENNA COLLEGE

Robert Day School of Economics and Finance

Program of Study

The Robert Day School of Economics and Finance at Claremont McKenna College (CMC) offers a one-year, intensive master's program in finance. The program, established by a record gift of $200 million by CMC alumnus Robert Day, seeks to provide well-rounded students with strong academic backgrounds and demonstrated leadership potential the essential skills to be an effective financial decision maker. The applied finance curriculum is coupled with co-curricular activities and career service support designed to enable immediate entry-level success progressing to positions of leadership in the global marketplace.

During the nine-month experience, which begins in mid-August, students participate in a comprehensive program of professional development and career preparation. Workshops on communication and other leadership skills, and industry-leading training occur regularly throughout both semesters. Students also attend presentations by finance industry leaders followed by small-group discussions with those leaders. A dedicated career service specialist works with each student to determine career plans and to hone interviewing and job acquisition skills. Numerous networking opportunities provide students with access to tremendously successful and active Claremont McKenna College alumni as well as recruiters in the leading financial institutions in and outside the United States.

Research Facilities

Students in the Robert Day School of Economics and Finance have access to state-of-the-art classroom technology, financial databases, and analytic software. CMC is also a member of the Claremont Colleges consortium, consisting of four other undergraduate colleges (Pomona, Scripps, Harvey Mudd, and Pitzer) and two graduate institutions (Claremont Graduate University and Keck Graduate Institute of Applied Life Sciences) which gives students access to a wide range of facilities and resources.

Financial Aid

The landmark gift which created this program includes substantial merit-based scholarship support. Through the first two years of the program, admitted students were offered scholarships averaging nearly three-quarters of total tuition. The scholarship decision is made as part of the admission process and does not require an additional application.

Cost of Study

Tuition for the 2010–11 academic year is $46,725. Health insurance is required, but all additional fees, including parking, total less than $300. The cost of all co-curricular events, including class and small-group networking trips is included in the cost of tuition.

Living and Housing Costs

With rare exceptions, graduate students live in the immediate area off campus. Rental options range from economical dormitory rooms to first-class apartments. The total cost of housing is estimated to be $15,000 for the nine months of classes.

Student Group

Claremont McKenna College is a preeminent liberal arts college with a distinguished reputation for its focus on economics, accounting, and finance. The small class of graduate students joins approximately 1,200 CMC undergraduates. The Claremont Colleges consortium (Pomona, Scripps, Harvey Mudd, Pitzer, Claremont Graduate University, and Keck Graduate Institute of Applied Life Sciences) includes over 6,300 students, 700 faculty members, and 1,600 staff members. CMC graduate students enjoy a distinctive place among a wealth of potential friends, and resources that include common access to dining, library, fitness, and health facilities.

Student Outcomes

The inaugural class of 20 graduates in 2010 reflects the intimate nature and high expectations of this unique program. Nineteen of these 20 students accepted full-time offers or were enrolled in doctoral programs within thirty days of graduation.

Location

CMC and the Claremont Colleges are located in the city of Claremont, just 35 miles east of Los Angeles; minutes from the mountains; and about a 1-hour drive from Southern California beaches, Joshua Tree National Park, and Disneyland. Claremont is famous for its tree-lined streets, world-renowned colleges, and award-winning school system. Its vitality charms residents and visitors alike with a unique warmth and community spirit.

The University

Claremont McKenna College is a highly selective, independent, coeducational liberal arts college. Its mission, within the mutually supportive framework of the Claremont Colleges, is to educate its students for thoughtful and productive lives and responsible leadership in business, government, and the professions, and to support faculty and student scholarship that contributes to intellectual vitality and the understanding of public policy issues. The College pursues this mission by providing a liberal arts education that emphasizes economics and political science, a professoriat that is dedicated to effective undergraduate teaching, a close student-teacher relationship that fosters critical inquiry, an active residential and intellectual environment that promotes responsible citizenship, and a program of research institutes and scholarly support that makes possible a faculty of teacher-scholars.

The CMC motto is "Crescit cum commercio civitas" (civilization prospers with commerce).

Established in 1946 as the Claremont Men's College, over 8,000 alumni have bolstered a reputation for success. Fully 70 percent of CMC graduates go on to advanced degrees at prestigious institutions. One in 8 graduates now holds a position in top management.

In September 2007, Robert A. Day, founder and chairman of the TCW Group, Inc., pledged a $200 million personal gift to establish the Robert Day School of Economics and Finance, and its unique programs. This was the largest recorded gift to a liberal arts institution, the largest gift in the field of finance and economics, and among the top 20 largest gifts ever given to a college or university. Through his generosity, the Robert Day School of Economics and Finance now offers multiple programs, including the Master of Arts degree in finance.

Applying

Priority applications to CMC must be submitted by November 3, 2010. Spring deadlines of January 14, February 11, and March 10 allow the graduate admission committee an appropriate window of time to review completed applications. Because graduate admissions are limited and competitive, applicants are encouraged to apply early and to be sure that all required materials (application, fee, official transcripts, two letters of recommendation, and all required test scores) have been received before the appropriate deadline. CMC accepts either the GRE or GMAT. International students must complete the TOEFL unless they have completed an undergraduate program taught in English.

Correspondence and Information

Graduate Admissions Office
Claremont McKenna College
Bauer Building, Room 221
Claremont, California 91711
Phone: 909-607-3347
Fax: 909-607-6955
E-mail: rdsadmission@claremontmckenna.edu
Web site: FinanceMastersDegree@cmc.edu

Claremont McKenna College

THE FACULTY

Brock Blomberg, Dean.
Darren Filson, Graduate Program Director.

Robert Day School faculty members are active researchers who publish regularly in top academic journals in economics, finance, and accounting. The Robert Day School faculty constitutes one of if not the largest and most productive department at any liberal arts college. Faculty members also host a weekly seminar series that brings in noted economics researchers from around the country to present their new research projects.

For more information about the faculty of the Robert Day School of Economics and Finance at Claremont McKenna College, visit the Web site at http://www.claremontmckenna.edu/rdschool/faculty-research/.

Claremont McKenna College graduate students.

CMC master's Asia networking trip.

Faculty of the Robert Day School of Economics and Finance.

Section 3
Advertising and Public Relations

This section contains a directory of institutions offering graduate work in advertising and public relations. Additional information about programs listed in the directory may be obtained by writing directly to the dean of a graduate school or chair of a department at the address given in the directory.

For programs offering related work, see also in this book *Business Administration and Management* and *Marketing.* In another guide in this series:

Graduate Programs in the Humanities, Arts & Social Sciences
See *Communication and Media*

CONTENTS

Program Directory

Advertising and Public Relations

Academy of Art University, Graduate Program, School of Advertising, San Francisco, CA 94105-3410. Offers MFA. Part-time programs available. Postbaccalaureate distance learning degree programs offered (no on-campus study). *Degree requirements:* For master's, thesis, final review. *Entrance requirements:* For master's, minimum GPA of 3.0, portfolio. Electronic applications accepted.

Ball State University, Graduate School, College of Communication, Information, and Media, Department of Journalism, Muncie, IN 47306-1099. Offers journalism (MA); public relations (MA). *Accreditation:* ACEJMC. *Entrance requirements:* For master's, resume. *Faculty research:* Image studies, readership surveys, audience perception studies.

Boston University, College of Communication, Department of Mass Communication, Advertising, and Public Relations, Boston, MA 02215. Offers advertising (MS); communication research (MS); communication studies (MS); public relations (MS); JD/MS. Part-time programs available. *Faculty:* 21 full-time, 28 part-time/adjunct. *Students:* 84 full-time (68 women), 72 part-time (57 women); includes 12 minority (5 African Americans, 3 Asian Americans or Pacific Islanders, 4 Hispanic Americans), 26 international. Average age 30. In 2009, 58 master's awarded. *Degree requirements:* For master's, comprehensive exam (for some programs), thesis (for some programs). *Entrance requirements:* For master's, GRE General Test, samples of written work. Additional exam requirements/recommendations for international students: Required—TOEFL (minimum score 600 paper-based; 250 computer-based; 100 iBT). *Application deadline:* For fall admission, 2/1 for domestic and international students. Application fee: $70. Electronic applications accepted. *Expenses:* Tuition: Full-time $37,910; part-time $1184 per credit hour. Required fees: $386; $40 per semester. Part-time tuition and fees vary according to class time, course level, degree level and program. *Financial support:* Research assistantships, teaching assistantships with partial tuition reimbursements, career-related internships or fieldwork, Federal Work-Study, institutionally sponsored loans, scholarships/grants, and unspecified assistantships available. Support available to part-time students. Financial award application deadline: 2/1; financial award applicants required to submit FAFSA. *Unit head:* T. Barton Carter, Chairman, 617-353-3482, E-mail: comlaw@bu.edu. *Application contact:* Kate Iserman, Administrator of Graduate Services, 617-353-3481, Fax: 617-358-0399, E-mail: comgrad@bu.edu.

Boston University, Metropolitan College, Program in Advertising, Boston, MA 02215. Offers MS. Part-time and evening/weekend programs available. *Faculty:* 4 part-time/adjunct (2 women). In 2009, 16 master's awarded. *Entrance requirements:* For master's, undergraduate degree in appropriate field of study. *Application deadline:* Applications are processed on a rolling basis. Application fee: $70. Electronic applications accepted. *Expenses:* Tuition: Full-time $37,910; part-time $1184 per credit hour. Required fees: $386; $40 per semester. Part-time tuition and fees vary according to class time, course level, degree level and program. *Financial support:* In 2009–10, 4 students received support. Institutionally sponsored loans and unspecified assistantships available. *Faculty research:* Communication and advertising. *Unit head:* Dr. Christopher Cakebread, Associate Professor, 617-353-3476, E-mail: ccakebr@bu.edu. *Application contact:* Sonia M. Parker, Assistant Dean, 617-353-2975, Fax: 617-353-2686, E-mail: soparker@bu.edu.

California State University, Fullerton, Graduate Studies, College of Communications, Department of Communications, Fullerton, CA 92834-9480. Offers communications—advertising (MA); communications—entertainment and tourism (MA); communications—journalism (MA); communications—public relations (MA). Part-time programs available. *Students:* 18 full-time (14 women), 38 part-time (30 women); includes 21 minority (2 African Americans, 8 Asian Americans or Pacific Islanders, 11 Hispanic Americans), 4 international. Average age 28. 121 applicants, 23% accepted, 17 enrolled. In 2009, 33 master's awarded. *Degree requirements:* For master's, project or thesis. *Entrance requirements:* For master's, GRE General Test. Application fee: $55. *Expenses:* Tuition, nonresident: full-time $11,160; part-time $373 per credit. Required fees: $1440 per term. Tuition and fees vary according to course load, degree level and program. *Financial support:* Teaching assistantships, career-related internships or fieldwork, Federal Work-Study, institutionally sponsored loans, and scholarships/grants available. Support available to part-time students. Financial award application deadline: 3/1; financial award applicants required to submit FAFSA. *Unit head:* Dr. Tony Fellow, Chair, 657-278-3517. *Application contact:* Coordinator, 657-278-3832.

Central Connecticut State University, School of Graduate Studies, School of Arts and Sciences, Department of Communication, New Britain, CT 06050-4010. Offers organizational communication (MS); public relations/promotions (Certificate). Part-time and evening/weekend programs available. *Faculty:* 12 full-time (4 women), 8 part-time/adjunct (2 women). *Students:* 10 full-time (5 women), 23 part-time (13 women); includes 7 minority (4 African Americans, 1 Asian American or Pacific Islander, 2 Hispanic Americans), 1 international. Average age 29. 30 applicants, 50% accepted, 15 enrolled. In 2009, 9 master's awarded. *Degree requirements:* For master's, comprehensive exam, thesis or alternative; for Certificate, qualifying exam. *Entrance requirements:* For master's, minimum undergraduate GPA of 3.0. Additional exam requirements/recommendations for international students: Required—TOEFL. *Application deadline:* For fall admission, 7/1 for domestic students; for spring admission, 12/1 for domestic students. Applications are processed on a rolling basis. Application fee: $50. Electronic applications accepted. *Expenses:* Tuition, area resident: Full-time $4662; part-time $440 per credit. Tuition, state resident: full-time $6994; part-time $440 per credit. Tuition, nonresident: full-time $12,988; part-time $440 per credit. Required fees: $3606. One-time fee: $62 part-time. *Financial support:* In 2009–10, 5 students received support, including 1 research assistantship; career-related internships or fieldwork, Federal Work-Study, scholarships/grants, and unspecified assistantships also available. Support available to part-time students. Financial award application deadline: 3/1; financial award applicants required to submit FAFSA. *Faculty research:* Organizational communication, mass communication, intercultural communication, political communication, information management. *Unit head:* Dr. Serafin Mendez-Mendez, Chair, 860-832-2690. *Application contact:* Dr. Serafin Mendez-Mendez, Chair, 860-832-2690.

Colorado State University, Graduate School, College of Liberal Arts, Department of Journalism and Technical Communication, Fort Collins, CO 80523-1785. Offers public communication and technology (MS, PhD); technical communication (MS). Part-time programs available. *Faculty:* 19 full-time (8 women). *Students:* 26 full-time (21 women), 38 part-time (28 women); includes 5 minority (1 American Indian/Alaska Native, 1 Asian American or Pacific Islander, 3 Hispanic Americans), 3 international. Average age 33. 60 applicants, 48% accepted, 15 enrolled. In 2009, 13 master's awarded. *Degree requirements:* For master's, variable foreign language requirement, comprehensive exam (for some programs), thesis (for some programs); for doctorate, variable foreign language requirement, comprehensive exam (for some programs), thesis/dissertation (for some programs). *Entrance requirements:* For master's, GRE General Test, samples of written work, letters of recommendation, resume or curriculum vitae, 3 writing/communication projects; for doctorate, GRE General Test, master's degree, minimum GPA of 3.0, scholarly/professional work, letters of recommendation, statement of career plans, resume. Additional exam requirements/recommendations for international students: Required—TOEFL (minimum score 600 paper-based; 250 computer-based). *Application deadline:* For fall admission, 2/15 priority date for domestic students, 12/15 priority date for international students; for spring admission, 6/15 priority date for domestic students. Applications are processed on a rolling basis. Application fee: $50. Electronic applications accepted. *Expenses:* Tuition, state resident: full-time $6434; part-time $359.10 per credit. Tuition, nonresident: full-time $18,116; part-time $1006.45 per credit. Required fees: $1496; $83 per credit. *Financial support:* In 2009–10, 21 students received support, including 21 teaching assistantships with partial tuition reimbursements available (averaging $9,428 per year); fellowships with partial tuition reimbursements available, research assistantships with full and partial tuition reimbursements available, career-related internships or fieldwork, Federal Work-Study, institutionally sponsored loans, scholarships/grants, traineeships, and unspecified assistantships also available. Support available to part-time students. Financial award application deadline: 3/1; financial award applicants required to submit FAFSA. *Faculty research:* Technical/science communication, public relations, health/risk communication, web/new media technologies, environmental communication. Total annual research expenditures: $133,759. *Unit head:* Dr. Greg Luft, Chair, 970-491-1979, Fax: 970-491-2908, E-mail: greg.luft@colostate.edu. *Application contact:* Dr. Craig Trumbo, Graduate Program Coordinator, 970-491-2077, Fax: 970-491-2908, E-mail: craig.trumbo@colostate.edu.

DePaul University, College of Communication, Chicago, IL 60614. Offers journalism (MA); media, culture and society (MA); organizational and multicultural communication (MA); public relations and advertising (MA). Part-time and evening/weekend programs available. *Faculty:* 31 full-time (17 women), 15 part-time/adjunct (7 women). *Students:* 159 full-time (127 women), 50 part-time (40 women); includes 56 minority (29 African Americans, 9 Asian Americans or Pacific Islanders, 18 Hispanic Americans), 11 international. Average age 29. 354 applicants, 44% accepted, 79 enrolled. In 2009, 64 master's awarded. *Degree requirements:* For master's, comprehensive exam (for some programs), final exam or thesis/project. *Entrance requirements:* For master's, GRE General Test (public relations and advertising), minimum GPA of 3.0, writing sample, letters of recommendation, resume. Additional exam requirements/recommendations for international students: Required—TOEFL (minimum score 590 paper-based; 243 computer-based; 96 iBT). Application fee: $40. Electronic applications accepted. *Expenses:* Tuition: Full-time $37,525; part-time $620 per credit hour. *Financial support:* In 2009–10, 8 students received support, including 4 research assistantships with partial tuition reimbursements available, 2 teaching assistantships with full tuition reimbursements available (averaging $12,000 per year); fellowships with full tuition reimbursements available, career-related internships or fieldwork, scholarships/grants, and tuition waivers (partial) also available. Support available to part-time students. Financial award applicants required to submit FAFSA. *Faculty research:* Intercultural communication, corporate culture, diversity in the working place, organizational socialization, critical cultural studies. *Unit head:* Dr. Jacqueline Taylor, Dean, 773-325-7216, Fax: 773-325-7584, E-mail: jtaylor@depaul.edu. *Application contact:* Ann Spittle, Director of Graduate Admission, 773-325-7315, Fax: 773-325-2395, E-mail: gradcom@depaul.edu.

Emerson College, Graduate Studies, School of Communication, Department of Marketing Communication, Boston, MA 02116-4624. Offers global marketing communication and advertising (MA); integrated marketing communication (MA). *Faculty:* 12 full-time (5 women), 17 part-time/adjunct (8 women). *Students:* 152 full-time (125 women), 19 part-time (13 women); includes 20 minority (9 African Americans, 4 Asian Americans or Pacific Islanders, 7 Hispanic Americans), 65 international. Average age 24. 343 applicants, 66% accepted, 107 enrolled. In 2009, 94 master's awarded. *Entrance requirements:* For master's, GMAT or GRE General Test. Additional exam requirements/recommendations for international students: Required—TOEFL (minimum score 550 paper-based; 213 computer-based; 80 iBT), IELTS (minimum score 6.5). *Application deadline:* For fall admission, 6/1 priority date for domestic students, 5/1 priority date for international students; for spring admission, 11/1 priority date for domestic and international students. Applications are processed on a rolling basis. Application fee: $60 ($75 for international students). Electronic applications accepted. *Expenses:* Tuition: Full-time $22,056; part-time $919 per credit. Required fees: $120. One-time fee: $170 full-time. *Financial support:* In 2009–10, 48 students received support, including 5 fellowships with partial tuition reimbursements available (averaging $14,000 per year), 28 research assistantships with partial tuition reimbursements available (averaging $10,000 per year); Federal Work-Study, scholarships/grants, and unspecified assistantships also available. Financial award application deadline: 3/1; financial award applicants required to submit FAFSA. *Unit head:* John Davis, Chair, E-mail: john_davis@emerson.edu. *Application contact:* Office of Graduate Admission, 617-824-8610, Fax: 617-824-8614.

George Mason University, College of Visual and Performing Arts, Program in Arts Management, Fairfax, VA 22030. Offers arts entrepreneurship (Certificate); arts management (MA); fund raising and development in the arts (Certificate); public relations and marketing in the arts (Certificate); special events management in the arts (Certificate). *Faculty:* 1 (woman) full-time, 3 part-time/adjunct (2 women). *Students:* 39 full-time (37 women), 48 part-time (40 women); includes 7 minority (4 African Americans, 2 Asian Americans or Pacific Islanders, 1 Hispanic American), 11 international. Average age 30. 76 applicants, 71% accepted, 37 enrolled. In 2009, 27 master's awarded. *Entrance requirements:* For master's, GRE (recommended), minimum GPA of 3.0, 2 letters of recommendation, personal interview, resume, work experience. Additional exam requirements/recommendations for international students: Required—TOEFL. *Application deadline:* For fall admission, 3/1 priority date for domestic students; for spring admission, 10/1 for domestic students. Applications are processed on a rolling basis. Application fee: $75. Electronic applications accepted. *Expenses:* Tuition, state resident: full-time $7568; part-time $315.33 per credit hour. Tuition, nonresident: full-time $21,704; part-time $904.33 per credit hour. Required fees: $2184; $91 per credit hour. *Financial support:* Application deadline: 3/1. *Faculty research:* Information technology for arts managers, special topics in arts management, directions in gallery management, arts in society, public relations/marketing strategies for art organizations. *Unit head:* William Reeder, Dean, 703-993-8624, Fax: 703-993-8883. *Application contact:* Richard Kamenitzer, Director, 703-993-9194, E-mail: rkamenit@gmu.edu.

Georgetown University, Graduate School of Arts and Sciences, School of Continuing Studies, Washington, DC 20057. Offers American studies (MALS); Catholic studies (MALS); classical civilizations (MALS); ethics and the professions (MALS); human resources management (MPS); humanities (MALS); individualized study (MALS); international affairs (MALS); Islam and Muslim-Christian relations (MALS); journalism (MPS); liberal studies (DLS); literature and society (MALS); medieval and early modern European studies (MALS); public relations (MPS); real estate (MPS); religious studies (MALS); social and public policy (MALS); sports industry management (MPS); the theory and practice of American democracy (MALS); visual culture (MALS). *Entrance requirements:* Additional exam requirements/recommendations for international students: Required—TOEFL.

Golden Gate University, Ageno School of Business, San Francisco, CA 94105-2968. Offers accounting (MBA); business administration (EMBA, MBA, PMBA, DBA); finance (MBA, MS, Certificate); financial planning (MS, Certificate); human resource management (MBA, MS); human resources management (Certificate); information systems (MS); information technology (MBA); information technology management (Certificate); integrated marketing and communications (MS, Certificate); international business (MBA); management (MBA); marketing (MBA, MS, Certificate); operations management (Certificate); psychology (MA, Certificate); public relations (MS, Certificate); JD/MBA. Part-time and evening/weekend programs available. *Faculty:* 16 full-time (4 women), 241 part-time/adjunct (72 women). *Students:* 380 full-time (193 women), 750 part-time (414 women); includes 480 minority (98 African Americans, 2 American Indian/Alaska Native, 298 Asian Americans or Pacific Islanders, 82 Hispanic Americans), 166 international. Average age 33. 681 applicants, 78% accepted, 270 enrolled. In 2009, 550 master's, 13 doctorates awarded. *Degree requirements:* For doctorate, thesis/dissertation. *Entrance requirements:* For master's, GMAT (MBA), minimum GPA of 2.5 (MS). Additional exam requirements/recommendations for international students: Required—TOEFL. *Application deadline:* For fall admission, 5/15 for international students; for winter admission, 1/15 for international students; for spring admission, 9/15 for international students. Applications are processed on a rolling basis. Application fee: $70 ($110 for international students). Electronic applications accepted. *Expenses:* Contact institution. *Financial support:* Career-related internships or fieldwork, Federal Work-Study, institutionally sponsored loans, and scholarships/grants available. Support available to part-time students. Financial award applicants required to submit FAFSA. *Unit head:* Terry Connelly, Dean, 415-442-6519, Fax: 415-442-5369. *Application contact:* Angela Melero, Enrollment Services, 415-442-7800, Fax: 415-442-7807, E-mail: info@ggu.edu.

Immaculata University, College of Graduate Studies, Program in Applied Communication, Immaculata, PA 19345. Offers MA.

Iona College, School of Arts and Science, Department of Mass Communication, New Rochelle, NY 10801-1890. Offers journalism (MS); public relations (MA). *Accreditation:* ACEJMC (one or more programs are accredited). Part-time and evening/weekend programs available. *Faculty:* 6 full-time (1 woman), 6 part-time/adjunct (3 women). *Students:* 14 full-time (all women), 40 part-time (33 women); includes 15 minority (5 African Americans, 2 Asian Americans or Pacific Islanders, 8 Hispanic Americans), 4 international. Average age 27. 46 applicants, 50% accepted, 15 enrolled. In 2009, 23 master's awarded. *Degree requirements:* For master's, comprehensive exam or thesis. *Entrance requirements:* For master's, GRE General Test, minimum GPA of 3.0. Additional exam requirements/recommendations for international students: Required—TOEFL (minimum score 550 paper-based; 213 computer-based). *Application deadline:* Applications are processed on a rolling basis. Application fee: $50. Electronic applications accepted. *Expenses:* Contact institution. *Financial support:* Career-related internships or fieldwork, tuition waivers (partial), and unspecified assistantships available. Support available to part-time students. Financial award application deadline: 4/15; financial award applicants required to submit FAFSA. *Faculty research:* Media ecology, new media, corporate communication, media images, organizational learning in public relations. *Unit head:* Br. Raymond Smith, Chair, 914-633-2354, E-mail: rrsmith@iona.edu. *Application contact:* Veronica Jarek-Prinz, Director of Graduate Admissions, 914-633-2420, Fax: 914-633-2277, E-mail: vjarekprinz@iona.edu.

Lasell College, Graduate and Professional Studies in Communication, Newton, MA 02466-2709. Offers integrated marketing communication (MSC, Graduate Certificate); public relations (MSC, Graduate Certificate). Part-time and evening/weekend programs available. Postbaccalaureate distance learning degree programs offered (minimal on-campus study). *Faculty:* 3 full-time (all women), 1 part-time/adjunct (0 women). *Students:* 5 full-time (all women), 13 part-time (12 women); includes 3 minority (all African Americans). Average age 29. 19 applicants, 89% accepted, 11 enrolled. *Entrance requirements:* For master's and Graduate Certificate, bachelor's degree from an accredited institution. Additional exam requirements/recommendations for international students: Required—TOEFL (minimum score 550 paper-based; 213 computer-based; 75 iBT) or IELTS. *Application deadline:* For fall admission, 8/31 priority date for domestic students, 6/30 priority date for international students; for spring admission, 12/31 priority date for domestic students, 10/31 priority date for international students. Applications are processed on a rolling basis. Application fee: $40. Electronic applications accepted. *Expenses:* Tuition: Full-time $4890; part-time $525 per credit hour. Required fees: $55 per term. *Financial support:* Available to part-time students. Application deadline: 8/30. *Unit head:* Dr. Joan Dolamore, Dean of Graduate and Professional Studies, 617-243-2485, Fax: 617-243-2450, E-mail: gradinfo@lasell.edu. *Application contact:* Adrienne Franciosi, Director of Graduate Admission, 617-243-2214, Fax: 617-243-2450, E-mail: gradinfo@lasell.edu.

La Sierra University, College of Arts and Sciences, Department of English and Communication, Riverside, CA 92515. Offers communication (MA), including public relations/advertising, theory emphasis; English (MA), including literary emphasis, writing emphasis. Part-time programs available. *Degree requirements:* For master's, one foreign language. *Entrance requirements:* For master's, GRE General Test.

Marquette University, Graduate School, College of Communication, Milwaukee, WI 53201-1881. Offers advertising and public relations (MA); broadcasting and electronic communications (MA); communications studies (MA); journalism (MA); mass communications (MA); religious communications (MA); science, health and environmental communications (MA). *Accreditation:* ACEJMC. Part-time and evening/weekend programs available. *Faculty:* 31 full-time (17 women), 35 part-time/adjunct (16 women). *Students:* 28 full-time (21 women), 30 part-time (24 women); includes 3 minority (1 African American, 2 American Indian/Alaska Native), 7 international. Average age 26. 81 applicants, 47% accepted, 22 enrolled. In 2009, 17 master's awarded. *Degree requirements:* For master's, comprehensive exam. *Entrance requirements:* For master's, GRE. Additional exam requirements/recommendations for international students: Required—TOEFL. Application fee: $40. *Financial support:* In 2009–10, 6 research assistantships, 12 teaching assistantships were awarded; career-related internships or fieldwork, Federal Work-Study, institutionally sponsored loans, scholarships/grants, and tuition waivers (full and partial) also available. Support available to part-time students. Financial award application deadline: 2/15. *Faculty research:* Urban journalism, gender and communication, intercultural communication, religious communication. *Unit head:* Dr. Ana Garner, Dean, 414-288-3588, Fax: 414-288-1578. *Application contact:* Erin Fox, Assistant Director for Recruitment, 414-288-5319, Fax: 414-288-1902, E-mail: erin.fox@marquette.edu.

Michigan State University, The Graduate School, College of Communication Arts and Sciences, Department of Advertising, Public Relations and Retailing, East Lansing, MI 48824. Offers advertising (MA); public relations (MA); retailing (MS, PhD). *Faculty:* 12 full-time (8 women), 1 part-time/adjunct (0 women). *Students:* 92 full-time (82 women), 42 part-time (34 women); includes 12 minority (8 African Americans, 2 Asian Americans or Pacific Islanders, 2 Hispanic Americans), 80 international. Average age 26. 211 applicants, 51% accepted. In 2009, 56 master's, 1 doctorate awarded. *Entrance requirements:* Additional exam requirements/recommendations for international students: Required—TOEFL. Electronic applications accepted. *Expenses:* Tuition, state resident: part-time $478.25 per credit hour. Tuition, nonresident: part-time $966.50 per credit hour. Part-time tuition and fees vary according to program. *Financial support:* In 2009–10, 4 research assistantships with tuition reimbursements (averaging $7,263 per year), 5 teaching assistantships with tuition reimbursements (averaging $8,264 per year) were awarded; career-related internships or fieldwork, scholarships/grants, and unspecified assistantships also available. Total annual research expenditures: $635,040. *Unit head:* Dr. Richard T. Cole, Chairperson, 517-353-5020, Fax: 517-432-2589, E-mail: rcole1@msu.edu. *Application contact:* Pamela Brock, Graduate Secretary, 517-355-2314, Fax: 517-432-2589, E-mail: brockp@msu.edu.

Mississippi College, Graduate School, College of Arts and Sciences, School of Christian Studies and the Arts, Department of Communication, Clinton, MS 39058. Offers applied communication (MSC); public relations and corporate communication (MSC). Part-time programs available. *Faculty:* 6 full-time (2 women), 1 part-time/adjunct (0 women). *Students:* 14 full-time (7 women), 18 part-time (13 women); includes 5 minority (all African Americans), 10 international. Average age 28. In 2009, 6 master's awarded. *Degree requirements:* For master's, comprehensive exam, thesis optional. *Entrance requirements:* For master's, GRE or NTE, minimum GPA of 2.5. Additional exam requirements/recommendations for international students: Recommended—IELTS. *Application deadline:* For fall admission, 8/15 priority date for domestic and international students. Applications are processed on a rolling basis. Application fee: $30. Electronic applications accepted. *Expenses:* Tuition: Part-time $452 per credit hour. Required fees: $101 per semester. Tuition and fees vary according to degree level, campus/location, program and student level. *Financial support:* Career-related internships or fieldwork, Federal Work-Study, and unspecified assistantships available. Support available to part-time students. Financial award application deadline: 4/1; financial award applicants required to submit FAFSA. *Unit head:* Dr. Cliff Fortenberry, Chair, 601-925-3457, E-mail: fortenbe@mc.edu. *Application contact:* Elnora Lewis, Secretary, 601-925-3225, Fax: 601-925-3889, E-mail: lewis09@mc.edu.

Monmouth University, Graduate School, Department of Corporate and Public Communication, West Long Branch, NJ 07764-1898. Offers corporate and public communication (MA); human resources communication (Certificate); public relations (Certificate); public service communication specialist (Certificate). Part-time and evening/weekend programs available. *Faculty:* 8 full-time (4 women), 2 part-time/adjunct (1 woman). *Students:* 6 full-time (3 women), 45 part-time (31 women); includes 8 minority (3 African Americans, 1 Asian American or Pacific Islander, 4 Hispanic Americans), 3 international. Average age 31. 39 applicants, 95% accepted, 20 enrolled. In 2009, 19 master's awarded. *Degree requirements:* For master's, comprehensive exam, project. *Entrance requirements:* For master's, GRE, minimum GPA of 3.0 in major, 2.75 overall. Additional exam requirements/recommendations for international students: Required—TOEFL (minimum score 550 paper-based; 213 computer-based; 79 iBT), IELTS (minimum score 5), Michigan English Language Assessment Battery (minimum score 77), Cambridge A, B, C. *Application deadline:* For fall admission, 7/15 priority date for domestic students, 6/1 for international students; for spring admission, 11/15 priority date for domestic students, 11/1 for international students. Applications are processed on a rolling basis. Application fee: $50. Electronic applications accepted. *Expenses:* Tuition: Part-time $773 per credit. Required fees: $157 per semester. *Financial support:* In 2009–10, 37 students received support, including 24 fellowships (averaging $1,242 per year), 7 research assistantships (averaging $5,715 per year); scholarships/grants and unspecified assistantships also available. Support available to part-time students. Financial award applicants required to submit FAFSA. *Faculty research:* Service-learning, history of television, feminism and the media, executive communication, public relations pedagogy. *Unit head:* Dr. Sherry Wien, Program Director, 732-263-5354, Fax: 732-571-3609, E-mail: swien@monmouth.edu. *Application contact:* Kevin Roane, Director, Office of Graduate Admission, 732-571-3452, Fax: 732-263-5123, E-mail: gradadm@monmouth.edu.

Montana State University Billings, College of Arts and Sciences, Department of Communication and Theater, Billings, MT 59101-0298. Offers public relations (MS). Part-time programs available. Postbaccalaureate distance learning degree programs offered. *Degree requirements:* For master's, thesis optional. *Entrance requirements:* For master's, GRE General Test, minimum undergraduate GPA of 3.0, 3 letters of recommendation.

Montclair State University, The Graduate School, School of the Arts, Department of Communication Studies, Montclair, NJ 07043-1624. Offers organizational communication (MA); public relations (MA); speech communication (MA). Part-time and evening/weekend programs available. *Faculty:* 5 full-time (2 women), 41 part-time/adjunct (24 women). *Students:* 16 full-time (15 women), 20 part-time (17 women). Average age 30. 23 applicants, 65% accepted, 12 enrolled. In 2009, 12 master's awarded. *Degree requirements:* For master's, comprehensive exam. *Entrance requirements:* For master's, GRE General Test, 2 letters of recommendation. Additional exam requirements/recommendations for international students: Required—TOEFL (minimum score 83 computer-based), or IELTS. *Application deadline:* For fall admission, 6/1 for international students; for spring admission, 10/1 for international students. Applications are processed on a rolling basis. Application fee: $60. Electronic applications accepted. *Expenses:* Tuition, area resident: Part-time $486.74 per credit. Tuition, state resident: part-time $486.74 per credit. Tuition, nonresident: part-time $751.34 per credit. Tuition and fees vary according to degree level and program. *Financial support:* In 2009–10, 3 research assistantships with full tuition reimbursements (averaging $7,000 per year) were awarded; Federal Work-Study, scholarships/grants, and unspecified assistantships also available. Support available to part-time students. Financial award application deadline: 3/1; financial award applicants required to submit FAFSA. *Unit head:* Dr. Harry Haines, Chair, 973-655-4200. *Application contact:* Amy Aiello, Director of Graduate Admissions and Operations, 973-655-5147, Fax: 973-655-7869, E-mail: graduate.school@montclair.edu.

New York University, School of Continuing and Professional Studies, Division of Programs in Business, Program in Public Relations and Corporate Communications, New York, NY 10012-1019. Offers corporate and organizational communications (MS); public relations management (MS). Part-time and evening/weekend programs available. *Faculty:* 2 full-time (0 women), 28 part-time/adjunct (13 women). *Students:* 46 full-time (39 women), 93 part-time (67 women). Average age 28. 169 applicants, 52% accepted, 47 enrolled. In 2009, 81 master's awarded. *Degree requirements:* For master's, capstone project. *Entrance requirements:* For master's, GRE General Test or GMAT (for recent graduates), 2 letters of recommendation, resume. Additional exam requirements/recommendations for international students: Required—TOEFL (minimum score 600 paper-based; 250 computer-based; 100 iBT), TWE. *Application deadline:* For fall admission, 2/1 priority date for domestic and international students; for spring admission, 10/15 priority date for domestic students, 8/15 priority date for international students. Applications are processed on a rolling basis. Application fee: $75. Electronic applications accepted. *Expenses:* Tuition: Full-time $30,528; part-time $1272 per credit. Required fees: $2177. *Financial support:* In 2009–10, 67 students received support, including 67 fellowships (averaging $2,735 per year); institutionally sponsored loans and scholarships/grants also available. Financial award application deadline: 3/1; financial award applicants required to submit FAFSA. *Unit head:* John Doorley, Director, 212-992-3600, Fax: 212-992-3650. *Application contact:* Angrand Fadia, Assistant Director, 212-992-3600, Fax: 212-992-3650, E-mail: fs20@nyu.edu.

Northern Kentucky University, Office of Graduate Programs, College of Informatics, Program in Communication, Highland Heights, KY 41099. Offers communication (MA); communication teaching (Certificate); documentary studies (Certificate); public relations (Certificate); relationships (Certificate). Part-time and evening/weekend programs available. *Students:* 9 full-time (8 women), 42 part-time (32 women); includes 5 minority (4 African Americans, 1 Asian American or Pacific Islander), 1 international. Average age 31. 48 applicants, 63% accepted, 23 enrolled. In 2009, 20 master's awarded. *Degree requirements:* For master's, thesis (for some programs), capstone experience, internship. *Entrance requirements:* For master's, GRE, minimum GPA of 3.0, 3 letters of recommendation. Additional exam requirements/recommendations for international students: Required—TOEFL (minimum score 550 paper-based; 213 computer-based; 79 iBT); Recommended—IELTS (minimum score 6.5). *Application deadline:* For fall admission, 2/1 priority date for domestic students, 6/1 for international students; for spring admission, 7/1 priority date for domestic students, 10/1 for international students. Applications are processed on a rolling basis. Application fee: $40. Electronic applications accepted. *Expenses:* Tuition, state resident: full-time $6912; part-time $384 per credit hour. Tuition, nonresident: full-time $12,150; part-time $675 per credit hour. Tuition and fees vary according to course load, program and reciprocity agreements. *Financial support:* Unspecified assistantships available. Financial award applicants required to submit FAFSA. *Faculty research:* Business/organizational communication, interpersonal/relational communication, public relations, communication teaching/pedagogy, media (production, criticism, popular culture). Total annual research expenditures: $29,000. *Unit head:* Dr. Jimmy Manning, Graduate Program Director, 859-572-1329, E-mail: manningj1@nku.edu. *Application contact:* Dr. Peg Griffin, Director of Graduate Programs, 859-572-6934, Fax: 859-572-6670, E-mail: griffinp@nku.edu.

Northwestern University, Medill School of Journalism, Integrated Marketing Communications Program, Evanston, IL 60208. Offers advertising/sales promotion (MSIMC); direct database and e-commerce marketing (MSIMC); general studies (MSIMC); public relations (MSIMC). Part-time programs available. *Entrance requirements:* For master's, GRE General Test or GMAT, full-time work experience (preferred). Additional exam requirements/recommendations for international students: Required—TOEFL. Electronic applications accepted. *Faculty research:* Data mining, business to business marketing, values in advertising, political advertising.

Quinnipiac University, School of Communications, Program in Public Relations, Hamden, CT 06518-1940. Offers MS. Part-time programs available. *Faculty:* 6 full-time (3 women), 2 part-time/adjunct (0 women). *Students:* 3 full-time (1 woman), 2 part-time (both women); includes 1 minority (African American). 8 applicants, 100% accepted. *Entrance requirements:* For master's, GRE. *Expenses:* Tuition: Full-time $16,030; part-time $770 per credit. Required fees: $630; $35 per credit. *Financial support:* Federal Work-Study and unspecified assistantships available. Financial award application deadline: 4/30; financial award applicants required to submit FAFSA. *Unit head:* Prof. Kathy Fitzpatrick, Professor, 203-582-3808, Fax: 203-582-3443, E-mail: graduate@quinnipiac.edu. *Application contact:* Scott Farber, Information Contact, 203-582-8672, E-mail: graduate@quinnipiac.edu.

Rowan University, Graduate School, College of Communication, Program in Public Relations, Glassboro, NJ 08028-1701. Offers MA. Part-time and evening/weekend programs available. *Students:* 18 full-time (13 women), 15 part-time (11 women); includes 5 minority (all African Americans). Average age 27. 23 applicants, 83% accepted, 13 enrolled. In 2009, 10 master's awarded. *Degree requirements:* For master's, thesis. *Entrance requirements:* For master's, GRE General Test. Additional exam requirements/recommendations for international students: Required—TOEFL. *Application deadline:* Applications are processed on a rolling basis. Application fee: $50. Electronic applications accepted. *Expenses:* Tuition, state resident: full-time $10,624; part-time $590 per semester hour. Tuition, nonresident: full-time $10,624; part-time $590 per semester hour. Required fees: $2320; $125 per semester hour. *Financial support:* Career-related internships or fieldwork available. Support available to part-time students.

Advertising and Public Relations

Rowan University (continued)

Unit head: Dr. Mira Lalovic-Hand, Interim Associate Provost/Director of Graduate School, 856-256-5120, E-mail: lalovic-hand@rowan.edu. *Application contact:* Karen Haynes, Graduate Coordinator, 856-256-4052, E-mail: haynesk@rowan.edu.

Royal Roads University, Graduate Studies, Applied Leadership and Management Program, Victoria, BC V9B 5Y2, Canada. Offers executive coaching (Graduate Certificate); health systems leadership (Graduate Certificate); project management (Graduate Certificate); public relations management (Graduate Certificate); strategic human resources management (Graduate Certificate).

San Diego State University, Graduate and Research Affairs, College of Professional Studies and Fine Arts, School of Communication, San Diego, CA 92182. Offers advertising and public relations (MA); critical-cultural studies (MA); interaction studies (MA); intercultural and international studies (MA); new media studies (MA); news and information studies (MA); telecommunications and media management (MA). *Degree requirements:* For master's, thesis. *Entrance requirements:* For master's, GRE General Test, 3 letters of recommendation. Additional exam requirements/recommendations for international students: Required—TOEFL. Electronic applications accepted.

Savannah College of Art and Design, Graduate School, Program in Advertising Design, Savannah, GA 31402-3146. Offers MA, MFA. Part-time programs available. *Degree requirements:* For master's, thesis, internships. *Entrance requirements:* For master's, interview, portfolio. Additional exam requirements/recommendations for international students: Required—TOEFL (minimum score 450 paper-based; 133 computer-based). Electronic applications accepted. *Expenses:* Tuition: Full-time $28,515; part-time $627 per credit hour. One-time fee: $500. Tuition and fees vary according to course load.

Seton Hall University, College of Arts and Sciences, Department of Communication, South Orange, NJ 07079-2697. Offers corporate and professional communication (MA); intercultural communication (MA); organizational communication (MA); public relations (MA); strategic communication and leadership (MA); strategic communication planning (MA). Part-time and evening/weekend programs available. Postbaccalaureate distance learning degree programs offered (minimal on-campus study). *Faculty:* 3 full-time (1 woman), 15 part-time/adjunct (6 women). *Students:* 30 full-time (19 women), 92 part-time (56 women); includes 42 minority (33 African Americans, 1 Asian American or Pacific Islander, 8 Hispanic Americans), 3 international. Average age 33. 66 applicants, 97% accepted, 39 enrolled. In 2009, 64 master's awarded. *Degree requirements:* For master's, thesis. *Entrance requirements:* Additional exam requirements/recommendations for international students: Required—TOEFL. *Application deadline:* For fall admission, 7/1 priority date for domestic and international students; for spring admission, 11/1 priority date for domestic and international students. Applications are processed on a rolling basis. Application fee: $50. Electronic applications accepted. *Financial support:* Research assistantships, career-related internships or fieldwork, Federal Work-Study, and unspecified assistantships available. Financial award applicants required to submit FAFSA. *Faculty research:* Managerial communication, communication consulting, communication and development. *Unit head:* Prof. Peter Reader, Chair, 973-761-9474, Fax: 973-761-9234, E-mail: readerpe@shu.edu. *Application contact:* Dr. Richard Dool, Director of Graduate Studies, 973-275-2794, Fax: 973-761-9234, E-mail: doolrich@shu.edu.

Southern Methodist University, Meadows School of the Arts, Temerlin Advertising Institute, Dallas, TX 75275. Offers MA. *Faculty:* 10 full-time (2 women), 5 part-time/adjunct (4 women). *Students:* 18 full-time (15 women); includes 4 minority (all Hispanic Americans), 2 international. Average age 24. 33 applicants, 61% accepted. *Entrance requirements:* For master's, GRE, GMAT. Additional exam requirements/recommendations for international students: Required—TOEFL (minimum score 550 paper-based; 213 computer-based; 80 iBT). *Application deadline:* For fall admission, 3/15 for domestic students. Application fee: $75. Electronic applications accepted. *Financial support:* In 2009–10, 12 students received support, including 5 research assistantships (averaging $8,000 per year). Financial award application deadline: 4/1; financial award applicants required to submit FAFSA. *Unit head:* Dr. Patricia Alvey, Director, 214-768-3090, E-mail: palvey@mail.smu.edu. *Application contact:* Joe S. Hoselton, Graduate Admissions and Records Coordinator, 214-768-3765, Fax: 214-768-3272, E-mail: hoselton@smu.edu.

Suffolk University, College of Arts and Sciences, Department of Communication, Boston, MA 02108-2770. Offers communication studies (MAC); integrated marketing communication (MAC); organizational communication (MAC); public relations and advertising (MAC). Part-time and evening/weekend programs available. *Faculty:* 20 full-time (10 women). *Students:* 14 full-time (12 women), 28 part-time (22 women), 2 international. Average age 27. 85 applicants, 58% accepted, 8 enrolled. In 2009, 21 master's awarded. *Degree requirements:* For master's, thesis optional. *Entrance requirements:* For master's, GRE General Test, MAT, or GMAT, 2 letters of recommendation, resume. Additional exam requirements/recommendations for international students: Required—TOEFL (minimum score 550 paper-based; 213 computer-based; 80 iBT). *Application deadline:* For fall admission, 6/15 priority date for domestic students, 6/15 for international students; for spring admission, 11/1 priority date for domestic students, 11/1 for international students. Applications are processed on a rolling basis. Application fee: $50. Electronic applications accepted. *Expenses:* Contact institution. *Financial support:* In 2009–10, 30 students received support, including 20 fellowships with partial tuition reimbursements available (averaging $3,413 per year); career-related internships or fieldwork, Federal Work-Study, and institutionally sponsored loans also available. Support available to part-time students. Financial award application deadline: 4/1; financial award applicants required to submit FAFSA. *Faculty research:* New media and new markets for advertising, First Amendment issues with the Internet, gender and intercultural communication, organizational development. *Unit head:* Dr. Robert Rosenthal, Chair, 617-573-8502, Fax: 617-742-6982, E-mail: rrosenth@suffolk.edu. *Application contact:* Judith Reynolds, Director of Graduate Admissions, 617-573-8302, Fax: 617-305-1733, E-mail: grad.admission@suffolk.edu.

Syracuse University, S. I. Newhouse School of Public Communications, Program in Advertising, Syracuse, NY 13244. Offers MA. *Students:* 19 full-time (14 women), 1 (woman) part-time; includes 5 minority (3 African Americans, 2 Asian Americans or Pacific Islanders), 4 international. Average age 24. 76 applicants, 49% accepted, 19 enrolled. In 2009, 18 master's awarded. *Degree requirements:* For master's, capstone course. *Entrance requirements:* For master's, GRE General Test. Additional exam requirements/recommendations for international students: Required—TOEFL (minimum score 600 paper-based; 250 computer-based; 100 iBT). *Application deadline:* For fall admission, 2/1 priority date for domestic and international students. Application fee: $45. Electronic applications accepted. *Expenses:* Tuition: Full-time $26,808; part-time $1117 per credit. Required fees: $1024. *Financial support:* Fellowships with full and partial tuition reimbursements, research assistantships with full and partial tuition reimbursements, teaching assistantships with full and partial tuition reimbursements, tuition waivers (partial) available. Financial award application deadline: 1/1. *Unit head:* James Tsao, Chair, 315-443-7401, Fax: 315-443-3946, E-mail: pcgrad@syr.edu. *Application contact:* Graduate Records Office, 315-443-5749, Fax: 315-443-1834, E-mail: pcgrad@syr.edu.

Syracuse University, S. I. Newhouse School of Public Communications, Program in Public Relations, Syracuse, NY 13244. Offers MS. *Students:* 30 full-time (24 women), 2 part-time (both women); includes 8 minority (4 African Americans, 3 Asian Americans or Pacific Islanders, 1 Hispanic American), 10 international. Average age 24. 163 applicants, 35% accepted, 24 enrolled. In 2009, 32 master's awarded. *Entrance requirements:* For master's, GRE General Test. Additional exam requirements/recommendations for international students: Required—TOEFL (minimum score 600 paper-based; 250 computer-based; 100 iBT). *Application deadline:* For fall admission, 2/1 priority date for domestic and international students. Application fee: $45. Electronic applications accepted. *Expenses:* Tuition: Full-time $26,808; part-time $1117 per credit. Required fees: $1024. *Financial support:* Fellowships with tuition reimbursements, research assistantships with tuition reimbursements, teaching assistantships with tuition reimbursements, tuition waivers (partial) available. Financial award application deadline: 2/1. *Unit head:* Brenda M. Wrigley, Chair, 315-443-1911, E-mail: newhouse@syr.edu. *Application contact:* Martha Coria, Graduate Records Office, 315-443-5749, Fax: 315-443-1834, E-mail: pcgrad@syr.edu.

Texas Christian University, College of Communication, Schieffer School of Journalism, Fort Worth, TX 76129-0002. Offers advertising/public relations (MS); news-editorial (MS). *Accreditation:* ACEJMC. Part-time and evening/weekend programs available. *Degree requirements:* For master's, thesis, written exam. *Entrance requirements:* For master's, GRE General Test. Additional exam requirements/recommendations for international students: Required—TOEFL. *Application deadline:* For fall admission, 3/1 for domestic students; for spring admission, 12/1 for domestic students. Applications are processed on a rolling basis. Application fee: $0. *Expenses:* Tuition: Full-time $17,640; part-time $980 per credit hour. Tuition and fees vary according to program. *Financial support:* Tuition waivers (full and partial) and unspecified assistantships available. Financial award application deadline: 3/1. *Unit head:* John Lumpkin, Director, 817-257-4908, E-mail: j.lumpkin@tcu.edu. *Application contact:* Dr. John Tisdale, Associate Director, 817-257-7425, E-mail: j.tisdale@tcu.edu.

Towson University, College of Graduate Studies and Research, Program in Strategic Public Relations and Integrated Communications, Towson, MD 21252-0001. Offers Certificate. Evening/weekend programs available. Postbaccalaureate distance learning degree programs offered (no on-campus study). *Entrance requirements:* For degree, 24 credits in related course work, minimum GPA of 3.0. Electronic applications accepted.

Universidad Autonoma de Guadalajara, Graduate Programs, Guadalajara, Mexico. Offers administrative law and justice (LL M); advertising and corporate communications (MA); architecture (M Arch); business (MBA); computational science (MCC); education (Ed M, Ed D); English-Spanish translation (MA); fiscal law (MA); integrated management of digital animation (MA); international business (MIB); international corporate law (LL M); internet technologies (MS); labor health (MS); manufacturing systems (MMS); philosophy (MA, PhD); power electronics (MS); quality systems (MQS); renewable energy (MS); social evaluation of projects (MBA); strategic market research (MBA); teaching mathematics (MA).

Universidad Iberoamericana, Graduate School, Santo Domingo D.N., Dominican Republic. Offers advertising management (MM); business (MBA); constitutional law (MA); dentistry (DMD); educational management (MA); integrated marketing communication (MA); psychopedagogical intervention (M Ed); strategic management of human talent (MM).

Université Laval, Faculty of Letters, Program in Public Relations, Québec, QC G1K 7P4, Canada. Offers Diploma. Part-time and evening/weekend programs available. *Entrance requirements:* For degree, knowledge of French, comprehension of written English. Electronic applications accepted.

The University of Alabama, Graduate School, College of Communication and Information Sciences, Department of Advertising and Public Relations, Tuscaloosa, AL 35487. Offers MA. Part-time programs available. *Faculty:* 14 full-time (7 women). *Students:* 25 full-time (19 women), 7 part-time (5 women); includes 4 minority (all African Americans), 1 international. Average age 23. 104 applicants, 29% accepted, 19 enrolled. In 2009, 16 degrees awarded. *Degree requirements:* For master's, comprehensive exam, thesis or alternative. *Entrance requirements:* For master's, GRE (minimum 1000 verbal and quantitative, 400 writing), minimum undergraduate GPA of 3.0 (for last 60 hours). Additional exam requirements/recommendations for international students: Required—TOEFL (minimum score 600 paper-based; 100 computer-based). *Application deadline:* For fall admission, 3/1 priority date for domestic and international students. Applications are processed on a rolling basis. Application fee: $50 ($60 for international students). Electronic applications accepted. *Expenses:* Tuition, state resident: full-time $7000. Tuition, nonresident: full-time $19,200. *Financial support:* In 2009–10, 7 students received support, including 4 research assistantships with partial tuition reimbursements available, 2 teaching assistantships with full tuition reimbursements available; career-related internships or fieldwork, scholarships/grants, health care benefits, and unspecified assistantships also available. Financial award application deadline: 3/1. *Faculty research:* Advertising and public relations management, public opinion, political communication, advertising media, international communication. Total annual research expenditures: $3,709. *Unit head:* Dr. Joseph Edward Phelps, Professor and Chairman, 205-348-8646, Fax: 205-348-2401, E-mail: phelps@apr.ua.edu. *Application contact:* Dr. Yorgo Pasadeos, Professor, 205-348-8641, Fax: 205-348-2401, E-mail: gower@apr.ua.edu.

University of Denver, Division of Arts, Humanities and Social Sciences, Department of Mass Communications, Denver, CO 80208. Offers advertising management (MS); digital media studies (MA); mass communications (MA); public relations (MS); video production (MA). Part-time programs available. *Faculty:* 14 full-time (8 women), 4 part-time/adjunct (3 women). *Students:* 37 full-time (28 women), 32 part-time (27 women); includes 8 minority (1 African American, 2 Asian Americans or Pacific Islanders, 5 Hispanic Americans), 3 international. Average age 26. 163 applicants, 64% accepted, 45 enrolled. In 2009, 24 master's awarded. *Degree requirements:* For master's, thesis (for some programs). *Entrance requirements:* For master's, GRE General Test. Additional exam requirements/recommendations for international students: Required—TOEFL, TWE. *Application deadline:* Applications are processed on a rolling basis. Application fee: $50. Electronic applications accepted. *Expenses:* Tuition: Full-time $34,596; part-time $961 per quarter hour. Required fees: $4 per quarter hour. Tuition and fees vary according to course load, campus/location and program. *Financial support:* In 2009–10, 10 research assistantships with full and partial tuition reimbursements (averaging $14,000 per year), 5 teaching assistantships with full and partial tuition reimbursements (averaging $11,500 per year) were awarded; career-related internships or fieldwork, Federal Work-Study, institutionally sponsored loans, and scholarships/grants also available. Support available to part-time students. Financial award application deadline: 3/1; financial award applicants required to submit FAFSA. *Faculty research:* Youth and civic engagement. Total annual research expenditures: $162,000. *Unit head:* Dr. Diane Waldman, Chair, 303-871-2008. *Application contact:* Information Contact, 303-871-2008, E-mail: mcom@du.edu.

University of Florida, Graduate School, College of Journalism and Communications, Department of Advertising, Gainesville, FL 32611. Offers M Adv. *Degree requirements:* For master's, thesis optional. *Entrance requirements:* For master's, GRE General Test, minimum GPA of 3.0. Additional exam requirements/recommendations for international students: Required—TOEFL (minimum score 550 paper-based; 213 computer-based).

University of Florida, Graduate School, College of Journalism and Communications, Department of Public Relations, Gainesville, FL 32611. Offers MAMC. *Degree requirements:* For master's, thesis optional. *Entrance requirements:* For master's, GRE General Test, minimum GPA of 3.0.

University of Houston, College of Liberal Arts and Social Sciences, School of Communication, Houston, TX 77204. Offers health communication (MA); mass communication studies (MA); public relations studies (MA); speech communication (MA). Part-time and evening/weekend programs available. *Faculty:* 9 full-time (5 women), 2 part-time/adjunct (0 women). *Students:* 42 full-time (38 women), 49 part-time (44 women); includes 31 minority (17 African Americans, 2 American Indian/Alaska Native, 2 Asian Americans or Pacific Islanders, 10 Hispanic Americans), 24 international. Average age 28. 92 applicants, 47% accepted, 28 enrolled. In 2009, 19 master's awarded. *Degree requirements:* For master's, comprehensive exam, thesis. *Entrance requirements:* For master's, GRE. Additional exam requirements/recommendations for international students: Required—TOEFL. *Application deadline:* For fall admission, 6/1 for domestic students, 4/1 for international students; for spring admission, 11/1 for domestic students, 10/1 for international students. Application fee: $25 ($75 for international students). Electronic applications accepted. *Expenses:* Tuition, state resident: full-time $7676; part-time $320 per credit hour. Tuition, nonresident: full-time $14,324; part-time $597 per credit hour. Required fees: $3034. *Financial support:* In 2009–10, 2 fellowships with full tuition reimbursements (averaging $9,750 per year), 5 teaching assistantships with full tuition reimbursements (averaging $9,750 per year) were awarded; career-related internships or fieldwork, Federal Work-Study, institutionally sponsored loans, scholarships/grants, health

care benefits, and unspecified assistantships also available. Support available to part-time students. Financial award application deadline: 2/1. *Unit head:* Dr. Beth Olson, Chairperson, 713-743-2873, Fax: 713-743-2876, E-mail: bolson@uh.edu. *Application contact:* Salima B. Haji, Academic Advisor, 713-743-2575, Fax: 713-743-2876, E-mail: sbhaji@central.uh.edu.

University of Illinois at Urbana–Champaign, Graduate College, College of Media, Department of Advertising, Champaign, IL 61820. Offers MS. *Accreditation:* ACEJMC. *Faculty:* 6 full-time (3 women), 2 part-time/adjunct (1 woman). *Students:* 15 full-time (12 women), 1 part-time (0 women); includes 3 minority (1 African American, 2 Asian Americans or Pacific Islanders), 5 international. 75 applicants, 12% accepted, 5 enrolled. In 2009, 16 master's awarded. *Entrance requirements:* For master's, GMAT or GRE General Test, minimum GPA of 3.0. Additional exam requirements/recommendations for international students: Required—TOEFL (minimum score 610 paper-based; 253 computer-based; 102 iBT), or IELTS (minimum score 6.5). *Application deadline:* Applications are processed on a rolling basis. Application fee: $60 ($75 for international students). Electronic applications accepted. *Financial support:* In 2009–10, 1 fellowship, 1 research assistantship, 9 teaching assistantships were awarded; tuition waivers (full and partial) also available. *Faculty research:* Consumer behavior, persuasive communication. *Unit head:* Janet S. Slater, Interim Head, 217-333-1602, Fax: 217-244-3348, E-mail: slaterj@illinois.edu. *Application contact:* Janet Bradley Wright, Office Administrator, 217-333-1602, Fax: 217-244-3348, E-mail: wjbradle@illinois.edu.

University of Maryland, College Park, Academic Affairs, College of Arts and Humanities, Department of Communication, College Park, MD 20742. Offers MA, PhD. *Faculty:* 24 full-time (14 women), 5 part-time/adjunct (3 women). *Students:* 68 full-time (50 women), 3 part-time (all women); includes 6 minority (1 African American, 4 Asian Americans or Pacific Islanders, 1 Hispanic American), 18 international. 194 applicants, 10% accepted, 17 enrolled. In 2009, 3 master's, 7 doctorates awarded. *Degree requirements:* For master's, thesis optional; for doctorate, comprehensive exam, thesis/dissertation. *Entrance requirements:* For master's, GRE General Test, minimum GPA of 3.0, sample of scholarly writing, 3 letters of recommendation; for doctorate, GRE General Test. Additional exam requirements/recommendations for international students: Required—TOEFL. *Application deadline:* For fall admission, 2/1 for domestic and international students. Applications are processed on a rolling basis. Application fee: $60. Electronic applications accepted. *Expenses:* Tuition, area resident: Part-time $471 per credit hour. Tuition, state resident: part-time $471 per credit hour. Tuition, nonresident: part-time $1016 per credit hour. Required fees: $337.04 per term. *Financial support:* In 2009–10, 6 fellowships with partial tuition reimbursements (averaging $7,917 per year), 56 teaching assistantships with tuition reimbursements (averaging $16,047 per year) were awarded; Federal Work-Study, scholarships/grants, and unspecified assistantships also available. Support available to part-time students. Financial award applicants required to submit FAFSA. *Faculty research:* Health communication, interpersonal communication, persuasion, intercultural communication, contemporary rhetoric theory. Total annual research expenditures: $50,458. *Unit head:* Dr. Elizabeth L. Toth, Chair, 301-405-0870, Fax: 301-314-9471, E-mail: eltoth@umd.edu. *Application contact:* Dean of Graduate School, 301-405-0376, Fax: 301-314-9305.

University of Miami, Graduate School, School of Communication, Coral Gables, FL 33124. Offers communication (PhD); communication studies (MA); film studies (MA, PhD); motion pictures (MFA), including production, producing, and screenwriting; print journalism (MA); public relations (MA); Spanish language journalism (MA); television broadcast journalism (MA). *Accreditation:* ACEJMC. Part-time programs available. *Degree requirements:* For master's, comprehensive exam (for some programs), thesis (for some programs); for doctorate, comprehensive exam, thesis/dissertation. *Entrance requirements:* For master's, GRE General Test; for doctorate, GRE General Test, master's thesis or scholarly research. Additional exam requirements/recommendations for international students: Required—TOEFL (minimum score 600 paper-based; 250 computer-based; 100 iBT). Electronic applications accepted. *Faculty research:* Communication studies, mass communication, international/interpersonal communication, film studies, journalism.

University of Nebraska–Lincoln, Graduate College, College of Arts and Sciences, Department of Communication Studies, Lincoln, NE 68588. Offers instructional communication (MA, PhD); interpersonal communication (MA, PhD); marketing, communication studies, and advertising (MA, PhD); organizational communication (MA, PhD); rhetoric and culture (MA, PhD). *Degree requirements:* For master's, thesis optional; for doctorate, comprehensive exam, thesis/dissertation. *Entrance requirements:* For master's and doctorate, GRE General Test, writing sample. Additional exam requirements/recommendations for international students: Required—TOEFL (minimum score 600 paper-based; 250 computer-based). Electronic applications accepted. *Faculty research:* Message strategies, gender communication, political communication, organizational communication, instructional communication.

University of Nebraska–Lincoln, Graduate College, College of Journalism and Mass Communications, Lincoln, NE 68588. Offers marketing, communication and advertising (MA); professional journalism (MA). *Accreditation:* ACEJMC. Postbaccalaureate distance learning degree programs offered (no on-campus study). *Degree requirements:* For master's, thesis. *Entrance requirements:* For master's, samples of work. Additional exam requirements/recommendations for international students: Required—TOEFL (minimum score 600 paper-based; 250 computer-based). Electronic applications accepted. *Faculty research:* Interactive media and the Internet, community newspapers, children's radio, advertising involvement, telecommunications policy.

University of Oklahoma, Graduate College, Gaylord College of Journalism and Mass Communication, Program in Journalism and Mass Communication, Norman, OK 73019-0390. Offers advertising and public relations (MA); information gathering and distribution (MA); mass communication management and policy (MA); professional writing (MA); telecommunication and new technology (MA). Part-time programs available. *Students:* 34 full-time (18 women), 43 part-time (23 women); includes 13 minority (4 African Americans, 5 American Indian/Alaska Native, 4 Hispanic Americans), 9 international. 45 applicants, 42% accepted, 9 enrolled. *Degree requirements:* For master's, thesis optional. *Entrance requirements:* For master's, GRE General Test, minimum GPA of 3.2, 9 hours of course work in journalism, course work in statistics. Additional exam requirements/recommendations for international students: Required—TOEFL (minimum score 600 paper-based; 250 computer-based), TWE (minimum score 5). *Application deadline:* For fall admission, 2/1 for domestic students, 4/1 for international students; for spring admission, 11/1 for domestic students, 9/1 for international students. Application fee: $40 ($90 for international students). Electronic applications accepted. *Expenses:* Tuition, state resident: full-time $3744; part-time $156 per credit hour. Tuition, nonresident: full-time $13,577; part-time $565.70 per credit hour. Required fees: $2415; $90.10 per credit hour. *Financial support:* In 2009–10, 43 students received support, including 4 fellowships (averaging $5,000 per year); career-related internships or fieldwork, scholarships/grants, health care benefits, and unspecified assistantships also available. *Faculty research:* Organizational management, rhetorical analysis, international public relations, digital production, normative theory. *Unit head:* Dr. Joe Foote, Dean, 405-325-2721, Fax: 405-325-7565, E-mail: jfoote@ou.edu. *Application contact:* Kelly Storm, Graduate Advisor, 405-325-2722, Fax: 405-325-7565, E-mail: kstorm@ou.edu.

University of Southern California, Graduate School, Annenberg School for Communication and Journalism, School of Journalism, Program in Strategic Public Relations, Los Angeles, CA 90089. Offers MA. *Students:* 79 full-time (69 women), 6 part-time; includes 29 minority (8 African Americans, 9 Asian Americans or Pacific Islanders, 12 Hispanic Americans), 25 international. Average age 24. 146 applicants, 54% accepted, 49 enrolled. In 2009, 27 master's awarded. *Degree requirements:* For master's, comprehensive exam (for some programs), thesis optional. *Entrance requirements:* For master's, GRE General Test, resume, writing samples, letters of recommendation, statement of purpose. Additional exam requirements/recommendations for international students: Required—TOEFL (minimum score 280 computer-based; 114 iBT). *Application deadline:* For fall admission, 1/15 for domestic and international students. Application fee: $85. Electronic applications accepted. *Expenses:* Tuition: Full-time $25,980; part-time $1315 per unit. Required fees: $554. One-time fee: $35 full-time. Full-time tuition and fees vary according to degree level and program. *Financial support:* Teaching assistantships with full tuition reimbursements, career-related internships or fieldwork, Federal Work-Study, institutionally sponsored loans, scholarships/grants, health care benefits, and unspecified assistantships available. Support available to part-time students. Financial award application deadline: 1/15; financial award applicants required to submit FAFSA. *Unit head:* Jerry Swerling, Director, 213-821-1275, Fax: 7, E-mail: swerling@usc.edu. *Application contact:* Allyson Hill, Assistant Dean, Admissions, 213-821-0770, E-mail: ascadm@usc.edu.

University of Southern Mississippi, Graduate School, College of Arts and Letters, School of Mass Communication and Journalism, Hattiesburg, MS 39406-0001. Offers mass communication (MA, MS, PhD); public relations (MS). *Accreditation:* ACEJMC. *Faculty:* 10 full-time (3 women), 1 part-time/adjunct (0 women). *Students:* 28 full-time (18 women), 57 part-time (43 women); includes 13 minority (12 African Americans, 1 Hispanic American), 5 international. Average age 34. 44 applicants, 66% accepted, 18 enrolled. In 2009, 24 master's, 4 doctorates awarded. *Degree requirements:* For master's, comprehensive exam, thesis optional; for doctorate, comprehensive exam, thesis/dissertation. *Entrance requirements:* For master's, GRE General Test, minimum GPA of 3.0 in field of study, 2.75 in last 2 years; for doctorate, GRE General Test, minimum GPA of 3.5. Additional exam requirements/recommendations for international students: Required—TOEFL. *Application deadline:* For fall admission, 3/1 priority date for domestic students, 3/1 for international students. Applications are processed on a rolling basis. Application fee: $35. *Expenses:* Tuition, state resident: full-time $5096; part-time $284 per hour. Tuition, nonresident: full-time $13,052; part-time $726 per hour. Required fees: $402. Tuition and fees vary according to course level and course load. *Financial support:* In 2009–10, 18 students received support, including 12 teaching assistantships with full tuition reimbursements available (averaging $8,000 per year); fellowships with full tuition reimbursements available, research assistantships with full tuition reimbursements available, career-related internships or fieldwork, Federal Work-Study, and unspecified assistantships also available. Financial award application deadline: 3/15; financial award applicants required to submit FAFSA. *Unit head:* Dr. Christopher Campbell, Director, 601-266-5650, Fax: 601-266-4263. *Application contact:* Dr. Fei Xue, Graduate Coordinator, 601-266-5652, Fax: 601-266-6473, E-mail: fei.xue@usm.edu.

The University of Tennessee, Graduate School, College of Communication and Information, Knoxville, TN 37996. Offers advertising (MS, PhD); broadcasting (MS, PhD); communications (MS, PhD); information sciences (MS, PhD); journalism (MS, PhD); public relations (MS, PhD); speech communication (MS, PhD). *Accreditation:* ACEJMC (one or more programs are accredited at the [master's] level). Part-time and evening/weekend programs available. Postbaccalaureate distance learning degree programs offered (no on-campus study). *Degree requirements:* For master's, thesis or alternative; for doctorate, thesis/dissertation. *Entrance requirements:* For master's and doctorate, GRE General Test, minimum GPA of 2.7. Additional exam requirements/recommendations for international students: Required—TOEFL. Electronic applications accepted. *Expenses:* Tuition, state resident: full-time $6826; part-time $380 per semester hour. Tuition, nonresident: full-time $21,844; part-time $1147 per semester hour. Tuition and fees vary according to program.

The University of Texas at Austin, Graduate School, College of Communication, Department of Advertising, Austin, TX 78712-1111. Offers MA, PhD. *Entrance requirements:* For master's and doctorate, GRE General Test. Electronic applications accepted. *Faculty research:* Interactive advertising, advertising laws and ethics, advertising creativity, media planning and modeling, international advertising.

University of the Sacred Heart, Graduate Programs, Department of Communication, Program in Public Relations, San Juan, PR 00914-0383. Offers MA. Part-time and evening/weekend programs available. *Degree requirements:* For master's, thesis. *Entrance requirements:* For master's, EXADEP, minimum undergraduate GPA of 2.75, interview.

University of Wisconsin–Stevens Point, College of Fine Arts and Communication, Division of Communication, Stevens Point, WI 54481-3897. Offers interpersonal communication (MA); mass communication (MA); organizational communication (MA); public relations (MA). Part-time programs available. *Students:* 7 full-time (3 women), 19 part-time (11 women). *Degree requirements:* For master's, thesis or alternative. *Entrance requirements:* For master's, GRE. Additional exam requirements/recommendations for international students: Required—TOEFL (minimum score 575 paper-based). *Application deadline:* For fall admission, 3/1 priority date for domestic students. Applications are processed on a rolling basis. Application fee: $45. *Expenses:* Tuition, state resident: full-time $7740; part-time $430 per credit hour. Tuition, nonresident: full-time $17,804; part-time $989 per credit hour. Tuition and fees vary according to course load and reciprocity agreements. *Financial support:* In 2009–10, 9 teaching assistantships were awarded; career-related internships or fieldwork, Federal Work-Study, institutionally sponsored loans, and unspecified assistantships also available. Support available to part-time students. Financial award application deadline: 5/1; financial award applicants required to submit FAFSA. *Faculty research:* Communication theory and research, film history. *Unit head:* Dr. James Haney, Chair, 715-346-3409, E-mail: jhaney@uwsp.edu. *Application contact:* Dr. Chris Sadler, Graduate Coordinator, 715-346-3898, E-mail: csadler@uwsp.edu.

Virginia Commonwealth University, Graduate School, College of Humanities and Sciences, School of Mass Communications, Brandcenter, Richmond, VA 23284-9005. Offers account management (MS); account planning (MS); art direction (MS); copywriting (MS); creative brand management (MS); creative media planning (MS). *Degree requirements:* For master's, comprehensive exam, thesis optional. *Entrance requirements:* For master's, GRE General Test, screening test, interview, portfolio.

Virginia Commonwealth University, Graduate School, College of Humanities and Sciences, School of Mass Communications, Program in Mass Communications, Richmond, VA 23284-9005. Offers scholastic journalism (MS); strategic public relations (MS). *Accreditation:* ACEJMC. *Degree requirements:* For master's, comprehensive exam, thesis optional. *Entrance requirements:* For master's, GRE General Test.

Wayne State University, College of Fine, Performing and Communication Arts, Department of Communication, Detroit, MI 48202. Offers communication studies (MA, PhD); public relations and organizational communication (MA); radio-TV-film (MA, PhD); speech communication (MA, PhD). *Degree requirements:* For master's, thesis, essay, or comprehensive exam; for doctorate, thesis/dissertation. *Entrance requirements:* For master's, minimum GPA of 3.0, sample of academic writing; for doctorate, GRE, minimum GPA of 3.3, MA; letters of recommendation; personal statement; sample of written scholarship. Additional exam requirements/recommendations for international students: Required—TOEFL (minimum score 550 paper-based; 213 computer-based); Recommended—TWE (minimum score 6). Electronic applications accepted. *Faculty research:* Rhetorical theory and criticism; mass media theory and research; argumentation; organizational communication; risk and crisis communication; interpersonal, family, and health communication.

Webster University, School of Communications, Program in Advertising and Marketing Communications, St. Louis, MO 63119-3194. Offers MA. *Expenses:* Tuition: Part-time $565 per credit hour. Tuition and fees vary according to degree level, campus/location and program.

Webster University, School of Communications, Program in Public Relations, St. Louis, MO 63119-3194. Offers MA. *Expenses:* Tuition: Part-time $565 per credit hour. Tuition and fees vary according to degree level, campus/location and program.

Section 4
Electronic Commerce

This section contains a directory of institutions offering graduate work in electronic commerce. Additional information about programs listed in the directory may be obtained by writing directly to the dean of a graduate school or chair of a department at the address given in the directory.

CONTENTS

Program Directory

Close-Up

See:

Electronic Commerce

Adelphi University, School of Business, MBA Program, Garden City, NY 11530-0701. Offers finance (MBA); management information systems (MBA); management/human resource management (MBA); marketing/e-commerce (MBA). *Accreditation:* AACSB. Part-time and evening/weekend programs available. *Students:* 77 full-time (30 women), 183 part-time (91 women); includes 56 minority (29 African Americans, 17 Asian Americans or Pacific Islanders, 10 Hispanic Americans), 81 international. Average age 30. In 2009, 64 master's awarded. *Degree requirements:* For master's, capstone course. *Entrance requirements:* For master's, GMAT, 2 letters of recommendation. Additional exam requirements/recommendations for international students: Required—TOEFL (minimum score 550 paper-based; 213 computer-based; 80 iBT). *Application deadline:* For fall admission, 4/1 for international students; for spring admission, 11/1 for international students. Applications are processed on a rolling basis. Application fee: $50. Electronic applications accepted. *Expenses:* Tuition: Full-time $28,340; part-time $830 per credit. Required fees: $600; $250 per credit. Full-time tuition and fees vary according to course load and program. *Financial support:* Research assistantships with full and partial tuition reimbursements, career-related internships or fieldwork, Federal Work-Study, institutionally sponsored loans, scholarships/grants, and unspecified assistantships available. Financial award application deadline: 3/1; financial award applicants required to submit FAFSA. *Faculty research:* Supply chain management, distribution channels, productivity benchmark analysis, data envelopment analysis, financial portfolio analysis. *Unit head:* Rakesh Gupta, 516-877-4670, Fax: 516-877-4607, E-mail: gradbusinquiries@adelphi.edu. *Application contact:* Christine Murphy, Director of Admissions, 516-877-3050, Fax: 516-877-3039, E-mail: graduateadmissions@adelphi.edu.

Arkansas State University—Jonesboro, Graduate School, College of Business, Department of Computer and Information Technology, Jonesboro, State University, AR 72467. Offers business technology education (MSE); information systems and e-commerce (MS). Part-time programs available. *Faculty:* 11 full-time (2 women). *Students:* 6 full-time (2 women), 23 part-time (17 women); includes 9 minority (all African Americans), 3 international. Average age 35. 11 applicants, 82% accepted, 9 enrolled. In 2009, 17 master's awarded. *Degree requirements:* For master's, comprehensive exam, thesis or alternative. *Entrance requirements:* For master's, GRE General Test or MAT, appropriate bachelor's degree, official transcript, immunization records. Additional exam requirements/recommendations for international students: Required—TOEFL (minimum score 550 paper-based; 213 computer-based; 79 iBT), IELTS (minimum score 6). *Application deadline:* For fall admission, 7/15 for domestic students, 7/1 for international students; for spring admission, 12/1 for domestic students, 11/13 for international students. Applications are processed on a rolling basis. Application fee: $30 ($40 for international students). Electronic applications accepted. *Expenses:* Contact institution. *Financial support:* In 2009–10, 4 students received support. Career-related internships or fieldwork and unspecified assistantships available. Financial award application deadline: 7/1; financial award applicants required to submit FAFSA. *Unit head:* Dr. John Robertson, Chair, 870-972-3416, Fax: 870-972-3417, E-mail: jfrobert@astate.edu. *Application contact:* Dr. Andrew Sustich, Dean of the Graduate School, 870-972-3029, Fax: 870-972-3857, E-mail: sustich@astate.edu.

Boston University, Metropolitan College, Department of Administrative Sciences, Boston, MA 02215. Offers banking and financial management (MSM); business continuity in emergency management (MSM); economics development and tourism management (MSAS); electronic commerce, systems, and technology (MSAS); financial economics (MSAS); human resource management (MSM); innovation and technology (MSAS); insurance management (MSM); international market management (MSM); multinational commerce (MSAS); project management (MSM). *Accreditation:* AACSB. Part-time and evening/weekend programs available. Postbaccalaureate distance learning degree programs offered (no on-campus study). *Students:* 123 full-time (48 women), 204 part-time (92 women); includes 31 minority (10 African Americans, 1 American Indian/Alaska Native, 11 Asian Americans or Pacific Islanders, 9 Hispanic Americans), 146 international. Average age 30. In 2009, 154 master's awarded. *Degree requirements:* For master's, thesis optional. *Entrance requirements:* For master's, 1 year of work experience, minimum GPA of 3.0. Additional exam requirements/recommendations for international students: Required—TOEFL (minimum score 560 paper-based; 220 computer-based; 84 iBT). *Application deadline:* Applications are processed on a rolling basis. Application fee: $70. Electronic applications accepted. *Expenses:* Tuition: Full-time $37,910; part-time $1184 per credit hour. Required fees: $386; $40 per semester. Part-time tuition and fees vary according to class time, course level, degree level and program. *Financial support:* In 2009–10, 15 students received support, including 8 research assistantships (averaging $10,000 per year); career-related internships or fieldwork and Federal Work-Study also available. *Faculty research:* International business, innovative process. *Unit head:* Dr. Kip Becker, Chairman, 617-353-3016, E-mail: adminsc@bu.edu. *Application contact:* Lucille Dicker, Administrative Sciences Department, 617-353-3016, E-mail: adminsc@bu.edu.

California State University, Fullerton, Graduate Studies, College of Business and Economics, Department of Information Systems and Decision Sciences, Fullerton, CA 92834-9480. Offers information systems (MS); information systems (decision sciences) (MS); information systems (e-commerce) (MS); information technology (MS); management science (MBA). Part-time programs available. *Students:* 9 full-time (3 women), 72 part-time (13 women); includes 32 minority (3 African Americans, 22 Asian Americans or Pacific Islanders, 7 Hispanic Americans), 16 international. Average age 33. 105 applicants, 50% accepted, 38 enrolled. In 2009, 29 master's awarded. *Degree requirements:* For master's, project or thesis. *Entrance requirements:* For master's, GMAT, minimum AACSB index of 950. Application fee: $55. *Expenses:* Tuition, nonresident: full-time $11,160; part-time $373 per credit. Required fees: $1440 per term. Tuition and fees vary according to course load, degree level and program. *Financial support:* Career-related internships or fieldwork, Federal Work-Study, institutionally sponsored loans, and scholarships/grants available. Support available to part-time students. Financial award application deadline: 3/1; financial award applicants required to submit FAFSA. *Unit head:* Dr. Bhushan Kapoor, Chair, 657-278-2221. *Application contact:* Admissions/Applications, 657-278-2371.

California State University, Fullerton, Graduate Studies, College of Business and Economics, Program in Business Administration, Fullerton, CA 92834-9480. Offers e-commerce (MBA); international business (MBA). *Accreditation:* AACSB. Part-time programs available. *Students:* 65 full-time (30 women), 68 part-time (31 women); includes 59 minority (3 African Americans, 1 American Indian/Alaska Native, 43 Asian Americans or Pacific Islanders, 12 Hispanic Americans), 32 international. Average age 28. 238 applicants, 42% accepted, 39 enrolled. In 2009, 33 master's awarded. *Degree requirements:* For master's, project or thesis. *Entrance requirements:* For master's, GMAT. *Expenses:* Tuition, nonresident: full-time $11,160; part-time $373 per credit. Required fees: $1440 per term. Tuition and fees vary according to course load, degree level and program. *Financial support:* Career-related internships or fieldwork, Federal Work-Study, institutionally sponsored loans, and scholarships/grants available. Support available to part-time students. Financial award application deadline: 3/1; financial award applicants required to submit FAFSA. *Unit head:* Dr. Anil Puri, Dean, 657-773-2592. *Application contact:* Admissions/Applications, 657-278-2371.

Carnegie Mellon University, Tepper School of Business and School of Computer Science, Program in Electronic Commerce, Pittsburgh, PA 15213-3891. Offers MS. *Entrance requirements:* For master's, GRE General Test or GMAT. Additional exam requirements/recommendations for international students: Required—TOEFL.

Claremont Graduate University, Graduate Programs, School of Information Systems and Technology, Claremont, CA 91711-6160. Offers electronic commerce (MS, PhD); health information management (MS); information systems (Certificate); knowledge management (MS, PhD); systems development (MS, PhD); telecommunications and networking (MS, PhD); MBA/MS. Part-time programs available. *Faculty:* 6 full-time (1 woman), 1 part-time/adjunct (0 women). *Students:* 78 full-time (28 women), 35 part-time (11 women); includes 32 minority (8 African Americans, 1 American Indian/Alaska Native, 16 Asian Americans or Pacific Islanders, 7 Hispanic Americans), 32 international. Average age 38. In 2009, 31 master's, 11 doctorates, 1 other advanced degree awarded. *Degree requirements:* For doctorate, comprehensive exam, thesis/dissertation, portfolio. *Entrance requirements:* For master's and doctorate, GMAT, GRE General Test. Additional exam requirements/recommendations for international students: Required—TOEFL (minimum score 550 paper-based; 213 computer-based; 80 iBT). *Application deadline:* For fall admission, 2/1 priority date for domestic students. Applications are processed on a rolling basis. Application fee: $60. Electronic applications accepted. *Expenses:* Tuition: Full-time $35,046; part-time $1524 per credit. Required fees: $161 per semester. *Financial support:* Fellowships, research assistantships, teaching assistantships, Federal Work-Study, institutionally sponsored loans, and scholarships/grants available. Support available to part-time students. Financial award application deadline: 2/15; financial award applicants required to submit FAFSA. *Faculty research:* GPSS, man-machine interaction, organizational aspects of computing, implementation of information systems, information systems practice. *Unit head:* Terry Ryan, Dean, 909-607-9591, Fax: 909-621-8564, E-mail: terry.ryan@cgu.edu. *Application contact:* Matt Hutter, Director of External Affairs, 909-621-3180, Fax: 909-621-8564, E-mail: matt.hutter@cgu.edu.

Columbia Southern University, MBA Program, Orange Beach, AL 36561. Offers electronic business and technology (MBA); finance (MBA); general (MBA); healthcare management (MBA); hospitality and tourism (MBA); human resources management (MBA); international management (MBA); marketing (MBA); project management (MBA); public administration (MBA); sport management (MBA). Part-time and evening/weekend programs available. Postbaccalaureate distance learning degree programs offered (no on-campus study). *Entrance requirements:* For master's, bachelor's degree from accredited/approved institution. Additional exam requirements/recommendations for international students: Required—TOEFL. Electronic applications accepted.

Dalhousie University, Faculty of Computer Science, Halifax, NS B3H 1W5, Canada. Offers computational biology and bioinformatics (M Sc); computer science (PhD); computer science (project-based) (MA Sc); computer science (thesis-based) (MC Sc); electronic commerce (MEC); health informatics (MHI). *Degree requirements:* For master's, thesis (for some programs); for doctorate, thesis/dissertation. *Entrance requirements:* Additional exam requirements/recommendations for international students: Required—1 of the following 5 approved tests: TOEFL, IELTS, CANTEST, CAEL, Michigan English Language Assessment Battery. Electronic applications accepted.

Dallas Baptist University, College of Business, Business Administration Program, Dallas, TX 75211-9299. Offers accounting (MBA); business communication (MBA); conflict resolution management (MBA); e-business (MBA); entrepreneurship (MBA); finance (MBA); health care management (MBA); international business (MBA); leading the non-profit organization (MBA); management (MBA); management information systems (MBA); marketing (MBA); project management (MBA); technology and engineering management (MBA). *Accreditation:* ACBSP. Part-time and evening/weekend programs available. *Entrance requirements:* For master's, GMAT, minimum GPA of 3.0. Additional exam requirements/recommendations for international students: Required—TOEFL, IELTS. Electronic applications accepted. *Expenses:* Tuition: Full-time $10,674; part-time $593 per credit hour. *Faculty research:* Sports management, services marketing, retailing, strategic management, financial planning/investments.

DePaul University, Charles H. Kellstadt Graduate School of Business, School of Accountancy and Management Information Systems, Chicago, IL 60604-2287. Offers accountancy (M Acc, MSA); business information technology (MS); e-business (MBA, MS); financial management and control (MBA); management accounting (MBA); management information systems (MBA); taxation (MST). Part-time and evening/weekend programs available. *Faculty:* 30 full-time (9 women), 54 part-time/adjunct (7 women). *Students:* 167 full-time (82 women), 237 part-time (106 women); includes 52 minority (8 African Americans, 1 American Indian/Alaska Native, 30 Asian Americans or Pacific Islanders, 13 Hispanic Americans), 49 international. In 2009, 141 master's awarded. *Entrance requirements:* For master's, GMAT, 2 letters of recommendation, resume. Additional exam requirements/recommendations for international students: Required—TOEFL (minimum score 550 paper-based; 213 computer-based). *Application deadline:* For fall admission, 7/1 for domestic students; for winter admission, 10/1 for domestic students; for spring admission, 2/1 for domestic students. Applications are processed on a rolling basis. Application fee: $60. *Expenses:* Tuition: Full-time $37,525; part-time $620 per credit hour. *Financial support:* In 2009–10, 7 research assistantships with full tuition reimbursements (averaging $4,100 per year) were awarded; institutionally sponsored loans also available. Financial award application deadline: 4/2. *Faculty research:* Tax policy, property transactions, stock options as compensation, standards setting, activity-based costing in health care. *Unit head:* Kevin Stevens, Director, 312-362-6989, E-mail: kstevens@depaul.edu. *Application contact:* Christopher E. Kinsella, Director of Cohort MBA Programs, 312-362-8810, Fax: 312-362-6677, E-mail: kgsb@depaul.edu.

DePaul University, College of Computing and Digital Media, Chicago, IL 60604. Offers business information technology (MS); computational finance (MS); computer and information sciences (PhD); computer game development (MS); computer graphics and motion technology (MS); computer science (MS); computer, information and network security (MS), including applied technology; digital cinema (MFA, MS), including information technology project management (MS); e-commerce technology (MS); human-computer interaction (MS); information systems (MS); information technology (MA); information technology project management (MS); software engineering (MS); telecommunications systems (MS); JD/MS. Part-time and evening/weekend programs available. Postbaccalaureate distance learning degree programs offered (no on-campus study). *Faculty:* 78 full-time (16 women), 191 part-time/adjunct (51 women). *Students:* 922 full-time (239 women), 887 part-time (209 women); includes 466 minority (193 African Americans, 3 American Indian/Alaska Native, 162 Asian Americans or Pacific Islanders, 108 Hispanic Americans), 276 international. Average age 31. 853 applicants, 67% accepted, 294 enrolled. In 2009, 444 master's, 4 doctorates awarded. *Degree requirements:* For master's, thesis (for some programs); for doctorate, comprehensive exam, thesis/dissertation. *Entrance requirements:* For master's, GRE or GMAT (MS in computational finance only), bachelor's degree; for doctorate, GRE, master's degree in computer science. Additional exam requirements/recommendations for international students: Required—TOEFL (minimum score 550 paper-based; 213 computer-based), IELTS (minimum score 6.5), Pearson Test of English (minimum score 53). *Application deadline:* For fall admission, 8/15 priority date for domestic students, 6/1 priority date for international students; for winter admission, 12/15 priority date for domestic students, 9/15 priority date for international students; for spring admission, 3/1 priority date for domestic students, 12/15 priority date for international students. Applications are processed on a rolling basis. Application fee: $25. Electronic applications accepted. *Expenses:* Contact institution. *Financial support:* In 2009–10, 69 students received support, including 6 fellowships with full tuition reimbursements available (averaging $25,858 per year), 75 teaching assistantships with full and partial tuition reimbursements available (averaging $5,780 per year); research assistantships, Federal Work-Study, scholarships/grants, tuition waivers (full and partial), and unspecified assistantships also available. Support available to part-time students. Financial award application deadline: 4/30; financial award applicants required to submit FAFSA. *Faculty research:* Bioinformatics, visual computing, graphics and animation, high performance and scientific computing, databases. Total annual research expenditures: $790,000. *Unit head:* Dr. David Miller, Dean, 312-362-8381, Fax: 312-362-5185. *Application contact:* Dr. Liz Friedman, Assistant Dean of Student Services, 312-362-5384, Fax: 312-362-5327, E-mail: efriedm2@cdm.depaul.edu.

Eastern Michigan University, Graduate School, College of Business, Programs in Business Administration, Ypsilanti, MI 48197. Offers business administration (MBA, Graduate Certificate); computer information systems (Graduate Certificate); e-business (MBA, Graduate Certificate); enterprise business intelligence (MBA); entrepreneurship (MBA, Graduate Certificate); finance (MBA, Graduate Certificate); human resources (MBA); human resources management (Graduate

Certificate); information systems (MBA); internal auditing (MBA); international business (MBA, Graduate Certificate); marketing management (Graduate Certificate); nonprofit management (MBA); organizational development (Graduate Certificate); supply chain management (MBA, Graduate Certificate). *Accreditation:* AACSB. Part-time programs available. Postbaccalaureate distance learning degree programs offered (no on-campus study). *Students:* 166 full-time (80 women), 439 part-time (231 women); includes 150 minority (103 African Americans, 7 American Indian/Alaska Native, 31 Asian Americans or Pacific Islanders, 9 Hispanic Americans), 97 international. Average age 34. In 2009, 3 other advanced degrees awarded. *Entrance requirements:* For master's, GMAT (minimum score 450), minimum cumulative undergraduate GPA of 2.75. Additional exam requirements/recommendations for international students: Required—TOEFL. *Application deadline:* For fall admission, 5/15 for domestic students, 5/1 for international students; for winter admission, 10/15 for domestic students, 10/1 for international students; for spring admission, 3/15 for domestic students, 3/1 for international students. Applications are processed on a rolling basis. Application fee: $35. Tuition and fees vary according to course level. *Financial support:* Fellowships, research assistantships with full tuition reimbursements, teaching assistantships with full tuition reimbursements, career-related internships or fieldwork, Federal Work-Study, institutionally sponsored loans, scholarships/grants, tuition waivers (partial), and unspecified assistantships available. Support available to part-time students. Financial award applicants required to submit FAFSA. *Unit head:* K. Michelle Henry, Director of Academic Services, 734-487-4444, Fax: 734-483-1316, E-mail: cob.grad@emich.edu. *Application contact:* Beste Windes, Advisor, 734-487-4444, Fax: 734-483-1316, E-mail: cob.grad@emich.edu.

Fairleigh Dickinson University, Metropolitan Campus, University College: Arts, Sciences, and Professional Studies, School of Computer Sciences and Engineering, Program in E-Commerce, Teaneck, NJ 07666-1914. Offers MS. *Students:* 2 full-time (both women), 2 part-time (0 women), 2 international. Average age 39. 8 applicants, 25% accepted, 1 enrolled. In 2009, 1 master's awarded. *Application deadline:* Applications are processed on a rolling basis. Application fee: $40. *Application contact:* Susan Brooman, University Director of Graduate Admissions, 201-692-2554, Fax: 201-692-2560, E-mail: globaleducation@fdu.edu.

Ferris State University, College of Business, Big Rapids, MI 49307. Offers application development (MSISM); business intelligence and infomatics (MBA); database administration (MSISM); design and innovation management process (MBA); e-business (MSISM); networking (MSISM); quality management (MBA); security (MSISM). *Accreditation:* ACBSP. Part-time and evening/weekend programs available. *Faculty:* 10 full-time (3 women), 2 part-time/adjunct (both women). *Students:* 33 full-time (6 women), 134 part-time (65 women); includes 13 minority (8 African Americans, 2 American Indian/Alaska Native, 2 Asian Americans or Pacific Islanders, 1 Hispanic American), 33 international. Average age 30. 120 applicants, 31% accepted, 26 enrolled. In 2009, 66 master's awarded. *Entrance requirements:* For master's, GRE or GMAT (waived if GPA is 3.5 or better), minimum GPA of 3.0 in CIS and business core, 2.75 overall; writing sample; 3 letters of reference; resume. Additional exam requirements/recommendations for international students: Required—TOEFL (minimum score 500 paper-based; 173 computer-based; 64 iBT). *Application deadline:* For fall admission, 7/1 priority date for domestic students, 6/15 for international students; for winter admission, 11/1 priority date for domestic students, 10/15 for international students; for spring admission, 3/1 priority date for domestic students, 2/15 for international students. Applications are processed on a rolling basis. Application fee: $30 for international students. Electronic applications accepted. *Financial support:* In 2009–10, 14 teaching assistantships were awarded; career-related internships or fieldwork, Federal Work-Study, and unspecified assistantships also available. Support available to part-time students. Financial award applicants required to submit FAFSA. *Faculty research:* Quality improvement, client/server end-user computing, information management and policy, security, digital forensics. *Unit head:* Dr. David Steenstra, Department Chair, 231-591-2168, Fax: 231-591-2973, E-mail: yosts@ferris.edu. *Application contact:* Shannon Yost, Department Secretary, 231-591-2168, Fax: 231-591-2973, E-mail: yosts@ferris.edu.

Florida Institute of Technology, Graduate Programs, College of Business, Extended Studies Division, Melbourne, FL 32901-6975. Offers acquisition and contract management (PMBA); business administration (PMBA); computer information systems (MS); e-business (PMBA); human resource management (PMBA); human resources management (MS); logistics management (MS), including humanitarian and disaster relief logistics; management (MS), including acquisition and contract management, e-business, human resource management, information systems, logistics management, management, transportation management; material acquisition management (MS); project management (MS), including information systems, operations research; public administration (MPA); quality management (MS); space management (MS); space systems (MS); systems management (MS), including information systems, operations research, systems management. Part-time and evening/weekend programs available. Postbaccalaureate distance learning degree programs offered (no on-campus study). *Faculty:* 12 full-time (3 women), 117 part-time/adjunct (20 women). *Students:* 74 full-time (32 women), 1,041 part-time (484 women); includes 343 minority (240 African Americans, 12 American Indian/Alaska Native, 44 Asian Americans or Pacific Islanders, 47 Hispanic Americans), 22 international. Average age 35. 520 applicants, 72% accepted, 279 enrolled. In 2009, 509 master's awarded. *Degree requirements:* For master's, capstone course. *Entrance requirements:* For master's, GMAT or resume showing 8 years of supervised experience, minimum GPA of 3.0, 2 letters of recommendation, resume. Additional exam requirements/recommendations for international students: Required—TOEFL (minimum score 550 paper-based; 213 computer-based; 79 iBT). *Application deadline:* For fall admission, 4/1 for international students; for spring admission, 9/30 for international students. Applications are processed on a rolling basis. Application fee: $50. Electronic applications accepted. *Expenses:* Tuition: Part-time $1015 per credit. Tuition and fees vary according to campus/location and program. *Financial support:* Application deadline: 3/1. *Unit head:* Dr. Clifford Bragdon, Dean, 321-674-8821, Fax: 321-674-7597, E-mail: cbragdon@fit.edu. *Application contact:* Carolyn Farrior, Director of Graduate Admissions Online Learning and Off Campus Programs, 321-674-7118, Fax: 321-674-8216, E-mail: cfarrior@fit.edu.

George Mason University, Volgenau School of Information Technology and Engineering, Department of Computer Science, Fairfax, VA 22030. Offers biometrics (Certificate); computer games technology (Certificate); computer networking (Certificate); computer science (MS, PhD); data mining (Certificate); database management (Certificate); electronic commerce (Certificate); foundations of information systems (Certificate); information engineering (Certificate); information security and assurance (MS, Certificate); information systems (MS); intelligent agents (Certificate); software architecture (Certificate); software engineering (MS, Certificate); systems engineering (MS); Web-based software engineering (Certificate). Part-time and evening/weekend programs available. Postbaccalaureate distance learning degree programs offered. *Faculty:* 42 full-time (9 women), 18 part-time/adjunct (0 women). *Students:* 121 full-time (36 women), 489 part-time (118 women); includes 90 minority (11 African Americans, 70 Asian Americans or Pacific Islanders, 9 Hispanic Americans), 222 international. Average age 29. 882 applicants, 58% accepted, 147 enrolled. In 2009, 202 master's, 6 doctorates, 21 other advanced degrees awarded. *Degree requirements:* For master's, thesis optional; for doctorate, comprehensive exam, thesis/dissertation. *Entrance requirements:* For master's, GRE General Test, minimum GPA of 3.0 in last 60 hours, 3 letters of recommendation; for doctorate, GRE, 4-year BA, academic work in computer science, 3 letters of recommendation, statement of career goals and aspirations. Additional exam requirements/recommendations for international students: Required—TOEFL. *Application deadline:* For fall admission, 4/15 priority date for domestic students, 1/15 for international students; for spring admission, 11/15 for domestic students. Application fee: $75. Electronic applications accepted. *Expenses:* Tuition, state resident: full-time $7568; part-time $315.33 per credit hour. Tuition, nonresident: full-time $21,704; part-time $904.33 per credit hour. Required fees: $2184; $91 per credit hour. *Financial support:* In 2009–10, 106 students received support, including 3 fellowships (averaging $18,000 per year), 53 research assistantships (averaging $11,119 per year), 53 teaching assistantships (averaging $7,881 per year); unspecified assistantships and health care benefits (full-time research or teaching assistantship recipients) also available. Financial award application deadline: 3/1; financial award applicants required to submit FAFSA. *Faculty research:* Artificial

intelligence, image processing/graphics, parallel/distributed systems, software engineering systems. Total annual research expenditures: $1.3 million. *Unit head:* Dr. Arun Sood, Director, 703-993-1524, Fax: 703-993-1710, E-mail: asood@gmu.edu. *Application contact:* Jay Shapiro, Professor, 703-993-1485, E-mail: jshapiro@gmu.edu.

Georgia Institute of Technology, Graduate Studies and Research, College of Management, Program in Business Administration, Atlanta, GA 30332-0001. Offers accounting (MBA); e-commerce (Certificate); engineering entrepreneurship (MBA); entrepreneurship (Certificate); finance (MBA); information technology management (MBA); international business (MBA, Certificate); management of technology (Certificate); marketing (MBA); operations management (MBA); organizational behavior (MBA); strategic management (MBA). *Accreditation:* AACSB.

Hawai'i Pacific University, College of Business Administration, Honolulu, HI 96813. Offers accounting/CPA (MBA); e-business (MBA); economics (MBA); finance (MBA); human resource management (MA, MBA); information systems (MBA, MSIS), including knowledge management (MSIS), software engineering (MSIS); telecommunications security (MSIS); international business (MBA); management (MBA); marketing (MBA); organizational change (MA, MBA); travel industry management (MBA). Part-time and evening/weekend programs available. *Faculty:* 15 full-time (5 women), 11 part-time/adjunct (4 women). *Students:* 206 full-time (107 women), 197 part-time (105 women); includes 136 minority (18 African Americans, 3 American Indian/Alaska Native, 98 Asian Americans or Pacific Islanders, 17 Hispanic Americans), 151 international. Average age 30. 235 applicants, 90% accepted, 127 enrolled. In 2009, 141 master's awarded. *Degree requirements:* For master's, thesis. *Entrance requirements:* For master's, GMAT. Additional exam requirements/recommendations for international students: Recommended—TOEFL (minimum score 550 paper-based; 213 computer-based; 80 iBT), TWE (minimum score 5). *Application deadline:* For fall admission, 2/15 priority date for domestic students; for spring admission, 10/15 priority date for domestic students. Applications are processed on a rolling basis. Application fee: $50. Electronic applications accepted. *Expenses:* Tuition: Full-time $12,600; part-time $700 per credit hour. Tuition and fees vary according to program. *Financial support:* In 2009–10, 164 students received support; research assistantships, career-related internships or fieldwork, Federal Work-Study, scholarships/grants, and unspecified assistantships available. Support available to part-time students. Financial award application deadline: 3/1; financial award applicants required to submit FAFSA. *Faculty research:* Statistical control process as used by management, studies in comparative cross-cultural management styles, not-for-profit management. *Unit head:* Dr. Aytun Ozturk, Dean, 808-544-9301, Fax: 808-544-0283, E-mail: uozturk@hpu.edu. *Application contact:* Danny Lam, Assistant Director of Graduate Admissions, 808-544-1135, Fax: 808-544-0280, E-mail: graduate@hpu.edu.

See Close-Up on page 251.

HEC Montreal, School of Business Administration, Diploma Programs in Administration, Program in E-Business, Montréal, QC H3T 2A7, Canada. Offers Diploma. All courses are given in French. Part-time programs available. *Students:* 19 full-time (4 women), 53 part-time (14 women). 76 applicants, 38% accepted, 21 enrolled. In 2009, 27 Diplomas awarded. *Degree requirements:* For Diploma, one foreign language. *Application deadline:* For fall admission, 4/15 for domestic and international students; for winter admission, 10/1 for domestic and international students. Application fee: $77 Canadian dollars. Electronic applications accepted. Tuition and fees charges are reported in Canadian dollars. *Expenses:* Tuition, area resident: Part-time $65.60 Canadian dollars per credit. Tuition, state resident: full-time $2361.60 Canadian dollars; part-time $183.36 Canadian dollars per credit. Tuition, nonresident: full-time $6601 Canadian dollars; part-time $448.13 Canadian dollars per credit. International tuition: $16,132.68 Canadian dollars full-time. Required fees: $1254.15 Canadian dollars; $28.99 Canadian dollars per course. $91.68 Canadian dollars per term. Tuition and fees vary according to degree level and program. *Financial support:* Scholarships/grants available. *Unit head:* Louise Cote, Director, 514-340-7022, Fax: 514-340-5640, E-mail: louise.cote@hec.ca. *Application contact:* Marie Deshaies, Senior Student Advisor, 514-340-6135, Fax: 514-340-6411, E-mail: marie.deshaies@hec.ca.

HEC Montreal, School of Business Administration, Master of Science Programs in Administration, Program in Electronic Commerce, Montréal, QC H3T 2A7, Canada. Offers M Sc. Part-time programs available. *Students:* 31 full-time (10 women), 13 part-time (4 women). 31 applicants, 68% accepted, 15 enrolled. In 2009, 8 master's awarded. *Degree requirements:* For master's, one foreign language. *Entrance requirements:* For master's, bachelor's degree in law, management, information systems or related field. *Application deadline:* For fall admission, 3/1 for domestic and international students. Application fee: $77 Canadian dollars. Tuition and fees charges are reported in Canadian dollars. *Expenses:* Tuition, area resident: Part-time $65.60 Canadian dollars per credit. Tuition, state resident: full-time $2361.60 Canadian dollars; part-time $183.36 Canadian dollars per credit. Tuition, nonresident: full-time $6601 Canadian dollars; part-time $448.13 Canadian dollars per credit. International tuition: $16,132.68 Canadian dollars full-time. Required fees: $1254.15 Canadian dollars; $28.99 Canadian dollars per course. $91.68 Canadian dollars per term. Tuition and fees vary according to degree level and program. *Financial support:* Research assistantships, teaching assistantships available. Financial award application deadline: 10/2. *Unit head:* Claude Laurin, Director, 514-340-6205, Fax: 514-340-5640, E-mail: claude.laurin@hec.ca. *Application contact:* Francine Blais, Administrative Director, 514-340-6112, Fax: 514-340-6411, E-mail: francine.blais@hec.ca.

Instituto Tecnológico y de Estudios Superiores de Monterrey, Campus Central de Veracruz, Graduate Programs, Córdoba, Mexico. Offers administration (MA); administration of information technologies (MTI); computer sciences (MCC); education (MEE); educational institution administration (MAD); educational technology (MTE); electronic commerce (MCE); finance (MAF); humanistic studies (MEH); international business for Latin America (MNL); marketing (MMT); science (MCP); technology management (MTT). Part-time and evening/weekend programs available. Postbaccalaureate distance learning degree programs offered (minimal on-campus study). *Degree requirements:* For master's, thesis (for some programs). *Entrance requirements:* For master's, PAEP College Board. Electronic applications accepted.

Instituto Tecnológico y de Estudios Superiores de Monterrey, Campus Ciudad Juárez, Program in Electronic Commerce, Ciudad Juárez, Mexico. Offers MEC.

Instituto Tecnológico y de Estudios Superiores de Monterrey, Campus Estado de México, Professional and Graduate Division, Estado de Mexico, Mexico. Offers administration of information technologies (MITA); architecture (M Arch); business administration (GMBA, MBA); computer sciences (MCS, PhD); education (M Ed); educational institution administration (MAD); educational technology and innovation (PhD); electronic commerce (MEC); environmental systems (MS); finance (MAF); humanistic studies (MHS); information sciences and knowledge management (MISKM); information systems (MS); manufacturing systems (MS); marketing (MEM); quality systems and productivity (MS); science and materials engineering (PhD); telecommunications management (MTM). Part-time programs available. Postbaccalaureate distance learning degree programs offered (minimal on-campus study). *Degree requirements:* For master's, one foreign language, thesis (for some programs); for doctorate, one foreign language, thesis/dissertation. *Entrance requirements:* For master's, E-PAEP 500, interview; for doctorate, E-PAEP 500, research proposal. Additional exam requirements/recommendations for international students: Required—TOEFL (minimum score 550 paper-based). *Faculty research:* Surface treatments by plasmas, mechanical properties, robotics, graphical computing, mechatronics security protocols.

Instituto Tecnológico y de Estudios Superiores de Monterrey, Campus Irapuato, Graduate Programs, Irapuato, Mexico. Offers administration (MBA); administration of information technology (MAIT); administration of telecommunications (MAT); architecture (M Arch); computer science (MCS); education (M Ed); educational administration (MEA); educational innovation and technology (DEIT); educational technology (MET); electronic commerce (MBA); environmental administration and planning (MEAP); environmental systems (MES); finances (MBA); humanistic studies (MHS); international management for Latin American executives (MIMLAE); library and information science (MLIS); manufacturing quality management (MMQM); marketing research (MBA).

Electronic Commerce

Inter American University of Puerto Rico, Bayamón Campus, Graduate School, Bayamón, PR 00957. Offers biology (MS), including environmental sciences and ecology, molecular biotechnology; electronic commerce (MBA); human resources (MBA). Part-time and evening/weekend programs available. *Faculty:* 6 full-time (1 woman), 5 part-time/adjunct (2 women). *Students:* 99 part-time (61 women); includes all Hispanic Americans. Average age 31. *Degree requirements:* For master's, comprehensive exam, research project. *Entrance requirements:* For master's, EXADEP, GRE General Test, letters of recommendation. *Application deadline:* For fall admission, 7/1 for domestic students, 5/1 priority date for international students; for winter admission, 11/15 priority date for domestic and international students; for spring admission, 2/15 priority date for domestic and international students. Application fee: $31. *Expenses:* Tuition: Part-time $195 per credit. Required fees: $148 per trimester. *Unit head:* Prof. Juan F. Martinez, Rector, 787-279-1200 Ext. 2295, Fax: 787-279-2205, E-mail: jmartinez@bc.inter.edu. *Application contact:* Carlos Alicea, Director of Admission, 787-279-1200 Ext. 2017, Fax: 787-279-2205, E-mail: calicea@bc.inter.edu.

Lewis University, College of Business, Graduate School of Management, Program in Business Administration, Romeoville, IL 60446. Offers accounting (MBA); custom elective option (MBA); e-business (MBA); finance (MBA); healthcare management (MBA); human resources management (MBA); information security (MBA); international business (MBA); management information systems (MBA); marketing (MBA); project management (MBA); technology and operations management (MBA). Part-time and evening/weekend programs available. *Faculty:* 15 full-time (2 women), 18 part-time/adjunct (4 women). *Students:* 120 full-time (64 women), 222 part-time (103 women); includes 97 minority (62 African Americans, 4 Asian Americans or Pacific Islanders, 31 Hispanic Americans), 9 international. Average age 31. In 2009, 84 master's awarded. *Entrance requirements:* For master's, interview, bachelor's degree, resume, 2 recommendations. Additional exam requirements/recommendations for international students: Required—TOEFL (minimum score 550 paper-based; 213 computer-based). *Application deadline:* For fall admission, 8/15 priority date for domestic students, 5/1 priority date for international students; for spring admission, 11/15 priority date for international students. Applications are processed on a rolling basis. Application fee: $40. Electronic applications accepted. *Expenses:* Tuition: Full-time $6480; part-time $720 per credit. One-time fee: $40. Tuition and fees vary according to course load, degree level and program. *Financial support:* Career-related internships or fieldwork, Federal Work-Study, scholarships/grants, and unspecified assistantships available. Financial award application deadline: 5/1; financial award applicants required to submit FAFSA. *Unit head:* Dr. Maureen Culleeney, Academic Program Director, 815-838-0500 Ext. 5631, E-mail: culleema@lewisu.edu. *Application contact:* Michele King, Director of Admission, 815-838-0500 Ext. 5384, E-mail: gsm@lewisu.edu.

Maryville University of Saint Louis, The John E. Simon School of Business, St. Louis, MO 63141-7299. Offers accounting (MBA, PGC); business studies (PGC); internet marketing (MBA, PGC); management (MBA, PGC); marketing (MBA, PGC). *Accreditation:* ACBSP. Part-time and evening/weekend programs available. *Students:* 17 full-time (9 women), 133 part-time (70 women); includes 14 minority (6 African Americans, 1 American Indian/Alaska Native, 3 Asian Americans or Pacific Islanders, 4 Hispanic Americans), 4 international. Average age 30. In 2009, 68 master's awarded. *Entrance requirements:* For master's, GMAT (unless applicant possesses undergraduate business degree with minimum cumulative GPA of 3.0, or has completed master's degree from accredited university, or has completed one early access course prior to undergraduate degree). Additional exam requirements/recommendations for international students: Required—TOEFL (minimum score 550 paper-based). *Application deadline:* Applications are processed on a rolling basis. Application fee: $40 ($60 for international students). Electronic applications accepted. *Expenses:* Tuition: Full-time $20,384; part-time $627.50 per credit hour. Required fees: $100 per semester. *Financial support:* Career-related internships or fieldwork, Federal Work-Study, tuition waivers (partial), and campus employment available. Financial award application deadline: 3/1; financial award applicants required to submit FAFSA. *Faculty research:* International business, e-marketing, strategic planning, interpersonal management skills, financial analysis. *Unit head:* Dr. Pamela Horwitz, Dean, 314-529-9418, Fax: 314-529-9975, E-mail: horwitz@maryville.edu. *Application contact:* Kathy Dougherty, Director of MBA Admissions and Enrollment, 314-529-9382, Fax: 314-529-9975, E-mail: business@maryville.edu.

Marywood University, Academic Affairs, Insalaco College of Creative and Performing Arts, Department of Communication Arts, Program in Information Sciences, Scranton, PA 18509-1598. Offers corporate communication (Certificate); e-business (Certificate); health communication (Certificate); information sciences (MS), including library science/information specialist; instructional technology (Certificate). *Students:* 1 full-time (0 women), 4 part-time (3 women). Average age 32. In 2009, 3 master's awarded. *Entrance requirements:* Additional exam requirements/recommendations for international students: Required—TOEFL (minimum score 550 paper-based; 213 computer-based; 79 iBT). *Application deadline:* For fall admission, 4/1 priority date for domestic students, 3/31 priority date for international students; for spring admission, 11/1 priority date for domestic students, 8/31 priority date for international students. Applications are processed on a rolling basis. Application fee: $35. Electronic applications accepted. *Expenses:* Tuition: Part-time $715 per credit. Required fees: $270 per semester. Tuition and fees vary according to degree level, campus/location and program. *Financial support:* Career-related internships or fieldwork, scholarships/grants, and unspecified assistantships available. Support available to part-time students. Financial award application deadline: 6/30; financial award applicants required to submit FAFSA. *Application contact:* Tammy Manka, Assistant Director of Graduate Admissions, 866-279-9663, E-mail: tmanka@marywood.edu.

Mercy College, School of Liberal Arts, Program in Internet Business Systems, Dobbs Ferry, NY 10522-1189. Offers MS. Part-time and evening/weekend programs available. Postbaccalaureate distance learning degree programs offered (no on-campus study). *Students:* 25 part-time (15 women); includes 6 African Americans, 1 Hispanic American, 4 international. Average age 34. 33 applicants, 48% accepted, 15 enrolled. In 2009, 16 master's awarded. *Entrance requirements:* For master's, interview, resume, 2 letters of recommendation, 2-page written personal statement. Additional exam requirements/recommendations for international students: Required—TOEFL (minimum score 600 paper-based; 250 computer-based; 100 iBT). *Application deadline:* For fall admission, 8/1 for international students. Applications are processed on a rolling basis. Application fee: $40. Electronic applications accepted. *Expenses:* Contact institution. *Financial support:* Career-related internships or fieldwork, Federal Work-Study, scholarships/grants, and unspecified assistantships available. Support available to part-time students. Financial award applicants required to submit FAFSA. *Faculty research:* Internet business systems, Internet marketing, Web design, Internet technologies. *Unit head:* John DiElsi, Program Director, 914-674-7306, E-mail: jdielsi@mercy.edu. *Application contact:* John DiElsi, Program Director, 914-674-7306, E-mail: jdielsi@mercy.edu.

The National Graduate School of Quality Management, Program in Quality Systems Management, Falmouth, MA 02541. Offers e-commerce (MS); management (MS); six sigma (MS).

National University, Academic Affairs, School of Business and Management, Department of Leadership and Business Administration, La Jolla, CA 92037-1011. Offers alternative dispute resolution (MBA); e-business (MBA); financial management (MBA); human resource management (MBA); human resources management (MA); international business (MBA); knowledge management (MS); marketing (MBA); organizational leadership (MBA, MS); technology management (MBA). Part-time and evening/weekend programs available. Postbaccalaureate distance learning degree programs offered (no on-campus study). *Faculty:* 4 full-time (2 women), 22 part-time/adjunct (9 women). *Students:* 95 full-time (56 women), 228 part-time (129 women); includes 63 African Americans, 24 Asian Americans or Pacific Islanders, 61 Hispanic Americans, 6 international. Average age 38. 191 applicants, 100% accepted, 131 enrolled. In 2009, 62 master's awarded. *Degree requirements:* For master's, thesis. *Entrance requirements:* For master's, interview, minimum GPA of 2.5. Additional exam requirements/recommendations for international students: Required—TOEFL (minimum score 550 paper-based; 213 computer-based; 79 iBT), IELTS (minimum score 6). *Application deadline:* Applications are processed on a rolling basis. Application fee: $60 ($65 for international students). Electronic applications accepted. *Expenses:* Tuition: Part-time $338 per quarter hour. *Financial support:* Career-related internships or fieldwork, institutionally sponsored loans, scholarships/grants, and tuition waivers (partial) available. Support available to part-time students. Financial award application deadline: 6/30; financial award applicants required to submit FAFSA. *Unit head:* Dr. George Drops, Chair and Professor, 858-642-8438, Fax: 858-642-8406, E-mail: gdrops@nu.edu. *Application contact:* Dominick Giovanniello, Associate Regional Dean—San Diego, 800-NAT-UNIV, Fax: 858-541-7792, E-mail: dgiovann@nu.edu.

National University, Academic Affairs, School of Business and Management, Department of Management and Marketing, La Jolla, CA 92037-1011. Offers e-business (MS); knowledge management (MS); management (MA); organizational leadership (MS). Part-time and evening/weekend programs available. Postbaccalaureate distance learning degree programs offered (no on-campus study). *Faculty:* 18 full-time (3 women), 37 part-time/adjunct (8 women). *Students:* 465 full-time (230 women), 702 part-time (319 women). Average age 34. 654 applicants, 100% accepted, 423 enrolled. In 2009, 308 master's awarded. *Degree requirements:* For master's, thesis. *Entrance requirements:* For master's, interview, minimum GPA of 2.5. Additional exam requirements/recommendations for international students: Required—TOEFL (minimum score 550 paper-based; 213 computer-based; 79 iBT), IELTS (minimum score 6). *Application deadline:* Applications are processed on a rolling basis. Application fee: $60 ($65 for international students). Electronic applications accepted. *Expenses:* Tuition: Part-time $338 per quarter hour. *Financial support:* Career-related internships or fieldwork, institutionally sponsored loans, scholarships/grants, and tuition waivers (partial) available. Support available to part-time students. Financial award application deadline: 6/30; financial award applicants required to submit FAFSA. *Unit head:* Dr. Brian Simpson, Chair and Professor, 858-642-8431, Fax: 858-642-8406, E-mail: bsimpson@nu.edu. *Application contact:* Dominick Giovanniello, Associate Regional Dean—San Diego, 800-NAT-UNIV, Fax: 858-541-7792, E-mail: dgiovann@nu.edu.

Northwestern University, Medill School of Journalism, Integrated Marketing Communications Program, Evanston, IL 60208. Offers advertising/sales promotion (MSIMC); direct database and e-commerce marketing (MSIMC); general studies (MSIMC); public relations (MSIMC). Part-time programs available. *Entrance requirements:* For master's, GRE General Test or GMAT, full-time work experience (preferred). Additional exam requirements/recommendations for international students: Required—TOEFL. Electronic applications accepted. *Faculty research:* Data mining, business to business marketing, values in advertising, political advertising.

Pace University, Seidenberg School of Computer Science and Information Systems, New York, NY 10038. Offers computer communications and networks (Certificate); computer science (MS); computing studies (DPS); information systems (MS); Internet technologies for e-commerce (MS); Internet technology (MS); object-oriented programming (Certificate); security and information assurance (Certificate); software development and engineering (MS); telecommunications (MS, Certificate). Part-time and evening/weekend programs available. *Students:* 122 full-time (37 women), 424 part-time (131 women); includes 188 minority (76 African Americans, 1 American Indian/Alaska Native, 65 Asian Americans or Pacific Islanders, 46 Hispanic Americans), 110 international. Average age 35. 352 applicants, 89% accepted, 128 enrolled. In 2009, 137 master's, 11 doctorates, 3 other advanced degrees awarded. *Entrance requirements:* For master's, GRE General Test. Additional exam requirements/recommendations for international students: Required—TOEFL. *Application deadline:* For fall admission, 7/31 priority date for domestic students; for spring admission, 11/30 for domestic students. Applications are processed on a rolling basis. Application fee: $70. Electronic applications accepted. *Expenses:* Contact institution. *Financial support:* Research assistantships, career-related internships or fieldwork available. Support available to part-time students. Financial award applicants required to submit FAFSA. *Unit head:* Dr. Constance Knapp, Interim Dean, 914-773-3750, Fax: 914-773-3533, E-mail: cknapp@pace.edu. *Application contact:* Joanna Broda, Director of Graduate Admissions, 914-422-4283, Fax: 914-422-4287, E-mail: gradwp@pace.edu.

Polytechnic Institute of NYU, Department of Technology Management, Brooklyn, NY 11201-2990. Offers construction management (Advanced Certificate); electronic business management (Advanced Certificate); entrepreneurship (Advanced Certificate); human resources management (Advanced Certificate); information management (Advanced Certificate); management (MS); management of technology (MS); organizational behavior (MS, Advanced Certificate); project management (Advanced Certificate); technology management (MBA, PhD, Advanced Certificate); telecommunications and information management (MS); telecommunications management (Advanced Certificate). Part-time and evening/weekend programs available. *Faculty:* 5 full-time (1 woman), 26 part-time/adjunct (3 women). *Students:* 272 full-time (111 women), 103 part-time (41 women); includes 64 minority (20 African Americans, 1 American Indian/Alaska Native, 34 Asian Americans or Pacific Islanders, 9 Hispanic Americans), 193 international. Average age 30. 518 applicants, 57% accepted, 135 enrolled. In 2009, 148 master's awarded. *Degree requirements:* For master's, comprehensive exam (for some programs), thesis (for some programs); for doctorate, comprehensive exam, thesis/dissertation. *Entrance requirements:* For master's, GMAT, minimum B average in undergraduate course work. Additional exam requirements/recommendations for international students: Required—TOEFL (minimum score 550 paper-based; 213 computer-based; 80 iBT); Recommended—IELTS (minimum score 6.5). *Application deadline:* For fall admission, 7/31 priority date for domestic students, 4/30 priority date for international students; for spring admission, 12/31 priority date for domestic students, 11/30 priority date for international students. Applications are processed on a rolling basis. Application fee: $75. Electronic applications accepted. *Expenses:* Tuition: Full-time $21,492; part-time $1194 per credit hour. Required fees: $1160; $204 per course. *Financial support:* In 2009–10, 1 fellowship (averaging $26,400 per year) was awarded; research assistantships, teaching assistantships, institutionally sponsored loans, scholarships/grants, and unspecified assistantships also available. Support available to part-time students. *Unit head:* Prof. Bharadwaj Rao, Head, 718-260-3617, Fax: 718-260-3874, E-mail: brao@poly.edu. *Application contact:* JeanCarlo Bonilla, Director of Graduate Enrollment Management, 718-260-3182, Fax: 718-260-3624, E-mail: gradinfo@poly.edu.

Regis University, College for Professional Studies, School of Computer and Information Sciences, Denver, CO 80221-1099. Offers database administration with IBM DB2 (Certificate); database administration with Oracle (Certificate); database development (Certificate); database technologies (MA); enterprise Java software development (Certificate); executive information technologies (Certificate); information assurance (MA, Certificate); information technology management (MA); software and information systems (M Sc); software engineering (MA, Certificate); storage area networks (Certificate); systems engineering (MA, Certificate). Offered at Boulder Campus, Northwest Denver Campus, Southeast Denver Campus, Fort Collins Campus, Colorado Springs Campus, and Broomfield Campus. Part-time and evening/weekend programs available. Postbaccalaureate distance learning degree programs offered (no on-campus study). *Degree requirements:* For master's, thesis, final research project. *Entrance requirements:* For master's, 2 years of related experience, resume, interview; for Certificate, 2 years of related experience, resumé. Additional exam requirements/recommendations for international students: Required—TOEFL (minimum score 213 computer-based), TWE (minimum score 5), TOEFL or university-based test. Electronic applications accepted. *Expenses:* Contact institution. *Faculty research:* Secure Virtual Laboratory Architecture, Joint IA project with W2C06 Institute, Information Policy, OLTP and OLAP Technologies, knowledge management, software architectures.

Saint Xavier University, Graduate Studies, Graham School of Management, Chicago, IL 60655-3105. Offers e-commerce (MBA); employee health benefits (Certificate); finance (MBA, MS); financial analysis and investments (MBA); financial planning (MBA, Certificate); financial trading and practice (MBA, Certificate); generalist/administration (MBA); health administration (MBA, MS); managed care (Certificate); management (MBA, MS); marketing (MBA); public and non-profit management (MBA); public health (MPH); service management (MBA); training and performance management (MBA); MBA/MS. *Accreditation:* ACBSP. Part-time and evening/weekend programs available. *Entrance requirements:* For master's, GMAT, minimum GPA of 3.0, 2 years of work experience. Electronic applications accepted. *Expenses:* Contact institution.

Stevens Institute of Technology, Graduate School, Wesley J. Howe School of Technology Management, Program in Information Systems, Hoboken, NJ 07030. Offers computer science

(MS); e-commerce (MS); enterprise systems (MS); entrepreneurial information technology (MS); information architecture (MS); information management (MS, Certificate); information security (MS); information technology in financial services industry (MS); information technology in the pharmaceutical industry (MS); information technology outsourcing management (MS); project management (MS, Certificate); software engineering (MS); telecommunications (MS). *Degree requirements:* For master's, thesis optional. *Entrance requirements:* For master's, GMAT, GRE General Test. Additional exam requirements/recommendations for international students: Required—TOEFL. Electronic applications accepted. *Expenses:* Tuition: Full-time $9900; part-time $1100 per credit. Required fees: $286 per semester.

Universidad del Este, Graduate School, Carolina, PR 00984. Offers accounting (MBA); adult education (M Ed); agribusiness (MBA); bilingual education (M Ed); criminal justice and criminology (MA); early education (M Ed); elementary education (M Ed); human resources (MBA); information security management (MBA); information technology and Web business development (MBA); management (MBA); public policy (MPA); social work (MA), including clinical social work; special education (M Ed); strategic leadership (MBA); teaching English (M Ed); teaching Spanish (M Ed).

Université de Montréal, Faculty of Arts and Sciences, Department of Computer Science and Operational Research, Montréal, QC H3C 3J7, Canada. Offers computer systems (M Sc, PhD); electronic commerce (M Sc). Part-time programs available. *Faculty:* 55 full-time (6 women), 6 part-time/adjunct (0 women). *Students:* 86 full-time (17 women), 121 part-time (30 women). 234 applicants, 25% accepted, 43 enrolled. In 2009, 26 master's, 15 doctorates awarded. Terminal master's awarded for partial completion of doctoral program. *Degree requirements:* For master's, one foreign language, thesis; for doctorate, one foreign language, thesis/dissertation, general exam. *Entrance requirements:* For master's, B Sc in related field; for doctorate, MA or M Sc in related field. *Application deadline:* For fall admission, 2/1 priority date for domestic students; for winter admission, 11/1 priority date for domestic students; for spring admission, 2/1 priority date for domestic students. Application fee: $100. Electronic applications accepted. *Financial support:* Available to part-time students. Application deadline: 10/31. *Faculty research:* Optimization statistics, programming languages, telecommunications, theoretical computer science, artificial intelligence. *Unit head:* Patrice Marcotte, Chairperson, 514-343-7090, Fax: 514-343-5834, E-mail: patrice.marcotte@umontreal.ca. *Application contact:* Jean-Yves Potvin, Responsible for Graduate Studies, 514-343-5746, Fax: 514-343-5834, E-mail: potvin@iro.umontreal.ca.

Université Laval, Faculty of Administrative Sciences, Programs in Business Administration, Québec, QC G1K 7P4, Canada. Offers accounting (MBA); agri-food management (MBA); electronic business (MBA, Diploma); factory management and logistics (MBA); finance (MBA); firm management (MBA); geomatic management (MBA); information technology management (MBA); international management (MBA); management (MBA); management accounting (MBA, Diploma); marketing (MBA); modeling and organizational decision (MBA); occupational health and safety management (MBA); pharmacy management (MBA); social and environmental responsibility (MBA); technological entrepreneurship (Diploma). *Accreditation:* AACSB. Part-time and evening/weekend programs available. Postbaccalaureate distance learning degree programs offered (no on-campus study). *Entrance requirements:* For master's and Diploma, knowledge of French and English. Electronic applications accepted.

University at Buffalo, the State University of New York, Graduate School, College of Arts and Sciences, Department of Economics, Buffalo, NY 14260. Offers economics (MA, MS, PhD); financial economics (Certificate); health services (Certificate); information and Internet economics (Certificate); international economics (Certificate); law and regulation (Certificate); urban and regional economics (Certificate). Part-time programs available. *Faculty:* 22 full-time (4 women), 2 part-time/adjunct (0 women). *Students:* 243 full-time (98 women); includes 19 minority (5 African Americans, 13 Asian Americans or Pacific Islanders, 1 Hispanic American), 183 international. Average age 25. 538 applicants, 44% accepted, 93 enrolled. In 2009, 83 master's, 6 doctorates, 5 other advanced degrees awarded. Terminal master's awarded for partial completion of doctoral program. *Degree requirements:* For master's, comprehensive exam; for doctorate, thesis/dissertation, field and theory exams. *Entrance requirements:* For master's and doctorate, GRE General Test. Additional exam requirements/recommendations for international students: Required—TOEFL (minimum score 550 paper-based; 213 computer-based; 79 iBT). *Application deadline:* For fall admission, 1/15 priority date for domestic and international students; for spring admission, 11/1 priority date for domestic and international students. Applications are processed on a rolling basis. Application fee: $50. Electronic applications accepted. *Financial support:* In 2009–10, 26 students received support, including 13 fellowships with full tuition reimbursements available (averaging $2,115 per year), 1 research assistantship with full tuition reimbursement available (averaging $13,220 per year), 12 teaching assistantships with full tuition reimbursements available (averaging.$13,220 per year); Federal Work-Study, health care benefits, and unspecified assistantships also available. Financial award application deadline: 2/15; financial award applicants required to submit FAFSA. *Faculty research:* International economics, econometrics, applied economics, urban economics, economic growth and development. *Unit head:* Dr. Isaac Ehrlich, Chair, 716-645-8670, Fax: 716-645-2127, E-mail: mgtehrl@buffalo.edu. *Application contact:* Dr. Nagesh Revankar, Director of Graduate Studies, 716-645-2121 Ext. 428, Fax: 716-645-2127, E-mail: ecorevan@buffalo.edu.

The University of Akron, Graduate School, College of Business Administration, Department of Management, Program in Electronic Business, Akron, OH 44325. Offers MBA. *Students:* 3 full-time (1 woman), 2 part-time (0 women), 2 international. Average age 28. 1 applicant, 100% accepted, 1 enrolled. In 2009, 1 master's awarded. *Entrance requirements:* For master's, GMAT, minimum GPA of 2.75, letters of recommendation, resume. Additional exam requirements/recommendations for international students: Required—TOEFL (minimum score 550 paper-based; 213 computer-based; 79 iBT). *Application deadline:* For fall admission, 8/1 for domestic and international students; for spring admission, 12/1 for domestic and international students. Applications are processed on a rolling basis. Application fee: $30 ($40 for international students). Electronic applications accepted. *Expenses:* Tuition, state resident: full-time $6570; part-time $365 per credit hour. Tuition, nonresident: full-time $11,250; part-time $625 per credit hour. *Unit head:* Dr. B. S. Vijayaraman, Head, 330-972-5442, E-mail: bsv@uakron.edu. *Application contact:* Dr. Susan Hanlon, Director of Graduate Business Programs, 330-972-7043, Fax: 330-972-6588, E-mail: shanlon@uakron.edu.

University of Dayton, Graduate School, School of Business Administration, Dayton, OH 45469-1300. Offers accounting (MBA); business intelligence (MBA); entrepreneurship (MBA); finance (MBA); international business (MBA); marketing (MBA); MIS (MBA); operations management (MBA); technology-enhanced business/e-commerce (MBA); JD/MBA. *Accreditation:* AACSB. Part-time and evening/weekend programs available. *Faculty:* 29 full-time (8 women), 15 part-time/adjunct (2 women). *Students:* 134 full-time (48 women), 111 part-time (31 women); includes 14 minority (9 African Americans, 3 Asian Americans or Pacific Islanders, 2 Hispanic Americans), 29 international. Average age 29. 179 applicants, 63% accepted, 73 enrolled. In 2009, 102 master's awarded. *Entrance requirements:* For master's, GMAT. Additional exam requirements/recommendations for international students: Required—TOEFL (minimum score 550 paper-based; 213 computer-based; 79 iBT). *Application deadline:* For fall admission, 3/1 priority date for international students; for winter admission, 7/1 priority date for international students; for spring admission, 1/1 priority date for international students. Applications are processed on a rolling basis. Application fee: $0 ($50 for international students). Electronic applications accepted. *Expenses:* Contact institution. *Financial support:* In 2009–10, 13 fellowships with partial tuition reimbursements, 17 research assistantships with full and partial tuition reimbursements (averaging $7,020 per year) were awarded; career-related internships or fieldwork, institutionally sponsored loans, scholarships/grants, health care benefits, and unspecified assistantships also available. Support available to part-time students. Financial award application deadline: 3/15; financial award applicants required to submit FAFSA. *Faculty research:* Management information systems, economics, finance, entrepreneurship, marketing. *Unit head:* Janice M. Glynn, Director, MBA Program, 937-229-3733, Fax: 937-229-3882, E-mail: glynn@udayton.edu. *Application contact:* Jeffrey Carter, Assistant Director, MBA Program, 937-229-3733, Fax: 937-229-3882, E-mail: jeff.carter@notes.udayton.edu.

University of Denver, Daniels College of Business, Department of Information Technology and Electronic Commerce, Denver, CO 80208. Offers IMBA, MBA. Part-time and evening/weekend programs available. *Faculty:* 6 full-time (1 woman). *Students:* 4 part-time (0 women). Average age 31. In 2009, 4 master's awarded. *Entrance requirements:* For master's, GMAT. *Application deadline:* For fall admission, 1/15 priority date for domestic students. Applications are processed on a rolling basis. Application fee: $50. Electronic applications accepted. *Expenses:* Tuition: Full-time $34,596; part-time $961 per quarter hour. Required fees: $4 per quarter hour. Tuition and fees vary according to course load, campus/location and program. *Financial support:* Career-related internships or fieldwork, Federal Work-Study, institutionally sponsored loans, and scholarships/grants available. Support available to part-time students. Financial award application deadline: 2/15. *Faculty research:* Cross-cultural research in information systems, electronic commerce, distributed project management, strategic information systems, management of emerging technologies. *Unit head:* Dr. Dick Scudder, Chair, 303-871-2197. *Application contact:* Information Contact, 303-871-3416, Fax: 303-871-4466, E-mail: daniels@du.edu.

University of Florida, Graduate School, Warrington College of Business Administration, Hough Graduate School of Business, Programs in Business Administration, Gainesville, FL 32611. Offers accounting (MBA); arts administration (MBA); business strategy and public policy (MBA); competitive strategy (MBA); decision and information sciences (MBA); electronic commerce (MBA); finance (MBA); general business (MBA); global management (MBA); Graham-Buffett security analysis (MBA); health administration (MBA); human resources management (MBA); international studies (MBA); Latin American business (MBA); management (MBA); marketing (MBA); sports administration (MBA); JD/MBA; MBA/MS; MBA/PhD; MBA/Pharm D; MD/MBA. *Accreditation:* AACSB. Part-time and evening/weekend programs available. Postbaccalaureate distance learning degree programs offered. *Entrance requirements:* For master's, GMAT, minimum GPA of 3.0, interview. Additional exam requirements/recommendations for international students: Required—TOEFL (minimum score 550 paper-based; 213 computer-based). Electronic applications accepted. *Faculty research:* Accounting, finance, insurance, management, real estate and urban analysis marketing.

University of Massachusetts Dartmouth, Graduate School, Charlton College of Business, Program in Business Administration, North Dartmouth, MA 02747-2300. Offers accounting (Postbaccalaureate Certificate); business administration (MBA); e-commerce (PMC); finance (PMC); general management (PMC); leadership (PMC); management (Postbaccalaureate Certificate); marketing (PMC); supply chain management (PMC). *Accreditation:* AACSB. Part-time programs available. *Faculty:* 42 full-time (13 women), 26 part-time/adjunct (6 women). *Students:* 93 full-time (41 women), 132 part-time (64 women); includes 22 minority (5 African Americans, 2 American Indian/Alaska Native, 6 Asian Americans or Pacific Islanders, 9 Hispanic Americans), 42 international. Average age 30. 186 applicants, 82% accepted, 94 enrolled. In 2009, 55 master's, 19 other advanced degrees awarded. *Entrance requirements:* For master's, GMAT, resume, letters of recommendation. Additional exam requirements/recommendations for international students: Required—TOEFL (minimum score 500 paper-based; 200 computer-based; 72 iBT). *Application deadline:* For fall admission, 6/1 for domestic students, 5/1 for international students; for spring admission, 10/1 for domestic students, 8/1 for international students. Application fee: $40 ($60 for international students). Electronic applications accepted. *Expenses:* Tuition, state resident: full-time $2071; part-time $86.29 per credit. Tuition, nonresident: full-time $8099; part-time $337.46 per credit. Required fees: $9446. Tuition and fees vary according to class time, course load and reciprocity agreements. *Financial support:* In 2009–10, 1 research assistantship with full tuition reimbursement (averaging $6,000 per year) was awarded; teaching assistantships, Federal Work-Study and unspecified assistantships also available. Support available to part-time students. Financial award application deadline: 3/1; financial award applicants required to submit FAFSA. *Faculty research:* Competitiveness of south coast enterprises, global sales, key performance indicators, agile manufacturing, green business. Total annual research expenditures: $19,000. *Unit head:* Dr. Norm Barber, Assistant Dean, 508-999-8543, E-mail: nbarber@umassd.edu. *Application contact:* Elan Turcotte-Shamski, Graduate Admissions Officer, 508-999-8604, Fax: 508-999-8183, E-mail: graduate@umassd.edu.

University of New Brunswick Saint John, Faculty of Business, Saint John, NB E2L 4L5, Canada. Offers administration (MBA); electronic commerce (MBA); international business (MBA); natural resource management (MBA). Part-time programs available. *Faculty:* 19 full-time (4 women), 14 part-time/adjunct (8 women). *Students:* 45 full-time (14 women), 18 part-time (8 women). 93 applicants, 78% accepted, 25 enrolled. In 2009, 45 master's awarded. *Entrance requirements:* For master's, GMAT, minimum GPA of 3.0. Additional exam requirements/recommendations for international students: Required—TOEFL (minimum score 580 paper-based; 237 computer-based), IELTS (minimum score 7), TWE (minimum score 4.5). *Application deadline:* For fall admission, 5/15 for domestic and international students. Applications are processed on a rolling basis. Application fee: $100. Electronic applications accepted. *Expenses:* Contact institution. *Financial support:* In 2009–10, 4 students received support. Career-related internships or fieldwork and scholarships/grants available. *Faculty research:* Business use of weblogs and podcasts to communicate, corporate governance, high-involvement work systems, international competitiveness, supply chain management and logistics. *Unit head:* Henryk Sterniczuk, Director of Graduate Studies, 506-648-5573, Fax: 506-648-5574, E-mail: sternicz@unbsj.ca. *Application contact:* Tammy Morin, Secretary, 506-648-5746, Fax: 506-648-5574, E-mail: tmorin@unbsj.ca.

University of Ottawa, Faculty of Graduate and Postdoctoral Studies, Interdisciplinary Programs, Ottawa, ON K1N 6N5, Canada. Offers e-business (Certificate); e-commerce (Certificate); finance (Certificate); health services and policies research (Diploma); population health (PhD); population health risk assessment and management (Certificate); public management and governance (Certificate); systems science (Certificate).

University of Ottawa, Faculty of Graduate and Postdoctoral Studies, Program in E-Business Technologies, Ottawa, ON K1N 6N5, Canada. Offers M Sc, MEBT. *Degree requirements:* For master's, thesis or alternative, project. *Entrance requirements:* For master's, honours degree or equivalent, minimum B average.

University of Phoenix–Austin Campus, College of Graduate Business and Management, Austin, TX 78759. Offers accounting (MBA); business administration (MBA); business and management (MBA); e-business (MBA); global management (MBA); human resources management (MBA, MM); management (MM); marketing (MBA); public administration (MBA). Postbaccalaureate distance learning degree programs offered.

University of Phoenix–Bay Area Campus, John Sperling School of Business, College of Information Systems and Technology, Pleasanton, CA 94588-3677. Offers e-business (MBA); information systems (MIS); technology management (MBA). Evening/weekend programs available. *Degree requirements:* For master's, thesis (for some programs). *Entrance requirements:* For master's, minimum undergraduate GPA of 3.0, 3 years of work experience. Additional exam requirements/recommendations for international students: Required—TOEFL (minimum score 550 paper-based; 213 computer-based; 79 iBT). Electronic applications accepted.

University of Phoenix–Chicago Campus, John Sperling School of Business, College of Information Systems and Technology, Schaumburg, IL 60173-4399. Offers e-business (MBA); information systems (MIS); management (MM); technology management (MBA). Evening/weekend programs available. *Degree requirements:* For master's, thesis (for some programs). *Entrance requirements:* For master's, 3 years of work experience, minimum undergraduate GPA of 3.0. Additional exam requirements/recommendations for international students: Required—TOEFL (minimum score 550 paper-based; 213 computer-based; 79 iBT). Electronic applications accepted.

University of Phoenix–Cincinnati Campus, John Sperling School of Business, College of Information Systems and Technology, West Chester, OH 45069-4875. Offers electronic business (MBA); information systems (MIS); technology management (MBA). Evening/weekend programs

Electronic Commerce

University of Phoenix–Cincinnati Campus *(continued)*
available. Postbaccalaureate distance learning degree programs offered. *Degree requirements:* For master's, thesis (for some programs). *Entrance requirements:* For master's, minimum undergraduate GPA of 2.5, 3 years of work experience. Additional exam requirements/recommendations for international students: Required—TOEFL (minimum score 550 paper-based; 213 computer-based; 79 iBT). Electronic applications accepted.

University of Phoenix–Columbus Georgia Campus, John Sperling School of Business, College of Information Systems and Technology, Columbus, GA 31904-6321. Offers e-business (MBA); information systems (MIS); technology management (MBA). Evening/weekend programs available. Postbaccalaureate distance learning degree programs offered. *Degree requirements:* For master's, thesis (for some programs). *Entrance requirements:* For master's, minimum undergraduate GPA of 3.0, 3 years of work experience. Additional exam requirements/recommendations for international students: Required—TOEFL (minimum score 550 paper-based; 213 computer-based; 79 iBT). Electronic applications accepted.

University of Phoenix–Dallas Campus, John Sperling School of Business, College of Information Systems and Technology, Dallas, TX 75251-2009. Offers e-business (MBA); information systems (MIS); technology management (MBA). Evening/weekend programs available. *Degree requirements:* For master's, thesis (for some programs). *Entrance requirements:* For master's, minimum undergraduate GPA of 3.0, 3 years of work experience. Additional exam requirements/recommendations for international students: Required—TOEFL (minimum score 550 paper-based; 213 computer-based; 79 iBT). Electronic applications accepted.

University of Phoenix–Denver Campus, John Sperling School of Business, College of Graduate Business and Management, Lone Tree, CO 80124-5453. Offers accountancy (MSA); accounting (MBA); business administration (MBA); e-business (MBA); global management (MBA); human resources management (MBA, MM); management (MM); marketing (MBA); public administration (MBA, MM). Evening/weekend programs available. Postbaccalaureate distance learning degree programs offered. *Degree requirements:* For master's, thesis (for some programs). *Entrance requirements:* For master's, minimum undergraduate GPA of 3.0, 3 years work experience. Additional exam requirements/recommendations for international students: Required—TOEFL (minimum score 550 paper-based; 213 computer-based; 79 iBT). Electronic applications accepted.

University of Phoenix–Denver Campus, John Sperling School of Business, College of Information Systems and Technology, Lone Tree, CO 80124-5453. Offers e-business (MBA); management (MIS); technology management (MBA). Evening/weekend programs available. Postbaccalaureate distance learning degree programs offered. *Degree requirements:* For master's, thesis (for some programs). *Entrance requirements:* For master's, minimum undergraduate GPA of 3.0, 3 years of work experience. Additional exam requirements/recommendations for international students: Required—TOEFL (minimum score 550 paper-based; 213 computer-based; 79 iBT). Electronic applications accepted.

University of Phoenix–Houston Campus, John Sperling School of Business, College of Information Systems and Technology, Houston, TX 77079-2004. Offers e-business (MBA); information systems (MIS); technology management (MBA). Evening/weekend programs available. Postbaccalaureate distance learning degree programs offered. *Degree requirements:* For master's, comprehensive exam (for some programs), thesis. *Entrance requirements:* For master's, minimum undergraduate GPA of 3.0, 3 years of work experience. Additional exam requirements/recommendations for international students: Required—TOEFL (minimum score 550 paper-based; 213 computer-based; 79 iBT). Electronic applications accepted.

University of Phoenix–Louisville Campus, College of Graduate Business and Management, Louisville, KY 40223-3839. Offers business administration (MBA); e-business (MBA); management (MM). Postbaccalaureate distance learning degree programs offered.

University of Phoenix–Madison Campus, College of Graduate Business and Management, Madison, WI 53718-2416. Offers accounting (MBA); business and management (MBA); e-business (MBA); global management (MBA); human resources management (MBA, MM); management (MM); marketing (MBA); public administration (MBA).

University of Phoenix–Maryland Campus, John Sperling School of Business, College of Graduate Business and Management, Columbia, MD 21045-5424. Offers accounting (MBA); business administration (MBA); e-business (MBA); global management (MBA); human resources management (MBA, MM); management (MM); marketing (MBA); public administration (MBA, MM). Evening/weekend programs available. *Degree requirements:* For master's, thesis (for some programs). *Entrance requirements:* For master's, minimum undergraduate GPA of 3.0, 3 years of work experience. Additional exam requirements/recommendations for international students: Required—TOEFL (minimum score 550 paper-based; 213 computer-based; 79 iBT). Electronic applications accepted.

University of Phoenix–Memphis Campus, College of Graduate Business and Management, Cordova, TN 38018. Offers accounting (MBA); business and management (MBA); e-business (MBA); global management (MBA); human resources management (MBA, MM); management (MM); marketing (MBA); public administration (MBA, MM).

University of Phoenix–New Mexico Campus, John Sperling School of Business, College of Information Systems and Technology, Albuquerque, NM 87113-1570. Offers e-business (MBA); information systems (MS); technology management (MBA). Evening/weekend programs available. *Degree requirements:* For master's, thesis (for some programs). *Entrance*

requirements: For master's, minimum undergraduate GPA of 3.0, 3 years of work experience. Additional exam requirements/recommendations for international students: Required—TOEFL (minimum score 550 paper-based; 213 computer-based; 79 iBT). Electronic applications accepted.

University of Phoenix–Northern Virginia Campus, College of Graduate Business and Management, Reston, VA 20190. Offers accounting (MBA); business administration (MBA); e-business (MBA); global management (MBA); human resources management (MBA, MM); management (MM); marketing (MBA); public administration (MBA).

University of Phoenix–Oklahoma City Campus, John Sperling School of Business, College of Information Systems and Technology, Oklahoma City, OK 73116-8244. Offers e-business (MBA); technology management (MBA). Evening/weekend programs available. *Degree requirements:* For master's, thesis (for some programs). *Entrance requirements:* For master's, minimum undergraduate GPA of 3.0, 3 years of work experience. Additional exam requirements/recommendations for international students: Required—TOEFL (minimum score 550 paper-based; 213 computer-based; 79 iBT). Electronic applications accepted.

University of Phoenix–Pittsburgh Campus, John Sperling School of Business, College of Information Systems and Technology, Pittsburgh, PA 15276. Offers e-business (MBA); information systems (MIS); technology management (MBA). Evening/weekend programs available. *Degree requirements:* For master's, thesis (for some programs). *Entrance requirements:* For master's, minimum undergraduate GPA of 3.0, 3 years work experience. Additional exam requirements/recommendations for international students: Required—TOEFL (minimum score 550 paper-based; 213 computer-based; 79 iBT). Electronic applications accepted.

University of Phoenix–Raleigh Campus, College of Graduate Business and Management, Raleigh, NC 27606. Offers accounting (MBA); business administration (MBA); e-business (MBA); global management (MBA); human resources management (MBA); marketing (MBA).

University of Phoenix–San Antonio Campus, College of Graduate Business and Management, San Antonio, TX 78230. Offers accounting (MBA); business administration (MBA); e-business (MBA); global management (MBA); human resources management (MBA, MM); management (MM); marketing (MBA); public administration (MBA, MM).

University of San Francisco, School of Business and Professional Studies, Masagung Graduate School of Management, Program in Business Administration, San Francisco, CA 94117-1080. Offers business economics (MBA); e-business (MBA); entrepreneurship (MBA); finance (MBA); international business (MBA); management (MBA); marketing (MBA); telecommunications management and policy (MBA); JD/MBA; MSN/MBA. *Accreditation:* AACSB. *Faculty:* 17 full-time (4 women), 16 part-time/adjunct (7 women). *Students:* 278 full-time (140 women), 18 part-time (10 women); includes 94 minority (5 African Americans, 1 American Indian/Alaska Native, 69 Asian Americans or Pacific Islanders, 19 Hispanic Americans), 53 international. Average age 30. 410 applicants, 70% accepted, 133 enrolled. In 2009, 137 master's awarded. *Entrance requirements:* For master's, GMAT, minimum undergraduate GPA of 3.2. Additional exam requirements/recommendations for international students: Required—TOEFL. *Application deadline:* For fall admission, 7/1 priority date for domestic students; for spring admission, 11/30 for domestic students. Applications are processed on a rolling basis. Application fee: $55 ($65 for international students). *Expenses:* Tuition: Full-time $19,710; part-time $1095 per unit. Part-time tuition and fees vary according to degree level, campus/location and program. *Financial support:* In 2009–10, 155 students received support; fellowships available. Financial award application deadline: 3/2; financial award applicants required to submit FAFSA. *Faculty research:* International financial markets, technology transfer licensing, international marketing, strategic planning. Total annual research expenditures: $50,000. *Unit head:* Kelly Brookes, Director, 415-422-2221, Fax: 415-422-6315. *Application contact:* Director, MBA Program, 415-422-2221, Fax: 415-422-6315, E-mail: mba@usfca.edu.

The University of Texas at Dallas, School of Management, Program in Management and Administrative Sciences, Richardson, TX 75080. Offers e-commerce (MS); health care management (MS); innovation and entrepreneurship (MS); organizations and strategy (MS). *Accreditation:* AACSB. Part-time and evening/weekend programs available. *Faculty:* 12 full-time (3 women), 13 part-time/adjunct (3 women). *Students:* 46 full-time (29 women), 103 part-time (47 women); includes 53 minority (12 African Americans, 34 Asian Americans or Pacific Islanders, 7 Hispanic Americans), 32 international. Average age 33. 156 applicants, 66% accepted, 47 enrolled. In 2009, 83 master's awarded. *Degree requirements:* For master's, thesis optional. *Entrance requirements:* For master's, GMAT. Additional exam requirements/recommendations for international students: Required—TOEFL (minimum score 550 paper-based; 213 computer-based). *Application deadline:* For fall admission, 7/15 for domestic students, 5/1 priority date for international students; for spring admission, 11/15 for domestic students, 9/1 priority date for international students. Applications are processed on a rolling basis. Application fee: $50 ($100 for international students). Electronic applications accepted. *Expenses:* Tuition, state resident: full-time $11,068; part-time $461 per credit hour. Tuition, nonresident: full-time $21,178; part-time $882 per credit hour. Tuition and fees vary according to course load. *Financial support:* In 2009–10, 25 teaching assistantships with full tuition reimbursements (averaging $14,400 per year) were awarded; fellowships, research assistantships, career-related internships or fieldwork, Federal Work-Study, institutionally sponsored loans, scholarships/grants, and unspecified assistantships also available. Support available to part-time students. Financial award application deadline: 4/30; financial award applicants required to submit FAFSA. *Faculty research:* Integrated and detailed knowledge of functional areas of management, analytical tools for effective appraisal and decision making. *Unit head:* Dr. Doug Eckel, Assistant Dean, 972-883-5923, E-mail: dogb.eckel@utdallas.edu. *Application contact:* James Parker, Assistant Director, 972-883-5842, E-mail: jparker@utdallas.edu.

Section 5
Entrepreneurship

This section contains a directory of institutions offering graduate work in entrepreneurship. Additional information about programs listed in the directory may be obtained by writing directly to the dean of a graduate school or chair of a department at the address given in the directory.

For programs offering related work, see also in this book *Business Administration and Management, International Business,* and *Education (Business Education).*

CONTENTS

Program Directory

Close-Up

Entrepreneurship

American College of Thessaloniki, Department of Business Administration, Pylea, Greece. Offers banking and finance (MBA); entrepreneurship (MBA, Certificate); finance (Certificate); management (MBA, Certificate); marketing (MBA, Certificate). Part-time and evening/weekend programs available. *Faculty:* 6 full-time (1 woman), 10 part-time/adjunct (2 women). *Students:* 6 full-time (3 women), 44 part-time (30 women), 17 international. 25 applicants, 96% accepted, 24 enrolled. *Degree requirements:* For master's, thesis. *Entrance requirements:* For master's, bachelor's degree. *Application deadline:* For fall admission, 9/30 priority date for domestic students; for spring admission, 2/18 priority date for domestic students. Applications are processed on a rolling basis. Application fee: $70. Electronic applications accepted. *Unit head:* Dr. Nikolaos Kourkoumelis, Chair, Business Division, 30-310-398386, E-mail: nikolaos@act.edu. *Application contact:* Elli Konstantinou, Director of Student Recruitment, 30-310-398238, E-mail: elli@act.edu.

American University, Kogod School of Business, Master of Business Administration Program, Washington, DC 20016-8044. Offers accounting (MBA); consulting (MBA), including information technology, international business, management; corporate finance: commercial banking (MBA); corporate finance: corporate financial management (MBA); corporate finance: investment banking (MBA), including corporate finance and private equity, trading and selling; entrepreneurship (MBA); global emerging markets (MBA), including business, finance, information technology; international trade and global supply chain management (MBA); leadership (MBA); marketing management (MBA); marketing research (MBA); real estate (MBA); MBA/JD; MBA/LL M. Part-time and evening/weekend programs available. *Faculty:* 14 full-time (6 women). *Students:* 133 full-time (56 women), 121 part-time (48 women); includes 54 minority (23 African Americans, 1 American Indian/Alaska Native, 16 Asian Americans or Pacific Islanders, 14 Hispanic Americans), 43 international. Average age 29. 539 applicants, 51% accepted, 86 enrolled. In 2009, 114 master's awarded. *Entrance requirements:* For master's, GMAT. Additional exam requirements/recommendations for international students: Required—TOEFL. *Application deadline:* For fall admission, 2/1 priority date for domestic students; for spring admission, 10/1 priority date for domestic students. Applications are processed on a rolling basis. Application fee: $100. *Expenses:* Contact institution. *Financial support:* In 2009–10, 19 students received support; fellowships, research assistantships with partial tuition reimbursements available, career-related internships or fieldwork, Federal Work-Study, and institutionally sponsored loans available. Support available to part-time students. Financial award application deadline: 2/1. *Faculty research:* Information technology, decision-aiding methodology, negotiation. *Unit head:* Dr. Stevan Holmberg, Chair, 202-885-6193, E-mail: sholmbe@american.edu. *Application contact:* Shannon Demko, Associate Director of Graduate Admissions, 202-885-1994, Fax: 202-885-1108, E-mail: demko@american.edu.

Andrew Jackson University, Brian Tracy College of Business and Entrepreneurship, Birmingham, AL 35244. Offers entrepreneurship (MBA); finance (MBA); health services management (MBA); hospitality and tourism management (MBA); human resource management (MBA); international business (MBA); management (MBA); marketing (MBA). Part-time and evening/weekend programs available. Postbaccalaureate distance learning degree programs offered (no on-campus study). *Entrance requirements:* For master's, course work in calculus, statistics, macroeconomics. Additional exam requirements/recommendations for international students: Required—TOEFL (minimum score 550 paper-based; 213 computer-based). Electronic applications accepted.

Babson College, F. W. Olin Graduate School of Business, Wellesley, Babson Park, MA 02457-0310. Offers accounting (MSA); advanced management (Certificate); business administration (MBA); global entrepreneurship (MS); technological entrepreneurship (MS). *Accreditation:* AACSB. Part-time and evening/weekend programs available. Postbaccalaureate distance learning degree programs offered (minimal on-campus study). *Faculty:* 144 full-time (37 women), 46 part-time/adjunct (10 women). *Students:* 503 full-time (171 women), 1,019 part-time (276 women); includes 221 minority (28 African Americans, 152 Asian Americans or Pacific Islanders, 41 Hispanic Americans), 285 international. Average age 32. 1,102 applicants, 57% accepted, 407 enrolled. In 2009, 712 master's, 2 other advanced degrees awarded. *Entrance requirements:* For master's, GMAT, 2 years of work experience, resume, letters of recommendation. Additional exam requirements/recommendations for international students: Required—TOEFL (minimum score 600 paper-based; 250 computer-based; 100 iBT). *Application deadline:* For fall admission, 4/15 priority date for domestic students, 1/15 priority date for international students. Application fee: $100. Electronic applications accepted. *Expenses:* Tuition: Full-time $40,600; part-time $1137 per credit. One-time fee: $1270. Full-time tuition and fees vary according to course load, program and student level. *Financial support:* In 2009–10, 317 students received support, including 43 fellowships (averaging $33,969 per year); career-related internships or fieldwork, Federal Work-Study, institutionally sponsored loans, scholarships/grants, and unspecified assistantships also available. Financial award application deadline: 4/15. *Faculty research:* Entrepreneurship, innovation and quality management, global management, e-commerce marketing, leadership and change management. Total annual research expenditures: $89,516. *Unit head:* Dr. Raghu Tadepalli, Dean, E-mail: rtadepalli@babson.edu. *Application contact:* Martha Snelling, Admission Services Team, 781-239-4317, Fax: 781-239-4194, E-mail: mbaadmission@babson.edu.

Bakke Graduate University, Programs in Pastoral Ministry and Business, Seattle, WA 98104. Offers business (MBA); global urban ministry (MA); social and civic entrepreneurship (MA); transformational leadership for the global city (D Min). Part-time programs available. Postbaccalaureate distance learning degree programs offered (minimal on-campus study). *Faculty:* 7 full-time (2 women), 30 part-time/adjunct (4 women). *Students:* 84 full-time (24 women), 284 part-time (74 women); includes 199 minority (99 African Americans, 1 American Indian/Alaska Native, 90 Asian Americans or Pacific Islanders, 9 Hispanic Americans). Average age 38. 41 applicants, 98% accepted, 25 enrolled. In 2009, 11 master's, 37 doctorates awarded. *Degree requirements:* For master's, thesis; for doctorate, thesis/dissertation. *Entrance requirements:* For master's, 2 years of ministry experience, BA in Biblical studies or theology; for doctorate, 3 years of ministry experience, M Div. Additional exam requirements/recommendations for international students: Required—TOEFL (minimum score 60 computer-based). *Application deadline:* For fall admission, 7/1 priority date for domestic students; for winter admission, 12/1 for domestic students; for spring admission, 3/15 for domestic students. Applications are processed on a rolling basis. Application fee: $75 ($25 for international students). Electronic applications accepted. *Expenses:* Tuition: Full-time $8000; part-time $2000 per course. Required fees: $175; $50 per course. *Financial support:* In 2009–10, 140 students received support. Scholarships/grants and tuition waivers (partial) available. Financial award applicants required to submit FAFSA. *Faculty research:* Theological systems, church management, worship. *Unit head:* Dr. Gwen Dewey, Academic Dean, 206-264-9100 Ext. 119, Fax: 206-264-8828, E-mail: gwend@bgu.edu. *Application contact:* Lauren Geiser, Assistant Registrar, 206-246-9100 Ext. 110, Fax: 206-264-8828, E-mail: laureng@bgu.edu.

Baldwin-Wallace College, Graduate Programs, Division of Business, Program in Entrepreneurship, Berea, OH 44017-2088. Offers MBA. Part-time and evening/weekend programs available. *Students:* 12 full-time (3 women), 26 part-time (8 women); includes 8 minority (6 African Americans, 1 Asian American or Pacific Islander, 1 Hispanic American), 2 international. Average age 34. 8 applicants, 63% accepted, 1 enrolled. In 2009, 8 master's awarded. *Entrance requirements:* For master's, GMAT, bachelor's degree in any field, work experience, minimum GPA of 3.0. Additional exam requirements/recommendations for international students: Required—TOEFL (minimum score 523 paper-based; 193 computer-based; 70 iBT). *Application deadline:* For fall admission, 7/25 priority date for domestic students, 4/30 priority date for international students; for spring admission, 12/15 priority date for domestic students, 9/30 priority date for international students. Applications are processed on a rolling basis. Application fee: $25. Electronic applications accepted. *Expenses:* Tuition: Full-time $14,174; part-time $682 per credit. Tuition and fees vary according to program. *Financial support:* Career-related internships or fieldwork available. Support available to part-time students. Financial award application deadline: 5/1. *Unit head:* Ven Ochaya, Director, 440-826-2392, Fax: 440-826-3868, E-mail: vochaya@bw.edu. *Application contact:* Peggy Shepard, Graduate Business Coordinator, 440-826-2196, Fax: 440-826-3868, E-mail: pshepard@bw.edu.

Bay Path College, Program in Entrepreneurial Thinking and Innovative Practices, Longmeadow, MA 01106-2292. Offers MBA. Part-time and evening/weekend programs available. *Entrance requirements:* Additional exam requirements/recommendations for international students: Recommended—TOEFL (minimum score 500 paper-based). Electronic applications accepted.

Benedictine University, Graduate Programs, Program in Business Administration, Lisle, IL 60532-0900. Offers accounting (MBA); entrepreneurship and managing innovation (MBA); financial management (MBA); health administration (MBA); human resource management (MBA); information systems security (MBA); international business (MBA); management consulting (MBA); management information systems (MBA); marketing management (MBA); operations management and logistics (MBA); organizational leadership (MBA); MBA/MPH; MBA/MS. Part-time and evening/weekend programs available. Postbaccalaureate distance learning degree programs offered (minimal on-campus study). *Faculty:* 4 full-time (2 women), 24 part-time/adjunct (3 women). *Students:* 247 full-time (141 women), 644 part-time (339 women); includes 223 minority (134 African Americans, 5 American Indian/Alaska Native, 44 Asian Americans or Pacific Islanders, 40 Hispanic Americans), 25 international. Average age 34. 287 applicants, 92% accepted, 229 enrolled. In 2009, 219 master's awarded. *Entrance requirements:* For master's, GMAT. Additional exam requirements/recommendations for international students: Required—TOEFL (minimum score 550 paper-based; 213 computer-based). *Application deadline:* For fall admission, 9/1 for domestic students; for winter admission, 12/1 for domestic students; for spring admission, 2/15 for domestic students. Applications are processed on a rolling basis. Application fee: $40. Electronic applications accepted. *Expenses:* Tuition: Part-time $750 per credit hour. Tuition and fees vary according to campus/location and program. *Financial support:* Career-related internships or fieldwork and health care benefits available. Support available to part-time students. *Faculty research:* Strategic leadership in professional organizations, sociology of professions, organizational change, social identity theory, applications to change management. *Unit head:* Dr. Sharon Borowicz, Director, 630-829-6219, E-mail: sborowicz@ben.edu. *Application contact:* Kari Gibbons, Director, Admissions, 630-829-6200, Fax: 630-829-6584, E-mail: kgibbons@ben.edu.

Bernard M. Baruch College of the City University of New York, Zicklin School of Business, Department of Management, New York, NY 10010-5585. Offers entrepreneurship (MBA); general management and policy (MBA); human resources management (MBA); management planning systems (PhD); management science (MBA); organization and policy studies (PhD); organizational behavior (MBA). Part-time and evening/weekend programs available. *Degree requirements:* For doctorate, comprehensive exam, thesis/dissertation. *Entrance requirements:* For master's, GMAT, 2 letters of recommendation, resume, 2 years of work experience; for doctorate, GMAT. Additional exam requirements/recommendations for international students: Required—TOEFL (minimum score 590 paper-based; 243 computer-based), TWE.

Boston University, School of Management, Master of Business Administration Program, Boston, MA 02215. Offers entrepreneurship (MBA); finance (MBA); health sector management (MBA); international management (MBA); marketing (MBA); operations and technology management (MBA); public and nonprofit management (MBA); strategy and business analysis (MBA); JD/MBA; MBA/MA; MBA/MPH; MBA/MS; MBA/MSIS; MS/MBA. Part-time and evening/weekend programs available. *Faculty:* 119 full-time (31 women), 99 part-time/adjunct (30 women). *Students:* 326 full-time (138 women), 677 part-time (257 women); includes 149 minority (13 African Americans, 119 Asian Americans or Pacific Islanders, 17 Hispanic Americans), 149 international. Average age 30. 1,617 applicants, 38% accepted, 317 enrolled. In 2009, 284 master's awarded. *Entrance requirements:* For master's, GMAT, resume, 2 letters of recommendation. Additional exam requirements/recommendations for international students: Required—TOEFL or IELTS. *Application deadline:* For fall admission, 3/15 for domestic and international students; for spring admission, 11/15 for domestic students. Application fee: $125. Electronic applications accepted. *Expenses:* Tuition: Full-time $37,910; part-time $1184 per credit hour. Required fees: $386; $40 per semester. Part-time tuition and fees vary according to class time, course level, degree level and program. *Financial support:* Career-related internships or fieldwork, Federal Work-Study, institutionally sponsored loans, and scholarships/grants available. Support available to part-time students. Financial award applicants required to submit FAFSA. *Unit head:* Katherine Nolan, Assistant Dean, Graduate Programs, 617-353-4157, Fax: 617-353-5003, E-mail: mba@bu.edu. *Application contact:* Hayden Estrada, Assistant Dean, Admissions, 617-353-2670, Fax: 617-353-7368, E-mail: mba@bu.edu.

Brandeis University, Graduate School of Arts and Sciences, Program in Computer Science and IT Entrepreneurship, Waltham, MA 02454-9110. Offers MA. Part-time programs available. *Entrance requirements:* For master's, official transcript(s), 3 letters of recommendation, curriculum vitae or resume, statement of purpose. Additional exam requirements/recommendations for international students: Required—TOEFL (minimum score 600 paper-based; 250 computer-based; 100 iBT); Recommended—IELTS (minimum score 7). *Application deadline:* Applications are processed on a rolling basis. Application fee: $75. Electronic applications accepted. *Financial support:* Scholarships/grants available. Financial award application deadline: 4/15; financial award applicants required to submit FAFSA. *Faculty research:* Software development, IT entrepreneurship, business, computer science. *Unit head:* Prof. Fernando Colon Osorio, 781-736-4586, E-mail: fcco@brandeis.edu. *Application contact:* David F. Cotter, Assistant Dean, Graduate School of Arts and Sciences, 781-736-3410, Fax: 781-736-3412, E-mail: gradschool@brandeis.edu.

California Intercontinental University, School of Business, Diamond Bar, CA 91765. Offers banking and finance (MBA); entrepreneurship and business management (DBA); global business leadership (DBA); international management and marketing (MBA); organizational management and human resource management (MBA).

California Lutheran University, Graduate Studies, School of Business, Thousand Oaks, CA 91360-2787. Offers business (IMBA); entrepreneurship (MBA, Certificate); finance (MBA, Certificate); financial planning (MBA, Certificate); information systems and technology (MS); information technology management (MBA, Certificate); international business (MBA, Certificate); management and organization behavior (MBA); management and organizational behavior (Certificate); marketing (MBA, Certificate). Evening/weekend programs available. Postbaccalaureate distance learning degree programs offered. *Entrance requirements:* For master's, GMAT, interview, minimum GPA of 3.0. *Expenses:* Contact institution.

California State University, East Bay, Graduate Programs, College of Business and Economics, Department of Marketing, Option in Entrepreneurship, Hayward, CA 94542-3000. Offers MBA. *Entrance requirements:* Additional exam requirements/recommendations for international students: Required—TOEFL (minimum score 550 paper-based; 213 computer-based). *Application deadline:* For fall admission, 6/30 for domestic and international students. *Financial support:* Career-related internships or fieldwork, Federal Work-Study, institutionally sponsored loans, and scholarships/grants available. Support available to part-time students. Financial award applicants required to submit FAFSA. *Unit head:* Dr. Nan Maxwell, Chair, 510-885-4336, Fax: 510-885-4796, E-mail: nan.maxwell@csueastbay.edu. *Application contact:* Donna Wiley, Interim Associate Director, 510-885-2928, Fax: 510-885-4777, E-mail: donna.wiley@csueastbay.edu.

California State University, Fullerton, Graduate Studies, College of Business and Economics, Department of Management, Fullerton, CA 92834-9480. Offers entrepreneurship (MBA); management (MBA). *Accreditation:* AACSB. Part-time programs available. *Students:* 31 full-time (17 women), 42 part-time (13 women); includes 30 minority (2 African Americans, 1 American Indian/Alaska Native, 15 Asian Americans or Pacific Islanders, 12 Hispanic Americans), 12 international. Average age 29. 94 applicants, 36% accepted, 21 enrolled. In 2009, 23 master's

awarded. *Degree requirements:* For master's, project or thesis. *Entrance requirements:* For master's, GMAT, minimum AACSB index of 950. Application fee: $55. *Expenses:* Tuition, nonresident: full-time $11,160; part-time $373 per credit. Required fees: $1440 per term. Tuition and fees vary according to course load, degree level and program. *Financial support:* Career-related internships or fieldwork, Federal Work-Study, institutionally sponsored loans, and scholarships/grants available. Support available to part-time students. Financial award application deadline: 3/1; financial award applicants required to submit FAFSA. *Unit head:* Dr. Ellen Dumond, Chair, 657-278-2251. *Application contact:* Admissions/Applications, 657-278-2371.

Cambridge College, School of Management, Cambridge, MA 02138-5304. Offers business negotiation and conflict resolution (M Mgt); general business (M Mgt); health care informatics (M Mgt); health care management (M Mgt); leadership in human and organizational dynamics (M Mgt); non-profit and public organization management (M Mgt); small business development (M Mgt); technology management (M Mgt). Part-time and evening/weekend programs available. *Faculty:* 4 full-time (3 women), 65 part-time/adjunct (32 women). *Students:* 297 full-time (178 women), 234 part-time (155 women); includes 217 minority (122 African Americans, 53 Asian Americans or Pacific Islanders, 42 Hispanic Americans), 135 international. Average age 39. In 2009, 259 master's awarded. *Degree requirements:* For master's, thesis, seminars. *Entrance requirements:* For master's, resume, 2 professional references. Additional exam requirements/recommendations for international students: Required—TOEFL (minimum score 550 paper-based; 213 computer-based; 79 iBT); Recommended—IELTS (minimum score 6). *Application deadline:* Applications are processed on a rolling basis. Application fee: $30. Electronic applications accepted. *Expenses:* Contact institution. *Financial support:* In 2009–10, 170 students received support. Career-related internships or fieldwork, Federal Work-Study, and scholarships/grants available. Financial award applicants required to submit FAFSA. *Faculty research:* Negotiation, mediation and conflict resolution; leadership; management of diverse organizations; case studies and simulation methodologies for management education, digital as a second language: social networking for digital immigrants. *Unit head:* Dr. Mary Ann Joseph, Acting Dean, 617-873-0227, E-mail: maryann.joseph@cambridgecollege.edu. *Application contact:* Stephen Lyons, Director of Enrollment, Graduate and N.I.T.E. Programs, 617-868-1000, Fax: 617-349-3561, E-mail: stephen.lyons@cambridgecollege.edu.

Cameron University, Office of Graduate Studies, Program in Entrepreneurial Studies, Lawton, OK 73505-6377. Offers MS. Part-time and evening/weekend programs available. Postbaccalaureate distance learning degree programs offered (no on-campus study). *Degree requirements:* For master's, comprehensive exam. *Entrance requirements:* Additional exam requirements/recommendations for international students: Required—TOEFL (minimum score 550 paper-based; 213 computer-based). Electronic applications accepted. *Faculty research:* Entrepreneurial competition, new venture creation, legal issues, electronic commerce.

Carlos Albizu University, Miami Campus, Graduate Programs, Miami, FL 33172-2209. Offers clinical psychology (Psy D); entrepreneurship (MBA); exceptional student education (MS); industrial/organizational psychology (MS); marriage and family therapy (MS); mental health counseling (MS); nonprofit management (MBA); organizational management (MBA); psychology (MS); school counseling (MS); teaching English as a second language (MS). *Accreditation:* APA. Part-time and evening/weekend programs available. *Faculty:* 23 full-time (13 women), 41 part-time/adjunct (21 women). *Students:* 529 full-time (420 women), 171 part-time (139 women); includes 551 minority (55 African Americans, 1 American Indian/Alaska Native, 5 Asian Americans or Pacific Islanders, 490 Hispanic Americans). Average age 37. 278 applicants, 57% accepted, 142 enrolled. In 2009, 139 master's, 26 doctorates awarded. Terminal master's awarded for partial completion of doctoral program. *Degree requirements:* For master's, one foreign language, comprehensive exam, integrative project (MBA), research project (exceptional student education, teaching English as a second language); for doctorate, one foreign language, comprehensive exam, internship, project. *Entrance requirements:* For master's, 3 letters of recommendation, interview, minimum GPA of 3.0, resume; for doctorate, 3 letters of recommendation, minimum GPA of 3.0, resume, interview. *Application deadline:* For fall admission, 8/1 priority date for domestic students; for spring admission, 11/30 priority date for domestic students. Applications are processed on a rolling basis. Application fee: $50. Electronic applications accepted. *Expenses:* Tuition: Full-time $9090; part-time $505 per credit hour. Required fees: $298 per term. Tuition and fees vary according to course load, degree level and program. *Financial support:* In 2009–10, 127 students received support. Federal Work-Study, scholarships/grants, and tuition discounts available. Financial award application deadline: 6/1; financial award applicants required to submit FAFSA. *Faculty research:* Psychotherapy, forensic psychology, neuropsychology, marketing strategy, entrepreneurship, special education. *Unit head:* Dr. Carmen S. Roca, Chancellor, 305-593-1223 Ext. 120, Fax: 305-629-8052, E-mail: croca@albizu.edu. *Application contact:* Annalye Alonso, Secretary, 305-593-1223 Ext. 137, Fax: 305-593-1854, E-mail: aalonso@albizu.edu.

Carnegie Mellon University, College of Humanities and Social Sciences, Department of Social and Decision Sciences, Pittsburgh, PA 15213-3891. Offers behavioral decision research (PhD); behavioral decision research and psychology (PhD); social and decision science (PhD); strategy, entrepreneurship, and technological change (PhD). Terminal master's awarded for partial completion of doctoral program. *Degree requirements:* For doctorate, comprehensive exam, thesis/dissertation, research paper. *Entrance requirements:* For doctorate, GRE General Test. Additional exam requirements/recommendations for international students: Required—TOEFL. Electronic applications accepted. *Faculty research:* Organization theory, political science, sociology, technology studies.

Columbia University, Graduate School of Business, MBA Program, New York, NY 10027. Offers accounting (MBA); decision, risk, and operations (MBA); entrepreneurship (MBA); finance and economics (MBA); healthcare and pharmaceutical management (MBA); human resource management (MBA); international business (MBA); leadership and ethics (MBA); management (MBA); marketing (MBA); media (MBA); private equity (MBA); real estate (MBA); social enterprise (MBA); value investing (MBA); DDS/MBA; JD/MBA; MBA/MIA; MBA/MPH; MBA/MS; MD/MBA. *Faculty:* 149 full-time (23 women), 134 part-time/adjunct (16 women). *Students:* 1,293 full-time (435 women); includes 235 minority (65 African Americans, 4 American Indian/Alaska Native, 135 Asian Americans or Pacific Islanders, 31 Hispanic Americans), 417 international. Average age 28. 6,885 applicants, 15% accepted, 737 enrolled. In 2009, 696 master's awarded. *Entrance requirements:* For master's, GMAT, 2 letters of recommendation. Additional exam requirements/recommendations for international students: Required—TOEFL. *Application deadline:* For fall admission, 4/14 for domestic students; 3/3 for international students; for spring admission, 10/7 for domestic and international students. Applications are processed on a rolling basis. Application fee: $250. Electronic applications accepted. *Expenses:* Contact institution. *Financial support:* In 2009–10, 358 students received support, including 101 fellowships (averaging $23,250 per year); research assistantships, teaching assistantships, career-related internships or fieldwork, institutionally sponsored loans, and scholarships/grants also available. Financial award application deadline: 3/1; financial award applicants required to submit CSS PROFILE or FAFSA. *Faculty research:* Human decision making and behavioral research; real estate market and mortgage defaults; financial crisis and corporate governance; international business; security analysis and accounting. *Unit head:* Prof. Amir Ziv, Vice Dean of Students and the MBA Program, 212-854-3485, Fax: 212-932-0545, E-mail: az50@columbia.edu. *Application contact:* Mary J. Miller, Assistant Dean of Admissions, 212-854-1961, Fax: 212-662-6754, E-mail: apply@gsb.columbia.edu.

Dallas Baptist University, College of Business, Business Administration Program, Dallas, TX 75211-9299. Offers accounting (MBA); business communication (MBA); conflict resolution management (MBA); e-business (MBA); entrepreneurship (MBA); finance (MBA); health care management (MBA); international business (MBA); leading the non-profit organization (MBA); management (MBA); management information systems (MBA); marketing (MBA); project management (MBA); technology and engineering management (MBA). *Accreditation:* ACBSP. Part-time and evening/weekend programs available. *Entrance requirements:* For master's, GMAT, minimum GPA of 3.0. Additional exam requirements/recommendations for international students: Required—TOEFL, IELTS. Electronic applications accepted. *Expenses:* Tuition:

Full-time $10,674; part-time $593 per credit hour. *Faculty research:* Sports management, services marketing, retailing, strategic management, financial planning/investments.

DePaul University, Charles H. Kellstadt Graduate School of Business, Department of Management, Chicago, IL 60604-2287. Offers entrepreneurship (MBA); health sector management (MBA); human resource management (MBA, MSHR); leadership/change management (MBA); management planning and strategy (MBA); operations management (MBA). Part-time and evening/weekend programs available. *Faculty:* 36 full-time (7 women), 35 part-time/adjunct (16 women). *Students:* 284 full-time (115 women), 147 part-time (69 women); includes 75 minority (20 African Americans, 1 American Indian/Alaska Native, 37 Asian Americans or Pacific Islanders, 17 Hispanic Americans), 18 international. In 2009, 112 master's awarded. *Entrance requirements:* For master's, GMAT, GRE (MSHR), 2 letters of recommendation, resume. Additional exam requirements/recommendations for international students: Required—TOEFL (minimum score 550 paper-based; 213 computer-based). *Application deadline:* For fall admission, 7/1 for domestic students; for winter admission, 10/1 for domestic students; for spring admission, 2/1 for domestic students. Applications are processed on a rolling basis. Application fee: $60. Electronic applications accepted. *Expenses:* Tuition: Full-time $37,525; part-time $620 per credit hour. *Financial support:* Research assistantships available. Financial award application deadline: 4/1. *Faculty research:* Growth management, creativity and innovation, quality management and business process design, entrepreneurship. *Application contact:* Christopher E. Kinsella, Director of Cohort MBA Programs, 312-362-8810, Fax: 312-362-6677, E-mail: kgsb@depaul.edu.

Eastern Michigan University, Graduate School, College of Business, Programs in Business Administration, Ypsilanti, MI 48197. Offers business administration (MBA, Graduate Certificate); computer information systems (Graduate Certificate); e-business (MBA, Graduate Certificate); enterprise business intelligence (MBA); entrepreneurship (MBA, Graduate Certificate); finance (MBA, Graduate Certificate); human resources (MBA); human resources management (Graduate Certificate); information systems (MBA); internal auditing (MBA); international business (MBA, Graduate Certificate); marketing management (Graduate Certificate); nonprofit management (MBA); organizational development (Graduate Certificate); supply chain management (MBA, Graduate Certificate). *Accreditation:* AACSB. Part-time programs available. Postbaccalaureate distance learning degree programs offered (no on-campus study). *Students:* 166 full-time (80 women), 439 part-time (231 women); includes 150 minority (103 African Americans, 7 American Indian/Alaska Native, 31 Asian Americans or Pacific Islanders, 9 Hispanic Americans), 97 international. Average age 34. In 2009, 3 other advanced degrees awarded. *Entrance requirements:* For master's, GMAT (minimum score 450), minimum cumulative undergraduate GPA of 2.75. Additional exam requirements/recommendations for international students: Required—TOEFL. *Application deadline:* For fall admission, 5/15 for domestic students, 5/1 for international students; for winter admission, 10/15 for domestic students, 10/1 for international students; for spring admission, 3/15 for domestic students, 3/1 for international students. Applications are processed on a rolling basis. Application fee: $35. Tuition and fees vary according to course level. *Financial support:* Fellowships, research assistantships with full tuition reimbursements, teaching assistantships with full tuition reimbursements, career-related internships or fieldwork, Federal Work-Study, institutionally sponsored loans, scholarships/grants, tuition waivers (partial), and unspecified assistantships available. Support available to part-time students. Financial award applicants required to submit FAFSA. *Unit head:* K. Michelle Henry, Director of Academic Services, 734-487-4444, Fax: 734-483-1316, E-mail: cob.grad@emich.edu. *Application contact:* Beste Windes, Advisor, 734-487-4444, Fax: 734-483-1316, E-mail: cob.grad@emich.edu.

Fairleigh Dickinson University, College at Florham, Silberman College of Business, Departments of Management, Marketing, and Entrepreneurial Studies, Program in Entrepreneurial Studies, Madison, NJ 07940-1099. Offers MBA, Certificate. *Students:* 4 full-time (2 women), 9 part-time (2 women), 1 international. Average age 29. 8 applicants, 63% accepted, 2 enrolled. In 2009, 2 master's awarded. *Application deadline:* Applications are processed on a rolling basis. Application fee: $40.

Fairleigh Dickinson University, Metropolitan Campus, Silberman College of Business, Departments of Management, Marketing, and Entrepreneurial Studies, Program in Entrepreneurial Studies, Teaneck, NJ 07666-1914. Offers MBA, Certificate. *Students:* 6 full-time (2 women), 5 part-time (1 woman), 6 international. Average age 26. 16 applicants, 50% accepted, 4 enrolled. In 2009, 3 master's awarded. *Application deadline:* Applications are processed on a rolling basis. Application fee: $40. *Application contact:* Susan Brooman, University Director of Graduate Admissions, 201-692-2554, Fax: 201-692-2560, E-mail: globaleducation@fdu.edu.

Felician College, Program in Business, Lodi, NJ 07644-2117. Offers accounting (MBA); business administration (MBA); innovation and entrepreneurship (MBA); management (MBA). Part-time and evening/weekend programs available. *Students:* 3 full-time (2 women), 80 part-time (46 women); includes 16 minority (8 African Americans, 3 Asian Americans or Pacific Islanders, 5 Hispanic Americans), 5 international. 28 applicants, 89% accepted, 24 enrolled. *Entrance requirements:* For master's, GMAT. *Application deadline:* Applications are processed on a rolling basis. Application fee: $40. *Unit head:* Dr. Beth Castiglia, Dean, Division of Business and Management Services, 201-559-6140, E-mail: mctaggartp@felician.edu. *Application contact:* Tamara Vaughn, Senior Assistant Director, Graduate Admissions, 201-559-6097, Fax: 201-559-6138, E-mail: vaughant@felician.edu.

See Close-Up on page 243.

Florida Atlantic University, College of Business, Department of Management Programs, Boca Raton, FL 33431-0991. Offers global entrepreneurship (MBA); international business (MBA, MS); management (PhD). *Faculty:* 24 full-time (9 women), 9 part-time/adjunct (3 women). *Students:* 286 full-time (123 women), 452 part-time (206 women); includes 238 minority (79 African Americans, 1 American Indian/Alaska Native, 53 Asian Americans or Pacific Islanders, 105 Hispanic Americans), 52 international. Average age 32. 677 applicants, 49% accepted, 98 enrolled. In 2009, 221 master's, 7 doctorates awarded. *Entrance requirements:* For master's, GMAT or GRE General Test, minimum GPA of 3.0 in last 60 hours of course work. Additional exam requirements/recommendations for international students: Required—TOEFL (minimum score 600 paper-based; 250 computer-based). *Application deadline:* For fall admission, 7/25 for domestic students, 2/15 for international students; for spring admission, 12/10 for domestic students, 7/15 for international students. Applications are processed on a rolling basis. Application fee: $30. Electronic applications accepted. *Expenses:* Tuition, state resident: full-time $7055; part-time $293.94 per credit hour. Tuition, nonresident: full-time $22,096; part-time $920.66 per credit hour. *Financial support:* Research assistantships with full tuition reimbursements, career-related internships or fieldwork, tuition waivers (partial), and unspecified assistantships available. *Faculty research:* Sports administration, healthcare, policy, finance, real estate, senior living. *Unit head:* Dr. Peggy Golden, Chair, 561-297-2675, E-mail: golden@fau.edu. *Application contact:* Dr. Peggy Golden, Chair, 561-297-2675, E-mail: golden@fau.edu.

George Mason University, College of Visual and Performing Arts, Program in Arts Management, Fairfax, VA 22030. Offers arts entrepreneurship (Certificate); arts management (MA); fund raising and development in the arts (Certificate); public relations and marketing in the arts (Certificate); special events management in the arts (Certificate). *Faculty:* 1 (woman) full-time, 3 part-time/adjunct (2 women). *Students:* 39 full-time (37 women), 48 part-time (40 women); includes 7 minority (4 African Americans, 2 Asian Americans or Pacific Islanders, 1 Hispanic American), 11 international. Average age 30. 76 applicants, 71% accepted, 37 enrolled. In 2009, 27 master's awarded. *Entrance requirements:* For master's, GRE (recommended), minimum GPA of 3.0, 2 letters of recommendation, personal interview, resume, work experience. Additional exam requirements/recommendations for international students: Required—TOEFL. *Application deadline:* For fall admission, 3/1 priority date for domestic students; for spring admission, 10/1 for domestic students. Applications are processed on a rolling basis. Application fee: $75. Electronic applications accepted. *Expenses:* Tuition, state resident: full-time $7568; part-time $315.33 per credit hour. Tuition, nonresident: full-time $21,704; part-time $904.33 per credit hour. Required fees: $2184; $91 per credit hour. *Financial*

Entrepreneurship

George Mason University (continued)

support: Application deadline: 3/1. *Faculty research:* Information technology for arts managers, special topics in arts management, directions in gallery management, arts in society, public relations/marketing strategies for art organizations. *Unit head:* William Reeder, Dean, 703-993-8624, Fax: 703-993-8883. *Application contact:* Richard Kamenitzer, Director, 703-993-9194, E-mail: rkamenit@gmu.edu.

Georgia Institute of Technology, Graduate Studies and Research, College of Management, Program in Business Administration, Atlanta, GA 30332-0001. Offers accounting (MBA); e-commerce (Certificate); engineering entrepreneurship (MBA); entrepreneurship (Certificate); finance (MBA); information technology management (MBA); international business (MBA, Certificate); management of technology (Certificate); marketing (MBA); operations management (MBA); organizational behavior (MBA); strategic management (MBA). *Accreditation:* AACSB.

Georgia State University, J. Mack Robinson College of Business, Department of Managerial Sciences, Atlanta, GA 30302-3083. Offers business analysis (MBA, MS); decision sciences (PhD); entrepreneurship (MBA); human resources management (MBA, MS); management (MBA, PhD); operations management (MBA, MS); organization change (MS); personnel employee relations (PhD); strategic management (PhD). Part-time and evening/weekend programs available. *Degree requirements:* For doctorate, thesis/dissertation. *Entrance requirements:* For master's and doctorate, GMAT. Additional exam requirements/recommendations for international students: Required—TOEFL (minimum score 610 paper-based; 255 computer-based; 101 iBT). Electronic applications accepted. *Faculty research:* Abusive supervision, entrepreneurship, time series and neural networks, organizational controls, inventory control systems.

Georgia State University, J. Mack Robinson College of Business, Program in General Business Administration, Atlanta, GA 30302-3083. Offers accounting/information systems (MBA); economics (MBA, MS); enterprise risk management (MBA); general business (MBA); general business administration (EMBA, PMBA); information systems consulting (MBA); information systems risk management (MBA); international business and information technology (MBA); international entrepreneurship (MBA); MBA/JD. *Accreditation:* AACSB. Part-time and evening/weekend programs available. *Entrance requirements:* For master's, GMAT. Additional exam requirements/recommendations for international students: Required—TOEFL (minimum score 610 paper-based; 255 computer-based; 101 iBT). Electronic applications accepted.

Harrisburg University of Science and Technology, Program in Information Systems Engineering and Management, Harrisburg, PA 17101. Offers digital government specialization (MS); digital health specialization (MS); entrepreneurship specialization (MS). Part-time programs available. *Faculty:* 1 full-time (0 women), 2 part-time/adjunct (0 women). *Degree requirements:* For master's, comprehensive exam, thesis optional. *Entrance requirements:* Additional exam requirements/recommendations for international students: Required—TOEFL (minimum score 520 paper-based; 200 computer-based; 80 iBT). *Application deadline:* For fall admission, 8/1 priority date for domestic students, 7/1 priority date for international students. Applications are processed on a rolling basis. Application fee: $0. Electronic applications accepted. *Expenses:* Tuition: Full-time $18,000; part-time $650 per semester hour. *Financial support:* Scholarships/grants available. Financial award applicants required to submit FAFSA. *Unit head:* Dr. Amjad Umar, Director and Professor, 717-901-5141, Fax: 717-901-3141, E-mail: aumar@harrisburgu.edu. *Application contact:* Julie Cullings, Information Contact, 717-901-5163, Fax: 717-901-3163, E-mail: admissions@harrisburgu.edu.

Hult International Business School, Program in Business Administration—Hult London Campus, London, MA WC 1B 4JP, United Kingdom. Offers entrepreneurship (MBA); international business (MBA); international finance (MBA); marketing (MBA). Part-time programs available. *Degree requirements:* For master's, comprehensive exam, thesis, internship. *Entrance requirements:* Additional exam requirements/recommendations for international students: Required—TOEFL (minimum score 580 paper-based; 237 computer-based), TWE (minimum score 5). Electronic applications accepted.

Inter American University of Puerto Rico, San Germán Campus, Graduate Studies Center, Program in Entrepreneurial and Managerial Development, San Germán, PR 00683-5008. Offers interregional and international business (PhD). Part-time and evening/weekend programs available. *Degree requirements:* For doctorate, comprehensive exam, thesis/dissertation. *Entrance requirements:* For doctorate, EXADEP or GMAT, minimum graduate GPA of 3.25.

The International University of Monaco, Graduate Programs, Monte Carlo, Monaco. Offers entrepreneurship (EMBA, MBA); financial engineering (M Sc); hedge fund and private equity (M Sc); international marketing (EMBA, MBA); international wealth management (M Sc); luxury goods and services (EMBA, M Sc, MBA); wealth and asset management (EMBA, MBA). Part-time programs available. *Degree requirements:* For master's, comprehensive exam (for some programs), applied research project. *Entrance requirements:* Additional exam requirements/recommendations for international students: Required—TOEFL (minimum score 550 paper-based; 213 computer-based), IELTS. Electronic applications accepted. *Faculty research:* Gaming, leadership, disintermediation.

Jones International University, School of Business, Centennial, CO 80112. Offers accounting (MBA); business communication (MABC); entrepreneurship (MABC, MBA); finance (MBA); global enterprise management (MBA); health care management (MBA); information security management (MBA); information technology management (MBA); leadership and influence (MABC); leading the customer-driven organization (MABC); negotiation and conflict management (MBA); project management (MABC, MBA). Program only offered online. Part-time and evening/weekend programs available. Postbaccalaureate distance learning degree programs offered (no on-campus study). *Degree requirements:* For master's, capstone project. *Entrance requirements:* For master's, minimum cumulative GPA of 2.5. Additional exam requirements/recommendations for international students: Recommended—TOEFL (minimum score 550 paper-based; 213 computer-based). Electronic applications accepted.

Kaplan University, Davenport Campus, School of Business, Davenport, IA 52807-2095. Offers business administration (MBA); change leadership (MS); entrepreneurship (MBA); finance (MBA); health care management (MBA, MS); human resource (MBA); international business (MBA); management (MS); marketing (MBA); project management (MBA, MS); supply chain management and logistics (MBA, MS). Part-time and evening/weekend programs available. Postbaccalaureate distance learning degree programs offered (no on-campus study). *Entrance requirements:* Additional exam requirements/recommendations for international students: Required—TOEFL (minimum score 550 paper-based; 218 computer-based; 80 iBT). Electronic applications accepted.

Lamar University, College of Graduate Studies, College of Business, Beaumont, TX 77710. Offers accounting (MBA); experiential business and entrepreneurship (MBA); financial management (MBA); healthcare administration (MBA); information systems (MBA); management (MBA). *Accreditation:* AACSB. Part-time and evening/weekend programs available. *Faculty:* 18 full-time (4 women), 4 part-time/adjunct (0 women). *Students:* 62 full-time (27 women), 59 part-time (16 women); includes 19 minority (8 African Americans, 6 Asian Americans or Pacific Islanders, 5 Hispanic Americans), 19 international. Average age 29. 210 applicants, 34% accepted, 33 enrolled. In 2009, 41 master's awarded. *Degree requirements:* For master's, comprehensive exam (for some programs), thesis optional. *Entrance requirements:* For master's, GMAT. Additional exam requirements/recommendations for international students: Required—TOEFL (minimum score 525 paper-based; 197 computer-based). *Application deadline:* For fall admission, 3/15 priority date for domestic students; for spring admission, 10/1 priority date for domestic students. Applications are processed on a rolling basis. Application fee: $25 ($50 for international students). *Financial support:* In 2009–10, 12 students received support, including 4 research assistantships with partial tuition reimbursements available; fellowships with tuition reimbursements available, career-related internships or fieldwork, Federal Work-Study, institutionally sponsored loans, scholarships/grants, and tuition waivers (partial) also available. Support available to part-time students. Financial award application deadline: 4/1; financial award applicants required to submit FAFSA. *Faculty research:* Marketing, finance, quantitative methods, management information systems, legal, environmental. *Unit head:* Dr. Enrique R. Venta, Dean, 409-880-8604, Fax: 409-880-8088, E-mail: henry.venta@lamar.edu. *Application contact:* Dr. Brad Mayer, Professor and Associate Dean, 409-880-2383, Fax: 409-880-8605, E-mail: bradley.mayer@lamar.edu.

Lenoir-Rhyne University, Graduate Programs, Charles M. Snipes School of Business, Hickory, NC 28601. Offers accounting (MBA); entrepreneurship (MBA); global leadership (MBA); leadership development (MBA). *Accreditation:* ACBSP. Part-time and evening/weekend programs available. *Degree requirements:* For master's, capstone course. *Entrance requirements:* For master's, GMAT, minimum undergraduate GPA of 2.7, graduate 3.0. Additional exam requirements/recommendations for international students: Required—TOEFL (minimum score 600 paper-based). Electronic applications accepted. *Expenses:* Contact institution.

LIM College, MBA Program, New York, NY 10022-5268. Offers entrepreneurship (MBA); fashion management (MBA).

Lincoln University, School of Graduate Studies and Continuing Education, Jefferson City, MO 65102. Offers business administration (MBA), including accounting, entrepreneurship, management, public administration and policy; educational leadership (Ed S), including elementary leadership, secondary leadership, superintendency; guidance and counseling (M Ed), including community/agency counseling, elementary school, secondary school; history (MA); school administration and supervision (M Ed), including elementary school administration, secondary school administration, special education administration; school teaching (M Ed), including elementary school teaching, secondary school teaching; social science (MA), including history, political science, sociology; sociology (MA); sociology/criminal justice (MA). Part-time and evening/weekend programs available. *Students:* 52 full-time (27 women), 146 part-time (107 women); includes 40 minority (39 African Americans, 1 Asian American or Pacific Islander), 15 international. Average age 35. 76 applicants, 95% accepted, 46 enrolled. In 2009, 60 master's, 6 other advanced degrees awarded. *Degree requirements:* For master's and Ed S, comprehensive exam, thesis optional. *Entrance requirements:* For master's and Ed S, GRE, MAT or GMAT, minimum GPA of 2.75 in major, 2.5 overall; 3 letters of recommendation; minimum C average in English composition; personal statement of purpose. Additional exam requirements/recommendations for international students: Required—TOEFL (minimum score 500 paper-based; 173 computer-based; 61 iBT). *Application deadline:* For fall admission, 7/1 priority date for domestic and international students; for spring admission, 12/1 priority date for domestic and international students. Applications are processed on a rolling basis. Application fee: $20. *Expenses:* Tuition, state resident: full-time $4185; part-time $232.50 per credit hour. Tuition, nonresident: full-time $7767; part-time $431.50 per credit hour. Required fees: $270; $15 per credit hour. $20 per term. *Financial support:* Federal Work-Study and scholarships/grants available. Financial award application deadline: 4/1; financial award applicants required to submit FAFSA. *Faculty research:* Suicide prevention. *Unit head:* Dr. Linda S. Bickel, Dean, 573-681-5247, Fax: 573-681-5106, E-mail: gradschool@lincolnu.edu. *Application contact:* Irasema Steck, Administrative Assistant, 573-681-5247, Fax: 573-681-5106, E-mail: gradschool@lincolnu.edu.

Lindenwood University, Graduate Programs, School of Business and Entrepreneurship, St. Charles, MO 63301-1695. Offers accounting (MBA, MS); business administration (MBA); entrepreneurial studies (MBA, MS); finance (MBA, MS); human resource management (MBA); human resources (MS); international business (MBA, MS); management (MBA, MS); management information systems (MBA, MS); marketing (MBA, MS); public management (MBA, MS); sport management (MA). *Accreditation:* ACBSP. Part-time and evening/weekend programs available. *Faculty:* 20 full-time (8 women), 17 part-time/adjunct (5 women). *Students:* 129 full-time (60 women), 138 part-time (61 women); includes 15 minority (11 African Americans, 2 Asian Americans or Pacific Islanders, 2 Hispanic Americans), 84 international. Average age 28. 149 applicants, 73 enrolled. In 2009, 142 master's awarded. *Degree requirements:* For master's, comprehensive exam (for some programs), thesis (for some programs). *Entrance requirements:* For master's, interview, minimum GPA of 3.0, letter of recommendation. Additional exam requirements/recommendations for international students: Required—TOEFL (minimum score 550 paper-based; 213 computer-based; 80 iBT). *Application deadline:* For fall admission, 7/30 priority date for domestic students, 9/16 priority date for international students; for winter admission, 12/19 priority date for domestic students, 12/17 priority date for international students; for spring admission, 2/25 priority date for domestic students, 2/11 priority date for international students. Applications are processed on a rolling basis. Application fee: $30 ($100 for international students). Electronic applications accepted. *Expenses:* Tuition: Full-time $12,960; part-time $370 per credit hour. Required fees: $340. One-time fee: $30 full-time. Tuition and fees vary according to course level and course load. *Financial support:* In 2009–10, 209 students received support. Career-related internships or fieldwork, Federal Work-Study, institutionally sponsored loans, and tuition waivers (partial) available. Financial award application deadline: 6/30; financial award applicants required to submit FAFSA. *Unit head:* Ed Morris, Dean of Management, 636-949-4832, E-mail: emorris@lindenwood.edu. *Application contact:* Brett Barger, Dean of Evening Admissions and Extension Campuses, 636-949-4934, Fax: 636-949-4109, E-mail: adultadmissions@lindenwood.edu.

Long Island University, Rockland Graduate Campus, Graduate School, Masters of Business Administration Program, Orangeburg, NY 10962. Offers business administration (Post Master's Certificate); entrepreneurship (MBA); finance (MBA); management (MBA). Part-time and evening/weekend programs available. *Faculty:* 12 part-time/adjunct (2 women). *Students:* 35 part-time (21 women). 51 applicants, 67% accepted, 22 enrolled. In 2009, 14 master's awarded. *Entrance requirements:* For master's, GMAT. Additional exam requirements/recommendations for international students: Required—TOEFL. *Application deadline:* Applications are processed on a rolling basis. Application fee: $30. *Expenses:* Tuition: Part-time $930 per credit. Required fees: $200 per semester. *Financial support:* In 2009–10, 34 students received support. Scholarships/grants available. Support available to part-time students. Financial award applicants required to submit FAFSA. *Unit head:* Dr. Lynn Johnson, Program Director, 845-359-7200 Ext. 5410, Fax: 845-359-7248, E-mail: ken.reilly@liu.edu. *Application contact:* Peter S. Reiner, Director of Admissions and Marketing, 845-359-7200, Fax: 845-359-7248, E-mail: peter.reiner@liu.edu.

Marquette University, Graduate School of Management, Program in Entrepreneurship, Milwaukee, WI 53201-1881. Offers Graduate Certificate. *Unit head:* Dr. David Shrock, Dean, 414-288-7141, Fax: 414-288-1578. *Application contact:* Erin Fox, Assistant Director for Recruitment, 414-288-5319, Fax: 414-288-1902, E-mail: erin.fox@marquette.edu.

McGill University, Faculty of Graduate and Postdoctoral Studies, Desautels Faculty of Management, Montréal, QC H3A 2T5, Canada. Offers administration (PhD); entrepreneurial studies (MBA); finance (MBA); general management (Post Master's Certificate); information systems (MBA); international business (exchange program) (MBA); international Master's program in practicing management (MM); management (MBA); management for development (MBA); manufacturing management (MMM); marketing (MBA); operations management (MBA); public accountancy (Diploma); strategic management (MBA); MBA/LL B; MD/MBA.

North Carolina State University, Graduate School, College of Management, Program in Business Administration, Raleigh, NC 27695. Offers biosciences management (MBA); entrepreneurship and technology commercialization (MBA); financial management (MBA); innovation management (MBA); marketing management (MBA); services management and consulting (MBA); supply chain management (MBA). *Accreditation:* AACSB. Part-time programs available. *Degree requirements:* For master's, thesis optional. *Entrance requirements:* For master's, GMAT, interview, 3 letters of recommendation. Additional exam requirements/recommendations for international students: Required—TOEFL (minimum score 600 paper-based; 250 computer-based; 100 iBT). Electronic applications accepted. *Faculty research:* Manufacturing strategy, information systems, technology commercialization, managing research and development, historical stock returns.

Northeastern University, School of Technological Entrepreneurship, Boston, MA 02115. Offers MS. Part-time programs available. *Faculty:* 7 full-time (2 women), 3 part-time/adjunct (0 women). *Students:* 33 full-time (8 women), 5 part-time (0 women); includes 1 African American, 19 international. 45 applicants, 87% accepted, 33 enrolled. In 2009, 19 master's awarded. *Entrance requirements:* For master's, GRE or GMAT, BS, minimum GPA of 3.0. Additional exam requirements/recommendations for international students: Required—TOEFL. *Application deadline:* For fall admission, 7/1 for international students. Applications are processed on a rolling basis. Application fee: $50. Electronic applications accepted. *Unit head:* Dr. Paul M. Zavracky, Dean, 617-373-2788, Fax: 617-373-7490, E-mail: ste@neu.edu. *Application contact:* Information Contact, 617-373-2788, Fax: 617-373-7490, E-mail: ste@neu.edu.

Northern Kentucky University, Office of Graduate Programs, College of Business, Program in Business Administration, Highland Heights, KY 41099. Offers business administration (MBA); entrepreneurship (Certificate); finance (Certificate); international business (Certificate); marketing (Certificate); project management (Certificate); JD/MBA. *Accreditation:* AACSB. Part-time and evening/weekend programs available. *Students:* 33 full-time (16 women), 155 part-time (63 women); includes 16 minority (9 African Americans, 7 Asian Americans or Pacific Islanders), 7 international. Average age 30. 105 applicants, 65% accepted, 34 enrolled. In 2009, 42 master's, 31 other advanced degrees awarded. *Degree requirements:* For master's, thesis optional. *Entrance requirements:* For master's, GMAT (minimum score 450), minimum GPA of 2.5. Additional exam requirements/recommendations for international students: Required—TOEFL (minimum score 550 paper-based; 213 computer-based; 79 iBT); Recommended—IELTS (minimum score 6.5). *Application deadline:* For fall admission, 8/1 priority date for domestic students, 6/1 priority date for international students; for spring admission, 12/1 priority date for domestic students, 10/1 priority date for international students. Applications are processed on a rolling basis. Application fee: $40. Electronic applications accepted. *Expenses:* Tuition, state resident: full-time $6912; part-time $384 per credit hour. Tuition, nonresident: full-time $12,150; part-time $675 per credit hour. Tuition and fees vary according to course load, program and reciprocity agreements. *Financial support:* Unspecified assistantships available. Financial award applicants required to submit FAFSA. *Unit head:* James Bast, Director of MBA Programs, 859-572-7695, Fax: 859-572-7694, E-mail: mbusiness@nku.edu. *Application contact:* Dr. Peg Griffin, Director of Graduate Programs, 859-572-6934, Fax: 859-572-6670, E-mail: griffinp@nku.edu.

Nova Southeastern University, H. Wayne Huizenga School of Business and Entrepreneurship, Program in Entrepreneurship, Fort Lauderdale, FL 33314-7796. Offers MBA. Part-time and evening/weekend programs available. Postbaccalaureate distance learning degree programs offered (minimal on-campus study). *Students:* 2 part-time (1 woman). Average age 32. 137 applicants, 61% accepted. *Degree requirements:* For master's, thesis optional. *Entrance requirements:* Additional exam requirements/recommendations for international students: Required—TOEFL (minimum score 550 paper-based; 213 computer-based; 79 iBT), IELTS (minimum score 6). *Application deadline:* For fall admission, 8/5 for domestic students, 8/15 for international students; for winter admission, 12/10 for domestic and international students; for spring admission, 2/10 for domestic and international students. Applications are processed on a rolling basis. Application fee: $50. Electronic applications accepted. *Financial support:* Federal Work-Study and scholarships/grants available. Support available to part-time students. Financial award applicants required to submit FAFSA. *Unit head:* Steve Harvey, Assistant Dean of Program Administration, 954-262-5047, Fax: 954-262-3829, E-mail: harvey@nsu.nova.edu. *Application contact:* Karen Goldberg, Associate Director of Recruitment and Special Events, 954-262-5039, Fax: 954-262-3822, E-mail: karen@nova.edu.

Oakland University, Graduate Study and Lifelong Learning, School of Business Administration, Department of Management and Marketing, Rochester, MI 48309-4401. Offers business administration (MBA); entrepreneurship (Certificate); general management (Certificate); human resource management (Certificate); international business (Certificate); marketing (Certificate).

Oral Roberts University, School of Business, Tulsa, OK 74171. Offers accounting (MBA); entrepreneurship (MBA); finance (MBA); international business (MBA); management (MBA); marketing (MBA); non-profit management (MBA); not for profit management (MNM). *Accreditation:* ACBSP. Part-time programs available. Postbaccalaureate distance learning degree programs offered (minimal on-campus study). *Faculty:* 7 full-time (0 women), 5 part-time/adjunct (4 women). *Students:* 68 full-time (30 women), 55 part-time (27 women); includes 54 minority (32 African Americans, 5 American Indian/Alaska Native, 8 Asian Americans or Pacific Islanders, 9 Hispanic Americans), 3 international. Average age 28. 71 applicants, 94% accepted, 56 enrolled. In 2009, 36 master's awarded. *Degree requirements:* For master's, thesis optional. *Entrance requirements:* For master's, minimum cumulative GPA of 3.0. Additional exam requirements/recommendations for international students: Required—TOEFL (minimum score 550 paper-based; 213 computer-based; 79 iBT). *Application deadline:* For fall admission, 7/1 priority date for domestic and international students; for spring admission, 12/1 priority date for domestic students, 10/15 priority date for international students. Applications are processed on a rolling basis. Application fee: $35. Electronic applications accepted. *Financial support:* In 2009–10, 39 students received support. Federal Work-Study, scholarships/grants, and unspecified assistantships available. Financial award application deadline: 6/1; financial award applicants required to submit FAFSA. *Faculty research:* Social media, international business and marketing. *Unit head:* Dr. Steven Greene, Dean, 918-495-7040, Fax: 918-495-7876, E-mail: businessdean@oru.edu. *Application contact:* Rebecca Gunn, Representative/Recruiter, 918-495-6117, Fax: 918-495-6500, E-mail: gradbusiness@oru.edu.

Park University, College of Graduate and Professional Studies, Kansas City, MO 54105. Offers adult education (M Ed); at-risk students (M Ed); disaster and emergency management (MPA); educational administration (M Ed); entrepreneurship (MBA); general business (MBA); general education (M Ed); government/business relations (MPA); healthcare/services management (MBA, MPA); international business (MBA); K-12 certification (MAT); management information systems (MBA); management of information systems (MPA); middle school certification (MAT); multi-cultural education (M Ed); nonprofit management (MPA); public management (MPA); school law (M Ed); secondary school certification (MAT); special education (M Ed). Part-time and evening/weekend programs available. Postbaccalaureate distance learning degree programs offered (no on-campus study). *Degree requirements:* For master's, comprehensive exam, thesis (for some programs). *Entrance requirements:* For master's, GRE, GMAT, teacher certification (M Ed). Additional exam requirements/recommendations for international students: Required—TOEFL (minimum score 550 paper-based). Electronic applications accepted. *Faculty research:* Literacy, leadership, brain based research, multicultural education, diversity.

Peru State College, Graduate Programs, Program in Organizational Management, Peru, NE 68421. Offers MS. Program offered online only. Part-time programs available. *Degree requirements:* For master's, thesis (for some programs). *Expenses:* Contact institution. *Faculty research:* Emotional intelligence.

Polytechnic Institute of NYU, Department of Chemical and Biological Sciences, Major in Biotechnology and Entrepreneurship, Brooklyn, NY 11201-2990. Offers MS. *Students:* 25 full-time (6 women), 7 part-time (1 woman); includes 1 minority (Asian American or Pacific Islander), 31 international. 80 applicants, 46% accepted, 8 enrolled. In 2009, 14 master's awarded. *Entrance requirements:* Additional exam requirements/recommendations for international students: Required—TOEFL (minimum score 550 paper-based; 213 computer-based; 80 iBT); Recommended—IELTS (minimum score 6.5). *Application deadline:* For fall admission, 7/31 priority date for domestic students, 4/30 priority date for international students; for spring admission, 12/31 priority date for domestic students, 10/30 priority date for international students. Applications are processed on a rolling basis. Application fee: $75. Electronic applications accepted. *Expenses:* Tuition: Full-time $21,492; part-time $1194 per credit hour. Required fees: $1160; $204 per course. *Financial support:* Institutionally sponsored loans, scholarships/grants, and unspecified assistantships available. Support available to part-time students. *Unit head:* Dr. Bruce Garetz, Department Head, 718-260-3600. *Application contact:* JeanCarlo Bonilla, Director of Graduate Enrollment Management, 718-260-3182, Fax: 718-260-3624, E-mail: gradinfo@poly.edu.

Polytechnic Institute of NYU, Department of Technology Management, Brooklyn, NY 11201-2990. Offers construction management (Advanced Certificate); electronic business management (Advanced Certificate); entrepreneurship (Advanced Certificate); human resources management (Advanced Certificate); information management (Advanced Certificate); management (MS); management of technology (MS); organizational behavior (MS, Advanced Certificate); project management (Advanced Certificate); technology management (MBA, PhD, Advanced Certificate); telecommunications and information management (MS); telecommunications management (Advanced Certificate). Part-time and evening/weekend programs available. *Faculty:* 5 full-time (1 woman), 26 part-time/adjunct (3 women). *Students:* 272 full-time (111 women), 103 part-time (41 women); includes 64 minority (20 African Americans, 1 American Indian/Alaska Native, 34 Asian Americans or Pacific Islanders, 9 Hispanic Americans), 193 international. Average age 30. 518 applicants, 57% accepted, 135 enrolled. In 2009, 148 master's awarded. *Degree requirements:* For master's, comprehensive exam (for some programs), thesis (for some programs); for doctorate, comprehensive exam, thesis/dissertation. *Entrance requirements:* For master's, GMAT, minimum B average in undergraduate course work. Additional exam requirements/recommendations for international students: Required—TOEFL (minimum score 550 paper-based; 213 computer-based; 80 iBT); Recommended—IELTS (minimum score 6.5). *Application deadline:* For fall admission, 7/31 priority date for domestic students, 4/30 priority date for international students; for spring admission, 12/31 priority date for domestic students, 11/30 priority date for international students. Applications are processed on a rolling basis. Application fee: $75. Electronic applications accepted. *Expenses:* Tuition: Full-time $21,492; part-time $1194 per credit hour. Required fees: $1160; $204 per course. *Financial support:* In 2009–10, 1 fellowship (averaging $26,400 per year) was awarded; research assistantships, teaching assistantships, institutionally sponsored loans, scholarships/grants, and unspecified assistantships also available. Support available to part-time students. *Unit head:* Prof. Bharadwaj Rao, Head, 718-260-3617, Fax: 718-260-3874, E-mail: brao@poly.edu. *Application contact:* JeanCarlo Bonilla, Director of Graduate Enrollment Management, 718-260-3182, Fax: 718-260-3624, E-mail: gradinfo@poly.edu.

Post University, Program in Business Administration, Waterbury, CT 06723-2540. Offers business administration (MBA); corporate innovation (MBA); entrepreneurship (MBA); finance (MBA); leadership (MBA); marketing (MBA). Postbaccalaureate distance learning degree programs offered.

Providence College, Graduate Studies, School of Business, Providence, RI 02918. Offers accountancy (MBA); economics (MBA); entrepreneurship (MBA); finance (MBA); international business (MBA); management (MBA); marketing (MBA); not-for-profit (MBA); quantitative (MBA). Part-time and evening/weekend programs available. *Faculty:* 14 full-time (8 women), 7 part-time/adjunct (3 women). *Students:* 63 full-time (18 women), 46 part-time (19 women); includes 4 minority (2 African Americans, 2 Asian Americans or Pacific Islanders), 7 international. Average age 26. 43 applicants, 88% accepted. In 2009, 40 master's awarded. *Degree requirements:* For master's, thesis optional. *Entrance requirements:* For master's, GMAT. Additional exam requirements/recommendations for international students: Required—TOEFL (minimum score 550 paper-based; 213 computer-based; 80 iBT). *Application deadline:* For fall admission, 8/1 priority date for domestic and international students; for spring admission, 12/1 priority date for domestic and international students. Applications are processed on a rolling basis. Application fee: $55. *Expenses:* Contact institution. *Financial support:* In 2009–10, 34 research assistantships with full tuition reimbursements (averaging $8,400 per year) were awarded; Federal Work-Study, institutionally sponsored loans, and unspecified assistantships also available. Support available to part-time students. Financial award application deadline: 8/1; financial award applicants required to submit FAFSA. *Unit head:* Dr. MaryJane Lenon, Director, MBA Program, 401-865-2566, Fax: 401-865-2978, E-mail: mjlenon@providence.edu. *Application contact:* Katherine A. Follett, Administrative Coordinator, 401-865-2333, Fax: 401-865-2978, E-mail: kfollett@providence.edu.

Queen's University at Kingston, Queens School of Business, Program in Business Administration, Kingston, ON K7L 3N6, Canada. Offers consulting and project management (MBA); finance (MBA); innovation and entrepreneurship (MBA); marketing (MBA). *Accreditation:* AACSB. *Degree requirements:* For master's, thesis optional, research project. *Entrance requirements:* For master's, GMAT, minimum B+ average. Additional exam requirements/recommendations for international students: Required—TOEFL. Electronic applications accepted. *Faculty research:* Management fundamentals, strategic thinking, global business, innovation and change, leadership.

Regent University, Graduate School, School of Global Leadership and Entrepreneurship, Virginia Beach, VA 23464-9800. Offers business administration (MBA); management (MA); organizational leadership (MA, PhD, Certificate); strategic foresight (MA); strategic leadership (DSL). Part-time and evening/weekend programs available. Postbaccalaureate distance learning degree programs offered (minimal on-campus study). *Faculty:* 15 full-time (3 women), 10 part-time/adjunct (3 women). *Students:* 14 full-time (4 women), 407 part-time (156 women); includes 123 minority (97 African Americans, 3 American Indian/Alaska Native, 6 Asian Americans or Pacific Islanders, 17 Hispanic Americans), 59 international. Average age 41. 153 applicants, 55% accepted, 31 enrolled. In 2009, 110 master's, 52 doctorates awarded. *Degree requirements:* For master's, thesis or alternative, 3 credit hour culminating experience; for doctorate, thesis/dissertation. *Entrance requirements:* For master's, GRE, GMAT, minimum undergraduate GPA of 2.75, computer literacy survey, 2 recommendations, resume, transcripts, essay; for doctorate, GRE, GMAT, sample of writing, minimum 3 years of relevant experience, computer literacy survey, 2 recommendations, resume, essay, transcripts; for Certificate, writing sample, resume, transcripts. Additional exam requirements/recommendations for international students: Required—TOEFL (minimum score 577 paper-based; 233 computer-based). *Application deadline:* For fall admission, 5/1 priority date for domestic students; for spring admission, 10/1 priority date for domestic students. Applications are processed on a rolling basis. Application fee: $50. Electronic applications accepted. *Expenses:* Contact institution. *Financial support:* In 2009–10, 258 students received support. Career-related internships or fieldwork, scholarships/grants, and tuition waivers (full and partial) available. Support available to part-time students. Financial award application deadline: 9/1. *Faculty research:* Servant leadership, ethics and values, telecommuting and family values, organizational communications, distance education. *Unit head:* Dr. Bruce Winston, Dean, 757-352-4306, Fax: 757-352-4634, E-mail: brucwin@regent.edu. *Application contact:* Matthew Chadwick, Director of Admissions, 800-373-5504, Fax: 757-352-4381, E-mail: admissions@regent.edu.

Rensselaer Polytechnic Institute, Graduate School, Lally School of Management and Technology, Program in Technology, Commercialization, and Entrepreneurship, Troy, NY 12180-3590. Offers MS. *Expenses:* Tuition: Full-time $38,100.

Rollins College, Crummer Graduate School of Business, Winter Park, FL 32789-4499. Offers entrepreneurship (MBA); finance (MBA); international business (MBA); management (MBA); marketing (MBA); operations and technology management (MBA). *Accreditation:* AACSB. Part-time and evening/weekend programs available. Postbaccalaureate distance learning degree programs offered (minimal on-campus study). *Faculty:* 25 full-time (3 women), 8 part-time/adjunct (2 women). *Students:* 277 full-time (105 women), 192 part-time (79 women); includes 95 minority (26 African Americans, 31 Asian Americans or Pacific Islanders, 38 Hispanic Americans), 48 international. Average age 29. 373 applicants, 53% accepted, 140 enrolled. In 2009, 220 master's awarded. *Entrance requirements:* For master's, GMAT. Additional exam requirements/recommendations for international students: Required—TOEFL. *Application deadline:* For fall admission, 6/1 priority date for domestic students; for spring admission, 12/1 for domestic students. Applications are processed on a rolling basis. Application fee: $50. Electronic applications accepted. *Expenses:* Contact institution. *Financial support:* In 2009–10, 95 students received support, including 95 fellowships, 56 research assistantships (averaging $2,400 per year); career-related internships or fieldwork, scholarships/grants, tuition waivers (full), and unspecified assistantships also available. *Faculty research:* Sustainability, world financial markets, international business, market research, strategic marketing. *Unit head:* Dr. Craig M. McAllaster, Dean, 407-646-2249, Fax: 407-646-1550, E-mail: cmcallaster@rollins.edu.

Entrepreneurship

Rollins College (continued)

Application contact: Linda Puritz, Student Admissions Office, 407-646-2405, Fax: 407-646-1550, E-mail: mbaadmissions@rollins.edu.

Rowan University, Graduate School, William G. Rohrer College of Business, Department of Management, Program in Entrepreneurship, Glassboro, NJ 08028-1701. Offers MBA. Part-time and evening/weekend programs available. *Students:* 3 full-time (2 women). Average age 22. 5 applicants, 80% accepted, 3 enrolled. *Degree requirements:* For master's, comprehensive exam, thesis. *Entrance requirements:* For master's, GRE General Test. Additional exam requirements/recommendations for international students: Required—TOEFL. *Application deadline:* Applications are processed on a rolling basis. Electronic applications accepted. *Expenses:* Tuition, state resident: full-time $10,624; part-time $590 per semester hour. Tuition, nonresident: full-time $10,624; part-time $590 per semester hour. Required fees: $2320; $125 per semester hour. *Financial support:* Career-related internships or fieldwork, Federal Work-Study, and unspecified assistantships available. Support available to part-time students. *Unit head:* Dr. Mira Lalovic-Hand, Interim Associate Provost/Director of Graduate School, 856-256-5120, E-mail: lalovic-hand@rowan.edu. *Application contact:* Karen Haynes, Graduate Coordinator, 856-256-4052, E-mail: haynes@rowan.edu.

San Diego State University, Graduate and Research Affairs, College of Business Administration, Department of Management, San Diego, CA 92182. Offers entrepreneurship (MS); human resources management (MS); management science (MS). Part-time and evening/weekend programs available. *Degree requirements:* For master's, thesis or alternative. *Entrance requirements:* For master's, GMAT, resume, letters of reference. Additional exam requirements/recommendations for international students: Required—TOEFL. Electronic applications accepted.

Santa Clara University, Leavey School of Business, Program in Business Administration, Santa Clara, CA 95053. Offers accounting (MBA); entrepreneurship (MBA); executive MBA (EMBA); finance (MBA); food and agribusiness (MBA); international business (MBA); leading people and organizations (MBA); managing technology and innovation (MBA); marketing management (MBA); supply chain management (MBA). *Accreditation:* AACSB. Part-time and evening/weekend programs available. *Students:* 228 full-time (88 women), 838 part-time (265 women); includes 388 minority (17 African Americans, 2 American Indian/Alaska Native, 326 Asian Americans or Pacific Islanders, 43 Hispanic Americans), 218 international. Average age 31. 486 applicants, 77% accepted, 263 enrolled. In 2009, 317 master's awarded. *Degree requirements:* For master's, thesis or alternative. *Entrance requirements:* For master's, GMAT, GRE. Additional exam requirements/recommendations for international students: Required—TOEFL (minimum score 600 paper-based; 250 computer-based; 100 iBT). *Application deadline:* For fall admission, 6/1 for domestic and international students; for spring admission, 1/19 for domestic students, 1/17 for international students. Applications are processed on a rolling basis. Application fee: $75 ($100 for international students). Electronic applications accepted. *Expenses:* Contact institution. *Financial support:* Fellowships with partial tuition reimbursements, research assistantships with partial tuition reimbursements, career-related internships or fieldwork, Federal Work-Study, institutionally sponsored loans, scholarships/grants, health care benefits, and unspecified assistantships available. Support available to part-time students. Financial award applicants required to submit FAFSA. *Unit head:* Elizabeth B. Ford, Senior Assistant Dean, 408-554-2752, Fax: 408-554-4571, E-mail: eford@scu.edu. *Application contact:* Jennifer W. Taylor, Senior Director, 408-554-4539, Fax: 408-554-4571, E-mail: mbaadmissions@scu.edu.

Seton Hill University, Program in Business Administration, Greensburg, PA 15601. Offers entrepreneurship (MBA); management (MBA). Part-time and evening/weekend programs available. *Entrance requirements:* For master's, resume, minimum GPA of 3.0. Additional exam requirements/recommendations for international students: Required—TOEFL (minimum score 600 paper-based; 250 computer-based). *Application deadline:* For fall admission, 8/15 priority date for domestic students; for spring admission, 12/15 for domestic students. Applications are processed on a rolling basis. Application fee: $35. Electronic applications accepted. *Expenses:* Tuition: Full-time $12,780; part-time $710 per credit. Required fees: $300; $150 per semester. Tuition and fees vary according to course load and program. *Financial support:* Scholarships/grants, tuition waivers (partial), and unspecified assistantships available. Support available to part-time students. Financial award application deadline: 8/15; financial award applicants required to submit FAFSA. *Faculty research:* Women in business, entrepreneurship. *Unit head:* Dr. Lloyd Gibson, Director, 724-830-4738, E-mail: gibson@setonhill.edu. *Application contact:* Christine Schaeffer, Director of Graduate and Adult Studies, 724-838-4283, Fax: 724-830-1891, E-mail: schaeffer@setonhill.edu.

SIT Graduate Institute, Graduate Programs, Program in Global Management (Oman), Brattleboro, VT 05302-0676. Offers MGM. Program offered in the Sultanate of Oman. Part-time programs available. *Degree requirements:* For master's, capstone project. *Entrance requirements:* Additional exam requirements/recommendations for international students: Required—TOEFL (minimum score of 550 paper-based, 213 computer-based, 79 iBT) or IELTS (minimum score of 6.0).

South Carolina State University, School of Graduate Studies, Department of Accounting, Agribusiness and Economics, Orangeburg, SC 29117-0001. Offers agribusiness (MS); agribusiness and entrepreneurship (MBA). Part-time and evening/weekend programs available. *Degree requirements:* For master's, comprehensive exam, business plan. *Entrance requirements:* For master's, GMAT, minimum GPA of 2.8. Additional exam requirements/recommendations for international students: Required—TOEFL. Electronic applications accepted. *Expenses:* Tuition, state resident: part-time $470 per credit hour. Tuition, nonresident: part-time $924 per credit hour. *Faculty research:* Small farm income and profitability, agricultural credit, aquaculture, low-input sustainable agriculture, rural development.

Southeast Missouri State University, School of Graduate Studies, Harrison College of Business, Cape Girardeau, MO 63701-4799. Offers accounting (MBA); entrepreneurship (MBA); environmental management (MBA); financial management (MBA); general management (MBA); health administration (MBA); industrial management (MBA); international business (MBA); sport management (MBA). *Accreditation:* AACSB. Part-time and evening/weekend programs available. Postbaccalaureate distance learning degree programs offered (no on-campus study). *Degree requirements:* For master's, applied research project. *Entrance requirements:* For master's, GMAT, minimum undergraduate GPA of 2.5. Additional exam requirements/recommendations for international students: Required—TOEFL (minimum score 550 paper-based; 213 computer-based); Recommended—IELTS (minimum score 6). *Expenses:* Tuition, state resident: full-time $4266; part-time $237 per credit hour. Tuition, nonresident: full-time $7506; part-time $417 per credit hour. Required fees: $427; $427. *Faculty research:* Human resources, laws impacting accounting, advertising.

Southern Methodist University, Cox School of Business, MBA Program, Dallas, TX 75275. Offers accounting (MBA); finance (MBA); information technology and operations management (MBA); management (MBA); marketing (MBA); strategy and entrepreneurship (MBA). *Students:* 396 full-time (91 women), 401 part-time (109 women); includes 185 minority (34 African Americans, 5 American Indian/Alaska Native, 102 Asian Americans or Pacific Islanders, 44 Hispanic Americans), 76 international. Average age 31. In 2009, 363 master's awarded. *Unit head:* Dr. Albert W. Niemi, Dean, 214-768-3012, Fax: 214-768-3713, E-mail: aniemi@mail.cox.smu.edu. *Application contact:* Path Cudney, Director of MBA Admissions, 214-768-3001, Fax: 214-768-3956, E-mail: pcudney@mail.cox.smu.edu.

Southern Methodist University, Cox School of Business, Program in Entrepreneurship, Dallas, TX 75275. Offers MS. *Faculty:* 7 full-time (3 women), 2 part-time/adjunct (0 women). *Students:* 13 part-time (5 women); includes 5 minority (1 African American, 2 Asian Americans or Pacific Islanders, 2 Hispanic Americans). Average age 33. In 2009, 11 master's awarded. *Unit head:* Dr. Albert W. Niemi, Dean, 214-768-3012, Fax: 214-768-3713, E-mail: aniemi@mail.cox.smu.edu. *Application contact:* Path Cudney, Director of MBA Admissions, 214-768-3001, Fax: 214-768-3956, E-mail: pcudney@mail.cox.smu.edu.

South University, Graduate Programs, College of Business, Savannah, GA 31406. Offers corrections (MBA); entrepreneurship and small business (MBA); hospitality management (MBA); sustainability (MBA).

Stevens Institute of Technology, Graduate School, Wesley J. Howe School of Technology Management, Program in Information Systems, Hoboken, NJ 07030. Offers computer science (MS); e-commerce (MS); enterprise systems (MS); entrepreneurial information technology (MS); information architecture (MS); information management (MS, Certificate); information security (MS); information technology in financial services industry (MS); information technology in the pharmaceutical industry (MS); information technology outsourcing management (MS); project management (MS, Certificate); software engineering (MS); telecommunications (MS). *Degree requirements:* For master's, thesis optional. *Entrance requirements:* For master's, GMAT, GRE General Test. Additional exam requirements/recommendations for international students: Required—TOEFL. Electronic applications accepted. *Expenses:* Tuition: Full-time $9900; part-time $1100 per credit. Required fees: $286 per semester.

Stratford University, School of Graduate Studies, Falls Church, VA 22043. Offers accounting (MS); business administration (IMBA, MBA); enterprise business management (MS); entrepreneurial management (MS); information assurance (MS); information systems (MS); software engineering (MS); telecommunications (MS). Part-time and evening/weekend programs available. Postbaccalaureate distance learning degree programs offered (no on-campus study). *Faculty:* 35 full-time (15 women), 115 part-time/adjunct (25 women). *Students:* 944 full-time (430 women), 15 part-time (5 women). Average age 26. 950 applicants, 45% accepted, 415 enrolled. In 2009, 412 master's awarded. *Degree requirements:* For master's, comprehensive exam, capstone project. *Entrance requirements:* For master's, baccalaureate degree. Additional exam requirements/recommendations for international students: Required—TOEFL (minimum score 500 paper-based; 173 computer-based; 61 iBT). *Application deadline:* Applications are processed on a rolling basis. Application fee: $50. Electronic applications accepted. *Expenses:* Tuition: Full-time $10,530; part-time $390 per credit. Tuition and fees vary according to course load. *Financial support:* Federal Work-Study available. Financial award applicants required to submit FAFSA. *Unit head:* Dr. Habib Khan, Chief Academic Officer, 703-821-8570 Ext. 3305, Fax: 703-734-5335, E-mail: hkhan@stratford.edu. *Application contact:* James Ray, Director of Admissions, 703-821-8570 Ext. 3021, Fax: 703-734-5339, E-mail: jray@stratford.edu.

Suffolk University, Sawyer Business School, Master of Business Administration Program, Boston, MA 02108-2770. Offers accounting (MBA); business administration (APC); corporate financial executive track (MBA); entrepreneurship (MBA); executive business administration (EMBA); finance (MBA); global business administration (GMBA); health administration (MBA); international business (MBA); marketing (MBA); organizational behavior (MBA); strategic management (MBA); taxation (MBA); JD/MBA; MBA/GDPA; MBA/MHA; MBA/MSA; MBA/MSF; MBA/MST. *Accreditation:* AACSB. Part-time and evening/weekend programs available. Postbaccalaureate distance learning degree programs offered (no on-campus study). *Faculty:* 103 full-time (30 women), 63 part-time/adjunct (19 women). *Students:* 173 full-time (68 women), 406 part-time (178 women); includes 51 minority (16 African Americans, 3 American Indian/Alaska Native, 22 Asian Americans or Pacific Islanders, 10 Hispanic Americans), 90 international. Average age 29. 460 applicants, 72% accepted, 157 enrolled. In 2009, 245 master's awarded. *Entrance requirements:* For master's, GMAT, minimum undergraduate GPA of 2.75 (MBA), 5 years of managerial experience (EMBA). Additional exam requirements/recommendations for international students: Required—TOEFL (minimum score 550 paper-based; 213 computer-based). *Application deadline:* For fall admission, 6/15 priority date for domestic students, 6/15 for international students; for spring admission, 11/1 priority date for domestic students, 11/1 for international students. Applications are processed on a rolling basis. Application fee: $50. Electronic applications accepted. *Expenses:* Tuition: Full-time $33,000; part-time $1100 per credit. Required fees: $20. Tuition and fees vary according to program. *Financial support:* In 2009–10, 284 students received support, including 99 fellowships with full and partial tuition reimbursements available (averaging $13,599 per year); career-related internships or fieldwork, Federal Work-Study, and institutionally sponsored loans also available. Support available to part-time students. Financial award application deadline: 4/1; financial award applicants required to submit FAFSA. *Faculty research:* Foreign investments; career strategies and boundaryless careers; corporate ethics codes; interest rates, inflation, and growth options; innovation and product development performance. *Unit head:* Lillian Hallberg, Assistant Dean of Graduate Programs/Director of MBA Programs, 617-573-8306, E-mail: lhallber@suffolk.edu. *Application contact:* Judith Reynolds, Director of Graduate Admissions, 617-573-8302, Fax: 617-305-1733, E-mail: grad.admission@suffolk.edu.

Syracuse University, Martin J. Whitman School of Management, Program in Business Administration, Syracuse, NY 13244. Offers accounting (MBA); entrepreneurship (MBA); finance (MBA); marketing (MBA); supply chain management (MBA). Postbaccalaureate distance learning degree programs offered (minimal on-campus study). *Entrance requirements:* For master's, GMAT, 2 letters of recommendation. Additional exam requirements/recommendations for international students: Required—TOEFL (minimum score 600 paper-based; 250 computer-based; 100 iBT). Electronic applications accepted. *Expenses:* Tuition: Full-time $26,808; part-time $1117 per credit. Required fees: $1024.

Syracuse University, Martin J. Whitman School of Management, Program in Entrepreneurship and Emerging Enterprises, Syracuse, NY 13244. Offers MS. *Expenses:* Tuition: Full-time $26,808; part-time $1117 per credit. Required fees: $1024.

Temple University, Graduate School, Fox School of Business, Doctoral Programs in Business, Philadelphia, PA 19122-6096. Offers accounting (PhD); entrepreneurship (PhD); finance (PhD); human resource administration (PhD); international business (PhD); management information systems (PhD); marketing (PhD); risk management and insurance (PhD); statistics (PhD); strategic management (PhD); tourism and sport (PhD). *Accreditation:* AACSB. *Degree requirements:* For doctorate, thesis/dissertation. *Entrance requirements:* For doctorate, GRE General Test, GMAT, minimum GPA of 3.0, master's degree. Additional exam requirements/recommendations for international students: Required—TOEFL (minimum score 600 paper-based; 250 computer-based; 100 iBT), IELTS (minimum score 7.5). Electronic applications accepted.

Texas Tech University, Jerry S. Rawls College of Business Administration, Programs in Business Administration, Lubbock, TX 79409. Offers agricultural business (MBA); business administration (IMBA); entrepreneurship (MBA); finance (MBA); general business (MBA); health organization management (MBA); international business (MBA); management and leadership skills (MBA); management information systems (MBA); marketing (MBA); statistics (MBA); JD/MBA; MBA/M Arch; MBA/MA; MBA/MD; MBA/MS; MBA/Pharm D. Part-time and evening/weekend programs available. *Faculty:* 54 full-time (9 women), 5 part-time/adjunct (0 women). *Students:* 59 full-time (15 women), 487 part-time (148 women); includes 107 minority (24 African Americans, 4 American Indian/Alaska Native, 30 Asian Americans or Pacific Islanders, 49 Hispanic Americans), 51 international. Average age 30. 477 applicants, 81% accepted, 302 enrolled. In 2009, 185 degrees awarded. *Degree requirements:* For master's, capstone course. *Entrance requirements:* For master's, GMAT, holistic review of academic credentials. Additional exam requirements/recommendations for international students: Required—TOEFL (minimum score 550 paper-based; 213 computer-based; 79 iBT). *Application deadline:* For fall admission, 4/1 priority date for domestic students, 1/15 priority date for international students; for spring admission, 9/1 priority date for domestic students, 7/15 priority date for international students. Applications are processed on a rolling basis. Application fee: $50 ($75 for international students). Electronic applications accepted. *Expenses:* Tuition, state resident: full-time $5100; part-time $213 per credit hour. Tuition, nonresident: full-time $11,748; part-time $490 per credit hour. Required fees: $2298; $50 per credit hour. $555 per semester. *Financial support:* In 2009–10, 13 research assistantships (averaging $8,000 per year) were awarded; teaching assistantships, career-related internships or fieldwork, Federal Work-Study, scholarships/grants, health care benefits, and unspecified assistantships also available. Support available to part-time students. Financial award applicants required to submit FAFSA. *Unit head:* Dr. W. Jay Conover, Director, 806-742-1546, Fax: 806-742-3958,

E-mail: jay.conover@ttu.edu. *Application contact:* Cynthia D. Barnes, Director, Graduate Services Center, 806-742-3184, Fax: 806-742-3958, E-mail: ba_grad@ttu.edu.

Université Laval, Faculty of Administrative Sciences, Programs in Business Administration, Québec, QC G1K 7P4, Canada. Offers accounting (MBA); agri-food management (MBA); electronic business (MBA, Diploma); factory management and logistics (MBA); finance (MBA); firm management (MBA); geomatic management (MBA); information technology management (MBA); international management (MBA); management (MBA); management accounting (MBA, Diploma); marketing (MBA); modeling and organizational decision (MBA); occupational health and safety management (MBA); pharmacy management (MBA); social and environmental responsibility (MBA); technological entrepreneurship (Diploma). *Accreditation:* AACSB. Part-time and evening/weekend programs available. Postbaccalaureate distance learning degree programs offered (no on-campus study). *Entrance requirements:* For master's and Diploma, knowledge of French and English. Electronic applications accepted.

The University of Akron, Graduate School, College of Business Administration, Department of Management, Program in Entrepreneurship, Akron, OH 44325. Offers MBA. *Students:* 6 full-time (5 women), 3 part-time (1 woman); includes 1 minority (Asian American or Pacific Islander), 3 international. Average age 27. 7 applicants, 57% accepted, 1 enrolled. In 2009, 1 master's awarded. *Entrance requirements:* For master's, GMAT, minimum GPA of 2.75, letters of recommendation, resume. Additional exam requirements/recommendations for international students: Required—TOEFL (minimum score 550 paper-based; 213 computer-based; 79 iBT). *Application deadline:* For fall admission, 8/1 for domestic and international students; for spring admission, 12/1 for domestic and international students. Application fee: $30 ($40 for international students). Electronic applications accepted. *Expenses:* Tuition, state resident: full-time $6570; part-time $365 per credit hour. Tuition, nonresident: full-time $11,250; part-time $625 per credit hour. *Unit head:* Dr. Steven Ash, Head, 330-972-6429, E-mail: ash@uakron.edu. *Application contact:* Dr. Susan Hanlon, Director of Graduate Business Programs, 330-972-7043, Fax: 330-972-6588, E-mail: shanlon@uakron.edu.

University of Central Florida, College of Business Administration, Department of Management, Orlando, FL 32816. Offers entrepreneurship (Graduate Certificate); management (MSM); technology ventures (Graduate Certificate). *Accreditation:* AACSB. *Faculty:* 25 full-time (8 women), 2 part-time/adjunct (both women). *Students:* 3 full-time (2 women), 24 part-time (21 women); includes 5 minority (2 African Americans, 1 Asian American or Pacific Islander, 2 Hispanic Americans). Average age 34. 11 applicants, 82% accepted, 9 enrolled. In 2009, 2 master's, 4 other advanced degrees awarded. *Entrance requirements:* For master's, GMAT, minimum GPA of 3.0 in last 60 hours. *Application deadline:* For fall admission, 2/1 priority date for domestic students; for spring admission, 11/1 priority date for domestic students. Application fee: $30. Electronic applications accepted. *Expenses:* Tuition, state resident: part-time $306.31 per credit hour. Tuition, nonresident: part-time $1099.01 per credit hour. Part-time tuition and fees vary according to degree level and program. *Financial support:* Fellowships, research assistantships, teaching assistantships available. *Unit head:* Dr. Foard Jones, Chair, 407-823-2925, Fax: 407-823-3725, E-mail: foard.jones@bus.ucf.edu. *Application contact:* Dr. Foard Jones, Chair, 407-823-2925, Fax: 407-823-3725, E-mail: foard.jones@bus.ucf.edu.

University of Colorado at Boulder, Leeds School of Business, Division of Business Administration, Boulder, CO 80309. Offers accounting (MS, PhD); finance (PhD); information systems (PhD); marketing (PhD); operations (PhD); strategic, organizational, and entrepreneurial studies (PhD). Part-time and evening/weekend programs available. *Students:* 74 full-time (27 women), 15 part-time (8 women); includes 6 minority (1 African American, 3 Asian Americans or Pacific Islanders, 2 Hispanic Americans), 21 international. Average age 28. 271 applicants, 8% accepted, 19 enrolled. In 2009, 40 master's, 6 doctorates awarded. *Entrance requirements:* For master's, GMAT, minimum undergraduate GPA of 3.0. *Application deadline:* For fall admission, 3/31 for domestic and international students; for spring admission, 10/31 for domestic and international students. Application fee: $50 ($60 for international students). Electronic applications accepted. *Financial support:* In 2009–10, 16 fellowships (averaging $1,038 per year), 26 research assistantships (averaging $17,558 per year), 11 teaching assistantships (averaging $12,576 per year) were awarded; career-related internships or fieldwork, Federal Work-Study, scholarships/grants, and unspecified assistantships also available. Financial award applicants required to submit FAFSA.

University of Dayton, Graduate School, School of Business Administration, Dayton, OH 45469-1300. Offers accounting (MBA); business intelligence (MBA); entrepreneurship (MBA); finance (MBA); international business (MBA); marketing (MBA); MIS (MBA); operations management (MBA); technology-enhanced business/e-commerce (MBA); JD/MBA. *Accreditation:* AACSB. Part-time and evening/weekend programs available. *Faculty:* 29 full-time (8 women), 15 part-time/adjunct (2 women). *Students:* 134 full-time (48 women), 111 part-time (31 women); includes 14 minority (9 African Americans, 3 Asian Americans or Pacific Islanders, 2 Hispanic Americans), 29 international. Average age 29. 179 applicants, 63% accepted, 73 enrolled. In 2009, 102 master's awarded. *Entrance requirements:* For master's, GMAT. Additional exam requirements/recommendations for international students: Required—TOEFL (minimum score 550 paper-based; 213 computer-based; 79 iBT). *Application deadline:* For fall admission, 3/1 priority date for international students; for winter admission, 7/1 priority date for international students; for spring admission, 1/1 priority date for international students. Applications are processed on a rolling basis. Application fee: $0 ($50 for international students). Electronic applications accepted. *Expenses:* Contact institution. *Financial support:* In 2009–10, 13 fellowships with partial tuition reimbursements, 17 research assistantships with full and partial tuition reimbursements (averaging $7,020 per year) were awarded; career-related internships or fieldwork, institutionally sponsored loans, scholarships/grants, health care benefits, and unspecified assistantships also available. Support available to part-time students. Financial award application deadline: 3/15; financial award applicants required to submit FAFSA. *Faculty research:* Management information systems, economics, finance, entrepreneurship, marketing. *Unit head:* Janice M. Glynn, Director, MBA Program, 937-229-3733, Fax: 937-229-3882, E-mail: glynn@udayton.edu. *Application contact:* Jeffrey Carter, Assistant Director, MBA Program, 937-229-3733, Fax: 937-229-3882, E-mail: jeff.carter@notes.udayton.edu.

University of Delaware, Alfred Lerner College of Business and Economics, Department of Economics, Newark, DE 19716. Offers economics (MA, MS, PhD); economics for entrepreneurship and educators (MA); MA/MBA. Part-time programs available. *Degree requirements:* For master's, comprehensive exam, thesis (for some programs), mathematics review exam, research project; for doctorate, comprehensive exam, thesis/dissertation, field exam. *Entrance requirements:* For master's, GMAT or GRE General Test, minimum GPA of 2.5; for doctorate, GRE General Test, minimum GPA of 3.5 in graduate economics course work. Additional exam requirements/recommendations for international students: Required—TOEFL (minimum score 550 paper-based; 225 computer-based). Electronic applications accepted. *Faculty research:* Applied quantitative economics, industrial organization, resource economics, monetary economics, labor economics.

University of Florida, Graduate School, Warrington College of Business Administration, Hough Graduate School of Business, Department of Finance, Insurance and Real Estate, Gainesville, FL 32611. Offers business administration (MS), including entrepreneurship, insurance, real estate and urban analysis, retailing; finance (PhD); financial services (Certificate); insurance (PhD); real estate and urban analysis (PhD); JD/MS. Terminal master's awarded for partial completion of doctoral program. *Degree requirements:* For doctorate, thesis/dissertation. *Entrance requirements:* For master's, GMAT or GRE General Test, minimum GPA of 3.0 for last 60 hours of undergraduate degree, work experience (preferred); for doctorate, GMAT or GRE General Test, minimum GPA of 3.0. Additional exam requirements/recommendations for international students: Required—TOEFL (minimum score 550 paper-based; 213 computer-based). Electronic applications accepted. *Faculty research:* Financial management, financial markets and institutions, investments, risk and insurance, real estate development.

University of Hawaii at Manoa, Graduate Division, Shidler College of Business, Program in Business Administration, Honolulu, HI 96822. Offers Asian business studies (MBA); Chinese business studies (MBA); decision sciences (MBA); entrepreneurship (MBA); finance (MBA); finance and banking (MBA); human resources management (MBA); information management (MBA); information technology (MBA); international business (MBA); Japanese business studies (MBA); marketing (MBA); organizational behavior (MBA); organizational management (MBA); real estate (MBA); student-designed track (MBA). *Accreditation:* AACSB. Part-time and evening/weekend programs available. *Faculty:* 46 full-time (8 women), 9 part-time/adjunct (4 women). *Students:* 259 full-time (90 women), 105 part-time (43 women); includes 123 minority (118 Asian Americans or Pacific Islanders, 5 Hispanic Americans), 119 international. Average age 32. 336 applicants, 52% accepted, 150 enrolled. In 2009, 113 master's awarded. *Degree requirements:* For master's, thesis optional. *Entrance requirements:* For master's, GMAT, minimum GPA of 3.0. Additional exam requirements/recommendations for international students: Required—TOEFL (minimum score 600 paper-based; 250 computer-based; 100 iBT), IELTS (minimum score 7). *Application deadline:* For fall admission, 5/1 for domestic students, 3/1 for international students. Application fee: $60. *Expenses:* Contact institution. *Financial support:* In 2009–10, 24 students received support, including 98 fellowships (averaging $3,481 per year), 3 research assistantships (averaging $16,626 per year). Total annual research expenditures: $427,000. *Application contact:* Tung Bui, Graduate Chair, 808-956-5565, Fax: 808-956-9889, E-mail: tung.bui@hawaii.edu.

University of Houston–Victoria, School of Business Administration, Victoria, TX 77901-4450. Offers accounting (MBA); economic development and entrepreneurship (MS); finance (GMBA, MBA); general business (MBA); international business (MBA); management (GMBA, MBA); marketing (MBA). *Accreditation:* AACSB. Part-time and evening/weekend programs available. Postbaccalaureate distance learning degree programs offered (no on-campus study). *Entrance requirements:* For master's, GMAT. Additional exam requirements/recommendations for international students: Required—TOEFL (minimum score 550 paper-based; 213 computer-based). Electronic applications accepted. *Faculty research:* Economic development, marketing, finance.

University of Louisville, Graduate School, College of Business, MBA Programs, Louisville, KY 40292-0001. Offers business administration (MBA); entrepreneurship (MBA). *Accreditation:* AACSB. Part-time and evening/weekend programs available. *Faculty:* 25 full-time (4 women), 1 (woman) part-time/adjunct. *Students:* 211 part-time (54 women); includes 29 minority (10 African Americans, 2 American Indian/Alaska Native, 11 Asian Americans or Pacific Islanders, 6 Hispanic Americans), 8 international. Average age 30. 90 applicants, 67% accepted, 48 enrolled. In 2009, 156 master's awarded. *Entrance requirements:* For master's, GMAT, 2 letters of reference, personal interview, resume. Additional exam requirements/recommendations for international students: Required—TOEFL (minimum score 557 paper-based; 213 computer-based; 79 iBT). *Application deadline:* For fall admission, 7/31 for domestic students; for spring admission, 12/1 for domestic students. Applications are processed on a rolling basis. Application fee: $50. *Financial support:* In 2009–10, 10 research assistantships with full tuition reimbursements (averaging $12,000 per year) were awarded; health care benefits and unspecified assistantships also available. Financial award application deadline: 3/31; financial award applicants required to submit FAFSA. *Faculty research:* Entrepreneurship, supply chain management, venture capital, retailing/franchising, corporate governance. Total annual research expenditures: $297,040. *Unit head:* Dr. Charles Moyer, Dean, 502-852-6443, Fax: 502-852-7557, E-mail: charlie.moyer@louisville.edu. *Application contact:* Joshua M. Philpot, Graduate Programs Manager, 502-852-7257, Fax: 502-852-4901, E-mail: josh.philpot@louisville.edu.

University of Louisville, Graduate School, College of Business, PhD Program in Entrepreneurship, Louisville, KY 40292-0001. Offers PhD. *Faculty:* 9 full-time (3 women), 6 part-time/adjunct (0 women). *Students:* 9 full-time (1 woman), 3 international. Average age 36. 6 applicants, 0% accepted, 0 enrolled. In 2009, 2 doctorates awarded. *Degree requirements:* For doctorate, comprehensive exam, thesis/dissertation, paper of sufficient quality for journal publication. *Entrance requirements:* For doctorate, GMAT, 3 letters of recommendation, curriculum vitae, personal interview. Additional exam requirements/recommendations for international students: Required—TOEFL (minimum score 550 paper-based; 213 computer-based; 79 iBT). *Application deadline:* For fall admission, 3/15 priority date for domestic and international students. Applications are processed on a rolling basis. Application fee: $50. Electronic applications accepted. *Financial support:* In 2009–10, 8 students received support, including 6 fellowships with full tuition reimbursements available (averaging $21,000 per year), 2 teaching assistantships with full tuition reimbursements available (averaging $18,000 per year); scholarships/grants, health care benefits, and unspecified assistantships also available. Financial award application deadline: 3/15; financial award applicants required to submit FAFSA. *Faculty research:* Entrepreneurship, supply chain management, venture capital, retailing/franchising, corporate governance. *Unit head:* Dr. Charles Moyer, Dean, 502-852-6443, Fax: 502-852-7557, E-mail: charlie.moyer@louisville.edu. *Application contact:* Dr. David Dubofsky, Director, 502-852-3016, Fax: 502-852-6072, E-mail: d.dubofsky@louisville.edu.

University of Massachusetts Lowell, College of Management, Lowell, MA 01854-2881. Offers business administration (MBA); foundations of business (Graduate Certificate); new venture creation (Graduate Certificate). *Accreditation:* AACSB. Part-time and evening/weekend programs available. *Entrance requirements:* For master's, GMAT.

University of Missouri–Kansas City, Henry W. Bloch School of Business and Public Administration, Kansas City, MO 64110-2499. Offers accounting (MS); business administration (MBA); entrepreneurship and innovation (PhD); public affairs (MPA, PhD); JD/MBA; LL M/MPA. PhD (interdisciplinary) offered through the School of Graduate Studies. *Accreditation:* AACSB; NASPAA. Part-time and evening/weekend programs available. *Faculty:* 43 full-time (14 women), 22 part-time/adjunct (7 women). *Students:* 234 full-time (108 women), 437 part-time (193 women); includes 79 minority (33 African Americans, 27 Asian Americans or Pacific Islanders, 19 Hispanic Americans), 51 international. Average age 30. 387 applicants, 65% accepted, 222 enrolled. In 2009, 240 master's awarded. Terminal master's awarded for partial completion of doctoral program. *Entrance requirements:* For master's, GMAT, GRE, 2 writing essays, 2 references and support of employer; for doctorate, GRE, minimum GPA of 3.0. Additional exam requirements/recommendations for international students: Required—TOEFL (minimum score 550 paper-based; 213 computer-based; 80 iBT). *Application deadline:* For fall admission, 5/1 priority date for domestic and international students; for spring admission, 10/1 priority date for domestic and international students. Applications are processed on a rolling basis. Application fee: $45 ($50 for international students). Electronic applications accepted. *Expenses:* Tuition, state resident: full-time $5378; part-time $299 per credit hour. Tuition, nonresident: full-time $13,881; part-time $771 per credit hour. Required fees: $641; $71 per credit hour. Tuition and fees vary according to course load and program. *Financial support:* In 2009–10, 18 research assistantships with partial tuition reimbursements (averaging $8,766 per year), 5 teaching assistantships with partial tuition reimbursements (averaging $8,430 per year) were awarded; career-related internships or fieldwork, Federal Work-Study, institutionally sponsored loans, scholarships/grants, tuition waivers (full and partial), and unspecified assistantships also available. Support available to part-time students. Financial award application deadline: 3/1; financial award applicants required to submit FAFSA. *Faculty research:* Entrepreneurship, finance, non-profit, risk management. Total annual research expenditures: $751,788. *Unit head:* Dr. Teng-Kee Tan, Dean, 816-235-2215, Fax: 816-235-2206. *Application contact:* 816-235-1111, E-mail: admit@umkc.edu.

University of New Brunswick Fredericton, School of Graduate Studies, Faculty of Business Administration, Fredericton, NB E3B 5A3, Canada. Offers business administration (MBA); engineering management (MBA); entrepreneurship (MBA); sports and recreation management (MBA); MBA/LL B. Part-time programs available. *Faculty:* 37 full-time (13 women). *Students:* 27 full-time (10 women), 51 part-time (25 women). In 2009, 72 master's awarded. *Degree requirements:* For master's, thesis optional. *Entrance requirements:* For master's, GMAT (550 minimum score), minimum GPA of 3.0; 3-5 years work experience. Additional exam requirements/recommendations for international students: Required—TOEFL (minimum score 580 paper-based; 92 iBT), IELTS (minimum score 7), TOEFL or IELTS. *Application deadline:* For fall admission, 3/1 priority date for domestic students. Applications are processed on a rolling basis. Application fee: $50 Canadian dollars. Tuition and fees charges are reported in Canadian dollars. *Expenses:* Tuition, area resident: Full-time $5562 Canadian dollars; part-time $2781

Entrepreneurship

University of New Brunswick Fredericton (continued)

Canadian dollars per year. Required fees: $49.75 Canadian dollars per term. *Financial support:* In 2009–10, 4 research assistantships (averaging $4,500 per year), 11 teaching assistantships (averaging $2,250 per year) were awarded. *Faculty research:* Strategic management, entrepreneurship, investment practices, marketing and supply chain management, operations management. *Unit head:* Judy Roy, Director of Graduate Studies, 506-458-7307, Fax: 506-453-3561, E-mail: jroy@unb.ca. *Application contact:* Marilyn Davis, Acting Graduate Secretary, 506-453-4766, Fax: 506-453-3561, E-mail: mbacontact@unb.ca.

University of Rochester, The College, School of Engineering and Applied Sciences, Center for Entrepreneurship, Rochester, NY 14627. Offers technical entrepreneurship and management (TEAM) (MS). *Entrance requirements:* For master's, GRE or GMAT, technical concentration of interest, 3 letters of recommendation. Additional exam requirements/recommendations for international students: Required—TOEFL.

University of San Francisco, College of Arts and Sciences, Department of Computer Science, Program in Web Science, San Francisco, CA 94117-1080. Offers MS. *Faculty:* 5 full-time (1 woman). *Students:* 18 full-time (2 women), 3 part-time (0 women), 13 international. Average age 29. 28 applicants, 71% accepted, 8 enrolled. In 2009, 4 master's awarded. *Expenses:* Tuition: Full-time $19,710; part-time $1095 per unit. Part-time tuition and fees vary according to degree level, campus/location and program. *Financial support:* In 2009–10, 12 students received support. *Unit head:* Terence Parr, Graduate Director, 415-422-6530, Fax: 415-422-5800. *Application contact:* Mark Landerghini, Graduate Adviser, 415-422-5135, E-mail: asgraduate@usfca.edu.

University of San Francisco, School of Business and Professional Studies, Masagung Graduate School of Management, Joint Master of Global Entrepreneurship and Management Program, San Francisco, CA 94117-1080. Offers MGEM. Program offered jointly with IQS in Barcelona, Spain and Fu Jen Catholic University in Taipei, Taiwan. *Faculty:* 2 full-time (both women), 2 part-time/adjunct (0 women). *Students:* 32 full-time (19 women); includes 7 minority (1 African American, 2 Asian Americans or Pacific Islanders, 4 Hispanic Americans), 19 international. Average age 23. 38 applicants, 95% accepted, 32 enrolled. *Expenses:* Tuition: Full-time $19,710; part-time $1095 per unit. Part-time tuition and fees vary according to degree level, campus/location and program. *Financial support:* In 2009–10, 8 students received support. *Unit head:* Dr. Shenzhao Fu, 415-422-6771, Fax: 415-422-2502. *Application contact:* Kelly Brookes, Director, MBA Program, 415-422-2221, Fax: 415-422-6315, E-mail: mba@usfca.edu.

University of San Francisco, School of Business and Professional Studies, Masagung Graduate School of Management, Program in Business Administration, San Francisco, CA 94117-1080. Offers business economics (MBA); e-business (MBA); entrepreneurship (MBA); finance (MBA); international business (MBA); management (MBA); marketing (MBA); telecommunications management and policy (MBA); JD/MBA; MSN/MBA. *Accreditation:* AACSB. *Faculty:* 17 full-time (4 women), 16 part-time/adjunct (7 women). *Students:* 278 full-time (140 women), 18 part-time (10 women); includes 94 minority (5 African Americans, 1 American Indian/Alaska Native, 69 Asian Americans or Pacific Islanders, 19 Hispanic Americans), 53 international. Average age 30. 410 applicants, 70% accepted, 133 enrolled. In 2009, 137 master's awarded. *Entrance requirements:* For master's, GMAT, minimum undergraduate GPA of 3.2. Additional exam requirements/recommendations for international students: Required—TOEFL. *Application deadline:* For fall admission, 7/1 priority date for domestic students; for spring admission, 11/30 for domestic students. Applications are processed on a rolling basis. Application fee: $55 ($65 for international students). *Expenses:* Tuition: Full-time $19,710; part-time $1095 per unit. Part-time tuition and fees vary according to degree level, campus/ location and program. *Financial support:* In 2009–10, 155 students received support; fellowships available. Financial award application deadline: 3/2; financial award applicants required to submit FAFSA. *Faculty research:* International financial markets, technology transfer licensing, international marketing, strategic planning. Total annual research expenditures: $50,000. *Unit head:* Kelly Brookes, Director, 415-422-2221, Fax: 415-422-6315. *Application contact:* Director, MBA Program, 415-422-2221, Fax: 415-422-6315, E-mail: mba@usfca.edu.

University of South Florida, Graduate School, College of Business, Center for Entrepreneurship, Tampa, FL 33620-9951. Offers MS, Graduate Certificate. Part-time and evening/weekend programs available. *Faculty:* 11 full-time (3 women). *Students:* 32 full-time (13 women), 43 part-time (9 women); includes 17 minority (8 African Americans, 3 Asian Americans or Pacific Islanders, 6 Hispanic Americans), 5 international. 68 applicants, 71% accepted, 34 enrolled. *Degree requirements:* For master's, thesis (for some programs). *Entrance requirements:* For master's, GMAT, minimum undergraduate GPA of 3.0 in last 2 years, recommendations, interview. Additional exam requirements/recommendations for international students: Required—TOEFL (minimum score 550 paper-based; 213 computer-based; 79 iBT). *Application deadline:* For fall admission, 2/15 for domestic students, 1/2 for international students; for spring admission, 10/15 for domestic students, 6/1 for international students. Applications are processed on a rolling basis. Application fee: $30. Electronic applications accepted. *Financial support:* Applicants required to submit FAFSA. *Unit head:* Dr. Michael W. Fountain, Director, 813-974-7900, Fax: 813-974-7663, E-mail: fountain@coba.usf.edu. *Application contact:* Dr. Michael W. Fountain, Director, 813-974-7900, Fax: 813-974-7663, E-mail: fountain@coba.usf.edu.

The University of Tampa, John H. Sykes College of Business, Tampa, FL 33606-1490. Offers accounting (MBA, MS); economics (MBA); entrepreneurship and innovation (MBA); finance (MBA, MS); information systems management (MBA); international business (MBA); management (MBA); marketing (MBA, MS); nonprofit management (MBA). *Accreditation:* AACSB. Part-time and evening/weekend programs available. *Faculty:* 62 full-time (22 women), 11 part-time/adjunct (4 women). *Students:* 240 full-time (101 women), 338 part-time (133 women); includes 95 minority (16 African Americans, 4 American Indian/Alaska Native, 24 Asian Americans or Pacific Islanders, 51 Hispanic Americans), 122 international. Average age 29. 564 applicants, 51% accepted, 186 enrolled. In 2009, 234 master's awarded. *Entrance requirements:* For master's, GMAT. Additional exam requirements/recommendations for international students: Required—TOEFL (minimum score 577 paper-based; 230 computer-based; 90 iBT), IELTS. *Application deadline:* For fall admission, 7/15 for domestic students, 6/1 for international students; for spring admission, 12/15 for domestic students, 11/1 for international students. Applications are processed on a rolling basis. Application fee: $40. Electronic applications accepted. *Expenses:* Tuition: Part-time $488 per credit hour. *Financial support:* In 2009–10, 332 students received support, including 71 research assistantships with full tuition reimbursements available (averaging $6,757 per year); career-related internships or fieldwork, scholarships/ grants, and unspecified assistantships also available. Support available to part-time students. Financial award applicants required to submit FAFSA. *Faculty research:* Information systems, leadership, corporate governance, entrepreneurship, hedonic price estimation. *Unit head:* Dr. Don Morrill, Associate Dean, Graduate and Continuing Studies, 813-257-3557, E-mail: dmorrill@ut.edu. *Application contact:* Karen Full, Director of Admissions, Graduate and Continuing Studies, 813-257-3642, E-mail: kfull@ut.edu.

The University of Texas at Austin, Graduate School, Program in Technology Commercialization, Austin, TX 78712-1111. Offers MS. Twelve month program, beginning in May, with classes held every other Friday and Saturday. Evening/weekend programs available. Postbaccalaureate distance learning degree programs offered (no on-campus study). *Degree requirements:* For master's, year-long global teaming project. *Entrance requirements:* For master's, GRE General Test, or GMAT. Additional exam requirements/recommendations for international students: Required—TOEFL (minimum score 550 paper-based; 213 computer-based; 79 iBT). Electronic applications accepted. *Expenses:* Contact institution. *Faculty research:* Technology transfer; entrepreneurship; commercialization; research, development and innovation.

The University of Texas at Dallas, School of Management, Program in Management and Administrative Sciences, Richardson, TX 75080. Offers e-commerce (MS); health care management (MS); innovation and entrepreneurship (MS); organizations and strategy (MS).

Accreditation: AACSB. Part-time and evening/weekend programs available. *Faculty:* 12 full-time (3 women), 13 part-time/adjunct (3 women). *Students:* 46 full-time (29 women), 103 part-time (47 women); includes 53 minority (12 African Americans, 34 Asian Americans or Pacific Islanders, 7 Hispanic Americans), 32 international. Average age 33. 156 applicants, 66% accepted, 47 enrolled. In 2009, 83 master's awarded. *Degree requirements:* For master's, thesis optional. *Entrance requirements:* For master's, GMAT. Additional exam requirements/ recommendations for international students: Required—TOEFL (minimum score 550 paper-based; 213 computer-based). *Application deadline:* For fall admission, 7/15 for domestic students, 5/1 priority date for international students; for spring admission, 11/15 for domestic students, 9/1 priority date for international students. Applications are processed on a rolling basis. Application fee: $50 ($100 for international students). Electronic applications accepted. *Expenses:* Tuition, state resident: full-time $11,068; part-time $461 per credit hour. Tuition, nonresident: full-time $21,178; part-time $882 per credit hour. Tuition and fees vary according to course load. *Financial support:* In 2009–10, 25 teaching assistantships with full tuition reimbursements (averaging $14,400 per year) were awarded; fellowships, research assistantships, career-related internships or fieldwork, Federal Work-Study, institutionally sponsored loans, scholarships/grants, and unspecified assistantships also available. Support available to part-time students. Financial award application deadline: 4/30; financial award applicants required to submit FAFSA. *Faculty research:* Integrated and detailed knowledge of functional areas of management, analytical tools for effective appraisal and decision making. *Unit head:* Dr. Doug Eckel, Assistant Dean, 972-883-5923, E-mail: dogb.eckel@utdallas.edu. *Application contact:* James Parker, Assistant Director, 972-883-5842, E-mail: jparker@utdallas.edu.

University of the Incarnate Word, School of Graduate Studies and Research, Dreeben School of Education, Programs in Education, San Antonio, TX 78209-6397. Offers adult education (M Ed, MA); cross-cultural education (M Ed, MA); early childhood literacy (M Ed, MA); general education (M Ed, MA); Higher Education (PhD); instructional technology (M Ed, MA); international education and entrepreneurship (PhD); kinesiology (M Ed, MA); literacy (M Ed, MA); organizational leadership (PhD); organizational learning and leading (M Ed, MA); reading (M Ed, MA); special education (M Ed, MA); teacher leadership (M Ed, MA). Part-time and evening/weekend programs available. *Students:* 20 full-time (11 women), 201 part-time (122 women); includes 113 minority (29 African Americans, 2 American Indian/Alaska Native, 2 Asian Americans or Pacific Islanders, 80 Hispanic Americans), 30 international. Average age 41. In 2009, 26 master's, 19 doctorates awarded. *Degree requirements:* For master's, capstone; for doctorate, thesis/dissertation, qualifying exam. *Entrance requirements:* For master's, baccalaureate degree; minimum foundation GPA of 2.5; interview; for doctorate, master's degree; interview; supervised writing sample. Additional exam requirements/recommendations for international students: Required—TOEFL (minimum score 560 paper-based; 220 computer-based; 83 iBT). *Application deadline:* Applications are processed on a rolling basis. Application fee: $20. Electronic applications accepted. *Expenses:* Tuition: Full-time $12,150; part-time $675 per credit hour. Required fees: $83 per credit hour. *Financial support:* Federal Work-Study and scholarships/grants available. Financial award applicants required to submit FAFSA. *Unit head:* Dr. Denise Staudt, Dean, Dreeben School of Education, 210-829-2762, E-mail: staudt@uiwtx.edu. *Application contact:* Andrea Cyterski-Acosta, Dean of Enrollment, 210-829-6005, Fax: 210-829-3921, E-mail: admis@uiwtx.edu.

University of Waterloo, Graduate Studies, Centre for Business, Entrepreneurship and Technology, Waterloo, ON N2L 3G1, Canada. Offers MBET. *Entrance requirements:* For master's, honors degree. Additional exam requirements/recommendations for international students: Required—TOEFL (minimum score 550 paper-based; 213 computer-based), TWE. Electronic applications accepted.

The University of Western Ontario, Richard Ivey School of Business, London, ON N6A 3K7, Canada. Offers business (EMBA, PhD); corporate strategy and leadership elective (MBA); entrepreneurship elective (MBA); finance elective (MBA); health sector stream (MBA); international management elective (MBA); marketing elective (MBA); JD/MBA. *Faculty:* 61 full-time (13 women). *Students:* 164 full-time (50 women). Average age 29. In 2009, 167 master's awarded. *Degree requirements:* For master's, thesis (for some programs); for doctorate, thesis/dissertation. *Entrance requirements:* For master's, GMAT, 2 years of full-time work experience, interview. Additional exam requirements/recommendations for international students: Required—TOEFL (minimum score 100 computer-based; 100 iBT), IELTS (minimum score 6), IELTS or TOEFL. *Application deadline:* For fall admission, 10/12 for domestic students, 8/16 for international students; for winter admission, 12/16 for domestic students, 10/12 for international students; for spring admission, 1/10 priority date for domestic students, 12/16 for international students. Applications are processed on a rolling basis. Application fee: $150 Canadian dollars. Electronic applications accepted. *Financial support:* Scholarships/grants and health care benefits available. Financial award application deadline: 1/10. *Faculty research:* Strategy, organizational behavior, international business, finance, operations management. *Unit head:* Carol Stephenson, Dean, 519-661-3285, Fax: 519-661-4126, E-mail: cstephenson@ivey.ca. *Application contact:* Niki da Silva, Director, MBA Program Services, 519-661-3419, Fax: 519-661-3431, E-mail: ndasilva@ivey.ca.

University of Wisconsin–Madison, Graduate School, Wisconsin School of Business, Wisconsin Full-Time MBA Program, Madison, WI 53706-1380. Offers applied corporate finance (MBA); applied security analysis (MBA); arts administration (MBA); brand and product management (MBA); entrepreneurial management (MBA); marketing research (MBA); operations and technology management (MBA); real estate (MBA); risk management and insurance (MBA); strategic human resource management (MBA); strategic management in the life and engineering sciences (MBA); supply chain management (MBA). *Faculty:* 32 full-time (5 women). *Students:* 242 full-time (74 women); includes 47 minority (16 African Americans, 3 American Indian/ Alaska Native, 16 Asian Americans or Pacific Islanders, 12 Hispanic Americans), 29 international. Average age 28. 526 applicants, 32% accepted, 117 enrolled. In 2009, 106 master's awarded. *Entrance requirements:* For master's, GMAT, bachelor's or equivalent degree, 2 years of work experience, letters of recommendation. Additional exam requirements/recommendations for international students: Required—TOEFL (minimum score 600 paper-based; 250 computer-based; 100 iBT), IELTS. *Application deadline:* For fall admission, 11/4 for domestic and international students; for winter admission, 2/5 for domestic and international students; for spring admission, 5/26 for domestic students, 4/5 for international students. Applications are processed on a rolling basis. Application fee: $56. Electronic applications accepted. *Expenses:* Tuition, state resident: part-time $594 per credit. Tuition, nonresident: part-time $1504 per credit. Required fees: $65 per credit. Tuition and fees vary according to course load, program and reciprocity agreements. *Financial support:* In 2009–10, 103 students received support, including 13 fellowships with full and partial tuition reimbursements available (averaging $15,000 per year), 53 research assistantships with full tuition reimbursements available (averaging $8,000 per year), 35 teaching assistantships with full tuition reimbursements available (averaging $11,000 per year); scholarships/grants, health care benefits, and unspecified assistantships also available. Financial award application deadline: 4/5; financial award applicants required to submit FAFSA. *Unit head:* Prof. Kenneth A. Kavajecz, Associate Dean, 608-265-3494, Fax: 608-265-4192, E-mail: kkavajecz@bus.wisc.edu. *Application contact:* Maria Reis, Assistant Director of MBA Marketing and Recruiting, 608-262-4000, Fax: 608-265-4192, E-mail: mreis@bus.wisc.edu.

Wake Forest University, Babcock Graduate School of Management, Full-time MBA Program, Winston-Salem, NC 27106. Offers consulting/general management (MBA); entrepreneurship (MBA); finance (MBA); health (MBA); marketing (MBA); operations management (MBA); JD/MBA; MBA/MSA; MD/MBA. *Accreditation:* AACSB. *Faculty:* 62 full-time (13 women), 36 part-time/adjunct (14 women). *Students:* 144 full-time (36 women); includes 17 minority (8 African Americans, 9 Asian Americans or Pacific Islanders), 22 international. Average age 28. In 2009, 81 master's awarded. *Entrance requirements:* For master's, GMAT or GRE, letters of recommendation, official transcripts, current resume or curriculum vitae, 2 years of work experience with the exception of joint-degree candidates. Additional exam requirements/ recommendations for international students: Required—TOEFL (minimum score 600 paper-based; 250 computer-based; 100 iBT), Pearson Test of English (PTE). *Application deadline:*

For fall admission, 6/1 for domestic and international students. Applications are processed on a rolling basis. Application fee: $75. Electronic applications accepted. *Expenses:* Contact institution. *Financial support:* In 2009–10, 95 students received support. Career-related internships or fieldwork, scholarships/grants, and unspecified assistantships available. Financial award application deadline: 3/1; financial award applicants required to submit FAFSA. *Faculty research:* The influence of personal relationships on business decision making and management of change; drivers of perceived value and consumer behavior; impact of accounting on auditing, financial, managerial, systems and taxation stakeholders; corporate governance and executive compensation; impact of operations strategies on competitiveness. *Unit head:* Sherry Moss, Director, Full-time MBA Program, 336-758-5422, Fax: 336-758-5830, E-mail: admissions@mba.wfu.edu. *Application contact:* LaKesha Alston, Administrative Assistant, 336-758-5422, Fax: 336-758-5830, E-mail: admissions@mba.wfu.edu.

Walden University, Graduate Programs, School of Management, Minneapolis, MN 55401. Offers applied management and decision sciences (PhD), including accounting, engineering management, finance, general applied management and decision sciences, information systems management, knowledge management, leadership and organizational change, learning management, operations research, self-designed program in applied management and design sciences; business information management (MISM); enterprise information security (MISM); entrepreneurship (MBA, DBA); finance (MBA, DBA); global supply chain management (DBA); healthcare management (MBA); healthcare system improvement (MBA); human resource management (MBA); information systems management (DBA); international business (MBA, DBA); IT strategy and governance (MISM); leadership (MBA, MS, DBA), including entrepreneurship (MS); general management (MS), human resources leadership (MS), innovation and technology (MS), leader development (MS), project management (MS), self-designed (MS), sustainable futures (MS); managing global software and service supply chains (MISM); marketing (MBA, DBA); project management (MBA, MS); risk management (MBA); self-designed (MBA, DBA); social impact management (DBA); sustainable futures (MBA); technology (MBA); technology entrepreneurship (DBA). Part-time and evening/weekend programs available. Postbaccalaureate distance learning degree programs offered (minimal on-campus study). *Faculty:* 17 full-time, 211 part-time/adjunct. *Students:* 3,389 full-time (1,774 women), 815 part-time (482 women); includes 1,969 minority (1,640 African Americans, 36 American Indian/Alaska Native, 123 Asian Americans or Pacific Islanders, 170 Hispanic Americans), 95 international. Average age 41. In 2009, 699 master's, 42 doctorates awarded. *Degree requirements:* For doctorate, thesis/dissertation (for some programs), residency. *Entrance requirements:* For master's, bachelor's degree or equivalent in related field; minimum GPA of 2.5; official transcripts; goal statement; access to computer and Internet; for doctorate, master's degree or equivalent in related field; minimum GPA of 3.0; 3 years of related professional/academic experience (preferred). Additional exam requirements/recommendations for international students: Required—TOEFL (minimum score 550 paper-based; 213 computer-based), IELTS (minimum score 6.5), TOEFL, IELTS, or Michigan English Language Assessment Battery (minimum score 82). *Application deadline:* Applications are processed on a rolling basis. Application fee: $50. Electronic applications accepted. *Expenses:* Tuition: Full-time $13,665; part-time $560 per credit. Required fees: $1375. Tuition and fees vary according to course load, degree level and program. *Financial support:* In 2009–10, 466 students received support; fellowships, Federal Work-Study, scholarships/grants, unspecified assistantships, and family tuition reduction, active duty/veteran tuition reduction, group tuition reduction, interest-free payment plans available. Support available to part-time students. Financial award applicants required to submit FAFSA. *Unit head:* William Schulz, Interim Associate Dean, 800-925-3368. *Application contact:* Jennifer Hall, Director of Enrollment, 866-4-WALDEN, E-mail: info@waldenu.edu.

West Chester University of Pennsylvania, Office of Graduate Studies, College of Education, Department of Professional and Secondary Education, West Chester, PA 19383. Offers education for sustainability (Certificate); entrepreneurial education (Certificate); secondary education (M Ed, Teaching Certificate); teaching and learning with technology (Certificate). Part-time and evening/weekend programs available. *Students:* 4 full-time (3 women), 39 part-time (27 women); includes 2 minority (both Asian Americans or Pacific Islanders). Average age 30. 33 applicants, 97% accepted, 16 enrolled. In 2009, 13 master's, 3 Certificates awarded. *Degree requirements:* For master's, comprehensive exam, thesis (for some programs). *Entrance requirements:* For master's, GRE or MAT, teaching certificate. Additional exam requirements/recommendations for international students: Required—TOEFL (minimum score 550 paper-based; 213 computer-based; 80 iBT). *Application deadline:* For fall admission, 4/15 priority date for domestic students, 3/15 for international students; for spring admission, 10/15 priority date for domestic students, 9/1 for international students. Applications are processed on a rolling basis. Application fee: $35. Electronic applications accepted. *Expenses:* Tuition, state resident: full-time $6666; part-time $370 per credit. Tuition, nonresident: full-time $10,666; part-time $593 per credit. Required fees: $122.56 per credit. *Financial support:* In 2009–10, research assistantships with full and partial tuition reimbursements (averaging $5,000 per year); unspecified assistantships also available. Support available to part-time students. Financial award application deadline: 2/15; financial award applicants required to submit FAFSA. *Faculty research:* Technology integration: preparing our teachers for the twenty-first century. *Unit head:* Dr. John Kinslow, Chair, 610-436-3108, E-mail: jkinslow@wcupa.edu. *Application contact:* Dr. Cynthia Haggard, Graduate Coordinator, 610-436-6934, E-mail: chaggard@wcupa.edu.

Western Carolina University, Graduate School, College of Business, Program in Entrepreneurship, Cullowhee, NC 28723. Offers ME. Part-time and evening/weekend programs available. Postbaccalaureate distance learning degree programs offered (no on-campus study). *Students:* 3 full-time (2 women), 51 part-time (21 women). Average age 37. 45 applicants, 96% accepted, 35 enrolled. In 2009, 38 master's awarded. *Entrance requirements:* For master's, GMAT or GRE General Test. Additional exam requirements/recommendations for international students: Required—TOEFL (minimum score 550 paper-based; 270 computer-based; 79 iBT). *Application deadline:* For fall admission, 5/1 priority date for domestic students; for spring admission, 9/1 priority date for domestic students. Applications are processed on a rolling basis. Application fee: $45. *Financial support:* In 2009–10, 1 student received support, including 1 research assistantship with full and partial tuition reimbursement available (averaging $7,500 per year); fellowships, teaching assistantships with full and partial tuition reimbursements available, institutionally sponsored loans, scholarships/grants, and unspecified assistantships also available. Financial award application deadline: 3/31; financial award applicants required to submit FAFSA. *Unit head:* Dr. Frank Lockwood, Director, 828-227-3390, Fax: 828-227-7414, E-mail: lockwood@email.wcu.edu. *Application contact:* Admissions Specialist for Entrepreneurship, 828-227-7398, Fax: 828-227-7480, E-mail: gradsch@email.wcu.edu.

Wilkes University, College of Graduate and Professional Studies, Jay S. Sidhu School of Business and Leadership, Wilkes-Barre, PA 18766-0002. Offers accounting (MBA); entrepreneurship (MBA); finance (MBA); human resource management (MBA); international business (MBA); management (MBA); marketing (MBA). *Accreditation:* ACBSP. Part-time and evening/weekend programs available. *Students:* 86 full-time (41 women), 118 part-time (59 women); includes 7 minority (4 African Americans, 1 Asian American or Pacific Islander, 2 Hispanic Americans), 48 international. Average age 29. In 2009, 59 master's awarded. *Entrance requirements:* For master's, GMAT. Additional exam requirements/recommendations for international students: Required—TOEFL (minimum score 500 paper-based; 173 computer-based; 79 iBT). *Application deadline:* Applications are processed on a rolling basis. Application fee: $45. *Expenses:* Contact institution. *Financial support:* Federal Work-Study and unspecified assistantships available. Financial award application deadline: 3/1; financial award applicants required to submit FAFSA. *Unit head:* Dr. Paul Browne, Dean, 570-408-4701, Fax: 570-408-7846, E-mail: paul.browne@wilkes.edu. *Application contact:* Kathleen Houlihan, Director of Graduate Studies, 570-408-3235, Fax: 570-408-7846, E-mail: kathleen.houlihan@wilkes.edu.

Section 6
Facilities and Entertainment Management

This section contains a directory of institutions offering graduate work in facilities and entertainment management. Additional information about programs listed in the directory may be obtained by writing directly to the dean of a graduate school or chair of a department at the address given in the directory.

For programs offering related work, see also in this book *Business Administration and Management*.

CONTENTS

Program Directories

Entertainment Management

California Intercontinental University, Hollywood College of the Entertainment Industry, Diamond Bar, CA 91765. Offers Hollywood and entertainment management (MBA).

Carnegie Mellon University, H. John Heinz III College, Institute for the Management of Creative Enterprises, Program in Entertainment Industry Management, Pittsburgh, PA 15213-3891. Offers MEIM. *Accreditation:* AACSB.

Columbia College Chicago, Graduate School, Department of Arts, Entertainment and Media Management, Chicago, IL 60605-1996. Offers arts, entertainment and media management (MA), including media management, music business management, performing arts management, visual arts management. Evening/weekend programs available. *Degree requirements:* For master's, thesis, internship. *Entrance requirements:* For master's, self-assessment essay. Additional exam requirements/recommendations for international students: Required—TOEFL (minimum score 550 paper-based; 213 computer-based). Electronic applications accepted. *Expenses:* Tuition: Part-time $651 per credit hour. Required fees: $205 per semester. One-time fee: $285 part-time. Tuition and fees vary according to program.

Full Sail University, Entertainment Business Master of Science Program—Campus, Winter Park, FL 32792-7437. Offers MS.

Full Sail University, Entertainment Business Master of Science Program—Online, Winter Park, FL 32792-7437. Offers MS. Postbaccalaureate distance learning degree programs offered. *Entrance requirements:* Additional exam requirements/recommendations for international students: Required—TOEFL (minimum score 550 paper-based; 213 computer-based; 79 iBT).

Hofstra University, Frank G. Zarb School of Business, Department of Management, Entrepreneurship and General Management, Hempstead, NY 11549. Offers business administration (MBA), including health services management, management, sports and entertainment management; human resource management (MS). Part-time and evening/weekend programs available. *Faculty:* 6 full-time (2 women), 4 part-time/adjunct (0 women). *Students:* 75 full-time (35 women), 185 part-time (72 women); includes 55 minority (19 African Americans, 24 Asian Americans or Pacific Islanders, 12 Hispanic Americans), 26 international. Average age 33. 215 applicants, 61% accepted, 71 enrolled. In 2009, 53 master's awarded. *Degree requirements:* For master's, capstone course (MBA), thesis (MS). *Entrance requirements:* For master's, GMAT or GRE, 2 letters of recommendation, resume. Additional exam requirements/recommendations for international students: Required—TOEFL (minimum score 550 paper-based; 213 computer-based; 80 iBT); Recommended—IELTS (minimum score 6). *Application deadline:* Applications are processed on a rolling basis. Application fee: $60. Electronic applications accepted. *Expenses:* Contact institution. *Financial support:* In 2009–10, 23 students received support, including 20 fellowships with full and partial tuition reimbursements available (averaging $10,251 per year), 2 research assistantships with full and partial tuition reimbursements available (averaging $20,788 per year); career-related internships or fieldwork, Federal Work-Study, institutionally sponsored loans, scholarships/grants, tuition waivers (full and partial), and unspecified assistantships also available. Support available to part-time students. Financial award applicants required to submit FAFSA. *Faculty research:* Business/personal ethics; emotion in workplace; gender issues; learning and pedagogical issues; family business. *Unit head:* Dr. Mamdouh I. Farid, Chairperson, 516-463-5735, Fax: 516-463-4834, E-mail: mgbmif@hofstra.edu. *Application contact:* Carol Drummer, Dean of Graduate Admissions, 516-463-4876, Fax: 516-463-4664, E-mail: gradstudent@hofstra.edu.

University of Dallas, Graduate School of Management, Irving, TX 75062-4736. Offers accounting (MBA, MM, MS); business management (MBA, MM); corporate finance (MBA, MM); financial services (MBA); global business (MBA, MM); health services management (MBA, MM); human resource management (MBA, MM); information assurance (MBA, MM, MS); information technology (MBA, MM, MS); information technology service management (MBA, MM, MS); marketing management (MBA, MM); organization development (MBA, MM); project management (MBA, MM); sports and entertainment management (MBA, MM); strategic leadership (MBA, MM); supply chain management (MBA); supply chain management and market logistics (MM). *Accreditation:* ACBSP. Part-time and evening/weekend programs available. Postbaccalaureate distance learning degree programs offered (no on-campus study). *Faculty:* 25 full-time (6 women), 31 part-time/adjunct (6 women). *Students:* 232 full-time (95 women), 923 part-time (365 women); includes 462 minority (184 African Americans, 14 American Indian/Alaska Native, 153 Asian Americans or Pacific Islanders, 111 Hispanic Americans), 184 international. Average age 34. 474 applicants, 85% accepted, 237 enrolled. In 2009, 399 master's awarded. *Entrance requirements:* Additional exam requirements/recommendations for international students: Required—TOEFL. *Application deadline:* Applications are processed on a rolling basis. Application fee: $50. Electronic applications accepted. *Expenses:* Contact institution. *Financial support:* In 2009–10, 399 students received support. Scholarships/grants and unspecified assistantships available. Financial award application deadline: 2/15; financial award applicants required to submit FAFSA. *Unit head:* Alounda Joseph, Director of Enrollment Processes, 972-721-5356, E-mail: admiss@gsm.udallas.edu. *Application contact:* Alounda Joseph, Director of Enrollment Processes, 972-721-5356, E-mail: admiss@gsm.udallas.edu.

University of South Carolina, The Graduate School, College of Hospitality, Retail, and Sport Management, Department of Sport and Entertainment Management, Columbia, SC 29208. Offers live sport and entertainment events (MS); public assembly facilities management (MS). Part-time programs available. *Degree requirements:* For master's, comprehensive exam, thesis optional. *Entrance requirements:* For master's, GRE General Test or GMAT (preferred), minimum GPA of 3.0. Additional exam requirements/recommendations for international students: Required—TOEFL (minimum score 570 paper-based; 230 computer-based; 70 iBT). Electronic applications accepted. *Expenses:* Contact institution. *Faculty research:* Public assembly marketing, operations, box office, booking and scheduling, law/economic impacts.

Facilities Management

Cornell University, Graduate School, Graduate Fields of Human Ecology, Field of Design and Environmental Analysis, Ithaca, NY 14853-0001. Offers applied research in human-environment relations (MS); facilities planning and management (MS); housing and design (MS); human factors and ergonomics (MS); human-environment relations (MS); interior design (MA, MPS). *Faculty:* 14 full-time (6 women). *Students:* 20 full-time (16 women); includes 3 minority (2 Asian Americans or Pacific Islanders, 1 Hispanic American), 2 international. Average age 27. 43 applicants, 30% accepted, 12 enrolled. In 2009, 3 master's awarded. *Degree requirements:* For master's, thesis. *Entrance requirements:* For master's, GRE General Test, portfolio or slides of recent work; bachelor's degree in interior design, architecture or related design discipline; 2 letters of recommendation. Additional exam requirements/recommendations for international students: Required—TOEFL (minimum score 600 paper-based; 250 computer-based; 105 iBT). *Application deadline:* For fall admission, 2/1 priority date for domestic students. Application fee: $70. Electronic applications accepted. *Expenses:* Tuition: Full-time $29,500. Required fees: $70. Full-time tuition and fees vary according to degree level, program and student level. *Financial support:* In 2009–10, 13 students received support, including 1 fellowship with full tuition reimbursement available, 5 teaching assistantships with full tuition reimbursements available; research assistantships with full tuition reimbursements available, institutionally sponsored loans, scholarships/grants, health care benefits, tuition waivers (full and partial), and unspecified assistantships also available. Financial award applicants required to submit FAFSA. *Faculty research:* Facility planning and management, environmental psychology, housing, interior design, ergonomics and human factors. *Unit head:* Director of Graduate Studies, 607-255-2168, Fax: 607-255-0305. *Application contact:* Graduate Field Assistant, 607-255-2168, Fax: 607-255-0305, E-mail: deagrad@cornell.edu.

Indiana University of Pennsylvania, School of Graduate Studies and Research, College of Health and Human Services, Department of Health and Physical Education, Indiana, PA 15705-1087. Offers aquatics administration and facilities management (MS); exercise science (MS); sport management (MS); sport science (MS). Part-time programs available. *Faculty:* 8 full-time (4 women). *Students:* 55 full-time (24 women), 33 part-time (10 women); includes 8 minority (all African Americans), 14 international. Average age 25. 154 applicants, 48% accepted, 48 enrolled. In 2009, 54 master's awarded. *Degree requirements:* For master's, thesis optional. *Entrance requirements:* For master's, 2 letters of recommendation. Additional exam requirements/recommendations for international students: Required—TOEFL. *Application deadline:* For fall admission, 7/1 priority date for domestic students; for spring admission, 11/1 for domestic students. Applications are processed on a rolling basis. Application fee: $40. *Expenses:* Tuition, state resident: full-time $6666; part-time $370 per credit hour. Tuition, nonresident: full-time $10,666; part-time $593 per credit hour. Required fees: $813 per semester. *Financial support:* In 2009–10, 1 fellowship (averaging $500 per year), 16 research assistantships with full and partial tuition reimbursements (averaging $4,335 per year) were awarded. Financial award application deadline: 3/15; financial award applicants required to submit FAFSA. *Unit head:* Dr. Elaine Blair, Chairperson, 724-357-2770, E-mail: eblair@iup.edu. *Application contact:* Dr. Elaine Blair, Chairperson, 724-357-2770, E-mail: eblair@iup.edu.

Indiana University–Purdue University Fort Wayne, College of Engineering, Technology, and Computer Science, Program in Technology, Fort Wayne, IN 46805-1499. Offers facilities and construction management (MS); industrial technology/manufacturing (MS); information technology/advanced computer applications (MS). Part-time programs available. *Faculty:* 10 full-time (6 women), 2 part-time/adjunct (0 women). *Students:* 6 full-time (3 women), 18 part-time (1 woman); includes 4 minority (3 Asian Americans or Pacific Islanders, 1 Hispanic American), 3 international. Average age 33. 13 applicants, 100% accepted, 12 enrolled. *Entrance requirements:* For master's, minimum GPA of 3.0. Additional exam requirements/recommendations for international students: Required—TOEFL (minimum score 550 paper-based; 213 computer-based; 77 iBT), TWE. *Application deadline:* For fall admission, 7/15 for domestic students, 5/15 for international students; for spring admission, 12/1 for domestic students, 10/15 for international students. Applications are processed on a rolling basis. Application fee: $55 ($60 for international students). Electronic applications accepted. *Expenses:* Tuition, state resident: full-time $4595; part-time $255 per credit. Tuition, nonresident: full-time $10,963; part-time $609 per credit. Required fees: $528; $29.35 per credit. Tuition and fees vary according to course load. *Financial support:* Career-related internships or fieldwork, scholarships/grants, and unspecified assistantships also available. Support available to part-time students. Financial award application deadline: 3/1; financial award applicants required to submit FAFSA. *Unit head:* Dr. Gerard Voland, Dean, 260-481-6839, Fax: 260-481-5734, E-mail: volandg@ipfw.edu. *Application contact:* Dr. Paul Lin, Graduate Program Director, 260-481-6339, Fax: 260-481-5734, E-mail: lin@ipfw.edu.

Massachusetts Maritime Academy, Program in Facilities Management, Buzzards Bay, MA 02532-1803. Offers MS. Part-time and evening/weekend programs available. *Entrance requirements:* For master's, GRE or GMAT, interview.

Pratt Institute, School of Architecture, Program in Facilities Management, New York, NY 10011. Offers MS. Part-time programs available. *Faculty:* 1 (woman) full-time, 5 part-time/adjunct (0 women). *Students:* 12 full-time (4 women), 4 part-time (1 woman); includes 6 minority (5 African Americans, 1 Hispanic American), 4 international. Average age 33. 21 applicants, 86% accepted, 7 enrolled. In 2009, 7 master's awarded. *Degree requirements:* For master's, thesis. *Entrance requirements:* For master's, writing sample, bachelor's degree, transcripts, letters of recommendation, portfolio. Additional exam requirements/recommendations for international students: Required—TOEFL (minimum score 550 paper-based; 213 computer-based; 79 iBT). *Application deadline:* For fall admission, 1/5 for domestic and international students; for spring admission, 10/1 for domestic and international students. Applications are processed on a rolling basis. Application fee: $50 ($90 for international students). Electronic applications accepted. *Expenses:* Tuition: Full-time $22,734. Required fees: $1280. *Financial support:* Career-related internships or fieldwork, Federal Work-Study, institutionally sponsored loans, scholarships/grants, health care benefits, and unspecified assistantships available. Support available to part-time students. Financial award application deadline: 2/1; financial award applicants required to submit FAFSA. *Faculty research:* Benchmarking, organizational studies, resource planning and management, computer-aided facilities management, value analysis. *Unit head:* Harriet Markis, Chairperson, 212-647-7524, Fax: 212-367-2497, E-mail: hmarkis@pratt.edu. *Application contact:* Young Hah, Director of Graduate Admissions, 718-636-3683, Fax: 718-399-4242, E-mail: yhah@pratt.edu.

Southern Methodist University, Bobby B. Lyle School of Engineering, Department of Environmental and Civil Engineering, Dallas, TX 75275-0340. Offers applied science (MS, PhD); civil engineering (MS, PhD); environmental engineering (MS); environmental science (MS), including environmental systems management, hazardous and waste materials management; facilities management (MS). Part-time and evening/weekend programs available. Postbaccalaureate distance learning degree programs offered (no on-campus study). *Faculty:* 7 full-time (0 women), 13 part-time/adjunct (4 women). *Students:* 19 full-time (8 women), 50 part-time (17 women); includes 13 minority (9 African Americans, 2 Asian Americans or Pacific Islanders, 2 Hispanic Americans), 7 international. Average age 34. 50 applicants, 86% accepted, 28 enrolled. In 2009, 17 master's, 1 doctorate awarded. Terminal master's awarded for partial completion of doctoral program. *Degree requirements:* For master's, thesis optional; for doctorate, thesis/dissertation, oral and written qualifying exams. *Entrance requirements:* For master's, GRE General Test, minimum GPA of 3.0 in last 2 years; bachelor's degree in engineering, mathematics, or sciences; for doctorate, GRE, BS and MS in related field, minimum GPA of 3.3. Additional exam requirements/recommendations for international students: Required—TOEFL. *Application deadline:* For fall admission, 7/1 for domestic students, 5/15 for international students; for spring admission, 11/15 for domestic students, 9/1 for international students. Applications are processed on a rolling basis. Application fee: $75. Electronic applications accepted. *Financial support:* In 2009–10, 9 students received support, including 2 research assistantships with full tuition reimbursements available (averaging $18,000 per year), 7 teaching assistantships with full tuition reimbursements available (averaging $18,000 per year); career-related internships or fieldwork, tuition waivers (full and partial), and unspecified assistantships also available. *Faculty research:* Human and environmental health effects of endocrine disrupters, development of air pollution control systems for diesel engines, structural analysis and design, modeling and design of waste treatment systems. Total annual research expenditures: $100,000. *Unit head:* Prof. Bijan Mohraz, Chair, 214-768-3894, Fax: 214-768-

2164, E-mail: bmohraz@lyle.smu.edu. *Application contact:* Marc Valerin, Director of Graduate and Executive Admissions, 214-768-3042, Fax: 214-768-3778, E-mail: valerin@lyle.smu.edu.

Université Laval, Faculty of Administrative Sciences, Programs in Business Administration, Québec, QC G1K 7P4, Canada. Offers accounting (MBA); agri-food management (MBA); electronic business (MBA, Diploma); factory management and logistics (MBA); finance (MBA); firm management (MBA); geomatic management (MBA); information technology management (MBA); international management (MBA); management (MBA); management accounting (MBA, Diploma); marketing (MBA); modeling and organizational decision (MBA); occupational health and safety management (MBA); pharmacy management (MBA); social and environmental responsibility (MBA); technological entrepreneurship (Diploma). *Accreditation:* AACSB. Part-time and evening/weekend programs available. Postbaccalaureate distance learning degree programs offered (no on-campus study). *Entrance requirements:* For master's and Diploma, knowledge of French and English. Electronic applications accepted.

University of California, Berkeley, UC Berkeley Extension, Certificate Programs in Engineering, Construction and Facilities Management, Berkeley, CA 94720-1500. Offers construction management (Certificate); HVAC (Certificate); integrated circuit design and techniques (online) (Certificate). Postbaccalaureate distance learning degree programs offered. *Unit head:* Diana Wu, Dean, 510-642-4181. *Application contact:* Engineering, Construction, and Facilities Management, 510-642-4151, E-mail: course@unex.berkeley.edu.

The University of Kansas, Graduate Studies, School of Architecture, Design, and Planning, Program in Architecture, Lawrence, KS 66045. Offers architecture (PhD); facility management (AC); management option (M Arch); professional track (M Arch); M Arch/MBA; M Arch/MUP. *Faculty:* 20 full-time (5 women). *Students:* 122 full-time (48 women), 19 part-time (11 women); includes 14 minority (6 African Americans, 2 American Indian/Alaska Native, 2 Asian Americans or Pacific Islanders, 4 Hispanic Americans), 11 international. Average age 25. 113 applicants, 65% accepted, 37 enrolled. In 2009, 76 master's awarded. Terminal master's awarded for partial completion of doctoral program. *Degree requirements:* For master's, thesis or alternative, 1 summer abroad; for doctorate, comprehensive exam, thesis/dissertation. *Entrance requirements:* For master's, portfolio, minimum GPA of 3.0; for doctorate, GRE, portfolio. Additional exam requirements/recommendations for international students: Required—TOEFL. *Application deadline:* For fall admission, 3/1 priority date for domestic and international students; for spring admission, 11/1 priority date for domestic and international students. Applications are processed on a rolling basis. Application fee: $45 ($55 for international students). Electronic applications accepted. *Expenses:* Tuition, state resident: full-time $6492; part-time $270.50 per credit hour. Tuition, nonresident: full-time $15,510; part-time $646.25 per credit hour. Required fees: $847; $70.56 per credit hour. Tuition and fees vary according to course load and program. *Financial support:* Design assistantships with partial tuition reimbursements, teaching assistantships with full and partial tuition reimbursements, scholarships/grants, health care benefits, and unspecified assistantships available. Financial award application deadline: 2/1; financial award applicants required to submit FAFSA. *Faculty research:* Design build, sustainability, emergent technology, healthy places, urban design. *Unit head:* Prof. Keith Diaz Moore, Chair, 785-864-5088, Fax: 785-864-5185, E-mail: archku@ku.edu. *Application contact:* Gera Elliott, Admissions Coordinator, 785-864-3167, Fax: 785-864-5185, E-mail: archku@ku.edu.

University of New Haven, Graduate School, School of Business, Program in Sports Management, West Haven, CT 06516-1916. Offers facility management (MS); management of sports industries (Certificate); sports management (MS). *Faculty:* 2 full-time (0 women), 11 part-time/adjunct (4 women). *Students:* 19 full-time (7 women), 12 part-time (5 women); includes 2 minority (both African Americans), 5 international. Average age 26. 31 applicants, 94% accepted, 15 enrolled. In 2009, 17 master's awarded. *Entrance requirements:* For master's, GMAT, minimum GPA of 2.7. Additional exam requirements/recommendations for international students: Required—TOEFL (minimum score 520 paper-based; 190 computer-based; 70 iBT); Recommended—IELTS (minimum score 5.5). *Application deadline:* For fall admission, 5/31 for international students; for winter admission, 10/15 for international students; for spring admission, 1/15 for international students. Applications are processed on a rolling basis. Application fee: $50. Electronic applications accepted. *Expenses:* Tuition: Part-time $700 per credit. Required fees: $45 per term. One-time fee: $390 part-time. *Financial support:* Research assistantships with partial tuition reimbursements, teaching assistantships with partial tuition reimbursements, career-related internships or fieldwork, Federal Work-Study, scholarships/grants, tuition waivers, and unspecified assistantships available. Support available to part-time students. Financial award applicants required to submit FAFSA. *Unit head:* Dr. Gil B. Fried, Head, 203-932-7081. *Application contact:* Eloise Gormley, Director of Graduate Admissions, 203-932-7449, Fax: 203-932-7137, E-mail: gradinfo@newhaven.edu.

Section 7
Hospitality Management

This section contains a directory of institutions offering graduate work in hospitality management, including a display ad submitted by an institution that chose to submit it. Additional information about programs listed in the directory may be obtained by writing directly to the dean of a graduate school or chair of a department at the address given in the directory.

For programs offering related work, see also in this book *Business Administration and Management, Advertising and Public Relations,* and *Health Services.* In another guide in this series:
Graduate Programs in the Physical Sciences, Mathematics, Agricultural Sciences, the Environment & Natural Resources
See *Agricultural and Food Sciences (Food Science and Technology)*

CONTENTS

Hospitality Management

American International College, School of Business Administration, MBA Program, Springfield, MA 01109-3189. Offers accounting (MBA); corporate/public communication (MBA); finance (MBA); general business (MBA); hospitality, hotel and service management (MBA); international business (MBA); international business practice (MBA); management (MBA); management information systems (MBA); marketing (MBA). International business practice program developed in cooperation with the Mountbatten Institute. *Expenses:* Tuition: Full-time $12,510; part-time $695 per credit hour. Required fees: $35 per term.

Andrew Jackson University, Brian Tracy College of Business and Entrepreneurship, Birmingham, AL 35244. Offers entrepreneurship (MBA); finance (MBA); health services management (MBA); hospitality and tourism management (MBA); human resource management (MBA); international business (MBA); management (MBA); marketing (MBA). Part-time and evening/weekend programs available. Postbaccalaureate distance learning degree programs offered (no on-campus study). *Entrance requirements:* For master's, course work in calculus, statistics, macroeconomics. Additional exam requirements/recommendations for international students: Required—TOEFL (minimum score 550 paper-based; 213 computer-based). Electronic applications accepted.

California State University, Long Beach, Graduate Studies, College of Health and Human Services, Department of Family and Consumer Sciences, Master of Science in Nutritional Science Program, Long Beach, CA 90840. Offers food science (MS); hospitality foodservice and hotel management (MS); nutritional science (MS). Part-time programs available. *Students:* 25 full-time (24 women), 22 part-time (all women); includes 14 minority (1 African American, 10 Asian Americans or Pacific Islanders, 3 Hispanic Americans), 1 international. Average age 26. 50 applicants, 62% accepted, 17 enrolled. *Degree requirements:* For master's, thesis, oral presentation of thesis or directed project. *Entrance requirements:* For master's, GRE, minimum GPA of 2.5 in last 60 units. *Application deadline:* For fall admission, 5/1 for domestic students. Applications are processed on a rolling basis. Application fee: $55. Electronic applications accepted. *Expenses:* Required fees: $1802 per semester. Part-time tuition and fees vary according to course load. *Financial support:* Federal Work-Study, institutionally sponsored loans, and scholarships/grants available. Financial award application deadline: 3/2. *Faculty research:* Protein and water-soluble vitamins, sensory evaluation of foods, mineral deficiencies in humans, child nutrition, minerals and blood pressure. *Unit head:* Dr. M. Sue Stanley, Chair, 562-985-4484, Fax: 562-985-4414, E-mail: stanleym@csulb.edu. *Application contact:* Dr. Mary Jacob, Graduate Coordinator, 562-985-4484, Fax: 562-985-4414, E-mail: marjacob@csulb.edu.

California State University, Northridge, Graduate Studies, College of Health and Human Development, Department of Recreation and Tourism Management, Northridge, CA 91330. Offers hospitality and tourism (MS); recreational sport management/campus recreation (MS). *Faculty:* 6 full-time (4 women), 11 part-time/adjunct (7 women). *Students:* 29 full-time (17 women), 21 part-time (11 women); includes 6 minority (4 African Americans, 1 Asian American or Pacific Islander, 1 Hispanic American), 9 international. Average age 27. 53 applicants, 77% accepted, 31 enrolled. In 2009, 8 master's awarded. *Degree requirements:* For master's, thesis (for some programs). *Entrance requirements:* For master's, GRE (if cumulative undergraduate GPA less than 3.0). Additional exam requirements/recommendations for international students: Required—TOEFL. *Application deadline:* For fall admission, 11/30 for domestic students. Application fee: $55. *Financial support:* Application deadline: 3/1. *Unit head:* Dr. Craig Finney, Chair, 818-677-3202, E-mail: cfinney@csun.edu. *Application contact:* Dr. Craig Finney, Chair, 818-677-3202, E-mail: cfinney@csun.edu.

Central Michigan University, College of Graduate Studies, College of Business Administration, Department of Marketing and Hospitality Services Administration, Mount Pleasant, MI 48859. Offers marketing (MBA). Part-time and evening/weekend programs available. *Degree requirements:* For master's, thesis or alternative. *Entrance requirements:* For master's, GMAT. Electronic applications accepted. *Faculty research:* Consumer preferences and market assessment; marketing research and new product development; business economics and forecasting; SAP/marketing and logistics; services marketing and hospitality organizations.

Columbia Southern University, MBA Program, Orange Beach, AL 36561. Offers electronic business and technology (MBA); finance (MBA); general (MBA); healthcare management (MBA); hospitality and tourism (MBA); human resources management (MBA); international management (MBA); marketing (MBA); project management (MBA); public administration (MBA); sport management (MBA). Part-time and evening/weekend programs available. Postbaccalaureate distance learning degree programs offered (no on-campus study). *Entrance requirements:* For master's, bachelor's degree from accredited/approved institution. Additional exam requirements/recommendations for international students: Required—TOEFL. Electronic applications accepted.

Cornell University, Graduate School, Field of Hotel Administration, Ithaca, NY 14853-0001. Offers hospitality management (MMH); hotel administration (MS, PhD). *Faculty:* 52 full-time (15 women). *Students:* 82 full-time (43 women); includes 17 minority (14 Asian Americans or Pacific Islanders, 3 Hispanic Americans), 41 international. Average age 28. 179 applicants, 47% accepted, 68 enrolled. In 2009, 62 master's, 3 doctorates awarded. Terminal master's awarded for partial completion of doctoral program. *Degree requirements:* For master's, thesis (MS); for doctorate, comprehensive exam, thesis/dissertation. *Entrance requirements:* For master's and doctorate, GMAT, 1 academic and 1 employer letter of recommendation, 2 interviews. Additional exam requirements/recommendations for international students: Required—TOEFL (minimum score 600 paper-based; 250 computer-based). *Application deadline:* For fall admission, 2/1 for domestic students. Application fee: $70. Electronic applications accepted. *Expenses:* Tuition: Full-time $29,500. Required fees: $70. Full-time tuition and fees vary according to degree level, program and student level. *Financial support:* In 2009–10, 12 students received support; fellowships with full tuition reimbursements available, research assistantships with full tuition reimbursements available, teaching assistantships with full tuition reimbursements available, institutionally sponsored loans, scholarships/grants, health care benefits, tuition waivers (full and partial), and unspecified assistantships available. Financial award applicants required to submit FAFSA. *Faculty research:* Hospitality finance; property-asset management; real estate; management, strategy, and human resources; organizational communication. *Unit head:* Director of Graduate Studies, 607-255-7245. *Application contact:* Graduate Field Assistant, 607-255-6376, E-mail: mmh@cornell.edu.

Drexel University, School of Technology and Professional Studies, Philadelphia, PA 19104-2875. Offers construction management (MS); engineering technology (MS); food science (MS); hospitality management (MS); professional studies: creativity studies (MS); professional studies: e-learning leadership (MS); professional studies: homeland security management (MS); project management (MS); property management (MS); sport management (MS). Postbaccalaureate distance learning degree programs offered.

Eastern Michigan University, Graduate School, College of Technology, School of Technology Studies, Program in Hotel and Restaurant Management, Ypsilanti, MI 48197. Offers MS, Graduate Certificate. Part-time and evening/weekend programs available. Postbaccalaureate distance learning degree programs offered (minimal on-campus study). *Students:* 4 full-time (all women), 9 part-time (6 women); includes 6 minority (2 African Americans, 2 Asian Americans or Pacific Islanders, 2 Hispanic Americans), 6 international. Average age 30. In 2009, 2 master's awarded. *Entrance requirements:* Additional exam requirements/recommendations for international students: Required—TOEFL. *Application deadline:* Applications are processed on a rolling basis. Application fee: $35. Tuition and fees vary according to course level. *Financial support:* Fellowships, research assistantships with full tuition reimbursements, teaching assistantships with full tuition reimbursements, career-related internships or fieldwork, Federal Work-Study, institutionally sponsored loans, scholarships/grants, tuition waivers (partial), and unspecified assistantships available. Support available to part-time students. Financial award applicants required to submit FAFSA. *Unit head:* Dr. Susan Gregory, Program Coordinator, 734-487-0845, Fax: 734-487-7690, E-mail: susan.gregory@emich.edu. *Application contact:* Dr. Susan Gregory, Program Coordinator, 734-487-0845, Fax: 734-487-7690, E-mail: susan.gregory@emich.edu.

East Stroudsburg University of Pennsylvania, Graduate School, College of Business and Management, Department of Hotel, Restaurant and Tourism Management, East Stroudsburg, PA 18301-2999. Offers management and leadership (MS). Part-time and evening/weekend programs available. *Faculty:* 3 full-time (1 woman). *Students:* 9 full-time (3 women); includes 3 minority (all African Americans), 2 international. Average age 28. In 2009, 4 master's awarded. *Degree requirements:* For master's, comprehensive exam. *Entrance requirements:* For master's, GRE or GMAT, 3 letters of recommendation. Additional exam requirements/recommendations for international students: Required—TOEFL (minimum score 560 paper-based; 220 computer-based; 83 iBT). *Application deadline:* For fall admission, 7/31 priority date for domestic students, 5/1 priority date for international students; for spring admission, 11/30 for domestic students, 10/1 for international students. Applications are processed on a rolling basis. Application fee: $50. *Expenses:* Tuition, state resident: full-time $9942; part-time $387 per credit. Tuition, nonresident: full-time $14,240; part-time $619 per credit. *Financial support:* Federal Work-Study and unspecified assistantships available. Financial award application deadline: 3/1; financial award applicants required to submit FAFSA. *Unit head:* Prof. Al Moranville, Graduate Coordinator, 570-422-3049, E-mail: moranville@po-box.esu.edu. *Application contact:* Kevin Quintero, Graduate Admissions Coordinator, 570-422-3890, Fax: 570-422-2711, E-mail: kquintero@po-box.esu.edu.

Ecole Hôtelière de Lausanne, Program in Hospitality Administration, Lausanne, Switzerland. Offers MHA. *Degree requirements:* For master's, project.

Endicott College, Apicius International School of Hospitality, Florence, MA 50122, Italy. Offers organizational management (M Ed). Program held entirely in Florence, Italy. *Entrance requirements:* For master's, MAT or GRE, 250-500 word essay explaining professional goals, official transcripts of all academic work, bachelor's degree, two letters of recommendation, personal interview. *Expenses:* Tuition: Part-time $389 per credit. One-time fee: $1350.

See Display on page 393.

Fairleigh Dickinson University, College at Florham, Anthony J. Petrocelli College of Continuing Studies, International School of Hospitality and Tourism Management, Madison, NJ 07940-1099. Offers hospitality management studies (MS). *Students:* 7 full-time (5 women), 32 part-time (18 women), 3 international. Average age 33. In 2009, 10 master's awarded. *Application deadline:* Applications are processed on a rolling basis. Application fee: $40. *Application contact:* Susan Brooman, University Director, Graduate Admissions, 973-443-8905, Fax: 973-443-8088, E-mail: grad@fdu.edu.

Fairleigh Dickinson University, Metropolitan Campus, Anthony J. Petrocelli College of Continuing Studies, International School of Hospitality and Tourism Management, Teaneck, NJ 07666-1914. Offers hospitality management (MS). *Students:* 12 full-time (10 women), 13 part-time (6 women), 14 international. Average age 30. 14 applicants, 79% accepted, 4 enrolled. In 2009, 6 master's awarded. *Application deadline:* Applications are processed on a rolling basis. Application fee: $40. *Unit head:* Dr. Richard Wisch, Director, 201-692-2000. *Application contact:* Susan Brooman, University Director of Graduate Admissions, 201-692-2554, Fax: 201-692-2560, E-mail: globaleducation@fdu.edu.

Florida International University, School of Hospitality and Tourism Management, Hospitality Management Program, Miami, FL 33199. Offers MS. Part-time and evening/weekend programs available. Postbaccalaureate distance learning degree programs offered. *Entrance requirements:* For master's, minimum GPA of 3.0, letters of recommendation, 5 years of management experience (for executive track). Additional exam requirements/recommendations for international students: Required—TOEFL (minimum score 550 paper-based; 213 computer-based). *Application deadline:* For fall admission, 6/1 for domestic students, 4/1 for international students; for spring admission, 10/1 for domestic students, 9/1 for international students. Applications are processed on a rolling basis. Electronic applications accepted. *Expenses:* Tuition, state resident: full-time $8008; part-time $4004 per year. Tuition, nonresident: full-time $20,104; part-time $10,052 per year. Required fees: $298; $149 per term. *Financial support:* Scholarships/grants available. *Unit head:* Dr. Joseph West, Dean, 305-919-4500, Fax: 305-919-4555, E-mail: jwest@fiu.edu. *Application contact:* Nanett Rojas, Coordinator of Graduate Admissions, 305-348-7442, Fax: 305-348-7441, E-mail: gradadm@fiu.edu.

The George Washington University, School of Business, Department of Tourism and Hospitality Management, Washington, DC 20052. Offers event and meeting management (MTA); event management (Professional Certificate); hospitality management (MTA, Professional Certificate); sports business management (Professional Certificate); sports management (MTA); sustainable destination management (MTA); tourism administration (MTA); tourism and hospitality management (MBA); tourism destination management (Professional Certificate). Part-time programs available. Postbaccalaureate distance learning degree programs offered. *Faculty:* 8 full-time (3 women), 5 part-time/adjunct (2 women). *Students:* 71 full-time (51 women), 110 part-time (86 women); includes 43 minority (23 African Americans, 3 American Indian/Alaska Native, 4 Asian Americans or Pacific Islanders, 13 Hispanic Americans), 42 international. Average age 30. 115 applicants, 83% accepted, 59 enrolled. In 2009, 74 master's awarded. *Degree requirements:* For master's, comprehensive exam, thesis. *Entrance requirements:* For master's, GRE General Test. Additional exam requirements/recommendations for international students: Required—TOEFL. *Application deadline:* For fall admission, 4/1 priority date for domestic students; for spring admission, 10/1 for domestic students. Applications are processed on a rolling basis. Application fee: $60. *Financial support:* In 2009–10, 32 students received support; fellowships, teaching assistantships, career-related internships or fieldwork, Federal Work-Study, institutionally sponsored loans, and tuition waivers (partial) available. Financial award application deadline: 4/1. *Faculty research:* Tourism policy, tourism impact forecasting, geotourism. *Unit head:* Susan M. Phillips, Dean, 202-994-6380, E-mail: gwsbdean@gwu.edu. *Application contact:* Kristin Williams, Assistant Vice President for Graduate and Special Enrollment Management, 202-994-0467, Fax: 202-994-0371, E-mail: ksw@gwu.edu.

Iowa State University of Science and Technology, Graduate College, College of Human Sciences, Department of Apparel, Education Studies, and Hospitality Management, Program in Foodservice and Lodging Management, Ames, IA 50011. Offers MFCS, MS, PhD. *Students:* 16 full-time (11 women), 16 part-time (10 women); includes 3 minority (1 African American, 1 Asian American or Pacific Islander, 1 Hispanic American), 14 international. In 2009, 2 master's, 6 doctorates awarded. *Degree requirements:* For master's, thesis or alternative; for doctorate, thesis/dissertation. *Entrance requirements:* For master's and doctorate, GMAT or GRE General Test. Additional exam requirements/recommendations for international students: Required—TOEFL (minimum score 550 paper-based; 80 iBT) or IELTS (minimum score 6.5). *Application deadline:* For fall admission, 2/1 priority date for domestic and international students. Application fee: $40 ($90 for international students). Electronic applications accepted. *Expenses:* Tuition, state resident: full-time $6716. Tuition, nonresident: full-time $8908. Tuition and fees vary according to course level, course load, program and student level. *Financial support:* In 2009–10, 6 research assistantships with full and partial tuition reimbursements (averaging $14,750 per year), 5 teaching assistantships with full and partial tuition reimbursements (averaging $14,750 per year) were awarded; scholarships/grants also available. *Unit head:* Dr. Ann-Marie Fiore, Director of Graduate Education, 515-294-9303. *Application contact:* Dr. Ann-Marie Fiore, Director of Graduate Education, 515-294-9303.

Johnson & Wales University, The Alan Shawn Feinstein Graduate School, MBA Program in Hospitality, Providence, RI 02903-3703. Offers event leadership (MBA); marketing (MBA). Part-time programs available. *Faculty:* 13 full-time (3 women), 17 part-time/adjunct (4 women). *Students:* 217 full-time (144 women), 25 part-time (15 women); includes 11 minority (7 African Americans, 1 Asian American or Pacific Islander, 3 Hispanic Americans), 186 international. Average age 25. 129 applicants, 80% accepted, 70 enrolled. In 2009, 48 master's awarded. *Entrance requirements:* For master's, minimum GPA of 2.85. Additional exam requirements/

recommendations for international students: Required—TOEFL, TOEFL (minimum score 550 paper-based; 210 computer-based; 80 iBT) or IELTS (minimum score 6.5); Recommended—TWE. *Application deadline:* For fall admission, 8/15 priority date for domestic students, 6/28 priority date for international students; for winter admission, 11/10 priority date for domestic students, 9/20 priority date for international students; for spring admission, 2/15 priority date for domestic students, 12/20 priority date for international students. Applications are processed on a rolling basis. Application fee: $0. Electronic applications accepted. *Expenses:* Required fees: $340 per quarter hour. *Financial support:* Tuition waivers (partial) and unspecified assistantships available. Support available to part-time students. Financial award application deadline: 5/1. *Faculty research:* Trade and tourism, hotel marketing, personal budget assessments, international ventures. *Unit head:* Dr. Frank Pontarelli, Dean, 401-598-1333, Fax: 401-598-1125. *Application contact:* Dr. Allan G. Freedman, Director of Graduate Admissions, 401-598-1015, Fax: 401-598-1286, E-mail: gradadm@jwu.edu.

Kansas State University, Graduate School, College of Human Ecology, Department of Hospitality Management and Dietetics, Manhattan, KS 66506. Offers dietetics (MS); food service hospitality management and dietetics administration (MS). Part-time programs available. *Faculty:* 6 full-time (3 women). *Students:* 19 full-time (14 women), 1 (woman) part-time, 2 international. Average age 29. 15 applicants, 93% accepted, 6 enrolled. *Degree requirements:* For master's, thesis or alternative, residency. *Entrance requirements:* Additional exam requirements/recommendations for international students: Required—TOEFL. *Application deadline:* For fall admission, 2/1 priority date for domestic and international students; for spring admission, 8/1 priority date for domestic and international students. Applications are processed on a rolling basis. Application fee: $40 ($55 for international students). Electronic applications accepted. *Financial support:* In 2009–10, 7 research assistantships (averaging $12,786 per year), 3 teaching assistantships with full and partial tuition reimbursements (averaging $11,523 per year) were awarded; Federal Work-Study, institutionally sponsored loans, and scholarships/grants also available. Support available to part-time students. Financial award application deadline: 3/1; financial award applicants required to submit FAFSA. *Faculty research:* Customer satisfaction, brand loyalty, food safety and biosecurity issues in foodservice operations; gerontology and the hospitality industry; education, training, and career development in dietetics and hospitality. Total annual research expenditures: $128,631. *Unit head:* Deborah Canter, Head, 785-532-5507, Fax: 785-532-5522, E-mail: canter@ksu.edu. *Application contact:* Judy Jensen, Application Contact, 785-532-2204, Fax: 785-532-5522, E-mail: jdj@ksu.edu.

Kansas State University, Graduate School, College of Human Ecology, Program in Human Ecology, Manhattan, KS 66506. Offers apparel and textiles (PhD); family life education and consultation (PhD); food service and hospitality management (PhD); lifespan and human development (PhD); marriage and family therapy (PhD); personal financial planning (PhD). *Faculty:* 3 full-time (all women). *Students:* 29 full-time (19 women), 43 part-time (23 women); includes 15 minority (13 African Americans, 1 American Indian/Alaska Native, 1 Asian American or Pacific Islander), 16 international. Average age 37. 29 applicants, 66% accepted, 16 enrolled. In 2009, 10 doctorates awarded. *Degree requirements:* For doctorate, thesis/dissertation. *Application deadline:* For fall admission, 2/1 priority date for domestic and international students; for spring admission, 8/1 priority date for domestic and international students. Applications are processed on a rolling basis. Application fee: $40 ($55 for international students). Electronic applications accepted. *Financial support:* Application deadline: 3/1. *Application contact:* Connie Fechter, Application Contact, 785-532-1473, Fax: 785-532-3796, E-mail: fechter@ksu.edu.

Kent State University, Graduate School of Education, Health, and Human Services, School of Foundations, Leadership and Administration, Program in Hospitality and Tourism Management, Kent, OH 44242-0001. Offers MS. Part-time programs available. *Faculty:* 5 full-time (3 women). *Students:* 8 full-time (4 women), 3 part-time (all women), 1 international. 13 applicants, 85% accepted. *Degree requirements:* For master's, thesis (for some programs). *Entrance requirements:* For master's, GRE, minimum GPA of 3.0, 3 letters of recommendation. Additional exam requirements/recommendations for international students: Required—TOEFL. *Application deadline:* Applications are processed on a rolling basis. Application fee: $30. Electronic applications accepted. *Financial support:* In 2009–10, 4 students received support, including 2 research assistantships with full tuition reimbursements available (averaging $8,500 per year); Federal Work-Study, scholarships/grants, and unspecified assistantships also available. Financial award application deadline: 2/1; financial award applicants required to submit FAFSA. *Faculty research:* Training human service workers, health care services for older adults, early adolescent development, caregiving arrangements with aging families, peace and war. *Unit head:* Barb Scheule, Coordinator, 330-672-3796, E-mail: bscheule@kent.edu. *Application contact:* Nancy Miller, Academic Program Coordinator, 330-672-2576, Fax: 330-672-9162, E-mail: ogs@kent.edu.

Lasell College, Graduate and Professional Studies in Sport Management, Newton, MA 02466-2709. Offers sport hospitality management (MS, Graduate Certificate); sport leadership (MS, Graduate Certificate); sport non-profit management (MS, Graduate Certificate). Part-time programs available. Postbaccalaureate distance learning degree programs offered (no on-campus study). *Entrance requirements:* For master's and Graduate Certificate, bachelor's degree from an accredited institution. Additional exam requirements/recommendations for international students: Required—TOEFL (minimum score 550 paper-based; 213 computer-based; 75 iBT) or IELTS. *Application deadline:* For fall admission, 8/31 priority date for domestic students, 6/30 priority date for international students; for spring admission, 12/31 priority date for domestic students, 10/31 priority date for international students. Applications are processed on a rolling basis. Electronic applications accepted. *Expenses:* Tuition: Full-time $4890; part-time $525 per credit hour. Required fees: $55 per term. *Financial support:* Available to part-time students. Application deadline: 8/31. *Unit head:* Dr. Joan Dolamore, Dean of Graduate and Professional Studies, 617-243-2485, Fax: 617-243-2450, E-mail: gradinfo@lasell.edu. *Application contact:* Adrienne Franciosi, Director of Graduate Admission, 617-243-2214, Fax: 617-243-2450, E-mail: gradinfo@lasell.edu.

Lynn University, College of Business and Management, Boca Raton, FL 33431-5598. Offers aviation management (MBA); financial valuation and investment management (MBA); hospitality management (MBA); international business (MBA); marketing (MBA); mass communication and media management (MBA); sports and athletics administration (MBA). Part-time and evening/weekend programs available. Postbaccalaureate distance learning degree programs offered. *Degree requirements:* For master's, project. *Entrance requirements:* For master's, GMAT or GRE, minimum undergraduate GPA of 3.0, resume, 2 letters of recommendation. Additional exam requirements/recommendations for international students: Required—TOEFL (minimum score 550 paper-based; 213 computer-based). *Application deadline:* Applications are processed on a rolling basis. Application fee: $50. Electronic applications accepted. *Expenses:* Tuition: Part-time $580 per credit. One-time fee: $200 part-time. Part-time tuition and fees vary according to degree level. *Financial support:* Career-related internships or fieldwork, Federal Work-Study, institutionally sponsored loans, scholarships/grants, tuition waivers (full and partial), and unspecified assistantships available. Support available to part-time students. Financial award application deadline: 8/1; financial award applicants required to submit FAFSA. *Faculty research:* Labor relations, dynamic balance in leisure-time skills, ethics in athletics, hotel development. *Unit head:* Dr. Ralph Norcio, Associate Dean, 561-237-7010, Fax: 561-237-7014, E-mail: rnorcio@lynn.edu. *Application contact:* Dr. Larissa Baia, Assistant Director of Graduate Admissions, 561-237-7916, Fax: 561-237-7100, E-mail: admissionpm@lynn.edu.

Michigan State University, The Graduate School, Eli Broad Graduate School of Management, The School of Hospitality Business, East Lansing, MI 48824. Offers foodservice business management (MS); hospitality business management (MS). *Faculty:* 11 full-time (2 women), 1 part-time/adjunct (0 women). *Students:* 31 full-time (21 women), 4 part-time (3 women); includes 1 minority (African American), 26 international. Average age 25. 60 applicants, 63% accepted. In 2009, 9 master's awarded. *Degree requirements:* For master's, research project. *Entrance requirements:* For master's, GRE General Test, minimum GPA of 3.0 in last 2 years of undergraduate course work, working knowledge of computers, resume, 3 letters of recommendation, specified college-level coursework or work experience. Additional exam

Hospitality Management

Michigan State University (continued)

requirements/recommendations for international students: Required—TOEFL (minimum score 580 paper-based; 237 computer-based). *Application deadline:* For fall admission, 12/27 priority date for domestic students. Electronic applications accepted. *Expenses:* Tuition, state resident: part-time $478.25 per credit hour. Tuition, nonresident: part-time $966.50 per credit hour. Part-time tuition and fees vary according to program. *Financial support:* Career-related internships or fieldwork, Federal Work-Study, scholarships/grants, and unspecified assistantships available. Support available to part-time students. *Faculty research:* Corporate food service management, entrepreneurial and food service management, hospitality business. Total annual research expenditures: $1,237. *Unit head:* Dr. Ronald F. Cichy, Director, 517-355-5080, Fax: 517-432-1170, E-mail: cichy@msu.edu. *Application contact:* Melissa Bankroff, Graduate Programs Coordinator, 517-353-9211, Fax: 517-432-1170, E-mail: mshb@bus.msu.edu.

New York University, School of Continuing and Professional Studies, The Preston Robert Tisch Center for Hospitality, Tourism, and Sports Management, Program in Hospitality Industry Studies, New York, NY 10012-1019. Offers customer relationship management (MS); hospitality industry studies (Advanced Certificate); hospitality investments (MS); hotel operations (MS); revenue management (MS). Part-time and evening/weekend programs available. *Faculty:* 13 full-time (5 women), 14 part-time/adjunct (2 women). *Students:* 19 full-time (16 women), 25 part-time (17 women); includes 10 minority (1 African American, 1 American Indian/Alaska Native, 6 Asian Americans or Pacific Islanders, 2 Hispanic Americans), 12 international. Average age 28. 78 applicants, 36% accepted, 12 enrolled. In 2009, 21 master's, 3 other advanced degrees awarded. *Degree requirements:* For master's, comprehensive exam (for some programs), thesis. *Entrance requirements:* For master's, GMAT or GRE General Test (for recent graduates), resume, 2 letters of recommendation. Additional exam requirements/recommendations for international students: Required—TOEFL (minimum score 600 paper-based; 250 computer-based; 100 iBT), TWE. *Application deadline:* For fall admission, 2/1 priority date for domestic and international students; for spring admission, 10/15 priority date for domestic students, 8/15 priority date for international students. Applications are processed on a rolling basis. Application fee: $75. Electronic applications accepted. *Expenses:* Tuition: Full-time $30,528; part-time $1272 per credit. Required fees: $2177. *Financial support:* In 2009–10, 17 students received support, including 17 fellowships (averaging $3,088 per year); career-related internships or fieldwork, Federal Work-Study, institutionally sponsored loans, and scholarships/grants also available. Support available to part-time students. Financial award application deadline: 3/1; financial award applicants required to submit FAFSA. *Unit head:* Lalia Rach, Divisional Dean, 212-998-9100, Fax: 212-995-4676, E-mail: lalia.rach@nyu.edu. *Application contact:* Sandra Dove-Lowther, Academic Services Director, 212-998-9106, Fax: 212-995-4676, E-mail: sd2@nyu.edu.

New York University, Steinhardt School of Culture, Education, and Human Development, Department of Nutrition, Food Studies, and Public Health, Program in Food Studies and Food Management, New York, NY 10012-1019. Offers food studies (MA), including food culture, food systems; food studies and food management (PhD). Part-time programs available. *Students:* 28 full-time (26 women), 107 part-time (89 women); includes 24 minority (5 African Americans, 13 Asian Americans or Pacific Islanders, 6 Hispanic Americans), 15 international. Average age 31. 107 applicants, 66% accepted, 50 enrolled. In 2009, 25 master's, 1 doctorate awarded. *Degree requirements:* For master's, thesis (for some programs); for doctorate, thesis/dissertation. *Entrance requirements:* For doctorate, GRE General Test, interview. Additional exam requirements/recommendations for international students: Required—TOEFL. *Application deadline:* For fall admission, 12/15 priority date for domestic students, 12/15 for international students; for spring admission, 11/1 for domestic and international students. Applications are processed on a rolling basis. Application fee: $75. Electronic applications accepted. *Expenses:* Tuition: Full-time $30,528; part-time $1272 per credit. Required fees: $2177. *Financial support:* Fellowships with full and partial tuition reimbursements, career-related internships or fieldwork, Federal Work-Study, institutionally sponsored loans, scholarships/grants, tuition waivers (partial), and unspecified assistantships available. Financial award application deadline: 2/1; financial award applicants required to submit FAFSA. *Faculty research:* Cultural and social history of food; food systems and agriculture; food and aesthetics; political economy of food. *Unit head:* Dr. Jennifer Berg, Director, 212-998-5580, Fax: 212-995-4194. *Application contact:* 212-998-5030, Fax: 212-995-4328, E-mail: steinhardt.gradadmissions@nyu.edu.

The Ohio State University, Graduate School, College of Education and Human Ecology, Department of Human Nutrition, Columbus, OH 43210. Offers food service management (MS, PhD); foods (MS, PhD); nutrition (MS, PhD). *Accreditation:* ADtA. *Faculty:* 18. *Students:* 8 full-time (7 women), 4 part-time (3 women); includes 2 minority (both African Americans), 3 international. Average age 30. In 2009, 9 master's awarded. *Degree requirements:* For master's, thesis optional; for doctorate, thesis/dissertation. *Entrance requirements:* For master's and doctorate, GRE General Test. Additional exam requirements/recommendations for international students: Required—TOEFL (minimum score 577 paper-based; 233 computer-based). *Application deadline:* For fall admission, 8/15 priority date for domestic students, 7/1 priority date for international students; for winter admission, 12/1 priority date for domestic students, 11/1 priority date for international students; for spring admission, 3/1 priority date for domestic students, 2/1 priority date for international students. Applications are processed on a rolling basis. Application fee: $40 ($50 for international students). Electronic applications accepted. *Expenses:* Tuition, state resident: full-time $10,683. Tuition, nonresident: full-time $25,923. Tuition and fees vary according to course load and program. *Financial support:* Fellowships, research assistantships, teaching assistantships, Federal Work-Study and institutionally sponsored loans available. Support available to part-time students. *Unit head:* James E. Kinder, Chair, 614-292-4485, Fax: 614-292-8880, E-mail: kinder.15@osu.edu. *Application contact:* 614-292-9444, Fax: 614-292-3895, E-mail: domestic.grad@osu.edu.

The Ohio State University, Graduate School, College of Education and Human Ecology, Program in Hospitality Management, Columbus, OH 43210. Offers MS, PhD. *Students:* 4 full-time (3 women), 1 (woman) part-time, 4 international. Average age 34. In 2009, 2 master's awarded. *Entrance requirements:* For master's and doctorate, GRE. *Application deadline:* For fall admission, 1/14 for domestic students, 12/1 for international students. Applications are processed on a rolling basis. Application fee: $40 ($50 for international students). Electronic applications accepted. *Expenses:* Tuition, state resident: full-time $10,683. Tuition, nonresident: full-time $25,923. Tuition and fees vary according to course load and program. *Unit head:* Jay Kandampully, Graduate Studies Committee Chair, 614-688-4583, Fax: 614-292-2581, E-mail: kandampully.1@osu.edu. *Application contact:* Graduate Admissions, 614-292-94444, Fax: 614-292-3895, E-mail: domestic.grad@osu.edu.

Oklahoma State University, College of Human Environmental Sciences, School of Hotel and Restaurant Administration, Stillwater, OK 74078. Offers MS, PhD. *Faculty:* 12 full-time (3 women), 4 part-time/adjunct (0 women). *Students:* 29 full-time (20 women), 31 part-time (18 women); includes 9 minority (2 African Americans, 2 American Indian/Alaska Native, 1 Asian American or Pacific Islander, 4 Hispanic Americans), 39 international. Average age 37. 28 applicants, 32% accepted, 5 enrolled. In 2009, 9 master's, 7 doctorates awarded. *Degree requirements:* For master's, thesis (for some programs); for doctorate, comprehensive exam, thesis/dissertation. *Entrance requirements:* For master's and doctorate, GRE or GMAT. Additional exam requirements/recommendations for international students: Required—TOEFL (minimum score 550 paper-based; 79 iBT). *Application deadline:* For fall admission, 3/1 priority date for international students; for spring admission, 8/1 priority date for international students. Applications are processed on a rolling basis. Application fee: $40 ($75 for international students). Electronic applications accepted. *Expenses:* Tuition, state resident: full-time $3716; part-time $154.85 per credit hour. Tuition, nonresident: full-time $14,448; part-time $602 per credit hour. Required fees: $1772; $73.85 per credit hour. One-time fee: $50. Tuition and fees vary according to course load and campus/location. *Financial support:* In 2009–10, 9 research assistantships (averaging $7,697 per year), 12 teaching assistantships (averaging $9,968 per year) were awarded; career-related internships or fieldwork, Federal Work-Study, scholarships/grants, health care benefits, tuition waivers (partial), and unspecified assistantships also available. Support available to part-time students. Financial award application deadline: 3/1; financial award applicants required to submit FAFSA. *Faculty research:* Hotel operations and management, restaurant/food service management, hospitality education, hospitality human resources management, tourism. *Unit head:* Dr. Bill Ryan, Director, 405-744-6713, Fax: 405-744-6299. *Application contact:* Dr. Gordon Emslie, Dean, 405-744-6368, Fax: 405-744-0355, E-mail: grad-i@okstate.edu.

Penn State University Park, Graduate School, College of Health and Human Development, School of Hospitality Management, State College, University Park, PA 16802-1503. Offers MS, PhD.

Purdue University, Graduate School, College of Consumer and Family Sciences, Department of Hospitality and Tourism Management, West Lafayette, IN 47907. Offers MS, PhD. *Degree requirements:* For master's, thesis optional; for doctorate, thesis/dissertation optional. *Entrance requirements:* For master's, GMAT or GRE General Test, minimum GPA of 3.0; for doctorate, GMAT or GRE. Additional exam requirements/recommendations for international students: Required—TOEFL. Electronic applications accepted. *Faculty research:* Human resources, marketing, hotel and restaurant operations, food product and equipment development, tourism development.

Rochester Institute of Technology, Graduate Enrollment Services, College of Applied Science and Technology, Department of Hospitality and Service Management, Program in Hospitality-Tourism Management, Rochester, NY 14623-5603. Offers MS. *Students:* 10 full-time (6 women), 3 part-time (2 women), 10 international. Average age 27. 30 applicants, 77% accepted, 5 enrolled. In 2009, 3 master's awarded. *Degree requirements:* For master's, thesis or project. *Entrance requirements:* For master's, minimum GPA of 3.0. Additional exam requirements/recommendations for international students: Required—TOEFL (minimum score 550 paper-based; 213 computer-based; 79 iBT) or IELTS (minimum score 6.5). *Application deadline:* For fall admission, 2/15 priority date for domestic and international students; for winter admission, 11/1 priority date for domestic students, 10/1 priority date for international students; for spring admission, 2/1 priority date for domestic students, 1/1 priority date for international students. Applications are processed on a rolling basis. Application fee: $50. *Expenses:* Tuition: Full-time $31,533; part-time $876 per credit hour. Required fees: $210. *Financial support:* In 2009–10, 6 students received support; research assistantships with partial tuition reimbursements available, teaching assistantships with partial tuition reimbursements available, career-related internships or fieldwork, scholarships/grants, and unspecified assistantships available. Support available to part-time students. Financial award application deadline: 2/15; financial award applicants required to submit FAFSA. *Unit head:* Dr. Linda Underhill, Chair, 585-475-7359, Fax: 585-475-5099, E-mail: lmuism@rit.edu. *Application contact:* Diane Ellison, Assistant Vice President, Graduate Enrollment Services, 585-475-2229, Fax: 585-475-7164, E-mail: gradinfo@rit.edu.

Rochester Institute of Technology, Graduate Enrollment Services, College of Applied Science and Technology, Department of Hospitality and Service Management, Program in Service Leadership and Innovation, Rochester, NY 14623-5603. Offers MS. Part-time and evening/weekend programs available. *Students:* 13 full-time (9 women), 49 part-time (29 women); includes 5 African Americans, 1 Hispanic American, 7 international. Average age 32. 68 applicants, 81% accepted, 36 enrolled. In 2009, 22 master's awarded. *Degree requirements:* For master's, thesis or alternative. *Entrance requirements:* For master's, minimum GPA of 3.0. Additional exam requirements/recommendations for international students: Required—TOEFL (minimum score 550 paper-based; 213 computer-based; 79 iBT), or IELTS (minimum score 6.5). *Application deadline:* For fall admission, 2/15 priority date for domestic and international students; for winter admission, 11/1 for domestic and international students; for spring admission, 2/1 for domestic and international students. Applications are processed on a rolling basis. Application fee: $50. *Expenses:* Tuition: Full-time $31,533; part-time $876 per credit hour. Required fees: $210. *Financial support:* In 2009–10, 23 students received support; research assistantships with partial tuition reimbursements available, teaching assistantships with partial tuition reimbursements available, career-related internships or fieldwork, institutionally sponsored loans, scholarships/grants, and unspecified assistantships available. Support available to part-time students. Financial award application deadline: 2/15; financial award applicants required to submit FAFSA. *Faculty research:* Global resource development, service/product innovation and implementation. *Unit head:* Dr. Linda Underhill, Chair, 585-475-7359, Fax: 585-475-5099, E-mail: lmuism@rit.edu. *Application contact:* Diane Ellison, Assistant Vice President, Graduate Enrollment Services, 585-475-2229, Fax: 585-475-7164, E-mail: gradinfo@rit.edu.

Roosevelt University, Graduate Division, College of Professional Studies, Program in Hospitality Management, Chicago, IL 60605. Offers MS. *Degree requirements:* For master's, thesis. *Entrance requirements:* For master's, minimum GPA of 2.75, work experience.

Royal Roads University, Graduate Studies, Tourism and Hotel Management Program, Victoria, BC V9B 5Y2, Canada. Offers destination development (Graduate Certificate); international hotel management (MA); sustainable tourism (Graduate Certificate); tourism leadership (Graduate Certificate); tourism management (MA).

Schiller International University, Graduate Programs, London, Program in International Hotel and Tourism Management, London, United Kingdom. Offers MA, MBA. Part-time and evening/weekend programs available. *Degree requirements:* For master's, thesis optional, GMAT before graduation. *Entrance requirements:* Additional exam requirements/recommendations for international students: Required—TOEFL (minimum score 550 paper-based; 213 computer-based).

Schiller International University, MBA Programs, Florida, Program in International Hotel and Tourism Management, Largo, FL 33770. Offers MBA. *Degree requirements:* For master's, thesis optional. *Entrance requirements:* Additional exam requirements/recommendations for international students: Required—TOEFL (minimum score 550 paper-based; 213 computer-based).

South Dakota State University, Graduate School, College of Education and Human Sciences, Department of Nutrition, Food Science and Hospitality, Brookings, SD 57007. Offers dietetics (MS); nutrition, food science and hospitality (MFCS); nutritional sciences (MS, PhD). Part-time programs available. *Degree requirements:* For master's, comprehensive exam (for some programs), thesis (for some programs), oral exam. *Entrance requirements:* Additional exam requirements/recommendations for international students: Required—TOEFL (minimum score 525 paper-based). *Faculty research:* Food chemistry, bone density, functional food, nutrition education, nutrition biochemistry.

Southern New Hampshire University, School of Business, Manchester, NH 03106-1045. Offers accounting (MS); business administration (MBA, Certificate), including accounting (Certificate), business administration (MBA), finance (Certificate), forensic accounting (Certificate), human resources management (Certificate), international business (Certificate), international sport management (Certificate), leadership of not for profit organizations (Certificate), marketing (Certificate), operations management (Certificate), sport management (Certificate), taxation (Certificate); finance (MS); hospitality and tourism leadership (Certificate); information technology (MS, Certificate); information technology/international business (Certificate); integrated marketing communications (Certificate); international business (MS, DBA); marketing (MS); operations and project management (MS); organizational leadership (MS); project management (Certificate); sport management (MS); MBA/Certificate. *Accreditation:* ACBSP. Part-time and evening/weekend programs available. Postbaccalaureate distance learning degree programs offered (no on-campus study). Terminal master's awarded for partial completion of doctoral program. *Degree requirements:* For master's, one foreign language, comprehensive exam (for some programs), thesis or alternative; for doctorate, one foreign language, comprehensive exam, thesis/dissertation. *Entrance requirements:* For master's, minimum GPA of 2.5; for doctorate, GMAT. Additional exam requirements/recommendations for international students: Required—TOEFL (minimum score 500 paper-based). Electronic applications accepted.

South University, Graduate Programs, College of Business, Savannah, GA 31406. Offers corrections (MBA); entrepreneurship and small business (MBA); hospitality management (MBA); sustainability (MBA).

Strayer University, Graduate Studies, Washington, DC 20005-2603. Offers accounting (MS); acquisition (MBA); business administration (MBA); communications technology (MS); educational management (M Ed); finance (MBA); health services administration (MHSA); hospitality and tourism management (MBA); human resource management (MBA); information systems (MS), including computer security management, decision support system management, enterprise resource management, network management, software engineering management, systems development management; management (MBA); management information systems (MS); marketing (MBA); professional accounting (MS), including accounting information systems, controllership, taxation; public administration (MPA); supply chain management (MBA); technology in education (M Ed). Programs also offered at campus locations in Birmingham, AL; Chamblee, GA; Cobb County, GA; Morrow, GA; White Marsh, MD; Charleston, SC; Columbia, SC; Greensboro, NC; Greenville, SC; Lexington, KY; Louisville, KY; Nashville, TN; North Raleigh, NC; Washington, DC. Part-time and evening/weekend programs available. Postbaccalaureate distance learning degree programs offered (minimal on-campus study). *Degree requirements:* For master's, thesis. *Entrance requirements:* For master's, GMAT, GRE General Test, bachelor's degree from an accredited college or university, minimum undergraduate GPA of 2.75. Electronic applications accepted.

Temple University, Graduate School, Fox School of Business, Doctoral Programs in Business, Philadelphia, PA 19122-6096. Offers accounting (PhD); entrepreneurship (PhD); finance (PhD); human resource administration (PhD); international business (PhD); management information systems (PhD); marketing (PhD); risk management and insurance (PhD); statistics (PhD); strategic management (PhD); tourism and sport (PhD). *Accreditation:* AACSB. *Degree requirements:* For doctorate, thesis/dissertation. *Entrance requirements:* For doctorate, GRE General Test, GMAT, minimum GPA of 3.0, master's degree. Additional exam requirements/recommendations for international students: Required—TOEFL (minimum score 600 paper-based; 250 computer-based; 100 iBT), IELTS (minimum score 7.5). Electronic applications accepted.

Temple University, Graduate School, School of Tourism and Hospitality Management, Program in Tourism and Hospitality Management, Philadelphia, PA 19122-6096. Offers MTHM. Part-time and evening/weekend programs available. *Entrance requirements:* For master's, GRE General Test or MAT, minimum of 2 years professional experience, minimum undergraduate GPA of 3.0. Additional exam requirements/recommendations for international students: Required—TOEFL (minimum score 550 paper-based; 213 computer-based; 79 iBT). Electronic applications accepted.

Texas Tech University, Graduate School, College of Human Sciences, Department of Nutrition, Hospitality, and Retailing, Program in Restaurant, Hotel, and Institutional Management, Lubbock, TX 79409. Offers hospitality administration (PhD); restaurant, hotel and institutional management (MS). Part-time programs available. Postbaccalaureate distance learning degree programs offered (minimal on-campus study). *Students:* 26 full-time (15 women), 6 part-time (5 women); includes 5 minority (1 Asian American or Pacific Islander, 4 Hispanic Americans), 5 international. Average age 28. 34 applicants, 71% accepted, 13 enrolled. In 2009, 12 master's awarded. *Degree requirements:* For master's, thesis or alternative; for doctorate, thesis/dissertation. *Entrance requirements:* For master's, GRE General Test; for doctorate, GRE. Additional exam requirements/recommendations for international students: Required—TOEFL (minimum score 550 paper-based; 213 computer-based). *Application deadline:* For fall admission, 3/1 priority date for international students; for spring admission, 11/1 priority date for international students. Applications are processed on a rolling basis. Application fee: $50 ($75 for international students). Electronic applications accepted. *Expenses:* Tuition, state resident: full-time $5100; part-time $213 per credit hour. Tuition, nonresident: full-time $11,748; part-time $490 per credit hour. Required fees: $2298; $50 per credit hour. $555 per semester. *Financial support:* Research assistantships with partial tuition reimbursements, teaching assistantships with partial tuition reimbursements, career-related internships or fieldwork, Federal Work-Study, institutionally sponsored loans, and scholarships/grants available. Support available to part-time students. Financial award application deadline: 4/15; financial award applicants required to submit FAFSA. *Faculty research:* Community engagement and food supply development and security, tourism, lodging and human resource management, rural tourism. *Unit head:* Dr. Shane Blum, Chairperson, 806-742-3068 Ext. 253, Fax: 806-742-3042, E-mail: shane.blum@ttu.edu. *Application contact:* Dr. Betty Stout, Graduate Advisor, Doctoral Program in Hospitality Administration, 806-742-3068 Ext. 233, Fax: 806-742-3042, E-mail: betty.stout@ttu.edu.

Troy University, Graduate School, College of Business, Program in Management, Troy, AL 36082. Offers healthcare management (MSM); human resources management (MSM); information systems (MSM); international hospitality management (MSM); international management (MSM); leadership and organizational effectiveness (MSM); public management (MS, MSM). *Accreditation:* ACBSP. Evening/weekend programs available. *Students:* 193 full-time (130 women), 575 part-time (374 women); includes 473 minority (417 African Americans, 12 American Indian/Alaska Native, 20 Asian Americans or Pacific Islanders, 24 Hispanic Americans). Average age 35. 275 applicants, 91% accepted. In 2009, 332 master's awarded. *Degree requirements:* For master's, thesis or alternative. *Entrance requirements:* For master's, GMAT (minimum score 500) or GRE General Test (minimum score 900), minimum GPA of 2.5; letter of recommendation. Additional exam requirements/recommendations for international students: Required—TOEFL (minimum score 523 paper-based; 193 computer-based; 70 iBT), IELTS, or ACT Compass ESL (minimum score 270 on Listening, Reading, and Grammar with no individual score below 85 and a minimum score of 8 out of 12 on writing test). *Application deadline:* Applications are processed on a rolling basis. Application fee: $50. Electronic applications accepted. *Expenses:* Contact institution. *Unit head:* Dr. Henry M. Findley, Interim Chair/Professor, 334-670-3271, Fax: 334-670-3599, E-mail: hfindley@troy.edu. *Application contact:* Brenda K. Campbell, Director of Graduate Admissions, 334-670-3178, Fax: 334-670-3733, E-mail: bcamp@troy.edu.

The University of Alabama, Graduate School, College of Human Environmental Sciences, Department of Human Nutrition and Hospitality Management, Tuscaloosa, AL 35487. Offers MSHES. Part-time programs available. Postbaccalaureate distance learning degree programs offered (no on-campus study). *Faculty:* 4 full-time (3 women). *Students:* 18 full-time (17 women), 59 part-time (58 women); includes 6 minority (5 African Americans, 1 Asian American or Pacific Islander), 1 international. Average age 31. 66 applicants, 52% accepted, 28 enrolled. In 2009, 22 degrees awarded. *Degree requirements:* For master's, comprehensive exam, thesis optional. *Entrance requirements:* For master's, minimum GPA of 3.0. Additional exam requirements/recommendations for international students: Required—TOEFL. *Application deadline:* For fall admission, 7/6 for domestic students. Applications are processed on a rolling basis. Application fee: $50 ($60 for international students). Electronic applications accepted. *Expenses:* Tuition, state resident: full-time $7000. Tuition, nonresident: full-time $19,200. *Financial support:* In 2009–10, 4 students received support, including 2 research assistantships (averaging $8,100 per year), 2 teaching assistantships (averaging $8,100 per year); career-related internships or fieldwork also available. Financial award application deadline: 3/15. *Faculty research:* Maternal and child nutrition, childhood obesity, community nutrition interventions, geriatric nutrition, family eating patterns. Total annual research expenditures: $11,473. *Unit head:* Dr. Olivia W. Kendrick, Chair and Associate Professor, 205-348-6150, Fax: 205-348-3789, E-mail: okendric@ches.ua.edu. *Application contact:* Dr. Olivia W. Kendrick, Chair and Associate Professor, 205-348-6150, Fax: 205-348-3789, E-mail: okendric@ches.ua.edu.

The University of Alabama, Graduate School, College of Human Environmental Sciences, Program in Human Environmental Science, Tuscaloosa, AL 35487. Offers family financial planning and counseling (MS); interactive technology (MS); quality management (MS); restaurant and meeting management (MS); rural community health (MS); sport management (MS). *Students:* 70 full-time (40 women), 99 part-time (45 women); includes 44 minority (42 African Americans, 2 Hispanic Americans), 1 international. Average age 33. 124 applicants, 71% accepted, 71 enrolled. In 2009, 70 degrees awarded. *Degree requirements:* For master's, comprehensive exam. *Entrance requirements:* For master's, GRE (for some specializations), minimum GPA of 3.0. Additional exam requirements/recommendations for international students: Required—TOEFL. *Application deadline:* Applications are processed on a rolling basis. Application fee: $50 ($60 for international students). Electronic applications accepted. *Expenses:* Tuition, state resident: full-time $7000. Tuition, nonresident: full-time $19,200. *Faculty research:* Hospitality management, sports medicine education, technology and education. *Unit head:* Dr. Milla D. Boschung, Dean, 205-348-6250, Fax: 205-348-1786, E-mail: mboschun@ches.ua.edu. *Application contact:* Dr. Stuart Usdan, Associate Dean, 205-348-6150, Fax: 205-348-3789, E-mail: susdan@ches.ua.edu.

University of Central Florida, Rosen College of Hospitality Management, Orlando, FL 32816. Offers hospitality and tourism management (MS). *Faculty:* 35 full-time (10 women), 27 part-time/adjunct (11 women). *Students:* 33 full-time (28 women), 41 part-time (24 women); includes 16 minority (5 African Americans, 3 Asian Americans or Pacific Islanders, 8 Hispanic Americans), 8 international. Average age 28. 60 applicants, 62% accepted, 25 enrolled. In 2009, 24 master's awarded. *Degree requirements:* For master's, thesis or alternative. *Entrance requirements:* For master's, GMAT or GRE, minimum GPA of 3.0 in last 60 hours. Additional exam requirements/recommendations for international students: Required—TOEFL. *Application deadline:* For fall admission, 2/1 for domestic students. Application fee: $30. Electronic applications accepted. *Expenses:* Tuition, state resident: part-time $306.31 per credit hour. Tuition, nonresident: part-time $1099.01 per credit hour. Part-time tuition and fees vary according to degree level and program. *Financial support:* In 2009–10, 1 student received support, including 1 fellowship with partial tuition reimbursement available (averaging $10,000 per year). *Unit head:* Dr. Abraham C. Pizam, Dean, 407-903-8010, E-mail: apizam@mail.ucf.edu. *Application contact:* Dr. Abraham C. Pizam, Dean, 407-903-8010, E-mail: apizam@mail.ucf.edu.

University of Delaware, Alfred Lerner College of Business and Economics, Program in Hospitality Information Management, Newark, DE 19716. Offers MS. *Entrance requirements:* Additional exam requirements/recommendations for international students: Required—TOEFL (minimum score 550 paper-based; 213 computer-based). Electronic applications accepted. *Faculty research:* Foodservice, lodging and tourism management.

University of Guelph, Graduate Program Services, College of Management and Economics, MBA Program, Guelph, ON N1G 2W1, Canada. Offers food and agribusiness management (MBA); hospitality and tourism management (MBA). Part-time and evening/weekend programs available. Postbaccalaureate distance learning degree programs offered (minimal on-campus study). *Entrance requirements:* For master's, minimum B-average, minimum of 3 years of relevant work experience. Additional exam requirements/recommendations for international students: Required—TOEFL (minimum score 550 paper-based; 213 computer-based). Electronic applications accepted. *Faculty research:* Marketing, operations management, business policy, financial management, organizational behavior.

University of Houston, Conrad N. Hilton College of Hotel and Restaurant Management, Houston, TX 77204. Offers MS. Part-time programs available. *Faculty:* 11 full-time (3 women), 9 part-time/adjunct (4 women). *Students:* 60 full-time (41 women), 12 part-time (8 women); includes 15 minority (5 African Americans, 4 Asian Americans or Pacific Islanders, 6 Hispanic Americans), 34 international. Average age 26. 59 applicants, 81% accepted, 28 enrolled. In 2009, 18 master's awarded. *Degree requirements:* For master's, practicum or thesis. *Entrance requirements:* For master's, GMAT or GRE General Test. Additional exam requirements/recommendations for international students: Required—TOEFL (minimum score 100 iBT) or IELTS (minimum score 7). *Application deadline:* For fall admission, 5/1 for domestic students, 4/1 for international students; for spring admission, 11/1 for domestic students, 10/1 for international students. Applications are processed on a rolling basis. Application fee: $50 ($75 for international students). Electronic applications accepted. *Expenses:* Tuition, state resident: full-time $7676; part-time $320 per credit hour. Tuition, nonresident: full-time $14,324; part-time $597 per credit hour. Required fees: $3034. *Financial support:* In 2009–10, 18 fellowships with full tuition reimbursements (averaging $9,200 per year), 5 research assistantships with full tuition reimbursements (averaging $9,200 per year), 21 teaching assistantships with full tuition reimbursements (averaging $9,200 per year) were awarded; career-related internships or fieldwork, Federal Work-Study, institutionally sponsored loans, scholarships/grants, health care benefits, and unspecified assistantships also available. Support available to part-time students. Financial award application deadline: 2/1. *Faculty research:* Catering, tourism, hospitality marketing, security and risk management, purchasing and financial information usage. *Unit head:* Dr. John Bowen, Dean, 713-743-2607, Fax: 713-743-2482, E-mail: jbowen@uh.edu. *Application contact:* Laura S. Gonzalez, Graduate Program Coordinator, 713-743-2457, Fax: 713-743-2218, E-mail: lgonzal3@central.uh.edu.

University of Kentucky, Graduate School, College of Agriculture, Program in Hospitality and Dietetic Administration, Lexington, KY 40506-0032. Offers MS. *Degree requirements:* For master's, comprehensive exam, thesis optional. *Entrance requirements:* For master's, GRE General Test, minimum undergraduate GPA of 2.75. Additional exam requirements/recommendations for international students: Required—TOEFL (minimum score 550 paper-based; 213 computer-based). Electronic applications accepted.

University of Massachusetts Amherst, Graduate School, Interdisciplinary Programs, Program in Hospitality and Tourism Management and Business Administration, Amherst, MA 01003. Offers MS/MBA. Part-time programs available. *Students:* 2 applicants, 100% accepted, 0 enrolled. *Entrance requirements:* Additional exam requirements/recommendations for international students: Required—TOEFL (minimum score 550 paper-based; 213 computer-based; 80 iBT), IELTS (minimum score 6.5). *Application deadline:* For fall admission, 2/1 for domestic and international students. Applications are processed on a rolling basis. Application fee: $50 ($65 for international students). Electronic applications accepted. *Expenses:* Tuition, state resident: full-time $2640; part-time $110 per credit. Tuition, nonresident: full-time $9936; part-time $414 per credit. Tuition and fees vary according to course load. *Financial support:* Career-related internships or fieldwork, Federal Work-Study, scholarships/grants, traineeships, health care benefits, tuition waivers (full), and unspecified assistantships available. Support available to part-time students. *Unit head:* Dr. Atul Sheel, Graduate Program Director, 413-545-1389, Fax: 413-545-1235. *Application contact:* Jean M. Ames, Supervisor of Admissions, 413-545-0722, Fax: 413-577-0010, E-mail: gradadm@grad.umass.edu.

University of Massachusetts Amherst, Graduate School, Isenberg School of Management, Department of Hospitality and Tourism Management, Amherst, MA 01003. Offers MS, MS/MBA. Part-time programs available. *Faculty:* 13 full-time (4 women). *Students:* 15 full-time (7 women), 9 international. Average age 26. 34 applicants, 79% accepted, 5 enrolled. In 2009, 9 master's awarded. *Degree requirements:* For master's, thesis or alternative. *Entrance requirements:* For master's, GMAT. Additional exam requirements/recommendations for international students: Required—TOEFL (minimum score 550 paper-based; 213 computer-based; 80 iBT), IELTS (minimum score 6.5). *Application deadline:* For fall admission, 2/1 for domestic and international students; for spring admission, 10/1 for domestic and international students. Applications are processed on a rolling basis. Application fee: $50 ($65 for international students). Electronic applications accepted. *Expenses:* Tuition, state resident: full-time $2640; part-time $110 per credit. Tuition, nonresident: full-time $9936; part-time $414 per credit. Tuition and fees vary according to course load. *Financial support:* In 2009–10, 1 research assistantship with full tuition reimbursement (averaging $3,682 per year), 13 teaching assistantships with full tuition reimbursements (averaging $6,303 per year) were awarded; fellowships, career-related internships or fieldwork, Federal Work-Study, scholarships/grants, traineeships, health care benefits, tuition waivers (full), and unspecified assistantships also available. Support available to part-time students. Financial award application deadline: 2/1. *Unit head:* Dr. Atul Sheel, Graduate Program Director, 413-545-1389, Fax: 413-545-1235. *Application contact:* Jean M. Ames, Supervisor of Admissions, 413-545-0722, Fax: 413-577-0010, E-mail: gradadm@grad.umass.edu.

University of Missouri, Graduate School, College of Agriculture, Food and Natural Resources, Department of Food and Hospitality Systems, Columbia, MO 65211. Offers food science (MS, PhD); foods and food systems management (MS); human nutrition (MS). *Faculty:* 17 full-time (4 women), 2 part-time/adjunct (0 women). *Students:* 18 full-time (11 women), 13 part-time (6 women), 15 international. Average age 27. 44 applicants, 36% accepted, 9 enrolled. In 2009, 1 master's awarded. Terminal master's awarded for partial completion of doctoral program. *Degree requirements:* For doctorate, comprehensive exam, thesis/dissertation. *Entrance*

Hospitality Management

University of Missouri (continued)

requirements: For master's, GRE General Test (minimum score: Verbal and Quantitative 1000 with neither section below 400, Analytical 3.5), minimum GPA of 3.0; BS in food science from accredited university; for doctorate, GRE General Test (minimum score: Verbal and Quantitative 1000 with neither section below 400, Analytical 3.5), minimum GPA of 3.0; BS and MS in food science from accredited university. Additional exam requirements/recommendations for international students: Required—TOEFL (minimum score 550 paper-based; 79 iBT). *Application deadline:* For fall admission, 4/1 priority date for domestic students; for winter admission, 10/1 priority date for domestic students. Applications are processed on a rolling basis. Application fee: $45 ($60 for international students). Electronic applications accepted. *Financial support:* Research assistantships with tuition reimbursements, teaching assistantships with tuition reimbursements, institutionally sponsored loans available. *Unit head:* Dr. Jinglu Tan, Department Chair, E-mail: tanj@missouri.edu. *Application contact:* JoAnn Lewis, 573-882-4113, E-mail: lewisj@missouri.edu.

University of Nevada, Las Vegas, Graduate College, William F. Harrah College of Hotel Administration, Program in Hotel Administration, Las Vegas, NV 89154-6013. Offers food and beverage management (Certificate); hospitality administration (MHA, PhD); hotel administration (MS). Part-time programs available. Postbaccalaureate distance learning degree programs offered (no on-campus study). *Faculty:* 36 full-time (14 women), 7 part-time/adjunct (3 women). *Students:* 51 full-time (30 women), 59 part-time (33 women); includes 15 minority (5 African Americans, 5 Asian Americans or Pacific Islanders, 5 Hispanic Americans), 29 international. Average age 35. 126 applicants, 44% accepted, 35 enrolled. In 2009, 48 master's, 6 doctorates awarded. *Degree requirements:* For master's, comprehensive exam, thesis (for some programs), professional paper; for doctorate, comprehensive exam, thesis/dissertation, dissertation defense, seminar. *Entrance requirements:* Additional exam requirements/recommendations for international students: Required—TOEFL (minimum score 550 paper-based; 213 computer-based; 80 iBT), IELTS (minimum score 7). *Application deadline:* For fall admission, 3/1 priority date for domestic and international students; for spring admission, 10/1 priority date for domestic and international students. Applications are processed on a rolling basis. Application fee: $60 ($95 for international students). Electronic applications accepted. *Financial support:* In 2009–10, 27 students received support, including 26 research assistantships with partial tuition reimbursements available (averaging $11,961 per year), 1 teaching assistantship with partial tuition reimbursement available (averaging $12,000 per year); institutionally sponsored loans, scholarships/grants, health care benefits, and unspecified assistantships also available. Financial award application deadline: 3/1. *Faculty research:* Hotel branding in China, managing the distribution channel relationship in hotels, costs in customer satisfaction and loyalty, hotel/restaurant valuation, customer/traveler satisfaction, loyalty. *Unit head:* Dr. Pearl Brewer, Chair/Professor, 702-895-3643, Fax: 702-895-4872, E-mail: pearl.brewer@unlv.edu. *Application contact:* Graduate College Admissions Evaluator, 702-895-3320, Fax: 702-895-4180, E-mail: gradcollege@unlv.edu.

University of New Orleans, Graduate School, College of Business Administration, School of Hotel, Restaurant, and Tourism Administration, Program in Hospitality and Tourism Management, New Orleans, LA 70148. Offers MS. *Entrance requirements:* Additional exam requirements/recommendations for international students: Required—TOEFL (minimum score 550 paper-based; 213 computer-based; 79 iBT).

University of North Texas, Robert B. Toulouse School of Graduate Studies, School of Merchandising and Hospitality Management, Denton, TX 76203. Offers hospitality management (MS); merchandising (MS). Part-time programs available. Postbaccalaureate distance learning degree programs offered (no on-campus study). *Degree requirements:* For master's, comprehensive exam, thesis or alternative. *Entrance requirements:* For master's, GRE General Test or GMAT, minimum GPA of 2.8, course work in major area, 3 references, resume. Additional exam requirements/recommendations for international students: Required—proof of English language proficiency required for non-native English speakers; Recommended—TOEFL (minimum score 550 paper-based; 213 computer-based; 79 iBT). *Application deadline:* Applications are processed on a rolling basis. Application fee: $50 ($75 for international students). Electronic applications accepted. *Expenses:* Tuition, state resident: full-time $4298; part-time $239 per contact hour. Tuition, nonresident: full-time $9878; part-time $549 per contact hour. Required fees: $265 per contact hour. *Financial support:* Fellowships, research assistantships, teaching assistantships, career-related internships or fieldwork, Federal Work-Study, and institutionally sponsored loans available. Financial award application deadline: 4/1; financial award applicants required to submit FAFSA. *Faculty research:* Management, hospitality, merchandising, globalization, consumer behavior and experiences. *Application contact:* Coordinator, 940-565-4757, Fax: 940-565-4348, E-mail: kennon@smhm.unt.edu.

University of South Carolina, The Graduate School, College of Hospitality, Retail, and Sport Management, School of Hotel, Restaurant and Tourism Management, Columbia, SC 29208. Offers MIHTM. *Entrance requirements:* For master's, GMAT or GRE General Test, minimum GPA of 3.0, 2 letters of recommendation. Electronic applications accepted. *Faculty research:* Corporate strategy and management practices, sustainable tourism, club management, tourism technology, revenue management.

The University of Tennessee, Graduate School, College of Education, Health and Human Sciences, Department of Consumer and Industry Services Management, Program in Hotel, Restaurant, and Tourism Management, Knoxville, TN 37996. Offers hospitality management (MS); tourism (MS). Part-time programs available. *Degree requirements:* For master's, thesis or alternative. *Entrance requirements:* For master's, GRE General Test, minimum GPA of 2.7. Additional exam requirements/recommendations for international students: Required—TOEFL. Electronic applications accepted. *Expenses:* Tuition, state resident: full-time $6826; part-time $380 per semester hour. Tuition, nonresident: full-time $21,844; part-time $1147 per semester hour. Tuition and fees vary according to program.

Virginia Polytechnic Institute and State University, Graduate School, Pamplin College of Business, Department of Hospitality and Tourism Management, Blacksburg, VA 24061. Offers MS, PhD. *Faculty:* 11 full-time (4 women), 1 part-time/adjunct (0 women). *Students:* 18 full-time (9 women), 3 part-time (2 women); includes 14 minority (12 American Indian/Alaska Native, 1 Asian American or Pacific Islander, 1 Hispanic American). Average age 30. 54 applicants, 19% accepted, 4 enrolled. In 2009, 7 master's, 1 doctorate awarded. *Entrance requirements:* For master's and doctorate, GRE, GMAT. Additional exam requirements/recommendations for international students: Required—TOEFL (minimum score 550 paper-based; 213 computer-based). *Application deadline:* For fall admission, 5/15 for international students; for spring admission, 10/15 for international students. Applications are processed on a rolling basis. Application fee: $65. Electronic applications accepted. *Expenses:* Tuition, area resident: Full-time $10,228; part-time $459 per credit hour. Tuition, nonresident: full-time $17,892; part-time $865 per credit hour. Required fees: $1966; $451 per semester. *Financial support:* In 2009–10, 1 research assistantship with full tuition reimbursement (averaging $8,508 per year), 13 teaching assistantships with full tuition reimbursements (averaging $14,052 per year) were awarded; career-related internships or fieldwork, Federal Work-Study, scholarships/grants, and unspecified assistantships also available. Financial award application deadline: 1/15. *Faculty research:* Human resource management, service management, marketing, strategy and finance tourist behavior. Total annual research expenditures: $59,740. *Unit head:* Dr. Rick R. Perdue, Dean, 540-231-3287, Fax: 540-231-8313, E-mail: perduerr@vt.edu. *Application contact:* Nancy McGehee, Information Contact, 540-231-1201, Fax: 540-231-8313, E-mail: nmcgehee@vt.edu.

Travel and Tourism

Arizona State University, Graduate College, College of Public Programs, School of Community Resources and Development, Tempe, AZ 85287. Offers community resources and development (PhD); nonprofit studies (MNpS); recreation and tourism studies (MS). *Degree requirements:* For master's, thesis or alternative.

Boston University, Metropolitan College, Department of Administrative Sciences, Boston, MA 02215. Offers banking and financial management (MSM); business continuity in emergency management (MSM); economics development and tourism management (MSAS); electronic commerce, systems, and technology (MSAS); financial economics (MSAS); human resource management (MSM); innovation and technology (MSAS); insurance management (MSM); international market management (MSM); multinational commerce (MSAS); project management (MSM). *Accreditation:* AACSB. Part-time and evening/weekend programs available. Postbaccalaureate distance learning degree programs offered (no on-campus study). *Students:* 123 full-time (48 women), 204 part-time (92 women); includes 31 minority (10 African Americans, 1 American Indian/Alaska Native, 11 Asian Americans or Pacific Islanders, 9 Hispanic Americans), 146 international. Average age 30. In 2009, 154 master's awarded. *Degree requirements:* For master's, thesis optional. *Entrance requirements:* For master's, 1 year of work experience, minimum GPA of 3.0. Additional exam requirements/recommendations for international students: Required—TOEFL (minimum score 560 paper-based; 220 computer-based; 84 iBT). *Application deadline:* Applications are processed on a rolling basis. Application fee: $70. Electronic applications accepted. *Expenses:* Tuition: Full-time $37,910; part-time $1184 per credit hour. Required fees: $386; $40 per semester. Part-time tuition and fees vary according to class time, course level, degree level and program. *Financial support:* In 2009–10, 15 students received support, including 8 research assistantships (averaging $10,000 per year); career-related internships or fieldwork and Federal Work-Study also available. *Faculty research:* International business, innovative process. *Unit head:* Dr. Kip Becker, Chairman, 617-353-3016, E-mail: adminsc@bu.edu. *Application contact:* Lucille Dicker, Administrative Sciences Department, 617-353-3016, E-mail: adminsc@bu.edu.

California State University, East Bay, Graduate Programs, College of Education and Allied Studies, Department of Hospitality, Recreation and Tourism, Hayward, CA 94542-3000. Offers recreation and tourism (MS). Part-time and evening/weekend programs available. Postbaccalaureate distance learning degree programs offered (no on-campus study). *Faculty:* 7 full-time (4 women). *Students:* 16 full-time (12 women), 8 part-time (5 women); includes 19 minority (1 African American, 17 Asian Americans or Pacific Islanders, 1 Hispanic American). Average age 31. 18 applicants, 44% accepted, 4 enrolled. *Entrance requirements:* For master's, minimum GPA of 2.75; 2 years' related work experience. Additional exam requirements/recommendations for international students: Required—TOEFL (minimum score 550 paper-based; 237 computer-based). *Application deadline:* For fall admission, 6/30 for domestic and international students. Applications are processed on a rolling basis. Application fee: $55. Electronic applications accepted. *Financial support:* Federal Work-Study, institutionally sponsored loans, and scholarships/grants available. Support available to part-time students. Financial award application deadline: 3/1; financial award applicants required to submit FAFSA. *Unit head:* Dr. Melany Spielman, Chair, 510-885-3043, E-mail: melany.spielman@csueastbay.edu. *Application contact:* Donna Wiley, Interim Associate Director, 510-885-2928, Fax: 510-885-4777, E-mail: donna.wiley@csueastbay.edu.

California State University, Fullerton, Graduate Studies, College of Communications, Department of Communications, Fullerton, CA 92834-9480. Offers communications—advertising (MA); communications—entertainment and tourism (MA); communications—journalism (MA); communications—public relations (MA). Part-time programs available. *Students:* 18 full-time (14 women), 38 part-time (30 women); includes 21 minority (2 African Americans, 8 Asian Americans or Pacific Islanders, 11 Hispanic Americans), 4 international. Average age 28. 121 applicants, 23% accepted, 17 enrolled. In 2009, 33 master's awarded. *Degree requirements:* For master's, project or thesis. *Entrance requirements:* For master's, GRE General Test. Application fee: $55. *Expenses:* Tuition, nonresident: full-time $11,160; part-time $373 per credit. Required fees: $1440 per term. Tuition and fees vary according to course load, degree level and program. *Financial support:* Teaching assistantships, career-related internships or fieldwork, Federal Work-Study, institutionally sponsored loans, and scholarships/grants available. Support available to part-time students. Financial award application deadline: 3/1; financial award applicants required to submit FAFSA. *Unit head:* Dr. Tony Fellow, Chair, 657-278-3517. *Application contact:* Coordinator, 657-278-3832.

California State University, Northridge, Graduate Studies, College of Health and Human Development, Department of Recreation and Tourism Management, Northridge, CA 91330. Offers hospitality and tourism (MS); recreational sport management/campus recreation (MS). *Faculty:* 6 full-time (4 women), 11 part-time/adjunct (7 women). *Students:* 29 full-time (17 women), 21 part-time (11 women); includes 6 minority (4 African Americans, 1 Asian American or Pacific Islander, 1 Hispanic American), 9 international. Average age 27. 53 applicants, 77% accepted, 31 enrolled. In 2009, 8 master's awarded. *Degree requirements:* For master's, thesis (for some programs). *Entrance requirements:* For master's, GRE (if cumulative undergraduate GPA less than 3.0). Additional exam requirements/recommendations for international students: Required—TOEFL. *Application deadline:* For fall admission, 11/30 for domestic students. Application fee: $55. *Financial support:* Application deadline: 3/1. *Unit head:* Dr. Craig Finney, Chair, 818-677-3202, E-mail: cfinney@csun.edu. *Application contact:* Dr. Craig Finney, Chair, 818-677-3202, E-mail: cfinney@csun.edu.

Clemson University, Graduate School, College of Health, Education, and Human Development, Department of Parks, Recreation, and Tourism Management, Clemson, SC 29634. Offers MPRTM, MS, PhD. Part-time programs available. *Faculty:* 16 full-time (6 women). *Students:* 49 full-time (27 women), 14 part-time (8 women); includes 4 minority (2 African Americans, 2 American Indian/Alaska Native), 14 international. Average age 32. 60 applicants, 42% accepted, 12 enrolled. In 2009, 3 master's, 5 doctorates awarded. *Degree requirements:* For master's, thesis (for some programs); for doctorate, thesis/dissertation. *Entrance requirements:* For master's, GRE General Test, minimum undergraduate GPA of 3.0; for doctorate, GRE General Test, minimum graduate GPA of 3.0. Additional exam requirements/recommendations for international students: Required—TOEFL. *Application deadline:* For fall admission, 5/1 priority date for domestic students; for spring admission, 10/1 for domestic students. Applications are processed on a rolling basis. Application fee: $70 ($80 for international students). Electronic applications accepted. *Expenses:* Tuition, state resident: full-time $8684; part-time $528 per credit hour. Tuition, nonresident: full-time $15,330; part-time $1078 per credit hour. Required fees: $736; $37 per semester. Part-time tuition and fees vary according to course load and program. *Financial support:* In 2009–10, 41 students received support, including 3 research assistantships with partial tuition reimbursements available (averaging $19,587 per year), 16 teaching assistantships with partial tuition reimbursements available (averaging $10,735 per year); fellowships with full and partial tuition reimbursements available, career-related internships or fieldwork, scholarships/grants, health care benefits, tuition waivers (partial), and unspecified assistantships also available. Support available to part-time students. Financial award application deadline: 4/15; financial award applicants required to submit FAFSA. *Faculty research:* Recreation resource management, leisure behavior, therapeutic recreation, com-

munity leisure services. Total annual research expenditures: $370,389. *Unit head:* Dr. Brett A. Wright, Chair, 864-656-3036, Fax: 864-656-2226, E-mail: wright@clemson.edu. *Application contact:* Dr. Denise M. Anderson, Graduate Coordinator, 864-656-5679, Fax: 864-656-2226, E-mail: dander2@clemson.edu.

Eastern Michigan University, Graduate School, College of Arts and Sciences, Department of Geography and Geology, Program in Historic Preservation, Ypsilanti, MI 48197. Offers heritage interpretation and tourism (MS); historic preservation (MS, Graduate Certificate). Part-time and evening/weekend programs available. Postbaccalaureate distance learning degree programs offered (minimal on-campus study). *Students:* 23 full-time (15 women), 61 part-time (43 women); includes 2 minority (both African Americans), 1 international. Average age 36. In 2009, 26 master's, 5 other advanced degrees awarded. *Entrance requirements:* Additional exam requirements/recommendations for international students: Required—TOEFL. *Application deadline:* Applications are processed on a rolling basis. Application fee: $35. Tuition and fees vary according to course level. *Financial support:* Fellowships, research assistantships with full tuition reimbursements, teaching assistantships with full tuition reimbursements, career-related internships or fieldwork, Federal Work-Study, institutionally sponsored loans, scholarships/grants, tuition waivers (partial), and unspecified assistantships available. Support available to part-time students. Financial award applicants required to submit FAFSA. *Application contact:* Dr. Ted Ligibel, Program Advisor, 734-487-0232, Fax: 734-487-6979, E-mail: tligibel@emich.edu.

East Stroudsburg University of Pennsylvania, Graduate School, College of Business and Management, Department of Hotel, Restaurant and Tourism Management, East Stroudsburg, PA 18301-2999. Offers management and leadership (MS). Part-time and evening/weekend programs available. *Faculty:* 3 full-time (1 woman). *Students:* 9 full-time (3 women); includes 3 minority (all African Americans), 2 international. Average age 28. In 2009, 4 master's awarded. *Degree requirements:* For master's, comprehensive exam. *Entrance requirements:* For master's, GRE or GMAT, 3 letters of recommendation. Additional exam requirements/recommendations for international students: Required—TOEFL (minimum score 560 paper-based; 220 computer-based; 83 iBT). *Application deadline:* For fall admission, 7/31 priority date for domestic students, 5/1 priority date for international students; for spring admission, 11/30 for domestic students, 10/1 for international students. Applications are processed on a rolling basis. Application fee: $50. *Expenses:* Tuition, state resident: full-time $9942; part-time $387 per credit. Tuition, nonresident: full-time $14,240; part-time $619 per credit. *Financial support:* Federal Work-Study and unspecified assistantships available. Financial award application deadline: 3/1; financial award applicants required to submit FAFSA. *Unit head:* Prof. Al Moranville, Graduate Coordinator, 570-422-3049, E-mail: moranville@po-box.esu.edu. *Application contact:* Kevin Quintero, Graduate Admissions Coordinator, 570-422-3890, Fax: 570-422-2711, E-mail: kquintero@po-box.esu.edu.

Florida Atlantic University, College of Architecture, Urban and Public Affairs, School of Urban and Regional Planning, Boca Raton, FL 33431-0991. Offers economic development and tourism (Certificate); environmental planning (Certificate); sustainable community planning (Certificate); urban and regional planning (MURP); visual planning technology (Certificate). *Accreditation:* ACSP. Part-time and evening/weekend programs available. *Faculty:* 8 full-time (6 women), 1 (woman) part-time/adjunct. *Students:* 28 full-time (17 women), 12 part-time (4 women); includes 11 minority (2 African Americans, 1 Asian American or Pacific Islander, 8 Hispanic Americans), 3 international. Average age 31. 70 applicants, 47% accepted, 7 enrolled. In 2009, 14 master's awarded. *Entrance requirements:* For master's, GRE General Test, minimum GPA of 3.0. Additional exam requirements/recommendations for international students: Required—TOEFL. *Application deadline:* For fall admission, 7/1 priority date for domestic students, 2/15 for international students; for spring admission, 11/1 priority date for domestic students, 7/15 for international students. Applications are processed on a rolling basis. Application fee: $30. *Expenses:* Tuition, state resident: full-time $7055; part-time $293.94 per credit hour. Tuition, nonresident: full-time $22,096; part-time $920.66 per credit hour. *Financial support:* Fellowships with full tuition reimbursements, research assistantships, career-related internships or fieldwork, Federal Work-Study, institutionally sponsored loans, and tuition waivers (partial) available. Financial award application deadline: 4/1. *Faculty research:* Growth management, urban design, computer applications/geographical information systems, environmental planning. *Unit head:* Dr. Jaap Vos, Chair, 954-762-5653, Fax: 954-762-5673, E-mail: jvos@fau.edu. *Application contact:* Dr. Jaap Vos, Chair, 954-762-5653, Fax: 954-762-5673, E-mail: jvos@fau.edu.

The George Washington University, School of Business, Department of Tourism and Hospitality Management, Washington, DC 20052. Offers event and meeting management (MTA); event management (Professional Certificate); hospitality management (MTA, Professional Certificate); sports business management (Professional Certificate); sports management (MTA); sustainable destination management (MTA); tourism administration (MTA); tourism and hospitality management (MBA); tourism destination management (Professional Certificate). Part-time programs available. Postbaccalaureate distance learning degree programs offered. *Faculty:* 8 full-time (3 women), 5 part-time/adjunct (2 women). *Students:* 71 full-time (51 women), 110 part-time (86 women); includes 43 minority (23 African Americans, 3 American Indian/Alaska Native, 4 Asian Americans or Pacific Islanders, 13 Hispanic Americans), 42 international. Average age 30. 115 applicants, 83% accepted, 59 enrolled. In 2009, 74 master's awarded. *Degree requirements:* For master's, comprehensive exam, thesis. *Entrance requirements:* For master's, GRE General Test. Additional exam requirements/recommendations for international students: Required—TOEFL. *Application deadline:* For fall admission, 4/1 priority date for domestic students; for spring admission, 10/1 for domestic students. Applications are processed on a rolling basis. Application fee: $60. *Financial support:* In 2009–10, 32 students received support; fellowships, teaching assistantships, career-related internships or fieldwork, Federal Work-Study, institutionally sponsored loans, and tuition waivers (partial) available. Financial award application deadline: 4/1. *Faculty research:* Tourism policy, tourism impact forecasting, geotourism. *Unit head:* Susan M. Phillips, Dean, 202-994-6380, E-mail: gwsbdean@gwu.edu. *Application contact:* Kristin Williams, Assistant Vice President for Graduate and Special Enrollment Management, 202-994-0467, Fax: 202-994-0371, E-mail: ksw@gwu.edu.

Hawai'i Pacific University, College of Business Administration, Honolulu, HI 96813. Offers accounting/CPA (MBA); e-business (MBA); economics (MBA); finance (MBA); human resource management (MA, MBA); information systems (MBA, MSIS), including knowledge management (MSIS), software engineering (MSIS), telecommunications security (MSIS); international business (MBA); management (MBA); marketing (MBA); organizational change (MA, MBA); travel industry management (MBA). Part-time and evening/weekend programs available. *Faculty:* 15 full-time (5 women), 11 part-time/adjunct (4 women). *Students:* 206 full-time (107 women), 197 part-time (105 women); includes 136 minority (18 African Americans, 3 American Indian/Alaska Native, 98 Asian Americans or Pacific Islanders, 17 Hispanic Americans), 151 international. Average age 30. 235 applicants, 90% accepted, 127 enrolled. In 2009, 141 master's awarded. *Degree requirements:* For master's, thesis. *Entrance requirements:* For master's, GMAT. Additional exam requirements/recommendations for international students: Recommended—TOEFL (minimum score 550 paper-based; 213 computer-based; 80 iBT), TWE (minimum score 5). *Application deadline:* For fall admission, 2/15 priority date for domestic students; for spring admission, 10/15 priority date for domestic students. Applications are processed on a rolling basis. Application fee: $50. Electronic applications accepted. *Expenses:* Tuition: Full-time $12,600; part-time $700 per credit hour. Tuition and fees vary according to program. *Financial support:* In 2009–10, 164 students received support; research assistantships, career-related internships or fieldwork, Federal Work-Study, scholarships/grants, and unspecified assistantships available. Support available to part-time students. Financial award application deadline: 3/1; financial award applicants required to submit FAFSA. *Faculty research:* Statistical control process as used by management, studies in comparative cross-cultural management styles, not-for-profit management. *Unit head:* Dr. Aytun Ozturk, Dean, 808-544-9301, Fax: 808-544-0283, E-mail: uozturk@hpu.edu. *Application contact:* Danny Lam, Assistant Director of Graduate Admissions, 808-544-1135, Fax: 808-544-0280, E-mail: graduate@hpu.edu.

See Close-Up on page 251.

Indiana University Bloomington, School of Health, Physical Education and Recreation, Department of Recreation, Park, and Tourism Studies, Bloomington, IN 47405-7000. Offers leisure behavior (PhD); outdoor recreation (MS); recreation (Re Dir); recreation administration (MS); recreational sports administration (MS); therapeutic recreation (MS); tourism management (MS). *Faculty:* 16 full-time (6 women), 2 part-time/adjunct (both women). *Students:* 55 full-time (29 women), 17 part-time (15 women); includes 8 minority (2 African Americans, 2 American Indian/Alaska Native, 3 Asian Americans or Pacific Islanders, 1 Hispanic American), 22 international. Average age 31. 62 applicants, 69% accepted, 23 enrolled. In 2009, 11 master's, 5 doctorates awarded. Terminal master's awarded for partial completion of doctoral program. *Degree requirements:* For master's and Re Dir, thesis optional; for doctorate, thesis/dissertation. *Entrance requirements:* For master's, GRE General Test, minimum GPA of 2.8; for doctorate, GRE General Test, minimum GPA of 3.0 (undergraduate), 3.5 (graduate). Additional exam requirements/recommendations for international students: Required—TOEFL. *Application deadline:* For fall admission, 1/1 for international students; for spring admission, 9/1 for international students. Applications are processed on a rolling basis. Application fee: $55 ($65 for international students). *Financial support:* In 2009–10, 30 students received support, including 7 fellowships (averaging $4,723 per year), 17 research assistantships (averaging $10,002 per year), 13 teaching assistantships with partial tuition reimbursements available (averaging $11,565 per year); career-related internships or fieldwork, Federal Work-Study, institutionally sponsored loans, scholarships/grants, tuition waivers (partial), unspecified assistantships, and fee remissions also available. Financial award application deadline: 3/1. *Faculty research:* Leisure counseling, gerontology, special populations, planning and development. *Unit head:* Dr. Craig Ross, Chairperson, 812-855-4711, E-mail: cmross@indiana.edu. *Application contact:* Program Office, 812-855-4711, Fax: 812-855-3998, E-mail: recpark@indiana.edu.

Kent State University, Graduate School of Education, Health, and Human Services, School of Foundations, Leadership and Administration, Program in Hospitality and Tourism Management, Kent, OH 44242-0001. Offers MS. Part-time programs available. *Faculty:* 5 full-time (3 women). *Students:* 8 full-time (4 women), 3 part-time (all women), 1 international. 13 applicants, 85% accepted. *Degree requirements:* For master's, thesis (for some programs). *Entrance requirements:* For master's, GRE, minimum GPA of 3.0, 3 letters of recommendation. Additional exam requirements/recommendations for international students: Required—TOEFL. *Application deadline:* Applications are processed on a rolling basis. Application fee: $30. Electronic applications accepted. *Financial support:* In 2009–10, 4 students received support, including 2 research assistantships with full tuition reimbursements available (averaging $8,500 per year); Federal Work-Study, scholarships/grants, and unspecified assistantships also available. Financial award application deadline: 2/1; financial award applicants required to submit FAFSA. *Faculty research:* Training human service workers, health care services for older adults, early adolescent development, caregiving arrangements with aging families, peace and war. *Unit head:* Barb Scheule, Coordinator, 330-672-3796, E-mail: bscheule@kent.edu. *Application contact:* Nancy Miller, Academic Program Coordinator, 330-672-2576, Fax: 330-672-9162, E-mail: ogs@kent.edu.

New York University, School of Continuing and Professional Studies, The Preston Robert Tisch Center for Hospitality, Tourism, and Sports Management, Program in Tourism and Travel Management, New York, NY 10012-1019. Offers customer relationship management (MS); strategic marketing (MS); tourism and travel management (Advanced Certificate); tourism development (MS); tourism planning and analysis (MS). Part-time and evening/weekend programs available. *Faculty:* 13 full-time (5 women), 11 part-time/adjunct (5 women). *Students:* 1 (woman) full-time, 6 part-time (4 women); includes 1 minority (Asian American or Pacific Islander). Average age 30. In 2009, 8 master's, 1 other advanced degree awarded. *Entrance requirements:* For master's, GMAT or GRE General Test (for recent graduates), resume, 2 letters of recommendation, essay. Additional exam requirements/recommendations for international students: Required—TOEFL (minimum score 600 paper-based; 250 computer-based; 100 iBT), TWE. *Application deadline:* For fall admission, 2/1 priority date for domestic and international students; for spring admission, 10/15 priority date for domestic students, 8/15 priority date for international students. Applications are processed on a rolling basis. Application fee: $75. Electronic applications accepted. *Expenses:* Tuition: Full-time $30,528; part-time $1272 per credit. Required fees: $2177. *Financial support:* In 2009–10, 4 students received support, including 4 fellowships (averaging $2,109 per year); research assistantships, career-related internships or fieldwork, Federal Work-Study, institutionally sponsored loans, and scholarships/grants also available. Support available to part-time students. Financial award application deadline: 3/1; financial award applicants required to submit FAFSA. *Faculty research:* Tourism planning for national parks and protected areas, leadership and organizational behavior issues. *Unit head:* Lalia Rach, 212-998-9100, Fax: 212-995-4676, E-mail: lalia.rach@nyu.edu. *Application contact:* Sandra Dove-Lowther, Office of Admissions, 212-998-9106, Fax: 212-995-4676, E-mail: sd2@nyu.edu.

North Carolina State University, Graduate School, College of Natural Resources, Department of Parks, Recreation and Tourism Management, Raleigh, NC 27695. Offers natural resource management (MPRTM, MS); park and recreation management (MPRTM, MS); parks, recreation and tourism management (PhD); recreational sport management (MPRTM, MS); spatial information science (MPRTM, MS); tourism policy and development (MPRTM, MS). *Degree requirements:* For master's, thesis (for some programs); for doctorate, thesis/dissertation. *Entrance requirements:* For master's and doctorate, GRE General Test. Additional exam requirements/recommendations for international students: Required—TOEFL. Electronic applications accepted. *Faculty research:* Tourism policy and development, spatial information systems, natural resource management, recreational sports management, park and recreation management.

Old Dominion University, Darden College of Education, Program in Physical Education, Recreation and Tourism Studies Emphasis, Norfolk, VA 23529. Offers MS Ed. Part-time and evening/weekend programs available. Postbaccalaureate distance learning degree programs offered (minimal on-campus study). *Faculty:* 1 full-time (0 women). *Students:* 9 full-time (6 women), 6 part-time (4 women); includes 5 minority (4 African Americans, 1 Asian American or Pacific Islander). Average age 26. 10 applicants, 60% accepted, 5 enrolled. In 2009, 1 master's awarded. *Degree requirements:* For master's, comprehensive exam, thesis or alternative, internship, research project. *Entrance requirements:* For master's, GRE, minimum GPA of 2.8 overall, 3.0 in major. Additional exam requirements/recommendations for international students: Required—TOEFL (minimum score 500 paper-based; 200 computer-based). *Application deadline:* For fall admission, 6/1 for domestic students. Application fee: $40. Electronic applications accepted. *Expenses:* Tuition, state resident: full-time $8112; part-time $338 per credit. Tuition, nonresident: full-time $20,256; part-time $844 per credit. Required fees: $119 per semester. One-time fee: $50. *Financial support:* In 2009–10, 1 student received support, including 1 research assistantship with partial tuition reimbursement available (averaging $9,000 per year); career-related internships or fieldwork, scholarships/grants, and unspecified assistantships also available. Financial award application deadline: 3/1; financial award applicants required to submit FAFSA. *Faculty research:* Ethnicity and recreation, recreation programming, recreation and resiliency, tourism development, dog parks, sense of community and urban parks. Total annual research expenditures: $12,000. *Unit head:* Dr. Edwin Gomez, Graduate Program Director, 757-683-4995, Fax: 757-683-4270, E-mail: egomez@odu.edu. *Application contact:* Dr. Edwin Gomez, Graduate Program Director, 757-683-4995, Fax: 757-683-4270, E-mail: egomez@odu.edu.

Purdue University, Graduate School, College of Consumer and Family Sciences, Department of Hospitality and Tourism Management, West Lafayette, IN 47907. Offers MS, PhD. *Degree requirements:* For master's, thesis optional; for doctorate, thesis/dissertation optional. *Entrance requirements:* For master's, GMAT or GRE General Test, minimum GPA of 3.0; for doctorate, GMAT or GRE. Additional exam requirements/recommendations for international students: Required—TOEFL. Electronic applications accepted. *Faculty research:* Human resources, marketing, hotel and restaurant operations, food product and equipment development, tourism development.

Rochester Institute of Technology, Graduate Enrollment Services, College of Applied Science and Technology, Department of Hospitality and Service Management, Program in Hospitality-

Travel and Tourism

Rochester Institute of Technology (continued)

Tourism Management, Rochester, NY 14623-5603. Offers MS. *Students:* 10 full-time (6 women), 3 part-time (2 women), 10 international. Average age 27. 30 applicants, 77% accepted, 5 enrolled. In 2009, 3 master's awarded. *Degree requirements:* For master's, thesis or project. *Entrance requirements:* For master's, minimum GPA of 3.0. Additional exam requirements/recommendations for international students: Required—TOEFL (minimum score 550 paper-based; 213 computer-based; 79 iBT) or IELTS (minimum score 6.5). *Application deadline:* For fall admission, 2/15 priority date for domestic and international students; for winter admission, 11/1 priority date for domestic students, 10/1 priority date for international students; for spring admission, 2/1 priority date for domestic students, 1/1 priority date for international students. Applications are processed on a rolling basis. Application fee: $50. *Expenses:* Tuition: Full-time $31,533; part-time $876 per credit hour. Required fees: $210. *Financial support:* In 2009–10, 6 students received support; research assistantships with partial tuition reimbursements available, teaching assistantships with partial tuition reimbursements available, career-related internships or fieldwork, scholarships/grants, and unspecified assistantships available. Support available to part-time students. Financial award application deadline: 2/15; financial award applicants required to submit FAFSA. *Unit head:* Dr. Linda Underhill, Chair, 585-475-7359, Fax: 585-475-5099, E-mail: lmuism@rit.edu. *Application contact:* Diane Ellison, Assistant Vice President, Graduate Enrollment Services, 585-475-2229, Fax: 585-475-7164, E-mail: gradinfo@rit.edu.

Rochester Institute of Technology, Graduate Enrollment Services, College of Applied Science and Technology, Department of Hospitality and Service Management, Program in Service Leadership and Innovation, Rochester, NY 14623-5603. Offers MS. Part-time and evening/weekend programs available. *Students:* 13 full-time (9 women), 49 part-time (29 women); includes 5 African Americans, 1 Hispanic American, 7 international. Average age 32. 68 applicants, 81% accepted, 36 enrolled. In 2009, 22 master's awarded. *Degree requirements:* For master's, thesis or alternative. *Entrance requirements:* For master's, minimum GPA of 3.0. Additional exam requirements/recommendations for international students: Required—TOEFL (minimum score 550 paper-based; 213 computer-based; 79 iBT), or IELTS (minimum score 6.5). *Application deadline:* For fall admission, 2/15 priority date for domestic and international students; for winter admission, 11/1 for domestic and international students; for spring admission, 2/1 for domestic and international students. Applications are processed on a rolling basis. Application fee: $50. *Expenses:* Tuition: Full-time $31,533; part-time $876 per credit hour. Required fees: $210. *Financial support:* In 2009–10, 23 students received support; research assistantships with partial tuition reimbursements available, teaching assistantships with partial tuition reimbursements available, career-related internships or fieldwork, institutionally sponsored loans, scholarships/grants, and unspecified assistantships available. Support available to part-time students. Financial award application deadline: 2/15; financial award applicants required to submit FAFSA. *Faculty research:* Global resource development, service/product innovation and implementation. *Unit head:* Dr. Linda Underhill, Chair, 585-475-7359, Fax: 585-475-5099, E-mail: lmuism@rit.edu. *Application contact:* Diane Ellison, Assistant Vice President, Graduate Enrollment Services, 585-475-2229, Fax: 585-475-7164, E-mail: gradinfo@rit.edu.

Royal Roads University, Graduate Studies, Tourism and Hotel Management Program, Victoria, BC V9B 5Y2, Canada. Offers destination development (Graduate Certificate); international hotel management (MA); sustainable tourism (Graduate Certificate); tourism leadership (Graduate Certificate); tourism management (MA).

Saint Xavier University, Graduate Studies, Graham School of Management, Chicago, IL 60655-3105. Offers e-commerce (MBA); employee health benefits (Certificate); finance (MBA, MS); financial analysis and investments (MBA); financial planning (MBA, Certificate); financial trading and practice (MBA, Certificate); generalist/administration (MBA); health administration (MBA, MS); managed care (Certificate); management (MBA, MS); marketing (MBA); public and non-profit management (MBA); public health (MPH); service management (MBA); training and performance management (MBA); MBA/MS. *Accreditation:* ACBSP. Part-time and evening/weekend programs available. *Entrance requirements:* For master's, GMAT, minimum GPA of 3.0, 2 years of work experience. Electronic applications accepted. *Expenses:* Contact institution.

Schiller International University, Graduate Programs, London, Program in International Hotel and Tourism Management, London, United Kingdom. Offers MA, MBA. Part-time and evening/weekend programs available. *Degree requirements:* For master's, thesis optional, GMAT before graduation. *Entrance requirements:* Additional exam requirements/recommendations for international students: Required—TOEFL (minimum score 550 paper-based; 213 computer-based).

Schiller International University, MBA Programs, Florida, Program in International Hotel and Tourism Management, Largo, FL 33770. Offers MBA. *Degree requirements:* For master's, thesis optional. *Entrance requirements:* Additional exam requirements/recommendations for international students: Required—TOEFL (minimum score 550 paper-based; 213 computer-based).

Strayer University, Graduate Studies, Washington, DC 20005-2603. Offers accounting (MS); acquisition (MBA); business administration (MBA); communications technology (MS); educational management (M Ed); finance (MBA); health services administration (MHSA); hospitality and tourism management (MBA); human resource management (MBA); information systems (MS), including computer security management, decision support system management, enterprise resource management, network management, software engineering management, systems development management; management (MBA); management information systems (MS); marketing (MBA); professional accounting (MS), including accounting information systems, controllership, taxation; public administration (MPA); supply chain management (MBA); technology in education (M Ed). Programs also offered at campus locations in Birmingham, AL; Chamblee, GA; Cobb County, GA; Morrow, GA; White Marsh, MD; Charleston, SC; Columbia, SC; Greensboro, NC; Greenville, SC; Lexington, KY; Louisville, KY; Nashville, TN; North Raleigh, NC; Washington, DC. Part-time and evening/weekend programs available. Postbaccalaureate distance learning degree programs offered (minimal on-campus study). *Degree requirements:* For master's, thesis. *Entrance requirements:* For master's, GMAT, GRE General Test, bachelor's degree from an accredited college or university, minimum undergraduate GPA of 2.75. Electronic applications accepted.

Temple University, Graduate School, School of Tourism and Hospitality Management, Program in Tourism and Hospitality Management, Philadelphia, PA 19122-6096. Offers MTHM. Part-time and evening/weekend programs available. *Entrance requirements:* For master's, GRE General Test or MAT, minimum of 2 years professional experience, minimum undergraduate GPA of 3.0. Additional exam requirements/recommendations for international students: Required—TOEFL (minimum score 550 paper-based; 213 computer-based; 79 iBT). Electronic applications accepted.

Université du Québec à Trois-Rivières, Graduate Programs, Program in Leisure, Culture and Tourism Sciences, Trois-Rivières, QC G9A 5H7, Canada. Offers MA, DESS. Part-time programs available. *Degree requirements:* For master's, thesis optional. *Entrance requirements:* For master's, appropriate bachelor's degree, proficiency in French.

University of Central Florida, Rosen College of Hospitality Management, Orlando, FL 32816. Offers hospitality and tourism management (MS). *Faculty:* 35 full-time (10 women), 27 part-time/adjunct (11 women). *Students:* 33 full-time (28 women), 41 part-time (24 women); includes 16 minority (5 African Americans, 3 Asian Americans or Pacific Islanders, 8 Hispanic Americans), 8 international. Average age 28. 60 applicants, 62% accepted, 25 enrolled. In 2009, 24 master's awarded. *Degree requirements:* For master's, thesis or alternative. *Entrance requirements:* For master's, GMAT or GRE, minimum GPA of 3.0 in last 60 hours. Additional exam requirements/recommendations for international students: Required—TOEFL. *Application deadline:* For fall admission, 2/1 for domestic students. Application fee: $30. Electronic applications accepted. *Expenses:* Tuition, state resident: part-time $306.31 per credit hour. Tuition, nonresident: part-time $1099.01 per credit hour. Part-time tuition and fees vary according to degree level and program. *Financial support:* In 2009–10, 1 student received support, including 1 fellowship with partial tuition reimbursement available (averaging $10,000 per year). *Unit head:* Dr. Abraham C. Pizam, Dean, 407-903-8010, E-mail: apizam@mail.ucf.edu. *Application contact:* Dr. Abraham C. Pizam, Dean, 407-903-8010, E-mail: apizam@mail.ucf.edu.

University of Hawaii at Manoa, Graduate Division, School of Travel Industry Management, Honolulu, HI 96822. Offers MS. Part-time programs available. *Faculty:* 4 full-time (2 women), 7 part-time/adjunct (3 women). *Students:* 7 full-time (4 women), 3 part-time (2 women); includes 5 minority (all Asian Americans or Pacific Islanders), 2 international. Average age 29. 47 applicants, 36% accepted, 8 enrolled. In 2009, 6 master's awarded. *Degree requirements:* For master's, thesis optional. *Entrance requirements:* For master's, GRE General Test, minimum GPA of 3.0. Additional exam requirements/recommendations for international students: Required—TOEFL (minimum score 560 paper-based; 220 computer-based; 83 iBT), IELTS (minimum score 5). *Application deadline:* For fall admission, 3/1 for domestic and international students. Applications are processed on a rolling basis. Application fee: $60. Electronic applications accepted. *Expenses:* Tuition, state resident: full-time $8900; part-time $372 per credit. Tuition, nonresident: full-time $21,400; part-time $898 per credit. Required fees: $207 per semester. *Financial support:* In 2009–10, 1 student received support, including 1 fellowship with partial tuition reimbursement available (averaging $12,350 per year); career-related internships or fieldwork, scholarships/grants, tuition waivers (full and partial), and student assistantships also available. Financial award application deadline: 3/1. *Faculty research:* Travel information technology, tourism development and policy, transportation management and policy, hospitality management, sustainable tourism development. Total annual research expenditures: $85,000. *Application contact:* Dexter J. L. Choy, Graduate Chair, 808-956-9840, Fax: 808-956-5378, E-mail: djlchoy@hawaii.edu.

University of Massachusetts Amherst, Graduate School, Interdisciplinary Programs, Program in Hospitality and Tourism Management and Business Administration, Amherst, MA 01003. Offers MS/MBA. Part-time programs available. *Students:* 2 applicants, 100% accepted, 0 enrolled. *Entrance requirements:* Additional exam requirements/recommendations for international students: Required—TOEFL (minimum score 550 paper-based; 213 computer-based; 80 iBT), IELTS (minimum score 6.5). *Application deadline:* For fall admission, 2/1 for domestic and international students. Applications are processed on a rolling basis. Application fee: $50 ($65 for international students). Electronic applications accepted. *Expenses:* Tuition, state resident: full-time $2640; part-time $110 per credit. Tuition, nonresident: full-time $9936; part-time $414 per credit. Tuition and fees vary according to course load. *Financial support:* Career-related internships or fieldwork, Federal Work-Study, scholarships/grants, traineeships, health care benefits, tuition waivers (full), and unspecified assistantships available. Support available to part-time students. *Unit head:* Dr. Atul Sheel, Graduate Program Director, 413-545-1389, Fax: 413-545-1235. *Application contact:* Jean M. Ames, Supervisor of Admissions, 413-545-0722, Fax: 413-577-0010, E-mail: gradadm@grad.umass.edu.

University of Massachusetts Amherst, Graduate School, Isenberg School of Management, Department of Hospitality and Tourism Management, Amherst, MA 01003. Offers MS, MS/MBA. Part-time programs available. *Faculty:* 13 full-time (4 women). *Students:* 15 full-time (7 women), 9 international. Average age 26. 34 applicants, 79% accepted, 5 enrolled. In 2009, 9 master's awarded. *Degree requirements:* For master's, thesis or alternative. *Entrance requirements:* For master's, GMAT. Additional exam requirements/recommendations for international students: Required—TOEFL (minimum score 550 paper-based; 213 computer-based; 80 iBT), IELTS (minimum score 6.5). *Application deadline:* For fall admission, 2/1 for domestic and international students; for spring admission, 10/1 for domestic and international students. Applications are processed on a rolling basis. Application fee: $50 ($65 for international students). Electronic applications accepted. *Expenses:* Tuition, state resident: full-time $2640; part-time $110 per credit. Tuition, nonresident: full-time $9936; part-time $414 per credit. Tuition and fees vary according to course load. *Financial support:* In 2009–10, 1 research assistantship with full tuition reimbursement (averaging $3,682 per year), 13 teaching assistantships with full tuition reimbursements (averaging $6,303 per year) were awarded; fellowships, career-related internships or fieldwork, Federal Work-Study, scholarships/grants, traineeships, health care benefits, tuition waivers (full), and unspecified assistantships also available. Support available to part-time students. Financial award application deadline: 2/1. *Unit head:* Dr. Atul Sheel, Graduate Program Director, 413-545-1389, Fax: 413-545-1235. *Application contact:* Jean M. Ames, Supervisor of Admissions, 413-545-0722, Fax: 413-577-0010, E-mail: gradadm@grad.umass.edu.

University of New Orleans, Graduate School, College of Business Administration, School of Hotel, Restaurant, and Tourism Administration, Program in Hospitality and Tourism Management, New Orleans, LA 70148. Offers MS. *Entrance requirements:* Additional exam requirements/recommendations for international students: Required—TOEFL (minimum score 550 paper-based; 213 computer-based; 79 iBT).

University of South Africa, College of Economic and Management Sciences, Pretoria, South Africa. Offers accounting (D Admin, D Com); accounting science (DA); auditing (D Admin, D Com); business administration (M Tech); business economics (D Admin); business leadership (DBL); business management (D Admin, D Com); economic management analysis (M Tech); economics (D Admin, D Com, PhD); human resource development (M Tech); industrial psychology (D Admin, D Com, PhD); logistics (D Com); marketing (M Tech); public administration (D Admin, D Com, DPA, PhD); public management (M Tech); quantitative management (D Admin, D Com); real estate (M Tech); statistics (D Admin, PhD); tourism management (D Admin, D Com); transport economics (D Admin, D Com).

University of South Carolina, The Graduate School, College of Hospitality, Retail, and Sport Management, School of Hotel, Restaurant and Tourism Management, Columbia, SC 29208. Offers MIHTM. *Entrance requirements:* For master's, GMAT or GRE General Test, minimum GPA of 3.0, 2 letters of recommendation. Electronic applications accepted. *Faculty research:* Corporate strategy and management practices, sustainable tourism, club management, tourism technology, revenue management.

The University of Tennessee, Graduate School, College of Education, Health and Human Sciences, Department of Consumer and Industry Services Management, Program in Hotel, Restaurant, and Tourism Management, Knoxville, TN 37996. Offers hospitality management (MS); tourism (MS). Part-time programs available. *Degree requirements:* For master's, thesis or alternative. *Entrance requirements:* For master's, GRE General Test, minimum GPA of 2.7. Additional exam requirements/recommendations for international students: Required—TOEFL. Electronic applications accepted. *Expenses:* Tuition, state resident: full-time $6826; part-time $380 per semester hour. Tuition, nonresident: full-time $21,844; part-time $1147 per semester hour. Tuition and fees vary according to program.

University of Waterloo, Graduate Studies, Faculty of Environmental Studies, Program in Tourism Policy and Planning, Waterloo, ON N2L 3G1, Canada. Offers MAES. Part-time programs available. *Degree requirements:* For master's, research paper. *Entrance requirements:* For master's, honors degree in related field, minimum B average. Additional exam requirements/recommendations for international students: Required—TOEFL, TWE. Electronic applications accepted. *Faculty research:* Urban and regional economics, regional economic development, strategic planning, environmental economics, economic geography.

Virginia Polytechnic Institute and State University, Graduate School, Pamplin College of Business, Department of Hospitality and Tourism Management, Blacksburg, VA 24061. Offers MS, PhD. *Faculty:* 11 full-time (4 women), 1 part-time/adjunct (0 women). *Students:* 18 full-time (9 women), 3 part-time (2 women); includes 14 minority (12 American Indian/Alaska Native, 1 Asian American or Pacific Islander, 1 Hispanic American). Average age 30. 54 applicants, 19% accepted, 4 enrolled. In 2009, 7 master's, 1 doctorate awarded. *Entrance requirements:* For master's and doctorate, GRE, GMAT. Additional exam requirements/recommendations for international students: Required—TOEFL (minimum score 550 paper-based; 213 computer-based). *Application deadline:* For fall admission, 5/15 for international students; for spring admission, 10/15 for international students. Applications are processed on a rolling basis. Application fee: $65. Electronic applications accepted. *Expenses:* Tuition, area resident: Full-time $10,228; part-time $459 per credit hour. Tuition, nonresident: full-time $17,892; part-time $865 per credit hour. Required fees: $1966; $451 per semester. *Financial*

support: In 2009–10, 1 research assistantship with full tuition reimbursement (averaging $8,508 per year), 13 teaching assistantships with full tuition reimbursements (averaging $14,052 per year) were awarded; career-related internships or fieldwork, Federal Work-Study, scholarships/grants, and unspecified assistantships also available. Financial award application deadline: 1/15. *Faculty research:* Human resource management, service management, marketing, strategy and finance tourist behavior. Total annual research expenditures: $59,740. *Unit head:* Dr. Rick R. Perdue, Dean, 540-231-3287, Fax: 540-231-8313, E-mail: perduerr@vt.edu. *Application contact:* Nancy McGehee, Information Contact, 540-231-1201, Fax: 540-231-8313, E-mail: nmcgehee@vt.edu.

Western Illinois University, School of Graduate Studies, College of Education and Human Services, Department of Recreation, Park, and Tourism Administration, Macomb, IL 61455-1390. Offers MS. Part-time programs available. *Students:* 35 full-time (19 women), 10 part-time (9 women); includes 4 minority (2 African Americans, 2 Hispanic Americans), 3 international. Average age 27. 34 applicants, 74% accepted. In 2009, 25 master's awarded. *Degree requirements:* For master's, thesis or alternative. *Entrance requirements:* Additional exam requirements/recommendations for international students: Required—TOEFL (minimum score 550 paper-based; 213 computer-based; 80 iBT). *Application deadline:* Applications are processed on a rolling basis. Application fee: $30. Electronic applications accepted. *Expenses:* Tuition, state resident: full-time $4486; part-time $249.21 per credit hour. Tuition, nonresident: full-time $8972; part-time $498.42 per credit hour. Required fees: $72.62 per credit hour. *Financial support:* In 2009–10, 28 students received support, including 28 research assistantships with full tuition reimbursements available (averaging $7,280 per year). Financial award applicants required to submit FAFSA. *Unit head:* Dr. K. Dale Adkins, Chairperson, 309-298-1967. *Application contact:* Evelyn Hoing, Assistant Director of Graduate Studies, 309-298-1806, Fax: 309-298-2345, E-mail: grad-office@wiu.edu.

Section 8
Human Resources

This section contains a directory of institutions offering graduate work in human resources, followed by in-depth entries submitted by institutions that chose to prepare detailed program descriptions. Additional information about programs listed in the directory but not augmented by an in-depth entry may be obtained by writing directly to the dean of a graduate school or chair of a department at the address given in the directory.

For programs offering related work, see also in this book *Business Administration and Management, Advertising and Public Relations, Hospitality Management, Industrial and Manufacturing Management,* and *Organizational Behavior.* In another guide in this series:

Graduate Programs in the Humanities, Arts & Social Sciences
See *Public, Regional, and Industrial Affairs (Industrial and Labor Relations)*

CONTENTS

Program Directories

Close-Ups

See also:

Human Resources Development

Abilene Christian University, Graduate School, College of Arts and Sciences, Department of Communication, Program in Organizational and Human Resource Development, Abilene, TX 79699-9100. Offers MS. Part-time and evening/weekend programs available. *Students:* 12 full-time (9 women), 93 part-time (68 women); includes 16 minority (10 African Americans, 2 Asian Americans or Pacific Islanders, 4 Hispanic Americans), 1 international. 82 applicants, 40% accepted, 30 enrolled. In 2009, 10 master's awarded. *Degree requirements:* For master's, comprehensive exam. *Entrance requirements:* For master's, GMAT, GRE General Test, or MAT. *Application deadline:* For fall admission, 4/1 priority date for domestic students; for spring admission, 11/1 for domestic students. Applications are processed on a rolling basis. Application fee: $40. Electronic applications accepted. *Expenses:* Tuition: Full-time $11,520; part-time $640 per hour. Required fees: $1090; $53.50 per hour. $10 per term. Tuition and fees vary according to program. *Financial support:* In 2009–10, 81 students received support. Federal Work-Study available. Support available to part-time students. Financial award application deadline: 4/1; financial award applicants required to submit FAFSA. *Unit head:* Dr. Jonathan Camp, Graduate Advisor, 325-674-2136, E-mail: jwc03b@acu.edu. *Application contact:* William Horn, Graduate Admissions Counselor, 325-674-2656, Fax: 325-674-6717, E-mail: gradinfo@acu.edu.

Amberton University, Graduate School, Program in Human Relations and Business, Garland, TX 75041-5595. Offers MA, MS. Part-time and evening/weekend programs available. *Entrance requirements:* For master's, minimum GPA of 3.0.

American International College, School of Arts, Education and Sciences, Center for Human Resource Development, Springfield, MA 01109-3189. Offers MA. Evening/weekend programs available. *Degree requirements:* For master's, practicum, project. *Entrance requirements:* For master's, minimum B- average in undergraduate course work, writing sample. Additional exam requirements/recommendations for international students: Required—TOEFL. Electronic applications accepted. *Expenses:* Tuition: Full-time $12,510; part-time $695 per credit hour. Required fees: $35 per term. *Faculty research:* Faculty development, teaching/training effectiveness.

Antioch University Los Angeles, Graduate Programs, Program in Organizational Management, Culver City, CA 90230. Offers human resource development (MA); leadership (MA); organizational development (MA). Part-time and evening/weekend programs available. *Entrance requirements:* For master's, interview. Additional exam requirements/recommendations for international students: Required—TOEFL. *Faculty research:* Systems thinking and chaos theory, technology and organizational structure, nonprofit management, power and empowerment.

Azusa Pacific University, School of Business and Management, Program in Human and Organizational Development, Azusa, CA 91702-7000. Offers MA. Part-time and evening/weekend programs available. *Degree requirements:* For master's, comprehensive exam, final project. *Entrance requirements:* For master's, minimum GPA of 3.0.

Barry University, School of Education, Program in Human Resource Development and Administration, Miami Shores, FL 33161-6695. Offers MS. Part-time and evening/weekend programs available. *Degree requirements:* For master's, comprehensive exam, practicum. *Entrance requirements:* For master's, GRE General Test or MAT, minimum GPA of 3.0. Electronic applications accepted.

Barry University, School of Education, Program in Leadership and Education, Miami Shores, FL 33161-6695. Offers educational technology (PhD); exceptional student education (PhD); higher education administration (PhD); human resource development (PhD); leadership (PhD). Part-time and evening/weekend programs available. *Degree requirements:* For doctorate, thesis/dissertation. *Entrance requirements:* For doctorate, GRE General Test, minimum GPA of 3.25. Electronic applications accepted.

Bowie State University, Graduate Programs, Program in Human Resource Development, Bowie, MD 20715-9465. Offers MA. Part-time and evening/weekend programs available. *Degree requirements:* For master's, comprehensive exam, thesis optional, research paper. *Entrance requirements:* For master's, minimum GPA of 2.5. Electronic applications accepted.

California State University, Sacramento, Graduate Studies, College of Business Administration, Sacramento, CA 95819. Offers accountancy (MS); business administration (MBA); human resources (MBA); management information science (MS); urban land development (MBA). *Accreditation:* AACSB. Part-time and evening/weekend programs available. *Degree requirements:* For master's, thesis or alternative, writing proficiency exam. *Entrance requirements:* For master's, GMAT. Additional exam requirements/recommendations for international students: Required—TOEFL. Electronic applications accepted.

Claremont Graduate University, Graduate Programs, School of Behavioral and Organizational Sciences, Department of Psychology, Claremont, CA 91711-6160. Offers advanced study in evaluation (Certificate); cognitive psychology (MA, PhD); developmental psychology (MA, PhD); evaluation and applied research methods (MA, PhD); health behavior research and evaluation (MA, PhD); human resource development and evaluation (MA); industrial/organizational psychology (MA, PhD); organizational behavior (MA, PhD); organizational psychology (MA, PhD); social psychology (MA, PhD); MBA/PhD. Part-time programs available. *Faculty:* 17 full-time (7 women), 1 part-time/adjunct (0 women). *Students:* 231 full-time (155 women), 25 part-time (18 women); includes 62 minority (13 African Americans, 1 American Indian/Alaska Native, 31 Asian Americans or Pacific Islanders, 17 Hispanic Americans), 21 international. Average age 30. In 2009, 37 master's, 12 doctorates, 8 other advanced degrees awarded. Terminal master's awarded for partial completion of doctoral program. *Entrance requirements:* For master's and doctorate, GRE General Test. Additional exam requirements/recommendations for international students: Required—TOEFL (minimum score 550 paper-based; 213 computer-based; 80 iBT). *Application deadline:* For fall admission, 1/15 priority date for domestic students. Applications are processed on a rolling basis. Application fee: $60. Electronic applications accepted. *Expenses:* Tuition: Full-time $35,046; part-time $1524 per credit. Required fees: $161 per semester. *Financial support:* Fellowships, research assistantships, teaching assistantships, Federal Work-Study, institutionally sponsored loans, scholarships/grants, and tuition waivers (full and partial) available. Support available to part-time students. Financial award application deadline: 2/15; financial award applicants required to submit FAFSA. *Faculty research:* Social intervention, diversity in organizations, eyewitness memory, aging and cognition, drug policy. *Unit head:* Stewart Donaldson, Dean, 909-607-9001, Fax: 909-621-8905, E-mail: stewart.donaldson@cgu.edu. *Application contact:* Paul Thomas, Director, External Affairs, 909-607-9016, Fax: 909-621-8905, E-mail: paul.thomas@cgu.edu.

Clemson University, Graduate School, College of Health, Education, and Human Development, School of Education, Program in Human Resource Development, Clemson, SC 29634. Offers MHRD. Part-time programs available. *Students:* 2 full-time (1 woman), 73 part-time (43 women); includes 14 minority (12 African Americans, 1 American Indian/Alaska Native, 1 Hispanic American), 1 international. Average age 34. 49 applicants, 86% accepted, 34 enrolled. In 2009, 21 master's awarded. *Entrance requirements:* For master's, GRE General Test. Additional exam requirements/recommendations for international students: Required—TOEFL. *Application deadline:* For fall admission, 7/1 for domestic students. Applications are processed on a rolling basis. Application fee: $70 ($80 for international students). Electronic applications accepted. *Expenses:* Contact institution. *Financial support:* Application deadline: 6/1. *Unit head:* Dr. Michael J. Padilla, Director/Associate Dean, 864-656-4444, Fax: 864-656-0311, E-mail: pmcgee@clemson.edu. *Application contact:* Dr. David Fleming, Graduate Coordinator, 864-656-1881, Fax: 864-656-0311, E-mail: dflemin@clemson.edu.

The College of New Rochelle, Graduate School, Division of Human Services, Program in Career Development, New Rochelle, NY 10805-2308. Offers MS. Part-time programs available. *Degree requirements:* For master's, fieldwork, internship. *Entrance requirements:* For master's, interview, minimum GPA of 3.0, writing sample. *Faculty research:* Technology.

Florida International University, College of Education, Department of Educational Leadership and Policy Studies, Program in Adult Education in Human Resource Development, Miami, FL 33199. Offers Ed D. Part-time and evening/weekend programs available. *Degree requirements:* For doctorate, thesis/dissertation. *Entrance requirements:* For doctorate, GRE General Test. Additional exam requirements/recommendations for international students: Required—TOEFL (minimum score 550 paper-based; 213 computer-based; 80 iBT), IELTS (minimum score 6.3). Electronic applications accepted. *Expenses:* Tuition, state resident: full-time $8008; part-time $4004 per year. Tuition, nonresident: full-time $20,104; part-time $10,052 per year. Required fees: $298; $149 per term. *Faculty research:* Adult education, family literacy, learning technologies.

Florida International University, College of Education, Department of Educational Leadership and Policy Studies, Program in Human Resource Development, Miami, FL 33199. Offers MS. Part-time and evening/weekend programs available. *Entrance requirements:* Additional exam requirements/recommendations for international students: Required—TOEFL (minimum score 550 paper-based; 213 computer-based; 80 iBT), IELTS (minimum score 6.3). Electronic applications accepted. *Expenses:* Tuition, state resident: full-time $8008; part-time $4004 per year. Tuition, nonresident: full-time $20,104; part-time $10,052 per year. Required fees: $298; $149 per term.

Florida State University, The Graduate School, College of Education, Department of Educational Psychology and Learning Systems, Program in Instructional Systems, Tallahassee, FL 32306. Offers instructional systems (MS, PhD, Ed S); open and distance learning (MS); performance improvement and human resources (MS). *Faculty:* 6 full-time (3 women), 4 part-time/adjunct (1 woman). *Students:* 51 full-time (34 women), 60 part-time (35 women); includes 19 minority (9 African Americans, 2 American Indian/Alaska Native, 5 Asian Americans or Pacific Islanders, 3 Hispanic Americans), 26 international. 68 applicants, 16% accepted, 11 enrolled. In 2009, 25 master's, 9 doctorates awarded. *Degree requirements:* For master's and Ed S, comprehensive exam, thesis optional; for doctorate, comprehensive exam, thesis/dissertation. *Entrance requirements:* For master's, doctorate, and Ed S, GRE General Test, minimum GPA of 3.0. Additional exam requirements/recommendations for international students: Required—TOEFL (minimum score 550 paper-based; 213 computer-based; 80 iBT). *Application deadline:* For fall admission, 6/1 priority date for domestic and international students; for spring admission, 10/1 priority date for domestic and international students. Applications are processed on a rolling basis. Application fee: $30. *Expenses:* Tuition, state resident: full-time $7413. Tuition, nonresident: full-time $22,567. *Financial support:* In 2009–10, 3 fellowships with full and partial tuition reimbursements, 8 research assistantships with full and partial tuition reimbursements, 6 teaching assistantships with full and partial tuition reimbursements were awarded; career-related internships or fieldwork and Federal Work-Study also available. Financial award applicants required to submit FAFSA. *Faculty research:* Human performance improvement, educational semiotics, development of software tools to measure online interaction among learners. *Unit head:* Dr. Vanessa Dennen, Program Coordinator, 850-644-8783, Fax: 850-644-8776, E-mail: vdennen@fsu.edu. *Application contact:* Mary Kate McKee, Program Coordinator, 850-644-8792, Fax: 850-644-8776, E-mail: mmckee@oddl.fsu.edu.

Friends University, Graduate School, Division of Business, Technology, and Leadership, Program in Organization Development, Wichita, KS 67213. Offers MSOD. Evening/weekend programs available. *Entrance requirements:* Additional exam requirements/recommendations for international students: Required—TOEFL (minimum score 560 paper-based; 220 computer-based). Electronic applications accepted.

The George Washington University, Graduate School of Education and Human Development, Department of Counseling/Human and Organizational Studies, Programs in Human and Organizational Learning, Washington, DC 20052. Offers human and organizational learning (Ed D); human resource development (MA Ed); leadership development (Graduate Certificate). MA Ed program also offered in Alexandria and Newport News, VA, as well as in Singapore and Hong Kong. *Students:* 57 full-time (32 women), 46 part-time (30 women); includes 32 minority (24 African Americans, 5 Asian Americans or Pacific Islanders, 3 Hispanic Americans), 4 international. Average age 43. 69 applicants, 94% accepted, 33 enrolled. In 2009, 5 other advanced degrees awarded. *Degree requirements:* For master's and Graduate Certificate, comprehensive exam; for doctorate, comprehensive exam, thesis/dissertation. *Entrance requirements:* For master's, GRE General Test or MAT, minimum GPA of 2.75; for doctorate, GRE General Test or MAT, interview, minimum GPA of 3.3; for Graduate Certificate, GRE General Test or MAT, minimum GPA of 3.3. *Application deadline:* For fall admission, 1/15 priority date for domestic students; for spring admission, 10/1 for domestic students. Applications are processed on a rolling basis. Application fee: $60. *Financial support:* Fellowships, research assistantships, teaching assistantships, career-related internships or fieldwork, Federal Work-Study, and tuition waivers (partial) available. Financial award application deadline: 1/15; financial award applicants required to submit FAFSA. *Faculty research:* Organizational learning, program evaluation. *Unit head:* David Schwandt, Program Manager, E-mail: chwandt@gwu.edu. *Application contact:* Sarah Lang, Director of Graduate Admissions, 202-994-1447, E-mail: slang@gwu.edu.

Illinois Institute of Technology, Graduate College, Institute of Psychology, Chicago, IL 60616-3793. Offers clinical psychology (PhD); industrial/organizational psychology (PhD); personnel/human resource development (MS); psychology (MS); rehabilitation counseling (MS); rehabilitation counselor education (PhD). *Accreditation:* APA (one or more programs are accredited); CORE. Part-time and evening/weekend programs available. *Faculty:* 19 full-time (8 women), 5 part-time/adjunct (all women). *Students:* 118 full-time (88 women), 82 part-time (62 women); includes 33 minority (10 African Americans, 1 American Indian/Alaska Native, 14 Asian Americans or Pacific Islanders, 8 Hispanic Americans), 24 international. Average age 29. 281 applicants, 33% accepted, 28 enrolled. In 2009, 37 master's, 13 doctorates awarded. Terminal master's awarded for partial completion of doctoral program. *Degree requirements:* For master's, thesis (for some programs); for doctorate, comprehensive exam, thesis/dissertation, 96-108 credit hours, internship for Clinical and I/O specializations. *Entrance requirements:* For master's, GRE General Test, minimum high school GPA of 3.0, official transcripts, 3 letters of recommendation, personal statement; for doctorate, GRE General Test, minimum high school GPA of 3.0, official transcriptions, 3 letters of recommendation, personal statement. Additional exam requirements/recommendations for international students: Required—TOEFL (minimum score 550 paper-based; 80 iBT). *Application deadline:* For fall admission, 2/15 for domestic and international students. Application fee: $40. Electronic applications accepted. *Expenses:* Tuition: Full-time $17,550; part-time $888 per credit hour. Required fees: $850; $7.50 per credit hour. One-time fee: $50 full-time. Full-time tuition and fees vary according to program. *Financial support:* In 2009–10, 39 fellowships with partial tuition reimbursements (averaging $2,798 per year), 1 research assistantship with partial tuition reimbursement, 24 teaching assistantships with partial tuition reimbursements (averaging $4,405 per year) were awarded; career-related internships or fieldwork, Federal Work-Study, institutionally sponsored loans, scholarships/grants, traineeships, health care benefits, tuition waivers (partial), and unspecified assistantships also available. Support available to part-time students. Financial award application deadline: 1/15; financial award applicants required to submit FAFSA. *Faculty research:* Stigma and mental illness, depression, couples communication, leadership, psychometric theory. Total annual research expenditures: $426,090. *Unit head:* Dr. M. Ellen Mitchell, Dean, 312-567-3362, Fax: 312-567-3493, E-mail: mitchelle@iit.edu. *Application contact:* Institute of Psychology Graduate Admissions, 312-567-3500, Fax: 312-567-3493, E-mail: psychology@iit.edu.

Indiana State University, School of Graduate Studies, College of Technology, Department of Industrial Technology Education, Terre Haute, IN 47809. Offers career and technical education (MS); human resource development (MS); technology education (MS); MA/MS. *Accreditation:* NCATE (one or more programs are accredited). *Entrance requirements:* For master's, bachelor's degree in industrial technology or related field. Additional exam requirements/recommendations for international students: Required—TOEFL. Electronic applications accepted.

Indiana Tech, Program in Business Administration, Fort Wayne, IN 46803-1297. Offers accounting (MBA); health care administration (MBA); human resources (MBA); management (MBA); marketing (MBA). Part-time and evening/weekend programs available. Postbaccalaureate distance learning degree programs offered (no on-campus study). *Students:* 202 full-time (97 women), 37 part-time (18 women); includes 60 minority (45 African Americans, 2 American Indian/Alaska Native, 7 Asian Americans or Pacific Islanders, 6 Hispanic Americans), 5 international. Average age 38. *Entrance requirements:* For master's, GMAT, minimum undergraduate GPA of 2.5, 3 letters of recommendation. *Application deadline:* Applications are processed on a rolling basis. Application fee: $25. Electronic applications accepted. *Expenses:* Tuition: Full-time $5160; part-time $430 per credit hour. Tuition and fees vary according to degree level and program. *Financial support:* Applicants required to submit FAFSA. *Unit head:* Dr. Andrew Nwanne, Associate Dean of College of Professional Studies, 260-422-5561 Ext. 2214, E-mail: ainwanne@indianatech.edu. *Application contact:* Steve Herendeen, Manager of Campus Development and Support, 260-422-5561 Ext. 2121, E-mail: saherendeen@indianatech.edu.

Indiana University of Pennsylvania, School of Graduate Studies and Research, Eberly College of Business and Information Technology, Department of Technology Support and Training, Program in Business/Workforce Development, Indiana, PA 15705-1087. Offers M Ed. *Faculty:* 4 full-time (3 women). *Students:* 16 full-time (8 women), 24 part-time (13 women); includes 3 minority (all African Americans). Average age 34. 39 applicants, 62% accepted, 18 enrolled. In 2009, 18 master's awarded. *Degree requirements:* For master's, thesis optional. *Entrance requirements:* For master's, 2 letters of recommendation. Additional exam requirements/recommendations for international students: Required—TOEFL. *Application deadline:* For fall admission, 7/1 priority date for domestic students; for spring admission, 11/1 for domestic students. Applications are processed on a rolling basis. Application fee: $40. *Expenses:* Tuition, state resident: full-time $6666; part-time $370 per credit hour. Tuition, nonresident: full-time $10,666; part-time $593 per credit hour. Required fees: $813 per semester. *Financial support:* In 2009–10, 11 research assistantships with full and partial tuition reimbursements (averaging $2,160 per year) were awarded; career-related internships or fieldwork and Federal Work-Study also available. Support available to part-time students. Financial award application deadline: 3/15; financial award applicants required to submit FAFSA. *Unit head:* Dr. Dawn Woodland, Graduate Coordinator, 724-357-5736, E-mail: woodland@iup.edu. *Application contact:* Dr. Dawn Woodland, Graduate Coordinator, 724-357-5736, E-mail: woodland@iup.edu.

Inter American University of Puerto Rico, Metropolitan Campus, Graduate Programs, Program in Human Resources, San Juan, PR 00919-1293. Offers MBA. *Degree requirements:* For master's, comprehensive exam. *Entrance requirements:* For master's, GRE or EXADEP, interview. Electronic applications accepted.

Inter American University of Puerto Rico, San Germán Campus, Graduate Studies Center, Program in Business Administration, San Germán, PR 00683-5008. Offers accounting (MBA); finance (MBA); human resources (PhD); human resources management (MBA); industrial management (MBA); international business (PhD); management information systems (MBA); marketing management (MBA). Part-time and evening/weekend programs available. *Degree requirements:* For master's, comprehensive exam. *Entrance requirements:* For master's, GRE General Test or EXADEP, minimum GPA of 3.0.

Iowa State University of Science and Technology, Graduate College, College of Human Sciences, Department of Educational Leadership and Policy Studies, Ames, IA 50011. Offers counselor education (M Ed, MS); educational administration (M Ed, MS); educational leadership (PhD); higher education (M Ed, MS); organizational learning and human resource development (M Ed, MS); research and evaluation (MS). *Faculty:* 21 full-time (10 women), 14 part-time/adjunct (8 women). *Students:* 116 full-time (68 women), 218 part-time (130 women); includes 58 minority (34 African Americans, 3 American Indian/Alaska Native, 4 Asian Americans or Pacific Islanders, 17 Hispanic Americans), 7 international. 138 applicants, 78% accepted, 74 enrolled. In 2009, 77 master's, 18 doctorates awarded. *Degree requirements:* For master's, thesis or alternative; for doctorate, thesis/dissertation. *Entrance requirements:* For doctorate, GRE General Test. Additional exam requirements/recommendations for international students: Required—TOEFL (minimum score 560 paper-based; 83 iBT) or IELTS (minimum score 6.5). *Application deadline:* For fall admission, 1/1 priority date for domestic and international students. Applications are processed on a rolling basis. Application fee: $40 ($90 for international students). Electronic applications accepted. *Expenses:* Tuition, state resident: full-time $6716. Tuition, nonresident: full-time $8908. Tuition and fees vary according to course level, course load, program and student level. *Financial support:* In 2009–10, 104 research assistantships with full and partial tuition reimbursements (averaging $13,500 per year), 2 teaching assistantships with full and partial tuition reimbursements (averaging $13,500 per year) were awarded; fellowships, scholarships/grants, health care benefits, and unspecified assistantships also available. *Unit head:* Dr. Laura Rendon, Chair, 515-294-7093, E-mail: lrendon@iastate.edu. *Application contact:* Dr. Daniel Robinson, Information Contact, 515-294-1241, E-mail: eldrshp@iastate.edu.

John F. Kennedy University, School of Management, Program in Career Development, Pleasant Hill, CA 94523-4817. Offers career coaching (Certificate); career development (MA, Certificate). Part-time and evening/weekend programs available. *Degree requirements:* For master's, thesis or alternative. *Entrance requirements:* For master's, interview. Additional exam requirements/recommendations for international students: Required—TOEFL.

The Johns Hopkins University, Carey Business School, Management Programs, Baltimore, MD 21218-2699. Offers leadership development (Certificate); organization development and human resources (MS); skilled facilitator (Certificate). Evening/weekend programs available. *Faculty:* 29 full-time (6 women), 135 part-time/adjunct (29 women). *Students:* 2 full-time (both women), 65 part-time (44 women); includes 40 minority (30 African Americans, 4 Asian Americans or Pacific Islanders, 6 Hispanic Americans), 4 international. Average age 35. 35 applicants, 94% accepted, 29 enrolled. In 2009, 93 master's, 37 other advanced degrees awarded. *Degree requirements:* For master's, 36 credits including final project. *Entrance requirements:* For master's and Certificate, minimum GPA of 3.0, resume, work experience, two letters of recommendation. Additional exam requirements/recommendations for international students: Required—TOEFL (minimum score 600 paper-based; 250 computer-based; 100 iBT). *Application deadline:* For fall admission, 5/1 for international students; for spring admission, 10/15 for international students. Applications are processed on a rolling basis. Application fee: $100. Electronic applications accepted. *Financial support:* Scholarships/grants available. Support available to part-time students. Financial award application deadline: 4/1; financial award applicants required to submit FAFSA. *Faculty research:* Agency theory and theory of the firm, technological entrepreneurship, technology policy and economic development, strategic human resources management, ethics and stakeholder theory. Total annual research expenditures: $57,832. *Unit head:* Dr. Dipankar Chakravarti, Vice Dean of Programs, 410-516-8561, E-mail: dipankar.chakravarti@jhu.edu. *Application contact:* Robin Greeberg, Admissions Coordinator, 410-516-4234, Fax: 410-516-0826, E-mail: carey.admissions@jhu.edu.

Kentucky State University, College of Professional Studies, Frankfort, KY 40601. Offers business administration (MBA), including accounting, finance, management, marketing; public administration (MPA), including human resource management, international administration and development, management information systems, nonprofit management; special education (MA). Part-time and evening/weekend programs available. Postbaccalaureate distance learning degree programs offered (minimal on-campus study). *Faculty:* 11 full-time (3 women), 2 part-time/adjunct (both women). *Students:* 79 full-time (51 women), 66 part-time (34 women); includes 88 minority (85 African Americans, 2 Asian Americans or Pacific Islanders, 1 Hispanic American), 4 international. Average age 34. 92 applicants, 75% accepted, 52 enrolled. In 2009, 32 master's awarded. *Degree requirements:* For master's, comprehensive exam, thesis optional. *Entrance requirements:* For master's, GMAT, GRE. Additional exam requirements/recommendations for international students: Required—TOEFL (minimum score 525 paper-based; 173 computer-based). *Application deadline:* For fall admission, 7/1 priority date for domestic students, 4/15 priority date for international students; for spring admission, 11/15 priority date for domestic students, 8/1 priority date for international students. Applications are processed on a rolling basis. Application fee: $30 ($100 for international students). Electronic applications accepted. *Expenses:* Tuition, state resident: full-time $5634; part-time $313 per credit hour. Tuition, nonresident: full-time $14,598; part-time $811 per credit hour. Required fees: $450; $25 per credit hour. *Financial support:* In 2009–10, 113 students received support, including 4 research assistantships (averaging $14,035 per year); career-related internships or fieldwork, scholarships/grants, tuition waivers (partial), and unspecified assistantships also available. Financial award application deadline: 4/15; financial award applicants required to submit FAFSA. *Unit head:* Dr. Gashaw Lake, Dean, College of Professional Studies, 502-597-6105, Fax: 502-597-6715, E-mail: gashaw.lake@kysu.edu. *Application contact:* Cedric Cunningham, Administrative Assistant, Office of Graduate Studies, 502-597-6536, E-mail: cedric.cunningham@kysu.edu.

Louisiana State University and Agricultural and Mechanical College, Graduate School, College of Agriculture, School of Human Resource Education and Workforce Development, Baton Rouge, LA 70803. Offers agriculture and extension education and youth development (MS, PhD); career and technical education (MS, PhD); comprehensive vocational education (MS, PhD); extension and international education (MS, PhD); human resource and leadership development (MS, PhD); industrial education (MS); vocational agriculture education (MS, PhD); vocational business education (MS); vocational home economics education (MS). *Accreditation:* NCATE. Part-time programs available. *Faculty:* 11 full-time (5 women), 2 part-time/adjunct (both women). *Students:* 39 full-time (22 women), 75 part-time (51 women); includes 14 African Americans, 1 Asian American or Pacific Islander, 2 Hispanic Americans, 7 international. Average age 37. 40 applicants, 93% accepted, 18 enrolled. In 2009, 16 master's, 13 doctorates awarded. Terminal master's awarded for partial completion of doctoral program. *Degree requirements:* For master's, thesis (for some programs); for doctorate, thesis/dissertation. *Entrance requirements:* For master's and doctorate, GRE General Test, minimum GPA of 3.0. Additional exam requirements/recommendations for international students: Required—TOEFL (minimum score 550 paper-based; 213 computer-based; 79 iBT) or IELTS (minimum score 6.5). *Application deadline:* For fall admission, 1/25 priority date for domestic students, 5/15 for international students; for spring admission, 10/15 for international students. Applications are processed on a rolling basis. Application fee: $50 ($70 for international students). Electronic applications accepted. *Financial support:* In 2009–10, 63 students received support, including 3 fellowships with full and partial tuition reimbursements available (averaging $24,885 per year), 5 research assistantships with full and partial tuition reimbursements available (averaging $14,440 per year), 4 teaching assistantships with partial tuition reimbursements available (averaging $13,750 per year); career-related internships or fieldwork, Federal Work-Study, institutionally sponsored loans, health care benefits, tuition waivers (full and partial), and unspecified assistantships also available. Financial award application deadline: 3/1; financial award applicants required to submit FAFSA. *Faculty research:* Adult education, history and philosophy of vocational education, curriculum and instruction, career decision making. Total annual research expenditures: $21,538. *Unit head:* Dr. Michael F. Burnett, Director, 225-578-5748, Fax: 225-578-2526, E-mail: vocbur@lsu.edu. *Application contact:* Paula Beecher, Recruiting Coordinator, 225-578-2468, E-mail: pbeeche@lsu.edu.

Manhattanville College, Graduate Programs, Humanities and Social Sciences Programs, Program in Organizational Management and Human Resource Development, Purchase, NY 10577-2132. Offers MS. Part-time and evening/weekend programs available. In 2009, 25 master's awarded. *Degree requirements:* For master's, thesis. *Entrance requirements:* For master's, interview, 2 letters of recommendation. Additional exam requirements/recommendations for international students: Required—TOEFL. *Application deadline:* Applications are processed on a rolling basis. Application fee: $70. *Financial support:* Career-related internships or fieldwork, Federal Work-Study, institutionally sponsored loans, and unspecified assistantships available. Financial award application deadline: 3/1; financial award applicants required to submit FAFSA. *Unit head:* Dr. Don Richards, Interim Dean, School of Graduate and Professional Studies, 914-323-5469, Fax: 914-694-3488, E-mail: gps@mivlle.edu. *Application contact:* Office of Admissions for Graduate and Professional Studies, 914-323-5418, E-mail: gps@mville.edu.

Marquette University, Graduate School of Management, Program in Human Resources, Milwaukee, WI 53201-1881. Offers MSHR. Part-time and evening/weekend programs available. *Faculty:* 4 full-time (3 women), 3 part-time/adjunct (2 women). *Students:* 10 full-time (5 women), 12 part-time (9 women); includes 3 minority (1 African American, 2 Asian Americans or Pacific Islanders), 8 international. Average age 27. 38 applicants, 63% accepted, 10 enrolled. In 2009, 11 master's awarded. *Entrance requirements:* For master's, GMAT or GRE General Test. Additional exam requirements/recommendations for international students: Required—TOEFL. Application fee: $40. *Financial support:* Research assistantships, teaching assistantships, Federal Work-Study, institutionally sponsored loans, and tuition waivers (full and partial) available. Support available to part-time students. Financial award application deadline: 2/15. *Faculty research:* Diversity, mentoring. *Unit head:* Dr. Timothy Keaveny, Management Chair, 414-288-3643. *Application contact:* Dr. Timothy Keaveny, Management Chair, 414-288-3643.

McDaniel College, Graduate and Professional Studies, Program in Human Resources Development, Westminster, MD 21157-4390. Offers MS. Part-time and evening/weekend programs available. *Degree requirements:* For master's, portfolio, internship. *Entrance requirements:* For master's, letters of reference (3). Additional exam requirements/recommendations for international students: Required—TOEFL (minimum score 213 computer-based). *Expenses:* Tuition: Part-time $325 per credit hour.

Midwestern State University, Graduate Studies, College of Education, Program in Counseling, Wichita Falls, TX 76308. Offers general counseling (MA); human resource development (MA); school counseling (M Ed); training and development (MA). Part-time and evening/weekend programs available. *Degree requirements:* For master's, comprehensive exam, thesis (for some programs). *Entrance requirements:* For master's, GRE General Test, MAT, or GMAT, valid teaching certificate (M Ed). Additional exam requirements/recommendations for international students: Required—TOEFL (minimum score 550 paper-based; 213 computer-based). Electronic applications accepted. *Expenses:* Tuition, state resident: full-time $1620; part-time $90 per credit hour. Tuition, nonresident: full-time $2160; part-time $120 per credit hour. International tuition: $7506 full-time. Required fees: $3068.80; $145.60 per credit hour. $179 per semester.

Mississippi State University, College of Education, Department of Instructional Systems and Workforce Development, Mississippi State, MS 39762. Offers education (Ed D, Ed S), including technology; instructional systems and workforce development (PhD); instructional technology (MSIT); technology (MS). *Faculty:* 10 full-time (7 women). *Students:* 29 full-time (14 women), 115 part-time (97 women); includes 69 minority (all African Americans), 5 international. Average age 36. 35 applicants, 74% accepted, 19 enrolled. In 2009, 30 master's, 11 doctorates, 1 other advanced degree awarded. *Degree requirements:* For master's, comprehensive exam, thesis optional, comprehensive oral or written exam; for doctorate, comprehensive exam, thesis/dissertation, comprehensive oral and written exam; for Ed S, comprehensive exam, thesis, comprehensive written exam. *Entrance requirements:* For master's, GRE, minimum GPA of 2.75 in junior and senior courses; for doctorate and Ed S, GRE. Additional exam requirements/recommendations for international students: Required—TOEFL (minimum score 550 paper-based; 213 computer-based; 79 iBT); Recommended—IELTS (minimum score 6.5). *Application deadline:* For fall admission, 7/1 for domestic students, 5/1 for international students; for spring admission, 11/1 for domestic students, 9/1 for international students. Applications are processed on a rolling basis. Application fee: $40. Electronic applications accepted. *Expenses:* Tuition, state resident: full-time $2575.50; part-time $286.25 per credit hour. Tuition, nonresident: full-time $6510; part-time $723.50 per credit hour. Tuition and fees vary according to course load. *Financial support:* In 2009–10, 5 teaching assistantships with full tuition reimbursements (averaging $10,078 per year) were awarded; Federal Work-Study, institutionally sponsored loans, and unspecified assistantships also available. Financial award application deadline: 4/1; financial award applicants required to submit FAFSA. *Faculty research:* Computer technology,

Human Resources Development

Mississippi State University (continued)

nontraditional students, interactive video, instructional technology, educational leadership. *Unit head:* Dr. Linda Cornelius, Professor and Interim Head, 662-325-2281, Fax: 662-325-7599, E-mail: lcornelius@colled.msstate.edu. *Application contact:* Interim Associate Vice President for Academic Affairs/Interim Dean of Graduate Studies.

Moravian College, Moravian College Comenius Center, Business and Management Programs, Bethlehem, PA 18018-6650. Offers general management (MBA); health care management (MBA); leadership (MSHRM); learning and performance management (MSHRM); supply chain management (MBA). Part-time and evening/weekend programs available. *Faculty:* 6 full-time (2 women), 10 part-time/adjunct (3 women). *Students:* 59 part-time (30 women). Average age 29. 27 applicants, 74% accepted, 10 enrolled. In 2009, 20 master's awarded. *Entrance requirements:* For master's, GMAT. Additional exam requirements/recommendations for international students: Required—TOEFL (minimum score 550 paper-based; 260 computer-based; 90 iBT). *Application deadline:* Applications are processed on a rolling basis. Application fee: $40. *Expenses:* Contact institution. *Financial support:* In 2009–10, 1 fellowship with full tuition reimbursement was awarded. *Faculty research:* Leadership, change management, human resources. *Unit head:* Dr. William A. Kleintop, Associate Dean for Business and Management Programs, 610-507-1400, Fax: 610-861-1400, E-mail: comenius@moravian.edu. *Application contact:* Linda J. Doyle, Information Contact, 610-861-1400, Fax: 610-861-1466, E-mail: mba@moravian.edu.

National-Louis University, College of Management and Business, Program in Human Resource Management and Development, Chicago, IL 60603. Offers MS. Part-time programs available. *Entrance requirements:* For master's, college-administered critical thinking and writing skills test, minimum GPA of 3.0, resume. *Expenses:* Contact institution.

Naval Postgraduate School, Graduate Programs, School of Business and Public Policy, Monterey, CA 93943. Offers contract management (MS); defense-focused business administration (MBA); executive business administration (MBA); leadership and human resource development (MS); management (MS); program management (MS); systems engineering management (MS). Program only open to commissioned officers of the United States and friendly nations and selected United States federal civilian employees. *Accreditation:* AACSB; NASPAA. Part-time programs available. Postbaccalaureate distance learning degree programs offered (minimal on-campus study). *Degree requirements:* For master's, thesis.

New York University, School of Continuing and Professional Studies, Division of Programs in Business, Program in Leadership and Human Capital Management, New York, NY 10012-1019. Offers benefits and compensation (Advanced Certificate); human resource development (MS); human resource management (MS, Advanced Certificate); organizational and executive coaching (Advanced Certificate); organizational effectiveness (MS). Part-time and evening/weekend programs available. Postbaccalaureate distance learning degree programs offered (no on-campus study). *Faculty:* 37 part-time/adjunct (12 women). *Students:* 32 full-time (27 women), 224 part-time (190 women); includes 71 minority (27 African Americans, 2 American Indian/Alaska Native, 24 Asian Americans or Pacific Islanders, 18 Hispanic Americans). Average age 31. 166 applicants, 82% accepted, 78 enrolled. In 2009, 56 master's, 19 other advanced degrees awarded. *Entrance requirements:* For master's, GRE General Test or GMAT (for recent graduates), 2 letters of recommendation, resume. Additional exam requirements/recommendations for international students: Required—TOEFL (minimum score 600 paper-based; 250 computer-based; 100 iBT), TWE. *Application deadline:* For fall admission, 2/1 priority date for domestic and international students; for spring admission, 10/15 priority date for domestic students, 8/15 priority date for international students. Applications are processed on a rolling basis. Application fee: $75. Electronic applications accepted. *Expenses:* Tuition: Full-time $30,528; part-time $1272 per credit. Required fees: $2177. *Financial support:* In 2009–10, 115 students received support, including 115 fellowships (averaging $2,462 per year); career-related internships or fieldwork, institutionally sponsored loans, and scholarships/grants also available. Support available to part-time students. Financial award application deadline: 3/1; financial award applicants required to submit FAFSA. *Unit head:* Stephanie Bonadio, Head, 212-992-3632, Fax: 212-992-3650, E-mail: sgb259@nyu.edu. *Application contact:* Assistant Director, 212-992-3632, Fax: 212-992-3650, E-mail: scpshrmdstudent@nyu.edu.

North Carolina Agricultural and Technical State University, Graduate School, School of Education, Department of Human Development and Services, Greensboro, NC 27411. Offers adult education (MS); counselor education (MS); human resources-agency counseling (MS); human resources-rehabilitation counseling (MS); leadership studies (PhD); school administration (MS). *Accreditation:* ACA. Part-time and evening/weekend programs available. *Degree requirements:* For master's, comprehensive exam, thesis, qualifying exam. *Entrance requirements:* For master's, GRE General Test, minimum GPA of 3.0.

North Carolina Agricultural and Technical State University, Graduate School, School of Technology, Department of Graphic Communication Systems and Technological Studies, Greensboro, NC 27411. Offers industrial arts education (MS); technology education (MS); technology management (PhD); vocational-industrial education (MS); workforce development director (MS). *Accreditation:* NCATE (one or more programs are accredited). Part-time and evening/weekend programs available. *Degree requirements:* For master's, comprehensive exam, thesis or alternative, qualifying exam. *Entrance requirements:* For master's, GRE General Test, minimum GPA of 3.0.

North Carolina State University, Graduate School, College of Education, Department of Adult and Higher Education, Program in Human Resource Development, Raleigh, NC 27695. Offers MS. *Degree requirements:* For master's, thesis. *Entrance requirements:* For master's, GRE, 3 letters of recommendation, resume.

Northeastern Illinois University, Graduate College, College of Education, Department of Educational Leadership and Development, Program in Human Resource Development, Chicago, IL 60625-4699. Offers MA. Part-time and evening/weekend programs available. *Degree requirements:* For master's, comprehensive papers. *Entrance requirements:* For master's, minimum GPA of 2.75, BA in human resource development. Additional exam requirements/recommendations for international students: Required—TOEFL (minimum score 550 paper-based; 213 computer-based; 80 iBT). Electronic applications accepted. *Faculty research:* Analogics, development of expertise, case-based instruction, action science organizational development, theoretical model building.

Oakland University, Graduate Study and Lifelong Learning, School of Education and Human Services, Department of Human Resource Development, Rochester, MI 48309-4401. Offers MTD. *Entrance requirements:* For master's, minimum GPA of 3.0 for unconditional admission. Additional exam requirements/recommendations for international students: Required—TOEFL (minimum score 550 paper-based; 213 computer-based). Electronic applications accepted.

Ottawa University, Graduate Studies-Kansas City, Overland Park, KS 66211. Offers business administration (MBA); human resources (MA). Part-time and evening/weekend programs available. Postbaccalaureate distance learning degree programs offered (minimal on-campus study). *Degree requirements:* For master's, thesis or alternative. *Entrance requirements:* For master's, resume, 3 letters of recommendation. Additional exam requirements/recommendations for international students: Required—TOEFL (minimum score 550 paper-based; 213 computer-based). Electronic applications accepted. *Expenses:* Contact institution.

Penn State University Park, Graduate School, College of the Liberal Arts, Department of Labor Studies and Industrial Relations, State College, University Park, PA 16802-1503. Offers MPS, MS, Postbaccalaureate Certificate. Postbaccalaureate distance learning degree programs offered.

Pittsburg State University, Graduate School, College of Technology, Departments of Graphics and Imaging Technologies and Technology Management, Program in Human Resource Development, Pittsburg, KS 66762. Offers MS. *Degree requirements:* For master's, thesis or alternative. *Expenses:* Tuition, state resident: full-time $4212; part-time $176 per credit. Tuition, nonresident: full-time $11,530; part-time $480 per credit. Required fees: $940; $43 per credit. Tuition and fees vary according to course level, course load, degree level, campus/location, reciprocity agreements and student level.

Rochester Institute of Technology, Graduate Enrollment Services, College of Applied Science and Technology, Department of Hospitality and Service Management, Program in Human Resources Development, Rochester, NY 14623-5603. Offers MS. Part-time and evening/weekend programs available. *Students:* 13 full-time (9 women), 20 part-time (17 women); includes 8 African Americans, 1 Hispanic American, 10 international. Average age 33. 32 applicants, 50% accepted, 10 enrolled. In 2009, 23 master's awarded. *Degree requirements:* For master's, thesis or alternative. *Entrance requirements:* For master's, minimum GPA of 3.0. Additional exam requirements/recommendations for international students: Required—TOEFL (minimum score 550 paper-based; 213 computer-based; 79 iBT), or IELTS (minimum score 6.5). *Application deadline:* For fall admission, 2/15 priority date for domestic and international students; for winter admission, 11/1 for domestic and international students; for spring admission, 2/1 for domestic and international students. Applications are processed on a rolling basis. Application fee: $50. *Expenses:* Tuition: Full-time $31,533; part-time $876 per credit hour. Required fees: $210. *Financial support:* In 2009–10, 31 students received support; research assistantships with partial tuition reimbursements available, teaching assistantships with partial tuition reimbursements available, career-related internships or fieldwork, scholarships/grants, and unspecified assistantships available. Support available to part-time students. Financial award application deadline: 2/15; financial award applicants required to submit FAFSA. *Faculty research:* Global resource development, service/product innovation and implementation. *Unit head:* Dr. Linda Underhill, Chair, 585-475-7359, Fax: 585-475-5099, E-mail: lmuism@rit.edu. *Application contact:* Diane Ellison, Assistant Vice President, Graduate Enrollment Services, 585-475-2229, Fax: 585-475-7164, E-mail: gradinfo@rit.edu.

Rollins College, Hamilton Holt School, Program in Human Resources, Winter Park, FL 32789-4499. Offers MA. Part-time and evening/weekend programs available. *Faculty:* 6 full-time (0 women), 1 part-time/adjunct (0 women). *Students:* 53 part-time (42 women); includes 21 minority (9 African Americans, 2 Asian Americans or Pacific Islanders, 10 Hispanic Americans), 1 international. Average age 32. 122 applicants, 53% accepted, 41 enrolled. In 2009, 25 master's awarded. *Degree requirements:* For master's, thesis optional. *Entrance requirements:* For master's, GMAT, GRE, or MAT, interview. Additional exam requirements/recommendations for international students: Required—TOEFL. *Application deadline:* For fall admission, 4/1 for domestic students; for winter admission, 12/1 for domestic students. Applications are processed on a rolling basis. Application fee: $50. *Expenses:* Contact institution. *Financial support:* Available to part-time students. *Unit head:* Dr. Donald Rogers, Director, 407-646-2348, E-mail: drogers@rollins.edu. *Application contact:* Christian Ricaurte, Coordinator of Records and Registration, 407-646-2653, Fax: 407-646-1551, E-mail: cricaurte@rollins.edu.

Roosevelt University, Graduate Division, College of Professional Studies, Program in Training and Development, Chicago, IL 60605. Offers MA. *Degree requirements:* For master's, thesis. *Entrance requirements:* For master's, minimum GPA of 2.75, relevant work experience.

St. John Fisher College, Ralph C. Wilson Jr. School of Education, Program in Organizational Learning and Human Resource Development, Rochester, NY 14618-3597. Offers MS. Part-time and evening/weekend programs available. *Faculty:* 4 part-time/adjunct (2 women). *Students:* 5 full-time (all women), 32 part-time (29 women); includes 7 minority (6 African Americans, 1 Hispanic American). Average age 32. 33 applicants, 70% accepted, 18 enrolled. In 2009, 12 master's awarded. *Degree requirements:* For master's, capstone project, professional portfolio. *Entrance requirements:* For master's, 2 letters of recommendation, personal statement, current resume. Additional exam requirements/recommendations for international students: Required—TOEFL (minimum score 575 paper-based; 233 computer-based; 80 iBT). *Application deadline:* Applications are processed on a rolling basis. Application fee: $30. Electronic applications accepted. *Expenses:* Tuition: Part-time $680 per credit hour. Required fees: $25 per semester. Tuition and fees vary according to degree level and program. *Financial support:* In 2009–10, 33 students received support. Federal Work-Study and scholarships/grants available. Financial award applicants required to submit FAFSA. *Faculty research:* Empowerment, leadership, group dynamics, team learning, project management. *Unit head:* Edward Ciaschi, Program Director, 585-385-5266, E-mail: eciaschi@sjfc.edu. *Application contact:* Jose Perales, Director of Graduate Admissions, 585-385-8067, E-mail: jperales@sjfc.edu.

Salve Regina University, Graduate Studies, Program in Business Administration, Newport, RI 02840-4192. Offers business administration (MBA); business studies (Certificate); human resources management (Certificate); management (Certificate); organizational development (Certificate). Part-time and evening/weekend programs available. Postbaccalaureate distance learning degree programs offered (minimal on-campus study). *Faculty:* 4 full-time (2 women), 13 part-time/adjunct (4 women). *Students:* 39 full-time (17 women), 89 part-time (39 women); includes 10 minority (5 African Americans, 3 Asian Americans or Pacific Islanders, 2 Hispanic Americans), 3 international. Average age 33. 62 applicants, 82% accepted, 45 enrolled. In 2009, 50 master's awarded. *Entrance requirements:* For master's, GMAT, GRE General Test, or MAT, 6 undergraduate credits each in accounting, economics, quantitative analysis and calculus or statistics. Additional exam requirements/recommendations for international students: Required—TOEFL (minimum score 600 paper-based; 250 computer-based; 100 iBT), or IELTS. *Application deadline:* For fall admission, 3/15 priority date for domestic and international students; for spring admission, 9/15 priority date for domestic and international students. Applications are processed on a rolling basis. Application fee: $60. Electronic applications accepted. *Expenses:* Tuition: Part-time $395 per credit. Part-time tuition and fees vary according to degree level. *Financial support:* Career-related internships or fieldwork and Federal Work-Study available. Support available to part-time students. Financial award application deadline: 3/1; financial award applicants required to submit FAFSA. *Unit head:* Dr. Myra Edelstein, Director, 401-341-3139, E-mail: edelstem@salve.edu. *Application contact:* Kelly Alverson, Graduate Admissions Counselor, 401-341-2153, Fax: 401-341-2973, E-mail: kelly.alverson@salve.edu.

Southern New Hampshire University, School of Education, Manchester, NH 03106-1045. Offers business education (MS); child development (M Ed); computer technology education (Certificate); curriculum and instruction (M Ed); education (M Ed, CAS); elementary education (M Ed); general special education (Certificate); school business administrator (Certificate); secondary education (M Ed); training and development (Certificate). Part-time and evening/weekend programs available. Postbaccalaureate distance learning degree programs offered (no on-campus study). *Degree requirements:* For master's, comprehensive exam (for some programs), thesis or alternative. *Entrance requirements:* For master's, PRAXIS I, minimum GPA of 2.75. Additional exam requirements/recommendations for international students: Required—TOEFL (minimum score 550 paper-based; 213 computer-based). Electronic applications accepted. *Expenses:* Contact institution.

Suffolk University, College of Arts and Sciences, Department of Education and Human Services, Programs in Human Resource, Learning and Performance, Boston, MA 02108-2770. Offers global human resources (Graduate Certificate); human resources (MS, Graduate Certificate); organizational development (CAGS, Graduate Certificate); organizational learning and development (MS, Graduate Certificate); MS/Certificate. Part-time and evening/weekend programs available. *Entrance requirements:* For master's, GRE General Test or MAT, 2 letters of recommendation, resume. *Application deadline:* For fall admission, 6/15 priority date for domestic students, 6/15 for international students; for spring admission, 11/15 priority date for domestic students, 11/15 for international students. Applications are processed on a rolling basis. Application fee: $50. *Expenses:* Tuition: Full-time $33,000; part-time $1100 per credit. Required fees: $20. Tuition and fees vary according to program. *Financial support:* Fellowships available. Financial award application deadline: 4/1. *Faculty research:* Adult training methods, adult learning theory, instructional design, learning and teaching styles, systems thinking. *Unit head:* Christine M. Westphal, Graduate Program Director, 617-994-6455, Fax:

617-305-1743, E-mail: cwestpha@suffolk.edu. *Application contact:* Judith Reynolds, Director of Graduate Admissions, 617-573-8302, Fax: 617-305-1733, E-mail: grad.admission@suffolk.edu.

Syracuse University, Martin J. Whitman School of Management, PhD Program in Business Administration, Syracuse, NY 13244. Offers accounting (PhD); finance (PhD); management information systems (PhD); managerial statistics (PhD); marketing (PhD); operations management (PhD); organizational behavior (PhD); strategy and human resources (PhD); supply chain management (PhD). *Degree requirements:* For doctorate, comprehensive exam, thesis/dissertation, summer research paper. *Entrance requirements:* For doctorate, GMAT or GRE General Test, 3 recommendations. Additional exam requirements/recommendations for international students: Required—TOEFL (minimum score 600 paper-based; 250 computer-based; 100 iBT). Electronic applications accepted. *Expenses:* Tuition: Full-time $26,808; part-time $1117 per credit. Required fees: $1024. *Faculty research:* Marketing models, market microstructure, supply chain, auditing, corporate governance.

Texas A&M University, College of Education and Human Development, Department of Educational Administration and Human Resource Development, College Station, TX 77843. Offers M Ed, MS, Ed D, PhD. Part-time programs available. *Faculty:* 30. *Students:* 132 full-time (90 women), 323 part-time (197 women); includes 165 minority (70 African Americans, 3 American Indian/Alaska Native, 9 Asian Americans or Pacific Islanders, 83 Hispanic Americans), 28 international. Average age 37. In 2009, 54 master's, 29 doctorates awarded. *Degree requirements:* For master's, thesis optional; for doctorate, thesis/dissertation. *Entrance requirements:* For master's, GRE General Test, writing exam, interview, professional experience; for doctorate, GRE General Test, writing exam, interview/presentation, professional experience. Additional exam requirements/recommendations for international students: Required—TOEFL. *Application deadline:* For fall admission, 12/1 for domestic and international students; for spring admission, 8/15 for domestic and international students. Application fee: $50 ($75 for international students). Electronic applications accepted. *Expenses:* Tuition, state resident: full-time $3991; part-time $221.74 per credit hour. Tuition, nonresident: full-time $9049; part-time $502.74 per credit hour. *Financial support:* In 2009–10, fellowships (averaging $20,000 per year), research assistantships (averaging $12,000 per year) were awarded; career-related internships or fieldwork and institutionally sponsored loans also available. Support available to part-time students. Financial award application deadline: 3/1; financial award applicants required to submit FAFSA. *Faculty research:* Higher education administration, public school administration, student affairs. *Application contact:* Joyce Nelson, Senior Academic Advisor, 979-847-9098, Fax: 979-862-4347, E-mail: jnelson@tamu.edu.

Towson University, College of Graduate Studies and Research, Program in Human Resource Development, Towson, MD 21252-0001. Offers MS. Part-time and evening/weekend programs available. *Degree requirements:* For master's, comprehensive exam, internship (educational leadership track). *Entrance requirements:* For master's, 2 letters of recommendation, minimum GPA of 3.0. Additional exam requirements/recommendations for international students: Required—TOEFL. Electronic applications accepted. *Faculty research:* Workforce training and development.

Universidad Central del Este, Graduate School, San Pedro de Macoris, Dominican Republic. Offers administration (M Ad); dentistry (DMD); development of educational and social policies (PhD); environmental engineering (ME); financial management (M Ad); higher education (M Ed); human resources (M Ad); public health (MPH). *Entrance requirements:* For master's, letters of recommendation.

Universidad Iberoamericana, Graduate School, Santo Domingo D.N., Dominican Republic. Offers advertising management (MM); business (MBA); constitutional law (MA); dentistry (DMD); educational management (MA); integrated marketing communication (MA); psychopedagogical intervention (M Ed); strategic management of human talent (MM).

University of Bridgeport, School of Education and Human Resources, Division of Human Resources, Bridgeport, CT 06604. Offers college student personnel (MS); community counseling (MS); human resource development (MS); human service (MS). Part-time and evening/weekend programs available. *Degree requirements:* For master's, thesis, project. *Entrance requirements:* Additional exam requirements/recommendations for international students: Recommended—TOEFL (minimum score 550 paper-based; 213 computer-based; 80 iBT), IELTS (minimum score 6.5). Electronic applications accepted. *Faculty research:* Corporate elder care programs.

University of Connecticut, Graduate School, Center for Continuing Studies, Program in Human Resource Management, Storrs, CT 06269. Offers labor relations (MPS); personnel (MPS). *Students:* 2 full-time (1 woman), 51 part-time (40 women); includes 11 minority (4 African Americans, 1 Asian American or Pacific Islander, 6 Hispanic Americans). Average age 37. 19 applicants, 47% accepted, 9 enrolled. In 2009, 4 master's awarded. *Expenses:* Tuition, state resident: full-time $4725; part-time $525 per credit. Tuition, nonresident: full-time $12,267; part-time $1363 per credit. Required fees: $346 per semester. Tuition and fees vary according to course load. *Unit head:* Susan W. Nesbitt, Director, 860-486-5941. *Application contact:* Peter Diplock, Information Contact, 860-486-2915, E-mail: peter.diplock@uconn.edu.

University of Illinois at Urbana–Champaign, Graduate College, College of Education, Department of Human Resource Education, Champaign, IL 61820. Offers Ed M, MS, Ed D, PhD, CAS, MBA/M Ed. Part-time and evening/weekend programs available. Postbaccalaureate distance learning degree programs offered (no on-campus study). *Faculty:* 6 full-time (1 woman). *Students:* 48 full-time (21 women), 118 part-time (81 women); includes 30 minority (19 African Americans, 6 Asian Americans or Pacific Islanders, 5 Hispanic Americans), 38 international. 104 applicants, 63% accepted, 29 enrolled. In 2009, 87 master's, 9 doctorates, 3 other advanced degrees awarded. *Entrance requirements:* For master's, minimum GPA of 3.0; for doctorate, GRE, minimum GPA of 3.0. Additional exam requirements/recommendations for international students: Required—TOEFL (minimum score 96 iBT). *Application deadline:* Applications are processed on a rolling basis. Application fee: $60 ($75 for international students). Electronic applications accepted. *Financial support:* In 2009–10, 3 fellowships, 8 research assistantships, 11 teaching assistantships were awarded; tuition waivers (full and partial) also available. *Unit head:* Steven R. Aragon, Interim Head, 217-333-0807, Fax: 217-244-5632, E-mail: aragon@illinois.edu. *Application contact:* Laura Ketchum, Secretary, 217-333-0807, Fax: 217-244-5632, E-mail: lirle@illinois.edu.

University of Louisville, Graduate School, College of Education and Human Development, Department of Leadership, Foundations and Human Resource Education, Louisville, KY 40292-0001. Offers educational leadership and organizational development (Ed D, PhD); higher education (MA); human resource education (MS); p-12 educational administration (M Ed, Ed S). *Accreditation:* NCATE. Part-time and evening/weekend programs available. Postbaccalaureate distance learning degree programs offered. *Faculty:* 23 full-time (11 women), 14 part-time/adjunct (7 women). *Students:* 57 full-time (37 women), 189 part-time (125 women); includes 32 minority (28 African Americans, 2 Asian Americans or Pacific Islanders, 2 Hispanic Americans), 7 international. Average age 39. 103 applicants, 63% accepted, 59 enrolled. In 2009, 35 master's, 27 doctorates, 12 other advanced degrees awarded. *Entrance requirements:* For master's, doctorate, and Ed S, GRE General Test. Additional exam requirements/recommendations for international students: Required—TOEFL (minimum score 560 paper-based; 210 computer-based; 83 iBT). *Application deadline:* Applications are processed on a rolling basis. Application fee: $50. Electronic applications accepted. *Financial support:* In 2009–10, 28 students received support; fellowships, research assistantships, teaching assistantships, career-related internships or fieldwork, Federal Work-Study, scholarships/grants, and unspecified assistantships available. Financial award application deadline: 6/1; financial award applicants required to submit FAFSA. *Faculty research:* Evaluation of programs to improve elementary and secondary education; research on organizational and human resource development; student access, retention and success in post-secondary education; educational policy analysis; multivariate quantitative research methods. Total annual research expenditures: $4.2 million. *Unit head:* Dr. Bridgette Pregliasco, Acting Chair, 502-852-6204, Fax: 502-852-4563, E-mail: bridgette.pregliasco@louisville.edu. *Application contact:* Libby Leggett, Director, Graduate Admissions, 502-852-3101, Fax: 502-852-6536, E-mail: gradadm@louisville.edu.

University of Minnesota, Twin Cities Campus, Graduate School, College of Education and Human Development, Department of Organizational Leadership, Policy and Development, Program in Human Resource Development, Minneapolis, MN 55455-0213. Offers M Ed, MA, Ed D, PhD, Certificate. *Students:* 42 full-time (32 women), 28 part-time (21 women); includes 12 minority (7 African Americans, 3 Asian Americans or Pacific Islanders, 2 Hispanic Americans), 5 international. Average age 31. 99 applicants, 81% accepted. In 2009, 28 master's, 76 other advanced degrees awarded. *Unit head:* Ken Bartlett, Chair, 612-624-4935, Fax: 612-624-2231. *Application contact:* Dr. Mary Trettin, Associate Dean, 612-625-6501, Fax: 612-626-1580, E-mail: mtrettin@umn.edu.

University of Missouri–St. Louis, Graduate School, Program in Public Policy Administration, St. Louis, MO 63121. Offers health policy (MPPA); local government management (MPPA); managing human resources and organization (MPPA); nonprofit organization management (MPPA); nonprofit organization management and leadership (Certificate); policy research and analysis (MPPA). *Accreditation:* NASPAA. Part-time and evening/weekend programs available. *Faculty:* 7 full-time (4 women), 6 part-time/adjunct (1 woman). *Students:* 20 full-time (8 women), 69 part-time (45 women); includes 13 minority (11 African Americans, 2 Hispanic Americans), 8 international. Average age 31. 85 applicants, 58% accepted, 28 enrolled. In 2009, 12 master's, 34 Certificates awarded. *Degree requirements:* For master's, exit project. *Entrance requirements:* For master's, 3 letters of recommendation. Additional exam requirements/recommendations for international students: Required—TOEFL (minimum score 550 paper-based; 213 computer-based). *Application deadline:* For fall admission, 7/1 priority date for domestic and international students; for spring admission, 12/1 priority date for domestic and international students. Applications are processed on a rolling basis. Application fee: $35 ($40 for international students). Electronic applications accepted. *Expenses:* Tuition, state resident: full-time $5377; part-time $297.70 per credit hour. Tuition, nonresident: full-time $13,882; part-time $771.20 per credit hour. Required fees: $220; $12.20 per credit hour. One-time fee: $12. Tuition and fees vary according to course level, campus/location and program. *Financial support:* In 2009–10, 2 research assistantships with full and partial tuition reimbursements (averaging $12,000 per year) were awarded; career-related internships or fieldwork also available. Financial award application deadline: 4/1; financial award applicants required to submit FAFSA. *Faculty research:* Urban policy, public finance, evaluation. *Unit head:* Dr. Brady Baybeck, Director, 314-516-5145, Fax: 314-516-5210, E-mail: baybeck@umsl.edu. *Application contact:* 314-516-5458, Fax: 314-516-6996, E-mail: gradadm@umsl.edu.

University of Regina, Faculty of Graduate Studies and Research, Faculty of Education, Department of Human Resources Development, Regina, SK S4S 0A2, Canada. Offers MHRD. Part-time programs available. *Faculty:* 3 full-time (2 women). *Students:* 7 full-time (4 women), 11 part-time (10 women). 18 applicants, 83% accepted. In 2009, 8 master's awarded. *Degree requirements:* For master's, thesis optional, practicum, project, course-based thesis. *Entrance requirements:* Additional exam requirements/recommendations for international students: Required—TOEFL (minimum score 580 paper-based; 237 computer-based; 80 iBT). *Application deadline:* For fall admission, 2/15 for domestic students; for winter admission, 2/15 for domestic students; for spring admission, 2/15 for domestic students. Application fee: $90 ($100 for international students). Electronic applications accepted. *Financial support:* In 2009–10, 2 research assistantships (averaging $16,910 per year), 3 teaching assistantships (averaging $6,650 per year) were awarded; fellowships also available. Financial award application deadline: 6/15. *Unit head:* Dr. Warren Wessel, 306-585-4555, E-mail: warren.wessel@uregina.ca. *Application contact:* Tania Gates, Graduate Program Coordinator, 306-585-4506, Fax: 306-585-5387, E-mail: edgrad@uregina.ca.

University of St. Thomas, Graduate Studies, School of Education, Program in Organization Learning and Development, St. Paul, MN 55105-1096. Offers career development (Certificate); e-learning (Certificate); human resource management (Certificate); human resources and change leadership (MA); learning technology (Certificate); learning technology for learning development and change (MA); organization development (Ed D, Certificate). Part-time and evening/weekend programs available. Postbaccalaureate distance learning degree programs offered (minimal on-campus study). *Faculty:* 5 full-time (4 women), 6 part-time/adjunct (2 women). *Students:* 6 full-time (5 women), 161 part-time (130 women); includes 24 minority (13 African Americans, 7 Asian Americans or Pacific Islanders, 4 Hispanic Americans), 1 international. Average age 37. 115 applicants, 75% accepted, 85 enrolled. In 2009, 29 master's, 7 doctorates, 18 other advanced degrees awarded. *Degree requirements:* For doctorate, comprehensive exam, thesis/dissertation. *Entrance requirements:* For master's, minimum GPA of 3.0, 2 letters of reference, personal statement; for doctorate, minimum GPA of 3.5, interview; for Certificate, minimum graduate GPA of 3.25. Additional exam requirements/recommendations for international students: Required—TOEFL (minimum score 550 paper-based; 213 computer-based). *Application deadline:* For fall admission, 8/1 priority date for domestic and international students; for winter admission, 12/1 priority date for domestic students, 12/1 for international students; for spring admission, 12/1 priority date for domestic and international students. Applications are processed on a rolling basis. Application fee: $50. *Expenses:* Contact institution. *Financial support:* Fellowships, research assistantships, institutionally sponsored loans and scholarships/grants available. Support available to part-time students. Financial award applicants required to submit FAFSA. *Faculty research:* Workplace conflict, physician leaders, entrepreneurship education, mentoring. *Unit head:* Dr. Christopher S. Vye, Acting Department Chair, 651-962-4666, Fax: 651-962-4169, E-mail: csvye@stthomas.edu. *Application contact:* Liz G. Knight, Department Coordinator, 651-962-4459, Fax: 651-962-4169, E-mail: egknight@stthomas.edu.

The University of Scranton, College of Graduate and Continuing Education, Department of Health Administration and Human Resources, Program in Human Resources, Scranton, PA 18510. Offers MS. Part-time and evening/weekend programs available. *Students:* 13 full-time (8 women), 1 (woman) part-time; includes 2 minority (both Hispanic Americans). Average age 33. 16 applicants, 100% accepted. *Degree requirements:* For master's, capstone experience. *Entrance requirements:* Additional exam requirements/recommendations for international students: Required—TOEFL (minimum score 550 paper-based; 173 computer-based), IELTS (minimum score 5.5). Application fee: $0. *Financial support:* Fellowships, teaching assistantships, career-related internships or fieldwork available. Financial award application deadline: 3/1. *Unit head:* Dr. Daniel J. West, Chair, 570-941-4126, Fax: 570-941-4201, E-mail: westd1@scranton.edu. *Application contact:* Joseph M. Roback, Director of Admissions, 570-941-4385, Fax: 570-941-5928, E-mail: robackj2@scranton.edu.

The University of Scranton, College of Graduate and Continuing Education, Department of Health Administration and Human Resources, Program in Human Resources Administration, Scranton, PA 18510. Offers human resources (MS); human resources development (MS); organizational leadership (MS). Part-time and evening/weekend programs available. *Students:* 10 full-time (6 women), 8 part-time (5 women); includes 2 minority (1 African American, 1 Hispanic American), 8 international. Average age 34. 1 applicant, 0% accepted. In 2009, 21 master's awarded. *Degree requirements:* For master's, capstone experience. *Entrance requirements:* For master's, minimum GPA of 2.75. Additional exam requirements/recommendations for international students: Required—TOEFL (minimum score 500 paper-based; 173 computer-based), IELTS (minimum score 5.5). *Application deadline:* Applications are processed on a rolling basis. Application fee: $0. *Financial support:* Fellowships, teaching assistantships, career-related internships or fieldwork, Federal Work-Study, and unspecified assistantships available. Support available to part-time students. Financial award application deadline: 3/1. *Unit head:* Dr. Daniel West, Director, 570-941-6218, E-mail: westd1@scranton.edu. *Application contact:* Joseph M. Roback, Director of Admissions, 570-941-4385, Fax: 570-941-5928, E-mail: roback j2@scranton.edu.

University of South Africa, College of Economic and Management Sciences, Pretoria, South Africa. Offers accounting (D Admin, D Com); accounting science (DA); auditing (D Admin, D Com); business administration (M Tech); business economics (D Admin); business leadership (DBL); business management (D Admin, D Com); economic management analysis (M Tech);

Human Resources Development

University of South Africa (continued)
economics (D Admin, D Com, PhD); human resource development (M Tech); industrial psychology (D Admin, D Com, PhD); logistics (D Com); marketing (M Tech); public administration (D Admin, D Com, DPA, PhD); public management (M Tech); quantitative management (D Admin, D Com); real estate (M Tech); statistics (D Admin, PhD); tourism management (D Admin, D Com); transport economics (D Admin, D Com).

The University of Tennessee, Graduate School, College of Business Administration, Program in Human Resource Development, Knoxville, TN 37996. Offers teacher licensure (MS); training and development (MS). Part-time programs available. *Degree requirements:* For master's, thesis. *Entrance requirements:* For master's, GRE General Test, minimum GPA of 2.7. Electronic applications accepted. *Expenses:* Tuition, state resident: full-time $6826; part-time $380 per semester hour. Tuition, nonresident: full-time $21,844; part-time $1147 per semester hour. Tuition and fees vary according to program.

The University of Texas at Tyler, College of Business and Technology, School of Human Resource Development and Technology, Tyler, TX 75799-0001. Offers human resource development (MS, PhD); industrial management (MS). Part-time and evening/weekend programs available. Postbaccalaureate distance learning degree programs offered (no on-campus study). *Faculty:* 5 full-time (1 woman). *Students:* 28 full-time (14 women), 51 part-time (29 women); includes 24 minority (14 African Americans, 10 Hispanic Americans), 3 international. Average age 35. 34 applicants, 97% accepted, 23 enrolled. In 2009, 31 master's awarded. *Degree requirements:* For master's, comprehensive exam. *Entrance requirements:* For master's, GRE General Test or MAT. Additional exam requirements/recommendations for international students: Required—TOEFL (minimum score 79 computer-based). *Application deadline:* For fall admission, 8/17 priority date for domestic students, 5/30 for international students; for spring admission, 12/21 priority date for domestic students, 10/30 for international students. Application fee: $25 ($50 for international students). Electronic applications accepted. *Expenses:* Tuition, state resident: part-time $665 per semester hour. Tuition, nonresident: part-time $942 per semester hour. Part-time tuition and fees vary according to degree level and program. *Financial support:* Career-related internships or fieldwork, institutionally sponsored loans, scholarships/grants, and health care benefits available. Support available to part-time students. Financial award application deadline: 7/1. *Faculty research:* Human resource development. *Unit head:* Dr. Paul B. Roberts, Interim Chair, 903-566-7334, Fax: 903-565-5650, E-mail: proberts@uttyler.edu. *Application contact:* Dr. Greg Wang, Director of Graduate Studies, 903-565-5910, Fax: 903-565-5650, E-mail: gwang@uttyler.edu.

University of Wisconsin–Milwaukee, Graduate School, College of Letters and Sciences, Interdepartmental Program in Human Resources and Labor Relations, Milwaukee, WI 53201-0413. Offers human resources and labor relations (MHRLR); international human resources and labor relations (Certificate); mediation and negotiation (Certificate). Part-time programs available. *Students:* 14 full-time (10 women), 44 part-time (34 women); includes 12 minority (5 African Americans, 2 Asian Americans or Pacific Islanders, 5 Hispanic Americans), 2 international. Average age 31. 37 applicants, 51% accepted, 5 enrolled. In 2009, 22 master's awarded. *Entrance requirements:* For master's, GMAT or GRE General Test. Additional exam requirements/recommendations for international students: Required—TOEFL (minimum score 550 paper-based; 79 iBT), IELTS (minimum score 6.5). *Application deadline:* For fall admission, 1/1 priority date for domestic students; for spring admission, 9/1 for domestic students. Applications are processed on a rolling basis. Application fee: $45 ($75 for international students). *Expenses:* Tuition, state resident: full-time $8800. Tuition, nonresident: full-time $20,760. Tuition and fees vary according to program and reciprocity agreements. *Financial support:* Career-related internships or fieldwork available. Support available to part-time students. Financial award application deadline: 4/15. *Unit head:* Susan M. Donohue-Davies, Representative, 414-299-4009, Fax: 414-229-5915, E-mail: suedono@uwm.edu. *Application contact:* General Information Contact, 414-229-4982, Fax: 414-229-6967, E-mail: gradschool@uwm.edu.

University of Wisconsin–Stout, Graduate School, College of Technology, Engineering, and Management, Program in Training and Development, Menomonie, WI 54751. Offers MS. Part-time programs available. *Degree requirements:* For master's, thesis. *Entrance requirements:* For master's, minimum GPA of 2.75. Additional exam requirements/recommendations for international students: Required—TOEFL (minimum score 500 paper-based; 173 computer-based; 61 iBT). Electronic applications accepted. *Faculty research:* Organizational behavior, performance, learning and performance, strategic planning.

Vanderbilt University, Peabody College, Department of Leadership, Policy, and Organizations, Nashville, TN 37240-1001. Offers education policy (MPP); educational leadership and policy (Ed D); higher education (M Ed); higher education, leadership and policy (Ed D); human resource development (M Ed); international education policy and management (M Ed); organizational leadership (M Ed). Part-time and evening/weekend programs available. *Faculty:* 28 full-time (13 women), 8 part-time/adjunct (3 women). *Students:* 155 full-time (111 women), 95 part-time (52 women); includes 36 minority (27 African Americans, 6 Asian Americans or Pacific Islanders, 3 Hispanic Americans), 21 international. Average age 31. 298 applicants, 76% accepted, 94 enrolled. In 2009, 65 master's, 21 doctorates awarded. *Degree requirements:* For master's, comprehensive exam, thesis optional; for doctorate, thesis/dissertation, qualifying exams, residency. *Entrance requirements:* For master's and doctorate, GRE General Test. Additional exam requirements/recommendations for international students: Required—TOEFL (minimum score 550 paper-based; 213 computer-based). *Application deadline:* For fall admission, 12/31 priority date for domestic and international students; for spring admission, 11/1 priority date for domestic and international students. Applications are processed on a rolling basis. Application fee: $0. Electronic applications accepted. *Financial support:* In 2009–10, 155 students received support, including 3 fellowships with full and partial tuition reimbursements available, 61 research assistantships with full and partial tuition reimbursements available, 1 teaching assistantship with full and partial tuition reimbursement available; Federal Work-Study, institutionally sponsored loans, scholarships/grants, tuition waivers (partial), and unspecified assistantships also available. Support available to part-time students. Financial award application deadline: 2/1; financial award applicants required to submit FAFSA. *Faculty research:* Education and leadership policy, education finances/economics of education, higher education leadership and policy, educator pay for performance and school choice, international and comparative education and policy management. *Unit head:* Dr. Ellen B. Goldring, Chair, 615-322-8000, Fax: 615-343-7094, E-mail: ellen.b.goldring@vanderbilt.edu. *Application contact:* Rosie Moody, Educational Coordinator, 615-322-8019, Fax: 615-343-7094, E-mail: rosie.moody@vanderbilt.edu.

Villanova University, Graduate School of Liberal Arts and Sciences, Department of Human Resource Development, Villanova, PA 19085-1699. Offers MS. Part-time and evening/weekend programs available. *Faculty:* 3 full-time (1 woman), 9 part-time/adjunct (4 women). *Students:* 19 full-time (15 women), 61 part-time (52 women); includes 14 minority (7 African Americans, 5 Asian Americans or Pacific Islanders, 2 Hispanic Americans), 3 international. Average age 30. 22 applicants, 100% accepted, 12 enrolled. In 2009, 26 master's awarded. *Degree requirements:* For master's, comprehensive exam. *Entrance requirements:* For master's, GRE General Test, minimum GPA of 3.0. Additional exam requirements/recommendations for international students: Required—TOEFL. *Application deadline:* For fall admission, 2/1 priority date for domestic and international students; for spring admission, 11/15 priority date for domestic and international students. Applications are processed on a rolling basis. Application fee: $50. Electronic applications accepted. *Expenses:* Tuition: Part-time $630 per credit. Required fees: $60 per credit. Part-time tuition and fees vary according to degree level and program. *Financial support:* Research assistantships, career-related internships or fieldwork and Federal Work-Study available. Financial award applicants required to submit FAFSA. *Unit head:* Dr. David F. Bush, Director, 610-519-4746, E-mail: david.bush@villanova.edu. *Application contact:* Dr. Adele Lindenmeyr, Dean, Graduate School of Liberal Arts and Sciences, 610-519-7093, Fax: 610-519-7096.

See Close-Up on page 1357.

Virginia Commonwealth University, Graduate School, School of Education, Program in Adult and Organizational Learning, Richmond, VA 23284-9005. Offers adult literacy (M Ed); adults with disabilities (M Ed); human resource development (M Ed). *Accreditation:* NCATE. Part-time programs available. *Entrance requirements:* For master's, GRE General Test or MAT. *Faculty research:* Adult development and learning, program planning and evaluation.

Virginia Polytechnic Institute and State University, Graduate School, College of Liberal Arts and Human Sciences, Department of Human Development, Blacksburg, VA 24061. Offers adult development and aging (MS, PhD); adult learning and human resource development (MS, PhD); child development (MS, PhD); family studies (MS, PhD); marriage and family therapy (MS, PhD). *Accreditation:* AAMFT/COAMFTE (one or more programs are accredited). *Faculty:* 22 full-time (18 women). *Students:* 49 full-time (38 women), 64 part-time (44 women); includes 30 minority (1 African American, 7 American Indian/Alaska Native, 16 Asian Americans or Pacific Islanders, 6 Hispanic Americans), 2 international. Average age 34. 64 applicants, 34% accepted, 16 enrolled. In 2009, 10 master's, 14 doctorates awarded. *Entrance requirements:* For master's and doctorate, GRE, GMAT. Additional exam requirements/recommendations for international students: Required—TOEFL (minimum score 550 paper-based; 213 computer-based). *Application deadline:* For fall admission, 5/15 for international students; for spring admission, 10/15 for international students. Applications are processed on a rolling basis. Application fee: $65. Electronic applications accepted. *Expenses:* Tuition, area resident: Full-time $10,228; part-time $459 per credit hour. Tuition, nonresident: full-time $17,892; part-time $865 per credit hour. Required fees: $1966; $451 per semester. *Financial support:* In 2009–10, 7 research assistantships with full tuition reimbursements (averaging $10,933 per year), 25 teaching assistantships with full tuition reimbursements (averaging $9,387 per year) were awarded; career-related internships or fieldwork, Federal Work-Study, scholarships/grants, and unspecified assistantships also available. Financial award application deadline: 1/15. *Faculty research:* Stress management, children's play, dual-career families, social cognition, relationships of elderly. Total annual research expenditures: $823,581. *Unit head:* Dr. Shannon E. Jarrott, Head, 540-231-4794, Fax: 540-231-7012, E-mail: sjarrott@vt.edu. *Application contact:* Mark Benson, Information Contact, 540-231-5720, Fax: 540-231-7012, E-mail: mbenson@vt.edu.

Webster University, George Herbert Walker School of Business and Technology, Department of Business, St. Louis, MO 63119-3194. Offers business (MA); business and organizational security management (MBA); computer resources and information management (MBA); environmental management (MBA); finance (MA, MBA); health services management (MBA); human resources development (MBA); human resources management (MBA); international business (MA, MBA); management and leadership (MBA); marketing (MBA); procurement and acquisitions management (MBA); telecommunications management (MBA). *Accreditation:* ACBSP. Part-time and evening/weekend programs available. Postbaccalaureate distance learning degree programs offered (no on-campus study). *Faculty:* 9 full-time, 430 part-time/adjunct. *Students:* 1,190 full-time (543 women), 4,226 part-time (2,159 women). Average age 34. In 2009, 2,021 master's awarded. *Degree requirements:* For master's, comprehensive exam (for some programs), thesis (for some programs). *Entrance requirements:* Additional exam requirements/recommendations for international students: Required—TOEFL. *Application deadline:* Applications are processed on a rolling basis. Application fee: $35 ($50 for international students). *Expenses:* Tuition: Part-time $565 per credit hour. Tuition and fees vary according to degree level, campus/location and program. *Financial support:* Federal Work-Study available. Support available to part-time students. Financial award application deadline: 4/1; financial award applicants required to submit FAFSA. *Unit head:* Dr. Debbie Psihountas, Chair, 314-246-7553 Ext. 7017, Fax: 314-968-7077, E-mail: buschair@webster.edu. *Application contact:* Matt Nolan, Associate Vice President for Enrollment Management/Dean of Admissions, Fax: 314-968-7116, E-mail: gadmit@webster.edu.

Webster University, George Herbert Walker School of Business and Technology, Department of Management, St. Louis, MO 63119-3194. Offers business and organizational security management (MA); computer resources and information management (MA); environmental management (MS); government contracting (Certificate); health care management (MA); health services management (MA); human resources development (MA); human resources management (MA); management (DM); management and leadership (MA); marketing (MA); nonprofit management (Certificate); procurement and acquisitions management (MA); public administration (MA); quality management (MA); space systems operations management (MS); telecommunications management (MA). *Accreditation:* ACBSP. Part-time and evening/weekend programs available. Postbaccalaureate distance learning degree programs offered (no on-campus study). *Faculty:* 16 full-time, 781 part-time/adjunct. *Students:* 1,369 full-time (610 women), 5,182 part-time (3,047 women); includes 3,460 minority (2,835 African Americans, 38 American Indian/Alaska Native, 169 Asian Americans or Pacific Islanders, 418 Hispanic Americans), 80 international. Average age 37. In 2009, 2,491 master's, 13 doctorates, 68 other advanced degrees awarded. *Degree requirements:* For master's, thesis (for some programs); for doctorate, thesis/dissertation, written exam. *Entrance requirements:* For doctorate, GMAT, 3 years of work experience, MBA. Additional exam requirements/recommendations for international students: Required—TOEFL. *Application deadline:* Applications are processed on a rolling basis. Application fee: $25 ($50 for international students). *Expenses:* Tuition: Part-time $565 per credit hour. Tuition and fees vary according to degree level, campus/location and program. *Financial support:* Federal Work-Study available. Support available to part-time students. Financial award application deadline: 4/1; financial award applicants required to submit FAFSA. *Unit head:* Jim Brasfield, Chair, 314-961-2660 Ext. 7063, Fax: 314-968-7077, E-mail: mgtchair@webster.edu. *Application contact:* Matt Nolan, Associate Vice President for Enrollment Management/Dean of Admissions, Fax: 314-968-7116, E-mail: gadmit@webster.edu.

Western Carolina University, Graduate School, College of Education and Allied Professions, Department of Human Services, Program in Human Resources, Cullowhee, NC 28723. Offers MS. Part-time and evening/weekend programs available. Postbaccalaureate distance learning degree programs offered. *Students:* 10 full-time (all women), 81 part-time (55 women). Average age 35. 49 applicants, 71% accepted, 27 enrolled. In 2009, 9 master's awarded. *Degree requirements:* For master's, comprehensive exam. *Entrance requirements:* For master's, GRE General Test, appropriate undergraduate degree with minimum GPA of 3.0, 3 letters of recommendation. Additional exam requirements/recommendations for international students: Required—TOEFL (minimum score 550 paper-based; 270 computer-based; 79 iBT). *Application deadline:* For fall admission, 4/1 for domestic students; for spring admission, 11/1 for domestic students. Applications are processed on a rolling basis. Application fee: $45. *Financial support:* Fellowships, research assistantships with full and partial tuition reimbursements, teaching assistantships with full and partial tuition reimbursements, career-related internships or fieldwork, institutionally sponsored loans, scholarships/grants, and unspecified assistantships available. Financial award application deadline: 3/31; financial award applicants required to submit FAFSA. *Faculty research:* Employee recruitment and retention, human resource development, leadership, phenomenological research methods, employment counseling. *Unit head:* Dr. John Sherlock, Director, 828-227-3380, E-mail: sherlock@email.wcu.edu. *Application contact:* Admissions Specialist for Human Resources, 828-227-7398, Fax: 828-227-7480, E-mail: gradsch@email.wcu.edu.

Western Michigan University, Graduate College, College of Education, Department of Counselor Education and Counseling Psychology, Kalamazoo, MI 49008. Offers counseling psychology (MA, PhD); counselor education (MA, PhD); human resources development (MA). *Accreditation:* ACA (one or more programs are accredited); APA (one or more programs are accredited); CORE; NCATE. *Faculty:* 19 full-time (5 women). *Students:* 328 full-time (258 women), 201 part-time (158 women); includes 57 minority (45 African Americans, 2 American Indian/Alaska Native, 4 Asian Americans or Pacific Islanders, 6 Hispanic Americans), 19 international. 294 applicants, 81% accepted, 101 enrolled. In 2009, 108 master's, 13 doctorates awarded. *Degree requirements:* For doctorate, thesis/dissertation, oral exams. *Entrance requirements:* For doctorate, GRE General Test. *Application deadline:* For fall admission, 1/15 for domestic students. Applications are processed on a rolling basis. Application fee: $25. *Financial support:* Fellowships, research assistantships, teaching assistantships, Federal Work-

Study available. Financial award application deadline: 2/15; financial award applicants required to submit FAFSA. *Unit head:* Patrick Munley, Chair, 269-387-5120. *Application contact:* Admissions and Orientation, 269-387-2000, Fax: 269-387-2355.

Western Seminary, Graduate Programs, Program in Ministry and Leadership, Portland, OR 97215-3367. Offers chaplaincy (MA); coaching (MA); Jewish ministry (MA); pastoral care to women (MA); youth ministry (MA). *Students:* 93 full-time (38 women), 586 part-time (198 women); includes 20 minority (5 African Americans, 1 American Indian/Alaska Native, 11 Asian Americans or Pacific Islanders, 3 Hispanic Americans). Average age 29. 132 applicants, 92% accepted, 86 enrolled. *Degree requirements:* For master's, practicum. *Entrance requirements:* Additional exam requirements/recommendations for international students: Required—TOEFL. *Application deadline:* For fall admission, 7/19 priority date for domestic students; for winter admission, 11/8 priority date for domestic students; for spring admission, 3/14 priority date for domestic students. Applications are processed on a rolling basis. Application fee: $50. *Expenses:* Tuition: Full-time $3280; part-time $410 per credit hour. *Financial support:* Applicants required to submit FAFSA. *Unit head:* Beverly Hislop, Director, 503-517-1881, E-mail: bhislop@westernseminary.edu. *Application contact:* Dr. Robert W. Wiggins, Registrar/Dean of Student Development, 503-517-1820, Fax: 503-517-1801, E-mail: rwiggins@westernseminary.edu.

William Woods University, Graduate and Adult Studies, Fulton, MO 65251-1098. Offers administration (Ed S); agriculture (MBA); athletic/activities administration (M Ed); curriculum and instruction (M Ed); curriculum leadership (Ed S); elementary administration (M Ed); health management (MBA); human resources (MBA); principalship (Ed S); secondary administration (M Ed); special education director (M Ed). Evening/weekend programs available. *Degree*

requirements: For master's, capstone course (MBA), action research (M Ed); for Ed S, field experience. *Entrance requirements:* For master's, 2 recommendations, resumé, BA/BS; teaching certification (M Ed); course work in economics and accounting (MBA); for Ed S, M Ed, 2 letters of recommendation, resume, teaching certification. Additional exam requirements/recommendations for international students: Required—TOEFL (minimum score 550 paper-based). Electronic applications accepted.

Xavier University, College of Social Sciences, Health and Education, School of Education, Department of Educational Leadership and Human Resource Development, Program in Human Resource Development, Cincinnati, OH 45207. Offers MS. Part-time and evening/weekend programs available. *Faculty:* 2 full-time (both women), 3 part-time/adjunct (1 woman). *Students:* 30 full-time (22 women), 31 part-time (25 women); includes 11 minority (10 African Americans, 1 Asian American or Pacific Islander). Average age 36. 39 applicants, 100% accepted, 27 enrolled. In 2009, 38 master's awarded. *Entrance requirements:* For master's, GRE or MAT, resume, 2 references. Additional exam requirements/recommendations for international students: Required—TOEFL (minimum score 550 paper-based; 213 computer-based; 79 iBT). *Application deadline:* Applications are processed on a rolling basis. Application fee: $35. Electronic applications accepted. *Expenses:* Contact institution. *Financial support:* In 2009–10, 18 students received support; teaching assistantships, unspecified assistantships available. Financial award applicants required to submit FAFSA. *Faculty research:* Graduate education, group dynamics, organizational behavior, reflection-in-action. *Unit head:* Dr. Brenda Levya-Gardner, Associate Professor/Director, 513-745-4287, Fax: 513-745-1048, E-mail: gardner@xavier.edu. *Application contact:* Dr. Brenda Levya-Gardner, Associate Professor/Director, 513-745-4287, Fax: 513-745-1048, E-mail: gardner@xavier.edu.

Human Resources Management

Adelphi University, School of Business, Certificate Programs in Human Resources Management, Garden City, NY 11530-0701. Offers Certificate. Part-time and evening/weekend programs available. *Students:* 4 part-time (3 women); includes 1 minority (African American). Average age 40. In 2009, 3 Certificates awarded. *Entrance requirements:* For degree, GMAT or master's degree. Additional exam requirements/recommendations for international students: Required—TOEFL (minimum score 550 paper-based; 213 computer-based; 80 iBT). *Application deadline:* For fall admission, 4/1 for international students; for spring admission, 11/1 for international students. Applications are processed on a rolling basis. Application fee: $50. Electronic applications accepted. *Expenses:* Tuition: Full-time $28,340; part-time $830 per credit. Required fees: $600; $250 per credit. Full-time tuition and fees vary according to course load and program. *Financial support:* Application deadline: 3/1. *Unit head:* Brian Rothschild, Assistant Dean, 516-877-4670, Fax: 516-877-4607, E-mail: gradbusinquiries@adelphi.edu. *Application contact:* Christine Murphy, Director of Admissions, 516-877-3050, Fax: 516-877-3039, E-mail: graduateadmissions@adelphi.edu.

Adelphi University, School of Business, MBA Program, Garden City, NY 11530-0701. Offers finance (MBA); management information systems (MBA); management/human resource management (MBA); marketing/e-commerce (MBA). *Accreditation:* AACSB. Part-time and evening/weekend programs available. *Students:* 77 full-time (30 women), 183 part-time (91 women); includes 56 minority (29 African Americans, 17 Asian Americans or Pacific Islanders, 10 Hispanic Americans), 81 international. Average age 30. In 2009, 64 master's awarded. *Degree requirements:* For master's, capstone course. *Entrance requirements:* For master's, GMAT, 2 letters of recommendation. Additional exam requirements/recommendations for international students: Required—TOEFL (minimum score 550 paper-based; 213 computer-based; 80 iBT). *Application deadline:* For fall admission, 4/1 for international students; for spring admission, 11/1 for international students. Applications are processed on a rolling basis. Application fee: $50. Electronic applications accepted. *Expenses:* Tuition: Full-time $28,340; part-time $830 per credit. Required fees: $600; $250 per credit. Full-time tuition and fees vary according to course load and program. *Financial support:* Research assistantships with full and partial tuition reimbursements, career-related internships or fieldwork, Federal Work-Study, institutionally sponsored loans, scholarships/grants, and unspecified assistantships available. Financial award application deadline: 3/1; financial award applicants required to submit FAFSA. *Faculty research:* Supply chain management, distribution channels, productivity benchmark analysis, data envelopment analysis, financial portfolio analysis. *Unit head:* Rakesh Gupta, 516-877-4670, Fax: 516-877-4607, E-mail: gradbusinquiries@adelphi.edu. *Application contact:* Christine Murphy, Director of Admissions, 516-877-3050, Fax: 516-877-3039, E-mail: graduateadmissions@adelphi.edu.

Alabama Agricultural and Mechanical University, School of Graduate Studies, School of Education, Department of Counseling and Special Education, Huntsville, AL 35811. Offers communicative disorders (M Ed, MS); psychology and counseling (MS, Ed S), including clinical psychology (MS), counseling and guidance, counseling psychology (MS), personnel management (MS), psychometry (MS), school psychology (MS); special education (M Ed, MS). *Accreditation:* CORE; NCATE. Part-time and evening/weekend programs available. *Degree requirements:* For master's, comprehensive exam. *Entrance requirements:* For master's, GRE General Test. Additional exam requirements/recommendations for international students: Required—TOEFL (minimum score 500 paper-based; 173 computer-based; 61 iBT). *Faculty research:* Increasing numbers of minorities in special education and speech-language pathology.

Albany State University, College of Arts and Humanities, Department of History, Political Science and Public Administration, Albany, GA 31705-2717. Offers community and economic development administration (MPA); criminal justice administration (MPA); fiscal management (MPA); general management (MPA); health administration and policy (MPA); human resources management (MPA); public policy (MPA); water resource management and policy (MPA). *Accreditation:* NASPAA. *Students:* 17 full-time (11 women), 43 part-time (29 women); includes 57 minority (56 African Americans, 1 Asian American or Pacific Islander). Average age 34. 21 applicants, 100% accepted, 17 enrolled. In 2009, 17 master's awarded. *Entrance requirements:* For master's, GRE or MAT. *Application deadline:* For fall admission, 11/16 for domestic students, 9/16 for international students; for spring admission, 4/19 for domestic students, 2/19 for international students. Applications are processed on a rolling basis. Application fee: $20. Electronic applications accepted. *Expenses:* Tuition, state resident: full-time $2970; part-time $162 per credit hour. Tuition, nonresident: full-time $12,168; part-time $676 per credit hour. Required fees: $962; $75 per credit hour. *Financial support:* Application deadline: 6/30. *Faculty research:* Public policy, strategic public human resources and human capital management, diversity management in the public sector and collective bargaining and labor relations in the public sector, e-government and public sector information systems, public administration pedagogy and business process modeling simulation, funded research- community development, non profit organizations, civic engagement and civic participation, health care disparities among minorities and poverty. Total annual research expenditures: $26,000. *Unit head:* Dr. Peter Ngwafu, Director, 229-430-4873, Fax: 229-430-7895, E-mail: peter.ngwafu@asurams.edu. *Application contact:* Nicole Lane, Interim Graduate Admissions Officer, 229-430-4862, Fax: 229-430-6398, E-mail: nicole.lane@asurams.edu.

Amberton University, Graduate School, Program in Human Relations and Business, Garland, TX 75041-5595. Offers MA, MS. Part-time and evening/weekend programs available. *Entrance requirements:* For master's, minimum GPA of 3.0.

American InterContinental University Online, Program in Business Administration, Hoffman Estates, IL 60192. Offers accounting and finance (MBA); finance (MBA); healthcare management

(MBA); human resource management (MBA); international business (MBA); management (MBA); marketing (MBA); operations management (MBA); organizational psychology and development (MBA); project management (MBA). Evening/weekend programs available. Post-baccalaureate distance learning degree programs offered (no on-campus study). *Entrance requirements:* Additional exam requirements/recommendations for international students: Required—TOEFL (minimum score 550 paper-based; 213 computer-based). Electronic applications accepted.

American InterContinental University South Florida, Program in International Business, Weston, FL 33326. Offers accounting and finance (MBA); human resource management (MBA); management (MBA); marketing (MBA). Part-time and evening/weekend programs available. Postbaccalaureate distance learning degree programs offered. Electronic applications accepted.

Andrew Jackson University, Brian Tracy College of Business and Entrepreneurship, Birmingham, AL 35244. Offers entrepreneurship (MBA); finance (MBA); health services management (MBA); hospitality and tourism management (MBA); human resource management (MBA); international business (MBA); management (MBA); marketing (MBA). Part-time and evening/weekend programs available. Postbaccalaureate distance learning degree programs offered (no on-campus study). *Entrance requirements:* For master's, course work in calculus, statistics, macroeconomics. Additional exam requirements/recommendations for international students: Required—TOEFL (minimum score 550 paper-based; 213 computer-based). Electronic applications accepted.

Assumption College, Graduate School, Department of Business Studies, Worcester, MA 01609-1296. Offers accounting (MBA); business administration (CAGS); finance/economics (MBA); general business (MBA); human resources (MBA); international business (MBA); management (MBA); marketing (MBA); nonprofit leadership (MBA). Part-time and evening/weekend programs available. *Faculty:* 6 full-time (1 woman), 14 part-time/adjunct (2 women). *Students:* 19 full-time (11 women), 127 part-time (68 women); includes 22 minority (13 African Americans, 3 Asian Americans or Pacific Islanders, 6 Hispanic Americans). Average age 27. 88 applicants, 99% accepted. In 2009, 40 master's, 2 other advanced degrees awarded. *Entrance requirements:* For master's, 3 letters of recommendation, resume; for CAGS, 3 letters of recommendation, resume, essay. Additional exam requirements/recommendations for international students: Required—TOEFL (minimum score 540 paper-based; 200 computer-based; 76 iBT), IELTS (minimum score 6). *Application deadline:* For fall admission, 6/1 priority date for domestic students, 5/1 priority date for international students; for spring admission, 11/1 priority date for domestic students, 9/1 priority date for international students. Applications are processed on a rolling basis. Application fee: $30. Electronic applications accepted. *Expenses:* Tuition: Part-time $503 per credit. Required fees: $20 per semester. One-time fee: $100 part-time. Part-time tuition and fees vary according to campus/location. *Financial support:* In 2009–10, 47 students received support. Application deadline: 6/1. *Faculty research:* Workplace diversity, dynamics of team interaction, utilization of leased employees. *Unit head:* Michael Lewis, Director, 508-767-7372, Fax: 508-767-7252, E-mail: jhunter@assumption.edu. *Application contact:* Adrian O. Dumas, Director of Graduate Enrollment Management and Services, 508-767-7365, Fax: 508-767-7030, E-mail: adumas@assumption.edu.

Auburn University, Graduate School, College of Business, Department of Management, Auburn University, AL 36849. Offers human resource management (PhD); management (MS, PhD); management information systems (MS, PhD). *Accreditation:* AACSB. Part-time programs available. *Faculty:* 34 full-time (7 women), 5 part-time/adjunct (0 women). *Students:* 12 full-time (4 women), 12 part-time (2 women); includes 3 minority (1 African American, 2 Asian Americans or Pacific Islanders), 5 international. Average age 34. 137 applicants, 28% accepted, 20 enrolled. In 2009, 9 master's, 6 doctorates awarded. *Degree requirements:* For master's, thesis (for some programs); for doctorate, thesis/dissertation. *Entrance requirements:* For master's, GMAT, GRE General Test (MS); for doctorate, GMAT, GRE General Test. Additional exam requirements/recommendations for international students: Required—TOEFL. *Application deadline:* For fall admission, 7/7 for domestic students; for spring admission, 11/24 for domestic students. Applications are processed on a rolling basis. Application fee: $50 ($60 for international students). Electronic applications accepted. *Expenses:* Tuition, state resident: full-time $6240. Tuition, nonresident: full-time $18,720. International tuition: $18,938 full-time. Required fees: $492. Tuition and fees vary according to course load, program and reciprocity agreements. *Financial support:* Teaching assistantships, Federal Work-Study available. Support available to part-time students. Financial award application deadline: 3/15; financial award applicants required to submit FAFSA. *Unit head:* Dr. Sharon Oswald, Head, 334-844-4071. *Application contact:* Dr. George Flowers, Dean of the Graduate School, 334-844-2125.

Baker College Center for Graduate Studies—Online, Graduate Programs—Online, Flint, MI 48507-9843. Offers accounting (MBA); business administration (DBA); finance (MBA); general business (MBA); health care management (MBA); human resources management (MBA); information management (MBA); leadership studies (MBA); management information systems (MSIS); marketing (MBA). Part-time and evening/weekend programs available. Post-baccalaureate distance learning degree programs offered. *Faculty:* 750. *Students:* 500 full-time, 500 part-time. Average age 37. *Degree requirements:* For master's, portfolio. *Entrance requirements:* For master's, 3 years of work experience, minimum undergraduate GPA of 2.5, writing sample, 3 letters of recommendation; for doctorate, MBA or acceptable related master's degree from accredited association, 5 years work experience, minimum graduate GPA of 3.25, writing sample, 3 professional references. Additional exam requirements/recommendations for international students: Required—TOEFL (minimum score 550 paper-based; 213 computer-

Human Resources Management

Baker College Center for Graduate Studies—Online (continued)
based). *Application deadline:* For fall admission, 8/6 priority date for domestic students; for winter admission, 12/15 priority date for domestic students; for spring admission, 2/15 priority date for domestic students. Applications are processed on a rolling basis. Application fee: $25. Electronic applications accepted. *Expenses:* Tuition: Part-time $330 per credit hour. Tuition and fees vary according to degree level. *Financial support:* Scholarships/grants available. Support available to part-time students. Financial award applicants required to submit FAFSA. *Unit head:* Dr. Julia Teahen, President, 810-766-4023, Fax: 810-766-4399, E-mail: julia@baker.edu. *Application contact:* Chuck J. Gurden, Vice President for Graduate and Online Admissions, 800-469-3165, Fax: 810-766-4399, E-mail: adm-ol@baker.edu.

Baldwin-Wallace College, Graduate Programs, Division of Business, Program in Human Resources, Berea, OH 44017-2088. Offers MBA. Part-time and evening/weekend programs available. *Students:* 19 full-time (all women), 20 part-time (17 women); includes 6 minority (4 African Americans, 2 Hispanic Americans), 2 international. Average age 34. 8 applicants, 88% accepted, 5 enrolled. In 2009, 13 master's awarded. *Entrance requirements:* For master's, GMAT, bachelor's degree in field, work experience, minimum GPA of 3.4. Additional exam requirements/recommendations for international students: Required—TOEFL (minimum score 523 paper-based; 193 computer-based; 70 iBT). *Application deadline:* For fall admission, 7/25 priority date for domestic students, 4/30 priority date for international students; for spring admission, 12/15 priority date for domestic students, 9/30 priority date for international students. Applications are processed on a rolling basis. Application fee: $25. Electronic applications accepted. *Expenses:* Tuition: Full-time $14,174; part-time $682 per credit. Tuition and fees vary according to program. *Financial support:* Career-related internships or fieldwork available. Support available to part-time students. Financial award application deadline: 5/1. *Unit head:* Dr. Mary Pisnar, Director, 440-826-2392, Fax: 440-826-3868, E-mail: mpisnar@bw.edu. *Application contact:* Peggy Shepard, Graduate Business Coordinator, 440-826-2196, Fax: 440-826-3868, E-mail: pshepard@bw.edu.

Barry University, School of Education, Graduate Certificate Programs, Miami Shores, FL 33161-6695. Offers advanced teaching and learning with technology (Certificate); distance education (Certificate); higher education technology integration (Certificate); human resources: not for profit and religious organizations (Certificate); K-12 technology integration (Certificate).

Benedictine University, Graduate Programs, Program in Business Administration, Lisle, IL 60532-0900. Offers accounting (MBA); entrepreneurship and managing innovation (MBA); financial management (MBA); health administration (MBA); human resource management (MBA); information systems security (MBA); international business (MBA); management consulting (MBA); management information systems (MBA); marketing management (MBA); operations management and logistics (MBA); organizational leadership (MBA); MBA/MPH; MBA/MS. Part-time and evening/weekend programs available. Postbaccalaureate distance learning degree programs offered (minimal on-campus study). *Faculty:* 4 full-time (2 women), 24 part-time/adjunct (3 women). *Students:* 247 full-time (141 women), 644 part-time (339 women); includes 223 minority (134 African Americans, 5 American Indian/Alaska Native, 44 Asian Americans or Pacific Islanders, 40 Hispanic Americans), 25 international. Average age 34. 287 applicants, 92% accepted, 229 enrolled. In 2009, 219 master's awarded. *Entrance requirements:* For master's, GMAT. Additional exam requirements/recommendations for international students: Required—TOEFL (minimum score 550 paper-based; 213 computer-based). *Application deadline:* For fall admission, 9/1 for domestic students; for winter admission, 12/1 for domestic students; for spring admission, 2/15 for domestic students. Applications are processed on a rolling basis. Application fee: $40. Electronic applications accepted. *Expenses:* Tuition: Part-time $750 per credit hour. Tuition and fees vary according to campus/location and program. *Financial support:* Career-related internships or fieldwork and health care benefits available. Support available to part-time students. *Faculty research:* Strategic leadership in professional organizations, sociology of professions, organizational change, social identity theory, applications to change management. *Unit head:* Dr. Sharon Borowicz, Director, 630-829-6219, E-mail: sborowicz@ben.edu. *Application contact:* Kari Gibbons, Director, Admissions, 630-829-6200, Fax: 630-829-6584, E-mail: kgibbons@ben.edu.

Bernard M. Baruch College of the City University of New York, Zicklin School of Business, Department of Management, New York, NY 10010-5585. Offers entrepreneurship (MBA); general management and policy (MBA); human resources management (MBA); management planning systems (PhD); management science (MBA); organization and policy studies (PhD); organizational behavior (MBA). Part-time and evening/weekend programs available. *Degree requirements:* For doctorate, comprehensive exam, thesis/dissertation. *Entrance requirements:* For master's, GMAT, 2 letters of recommendation, resume, 2 years of work experience; for doctorate, GMAT. Additional exam requirements/recommendations for international students: Required—TOEFL (minimum score 590 paper-based; 243 computer-based), TWE.

Boston University, Metropolitan College, Department of Administrative Sciences, Boston, MA 02215. Offers banking and financial management (MSM); business continuity in emergency management (MSM); economics development and tourism management (MSAS); electronic commerce, systems, and technology (MSAS); financial economics (MSAS); human resource management (MSM); innovation and technology (MSAS); insurance management (MSM); international market management (MSM); multinational commerce (MSAS); project management (MSM). *Accreditation:* AACSB. Part-time and evening/weekend programs available. Postbaccalaureate distance learning degree programs offered (no on-campus study). *Students:* 123 full-time (48 women), 204 part-time (92 women); includes 31 minority (10 African Americans, 1 American Indian/Alaska Native, 11 Asian Americans or Pacific Islanders, 9 Hispanic Americans), 146 international. Average age 30. In 2009, 154 master's awarded. *Degree requirements:* For master's, thesis optional. *Entrance requirements:* For master's, 1 year of work experience, minimum GPA of 3.0. Additional exam requirements/recommendations for international students: Required—TOEFL (minimum score 560 paper-based; 220 computer-based; 84 iBT). *Application deadline:* Applications are processed on a rolling basis. Application fee: $70. Electronic applications accepted. *Expenses:* Tuition: Full-time $37,910; part-time $1184 per credit hour. Required fees: $386; $40 per semester. Part-time tuition and fees vary according to class time, course level, degree level and program. *Financial support:* In 2009–10, 15 students received support, including 8 research assistantships (averaging $10,000 per year); career-related internships or fieldwork and Federal Work-Study also available. *Faculty research:* International business, innovative process. *Unit head:* Dr. Kip Becker, Chairman, 617-353-3016, E-mail: adminsc@bu.edu. *Application contact:* Lucille Dicker, Administrative Sciences Department, 617-353-3016, E-mail: adminsc@bu.edu.

Boston University, School of Education, Department of Administration, Training, and Policy Studies, Program in Human Resource Education, Boston, MA 02215. Offers Ed M, CAGS. Part-time programs available. *Degree requirements:* For master's, thesis optional; for CAGS, comprehensive exam. *Entrance requirements:* For master's and CAGS, GRE General Test or MAT. Additional exam requirements/recommendations for international students: Required—TOEFL. Electronic applications accepted. *Expenses:* Tuition: Full-time $37,910; part-time $1184 per credit hour. Required fees: $386; $40 per semester. Part-time tuition and fees vary according to class time, course level, degree level and program.

Briar Cliff University, Program in Human Resource Management, Sioux City, IA 51104-0100. Offers MA. Part-time and evening/weekend programs available. *Faculty:* 3 full-time (2 women), 5 part-time/adjunct (4 women). *Students:* 9 full-time (5 women), 27 part-time (19 women); includes 4 minority (1 African American, 1 Asian American or Pacific Islander, 2 Hispanic Americans). Average age 36. In 2009, 13 master's awarded. *Degree requirements:* For master's, thesis optional. *Entrance requirements:* For master's, minimum undergraduate GPA of 2.77. *Application deadline:* For fall admission, 8/1 for domestic students. Application fee: $25. *Expenses:* Tuition: Full-time $8856; part-time $492 per credit hour. Required fees: $23 per credit hour. *Financial support:* Application deadline: 8/1. *Faculty research:* Diversity in the workplace. *Unit head:* Barb Redmond, Director, 712-279-5561, Fax: 712-279-1698, E-mail: barb.redmond@briarcliff.edu. *Application contact:* Cheryl Olson, Continuing Studies Admissions Representative, 712-279-1777, Fax: 712-279-1632, E-mail: cheryl.olson@briarcliff.edu.

Brigham Young University, Graduate Studies, Marriott School of Management, Master of Public Administration Program, Provo, UT 84602. Offers finance (MPA); human resources (MPA); local government (MPA); nonprofit management (MPA); JD/MPA. *Faculty:* 10 full-time (4 women), 18 part-time/adjunct (1 woman). *Students:* 128 full-time (54 women); includes 26 minority (3 African Americans, 13 Asian Americans or Pacific Islanders, 10 Hispanic Americans). Average age 27. 136 applicants, 66% accepted, 62 enrolled. In 2009, 53 master's awarded. *Entrance requirements:* For master's, GRE, GMAT, minimum GPA of 3.0. Additional exam requirements/recommendations for international students: Required—TOEFL (minimum score 580 paper-based; 85 iBT), IELTS (minimum score 7). *Application deadline:* For fall admission, 2/1 for domestic and international students. Application fee: $50. Electronic applications accepted. *Expenses:* Tuition: Full-time $5580; part-time $301 per credit hour. Tuition and fees vary according to student's religious affiliation. *Financial support:* In 2009–10, 96 students received support. Career-related internships or fieldwork and scholarships/grants available. Financial award application deadline: 4/15; financial award applicants required to submit FAFSA. *Faculty research:* Taxes, budgeting, nonprofit, ethics, decision modeling, work balance, organizational behavior. *Unit head:* Dr. David W. Hart, Director, 801-422-4221, Fax: 801-422-0311, E-mail: mpa@byu.edu. *Application contact:* Catherine Cooper, Director of Student Services, E-mail: mpa@byu.edu.

Buffalo State College, State University of New York, The Graduate School, Faculty of Applied Science and Education, Department of Educational Foundations, Program in Adult Education, Buffalo, NY 14222-1095. Offers adult education (MS, Certificate); human resources development (Certificate). Part-time and evening/weekend programs available. Postbaccalaureate distance learning degree programs offered (no on-campus study). *Degree requirements:* For master's, comprehensive exam. *Entrance requirements:* Additional exam requirements/recommendations for international students: Required—TOEFL (minimum score 550 paper-based; 213 computer-based).

California Coast University, Programs in Business Administration, Santa Ana, CA 92701. Offers human resources management (MBA); management (MBA); marketing (MBA). Part-time and evening/weekend programs available. Postbaccalaureate distance learning degree programs offered (no on-campus study). Application fee: $75. Electronic applications accepted. *Application contact:* Christi Okuma, 714-547-9625, Fax: 714-547-5777, E-mail: ccu@calcoast.edu.

California Intercontinental University, School of Business, Diamond Bar, CA 91765. Offers banking and finance (MBA); entrepreneurship and business management (DBA); global business leadership (DBA); international management and marketing (MBA); organizational management and human resource management (MBA).

California State University, East Bay, Graduate Programs, College of Business and Economics, Department of Information Technology Management, Option in Human Resources and Organizational Behavior, Hayward, CA 94542-3000. Offers MBA. Part-time and evening/weekend programs available. *Degree requirements:* For master's, comprehensive exam or thesis. *Entrance requirements:* For master's, GMAT, minimum GPA of 2.75. Additional exam requirements/recommendations for international students: Required—TOEFL (minimum score 550 paper-based; 213 computer-based). *Application deadline:* For fall admission, 6/30 for domestic and international students. Application fee: $55. Electronic applications accepted. *Financial support:* Fellowships, career-related internships or fieldwork, Federal Work-Study, institutionally sponsored loans, and scholarships/grants available. Support available to part-time students. Financial award application deadline: 3/1; financial award applicants required to submit FAFSA. *Unit head:* Prof. Xinjian Lu, Chair, 510-885-3307, Fax: 510-885-2660, E-mail: xinjian.lu@csueastbay.edu. *Application contact:* Donna Wiley, Interim Associate Director, 510-885-2928, Fax: 510-885-4777, E-mail: donna.wiley@csueastbay.edu.

California State University, Sacramento, Graduate Studies, College of Business Administration, Sacramento, CA 95819. Offers accountancy (MS); business administration (MBA); human resources (MBA); management information science (MS); urban land development (MBA). *Accreditation:* AACSB. Part-time and evening/weekend programs available. *Degree requirements:* For master's, thesis or alternative, writing proficiency exam. *Entrance requirements:* For master's, GMAT. Additional exam requirements/recommendations for international students: Required—TOEFL. Electronic applications accepted.

Capella University, School of Business and Technology, Minneapolis, MN 55402. Offers accounting (MBA), including system design and programming; business (Certificate), including human resource management (MS, PhD, Certificate), information technology management (MS, PhD, Certificate), leadership (MBA, MS, PhD, Certificate); finance (MBA); general business (MBA); health care management (MBA); information technology (MS, Certificate), including general information technology (MS), information security, network architecture and design (MS), professional projects management (Certificate), project management and leadership (MS), system design and development (MS),); information technology management (MBA); marketing (MBA); organization and management (MBA, MS, PhD), including general business (PhD), general organization and management (MBA, MS), human resource management (MS, PhD, Certificate), information technology management (MS, PhD, Certificate), leadership (MBA, MS, PhD, Certificate); project management (MBA). Part-time and evening/weekend programs available. Postbaccalaureate distance learning degree programs offered (minimal on-campus study). Terminal master's awarded for partial completion of doctoral program. *Degree requirements:* For master's, thesis optional, integrative project; for doctorate, comprehensive exam, thesis/dissertation. *Entrance requirements:* Additional exam requirements/recommendations for international students: Required—TOEFL (minimum score 550 paper-based; 213 computer-based), TWE (minimum score 4). Electronic applications accepted. *Faculty research:* Business policies: strategic, corporate, and financial management; interplay of technological, organizational and social change.

Caribbean University, Graduate School, Bayamón, PR 00960-0493. Offers administration and supervision (MA Ed); criminal justice (MA); curriculum and instruction (MA Ed), including elementary education, English education, history education, mathematics education, primary education, science education, Spanish education; education (PhD); gerontology (MSN); human resources (MBA); museology, archiving and art history (MA Ed); neonatal pediatrics (MSN); physical education (MA Ed); special education (MA Ed). *Entrance requirements:* For master's, interview, minimum GPA of 2.5.

Case Western Reserve University, Weatherhead School of Management, Department of Marketing and Policy Studies, Division of Labor and Human Resource Policy, Cleveland, OH 44106. Offers MBA. Part-time and evening/weekend programs available. *Entrance requirements:* For master's, GMAT. *Application deadline:* Applications are processed on a rolling basis. Application fee: $100. *Financial support:* Career-related internships or fieldwork, Federal Work-Study, institutionally sponsored loans, and tuition waivers (full and partial) available. Financial award application deadline: 5/1. *Faculty research:* Strategic human resource management, negotiations and conflict management, human resources in high performance organizations, international human resources management, union management relations and collective bargaining. *Unit head:* Dr. Paul F. Gerhart, Head, 216-368-2045, E-mail: pfg2@po.cwru.edu. *Application contact:* Dr. Paul F. Gerhart, Head, 216-368-2045, E-mail: pfg2@po.cwru.edu.

The Catholic University of America, Metropolitan School of Professional Studies, Washington, DC 20064. Offers human resource management (MA); management (MSM). Part-time and evening/weekend programs available. *Faculty:* 75 part-time/adjunct (41 women). *Students:* 21 full-time, 152 part-time, 26 international. Average age 34. 198 applicants, 69% accepted, 106 enrolled. In 2009, 8 degrees awarded. *Degree requirements:* For master's, minimum GPA of 3.0, capstone course. *Entrance requirements:* For master's, statement of purpose, official copies of academic transcripts, three letters of recommendation, resume. Additional exam requirements/recommendations for international students: Required—TOEFL (minimum score 237 computer-based; 93 iBT). *Application deadline:* For fall admission, 8/1 priority date for domestic students, 7/15 for international students; for spring admission, 12/1 priority date for domestic students, 10/15 for international students. *Expenses:* Tuition: Full-time $31,740;

part-time $1245 per credit hour. Required fees: $50; $25 per semester hour. One-time fee: $425. *Unit head:* Dr. Sara Thompson, Dean, 202-319-5256, Fax: 202-319-6032, E-mail: thompson@cua.edu. *Application contact:* Julie Schwing, Director of Graduate Admissions, 202-319-5057, Fax: 202-319-6533, E-mail: cua-admissions@cua.edu.

See Display below and Close-Up on page 427.

Central Michigan University, Central Michigan University Off-Campus Programs, Program in Administration, Mount Pleasant, MI 48859. Offers acquisitions administration (MSA, Certificate); general administration (MSA, Certificate); health services administration (MSA, Certificate); human resources administration (MSA, Certificate); information resource management (MSA, Certificate); international administration (MSA, Certificate); leadership (MSA, Certificate); public administration (MSA, Certificate); vehicle design and manufacturing administration (MSA, Certificate). Part-time and evening/weekend programs available. Postbaccalaureate distance learning degree programs offered (no on-campus study). *Students:* Average age 38. *Entrance requirements:* For master's, minimum GPA of 2.7 in major. *Application deadline:* Applications are processed on a rolling basis. Application fee: $50. Electronic applications accepted. *Financial support:* Scholarships/grants available. Support available to part-time students. Financial award applicants required to submit FAFSA. *Unit head:* Dr. Nana Korsah, Director, MSA Programs, 989-774-6525, E-mail: korsa1na@cmich.edu. *Application contact:* 877-268-4636, E-mail: cmuoffcampus@cmich.edu.

Central Michigan University, College of Graduate Studies, College of Business Administration, Department of Management, Mount Pleasant, MI 48859. Offers human resource management (MBA); international business (MBA). *Degree requirements:* For master's, thesis or alternative. *Entrance requirements:* For master's, GMAT. Electronic applications accepted. *Faculty research:* Human resource accounting, valuation, and liability; international business and economic issues; entrepreneurial leadership; technology management and strategy; electronic commerce and neural networks.

Central Michigan University, College of Graduate Studies, Interdisciplinary Administration Programs, Mount Pleasant, MI 48859. Offers acquisitions administration (MSA, Graduate Certificate); general administration (MSA, Graduate Certificate); health services administration (MSA, Graduate Certificate); human resource administration (Graduate Certificate); human resources administration (MSA); information resource management (MSA, Graduate Certificate); international administration (MSA, Graduate Certificate); leadership (MSA); organizational communication (MSA, Graduate Certificate); public administration (MSA, Graduate Certificate); recreation and park administration (MSA); sport administration (MSA). *Accreditation:* AACSB. Part-time and evening/weekend programs available. Postbaccalaureate distance learning degree programs offered (no on-campus study). *Degree requirements:* For master's, thesis or alternative. *Entrance requirements:* For master's, bachelor's degree with minimum GPA of 2.7. Electronic applications accepted. *Faculty research:* Interdisciplinary studies in acquisitions administration, health services administration, sport administration, recreation and park administration, and international administration.

Claremont Graduate University, Graduate Programs, School of Behavioral and Organizational Sciences, Program in Human Resources Design, Claremont, CA 91711-6160. Offers MS. Part-time and evening/weekend programs available. *Students:* 31 full-time (17 women), 7 part-time (all women); includes 12 minority (3 African Americans, 2 Asian Americans or Pacific Islanders, 7 Hispanic Americans), 17 international. Average age 29. In 2009, 4 master's awarded. *Entrance requirements:* For master's, GMAT or GRE General Test. Additional exam requirements/recommendations for international students: Required—TOEFL (minimum score 550 paper-based; 213 computer-based; 80 iBT). *Application deadline:* For fall admission, 1/15 priority date for domestic students. Applications are processed on a rolling basis. Application fee: $60. Electronic applications accepted. *Expenses:* Tuition: Full-time $35,046; part-time

$1524 per credit. Required fees: $161 per semester. *Financial support:* Fellowships, Federal Work-Study, institutionally sponsored loans, and scholarships/grants available. Support available to part-time students. Financial award application deadline: 2/15; financial award applicants required to submit FAFSA. *Unit head:* Katie Ear, Administrative Director, 909-607-1916, Fax: 909-621-8905, E-mail: katie.ear@cgu.edu. *Application contact:* Deryn Dudley, Program Assistant, 909-607-3286, Fax: 909-621-8905, E-mail: hrd@cgu.edu.

Cleveland State University, College of Graduate Studies, Nance College of Business Administration, Department of Management and Labor Relations, Cleveland, OH 44115. Offers labor relations and human resources (MLRHR). Part-time programs available. *Entrance requirements:* For master's, GMAT or GRE. Additional exam requirements/recommendations for international students: Required—TOEFL (minimum score 525 paper-based; 197 computer-based). Electronic applications accepted.

College of Santa Fe, Department of Business Administration, Santa Fe, NM 87505-7634. Offers finance (MBA); human resources (MBA). Program also available at Albuquerque campus. Part-time and evening/weekend programs available. *Entrance requirements:* For master's, minimum GPA of 3.0 in last 60 hours (preferred).

Colorado Technical University Colorado Springs, Graduate Studies, Program in Management, Colorado Springs, CO 80907-3896. Offers accounting (MBA, MSA); business administration (MBA); finance (MBA); human resources management (MBA); logistics/supply chain management (MBA); management (DM); marketing (MBA); mediation and dispute resolution (MBA); operations management (MBA); project management (MBA); technology management (MBA). Part-time and evening/weekend programs available. *Degree requirements:* For master's, thesis or alternative; for doctorate, thesis/dissertation. *Entrance requirements:* For doctorate, minimum graduate GPA of 3.0, 5 years of related work experience. *Faculty research:* Sexual harassment, performance evaluation, critical thinking.

Colorado Technical University Denver, Programs in Business Administration and Management, Greenwood Village, CO 80111. Offers accounting (MBA); business administration (MBA); business administration and management (EMBA); finance (MBA); human resource management (MBA); marketing (MBA); mediation and dispute resolution (MBA); operations management (MBA); project management (MBA); technology management (MBA). Part-time and evening/weekend programs available. *Degree requirements:* For master's, thesis or alternative. *Entrance requirements:* For master's, minimum undergraduate GPA of 3.0, resume.

Colorado Technical University Sioux Falls, Programs in Business Administration and Management, Sioux Falls, SD 57108. Offers business administration (MBA); business management (MSM); health science management (MSM); human resources management (MSM); information technology (MSM); organizational leadership (MSM); project management (MBA); technology management (MBA). Evening/weekend programs available. *Degree requirements:* For master's, thesis optional. *Entrance requirements:* For master's, minimum 2 years work experience, resume.

Columbia Southern University, MBA Program, Orange Beach, AL 36561. Offers electronic business and technology (MBA); finance (MBA); general (MBA); healthcare management (MBA); hospitality and tourism (MBA); human resources management (MBA); international management (MBA); marketing (MBA); project management (MBA); public administration (MBA); sport management (MBA). Part-time and evening/weekend programs available. Postbaccalaureate distance learning degree programs offered (no on-campus study). *Entrance requirements:* For master's, bachelor's degree from accredited/approved institution. Additional exam requirements/recommendations for international students: Required—TOEFL. Electronic applications accepted.

Human Resources Management

Columbia University, Graduate School of Business, MBA Program, New York, NY 10027. Offers accounting (MBA); decision, risk, and operations (MBA); entrepreneurship (MBA); finance and economics (MBA); healthcare and pharmaceutical management (MBA); human resource management (MBA); international business (MBA); leadership and ethics (MBA); management (MBA); marketing (MBA); media (MBA); private equity (MBA); real estate (MBA); social enterprise (MBA); value investing (MBA); DDS/MBA; JD/MBA; MBA/MIA; MBA/MPH; MBA/MS; MD/MBA. *Faculty:* 149 full-time (23 women), 134 part-time/adjunct (16 women). *Students:* 1,293 full-time (435 women); includes 235 minority (65 African Americans, 4 American Indian/Alaska Native, 135 Asian Americans or Pacific Islanders, 31 Hispanic Americans), 417 international. Average age 28. 6,885 applicants, 15% accepted, 737 enrolled. In 2009, 696 master's awarded. *Entrance requirements:* For master's, GMAT, 2 letters of recommendation. Additional exam requirements/recommendations for international students: Required—TOEFL. *Application deadline:* For fall admission, 4/14 for domestic students, 3/3 for international students; for spring admission, 10/7 for domestic and international students. Applications are processed on a rolling basis. Application fee: $250. Electronic applications accepted. *Expenses:* Contact institution. *Financial support:* In 2009–10, 358 students received support, including 101 fellowships (averaging $23,250 per year); research assistantships, teaching assistantships, career-related internships or fieldwork, institutionally sponsored loans, and scholarships/grants also available. Financial award application deadline: 3/1; financial award applicants required to submit CSS PROFILE or FAFSA. *Faculty research:* Human decision making and behavioral research; real estate market and mortgage defaults; financial crisis and corporate governance; international business; security analysis and accounting. *Unit head:* Prof. Amir Ziv, Vice Dean of Students and the MBA Program, 212-854-3485, Fax: 212-932-0545, E-mail: az50@columbia.edu. *Application contact:* Mary J. Miller, Assistant Dean of Admissions, 212-854-1961, Fax: 212-662-6754, E-mail: apply@gsb.columbia.edu.

Concordia University, St. Paul, College of Business and Organizational Leadership, St. Paul, MN 55104-5494. Offers business and organizational leadership (MBA); criminal justice leadership (MA); health care management (MBA); human resources management (MA); leadership and management (MA). *Accreditation:* ACBSP. Evening/weekend programs available. Postbaccalaureate distance learning degree programs offered (minimal on-campus study). *Faculty:* 10 full-time (5 women), 19 part-time/adjunct (4 women). *Students:* 295 full-time (169 women), 3 part-time (2 women); includes 30 minority (19 African Americans, 2 American Indian/Alaska Native, 5 Asian Americans or Pacific Islanders, 4 Hispanic Americans), 3 international. Average age 32. In 2009, 114 master's awarded. *Application deadline:* Applications are processed on a rolling basis. Application fee: $50. Electronic applications accepted. *Financial support:* Applicants required to submit FAFSA. *Unit head:* Dr. Bruce Corrie, Dean, 651-641-8226, Fax: 651-641-8807, E-mail: corrie@csp.edu. *Application contact:* Kimberly Craig, Director of Graduate and Cohort Admission, 651-603-6223, Fax: 651-603-6320, E-mail: craig@csp.edu.

Concordia University Wisconsin, Graduate Programs, School of Business and Legal Studies, MBA Program, Mequon, WI 53097-2402. Offers finance (MBA); health care administration (MBA); human resource management (MBA); international business (MBA); international business-bilingual English/Chinese (MBA); management (MBA); management information systems (MBA); managerial communications (MBA); marketing (MBA); public administration (MBA); risk management (MBA). Postbaccalaureate distance learning degree programs offered (minimal on-campus study). *Degree requirements:* For master's, comprehensive exam, thesis or alternative. *Entrance requirements:* Additional exam requirements/recommendations for international students: Required—TOEFL. *Expenses:* Contact institution.

Cornell University, Graduate School, Graduate Fields of Industrial and Labor Relations, Ithaca, NY 14853-0001. Offers collective bargaining, labor law and labor history (MILR, MPS, MS, PhD); economic and social statistics (MILR); human resource studies (MILR, MPS, MS, PhD); industrial and labor relations problems (MILR, MPS, MS, PhD); international and comparative labor (MILR, MPS, MS, PhD); labor economics (MILR, MPS, MS, PhD); organizational behavior (MILR, MPS, MS, PhD). *Faculty:* 60 full-time (19 women). *Students:* 165 full-time (100 women); includes 35 minority (16 African Americans, 2 American Indian/Alaska Native, 11 Asian Americans or Pacific Islanders, 6 Hispanic Americans), 58 international. Average age 30. 271 applicants, 34% accepted, 69 enrolled. In 2009, 72 master's, 4 doctorates awarded. *Degree requirements:* For master's, thesis (MS); for doctorate, comprehensive exam, thesis/dissertation, teaching experience. *Entrance requirements:* For master's and doctorate, GMAT or GRE General Test, 2 academic recommendations. Additional exam requirements/recommendations for international students: Required—TOEFL (minimum score 550 paper-based; 213 computer-based; 77 iBT). Application fee: $70. Electronic applications accepted. *Expenses:* Contact institution. *Financial support:* In 2009–10, 73 students received support, including 7 fellowships with full tuition reimbursements available, 2 research assistantships with full tuition reimbursements available, 5 teaching assistantships with full tuition reimbursements available; institutionally sponsored loans, scholarships/grants, health care benefits, tuition waivers (full and partial), and unspecified assistantships also available. Financial award applicants required to submit FAFSA. *Unit head:* Director of Graduate Studies, 607-255-1522. *Application contact:* Graduate Field Assistant, 607-255-1522, E-mail: ilrgradapplicant@cornell.edu.

Cumberland University, Program in Organizational Leadership and Human Relations Management, Lebanon, TN 37087. Offers MS. Part-time and evening/weekend programs available. *Degree requirements:* For master's, comprehensive exam. *Entrance requirements:* For master's, MAT, 3 letters of recommendation. Additional exam requirements/recommendations for international students: Required—TOEFL (minimum score 500 paper-based; 173 computer-based).

Dallas Baptist University, College of Business, Management Program, Dallas, TX 75211-9299. Offers business communication (MA); conflict resolution management (MA); general management (MA); health care management (MA); human resource management (MA); performance management (MA). Part-time and evening/weekend programs available. *Entrance requirements:* For master's, GRE General Test, minimum GPA of 3.0. Additional exam requirements/recommendations for international students: Required—TOEFL, IELTS. Electronic applications accepted. *Expenses:* Tuition: Full-time $10,674; part-time $593 per credit hour. *Faculty research:* Organizational behavior, conflict personalities.

Davenport University, Sneden Graduate School, Grand Rapids, MI 49503. Offers accounting (MBA); business administration (EMBA); finance (MBA); health care management (MBA); human resources (MBA); information assurance (MS); public health (MPH); strategic management (MBA). Evening/weekend programs available. *Entrance requirements:* For master's, GMAT, minimum undergraduate GPA of 2.75. Additional exam requirements/recommendations for international students: Required—TOEFL. Electronic applications accepted. *Faculty research:* Leadership, management, marketing, organizational culture.

Davenport University, Sneden Graduate School, Warren, MI 48092-5209. Offers accounting (MBA); business administration (EMBA); finance (MBA); health care management (MBA); human resources management (MBA); information assurance (MS); public health (MPH); strategic management (MBA). *Entrance requirements:* For master's, minimum undergraduate GPA of 2.7.

Davenport University, Sneden Graduate School, Dearborn, MI 48126-3799. Offers accounting (MBA); business administration (EMBA); finance (MBA); health care management (MBA); human resources management (MBA); information assurance (MS); marketing (MBA); public health (MPH); strategic management (MBA). Part-time and evening/weekend programs available. Postbaccalaureate distance learning degree programs offered (no on-campus study). *Entrance requirements:* For master's, minimum GPA of 2.7, previous course work in accounting and statistics. *Faculty research:* Accounting, international accounting, social and environmental accounting, finance.

DePaul University, Charles H. Kellstadt Graduate School of Business, Department of Management, Chicago, IL 60604-2287. Offers entrepreneurship (MBA); health sector management (MBA); human resource management (MBA, MSHR); leadership/change management (MBA); management planning and strategy (MBA); operations management (MBA). Part-time and evening/weekend programs available. *Faculty:* 36 full-time (7 women), 35 part-time/adjunct (16 women). *Students:* 284 full-time (115 women), 147 part-time (69 women); includes 75 minority (20 African Americans, 1 American Indian/Alaska Native, 37 Asian Americans or Pacific Islanders, 17 Hispanic Americans), 18 international. In 2009, 112 master's awarded. *Entrance requirements:* For master's, GMAT, GRE (MSHR), 2 letters of recommendation, resume. Additional exam requirements/recommendations for international students: Required—TOEFL (minimum score 550 paper-based; 213 computer-based). *Application deadline:* For fall admission, 7/1 for domestic students; for winter admission, 10/1 for domestic students; for spring admission, 2/1 for domestic students. Applications are processed on a rolling basis. Application fee: $60. Electronic applications accepted. *Expenses:* Tuition: Full-time $37,525; part-time $620 per credit hour. *Financial support:* Research assistantships available. Financial award application deadline: 4/1. *Faculty research:* Growth management, creativity and innovation, quality management and business process design, entrepreneurship. *Application contact:* Christopher E. Kinsella, Director of Cohort MBA Programs, 312-362-8810, Fax: 312-362-6677, E-mail: kgsb@depaul.edu.

DeVry University, Keller Graduate School of Management, Downers Grove, IL 60515. Offers accounting and financial management (MAFM); business administration (MBA); human resources management (MHRM); information systems management (MISM); network and communications management (MNCM); project management (MPM); public administration (MPA).

Dowling College, School of Business, Oakdale, NY 11769-1999. Offers aviation management (MBA, Certificate); banking and finance (MBA, Certificate); financial planning (Certificate); general management (MBA); health care management (MBA, Certificate); human resource management (Certificate); management and leadership (MBA); marketing (Certificate); project management (Certificate); public management (MBA, Certificate); total quality management (MBA, Certificate); JD/MBA. Part-time and evening/weekend programs available. *Faculty:* 14 full-time (5 women), 58 part-time/adjunct (5 women). *Students:* 324 full-time (142 women), 479 part-time (237 women); includes 238 minority (82 African Americans, 1 American Indian/Alaska Native, 117 Asian Americans or Pacific Islanders, 38 Hispanic Americans), 2 international. Average age 33. 457 applicants, 91% accepted, 153 enrolled. In 2009, 341 master's, 2 other advanced degrees awarded. *Degree requirements:* For master's, comprehensive exam, thesis optional. *Entrance requirements:* For master's, minimum GPA of 2.8, 2 letters of recommendation, courses in accounting and finance or seminar in accounting/finance, resume. Additional exam requirements/recommendations for international students: Required—TOEFL (minimum score 550 paper-based). *Application deadline:* For fall admission, 9/1 priority date for domestic students; for winter admission, 1/1 priority date for domestic students; for spring admission, 2/1 priority date for domestic students. Applications are processed on a rolling basis. Application fee: $50. Electronic applications accepted. *Expenses:* Tuition: Full-time $14,490; part-time $805 per credit. Required fees: $346 per term. *Financial support:* Career-related internships or fieldwork and Federal Work-Study available. Support available to part-time students. Financial award application deadline: 6/30; financial award applicants required to submit FAFSA. *Faculty research:* International finance, computer applications, labor relations, executive development. *Unit head:* Mathew Cordaro, Dean, 631-244-3162, Fax: 631-244-1018, E-mail: cordarom@dowling.edu. *Application contact:* Glenn M. Berman, Director of Admissions Operations, 631-244-3357, Fax: 631-244-1059, E-mail: glenn.berman@dowling.edu.

East Central University, School of Graduate Studies, Department of Human Resources, Ada, OK 74820-6899. Offers administration (MSHR); counseling (MSHR); criminal justice (MSHR); rehabilitation counseling (MSHR). *Accreditation:* CORE. Part-time and evening/weekend programs available. *Degree requirements:* For master's, thesis optional. *Entrance requirements:* For master's, GRE General Test, MAT, minimum GPA of 2.5. Electronic applications accepted.

Eastern Michigan University, Graduate School, College of Arts and Sciences, Department of Political Science, Programs in Public Administration, Ypsilanti, MI 48197. Offers local government management (Graduate Certificate); management of public healthcare services (Graduate Certificate); public administration (MPA, Graduate Certificate); public budget management (Graduate Certificate); public land planning (Graduate Certificate); public management (Graduate Certificate); public personnel management (Graduate Certificate); public policy analysis (Graduate Certificate). *Accreditation:* NASPAA. *Students:* 18 full-time (7 women), 130 part-time (72 women); includes 53 minority (46 African Americans, 2 American Indian/Alaska Native, 1 Asian American or Pacific Islander, 4 Hispanic Americans), 5 international. Average age 34. In 2009, 17 master's, 37 other advanced degrees awarded. Application fee: $35. Tuition and fees vary according to course level. *Unit head:* Dr. Joseph Ohren, Program Director, 734-487-2522, Fax: 734-487-3340, E-mail: joseph.ohren@emich.edu. *Application contact:* Dr. Sukru Koyuoglu, Program Coordinator, 734-487-0063, Fax: 734-487-3340, E-mail: sukru.koyuoglu@emich.edu.

Eastern Michigan University, Graduate School, College of Business, Department of Management, Program in Human Resources Management and Organizational Development, Ypsilanti, MI 48197. Offers MSHROD. Part-time and evening/weekend programs available. Postbaccalaureate distance learning degree programs offered (minimal on-campus study). *Students:* 23 full-time (11 women), 64 part-time (40 women); includes 12 minority (6 African Americans, 2 American Indian/Alaska Native, 1 Asian American or Pacific Islander, 3 Hispanic Americans), 44 international. Average age 30. In 2009, 54 master's awarded. *Degree requirements:* For master's, thesis optional. *Entrance requirements:* For master's, GMAT. Additional exam requirements/recommendations for international students: Required—TOEFL. *Application deadline:* Applications are processed on a rolling basis. Application fee: $35. Tuition and fees vary according to course level. *Financial support:* Fellowships, research assistantships with full tuition reimbursements, teaching assistantships with full tuition reimbursements, career-related internships or fieldwork, Federal Work-Study, institutionally sponsored loans, scholarships/grants, tuition waivers (partial), and unspecified assistantships available. Support available to part-time students. Financial award applicants required to submit FAFSA.

Eastern Michigan University, Graduate School, College of Business, Programs in Business Administration, Ypsilanti, MI 48197. Offers business administration (MBA, Graduate Certificate); computer information systems (Graduate Certificate); e-business (MBA, Graduate Certificate); enterprise business intelligence (MBA); entrepreneurship (MBA, Graduate Certificate); finance (MBA, Graduate Certificate); human resources (MBA); human resources management (Graduate Certificate); information systems (MBA); internal auditing (MBA); international business (MBA, Graduate Certificate); marketing management (Graduate Certificate); nonprofit management (MBA); organizational development (Graduate Certificate); supply chain management (MBA, Graduate Certificate). *Accreditation:* AACSB. Part-time programs available. Postbaccalaureate distance learning degree programs offered (no on-campus study). *Students:* 166 full-time (80 women), 439 part-time (231 women); includes 150 minority (103 African Americans, 7 American Indian/Alaska Native, 31 Asian Americans or Pacific Islanders, 9 Hispanic Americans), 97 international. Average age 34. In 2009, 3 other advanced degrees awarded. *Entrance requirements:* For master's, GMAT (minimum score 450), minimum cumulative undergraduate GPA of 2.75. Additional exam requirements/recommendations for international students: Required—TOEFL. *Application deadline:* For fall admission, 5/15 for domestic students, 5/1 for international students; for winter admission, 10/15 for domestic students, 10/1 for international students; for spring admission, 3/15 for domestic students, 3/1 for international students. Applications are processed on a rolling basis. Application fee: $35. Tuition and fees vary according to course level. *Financial support:* Fellowships, research assistantships with full tuition reimbursements, teaching assistantships with full tuition reimbursements, career-related internships or fieldwork, Federal Work-Study, institutionally sponsored loans, scholarships/grants, tuition waivers (partial), and unspecified assistantships available. Support available to part-time students. Financial award applicants required to submit FAFSA. *Unit head:* K. Michelle Henry, Director of Academic Services, 734-487-4444, Fax: 734-483-1316, E-mail: cob.grad@emich.edu. *Application contact:* Beste Windes, Advisor, 734-487-4444, Fax: 734-483-1316, E-mail: cob.grad@emich.edu.

Emmanuel College, Graduate Programs, Program in Human Resource Management, Boston, MA 02115. Offers MS, Certificate. Part-time and evening/weekend programs available. *Faculty:* 1 (woman) full-time, 15 part-time/adjunct (4 women). *Students:* 4 full-time (all women), 75 part-time (58 women); includes 17 minority (11 African Americans, 1 American Indian/Alaska Native, 1 Asian American or Pacific Islander, 4 Hispanic Americans). Average age 32. 28 applicants, 82% accepted, 23 enrolled. In 2009, 16 master's, 5 other advanced degrees awarded. *Entrance requirements:* For master's, interview, resume, 2 letters of recommendation, essay, bachelor's degree; for Certificate, interview, resume, letter of recommendation. Additional exam requirements/recommendations for international students: Required—TOEFL (minimum score 600 paper-based; 250 computer-based). *Application deadline:* For fall admission, 8/15 priority date for domestic students; for spring admission, 12/8 priority date for domestic students. Applications are processed on a rolling basis. Application fee: $50. Electronic applications accepted. *Expenses:* Tuition: Part-time $665 per credit. *Unit head:* Dr. Judith Marley, Dean, Graduate and Professional Programs, 617-735-9700, Fax: 617-507-0434, E-mail: gpp@emmanuel.edu. *Application contact:* Enrollment Counselor, 617-735-9700, Fax: 617-507-0434, E-mail: gpp@emmanuel.edu.

Everest University, Department of Business Administration, Tampa, FL 33614-5899. Offers accounting (MBA); human resources (MBA); international business (MBA). Part-time and evening/weekend programs available. *Degree requirements:* For master's, thesis optional. *Entrance requirements:* For master's, GMAT or GRE General Test, minimum GPA of 3.0.

Everest University, Program in Business Administration, Orlando, FL 32819. Offers accounting (MBA); general management (MBA); human resources (MBA); international management (MBA).

Fairfield University, Charles F. Dolan School of Business, Fairfield, CT 06824-5195. Offers accounting (MBA, MS, CAS); finance (MBA, MS, CAS); general management (MBA); human resource management (MBA, CAS); information systems and operations (MBA); information systems and operations management (CAS); international business (MBA, CAS); marketing (MBA, CAS); taxation (MBA, MS). *Accreditation:* AACSB. Part-time and evening/weekend programs available. *Degree requirements:* For master's, capstone course. *Entrance requirements:* For master's, GMAT (minimum score 500), 2 letters of reference, resume, minimum GPA of 3.0. Additional exam requirements/recommendations for international students: Required—TOEFL (minimum score 550 paper-based; 213 computer-based; 80 iBT). Electronic applications accepted. *Expenses:* Contact institution. *Faculty research:* Optimization strategies, international finance, consumer behavior, financial market volatility, Internet marketing, supply chain analysis, tax issues.

Fairleigh Dickinson University, College at Florham, Silberman College of Business, Center for Human Resource Management Studies, Program in Human Resource Management, Madison, NJ 07940-1099. Offers MBA, MA/MBA. *Students:* 10 full-time (8 women), 8 part-time (5 women), 4 international. Average age 29. 19 applicants, 63% accepted, 6 enrolled. In 2009, 6 master's awarded. *Application deadline:* Applications are processed on a rolling basis. Application fee: $40.

Fairleigh Dickinson University, Metropolitan Campus, Silberman College of Business, Center for Human Resources Management Studies, Program in Human Resource Management, Teaneck, NJ 07666-1914. Offers MBA, Certificate. *Students:* 7 full-time (all women), 7 part-time (5 women), 6 international. Average age 30. 16 applicants, 38% accepted, 2 enrolled. In 2009, 2 master's awarded. *Application deadline:* Applications are processed on a rolling basis. Application fee: $40. *Application contact:* Susan Brooman, University Director of Graduate Admissions, 201-692-2554, Fax: 201-692-2560, E-mail: globaleducation@fdu.edu.

Fitchburg State University, Division of Graduate and Continuing Education, Program in Business Administration, Fitchburg, MA 01420-2697. Offers accounting (MBA); human resource management (MBA); management (MBA). Part-time and evening/weekend programs available. Postbaccalaureate distance learning degree programs offered (no on-campus study). *Students:* 24 full-time (9 women), 58 part-time (33 women); includes 10 minority (4 African Americans, 1 Asian American or Pacific Islander, 5 Hispanic Americans), 15 international. Average age 32. 64 applicants, 91% accepted, 27 enrolled. In 2009, 56 master's awarded. *Entrance requirements:* For master's, GMAT, minimum GPA of 2.8, letters of recommendation, resume. Additional exam requirements/recommendations for international students: Required—TOEFL (minimum score 550 paper-based; 213 computer-based; 79 iBT). *Application deadline:* Applications are processed on a rolling basis. Application fee: $25 ($50 for international students). *Expenses:* Tuition, area resident: Part-time $150 per credit. Tuition, state resident: part-time $150 per credit. Tuition, nonresident: part-time $150 per credit. Required fees: $120 per credit. *Financial support:* In 2009–10, research assistantships with partial tuition reimbursements (averaging $5,500 per year); Federal Work-Study, scholarships/grants, and unspecified assistantships also available. Support available to part-time students. Financial award application deadline: 3/1; financial award applicants required to submit FAFSA. *Unit head:* Joseph McAloon, Chair, 978-665-3745, Fax: 978-665-3658, E-mail: gce@fsc.edu. *Application contact:* Director of Admissions, 978-665-3144, Fax: 978-665-4540, E-mail: admissions@fsc.edu.

Florida Institute of Technology, Graduate Programs, College of Business, Extended Studies Division, Melbourne, FL 32901-6975. Offers acquisition and contract management (PMBA); business administration (PMBA); computer information systems (MS); e-business (PMBA); human resource management (PMBA); human resources management (MS); logistics management (MS), including humanitarian and disaster relief logistics; management (MS), including acquisition and contract management, e-business, human resource management, information systems, logistics management, management, transportation management; material acquisition management (MS); project management (MS), including information systems, operations research; public administration (MPA); quality management (MS); space management (MS); space systems (MS); systems management (MS), including information systems, operations research, systems management. Part-time and evening/weekend programs available. Postbaccalaureate distance learning degree programs offered (no on-campus study). *Faculty:* 12 full-time (3 women), 117 part-time/adjunct (20 women). *Students:* 74 full-time (32 women), 1,041 part-time (484 women); includes 343 minority (240 African Americans, 12 American Indian/Alaska Native, 44 Asian Americans or Pacific Islanders, 47 Hispanic Americans), 22 international. Average age 35. 520 applicants, 72% accepted, 279 enrolled. In 2009, 509 master's awarded. *Degree requirements:* For master's, capstone course. *Entrance requirements:* For master's, GMAT or resume showing 8 years of supervised experience, minimum GPA of 3.0, 2 letters of recommendation, resume. Additional exam requirements/recommendations for international students: Required—TOEFL (minimum score 550 paper-based; 213 computer-based; 79 iBT). *Application deadline:* For fall admission, 4/1 for international students; for spring admission, 9/30 for international students. Applications are processed on a rolling basis. Application fee: $50. Electronic applications accepted. *Expenses:* Tuition: Part-time $1015 per credit. Tuition and fees vary according to campus/location and program. *Financial support:* Application deadline: 3/1. *Unit head:* Dr. Clifford Bragdon, Dean, 321-674-8821, Fax: 321-674-7597, E-mail: cbragdon@fit.edu. *Application contact:* Carolyn Farrior, Director of Graduate Admissions Online Learning and Off Campus Programs, 321-674-7118, Fax: 321-674-8216, E-mail: cfarrior@fit.edu.

Florida International University, Alvah H. Chapman, Jr. Graduate School of Business, Department of Management and International Business, Human Resources Management Program, Miami, FL 33199. Offers MSHRM. Part-time and evening/weekend programs available. *Students:* 31 full-time (26 women), 2 part-time (0 women); includes 27 minority (4 African Americans, 3 Asian Americans or Pacific Islanders, 20 Hispanic Americans), 1 international. Average age 34. 60 applicants, 37% accepted, 22 enrolled. In 2009, 63 master's awarded. *Entrance requirements:* For master's, GRE (minimum score of 1000) or GMAT (minimum score of 500), minimum GPA of 3.0 (upper-level coursework); two letters of recommendation; letter of intent; minimum of five years of professional (exempt) experience, of which at least two years are in HR field. Additional exam requirements/recommendations for international students: Required—TOEFL (minimum score 550 paper-based; 213 computer-based; 80 iBT), or IELTS (minimum score 6.5). *Application deadline:* For fall admission, 6/1 for domestic students, 4/1 for international students; for spring admission, 10/1 for domestic students, 9/1 for international students. Applications are processed on a rolling basis. Application fee: $30. Electronic applications accepted. *Expenses:* Contact institution. *Financial support:* Institutionally sponsored loans and scholarships/grants available. Financial award application deadline: 3/1; financial award applicants required to submit FAFSA. *Faculty research:* Compensation, labor issues, labor law, HR strategy. *Unit head:* Dr. Galen Kroeck, Chair, Management and International Business Department, 305-348-2791, Fax: 305-348-6146, E-mail: kroeck@fiu.edu. *Application contact:* Zuzana Hlavacova, Assistant Director, 305-348-5945, Fax: 305-348-7204, E-mail: zuzana.hlavacova@fiu.edu.

Fordham University, Graduate School of Education, Division of Educational Leadership, Administration and Policy, New York, NY 10023. Offers administration and supervision (MSE, Adv C); administration and supervision for church leaders (PhD); educational administration and supervision (Ed D, PhD); human resource program administration (MS). *Accreditation:* NCATE. *Degree requirements:* For doctorate, thesis/dissertation. *Entrance requirements:* For doctorate, MAT, GRE General Test.

Framingham State University, Division of Graduate and Continuing Education, Program in Human Resource Management, Framingham, MA 01701-9101. Offers MA. Part-time and evening/weekend programs available.

Franklin Pierce University, Graduate Studies, Rindge, NH 03461-0060. Offers emerging network technology (Graduate Certificate); health practice management (MBA, Graduate Certificate); human resource management (MBA); human resources management (Graduate Certificate); information technology management (MS); leadership (MBA, DA), including transformational leadership (DA); nursing (MS); physical therapy (DPT); physician assistant (MPAS); sports facilities management (MS); teacher education (M Ed). *Accreditation:* APTA. Part-time programs available. Postbaccalaureate distance learning degree programs offered (no on-campus study). *Faculty:* 27 full-time (16 women), 18 part-time/adjunct (4 women). *Students:* 296 full-time (172 women), 249 part-time (165 women); includes 18 minority (5 African Americans, 7 Asian Americans or Pacific Islanders, 6 Hispanic Americans), 31 international. Average age 38. 227 applicants, 97% accepted, 185 enrolled. In 2009, 76 master's, 46 doctorates awarded. *Degree requirements:* For master's, concentrated original research projects; student teaching; fieldwork and/or internship; leadership project; for doctorate, concentrated original research projects, clinical fieldwork and/or internship, leadership project. *Entrance requirements:* For master's, minimum GPA of 2.5, 3 letters of recommendation; for doctorate, demonstrated success at previous academic institutions (minimum GPA of 2.5), 3 letters of recommendation, personal mission statement, interview; writing sample (for DA program). Additional exam requirements/recommendations for international students: Required—TOEFL (minimum score 550 paper-based; 195 computer-based). *Application deadline:* Applications are processed on a rolling basis. Application fee: $0. Electronic applications accepted. *Expenses:* Tuition: Part-time $1560 per course. Part-time tuition and fees vary according to degree level, campus/location and program. *Financial support:* In 2009–10, 36 students received support, including 22 teaching assistantships with full and partial tuition reimbursements available; career-related internships or fieldwork and unspecified assistantships also available. Support available to part-time students. Financial award applicants required to submit FAFSA. *Faculty research:* Evidence based practice in sports physical therapy, human resource management in economic crisis, leadership in nursing, innovation in sports facility management, differentiated learning and understanding by design. *Unit head:* Dr. Robert G. Goddard, Assistant Dean, 603-899-4361, Fax: 603-229-4580, E-mail: goddardr@franklinpierce.edu. *Application contact:* 800-325-1090, Fax: 603-898-0827, E-mail: gpsadmin@franklinpierce.edu.

Gannon University, School of Graduate Studies, College of Engineering and Business, School of Business, Program in Human Resources Management, Erie, PA 16541-0001. Offers Certificate. Part-time and evening/weekend programs available. *Students:* 1 (woman) part-time. Average age 30. 1 applicant, 100% accepted, 0 enrolled. In 2009, 1 Certificate awarded. *Entrance requirements:* For degree, GMAT. Additional exam requirements/recommendations for international students: Required—TOEFL (minimum score 79 iBT). *Application deadline:* Applications are processed on a rolling basis. Application fee: $25. Electronic applications accepted. *Expenses:* Tuition: Full-time $13,590; part-time $755 per credit. Required fees: $524; $17 per credit. Tuition and fees vary according to course load, degree level, campus/location and program. *Financial support:* Application deadline: 7/1. *Unit head:* Scott Miller, Associate Director, 814-871-7397, E-mail: miller032@gannon.edu. *Application contact:* Kara Morgan, Assistant Director of Graduate Admissions, 814-871-5831, Fax: 814-871-5827, E-mail: graduate@gannon.edu.

George Fox University, School of Business, Newberg, OR 97132-2697. Offers finance (MBA); management (DBA); management/general (MBA); marketing (DBA); organizational strategy (MBA); strategic human resource management (MBA). MBA offered in part-time and full-time formats. Also offered in Portland, OR and Boise, ID. Part-time and evening/weekend programs available. Postbaccalaureate distance learning degree programs offered (minimal on-campus study). *Faculty:* 15 full-time (5 women), 7 part-time/adjunct (0 women). *Students:* 14 full-time (3 women), 223 part-time (77 women); includes 28 minority (7 African Americans, 3 American Indian/Alaska Native, 9 Asian Americans or Pacific Islanders, 9 Hispanic Americans), 2 international. Average age 38. 88 applicants, 86% accepted, 63 enrolled. In 2009, 66 master's, 2 doctorates awarded. *Degree requirements:* For master's, capstone project; for doctorate, credit-applied research project. *Entrance requirements:* For master's, resume (5 years professional experience required); 3 professional references; interview; financial e-learning course; for doctorate, GRE or GMAT, resume; personal mission statement; academic research writing sample; official transcript from each college/university attended; three professional references. Additional exam requirements/recommendations for international students: Required—TOEFL (minimum score 577 paper-based; 233 computer-based; 90 iBT), or IELTS (minimum score 7). *Application deadline:* For fall admission, 8/1 for domestic and international students; for spring admission, 12/1 for domestic and international students. Applications are processed on a rolling basis. Application fee: $40. Electronic applications accepted. *Expenses:* Contact institution. *Financial support:* In 2009–10, 2 students received support. Applicants required to submit FAFSA. *Unit head:* Dr. Ken Armstrong, Professor of Management and Dean, School of Management, 800-631-0921. *Application contact:* Robin Halverson, Admissions Counselor, 800-493-4937, Fax: 503-554-6111, E-mail: mba@georgefox.edu.

George Mason University, School of Public Policy, Program in Organization Development and Knowledge Management, Arlington, VA 22201. Offers MS. Evening/weekend programs available. *Faculty:* 61 full-time (14 women), 30 part-time/adjunct (4 women). *Students:* 73 full-time (50 women), 10 part-time (7 women); includes 13 minority (6 African Americans, 1 Asian American or Pacific Islander, 6 Hispanic Americans), 4 international. 60 applicants, 75% accepted, 33 enrolled. In 2009, 31 master's awarded. *Degree requirements:* For master's, thesis or alternative. *Entrance requirements:* For master's, GRE (for students seeking merit-based scholarships), minimum GPA of 3.0, 2 letters of recommendation, resume. Additional exam requirements/recommendations for international students: Required—TOEFL (minimum score 575 paper-based; 230 computer-based; 88 iBT). *Application deadline:* For fall admission, 6/1 priority date for domestic students, 5/1 priority date for international students. Applications are processed on a rolling basis. Application fee: $60. Electronic applications accepted. *Expenses:* Contact institution. *Financial support:* Career-related internships or fieldwork, Federal Work-Study, scholarships/grants, tuition waivers (partial), and unspecified assistantships available. Support available to part-time students. Financial award application deadline: 3/1; financial award applicants required to submit FAFSA. *Unit head:* Dr. Ann Baker, Director, 703-993-8099, E-mail: spp@gmu.edu. *Application contact:* Leslie Metzger Levin, Assistant Dean of Graduate Admissions and Marketing, 703-993-8099, Fax: 703-993-4876, E-mail: lmetzger@gmu.edu.

Georgetown University, Graduate School of Arts and Sciences, School of Continuing Studies, Washington, DC 20057. Offers American studies (MALS); Catholic studies (MALS); classical civilizations (MALS); ethics and the professions (MALS); human resources management (MPS); humanities (MALS); individualized study (MALS); international affairs (MALS); Islam

Human Resources Management

Georgetown University (continued)
and Muslim-Christian relations (MALS); journalism (MPS); liberal studies (DLS); literature and society (MALS); medieval and early modern European studies (MALS); public relations (MPS); real estate (MPS); religious studies (MALS); social and public policy (MALS); sports industry management (MPS); the theory and practice of American democracy (MALS); visual culture (MALS). *Entrance requirements:* Additional exam requirements/recommendations for international students: Required—TOEFL.

The George Washington University, Columbian College of Arts and Sciences, Department of Organizational Sciences and Communication, Washington, DC 20052. Offers human resources management (MA); industrial/organizational psychology (PhD); organizational management (MA). Part-time and evening/weekend programs available. *Faculty:* 10 full-time (6 women), 18 part-time/adjunct (15 women). *Students:* 23 full-time (13 women), 41 part-time (34 women); includes 15 minority (7 African Americans, 2 Asian Americans or Pacific Islanders, 6 Hispanic Americans), 8 international. Average age 29. 74 applicants, 84% accepted, 32 enrolled. In 2009, 28 master's awarded. *Degree requirements:* For master's, comprehensive exam. *Entrance requirements:* For master's, GRE General Test, minimum GPA of 3.0. Additional exam requirements/recommendations for international students: Required—TOEFL (minimum score 500 paper-based; 213 computer-based; 80 iBT). *Application deadline:* For fall admission, 1/15 priority date for domestic and international students; for spring admission, 10/1 priority date for domestic students, 9/1 priority date for international students. Applications are processed on a rolling basis. Application fee: $60. Electronic applications accepted. *Financial support:* Federal Work-Study and institutionally sponsored loans available. *Unit head:* Dr. David Costanza, Acting Director, 202-994-1875, Fax: 202-994-1881, E-mail: dconstanz@gwu.edu. *Application contact:* Information Contact, 202-994-1880, Fax: 202-994-1881.

Georgia State University, J. Mack Robinson College of Business, Department of Managerial Sciences, Atlanta, GA 30302-3083. Offers business analysis (MBA, MS); decision sciences (PhD); entrepreneurship (MBA); human resources management (MBA, MS); management (MBA, PhD); operations management (MBA, MS); organization change (MS); personnel employee relations (PhD); strategic management (PhD). Part-time and evening/weekend programs available. *Degree requirements:* For doctorate, thesis/dissertation. *Entrance requirements:* For master's and doctorate, GMAT. Additional exam requirements/recommendations for international students: Required—TOEFL (minimum score 610 paper-based; 255 computer-based; 101 iBT). Electronic applications accepted. *Faculty research:* Abusive supervision, entrepreneurship, time series and neural networks, organizational controls, inventory control systems.

Golden Gate University, Ageno School of Business, San Francisco, CA 94105-2968. Offers accounting (MBA); business administration (EMBA, MBA, PMBA, DBA); finance (MBA, MS, Certificate); financial planning (MS, Certificate); human resource management (MBA, MS); human resources management (Certificate); information systems (MS); information technology (MBA); information technology management (Certificate); integrated marketing and communications (MS, Certificate); international business (MBA); management (MBA); marketing (MBA, MS, Certificate); operations management (Certificate); psychology (MA, Certificate); public relations (MS, Certificate); JD/MBA. Part-time and evening/weekend programs available. *Faculty:* 16 full-time (4 women), 241 part-time/adjunct (72 women). *Students:* 380 full-time (193 women), 750 part-time (414 women); includes 480 minority (98 African Americans, 2 American Indian/Alaska Native, 298 Asian Americans or Pacific Islanders, 82 Hispanic Americans), 166 international. Average age 33. 681 applicants, 78% accepted, 270 enrolled. In 2009, 550 master's, 13 doctorates awarded. *Degree requirements:* For doctorate, thesis/dissertation. *Entrance requirements:* For master's, GMAT (MBA), minimum GPA of 2.5 (MS). Additional exam requirements/recommendations for international students: Required—TOEFL. *Application deadline:* For fall admission, 5/15 for international students; for winter admission, 1/15 for international students; for spring admission, 9/15 for international students. Applications are processed on a rolling basis. Application fee: $70 ($110 for international students). Electronic applications accepted. *Expenses:* Contact institution. *Financial support:* Career-related internships or fieldwork, Federal Work-Study, institutionally sponsored loans, and scholarships/grants available. Support available to part-time students. Financial award applicants required to submit FAFSA. *Unit head:* Terry Connelly, Dean, 415-442-6519, Fax: 415-442-5369. *Application contact:* Angela Melero, Enrollment Services, 415-442-7800, Fax: 415-442-7807, E-mail: info@ggu.edu.

Goldey-Beacom College, Graduate Program, Wilmington, DE 19808-1999. Offers business administration (MBA); finance (MS); financial management (MBA); human resource management (MBA); information technology (MBA); international business management (MBA); management (MM); marketing management (MBA); taxation (MBA, MS). *Accreditation:* ACBSP. Part-time and evening/weekend programs available. *Faculty:* 20 full-time (8 women), 28 part-time/adjunct (10 women). *Students:* 38 full-time (18 women), 486 part-time (184 women); includes 350 minority (38 African Americans, 300 Asian Americans or Pacific Islanders, 12 Hispanic Americans). Average age 27. In 2009, 130 master's awarded. *Entrance requirements:* For master's, GMAT, MAT, GRE, minimum GPA of 3.0. Additional exam requirements/recommendations for international students: Required—TOEFL (minimum score 65 computer-based); Recommended—IELTS (minimum score 5). *Application deadline:* Applications are processed on a rolling basis. Electronic applications accepted. *Expenses:* Tuition: Full-time $14,166; part-time $787 per credit. Required fees: $180; $10 per credit. *Financial support:* In 2009–10, 486 students received support. Scholarships/grants available. Support available to part-time students. Financial award application deadline: 4/1; financial award applicants required to submit FAFSA. *Unit head:* Larry W. Eby, Director of Admissions, 302-225-6289, Fax: 302-996-5408, E-mail: ebylw@gbc.edu. *Application contact:* Ashley E. Mashington, Graduate Admissions Representative, 302-225-6259, Fax: 302-996-5408, E-mail: mashina@gbc.edu.

Grambling State University, School of Graduate Studies and Research, College of Arts and Sciences, Program in Public Administration, Grambling, LA 71270. Offers health service administration (MPA); human resource management (MPA); public management (MPA); state and local government (MPA). *Accreditation:* NASPAA. Part-time programs available. *Faculty:* 5 full-time (2 women), 2 part-time/adjunct (0 women). *Students:* 25 full-time (16 women), 14 part-time (12 women); includes 32 minority (all African Americans), 5 international. Average age 29. 30 applicants, 53% accepted, 11 enrolled. In 2009, 12 master's awarded. *Degree requirements:* For master's, comprehensive exam (for some programs), thesis optional. *Entrance requirements:* For master's, GRE, minimum GPA of 2.75 on last degree. Additional exam requirements/recommendations for international students: Required—TOEFL (minimum score 500 paper-based; 173 computer-based; 61 iBT). *Application deadline:* For fall admission, 7/1 for domestic and international students; for spring admission, 12/1 for domestic and international students. Applications are processed on a rolling basis. Application fee: $20 ($30 for international students). Electronic applications accepted. *Expenses:* Tuition, state resident: full-time $2610. Tuition, nonresident: full-time $2610. *Financial support:* In 2009–10, 6 research assistantships (averaging $5,958 per year) were awarded; health care benefits, tuition waivers (full), and unspecified assistantships also available. Financial award application deadline: 5/31. *Unit head:* Dr. Rose Harris, Director, 318-274-2310, Fax: 318-274-3427, E-mail: harrisr@gram.edu. *Application contact:* Sarah Dennis, Admissions Coordinator, 318-274-2319, Fax: 318-274-3427, E-mail: denniss@alpha0.gram.edu.

Hawai'i Pacific University, College of Business Administration, Program in Human Resource Management, Honolulu, HI 96813. Offers MA. *Faculty:* 2 full-time (1 woman). *Students:* 31 full-time (19 women), 35 part-time (23 women); includes 11 African Americans, 19 Asian Americans or Pacific Islanders, 3 Hispanic Americans, 15 international. Average age 31. 33 applicants, 91% accepted, 22 enrolled. In 2009, 22 master's awarded. *Entrance requirements:* Additional exam requirements/recommendations for international students: Required—TOEFL (minimum score 550 paper-based; 213 computer-based; 80 iBT), IELTS (minimum score 6), TWE (minimum score 5). *Application deadline:* Applications are processed on a rolling basis. Application fee: $50. Electronic applications accepted. *Expenses:* Tuition: Full-time $12,600; part-time $700 per credit hour. Tuition and fees vary according to program. *Unit head:* Dr. Cheryl Crozier Garcia, Program Chair, 808-544-1178, Fax: 808-566-2403, E-mail: ccrozier@campus.hpu.edu. *Application contact:* Danny Lam, Assistant Director of Graduate Admissions, 808-544-1135, Fax: 808-544-0280, E-mail: graduate@hpu.edu.

HEC Montreal, School of Business Administration, Master of Science Programs in Administration, Program in Human Resources Management, Montréal, QC H3T 2A7, Canada. Offers M Sc. All courses are given in French. Part-time programs available. *Students:* 51 full-time (40 women), 9 part-time (7 women). 60 applicants, 47% accepted, 16 enrolled. In 2009, 7 master's awarded. *Degree requirements:* For master's, one foreign language, thesis. *Application deadline:* For fall admission, 3/15 for domestic and international students; for winter admission, 9/15 for domestic and international students. Application fee: $77 Canadian dollars. Electronic applications accepted. Tuition and fees charges are reported in Canadian dollars. *Expenses:* Tuition, area resident: Part-time $65.60 Canadian dollars per credit. Tuition, state resident: full-time $2361.60 Canadian dollars; part-time $183.36 Canadian dollars per credit. Tuition, nonresident: full-time $6601 Canadian dollars; part-time $448.13 Canadian dollars per credit. International tuition: $16,132.68 Canadian dollars full-time. Required fees: $1254.15 Canadian dollars; $28.99 Canadian dollars per course. $91.68 Canadian dollars per term. Tuition and fees vary according to degree level and program. *Financial support:* Fellowships, research assistantships, teaching assistantships, scholarships/grants available. Financial award application deadline: 10/2. *Unit head:* Dr. Claude Laurin, Director, 514-340-6485, Fax: 514-340-5690, E-mail: claude.laurin@hec.ca. *Application contact:* Francine Blais, Administrative Director, 514-340-6112, Fax: 514-340-6411, E-mail: francine.blais@hec.ca.

Hofstra University, Frank G. Zarb School of Business, Department of Management, Entrepreneurship and General Management, Hempstead, NY 11549. Offers business administration (MBA), including health services management, management, sports and entertainment management; human resource management (MS). Part-time and evening/weekend programs available. *Faculty:* 6 full-time (2 women), 4 part-time/adjunct (0 women). *Students:* 75 full-time (35 women), 185 part-time (72 women); includes 55 minority (19 African Americans, 24 Asian Americans or Pacific Islanders, 12 Hispanic Americans), 26 international. Average age 33. 215 applicants, 61% accepted, 71 enrolled. In 2009, 53 master's awarded. *Degree requirements:* For master's, capstone course (MBA), thesis (MS). *Entrance requirements:* For master's, GMAT or GRE, 2 letters of recommendation, resume. Additional exam requirements/recommendations for international students: Required—TOEFL (minimum score 550 paper-based; 213 computer-based; 80 iBT); Recommended—IELTS (minimum score 6). *Application deadline:* Applications are processed on a rolling basis. Application fee: $60. Electronic applications accepted. *Expenses:* Contact institution. *Financial support:* In 2009–10, 23 students received support, including 20 fellowships with full and partial tuition reimbursements available (averaging $10,251 per year), 2 research assistantships with full and partial tuition reimbursements available (averaging $20,788 per year); career-related internships or fieldwork, Federal Work-Study, institutionally sponsored loans, scholarships/grants, tuition waivers (full and partial), and unspecified assistantships also available. Support available to part-time students. Financial award applicants required to submit FAFSA. *Faculty research:* Business/personal ethics; emotion in workplace; gender issues; learning and pedagogical issues; family business. *Unit head:* Dr. Mamdouh I. Farid, Chairperson, 516-463-5735, Fax: 516-463-4834, E-mail: mgbmif@hofstra.edu. *Application contact:* Carol Drummer, Dean of Graduate Admissions, 516-463-4876, Fax: 516-463-4664, E-mail: gradstudent@hofstra.edu.

Holy Family University, Graduate School, School of Business, Philadelphia, PA 19114. Offers human resources management (MS); information systems management (MS). Part-time and evening/weekend programs available. *Faculty:* 3 full-time (0 women), 3 part-time/adjunct (0 women). *Students:* 7 full-time (6 women), 49 part-time (32 women); includes 9 minority (4 African Americans, 3 Asian Americans or Pacific Islanders, 2 Hispanic Americans), 5 international. Average age 35. 18 applicants, 94% accepted, 15 enrolled. In 2009, 24 master's awarded. *Degree requirements:* For master's, comprehensive exam, thesis optional. *Entrance requirements:* For master's, GMAT, GRE, or MAT, minimum GPA of 3.0. *Application deadline:* For fall admission, 7/1 priority date for domestic students; for winter admission, 11/1 priority date for domestic students. Applications are processed on a rolling basis. Application fee: $25. *Expenses:* Tuition: Part-time $600 per credit. Required fees: $58 per semester. *Financial support:* Federal Work-Study available. Support available to part-time students. Financial award application deadline: 2/15; financial award applicants required to submit FAFSA. *Unit head:* Dr. Jan Duggar, Dean, 267-341-3373, Fax: 215-637-5937, E-mail: jduggar@holyfamily.edu. *Application contact:* Gidget Marie Montelibano, Graduate Admissions Counselor, 267-341-3558, Fax: 215-637-1478, E-mail: gmontelibano@holyfamily.edu.

Hood College, Graduate School, Department of Economics and Management, Frederick, MD 21701-8575. Offers accounting (MBA); administration and management (MBA); finance (MBA); human resource management (MBA); information systems (MBA); marketing (MBA); public management (MBA). Part-time and evening/weekend programs available. *Faculty:* 5 full-time (1 woman), 9 part-time/adjunct (1 woman). *Students:* 21 full-time (16 women), 166 part-time (85 women); includes 33 minority (18 African Americans, 8 Asian Americans or Pacific Islanders, 7 Hispanic Americans), 15 international. Average age 32. 47 applicants, 87% accepted, 32 enrolled. In 2009, 31 master's awarded. *Degree requirements:* For master's, capstone/final research project. *Entrance requirements:* For master's, minimum GPA of 2.75, resume, letters of recommendation. *Application deadline:* For fall admission, 7/15 for domestic and international students; for spring admission, 12/15 for domestic and international students. Applications are processed on a rolling basis. Application fee: $35. Electronic applications accepted. *Expenses:* Tuition: Full-time $6480; part-time $360 per credit. Required fees: $100; $50 per term. *Financial support:* Applicants required to submit FAFSA. *Faculty research:* Corporate strategy and sustainable competitive advantages, business ethics, entrepreneurship, investments management, economic development. *Unit head:* Dr. Anita Jose, Program Director, 301-696-3691, Fax: 301-696-3597, E-mail: jose@hood.edu. *Application contact:* Dr. Allen P. Flora, Dean of Graduate School, 301-696-3811, Fax: 301-696-3597, E-mail: gofurther@hood.edu.

Houston Baptist University, College of Business and Economics, Program in Human Resources Management, Houston, TX 77074-3298. Offers MSHRM. Part-time and evening/weekend programs available. *Entrance requirements:* For master's, GMAT, minimum GPA of 2.5. Additional exam requirements/recommendations for international students: Required—TOEFL (minimum score 550 paper-based; 213 computer-based). *Expenses:* Contact institution.

Howard University, School of Business, Graduate Programs in Business, Washington, DC 20059-0002. Offers accounting (MBA); entrepreneurship (MBA); finance (MBA); general management (MBA); human resources management (MBA); information systems (MBA); international business (MBA); marketing (MBA); supply chain management (MBA); JD/MBA. *Accreditation:* AACSB. Part-time and evening/weekend programs available. Postbaccalaureate distance learning degree programs offered (no on-campus study). *Entrance requirements:* For master's, GMAT, minimum 1 year post undergraduate work experience, resume, 3 letters of recommendation, advanced college algebra. Additional exam requirements/recommendations for international students: Required—TOEFL. *Faculty research:* Marketing research in multi-ethnic populations, U.S. trade policies and international relations, risk management (finance).

Indiana Tech, Program in Business Administration, Fort Wayne, IN 46803-1297. Offers accounting (MBA); health care administration (MBA); human resources (MBA); management (MBA); marketing (MBA). Part-time and evening/weekend programs available. Postbaccalaureate distance learning degree programs offered (no on-campus study). *Students:* 202 full-time (97 women), 37 part-time (18 women); includes 60 minority (45 African Americans, 2 American Indian/Alaska Native, 7 Asian Americans or Pacific Islanders, 6 Hispanic Americans), 5 international. Average age 38. *Entrance requirements:* For master's, GMAT, minimum undergraduate GPA of 2.5, 3 letters of recommendation. *Application deadline:* Applications are processed on a rolling basis. Application fee: $25. Electronic applications accepted. *Expenses:* Tuition: Full-time $5160; part-time $430 per credit hour. Tuition and fees vary according to degree level and program. *Financial support:* Applicants required to submit FAFSA. *Unit head:* Dr. Andrew Nwanne, Associate Dean of College of Professional Studies, 260-422-5561 Ext.

2214, E-mail: ainwanne@indianatech.edu. *Application contact:* Steve Herendeen, Manager of Campus Development and Support, 260-422-5561 Ext. 2121, E-mail: saherendeen@indianatech.edu.

Indiana Wesleyan University, College of Adult and Professional Studies, Department of Graduate Studies in Business, Marion, IN 46953. Offers accounting (MBA); applied management (MBA); business administration (MBA); health care (MBA); human resources (MBA); management (MS). Part-time and evening/weekend programs available. Postbaccalaureate distance learning degree programs offered (no on-campus study). *Degree requirements:* For master's, applied business or management project. *Entrance requirements:* For master's, minimum GPA of 2.5, 2 years of related work experience. Additional exam requirements/recommendations for international students: Required—TOEFL (minimum score 550 paper-based; 213 computer-based). Electronic applications accepted. *Expenses:* Tuition: Full-time $7380; part-time $410 per credit. One-time fee: $85. Tuition and fees vary according to campus/location.

Instituto Tecnologico de Santo Domingo, Graduate School, Santo Domingo, Dominican Republic. Offers applied linguistics (MA); construction administration (M Mgmt); corporate finance (M Mgmt); education (M Ed); engineering (M Eng), including data telecommunications, industrial engineering, logistics and supply chain, maintenance engineering, sanitary and environmental engineering, structural engineering; environmental science (M En S), including environmental education, environmental management, marine and coastal ecosystems, natural resources management; family therapy (MA); food science and technology (MS); human development (MA); human resources administration (M Mgmt); international business (M Mgmt); labor risks (M Mgmt); management (M Mgmt); marketing (M Mgmt); mathematics (MS); organizational development (M Mgmt); planning and taxation (M Mgmt); psychology (MA); social science (M Ed); upper management (M Mgmt). *Entrance requirements:* For master's, birth certificate, minimum GPA of 2.0.

Instituto Tecnológico y de Estudios Superiores de Monterrey, Campus Cuernavaca, Programs in Business Administration, Temixco, Mexico. Offers finance (MA); human resources management (MA); international business (MA); marketing (MA).

Inter American University of Puerto Rico, Aguadilla Campus, Graduate School, Aguadilla, PR 00605. Offers accounting (MBA); business information systems (MBA); counseling psychology with an emphasis in family (MS); criminal justice (MA); educative management and leadership (MA); elementary education (MA); finance (MBA); human resources (MBA); industrial management (MBA); marketing (MBA). Part-time and evening/weekend programs available. *Degree requirements:* For master's, comprehensive exam. *Entrance requirements:* For master's, EXADEP, 2 letters of recommendation, minimum GPA of 2.5. Electronic applications accepted.

Inter American University of Puerto Rico, Arecibo Campus, Program in Business Administration, Arecibo, PR 00614-4050. Offers accounting (MBA); finance (MBA); human resources (MBA).

Inter American University of Puerto Rico, Bayamón Campus, Graduate School, Bayamón, PR 00957. Offers biology (MS), including environmental sciences and ecology, molecular biotechnology; electronic commerce (MBA); human resources (MBA). Part-time and evening/weekend programs available. *Faculty:* 6 full-time (1 woman), 5 part-time/adjunct (2 women). *Students:* 99 part-time (61 women); includes all Hispanic Americans. Average age 31. *Degree requirements:* For master's, comprehensive exam, research project. *Entrance requirements:* For master's, EXADEP, GRE General Test, letters of recommendation. *Application deadline:* For fall admission, 7/1 for domestic students, 5/1 priority date for international students; for winter admission, 11/15 priority date for domestic and international students; for spring admission, 2/15 priority date for domestic and international students. Application fee: $31. *Expenses:* Tuition: Part-time $195 per credit. Required fees: $148 per trimester. *Unit head:* Prof. Juan F. Martinez, Rector, 787-279-1200 Ext. 2295, Fax: 787-279-2205, E-mail: jmartinez@bc.inter.edu. *Application contact:* Carlos Alicea, Director of Admission, 787-279-1200 Ext. 2017, Fax: 787-279-2205, E-mail: calicea@bc.inter.edu.

Inter American University of Puerto Rico, Metropolitan Campus, Graduate Programs, Program in Human Resources, San Juan, PR 00919-1293. Offers MBA. *Degree requirements:* For master's, comprehensive exam. *Entrance requirements:* For master's, GRE or EXADEP, interview. Electronic applications accepted.

Inter American University of Puerto Rico, Ponce Campus, Graduate School, Mercedita, PR 00715-1602. Offers accounting (MBA); biology (M Ed); chemistry (M Ed); criminal justice (MA); elementary education (M Ed); English as a Second Language (M Ed); finance (MBA); history (M Ed); human resources (MBA); marketing (MBA); mathematics (M Ed); Spanish (M Ed). *Entrance requirements:* For master's, minimum GPA of 2.5.

Inter American University of Puerto Rico, San Germán Campus, Graduate Studies Center, Program in Business Administration, San Germán, PR 00683-5008. Offers accounting (MBA); finance (MBA); human resources (PhD); human resources management (MBA); industrial management (MBA); international business (PhD); management information systems (MBA); marketing management (MBA). Part-time and evening/weekend programs available. *Degree requirements:* For master's, comprehensive exam. *Entrance requirements:* For master's, GRE General Test or EXADEP, minimum GPA of 3.0.

International College of the Cayman Islands, Graduate Program in Management, Newlands, Cayman Islands. Offers business administration (MBA); management (MS), including education, human resources. Part-time and evening/weekend programs available. *Degree requirements:* For master's, comprehensive exam. *Faculty research:* International human resources administration.

Iona College, Hagan School of Business, Department of Management, New Rochelle, NY 10801-1890. Offers business administration (MBA); health care management (MBA); human resource management (MBA, PMC); management (MBA, PMC). Part-time and evening/weekend programs available. *Faculty:* 7 full-time (2 women), 4 part-time/adjunct (2 women). *Students:* 23 full-time (12 women), 133 part-time (76 women); includes 19 minority (7 African Americans, 1 American Indian/Alaska Native, 3 Asian Americans or Pacific Islanders, 8 Hispanic Americans), 4 international. Average age 33. 71 applicants, 75% accepted, 34 enrolled. In 2009, 57 master's, 1 other advanced degree awarded. *Entrance requirements:* For master's, GMAT, 2 letters of recommendation; for PMC, GMAT. Additional exam requirements/recommendations for international students: Required—TOEFL (minimum score 550 paper-based; 213 computer-based). *Application deadline:* Applications are processed on a rolling basis. Application fee: $50. Electronic applications accepted. *Expenses:* Contact institution. *Financial support:* Scholarships/grants, tuition waivers (partial), and unspecified assistantships available. Support available to part-time students. Financial award application deadline: 4/15; financial award applicants required to submit FAFSA. *Faculty research:* Information systems, strategic management, corporate values and ethics. *Unit head:* Dr. Fredrica Rudell, Acting Chair, 914-637-2748, E-mail: frudell@iona.edu. *Application contact:* Jude Fleurismond, Director of MBA Admissions, 914-633-2289, Fax: 914-637-2708, E-mail: jfleurismond@iona.edu.

Kaplan University, Davenport Campus, School of Business, Davenport, IA 52807-2095. Offers business administration (MBA); change leadership (MS); entrepreneurship (MBA); finance (MBA); health care management (MBA, MS); human resource (MBA); international business (MBA); management (MS); marketing (MBA); project management (MBA, MS); supply chain management and logistics (MBA, MS). Part-time and evening/weekend programs available. Postbaccalaureate distance learning degree programs offered (no on-campus study). *Entrance requirements:* Additional exam requirements/recommendations for international students: Required—TOEFL (minimum score 550 paper-based; 218 computer-based; 80 iBT). Electronic applications accepted.

La Roche College, School of Graduate Studies and Adult Education, Program in Human Resources Management, Pittsburgh, PA 15237-5898. Offers MS, Certificate. *Accreditation:* ACBSP. Part-time and evening/weekend programs available. *Faculty:* 2 full-time (both women), 5 part-time/adjunct (3 women). *Students:* 16 full-time (10 women), 62 part-time (56 women); includes 6 minority (4 African Americans, 1 Asian American or Pacific Islander, 1 Hispanic American), 7 international. Average age 34. 15 applicants, 67% accepted, 7 enrolled. In 2009, 21 master's awarded. *Entrance requirements:* For master's, GMAT, GRE or MAT, minimum GPA of 3.0 during previous 2 years. Additional exam requirements/recommendations for international students: Recommended—TOEFL (minimum score 550 paper-based; 220 computer-based). *Application deadline:* For fall admission, 8/15 priority date for domestic students, 8/15 for international students; for spring admission, 12/15 priority date for domestic students, 12/15 for international students. Applications are processed on a rolling basis. Application fee: $50. Electronic applications accepted. *Expenses:* Tuition: Full-time $10,350; part-time $575 per credit hour. *Financial support:* Unspecified assistantships available. Financial award application deadline: 3/31; financial award applicants required to submit FAFSA. *Faculty research:* Personnel administration, human resources development. *Unit head:* Dr. Jean Forti, Coordinator, 412-536-1193, Fax: 412-536-1179, E-mail: fortij1@laroche.edu. *Application contact:* Hope Schiffgens, Director of Graduate Studies and Adult Education, 412-536-1266, Fax: 412-536-1283, E-mail: schombh1@laroche.edu.

Lasell College, Graduate and Professional Studies in Management, Newton, MA 02466-2709. Offers elder care administration (MSM, Graduate Certificate); elder care marketing (MSM, Graduate Certificate); fundraising management (MSM, Graduate Certificate); human resource management (MSM, Graduate Certificate); management (MSM, Graduate Certificate); marketing (MSM, Graduate Certificate); non-profit management (MSM, Graduate Certificate); project management (MSM, Graduate Certificate). Part-time and evening/weekend programs available. Postbaccalaureate distance learning degree programs offered (no on-campus study). *Faculty:* 2 full-time (both women), 8 part-time/adjunct (6 women). *Students:* 26 full-time (18 women), 85 part-time (60 women); includes 10 African Americans, 4 Asian Americans or Pacific Islanders, 9 Hispanic Americans, 17 international. Average age 31. 55 applicants, 80% accepted, 31 enrolled. In 2009, 31 master's awarded. *Entrance requirements:* For master's and Graduate Certificate, bachelor's degree from an accredited institution. Additional exam requirements/recommendations for international students: Required—TOEFL (minimum score 550 paper-based; 213 computer-based; 75 iBT) or IELTS. *Application deadline:* For fall admission, 8/31 priority date for domestic students, 6/30 priority date for international students; for spring admission, 12/31 priority date for domestic students, 10/31 priority date for international students. Applications are processed on a rolling basis. Application fee: $40. Electronic applications accepted. *Expenses:* Tuition: Full-time $4890; part-time $525 per credit hour. Required fees: $55 per term. *Financial support:* Available to part-time students. Application deadline: 8/31. *Unit head:* Dr. Joan Dolamore, Dean of Graduate and Professional Studies, 617-243-2485, Fax: 617-243-2450, E-mail: gradinfo@lasell.edu. *Application contact:* Adrienne Franciosi, Director of Graduate Admission, 617-243-2214, Fax: 617-243-2450, E-mail: gradinfo@lasell.edu.

La Sierra University, School of Business and Management, Riverside, CA 92515. Offers accounting (MBA); finance (MBA); general management (MBA); human resources management (MBA); leadership, values, and ethics for business and management (Certificate); marketing (MBA). *Degree requirements:* For master's, research project. *Entrance requirements:* For master's, GMAT, minimum GPA of 3.0. Additional exam requirements/recommendations for international students: Required—TOEFL. *Faculty research:* Financial econometrics, institutional assessment and strategic planning, legal issues in management, behavioral finance, content of financial reports.

Lewis University, College of Business, Graduate School of Management, Program in Business Administration, Romeoville, IL 60446. Offers accounting (MBA); custom elective option (MBA); e-business (MBA); finance (MBA); healthcare management (MBA); human resources management (MBA); information security (MBA); international business (MBA); management information systems (MBA); marketing (MBA); project management (MBA); technology and operations management (MBA). Part-time and evening/weekend programs available. *Faculty:* 15 full-time (2 women), 18 part-time/adjunct (4 women). *Students:* 120 full-time (64 women), 222 part-time (103 women); includes 97 minority (62 African Americans, 4 Asian Americans or Pacific Islanders, 31 Hispanic Americans), 9 international. Average age 31. In 2009, 84 master's awarded. *Entrance requirements:* For master's, interview, bachelor's degree, resume, 2 recommendations. Additional exam requirements/recommendations for international students: Required—TOEFL (minimum score 550 paper-based; 213 computer-based). *Application deadline:* For fall admission, 8/15 priority date for domestic students, 5/1 priority date for international students; for spring admission, 11/15 priority date for international students. Applications are processed on a rolling basis. Application fee: $40. Electronic applications accepted. *Expenses:* Tuition: Full-time $6480; part-time $720 per credit. One-time fee: $40. Tuition and fees vary according to course load, degree level and program. *Financial support:* Career-related internships or fieldwork, Federal Work-Study, scholarships/grants, and unspecified assistantships available. Financial award application deadline: 5/1; financial award applicants required to submit FAFSA. *Unit head:* Dr. Maureen Culleeney, Academic Program Director, 815-838-0500 Ext. 5631, E-mail: culleema@lewisu.edu. *Application contact:* Michele King, Director of Admission, 815-838-0500 Ext. 5384, E-mail: gsm@lewisu.edu.

Lincoln University, Graduate Center, Lincoln University, PA 19352. Offers administration (MSA), including finance, human resources management; early childhood education (M Ed); elementary education (M Ed); human services (M Hum Svcs); reading (MSR). Evening/weekend programs available. *Degree requirements:* For master's, thesis. *Entrance requirements:* For master's, 5 years of work experience in human services. *Faculty research:* Gerontology/minority aging, computers in composition instruction.

Lincoln University, Graduate Degree Programs, Oakland, CA 94612. Offers finance and investments (DBA); finance management and investment banking (MBA); general business (MBA); human resource management (MBA); international business (MBA); management information systems (MBA). Part-time and evening/weekend programs available. *Faculty:* 7 full-time (2 women), 13 part-time/adjunct (1 woman). *Students:* 295 full-time (133 women), 3 part-time (0 women). 177 applicants, 100% accepted, 71 enrolled. In 2009, 98 master's awarded. *Degree requirements:* For master's, research project (thesis) or internship report, or comprehensive exam; for doctorate, comprehensive exam, thesis/dissertation. *Entrance requirements:* For master's, minimum GPA of 2.7; for doctorate, GMAT (minimum score: 550), GRE (minimum score: 1000), or equivalent test results (waived for master's degree with cumulative GPA of 3.3). Additional exam requirements/recommendations for international students: Required—TOEFL or IELTS. *Application deadline:* For fall admission, 7/3 priority date for domestic students; for spring admission, 11/27 priority date for domestic students. Applications are processed on a rolling basis. Application fee: $75. Electronic applications accepted. *Expenses:* Tuition: Full-time $6750. Required fees: $190 per term. *Financial support:* In 2009–10, 1 teaching assistantship was awarded; career-related internships or fieldwork and scholarships/grants also available. *Unit head:* Dr. Marshall Burak, Director of Graduate Programs, 510-628-8016, Fax: 510-628-8012, E-mail: mburak@lincolnuca.edu. *Application contact:* Peggy Au, Director of Admissions and Records, 510-628-8010, Fax: 510-628-8012, E-mail: admissions@lincolnuca.edu.

Lindenwood University, Graduate Programs, College of Individualized Education, St. Charles, MO 63301-1695. Offers administration (MSA); business administration (MBA); communications (MA); criminal justice and administration (MS); gerontology (MA); health management (MS); human resource management (MS); information technology (MBA, Certificate); management (MSA); managing information technology (MS); marketing (MSA); writing (MFA). Part-time and evening/weekend programs available. *Faculty:* 15 full-time (8 women), 128 part-time/adjunct (53 women). *Students:* 679 full-time (432 women), 90 part-time (57 women); includes 138 minority (121 African Americans, 2 American Indian/Alaska Native, 5 Asian Americans or Pacific Islanders, 10 Hispanic Americans), 18 international. Average age 34. 223 applicants, 44% accepted, 87 enrolled. In 2009, 478 master's awarded. *Degree requirements:* For master's, thesis (for some programs), 1 colloquium per term. *Entrance requirements:* For master's, interview, minimum GPA of 3.0. Additional exam requirements/recommendations for international students: Required—TOEFL (minimum score 550 paper-based; 213 computer-

Human Resources Management

Lindenwood University (continued)

based; 80 iBT). *Application deadline:* For fall admission, 10/2 priority date for domestic and international students; for winter admission, 1/8 priority date for domestic and international students; for spring admission, 4/8 priority date for domestic and international students. Applications are processed on a rolling basis. Application fee: $30 ($100 for international students). *Expenses:* Tuition: Full-time $12,960; part-time $370 per credit hour. Required fees: $340. One-time fee: $30 full-time. Tuition and fees vary according to course level and course load. *Financial support:* In 2009–10, 631 students received support. Career-related internships or fieldwork, institutionally sponsored loans, tuition waivers (partial), and unspecified assistantships available. Financial award application deadline: 6/30; financial award applicants required to submit FAFSA. *Unit head:* Dan Kemper, Dean, 636-949-4501, Fax: 636-949-4505, E-mail: dkemper@lindenwood.edu. *Application contact:* Brett Barger, Dean of Evening Admissions and Extension Campuses, 636-949-4934, Fax: 636-949-4109, E-mail: adultadmissions@lindenwood.edu.

Lindenwood University, Graduate Programs, School of Business and Entrepreneurship, St. Charles, MO 63301-1695. Offers accounting (MBA, MS); business administration (MBA); entrepreneurial studies (MBA, MS); finance (MBA, MS); human resource management (MBA); human resources (MS); international business (MBA, MS); management (MBA, MS); management information systems (MBA, MS); marketing (MBA, MS); public management (MBA, MS); sport management (MA). *Accreditation:* ACBSP. Part-time and evening/weekend programs available. *Faculty:* 20 full-time (8 women), 17 part-time/adjunct (5 women). *Students:* 129 full-time (60 women), 138 part-time (61 women); includes 15 minority (11 African Americans, 2 Asian Americans or Pacific Islanders, 2 Hispanic Americans), 84 international. Average age 28. 149 applicants, 73 enrolled. In 2009, 142 master's awarded. *Degree requirements:* For master's, comprehensive exam (for some programs), thesis (for some programs). *Entrance requirements:* For master's, interview, minimum GPA of 3.0, letter of recommendation. Additional exam requirements/recommendations for international students: Required—TOEFL (minimum score 550 paper-based; 213 computer-based; 80 iBT). *Application deadline:* For fall admission, 7/30 priority date for domestic students, 9/16 priority date for international students; for winter admission, 12/19 priority date for domestic students, 12/17 priority date for international students; for spring admission, 2/25 priority date for domestic students, 2/11 priority date for international students. Applications are processed on a rolling basis. Application fee: $30 ($100 for international students). Electronic applications accepted. *Expenses:* Tuition: Full-time $12,960; part-time $370 per credit hour. Required fees: $340. One-time fee: $30 full-time. Tuition and fees vary according to course level and course load. *Financial support:* In 2009–10, 209 students received support. Career-related internships or fieldwork, Federal Work-Study, institutionally sponsored loans, and tuition waivers (partial) available. Financial award application deadline: 6/30; financial award applicants required to submit FAFSA. *Unit head:* Ed Morris, Dean of Management, 636-949-4832, E-mail: emorris@lindenwood.edu. *Application contact:* Brett Barger, Dean of Evening Admissions and Extension Campuses, 636-949-4934, Fax: 636-949-4109, E-mail: adultadmissions@lindenwood.edu.

Long Island University, Brooklyn Campus, School of Business, Public Administration and Information Sciences, Program in Human Resources Management, Brooklyn, NY 11201-8423. Offers MS. *Entrance requirements:* For master's, GMAT or GRE, 2 letters of recommendation. Additional exam requirements/recommendations for international students: Required—TOEFL (minimum score 500 paper-based; 173 computer-based).

Loyola University Chicago, Graduate School of Business, Institute of Human Resources and Employee Relations, Chicago, IL 60660. Offers MSHR. Part-time programs available. *Entrance requirements:* For master's, GMAT or GRE General Test, letters of recommendation. Additional exam requirements/recommendations for international students: Required—TOEFL (minimum score 550 paper-based; 213 computer-based; 80 iBT). *Expenses:* Contact institution. *Faculty research:* Human resource management, labor relations, global human resource management, organizational development, compensation.

Marquette University, Graduate School of Management, Program in Human Resources, Milwaukee, WI 53201-1881. Offers MSHR. Part-time and evening/weekend programs available. *Faculty:* 4 full-time (3 women), 3 part-time/adjunct (2 women). *Students:* 10 full-time (5 women), 12 part-time (9 women); includes 3 minority (1 African American, 2 Asian Americans or Pacific Islanders), 8 international. Average age 27. 38 applicants, 63% accepted, 10 enrolled. In 2009, 11 master's awarded. *Entrance requirements:* For master's, GMAT or GRE General Test. Additional exam requirements/recommendations for international students: Required—TOEFL. Application fee: $40. *Financial support:* Research assistantships, teaching assistantships, Federal Work-Study, institutionally sponsored loans, and tuition waivers (full and partial) available. Support available to part-time students. Financial award application deadline: 2/15. *Faculty research:* Diversity, mentoring. *Unit head:* Dr. Timothy Keaveny, Management Chair, 414-288-3643. *Application contact:* Dr. Timothy Keaveny, Management Chair, 414-288-3643.

Marshall University, Academic Affairs Division, Lewis College of Business, Program in Human Resource Management, Huntington, WV 25755. Offers MS. Part-time and evening/weekend programs available. *Students:* 59 full-time (31 women), 28 part-time (18 women); includes 11 minority (8 African Americans, 3 Asian Americans or Pacific Islanders), 13 international. Average age 28. In 2009, 34 master's awarded. *Degree requirements:* For master's, comprehensive assessment. *Entrance requirements:* For master's, GMAT or GRE General Test. *Application deadline:* Applications are processed on a rolling basis. Application fee: $40. *Financial support:* Tuition waivers (full) available. Support available to part-time students. Financial award applicants required to submit FAFSA. *Unit head:* Dr. Andrew Sikula, Associate Dean, 304-746-1956, E-mail: sikula@marshall.edu. *Application contact:* Steven Shumlas, Information Contact, 304-746-8964, Fax: 304-746-1902, E-mail: shumlas@marshall.edu.

Marygrove College, Graduate Division, Program in Human Resource Management, Detroit, MI 48221-2599. Offers MA. *Entrance requirements:* For master's, interview, writing sample.

Marymount University, School of Business Administration, Program in Human Resource Management, Arlington, VA 22207-4299. Offers human resource management (MA, Certificate); instructional design (Certificate); organization development (Certificate). Part-time and evening/weekend programs available. *Students:* 9 full-time (7 women), 64 part-time (55 women); includes 28 minority (19 African Americans, 1 American Indian/Alaska Native, 4 Asian Americans or Pacific Islanders, 4 Hispanic Americans), 6 international. Average age 33. 40 applicants, 98% accepted, 22 enrolled. In 2009, 15 master's, 2 other advanced degrees awarded. *Entrance requirements:* For master's, GMAT or GRE General Test, resume; for Certificate, resume. Additional exam requirements/recommendations for international students: Required—TOEFL (minimum score 600 paper-based; 250 computer-based; 96 iBT), IELTS (minimum score 6.5). *Application deadline:* For fall admission, 7/15 for domestic students, 7/1 for international students; for spring admission, 11/15 for domestic students, 10/15 for international students. Applications are processed on a rolling basis. Application fee: $40. Electronic applications accepted. *Expenses:* Tuition: Full-time $13,050; part-time $725 per credit hour. Required fees: $135; $7.50 per credit hour. *Financial support:* In 2009–10, 9 students received support; research assistantships with full tuition reimbursements available, career-related internships or fieldwork, Federal Work-Study, scholarships/grants, and unspecified assistantships available. Support available to part-time students. Financial award applicants required to submit FAFSA. *Unit head:* Dr. Virginia Bianco-Mathis, Chair/Director, 703-284-5957, Fax: 703-527-3830, E-mail: virginia.bianco-mathis@marymount.edu. *Application contact:* Francesca Reed, Director, Graduate Admissions, 703-284-5901, Fax: 703-527-3815, E-mail: grad.admissions@marymount.edu.

McKendree University, Graduate Programs, Master of Business Administration Program, Lebanon, IL 62254-1299. Offers business administration (MBA); human resource management (MBA); international business (MBA). Part-time and evening/weekend programs available. Postbaccalaureate distance learning degree programs offered (no on-campus study). *Faculty:* 8 full-time (1 woman), 18 part-time/adjunct (6 women). *Students:* 68 full-time (26 women), 122 part-time (63 women); includes 23 minority (17 African Americans, 1 Asian American or Pacific Islander, 5 Hispanic Americans), 1 international. Average age 34. 80 applicants, 68% accepted, 47 enrolled. In 2009, 37 master's awarded. *Entrance requirements:* For master's, official transcripts from all institutions attended, essay, minimum GPA of 3.0, three references, resume. Additional exam requirements/recommendations for international students: Required—TOEFL. *Application deadline:* Applications are processed on a rolling basis. Application fee: $0. Electronic applications accepted. *Expenses:* Tuition: Full-time $6300; part-time $350 per credit hour. One-time fee: $125. *Financial support:* Applicants required to submit FAFSA. *Unit head:* Dr. Frank Spreng, Director of MBA Program, 618-537-6902, E-mail: fspreng@mckendree.edu. *Application contact:* Patty Aubel, Graduate Admission Counselor, 618-537-6943, Fax: 618-537-6410, E-mail: plaubel@mckendree.edu.

McMaster University, School of Graduate Studies, Faculty of Business, Program in Human Resources and Management, Hamilton, ON L8S 4M2, Canada. Offers MBA, PhD. Part-time programs available. *Degree requirements:* For doctorate, comprehensive exam, thesis/dissertation. *Entrance requirements:* For master's, GMAT; for doctorate, GMAT or GRE, master's degree, minimum B+ average. Additional exam requirements/recommendations for international students: Required—TOEFL (minimum score 580 paper-based; 237 computer-based). *Faculty research:* Leadership, occupational mental health, work attitudes, human resources recruitment, change and stress management strategies.

Mercy College, School of Business, Program in Human Resource Management, Dobbs Ferry, NY 10522-1189. Offers MS, AC. Part-time and evening/weekend programs available. Postbaccalaureate distance learning degree programs offered (minimal on-campus study). *Students:* 1 (woman) full-time, 95 part-time (80 women); includes 38 African Americans, 2 Asian Americans or Pacific Islanders, 9 Hispanic Americans, 10 international. Average age 34. 62 applicants, 65% accepted, 33 enrolled. In 2009, 12 master's awarded. *Degree requirements:* For master's, thesis or alternative, capstone experience. *Entrance requirements:* For master's, undergraduate transcripts, interview, two letters of reference, resume. Additional exam requirements/recommendations for international students: Required—TOEFL (minimum score 600 paper-based; 250 computer-based; 100 iBT). *Application deadline:* For fall admission, 8/1 for international students. Applications are processed on a rolling basis. Application fee: $40. Electronic applications accepted. *Expenses:* Contact institution. *Financial support:* Career-related internships or fieldwork, Federal Work-Study, scholarships/grants, and unspecified assistantships available. Support available to part-time students. Financial award applicants required to submit FAFSA. *Faculty research:* Team building, motivation, leadership, training, productivity. *Unit head:* Frederick Collett, Program Director, 914-674-7632, E-mail: hrprogram@mercy.edu. *Application contact:* Beverly Bennett, Administrative Assistant, 914-674-7632, E-mail: bbennett@mercy.edu.

Meritus University, School of Business, Fredericton, NB E3C 2R2, Canada. Offers global management (MBA); health care management (MBA); human resources management (MBA); information technology management (MBA); marketing (MBA); technology management (MBA). Evening/weekend programs available. Postbaccalaureate distance learning degree programs offered (no on-campus study). *Faculty:* 5 full-time (1 woman), 50 part-time/adjunct (15 women). *Students:* 77 full-time (29 women). Average age 35. *Entrance requirements:* For master's, undergraduate degree or comparable equivalent with minimum cumulative GPA of 2.5; minimum equivalent of two years of full-time, post high-school work experience; current employment. Additional exam requirements/recommendations for international students: Required—TOEFL (minimum score 213 computer-based; 79 iBT), IELTS (minimum score 6.5), or TOEIC (minimum score 750) or Berlitz (minimum score 550). *Application deadline:* Applications are processed on a rolling basis. Application fee: $45. Electronic applications accepted. Tuition and fees charges are reported in Canadian dollars. *Expenses:* Tuition: Full-time $14,400 Canadian dollars. Required fees: $720 Canadian dollars. *Unit head:* Dr. Albert K. S. Wong, Program Chair, Business Administration, 604-657-5465, Fax: 602-643-4624, E-mail: albert.wong@staff.meritusu.ca. *Application contact:* Jeremy S. DeMerchant, Enrolment Manager, 506-443-8413, Fax: 602-759-3688, E-mail: jeremy.demerchant@staff.meritusu.ca.

Michigan State University, The Graduate School, College of Social Science, School of Labor and Industrial Relations, East Lansing, MI 48824. Offers human resources and labor relations (MLRHR); industrial relations and human resources (PhD). *Faculty:* 16 full-time (4 women). *Students:* 110 full-time (69 women), 37 part-time (25 women); includes 15 minority (8 African Americans, 1 American Indian/Alaska Native, 4 Asian Americans or Pacific Islanders, 2 Hispanic Americans), 37 international. Average age 26. 226 applicants, 44% accepted. In 2009, 67 master's, 1 doctorate awarded. *Entrance requirements:* Additional exam requirements/recommendations for international students: Required—TOEFL. *Application deadline:* For fall admission, 12/27 priority date for domestic students. *Expenses:* Tuition, state resident: part-time $478.25 per credit hour. Tuition, nonresident: part-time $966.50 per credit hour. Part-time tuition and fees vary according to program. *Financial support:* In 2009–10, 5 research assistantships with tuition reimbursements (averaging $6,879 per year), 1 teaching assistantship with tuition reimbursement (averaging $6,061 per year) were awarded. Total annual research expenditures: $257,815. *Unit head:* Dr. William N. Cooke, Director, 517-355-1801, Fax: 517-432-9443, E-mail: cookew@msu.edu. *Application contact:* Cheryl Mollitor, Graduate Program Administrator, 517-355-3285, Fax: 517-355-7656, E-mail: graduate@lir.msu.edu.

Moravian College, Moravian College Comenius Center, Business and Management Programs, Bethlehem, PA 18018-6650. Offers general management (MBA); health care management (MBA); leadership (MSHRM); learning and performance management (MSHRM); supply chain management (MBA). Part-time and evening/weekend programs available. *Faculty:* 6 full-time (2 women), 10 part-time/adjunct (3 women). *Students:* 59 part-time (30 women). Average age 29. 27 applicants, 74% accepted, 10 enrolled. In 2009, 20 master's awarded. *Entrance requirements:* For master's, GMAT. Additional exam requirements/recommendations for international students: Required—TOEFL (minimum score 550 paper-based; 260 computer-based; 90 iBT). *Application deadline:* Applications are processed on a rolling basis. Application fee: $40. *Expenses:* Contact institution. *Financial support:* In 2009–10, 1 fellowship with full tuition reimbursement was awarded. *Faculty research:* Leadership, change management, human resources. *Unit head:* Dr. William A. Kleintop, Associate Dean for Business and Management Programs, 610-507-1400, Fax: 610-861-1400, E-mail: comenius@moravian.edu. *Application contact:* Linda J. Doyle, Information Contact, 610-861-1400, Fax: 610-861-1466, E-mail: mba@moravian.edu.

National-Louis University, College of Management and Business, Program in Human Resource Management and Development, Chicago, IL 60603. Offers MS. Part-time programs available. *Entrance requirements:* For master's, college-administered critical thinking and writing skills test, minimum GPA of 3.0, resume. *Expenses:* Contact institution.

National University, Academic Affairs, College of Letters and Sciences, Department of Professional Studies, La Jolla, CA 92037-1011. Offers forensic science (MFS), including criminalistics and investigation; public administration (MPA), including alternative dispute resolution, human resource management, organizational leadership, public finance. Part-time and evening/weekend programs available. Postbaccalaureate distance learning degree programs offered (no on-campus study). *Faculty:* 5 full-time (3 women), 27 part-time/adjunct (7 women). *Students:* 167 full-time (95 women), 246 part-time (133 women); includes 188 minority (71 African Americans, 2 American Indian/Alaska Native, 41 Asian Americans or Pacific Islanders, 74 Hispanic Americans). Average age 38. 284 applicants, 100% accepted, 206 enrolled. In 2009, 104 master's awarded. *Degree requirements:* For master's, thesis. *Entrance requirements:* For master's, interview, minimum GPA of 2.5. Additional exam requirements/recommendations for international students: Required—TOEFL (minimum score 550 paper-based; 213 computer-based; 79 iBT), IELTS (minimum score 6). *Application deadline:* Applications are processed on a rolling basis. Application fee: $60 ($65 for international students). Electronic applications accepted. *Expenses:* Tuition: Part-time $338 per quarter hour. *Financial support:* Career-related internships or fieldwork, institutionally sponsored loans, scholarships/grants, and tuition waivers (partial) available. Support available to part-time students. Financial award application deadline: 6/30; financial award applicants required to submit FAFSA. *Unit head:* Chandrika M.

Kelso, Associate Professor and Chair, 858-642-8433, Fax: 858-642-8715, E-mail: ckelso@nu.edu. *Application contact:* Dominick Giovanniello, Associate Regional Dean—San Diego, 800-NAT-UNIV, Fax: 858-541-7792, E-mail: dgiovann@nu.edu.

National University, Academic Affairs, School of Business and Management, Department of Leadership and Business Administration, La Jolla, CA 92037-1011. Offers alternative dispute resolution (MBA); e-business (MBA); financial management (MBA); human resource management (MBA); human resources management (MA); international business (MBA); knowledge management (MS); marketing (MBA); organizational leadership (MBA, MS); technology management (MBA). Part-time and evening/weekend programs available. Postbaccalaureate distance learning degree programs offered (no on-campus study). *Faculty:* 4 full-time (2 women), 22 part-time/adjunct (9 women). *Students:* 95 full-time (56 women), 228 part-time (129 women); includes 63 African Americans, 24 Asian Americans or Pacific Islanders, 61 Hispanic Americans, 6 international. Average age 38. 191 applicants, 100% accepted, 131 enrolled. In 2009, 62 master's awarded. *Degree requirements:* For master's, thesis. *Entrance requirements:* For master's, interview, minimum GPA of 2.5. Additional exam requirements/recommendations for international students: Required—TOEFL (minimum score 550 paper-based; 213 computer-based; 79 iBT), IELTS (minimum score 6). *Application deadline:* Applications are processed on a rolling basis. Application fee: $60 ($65 for international students). Electronic applications accepted. *Expenses:* Tuition: Part-time $338 per quarter hour. *Financial support:* Career-related internships or fieldwork, institutionally sponsored loans, scholarships/grants, and tuition waivers (partial) available. Support available to part-time students. Financial award application deadline: 6/30; financial award applicants required to submit FAFSA. *Unit head:* Dr. George Drops, Chair and Professor, 858-642-8438, Fax: 858-642-8406, E-mail: gdrops@nu.edu. *Application contact:* Dominick Giovanniello, Associate Regional Dean—San Diego, 800-NAT-UNIV, Fax: 858-541-7792, E-mail: dgiovann@nu.edu.

Nazareth College of Rochester, Graduate Studies, Department of Business, Program in Human Resource Management, Rochester, NY 14618-3790. Offers MS. *Entrance requirements:* For master's, minimum GPA of 3.0.

New Mexico Highlands University, Graduate Studies, School of Business, Las Vegas, NM 87701. Offers business administration (MBA), including government nonprofit management, human resource management, international business, management, management information systems. *Accreditation:* ACBSP. *Degree requirements:* For master's, comprehensive exam, thesis or alternative. *Entrance requirements:* For master's, minimum undergraduate GPA of 3.0. Additional exam requirements/recommendations for international students: Required—TOEFL (minimum score 540 paper-based; 207 computer-based). *Faculty research:* Real estate valuation, studying expert judgments in complex accounting, decision environments, green marketing, environmentalism, marketing research methodology.

New York Institute of Technology, Graduate Division, School of Management, Program in Human Resources Management and Labor Relations, Old Westbury, NY 11568-8000. Offers human resources administration (Advanced Certificate); human resources management and labor relations (MS); labor relations (Advanced Certificate). Part-time and evening/weekend programs available. *Students:* 21 full-time (13 women), 71 part-time (54 women); includes 24 minority (13 African Americans, 6 Asian Americans or Pacific Islanders, 5 Hispanic Americans), 19 international. Average age 31. In 2009, 32 master's awarded. *Degree requirements:* For master's, comprehensive exam, thesis optional. *Entrance requirements:* For master's, GRE, minimum QPA of 2.85, interview, 2 letters of recommendation. *Application deadline:* For fall admission, 7/1 priority date for domestic students; for spring admission, 12/1 priority date for domestic students. Applications are processed on a rolling basis. Application fee: $50. Electronic applications accepted. *Expenses:* Tuition: Part-time $825 per credit. *Financial support:* Fellowships, research assistantships, career-related internships or fieldwork, institutionally sponsored loans, and tuition waivers (full and partial) available. Support available to part-time students. Financial award applicants required to submit FAFSA. *Faculty research:* Ethics in industrial relations, employee relations, public sector labor relations, benefits. *Unit head:* William Ninehan, Director, 646-273-6071, Fax: 516-686-7425, E-mail: wninehan@nyit.edu. *Application contact:* Dr. Jacquelyn Nealon, Vice President for Enrollment Services, 516-686-7925, Fax: 516-686-7597, E-mail: jnealon@nyit.edu.

New York University, Robert F. Wagner Graduate School of Public Service, Program in Public Administration, New York, NY 10012-1019. Offers public administration (PhD); public and nonprofit management and policy (MPA, Advanced Certificate), including developmental administration (Advanced Certificate), financial management and public finance, human resources management (Advanced Certificate), international administration (Advanced Certificate), management (MPA), management for public and nonprofit organizations (Advanced Certificate), public policy analysis, quantitative analysis and computer applications (Advanced Certificate), urban public policy (Advanced Certificate); JD/MPA; MBA/MPA; MPA/MA. *Accreditation:* NASPAA (one or more programs are accredited). Part-time and evening/weekend programs available. *Faculty:* 31 full-time (13 women), 33 part-time/adjunct (16 women). *Students:* 363 full-time (270 women), 228 part-time (171 women); includes 146 minority (46 African Americans, 64 Asian Americans or Pacific Islanders, 36 Hispanic Americans), 76 international. Average age 28. 1,117 applicants, 57% accepted, 225 enrolled. In 2009, 236 master's, 3 doctorates awarded. *Degree requirements:* For master's, thesis or alternative, capstone end event; for doctorate, one foreign language, thesis/dissertation. *Entrance requirements:* For master's, minimum undergraduate GPA of 3.0; for doctorate, GMAT or GRE General Test, minimum GPA of 3.5. Additional exam requirements/recommendations for international students: Required—TOEFL (minimum score 600 paper-based; 250 computer-based; 100 iBT), TWE (minimum score 4). *Application deadline:* For fall admission, 6/1 for domestic students, 1/15 for international students; for spring admission, 11/15 for domestic students, 10/1 for international students. Applications are processed on a rolling basis. Application fee: $80. Electronic applications accepted. *Expenses:* Contact institution. *Financial support:* In 2009–10, 155 students received support, including 150 fellowships (averaging $11,335 per year), 5 research assistantships with full tuition reimbursements available (averaging $22,440 per year); career-related internships or fieldwork, Federal Work-Study, institutionally sponsored loans, scholarships/grants, health care benefits, and unspecified assistantships also available. Support available to part-time students. Financial award application deadline: 12/1; financial award applicants required to submit FAFSA. *Unit head:* Katty Jones, Director, Program Services, 212-998-7411, Fax: 212-995-4164, E-mail: katty.jones@nyu.edu. *Application contact:* Christopher Alexander, Administrative Aide, Enrollment, 212-998-7414, Fax: 212-995-4611, E-mail: wagner.admissions@nyu.edu.

New York University, School of Continuing and Professional Studies, Division of Programs in Business, Program in Leadership and Human Capital Management, New York, NY 10012-1019. Offers benefits and compensation (Advanced Certificate); human resource development (MS); human resource management (MS, Advanced Certificate); organizational and executive coaching (Advanced Certificate); organizational effectiveness (MS). Part-time and evening/weekend programs available. Postbaccalaureate distance learning degree programs offered (no on-campus study). *Faculty:* 37 part-time/adjunct (12 women). *Students:* 32 full-time (27 women), 224 part-time (190 women); includes 71 minority (27 African Americans, 2 American Indian/Alaska Native, 24 Asian Americans or Pacific Islanders, 18 Hispanic Americans). Average age 31. 166 applicants, 82% accepted, 78 enrolled. In 2009, 56 master's, 19 other advanced degrees awarded. *Entrance requirements:* For master's, GRE General Test or GMAT (for recent graduates), 2 letters of recommendation, resume. Additional exam requirements/recommendations for international students: Required—TOEFL (minimum score 600 paper-based; 250 computer-based; 100 iBT), TWE. *Application deadline:* For fall admission, 2/1 priority date for domestic and international students; for spring admission, 10/15 priority date for domestic students, 8/15 priority date for international students. Applications are processed on a rolling basis. Application fee: $75. Electronic applications accepted. *Expenses:* Tuition: Full-time $30,528; part-time $1272 per credit. Required fees: $2177. *Financial support:* In 2009–10, 115 students received support, including 115 fellowships (averaging $2,462 per year); career-related internships or fieldwork, institutionally sponsored loans, and scholarships/grants also available. Support available to part-time students. Financial award application deadline: 3/1; financial award applicants required to submit FAFSA. *Unit head:* Stephanie Bonadio, Head, 212-992-3632, Fax: 212-992-3650, E-mail: sgb259@nyu.edu. *Application contact:* Assistant Director, 212-992-3632, Fax: 212-992-3650, E-mail: scpshrmdstudent@nyu.edu.

North Greenville University, T. Walter Brashier Graduate School, Greer, SC 29651. Offers Christian ministry (MCM); human resources (MBA). Part-time and evening/weekend programs available. Postbaccalaureate distance learning degree programs offered (no on-campus study). *Faculty:* 4 full-time (1 woman), 16 part-time/adjunct (1 woman). *Students:* 69 full-time (29 women), 104 part-time (33 women); includes 30 minority (27 African Americans, 3 Hispanic Americans), 2 international. Average age 32. 180 applicants, 98% accepted, 173 enrolled. In 2009, 34 master's awarded. *Degree requirements:* For master's, comprehensive exam (for some programs), thesis or alternative, capstone course. *Entrance requirements:* For master's, GMAT, GRE, minimum GPA of 2.25 overall, 2.5 in major. Additional exam requirements/recommendations for international students: Required—TOEFL (minimum score 550 paper-based; 213 computer-based). *Application deadline:* For fall admission, 8/1 for domestic students, 6/1 for international students; for winter admission, 1/1 for domestic students, 10/1 for international students; for spring admission, 3/1 for domestic students, 1/1 for international students. Applications are processed on a rolling basis. Application fee: $30. Electronic applications accepted. *Financial support:* In 2009–10, 86 students received support. Federal Work-Study, institutionally sponsored loans, scholarships/grants, and tuition waivers (partial) available. Support available to part-time students. Financial award applicants required to submit FAFSA. *Faculty research:* Organizational behavior, church growth, homiletics, human resources, business strategy. *Unit head:* Dr. Joseph Samuel Isgett, Vice President for Graduate Studies, 864-877-3052, Fax: 864-877-1653, E-mail: sisgett@ngu.edu. *Application contact:* Tawana P. Scott, Director of Graduate Enrollment, 864-877-1598, Fax: 864-877-1653, E-mail: tscott@ngu.edu.

Notre Dame de Namur University, Division of Academic Affairs, School of Business and Management, Department of Business Administration, Belmont, CA 94002-1908. Offers business administration (MBA); finance (MBA); human resource management (MBA); marketing (MBA). Part-time and evening/weekend programs available. *Faculty:* 7 full-time (1 woman), 6 part-time/adjunct (0 women). *Students:* 21 full-time (17 women), 87 part-time (49 women); includes 47 minority (3 African Americans, 4 American Indian/Alaska Native, 21 Asian Americans or Pacific Islanders, 19 Hispanic Americans), 9 international. Average age 34. 27 applicants, 100% accepted, 20 enrolled. In 2009, 43 master's awarded. *Entrance requirements:* For master's, minimum GPA of 2.5. Additional exam requirements/recommendations for international students: Required—TOEFL (minimum score 550 paper-based; 213 computer-based; 79 iBT). *Application deadline:* For fall admission, 8/1 priority date for domestic students; for spring admission, 12/1 priority date for domestic students. Applications are processed on a rolling basis. Application fee: $60. Electronic applications accepted. *Expenses:* Tuition: Part-time $720 per credit. Required fees: $35 per semester hour. *Financial support:* Career-related internships or fieldwork available. Support available to part-time students. Financial award applicants required to submit FAFSA. *Unit head:* Henry Roth, Director, 650-508-3721, E-mail: hroth@ndnu.edu. *Application contact:* Candace Hallmark, Associate Director of Admissions, 650-508-3592, Fax: 650-508-3426, E-mail: grad.admit@ndnu.edu.

Notre Dame de Namur University, Division of Academic Affairs, School of Business and Management, Department of Public Administration, Belmont, CA 94002-1908. Offers human resource management (MPA); public administration (MPA); public affairs administration (MPA). Part-time and evening/weekend programs available. *Faculty:* 2 full-time (1 woman), 4 part-time/adjunct (2 women). *Students:* 2 full-time (both women), 30 part-time (25 women); includes 18 minority (2 African Americans, 1 Asian American or Pacific Islander, 15 Hispanic Americans), 1 international. Average age 31. 20 applicants, 100% accepted, 11 enrolled. In 2009, 7 master's awarded. *Entrance requirements:* For master's, interview, minimum GPA of 2.5. Additional exam requirements/recommendations for international students: Required—TOEFL (minimum score 550 paper-based; 213 computer-based; 79 iBT). *Application deadline:* For fall admission, 8/1 priority date for domestic students; for spring admission, 12/1 priority date for domestic students. Applications are processed on a rolling basis. Application fee: $60. Electronic applications accepted. *Expenses:* Tuition: Part-time $720 per credit. Required fees: $35 per semester hour. *Financial support:* Career-related internships or fieldwork available. Support available to part-time students. Financial award applicants required to submit FAFSA. *Unit head:* Henry Roth, Director, 650-508-3721, E-mail: hroth@ndnu.edu. *Application contact:* Candace Hallmark, Associate Director of Admissions, 650-508-3592, Fax: 650-508-3426, E-mail: grad.admit@ndnu.edu.

Nova Southeastern University, H. Wayne Huizenga School of Business and Entrepreneurship, Doctoral Program in Business Administration, Fort Lauderdale, FL 33314-7796. Offers accounting (DBA); decision sciences (DBA); finance (DBA); human resource management (DBA); international business (DBA); management (DBA); marketing (DBA). Part-time and evening/weekend programs available. *Faculty:* 34 full-time (11 women), 2 part-time/adjunct (1 woman). *Students:* 6 full-time (1 woman), 129 part-time (41 women); includes 33 minority (17 African Americans, 6 Asian Americans or Pacific Islanders, 10 Hispanic Americans), 12 international. Average age 47. 58 applicants, 14% accepted, 5 enrolled. In 2009, 32 doctorates awarded. *Degree requirements:* For doctorate, comprehensive exam, thesis/dissertation. *Entrance requirements:* For doctorate, GMAT. Additional exam requirements/recommendations for international students: Required—TOEFL (minimum score 600 paper-based; 250 computer-based; 100 iBT), IELTS (minimum score 7). *Application deadline:* Applications are processed on a rolling basis. Application fee: $50. Electronic applications accepted. *Financial support:* Available to part-time students. Applicants required to submit FAFSA. *Faculty research:* Reputation management, call centers, international social capital, corporate earnings guidance, corporate governance. *Unit head:* Kristie Tetrault, Director of Program Administration, 954-262-5120, Fax: 954-262-3849, E-mail: kristie@huizenga.nova.edu. *Application contact:* Karen Goldberg, Associate Director of Recruitment and Special Events, 954-262-5039, Fax: 954-262-3822, E-mail: karen@huizenga.nova.edu.

Nova Southeastern University, H. Wayne Huizenga School of Business and Entrepreneurship, Master's Program in Human Resources Management, Fort Lauderdale, FL 33314-7796. Offers MSHRM. Part-time and evening/weekend programs available. Postbaccalaureate distance learning degree programs offered (minimal on-campus study). *Faculty:* 12 part-time/adjunct (3 women). *Students:* 15 full-time (12 women), 310 part-time (263 women); includes 228 minority (137 African Americans, 10 Asian Americans or Pacific Islanders, 81 Hispanic Americans), 11 international. Average age 33. 129 applicants, 62% accepted, 60 enrolled. In 2009, 85 master's awarded. *Degree requirements:* For master's, thesis or alternative. *Entrance requirements:* Additional exam requirements/recommendations for international students: Required—TOEFL (minimum score 550 paper-based; 213 computer-based; 79 iBT), IELTS (minimum score 6). *Application deadline:* For fall admission, 8/15 for domestic and international students; for winter admission, 12/10 for domestic and international students; for spring admission, 2/10 for domestic and international students. Applications are processed on a rolling basis. Application fee: $50. Electronic applications accepted. *Financial support:* Federal Work-Study and scholarships/grants available. Support available to part-time students. Financial award applicants required to submit FAFSA. *Unit head:* Steve Harvey, Assistant Dean of Program Administration, 954-262-5047, Fax: 954-262-3829, E-mail: harvey@nsu.nova.edu. *Application contact:* Karen Goldberg, Associate Director of Recruitment and Special Events, 954-262-5039, Fax: 954-262-3822, E-mail: karen@nova.edu.

Oakland University, Graduate Study and Lifelong Learning, School of Business Administration, Department of Management and Marketing, Rochester, MI 48309-4401. Offers business administration (MBA); entrepreneurship (Certificate); general management (Certificate); human resource management (Certificate); international business (Certificate); marketing (Certificate).

The Ohio State University, Graduate School, Max M. Fisher College of Business, Program in Labor and Human Resources, Columbus, OH 43210. Offers MLHR, PhD. *Faculty:* 28. *Students:* 62 full-time (48 women), 39 part-time (34 women); includes 18 minority (6 African Americans, 1 American Indian/Alaska Native, 5 Asian Americans or Pacific Islanders, 6 Hispanic Americans),

Human Resources Management

The Ohio State University (continued)

14 international. Average age 28. In 2009, 44 master's, 1 doctorate awarded. *Degree requirements:* For master's, thesis optional; for doctorate, thesis/dissertation. *Entrance requirements:* For master's and doctorate, GRE General Test. Additional exam requirements/recommendations for international students: Recommended—TOEFL (minimum score 600 paper-based; 250 computer-based). *Application deadline:* For fall admission, 8/15 priority date for domestic students, 7/1 priority date for international students; for winter admission, 12/1 priority date for domestic students, 11/1 priority date for international students; for spring admission, 3/1 priority date for domestic students, 2/1 priority date for international students. Applications are processed on a rolling basis. Application fee: $40 ($50 for international students). Electronic applications accepted. *Expenses:* Tuition, state resident: full-time $10,683. Tuition, nonresident: full-time $25,923. Tuition and fees vary according to course load and program. *Financial support:* Fellowships, research assistantships, teaching assistantships, Federal Work-Study and institutionally sponsored loans available. Support available to part-time students. *Unit head:* Robert L. Heneman, Graduate Studies Committee Chair, 614-292-4587, Fax: 614-292-9006, E-mail: heneman.1@osu.edu. *Application contact:* 614-292-9444, Fax: 614-292-3895, E-mail: domestic.grad@osu.edu.

Ottawa University, Graduate Studies-Arizona, Programs in Business, Ottawa, KS 66067-3399. Offers business administration (MBA); finance (MBA); human resources (MA, MBA); leadership (MBA); marketing (MBA). Programs offered in Mesa, Phoenix, Tempe and West Valley, AZ. Part-time and evening/weekend programs available. Postbaccalaureate distance learning degree programs offered. *Degree requirements:* For master's, thesis or alternative. *Entrance requirements:* For master's, minimum undergraduate GPA of 3.0. Additional exam requirements/recommendations for international students: Required—TOEFL (minimum score 550 paper-based; 213 computer-based). Electronic applications accepted.

Penn State University Park, Graduate School, College of the Liberal Arts, Department of Labor Studies and Industrial Relations, State College, University Park, PA 16802-1503. Offers MPS, MS, Postbaccalaureate Certificate. Postbaccalaureate distance learning degree programs offered.

Polytechnic Institute of NYU, Department of Technology Management, Brooklyn, NY 11201-2990. Offers construction management (Advanced Certificate); electronic business management (Advanced Certificate); entrepreneurship (Advanced Certificate); human resources management (Advanced Certificate); information management (Advanced Certificate); management (MS); management of technology (MS); organizational behavior (MS, Advanced Certificate); project management (Advanced Certificate); technology management (MBA, PhD, Advanced Certificate); telecommunications and information management (MS); telecommunications management (Advanced Certificate). Part-time and evening/weekend programs available. *Faculty:* 5 full-time (1 woman), 26 part-time/adjunct (3 women). *Students:* 272 full-time (111 women), 103 part-time (41 women); includes 64 minority (20 African Americans, 1 American Indian/Alaska Native, 34 Asian Americans or Pacific Islanders, 9 Hispanic Americans), 193 international. Average age 30. 518 applicants, 57% accepted, 135 enrolled. In 2009, 148 master's awarded. *Degree requirements:* For master's, comprehensive exam (for some programs), thesis (for some programs); for doctorate, comprehensive exam, thesis/dissertation. *Entrance requirements:* For master's, GMAT, minimum B average in undergraduate course work. Additional exam requirements/recommendations for international students: Required—TOEFL (minimum score 550 paper-based; 213 computer-based; 80 iBT); Recommended—IELTS (minimum score 6.5). *Application deadline:* For fall admission, 7/31 priority date for domestic students, 4/30 priority date for international students; for spring admission, 12/31 priority date for domestic students, 11/30 priority date for international students. Applications are processed on a rolling basis. Application fee: $75. Electronic applications accepted. *Expenses:* Tuition: Full-time $21,492; part-time $1194 per credit hour. Required fees: $1160; $204 per course. *Financial support:* In 2009–10, 1 fellowship (averaging $26,400 per year) was awarded; research assistantships, teaching assistantships, institutionally sponsored loans, scholarships/grants, and unspecified assistantships also available. Support available to part-time students. *Unit head:* Prof. Bharadwaj Rao, Head, 718-260-3617, Fax: 718-260-3874, E-mail: brao@poly.edu. *Application contact:* JeanCarlo Bonilla, Director of Graduate Enrollment Management, 718-260-3182, Fax: 718-260-3624, E-mail: gradinfo@poly.edu.

Pontifical Catholic University of Puerto Rico, College of Business Administration, Program in Human Resources, Ponce, PR 00717-0777. Offers MBA. Part-time and evening/weekend programs available. *Degree requirements:* For master's, thesis. *Entrance requirements:* For master's, GRE, interview, minimum GPA of 2.75.

Pontificia Universidad Catolica Madre y Maestra, Graduate School, Santiago, Dominican Republic. Offers administration (M Adm); architecture of interiors (M Arch); architecture of tourist lodgings (M Arch); banking and financial management (M Mgmt); civil law (LL M); construction administration (ME); corporate business law (LL M); criminal procedure law (LL M); environmental engineering (ME, MEE); finance (M Mgmt); history applied to education (M Ed); human resources (EMBA); insurance (M Mgmt); international business (M Mgmt); labor law and Social Security (LL M); logistics management (ME); marketing (M Mgmt); renewable energy (ME); strategic cost management (M Mgmt). *Entrance requirements:* For master's, curriculum vitae, interview.

Portland State University, Graduate Studies, School of Business Administration, Program in Human Resource Management, Portland, OR 97207-0751. Offers MBA. Part-time and evening/weekend programs available. *Degree requirements:* For master's, one foreign language, project. *Entrance requirements:* For master's, GMAT, minimum GPA of 3.0 in upper-division course work, 2 recommendations, resume, interview. Additional exam requirements/recommendations for international students: Required—TOEFL (minimum score 550 paper-based; 213 computer-based). *Faculty research:* Quality management and organizational excellence, performance measurement, customer satisfaction, values, technology management and technology transfer.

Purdue University, Graduate School, Krannert School of Management, Doctoral Program in Organizational Behavior and Human Resource Management, West Lafayette, IN 47907-2056. Offers PhD. *Students:* 7 full-time (2 women); includes 1 African American, 2 American Indian/Alaska Native. Average age 34. 101 applicants, 4% accepted, 2 enrolled. In 2009, 2 doctorates awarded. *Degree requirements:* For doctorate, comprehensive exam, thesis/dissertation, dissertation proposal. *Entrance requirements:* For doctorate, GMAT or GRE, bachelor's degree, two semesters of calculus, one semester each of linear algebra and statistics. Additional exam requirements/recommendations for international students: Required—TOEFL (minimum score 575 paper-based; 233 computer-based); Recommended—TWE. *Application deadline:* For fall admission, 1/15 priority date for domestic and international students. Application fee: $55. *Financial support:* In 2009–10, fellowships with full tuition reimbursements (averaging $25,000 per year), research assistantships with partial tuition reimbursements (averaging $18,000 per year), teaching assistantships with partial tuition reimbursements (averaging $18,000 per year) were awarded; scholarships/grants, health care benefits, tuition waivers (full and partial), unspecified assistantships, and travel funds to present at a major conference also available. Support available to part-time students. Financial award application deadline: 1/15. *Faculty research:* Human research management, organizational behavior. *Unit head:* Dr. R. A. Cosier, Dean, 765-494-4366. *Application contact:* Krannert PhD Admissions, 765-494-4375, Fax: 765-494-0136, E-mail: krannertphd@purdue.edu.

Purdue University, Graduate School, Krannert School of Management, Master of Science in Human Resource Management Program, West Lafayette, IN 47907. Offers MSHRM. *Faculty:* 102 full-time (29 women), 16 part-time/adjunct (1 woman). *Students:* 42 full-time (30 women); includes 13 minority (8 African Americans, 2 Asian Americans or Pacific Islanders, 3 Hispanic Americans), 15 international. Average age 26. 180 applicants, 33% accepted, 17 enrolled. In 2009, 26 master's awarded. *Entrance requirements:* For master's, GMAT or GRE, essays, recommendation letters, work experience/internship, minimum GPA of 3.0, four-year baccalaureate degree. Additional exam requirements/recommendations for international students: Required—TOEFL (minimum score 550 paper-based; 213 computer-based; 77 iBT). *Application deadline:* For fall admission, 1/10 priority date for domestic students, 2/1 for international students. Applications are processed on a rolling basis. Application fee: $55. Electronic applications accepted. *Financial support:* In 2009–10, 11 students received support, including 9 research assistantships, 2 teaching assistantships; scholarships/grants and unspecified assistantships also available. Financial award application deadline: 2/1; financial award applicants required to submit FAFSA. *Unit head:* Dr. R. A. Cosier, Dean, 765-494-4366. *Application contact:* Brenda Knebel, Director, Master's and Executive Admissions, 765-494-0773, Fax: 765-494-9841, E-mail: krannertmasters@purdue.edu.

Quincy University, Program in Business Administration, Quincy, IL 62301-2699. Offers business administration (MBA); human resource management (MBA). Part-time and evening/weekend programs available. *Faculty:* 4 full-time (3 women). *Students:* 4 full-time (2 women), 26 part-time (7 women); includes 1 African American, 1 Hispanic American. In 2009, 24 master's awarded. *Entrance requirements:* For master's, GMAT, previous course work in accounting, economics, finance, management, marketing, and statistics. Additional exam requirements/recommendations for international students: Required—TOEFL. *Application deadline:* Applications are processed on a rolling basis. Application fee: $25. Electronic applications accepted. *Expenses:* Contact institution. *Financial support:* Available to part-time students. Applicants required to submit FAFSA. *Faculty research:* Macroeconomic forecasting, business ethics/social responsibility. *Unit head:* Dr. John Palmer, Director, 217-228-5432 Ext. 3070, E-mail: palmejo@quincy.edu. *Application contact:* Jennifer O'Donnell, Coordinator of Adult Studies, 217-228-5404, Fax: 217-228-5479, E-mail: admissions@quincy.edu.

Regent's American College London, Webster Graduate School, London, United Kingdom. Offers business (MBA); finance (MS); human resources (MA); information technology management (MA); international business (MA); international non-governmental organizations (MA); international relations (MA); management and leadership (MA); marketing (MA). Part-time programs available.

Regis University, College for Professional Studies, School of Management, Denver, CO 80221-1099. Offers accounting (MS); business administration (MBA); computer information technology (MSOL); executive internal management (Certificate); executive leadership (Certificate); finance (MBA); finance and accounting (MBA); human resource management (MSOL); international business (MBA); marketing (MBA); operations management (MBA); organization leadership (MS); organizational leadership (MSOL); project leadership and management (MSOL, Certificate); project management (Certificate); strategic business (Certificate); strategic human resource (Certificate); technical management (Certificate). Offered at Colorado Springs Campus, Northwest Denver Campus, Southeast Denver Campus, Fort Collins Campus, Broomfield Campus, Henderson (Nevada) Campus, and Summerlin (Nevada) Campus and online. Part-time and evening/weekend programs available. Postbaccalaureate distance learning degree programs offered (no on-campus study). *Degree requirements:* For master's, thesis optional, capstone project. *Entrance requirements:* For master's, GMAT or essays, interview, 2 years of full-time business work experience, resume; for Certificate, GMAT. Additional exam requirements/recommendations for international students: Required—TOEFL, TOEFL or university-based test; Recommended—TWE (minimum score 5). Electronic applications accepted. *Faculty research:* Impact of Info Technology on Small Business Regulation of Accounting, International Project financing, Mineral Development, Delivery of Healthcare to rural indigenos communities.

Robert Morris University, Graduate Studies, School of Business, Moon Township, PA 15108-1189. Offers business administration and management (MBA); human resource management (MS); nonprofit management (MS); taxation (MS). *Accreditation:* AACSB. Part-time and evening/weekend programs available. *Faculty:* 29 full-time (11 women), 3 part-time/adjunct (0 women). *Students:* 209 part-time (97 women); includes 11 minority (9 African Americans, 1 Asian American or Pacific Islander, 1 Hispanic American), 4 international. Average age 31. 126 applicants, 70% accepted, 54 enrolled. In 2009, 85 master's awarded. *Entrance requirements:* For master's, GMAT, letters of recommendation. Additional exam requirements/recommendations for international students: Required—TOEFL (minimum score 550 paper-based; 213 computer-based; 79 iBT). *Application deadline:* For fall admission, 7/1 priority date for domestic and international students; for spring admission, 11/1 priority date for domestic and international students. Applications are processed on a rolling basis. Application fee: $35. Electronic applications accepted. *Expenses:* Tuition: Part-time $765 per credit. Required fees: $15 per credit. Full-time tuition and fees vary according to degree level. Part-time tuition and fees vary according to program. *Financial support:* Research assistantships with partial tuition reimbursements, Federal Work-Study, institutionally sponsored loans, and unspecified assistantships available. Support available to part-time students. Financial award application deadline: 5/1; financial award applicants required to submit FAFSA. *Unit head:* Dr. Derya A. Jacobs, Dean, 412-397-2191, Fax: 412-397-2585, E-mail: jacobs@rmu.edu. *Application contact:* Deborah Roach, Assistant Dean, Graduate Admissions, 412-397-5200, Fax: 412-397-2425, E-mail: graduateadmissions@rmu.edu.

Robert Morris University Illinois, Morris Graduate School of Management, Chicago, IL 60605. Offers accounting (MBA); accounting/finance (MBA); human resource management (MBA); information technology (MIS); leadership (MBA); management/finance (MIS); management/human resource management (MBA). Part-time and evening/weekend programs available. *Faculty:* 16 full-time (6 women), 25 part-time/adjunct (9 women). *Students:* 275 full-time (169 women), 194 part-time (134 women); includes 267 minority (176 African Americans, 1 American Indian/Alaska Native, 26 Asian Americans or Pacific Islanders, 64 Hispanic Americans), 17 international. Average age 32. 202 applicants, 84% accepted, 135 enrolled. In 2009, 161 master's awarded. *Degree requirements:* For master's, 44 residency hours. *Entrance requirements:* Additional exam requirements/recommendations for international students: Required—TOEFL (minimum score 500 paper-based; 173 computer-based). *Application deadline:* Applications are processed on a rolling basis. Application fee: $30 ($100 for international students). Electronic applications accepted. *Expenses:* Tuition: Full-time $18,000; part-time $2000 per course. *Financial support:* In 2009–10, 420 students received support. Federal Work-Study, scholarships/grants, and tuition waivers available. Support available to part-time students. *Unit head:* Kayed Akkawi, Dean, 312-935-4244, Fax: 312-935-4248, E-mail: kakkawi@robertmorris.edu. *Application contact:* Courtney A. Kohn Sanders, Dean of Graduate Admissions, 312-935-4240, Fax: 312-935-4248, E-mail: ckohn@robertmorris.edu.

Rollins College, Hamilton Holt School, Program in Human Resources, Winter Park, FL 32789-4499. Offers MA. Part-time and evening/weekend programs available. *Faculty:* 6 full-time (0 women), 1 part-time/adjunct (0 women). *Students:* 53 part-time (42 women); includes 21 minority (9 African Americans, 2 Asian Americans or Pacific Islanders, 10 Hispanic Americans), 1 international. Average age 32. 122 applicants, 53% accepted, 41 enrolled. In 2009, 25 master's awarded. *Degree requirements:* For master's, thesis optional. *Entrance requirements:* For master's, GMAT, GRE, or MAT, interview. Additional exam requirements/recommendations for international students: Required—TOEFL. *Application deadline:* For fall admission, 4/1 for domestic students; for winter admission, 12/1 for domestic students. Applications are processed on a rolling basis. Application fee: $50. *Expenses:* Contact institution. *Financial support:* Available to part-time students. *Unit head:* Dr. Donald Rogers, Director, 407-646-2348, E-mail: drogers@rollins.edu. *Application contact:* Christian Ricaurte, Coordinator of Records and Registration, 407-646-2653, Fax: 407-646-1551, E-mail: cricaurte@rollins.edu.

Roosevelt University, Graduate Division, Walter E. Heller College of Business Administration, Program in Human Resource Management, Chicago, IL 60605. Offers MSHRM.

Royal Roads University, Graduate Studies, Applied Leadership and Management Program, Victoria, BC V9B 5Y2, Canada. Offers executive coaching (Graduate Certificate); health systems leadership (Graduate Certificate); project management (Graduate Certificate); public relations management (Graduate Certificate); strategic human resources management (Graduate Certificate).

Royal Roads University, Graduate Studies, Faculty of Management, Victoria, BC V9B 5Y2, Canada. Offers digital technologies management (MBA); executive management (MBA), including global aviation management, knowledge management, leadership; human resources management (MBA). Postbaccalaureate distance learning degree programs offered (minimal on-campus study). *Degree requirements:* For master's, thesis. *Entrance requirements:* For master's, 5-7 years of related work experience. Additional exam requirements/recommendations for international students: Required—TOEFL (paper-based 570; computer-based 233) or IELTS (paper-based 7) (recommended). Electronic applications accepted. *Expenses:* Contact institution. *Faculty research:* Global venture analysis standards; computer assisted venture opportunity screening; teaching philosophies, instructions and methods.

Rutgers, The State University of New Jersey, Newark, Graduate School, Program in Public Administration, Newark, NJ 07102. Offers health care administration (MPA); human resources administration (MPA); public administration (PhD); public management (MPA); public policy analysis (MPA); urban systems and issues (MPA). *Accreditation:* NASPAA (one or more programs are accredited). Part-time and evening/weekend programs available. *Degree requirements:* For master's, comprehensive exam, thesis or alternative; for doctorate, thesis/dissertation. *Entrance requirements:* For master's, GRE, minimum undergraduate B average; for doctorate, GRE, MPA, minimum B average. Electronic applications accepted. *Faculty research:* Government finance, municipal and state government, public productivity.

Rutgers, The State University of New Jersey, New Brunswick, School of Management and Labor Relations, Program in Human Resource Management, Piscataway, NJ 08854-8097. Offers MHRM. Part-time and evening/weekend programs available. *Entrance requirements:* For master's, GMAT or GRE General Test, 3 letters of recommendation. Additional exam requirements/recommendations for international students: Required—TOEFL (minimum score 575 paper-based; 233 computer-based). Electronic applications accepted. *Expenses:* Contact institution. *Faculty research:* Human resource policy and planning, employee ownership and profit sharing, compensation and appraisal of performance, law and public policy, computers and decision making.

See Close-Up on page 429.

Rutgers, The State University of New Jersey, New Brunswick, School of Management and Labor Relations, Program in Industrial Relations and Human Resources, Piscataway, NJ 08854-8097. Offers PhD. Part-time programs available. *Degree requirements:* For doctorate, comprehensive exam, thesis/dissertation. *Entrance requirements:* For doctorate, GRE. Additional exam requirements/recommendations for international students: Required—TOEFL (minimum score 575 paper-based; 233 computer-based; 91 iBT). Electronic applications accepted. *Faculty research:* Strategic human resources, labor relations, organizational change, worker representation.

See Close-Up on page 429.

Sage Graduate School, Graduate School, School of Management, Program in Business Administration, Troy, NY 12180-4115. Offers business strategy (MBA); finance (MBA); human resources (MBA); marketing (MBA); JD/MBA. Part-time and evening/weekend programs available. *Faculty:* 4 full-time (2 women), 6 part-time/adjunct (0 women). *Students:* 9 full-time (7 women), 68 part-time (44 women); includes 11 minority (5 African Americans, 2 Asian Americans or Pacific Islanders, 4 Hispanic Americans), 2 international. Average age 31. 50 applicants, 60% accepted, 17 enrolled. In 2009, 19 master's awarded. *Entrance requirements:* For master's, minimum GPA of 2.75, resume, 2 letters of recommendation. Additional exam requirements/recommendations for international students: Required—TOEFL (minimum score 550 paper-based; 213 computer-based). *Application deadline:* Applications are processed on a rolling basis. Application fee: $40. *Expenses:* Tuition: Full-time $10,620; part-time $590 per credit hour. *Financial support:* Fellowships, research assistantships, Federal Work-Study, scholarships/grants, and unspecified assistantships available. Support available to part-time students. Financial award application deadline: 3/1; financial award applicants required to submit FAFSA. *Unit head:* Daniel Robeson, Chair, Management Department, 518-292-1770, Fax: 518-292-5414, E-mail: robesd@sage.edu. *Application contact:* Wendy D. Diefendorf, Director of Graduate and Adult Admission, 518-244-2443, Fax: 518-244-6880, E-mail: diefew@sage.edu.

St. Ambrose University, College of Business, Program in Business Administration, Davenport, IA 52803-2898. Offers business administration (DBA); health care (MBA); human resources (MBA). *Accreditation:* ACBSP. Part-time and evening/weekend programs available. *Faculty:* 19 full-time (4 women), 8 part-time/adjunct (3 women). *Students:* 29 full-time (11 women), 279 part-time (146 women); includes 16 minority (6 African Americans, 3 Asian Americans or Pacific Islanders, 7 Hispanic Americans). Average age 36. 95 applicants, 86% accepted, 82 enrolled. In 2009, 146 master's, 3 doctorates awarded. *Degree requirements:* For master's, comprehensive exam (for some programs), thesis or alternative, capstone seminar; for doctorate, comprehensive exam, thesis/dissertation, oral and written exams. *Entrance requirements:* For master's, GMAT; for doctorate, GMAT, master's degree. Additional exam requirements/recommendations for international students: Required—TOEFL. *Application deadline:* For fall admission, 8/15 priority date for domestic students; for winter admission, 12/15 for domestic students; for spring admission, 1/1 for domestic students. Applications are processed on a rolling basis. Application fee: $25. Electronic applications accepted. *Expenses:* Contact institution. *Financial support:* In 2009–10, 48 students received support, including 5 research assistantships with partial tuition reimbursements available (averaging $3,600 per year); career-related internships or fieldwork, scholarships/grants, tuition waivers (partial), and unspecified assistantships also available. Financial award application deadline: 3/15; financial award applicants required to submit FAFSA. *Unit head:* Joseph L. Kehoe, Director of MBA, 563-322-1142, Fax: 563-333-6268, E-mail: kehoejosephl@sau.edu. *Application contact:* Erin E. Leifker, Assistant MBA Director, 563-322-1165, Fax: 563-333-6268, E-mail: leifkererine@sau.edu.

St. Edward's University, School of Management and Business, Area of Business Administration, Austin, TX 78704. Offers accounting (MBA); business management (MBA); corporate finance (MBA, Certificate); global entrepreneurship (MBA); human resource management (MBA, Certificate); management information systems (MBA, Certificate); marketing (MBA, Certificate); operations management (MBA, Certificate). Part-time and evening/weekend programs available. *Faculty:* 20 full-time (9 women), 13 part-time/adjunct (4 women). *Students:* 29 full-time (16 women), 307 part-time (152 women); includes 116 minority (27 African Americans, 1 American Indian/Alaska Native, 16 Asian Americans or Pacific Islanders, 72 Hispanic Americans), 9 international. Average age 33. 129 applicants, 75% accepted, 74 enrolled. In 2009, 108 master's awarded. *Degree requirements:* For master's, minimum of 24 resident hours. *Entrance requirements:* For master's, GMAT or GRE General Test, minimum GPA of 2.75 in last 60 hours of course work. Additional exam requirements/recommendations for international students: Required—TOEFL (minimum score 550 paper-based; 213 computer-based; 79 iBT) or IELTS (minimum score 6). *Application deadline:* For fall admission, 7/1 for domestic and international students; for spring admission, 11/1 for domestic and international students. Applications are processed on a rolling basis. Application fee: $45 ($50 for international students). Electronic applications accepted. *Expenses:* Tuition: Full-time $14,922; part-time $829 per credit hour. Required fees: $50 per trimester. Full-time tuition and fees vary according to course load and program. *Financial support:* In 2009–10, 14 students received support. Scholarships/grants available. *Faculty research:* Operations management, minority entrepreneurship, globalization, professional services marketing. *Unit head:* Dr. Dianne Hill, Director, 512-428-1295, Fax: 512-448-8492,, E-mail: dianneh@stedwards.edu. *Application contact:* Kelly Luna, Graduate Admissions Coordinator, 512-233-1697, Fax: 512-428-1032, E-mail: kellyl@stedwards.edu.

St. Edward's University, School of Management and Business, Program in Human Services, Austin, TX 78704. Offers administration (Certificate); conflict resolution (Certificate); family mediation (Certificate); human services (MA), including administration, conflict resolution, human resource management, organization development and training, social and psychological services; mediation (Certificate); organization development and training (Certificate). Part-time and evening/weekend programs available. *Students:* 4 full-time (3 women), 51 part-time (43 women); includes 24 minority (9 African Americans, 2 Asian Americans or Pacific Islanders, 13 Hispanic Americans). Average age 34. 23 applicants, 96% accepted, 18 enrolled. In 2009, 19 master's awarded. *Degree requirements:* For master's, minimum of 24 resident hours. *Entrance requirements:* For master's, GRE General Test, GMAT, minimum GPA of 2.75 in last 60 hours of course work. Additional exam requirements/recommendations for international students: Required—TOEFL (minimum score 550 paper-based; 213 computer-based; 79 iBT) or IELTS (minimum score 6). *Application deadline:* For fall admission, 7/1 for domestic and international students; for spring admission, 11/1 for domestic and international students. Applications are processed on a rolling basis. Application fee: $45 ($50 for international students). Electronic applications accepted. *Expenses:* Tuition: Full-time $14,922; part-time $829 per credit hour. Required fees: $50 per trimester. Full-time tuition and fees vary according to course load and program. *Financial support:* In 2009–10, 2 students received support. Scholarships/grants available. *Faculty research:* Leadership development, organizational management, public policy. *Unit head:* Dr. Constance D. Porter, Director, 512-416-5827, Fax: 512-448-8492, E-mail: constanp@stedwards.edu. *Application contact:* Kay L. Arnold, Assistant Director of Admissions, 512-233-1636, Fax: 512-428-1032, E-mail: kayla@stedwards.edu.

Saint Francis University, Graduate School of Business and Human Resource Management, Loretto, PA 15940-0600. Offers business administration (MBA); human resource management (MHRM). Part-time and evening/weekend programs available. *Faculty:* 8 full-time (2 women), 25 part-time/adjunct (12 women). *Students:* 16 full-time (8 women), 141 part-time (66 women); includes 2 minority (both African Americans). Average age 32. 40 applicants, 88% accepted, 25 enrolled. In 2009, 67 master's awarded. *Entrance requirements:* For master's, 2 letters of recommendation, minimum GPA of 2.75. Additional exam requirements/recommendations for international students: Required—TOEFL (minimum score 550 paper-based; 213 computer-based; 57 iBT). *Application deadline:* For fall admission, 8/1 priority date for domestic and international students; for spring admission, 12/1 priority date for domestic students, 12/1 for international students. Applications are processed on a rolling basis. Application fee: $30. *Expenses:* Contact institution. *Financial support:* Fellowships with partial tuition reimbursements, career-related internships or fieldwork and unspecified assistantships available. *Unit head:* Dr. Randy Frye, Director, 814-472-3041, Fax: 814-472-3174, E-mail: rfrye@francis.edu. *Application contact:* Dr. Peter Raymond Skoner, Associate Vice President for Academic Affairs, 814-472-3085, Fax: 814-472-3365, E-mail: pskoner@francis.edu.

St. Joseph's College, Long Island Campus, Program in Management, Patchogue, NY 11772-2399. Offers health care (AC); health care management (MS); human resource management (AC); human resources management (MS); organizational management (MS).

Saint Joseph's University, Erivan K. Haub School of Business, MS Program in Human Resources Management, Philadelphia, PA 19131-1395. Offers human resource management (MS). Part-time and evening/weekend programs available. *Students:* 39 part-time (30 women); includes 8 minority (7 African Americans, 1 Hispanic American). Average age 32. In 2009, 4 master's awarded. *Entrance requirements:* For master's, MAT, GRE, or GMAT, 2 letters of recommendation, resume, essay. Additional exam requirements/recommendations for international students: Required—TOEFL (minimum score 550 paper-based; 213 computer-based; 79 iBT) or IELTS (minimum score 6.5). *Application deadline:* For fall admission, 7/15 priority date for domestic students, 5/15 priority date for international students; for spring admission, 11/15 priority date for domestic students, 10/15 priority date for international students. Applications are processed on a rolling basis. Application fee: $35. Electronic applications accepted. *Expenses:* Tuition: Part-time $729 per credit hour. Tuition and fees vary according to degree level and program. *Financial support:* Unspecified assistantships available. Financial award application deadline: 5/1. *Unit head:* Patricia Rafferty, Director, MS in Business Intelligence and MS in Human Resource Management Programs, 610-660-1318, Fax: 610-660-1229, E-mail: patricia.rafferty@sju.edu. *Application contact:* Patricia Rafferty, Director, MS in Business Intelligence and MS in Human Resource Management Programs, 610-660-1318, Fax: 610-660-1229, E-mail: patricia.rafferty@sju.edu.

Saint Joseph's University, Erivan K. Haub School of Business, Professional MBA Program, Philadelphia, PA 19131-1395. Offers accounting (MBA); finance (MBA), including finance; general business (MBA); health and medical services administration (MBA); human resource management (MBA); international business (MBA); international marketing (MBA); management (MBA); marketing (MBA); DO/MBA. Part-time and evening/weekend programs available. *Students:* 51 full-time (24 women), 480 part-time (184 women); includes 71 minority (32 African Americans, 1 American Indian/Alaska Native, 30 Asian Americans or Pacific Islanders, 8 Hispanic Americans), 38 international. Average age 30. In 2009, 190 master's awarded. *Entrance requirements:* For master's, GMAT or GRE, 2 letters of recommendation, resume. Additional exam requirements/recommendations for international students: Required—TOEFL (minimum score 550 paper-based; 213 computer-based; 79 iBT) or IELTS (minimum score 6.5). *Application deadline:* For fall admission, 7/15 priority date for domestic students, 4/15 priority date for international students; for spring admission, 11/15 priority date for domestic students, 10/15 priority date for international students. Applications are processed on a rolling basis. Application fee: $35. Electronic applications accepted. *Expenses:* Tuition: Part-time $729 per credit hour. Tuition and fees vary according to degree level and program. *Financial support:* Scholarships/grants and unspecified assistantships available. Financial award application deadline: 5/1. *Unit head:* Adele C. Foley, Associate Dean/Director, Graduate Business Programs, 610-660-1691, Fax: 610-660-1599, E-mail: afoley@sju.edu. *Application contact:* Janine N. Guerra, Esq., Assistant Director, MBA Program, 610-660-1695, Fax: 610-660-1599, E-mail: jguerra@sju.edu.

Saint Leo University, Graduate Business Studies, Saint Leo, FL 33574-6665. Offers accounting (MBA); business (MBA); criminal justice (MBA); health services management (MBA); human resource administration (MBA); information security management (MBA); marketing (MBA); sport business (MBA). Part-time and evening/weekend programs available. Postbaccalaureate distance learning degree programs offered (no on-campus study). *Faculty:* 31 full-time (5 women), 48 part-time/adjunct (17 women). *Students:* 1,433 full-time (856 women), 3 part-time (1 woman); includes 601 minority (429 African Americans, 8 American Indian/Alaska Native, 75 Asian Americans or Pacific Islanders, 89 Hispanic Americans), 11 international. Average age 37. In 2009, 405 master's awarded. *Entrance requirements:* For master's, GMAT (minimum score 500 if applicant does not have 5 years of professional work experience), bachelor's degree from regionally-accredited college or university with minimum GPA of 3.0 in the last 60 hours of coursework; 5 years of professional work experience; resume; 2 letters of recommendation. Additional exam requirements/recommendations for international students: Required—TOEFL (minimum score 550 paper-based; 213 computer-based; 80 iBT). *Application deadline:* For fall admission, 7/1 priority date for domestic students; for spring admission, 11/12 priority date for domestic students. Applications are processed on a rolling basis. Application fee: $75. Electronic applications accepted. *Expenses:* Contact institution. *Financial support:* In 2009–10, 1 student received support. Career-related internships or fieldwork, Federal Work-Study, and health care benefits available. Financial award application deadline: 3/1; financial award applicants required to submit FAFSA. *Unit head:* Dr. Robert Robertson, Director, 352-588-7390, Fax: 352-588-8585, E-mail: mba@saintleo.edu. *Application contact:* Jared Welling, Director, Graduate/Weekend and Evening Admission, 800-707-8846, Fax: 352-588-7873, E-mail: grad.admissions@saintleo.edu.

Saint Mary's University of Minnesota, Schools of Graduate and Professional Programs, Graduate School of Business and Technology, Human Resource Management Program, Winona, MN 55987-1399. Offers MA. *Unit head:* Janet Dunn, Director, 612-238-4546, E-mail: jdunn@smumn.edu. *Application contact:* Yasin Alsaidi, Director of Admissions for Graduate and Professional Programs, 612-728-5207, Fax: 612-728-5121, E-mail: yalsaidi@smumn.edu.

St. Thomas University, School of Business, Department of Management, Miami Gardens, FL 33054-6459. Offers accounting (MBA); general management (MSM, Certificate); health management (MBA, MSM, Certificate); human resource management (MBA, MSM, Certificate); international business (MBA, MIB, MSM, Certificate); justice administration (MSM, Certificate); management accounting (MSM, Certificate); public management (MSM, Certificate); sports administration (MS). Part-time and evening/weekend programs available. *Degree requirements:* For master's, comprehensive exam. *Entrance requirements:* For master's, interview, minimum

Human Resources Management

St. Thomas University (continued)
GPA of 3.0 or GMAT. Additional exam requirements/recommendations for international students: Required—TOEFL (minimum score 550 paper-based; 213 computer-based; 79 iBT). Electronic applications accepted.

Salve Regina University, Graduate Studies, Program in Business Administration, Newport, RI 02840-4192. Offers business administration (MBA); business studies (Certificate); human resources management (Certificate); management (Certificate); organizational development (Certificate). Part-time and evening/weekend programs available. Postbaccalaureate distance learning degree programs offered (minimal on-campus study). *Faculty:* 4 full-time (2 women), 13 part-time/adjunct (4 women). *Students:* 39 full-time (17 women), 89 part-time (39 women); includes 10 minority (5 African Americans, 3 Asian Americans or Pacific Islanders, 2 Hispanic Americans), 3 international. Average age 33. 62 applicants, 82% accepted, 45 enrolled. In 2009, 50 master's awarded. *Entrance requirements:* For master's, GMAT, GRE General Test, or MAT, 6 undergraduate credits each in accounting, economics, quantitative analysis and calculus or statistics. Additional exam requirements/recommendations for international students: Required—TOEFL (minimum score 600 paper-based; 250 computer-based; 100 iBT), or IELTS. *Application deadline:* For fall admission, 3/15 priority date for domestic and international students; for spring admission, 9/15 priority date for domestic and international students. Applications are processed on a rolling basis. Application fee: $60. Electronic applications accepted. *Expenses:* Tuition: Part-time $395 per credit. Part-time tuition and fees vary according to degree level. *Financial support:* Career-related internships or fieldwork and Federal Work-Study available. Support available to part-time students. Financial award application deadline: 3/1; financial award applicants required to submit FAFSA. *Unit head:* Dr. Myra Edelstein, Director, 401-341-3139, E-mail: edelstem@salve.edu. *Application contact:* Kelly Alverson, Graduate Admissions Counselor, 401-341-2153, Fax: 401-341-2973, E-mail: kelly.alverson@salve.edu.

San Diego State University, Graduate and Research Affairs, College of Business Administration, Department of Management, San Diego, CA 92182. Offers entrepreneurship (MS); human resources management (MS); management science (MS). Part-time and evening/weekend programs available. *Degree requirements:* For master's, thesis or alternative. *Entrance requirements:* For master's, GMAT, resume, letters of reference. Additional exam requirements/recommendations for international students: Required—TOEFL. Electronic applications accepted.

Southern New Hampshire University, School of Business, Manchester, NH 03106-1045. Offers accounting (MS); business administration (MBA, Certificate), including accounting (Certificate), business administration (MBA), finance (Certificate), forensic accounting (Certificate), human resources management (Certificate), international business (Certificate), international sport management (Certificate), leadership of not for profit organizations (Certificate), marketing (Certificate), operations management (Certificate), sport management (Certificate), taxation (Certificate); finance (MS); hospitality and tourism leadership (Certificate); information technology (MS, Certificate); information technology/international business (Certificate); integrated marketing communications (Certificate); international business (MS, DBA); marketing (MS); operations and project management (MS); organizational leadership (MS); project management (Certificate); sport management (MS); MBA/Certificate. *Accreditation:* ACBSP. Part-time and evening/weekend programs available. Postbaccalaureate distance learning degree programs offered (no on-campus study). Terminal master's awarded for partial completion of doctoral program. *Degree requirements:* For master's, one foreign language, comprehensive exam (for some programs), thesis or alternative; for doctorate, one foreign language, comprehensive exam, thesis/dissertation. *Entrance requirements:* For master's, minimum GPA of 2.5; for doctorate, GMAT. Additional exam requirements/recommendations for international students: Required—TOEFL (minimum score 500 paper-based). Electronic applications accepted.

Stevens Institute of Technology, Graduate School, Wesley J. Howe School of Technology Management, Program in Management, Hoboken, NJ 07030. Offers general management (MS); global innovation management (MS); human resource management (MS); information management (MS); project management (MS); technology commercialization (MS); technology management (MS). Part-time programs available. *Degree requirements:* For master's, thesis optional. *Entrance requirements:* For master's, GMAT, GRE General Test. Additional exam requirements/recommendations for international students: Required—TOEFL. Electronic applications accepted. *Expenses:* Tuition: Full-time $9900; part-time $1100 per credit. Required fees: $286 per semester. *Faculty research:* Industrial economics.

Stony Brook University, State University of New York, Graduate School, College of Business, Program in Business Administration, Stony Brook, NY 11794. Offers finance (MBA, Certificate); health care management (MBA, Certificate); human resource management (Certificate); human resources (MBA); information systems management (MBA, Certificate); management (MBA); marketing (MBA). *Faculty:* 17 full-time (2 women), 25 part-time/adjunct (5 women). *Students:* 134 full-time (64 women), 112 part-time (44 women); includes 54 minority (8 African Americans, 1 American Indian/Alaska Native, 35 Asian Americans or Pacific Islanders, 10 Hispanic Americans), 56 international. 222 applicants, 55% accepted. In 2009, 134 master's, 5 other advanced degrees awarded. Application fee: $60. *Expenses:* Tuition, state resident: full-time $8370; part-time $349 per credit. Tuition, nonresident: full-time $13,250; part-time $552 per credit. Required fees: $933. *Financial support:* In 2009–10, 2 teaching assistantships were awarded. *Unit head:* Joseph McDonnell, Interim Dean, 631-632-7180. *Application contact:* Dr. Aristotle Lekacos, Director, Graduate Program, 631-632-7171, E-mail: aristotle.lekacost@notes.cc.sunysb.edu.

Stony Brook University, State University of New York, School of Professional Development, Stony Brook, NY 11794. Offers biology-grade 7-12 (MAT); chemistry-grade 7-12 (MAT); coaching (Graduate Certificate); computer integrated engineering (Graduate Certificate); earth science-grade 7-12 (MAT); educational computing (Graduate Certificate); educational leadership (Advanced Certificate); English-grade 7-12 (MAT); environmental management (Graduate Certificate); environmental/occupational health and safety (Graduate Certificate); French-grade 7-12 (MAT); German-grade 7-12 (MAT); human resource management (Graduate Certificate); information systems management (Graduate Certificate); Italian-grade 7-12 (MAT); liberal studies (MA); mathematics-grade 7-12 (MAT); operation research (Graduate Certificate); physics-grade 7-12 (MAT); school administration and supervision (Graduate Certificate); school building leadership (Graduate Certificate); school district administration (Graduate Certificate); school district business leadership (Advanced Certificate); school district leadership (Graduate Certificate); social science and the professions (MPS), including environmental waste management, human resource management; social studies-grade 7-12 (MAT); Spanish-grade 7-12 (MAT); waste management (Graduate Certificate). Part-time and evening/weekend programs available. Postbaccalaureate distance learning degree programs offered. *Faculty:* 5 full-time (3 women), 131 part-time/adjunct (53 women). *Students:* 317 full-time (187 women), 1,200 part-time (773 women); includes 187 minority (77 African Americans, 2 American Indian/Alaska Native, 22 Asian Americans or Pacific Islanders, 86 Hispanic Americans), 11 international. Average age 28. In 2009, 597 master's, 234 other advanced degrees awarded. *Degree requirements:* For master's, one foreign language, thesis or alternative. *Application deadline:* Applications are processed on a rolling basis. Application fee: $62. *Expenses:* Tuition, state resident: full-time $8370; part-time $349 per credit. Tuition, nonresident: full-time $13,250; part-time $552 per credit. Required fees: $933. *Financial support:* Fellowships, research assistantships, teaching assistantships, career-related internships or fieldwork available. Support available to part-time students. *Unit head:* Dr. Paul J. Edelson, Dean, 631-632-7052, Fax: 631-632-9046, E-mail: paul.edelson@stonybrook.edu. *Application contact:* Dr. Paul J. Edelson, Dean, 631-632-7052, Fax: 631-632-9046, E-mail: paul.edelson@stonybrook.edu.

Strayer University, Graduate Studies, Washington, DC 20005-2603. Offers accounting (MS); acquisition (MBA); business administration (MBA); communications technology (MS); educational management (M Ed); finance (MBA); health services administration (MHSA); hospitality and tourism management (MBA); human resource management (MBA); information systems (MS), including computer security management, decision support system management, enterprise resource management, network management, software engineering management, systems development management; management (MBA); management information systems (MS); marketing (MBA); professional accounting (MS), including accounting information systems, controllership, taxation; public administration (MPA); supply chain management (MBA); technology in education (M Ed). Programs also offered at campus locations in Birmingham, AL; Chamblee, GA; Cobb County, GA; Morrow, GA; White Marsh, MD; Charleston, SC; Columbia, SC; Greensboro, NC; Greenville, SC; Lexington, KY; Louisville, KY; Nashville, TN; North Raleigh, NC; Washington, DC. Part-time and evening/weekend programs available. Postbaccalaureate distance learning degree programs offered (minimal on-campus study). *Degree requirements:* For master's, thesis. *Entrance requirements:* For master's, GMAT, GRE General Test, bachelor's degree from an accredited college or university, minimum undergraduate GPA of 2.75. Electronic applications accepted.

Tarleton State University, College of Graduate Studies, College of Business Administration, Department of Management, Marketing, and Administrative Systems, Stephenville, TX 76402. Offers human resource management (MS); management and leadership (MS). Part-time and evening/weekend programs available. Postbaccalaureate distance learning degree programs offered. *Degree requirements:* For master's, comprehensive exam. *Entrance requirements:* For master's, GRE, minimum GPA of 3.0. Additional exam requirements/recommendations for international students: Required—TOEFL (minimum score 550 paper-based; 213 computer-based; 80 iBT). Electronic applications accepted.

Temple University, Graduate School, Fox School of Business, Doctoral Programs in Business, Philadelphia, PA 19122-6096. Offers accounting (PhD); entrepreneurship (PhD); finance (PhD); human resource administration (PhD); international business (PhD); management information systems (PhD); marketing (PhD); risk management and insurance (PhD); statistics (PhD); strategic management (PhD); tourism and sport (PhD). *Accreditation:* AACSB. *Degree requirements:* For doctorate, thesis/dissertation. *Entrance requirements:* For doctorate, GRE General Test, GMAT, minimum GPA of 3.0, master's degree. Additional exam requirements/recommendations for international students: Required—TOEFL (minimum score 600 paper-based; 250 computer-based; 100 iBT), IELTS (minimum score 7.5). Electronic applications accepted.

Temple University, Graduate School, Fox School of Business, MBA Programs, Philadelphia, PA 19122-6096. Offers accounting (MBA); business management (MBA); financial management (MBA); healthcare and life sciences innovation (MBA); human resource management (MBA); international business (IMBA); IT management (MBA); marketing management (MBA); pharmaceutical management (MBA); strategic management (EMBA, MBA). EMBA offered in Philadelphia, PA and Tokyo, Japan. *Accreditation:* AACSB. Part-time and evening/weekend programs available. Postbaccalaureate distance learning degree programs offered (minimal on-campus study). *Entrance requirements:* For master's, GMAT, minimum undergraduate GPA of 3.0. Additional exam requirements/recommendations for international students: Required—TOEFL (minimum score 600 paper-based; 250 computer-based; 100 iBT), IELTS (minimum score 7.5).

Temple University, Graduate School, Fox School of Business, Specialized Master's Programs, Philadelphia, PA 19122-6096. Offers accounting and financial management (MS); actuarial science (MS); finance (MS); financial engineering (MS); healthcare financial management (MS); healthcare management (MHM); human resource management (MS); management information systems (MS); marketing (MS); statistics (MS). *Accreditation:* AACSB. Part-time programs available. *Entrance requirements:* For master's, GRE General Test or GMAT, minimum undergraduate GPA of 3.0. Additional exam requirements/recommendations for international students: Required—TOEFL (minimum score 600 paper-based; 250 computer-based; 100 iBT), IELTS (minimum score 7.5).

Tennessee Technological University, Graduate School, College of Business, Cookeville, TN 38505. Offers accounting (MBA); finance (MBA); human resource management (MBA); international business (MBA); management information systems (MBA); risk management & insurance (MBA). *Accreditation:* AACSB. Part-time and evening/weekend programs available. *Faculty:* 28 full-time (5 women). *Students:* 64 full-time (26 women), 163 part-time (70 women); includes 17 minority (6 African Americans, 8 Asian Americans or Pacific Islanders, 3 Hispanic Americans). Average age 25. 203 applicants, 52% accepted, 75 enrolled. In 2009, 105 master's awarded. *Entrance requirements:* For master's, GMAT. Additional exam requirements/recommendations for international students: Required—TOEFL (minimum score 550 paper-based; 79 iBT), IELTS (minimum score 5.5). *Application deadline:* For fall admission, 8/1 for domestic and international students; for spring admission, 12/1 for domestic students, 10/1 for international students. Application fee: $25 ($30 for international students). Electronic applications accepted. *Expenses:* Tuition, state resident: full-time $7034; part-time $368 per credit hour. *Financial support:* In 2009–10, 5 fellowships (averaging $10,000 per year), 18 research assistantships (averaging $4,000 per year), teaching assistantships (averaging $4,000 per year) were awarded. Support available to part-time students. Financial award application deadline: 4/1. *Unit head:* Dr. Bob G. Wood, Director, 931-372-3600, Fax: 931-372-6249. *Application contact:* Shelia K. Kendrick, Coordinator of Graduate Studies, 931-372-3808, Fax: 931-372-3497, E-mail: skendrick@tntech.edu.

Tennessee Technological University, Graduate School, Program of Professional Studies, Cookeville, TN 38505. Offers human resources leadership (MPS); strategic leadership (MPS); training and development (MPS). *Students:* 4 full-time (2 women), 27 part-time (20 women); includes 5 minority (4 African Americans, 1 Hispanic American). 14 applicants, 57% accepted, 7 enrolled. In 2009, 1 master's awarded. *Degree requirements:* For master's, comprehensive exam, thesis or alternative. *Entrance requirements:* For master's, GRE. Additional exam requirements/recommendations for international students: Required—TOEFL (minimum score 550 paper-based; 79 iBT), IELTS (minimum score 5.5). *Application deadline:* For fall admission, 8/1 for domestic students, 5/1 for international students; for spring admission, 12/1 for domestic students, 10/1 for international students. Application fee: $25 ($30 for international students). Electronic applications accepted. *Expenses:* Tuition, state resident: full-time $7034; part-time $368 per credit hour. *Financial support:* Application deadline: 4/1. *Unit head:* Dr. Susan A. Elkins, Dean, School of Interdisciplinary Studies and Extended Education, 931-372-3394, Fax: 372-372-3499, E-mail: selkins@tntech.edu. *Application contact:* Shelia K. Kendrick, Coordinator of Graduate Studies, 931-372-3808, Fax: 931-372-3497, E-mail: skendrick@tntech.edu.

Texas A&M University, Mays Business School, Department of Management, College Station, TX 77843. Offers human resource management (MS); management (PhD). Terminal master's awarded for partial completion of doctoral program. *Degree requirements:* For master's, comprehensive exam; for doctorate, thesis/dissertation. *Entrance requirements:* For master's, GMAT or GRE; for doctorate, GMAT or GRE General Test. Additional exam requirements/recommendations for international students: Required—TOEFL. *Expenses:* Tuition, state resident: full-time $3991; part-time $221.74 per credit hour. Tuition, nonresident: full-time $9049; part-time $502.74 per credit hour. *Faculty research:* Strategic and human resource management, business and public policy, organizational behavior, organizational theory.

Thomas College, Graduate School, Programs in Business, Waterville, ME 04901-5097. Offers business (MBA); computer technology education (MS); education (MS); human resource management (MBA). Part-time and evening/weekend programs available. *Entrance requirements:* For master's, GMAT, GRE, MAT or minimum GPA of 3.3 in first 3 graduate-level courses.

Thomas Edison State College, School of Business and Management, Program in Human Resources Management, Trenton, NJ 08608-1176. Offers MSHRM, Graduate Certificate. Part-time programs available. Postbaccalaureate distance learning degree programs offered (no on-campus study). *Students:* 78 part-time (54 women); includes 22 minority (12 African Americans, 1 American Indian/Alaska Native, 1 Asian American or Pacific Islander, 8 Hispanic Americans), 2 international. Average age 38. In 2009, 9 master's, 4 other advanced degrees awarded. *Degree requirements:* For master's, final project/capstone project. *Entrance requirements:* For master's, bachelor's degree from a regionally-accredited college or university; minimum 2 letters of recommendation; 3-5 years of related working experience; current

resume. Additional exam requirements/recommendations for international students: Required—TOEFL (minimum score 550 paper-based; 213 computer-based; 79 iBT). *Application deadline:* For fall admission, 8/15 priority date for domestic and international students; for winter admission, 11/15 priority date for domestic and international students; for spring admission, 2/15 priority date for domestic and international students. Applications are processed on a rolling basis. Application fee: $75. Electronic applications accepted. *Expenses:* Tuition, area resident: Part-time $479 per credit. Tuition, state resident: part-time $479 per credit. Tuition, nonresident: part-time $479 per credit. *Financial support:* Applicants required to submit FAFSA. *Unit head:* Dr. Joseph Santora, Dean, School of Business and Management, 609-984-1130, Fax: 609-984-3898, E-mail: info@tesc.edu. *Application contact:* David Hoftiezer, Director of Admissions, 888-442-8372, Fax: 609-984-8447, E-mail: admissions@tesc.edu.

Trinity (Washington) University, School of Professional Studies, Washington, DC 20017-1094. Offers business administration (MBA); communication (MA); international security studies (MA); organizational management (MSA), including federal program management, human resource management, nonprofit management, organizational development, public and community health. Part-time and evening/weekend programs available. *Degree requirements:* For master's, thesis (for some programs), capstone project (MSA). *Entrance requirements:* For master's, minimum GPA of 2.5. Additional exam requirements/recommendations for international students: Required—TOEFL (minimum score 550 paper-based; 213 computer-based).

Troy University, Graduate School, College of Arts and Sciences, Program in Public Administration, Troy, AL 36082. Offers education (MPA); environmental management (MPA); government contracting (MPA); health care administration (MPA); justice administration (MPA); management information systems (MPA); national security affairs (MPA); nonprofit management (MPA); public human resources management (MPA); public management (MPA). *Accreditation:* NASPAA. Part-time and evening/weekend programs available. Postbaccalaureate distance learning degree programs offered (no on-campus study). *Students:* 239 full-time (161 women), 652 part-time (416 women); includes 596 minority (547 African Americans, 11 American Indian/Alaska Native, 6 Asian Americans or Pacific Islanders, 32 Hispanic Americans). Average age 34. 415 applicants, 80% accepted. In 2009, 247 master's awarded. *Degree requirements:* For master's, capstone course, research methodologies course. *Entrance requirements:* For master's, GRE, MAT or GMAT, minimum undergraduate GPA of 2.5, letter of recommendation. Additional exam requirements/recommendations for international students: Required—TOEFL (minimum score 523 paper-based; 193 computer-based; 70 iBT), IELTS (minimum score 6). *Application deadline:* Applications are processed on a rolling basis. Application fee: $50. Electronic applications accepted. *Financial support:* Available to part-time students. Applicants required to submit FAFSA. *Unit head:* Dr. Ellen Rosell, Chairman, 334-670-3758, Fax: 334-670-5647, E-mail: erosell@troy.edu. *Application contact:* Brenda K. Campbell, Director of Graduate Admissions, 334-670-3178, Fax: 334-670-3733, E-mail: bcamp@troy.edu.

Troy University, Graduate School, College of Business, Program in Human Resources Management, Troy, AL 36082. Offers MS. Part-time and evening/weekend programs available. *Students:* 144 full-time (111 women), 447 part-time (356 women); includes 455 minority (438 African Americans, 4 American Indian/Alaska Native, 3 Asian Americans or Pacific Islanders, 10 Hispanic Americans). Average age 34. 219 applicants, 88% accepted. In 2009, 227 master's awarded. *Degree requirements:* For master's, thesis or alternative. *Entrance requirements:* For master's, GMAT (minimum score 500) or GRE General Test (minimum score 900), minimum GPA of 2.5; letter of recommendation. Additional exam requirements/recommendations for international students: Required—TOEFL (minimum score 523 paper-based; 193 computer-based; 70 iBT), IELTS (minimum score 6), or ACT Compass ESL (minimum score 270 on Listening, Reading, and Grammar with no individual score below 85 and a minimum score of 8 out of 12 on writing test). *Application deadline:* Applications are processed on a rolling basis. Application fee: $50. *Unit head:* Dr. Charles Durham, Associate Professor of Management, 334-241-9727, E-mail: cdurham@troy.edu. *Application contact:* Brenda K. Campbell, Director of Graduate Admissions, 334-670-3178, Fax: 334-670-3733, E-mail: bcamp@troy.edu.

Troy University, Graduate School, College of Business, Program in Management, Troy, AL 36082. Offers healthcare management (MSM); human resources management (MSM); information systems (MSM); international hospitality management (MSM); international management (MSM); leadership and organizational effectiveness (MSM); public management (MS, MSM). *Accreditation:* ACBSP. Evening/weekend programs available. *Students:* 193 full-time (130 women), 575 part-time (374 women); includes 473 minority (417 African Americans, 12 American Indian/Alaska Native, 20 Asian Americans or Pacific Islanders, 24 Hispanic Americans). Average age 35. 275 applicants, 91% accepted. In 2009, 332 master's awarded. *Degree requirements:* For master's, thesis or alternative. *Entrance requirements:* For master's, GMAT (minimum score 500) or GRE General Test (minimum score 900), minimum GPA of 2.5; letter of recommendation. Additional exam requirements/recommendations for international students: Required—TOEFL (minimum score 523 paper-based; 193 computer-based; 70 iBT), IELTS, or ACT Compass ESL (minimum score 270 on Listening, Reading, and Grammar with no individual score below 85 and a minimum score of 8 out of 12 on writing test). *Application deadline:* Applications are processed on a rolling basis. Application fee: $50. Electronic applications accepted. *Expenses:* Contact institution. *Unit head:* Dr. Henry M. Findley, Interim Chair/Professor, 334-670-3271, Fax: 334-670-3599, E-mail: hfindley@troy.edu. *Application contact:* Brenda K. Campbell, Director of Graduate Admissions, 334-670-3178, Fax: 334-670-3733, E-mail: bcamp@troy.edu.

TUI University, College of Business Administration, Program in Business Administration, Cypress, CA 90630. Offers business administration (PhD); conflict and negotiation management (MBA); criminal justice administration (MBA); entrepreneurship (MBA); finance (MBA); general management (MBA); government accounting (MBA); human resource management (MBA); information security and digital assurance management (MBA); information technology management (MBA); international business (MBA); logistics management (MBA); marketing (MBA); project management (MBA); public management (MBA); quality management (MBA); strategic leadership (MBA). Part-time and evening/weekend programs available. Postbaccalaureate distance learning degree programs offered (no on-campus study). *Degree requirements:* For doctorate, comprehensive exam, thesis/dissertation, defense of dissertation. *Entrance requirements:* For master's, minimum GPA of 2.5 (students with GPA 3.0 or greater may transfer up to 30% of graduate level credits); for doctorate, minimum GPA of 3.4, curriculum vitae, course work in research methods or statistics. Additional exam requirements/recommendations for international students: Required—TOEFL. Electronic applications accepted.

Union Graduate College, School of Management, Schenectady, NY 12308-3107. Offers Business Administration (MBA); Financial Management (Certificate); General Management (Certificate); Health Systems Administration (MBA, Certificate); Human Resources (Certificate). *Accreditation:* AACSB. Part-time and evening/weekend programs available. *Faculty:* 9 full-time (1 woman), 25 part-time/adjunct (9 women). *Students:* 112 full-time (53 women), 86 part-time (38 women); includes 24 minority (4 African Americans, 16 Asian Americans or Pacific Islanders, 4 Hispanic Americans), 13 international. Average age 26. 173 applicants, 61% accepted, 93 enrolled. In 2009, 76 master's, 15 other advanced degrees awarded. *Degree requirements:* For master's, internship, capstone course. *Entrance requirements:* For master's, GMAT, minimum GPA of 3.0, 3 letters of recommendation. Additional exam requirements/recommendations for international students: Required—TOEFL (minimum score 550 paper-based; 213 computer-based). *Application deadline:* Applications are processed on a rolling basis. Application fee: $60. *Financial support:* Research assistantships, career-related internships or fieldwork, Federal Work-Study, scholarships/grants, health care benefits, and tuition waivers (partial) available. Support available to part-time students. Financial award applicants required to submit FAFSA. *Unit head:* Dr. Eric Lewis, Dean, 518-631-9890, Fax: 518-631-9902, E-mail: lewise@uniongraduatecollege.edu. *Application contact:* Diane Trzaskos, Admissions Coordinator, 518-631-9837, Fax: 518-631-9901, E-mail: trzaskod@uniongraduatecollege.edu.

Universidad del Este, Graduate School, Carolina, PR 00984. Offers accounting (MBA); adult education (M Ed); agribusiness (MBA); bilingual education (M Ed); criminal justice and criminology (MA); early education (M Ed); elementary education (M Ed); human resources (MBA); information security management (MBA); information technology and Web business development (MBA); management (MBA); public policy (MPA); social work (MA), including clinical social work; special education (M Ed); strategic leadership (MBA); teaching English (M Ed); teaching Spanish (M Ed).

Universidad del Turabo, Graduate Programs, School in Business Administration, Online Business Administration Program, Gurabo, PR 00778-3030. Offers human resources (MBA); management (MBA); marketing (MBA); materials management (MBA).

Universidad del Turabo, Graduate Programs, School in Business Administration, Program in Human Resources, Gurabo, PR 00778-3030. Offers MBA. *Students:* 60 full-time (49 women), 79 part-time (67 women); includes 125 Hispanic Americans. Average age 32. 67 applicants, 85% accepted, 48 enrolled. In 2009, 111 master's awarded. *Unit head:* Marcelino Rivera, Dean, 787-743-7979 Ext. 4117. *Application contact:* Virginia Gonzalez, Admissions Officer, 787-746-3009.

Universidad Metropolitana, School of Business Administration, Program in Human Resources Management, San Juan, PR 00928-1150. Offers MBA. Part-time programs available.

University at Albany, State University of New York, School of Business, Department of Management, Albany, NY 12222-0001. Offers human resource systems (MBA). *Degree requirements:* For master's, field study project. *Entrance requirements:* For master's, GMAT. Additional exam requirements/recommendations for international students: Required—TOEFL (minimum score 550 paper-based; 213 computer-based). Electronic applications accepted. *Faculty research:* Leadership, strategic management, performance appraisal, franchising, job satisfaction.

University at Buffalo, the State University of New York, Graduate School, Graduate School of Education, Department of Educational Leadership and Policy, Buffalo, NY 14260. Offers educational administration (Ed M, Ed D, PhD); general education (Ed M); higher education administration (Ed M, Ed D, PhD), including student affairs (Ed D); school building leadership (LIFTS) (Certificate); school business and human resource administration (Certificate); school district business leadership (LIFTS) (Certificate); school district leadership (LIFTS) (Certificate); social foundations (PhD). Part-time and evening/weekend programs available. *Faculty:* 12 full-time (6 women), 13 part-time/adjunct (7 women). *Students:* 71 full-time (53 women), 159 part-time (99 women); includes 42 minority (27 African Americans, 1 American Indian/Alaska Native, 4 Asian Americans or Pacific Islanders, 10 Hispanic Americans), 20 international. Average age 36.7. 170 applicants, 59% accepted, 65 enrolled. In 2009, 29 master's, 24 doctorates, 29 other advanced degrees awarded. *Degree requirements:* For master's, comprehensive exam (for some programs), thesis optional; for doctorate, comprehensive exam, thesis/dissertation. *Entrance requirements:* For doctorate, GRE General Test or MAT, writing sample. Additional exam requirements/recommendations for international students: Required—TOEFL (minimum score 550 paper-based; 213 computer-based; 79 iBT). *Application deadline:* For fall admission, 3/1 priority date for domestic students, 3/1 for international students; for spring admission, 11/15 priority date for domestic students, 10/1 for international students. Applications are processed on a rolling basis. Application fee: $50. Electronic applications accepted. *Financial support:* In 2009–10, 6 fellowships with full tuition reimbursements (averaging $9,000 per year), 12 research assistantships with full tuition reimbursements (averaging $9,000 per year) were awarded; career-related internships or fieldwork, Federal Work-Study, institutionally sponsored loans, health care benefits, tuition waivers (full and partial), and unspecified assistantships also available. Financial award application deadline: 3/15; financial award applicants required to submit FAFSA. *Faculty research:* College access and choice, school leadership preparation and practice, public policy, curriculum and pedagogy, comparative and international education. Total annual research expenditures: $34,848. *Unit head:* Dr. William C. Barba, Chairman, 716-645-2471, Fax: 716-645-2481, E-mail: barba@buffalo.edu. *Application contact:* Bonnie Fisher, Admissions Assistant, 716-645-2110, Fax: 716-645-7937, E-mail: brfisher@buffalo.edu.

The University of Akron, Graduate School, College of Business Administration, Department of Management, Program in Management-Human Resources, Akron, OH 44325. Offers MSM. *Students:* 1 (woman) full-time, 16 part-time (10 women); includes 7 minority (4 African Americans, 2 Asian Americans or Pacific Islanders, 1 Hispanic American), 1 international. Average age 30. 7 applicants, 57% accepted, 2 enrolled. In 2009, 4 master's awarded. *Entrance requirements:* For master's, GMAT, minimum GPA of 2.75, letters of recommendation, resume. Additional exam requirements/recommendations for international students: Required—TOEFL (minimum score 550 paper-based; 213 computer-based; 79 iBT). *Application deadline:* For fall admission, 8/1 for domestic and international students; for spring admission, 12/1 for domestic and international students. Application fee: $30 ($40 for international students). Electronic applications accepted. *Expenses:* Tuition, state resident: full-time $6570; part-time $365 per credit hour. Tuition, nonresident: full-time $11,250; part-time $625 per credit hour. *Application contact:* Dr. Susan Hanlon, Director of Graduate Business Programs, 330-972-7043, Fax: 330-972-6588, E-mail: shanlon@uakron.edu.

The University of Alabama in Huntsville, School of Graduate Studies, College of Business Administration, Department of Management and Marketing, Huntsville, AL 35899. Offers management (MBA), including acquisition management, finance, human resource management, logistics and supply chain management, marketing, project management. *Accreditation:* AACSB. Part-time and evening/weekend programs available. *Faculty:* 7 full-time (1 woman), 1 part-time/adjunct (0 women). *Students:* 41 full-time (19 women), 155 part-time (59 women); includes 30 minority (15 African Americans, 5 American Indian/Alaska Native, 7 Asian Americans or Pacific Islanders, 3 Hispanic Americans), 20 international. Average age 32. 138 applicants, 63% accepted, 68 enrolled. In 2009, 38 master's awarded. *Degree requirements:* For master's, comprehensive exam, thesis or alternative. *Entrance requirements:* For master's, GMAT (minimum score 500), minimum AACSB index of 1080. Additional exam requirements/recommendations for international students: Required—TOEFL (minimum score 550 paper-based; 213 computer-based; 62 iBT). *Application deadline:* For fall admission, 8/1 for domestic students, 4/1 for international students; for spring admission, 12/1 for domestic students, 9/1 for international students. Applications are processed on a rolling basis. Application fee: $40 ($50 for international students). Electronic applications accepted. *Expenses:* Tuition, state resident: part-time $355.75 per credit hour. Tuition, nonresident: part-time $847.10 per credit hour. Required fees: $210.80 per semester. Tuition and fees vary according to course load and program. *Financial support:* In 2009–10, 3 students received support, including 2 research assistantships with full tuition reimbursements available (averaging $14,400 per year), 1 teaching assistantship with full tuition reimbursement available (averaging $11,800 per year); career-related internships or fieldwork, Federal Work-Study, institutionally sponsored loans, scholarships/grants, health care benefits, and unspecified assistantships also available. Support available to part-time students. Financial award application deadline: 4/1; financial award applicants required to submit FAFSA. *Unit head:* Dr. Brent Wren, Chair, 256-824-6408, Fax: 256-824-6328, E-mail: wrenb@uah.edu. *Application contact:* Jennifer Pettitt, Director of Graduate Programs, 256-824-6681, Fax: 256-824-7571, E-mail: jennifer.pettitt@uah.edu.

University of California, Berkeley, UC Berkeley Extension, Certificate Programs in Business, Berkeley, CA 94720-1500. Offers accounting (Certificate); business administration (Certificate); finance (Certificate); human resource management (Certificate); management (Certificate); marketing (Certificate); project management (Certificate). Postbaccalaureate distance learning degree programs offered. *Unit head:* Diana Wu, Dean, 510-642-4181. *Application contact:* Business, 510-642-4231, E-mail: business@unex.berkeley.edu.

University of Connecticut, Graduate School, Center for Continuing Studies, Program in Human Resource Management, Storrs, CT 06269. Offers labor relations (MPS); personnel (MPS). *Students:* 2 full-time (1 woman), 51 part-time (40 women); includes 11 minority (4 African Americans, 1 Asian American or Pacific Islander, 6 Hispanic Americans). Average age 37. 19 applicants, 47% accepted, 9 enrolled. In 2009, 4 master's awarded. *Expenses:* Tuition, state resident: full-time $4725; part-time $525 per credit. Tuition, nonresident: full-time $12,267;

Human Resources Management

University of Connecticut (continued)
part-time $1363 per credit. Required fees: $346 per semester. Tuition and fees vary according to course load. *Unit head:* Susan W. Nesbitt, Director, 860-486-5941. *Application contact:* Peter Diplock, Information Contact, 860-486-2915, E-mail: peter.diplock@uconn.edu.

University of Dallas, Graduate School of Management, Irving, TX 75062-4736. Offers accounting (MBA, MM, MS); business management (MBA, MM); corporate finance (MBA, MM); financial services (MBA); global business (MBA, MM); health services management (MBA, MM); human resource management (MBA, MM); information assurance (MBA, MM, MS); information technology (MBA, MM, MS); information technology service management (MBA, MM, MS); marketing management (MBA, MM); organization development (MBA, MM); project management (MBA, MM); sports and entertainment management (MBA, MM); strategic leadership (MBA, MM); supply chain management (MBA); supply chain management and market logistics (MM). *Accreditation:* ACBSP. Part-time and evening/weekend programs available. Postbaccalaureate distance learning degree programs offered (no on-campus study). *Faculty:* 25 full-time (6 women), 31 part-time/adjunct (6 women). *Students:* 232 full-time (95 women), 923 part-time (365 women); includes 462 minority (184 African Americans, 14 American Indian/Alaska Native, 153 Asian Americans or Pacific Islanders, 111 Hispanic Americans), 184 international. Average age 34. 474 applicants, 85% accepted, 237 enrolled. In 2009, 399 master's awarded. *Entrance requirements:* Additional exam requirements/recommendations for international students: Required—TOEFL. *Application deadline:* Applications are processed on a rolling basis. Application fee: $50. Electronic applications accepted. *Expenses:* Contact institution. *Financial support:* In 2009–10, 399 students received support. Scholarships/grants and unspecified assistantships available. Financial award application deadline: 2/15; financial award applicants required to submit FAFSA. *Unit head:* Alounda Joseph, Director of Enrollment Processes, 972-721-5356, E-mail: admiss@gsm.udallas.edu. *Application contact:* Alounda Joseph, Director of Enrollment Processes, 972-721-5356, E-mail: admiss@gsm.udallas.edu.

University of Denver, University College, Denver, CO 80208. Offers applied communication (MAS, MPS, Certificate); computer information systems (MAS, Certificate); environmental policy and management (MAS, Certificate); geographic information systems (MAS, Certificate); human resource administration (MPS, Certificate); knowledge and information technologies (MAS); liberal studies (MLS, Certificate); modern languages (MLS, Certificate); organizational leadership (MPS, Certificate); security management (Certificate); technology management (MAS, Certificate), including 21st century strategic management (MAS), international markets (MAS), project management (MAS), research and development management (MAS); telecommunications (MAS, Certificate), including broadband (MAS), telecommunications management and policy (MAS), telecommunications technology (MAS), wireless networks (MAS). Part-time and evening/weekend programs available. Postbaccalaureate distance learning degree programs offered (no on-campus study). *Faculty:* 160 part-time/adjunct (64 women). *Students:* 53 full-time (25 women), 984 part-time (551 women); includes 171 minority (72 African Americans, 10 American Indian/Alaska Native, 33 Asian Americans or Pacific Islanders, 56 Hispanic Americans), 75 international. Average age 36. 537 applicants, 96% accepted, 494 enrolled. In 2009, 229 master's, 109 Certificates awarded. *Entrance requirements:* Additional exam requirements/recommendations for international students: Required—TOEFL (minimum score 550 paper-based; 213 computer-based). *Application deadline:* Applications are processed on a rolling basis. Application fee: $75. Electronic applications accepted. *Expenses:* Contact institution. *Financial support:* Applicants required to submit FAFSA. *Unit head:* Dr. James Davis, Dean, 303-871-2291, Fax: 303-871-4047, E-mail: jdavis@du.edu. *Application contact:* Information Contact, 303-871-3155.

The University of Findlay, Graduate and Professional Studies, College of Business, Findlay, OH 45840-3653. Offers financial management (MBA); human resource management (MBA); international management (MBA); management (MBA); marketing (MBA); public management (MBA). Part-time and evening/weekend programs available. Postbaccalaureate distance learning degree programs offered (no on-campus study). *Degree requirements:* For master's, thesis, cumulative project. *Entrance requirements:* For master's, GMAT, minimum undergraduate GPA of 3.0 in last 64 hours of course work. Additional exam requirements/recommendations for international students: Required—TOEFL (minimum score 550 paper-based; 213 computer-based; 80 iBT). Electronic applications accepted. *Expenses:* Contact institution. *Faculty research:* Health care management, operations and logistics management.

University of Florida, Graduate School, Warrington College of Business Administration, Hough Graduate School of Business, Programs in Business Administration, Gainesville, FL 32611. Offers accounting (MBA); arts administration (MBA); business strategy and public policy (MBA); competitive strategy (MBA); decision and information sciences (MBA); electronic commerce (MBA); finance (MBA); general business (MBA); global management (MBA); Graham-Buffett security analysis (MBA); health administration (MBA); human resources management (MBA); international studies (MBA); Latin American business (MBA); management (MBA); marketing (MBA); sports administration (MBA); JD/MBA; MBA/MS; MBA/PhD; MBA/Pharm D; MD/MBA. *Accreditation:* AACSB. Part-time and evening/weekend programs available. Postbaccalaureate distance learning degree programs offered. *Entrance requirements:* For master's, GMAT, minimum GPA of 3.0, interview. Additional exam requirements/recommendations for international students: Required—TOEFL (minimum score 550 paper-based; 213 computer-based). Electronic applications accepted. *Faculty research:* Accounting, finance, insurance, management, real estate and urban analysis marketing.

University of Georgia, Graduate School, College of Education, Department of Lifelong Education, Administration and Policy, Athens, GA 30602. Offers adult education (M Ed, Ed D, PhD, Ed S); educational administration and policy (M Ed, PhD, Ed S); educational leadership (Ed D); human resource and organizational design (M Ed). *Accreditation:* NCATE. *Faculty:* 26 full-time (17 women). *Students:* 77 full-time (55 women), 181 part-time (124 women); includes 64 minority (54 African Americans, 1 American Indian/Alaska Native, 4 Asian Americans or Pacific Islanders, 5 Hispanic Americans), 28 international. 199 applicants, 60% accepted, 77 enrolled. In 2009, 43 master's, 21 doctorates, 5 other advanced degrees awarded. *Entrance requirements:* For master's and Ed S, GRE General Test or MAT; for doctorate, GRE General Test. *Application deadline:* For fall admission, 7/1 priority date for domestic students; for spring admission, 11/15 for domestic students. Application fee: $50. Electronic applications accepted. *Expenses:* Tuition, state resident: full-time $6000; part-time $250 per credit hour. Tuition, nonresident: full-time $20,904; part-time $871 per credit hour. Required fees: $730 per semester. *Unit head:* Dr. Ronald M. Cervero, Head, 706-542-2221, Fax: 706-542-5873, E-mail: rcervero@uga.edu. *Application contact:* Dr. Kathryn Roulston, Graduate Coordinator, 706-542-4060, Fax: 706-542-5873, E-mail: roulston@uga.edu.

University of Georgia, Graduate School, College of Education, Department of Workforce Education, Leadership and Social Foundations, Athens, GA 30602. Offers educational leadership (Ed D); human resources and organization design (M Ed); occupational studies (MAT, Ed D, PhD, Ed S); social foundations of education (PhD). *Accreditation:* NCATE. *Faculty:* 19 full-time (8 women). *Students:* 33 full-time (20 women), 127 part-time (81 women); includes 24 minority (19 African Americans, 2 American Indian/Alaska Native, 1 Asian American or Pacific Islander, 2 Hispanic Americans), 6 international. 140 applicants, 71% accepted, 46 enrolled. In 2009, 18 master's, 11 doctorates, 9 other advanced degrees awarded. *Entrance requirements:* For master's, GRE General Test, MAT; for doctorate, GRE General Test; for Ed S, GRE General Test or MAT. *Application deadline:* For fall admission, 7/1 priority date for domestic students; for spring admission, 11/15 for domestic students. Application fee: $50. Electronic applications accepted. *Expenses:* Tuition, state resident: full-time $6000; part-time $250 per credit hour. Tuition, nonresident: full-time $20,904; part-time $871 per credit hour. Required fees: $730 per semester. *Financial support:* Fellowships, research assistantships, teaching assistantships, unspecified assistantships available. *Unit head:* Dr. Roger B. Hill, Interim Head, 706-542-4100, Fax: 706-542-4054, E-mail: rbhill@uga.edu. *Application contact:* Dr. Myra N. Womble, Graduate Coordinator, 706-542-4091, Fax: 706-542-4054, E-mail: mwomble@uga.edu.

University of Hawaii at Manoa, Graduate Division, Shidler College of Business, Program in Business Administration, Honolulu, HI 96822. Offers Asian business studies (MBA); Chinese business studies (MBA); decision sciences (MBA); entrepreneurship (MBA); finance (MBA); finance and banking (MBA); human resources management (MBA); information management (MBA); information technology (MBA); international business (MBA); Japanese business studies (MBA); marketing (MBA); organizational behavior (MBA); organizational management (MBA); real estate (MBA); student-designed track (MBA). *Accreditation:* AACSB. Part-time and evening/weekend programs available. *Faculty:* 46 full-time (8 women), 9 part-time/adjunct (4 women). *Students:* 259 full-time (90 women), 105 part-time (43 women); includes 123 minority (118 Asian Americans or Pacific Islanders, 5 Hispanic Americans), 119 international. Average age 32. 336 applicants, 52% accepted, 150 enrolled. In 2009, 113 master's awarded. *Degree requirements:* For master's, thesis optional. *Entrance requirements:* For master's, GMAT, minimum GPA of 3.0. Additional exam requirements/recommendations for international students: Required—TOEFL (minimum score 600 paper-based; 250 computer-based; 100 iBT), IELTS (minimum score 7). *Application deadline:* For fall admission, 5/1 for domestic students, 3/1 for international students. Application fee: $60. *Expenses:* Contact institution. *Financial support:* In 2009–10, 24 students received support, including 98 fellowships (averaging $3,481 per year), 3 research assistantships (averaging $16,626 per year). Total annual research expenditures: $427,000. *Application contact:* Tung Bui, Graduate Chair, 808-956-5565, Fax: 808-956-9889, E-mail: tung.bui@hawaii.edu.

University of Hawaii at Manoa, Graduate Division, Shidler College of Business, Program in Human Resources Management, Honolulu, HI 96822. Offers MHRM. Part-time programs available. *Students:* 45 part-time (34 women); includes 31 minority (29 Asian Americans or Pacific Islanders, 2 Hispanic Americans). Average age 34. 1 applicant, 0% accepted, 0 enrolled. In 2009, 42 master's awarded. *Entrance requirements:* Additional exam requirements/recommendations for international students: Required—TOEFL (minimum score 600 paper-based; 250 computer-based; 100 iBT), IELTS (minimum score 7). *Application deadline:* For fall admission, 7/1 for domestic and international students. Application fee: $60. *Expenses:* Contact institution. *Financial support:* In 2009–10, 2 students received support, including 1 fellowship (averaging $1,500 per year). *Application contact:* Elaine Bailey, Director, 808-956-8135, Fax: 808-956-2774, E-mail: elaine@cba.hawaii.edu.

University of Houston–Clear Lake, School of Business, Program in Administrative Science, Houston, TX 77058-1098. Offers environmental management (MS); human resource management (MA). *Accreditation:* CAHME (one or more programs are accredited). Part-time and evening/weekend programs available. *Degree requirements:* For master's, thesis optional. *Entrance requirements:* For master's, GMAT. Additional exam requirements/recommendations for international students: Required—TOEFL (minimum score 550 paper-based; 213 computer-based). Electronic applications accepted.

University of Illinois at Urbana–Champaign, Graduate College, School of Labor and Employment Relations, Champaign, IL 61820. Offers human resources and industrial relations (MHRIR, PhD); MHRIR/JD; MHRIR/MBA. Part-time programs available. *Faculty:* 14 full-time (5 women), 1 part-time/adjunct (0 women). *Students:* 180 full-time (126 women), 11 part-time (7 women); includes 39 minority (14 African Americans, 16 Asian Americans or Pacific Islanders, 9 Hispanic Americans), 55 international. 272 applicants, 44% accepted, 74 enrolled. In 2009, 95 master's, 6 doctorates awarded. Terminal master's awarded for partial completion of doctoral program. *Entrance requirements:* For master's and doctorate, GRE or GMAT, minimum GPA of 3.0. Additional exam requirements/recommendations for international students: Required—TOEFL (minimum score 590 paper-based; 243 computer-based; 96 iBT), or IELTS (minimum score 6.5). Application fee: $60 ($75 for international students). Electronic applications accepted. *Financial support:* In 2009–10, 23 fellowships, 12 research assistantships, 3 teaching assistantships were awarded; tuition waivers (full and partial) also available. *Unit head:* Dr. Joel E. Cutcher-Gershenfeld, Dean, 217-333-1482, Fax: 217-244-9290, E-mail: joelcg@illinois.edu. *Application contact:* Elizabeth Barker, Director of Student Services, 217-333-2381, Fax: 217-244-9290, E-mail: ebarker@illinois.edu.

See Close-Up on page 431.

University of Lethbridge, School of Graduate Studies, Lethbridge, AB T1K 3M4, Canada. Offers accounting (MScM); addictions counseling (M Sc); agricultural biotechnology (M Sc); agricultural studies (M Sc, MA); anthropology (MA); archaeology (MA); art (MA, MFA); biochemistry (M Sc); biological sciences (M Sc); biomolecular science (PhD); biosystems and biodiversity (PhD); Canadian studies (MA); chemistry (M Sc); computer science (M Sc); computer science and geographical information science (M Sc); counseling psychology (M Ed); dramatic arts (MA); earth, space, and physical science (PhD); economics (MA); educational leadership (M Ed); English (MA); environmental science (M Sc); evolution and behavior (PhD); exercise science (M Sc); finance (MScM); French (MA); French/German (MA); French/Spanish (MA); general education (M Ed); general management (MScM); geography (M Sc, MA); German (MA); health science (M Sc); health sciences (MA); history (MA); human resource management and labour relations (MScM); individualized multidisciplinary (M Sc, MA); information systems (MScM); international management (MScM); kinesiology (M Sc, MA); management (M Sc, MA); marketing (MScM); mathematics (M Sc); music (M Mus, MA); Native American studies (MA); neuroscience (M Sc, PhD); new media (MA); nursing (M Sc); philosophy (MA); physics (M Sc); policy and strategy (MScM); political science (MA); psychology (M Sc, MA); religious studies (MA); social sciences (MA); sociology (MA); theatre and dramatic arts (MFA); theoretical and computational science (PhD); urban and regional studies (MA); women's studies (MA). Part-time and evening/weekend programs available. *Degree requirements:* For doctorate, comprehensive exam, thesis/dissertation. *Entrance requirements:* For master's, GMAT (M Sc in management), bachelor's degree in related field, minimum GPA of 3.0 during previous 20 graded semester courses, 2 years teaching or related experience (M Ed); for doctorate, master's degree, minimum graduate GPA of 3.5. Additional exam requirements/recommendations for international students: Required—TOEFL. *Faculty research:* Movement and brain plasticity, gibberellin physiology, photosynthesis, carbon cycling, molecular properties of main-group ring components.

University of Louisville, Graduate School, College of Arts and Sciences, Department of Urban and Public Affairs, Louisville, KY 40208. Offers public administration (MPA), including human resources management, non-profit management, public policy and administration; urban and public affairs (PhD), including urban planning and development, urban policy and administration; urban planning (MUP), including administration of planning organizations, housing and community development, land use and environmental planning, spatial analysis. Part-time and evening/weekend programs available. *Faculty:* 22 full-time (7 women), 8 part-time/adjunct (1 woman). *Students:* 67 full-time (32 women), 35 part-time (20 women); includes 13 minority (10 African Americans, 1 Asian American or Pacific Islander, 2 Hispanic Americans), 6 international. Average age 31. 107 applicants, 57% accepted, 40 enrolled. In 2009, 25 master's, 5 doctorates awarded. Terminal master's awarded for partial completion of doctoral program. *Degree requirements:* For master's, internship; for doctorate, comprehensive exam, thesis/dissertation. *Entrance requirements:* For master's, GRE General Test, minimum GPA of 3.0; for doctorate, GRE General Test, master's degree in appropriate field. Additional exam requirements/recommendations for international students: Required—TOEFL (minimum score 550 paper-based; 213 computer-based; 79 iBT). *Application deadline:* For fall admission, 7/15 for domestic students; for spring admission, 11/15 for domestic students. Applications are processed on a rolling basis. Application fee: $50. Electronic applications accepted. *Financial support:* In 2009–10, 26 students received support; fellowships, research assistantships, health care benefits available. *Unit head:* Dr. David Simpson, Chair, 502-852-8019, Fax: 502-852-4558, E-mail: dave.simpson@louisville.edu. *Application contact:* Patty Sarley, Graduate Student Advisor, 502-852-7914, Fax: 502-852-4558, E-mail: plclea01@louisville.edu.

University of Mary, Gary Tharaldson School of Business, Bismarck, ND 58504-9652. Offers health care (MBA); human resource management (MBA); management (MBA); project management (MPM); strategic leadership (MSSL). Part-time and evening/weekend programs available. *Degree requirements:* For master's, strategic planning seminar. *Entrance requirements:* For master's, minimum GPA of 2.5. Additional exam requirements/recommendations for international students: Required—TOEFL. *Expenses:* Tuition: Full-time $10,062; part-time $430 per credit. Tuition and fees vary according to course load, degree level, program and student level.

Human Resources Management

University of Minnesota, Twin Cities Campus, Carlson School of Management, Program in Human Resources and Industrial Relations, Minneapolis, MN 55455-0213. Offers MA, PhD. *Accreditation:* AACSB. Part-time and evening/weekend programs available. *Faculty:* 12 full-time (6 women), 6 part-time/adjunct (1 woman). *Students:* 196 full-time (138 women), 92 part-time (68 women); includes 36 minority (13 African Americans, 18 Asian Americans or Pacific Islanders, 5 Hispanic Americans), 62 international. Average age 26. 306 applicants, 44% accepted, 85 enrolled. In 2009, 96 master's, 5 doctorates awarded. Terminal master's awarded for partial completion of doctoral program. *Degree requirements:* For master's, thesis optional; for doctorate, thesis/dissertation. *Entrance requirements:* For master's, GMAT or GRE General Test; for doctorate, GRE General Test. Additional exam requirements/recommendations for international students: Required—TOEFL (minimum score 580 paper-based; 85 iBT). *Application deadline:* For fall admission, 6/15 for domestic and international students; for spring admission, 10/15 for domestic and international students. Applications are processed on a rolling basis. Application fee: $75 ($95 for international students). *Expenses:* Contact institution. *Financial support:* In 2009–10, 60 students received support, including 39 fellowships with partial tuition reimbursements available (averaging $6,500 per year), 14 research assistantships with full and partial tuition reimbursements available (averaging $12,500 per year), 7 teaching assistantships with full tuition reimbursements available (averaging $9,000 per year); career-related internships or fieldwork, Federal Work-Study, institutionally sponsored loans, and tuition waivers (full and partial) also available. Support available to part-time students. Financial award application deadline: 2/1; financial award applicants required to submit FAFSA. *Faculty research:* Staffing, training, and development; compensation and benefits; organization theory; collective bargaining. Total annual research expenditures: $200,000. *Unit head:* Theresa Glomb, Director of Graduate Studies, 612-624-4863, Fax: 612-624-8360, E-mail: tglomb@umn.edu. *Application contact:* Celeste Pape, Admissions Coordinator, 612-624-5704, Fax: 612-624-8360, E-mail: cpape@umn.edu.

University of Missouri–St. Louis, College of Business Administration, Program in Business Administration, St. Louis, MO 63121. Offers accounting (MBA); business administration (Certificate); finance (MBA); human resource management (Certificate); logistics and supply chain management (MBA, Certificate); management (MBA); marketing (MBA); marketing management (Certificate); operations (MBA); quantitative management science (MBA). *Accreditation:* AACSB. Part-time and evening/weekend programs available. *Faculty:* 30 full-time (5 women), 11 part-time/adjunct (2 women). *Students:* 107 full-time (47 women), 310 part-time (120 women); includes 32 minority (17 African Americans, 6 Asian Americans or Pacific Islanders, 9 Hispanic Americans), 66 international. Average age 31. 285 applicants, 58% accepted, 130 enrolled. In 2009, 149 master's, 13 other advanced degrees awarded. *Entrance requirements:* For master's, GMAT, 2 letters of recommendation. Additional exam requirements/recommendations for international students: Required—TOEFL (minimum score 550 paper-based; 213 computer-based). *Application deadline:* For fall admission, 7/1 for domestic students; for spring admission, 11/1 for domestic students. Applications are processed on a rolling basis. Application fee: $35 ($40 for international students). Electronic applications accepted. *Expenses:* Tuition, state resident: full-time $5377; part-time $297.70 per credit hour. Tuition, nonresident: full-time $13,882; part-time $771.20 per credit hour. Required fees: $220; $12.20 per credit hour. One-time fee: $12. Tuition and fees vary according to course level, campus/location and program. *Financial support:* In 2009–10, 27 research assistantships with full and partial tuition reimbursements (averaging $8,525 per year), 6 teaching assistantships with full and partial tuition reimbursements (averaging $13,950 per year) were awarded; career-related internships or fieldwork, Federal Work-Study, and institutionally sponsored loans also available. Support available to part-time students. Financial award application deadline: 4/1; financial award applicants required to submit FAFSA. *Faculty research:* Human resources, strategic management, marketing strategy, consumer behavior product development, advertising. *Unit head:* Karl Kottemann, Assistant Director, 314-516-5885, Fax: 314-516-6420, E-mail: mba@umsl.edu. *Application contact:* 314-516-5458, Fax: 314-516-6996, E-mail: gradadm@umsl.edu.

University of New Haven, Graduate School, College of Arts and Sciences, Program in Industrial and Organizational Psychology, West Haven, CT 06516-1916. Offers conflict management (MA); human resource management (MA); industrial organizational psychology (MA); organizational development (MA); psychology of conflict management (Certificate). Part-time and evening/weekend programs available. *Faculty:* 5 full-time (3 women), 10 part-time/adjunct (5 women). *Students:* 97 full-time (59 women), 34 part-time (26 women); includes 20 minority (9 African Americans, 2 American Indian/Alaska Native, 2 Asian Americans or Pacific Islanders, 7 Hispanic Americans), 11 international. Average age 28. 85 applicants, 98% accepted, 48 enrolled. In 2009, 71 master's awarded. *Degree requirements:* For master's, thesis or alternative. *Entrance requirements:* Additional exam requirements/recommendations for international students: Required—TOEFL (minimum score 520 paper-based; 190 computer-based; 70 iBT); Recommended—IELTS (minimum score 5.5). *Application deadline:* For fall admission, 5/31 for international students; for winter admission, 10/15 for international students; for spring admission, 1/15 for international students. Applications are processed on a rolling basis. Application fee: $50. Electronic applications accepted. *Expenses:* Contact institution. *Financial support:* Research assistantships with partial tuition reimbursements, teaching assistantships with partial tuition reimbursements, career-related internships or fieldwork, Federal Work-Study, scholarships/grants, tuition waivers, and unspecified assistantships available. Support available to part-time students. Financial award applicants required to submit FAFSA. *Unit head:* Dr. Stuart D. Sidle, Coordinator, 203-932-7341. *Application contact:* Eloise Gormley, Information Contact, 203-932-7449.

University of New Haven, Graduate School, School of Business, Program in Business Administration, West Haven, CT 06516-1916. Offers accounting (MBA, Certificate), including CPA (MBA); business management (Certificate); business policy and strategy (MBA); finance (MBA), including CFA; global marketing (MBA); human resource management (Certificate); human resources management (MBA); international business (Certificate); marketing (Certificate); sports management (MBA); telecommunications management (Certificate); MBA/MPA. Part-time and evening/weekend programs available. *Faculty:* 26 full-time (3 women), 23 part-time/adjunct (5 women). *Students:* 302 full-time (120 women), 194 part-time (101 women); includes 109 minority (56 African Americans, 3 American Indian/Alaska Native, 28 Asian Americans or Pacific Islanders, 22 Hispanic Americans), 110 international. Average age 31. 372 applicants, 83% accepted, 172 enrolled. In 2009, 194 master's, 31 other advanced degrees awarded. *Degree requirements:* For master's, thesis or alternative. *Entrance requirements:* For master's, GMAT. Additional exam requirements/recommendations for international students: Required—TOEFL (minimum score 520 paper-based; 190 computer-based; 70 iBT), IELTS (minimum score 5.5). *Application deadline:* For fall admission, 5/31 for international students; for winter admission, 10/15 for international students; for spring admission, 1/15 for international students. Applications are processed on a rolling basis. Application fee: $50. Electronic applications accepted. *Expenses:* Contact institution. *Financial support:* Research assistantships with partial tuition reimbursements, teaching assistantships with partial tuition reimbursements, Federal Work-Study, scholarships/grants, health care benefits, tuition waivers, and unspecified assistantships available. Support available to part-time students. Financial award applicants required to submit FAFSA. *Unit head:* Charles Coleman, Chairman, 203-932-7375. *Application contact:* Eloise Gormley, Director of Graduate Admissions, 203-932-7449, Fax: 203-932-7137, E-mail: gradinfo@newhaven.edu.

University of New Haven, Graduate School, School of Business, Program in Public Administration, West Haven, CT 06516-1916. Offers personnel and labor relations (MPA); public administration (MPA, Certificate), including city management (MPA), community-clinical services (MPA), health care management (MPA), long-term health care (MPA), personnel and labor relations (MPA), public administration (Certificate), public management (Certificate), public personnel management (Certificate); MBA/MPA. Part-time and evening/weekend programs available. *Faculty:* 3 full-time (1 woman), 11 part-time/adjunct (5 women). *Students:* 17 full-time (9 women), 26 part-time (14 women); includes 11 minority (9 African Americans, 1 Asian American or Pacific Islander, 1 Hispanic American), 1 international. Average age 35. 35 applicants, 94% accepted, 8 enrolled. In 2009, 9 master's, 12 other advanced degrees awarded. *Degree requirements:* For master's, thesis or alternative. *Entrance requirements:* Additional exam requirements/recommendations for international students: Required—TOEFL (minimum score 520 paper-based; 190 computer-based; 70 iBT); Recommended—IELTS (minimum score 5.5). *Application deadline:* For fall admission, 5/31 for international students; for winter admission, 10/15 for international students; for spring admission, 1/15 for international students. Applications are processed on a rolling basis. Application fee: $50. Electronic applications accepted. *Expenses:* Contact institution. *Financial support:* Research assistantships with partial tuition reimbursements, teaching assistantships with partial tuition reimbursements, career-related internships or fieldwork, Federal Work-Study, scholarships/grants, tuition waivers, and unspecified assistantships available. Support available to part-time students. Financial award application deadline: 5/1; financial award applicants required to submit FAFSA. *Unit head:* Charles Coleman, Chairman, 203-932-7375. *Application contact:* Eloise Gormley, Director of Graduate Admissions, 203-932-7449, Fax: 203-932-7137, E-mail: gradinfo@newhaven.edu.

University of New Mexico, Robert O. Anderson Graduate School of Management, Department of Organizational Studies, Albuquerque, NM 87131. Offers human resources management (MBA); policy and planning (MBA). Part-time and evening/weekend programs available. *Faculty:* 14 full-time (10 women), 6 part-time/adjunct (2 women). *Students:* 25 full-time (23 women), 22 part-time (15 women); includes 25 minority (3 African Americans, 3 American Indian/Alaska Native, 2 Asian Americans or Pacific Islanders, 17 Hispanic Americans), 1 international. Average age 29. 28 applicants, 100% accepted, 28 enrolled. In 2009, 20 master's awarded. *Entrance requirements:* For master's, GMAT or GRE (can be waived in some instances). Additional exam requirements/recommendations for international students: Required—TOEFL (minimum score 550 paper-based; 213 computer-based; 79 iBT). *Application deadline:* For fall admission, 4/1 priority date for domestic students, 5/1 for international students; for spring admission, 10/1 priority date for domestic students, 10/1 for international students. Applications are processed on a rolling basis. Application fee: $50. Electronic applications accepted. *Expenses:* Tuition, state resident: full-time $2099; part-time $233.20 per credit hour. Tuition, nonresident: full-time $6650. Required fees: $25 per semester. Tuition and fees vary according to course load, program and reciprocity agreements. *Financial support:* Fellowships, research assistantships, teaching assistantships, career-related internships or fieldwork, Federal Work-Study, scholarships/grants, and unspecified assistantships available. Support available to part-time students. Financial award application deadline: 6/1. *Faculty research:* Business ethics and social corporate responsibility, diversity, human resources, organizational strategy, organizational behavior. *Unit head:* Dr. Jacqueline Hood, Chair, 505-277-6471, Fax: 505-277-7108. *Application contact:* Megan Conner, Academic Advisement Manager, 505-277-3290, Fax: 505-277-8436, E-mail: mconner@mgt.unm.edu.

University of Phoenix, School of Business, College of Graduate Business and Management, Phoenix, AZ 85034-7209. Offers accountancy (MSA); accounting (MBA); business administration (MBA); global management (MBA); human resources management (MBA, MM); management (MM); marketing (MBA); public administration (MBA, MM). *Accreditation:* ACBSP. Evening/weekend programs available. Postbaccalaureate distance learning degree programs offered. *Faculty:* 25 full-time (15 women), 4,861 part-time/adjunct (1,504 women). *Students:* 6,681 full-time (5,284 women); includes 2,558 minority (1,955 African Americans, 69 American Indian/Alaska Native, 90 Asian Americans or Pacific Islanders, 444 Hispanic Americans), 137 international. Average age 35. In 2009, 1,740 master's awarded. *Degree requirements:* For master's, thesis (for some programs). *Entrance requirements:* For master's, 3 years of work experience, minimum undergraduate GPA of 3.0. Additional exam requirements/recommendations for international students: Required—TOEFL (minimum score 550 paper-based; 213 computer-based; 79 iBT). *Application deadline:* Applications are processed on a rolling basis. Application fee: $45. Electronic applications accepted. *Expenses:* Tuition: Full-time $13,272. Required fees: $660. Full-time tuition and fees vary according to course level, degree level and program. *Financial support:* Institutionally sponsored loans and scholarships/grants available. Financial award applicants required to submit FAFSA. *Unit head:* Brian Lindquist, Dean/Executive Director and Associate Vice President, 480-557-1221, E-mail: brian.lindquist@phoenix.edu. *Application contact:* Chair, 602-387-7000, Fax: 602-387-6020.

University of Phoenix–Atlanta Campus, John Sperling School of Business, College of Graduate Business and Management, Sandy Springs, GA 30350-4153. Offers accounting (MBA); business administration (MBA); global management (MBA); human resources management (MBA, MM); management (MM); marketing (MBA); public administration (MM). Evening/weekend programs available. Postbaccalaureate distance learning degree programs offered. *Degree requirements:* For master's, thesis (for some programs). *Entrance requirements:* For master's, minimum undergraduate GPA of 3.0, 3 years of work experience. Additional exam requirements/recommendations for international students: Required—TOEFL (minimum score 550 paper-based; 213 computer-based; 79 iBT).

University of Phoenix–Augusta Campus, College of Graduate Business and Management, Augusta, GA 30909-4583. Offers accounting (MBA); business administration (MBA); business and management (MBA, MM); global management (MBA); human resources management (MBA, MM); management (MM); marketing (MBA); public administration (MBA, MM). Postbaccalaureate distance learning degree programs offered.

University of Phoenix–Austin Campus, College of Graduate Business and Management, Austin, TX 78759. Offers accounting (MBA); business administration (MBA); business and management (MBA); e-business (MBA); global management (MBA); human resources management (MBA, MM); management (MM); marketing (MBA); public administration (MBA). Postbaccalaureate distance learning degree programs offered.

University of Phoenix–Bay Area Campus, John Sperling School of Business, College of Graduate Business and Management, Pleasanton, CA 94588-3677. Offers accounting (MBA); business administration (MBA); global management (MBA); human resources management (MBA, MM); marketing (MBA); public administration (MBA, MM). Evening/weekend programs available. Postbaccalaureate distance learning degree programs offered (no on-campus study). *Degree requirements:* For master's, thesis (for some programs). *Entrance requirements:* For master's, minimum undergraduate GPA of 3.0, 3 years of work experience. Additional exam requirements/recommendations for international students: Required—TOEFL (minimum score 550 paper-based; 213 computer-based; 79 iBT). Electronic applications accepted.

University of Phoenix–Birmingham Campus, College of Graduate Business and Management, Birmingham, AL 35244. Offers accounting (MBA); business administration (MBA); global management (MBA); human resources management (MBA, MM); management (MM); marketing (MBA); public administration (MM).

University of Phoenix–Central Florida Campus, John Sperling School of Business, College of Graduate Business and Management, Maitland, FL 32751-7057. Offers accounting (MBA); business administration (MBA); business and management (MM); global management (MBA); human resources management (MBA, MM); management (MM); marketing (MBA); public administration (MBA, MM). Evening/weekend programs available. *Degree requirements:* For master's, thesis (for some programs). *Entrance requirements:* For master's, minimum undergraduate GPA of 3.0, 3 years work experience. Additional exam requirements/recommendations for international students: Required—TOEFL (minimum score 550 paper-based; 213 computer-based; 79 iBT). Electronic applications accepted.

University of Phoenix–Central Valley Campus, College of Graduate Business and Management, Fresno, CA 93720-1562. Offers accounting (MBA); business administration (MBA); global management (MBA); human resources management (MBA, MM); management (MM); marketing (MBA); public administration (MBA, MM).

University of Phoenix–Chattanooga Campus, College of Graduate Business and Management, Chattanooga, TN 37421-3707. Offers accounting (MBA); business administration (MBA); business and management (MBA); global management (MBA); human resources management (MBA, MM); management (MM); marketing (MBA); public administration (MBA, MM). Postbaccalaureate distance learning degree programs offered.

Human Resources Management

University of Phoenix–Cheyenne Campus, College of Graduate Business and Management, Cheyenne, WY 82009. Offers global management (MBA); human resources management (MBA, MM); management (MM); marketing (MBA); public administration (MBA, MM). Postbaccalaureate distance learning degree programs offered.

University of Phoenix–Chicago Campus, John Sperling School of Business, College of Graduate Business and Management, Schaumburg, IL 60173-4399. Offers business administration (MBA); global management (MBA); human resources management (MBA); information systems (MIS); management (MM). Evening/weekend programs available. *Degree requirements:* For master's, thesis (for some programs). *Entrance requirements:* For master's, minimum undergraduate GPA of 3.0, 3 years of work experience. Additional exam requirements/recommendations for international students: Required—TOEFL (minimum score 550 paper-based; 213 computer-based; 79 iBT). Electronic applications accepted.

University of Phoenix–Cincinnati Campus, John Sperling School of Business, College of Graduate Business and Management, West Chester, OH 45069-4875. Offers accounting (MBA); business administration (MBA); global management (MBA); human resources management (MBA, MM); management (MM); marketing (MBA); public administration (MM). Evening/weekend programs available. *Degree requirements:* For master's, thesis (for some programs). *Entrance requirements:* For master's, minimum undergraduate GPA of 3.0, 3 years of work experience. Additional exam requirements/recommendations for international students: Required—TOEFL (minimum score 550 paper-based; 213 computer-based; 79 iBT). Electronic applications accepted.

University of Phoenix–Cleveland Campus, John Sperling School of Business, College of Graduate Business and Management, Independence, OH 44131-2194. Offers accounting (MBA); business administration (MBA); global management (MBA); human resources management (MBA, MM); management (MM); marketing (MBA); public administration (MBA, MM). Evening/weekend programs available. Postbaccalaureate distance learning degree programs offered (no on-campus study). *Degree requirements:* For master's, thesis (for some programs). *Entrance requirements:* For master's, minimum undergraduate GPA of 3.0, 3 years of work experience. Additional exam requirements/recommendations for international students: Required—TOEFL (minimum score 550 paper-based; 213 computer-based; 79 iBT). Electronic applications accepted.

University of Phoenix–Columbus Georgia Campus, John Sperling School of Business, College of Graduate Business and Management, Columbus, GA 31904-6321. Offers accounting (MBA); business administration (MBA); global management (MBA); human resources management (MBA, MM); management (MM); marketing (MBA); public administration (MBA). Evening/weekend programs available. *Degree requirements:* For master's, thesis (for some programs). *Entrance requirements:* For master's, minimum undergraduate GPA of 3.0, 3 years of work experience. Additional exam requirements/recommendations for international students: Required—TOEFL (minimum score 550 paper-based; 213 computer-based; 79 iBT). Electronic applications accepted.

University of Phoenix–Columbus Ohio Campus, John Sperling School of Business, College of Graduate Business and Management, Columbus, OH 43240-4032. Offers accounting (MBA); business administration (MBA); global management (MBA); human resources management (MBA, MM); management (MM); marketing (MBA); public administration (MM). Evening/weekend programs available. Postbaccalaureate distance learning degree programs offered. *Degree requirements:* For master's, thesis (for some programs). *Entrance requirements:* For master's, minimum undergraduate GPA of 3.0, 3 years of work experience. Additional exam requirements/recommendations for international students: Required—TOEFL (minimum score 550 paper-based; 213 computer-based; 79 iBT). Electronic applications accepted.

University of Phoenix–Dallas Campus, John Sperling School of Business, College of Graduate Business and Management, Dallas, TX 75251-2009. Offers accounting (MBA); business administration (MBA); global management (MBA); human resources management (MBA, MM); management (MM); marketing (MBA); public administration (MBA, MM). Evening/weekend programs available. Postbaccalaureate distance learning degree programs offered. *Degree requirements:* For master's, thesis (for some programs). *Entrance requirements:* For master's, 3 years of work experience, minimum undergraduate GPA of 3.0. Additional exam requirements/recommendations for international students: Required—TOEFL (minimum score 550 paper-based; 213 computer-based; 79 iBT). Electronic applications accepted.

University of Phoenix–Denver Campus, John Sperling School of Business, College of Graduate Business and Management, Lone Tree, CO 80124-5453. Offers accountancy (MSA); accounting (MBA); business administration (MBA); e-business (MBA); global management (MBA); human resources management (MBA, MM); management (MM); marketing (MBA); public administration (MBA, MM). Evening/weekend programs available. Postbaccalaureate distance learning degree programs offered. *Degree requirements:* For master's, thesis (for some programs). *Entrance requirements:* For master's, minimum undergraduate GPA of 3.0, 3 years work experience. Additional exam requirements/recommendations for international students: Required—TOEFL (minimum score 550 paper-based; 213 computer-based; 79 iBT). Electronic applications accepted.

University of Phoenix–Des Moines Campus, College of Graduate Business and Management, Des Moines, IA 50266. Offers accounting (MBA); business administration (MBA); global management (MBA); human resources management (MBA, MM); management (MM); marketing (MBA); public administration (MBA, MM). Postbaccalaureate distance learning degree programs offered.

University of Phoenix–Eastern Washington Campus, John Sperling School of Business, College of Graduate Business and Management, Spokane Valley, WA 99212-2531. Offers accounting (MBA); business administration (MBA); human resources management (MBA); marketing (MBA); public administration (MBA). Evening/weekend programs available. *Degree requirements:* For master's, thesis (for some programs). *Entrance requirements:* For master's, minimum undergraduate GPA of 3.0, 3 years of work experience. Additional exam requirements/recommendations for international students: Required—TOEFL (minimum score 550 paper-based; 213 computer-based; 79 iBT). Electronic applications accepted.

University of Phoenix–Harrisburg Campus, College of Graduate Business and Management, Harrisburg, PA 17112. Offers accounting (MBA); business administration (MBA); business and management (MBA); global management (MBA); human resources management (MBA, MM); management (MM); marketing (MBA); public administration (MBA, MM). Postbaccalaureate distance learning degree programs offered.

University of Phoenix–Hawaii Campus, John Sperling School of Business, College of Graduate Business and Management, Honolulu, HI 96813-4317. Offers accounting (MBA); business administration (MBA); global management (MBA); human resources management (MBA, MM); management (MM); marketing (MBA); public administration (MBA, MM). Evening/weekend programs available. *Degree requirements:* For master's, thesis (for some programs). *Entrance requirements:* For master's, minimum undergraduate GPA of 3.0, 3 years of work experience. Additional exam requirements/recommendations for international students: Required—TOEFL (minimum score 550 paper-based; 213 computer-based; 79 iBT). Electronic applications accepted.

University of Phoenix–Houston Campus, John Sperling School of Business, College of Graduate Business and Management, Houston, TX 77079-2004. Offers accounting (MBA); business administration (MBA); global management (MBA); human resources management (MBA, MM); management (MM); marketing (MBA); public administration (MBA, MM). Evening/weekend programs available. Postbaccalaureate distance learning degree programs offered. *Degree requirements:* For master's, thesis (for some programs). *Entrance requirements:* For master's, 3 years of work experience, minimum undergraduate GPA of 3.0. Additional exam requirements/recommendations for international students: Required—TOEFL (minimum score 550 paper-based; 213 computer-based; 79 iBT). Electronic applications accepted.

University of Phoenix–Idaho Campus, John Sperling School of Business, College of Graduate Business and Management, Meridian, ID 83642-3014. Offers accounting (MBA); administration (MBA); global management (MBA); human resources management (MBA, MM); management (MM); marketing (MBA); public administration (MM). Evening/weekend programs available. Postbaccalaureate distance learning degree programs offered. *Degree requirements:* For master's, thesis (for some programs). *Entrance requirements:* For master's, 3 years of work experience, minimum undergraduate GPA of 3.0. Additional exam requirements/recommendations for international students: Required—TOEFL (minimum score 550 paper-based; 213 computer-based). Electronic applications accepted.

University of Phoenix–Indianapolis Campus, John Sperling School of Business, College of Graduate Business and Management, Indianapolis, IN 46250-932. Offers accounting (MBA); business administration (MBA); global management (MBA); human resources management (MBA, MM); management (MM); marketing (MBA); public administration (MM). Evening/weekend programs available. *Degree requirements:* For master's, thesis (for some programs). *Entrance requirements:* For master's, minimum undergraduate GPA of 3.0, 3 years of work experience. Additional exam requirements/recommendations for international students: Required—TOEFL (minimum score 550 paper-based; 213 computer-based). Electronic applications accepted.

University of Phoenix–Jersey City Campus, College of Graduate Business and Management, Jersey City, NJ 07310. Offers accounting (MBA); business administration (MBA); global management (MBA); human resources management (MBA, MM); management (MM); marketing (MBA); public administration (MBA, MM).

University of Phoenix–Kansas City Campus, John Sperling School of Business, College of Graduate Business and Management, Kansas City, MO 64131-4517. Offers accounting (MBA); business administration (MBA); global management (MBA); human resources management (MBA, MM); management (MM); marketing (MBA); public administration (MBA). Evening/weekend programs available. *Degree requirements:* For master's, thesis (for some programs). *Entrance requirements:* For master's, minimum undergraduate GPA of 3.0, 3 years of work experience. Additional exam requirements/recommendations for international students: Required—TOEFL (minimum score 550 paper-based; 213 computer-based). Electronic applications accepted.

University of Phoenix–Las Vegas Campus, John Sperling School of Business, College of Graduate Business and Management, Las Vegas, NV 89128. Offers accounting (MBA); business administration (MBA); global management (MBA); human resources management (MBA, MM); management (MM); marketing (MBA); public administration (MM). Evening/weekend programs available. Postbaccalaureate distance learning degree programs offered (no on-campus study). *Degree requirements:* For master's, thesis (for some programs). *Entrance requirements:* For master's, minimum undergraduate GPA of 3.0, 3 years of work experience. Additional exam requirements/recommendations for international students: Required—TOEFL (minimum score 550 paper-based; 213 computer-based; 79 iBT). Electronic applications accepted.

University of Phoenix–Louisiana Campus, John Sperling School of Business, College of Graduate Business and Management, Metairie, LA 70001-2082. Offers accounting (MBA); business administration (MBA); global management (MBA); human resources management (MBA, MM); management (MM); marketing (MBA); public administration (MBA). Evening/weekend programs available. *Degree requirements:* For master's, thesis (for some programs). *Entrance requirements:* For master's, minimum undergraduate GPA of 3.0, 3 years work experience. Additional exam requirements/recommendations for international students: Required—TOEFL (minimum score 550 paper-based; 213 computer-based; 79 iBT). Electronic applications accepted.

University of Phoenix–Madison Campus, College of Graduate Business and Management, Madison, WI 53718-2416. Offers accounting (MBA); business and management (MBA); e-business (MBA); global management (MBA); human resources management (MBA, MM); management (MM); marketing (MBA); public administration (MBA).

University of Phoenix–Madison Campus, John Sperling School of Business, College of Graduate Business and Management, Madison, WI 53718-2416. Offers accounting (MBA); administration (MBA); global management (MBA); human resources management (MBA); management (MM); marketing (MBA); public administration (MBA). Evening/weekend programs available. *Degree requirements:* For master's, thesis (for some programs). *Entrance requirements:* For master's, 3 years of work experience, minimum undergraduate GPA of 3.0. Additional exam requirements/recommendations for international students: Required—TOEFL (minimum score 550 paper-based; 213 computer-based; 79 iBT). Electronic applications accepted.

University of Phoenix–Maryland Campus, John Sperling School of Business, College of Graduate Business and Management, Columbia, MD 21045-5424. Offers accounting (MBA); business administration (MBA); e-business (MBA); global management (MBA); human resources management (MBA, MM); management (MM); marketing (MBA); public administration (MBA, MM). Evening/weekend programs available. *Degree requirements:* For master's, thesis (for some programs). *Entrance requirements:* For master's, minimum undergraduate GPA of 3.0, 3 years of work experience. Additional exam requirements/recommendations for international students: Required—TOEFL (minimum score 550 paper-based; 213 computer-based; 79 iBT). Electronic applications accepted.

University of Phoenix–Memphis Campus, College of Graduate Business and Management, Cordova, TN 38018. Offers accounting (MBA); business and management (MBA); e-business (MBA); global management (MBA); human resources management (MBA, MM); management (MM); marketing (MBA); public administration (MBA, MM).

University of Phoenix–Metro Detroit Campus, School of Business, College of Graduate Business and Management, Troy, MI 48098-2623. Offers accountancy (MS); accounting (MBA); business administration (MBA); global management (MBA); human resources management (MBA, MM); management (MM); marketing (MBA). Evening/weekend programs available. *Degree requirements:* For master's, thesis (for some programs). *Entrance requirements:* For master's, minimum undergraduate GPA of 3.0, 3 years work experience. Additional exam requirements/recommendations for international students: Required—TOEFL (minimum score 550 paper-based; 213 computer-based; 79 iBT). Electronic applications accepted. *Expenses:* Tuition: Full-time $14,136. Required fees: $660.

University of Phoenix–Minneapolis/St. Louis Park Campus, College of Graduate Business and Management, St. Louis Park, MN 55426. Offers accounting (MBA); business administration (MBA); global management (MBA); human resources management (MBA); management (MM); marketing (MBA); public administration (MBA).

University of Phoenix–Nashville Campus, John Sperling School of Business, College of Graduate Business and Management, Nashville, TN 37214-5048. Offers business administration (MBA); human resources management (MBA); management (MM). Evening/weekend programs available. *Degree requirements:* For master's, thesis (for some programs). *Entrance requirements:* For master's, minimum undergraduate GPA of 3.0, 3 years of work experience. Additional exam requirements/recommendations for international students: Required—TOEFL (minimum score 550 paper-based; 213 computer-based; 79 iBT). Electronic applications accepted.

University of Phoenix–New Mexico Campus, John Sperling School of Business, College of Graduate Business and Management, Albuquerque, NM 87113-1570. Offers accounting (MBA); business administration (MBA); global management (MBA); human resource management (MBA); human resources management (MM); management (MM); marketing (MBA). Evening/weekend programs available. *Degree requirements:* For master's, thesis (for some programs). *Entrance requirements:* For master's, 3 years of work experience, minimum undergraduate GPA of 3.0. Additional exam requirements/recommendations for international students:

Required—TOEFL (minimum score 550 paper-based; 213 computer-based; 79 iBT). Electronic applications accepted.

University of Phoenix–Northern Nevada Campus, College of Graduate Business and Management, Reno, NV 89521-5862. Offers accounting (MBA); business administration (MBA); global management (MBA); human resources management (MBA, MM); management (MM); marketing (MBA); public administration (MBA, MM).

University of Phoenix–Northern Virginia Campus, College of Graduate Business and Management, Reston, VA 20190. Offers accounting (MBA); business administration (MBA); e-business (MBA); global management (MBA); human resources management (MBA, MM); management (MM); marketing (MBA); public administration (MBA).

University of Phoenix–North Florida Campus, John Sperling School of Business, College of Graduate Business and Management, Jacksonville, FL 32216-0959. Offers accounting (MBA); business administration (MBA); global management (MBA); human resources management (MBA, MM); management (MM); marketing (MBA); public administration (MBA, MM). Evening/weekend programs available. *Degree requirements:* For master's, thesis (for some programs). *Entrance requirements:* For master's, minimum undergraduate GPA of 3.0, 3 years work experience. Additional exam requirements/recommendations for international students: Required—TOEFL (minimum score 550 paper-based; 213 computer-based; 79 iBT). Electronic applications accepted.

University of Phoenix–Northwest Arkansas Campus, College of Graduate Business and Management, Rogers, AR 72756-9615. Offers accounting (MBA); business and management (MBA); global management (MBA); human resources management (MBA, MM); management (MM); marketing (MBA); public administration (MBA, MM).

University of Phoenix–Oklahoma City Campus, John Sperling School of Business, College of Graduate Business and Management, Oklahoma City, OK 73116-8244. Offers accounting (MBA); business administration (MBA); global management (MBA); human resource management (MBA); management (MM); marketing (MBA). Evening/weekend programs available. *Degree requirements:* For master's, thesis (for some programs). *Entrance requirements:* For master's, minimum undergraduate GPA of 3.0, 3 years of work experience. Additional exam requirements/recommendations for international students: Required—TOEFL (minimum score 550 paper-based; 213 computer-based; 79 iBT). Electronic applications accepted.

University of Phoenix–Omaha Campus, College of Graduate Business and Management, Omaha, NE 68154-5240. Offers accounting (MBA); business and management (MBA); global management (MBA); human resources management (MBA, MM); management (MM); marketing (MBA); public administration (MBA, MM).

University of Phoenix–Oregon Campus, The John Sperling School of Business, College of Graduate Business and Management, Tigard, OR 97223. Offers accounting (MBA); business administration (MBA); global management (MBA); human resource management (MM); human resources management (MM); management (MM); marketing (MBA); public administration (MM). Evening/weekend programs available. *Degree requirements:* For master's, thesis (for some programs). *Entrance requirements:* For master's, minimum undergraduate GPA of 3.0, 3 years of work experience. Additional exam requirements/recommendations for international students: Required—TOEFL (minimum score 550 paper-based; 213 computer-based; 79 iBT). Electronic applications accepted.

University of Phoenix–Philadelphia Campus, The John Sperling School of Business, College of Graduate Business and Management, Wayne, PA 19087-2121. Offers accounting (MBA); business administration (MBA); global management (MBA); human resources management (MBA, MM); management (MM); marketing (MBA); public administration (MM). Evening/weekend programs available. *Degree requirements:* For master's, thesis (for some programs). *Entrance requirements:* For master's, minimum undergraduate GPA of 3.0, 3 years work experience. Additional exam requirements/recommendations for international students: Required—TOEFL (minimum score 550 paper-based; 213 computer-based; 79 iBT). Electronic applications accepted.

University of Phoenix–Pittsburgh Campus, John Sperling School of Business, College of Graduate Business and Management, Pittsburgh, PA 15276. Offers accounting (MBA); business administration (MBA); global management (MBA); human resources management (MBA, MM); management (MM); marketing (MBA); public administration (MBA, MM). Evening/weekend programs available. *Degree requirements:* For master's, thesis (for some programs). *Entrance requirements:* For master's, minimum undergraduate GPA of 3.0, 3 years work experience. Additional exam requirements/recommendations for international students: Required—TOEFL (minimum score 550 paper-based; 213 computer-based; 79 iBT). Electronic applications accepted.

University of Phoenix–Puerto Rico Campus, John Sperling School of Business, College of Graduate Business and Management, Guaynabo, PR 00968. Offers accounting (MBA); business administration (MBA); global management (MBA); human resource management (MBA); marketing (MBA). Evening/weekend programs available. *Degree requirements:* For master's, thesis (for some programs). *Entrance requirements:* For master's, minimum undergraduate GPA of 3.0, 3 years work experience. Additional exam requirements/recommendations for international students: Required—TOEFL (minimum score 550 paper-based; 213 computer-based; 79 iBT). Electronic applications accepted.

University of Phoenix–Raleigh Campus, College of Graduate Business and Management, Raleigh, NC 27606. Offers accounting (MBA); business administration (MBA); e-business (MBA); global management (MBA); human resources management (MBA); marketing (MBA).

University of Phoenix–Richmond Campus, John Sperling School of Business, College of Graduate Business and Management, Richmond, VA 23230. Offers accounting (MBA); business administration (MBA); global management (MBA); human resources management (MBA, MM); management (MM); marketing (MBA); public administration (MBA, MM). Evening/weekend programs available. *Degree requirements:* For master's, thesis (for some programs). *Entrance requirements:* For master's, minimum undergraduate GPA of 3.0, 3 years work experience. Additional exam requirements/recommendations for international students: Required—TOEFL (minimum score 550 paper-based; 213 computer-based; 79 iBT). Electronic applications accepted.

University of Phoenix–Sacramento Valley Campus, John Sperling School of Business, College of Graduate Business and Management, Sacramento, CA 95833-3632. Offers accounting (MBA); business administration (MBA); global management (MBA); human resources management (MBA, MM); management (MM); marketing (MBA); public administration (MBA, MM). Evening/weekend programs available. *Degree requirements:* For master's, thesis (for some programs). *Entrance requirements:* For master's, minimum undergraduate GPA of 3.0, 3 years work experience. Additional exam requirements/recommendations for international students: Required—TOEFL (minimum score 550 paper-based; 213 computer-based; 79 iBT). Electronic applications accepted.

University of Phoenix–St. Louis Campus, John Sperling School of Business, College of Graduate Business and Management, St. Louis, MO 63043-4828. Offers accounting (MBA); business administration (MBA); global management (MBA); human resources management (MBA, MM); management (MM); marketing (MBA); public administration (MM). Evening/weekend programs available. *Degree requirements:* For master's, thesis (for some programs). *Entrance requirements:* For master's, 3 years of work experience, minimum undergraduate GPA of 3.0. Additional exam requirements/recommendations for international students: Required—TOEFL (minimum score 550 paper-based; 213 computer-based; 79 iBT). Electronic applications accepted.

University of Phoenix–San Antonio Campus, College of Graduate Business and Management, San Antonio, TX 78230. Offers accounting (MBA); business administration (MBA); e-business (MBA); global management (MBA); human resources management (MBA, MM); management (MM); marketing (MBA); public administration (MBA, MM).

University of Phoenix–San Diego Campus, John Sperling School of Business, College of Graduate Business and Management, San Diego, CA 92123. Offers accounting (MBA); business administration (MBA); global management (MBA); human resources management (MBA, MM); management (MM); marketing (MBA); public administration (MBA). Evening/weekend programs available. *Degree requirements:* For master's, thesis (for some programs). *Entrance requirements:* For master's, 3 years of work experience, minimum undergraduate GPA of 3.0. Additional exam requirements/recommendations for international students: Required—TOEFL (minimum score 550 paper-based; 213 computer-based; 79 iBT). Electronic applications accepted.

University of Phoenix–Savannah Campus, College of Graduate Business and Management, Savannah, GA 31405-7400. Offers accounting (MBA); business administration (MBA); global management (MBA); human resources management (MBA, MM); management (MM); marketing (MBA); public administration (MBA, MM).

University of Phoenix–Southern Arizona Campus, John Sperling School of Business, College of Graduate Business and Management, Tucson, AZ 85711. Offers accountancy (MS); accounting (MBA); business administration (MBA); global management (MBA); human resources management (MBA); management (MM); marketing (MBA). Evening/weekend programs available. *Degree requirements:* For master's, thesis (for some programs). *Entrance requirements:* For master's, minimum undergraduate GPA of 3.0, 3 years of work experience. Additional exam requirements/recommendations for international students: Required—TOEFL (minimum score 550 paper-based; 213 computer-based; 79 iBT). Electronic applications accepted.

University of Phoenix–Southern Colorado Campus, John Sperling School of Business, College of Graduate Business and Management, Colorado Springs, CO 80919-2335. Offers accounting (MBA); business administration (MBA); global management (MBA); human resources management (MBA, MM); management (MM); marketing (MBA); public administration (MM). Evening/weekend programs available. *Degree requirements:* For master's, thesis (for some programs). *Entrance requirements:* For master's, minimum undergraduate GPA of 3.0, 3 years of work experience. Additional exam requirements/recommendations for international students: Required—TOEFL (minimum score 550 paper-based; 213 computer-based; 79 iBT). Electronic applications accepted.

University of Phoenix–South Florida Campus, John Sperling School of Business, College of Graduate Business and Management, Fort Lauderdale, FL 33309. Offers accounting (MBA); business administration (MBA); global management (MBA); human resource management (MBA); human resources management (MM); management (MM); marketing (MBA); public administration (MBA, MM). Evening/weekend programs available. *Degree requirements:* For master's, thesis (for some programs). *Entrance requirements:* For master's, minimum undergraduate GPA of 3.0, 3 years work experience. Additional exam requirements/recommendations for international students: Required—TOEFL (minimum score 550 paper-based; 213 computer-based; 79 iBT). Electronic applications accepted.

University of Phoenix–Springfield Campus, College of Graduate Business and Management, Springfield, MO 65804-7211. Offers accounting (MBA); business administration (MBA); global management (MBA); human resources management (MBA, MM); management (MM); marketing (MBA); public administration (MBA, MM).

University of Phoenix–Tulsa Campus, John Sperling School of Business, College of Graduate Business and Management, Tulsa, OK 74134-1412. Offers accounting (MBA); business (MM); business administration (MBA); global management (MBA); human resources management (MBA); marketing (MBA). Evening/weekend programs available. *Degree requirements:* For master's, thesis (for some programs). *Entrance requirements:* For master's, minimum undergraduate GPA of 3.0, 3 years work experience. Additional exam requirements/recommendations for international students: Required—TOEFL (minimum score 550 paper-based; 213 computer-based; 79 iBT).

University of Phoenix–Utah Campus, John Sperling School of Business, College of Graduate Business and Management, Salt Lake City, UT 84123-4617. Offers accounting (MBA); business administration (MBA); global management (MBA); human resource management (MBA, MM); management (MM); marketing (MBA); technology management (MBA). Evening/weekend programs available. *Degree requirements:* For master's, thesis (for some programs). *Entrance requirements:* For master's, minimum undergraduate GPA of 3.0, 3 years of work experience. Additional exam requirements/recommendations for international students: Required—TOEFL (minimum score 550 paper-based; 213 computer-based; 79 iBT). Electronic applications accepted.

University of Phoenix–Vancouver Campus, John Sperling School of Business, College of Graduate Business and Management, Burnaby, BC V5C 6G9, Canada. Offers accounting (MBA); business administration (MBA); global management (MBA); human resources management (MBA, MM); marketing (MBA). Evening/weekend programs available. *Degree requirements:* For master's, thesis (for some programs). *Entrance requirements:* For master's, minimum undergraduate GPA of 3.0, 3 years of work experience. Additional exam requirements/recommendations for international students: Required—TOEFL (minimum score 550 paper-based; 213 computer-based; 79 iBT). Electronic applications accepted.

University of Phoenix–Western Washington Campus, College of Graduate Business and Management, Tukwila, WA 98188. Offers accounting (MBA); business and management (MBA, MM); global management (MBA); human resources management (MBA, MM); marketing (MBA); public administration (MBA, MM). Evening/weekend programs available. *Degree requirements:* For master's, thesis (for some programs). *Entrance requirements:* For master's, minimum undergraduate GPA of 3.0, 3 years of work experience. Additional exam requirements/recommendations for international students: Required—TOEFL (minimum score 550 paper-based; 213 computer-based; 79 iBT). Electronic applications accepted.

University of Phoenix–West Florida Campus, The John Sperling School of Business, College of Graduate Business and Management, Temple Terrace, FL 33637. Offers accounting (MBA); business administration (MBA); global management (MBA); human resources management (MBA, MM); management (MM); marketing (MBA); public administration (MBA, MM). Evening/weekend programs available. *Degree requirements:* For master's, thesis (for some programs). *Entrance requirements:* For master's, 3 years of work experience, minimum undergraduate GPA of 3.0. Additional exam requirements/recommendations for international students: Required—TOEFL (minimum score 550 paper-based; 213 computer-based; 79 iBT). Electronic applications accepted.

University of Pittsburgh, Katz Graduate School of Business, Doctoral Program in Business Administration, Pittsburgh, PA 15260. Offers accounting (PhD); finance (PhD); information systems (PhD); marketing (PhD); operations/decision sciences/artificial intelligence (PhD); organizational behavior and human resource management (PhD); strategic planning (PhD). *Accreditation:* AACSB. *Faculty:* 50 full-time (15 women). *Students:* 53 full-time (21 women); includes 8 minority (4 African Americans, 2 Asian Americans or Pacific Islanders, 2 Hispanic Americans), 22 international. 324 applicants, 4% accepted, 12 enrolled. In 2009, 11 doctorates awarded. *Degree requirements:* For doctorate, comprehensive exam, thesis/dissertation. *Entrance requirements:* For doctorate, GMAT or GRE, references, work experience relevant for individual program. Additional exam requirements/recommendations for international students: Required—TOEFL or IELTS. *Application deadline:* For fall admission, 2/1 priority date for domestic and international students. Applications are processed on a rolling basis. Application fee: $50. Electronic applications accepted. *Expenses:* Tuition, state resident: full-time $16,402; part-time $665 per credit. Tuition, nonresident: full-time $28,694; part-time $1175 per credit. Required fees: $690; $175 per term. Tuition and fees vary according to program. *Financial support:* In 2009–10, 36 students received support, including 31 research assistantships with full tuition reimbursements available (averaging $18,450 per year), 5 teaching assistantships

Human Resources Management

University of Pittsburgh (continued)
with full tuition reimbursements available (averaging $23,511 per year); fellowships, Federal Work-Study, scholarships/grants, health care benefits, and unspecified assistantships also available. Financial award application deadline: 2/1. *Faculty research:* Accounting statements and reporting, incentives and governance; corporate finance, mergers and acquisitions; information systems processes, structures, OR, supply chain, and decision-making; organizational structure, knowledge management, and corporate strategy; consumer behavior and marketing models. Total annual research expenditures: $362,777. *Unit head:* Dr. John E. Hulland, Director, 412-648-1534, Fax: 412-624-3633, E-mail: jhulland@katz.pitt.edu. *Application contact:* Carrie Woods, Assistant Director, 412-648-1525, Fax: 412-624-3633, E-mail: cawoods@katz.pitt.edu.

University of Pittsburgh, Katz Graduate School of Business, Masters of Business Administration Programs, Pittsburgh, PA 15260. Offers accounting (MS); finance (MBA); general management (MBA); information systems (MBA, MSIS); marketing (MBA); organizational behavior and human resource management (MBA); organizational leadership (Certificate); six sigma (Certificate); strategy (MBA); technology, innovation and entrepreneurship (Certificate); MBA/JD; MBA/MIB; MBA/MPIA; MBA/MSE; MBA/MSIS. *Accreditation:* AACSB. Part-time and evening/weekend programs available. *Faculty:* 58 full-time (12 women), 23 part-time/adjunct (7 women). *Students:* 192 full-time (62 women), 506 part-time (179 women); includes 58 minority (29 African Americans, 1 American Indian/Alaska Native, 24 Asian Americans or Pacific Islanders, 4 Hispanic Americans), 101 international. Average age 29. 674 applicants, 52% accepted, 204 enrolled. In 2009, 263 master's awarded. *Entrance requirements:* For master's, GMAT, references, work experience relevant for individual programs. Additional exam requirements/recommendations for international students: Required—TOEFL (minimum score 600 paper-based; 250 computer-based; 100 iBT), or IELTS. *Application deadline:* For fall admission, 7/1 for domestic and international students; for winter admission, 11/1 for domestic and international students; for spring admission, 3/1 for domestic and international students. Applications are processed on a rolling basis. Application fee: $50. Electronic applications accepted. *Expenses:* Tuition, state resident: full-time $16,402; part-time $665 per credit. Tuition, nonresident: full-time $28,694; part-time $1175 per credit. Required fees: $690; $175 per term. Tuition and fees vary according to program. *Financial support:* In 2009–10, 75 students received support. Career-related internships or fieldwork and scholarships/grants available. Financial award application deadline: 6/1; financial award applicants required to submit FAFSA. *Faculty research:* Accounting statements and reporting, incentives and governance; corporate finance, mergers and acquisitions; information systems processes, structures, and decision-making; organizational structure, knowledge management, and corporate strategy; consumer behavior and marketing models. *Unit head:* William T. Valenta, Assistant Dean/MBA Program Director, 412-648-1610, Fax: 412-648-1659, E-mail: wtvalenta@katz.pitt.edu. *Application contact:* Cliff McCormick, Director of MBA Admissions, 412-648-1700, Fax: 412-648-1659, E-mail: mba@katz.pitt.edu.

University of Puerto Rico, Mayagüez Campus, Graduate Studies, College of Business Administration, Mayagüez, PR 00681-9000. Offers business administration (MBA); finance (MBA); human resources (MBA); industrial management (MBA). Part-time and evening/weekend programs available. *Degree requirements:* For master's, comprehensive exam. *Entrance requirements:* For master's, GMAT or EXADEP, bachelor's degree with courses in calculus, microeconomics, accounting and statistics. Additional exam requirements/recommendations for international students: Required—TOEFL (minimum score 500 paper-based; 173 computer-based). *Faculty research:* Organizational studies, management, accounting.

University of Puerto Rico, Río Piedras, College of Business Administration, San Juan, PR 00931-3300. Offers accounting (MBA); finance (MBA, PhD); general business (MBA); human resources management (MBA); international trade and business (MBA, PhD); marketing (MBA); operations management (MBA); quantitative methods (MBA). *Accreditation:* ACBSP. Part-time programs available. *Degree requirements:* For master's, comprehensive exam, thesis or alternative, research project. *Entrance requirements:* For master's, GMAT or PAEG, minimum GPA of 3.0, letter of recommendation; for doctorate, GMAT, PAEG, minimum GPA of 3.0, master degree. *Faculty research:* Management.

University of Regina, Faculty of Graduate Studies and Research, Kenneth Levene Graduate School of Business, Program in Human Resources Management, Regina, SK S4S 0A2, Canada. Offers MHRM, Master's Certificate. *Faculty:* 25 full-time (5 women), 3 part-time/adjunct (0 women). *Students:* 18 full-time (11 women), 31 part-time (22 women). 41 applicants, 71% accepted. In 2009, 12 master's awarded. *Degree requirements:* For master's, project. *Entrance requirements:* For master's, 2 years of relevant work experience. Additional exam requirements/recommendations for international students: Required—TOEFL (minimum score 580 paper-based; 237 computer-based; 80 iBT). *Application deadline:* Applications are processed on a rolling basis. Application fee: $90 ($100 for international students). Electronic applications accepted. *Expenses:* Contact institution. *Financial support:* In 2009–10, 4 fellowships (averaging $19,000 per year), 2 research assistantships (averaging $16,910 per year), 6 teaching assistantships (averaging $6,650 per year) were awarded. Financial award application deadline: 6/15. *Unit head:* Ann Lavack, 306-585-4716, E-mail: ann.lavack@uregina.ca. *Application contact:* Dr. Ronald Crump, Professor, 306-337-2387, Fax: 306-585-4805, E-mail: ronald.crump@uregina.ca.

University of Rhode Island, Graduate School, Labor Research Center, Kingston, RI 02881. Offers labor relations and human resources (MS); MS/JD. Part-time and evening/weekend programs available. *Faculty:* 2 full-time (0 women), 2 part-time/adjunct (1 woman). *Students:* 6 full-time (3 women), 25 part-time (21 women); includes 3 minority (2 African Americans, 1 Hispanic American), 2 international. In 2009, 4 master's awarded. *Entrance requirements:* For master's, GRE, MAT, GMAT, or LSAT, 2 letters of recommendation. Additional exam requirements/recommendations for international students: Required—TOEFL (minimum score 550 paper-based; 213 computer-based). *Application deadline:* For fall admission, 7/15 for domestic students, 2/1 for international students; for spring admission, 11/15 for domestic students, 7/15 for international students. Application fee: $65. Electronic applications accepted. *Expenses:* Tuition, state resident: full-time $8828; part-time $490 per credit hour. Tuition, nonresident: full-time $22,100; part-time $1228 per credit hour. Required fees: $1118; $57 per semester. Tuition and fees vary according to program. *Financial support:* In 2009–10, 1 teaching assistantship with full tuition reimbursement (averaging $13,894 per year) was awarded; institutionally sponsored loans also available. Financial award application deadline: 2/1; financial award applicants required to submit FAFSA. Total annual research expenditures: $11,637. *Unit head:* Dr. Richard W. Scholl, Director, 401-874-4347, Fax: 401-874-2954, E-mail: rscholl@uri.edu. *Application contact:* Dr. Richard W. Scholl, Director, 401-874-4347, Fax: 401-874-2954, E-mail: rscholl@uri.edu.

University of St. Thomas, Graduate Studies, School of Education, Program in Organization Learning and Development, St. Paul, MN 55105-1096. Offers career development (Certificate); e-learning (Certificate); human resource management (Certificate); human resources and change leadership (MA); learning technology (Certificate); learning technology for learning development and change (MA); organization development (Ed D, Certificate). Part-time and evening/weekend programs available. Postbaccalaureate distance learning degree programs offered (minimal on-campus study). *Faculty:* 5 full-time (4 women), 6 part-time/adjunct (2 women). *Students:* 6 full-time (5 women), 161 part-time (130 women); includes 24 minority (13 African Americans, 7 Asian Americans or Pacific Islanders, 4 Hispanic Americans), 1 international. Average age 37. 115 applicants, 75% accepted, 85 enrolled. In 2009, 29 master's, 7 doctorates, 18 other advanced degrees awarded. *Degree requirements:* For doctorate, comprehensive exam, thesis/dissertation. *Entrance requirements:* For master's, minimum GPA of 3.0, 2 letters of reference, personal statement; for doctorate, minimum GPA of 3.5, interview; for Certificate, minimum graduate GPA of 3.25. Additional exam requirements/recommendations for international students: Required—TOEFL (minimum score 550 paper-based; 213 computer-based). *Application deadline:* For fall admission, 8/1 priority date for domestic and international

students; for winter admission, 12/1 priority date for domestic students, 12/1 for international students; for spring admission, 12/1 priority date for domestic and international students. Applications are processed on a rolling basis. Application fee: $50. *Expenses:* Contact institution. *Financial support:* Fellowships, research assistantships, institutionally sponsored loans and scholarships/grants available. Support available to part-time students. Financial award applicants required to submit FAFSA. *Faculty research:* Workplace conflict, physician leaders, entrepreneurship education, mentoring. *Unit head:* Dr. Christopher S. Vye, Acting Department Chair, 651-962-4666, Fax: 651-962-4169, E-mail: csvye@stthomas.edu. *Application contact:* Liz G. Knight, Department Coordinator, 651-962-4459, Fax: 651-962-4169, E-mail: egknight@stthomas.edu.

The University of Scranton, College of Graduate and Continuing Education, Department of Health Administration and Human Resources, Program in Human Resources Administration, Scranton, PA 18510. Offers human resources (MS); human resources development (MS); organizational leadership (MS). Part-time and evening/weekend programs available. *Students:* 10 full-time (6 women), 8 part-time (5 women); includes 2 minority (1 African American, 1 Hispanic American), 8 international. Average age 34. 1 applicant, 0% accepted. In 2009, 21 master's awarded. *Degree requirements:* For master's, capstone experience. *Entrance requirements:* For master's, minimum GPA of 2.75. Additional exam requirements/recommendations for international students: Required—TOEFL (minimum score 500 paper-based; 173 computer-based), IELTS (minimum score 5.5). *Application deadline:* Applications are processed on a rolling basis. Application fee: $0. *Financial support:* Fellowships, teaching assistantships, career-related internships or fieldwork, Federal Work-Study, and unspecified assistantships available. Support available to part-time students. Financial award application deadline: 3/1. *Unit head:* Dr. Daniel West, Director, 570-941-6218, E-mail: westd1@scranton.edu. *Application contact:* Joseph M. Roback, Director of Admissions, 570-941-4385, Fax: 570-941-5928, E-mail: roback j2@scranton.edu.

University of South Carolina, The Graduate School, Moore School of Business, Human Resources Program, Columbia, SC 29208. Offers MHR, JD/MHR. Part-time programs available. *Degree requirements:* For master's, thesis optional, internship. *Entrance requirements:* For master's, GMAT or GRE, minimum GPA of 3.0. Additional exam requirements/recommendations for international students: Required—TOEFL (minimum score 600 paper-based; 250 computer-based). Electronic applications accepted. *Faculty research:* Performance appraisal, work values, grievance systems, union formation, group behavior.

The University of Texas at Arlington, Graduate School, College of Business, Department of Management, Arlington, TX 76019. Offers human resources (MSHRM). Part-time and evening/weekend programs available. *Faculty:* 16 full-time (6 women). *Students:* 25 full-time (15 women), 37 part-time (25 women); includes 12 minority (7 African Americans, 1 Asian American or Pacific Islander, 4 Hispanic Americans), 12 international. 42 applicants, 95% accepted, 13 enrolled. In 2009, 17 master's awarded. *Degree requirements:* For master's, thesis optional. *Entrance requirements:* For master's, GMAT. Additional exam requirements/recommendations for international students: Required—TOEFL (minimum score 550 paper-based; 213 computer-based; 79 iBT). *Application deadline:* For fall admission, 6/5 priority date for domestic students, 4/1 for international students; for spring admission, 10/15 for domestic students, 9/1 for international students. Applications are processed on a rolling basis. Application fee: $35 ($50 for international students). *Financial support:* In 2009–10, 4 fellowships (averaging $1,000 per year), 1 research assistantship (averaging $6,000 per year), 12 teaching assistantships (averaging $13,000 per year) were awarded; career-related internships or fieldwork, scholarships/grants, and unspecified assistantships also available. Support available to part-time students. Financial award application deadline: 6/1; financial award applicants required to submit FAFSA. *Faculty research:* Compensations, training, diversity, strategic human resources. *Unit head:* Dr. Jeffrey McGee, Chair, 817-272-3166, Fax: 817-272-3122, E-mail: jmcgee@uta.edu. *Application contact:* Dennis Veit, Graduate Advisor, 817-272-3865, Fax: 817-272-3122, E-mail: dveit@uta.edu.

University of the Sacred Heart, Graduate Programs, Department of Business Administration, Program in Human Resource Management, San Juan, PR 00914-0383. Offers MBA. Part-time and evening/weekend programs available. *Degree requirements:* For master's, thesis. *Entrance requirements:* For master's, EXADEP, minimum undergraduate GPA of 2.75, interview.

The University of Toledo, College of Graduate Studies, College of Business Administration, Department of Management, Program in Human Resource Management, Toledo, OH 43606-3390. Offers MBA. *Entrance requirements:* For master's, GMAT.

University of Toronto, School of Graduate Studies, Social Sciences Division, Centre for Industrial Relations and Human Resources, Toronto, ON M5S 1A1, Canada. Offers MHRIR, PhD. Part-time programs available. *Degree requirements:* For doctorate, thesis/dissertation. *Entrance requirements:* For master's, GRE or GMAT (for applicants who completed degree outside of Canada), minimum B+ in final 2 years of bachelor's degree completion, 2 letters of reference, resume; for doctorate, GRE or GMAT, MIR degree or equivalent, minimum B+ average, 3 letters of reference, resumé. Additional exam requirements/recommendations for international students: Required—TOEFL (minimum score 600 paper-based; 250 computer-based), TWE (minimum score 5), Michigan English Language Assessment Battery, IELTS, or COPE. *Expenses:* Contact institution.

University of Wisconsin–Madison, Graduate School, Wisconsin School of Business, Doctoral Program in Management and Human Resources, Madison, WI 53706-1380. Offers PhD. *Faculty:* 13 full-time (4 women), 2 part-time/adjunct (0 women). *Students:* 10 full-time (4 women), 4 international. Average age 31. 44 applicants, 9% accepted, 3 enrolled. In 2009, 1 doctorate awarded. *Degree requirements:* For doctorate, comprehensive exam, thesis/dissertation. *Entrance requirements:* For doctorate, GMAT or GRE. Additional exam requirements/recommendations for international students: Required—Pearson Test of English (minimum score 73, written 80); Recommended—TOEFL (minimum score 623 paper-based; 263 computer-based; 106 iBT), IELTS (minimum score 7.5). *Application deadline:* For fall admission, 12/15 priority date for domestic and international students. Application fee: $56. Electronic applications accepted. *Expenses:* Tuition, state resident: part-time $594 per credit. Tuition, nonresident: part-time $1504 per credit. Required fees: $65 per credit. Tuition and fees vary according to course load, program and reciprocity agreements. *Financial support:* In 2009–10, 10 students received support, including fellowships with tuition reimbursements available (averaging $18,567 per year), research assistantships with full tuition reimbursements available (averaging $16,506 per year), 7 teaching assistantships with full tuition reimbursements available (averaging $14,088 per year); Federal Work-Study, institutionally sponsored loans, scholarships/grants, health care benefits, and unspecified assistantships also available. Financial award application deadline: 2/1; financial award applicants required to submit FAFSA. *Faculty research:* Employee compensation, performance for work groups, small business management, venture financing, arts industry. *Unit head:* Prof. Barry Gerhart, Chair, 608-262-3895, E-mail: bgerhart@bus.wisc.edu. *Application contact:* Belle Heberling, Assistant Director for Research Programs, 608-262-3749, Fax: 608-890-0180, E-mail: phd@bus.wisc.edu.

University of Wisconsin–Madison, Graduate School, Wisconsin School of Business, Wisconsin Full-Time MBA Program, Madison, WI 53706-1380. Offers applied corporate finance (MBA); applied security analysis (MBA); arts administration (MBA); brand and product management (MBA); entrepreneurial management (MBA); marketing research (MBA); operations and technology management (MBA); real estate (MBA); risk management and insurance (MBA); strategic human resource management (MBA); strategic management in the life and engineering sciences (MBA); supply chain management (MBA). *Faculty:* 32 full-time (5 women). *Students:* 242 full-time (74 women); includes 47 minority (16 African Americans, 3 American Indian/Alaska Native, 16 Asian Americans or Pacific Islanders, 12 Hispanic Americans), 29 international. Average age 28. 526 applicants, 32% accepted, 117 enrolled. In 2009, 106 master's awarded. *Entrance requirements:* For master's, GMAT, bachelor's or equivalent degree, 2 years of work experience, letters of recommendation. Additional exam requirements/recommendations for international students: Required—TOEFL (minimum score 600 paper-based; 250 computer-based; 100 iBT), IELTS. *Application deadline:* For fall admission, 11/4 for domestic and

international students; for winter admission, 2/5 for domestic and international students; for spring admission, 5/26 for domestic students, 4/5 for international students. Applications are processed on a rolling basis. Application fee: $56. Electronic applications accepted. *Expenses:* Tuition, state resident: part-time $594 per credit. Tuition, nonresident: part-time $1504 per credit. Required fees: $65 per credit. Tuition and fees vary according to course load, program and reciprocity agreements. *Financial support:* In 2009–10, 103 students received support, including 13 fellowships with full and partial tuition reimbursements available (averaging $15,000 per year), 53 research assistantships with full tuition reimbursements available (averaging $8,000 per year), 35 teaching assistantships with full tuition reimbursements available (averaging $11,000 per year); scholarships/grants, health care benefits, and unspecified assistantships also available. Financial award application deadline: 4/5; financial award applicants required to submit FAFSA. *Unit head:* Prof. Kenneth A. Kavajecz, Associate Dean, 608-265-3494, Fax: 608-265-4192, E-mail: kkavajecz@bus.wisc.edu. *Application contact:* Maria Reis, Assistant Director of MBA Marketing and Recruiting, 608-262-4000, Fax: 608-265-4192, E-mail: mreis@bus.wisc.edu.

University of Wisconsin–Whitewater, School of Graduate Studies, College of Business and Economics, Program in Business Administration, Whitewater, WI 53190-1790. Offers finance (MBA); human resource management (MBA); information technology management (MBA); international business (MBA); management (MBA); marketing (MBA); operations and supply chain management (MBA); technology and training (MBA). *Accreditation:* AACSB. Part-time and evening/weekend programs available. Postbaccalaureate distance learning degree programs offered (no on-campus study). *Degree requirements:* For master's, thesis or alternative. *Entrance requirements:* For master's, GMAT, minimum AACSB index of 1000, minimum GPA of 2.75. Additional exam requirements/recommendations for international students: Required—TOEFL (minimum score 550 paper-based; 213 computer-based). Electronic applications accepted. *Faculty research:* Interface between social institutions and individual behavior, technology and innovation management, occupational mental health, workplace deviance and workplace romance.

See Display on page 190.

Upper Iowa University, Online Master's Programs, Fayette, IA 52142-1857. Offers accounting (MBA); corporate financial management (MBA); global business (MBA); health and human services (MPA); higher education administration (MHEA); homeland security (MPA); human resources management (MBA); justice administration (MPA); organizational development (MBA); public personnel management (MPA); quality management (MBA). MBA also available at Madison, WI campus. Part-time programs available. Postbaccalaureate distance learning degree programs offered (no on-campus study). *Faculty:* 3 full-time (0 women), 66 part-time/adjunct (27 women). *Students:* 723 full-time (442 women). *Degree requirements:* For master's, research project. *Entrance requirements:* For master's, GMAT, GRE, or minimum GPA of 2.7 during last 60 hours. Additional exam requirements/recommendations for international students: Required—TOEFL (minimum score 570 paper-based; 230 computer-based). *Application deadline:* Applications are processed on a rolling basis. Application fee: $50. Electronic applications accepted. *Expenses:* Tuition: Full-time $6948; part-time $386 per credit hour. *Financial support:* Available to part-time students. Applicants required to submit FAFSA. *Faculty research:* Total quality management, CQI, teams, organization culture and climate, management. *Application contact:* David Hannum, Admissions Advisor, 800-603-3756, E-mail: hannumd@uiu.edu.

Utah State University, School of Graduate Studies, College of Business, Program in Human Resource Management, Logan, UT 84322. Offers MS. Part-time and evening/weekend programs available. Postbaccalaureate distance learning degree programs offered. *Entrance requirements:* For master's, GMAT or GRE, minimum GPA of 3.0. Additional exam requirements/recommendations for international students: Required—TOEFL. Electronic applications accepted. *Expenses:* Contact institution. *Faculty research:* International human resources, aging workforce.

Virginia International University, Business Programs Department, Fairfax, VA 22030. Offers accounting (MBA); executive management (Graduate Certificate); global logistics (MBA); health care management (MBA); human resources management (MBA); international business management (MBA); international finance (MBA); marketing management (MBA). Part-time programs available. *Faculty:* 12 part-time/adjunct (1 woman). *Students:* 138 full-time (63 women), 7 part-time (5 women); includes 7 minority (1 African American, 5 Asian Americans or Pacific Islanders, 1 Hispanic American), 136 international. Average age 27. 331 applicants, 31% accepted, 40 enrolled. In 2009, 42 master's awarded. *Entrance requirements:* For master's and Graduate Certificate, bachelor's degree. Additional exam requirements/recommendations for international students: Required—TOEFL (minimum score 550 paper-based; 213 computer-based; 80 iBT), IELTS (minimum score 6). *Application deadline:* For fall admission, 7/31 for domestic students, 7/3 for international students; for spring admission, 12/18 for domestic students, 11/20 for international students. Applications are processed on a rolling basis. Application fee: $100. Electronic applications accepted. *Expenses:* Tuition: Full-time $10,044; part-time $569 per credit. One-time fee: $75. Tuition and fees vary according to degree level. *Financial support:* In 2009–10, 10 students received support. Scholarships/grants available. Financial award application deadline: 7/1. *Unit head:* Dr. Gail Whitaker, Chair, 703-591-7042 Ext. 346, Fax: 703-591-7046, E-mail: gwhitaker@viu.edu. *Application contact:* Emily L. Kraus, Director of Admissions, 703-591-7042 Ext. 309, Fax: 703-591-7048, E-mail: admissions@viu.edu.

Walden University, Graduate Programs, School of Management, Minneapolis, MN 55401. Offers applied management and decision sciences (PhD), including accounting, engineering management, finance, general applied management and decision sciences, information systems management, knowledge management, leadership and organizational change, learning management, operations research, self-designed program in applied management and design sciences; business information management (MISM); enterprise information security (MISM); entrepreneurship (MBA, DBA); finance (MBA, DBA); global supply chain management (DBA); healthcare management (MBA); healthcare system improvement (MBA); human resource management (MBA); information systems management (DBA); international business (MBA, DBA); IT strategy and governance (MISM); leadership (MBA, MS, DBA), including entrepreneurship (MS), general management (MS), human resources leadership (MS), innovation and technology (MS), leader development (MS), project management (MS), self-designed (MS), sustainable futures (MS); managing global software and service supply chains (MISM); marketing (MBA, DBA); project management (MBA, MS); risk management (MBA); self-designed (MBA, DBA); social impact management (DBA); sustainable futures (MBA); technology (MBA); technology entrepreneurship (DBA). Part-time and evening/weekend programs available. Postbaccalaureate distance learning degree programs offered (minimal on-campus study). *Faculty:* 17 full-time, 211 part-time/adjunct. *Students:* 3,389 full-time (1,774 women), 815 part-time (482 women); includes 1,969 minority (1,640 African Americans, 36 American Indian/Alaska Native, 123 Asian Americans or Pacific Islanders, 170 Hispanic Americans), 95 international. Average age 41. In 2009, 699 master's, 42 doctorates awarded. *Degree requirements:* For doctorate, thesis/dissertation (for some programs), residency. *Entrance requirements:* For master's, bachelor's degree or equivalent in related field; minimum GPA of 2.5; official transcripts; goal statement; access to computer and Internet; for doctorate, master's degree or equivalent in related field; minimum GPA of 3.0; 3 years of related professional/academic experience (preferred). Additional exam requirements/recommendations for international students: Required—TOEFL (minimum score 550 paper-based; 213 computer-based), IELTS (minimum score 6.5), TOEFL, IELTS, or Michigan English Language Assessment Battery (minimum score 82). *Application deadline:* Applications are processed on a rolling basis. Application fee: $50. Electronic applications accepted. *Expenses:* Tuition: Full-time $13,665; part-time $560 per credit. Required fees: $1375. Tuition and fees vary according to course load, degree level and program. *Financial support:* In 2009–10, 466 students received support; fellowships, Federal Work-Study, scholarships/grants, unspecified assistantships, and family tuition reduction, active duty/veteran tuition reduction, group tuition reduction, interest-free payment plans available. Support available to part-time students. Financial award applicants required to submit FAFSA. *Unit head:* William Schulz, Interim Associate Dean, 800-925-3368. *Application contact:* Jennifer Hall, Director of Enrollment, 866-4-WALDEN, E-mail: info@waldenu.edu.

Wayland Baptist University, Graduate Programs, Programs in Business Administration/Management, Plainview, TX 79072-6998. Offers general business (MBA); health care administration (MBA); human resource management (MBA); international management (MBA); management (MA, MBA), including health care administration (MA), human resource management (MA), organization management (MA); management information systems (MBA). Part-time and evening/weekend programs available. Postbaccalaureate distance learning degree programs offered (no on-campus study). *Faculty:* 10 full-time (3 women). *Students:* 6 full-time (1 woman), 55 part-time (31 women); includes 24 minority (9 African Americans, 1 American Indian/Alaska Native, 14 Hispanic Americans). Average age 34. 25 applicants, 76% accepted, 10 enrolled. In 2009, 8 master's awarded. *Degree requirements:* For master's, capstone course. *Entrance requirements:* For master's, GMAT, GRE or MAT. Additional exam requirements/recommendations for international students: Required—TOEFL (minimum score 500 paper-based; 173 computer-based; 61 iBT). *Application deadline:* Applications are processed on a rolling basis. Application fee: $50. Electronic applications accepted. *Expenses:* Tuition: Full-time $5796; part-time $322 per credit hour. Required fees: $782; $9 per credit hour. $60 per semester. Tuition and fees vary according to course load and campus/location. *Financial support:* Federal Work-Study, institutionally sponsored loans, and scholarships/grants available. Support available to part-time students. Financial award application deadline: 5/1; financial award applicants required to submit FAFSA. *Unit head:* Dr. Otto Schacht, Chairman, 806-291-1020, Fax: 806-291-1957. *Application contact:* Amanda Stanton, Graduate Studies, 806-291-3423, Fax: 806-291-1950, E-mail: stanton@wbu.edu.

Waynesburg University, Graduate and Professional Studies, Waynesburg, PA 15370-1222. Offers business (MBA), including finance, health systems, human resources, leadership, market development; counseling (MA), including addictions counseling, clinical mental health; education (MAT); nursing (MSN), including administration, education, informatics, palliative care; nursing practice (DNP); special education (M Ed); technology (M Ed); MSN/MBA. *Accreditation:* AACN. Part-time and evening/weekend programs available. *Faculty:* 11 full-time (5 women), 136 part-time/adjunct (80 women). *Students:* 116 full-time (85 women), 984 part-time (682 women). 711 applicants, 80% accepted, 485 enrolled. In 2009, 320 master's, 41 doctorates awarded. *Degree requirements:* For doctorate, thesis/dissertation. *Entrance requirements:* Additional exam requirements/recommendations for international students: Required—TOEFL. *Application deadline:* For fall admission, 8/1 priority date for domestic students. Applications are processed on a rolling basis. Electronic applications accepted. *Expenses:* Tuition: Part-time $520 per credit. *Financial support:* Available to part-time students. Application deadline: 5/1. *Unit head:* David Mariner, Dean, 724-743-4420, Fax: 724-743-4425, E-mail: dmariner@waynesburg.edu. *Application contact:* Michael Bednarski, Director of Admissions, 724-743-4420, Fax: 724-743-4425, E-mail: mbednars@waynesburg.edu.

Webster University, George Herbert Walker School of Business and Technology, Department of Business, St. Louis, MO 63119-3194. Offers business (MA); business and organizational security management (MBA); computer resources and information management (MBA); environmental management (MBA); finance (MA, MBA); health services management (MBA); human resources development (MBA); human resources management (MBA); international business (MA, MBA); management and leadership (MBA); marketing (MBA); procurement and acquisitions management (MBA); telecommunications management (MBA). *Accreditation:* ACBSP. Part-time and evening/weekend programs available. Postbaccalaureate distance learning degree programs offered (no on-campus study). *Faculty:* 9 full-time, 430 part-time/adjunct. *Students:* 1,190 full-time (543 women), 4,226 part-time (2,159 women). Average age 34. In 2009, 2,021 master's awarded. *Degree requirements:* For master's, comprehensive exam (for some programs), thesis (for some programs). *Entrance requirements:* Additional exam requirements/recommendations for international students: Required—TOEFL. *Application deadline:* Applications are processed on a rolling basis. Application fee: $35 ($50 for international students). *Expenses:* Tuition: Part-time $565 per credit hour. Tuition and fees vary according to degree level, campus/location and program. *Financial support:* Federal Work-Study available. Support available to part-time students. Financial award application deadline: 4/1; financial award applicants required to submit FAFSA. *Unit head:* Dr. Debbie Psihountas, Chair, 314-246-7553 Ext. 7017, Fax: 314-968-7077, E-mail: buschair@webster.edu. *Application contact:* Matt Nolan, Associate Vice President for Enrollment Management/Dean of Admissions, Fax: 314-968-7116, E-mail: gadmit@webster.edu.

Webster University, George Herbert Walker School of Business and Technology, Department of Management, St. Louis, MO 63119-3194. Offers business and organizational security management (MA); computer resources and information management (MA); environmental management (MS); government contracting (Certificate); health care management (MA); health services management (MA); human resources development (MA); human resources management (MA); management (DM); management and leadership (MA); marketing (MA); nonprofit management (Certificate); procurement and acquisitions management (MA); public administration (MA); quality management (MA); space systems operations management (MS); telecommunications management (MA). *Accreditation:* ACBSP. Part-time and evening/weekend programs available. Postbaccalaureate distance learning degree programs offered (no on-campus study). *Faculty:* 16 full-time, 781 part-time/adjunct. *Students:* 1,369 full-time (610 women), 5,182 part-time (3,047 women); includes 3,460 minority (2,835 African Americans, 38 American Indian/Alaska Native, 169 Asian Americans or Pacific Islanders, 418 Hispanic Americans), 80 international. Average age 37. In 2009, 2,491 master's, 13 doctorates, 68 other advanced degrees awarded. *Degree requirements:* For master's, thesis (for some programs); for doctorate, thesis/dissertation, written exam. *Entrance requirements:* For doctorate, GMAT, 3 years of work experience, MBA. Additional exam requirements/recommendations for international students: Required—TOEFL. *Application deadline:* Applications are processed on a rolling basis. Application fee: $25 ($50 for international students). *Expenses:* Tuition: Part-time $565 per credit hour. Tuition and fees vary according to degree level, campus/location and program. *Financial support:* Federal Work-Study available. Support available to part-time students. Financial award application deadline: 4/1; financial award applicants required to submit FAFSA. *Unit head:* Jim Brasfield, Chair, 314-961-2660 Ext. 7063, Fax: 314-968-7077, E-mail: mgtchair@webster.edu. *Application contact:* Matt Nolan, Associate Vice President for Enrollment Management/Dean of Admissions, Fax: 314-968-7116, E-mail: gadmit@webster.edu.

West Chester University of Pennsylvania, Office of Graduate Studies, College of Business and Public Affairs, Department of Political Science, West Chester, PA 19383. Offers administration (Certificate); human resource management (MSA, Certificate); individualized (MSA); non profit administration (Certificate); nonprofit administration (MSA); public administration (MSA); training and development (MSA). Part-time and evening/weekend programs available. *Students:* 3 full-time (2 women), 42 part-time (31 women); includes 8 minority (6 African Americans, 2 Hispanic Americans), 2 international. Average age 28. 28 applicants, 96% accepted, 11 enrolled. In 2009, 12 master's awarded. *Degree requirements:* For master's, comprehensive exam (for some programs). *Entrance requirements:* For master's, GMAT, GRE General Test, or MAT; for Certificate, GMAT, GRE General Test, or MAT, statement of professional goals, resume, two letters of reference. Additional exam requirements/recommendations for international students: Required—TOEFL (minimum score 550 paper-based; 213 computer-based; 80 iBT). *Application deadline:* For fall admission, 4/15 priority date for domestic students, 3/15 for international students; for spring admission, 10/15 for domestic students, 9/1 for international students. Applications are processed on a rolling basis. Application fee: $35. Electronic applications accepted. *Expenses:* Tuition, state resident: full-time $6666; part-time $370 per credit. Tuition, nonresident: full-time $10,666; part-time $593 per credit. Required fees: $122.56 per credit. *Financial support:* In 2009–10, 5 research assistantships with full and partial tuition reimbursements (averaging $5,000 per year) were awarded; unspecified assistantships also available. Support available to part-time students. Financial award application deadline: 2/15; financial award applicants required to submit FAFSA. *Unit head:* Dr. Christopher Fiorentino, Dean, College of Business and Public Affairs, 610-436-2930, E-mail: cfiorentino@wcupa.edu. *Application contact:* Dr. Lorraine Bernotsky, Graduate Coordinator, 610-738-0576, E-mail: lbernotsky@wcupa.edu.

Human Resources Management

Widener University, School of Business Administration, Program in Human Resource Management, Chester, PA 19013-5792. Offers MHR, MS, Psy D/MHR. Part-time and evening/weekend programs available. *Faculty:* 5 full-time (1 woman), 5 part-time/adjunct (3 women). *Students:* 1 full-time (0 women), 7 part-time (5 women); includes 1 minority (Asian American or Pacific Islander), 1 international. Average age 30. 38 applicants, 87% accepted. In 2009, 3 master's awarded. *Entrance requirements:* For master's, GMAT, GRE, or MAT, minimum GPA of 2.5. *Application deadline:* For fall admission, 8/1 priority date for domestic students; for spring admission, 12/1 for domestic students. Applications are processed on a rolling basis. Application fee: $25 ($300 for international students). Electronic applications accepted. *Financial support:* Research assistantships, Federal Work-Study available. Support available to part-time students. Financial award application deadline: 5/1. *Faculty research:* Training and development, collective bargaining and arbitration, business communication. *Unit head:* Dr. Caryl Carpenter, Director, 610-499-4109. *Application contact:* Ann Seltzer, Graduate Enrollment Administrator, 610-499-4305, E-mail: apseltzer@widener.edu.

Wilkes University, College of Graduate and Professional Studies, Jay S. Sidhu School of Business and Leadership, Wilkes-Barre, PA 18766-0002. Offers accounting (MBA); entrepreneurship (MBA); finance (MBA); human resource management (MBA); international business (MBA); management (MBA); marketing (MBA). *Accreditation:* ACBSP. Part-time and evening/weekend programs available. *Students:* 86 full-time (41 women), 118 part-time (59 women); includes 7 minority (4 African Americans, 1 Asian American or Pacific Islander, 2 Hispanic Americans), 48 international. Average age 29. In 2009, 59 master's awarded. *Entrance requirements:* For master's, GMAT. Additional exam requirements/recommendations for international students: Required—TOEFL (minimum score 500 paper-based; 173 computer-based; 79 iBT). *Application deadline:* Applications are processed on a rolling basis. Application fee: $45. *Expenses:* Contact institution. *Financial support:* Federal Work-Study and unspecified assistantships available. Financial award application deadline: 3/1; financial award applicants required to submit FAFSA. *Unit head:* Dr. Paul Browne, Dean, 570-408-4701, Fax: 570-408-7846, E-mail: paul.browne@wilkes.edu. *Application contact:* Kathleen Houlihan, Director of Graduate Studies, 570-408-3235, Fax: 570-408-7846, E-mail: kathleen.houlihan@wilkes.edu.

Wilmington University, College of Business, New Castle, DE 19720-6491. Offers business administration (MBA); finance (MBA); health care administration (MBA, MS); homeland security (MBA, MS); human resource management (MS); management (MS); management information systems (MBA); organizational leadership (MS); public administration (MS); transportation and logistics (MBA, MS). Part-time and evening/weekend programs available. *Entrance requirements:* Additional exam requirements/recommendations for international students: Required—TOEFL (minimum score 500 paper-based; 173 computer-based). Electronic applications accepted.

York University, Faculty of Graduate Studies, Atkinson Faculty of Liberal and Professional Studies, Program in Human Resources Management, Toronto, ON M3J 1P3, Canada. Offers MHRM, PhD. Part-time programs available. *Degree requirements:* For master's, thesis or alternative. *Entrance requirements:* Additional exam requirements/recommendations for international students: Required—TOEFL (minimum score 600 paper-based; 250 computer-based). Electronic applications accepted.

THE CATHOLIC UNIVERSITY OF AMERICA

Programs in Management and Human Resource Management

Programs of Study

The Metropolitan School of Professional Studies (MSPS) is one of twelve academic schools within The Catholic University of America (CUA). MSPS's mission is to provide career-oriented, educational opportunities to working adults, with program offerings ranging from exam preparation courses to master's degrees. MSPS offers two master's degree programs: the Master of Arts (M.A.) in human resource management and the Master of Science in Management (M.S.M.).

MSPS's graduate programs consist of a total of twelve courses, or 36 semester credits, and require approximately twenty-two months to complete on a part-time basis, or as little as one calendar year on a full-time basis. Students must earn at least a B grade point average (3.0 on a 4.0 scale) both overall and on the final project completed as part of the master's capstone course.

The highly-regarded M.A. in human resource management program is the flagship in MSPS's comprehensive collection of graduate, undergraduate, and non-credit human resource (HR) offerings. The program focuses on concepts, principles, and issues in human resource management as experienced by HR managers and practitioners. The emphasis is on providing an academic foundation that equips practicing HR professionals with the skills and knowledge to both perform their jobs more effectively and better understand the organizational context in which they operate. Consistent with this orientation, graduate HR courses are led by faculty-practitioners who are particularly skilled at teaching the theoretical concepts of HR with an emphasis on practical applications.

Two versions of this program are offered to ensure relevance to students' particular interests and needs: the HR generalist track, for students pursuing HR careers in corporations and nonprofit organizations; and the federal HR track, for those interested in an HR career in the federal government. Both versions of the program are designed for current and aspiring HR professionals who seek to pursue their academic goals while balancing personal and professional demands. The program offers an extensive array of evening courses each semester to help students complete the program on either a part-time or full-time basis.

The M.S.M. degree program provides working adults with the skills, knowledge, and credentials necessary to progress in their management careers. The program focuses on concepts, principles, and issues experienced by managers in all types of organizations: commercial, government, educational, community, and nonprofit. The program combines a strong academic foundation with practical knowledge and skills in management, and, therefore, is of potential relevance to anyone who has, or is assuming, managerial responsibilities. Students are able to pursue specific tracks in the M.S.M. program to make it more relevant to their personal interests and professional goals. Tracks are currently offered in professional communication, leadership, human resource management, and federal acquisition and contract management. Students may also opt to pursue a general M.S.M. degree with no track.

Student Services and Involvement: MSPS strives to deliver an unparalleled level of service to adult students. As part of this commitment, the School offers the Student Development Series—a robust selection of workshops, seminars, speakers, and programs aimed at providing opportunities for personal, professional, and academic/scholarly development. MSPS also offers its students the opportunity to become involved and assume leadership roles in two student organizations: Metropolitan Connection and the student chapter of the Society for Human Resource Management (SHRM). In addition, CUA offers eighty other student organizations, as well as campus-produced musicals and performances, community service projects, and opportunities for individual leadership development.

Other resources available to MSPS students include the University's new 7,000-square-foot fitness center, a writing center, disability support services, career services, a student union (housing a food court, other dining facilities, and a convenience store), and the Center for Global Education.

Research Facilities

The CUA library system supports and enriches the instructional, research, and service programs of the University. The library system is comprised of a central library, four branch (subject-specific) libraries, and several other small, specialized libraries and collections. Students have access to over 130 online databases, various worldwide libraries through an interlibrary loan program, and the resources of other D.C.-area universities through the Washington Research Library Consortium. Of particular use to students who are working professionals, the libraries offer an instant messaging reference service to provide research assistance to students unable to visit the library.

Financial Aid

Catholic University participates in a wide variety of financial aid programs to assist students in paying for their graduate education. Information on federal loan programs, tuition payment plans, and other options may be obtained by visiting http://financialaid.cua.edu or contacting the CUA Office of Financial Aid at 202-319-5307, 888-635-7788 (toll-free), or cua-finaid@cua.edu.

Cost of Study

The official source for tuition and expense information is CUA's Office of Enrollment Services. The information is available online at http://enrollmentservices.cua.edu, and should be consulted for current, reliable cost information. For the 2010–11 academic year, MSPS graduate students pay $720 per credit for tuition (with all classes awarding 3 credits) and a one-time, new-student fee of $120. Additional expenses include the cost of textbooks, parking permits, and other incidentals.

Living and Housing Costs

Because the majority of students pursuing these degree programs are working professionals, most have existing living arrangements. Should a student choose to relocate to study at CUA, information on housing options is available at the Office of Housing Services, http://housing.cua.edu.

Student Group

CUA enrolls approximately 3,470 undergraduate and 3,240 graduate students from all fifty states and ninety-seven other countries. Of these, MSPS enrolls approximately 175 graduate students in the M.A. in human resource management and M.S.M. programs. The student body is diverse and includes numerous international students. Most MSPS graduate students work full-time and attend school part-time, but about 15% of the students pursue their degrees on a full-time basis.

Location

Students at CUA have the best of both worlds. They study and live on the largest campus (193 acres) in Washington, D.C., where they can enjoy a complete collegiate experience in the heart of the nation's capital. Traveling by Metrorail (subway), which is near the edge of campus, students are only a 10-minute ride from Union Station, Capitol Hill and the Library of Congress, and within easy reach of the abundant array of educational, cultural, social, political, and professional opportunities that Washington has to offer.

Many first-time visitors to campus are captivated by the University's expansive setting among tree-lined rolling hills where the skyline is dominated by the adjacent majestic Basilica of the National Shrine of the Immaculate Conception, the largest Catholic church in the United States.

The University and The School

Established as a papally-chartered graduate and research center, The Catholic University of America officially opened as an institution of higher education in 1889. Accredited by the Commission on Higher Education of the Middle States Association of Colleges and Schools, as well as many disciplinary accrediting organizations, CUA has a distinguished history and fills several important niches: doctoral programs in philosophy and social work that are among the nation's oldest; the only university library science and music schools in Washington, D.C.; the largest architecture school in the area; a law school that is a pioneer in clinical education; and a drama department that has been the educational incubator for acclaimed playwrights, directors, and actors.

Applying

In order to be considered for admission into one of the master's degree programs offered by MSPS, applicants must submit the following materials: a completed CUA graduate application for admission; official transcripts (with institutional seal) from all post-secondary institutions attended (one transcript must be from a regionally-accredited U.S. college or university showing completion of a four-year baccalaureate degree, or the international equivalent); three letters of recommendation, including at least one academic recommendation (from a former faculty member) and one professional recommendation (preferably from a former or current supervisor); a statement of purpose, approximately 500 words in length, stating purpose for undertaking graduate studies, qualifications, personal, and professional goals, and how participation in the program will help attain these goals; a $55 nonrefundable application fee; and a resume, detailing professional experiences (e.g., work, awards, and memberships). Additional credentials required for international applicants include an official TOEFL score report (minimum scores: 237 on the older TOEFL or 92–93 on the reformatted TOEFL) and confirmation of financial support.

Admission decisions are based on grade point average, undergraduate major, years and relevance of work experience, recommendations, writing ability, relevance/usefulness of program to meeting personal and professional objectives, and other relevant criteria. The priority deadline for applying for the fall semester is August 1 (July 15 for international applicants), spring semester is December 1 (November 15 for international applicants), and summer semester is April 1 for all applicants.

For more information on applying, application deadlines, and access to online application materials, prospective students should visit the Web site at http://metro.cua.edu/masters/admissions.cfm.

Correspondence and Information

CUA Office of Graduate Admissions
McMahon Hall, Room 102
The Catholic University of America
620 Michigan Avenue, N.E.
Washington, D.C. 20064

Phone: 202-319-5057
    800-673-2772 (toll-free)
Fax: 202-319-6533
E-mail: cua-admissions@cua.edu
Web site: http://admissions.cua.edu

Metropolitan School of Professional Studies
Pangborn Hall, Room 334
The Catholic University of America
620 Michigan Avenue, N.E.
Washington, D.C. 20064

Phone: 202-319-5256
Fax: 202-319-6032
E-mail: metropolitan@cua.edu
Web site: http://metro.cua.edu

The Catholic University of America

THE FACULTY

Because MSPS's graduate programs emphasize practical applications of managerial concepts and principles, each faculty member must offer a background that combines strong academic credentials with extensive professional experience. The MSPS faculty currently has about 75 members, with all members holding a master's degree or doctorate in a field relevant to the courses they teach. In addition, all of the graduate faculty members bring solid professional experience into the classroom, holding positions such as vice president, senior consultant, business owner, or government executive.

More specific details regarding individual faculty members at MSPS is available online at http://metro.cua.edu/faculty/index.cfm.

RUTGERS, THE STATE UNIVERSITY OF NEW JERSEY, NEW BRUNSWICK
Graduate Programs in Human Resource Management, Labor and Employment Relations

Programs of Study

The School of Management and Labor Relations (SMLR) offers a Ph.D. in industrial relations and human resources (IRHR), a Master of Human Resources Management (M.H.R.M.), and a Master of Labor and Employment Relations (M.L.E.R.).

The Ph.D. program is designed to prepare students for research careers in colleges, universities, and other relevant institutions. It normally consists of 48 credit hours of course work, 6 hours of master's thesis credits, and 18 credit hours of dissertation study. All students take three Ph.D. seminars, five courses in their primary field, a minimum of four statistics and research methods courses, and the Pro-Seminar. Most Ph.D. students are full-time, but it is possible for an individual who is interested in a research career to pursue the degree on a less than full-time basis.

The M.H.R.M. degree, which requires 48 credits of course work, focuses on the strategic role of human resource management in shaping and supporting the organization's business plan. It is a professional program integrating theory and practice, training students to become internal consultants and business partners. Students are accepted into the program on a full-time or part-time basis, and courses are scheduled in the late afternoon and evening for the convenience of working adults. The proximity of Rutgers to a wide variety of the nation's leading businesses provides excellent opportunities for internships, research, and eventual job placement. The M.H.R.M. program offers a one-year executive master's option to high-level HR managers or professionals who meet the program's criteria.

The M.L.E.R. degree, which requires 39 credits of course work, affords students the opportunity to both explore the causes and consequences of changes in employment relations and develop the professional skills necessary to function as an employment relations professional. The program combines the study of labor relations, organizational change, employee diversity, and related public policy with a broad approach to the study of work-related issues. Students prepare to pursue careers in labor or community organizations, employment relations for private and public sector employers, or government agencies that regulate employment.

Research Facilities

The School of Management and Labor Relations conducts programs of graduate instruction, research, and continuing professional education for both management and labor to further their understanding of human resources management, the process of labor relations, and public policy related to work.

SMLR has a specialized library within the 3-million-volume Rutgers University library system. The SMLR library provides access to leading journals, reporting services, and databases in labor relations and human resources. Graduate students have access to the Rutgers Center for Computer and Information Services, which contains some of the most powerful and innovative computer equipment in the country. Students are encouraged to develop computer skills through courses that rely heavily on the computer and its application to human resource issues.

Financial Aid

Research and teaching assistantships are available on a competitive basis. There are also opportunities for paid employment and paid or unpaid internships in the New Jersey–New York–Pennsylvania area. Work-study programs and Federal Stafford Student Loans are offered by the Financial Aid Office. The University offers Graduate Scholar Awards, Garden State Fellowships, and Ralph J. Bunche Fellowships.

Cost of Study

New Jersey residents pursuing full-time graduate study without financial assistance from the University paid tuition and associated fees totaling approximately $18,000 for the 2009–10 academic year. Nonresidents and international students paid $26,300. For students pursuing part-time graduate study, per-credit tuition rates for 2009–10 were $686 for residents and $1030 for nonresidents and international students.

Living and Housing Costs

Dormitory housing in 2009–10 ranged from approximately $6600 to $8900. A full meal plan for the same year cost approximately $4100 with partial meal plans available as well. Off-campus housing is generally more costly; average rents for studio and one-bedroom apartments are $800 and $925 per month respectively.

Student Group

One to 4 students are generally admitted to the Ph.D. program each fall, about 150 students are enrolled in the M.H.R.M. program, and 90 are enrolled in the M.L.E.R. program. Two thirds are women and the average age is 31. Both the M.H.R.M. and M.L.E.R. programs have a diverse student population.

Student Outcomes

Because the programs provide students with a broad theoretical foundation and an impressive array of professional skills, graduates have consistently obtained excellent positions in a variety of organizations. Recent placements of IRHR doctoral students include the University of Illinois, California State University, McMaster University, Pennsylvania State University, Pace University, Simon Fraser University, and Meredith College, among others. Recent placements of SMLR master's students include IBM, Bristol-Myers Squibb, GE, Anheuser-Busch, Pfizer (Wyeth), L'Oreal, Johnson & Johnson, Chevron, Lockheed Martin, American Express, Merck, Tyco, Ford, CWA, SEIU, and the National Labor Relations Board.

Location

New Brunswick, with a population of about 51,000, is located in central New Jersey at Exit 9 of the New Jersey Turnpike and along the New York–Philadelphia railroad line. It is approximately 35 miles from New York City, 16 miles from Princeton, 60 miles from Philadelphia, and less than 200 miles from Washington, D.C. The many educational, cultural, and recreational resources of the New York–Philadelphia region are easily accessible to students, and Rutgers attracts many distinguished visitors, lecturers, and performing artists not always available to less favorably situated institutions.

The University

As a university strongly committed to graduate education and research, Rutgers, The State University of New Jersey, provides graduate programs of exceptional academic quality taught by a distinguished faculty. Chartered in 1766, Rutgers is now one of the nation's largest state university systems; combined enrollment at the New Brunswick, Newark, and Camden campuses is approximately 54,000 students.

Applying

The M.H.R.M. program application deadlines are February 1 for the summer semester; March 1 for the fall semester; and October 1 for the spring semester. The M.L.E.R. application deadlines are March 1 for the summer semester; July 1 for the fall semester; and November 1 for the spring semester. International students applying from abroad must submit application materials by July 1 for the spring semester and February 1 for the fall semester. The Ph.D. program deadline is February 1 for fall admission. The Graduate Record Examinations (GRE) General Test or the Law School Aptitude Test (LSAT) is required for the M.L.E.R. program unless the applicant's bachelor's degree is more than five years old. The GRE General Test or the Graduate Management Admissions Test (GMAT) is required for the M.H.R.M. program. Both the M.H.R.M. and M.L.E.R. programs have a rolling admission policy. Admission decisions are made by judgment, not formula, but successful applicants are expected to achieve competitive grades and scores and provide letters of recommendation that indicate potential for graduate study. Additional requirements for each program can be found at http://smlr.rutgers.edu.

Correspondence and Information

Director
Graduate Programs in HRM and IRHR
Janice H. Levin Building
Rutgers, The State University of New Jersey
94 Rockafeller Road, Room 216
Piscataway, New Jersey 08854
Phone: 732-445-5973
E-mail: mhrm@smlr.rutgers.edu (M.H.R.M.)
irhrphd@smlr.rutgers.edu (Ph.D.)
http://smlr.rutgers.edu

Director
Graduate Program in Labor and Employment Relations
Labor Education Center
Rutgers, The State University of New Jersey
50 Labor Center Way
New Brunswick, New Jersey 08903
Phone: 732-932-8559
E-mail: MLER@work.rutgers.edu
Web site: http://smlr.rutgers.edu

Rutgers, The State University of New Jersey, New Brunswick

THE FACULTY

John R. Aiello, Ph.D., Michigan State.
Eileen Appelbaum, Ph.D. (economics), Pennsylvania.
Amy Bahruth, M.S., I.H. (environmental and occupational health services), CUNY, Hunter.
Richard W. Beatty, Ph.D. (organizational behavior), Washington (St. Louis).
David Bensman, Ph.D. (history), Columbia.
Joseph R. Blasi, Ed.D. (sociology of organizations), Harvard.
Paula Caligiuri, Ph.D. (industrial/organizational psychology), Penn State.
William Castellano, Ph.D. (industrial relations and human resources), Rutgers.
Cary Cherniss, Ph.D., Yale.
Dorothy Sue Cobble, Ph.D. (history), Stanford.
Niki T. Dickerson, Ph.D. (sociology), Michigan.
Steven M. Director, Associate Dean; Ph.D. (management), Northwestern.
Adrienne Eaton, Chair LSER; Ph.D. (industrial relations), Wisconsin.
Charles H. Fay, Ph.D. (management and organization behavior), Washington (Seattle).
David Ferio, Director, M.H.R.M.; M.S., PH.D. candidate, Stevens.
Janice Fine, Ph.D. (American politics, public policy, political economy), MIT.
David L. Finegold, Dean of the School; D.Phil. (political science), Oxford.
Mary Gatta, Ph.D. (sociology), Rutgers.
Stanley M. Gully, Ph.D. (industrial/organizational psychology), Michigan State.
Charles Heckscher, Ph.D. (sociology), Harvard.
Mark A. Huselid, Ph.D. (human resource management), SUNY at Buffalo.
Susan E. Jackson, Ph.D. (organizational and social psychology), Berkeley.
Jeffrey H. Keefe, Ph.D. (industrial and labor relations), Cornell.
Mark R. Killingsworth, D. Phil. (labor and human resources, discrimination), Oxford.
Douglas Kruse, Ph.D. (economics), Harvard.
Barbara A. Lee, Ph.D. (higher education administration), Ohio State; J.D., Georgetown.
David Lepak, Chair HRM program, Ph.D. (strategic management), Penn State.
Mingwei Liu, Ph.D. (industrial and labor relations), Cornell.
Joseph T. McCune, Director, Global Executive Master's in HR Leadership; Ph.D. (industrial and organizational psychology), Michigan State.
Patrick F. McKay, Director Ph.D. program Ph.D. (industrial and organizational psychology), Akron.
Claudia G. Meer, Ed.D. (adult education), Rutgers.
Jean M. Phillips, Ph.D. (business management and organizational behavior), Michigan State.
William Rodgers III, Ph.D. (economics), Harvard.
Patricia Roos, Ph.D. (sociology), UCLA.
Saul Rubinstein, Ph.D. (industrial relations and management), MIT; M.B.A., Ed.M., Harvard.
Randall S. Schuler, Ph.D. (organizational strategy and human resource management), Michigan State.
Donna Schulman, Director, James Carey Library; M.S. (library science), Columbia; M.S. (women's studies), CUNY.
Lisa Schur, J.D., Northeastern; Ph.D. (political science), Berkeley.
Susan Schurman, Dean, University College Community and Director of Lifelong Learning for the Division of Continuous Education; Ph.D. (higher adult continuing education), Michigan.
Carl Edward Van Horn, Ph.D., Ohio State.
Paula B. Voos, Director, M.L.E.R.; Ph.D. (economics), Harvard.
John D. Worrall, Ph.D. (economics), Rutgers.

UNIVERSITY OF ILLINOIS AT URBANA-CHAMPAIGN

School of Labor and Employment Relations

Program of Study

The School of Labor and Employment Relations (LER) at the University of Illinois at Urbana-Champaign is a graduate program offering both the Master of Human Resources and Industrial Relations (M.H.R.I.R.) and the Doctor of Philosophy (Ph.D.) in human resources and industrial relations. Human resource management and industrial/employment relations concerns itself with many diverse employee and employment issues. Career opportunities in business firms include human resource generalist, employment relations specialist, compensation and benefits analyst, training and development specialist, labor relations administrator, and other human resource functions. Employment opportunities with government agencies, educational institutions, municipalities, and union organizations offer other career alternatives.

Graduate work for the master's degree program includes twelve to fourteen courses (depending on the number of hours each course is worth, 48 hours of total course work) and usually takes three semesters to complete. Required courses in the master's program include employment relations systems and quantitative methods. Students must also choose at least one class from the following four distribution requirements: Human Resource Management and Organizational Behavior, International Human Resources, Labor Markets and Employment, and Union-Management Relations and Labor Relations Policy. The student's electives are driven by his or her interests and professional goals.

Most students attend the School on a full-time basis and complete their M.H.R.I.R. degree in three semesters. In addition, most students obtain a summer internship to make use of the knowledge and skills gained in the classroom. Other program options include part-time enrollment and joint-degree programs with the College of Law or the College of Business.

Graduate work at the Ph.D. level leads primarily to academic research and teaching careers in business schools that teach human resource management or labor relations. The program can be completed in three to four years beyond the master's degree. The doctoral degree requires 48 hours of course work and additional thesis hours for a total of 96 hours. Candidates who enter the Ph.D. program having obtained a master's degree are considered to have completed the first stage of doctoral course work and must take the 48 hours of course work, but need only 64 completed hours from the University of Illinois, including thesis hours.

Research Facilities

The University Library's extensive collection contains more than 22 million items, including nearly 9.8 million volumes, over 13 million print and nonprint materials, and more than 90,000 periodicals and journals. The School computer laboratory is equipped with personal computers, networked for worldwide access by scholars and practitioners in the field.

Financial Aid

Extremely competitive financial aid awards are available from the School. Award recipients are selected on the basis of academic excellence. Fellowships that include full tuition and service-fee waiver are available to highly qualified students. In addition, tuition scholarships that are sponsored by various organizations, corporations, and alumni funds, designated for students in a particular area of interest or from a minority group, are available. Fellowships combined with tuition and fee waivers from the School make up an entire aid package totaling between $28,000 and $36,000, depending on in-state versus out-of-state tuition. Tuition scholarships range from $5,000 to $15,000. There is no separate form on which to apply for financial aid. For information on loans, grants, and need-based financial aid from the government or other University sources, students should contact the Student Financial Aid Office (620 East John Street, Champaign, Illinois 61820; telephone: 217-333-0100; Web: http://www.osfa.uiuc.edu). All students pursuing a Ph.D. are given a generous financial aid package, including financial support for travel to professional conferences.

Cost of Study

For the 2010–11 academic year, in-state tuition is $16,700 and out-of-state tuition is $24,700. Textbook expenses range from $800 to $1200 per year.

Living and Housing Costs

Graduate student housing includes two residence halls for 750 students and two University-owned apartment complexes for 975 students with families or for single graduate students. In 2010–11, graduate residence hall rates are $4838 to $6130 for a single room per person per year and $4630 to $5594 for a double room per person per year. The board contract for meal plans ranges from $1938 to $5267 per year. Students should contact the University Housing Office (telephone: 217-333-7111; e-mail: housing@uiuc.edu) for more complete information. Privately owned on- or off-campus housing is abundant and available at similar or higher rates.

Student Group

The School strives to maintain a student body balanced in geographic, gender, and ethnic composition. At any one time, there are about 190 students enrolled in the master's program and 12–16 students enrolled in the doctoral program. In 2009–10, LER students came from seventy undergraduate institutions in seventeen states and nine other countries. Of the student body, 64 percent are women, 12 percent are members of minority groups, and 28 percent are international.

Student Outcomes

LER Career Services provides a wide variety of career development services, including presentations and workshops covering cover letters and resumes, interviewing skills, off-campus job searches, internship searches, job offer evaluation, and networking with alumni and employers; etiquette dinners and plant tours; and individual advising. The office sponsors on-campus recruiting throughout the academic year with representatives of numerous corporations, labor unions, and government agencies interviewing students for positions in human resources, labor relations, and governmental positions. Further career information is available from LER Career Services, School of Labor and Employment Relations (147 LER, 504 East Armory Avenue, Champaign, Illinois 61820; telephone: 217-333-1534; Web site: http://www.ler.illinois.edu/career/index.html).

Leading employers of 2008–09 graduates include Coca-Cola Enterprises, Northrop Grumman, Conoco Phillips, Cooper Industries, Cummins, Lockheed Martin, Microsoft, and Texas Instruments. The average salary for last year's graduating class was $70,325, with an average signing bonus of $7664 (not including relocation and housing allowances).

Location

The University is located in the twin cities of Urbana and Champaign, with a combined population of about 110,000. The University enhances the community through a large variety of performing arts and entertainment bookings, in addition to various museums and intramural and intercollegiate athletic facilities. The University is located 140 miles south of Chicago, 120 miles west of Indianapolis, and 170 miles north of St. Louis. Three interstate highways, several airlines, Amtrak, and an excellent mass-transit system serve the twin cities. The community has excellent public school and park systems and numerous shopping facilities.

The University

The University of Illinois at Urbana-Champaign, founded in 1867 as one of the original thirty-seven public land-grant institutions, today ranks among the world's finest universities. It offers more than 150 fields of study for its 28,000 undergraduates and over 100 disciplines for more than 10,000 graduate students.

Applying

Students enter the School with a wide range of social science backgrounds. Psychology, business administration, history, economics, political science, and speech communications are typical undergraduate areas of study. To be accepted to the School of Labor and Employment Relations, students must meet the general entrance requirements of the Graduate College at the University of Illinois at Urbana-Champaign as well as the School's specific requirements. Entering students at LER have an average GPA of 3.5, based on the last 60 hours of undergraduate work.

Application deadlines are November 1 for spring semester enrollment and February 1 for fall semester enrollment for M.H.R.I.R. candidates. For Ph.D. applicants, the deadline is January 7. Applicants are notified by March 15 for fall admission and by December 1 for spring admission. All applicants must submit a completed application form plus the application fee, academic transcripts, three letters of professional and personal recommendation, and Graduate Record Examinations (GRE) or Graduate Management Admission Test (GMAT) scores. International students are required to submit scores of the Test of English as a Foreign Language (TOEFL) or the International English Language Testing System (IELTS).

Correspondence and Information

Becky Barker, Director of Student Services
School of Labor and Employment Relations
University of Illinois at Urbana-Champaign
504 East Armory Avenue
Champaign, Illinois 61820

Phone: 217-333-1482
Fax: 217-244-9290
E-mail: ebarker@illinois.edu
Web site: http://www.ler.illinois.edu

University of Illinois at Urbana-Champaign

THE FACULTY AND THEIR RESEARCH

Steven K. Ashby, Clinical Professor of LER assigned to the Chicago Labor Education Program; Ph.D., Chicago. Labor movement and distance learning.

Ariel Avgar, Assistant Professor of LER; Ph.D., Cornell. Conflict management systems, alternative dispute resolution, organizational conflict.

Betty J. Barrett, Clinical Assistant Professor of LER; Ph.D., Michigan State. Socio-technical systems, large-scale systems change, work systems.

Monica Bielski Boris, Assistant Professor of LER, Labor Education Program; Ph.D., Rutgers. Women's issues in the labor movement; lesbian, gay, and transgender challenges and issues in American labor.

Kristine M. Brown, Assistant Professor of LER and Economics; Ph.D., Berkeley. Retirement decisions, economics of aging, health economics.

Robert Bruno, Professor of LER and Head, Labor Education Program; Ph.D., NYU. Unions and political action, union democracy, working-class culture and consciousness.

Joel Cutcher-Gershenfeld, Professor and Dean of LER; Ph.D., MIT. New work systems, labor-management relations, negotiations and conflict resolution, organizational learning and change, public policy, economic development, engineering systems.

John C. Dencker, Associate Professor of LER; Ph.D., Harvard. Corporate reorganization and workforce reductions, labor markets and international human resource management.

Fritz Drasgow, Professor of LER and Psychology; Ph.D., Illinois at Urbana-Champaign. Psychological measurement, computerized testing and sexual harassment.

Peter Feuille, Professor Emeritus of LER; Ph.D., Berkeley. Workplace disputed resolution; human resource practices in multinational firms, human resource practices and firm performance.

Matthew Finkin, Albert J. Harno and Edward W. Cleary Chair in Law, Center for Advanced Study Professor, and Professor of LER; LL.M., Yale. Labor and employment law, in both domestic and comparative context.

Wallace Hendricks, Professor Emeritus of LER and Economics; Ph.D., Berkeley. Performance evaluations and statistical discrimination.

Edward J. Hertenstein, Assistant Professor of LER, Labor Education Program; Ph.D., Illinois at Urbana-Champaign. Training and development, especially with distance learning technologies and collective bargaining.

Aparna Joshi, Associate Professor of LER; Ph.D., Rutgers. Work team diversity, and global cross-cultural teams.

Ron Laschever, Assistant Professor of LER and Economics; Ph.D., Northwestern. How personal interaction in social networks affect labor market outcomes.

John Lawler, Professor of LER; Ph.D., Berkeley. Human resource information systems, international human resource management.

Michael LeRoy, Professor of LER and Law; J.D., North Carolina at Chapel Hill. Government regulation, collective bargaining, grievance arbitration.

Darren Lubotsky, Associate Professor of LER and Economics; Ph.D., Berkeley. Labor and health economics, econometrics.

Joseph J. Martocchio, Associate Dean and Professor of LER and Psychology; Ph.D., Michigan State. Training effectiveness and evaluation, absence motivation and control policies, incentive compensation systems.

Craig Olson, LER Alumni Professor; Ph.D., Wisconsin–Madison. Effects of human resources and human resource policies on organizational performance, impact of employer-provided health insurance on labor market behaviors, causes of the decline in employer-provided health insurance in the United States.

Deborah Rupp, Associate Professor of LER and Psychology; Ph.D., Colorado State. Antecedents and consequences of organizational justice, impact of job attitudes on task and contextual performance, use of assessment centers for both personal decision making and development.

Taekjin Shin, Assistant Professor of LER; Ph.D., Berkeley. Organizational theory, corporate governance, executive compensation, organizational labor market, wage distribution, career mobility.

Section 9
Industrial and Manufacturing Management

This section contains a directory of institutions offering graduate work in industrial and manufacturing management. Additional information about programs listed in the directory may be obtained by writing directly to the dean of a graduate school or chair of a department at the address given in the directory.

For programs offering related work, see also in this book *Business Administration and Management* and *Human Resources.* In another guide in this series:

Graduate Programs in the Humanities, Arts & Social Sciences
See *Public, Regional, and Industrial Affairs (Industrial and Labor Relations)*

CONTENTS

Program Directory

Display

Industrial and Manufacturing Management

American InterContinental University Online, Program in Business Administration, Hoffman Estates, IL 60192. Offers accounting and finance (MBA); finance (MBA); healthcare management (MBA); human resource management (MBA); international business (MBA); management (MBA); marketing (MBA); operations management (MBA); organizational psychology and development (MBA); project management (MBA). Evening/weekend programs available. Post-baccalaureate distance learning degree programs offered (no on-campus study). *Entrance requirements:* Additional exam requirements/recommendations for international students: Required—TOEFL (minimum score 550 paper-based; 213 computer-based). Electronic applications accepted.

Boston University, School of Management, Doctorate in Business Administration Program, Boston, MA 02215. Offers accounting (PhD); information systems (PhD); marketing (PhD); operations and technology management (PhD); organizational behavior (PhD); strategy and innovation (PhD). *Students:* 31 full-time (18 women), 21 international. Average age 32. 158 applicants, 7% accepted, 6 enrolled. In 2009, 12 doctorates awarded. *Degree requirements:* For doctorate, comprehensive exam, thesis/dissertation, curriculum paper. *Entrance requirements:* For doctorate, GMAT or GRE General Test, resume, 3 letters of evaluation. Additional exam requirements/recommendations for international students: Required—TOEFL or IELTS. *Application deadline:* For fall admission, 1/5 for domestic and international students. Application fee: $125. *Expenses:* Tuition: Full-time $37,910; part-time $1184 per credit hour. Required fees: $386; $40 per semester. Part-time tuition and fees vary according to class time, course level, degree level and program. *Financial support:* Fellowships, research assistantships, teaching assistantships, career-related internships or fieldwork, Federal Work-Study, institutionally sponsored loans, scholarships/grants, and tuition waivers available. Support available to part-time students. Financial award applicants required to submit FAFSA. *Unit head:* Dr. Lloyd Baird, Director, 617-353-2670, E-mail: dba@bu.edu. *Application contact:* Hayden Estrada, Assistant Dean, Admissions, 617-353-2670, Fax: 617-353-7368, E-mail: dba@bu.edu.

California Polytechnic State University, San Luis Obispo, Orfalea College of Business, Department of Business and Technology, San Luis Obispo, CA 93407. Offers MS. Part-time programs available. *Faculty:* 2 full-time (0 women). *Students:* 1 part-time (0 women). Average age 30. 5 applicants, 0% accepted, 0 enrolled. In 2009, 12 master's awarded. *Degree requirements:* For master's, thesis or alternative. *Entrance requirements:* For master's, GRE General Test or GMAT, minimum GPA of 2.8 in last 90 quarter units of course work, 2 letters of recommendation. Additional exam requirements/recommendations for international students: Required—TOEFL (minimum score 550 paper-based; 213 computer-based), or IELTS (minimum score 6). *Application deadline:* For fall admission, 7/1 for domestic students, 11/30 for international students. Applications are processed on a rolling basis. Application fee: $55. Electronic applications accepted. *Expenses:* Tuition, nonresident: full-time $11,160; part-time $248 per unit. Required fees: $7134; $1553 per quarter. *Financial support:* Career-related internships or fieldwork, Federal Work-Study, institutionally sponsored loans, and scholarships/grants available. Support available to part-time students. Financial award application deadline: 3/2; financial award applicants required to submit FAFSA. *Faculty research:* Valve chain management, packing science and technology, technology entrepreneurship and innovation, industrial processes and systems. *Unit head:* Dr. Lou Tornatzky, Associate Dean/Graduate Coordinator, 805-756-2676, Fax: 805-756-6111, E-mail: ltornatzk@calpoly.edu. *Application contact:* Dr. Lou Tornatzky, Associate Dean/Graduate Coordinator, 805-756-2676, Fax: 805-756-6111, E-mail: ltornatzk@calpoly.edu.

California State University, East Bay, Graduate Programs, College of Business and Economics, Department of Information Technology Management, Option in Operations and Supply Chain Management, Hayward, CA 94542-3000. Offers MBA. *Degree requirements:* For master's, comprehensive exam or thesis. *Entrance requirements:* For master's, GMAT, minimum GPA of 2.75. Additional exam requirements/recommendations for international students: Required—TOEFL (minimum score 550 paper-based; 213 computer-based). *Application deadline:* For fall admission, 6/30 for domestic and international students. Application fee: $55. Electronic applications accepted. *Financial support:* Fellowships, career-related internships or fieldwork, Federal Work-Study, institutionally sponsored loans, and scholarships/grants available. Support available to part-time students. Financial award application deadline: 3/1; financial award applicants required to submit FAFSA. *Unit head:* Prof. Xinjian Lu, Chair, 510-885-3307, E-mail: xinjian.lu@csueastbay.edu. *Application contact:* Donna Wiley, Interim Associate Director, 510-885-2928, Fax: 510-885-4777, E-mail: donna.wiley@csueastbay.edu.

Carnegie Mellon University, Carnegie Institute of Technology and School of Design, Program in Product Development, Pittsburgh, PA 15213-3891. Offers MPD. *Entrance requirements:* For master's, GRE General Test, undergraduate degree in engineering, industrial design, or related fields, 3 letters of reference, 2 years of professional experience. Additional exam requirements/recommendations for international students: Required—TOEFL or TSE.

Carnegie Mellon University, College of Fine Arts, School of Design, Pittsburgh, PA 15213-3891. Offers communication planning and information design (M Des); design (PhD); design theory (PhD); interaction design (M Des, PhD); new product development (PhD); product development (MPD); typography and information design (PhD). *Accreditation:* NASAD.

Carnegie Mellon University, Tepper School of Business, Program in Management of Manufacturing and Automation, Pittsburgh, PA 15213-3891. Offers PhD. *Degree requirements:* For doctorate, thesis/dissertation.

Case Western Reserve University, Weatherhead School of Management, Department of Operations, Cleveland, OH 44106. Offers management (MS, MSM), including finance (MS), information systems (MS), marketing (MS), operations research, quality management (MS), supply chain (MSM); management for liberal arts graduates (MSM); operations research (PhD); MBA/MSM. Part-time programs available. *Degree requirements:* For doctorate, thesis/dissertation. *Entrance requirements:* For master's, GRE General Test; for doctorate, GMAT, GRE General Test. *Application deadline:* Applications are processed on a rolling basis. Application fee: $100. *Financial support:* Tuition waivers (full and partial) available. Financial award application deadline: 5/1. *Faculty research:* Mathematical finance, mathematical programming, scheduling, stochastic optimization, environmental/energy models. *Unit head:* Kamlesh Mathur, Chairman, 216-368-3857, E-mail: kamlesh.mathur@case.edu. *Application contact:* Kamlesh Mathur, Chairman, 216-368-3857, E-mail: kamlesh.mathur@case.edu.

Central Connecticut State University, School of Graduate Studies, School of Technology, Department of Manufacturing and Construction Management, New Britain, CT 06050-4010. Offers construction management (MS, Certificate); lean manufacturing and six sigma (Certificate); supply chain and logistics (Certificate); technology management (MS). Part-time and evening/weekend programs available. *Faculty:* 17 full-time (5 women), 25 part-time/adjunct (1 woman). *Students:* 13 full-time (4 women), 66 part-time (9 women); includes 11 minority (4 African Americans, 4 Asian Americans or Pacific Islanders, 3 Hispanic Americans), 4 international. Average age 33. 46 applicants, 50% accepted, 17 enrolled. In 2009, 27 master's, 1 other advanced degree awarded. *Degree requirements:* For master's, comprehensive exam, thesis or alternative; for Certificate, qualifying exam. *Entrance requirements:* For master's, minimum undergraduate GPA of 2.7. Additional exam requirements/recommendations for international students: Required—TOEFL. *Application deadline:* For fall admission, 7/1 for domestic students; for spring admission, 12/1 for domestic students. Applications are processed on a rolling basis. Application fee: $50. Electronic applications accepted. *Expenses:* Tuition, area resident: Full-time $4662; part-time $440 per credit. Tuition, state resident: full-time $6994; part-time $440 per credit. Tuition, nonresident: full-time $12,988; part-time $440 per credit. Required fees: $3606. One-time fee: $62 part-time. *Financial support:* In 2009–10, 5 students received support, including 3 research assistantships; career-related internships or fieldwork, Federal Work-Study, scholarships/grants, and unspecified assistantships also available. Support available to part-time students. Financial award application deadline: 3/1; financial award applicants required to submit FAFSA. *Faculty research:* All aspects of middle management, technical supervision in the workplace. *Unit head:* Dr. Jacob Kovel, Chair, 860-832-1830. *Application contact:* Dr. Jacob Kovel, Chair, 860-832-1830.

Central Michigan University, College of Graduate Studies, College of Science and Technology, Department of Engineering Technology, Mount Pleasant, MI 48859. Offers industrial management and technology (MA). Part-time programs available. *Degree requirements:* For master's, thesis or alternative. Electronic applications accepted. *Faculty research:* Computer applications, manufacturing process control, mechanical engineering automation, industrial technology.

Cleveland State University, College of Graduate Studies, Nance College of Business Administration, Doctor of Business Administration (DBA) Program, Cleveland, OH 44115. Offers business administration (DBA); finance (DBA); information systems (DBA); marketing (DBA); operations management (DBA). *Accreditation:* AACSB. Part-time and evening/weekend programs available. *Degree requirements:* For doctorate, comprehensive exam, thesis/dissertation, oral dissertation defense. *Entrance requirements:* For doctorate, GMAT, MBA or equivalent. Additional exam requirements/recommendations for international students: Required—TOEFL (minimum score 550 paper-based; 213 computer-based; 79 iBT). Electronic applications accepted. *Faculty research:* Supply chain management, international business, strategic management, risk analysis.

Colorado Technical University Colorado Springs, Graduate Studies, Program in Management, Colorado Springs, CO 80907-3896. Offers accounting (MBA, MSA); business administration (MBA); finance (MBA); human resources management (MBA); logistics/supply chain management (MBA); management (DM); marketing (MBA); mediation and dispute resolution (MBA); operations management (MBA); project management (MBA); technology management (MBA). Part-time and evening/weekend programs available. Postbaccalaureate distance learning degree programs offered. *Degree requirements:* For master's, thesis or alternative; for doctorate, thesis/dissertation. *Entrance requirements:* For doctorate, minimum graduate GPA of 3.0, 5 years of related work experience. *Faculty research:* Sexual harassment, performance evaluation, critical thinking.

Colorado Technical University Denver, Programs in Business Administration and Management, Greenwood Village, CO 80111. Offers accounting (MBA); business administration (MBA); business administration and management (EMBA); finance (MBA); human resource management (MBA); marketing (MBA); mediation and dispute resolution (MBA); operations management (MBA); project management (MBA); technology management (MBA). Part-time and evening/weekend programs available. *Degree requirements:* For master's, thesis or alternative. *Entrance requirements:* For master's, minimum undergraduate GPA of 3.0, resume.

DePaul University, Charles H. Kellstadt Graduate School of Business, Department of Management, Chicago, IL 60604-2287. Offers entrepreneurship (MBA); health sector management (MBA); human resource management (MBA, MSHR); leadership/change management (MBA); management planning and strategy (MBA); operations management (MBA). Part-time and evening/weekend programs available. *Faculty:* 36 full-time (7 women), 35 part-time/adjunct (16 women). *Students:* 284 full-time (115 women), 147 part-time (69 women); includes 75 minority (20 African Americans, 1 American Indian/Alaska Native, 37 Asian Americans or Pacific Islanders, 17 Hispanic Americans), 18 international. In 2009, 112 master's awarded. *Entrance requirements:* For master's, GMAT, GRE (MSHR), 2 letters of recommendation, resume. Additional exam requirements/recommendations for international students: Required—TOEFL (minimum score 550 paper-based; 213 computer-based). *Application deadline:* For fall admission, 7/1 for domestic students; for winter admission, 10/1 for domestic students; for spring admission, 2/1 for domestic students. Applications are processed on a rolling basis. Application fee: $60. Electronic applications accepted. *Expenses:* Tuition: Full-time $37,525; part-time $620 per credit hour. *Financial support:* Research assistantships available. Financial award application deadline: 4/1. *Faculty research:* Growth management, creativity and innovation, quality management and business process design, entrepreneurship. *Application contact:* Christopher E. Kinsella, Director of Cohort MBA Programs, 312-362-8810, Fax: 312-362-6677, E-mail: kgsb@depaul.edu.

Friends University, Graduate School, Division of Business, Technology, and Leadership, Program in Operations Management, Wichita, KS 67213. Offers MSOM. Evening/weekend programs available. *Entrance requirements:* Additional exam requirements/recommendations for international students: Required—TOEFL (minimum score 560 paper-based; 220 computer-based). Electronic applications accepted.

Georgetown University, Graduate School of Arts and Sciences, Department of Economics, Washington, DC 20057. Offers econometrics (PhD); economic development (PhD); economic theory (PhD); industrial organization (PhD); international macro and finance (PhD); international trade (PhD); labor economics (PhD); macroeconomics (PhD); public economics and political economics (PhD); MA/PhD; MS/MA. *Degree requirements:* For doctorate, comprehensive exam, thesis/dissertation. *Entrance requirements:* For doctorate, GRE General Test. Additional exam requirements/recommendations for international students: Required—TOEFL. *Faculty research:* International economics, economic development.

Harvard University, Harvard Business School, Doctoral Programs in Management, Boston, MA 02163. Offers accounting and management (DBA); business economics (PhD); health policy management (PhD); management (DBA); marketing (DBA); organizational behavior (PhD); science, technology and management (PhD); strategy (DBA); technology and operations management (DBA). *Degree requirements:* For doctorate, comprehensive exam (for some programs), thesis/dissertation. *Entrance requirements:* For doctorate, GRE General Test or GMAT. Additional exam requirements/recommendations for international students: Required—TOEFL. *Expenses:* Tuition: Full-time $33,696. Required fees: $1126. Full-time tuition and fees vary according to program.

HEC Montreal, School of Business Administration, Master of Science Programs in Administration, Program in Production and Operations Management, Montréal, QC H3T 2A7, Canada. Offers M Sc. All courses are given in French. Part-time programs available. *Students:* 24 full-time (16 women), 5 part-time (4 women). 24 applicants, 71% accepted, 12 enrolled. In 2009, 14 master's awarded. *Degree requirements:* For master's, one foreign language, thesis. *Application deadline:* For fall admission, 3/15 for domestic and international students; for winter admission, 9/15 for domestic and international students. Application fee: $77 Canadian dollars. Electronic applications accepted. Tuition and fees charges are reported in Canadian dollars. *Expenses:* Tuition, area resident: Part-time $65.60 Canadian dollars per credit. Tuition, state resident: full-time $2361.60 Canadian dollars; part-time $183.36 Canadian dollars per credit. Tuition, nonresident: full-time $6601 Canadian dollars; part-time $448.13 Canadian dollars per credit. International tuition: $16,132.68 Canadian dollars full-time. Required fees: $1254.15 Canadian dollars; $28.99 Canadian dollars per course. $91.68 Canadian dollars per term. Tuition and fees vary according to degree level and program. *Financial support:* Fellowships, research assistantships, teaching assistantships, scholarships/grants available. Financial award application deadline: 10/2. *Unit head:* Dr. Claude Laurin, Director, 514-340-6485, Fax: 514-340-5690, E-mail: claude.laurin@hec.ca. *Application contact:* Francine Blais, Administrative Director, 514-340-6112, Fax: 514-340-6411, E-mail: francine.blais@hec.ca.

Illinois Institute of Technology, Graduate College, School of Applied Technology, Program in Industrial Technology and Management, Chicago, IL 60616-3793. Offers MITO. Part-time and evening/weekend programs available. Postbaccalaureate distance learning degree programs offered (no on-campus study). *Faculty:* 2 full-time (0 women), 16 part-time/adjunct (1 woman). *Students:* 27 full-time (6 women), 28 part-time (5 women); includes 11 minority (3 African Americans, 2 Asian Americans or Pacific Islanders, 6 Hispanic Americans), 28 international. Average age 31. 48 applicants, 60% accepted, 9 enrolled. In 2009, 18 master's awarded. *Entrance requirements:* For master's, minimum undergraduate GPA of 3.0. Additional exam requirements/recommendations for international students: Required—TOEFL (minimum score 523 paper-based; 70 iBT). *Application deadline:* For fall admission, 8/1 for domestic students,

5/1 for international students; for spring admission, 12/15 for domestic students, 10/15 for international students. Applications are processed on a rolling basis. Application fee: $50. Electronic applications accepted. *Expenses:* Tuition: Full-time $17,550; part-time $888 per credit hour. Required fees: $850; $7.50 per credit hour. One-time fee: $50 full-time. Full-time tuition and fees vary according to program. *Financial support:* In 2009–10, 6 fellowships with partial tuition reimbursements, 8 teaching assistantships (averaging $2,500 per year) were awarded; career-related internships or fieldwork, Federal Work-Study, institutionally sponsored loans, scholarships/grants, traineeships, health care benefits, tuition waivers (partial), and unspecified assistantships also available. Support available to part-time students. Financial award applicants required to submit FAFSA. *Faculty research:* Industrial logistics, industrial facilities, manufacturing technology, entrepreneurship, energy options. *Unit head:* Mazin Safit, Associate Director, 312-567-3624, Fax: 312-567-3655, E-mail: safar@iit.edu. *Application contact:* Mazin Safit, Associate Director, 312-567-3624, Fax: 312-567-3655, E-mail: safar@iit.edu.

Instituto Tecnológico y de Estudios Superiores de Monterrey, Campus Estado de México, Professional and Graduate Division, Estado de Mexico, Mexico. Offers administration of information technologies (MITA); architecture (M Arch); business administration (GMBA, MBA); computer sciences (MCS, PhD); education (M Ed); educational institution administration (MAD); educational technology and innovation (PhD); electronic commerce (MEC); environmental systems (MS); finance (MAF); humanistic studies (MHS); information sciences and knowledge management (MISKM); information systems (MS); manufacturing systems (MS); marketing (MEM); quality systems and productivity (MS); science and materials engineering (PhD); telecommunications management (MTM). Part-time programs available. Postbaccalaureate distance learning degree programs offered (minimal on-campus study). *Degree requirements:* For master's, one foreign language, thesis (for some programs); for doctorate, one foreign language, thesis/dissertation. *Entrance requirements:* For master's, E-PAEP 500, interview; for doctorate, E-PAEP 500, research proposal. Additional exam requirements/recommendations for international students: Required—TOEFL (minimum score 550 paper-based). *Faculty research:* Surface treatments by plasmas, mechanical properties, robotics, graphical computing, mechatronics security protocols.

Instituto Tecnológico y de Estudios Superiores de Monterrey, Campus Irapuato, Graduate Programs, Irapuato, Mexico. Offers administration (MBA); administration of information technology (MAIT); administration of telecommunications (MAT); architecture (M Arch); computer science (MCS); education (M Ed); educational administration (MEA); educational innovation and technology (DEIT); educational technology (MET); electronic commerce (MBA); environmental administration and planning (MEAP); environmental systems (MES); finances (MBA); humanistic studies (MHS); international management for Latin American executives (MIMLAE); library and information science (MLIS); manufacturing quality management (MMQM); marketing research (MBA).

Inter American University of Puerto Rico, Metropolitan Campus, Graduate Programs, Program in Industrial Management, San Juan, PR 00919-1293. Offers MBA. *Degree requirements:* For master's, comprehensive exam. *Entrance requirements:* For master's, GRE or EXADEP, interview. Electronic applications accepted.

Inter American University of Puerto Rico, San Germán Campus, Graduate Studies Center, Program in Business Administration, San Germán, PR 00683-5008. Offers accounting (MBA); finance (MBA); human resources (PhD); human resources management (MBA); industrial management (MBA); international business (PhD); management information systems (MBA); marketing management (MBA). Part-time and evening/weekend programs available. *Degree requirements:* For master's, comprehensive exam. *Entrance requirements:* For master's, GRE General Test or EXADEP, minimum GPA of 3.0.

International Technological University, Program in Industrial Management, Santa Clara, CA 95050. Offers MIM.

Kansas State University, Graduate School, College of Human Ecology, Department of Apparel, Textiles, and Interior Design, Manhattan, KS 66506. Offers design (MS); general apparel and textile (MS); marketing (MS); merchandising (MS); product development (MS). *Faculty:* 10 full-time (8 women), 1 (woman) part-time/adjunct. *Students:* 7 full-time (5 women), 15 part-time (12 women); includes 3 minority (1 African American, 1 Asian American or Pacific Islander, 1 Hispanic American). Average age 29. 13 applicants, 85% accepted, 7 enrolled. In 2009, 3 master's awarded. *Degree requirements:* For master's, thesis optional, residency. *Entrance requirements:* For master's, GRE General Test, minimum undergraduate GPA of 3.0. Additional exam requirements/recommendations for international students: Required—TOEFL (minimum score 600 paper-based; 250 computer-based). *Application deadline:* For fall admission, 2/1 priority date for domestic and international students; for spring admission, 8/1 priority date for domestic and international students. Applications are processed on a rolling basis. Application fee: $40 ($55 for international students). Electronic applications accepted. *Financial support:* In 2009–10, 3 research assistantships (averaging $14,460 per year), 5 teaching assistantships with full tuition reimbursements (averaging $10,590 per year) were awarded; career-related internships or fieldwork, Federal Work-Study, institutionally sponsored loans, and scholarships/grants also available. Support available to part-time students. Financial award application deadline: 3/1; financial award applicants required to submit FAFSA. *Faculty research:* Apparel marketing and consumer behavior, protective and functional clothing and textiles, social and environmental responsibility, apparel design, new product development. Total annual research expenditures: $40,303. *Unit head:* Jana Hawley, Head, 785-532-6993, Fax: 785-532-3796, E-mail: hawleyj@ksu.edu. *Application contact:* Gina Jackson, Application Contact, 785-532-6693, Fax: 785-532-3796, E-mail: gjackson@ksu.edu.

Kettering University, Graduate School, Department of Business, Flint, MI 48504. Offers business administration (MBA); engineering management (MSEM); information technology (MSIT); manufacturing management (MSMM); manufacturing operations (MSMO); operations management (MSOM). *Accreditation:* ACBSP. Part-time and evening/weekend programs available. Postbaccalaureate distance learning degree programs offered (no on-campus study). *Faculty:* 9 full-time (3 women), 4 part-time/adjunct (0 women). *Students:* 12 full-time (5 women), 251 part-time (79 women); includes 42 minority (27 African Americans, 1 American Indian/Alaska Native, 9 Asian Americans or Pacific Islanders, 5 Hispanic Americans), 15 international. Average age 32. 74 applicants, 78% accepted, 31 enrolled. In 2009, 123 master's awarded. *Entrance requirements:* Additional exam requirements/recommendations for international students: Required—TOEFL (minimum score 550 paper-based; 213 computer-based; 79 iBT). *Application deadline:* For fall admission, 9/15 for domestic students, 6/15 for international students; for winter admission, 12/15 for domestic students, 9/15 for international students; for spring admission, 3/15 for domestic students, 12/15 for international students. Applications are processed on a rolling basis. Electronic applications accepted. *Expenses:* Tuition: Full-time $11,120; part-time $695 per credit hour. *Financial support:* In 2009–10, 101 students received support, including fellowships with full tuition reimbursements available (averaging $13,000 per year), research assistantships with full tuition reimbursements available (averaging $13,000 per year), teaching assistantships with full tuition reimbursements available (averaging $13,000 per year); Federal Work-Study, scholarships/grants, and tuition waivers (partial) also available. Support available to part-time students. Financial award application deadline: 7/15. *Unit head:* Dr. Tony Hain, Vice President of Graduate Studies and Corporate Connections, 810-762-9616, Fax: 810-762-9935, E-mail: thain@kettering.edu. *Application contact:* Bonnie Switzer, Admissions Representative, 810-762-7953, Fax: 810-762-9935, E-mail: bswitzer@kettering.edu.

Lawrence Technological University, College of Management, Southfield, MI 48075-1058. Offers business administration (MBA, DBA); information systems (MS); information technology (DM); operations management (MS). *Accreditation:* ACBSP. Part-time and evening/weekend programs available. *Faculty:* 14 full-time (6 women), 53 part-time/adjunct (14 women). *Students:* 17 full-time (6 women), 565 part-time (234 women); includes 149 minority (103 African Americans, 2 American Indian/Alaska Native, 37 Asian Americans or Pacific Islanders, 7 Hispanic Americans), 96 international. Average age 34. 353 applicants, 58% accepted, 125 enrolled. In 2009, 263 master's, 5 doctorates awarded. *Degree requirements:* For master's, thesis (for some programs). *Entrance requirements:* For master's, GMAT. Additional exam requirements/recommendations for international students: Required—TOEFL (minimum score 550 paper-based; 213 computer-based; 79 iBT). *Application deadline:* For fall admission, 8/1 priority date for domestic students, 6/1 for international students; for winter admission, 12/1 priority date for domestic students, 10/1 for international students; for spring admission, 5/1 priority date for domestic students, 3/1 for international students. Applications are processed on a rolling basis. Application fee: $50. Electronic applications accepted. *Expenses:* Tuition: Full-time $11,320; part-time $798 per credit hour. *Financial support:* Federal Work-Study and institutionally sponsored loans available. Support available to part-time students. Financial award application deadline: 4/1; financial award applicants required to submit FAFSA. *Unit head:* Dr. Lou DeGennaro, Dean, 248-204-3050, E-mail: degennaro@ltu.edu. *Application contact:* Jane Rohrback, Director of Admissions, 248-204-3160, Fax: 248-204-3188, E-mail: admissions@ltu.edu.

Marist College, Graduate Programs, School of Management, Poughkeepsie, NY 12601-1387. Offers business administration (MBA, Adv C), including business administration (MBA), executive leadership (Adv C), production management (Adv C); public administration (MPA); technology management (MS). Part-time and evening/weekend programs available. Postbaccalaureate distance learning degree programs offered (no on-campus study). *Entrance requirements:* For master's, GMAT (MBA), GRE General Test(MPA), resume, letters of recommendation. Additional exam requirements/recommendations for international students: Required—TOEFL (minimum score 550 paper-based; 213 computer-based; 80 iBT); Recommended—IELTS (minimum score 6.5). Electronic applications accepted. *Expenses:* Tuition: Full-time $12,510; part-time $695 per credit hour.

McGill University, Faculty of Graduate and Postdoctoral Studies, Desautels Faculty of Management, Montréal, QC H3A 2T5, Canada. Offers administration (PhD); entrepreneurial studies (MBA); finance (MBA); general management (Post Master's Certificate); information systems (MBA); international business (exchange program) (MBA); international Master's program in practicing management (MM); management (MBA); management for development (MBA); manufacturing management (MMM); marketing (MBA); operations management (MBA); public accountancy (Diploma); strategic management (MBA); MBA/LL B; MD/MBA.

McGill University, Faculty of Graduate and Postdoctoral Studies, Faculty of Engineering, Department of Mechanical Engineering and Desautels Faculty of Management, Master in Manufacturing Management, Montréal, QC H3A 2T5, Canada. Offers MMM.

Milwaukee School of Engineering, Rader School of Business, Program in New Product Management, Milwaukee, WI 53202-3109. Offers MS. *Faculty:* 1 full-time (0 women), 2 part-time/adjunct (1 woman). *Students:* 2 full-time (0 women), 9 part-time (3 women); includes 2 minority (1 African American, 1 Asian American or Pacific Islander). 11 applicants, 82% accepted, 2 enrolled. *Degree requirements:* For master's, thesis optional, thesis defense or capstone project. *Entrance requirements:* For master's, GRE General Test or GMAT, 2 letters of recommendation. Additional exam requirements/recommendations for international students: Recommended—TOEFL (minimum score 550 paper-based; 213 computer-based; 79 iBT), IELTS. *Application deadline:* Applications are processed on a rolling basis. Application fee: $30. Electronic applications accepted. *Expenses:* Tuition: Part-time $603 per credit. *Financial support:* In 2009–10, 3 students received support. Applicants required to submit FAFSA. *Faculty research:* New product development, product research and design, product development. *Unit head:* Dr. Bruce Thompson, Director, 414-277-7378, Fax: 414-277-7279, E-mail: thomson@msoe.com. *Application contact:* David E. Tietyen, Graduate Admissions Director, 800-332-6763, Fax: 414-277-7475, E-mail: wp@msoe.edu.

Northeastern State University, Graduate College, College of Business and Technology, Program in Industrial Management, Tahlequah, OK 74464-2399. Offers MS. Part-time and evening/weekend programs available. *Degree requirements:* For master's, synergistic experience. *Entrance requirements:* For master's, GRE, MAT, minimum GPA of 2.5. Additional exam requirements/recommendations for international students: Required—TOEFL (minimum score 213 computer-based). Electronic applications accepted.

Northern Illinois University, Graduate School, College of Engineering and Engineering Technology, Department of Technology, De Kalb, IL 60115-2854. Offers industrial management (MS). Part-time and evening/weekend programs available. *Faculty:* 14 full-time (1 woman), 1 part-time/adjunct (0 women). *Students:* 13 full-time (1 woman), 31 part-time (5 women); includes 5 minority (3 African Americans, 1 American Indian/Alaska Native, 1 Asian American or Pacific Islander), 8 international. Average age 31. 18 applicants, 72% accepted, 10 enrolled. In 2009, 21 master's awarded. *Degree requirements:* For master's, thesis optional. *Entrance requirements:* For master's, GRE General Test, minimum GPA of 2.75. Additional exam requirements/recommendations for international students: Required—TOEFL (minimum score 550 paper-based; 213 computer-based). *Application deadline:* For fall admission, 6/1 for domestic students, 5/1 for international students; for spring admission, 11/1 for domestic students, 10/1 for international students. Applications are processed on a rolling basis. Application fee: $30. Electronic applications accepted. *Expenses:* Tuition, state resident: full-time $6576; part-time $274 per credit hour. Tuition, nonresident: full-time $13,152; part-time $548 per credit hour. Required fees: $1813; $75.53 per credit hour. Part-time tuition and fees vary according to course load. *Financial support:* In 2009–10, 11 teaching assistantships with full tuition reimbursements were awarded; fellowships with full tuition reimbursements, research assistantships with full tuition reimbursements, career-related internships or fieldwork, Federal Work-Study, scholarships/grants, tuition waivers (full), and unspecified assistantships also available. Support available to part-time students. Financial award applicants required to submit FAFSA. *Faculty research:* Digital control, intelligent systems, engineering graphic design, occupational safety, ergonomics. *Unit head:* Dr. Clifford Mirman, Chair, 815-753-1349, Fax: 815-753-3702, E-mail: mirman@ceet.niu.edu. *Application contact:* Graduate School Office, 815-753-0395, E-mail: gradsch@niu.edu.

Oakland University, Graduate Study and Lifelong Learning, School of Business Administration, Department of Decision and Information Sciences, Rochester, MI 48309-4401. Offers information technology management (MS); management information systems (Certificate); production and operations management (Certificate).

Penn State University Park, Graduate School, Intercollege Graduate Programs, Intercollege Program in Quality and Manufacturing Management, State College, University Park, PA 16802-1503. Offers MMM. *Unit head:* Dr. Jose A. Ventura, Co-Director, 814-865-5802, Fax: 814-863-4745, E-mail: jav1@psu.edu. *Application contact:* Cynthia E. Nicosia, Director, Graduate Enrollment Services, 814-865-1795, Fax: 814-865-4627, E-mail: cey1@psu.edu.

Polytechnic University of Puerto Rico, Graduate School, Hato Rey, PR 00919. Offers business administration (MBA), including general studies, management of information systems, management of international enterprises; civil engineering (ME, MS); computer engineering (ME, MS); computer science (MS); electrical engineering (ME, MS); engineering management (MEM); environmental management (MEPM); landscape architecture (M Land Arch); manufacturing competitiveness (MMC, MS); manufacturing engineering (ME, MS). Part-time and evening/weekend programs available. *Entrance requirements:* For master's, 3 letters of recommendation.

Portland State University, Graduate Studies, Maseeh College of Engineering and Computer Science, Department of Engineering and Technology Management, Portland, OR 97207-0751. Offers engineering and technology management (M Eng); engineering management (MS); manufacturing engineering (ME); manufacturing management (M Eng); systems science/engineering management (PhD); MS/MBA; MS/MS. Part-time and evening/weekend programs available. *Degree requirements:* For master's, thesis optional; for doctorate, one foreign language, thesis/dissertation, oral and written exams. *Entrance requirements:* For master's, minimum GPA of 3.0 in upper-division course work, BS degree in civil engineering; for doctorate, GRE General Test, GRE Subject Test, minimum GPA of 3.0 in upper-division course work. Additional exam requirements/recommendations for international students: Required—TOEFL (minimum score 550 paper-based; 213 computer-based). *Faculty research:* Scheduling, hierarchical decision modeling, operations research, knowledge-based information systems.

Industrial and Manufacturing Management

Purdue University, Graduate School, Krannert School of Management, Master of Science in Industrial Administration Program, West Lafayette, IN 47907. Offers MSIA. *Faculty:* 102 full-time (29 women), 16 part-time/adjunct (1 woman). *Students:* 21 full-time (10 women); includes 2 minority (both Asian Americans or Pacific Islanders), 13 international. Average age 29. 68 applicants, 69% accepted. In 2009, 21 master's awarded. *Entrance requirements:* For master's, GMAT or GRE, work experience, essays, minimum GPA of 3.0, four-year baccalaureate degree, letters of recommendation. Additional exam requirements/recommendations for international students: Required—TOEFL (minimum score 550 paper-based; 213 computer-based; 77 iBT). *Application deadline:* For fall admission, 1/10 priority date for domestic students, 2/1 for international students. Applications are processed on a rolling basis. Application fee: $55. Electronic applications accepted. *Financial support:* Application deadline: 2/1. *Unit head:* Dr. R. A. Cosier, Dean, 765-494-4366. *Application contact:* Brenda Knebel, Director, Master's and Executive Programs, 765-494-0773, Fax: 765-494-9841, E-mail: krannertmasters@purdue.edu.

Regis University, College for Professional Studies, School of Management, Denver, CO 80221-1099. Offers accounting (MS); business administration (MBA); computer information technology (MSOL); executive internal management (Certificate); executive leadership (Certificate); finance (MBA); finance and accounting (MBA); human resource management (MSOL); international business (MBA); marketing (MBA); operations management (MBA); organization leadership (MS); organizational leadership (MSOL); project leadership and management (MSOL, Certificate); project management (Certificate); strategic business (Certificate); strategic human resource (Certificate); technical management (Certificate). Offered at Colorado Springs Campus, Northwest Denver Campus, Southeast Denver Campus, Fort Collins Campus, Broomfield Campus, Henderson (Nevada) Campus, and Summerlin (Nevada) Campus and online. Part-time and evening/weekend programs available. Postbaccalaureate distance learning degree programs offered (no on-campus study). *Degree requirements:* For master's, thesis optional, capstone project. *Entrance requirements:* For master's, GMAT or essays, interview, 2 years of full-time business work experience, resume; for Certificate, GMAT. Additional exam requirements/recommendations for international students: Required—TOEFL, TOEFL or university-based test; Recommended—TWE (minimum score 5). Electronic applications accepted. *Faculty research:* Impact of Info Technology on Small Business Regulation of Accounting, International Project financing, Mineral Development, Delivery of Healthcare to rural indigenos communities.

Rochester Institute of Technology, Graduate Enrollment Services, College of Applied Science and Technology, Department of Electrical, Computer and Telecommunications Engineering Technology, Program in Facility Management, Rochester, NY 14623-5603. Offers MS. Part-time programs available. Postbaccalaureate distance learning degree programs offered (no on-campus study). *Students:* 4 full-time (3 women), 13 part-time (2 women); includes 1 African American. Average age 39. 9 applicants, 56% accepted, 5 enrolled. In 2009, 5 master's awarded. *Degree requirements:* For master's, thesis or alternative, project. *Entrance requirements:* For master's, minimum GPA of 3.0. Additional exam requirements/recommendations for international students: Required—TOEFL (minimum score 550 paper-based; 213 computer-based; 79 iBT), or IELTS (minimum score 6.5). *Application deadline:* For fall admission, 2/15 priority date for domestic and international students; for winter admission, 11/1 priority date for domestic students, 10/1 priority date for international students; for spring admission, 2/1 priority date for domestic students, 1/1 priority date for international students. Applications are processed on a rolling basis. Application fee: $50. Electronic applications accepted. *Expenses:* Tuition: Full-time $31,533; part-time $876 per credit hour. Required fees: $210. *Financial support:* In 2009–10, 11 students received support. Career-related internships or fieldwork and scholarships/grants available. Support available to part-time students. Financial award applicants required to submit FAFSA. *Faculty research:* Sustainability. *Unit head:* Joseph Rosenbeck, Program Chair, 585-475-6469, Fax: 585-475-2178, E-mail: jmrcem@rit.edu. *Application contact:* Diane Ellison, Assistant Vice President, Graduate Enrollment Services, 585-475-2229, Fax: 585-475-7164, E-mail: gradinfo@rit.edu.

Rochester Institute of Technology, Graduate Enrollment Services, Kate Gleason College of Engineering, Department of Design, Development and Manufacturing, Program in Manufacturing Leadership, Rochester, NY 14623-5603. Offers MS. Part-time and evening/weekend programs available. Postbaccalaureate distance learning degree programs offered (minimal on-campus study). *Students:* 5 full-time (2 women), 13 part-time (4 women); includes 2 African Americans, 1 Hispanic American, 5 international. Average age 37. 28 applicants, 32% accepted, 8 enrolled. In 2009, 8 master's awarded. *Degree requirements:* For master's, capstone. *Entrance requirements:* For master's, GMAT, minimum GPA of 2.5. Additional exam requirements/recommendations for international students: Required—TOEFL (minimum score 570 paper-based; 230 computer-based; 88 iBT), or IELTS (minimum score 6.5). *Application deadline:* For fall admission, 2/15 priority date for domestic and international students. Applications are processed on a rolling basis. Application fee: $50. *Expenses:* Tuition: Full-time $31,533; part-time $876 per credit hour. Required fees: $210. *Financial support:* In 2009–10, 7 students received support. Institutionally sponsored loans and scholarships/grants available. Support available to part-time students. Financial award applicants required to submit FAFSA. *Unit head:* Mark Smith, Director, 585-475-7974, Fax: 585-475-7955, E-mail: mml@rit.edu. *Application contact:* Diane Ellison, Assistant Vice President, Graduate Enrollment Services, 585-475-2229, Fax: 585-475-7164, E-mail: gradinfo@rit.edu.

San Diego State University, Graduate and Research Affairs, College of Business Administration, Department of Information and Decision Systems, San Diego, CA 92182. Offers information and decision systems (MS); production and operations management (MS). Evening/weekend programs available. *Degree requirements:* For master's, thesis or alternative. *Entrance requirements:* For master's, GMAT, resume, letters of reference. Additional exam requirements/recommendations for international students: Required—TOEFL. Electronic applications accepted.

San Jose State University, Graduate Studies and Research, Lucas Graduate School of Business, Programs in Business Administration, San Jose, CA 95192-0001. Offers MBA. *Accreditation:* AACSB. *Degree requirements:* For master's, comprehensive exam, thesis or alternative. *Entrance requirements:* For master's, GMAT, minimum GPA of 3.0. *Application deadline:* For fall admission, 6/29 for domestic students; for spring admission, 11/30 for domestic students. Applications are processed on a rolling basis. Application fee: $59. Electronic applications accepted. *Financial support:* Applicants required to submit FAFSA.

Southeast Missouri State University, School of Graduate Studies, Harrison College of Business, Cape Girardeau, MO 63701-4799. Offers accounting (MBA); entrepreneurship (MBA); environmental management (MBA); financial management (MBA); general management (MBA); health administration (MBA); industrial management (MBA); international business (MBA); sport management (MBA). *Accreditation:* AACSB. Part-time and evening/weekend programs available. Postbaccalaureate distance learning degree programs offered (no on-campus study). *Degree requirements:* For master's, applied research project. *Entrance requirements:* For master's, GMAT, minimum undergraduate GPA of 2.5. Additional exam requirements/recommendations for international students: Required—TOEFL (minimum score 550 paper-based; 213 computer-based); Recommended—IELTS (minimum score 6). *Expenses:* Tuition: state resident: full-time $4266; part-time $237 per credit hour. Tuition, nonresident: full-time $7506; part-time $417 per credit hour. Required fees: $427; $427. *Faculty research:* Human resources, laws impacting accounting, advertising.

Stevens Institute of Technology, Graduate School, Charles V. Schaefer Jr. School of Engineering, Department of Mechanical Engineering, Program in Integrated Product Development, Hoboken, NJ 07030. Offers armament engineering (M Eng); computer and electrical engineering (M Eng); manufacturing technologies (M Eng); systems reliability and design (M Eng). *Expenses:* Tuition: Full-time $9900; part-time $1100 per credit. Required fees: $286 per semester.

Syracuse University, Martin J. Whitman School of Management, PhD Program in Business Administration, Syracuse, NY 13244. Offers accounting (PhD); finance (PhD); management information systems (PhD); managerial statistics (PhD); marketing (PhD); operations management (PhD); organizational behavior (PhD); strategy and human resources (PhD); supply chain management (PhD). *Degree requirements:* For doctorate, comprehensive exam, thesis/dissertation, summer research paper. *Entrance requirements:* For doctorate, GMAT or GRE General Test, 3 recommendations. Additional exam requirements/recommendations for international students: Required—TOEFL (minimum score 600 paper-based; 250 computer-based; 100 iBT). Electronic applications accepted. *Expenses:* Tuition: Full-time $26,808; part-time $1117 per credit. Required fees: $1024. *Faculty research:* Marketing models, market microstructure, supply chain, auditing, corporate governance.

Texas A&M University, Mays Business School, Department of Information and Operations Management, College Station, TX 77843. Offers management information systems (MS, PhD); management science (PhD); production and operations management (PhD). Terminal master's awarded for partial completion of doctoral program. *Degree requirements:* For master's, comprehensive exam; for doctorate, thesis/dissertation. *Entrance requirements:* For master's, GMAT; for doctorate, GMAT or GRE General Test. Additional exam requirements/recommendations for international students: Required—TOEFL. *Expenses:* Tuition, state resident: full-time $3991; part-time $221.74 per credit hour. Tuition, nonresident: full-time $9049; part-time $502.74 per credit hour.

Texas Tech University, Jerry S. Rawls College of Business Administration, Area of Information Systems and Quantitative Sciences, Lubbock, TX 79409. Offers business statistics (MS, PhD); healthcare management (MS); management information systems (MS, PhD); production and operations management (MS, PhD); risk management (MS). Part-time programs available. *Faculty:* 14 full-time (0 women). *Students:* 61 full-time (14 women), 5 part-time (1 woman); includes 2 minority (1 African American, 1 Asian American or Pacific Islander), 52 international. Average age 27. 94 applicants, 84% accepted, 35 enrolled. In 2009, 6 master's, 6 doctorates awarded. Terminal master's awarded for partial completion of doctoral program. *Degree requirements:* For master's, comprehensive exam or capstone course; for doctorate, thesis/ dissertation, qualifying exams. *Entrance requirements:* For master's and doctorate, GMAT, holistic profile of academic credentials. Additional exam requirements/recommendations for international students: Required—TOEFL (minimum score 550 paper-based; 213 computer-based; 79 iBT). *Application deadline:* For fall admission, 4/1 priority date for domestic students, 1/15 priority date for international students; for spring admission, 9/1 priority date for domestic students, 7/15 priority date for international students. Applications are processed on a rolling basis. Application fee: $50 ($75 for international students). Electronic applications accepted. *Expenses:* Tuition, state resident: full-time $5100; part-time $213 per credit hour. Tuition, nonresident: full-time $11,748; part-time $490 per credit hour. Required fees: $2298; $50 per credit hour. $555 per semester. *Financial support:* In 2009–10, 4 research assistantships (averaging $8,000 per year), 8 teaching assistantships (averaging $17,000 per year) were awarded; Federal Work-Study, scholarships/grants, and unspecified assistantships also available. *Faculty research:* Database management systems, systems management and engineering, expert systems and adaptive knowledge-based sciences, statistical analysis and design. *Unit head:* Dr. Bradley Ewing, Area Coordinator, 806-742-3939, Fax: 806-742-3193, E-mail: bradley. ewing@ttu.edu. *Application contact:* Cynthia D. Barnes, Director, Graduate Services Center, 806-742-3184, Fax: 806-742-3958, E-mail: ba_grad@ttu.edu.

Universidad de las Américas–Puebla, Division of Graduate Studies, School of Engineering, Program in Industrial Engineering, Puebla, Mexico. Offers industrial engineering (MS); production management (M Adm). Part-time and evening/weekend programs available. *Degree requirements:* For master's, one foreign language, thesis. *Faculty research:* Textile industry, quality control.

Universidad de las Américas–Puebla, Division of Graduate Studies, School of Engineering, Program in Manufacturing Administration, Puebla, Mexico. Offers MS. *Faculty research:* Operations research, construction.

University of Arkansas, Graduate School, College of Engineering, Department of Industrial Engineering, Operations Management Program, Fayetteville, AR 72701-1201. Offers MS. Part-time and evening/weekend programs available. Postbaccalaureate distance learning degree programs offered. *Students:* 21 full-time (8 women), 361 part-time (95 women); includes 84 minority (58 African Americans, 5 American Indian/Alaska Native, 12 Asian Americans or Pacific Islanders, 9 Hispanic Americans), 17 international. In 2009, 188 master's awarded. *Degree requirements:* For master's, thesis optional. Application fee: $0. *Expenses:* Tuition, state resident: full-time $7355; part-time $356.58 per hour. Tuition, nonresident: full-time $17,401; part-time $775.17 per hour. Required fees: $1203. *Financial support:* Fellowships, research assistantships, teaching assistantships, institutionally sponsored loans available. *Unit head:* Dr. Kim Needy, Department Chair, 479-575-7426, E-mail: kneedy@uark.edu. *Application contact:* Nancy Sloan, Program Manager, 479-575-2082, E-mail: ncsloan@uark.edu.

University of California, Berkeley, Graduate Division, Haas School of Business, PhD in Business Administration Program, Berkeley, CA 94720-1500. Offers accounting (PhD); business and public policy (PhD); finance (PhD); management of organizations (PhD); marketing (PhD); operations management (PhD); real estate (PhD). *Accreditation:* AACSB. *Faculty:* 80 full-time (20 women), 130 part-time/adjunct (22 women). *Students:* 82 full-time (23 women); includes 22 minority (18 Asian Americans or Pacific Islanders, 4 Hispanic Americans), 29 international. Average age 30. 511 applicants, 5% accepted, 16 enrolled. In 2009, 8 doctorates awarded. *Degree requirements:* For doctorate, comprehensive exam, thesis/dissertation, oral exam, written preliminary exams. *Entrance requirements:* For doctorate, GMAT or GRE, minimum GPA of 3.0 in undergraduate and graduate coursework. Additional exam requirements/recommendations for international students: Required—TOEFL (minimum score 570 paper-based; 230 computer-based; 68 iBT), IELTS (minimum score 7). *Application deadline:* For fall admission, 12/10 for domestic and international students. Application fee: $70 ($90 for international students). Electronic applications accepted. *Financial support:* Fellowships with full and partial tuition reimbursements, research assistantships with full and partial tuition reimbursements, teaching assistantships with full and partial tuition reimbursements, career-related internships or fieldwork, Federal Work-Study, scholarships/grants, health care benefits, tuition waivers (full), unspecified assistantships, and transit pass, travel grants available. Financial award application deadline: 12/10; financial award applicants required to submit FAFSA. *Faculty research:* Accounting, business and public policy, finance, management of organizations, marketing, operations and information technology management, real estate. *Unit head:* Sunil Dutta, Director, 510-642-1229, Fax: 510-643-4255, E-mail: kimg@haas.berkeley.edu. *Application contact:* Kim Guilfoyle, Director, Student Affairs, 510-642-3944, Fax: 510-643-4255, E-mail: kimg@haas.berkeley.edu.

University of Central Missouri, The Graduate School, College of Science and Technology, Warrensburg, MO 64093. Offers applied mathematics (MS); aviation safety (MS); biology (MS); computer science (MS); environmental studies (MA); industrial management (MS); mathematics (MS); technology (MS); technology management (PhD). Part-time programs available. Postbaccalaureate distance learning degree programs offered. *Faculty:* 59. *Students:* 99 full-time (31 women), 85 part-time (37 women). Average age 33. 45 applicants, 96% accepted, 42 enrolled. In 2009, 68 master's awarded. *Entrance requirements:* Additional exam requirements/recommendations for international students: Required—TOEFL (minimum score 550 paper-based; 79 computer-based). *Application deadline:* For fall admission, 6/1 priority date for domestic students, 5/1 for international students; for spring admission, 10/1 priority date for domestic students, 10/1 for international students. Applications are processed on a rolling basis. Application fee: $30 ($75 for international students). Electronic applications accepted. *Expenses:* Tuition, area resident: Part-time $245.80 per credit hour. Tuition, nonresident: part-time $491.60 per credit hour. Required fees: $24.20 per credit hour. Full-time tuition and fees vary according to course load, degree level, campus/location and reciprocity agreements. *Financial support:* In 2009–10, 15 students received support; fellowships with full and partial tuition reimbursements available, research assistantships with full and partial tuition reimbursements available, teaching assistantships with full and partial tuition reimbursements available, career-related internships or fieldwork, Federal Work-Study, scholarships/grants, and administrative and laboratory assistantships available. Support available to part-time students. Financial award application deadline: 3/1; financial award applicants required to submit FAFSA. *Unit head:* Dr. Alice Greife, Dean, 660-543-4450, Fax: 660-543-8031, E-mail:

greife@ucmo.edu. *Application contact:* Laurie Delap, Admissions Coordinator, 660-543-4621, Fax: 660-543-4778, E-mail: gradinfo@ucmo.edu.

University of Cincinnati, Graduate School, College of Business, PhD Program, Cincinnati, OH 45221. Offers accounting (PhD); finance (PhD); information systems (PhD); management (PhD); marketing (PhD); quantitative analysis and operations management (PhD). *Degree requirements:* For doctorate, comprehensive exam, thesis/dissertation. *Entrance requirements:* For doctorate, GMAT, GRE, resume, letters of recommendation. Additional exam requirements/recommendations for international students: Required—TOEFL (minimum score 600 paper-based; 250 computer-based; 100 iBT). Electronic applications accepted. *Expenses:* Contact institution.

University of Dayton, Graduate School, School of Business Administration, Dayton, OH 45469-1300. Offers accounting (MBA); business intelligence (MBA); entrepreneurship (MBA); finance (MBA); international business (MBA); marketing (MBA); MIS (MBA); operations management (MBA); technology-enhanced business/e-commerce (MBA); JD/MBA. *Accreditation:* AACSB. Part-time and evening/weekend programs available. *Faculty:* 29 full-time (8 women), 15 part-time/adjunct (2 women). *Students:* 134 full-time (48 women), 111 part-time (31 women); includes 14 minority (9 African Americans, 3 Asian Americans or Pacific Islanders, 2 Hispanic Americans), 29 international. Average age 29. 179 applicants, 63% accepted, 73 enrolled. In 2009, 102 master's awarded. *Entrance requirements:* For master's, GMAT. Additional exam requirements/recommendations for international students: Required—TOEFL (minimum score 550 paper-based; 213 computer-based; 79 iBT). *Application deadline:* For fall admission, 3/1 priority date for international students; for winter admission, 7/1 priority date for international students; for spring admission, 1/1 priority date for international students. Applications are processed on a rolling basis. Application fee: $0 ($50 for international students). Electronic applications accepted. *Expenses:* Contact institution. *Financial support:* In 2009–10, 13 fellowships with partial tuition reimbursements, 17 research assistantships with full and partial tuition reimbursements (averaging $7,020 per year) were awarded; career-related internships or fieldwork, institutionally sponsored loans, scholarships/grants, health care benefits, and unspecified assistantships also available. Support available to part-time students. Financial award application deadline: 3/15; financial award applicants required to submit FAFSA. *Faculty research:* Management information systems, economics, finance, entrepreneurship, marketing. *Unit head:* Janice M. Glynn, Director, MBA Program, 937-229-3733, Fax: 937-229-3882, E-mail: glynn@udayton.edu. *Application contact:* Jeffrey Carter, Assistant Director, MBA Program, 937-229-3733, Fax: 937-229-3882, E-mail: jeff.carter@notes.udayton.edu.

University of Minnesota, Twin Cities Campus, Carlson School of Management, Doctoral Program in Business Administration, Minneapolis, MN 55455-0213. Offers accounting (PhD); finance (PhD); information and decision sciences (PhD); marketing and logistics management (PhD); operations and management science (PhD); strategic management and organization (PhD). *Faculty:* 74 full-time (19 women). *Students:* 68 full-time (28 women); includes 7 minority (1 African American, 3 Asian Americans or Pacific Islanders, 3 Hispanic Americans), 46 international. Average age 29. 250 applicants, 5% accepted, 9 enrolled. In 2009, 11 doctorates awarded. *Degree requirements:* For doctorate, comprehensive exam, thesis/dissertation, written and oral preliminary exams, proposal defense. *Entrance requirements:* For doctorate, GMAT, GRE General Test. Additional exam requirements/recommendations for international students: Required—TOEFL (minimum score 600 paper-based; 250 computer-based; 100 iBT), IELTS (minimum score 7.5). *Application deadline:* For fall admission, 12/31 for domestic students, 12/31 priority date for international students. Applications are processed on a rolling basis. Application fee: $55 ($75 for international students). Electronic applications accepted. *Financial support:* In 2009–10, 68 fellowships with full tuition reimbursements (averaging $11,500 per year), 63 research assistantships with full tuition reimbursements (averaging $6,750 per year), 53 teaching assistantships with full tuition reimbursements (averaging $6,750 per year) were awarded; institutionally sponsored loans, scholarships/grants, health care benefits, and unspecified assistantships also available. Financial award application deadline: 12/31. *Faculty research:* Corporate strategy, finance, entrepreneurship, marketing, information and decision science, operations, accounting. Total annual research expenditures: $300,000. *Unit head:* Dr. Shawn P. Curley, Director of Graduate Studies/Program Director, 612-624-6546, Fax: 612-624-8221, E-mail: curley@umn.edu. *Application contact:* Earlene K. Bronson, Assistant Director, 612-624-0875, Fax: 612-624-8221, E-mail: brons003@umn.edu.

University of Missouri–St. Louis, College of Business Administration, Program in Business Administration, St. Louis, MO 63121. Offers accounting (MBA); business administration (Certificate); finance (MBA); human resource management (Certificate); logistics and supply chain management (MBA, Certificate); management (MBA); marketing (MBA); marketing management (Certificate); operations (MBA); quantitative management science (MBA). *Accreditation:* AACSB. Part-time and evening/weekend programs available. *Faculty:* 30 full-time (5 women), 11 part-time/adjunct (2 women). *Students:* 107 full-time (47 women), 310 part-time (120 women); includes 32 minority (17 African Americans, 6 Asian Americans or Pacific Islanders, 9 Hispanic Americans), 66 international. Average age 31. 285 applicants, 58% accepted, 130 enrolled. In 2009, 149 master's, 13 other advanced degrees awarded. *Entrance requirements:* For master's, GMAT, 2 letters of recommendation. Additional exam requirements/recommendations for international students: Required—TOEFL (minimum score 550 paper-based; 213 computer-based). *Application deadline:* For fall admission, 7/1 for domestic students; for spring admission, 11/1 for domestic students. Applications are processed on a rolling basis. Application fee: $35 ($40 for international students). Electronic applications accepted. *Expenses:* Tuition, state resident: full-time $5377; part-time $297.70 per credit hour. Tuition, nonresident: full-time $13,882; part-time $771.20 per credit hour. Required fees: $220; $12.20 per credit hour. One-time fee: $12. Tuition and fees vary according to course level, campus/location and program. *Financial support:* In 2009–10, 27 research assistantships with full and partial tuition reimbursements (averaging $8,525 per year), 6 teaching assistantships with full and partial tuition reimbursements (averaging $13,950 per year) were awarded; career-related internships or fieldwork, Federal Work-Study, and institutionally sponsored loans also available. Support available to part-time students. Financial award application deadline: 4/1; financial award applicants required to submit FAFSA. *Faculty research:* Human resources, strategic management, marketing strategy, consumer behavior product development, advertising. *Unit head:* Karl Kottemann, Assistant Director, 314-516-5885, Fax: 314-516-6420, E-mail: mba@umsl.edu. *Application contact:* 314-516-5458, Fax: 314-516-6996, E-mail: gradadm@umsl.edu.

University of Puerto Rico, Mayagüez Campus, Graduate Studies, College of Business Administration, Mayagüez, PR 00681-9000. Offers business administration (MBA); finance (MBA); human resources (MBA); industrial management (MBA). Part-time and evening/weekend programs available. *Degree requirements:* For master's, comprehensive exam. *Entrance requirements:* For master's, GMAT or EXADEP, bachelor's degree with courses in calculus, microeconomics, accounting and statistics. Additional exam requirements/recommendations for international students: Required—TOEFL (minimum score 500 paper-based; 173 computer-based). *Faculty research:* Organizational studies, management, accounting.

University of Puerto Rico, Río Piedras, College of Business Administration, San Juan, PR 00931-3300. Offers accounting (MBA); finance (MBA, PhD); general business (MBA); human resources management (MBA); international trade and business (MBA, PhD); marketing (MBA); operations management (MBA); quantitative methods (MBA). *Accreditation:* ACBSP. Part-time programs available. *Degree requirements:* For master's, comprehensive exam, thesis or alternative, research project. *Entrance requirements:* For master's, GMAT or PAEG, minimum GPA of 3.0, letter of recommendation; for doctorate, GMAT, PAEG, minimum GPA of 3.0, master degree. *Faculty research:* Management.

University of Rhode Island, Graduate School, College of Business Administration, Kingston, RI 02881. Offers accounting (MS); business administration (MBA, PhD), including finance and insurance (PhD), management (PhD), marketing (PhD), operations and supply chain management (MBA); finance (MBA); general business (MBA); management (MBA); marketing (MBA); supply chain management (MBA). *Accreditation:* AACSB. Part-time and evening/weekend programs available. *Faculty:* 54 full-time (15 women), 2 part-time/adjunct (1 woman). *Students:* 71 full-time (27 women), 157 part-time (56 women); includes 24 minority (6 African Americans, 10 Asian Americans or Pacific Islanders, 8 Hispanic Americans), 23 international. In 2009, 86 master's, 3 doctorates awarded. *Degree requirements:* For master's, comprehensive exam (for some programs), thesis optional; for doctorate, comprehensive exam, thesis/dissertation. *Entrance requirements:* For master's, GMAT or GRE, 2 letters of recommendation, resume; for doctorate, GMAT or GRE, 3 letters of recommendation, resume. Additional exam requirements/recommendations for international students: Required—TOEFL (minimum score 575 paper-based; 233 computer-based; 91 iBT). Application fee: $65. Electronic applications accepted. *Expenses:* Tuition, state resident: full-time $8828; part-time $490 per credit hour. Tuition, nonresident: full-time $22,100; part-time $1228 per credit hour. Required fees: $1118; $57 per semester. Tuition and fees vary according to program. *Financial support:* In 2009–10, 13 teaching assistantships with full and partial tuition reimbursements (averaging $13,095 per year) were awarded. Financial award applicants required to submit FAFSA. Total annual research expenditures: $245,746. *Unit head:* Dr. Mark Higgins, Dean, 401-874-4244, Fax: 401-874-4312, E-mail: markhiggins@uri.edu. *Application contact:* Lisa Lancellotta, Coordinator, MBA Programs, 401-874-4241, Fax: 401-874-4312, E-mail: mba@uri.edu.

University of St. Thomas, Graduate Studies, School of Engineering, St. Paul, MN 55105-1096. Offers engineering and technology management (Certificate); manufacturing systems (MS); manufacturing systems engineering (MMSE); systems engineering (MS); technology management (MS). *Accreditation:* ABET (one or more programs are accredited). Electronic applications accepted. *Expenses:* Contact institution.

University of Southern Indiana, Graduate Studies, College of Science and Engineering, Program in Industrial Management, Evansville, IN 47712-3590. Offers MS. Part-time and evening/weekend programs available. *Faculty:* 2 full-time (0 women). *Students:* 12 part-time (4 women). Average age 33. 1 applicant, 100% accepted, 1 enrolled. In 2009, 2 master's awarded. *Degree requirements:* For master's, project. *Entrance requirements:* For master's, minimum GPA of 2.5, BS in engineering or engineering technology. Additional exam requirements/recommendations for international students: Required—TOEFL (minimum score 550 paper-based; 213 computer-based; 79 iBT), IELTS (minimum score 6). *Application deadline:* For fall admission, 8/15 priority date for domestic students, 3/1 priority date for international students. Applications are processed on a rolling basis. Application fee: $25. Electronic applications accepted. *Expenses:* Tuition, state resident: full-time $4592; part-time $255 per credit hour. Tuition, nonresident: full-time $9060; part-time $503 per credit hour. Required fees: $220; $22.75 per term. Tuition and fees vary according to course load and reciprocity agreements. *Financial support:* In 2009–10, 2 students received support. Federal Work-Study, scholarships/grants, tuition waivers (full and partial), and unspecified assistantships available. Financial award application deadline: 3/1; financial award applicants required to submit FAFSA. *Unit head:* Dr. David E. Schultz, Director, 812-464-1881, E-mail: dschultz@usi.edu. *Application contact:* Dr. Peggy F. Harrel, Director, Graduate Studies, 812-465-7015, Fax: 812-464-1956, E-mail: pharrel@usi.edu.

The University of Tennessee, Graduate School, College of Business Administration, Program in Business Administration, Knoxville, TN 37996. Offers accounting (PhD); finance (MBA, PhD); logistics and transportation (MBA, PhD); management (PhD); marketing (MBA, PhD); operations management (MBA); professional business administration (MBA); statistics (PhD); JD/MBA; MS/MBA. *Accreditation:* AACSB. Postbaccalaureate distance learning degree programs offered. *Degree requirements:* For master's, thesis or alternative; for doctorate, thesis/dissertation. *Entrance requirements:* For master's and doctorate, GMAT, minimum GPA of 2.7. Additional exam requirements/recommendations for international students: Required—TOEFL. Electronic applications accepted. *Expenses:* Tuition, state resident: full-time $6826; part-time $380 per semester hour. Tuition, nonresident: full-time $21,844; part-time $1147 per semester hour. Tuition and fees vary according to program.

The University of Texas at Austin, Graduate School, McCombs School of Business, Department of Information, Risk, and Operations Management, Austin, TX 78712-1111. Offers information systems (PhD); risk analysis and decision making (PhD); supply chain and operations management (PhD). *Degree requirements:* For doctorate, thesis/dissertation. *Entrance requirements:* For doctorate, GMAT or GRE. Electronic applications accepted. *Faculty research:* Stochastic processing and queuing, discrete nonlinear and large-scale optimization simulation, quality assurance logistics, distributed artificial intelligence, organizational modeling.

The University of Texas at Tyler, College of Business and Technology, School of Human Resource Development and Technology, Tyler, TX 75799-0001. Offers human resource development (MS, PhD); industrial management (MS). Part-time and evening/weekend programs available. Postbaccalaureate distance learning degree programs offered (no on-campus study). *Faculty:* 5 full-time (1 woman). *Students:* 28 full-time (14 women), 51 part-time (29 women); includes 24 minority (14 African Americans, 10 Hispanic Americans), 3 international. Average age 35. 34 applicants, 97% accepted, 23 enrolled. In 2009, 31 master's awarded. *Degree requirements:* For master's, comprehensive exam. *Entrance requirements:* For master's, GRE General Test or MAT. Additional exam requirements/recommendations for international students: Required—TOEFL (minimum score 79 computer-based). *Application deadline:* For fall admission, 8/17 priority date for domestic students, 5/30 for international students; for spring admission, 12/21 priority date for domestic students, 10/30 for international students. Application fee: $25 ($50 for international students). Electronic applications accepted. *Expenses:* Tuition, state resident: part-time $665 per semester hour. Tuition, nonresident: part-time $942 per semester hour. Part-time tuition and fees vary according to degree level and program. *Financial support:* Career-related internships or fieldwork, institutionally sponsored loans, scholarships/grants, and health care benefits available. Support available to part-time students. Financial award application deadline: 7/1. *Faculty research:* Human resource development. *Unit head:* Dr. Paul B. Roberts, Interim Chair, 903-566-7334, Fax: 903-565-5650, E-mail: proberts@uttyler.edu. *Application contact:* Dr. Greg Wang, Director of Graduate Studies, 903-565-5910, Fax: 903-565-5650, E-mail: gwang@uttyler.edu.

The University of Toledo, College of Graduate Studies, College of Business Administration, Department of Information Systems, Marketing, E-Commerce, and Sales, Program in Manufacturing Management, Toledo, OH 43606-3390. Offers MBA, DME. *Degree requirements:* For doctorate, thesis/dissertation. *Entrance requirements:* For master's, GMAT. Additional exam requirements/recommendations for international students: Required—TOEFL.

Wake Forest University, Babcock Graduate School of Management, Full-time MBA Program, Winston-Salem, NC 27106. Offers consulting/general management (MBA); entrepreneurship (MBA); finance (MBA); health (MBA); marketing (MBA); operations management (MBA); JD/MBA; MBA/MSA; MD/MBA. *Accreditation:* AACSB. *Faculty:* 62 full-time (13 women), 36 part-time/adjunct (14 women). *Students:* 144 full-time (36 women); includes 17 minority (8 African Americans, 9 Asian Americans or Pacific Islanders), 22 international. Average age 28. In 2009, 81 master's awarded. *Entrance requirements:* For master's, GMAT or GRE, letters of recommendation, official transcripts, current resume or curriculum vitae, 2 years of work experience with the exception of joint-degree candidates. Additional exam requirements/recommendations for international students: Required—TOEFL (minimum score 600 paper-based; 250 computer-based; 100 iBT), Pearson Test of English (PTE). *Application deadline:* For fall admission, 6/1 for domestic and international students. Applications are processed on a rolling basis. Application fee: $75. Electronic applications accepted. *Expenses:* Contact institution. *Financial support:* In 2009–10, 95 students received support. Career-related internships or fieldwork, scholarships/grants, and unspecified assistantships available. Financial award application deadline: 3/1; financial award applicants required to submit FAFSA. *Faculty research:* The influence of personal relationships on business decision making and management of change; drivers of perceived value and consumer behavior; impact of accounting on auditing, financial, managerial, systems and taxation stakeholders; corporate governance and executive compensation; impact of operations strategies on competitiveness. *Unit head:* Sherry Moss, Director, Full-time MBA Program, 336-758-5422, Fax: 336-758-5830, E-mail: admissions@

Industrial and Manufacturing Management

Wake Forest University (continued)
mba.wfu.edu. *Application contact:* LaKesha Alston, Administrative Assistant, 336-758-5422, Fax: 336-758-5830, E-mail: admissions@mba.wfu.edu.

Washington State University, Graduate School, College of Business, Graduate Programs in Business, Pullman, WA 99164. Offers accounting and business law (M Acc); business administration (MBA, PhD), including accounting (PhD), finance (PhD), management and operations (PhD), management information systems (PhD), marketing (PhD). *Accreditation:* AACSB. *Degree requirements:* For master's, comprehensive exam (for some programs), thesis (for some programs), final presentation; for doctorate, comprehensive exam, thesis/dissertation, oral and written exams. *Entrance requirements:* For master's and doctorate, GMAT, minimum GPA of 3.0, 3 letters of recommendation. Additional exam requirements/recommendations for international students: Required—TOEFL. Electronic applications accepted.
See Display on page 193.

Section 10
Insurance and Actuarial Science

This section contains a directory of institutions offering graduate work in insurance and actuarial science. Additional information about programs listed in the directory may be obtained by writing directly to the dean of a graduate school or chair of a department at the address given in the directory.

For programs offering related work, see also in this book *Business Administration and Management*.

CONTENTS

Program Directories

Actuarial Science

Ball State University, Graduate School, College of Sciences and Humanities, Department of Mathematical Sciences, Program in Actuarial Science, Muncie, IN 47306-1099. Offers MA. *Entrance requirements:* For master's, GMAT.

Boston University, Metropolitan College, Department of Actuarial Science, Boston, MA 02215. Offers MS. Part-time and evening/weekend programs available. *Students:* 40 full-time (24 women), 26 part-time (15 women); includes 9 minority (3 African Americans, 5 Asian Americans or Pacific Islanders, 1 Hispanic American), 43 international. Average age 27. In 2009, 24 master's awarded. *Entrance requirements:* For master's, prerequisite coursework in calculus. Additional exam requirements/recommendations for international students: Required—TOEFL (minimum score 550 paper-based; 213 computer-based; 84 iBT). *Application deadline:* For fall admission, 5/31 priority date for domestic students, 5/15 priority date for international students; for spring admission, 10/31 priority date for domestic students, 10/15 priority date for international students. Applications are processed on a rolling basis. Application fee: $70. Electronic applications accepted. *Expenses:* Tuition: Full-time $37,910; part-time $1184 per credit hour. Required fees: $386; $40 per semester. Part-time tuition and fees vary according to class time, course level, degree level and program. *Financial support:* In 2009–10, 3 fellowships with tuition reimbursements (averaging $18,000 per year), 9 teaching assistantships (averaging $5,000 per year) were awarded; research assistantships with tuition reimbursements, career-related internships or fieldwork, institutionally sponsored loans, scholarships/grants, and unspecified assistantships also available. *Faculty research:* Survival models, life contingencies, numerical analysis, operations research, compound interest. *Unit head:* Lois K. Horwitz, Chairman, 617-353-8758, Fax: 617-353-8757, E-mail: lhorwitz@bu.edu. *Application contact:* Andrea Cozzi, Administrative Coordinator, 617-353-8758, Fax: 617-353-8757, E-mail: actuary@bu.edu.

Central Connecticut State University, School of Graduate Studies, School of Arts and Sciences, Department of Mathematical Sciences, New Britain, CT 06050-4010. Offers data mining (MS, Certificate); mathematics (MA, MS, Certificate, Sixth Year Certificate), including actuarial science (MA), computer science (MA), statistics (MA). Part-time and evening/weekend programs available. *Faculty:* 33 full-time (12 women), 60 part-time/adjunct (30 women). *Students:* 21 full-time (10 women), 129 part-time (76 women); includes 13 minority (4 African Americans, 1 American Indian/Alaska Native, 4 Asian Americans or Pacific Islanders, 4 Hispanic Americans), 13 international. Average age 37. 78 applicants, 64% accepted, 37 enrolled. In 2009, 27 master's, 13 other advanced degrees awarded. *Degree requirements:* For master's, comprehensive exam, thesis or alternative; for other advanced degree, qualifying exam. *Entrance requirements:* For master's, minimum undergraduate GPA of 2.7. Additional exam requirements/recommendations for international students: Required—TOEFL. *Application deadline:* For fall admission, 7/1 for domestic students; for spring admission, 12/1 for domestic students. Applications are processed on a rolling basis. Application fee: $50. Electronic applications accepted. *Expenses:* Tuition, area resident: Full-time $4662; part-time $440 per credit. Tuition, state resident: full-time $6994; part-time $440 per credit. Tuition, nonresident: full-time $12,988; part-time $440 per credit. Required fees: $3606. One-time fee: $62 part-time. *Financial support:* In 2009–10, 7 students received support, including 3 research assistantships; career-related internships or fieldwork, Federal Work-Study, scholarships/grants, and unspecified assistantships also available. Support available to part-time students. Financial award application deadline: 3/1; financial award applicants required to submit FAFSA. *Faculty research:* Statistics, actuarial mathematics, computer systems and engineering, computer programming techniques, operations research. *Unit head:* Dr. Jeffrey McGowan, Chair, 860-832-2835. *Application contact:* Dr. Jeffrey McGowan, Chair, 860-832-2835.

Columbia University, School of Continuing Education, Program in Actuarial Science, New York, NY 10027. Offers MS. Part-time programs available. *Faculty:* 7 part-time/adjunct (1 woman). *Students:* 22 full-time (8 women), 40 part-time (20 women); includes 12 minority (1 African American, 9 Asian Americans or Pacific Islanders, 2 Hispanic Americans), 34 international. Average age 26. 77 applicants, 60% accepted, 30 enrolled. *Degree requirements:* For master's, comprehensive exam. *Entrance requirements:* For master's, minimum GPA of 3.0, knowledge of economics, linear algebra, calculus. Additional exam requirements/recommendations for international students: Required—American Language Program placement test. *Application deadline:* For fall admission, 4/15 priority date for domestic students. Application fee: $50. Electronic applications accepted. *Financial support:* Institutionally sponsored loans available. Financial award applicants required to submit FAFSA. *Unit head:* Dr. Michael Hogan, Program Director, 212-851-2161, E-mail: mh2422@columbia.edu. *Application contact:* Bryce Weinert, Admissions Adviser, 212-854-9666, E-mail: sce-apply@columbia.edu.

DePaul University, College of Liberal Arts and Sciences, Department of Mathematical Sciences, Chicago, IL 60614. Offers applied mathematics (MS), including actuarial science or statistics; applied statistics (MS, Certificate); mathematics education (MA). Part-time and evening/weekend programs available. *Faculty:* 23 full-time (6 women), 18 part-time/adjunct (5 women). *Students:* 117 full-time (64 women), 67 part-time (37 women); includes 47 minority (22 African Americans, 15 Asian Americans or Pacific Islanders, 10 Hispanic Americans), 13 international. Average age 30. 40 applicants, 100% accepted. In 2009, 30 master's awarded. *Degree requirements:* For master's, comprehensive exam. *Entrance requirements:* Additional exam requirements/recommendations for international students: Required—TOEFL. *Application deadline:* For fall admission, 7/30 for domestic students, 6/30 for international students; for winter admission, 11/30 for domestic students, 10/31 for international students; for spring admission, 2/15 for domestic students. Applications are processed on a rolling basis. Application fee: $25. *Expenses:* Tuition: Full-time $37,525; part-time $620 per credit hour. *Financial support:* In 2009–10, 12 students received support, including research assistantships with partial tuition reimbursements available (averaging $6,000 per year); teaching assistantships, tuition waivers (full) also available. Financial award application deadline: 4/30. *Faculty research:* Verbally prime algebras, enveloping algebras of Lie, superalgebras and related rings, harmonic analysis, estimation theory. *Unit head:* Dr. Ahmed I. Zayed, Chairperson, 773-325-7806, Fax: 773-325-7807, E-mail: azayed@depaul.edu. *Application contact:* Ann Spittle, Director of Graduate Admissions, 312-362-8300, Fax: 312-362-5749, E-mail: admitdpu@depaul.edu.

Georgia State University, J. Mack Robinson College of Business, Department of Risk Management and Insurance, Program in Actuarial Science, Atlanta, GA 30302-3083. Offers MAS, MBA. Part-time and evening/weekend programs available. *Entrance requirements:* For master's, GMAT, GRE. Additional exam requirements/recommendations for international students: Required—TOEFL (minimum score 610 paper-based; 255 computer-based; 101 iBT). Electronic applications accepted.

Maryville University of Saint Louis, College of Arts and Sciences, Actuarial Science Program, St. Louis, MO 63141-7299. Offers MS. Part-time and evening/weekend programs available. *Students:* 11 full-time (7 women), 3 part-time (2 women), 5 international. Average age 29. In 2009, 5 master's awarded. *Entrance requirements:* For master's, GRE (minimum score: 600 on mathematics quantitative section), minimum GPA of 3.0 in last 2 years of baccalaureate degree, 2 letters of recommendation, letter of intent. Additional exam requirements/recommendations for international students: Required—TOEFL (minimum score 550 paper-based). *Application deadline:* Applications are processed on a rolling basis. Application fee: $40 ($60 for international students). Electronic applications accepted. *Expenses:* Tuition: Full-time $20,384; part-time $627.50 per credit hour. Required fees: $100 per semester. *Financial support:* Application deadline: 3/1. *Unit head:* Dr. Min Deng, Director, 314-529-9433, Fax: 314-529-9965, E-mail: mdeng@maryville.edu. *Application contact:* Denise Evans, Assistant Vice President, Adult and Continuing Education, 314-529-9676, Fax: 314-529-9927, E-mail: devans1@maryville.edu.

Roosevelt University, Graduate Division, College of Arts and Sciences, Department of Mathematics and Actuarial Science, Program in Mathematics, Chicago, IL 60605. Offers mathematical sciences (MS), including actuarial science. Part-time and evening/weekend programs available. *Faculty research:* Statistics, mathematics education, finite groups, computers in mathematics.

St. John's University, The Peter J. Tobin College of Business, School of Risk Management and Actuarial Science, Queens, NY 11439. Offers MBA, MS. *Students:* 46 full-time (17 women), 37 part-time (17 women); includes 12 minority (6 African Americans, 4 Asian Americans or Pacific Islanders, 2 Hispanic Americans), 47 international. Average age 26. 81 applicants, 69% accepted, 30 enrolled. In 2009, 35 master's awarded. *Degree requirements:* For master's, comprehensive exam (for some programs), thesis optional. *Entrance requirements:* For master's, GMAT or GRE (MS in management of risk), 2 letters of recommendation, resume. Additional exam requirements/recommendations for international students: Required—TOEFL (minimum score 500 paper-based; 173 computer-based; 61 iBT), IELTS (minimum score 5.5). *Application deadline:* For fall admission, 5/1 priority date for domestic and international students; for spring admission, 11/1 priority date for domestic and international students. Applications are processed on a rolling basis. Application fee: $70. Electronic applications accepted. *Expenses:* Contact institution. *Financial support:* Research assistantships available. *Faculty research:* Insurance company operations, regulation, and contracting; governance and enterprise risk management; risk theory and risk modeling; credibility theory and copula applications; international, Islamic and microinsurance. *Unit head:* Dr. James Barrese, Chair, 212-277-5191, E-mail: barresej@stjohns.edu. *Application contact:* Nicole T. Bryan, Assistant Dean, 718-990-2599, Fax: 718-990-5242, E-mail: tcbgradadmissions@stjohns.edu.

Simon Fraser University, Graduate Studies, Faculty of Science, Department of Statistics and Actuarial Science, Burnaby, BC V5A 1S6, Canada. Offers M Sc, PhD. Part-time programs available. *Degree requirements:* For master's, participation in consulting, project; for doctorate, comprehensive exam, thesis/dissertation. *Entrance requirements:* For master's, minimum GPA of 3.0; for doctorate, minimum GPA of 3.5. Additional exam requirements/recommendations for international students: Required—TOEFL. Electronic applications accepted. *Faculty research:* Biostatistics, experimental design, envirometrics, statistical computing, statistical theory.

Temple University, Graduate School, Fox School of Business, Specialized Master's Programs, Philadelphia, PA 19122-6096. Offers accounting and financial management (MS); actuarial science (MS); finance (MS); financial engineering (MS); healthcare financial management (MS); healthcare management (MHM); human resource management (MS); management information systems (MS); marketing (MS); statistics (MS). *Accreditation:* AACSB. Part-time programs available. *Entrance requirements:* For master's, GRE General Test or GMAT, minimum undergraduate GPA of 3.0. Additional exam requirements/recommendations for international students: Required—TOEFL (minimum score 600 paper-based; 250 computer-based; 100 iBT), IELTS (minimum score 7.5).

Université du Québec à Montréal, Graduate Programs, Program in Actuarial Sciences, Montréal, QC H3C 3P8, Canada. Offers Diploma. Part-time programs available. *Entrance requirements:* For degree, appropriate bachelor's degree or equivalent and proficiency in French.

University of Central Florida, College of Sciences, Department of Statistics and Actuarial Science, Orlando, FL 32816. Offers SAS data mining (Certificate); statistical computing (MS). Part-time and evening/weekend programs available. *Faculty:* 11 full-time (3 women), 2 part-time/adjunct (0 women). *Students:* 30 full-time (14 women), 19 part-time (5 women); includes 8 minority (5 African Americans, 1 Asian American or Pacific Islander, 2 Hispanic Americans), 26 international. Average age 30. 62 applicants, 74% accepted, 21 enrolled. In 2009, 18 master's, 1 other advanced degree awarded. *Degree requirements:* For master's, comprehensive exam. *Entrance requirements:* For master's, GRE General Test, minimum GPA of 3.0 in last 60 hours. Additional exam requirements/recommendations for international students: Required—TOEFL. *Application deadline:* For fall admission, 7/15 for domestic students; for spring admission, 12/1 for domestic students. Application fee: $30. Electronic applications accepted. *Expenses:* Tuition, state resident: part-time $306.31 per credit hour. Tuition, nonresident: part-time $1099.01 per credit hour. Part-time tuition and fees vary according to degree level and program. *Financial support:* In 2009–10, 14 students received support, including 2 fellowships with partial tuition reimbursements available (averaging $5,300 per year), 1 research assistantship with partial tuition reimbursement available (averaging $12,600 per year), 11 teaching assistantships with partial tuition reimbursements available (averaging $10,500 per year); career-related internships or fieldwork, Federal Work-Study, institutionally sponsored loans, tuition waivers (partial), and unspecified assistantships also available. Financial award application deadline: 3/1; financial award applicants required to submit FAFSA. *Faculty research:* Multivariate analysis, quality control, shrinkage estimation. *Unit head:* Dr. David Nickerson, Chair, 407-823-2289, Fax: 407-823-5419, E-mail: nickerson@mail.ucf.edu. *Application contact:* Dr. David Nickerson, Chair, 407-823-2289, Fax: 407-823-5419, E-mail: nickerson@mail.ucf.edu.

University of Connecticut, Graduate School, College of Liberal Arts and Sciences, Department of Mathematics, Storrs, CT 06269. Offers applied financial mathematics (MS); mathematics (MS, PhD), including actuarial science, mathematics. *Faculty:* 51 full-time (10 women). *Students:* 111 full-time (44 women), 21 part-time (6 women); includes 10 minority (4 African Americans, 6 Asian Americans or Pacific Islanders), 76 international. Average age 27. 342 applicants, 13% accepted, 31 enrolled. In 2009, 40 master's, 10 doctorates awarded. *Degree requirements:* For doctorate, thesis/dissertation. *Entrance requirements:* For master's and doctorate, GRE General Test, GRE Subject Test. Additional exam requirements/recommendations for international students: Required—TOEFL (minimum score 550 paper-based; 213 computer-based). *Application deadline:* For fall admission, 2/1 priority date for domestic and international students; for spring admission, 11/1 for domestic students, 10/1 for international students. Applications are processed on a rolling basis. Application fee: $55. Electronic applications accepted. *Expenses:* Tuition, state resident: full-time $4725; part-time $525 per credit. Tuition, nonresident: full-time $12,267; part-time $1363 per credit. Required fees: $346 per semester. Tuition and fees vary according to course load. *Financial support:* In 2009–10, 19 research assistantships with full tuition reimbursements, 53 teaching assistantships with full tuition reimbursements were awarded; fellowships, Federal Work-Study, scholarships/grants, health care benefits, and unspecified assistantships also available. Financial award application deadline: 2/1; financial award applicants required to submit FAFSA. *Unit head:* Michael Neumann, Head, 860-486-1290, Fax: 860-486-4283. *Application contact:* Sharon McDermott, Administrative Assistant, 860-486-6452, Fax: 860-486-4283, E-mail: gradadm@math.uconn.edu.

University of Connecticut, Graduate School, College of Liberal Arts and Sciences, Department of Mathematics, Field of Mathematics, Program in Actuarial Science, Storrs, CT 06269. Offers MS, PhD. *Faculty:* 51 full-time (10 women). *Students:* 42 full-time (24 women), 13 part-time (4 women); includes 3 minority (2 African Americans, 1 Asian American or Pacific Islander), 38 international. Average age 26. 105 applicants, 16% accepted, 10 enrolled. In 2009, 17 master's awarded. *Degree requirements:* For master's, comprehensive exam. *Entrance requirements:* Additional exam requirements/recommendations for international students: Required—TOEFL (minimum score 550 paper-based; 213 computer-based). *Application deadline:* For fall admission, 2/1 priority date for domestic and international students; for spring admission, 11/1 for domestic students, 10/1 for international students. Applications are processed on a rolling basis. Application fee: $55. Electronic applications accepted. *Expenses:* Tuition, state resident: full-time $4725; part-time $525 per credit. Tuition, nonresident: full-time $12,267; part-time $1363 per credit. Required fees: $346 per semester. Tuition and fees vary according to course load. *Financial support:* In 2009–10, 7 research assistantships with full tuition reimbursements, 6 teaching assistantships with full tuition reimbursements were awarded; career-related internships or fieldwork, Federal Work-Study, scholarships/grants, health care benefits, and unspecified assistantships also available. Financial award application deadline: 2/1; financial award applicants required to submit FAFSA. *Application contact:* Sharon McDermott, Administrative Assistant, 860-486-6452, Fax: 860-486-4283, E-mail: gradadm@math.uconn.edu.

University of Illinois at Urbana–Champaign, Graduate College, College of Liberal Arts and Sciences, Department of Mathematics, Champaign, IL 61820. Offers applied mathematics (MS); applied mathematics: actuarial science (MS); mathematics (MA, MS, PhD); teaching of mathematics (MS). *Faculty:* 67 full-time (5 women), 3 part-time/adjunct (0 women). *Students:* 161 full-time (40 women), 25 part-time (8 women); includes 13 minority (1 African American, 10 Asian Americans or Pacific Islanders, 2 Hispanic Americans), 107 international. 361 applicants, 25% accepted, 37 enrolled. In 2009, 41 master's, 23 doctorates awarded. *Entrance requirements:* For master's, GRE General Test, GRE Subject Test (mathematics), minimum GPA of 3.0; for doctorate, GRE General Test, GRE Subject Test (math), minimum GPA of 3.0. Additional exam requirements/recommendations for international students: Required—TOEFL (minimum score 550 paper-based; 213 computer-based). *Application deadline:* Applications are processed on a rolling basis. Application fee: $60 ($75 for international students). Electronic applications accepted. *Financial support:* In 2009–10, 22 fellowships, 44 research assistantships, 148 teaching assistantships were awarded; tuition waivers (full and partial) also available. *Unit head:* Sheldon Katz, Chair, 217-265-6258, Fax: 217-333-9576, E-mail: katzs@illinois.edu. *Application contact:* Marci Blocher, Office Support Specialist, 217-333-3350, Fax: 217-333-9576, E-mail: mblocher@illinois.edu.

The University of Iowa, Graduate College, College of Liberal Arts and Sciences, Department of Statistics and Actuarial Science, Iowa City, IA 52242-1316. Offers MS, PhD. *Degree requirements:* For master's, thesis optional, exam; for doctorate, comprehensive exam, thesis/dissertation. *Entrance requirements:* For master's and doctorate, GRE General Test, minimum GPA of 3.0. Additional exam requirements/recommendations for international students: Required—TOEFL (minimum score 550 paper-based; 213 computer-based; 81 iBT). Electronic applications accepted.

University of Nebraska–Lincoln, Graduate College, College of Business Administration, Interdepartmental Area of Actuarial Science, Lincoln, NE 68588. Offers MS. *Entrance requirements:* For master's, GRE. Additional exam requirements/recommendations for international students: Required—TOEFL (minimum score 550 paper-based; 213 computer-based). Electronic applications accepted. *Faculty research:* Risk theory, pensions, actuarial finance, decision theory, stochastic calculus.

The University of Texas at Austin, Graduate School, College of Natural Sciences, Department of Mathematics, Austin, TX 78712-1111. Offers mathematics (MA, PhD); statistics (MS Stat). *Entrance requirements:* For master's and doctorate, GRE General Test. Electronic applications accepted.

University of Waterloo, Graduate Studies, Faculty of Mathematics, Department of Statistics and Actuarial Science, Waterloo, ON N2L 3G1, Canada. Offers actuarial science (M Math, PhD); biostatistics (PhD); statistics (M Math, PhD); statistics-biostatistics (M Math); statistics-computing (M Math); statistics-finance (M Math). *Degree requirements:* For master's, research paper or thesis; for doctorate, comprehensive exam, thesis/dissertation. *Entrance requirements:* For master's, honors degree in field, minimum B+ average; for doctorate, master's degree, minimum B+ average. Additional exam requirements/recommendations for international students: Required—TOEFL (minimum score 600 paper-based; 250 computer-based; 90 iBT), TWE (minimum score 4.5). Electronic applications accepted. *Faculty research:* Data analysis, risk theory, inference, stochastic processes, quantitative finance.

University of Wisconsin–Madison, Graduate School, Wisconsin School of Business, MS Program in Actuarial Science, Madison, WI 53706-1380. Offers MS. *Faculty:* 5 full-time (2 women), 1 part-time/adjunct (0 women). *Students:* 14 full-time (5 women); includes 1 minority (African American), 10 international. Average age 25. 99 applicants, 9% accepted, 6 enrolled. In 2009, 7 master's awarded. *Entrance requirements:* For master's, GMAT or GRE. Additional exam requirements/recommendations for international students: Required—Pearson Test of English (minimum score 73, written 80); Recommended—TOEFL (minimum score 623 paper-based; 263 computer-based; 106 iBT), IELTS (minimum score 7.5). *Application deadline:* For fall admission, 3/15 for domestic and international students. Application fee: $56. Electronic applications accepted. *Expenses:* Contact institution. *Financial support:* In 2009–10, 2 students received support, including 2 teaching assistantships with full tuition reimbursements available (averaging $9,392 per year); Federal Work-Study, institutionally sponsored loans, scholarships/grants, health care benefits, and unspecified assistantships also available. Financial award application deadline: 3/15; financial award applicants required to submit FAFSA. *Faculty research:* Fuzzy logic, business forecasting, health insurance, international insurance. *Unit head:* Prof. Marjorie Rosenberg, Chair, 608-262-1683, E-mail: mrosenberg@bus.wisc.edu. *Application contact:* Belle Heberling, Assistant Director for Research Programs, 608-262-3749, Fax: 608-890-0180, E-mail: ms@bus.wisc.edu.

Insurance

Florida State University, The Graduate School, College of Business, Tallahassee, FL 32306-1110. Offers accounting (M Acc), including accounting information services, assurance services, corporate accounting, taxation; business administration (MBA, PhD), including accounting (PhD), finance (PhD), management information systems (PhD), marketing (PhD), organizational behavior (PhD), risk management and insurance (PhD), strategic management (PhD); finance (MS); insurance (MSM); management information systems (MS); JD/MBA; MSW/MBA. *Accreditation:* AACSB. Part-time programs available. Postbaccalaureate distance learning degree programs offered (no on-campus study). *Faculty:* 107 full-time (31 women), 2 part-time/adjunct (0 women). *Students:* 212 full-time (73 women), 345 part-time (107 women); includes 123 minority (37 African Americans, 2 American Indian/Alaska Native, 48 Asian Americans or Pacific Islanders, 36 Hispanic Americans). Average age 30. 908 applicants, 43% accepted, 307 enrolled. In 2009, 257 master's, 18 doctorates awarded. Terminal master's awarded for partial completion of doctoral program. *Degree requirements:* For doctorate, comprehensive exam, thesis/dissertation. *Entrance requirements:* For master's, GMAT, work experience (MBA, MS), minimum GPA of 3.0, letters of recommendation; for doctorate, GMAT, minimum graduate GPA of 3.5, letters of recommendation. Additional exam requirements/recommendations for international students: Required—TOEFL (minimum score 600 paper-based; 80 computer-based); Recommended—IELTS (minimum score 6.5). *Application deadline:* For fall admission, 6/1 for domestic students, 5/1 for international students; for spring admission, 10/1 for domestic students, 9/1 for international students. Applications are processed on a rolling basis. Application fee: $30. Electronic applications accepted. *Expenses:* Tuition, state resident: full-time $7413. Tuition, nonresident: full-time $22,567. *Financial support:* In 2009–10, 102 students received support, including 32 fellowships with full tuition reimbursements available (averaging $6,900 per year), 30 research assistantships with full tuition reimbursements available (averaging $4,500 per year), 40 teaching assistantships with full tuition reimbursements available (averaging $11,500 per year); career-related internships or fieldwork, scholarships/grants, health care benefits, tuition waivers (full and partial), and unspecified assistantships also available. Support available to part-time students. Financial award application deadline: 1/1. *Unit head:* Dr. Caryn Beck-Dudley, Dean, 850-644-3090, Fax: 850-644-0915. *Application contact:* Lisa Beverly, Director, Graduate Programs Admissions, 850-644-6458, Fax: 850-644-0588, E-mail: lbeverly@cob.fsu.edu.

Georgia State University, J. Mack Robinson College of Business, Department of Risk Management and Insurance, Program in Risk Management and Insurance, Atlanta, GA 30302-3083. Offers MBA, MS, PhD, Certificate. Part-time and evening/weekend programs available. *Degree requirements:* For doctorate, comprehensive exam, thesis/dissertation. *Entrance requirements:* For master's and doctorate, GMAT, GRE. Additional exam requirements/recommendations for international students: Required—TOEFL (minimum score 610 paper-based; 255 computer-based; 101 iBT). Electronic applications accepted.

Pontificia Universidad Catolica Madre y Maestra, Graduate School, Santiago, Dominican Republic. Offers administration (M Adm); architecture of interiors (M Arch); architecture of tourist lodgings (M Arch); banking and financial management (M Mgmt); civil law (LL M); construction administration (ME); corporate business law (LL M); criminal procedure law (LL M); environmental engineering (ME, MEE); finance (M Mgmt); history applied to education (M Ed); human resources (EMBA); insurance (M Mgmt); international business (M Mgmt); labor law and Social Security (LL M); logistics management (ME); marketing (M Mgmt); renewable energy (ME); strategic cost management (M Mgmt). *Entrance requirements:* For master's, curriculum vitae, interview.

St. John's University, The Peter J. Tobin College of Business, School of Risk Management and Actuarial Science, Queens, NY 11439. Offers MBA, MS. *Students:* 46 full-time (17 women), 37 part-time (17 women); includes 12 minority (6 African Americans, 4 Asian Americans or Pacific Islanders, 2 Hispanic Americans), 47 international. Average age 26. 81 applicants, 69% accepted, 30 enrolled. In 2009, 35 master's awarded. *Degree requirements:* For master's, comprehensive exam (for some programs), thesis optional. *Entrance requirements:* For master's, GMAT or GRE (MS in management of risk), 2 letters of recommendation, resume. Additional exam requirements/recommendations for international students: Required—TOEFL (minimum score 500 paper-based; 173 computer-based; 61 iBT), IELTS (minimum score 5.5). *Application deadline:* For fall admission, 5/1 priority date for domestic and international students; for spring admission, 11/1 priority date for domestic and international students. Applications are processed on a rolling basis. Application fee: $70. Electronic applications accepted. *Expenses:* Contact institution. *Financial support:* Research assistantships available. *Faculty research:* Insurance company operations, regulation, and contracting; governance and enterprise risk management; risk theory and risk modeling; credibility theory and copula applications; international, Islamic and microinsurance. *Unit head:* Dr. James Barrese, Chair, 212-277-5191, E-mail: barresej@stjohns.edu. *Application contact:* Nicole T. Bryan, Assistant Dean, 718-990-2599, Fax: 718-990-5242, E-mail: tcbgradadmissions@stjohns.edu.

Temple University, Graduate School, Fox School of Business, Doctoral Programs in Business, Philadelphia, PA 19122-6096. Offers accounting (PhD); entrepreneurship (PhD); finance (PhD); human resource administration (PhD); international business (PhD); management information systems (PhD); marketing (PhD); risk management and insurance (PhD); statistics (PhD); strategic management (PhD); tourism and sport (PhD). *Accreditation:* AACSB. *Degree requirements:* For doctorate, thesis/dissertation. *Entrance requirements:* For doctorate, GRE General Test, GMAT, minimum GPA of 3.0, master's degree. Additional exam requirements/recommendations for international students: Required—TOEFL (minimum score 600 paper-based; 250 computer-based; 100 iBT), IELTS (minimum score 7.5). Electronic applications accepted.

Tennessee Technological University, Graduate School, College of Business, Cookeville, TN 38505. Offers accounting (MBA); finance (MBA); human resource management (MBA); international business (MBA); management information systems (MBA); risk management & insurance (MBA). *Accreditation:* AACSB. Part-time and evening/weekend programs available. *Faculty:* 28 full-time (5 women). *Students:* 64 full-time (26 women), 163 part-time (70 women); includes 17 minority (6 African Americans, 8 Asian Americans or Pacific Islanders, 3 Hispanic Americans). Average age 25. 203 applicants, 52% accepted, 75 enrolled. In 2009, 105 master's awarded. *Entrance requirements:* For master's, GMAT. Additional exam requirements/recommendations for international students: Required—TOEFL (minimum score 550 paper-based; 79 iBT), IELTS (minimum score 5.5). *Application deadline:* For fall admission, 8/1 for domestic and international students; for spring admission, 12/1 for domestic students, 10/1 for international students. Application fee: $25 ($30 for international students). Electronic applications accepted. *Expenses:* Tuition, state resident: full-time $7034; part-time $368 per credit hour. *Financial support:* In 2009–10, 5 fellowships (averaging $10,000 per year), 18 research assistantships (averaging $4,000 per year), teaching assistantships (averaging $4,000 per year) were awarded. Support available to part-time students. Financial award application deadline: 4/1. *Unit head:* Dr. Bob G. Wood, Director, 931-372-3600, Fax: 931-372-6249. *Application contact:* Shelia K. Kendrick, Coordinator of Graduate Studies, 931-372-3808, Fax: 931-372-3497, E-mail: skendrick@tntech.edu.

University of Florida, Graduate School, Warrington College of Business Administration, Hough Graduate School of Business, Department of Finance, Insurance and Real Estate, Gainesville, FL 32611. Offers business administration (MS), including entrepreneurship, insurance, real estate and urban analysis, retailing; finance (PhD); financial services (Certificate); insurance (PhD); real estate and urban analysis (PhD); JD/MS. Terminal master's awarded for partial completion of doctoral program. *Degree requirements:* For doctorate, thesis/dissertation. *Entrance requirements:* For master's, GMAT or GRE General Test, minimum GPA of 3.0 for last 60 hours of undergraduate degree, work experience (preferred); for doctorate, GMAT or GRE General Test, minimum GPA of 3.0. Additional exam requirements/recommendations for international students: Required—TOEFL (minimum score 550 paper-based; 213 computer-based). Electronic applications accepted. *Faculty research:* Financial management, financial markets and institutions, investments, risk and insurance, real estate development.

University of Pennsylvania, Wharton School, Insurance and Risk Management Department, Philadelphia, PA 19104. Offers MBA, PhD. *Degree requirements:* For doctorate, thesis/dissertation. *Entrance requirements:* For master's, GMAT; for doctorate, GMAT or GRE. *Expenses:* Tuition: Full-time $25,660; part-time $4758 per course. Required fees: $2152; $270 per course. Tuition and fees vary according to course load, degree level and program. *Faculty research:* Fair rate of return in insurance economics of pension plans, insurance regulation, malpractice insurance, actuarial science, genetic testing and life insurance.

University of Wisconsin–Madison, Graduate School, Wisconsin School of Business, Doctoral Program in Actuarial Science, Risk Management and Insurance, Madison, WI 53706-1380. Offers PhD. *Faculty:* 5 full-time (2 women). *Students:* 8 full-time (6 women); includes 1 minority (African American), 7 international. Average age 32. 20 applicants, 25% accepted, 2 enrolled. In 2009, 1 doctorate awarded. *Degree requirements:* For doctorate, comprehensive exam, thesis/dissertation. *Entrance requirements:* For doctorate, GMAT or GRE General Test. Additional exam requirements/recommendations for international students: Required—Pearson Test of English (minimum score 73, written 80); Recommended—TOEFL (minimum score 623 paper-based; 263 computer-based; 106 iBT), IELTS (minimum score 7.5). *Application deadline:* For fall admission, 12/15 priority date for domestic and international students. Application fee: $56. Electronic applications accepted. *Expenses:* Tuition, state resident: part-time $594 per credit. Tuition, nonresident: part-time $1504 per credit. Required fees: $65 per credit. Tuition and fees vary according to course load, program and reciprocity agreements. *Financial support:* In 2009–10, 6 students received support, including fellowships with full tuition reimbursements available (averaging $18,567 per year), research assistantships with full tuition reimbursements available (averaging $16,506 per year), 6 teaching assistantships with full tuition reimbursements available (averaging $14,088 per year); Federal Work-Study, institutionally

Insurance

University of Wisconsin–Madison (continued)

sponsored loans, scholarships/grants, health care benefits, and unspecified assistantships also available. Financial award application deadline: 2/1; financial award applicants required to submit FAFSA. *Faculty research:* Superfund, health insurance, workers compensation, employee benefits, fuzzy logic. *Unit head:* Prof. Marjorie Rosenberg, Chair, 608-262-1683, E-mail: mrosenberg@bus.wisc.edu. *Application contact:* Belle Heberling, Assistant Director for Research Programs, 608-262-3749, Fax: 608-890-0180, E-mail: phd@bus.wisc.edu.

University of Wisconsin–Madison, Graduate School, Wisconsin School of Business, Wisconsin Full-Time MBA Program, Madison, WI 53706-1380. Offers applied corporate finance (MBA); applied security analysis (MBA); arts administration (MBA); brand and product management (MBA); entrepreneurial management (MBA); marketing research (MBA); operations and technology management (MBA); real estate (MBA); risk management and insurance (MBA); strategic human resource management (MBA); strategic management in the life and engineering sciences (MBA); supply chain management (MBA). *Faculty:* 32 full-time (5 women). *Students:* 242 full-time (74 women); includes 47 minority (16 African Americans, 3 American Indian/Alaska Native, 16 Asian Americans or Pacific Islanders, 12 Hispanic Americans), 29 international. Average age 28. 526 applicants, 32% accepted, 117 enrolled. In 2009, 106 master's awarded. *Entrance requirements:* For master's, GMAT, bachelor's or equivalent degree, 2 years of work experience, letters of recommendation. Additional exam requirements/recommendations for international students: Required—TOEFL (minimum score 600 paper-based; 250 computer-based; 100 iBT), IELTS. *Application deadline:* For fall admission, 11/4 for domestic and international students; for winter admission, 2/5 for domestic and international students; for spring admission, 5/26 for domestic and international students. Applications are processed on a rolling basis. Application fee: $56. Electronic applications accepted. *Expenses:* Tuition, state resident: part-time $594 per credit. Tuition, nonresident: part-time $1504 per credit. Required fees: $65 per credit. Tuition and fees vary according to course load, program and reciprocity agreements. *Financial support:* In 2009–10, 103 students received support, including 13 fellowships with full and partial tuition reimbursements available (averaging $15,000 per year), 53 research assistantships with full tuition reimbursements available (averaging $8,000 per year), 35 teaching assistantships with full tuition reimbursements available (averaging $11,000 per year); scholarships/grants, health care benefits, and unspecified assistantships also available. Financial award application deadline: 4/5; financial award applicants required to submit FAFSA. *Unit head:* Prof. Kenneth A. Kavajecz, Associate Dean, 608-265-3494, Fax: 608-265-4192, E-mail: kkavajecz@bus.wisc.edu. *Application contact:* Maria Reis, Assistant Director of MBA Marketing and Recruiting, 608-262-4000, Fax: 608-265-4192, E-mail: mreis@bus.wisc.edu.

Virginia Commonwealth University, Graduate School, School of Business, Program in Finance, Insurance, and Real Estate, Richmond, VA 23284-9005. Offers MS. *Entrance requirements:* For master's, GMAT.

Washington State University, Graduate School, College of Business, Department of Finance, Insurance and Real Estate, Pullman, WA 99164. Offers PhD.

Section 11
International Business

This section contains a directory of institutions offering graduate work in international business, followed by an in-depth entry submitted by an institution that chose to prepare a detailed program description. Additional information about programs listed in the directory but not augmented by an in-depth entry may be obtained by writing directly to the dean of a graduate school or chair of a department at the address given in the directory.

For programs offering related work, see also in this book *Business Administration and Management, Entrepreneurship, Industrial and Manufacturing Management,* and *Organizational Behavior.* In another guide in this series:

Graduate Programs in the Humanities, Arts & Social Sciences
See *Political Science and International Affairs* and *Public, Regional, and Industrial Affairs*

CONTENTS

Program Directory

Close-Up

International Business

Alliant International University–México City, Marshall Goldsmith School of Management, Mexico City, Mexico. Offers international business administration (MIBA); international relations (MA). Part-time and evening/weekend programs available. *Entrance requirements:* For master's, GMAT, minimum GPA of 3.0. Additional exam requirements/recommendations for international students: Required—TOEFL (minimum score 550 paper-based; 213 computer-based), TWE (minimum score 5). Electronic applications accepted. *Faculty research:* Environmental impact and business in Mexico.

Alliant International University–San Diego, Marshall Goldsmith School of Management, Business and Management Division, San Diego, CA 92131-1799. Offers business administration (MBA); information and technology management (DBA); international business (MIBA, DBA), including finance (DBA), marketing (DBA); strategic business (DBA); sustainable management (MBA); MBA/MA; MBA/PhD. Part-time and evening/weekend programs available. *Degree requirements:* For doctorate, thesis/dissertation. *Entrance requirements:* For master's, GMAT, minimum GPA of 3.0; for doctorate, GMAT, minimum GPA of 3.3. Additional exam requirements/recommendations for international students: Required—TOEFL (minimum score 550 paper-based; 213 computer-based), TWE (minimum score 5). Electronic applications accepted. *Faculty research:* Consumer behavior, international business, strategic management, information systems.

American InterContinental University Dunwoody Campus, Program in Global Technology Management, Atlanta, GA 30328. Offers MBA. Part-time and evening/weekend programs available. Postbaccalaureate distance learning degree programs offered. *Entrance requirements:* For master's, interview. Electronic applications accepted. *Faculty research:* E-commerce, service quality leadership, human resources management.

American InterContinental University–London, Program in Business Administration, London, United Kingdom. Offers international business (MBA). *Degree requirements:* For master's, thesis optional. *Entrance requirements:* For master's, interview, professional experience. Additional exam requirements/recommendations for international students: Required—TOEFL or IELTS recommended. Electronic applications accepted.

American InterContinental University Online, Program in Business Administration, Hoffman Estates, IL 60192. Offers accounting and finance (MBA); finance (MBA); healthcare management (MBA); human resource management (MBA); international business (MBA); management (MBA); marketing (MBA); operations management (MBA); organizational psychology and development (MBA); project management (MBA). Evening/weekend programs available. Postbaccalaureate distance learning degree programs offered (no on-campus study). *Entrance requirements:* Additional exam requirements/recommendations for international students: Required—TOEFL (minimum score 550 paper-based; 213 computer-based). Electronic applications accepted.

American InterContinental University South Florida, Program in International Business, Weston, FL 33326. Offers accounting and finance (MBA); human resource management (MBA); management (MBA); marketing (MBA). Part-time and evening/weekend programs available. Postbaccalaureate distance learning degree programs offered. Electronic applications accepted.

American International College, School of Business Administration, MBA Program, Springfield, MA 01109-3189. Offers accounting (MBA); corporate/public communication (MBA); finance (MBA); general business (MBA); hospitality, hotel and service management (MBA); international business (MBA); international business practice (MBA); management (MBA); management information systems (MBA); marketing (MBA). International business practice program developed in cooperation with the Mountbatten Institute. *Expenses:* Tuition: Full-time $12,510; part-time $695 per credit hour. Required fees: $35 per term.

American University, Kogod School of Business, Department of International Business, Washington, DC 20016-8044. Offers international business (Certificate). Part-time and evening/weekend programs available. *Faculty:* 11 full-time (2 women). *Students:* 4 part-time (3 women), 1 international. Average age 26. In 2009, 2 Certificates awarded. *Entrance requirements:* For degree, bachelor's degree. Additional exam requirements/recommendations for international students: Required—TOEFL. *Application deadline:* For fall admission, 2/1 priority date for domestic students; for spring admission, 10/1 priority date for domestic students. Applications are processed on a rolling basis. Application fee: $100. *Expenses:* Contact institution. *Financial support:* Fellowships, research assistantships with partial tuition reimbursements, career-related internships or fieldwork, Federal Work-Study, and institutionally sponsored loans available. Support available to part-time students. Financial award application deadline: 2/1; financial award applicants required to submit FAFSA. *Faculty research:* Financial risk in the multinational corporation, emerging security markets, import/export issues, joint ventures in China, Japanese management. *Unit head:* Dr. Frank DuBois, Chair, 202-885-1967, Fax: 202-885-1992, E-mail: fdubois@american.edu. *Application contact:* Shannon Demko, Associate Director of Graduate Admissions, 202-885-1994, Fax: 202-885-1108, E-mail: demko@american.edu.

American University, Kogod School of Business, Master of Business Administration Program, Washington, DC 20016-8044. Offers accounting (MBA); consulting (MBA), including information technology, international business, management; corporate finance: commercial banking (MBA); corporate finance: corporate financial management (MBA); corporate finance: investment banking (MBA), including corporate finance and private equity, trading and selling; entrepreneurship (MBA); global emerging markets (MBA), including business, finance, information technology; international trade and global supply chain management (MBA); leadership (MBA); marketing management (MBA); marketing research (MBA); real estate (MBA); MBA/JD; MBA/LL M. Part-time and evening/weekend programs available. *Faculty:* 14 full-time (6 women). *Students:* 133 full-time (56 women), 121 part-time (48 women); includes 54 minority (23 African Americans, 1 American Indian/Alaska Native, 16 Asian Americans or Pacific Islanders, 14 Hispanic Americans), 43 international. Average age 29. 539 applicants, 51% accepted, 86 enrolled. In 2009, 114 master's awarded. *Entrance requirements:* For master's, GMAT. Additional exam requirements/recommendations for international students: Required—TOEFL. *Application deadline:* For fall admission, 2/1 priority date for domestic students; for spring admission, 10/1 priority date for domestic students. Applications are processed on a rolling basis. Application fee: $100. *Expenses:* Contact institution. *Financial support:* In 2009–10, 19 students received support; fellowships, research assistantships with partial tuition reimbursements available, career-related internships or fieldwork, Federal Work-Study, and institutionally sponsored loans available. Support available to part-time students. Financial award application deadline: 2/1. *Faculty research:* Information technology, decision-aiding methodology, negotiation. *Unit head:* Dr. Stevan Holmberg, Chair, 202-885-6193, E-mail: sholmbe@american.edu. *Application contact:* Shannon Demko, Associate Director of Graduate Admissions, 202-885-1994, Fax: 202-885-1108, E-mail: demko@american.edu.

The American University in Dubai, Master in Business Administration Program, Dubai, United Arab Emirates. Offers general (MBA); healthcare management (MBA); international finance (MBA); international marketing (MBA); management of construction enterprises (MBA). Part-time and evening/weekend programs available. *Degree requirements:* For master's, thesis optional. *Entrance requirements:* For master's, GMAT, Interview. Additional exam requirements/recommendations for international students: Required—TOEFL (minimum score 550 paper-based; 213 computer-based; 79 iBT). Electronic applications accepted.

The American University of Paris, Graduate Programs, Paris, France. Offers cross-cultural and sustainable business management (MA); cultural translation (MA); global communications (MA); global communications and civil society (MA); international affairs, conflict resolution and civil society development (MA); Middle East and Islamic studies (MA); Middle East and Islamic studies and international affairs (MA); public policy and international affairs (MA); public policy and international law (MA). *Faculty:* 14 full-time (3 women). *Students:* 143 full-time (109 women). 71 applicants, 92% accepted, 34 enrolled. *Degree requirements:* For master's, thesis. *Entrance requirements:* For master's, minimum undergraduate GPA of 3.0. *Application deadline:* For fall admission, 4/15 priority date for international students; for spring admission, 11/15 priority date for international students. Applications are processed on a rolling basis. Application fee: $75. Tuition charges are reported in euros. *Expenses:* Tuition: Full-time 23,460 euros. *Financial support:* Scholarships/grants available. Financial award applicants required to submit FAFSA. *Unit head:* Celeste Schenk, President, 33 1-40620659, E-mail: president@aup.fr. *Application contact:* International Admissions Counselor, 33 1-40620720, Fax: 33 1-47053432, E-mail: admissions@aup.edu.

Andrew Jackson University, Brian Tracy College of Business and Entrepreneurship, Birmingham, AL 35244. Offers entrepreneurship (MBA); finance (MBA); health services management (MBA); hospitality and tourism management (MBA); human resource management (MBA); international business (MBA); management (MBA); marketing (MBA). Part-time and evening/weekend programs available. Postbaccalaureate distance learning degree programs offered (no on-campus study). *Entrance requirements:* For master's, course work in calculus, statistics, macroeconomics. Additional exam requirements/recommendations for international students: Required—TOEFL (minimum score 550 paper-based; 213 computer-based). Electronic applications accepted.

Argosy University, Atlanta, College of Business, Atlanta, GA 30328. Offers accounting (DBA); corporate compliance (MBA); customized professional concentration (MBA, DBA); finance (MBA); healthcare administration (MBA); information systems (DBA); information systems management (MBA); international business (MBA, DBA); management (MBA, MSM, DBA); marketing (MBA, DBA).

See Close-Up on page 197.

Argosy University, Chicago, College of Business, Chicago, IL 60601. Offers accounting (DBA); customized professional concentration (MBA, DBA); finance (MBA); fraud examination (MBA); global business sustainability (DBA); healthcare administration (MBA); information systems (DBA); information systems management (MBA); international business (MBA, DBA); management (MBA, MSM, DBA); marketing (MBA, DBA); organizational leadership (Ed D); public administration (MBA); sustainable management (MBA). Postbaccalaureate distance learning degree programs offered (minimal on-campus study).

See Close-Up on page 199.

Argosy University, Dallas, College of Business, Farmers Branch, TX 75244. Offers accounting (DBA, AGC); corporate compliance (MBA, Graduate Certificate); customized professional concentration (MBA); finance (MBA, Graduate Certificate); fraud examination (MBA, Graduate Certificate); global business sustainability (DBA, AGC); healthcare administration (Graduate Certificate); healthcare management (MBA); information systems (MBA, DBA, AGC); information systems management (Graduate Certificate); international business (MBA, DBA, AGC, Graduate Certificate); management (MBA, DBA, AGC, Graduate Certificate); marketing (MBA, DBA, AGC, Graduate Certificate); public administration (MBA, Graduate Certificate); sustainable management (MBA, Graduate Certificate).

See Close-Up on page 201.

Argosy University, Denver, College of Business, Denver, CO 80231. Offers accounting (DBA); corporate compliance (MBA); customized professional concentration (MBA, DBA); finance (MBA); fraud examination (MBA); global business sustainability (DBA); healthcare administration (MBA); information systems (DBA); information systems management (MBA); international business (MBA, DBA); management (MBA, MSM, DBA); marketing (MBA, DBA); organizational leadership (Ed D); public administration (MBA); sustainable management (MBA).

See Close-Up on page 203.

Argosy University, Hawai'i, College of Business, Honolulu, HI 96813. Offers accounting (DBA); corporate compliance (MBA); customized professional concentration (MBA, DBA); finance (MBA, Certificate); fraud examination (MBA); global business sustainability (DBA); healthcare administration (MBA, Certificate); information systems (DBA); information systems management (MBA, Certificate); international business (MBA, DBA, Certificate); management (MBA, MSM, DBA); marketing (MBA, DBA, Certificate); organizational leadership (Ed D); public administration (MBA); sustainable management (MBA).

See Close-Up on page 205.

Argosy University, Inland Empire, College of Business, San Bernardino, CA 92408. Offers accounting (DBA); corporate compliance (MBA); customized professional concentration (MBA, DBA); finance (MBA); fraud examination (MBA); global business sustainability (DBA); healthcare administration (MBA); information systems (DBA); information systems management (MBA); international business (MBA, DBA); management (MBA, MSM, DBA); marketing (MBA, DBA); organizational leadership (Ed D); public administration (MBA); sustainable management (MBA).

See Close-Up on page 207.

Argosy University, Los Angeles, College of Business, Santa Monica, CA 90045. Offers accounting (DBA); corporate compliance (MBA); customized professional concentration (MBA, DBA); finance (MBA); fraud examination (MBA); global business sustainability (DBA); healthcare administration (MBA); information systems (DBA); information systems management (MBA); international business (MBA, DBA); management (MBA, MSM, DBA); marketing (MBA, DBA); organizational leadership (Ed D); public administration (MBA); sustainable management (MBA).

See Close-Up on page 209.

Argosy University, Nashville, College of Business, Nashville, TN 37214. Offers accounting (DBA); customized professional concentration (MBA, DBA); finance (MBA); healthcare administration (MBA); information systems (MBA, DBA); international business (MBA, DBA); management (MBA, MSM, DBA); marketing (MBA, DBA).

See Close-Up on page 211.

Argosy University, Orange County, College of Business, Orange, CA 92868. Offers accounting (DBA, Adv C); corporate compliance (MBA); customized professional concentration (MBA, DBA); finance (MBA, Certificate); fraud examination (MBA); global business sustainability (DBA); healthcare administration (MBA, Certificate); information systems (DBA, Adv C, Certificate); information systems management (MBA); international business (MBA, DBA, Adv C, Certificate); management (MBA, MSM, DBA, Adv C); marketing (MBA, DBA, Adv C, Certificate); organizational leadership (Ed D); public administration (MBA, Certificate); sustainable management (MBA).

See Close-Up on page 213.

Argosy University, Phoenix, College of Business, Phoenix, AZ 85021. Offers accounting (DBA); corporate compliance (MBA); customized professional concentration (MBA, DBA); finance (MBA); fraud examination (MBA); global business sustainability (DBA); healthcare administration (MBA); information systems (DBA); information systems management (MBA); international business (MBA, DBA); management (MBA, DBA); marketing (MBA, DBA); public administration (MBA); sustainable management (MBA).

See Close-Up on page 215.

Argosy University, Salt Lake City, College of Business, Draper, UT 84020. Offers accounting (DBA); corporate compliance (MBA); customized professional concentration (MBA, DBA); finance (MBA); fraud examination (MBA); global business sustainability (DBA); healthcare administration (MBA); information systems (DBA); information systems management (MBA); international business (MBA, DBA); management (MBA, DBA); marketing (MBA, DBA); public administration (MBA); sustainable management (MBA).

See Close-Up on page 217.

Argosy University, San Diego, College of Business, San Diego, CA 92108. Offers accounting (DBA); corporate compliance (MBA); customized professional concentration (MBA, DBA);

finance (MBA); fraud examination (MBA); global business sustainability (DBA); information systems (DBA); information systems management (MBA); international business (MBA, DBA); management (MBA, MSM, DBA); marketing (MBA, DBA); organizational leadership (Ed D); public administration (MBA).

See Close-Up on page 219.

Argosy University, San Francisco Bay Area, College of Business, Alameda, CA 94501. Offers accounting (DBA); corporate compliance (MBA); customized professional concentration (MBA, DBA); finance (MBA); fraud examination (MBA); global business sustainability (DBA); healthcare administration (MBA); information systems (DBA); information systems management (MBA); international business (MBA, DBA); management (MBA, MSM, DBA); marketing (MBA, DBA); organizational leadership (Ed D); public administration (MBA); sustainable management (MBA).

See Close-Up on page 221.

Argosy University, Sarasota, College of Business, Sarasota, FL 34235. Offers accounting (DBA, Adv C); corporate compliance (MBA, DBA, Certificate); customized professional concentration (MBA, DBA); finance (MBA, Certificate); fraud examination (MBA, Certificate); global business sustainability (DBA, Adv C); healthcare administration (MBA, Certificate); information systems (DBA, Adv C, Certificate); information systems management (MBA); international business (MBA, DBA, Adv C, Certificate); management (MBA, MSM, DBA, Adv C, Certificate); marketing (MBA, DBA, Adv C, Certificate); organizational leadership (Ed D); public administration (MBA, Certificate); sustainable management (MBA, Certificate).

See Close-Up on page 223.

Argosy University, Schaumburg, College of Business, Schaumburg, IL 60173-5403. Offers accounting (DBA, Adv C); customized professional concentration (MBA, DBA); finance (MBA, Certificate); fraud examination (MBA); global business sustainability (DBA); healthcare administration (MBA, Certificate); information systems (DBA, Adv C, Certificate); information systems management (MBA); international business (MBA, DBA, Adv C, Certificate); management (MBA, MSM, DBA, Adv C, Certificate); marketing (MBA, DBA, Adv C, Certificate); organizational leadership (Ed D); public administration (MBA); sustainable management (MBA).

See Close-Up on page 225.

Argosy University, Seattle, College of Business, Seattle, WA 98121. Offers accounting (DBA); corporate compliance (MBA); customized professional concentration (MBA, DBA); finance (MBA); fraud examination (MBA); global business sustainability (DBA); healthcare administration (MBA); information systems (DBA); information systems management (MBA); international business (MBA, DBA); management (MBA, MSM, DBA); marketing (MBA, DBA); organizational leadership (Ed D); public administration (MBA); sustainable management (MBA).

See Close-Up on page 227.

Argosy University, Tampa, College of Business, Tampa, FL 33607. Offers accounting (DBA); corporate compliance (MBA); customized professional concentration (MBA, DBA); finance (MBA); fraud examination (MBA); global business sustainability (DBA); healthcare administration (MBA); information systems (DBA); information systems management (MBA); international business (MBA, DBA); management (MBA, MSM, DBA); marketing (MBA, DBA); organizational leadership (Ed D); public administration (MBA); sustainable management (MBA).

See Close-Up on page 229.

Argosy University, Twin Cities, College of Business, Eagan, MN 55121. Offers accounting (DBA); customized professional concentration (MBA, DBA); finance (MBA); fraud examination (MBA); global business sustainability (DBA); healthcare administration (MBA); information systems (DBA); information systems management (MBA); international business (MBA, DBA); management (MBA, MSM, DBA); marketing (MBA, DBA); organizational leadership (Ed D); public administration (MBA); sustainable management (MBA).

See Close-Up on page 231.

Argosy University, Washington DC, College of Business, Arlington, VA 22209. Offers accounting (DBA); customized professional concentration (MBA, DBA); finance (MBA); fraud examination (MBA); global business sustainability (DBA); healthcare administration (MBA); information systems (DBA); information systems management (MBA); international business (MBA, DBA, Certificate); management (MBA, MSM, DBA); marketing (MBA, DBA, Certificate); organizational leadership (Ed D); public administration (MBA); sustainable management (MBA).

See Close-Up on page 233.

Assumption College, Graduate School, Department of Business Studies, Worcester, MA 01609-1296. Offers accounting (MBA); business administration (CAGS); finance/economics (MBA); general business (MBA); human resources (MBA); international business (MBA); management (MBA); marketing (MBA); nonprofit leadership (MBA). Part-time and evening/weekend programs available. *Faculty:* 6 full-time (1 woman), 14 part-time/adjunct (2 women). *Students:* 19 full-time (11 women), 127 part-time (68 women); includes 22 minority (13 African Americans, 3 Asian Americans or Pacific Islanders, 6 Hispanic Americans). Average age 27. 88 applicants, 99% accepted. In 2009, 40 master's, 2 other advanced degrees awarded. *Entrance requirements:* For master's, 3 letters of recommendation, resume; for CAGS, 3 letters of recommendation, resume, essay. Additional exam requirements/recommendations for international students: Required—TOEFL (minimum score 540 paper-based; 200 computer-based; 76 iBT), IELTS (minimum score 6). *Application deadline:* For fall admission, 6/1 priority date for domestic students, 5/1 priority date for international students; for spring admission, 11/1 priority date for domestic students, 9/1 priority date for international students. Applications are processed on a rolling basis. Application fee: $30. Electronic applications accepted. *Expenses:* Tuition: Part-time $503 per credit. Required fees: $20 per semester. One-time fee: $100 part-time. Part-time tuition and fees vary according to campus/location. *Financial support:* In 2009–10, 47 students received support. Application deadline: 6/1. *Faculty research:* Workplace diversity, dynamics of team interaction, utilization of leased employees. *Unit head:* Michael Lewis, Director, 508-767-7372, Fax: 508-767-7252, E-mail: jhunter@assumption.edu. *Application contact:* Adrian O. Dumas, Director of Graduate Enrollment Management and Services, 508-767-7365, Fax: 508-767-7030, E-mail: adumas@assumption.edu.

Avila University, School of Business, Kansas City, MO 64145-1698. Offers accounting (MBA); finance (MBA); general management (MBA); health care administration (MBA); international business (MBA); management information systems (MBA); marketing (MBA). Part-time and evening/weekend programs available. *Faculty:* 9 full-time (3 women), 24 part-time/adjunct (5 women). *Students:* 148 full-time (71 women), 86 part-time (47 women); includes 56 minority (36 African Americans, 2 American Indian/Alaska Native, 13 Asian Americans or Pacific Islanders, 5 Hispanic Americans), 63 international. Average age 32. 53 applicants, 75% accepted, 40 enrolled. In 2009, 93 master's awarded. *Degree requirements:* For master's, comprehensive exam, capstone course. *Entrance requirements:* For master's, GMAT, minimum GPA of 3.0, interview. Additional exam requirements/recommendations for international students: Required—TOEFL (minimum score 550 paper-based). *Application deadline:* For fall admission, 7/30 priority date for domestic students, 7/30 for international students; for winter admission, 11/30 priority date for domestic students, 11/30 for international students; for spring admission, 2/28 priority date for domestic students, 2/28 for international students. Applications are processed on a rolling basis. Application fee: $0. Electronic applications accepted. *Expenses:* Contact institution. *Financial support:* In 2009–10, 102 students received support. Career-related internships or fieldwork available. Support available to part-time students. Financial award applicants required to submit FAFSA. *Faculty research:* Leadership characteristics, financial hedging, group dynamics. *Unit head:* Dr. Richard Woodall, Dean, 816-501-3720, Fax: 816-501-2463, E-mail: richard.woodall@avila.edu. *Application contact:* JoAnna Giffin, MBA Admissions Director, 816-501-3601, Fax: 816-501-2463, E-mail: joanna.giffin@avila.edu.

Azusa Pacific University, School of Business and Management, Azusa, CA 91702-7000. Offers business administration (MBA); human and organizational development (MA); international business (MBA); strategic management (MBA). Part-time and evening/weekend programs available. *Degree requirements:* For master's, thesis (for some programs), final project. *Entrance requirements:* For master's, GMAT, minimum GPA of 3.0. Additional exam requirements/recommendations for international students: Required—TOEFL (minimum score 600 paper-based). *Expenses:* Contact institution. *Faculty research:* Gender issues, financial risk, leadership and ethics, marketing strategy.

Baldwin-Wallace College, Graduate Programs, Division of Business, Program in International Management, Berea, OH 44017-2088. Offers MBA. Part-time and evening/weekend programs available. *Students:* 30 full-time (15 women), 26 part-time (13 women); includes 11 minority (4 African Americans, 5 Asian Americans or Pacific Islanders, 2 Hispanic Americans), 7 international. Average age 33. 34 applicants, 76% accepted, 10 enrolled. In 2009, 22 master's awarded. *Degree requirements:* For master's, one foreign language. *Entrance requirements:* For master's, GMAT, interview, work experience, bachelor's degree in field. Additional exam requirements/recommendations for international students: Required—TOEFL (minimum score 523 paper-based; 193 computer-based; 70 iBT). *Application deadline:* For fall admission, 7/25 priority date for domestic students, 4/30 priority date for international students; for spring admission, 12/15 priority date for domestic students, 9/30 priority date for international students. Applications are processed on a rolling basis. Application fee: $25. Electronic applications accepted. *Expenses:* Contact institution. *Financial support:* Career-related internships or fieldwork available. Support available to part-time students. Financial award application deadline: 5/1; financial award applicants required to submit FAFSA. *Faculty research:* International finance, systems approach, international marketing. *Unit head:* Harvey Hopson, Director, 440-826-2137, Fax: 440-826-3868, E-mail: hhopson@bw.edu. *Application contact:* Peggy Shepard, Graduate Business Coordinator, 440-826-2196, Fax: 440-826-3868, E-mail: pshepard@bw.edu.

Barry University, Andreas School of Business, Graduate Certificate Programs, Miami Shores, FL 33161-6695. Offers finance (Certificate); health services administration (Certificate); international business (Certificate); management (Certificate); management information systems (Certificate); marketing (Certificate).

Benedictine University, Graduate Programs, Program in Business Administration, Lisle, IL 60532-0900. Offers accounting (MBA); entrepreneurship and managing innovation (MBA); financial management (MBA); health administration (MBA); human resource management (MBA); information systems security (MBA); international business (MBA); management consulting (MBA); management information systems (MBA); marketing management (MBA); operations management and logistics (MBA); organizational leadership (MBA); MBA/MPH; MBA/MS. Part-time and evening/weekend programs available. Postbaccalaureate distance learning degree programs offered (minimal on-campus study). *Faculty:* 4 full-time (2 women), 24 part-time/adjunct (3 women). *Students:* 247 full-time (141 women), 644 part-time (339 women); includes 223 minority (134 African Americans, 5 American Indian/Alaska Native, 44 Asian Americans or Pacific Islanders, 40 Hispanic Americans), 25 international. Average age 34. 287 applicants, 92% accepted, 229 enrolled. In 2009, 219 master's awarded. *Entrance requirements:* For master's, GMAT. Additional exam requirements/recommendations for international students: Required—TOEFL (minimum score 550 paper-based; 213 computer-based). *Application deadline:* For fall admission, 9/1 for domestic students; for winter admission, 12/1 for domestic students; for spring admission, 2/15 for domestic students. Applications are processed on a rolling basis. Application fee: $40. Electronic applications accepted. *Expenses:* Tuition: Part-time $750 per credit hour. Tuition and fees vary according to campus/location and program. *Financial support:* Career-related internships or fieldwork and health care benefits available. Support available to part-time students. *Faculty research:* Strategic leadership in professional organizations, sociology of professions, organizational change, social identity theory, applications to change management. *Unit head:* Dr. Sharon Borowicz, Director, 630-829-6219, E-mail: sborowicz@ben.edu. *Application contact:* Kari Gibbons, Director, Admissions, 630-829-6200, Fax: 630-829-6584, E-mail: kgibbons@ben.edu.

Bernard M. Baruch College of the City University of New York, Zicklin School of Business, International Executive Programs, New York, NY 10010-5585. Offers MBA. Part-time and evening/weekend programs available. *Entrance requirements:* For master's, GMAT, 2 letters of recommendation, resume, 2 years of work experience. Additional exam requirements/recommendations for international students: Required—TOEFL (minimum score 590 paper-based; 243 computer-based), TWE (minimum score 5).

Boston University, Metropolitan College, Department of Administrative Sciences, Boston, MA 02215. Offers banking and financial management (MSM); business continuity in emergency management (MSM); economics development and tourism management (MSAS); electronic commerce, systems, and technology (MSAS); financial economics (MSAS); human resource management (MSM); innovation and technology (MSAS); insurance management (MSM); international market management (MSM); multinational commerce (MSAS); project management (MSM). *Accreditation:* AACSB. Part-time and evening/weekend programs available. Postbaccalaureate distance learning degree programs offered (no on-campus study). *Students:* 123 full-time (48 women), 204 part-time (92 women); includes 31 minority (10 African Americans, 1 American Indian/Alaska Native, 11 Asian Americans or Pacific Islanders, 9 Hispanic Americans), 146 international. Average age 30. In 2009, 154 master's awarded. *Degree requirements:* For master's, thesis optional. *Entrance requirements:* For master's, 1 year of work experience, minimum GPA of 3.0. Additional exam requirements/recommendations for international students: Required—TOEFL (minimum score 560 paper-based; 220 computer-based; 84 iBT). *Application deadline:* Applications are processed on a rolling basis. Application fee: $70. Electronic applications accepted. *Expenses:* Tuition: Full-time $37,910; part-time $1184 per credit hour. Required fees: $386; $40 per semester. Part-time tuition and fees vary according to class time, course level, degree level and program. *Financial support:* In 2009–10, 15 students received support, including 8 research assistantships (averaging $10,000 per year); career-related internships or fieldwork and Federal Work-Study also available. *Faculty research:* International business, innovative process. *Unit head:* Dr. Kip Becker, Chairman, 617-353-3016, E-mail: adminsc@bu.edu. *Application contact:* Lucille Dicker, Administrative Sciences Department, 617-353-3016, E-mail: adminsc@bu.edu.

Boston University, School of Management, Master of Business Administration Program, Boston, MA 02215. Offers entrepreneurship (MBA); finance (MBA); health sector management (MBA); international management (MBA); marketing (MBA); operations and technology management (MBA); public and nonprofit management (MBA); strategy and business analysis (MBA); JD/MBA; MBA/MA; MBA/MPH; MBA/MS; MBA/MSIS; MS/MBA. Part-time and evening/weekend programs available. *Faculty:* 119 full-time (31 women), 99 part-time/adjunct (30 women). *Students:* 326 full-time (138 women), 677 part-time (257 women); includes 149 minority (13 African Americans, 119 Asian Americans or Pacific Islanders, 17 Hispanic Americans), 149 international. Average age 30. 1,617 applicants, 38% accepted, 317 enrolled. In 2009, 284 master's awarded. *Entrance requirements:* For master's, GMAT, resume, 2 letters of recommendation. Additional exam requirements/recommendations for international students: Required—TOEFL or IELTS. *Application deadline:* For fall admission, 3/15 for domestic and international students; for spring admission, 11/15 for domestic students. Application fee: $125. Electronic applications accepted. *Expenses:* Tuition: Full-time $37,910; part-time $1184 per credit hour. Required fees: $386; $40 per semester. Part-time tuition and fees vary according to class time, course level, degree level and program. *Financial support:* Career-related internships or fieldwork, Federal Work-Study, institutionally sponsored loans, and scholarships/grants available. Support available to part-time students. Financial award applicants required to submit FAFSA. *Unit head:* Katherine Nolan, Assistant Dean, Graduate Programs, 617-353-4157, Fax: 617-353-5003, E-mail: mba@bu.edu. *Application contact:* Hayden Estrada, Assistant Dean, Admissions, 617-353-2670, Fax: 617-353-7368, E-mail: mba@bu.edu.

Brandeis University, International Business School, Waltham, MA 02454-9110. Offers finance (MSF); international business (MBAi); international economics and finance (MA, PhD); international finance/international economics (MBAi). Part-time and evening/weekend programs available. Terminal master's awarded for partial completion of doctoral program. *Degree requirements:* For master's, one foreign language, semester abroad; for doctorate, thesis/dissertation. *Entrance requirements:* For master's, GMAT or GRE General Test (MA), GMAT

International Business

Brandeis University (continued)

(MBAi, MSF); for doctorate, GRE General Test. Additional exam requirements/recommendations for international students: Required—TOEFL (minimum score 600 paper-based; 250 computer-based), IELTS (minimum score 7). Electronic applications accepted. *Faculty research:* International finance and business, trade policy, macroeconomics, Asian economic issues, developmental economics.

California Intercontinental University, School of Business, Diamond Bar, CA 91765. Offers banking and finance (MBA); entrepreneurship and business management (DBA); global business leadership (DBA); international management and marketing (MBA); organizational management and human resource management (MBA).

California Lutheran University, Graduate Studies, School of Business, Thousand Oaks, CA 91360-2787. Offers business (IMBA); entrepreneurship (MBA, Certificate); finance (MBA, Certificate); financial planning (MBA, Certificate); information systems and technology (MS); information technology management (MBA, Certificate); international business (MBA, Certificate); management and organization behavior (MBA); management and organizational behavior (Certificate); marketing (MBA, Certificate). Evening/weekend programs available. Postbaccalaureate distance learning degree programs offered. *Entrance requirements:* For master's, GMAT, interview, minimum GPA of 3.0. *Expenses:* Contact institution.

California State University, East Bay, Graduate Programs, College of Business and Economics, Department of Information Technology Management, Option in Strategy and International Business, Hayward, CA 94542-3000. Offers MBA. Part-time and evening/weekend programs available. *Degree requirements:* For master's, comprehensive exam or thesis. *Entrance requirements:* For master's, GMAT, minimum GPA of 2.75. Additional exam requirements/recommendations for international students: Required—TOEFL (minimum score 550 paper-based; 213 computer-based). *Application deadline:* For fall admission, 6/30 for domestic and international students. Application fee: $55. *Financial support:* Career-related internships or fieldwork, Federal Work-Study, institutionally sponsored loans, and scholarships/grants available. Support available to part-time students. Financial award application deadline: 3/1. *Unit head:* Dr. Xinjian Lu, Chair, 510-885-3307, E-mail: xinjian.lu@csueastbay.edu. *Application contact:* Donna Wiley, Interim Associate Director, 510-885-2928, Fax: 510-885-4777, E-mail: donna.wiley@csueastbay.edu.

California State University, Fullerton, Graduate Studies, College of Business and Economics, Program in Business Administration, Fullerton, CA 92834-9480. Offers e-commerce (MBA); international business (MBA). *Accreditation:* AACSB. Part-time programs available. *Students:* 65 full-time (30 women), 68 part-time (31 women); includes 59 minority (3 African Americans, 1 American Indian/Alaska Native, 43 Asian Americans or Pacific Islanders, 12 Hispanic Americans), 32 international. Average age 28. 238 applicants, 42% accepted, 39 enrolled. In 2009, 33 master's awarded. *Degree requirements:* For master's, project or thesis. *Entrance requirements:* For master's, GMAT. *Expenses:* Tuition, nonresident: full-time $11,160; part-time $373 per credit. Required fees: $1440 per term. Tuition and fees vary according to course load, degree level and program. *Financial support:* Career-related internships or fieldwork, Federal Work-Study, institutionally sponsored loans, and scholarships/grants available. Support available to part-time students. Financial award application deadline: 3/1; financial award applicants required to submit FAFSA. *Unit head:* Dr. Anil Puri, Dean, 657-773-2592. *Application contact:* Admissions/Applications, 657-278-2371.

California State University, Los Angeles, Graduate Studies, College of Business and Economics, Department of Marketing, Los Angeles, CA 90032-8530. Offers international business (MBA, MS); marketing management (MBA, MS). Part-time and evening/weekend programs available. *Students:* 4 full-time (3 women), 10 part-time (6 women); includes 3 minority (1 African American, 1 Asian American or Pacific Islander, 1 Hispanic American), 10 international. Average age 28. 15 applicants, 100% accepted, 4 enrolled. In 2009, 18 master's awarded. *Degree requirements:* For master's, comprehensive exam (MBA), thesis (MS). *Entrance requirements:* For master's, GMAT, minimum GPA of 2.5 during previous 2 years of course work. Additional exam requirements/recommendations for international students: Required—TOEFL (minimum score 550 paper-based; 213 computer-based). *Application deadline:* For fall admission, 5/1 for domestic and international students. Applications are processed on a rolling basis. Application fee: $55. Electronic applications accepted. *Financial support:* Career-related internships or fieldwork and Federal Work-Study available. Support available to part-time students. Financial award application deadline: 3/1. *Unit head:* Dr. Paul Washburn, Acting Chair, 323-343-2960, Fax: 323-343-5462, E-mail: pwashbu@calstatela.edu. *Application contact:* Dr. Cheryl L. Ney, Associate Vice President for Academic Affairs and Dean of Graduate Studies, 323-343-3820, Fax: 323-343-5653, E-mail: cney@cslanet.calstatela.edu.

California State University, Stanislaus, College of Business Administration, Department of Accounting and Finance, Turlock, CA 95382. Offers finance and international finance (MSBA). *Degree requirements:* For master's, comprehensive exam. *Entrance requirements:* For master's, GMAT, minimum GPA 2.50, 3 letters of reference. Additional exam requirements/recommendations for international students: Required—TOEFL (minimum score 550 paper-based; 213 computer-based). Electronic applications accepted. *Expenses:* Contact institution. *Faculty research:* Marketing valuation and corporate investment, investment and cash-flow from Asian countries.

Canisius College, Graduate Division, Richard J. Wehle School of Business, Program in International Business, Buffalo, NY 14208-1098. Offers MS. *Faculty:* 1 (woman) full-time. *Students:* 4 full-time (1 woman), 3 part-time (2 women), 1 international. Average age 28. 10 applicants, 70% accepted, 7 enrolled.Application fee: $25. *Unit head:* Dr. Antone Alber, Dean, 716-888-2160, Fax: 716-888-2145, E-mail: gradubus@canisius.edu. *Application contact:* Laura McEwen, Director, Graduate Business Programs, 716-888-2142, Fax: 716-888-2145, E-mail: mcewenl@canisius.edu.

Central European University, Graduate Studies, Department of Legal Studies, Budapest, Hungary. Offers comparative constitutional law (LL M); economic and legal studies (LL M, MA); human rights (LL M, MA); international business law (LL M); legal studies (SJD). Terminal master's awarded for partial completion of doctoral program. *Degree requirements:* For master's, one foreign language, thesis; for doctorate, one foreign language, comprehensive exam, thesis/dissertation. *Entrance requirements:* For master's and doctorate, LSAT, CEU admissions exams. Additional exam requirements/recommendations for international students: Required—TOEFL (minimum score 570 paper-based; 230 computer-based). Electronic applications accepted. *Expenses:* Contact institution. *Faculty research:* Institutional, constitutional and human rights in European Union law, biomedical law and reproductive rights, data protection law, Islamic banking and finance.

Central Michigan University, College of Graduate Studies, College of Business Administration, Department of Management, Mount Pleasant, MI 48859. Offers human resource management (MBA); international business (MBA). *Degree requirements:* For master's, thesis or alternative. *Entrance requirements:* For master's, GMAT. Electronic applications accepted. *Faculty research:* Human resource accounting, valuation, and liability; international business and economic issues; entrepreneurial leadership; technology management and strategy; electronic commerce and neural networks.

Central Michigan University, College of Graduate Studies, Interdisciplinary Administration Programs, Mount Pleasant, MI 48859. Offers acquisitions administration (MSA, Graduate Certificate); general administration (MSA, Graduate Certificate); health services administration (MSA, Graduate Certificate); human resource administration (Graduate Certificate); human resources administration (MSA); information resource management (MSA, Graduate Certificate); international administration (MSA, Graduate Certificate); leadership (MSA); organizational communication (MSA, Graduate Certificate); public administration (MSA, Graduate Certificate); recreation and park administration (MSA); sport administration (MSA). *Accreditation:* AACSB. Part-time and evening/weekend programs available. Postbaccalaureate distance learning degree programs offered (no on-campus study). *Degree requirements:* For master's, thesis or alternative. *Entrance requirements:* For master's, bachelor's degree with minimum GPA of 2.7. Electronic applications accepted. *Faculty research:* Interdisciplinary studies in acquisitions administration, health services administration, sport administration, recreation and park administration, and international administration.

City University of Seattle, Graduate Division, School of Management, Bellevue, WA 98005. Offers accounting (Certificate); change leadership (MBA, Certificate); financial management (MBA, Certificate); general management (MBA); general management-Europe (MBA); global leadership (Certificate); global marketing (MBA); individualized study (MBA); information security (MS); information systems (MBA); leadership (MA); marketing (MBA, Certificate); project management (MBA, MS, Certificate); sustainable business (Certificate); technology management (MBA, MS, Certificate). Part-time and evening/weekend programs available. Postbaccalaureate distance learning degree programs offered (no on-campus study). *Entrance requirements:* Additional exam requirements/recommendations for international students: Required—TOEFL (minimum score 540 paper-based; 207 computer-based); Recommended—IELTS. Electronic applications accepted. *Expenses:* Tuition: Full-time $14,760; part-time $615 per credit. Tuition and fees vary according to program.

Clark University, Graduate School, Graduate School of Management, Business Administration Program, Worcester, MA 01610-1477. Offers accounting (MBA); finance (MBA); global business (MBA); health care management (MBA); management (MBA); management of information technology (MBA); marketing (MBA). *Accreditation:* AACSB. Part-time and evening/weekend programs available. *Students:* 148 full-time (67 women), 120 part-time (52 women); includes 27 minority (12 African Americans, 2 American Indian/Alaska Native, 9 Asian Americans or Pacific Islanders, 4 Hispanic Americans), 108 international. Average age 29. 340 applicants, 57% accepted, 63 enrolled. In 2009, 118 master's awarded. *Degree requirements:* For master's, thesis optional. *Application deadline:* For fall admission, 6/1 priority date for domestic students; for spring admission, 12/1 priority date for domestic students. Applications are processed on a rolling basis. Application fee: $50. Electronic applications accepted. *Expenses:* Tuition: Full-time $34,900; part-time $4362.50 per course. *Financial support:* In 2009–10, research assistantships with partial tuition reimbursements (averaging $4,800 per year), teaching assistantships with partial tuition reimbursements (averaging $4,800 per year) were awarded; fellowships, career-related internships or fieldwork, Federal Work-Study, institutionally sponsored loans, and tuition waivers (partial) also available. Support available to part-time students. Financial award application deadline: 5/31. *Faculty research:* Organizational development, accounting, marketing, finance, human resource management. *Application contact:* Lynn Davis, Enrollment and Marketing Director, 508-793-7406, Fax: 508-793-8822, E-mail: clarkmba@clarku.edu.

Cleveland State University, College of Graduate Studies, Nance College of Business Administration, Department of Marketing, Cleveland, OH 44115. Offers global business (Graduate Certificate); marketing (MBA, DBA); marketing analytics (Graduate Certificate).

Columbia Southern University, MBA Program, Orange Beach, AL 36561. Offers electronic business and technology (MBA); finance (MBA); general (MBA); healthcare management (MBA); hospitality and tourism (MBA); human resources management (MBA); international management (MBA); marketing (MBA); project management (MBA); public administration (MBA); sport management (MBA). Part-time and evening/weekend programs available. Postbaccalaureate distance learning degree programs offered (no on-campus study). *Entrance requirements:* For master's, bachelor's degree from accredited/approved institution. Additional exam requirements/recommendations for international students: Required—TOEFL. Electronic applications accepted.

Columbia University, Graduate School of Business, Executive MBA Global Program, New York, NY 10027. Offers EMBA. Program offered jointly with London Business School. *Students:* 169 full-time (43 women); includes 12 minority (all Asian Americans or Pacific Islanders), 110 international. Average age 32. In 2009, 67 master's awarded. *Entrance requirements:* For master's, GMAT, 2 letters of reference, interview, minimum 5 years of work experience, curriculum vitae or resume, employer support. Additional exam requirements/recommendations for international students: Recommended—IELTS. *Application deadline:* For spring admission, 3/8 for domestic and international students. Applications are processed on a rolling basis. Application fee: $200. Electronic applications accepted. *Expenses:* Contact institution. *Unit head:* Kelley Martin Blanco, Assistant Dean, 212-854-2211, Fax: 212-854-8998, E-mail: embainfo@columbia.edu. *Application contact:* Mary J. Miller, Assistant Dean of Admissions, 212-854-1961, Fax: 212-662-6754, E-mail: apply@gsb.columbia.edu.

Columbia University, Graduate School of Business, MBA Program, New York, NY 10027. Offers accounting (MBA); decision, risk, and operations (MBA); entrepreneurship (MBA); finance and economics (MBA); healthcare and pharmaceutical management (MBA); human resource management (MBA); international business (MBA); leadership and ethics (MBA); management (MBA); marketing (MBA); media (MBA); private equity (MBA); real estate (MBA); social enterprise (MBA); value investing (MBA); DDS/MBA; JD/MBA; MBA/MIA; MBA/MPH; MBA/MS; MD/MBA. *Faculty:* 149 full-time (23 women), 134 part-time/adjunct (16 women). *Students:* 1,293 full-time (435 women); includes 235 minority (65 African Americans, 4 American Indian/Alaska Native, 135 Asian Americans or Pacific Islanders, 31 Hispanic Americans), 417 international. Average age 28. 6,885 applicants, 15% accepted, 737 enrolled. In 2009, 696 master's awarded. *Entrance requirements:* For master's, GMAT, 2 letters of recommendation. Additional exam requirements/recommendations for international students: Required—TOEFL. *Application deadline:* For fall admission, 4/14 for domestic students, 3/3 for international students; for spring admission, 10/7 for domestic and international students. Applications are processed on a rolling basis. Application fee: $250. Electronic applications accepted. *Expenses:* Contact institution. *Financial support:* In 2009–10, 358 students received support, including 101 fellowships (averaging $23,250 per year); research assistantships, teaching assistantships, career-related internships or fieldwork, institutionally sponsored loans, and scholarships/grants also available. Financial award application deadline: 3/1; financial award applicants required to submit CSS PROFILE or FAFSA. *Faculty research:* Human decision making and behavioral research; real estate market and mortgage defaults; financial crisis and corporate governance; international business; security analysis and accounting. *Unit head:* Prof. Amir Ziv, Vice Dean of Students and the MBA Program, 212-854-3485, Fax: 212-932-0545, E-mail: az50@columbia.edu. *Application contact:* Mary J. Miller, Assistant Dean of Admissions, 212-854-1961, Fax: 212-662-6754, E-mail: apply@gsb.columbia.edu.

Concordia University Wisconsin, Graduate Programs, School of Business and Legal Studies, MBA Program, Mequon, WI 53097-2402. Offers finance (MBA); health care administration (MBA); human resource management (MBA); international business (MBA); international business-bilingual English/Chinese (MBA); management (MBA); management information systems (MBA); managerial communications (MBA); marketing (MBA); public administration (MBA); risk management (MBA). Postbaccalaureate distance learning degree programs offered (minimal on-campus study). *Degree requirements:* For master's, comprehensive exam, thesis or alternative. *Entrance requirements:* Additional exam requirements/recommendations for international students: Required—TOEFL. *Expenses:* Contact institution.

Daemen College, Department of Accounting/Information Systems, Amherst, NY 14226-3592. Offers global business (MS). Part-time and evening/weekend programs available. *Faculty:* 3 full-time (1 woman), 4 part-time/adjunct (0 women). *Students:* 15 full-time (9 women), 6 part-time (1 woman); includes 4 minority (1 African American, 1 Asian American or Pacific Islander, 2 Hispanic Americans), 9 international. Average age 26. 22 applicants, 68% accepted, 13 enrolled. In 2009, 9 master's awarded. *Degree requirements:* For master's, thesis, completion of degree within 5 years. *Entrance requirements:* For master's, minimum undergraduate business program GPA of 3.0 or GMAT, interview, 2 letters of recommendation. Additional exam requirements/recommendations for international students: Required—TOEFL (minimum score 500 paper-based; 173 computer-based; 61 iBT). *Application deadline:* For fall admission, 3/1 priority date for domestic and international students; for spring admission, 10/1 priority date for domestic and international students. Applications are processed on a rolling basis. Application fee: $25. Electronic applications accepted. *Expenses:* Tuition: Part-time $770 per credit hour. Tuition and fees vary according to course load, program and reciprocity agreements. *Financial*

support: Institutionally sponsored loans and scholarships/grants available. Financial award application deadline: 2/15; financial award applicants required to submit FAFSA. *Faculty research:* Internationalization of small business, cultural influences on business practices, international human resource practices. *Unit head:* Dr. Linda J. Kuechler, Chair, 716-839-8398, Fax: 716-839-8261, E-mail: lkuechle@daemen.edu. *Application contact:* Scott Rowe, Associate Director of Graduate Admissions, 716-839-8225, Fax: 716-839-8229, E-mail: srowe@daemen.edu.

Dallas Baptist University, College of Business, Business Administration Program, Dallas, TX 75211-9299. Offers accounting (MBA); business communication (MBA); conflict resolution management (MBA); e-business (MBA); entrepreneurship (MBA); finance (MBA); health care management (MBA); international business (MBA); leading the non-profit organization (MBA); management (MBA); management information systems (MBA); marketing (MBA); project management (MBA); technology and engineering management (MBA). *Accreditation:* ACBSP. Part-time and evening/weekend programs available. *Entrance requirements:* For master's, GMAT, minimum GPA of 3.0. Additional exam requirements/recommendations for international students: Required—TOEFL, IELTS. Electronic applications accepted. *Expenses:* Tuition: Full-time $10,674; part-time $593 per credit hour. *Faculty research:* Sports management, services marketing, retailing, strategic management, financial planning/investments.

Dallas Baptist University, Gary Cook School of Leadership, Program in Global Leadership, Dallas, TX 75211-9299. Offers business communication (MA); Christian education/missions (MA); ESL (MA); general studies (MA); global studies (MA); international business (MA); missions (MA); worship/missions (MA). Part-time and evening/weekend programs available. *Entrance requirements:* For master's, minimum GPA of 3.0. Additional exam requirements/recommendations for international students: Required—TOEFL, IELTS. *Expenses:* Tuition: Full-time $10,674; part-time $593 per credit hour.

Delaware Valley College, Program in Business Administration (MBA), Doylestown, PA 18901-2697. Offers accounting (MBA); food and agribusiness (MBA); general business (MBA); online global executive leadership (MBA). Part-time and evening/weekend programs available. Post-baccalaureate distance learning degree programs offered (no on-campus study). *Faculty:* 24 part-time/adjunct (10 women). *Students:* 25 full-time (16 women), 74 part-time (37 women); includes 7 minority (4 African Americans, 2 Asian Americans or Pacific Islanders, 1 Hispanic American). Average age 37. 18 applicants, 100% accepted, 18 enrolled. In 2009, 12 master's awarded. *Entrance requirements:* For master's, minimum undergraduate GPA of 3.0. *Application deadline:* Applications are processed on a rolling basis. Application fee: $50. *Expenses:* Contact institution. *Financial support:* Applicants required to submit FAFSA. *Unit head:* Thomas Kennedy, Director of MBA Program, 215-489-2322, E-mail: thomas.kennedy@delval.edu. *Application contact:* Pamela Heffner, Graduate and Continuing Studies Enrollment Manager, 215-489-4469, Fax: 215-489-4832, E-mail: pamela.heffner@deval.edu.

DePaul University, Charles H. Kellstadt Graduate School of Business and College of Liberal Arts and Sciences, Department of Economics, Chicago, IL 60604-2287. Offers applied economics (MBA); business strategy (MBA); economics and policy analysis (MA); international business (MBA). Part-time and evening/weekend programs available. *Faculty:* 26 full-time (5 women), 21 part-time/adjunct (5 women). *Students:* 67 full-time (32 women), 28 part-time (16 women); includes 14 minority (3 African Americans, 6 Asian Americans or Pacific Islanders, 5 Hispanic Americans), 8 international. 47 applicants, 47 enrolled. In 2009, 7 master's awarded. *Degree requirements:* For master's, thesis optional. *Entrance requirements:* For master's, GMAT (MBA), GRE (MS). Additional exam requirements/recommendations for international students: Required—TOEFL. *Application deadline:* For fall admission, 7/1 for domestic students; for winter admission, 10/1 for domestic students; for spring admission, 2/1 for domestic students. Applications are processed on a rolling basis. Application fee: $40. Electronic applications accepted. *Expenses:* Tuition: Full-time $37,525; part-time $620 per credit hour. *Financial support:* In 2009–10, 3 students received support, including 2 research assistantships with partial tuition reimbursements available (averaging $9,999 per year). Support available to part-time students. *Faculty research:* Forensic economics, game theory sports, economics of education, banking in Poland and Thailand. *Unit head:* Dr. Thomas D. Donley, Chairperson, 312-362-8887, Fax: 312-362-5452, E-mail: tdonley@depaul.edu. *Application contact:* Gabriella Bucci, Director of Graduate Program in Economics, 773-362-6787, Fax: 312-362-5452, E-mail: gbucci@depaul.edu.

Dominican University of California, Graduate Programs, School of Business and Leadership, Program in Global Strategic Management, San Rafael, CA 94901-2298. Offers MBA. Part-time programs available. *Entrance requirements:* For master's, minimum GPA of 3.0. Additional exam requirements/recommendations for international students: Required—TOEFL (minimum score 550 paper-based; 213 computer-based). Electronic applications accepted.

Duquesne University, School of Leadership and Professional Advancement, Pittsburgh, PA 15282-0001. Offers leadership (MS), including business ethics, community leadership, global leadership, information technology, leadership, liberal studies, professional administration, sports leadership. Part-time and evening/weekend programs available. Postbaccalaureate distance learning degree programs offered (no on-campus study). *Faculty:* 1 full-time (0 women), 70 part-time/adjunct (35 women). *Students:* 654 (307 women); includes 68 minority (57 African Americans, 1 American Indian/Alaska Native, 6 Asian Americans or Pacific Islanders, 4 Hispanic Americans). 161 applicants, 73% accepted, 103 enrolled. In 2009, 108 master's awarded. *Degree requirements:* For master's, capstone course. *Entrance requirements:* For master's, professional work experience, 500-word essay. Additional exam requirements/recommendations for international students: Required—TOEFL. *Application deadline:* Applications are processed on a rolling basis. Application fee: $0. Electronic applications accepted. *Expenses:* Tuition: Part-time $851 per credit. Required fees: $81 per credit. *Financial support:* Applicants required to submit FAFSA. *Unit head:* Dr. Dorothy Bassett, Dean, 412-396-2141, Fax: 412-396-4711, E-mail: bassettd@duq.edu. *Application contact:* Marianne Leister, Director of Student Services, 412-396-4933, Fax: 412-396-5072, E-mail: leister@duq.edu.

D'Youville College, Department of Business, Buffalo, NY 14201-1084. Offers business administration (MBA); international business (MS). Part-time and evening/weekend programs available. *Degree requirements:* For master's, one foreign language, project or thesis. *Entrance requirements:* For master's, minimum GPA of 3.0. Additional exam requirements/recommendations for international students: Required—TOEFL (minimum score 500 paper-based; 173 computer-based). Electronic applications accepted. *Faculty research:* Assessment, accreditation, supply chain, online learning, adult learning.

Eastern Michigan University, Graduate School, College of Arts and Sciences, Department of World Languages, Program in Language and International Trade, Ypsilanti, MI 48197. Offers MA. Evening/weekend programs available. *Students:* 1 (woman) full-time. Average age 32. In 2009, 1 master's awarded. *Degree requirements:* For master's, one foreign language. *Entrance requirements:* Additional exam requirements/recommendations for international students: Required—TOEFL. *Application deadline:* Applications are processed on a rolling basis. Application fee: $35. Tuition and fees vary according to course level. *Financial support:* Fellowships, research assistantships with full tuition reimbursements, teaching assistantships with full tuition reimbursements, career-related internships or fieldwork, Federal Work-Study, institutionally sponsored loans, scholarships/grants, tuition waivers (partial), and unspecified assistantships available. Support available to part-time students. Financial award applicants required to submit FAFSA. *Unit head:* Program Advisor. *Application contact:* Dr. Genevieve Peden, Program Advisor, 734-487-2283, Fax: 734-487-3411, E-mail: gpeden@emich.edu.

Eastern Michigan University, Graduate School, College of Arts and Sciences, Department of World Languages, Programs in Foreign Languages, Ypsilanti, MI 48197. Offers French (MA); German (MA); German for business (Graduate Certificate); Hispanic language and cultures (Graduate Certificate); Japanese business practices (Graduate Certificate); Spanish (MA). Part-time and evening/weekend programs available. Postbaccalaureate distance learning degree programs offered (minimal on-campus study). *Students:* 1 full-time (0 women), 15 part-time (14 women); includes 4 minority (1 African American, 3 Hispanic Americans), 1 international.

Average age 39. In 2009, 6 master's awarded. *Degree requirements:* For master's, one foreign language, thesis optional. *Entrance requirements:* Additional exam requirements/recommendations for international students: Required—TOEFL. *Application deadline:* Applications are processed on a rolling basis. Application fee: $35. Tuition and fees vary according to course level. *Financial support:* Fellowships, research assistantships with full tuition reimbursements, teaching assistantships with full tuition reimbursements, career-related internships or fieldwork, Federal Work-Study, institutionally sponsored loans, scholarships/grants, tuition waivers (partial), and unspecified assistantships available. Support available to part-time students. Financial award applicants required to submit FAFSA. *Application contact:* Dr. Genevieve Peden, Program Advisor, 734-487-2283, Fax: 734-487-3411, E-mail: gpeden@emich.edu.

Eastern Michigan University, Graduate School, College of Business, Programs in Business Administration, Ypsilanti, MI 48197. Offers business administration (MBA, Graduate Certificate); computer information systems (Graduate Certificate); e-business (MBA, Graduate Certificate); enterprise business intelligence (MBA); entrepreneurship (MBA, Graduate Certificate); finance (MBA, Graduate Certificate); human resources (MBA); human resources management (Graduate Certificate); information systems (MBA); internal auditing (MBA); international business (MBA, Graduate Certificate); marketing management (Graduate Certificate); nonprofit management (MBA); organizational development (Graduate Certificate); supply chain management (MBA, Graduate Certificate). *Accreditation:* AACSB. Part-time programs available. Postbaccalaureate distance learning degree programs offered (no on-campus study). *Students:* 166 full-time (80 women), 439 part-time (231 women); includes 150 minority (103 African Americans, 7 American Indian/Alaska Native, 31 Asian Americans or Pacific Islanders, 9 Hispanic Americans), 97 international. Average age 34. In 2009, 3 other advanced degrees awarded. *Entrance requirements:* For master's, GMAT (minimum score 450), minimum cumulative undergraduate GPA of 2.75. Additional exam requirements/recommendations for international students: Required—TOEFL. *Application deadline:* For fall admission, 5/15 for domestic students, 5/1 for international students; for winter admission, 10/15 for domestic students, 10/1 for international students; for spring admission, 3/15 for domestic students, 3/1 for international students. Applications are processed on a rolling basis. Application fee: $35. Tuition and fees vary according to course level. *Financial support:* Fellowships, research assistantships with full tuition reimbursements, teaching assistantships with full tuition reimbursements, career-related internships or fieldwork, Federal Work-Study, institutionally sponsored loans, scholarships/grants, tuition waivers (partial), and unspecified assistantships available. Support available to part-time students. Financial award applicants required to submit FAFSA. *Unit head:* K. Michelle Henry, Director of Academic Services, 734-487-4444, Fax: 734-483-1316, E-mail: cob.grad@emich.edu. *Application contact:* Beste Windes, Advisor, 734-487-4444, Fax: 734-483-1316, E-mail: cob.grad@emich.edu.

Emerson College, Graduate Studies, School of Communication, Department of Marketing Communication, Program in Global Marketing Communication and Advertising, Boston, MA 02116-4624. Offers MA. *Faculty:* 12 full-time (5 women). *Students:* 40 full-time (34 women), 1 (woman) part-time; includes 5 minority (2 Asian Americans or Pacific Islanders, 3 Hispanic Americans), 18 international. Average age 24. 97 applicants, 66% accepted. In 2009, 36 master's awarded. *Entrance requirements:* For master's, GMAT or GRE General Test. Additional exam requirements/recommendations for international students: Required—TOEFL (minimum score 550 paper-based; 213 computer-based; 80 iBT), IELTS (minimum score 6.5). *Application deadline:* For fall admission, 5/1 priority date for domestic and international students. Applications are processed on a rolling basis. Application fee: $60 ($75 for international students). Electronic applications accepted. *Expenses:* Tuition: Full-time $22,056; part-time $919 per credit. Required fees: $120. One-time fee: $170 full-time. *Financial support:* In 2009–10, 13 students received support, including 9 research assistantships with partial tuition reimbursements available (averaging $10,000 per year); Federal Work-Study, scholarships/grants, and unspecified assistantships also available. Financial award application deadline: 3/1; financial award applicants required to submit FAFSA. *Faculty research:* International business, marketing. *Unit head:* Thomas Vogel, Graduate Program Director, 617-824-8492, E-mail: thomas_vogel@emerson.edu. *Application contact:* Office of Graduate Admission, 617-824-8610, Fax: 617-824-8614, E-mail: gradapp@emerson.edu.

Everest University, Department of Business Administration, Tampa, FL 33614-5899. Offers accounting (MBA); human resources (MBA); international business (MBA). Part-time and evening/weekend programs available. *Degree requirements:* For master's, thesis optional. *Entrance requirements:* For master's, GMAT or GRE General Test, minimum GPA of 3.0.

Everest University, Program in Business Administration, Orlando, FL 32819. Offers accounting (MBA); general management (MBA); human resources (MBA); international management (MBA).

Fairfield University, Charles F. Dolan School of Business, Fairfield, CT 06824-5195. Offers accounting (MBA, MS, CAS); finance (MBA, MS, CAS); general management (MBA); human resource management (MBA, CAS); information systems and operations (MBA); information systems and operations management (CAS); international business (MBA, CAS); marketing (MBA, CAS); taxation (MBA, MS). *Accreditation:* AACSB. Part-time and evening/weekend programs available. *Degree requirements:* For master's, capstone course. *Entrance requirements:* For master's, GMAT (minimum score 500), 2 letters of reference, resume, minimum GPA of 3.0. Additional exam requirements/recommendations for international students: Required—TOEFL (minimum score 550 paper-based; 213 computer-based; 80 iBT). Electronic applications accepted. *Expenses:* Contact institution. *Faculty research:* Optimization strategies, international finance, consumer behavior, financial market volatility, Internet marketing, supply chain analysis, tax issues.

Fairleigh Dickinson University, College at Florham, Silberman College of Business, Department of Economics, Finance, and International Business, Program in International Business, Madison, NJ 07940-1099. Offers MBA, Certificate. *Students:* 6 full-time (4 women), 3 part-time (2 women), 1 international. Average age 26. 11 applicants, 36% accepted, 2 enrolled. In 2009, 4 master's awarded. *Application deadline:* Applications are processed on a rolling basis. Application fee: $40.

Fairleigh Dickinson University, Metropolitan Campus, Silberman College of Business, Department of Economics, Finance and International Business, Program in International Business, Teaneck, NJ 07666-1914. Offers MBA. *Students:* 10 full-time (7 women), 2 part-time (both women), 9 international. Average age 24. 34 applicants, 53% accepted, 6 enrolled. In 2009, 5 master's awarded. *Application deadline:* Applications are processed on a rolling basis. Application fee: $40.

Florida Atlantic University, College of Business, Department of Management Programs, Boca Raton, FL 33431-0991. Offers global entrepreneurship (MBA); international business (MBA, MS); management (PhD). *Faculty:* 24 full-time (9 women), 9 part-time/adjunct (3 women). *Students:* 286 full-time (123 women), 452 part-time (206 women); includes 238 minority (79 African Americans, 1 American Indian/Alaska Native, 53 Asian Americans or Pacific Islanders, 105 Hispanic Americans), 52 international. Average age 32. 677 applicants, 49% accepted, 98 enrolled. In 2009, 221 master's, 7 doctorates awarded. *Entrance requirements:* For master's, GMAT or GRE General Test, minimum GPA of 3.0 in last 60 hours of course work. Additional exam requirements/recommendations for international students: Required—TOEFL (minimum score 600 paper-based; 250 computer-based). *Application deadline:* For fall admission, 7/25 for domestic students, 2/15 for international students; for spring admission, 12/10 for domestic students, 7/15 for international students. Applications are processed on a rolling basis. Application fee: $30. Electronic applications accepted. *Expenses:* Tuition, state resident: full-time $7055; part-time $293.94 per credit hour. Tuition, nonresident: full-time $22,096; part-time $920.66 per credit hour. *Financial support:* Research assistantships with full tuition reimbursements, career-related internships or fieldwork, tuition waivers (partial), and unspecified assistantships available. *Faculty research:* Sports administration, healthcare, policy,

International Business

Florida Atlantic University (continued)
finance, real estate, senior living. *Unit head:* Dr. Peggy Golden, Chair, 561-297-2675, E-mail: golden@fau.edu. *Application contact:* Dr. Peggy Golden, Chair, 561-297-2675, E-mail: golden@fau.edu.

Florida International University, Alvah H. Chapman, Jr. Graduate School of Business, Department of Management and International Business, International Business Program, Miami, FL 33199. Offers MIB. Part-time and evening/weekend programs available. *Students:* 76 full-time (38 women), 43 part-time (24 women); includes 54 minority (2 African Americans, 4 Asian Americans or Pacific Islanders, 48 Hispanic Americans), 50 international. Average age 29. 58 applicants, 60% accepted, 35 enrolled. In 2009, 47 master's awarded. *Entrance requirements:* For master's, GRE or GMAT, minimum GPA of 3.0 (upper-level coursework), letter of intent, bachelor's degree in business administration or related area, resume, at least two years of work experience. Additional exam requirements/recommendations for international students: Required—TOEFL (minimum score 550 paper-based; 213 computer-based; 80 iBT), or IELTS (minimum score 6.5). *Application deadline:* For fall admission, 6/1 for domestic students, 4/1 for international students; for spring admission, 10/1 for domestic students, 9/1 for international students. Applications are processed on a rolling basis. Application fee: $30. Electronic applications accepted. *Expenses:* Contact institution. *Financial support:* Institutionally sponsored loans and scholarships/grants available. Financial award application deadline: 3/1; financial award applicants required to submit FAFSA. *Faculty research:* Strategy, international business, multinational corporations. *Unit head:* Dr. Galen Kroeck, Chair, Management and International Business Department, 305-348-2791, Fax: 305-348-6146, E-mail: kroeck@fiu.edu. *Application contact:* Yusimit Martinez, Coordinator, 305-348-3279, E-mail: yusimit.martinez@business.fiu.edu.

Florida Southern College, Program in Business Administration, Lakeland, FL 33801-5698. Offers accounting (MBA); business administration (MBA); international business (MBA). Part-time and evening/weekend programs available. *Entrance requirements:* For master's, GMAT or GRE General Test, minimum GPA of 2.75. Additional exam requirements/recommendations for international students: Required—TOEFL (minimum score 550 paper-based). *Expenses:* Contact institution.

See Close-Up on page 247.

Georgetown University, Graduate School of Arts and Sciences, Department of Economics, Washington, DC 20057. Offers econometrics (PhD); economic development (PhD); economic theory (PhD); industrial organization (PhD); international macro and finance (PhD); international trade (PhD); labor economics (PhD); macroeconomics (PhD); public economics and political economics (PhD); MA/PhD; MS/MA. *Degree requirements:* For doctorate, comprehensive exam, thesis/dissertation. *Entrance requirements:* For doctorate, GRE General Test. Additional exam requirements/recommendations for international students: Required—TOEFL. *Faculty research:* International economics, economic development.

Georgetown University, Graduate School of Arts and Sciences, McDonough School of Business, Washington, DC 20057. Offers business administration (IEMBA, MBA). *Accreditation:* AACSB. *Entrance requirements:* For master's, GMAT. Additional exam requirements/recommendations for international students: Required—TOEFL. *Expenses:* Contact institution.

Georgetown University, Law Center, Washington, DC 20001. Offers general (LL M); global health law (LL M); international and comparative law (LL M); international business and economic law (LL M); international legal studies (LL M); law (JD, SJD); securities and financial regulation (LL M); taxation (LL M); JD/LL M; JD/MA; JD/MBA; JD/MPH; JD/PhD. *Accreditation:* ABA. Part-time and evening/weekend programs available. *Degree requirements:* For master's, thesis; for doctorate, thesis/dissertation. *Entrance requirements:* For JD, LSAT; for master's and doctorate, JD, LL B, or first law degree earned in country of origin. Additional exam requirements/recommendations for international students: Required—TOEFL. *Expenses:* Contact institution. *Faculty research:* Constitutional law, legal history, jurisprudence.

The George Washington University, Elliott School of International Affairs, Program in International Trade and Investment Policy, Washington, DC 20052. Offers MA, JD/MA, MBA/MA. Part-time and evening/weekend programs available. *Students:* 36 full-time (21 women), 13 part-time (10 women); includes 7 minority (1 African American, 3 Asian Americans or Pacific Islanders, 3 Hispanic Americans), 9 international. Average age 26. 93 applicants, 73% accepted, 23 enrolled. In 2009, 19 master's awarded. *Degree requirements:* For master's, one foreign language, capstone project. *Entrance requirements:* For master's, GRE General Test, 2 years of a modern foreign language, 2 semesters of introductory economics. Additional exam requirements/recommendations for international students: Required—TOEFL. *Application deadline:* For fall admission, 2/1 for domestic students; for spring admission, 10/1 for domestic students. Application fee: $60. Electronic applications accepted. *Financial support:* In 2009–10, 11 students received support; fellowships with tuition reimbursements available, research assistantships with tuition reimbursements available, career-related internships or fieldwork, Federal Work-Study, institutionally sponsored loans, and tuition waivers available. Financial award application deadline: 1/15. *Unit head:* Steven Suranovic, Director, 202-994-7579, Fax: 202-994-5477, E-mail: smsuran@gwu.edu. *Application contact:* Jeff V. Miles, Director of Graduate Admissions, 202-994-7050, Fax: 202-994-9537, E-mail: esiagrad@gwu.edu.

The George Washington University, School of Business, Department of International Business, Washington, DC 20052. Offers MBA, PhD, MBA/MA. Part-time and evening/weekend programs available. *Faculty:* 15 full-time (8 women), 2 part-time/adjunct (both women). *Degree requirements:* For doctorate, thesis/dissertation. *Entrance requirements:* For master's, GMAT; for doctorate, GMAT or GRE. Additional exam requirements/recommendations for international students: Required—TOEFL. *Application deadline:* For fall admission, 4/1 priority date for domestic students; for spring admission, 10/1 for domestic students. Applications are processed on a rolling basis. Application fee: $60. *Financial support:* Fellowships, teaching assistantships, career-related internships or fieldwork, Federal Work-Study, and institutionally sponsored loans available. Financial award application deadline: 4/1. *Faculty research:* International trade, competitiveness, business management. *Unit head:* Reid Click, Chair, 202-994-7130, E-mail: rclick@gwu.edu. *Application contact:* Kristin Williams, Assistant Vice President for Graduate and Special Enrollment Management, 202-994-0467, Fax: 202-994-0371, E-mail: ksw@gwu.edu.

Georgia Institute of Technology, Graduate Studies and Research, College of Management, Program in Business Administration, Atlanta, GA 30332-0001. Offers accounting (MBA); e-commerce (Certificate); engineering entrepreneurship (MBA); entrepreneurship (Certificate); finance (MBA); information technology management (MBA); international business (MBA, Certificate); management of technology (Certificate); marketing (MBA); operations management (MBA); organizational behavior (MBA); strategic management (MBA). *Accreditation:* AACSB.

Georgia State University, J. Mack Robinson College of Business, Institute of International Business, Atlanta, GA 30303. Offers MBA, MIB, MIB/MAPOLS. Part-time and evening/weekend programs available. *Entrance requirements:* For master's, GMAT. Additional exam requirements/recommendations for international students: Required—TOEFL (minimum score 610 paper-based; 255 computer-based; 101 iBT). Electronic applications accepted. *Faculty research:* Emerging markets, international business strategy, international business transactions, multi-international enterprise, international buyer seller relations.

Georgia State University, J. Mack Robinson College of Business, Program in General Business Administration, Atlanta, GA 30302-3083. Offers accounting/information systems (MBA); economics (MBA, MS); enterprise risk management (MBA); general business (MBA); general business administration (EMBA, PMBA); information systems consulting (MBA); information systems risk management (MBA); international business and information technology (MBA); international entrepreneurship (MBA); MBA/JD. *Accreditation:* AACSB. Part-time and evening/weekend programs available. *Entrance requirements:* For master's, GMAT. Additional exam requirements/recommendations for international students: Required—TOEFL (minimum score 610 paper-based; 255 computer-based; 101 iBT). Electronic applications accepted.

Golden Gate University, Ageno School of Business, San Francisco, CA 94105-2968. Offers accounting (MBA); business administration (EMBA, MBA, PMBA, DBA); finance (MBA, MS, Certificate); financial planning (MS, Certificate); human resource management (MBA, MS); human resources management (Certificate); information systems (MS); information technology (MBA); information technology management (Certificate); integrated marketing and communications (MS, Certificate); international business (MBA); management (MBA); marketing (MBA, MS, Certificate); operations management (Certificate); psychology (MA, Certificate); public relations (MS, Certificate); JD/MBA. Part-time and evening/weekend programs available. *Faculty:* 16 full-time (4 women), 241 part-time/adjunct (72 women). *Students:* 380 full-time (193 women), 750 part-time (414 women); includes 480 minority (98 African Americans, 2 American Indian/Alaska Native, 298 Asian Americans or Pacific Islanders, 82 Hispanic Americans), 166 international. Average age 33. 681 applicants, 78% accepted, 270 enrolled. In 2009, 550 master's, 13 doctorates awarded. *Degree requirements:* For doctorate, thesis/dissertation. *Entrance requirements:* For master's, GMAT (MBA), minimum GPA of 2.5 (MS). Additional exam requirements/recommendations for international students: Required—TOEFL. *Application deadline:* For fall admission, 5/15 for international students; for winter admission, 1/15 for international students; for spring admission, 9/15 for international students. Applications are processed on a rolling basis. Application fee: $70 ($110 for international students). Electronic applications accepted. *Expenses:* Contact institution. *Financial support:* Career-related internships or fieldwork, Federal Work-Study, institutionally sponsored loans, and scholarships/grants available. Support available to part-time students. Financial award applicants required to submit FAFSA. *Unit head:* Terry Connelly, Dean, 415-442-6519, Fax: 415-442-5369. *Application contact:* Angela Melero, Enrollment Services, 415-442-7800, Fax: 415-442-7807, E-mail: info@ggu.edu.

Goldey-Beacom College, Graduate Program, Wilmington, DE 19808-1999. Offers business administration (MBA); finance (MS); financial management (MBA); human resource management (MBA); information technology (MBA); international business management (MBA); management (MM); marketing management (MBA); taxation (MBA, MS). *Accreditation:* ACBSP. Part-time and evening/weekend programs available. *Faculty:* 20 full-time (8 women), 28 part-time/adjunct (10 women). *Students:* 38 full-time (18 women), 486 part-time (184 women); includes 350 minority (38 African Americans, 300 Asian Americans or Pacific Islanders, 12 Hispanic Americans). Average age 27. In 2009, 130 master's awarded. *Entrance requirements:* For master's, GMAT, MAT, GRE, minimum GPA of 3.0. Additional exam requirements/recommendations for international students: Required—TOEFL (minimum score 65 computer-based); Recommended—IELTS (minimum score 5). *Application deadline:* Applications are processed on a rolling basis. Electronic applications accepted. *Expenses:* Tuition: Full-time $14,166; part-time $787 per credit. Required fees: $180; $10 per credit. *Financial support:* In 2009–10, 486 students received support. Scholarships/grants available. Support available to part-time students. Financial award application deadline: 4/1; financial award applicants required to submit FAFSA. *Unit head:* Larry W. Eby, Director of Admissions, 302-225-6289, Fax: 302-996-5408, E-mail: ebylw@gbc.edu. *Application contact:* Ashley E. Mashington, Graduate Admissions Representative, 302-225-6259, Fax: 302-996-5408, E-mail: mashina@gbc.edu.

Harding University, College of Business Administration, Searcy, AR 72149-0001. Offers accounting (MBA); health care management (MBA); information technology management (MBA); international business (MBA); leadership and organizational management (MBA). *Accreditation:* ACBSP. Part-time and evening/weekend programs available. Postbaccalaureate distance learning degree programs offered (no on-campus study). *Faculty:* 27 part-time/adjunct (6 women). *Students:* 105 full-time (46 women), 140 part-time (66 women); includes 31 minority (18 African Americans, 3 American Indian/Alaska Native, 6 Asian Americans or Pacific Islanders, 4 Hispanic Americans), 43 international. Average age 31. 82 applicants, 96% accepted, 66 enrolled. In 2009, 130 master's awarded. *Degree requirements:* For master's, portfolio. *Entrance requirements:* For master's, minimum GPA of 3.0, 2 letters of recommendation, resume. Additional exam requirements/recommendations for international students: Required—TOEFL (minimum score 550 paper-based; 213 computer-based; 80 iBT). *Application deadline:* For fall admission, 8/1 priority date for domestic and international students; for spring admission, 12/1 priority date for domestic and international students. Applications are processed on a rolling basis. Application fee: $35. *Expenses:* Tuition: Full-time $9720; part-time $540 per credit hour. Required fees: $22 per credit hour. Tuition and fees vary according to course load and program. *Financial support:* In 2009–10, 27 students received support. Unspecified assistantships available. Financial award application deadline: 7/30; financial award applicants required to submit FAFSA. *Unit head:* Glen Metheny, Director of Graduate Studies, 501-279-5851, Fax: 501-279-4805, E-mail: gmetheny@harding.edu. *Application contact:* Melanie Kiihnl, Recruiting Manager/Director of Marketing, 501-279-4523, Fax: 501-279-4805, E-mail: mba@harding.edu.

Hawai'i Pacific University, College of Business Administration, Honolulu, HI 96813. Offers accounting/CPA (MBA); e-business (MBA); economics (MBA); finance (MBA); human resource management (MA, MBA); information systems (MBA, MSIS), including knowledge management (MSIS), software engineering (MSIS), telecommunications security (MSIS); international business (MBA); management (MBA); marketing (MBA); organizational change (MA, MBA); travel industry management (MBA). Part-time and evening/weekend programs available. *Faculty:* 15 full-time (5 women), 11 part-time/adjunct (4 women). *Students:* 206 full-time (107 women), 197 part-time (105 women); includes 136 minority (18 African Americans, 3 American Indian/Alaska Native, 98 Asian Americans or Pacific Islanders, 17 Hispanic Americans), 151 international. Average age 30. 235 applicants, 90% accepted, 127 enrolled. In 2009, 141 master's awarded. *Degree requirements:* For master's, thesis. *Entrance requirements:* For master's, GMAT. Additional exam requirements/recommendations for international students: Recommended—TOEFL (minimum score 550 paper-based; 213 computer-based; 80 iBT), TWE (minimum score 5). *Application deadline:* For fall admission, 2/15 priority date for domestic students; for spring admission, 10/15 priority date for domestic students. Applications are processed on a rolling basis. Application fee: $50. Electronic applications accepted. *Expenses:* Tuition: Full-time $12,600; part-time $700 per credit hour. Tuition and fees vary according to program. *Financial support:* In 2009–10, 164 students received support; research assistantships, career-related internships or fieldwork, Federal Work-Study, scholarships/grants, and unspecified assistantships available. Support available to part-time students. Financial award application deadline: 3/1; financial award applicants required to submit FAFSA. *Faculty research:* Statistical control process as used by management, studies in comparative cross-cultural management styles, not-for-profit management. *Unit head:* Dr. Aytun Ozturk, Dean, 808-544-9301, Fax: 808-544-0283, E-mail: uozturk@hpu.edu. *Application contact:* Danny Lam, Assistant Director of Graduate Admissions, 808-544-1135, Fax: 808-544-0280, E-mail: graduate@hpu.edu.

See Close-Up on page 251.

HEC Montreal, School of Business Administration, Master of Science Programs in Administration, Program in International Business, Montréal, QC H3T 2A7, Canada. Offers M Sc. Part-time programs available. *Students:* 73 full-time (43 women), 10 part-time (5 women). 102 applicants, 56% accepted, 32 enrolled. In 2009, 31 master's awarded. *Degree requirements:* For master's, one foreign language, thesis. *Application deadline:* For fall admission, 3/15 for domestic and international students; for winter admission, 9/15 for domestic and international students. Application fee: $77. Electronic applications accepted. Tuition and fees charges are reported in Canadian dollars. *Expenses:* Tuition, area resident: Part-time $65.60 Canadian dollars per credit. Tuition, state resident: full-time $2361.60 Canadian dollars; part-time $183.36 Canadian dollars per credit. Tuition, nonresident: full-time $6601 Canadian dollars; part-time $448.13 Canadian dollars per credit. International tuition: $16,132.68 Canadian dollars full-time. Required fees: $1254.15 Canadian dollars; $28.99 Canadian dollars per course. $91.68 Canadian dollars per term. Tuition and fees vary according to degree level and program. *Financial support:* Research assistantships, teaching assistantships available. Financial award application deadline: 10/2. *Unit head:* Dr. Claude Laurin, Director, 514-340-6485, Fax: 514-340-5690, E-mail: claude.laurin@hec.ca. *Application contact:* Francine Blais, Administrative Director, 514-340-6112, Fax: 514-340-6411, E-mail: francine.blais@hec.ca.

HEC Montreal, School of Business Administration, Master of Science Programs in Administration, Program in International Management, Montréal, QC H3T 2A7, Canada. Offers M Sc. All

courses are given in French. Part-time programs available. *Students:* 4 full-time (1 woman). In 2009, 24 master's awarded. *Degree requirements:* For master's, one foreign language, thesis. Application fee: $76 Canadian dollars. Electronic applications accepted. Tuition and fees charges are reported in Canadian dollars. *Expenses:* Tuition, area resident: Part-time $65.60 Canadian dollars per credit. Tuition, state resident: full-time $2361.60 Canadian dollars; part-time $183.36 Canadian dollars per credit. Tuition, nonresident: full-time $6601 Canadian dollars; part-time $448.13 Canadian dollars per credit. International tuition: $16,132.68 Canadian dollars full-time. Required fees: $1254.15 Canadian dollars; $28.99 Canadian dollars per course. $91.68 Canadian dollars per term. Tuition and fees vary according to degree level and program. *Financial support:* Fellowships, research assistantships, teaching assistantships, scholarships/grants available. *Unit head:* Dr. Francois Bellavance, Director, 514-340-6485, Fax: 514-340-5690, E-mail: francois.bellavance@hec.ca. *Application contact:* Francine Blais, Administrative Director, 514-340-6112, Fax: 514-340-6411, E-mail: francine.blais@hec.ca.

Hofstra University, Frank G. Zarb School of Business, Department of Marketing and International Business, Hempstead, NY 11549. Offers business administration (MBA), including international business, marketing; marketing (MS); marketing research (MS). Part-time and evening/weekend programs available. *Faculty:* 9 full-time (0 women), 1 part-time/adjunct (0 women). *Students:* 52 full-time (28 women), 38 part-time (21 women); includes 9 minority (2 African Americans, 3 Asian Americans or Pacific Islanders, 4 Hispanic Americans), 40 international. Average age 27. 114 applicants, 71% accepted, 26 enrolled. In 2009, 29 master's awarded. *Degree requirements:* For master's, capstone course (MBA), thesis (MS). *Entrance requirements:* For master's, GMAT or GRE, 2 letters of recommendation, resume. Additional exam requirements/recommendations for international students: Required—TOEFL (minimum score 550 paper-based; 213 computer-based; 80 iBT); Recommended—IELTS (minimum score 6). *Application deadline:* Applications are processed on a rolling basis. Application fee: $60. Electronic applications accepted. *Expenses:* Contact institution. *Financial support:* In 2009–10, 24 students received support, including 21 fellowships with full and partial tuition reimbursements available (averaging $9,582 per year), 2 research assistantships with full and partial tuition reimbursements available (averaging $14,187 per year); career-related internships or fieldwork, Federal Work-Study, institutionally sponsored loans, scholarships/grants, tuition waivers (full and partial), and unspecified assistantships also available. Support available to part-time students. Financial award applicants required to submit FAFSA. *Faculty research:* Outsourcing, global alliances, retailing, web marketing, cross-cultural age research. *Unit head:* Dr. Benny Barak, Chairperson, 516-463-5707, Fax: 516-463-4834, E-mail: mktbzb@hofstra.edu. *Application contact:* Carol Drummer, Dean of Graduate Admissions, 516-463-4876, Fax: 516-463-4664, E-mail: gradstudent@hofstra.edu.

Hope International University, School of Graduate and Professional Studies, Program in Business Administration, Fullerton, CA 92831-3138. Offers business administration (MBA); educational administration (MSM); international development (MBA, MSM); management (MBA); nonprofit management (MBA). Part-time programs available. Postbaccalaureate distance learning degree programs offered (no on-campus study). *Degree requirements:* For master's, comprehensive exam (for some programs), thesis (for some programs), project. *Entrance requirements:* For master's, minimum GPA of 3.0; 2 references. Additional exam requirements/recommendations for international students: Required—TOEFL (minimum score 550 paper-based; 213 computer-based; 86 iBT); Recommended—IELTS (minimum score 6.5). Electronic applications accepted. *Expenses:* Contact institution.

Howard University, School of Business, Graduate Programs in Business, Washington, DC 20059-0002. Offers accounting (MBA); entrepreneurship (MBA); finance (MBA); general management (MBA); human resources management (MBA); information systems (MBA); international business (MBA); marketing (MBA); supply chain management (MBA); JD/MBA. *Accreditation:* AACSB. Part-time and evening/weekend programs available. Postbaccalaureate distance learning degree programs offered (no on-campus study). *Entrance requirements:* For master's, GMAT, minimum 1 year post undergraduate work experience, resume, 3 letters of recommendation, advanced college algebra. Additional exam requirements/recommendations for international students: Required—TOEFL. *Faculty research:* Marketing research in multi-ethnic populations, U.S. trade policies and international relations, risk management (finance).

Hult International Business School, Program in Business Administration—Hult London Campus, London, MA WC 1B 4JP, United Kingdom. Offers entrepreneurship (MBA); international business (MBA); international finance (MBA); marketing (MBA). Part-time programs available. *Degree requirements:* For master's, comprehensive exam, thesis, internship. *Entrance requirements:* Additional exam requirements/recommendations for international students: Required—TOEFL (minimum score 580 paper-based; 237 computer-based), TWE (minimum score 5). Electronic applications accepted.

Hult International Business School, Program in International Business, Cambridge, MA 02141. Offers MIB.

Hult International Business School, Program in International Business—Hult Dubai Campus, Dubai, MA 02141, United Arab Emirates. Offers MIB.

Hult International Business School, Program in International Business—Hult London Campus, London, MA WC 1B 4JP, United Kingdom. Offers MIB.

Hult International Business School, Program in International Business—Hult San Francisco Campus, San Francisco, CA 94133. Offers MIB.

Indiana Tech, Program in Global Leadership, Fort Wayne, IN 46803-1297. Offers PhD. Part-time and evening/weekend programs available. Postbaccalaureate distance learning degree programs offered (minimal on-campus study). *Students:* 25 full-time (16 women), 6 part-time (0 women); includes 8 minority (6 African Americans, 2 Hispanic Americans). Average age 43. *Entrance requirements:* For doctorate, GMAT, LSAT, GRE, or MAT, transcripts from accredited institutions, essay, resume, interview. *Application deadline:* Applications are processed on a rolling basis. Application fee: $50. Electronic applications accepted. *Expenses:* Tuition: Full-time $5160; part-time $430 per credit hour. Tuition and fees vary according to degree level and program. *Unit head:* Dr. Kenneth E. Rauch, Director, 260-422-5561 Ext. 2446, E-mail: kerauch@indianatech.edu. *Application contact:* Steve Herendeen, Associate Vice President of College of Professional Studies Admissions, 260-422-5561 Ext. 2121, Fax: 260-422-1518, E-mail: saherendeen@indianatech.edu.

Instituto Tecnologico de Santo Domingo, Graduate School, Santo Domingo, Dominican Republic. Offers applied linguistics (MA); construction administration (M Mgmt); corporate finance (M Mgmt); education (M Ed); engineering (M Eng), including data telecommunications, industrial engineering, logistics and supply chain, maintenance engineering, sanitary and environmental engineering, structural engineering; environmental science (M En S), including environmental education, environmental management, marine and coastal ecosystems, natural resources management; family therapy (MA); food science and technology (MS); human development (MA); human resources administration (M Mgmt); international business (M Mgmt); labor risks (M Mgmt); management (M Mgmt); marketing (M Mgmt); mathematics (MS); organizational development (M Mgmt); planning and taxation (M Mgmt); psychology (MA); social science (M Ed); upper management (M Mgmt). *Entrance requirements:* For master's, birth certificate, minimum GPA of 2.0.

Instituto Tecnológico y de Estudios Superiores de Monterrey, Campus Central de Veracruz, Graduate Programs, Córdoba, Mexico. Offers administration (MA); administration of information technologies (MTI); computer sciences (MCC); education (MEE); educational institution administration (MAD); educational technology (MTE); electronic commerce (MCE); finance (MAF); humanistic studies (MEH); international business for Latin America (MNL); marketing (MMT); science (MCP); technology management (MTT). Part-time and evening/weekend programs available. Postbaccalaureate distance learning degree programs offered (minimal on-campus study). *Degree requirements:* For master's, thesis (for some programs). *Entrance requirements:* For master's, PAEP College Board. Electronic applications accepted.

Instituto Tecnológico y de Estudios Superiores de Monterrey, Campus Chihuahua, Graduate Programs, Chihuahua, Mexico. Offers computer systems engineering (Ingeniero); electrical engineering (Ingeniero); electromechanical engineering (Ingeniero); electronic engineering (Ingeniero); engineering administration (MEA); industrial engineering (MIE, Ingeniero); international trade (MIT); mechanical engineering (Ingeniero).

Instituto Tecnológico y de Estudios Superiores de Monterrey, Campus Ciudad de México, Virtual University Division, Ciudad de Mexico, Mexico. Offers administration of information technologies (MA); computer sciences (MA); education (MA, PhD); educational technology (MA); environmental engineering (MA); environmental systems (MA); humanistic studies (MA); industrial engineering (MA); international business for Latin America (MA); quality systems (MA); quality systems and productivity (MA). Part-time and evening/weekend programs available. Postbaccalaureate distance learning degree programs offered (minimal on-campus study). *Entrance requirements:* For master's and doctorate, Instituto entrance exam. Additional exam requirements/recommendations for international students: Required—TOEFL.

Instituto Tecnológico y de Estudios Superiores de Monterrey, Campus Cuernavaca, Programs in Business Administration, Temixco, Mexico. Offers finance (MA); human resources management (MA); international business (MA); marketing (MA).

Instituto Tecnológico y de Estudios Superiores de Monterrey, Campus Irapuato, Graduate Programs, Irapuato, Mexico. Offers administration (MBA); administration of information technology (MAIT); administration of telecommunications (MAT); architecture (M Arch); computer science (MCS); education (M Ed); educational administration (MEA); educational innovation and technology (DEIT); educational technology (MET); electronic commerce (MBA); environmental administration and planning (MEAP); environmental systems (MES); finances (MBA); humanistic studies (MHS); international management for Latin American executives (MIMLAE); library and information science (MLIS); manufacturing quality management (MMQM); marketing research (MBA).

Instituto Tecnológico y de Estudios Superiores de Monterrey, Campus Monterrey, Graduate School of Business Administration and Leadership, Program in Business Administration, Monterrey, Mexico. Offers business administration (MA, MBA); finance (M Sc); international business (M Sc); marketing (M Sc). *Accreditation:* AACSB. Part-time programs available. *Degree requirements:* For master's, one foreign language, thesis. *Entrance requirements:* For master's, GMAT. Additional exam requirements/recommendations for international students: Required—TOEFL. *Faculty research:* Technology management, quality management, organizational theory and behavior.

Inter American University of Puerto Rico, Metropolitan Campus, Graduate Programs, Program in International Business, San Juan, PR 00919-1293. Offers MIB.

Inter American University of Puerto Rico, San Germán Campus, Graduate Studies Center, Program in Business Administration, San Germán, PR 00683-5008. Offers accounting (MBA); finance (MBA); human resources (PhD); human resources management (MBA); industrial management (MBA); international business (PhD); management information systems (MBA); marketing management (MBA). Part-time and evening/weekend programs available. *Degree requirements:* For master's, comprehensive exam. *Entrance requirements:* For master's, GRE General Test or EXADEP, minimum GPA of 3.0.

Inter American University of Puerto Rico, San Germán Campus, Graduate Studies Center, Program in Entrepreneurial and Managerial Development, San Germán, PR 00683-5008. Offers interregional and international business (PhD). Part-time and evening/weekend programs available. *Degree requirements:* For doctorate, comprehensive exam, thesis/dissertation. *Entrance requirements:* For doctorate, EXADEP or GMAT, minimum graduate GPA of 3.25.

International University in Geneva, Master of Business Administration Program, Geneva, Switzerland. Offers finance (MBA); international business (MIB); investment management (MBA); luxury management (MBA); marketing (MBA); wealth management (MBA). *Accreditation:* ACBSP. Part-time and evening/weekend programs available. *Degree requirements:* For master's, comprehensive exam. *Entrance requirements:* For master's, GMAT. Additional exam requirements/recommendations for international students: Required—TOEFL. Electronic applications accepted.

The International University of Monaco, Graduate Programs, Monte Carlo, Monaco. Offers entrepreneurship (EMBA, MBA); financial engineering (M Sc); hedge fund and private equity (M Sc); international marketing (EMBA, MBA); international wealth management (M Sc); luxury goods and services (EMBA, M Sc, MBA); wealth and asset management (EMBA, MBA). Part-time programs available. *Degree requirements:* For master's, comprehensive exam (for some programs), applied research project. *Entrance requirements:* Additional exam requirements/recommendations for international students: Required—TOEFL (minimum score 550 paper-based; 213 computer-based), IELTS. Electronic applications accepted. *Faculty research:* Gaming, leadership, disintermediation.

Iona College, Hagan School of Business, Department of Marketing and International Business, New Rochelle, NY 10801-1890. Offers international business (PMC); marketing (MBA). Part-time and evening/weekend programs available. *Faculty:* 4 full-time (2 women), 3 part-time/adjunct (0 women). *Students:* 13 full-time (9 women), 41 part-time (26 women); includes 8 minority (4 African Americans, 1 Asian American or Pacific Islander, 3 Hispanic Americans), 1 international. Average age 29. 20 applicants, 90% accepted, 13 enrolled. In 2009, 14 master's, 38 other advanced degrees awarded. *Entrance requirements:* For master's, GMAT, 2 letters of recommendation; for PMC, GMAT. Additional exam requirements/recommendations for international students: Required—TOEFL (minimum score 550 paper-based; 213 computer-based). *Application deadline:* Applications are processed on a rolling basis. Application fee: $50. Electronic applications accepted. *Expenses:* Contact institution. *Financial support:* Scholarships/grants, tuition waivers (partial), and unspecified assistantships available. Support available to part-time students. Financial award application deadline: 4/15; financial award applicants required to submit FAFSA. *Faculty research:* Business ethics, international retailing, mega-marketing, consumer behavior and consumer confidence. *Unit head:* Dr. Frederica E. Rudell, Chair, 914-637-2748, E-mail: frudell@iona.edu. *Application contact:* Jude Fleurismond, Director of MBA Admissions, 914-633-2289, Fax: 914-637-2708, E-mail: jfleurismond@iona.edu.

John Brown University, Graduate Business Division, Siloam Springs, AR 72761-2121. Offers business administration (MBA), including international business, leadership and ethics; leadership and ethics (MS), including higher education. Part-time and evening/weekend programs available. Postbaccalaureate distance learning degree programs offered (minimal on-campus study). *Faculty:* 2 full-time (0 women), 13 part-time/adjunct (6 women). *Students:* 13 full-time (6 women), 143 part-time (56 women); includes 19 minority (6 African Americans, 2 American Indian/Alaska Native, 6 Asian Americans or Pacific Islanders, 5 Hispanic Americans), 5 international. Average age 35. 94 applicants, 85% accepted, 71 enrolled. In 2009, 54 master's awarded. *Entrance requirements:* For master's, GRE General Test, MAT, minimum GPA of 3.0. Additional exam requirements/recommendations for international students: Required—TOEFL (minimum score 550 paper-based; 173 computer-based). *Application deadline:* For fall admission, 8/11 priority date for domestic students; for spring admission, 1/12 priority date for domestic students. Applications are processed on a rolling basis. Application fee: $35 ($100 for international students). Electronic applications accepted. *Expenses:* Tuition: Full-time $8100; part-time $450 per credit. *Financial support:* In 2009–10, 8 students received support, including 8 fellowships (averaging $5,500 per year); scholarships/grants, tuition waivers (full), and unspecified assistantships also available. Financial award application deadline: 3/1; financial award applicants required to submit FAFSA. *Unit head:* Dr. Joe Walenciak, Program Director, 479-524-7170, Fax: 479-524-9548. *Application contact:* Brent Young, Graduate Business Representative, 479-631-0496, E-mail: byoung@jbu.edu.

John Marshall Law School, Graduate and Professional Programs, Chicago, IL 60604-3968. Offers comparative legal studies (LL M); employee benefits (LL M, MS); information technology (LL M, MS); intellectual property (LL M); international business and trade (LL M); law (JD); real estate (LL M, MS); taxation (LL M, MS); JD/LL M; JD/MA; JD/MBA; JD/MPA. *Accreditation:* ABA. Part-time and evening/weekend programs available. *Faculty:* 73 full-time (26 women),

International Business

John Marshall Law School (continued)

110 part-time/adjunct (33 women). *Students:* 1,139 full-time (505 women), 407 part-time (204 women); includes 353 minority (130 African Americans, 15 American Indian/Alaska Native, 91 Asian Americans or Pacific Islanders, 117 Hispanic Americans), 43 international. Average age 27. 3,027 applicants, 44% accepted, 385 enrolled. In 2009, 401 first professional degrees, 16 master's awarded. *Degree requirements:* For JD, 90 credits. *Entrance requirements:* For JD, LSAT; for master's, JD. Additional exam requirements/recommendations for international students: Required—TOEFL. *Application deadline:* For fall admission, 3/1 priority date for domestic and international students; for spring admission, 10/15 priority date for domestic and international students. Applications are processed on a rolling basis. Application fee: $60. Electronic applications accepted. *Expenses:* Contact institution. *Financial support:* In 2009–10, 1,350 students received support. Scholarships/grants and tuition waivers (full and partial) available. Support available to part-time students. Financial award application deadline: 6/1; financial award applicants required to submit FAFSA. *Unit head:* John Corkery, Dean, 312-427-2737. *Application contact:* William B. Powers, Associate Dean of Admission and Student Affairs, 800-537-4280, Fax: 312-427-5136, E-mail: admission@jmls.edu.

Johnson & Wales University, The Alan Shawn Feinstein Graduate School, MBA Program in Global Business Leadership, Providence, RI 02903-3703. Offers accounting (MBA); enhanced accounting (MBA); financial management (MBA); international trade (MBA); marketing (MBA); organizational leadership (MBA). Part-time programs available. *Faculty:* 13 full-time (3 women), 17 part-time/adjunct (4 women). *Students:* 523 full-time (272 women), 162 part-time (85 women); includes 29 minority (18 African Americans, 4 Asian Americans or Pacific Islanders, 7 Hispanic Americans), 385 international. Average age 27. 330 applicants, 82% accepted, 151 enrolled. In 2009, 274 master's awarded. *Entrance requirements:* For master's, minimum GPA of 2.75. Additional exam requirements/recommendations for international students: Required—TOEFL, TOEFL (minimum score 550 paper-based; 210 computer-based) or IELTS recommended; Recommended—TWE. *Application deadline:* For fall admission, 8/15 priority date for domestic students, 6/28 priority date for international students; for winter admission, 11/10 priority date for domestic students, 9/20 priority date for international students; for spring admission, 2/5 priority date for domestic students, 12/20 priority date for international students. Applications are processed on a rolling basis. *Expenses:* Required fees: $340 per quarter hour. *Financial support:* Tuition waivers (partial) and unspecified assistantships available. Support available to part-time students. Financial award application deadline: 5/1. *Faculty research:* International banking, global economy, international trade, cultural differences. *Unit head:* Dr. Frank Pontarelli, Dean, 401-598-1333, Fax: 401-598-1125. *Application contact:* Dr. Allan G. Freedman, Director of Graduate Admissions, 401-598-1015, Fax: 401-598-1286, E-mail: gradadm@jwu.edu.

Kaplan University, Davenport Campus, School of Business, Davenport, IA 52807-2095. Offers business administration (MBA); change leadership (MS); entrepreneurship (MBA); finance (MBA); health care management (MBA, MS); human resource (MBA); international business (MBA); management (MS); marketing (MBA); project management (MBA, MS); supply chain management and logistics (MBA, MS). Part-time and evening/weekend programs available. Postbaccalaureate distance learning degree programs offered (no on-campus study). *Entrance requirements:* Additional exam requirements/recommendations for international students: Required—TOEFL (minimum score 550 paper-based; 218 computer-based; 80 iBT). Electronic applications accepted.

Kean University, Nathan Weiss Graduate College, Program in Global Management, Union, NJ 07083. Offers executive management (MBA); global management (MBA), including information management. *Faculty:* 3 full-time (2 women). *Students:* 46 full-time (30 women), 66 part-time (33 women); includes 61 minority (33 African Americans, 8 Asian Americans or Pacific Islanders, 20 Hispanic Americans), 14 international. Average age 33. 66 applicants, 88% accepted, 37 enrolled. In 2009, 49 master's awarded. *Degree requirements:* For master's, one foreign language, internship or study abroad. *Entrance requirements:* For master's, GMAT, minimum GPA of 3.0, 3 letters of recommendation, prerequisite business courses. *Application deadline:* For fall admission, 5/1 for domestic students; for spring admission, 11/1 for domestic students. Applications are processed on a rolling basis. Application fee: $60 ($150 for international students). Electronic applications accepted. *Expenses:* Tuition, state resident: full-time $10,440; part-time $435 per credit. Tuition, nonresident: full-time $14,160; part-time $590 per credit. Required fees: $2642; $110 per credit. Part-time tuition and fees vary according to course load and degree level. *Financial support:* In 2009–10, 13 research assistantships with full tuition reimbursements (averaging $3,263 per year) were awarded; unspecified assistantships also available. *Unit head:* Dr. David Shani, Program Coordinator, 908-737-5980, E-mail: dshani@kean.edu. *Application contact:* Reenat Hasan, Pre-Admissions Coordinator, 908-737-5923, Fax: 908-737-5965, E-mail: rhasan@exchange.kean.edu.

Keiser University, MBA, Master of Business Administration Program, Fort Lauderdale, FL 33309. Offers international business (MBA); leadership for managers (MBA); marketing (MBA). Part-time programs available. Postbaccalaureate distance learning degree programs offered (minimal on-campus study). *Faculty:* 8 full-time (3 women), 7 part-time/adjunct (2 women). *Students:* 18 full-time (14 women), 83 part-time (51 women); includes 51 minority (30 African Americans, 2 American Indian/Alaska Native, 2 Asian Americans or Pacific Islanders, 17 Hispanic Americans), 1 international. Average age 42. 30 applicants, 77% accepted, 18 enrolled. In 2009, 21 master's awarded. *Entrance requirements:* For master's, minimum GPA of 2.7 from an accredited institution. Additional exam requirements/recommendations for international students: Required—TOEFL. *Application deadline:* Applications are processed on a rolling basis. Application fee: $50. Electronic applications accepted. *Financial support:* In 2009–10, 95 students received support. Federal Work-Study available. Financial award applicants required to submit FAFSA. *Unit head:* Dr. Sara Malmstrom, Dean, 954-318-1620. *Application contact:* Manuel Christiansen, Associate Director of Admissions, 954-318-1620 Ext. 309, E-mail: mchristiansen@keiseruniversity.edu.

Lewis University, College of Business, Graduate School of Management, Program in Business Administration, Romeoville, IL 60446. Offers accounting (MBA); custom elective option (MBA); e-business (MBA); finance (MBA); healthcare management (MBA); human resources management (MBA); information security (MBA); international business (MBA); management information systems (MBA); marketing (MBA); project management (MBA); technology and operations management (MBA). Part-time and evening/weekend programs available. *Faculty:* 15 full-time (2 women), 18 part-time/adjunct (4 women). *Students:* 120 full-time (64 women), 222 part-time (103 women); includes 97 minority (62 African Americans, 4 Asian Americans or Pacific Islanders, 31 Hispanic Americans), 9 international. Average age 31. In 2009, 84 master's awarded. *Entrance requirements:* For master's, interview, bachelor's degree, resume, 2 recommendations. Additional exam requirements/recommendations for international students: Required—TOEFL (minimum score 550 paper-based; 213 computer-based). *Application deadline:* For fall admission, 8/15 priority date for domestic students, 5/1 priority date for international students; for spring admission, 11/15 priority date for international students. Applications are processed on a rolling basis. Application fee: $40. Electronic applications accepted. *Expenses:* Tuition: Full-time $6480; part-time $720 per credit. One-time fee: $40. Tuition and fees vary according to course load, degree level and program. *Financial support:* Career-related internships or fieldwork, Federal Work-Study, scholarships/grants, and unspecified assistantships available. Financial award application deadline: 5/1; financial award applicants required to submit FAFSA. *Unit head:* Dr. Maureen Culleeney, Academic Program Director, 815-838-0500 Ext. 5631, E-mail: culleema@lewisu.edu. *Application contact:* Michele King, Director of Admission, 815-838-0500 Ext. 5384, E-mail: gsm@lewisu.edu.

Lincoln University, Graduate Degree Programs, Oakland, CA 94612. Offers finance and investments (DBA); finance management and investment banking (MBA); general business (MBA); human resource management (MBA); international business (MBA); management information systems (MBA). Part-time and evening/weekend programs available. *Faculty:* 7 full-time (2 women), 13 part-time/adjunct (1 woman). *Students:* 295 full-time (133 women), 3 part-time (0 women). 177 applicants, 100% accepted, 71 enrolled. In 2009, 98 master's awarded. *Degree requirements:* For master's, research project (thesis) or internship report, or comprehensive exam; for doctorate, comprehensive exam, thesis/dissertation. *Entrance requirements:* For master's, minimum GPA of 2.7; for doctorate, GMAT (minimum score: 550), GRE (minimum score: 1000), or equivalent test results (waived for master's degree with cumulative GPA of 3.3). Additional exam requirements/recommendations for international students: Required—TOEFL or IELTS. *Application deadline:* For fall admission, 7/3 priority date for domestic students; for spring admission, 11/27 priority date for domestic students. Applications are processed on a rolling basis. Application fee: $75. Electronic applications accepted. *Expenses:* Tuition: Full-time $6750. Required fees: $190 per term. *Financial support:* In 2009–10, 1 teaching assistantship was awarded; career-related internships or fieldwork and scholarships/grants also available. *Unit head:* Dr. Marshall Burak, Director of Graduate Programs, 510-628-8016, Fax: 510-628-8012, E-mail: mburak@lincolnuca.edu. *Application contact:* Peggy Au, Director of Admissions and Records, 510-628-8010, Fax: 510-628-8012, E-mail: admissions@lincolnuca.edu.

Lindenwood University, Graduate Programs, School of Business and Entrepreneurship, St. Charles, MO 63301-1695. Offers accounting (MBA, MS); business administration (MBA); entrepreneurial studies (MBA, MS); finance (MBA, MS); human resource management (MBA); human resources (MS); international business (MBA, MS); management (MBA, MS); management information systems (MBA, MS); marketing (MBA, MS); public management (MBA, MS); sport management (MA). *Accreditation:* ACBSP. Part-time and evening/weekend programs available. *Faculty:* 20 full-time (8 women), 17 part-time/adjunct (5 women). *Students:* 129 full-time (60 women), 138 part-time (61 women); includes 15 minority (11 African Americans, 2 Asian Americans or Pacific Islanders, 2 Hispanic Americans), 84 international. Average age 28. 149 applicants, 73 enrolled. In 2009, 142 master's awarded. *Degree requirements:* For master's, comprehensive exam (for some programs), thesis (for some programs). *Entrance requirements:* For master's, interview, minimum GPA of 3.0, letter of recommendation. Additional exam requirements/recommendations for international students: Required—TOEFL (minimum score 550 paper-based; 213 computer-based; 80 iBT). *Application deadline:* For fall admission, 7/30 priority date for domestic students, 9/16 priority date for international students; for winter admission, 12/19 priority date for domestic students, 12/17 priority date for international students; for spring admission, 2/25 priority date for domestic students, 2/11 priority date for international students. Applications are processed on a rolling basis. Application fee: $30 ($100 for international students). Electronic applications accepted. *Expenses:* Tuition: Full-time $12,960; part-time $370 per credit hour. Required fees: $340. One-time fee: $30 full-time. Tuition and fees vary according to course level and course load. *Financial support:* In 2009–10, 209 students received support. Career-related internships or fieldwork, Federal Work-Study, institutionally sponsored loans, and tuition waivers (partial) available. Financial award application deadline: 6/30; financial award applicants required to submit FAFSA. *Unit head:* Ed Morris, Dean of Management, 636-949-4832, E-mail: emorris@lindenwood.edu. *Application contact:* Brett Barger, Dean of Evening Admissions and Extension Campuses, 636-949-4934, Fax: 636-949-4109, E-mail: adultadmissions@lindenwood.edu.

Long Island University, C.W. Post Campus, College of Management, School of Business, Brookville, NY 11548-1300. Offers accounting and taxation (Certificate); business administration (Certificate); finance (MBA, Certificate); general business administration (MBA); international business (MBA, Certificate); management (MBA, Certificate); management information systems (MBA, Certificate); marketing (MBA, Certificate). *Accreditation:* AACSB. Part-time and evening/weekend programs available. *Entrance requirements:* For master's, GMAT, resume, minimum GPA of 3.0, 2 letters of recommendation. Additional exam requirements/recommendations for international students: Required—TOEFL (minimum score 527 paper-based; 197 computer-based). Electronic applications accepted. *Faculty research:* Financial markets, consumer behavior.

Loyola University Maryland, Graduate Programs, Sellinger School of Business and Management, Program in Business Administration, Baltimore, MD 21210-2699. Offers accounting (MBA); finance (MBA); general business (MBA); international business (MBA); management (MBA); management information systems (MBA); marketing (MBA). *Accreditation:* AACSB. Part-time and evening/weekend programs available. *Entrance requirements:* For master's, GMAT. Additional exam requirements/recommendations for international students: Required—TOEFL (minimum score 550 paper-based; 213 computer-based).

Lynn University, College of Business and Management, Boca Raton, FL 33431-5598. Offers aviation management (MBA); financial valuation and investment management (MBA); hospitality management (MBA); international business (MBA); marketing (MBA); mass communication and media management (MBA); sports and athletics administration (MBA). Part-time and evening/weekend programs available. Postbaccalaureate distance learning degree programs offered. *Degree requirements:* For master's, project. *Entrance requirements:* For master's, GMAT or GRE, minimum undergraduate GPA of 3.0, resume, 2 letters of recommendation. Additional exam requirements/recommendations for international students: Required—TOEFL (minimum score 550 paper-based; 213 computer-based). *Application deadline:* Applications are processed on a rolling basis. Application fee: $50. Electronic applications accepted. *Expenses:* Tuition: Part-time $580 per credit. One-time fee: $200 part-time. Part-time tuition and fees vary according to degree level. *Financial support:* Career-related internships or fieldwork, Federal Work-Study, institutionally sponsored loans, scholarships/grants, tuition waivers (full and partial), and unspecified assistantships available. Support available to part-time students. Financial award application deadline: 8/1; financial award applicants required to submit FAFSA. *Faculty research:* Labor relations, dynamic balance in leisure-time skills, ethics in athletics, hotel development. *Unit head:* Dr. Ralph Norcio, Associate Dean, 561-237-7010, Fax: 561-237-7014, E-mail: rnorcio@lynn.edu. *Application contact:* Dr. Larissa Baia, Assistant Director of Graduate Admissions, 561-237-7916, Fax: 561-237-7100, E-mail: admissionpm@lynn.edu.

Madonna University, School of Business, Livonia, MI 48150-1173. Offers business administration (MBA); international business (MSBA); leadership studies (MSBA); leadership studies in criminal justice (MSBA); quality and operations management (MSBA). Part-time and evening/weekend programs available. Postbaccalaureate distance learning degree programs offered (minimal on-campus study). *Degree requirements:* For master's, thesis (for some programs), foreign language proficiency (international business). *Entrance requirements:* For master's, GMAT, GRE General Test, minimum GPA of 3.0. Electronic applications accepted. *Faculty research:* Management, women in management, future studies.

Maine Maritime Academy, Department of Graduate Studies, Program in Global Supply Chain Management, Castine, ME 04420. Offers MS, Certificate, Diploma. Part-time programs available. *Degree requirements:* For master's, capstone course. *Entrance requirements:* For master's, GMAT or GRE, letters of recommendation. Additional exam requirements/recommendations for international students: Required—TOEFL.

Maine Maritime Academy, Department of Graduate Studies, Program in International Business, Castine, ME 04420. Offers MS, Certificate, Diploma. Part-time programs available. *Degree requirements:* For master's, thesis optional, capstone course. *Entrance requirements:* Additional exam requirements/recommendations for international students: Required—TOEFL.

Manhattanville College, Graduate Programs, Humanities and Social Sciences Programs, Program in International Management, Purchase, NY 10577-2132. Offers MS. Part-time and evening/weekend programs available. *Entrance requirements:* Additional exam requirements/recommendations for international students: Required—TOEFL. *Application deadline:* Applications are processed on a rolling basis. Application fee: $70. *Financial support:* Career-related internships or fieldwork, Federal Work-Study, institutionally sponsored loans, and unspecified assistantships available. Financial award application deadline: 3/1; financial award applicants required to submit FAFSA. *Unit head:* Donald Richards, Dean, School of Graduate and Professional Studies, 914-323-5469, Fax: 914-694-3488, E-mail: gps@mville.edu. *Application contact:* Office of Admissions for Graduate and Professional Studies, 914-323-5418, E-mail: gps@mville.edu.

McGill University, Faculty of Graduate and Postdoctoral Studies, Desautels Faculty of Management, Montréal, QC H3A 2T5, Canada. Offers administration (PhD); entrepreneurial studies (MBA); finance (MBA); general management (Post Master's Certificate); information systems (MBA); international business (exchange program) (MBA); international Master's program in practicing management (MM); management (MBA); management for development (MBA); manufacturing management (MMM); marketing (MBA); operations management (MBA); public accountancy (Diploma); strategic management (MBA); MBA/LL B; MD/MBA.

McKendree University, Graduate Programs, Master of Business Administration Program, Lebanon, IL 62254-1299. Offers business administration (MBA); human resource management (MBA); international business (MBA). Part-time and evening/weekend programs available. Postbaccalaureate distance learning degree programs offered (no on-campus study). *Faculty:* 8 full-time (1 woman), 18 part-time/adjunct (6 women). *Students:* 68 full-time (26 women), 122 part-time (63 women); includes 23 minority (17 African Americans, 1 Asian American or Pacific Islander, 5 Hispanic Americans), 1 international. Average age 34. 80 applicants, 68% accepted, 47 enrolled. In 2009, 37 master's awarded. *Entrance requirements:* For master's, official transcripts from all institutions attended, essay, minimum GPA of 3.0, three references, resume. Additional exam requirements/recommendations for international students: Required—TOEFL. *Application deadline:* Applications are processed on a rolling basis. Application fee: $0. Electronic applications accepted. *Expenses:* Tuition: Full-time $6300; part-time $350 per credit hour. One-time fee: $125. *Financial support:* Applicants required to submit FAFSA. *Unit head:* Dr. Frank Spreng, Director of MBA Program, 618-537-6902, E-mail: fspreng@mckendree.edu. *Application contact:* Patty Aubel, Graduate Admission Counselor, 618-537-6943, Fax: 618-537-6410, E-mail: plaubel@mckendree.edu.

Meritus University, School of Business, Fredericton, NB E3C 2R2, Canada. Offers global management (MBA); health care management (MBA); human resources management (MBA); information technology management (MBA); marketing (MBA); technology management (MBA). Evening/weekend programs available. Postbaccalaureate distance learning degree programs offered (no on-campus study). *Faculty:* 5 full-time (1 woman), 50 part-time/adjunct (15 women). *Students:* 77 full-time (29 women). Average age 35. *Entrance requirements:* For master's, undergraduate degree or comparable equivalent with minimum cumulative GPA of 2.5; minimum equivalent of two years of full-time, post high-school work experience; current employment. Additional exam requirements/recommendations for international students: Required—TOEFL (minimum score 213 computer-based; 79 iBT), IELTS (minimum score 6.5), or TOEIC (minimum score 750) or Berlitz (minimum score 550). *Application deadline:* Applications are processed on a rolling basis. Application fee: $45. Electronic applications accepted. Tuition and fees charges are reported in Canadian dollars. *Expenses:* Tuition: Full-time $14,400 Canadian dollars. Required fees: $720 Canadian dollars. *Unit head:* Dr. Albert K. S. Wong, Program Chair, Business Administration, 604-657-5465, Fax: 602-643-4624, E-mail: albert.wong@staff.meritusu.ca. *Application contact:* Jeremy S. DeMerchant, Enrolment Manager, 506-443-8413, Fax: 602-759-3688, E-mail: jeremy.demerchant@staff.meritusu.ca.

MidAmerica Nazarene University, Graduate Studies in Management, Olathe, KS 66062-1899. Offers management (MBA); organizational administration (MA), including finance, international business, leadership, non-profit. Evening/weekend programs available. *Faculty:* 6 full-time (2 women), 18 part-time/adjunct (7 women). *Students:* 107 full-time (49 women), 7 part-time (3 women); includes 25 minority (18 African Americans, 1 Asian American or Pacific Islander, 6 Hispanic Americans). Average age 36. In 2009, 81 master's awarded. *Entrance requirements:* For master's, mathematical assessment, minimum undergraduate GPA of 3.0, letters of recommendation. Additional exam requirements/recommendations for international students: Required—TOEFL. *Application deadline:* For fall admission, 9/1 priority date for domestic students; for spring admission, 5/1 priority date for domestic students. Applications are processed on a rolling basis. Application fee: $100. Electronic applications accepted. *Financial support:* Application deadline: 5/1. *Faculty research:* Economic development, international finance, business development, employee evaluation. *Unit head:* Dr. Willadee Wehmeyer, Director, 913-971-3276, Fax: 913-791-3409, E-mail: wwehmeye@mnu.edu. *Application contact:* Melanie Sutherland, Administrative Assistant, 913-971-3276, Fax: 913-971-3409, E-mail: mba@mnu.edu.

Milwaukee School of Engineering, Rader School of Business, Program in Marketing and Export Management, Milwaukee, WI 53202-3109. Offers MS. *Faculty:* 1 full-time (0 women), 1 part-time/adjunct (0 women). *Students:* 2 full-time (1 woman), 7 part-time (3 women); includes 1 Asian American or Pacific Islander, 1 Hispanic American. Average age 28. 2 applicants, 100% accepted, 1 enrolled. *Degree requirements:* For master's, thesis optional, thesis defense or capstone project. *Entrance requirements:* For master's, GRE General Test or GMAT, 2 letters of recommendation. Additional exam requirements/recommendations for international students: Recommended—TOEFL (minimum score 550 paper-based; 213 computer-based; 79 iBT), IELTS. *Application deadline:* Applications are processed on a rolling basis. Application fee: $30. Electronic applications accepted. *Expenses:* Tuition: Part-time $603 per credit. *Financial support:* In 2009–10, 6 students received support. Applicants required to submit FAFSA. *Unit head:* Dr. Bruce Thompson, Director, 414-277-7378, Fax: 414-277-7279, E-mail: thomson@msoe.com. *Application contact:* David E. Tietyen, Graduate Admissions Director, 800-332-6763, Fax: 414-277-7475, E-mail: wp@msoe.edu.

Montclair State University, The Graduate School, School of Business, Department of International Business, Montclair, NJ 07043-1624. Offers MBA, Certificate. *Faculty:* 10 full-time (2 women), 1 part-time/adjunct (0 women). *Students:* 14 full-time (7 women), 20 part-time (11 women). Average age 29. 16 applicants, 56% accepted, 8 enrolled. In 2009, 5 master's awarded. *Degree requirements:* For master's, comprehensive project. *Entrance requirements:* For master's, GMAT, 2 letters of recommendation, resume. Additional exam requirements/recommendations for international students: Required—TOEFL (minimum score 83 computer-based), or IELTS. *Application deadline:* For fall admission, 6/1 for international students; for spring admission, 10/1 for international students. Applications are processed on a rolling basis. Application fee: $60. Electronic applications accepted. *Expenses:* Tuition, area resident: Part-time $486.74 per credit. Tuition, state resident: part-time $486.74 per credit. Tuition, nonresident: part-time $751.34 per credit. Tuition and fees vary according to degree level and program. *Financial support:* In 2009–10, 3 research assistantships with full tuition reimbursements (averaging $7,000 per year) were awarded; Federal Work-Study, scholarships/grants, and unspecified assistantships also available. Support available to part-time students. Financial award application deadline: 3/1; financial award applicants required to submit FAFSA. *Unit head:* Dr. Chandana Chakraborty, Head, 973-655-4280. *Application contact:* Amy Aiello, Director of Graduate Admissions and Operations, 973-655-5147, Fax: 973-655-7869, E-mail: graduate.school@montclair.edu.

Monterey Institute of International Studies, Graduate School of International Policy and Management, Fisher International MBA Program, Monterey, CA 93940-2691. Offers MBA. *Accreditation:* AACSB. *Students:* 67 full-time (27 women), 4 part-time (1 woman); includes 13 minority (1 African American, 7 Asian Americans or Pacific Islanders, 5 Hispanic Americans), 15 international. Average age 28. In 2009, 66 master's awarded. *Degree requirements:* For master's, one foreign language, thesis. *Entrance requirements:* For master's, GMAT, minimum GPA of 3.0, proficiency in a foreign language. Additional exam requirements/recommendations for international students: Required—TOEFL (minimum score 550 paper-based; 213 computer-based; 80 iBT). *Application deadline:* For fall admission, 3/15 priority date for domestic students, 3/5 priority date for international students; for spring admission, 10/1 priority date for domestic and international students. Applications are processed on a rolling basis. Application fee: $50. Electronic applications accepted. *Expenses:* Tuition: Full-time $31,000; part-time $1500 per credit. Required fees: $56. *Financial support:* Career-related internships or fieldwork, Federal Work-Study, institutionally sponsored loans, scholarships/grants, tuition waivers (partial), and unspecified assistantships available. Support available to part-time students. Financial award application deadline: 3/15; financial award applicants required to submit FAFSA. *Faculty research:* Cross-cultural consumer behavior, foreign direct investment, marketing and entrepreneurial orientation, political risk analysis and area studies, managing international human resources. *Application contact:* 831-647-4123, Fax: 831-647-6405, E-mail: admit@miis.edu.

See Close-Up on page 465.

Monterey Institute of International Studies, Graduate School of International Policy and Management, Program in International Trade Policy, Monterey, CA 93940-2691. Offers MA. *Students:* 13 full-time (6 women), 3 part-time (1 woman); includes 3 minority (2 African Americans, 1 Asian American or Pacific Islander), 4 international. Average age 27. In 2009, 17 master's awarded. *Degree requirements:* For master's, one foreign language. *Entrance requirements:* For master's, minimum GPA of 3.0, proficiency in a foreign language. Additional exam requirements/recommendations for international students: Required—TOEFL (minimum score 550 paper-based; 213 computer-based; 80 iBT). *Application deadline:* For fall admission, 3/15 priority date for domestic and international students; for spring admission, 10/1 priority date for domestic and international students. Applications are processed on a rolling basis. Application fee: $50. Electronic applications accepted. *Expenses:* Tuition: Full-time $31,000; part-time $1500 per credit. Required fees: $56. *Financial support:* Application deadline: 3/15. *Application contact:* 831-647-4123, Fax: 831-647-6405, E-mail: admit@miis.edu.

National University, Academic Affairs, School of Business and Management, Department of Accounting and Finance, La Jolla, CA 92037-1011. Offers accountancy (MS); corporate and international finance (MS). Part-time and evening/weekend programs available. Postbaccalaureate distance learning degree programs offered (no on-campus study). *Faculty:* 8 full-time (1 woman), 37 part-time/adjunct (10 women). *Students:* 67 full-time (32 women), 68 part-time (27 women); includes 41 minority (10 African Americans, 2 American Indian/Alaska Native, 13 Asian Americans or Pacific Islanders, 16 Hispanic Americans), 23 international. Average age 33. 145 applicants, 100% accepted, 75 enrolled. In 2009, 14 master's awarded. *Degree requirements:* For master's, thesis. *Entrance requirements:* For master's, interview, minimum GPA of 2.5. Additional exam requirements/recommendations for international students: Required—TOEFL (minimum score 550 paper-based; 213 computer-based; 79 iBT), IELTS (minimum score 6). *Application deadline:* Applications are processed on a rolling basis. Application fee: $60 ($65 for international students). Electronic applications accepted. *Expenses:* Tuition: Part-time $338 per quarter hour. *Financial support:* Career-related internships or fieldwork, institutionally sponsored loans, scholarships/grants, and tuition waivers (partial) available. Support available to part-time students. Financial award application deadline: 6/30; financial award applicants required to submit FAFSA. *Unit head:* Prof. Donald A. Schwartz, Chair and Associate Professor, 858-642-8420, Fax: 858-642-8740, E-mail: dschwartz@nu.edu. *Application contact:* Dominick Giovanniello, Associate Regional Dean—San Diego, 800-NAT-UNIV, Fax: 858-541-7792, E-mail: dgiovann@nu.edu.

National University, Academic Affairs, School of Business and Management, Department of Leadership and Business Administration, La Jolla, CA 92037-1011. Offers alternative dispute resolution (MBA); e-business (MBA); financial management (MBA); human resource management (MBA); human resources management (MA); international business (MBA); knowledge management (MS); marketing (MBA); organizational leadership (MBA, MS); technology management (MBA). Part-time and evening/weekend programs available. Postbaccalaureate distance learning degree programs offered (no on-campus study). *Faculty:* 4 full-time (2 women), 22 part-time/adjunct (9 women). *Students:* 95 full-time (56 women), 228 part-time (129 women); includes 63 African Americans, 24 Asian Americans or Pacific Islanders, 61 Hispanic Americans, 6 international. Average age 38. 191 applicants, 100% accepted, 131 enrolled. In 2009, 62 master's awarded. *Degree requirements:* For master's, thesis. *Entrance requirements:* For master's, interview, minimum GPA of 2.5. Additional exam requirements/recommendations for international students: Required—TOEFL (minimum score 550 paper-based; 213 computer-based; 79 iBT), IELTS (minimum score 6). *Application deadline:* Applications are processed on a rolling basis. Application fee: $60 ($65 for international students). Electronic applications accepted. *Expenses:* Tuition: Part-time $338 per quarter hour. *Financial support:* Career-related internships or fieldwork, institutionally sponsored loans, scholarships/grants, and tuition waivers (partial) available. Support available to part-time students. Financial award application deadline: 6/30; financial award applicants required to submit FAFSA. *Unit head:* Dr. George Drops, Chair and Professor, 858-642-8438, Fax: 858-642-8406, E-mail: gdrops@nu.edu. *Application contact:* Dominick Giovanniello, Associate Regional Dean—San Diego, 800-NAT-UNIV, Fax: 858-541-7792, E-mail: dgiovann@nu.edu.

Newman University, School of Business, Wichita, KS 67213-2097. Offers finance (MBA); international business (MBA); leadership (MBA); management (MBA); technology (MBA). Part-time programs available. *Faculty:* 5 full-time (1 woman), 8 part-time/adjunct (2 women). *Students:* 29 full-time (13 women), 105 part-time (52 women); includes 30 minority (9 African Americans, 1 American Indian/Alaska Native, 10 Asian Americans or Pacific Islanders, 10 Hispanic Americans), 23 international. Average age 32. 80 applicants, 76% accepted, 47 enrolled. In 2009, 76 master's awarded. *Degree requirements:* For master's, thesis optional. *Entrance requirements:* For master's, interview; minimum GPA of 3.0; 3 letters of recommendation; course work in algebra, statistics, macroeconomics, and financial accounting. Additional exam requirements/recommendations for international students: Required—TOEFL (minimum score 600 paper-based; 250 computer-based; 100 iBT). *Application deadline:* For fall admission, 8/1 priority date for domestic students, 7/15 priority date for international students; for winter admission, 1/1 priority date for domestic students; for spring admission, 1/1 priority date for domestic students, 11/15 priority date for international students. Applications are processed on a rolling basis. Application fee: $25 ($40 for international students). Electronic applications accepted. *Expenses:* Contact institution. *Financial support:* In 2009–10, 3 students received support. Federal Work-Study available. Financial award application deadline: 8/15; financial award applicants required to submit FAFSA. *Unit head:* Dr. Joe Goetz, Dean of the College of Professional Studies/Director, 316-942-4291 Ext. 2111, Fax: 316-942-4486, E-mail: goetzj@newmanu.edu. *Application contact:* Linda Kay Sabala, Director of Graduate Admissions, 316-942-4291 Ext. 2230, Fax: 316-942-4483, E-mail: sabalal@newmanu.edu.

New Mexico Highlands University, Graduate Studies, School of Business, Las Vegas, NM 87701. Offers business administration (MBA), including government nonprofit management, human resource management, international business, management, management information systems. *Accreditation:* ACBSP. *Degree requirements:* For master's, comprehensive exam, thesis or alternative. *Entrance requirements:* For master's, minimum undergraduate GPA of 3.0. Additional exam requirements/recommendations for international students: Required—TOEFL (minimum score 540 paper-based; 207 computer-based). *Faculty research:* Real estate valuation, studying expert judgments in complex accounting, decision environments, green marketing, environmentalism, marketing research methodology.

New York Institute of Technology, Graduate Division, School of Management, Program in Business Administration, Old Westbury, NY 11568-8000. Offers accounting (Advanced Certificate); business administration (MBA); finance (Advanced Certificate); international business (Advanced Certificate); management of information systems (Advanced Certificate); marketing (Advanced Certificate). Part-time and evening/weekend programs available. *Students:* 599 full-time (262 women), 528 part-time (200 women); includes 51 minority (17 African Americans, 24 Asian Americans or Pacific Islanders, 10 Hispanic Americans), 324 international. Average age 29. In 2009, 691 master's, 7 other advanced degrees awarded. *Degree requirements:* For master's, thesis (for some programs). *Entrance requirements:* For master's, minimum QPA of 2.85. Additional exam requirements/recommendations for international students: Required—TOEFL (minimum score 550 paper-based; 213 computer-based). *Application deadline:* For fall admission, 7/1 priority date for domestic students; for spring admission, 12/1 priority date for domestic students. Applications are processed on a rolling basis. Application fee: $50. Electronic applications accepted. *Expenses:* Tuition: Part-time $825 per credit. *Financial support:* Fellowships, research assistantships with partial tuition reimbursements, institutionally sponsored loans, tuition waivers (full and partial), and unspecified assistantships available. Support available to part-time students. Financial award applicants required to submit FAFSA. *Faculty research:* Instructor performance appraisal; relationship between TOEFL, GMAT, GRE, and performance in foreign students. *Unit head:* Dr. Diamando Afxentiou, Acting Associate Dean,

International Business

New York Institute of Technology (continued)
516-686-3937, Fax: 516-686-7430, E-mail: dafxenti@nyit.edu. *Application contact:* Dr. Jacquelyn Nealon, Vice President for Enrollment Services, 516-686-7925, Fax: 516-686-7597, E-mail: jnealon@nyit.edu.

New York University, Graduate School of Arts and Science, Department of Politics, New York, NY 10012-1019. Offers political campaign management (MA); politics (MA, PhD); JD/MA; MBA/MA. Part-time programs available. *Faculty:* 30 full-time (4 women). *Students:* 186 full-time (92 women), 56 part-time (37 women); includes 27 minority (3 African Americans, 13 Asian Americans or Pacific Islanders, 11 Hispanic Americans), 118 international. Average age 28. 633 applicants, 42% accepted, 97 enrolled. In 2009, 78 master's, 5 doctorates awarded. Terminal master's awarded for partial completion of doctoral program. *Degree requirements:* For master's, one foreign language, thesis or alternative; for doctorate, 2 foreign languages, comprehensive exam, thesis/dissertation. *Entrance requirements:* For master's, GRE General Test; for doctorate, GRE General Test, master's degree in political science, minimum GPA of 2.5. Additional exam requirements/recommendations for international students: Required—TOEFL. *Application deadline:* For fall admission, 12/18 priority date for domestic students. Application fee: $90. *Expenses:* Tuition: Full-time $30,528; part-time $1272 per credit. Required fees: $2177. *Financial support:* Fellowships with tuition reimbursements, teaching assistantships with tuition reimbursements, career-related internships or fieldwork, Federal Work-Study, and institutionally sponsored loans available. Financial award application deadline: 12/18; financial award applicants required to submit FAFSA. *Faculty research:* Comparative politics, democratic theory and practice, rational choice, political economy; international relations. *Unit head:* Michael Gilligan, Director of PhD Program, 212-998-8500, Fax: 212-995-4184, E-mail: politics.phd@nyu.edu. *Application contact:* Shinasi Rama, Director of Master's Program, 212-998-8500, Fax: 212-995-4184, E-mail: politics.masters@nyu.edu.

Northern Kentucky University, Office of Graduate Programs, College of Business, Program in Business Administration, Highland Heights, KY 41099. Offers business administration (MBA); entrepreneurship (Certificate); finance (Certificate); international business (Certificate); marketing (Certificate); project management (Certificate); JD/MBA. *Accreditation:* AACSB. Part-time and evening/weekend programs available. *Students:* 33 full-time (16 women), 155 part-time (63 women); includes 16 minority (9 African Americans, 7 Asian Americans or Pacific Islanders), 7 international. Average age 30. 105 applicants, 65% accepted, 34 enrolled. In 2009, 42 master's, 31 other advanced degrees awarded. *Degree requirements:* For master's, thesis optional. *Entrance requirements:* For master's, GMAT (minimum score 450), minimum GPA of 2.5. Additional exam requirements/recommendations for international students: Required—TOEFL (minimum score 550 paper-based; 213 computer-based; 79 iBT); Recommended—IELTS (minimum score 6.5). *Application deadline:* For fall admission, 8/1 priority date for domestic students, 6/1 priority date for international students; for spring admission, 12/1 priority date for domestic students, 10/1 priority date for international students. Applications are processed on a rolling basis. Application fee: $40. Electronic applications accepted. *Expenses:* Tuition, state resident: full-time $6912; part-time $384 per credit hour. Tuition, nonresident: full-time $12,150; part-time $675 per credit hour. Tuition and fees vary according to course load, program and reciprocity agreements. *Financial support:* Unspecified assistantships available. Financial award applicants required to submit FAFSA. *Unit head:* James Bast, Director of MBA Programs, 859-572-7695, Fax: 859-572-7694, E-mail: mbusiness@nku.edu. *Application contact:* Dr. Peg Griffin, Director of Graduate Programs, 859-572-6934, Fax: 859-572-6670, E-mail: griffinp@nku.edu.

Norwich University, School of Graduate and Continuing Studies, Program in Diplomacy, Northfield, VT 05663. Offers international commerce (MA); international conflict management (MA); international terrorism (MA). Evening/weekend programs available. *Faculty:* 48 part-time/adjunct (8 women). *Students:* 798 full-time (233 women); includes 133 minority (55 African Americans, 23 Asian Americans or Pacific Islanders, 55 Hispanic Americans). Average age 38. 1,112 applicants, 77% accepted. In 2009, 145 master's awarded. *Degree requirements:* For master's, comprehensive exam, thesis optional. *Entrance requirements:* For master's, minimum undergraduate GPA of 2.75. Additional exam requirements/recommendations for international students: Required—TOEFL. *Application deadline:* For fall admission, 8/10 for domestic and international students; for winter admission, 11/7 for domestic and international students; for spring admission, 2/6 for domestic and international students. Application fee: $50. Electronic applications accepted. Full-time tuition and fees vary according to course level and course load. *Financial support:* Scholarships/grants available. Financial award applicants required to submit FAFSA. *Unit head:* Dr. Harold Kearsley, Program Director, 802-485-2730, E-mail: hkearsley@norwich.edu. *Application contact:* Lars Nielsen, Associate Program Director, 802-485-2853, Fax: 802-485-2533, E-mail: lnielsen@norwich.edu.

Nova Southeastern University, H. Wayne Huizenga School of Business and Entrepreneurship, Doctoral Program in Business Administration, Fort Lauderdale, FL 33314-7796. Offers accounting (DBA); decision sciences (DBA); finance (DBA); human resource management (DBA); international business (DBA); management (DBA); marketing (DBA). Part-time and evening/weekend programs available. *Faculty:* 34 full-time (11 women), 2 part-time/adjunct (1 woman). *Students:* 6 full-time (1 woman), 129 part-time (41 women); includes 33 minority (17 African Americans, 6 Asian Americans or Pacific Islanders, 10 Hispanic Americans), 12 international. Average age 47. 58 applicants, 14% accepted, 5 enrolled. In 2009, 32 doctorates awarded. *Degree requirements:* For doctorate, comprehensive exam, thesis/dissertation. *Entrance requirements:* For doctorate, GMAT. Additional exam requirements/recommendations for international students: Required—TOEFL (minimum score 600 paper-based; 250 computer-based; 100 iBT), IELTS (minimum score 7). *Application deadline:* Applications are processed on a rolling basis. Application fee: $50. Electronic applications accepted. *Financial support:* Available to part-time students. Applicants required to submit FAFSA. *Faculty research:* Reputation management, call centers, international social capital, corporate earnings guidance, corporate governance. *Unit head:* Kristie Tetrault, Director of Program Administration, 954-262-5120, Fax: 954-262-3849, E-mail: kristie@huizenga.nova.edu. *Application contact:* Karen Goldberg, Associate Director of Recruitment and Special Events, 954-262-5039, Fax: 954-262-3822, E-mail: karen@huizenga.nova.edu.

Nova Southeastern University, H. Wayne Huizenga School of Business and Entrepreneurship, Program in International Business Administration, Fort Lauderdale, FL 33314-7796. Offers MIBA. Part-time and evening/weekend programs available. Postbaccalaureate distance learning degree programs offered (minimal on-campus study). *Faculty:* 4 full-time (2 women), 6 part-time/adjunct (2 women). *Students:* 21 full-time (16 women), 235 part-time (116 women); includes 162 minority (38 African Americans, 9 Asian Americans or Pacific Islanders, 115 Hispanic Americans), 39 international. Average age 32. 109 applicants, 54% accepted, 43 enrolled. In 2009, 71 master's awarded. *Degree requirements:* For master's, thesis optional. *Entrance requirements:* Additional exam requirements/recommendations for international students: Required—TOEFL (minimum score 550 paper-based; 213 computer-based; 79 iBT), IELTS (minimum score 6). *Application deadline:* For fall admission, 8/15 for domestic and international students; for winter admission, 12/10 for domestic and international students; for spring admission, 2/10 for domestic and international students. Applications are processed on a rolling basis. Application fee: $50. Electronic applications accepted. *Financial support:* Career-related internships or fieldwork, Federal Work-Study, and scholarships/grants available. Support available to part-time students. Financial award applicants required to submit FAFSA. *Unit head:* Steve Harvey, Assistant Dean of Program Administration, 954-262-5047, Fax: 954-262-3829, E-mail: harvey@nsu.nova.edu. *Application contact:* Karen Goldberg, Associate Director of Recruitment and Special Events, 954-262-5039, Fax: 954-262-3822, E-mail: karen@nova.edu.

Oakland University, Graduate Study and Lifelong Learning, School of Business Administration, Department of Management and Marketing, Rochester, MI 48309-4401. Offers business administration (MBA); entrepreneurship (Certificate); general management (Certificate); human resource management (Certificate); international business (Certificate); marketing (Certificate).

Oklahoma City University, Meinders School of Business, Program in Business Administration, Oklahoma City, OK 73106-1402. Offers finance (MBA); health administration (MBA); information technology (MBA); integrated marketing communications (MBA); international business (MBA); marketing (MBA); JD/MBA. *Accreditation:* ACBSP. Part-time and evening/weekend programs available. *Faculty:* 24 full-time (7 women), 11 part-time/adjunct (1 woman). *Students:* 268 full-time (91 women), 180 part-time (62 women); includes 51 minority (20 African Americans, 7 American Indian/Alaska Native, 11 Asian Americans or Pacific Islanders, 13 Hispanic Americans), 257 international. Average age 30. 158 applicants, 90% accepted, 35 enrolled. In 2009, 236 master's awarded. *Degree requirements:* For master's, comprehensive exam. *Entrance requirements:* Additional exam requirements/recommendations for international students: Required—TOEFL (minimum score 560 paper-based; 220 computer-based; 83 iBT). *Application deadline:* For fall admission, 8/20 for domestic students; for spring admission, 1/6 for domestic students. Applications are processed on a rolling basis. Application fee: $50 ($70 for international students). *Expenses:* Tuition: Full-time $15,930; part-time $885 per hour. *Financial support:* Fellowships with partial tuition reimbursements, career-related internships or fieldwork, Federal Work-Study, institutionally sponsored loans, and tuition waivers (partial) available. Support available to part-time students. Financial award application deadline: 8/1. *Faculty research:* Management information systems, international business strategies. *Unit head:* Dr. Mahmood Shandiz, Senior Associate Dean, 405-208-5130, Fax: 405-208-5098, E-mail: mshandiz@okcu.edu. *Application contact:* Michelle Lockhart, Director, Graduate Admissions, 800-633-7242, Fax: 405-208-5916, E-mail: gadmissions@okcu.edu.

Old Dominion University, College of Business and Public Administration, MBA Program, Norfolk, VA 23529. Offers business and economic forecasting (MBA); financial analysis and valuation (MBA); information technology and enterprise integration (MBA); international business (MBA); maritime and port management (MBA); public administration (MBA). *Accreditation:* AACSB. Part-time and evening/weekend programs available. *Faculty:* 66 full-time (15 women), 6 part-time/adjunct (1 woman). *Students:* 81 full-time (27 women), 198 part-time (92 women); includes 46 minority (25 African Americans, 1 American Indian/Alaska Native, 13 Asian Americans or Pacific Islanders, 7 Hispanic Americans), 31 international. Average age 30. 169 applicants, 52% accepted, 61 enrolled. In 2009, 81 master's awarded. *Entrance requirements:* For master's, GMAT, letters of reference, resume, coursework in calculus. Additional exam requirements/recommendations for international students: Required—TOEFL (minimum score 550 paper-based; 213 computer-based; 80 iBT). *Application deadline:* For fall admission, 6/1 priority date for domestic students, 4/15 priority date for international students; for spring admission, 11/1 priority date for domestic students, 10/1 priority date for international students. Applications are processed on a rolling basis. Application fee: $50. Electronic applications accepted. *Expenses:* Tuition, state resident: full-time $8112; part-time $338 per credit. Tuition, nonresident: full-time $20,256; part-time $844 per credit. Required fees: $119 per semester. One-time fee: $50. *Financial support:* In 2009–10, 46 students received support, including 31 research assistantships with partial tuition reimbursements available (averaging $7,000 per year), 3 teaching assistantships with partial tuition reimbursements available (averaging $6,300 per year); career-related internships or fieldwork, scholarships/grants, and unspecified assistantships also available. Support available to part-time students. Financial award application deadline: 2/15; financial award applicants required to submit FAFSA. *Faculty research:* International business, buyer behavior, financial markets, strategy, operations research. *Unit head:* Dr. Bruce Rubin, Graduate Program Director, 757-683-3585, E-mail: mbainfo@odu.edu. *Application contact:* Shanna Wood, MBA Program Manager, 757-683-3585, Fax: 757-683-5750, E-mail: mbainfo@odu.edu.

Oral Roberts University, School of Business, Tulsa, OK 74171. Offers accounting (MBA); entrepreneurship (MBA); finance (MBA); international business (MBA); management (MBA); marketing (MBA); non-profit management (MBA); not for profit management (MNM). *Accreditation:* ACBSP. Part-time programs available. Postbaccalaureate distance learning degree programs offered (minimal on-campus study). *Faculty:* 7 full-time (0 women), 5 part-time/adjunct (4 women). *Students:* 68 full-time (30 women), 55 part-time (27 women); includes 54 minority (32 African Americans, 5 American Indian/Alaska Native, 8 Asian Americans or Pacific Islanders, 9 Hispanic Americans), 3 international. Average age 28. 71 applicants, 94% accepted, 56 enrolled. In 2009, 36 master's awarded. *Degree requirements:* For master's, thesis optional. *Entrance requirements:* For master's, minimum cumulative GPA of 3.0. Additional exam requirements/recommendations for international students: Required—TOEFL (minimum score 550 paper-based; 213 computer-based; 79 iBT). *Application deadline:* For fall admission, 7/1 priority date for domestic and international students; for spring admission, 12/1 priority date for domestic students, 10/15 priority date for international students. Applications are processed on a rolling basis. Application fee: $35. Electronic applications accepted. *Financial support:* In 2009–10, 39 students received support. Federal Work-Study, scholarships/grants, and unspecified assistantships available. Financial award application deadline: 6/1; financial award applicants required to submit FAFSA. *Faculty research:* Social media, international business and marketing. *Unit head:* Dr. Steven Greene, Dean, 918-495-7040, Fax: 918-495-7876, E-mail: businessdean@oru.edu. *Application contact:* Rebecca Gunn, Representative/Recruiter, 918-495-6117, Fax: 918-495-6500, E-mail: gradbusiness@oru.edu.

Pace University, Lubin School of Business, International Business Program, New York, NY 10038. Offers MBA. Part-time and evening/weekend programs available. *Students:* 22 full-time (9 women), 53 part-time (22 women); includes 14 minority (3 African Americans, 8 Asian Americans or Pacific Islanders, 3 Hispanic Americans), 26 international. Average age 27. 117 applicants, 66% accepted, 25 enrolled. In 2009, 11 master's awarded. *Entrance requirements:* For master's, GMAT. Additional exam requirements/recommendations for international students: Required—TOEFL. *Application deadline:* For fall admission, 7/31 priority date for domestic students; for spring admission, 11/30 for domestic students. Applications are processed on a rolling basis. Application fee: $70. Electronic applications accepted. *Expenses:* Tuition: Part-time $954 per credit. Tuition and fees vary according to course load, degree level and program. *Financial support:* Research assistantships, career-related internships or fieldwork and Federal Work-Study available. Support available to part-time students. Financial award applicants required to submit FAFSA. *Unit head:* Dr. Lawrence Bridwell, Chairperson, 914-422-4165. *Application contact:* Susan Ford-Goldschein, Director of Admissions, 212-346-1652, Fax: 212-346-1585, E-mail: gradnyc@pace.edu.

Pacific States University, College of Business, Los Angeles, CA 90006. Offers accounting (MBA); business administration (DBA); finance (MBA); international business (MBA); management of information technology (MBA); real estate management (MBA). Part-time and evening/weekend programs available. Postbaccalaureate distance learning degree programs offered (no on-campus study). *Entrance requirements:* For master's, minimum undergraduate GPA of 2.5 during last 90 hours of course work. Additional exam requirements/recommendations for international students: Required—TOEFL (minimum score 133 computer-based).

Park University, College of Graduate and Professional Studies, Kansas City, MO 54105. Offers adult education (M Ed); at-risk students (M Ed); disaster and emergency management (MPA); educational administration (M Ed); entrepreneurship (MBA); general business (MBA); general education (M Ed); government/business relations (MPA); healthcare/services management (MBA, MPA); international business (MBA); K-12 certification (MAT); management information systems (MBA); management of information systems (MPA); middle school certification (MAT); multi-cultural education (M Ed); nonprofit management (MPA); public management (MPA); school law (M Ed); secondary school certification (MAT); special education (M Ed). Part-time and evening/weekend programs available. Postbaccalaureate distance learning degree programs offered (no on-campus study). *Degree requirements:* For master's, comprehensive exam, thesis (for some programs). *Entrance requirements:* For master's, GRE, GMAT, teacher certification (M Ed). Additional exam requirements/recommendations for international students: Required—TOEFL (minimum score 550 paper-based). Electronic applications accepted. *Faculty research:* Literacy, leadership, brain based research, multicultural education, diversity.

Pepperdine University, Graziadio School of Business and Management, Malibu, CA 90263. Offers applied finance (MS); business administration (MBA); fully-employed (MBA); international business administration (IMBA); management and leadership (MS); organizational

development (MSOD); presidential and key executive business administration (Exec MBA). *Accreditation:* AACSB. Part-time and evening/weekend programs available. *Faculty:* 86 full-time (18 women), 49 part-time/adjunct (12 women). *Students:* 872 full-time (343 women), 804 part-time (357 women); includes 530 minority (76 African Americans, 7 American Indian/Alaska Native, 306 Asian Americans or Pacific Islanders, 141 Hispanic Americans), 162 international. *Entrance requirements:* For master's, GMAT or MAT. Additional exam requirements/recommendations for international students: Required—TOEFL (minimum score 550 paper-based). *Application deadline:* For fall admission, 6/28 for domestic students. Applications are processed on a rolling basis. Application fee: $45. *Expenses:* Contact institution. *Financial support:* Career-related internships or fieldwork, institutionally sponsored loans, scholarships/grants, and unspecified assistantships available. Support available to part-time students. Financial award applicants required to submit FAFSA. *Unit head:* Dr. Linda A. Livingstone, Dean, 310-568-5689, Fax: 310-568-5766, E-mail: linda.livingstone@pepperdine.edu. *Application contact:* Darrell Eriksen, Director of Admission and Student Accounts, 310-568-5525, E-mail: darrell.eriksen@pepperdine.edu.

Philadelphia University, School of Business Administration, Program in Business Administration, Philadelphia, PA 19144. Offers business administration (MBA); finance (MBA); health care management (MBA); international business (MBA); marketing (MBA); MBA/MS. Part-time and evening/weekend programs available. Postbaccalaureate distance learning degree programs offered (no on-campus study). *Entrance requirements:* For master's, GMAT. Additional exam requirements/recommendations for international students: Required—TOEFL (minimum score 550 paper-based; 213 computer-based; 79 iBT).

Polytechnic University of Puerto Rico, Graduate School, Hato Rey, PR 00919. Offers business administration (MBA), including general studies, management of information systems, management of international enterprises; civil engineering (ME, MS); computer engineering (ME, MS); computer science (MS); electrical engineering (ME, MS); engineering management (MEM); environmental management (MEPM); landscape architecture (M Land Arch); manufacturing competitiveness (MMC, MS); manufacturing engineering (ME, MS). Part-time and evening/weekend programs available. *Entrance requirements:* For master's, 3 letters of recommendation.

Pontifical Catholic University of Puerto Rico, College of Business Administration, Program in International Business, Ponce, PR 00717-0777. Offers MBA. Part-time and evening/weekend programs available. *Entrance requirements:* For master's, GRE, interview, minimum GPA of 2.75.

Pontificia Universidad Catolica Madre y Maestra, Graduate School, Santiago, Dominican Republic. Offers administration (M Adm); architecture of interiors (M Arch); architecture of tourist lodgings (M Arch); banking and financial management (M Mgmt); civil law (LL M); construction administration (ME); corporate business law (LL M); criminal procedure law (LL M); environmental engineering (ME, MEE); finance (M Mgmt); history applied to education (M Ed); human resources (EMBA); insurance (M Mgmt); international business (M Mgmt); labor law and Social Security (LL M); logistics management (ME); marketing (M Mgmt); renewable energy (ME); strategic cost management (M Mgmt). *Entrance requirements:* For master's, curriculum vitae, interview.

Portland State University, Graduate Studies, School of Business Administration, Program in International Management, Portland, OR 97207-0751. Offers MIM. Part-time and evening/weekend programs available. *Degree requirements:* For master's, field study trip to China and Japan. *Entrance requirements:* For master's, GMAT, GRE General Test, minimum GPA of 2.75, resume, 2 letters of recommendation. Additional exam requirements/recommendations for international students: Required—TOEFL (minimum score 550 paper-based; 213 computer-based).

Providence College, Graduate Studies, School of Business, Providence, RI 02918. Offers accountancy (MBA); economics (MBA); entrepreneurship (MBA); finance (MBA); international business (MBA); management (MBA); marketing (MBA); not-for-profit (MBA); quantitative (MBA). Part-time and evening/weekend programs available. *Faculty:* 14 full-time (8 women), 7 part-time/adjunct (3 women). *Students:* 63 full-time (18 women), 46 part-time (19 women); includes 4 minority (2 African Americans, 2 Asian Americans or Pacific Islanders), 7 international. Average age 26. 43 applicants, 88% accepted. In 2009, 40 master's awarded. *Degree requirements:* For master's, thesis optional. *Entrance requirements:* For master's, GMAT. Additional exam requirements/recommendations for international students: Required—TOEFL (minimum score 550 paper-based; 213 computer-based; 80 iBT). *Application deadline:* For fall admission, 8/1 priority date for domestic and international students; for spring admission, 12/1 priority date for domestic and international students. Applications are processed on a rolling basis. Application fee: $55. *Expenses:* Contact institution. *Financial support:* In 2009–10, 34 research assistantships with full tuition reimbursements (averaging $8,400 per year) were awarded; Federal Work-Study, institutionally sponsored loans, and unspecified assistantships also available. Support available to part-time students. Financial award application deadline: 8/1; financial award applicants required to submit FAFSA. *Unit head:* Dr. MaryJane Lenon, Director, MBA Program, 401-865-2566, Fax: 401-865-2978, E-mail: mjlenon@providence.edu. *Application contact:* Katherine A. Follett, Administrative Coordinator, 401-865-2333, Fax: 401-865-2978, E-mail: kfollett@providence.edu.

Purdue University, Graduate School, Krannert School of Management, International Master's in Management Program, West Lafayette, IN 47907. Offers MBA. *Faculty:* 12 full-time (3 women), 4 part-time/adjunct (0 women). *Students:* 48 full-time (8 women); includes 2 Asian Americans or Pacific Islanders. Average age 37. 57 applicants, 88% accepted, 46 enrolled. In 2009, 38 master's awarded. *Entrance requirements:* Additional exam requirements/recommendations for international students: Required—TOEFL. *Application deadline:* For fall admission, 12/1 for domestic and international students. Applications are processed on a rolling basis. Application fee: $55. Electronic applications accepted. *Financial support:* Applicants required to submit FAFSA. *Unit head:* Charles R. Johnson, Executive Director, 877-629-0002. *Application contact:* JoAnn Whitford, Director of Admissions, 877-629-0002, E-mail: jwhitfor@purdue.edu.

Quinnipiac University, School of Business, Program in Business Administration, Hamden, CT 06518-1940. Offers chartered financial analyst (MBA); finance (MBA); healthcare management (MBA); information systems management (MBA); international business (MBA); management (MBA); marketing (MBA); JD/MBA. *Accreditation:* AACSB. Part-time and evening/weekend programs available. *Faculty:* 24 full-time (6 women), 12 part-time/adjunct (4 women). *Students:* 83 full-time (30 women), 106 part-time (36 women); includes 11 minority (2 African Americans, 1 American Indian/Alaska Native, 6 Asian Americans or Pacific Islanders, 2 Hispanic Americans), 13 international. Average age 29. 124 applicants, 79% accepted, 77 enrolled. In 2009, 63 master's awarded. *Entrance requirements:* For master's, GMAT, minimum GPA of 3.0. Additional exam requirements/recommendations for international students: Required—TOEFL (minimum score 575 paper-based; 233 computer-based; 90 iBT), IELTS (minimum score 6.5). *Application deadline:* For fall admission, 7/30 priority date for domestic students, 4/30 priority date for international students; for spring admission, 12/15 priority date for domestic students, 9/15 priority date for international students. Applications are processed on a rolling basis. Application fee: $45. Electronic applications accepted. *Expenses:* Tuition: Full-time $16,030; part-time $770 per credit. Required fees: $630; $35 per credit. *Financial support:* In 2009–10, 110 students received support. Federal Work-Study, tuition waivers (partial), and unspecified assistantships available. Support available to part-time students. Financial award application deadline: 4/15; financial award applicants required to submit FAFSA. *Faculty research:* Equity compensation, marketing relationships and public policy, corporate governance, international business, supply chain management. *Unit head:* Kimberly McKeage, MBA Program Director, 203-582-3676. *Application contact:* Jennifer Boutin, 800-462-1944, Fax: 203-582-3443, E-mail: jennifer.boutin@quinnipiac.edu.

Regent's American College London, Webster Graduate School, London, United Kingdom. Offers business (MBA); finance (MS); human resources (MA); information technology management (MA); international business (MA); international non-governmental organizations (MA); international relations (MA); management and leadership (MA); marketing (MA). Part-time programs available.

Regis University, College for Professional Studies, School of Management, Denver, CO 80221-1099. Offers accounting (MS); business administration (MBA); computer information technology (MSOL); executive internal management (Certificate); executive leadership (Certificate); finance (MBA); finance and accounting (MBA); human resource management (MSOL); international business (MBA); marketing (MBA); operations management (MBA); organization leadership (MS); organizational leadership (MSOL); project leadership and management (MSOL, Certificate); project management (Certificate); strategic business (Certificate); strategic human resource (Certificate); technical management (Certificate). Offered at Colorado Springs Campus, Northwest Denver Campus, Southeast Denver Campus, Fort Collins Campus, Broomfield Campus, Henderson (Nevada) Campus, and Summerlin (Nevada) Campus and online. Part-time and evening/weekend programs available. Postbaccalaureate distance learning degree programs offered (no on-campus study). *Degree requirements:* For master's, thesis optional, capstone project. *Entrance requirements:* For master's, GMAT or essays, interview, 2 years of full-time business work experience, resume; for Certificate, GMAT. Additional exam requirements/recommendations for international students: Required—TOEFL, TOEFL or university-based test; Recommended—TWE (minimum score 5). Electronic applications accepted. *Faculty research:* Impact of Info Technology on Small Business Regulation of Accounting, International Project financing, Mineral Development, Delivery of Healthcare to rural indigenos communities.

Rochester Institute of Technology, Graduate Enrollment Services, E. Philip Saunders College of Business, Graduate Business Programs, Program in Management, Rochester, NY 14623-5603. Offers MS. Part-time and evening/weekend programs available. *Students:* 4 full-time (1 woman), 2 part-time (1 woman), 2 international. Average age 27. 34 applicants, 15% accepted, 3 enrolled. In 2009, 1 master's awarded. *Degree requirements:* For master's, comprehensive exam (for some programs), thesis (for some programs). *Entrance requirements:* For master's, GMAT, minimum GPA of 2.5. Additional exam requirements/recommendations for international students: Required—TOEFL (minimum score 580 paper-based; 237 computer-based; 92 iBT), or IELTS (minimum score 7). *Application deadline:* For fall admission, 2/15 priority date for domestic and international students; for winter admission, 11/1 priority date for domestic students, 10/1 priority date for international students; for spring admission, 2/1 priority date for domestic students, 1/1 priority date for international students. Applications are processed on a rolling basis. Application fee: $50. *Expenses:* Tuition: Full-time $31,533; part-time $876 per credit hour. Required fees: $210. *Financial support:* In 2009–10, 2 students received support; research assistantships with partial tuition reimbursements available, teaching assistantships with partial tuition reimbursements available, career-related internships or fieldwork, scholarships/grants, and unspecified assistantships available. Support available to part-time students. Financial award applicants required to submit FAFSA. *Faculty research:* Strategic and managerial issues associated with manufacturing and production systems, total quality management (TQM), technology-based entrepreneurship. *Unit head:* Kathy Ozminkowski, Assistant Dean for Student Services, 585-475-6985, Fax: 585-475-7450, E-mail: kozminkowski@saunders.rit.edu. *Application contact:* Diane Ellison, Assistant Vice President, Graduate Enrollment Services, 585-475-2229, Fax: 585-475-7164, E-mail: gradinfo@rit.edu.

Rollins College, Crummer Graduate School of Business, Winter Park, FL 32789-4499. Offers entrepreneurship (MBA); finance (MBA); international business (MBA); management (MBA); marketing (MBA); operations and technology management (MBA). *Accreditation:* AACSB. Part-time and evening/weekend programs available. Postbaccalaureate distance learning degree programs offered (minimal on-campus study). *Faculty:* 25 full-time (3 women), 8 part-time/adjunct (2 women). *Students:* 277 full-time (105 women), 192 part-time (79 women); includes 95 minority (26 African Americans, 31 Asian Americans or Pacific Islanders, 38 Hispanic Americans), 48 international. Average age 29. 373 applicants, 53% accepted, 140 enrolled. In 2009, 220 master's awarded. *Entrance requirements:* For master's, GMAT. Additional exam requirements/recommendations for international students: Required—TOEFL. *Application deadline:* For fall admission, 6/1 priority date for domestic students; for spring admission, 12/1 for domestic students. Applications are processed on a rolling basis. Application fee: $50. Electronic applications accepted. *Expenses:* Contact institution. *Financial support:* In 2009–10, 95 students received support, including 95 fellowships, 56 research assistantships (averaging $2,400 per year); career-related internships or fieldwork, scholarships/grants, tuition waivers (full), and unspecified assistantships also available. *Faculty research:* Sustainability, world financial markets, international business, market research, strategic marketing. *Unit head:* Dr. Craig M. McAllaster, Dean, 407-646-2249, Fax: 407-646-1550, E-mail: cmcallaster@rollins.edu. *Application contact:* Linda Puritz, Student Admissions Office, 407-646-2405, Fax: 407-646-1550, E-mail: mbaadmissions@rollins.edu.

Roosevelt University, Graduate Division, Walter E. Heller College of Business Administration, Program in International Business, Chicago, IL 60605. Offers MSIB. Part-time and evening/weekend programs available. *Degree requirements:* For master's, one foreign language. *Entrance requirements:* For master's, GMAT.

Rutgers, The State University of New Jersey, Newark, Graduate School, Program in Management, Newark, NJ 07102. Offers accounting (PhD); accounting information systems (PhD); computer information systems (PhD); finance (PhD); information technology (PhD); international business (PhD); management science (PhD); marketing (PhD); organization management (PhD). *Accreditation:* AACSB. *Degree requirements:* For doctorate, thesis/dissertation, cumulative exams. *Entrance requirements:* For doctorate, GMAT or GRE General Test, minimum undergraduate B average. Additional exam requirements/recommendations for international students: Required—TOEFL. Electronic applications accepted. *Faculty research:* Technology management, leadership and teams, consumer behavior, financial and markets, logistics.

Rutgers, The State University of New Jersey, Newark, Rutgers Business School–Newark and New Brunswick, Department of Business Environment, Newark, NJ 07102. Offers MBA. *Entrance requirements:* For master's, GMAT. Additional exam requirements/recommendations for international students: Required—TOEFL.

Rutgers, The State University of New Jersey, Newark, Rutgers Business School–Newark and New Brunswick, Department of Management and Global Business, Newark, NJ 07102. Offers customized concentration (MBA); global business (MBA); management and business strategy (MBA). *Entrance requirements:* For master's, GMAT. Additional exam requirements/recommendations for international students: Required—TOEFL.

Rutgers, The State University of New Jersey, Newark, Rutgers Business School–Newark and New Brunswick, Doctoral Programs in Business, Newark, NJ 07102. Offers accounting (PhD); accounting information systems (PhD); finance (PhD); individualized study (PhD); information technology (PhD); international business (PhD); management science (PhD); organizational management (PhD); supply chain management (PhD).

St. Edward's University, School of Management and Business, Area of Business Administration, Austin, TX 78704. Offers accounting (MBA); business management (MBA); corporate finance (MBA, Certificate); global entrepreneurship (MBA); human resource management (MBA, Certificate); management information systems (MBA, Certificate); marketing (MBA, Certificate); operations management (MBA, Certificate). Part-time and evening/weekend programs available. *Faculty:* 20 full-time (9 women), 13 part-time/adjunct (4 women). *Students:* 29 full-time (16 women), 307 part-time (152 women); includes 116 minority (27 African Americans, 1 American Indian/Alaska Native, 16 Asian Americans or Pacific Islanders, 72 Hispanic Americans), 9 international. Average age 33. 129 applicants, 75% accepted, 74 enrolled. In 2009, 108 master's awarded. *Degree requirements:* For master's, minimum of 24 resident hours. *Entrance requirements:* For master's, GMAT or GRE General Test, minimum GPA of 2.75 in last 60 hours of course work. Additional exam requirements/recommendations for international students: Required—TOEFL (minimum score 550 paper-based; 213 computer-based; 79 iBT) or IELTS (minimum score 6). *Application deadline:* For fall admission, 7/1 for domestic and international

International Business

St. Edward's University (continued)

students; for spring admission, 11/1 for domestic and international students. Applications are processed on a rolling basis. Application fee: $45 ($50 for international students). Electronic applications accepted. *Expenses:* Tuition: Full-time $14,922; part-time $829 per credit hour. Required fees: $50 per trimester. Full-time tuition and fees vary according to course load and program. *Financial support:* In 2009–10, 14 students received support. Scholarships/grants available. *Faculty research:* Operations management, minority entrepreneurship, globalization, professional services marketing. *Unit head:* Dr. Dianne Hill, Director, 512-428-1295, Fax: 512-448-8492, E-mail: dianneh@stedwards.edu. *Application contact:* Kelly Luna, Graduate Admissions Coordinator, 512-233-1697, Fax: 512-428-1032, E-mail: kellyl@stedwards.edu.

St. John's University, The Peter J. Tobin College of Business, Program in International Business, Queens, NY 11439. Offers MBA, Adv C. Part-time and evening/weekend programs available. *Students:* 43 full-time (22 women), 11 part-time (5 women); includes 13 minority (6 African Americans, 2 Asian Americans or Pacific Islanders, 5 Hispanic Americans), 18 international. Average age 26. 70 applicants, 69% accepted, 26 enrolled. In 2009, 19 master's awarded. *Degree requirements:* For master's, comprehensive exam (for some programs), thesis optional. *Entrance requirements:* For master's, GMAT, 2 letters of recommendation, resume; for Adv C, GMAT, 2 letters of recommendation, resume, undergraduate transcripts, essay. Additional exam requirements/recommendations for international students: Required—TOEFL (minimum score 500 paper-based; 173 computer-based; 61 iBT), IELTS (minimum score 5.5). *Application deadline:* For fall admission, 5/1 priority date for domestic and international students; for spring admission, 11/1 priority date for domestic and international students. Applications are processed on a rolling basis. Application fee: $70. Electronic applications accepted. *Expenses:* Contact institution. *Financial support:* Research assistantships, scholarships/grants available. Support available to part-time students. Financial award application deadline: 3/1; financial award applicants required to submit FAFSA. *Unit head:* Dr. Victoria L. Shoaf, Acting Dean, 718-990-6458, E-mail: shoafv@stjohns.edu. *Application contact:* Nicole T. Bryan, Assistant Dean, 718-990-2599, Fax: 718-990-5242, E-mail: tcbgradadmissions@stjohns.edu.

Saint Joseph's University, Erivan K. Haub School of Business, MS Program in International Marketing, Philadelphia, PA 19131. Offers MS. Part-time and evening/weekend programs available. *Students:* 33 full-time (27 women), 11 part-time (6 women); includes 3 minority (1 African American, 1 Asian American or Pacific Islander, 1 Hispanic American), 24 international. Average age 25. In 2009, 19 master's awarded. *Entrance requirements:* For master's, GMAT, 2 letters of recommendation, resume. Additional exam requirements/recommendations for international students: Required—TOEFL (minimum score 550 paper-based; 213 computer-based; 79 iBT) or IELTS (minimum score 6.5). *Application deadline:* For fall admission, 7/15 priority date for domestic students; for spring admission, 11/15 priority date for domestic students. Applications are processed on a rolling basis. Application fee: $35. Electronic applications accepted. *Expenses:* Tuition: Part-time $729 per credit hour. Tuition and fees vary according to degree level and program. *Financial support:* In 2009–10, 2 research assistantships with partial tuition reimbursements (averaging $8,000 per year) were awarded; unspecified assistantships also available. Financial award application deadline: 5/1; financial award applicants required to submit FAFSA. *Faculty research:* Export marketing, global marketing, international marketing research, new product development, emerging markets, international consumer behavior. *Unit head:* Christine Kaczmar-Russo, Director, 610-660-1238, Fax: 610-660-3239, E-mail: ckaczmar@sju.edu. *Application contact:* Christine Kaczmar-Russo, Director, 610-660-1238, Fax: 610-660-3239, E-mail: ckaczmar@sju.edu.

Saint Joseph's University, Erivan K. Haub School of Business, Professional MBA Program, Philadelphia, PA 19131-1395. Offers accounting (MBA); finance (MBA), including finance; general business (MBA); health and medical services administration (MBA); human resource management (MBA); international business (MBA); international marketing (MBA); management (MBA); marketing (MBA); DO/MBA. Part-time and evening/weekend programs available. *Students:* 51 full-time (24 women), 480 part-time (184 women); includes 71 minority (32 African Americans, 1 American Indian/Alaska Native, 30 Asian Americans or Pacific Islanders, 8 Hispanic Americans), 38 international. Average age 30. In 2009, 190 master's awarded. *Entrance requirements:* For master's, GMAT or GRE, 2 letters of recommendation, resume. Additional exam requirements/recommendations for international students: Required—TOEFL (minimum score 550 paper-based; 213 computer-based; 79 iBT) or IELTS (minimum score 6.5). *Application deadline:* For fall admission, 7/15 priority date for domestic students, 4/15 priority date for international students; for spring admission, 11/15 priority date for domestic students, 10/15 priority date for international students. Applications are processed on a rolling basis. Application fee: $35. Electronic applications accepted. *Expenses:* Tuition: Part-time $729 per credit hour. Tuition and fees vary according to degree level and program. *Financial support:* Scholarships/grants and unspecified assistantships available. Financial award application deadline: 5/1. *Unit head:* Adele C. Foley, Associate Dean/Director, Graduate Business Programs, 610-660-1691, Fax: 610-660-1599, E-mail: afoley@sju.edu. *Application contact:* Janine N. Guerra, Esq., Assistant Director, MBA Program, 610-660-1695, Fax: 610-660-1599, E-mail: jguerra@sju.edu.

Saint Louis University, Graduate School, John Cook School of Business, Boeing Institute of International Business, St. Louis, MO 63103-2097. Offers business administration (PhD), including international business and marketing; executive international business (EMIB); international business (MBA). Part-time and evening/weekend programs available. *Degree requirements:* For master's, thesis, study abroad; for doctorate, comprehensive exam, thesis/dissertation. *Entrance requirements:* For master's, GMAT, work experience. Additional exam requirements/recommendations for international students: Required—TOEFL (minimum score 525 paper-based; 194 computer-based). *Expenses:* Contact institution. *Faculty research:* Foreign direct investment, technology transfer, emerging markets, Asian business, Latin American business.

St. Mary's University, Graduate School, Bill Greehey School of Business, MBA Program, San Antonio, TX 78228-8507. Offers finance (MBA); international business (MBA); management (MBA). Part-time and evening/weekend programs available. Postbaccalaureate distance learning degree programs offered (minimal on-campus study). *Degree requirements:* For master's, comprehensive exam. *Entrance requirements:* For master's, GMAT. Additional exam requirements/recommendations for international students: Required—TOEFL (minimum score 570 paper-based; 230 computer-based; 80 iBT). *Expenses:* Tuition: Full-time $8004. Required fees: $536. One-time fee: $5 full-time. Full-time tuition and fees vary according to program.

Saint Mary's University of Minnesota, Schools of Graduate and Professional Programs, Graduate School of Business and Technology, International Business Program, Winona, MN 55987-1399. Offers MA. *Unit head:* Jay Skranka, Director, 507-457-6696, E-mail: jskranka@smumn.edu. *Application contact:* Jami Spitzer, Information Contact, 507-457-7500, E-mail: jspitzer@smumn.edu.

Saint Peter's College, Graduate Business Programs, MBA Program, Jersey City, NJ 07306-5997. Offers finance (MBA); health care administration (MBA); international business (MBA); management (MBA); management information systems (MBA); marketing (MBA); MBA/MS. Part-time and evening/weekend programs available. *Entrance requirements:* Additional exam requirements/recommendations for international students: Required—TOEFL. *Application deadline:* Applications are processed on a rolling basis. Electronic applications accepted. *Expenses:* Tuition: Part-time $971 per credit. *Financial support:* Career-related internships or fieldwork, Federal Work-Study, and institutionally sponsored loans available. *Faculty research:* Finance, health care management, human resource management, international business, management, management information systems, marketing, risk management.

St. Thomas University, School of Business, Department of Management, Miami Gardens, FL 33054-6459. Offers accounting (MBA); general management (MSM, Certificate); health management (MBA, MSM, Certificate); human resource management (MBA, MSM, Certificate); international business (MBA, MIB, MSM, Certificate); justice administration (MSM, Certificate);

management accounting (MSM, Certificate); public management (MSM, Certificate); sports administration (MS). Part-time and evening/weekend programs available. *Degree requirements:* For master's, comprehensive exam. *Entrance requirements:* For master's, interview, minimum GPA of 3.0 or GMAT. Additional exam requirements/recommendations for international students: Required—TOEFL (minimum score 550 paper-based; 213 computer-based; 79 iBT). Electronic applications accepted.

Salem International University, School of Business, Salem, WV 26426-0500. Offers information security (MBA); international business (MBA). Part-time programs available. Postbaccalaureate distance learning degree programs offered (no on-campus study). *Entrance requirements:* For master's, minimum undergraduate GPA of 2.5, course work in business, resume. Additional exam requirements/recommendations for international students: Recommended—TOEFL (minimum score 550 paper-based; 213 computer-based), IELTS (minimum score 6.5). Electronic applications accepted. *Expenses:* Contact institution. *Faculty research:* Organizational behavior strategy, marketing services.

San Diego State University, Graduate and Research Affairs, College of Business Administration, Program in International Business, San Diego, CA 92182. Offers MS. Evening/weekend programs available. *Degree requirements:* For master's, thesis or alternative. *Entrance requirements:* For master's, GMAT, resume, letters of reference. Additional exam requirements/recommendations for international students: Required—TOEFL. Electronic applications accepted. *Faculty research:* International management.

Santa Clara University, Leavey School of Business, Program in Business Administration, Santa Clara, CA 95053. Offers accounting (MBA); entrepreneurship (MBA); executive MBA (EMBA); finance (MBA); food and agribusiness (MBA); international business (MBA); leading people and organizations (MBA); managing technology and innovation (MBA); marketing management (MBA); supply chain management (MBA). *Accreditation:* AACSB. Part-time and evening/weekend programs available. *Students:* 228 full-time (88 women), 838 part-time (265 women); includes 388 minority (17 African Americans, 2 American Indian/Alaska Native, 326 Asian Americans or Pacific Islanders, 43 Hispanic Americans), 218 international. Average age 31. 486 applicants, 77% accepted, 263 enrolled. In 2009, 317 master's awarded. *Degree requirements:* For master's, thesis or alternative. *Entrance requirements:* For master's, GMAT, GRE. Additional exam requirements/recommendations for international students: Required—TOEFL (minimum score 600 paper-based; 250 computer-based; 100 iBT). *Application deadline:* For fall admission, 6/1 for domestic and international students; for spring admission, 1/19 for domestic students, 1/17 for international students. Applications are processed on a rolling basis. Application fee: $75 ($100 for international students). Electronic applications accepted. *Expenses:* Contact institution. *Financial support:* Fellowships with partial tuition reimbursements, research assistantships with partial tuition reimbursements, career-related internships or fieldwork, Federal Work-Study, institutionally sponsored loans, scholarships/grants, health care benefits, and unspecified assistantships available. Support available to part-time students. Financial award applicants required to submit FAFSA. *Unit head:* Elizabeth B. Ford, Senior Assistant Dean, 408-554-2752, Fax: 408-554-4571, E-mail: eford@scu.edu. *Application contact:* Jennifer W. Taylor, Senior Director, 408-554-4539, Fax: 408-554-4571, E-mail: mbaadmissions@scu.edu.

Schiller International University, Graduate Programs, London, Program in International Business, London, United Kingdom. Offers international business (MBA); management of information technology (MBA). Part-time programs available. Postbaccalaureate distance learning degree programs offered (no on-campus study). *Degree requirements:* For master's, thesis optional, GMAT before graduation. *Entrance requirements:* Additional exam requirements/recommendations for international students: Required—TOEFL (minimum score 550 paper-based; 213 computer-based).

Schiller International University, Graduate Programs, London, Program in International Management, London, United Kingdom. Offers MIM. *Accreditation:* ASHA. Part-time programs available. *Degree requirements:* For master's, thesis optional. *Entrance requirements:* Additional exam requirements/recommendations for international students: Required—TOEFL (minimum score 550 paper-based; 213 computer-based).

Schiller International University, MBA Program, Madrid, Spain, Madrid, Spain. Offers international business (MBA). Part-time programs available. *Degree requirements:* For master's, comprehensive exam, thesis optional. *Entrance requirements:* Additional exam requirements/recommendations for international students: Required—TOEFL (minimum score 550 paper-based; 213 computer-based).

Schiller International University, MBA Program Paris, France, Paris, France. Offers international business (MBA). Bilingual French/English MBA available for native French speakers. Part-time and evening/weekend programs available. Postbaccalaureate distance learning degree programs offered (no on-campus study). *Degree requirements:* For master's, comprehensive exam, thesis or alternative. *Entrance requirements:* Additional exam requirements/recommendations for international students: Required—TOEFL (minimum score 550 paper-based; 213 computer-based).

Schiller International University, MBA Programs, Florida, Program in International Business, Largo, FL 33770. Offers MBA. Part-time and evening/weekend programs available. Postbaccalaureate distance learning degree programs offered (no on-campus study). *Degree requirements:* For master's, thesis optional. *Entrance requirements:* Additional exam requirements/recommendations for international students: Required—TOEFL (minimum score 550 paper-based; 213 computer-based).

Schiller International University, MBA Programs, Heidelberg, Germany, Heidelberg, Germany. Offers international business (MBA, MIM); management of information technology (MBA). Part-time and evening/weekend programs available. *Degree requirements:* For master's, thesis optional. *Entrance requirements:* Additional exam requirements/recommendations for international students: Required—TOEFL (minimum score 550 paper-based; 213 computer-based). *Faculty research:* Leadership, international economy, foreign direct investment.

Schiller International University, MBA Program, Strasbourg, France Campus, Strasbourg, France. Offers international business (MBA). Part-time and evening/weekend programs available. Postbaccalaureate distance learning degree programs offered (no on-campus study). *Degree requirements:* For master's, oral comprehensive exam or thesis. *Entrance requirements:* Additional exam requirements/recommendations for international students: Recommended—TOEFL (minimum score 550 paper-based; 213 computer-based).

Seton Hall University, Stillman School of Business, Department of International Business, South Orange, NJ 07079-2697. Offers MBA, Certificate. Part-time and evening/weekend programs available. *Faculty:* 3 full-time (0 women), 3 part-time/adjunct (1 woman). *Students:* 11 full-time (5 women), 6 part-time (2 women); includes 5 minority (3 Asian Americans or Pacific Islanders, 2 Hispanic Americans). Average age 26. 27 applicants, 81% accepted, 17 enrolled. In 2009, 11 master's awarded. *Entrance requirements:* For master's, GMAT, minimum GPA of 3.0; for Certificate, master's degree. Additional exam requirements/recommendations for international students: Required—TOEFL (minimum score 607 paper-based; 254 computer-based; 102 iBT), or IELTS, or Pearson Test of English (PTE). *Application deadline:* For fall admission, 5/31 priority date for domestic students, 3/31 priority date for international students; for spring admission, 10/31 priority date for domestic students. Applications are processed on a rolling basis. Application fee: $75. Electronic applications accepted. *Expenses:* Contact institution. *Financial support:* In 2009–10, research assistantships with full tuition reimbursements (averaging $34,404 per year); career-related internships or fieldwork, Federal Work-Study, scholarships/grants, and unspecified assistantships also available. Support available to part-time students. Financial award application deadline: 6/30; financial award applicants required to submit FAFSA. *Faculty research:* International marketing, Asian financial markets, economics in eastern Europe and accounting in the Middle East. *Unit head:* Dr. Laurence McCarthy, 973-275-2957, Fax: 973-761-9217, E-mail: laurence.mccarthy@shu.edu. *Application

contact: Catherine Bianchi, Director of Graduate Admissions, 973-761-9262, Fax: 973-761-9208, E-mail: catherine.bianchi@shu.edu.

Seton Hall University, Stillman School of Business, Programs in Business Administration, South Orange, NJ 07079-2697. Offers accounting (MBA); finance (MBA); information technology management (MBA); international business (MBA); management (MBA); marketing (MBA); sport management (MBA). Part-time and evening/weekend programs available. *Faculty:* 57 full-time (13 women), 30 part-time/adjunct (3 women). *Students:* 69 full-time (26 women), 217 part-time (91 women); includes 53 minority (11 African Americans, 35 Asian Americans or Pacific Islanders, 7 Hispanic Americans), 38 international. Average age 29. 286 applicants, 70% accepted, 130 enrolled. In 2009, 110 master's awarded. *Degree requirements:* For master's, 20 hours of community service (Social Responsibility Project). *Entrance requirements:* For master's, GMAT, minimum GPA of 3.0. Additional exam requirements/recommendations for international students: Required—TOEFL (minimum score 607 paper-based; 254 computer-based; 102 iBT), or IELTS, or Pearson Test of English (PTE). *Application deadline:* For fall admission, 5/31 priority date for domestic students, 3/31 priority date for international students; for spring admission, 10/31 priority date for domestic students, 4/30 priority date for international students. Applications are processed on a rolling basis. Application fee: $75. Electronic applications accepted. *Financial support:* In 2009–10, research assistantships with full tuition reimbursements (averaging $34,404 per year); career-related internships or fieldwork, Federal Work-Study, scholarships/grants, and unspecified assistantships also available. Support available to part-time students. Financial award application deadline: 6/30; financial award applicants required to submit FAFSA. *Faculty research:* Financial, hedge funds, international business, legal issues, disclosure and branding. *Unit head:* Dr. Joyce A. Strawser, Associate Dean for Undergraduate and MBA Curricula, 973-761-9225, Fax: 973-761-9217, E-mail: strawsjo@shu.edu. *Application contact:* Catherine Bianchi, Director of Graduate Admissions, 973-761-9262, Fax: 973-761-9208, E-mail: catherine.bianchi@shu.edu.

Simon Fraser University, Graduate Studies, Faculty of Business Administration, Burnaby, BC V5A 1S6, Canada. Offers business administration (EMBA, PhD); financial management (MA); general business (MBA); global asset and wealth management (MBA); management of technology/biotechnology (MBA); MBA/MRM. *Accreditation:* AACSB. Postbaccalaureate distance learning degree programs offered. *Degree requirements:* For master's, thesis or written project. *Entrance requirements:* For master's, minimum GPA of 3.0. Additional exam requirements/recommendations for international students: Required—TOEFL. *Expenses:* Contact institution. *Faculty research:* Leadership, marketing and technology, wealth management.

SIT Graduate Institute, Graduate Programs, Master's Programs in Intercultural Service, Leadership, and Management, Brattleboro, VT 05302-0676. Offers conflict transformation (MA); intercultural service, leadership, and management (MA); international education (MA); management (MS); social justice in intercultural relations (MA); sustainable development (MA). Postbaccalaureate distance learning degree programs offered (minimal on-campus study). *Degree requirements:* For master's, one foreign language, thesis. *Entrance requirements:* For master's, 3 letters of reference. Additional exam requirements/recommendations for international students: Required—TOEFL. *Faculty research:* Intercultural communication, conflict resolution, advising and training, world issues, international business.

SIT Graduate Institute, Graduate Programs, Program in Global Management (Oman), Brattleboro, VT 05302-0676. Offers MGM. Program offered in the Sultanate of Oman. Part-time programs available. *Degree requirements:* For master's, capstone project. *Entrance requirements:* Additional exam requirements/recommendations for international students: Required—TOEFL (minimum score of 550 paper-based, 213 computer-based, 79 iBT) or IELTS (minimum score of 6.0).

Southeast Missouri State University, School of Graduate Studies, Harrison College of Business, Cape Girardeau, MO 63701-4799. Offers accounting (MBA); entrepreneurship (MBA); environmental management (MBA); financial management (MBA); general management (MBA); health administration (MBA); industrial management (MBA); international business (MBA); sport management (MBA). *Accreditation:* AACSB. Part-time and evening/weekend programs available. Postbaccalaureate distance learning degree programs offered (no on-campus study). *Degree requirements:* For master's, applied research project. *Entrance requirements:* For master's, GMAT, minimum undergraduate GPA of 2.5. Additional exam requirements/recommendations for international students: Required—TOEFL (minimum score 550 paper-based; 213 computer-based); Recommended—IELTS (minimum score 6). *Expenses:* Tuition, state resident: full-time $4266; part-time $237 per credit hour. Tuition, nonresident: full-time $7506; part-time $417 per credit hour. Required fees: $427; $427. *Faculty research:* Human resources, laws impacting accounting, advertising.

Southern New Hampshire University, School of Business, Manchester, NH 03106-1045. Offers accounting (MS); business administration (MBA, Certificate), including accounting (Certificate), business administration (MBA), finance (Certificate), forensic accounting (Certificate), human resources management (Certificate), international business (Certificate), international sport management (Certificate), leadership of not for profit organizations (Certificate), marketing (Certificate), operations management (Certificate), sport management (Certificate), taxation (Certificate); finance (MS); hospitality and tourism leadership (Certificate); information technology (MS, Certificate); information technology/international business (Certificate); integrated marketing communications (Certificate); international business (MS, DBA); marketing (MS); operations and project management (MS); organizational leadership (MS); project management (Certificate); sport management (MS); MBA/Certificate. *Accreditation:* ACBSP. Part-time and evening/weekend programs available. Postbaccalaureate distance learning degree programs offered (no on-campus study). Terminal master's awarded for partial completion of doctoral program. *Degree requirements:* For master's, one foreign language, comprehensive exam (for some programs), thesis or alternative; for doctorate, one foreign language, comprehensive exam, thesis/dissertation. *Entrance requirements:* For master's, minimum GPA of 2.5; for doctorate, GMAT. Additional exam requirements/recommendations for international students: Required—TOEFL (minimum score 500 paper-based). Electronic applications accepted.

Stevens Institute of Technology, Graduate School, Wesley J. Howe School of Technology Management, Program in Management, Hoboken, NJ 07030. Offers general management (MS); global innovation management (MS); human resource management (MS); information management (MS); project management (MS); technology commercialization (MS); technology management (MS). Part-time programs available. *Degree requirements:* For master's, thesis optional. *Entrance requirements:* For master's, GMAT, GRE General Test. Additional exam requirements/recommendations for international students: Required—TOEFL. Electronic applications accepted. *Expenses:* Tuition: Full-time $9900; part-time $1100 per credit. Required fees: $286 per semester. *Faculty research:* Industrial economics.

Suffolk University, College of Arts and Sciences, Department of Economics, Boston, MA 02108-2770. Offers economic policy (MSEP); economics (MSE, PhD); international economics (MSIE); JD/MSIE. Part-time and evening/weekend programs available. *Faculty:* 13 full-time (3 women). *Students:* 24 full-time (7 women), 15 part-time (12 women); includes 2 minority (both Asian Americans or Pacific Islanders), 17 international. Average age 26. 103 applicants, 62% accepted, 26 enrolled. In 2009, 8 master's awarded. *Degree requirements:* For doctorate, comprehensive exam, thesis/dissertation. *Entrance requirements:* For master's, GRE General Test or GMAT, 2 letters of recommendation, resume; for doctorate, GRE General Test, 3 letters of recommendation. Additional exam requirements/recommendations for international students: Required—TOEFL (minimum score 550 paper-based; 213 computer-based; 80 iBT). *Application deadline:* For fall admission, 6/15 priority date for domestic students, 6/15 for international students; for spring admission, 11/1 priority date for domestic students, 11/1 for international students. Applications are processed on a rolling basis. Application fee: $50. Electronic applications accepted. *Expenses:* Contact institution. *Financial support:* In 2009–10, 32 students received support, including 21 fellowships with full and partial tuition reimbursements available (averaging $15,596 per year); career-related internships or fieldwork, Federal Work-Study, and institutionally sponsored loans also available. Support available to part-time students. Financial award application deadline: 4/1; financial award applicants required to submit FAFSA. *Faculty research:* Trade demands, fair tax, smoking, multinational firms, charitable giving, fair tax. *Unit head:* Dr. David Tuerck, Chairperson, 617-573-8259, Fax: 617-994-4216, E-mail: dtuerck@suffolk.edu. *Application contact:* Judith Reynolds, Director of Graduate Admissions, 617-573-8302, Fax: 617-305-1733, E-mail: grad.admission@suffolk.edu.

Suffolk University, Sawyer Business School, Master of Business Administration Program, Boston, MA 02108-2770. Offers accounting (MBA); business administration (APC); corporate financial executive track (MBA); entrepreneurship (MBA); executive business administration (EMBA); finance (MBA); global business administration (GMBA); health administration (MBA); international business (MBA); marketing (MBA); organizational behavior (MBA); strategic management (MBA); taxation (MBA); JD/MBA; MBA/GDPA; MBA/MHA; MBA/MSA; MBA/MSF; MBA/MST. *Accreditation:* AACSB. Part-time and evening/weekend programs available. Postbaccalaureate distance learning degree programs offered (no on-campus study). *Faculty:* 103 full-time (30 women), 63 part-time/adjunct (19 women). *Students:* 173 full-time (68 women), 406 part-time (178 women); includes 51 minority (16 African Americans, 3 American Indian/Alaska Native, 22 Asian Americans or Pacific Islanders, 10 Hispanic Americans), 90 international. Average age 29. 460 applicants, 72% accepted, 157 enrolled. In 2009, 245 master's awarded. *Entrance requirements:* For master's, GMAT, minimum undergraduate GPA of 2.75 (MBA), 5 years of managerial experience (EMBA). Additional exam requirements/recommendations for international students: Required—TOEFL (minimum score 550 paper-based; 213 computer-based). *Application deadline:* For fall admission, 6/15 priority date for domestic students, 6/15 for international students; for spring admission, 11/1 priority date for domestic students, 11/1 for international students. Applications are processed on a rolling basis. Application fee: $50. Electronic applications accepted. *Expenses:* Tuition: Full-time $33,000; part-time $1100 per credit. Required fees: $20. Tuition and fees vary according to program. *Financial support:* In 2009–10, 284 students received support, including 99 fellowships with full and partial tuition reimbursements available (averaging $13,599 per year); career-related internships or fieldwork, Federal Work-Study, and institutionally sponsored loans also available. Support available to part-time students. Financial award application deadline: 4/1; financial award applicants required to submit FAFSA. *Faculty research:* Foreign investments; career strategies and boundaryless careers; corporate ethics codes; interest rates, inflation, and growth options; innovation and product development performance. *Unit head:* Lillian Hallberg, Assistant Dean of Graduate Programs/Director of MBA Programs, 617-573-8306, E-mail: lhallber@suffolk.edu. *Application contact:* Judith Reynolds, Director of Graduate Admissions, 617-573-8302, Fax: 617-305-1733, E-mail: grad.admission@suffolk.edu.

Taylor University, Master of Business Administration Program, Upland, IN 46989-1001. Offers emerging business strategies (MBA); global leadership (MBA). Part-time programs available. *Faculty:* 1 full-time (0 women), 9 part-time/adjunct (0 women). *Students:* 57 full-time (21 women), 4 part-time (1 woman); includes 3 African Americans, 1 Asian American or Pacific Islander, 2 Hispanic Americans. Average age 36. 55 applicants, 100% accepted, 52 enrolled. In 2009, 27 master's awarded. *Application deadline:* Applications are processed on a rolling basis. Application fee: $100. *Expenses:* Tuition: Full-time $10,800. *Financial support:* In 2009–10, 2 students received support. Applicants required to submit FAFSA. *Unit head:* Dr. Larry Rottmeyer, Graduate Chair, 260-399-1622, E-mail: lrrottmeyer@taylor.edu. *Application contact:* Wendy Speakman, Program Director, 866-471-6062, Fax: 260-492-0452, E-mail: wnspeakman@taylor.edu.

See Display on page 162 and Close-Up on page 257.

Temple University, Graduate School, Fox School of Business, Doctoral Programs in Business, Philadelphia, PA 19122-6096. Offers accounting (PhD); entrepreneurship (PhD); finance (PhD); human resource administration (PhD); international business (PhD); management information systems (PhD); marketing (PhD); risk management and insurance (PhD); statistics (PhD); strategic management (PhD); tourism and sport (PhD). *Accreditation:* AACSB. *Degree requirements:* For doctorate, thesis/dissertation. *Entrance requirements:* For doctorate, GRE General Test, GMAT, minimum GPA of 3.0, master's degree. Additional exam requirements/recommendations for international students: Required—TOEFL (minimum score 600 paper-based; 250 computer-based; 100 iBT), IELTS (minimum score 7.5). Electronic applications accepted.

Temple University, Graduate School, Fox School of Business, MBA Programs, Philadelphia, PA 19122-6096. Offers accounting (MBA); business management (MBA); financial management (MBA); healthcare and life sciences innovation (MBA); human resource management (MBA); international business (IMBA); IT management (MBA); marketing management (MBA); pharmaceutical management (MBA); strategic management (EMBA, MBA). EMBA offered in Philadelphia, PA and Tokyo, Japan. *Accreditation:* AACSB. Part-time and evening/weekend programs available. Postbaccalaureate distance learning degree programs offered (minimal on-campus study). *Entrance requirements:* For master's, GMAT, minimum undergraduate GPA of 3.0. Additional exam requirements/recommendations for international students: Required—TOEFL (minimum score 600 paper-based; 250 computer-based; 100 iBT), IELTS (minimum score 7.5).

Tennessee Technological University, Graduate School, College of Business, Cookeville, TN 38505. Offers accounting (MBA); finance (MBA); human resource management (MBA); international business (MBA); management information systems (MBA); risk management & insurance (MBA). *Accreditation:* AACSB. Part-time and evening/weekend programs available. *Faculty:* 28 full-time (5 women). *Students:* 64 full-time (26 women), 163 part-time (70 women); includes 17 minority (6 African Americans, 8 Asian Americans or Pacific Islanders, 3 Hispanic Americans). Average age 25. 203 applicants, 52% accepted, 75 enrolled. In 2009, 105 master's awarded. *Entrance requirements:* For master's, GMAT. Additional exam requirements/recommendations for international students: Required—TOEFL (minimum score 550 paper-based; 79 iBT), IELTS (minimum score 5.5). *Application deadline:* For fall admission, 8/1 for domestic and international students; for spring admission, 12/1 for domestic students, 10/1 for international students. Application fee: $25 ($30 for international students). Electronic applications accepted. *Expenses:* Tuition, state resident: full-time $7034; part-time $368 per credit hour. *Financial support:* In 2009–10, 5 fellowships (averaging $10,000 per year), 18 research assistantships (averaging $4,000 per year), teaching assistantships (averaging $4,000 per year) were awarded. Support available to part-time students. Financial award application deadline: 4/1. *Unit head:* Dr. Bob G. Wood, Director, 931-372-3600, Fax: 931-372-6249. *Application contact:* Shelia K. Kendrick, Coordinator of Graduate Studies, 931-372-3808, Fax: 931-372-3497, E-mail: skendrick@tntech.edu.

Texas A&M International University, Office of Graduate Studies and Research, College of Business Administration, Division of International Business and Technology Studies, Laredo, TX 78041-1900. Offers information systems (MSIS); international trade (MBA). *Faculty:* 12 full-time (0 women). *Students:* 50 full-time (7 women), 45 part-time (11 women); includes 20 minority (3 African Americans, 2 Asian Americans or Pacific Islanders, 15 Hispanic Americans), 69 international. Average age 28. 133 applicants, 35% accepted, 26 enrolled. In 2009, 42 master's awarded. *Degree requirements:* For master's, thesis (for some programs). *Entrance requirements:* For master's, GMAT or GRE General Test. Additional exam requirements/recommendations for international students: Required—TOEFL (minimum score 550 paper-based; 213 computer-based). *Application deadline:* For fall admission, 4/30 priority date for domestic students; for spring admission, 11/30 for domestic students. Applications are processed on a rolling basis. Application fee: $25. *Financial support:* In 2009–10, 33 students received support; fellowships, Federal Work-Study, institutionally sponsored loans, and scholarships/grants available. Support available to part-time students. *Unit head:* Dr. Ananda Mukhergi, Interim Chair, 956-326-2526, Fax: 956-326-2494, E-mail: max@tamiu.edu. *Application contact:* Imelda Lopez, Graduate Admissions Counselor, 956-326-2485, Fax: 956-326-2459, E-mail: lopez@tamiu.edu.

Texas A&M University–Corpus Christi, Graduate Studies and Research, College of Business, Corpus Christi, TX 78412-5503. Offers accounting (M Acc); health care administration (MBA); international business (MBA). *Accreditation:* AACSB. Part-time and evening/weekend programs

International Business

Texas A&M University–Corpus Christi (continued)

available. *Degree requirements:* For master's, comprehensive exam, thesis (for some programs). *Entrance requirements:* For master's, GMAT. Additional exam requirements/recommendations for international students: Required—TOEFL. Electronic applications accepted.

Texas Christian University, The Neeley School of Business at TCU, Program in International Management, Fort Worth, TX 76129-0002. Offers MIM. Application fee: $75. *Expenses:* Tuition: Full-time $17,640; part-time $980 per credit hour. Tuition and fees vary according to program. *Unit head:* Dr. Bill Cron, Associate Dean, Graduate Programs, 817-257-7531, Fax: 817-257-6431. *Application contact:* Peggy Conway, Director, MBA Admissions, 817-257-7531, Fax: 817-257-6431, E-mail: mbainfo@tcu.edu.

Texas Tech University, Jerry S. Rawls College of Business Administration, Programs in Business Administration, Lubbock, TX 79409. Offers agricultural business (MBA); business administration (IMBA); entrepreneurship (MBA); finance (MBA); general business (MBA); health organization management (MBA); international business (MBA); management and leadership skills (MBA); management information systems (MBA); marketing (MBA); statistics (MBA); JD/MBA; MBA/M Arch; MBA/MA; MBA/MD; MBA/MS; MBA/Pharm D. Part-time and evening/weekend programs available. *Faculty:* 54 full-time (9 women), 5 part-time/adjunct (0 women). *Students:* 59 full-time (15 women), 487 part-time (148 women); includes 107 minority (24 African Americans, 4 American Indian/Alaska Native, 30 Asian Americans or Pacific Islanders, 49 Hispanic Americans), 51 international. Average age 30. 477 applicants, 81% accepted, 302 enrolled. In 2009, 185 degrees awarded. *Degree requirements:* For master's, capstone course. *Entrance requirements:* For master's, GMAT, holistic review of academic credentials. Additional exam requirements/recommendations for international students: Required—TOEFL (minimum score 550 paper-based; 213 computer-based; 79 iBT). *Application deadline:* For fall admission, 4/1 priority date for domestic students, 1/15 priority date for international students; for spring admission, 9/1 priority date for domestic students, 7/15 priority date for international students. Applications are processed on a rolling basis. Application fee: $50 ($75 for international students). Electronic applications accepted. *Expenses:* Tuition, state resident: full-time $5100; part-time $213 per credit hour. Tuition, nonresident: full-time $11,748; part-time $490 per credit hour. Required fees: $2298; $50 per credit hour. $555 per semester. *Financial support:* In 2009–10, 13 research assistantships (averaging $8,000 per year) were awarded; teaching assistantships, career-related internships or fieldwork, Federal Work-Study, scholarships/grants, health care benefits, and unspecified assistantships also available. Support available to part-time students. Financial award applicants required to submit FAFSA. *Unit head:* Dr. W. Jay Conover, Director, 806-742-1546, Fax: 806-742-3958, E-mail: jay.conover@ttu.edu. *Application contact:* Cynthia D. Barnes, Director, Graduate Services Center, 806-742-3184, Fax: 806-742-3958, E-mail: ba_grad@ttu.edu.

Thunderbird School of Global Management, Executive MBA Program–Glendale, Glendale, AZ 85306-6000. Offers global management (MBA). Part-time and evening/weekend programs available. *Faculty:* 47 full-time (13 women). *Students:* 94 part-time (22 women); includes 10 minority (3 Asian Americans or Pacific Islanders, 7 Hispanic Americans), 19 international. Average age 37. In 2009, 48 master's awarded. *Degree requirements:* For master's, one foreign language. *Entrance requirements:* For master's, 8 years of full-time work experience, 3 years of management experience, company sponsorship, mid-management position. *Application deadline:* For fall admission, 6/10 priority date for domestic students, 4/30 priority date for international students. Applications are processed on a rolling basis. Application fee: $125. Electronic applications accepted. *Expenses:* Contact institution. *Financial support:* In 2009–10, 25 students received support. Application deadline: 6/7. *Faculty research:* Management, social enterprise, cross-cultural communication, finance, marketing. *Unit head:* Barbara Carpenter, Associate Vice President, 602-978-7921, Fax: 602-978-7463, E-mail: barbara.carpenter@thunderbird.edu.

Thunderbird School of Global Management, Global MBA—Latin American Managers Program, Glendale, AZ 85306-6000. Offers GMBA. Offered jointly with Instituto Tecnológico y de Estudios Superiores de Monterrey. Part-time and evening/weekend programs available. Postbaccalaureate distance learning degree programs offered. *Faculty:* 47 full-time (13 women). *Students:* 303 part-time (86 women); includes 1 minority (Hispanic American), 291 international. Average age 31. 185 applicants, 72% accepted, 133 enrolled. In 2009, 146 master's awarded. *Entrance requirements:* For master's, GMAT or PAEP (Pruebade Admisiona Estudios Posgrado), minimum GPA of 3.0, 2 years of work experience. Additional exam requirements/recommendations for international students: Required—TOEFL (minimum score 550 paper-based; 213 computer-based; 79 iBT). *Application deadline:* For spring admission, 4/25 priority date for domestic and international students. Application fee: $125. *Expenses:* Contact institution. *Financial support:* In 2009–10, 110 students received support. Scholarships/grants available. Financial award application deadline: 4/30. *Faculty research:* Globalization impact on Latin American business, doing business in Latin America, international marketing in Latin America. *Unit head:* Dr. Bert Valencia, Vice President, 602-978-7534, Fax: 602-978-7729, E-mail: globalmba@thunderbird.edu. *Application contact:* Dr. Bert Valencia, Vice President, 602-978-7534, Fax: 602-978-7729, E-mail: globalmba@thunderbird.edu.

Thunderbird School of Global Management, GMBA—On Demand Program, Glendale, AZ 85306-6000. Offers GMBA. Part-time programs available. Postbaccalaureate distance learning degree programs offered (minimal on-campus study). *Faculty:* 47 full-time (13 women). *Students:* 118 part-time (41 women); includes 5 minority (1 African American, 3 Asian Americans or Pacific Islanders, 1 Hispanic American), 22 international. Average age 32. 96 applicants, 51% accepted, 44 enrolled. In 2009, 68 master's awarded. *Entrance requirements:* For master's, GMAT. Additional exam requirements/recommendations for international students: Required—TOEFL. *Application deadline:* For fall admission, 6/10 for domestic students, 4/30 for international students. Application fee: $125. *Expenses:* Tuition: Full-time $38,970; part-time $1299 per credit. Required fees: $1330. One-time fee: $625 full-time. *Financial support:* In 2009–10, 65 students received support. Scholarships/grants available. Financial award application deadline: 2/15. *Unit head:* Dr. Bert Valencia, Vice President, 602-978-7534, Fax: 602-978-7729, E-mail: globalmba@thunderbird.edu. *Application contact:* Jay Bryant, Director of Admissions, 602-978-7294, Fax: 602-439-5432, E-mail: jay.bryant@thunderbird.edu.

Thunderbird School of Global Management, Master's Programs in Global Management, Glendale, AZ 85306-6000. Offers global affairs and management (MA); global management (MS). *Accreditation:* AACSB. *Faculty:* 47 full-time (13 women). *Students:* 109 full-time (60 women); includes 6 minority (3 Asian Americans or Pacific Islanders, 3 Hispanic Americans), 44 international. 153 applicants, 80% accepted, 69 enrolled. In 2009, 43 master's awarded. *Degree requirements:* For master's, one foreign language. *Entrance requirements:* For master's, GMAT/GRE. Additional exam requirements/recommendations for international students: Required—TOEFL. *Application deadline:* For fall admission, 6/10 for domestic students, 4/30 for international students. Application fee: $125. *Expenses:* Tuition: Full-time $38,970; part-time $1299 per credit. Required fees: $1330. One-time fee: $625 full-time. *Financial support:* Career-related internships or fieldwork, Federal Work-Study, scholarships/grants, and unspecified assistantships available. *Unit head:* Dr. Glenn Fong, Unit Head, 602-978-7156. *Application contact:* Jay Bryant, Director of Admissions, 602-978-7294, Fax: 602-439-5432, E-mail: jay.bryant@thunderbird.edu.

Trinity Western University, School of Graduate Studies, Program in Business Administration, Langley, BC V2Y 1Y1, Canada. Offers international business (MBA); managing the growing enterprise (MBA); non-profit and charitable organization management (MBA). Part-time programs available. Postbaccalaureate distance learning degree programs offered (minimal on-campus study). *Degree requirements:* For master's, thesis or alternative, applied project. *Entrance requirements:* For master's, GMAT (minimum score of 550 recommended). Additional exam requirements/recommendations for international students: Required—TOEFL (minimum score 600 paper-based; 250 computer-based; 100 iBT), IELTS. Electronic applications accepted.

Troy University, Graduate School, College of Business, Program in Management, Troy, AL 36082. Offers healthcare management (MSM); human resources management (MSM); information systems (MSM); international hospitality management (MSM); international management (MSM); leadership and organizational effectiveness (MSM); public management (MS, MSM). *Accreditation:* ACBSP. Evening/weekend programs available. *Students:* 193 full-time (130 women), 575 part-time (374 women); includes 473 minority (417 African Americans, 12 American Indian/Alaska Native, 20 Asian Americans or Pacific Islanders, 24 Hispanic Americans). Average age 35. 275 applicants, 91% accepted. In 2009, 332 master's awarded. *Degree requirements:* For master's, thesis or alternative. *Entrance requirements:* For master's, GMAT (minimum score 500) or GRE General Test (minimum score 900), minimum GPA of 2.5; letter of recommendation. Additional exam requirements/recommendations for international students: Required—TOEFL (minimum score 523 paper-based; 193 computer-based; 70 iBT), IELTS, or ACT Compass ESL (minimum score 270 on Listening, Reading, and Grammar with no individual score below 85 and a minimum score of 8 out of 12 on writing test). *Application deadline:* Applications are processed on a rolling basis. Application fee: $50. Electronic applications accepted. *Expenses:* Contact institution. *Unit head:* Dr. Henry M. Findley, Interim Chair/Professor, 334-670-3271, Fax: 334-670-3599, E-mail: hfindley@troy.edu. *Application contact:* Brenda K. Campbell, Director of Graduate Admissions, 334-670-3178, Fax: 334-670-3733, E-mail: bcamp@troy.edu.

Troy University, Graduate School, College of Education, Program in Teacher Education-Multiple Levels, Troy, AL 36082. Offers alternative 5th year art education (MS); alternative 5th year instrumental (MS); alternative 5th year physical education (MS); alternative 5th year vocal/choral (MS); traditional art education (MS); traditional gifted education (MS); traditional instrumental (MS); traditional physical education (MS); traditional reading specialist (MS); traditional vocal/choral (MS). Part-time and evening/weekend programs available. *Students:* 5 full-time (3 women), 21 part-time (12 women); includes 11 minority (9 African Americans, 1 American Indian/Alaska Native, 1 Asian American or Pacific Islander). Average age 30. 2 applicants, 50% accepted. In 2009, 8 master's awarded. *Degree requirements:* For master's, comprehensive exam, thesis. *Entrance requirements:* For master's, minimum GPA of 2.5. Additional exam requirements/recommendations for international students: Required—TOEFL (minimum score 523 paper-based; 193 computer-based; 70 iBT), IELTS (minimum score 6). *Application deadline:* Applications are processed on a rolling basis. Application fee: $50. Electronic applications accepted. *Financial support:* Available to part-time students. Applicants required to submit FAFSA. *Unit head:* Dr. Marian Parker, Coordinator, 334-670-5661, Fax: 334-670-3548, E-mail: mjparker@troy.edu. *Application contact:* Brenda K. Campbell, Director of Graduate Admissions, 334-670-3178, Fax: 334-670-3733, E-mail: bcamp@troy.edu.

Tufts University, Fletcher School of Law and Diplomacy, Medford, MA 02155. Offers LL M, MA, MAHA, MALD, MIB, PhD, DVM/MA, JD/MALD, MALD/MA, MALD/MBA, MALD/MS, MD/MA. Postbaccalaureate distance learning degree programs offered (minimal on-campus study). *Faculty:* 34 full-time (7 women), 31 part-time/adjunct (8 women). *Students:* 443 full-time (224 women), 7 part-time (4 women); includes 51 minority (6 African Americans, 1 American Indian/Alaska Native, 26 Asian Americans or Pacific Islanders, 18 Hispanic Americans), 165 international. Average age 31. 1,866 applicants, 40% accepted, 292 enrolled. In 2009, 364 master's, 12 doctorates awarded. *Degree requirements:* For master's, one foreign language, thesis; for doctorate, one foreign language, comprehensive exam, thesis/dissertation, dissertation defense. *Entrance requirements:* For master's and doctorate, GMAT or GRE General Test. Additional exam requirements/recommendations for international students: Required—TOEFL (minimum score 600 paper-based; 250 computer-based; 100 iBT), IELTS (minimum score 7). *Application deadline:* For fall admission, 1/15 for domestic and international students; for spring admission, 10/15 for domestic and international students. Application fee: $70. Electronic applications accepted. *Expenses:* Contact institution. *Financial support:* Federal Work-Study, institutionally sponsored loans, scholarships/grants, and tuition waivers (partial) available. Financial award application deadline: 1/15; financial award applicants required to submit FAFSA. *Faculty research:* Negotiation and conflict resolution, international organizations, international business and economic law, security studies, development economics. *Unit head:* Stephen W. Bosworth, Dean, 617-627-3050, Fax: 617-627-3712. *Application contact:* Laurie A. Hurley, E-mail: fletcheradmissions@tufts.edu.

TUI University, College of Business Administration, Program in Business Administration, Cypress, CA 90630. Offers business administration (PhD); conflict and negotiation management (MBA); criminal justice administration (MBA); entrepreneurship (MBA); finance (MBA); general management (MBA); government accounting (MBA); human resource management (MBA); information security and digital assurance management (MBA); information technology management (MBA); international business (MBA); logistics management (MBA); marketing (MBA); project management (MBA); public management (MBA); quality management (MBA); strategic leadership (MBA). Part-time and evening/weekend programs available. Postbaccalaureate distance learning degree programs offered (no on-campus study). *Degree requirements:* For doctorate, comprehensive exam, thesis/dissertation, defense of dissertation. *Entrance requirements:* For master's, minimum GPA of 2.5 (students with GPA 3.0 or greater may transfer up to 30% of graduate level credits); for doctorate, minimum GPA of 3.4, curriculum vitae, course work in research methods or statistics. Additional exam requirements/recommendations for international students: Required—TOEFL. Electronic applications accepted.

Universidad Autonoma de Guadalajara, Graduate Programs, Guadalajara, Mexico. Offers administrative law and justice (LL M); advertising and corporate communications (MA); architecture (M Arch); business (MBA); computational science (MCC); education (Ed M, Ed D); English-Spanish translation (MA); fiscal law (MA); integrated management of digital animation (MA); international business (MIB); international corporate law (LL M); internet technologies (MS); labor health (MS); manufacturing systems (MMS); philosophy (MA, PhD); power electronics (MS); quality systems (MQS); renewable energy (MS); social evaluation of projects (MBA); strategic market research (MBA); teaching mathematics (MA).

Universidad Metropolitana, School of Business Administration, Program in International Business, San Juan, PR 00928-1150. Offers MBA.

Université de Sherbrooke, Faculty of Administration, Program in International Business, Sherbrooke, QC J1K 2R1, Canada. Offers M Sc. *Entrance requirements:* For master's, bachelor's degree. Electronic applications accepted.

Université du Québec, École nationale d'administration publique, Graduate Program in Public Administration, Program in International Administration, Quebec, QC G1K 9E5, Canada. Offers MAP, Diploma. Part-time programs available. *Entrance requirements:* For degree, appropriate bachelor's degree, proficiency in French.

Université Laval, Faculty of Administrative Sciences, Programs in Business Administration, Québec, QC G1K 7P4, Canada. Offers accounting (MBA); agri-food management (MBA); electronic business (MBA, Diploma); factory management and logistics (MBA); finance (MBA); firm management (MBA); geomatic management (MBA); information technology management (MBA); international management (MBA); management (MBA); management accounting (MBA, Diploma); marketing (MBA); modeling and organizational decision (MBA); occupational health and safety management (MBA); pharmacy management (MBA); social and environmental responsibility (MBA); technological entrepreneurship (Diploma). *Accreditation:* AACSB. Part-time and evening/weekend programs available. Postbaccalaureate distance learning degree programs offered (no on-campus study). *Entrance requirements:* For master's and Diploma, knowledge of French and English. Electronic applications accepted.

University at Buffalo, the State University of New York, Graduate School, College of Arts and Sciences, Department of Geography, Buffalo, NY 14260. Offers earth systems science (MA); economic geography and international business and world trade (MA); environmental and earth systems science (MS); environmental modeling and analysis (MA); geographic information science (MA, Certificate); geographic information systems and science (MS); geography (MA, PhD); urban and regional geography (MA); MA/MBA. *Faculty:* 14 full-time (6 women), 2 part-time/adjunct (0 women). *Students:* 63 full-time (16 women), 32 part-time (8 women); includes 31 minority (3 African Americans, 26 Asian Americans or Pacific Islanders, 2 Hispanic Americans), 3 international. Average age 29. 154 applicants, 42% accepted, 24

enrolled. In 2009, 18 master's, 6 doctorates awarded. *Degree requirements:* For master's, thesis (for some programs), project; for doctorate, thesis/dissertation. *Entrance requirements:* For master's, GRE General Test, minimum GPA of 2.9; for doctorate, GRE General Test, minimum GPA of 3.0. Additional exam requirements/recommendations for international students: Required—TOEFL (minimum score 550 paper-based; 213 computer-based; 79 iBT). *Application deadline:* For fall admission, 7/1 priority date for domestic students, 1/10 priority date for international students; for spring admission, 12/1 priority date for domestic students, 10/1 priority date for international students. Applications are processed on a rolling basis. Application fee: $75. Electronic applications accepted. *Financial support:* In 2009–10, 19 students received support, including 6 fellowships with full tuition reimbursements available (averaging $4,333 per year), 14 teaching assistantships with full tuition reimbursements available (averaging $13,361 per year); research assistantships with full tuition reimbursements available, career-related internships or fieldwork, Federal Work-Study, institutionally sponsored loans, traineeships, health care benefits, and unspecified assistantships also available. Financial award application deadline: 1/10. *Faculty research:* International business and world trade, geographic information systems and cartography, transportation, urban and regional analysis, physical and environmental geography. Total annual research expenditures: $944,614. *Unit head:* Dr. Peter Rogerson, Chairman, 716-645-0473, Fax: 716-645-2329, E-mail: rogerson@buffalo.edu. *Application contact:* Betsy Abraham, Graduate Secretary, 716-645-0471, Fax: 716-645-2329, E-mail: babraham@buffalo.edu.

The University of Akron, Graduate School, College of Business Administration, Department of Marketing, Akron, OH 44325. Offers international business (MBA); international business for international executive (MBA); strategic marketing (MBA); JD/MBA. Part-time and evening/weekend programs available. *Faculty:* 9 full-time (2 women), 10 part-time/adjunct (2 women). *Students:* 20 full-time (7 women), 40 part-time (21 women); includes 2 minority (1 African American, 1 Asian American or Pacific Islander), 12 international. Average age 31. 40 applicants, 60% accepted, 16 enrolled. In 2009, 16 master's awarded. *Entrance requirements:* For master's, GMAT, minimum GPA of 2.75, letters of recommendation, resume. Additional exam requirements/recommendations for international students: Required—TOEFL (minimum score 550 paper-based; 213 computer-based; 79 iBT). *Application deadline:* For fall admission, 8/1 for domestic and international students; for spring admission, 12/1 for domestic and international students. Application fee: $30 ($40 for international students). Electronic applications accepted. *Expenses:* Tuition, state resident: full-time $6570; part-time $365 per credit hour. Tuition, nonresident: full-time $11,250; part-time $625 per credit hour. *Financial support:* In 2009–10, 7 research assistantships with full tuition reimbursements were awarded. *Faculty research:* Multi-channel marketing, direct interactive marketing, strategic retailing, marketing strategy and telemarketing. Total annual research expenditures: $38,705. *Unit head:* Dr. Douglas Hausknecht, Interim Chair, 330-972-5798, E-mail: hauskne@uakron.edu. *Application contact:* Dr. Susan Hanlon, Director of Graduate Business Programs, 330-972-7043, Fax: 330-972-6588, E-mail: shanlon@uakron.edu.

The University of Akron, Graduate School, College of Business Administration, Program in International Business, Akron, OH 44325. Offers MBA, JD/MBA. Part-time and evening/weekend programs available. *Students:* 8 full-time (3 women), 18 part-time (11 women); includes 1 minority (Asian American or Pacific Islander), 7 international. Average age 36. 16 applicants, 75% accepted, 8 enrolled. In 2009, 6 master's awarded. *Entrance requirements:* For master's, GMAT, minimum GPA of 2.75, letters of recommendation, resume. Additional exam requirements/recommendations for international students: Required—TOEFL (minimum score 550 paper-based; 213 computer-based; 79 iBT). *Application deadline:* For fall admission, 8/1 for domestic and international students; for spring admission, 12/1 for domestic and international students. Application fee: $30 ($40 for international students). Electronic applications accepted. *Expenses:* Tuition, state resident: full-time $6570; part-time $365 per credit hour. Tuition, nonresident: full-time $11,250; part-time $625 per credit hour. *Financial support:* In 2009–10, 2 research assistantships with full tuition reimbursements, 1 teaching assistantship with tuition reimbursement were awarded. *Unit head:* Dr. Douglas Hausknecht, Head, 330-972-5892. *Application contact:* Dr. Susan Hanlon, Director of Graduate Business Programs, 330-972-7043, Fax: 330-972-6588, E-mail: shanlon@uakron.edu.

University of Alberta, Faculty of Graduate Studies and Research, Program in Business Administration, Edmonton, AB T6G 2E1, Canada. Offers international business (MBA); leisure and sport management (MBA); natural resources and energy (MBA); technology commercialization (MBA); MBA/LL B; MBA/M Ag; MBA/M Eng; MBA/MF; MBA/PhD. *Accreditation:* AACSB. Part-time and evening/weekend programs available. *Faculty:* 77 full-time, 20 part-time/adjunct. *Students:* 131 full-time (56 women), 109 part-time (51 women). Average age 29. 525 applicants, 30% accepted, 90 enrolled. In 2009, 114 master's awarded. *Degree requirements:* For master's, thesis or alternative. *Entrance requirements:* For master's, GMAT. Additional exam requirements/recommendations for international students: Required—TOEFL (minimum score 600 paper-based; 250 computer-based). *Application deadline:* For fall admission, 4/30 priority date for domestic students, 4/30 for international students. Applications are processed on a rolling basis. Application fee: $0. Electronic applications accepted. Tuition and fees charges are reported in Canadian dollars. *Expenses:* Tuition, area resident: Full-time $4626 Canadian dollars; part-time $99.72 Canadian dollars per unit. International tuition: $8216 Canadian dollars full-time. Required fees: $3590 Canadian dollars; $99.72 Canadian dollars per unit. $215 Canadian dollars per term. *Financial support:* Fellowships, research assistantships, teaching assistantships, career-related internships or fieldwork, scholarships/grants, health care benefits, and unspecified assistantships available. *Faculty research:* Natural resources and energy/management and policy/family enterprise/international business/healthcare research management. Total annual research expenditures: $1 million. *Unit head:* Dr. Douglas Olsen, Associate Dean, 780-492-5412, Fax: 780-492-7825. *Application contact:* Joan A. White, Secretary, 780-492-3679, Fax: 780-492-2024, E-mail: mba@ualberta.ca.

The University of British Columbia, Sauder School of Business, Doctoral Program in Commerce and Business Administration, Vancouver, BC V6T 1Z1, Canada. Offers accounting (PhD); finance (PhD); international business (PhD); management information systems (PhD); management science (PhD); marketing (PhD); organizational behavior (PhD); strategy and business economics (PhD); transportation and logistics (PhD); urban land economics (PhD). *Degree requirements:* For doctorate, comprehensive exam, thesis/dissertation. *Entrance requirements:* For doctorate, GMAT or GRE. Additional exam requirements/recommendations for international students: Required—TOEFL (minimum score 600 paper-based; 250 computer-based; 100 iBT). Electronic applications accepted.

University of California, Berkeley, UC Berkeley Extension, International Diploma Programs, Berkeley, CA 94720-1500. Offers business administration (Certificate); finance (Certificate); global business management (Certificate); marketing (Certificate); project management (Certificate). *Unit head:* Diana Wu, Dean, 510-642-4181. *Application contact:* International Diploma Programs, 510-642-2564, E-mail: diploma@unex.berkeley.edu.

University of Chicago, Booth School of Business, Executive MBA Program Asia, Singapore, IL 238466, Singapore. Offers MBA. Part-time programs available. *Faculty:* 144 full-time, 36 part-time/adjunct. *Students:* 200 part-time (41 women). Average age 36. In 2009, 97 master's awarded. *Entrance requirements:* For master's, interview, letter of company support, 3 letters of recommendation, resume. Additional exam requirements/recommendations for international students: Recommended—TOEFL (minimum score 600 paper-based; 250 computer-based). *Application deadline:* For spring admission, 4/1 for domestic and international students. Application fee: $100. Electronic applications accepted. *Expenses:* Contact institution. *Faculty research:* Finance, marketing, international business, general management, strategy. *Unit head:* Glenn Sykes, Managing Director, 65-(68) 356482, Fax: 65-(68) 356483, E-mail: singapore.inquiries@chicagobooth.edu. *Application contact:* Glenn Sykes, Managing Director, 65-(68) 356482, Fax: 65-(68) 356483, E-mail: singapore.inquiries@chicagobooth.edu.

University of Chicago, Booth School of Business, Executive MBA Program Europe, London, IL EC2V 5HA, United Kingdom. Offers MBA. Part-time programs available. *Faculty:* 147 full-time, 29 part-time/adjunct. *Students:* 183 part-time (34 women); includes 2 minority (both Asian Americans or Pacific Islanders), 169 international. Average age 35. In 2009, 84 master's awarded. *Entrance requirements:* For master's, interview, 3 letters of recommendation, letter of company support, resume. Additional exam requirements/recommendations for international students: Recommended—TOEFL (minimum score 600 paper-based; 250 computer-based). *Application deadline:* For spring admission, 4/1 for domestic and international students. Application fee: $100. Electronic applications accepted. *Expenses:* Contact institution. *Faculty research:* Finance, marketing, international business, general management, strategy. *Unit head:* Glenn Sykes, Associate Dean, Europe and Asia Executive MBA Programs, (44) 20-7070-2220, E-mail: glenn.sykes@chicagogbooth.edu. *Application contact:* Arnold Longboy, Managing Director, External Relations and Executive Education, (44) 207 070 2224, E-mail: europeinquiries@chicagobooth.edu.

University of Chicago, Booth School of Business, Executive MBA Program North America, Chicago, IL 60611. Offers MBA. Part-time programs available. *Faculty:* 147 full-time, 29 part-time/adjunct. *Students:* 186 part-time (37 women); includes 68 minority (14 African Americans, 46 Asian Americans or Pacific Islanders, 8 Hispanic Americans), 11 international. Average age 37. *Entrance requirements:* For master's, interview, company-sponsored letter, 3 letters of recommendation, resume. Additional exam requirements/recommendations for international students: Required—TOEFL (minimum score 600 paper-based; 250 computer-based), IELTS. *Application deadline:* For spring admission, 4/1 for domestic students, 3/1 for international students. Application fee: $100. Electronic applications accepted. *Expenses:* Contact institution. *Faculty research:* Finance, marketing, international business, general management, strategy. *Unit head:* Patty Keegan, Managing Director, 312-464-8751, Fax: 312-464-8755, E-mail: patty.keegan@chicagobooth.edu. *Application contact:* Information Contact, 312-464-8750, Fax: 312-464-8755, E-mail: xp@chicagobooth.edu.

University of Chicago, Booth School of Business, International MBA Program, Chicago, IL 60637-1513. Offers IMBA. *Accreditation:* AACSB. *Degree requirements:* For master's, one foreign language, study abroad. *Entrance requirements:* For master's, GMAT, 2 letters of recommendation. Additional exam requirements/recommendations for international students: Required—TOEFL (minimum score 600 paper-based; 250 computer-based), IELTS. Electronic applications accepted.

University of Colorado Denver, Business School, Program in International Business, Denver, CO 80217-3364. Offers MSIB. Part-time and evening/weekend programs available. *Students:* 18 full-time (12 women), 27 part-time (15 women); includes 4 minority (1 Asian American or Pacific Islander, 3 Hispanic Americans), 8 international. 24 applicants, 54% accepted, 9 enrolled. In 2009, 7 master's awarded. *Degree requirements:* For master's, one foreign language. *Entrance requirements:* For master's, GMAT. Additional exam requirements/recommendations for international students: Required—TOEFL (minimum score 525 paper-based; 197 computer-based). *Application deadline:* For fall admission, 6/1 for domestic students, 3/15 for international students; for spring admission, 11/1 priority date for domestic students, 10/1 for international students. Applications are processed on a rolling basis. Application fee: $50 ($75 for international students). Electronic applications accepted. *Financial support:* Federal Work-Study, institutionally sponsored loans, and scholarships/grants available. Support available to part-time students. Financial award application deadline: 4/1; financial award applicants required to submit FAFSA. *Unit head:* Dr. Manuel Serapio, Director, 303-556-5832, Fax: 303-556-5899, E-mail: manuel.serapio@ucdenver.edu. *Application contact:* Shelly Townley, Admissions Coordinator, 303-556-5956, Fax: 303-556-5904, E-mail: shelly.townley@ucdenver.edu.

University of Dallas, Graduate School of Management, Irving, TX 75062-4736. Offers accounting (MBA, MM, MS); business management (MBA, MM); corporate finance (MBA, MM); financial services (MBA); global business (MBA, MM); health services management (MBA, MM); human resource management (MBA, MM); information assurance (MBA, MM, MS); information technology (MBA, MM, MS); information technology service management (MBA, MM, MS); marketing management (MBA, MM); organization development (MBA, MM); project management (MBA, MM); sports and entertainment management (MBA, MM); strategic leadership (MBA, MM); supply chain management (MBA); supply chain management and market logistics (MM). *Accreditation:* ACBSP. Part-time and evening/weekend programs available. Postbaccalaureate distance learning degree programs offered (no on-campus study). *Faculty:* 25 full-time (6 women), 31 part-time/adjunct (6 women). *Students:* 232 full-time (95 women), 923 part-time (365 women); includes 462 minority (184 African Americans, 14 American Indian/Alaska Native, 153 Asian Americans or Pacific Islanders, 111 Hispanic Americans), 184 international. Average age 34. 474 applicants, 85% accepted, 237 enrolled. In 2009, 399 master's awarded. *Entrance requirements:* Additional exam requirements/recommendations for international students: Required—TOEFL. *Application deadline:* Applications are processed on a rolling basis. Application fee: $50. Electronic applications accepted. *Expenses:* Contact institution. *Financial support:* In 2009–10, 399 students received support. Scholarships/grants and unspecified assistantships available. Financial award application deadline: 2/15; financial award applicants required to submit FAFSA. *Unit head:* Alounda Joseph, Director of Enrollment Processes, 972-721-5356, E-mail: admiss@gsm.udallas.edu. *Application contact:* Alounda Joseph, Director of Enrollment Processes, 972-721-5356, E-mail: admiss@gsm.udallas.edu.

University of Dayton, Graduate School, School of Business Administration, Dayton, OH 45469-1300. Offers accounting (MBA); business intelligence (MBA); entrepreneurship (MBA); finance (MBA); international business (MBA); marketing (MBA); MIS (MBA); operations management (MBA); technology-enhanced business/e-commerce (MBA); JD/MBA. *Accreditation:* AACSB. Part-time and evening/weekend programs available. *Faculty:* 29 full-time (8 women), 15 part-time/adjunct (2 women). *Students:* 134 full-time (48 women), 111 part-time (31 women); includes 14 minority (9 African Americans, 3 Asian Americans or Pacific Islanders, 2 Hispanic Americans), 29 international. Average age 29. 179 applicants, 63% accepted, 73 enrolled. In 2009, 102 master's awarded. *Entrance requirements:* For master's, GMAT. Additional exam requirements/recommendations for international students: Required—TOEFL (minimum score 550 paper-based; 213 computer-based; 79 iBT). *Application deadline:* For fall admission, 3/1 priority date for international students; for winter admission, 7/1 priority date for international students; for spring admission, 1/1 priority date for international students. Applications are processed on a rolling basis. Application fee: $0 ($50 for international students). Electronic applications accepted. *Expenses:* Contact institution. *Financial support:* In 2009–10, 13 fellowships with partial tuition reimbursements, 17 research assistantships with full and partial tuition reimbursements (averaging $7,020 per year) were awarded; career-related internships or fieldwork, institutionally sponsored loans, scholarships/grants, health care benefits, and unspecified assistantships also available. Support available to part-time students. Financial award application deadline: 3/15; financial award applicants required to submit FAFSA. *Faculty research:* Management information systems, economics, finance, entrepreneurship, marketing. *Unit head:* Janice M. Glynn, Director, MBA Program, 937-229-3733, Fax: 937-229-3882, E-mail: glynn@udayton.edu. *Application contact:* Jeffrey Carter, Assistant Director, MBA Program, 937-229-3733, Fax: 937-229-3882, E-mail: jeff.carter@notes.udayton.edu.

University of Denver, Daniels College of Business, Programs in International Business/Management, Denver, CO 80208. Offers IMBA, MBA. *Accreditation:* AACSB. *Students:* 49 full-time (16 women), 20 part-time (10 women); includes 7 minority (1 African American, 4 Asian Americans or Pacific Islanders, 2 Hispanic Americans), 4 international. Average age 28. 76 applicants, 67% accepted, 18 enrolled. In 2009, 29 master's awarded. *Entrance requirements:* For master's, GMAT. *Application deadline:* For fall admission, 1/15 priority date for domestic students. Applications are processed on a rolling basis. Application fee: $50. Electronic applications accepted. *Expenses:* Tuition: Full-time $34,596; part-time $961 per quarter hour. Required fees: $4 per quarter hour. Tuition and fees vary according to course load, campus/location and program. *Financial support:* Career-related internships or fieldwork, Federal Work-Study, institutionally sponsored loans, and scholarships/grants available. Support available to part-time students. Financial award application deadline: 2/15. *Unit head:* Dr. Doug Allen, Director, 303-871-2428. *Application contact:* Information Contact, 303-871-3416, E-mail: daniels@du.edu.

International Business

The University of Findlay, Graduate and Professional Studies, College of Business, Findlay, OH 45840-3653. Offers financial management (MBA); human resource management (MBA); international management (MBA); management (MBA); marketing (MBA); public management (MBA). Part-time and evening/weekend programs available. Postbaccalaureate distance learning degree programs offered (no on-campus study). *Degree requirements:* For master's, thesis, cumulative project. *Entrance requirements:* For master's, GMAT, minimum undergraduate GPA of 3.0 in last 64 hours of course work. Additional exam requirements/recommendations for international students: Required—TOEFL (minimum score 550 paper-based; 213 computer-based; 80 iBT). Electronic applications accepted. *Expenses:* Contact institution. *Faculty research:* Health care management, operations and logistics management.

University of Florida, Graduate School, Warrington College of Business Administration, Hough Graduate School of Business, Department of Management, Gainesville, FL 32611. Offers international business (MAIB); management (MS, PhD). *Accreditation:* AACSB. Terminal master's awarded for partial completion of doctoral program. *Degree requirements:* For master's, thesis; for doctorate, thesis/dissertation. *Entrance requirements:* For master's and doctorate, GMAT or GRE General Test, minimum GPA of 3.0. Additional exam requirements/recommendations for international students: Required—TOEFL (minimum score 550 paper-based; 213 computer-based). Electronic applications accepted. *Faculty research:* Organizational behavior, organizational theory, strategy and business policy.

University of Florida, Graduate School, Warrington College of Business Administration, Hough Graduate School of Business, Programs in Business Administration, Gainesville, FL 32611. Offers accounting (MBA); arts administration (MBA); business strategy and public policy (MBA); competitive strategy (MBA); decision and information sciences (MBA); electronic commerce (MBA); finance (MBA); general business (MBA); global management (MBA); Graham-Buffett security analysis (MBA); health administration (MBA); human resources management (MBA); international studies (MBA); Latin American business (MBA); management (MBA); marketing (MBA); sports administration (MBA); JD/MBA; MBA/MS; MBA/PhD; MBA/Pharm D; MD/MBA. *Accreditation:* AACSB. Part-time and evening/weekend programs available. Postbaccalaureate distance learning degree programs offered. *Entrance requirements:* For master's, GMAT, minimum GPA of 3.0, interview. Additional exam requirements/recommendations for international students: Required—TOEFL (minimum score 550 paper-based; 213 computer-based). Electronic applications accepted. *Faculty research:* Accounting, finance, insurance, management, real estate and urban analysis marketing.

University of Florida, Levin College of Law, Gainesville, FL 32611. Offers comparative law (LL M); environmental law (LL M); international taxation (LL M); law (JD); taxation (LL M, SJD). *Accreditation:* ABA. *Faculty:* 77 full-time (37 women), 36 part-time/adjunct (10 women). *Students:* 1,369 full-time (620 women); includes 279 minority (69 African Americans, 8 American Indian/Alaska Native, 77 Asian Americans or Pacific Islanders, 125 Hispanic Americans), 71 international. Average age 24. 3,170 applicants, 25% accepted, 307 enrolled. In 2009, 497 JDs, 1 doctorate awarded. *Degree requirements:* For JD, thesis/dissertation or alternative. *Entrance requirements:* LSAT. Additional exam requirements/recommendations for international students: Required—TOEFL (minimum score 250 computer-based; 100 iBT). *Application deadline:* For fall admission, 1/15 for domestic and international students. Applications are processed on a rolling basis. Application fee: $30. Electronic applications accepted. *Expenses:* Contact institution. *Financial support:* In 2009–10, 299 students received support, including 25 fellowships (averaging $2,400 per year), 30 research assistantships with partial tuition reimbursements available (averaging $4,125 per year); career-related internships or fieldwork, Federal Work-Study, institutionally sponsored loans, scholarships/grants, traineeships, health care benefits, and unspecified assistantships also available. Financial award application deadline: 4/7; financial award applicants required to submit FAFSA. *Faculty research:* Environmental and land use law, taxation, family law, international law, constitutional law. *Unit head:* Robert Jerry, Dean, 352-273-0600, Fax: 352-392-8727, E-mail: jerryr@law.ufl.edu. *Application contact:* Michelle Adorno, Assistant Dean for Admissions, 352-273-0890, Fax: 352-392-4087, E-mail: madorno@law.ufl.edu.

University of Hawaii at Manoa, Graduate Division, Shidler College of Business, Program in Business Administration, Honolulu, HI 96822. Offers Asian business studies (MBA); Chinese business studies (MBA); decision sciences (MBA); entrepreneurship (MBA); finance (MBA); finance and banking (MBA); human resources management (MBA); information management (MBA); information technology (MBA); international business (MBA); Japanese business studies (MBA); marketing (MBA); organizational behavior (MBA); organizational management (MBA); real estate (MBA); student-designed track (MBA). *Accreditation:* AACSB. Part-time and evening/weekend programs available. *Faculty:* 46 full-time (8 women), 9 part-time/adjunct (4 women). *Students:* 259 full-time (90 women), 105 part-time (43 women); includes 123 minority (118 Asian Americans or Pacific Islanders, 5 Hispanic Americans), 119 international. Average age 32. 336 applicants, 52% accepted, 150 enrolled. In 2009, 113 master's awarded. *Degree requirements:* For master's, thesis optional. *Entrance requirements:* For master's, GMAT, minimum GPA of 3.0. Additional exam requirements/recommendations for international students: Required—TOEFL (minimum score 600 paper-based; 250 computer-based; 100 iBT), IELTS (minimum score 7). *Application deadline:* For fall admission, 5/1 for domestic students, 3/1 for international students. Application fee: $60. *Expenses:* Contact institution. *Financial support:* In 2009–10, 24 students received support, including 98 fellowships (averaging $3,481 per year), 3 research assistantships (averaging $16,626 per year). Total annual research expenditures: $427,000. *Application contact:* Tung Bui, Graduate Chair, 808-956-5565, Fax: 808-956-9889, E-mail: tung.bui@hawaii.edu.

University of Hawaii at Manoa, Graduate Division, Shidler College of Business, Program in International Management, Honolulu, HI 96822. Offers Asian finance (PhD); global information technology management (PhD); international accounting (PhD); international marketing (PhD); international organization and strategy (PhD). Part-time programs available. *Students:* 28 full-time (12 women), 5 part-time (0 women); includes 7 minority (all Asian Americans or Pacific Islanders), 17 international. Average age 33. 65 applicants, 18% accepted, 5 enrolled. In 2009, 1 doctorate awarded. *Degree requirements:* For doctorate, comprehensive exam, thesis/dissertation. *Entrance requirements:* For doctorate, GMAT or GRE General Test, minimum GPA of 3.0. Additional exam requirements/recommendations for international students: Required—TOEFL (minimum score 600 paper-based; 250 computer-based; 100 iBT), IELTS (minimum score 7). *Application deadline:* For fall admission, 3/1 for domestic and international students. Application fee: $60. *Expenses:* Contact institution. *Financial support:* In 2009–10, 2 fellowships (averaging $6,945 per year), 21 research assistantships (averaging $17,766 per year) were awarded. *Application contact:* Erica Okada, Graduate Chair, 808-956-6723, Fax: 808-956-6889, E-mail: emokada@hawaii.edu.

University of Houston–Victoria, School of Business Administration, Victoria, TX 77901-4450. Offers accounting (MBA); economic development and entrepreneurship (MS); finance (GMBA, MBA); general business (MBA); international business (MBA); management (GMBA, MBA); marketing (MBA). *Accreditation:* AACSB. Part-time and evening/weekend programs available. Postbaccalaureate distance learning degree programs offered (no on-campus study). *Entrance requirements:* For master's, GMAT. Additional exam requirements/recommendations for international students: Required—TOEFL (minimum score 550 paper-based; 213 computer-based). Electronic applications accepted. *Faculty research:* Economic development, marketing, finance.

University of Kentucky, Graduate School, Patterson School of Diplomacy and International Commerce, Lexington, KY 40506-0027. Offers MA. *Degree requirements:* For master's, one foreign language, comprehensive exam, statistics. *Entrance requirements:* For master's, GRE General Test, minimum undergraduate GPA of 3.0. Additional exam requirements/recommendations for international students: Required—TOEFL (minimum score 550 paper-based; 213 computer-based; 79 iBT). Electronic applications accepted. *Faculty research:* International relations, foreign and defense policy, cross-cultural negotiation, international science and technology, diplomacy, international economics and development, geopolitical modeling.

University of La Verne, College of Business and Public Management, Graduate Programs in Business Administration, La Verne, CA 91750-4443. Offers accounting (MBA); executive management (MBA-EP); finance (MBA, MBA-EP); health services management (MBA); information technology (MBA, MBA-EP); international business (MBA, MBA-EP); leadership (MBA-EP); managed care (MBA); management (MBA, MBA-EP); marketing (MBA, MBA-EP). Part-time and evening/weekend programs available. *Faculty:* 22 full-time (11 women), 41 part-time/adjunct (8 women). *Students:* 409 full-time (213 women), 156 part-time (74 women); includes 371 minority (23 African Americans, 7 American Indian/Alaska Native, 259 Asian Americans or Pacific Islanders, 82 Hispanic Americans), 9 international. Average age 29. In 2009, 356 master's awarded. *Entrance requirements:* For master's, minimum undergraduate GPA of 3.0, 2 letters of recommendation, resume. Additional exam requirements/recommendations for international students: Required—TOEFL (minimum score 550 paper-based; 213 computer-based). *Application deadline:* Applications are processed on a rolling basis. Application fee: $50. *Expenses:* Contact institution. *Financial support:* Career-related internships or fieldwork, institutionally sponsored loans, and scholarships/grants available. Financial award application deadline: 3/2; financial award applicants required to submit FAFSA. *Unit head:* Dr. Abe Helou, Chairperson, 909-593-3511 Ext. 4211, Fax: 909-392-2704, E-mail: ihelou@laverne.edu. *Application contact:* Rina Lazarian, Program and Admission Specialist, 909-593-3511 Ext. 4819, Fax: 909-392-2704, E-mail: cbpm@ulv.edu.

University of Lethbridge, School of Graduate Studies, Lethbridge, AB T1K 3M4, Canada. Offers accounting (MScM); addictions counseling (M Sc); agricultural biotechnology (M Sc); agricultural studies (M Sc, MA); anthropology (MA); archaeology (MA); art (MA, MFA); biochemistry (M Sc); biological sciences (M Sc); biomolecular science (PhD); biosystems and biodiversity (PhD); Canadian studies (MA); chemistry (M Sc); computer science (M Sc); computer science and geographical information science (M Sc); counseling psychology (M Ed); dramatic arts (MA); earth, space, and physical science (PhD); economics (MA); educational leadership (M Ed); English (MA); environmental science (M Sc); evolution and behavior (PhD); exercise science (M Sc); finance (MScM); French (MA); French/German (MA); French/Spanish (MA); general education (M Ed); general management (MScM); geography (M Sc, MA); German (MA); health science (M Sc); health sciences (MA); history (MA); human resource management and labour relations (MScM); individualized multidisciplinary (M Sc, MA); information systems (MScM); international management (MScM); kinesiology (M Sc, MA); management (M Sc, MA); marketing (MScM); mathematics (M Sc); music (M Mus, MA); Native American studies (MA); neuroscience (M Sc, PhD); new media (MA); nursing (M Sc); philosophy (MA); physics (M Sc); policy and strategy (MScM); political science (MA); psychology (M Sc, MA); religious studies (MA); social sciences (MA); sociology (MA); theatre and dramatic arts (MFA); theoretical and computational science (PhD); urban and regional studies (MA); women's studies (MA). Part-time and evening/weekend programs available. *Degree requirements:* For doctorate, comprehensive exam, thesis/dissertation. *Entrance requirements:* For master's, GMAT (M Sc in management), bachelor's degree in related field, minimum GPA of 3.0 during previous 20 graded semester courses, 2 years teaching or related experience (M Ed); for doctorate, master's degree, minimum graduate GPA of 3.5. Additional exam requirements/recommendations for international students: Required—TOEFL. *Faculty research:* Movement and brain plasticity, gibberellin physiology, photosynthesis, carbon cycling, molecular properties of main-group ring components.

University of Maryland University College, Graduate School of Management and Technology, Program in International Management, Adelphi, MD 20783. Offers MIM, Certificate. Offered evenings and weekends only. Part-time and evening/weekend programs available. Postbaccalaureate distance learning degree programs offered (no on-campus study). *Students:* 2 full-time (both women), 250 part-time (139 women); includes 128 minority (90 African Americans, 2 American Indian/Alaska Native, 13 Asian Americans or Pacific Islanders, 23 Hispanic Americans), 8 international. Average age 35. 51 applicants, 100% accepted, 31 enrolled. In 2009, 47 master's, 5 Certificates awarded. *Degree requirements:* For master's, thesis or alternative. *Application deadline:* Applications are processed on a rolling basis. Application fee: $50. Electronic applications accepted. *Expenses:* Tuition, state resident: full-time $7704; part-time $428 per credit hour. Tuition, nonresident: full-time $11,862; part-time $659 per credit hour. *Financial support:* Federal Work-Study and scholarships/grants available. Support available to part-time students. Financial award application deadline: 6/1; financial award applicants required to submit FAFSA. *Unit head:* Dr. Robert Jerome, Director, 240-684-2400, Fax: 240-684-2401, E-mail: rjerome@umuc.edu. *Application contact:* Coordinator, Graduate Admissions, 800-888-UMUC, Fax: 240-684-2151, E-mail: newgrad@umuc.edu.

University of Memphis, Graduate School, Fogelman College of Business and Economics, Program in Business Administration, Memphis, TN 38152. Offers accounting (MBA, PhD); economics (MBA, PhD); executive business administration (MBA); finance (PhD); finance, insurance, and real estate (MBA, MS); international business administration (IMBA); management (MBA, MS, PhD); management information systems (MBA, MS, PhD); management science (MBA); marketing (MBA, MS); marketing and supply chain management (PhD); real estate development (MS); JD/MBA. *Accreditation:* AACSB. *Faculty:* 44 full-time (9 women), 5 part-time/adjunct (0 women). *Students:* 263 full-time (106 women), 181 part-time (66 women); includes 70 minority (46 African Americans, 3 American Indian/Alaska Native, 16 Asian Americans or Pacific Islanders, 5 Hispanic Americans), 109 international. Average age 31. 374 applicants, 73% accepted, 119 enrolled. In 2009, 140 master's, 17 doctorates awarded. *Degree requirements:* For master's, comprehensive exam; for doctorate, comprehensive exam, thesis/dissertation. *Entrance requirements:* For master's, GMAT, resume; for doctorate, GMAT, interview, minimum GPA of 3.4, resume, letter of recommendation. Additional exam requirements/recommendations for international students: Required—TOEFL (minimum score 550 paper-based; 220 computer-based). *Application deadline:* For fall admission, 8/1 for domestic students; for spring admission, 12/1 for domestic students. Application fee: $35 ($60 for international students). *Expenses:* Tuition, state resident: full-time $6246; part-time $347 per credit hour. Tuition, nonresident: full-time $15,894; part-time $883 per credit hour. Required fees: $1160. Full-time tuition and fees vary according to course load, degree level and program. *Financial support:* In 2009–10, 164 students received support; research assistantships with full tuition reimbursements available, teaching assistantships with full tuition reimbursements available, career-related internships or fieldwork, Federal Work-Study, scholarships/grants, and unspecified assistantships available. Financial award application deadline: 2/15; financial award applicants required to submit FAFSA. *Faculty research:* Competitive business strategy, finance microstructures, supply chain management innovations, health care economics, litigation risks and corporate audits. *Unit head:* Rajiv Grover, Dean, 901-678-3759, E-mail: rgrover@memphis.edu. *Application contact:* Dr. Carol V. Danehower, Associate Dean for Programs, 901-678-5402, Fax: 901-678-3579, E-mail: fcbegp@memphis.edu.

University of Miami, Graduate School, School of Business Administration, Program in Business Administration, Coral Gables, FL 33124. Offers accounting (MBA); computer information systems (MBA); executive and professional (MBA), including international business, management; finance (MBA); international business (MBA); management (MBA); management science (MBA); marketing (MBA); professional management (MSPM); JD/MBA; MBA/MSIE. *Accreditation:* AACSB. Evening/weekend programs available. *Degree requirements:* For master's, comprehensive exam. *Entrance requirements:* For master's, GMAT. Additional exam requirements/recommendations for international students: Required—TOEFL (minimum score 550 paper-based; 213 computer-based; 59 iBT). Electronic applications accepted. *Faculty research:* Leadership, e-commerce, supply chain management.

University of Michigan–Dearborn, School of Management, Dearborn, MI 48128-1491. Offers accounting (MBA, MS); finance (MBA, MS); information systems (MS); international business (MBA); management (MBA); management information systems (MBA); marketing (MBA); supply chain management (MBA); MBA/MHSA; MBA/MSE; MBA/MSF. *Accreditation:* AACSB. Part-time and evening/weekend programs available. Postbaccalaureate distance learning degree programs offered (no on-campus study). *Faculty:* 26 full-time (6 women), 8 part-time/adjunct (4 women). *Students:* 73 full-time (30 women), 412 part-time (134 women); includes 65 minority (20 African Americans, 1 American Indian/Alaska Native, 38 Asian Americans or Pacific

Islanders, 6 Hispanic Americans), 76 international. Average age 30. 185 applicants, 56% accepted, 78 enrolled. In 2009, 151 master's awarded. *Entrance requirements:* For master's, GMAT, 2 years of work experience (MBA); course work in computer applications, statistics, and pre-calculus or finite mathematics; 18 credits of accounting course work beyond introductory courses (MS in accounting). Additional exam requirements/recommendations for international students: Required—TOEFL (minimum score 560 paper-based; 220 computer-based; 84 iBT). *Application deadline:* For fall admission, 8/1 priority date for domestic students, 6/1 for international students; for winter admission, 12/1 priority date for domestic students, 10/1 for international students; for spring admission, 4/1 priority date for domestic students, 2/1 for international students. Applications are processed on a rolling basis. Application fee: $60. Electronic applications accepted. *Expenses:* Contact institution. *Financial support:* Career-related internships or fieldwork, Federal Work-Study, and scholarships/grants available. Support available to part-time students. Financial award application deadline: 9/1; financial award applicants required to submit FAFSA. *Faculty research:* Cultural diversity, buyer-supplier relations, error detection in data, economic evolution. *Unit head:* Dr. Kim Schatzel, Dean, 313-593-5248, Fax: 313-271-9835, E-mail: schatzel@umd.umich.edu. *Application contact:* Joan Doherty, Academic Advisor/Counselor, 313-593-5460, Fax: 313-271-9838, E-mail: gradbusiness@umd.umich.edu.

University of New Brunswick Saint John, Faculty of Business, Saint John, NB E2L 4L5, Canada. Offers administration (MBA); electronic commerce (MBA); international business (MBA); natural resource management (MBA). Part-time programs available. *Faculty:* 19 full-time (4 women), 14 part-time/adjunct (8 women). *Students:* 45 full-time (14 women), 18 part-time (8 women). 93 applicants, 78% accepted, 25 enrolled. In 2009, 45 master's awarded. *Entrance requirements:* For master's, GMAT, minimum GPA of 3.0. Additional exam requirements/recommendations for international students: Required—TOEFL (minimum score 580 paper-based; 237 computer-based), IELTS (minimum score 7), TWE (minimum score 4.5). *Application deadline:* For fall admission, 5/15 for domestic and international students. Applications are processed on a rolling basis. Application fee: $100. Electronic applications accepted. *Expenses:* Contact institution. *Financial support:* In 2009–10, 4 students received support. Career-related internships or fieldwork and scholarships/grants available. *Faculty research:* Business use of weblogs and podcasts to communicate, corporate governance, high-involvement work systems, international competitiveness, supply chain management and logistics. *Unit head:* Henryk Sterniczuk, Director of Graduate Studies, 506-648-5573, Fax: 506-648-5574, E-mail: sternicz@unbsj.ca. *Application contact:* Tammy Morin, Secretary, 506-648-5746, Fax: 506-648-5574, E-mail: tmorin@unbsj.ca.

University of New Haven, Graduate School, School of Business, Program in Business Administration, West Haven, CT 06516-1916. Offers accounting (MBA, Certificate), including CPA (MBA); business management (Certificate); business policy and strategy (MBA); finance (MBA), including CFA; global marketing (MBA); human resource management (Certificate); human resources management (MBA); international business (Certificate); marketing (Certificate); sports management (MBA); telecommunications management (Certificate); MBA/MPA. Part-time and evening/weekend programs available. *Faculty:* 26 full-time (3 women), 23 part-time/adjunct (5 women). *Students:* 302 full-time (120 women), 194 part-time (101 women); includes 109 minority (56 African Americans, 3 American Indian/Alaska Native, 28 Asian Americans or Pacific Islanders, 22 Hispanic Americans), 110 international. Average age 31. 372 applicants, 83% accepted, 172 enrolled. In 2009, 194 master's, 31 other advanced degrees awarded. *Degree requirements:* For master's, thesis or alternative. *Entrance requirements:* For master's, GMAT. Additional exam requirements/recommendations for international students: Required—TOEFL (minimum score 520 paper-based; 190 computer-based; 70 iBT), IELTS (minimum score 5.5). *Application deadline:* For fall admission, 5/31 for international students; for winter admission, 10/15 for international students; for spring admission, 1/15 for international students. Applications are processed on a rolling basis. Application fee: $50. Electronic applications accepted. *Expenses:* Contact institution. *Financial support:* Research assistantships with partial tuition reimbursements, teaching assistantships with partial tuition reimbursements, Federal Work-Study, scholarships/grants, health care benefits, tuition waivers, and unspecified assistantships available. Support available to part-time students. Financial award applicants required to submit FAFSA. *Unit head:* Charles Coleman, Chairman, 203-932-7375. *Application contact:* Eloise Gormley, Director of Graduate Admissions, 203-932-7449, Fax: 203-932-7137, E-mail: gradinfo@newhaven.edu.

University of New Mexico, Robert O. Anderson Graduate School of Management, Department of Finance, International, Technology and Entrepreneurship, Albuquerque, NM 87131-1221. Offers finance (MBA); international management (MBA); international management in Latin America (MBA); management of technology (MBA). Part-time and evening/weekend programs available. *Faculty:* 12 full-time (0 women), 5 part-time/adjunct (1 woman). *Students:* 46 full-time (18 women), 28 part-time (9 women); includes 31 minority (1 African American, 2 American Indian/Alaska Native, 10 Asian Americans or Pacific Islanders, 18 Hispanic Americans), 7 international. Average age 30. 30 applicants, 97% accepted, 27 enrolled. In 2009, 43 master's awarded. *Entrance requirements:* For master's, GMAT or GRE (can be waived in some instances). Additional exam requirements/recommendations for international students: Required—TOEFL (minimum score 550 paper-based; 213 computer-based; 79 iBT). *Application deadline:* For fall admission, 4/1 priority date for domestic students, 5/1 for international students; for spring admission, 10/1 priority date for domestic students, 10/1 for international students. Applications are processed on a rolling basis. Application fee: $50. Electronic applications accepted. *Expenses:* Tuition, state resident: full-time $2099; part-time $233.20 per credit hour. Tuition, nonresident: full-time $6650. Required fees: $25 per semester. Tuition and fees vary according to course load, program and reciprocity agreements. *Financial support:* Fellowships, research assistantships, teaching assistantships, career-related internships or fieldwork, Federal Work-Study, scholarships/grants, and unspecified assistantships available. Support available to part-time students. Financial award application deadline: 6/1. *Faculty research:* Corporate finance, investments, management in Latin America, management of technology, entrepreneurship. *Unit head:* Dr. Raul de Gouvea, Chair, 505-277-6471, Fax: 505-277-7108. *Application contact:* Megan Conner, Academic Advisement Manager, 505-277-3290, Fax: 505-277-8436, E-mail: mconner@mgt.unm.edu.

University of Oklahoma, Graduate College, School of International and Area Studies, Norman, OK 73019-0390. Offers international studies (MA), including global affairs, global management. *Faculty:* 17 full-time (5 women), 1 part-time/adjunct (0 women). *Students:* 15 full-time (10 women), 4 part-time (2 women); includes 3 minority (1 Asian American or Pacific Islander, 2 Hispanic Americans). 13 applicants, 69% accepted, 5 enrolled. In 2009, 2 master's awarded. *Degree requirements:* For master's, one foreign language, thesis optional. *Entrance requirements:* For master's, GMAT or GRE. Additional exam requirements/recommendations for international students: Required—TOEFL (minimum score 550 paper-based; 213 computer-based). *Application deadline:* For fall admission, 2/15 for domestic students, 4/1 for international students; for spring admission, 10/15 for domestic students, 9/1 for international students. Applications are processed on a rolling basis. Application fee: $40 ($90 for international students). Electronic applications accepted. *Expenses:* Tuition, state resident: full-time $3744; part-time $156 per credit hour. Tuition, nonresident: full-time $13,577; part-time $565.70 per credit hour. Required fees: $2415; $90.10 per credit hour. *Financial support:* In 2009–10, 19 students received support, including 7 research assistantships (averaging $11,302 per year), 6 teaching assistantships with partial tuition reimbursements available (averaging $13,590 per year); tuition waivers (full) and unspecified assistantships also available. Financial award applicants required to submit FAFSA. *Faculty research:* Political economy, foreign policy, linguistics, environmental affairs, international law. Total annual research expenditures: $379,964. *Unit head:* Mark Fraizer, Director, 405-325-1584, Fax: 405-325-7738, E-mail: markfrazier@ou.edu. *Application contact:* Mitchell Smith, Associate Professor, 405-325-8893, Fax: 405-325-0718, E-mail: mps@ou.edu.

University of Pennsylvania, School of Arts and Sciences and Wharton School, Joseph H. Lauder Institute of Management and International Studies, Philadelphia, PA 19104. Offers international studies (MA); management and international studies (MBA); MBA/MA. Applica-

tions made concurrently and separately to Lauder Institute and Wharton MBA program. *Degree requirements:* For master's, one foreign language, thesis. *Entrance requirements:* For master's, GMAT, advanced proficiency in a non-native language. Additional exam requirements/recommendations for international students: Required—TOEFL. Electronic applications accepted. *Expenses:* Contact institution. *Faculty research:* Finance, marketing, strategy, operations management, multinational management.

University of Phoenix–Atlanta Campus, John Sperling School of Business, College of Graduate Business and Management, Sandy Springs, GA 30350-4153. Offers accounting (MBA); business administration (MBA); global management (MBA); human resources management (MBA, MM); management (MM); marketing (MBA); public administration (MM). Evening/weekend programs available. Postbaccalaureate distance learning degree programs offered. *Degree requirements:* For master's, thesis (for some programs). *Entrance requirements:* For master's, minimum undergraduate GPA of 3.0, 3 years of work experience. Additional exam requirements/recommendations for international students: Required—TOEFL (minimum score 550 paper-based; 213 computer-based; 79 iBT).

University of Phoenix–Augusta Campus, College of Graduate Business and Management, Augusta, GA 30909-4583. Offers accounting (MBA); business administration (MBA); business and management (MBA, MM); global management (MBA); human resources management (MBA, MM); management (MM); marketing (MBA); public administration (MBA, MM). Postbaccalaureate distance learning degree programs offered.

University of Phoenix–Austin Campus, College of Graduate Business and Management, Austin, TX 78759. Offers accounting (MBA); business administration (MBA); business and management (MBA); e-business (MBA); global management (MBA); human resources management (MBA, MM); management (MM); marketing (MBA); public administration (MBA). Postbaccalaureate distance learning degree programs offered.

University of Phoenix–Bay Area Campus, John Sperling School of Business, College of Graduate Business and Management, Pleasanton, CA 94588-3677. Offers accounting (MBA); business administration (MBA); global management (MBA); human resources management (MBA, MM); marketing (MBA); public administration (MBA, MM). Evening/weekend programs available. Postbaccalaureate distance learning degree programs offered (no on-campus study). *Degree requirements:* For master's, thesis (for some programs). *Entrance requirements:* For master's, minimum undergraduate GPA of 3.0, 3 years of work experience. Additional exam requirements/recommendations for international students: Required—TOEFL (minimum score 550 paper-based; 213 computer-based; 79 iBT). Electronic applications accepted.

University of Phoenix–Birmingham Campus, College of Graduate Business and Management, Birmingham, AL 35244. Offers accounting (MBA); business administration (MBA); global management (MBA); human resources management (MBA, MM); management (MM); marketing (MBA); public administration (MM).

University of Phoenix–Boston Campus, John Sperling School of Business, College of Graduate Business and Management, Braintree, MA 02184-4949. Offers administration (MBA); global management (MBA). Evening/weekend programs available. *Degree requirements:* For master's, thesis (for some programs). *Entrance requirements:* For master's, 3 years of work experience, minimum undergraduate GPA of 3.0. Additional exam requirements/recommendations for international students: Required—TOEFL (minimum score 550 paper-based; 213 computer-based; 79 iBT).

University of Phoenix–Central Florida Campus, John Sperling School of Business, College of Graduate Business and Management, Maitland, FL 32751-7057. Offers accounting (MBA); business administration (MBA); business and management (MM); global management (MBA); human resources management (MBA, MM); management (MM); marketing (MBA); public administration (MBA, MM). Evening/weekend programs available. *Degree requirements:* For master's, thesis (for some programs). *Entrance requirements:* For master's, minimum undergraduate GPA of 3.0, 3 years work experience. Additional exam requirements/recommendations for international students: Required—TOEFL (minimum score 550 paper-based; 213 computer-based; 79 iBT). Electronic applications accepted.

University of Phoenix–Central Valley Campus, College of Graduate Business and Management, Fresno, CA 93720-1562. Offers accounting (MBA); business administration (MBA); global management (MBA); human resources management (MBA, MM); management (MM); marketing (MBA); public administration (MBA, MM).

University of Phoenix–Charlotte Campus, John Sperling School of Business, College of Graduate Business and Management, Charlotte, NC 28273-3409. Offers accounting (MBA); business administration (MBA); global management (MBA). Evening/weekend programs available. *Degree requirements:* For master's, thesis (for some programs). *Entrance requirements:* For master's, minimum undergraduate GPA of 3.0, 3 years work experience. Additional exam requirements/recommendations for international students: Required—TOEFL (minimum score 550 paper-based; 213 computer-based; 79 iBT). Electronic applications accepted.

University of Phoenix–Chattanooga Campus, College of Graduate Business and Management, Chattanooga, TN 37421-3707. Offers accounting (MBA); business administration (MBA); business and management (MBA); global management (MBA); human resources management (MBA, MM); management (MM); marketing (MBA); public administration (MBA, MM). Postbaccalaureate distance learning degree programs offered.

University of Phoenix–Cheyenne Campus, College of Graduate Business and Management, Cheyenne, WY 82009. Offers global management (MBA); human resources management (MBA, MM); management (MM); marketing (MBA); public administration (MBA, MM). Postbaccalaureate distance learning degree programs offered.

University of Phoenix–Chicago Campus, John Sperling School of Business, College of Graduate Business and Management, Schaumburg, IL 60173-4399. Offers business administration (MBA); global management (MBA); human resources management (MBA); information systems (MIS); management (MM). Evening/weekend programs available. *Degree requirements:* For master's, thesis (for some programs). *Entrance requirements:* For master's, minimum undergraduate GPA of 3.0, 3 years of work experience. Additional exam requirements/recommendations for international students: Required—TOEFL (minimum score 550 paper-based; 213 computer-based; 79 iBT). Electronic applications accepted.

University of Phoenix–Cincinnati Campus, John Sperling School of Business, College of Graduate Business and Management, West Chester, OH 45069-4875. Offers accounting (MBA); business administration (MBA); global management (MBA); human resources management (MBA, MM); management (MM); marketing (MBA); public administration (MM). Evening/weekend programs available. *Degree requirements:* For master's, thesis (for some programs). *Entrance requirements:* For master's, minimum undergraduate GPA of 3.0, 3 years of work experience. Additional exam requirements/recommendations for international students: Required—TOEFL (minimum score 550 paper-based; 213 computer-based; 79 iBT). Electronic applications accepted.

University of Phoenix–Cleveland Campus, John Sperling School of Business, College of Graduate Business and Management, Independence, OH 44131-2194. Offers accounting (MBA); business administration (MBA); global management (MBA); human resources management (MBA, MM); management (MM); marketing (MBA); public administration (MBA, MM). Evening/weekend programs available. Postbaccalaureate distance learning degree programs offered (no on-campus study). *Degree requirements:* For master's, thesis (for some programs). *Entrance requirements:* For master's, minimum undergraduate GPA of 3.0, 3 years of work experience. Additional exam requirements/recommendations for international students: Required—TOEFL (minimum score 550 paper-based; 213 computer-based; 79 iBT). Electronic applications accepted.

International Business

University of Phoenix–Columbus Georgia Campus, John Sperling School of Business, College of Graduate Business and Management, Columbus, GA 31904-6321. Offers accounting (MBA); business administration (MBA); global management (MBA); human resources management (MBA, MM); management (MM); marketing (MBA); public administration (MBA). Evening/weekend programs available. *Degree requirements:* For master's, thesis (for some programs). *Entrance requirements:* For master's, minimum undergraduate GPA of 3.0, 3 years of work experience. Additional exam requirements/recommendations for international students: Required—TOEFL (minimum score 550 paper-based; 213 computer-based; 79 iBT). Electronic applications accepted.

University of Phoenix–Columbus Ohio Campus, John Sperling School of Business, College of Graduate Business and Management, Columbus, OH 43240-4032. Offers accounting (MBA); business administration (MBA); global management (MBA); human resources management (MBA, MM); management (MM); marketing (MBA); public administration (MM). Evening/weekend programs available. Postbaccalaureate distance learning degree programs offered. *Degree requirements:* For master's, thesis (for some programs). *Entrance requirements:* For master's, minimum undergraduate GPA of 3.0, 3 years of work experience. Additional exam requirements/recommendations for international students: Required—TOEFL (minimum score 550 paper-based; 213 computer-based; 79 iBT). Electronic applications accepted.

University of Phoenix–Dallas Campus, John Sperling School of Business, College of Graduate Business and Management, Dallas, TX 75251-2009. Offers accounting (MBA); business administration (MBA); global management (MBA); human resources management (MBA, MM); management (MM); marketing (MBA); public administration (MBA, MM). Evening/weekend programs available. Postbaccalaureate distance learning degree programs offered. *Degree requirements:* For master's, thesis (for some programs). *Entrance requirements:* For master's, 3 years of work experience, minimum undergraduate GPA of 3.0. Additional exam requirements/recommendations for international students: Required—TOEFL (minimum score 550 paper-based; 213 computer-based; 79 iBT). Electronic applications accepted.

University of Phoenix–Denver Campus, John Sperling School of Business, College of Graduate Business and Management, Lone Tree, CO 80124-5453. Offers accountancy (MSA); accounting (MBA); business administration (MBA); e-business (MBA); global management (MBA); human resources management (MBA, MM); management (MM); marketing (MBA); public administration (MBA, MM). Evening/weekend programs available. Postbaccalaureate distance learning degree programs offered. *Degree requirements:* For master's, thesis (for some programs). *Entrance requirements:* For master's, minimum undergraduate GPA of 3.0, 3 years work experience. Additional exam requirements/recommendations for international students: Required—TOEFL (minimum score 550 paper-based; 213 computer-based; 79 iBT). Electronic applications accepted.

University of Phoenix–Des Moines Campus, College of Graduate Business and Management, Des Moines, IA 50266. Offers accounting (MBA); business administration (MBA); global management (MBA); human resources management (MBA, MM); management (MM); marketing (MBA); public administration (MBA, MM). Postbaccalaureate distance learning degree programs offered.

University of Phoenix–Harrisburg Campus, College of Graduate Business and Management, Harrisburg, PA 17112. Offers accounting (MBA); business administration (MBA); business and management (MBA); global management (MBA); human resources management (MBA, MM); management (MM); marketing (MBA); public administration (MBA, MM). Postbaccalaureate distance learning degree programs offered.

University of Phoenix–Hawaii Campus, John Sperling School of Business, College of Graduate Business and Management, Honolulu, HI 96813-4317. Offers accounting (MBA); business administration (MBA); global management (MBA); human resources management (MBA, MM); management (MM); marketing (MBA); public administration (MBA, MM). Evening/weekend programs available. *Degree requirements:* For master's, thesis (for some programs). *Entrance requirements:* For master's, minimum undergraduate GPA of 3.0, 3 years of work experience. Additional exam requirements/recommendations for international students: Required—TOEFL (minimum score 550 paper-based; 213 computer-based; 79 iBT). Electronic applications accepted.

University of Phoenix–Houston Campus, John Sperling School of Business, College of Graduate Business and Management, Houston, TX 77079-2004. Offers accounting (MBA); business administration (MBA); global management (MBA); human resources management (MBA, MM); management (MM); marketing (MBA); public administration (MBA, MM). Evening/weekend programs available. Postbaccalaureate distance learning degree programs offered. *Degree requirements:* For master's, thesis (for some programs). *Entrance requirements:* For master's, 3 years of work experience, minimum undergraduate GPA of 3.0. Additional exam requirements/recommendations for international students: Required—TOEFL (minimum score 550 paper-based; 213 computer-based; 79 iBT). Electronic applications accepted.

University of Phoenix–Idaho Campus, John Sperling School of Business, College of Graduate Business and Management, Meridian, ID 83642-3014. Offers accounting (MBA); administration (MBA); global management (MBA); human resources management (MBA, MM); management (MM); marketing (MBA); public administration (MM). Evening/weekend programs available. Postbaccalaureate distance learning degree programs offered. *Degree requirements:* For master's, thesis (for some programs). *Entrance requirements:* For master's, 3 years of work experience, minimum undergraduate GPA of 3.0. Additional exam requirements/recommendations for international students: Required—TOEFL (minimum score 550 paper-based; 213 computer-based). Electronic applications accepted.

University of Phoenix–Indianapolis Campus, John Sperling School of Business, College of Graduate Business and Management, Indianapolis, IN 46250-932. Offers accounting (MBA); business administration (MBA); global management (MBA); human resources management (MBA, MM); management (MM); marketing (MBA); public administration (MM). Evening/weekend programs available. *Degree requirements:* For master's, thesis (for some programs). *Entrance requirements:* For master's, minimum undergraduate GPA of 3.0, 3 years of work experience. Additional exam requirements/recommendations for international students: Required—TOEFL (minimum score 550 paper-based; 213 computer-based). Electronic applications accepted.

University of Phoenix–Jersey City Campus, College of Graduate Business and Management, Jersey City, NJ 07310. Offers accounting (MBA); business administration (MBA); global management (MBA); human resources management (MBA, MM); management (MM); marketing (MBA); public administration (MBA, MM).

University of Phoenix–Kansas City Campus, John Sperling School of Business, College of Graduate Business and Management, Kansas City, MO 64131-4517. Offers accounting (MBA); business administration (MBA); global management (MBA); human resources management (MBA, MM); management (MM); marketing (MBA); public administration (MBA). Evening/weekend programs available. *Degree requirements:* For master's, thesis (for some programs). *Entrance requirements:* For master's, minimum undergraduate GPA of 3.0, 3 years of work experience. Additional exam requirements/recommendations for international students: Required—TOEFL (minimum score 550 paper-based; 213 computer-based). Electronic applications accepted.

University of Phoenix–Las Vegas Campus, John Sperling School of Business, College of Graduate Business and Management, Las Vegas, NV 89128. Offers accounting (MBA); business administration (MBA); global management (MBA); human resources management (MBA, MM); management (MM); marketing (MBA); public administration (MM). Evening/weekend programs available. Postbaccalaureate distance learning degree programs offered (no on-campus study). *Degree requirements:* For master's, thesis (for some programs). *Entrance requirements:* For master's, minimum undergraduate GPA of 3.0, 3 years of work experience. Additional exam requirements/recommendations for international students: Required—TOEFL (minimum score 550 paper-based; 213 computer-based; 79 iBT). Electronic applications accepted.

University of Phoenix–Louisiana Campus, John Sperling School of Business, College of Graduate Business and Management, Metairie, LA 70001-2082. Offers accounting (MBA); business administration (MBA); global management (MBA); human resources management (MBA, MM); management (MM); marketing (MBA); public administration (MBA). Evening/weekend programs available. *Degree requirements:* For master's, thesis (for some programs). *Entrance requirements:* For master's, minimum undergraduate GPA of 3.0, 3 years work experience. Additional exam requirements/recommendations for international students: Required—TOEFL (minimum score 550 paper-based; 213 computer-based; 79 iBT). Electronic applications accepted.

University of Phoenix–Madison Campus, College of Graduate Business and Management, Madison, WI 53718-2416. Offers accounting (MBA); business and management (MBA); e-business (MBA); global management (MBA); human resources management (MBA, MM); management (MM); marketing (MBA); public administration (MBA).

University of Phoenix–Madison Campus, John Sperling School of Business, College of Graduate Business and Management, Madison, WI 53718-2416. Offers accounting (MBA); administration (MBA); global management (MBA); human resources management (MBA); management (MM); marketing (MBA); public administration (MBA). Evening/weekend programs available. *Degree requirements:* For master's, thesis (for some programs). *Entrance requirements:* For master's, 3 years of work experience, minimum undergraduate GPA of 3.0. Additional exam requirements/recommendations for international students: Required—TOEFL (minimum score 550 paper-based; 213 computer-based; 79 iBT). Electronic applications accepted.

University of Phoenix–Maryland Campus, John Sperling School of Business, College of Graduate Business and Management, Columbia, MD 21045-5424. Offers accounting (MBA); business administration (MBA); e-business (MBA); global management (MBA); human resources management (MBA, MM); management (MM); marketing (MBA); public administration (MBA, MM). Evening/weekend programs available. *Degree requirements:* For master's, thesis (for some programs). *Entrance requirements:* For master's, minimum undergraduate GPA of 3.0, 3 years of work experience. Additional exam requirements/recommendations for international students: Required—TOEFL (minimum score 550 paper-based; 213 computer-based; 79 iBT). Electronic applications accepted.

University of Phoenix–Memphis Campus, College of Graduate Business and Management, Cordova, TN 38018. Offers accounting (MBA); business and management (MBA); e-business (MBA); global management (MBA); human resources management (MBA, MM); management (MM); marketing (MBA); public administration (MBA, MM).

University of Phoenix–Metro Detroit Campus, School of Business, College of Graduate Business and Management, Troy, MI 48098-2623. Offers accountancy (MS); accounting (MBA); business administration (MBA); global management (MBA); human resources management (MBA, MM); management (MM); marketing (MBA). Evening/weekend programs available. *Degree requirements:* For master's, thesis (for some programs). *Entrance requirements:* For master's, minimum undergraduate GPA of 3.0, 3 years work experience. Additional exam requirements/recommendations for international students: Required—TOEFL (minimum score 550 paper-based; 213 computer-based; 79 iBT). Electronic applications accepted. *Expenses:* Tuition: Full-time $14,136. Required fees: $660.

University of Phoenix–Minneapolis/St. Louis Park Campus, College of Graduate Business and Management, St. Louis Park, MN 55426. Offers accounting (MBA); business administration (MBA); global management (MBA); human resources management (MBA); management (MM); marketing (MBA); public administration (MBA).

University of Phoenix–New Mexico Campus, John Sperling School of Business, College of Graduate Business and Management, Albuquerque, NM 87113-1570. Offers accounting (MBA); business administration (MBA); global management (MBA); human resource management (MBA); human resources management (MM); management (MM); marketing (MBA). Evening/weekend programs available. *Degree requirements:* For master's, thesis (for some programs). *Entrance requirements:* For master's, 3 years of work experience, minimum undergraduate GPA of 3.0. Additional exam requirements/recommendations for international students: Required—TOEFL (minimum score 550 paper-based; 213 computer-based; 79 iBT). Electronic applications accepted.

University of Phoenix–Northern Nevada Campus, College of Graduate Business and Management, Reno, NV 89521-5862. Offers accounting (MBA); business administration (MBA); global management (MBA); human resources management (MBA, MM); management (MM); marketing (MBA); public administration (MBA, MM).

University of Phoenix–Northern Virginia Campus, College of Graduate Business and Management, Reston, VA 20190. Offers accounting (MBA); business administration (MBA); e-business (MBA); global management (MBA); human resources management (MBA, MM); management (MM); marketing (MBA); public administration (MBA).

University of Phoenix–North Florida Campus, John Sperling School of Business, College of Graduate Business and Management, Jacksonville, FL 32216-0959. Offers accounting (MBA); business administration (MBA); global management (MBA); human resources management (MBA, MM); management (MM); marketing (MBA); public administration (MBA, MM). Evening/weekend programs available. *Degree requirements:* For master's, thesis (for some programs). *Entrance requirements:* For master's, minimum undergraduate GPA of 3.0, 3 years work experience. Additional exam requirements/recommendations for international students: Required—TOEFL (minimum score 550 paper-based; 213 computer-based; 79 iBT). Electronic applications accepted.

University of Phoenix–Northwest Arkansas Campus, College of Graduate Business and Management, Rogers, AR 72756-9615. Offers accounting (MBA); business and management (MBA); global management (MBA); human resources management (MBA, MM); management (MM); marketing (MBA); public administration (MBA, MM).

University of Phoenix–Oklahoma City Campus, John Sperling School of Business, College of Graduate Business and Management, Oklahoma City, OK 73116-8244. Offers accounting (MBA); business administration (MBA); global management (MBA); human resource management (MBA); management (MM); marketing (MBA). Evening/weekend programs available. *Degree requirements:* For master's, thesis (for some programs). *Entrance requirements:* For master's, minimum undergraduate GPA of 3.0, 3 years of work experience. Additional exam requirements/recommendations for international students: Required—TOEFL (minimum score 550 paper-based; 213 computer-based; 79 iBT). Electronic applications accepted.

University of Phoenix–Omaha Campus, College of Graduate Business and Management, Omaha, NE 68154-5240. Offers accounting (MBA); business and management (MBA); global management (MBA); human resources management (MBA, MM); management (MM); marketing (MBA); public administration (MBA, MM).

University of Phoenix–Oregon Campus, The John Sperling School of Business, College of Graduate Business and Management, Tigard, OR 97223. Offers accounting (MBA); business administration (MBA); global management (MBA); human resource management (MM); human resources management (MBA); management (MM); marketing (MBA); public administration (MM). Evening/weekend programs available. *Degree requirements:* For master's, thesis (for some programs). *Entrance requirements:* For master's, minimum undergraduate GPA of 3.0, 3 years of work experience. Additional exam requirements/recommendations for international students: Required—TOEFL (minimum score 550 paper-based; 213 computer-based; 79 iBT). Electronic applications accepted.

University of Phoenix–Philadelphia Campus, The John Sperling School of Business, College of Graduate Business and Management, Wayne, PA 19087-2121. Offers accounting (MBA); business administration (MBA); global management (MBA); human resources management (MBA, MM); management (MM); marketing (MBA); public administration (MM). Evening/weekend programs available. *Degree requirements:* For master's, thesis (for some programs). *Entrance requirements:* For master's, minimum undergraduate GPA of 3.0, 3 years work experience. Additional exam requirements/recommendations for international students: Required—TOEFL (minimum score 550 paper-based; 213 computer-based; 79 iBT). Electronic applications accepted.

University of Phoenix–Pittsburgh Campus, John Sperling School of Business, College of Graduate Business and Management, Pittsburgh, PA 15276. Offers accounting (MBA); business administration (MBA); global management (MBA); human resources management (MBA, MM); management (MM); marketing (MBA); public administration (MBA, MM). Evening/weekend programs available. *Degree requirements:* For master's, thesis (for some programs). *Entrance requirements:* For master's, minimum undergraduate GPA of 3.0, 3 years work experience. Additional exam requirements/recommendations for international students: Required—TOEFL (minimum score 550 paper-based; 213 computer-based; 79 iBT). Electronic applications accepted.

University of Phoenix–Puerto Rico Campus, John Sperling School of Business, College of Graduate Business and Management, Guaynabo, PR 00968. Offers accounting (MBA); business administration (MBA); global management (MBA); human resource management (MBA); marketing (MBA). Evening/weekend programs available. *Degree requirements:* For master's, thesis (for some programs). *Entrance requirements:* For master's, minimum undergraduate GPA of 3.0, 3 years work experience. Additional exam requirements/recommendations for international students: Required—TOEFL (minimum score 550 paper-based; 213 computer-based; 79 iBT). Electronic applications accepted.

University of Phoenix–Raleigh Campus, College of Graduate Business and Management, Raleigh, NC 27606. Offers accounting (MBA); business administration (MBA); e-business (MBA); global management (MBA); human resources management (MBA); marketing (MBA).

University of Phoenix–Richmond Campus, John Sperling School of Business, College of Graduate Business and Management, Richmond, VA 23230. Offers accounting (MBA); business administration (MBA); global management (MBA); human resources management (MBA, MM); management (MM); marketing (MBA); public administration (MBA, MM). Evening/weekend programs available. *Degree requirements:* For master's, thesis (for some programs). *Entrance requirements:* For master's, minimum undergraduate GPA of 3.0, 3 years work experience. Additional exam requirements/recommendations for international students: Required—TOEFL (minimum score 550 paper-based; 213 computer-based; 79 iBT). Electronic applications accepted.

University of Phoenix–Sacramento Valley Campus, John Sperling School of Business, College of Graduate Business and Management, Sacramento, CA 95833-3632. Offers accounting (MBA); business administration (MBA); global management (MBA); human resources management (MBA, MM); management (MM); marketing (MBA); public administration (MBA, MM). Evening/weekend programs available. *Degree requirements:* For master's, thesis (for some programs). *Entrance requirements:* For master's, minimum undergraduate GPA of 3.0, 3 years work experience. Additional exam requirements/recommendations for international students: Required—TOEFL (minimum score 550 paper-based; 213 computer-based; 79 iBT). Electronic applications accepted.

University of Phoenix–St. Louis Campus, John Sperling School of Business, College of Graduate Business and Management, St. Louis, MO 63043-4828. Offers accounting (MBA); business administration (MBA); global management (MBA); human resources management (MBA, MM); management (MM); marketing (MBA); public administration (MM). Evening/weekend programs available. *Degree requirements:* For master's, thesis (for some programs). *Entrance requirements:* For master's, 3 years of work experience, minimum undergraduate GPA of 3.0. Additional exam requirements/recommendations for international students: Required—TOEFL (minimum score 550 paper-based; 213 computer-based; 79 iBT). Electronic applications accepted.

University of Phoenix–San Antonio Campus, College of Graduate Business and Management, San Antonio, TX 78230. Offers accounting (MBA); business administration (MBA); e-business (MBA); global management (MBA); human resources management (MBA, MM); management (MM); marketing (MBA); public administration (MBA, MM).

University of Phoenix–San Diego Campus, John Sperling School of Business, College of Graduate Business and Management, San Diego, CA 92123. Offers accounting (MBA); business administration (MBA); global management (MBA); human resources management (MBA, MM); management (MM); marketing (MBA); public administration (MBA). Evening/weekend programs available. *Degree requirements:* For master's, thesis (for some programs). *Entrance requirements:* For master's, 3 years of work experience, minimum undergraduate GPA of 3.0. Additional exam requirements/recommendations for international students: Required—TOEFL (minimum score 550 paper-based; 213 computer-based; 79 iBT). Electronic applications accepted.

University of Phoenix–Savannah Campus, College of Graduate Business and Management, Savannah, GA 31405-7400. Offers accounting (MBA); business administration (MBA); global management (MBA); human resources management (MBA, MM); management (MM); marketing (MBA); public administration (MBA, MM).

University of Phoenix–Southern Arizona Campus, John Sperling School of Business, College of Graduate Business and Management, Tucson, AZ 85711. Offers accountancy (MS); accounting (MBA); business administration (MBA); global management (MBA); human resources management (MBA); management (MM); marketing (MBA). Evening/weekend programs available. *Degree requirements:* For master's, thesis (for some programs). *Entrance requirements:* For master's, minimum undergraduate GPA of 3.0, 3 years of work experience. Additional exam requirements/recommendations for international students: Required—TOEFL (minimum score 550 paper-based; 213 computer-based; 79 iBT). Electronic applications accepted.

University of Phoenix–Southern Colorado Campus, John Sperling School of Business, College of Graduate Business and Management, Colorado Springs, CO 80919-2335. Offers accounting (MBA); business administration (MBA); global management (MBA); human resources management (MBA, MM); management (MM); marketing (MBA); public administration (MM). Evening/weekend programs available. *Degree requirements:* For master's, thesis (for some programs). *Entrance requirements:* For master's, minimum undergraduate GPA of 3.0, 3 years of work experience. Additional exam requirements/recommendations for international students: Required—TOEFL (minimum score 550 paper-based; 213 computer-based; 79 iBT). Electronic applications accepted.

University of Phoenix–South Florida Campus, John Sperling School of Business, College of Graduate Business and Management, Fort Lauderdale, FL 33309. Offers accounting (MBA); business administration (MBA); global management (MBA); human resource management (MBA); human resources management (MM); management (MM); marketing (MBA); public administration (MBA, MM). Evening/weekend programs available. *Degree requirements:* For master's, thesis (for some programs). *Entrance requirements:* For master's, minimum undergraduate GPA of 3.0, 3 years work experience. Additional exam requirements/recommendations for international students: Required—TOEFL (minimum score 550 paper-based; 213 computer-based; 79 iBT). Electronic applications accepted.

University of Phoenix–Springfield Campus, College of Graduate Business and Management, Springfield, MO 65804-7211. Offers accounting (MBA); business administration (MBA); global management (MBA); human resources management (MBA, MM); management (MM); marketing (MBA); public administration (MBA, MM).

University of Phoenix–Tulsa Campus, John Sperling School of Business, College of Graduate Business and Management, Tulsa, OK 74134-1412. Offers accounting (MBA); business (MM); business administration (MBA); global management (MBA); human resources management (MBA); marketing (MBA). Evening/weekend programs available. *Degree requirements:* For master's, thesis (for some programs). *Entrance requirements:* For master's, minimum undergraduate GPA of 3.0, 3 years work experience. Additional exam requirements/recommendations for international students: Required—TOEFL (minimum score 550 paper-based; 213 computer-based; 79 iBT).

University of Phoenix–Utah Campus, John Sperling School of Business, College of Graduate Business and Management, Salt Lake City, UT 84123-4617. Offers accounting (MBA); business administration (MBA); global management (MBA); human resource management (MBA, MM); management (MM); marketing (MBA); technology management (MBA). Evening/weekend programs available. *Degree requirements:* For master's, thesis (for some programs). *Entrance requirements:* For master's, minimum undergraduate GPA of 3.0, 3 years of work experience. Additional exam requirements/recommendations for international students: Required—TOEFL (minimum score 550 paper-based; 213 computer-based; 79 iBT). Electronic applications accepted.

University of Phoenix–Vancouver Campus, John Sperling School of Business, College of Graduate Business and Management, Burnaby, BC V5C 6G9, Canada. Offers accounting (MBA); business administration (MBA); global management (MBA); human resources management (MBA, MM); marketing (MBA). Evening/weekend programs available. *Degree requirements:* For master's, thesis (for some programs). *Entrance requirements:* For master's, minimum undergraduate GPA of 3.0, 3 years of work experience. Additional exam requirements/recommendations for international students: Required—TOEFL (minimum score 550 paper-based; 213 computer-based; 79 iBT). Electronic applications accepted.

University of Phoenix–Western Washington Campus, College of Graduate Business and Management, Tukwila, WA 98188. Offers accounting (MBA); business and management (MBA, MM); global management (MBA); human resources management (MBA, MM); marketing (MBA); public administration (MBA, MM). Evening/weekend programs available. *Degree requirements:* For master's, thesis (for some programs). *Entrance requirements:* For master's, minimum undergraduate GPA of 3.0, 3 years of work experience. Additional exam requirements/recommendations for international students: Required—TOEFL (minimum score 550 paper-based; 213 computer-based; 79 iBT). Electronic applications accepted.

University of Phoenix–West Florida Campus, The John Sperling School of Business, College of Graduate Business and Management, Temple Terrace, FL 33637. Offers accounting (MBA); business administration (MBA); global management (MBA); human resources management (MBA, MM); management (MM); marketing (MBA); public administration (MBA, MM). Evening/weekend programs available. *Degree requirements:* For master's, thesis (for some programs). *Entrance requirements:* For master's, 3 years of work experience, minimum undergraduate GPA of 3.0. Additional exam requirements/recommendations for international students: Required—TOEFL (minimum score 550 paper-based; 213 computer-based; 79 iBT). Electronic applications accepted.

University of Pittsburgh, Katz Graduate School of Business, Augsburg Executive Fellows Program, Pittsburgh, PA 15260. Offers MBA. *Students:* 26 full-time (1 woman), all international. Average age 34. *Degree requirements:* For master's, one foreign language, 7 week stay at Katz Graduate School as full-time student. *Entrance requirements:* For master's, admission to the MBA program at the University of Augsburg, Germany. Additional exam requirements/recommendations for international students: Required—TOEFL (minimum score 600 paper-based; 250 computer-based; 100 iBT), or IELTS. *Application deadline:* For spring admission, 7/1 priority date for international students. *Expenses:* Contact institution. *Faculty research:* Accounting statements and reporting, incentives and governance; corporate finance, mergers and acquisitions; information systems processes, structures, and decision-making; organizational structure, knowledge management, and corporate strategy; consumer behavior and marketing models. *Unit head:* William T. Valenta, Assistant Dean, MBA Programs, 412-648-1610, Fax: 412-648-1659, E-mail: wtvalenta@katz.pitt.edu. *Application contact:* Patricia Hermenault, Director, Special International and Dual Degree Programs, 412-383-8835, Fax: 412-648-1659, E-mail: hermenault@katz.pitt.edu.

University of Pittsburgh, Katz Graduate School of Business, MBA/Masters of International Business Dual Degree Program, Pittsburgh, PA 15260. Offers MBA/MIB. Part-time and evening/weekend programs available. *Students:* 6 full-time (1 woman), 2 part-time (both women); includes 5 minority (2 African Americans, 2 Asian Americans or Pacific Islanders, 1 Hispanic American). Average age 25. 22 applicants, 59% accepted, 7 enrolled. *Entrance requirements:* Additional exam requirements/recommendations for international students: Required—TOEFL (minimum score 600 paper-based; 250 computer-based; 100 iBT), or IELTS. *Application deadline:* For fall admission, 7/1 priority date for domestic students, 7/1 for international students; for winter admission, 11/1 for domestic and international students; for spring admission, 3/1 for international students. Applications are processed on a rolling basis. Application fee: $50. Electronic applications accepted. *Expenses:* Tuition, state resident: full-time $16,402; part-time $665 per credit. Tuition, nonresident: full-time $28,694; part-time $1175 per credit. Required fees: $690; $175 per term. Tuition and fees vary according to program. *Financial support:* In 2009–10, 3 students received support. Career-related internships or fieldwork and scholarships/grants available. Financial award application deadline: 6/1; financial award applicants required to submit FAFSA. *Faculty research:* Transitional economies, incentives and governance; corporate finance, mergers and acquisitions; global information systems and structures; consumer behavior and marketing models; entrepreneurship and globalization. *Unit head:* William T. Valenta, Assistant Dean/Director of MBA Programs, 412-648-1610, Fax: 412-648-1659, E-mail: wtvalenta@katz.pitt.edu. *Application contact:* Cliff McCormick, Director of MBA Admissions, 412-648-1700, Fax: 412-648-1659, E-mail: mba@katz.pitt.edu.

University of Puerto Rico, Río Piedras, College of Business Administration, San Juan, PR 00931-3300. Offers accounting (MBA); finance (MBA, PhD); general business (MBA); human resources management (MBA); international trade and business (MBA, PhD); marketing (MBA); operations management (MBA); quantitative methods (MBA). *Accreditation:* ACBSP. Part-time programs available. *Degree requirements:* For master's, comprehensive exam, thesis or alternative, research project. *Entrance requirements:* For master's, GMAT or PAEG, minimum GPA of 3.0, letter of recommendation; for doctorate, GMAT, PAEG, minimum GPA of 3.0, master degree. *Faculty research:* Management.

University of Regina, Faculty of Graduate Studies and Research, Kenneth Levene Graduate School of Business, Program in Business Administration, Regina, SK S4S 0A2, Canada. Offers business administration (MBA); business fundamentals (Master's Certificate); general management (Master's Certificate); international business (Master's Certificate). Part-time and evening/weekend programs available. *Faculty:* 25 full-time (5 women), 3 part-time/adjunct (0 women). *Students:* 53 full-time (11 women), 26 part-time (11 women). 104 applicants, 91% accepted. In 2009, 37 master's awarded. *Entrance requirements:* For master's, GMAT, 2 years of full-time relevant work experience. Additional exam requirements/recommendations for international students: Required—TOEFL (minimum score 580 paper-based; 237 computer-based; 80 iBT). *Application deadline:* Applications are processed on a rolling basis. Application fee: $90 ($100 for international students). Electronic applications accepted. *Expenses:* Contact institution. *Financial support:* In 2009–10, 4 fellowships (averaging $19,000 per year) were awarded; research assistantships, teaching assistantships. Financial award application deadline: 6/15. *Faculty research:* Accounting, finance, marketing, management science, operations management. *Unit head:* Ann Lavack, 306-585-4716. *Application contact:* Dr. David Senkow, Professor, 306-585-4719, Fax: 306-585-4805, E-mail: david.senkow@uregina.ca.

University of San Francisco, School of Business and Professional Studies, Masagung Graduate School of Management, Joint Master of Global Entrepreneurship and Management Program, San Francisco, CA 94117-1080. Offers MGEM. Program offered jointly with IQS in Barcelona, Spain and Fu Jen Catholic University in Taipei, Taiwan. *Faculty:* 2 full-time (both

International Business

University of San Francisco (continued)
women), 2 part-time/adjunct (0 women). *Students:* 32 full-time (19 women); includes 7 minority (1 African American, 2 Asian Americans or Pacific Islanders, 4 Hispanic Americans), 19 international. Average age 23. 38 applicants, 95% accepted, 32 enrolled. *Expenses:* Tuition: Full-time $19,710; part-time $1095 per unit. Part-time tuition and fees vary according to degree level, campus/location and program. *Financial support:* In 2009–10, 8 students received support. *Unit head:* Dr. Shenzhao Fu, 415-422-6771, Fax: 415-422-2502. *Application contact:* Kelly Brookes, Director, MBA Program, 415-422-2221, Fax: 415-422-6315, E-mail: mba@usfca.edu.

University of San Francisco, School of Business and Professional Studies, Masagung Graduate School of Management, Program in Business Administration, San Francisco, CA 94117-1080. Offers business economics (MBA); e-business (MBA); entrepreneurship (MBA); finance (MBA); international business (MBA); management (MBA); marketing (MBA); telecommunications management and policy (MBA); JD/MBA; MSN/MBA. *Accreditation:* AACSB. *Faculty:* 17 full-time (4 women), 16 part-time/adjunct (7 women). *Students:* 278 full-time (140 women), 18 part-time (10 women); includes 94 minority (5 African Americans, 1 American Indian/Alaska Native, 69 Asian Americans or Pacific Islanders, 19 Hispanic Americans), 53 international. Average age 30. 410 applicants, 70% accepted, 133 enrolled. In 2009, 137 master's awarded. *Entrance requirements:* For master's, GMAT, minimum undergraduate GPA of 3.2. Additional exam requirements/recommendations for international students: Required—TOEFL. *Application deadline:* For fall admission, 7/1 priority date for domestic students; for spring admission, 11/30 for domestic students. Applications are processed on a rolling basis. Application fee: $55 ($65 for international students). *Expenses:* Tuition: Full-time $19,710; part-time $1095 per unit. Part-time tuition and fees vary according to degree level, campus/location and program. *Financial support:* In 2009–10, 155 students received support; fellowships available. Financial award application deadline: 3/2; financial award applicants required to submit FAFSA. *Faculty research:* International financial markets, technology transfer licensing, international marketing, strategic planning. Total annual research expenditures: $50,000. *Unit head:* Kelly Brookes, Director, 415-422-2221, Fax: 415-422-6315. *Application contact:* Director, MBA Program, 415-422-2221, Fax: 415-422-6315, E-mail: mba@usfca.edu.

University of San Francisco, School of Law, Program in Law, San Francisco, CA 94117-1080. Offers intellectual property and technology law (LL M); international transactions and comparative law (LL M). *Faculty:* 15 full-time (7 women), 49 part-time/adjunct (18 women). *Students:* 14 full-time (9 women), 2 part-time (1 woman), 11 international. Average age 30. 106 applicants, 69% accepted, 15 enrolled. In 2009, 27 master's awarded. *Entrance requirements:* For master's, law degree from U.S. or foreign school (intellectual property and technology law), law degree from foreign school (international transactions and comparative law). Application fee: $60. *Expenses:* Tuition: Full-time $19,710; part-time $1095 per unit. Part-time tuition and fees vary according to degree level, campus/location and program. *Financial support:* In 2009–10, 12 students received support. *Unit head:* Eldon Reiley, Director, Fax: 415-422-5440. *Application contact:* Program Assistant, 415-422-5100, E-mail: masterlaws@usfca.edu.

University of Saskatchewan, College of Graduate Studies and Research, Edwards School of Business, Program in Business Administration, Saskatoon, SK S7N 5A2, Canada. Offers agribusiness management (MBA); biotechnology management (MBA); health services management (MBA); indigenous management (MBA); international business management (MBA). Tuition and fees charges are reported in Canadian dollars. *Expenses:* Tuition, area resident: Full-time $3000 Canadian dollars; part-time $500 Canadian dollars per term. Required fees: $700 Canadian dollars; $100 Canadian dollars per term.

University of Saskatchewan, College of Graduate Studies and Research, School of Public Policy, Saskatoon, SK S7N 5A2, Canada. Offers MIT, MPA, MPP, PhD. Tuition and fees charges are reported in Canadian dollars. *Expenses:* Tuition, area resident: Full-time $3000 Canadian dollars; part-time $500 Canadian dollars per term. Required fees: $700 Canadian dollars; $100 Canadian dollars per term.

The University of Scranton, College of Graduate and Continuing Education, Program in Business Administration, Scranton, PA 18510. Offers accounting (MBA); finance (MBA); general business administration (MBA); health care management (MBA); international business (MBA); management information systems (MBA); marketing (MBA); operations management (MBA). *Accreditation:* AACSB. Part-time and evening/weekend programs available. Postbaccalaureate distance learning degree programs offered (no on-campus study). *Faculty:* 34 full-time (8 women). *Students:* 92 full-time (38 women), 137 part-time (58 women); includes 27 minority (15 African Americans, 5 Asian Americans or Pacific Islanders, 7 Hispanic Americans), 21 international. Average age 31. 255 applicants, 79% accepted. In 2009, 33 master's awarded. *Degree requirements:* For master's, capstone experience. *Entrance requirements:* For master's, GMAT, minimum GPA of 2.75. Additional exam requirements/recommendations for international students: Required—TOEFL (minimum score 500 paper-based; 173 computer-based), IELTS (minimum score 5.5). *Application deadline:* Applications are processed on a rolling basis. Application fee: $0. *Financial support:* In 2009–10, 10 students received support, including 10 teaching assistantships with full and partial tuition reimbursements available (averaging $6,600 per year); fellowships, career-related internships or fieldwork, Federal Work-Study, and unspecified assistantships also available. Support available to part-time students. Financial award application deadline: 3/1. *Faculty research:* Financial markets, strategic impact of total quality management, internal accounting controls, consumer preference, information systems and the Internet. *Unit head:* Dr. Murli Rajan, Director, 570-941-4043, Fax: 570-941-4342. *Application contact:* Joseph M. Roback, Director of Admissions, 570-941-4385, Fax: 570-941-5928, E-mail: robackj2@scranton.edu.

University of South Carolina, The Graduate School, Moore School of Business, International Business Administration Program, Columbia, SC 29208. Offers IMBA. *Degree requirements:* For master's, one foreign language, field consulting project. *Entrance requirements:* For master's, GMAT, minimum GPA of 3.0, minimum two years of work experience. Additional exam requirements/recommendations for international students: Required—TOEFL (minimum score 600 paper-based; 250 computer-based; 100 iBT); Recommended—IELTS. Electronic applications accepted.

The University of Tampa, John H. Sykes College of Business, Tampa, FL 33606-1490. Offers accounting (MBA, MS); economics (MBA); entrepreneurship and innovation (MBA); finance (MBA, MS); information systems management (MBA); international business (MBA); management (MBA); marketing (MBA, MS); nonprofit management (MBA). *Accreditation:* AACSB. Part-time and evening/weekend programs available. *Faculty:* 62 full-time (22 women), 11 part-time/adjunct (4 women). *Students:* 240 full-time (101 women), 338 part-time (133 women); includes 95 minority (16 African Americans, 4 American Indian/Alaska Native, 24 Asian Americans or Pacific Islanders, 51 Hispanic Americans), 122 international. Average age 29. 564 applicants, 51% accepted, 186 enrolled. In 2009, 234 master's awarded. *Entrance requirements:* For master's, GMAT. Additional exam requirements/recommendations for international students: Required—TOEFL (minimum score 577 paper-based; 230 computer-based; 90 iBT), IELTS. *Application deadline:* For fall admission, 7/15 for domestic students, 6/1 for international students; for spring admission, 12/15 for domestic students, 11/1 for international students. Applications are processed on a rolling basis. Application fee: $40. Electronic applications accepted. *Expenses:* Tuition: Part-time $488 per credit hour. *Financial support:* In 2009–10, 332 students received support, including 71 research assistantships with full tuition reimbursements available (averaging $6,757 per year); career-related internships or fieldwork, scholarships/grants, and unspecified assistantships also available. Support available to part-time students. Financial award applicants required to submit FAFSA. *Faculty research:* Information systems, leadership, corporate governance, entrepreneurship, hedonic price estimation. *Unit head:* Dr. Don Morrill, Associate Dean, Graduate and Continuing Studies, 813-257-3557, E-mail: dmorrill@ut.edu. *Application contact:* Karen Full, Director of Admissions, Graduate and Continuing Studies, 813-257-3642, E-mail: kfull@ut.edu.

The University of Texas at Dallas, School of Management, Program in Business Administration, Richardson, TX 75080. Offers cohort (MBA); executive business administration (EMBA); global leadership (EMBA); global online (MBA); healthcare management (EMBA); professional business administration (MBA); project management (EMBA). *Accreditation:* AACSB. Part-time and evening/weekend programs available. Postbaccalaureate distance learning degree programs offered. *Faculty:* 79 full-time (13 women), 29 part-time/adjunct (9 women). *Students:* 314 full-time (104 women), 857 part-time (244 women); includes 377 minority (52 African Americans, 5 American Indian/Alaska Native, 231 Asian Americans or Pacific Islanders, 89 Hispanic Americans), 211 international. Average age 32. 712 applicants, 48% accepted, 317 enrolled. In 2009, 409 master's awarded. *Degree requirements:* For master's, thesis optional. *Entrance requirements:* For master's, GMAT, 10 years of business experience (EMBA), minimum GPA of 3.0. Additional exam requirements/recommendations for international students: Required—TOEFL (minimum score 550 paper-based; 213 computer-based). *Application deadline:* For fall admission, 7/15 for domestic students, 5/1 priority date for international students; for spring admission, 11/15 for domestic students, 9/1 priority date for international students. Applications are processed on a rolling basis. Application fee: $50 ($100 for international students). Electronic applications accepted. *Expenses:* Contact institution. *Financial support:* In 2009–10, 5 research assistantships with full tuition reimbursements (averaging $10,692 per year), 23 teaching assistantships with full tuition reimbursements (averaging $10,050 per year) were awarded; fellowships, career-related internships or fieldwork, Federal Work-Study, institutionally sponsored loans, scholarships/grants, and unspecified assistantships also available. Support available to part-time students. Financial award application deadline: 4/30; financial award applicants required to submit FAFSA. *Faculty research:* Production scheduling, trade and finance, organizational decision making, life/work planning. *Unit head:* Lisa Shatz, Director, 972-883-6191, E-mail: mba@utdallas.edu. *Application contact:* James Parker, Assistant Director, 972-883-5842, E-mail: jparker@utdallas.edu.

The University of Texas at Dallas, School of Management, Program in International Management, Richardson, TX 75080. Offers MA, PhD. Part-time and evening/weekend programs available. *Faculty:* 12 full-time (3 women), 7 part-time/adjunct (0 women). *Students:* 18 full-time (8 women), 12 part-time (7 women); includes 5 minority (4 Asian Americans or Pacific Islanders, 1 Hispanic American), 15 international. Average age 30. 61 applicants, 23% accepted, 9 enrolled. In 2009, 11 master's, 3 doctorates awarded. *Degree requirements:* For doctorate, thesis/dissertation. *Entrance requirements:* For master's and doctorate, GMAT. Additional exam requirements/recommendations for international students: Required—TOEFL (minimum score 550 paper-based; 213 computer-based). *Application deadline:* For fall admission, 7/15 for domestic students, 5/1 priority date for international students; for spring admission, 11/15 for domestic students, 9/1 priority date for international students. Applications are processed on a rolling basis. Application fee: $50 ($100 for international students). Electronic applications accepted. *Expenses:* Tuition, state resident: full-time $11,068; part-time $461 per credit hour. Tuition, nonresident: full-time $21,178; part-time $882 per credit hour. Tuition and fees vary according to course load. *Financial support:* In 2009–10, 10 teaching assistantships with full tuition reimbursements (averaging $14,580 per year) were awarded; fellowships, research assistantships, Federal Work-Study, institutionally sponsored loans, scholarships/grants, and unspecified assistantships also available. Support available to part-time students. Financial award application deadline: 4/30; financial award applicants required to submit FAFSA. *Faculty research:* International accounting, international trade and finance, economic development, international economics. *Unit head:* Dr. Sumit Sarkar, Program Director, 972-883-2745, Fax: 972-883-5977, E-mail: som_phd@utdallas.edu. *Application contact:* Mike Peng, Coordinator, 972-883-2714, E-mail: mikepeng@utdallas.edu.

The University of Texas at El Paso, Graduate School, College of Business Administration, Programs in Business Administration, El Paso, TX 79968-0001. Offers international business (PhD). *Accreditation:* AACSB. Part-time and evening/weekend programs available. Postbaccalaureate distance learning degree programs offered (no on-campus study). *Entrance requirements:* For master's, GMAT, minimum GPA of 2.7. Additional exam requirements/recommendations for international students: Required—TOEFL. Electronic applications accepted.

The University of Texas at San Antonio, College of Business, Department of Management, San Antonio, TX 78249-0617. Offers business administration-organizational management (PhD); international business (MBA); management science (MBA). *Accreditation:* AACSB. Part-time and evening/weekend programs available. *Faculty:* 12 full-time (4 women), 4 part-time/adjunct (2 women). *Students:* 3 full-time (1 woman), 6 part-time (2 women); includes 3 minority (1 African American, 1 Asian American or Pacific Islander, 1 Hispanic American). Average age 34. 29 applicants, 59% accepted. In 2009, 1 master's awarded. *Degree requirements:* For master's, comprehensive exam (for some programs), thesis (for some programs). *Entrance requirements:* For master's, GMAT, minimum GPA of 3.0. Additional exam requirements/recommendations for international students: Required—TOEFL (minimum score 500 paper-based; 173 computer-based; 61 iBT), IELTS (minimum score 5). *Application deadline:* For fall admission, 7/1 for domestic students, 4/1 for international students; for spring admission, 11/1 for domestic students, 9/1 for international students. Applications are processed on a rolling basis. Application fee: $45 ($80 for international students). Electronic applications accepted. *Expenses:* Tuition, state resident: full-time $3975; part-time $221 per contact hour. Tuition, nonresident: full-time $13,947; part-time $775 per contact hour. Required fees: $1853. *Financial support:* In 2009–10, 2 research assistantships (averaging $15,600 per year), 8 teaching assistantships (averaging $7,800 per year) were awarded; career-related internships or fieldwork, Federal Work-Study, scholarships/grants, and unspecified assistantships also available. Support available to part-time students. *Faculty research:* Business ethics, entrepreneurship, human resource management, knowledge management, international management. *Unit head:* Dr. Robert L. Cardy, Chair, 210-458-7480, Fax: 210-458-6335, E-mail: robert.cardy@utsa.edu. *Application contact:* Cynthia Lengnick-Hall, Graduate Advisor, 210-458-5387, E-mail: cynthia.lengnickhall@utsa.edu.

The University of Texas–Pan American, College of Business Administration, Program in International Business, Edinburg, TX 78539. Offers computer information systems (PhD); economics (PhD); finance (PhD); management (PhD); marketing (PhD). *Degree requirements:* For doctorate, comprehensive exam, thesis/dissertation. *Entrance requirements:* For doctorate, GMAT or GRE. Additional exam requirements/recommendations for international students: Required—TOEFL, IELTS. Electronic applications accepted. *Expenses:* Contact institution.

University of the Incarnate Word, School of Graduate Studies and Research, H-E-B School of Business and Administration, Programs in Administration, San Antonio, TX 78209-6397. Offers adult education (MAA); applied administration (MAA); communication arts (MAA); healthcare administration (MAA); instructional technology (MAA); international business (Certificate); nutrition (MAA); organizational development (MAA, Certificate); project management (Certificate); sports management (MAA). Part-time and evening/weekend programs available. Postbaccalaureate distance learning degree programs offered (no on-campus study). *Students:* 30 full-time (17 women), 163 part-time (114 women); includes 128 minority (18 African Americans, 3 Asian Americans or Pacific Islanders, 107 Hispanic Americans), 8 international. Average age 35. In 2009, 68 master's awarded. *Degree requirements:* For master's, capstone. *Entrance requirements:* For master's, GRE, GMAT, undergraduate degree, minimum GPA of 2.5. Additional exam requirements/recommendations for international students: Required—TOEFL (minimum score 560 paper-based; 220 computer-based; 83 iBT). *Application deadline:* Applications are processed on a rolling basis. Application fee: $20. Electronic applications accepted. *Expenses:* Tuition: Full-time $12,150; part-time $675 per credit hour. Required fees: $83 per credit hour. *Financial support:* Federal Work-Study and scholarships/grants available. Financial award applicants required to submit FAFSA. *Unit head:* Dr. Daniel Dominguez, MAA Director, 210-829-3180, Fax: 210-805-3564, E-mail: domingue@uiwtx.edu. *Application contact:* Andrea Cyterski-Acosta, Dean of Enrollment, 210-829-6005, Fax: 210-829-3921, E-mail: admis@uiwtx.edu.

University of the Incarnate Word, School of Graduate Studies and Research, H-E-B School of Business and Administration, Programs in Business Administration, San Antonio, TX 78209-6397. Offers general business (MBA); international business (MBA); international business

strategy (MBA); sports management (MBA). *Accreditation:* ACBSP. Part-time and evening/weekend programs available. Postbaccalaureate distance learning degree programs offered. *Students:* 100 full-time (55 women), 255 part-time (155 women); includes 196 minority (19 African Americans, 1 American Indian/Alaska Native, 14 Asian Americans or Pacific Islanders, 162 Hispanic Americans), 41 international. Average age 32. In 2009, 111 master's awarded. *Degree requirements:* For master's, capstone. *Entrance requirements:* For master's, GMAT (minimum score 450), undergraduate degree with minimum overall GPA of 2.5. Additional exam requirements/recommendations for international students: Required—TOEFL (minimum score 560 paper-based; 220 computer-based; 83 iBT). *Application deadline:* Applications are processed on a rolling basis. Application fee: $20. Electronic applications accepted. *Expenses:* Tuition: Full-time $12,150; part-time $675 per credit hour. Required fees: $83 per credit hour. *Financial support:* Federal Work-Study and scholarships/grants available. Financial award applicants required to submit FAFSA. *Unit head:* Dr. Jeannie Scott, MBA Director, 210-283-5002, Fax: 210-805-3564, E-mail: scott@uiwtx.edu. *Application contact:* Andrea Cyterski-Acosta, Dean of Enrollment, 210-829-6005, Fax: 210-829-3921, E-mail: admis@uiwtx.edu.

University of the West, Department of Business Administration, Rosemead, CA 91770. Offers business administration (EMBA); finance (MBA); information technology and management (MBA); international business (MBA); nonprofit organization management (MBA). Part-time and evening/weekend programs available. *Entrance requirements:* Additional exam requirements/recommendations for international students: Required—TOEFL.

The University of Toledo, College of Graduate Studies, College of Business Administration, Department of Marketing and International Business, Program in International Business, Toledo, OH 43606-3390. Offers MBA. *Entrance requirements:* For master's, GMAT.

University of Tulsa, Graduate School, Collins College of Business, Master of Business Administration Program, Tulsa, OK 74104-3189. Offers accounting (MBA); business administration (MBA); energy management (MBA); finance (MBA); international business (MBA); management information systems (MBA); taxation (MBA); JD/MBA; MBA/MSCS; MBA/MSF. *Accreditation:* AACSB. Part-time and evening/weekend programs available. *Faculty:* 32 full-time (6 women). *Students:* 59 full-time (26 women), 45 part-time (18 women); includes 13 minority (4 African Americans, 4 American Indian/Alaska Native, 1 Asian American or Pacific Islander, 4 Hispanic Americans), 9 international. Average age 25. 78 applicants, 53% accepted, 30 enrolled. In 2009, 36 master's awarded. *Entrance requirements:* For master's, GMAT. Additional exam requirements/recommendations for international students: Required—TOEFL (minimum score 575 paper-based; 232 computer-based; 90 iBT), IELTS (minimum score 6.5). *Application deadline:* Applications are processed on a rolling basis. Application fee: $40. Electronic applications accepted. *Expenses:* Tuition: Full-time $16,182; part-time $899 per credit hour. Required fees: $4 per credit hour. Tuition and fees vary according to course load. *Financial support:* In 2009–10, 42 students received support, including 5 fellowships (averaging $11,894 per year), 2 research assistantships (averaging $9,322 per year), 35 teaching assistantships (averaging $8,112 per year); institutionally sponsored loans, scholarships/grants, health care benefits, tuition waivers (full and partial), and unspecified assistantships also available. Support available to part-time students. Financial award application deadline: 2/1; financial award applicants required to submit FAFSA. *Faculty research:* Accounting, energy management, finance, international business, management information systems, taxation. *Unit head:* Dr. Markham Collins, Associate Dean of the Collins College of Business, 918-631-2783, Fax: 918-631-2142, E-mail: markham-collins@utulsa.edu. *Application contact:* Dr. Markham Collins, Associate Dean of the Collins College of Business, 918-631-2783, Fax: 918-631-2142, E-mail: markham-collins@utulsa.edu.

University of Washington, Graduate School, Interdisciplinary Program in Global Trade, Transportation and Logistics Studies, Seattle, WA 98195. Offers Certificate.

University of Washington, Graduate School, Michael G. Foster School of Business, Seattle, WA 98195-3200. Offers auditing and assurance (MP Acc); business (PhD); business administration (evening) (MBA); business administration (full-time) (MBA); executive business administration (MBA); global business administration (MBA); global executive business administration (MBA); taxation (MP Acc); technology management (MBA); JD/MBA; MBA/MAIS; MBA/MHA. *Accreditation:* AACSB. Part-time and evening/weekend programs available. Terminal master's awarded for partial completion of doctoral program. *Degree requirements:* For doctorate, comprehensive exam, thesis/dissertation. *Entrance requirements:* For master's, GMAT; for doctorate, GMAT, GRE. Additional exam requirements/recommendations for international students: Required—TOEFL (minimum score 600 paper-based; 250 computer-based). Electronic applications accepted. *Expenses:* Contact institution. *Faculty research:* Finance, marketing, organizational behavior, information technology, strategy.

The University of Western Ontario, Richard Ivey School of Business, London, ON N6A 3K7, Canada. Offers business (EMBA, PhD); corporate strategy and leadership elective (MBA); entrepreneurship elective (MBA); finance elective (MBA); health sector stream (MBA); international management elective (MBA); marketing elective (MBA); JD/MBA. *Faculty:* 61 full-time (13 women). *Students:* 164 full-time (50 women). Average age 29. In 2009, 167 master's awarded. *Degree requirements:* For master's, thesis (for some programs); for doctorate, thesis/dissertation. *Entrance requirements:* For master's, GMAT, 2 years of full-time work experience, interview. Additional exam requirements/recommendations for international students: Required—TOEFL (minimum score 100 computer-based; 100 iBT), IELTS (minimum score 6), IELTS or TOEFL. *Application deadline:* For fall admission, 10/12 for domestic students, 8/16 for international students; for winter admission, 12/16 for domestic students, 10/12 for international students; for spring admission, 1/10 priority date for domestic students, 12/16 for international students. Applications are processed on a rolling basis. Application fee: $150 Canadian dollars. Electronic applications accepted. *Financial support:* Scholarships/grants and health care benefits available. Financial award application deadline: 1/10. *Faculty research:* Strategy, organizational behavior, international business, finance, operations management. *Unit head:* Carol Stephenson, Dean, 519-661-3285, Fax: 519-661-4126, E-mail: cstephenson@ivey.ca. *Application contact:* Niki da Silva, Director, MBA Program Services, 519-661-3419, Fax: 519-661-3431, E-mail: ndasilva@ivey.ca.

University of Wisconsin–Milwaukee, Graduate School, College of Letters and Sciences, Interdepartmental Program in Human Resources and Labor Relations, Milwaukee, WI 53201-0413. Offers human resources and labor relations (MHRLR); international human resources and labor relations (Certificate); mediation and negotiation (Certificate). Part-time programs available. *Students:* 14 full-time (10 women), 44 part-time (34 women); includes 12 minority (5 African Americans, 2 Asian Americans or Pacific Islanders, 5 Hispanic Americans), 2 international. Average age 31. 37 applicants, 51% accepted, 5 enrolled. In 2009, 22 master's awarded. *Entrance requirements:* For master's, GMAT or GRE General Test. Additional exam requirements/recommendations for international students: Required—TOEFL (minimum score 550 paper-based; 79 iBT), IELTS (minimum score 6.5). *Application deadline:* For fall admission, 1/1 priority date for domestic students; for spring admission, 9/1 for domestic students. Applications are processed on a rolling basis. Application fee: $45 ($75 for international students). *Expenses:* Tuition, state resident: full-time $8800. Tuition, nonresident: full-time $20,760. Tuition and fees vary according to program and reciprocity agreements. *Financial support:* Career-related internships or fieldwork available. Support available to part-time students. Financial award application deadline: 4/15. *Unit head:* Susan M. Donohue-Davies, Representative, 414-299-4009, Fax: 414-229-5915, E-mail: suedono@uwm.edu. *Application contact:* General Information Contact, 414-229-4982, Fax: 414-229-6967, E-mail: gradschool@uwm.edu.

University of Wisconsin–Oshkosh, The Office of Graduate Studies, College of Business, Program in Global Business Administration, Oshkosh, WI 54901. Offers GMBA. *Degree requirements:* For master's, integrative seminar, study abroad. *Entrance requirements:* For master's, GMAT, GRE, letters of recommendation.

University of Wisconsin–Whitewater, School of Graduate Studies, College of Business and Economics, Program in Business Administration, Whitewater, WI 53190-1790. Offers finance (MBA); human resource management (MBA); information technology management (MBA);

international business (MBA); management (MBA); marketing (MBA); operations and supply chain management (MBA); technology and training (MBA). *Accreditation:* AACSB. Part-time and evening/weekend programs available. Postbaccalaureate distance learning degree programs offered (no on-campus study). *Degree requirements:* For master's, thesis or alternative. *Entrance requirements:* For master's, GMAT, minimum AACSB index of 1000, minimum GPA of 2.75. Additional exam requirements/recommendations for international students: Required—TOEFL (minimum score 550 paper-based; 213 computer-based). Electronic applications accepted. *Faculty research:* Interface between social institutions and individual behavior, technology and innovation management, occupational mental health, workplace deviance and workplace romance.

See Close-Up on page 0.

Upper Iowa University, Online Master's Programs, Fayette, IA 52142-1857. Offers accounting (MBA); corporate financial management (MBA); global business (MBA); health and human services (MPA); higher education administration (MHEA); homeland security (MPA); human resources management (MBA); justice administration (MPA); organizational development (MBA); public personnel management (MPA); quality management (MBA). MBA also available at Madison, WI campus. Part-time programs available. Postbaccalaureate distance learning degree programs offered (no on-campus study). *Faculty:* 3 full-time (0 women), 66 part-time/adjunct (27 women). *Students:* 723 full-time (442 women). *Degree requirements:* For master's, research project. *Entrance requirements:* For master's, GMAT, GRE, or minimum GPA of 2.7 during last 60 hours. Additional exam requirements/recommendations for international students: Required—TOEFL (minimum score 570 paper-based; 230 computer-based). *Application deadline:* Applications are processed on a rolling basis. Application fee: $50. Electronic applications accepted. *Expenses:* Tuition: Full-time $6948; part-time $386 per credit hour. *Financial support:* Available to part-time students. Applicants required to submit FAFSA. *Faculty research:* Total quality management, CQI, teams, organization culture and climate, management. *Application contact:* David Hannum, Admissions Advisor, 800-603-3756, E-mail: hannumd@uiu.edu.

Valparaiso University, Graduate School, Program in International Commerce and Policy, Valparaiso, IN 46383. Offers MS, JD/MS. Part-time and evening/weekend programs available. *Students:* 83 full-time (41 women), 11 part-time (6 women); includes 7 minority (4 African Americans, 3 Asian Americans or Pacific Islanders), 78 international. Average age 25. In 2009, 64 master's awarded. *Entrance requirements:* For master's, minimum GPA of 3.0. Additional exam requirements/recommendations for international students: Required—TOEFL (minimum score 550 paper-based; 213 computer-based; 80 iBT). *Application deadline:* Applications are processed on a rolling basis. Application fee: $30 ($50 for international students). Electronic applications accepted. *Financial support:* Available to part-time students. Applicants required to submit FAFSA. *Unit head:* Dr. David L. Rowland, Dean, Graduate Studies and Continuing Education/Associate Provost, 219-464-5313, Fax: 219-464-5381, E-mail: david.rowland@valpo.edu. *Application contact:* Jamie Haney, Coordinator of Graduate Admission, 219-464-5313, Fax: 219-464-5381, E-mail: jamie.haney@valpo.edu.

Villanova University, Villanova School of Business, MBA—Fast Track Program, Villanova, PA 19085. Offers finance (MBA); international business (MBA); management information systems (MBA); marketing (MBA). *Accreditation:* AACSB. Part-time and evening/weekend programs available. *Entrance requirements:* For master's, GMAT, minimum 4.5 years of professional work experience. Additional exam requirements/recommendations for international students: Required—TOEFL (minimum score 550 paper-based; 213 computer-based; 80 iBT). Electronic applications accepted. *Expenses:* Tuition: Part-time $630 per credit. Required fees: $60 per credit. Part-time tuition and fees vary according to degree level and program. *Faculty research:* Developing and leveraging technology, ethical business practices, managing for innovation and creativity, the global political economy, strategic marketing management.

Villanova University, Villanova School of Business, MBA—Flex Track Program, Villanova, PA 19085. Offers corporate management (general) (MBA); finance (MBA); international business (MBA); management information systems (MBA); marketing (MBA); JD/MBA. *Accreditation:* AACSB. Part-time and evening/weekend programs available. Postbaccalaureate distance learning degree programs offered (minimal on-campus study). *Entrance requirements:* For master's, GMAT, minimum 4.5 years work experience. Additional exam requirements/recommendations for international students: Required—TOEFL (minimum score 550 paper-based; 213 computer-based; 80 iBT). Electronic applications accepted. *Expenses:* Tuition: Part-time $630 per credit. Required fees: $60 per credit. Part-time tuition and fees vary according to degree level and program. *Faculty research:* Developing and leveraging technology, ethical business practices, managing for innovation and creativity, the global political economy, strategic marketing management.

Virginia International University, Business Programs Department, Fairfax, VA 22030. Offers accounting (MBA); executive management (Graduate Certificate); global logistics (MBA); health care management (MBA); human resources management (MBA); international business management (MBA); international finance (MBA); marketing management (MBA). Part-time programs available. *Faculty:* 12 part-time/adjunct (1 woman). *Students:* 138 full-time (63 women), 7 part-time (5 women); includes 7 minority (1 African American, 5 Asian Americans or Pacific Islanders, 1 Hispanic American), 136 international. Average age 27. 331 applicants, 31% accepted, 40 enrolled. In 2009, 42 master's awarded. *Entrance requirements:* For master's and Graduate Certificate, bachelor's degree. Additional exam requirements/recommendations for international students: Required—TOEFL (minimum score 550 paper-based; 213 computer-based; 80 iBT), IELTS (minimum score 6). *Application deadline:* For fall admission, 7/31 for domestic students, 7/3 for international students; for spring admission, 12/18 for domestic students, 11/20 for international students. Applications are processed on a rolling basis. Application fee: $100. Electronic applications accepted. *Expenses:* Tuition: Full-time $10,044; part-time $569 per credit. One-time fee: $75. Tuition and fees vary according to degree level. *Financial support:* In 2009–10, 10 students received support. Scholarships/grants available. Financial award application deadline: 7/1. *Unit head:* Dr. Gail Whitaker, Chair, 703-591-7042 Ext. 346, Fax: 703-591-7046, E-mail: gwhitaker@viu.edu. *Application contact:* Emily L. Kraus, Director of Admissions, 703-591-7042 Ext. 309, Fax: 703-591-7048, E-mail: admissions@viu.edu.

Wagner College, Division of Graduate Studies, Department of Business Administration, Program in International Business, Staten Island, NY 10301-4495. Offers MBA. Part-time and evening/weekend programs available. *Degree requirements:* For master's, thesis optional. *Entrance requirements:* For master's, GMAT, minimum GPA of 2.6. *Expenses:* Tuition: Full-time $15,570; part-time $865 per credit. Required fees: $2.

Walden University, Graduate Programs, School of Management, Minneapolis, MN 55401. Offers applied management and decision sciences (PhD), including accounting, engineering management, finance, general applied management and decision sciences, information systems management, knowledge management, leadership and organizational change, learning management, operations research, self-designed program in applied management and design sciences; business information management (MISM); enterprise information security (MISM); entrepreneurship (MBA, DBA); finance (MBA, DBA); global supply chain management (DBA); healthcare management (MBA); healthcare system improvement (MBA); human resource management (MBA); information systems management (DBA); international business (MBA, DBA); IT strategy and governance (MISM); leadership (MBA, MS, DBA), including entrepreneurship (MS), general management (MS), human resources leadership (MS), innovation and technology (MS), leader development (MS), project management (MS), self-designed (MS), sustainable futures (MS); managing global software and service supply chains (MISM); marketing (MBA, DBA); project management (MBA, MS); risk management (MBA); self-designed (MBA, DBA); social impact management (DBA); sustainable futures (MBA); technology (MBA); technology entrepreneurship (DBA). Part-time and evening/weekend programs available. Postbaccalaureate distance learning degree programs offered (minimal on-campus study). *Faculty:* 17 full-time, 211 part-time/adjunct. *Students:* 3,389 full-time (1,774 women), 815 part-time (482 women); includes 1,969 minority (1,640 African Americans, 36 American Indian/Alaska Native, 123

International Business

Walden University (continued)
Asian Americans or Pacific Islanders, 170 Hispanic Americans), 95 international. Average age 41. In 2009, 699 master's, 42 doctorates awarded. *Degree requirements:* For doctorate, thesis/dissertation (for some programs), residency. *Entrance requirements:* For master's, bachelor's degree or equivalent in related field; minimum GPA of 2.5; official transcripts; goal statement; access to computer and Internet; for doctorate, master's degree or equivalent in related field; minimum GPA of 3.0; 3 years of related professional/academic experience (preferred). Additional exam requirements/recommendations for international students: Required—TOEFL (minimum score 550 paper-based; 213 computer-based), IELTS (minimum score 6.5), TOEFL, IELTS, or Michigan English Language Assessment Battery (minimum score 82). *Application deadline:* Applications are processed on a rolling basis. Application fee: $50. Electronic applications accepted. *Expenses:* Tuition: Full-time $13,665; part-time $560 per credit. Required fees: $1375. Tuition and fees vary according to course load, degree level and program. *Financial support:* In 2009–10, 466 students received support; fellowships, Federal Work-Study, scholarships/grants, unspecified assistantships, and family tuition reduction, active duty/veteran tuition reduction, group tuition reduction, interest-free payment plans available. Support available to part-time students. Financial award applicants required to submit FAFSA. *Unit head:* William Schulz, Interim Associate Dean, 800-925-3368. *Application contact:* Jennifer Hall, Director of Enrollment, 866-4-WALDEN, E-mail: info@waldenu.edu.

Washington State University, Graduate School, College of Agricultural, Human, and Natural Resource Sciences, School of Economic Sciences, Department of Economics, Pullman, WA 99164. Offers applied economics (MA); economics (MA, PhD); international business economics (Certificate). *Faculty:* 34. *Students:* 50 full-time (16 women), 6 part-time (2 women); includes 2 minority (1 American Indian/Alaska Native, 1 Hispanic American), 30 international. Average age 30. 233 applicants, 26% accepted, 26 enrolled. In 2009, 9 master's, 8 doctorates awarded. *Degree requirements:* For master's, comprehensive exam (for some programs), thesis (for some programs), oral exam; for doctorate, comprehensive exam, thesis/dissertation, oral exam, written exam, field exams. *Entrance requirements:* For master's, GRE General Test, statement of purpose, three letters of reference, copies of all transcripts; for doctorate, GRE General Test or GMAT, statement of purpose, three letters of reference, copies of all transcripts. Additional exam requirements/recommendations for international students: Required—TOEFL, IELTS. *Application deadline:* For fall admission, 1/10 priority date for domestic students, 1/10 for international students. Applications are processed on a rolling basis. Application fee: $50. *Financial support:* In 2009–10, research assistantships (averaging $13,917 per year), 13 teaching assistantships (averaging $13,506 per year) were awarded; career-related internships or fieldwork, Federal Work-Study, institutionally sponsored loans, tuition waivers (partial), and teaching associateships also available. Financial award application deadline: 4/1; financial award applicants required to submit FAFSA. *Faculty research:* Economic theory and quantitative methods, applied microeconomics. Total annual research expenditures: $1 million. *Unit head:* Dr. Ron C. Mittelhammer, Director, 509-335-1706, Fax: 509-335-1173, E-mail: mittelha@wsu.edu. *Application contact:* Graduate School Admissions, 800-GRADWSU, Fax: 509-335-1949, E-mail: gradsch@wsu.edu.

Wayland Baptist University, Graduate Programs, Programs in Business Administration/Management, Plainview, TX 79072-6998. Offers general business (MBA); health care administration (MBA); human resource management (MBA); international management (MBA); management (MA, MBA), including health care administration (MA), human resource management (MA), organization management (MA); management information systems (MBA). Part-time and evening/weekend programs available. Postbaccalaureate distance learning degree programs offered (no on-campus study). *Faculty:* 10 full-time (3 women). *Students:* 6 full-time (1 woman), 55 part-time (31 women); includes 24 minority (9 African Americans, 1 American Indian/Alaska Native, 14 Hispanic Americans). Average age 34. 25 applicants, 76% accepted, 10 enrolled. In 2009, 8 master's awarded. *Degree requirements:* For master's, capstone course. *Entrance requirements:* For master's, GMAT, GRE or MAT. Additional exam requirements/recommendations for international students: Required—TOEFL (minimum score 500 paper-based; 173 computer-based; 61 iBT). *Application deadline:* Applications are processed on a rolling basis. Application fee: $50. Electronic applications accepted. *Expenses:* Tuition: Full-time $5796; part-time $322 per credit hour. Required fees: $782; $9 per credit hour. $60 per semester. Tuition and fees vary according to course load and campus/location. *Financial support:* Federal Work-Study, institutionally sponsored loans, and scholarships/grants available. Support available to part-time students. Financial award application deadline: 5/1; financial award applicants required to submit FAFSA. *Unit head:* Dr. Otto Schacht, Chairman, 806-291-1020, Fax: 806-291-1957. *Application contact:* Amanda Stanton, Graduate Studies, 806-291-3423, Fax: 806-291-1950, E-mail: stanton@wbu.edu.

Webster University, George Herbert Walker School of Business and Technology, Department of Business, St. Louis, MO 63119-3194. Offers business (MA); business and organizational security management (MBA); computer resources and information management (MBA); environmental management (MBA); finance (MA, MBA); health services management (MBA); human resources development (MBA); human resources management (MBA); international business (MA, MBA); management and leadership (MBA); marketing (MBA); procurement and acquisitions management (MBA); telecommunications management (MBA). *Accreditation:* ACBSP. Part-time and evening/weekend programs available. Postbaccalaureate distance learning degree programs offered (no on-campus study). *Faculty:* 9 full-time, 430 part-time/adjunct. *Students:* 1,190 full-time (543 women), 4,226 part-time (2,159 women). Average age 34. In 2009, 2,021 master's awarded. *Degree requirements:* For master's, comprehensive exam (for some programs), thesis (for some programs). *Entrance requirements:* Additional exam requirements/recommendations for international students: Required—TOEFL. *Application deadline:* Applications are processed on a rolling basis. Application fee: $35 ($50 for international students). *Expenses:* Tuition: Part-time $565 per credit hour. Tuition and fees vary according to degree level, campus/location and program. *Financial support:* Federal Work-Study available. Support available to part-time students. Financial award application deadline: 4/1; financial award applicants required to submit FAFSA. *Unit head:* Dr. Debbie Psihountas, Chair, 314-246-7553 Ext. 7017, Fax: 314-968-7077, E-mail: buschair@webster.edu. *Application contact:* Matt Nolan, Associate Vice President for Enrollment Management/Dean of Admissions, Fax: 314-968-7116, E-mail: gadmit@webster.edu.

Western International University, Graduate Programs in Business, Master of Business Administration Program in International Business, Phoenix, AZ 85021-2718. Offers MBA. Part-time and evening/weekend programs available. Postbaccalaureate distance learning degree programs offered (no on-campus study). *Faculty:* 21 part-time/adjunct (5 women). *Students:* 83 full-time (38 women); includes 24 minority (8 African Americans, 7 Asian Americans or Pacific Islanders, 9 Hispanic Americans), 13 international. Average age 34. In 2009, 23 master's awarded. *Entrance requirements:* For master's, minimum GPA of 2.75. Additional exam requirements/recommendations for international students: Required—TOEFL (minimum score 550 paper-based; 213 computer-based; 79 iBT), TWE (minimum score 5), or IELTS (minimum score 6.5). *Application deadline:* Applications are processed on a rolling basis. Application fee: $25. Electronic applications accepted. *Expenses:* Tuition: Full-time $12,600. One-time fee: $25 full-time. *Financial support:* Applicants required to submit FAFSA. *Unit head:* Dr. Deborah DeSimone, Chief Academic Officer, 602-429-1135, E-mail: deborah.desemone@west.edu. *Application contact:* Melissa Machuca, Director of Enrollment, 602-943-2311, Fax: 602-371-8637.

Whitworth University, School of Global Commerce and Management, Spokane, WA 99251-0001. Offers international management (MBA, MIM). Part-time and evening/weekend programs available. *Faculty:* 6 full-time (1 woman), 9 part-time/adjunct (2 women). *Students:* 39 full-time (22 women), 3 international. Average age 31. 36 applicants, 42% accepted, 15 enrolled. In 2009, 18 master's awarded. *Degree requirements:* For master's, one foreign language, foreign language (MBA in international management, MIM). *Entrance requirements:* For master's, GMAT or GRE, Minimum GPA of 3.0, two letters of recommendation, resume, completion of prerequisite courses in micro-economics, macro-economics, financial accounting, finance, marketing. Additional exam requirements/recommendations for international students: Required—TOEFL (minimum score 213 computer-based; 88 iBT), TWE. *Application deadline:* For fall admission, 8/20 priority date for domestic students, 8/20 for international students; for spring admission, 1/8 priority date for domestic students. Applications are processed on a rolling basis. Application fee: $35. Electronic applications accepted. Tuition and fees vary according to program. *Financial support:* In 2009–10, 9 students received support; fellowships with tuition reimbursements available, career-related internships or fieldwork, Federal Work-Study, institutionally sponsored loans, and scholarships/grants available. Support available to part-time students. Financial award application deadline: 3/1; financial award applicants required to submit FAFSA. *Faculty research:* International business (European, Central America and Asian topics), entrepreneurship and business plan development. *Unit head:* John Hengesh, Director, Graduate Studies in Business, 509-777-4455, Fax: 509-777-3723, E-mail: jhengesh@whitworth.edu. *Application contact:* Bonnie Wakefield, Assistant Director, Graduate Studies in Business, 509-777-4606, Fax: 509-777-3723, E-mail: bwakefield@whitworth.edu.

Wilkes University, College of Graduate and Professional Studies, Jay S. Sidhu School of Business and Leadership, Wilkes-Barre, PA 18766-0002. Offers accounting (MBA); entrepreneurship (MBA); finance (MBA); human resource management (MBA); international business (MBA); management (MBA); marketing (MBA). *Accreditation:* ACBSP. Part-time and evening/weekend programs available. *Students:* 86 full-time (41 women), 118 part-time (59 women); includes 7 minority (4 African Americans, 1 Asian American or Pacific Islander, 2 Hispanic Americans), 48 international. Average age 29. In 2009, 59 master's awarded. *Entrance requirements:* For master's, GMAT. Additional exam requirements/recommendations for international students: Required—TOEFL (minimum score 500 paper-based; 173 computer-based; 79 iBT). *Application deadline:* Applications are processed on a rolling basis. Application fee: $45. *Expenses:* Contact institution. *Financial support:* Federal Work-Study and unspecified assistantships available. Financial award application deadline: 3/1; financial award applicants required to submit FAFSA. *Unit head:* Dr. Paul Browne, Dean, 570-408-4701, Fax: 570-408-7846, E-mail: paul.browne@wilkes.edu. *Application contact:* Kathleen Houlihan, Director of Graduate Studies, 570-408-3235, Fax: 570-408-7846, E-mail: kathleen.houlihan@wilkes.edu.

Wright State University, School of Graduate Studies, Raj Soin College of Business, Department of Management, Dayton, OH 45435. Offers flexible business (MBA); health care management (MBA); international business (MBA); management, innovation and change (MBA); project management (MBA); supply chain management (MBA); MBA/MS. *Entrance requirements:* For master's, GMAT, minimum AACSB index of 1000. Additional exam requirements/recommendations for international students: Required—TOEFL.

Xavier University, Williams College of Business, Master of Business Administration Program, Cincinnati, OH 45207-3221. Offers business administration (Exec MBA, MBA); business intelligence (MBA); finance (MBA); international business (MBA); management information systems (MBA); marketing (MBA); MBA/MHSA; MSN/MBA. *Accreditation:* AACSB. Part-time and evening/weekend programs available. *Faculty:* 44 full-time (17 women), 9 part-time/adjunct (2 women). *Students:* 167 full-time (51 women), 862 part-time (283 women); includes 149 minority (60 African Americans, 62 Asian Americans or Pacific Islanders, 27 Hispanic Americans), 17 international. Average age 30. 355 applicants, 63% accepted, 187 enrolled. In 2009, 369 master's awarded. *Degree requirements:* For master's, capstone course. *Entrance requirements:* For master's, GMAT. Additional exam requirements/recommendations for international students: Required—TOEFL (minimum score 550 paper-based; 213 computer-based; 80 iBT). *Application deadline:* For fall admission, 8/1 priority date for domestic students, 5/1 for international students; for spring admission, 12/1 priority date for domestic students, 9/1 for international students. Applications are processed on a rolling basis. Application fee: $0. Electronic applications accepted. *Expenses:* Contact institution. *Financial support:* In 2009–10, 183 students received support. Scholarships/grants, tuition waivers (partial), and unspecified assistantships available. Financial award application deadline: 3/1; financial award applicants required to submit FAFSA. *Unit head:* Dr. Hema Krishnan, Associate Dean, 513-745-3206, Fax: 513-745-3455; E-mail: krishnan@xavier.edu. *Application contact:* Anna Marie Whelan, Assistant Director, MBA Programs, 513-745-3525, Fax: 513-745-2929, E-mail: whelana@xavier.edu.

York University, Faculty of Graduate Studies, Schulich School of Business, Toronto, ON M3J 1P3, Canada. Offers administration (PhD); business (MBA); finance (MF); international business (IMBA); public administration (MPA); MBA/JD; MBA/MA; MBA/MFA. Part-time and evening/weekend programs available. *Degree requirements:* For master's, advanced proficiency in a second language, work term (IMBA); for doctorate, comprehensive exam, thesis/dissertation. *Entrance requirements:* For master's, GMAT, minimum GPA of 3.0; for doctorate, GMAT, minimum GPA of 3.3. Electronic applications accepted.

See Close-Up on page 285.

Monterey Institute
of International Studies
A Graduate School of Middlebury College

MONTEREY INSTITUTE OF INTERNATIONAL STUDIES

Fisher International M.B.A. Program

Programs of Study	The Fisher International M.B.A. Program at the Monterey Institute of International Studies prepares professionals to operate successfully in the global business environment of the twenty-first century. Students from around the world choose this M.B.A. program because they are interested in international business ventures. The School's diverse student body, of which 50 percent is international students and 50 percent is women, as well as its 10:1 student-faculty ratio, makes this M.B.A. program unique and highly personalized.
	The Fisher International M.B.A. Program is located in the heart of California's beautiful central coast and only a short driving distance away from San Francisco and Silicon Valley. The School's strategic location and its ranking as one of the top M.B.A. programs in the United States for entrepreneurs is a very attractive mix for prospective M.B.A. students.
	The Fisher M.B.A. program offers diverse course work to assist students in developing the skills needed for today's business world. All students enroll in the international business core classes, comprised of International Organizational Behavior, Global Business Strategies, and the capstone, the International Business Plan. These courses build cross-cultural competency and an entrepreneurial mindset in graduates. Cross-cultural perspectives are integrated throughout the curriculum, and students customize their programs with multiple language courses and electives.
	Depending on students' background and experience, they may pursue one of several tracks in the Fisher M.B.A. program, described below.
	The traditional two-year M.B.A. program is designed for students from nonbusiness undergraduate programs looking to transition to business management opportunities. Students enroll in core business courses during the first two semesters, exploring key business functions. During the second year of the program, students apply these core skills to electives and the International Business Plan project.
	An advanced entry M.B.A. program is available for applicants with undergraduate degrees in business, significant business experience, and high-level language skills.
	The Peace Corps Master's International (PCMI) program is offered in conjunction with the U.S. Peace Corps. Students either may pursue a PCMI program in the two-year or advanced entry track. Students attend two or three semesters on campus and complete the International Business Plan. Then they complete a twenty-seven-month assignment with the U.S. Peace Corps during which they apply the M.B.A. curriculum to business and economic development opportunities in countries around the globe. Students return to campus for a final semester to complete a Business Development Project, which ties their M.B.A. curriculum to a business-related aspect of their Peace Corps assignment.
	Dual degree programs allow students to pursue a second master's degree by combining the M.B.A. curriculum with course work from international policy studies, international environmental policy, international trade policy, or translation localization management. Dual degree programs require careful planning and integration of courses from both programs in order to be completed within six semesters.
	M.B.A. specializations are for students who want to pursue a graduate degree in order to develop their resume, build networks, gain new skills, and position themselves for career development and advancement. The M.B.A. program provides a wealth of opportunities to help with these goals. Students may design specialization tracks displaying significant course work, projects, internships, and activities based around their topic area. Students may choose from the following list of specializations or design their own: entrepreneurship, international marketing, international finance, international trade management, international environmental management, globalization/localization management, corporate social responsibility/business sustainability, public and nonprofit management, global business management, or regional business emphases.
Research Facilities	The Center for Globalization and Localization of Business Exports (GLOBE) provides education, consulting, and research in the area of business globalization and localization, including the development of business plans and assessment of a company's globalization or localization needs. The Center for East Asian Studies sponsors research on the geopolitical and international issues in East Asia, including trade, investment, migration, and natural resource development. The Center for Russian and Eurasian Studies is focused on the political, social, and cultural developments in Russia and the newly independent states, including negotiating behavior, arms control, security issues, and nuclear regionalism.
	The William Tell Coleman Library includes 95,000 volumes, more than 500 print periodicals, over 50 online databases, more than 400 academic journals, about thirty-five newspapers, and approximately 15,000 electronic books. One third of the collection is in languages other than English.
	Innovative and challenging curricula at the Institute require appropriate facilities and cutting-edge technology. Classrooms vary in size from large halls, where plenary sessions with simultaneous interpretation can be held, to smaller classrooms and labs befitting seminar-style classes for 5 to 15 students.
	The Max Kade Language and Technology Center is a fully equipped language-learning center. It provides multimedia classrooms and conference rooms with state-of-the-art technology, including a multimedia resource center and the campus Teaching and Learning Collaborative.
	In addition to numerous computer labs, the campus is wireless. Every student is encouraged to have a personal laptop computer adapted for wireless connectivity.
Financial Aid	Candidates with a minimum grade point average of 3.3 on a 4.0 scale (or equivalent) are considered for merit scholarships that range from $4000 to $15,000. Veterans of military service or orphans/dependants of veterans may be eligible for veteran's benefits. Other scholarships may be awarded by outside foundations.
	Under the Federal Stafford Loan Program, students may borrow up to $8500 in subsidized loans or $20,500 in unsubsidized loans, less any subsidized amount. Graduate PLUS Loans cover the cost of attendance minus other financial aid resources. The Federal Work-Study Program allows students to work up to $3000 per academic year, working a maximum of 20 hours per week.
Cost of Study	Tuition and fees for 2010–11 are $32,056.
Living and Housing Costs	The estimated variable expenses for books, supplies, housing, food, location transportation, personal expenses, and health insurance is $17,792.
Student Group	The Fisher International M.B.A. Program is characterized by its diverse student body—50 percent are international students and 50 percent are women. Fisher M.B.A. students have a broad range of previous work experience; they include software engineers, entrepreneurs, linguists, nonprofit managers, accountants, former Peace Corps volunteers, and many others. As a microcosm of the world, the School is the ideal setting for aspiring business executives to acquire the skills necessary to succeed in today's complex, cross-cultural business environments.
Student Outcomes	Fisher alumni have built careers in every corner of the business world and are involved in key emerging markets. Nearly half of all recent graduates work in finance and accounting, and a quarter of them work in marketing and sales. Other career tracks pursued by Fisher M.B.A. graduates include consulting, international management, and entrepreneurship. The top employers of Fisher graduates include: HSBC, HP, Fujitsu, IBM, Intel, Microsoft, Deloitte & Touche, Accenture, Adobe Systems, and Cisco Systems.
Location	The Monterey Institute is situated in one of the most spectacular natural environments in the world. The Monterey Peninsula is 130 miles south of San Francisco, on California's central coast, surrounded by ocean and mountains. Silicon Valley is only a short drive away. With a population of 100,000, the area combines a variety of rich cultural resources and agricultural activities.
The Institute	Established in 1955 with summer classes in language and culture, the Monterey Institute of Foreign Studies was the first institute dedicated to the then-revolutionary concept that a living language should be taught as such: French in French, German in German, etc. Year-round degree programs began in 1961. By 1979, the Institute had grown to international distinction and was renamed the Monterey Institute of International Studies.
	The Monterey Institute is a graduate school of Middlebury College. Founded in 1800, Middlebury is one of the country's top liberal arts colleges. It offers students a broad curriculum embracing the arts, humanities, literature, foreign languages, social sciences, and natural sciences. The affiliation further enriches the curriculum, creates a bicoastal presence, and offers valuable connections to build greater global connection.
	The Fisher International M.B.A. Program at the Monterey Institute of International Studies has been providing M.B.A. degrees with an international emphasis for over thirty years. The Fisher International M.B.A. Program is accredited by AACSB International, the premier accrediting agency for schools of business. For the past three years, the Princeton Review and *Entrepreneur* magazine have ranked Fisher as one of the top graduate schools committed to success in entrepreneurial endeavors.
Applying	Prospective students must submit a completed application form, a statement of purpose of no more than 600 words stating career objectives, a current resume or curriculum vitae, official transcripts from all colleges previously attended, two letters of recommendation, GMAT score, and a nonrefundable $50 application fee.
	International students should apply three months before enrollment. For the two-year M.B.A. program, the minimum scores for TOEFL are: 550 for paper-based test (PBT), with 4.0 for the test of written English; 213 for computer-based test (CBT), with 4.0 for the test of written English; 80 for Internet-based test (iBT), with 23 for the test of written English, and no other subscore below 19. The minimum score for IELTS is 6.5 overall with no subscore below 6.0 on the Academic module. The one-year Advanced Entry M.B.A. Program requires minimum TOEFL scores of 600 (PBT), 250 (CBT), and 100 (iBT); the IELTS minimum scores required are 7.0 overall and 7.0 on listening and reading subscores, with no subscore below 6.5 on writing and speaking on the Academic module.
Correspondence and Information	Admissions Office Monterey Institute of International Studies 460 Pierce Street Monterey, California 93940 Phone: 831-647-4123 800-824-7235 (toll-free) Fax: 831-647-6405 E-mail: admit@miis.edu Web site: http://www.miis.edu

Monterey Institute of International Studies

THE FACULTY AND THEIR RESEARCH

Harvey Arbelaez, Professor; Ph.D., Temple. Business in Latin America, corporate finance, country analysis, currency substitution, foreign direct investment, international business planning.

William Brooks, Adjunct Professor. Cross-border leadership and management, leadership development, management of product development, operations management, strategic planning.

Canri Chan, Assistant Professor; Ph.D., Flinders (Australia). Financial and management accounting, international accounting.

Michael Czinkota, Adjunct Professor; Ph.D., M.B.A., Ohio State. International business-to-business marketing.

Eddine Dahel, Associate Professor; Ph.D., M.B.A., IIT. International supply chain management, logistics, management science, operations management.

Vassilis Dalakas, Adjunct Professor; Ph.D., Oregon. Advertising, cross-cultural consumer behavior, international marketing, marketing communications.

David Deninger, Adjunct Professor. Real estate investment.

Sandra Dow, Professor; Ph.D., Concordia University (Canada); M.A., Dalhousie. Corporate governance, international finance.

Greg Elofson, Adjunct Professor; Ph.D., Arizona. Artificial intelligence, information technology strategy, object-oriented systems analysis and design.

John Jenkins, Professor Emeritus; D.Phil., Oxford (England). Business in Pacific Rim countries, entrepreneurship, international marketing, marketing communications.

Fredric Kropp, Associate Professor; Ph.D., Oregon. Entrepreneurship, international marketing.

Steve Landry, Professor; Ph.D., M.B.A., Colorado at Boulder. Cost accounting, financial and management accounting, financial auditing, government and nonprofit accounting.

Leonard Lane, Adjunct Professor; M.B.A., USC. Leadership development, organizational structuring, strategic planning.

Janet Marks, Adjunct Professor; Ph.D., NYU. Anthropology, cross-cultural communication, leadership development, organizational behavior.

Hillel Maximon, Adjunct Professor; M.B.A., NYU; CPA. Financial and management accounting, financial statement analysis, real estate finance.

Hugh McAllister, Adjunct Professor; Ph.D., M.B.A., Rensselaer. Corporate finance, foreign direct investment, international capital markets, international finance.

Kevin McGibben, Adjunct Professor; M.B.A. Arizona, Globalization/localization of products and services, global strategic development, international marketing, market development, strategic marketing.

Lynn Metcalf, Adjunct Professor; Ph.D., South Carolina, International marketing.

R. Bruce Paton, Department Chair; Ph.D., USC; M.B.A., Stanford. Corporate social responsibility, environmental management, sustainability.

David Roberts, Professor; Ph.D., USC. Economic theory, modeling and forecasting, monetary policy.

Daniel Robin, Adjunct Professor; Berkeley. Corporate social responsibility, environmental management, information technology strategy, leadership development, sustainability.

Ernest J. Scalberg, Research Professor; Ph.D., UCLA. Globalization/localization of products and services, global leadership, leadership development, organizational behavior.

Ron Schill, Visiting Professor; Ph.D., Oregon; M.B.A., Utah. Global strategic development, international business-to-business marketing, international marketing, management of product development, marketing of high-tech products, strategic marketing.

Yuwei Shi, Dean; Ph.D., Texas. Business technology management, global strategic development, strategic management.

Dave Schiffman, Adjunct Faculty; M.S., Naval Postgraduate School. Operations management.

Cary Simon, Adjunct Faculty; Ph.D., US International; M.B.A., Brenau. Cross-border leadership and management, leadership development, strategic planning.

Luc Soenen, Adjunct Professor; D.B.A., Harvard. Corporate finance, foreign exchange management, international capital markets, international finance.

Eli Zelkha, Adjunct Professor; M.B.A., Stanford. Market development, strategic management, venture capital.

Section 12
Management Information Systems

This section contains a directory of institutions offering graduate work in management information systems, followed by an in-depth entry submitted by an institution that chose to prepare a detailed program description. Additional information about programs listed in the directory but not augmented by an in-depth entry may be obtained by writing directly to the dean of a graduate school or chair of a department at the address given in the directory.

For programs offering related work, see also in this book *Business Administration and Management.* In another guide in this series: **_Graduate Programs in Engineering & Applied Sciences_**

See *Computer Science and Information Technology* and *Management of Engineering and Technology*

CONTENTS

Program Directory

Close-Up

Management Information Systems

Abilene Christian University, Graduate School, School of Information Technology and Computing, Abilene, TX 79699-9100. Offers MS. Part-time programs available. *Faculty:* 8 part-time/adjunct (1 woman). *Students:* 7 full-time (2 women); includes 1 Hispanic American, 6 international. 21 applicants, 81% accepted, 7 enrolled. *Degree requirements:* For master's, comprehensive exam. *Entrance requirements:* For master's, GMAT or GRE General Test. Additional exam requirements/recommendations for international students: Required—TOEFL (minimum score 525 paper-based; 197 computer-based). *Application deadline:* For fall admission, 4/1 priority date for domestic students; for spring admission, 11/1 for domestic students. Applications are processed on a rolling basis. Application fee: $40. Electronic applications accepted. *Expenses:* Tuition: Full-time $11,520; part-time $640 per hour. Required fees: $1090; $53.50 per hour. $10 per term. Tuition and fees vary according to program. *Financial support:* In 2009–10, 3 students received support; teaching assistantships, Federal Work-Study available. Support available to part-time students. Financial award application deadline: 4/1. *Unit head:* Dr. Timothy Coburn, Graduate Advisor, 325-674-2206, Fax: 325-674-2507, E-mail: tim.coburn@coba.acu.edu. *Application contact:* William Horn, Graduate Admissions Counselor, 325-674-2656, Fax: 325-674-3717, E-mail: gradinfo@acu.edu.

Adelphi University, School of Business, MBA Program, Garden City, NY 11530-0701. Offers finance (MBA); management information systems (MBA); management/human resource management (MBA); marketing/e-commerce (MBA). *Accreditation:* AACSB. Part-time and evening/weekend programs available. *Students:* 77 full-time (30 women), 183 part-time (91 women); includes 56 minority (29 African Americans, 17 Asian Americans or Pacific Islanders, 10 Hispanic Americans), 81 international. Average age 30. In 2009, 64 master's awarded. *Degree requirements:* For master's, capstone course. *Entrance requirements:* For master's, GMAT, 2 letters of recommendation. Additional exam requirements/recommendations for international students: Required—TOEFL (minimum score 550 paper-based; 213 computer-based; 80 iBT). *Application deadline:* For fall admission, 4/1 for international students; for spring admission, 11/1 for international students. Applications are processed on a rolling basis. Application fee: $50. Electronic applications accepted. *Expenses:* Tuition: Full-time $28,340; part-time $830 per credit. Required fees: $600; $250 per credit. Full-time tuition and fees vary according to course load and program. *Financial support:* Research assistantships with full and partial tuition reimbursements, career-related internships or fieldwork, Federal Work-Study, institutionally sponsored loans, scholarships/grants, and unspecified assistantships available. Financial award application deadline: 3/1; financial award applicants required to submit FAFSA. *Faculty research:* Supply chain management, distribution channels, productivity benchmark analysis, data envelopment analysis, financial portfolio analysis. *Unit head:* Rakesh Gupta, 516-877-4670, Fax: 516-877-4607, E-mail: gradbusinquiries@adelphi.edu. *Application contact:* Christine Murphy, Director of Admissions, 516-877-3050, Fax: 516-877-3039, E-mail: graduateadmissions@adelphi.edu.

Air Force Institute of Technology, Graduate School of Engineering and Management, Department of Systems and Engineering Management, Dayton, OH 45433-7765. Offers cost analysis (MS); environmental and engineering management (MS); environmental engineering science (MS); information resource/systems management (MS). *Accreditation:* ABET. Part-time programs available. *Degree requirements:* For master's, thesis. *Entrance requirements:* For master's, GRE, GMAT, minimum GPA of 3.0.

Alliant International University–San Diego, Marshall Goldsmith School of Management, Business and Management Division, San Diego, CA 92131-1799. Offers business administration (MBA); information and technology management (DBA); international business (MIBA, DBA), including finance (DBA), marketing (DBA); strategic business (DBA); sustainable management (MBA); MBA/MA; MBA/PhD. Part-time and evening/weekend programs available. *Degree requirements:* For doctorate, thesis/dissertation. *Entrance requirements:* For master's, GMAT, minimum GPA of 3.0; for doctorate, GMAT, minimum GPA of 3.3. Additional exam requirements/recommendations for international students: Required—TOEFL (minimum score 550 paper-based; 213 computer-based), TWE (minimum score 5). Electronic applications accepted. *Faculty research:* Consumer behavior, international business, strategic management, information systems.

American InterContinental University Dunwoody Campus, Program in Information Technology, Atlanta, GA 30328. Offers MIT. Part-time and evening/weekend programs available. *Degree requirements:* For master's, technical proficiency demonstration. *Entrance requirements:* For master's, Computer Programmer Aptitude Battery Exam, interview. Electronic applications accepted. *Faculty research:* Operating systems, security issues, networks and routing, computer hardware.

American InterContinental University–London, Program in Information Technology, London, United Kingdom. Offers MIT. *Degree requirements:* For master's, thesis optional. *Entrance requirements:* For master's, interview, professional experience. Electronic applications accepted.

American International College, School of Business Administration, MBA Program, Springfield, MA 01109-3189. Offers accounting (MBA); corporate/public communication (MBA); finance (MBA); general business (MBA); hospitality, hotel and service management (MBA); international business (MBA); international business practice (MBA); management (MBA); management information systems (MBA); marketing (MBA). International business practice program developed in cooperation with the Mountbatten Institute. *Expenses:* Tuition: Full-time $12,510; part-time $695 per credit hour. Required fees: $35 per term.

American Sentinel University, Graduate Programs, Englewood, CO 80112. Offers business administration (MBA); business intelligence (MS); computer science (MSCS); health information management (MS); healthcare (MBA); information systems (MSIS); nursing (MSN). Part-time and evening/weekend programs available. Postbaccalaureate distance learning degree programs offered (no on-campus study). *Entrance requirements:* Additional exam requirements/recommendations for international students: Required—TOEFL (minimum score 600 paper-based; 215 computer-based). Electronic applications accepted.

American University, Kogod School of Business, Department of Information Technology, Washington, DC 20016-8044. Offers information systems (MS, Certificate). *Entrance requirements:* For master's, GMAT; for Certificate, bachelor's degree. Additional exam requirements/recommendations for international students: Required—TOEFL. *Expenses:* Contact institution.

American University, Kogod School of Business, Master of Business Administration Program, Washington, DC 20016-8044. Offers accounting (MBA); consulting (MBA), including information technology, international business, management; corporate finance: commercial banking (MBA); corporate finance: corporate financial management (MBA); corporate finance: investment banking (MBA), including corporate finance and private equity, trading and selling; entrepreneurship (MBA); global emerging markets (MBA), including business, finance, information technology; international trade and global supply chain management (MBA); leadership (MBA); marketing management (MBA); marketing research (MBA); real estate (MBA); MBA/JD; MBA/LL M. Part-time and evening/weekend programs available. *Faculty:* 14 full-time (6 women). *Students:* 133 full-time (56 women), 121 part-time (48 women); includes 54 minority (23 African Americans, 1 American Indian/Alaska Native, 16 Asian Americans or Pacific Islanders, 14 Hispanic Americans), 43 international. Average age 29. 539 applicants, 51% accepted, 86 enrolled. In 2009, 114 master's awarded. *Entrance requirements:* For master's, GMAT. Additional exam requirements/recommendations for international students: Required—TOEFL. *Application deadline:* For fall admission, 2/1 priority date for domestic students; for spring admission, 10/1 priority date for domestic students. Applications are processed on a rolling basis. Application fee: $100. *Expenses:* Contact institution. *Financial support:* In 2009–10, 19 students received support; fellowships, research assistantships with partial tuition reimbursements available, career-related internships or fieldwork, Federal Work-Study, and institutionally sponsored loans available. Support available to part-time students. Financial award application deadline: 2/1. *Faculty research:* Information technology, decision-aiding methodology, negotiation. *Unit head:* Dr. Stevan Holmberg, Chair, 202-885-6193, E-mail: sholmbe@american.edu. *Application contact:* Shannon Demko, Associate Director of Graduate Admissions, 202-885-1994, Fax: 202-885-1108, E-mail: demko@american.edu.

Argosy University, Atlanta, College of Business, Atlanta, GA 30328. Offers accounting (DBA); corporate compliance (MBA); customized professional concentration (MBA, DBA); finance (MBA); healthcare administration (MBA); information systems (DBA); information systems management (MBA); international business (MBA, DBA); management (MBA, MSM, DBA); marketing (MBA, DBA).

See Close-Up on page 197.

Argosy University, Chicago, College of Business, Chicago, IL 60601. Offers accounting (DBA); customized professional concentration (MBA, DBA); finance (MBA); fraud examination (MBA); global business sustainability (DBA); healthcare administration (MBA); information systems (DBA); information systems management (MBA); international business (MBA, DBA); management (MBA, MSM, DBA); marketing (MBA, DBA); organizational leadership (Ed D); public administration (MBA); sustainable management (MBA). Postbaccalaureate distance learning degree programs offered (minimal on-campus study).

See Close-Up on page 199.

Argosy University, Dallas, College of Business, Farmers Branch, TX 75244. Offers accounting (DBA, AGC); corporate compliance (MBA, Graduate Certificate); customized professional concentration (MBA); finance (MBA, Graduate Certificate); fraud examination (MBA, Graduate Certificate); global business sustainability (DBA, AGC); healthcare administration (Graduate Certificate); healthcare management (MBA); information systems (MBA, DBA, AGC); information systems management (Graduate Certificate); international business (MBA, DBA, AGC, Graduate Certificate); management (MBA, DBA, AGC, Graduate Certificate); marketing (MBA, DBA, AGC, Graduate Certificate); public administration (MBA, Graduate Certificate); sustainable management (MBA, Graduate Certificate).

See Close-Up on page 201.

Argosy University, Denver, College of Business, Denver, CO 80231. Offers accounting (DBA); corporate compliance (MBA); customized professional concentration (MBA, DBA); finance (MBA); fraud examination (MBA); global business sustainability (DBA); healthcare administration (MBA); information systems (DBA); information systems management (MBA); international business (MBA, DBA); management (MBA, MSM, DBA); marketing (MBA, DBA); organizational leadership (Ed D); public administration (MBA); sustainable management (MBA).

See Close-Up on page 203.

Argosy University, Hawai'i, College of Business, Honolulu, HI 96813. Offers accounting (DBA); corporate compliance (MBA); customized professional concentration (MBA, DBA); finance (MBA, Certificate); fraud examination (MBA); global business sustainability (DBA); healthcare administration (MBA, Certificate); information systems (DBA); information systems management (MBA, Certificate); international business (MBA, DBA, Certificate); management (MBA, MSM, DBA); marketing (MBA, DBA, Certificate); organizational leadership (Ed D); public administration (MBA); sustainable management (MBA).

See Close-Up on page 205.

Argosy University, Inland Empire, College of Business, San Bernardino, CA 92408. Offers accounting (DBA); corporate compliance (MBA); customized professional concentration (MBA, DBA); finance (MBA); fraud examination (MBA); global business sustainability (DBA); healthcare administration (MBA); information systems (DBA); information systems management (MBA); international business (MBA, DBA); management (MBA, MSM, DBA); marketing (MBA, DBA); organizational leadership (Ed D); public administration (MBA); sustainable management (MBA).

See Close-Up on page 207.

Argosy University, Los Angeles, College of Business, Santa Monica, CA 90045. Offers accounting (DBA); corporate compliance (MBA); customized professional concentration (MBA, DBA); finance (MBA); fraud examination (MBA); global business sustainability (DBA); healthcare administration (MBA); information systems (DBA); information systems management (MBA); international business (MBA, DBA); management (MBA, MSM, DBA); marketing (MBA, DBA); organizational leadership (Ed D); public administration (MBA); sustainable management (MBA).

See Close-Up on page 209.

Argosy University, Nashville, College of Business, Nashville, TN 37214. Offers accounting (DBA); customized professional concentration (MBA, DBA); finance (MBA); healthcare administration (MBA); information systems (MBA, DBA); international business (MBA, DBA); management (MBA, MSM, DBA); marketing (MBA, DBA).

See Close-Up on page 211.

Argosy University, Orange County, College of Business, Orange, CA 92868. Offers accounting (DBA, Adv C); corporate compliance (MBA); customized professional concentration (MBA, DBA); finance (MBA, Certificate); fraud examination (MBA); global business sustainability (DBA); healthcare administration (MBA, Certificate); information systems (DBA, Adv C, Certificate); information systems management (MBA); international business (MBA, DBA, Adv C, Certificate); management (MBA, MSM, DBA, Adv C); marketing (MBA, DBA, Adv C, Certificate); organizational leadership (Ed D); public administration (MBA, Certificate); sustainable management (MBA).

See Close-Up on page 213.

Argosy University, Phoenix, College of Business, Phoenix, AZ 85021. Offers accounting (DBA); corporate compliance (MBA); customized professional concentration (MBA, DBA); finance (MBA); fraud examination (MBA); global business sustainability (DBA); healthcare administration (MBA); information systems (DBA); information systems management (MBA); international business (MBA, DBA); management (MBA, DBA); marketing (MBA, DBA); public administration (MBA); sustainable management (MBA).

See Close-Up on page 215.

Argosy University, Salt Lake City, College of Business, Draper, UT 84020. Offers accounting (DBA); corporate compliance (MBA); customized professional concentration (MBA, DBA); finance (MBA); fraud examination (MBA); global business sustainability (DBA); healthcare administration (MBA); information systems (DBA); information systems management (MBA); international business (MBA, DBA); management (MBA, DBA); marketing (MBA, DBA); public administration (MBA); sustainable management (MBA).

See Close-Up on page 217.

Argosy University, San Diego, College of Business, San Diego, CA 92108. Offers accounting (DBA); corporate compliance (MBA); customized professional concentration (MBA, DBA); finance (MBA); fraud examination (MBA); global business sustainability (DBA); information systems (DBA); information systems management (MBA); international business (MBA, DBA); management (MBA, MSM, DBA); marketing (MBA, DBA); organizational leadership (Ed D); public administration (MBA).

See Close-Up on page 219.

Argosy University, San Francisco Bay Area, College of Business, Alameda, CA 94501. Offers accounting (DBA); corporate compliance (MBA); customized professional concentration (MBA, DBA); finance (MBA); fraud examination (MBA); global business sustainability (DBA); healthcare administration (MBA); information systems (DBA); information systems management

(MBA); international business (MBA, DBA); management (MBA, MSM, DBA); marketing (MBA, DBA); organizational leadership (Ed D); public administration (MBA); sustainable management (MBA).

See Close-Up on page 221.

Argosy University, Sarasota, College of Business, Sarasota, FL 34235. Offers accounting (DBA, Adv C); corporate compliance (MBA, DBA, Certificate); customized professional concentration (MBA, DBA); finance (MBA, Certificate); fraud examination (MBA, Certificate); global business sustainability (DBA, Adv C); healthcare administration (MBA, Certificate); information systems (DBA, Adv C, Certificate); information systems management (MBA); international business (MBA, DBA, Adv C, Certificate); management (MBA, MSM, DBA, Adv C, Certificate); marketing (MBA, DBA, Adv C, Certificate); organizational leadership (Ed D); public administration (MBA, Certificate); sustainable management (MBA, Certificate).

See Close-Up on page 223.

Argosy University, Schaumburg, College of Business, Schaumburg, IL 60173-5403. Offers accounting (DBA, Adv C); customized professional concentration (MBA, DBA); finance (MBA, Certificate); fraud examination (MBA); global business sustainability (DBA); healthcare administration (MBA, Certificate); information systems (DBA, Adv C, Certificate); information systems management (MBA); international business (MBA, DBA, Adv C, Certificate); management (MBA, MSM, DBA, Adv C, Certificate); marketing (MBA, DBA, Adv C, Certificate); organizational leadership (Ed D); public administration (MBA); sustainable management (MBA).

See Close-Up on page 225.

Argosy University, Seattle, College of Business, Seattle, WA 98121. Offers accounting (DBA); corporate compliance (MBA); customized professional concentration (MBA, DBA); finance (MBA); fraud examination (MBA); global business sustainability (DBA); healthcare administration (MBA); information systems (DBA); information systems management (MBA); international business (MBA, DBA); management (MBA, MSM, DBA); marketing (MBA, DBA); organizational leadership (Ed D); public administration (MBA); sustainable management (MBA).

See Close-Up on page 227.

Argosy University, Tampa, College of Business, Tampa, FL 33607. Offers accounting (DBA); corporate compliance (MBA); customized professional concentration (MBA, DBA); finance (MBA); fraud examination (MBA); global business sustainability (DBA); healthcare administration (MBA); information systems (DBA); information systems management (MBA); international business (MBA, DBA); management (MBA, MSM, DBA); marketing (MBA, DBA); organizational leadership (Ed D); public administration (MBA); sustainable management (MBA).

See Close-Up on page 229.

Argosy University, Twin Cities, College of Business, Eagan, MN 55121. Offers accounting (DBA); customized professional concentration (MBA, DBA); finance (MBA); fraud examination (MBA); global business sustainability (DBA); healthcare administration (MBA); information systems (DBA); information systems management (MBA); international business (MBA, DBA); management (MBA, MSM, DBA); marketing (MBA, DBA); organizational leadership (Ed D); public administration (MBA); sustainable management (MBA).

See Close-Up on page 231.

Argosy University, Washington DC, College of Business, Arlington, VA 22209. Offers accounting (DBA); customized professional concentration (MBA, DBA); finance (MBA); fraud examination (MBA); global business sustainability (DBA); healthcare administration (MBA); information systems (DBA); information systems management (MBA); international business (MBA, DBA, Certificate); management (MBA, MSM, DBA); marketing (MBA, DBA, Certificate); organizational leadership (Ed D); public administration (MBA); sustainable management (MBA).

See Close-Up on page 233.

Arizona State University, Graduate College, College of Technology and Innovation, Department of Technology Management, Tempe, AZ 85287. Offers MS. Part-time and evening/weekend programs available. *Degree requirements:* For master's, thesis or applied project and oral defense. *Entrance requirements:* For master's, GRE, 30 semester hours in technology or high school equivalent; 16 semester hours of physical science and math; adequate technical preparation in a selected technology; resume; industrial experience (strongly recommended); minimum GPA of 3.0. Additional exam requirements/recommendations for international students: Required—TOEFL (minimum score 550 paper-based; 213 computer-based; 83 iBT); Recommended—TWE. Electronic applications accepted. *Faculty research:* Digital imaging, digital publishing, Internet development/e-commerce, information databases, multimedia, commercial digital photography, digital workflow, computer graphics modeling and animation, information design, sociotechnology, visual and technical literacy, environmental management, quality mgmt, project mgmt, international environmental, industrial ethics, hazardous materials, environmental chemistry.

Arizona State University, Graduate College, W.P. Carey School of Business, Department of Information Systems, Tempe, AZ 85287. Offers information management (MS); MBA/MS.

Arizona State University, Graduate College, W.P. Carey School of Business, Program in Business Administration, Tempe, AZ 85287. Offers agribusiness (PhD); business administration (MBA); finance (MBA, PhD); health sector management (MBA); information systems (PhD); management (MBA, PhD); marketing (MBA, PhD); supply chain management (MBA, PhD); JD/MBA; MBA/M Arch; MBA/MHSM. *Accreditation:* AACSB. *Degree requirements:* For master's, thesis optional; for doctorate, thesis/dissertation. *Entrance requirements:* For master's, GMAT.

Arkansas State University—Jonesboro, Graduate School, College of Business, Department of Computer and Information Technology, Jonesboro, State University, AR 72467. Offers business technology education (MSE); information systems and e-commerce (MS). Part-time programs available. *Faculty:* 11 full-time (2 women). *Students:* 6 full-time (2 women), 23 part-time (17 women); includes 9 minority (all African Americans), 3 international. Average age 35. 11 applicants, 82% accepted, 9 enrolled. In 2009, 17 master's awarded. *Degree requirements:* For master's, comprehensive exam, thesis or alternative. *Entrance requirements:* For master's, GRE General Test or MAT, appropriate bachelor's degree, official transcript, immunization records. Additional exam requirements/recommendations for international students: Required—TOEFL (minimum score 550 paper-based; 213 computer-based; 79 iBT), IELTS (minimum score 6). *Application deadline:* For fall admission, 7/15 for domestic students, 7/1 for international students; for spring admission, 12/1 for domestic students, 11/13 for international students. Applications are processed on a rolling basis. Application fee: $30 ($40 for international students). Electronic applications accepted. *Expenses:* Contact institution. *Financial support:* In 2009–10, 4 students received support. Career-related internships or fieldwork and unspecified assistantships available. Financial award application deadline: 7/1; financial award applicants required to submit FAFSA. *Unit head:* Dr. John Robertson, Chair, 870-972-3416, Fax: 870-972-3417, E-mail: jfrobert@astate.edu. *Application contact:* Dr. Andrew Sustich, Dean of the Graduate School, 870-972-3029, Fax: 870-972-3857, E-mail: sustich@astate.edu.

Aspen University, Programs in Information Management, Denver, CO 80246. Offers information management (MS); information systems (Certificate). Part-time and evening/weekend programs available. Postbaccalaureate distance learning degree programs offered (no on-campus study). Electronic applications accepted.

Auburn University, Graduate School, College of Business, Department of Management, Auburn University, AL 36849. Offers human resource management (PhD); management (MS, PhD); management information systems (MS, PhD). *Accreditation:* AACSB. Part-time programs available. *Faculty:* 34 full-time (7 women), 5 part-time/adjunct (0 women). *Students:* 12 full-time (4 women), 12 part-time (2 women); includes 3 minority (1 African American, 2 Asian Americans or Pacific Islanders), 5 international. Average age 34. 137 applicants, 28% accepted, 20 enrolled. In 2009, 9 master's, 6 doctorates awarded. *Degree requirements:* For master's, thesis (for some programs); for doctorate, thesis/dissertation. *Entrance requirements:* For master's, GMAT, GRE General Test (MS); for doctorate, GMAT, GRE General Test. Additional exam requirements/recommendations for international students: Required—TOEFL. *Application deadline:* For fall admission, 7/7 for domestic students; for spring admission, 11/24 for domestic students. Applications are processed on a rolling basis. Application fee: $50 ($60 for international students). Electronic applications accepted. *Expenses:* Tuition, state resident: full-time $6240. Tuition, nonresident: full-time $18,720. International tuition: $18,938 full-time. Required fees: $492. Tuition and fees vary according to course load, program and reciprocity agreements. *Financial support:* Teaching assistantships, Federal Work-Study available. Support available to part-time students. Financial award application deadline: 3/15; financial award applicants required to submit FAFSA. *Unit head:* Dr. Sharon Oswald, Head, 334-844-4071. *Application contact:* Dr. George Flowers, Dean of the Graduate School, 334-844-2125.

Avila University, School of Business, Kansas City, MO 64145-1698. Offers accounting (MBA); finance (MBA); general management (MBA); health care administration (MBA); international business (MBA); management information systems (MBA); marketing (MBA). Part-time and evening/weekend programs available. *Faculty:* 9 full-time (3 women), 24 part-time/adjunct (5 women). *Students:* 148 full-time (71 women), 86 part-time (47 women); includes 56 minority (36 African Americans, 2 American Indian/Alaska Native, 13 Asian Americans or Pacific Islanders, 5 Hispanic Americans), 63 international. Average age 32. 53 applicants, 75% accepted, 40 enrolled. In 2009, 93 master's awarded. *Degree requirements:* For master's, comprehensive exam, capstone course. *Entrance requirements:* For master's, GMAT, minimum GPA of 3.0, interview. Additional exam requirements/recommendations for international students: Required—TOEFL (minimum score 550 paper-based). *Application deadline:* For fall admission, 7/30 priority date for domestic students, 7/30 for international students; for winter admission, 11/30 priority date for domestic students, 11/30 for international students; for spring admission, 2/28 priority date for domestic students, 2/28 for international students. Applications are processed on a rolling basis. Application fee: $0. Electronic applications accepted. *Expenses:* Contact institution. *Financial support:* In 2009–10, 102 students received support. Career-related internships or fieldwork available. Support available to part-time students. Financial award applicants required to submit FAFSA. *Faculty research:* Leadership characteristics, financial hedging, group dynamics. *Unit head:* Dr. Richard Woodall, Dean, 816-501-3720, Fax: 816-501-2463, E-mail: richard.woodall@avila.edu. *Application contact:* JoAnna Giffin, MBA Admissions Director, 816-501-3601, Fax: 816-501-2463, E-mail: joanna.giffin@avila.edu.

Baker College Center for Graduate Studies—Online, Graduate Programs—Online, Flint, MI 48507-9843. Offers accounting (MBA); business administration (DBA); finance (MBA); general business (MBA); health care management (MBA); human resources management (MBA); information management (MBA); leadership studies (MBA); management information systems (MSIS); marketing (MBA). Part-time and evening/weekend programs available. Postbaccalaureate distance learning degree programs offered. *Faculty:* 750. *Students:* 500 full-time, 500 part-time. Average age 37. *Degree requirements:* For master's, portfolio. *Entrance requirements:* For master's, 3 years of work experience, minimum undergraduate GPA of 2.5, writing sample, 3 letters of recommendation; for doctorate, MBA or acceptable related master's degree from accredited association, 5 years work experience, minimum graduate GPA of 3.25, writing sample, 3 professional references. Additional exam requirements/recommendations for international students: Required—TOEFL (minimum score 550 paper-based; 213 computer-based). *Application deadline:* For fall admission, 8/6 priority date for domestic students; for winter admission, 12/15 priority date for domestic students; for spring admission, 2/15 priority date for domestic students. Applications are processed on a rolling basis. Application fee: $25. Electronic applications accepted. *Expenses:* Tuition: Part-time $330 per credit hour. Tuition and fees vary according to degree level. *Financial support:* Scholarships/grants available. Support available to part-time students. Financial award applicants required to submit FAFSA. *Unit head:* Dr. Julia Teahen, President, 810-766-4023, Fax: 810-766-4399, E-mail: julia@baker.edu. *Application contact:* Chuck J. Gurden, Vice President for Graduate and Online Admissions, 800-469-3165, Fax: 810-766-4399, E-mail: adm-ol@baker.edu.

Barry University, Andreas School of Business, Graduate Certificate Programs, Miami Shores, FL 33161-6695. Offers finance (Certificate); health services administration (Certificate); international business (Certificate); management (Certificate); management information systems (Certificate); marketing (Certificate).

Baylor University, Graduate School, Hankamer School of Business, Department of Information Systems, Waco, TX 76798. Offers information systems (MSIS); information systems management (MBA); MBA/MSIS. *Faculty:* 12 full-time (4 women). *Students:* 13 full-time (9 women), 5 part-time (1 woman); includes 2 minority (1 African American, 1 Hispanic American), 8 international. In 2009, 5 master's awarded. *Entrance requirements:* For master's, GMAT. Additional exam requirements/recommendations for international students: Required—TOEFL. *Application deadline:* For fall admission, 8/1 for domestic students; for spring admission, 12/1 for domestic students. Applications are processed on a rolling basis. Application fee: $25. *Financial support:* Research assistantships, career-related internships or fieldwork and Federal Work-Study available. *Faculty research:* Computer personnel, group systems, information technology standards and infrastructure, international information systems, technology and the learning environment. *Unit head:* Dr. Gary Carini, Graduate Program Director, 254-710-4091, Fax: 254-710-1091, E-mail: gary_carini@baylor.edu. *Application contact:* Laurie Wilson, Director, Graduate Business Degree Programs, 254-710-4163, Fax: 254-710-1066, E-mail: laurie_wilson@baylor.edu.

Bay Path College, Program in Communications and Information Management, Longmeadow, MA 01106-2292. Offers information management (MS); information systems (MS). Part-time and evening/weekend programs available. *Entrance requirements:* Additional exam requirements/recommendations for international students: Recommended—TOEFL (minimum score 500 paper-based). Electronic applications accepted.

Bellarmine University, School of Continuing and Professional Studies, Louisville, KY 40205-0671. Offers MAIT. Part-time and evening/weekend programs available. *Faculty:* 2 full-time (0 women), 4 part-time/adjunct (1 woman). *Students:* 7 full-time (3 women), 13 part-time (5 women); includes 1 minority (African American). Average age 34. In 2009, 13 master's awarded. *Entrance requirements:* For master's, GRE or GMAT, minimum GPA of 2.75, two letters of recommendation. Additional exam requirements/recommendations for international students: Required—TOEFL (minimum score 550 paper-based; 213 computer-based; 80 iBT). Application fee: $25. *Expenses:* Contact institution. *Unit head:* Dr. Michael D. Mattei, Dean, 502-452-8441, E-mail: mmattei@bellarmine.edu. *Application contact:* Dr. Sara Yount, Dean of Graduate Admission, 502-452-8401, E-mail: syount@bellarmine.edu.

Bellevue University, Graduate School, Program in Computer Information Systems, Bellevue, NE 68005-3098. Offers MS.

Benedictine University, Graduate Programs, Program in Business Administration, Lisle, IL 60532-0900. Offers accounting (MBA); entrepreneurship and managing innovation (MBA); financial management (MBA); health administration (MBA); human resource management (MBA); information systems security (MBA); international business (MBA); management consulting (MBA); management information systems (MBA); marketing management (MBA); operations management and logistics (MBA); organizational leadership (MBA); MBA/MPH; MBA/MS. Part-time and evening/weekend programs available. Postbaccalaureate distance learning degree programs offered (minimal on-campus study). *Faculty:* 4 full-time (2 women), 24 part-time/adjunct (3 women). *Students:* 247 full-time (141 women), 644 part-time (339 women); includes 223 minority (134 African Americans, 5 American Indian/Alaska Native, 44 Asian Americans or Pacific Islanders, 40 Hispanic Americans), 25 international. Average age 34. 287 applicants, 92% accepted, 229 enrolled. In 2009, 219 master's awarded. *Entrance requirements:* For master's, GMAT. Additional exam requirements/recommendations for international students: Required—TOEFL (minimum score 550 paper-based; 213 computer-based). *Application deadline:* For fall admission, 9/1 for domestic students; for winter admission, 12/1 for domestic students; for spring admission, 2/15 for domestic students. Applications are processed on a rolling basis. Application fee: $40. Electronic applications accepted. *Expenses:* Tuition: Part-time $750 per credit hour. Tuition and fees vary according to campus/location and program. *Financial support:* Career-related internships or fieldwork and health care benefits available. Support available to part-time students. *Faculty research:* Strategic leadership in

Management Information Systems

Benedictine University (continued)
professional organizations, sociology of professions, organizational change, social identity theory, applications to change management. *Unit head:* Dr. Sharon Borowicz, Director, 630-829-6219, E-mail: sborowicz@ben.edu. *Application contact:* Kari Gibbons, Director, Admissions, 630-829-6200, Fax: 630-829-6584, E-mail: kgibbons@ben.edu.

Benedictine University, Graduate Programs, Program in Management Information Systems, Lisle, IL 60532-0900. Offers MS, MBA/MS, MPH/MS. Part-time programs available. *Faculty:* 2 full-time (1 woman), 6 part-time/adjunct (1 woman). *Students:* 1 full-time (0 women), 18 part-time (5 women); includes 6 minority (3 African Americans, 2 Asian Americans or Pacific Islanders, 1 Hispanic American), 5 international. Average age 36. 11 applicants, 55% accepted, 3 enrolled. In 2009, 10 master's awarded. *Entrance requirements:* For master's, GMAT. Additional exam requirements/recommendations for international students: Required—TOEFL (minimum score 550 paper-based; 213 computer-based). *Application deadline:* For fall admission, 9/1 for domestic students; for winter admission, 12/1 for domestic students; for spring admission, 2/15 for domestic students. Applications are processed on a rolling basis. Application fee: $40. Electronic applications accepted. *Expenses:* Tuition: Part-time $750 per credit hour. Tuition and fees vary according to campus/location and program. *Financial support:* Career-related internships or fieldwork and health care benefits available. Support available to part-time students. *Faculty research:* Technology management, knowledge management, electronic commerce, information security. *Unit head:* Dr. Barbara Ozog, Director, 630-829-6218, E-mail: bozog@ben.edu. *Application contact:* Kari Gibbons, Director, Admissions, 630-829-6200, Fax: 630-829-6584, E-mail: kgibbons@ben.edu.

Bernard M. Baruch College of the City University of New York, Zicklin School of Business, Department of Statistics and Computer Information Systems, Program in Computer Information Systems, New York, NY 10010-5585. Offers MBA, MS, PhD. Part-time and evening/weekend programs available. Terminal master's awarded for partial completion of doctoral program. *Degree requirements:* For master's, thesis or alternative; for doctorate, comprehensive exam, thesis/dissertation. *Entrance requirements:* For master's, GMAT, 2 letters of recommendation, resume, 2 years of work experience; for doctorate, GMAT. Additional exam requirements/recommendations for international students: Required—TOEFL (minimum score 590 paper-based; 243 computer-based), TWE (minimum score 5).

Boise State University, Graduate College, College of Business and Economics, Program in Information Technology Management, Boise, ID 83725-0399. Offers MBA. Part-time programs available. *Entrance requirements:* For master's, GMAT, minimum GPA of 3.0. Additional exam requirements/recommendations for international students: Required—TOEFL. Electronic applications accepted. *Expenses:* Tuition, state resident: full-time $3106; part-time $209 per credit. Tuition, nonresident: part-time $284 per credit.

Boston University, School of Management, Doctorate in Business Administration Program, Boston, MA 02215. Offers accounting (PhD); information systems (PhD); marketing (PhD); operations and technology management (PhD); organizational behavior (PhD); strategy and innovation (PhD). *Students:* 31 full-time (18 women), 21 international. Average age 32. 158 applicants, 7% accepted, 6 enrolled. In 2009, 12 doctorates awarded. *Degree requirements:* For doctorate, comprehensive exam, thesis/dissertation, curriculum paper. *Entrance requirements:* For doctorate, GMAT or GRE General Test, resume, 3 letters of evaluation. Additional exam requirements/recommendations for international students: Required—TOEFL or IELTS. *Application deadline:* For fall admission, 1/5 for domestic and international students. Application fee: $125. *Expenses:* Tuition: Full-time $37,910; part-time $1184 per credit hour. Required fees: $386; $40 per semester. Part-time tuition and fees vary according to class time, course level, degree level and program. *Financial support:* Fellowships, research assistantships, teaching assistantships, career-related internships or fieldwork, Federal Work-Study, institutionally sponsored loans, scholarships/grants, and tuition waivers available. Support available to part-time students. Financial award applicants required to submit FAFSA. *Unit head:* Dr. Lloyd Baird, Director, 617-353-2670, E-mail: dba@bu.edu. *Application contact:* Hayden Estrada, Assistant Dean, Admissions, 617-353-2670, Fax: 617-353-7368, E-mail: dba@bu.edu.

Bowie State University, Graduate Programs, Program in Management Information Systems, Bowie, MD 20715-9465. Offers information systems analyst (Certificate); management information systems (MS). Part-time and evening/weekend programs available. *Degree requirements:* For master's, comprehensive exam, thesis optional, research paper. *Entrance requirements:* For master's, minimum GPA of 2.5. Electronic applications accepted.

Brandeis University, Rabb School of Continuing Studies, Division of Graduate Professional Studies, Information Technology Management Program, Waltham, MA 02454-9110. Offers MS, Graduate Certificate. Part-time and evening/weekend programs available. Postbaccalaureate distance learning degree programs offered (no on-campus study). *Faculty:* 2 full-time (both women), 32 part-time/adjunct (8 women). *Students:* 2 full-time (1 woman), 58 part-time (14 women); includes 9 minority (3 African Americans, 6 Asian Americans or Pacific Islanders). Average age 35. 12 applicants, 100% accepted, 12 enrolled. In 2009, 38 master's, 4 other advanced degrees awarded. *Entrance requirements:* For master's, resume, letter of recommendation; for Graduate Certificate, resume, official transcripts, recommendations. Additional exam requirements/recommendations for international students: Recommended—TOEFL (minimum score 600 paper-based; 250 computer-based; 100 iBT). *Application deadline:* For fall admission, 6/15 priority date for domestic students; for winter admission, 10/15 priority date for domestic students; for spring admission, 2/15 priority date for domestic students. Applications are processed on a rolling basis. Application fee: $50. Electronic applications accepted. *Unit head:* Dr. Cynthia Phillips, Program Chair, 781-736-8787, Fax: 781-736-3420, E-mail: cynthiap@brandeis.edu. *Application contact:* Frances Stearns, Associate Director of Admissions and Student Services, 781-736-8785, Fax: 781-736-3420, E-mail: fstearns@brandeis.edu.

Brigham Young University, Graduate Studies, Marriott School of Management, Information Systems Program, Provo, UT 84602. Offers MISM. *Faculty:* 13 full-time (1 woman), 1 part-time/adjunct (0 women). *Students:* 41 full-time (1 woman); includes 4 minority (1 Asian American or Pacific Islander, 3 Hispanic Americans), 2 international. Average age 26. 60 applicants, 63% accepted, 38 enrolled. In 2009, 35 master's awarded. *Entrance requirements:* For master's, GMAT, minimum GPA of 3.0 in last 60 hours of course work. Additional exam requirements/recommendations for international students: Required—TOEFL (minimum score 580 paper-based; 237 computer-based). *Application deadline:* For fall admission, 3/1 for domestic and international students. Application fee: $50. Electronic applications accepted. *Expenses:* Tuition: Full-time $5580; part-time $301 per credit hour. Tuition and fees vary according to student's religious affiliation. *Financial support:* In 2009–10, 41 students received support; research assistantships, teaching assistantships, career-related internships or fieldwork and scholarships/grants available. Financial award application deadline: 2/19. *Faculty research:* Research standards—faculty career development in information systems; electronic commerce technology and standards; collaborative tools and methods; technology for fraud detection and prevention; ethical issues in the information systems field. *Unit head:* Dr. Marshall B. Romney, Director, 801-422-3247, Fax: 801-422-0573, E-mail: marshall_romney@byu.edu. *Application contact:* Ann E. Sumsion, Program Assistant, 801-422-3247, Fax: 801-422-0573, E-mail: mism@byu.edu.

California Intercontinental University, School of Information Technology, Diamond Bar, CA 91765. Offers information systems and enterprise resource management (DBA); information systems and knowledge management (MBA); project and quality management (MBA).

California Lutheran University, Graduate Studies, School of Business, Thousand Oaks, CA 91360-2787. Offers business (IMBA); entrepreneurship (MBA, Certificate); finance (MBA, Certificate); financial planning (MBA, Certificate); information systems and technology (MS); information technology management (MBA, Certificate); international business (MBA, Certificate); management and organization behavior (MBA); management and organizational behavior (Certificate); marketing (MBA, Certificate). Evening/weekend programs available. Postbaccalaureate distance learning degree programs offered. *Entrance requirements:* For master's, GMAT, interview, minimum GPA of 3.0. *Expenses:* Contact institution.

California State University, Fullerton, Graduate Studies, College of Business and Economics, Department of Information Systems and Decision Sciences, Fullerton, CA 92834-9480. Offers information systems (MS); information systems (decision sciences) (MS); information systems (e-commerce) (MS); information technology (MS); management science (MBA). Part-time programs available. *Students:* 9 full-time (3 women), 72 part-time (13 women); includes 32 minority (3 African Americans, 22 Asian Americans or Pacific Islanders, 7 Hispanic Americans), 16 international. Average age 33. 105 applicants, 50% accepted, 38 enrolled. In 2009, 29 master's awarded. *Degree requirements:* For master's, project or thesis. *Entrance requirements:* For master's, GMAT, minimum AACSB index of 950. Application fee: $55. *Expenses:* Tuition, nonresident: full-time $11,160; part-time $373 per credit. Required fees: $1440 per term. Tuition and fees vary according to course load, degree level and program. *Financial support:* Career-related internships or fieldwork, Federal Work-Study, institutionally sponsored loans, and scholarships/grants available. Support available to part-time students. Financial award application deadline: 3/1; financial award applicants required to submit FAFSA. *Unit head:* Dr. Bhushan Kapoor, Chair, 657-278-2221. *Application contact:* Admissions/Applications, 657-278-2371.

California State University, Los Angeles, Graduate Studies, College of Business and Economics, Department of Information Systems, Los Angeles, CA 90032-8530. Offers business information systems (MBA); management (MS); management information systems (MS); office management (MBA). Part-time and evening/weekend programs available. *Faculty:* 3 full-time (0 women), 2 part-time/adjunct (0 women). *Students:* 12 full-time (3 women), 18 part-time (3 women); includes 5 minority (1 African American, 4 Asian Americans or Pacific Islanders), 18 international. Average age 28. 11 applicants, 91% accepted, 7 enrolled. In 2009, 18 master's awarded. *Degree requirements:* For master's, comprehensive exam (MBA), thesis (MS). *Entrance requirements:* For master's, GMAT, minimum GPA of 2.5 during previous 2 years of course work. Additional exam requirements/recommendations for international students: Required—TOEFL (minimum score 550 paper-based; 213 computer-based). *Application deadline:* For fall admission, 5/1 for domestic and international students. Applications are processed on a rolling basis. Application fee: $55. Electronic applications accepted. *Financial support:* Career-related internships or fieldwork and Federal Work-Study available. Support available to part-time students. Financial award application deadline: 3/1. *Unit head:* Dr. Adam Huarng, Chair, 323-343-2983, E-mail: ahuarng@calstatela.edu. *Application contact:* Dr. Cheryl L. Ney, Associate Vice President for Academic Affairs and Dean of Graduate Studies, 323-343-3820, Fax: 323-343-5653, E-mail: cney@cslanet.calstatela.edu.

California State University, Monterey Bay, College of Science, Media Arts and Technology, School of Information Technology and Communication Design, Seaside, CA 93955-8001. Offers interdisciplinary studies (MA), including instructional science and technology; management and information technology (MA). *Degree requirements:* For master's, capstone or thesis. *Entrance requirements:* For master's, GRE, 2 letters of recommendation, minimum GPA of 3.0, technology screening assessment. Additional exam requirements/recommendations for international students: Required—TOEFL (minimum score 550 paper-based; 213 computer-based; 71 iBT). Electronic applications accepted. *Faculty research:* Electronic commerce, e-learning, knowledge management, international business, business and public policy.

California State University, Sacramento, Graduate Studies, College of Business Administration, Sacramento, CA 95819. Offers accountancy (MS); business administration (MBA); human resources (MBA); management information science (MS); urban land development (MBA). *Accreditation:* AACSB. Part-time and evening/weekend programs available. *Degree requirements:* For master's, thesis or alternative, writing proficiency exam. *Entrance requirements:* For master's, GMAT. Additional exam requirements/recommendations for international students: Required—TOEFL. Electronic applications accepted.

Capella University, School of Business and Technology, Minneapolis, MN 55402. Offers accounting (MBA), including system design and programming; business (Certificate), including human resource management (MS, PhD, Certificate), information technology management (MS, PhD, Certificate), leadership (MBA, MS, PhD, Certificate); finance (MBA); general business (MBA); health care management (MBA); information technology (MS, Certificate), including general information technology (MS), information security, network architecture and design (MS), professional projects management (Certificate), project management and leadership (MS), system design and development (MS),); information technology management (MBA); marketing (MBA); organization and management (MBA, MS, PhD), including general business (PhD), general organization and management (MBA, MS), human resource management (MS, PhD, Certificate), information technology management (MS, PhD, Certificate), leadership (MBA, MS, PhD, Certificate); project management (MBA). Part-time and evening/weekend programs available. Postbaccalaureate distance learning degree programs offered (minimal on-campus study). Terminal master's awarded for partial completion of doctoral program. *Degree requirements:* For master's, thesis optional, integrative project; for doctorate, comprehensive exam, thesis/dissertation. *Entrance requirements:* Additional exam requirements/recommendations for international students: Required—TOEFL (minimum score 550 paper-based; 213 computer-based), TWE (minimum score 4). Electronic applications accepted. *Faculty research:* Business policies: strategic, corporate, and financial management; interplay of technological, organizational and social change.

Capitol College, Graduate Programs, Laurel, MD 20708-9759. Offers business administration (MBA); computer science (MS); electrical engineering (MS); information and telecommunications systems management (MS); information architecture (MS); network security (MS). Part-time and evening/weekend programs available. Postbaccalaureate distance learning degree programs offered (no on-campus study). *Entrance requirements:* For master's, minimum GPA of 3.0. Electronic applications accepted.

Carnegie Mellon University, H. John Heinz III College, School of Information Systems and Management, Program in Information Security Policy and Management, Pittsburgh, PA 15213-3891. Offers MSISPM.

Carnegie Mellon University, H. John Heinz III College, School of Information Systems and Management, Program in Information Systems Management, Pittsburgh, PA 15213-3891. Offers MISM.

Carnegie Mellon University, H. John Heinz III College, School of Information Systems and Management, Program in Information Technology, Pittsburgh, PA 15213-3891. Offers MSIT.

Carnegie Mellon University, H. John Heinz III College, School of Information Systems and Management, Program in Information Technology–Australia, Adelaide, PA 5000, Australia. Offers MSIT.

Carnegie Mellon University, Tepper School of Business, Program in Information Systems, Pittsburgh, PA 15213-3891. Offers PhD. *Degree requirements:* For doctorate, thesis/dissertation. *Entrance requirements:* For doctorate, GRE General Test.

Case Western Reserve University, Weatherhead School of Management, Department of Information Systems, Cleveland, OH 44106. Offers MBA. Part-time and evening/weekend programs available. *Entrance requirements:* For master's, GMAT. *Application deadline:* Applications are processed on a rolling basis. Application fee: $75. *Financial support:* Career-related internships or fieldwork, Federal Work-Study, institutionally sponsored loans, and tuition waivers (full and partial) available. Financial award application deadline: 5/1. *Faculty research:* Decision support, business forecasting systems, design and use of information systems, artificial intelligence, executive information systems. *Unit head:* Fred Collopy, Chairman, 216-368-2144, Fax: 216-368-4776, E-mail: fred.collopy@case.edu. *Application contact:* Fred Collopy, Chairman, 216-368-2144, Fax: 216-368-4776, E-mail: fred.collopy@case.edu.

Case Western Reserve University, Weatherhead School of Management, Department of Operations, Cleveland, OH 44106. Offers management (MS, MSM), including finance (MS), information systems (MS), marketing (MS), operations research, quality management (MS), supply chain (MSM); management for liberal arts graduates (MSM); operations research (PhD); MBA/MSM. Part-time programs available. *Degree requirements:* For doctorate, thesis/

dissertation. *Entrance requirements:* For master's, GRE General Test; for doctorate, GMAT, GRE General Test. *Application deadline:* Applications are processed on a rolling basis. Application fee: $100. *Financial support:* Tuition waivers (full and partial) available. Financial award application deadline: 5/1. *Faculty research:* Mathematical finance, mathematical programming, scheduling, stochastic optimization, environmental/energy models. *Unit head:* Kamlesh Mathur, Chairman, 216-368-3857, E-mail: kamlesh.mathur@case.edu. *Application contact:* Kamlesh Mathur, Chairman, 216-368-3857, E-mail: kamlesh.mathur@case.edu.

Central European University, CEU Business School, Budapest, Hungary. Offers finance (MBA); general management (MBA); information technology (M Sc); information technology management (MBA); management (EMBA); marketing (MBA); real estate management (MBA). Part-time and evening/weekend programs available. *Entrance requirements:* For master's, GMAT. Additional exam requirements/recommendations for international students: Required—TOEFL (minimum score 570 paper-based; 230 computer-based). Electronic applications accepted. *Faculty research:* Social and ethical business, marketing.

Central Michigan University, Central Michigan University Off-Campus Programs, Program in Administration, Mount Pleasant, MI 48859. Offers acquisitions administration (MSA, Certificate); general administration (MSA, Certificate); health services administration (MSA, Certificate); human resources administration (MSA, Certificate); information resource management (MSA, Certificate); international administration (MSA, Certificate); leadership (MSA, Certificate); public administration (MSA, Certificate); vehicle design and manufacturing administration (MSA, Certificate). Part-time and evening/weekend programs available. Postbaccalaureate distance learning degree programs offered (no on-campus study). *Students:* Average age 38. *Entrance requirements:* For master's, minimum GPA of 2.7 in major. *Application deadline:* Applications are processed on a rolling basis. Application fee: $50. Electronic applications accepted. *Financial support:* Scholarships/grants available. Support available to part-time students. Financial award applicants required to submit FAFSA. *Unit head:* Dr. Nana Korsah, Director, MSA Programs, 989-774-6525, E-mail: korsa1na@cmich.edu. *Application contact:* 877-268-4636, E-mail: cmuoffcampus@cmich.edu.

Central Michigan University, College of Graduate Studies, College of Business Administration, Department of Business Information Systems, Mount Pleasant, MI 48859. Offers business computing (Graduate Certificate); information systems (MS), including enterprise software, general business, systems applications. Part-time and evening/weekend programs available. *Degree requirements:* For master's, thesis or alternative. Electronic applications accepted. *Faculty research:* Enterprise software, electronic commerce, decision support systems, ethical issues in information systems, information technology management and teaching issues.

Central Michigan University, College of Graduate Studies, Interdisciplinary Administration Programs, Mount Pleasant, MI 48859. Offers acquisitions administration (MSA, Graduate Certificate); general administration (MSA, Graduate Certificate); health services administration (MSA, Graduate Certificate); human resource administration (Graduate Certificate); human resources administration (MSA); information resource management (MSA, Graduate Certificate); international administration (MSA, Graduate Certificate); leadership (MSA); organizational communication (MSA, Graduate Certificate); public administration (MSA, Graduate Certificate); recreation and park administration (MSA); sport administration (MSA). *Accreditation:* AACSB. Part-time and evening/weekend programs available. Postbaccalaureate distance learning degree programs offered (no on-campus study). *Degree requirements:* For master's, thesis or alternative. *Entrance requirements:* For master's, bachelor's degree with minimum GPA of 2.7. Electronic applications accepted. *Faculty research:* Interdisciplinary studies in acquisitions administration, health services administration, sport administration, recreation and park administration, and international administration.

Charleston Southern University, Program in Business, Charleston, SC 29423-8087. Offers accounting (MBA); finance (MBA); health care administration (MBA); information systems (MBA); organizational development (MBA). Part-time and evening/weekend programs available. *Faculty:* 14 full-time (1 woman), 6 part-time/adjunct (1 woman). *Students:* 316 part-time (157 women); includes 67 minority (53 African Americans, 1 American Indian/Alaska Native, 7 Asian Americans or Pacific Islanders, 6 Hispanic Americans), 7 international. Average age 32. 173 applicants, 85% accepted, 97 enrolled. In 2009, 69 master's awarded. *Degree requirements:* For master's, thesis optional. *Entrance requirements:* For master's, GMAT. Additional exam requirements/recommendations for international students: Required—TOEFL (minimum score 550 paper-based; 213 computer-based; 79 iBT). *Application deadline:* Applications are processed on a rolling basis. Application fee: $30. *Expenses:* Tuition: Part-time $350 per credit hour. Required fees: $40 per semester. Tuition and fees vary according to program. *Financial support:* Research assistantships with full tuition reimbursements available. Financial award application deadline: 4/15; financial award applicants required to submit FAFSA. *Unit head:* Dr. Scott Pearson, Director of the MBA Program, 843-863-7038, Fax: 843-863-7922, E-mail: spearson@csuniv.edu. *Application contact:* Alison Harrison, Graduate Enrollment Counselor, 843-863-7534, Fax: 843-863-7070, E-mail: aharrison@cusniv.edu.

City University of Seattle, Graduate Division, School of Management, Bellevue, WA 98005. Offers accounting (Certificate); change leadership (MBA, Certificate); financial management (MBA, Certificate); general management (MBA); general management-Europe (MBA); global leadership (Certificate); global marketing (MBA); individualized study (MBA); information security (MS); information systems (MBA); leadership (MA); marketing (MBA, Certificate); project management (MBA, MS, Certificate); sustainable business (Certificate); technology management (MBA, MS, Certificate). Part-time and evening/weekend programs available. Postbaccalaureate distance learning degree programs offered (no on-campus study). *Entrance requirements:* Additional exam requirements/recommendations for international students: Required—TOEFL (minimum score 540 paper-based; 207 computer-based); Recommended—IELTS. Electronic applications accepted. *Expenses:* Tuition: Full-time $14,760; part-time $615 per credit. Tuition and fees vary according to program.

Claremont Graduate University, Graduate Programs, School of Information Systems and Technology, Claremont, CA 91711-6160. Offers electronic commerce (MS, PhD); health information management (MS); information systems (Certificate); knowledge management (MS, PhD); systems development (MS, PhD); telecommunications and networking (MS, PhD); MBA/MS. Part-time programs available. *Faculty:* 6 full-time (1 woman), 1 part-time/adjunct (0 women). *Students:* 78 full-time (28 women), 35 part-time (11 women); includes 32 minority (8 African Americans, 1 American Indian/Alaska Native, 16 Asian Americans or Pacific Islanders, 7 Hispanic Americans), 32 international. Average age 38. In 2009, 31 master's, 11 doctorates, 1 other advanced degree awarded. *Degree requirements:* For doctorate, comprehensive exam, thesis/dissertation, portfolio. *Entrance requirements:* For master's and doctorate, GMAT, GRE General Test. Additional exam requirements/recommendations for international students: Required—TOEFL (minimum score 550 paper-based; 213 computer-based; 80 iBT). *Application deadline:* For fall admission, 2/1 priority date for domestic students. Applications are processed on a rolling basis. Application fee: $60. Electronic applications accepted. *Expenses:* Tuition: Full-time $35,046; part-time $1524 per credit. Required fees: $161 per semester. *Financial support:* Fellowships, research assistantships, teaching assistantships, Federal Work-Study, institutionally sponsored loans, and scholarships/grants available. Support available to part-time students. Financial award application deadline: 2/15; financial award applicants required to submit FAFSA. *Faculty research:* GPSS, man-machine interaction, organizational aspects of computing, implementation of information systems, information systems practice. *Unit head:* Terry Ryan, Dean, 909-607-9591, Fax: 909-621-8564, E-mail: terry.ryan@cgu.edu. *Application contact:* Matt Hutter, Director of External Affairs, 909-621-3180, Fax: 909-621-8564, E-mail: matt.hutter@cgu.edu.

Clark University, Graduate School, Graduate School of Management, Business Administration Program, Worcester, MA 01610-1477. Offers accounting (MBA); finance (MBA); global business (MBA); health care management (MBA); management (MBA); management of information technology (MBA); marketing (MBA). *Accreditation:* AACSB. Part-time and evening/weekend programs available. *Students:* 148 full-time (67 women), 120 part-time (52 women); includes 27 minority (12 African Americans, 2 American Indian/Alaska Native, 9 Asian Americans or Pacific Islanders, 4 Hispanic Americans), 108 international. Average age 29. 340 applicants, 57% accepted, 63 enrolled. In 2009, 118 master's awarded. *Degree requirements:* For master's, thesis optional. *Application deadline:* For fall admission, 6/1 priority date for domestic students; for spring admission, 12/1 priority date for domestic students. Applications are processed on a rolling basis. Application fee: $50. Electronic applications accepted. *Expenses:* Tuition: Full-time $34,900; part-time $4362.50 per course. *Financial support:* In 2009–10, research assistantships with partial tuition reimbursements (averaging $4,800 per year), teaching assistantships with partial tuition reimbursements (averaging $4,800 per year) were awarded; fellowships, career-related internships or fieldwork, Federal Work-Study, institutionally sponsored loans, and tuition waivers (partial) also available. Support available to part-time students. Financial award application deadline: 5/31. *Faculty research:* Organizational development, accounting, marketing, finance, human resource management. *Application contact:* Lynn Davis, Enrollment and Marketing Director, 508-793-7406, Fax: 508-793-8822, E-mail: clarkmba@clarku.edu.

Cleveland State University, College of Graduate Studies, Nance College of Business Administration, Department of Computer and Information Science, Cleveland, OH 44115. Offers computer and information science (MCIS); information systems (DBA). Part-time and evening/weekend programs available. Terminal master's awarded for partial completion of doctoral program. *Degree requirements:* For master's, thesis optional; for doctorate, comprehensive exam, thesis/dissertation. *Entrance requirements:* For master's, GRE or GMAT, minimum GPA of 2.75; for doctorate, GRE or GMAT, MBA, MCIS or equivalent. Additional exam requirements/recommendations for international students: Required—TOEFL (minimum score 525 paper-based; 197 computer-based; 78 iBT). Electronic applications accepted. *Faculty research:* Artificial intelligence, object oriented analysis, database design, software efficiency, distributed system, geographical information systems.

Cleveland State University, College of Graduate Studies, Nance College of Business Administration, Doctor of Business Administration (DBA) Program, Cleveland, OH 44115. Offers business administration (DBA); finance (DBA); information systems (DBA); marketing (DBA); operations management (DBA). *Accreditation:* AACSB. Part-time and evening/weekend programs available. *Degree requirements:* For doctorate, comprehensive exam, thesis/dissertation, oral dissertation defense. *Entrance requirements:* For doctorate, GMAT, MBA or equivalent. Additional exam requirements/recommendations for international students: Required—TOEFL (minimum score 550 paper-based; 213 computer-based; 79 iBT). Electronic applications accepted. *Faculty research:* Supply chain management, international business, strategic management, risk analysis.

College of Charleston, Graduate School, School of Sciences and Mathematics, Program in Computer and Information Sciences, Charleston, SC 29424-0001. Offers MS. Part-time programs available. *Faculty:* 7 full-time (1 woman). *Students:* 9 full-time (2 women), 10 part-time (1 woman), 3 international. Average age 31. 10 applicants, 70% accepted, 7 enrolled. In 2009, 4 master's awarded. *Entrance requirements:* For master's, GRE. Additional exam requirements/recommendations for international students: Required—TOEFL. *Application deadline:* For fall admission, 7/1 for domestic students; for spring admission, 11/1 for domestic students. Application fee: $45. Electronic applications accepted. *Financial support:* Scholarships/grants and unspecified assistantships available. Financial award applicants required to submit FAFSA. *Unit head:* Dr. Paul Buhler, Director, 843-953-7146. *Application contact:* Susan Hallatt, Director of Graduate Admissions, 843-953-5614, Fax: 843-953-1434, E-mail: hallatts@cofc.edu.

The College of St. Scholastica, Graduate Studies, Department of Computer Information Systems, Duluth, MN 55811-4199. Offers MA, Certificate. Part-time programs available. Post-baccalaureate distance learning degree programs offered (minimal on-campus study). *Degree requirements:* For master's, thesis. *Entrance requirements:* For master's, minimum GPA of 2.8. Additional exam requirements/recommendations for international students: Required—TOEFL (minimum score 550 paper-based; 213 computer-based; 79 iBT). *Expenses:* Contact institution. *Faculty research:* Organization acceptance of software development methodologies.

Colorado State University, Graduate School, College of Business, Department of Computer Information Systems, Fort Collins, CO 80523-1277. Offers MSBA. Part-time programs available. *Faculty:* 11 full-time (2 women). *Students:* Average age 31. In 2009, 11 master's awarded. *Degree requirements:* For master's, thesis or alternative, project. *Entrance requirements:* For master's, GMAT, minimum GPA of 3.0. Additional exam requirements/recommendations for international students: Required—TOEFL (minimum score 565 paper-based; 227 computer-based; 86 iBT). *Application deadline:* For fall admission, 7/15 for domestic students; 4/1 for international students. Applications are processed on a rolling basis. Application fee: $50. Electronic applications accepted. *Expenses:* Tuition, state resident: full-time $6434; part-time $359.10 per credit. Tuition, nonresident: full-time $18,116; part-time $1006.45 per credit. Required fees: $1496; $83 per credit. *Financial support:* In 2009–10, 1 student received support, including 1 fellowship (averaging $1,500 per year); teaching assistantships with full and partial tuition reimbursements available, career-related internships or fieldwork, Federal Work-Study, scholarships/grants, traineeships, and unspecified assistantships also available. Support available to part-time students. Financial award application deadline: 3/1; financial award applicants required to submit FAFSA. *Faculty research:* Decision-making, object-oriented design, database research, electronic marketing, e-commerce. Total annual research expenditures: $202,772. *Unit head:* Dr. Jon D. Clark, Chair, 970-491-1618, Fax: 970-491-5205, E-mail: jon.clark@business.colostate.edu. *Application contact:* Dr. John Hoxmeier, Associate Dean of Graduate Programs, 970-491-2142, Fax: 970-491-5205, E-mail: john.hoxmeier@colostate.edu.

Colorado Technical University Sioux Falls, Programs in Business Administration and Management, Sioux Falls, SD 57108. Offers business administration (MBA); business management (MSM); health science management (MSM); human resources management (MSM); information technology (MSM); organizational leadership (MSM); project management (MBA); technology management (MBA). Evening/weekend programs available. *Degree requirements:* For master's, thesis optional. *Entrance requirements:* For master's, minimum 2 years work experience, resume.

Concordia University Wisconsin, Graduate Programs, School of Business and Legal Studies, MBA Program, Mequon, WI 53097-2402. Offers finance (MBA); health care administration (MBA); human resource management (MBA); international business (MBA); international business-bilingual English/Chinese (MBA); management (MBA); management information systems (MBA); managerial communications (MBA); marketing (MBA); public administration (MBA); risk management (MBA). Postbaccalaureate distance learning degree programs offered (minimal on-campus study). *Degree requirements:* For master's, comprehensive exam, thesis or alternative. *Entrance requirements:* Additional exam requirements/recommendations for international students: Required—TOEFL. *Expenses:* Contact institution.

Creighton University, Graduate School, Eugene C. Eppley College of Business Administration, Omaha, NE 68178-0001. Offers business administration (MBA); information technology management (MS); securities and portfolio management (MSAPM); JD/MBA; MBA/INR; MBA/MS-ITM; MBA/MSAPM; MS ITM/JD; Pharm D/MBA. *Accreditation:* AACSB. Part-time and evening/weekend programs available. Postbaccalaureate distance learning degree programs offered (minimal on-campus study). *Faculty:* 38 full-time (5 women). *Students:* 46 full-time (12 women), 222 part-time (36 women); includes 30 minority (12 African Americans, 13 Asian Americans or Pacific Islanders, 5 Hispanic Americans), 18 international. Average age 30. 160 applicants, 79% accepted, 118 enrolled. In 2009, 78 master's awarded. *Degree requirements:* For master's, thesis optional. *Entrance requirements:* For master's, GMAT, resume, 2 letters of recommendation. Additional exam requirements/recommendations for international students: Required—TOEFL (minimum score 550 paper-based; 213 computer-based; 80 iBT). *Application deadline:* For fall admission, 7/1 priority date for domestic students, 3/1 for international students; for winter admission, 10/1 priority date for domestic students, 7/1 for international students; for spring admission, 4/1 priority date for domestic students, 10/1 for international students. Applications are processed on a rolling basis. Application fee: $50. Electronic applications accepted. *Expenses:* Tuition: Full-time $11,700; part-time $650 per credit hour. Required fees: $126 per semester. *Financial support:* In 2009–10, 8 research assistantships with full

Management Information Systems

Creighton University (continued)
tuition reimbursements (averaging $8,650 per year) were awarded; career-related internships or fieldwork, tuition waivers (partial), and unspecified assistantships also available. Financial award application deadline: 3/1. *Faculty research:* Small business issues. *Unit head:* Dr. Deborah Wells, Associate Dean for Graduate Programs, 402-280-2841, E-mail: deborahwells@creighton.edu. *Application contact:* Gail Hafer, Assistant Dean, 402-280-2829, Fax: 402-280-2172, E-mail: ghafer@creighton.edu.

Dalhousie University, Faculty of Management, Centre for Advanced Management Education, Halifax, NS B3H 3J5, Canada. Offers financial services (MBA); information management (MIM); management (MPA); natural resources (MBA). Part-time programs available. Postbaccalaureate distance learning degree programs offered. *Faculty:* 10 full-time (5 women). *Students:* 19 part-time (4 women). Average age 27. 50 applicants, 42% accepted. *Entrance requirements:* For master's, GMAT, minimum GPA of 3.0, resume. Additional exam requirements/recommendations for international students: Required—TOEFL, IELTS, CANTEST, CAEL, or Michigan English Language Assessment Battery. *Application deadline:* Applications are processed on a rolling basis. Application fee: $70. Electronic applications accepted. *Unit head:* Michelle Hunter, Associate Director (Administration), 902-494-1828, Fax: 902-494-7154, E-mail: mhunter@dal.ca. *Application contact:* Deborah McColl, Admissions and Registration Coordinator, 902-494-6391, E-mail: mbafs@dal.ca.

Dallas Baptist University, College of Adult Education, Professional Development Program, Dallas, TX 75211-9299. Offers accounting (MA); church leadership (MA); counseling (MA); criminal justice (MA); English as a second language (MA); finance (MA); higher education (MA); leadership studies (MA); management (MA); management information systems (MA); marketing (MA); missions (MA). Part-time and evening/weekend programs available. *Entrance requirements:* For master's, minimum GPA of 3.0. Additional exam requirements/recommendations for international students: Required—TOEFL, IELTS. *Expenses:* Tuition: Full-time $10,674; part-time $593 per credit hour.

Dallas Baptist University, College of Business, Business Administration Program, Dallas, TX 75211-9299. Offers accounting (MBA); business communication (MBA); conflict resolution management (MBA); e-business (MBA); entrepreneurship (MBA); finance (MBA); health care management (MBA); international business (MBA); leading the non-profit organization (MBA); management (MBA); management information systems (MBA); marketing (MBA); project management (MBA); technology and engineering management (MBA). *Accreditation:* ACBSP. Part-time and evening/weekend programs available. *Entrance requirements:* For master's, GMAT, minimum GPA of 3.0. Additional exam requirements/recommendations for international students: Required—TOEFL, IELTS. Electronic applications accepted. *Expenses:* Tuition: Full-time $10,674; part-time $593 per credit hour. *Faculty research:* Sports management, services marketing, retailing, strategic management, financial planning/investments.

DePaul University, Charles H. Kellstadt Graduate School of Business, School of Accountancy and Management Information Systems, Chicago, IL 60604-2287. Offers accountancy (M Acc, MSA); business information technology (MS); e-business (MBA, MS); financial management and control (MBA); management accounting (MBA); management information systems (MBA); taxation (MST). Part-time and evening/weekend programs available. *Faculty:* 30 full-time (9 women), 54 part-time/adjunct (7 women). *Students:* 167 full-time (82 women), 237 part-time (106 women); includes 52 minority (8 African Americans, 1 American Indian/Alaska Native, 30 Asian Americans or Pacific Islanders, 13 Hispanic Americans), 49 international. In 2009, 141 master's awarded. *Entrance requirements:* For master's, GMAT, 2 letters of recommendation, resume. Additional exam requirements/recommendations for international students: Required—TOEFL (minimum score 550 paper-based; 213 computer-based). *Application deadline:* For fall admission, 7/1 for domestic students; for winter admission, 10/1 for domestic students; for spring admission, 2/1 for domestic students. Applications are processed on a rolling basis. Application fee: $60. *Expenses:* Tuition: Full-time $37,525; part-time $620 per credit hour. *Financial support:* In 2009–10, 7 research assistantships with full tuition reimbursements (averaging $4,100 per year) were awarded; institutionally sponsored loans also available. Financial award application deadline: 4/2. *Faculty research:* Tax policy, property transactions, stock options as compensation, standards setting, activity-based costing in health care. *Unit head:* Kevin Stevens, Director, 312-362-6989, E-mail: kstevens@depaul.edu. *Application contact:* Christopher E. Kinsella, Director of Cohort MBA Programs, 312-362-8810, Fax: 312-362-6677, E-mail: kgsb@depaul.edu.

DePaul University, College of Computing and Digital Media, Chicago, IL 60604. Offers business information technology (MS); computational finance (MS); computer and information sciences (PhD); computer game development (MS); computer graphics and motion technology (MS); computer science (MS); computer, information and network security (MS), including applied technology; digital cinema (MFA, MS), including information technology project management (MS); e-commerce technology (MS); human-computer interaction (MS); information systems (MS); information technology (MA); information technology project management (MS); software engineering (MS); telecommunications systems (MS); JD/MS. Part-time and evening/weekend programs available. Postbaccalaureate distance learning degree programs offered (no on-campus study). *Faculty:* 78 full-time (16 women), 191 part-time/adjunct (51 women). *Students:* 922 full-time (239 women), 887 part-time (209 women); includes 466 minority (193 African Americans, 3 American Indian/Alaska Native, 162 Asian Americans or Pacific Islanders, 108 Hispanic Americans), 276 international. Average age 31. 853 applicants, 67% accepted, 294 enrolled. In 2009, 444 master's, 4 doctorates awarded. *Degree requirements:* For master's, thesis (for some programs); for doctorate, comprehensive exam, thesis/dissertation. *Entrance requirements:* For master's, GRE or GMAT (MS in computational finance only), bachelor's degree; for doctorate, GRE, master's degree in computer science. Additional exam requirements/recommendations for international students: Required—TOEFL (minimum score 550 paper-based; 213 computer-based), IELTS (minimum score 6.5), Pearson Test of English (minimum score 53). *Application deadline:* For fall admission, 8/15 priority date for domestic students, 6/1 priority date for international students; for winter admission, 12/15 priority date for domestic students, 9/15 priority date for international students; for spring admission, 3/1 priority date for domestic students, 12/15 priority date for international students. Applications are processed on a rolling basis. Application fee: $25. Electronic applications accepted. *Expenses:* Contact institution. *Financial support:* In 2009–10, 69 students received support, including 6 fellowships with full tuition reimbursements available (averaging $25,858 per year), 75 teaching assistantships with full and partial tuition reimbursements available (averaging $5,780 per year); research assistantships, Federal Work-Study, scholarships/grants, tuition waivers (full and partial), and unspecified assistantships also available. Support available to part-time students. Financial award application deadline: 4/30; financial award applicants required to submit FAFSA. *Faculty research:* Bioinformatics, visual computing, graphics and animation, high performance and scientific computing, databases. Total annual research expenditures: $790,000. *Unit head:* Dr. David Miller, Dean, 312-362-8381, Fax: 312-362-5185. *Application contact:* Dr. Liz Friedman, Assistant Dean of Student Services, 312-362-5384, Fax: 312-362-5327, E-mail: efriedm2@cdm.depaul.edu.

DeSales University, Graduate Division, Program in Business Administration, Center Valley, PA 18034-9568. Offers accounting (MBA); business administration (MBA); computer information systems (MBA); finance (MBA); health care systems management (MBA); management (MBA); marketing (MBA); project management (MBA); self-design (MBA); MSN/MBA. *Accreditation:* ACBSP. Part-time programs available. Postbaccalaureate distance learning degree programs offered (no on-campus study). *Students:* 433 part-time. In 2009, 218 master's awarded. *Entrance requirements:* For master's, minimum GPA of 3.0, 2 years of work experience. Additional exam requirements/recommendations for international students: Required—TOEFL. *Application deadline:* Applications are processed on a rolling basis. Application fee: $35. Electronic applications accepted. *Expenses:* Tuition: Full-time $17,500; part-time $665 per credit. Full-time tuition and fees vary according to program. Part-time tuition and fees vary according to course load. *Faculty research:* Quality improvement, executive development, productivity, cross-cultural managerial differences, leadership. *Unit head:* Dr. David Gilfoil, Director, 610-282-1100 Ext. 1828, Fax: 610-282-2869, E-mail: david.gilfoil@desales.edu. *Application contact:* Caryn Stopper, Director of Graduate Admissions, 610-282-1100 Ext. 1768, Fax: 610-282-0525, E-mail: caryn.stopper@desales.edu.

DeVry University, Keller Graduate School of Management, Downers Grove, IL 60515. Offers accounting and financial management (MAFM); business administration (MBA); human resources management (MHRM); information systems management (MISM); network and communications management (MNCM); project management (MPM); public administration (MPA).

Duquesne University, John F. Donahue Graduate School of Business, Pittsburgh, PA 15282-0001. Offers accountancy (MS); business administration (MBA); information systems management (MSISM); sustainability (MBA); JD/MBA; MBA/MA; MBA/MES; MBA/MHMS; MBA/MLLS; MBA/MS; MBA/MSN. *Accreditation:* AACSB. Part-time and evening/weekend programs available. *Faculty:* 52 full-time (12 women), 39 part-time/adjunct (7 women). *Students:* 122 full-time (56 women), 252 part-time (93 women); includes 14 minority (5 African Americans, 4 Asian Americans or Pacific Islanders, 5 Hispanic Americans), 30 international. Average age 31. 195 applicants, 95% accepted, 136 enrolled. In 2009, 97 master's awarded. *Entrance requirements:* For master's, GMAT, 2 letters of recommendation, current resume. Additional exam requirements/recommendations for international students: Required—TOEFL (minimum score 577 paper-based; 233 computer-based; 90 iBT); Recommended—TWE. *Application deadline:* For fall admission, 5/1 priority date for domestic students, 5/1 for international students; for spring admission, 10/1 for domestic and international students. Applications are processed on a rolling basis. Application fee: $0. Electronic applications accepted. *Expenses:* Tuition: Part-time $851 per credit. Required fees: $81 per credit. *Financial support:* In 2009–10, 46 students received support, including 14 fellowships with partial tuition reimbursements available, 32 research assistantships with partial tuition reimbursements available; career-related internships or fieldwork and unspecified assistantships also available. Support available to part-time students. Financial award application deadline: 7/1; financial award applicants required to submit FAFSA. *Faculty research:* International business, investment management, business ethics, technology management, supply chain management, business strategy, finance. *Unit head:* Alan R. Miciak, Dean, 412-396-5848, Fax: 412-396-5304, E-mail: miciaka@duq.edu. *Application contact:* Patricia Moore, Assistant Director, 412-396-6276, Fax: 412-396-1726, E-mail: moorep@duq.edu.

See Close-Up on page 239.

Duquesne University, School of Leadership and Professional Advancement, Pittsburgh, PA 15282-0001. Offers leadership (MS), including business ethics, community leadership, global leadership, information technology, leadership, liberal studies, professional administration, sports leadership. Part-time and evening/weekend programs available. Postbaccalaureate distance learning degree programs offered (no on-campus study). *Faculty:* 1 full-time (0 women), 70 part-time/adjunct (35 women). *Students:* 654 (307 women); includes 68 minority (57 African Americans, 1 American Indian/Alaska Native, 6 Asian Americans or Pacific Islanders, 4 Hispanic Americans). 161 applicants, 73% accepted, 103 enrolled. In 2009, 108 master's awarded. *Degree requirements:* For master's, capstone course. *Entrance requirements:* For master's, professional work experience, 500-word essay. Additional exam requirements/recommendations for international students: Required—TOEFL. *Application deadline:* Applications are processed on a rolling basis. Application fee: $0. Electronic applications accepted. *Expenses:* Tuition: Part-time $851 per credit. Required fees: $81 per credit. *Financial support:* Applicants required to submit FAFSA. *Unit head:* Dr. Dorothy Bassett, Dean, 412-396-2141, Fax: 412-396-4711, E-mail: bassettd@duq.edu. *Application contact:* Marianne Leister, Director of Student Services, 412-396-4933, Fax: 412-396-5072, E-mail: leister@duq.edu.

East Carolina University, Graduate School, College of Technology and Computer Science, Department of Technology Systems, Greenville, NC 27858-4353. Offers computer network professional (Certificate); industrial technology (MS), including computer networking management, digital communications, industrial distribution and logistics, information security, manufacturing, performance improvement, planning; information assurance (Certificate); occupational safety (MS); technology management (PhD); Website developer (Certificate). *Entrance requirements:* For master's and Certificate, GRE General Test or MAT, minimum GPA of 2.5; for doctorate, GRE General Test, related work experience.

Eastern Michigan University, Graduate School, College of Business, Department of Computer Information Systems, Ypsilanti, MI 48197. Offers information systems (MSIS). Part-time and evening/weekend programs available. *Faculty:* 12 full-time (1 woman). *Students:* 21 full-time (9 women), 32 part-time (9 women); includes 4 minority (1 African American, 3 Asian Americans or Pacific Islanders), 45 international. Average age 25. 46 applicants, 67% accepted, 12 enrolled. In 2009, 28 master's awarded. *Entrance requirements:* Additional exam requirements/recommendations for international students: Required—TOEFL. *Application deadline:* For fall admission, 5/15 priority date for domestic students, 5/1 priority date for international students; for winter admission, 10/15 priority date for domestic students, 10/1 priority date for international students; for spring admission, 3/15 priority date for domestic students, 3/1 priority date for international students. Applications are processed on a rolling basis. Application fee: $35. Tuition and fees vary according to course level. *Financial support:* In 2009–10, 7 research assistantships with full tuition reimbursements (averaging $3,300 per year), 3 teaching assistantships with full tuition reimbursements (averaging $2,100 per year) were awarded; fellowships, career-related internships or fieldwork, Federal Work-Study, institutionally sponsored loans, scholarships/grants, tuition waivers (partial), and unspecified assistantships also available. Support available to part-time students. Financial award applicants required to submit FAFSA. *Unit head:* Dr. S. Imtiaz Ahmad, Department Head, 734-487-2454, Fax: 734-487-1941, E-mail: imtiaz.ahmad@emich.edu. *Application contact:* Dr. S. Imtiaz Ahmad, Department Head, 734-487-2454, Fax: 734-487-1941, E-mail: imtiaz.ahmad@emich.edu.

Eastern Michigan University, Graduate School, College of Business, Programs in Business Administration, Ypsilanti, MI 48197. Offers business administration (MBA, Graduate Certificate); computer information systems (Graduate Certificate); e-business (MBA, Graduate Certificate); enterprise business intelligence (MBA); entrepreneurship (MBA, Graduate Certificate); finance (MBA, Graduate Certificate); human resources (MBA); human resources management (Graduate Certificate); information systems (MBA); internal auditing (MBA); international business (MBA, Graduate Certificate); marketing management (Graduate Certificate); nonprofit management (MBA); organizational development (Graduate Certificate); supply chain management (MBA, Graduate Certificate). *Accreditation:* AACSB. Part-time programs available. Postbaccalaureate distance learning degree programs offered (no on-campus study). *Students:* 166 full-time (80 women), 439 part-time (231 women); includes 150 minority (103 African Americans, 7 American Indian/Alaska Native, 31 Asian Americans or Pacific Islanders, 9 Hispanic Americans), 97 international. Average age 34. In 2009, 3 other advanced degrees awarded. *Entrance requirements:* For master's, GMAT (minimum score 450), minimum cumulative undergraduate GPA of 2.75. Additional exam requirements/recommendations for international students: Required—TOEFL. *Application deadline:* For fall admission, 5/15 for domestic students, 5/1 for international students; for winter admission, 10/15 for domestic students, 10/1 for international students; for spring admission, 3/15 for domestic students, 3/1 for international students. Applications are processed on a rolling basis. Application fee: $35. Tuition and fees vary according to course level. *Financial support:* Fellowships, research assistantships with full tuition reimbursements, teaching assistantships with full tuition reimbursements, career-related internships or fieldwork, Federal Work-Study, institutionally sponsored loans, scholarships/grants, tuition waivers (partial), and unspecified assistantships available. Support available to part-time students. Financial award applicants required to submit FAFSA. *Unit head:* K. Michelle Henry, Director of Academic Services, 734-487-4444, Fax: 734-483-1316, E-mail: cob.grad@emich.edu. *Application contact:* Beste Windes, Advisor, 734-487-4444, Fax: 734-483-1316, E-mail: cob.grad@emich.edu.

Emory University, Goizueta Business School, Doctoral Program in Business, Atlanta, GA 30322-1100. Offers accounting (PhD); finance (PhD); information systems (PhD); marketing (PhD); organization and management (PhD). *Faculty:* 57 full-time (11 women). *Students:* 37

full-time (14 women); includes 8 minority (3 African Americans, 4 Asian Americans or Pacific Islanders, 1 Hispanic American), 19 international. Average age 30. 218 applicants, 9% accepted, 9 enrolled. In 2009, 11 doctorates awarded. *Degree requirements:* For doctorate, comprehensive exam, thesis/dissertation. *Entrance requirements:* For doctorate, GMAT (strongly preferred) or GRE. Additional exam requirements/recommendations for international students: Required—TOEFL (minimum score 250 computer-based). *Application deadline:* For fall admission, 1/3 priority date for domestic and international students. Application fee: $50. Electronic applications accepted. *Unit head:* Dr. Lawrence Benveniste, Dean, 404-727-6377, Fax: 404-727-0868, E-mail: larry_benveniste@bus.emory.edu. *Application contact:* Allison Gilmore, Director of Admissions and Student Services, 404-727-6353, Fax: 404-727-5337, E-mail: phd@bus.emory.edu.

Endicott College, Van Loan School of Graduate and Professional Studies, Program in Information Technology, Beverly, MA 01915-2096. Offers MSIT. *Faculty:* 4 part-time/adjunct (0 women). *Students:* 8 part-time (3 women). Average age 40. *Degree requirements:* For master's, thesis. *Entrance requirements:* For master's, GMAT. Additional exam requirements/recommendations for international students: Required—TOEFL. *Expenses:* Contact institution. *Unit head:* Dr. Richard Benedetto, Associate Dean of Graduate School, 978-232-2744, Fax: 978-232-3000, E-mail: rbenedet@endicott.edu. *Application contact:* Richard Benedetto, Associate Dean of Graduate School, 978-232-2744, Fax: 978-232-3000, E-mail: rbenedet@endicott.edu.

Fairfield University, Charles F. Dolan School of Business, Fairfield, CT 06824-5195. Offers accounting (MBA, MS, CAS); finance (MBA, MS, CAS); general management (MBA); human resource management (MBA, CAS); information systems and operations (MBA); information systems and operations management (CAS); international business (MBA, CAS); marketing (MBA, CAS); taxation (MBA, MS). *Accreditation:* AACSB. Part-time and evening/weekend programs available. *Degree requirements:* For master's, capstone course. *Entrance requirements:* For master's, GMAT (minimum score 500), 2 letters of reference, resume, minimum GPA of 3.0. Additional exam requirements/recommendations for international students: Required—TOEFL (minimum score 550 paper-based; 213 computer-based; 80 iBT). Electronic applications accepted. *Expenses:* Contact institution. *Faculty research:* Optimization strategies, international finance, consumer behavior, financial market volatility, Internet marketing, supply chain analysis, tax issues.

Fairleigh Dickinson University, Metropolitan Campus, Silberman College of Business, Departments of Management, Marketing, and Entrepreneurial Studies, Program in Management, Teaneck, NJ 07666-1914. Offers management (MBA); management information systems (Certificate). *Accreditation:* AACSB. *Students:* 34 full-time (12 women), 14 part-time (7 women), 29 international. Average age 27. 131 applicants, 43% accepted, 15 enrolled. In 2009, 19 master's awarded. *Application deadline:* Applications are processed on a rolling basis. Application fee: $40. *Application contact:* Susan Brooman, University Director of Graduate Admissions, 201-692-2554, Fax: 201-692-2560, E-mail: globaleducation@fdu.edu.

Fairleigh Dickinson University, Metropolitan Campus, University College: Arts, Sciences, and Professional Studies, School of Computer Sciences and Engineering, Program in Management Information Systems, Teaneck, NJ 07666-1914. Offers MS. *Students:* 9 full-time (2 women), 16 part-time (7 women), 10 international. Average age 33. 56 applicants, 59% accepted, 7 enrolled. In 2009, 11 master's awarded. *Application deadline:* Applications are processed on a rolling basis. Application fee: $40. *Application contact:* Susan Brooman, University Director of Graduate Admissions, 201-692-2554, Fax: 201-692-2560, E-mail: globaleducation@fdu.edu.

Ferris State University, College of Business, Big Rapids, MI 49307. Offers application development (MSISM); business intelligence and infomatics (MBA); database administration (MSISM); design and innovation management process (MBA); e-business (MSISM); networking (MSISM); quality management (MBA); security (MSISM). *Accreditation:* ACBSP. Part-time and evening/weekend programs available. *Faculty:* 10 full-time (3 women), 2 part-time/adjunct (both women). *Students:* 33 full-time (6 women), 134 part-time (65 women); includes 13 minority (8 African Americans, 2 American Indian/Alaska Native, 2 Asian Americans or Pacific Islanders, 1 Hispanic American), 33 international. Average age 30. 120 applicants, 31% accepted, 26 enrolled. In 2009, 66 master's awarded. *Entrance requirements:* For master's, GRE or GMAT (waived if GPA is 3.5 or better), minimum GPA of 3.0 in CIS and business core, 2.75 overall; writing sample; 3 letters of reference; resume. Additional exam requirements/recommendations for international students: Required—TOEFL (minimum score 500 paper-based; 173 computer-based; 64 iBT). *Application deadline:* For fall admission, 7/1 priority date for domestic students, 6/15 for international students; for winter admission, 11/1 priority date for domestic students, 10/15 for international students; for spring admission, 3/1 priority date for domestic students, 2/15 for international students. Applications are processed on a rolling basis. Application fee: $30 for international students. Electronic applications accepted. *Financial support:* In 2009–10, 14 teaching assistantships were awarded; career-related internships or fieldwork, Federal Work-Study, and unspecified assistantships also available. Support available to part-time students. Financial award applicants required to submit FAFSA. *Faculty research:* Quality improvement, client/server end-user computing, information management and policy, security, digital forensics. *Unit head:* Dr. David Steenstra, Department Chair, 231-591-2168, Fax: 231-591-2973, E-mail: yosts@ferris.edu. *Application contact:* Shannon Yost, Department Secretary, 231-591-2168, Fax: 231-591-2973, E-mail: yosts@ferris.edu.

Florida Agricultural and Mechanical University, Division of Graduate Studies, Research, and Continuing Education, School of Business and Industry, Tallahassee, FL 32307-3200. Offers accounting (MBA); finance (MBA); management information systems (MBA); marketing (MBA). *Faculty:* 42 full-time (28 women). *Students:* 71 full-time (45 women), 15 part-time (9 women); includes 80 minority (all African Americans), 4 international. In 2009, 90 master's awarded. *Degree requirements:* For master's, residency. *Entrance requirements:* For master's, GMAT, minimum GPA of 3.0. *Application deadline:* For fall admission, 5/18 for domestic students, 12/18 for international students; for spring admission, 11/12 for domestic students, 5/12 for international students. Application fee: $30. *Financial support:* Fellowships, Federal Work-Study and scholarships/grants available. *Unit head:* Dr. Amos Bradford, Interim Dean, 850-599-3565. *Application contact:* Dr. Amos Bradford, Interim Dean, 850-599-3565.

Florida Atlantic University, College of Business, Department of Information Technology and Operations Management, Boca Raton, FL 33431-0991. Offers management information systems (MS). *Faculty:* 19 full-time (7 women), 5 part-time/adjunct (2 women). *Students:* 19 full-time (13 women), 29 part-time (18 women); includes 18 minority (10 African Americans, 2 Asian Americans or Pacific Islanders, 6 Hispanic Americans), 3 international. Average age 30. 80 applicants, 43% accepted, 14 enrolled. In 2009, 15 master's awarded. *Degree requirements:* For master's, thesis optional. *Entrance requirements:* For master's, GMAT, minimum GPA of 3.0. Additional exam requirements/recommendations for international students: Required—TOEFL (minimum score 600 paper-based; 250 computer-based). *Application deadline:* For fall admission, 7/1 priority date for domestic students, 2/15 priority date for international students; for winter admission, 11/1 priority date for domestic students, 8/15 priority date for international students; for spring admission, 4/1 priority date for domestic students, 1/15 priority date for international students. Applications are processed on a rolling basis. Application fee: $30. Electronic applications accepted. *Expenses:* Tuition, state resident: full-time $7055; part-time $293.94 per credit hour. Tuition, nonresident: full-time $22,096; part-time $920.66 per credit hour. *Financial support:* Research assistantships, teaching assistantships, career-related internships or fieldwork, Federal Work-Study, institutionally sponsored loans, tuition waivers (partial), and unspecified assistantships available. Support available to part-time students. Financial award application deadline: 3/1; financial award applicants required to submit FAFSA. *Unit head:* Dr. Paul Hart, Chair, 561-297-3675, E-mail: hart@fau.edu. *Application contact:* Dr. Paul Hart, Chair, 561-297-3675, E-mail: hart@fau.edu.

Florida Institute of Technology, Graduate Programs, College of Business, Extended Studies Division, Melbourne, FL 32901-6975. Offers acquisition and contract management (PMBA); business administration (PMBA); computer information systems (MS); e-business (PMBA); human resource management (PMBA); human resources management (MS); logistics management (MS), including humanitarian and disaster relief logistics; management (MS), including acquisition and contract management, e-business, human resource management, information systems, logistics management, management, transportation management; material acquisition management (MS); project management (MS), including information systems, operations research; public administration (MPA); quality management (MS); space management (MS); space systems (MS); systems management (MS), including information systems, operations research, systems management. Part-time and evening/weekend programs available. Postbaccalaureate distance learning degree programs offered (no on-campus study). *Faculty:* 12 full-time (3 women), 117 part-time/adjunct (20 women). *Students:* 74 full-time (32 women), 1,041 part-time (484 women); includes 343 minority (240 African Americans, 12 American Indian/Alaska Native, 44 Asian Americans or Pacific Islanders, 47 Hispanic Americans), 22 international. Average age 35. 520 applicants, 72% accepted, 279 enrolled. In 2009, 509 master's awarded. *Degree requirements:* For master's, capstone course. *Entrance requirements:* For master's, GMAT or resume showing 8 years of supervised experience, minimum GPA of 3.0, 2 letters of recommendation, resume. Additional exam requirements/recommendations for international students: Required—TOEFL (minimum score 550 paper-based; 213 computer-based; 79 iBT). *Application deadline:* For fall admission, 4/1 for international students; for spring admission, 9/30 for international students. Applications are processed on a rolling basis. Application fee: $50. Electronic applications accepted. *Expenses:* Tuition: Part-time $1015 per credit. Tuition and fees vary according to campus/location and program. *Financial support:* Application deadline: 3/1. *Unit head:* Dr. Clifford Bragdon, Dean, 321-674-8821, Fax: 321-674-7597, E-mail: cbragdon@fit.edu. *Application contact:* Carolyn Farrior, Director of Graduate Admissions Online Learning and Off Campus Programs, 321-674-7118, Fax: 321-674-8216, E-mail: cfarrior@fit.edu.

Florida Institute of Technology, Graduate Programs, College of Business, Online Programs, Melbourne, FL 32901-6975. Offers accounting and finance (MBA); healthcare management (MBA); information technology (MS); information technology management (MBA); management (MBA); marketing (MBA); project management (MBA). Part-time and evening/weekend programs available. Postbaccalaureate distance learning degree programs offered (no on-campus study). *Faculty:* 30 part-time/adjunct (6 women). *Students:* 6 full-time (2 women), 875 part-time (387 women); includes 290 minority (194 African Americans, 6 American Indian/Alaska Native, 44 Asian Americans or Pacific Islanders, 46 Hispanic Americans), 32 international. Average age 37. 329 applicants, 64% accepted, 177 enrolled. In 2009, 33 master's awarded. *Entrance requirements:* For master's, GMAT or resume showing 8 years of supervised experience, 2 letters of recommendation, resume, competency in math past college algebra. Additional exam requirements/recommendations for international students: Required—TOEFL (minimum score 550 paper-based; 213 computer-based; 79 iBT). *Application deadline:* For fall admission, 4/1 for international students; for spring admission, 9/30 for international students. Applications are processed on a rolling basis. Application fee: $50. Electronic applications accepted. *Expenses:* Tuition: Part-time $1015 per credit. Tuition and fees vary according to campus/location and program. *Financial support:* Available to part-time students. Application deadline: 3/1. *Unit head:* Dr. Mary S. Bonhomme, Dean, Florida Tech Online/Associate Provost for Online Learning, 321-674-8883, Fax: 321-674-8216, E-mail: bonhomme@fit.edu. *Application contact:* Carolyn Farrior, Director of Graduate Admissions Online Learning and Off Campus Programs, 321-674-7118, Fax: 321-674-8216, E-mail: cfarrior@fit.edu.

Florida International University, Alvah H. Chapman, Jr. Graduate School of Business, Department of Decision Sciences and Information Systems, Miami, FL 33199. Offers MSMIS. Part-time and evening/weekend programs available. *Faculty:* 17 full-time (3 women). *Students:* 44 full-time (7 women), 2 part-time (0 women); includes 30 minority (4 African Americans, 1 American Indian/Alaska Native, 3 Asian Americans or Pacific Islanders, 22 Hispanic Americans), 8 international. Average age 30. 61 applicants, 34% accepted, 21 enrolled. In 2009, 73 master's awarded. *Entrance requirements:* For master's, GMAT or GRE, minimum GPA of 3.0 (upper-level coursework); letter of intent; resume. Additional exam requirements/recommendations for international students: Required—TOEFL (minimum score 550 paper-based; 213 computer-based; 80 iBT), or IELTS. *Application deadline:* For fall admission, 6/1 for domestic students, 4/1 for international students; for spring admission, 10/1 for domestic students, 9/1 for international students. Applications are processed on a rolling basis. Application fee: $30. Electronic applications accepted. *Expenses:* Contact institution. *Financial support:* Institutionally sponsored loans and scholarships/grants available. Financial award application deadline: 3/1; financial award applicants required to submit FAFSA. *Faculty research:* Artificial intelligence; data warehouses; operations management. *Unit head:* Dr. Christos Koulamas, Chair, 305-348-2830, Fax: 305-348-4126, E-mail: koulamas@fiu.edu. *Application contact:* Zuzana Hlavacova, Assistant Program Director, 305-348- 6852, Fax: 305-348-7204, E-mail: zuzana.hlavacova@business.fiu.edu.

Florida State University, The Graduate School, College of Business, Tallahassee, FL 32306-1110. Offers accounting (M Acc), including accounting information services, assurance services, corporate accounting, taxation; business administration (MBA, PhD), including accounting (PhD), finance (PhD), management information systems (PhD), marketing (PhD), organizational behavior (PhD), risk management and insurance (PhD), strategic management (PhD); finance (MS); insurance (MSM); management information systems (MS); JD/MBA; MSW/MBA. *Accreditation:* AACSB. Part-time programs available. Postbaccalaureate distance learning degree programs offered (no on-campus study). *Faculty:* 107 full-time (31 women), 2 part-time/adjunct (0 women). *Students:* 212 full-time (73 women), 345 part-time (107 women); includes 123 minority (37 African Americans, 2 American Indian/Alaska Native, 48 Asian Americans or Pacific Islanders, 36 Hispanic Americans). Average age 30. 908 applicants, 43% accepted, 307 enrolled. In 2009, 257 master's, 18 doctorates awarded. Terminal master's awarded for partial completion of doctoral program. *Degree requirements:* For doctorate, comprehensive exam, thesis/dissertation. *Entrance requirements:* For master's, GMAT, work experience (MBA, MS), minimum GPA of 3.0, letters of recommendation; for doctorate, GMAT, minimum graduate GPA of 3.5, letters of recommendation. Additional exam requirements/recommendations for international students: Required—TOEFL (minimum score 600 paper-based; 80 computer-based); Recommended—IELTS (minimum score 6.5). *Application deadline:* For fall admission, 6/1 for domestic students, 5/1 for international students; for spring admission, 10/1 for domestic students, 9/1 for international students. Applications are processed on a rolling basis. Application fee: $30. Electronic applications accepted. *Expenses:* Tuition, state resident: full-time $7413. Tuition, nonresident: full-time $22,567. *Financial support:* In 2009–10, 102 students received support, including 32 fellowships with full tuition reimbursements available (averaging $6,900 per year), 30 research assistantships with full tuition reimbursements available (averaging $4,500 per year), 40 teaching assistantships with full tuition reimbursements available (averaging $11,500 per year); career-related internships or fieldwork, scholarships/grants, health care benefits, tuition waivers (full and partial), and unspecified assistantships also available. Support available to part-time students. Financial award application deadline: 1/1. *Unit head:* Dr. Caryn Beck-Dudley, Dean, 850-644-3090, Fax: 850-644-0915. *Application contact:* Lisa Beverly, Director, Graduate Programs Admissions, 850-644-6458, Fax: 850-644-0588, E-mail: lbeverly@cob.fsu.edu.

Fordham University, Graduate School of Business Administration, New York, NY 10023. Offers accounting (MBA); communications and media management (MBA); executive business administration (EMBA); finance (MBA, MS); information systems (MBA, MS); management systems (MBA); marketing (MBA); media management (MS); taxation (MS); taxation and accounting (MTA);); JD/MBA; MBA/MIM; MS/MBA. *Accreditation:* AACSB. Part-time and evening/weekend programs available. *Entrance requirements:* For master's, GMAT, 2 letters of recommendation, resume. Additional exam requirements/recommendations for international students: Required—TOEFL (minimum score 600 paper-based; 250 computer-based; 100 iBT). Electronic applications accepted. *Expenses:* Contact institution.

Franklin Pierce University, Graduate Studies, Rindge, NH 03461-0060. Offers emerging network technology (Graduate Certificate); health practice management (MBA, Graduate Certificate); human resource management (MBA); human resources management (Graduate

Management Information Systems

Franklin Pierce University *(continued)*

Certificate); information technology management (MS); leadership (MBA, DA), including transformational leadership (DA); nursing (MS); physical therapy (DPT); physician assistant (MPAS); sports facilities management (MS); teacher education (M Ed). *Accreditation:* APTA. Part-time programs available. Postbaccalaureate distance learning degree programs offered (no on-campus study). *Faculty:* 27 full-time (16 women), 18 part-time/adjunct (4 women). *Students:* 296 full-time (172 women), 249 part-time (165 women); includes 18 minority (5 African Americans, 7 Asian Americans or Pacific Islanders, 6 Hispanic Americans), 31 international. Average age 38. 227 applicants, 97% accepted, 185 enrolled. In 2009, 76 master's, 46 doctorates awarded. *Degree requirements:* For master's, concentrated original research projects; student teaching; fieldwork and/or internship; leadership project; for doctorate, concentrated original research projects, clinical fieldwork and/or internship, leadership project. *Entrance requirements:* For master's, minimum GPA of 2.5, 3 letters of recommendation; for doctorate, demonstrated success at previous academic institutions (minimum GPA of 2.5), 3 letters of recommendation, personal mission statement, interview; writing sample (for DA program). Additional exam requirements/recommendations for international students: Required—TOEFL (minimum score 550 paper-based; 195 computer-based). *Application deadline:* Applications are processed on a rolling basis. Application fee: $0. Electronic applications accepted. *Expenses:* Tuition: Part-time $1560 per course. Part-time tuition and fees vary according to degree level, campus/location and program. *Financial support:* In 2009–10, 36 students received support, including 22 teaching assistantships with full and partial tuition reimbursements available; career-related internships or fieldwork and unspecified assistantships also available. Support available to part-time students. Financial award applicants required to submit FAFSA. *Faculty research:* Evidence based practice in sports physical therapy, human resource management in economic crisis, leadership in nursing, innovation in sports facility management, differentiated learning and understanding by design. *Unit head:* Dr. Robert G. Goddard, Assistant Dean, 603-899-4361, Fax: 603-229-4580, E-mail: goddardr@franklinpierce.edu. *Application contact:* 800-325-1090, Fax: 603-898-0827, E-mail: gpsadmin@franklinpierce.edu.

Friends University, Graduate School, Division of Business, Technology, and Leadership, Program in Management Information Systems, Wichita, KS 67213. Offers MMIS. Evening/weekend programs available. *Entrance requirements:* Additional exam requirements/recommendations for international students: Required—TOEFL (minimum score 560 paper-based; 220 computer-based; 83 iBT), IELTS (minimum score 6). Electronic applications accepted.

George Mason University, Volgenau School of Information Technology and Engineering, Department of Computer Science, Fairfax, VA 22030. Offers biometrics (Certificate); computer games technology (Certificate); computer networking (Certificate); computer science (MS, PhD); data mining (Certificate); database management (Certificate); electronic commerce (Certificate); foundations of information systems (Certificate); information engineering (Certificate); information security and assurance (MS, Certificate); information systems (MS); intelligent agents (Certificate); software architecture (Certificate); software engineering (MS, Certificate); systems engineering (MS); Web-based software engineering (Certificate). Part-time and evening/weekend programs available. Postbaccalaureate distance learning degree programs offered. *Faculty:* 42 full-time (9 women), 18 part-time/adjunct (0 women). *Students:* 121 full-time (36 women), 489 part-time (118 women); includes 90 minority (11 African Americans, 70 Asian Americans or Pacific Islanders, 9 Hispanic Americans), 222 international. Average age 29. 882 applicants, 58% accepted, 147 enrolled. In 2009, 202 master's, 6 doctorates, 21 other advanced degrees awarded. *Degree requirements:* For master's, thesis optional; for doctorate, comprehensive exam, thesis/dissertation. *Entrance requirements:* For master's, GRE General Test, minimum GPA of 3.0 in last 60 hours, 3 letters of recommendation; for doctorate, GRE, 4-year BA, academic work in computer science, 3 letters of recommendation, statement of career goals and aspirations. Additional exam requirements/recommendations for international students: Required—TOEFL. *Application deadline:* For fall admission, 4/15 priority date for domestic students, 1/15 for international students; for spring admission, 11/15 for domestic students. Application fee: $75. Electronic applications accepted. *Expenses:* Tuition, state resident: full-time $7568; part-time $315.33 per credit hour. Tuition, nonresident: full-time $21,704; part-time $904.33 per credit hour. Required fees: $2184; $91 per credit hour. *Financial support:* In 2009–10, 106 students received support, including 3 fellowships (averaging $18,000 per year), 53 research assistantships (averaging $11,119 per year), 53 teaching assistantships (averaging $7,881 per year); unspecified assistantships and health care benefits (full-time research or teaching assistantship recipients) also available. Financial award application deadline: 3/1; financial award applicants required to submit FAFSA. *Faculty research:* Artificial intelligence, image processing/graphics, parallel/distributed systems, software engineering systems. Total annual research expenditures: $1.3 million. *Unit head:* Dr. Arun Sood, Director, 703-993-1524, Fax: 703-993-1710, E-mail: asood@gmu.edu. *Application contact:* Jay Shapiro, Professor, 703-993-1485, E-mail: jshapiro@gmu.edu.

The George Washington University, School of Business, Department of Information Systems and Technology Management, Washington, DC 20052. Offers information and decision systems (PhD); information systems (MSIST); information systems development (MSIST); information systems management (MBA); information systems project management (MSIST); management information systems (MSIST); management of science, technology, and innovation (MBA, PhD). Programs also offered in Ashburn and Arlington, VA. Part-time and evening/weekend programs available. *Faculty:* 13 full-time (4 women), 3 part-time/adjunct (1 woman). *Students:* 76 full-time (27 women), 160 part-time (50 women); includes 83 minority (30 African Americans, 1 American Indian/Alaska Native, 39 Asian Americans or Pacific Islanders, 13 Hispanic Americans), 35 international. Average age 33. 217 applicants, 72% accepted, 77 enrolled. In 2009, 117 master's, 7 doctorates awarded. *Entrance requirements:* For master's, GMAT. Additional exam requirements/recommendations for international students: Required—TOEFL. *Application deadline:* For fall admission, 4/1 priority date for domestic students; for spring admission, 10/1 for domestic students. Applications are processed on a rolling basis. Application fee: $60. *Financial support:* In 2009–10, 35 students received support; fellowships, teaching assistantships, career-related internships or fieldwork, Federal Work-Study, institutionally sponsored loans, and tuition waivers available. Financial award application deadline: 4/1. *Faculty research:* Expert systems, decision support systems. *Unit head:* Richard G. Donnelly, Chair, 202-994-4364, E-mail: rgd@gwu.edu. *Application contact:* Kristin Williams, Assistant Vice President for Graduate and Special Enrollment Management, 202-994-0467, Fax: 202-994-0371, E-mail: ksw@gwu.edu.

Georgia College & State University, Graduate School, The J. Whitney Bunting School of Business, Milledgeville, GA 31061. Offers accountancy (MACCT); accounting (MBA); business (MBA); health services administration (MBA); information systems (MIS); management information services (MBA). *Accreditation:* AACSB. Part-time and evening/weekend programs available. Postbaccalaureate distance learning degree programs offered (no on-campus study). *Faculty:* 43 full-time (17 women). *Students:* 70 full-time (32 women), 166 part-time (63 women); includes 29 minority (20 African Americans, 7 Asian Americans or Pacific Islanders, 2 Hispanic Americans), 23 international. Average age 29. 134 applicants, 84% accepted, 78 enrolled. In 2009, 75 master's awarded. *Entrance requirements:* For master's, GMAT. Additional exam requirements/recommendations for international students: Recommended—TOEFL (minimum score 550 paper-based; 213 computer-based; 79 iBT). *Application deadline:* For fall admission, 7/1 priority date for domestic students; for spring admission, 11/15 priority date for domestic students. Applications are processed on a rolling basis. Application fee: $40. Electronic applications accepted. *Expenses:* Tuition, area resident: Part-time $241 per credit hour. Tuition, state resident: full-time $4338. Tuition, nonresident: full-time $17,352; part-time $964 per credit hour. Required fees: $609 per semester. Tuition and fees vary according to course load and campus/location. *Financial support:* In 2009–10, 30 research assistantships with full tuition reimbursements were awarded; career-related internships or fieldwork and unspecified assistantships also available. Support available to part-time students. Financial award application deadline: 3/1; financial award applicants required to submit FAFSA. *Unit head:* Dr. Dale Young, Interim Dean, 478-445-5497, E-mail: dale.young@gcsu.edu. *Application contact:* Lynn Hanson, Director of Graduate Programs, 478-445-5115, E-mail: lynn.hanson@gcsu.edu.

Georgia Institute of Technology, Graduate Studies and Research, College of Management, Program in Business Administration, Atlanta, GA 30332-0001. Offers accounting (MBA); e-commerce (Certificate); engineering entrepreneurship (MBA); entrepreneurship (Certificate); finance (MBA); information technology management (MBA); international business (MBA, Certificate); management of technology (Certificate); marketing (MBA); operations management (MBA); organizational behavior (MBA); strategic management (MBA). *Accreditation:* AACSB.

Georgia Institute of Technology, Graduate Studies and Research, College of Management, Program in Management, Atlanta, GA 30332-0001. Offers accounting (PhD); finance (PhD); information technology management (PhD); marketing (PhD); operations management (PhD); organizational behavior (PhD); quantitative and computational finance (MS); strategic management (PhD). *Accreditation:* AACSB. *Degree requirements:* For doctorate, comprehensive exam, thesis/dissertation, oral exams. *Entrance requirements:* For master's and doctorate, GMAT. Additional exam requirements/recommendations for international students: Required—TOEFL. *Faculty research:* MIS, management of technology, international business, entrepreneurship, operations management.

Georgia State University, J. Mack Robinson College of Business, Department of Computer Information Systems, Atlanta, GA 30302-3083. Offers MBA, MSIS, PhD. Part-time and evening/weekend programs available. Terminal master's awarded for partial completion of doctoral program. *Degree requirements:* For doctorate, thesis/dissertation. *Entrance requirements:* For master's and doctorate, GMAT. Additional exam requirements/recommendations for international students: Required—TOEFL (minimum score 610 paper-based; 255 computer-based; 101 iBT).

Georgia State University, J. Mack Robinson College of Business, Program in General Business Administration, Atlanta, GA 30302-3083. Offers accounting/information systems (MBA); economics (MBA, MS); enterprise risk management (MBA); general business (MBA); general business administration (EMBA, PMBA); information systems consulting (MBA); information systems risk management (MBA); international business and information technology (MBA); international entrepreneurship (MBA); MBA/JD. *Accreditation:* AACSB. Part-time and evening/weekend programs available. *Entrance requirements:* For master's, GMAT. Additional exam requirements/recommendations for international students: Required—TOEFL (minimum score 610 paper-based; 255 computer-based; 101 iBT). Electronic applications accepted.

Globe University, Minnesota School of Business, Woodbury, MN 55125. Offers business administration (MBA); health care management (MSM); information technology (MSM); managerial leadership (MSM).

Golden Gate University, Ageno School of Business, San Francisco, CA 94105-2968. Offers accounting (MBA); business administration (EMBA, MBA, PMBA, DBA); finance (MBA, MS, Certificate); financial planning (MS, Certificate); human resource management (MBA, MS); human resources management (Certificate); information systems (MS); information technology (MBA); information technology management (Certificate); integrated marketing and communications (MS, Certificate); international business (MBA); management (MBA); marketing (MBA, MS, Certificate); operations management (Certificate); psychology (MA, Certificate); public relations (MS, Certificate); JD/MBA. Part-time and evening/weekend programs available. *Faculty:* 16 full-time (4 women), 241 part-time/adjunct (72 women). *Students:* 380 full-time (193 women), 750 part-time (414 women); includes 480 minority (98 African Americans, 2 American Indian/Alaska Native, 298 Asian Americans or Pacific Islanders, 82 Hispanic Americans), 166 international. Average age 33. 681 applicants, 78% accepted, 270 enrolled. In 2009, 550 master's, 13 doctorates awarded. *Degree requirements:* For doctorate, thesis/dissertation. *Entrance requirements:* For master's, GMAT (MBA), minimum GPA of 2.5 (MS). Additional exam requirements/recommendations for international students: Required—TOEFL. *Application deadline:* For fall admission, 5/15 for international students; for winter admission, 1/15 for international students; for spring admission, 9/15 for international students. Applications are processed on a rolling basis. Application fee: $70 ($110 for international students). Electronic applications accepted. *Expenses:* Contact institution. *Financial support:* Career-related internships or fieldwork, Federal Work-Study, institutionally sponsored loans, and scholarships/grants available. Support available to part-time students. Financial award applicants required to submit FAFSA. *Unit head:* Terry Connelly, Dean, 415-442-6519, Fax: 415-442-5369. *Application contact:* Angela Melero, Enrollment Services, 415-442-7800, Fax: 415-442-7807, E-mail: info@ggu.edu.

Goldey-Beacom College, Graduate Program, Wilmington, DE 19808-1999. Offers business administration (MBA); finance (MS); financial management (MBA); human resource management (MBA); information technology (MBA); international business management (MBA); management (MM); marketing management (MBA); taxation (MBA, MS). *Accreditation:* ACBSP. Part-time and evening/weekend programs available. *Faculty:* 20 full-time (8 women), 28 part-time/adjunct (10 women). *Students:* 38 full-time (18 women), 486 part-time (184 women); includes 350 minority (38 African Americans, 300 Asian Americans or Pacific Islanders, 12 Hispanic Americans). Average age 27. In 2009, 130 master's awarded. *Entrance requirements:* For master's, GMAT, MAT, GRE, minimum GPA of 3.0. Additional exam requirements/recommendations for international students: Required—TOEFL (minimum score 65 computer-based); Recommended—IELTS (minimum score 5). *Application deadline:* Applications are processed on a rolling basis. Electronic applications accepted. *Expenses:* Tuition: Full-time $14,166; part-time $787 per credit. Required fees: $180; $10 per credit. *Financial support:* In 2009–10, 486 students received support. Scholarships/grants available. Support available to part-time students. Financial award application deadline: 4/1; financial award applicants required to submit FAFSA. *Unit head:* Larry W. Eby, Director of Admissions, 302-225-6289, Fax: 302-996-5408, E-mail: ebylw@gbc.edu. *Application contact:* Ashley E. Mashington, Graduate Admissions Representative, 302-225-6259, Fax: 302-996-5408, E-mail: mashina@gbc.edu.

Governors State University, College of Business and Public Administration, Program in Management Information Systems, University Park, IL 60466-0975. Offers MS.

Graduate School and University Center of the City University of New York, Graduate Studies, Program in Business, New York, NY 10016-4039. Offers accounting (PhD); behavioral science (PhD); finance (PhD); management planning systems (PhD). *Faculty:* 66 full-time (5 women). *Students:* 64 full-time (37 women); includes 7 minority (3 African Americans, 1 American Indian/Alaska Native, 2 Asian Americans or Pacific Islanders, 1 Hispanic American), 34 international. Average age 33. 89 applicants, 28% accepted, 18 enrolled. In 2009, 7 doctorates awarded. *Degree requirements:* For doctorate, thesis/dissertation. *Entrance requirements:* For doctorate, GMAT, writing sample (15 pages). Additional exam requirements/recommendations for international students: Required—TOEFL. *Application deadline:* For fall admission, 1/15 for domestic students. Application fee: $125. Electronic applications accepted. *Financial support:* In 2009–10, 50 students received support, including 54 fellowships, 5 teaching assistantships; research assistantships, career-related internships or fieldwork, Federal Work-Study, institutionally sponsored loans, and tuition waivers (full and partial) also available. Financial award application deadline: 2/1; financial award applicants required to submit FAFSA. *Unit head:* Dr. Joseph Weintrop, Executive Officer, 646-312-3092, Fax: 646-312-3031. *Application contact:* Les Gribben, Director of Admissions, 212-817-7470, Fax: 212-817-1624, E-mail: lgribben@gc.cuny.edu.

Grand Canyon University, College of Business, Phoenix, AZ 85017-1097. Offers accounting (MBA); executive fire service leadership (MS); finance (MBA); general management (MBA); health systems management (MBA); leadership (MBA, MS); management of information system (MBA); marketing (MBA); six sigma (MBA). *Accreditation:* ACBSP. Part-time and evening/weekend programs available. Postbaccalaureate distance learning degree programs offered (no on-campus study). *Entrance requirements:* For master's, equivalent of two years full-time professional work experience. Additional exam requirements/recommendations for international students: Required—TOEFL (minimum score 575 paper-based; 233 computer-based; 90 iBT), IELTS (minimum score 7). Electronic applications accepted.

Grand Valley State University, Padnos College of Engineering and Computing, School of Computing and Information Systems, Allendale, MI 49401-9403. Offers computer information

systems (MS), including databases, distributed systems, management of information systems, object-oriented systems, software engineering. Part-time and evening/weekend programs available. *Faculty:* 11 full-time (0 women). *Students:* 10 full-time (3 women), 52 part-time (12 women); includes 8 minority (1 African American, 6 Asian Americans or Pacific Islanders, 1 Hispanic American), 11 international. Average age 33. 32 applicants, 81% accepted, 16 enrolled. In 2009, 22 master's awarded. *Degree requirements:* For master's, thesis or alternative. *Entrance requirements:* For master's, GMAT or GRE General Test. Additional exam requirements/recommendations for international students: Required—TOEFL. *Application deadline:* For fall admission, 6/1 for international students; for winter admission, 9/1 for international students. Applications are processed on a rolling basis. Application fee: $30. Electronic applications accepted. *Expenses:* Tuition, state resident: part-time $471 per credit hour. Tuition, nonresident: part-time $646 per credit hour. Tuition and fees vary according to course level. *Financial support:* In 2009–10, 9 students received support, including 5 fellowships (averaging $3,380 per year), 5 research assistantships with full and partial tuition reimbursements available (averaging $4,626 per year). *Faculty research:* Object technology, distributed computing, information systems management database, software engineering. *Unit head:* Paul Leidig, Director, 616-331-2038, Fax: 616-331-2106, E-mail: leidigp@gvsu.edu. *Application contact:* D. Robert Adams, CIS Graduate Program Chair, 616-331-3885, Fax: 616-331-2106, E-mail: adams@cis.gvsu.edu.

Grantham University, Mark Skousen School of Business, Kansas City, MO 64153. Offers business administration (MBA); information management (MBA); information technology (MS); project management (MBA, MSIM). Part-time and evening/weekend programs available. Postbaccalaureate distance learning degree programs offered (no on-campus study). In 2009, 48 master's awarded. *Degree requirements:* For master's, capstone project. *Entrance requirements:* For master's, bachelor's degree from accredited degree-granting institution. Additional exam requirements/recommendations for international students: Required—TOEFL (minimum score 500 paper-based; 213 computer-based; 61 iBT). *Application deadline:* Applications are processed on a rolling basis. Application fee: $0. Electronic applications accepted. *Expenses:* Tuition: Part-time $265 per credit hour. One-time fee: $30 part-time. *Financial support:* Institutionally sponsored loans and scholarships/grants available. *Unit head:* Rhonda Corwin, Dean, 800-955-2527, Fax: 816-595-5757, E-mail: admissions@grantham.edu. *Application contact:* Matthew Hawes, Vice President of Enrollment Management, 800-955-2527, Fax: 816-595-5757, E-mail: admissions@grantham.edu.

Harrisburg University of Science and Technology, Program in Information Systems Engineering and Management, Harrisburg, PA 17101. Offers digital government specialization (MS); digital health specialization (MS); entrepreneurship specialization (MS). Part-time programs available. *Faculty:* 1 full-time (0 women), 2 part-time/adjunct (0 women). *Degree requirements:* For master's, comprehensive exam, thesis optional. *Entrance requirements:* Additional exam requirements/recommendations for international students: Required—TOEFL (minimum score 520 paper-based; 200 computer-based; 80 iBT). *Application deadline:* For fall admission, 8/1 priority date for domestic students, 7/1 priority date for international students. Applications are processed on a rolling basis. Application fee: $0. Electronic applications accepted. *Expenses:* Tuition: Full-time $18,000; part-time $650 per semester hour. *Financial support:* Scholarships/grants available. Financial award applicants required to submit FAFSA. *Unit head:* Dr. Amjad Umar, Director and Professor, 717-901-5141, Fax: 717-901-3141, E-mail: aumar@harrisburgu.edu. *Application contact:* Julie Cullings, Information Contact, 717-901-5163, Fax: 717-901-3163, E-mail: admissions@harrisburgu.edu.

Hawai'i Pacific University, College of Business Administration, Program in Information Systems, Honolulu, HI 96813. Offers knowledge management (MSIS); software engineering (MSIS); telecommunications security (MSIS). *Faculty:* 9 full-time (2 women), 3 part-time/adjunct (1 woman). *Students:* 54 full-time (14 women), 60 part-time (17 women); includes 50 minority (4 African Americans, 40 Asian Americans or Pacific Islanders, 6 Hispanic Americans), 49 international. Average age 32. In 2009, 52 master's awarded. *Expenses:* Tuition: Full-time $12,600; part-time $700 per credit hour. Tuition and fees vary according to program. *Unit head:* Dr. Gordon Jones, Dean, 808-544-1181, Fax: 808-544-0247, E-mail: gjones@hpu.edu. *Application contact:* Danny Lam, Assistant Director of Graduate Admissions, 808-544-1135, Fax: 808-544-0280, E-mail: graduate@hpu.edu.

See Close-Up on page 497.

HEC Montreal, School of Business Administration, Master of Science Programs in Administration, Program in Information Systems, Montréal, QC H3T 2A7, Canada. Offers M Sc. All courses are given in French. Part-time programs available. *Students:* 25 full-time (6 women), 4 part-time (all women). 20 applicants, 80% accepted, 8 enrolled. In 2009, 13 master's awarded. *Degree requirements:* For master's, one foreign language, thesis. *Application deadline:* For fall admission, 3/15 for domestic and international students; for winter admission, 9/15 for domestic and international students. Application fee: $77 Canadian dollars. Electronic applications accepted. Tuition and fees charges are reported in Canadian dollars. *Expenses:* Tuition, area resident: Part-time $65.60 Canadian dollars per credit. Tuition, state resident: full-time $2361.60 Canadian dollars; part-time $183.36 Canadian dollars per credit. Tuition, nonresident: full-time $6601 Canadian dollars; part-time $448.13 Canadian dollars per credit. International tuition: $16,132.68 Canadian dollars full-time. Required fees: $1254.15 Canadian dollars; $28.99 Canadian dollars per course. $91.68 Canadian dollars per term. Tuition and fees vary according to degree level and program. *Financial support:* Fellowships, research assistantships, teaching assistantships, scholarships/grants available. Financial award application deadline: 10/2. *Unit head:* Dr. Claude Laurin, Director, 514-340-6485, Fax: 514-340-5690, E-mail: claude.laurin@hec.ca. *Application contact:* Francine Blais, Administrative Director, 514-340-6112, Fax: 514-340-6411, E-mail: francine.blais@hec.ca.

Hodges University, Graduate Programs, Naples, FL 34119. Offers business administration (MBA); computer information technology (MS); criminal justice (MCJ); education (MPS); information systems management (MIS); interdisciplinary (MPS); law (MPS); management (MSM); professional studies (MPS); psychology (MPS); public administration (MPA). Part-time and evening/weekend programs available. Postbaccalaureate distance learning degree programs offered (no on-campus study). *Faculty:* 14 full-time (4 women), 4 part-time/adjunct (3 women). *Students:* 37 full-time (28 women), 217 part-time (142 women); includes 76 minority (35 African Americans, 5 Asian Americans or Pacific Islanders, 36 Hispanic Americans). Average age 36. 92 applicants, 91% accepted, 81 enrolled. In 2009, 92 master's awarded. *Degree requirements:* For master's, comprehensive exam (for some programs), thesis (for some programs). *Entrance requirements:* For master's, in-house entrance exam. *Application deadline:* Applications are processed on a rolling basis. Application fee: $50. Electronic applications accepted. *Expenses:* Tuition: Full-time $16,605; part-time $615 per credit hour. Required fees: $570. *Financial support:* In 2009–10, 200 students received support. Federal Work-Study and scholarships/grants available. Financial award application deadline: 7/9; financial award applicants required to submit FAFSA. *Unit head:* Terry McMahan, President, 239-513-1122, Fax: 239-598-6253, E-mail: tmcmahan@hodges.edu. *Application contact:* Rita Lampus, Vice President of Student Enrollment Management, 239-513-1122, Fax: 239-598-6253, E-mail: rlampus@hodges.edu.

Hofstra University, Frank G. Zarb School of Business, Department of Information Technology and Quantitative Methods, Hempstead, NY 11549. Offers business administration (MBA), including information technology, quality management; information technology (MS). Part-time and evening/weekend programs available. *Faculty:* 10 full-time (2 women), 1 part-time/adjunct (0 women). *Students:* 8 full-time (2 women), 16 part-time (4 women); includes 5 minority (1 African American, 3 Asian Americans or Pacific Islanders, 1 Hispanic American), 2 international. Average age 30. 22 applicants, 64% accepted, 9 enrolled. In 2009, 9 master's awarded. *Degree requirements:* For master's, capstone course (MBA), thesis (MS). *Entrance requirements:* For master's, GMAT or GRE, 2 letters of recommendation, resume. Additional exam requirements/recommendations for international students: Required—TOEFL (minimum score 550 paper-based; 213 computer-based; 80 iBT); Recommended—IELTS (minimum score 6). *Application deadline:* Applications are processed on a rolling basis. Application fee: $60. Electronic applications accepted. *Expenses:* Contact institution. *Financial support:* In 2009–10, 3 students received support, including 3 fellowships with full and partial tuition reimbursements available (averaging $14,483 per year); research assistantships with full and partial tuition reimbursements available, career-related internships or fieldwork, Federal Work-Study, institutionally sponsored loans, scholarships/grants, tuition waivers (full and partial), and unspecified assistantships also available. Support available to part-time students. Financial award applicants required to submit FAFSA. *Faculty research:* IT outsourcing: IT strategy; SAP and enterprise systems; data mining/electronic medical records; IT and crisis management; inventory theory and modeling, forecasting. *Unit head:* Dr. Mohammed H. Tafti, Chairperson, 516-463-5720, E-mail: acsmht@hofstra.edu. *Application contact:* Carol Drummer, Dean of Graduate Admissions, 516-463-4876, Fax: 516-463-4664, E-mail: gradstudent@hofstra.edu.

Holy Family University, Graduate School, School of Business, Philadelphia, PA 19114. Offers human resources management (MS); information systems management (MS). Part-time and evening/weekend programs available. *Faculty:* 3 full-time (0 women), 3 part-time/adjunct (0 women). *Students:* 7 full-time (6 women), 49 part-time (32 women); includes 9 minority (4 African Americans, 3 Asian Americans or Pacific Islanders, 2 Hispanic Americans), 5 international. Average age 35. 18 applicants, 94% accepted, 15 enrolled. In 2009, 24 master's awarded. *Degree requirements:* For master's, comprehensive exam, thesis optional. *Entrance requirements:* For master's, GMAT, GRE, or MAT, minimum GPA of 3.0. *Application deadline:* For fall admission, 7/1 priority date for domestic students; for winter admission, 11/1 priority date for domestic students. Applications are processed on a rolling basis. Application fee: $25. *Expenses:* Tuition: Part-time $600 per credit. Required fees: $58 per semester. *Financial support:* Federal Work-Study available. Support available to part-time students. Financial award application deadline: 2/15; financial award applicants required to submit FAFSA. *Unit head:* Dr. Jan Duggar, Dean, 267-341-3373, Fax: 215-637-5937, E-mail: jduggar@holyfamily.edu. *Application contact:* Gidget Marie Montelibano, Graduate Admissions Counselor, 267-341-3558, Fax: 215-637-1478, E-mail: gmontelibano@holyfamily.edu.

Hood College, Graduate School, Department of Economics and Management, Frederick, MD 21701-8575. Offers accounting (MBA); administration and management (MBA); finance (MBA); human resource management (MBA); information systems (MBA); marketing (MBA); public management (MBA). Part-time and evening/weekend programs available. *Faculty:* 5 full-time (1 woman), 9 part-time/adjunct (1 woman). *Students:* 21 full-time (16 women), 166 part-time (85 women); includes 33 minority (18 African Americans, 8 Asian Americans or Pacific Islanders, 7 Hispanic Americans), 15 international. Average age 32. 47 applicants, 87% accepted, 32 enrolled. In 2009, 31 master's awarded. *Degree requirements:* For master's, capstone/final research project. *Entrance requirements:* For master's, minimum GPA of 2.75, resume, letters of recommendation. *Application deadline:* For fall admission, 7/15 for domestic and international students; for spring admission, 12/15 for domestic and international students. Applications are processed on a rolling basis. Application fee: $35. Electronic applications accepted. *Expenses:* Tuition: Full-time $6480; part-time $360 per credit. Required fees: $100; $50 per term. *Financial support:* Applicants required to submit FAFSA. *Faculty research:* Corporate strategy and sustainable competitive advantages, business ethics, entrepreneurship, investments management, economic development. *Unit head:* Dr. Anita Jose, Program Director, 301-696-3691, Fax: 301-696-3597, E-mail: jose@hood.edu. *Application contact:* Dr. Allen P. Flora, Dean of Graduate School, 301-696-3811, Fax: 301-696-3597, E-mail: gofurther@hood.edu.

Howard University, School of Business, Graduate Programs in Business, Washington, DC 20059-0002. Offers accounting (MBA); entrepreneurship (MBA); finance (MBA); general management (MBA); human resources management (MBA); information systems (MBA); international business (MBA); marketing (MBA); supply chain management (MBA); JD/MBA. *Accreditation:* AACSB. Part-time and evening/weekend programs available. Postbaccalaureate distance learning degree programs offered (no on-campus study). *Entrance requirements:* For master's, GMAT, minimum 1 year post undergraduate work experience, resume, 3 letters of recommendation, advanced college algebra. Additional exam requirements/recommendations for international students: Required—TOEFL. *Faculty research:* Marketing research in multiethnic populations, U.S. trade policies and international relations, risk management (finance).

Idaho State University, Office of Graduate Studies, College of Business, Pocatello, ID 83209-8020. Offers business administration (MBA, Postbaccalaureate Certificate); computer information systems (MS, Postbaccalaureate Certificate). *Accreditation:* AACSB. Part-time programs available. *Faculty:* 27 full-time (5 women). *Students:* 49 full-time (15 women), 73 part-time (17 women); includes 7 minority (1 African American, 2 American Indian/Alaska Native, 1 Asian American or Pacific Islander, 3 Hispanic Americans), 7 international. Average age 32. 38 applicants, 74% accepted, 5 enrolled. In 2009, 39 master's, 2 other advanced degrees awarded. *Degree requirements:* For master's, comprehensive exam, thesis (for some programs), oral exam; for Postbaccalaureate Certificate, comprehensive exam, thesis (for some programs), 6 hours of clerkship. *Entrance requirements:* For master's, GMAT, GRE General Test, minimum GPA of 3.0, resume outlining work experience, 2 letters of reference; for Postbaccalaureate Certificate, GMAT, GRE General Test, minimum upper-level GPA of 3.0, resume of work experience. Additional exam requirements/recommendations for international students: Required—TOEFL (minimum score 550 paper-based; 213 computer-based; 80 iBT). *Application deadline:* For fall admission, 7/1 for domestic students, 6/1 for international students; for spring admission, 12/1 for domestic students, 11/1 for international students. Applications are processed on a rolling basis. Application fee: $55. Electronic applications accepted. *Expenses:* Tuition, state resident: full-time $3318; part-time $297 per credit hour. Tuition, nonresident: full-time $13,120; part-time $437 per credit hour. Required fees: $2530. Tuition and fees vary according to program. *Financial support:* In 2009–10, 10 teaching assistantships with full and partial tuition reimbursements (averaging $10,841 per year) were awarded; career-related internships or fieldwork, Federal Work-Study, institutionally sponsored loans, scholarships/grants, health care benefits, tuition waivers (full and partial), and unspecified assistantships also available. Support available to part-time students. Financial award application deadline: 1/1; financial award applicants required to submit FAFSA. *Faculty research:* Information assurance, computer information technology, finance management, marketing. *Unit head:* Dr. Ken Smith, Dean, 208-282-3585, Fax: 208-282-4367, E-mail: smithken@isu.edu. *Application contact:* Tami Carson, Graduate School Technical Records Specialist, 208-282-2150, Fax: 208-282-4847, E-mail: carstami@isu.edu.

Illinois Institute of Technology, Graduate College, College of Science and Letters, Lewis Department of Humanities, Chicago, IL 60616-3793. Offers information architecture (MS); technical communication (PhD); technical communication and information design (MS). Part-time and evening/weekend programs available. *Faculty:* 17 full-time (6 women), 11 part-time/adjunct (4 women). *Students:* 13 full-time (8 women), 34 part-time (24 women); includes 12 minority (11 African Americans, 1 Asian American or Pacific Islander), 6 international. Average age 34. 46 applicants, 52% accepted, 9 enrolled. In 2009, 9 master's, 2 doctorates awarded. *Degree requirements:* For master's, comprehensive exam, thesis or alternative, project; for doctorate, comprehensive exam, thesis/dissertation, qualifying exam. *Entrance requirements:* For master's, GRE General Test; for doctorate, GRE General Test, bachelor's degree in technical communication or other relevant field. Additional exam requirements/recommendations for international students: Required—TOEFL (minimum score 523 paper-based; 70 iBT). *Application deadline:* For fall admission, 5/1 for domestic and international students; for spring admission, 10/15 for domestic and international students. Applications are processed on a rolling basis. Application fee: $50. Electronic applications accepted. *Expenses:* Tuition: Full-time $17,550; part-time $888 per credit hour. Required fees: $850; $7.50 per credit hour. One-time fee: $50 full-time. Full-time tuition and fees vary according to program. *Financial support:* In 2009–10, 15 teaching assistantships with partial tuition reimbursements (averaging $9,000 per year) were awarded; career-related internships or fieldwork, Federal Work-Study, institutionally sponsored loans, scholarships/grants, health care benefits, tuition waivers (partial), and unspecified assistantships also available. Support available to part-time students. Financial award applicants required to submit FAFSA. *Faculty research:* Discourse analysis, linguistics, readability, ethics in professions, instructional and document design, knowledge management, usability testing and evaluation, history and philosophy of science. Total annual research

Management Information Systems

Illinois Institute of Technology (continued)

expenditures: $34,161. *Unit head:* Dr. Kathryn Riley, Professor and Chair, 312-567-3566, Fax: 312-567-5187, E-mail: riley@iit.edu. *Application contact:* Dr. Kathryn Riley, Professor and Chair, 312-567-3566, Fax: 312-567-5187, E-mail: riley@iit.edu.

Illinois Institute of Technology, Graduate College, School of Applied Technology, Program in Information Technology and Management, Chicago, IL 60616-3793. Offers MITM. Part-time and evening/weekend programs available. Postbaccalaureate distance learning degree programs offered (no on-campus study). *Faculty:* 2 full-time (0 women), 7 part-time/adjunct (1 woman). *Students:* 131 full-time (36 women), 77 part-time (21 women); includes 13 minority (3 African Americans, 9 Asian Americans or Pacific Islanders, 1 Hispanic American), 157 international. Average age 27. 195 applicants, 72% accepted, 51 enrolled. In 2009, 78 master's awarded. *Entrance requirements:* For master's, minimum undergraduate GPA of 3.0. Additional exam requirements/recommendations for international students: Required—TOEFL (minimum score 523 paper-based; 70 iBT). *Application deadline:* For fall admission, 8/1 for domestic students, 5/1 for international students; for spring admission, 12/15 for domestic students, 10/15 for international students. Applications are processed on a rolling basis. Application fee: $50. Electronic applications accepted. *Expenses:* Tuition: Full-time $17,550; part-time $888 per credit hour. Required fees: $850; $7.50 per credit hour. One-time fee: $50 full-time. Full-time tuition and fees vary according to program. *Financial support:* In 2009–10, 15 fellowships with partial tuition reimbursements, 1 research assistantship with full tuition reimbursement (averaging $1,200 per year), 10 teaching assistantships with partial tuition reimbursements (averaging $6,000 per year) were awarded; career-related internships or fieldwork, Federal Work-Study, institutionally sponsored loans, scholarships/grants, traineeships, health care benefits, tuition waivers (partial), and unspecified assistantships also available. Support available to part-time students. Financial award applicants required to submit FAFSA. *Faculty research:* Information, computer and network security; computer forensics; voice-over IP (VOIP) and telecommunications; web technologies; software engineering methodologies, testing maturity model; operating system virtualization; service oriented architecture. *Unit head:* C. Robert Carlson, Director, 630-682-6002, Fax: 630-682-6010, E-mail: carlson@iit.edu. *Application contact:* C. Robert Carlson, Director, 630-682-6002, Fax: 630-682-6010, E-mail: carlson@iit.edu.

Illinois State University, Graduate School, College of Applied Science and Technology, School of Information Technology, Normal, IL 61790-2200. Offers MS. *Entrance requirements:* For master's, GRE General Test, minimum GPA of 3.0 in last 60 hours; proficiency in COBOL, FORTRAN, Pascal, or P12. *Faculty research:* Graduate practicum training in network support.

Indiana University Bloomington, School of Public and Environmental Affairs, Public Affairs Programs, Bloomington, IN 47405-7000. Offers comparative and international affairs (MPA); economic development (MPA); environmental policy and natural resource management (MPA); information systems (MPA); local government management (MPA); nonprofit management (MPA); policy analysis (MPA); public affairs (PhD, Certificate); public financial administration (MPA); public management (MPA); sustainability and sustainable development (MPA); JD/MPA; MPA/MIS; MPA/MLS; MSES/MPA. *Accreditation:* NASPAA (one or more programs are accredited). Part-time programs available. *Faculty:* 75 full-time (22 women), 91 part-time/adjunct (24 women). *Students:* 389 full-time (222 women), 45 part-time (24 women); includes 38 minority (18 African Americans, 1 American Indian/Alaska Native, 12 Asian Americans or Pacific Islanders, 7 Hispanic Americans), 72 international. Average age 26. 474 applicants, 206 enrolled. In 2009, 190 master's, 11 doctorates, 3 other advanced degrees awarded. Terminal master's awarded for partial completion of doctoral program. *Degree requirements:* For master's, thesis optional; for doctorate, comprehensive exam, thesis/dissertation or alternative, A thesis is required for the Public Affairs and Public Policy degree. *Entrance requirements:* For master's, GRE, LSAT (if also applying for the Law School), 3 letters of recommendation, resume or curriculum vitae; for doctorate, GRE General Test. Additional exam requirements/recommendations for international students: Required—TOEFL (minimum score 590 paper-based; 243 computer-based; 96 iBT). *Application deadline:* For fall admission, 2/1 priority date for domestic students, 12/1 priority date for international students; for spring admission, 9/1 for international students. Application fee: $55 ($65 for international students). Electronic applications accepted. *Financial support:* Fellowships with full tuition reimbursements, research assistantships with partial tuition reimbursements, teaching assistantships with partial tuition reimbursements, career-related internships or fieldwork, Federal Work-Study, institutionally sponsored loans, unspecified assistantships, and Service Corps programs available. Financial award application deadline: 2/1; financial award applicants required to submit FAFSA. *Faculty research:* Comparative and international affairs, environmental policy and resource management, policy analysis, public finance, public management, urban management, nonprofit management. *Unit head:* Dean John Graham, Dean, School of Public and Environmental Affairs, 812-855-1432, E-mail: grahamjd@indiana.edu. *Application contact:* Jennifer Medlin, Assistant Director of Admissions and Financial Aid, 812-855-3784, Fax: 812-856-3665, E-mail: jlmedlin@indiana.edu.

Indiana University South Bend, School of Business and Economics, South Bend, IN 46634-7111. Offers accounting (MSA); business administration (MBA); management of information technologies (MS). Part-time and evening/weekend programs available. *Faculty:* 17 full-time (2 women), 3 part-time/adjunct (1 woman). *Students:* 67 full-time (34 women), 110 part-time (49 women); includes 12 minority (7 African Americans, 1 American Indian/Alaska Native, 1 Asian American or Pacific Islander, 3 Hispanic Americans), 56 international. Average age 32. In 2009, 58 master's awarded. *Entrance requirements:* For master's, GMAT. Additional exam requirements/recommendations for international students: Required—TOEFL (minimum score 550 paper-based; 213 computer-based). *Application deadline:* For fall admission, 7/1 priority date for domestic and international students; for spring admission, 11/1 priority date for domestic and international students. Applications are processed on a rolling basis. Application fee: $46 ($58 for international students). *Expenses:* Contact institution. *Financial support:* In 2009–10, 1 fellowship (averaging $3,846 per year) was awarded; Federal Work-Study and institutionally sponsored loans also available. Support available to part-time students. Financial award applicants required to submit FAFSA. *Faculty research:* Financial accounting, consumer research, capital budgeting research, business strategy research. *Unit head:* Robert H. Ducoffe, Dean, 574-520-4228, Fax: 574-520-4866. *Application contact:* Sharon Peterson, Secretary, Graduate Business, 574-520-4138, Fax: 574-520-4866, E-mail: spetersо@iusb.edu.

Instituto Tecnológico y de Estudios Superiores de Monterrey, Campus Central de Veracruz, Graduate Programs, Córdoba, Mexico. Offers administration (MA); administration of information technologies (MTI); computer sciences (MCC); education (MEE); educational institution administration (MAD); educational technology (MTE); electronic commerce (MCE); finance (MAF); humanistic studies (MEH); international business for Latin America (MNL); marketing (MMT); science (MCP); technology management (MTT). Part-time and evening/weekend programs available. Postbaccalaureate distance learning degree programs offered (minimal on-campus study). *Degree requirements:* For master's, thesis (for some programs). *Entrance requirements:* For master's, PAEP College Board. Electronic applications accepted.

Instituto Tecnológico y de Estudios Superiores de Monterrey, Campus Ciudad de México, Virtual University Division, Ciudad de Mexico, Mexico. Offers administration of information technologies (MA); computer sciences (MA); education (MA, PhD); educational technology (MA); environmental engineering (MA); environmental systems (MA); humanistic studies (MA); industrial engineering (MA); international business for Latin America (MA); quality systems (MA); quality systems and productivity (MA). Part-time and evening/weekend programs available. Postbaccalaureate distance learning degree programs offered (minimal on-campus study). *Entrance requirements:* For master's and doctorate, Instituto entrance exam. Additional exam requirements/recommendations for international students: Required—TOEFL.

Instituto Tecnológico y de Estudios Superiores de Monterrey, Campus Ciudad Juárez, Program in Administration of Information Technology, Ciudad Juárez, Mexico. Offers MAIT.

Instituto Tecnológico y de Estudios Superiores de Monterrey, Campus Ciudad Obregón, Program in Administration of Information Technology, Ciudad Obregón, Mexico. Offers MATI.

Instituto Tecnológico y de Estudios Superiores de Monterrey, Campus Estado de México, Professional and Graduate Division, Estado de Mexico, Mexico. Offers administration of information technologies (MITA); architecture (M Arch); business administration (GMBA, MBA); computer sciences (MCS, PhD); education (M Ed); educational institution administration (MAD); educational technology and innovation (PhD); electronic commerce (MEC); environmental systems (MS); finance (MAF); humanistic studies (MHS); information sciences and knowledge management (MISKM); information systems (MS); manufacturing systems (MS); marketing (MEM); quality systems and productivity (MS); science and materials engineering (PhD); telecommunications management (MTM). Part-time programs available. Postbaccalaureate distance learning degree programs offered (minimal on-campus study). *Degree requirements:* For master's, one foreign language, thesis (for some programs); for doctorate, one foreign language, thesis/dissertation. *Entrance requirements:* For master's, E-PAEP 500, interview; for doctorate, E-PAEP 500, research proposal. Additional exam requirements/recommendations for international students: Required—TOEFL (minimum score 550 paper-based). *Faculty research:* Surface treatments by plasmas, mechanical properties, robotics, graphical computing, mechatronics security protocols.

Instituto Tecnológico y de Estudios Superiores de Monterrey, Campus Irapuato, Graduate Programs, Irapuato, Mexico. Offers administration (MBA); administration of information technology (MAIT); administration of telecommunications (MAT); architecture (M Arch); computer science (MCS); education (M Ed); educational administration (MEA); educational innovation and technology (DEIT); educational technology (MET); electronic commerce (MBA); environmental administration and planning (MEAP); environmental systems (MES); finances (MBA); humanistic studies (MHS); international management for Latin American executives (MIMLAE); library and information science (MLIS); manufacturing quality management (MMQM); marketing research (MBA).

Instituto Tecnológico y de Estudios Superiores de Monterrey, Campus Laguna, Graduate School, Torreón, Mexico. Offers business administration (MBA); industrial engineering (MIE); management information systems (MS). Part-time programs available. *Entrance requirements:* For master's, GMAT. *Faculty research:* Computer communications from home to the university.

Inter American University of Puerto Rico, Aguadilla Campus, Graduate School, Aguadilla, PR 00605. Offers accounting (MBA); business information systems (MBA); counseling psychology with an emphasis in family (MS); criminal justice (MA); educative management and leadership (MA); elementary education (MA); finance (MBA); human resources (MBA); industrial management (MBA); marketing (MBA). Part-time and evening/weekend programs available. *Degree requirements:* For master's, comprehensive exam. *Entrance requirements:* For master's, EXADEP, 2 letters of recommendation, minimum GPA of 2.5. Electronic applications accepted.

Inter American University of Puerto Rico, Metropolitan Campus, Graduate Programs, Program in Management Information Systems, San Juan, PR 00919-1293. Offers MBA.

Inter American University of Puerto Rico, San Germán Campus, Graduate Studies Center, Program in Business Administration, San Germán, PR 00683-5008. Offers accounting (MBA); finance (MBA); human resources (PhD); human resources management (MBA); industrial management (MBA); international business (PhD); management information systems (MBA); marketing management (MBA). Part-time and evening/weekend programs available. *Degree requirements:* For master's, comprehensive exam. *Entrance requirements:* For master's, GRE General Test or EXADEP, minimum GPA of 3.0.

Iowa State University of Science and Technology, Graduate College, College of Business, Program in Logistics, Operations, and Management Information Systems, Ames, IA 50011. Offers information systems (MS). *Faculty:* 20 full-time (2 women). *Students:* 16 full-time (7 women), 9 part-time (1 woman); includes 2 minority (1 Asian American or Pacific Islander, 1 Hispanic American), 16 international. 35 applicants, 51% accepted, 8 enrolled. In 2009, 6 master's awarded. *Degree requirements:* For master's, thesis or alternative. *Entrance requirements:* For master's, GMAT. Additional exam requirements/recommendations for international students: Required—TOEFL (minimum score 570 paper-based; 88 iBT) or IELTS (minimum score 7). *Application deadline:* For fall admission, 6/1 priority date for domestic students, 3/1 priority date for international students; for spring admission, 11/1 for domestic and international students. Application fee: $40 ($90 for international students). Electronic applications accepted. *Expenses:* Tuition, state resident: full-time $6716. Tuition, nonresident: full-time $8908. Tuition and fees vary according to course level, course load, program and student level. *Financial support:* In 2009–10, 1 research assistantship with full and partial tuition reimbursement (averaging $7,600 per year) was awarded; teaching assistantships with full and partial tuition reimbursements, career-related internships or fieldwork, institutionally sponsored loans, scholarships/grants, health care benefits, and unspecified assistantships also available. *Unit head:* Dr. Qing Hu, Chair, 515-294-8118, E-mail: busgrad@iastate.edu. *Application contact:* Deb Johnson, Information Contact, 515-294-8118, E-mail: busgrad@iastate.edu.

John Marshall Law School, Graduate and Professional Programs, Chicago, IL 60604-3968. Offers comparative legal studies (LL M); employee benefits (LL M, MS); information technology (LL M, MS); intellectual property (LL M); international business and trade (LL M); law (JD); real estate (LL M, MS); taxation (LL M, MS); JD/LL M; JD/MA; JD/MBA; JD/MPA. *Accreditation:* ABA. Part-time and evening/weekend programs available. *Faculty:* 73 full-time (26 women), 110 part-time/adjunct (33 women). *Students:* 1,139 full-time (505 women), 407 part-time (204 women); includes 353 minority (130 African Americans, 15 American Indian/Alaska Native, 91 Asian Americans or Pacific Islanders, 117 Hispanic Americans), 43 international. Average age 27. 3,027 applicants, 44% accepted, 385 enrolled. In 2009, 401 first professional degrees, 16 master's awarded. *Degree requirements:* For JD, 90 credits. *Entrance requirements:* For JD, LSAT; for master's, JD. Additional exam requirements/recommendations for international students: Required—TOEFL. *Application deadline:* For fall admission, 3/1 priority date for domestic and international students; for spring admission, 10/15 priority date for domestic and international students. Applications are processed on a rolling basis. Application fee: $60. Electronic applications accepted. *Expenses:* Contact institution. *Financial support:* In 2009–10, 1,350 students received support. Scholarships/grants and tuition waivers (full and partial) available. Support available to part-time students. Financial award application deadline: 6/1; financial award applicants required to submit FAFSA. *Unit head:* John Corkery, Dean, 312-427-2737. *Application contact:* William B. Powers, Associate Dean of Admission and Student Affairs, 800-537-4280, Fax: 312-427-5136, E-mail: admission@jmls.edu.

The Johns Hopkins University, Carey Business School, Information Technology Programs, Baltimore, MD 21218-2699. Offers competitive intelligence (Certificate); information security management (Certificate); information systems (MS); MBA/MSIS. Part-time and evening/weekend programs available. *Faculty:* 29 full-time (6 women), 135 part-time/adjunct (29 women). *Students:* 25 full-time (11 women), 171 part-time (57 women); includes 74 minority (35 African Americans, 34 Asian Americans or Pacific Islanders, 5 Hispanic Americans), 10 international. Average age 34. 69 applicants, 77% accepted, 41 enrolled. In 2009, 131 master's, 45 other advanced degrees awarded. *Degree requirements:* For master's, 36 credits including final project. *Entrance requirements:* For master's and Certificate, minimum GPA of 3.0, resume, work experience, two letters of recommendation. Additional exam requirements/recommendations for international students: Required—TOEFL (minimum score 600 paper-based; 250 computer-based; 100 iBT). *Application deadline:* For fall admission, 5/1 for international students; for spring admission, 10/15 for international students. Applications are processed on a rolling basis. Application fee: $100. Electronic applications accepted. *Financial support:* Scholarships/grants available. Support available to part-time students. Financial award application deadline: 4/1; financial award applicants required to submit FAFSA. *Faculty research:* Information security, healthcare information systems. Total annual research expenditures: $89,653. *Unit head:* Dr. Dipankar Chakravarti, Vice Dean of Programs, 410-516-8561, E-mail: dipankar.chakravarti@jhu.edu. *Application contact:* Robin Greenberg, Admissions Coordinator, 410-516-4234, Fax: 410-516-0826, E-mail: carey.admissions@jhu.edu.

Management Information Systems

The Johns Hopkins University, Engineering for Professionals, Part-time Program in Information Systems and Technology, Baltimore, MD 21218-2699. Offers MS, Post-Master's Certificate. Part-time and evening/weekend programs available. *Faculty:* 9 part-time/adjunct (1 woman). *Students:* 3 full-time (1 woman), 147 part-time (30 women); includes 55 minority (23 African Americans, 20 Asian Americans or Pacific Islanders, 12 Hispanic Americans), 5 international. Average age 32. In 2009, 35 master's awarded. *Application deadline:* Applications are processed on a rolling basis. Application fee: $75. Electronic applications accepted. *Financial support:* Institutionally sponsored loans available. *Unit head:* Dr. Ralph D. Semmel, Program Chair, 443-778-6179, E-mail: ralph.semmel@jhuapl.edu. *Application contact:* Priyanka Dwivedi, Admissions Manager, 410-516-2300, Fax: 410-579-8049, E-mail: pdwived1@jhu.edu.

Kaplan University, Davenport Campus, School of Information Technology, Davenport, IA 52807-2095. Offers decision support systems (MS); information security and assurance (MS). Part-time and evening/weekend programs available. Postbaccalaureate distance learning degree programs offered (no on-campus study). *Entrance requirements:* Additional exam requirements/recommendations for international students: Required—TOEFL (minimum score 550 paper-based; 218 computer-based; 80 iBT).

Kean University, Nathan Weiss Graduate College, Program in Global Management, Union, NJ 07083. Offers executive management (MBA); global management (MBA), including information management. *Faculty:* 3 full-time (2 women). *Students:* 46 full-time (30 women), 66 part-time (33 women); includes 61 minority (33 African Americans, 8 Asian Americans or Pacific Islanders, 20 Hispanic Americans), 14 international. Average age 33. 66 applicants, 88% accepted, 37 enrolled. In 2009, 49 master's awarded. *Degree requirements:* For master's, one foreign language, internship or study abroad. *Entrance requirements:* For master's, GMAT, minimum GPA of 3.0, 3 letters of recommendation, prerequisite business courses. *Application deadline:* For fall admission, 5/1 for domestic students; for spring admission, 11/1 for domestic students. Applications are processed on a rolling basis. Application fee: $60 ($150 for international students). Electronic applications accepted. *Expenses:* Tuition, state resident: full-time $10,440; part-time $435 per credit. Tuition, nonresident: full-time $14,160; part-time $590 per credit. Required fees: $2642; $110 per credit. Part-time tuition and fees vary according to course load and degree level. *Financial support:* In 2009–10, 13 research assistantships with full tuition reimbursements (averaging $3,263 per year) were awarded; unspecified assistantships also available. *Unit head:* Dr. David Shani, Program Coordinator, 908-737-5980, E-mail: dshani@kean.edu. *Application contact:* Reenat Hasan, Pre-Admissions Coordinator, 908-737-5923, Fax: 908-737-5965, E-mail: rhasan@exchange.kean.edu.

Kent State University, Graduate School of Management, Doctoral Program in Management Systems, Kent, OH 44242-0001. Offers PhD. *Faculty:* 17 full-time (4 women). *Students:* 14 full-time (6 women), 11 international. Average age 33. 13 applicants, 54% accepted, 4 enrolled. In 2009, 2 doctorates awarded. *Degree requirements:* For doctorate, comprehensive exam, thesis/dissertation, oral defense. *Entrance requirements:* For doctorate, GMAT. Additional exam requirements/recommendations for international students: Required—TOEFL (minimum score 600 paper-based; 250 computer-based; 100 iBT). *Application deadline:* For fall admission, 2/1 for domestic students, 1/1 for international students. Application fee: $30 ($60 for international students). Electronic applications accepted. *Financial support:* In 2009–10, 12 students received support, including 12 teaching assistantships with full tuition reimbursements available (averaging $15,000 per year); fellowships with full tuition reimbursements available, Federal Work-Study and tuition waivers also available. Financial award application deadline: 2/1; financial award applicants required to submit FAFSA. *Unit head:* Dr. O. Felix Offodile, Chair and Professor, 330-672-2750, Fax: 330-672-2953, E-mail: foffodil@kent.edu. *Application contact:* Felecia A. Urbanek, Coordinator, Graduate Programs, 330-672-2282, Fax: 330-672-7303, E-mail: gradbus@kent.edu.

Kentucky State University, College of Professional Studies, Frankfort, KY 40601. Offers business administration (MBA), including accounting, finance, management, marketing; public administration (MPA), including human resource management, international administration and development, management information systems, nonprofit management; special education (MA). Part-time and evening/weekend programs available. Postbaccalaureate distance learning degree programs offered (minimal on-campus study). *Faculty:* 11 full-time (3 women), 2 part-time/adjunct (both women). *Students:* 79 full-time (51 women), 66 part-time (34 women); includes 88 minority (85 African Americans, 2 Asian Americans or Pacific Islanders, 1 Hispanic American), 4 international. Average age 34. 92 applicants, 75% accepted, 52 enrolled. In 2009, 32 master's awarded. *Degree requirements:* For master's, comprehensive exam, thesis optional. *Entrance requirements:* For master's, GMAT, GRE. Additional exam requirements/recommendations for international students: Required—TOEFL (minimum score 525 paper-based; 173 computer-based). *Application deadline:* For fall admission, 7/1 priority date for domestic students, 4/15 priority date for international students; for spring admission, 11/15 priority date for domestic students, 8/1 priority date for international students. Applications are processed on a rolling basis. Application fee: $30 ($100 for international students). Electronic applications accepted. *Expenses:* Tuition, state resident: full-time $5634; part-time $313 per credit hour. Tuition, nonresident: full-time $14,598; part-time $811 per credit hour. Required fees: $450; $25 per credit hour. *Financial support:* In 2009–10, 113 students received support, including 4 research assistantships (averaging $14,035 per year); career-related internships or fieldwork, scholarships/grants, tuition waivers (partial), and unspecified assistantships also available. Financial award application deadline: 4/15; financial award applicants required to submit FAFSA. *Unit head:* Dr. Gashaw Lake, Dean, College of Professional Studies, 502-597-6105, Fax: 502-597-6715, E-mail: gashaw.lake@kysu.edu. *Application contact:* Cedric Cunningham, Administrative Assistant, Office of Graduate Studies, 502-597-6536, E-mail: cedric.cunningham@kysu.edu.

Lawrence Technological University, College of Management, Southfield, MI 48075-1058. Offers business administration (MBA, DBA); information systems (MS); information technology (DM); operations management (MS). *Accreditation:* ACBSP. Part-time and evening/weekend programs available. *Faculty:* 14 full-time (6 women), 53 part-time/adjunct (14 women). *Students:* 17 full-time (6 women), 565 part-time (234 women); includes 149 minority (103 African Americans, 2 American Indian/Alaska Native, 37 Asian Americans or Pacific Islanders, 7 Hispanic Americans), 96 international. Average age 34. 353 applicants, 58% accepted, 125 enrolled. In 2009, 263 master's, 5 doctorates awarded. *Degree requirements:* For master's, thesis (for some programs). *Entrance requirements:* For master's, GMAT. Additional exam requirements/recommendations for international students: Required—TOEFL (minimum score 550 paper-based; 213 computer-based; 79 iBT). *Application deadline:* For fall admission, 8/1 priority date for domestic students, 6/1 for international students; for winter admission, 12/1 priority date for domestic students, 10/1 for international students; for spring admission, 5/1 priority date for domestic students, 3/1 for international students. Applications are processed on a rolling basis. Application fee: $50. Electronic applications accepted. *Expenses:* Tuition: Full-time $11,320; part-time $798 per credit hour. *Financial support:* Federal Work-Study and institutionally sponsored loans available. Support available to part-time students. Financial award application deadline: 4/1; financial award applicants required to submit FAFSA. *Unit head:* Dr. Lou DeGennaro, Dean, 248-204-3050, E-mail: degennaro@ltu.edu. *Application contact:* Jane Rohrback, Director of Admissions, 248-204-3160, Fax: 248-204-3188, E-mail: admissions@ltu.edu.

Lewis University, College of Business, Graduate School of Management, Program in Business Administration, Romeoville, IL 60446. Offers accounting (MBA); custom elective option (MBA); e-business (MBA); finance (MBA); healthcare management (MBA); human resources management (MBA); information security (MBA); international business (MBA); management information systems (MBA); marketing (MBA); project management (MBA); technology and operations management (MBA). Part-time and evening/weekend programs available. *Faculty:* 15 full-time (2 women), 18 part-time/adjunct (4 women). *Students:* 120 full-time (64 women), 222 part-time (103 women); includes 97 minority (62 African Americans, 4 Asian Americans or Pacific Islanders, 31 Hispanic Americans), 9 international. Average age 31. In 2009, 84 master's awarded. *Entrance requirements:* For master's, interview, bachelor's degree, resume, 2 recommendations. Additional exam requirements/recommendations for international students: Required—TOEFL (minimum score 550 paper-based; 213 computer-based). *Application deadline:* For fall admission, 8/15 priority date for domestic students, 5/1 priority date for international students; for spring admission, 11/15 priority date for international students. Applications are processed on a rolling basis. Application fee: $40. Electronic applications accepted. *Expenses:* Tuition: Full-time $6480; part-time $720 per credit. One-time fee: $40. Tuition and fees vary according to course load, degree level and program. *Financial support:* Career-related internships or fieldwork, Federal Work-Study, scholarships/grants, and unspecified assistantships available. Financial award application deadline: 5/1; financial award applicants required to submit FAFSA. *Unit head:* Dr. Maureen Culleeney, Academic Program Director, 815-838-0500 Ext. 5631, E-mail: culleema@lewisu.edu. *Application contact:* Michele King, Director of Admission, 815-838-0500 Ext. 5384, E-mail: gsm@lewisu.edu.

Lincoln University, Graduate Degree Programs, Oakland, CA 94612. Offers finance and investments (DBA); finance management and investment banking (MBA); general business (MBA); human resource management (MBA); international business (MBA); management information systems (MBA). Part-time and evening/weekend programs available. *Faculty:* 7 full-time (2 women), 13 part-time/adjunct (1 woman). *Students:* 295 full-time (133 women), 3 part-time (0 women). 177 applicants, 100% accepted, 71 enrolled. In 2009, 98 master's awarded. *Degree requirements:* For master's, research project (thesis) or internship report, or comprehensive exam; for doctorate, comprehensive exam, thesis/dissertation. *Entrance requirements:* For master's, minimum GPA of 2.7; for doctorate, GMAT (minimum score: 550), GRE (minimum score: 1000), or equivalent test results (waived for master's degree with cumulative GPA of 3.3). Additional exam requirements/recommendations for international students: Required—TOEFL or IELTS. *Application deadline:* For fall admission, 7/3 priority date for domestic students; for spring admission, 11/27 priority date for domestic students. Applications are processed on a rolling basis. Application fee: $75. Electronic applications accepted. *Expenses:* Tuition: Full-time $6750. Required fees: $190 per term. *Financial support:* In 2009–10, 1 teaching assistantship was awarded; career-related internships or fieldwork and scholarships/grants also available. *Unit head:* Dr. Marshall Burak, Director of Graduate Programs, 510-628-8016, Fax: 510-628-8012, E-mail: mburak@lincolnuca.edu. *Application contact:* Peggy Au, Director of Admissions and Records, 510-628-8010, Fax: 510-628-8012, E-mail: admissions@lincolnuca.edu.

Lindenwood University, Graduate Programs, College of Individualized Education, St. Charles, MO 63301-1695. Offers administration (MSA); business administration (MBA); communications (MA); criminal justice and administration (MS); gerontology (MA); health management (MS); human resource management (MS); information technology (MBA, Certificate); management (MSA); managing information technology (MS); marketing (MSA); writing (MFA). Part-time and evening/weekend programs available. *Faculty:* 15 full-time (8 women), 128 part-time/adjunct (53 women). *Students:* 679 full-time (432 women), 90 part-time (57 women); includes 138 minority (121 African Americans, 2 American Indian/Alaska Native, 5 Asian Americans or Pacific Islanders, 10 Hispanic Americans), 18 international. Average age 34. 223 applicants, 44% accepted, 87 enrolled. In 2009, 478 master's awarded. *Degree requirements:* For master's, thesis (for some programs), 1 colloquium per term. *Entrance requirements:* For master's, interview, minimum GPA of 3.0. Additional exam requirements/recommendations for international students: Required—TOEFL (minimum score 550 paper-based; 213 computer-based; 80 iBT). *Application deadline:* For fall admission, 10/2 priority date for domestic and international students; for winter admission, 1/8 priority date for domestic and international students; for spring admission, 4/8 priority date for domestic and international students. Applications are processed on a rolling basis. Application fee: $30 ($100 for international students). *Expenses:* Tuition: Full-time $12,960; part-time $370 per credit hour. Required fees: $340. One-time fee: $30 full-time. Tuition and fees vary according to course level and course load. *Financial support:* In 2009–10, 631 students received support. Career-related internships or fieldwork, institutionally sponsored loans, tuition waivers (partial), and unspecified assistantships available. Financial award application deadline: 6/30; financial award applicants required to submit FAFSA. *Unit head:* Dan Kemper, Dean, 636-949-4501, Fax: 636-949-4505, E-mail: dkemper@lindenwood.edu. *Application contact:* Brett Barger, Dean of Evening Admissions and Extension Campuses, 636-949-4934, Fax: 636-949-4109, E-mail: adultadmissions@lindenwood.edu.

Lindenwood University, Graduate Programs, School of Business and Entrepreneurship, St. Charles, MO 63301-1695. Offers accounting (MBA, MS); business administration (MBA); entrepreneurial studies (MBA, MS); finance (MBA, MS); human resource management (MBA); human resources (MS); international business (MBA, MS); management (MBA, MS); management information systems (MBA, MS); marketing (MBA, MS); public management (MBA, MS); sport management (MA). *Accreditation:* ACBSP. Part-time and evening/weekend programs available. *Faculty:* 20 full-time (8 women), 17 part-time/adjunct (5 women). *Students:* 129 full-time (60 women), 138 part-time (61 women); includes 15 minority (11 African Americans, 2 Asian Americans or Pacific Islanders, 2 Hispanic Americans), 84 international. Average age 28. 149 applicants, 73 enrolled. In 2009, 142 master's awarded. *Degree requirements:* For master's, comprehensive exam (for some programs), thesis (for some programs). *Entrance requirements:* For master's, interview, minimum GPA of 3.0, letter of recommendation. Additional exam requirements/recommendations for international students: Required—TOEFL (minimum score 550 paper-based; 213 computer-based; 80 iBT). *Application deadline:* For fall admission, 7/30 priority date for domestic students, 9/16 priority date for international students; for winter admission, 12/19 priority date for domestic students, 12/17 priority date for international students; for spring admission, 2/25 priority date for domestic students, 2/11 priority date for international students. Applications are processed on a rolling basis. Application fee: $30 ($100 for international students). Electronic applications accepted. *Expenses:* Tuition: Full-time $12,960; part-time $370 per credit hour. Required fees: $340. One-time fee: $30 full-time. Tuition and fees vary according to course level and course load. *Financial support:* In 2009–10, 209 students received support. Career-related internships or fieldwork, Federal Work-Study, institutionally sponsored loans, and tuition waivers (partial) available. Financial award application deadline: 6/30; financial award applicants required to submit FAFSA. *Unit head:* Ed Morris, Dean of Management, 636-949-4832, E-mail: emorris@lindenwood.edu. *Application contact:* Brett Barger, Dean of Evening Admissions and Extension Campuses, 636-949-4934, Fax: 636-949-4109, E-mail: adultadmissions@lindenwood.edu.

Long Island University, C.W. Post Campus, College of Management, School of Business, Brookville, NY 11548-1300. Offers accounting and taxation (Certificate); business administration (Certificate); finance (MBA, Certificate); general business administration (MBA); international business (MBA, Certificate); management (MBA, Certificate); management information systems (MBA, Certificate); marketing (MBA, Certificate). *Accreditation:* AACSB. Part-time and evening/weekend programs available. *Entrance requirements:* For master's, GMAT, resume, minimum GPA of 3.0, 2 letters of recommendation. Additional exam requirements/recommendations for international students: Required—TOEFL (minimum score 527 paper-based; 197 computer-based). Electronic applications accepted. *Faculty research:* Financial markets, consumer behavior.

Louisiana State University and Agricultural and Mechanical College, Graduate School, E. J. Ourso College of Business, Department of Information Systems and Decision Sciences, Baton Rouge, LA 70803. Offers information systems and decision sciences (MS, PhD). *Faculty:* 12 full-time (3 women). *Students:* 16 full-time (4 women), 4 part-time (0 women); includes 6 minority (3 African Americans, 1 Asian American or Pacific Islander, 2 Hispanic Americans), 6 international. Average age 33. 32 applicants, 31% accepted, 2 enrolled. In 2009, 6 master's, 2 doctorates awarded. Terminal master's awarded for partial completion of doctoral program. *Degree requirements:* For master's, comprehensive exam, thesis optional; for doctorate, comprehensive exam, thesis/dissertation. *Entrance requirements:* For master's, GMAT or GRE General Test; for doctorate, GMAT or GRE. Additional exam requirements/recommendations for international students: Required—TOEFL (minimum score 550 paper-based; 213 computer-based; 79 iBT). *Application deadline:* For fall admission, 1/25 priority date for domestic students, 5/15 for international students; for spring admission, 10/15 for international students. Applications are processed on a rolling basis. Application fee: $50 ($70 for international students). Electronic applications accepted. *Financial support:* In 2009–10, 18

Management Information Systems

Louisiana State University and Agricultural and Mechanical College (continued)

students received support, including 1 fellowship (averaging $5,099 per year), 12 research assistantships with full and partial tuition reimbursements available (averaging $18,208 per year), 1 teaching assistantship with full and partial tuition reimbursement available (averaging $9,000 per year); Federal Work-Study, institutionally sponsored loans, scholarships/grants, health care benefits, tuition waivers (full and partial), and unspecified assistantships also available. Support available to part-time students. Financial award applicants required to submit FAFSA. *Faculty research:* Healthcare informatics, outsourcing, information systems management, operations management. Total annual research expenditures: $366,618. *Unit head:* Dr. Helmut Schneider, Department Head, 225-578-2516, Fax: 225-578-2511, E-mail: hschnei@lsu.edu. *Application contact:* Dr. Rudy Hirschheim, Graduate Adviser, 225-578-2514, Fax: 225-578-2511, E-mail: rudy@lsu.edu.

Loyola University Chicago, Graduate School of Business, Information Systems and Operations Management Department, Chicago, IL 60660. Offers information systems management (MS). Part-time and evening/weekend programs available. *Entrance requirements:* For master's, GMAT, letters of recommendation. Additional exam requirements/recommendations for international students: Required—TOEFL (minimum score 550 paper-based; 213 computer-based; 80 iBT). Electronic applications accepted. *Expenses:* Contact institution. *Faculty research:* Strategic use of IT, database design data warehousing, e-business, applications of data mining.

Loyola University Maryland, Graduate Programs, Sellinger School of Business and Management, Program in Business Administration, Baltimore, MD 21210-2699. Offers accounting (MBA); finance (MBA); general business (MBA); international business (MBA); management (MBA); management information systems (MBA); marketing (MBA). *Accreditation:* AACSB. Part-time and evening/weekend programs available. *Entrance requirements:* For master's, GMAT. Additional exam requirements/recommendations for international students: Required—TOEFL (minimum score 550 paper-based; 213 computer-based).

Marist College, Graduate Programs, School of Computer Science and Mathematics, Poughkeepsie, NY 12601-1387. Offers information systems (MS, Adv C); software development (MS); technology management (MS). Part-time and evening/weekend programs available. Postbaccalaureate distance learning degree programs offered (minimal on-campus study). *Entrance requirements:* For master's, resume. Additional exam requirements/recommendations for international students: Required—TOEFL (minimum score 550 paper-based; 213 computer-based; 80 iBT); Recommended—IELTS (minimum score 6.5). Electronic applications accepted. *Expenses:* Tuition: Full-time $12,510; part-time $695 per credit hour. *Faculty research:* Data quality, artificial intelligence, imaging, analysis of algorithms, distributed systems and applications.

Marymount University, School of Business Administration, Program in Information Technology, Arlington, VA 22207-4299. Offers computer security and information assurance (Certificate); health care informatics (Certificate); information technology (MS, Certificate); information technology project management: technology leadership (Certificate). Part-time and evening/weekend programs available. *Faculty:* 6 full-time (3 women), 4 part-time/adjunct (0 women). *Students:* 28 full-time (11 women), 23 part-time (6 women); includes 15 minority (9 African Americans, 1 American Indian/Alaska Native, 4 Asian Americans or Pacific Islanders, 1 Hispanic American), 21 international. Average age 31. 45 applicants, 100% accepted, 26 enrolled. In 2009, 19 master's, 1 other advanced degree awarded. *Degree requirements:* For master's, thesis or alternative. *Entrance requirements:* For master's, GMAT or GRE General Test, interview, resume, bachelor's degree in computer-related field or degree in another subject with a post-baccalaureate certificate in a computer-related field; for Certificate, resume. Additional exam requirements/recommendations for international students: Required—TOEFL (minimum score 600 paper-based; 250 computer-based; 96 iBT), IELTS (minimum score 6.5). *Application deadline:* For fall admission, 7/15 for domestic students, 7/1 for international students; for spring admission, 11/15 for domestic students, 10/15 for international students. Applications are processed on a rolling basis. Application fee: $40. Electronic applications accepted. *Expenses:* Tuition: Full-time $13,050; part-time $725 per credit hour. Required fees: $135; $7.50 per credit hour. *Financial support:* In 2009–10, 5 students received support; research assistantships with full tuition reimbursements available, career-related internships or fieldwork, Federal Work-Study, scholarships/grants, and unspecified assistantships available. Support available to part-time students. Financial award applicants required to submit FAFSA. *Unit head:* Dr. Diane Murphy, Chair, 703-284-5958, Fax: 703-527-3830, E-mail: diane.murphy@marymount.edu. *Application contact:* Francesca Reed, Director, Graduate Admissions, 703-284-5901, Fax: 703-527-3815, E-mail: grad.admissions@marymount.edu.

Marywood University, Academic Affairs, College of Liberal Arts and Sciences, Department of Business and Managerial Science, Emphasis in Management Information Systems, Scranton, PA 18509-1598. Offers MBA, MS. *Students:* 1 (woman) full-time, 5 part-time (3 women), 1 international. Average age 35. *Entrance requirements:* Additional exam requirements/recommendations for international students: Required—TOEFL (minimum score 550 paper-based; 213 computer-based; 79 iBT). *Application deadline:* For fall admission, 4/1 priority date for domestic students, 3/31 priority date for international students; for spring admission, 11/1 priority date for domestic students, 8/31 priority date for international students. Applications are processed on a rolling basis. Application fee: $35. Electronic applications accepted. *Expenses:* Tuition: Part-time $715 per credit. Required fees: $270 per semester. Tuition and fees vary according to degree level, campus/location and program. *Financial support:* Career-related internships or fieldwork, scholarships/grants, and unspecified assistantships available. Support available to part-time students. Financial award application deadline: 6/30; financial award applicants required to submit FAFSA. *Faculty research:* Systems design. *Application contact:* Tammy Manka, Assistant Director of Graduate Admissions, 866-279-9663, E-mail: tmanka@marywood.edu.

McGill University, Faculty of Graduate and Postdoctoral Studies, Desautels Faculty of Management, Montréal, QC H3A 2T5, Canada. Offers administration (PhD); entrepreneurial studies (MBA); finance (MBA); general management (Post Master's Certificate); information systems (MBA); international business (exchange program) (MBA); international Master's program in practicing management (MM); management (MBA); management for development (MBA); manufacturing management (MMM); marketing (MBA); operations management (MBA); public accountancy (Diploma); strategic management (MBA); MBA/LL B; MD/MBA.

McMaster University, School of Graduate Studies, Faculty of Business, Program in Information Systems, Hamilton, ON L8S 4M2, Canada. Offers PhD. Part-time programs available. *Degree requirements:* For doctorate, comprehensive exam, thesis/dissertation. *Entrance requirements:* For doctorate, GMAT or GRE General Test, master's degree, minimum B+ average. Additional exam requirements/recommendations for international students: Required—TOEFL (minimum score 580 paper-based; 237 computer-based). *Faculty research:* Information systems, operations management, web-based decision support systems, web-based agents, financial engineering.

Meritus University, School of Business, Fredericton, NB E3C 2R2, Canada. Offers global management (MBA); health care management (MBA); human resources management (MBA); information technology management (MBA); marketing (MBA); technology management (MBA). Evening/weekend programs available. Postbaccalaureate distance learning degree programs offered (no on-campus study). *Faculty:* 5 full-time (1 woman), 50 part-time/adjunct (15 women). *Students:* 77 full-time (29 women). Average age 35. *Entrance requirements:* For master's, undergraduate degree or comparable equivalent with minimum cumulative GPA of 2.5; minimum equivalent of two years of full-time, post high-school work experience; current employment. Additional exam requirements/recommendations for international students: Required—TOEFL (minimum score 213 computer-based; 79 iBT), IELTS (minimum score 6.5), or TOEIC (minimum score 750) or Berlitz (minimum score 550). *Application deadline:* Applications are processed on a rolling basis. Application fee: $45. Electronic applications accepted. Tuition and fees charges are reported in Canadian dollars. *Expenses:* Tuition: Full-time $14,400 Canadian dollars. Required fees: $720 Canadian dollars. *Unit head:* Dr. Albert K. S. Wong, Program Chair, Business Administration, 604-657-5465, Fax: 602-643-4624, E-mail: albert.wong@staff.meritusu.ca. *Application contact:* Jeremy S. DeMerchant, Enrolment Manager, 506-443-8413, Fax: 602-759-3688, E-mail: jeremy.demerchant@staff.meritusu.ca.

Metropolitan State University, College of Management, St. Paul, MN 55106-5000. Offers business administration (MBA); information assurance security (Graduate Certificate); information management (MMIS); MIS generalist (Graduate Certificate); MIS systems analysis and design (Graduate Certificate); nonprofit management (MPNA); project management (Graduate Certificate); public administration (MPNA); systems management (MMIS). Part-time and evening/weekend programs available. *Degree requirements:* For master's, thesis optional, computer language (MMIS). *Entrance requirements:* For master's, GMAT (MBA), resume. Additional exam requirements/recommendations for international students: Required—TOEFL (minimum score 550 paper-based; 213 computer-based). *Expenses:* Tuition, state resident: full-time $5520; part-time $276 per credit hour. Tuition, nonresident: full-time $11,040; part-time $552 per credit hour. Required fees: $209; $10 per credit hour. Tuition and fees vary according to degree level. *Faculty research:* Yugoslav economic system, workers' cooperatives, participative management and job enrichment, global business systems.

Michigan State University, The Graduate School, College of Communication Arts and Sciences, Department of Telecommunication, Information Studies, and Media, East Lansing, MI 48824. Offers digital media arts and technology (MA); information and telecommunication management (MA); information, policy and society (MA); serious game design (MA). *Faculty:* 14 full-time (3 women). *Students:* 29 full-time (8 women), 32 part-time (8 women); includes 7 minority (3 African Americans, 3 Asian Americans or Pacific Islanders, 1 Hispanic American), 20 international. Average age 29. 53 applicants, 42% accepted. In 2009, 23 master's awarded. *Entrance requirements:* Additional exam requirements/recommendations for international students: Required—TOEFL. Electronic applications accepted. *Expenses:* Tuition, state resident: part-time $478.25 per credit hour. Tuition, nonresident: part-time $966.50 per credit hour. Part-time tuition and fees vary according to program. *Financial support:* In 2009–10, 6 research assistantships with tuition reimbursements (averaging $6,080 per year), 3 teaching assistantships with tuition reimbursements (averaging $6,061 per year) were awarded. Total annual research expenditures: $1.1 million. *Unit head:* Dr. Charles Steinfield, Chairperson, 517-355-8372, Fax: 517-355-1292, E-mail: steinfie@msu.edu. *Application contact:* Rachel Iseler, Academic Programs Coordinator, 517-432-3676, Fax: 517-355-1292, E-mail: tism@msu.edu.

Michigan State University, The Graduate School, Eli Broad Graduate School of Management, Department of Accounting and Information Systems, East Lansing, MI 48824. Offers accounting (MS); business administration (PhD). *Accreditation:* AACSB. *Faculty:* 27 full-time (10 women). *Students:* 175 full-time (69 women), 12 part-time (7 women); includes 16 minority (4 African Americans, 1 American Indian/Alaska Native, 8 Asian Americans or Pacific Islanders, 3 Hispanic Americans), 39 international. Average age 24. 472 applicants, 26% accepted. In 2009, 143 master's, 2 doctorates awarded. *Entrance requirements:* Additional exam requirements/recommendations for international students: Required—TOEFL. *Application deadline:* Applications are processed on a rolling basis. Electronic applications accepted. *Expenses:* Tuition, state resident: part-time $478.25 per credit hour. Tuition, nonresident: part-time $966.50 per credit hour. Part-time tuition and fees vary according to program. *Financial support:* In 2009–10, 11 research assistantships with tuition reimbursements (averaging $6,274 per year), 20 teaching assistantships with tuition reimbursements (averaging $5,920 per year) were awarded. Total annual research expenditures: $414,022. *Unit head:* Dr. Sanjay Gupta, Chairperson, 517-355-3388, Fax: 517-432-1101, E-mail: gupta@bus.msu.edu. *Application contact:* Program Information, 517-355-7486, Fax: 517-432-1101, E-mail: acct@bus.msu.edu.

Middle Tennessee State University, College of Graduate Studies, Jennings A. Jones College of Business, Department of Computer Information Systems, Murfreesboro, TN 37132. Offers MS. Part-time and evening/weekend programs available. Postbaccalaureate distance learning degree programs offered. *Faculty:* 12 full-time (3 women). *Students:* 15 full-time (5 women), 44 part-time (13 women); includes 19 minority (14 African Americans, 5 Asian Americans or Pacific Islanders). Average age 30. 21 applicants, 67% accepted, 14 enrolled. In 2009, 15 master's awarded. *Entrance requirements:* Additional exam requirements/recommendations for international students: Required—TOEFL (minimum score 525 paper-based; 195 computer-based; 71 iBT) or IELTS (minimum score 6). *Application deadline:* For fall admission, 6/1 for domestic and international students. Applications are processed on a rolling basis. Application fee: $25 ($30 for international students). Electronic applications accepted. *Expenses:* Tuition, state resident: full-time $4404. Tuition, nonresident: full-time $10,956. *Financial support:* In 2009–10, 8 students received support. Institutionally sponsored loans available. Support available to part-time students. Financial award application deadline: 5/1; financial award applicants required to submit FAFSA. *Faculty research:* Information technology assessment, information systems education, information technology job market, e-commerce, database technology. *Unit head:* Dr. Stanley Gambill, Chair, 615-898-2362. *Application contact:* Dr. Michael Allen, Dean and Vice Provost for Research, 615-898-2840, Fax: 615-904-8020, E-mail: mallen@mtsu.edu.

Minnesota State University Mankato, College of Graduate Studies, College of Science, Engineering and Technology, Department of Information Systems and Technology, Mankato, MN 56001. Offers database technologies (Certificate); information technology (MS). *Students:* 3 full-time (0 women), 2 part-time (both women). *Degree requirements:* For master's, comprehensive exam, thesis or alternative. *Entrance requirements:* For master's, GRE General Test, minimum GPA of 3.0 during previous 2 years. Additional exam requirements/recommendations for international students: Required—TOEFL (minimum score 550 paper-based; 213 computer-based; 80 iBT). *Application deadline:* For fall admission, 7/1 priority date for domestic students; for spring admission, 11/1 for domestic students. Applications are processed on a rolling basis. Electronic applications accepted. *Expenses:* Tuition, state resident: full-time $5364. Tuition, nonresident: full-time $8314. *Financial support:* Research assistantships with full tuition reimbursements, teaching assistantships with full tuition reimbursements, unspecified assistantships available. Financial award application deadline: 3/15; financial award applicants required to submit FAFSA. *Unit head:* Dr. Leon Tietz, Chairperson, 507-389-1412. *Application contact:* 507-389-2321, E-mail: grad@mnsu.edu.

Minot State University, Graduate School, Information Systems Program, Minot, ND 58707-0002. Offers MSIS. Part-time programs available. Postbaccalaureate distance learning degree programs offered (minimal on-campus study). *Expenses:* Tuition, state resident: full-time $5720; part-time $283 per credit hour. Tuition, nonresident: full-time $5720; part-time $283 per credit hour. Required fees: $1034; $1034 per year. Tuition and fees vary according to course load, degree level and program.

Mississippi State University, College of Business, Department of Management and Information Systems, Mississippi State, MS 39762. Offers business administration (PhD), including business information systems, management; information systems (MSIS). Part-time programs available. *Faculty:* 16 full-time (4 women), 1 part-time/adjunct (0 women). *Students:* 20 full-time (6 women), 5 part-time (2 women); includes 4 minority (2 African Americans, 1 American Indian/Alaska Native, 1 Asian American or Pacific Islander), 7 international. Average age 31. 49 applicants, 33% accepted, 12 enrolled. In 2009, 9 master's, 5 doctorates awarded. *Degree requirements:* For master's, comprehensive exam; for doctorate, comprehensive exam, thesis/dissertation. *Entrance requirements:* For master's, GMAT, minimum GPA of 3.0 in last 60 hours of course work; for doctorate, GMAT, minimum graduate GPA of 3.25 in last 60 hours. Additional exam requirements/recommendations for international students: Required—TOEFL (minimum score 575 paper-based; 233 computer-based; 90 iBT); Recommended—IELTS (minimum score 7). *Application deadline:* For fall admission, 7/1 for domestic students, 5/1 for international students; for spring admission, 11/1 for domestic students, 9/1 for international students. Applications are processed on a rolling basis. Application fee: $40. Electronic applications accepted. *Expenses:* Tuition, state resident: full-time $2575.50; part-time $286.25 per credit hour. Tuition, nonresident: full-time $6510; part-time $723.50 per credit hour. Tuition and fees vary according to course load. *Financial support:* In 2009–10, 6 teaching assistantships

(averaging $10,037 per year) were awarded; Federal Work-Study and institutionally sponsored loans also available. Financial award applicants required to submit FAFSA. *Faculty research:* Electronic commerce, management of information technology. *Unit head:* Dr. Rodney Pearson, Department Head and Professor of Information Systems, 662-325-3928, Fax: 662-325-8651, E-mail: rodney.pearson@msstate.edu. *Application contact:* Dr. Barbara Spencer, Associate Dean for Research and Outreach, 662-325-1891, Fax: 662-325-8161, E-mail: bspencer@cobian.msstate.edu.

Missouri State University, Graduate College, College of Business Administration, Department of Computer Information Systems, Springfield, MO 65897. Offers computer information systems (MS); secondary education (MS Ed), including business. Part-time and evening/weekend programs available. Postbaccalaureate distance learning degree programs offered (no on-campus study). *Faculty:* 13 full-time (3 women), 1 part-time/adjunct (0 women). *Students:* 34 full-time (7 women), 4 part-time (all women); includes 1 minority (Asian American or Pacific Islander), 1 international. Average age 41. 15 applicants, 100% accepted, 13 enrolled. In 2009, 16 master's awarded. *Degree requirements:* For master's, thesis optional. *Entrance requirements:* For master's, GMAT, 3 years of work experience in computer information systems, minimum GPA of 2.75 (MS), 9-12 teaching certification (MS Ed). Additional exam requirements/recommendations for international students: Required—TOEFL (minimum score 550 paper-based; 213 computer-based; 79 iBT). *Application deadline:* For fall admission, 7/20 priority date for domestic students, 5/1 for international students; for spring admission, 12/20 priority date for domestic students, 9/1 for international students. Applications are processed on a rolling basis. Application fee: $35 ($50 for international students). Electronic applications accepted. *Expenses:* Contact institution. *Financial support:* Federal Work-Study, institutionally sponsored loans, scholarships/grants, and unspecified assistantships available. Support available to part-time students. Financial award application deadline: 3/31; financial award applicants required to submit FAFSA. *Faculty research:* Decision support systems, algorithms in Visual Basic, end-user satisfaction, information security. *Unit head:* Dr. Jerry Chin, Head, 417-836-4131, Fax: 417-836-6907, E-mail: jerrychin@missouristate.edu. *Application contact:* Dr. Jerry Chin, Head, 417-836-4131, Fax: 417-836-6907, E-mail: jerrychin@missouristate.edu.

Montclair State University, The Graduate School, School of Business, Department of Accounting, Law and Taxation, Montclair, NJ 07043-1624. Offers accounting (MBA, Certificate); finance (Certificate); management information systems (Certificate); marketing (Certificate). Part-time and evening/weekend programs available. *Faculty:* 15 full-time (5 women), 11 part-time/adjunct (9 women). *Students:* 44 full-time (23 women), 94 part-time (40 women). Average age 30. 81 applicants, 56% accepted, 29 enrolled. In 2009, 31 master's, 1 other advanced degree awarded. *Entrance requirements:* For master's, GMAT, 2 letters of recommendation, resume. Additional exam requirements/recommendations for international students: Required—TOEFL (minimum score 83 computer-based), or IELTS. *Application deadline:* For fall admission, 6/1 for international students; for spring admission, 10/1 for international students. Applications are processed on a rolling basis. Application fee: $60. Electronic applications accepted. *Expenses:* Tuition, area resident: Part-time $486.74 per credit. Tuition, state resident: part-time $486.74 per credit. Tuition, nonresident: part-time $751.34 per credit. Tuition and fees vary according to degree level and program. *Financial support:* In 2009–10, 2 research assistantships with full tuition reimbursements (averaging $7,000 per year) were awarded; Federal Work-Study and scholarships/grants also available. Support available to part-time students. Financial award application deadline: 3/1; financial award applicants required to submit FAFSA. *Unit head:* Prof. Frank Aquilino, Head, 973-655-4174. *Application contact:* Amy Aiello, Director of Graduate Admissions and Operations, 973-655-5147, Fax: 973-655-7869, E-mail: graduate.school@montclair.edu.

Montclair State University, The Graduate School, School of Business, Department of Management Information Systems, Montclair, NJ 07043-1624. Offers management (MBA, Certificate); management information systems (MBA). Part-time and evening/weekend programs available. *Faculty:* 28 full-time (10 women), 14 part-time/adjunct (2 women). *Students:* 17 full-time (8 women), 55 part-time (22 women). Average age 29. 35 applicants, 54% accepted, 9 enrolled. In 2009, 17 master's awarded. *Degree requirements:* For master's, comprehensive project. *Entrance requirements:* For master's, GMAT, 2 letters of recommendation, resume. Additional exam requirements/recommendations for international students: Required—TOEFL (minimum score 83 computer-based), or IELTS. *Application deadline:* For fall admission, 6/1 for international students; for spring admission, 10/1 for international students. Applications are processed on a rolling basis. Application fee: $60. Electronic applications accepted. *Expenses:* Tuition, area resident: Part-time $486.74 per credit. Tuition, state resident: part-time $486.74 per credit. Tuition, nonresident: part-time $751.34 per credit. Tuition and fees vary according to degree level and program. *Financial support:* In 2009–10, 7 research assistantships (averaging $7,000 per year) were awarded; Federal Work-Study, scholarships/grants, and unspecified assistantships also available. Support available to part-time students. Financial award application deadline: 3/1; financial award applicants required to submit FAFSA. *Unit head:* Dr. Richard Peterson, Head, 973-655-4269. *Application contact:* Amy Aiello, Director of Graduate Admissions and Operations, 973-655-5147, Fax: 973-655-7869, E-mail: graduate.school@montclair.edu.

Morehead State University, Graduate Programs, College of Business and Public Affairs, Department of Information Systems, Morehead, KY 40351. Offers MSIS. *Faculty:* 7 full-time (2 women). *Students:* 4 full-time (2 women), 13 part-time (3 women); includes 1 minority (African American), 4 international. Average age 36. 9 applicants, 78% accepted, 3 enrolled. In 2009, 5 master's awarded. *Entrance requirements:* For master's, GRE, GMAT. Additional exam requirements/recommendations for international students: Required—TOEFL (minimum score 525 paper-based). *Application deadline:* For fall admission, 8/1 for domestic and international students; for spring admission, 12/1 for domestic and international students. Applications are processed on a rolling basis. Application fee: $30. Electronic applications accepted. *Expenses:* Tuition, state resident: full-time $6318; part-time $351 per credit hour. Tuition, nonresident: full-time $15,804; part-time $878 per credit hour. *Financial support:* In 2009–10, 4 teaching assistantships (averaging $6,000 per year) were awarded. Financial award application deadline: 3/15. *Unit head:* Dr. Betty Regan, Chair, 606-783-2730, Fax: 606-783-5025, E-mail: e.regan@moreheadstate.edu. *Application contact:* Michelle Barber, Graduate Recruitment and Retention Assistant Director, 606-783-5127, Fax: 606-783-5061, E-mail: m.barber@moreheadstate.edu.

Morehead State University, Graduate Programs, College of Business and Public Affairs, School of Business Administration, Morehead, KY 40351. Offers business administration (MBA); information systems (MSIS); sport management (MA). Part-time and evening/weekend programs available. *Faculty:* 21 full-time (8 women). *Students:* 41 full-time (17 women), 198 part-time (99 women); includes 16 minority (10 African Americans, 4 Asian Americans or Pacific Islanders, 2 Hispanic Americans), 4 international. Average age 32. 118 applicants, 71% accepted, 53 enrolled. In 2009, 60 master's awarded. *Entrance requirements:* For master's, GRE or GMAT. Additional exam requirements/recommendations for international students: Required—TOEFL (minimum score 500 paper-based; 173 computer-based). *Application deadline:* For fall admission, 8/1 priority date for domestic and international students; for spring admission, 12/1 priority date for domestic and international students. Applications are processed on a rolling basis. Application fee: $30. Electronic applications accepted. *Expenses:* Tuition, state resident: full-time $6318; part-time $351 per credit hour. Tuition, nonresident: full-time $15,804; part-time $878 per credit hour. *Financial support:* In 2009–10, 1 research assistantship (averaging $10,000 per year), 9 teaching assistantships (averaging $10,000 per year) were awarded; career-related internships or fieldwork, Federal Work-Study, and unspecified assistantships also available. Financial award application deadline: 3/15; financial award applicants required to submit FAFSA. *Unit head:* Dr. Robert L. Albert, Dean, 606-783-2174, Fax: 606-783-5025, E-mail: r.albert@moreheadstate.edu. *Application contact:* Michelle Barber, Graduate Recruitment and Retention Assistant Director, 606-783-5127, Fax: 606-783-5061, E-mail: m.barber@moreheadstate.edu.

National University, Academic Affairs, School of Engineering and Technology, Department of Applied Engineering, La Jolla, CA 92037-1011. Offers database administration (MS); engineering management (MS); environmental engineering (MS); homeland security and safety engineering

(MS); system engineering (MS); wireless communications (MS). Part-time and evening/weekend programs available. Postbaccalaureate distance learning degree programs offered (no on-campus study). *Faculty:* 6 full-time (1 woman), 7 part-time/adjunct (1 woman). *Students:* 61 full-time (16 women), 176 part-time (35 women); includes 54 minority (11 African Americans, 1 American Indian/Alaska Native, 23 Asian Americans or Pacific Islanders, 19 Hispanic Americans), 117 international. Average age 31. 133 applicants, 100% accepted, 83 enrolled. In 2009, 34 master's awarded. *Degree requirements:* For master's, thesis. *Entrance requirements:* For master's, interview, minimum GPA of 2.5. Additional exam requirements/recommendations for international students: Required—TOEFL (minimum score 550 paper-based; 213 computer-based; 79 iBT), IELTS (minimum score 6). *Application deadline:* Applications are processed on a rolling basis. Application fee: $60 ($65 for international students). Electronic applications accepted. *Expenses:* Tuition: Part-time $338 per quarter hour. *Financial support:* Career-related internships or fieldwork, institutionally sponsored loans, scholarships/grants, and tuition waivers (partial) available. Support available to part-time students. Financial award application deadline: 6/30; financial award applicants required to submit FAFSA. *Unit head:* Dr. Shekar Viswanathan, Chair and Associate Professor, 858-309-8416, Fax: 858-309-3420, E-mail: sviswana@nu.edu. *Application contact:* Dominick Giovanniello, Associate Regional Dean—San Diego, 800-NAT-UNIV, Fax: 858-541-7792, E-mail: dgiovann@nu.edu.

National University, Academic Affairs, School of Engineering and Technology, Department of Computer Science and Information Systems, La Jolla, CA 92037-1011. Offers computer science (MS); information systems (MS); software engineering (MS); technology management (MS). Part-time and evening/weekend programs available. Postbaccalaureate distance learning degree programs offered (no on-campus study). *Faculty:* 18 full-time (10 women), 30 part-time/adjunct (7 women). *Students:* 88 full-time (19 women), 163 part-time (31 women); includes 57 minority (24 African Americans, 24 Asian Americans or Pacific Islanders, 9 Hispanic Americans), 111 international. Average age 32. 146 applicants, 100% accepted, 89 enrolled. In 2009, 51 master's awarded. *Degree requirements:* For master's, thesis. *Entrance requirements:* For master's, interview, minimum GPA of 2.5. Additional exam requirements/recommendations for international students: Required—TOEFL (minimum score 550 paper-based; 213 computer-based; 79 iBT), IELTS (minimum score 6). *Application deadline:* Applications are processed on a rolling basis. Application fee: $60 ($65 for international students). Electronic applications accepted. *Expenses:* Tuition: Part-time $338 per quarter hour. *Financial support:* Career-related internships or fieldwork, institutionally sponsored loans, scholarships/grants, and tuition waivers (partial) available. Support available to part-time students. Financial award application deadline: 6/30; financial award applicants required to submit FAFSA. *Unit head:* Dr. Ron Uhlig, Interim Chair and Instructor, 858-309-3412, Fax: 858-309-3420, E-mail: ruhlig@nu.edu. *Application contact:* Dominick Giovanniello, Associate Regional Dean—San Diego, 800-NAT-UNIV, Fax: 858-541-7792, E-mail: dgiovann@nu.edu.

Naval Postgraduate School, Graduate Programs, Department of Information Sciences, Monterey, CA 93943. Offers information sciences (MS); knowledge superiority (MS, Certificate). Program open only to commissioned officers of the United States and friendly nations and selected United States federal civilian employees. Part-time programs available. *Degree requirements:* For master's, thesis.

Naval Postgraduate School, Graduate Programs, School of Business and Public Policy, Monterey, CA 93943. Offers contract management (MS); defense-focused business administration (MBA); executive business administration (MBA); leadership and human resource development (MS); management (MS); program management (MS); systems engineering management (MS). Program only open to commissioned officers of the United States and friendly nations and selected United States federal civilian employees. *Accreditation:* AACSB; NASPAA. Part-time programs available. Postbaccalaureate distance learning degree programs offered (minimal on-campus study). *Degree requirements:* For master's, thesis.

New Jersey Institute of Technology, Office of Graduate Studies, College of Computing Science, Department of Computer Science, Newark, NJ 07102. Offers bioinformatics (MS); computer science (MS, PhD); computing and business (MS); software engineering (MS). Part-time and evening/weekend programs available. Terminal master's awarded for partial completion of doctoral program. *Degree requirements:* For master's, thesis optional; for doctorate, thesis/dissertation. *Entrance requirements:* For master's, GRE General Test; for doctorate, GRE General Test, minimum graduate GPA of 3.5. Additional exam requirements/recommendations for international students: Required—TOEFL (minimum score 550 paper-based; 213 computer-based; 79 iBT). Electronic applications accepted.

New Jersey Institute of Technology, Office of Graduate Studies, College of Computing Science, Program in Information Systems, Newark, NJ 07102. Offers business and information systems (MS); emergency management and business continuity (MS); information systems (MS, PhD). Part-time and evening/weekend programs available. Terminal master's awarded for partial completion of doctoral program. *Degree requirements:* For master's, thesis optional; for doctorate, thesis/dissertation. *Entrance requirements:* For master's, GRE General Test; for doctorate, GRE General Test, minimum graduate GPA of 3.5. Additional exam requirements/recommendations for international students: Required—TOEFL (minimum score 550 paper-based; 213 computer-based; 79 iBT). Electronic applications accepted.

Newman University, School of Business, Wichita, KS 67213-2097. Offers finance (MBA); international business (MBA); leadership (MBA); management (MBA); technology (MBA). Part-time programs available. *Faculty:* 5 full-time (1 woman), 8 part-time/adjunct (2 women). *Students:* 29 full-time (13 women), 105 part-time (52 women); includes 30 minority (9 African Americans, 1 American Indian/Alaska Native, 10 Asian Americans or Pacific Islanders, 10 Hispanic Americans), 23 international. Average age 32. 80 applicants, 76% accepted, 47 enrolled. In 2009, 76 master's awarded. *Degree requirements:* For master's, thesis optional. *Entrance requirements:* For master's, interview, minimum GPA of 3.0; 3 letters of recommendation; course work in algebra, statistics, macroeconomics, and financial accounting. Additional exam requirements/recommendations for international students: Required—TOEFL (minimum score 600 paper-based; 250 computer-based; 100 iBT). *Application deadline:* For fall admission, 8/1 priority date for domestic students, 7/15 priority date for international students; for winter admission, 1/1 priority date for domestic students; for spring admission, 1/1 priority date for domestic students, 11/15 priority date for international students. Applications are processed on a rolling basis. Application fee: $25 ($40 for international students). Electronic applications accepted. *Expenses:* Contact institution. *Financial support:* In 2009–10, 3 students received support. Federal Work-Study available. Financial award application deadline: 8/15; financial award applicants required to submit FAFSA. *Unit head:* Dr. Joe Goetz, Dean of the College of Professional Studies/Director, 316-942-4291 Ext. 2111, Fax: 316-942-4486, E-mail: goetzj@newmanu.edu. *Application contact:* Linda Kay Sabala, Director of Graduate Admissions, 316-942-4291 Ext. 2230, Fax: 316-942-4483, E-mail: sabalal@newmanu.edu.

New Mexico Highlands University, Graduate Studies, School of Business, Las Vegas, NM 87701. Offers business administration (MBA), including government nonprofit management, human resource management, international business, management, management information systems. *Accreditation:* ACBSP. *Degree requirements:* For master's, comprehensive exam, thesis or alternative. *Entrance requirements:* For master's, minimum undergraduate GPA of 3.0. Additional exam requirements/recommendations for international students: Required—TOEFL (minimum score 540 paper-based; 207 computer-based). *Faculty research:* Real estate valuation, studying expert judgments in complex accounting, decision environments, green marketing, environmentalism, marketing research methodology.

New York Institute of Technology, Graduate Division, School of Management, Program in Business Administration, Old Westbury, NY 11568-8000. Offers accounting (Advanced Certificate); business administration (MBA); finance (Advanced Certificate); international business (Advanced Certificate); management of information systems (Advanced Certificate); marketing (Advanced Certificate). Part-time and evening/weekend programs available. *Students:* 599 full-time (262 women), 528 part-time (200 women); includes 51 minority (17 African Americans, 24 Asian Americans or Pacific Islanders, 10 Hispanic Americans), 324 international. Average

Management Information Systems

New York Institute of Technology (continued)

age 29. In 2009, 691 master's, 7 other advanced degrees awarded. *Degree requirements:* For master's, thesis (for some programs). *Entrance requirements:* For master's, minimum QPA of 2.85. Additional exam requirements/recommendations for international students: Required—TOEFL (minimum score 550 paper-based; 213 computer-based). *Application deadline:* For fall admission, 7/1 priority date for domestic students; for spring admission, 12/1 priority date for domestic students. Applications are processed on a rolling basis. Application fee: $50. Electronic applications accepted. *Expenses:* Tuition: Part-time $825 per credit. *Financial support:* Fellowships, research assistantships with partial tuition reimbursements, institutionally sponsored loans, tuition waivers (full and partial), and unspecified assistantships available. Support available to part-time students. Financial award applicants required to submit FAFSA. *Faculty research:* Instructor performance appraisal; relationship between TOEFL, GMAT, GRE, and performance in foreign students. *Unit head:* Dr. Diamando Afxentiou, Acting Associate Dean, 516-686-3937, Fax: 516-686-7430, E-mail: dafxenti@nyit.edu. *Application contact:* Dr. Jacquelyn Nealon, Vice President for Enrollment Services, 516-686-7925, Fax: 516-686-7597, E-mail: jnealon@nyit.edu.

New York University, Leonard N. Stern School of Business, Department of Information, Operations and Management Sciences, New York, NY 10012-1019. Offers information systems (MBA, PhD); operations management (MBA, PhD); statistics (MBA, PhD). *Expenses:* Tuition: Full-time $30,528; part-time $1272 per credit. Required fees: $2177. *Faculty research:* Knowledge management, economics of information, computer-supported groups and communities financial information systems, data mining and business intelligence.

New York University, School of Continuing and Professional Studies, Division of Programs in Business, Graduate Programs in Management and Systems, New York, NY 10012-1019. Offers core business competencies (Advanced Certificate); database technologies (MS); enterprise and risk management (Advanced Certificate); enterprise risk management (MS); information technologies (Advanced Certificate); strategy and leadership (MS, Advanced Certificate); systems management (MS). Part-time and evening/weekend programs available. Postbaccalaureate distance learning degree programs offered (no on-campus study). *Faculty:* 2 full-time (0 women), 21 part-time/adjunct (6 women). *Students:* 32 full-time (18 women), 197 part-time (78 women). Average age 34. 168 applicants, 80% accepted, 69 enrolled. In 2009, 51 master's, 7 other advanced degrees awarded. *Degree requirements:* For master's, thesis, capstone project. *Entrance requirements:* For master's, GMAT or GRE General Test (for recent graduates), resume, 2 letters of recommendation, essay. Additional exam requirements/recommendations for international students: Required—TOEFL (minimum score 600 paper-based; 250 computer-based; 100 iBT), TWE. *Application deadline:* For fall admission, 2/1 priority date for domestic and international students; for spring admission, 10/15 priority date for domestic students, 8/15 priority date for international students. Applications are processed on a rolling basis. Application fee: $75. Electronic applications accepted. *Expenses:* Tuition: Full-time $30,528; part-time $1272 per credit. Required fees: $2177. *Financial support:* In 2009–10, 61 students received support, including 61 fellowships (averaging $2,300 per year); scholarships/grants also available. Support available to part-time students. Financial award application deadline: 3/1; financial award applicants required to submit FAFSA. *Unit head:* Israel Moskowitz, Director, 212-992-3600, Fax: 212-992-3650, E-mail: im36@nyu.edu. *Application contact:* Helen Sapp, Assistant Director, 212-992-3600, Fax: 212-992-3650, E-mail: helen.sapp@nyu.edu.

North Central College, Graduate Programs, Department of Business, Program in Management Information Systems, Naperville, IL 60566-7063. Offers MS. Part-time and evening/weekend programs available. *Degree requirements:* For master's, project. *Entrance requirements:* For master's, interview. *Expenses:* Contact institution.

Northeastern University, College of Computer and Information Science, Boston, MA 02115-5096. Offers computer and information science (PhD); computer science (MS); health informatics (MS); information assurance (MS). Part-time and evening/weekend programs available. *Faculty:* 28 full-time (3 women), 3 part-time/adjunct (all women). *Students:* 180 full-time (48 women), 15 part-time (0 women); includes 4 minority (2 Asian Americans or Pacific Islanders, 2 Hispanic Americans), 154 international. 829 applicants, 52% accepted, 74 enrolled. In 2009, 97 master's, 5 doctorates awarded. Terminal master's awarded for partial completion of doctoral program. *Degree requirements:* For master's, thesis optional; for doctorate, comprehensive exam, thesis/dissertation. *Entrance requirements:* For master's and doctorate, GRE General Test. Additional exam requirements/recommendations for international students: Required—TOEFL or IELTS. *Application deadline:* For fall admission, 7/15 for domestic students, 5/1 for international students; for spring admission, 10/15 for domestic students, 9/1 for international students. Applications are processed on a rolling basis. Application fee: $50. Electronic applications accepted. *Expenses:* Contact institution. *Financial support:* In 2009–10, 59 students received support, including 1 fellowship, 35 research assistantships with full tuition reimbursements available (averaging $18,260 per year), 24 teaching assistantships with full tuition reimbursements available (averaging $18,260 per year); career-related internships or fieldwork, Federal Work-Study, institutionally sponsored loans, scholarships/grants, and unspecified assistantships also available. Financial award application deadline: 1/15. *Faculty research:* Programming languages, artificial intelligence, human-computer interaction, database management, network security. *Unit head:* Dr. Larry A. Finkelstein, Dean, 617-373-2462, Fax: 617-373-5121. *Application contact:* Dr. Agnes Chan, Associate Dean and Director of Graduate Program, 617-373-2462, Fax: 617-373-5121, E-mail: gradschool@ccs.neu.edu.

Northern Illinois University, Graduate School, College of Business, Department of Operations Management and Information Systems, De Kalb, IL 60115-2854. Offers management information systems (MS). Part-time programs available. *Faculty:* 11 full-time (3 women), 3 part-time/adjunct (0 women). *Students:* 25 full-time (9 women), 21 part-time (8 women); includes 8 minority (3 African Americans, 5 Asian Americans or Pacific Islanders), 21 international. Average age 28. 33 applicants, 61% accepted, 13 enrolled. In 2009, 18 master's awarded. *Degree requirements:* For master's, computer language. *Entrance requirements:* For master's, GMAT, minimum GPA of 2.75. Additional exam requirements/recommendations for international students: Required—TOEFL (minimum score 550 paper-based; 213 computer-based). *Application deadline:* For fall admission, 6/1 for domestic students, 5/1 for international students; for spring admission, 11/1 for domestic students, 10/1 for international students. Applications are processed on a rolling basis. Application fee: $30. Electronic applications accepted. *Expenses:* Tuition, state resident: full-time $6576; part-time $274 per credit hour. Tuition, nonresident: full-time $13,152; part-time $548 per credit hour. Required fees: $1813; $75.53 per credit hour. Part-time tuition and fees vary according to course load. *Financial support:* In 2009–10, 14 research assistantships with full tuition reimbursements were awarded; fellowships with full tuition reimbursements, teaching assistantships with full tuition reimbursements, career-related internships or fieldwork, Federal Work-Study, scholarships/grants, tuition waivers (full), and unspecified assistantships also available. Support available to part-time students. Financial award applicants required to submit FAFSA. *Faculty research:* Affordability of home ownership, Web portal competition intranet, electronic commerce, corporate-academic alliances. *Unit head:* Dr. Geoffrey Gordon, Interim Chair, 815-753-1285, Fax: 815-753-7460. *Application contact:* Steve Kispert, Office of Graduate Studies in Business, 815-753-6301, E-mail: skispert@niu.edu.

Northwestern University, The Graduate School, School of Communication, Department of Communication Studies, Communication Systems Strategy and Management Program, Evanston, IL 60208. Offers MSC. Part-time programs available. Electronic applications accepted.

Northwestern University, School of Continuing Studies, Program in Information Systems, Evanston, IL 60208. Offers database and Internet technologies (MS); information systems management (MS); information systems security (MS); software project management and development (MS).

Northwest Missouri State University, Graduate School, Melvin and Valorie Booth College of Business and Professional Studies, Program in Information Technology Management, Maryville, MO 64468-6001. Offers MBA. Part-time programs available. *Faculty:* 11 full-time (5 women). *Students:* 8 full-time (1 woman), 6 international. 17 applicants, 29% accepted, 2 enrolled. In 2009, 1 master's awarded. *Degree requirements:* For master's, comprehensive exam. *Entrance requirements:* For master's, GMAT, minimum GPA of 2.5. Additional exam requirements/recommendations for international students: Required—TOEFL (minimum score 550 paper-based; 213 computer-based). *Application deadline:* For fall admission, 7/1 for domestic and international students; for spring admission, 12/1 for domestic students, 11/15 for international students. Application fee: $0 ($50 for international students). *Expenses:* Tuition, state resident: part-time $296.34 per credit hour. Tuition, nonresident: part-time $510.43 per credit hour. *Financial support:* In 2009–10, 2 research assistantships with full tuition reimbursements (averaging $6,000 per year) were awarded. Financial award application deadline: 4/1; financial award applicants required to submit FAFSA. *Unit head:* Dr. Gary Ury, Head, 660-562-1185. *Application contact:* Dr. Gregory Haddock, Dean of Graduate School, 660-562-1145, Fax: 660-562-1096, E-mail: gradsch@nwmissouri.edu.

Norwich University, School of Graduate and Continuing Studies, Program in Information Assurance, Northfield, VT 05663. Offers business continuity management (MS); computer security incident response team management (MS); cyber forensic investigations (MS); managing cyber crime and digital incidents (MS). Evening/weekend programs available. *Faculty:* 18 part-time/adjunct (3 women). *Students:* 296 full-time (42 women); includes 31 minority (18 African Americans, 13 Hispanic Americans), 17 international. Average age 40. In 2009, 167 master's awarded. *Entrance requirements:* For master's, minimum undergraduate GPA of 2.75. Additional exam requirements/recommendations for international students: Required—TOEFL (minimum score 550 paper-based; 212 computer-based; 83 iBT). *Application deadline:* For fall admission, 8/10 for domestic and international students; for winter admission, 11/7 for domestic and international students; for spring admission, 2/6 for domestic and international students. Application fee: $50. Full-time tuition and fees vary according to course level and course load. *Financial support:* Scholarships/grants available. Financial award applicants required to submit FAFSA. *Unit head:* Dr. John Orlando, Program Director, 802-485-2730, E-mail: jorlando@norwich.edu. *Application contact:* Elizabeth Templeton, Administrative Director, 802-485-2757, Fax: 802-485-2533, E-mail: etemplet@norwich.edu.

Notre Dame College, Graduate Studies, South Euclid, OH 44121-4293. Offers accounting (Certificate); creative critical thinking (M Ed); financial services management (Certificate); information systems (Certificate); learning disabilities (M Ed); management (Certificate); paralegal (Certificate); pastoral ministry (Certificate); reading (M Ed); teacher education (Certificate). Part-time and evening/weekend programs available. *Degree requirements:* For master's, thesis. *Entrance requirements:* For master's, GRE General Test, MAT, minimum GPA of 2.75, valid teaching certificate. *Faculty research:* Cognitive psychology, teaching critical thinking in the classroom.

Nova Southeastern University, Graduate School of Computer and Information Sciences, Program in Information Security, Fort Lauderdale, FL 33314-7796. Offers MS. *Students:* 12 full-time (1 woman), 51 part-time (7 women); includes 28 minority (15 African Americans, 1 American Indian/Alaska Native, 2 Asian Americans or Pacific Islanders, 10 Hispanic Americans), 3 international. In 2009, 12 master's awarded. *Degree requirements:* For master's, thesis optional. *Application deadline:* Applications are processed on a rolling basis. Electronic applications accepted. *Unit head:* Dr. Amon Seagull, Interim Dean, 954-262-7300. *Application contact:* 954-262-2000, Fax: 954-262-2752, E-mail: scisinfo@nova.edu.

Nova Southeastern University, Graduate School of Computer and Information Sciences, Program in Information Systems, Fort Lauderdale, FL 33314-7796. Offers MS, PhD. *Students:* 44 full-time (14 women), 263 part-time (84 women); includes 115 minority (73 African Americans, 4 American Indian/Alaska Native, 18 Asian Americans or Pacific Islanders, 20 Hispanic Americans), 8 international. In 2009, 17 doctorates awarded. *Degree requirements:* For doctorate, thesis/dissertation. *Application deadline:* Applications are processed on a rolling basis. Electronic applications accepted. *Unit head:* Dr. Amon Seagull, Interim Dean, 954-262-7300. *Application contact:* 954-262-2000, Fax: 954-262-2752, E-mail: scisinfo@nova.edu.

Nova Southeastern University, Graduate School of Computer and Information Sciences, Program in Management Information Systems, Fort Lauderdale, FL 33314-7796. Offers information security (MS); management information systems (MS). Part-time and evening/weekend programs available. Postbaccalaureate distance learning degree programs offered (no on-campus study). *Students:* 19 full-time (4 women), 120 part-time (42 women); includes 71 minority (36 African Americans, 8 Asian Americans or Pacific Islanders, 27 Hispanic Americans), 8 international. In 2009, 75 master's awarded. *Degree requirements:* For master's, thesis optional. *Application deadline:* Applications are processed on a rolling basis. Electronic applications accepted. *Financial support:* Application deadline: 5/1. *Unit head:* Dr. Amon Seagull, Interim Dean. *Application contact:* 954-262-2000, Fax: 954-262-2752, E-mail: scisinfo@nova.edu.

Oakland University, Graduate Study and Lifelong Learning, School of Business Administration, Department of Decision and Information Sciences, Rochester, MI 48309-4401. Offers information technology management (MS); management information systems (Certificate); production and operations management (Certificate).

The Ohio State University, Graduate School, Max M. Fisher College of Business, Department of Accounting and Management Information Systems, Columbus, OH 43210. Offers accounting (M Acc, MA, MS, PhD); accounting and MIS (PhD). *Accreditation:* AACSB. *Faculty:* 25. *Students:* 96 full-time (42 women), 4 part-time (2 women); includes 9 minority (3 African Americans, 4 Asian Americans or Pacific Islanders, 2 Hispanic Americans), 30 international. Average age 24. In 2009, 84 master's, 2 doctorates awarded. Terminal master's awarded for partial completion of doctoral program. *Degree requirements:* For doctorate, thesis/dissertation. *Entrance requirements:* For master's, GMAT (preferred) or GRE General Test; for doctorate, GMAT (preferred) or GRE. Additional exam requirements/recommendations for international students: Required—TOEFL (minimum score 600 paper-based; 250 computer-based). *Application deadline:* For fall admission, 8/15 priority date for domestic students, 7/1 priority date for international students; for winter admission, 12/1 priority date for domestic students, 11/1 priority date for international students; for spring admission, 3/1 priority date for domestic students, 2/1 priority date for international students. Applications are processed on a rolling basis. Application fee: $40 ($50 for international students). Electronic applications accepted. *Expenses:* Tuition, state resident: full-time $10,683. Tuition, nonresident: full-time $25,923. Tuition and fees vary according to course load and program. *Financial support:* Fellowships, research assistantships, teaching assistantships, career-related internships or fieldwork, Federal Work-Study, and institutionally sponsored loans available. Support available to part-time students. *Faculty research:* Artificial intelligence, protocol analysis, database design in decision-supporting systems. *Unit head:* Annette Beatty, Graduate Studies Committee Chair, 614-292-2081, Fax: 614-292-2118, E-mail: beatty.86@osu.edu. *Application contact:* 614-292-9444, Fax: 614-292-3895, E-mail: domestic.grad@osu.edu.

Oklahoma City University, Meinders School of Business, Program in Business Administration, Oklahoma City, OK 73106-1402. Offers finance (MBA); health administration (MBA); information technology (MBA); integrated marketing communications (MBA); international business (MBA); marketing (MBA); JD/MBA. *Accreditation:* ACBSP. Part-time and evening/weekend programs available. *Faculty:* 24 full-time (7 women), 11 part-time/adjunct (1 woman). *Students:* 268 full-time (91 women), 180 part-time (62 women); includes 51 minority (20 African Americans, 7 American Indian/Alaska Native, 11 Asian Americans or Pacific Islanders, 13 Hispanic Americans), 257 international. Average age 30. 158 applicants, 90% accepted, 35 enrolled. In 2009, 236 master's awarded. *Degree requirements:* For master's, comprehensive exam. *Entrance requirements:* Additional exam requirements/recommendations for international students: Required—TOEFL (minimum score 560 paper-based; 220 computer-based; 83 iBT). *Application deadline:* For fall admission, 8/20 for domestic students; for spring admission, 1/6 for domestic students. Applications are processed on a rolling basis. Application fee: $50 ($70 for international students). *Expenses:* Tuition: Full-time $15,930; part-time $885 per hour. *Financial support:* Fellowships with partial tuition reimbursements, career-related internships or fieldwork,

Federal Work-Study, institutionally sponsored loans, and tuition waivers (partial) available. Support available to part-time students. Financial award application deadline: 8/1. *Faculty research:* Management information systems, international business strategies. *Unit head:* Dr. Mahmood Shandiz, Senior Associate Dean, 405-208-5130, Fax: 405-208-5098, E-mail: mshandiz@okcu.edu. *Application contact:* Michelle Lockhart, Director, Graduate Admissions, 800-633-7242, Fax: 405-208-5916, E-mail: gadmissions@okcu.edu.

Oklahoma State University, William S. Spears School of Business, Department of Management Science and Information Systems, Stillwater, OK 74078. Offers management information systems (MS); management science and information systems (PhD); telecommunications management (MS). Part-time programs available. Postbaccalaureate distance learning degree programs offered. *Faculty:* 15 full-time (2 women), 1 part-time/adjunct (0 women). *Students:* 75 full-time (25 women), 80 part-time (17 women); includes 7 minority (1 African American, 4 American Indian/Alaska Native, 2 Asian Americans or Pacific Islanders), 100 international. Average age 29. 251 applicants, 38% accepted, 41 enrolled. In 2009, 58 master's awarded. *Degree requirements:* For master's, thesis or alternative; for doctorate, comprehensive exam, thesis/dissertation. *Entrance requirements:* For master's and doctorate, GRE or GMAT. Additional exam requirements/recommendations for international students: Required—TOEFL (minimum score 550 paper-based; 79 iBT). *Application deadline:* For fall admission, 3/1 priority date for international students; for spring admission, 8/1 priority date for international students. Applications are processed on a rolling basis. Application fee: $40 ($75 for international students). Electronic applications accepted. *Expenses:* Tuition, state resident: full-time $3716; part-time $154.85 per credit hour. Tuition, nonresident: full-time $14,448; part-time $602 per credit hour. Required fees: $1772; $73.85 per credit hour. One-time fee: $50. Tuition and fees vary according to course load and campus/location. *Financial support:* In 2009–10, 2 research assistantships (averaging $6,720 per year), 14 teaching assistantships (averaging $13,962 per year) were awarded; career-related internships or fieldwork, Federal Work-Study, scholarships/grants, health care benefits, tuition waivers (partial), and unspecified assistantships also available. Support available to part-time students. Financial award application deadline: 3/1; financial award applicants required to submit FAFSA. *Unit head:* Dr. Rick Wilson, Head, 405-744-3551, Fax: 405-744-5180. *Application contact:* Dr. Gordon Emslie, Dean, 405-744-6368, Fax: 405-744-0355, E-mail: grad-i@okstate.edu.

Old Dominion University, College of Business and Public Administration, MBA Program, Norfolk, VA 23529. Offers business and economic forecasting (MBA); financial analysis and valuation (MBA); information technology and enterprise integration (MBA); international business (MBA); maritime and port management (MBA); public administration (MBA). *Accreditation:* AACSB. Part-time and evening/weekend programs available. *Faculty:* 66 full-time (15 women), 6 part-time/adjunct (1 woman). *Students:* 81 full-time (27 women), 198 part-time (92 women); includes 46 minority (25 African Americans, 1 American Indian/Alaska Native, 13 Asian Americans or Pacific Islanders, 7 Hispanic Americans), 31 international. Average age 30. 169 applicants, 52% accepted, 61 enrolled. In 2009, 81 master's awarded. *Entrance requirements:* For master's, GMAT, letters of reference, resume, coursework in calculus. Additional exam requirements/recommendations for international students: Required—TOEFL (minimum score 550 paper-based; 213 computer-based; 80 iBT). *Application deadline:* For fall admission, 6/1 priority date for domestic students, 4/15 priority date for international students; for spring admission, 11/1 priority date for domestic students, 10/1 priority date for international students. Applications are processed on a rolling basis. Application fee: $50. Electronic applications accepted. *Expenses:* Tuition, state resident: full-time $8112; part-time $338 per credit. Tuition, nonresident: full-time $20,256; part-time $844 per credit. Required fees: $119 per semester. One-time fee: $50. *Financial support:* In 2009–10, 46 students received support, including 31 research assistantships with partial tuition reimbursements available (averaging $7,000 per year), 3 teaching assistantships with partial tuition reimbursements available (averaging $6,300 per year); career-related internships or fieldwork, scholarships/grants, and unspecified assistantships also available. Support available to part-time students. Financial award application deadline: 2/15; financial award applicants required to submit FAFSA. *Faculty research:* International business, buyer behavior, financial markets, strategy, operations research. *Unit head:* Dr. Bruce Rubin, Graduate Program Director, 757-683-3585, E-mail: mbainfo@odu.edu. *Application contact:* Shanna Wood, MBA Program Manager, 757-683-3585, Fax: 757-683-5750, E-mail: mbainfo@odu.edu.

Our Lady of the Lake University of San Antonio, School of Business and Leadership, Program in Information Systems and Security, San Antonio, TX 78207-4689. Offers MS. *Students:* 7 part-time (3 women); includes 3 minority (all Hispanic Americans). Average age 32. In 2009, 6 master's awarded. *Expenses:* Tuition: Full-time $12,330; part-time $685 per contact hour. Required fees: $139; $12 per contact hour. $57 per semester. Tuition and fees vary according to campus/location. *Unit head:* Dr. Robert Bisking, Dean, 210-434-6711, Fax: 210-434-0821. *Application contact:* Dr. Robert Bisking, Dean, 210-434-6711, Fax: 210-434-0821.

Pace University, Lubin School of Business, Information Systems Program, New York, NY 10038. Offers MBA. Part-time and evening/weekend programs available. *Students:* 2 full-time (0 women), 17 part-time (3 women); includes 4 minority (all Asian Americans or Pacific Islanders), 4 international. Average age 31. 36 applicants, 78% accepted, 4 enrolled. In 2009, 9 master's awarded. *Entrance requirements:* For master's, GMAT. Additional exam requirements/recommendations for international students: Required—TOEFL. *Application deadline:* For fall admission, 7/31 priority date for domestic students; for spring admission, 11/30 for domestic students. Applications are processed on a rolling basis. Application fee: $70. Electronic applications accepted. *Expenses:* Tuition: Part-time $954 per credit. Tuition and fees vary according to course load, degree level and program. *Financial support:* Research assistantships, career-related internships or fieldwork and Federal Work-Study available. Support available to part-time students. Financial award applicants required to submit FAFSA. *Unit head:* Dr. John Molluzzo, Chair, 212-346-1780. *Application contact:* Susan Ford-Goldschein, Director of Admissions, 212-346-1652, Fax: 212-346-1585, E-mail: gradnyc@pace.edu.

Pacific States University, College of Business, Los Angeles, CA 90006. Offers accounting (MBA); business administration (DBA); finance (MBA); international business (MBA); management of information technology (MBA); real estate management (MBA). Part-time and evening/weekend programs available. Postbaccalaureate distance learning degree programs offered (no on-campus study). *Entrance requirements:* For master's, minimum undergraduate GPA of 2.5 during last 90 hours of course work. Additional exam requirements/recommendations for international students: Required—TOEFL (minimum score 133 computer-based).

Pacific States University, College of Computer Science, Los Angeles, CA 90006. Offers computer science (MSCS); information systems (MSCS). Part-time and evening/weekend programs available. *Entrance requirements:* For master's, bachelor's degree in physics, engineering, computer science, or applied mathematics; minimum undergraduate GPA of 2.5 during last 90 hours of course work. Additional exam requirements/recommendations for international students: Required—TOEFL (minimum score 133 computer-based).

Park University, College of Graduate and Professional Studies, Kansas City, MO 54105. Offers adult education (M Ed); at-risk students (M Ed); disaster and emergency management (MPA); educational administration (M Ed); entrepreneurship (MBA); general business (MBA); general education (M Ed); government/business relations (MPA); healthcare/services management (MBA, MPA); international business (MBA); K-12 certification (MAT); management information systems (MBA); management of information systems (MPA); middle school certification (MAT); multi-cultural education (M Ed); nonprofit management (MPA); public management (MPA); school law (M Ed); secondary school certification (MAT); special education (M Ed). Part-time and evening/weekend programs available. Postbaccalaureate distance learning degree programs offered (no on-campus study). *Degree requirements:* For master's, comprehensive exam, thesis (for some programs). *Entrance requirements:* For master's, GRE, GMAT, teacher certification (M Ed). Additional exam requirements/recommendations for international students: Required—TOEFL (minimum score 550 paper-based). Electronic applications accepted. *Faculty research:* Literacy, leadership, brain based research, multicultural education, diversity.

Polytechnic Institute of NYU, Department of Technology Management, Brooklyn, NY 11201-2990. Offers construction management (Advanced Certificate); electronic business management (Advanced Certificate); entrepreneurship (Advanced Certificate); human resources management (Advanced Certificate); information management (Advanced Certificate); management (MS); management of technology (MS); organizational behavior (MS, Advanced Certificate); project management (Advanced Certificate); technology management (MBA, PhD, Advanced Certificate); telecommunications and information management (MS); telecommunications management (Advanced Certificate). Part-time and evening/weekend programs available. *Faculty:* 5 full-time (1 woman), 26 part-time/adjunct (3 women). *Students:* 272 full-time (111 women), 103 part-time (41 women); includes 64 minority (20 African Americans, 1 American Indian/Alaska Native, 34 Asian Americans or Pacific Islanders, 9 Hispanic Americans), 193 international. Average age 30. 518 applicants, 57% accepted, 135 enrolled. In 2009, 148 master's awarded. *Degree requirements:* For master's, comprehensive exam (for some programs), thesis (for some programs); for doctorate, comprehensive exam, thesis/dissertation. *Entrance requirements:* For master's, GMAT, minimum B average in undergraduate course work. Additional exam requirements/recommendations for international students: Required—TOEFL (minimum score 550 paper-based; 213 computer-based; 80 iBT); Recommended—IELTS (minimum score 6.5). *Application deadline:* For fall admission, 7/31 priority date for domestic students, 4/30 priority date for international students; for spring admission, 12/31 priority date for domestic students, 11/30 priority date for international students. Applications are processed on a rolling basis. Application fee: $75. Electronic applications accepted. *Expenses:* Tuition: Full-time $21,492; part-time $1194 per credit hour. Required fees: $1160; $204 per course. *Financial support:* In 2009–10, 1 fellowship (averaging $26,400 per year) was awarded; research assistantships, teaching assistantships, institutionally sponsored loans, scholarships/grants, and unspecified assistantships also available. Support available to part-time students. *Unit head:* Prof. Bharadwaj Rao, Head, 718-260-3617, Fax: 718-260-3874, E-mail: brao@poly.edu. *Application contact:* JeanCarlo Bonilla, Director of Graduate Enrollment Management, 718-260-3182, Fax: 718-260-3624, E-mail: gradinfo@poly.edu.

Polytechnic Institute of NYU, Westchester Graduate Center, Graduate Programs, Department of Finance and Risk Engineering, Major in Financial Engineering, Hawthorne, NY 10532-1507. Offers capital markets (MS); computational finance (MS); financial engineering (AC); financial technology (MS); financial technology management (AC); information management (AC). *Students:* 9 full-time (6 women), 8 international. *Degree requirements:* For master's, comprehensive exam (for some programs), thesis (for some programs). *Entrance requirements:* Additional exam requirements/recommendations for international students: Required—TOEFL (minimum score 550 paper-based; 213 computer-based; 80 iBT); Recommended—IELTS (minimum score 6.5). *Application deadline:* For fall admission, 7/31 priority date for domestic students, 4/30 priority date for international students; for spring admission, 12/31 priority date for domestic students, 11/30 priority date for international students. Applications are processed on a rolling basis. Application fee: $75. Electronic applications accepted. *Financial support:* Institutionally sponsored loans, scholarships/grants, and unspecified assistantships available. Support available to part-time students. *Unit head:* Dr. Charles S. Tapiero, Department Head, 718-260-3653, E-mail: ctapiero@poly.edu. *Application contact:* JeanCarlo Bonilla, Director of Graduate Enrollment Management, 718-260-3182, Fax: 718-260-3624, E-mail: gradinfo@poly.edu.

Pontifical Catholic University of Puerto Rico, College of Business Administration, Program in Management Information Systems, Ponce, PR 00717-0777. Offers MBA. Part-time and evening/weekend programs available. *Degree requirements:* For master's, thesis. *Entrance requirements:* For master's, GRE, interview, minimum GPA of 2.75.

Prairie View A&M University, College of Engineering, Prairie View, TX 77446-0519. Offers computer information systems (MSCIS); computer science (MSCS); electrical engineering (MSEE, PhDEE); engineering (MS Engr). Part-time and evening/weekend programs available. *Faculty:* 19 full-time (0 women). *Students:* 64 full-time (18 women), 47 part-time (14 women); includes 43 minority (36 African Americans, 4 Asian Americans or Pacific Islanders, 3 Hispanic Americans), 51 international. Average age 24. 50 applicants, 84% accepted, 33 enrolled. In 2009, 26 master's, 3 doctorates awarded. *Degree requirements:* For master's, thesis (for some programs); for doctorate, comprehensive exam, thesis/dissertation. *Entrance requirements:* For master's, GRE General Test, bachelor's degree in engineering from an ABET accredited institution; for doctorate, GRE. Additional exam requirements/recommendations for international students: Required—TOEFL (minimum score 550 paper-based). *Application deadline:* For fall admission, 7/1 priority date for domestic and international students; for spring admission, 11/1 priority date for domestic and international students. Application fee: $50. Electronic applications accepted. *Expenses:* Tuition, state resident: full-time $2200. Tuition, nonresident: full-time $5600. Required fees: $1720. Tuition and fees vary according to course load. *Financial support:* In 2009–10, 80 students received support, including 14 fellowships (averaging $1,050 per year), 16 research assistantships (averaging $16,150 per year), 13 teaching assistantships (averaging $14,000 per year); career-related internships or fieldwork, institutionally sponsored loans, scholarships/grants, health care benefits, tuition waivers (partial), and unspecified assistantships also available. Financial award application deadline: 3/1; financial award applicants required to submit FAFSA. *Faculty research:* Applied radiation research, thermal science, computational fluid dynamics, analog mixed signal, aerial space battlefield. Total annual research expenditures: $439,054. *Unit head:* Dr. Kendall T. Harris, Dean, 936-261-9956, Fax: 936-261-9869, E-mail: tharris@pvamu.edu. *Application contact:* Barbara A. Thompson, Administrative Assistant, 936-261-9896, Fax: 936-261-9869, E-mail: bathompson@pvamu.edu.

Quinnipiac University, School of Business, Program in Information Systems Management, Hamden, CT 06518-1940. Offers MS. Part-time and evening/weekend programs available. *Faculty:* 3 full-time (1 woman), 1 part-time/adjunct (0 women). *Students:* 5 full-time (3 women), 21 part-time (5 women); includes 1 African American, 3 Asian Americans or Pacific Islanders, 1 Hispanic American, 2 international. Average age 24. 14 applicants, 93% accepted, 9 enrolled. In 2009, 15 master's awarded. *Entrance requirements:* For master's, minimum GPA of 2.75; course work in computer language programming, management, accounting foundation. Additional exam requirements/recommendations for international students: Required—TOEFL (minimum score 575 paper-based; 233 computer-based; 90 iBT), IELTS (minimum score 6.5). *Application deadline:* For fall admission, 7/30 priority date for domestic students, 4/30 priority date for international students; for spring admission, 12/15 priority date for domestic students, 9/15 priority date for international students. Applications are processed on a rolling basis. Application fee: $45. Electronic applications accepted. *Expenses:* Tuition: Full-time $16,030; part-time $770 per credit. Required fees: $630; $35 per credit. *Financial support:* Tuition waivers (partial) and unspecified assistantships available. Support available to part-time students. Financial award application deadline: 4/15. *Faculty research:* Data management and warehousing, peer-to-peer counseling, decision support systems. *Unit head:* Dr. Bruce White, Director, 203-582-3386, Fax: 203-582-8664, E-mail: bruce.white@quinnipiac.edu. *Application contact:* Jennifer Boutin, Associate Director of Graduate Admissions, 800-462-1944, Fax: 203-582-3443, E-mail: jennifer.boutin@quinnipiac.edu.

Regent's American College London, Webster Graduate School, London, United Kingdom. Offers business (MBA); finance (MS); human resources (MA); information technology management (MA); international business (MA); international non-governmental organizations (MA); international relations (MA); management and leadership (MA); marketing (MA). Part-time programs available.

Regis University, College for Professional Studies, School of Computer and Information Sciences, Denver, CO 80221-1099. Offers database administration with IBM DB2 (Certificate); database administration with Oracle (Certificate); database development (Certificate); database technologies (MA); enterprise Java software development (Certificate); executive information technologies (Certificate); information assurance (MA, Certificate); information technology management (MA); software and information systems (M Sc); software engineering (MA, Certificate); storage area networks (Certificate); systems engineering (MA, Certificate). Offered at Boulder Campus, Northwest Denver Campus, Southeast Denver Campus, Fort Collins

Management Information Systems

Regis University (continued)

Campus, Colorado Springs Campus, and Broomfield Campus. Part-time and evening/weekend programs available. Postbaccalaureate distance learning degree programs offered (no on-campus study). *Degree requirements:* For master's, thesis, final research project. *Entrance requirements:* For master's, 2 years of related experience, resume, interview; for Certificate, 2 years of related experience, resumé. Additional exam requirements/recommendations for international students: Required—TOEFL (minimum score 213 computer-based), TWE (minimum score 5), TOEFL or university-based test. Electronic applications accepted. *Expenses:* Contact institution. *Faculty research:* Secure Virtual Laboratory Architecture, Joint IA project with W2C06 Institute, Information Policy, OLTP and OLAP Technologies, knowledge management, software architectures.

Rivier College, School of Graduate Studies, Department of Computer Information Systems, Nashua, NH 03060. Offers MS. Part-time programs available. *Faculty:* 1 (woman) part-time/adjunct. *Students:* 12 full-time (8 women), 27 part-time (11 women); includes 24 minority (1 African American, 23 Asian Americans or Pacific Islanders), 1 international. Average age 36. 17 applicants, 100% accepted, 10 enrolled. In 2009, 9 master's awarded. Application fee: $25. *Expenses:* Tuition: Part-time $447 per credit. *Financial support:* Application deadline: 2/1. *Unit head:* Dr. Paul Cunningham, Director, 603-897-8272, E-mail: pcunningham@rivier.edu. *Application contact:* Mathew Kittredge, Director of Graduate Admissions, 603-897-8129, Fax: 603-897-8810, E-mail: mkittredge@rivier.edu.

Robert Morris University, Graduate Studies, School of Communications and Information Systems, Moon Township, PA 15108-1189. Offers communication and information systems (MS); competitive intelligence systems (MS); information security and assurance (MS); information systems and communications (D Sc); information systems management (MS); information technology project management (MS); Internet information systems (MS); organizational studies (MS). Part-time and evening/weekend programs available. *Faculty:* 28 full-time (9 women), 9 part-time/adjunct (3 women). *Students:* 257 part-time (76 women); includes 41 minority (31 African Americans, 8 Asian Americans or Pacific Islanders, 2 Hispanic Americans), 16 international. Average age 33. 106 applicants, 100% accepted, 106 enrolled. In 2009, 84 master's, 8 doctorates awarded. *Degree requirements:* For doctorate, thesis/dissertation. *Entrance requirements:* For doctorate, employer letter of endorsement, interview. Additional exam requirements/recommendations for international students: Required—TOEFL (minimum score 550 paper-based; 213 computer-based; 79 iBT). *Application deadline:* For fall admission, 7/1 priority date for domestic and international students; for spring admission, 11/1 priority date for domestic and international students. Applications are processed on a rolling basis. Application fee: $35. Electronic applications accepted. *Expenses:* Contact institution. *Financial support:* Research assistantships with partial tuition reimbursements, institutionally sponsored loans and unspecified assistantships available. Support available to part-time students. Financial award application deadline: 5/1. *Unit head:* Dr. Barbara J. Levine, Dean, 412-397-2591, Fax: 412-397-2481, E-mail: levine@rmu.edu. *Application contact:* Deborah Roach, Assistant Dean, Graduate Admissions, 412-397-5200, Fax: 412-397-2425, E-mail: graduateadmissions@rmu.edu.

Robert Morris University Illinois, Morris Graduate School of Management, Chicago, IL 60605. Offers accounting (MBA); accounting/finance (MBA); human resource management (MBA); information technology (MIS); leadership (MBA); management/finance (MIS); management/human resource management (MBA). Part-time and evening/weekend programs available. *Faculty:* 16 full-time (6 women), 25 part-time/adjunct (9 women). *Students:* 275 full-time (169 women), 194 part-time (134 women); includes 267 minority (176 African Americans, 1 American Indian/Alaska Native, 26 Asian Americans or Pacific Islanders, 64 Hispanic Americans), 17 international. Average age 32. 202 applicants, 84% accepted, 135 enrolled. In 2009, 161 master's awarded. *Degree requirements:* For master's, 44 residency hours. *Entrance requirements:* Additional exam requirements/recommendations for international students: Required—TOEFL (minimum score 500 paper-based; 173 computer-based). *Application deadline:* Applications are processed on a rolling basis. Application fee: $30 ($100 for international students). Electronic applications accepted. *Expenses:* Tuition: Full-time $18,000; part-time $2000 per course. *Financial support:* In 2009–10, 420 students received support. Federal Work-Study, scholarships/grants, and tuition waivers available. Support available to part-time students. *Unit head:* Kayed Akkawi, Dean, 312-935-4244, Fax: 312-935-4248, E-mail: kakkawi@robertmorris.edu. *Application contact:* Courtney A. Kohn Sanders, Dean of Graduate Admissions, 312-935-4240, Fax: 312-935-4248, E-mail: ckohn@robertmorris.edu.

Rochester Institute of Technology, Graduate Enrollment Services, B. Thomas Golisano College of Computing and Information Sciences, Department of Networking, Security and Systems Administration, Program in Security and Information Assurance, Rochester, NY 14623-5603. Offers MS. Part-time and evening/weekend programs available. Postbaccalaureate distance learning degree programs offered (no on-campus study). *Students:* 16 full-time (3 women), 8 part-time (1 woman), 10 international. Average age 28. 49 applicants, 71% accepted, 15 enrolled. In 2009, 5 master's awarded. *Degree requirements:* For master's, thesis. *Entrance requirements:* For master's, GRE, minimum GPA of 3.0. Additional exam requirements/recommendations for international students: Required—TOEFL (minimum score 570 paper-based; 230 computer-based; 88 iBT), or IELTS (minimum score 6.5). *Application deadline:* For fall admission, 8/1 for domestic students, 7/1 for international students; for spring admission, 2/1 for domestic students. Applications are processed on a rolling basis. Application fee: $50. Electronic applications accepted. *Expenses:* Tuition: Full-time $31,533; part-time $876 per credit hour. Required fees: $210. *Financial support:* In 2009–10, 19 students received support; research assistantships with partial tuition reimbursements available, teaching assistantships with partial tuition reimbursements available, career-related internships or fieldwork, scholarships/grants, and unspecified assistantships available. Support available to part-time students. Financial award applicants required to submit FAFSA. *Unit head:* Prof. Dianne Bills, Graduate Coordinator, 585-475-2700, Fax: 585-475-6584, E-mail: informaticsgrad@rit.edu. *Application contact:* Diane Ellison, Assistant Vice President, Graduate Enrollment Services, 585-475-2229, Fax: 585-475-7164, E-mail: gradinfo@rit.edu.

Roosevelt University, Graduate Division, Walter E. Heller College of Business Administration, Program in Information Systems, Chicago, IL 60605. Offers MSIS. Part-time and evening/weekend programs available. *Entrance requirements:* For master's, GMAT.

Rowan University, Graduate School, William G. Rohrer College of Business, Department of Marketing and Business Information Systems, Glassboro, NJ 08028-1701. Offers MBA. Part-time and evening/weekend programs available. *Faculty:* 2 full-time (1 woman), 2 part-time/adjunct (both women). *Students:* 1 (woman) full-time, 4 part-time (2 women). Average age 26. 4 applicants, 50% accepted, 1 enrolled. *Degree requirements:* For master's, comprehensive exam, thesis. *Entrance requirements:* For master's, GRE General Test. Additional exam requirements/recommendations for international students: Required—TOEFL. *Application deadline:* Applications are processed on a rolling basis. Application fee: $50. Electronic applications accepted. *Expenses:* Tuition, state resident: full-time $10,624; part-time $590 per semester hour. Tuition, nonresident: full-time $10,624; part-time $590 per semester hour. Required fees: $2320; $125 per semester hour. *Unit head:* Dr. Mira Lalovic-Hand, Interim Associate Provost/Director of Graduate School, 856-256-5120, E-mail: lalovic-hand@rowan.edu. *Application contact:* Karen Haynes, Graduate Coordinator, 856-256-4052, E-mail: haynes@rowan.edu.

Rutgers, The State University of New Jersey, Newark, Graduate School, Program in Management, Newark, NJ 07102. Offers accounting (PhD); accounting information systems (PhD); computer information systems (PhD); finance (PhD); information technology (PhD); international business (PhD); management science (PhD); marketing (PhD); organization management (PhD). *Accreditation:* AACSB. *Degree requirements:* For doctorate, thesis/dissertation, cumulative exams. *Entrance requirements:* For doctorate, GMAT or GRE General Test, minimum undergraduate B average. Additional exam requirements/recommendations for international students: Required—TOEFL. Electronic applications accepted. *Faculty research:* Technology management, leadership and teams, consumer behavior, financial and markets, logistics.

Rutgers, The State University of New Jersey, Newark, Rutgers Business School–Newark and New Brunswick, Department of Management Science and Information Systems, Newark, NJ 07102. Offers MBA. *Entrance requirements:* For master's, GMAT. Additional exam requirements/recommendations for international students: Required—TOEFL.

Rutgers, The State University of New Jersey, Newark, Rutgers Business School–Newark and New Brunswick, Doctoral Programs in Business, Newark, NJ 07102. Offers accounting (PhD); accounting information systems (PhD); finance (PhD); individualized study (PhD); information technology (PhD); international business (PhD); management science (PhD); organizational management (PhD); supply chain management (PhD).

Sacred Heart University, Graduate Programs, College of Arts and Sciences, Department of Computer Science and Information Technology, Fairfield, CT 06825-1000. Offers computer science (MS); database (CPS); information technology (MS, CPS); information technology and network security (CPS); interactive multimedia (CPS); Web development (CPS). Part-time and evening/weekend programs available. *Faculty:* 7 full-time (4 women). *Students:* 20 full-time (6 women), 79 part-time (25 women); includes 10 minority (2 African Americans, 1 American Indian/Alaska Native, 5 Asian Americans or Pacific Islanders, 2 Hispanic Americans), 30 international. Average age 33. 66 applicants, 97% accepted, 26 enrolled. In 2009, 17 master's awarded. *Degree requirements:* For master's, thesis optional. *Entrance requirements:* Additional exam requirements/recommendations for international students: Required—TOEFL (minimum score 550 paper-based; 213 computer-based). *Application deadline:* Applications are processed on a rolling basis. Application fee: $50 ($100 for international students). Electronic applications accepted. *Expenses:* Tuition: Full-time $24,000; part-time $650 per credit. Required fees: $248. *Financial support:* Career-related internships or fieldwork, institutionally sponsored loans, and unspecified assistantships available. Support available to part-time students. Financial award applicants required to submit FAFSA. *Faculty research:* Contemporary market software. *Unit head:* Domenick Pinto, Academic Director and Chairperson, 203-371-7789, Fax: 203-371-0506, E-mail: pintod@sacredheart.edu. *Application contact:* Dean Alexis Haakonsen, Office of Graduate Admissions, 203-365-7619, Fax: 203-365-4732, E-mail: gradstudies@sacredheart.edu.

St. Edward's University, School of Management and Business, Area of Business Administration, Austin, TX 78704. Offers accounting (MBA); business management (MBA); corporate finance (MBA, Certificate); global entrepreneurship (MBA); human resource management (MBA, Certificate); management information systems (MBA, Certificate); marketing (MBA, Certificate); operations management (MBA, Certificate). Part-time and evening/weekend programs available. *Faculty:* 20 full-time (9 women), 13 part-time/adjunct (4 women). *Students:* 29 full-time (16 women), 307 part-time (152 women); includes 116 minority (27 African Americans, 1 American Indian/Alaska Native, 16 Asian Americans or Pacific Islanders, 72 Hispanic Americans), 9 international. Average age 33. 129 applicants, 75% accepted, 74 enrolled. In 2009, 108 master's awarded. *Degree requirements:* For master's, minimum of 24 resident hours. *Entrance requirements:* For master's, GMAT or GRE General Test, minimum GPA of 2.75 in last 60 hours of course work. Additional exam requirements/recommendations for international students: Required—TOEFL (minimum score 550 paper-based; 213 computer-based; 79 iBT) or IELTS (minimum score 6). *Application deadline:* For fall admission, 7/1 for domestic and international students; for spring admission, 11/1 for domestic and international students. Applications are processed on a rolling basis. Application fee: $45 ($50 for international students). Electronic applications accepted. *Expenses:* Tuition: Full-time $14,922; part-time $829 per credit hour. Required fees: $50 per trimester. Full-time tuition and fees vary according to course load and program. *Financial support:* In 2009–10, 14 students received support. Scholarships/grants available. *Faculty research:* Operations management, minority entrepreneurship, globalization, professional services marketing. *Unit head:* Dr. Dianne Hill, Director, 512-428-1295, Fax: 512-448-8492, E-mail: dianneh@stedwards.edu. *Application contact:* Kelly Luna, Graduate Admissions Coordinator, 512-233-1697, Fax: 512-428-1032, E-mail: kellyl@stedwards.edu.

St. Edward's University, School of Management and Business, Program in Computer Information Systems, Austin, TX 78704. Offers MS. Part-time and evening/weekend programs available. *Students:* 2 full-time (1 woman), 30 part-time (5 women); includes 10 minority (3 African Americans, 2 Asian Americans or Pacific Islanders, 5 Hispanic Americans), 2 international. Average age 38. 13 applicants, 62% accepted, 6 enrolled. In 2009, 11 master's awarded. *Degree requirements:* For master's, minimum of 24 resident hours. *Entrance requirements:* For master's, GMAT or GRE General Test, minimum GPA of 2.75 in last 60 hours of course work. Additional exam requirements/recommendations for international students: Required—TOEFL (minimum score 550 paper-based; 213 computer-based; 79 iBT) or IELTS (minimum score 6). *Application deadline:* For fall admission, 7/1 for domestic and international students; for spring admission, 11/1 for domestic and international students. Applications are processed on a rolling basis. Application fee: $45 ($50 for international students). Electronic applications accepted. *Expenses:* Tuition: Full-time $14,922; part-time $829 per credit hour. Required fees: $50 per trimester. Full-time tuition and fees vary according to course load and program. *Financial support:* In 2009–10, 1 student received support. Scholarships/grants available. *Faculty research:* System design. *Unit head:* Dwight D. Daniel, Director, 512-448-8460, Fax: 512-428-8492, E-mail: dwightd@stedwards.edu. *Application contact:* Kelly Luna, Graduate Admissions Coordinator, 512-233-1697, Fax: 512-428-1032, E-mail: kellyl@stedwards.edu.

St. John's University, The Peter J. Tobin College of Business, Department of Computer Information Systems and Decision Sciences, Queens, NY 11439. Offers MBA, Adv C. Part-time and evening/weekend programs available. *Students:* 9 full-time (4 women), 2 part-time (0 women); includes 2 minority (both Asian Americans or Pacific Islanders), 6 international. Average age 26. 8 applicants, 75% accepted, 3 enrolled. In 2009, 5 master's awarded. *Degree requirements:* For master's, comprehensive exam (for some programs), thesis optional. *Entrance requirements:* For master's, GMAT, 2 letters of recommendation, resume; for Adv C, GMAT, 2 letters of recommendation, resume, undergraduate transcripts, essay. Additional exam requirements/recommendations for international students: Required—TOEFL (minimum score 500 paper-based; 173 computer-based; 61 iBT), IELTS (minimum score 5.5). *Application deadline:* For fall admission, 5/1 priority date for domestic and international students; for spring admission, 11/1 priority date for domestic and international students. Applications are processed on a rolling basis. Application fee: $70. Electronic applications accepted. *Expenses:* Contact institution. *Financial support:* Research assistantships, scholarships/grants available. Support available to part-time students. Financial award application deadline: 3/1; financial award applicants required to submit FAFSA. *Unit head:* Dr. Victor Lu, Chair, 718-990-6392, Fax: 718-990-1868, E-mail: luf@stjohns.edu. *Application contact:* Nicole T. Bryan, Assistant Dean, 718-990-2599, Fax: 718-990-5242, E-mail: tcbgradadmissions@stjohns.edu.

Saint Peter's College, Graduate Business Programs, MBA Program, Jersey City, NJ 07306-5997. Offers finance (MBA); health care administration (MBA); international business (MBA); management (MBA); management information systems (MBA); marketing (MBA); MBA/MS. Part-time and evening/weekend programs available. *Entrance requirements:* Additional exam requirements/recommendations for international students: Required—TOEFL. *Application deadline:* Applications are processed on a rolling basis. Electronic applications accepted. *Expenses:* Tuition: Part-time $971 per credit. *Financial support:* Career-related internships or fieldwork, Federal Work-Study, and institutionally sponsored loans available. *Faculty research:* Finance, health care management, human resource management, international business, management, management information systems, marketing, risk management.

San Diego State University, Graduate and Research Affairs, College of Business Administration, Department of Information and Decision Systems, San Diego, CA 92182. Offers information and decision systems (MS); production and operations management (MS). Evening/weekend programs available. *Degree requirements:* For master's, thesis or alternative. *Entrance requirements:* For master's, GMAT, resume, letters of reference. Additional exam requirements/recommendations for international students: Required—TOEFL. Electronic applications accepted.

San Jose State University, Graduate Studies and Research, Lucas Graduate School of Business, Programs in Business Administration, San Jose, CA 95192-0001. Offers MBA. *Accreditation:* AACSB. *Degree requirements:* For master's, comprehensive exam, thesis or alternative. *Entrance requirements:* For master's, GMAT, minimum GPA of 3.0. *Application deadline:* For fall admission, 6/29 for domestic students; for spring admission, 11/30 for domestic students. Applications are processed on a rolling basis. Application fee: $59. Electronic applications accepted. *Financial support:* Applicants required to submit FAFSA.

Santa Clara University, Leavey School of Business, Program in Information Systems, Santa Clara, CA 95053. Offers MS. Part-time and evening/weekend programs available. *Students:* 32 full-time (10 women), 42 part-time (14 women); includes 15 minority (13 Asian Americans or Pacific Islanders, 2 Hispanic Americans), 38 international. Average age 28. In 2009, 5 master's awarded. *Degree requirements:* For master's, thesis or alternative. *Entrance requirements:* For master's, GMAT, GRE. Additional exam requirements/recommendations for international students: Required—TOEFL (minimum score 600 paper-based; 250 computer-based; 100 iBT). *Application deadline:* For fall admission, 6/1 for domestic and international students; for spring admission, 1/19 for domestic and international students. Applications are processed on a rolling basis. Application fee: $75 ($100 for international students). Electronic applications accepted. *Expenses:* Contact institution. *Financial support:* Fellowships with partial tuition reimbursements, research assistantships with partial tuition reimbursements, career-related internships or fieldwork, Federal Work-Study, institutionally sponsored loans, scholarships/grants, health care benefits, and unspecified assistantships available. Support available to part-time students. Financial award applicants required to submit FAFSA. *Unit head:* Elizabeth B. Ford, Senior Assistant Dean, 408-554-2752, Fax: 408-554-4571, E-mail: eford@scu.edu. *Application contact:* Jennifer W. Taylor, Senior Director, 408-554-4539, Fax: 408-554-4571, E-mail: mbaadmissions@scu.edu.

Schiller International University, Graduate Programs, London, Program in International Business, London, United Kingdom. Offers international business (MBA); management of information technology (MBA). Part-time programs available. Postbaccalaureate distance learning degree programs offered (no on-campus study). *Degree requirements:* For master's, thesis optional, GMAT before graduation. *Entrance requirements:* Additional exam requirements/recommendations for international students: Required—TOEFL (minimum score 550 paper-based; 213 computer-based).

Schiller International University, MBA Programs, Florida, Program in Information Technology, Largo, FL 33770. Offers MBA. *Entrance requirements:* Additional exam requirements/recommendations for international students: Required—TOEFL.

Schiller International University, MBA Programs, Heidelberg, Germany, Heidelberg, Germany. Offers international business (MBA, MIM); management of information technology (MBA). Part-time and evening/weekend programs available. *Degree requirements:* For master's, thesis optional. *Entrance requirements:* Additional exam requirements/recommendations for international students: Required—TOEFL (minimum score 550 paper-based; 213 computer-based). *Faculty research:* Leadership, international economy, foreign direct investment.

Seattle Pacific University, Master's Degree in Information Systems Management (MS-ISM) Program, Seattle, WA 98119-1997. Offers MS. Part-time programs available. *Faculty:* 1 full-time (0 women), 1 part-time/adjunct (0 women). *Students:* 1 full-time (0 women), 19 part-time (6 women); includes 5 minority (2 African Americans, 2 Asian Americans or Pacific Islanders, 1 Hispanic American), 2 international. Average age 30. 9 applicants, 89% accepted, 8 enrolled. In 2009, 5 master's awarded. *Entrance requirements:* For master's, GMAT, minimum GPA of 3.0. Additional exam requirements/recommendations for international students: Required—TOEFL (minimum score 225 computer-based). *Application deadline:* For fall admission, 8/1 for domestic and international students; for winter admission, 11/1 for domestic and international students; for spring admission, 2/1 for domestic and international students. Applications are processed on a rolling basis. Application fee: $50. Electronic applications accepted. *Expenses:* Tuition: Part-time $485 per credit. Part-time tuition and fees vary according to course level, degree level and program. *Financial support:* In 2009–10, 4 students received support. Applicants required to submit FAFSA. *Unit head:* Gary Karns, Graduate Director, 206-281-2948, Fax: 206-281-2733. *Application contact:* The Grad Center, 206-281-2091.

Southeastern Oklahoma State University, School of Arts and Sciences, Durant, OK 74701-0609. Offers biology (MT); computer information systems (MT). Part-time and evening/weekend programs available. *Faculty:* 12 full-time (4 women), 1 part-time/adjunct (0 women). *Students:* 10 full-time (5 women), 7 part-time (1 woman); includes 5 minority (4 American Indian/Alaska Native, 1 Hispanic American). Average age 28. 1 applicant, 100% accepted, 1 enrolled. *Degree requirements:* For master's, thesis optional. *Entrance requirements:* For master's, minimum GPA of 3.0 in last 60 hours or 2.75 overall. Additional exam requirements/recommendations for international students: Required—TOEFL (minimum score 550 paper-based; 213 computer-based). *Application deadline:* For fall admission, 8/1 for domestic students, 6/1 for international students; for spring admission, 1/5 for domestic students, 11/1 for international students. Application fee: $20 ($55 for international students). Electronic applications accepted. *Financial support:* In 2009–10, 8 students received support; fellowships, research assistantships, teaching assistantships, Federal Work-Study and institutionally sponsored loans available. Support available to part-time students. Financial award application deadline: 6/15; financial award applicants required to submit FAFSA. *Unit head:* Dr. Teresa Golden, Graduate Coordinator, 580-745-2286, E-mail: tgolden@se.edu. *Application contact:* Carrie Williamson, Graduate Secretary, 580-745-2200, Fax: 580-745-7474, E-mail: cwilliamson@se.edu.

Southern Illinois University Edwardsville, Graduate Studies and Research, School of Business, Department of Computer Management and Information Systems, Edwardsville, IL 62026-0001. Offers MS. Part-time and evening/weekend programs available. *Faculty:* 9 full-time (5 women). *Students:* 7 full-time (2 women), 15 part-time (3 women); includes 2 minority (both African Americans), 6 international. Average age 26. 29 applicants, 28% accepted. In 2009, 9 master's awarded. *Degree requirements:* For master's, thesis or alternative, final exam. *Entrance requirements:* For master's, GMAT. Additional exam requirements/recommendations for international students: Required—TOEFL (minimum score 550 paper-based; 213 computer-based; 79 iBT), IELTS (minimum score 6.5). *Application deadline:* For fall admission, 7/23 for domestic students, 6/1 for international students; for spring admission, 12/11 for domestic students, 10/1 for international students. Applications are processed on a rolling basis. Application fee: $30. Electronic applications accepted. *Expenses:* Tuition, state resident: part-time $1252.50 per semester. Tuition, nonresident: part-time $3131.25 per semester. Required fees: $586.85 per semester. Tuition and fees vary according to course load. *Financial support:* In 2009–10, 6 teaching assistantships with full tuition reimbursements (averaging $8,064 per year) were awarded; fellowships, research assistantships, career-related internships or fieldwork, Federal Work-Study, institutionally sponsored loans, scholarships/grants, traineeships, and unspecified assistantships also available. Support available to part-time students. Financial award application deadline: 3/1; financial award applicants required to submit FAFSA. *Unit head:* Dr. Douglas Bock, Chair, 618-650-2504, E-mail: dbock@siue.edu. *Application contact:* Dr. Jo Ellen Moore, Director, 618-650-5816, E-mail: joemoor@siue.edu.

Southern Illinois University Edwardsville, Graduate Studies and Research, School of Business, Program in Business Administration, Specialization in Management Information Systems, Edwardsville, IL 62026-0001. Offers MBA. Part-time programs available. *Students:* 13 part-time (4 women); includes 1 minority (African American). Average age 26. In 2009, 6 master's awarded. *Degree requirements:* For master's, thesis or alternative, final exam. *Entrance requirements:* For master's, GMAT. Additional exam requirements/recommendations for international students: Required—TOEFL (minimum score 550 paper-based; 213 computer-based; 79 iBT), IELTS (minimum score 6.5). *Application deadline:* For fall admission, 7/23 for domestic students, 6/1 for international students; for spring admission, 12/11 for domestic students, 10/1 for international students. Applications are processed on a rolling basis. Application fee: $30. Electronic applications accepted. *Expenses:* Tuition, state resident: part-time $1252.50 per semester. Tuition, nonresident: part-time $3131.25 per semester. Required fees: $586.85 per semester. Tuition and fees vary according to course load. *Financial support:* Fellowships with full tuition reimbursements, research assistantships with full tuition reimbursements, teaching assistantships with full tuition reimbursements, career-related internships or fieldwork, Federal Work-Study, institutionally sponsored loans, scholarships/grants, traineeships, and unspecified assistantships available. Support available to part-time students. Financial award application deadline: 3/1; financial award applicants required to submit FAFSA. *Unit head:* Dr. Janice Joplin, Director, 618-650-3412, E-mail: jjoplin@siue.edu. *Application contact:* Dr. Janice Joplin, Director, 618-650-3412, E-mail: jjoplin@siue.edu.

Southern Methodist University, Cox School of Business, MBA Program, Dallas, TX 75275. Offers accounting (MBA); finance (MBA); information technology and operations management (MBA); management (MBA); marketing (MBA); strategy and entrepreneurship (MBA). *Students:* 396 full-time (91 women), 401 part-time (109 women); includes 185 minority (34 African Americans, 5 American Indian/Alaska Native, 102 Asian Americans or Pacific Islanders, 44 Hispanic Americans), 76 international. Average age 31. In 2009, 363 master's awarded. *Unit head:* Dr. Albert W. Niemi, Dean, 214-768-3012, Fax: 214-768-3713, E-mail: aniemi@mail.cox.smu.edu. *Application contact:* Path Cudney, Director of MBA Admissions, 214-768-3001, Fax: 214-768-3956, E-mail: pcudney@mail.cox.smu.edu.

Southern New Hampshire University, School of Business, Manchester, NH 03106-1045. Offers accounting (MS); business administration (MBA, Certificate), including accounting (Certificate), business administration (MBA), finance (Certificate), forensic accounting (Certificate), human resources management (Certificate), international business (Certificate), international sport management (Certificate), leadership of not for profit organizations (Certificate), marketing (Certificate), operations management (Certificate), sport management (Certificate), taxation (Certificate); finance (MS); hospitality and tourism leadership (Certificate); information technology (MS, Certificate); information technology/international business (Certificate); integrated marketing communications (Certificate); international business (MS, DBA); marketing (MS); operations and project management (MS); organizational leadership (MS); project management (Certificate); sport management (MS); MBA/Certificate. *Accreditation:* ACBSP. Part-time and evening/weekend programs available. Postbaccalaureate distance learning degree programs offered (no on-campus study). Terminal master's awarded for partial completion of doctoral program. *Degree requirements:* For master's, one foreign language, comprehensive exam (for some programs), thesis or alternative; for doctorate, one foreign language, comprehensive exam, thesis/dissertation. *Entrance requirements:* For master's, minimum GPA of 2.5; for doctorate, GMAT. Additional exam requirements/recommendations for international students: Required—TOEFL (minimum score 500 paper-based). Electronic applications accepted.

State University of New York College at Potsdam, School of Education and Professional Studies, Program in Information and Communication Technology, Potsdam, NY 13676. Offers educational technology specialist (MS Ed); human performance technology (MS Ed); information technology (MS Ed); organizational leadership (MS Ed); technology educator (MS Ed). Part-time and evening/weekend programs available. Postbaccalaureate distance learning degree programs offered. *Faculty:* 4 full-time (1 woman), 2 part-time/adjunct (1 woman). *Students:* 22 full-time (12 women), 28 part-time (17 women); includes 4 minority (3 African Americans, 1 Asian American or Pacific Islander), 7 international. 28 applicants, 100% accepted, 20 enrolled. In 2009, 21 master's awarded. *Degree requirements:* For master's, thesis optional, culminating experience. *Entrance requirements:* For master's, minimum GPA of 2.75 in last 60 hours of course work. Additional exam requirements/recommendations for international students: Required—TOEFL (minimum score 550 paper-based; 213 computer-based; 80 iBT), IELTS (minimum score 6). *Application deadline:* For fall admission, 4/1 priority date for domestic and international students; for spring admission, 10/15 priority date for domestic and international students. Applications are processed on a rolling basis. Application fee: $50. *Expenses:* Tuition, state resident: full-time $8370; part-time $349 per credit hour. Tuition, nonresident: full-time $13,250; part-time $552 per credit hour. Required fees: $942; $38.70 per credit hour. *Financial support:* In 2009–10, 1 student received support; fellowships, teaching assistantships, career-related internships or fieldwork, Federal Work-Study, scholarships/grants, and unspecified assistantships available. Support available to part-time students. Financial award application deadline: 3/1; financial award applicants required to submit FAFSA. *Unit head:* Dr. Anthony Betrus, Chairperson, 315-267-2535, Fax: 315-267-4802, E-mail: betrusak@potsdam.edu. *Application contact:* Peter Cutler, Graduate Admissions Counselor, 315-267-3154, Fax: 315-267-4802, E-mail: cutlerpj@potsdam.edu.

Stevens Institute of Technology, Graduate School, Wesley J. Howe School of Technology Management, Doctoral Program in Technology Management, Hoboken, NJ 07030. Offers information management (PhD); technology management (PhD); telecommunications management (PhD). Part-time and evening/weekend programs available. Postbaccalaureate distance learning degree programs offered (minimal on-campus study). *Entrance requirements:* Additional exam requirements/recommendations for international students: Required—TOEFL. Electronic applications accepted. *Expenses:* Tuition: Full-time $9900; part-time $1100 per credit. Required fees: $286 per semester.

Stevens Institute of Technology, Graduate School, Wesley J. Howe School of Technology Management, Program in Business Administration, Hoboken, NJ 07030. Offers engineering management (MBA); financial engineering (MBA); information management (MBA); information technology in financial services (MBA); information technology in the pharmaceutical industry (MBA); information technology outsourcing (MBA); pharmaceutical management (MBA); project management (MBA); technology management (MBA); telecommunications management (MBA). *Expenses:* Tuition: Full-time $9900; part-time $1100 per credit. Required fees: $286 per semester.

Stevens Institute of Technology, Graduate School, Wesley J. Howe School of Technology Management, Program in Information Systems, Hoboken, NJ 07030. Offers computer science (MS); e-commerce (MS); enterprise systems (MS); entrepreneurial information technology (MS); information architecture (MS); information management (MS, Certificate); information security (MS); information technology in financial services industry (MS); information technology in the pharmaceutical industry (MS); information technology outsourcing management (MS); project management (MS, Certificate); software engineering (MS); telecommunications (MS). *Degree requirements:* For master's, thesis optional. *Entrance requirements:* For master's, GMAT, GRE General Test. Additional exam requirements/recommendations for international students: Required—TOEFL. Electronic applications accepted. *Expenses:* Tuition: Full-time $9900; part-time $1100 per credit. Required fees: $286 per semester.

Stevens Institute of Technology, Graduate School, Wesley J. Howe School of Technology Management, Program in Management, Hoboken, NJ 07030. Offers general management (MS); global innovation management (MS); human resource management (MS); information management (MS); project management (MS); technology commercialization (MS); technology management (MS). Part-time programs available. *Degree requirements:* For master's, thesis optional. *Entrance requirements:* For master's, GMAT, GRE General Test. Additional exam requirements/recommendations for international students: Required—TOEFL. Electronic applications accepted. *Expenses:* Tuition: Full-time $9900; part-time $1100 per credit. Required fees: $286 per semester. *Faculty research:* Industrial economics.

Stony Brook University, State University of New York, Graduate School, College of Business, Program in Business Administration, Stony Brook, NY 11794. Offers finance (MBA, Certificate); health care management (MBA, Certificate); human resource management (Certificate); human resources (MBA); information systems management (MBA, Certificate); management (MBA); marketing (MBA). *Faculty:* 17 full-time (2 women), 25 part-time/adjunct (5 women). *Students:* 134 full-time (64 women), 112 part-time (44 women); includes 54 minority (8 African Americans, 1 American Indian/Alaska Native, 35 Asian Americans or Pacific Islanders, 10 Hispanic Americans), 56 international. 222 applicants, 55% accepted. In 2009, 134 master's, 5 other advanced degrees awarded. Application fee: $60. *Expenses:* Tuition, state resident: full-time $8370; part-time $349 per credit. Tuition, nonresident: full-time $13,250; part-time $552 per credit. Required fees: $933. *Financial support:* In 2009–10, 2 teaching assistantships were

Management Information Systems

Stony Brook University, State University of New York (continued)
awarded. *Unit head:* Joseph McDonnell, Interim Dean, 631-632-7180. *Application contact:* Dr. Aristotle Lekacos, Director, Graduate Program, 631-632-7171, E-mail: aristotle.lekacost@notes.cc.sunysb.edu.

Stony Brook University, State University of New York, Graduate School, College of Engineering and Applied Sciences, Department of Computer Science, Stony Brook, NY 11794. Offers computer science (MS, PhD); information systems (Certificate); information systems engineering (MS); software engineering (Certificate). *Faculty:* 34 full-time (6 women), 1 part-time/adjunct (0 women). *Students:* 239 full-time (61 women), 33 part-time (9 women); includes 16 minority (1 African American, 14 Asian Americans or Pacific Islanders, 1 Hispanic American), 221 international. Average age 25. 1,139 applicants, 25% accepted. In 2009, 84 master's, 20 doctorates awarded. *Degree requirements:* For master's, thesis or alternative; for doctorate, comprehensive exam, thesis/dissertation. *Entrance requirements:* For master's and doctorate, GRE General Test. Additional exam requirements/recommendations for international students: Required—TOEFL. *Application deadline:* For fall admission, 1/15 for domestic students. Application fee: $60. *Expenses:* Tuition, state resident: full-time $8370; part-time $349 per credit. Tuition, nonresident: full-time $13,250; part-time $552 per credit. Required fees: $933. *Financial support:* In 2009–10, 81 research assistantships, 30 teaching assistantships were awarded; fellowships also available. *Faculty research:* Artificial intelligence, computer architecture, database management systems, VLSI, operating systems. Total annual research expenditures: $5.1 million. *Unit head:* Prof. Arie Kauffman, Chairman, 631-632-8428. *Application contact:* Graduate Director, 631-632-8462, Fax: 631-632-8334.

Stony Brook University, State University of New York, School of Professional Development, Stony Brook, NY 11794. Offers biology-grade 7-12 (MAT); chemistry-grade 7-12 (MAT); coaching (Graduate Certificate); computer integrated engineering (Graduate Certificate); earth science-grade 7-12 (MAT); educational computing (Graduate Certificate); educational leadership (Advanced Certificate); English-grade 7-12 (MAT); environmental management (Graduate Certificate); environmental/occupational health and safety (Graduate Certificate); French-grade 7-12 (MAT); German-grade 7-12 (MAT); human resource management (Graduate Certificate); information systems management (Graduate Certificate); Italian-grade 7-12 (MAT); liberal studies (MA); mathematics-grade 7-12 (MAT); operation research (Graduate Certificate); physics-grade 7-12 (MAT); school administration and supervision (Graduate Certificate); school building leadership (Graduate Certificate); school district administration (Graduate Certificate); school district business leadership (Advanced Certificate); school district leadership (Graduate Certificate); social science and the professions (MPS), including environmental waste management, human resource management; social studies-grade 7-12 (MAT); Spanish-grade 7-12 (MAT); waste management (Graduate Certificate). Part-time and evening/weekend programs available. Postbaccalaureate distance learning degree programs offered. *Faculty:* 5 full-time (3 women), 131 part-time/adjunct (53 women). *Students:* 317 full-time (187 women), 1,200 part-time (773 women); includes 187 minority (77 African Americans, 2 American Indian/Alaska Native, 22 Asian Americans or Pacific Islanders, 86 Hispanic Americans), 11 international. Average age 28. In 2009, 597 master's, 234 other advanced degrees awarded. *Degree requirements:* For master's, one foreign language, thesis or alternative. *Application deadline:* Applications are processed on a rolling basis. Application fee: $62. *Expenses:* Tuition, state resident: full-time $8370; part-time $349 per credit. Tuition, nonresident: full-time $13,250; part-time $552 per credit. Required fees: $933. *Financial support:* Fellowships, research assistantships, teaching assistantships, career-related internships or fieldwork available. Support available to part-time students. *Unit head:* Dr. Paul J. Edelson, Dean, 631-632-7052, Fax: 631-632-9046, E-mail: paul.edelson@stonybrook.edu. *Application contact:* Dr. Paul J. Edelson, Dean, 631-632-7052, Fax: 631-632-9046, E-mail: paul.edelson@stonybrook.edu.

Stratford University, School of Graduate Studies, Falls Church, VA 22043. Offers accounting (MS); business administration (IMBA, MBA); enterprise business management (MS); entrepreneurial management (MS); information assurance (MS); information systems (MS); software engineering (MS); telecommunications (MS). Part-time and evening/weekend programs available. Postbaccalaureate distance learning degree programs offered (no on-campus study). *Faculty:* 35 full-time (15 women), 115 part-time/adjunct (25 women). *Students:* 944 full-time (430 women), 15 part-time (5 women). Average age 26. 950 applicants, 45% accepted, 415 enrolled. In 2009, 412 master's awarded. *Degree requirements:* For master's, comprehensive exam, capstone project. *Entrance requirements:* For master's, baccalaureate degree. Additional exam requirements/recommendations for international students: Required—TOEFL (minimum score 500 paper-based; 173 computer-based; 61 iBT). *Application deadline:* Applications are processed on a rolling basis. Application fee: $50. Electronic applications accepted. *Expenses:* Tuition: Full-time $10,530; part-time $390 per credit. Tuition and fees vary according to course load. *Financial support:* Federal Work-Study available. Financial award applicants required to submit FAFSA. *Unit head:* Dr. Habib Khan, Chief Academic Officer, 703-821-8570 Ext. 3305, Fax: 703-734-5335, E-mail: hkhan@stratford.edu. *Application contact:* James Ray, Director of Admissions, 703-821-8570 Ext. 3021, Fax: 703-734-5339, E-mail: jray@stratford.edu.

Strayer University, Graduate Studies, Washington, DC 20005-2603. Offers accounting (MS); acquisition (MBA); business administration (MBA); communications technology (MS); educational management (M Ed); finance (MBA); health services administration (MHSA); hospitality and tourism management (MBA); human resource management (MBA); information systems (MS), including computer security management, decision support system management, enterprise resource management, network management, software engineering management, systems development management; management (MBA); management information systems (MS); marketing (MBA); professional accounting (MS), including accounting information systems, controllership, taxation; public administration (MPA); supply chain management (MBA); technology in education (M Ed). Programs also offered at campus locations in Birmingham, AL; Chamblee, GA; Cobb County, GA; Morrow, GA; White Marsh, MD; Charleston, SC; Columbia, SC; Greensboro, NC; Greenville, SC; Lexington, KY; Louisville, KY; Nashville, TN; North Raleigh, NC; Washington, DC. Part-time and evening/weekend programs available. Postbaccalaureate distance learning degree programs offered (minimal on-campus study). *Degree requirements:* For master's, thesis. *Entrance requirements:* For master's, GMAT, GRE General Test, bachelor's degree from an accredited college or university, minimum undergraduate GPA of 2.75. Electronic applications accepted.

Sullivan University, School of Business, Louisville, KY 40205. Offers business administration (MBA); collaborative leadership (MSCL); conflict management (MSCM); dispute resolution (MSDR); executive business administration (EMBA); human resource leadership (MSHRL); information technology (MSMIT); management and information technology (MBIT); pharmacy (Pharm D). Part-time programs available. Postbaccalaureate distance learning degree programs offered (no on-campus study). *Entrance requirements:* Additional exam requirements/recommendations for international students: Required—TOEFL.

Syracuse University, Martin J. Whitman School of Management, PhD Program in Business Administration, Syracuse, NY 13244. Offers accounting (PhD); finance (PhD); management information systems (PhD); managerial statistics (PhD); marketing (PhD); operations management (PhD); organizational behavior (PhD); strategy and human resources (PhD); supply chain management (PhD). *Degree requirements:* For doctorate, comprehensive exam, thesis/dissertation, summer research paper. *Entrance requirements:* For doctorate, GMAT or GRE General Test, 3 recommendations. Additional exam requirements/recommendations for international students: Required—TOEFL (minimum score 600 paper-based; 250 computer-based; 100 iBT). Electronic applications accepted. *Expenses:* Tuition: Full-time $26,808; part-time $1117 per credit. Required fees: $1024. *Faculty research:* Marketing models, market microstructure, supply chain, auditing, corporate governance.

Syracuse University, School of Information Studies, Program in Information Management, Syracuse, NY 13244. Offers MS, DPS. Part-time and evening/weekend programs available. Postbaccalaureate distance learning degree programs offered (minimal on-campus study). *Students:* 166 full-time (58 women), 125 part-time (31 women); includes 43 minority (15 African Americans, 4 American Indian/Alaska Native, 15 Asian Americans or Pacific Islanders, 9 Hispanic Americans), 137 international. Average age 30. 534 applicants, 51% accepted, 108 enrolled. In 2009, 98 master's awarded. *Entrance requirements:* For master's, GRE General Test. Additional exam requirements/recommendations for international students: Required—TOEFL (minimum score 100 iBT). *Application deadline:* For fall admission, 2/14 priority date for domestic and international students; for spring admission, 10/15 priority date for domestic and international students. Applications are processed on a rolling basis. Application fee: $75. Electronic applications accepted. *Expenses:* Tuition: Full-time $26,808; part-time $1117 per credit. Required fees: $1024. *Financial support:* Fellowships with tuition reimbursements, research assistantships with tuition reimbursements, teaching assistantships with tuition reimbursements, scholarships/grants and tuition waivers (partial) available. Financial award application deadline: 1/1; financial award applicants required to submit FAFSA. *Unit head:* David Dischiave, Director, 315-443-4681, Fax: 315-443-6886, E-mail: ddischia@syr.edu. *Application contact:* Susan Corieri, Director of Enrollment Management, 315-443-2575, E-mail: ist@syr.edu.

See Close-Up on page 1723.

Syracuse University, School of Information Studies, Program in Information Security Management, Syracuse, NY 13244. Offers CAS. Part-time and evening/weekend programs available. Postbaccalaureate distance learning degree programs offered. *Students:* 1 full-time (0 women), 15 part-time (3 women); includes 5 minority (2 African Americans, 1 Asian American or Pacific Islander, 2 Hispanic Americans). Average age 38. 49 applicants, 86% accepted, 7 enrolled. In 2009, 15 CASs awarded. *Entrance requirements:* Additional exam requirements/recommendations for international students: Required—TOEFL (minimum score 100 iBT). *Application deadline:* For fall admission, 2/1 priority date for domestic and international students; for spring admission, 10/15 priority date for domestic and international students. Applications are processed on a rolling basis. Application fee: $75. Electronic applications accepted. *Expenses:* Tuition: Full-time $26,808; part-time $1117 per credit. Required fees: $1024. *Financial support:* Application deadline: 1/1. *Unit head:* Dave Dischiave, Head, 315-443-4681, E-mail: ddischia@syr.edu. *Application contact:* Susan Corieri, Director of Enrollment Management, 315-443-2575, E-mail: ist@syr.edu.

Syracuse University, School of Information Studies, Program in Information Systems and Telecommunications Management, Syracuse, NY 13244. Offers CAS. Part-time and evening/weekend programs available. Postbaccalaureate distance learning degree programs offered. *Students:* 1 full-time (0 women), 7 part-time (3 women); includes 3 minority (2 African Americans, 1 Hispanic American). Average age 36. 15 applicants, 80% accepted, 3 enrolled. In 2009, 5 CASs awarded. *Entrance requirements:* Additional exam requirements/recommendations for international students: Required—TOEFL (minimum score 100 iBT). *Application deadline:* For fall admission, 2/1 priority date for domestic and international students; for spring admission, 10/15 priority date for domestic and international students. Applications are processed on a rolling basis. Application fee: $75. Electronic applications accepted. *Expenses:* Tuition: Full-time $26,808; part-time $1117 per credit. Required fees: $1024. *Financial support:* Application deadline: 1/1. *Unit head:* David Dischiave, Director, 315-443-4681, Fax: 315-443-6886, E-mail: ddischia@syr.edu. *Application contact:* Susan Corieri, Director of Enrollment Management, 315-443-2575, E-mail: ist@syr.edu.

See Close-Up on page 1723.

Tarleton State University, College of Graduate Studies, College of Business Administration, Department of Computer Information Systems, Stephenville, TX 76402. Offers information systems (MS). Part-time and evening/weekend programs available. *Degree requirements:* For master's, comprehensive exam. *Entrance requirements:* For master's, GRE, minimum GPA of 3.0. Additional exam requirements/recommendations for international students: Required—TOEFL (minimum score 550 paper-based; 213 computer-based; 80 iBT). Electronic applications accepted.

Temple University, Graduate School, Fox School of Business, Doctoral Programs in Business, Philadelphia, PA 19122-6096. Offers accounting (PhD); entrepreneurship (PhD); finance (PhD); human resource administration (PhD); international business (PhD); management information systems (PhD); marketing (PhD); risk management and insurance (PhD); statistics (PhD); strategic management (PhD); tourism and sport (PhD). *Accreditation:* AACSB. *Degree requirements:* For doctorate, thesis/dissertation. *Entrance requirements:* For doctorate, GRE General Test, GMAT, minimum GPA of 3.0, master's degree. Additional exam requirements/recommendations for international students: Required—TOEFL (minimum score 600 paper-based; 250 computer-based; 100 iBT), IELTS (minimum score 7.5). Electronic applications accepted.

Temple University, Graduate School, Fox School of Business, Specialized Master's Programs, Philadelphia, PA 19122-6096. Offers accounting and financial management (MS); actuarial science (MS); finance (MS); financial engineering (MS); healthcare financial management (MS); healthcare management (MHM); human resource management (MS); management information systems (MS); marketing (MS); statistics (MS). *Accreditation:* AACSB. Part-time programs available. *Entrance requirements:* For master's, GRE General Test or GMAT, minimum undergraduate GPA of 3.0. Additional exam requirements/recommendations for international students: Required—TOEFL (minimum score 600 paper-based; 250 computer-based; 100 iBT), IELTS (minimum score 7.5).

Tennessee Technological University, Graduate School, College of Business, Cookeville, TN 38505. Offers accounting (MBA); finance (MBA); human resource management (MBA); international business (MBA); management information systems (MBA); risk management & insurance (MBA). *Accreditation:* AACSB. Part-time and evening/weekend programs available. *Faculty:* 28 full-time (5 women). *Students:* 64 full-time (26 women), 163 part-time (70 women); includes 17 minority (6 African Americans, 8 Asian Americans or Pacific Islanders, 3 Hispanic Americans). Average age 25. 203 applicants, 52% accepted, 75 enrolled. In 2009, 105 master's awarded. *Entrance requirements:* For master's, GMAT. Additional exam requirements/recommendations for international students: Required—TOEFL (minimum score 550 paper-based; 79 iBT), IELTS (minimum score 5.5). *Application deadline:* For fall admission, 8/1 for domestic and international students; for spring admission, 12/1 for domestic students, 10/1 for international students. Application fee: $25 ($30 for international students). Electronic applications accepted. *Expenses:* Tuition, state resident: full-time $7034; part-time $368 per credit hour. *Financial support:* In 2009–10, 5 fellowships (averaging $10,000 per year), 18 research assistantships (averaging $4,000 per year), teaching assistantships (averaging $4,000 per year) were awarded. Support available to part-time students. Financial award application deadline: 4/1. *Unit head:* Dr. Bob G. Wood, Director, 931-372-3600, Fax: 931-372-6249. *Application contact:* Shelia K. Kendrick, Coordinator of Graduate Studies, 931-372-3808, Fax: 931-372-3497, E-mail: skendrick@tntech.edu.

Texas A&M International University, Office of Graduate Studies and Research, College of Business Administration, Division of International Business and Technology Studies, Laredo, TX 78041-1900. Offers information systems (MSIS); international trade (MBA). *Faculty:* 12 full-time (0 women). *Students:* 50 full-time (7 women), 45 part-time (11 women); includes 20 minority (3 African Americans, 2 Asian Americans or Pacific Islanders, 15 Hispanic Americans), 69 international. Average age 28. 133 applicants, 35% accepted, 26 enrolled. In 2009, 42 master's awarded. *Degree requirements:* For master's, thesis (for some programs). *Entrance requirements:* For master's, GMAT or GRE General Test. Additional exam requirements/recommendations for international students: Required—TOEFL (minimum score 550 paper-based; 213 computer-based). *Application deadline:* For fall admission, 4/30 priority date for domestic students; for spring admission, 11/30 for domestic students. Applications are processed on a rolling basis. Application fee: $25. *Financial support:* In 2009–10, 33 students received support; fellowships, Federal Work-Study, institutionally sponsored loans, and scholarships/grants available. Support available to part-time students. *Unit head:* Dr. Ananda Mukhergi, Interim Chair, 956-326-2526, Fax: 956-326-2494, E-mail: max@tamiu.edu. *Application contact:* Imelda Lopez, Graduate Admissions Counselor, 956-326-2485, Fax: 956-326-2459, E-mail: lopez@tamiu.edu.

Management Information Systems

Texas A&M University, Mays Business School, Department of Information and Operations Management, College Station, TX 77843. Offers management information systems (MS, PhD); management science (PhD); production and operations management (PhD). Terminal master's awarded for partial completion of doctoral program. *Degree requirements:* For master's, comprehensive exam; for doctorate, thesis/dissertation. *Entrance requirements:* For master's, GMAT; for doctorate, GMAT or GRE General Test. Additional exam requirements/recommendations for international students: Required—TOEFL. *Expenses:* Tuition, state resident: full-time $3991; part-time $221.74 per credit hour. Tuition, nonresident: full-time $9049; part-time $502.74 per credit hour.

Texas Southern University, Jesse H. Jones School of Business, Program in Management Information Systems, Houston, TX 77004-4584. Offers MS. *Students:* 16 full-time (9 women), 12 part-time (8 women); includes 23 minority (20 African Americans, 2 Asian Americans or Pacific Islanders, 1 Hispanic American), 3 international. Average age 32. 22 applicants, 100% accepted, 14 enrolled. In 2009, 6 master's awarded. *Application deadline:* For fall admission, 7/1 for domestic and international students; for spring admission, 11/1 for domestic and international students. Applications are processed on a rolling basis. Application fee: $50 ($75 for international students). Electronic applications accepted. *Expenses:* Tuition, state resident: full-time $1805; part-time $100 per credit hour. Tuition, nonresident: full-time $6470; part-time $343 per credit hour. Tuition and fees vary according to course level, course load and degree level. *Financial support:* In 2009–10, 4 research assistantships (averaging $3,500 per year), 3 teaching assistantships (averaging $1,650 per year) were awarded; fellowships, career-related internships or fieldwork, scholarships/grants, and unspecified assistantships also available. Financial award applicants required to submit FAFSA. *Unit head:* Dr. K. V. Ramaswamy, Chair, 713-313-7309, Fax: 713-313-7705, E-mail: ramaswamy_kv@tsu.edu. *Application contact:* Bobbie J. Richardson, Executive Secretary, 713-313-7309, Fax: 713-313-7705, E-mail: richardson_bj@tsu.edu.

Texas State University–San Marcos, Graduate School, Emmett and Miriam McCoy College of Business Administration, Program in Accounting and Information Technology, San Marcos, TX 78666. Offers MS. *Faculty:* 7 full-time (2 women). *Students:* 15 full-time (5 women), 10 part-time (5 women); includes 9 minority (3 African Americans, 5 Asian Americans or Pacific Islanders, 1 Hispanic American), 2 international. Average age 29. 7 applicants, 100% accepted, 5 enrolled. In 2009, 2 master's awarded. *Degree requirements:* For master's, comprehensive exam. *Entrance requirements:* For master's, GMAT, official transcript from each college or university attended, 2 letters of recommendation, resume. Additional exam requirements/recommendations for international students: Required—TOEFL (minimum score 550 paper-based; 213 computer-based). *Application deadline:* For fall admission, 6/1 for domestic and international students; for spring admission, 10/1 for domestic and international students. Application fee: $40 ($90 for international students). *Expenses:* Tuition, state resident: full-time $5784; part-time $241 per credit hour. Tuition, nonresident: full-time $13,224; part-time $551 per credit hour. Required fees: $1728; $48 per credit hour. $306. Tuition and fees vary according to course load. *Financial support:* In 2009–10, 12 students received support, including 1 research assistantship (averaging $5,076 per year), 6 teaching assistantships (averaging $5,145 per year). *Unit head:* Dr. Robert Davis, Associate Dean, 512-245-3591, Fax: 512-245-7973, E-mail: rd23@txstate.edu. *Application contact:* Dr. J. Michael Willoughby, Dean of Graduate School, 512-245-2581, Fax: 512-245-8365, E-mail: gradcollege@txstate.edu.

Texas Tech University, Jerry S. Rawls College of Business Administration, Area of Information Systems and Quantitative Sciences, Lubbock, TX 79409. Offers business statistics (MS, PhD); healthcare management (MS); management information systems (MS, PhD); production and operations management (MS, PhD); risk management (MS). Part-time programs available. *Faculty:* 14 full-time (0 women). *Students:* 61 full-time (14 women), 5 part-time (1 woman); includes 2 minority (1 African American, 1 Asian American or Pacific Islander), 52 international. Average age 27. 94 applicants, 84% accepted, 35 enrolled. In 2009, 6 master's, 6 doctorates awarded. Terminal master's awarded for partial completion of doctoral program. *Degree requirements:* For master's, comprehensive exam or capstone course; for doctorate, thesis/dissertation, qualifying exams. *Entrance requirements:* For master's and doctorate, GMAT, holistic profile of academic credentials. Additional exam requirements/recommendations for international students: Required—TOEFL (minimum score 550 paper-based; 213 computer-based; 79 iBT). *Application deadline:* For fall admission, 4/1 priority date for domestic students, 1/15 priority date for international students; for spring admission, 9/1 priority date for domestic students, 7/15 priority date for international students. Applications are processed on a rolling basis. Application fee: $50 ($75 for international students). Electronic applications accepted. *Expenses:* Tuition, state resident: full-time $5100; part-time $213 per credit hour. Tuition, nonresident: full-time $11,748; part-time $490 per credit hour. Required fees: $2298; $50 per credit hour. $555 per semester. *Financial support:* In 2009–10, 4 research assistantships (averaging $8,000 per year), 8 teaching assistantships (averaging $17,000 per year) were awarded; Federal Work-Study, scholarships/grants, and unspecified assistantships also available. *Faculty research:* Database management systems, systems management and engineering, expert systems and adaptive knowledge-based sciences, statistical analysis and design. *Unit head:* Dr. Bradley Ewing, Area Coordinator, 806-742-3939, Fax: 806-742-3193, E-mail: bradley.ewing@ttu.edu. *Application contact:* Cynthia D. Barnes, Director, Graduate Services Center, 806-742-3184, Fax: 806-742-3958, E-mail: ba_grad@ttu.edu.

Texas Tech University, Jerry S. Rawls College of Business Administration, Programs in Business Administration, Lubbock, TX 79409. Offers agricultural business (MBA); business administration (IMBA); entrepreneurship (MBA); finance (MBA); general business (MBA); health organization management (MBA); international business (MBA); management and leadership skills (MBA); management information systems (MBA); marketing (MBA); statistics (MBA); JD/MBA; MBA/M Arch; MBA/MA; MBA/MD; MBA/MS; MBA/Pharm D. Part-time and evening/weekend programs available. *Faculty:* 54 full-time (9 women), 5 part-time/adjunct (0 women). *Students:* 59 full-time (15 women), 487 part-time (148 women); includes 107 minority (24 African Americans, 4 American Indian/Alaska Native, 30 Asian Americans or Pacific Islanders, 49 Hispanic Americans), 51 international. Average age 30. 477 applicants, 81% accepted, 302 enrolled. In 2009, 185 degrees awarded. *Degree requirements:* For master's, capstone course. *Entrance requirements:* For master's, GMAT, holistic review of academic credentials. Additional exam requirements/recommendations for international students: Required—TOEFL (minimum score 550 paper-based; 213 computer-based; 79 iBT). *Application deadline:* For fall admission, 4/1 priority date for domestic students, 1/15 priority date for international students; for spring admission, 9/1 priority date for domestic students, 7/15 priority date for international students. Applications are processed on a rolling basis. Application fee: $50 ($75 for international students). Electronic applications accepted. *Expenses:* Tuition, state resident: full-time $5100; part-time $213 per credit hour. Tuition, nonresident: full-time $11,748; part-time $490 per credit hour. Required fees: $2298; $50 per credit hour. $555 per semester. *Financial support:* In 2009–10, 13 research assistantships (averaging $8,000 per year) were awarded; teaching assistantships, career-related internships or fieldwork, Federal Work-Study, scholarships/grants, health care benefits, and unspecified assistantships also available. Support available to part-time students. Financial award applicants required to submit FAFSA. *Unit head:* Dr. W. Jay Conover, Director, 806-742-1546, Fax: 806-742-3958, E-mail: jay.conover@ttu.edu. *Application contact:* Cynthia D. Barnes, Director, Graduate Services Center, 806-742-3184, Fax: 806-742-3958, E-mail: ba_grad@ttu.edu.

Towson University, College of Graduate Studies and Research, Program in Applied Information Technology, Towson, MD 21252-0001. Offers applied information technology (D Sc); database management (Certificate); information security and assurance (Certificate); information systems management (Certificate); Internet application development (Certificate); networking technologies (Certificate); software engineering (Certificate). *Entrance requirements:* For doctorate, minimum GPA 3.0, letter of intent, resume, 2 letters of recommendation, personal assessment forms, official transcripts. Additional exam requirements/recommendations for international students: Required—TOEFL (minimum score 550 paper-based). Electronic applications accepted.

Towson University, College of Graduate Studies and Research, Program in Information Systems Management, Towson, MD 21252-0001. Offers Certificate. Part-time and evening/weekend programs available. Electronic applications accepted.

Troy University, Graduate School, College of Arts and Sciences, Program in Public Administration, Troy, AL 36082. Offers education (MPA); environmental management (MPA); government contracting (MPA); health care administration (MPA); justice administration (MPA); management information systems (MPA); national security affairs (MPA); nonprofit management (MPA); public human resources management (MPA); public management (MPA). *Accreditation:* NASPAA. Part-time and evening/weekend programs available. Postbaccalaureate distance learning degree programs offered (no on-campus study). *Students:* 239 full-time (161 women), 652 part-time (416 women); includes 596 minority (547 African Americans, 11 American Indian/Alaska Native, 6 Asian Americans or Pacific Islanders, 32 Hispanic Americans). Average age 34. 415 applicants, 80% accepted. In 2009, 247 master's awarded. *Degree requirements:* For master's, capstone course, research methodologies course. *Entrance requirements:* For master's, GRE, MAT or GMAT, minimum undergraduate GPA of 2.5, letter of recommendation. Additional exam requirements/recommendations for international students: Required—TOEFL (minimum score 523 paper-based; 193 computer-based; 70 iBT), IELTS (minimum score 6). *Application deadline:* Applications are processed on a rolling basis. Application fee: $50. Electronic applications accepted. *Financial support:* Available to part-time students. Applicants required to submit FAFSA. *Unit head:* Dr. Ellen Rosell, Chairman, 334-670-3758, Fax: 334-670-5647, E-mail: erosell@troy.edu. *Application contact:* Brenda K. Campbell, Director of Graduate Admissions, 334-670-3178, Fax: 334-670-3733, E-mail: bcamp@troy.edu.

Troy University, Graduate School, College of Business, Program in Business Administration, Troy, AL 36082. Offers accounting (EMBA, MBA); criminal justice (EMBA); finance (MBA); general management (EMBA); healthcare management (EMBA); information systems (EMBA, MBA); international economic development (MBA). *Accreditation:* ACBSP. Part-time and evening/weekend programs available. *Students:* 382 full-time (196 women), 732 part-time (457 women); includes 616 minority (483 African Americans, 14 American Indian/Alaska Native, 96 Asian Americans or Pacific Islanders, 23 Hispanic Americans). Average age 29. 869 applicants, 61% accepted. In 2009, 296 master's awarded. *Degree requirements:* For master's, thesis or alternative. *Entrance requirements:* For master's, GMAT (minimum score 500) or GRE General Test (minimum score 900), minimum GPA of 2.5; letter of recommendation. Additional exam requirements/recommendations for international students: Required—TOEFL (minimum score 523 paper-based; 193 computer-based; 70 iBT), IELTS (minimum score 6), or ACT Compass ESL (minimum score 270 on Listening, Reading, and Grammar with no individual score below 85 and a minimum score of 8 out of 12 on writing test). *Application deadline:* Applications are processed on a rolling basis. Application fee: $50. *Unit head:* Dr. Henry M. Findley, Interim Chair/Professor, 334-670-3271, Fax: 334-670-3599, E-mail: hfindley@troy.edu. *Application contact:* Brenda K. Campbell, Director of Graduate Admissions, 334-670-3178, Fax: 334-670-3733, E-mail: bcamp@troy.edu.

Troy University, Graduate School, College of Business, Program in Management, Troy, AL 36082. Offers healthcare management (MSM); human resources management (MSM); information systems (MSM); international hospitality management (MSM); international management (MSM); leadership and organizational effectiveness (MSM); public management (MS, MSM). *Accreditation:* ACBSP. Evening/weekend programs available. *Students:* 193 full-time (130 women), 575 part-time (374 women); includes 473 minority (417 African Americans, 12 American Indian/Alaska Native, 20 Asian Americans or Pacific Islanders, 24 Hispanic Americans). Average age 35. 275 applicants, 91% accepted. In 2009, 332 master's awarded. *Degree requirements:* For master's, thesis or alternative. *Entrance requirements:* For master's, GMAT (minimum score 500) or GRE General Test (minimum score 900), minimum GPA of 2.5; letter of recommendation. Additional exam requirements/recommendations for international students: Required—TOEFL (minimum score 523 paper-based; 193 computer-based; 70 iBT), IELTS, or ACT Compass ESL (minimum score 270 on Listening, Reading, and Grammar with no individual score below 85 and a minimum score of 8 out of 12 on writing test). *Application deadline:* Applications are processed on a rolling basis. Application fee: $50. Electronic applications accepted. *Expenses:* Contact institution. *Unit head:* Dr. Henry M. Findley, Interim Chair/Professor, 334-670-3271, Fax: 334-670-3599, E-mail: hfindley@troy.edu. *Application contact:* Brenda K. Campbell, Director of Graduate Admissions, 334-670-3178, Fax: 334-670-3733, E-mail: bcamp@troy.edu.

TUI University, College of Business Administration, Program in Business Administration, Cypress, CA 90630. Offers business administration (PhD); conflict and negotiation management (MBA); criminal justice administration (MBA); entrepreneurship (MBA); finance (MBA); general management (MBA); government accounting (MBA); human resource management (MBA); information security and digital assurance management (MBA); information technology management (MBA); international business (MBA); logistics management (MBA); marketing (MBA); project management (MBA); public management (MBA); quality management (MBA); strategic leadership (MBA). Part-time and evening/weekend programs available. Postbaccalaureate distance learning degree programs offered (no on-campus study). *Degree requirements:* For doctorate, comprehensive exam, thesis/dissertation, defense of dissertation. *Entrance requirements:* For master's, minimum GPA of 2.5 (students with GPA 3.0 or greater may transfer up to 30% of graduate level credits); for doctorate, minimum GPA of 3.4, curriculum vitae, course work in research methods or statistics. Additional exam requirements/recommendations for international students: Required—TOEFL. Electronic applications accepted.

TUI University, College of Information Systems, Cypress, CA 90630. Offers business intelligence (Certificate); information technology management (MS). Part-time and evening/weekend programs available. Postbaccalaureate distance learning degree programs offered (no on-campus study). *Entrance requirements:* For master's, minimum GPA of 2.5 (students with GPA 3.0 or greater may transfer up to 30% of graduate level credits); undergraduate degree completed within the past 5 years. Additional exam requirements/recommendations for international students: Required—TOEFL (minimum score 525 paper-based). Electronic applications accepted.

United States International University, School of Business Administration, Nairobi, Kenya. Offers finance (MBA); information technology management (MBA); integrated studies (MBA); management and organizational development (MS); marketing (MBA); strategic management (MBA). Part-time and evening/weekend programs available. *Degree requirements:* For master's, thesis. *Entrance requirements:* For master's, GMAT, 2 letters of reference, resume. Additional exam requirements/recommendations for international students: Required—TOEFL (minimum score 550 paper-based; 213 computer-based). *Faculty research:* Marketing in small business enterprises, total quality management in Kenya.

Universidad del Este, Graduate School, Carolina, PR 00984. Offers accounting (MBA); adult education (M Ed); agribusiness (MBA); bilingual education (M Ed); criminal justice and criminology (MA); early education (M Ed); elementary education (M Ed); human resources (MBA); information security management (MBA); information technology and Web business development (MBA); management (MBA); public policy (MPA); social work (MA), including clinical social work; special education (M Ed); strategic leadership (MBA); teaching English (M Ed); teaching Spanish (M Ed).

Universidad del Turabo, Graduate Programs, School in Business Administration, Program in Management of Information Systems, Gurabo, PR 00778-3030. Offers MBA. *Students:* 13 full-time (3 women), 21 part-time (8 women); includes 33 Hispanic Americans. Average age 33. 14 applicants, 36% accepted, 4 enrolled. In 2009, 11 master's awarded. *Unit head:* Marcelino Rivera, Dean, 787-743-7979 Ext. 4117. *Application contact:* Virginia Gonzalez, Admissions Officer, 787-746-3009.

Universidad del Turabo, Graduate Programs, School in Business Administration, Program in Office Systems Management, Gurabo, PR 00778-3030. Offers MBA, DBA. *Students:* 2 full-time (1 woman), 25 part-time (7 women); includes 20 Hispanic Americans. Average age 39. 13 applicants, 100% accepted, 12 enrolled. In 2009, 11 doctorates awarded. *Unit head:* Marcelino Rivera, Dean, 787-743-7979 Ext. 4117. *Application contact:* Virginia Gonzalez, Admissions Officer, 787-746-3009.

Management Information Systems

Universidad Metropolitana, School of Business Administration, Program in Management Information Systems, San Juan, PR 00928-1150. Offers MBA.

Université de Sherbrooke, Faculty of Administration, Program in Management Information Systems, Sherbrooke, QC J1K 2R1, Canada. Offers M Sc.

Université de Sherbrooke, Faculty of Sciences, Centre de Formation en Technologies de L'information, Sherbrooke, QC J1K 2R1, Canada. Offers M Sc, Diploma. Electronic applications accepted.

Université du Québec à Montréal, Graduate Programs, Program in Management Information Systems, Montréal, QC H3C 3P8, Canada. Offers M Sc, M Sc A. Part-time programs available. *Entrance requirements:* For master's, appropriate bachelor's degree or equivalent and proficiency in French.

Université Laval, Faculty of Administrative Sciences, Programs in Business Administration, Québec, QC G1K 7P4, Canada. Offers accounting (MBA); agri-food management (MBA); electronic business (MBA, Diploma); factory management and logistics (MBA); finance (MBA); firm management (MBA); geomatic management (MBA); information technology management (MBA); international management (MBA); management (MBA); management accounting (MBA, Diploma); marketing (MBA); modeling and organizational decision (MBA); occupational health and safety management (MBA); pharmacy management (MBA); social and environmental responsibility (MBA); technological entrepreneurship (Diploma). *Accreditation:* AACSB. Part-time and evening/weekend programs available. Postbaccalaureate distance learning degree programs offered (no on-campus study). *Entrance requirements:* For master's and Diploma, knowledge of French and English. Electronic applications accepted.

University at Buffalo, the State University of New York, Graduate School, School of Management, Buffalo, NY 14260. Offers accounting (MS); business administration (EMBA, MBA, PMBA); finance (MS), including financial engineering, financial management; information assurance (Certificate); management (PhD); management information systems (MS); supply chains and operations management (MS); Au D/MBA; JD/MBA; M Arch/MBA; MA/MBA; MD/MBA; MPH/MBA; MSW/MBA; Pharm D/MBA. *Accreditation:* AACSB. Part-time and evening/weekend programs available. *Faculty:* 66 full-time (19 women), 21 part-time/adjunct (4 women). *Students:* 502 full-time (176 women), 199 part-time (54 women); includes 29 minority (10 African Americans, 16 Asian Americans or Pacific Islanders, 3 Hispanic Americans), 306 international. Average age 27. 1,944 applicants, 31% accepted, 324 enrolled. In 2009, 363 master's, 7 doctorates, 3 other advanced degrees awarded. *Degree requirements:* For master's, thesis (for some programs); for doctorate, comprehensive exam, thesis/dissertation. *Entrance requirements:* For master's, GMAT (MBA, MS in accounting), GRE General Test (for all other MS concentrations); for doctorate, GMAT or GRE. Additional exam requirements/recommendations for international students: Required—TOEFL (minimum score 230 computer-based; 95 iBT). *Application deadline:* For fall admission, 6/2 priority date for domestic students, 3/1 priority date for international students. Applications are processed on a rolling basis. Application fee: $100. Electronic applications accepted. *Expenses:* Contact institution. *Financial support:* In 2009–10, 91 students received support, including 5 fellowships with full and partial tuition reimbursements available (averaging $4,000 per year), 41 research assistantships with full and partial tuition reimbursements available (averaging $16,000 per year), 28 teaching assistantships with full and partial tuition reimbursements available (averaging $15,000 per year); career-related internships or fieldwork, Federal Work-Study, institutionally sponsored loans, scholarships/grants, health care benefits, and unspecified assistantships also available. Financial award application deadline: 2/15; financial award applicants required to submit FAFSA. *Faculty research:* Earnings management and electronic information assurance, supply chains and operations management, corporate financing and asset pricing, consumer behavior and quantitative modeling of marketing behavior, leadership and politics in organizations. Total annual research expenditures: $230,000. *Unit head:* David W. Frasier, Assistant Dean, 716-645-3204, Fax: 716-645-2341, E-mail: davidf@buffalo.edu. *Application contact:* David W. Frasier, Assistant Dean, 716-645-3204, Fax: 716-645-2341, E-mail: davidf@buffalo.edu.

The University of Akron, Graduate School, College of Business Administration, Department of Management, Program in Management-Information Systems, Akron, OH 44325. Offers MSM. *Students:* 12 full-time (4 women), 8 part-time (2 women); includes 1 minority (Asian American or Pacific Islander), 10 international. Average age 27. 10 applicants, 70% accepted, 4 enrolled. In 2009, 4 master's awarded. *Entrance requirements:* For master's, GMAT, minimum GPA of 2.75, letters of recommendation, resume. Additional exam requirements/recommendations for international students: Required—TOEFL (minimum score 550 paper-based; 213 computer-based; 79 iBT). *Application deadline:* For fall admission, 8/1 for domestic and international students; for spring admission, 12/1 for domestic and international students. Application fee: $30 ($40 for international students). Electronic applications accepted. *Expenses:* Tuition, state resident: full-time $6570; part-time $365 per credit hour. Tuition, nonresident: full-time $11,250; part-time $625 per credit hour. *Unit head:* Dr. B. S. Vijayaraman, Head, 330-972-5442, E-mail: bsv@uakron.edu. *Application contact:* Dr. Susan Hanlon, Director of Graduate Business Programs, 330-972-7043, Fax: 330-972-6588, E-mail: shanlon@uakron.edu.

The University of Alabama in Huntsville, School of Graduate Studies, College of Business Administration, Department of Accounting and Finance, Huntsville, AL 35899. Offers accounting (M Acc, Certificate), including CPA preparatory with an emphasis in taxation (M Acc), CPA preparatory with emphasis in assurance and financial reporting (M Acc), general accounting (M Acc), information systems audit and control (ISAC) (M Acc). Part-time and evening/weekend programs available. *Faculty:* 5 full-time (3 women), 3 part-time/adjunct (0 women). *Students:* 16 full-time (10 women), 31 part-time (15 women); includes 5 minority (4 African Americans, 1 Asian American or Pacific Islander), 3 international. Average age 30. 42 applicants, 69% accepted, 21 enrolled. In 2009, 13 master's awarded. *Degree requirements:* For master's, comprehensive exam, thesis or alternative. *Entrance requirements:* For master's and Certificate, GMAT (minimum score 500), minimum AACSB index of 1080. Additional exam requirements/recommendations for international students: Required—TOEFL (minimum score 550 paper-based; 213 computer-based; 62 iBT). *Application deadline:* For fall admission, 8/1 for domestic students, 4/1 for international students; for spring admission, 12/1 for domestic students, 9/1 for international students. Applications are processed on a rolling basis. Application fee: $40 ($50 for international students). Electronic applications accepted. *Expenses:* Tuition, state resident: part-time $355.75 per credit hour. Tuition, nonresident: part-time $847.10 per credit hour. Required fees: $210.80 per semester. Tuition and fees vary according to course load and program. *Financial support:* Career-related internships or fieldwork, Federal Work-Study, institutionally sponsored loans, scholarships/grants, health care benefits, and unspecified assistantships available. Support available to part-time students. Financial award application deadline: 4/1; financial award applicants required to submit FAFSA. *Faculty research:* Accounting information systems, emerging technologies in accounting, behavioral accounting, state and local taxation, financial accounting. Total annual research expenditures: $67,010. *Unit head:* Dr. John Burnett, Interim Chair, 256-824-2923, Fax: 256-824-2929, E-mail: burnettj@uah.edu. *Application contact:* Jennifer Pettitt, Director of Graduate Programs, 256-824-6681, Fax: 256-824-7571, E-mail: jennifer.pettitt@uah.edu.

The University of Alabama in Huntsville, School of Graduate Studies, College of Business Administration, Department of Economics and Information Systems, Huntsville, AL 35899. Offers MSIS. Part-time and evening/weekend programs available. *Faculty:* 10 full-time (0 women), 2 part-time/adjunct (0 women). *Students:* 6 full-time (3 women), 29 part-time (9 women); includes 5 minority (3 African Americans, 1 American Indian/Alaska Native, 1 Asian American or Pacific Islander), 1 international. Average age 35. 25 applicants, 76% accepted, 14 enrolled. In 2009, 13 master's awarded. *Degree requirements:* For master's, comprehensive exam, thesis or alternative. *Entrance requirements:* For master's, GMAT (minimum score 500), minimum AACSB index of 1080. Additional exam requirements/recommendations for international students: Required—TOEFL (minimum score 550 paper-based; 213 computer-based; 62 iBT). *Application deadline:* For fall admission, 8/1 for domestic students, 4/1 for international students; for spring admission, 12/1 for domestic students, 9/1 for international students. Applications are processed on a rolling basis. Application fee: $40 ($50 for international students). Electronic applications accepted. *Expenses:* Tuition, state resident: part-time $355.75 per credit hour. Tuition, nonresident: part-time $847.10 per credit hour. Required fees: $210.80 per semester. Tuition and fees vary according to course load and program. *Financial support:* In 2009–10, 1 student received support, including 1 teaching assistantship with full tuition reimbursement available (averaging $8,000 per year); career-related internships or fieldwork, Federal Work-Study, institutionally sponsored loans, scholarships/grants, health care benefits, and unspecified assistantships also available. Support available to part-time students. Financial award application deadline: 4/1; financial award applicants required to submit FAFSA. Total annual research expenditures: $6.9 million. *Unit head:* Dr. Allen W. Wilhite, Chair, 256-824-6591, Fax: 256-824-6328, E-mail: wilhitea@uah.edu. *Application contact:* Jennifer Pettitt, Director of Graduate Programs, 256-824-6681, Fax: 256-824-7571, E-mail: jennifer.pettitt@uah.edu.

The University of Alabama in Huntsville, School of Graduate Studies, Interdisciplinary Studies, Interdisciplinary Program in Information Assurance and Cybersecurity, Huntsville, AL 35899. Offers Certificate. Part-time and evening/weekend programs available. *Faculty:* 2 full-time (0 women), 2 part-time/adjunct (0 women). *Students:* 13 part-time (1 woman); includes 3 minority (2 African Americans, 1 American Indian/Alaska Native). Average age 38. 6 applicants, 67% accepted, 4 enrolled. In 2009, 10 Certificates awarded. *Entrance requirements:* For degree, GMAT, minimum GPA of 3.0. Additional exam requirements/recommendations for international students: Required—TOEFL (minimum score 550 paper-based; 213 computer-based; 62 iBT). *Application deadline:* For fall admission, 7/15 for domestic students, 4/1 for international students; for spring admission, 11/30 for domestic students, 9/1 for international students. Applications are processed on a rolling basis. Application fee: $40 ($50 for international students). Electronic applications accepted. *Expenses:* Tuition, state resident: part-time $355.75 per credit hour. Tuition, nonresident: part-time $847.10 per credit hour. Required fees: $210.80 per semester. Tuition and fees vary according to course load and program. *Financial support:* Career-related internships or fieldwork, Federal Work-Study, institutionally sponsored loans, scholarships/grants, health care benefits, and unspecified assistantships available. Support available to part-time students. Financial award application deadline: 4/1; financial award applicants required to submit FAFSA. *Unit head:* Dr. Debra Moriarity, Dean of Graduate Studies, 256-824-6002, Fax: 256-824-6405, E-mail: deangrad@uah.edu. *Application contact:* Jennifer Pettitt, College of Business Administration Director of Graduate Programs, 256-824-6681, Fax: 256-824-7572, E-mail: jennifer.pettitt@uah.edu.

The University of Arizona, Graduate College, Eller College of Management, Department of Management Information Systems, Tucson, AZ 85721. Offers MS. *Faculty:* 11. *Students:* 74 full-time (25 women), 6 part-time (1 woman); includes 2 minority (1 Asian American or Pacific Islander, 1 Hispanic American), 69 international. Average age 26. 393 applicants, 66% accepted, 58 enrolled. In 2009, 47 master's awarded. *Degree requirements:* For master's, thesis or alternative. *Entrance requirements:* For master's, GMAT or GRE General Test, 2 letters of recommendation, resume. Additional exam requirements/recommendations for international students: Required—TOEFL (minimum score 550 paper-based; 213 computer-based; 80 iBT). *Application deadline:* For fall admission, 1/15 for domestic and international students. Applications are processed on a rolling basis. Application fee: $75. Electronic applications accepted. *Expenses:* Tuition, state resident: full-time $9028. Tuition, nonresident: full-time $24,890. *Financial support:* In 2009–10, 11 research assistantships with full tuition reimbursements (averaging $14,701 per year), 19 teaching assistantships with full tuition reimbursements (averaging $14,013 per year) were awarded; career-related internships or fieldwork, Federal Work-Study, scholarships/grants, health care benefits, tuition waivers (partial), and unspecified assistantships also available. Financial award application deadline: 3/15. *Faculty research:* Group decision support systems, domestic and international computing issues, expert systems, data management and structures. Total annual research expenditures: $1.2 million. *Unit head:* Dr. Paul Goes, Department Head, 520-621-2429, Fax: 520-621-2775, E-mail: pgoes@eller.arizona.edu. *Application contact:* Cinda Van Winkle, 520-621-2387, E-mail: admissions_mis@eller.arizona.edu.

University of Arkansas, Graduate School, Sam M. Walton College of Business Administration, Department of Information Systems, Fayetteville, AR 72701-1201. Offers MIS. Part-time and evening/weekend programs available. *Students:* 20 full-time (8 women), 37 part-time (13 women); includes 6 minority (1 African American, 2 American Indian/Alaska Native, 3 Hispanic Americans), 28 international. In 2009, 23 master's awarded. *Entrance requirements:* For master's, GMAT. Application fee: $40 ($50 for international students). *Expenses:* Tuition, state resident: full-time $7355; part-time $356.58 per hour. Tuition, nonresident: full-time $17,401; part-time $775.17 per hour. Required fees: $1203. *Financial support:* In 2009–10, 8 fellowships with tuition reimbursements, 15 research assistantships, 5 teaching assistantships were awarded. Financial award application deadline: 4/1. *Unit head:* Dr. Moez Limayem, Head, 479-575-4500, E-mail: mlimayem@uark.edu. *Application contact:* Dr. Paul Cronan, Graduate Coordinator, 479-575-6130, E-mail: cronan@uark.edu.

University of Arkansas at Little Rock, Graduate School, College of Business Administration, Little Rock, AR 72204-1099. Offers accountancy (M Acc, Graduate Certificate); business administration (MBA); construction management (Graduate Certificate); management (Graduate Certificate); management information system (MIS); management information systems (Graduate Certificate); management information systems leadership (Graduate Certificate); taxation (MS, Graduate Certificate). *Accreditation:* AACSB. Part-time and evening/weekend programs available. *Entrance requirements:* For master's, GMAT, minimum undergraduate GPA of 2.7. Additional exam requirements/recommendations for international students: Required—TOEFL (minimum score 525 paper-based; 195 computer-based).

University of Atlanta, Graduate Programs, Atlanta, GA 30360. Offers business (MS); business administration (Exec MBA, MBA); computer science (MS); educational leadership (MS, Ed D); healthcare administration (MS, D Sc, Graduate Certificate); information technology for management (Graduate Certificate); international project management (Graduate Certificate); law (JD); managerial science (DBA); project management (Graduate Certificate); social science (MS). Postbaccalaureate distance learning degree programs offered. *Faculty:* 54 part-time/adjunct (10 women). *Students:* 251 full-time. *Entrance requirements:* For master's, minimum cumulative GPA of 2.5. *Expenses:* Tuition: Part-time $1000 per course. Part-time tuition and fees vary according to course load and degree level.

University of Baltimore, Graduate School, Merrick School of Business, Department of Accounting and Management Information Systems, Baltimore, MD 21201-5779. Offers accounting and business advisory services (MS); accounting fundamentals (Graduate Certificate); forensic accounting (Graduate Certificate). Part-time and evening/weekend programs available. *Entrance requirements:* For master's, GMAT. Additional exam requirements/recommendations for international students: Required—TOEFL (minimum score 550 paper-based; 213 computer-based). Electronic applications accepted. *Faculty research:* Health care, accounting and administration, managerial accounting, financial accounting theory, accounting information.

The University of British Columbia, Sauder School of Business, Doctoral Program in Commerce and Business Administration, Vancouver, BC V6T 1Z1, Canada. Offers accounting (PhD); finance (PhD); international business (PhD); management information systems (PhD); management science (PhD); marketing (PhD); organizational behavior (PhD); strategy and business economics (PhD); transportation and logistics (PhD); urban land economics (PhD). *Degree requirements:* For doctorate, comprehensive exam, thesis/dissertation. *Entrance requirements:* For doctorate, GMAT or GRE. Additional exam requirements/recommendations for international students: Required—TOEFL (minimum score 600 paper-based; 250 computer-based; 100 iBT). Electronic applications accepted.

University of California, Berkeley, UC Berkeley Extension, Certificate Programs in Computer Technology and Information Management, Berkeley, CA 94720-1500. Offers information systems and management (Postbaccalaureate Certificate); UNIX/LINUX system administration (Certificate). Postbaccalaureate distance learning degree programs offered. *Unit head:* Diana Wu, Dean,

510-642-4181. *Application contact:* Computer Technology and Information Management, 510-642-4151, E-mail: course@unex.berkeley.edu.

University of Central Florida, College of Business Administration, Department of Management Information Systems, Orlando, FL 32816. Offers MS. *Faculty:* 8 full-time (1 woman). *Students:* 16 full-time (5 women), 54 part-time (17 women); includes 19 minority (9 African Americans, 3 Asian Americans or Pacific Islanders, 7 Hispanic Americans), 13 international. In 2009, 38 master's awarded. *Degree requirements:* For master's, thesis or alternative. *Entrance requirements:* For master's, GMAT or GRE General Test, minimum GPA of 3.0 in last 60 hours, letters of recommendation. Additional exam requirements/recommendations for international students: Required—TOEFL. *Application deadline:* For fall admission, 2/15 priority date for domestic students; for spring admission, 11/1 for domestic students. Application fee: $30. Electronic applications accepted. *Expenses:* Tuition, state resident: part-time $306.31 per credit hour. Tuition, nonresident: part-time $1099.01 per credit hour. Part-time tuition and fees vary according to degree level and program. *Financial support:* In 2009–10, 1 research assistantship with partial tuition reimbursement (averaging $5,200 per year), 1 teaching assistantship with partial tuition reimbursement (averaging $7,100 per year) were awarded; fellowships with partial tuition reimbursements also available. *Unit head:* Dr. Paul Cheney, Chair, 407-823-3107, E-mail: paul.cheney@bus.ucf.edu. *Application contact:* Judy Ryder, Director, Graduate Admissions, 407-823-2364, Fax: 407-823-0219, E-mail: judy.ryder@bus.ucf.edu.

University of Central Missouri, The Graduate School, Harmon College of Business Administration, Warrensburg, MO 64093. Offers accountancy (MA); accounting (MBA); ethical strategic leadership (MBA); finance (MBA); general business (MBA); information systems (MBA); information technology (MS); marketing (MBA). Part-time programs available. Post-baccalaureate distance learning degree programs offered. *Faculty:* 31. *Students:* 87 full-time (34 women), 62 part-time (25 women); includes 10 minority (3 African Americans, 1 American Indian/Alaska Native, 5 Asian Americans or Pacific Islanders, 1 Hispanic American), 66 international. Average age 27. 55 applicants, 64% accepted, 27 enrolled. In 2009, 83 master's awarded. *Entrance requirements:* Additional exam requirements/recommendations for international students: Required—TOEFL (minimum score 550 paper-based; 79 computer-based). *Application deadline:* For fall admission, 6/1 priority date for domestic students, 5/1 for international students; for spring admission, 10/1 priority date for domestic students, 10/1 for international students. Applications are processed on a rolling basis. Application fee: $30 ($75 for international students). Electronic applications accepted. *Expenses:* Tuition, area resident: Part-time $245.80 per credit hour. Tuition, nonresident: part-time $491.60 per credit hour. Required fees: $24.20 per credit hour. Full-time tuition and fees vary according to course load, degree level, campus/location and reciprocity agreements. *Financial support:* Research assistantships with full and partial tuition reimbursements, teaching assistantships with full and partial tuition reimbursements, career-related internships or fieldwork, Federal Work-Study, scholarships/grants, and administrative and laboratory assistantships available. Support available to part-time students. Financial award application deadline: 3/1; financial award applicants required to submit FAFSA. *Unit head:* Dr. Roger Best, Dean, 660-543-4560, Fax: 660-543-8350, E-mail: best@ucmo.edu. *Application contact:* Laurie Delap, Admissions Coordinator, 660-543-4621, Fax: 660-543-4778, E-mail: gradinfo@ucmo.edu.

University of Cincinnati, Graduate School, College of Business, MS Program, Cincinnati, OH 45221. Offers accounting (MS); information systems (MS); marketing (MS); quantitative analysis (MS). Part-time and evening/weekend programs available. *Degree requirements:* For master's, thesis (for some programs). *Entrance requirements:* For master's, GMAT, GRE, resume, letters of recommendation. Additional exam requirements/recommendations for international students: Required—TOEFL (minimum score 600 paper-based; 250 computer-based; 100 iBT). Electronic applications accepted. *Expenses:* Contact institution.

University of Cincinnati, Graduate School, College of Business, PhD Program, Cincinnati, OH 45221. Offers accounting (PhD); finance (PhD); information systems (PhD); management (PhD); marketing (PhD); quantitative analysis and operations management (PhD). *Degree requirements:* For doctorate, comprehensive exam, thesis/dissertation. *Entrance requirements:* For doctorate, GMAT, GRE, resume, letters of recommendation. Additional exam requirements/recommendations for international students: Required—TOEFL (minimum score 600 paper-based; 250 computer-based; 100 iBT). Electronic applications accepted. *Expenses:* Contact institution.

University of Colorado at Boulder, Leeds School of Business, Division of Business Administration, Boulder, CO 80309. Offers accounting (MS, PhD); finance (PhD); information systems (PhD); marketing (PhD); operations (PhD); strategic, organizational, and entrepreneurial studies (PhD). Part-time and evening/weekend programs available. *Students:* 74 full-time (27 women), 15 part-time (8 women); includes 6 minority (1 African American, 3 Asian Americans or Pacific Islanders, 2 Hispanic Americans), 21 international. Average age 28. 271 applicants, 8% accepted, 19 enrolled. In 2009, 40 master's, 6 doctorates awarded. *Entrance requirements:* For master's, GMAT, minimum undergraduate GPA of 3.0. *Application deadline:* For fall admission, 3/31 for domestic and international students; for spring admission, 10/31 for domestic and international students. Application fee: $50 ($60 for international students). Electronic applications accepted. *Financial support:* In 2009–10, 16 fellowships (averaging $1,038 per year), 26 research assistantships (averaging $17,558 per year), 11 teaching assistantships (averaging $12,576 per year) were awarded; career-related internships or fieldwork, Federal Work-Study, scholarships/grants, and unspecified assistantships also available. Financial award applicants required to submit FAFSA.

University of Colorado Denver, Business School, Program in Computer Science and Information Systems, Denver, CO 80217-3364. Offers PhD. *Students:* 3 full-time (1 woman), 13 part-time (2 women); includes 2 minority (1 Asian American or Pacific Islander, 1 Hispanic American), 6 international. 39 applicants, 100% accepted, 0 enrolled. In 2009, 1 doctorate awarded. *Degree requirements:* For doctorate, comprehensive exam, thesis/dissertation. *Entrance requirements:* For doctorate, GMAT or GRE General Test, minimum undergraduate GPA of 3.0, graduate 3.5; resume. Additional exam requirements/recommendations for international students: Required—TOEFL (minimum score 525 paper-based; 197 computer-based). *Application deadline:* For fall admission, 6/1 for domestic students, 3/15 for international students; for spring admission, 11/1 for domestic students, 10/1 for international students. Application fee: $50 ($75 for international students). Electronic applications accepted. *Financial support:* Federal Work-Study, institutionally sponsored loans, and scholarships/grants available. Support available to part-time students. Financial award application deadline: 4/1; financial award applicants required to submit FAFSA. *Unit head:* Dr. Jahangir Karimi, Head, 303-556-5881, E-mail: jahangir.karimi@ucdenver.edu. *Application contact:* Shelly Townley, Admissions Coordinator, 303-556-5956, Fax: 303-556-5904, E-mail: shelly.townley@ucdenver.edu.

University of Colorado Denver, Business School, Program in Information Systems, Denver, CO 80217-3364. Offers MS. Part-time and evening/weekend programs available. *Students:* 14 full-time (4 women), 46 part-time (22 women); includes 13 minority (10 Asian Americans or Pacific Islanders, 3 Hispanic Americans), 13 international. 31 applicants, 68% accepted, 17 enrolled. In 2009, 18 master's awarded. *Entrance requirements:* For master's, GMAT. Additional exam requirements/recommendations for international students: Required—TOEFL (minimum score 525 paper-based; 197 computer-based). *Application deadline:* For fall admission, 6/1 for domestic students, 3/15 for international students; for spring admission, 11/1 priority date for domestic students, 10/1 for international students. Applications are processed on a rolling basis. Application fee: $50 ($75 for international students). Electronic applications accepted. *Financial support:* Federal Work-Study, institutionally sponsored loans, and scholarships/grants available. Support available to part-time students. Financial award application deadline: 4/1; financial award applicants required to submit FAFSA. *Faculty research:* Human-computer interaction, expert systems, database management, electronic commerce, object-oriented software development. *Unit head:* Dr. Jahangir Karimi, Director, 303-556-5881, Fax: 303-556-5899, E-mail: jahangir.karimi@ucdenver.edu. *Application contact:* Shelly Townley, Admissions Coordinator, 303-556-5956, Fax: 303-556-5904, E-mail: shelly.townley@ucdenver.edu.

University of Dallas, Graduate School of Management, Irving, TX 75062-4736. Offers accounting (MBA, MM, MS); business management (MBA, MM); corporate finance (MBA, MM); financial services (MBA); global business (MBA, MM); health services management (MBA, MM); human resource management (MBA, MM); information assurance (MBA, MM, MS); information technology (MBA, MM, MS); information technology service management (MBA, MM, MS); marketing management (MBA, MM); organization development (MBA, MM); project management (MBA, MM); sports and entertainment management (MBA, MM); strategic leadership (MBA, MM); supply chain management (MBA); supply chain management and market logistics (MM). *Accreditation:* ACBSP. Part-time and evening/weekend programs available. Postbaccalaureate distance learning degree programs offered (no on-campus study). *Faculty:* 25 full-time (6 women), 31 part-time/adjunct (6 women). *Students:* 232 full-time (95 women), 923 part-time (365 women); includes 462 minority (184 African Americans, 14 American Indian/Alaska Native, 153 Asian Americans or Pacific Islanders, 111 Hispanic Americans), 184 international. Average age 34. 474 applicants, 85% accepted, 237 enrolled. In 2009, 399 master's awarded. *Entrance requirements:* Additional exam requirements/recommendations for international students: Required—TOEFL. *Application deadline:* Applications are processed on a rolling basis. Application fee: $50. Electronic applications accepted. *Expenses:* Contact institution. *Financial support:* In 2009–10, 399 students received support. Scholarships/grants and unspecified assistantships available. Financial award application deadline: 2/15; financial award applicants required to submit FAFSA. *Unit head:* Alounda Joseph, Director of Enrollment Processes, 972-721-5356, E-mail: admiss@gsm.udallas.edu. *Application contact:* Alounda Joseph, Director of Enrollment Processes, 972-721-5356, E-mail: admiss@gsm.udallas.edu.

University of Dayton, Graduate School, School of Business Administration, Dayton, OH 45469-1300. Offers accounting (MBA); business intelligence (MBA); entrepreneurship (MBA); finance (MBA); international business (MBA); marketing (MBA); MIS (MBA); operations management (MBA); technology-enhanced business/e-commerce (MBA); JD/MBA. *Accreditation:* AACSB. Part-time and evening/weekend programs available. *Faculty:* 29 full-time (8 women), 15 part-time/adjunct (2 women). *Students:* 134 full-time (48 women), 111 part-time (31 women); includes 14 minority (9 African Americans, 3 Asian Americans or Pacific Islanders, 2 Hispanic Americans), 29 international. Average age 29. 179 applicants, 63% accepted, 73 enrolled. In 2009, 102 master's awarded. *Entrance requirements:* For master's, GMAT. Additional exam requirements/recommendations for international students: Required—TOEFL (minimum score 550 paper-based; 213 computer-based; 79 iBT). *Application deadline:* For fall admission, 3/1 priority date for international students; for winter admission, 7/1 priority date for international students; for spring admission, 1/1 priority date for international students. Applications are processed on a rolling basis. Application fee: $0 ($50 for international students). Electronic applications accepted. *Expenses:* Contact institution. *Financial support:* In 2009–10, 13 fellowships with partial tuition reimbursements, 17 research assistantships with full and partial tuition reimbursements (averaging $7,020 per year) were awarded; career-related internships or fieldwork, institutionally sponsored loans, scholarships/grants, health care benefits, and unspecified assistantships also available. Support available to part-time students. Financial award application deadline: 3/15; financial award applicants required to submit FAFSA. *Faculty research:* Management information systems, economics, finance, entrepreneurship, marketing. *Unit head:* Janice M. Glynn, Director, MBA Program, 937-229-3733, Fax: 937-229-3882, E-mail: glynn@udayton.edu. *Application contact:* Jeffrey Carter, Assistant Director, MBA Program, 937-229-3733, Fax: 937-229-3882, E-mail: jeff.carter@notes.udayton.edu.

University of Delaware, Alfred Lerner College of Business and Economics, Department of Accounting and Management Information Systems and Department of Electrical and Computer Engineering, Program in Information Systems and Technology Management, Newark, DE 19716. Offers MS. Part-time and evening/weekend programs available. *Entrance requirements:* For master's, GRE or GMAT, 2 letters of recommendation, resume, minimum GPA of 2.75. Additional exam requirements/recommendations for international students: Required—TOEFL (minimum score 600 paper-based; 250 computer-based). *Faculty research:* Security, developer trust, XML.

University of Denver, Daniels College of Business, Department of Information Technology and Electronic Commerce, Denver, CO 80208. Offers IMBA, MBA. Part-time and evening/weekend programs available. *Faculty:* 6 full-time (1 woman). *Students:* 4 part-time (0 women). Average age 31. In 2009, 4 master's awarded. *Entrance requirements:* For master's, GMAT. *Application deadline:* For fall admission, 1/15 priority date for domestic students. Applications are processed on a rolling basis. Application fee: $50. Electronic applications accepted. *Expenses:* Tuition: Full-time $34,596; part-time $961 per quarter hour. Required fees: $4 per quarter hour. Tuition and fees vary according to course load, campus/location and program. *Financial support:* Career-related internships or fieldwork, Federal Work-Study, institutionally sponsored loans, and scholarships/grants available. Support available to part-time students. Financial award application deadline: 2/15. *Faculty research:* Cross-cultural research in information systems, electronic commerce, distributed project management, strategic information systems, management of emerging technologies. *Unit head:* Dr. Dick Scudder, Chair, 303-871-2197. *Application contact:* Information Contact, 303-871-3416, Fax: 303-871-4466, E-mail: daniels@du.edu.

University of Detroit Mercy, College of Business Administration, Program in Computer Information Systems, Detroit, MI 48221. Offers MSCIS. Part-time and evening/weekend programs available. *Degree requirements:* For master's, thesis or alternative. *Entrance requirements:* For master's, minimum GPA of 3.75.

University of Florida, Graduate School, Warrington College of Business Administration, Hough Graduate School of Business, Department of Information Systems and Operations Management, Gainesville, FL 32611. Offers decision and information sciences (MS, PhD); supply chain management (MS). Terminal master's awarded for partial completion of doctoral program. *Degree requirements:* For doctorate, thesis/dissertation. *Entrance requirements:* For master's and doctorate, GMAT or GRE General Test, minimum GPA of 3.0. Additional exam requirements/recommendations for international students: Required—TOEFL (minimum score 550 paper-based; 213 computer-based). *Faculty research:* Expert systems, nonconvex optimization, manufacturing management, production and operation management, telecommunication.

University of Hawaii at Manoa, Graduate Division, College of Social Sciences, School of Communications, Program in Telecommunication and Information Resource Management, Honolulu, HI 96822. Offers Graduate Certificate. Part-time programs available. *Students:* 1 part-time (0 women). Average age 32. In 2009, 5 Graduate Certificates awarded. *Entrance requirements:* Additional exam requirements/recommendations for international students: Required—TOEFL (minimum score 500 paper-based; 173 computer-based; 61 iBT), IELTS (minimum score 5). *Application deadline:* For fall admission, 5/1 for domestic and international students; for spring admission, 10/1 for domestic and international students. Application fee: $60. *Expenses:* Tuition, state resident: full-time $8900; part-time $372 per credit. Tuition, nonresident: full-time $21,400; part-time $898 per credit. Required fees: $207 per semester. *Application contact:* Norman Okamura, Director, 808-956-2895, Fax: 808-956-5591, E-mail: tirm@hawaii.edu.

University of Hawaii at Manoa, Graduate Division, Shidler College of Business, Program in Accounting, Honolulu, HI 96822. Offers accounting (M Acc); accounting law (M Acc); information systems (M Acc); taxation (M Acc). Part-time programs available. *Faculty:* 8 full-time (2 women), 1 part-time/adjunct (0 women). *Students:* 63 full-time (31 women), 30 part-time (18 women); includes 57 minority (1 African American, 53 Asian Americans or Pacific Islanders, 3 Hispanic Americans), 17 international. Average age 28. 83 applicants, 80% accepted, 42 enrolled. In 2009, 37 master's awarded. *Entrance requirements:* For master's, GMAT, bachelor's degree in accounting, minimum GPA of 3.0. Additional exam requirements/recommendations for international students: Required—TOEFL (minimum score 550 paper-based; 213 computer-based; 79 iBT), IELTS (minimum score 5). *Application deadline:* For fall admission, 5/1 for domestic students, 3/1 for international students; for spring admission, 11/1 for domestic students, 10/1 for international students. Application fee: $60. *Expenses:* Tuition, state resident: full-time

Management Information Systems

University of Hawaii at Manoa *(continued)*

$8900; part-time $372 per credit. Tuition, nonresident: full-time $21,400; part-time $898 per credit. Required fees: $207 per semester. *Financial support:* In 2009–10, 5 students received support, including 17 fellowships (averaging $3,470 per year), 5 research assistantships (averaging $16,592 per year); career-related internships or fieldwork, Federal Work-Study, and tuition waivers (full) also available. *Faculty research:* International accounting, current tax topics, insurance industry financial reporting, behavioral accounting, auditing. *Application contact:* Liming Guan, Graduate Chair, 808-956-7332, Fax: 808-956-9888, E-mail: lguan@hawaii.edu.

University of Hawaii at Manoa, Graduate Division, Shidler College of Business, Program in Business Administration, Honolulu, HI 96822. Offers Asian business studies (MBA); Chinese business studies (MBA); decision sciences (MBA); entrepreneurship (MBA); finance (MBA); finance and banking (MBA); human resources management (MBA); information management (MBA); information technology (MBA); international business (MBA); Japanese business studies (MBA); marketing (MBA); organizational behavior (MBA); organizational management (MBA); real estate (MBA); student-designed track (MBA). *Accreditation:* AACSB. Part-time and evening/weekend programs available. *Faculty:* 46 full-time (8 women), 9 part-time/adjunct (4 women). *Students:* 259 full-time (90 women), 105 part-time (43 women); includes 123 minority (118 Asian Americans or Pacific Islanders, 5 Hispanic Americans), 119 international. Average age 32. 336 applicants, 52% accepted, 150 enrolled. In 2009, 113 master's awarded. *Degree requirements:* For master's, thesis optional. *Entrance requirements:* For master's, GMAT, minimum GPA of 3.0. Additional exam requirements/recommendations for international students: Required—TOEFL (minimum score 600 paper-based; 250 computer-based; 100 iBT), IELTS (minimum score 7). *Application deadline:* For fall admission, 5/1 for domestic students, 3/1 for international students. Application fee: $60. *Expenses:* Contact institution. *Financial support:* In 2009–10, 24 students received support, including 98 fellowships (averaging $3,481 per year), 3 research assistantships (averaging $16,626 per year). Total annual research expenditures: $427,000. *Application contact:* Tung Bui, Graduate Chair, 808-956-5565, Fax: 808-956-9889, E-mail: tung.bui@hawaii.edu.

University of Hawaii at Manoa, Graduate Division, Shidler College of Business, Program in International Management, Honolulu, HI 96822. Offers Asian finance (PhD); global information technology management (PhD); international accounting (PhD); international marketing (PhD); international organization and strategy (PhD). Part-time programs available. *Students:* 28 full-time (12 women), 5 part-time (0 women); includes 7 minority (all Asian Americans or Pacific Islanders), 17 international. Average age 33. 65 applicants, 18% accepted, 5 enrolled. In 2009, 1 doctorate awarded. *Degree requirements:* For doctorate, comprehensive exam, thesis/dissertation. *Entrance requirements:* For doctorate, GMAT or GRE General Test, minimum GPA of 3.0. Additional exam requirements/recommendations for international students: Required—TOEFL (minimum score 600 paper-based; 250 computer-based; 100 iBT), IELTS (minimum score 7). *Application deadline:* For fall admission, 3/1 for domestic and international students. Application fee: $60. *Expenses:* Contact institution. *Financial support:* In 2009–10, 2 fellowships (averaging $6,945 per year), 21 research assistantships (averaging $17,766 per year) were awarded. *Application contact:* Erica Okada, Graduate Chair, 808-956-6723, Fax: 808-956-6889, E-mail: emokada@hawaii.edu.

University of Houston, Bauer College of Business, Decision and Information Sciences Program, Houston, TX 77204. Offers management information systems (MBA, PhD). Part-time and evening/weekend programs available. *Faculty:* 12 full-time (1 woman), 9 part-time/adjunct (0 women). *Expenses:* Tuition, state resident: full-time $7676; part-time $320 per credit hour. Tuition, nonresident: full-time $14,324; part-time $597 per credit hour. Required fees: $3034. *Financial support:* In 2009–10, 6 teaching assistantships with full tuition reimbursements (averaging $7,100 per year) were awarded; fellowships with full tuition reimbursements, research assistantships with full tuition reimbursements, career-related internships or fieldwork, Federal Work-Study, institutionally sponsored loans, scholarships/grants, health care benefits, and unspecified assistantships also available. Support available to part-time students. Financial award application deadline: 2/1; financial award applicants required to submit FAFSA. *Unit head:* Dr. Basheer Khumawala, Chair, 713-743-4747, E-mail: bkhumawala@uh.edu. *Application contact:* 713-743-4900, Fax: 713-743-4942, E-mail: oss@uh.edu.

University of Houston–Clear Lake, School of Business, Program in Management Information Systems, Houston, TX 77058-1098. Offers MS. Part-time programs available. *Entrance requirements:* For master's, GMAT. Additional exam requirements/recommendations for international students: Required—TOEFL (minimum score 550 paper-based; 213 computer-based).

University of Illinois at Chicago, Graduate College, Liautaud Graduate School of Business, Department of Information and Decision Sciences, Chicago, IL 60607-7128. Offers business statistics (PhD); management information systems (MS, PhD). Part-time and evening/weekend programs available. *Degree requirements:* For doctorate, thesis/dissertation. *Entrance requirements:* For doctorate, GMAT, minimum GPA of 2.75. Additional exam requirements/recommendations for international students: Required—TOEFL. Electronic applications accepted.

University of Illinois at Springfield, Graduate Programs, College of Business and Management, Program in Management Information Systems, Springfield, IL 62703-5407. Offers MS. Part-time and evening/weekend programs available. Postbaccalaureate distance learning degree programs offered (no on-campus study). *Faculty:* 7 full-time (0 women), 2 part-time/adjunct (0 women). *Students:* 26 full-time (8 women), 122 part-time (36 women); includes 33 minority (14 African Americans, 17 Asian Americans or Pacific Islanders, 2 Hispanic Americans), 28 international. Average age 35. 154 applicants, 67% accepted, 28 enrolled. In 2009, 42 master's awarded. *Degree requirements:* For master's, project, closure seminar. *Entrance requirements:* For master's, GMAT or GRE General Test, competency in a structured, high-level programming language; minimum undergraduate GPA of 3.0. Additional exam requirements/recommendations for international students: Required—TOEFL (minimum score 500 paper-based; 176 computer-based; 61 iBT). *Application deadline:* Applications are processed on a rolling basis. Application fee: $50 ($60 for international students). Electronic applications accepted. *Expenses:* Tuition, state resident: full-time $6390; part-time $266.25 per credit hour. Tuition, nonresident: full-time $14,226; part-time $592.75 per credit hour. Required fees: $2044; $14.36 per credit hour. $722.50 per term. *Financial support:* In 2009–10, research assistantships with full tuition reimbursements (averaging $8,109 per year), teaching assistantships with full tuition reimbursements (averaging $8,109 per year) were awarded; career-related internships or fieldwork, Federal Work-Study, scholarships/grants, health care benefits, and unspecified assistantships also available. Support available to part-time students. Financial award application deadline: 11/15; financial award applicants required to submit FAFSA. *Unit head:* Dr. Rassule Hadidi, Program Administrator, 217-206-6067, Fax: 217-206-7543, E-mail: hadidi.rassule@uis.edu. *Application contact:* Dr. Lynn Pardie, Office of Graduate Studies, 800-252-8533, Fax: 217-206-7623, E-mail: pardie.lynn@uis.edu.

The University of Kansas, Graduate Studies, School of Engineering, Department of Electrical Engineering and Computer Science, Program in Information Technology, Lawrence, KS 66045. Offers MS. Part-time and evening/weekend programs available. *Students:* 29 part-time (12 women); includes 6 minority (all Asian Americans or Pacific Islanders), 5 international. Average age 35. 16 applicants, 63% accepted, 5 enrolled. *Degree requirements:* For master's, thesis optional. *Entrance requirements:* For master's, GRE. Additional exam requirements/recommendations for international students: Required—TOEFL (minimum score 600 paper-based; 250 computer-based; 100 iBT). *Application deadline:* For fall admission, 3/1 priority date for domestic students, 3/1 for international students; for spring admission, 10/1 priority date for domestic students, 10/1 for international students. Applications are processed on a rolling basis. Application fee: $45 ($55 for international students). Electronic applications accepted. *Expenses:* Tuition, state resident: full-time $6492; part-time $270.50 per credit hour. Tuition, nonresident: full-time $15,510; part-time $646.25 per credit hour. Required fees: $847; $70.56 per credit hour. Tuition and fees vary according to course load and program. *Faculty research:* Information security and privacy, game theory, graph theory, software process

improvement, resilient and survivable networks, object orientation technology. *Unit head:* Dr. Glenn Prescott, Chairperson, 785-864-4620, Fax: 785-864-3226. *Application contact:* Pam Shadoin, Assistant to Graduate Director, 785-864-4487, Fax: 785-864-3226, E-mail: graduate@eecs.ku.edu.

University of La Verne, College of Business and Public Management, Graduate Programs in Business Administration, La Verne, CA 91750-4443. Offers accounting (MBA); executive management (MBA-EP); finance (MBA, MBA-EP); health services management (MBA); information technology (MBA, MBA-EP); international business (MBA, MBA-EP); leadership (MBA-EP); managed care (MBA); management (MBA, MBA-EP); marketing (MBA, MBA-EP). Part-time and evening/weekend programs available. *Faculty:* 22 full-time (11 women), 41 part-time/adjunct (8 women). *Students:* 409 full-time (213 women), 156 part-time (74 women); includes 371 minority (23 African Americans, 7 American Indian/Alaska Native, 259 Asian Americans or Pacific Islanders, 82 Hispanic Americans), 9 international. Average age 29. In 2009, 356 master's awarded. *Entrance requirements:* For master's, minimum undergraduate GPA of 3.0, 2 letters of recommendation, resume. Additional exam requirements/recommendations for international students: Required—TOEFL (minimum score 550 paper-based; 213 computer-based). *Application deadline:* Applications are processed on a rolling basis. Application fee: $50. *Expenses:* Contact institution. *Financial support:* Career-related internships or fieldwork, institutionally sponsored loans, and scholarships/grants available. Financial award application deadline: 3/2; financial award applicants required to submit FAFSA. *Unit head:* Dr. Abe Helou, Chairperson, 909-593-3511 Ext. 4211, Fax: 909-392-2704, E-mail: ihelou@laverne.edu. *Application contact:* Rina Lazarian, Program and Admission Specialist, 909-593-3511 Ext. 4819, Fax: 909-392-2704, E-mail: cbpm@ulv.edu.

University of La Verne, Regional Campus Administration, Graduate Programs, Central Coast/Vandenberg Air Force Base Campuses, La Verne, CA 91750-4443. Offers business (MBA-EP), including health services management, information technology; health administration (MHA); leadership and management (MS). *Faculty:* 18 part-time/adjunct (6 women). *Students:* 19 full-time (12 women), 35 part-time (14 women); includes 20 minority (7 African Americans, 2 American Indian/Alaska Native, 2 Asian Americans or Pacific Islanders, 9 Hispanic Americans). Average age 36. In 2009, 20 master's awarded. *Entrance requirements:* For master's, 2 letters of recommendation, resume. *Application deadline:* Applications are processed on a rolling basis. Application fee: $50. *Expenses:* Contact institution. *Financial support:* Institutionally sponsored loans available. Financial award application deadline: 3/2; financial award applicants required to submit FAFSA. *Unit head:* Kitt Vincent, Director, Central Coast Campus, 805-542-9690 Ext. 6043, Fax: 805-542-9735, E-mail: kvincent@laverne.edu. *Application contact:* Kitt Vincent, Director, Central Coast Campus, 805-542-9690 Ext. 6043, Fax: 805-542-9735, E-mail: kvincent@laverne.edu.

University of La Verne, Regional Campus Administration, Graduate Programs, Inland Empire Campus, Rancho Cucamonga, CA 91730. Offers business (MBA-EP), including health services management, information technology, management, marketing; leadership and management (MS). *Faculty:* 2 full-time (both women), 12 part-time/adjunct (2 women). *Students:* 20 full-time (13 women), 61 part-time (41 women); includes 50 minority (10 African Americans, 11 Asian Americans or Pacific Islanders, 29 Hispanic Americans). Average age 37. In 2009, 24 master's awarded. *Entrance requirements:* For master's, 2 letters of recommendation, resume. *Application deadline:* Applications are processed on a rolling basis. Application fee: $50. *Expenses:* Contact institution. *Financial support:* Institutionally sponsored loans available. Financial award application deadline: 3/2; financial award applicants required to submit FAFSA. *Unit head:* Allan Stout, Director, 909-484-3858 Ext. 6002, Fax: 909-484-9469, E-mail: astout@laverne.edu. *Application contact:* Allan Stout, Director, 909-484-3858 Ext. 6002, Fax: 909-484-9469, E-mail: astout@laverne.edu.

University of Lethbridge, School of Graduate Studies, Lethbridge, AB T1K 3M4, Canada. Offers accounting (MScM); addictions counseling (M Sc); agricultural biotechnology (M Sc); agricultural studies (M Sc, MA); anthropology (MA); archaeology (MA); art (MA, MFA); biochemistry (M Sc); biological sciences (M Sc); biomolecular science (PhD); biosystems and biodiversity (PhD); Canadian studies (MA); chemistry (M Sc); computer science (M Sc); computer science and geographical information science (M Sc); counseling psychology (M Ed); dramatic arts (MA); earth, space, and physical science (PhD); economics (MA); educational leadership (M Ed); English (MA); environmental science (M Sc); evolution and behavior (PhD); exercise science (M Sc); finance (MScM); French (MA); French/German (MA); French/Spanish (MA); general education (M Ed); general management (MScM); geography (M Sc, MA); German (MA); health science (M Sc); health sciences (MA); history (MA); human resource management and labour relations (MScM); individualized multidisciplinary (M Sc, MA); information systems (MScM); international management (MScM); kinesiology (M Sc, MA); management (M Sc, MA); marketing (MScM); mathematics (M Sc); music (M Mus, MA); Native American studies (MA); neuroscience (M Sc, PhD); new media (MA); nursing (M Sc); philosophy (MA); physics (M Sc); policy and strategy (MScM); political science (MA); psychology (M Sc, MA); religious studies (MA); social sciences (MA); sociology (MA); theatre and dramatic arts (MFA); theoretical and computational science (PhD); urban and regional studies (MA); women's studies (MA). Part-time and evening/weekend programs available. *Degree requirements:* For doctorate, comprehensive exam, thesis/dissertation. *Entrance requirements:* For master's, GMAT (M Sc in management), bachelor's degree in related field, minimum GPA of 3.0 during previous 20 graded semester courses, 2 years teaching or related experience (M Ed); for doctorate, master's degree, minimum graduate GPA of 3.5. Additional exam requirements/recommendations for international students: Required—TOEFL. *Faculty research:* Movement and brain plasticity, gibberellin physiology, photosynthesis, carbon cycling, molecular properties of main-group ring components.

University of Maine, Graduate School, Interdisciplinary Program in Information Systems, Orono, ME 04469. Offers MS. Part-time programs available. *Faculty:* 4 full-time (1 woman), 3 part-time/adjunct (1 woman). *Students:* 24 full-time (13 women); includes 1 minority (Asian American or Pacific Islander). Average age 32. 15 applicants, 87% accepted, 12 enrolled. *Entrance requirements:* For master's, GRE General Test or GMAT. Additional exam requirements/recommendations for international students: Required—TOEFL. *Application deadline:* For fall admission, 2/1 priority date for domestic students. Applications are processed on a rolling basis. Application fee: $65. Electronic applications accepted. *Financial support:* In 2009–10, 4 teaching assistantships with tuition reimbursements (averaging $12,790 per year) were awarded; Federal Work-Study also available. *Unit head:* Dr. Owen Smith, Associate Dean of the Graduate School, 207-581-4358, Fax: 207-581-4357, E-mail: graduate@maine.edu. *Application contact:* Dr. Owen Smith, Associate Dean of the Graduate School, 207-581-4358, Fax: 207-581-4357, E-mail: graduate@maine.edu.

University of Management and Technology, Program in Computer Science and Information Technology, Arlington, VA 22209. Offers computer science (MS); information technology (AC); information technology project management (MS); management information systems (MS); project management (AC); software engineering (MS). Part-time and evening/weekend programs available. Postbaccalaureate distance learning degree programs offered (no on-campus study). *Entrance requirements:* For master's, 3 recommendations, resume. Additional exam requirements/recommendations for international students: Required—TOEFL (minimum score 550 paper-based; 213 computer-based). Electronic applications accepted.

University of Mary Hardin-Baylor, Graduate Studies in Information Systems, Belton, TX 76513. Offers MS. Part-time and evening/weekend programs available. *Degree requirements:* For master's, comprehensive exam. *Entrance requirements:* For master's, GMAT, minimum GPA of 3.0, work experience, interview. Electronic applications accepted.

University of Maryland University College, Graduate School of Management and Technology, Program in Financial Management and Information Systems, Adelphi, MD 20783. Offers MS, Certificate. Part-time and evening/weekend programs available. Postbaccalaureate distance learning degree programs offered (no on-campus study). *Students:* 7 full-time (2 women), 177 part-time (88 women); includes 105 minority (87 African Americans, 11 Asian Americans or Pacific Islanders, 7 Hispanic Americans), 4 international. Average age 34. In 2009, 13 master's,

1 other advanced degree awarded. *Degree requirements:* For master's, thesis or alternative. *Application deadline:* Applications are processed on a rolling basis. Application fee: $50. Electronic applications accepted. *Expenses:* Tuition, state resident: full-time $7704; part-time $428 per credit hour. Tuition, nonresident: full-time $11,862; part-time $659 per credit hour. *Financial support:* Federal Work-Study and scholarships/grants available. Support available to part-time students. Financial award application deadline: 6/1; financial award applicants required to submit FAFSA. *Unit head:* Dr. Jayanta Sen, Program Director, Finance and Management, 240-684-2400, Fax: 240-684-2401, E-mail: jsen@umuc.edu. *Application contact:* Coordinator, Graduate Admissions, 800-888-UMUC, Fax: 240-684-2151, E-mail: newgrad@umuc.edu.

University of Mary Washington, College of Graduate and Professional Studies, Fredericksburg, VA 22406-7239. Offers business administration (MBA); education (M Ed); management information systems (MSMIS). Part-time and evening/weekend programs available. *Entrance requirements:* For master's, GMAT (MBA), PRAXIS I (M Ed), minimum GPA of 3.0. Additional exam requirements/recommendations for international students: Required—TOEFL (minimum score 600 paper-based; 250 computer-based; 100 iBT).

University of Memphis, Graduate School, Fogelman College of Business and Economics, Program in Business Administration, Memphis, TN 38152. Offers accounting (MBA, PhD); economics (MBA, PhD); executive business administration (MBA); finance (PhD); finance, insurance, and real estate (MBA, MS); international business administration (IMBA); management (MBA, MS, PhD); management information systems (MBA, MS, PhD); management science (MBA); marketing (MBA, MS); marketing and supply chain management (PhD); real estate development (MS); JD/MBA. *Accreditation:* AACSB. *Faculty:* 44 full-time (9 women), 5 part-time/adjunct (0 women). *Students:* 263 full-time (106 women), 181 part-time (66 women); includes 70 minority (46 African Americans, 3 American Indian/Alaska Native, 16 Asian Americans or Pacific Islanders, 5 Hispanic Americans), 109 international. Average age 31. 374 applicants, 73% accepted, 119 enrolled. In 2009, 140 master's, 17 doctorates awarded. *Degree requirements:* For master's, comprehensive exam; for doctorate, comprehensive exam, thesis/dissertation. *Entrance requirements:* For master's, GMAT, resume; for doctorate, GMAT, interview, minimum GPA of 3.4, resume, letter of recommendation. Additional exam requirements/recommendations for international students: Required—TOEFL (minimum score 550 paper-based; 220 computer-based). *Application deadline:* For fall admission, 8/1 for domestic students; for spring admission, 12/1 for domestic students. Application fee: $35 ($60 for international students). *Expenses:* Tuition, state resident: full-time $6246; part-time $347 per credit hour. Tuition, nonresident: full-time $15,894; part-time $883 per credit hour. Required fees: $1160. Full-time tuition and fees vary according to course load, degree level and program. *Financial support:* In 2009–10, 164 students received support; research assistantships with full tuition reimbursements available, teaching assistantships with full tuition reimbursements available, career-related internships or fieldwork, Federal Work-Study, scholarships/grants, and unspecified assistantships available. Financial award application deadline: 2/15; financial award applicants required to submit FAFSA. *Faculty research:* Competitive business strategy, finance microstructures, supply chain management innovations, health care economics, litigation risks and corporate audits. *Unit head:* Rajiv Grover, Dean, 901-678-3759, E-mail: rgrover@memphis.edu. *Application contact:* Dr. Carol V. Danehower, Associate Dean for Programs, 901-678-5402, Fax: 901-678-3579, E-mail: fcbegp@memphis.edu.

University of Miami, Graduate School, School of Business Administration, Program in Business Administration, Coral Gables, FL 33124. Offers accounting (MBA); computer information systems (MBA); executive and professional (MBA), including international business, management; finance (MBA); international business (MBA); management (MBA); management science (MBA); marketing (MBA); professional management (MSPM); JD/MBA; MBA/MSIE. *Accreditation:* AACSB. Evening/weekend programs available. *Degree requirements:* For master's, comprehensive exam. *Entrance requirements:* For master's, GMAT. Additional exam requirements/recommendations for international students: Required—TOEFL (minimum score 550 paper-based; 213 computer-based; 59 iBT). Electronic applications accepted. *Faculty research:* Leadership, e-commerce, supply chain management.

University of Michigan–Dearborn, School of Management, Dearborn, MI 48128-1491. Offers accounting (MBA, MS); finance (MBA, MS); information systems (MS); international business (MBA); management (MBA); management information systems (MBA); marketing (MBA); supply chain management (MBA); MBA/MHSA; MBA/MSE; MBA/MSF. *Accreditation:* AACSB. Part-time and evening/weekend programs available. Postbaccalaureate distance learning degree programs offered (no on-campus study). *Faculty:* 26 full-time (6 women), 8 part-time/adjunct (4 women). *Students:* 73 full-time (30 women), 412 part-time (134 women); includes 65 minority (20 African Americans, 1 American Indian/Alaska Native, 38 Asian Americans or Pacific Islanders, 6 Hispanic Americans), 76 international. Average age 30. 185 applicants, 56% accepted, 78 enrolled. In 2009, 151 master's awarded. *Entrance requirements:* For master's, GMAT, 2 years of work experience (MBA); course work in computer applications, statistics, and pre-calculus or finite mathematics; 18 credits of accounting course work beyond introductory courses (MS in accounting). Additional exam requirements/recommendations for international students: Required—TOEFL (minimum score 560 paper-based; 220 computer-based; 84 iBT). *Application deadline:* For fall admission, 8/1 priority date for domestic students, 6/1 for international students; for winter admission, 12/1 priority date for domestic students, 10/1 for international students; for spring admission, 4/1 priority date for domestic students, 2/1 for international students. Applications are processed on a rolling basis. Application fee: $60. Electronic applications accepted. *Expenses:* Contact institution. *Financial support:* Career-related internships or fieldwork, Federal Work-Study, and scholarships/grants available. Support available to part-time students. Financial award application deadline: 9/1; financial award applicants required to submit FAFSA. *Faculty research:* Cultural diversity, buyer-supplier relations, error detection in data, economic evolution. *Unit head:* Dr. Kim Schatzel, Dean, 313-593-5248, Fax: 313-271-9835, E-mail: schatzel@umd.umich.edu. *Application contact:* Joan Doherty, Academic Advisor/Counselor, 313-593-5460, Fax: 313-271-9838, E-mail: gradbusiness@umd.umich.edu.

University of Minnesota, Twin Cities Campus, Carlson School of Management, Carlson Full-Time MBA Program, Minneapolis, MN 55455. Offers finance (MBA); information technology (MBA); management (MBA); marketing (MBA); medical industry orientation (MBA); supply chain and operations (MBA); JD/MBA; MBA/MPP; MD/MBA; MHA/MBA; Pharm D/MBA. *Accreditation:* AACSB. *Faculty:* 60 full-time (11 women), 15 part-time/adjunct (7 women). *Students:* 217 full-time (78 women); includes 23 minority (6 African Americans, 1 American Indian/Alaska Native, 14 Asian Americans or Pacific Islanders, 2 Hispanic Americans), 41 international. Average age 28. 548 applicants, 41% accepted, 104 enrolled. In 2009, 91 master's awarded. *Entrance requirements:* For master's, GMAT. Additional exam requirements/recommendations for international students: Required—TOEFL (minimum score 580 paper-based; 240 computer-based; 82 iBT), or IELTS (minimum score 7), or Pearson Test of English (PTE). *Application deadline:* For fall admission, 4/1 for domestic students, 2/1 for international students. Application fee: $60 ($90 for international students). Electronic applications accepted. *Expenses:* Contact institution. *Financial support:* In 2009–10, 107 students received support, including 107 fellowships with full and partial tuition reimbursements available (averaging $22,174 per year); research assistantships with partial tuition reimbursements available, teaching assistantships with partial tuition reimbursements available, career-related internships or fieldwork, Federal Work-Study, institutionally sponsored loans, scholarships/grants, health care benefits, and unspecified assistantships also available. Financial award application deadline: 2/1; financial award applicants required to submit FAFSA. *Unit head:* Kathryn J. Carlson, Assistant Dean, MBA Programs and Graduate Business Career Center, 612-625-5555, Fax: 612-625-1012, E-mail: mba@umn.edu. *Application contact:* Tracy J. Keeling, Associate Director of Admissions, Full-Time and Part-Time MBA Programs, 612-625-5555, Fax: 612-625-1012, E-mail: mba@umn.edu.

University of Minnesota, Twin Cities Campus, Carlson School of Management, Carlson Part-Time MBA Program, Minneapolis, MN 55455. Offers finance (MBA); information technology (MBA); management (MBA); marketing (MBA); supply chain and operations (MBA); JD/MBA; MBA/MPP; MD/MBA; MHA/MBA; Pharm D/MBA. Part-time and evening/weekend programs available. *Faculty:* 72 full-time (15 women), 26 part-time/adjunct (5 women). *Students:* 1,861 part-time (606 women); includes 188 minority (31 African Americans, 1 American Indian/Alaska Native, 132 Asian Americans or Pacific Islanders, 24 Hispanic Americans), 121 international. Average age 29. 387 applicants, 67% accepted, 238 enrolled. In 2009, 393 master's awarded. *Entrance requirements:* For master's, GMAT. Additional exam requirements/recommendations for international students: Required—TOEFL (minimum score 580 paper-based; 240 computer-based; 82 iBT), IELTS (minimum score 7) or Pearson Test of English (PTE) Academic. *Application deadline:* For fall admission, 5/1 priority date for domestic and international students; for spring admission, 10/1 priority date for domestic and international students. Application fee: $60 ($90 for international students). Electronic applications accepted. *Expenses:* Contact institution. *Financial support:* Applicants required to submit FAFSA. *Faculty research:* Strategy, IT, finance, marketing, operations, supply chain, entrepreneurship, quality management, accounting. *Unit head:* Kathryn J. Carlson, Assistant Dean, MBA Programs and Graduate Business Career Center, 612-624-2039, Fax: 612-625-1012, E-mail: mba@umn.edu. *Application contact:* Tracy J. Keeling, Associate Director of Admissions, Full-Time and Part-Time MBA Programs, 612-625-5555, Fax: 612-625-1012, E-mail: mba@umn.edu.

University of Minnesota, Twin Cities Campus, Carlson School of Management, Doctoral Program in Business Administration, Minneapolis, MN 55455-0213. Offers accounting (PhD); finance (PhD); information and decision sciences (PhD); marketing and logistics management (PhD); operations and management science (PhD); strategic management and organization (PhD). *Faculty:* 74 full-time (19 women). *Students:* 68 full-time (28 women); includes 7 minority (1 African American, 3 Asian Americans or Pacific Islanders, 3 Hispanic Americans), 46 international. Average age 29. 250 applicants, 5% accepted, 9 enrolled. In 2009, 11 doctorates awarded. *Degree requirements:* For doctorate, comprehensive exam, thesis/dissertation, written and oral preliminary exams, proposal defense. *Entrance requirements:* For doctorate, GMAT, GRE General Test. Additional exam requirements/recommendations for international students: Required—TOEFL (minimum score 600 paper-based; 250 computer-based; 100 iBT), IELTS (minimum score 7.5). *Application deadline:* For fall admission, 12/31 for domestic students, 12/31 priority date for international students. Applications are processed on a rolling basis. Application fee: $55 ($75 for international students). Electronic applications accepted. *Financial support:* In 2009–10, 68 fellowships with full tuition reimbursements (averaging $11,500 per year), 63 research assistantships with full tuition reimbursements (averaging $6,750 per year), 53 teaching assistantships with full tuition reimbursements (averaging $6,750 per year) were awarded; institutionally sponsored loans, scholarships/grants, health care benefits, and unspecified assistantships also available. Financial award application deadline: 12/31. *Faculty research:* Corporate strategy, finance, entrepreneurship, marketing, information and decision science, operations, accounting. Total annual research expenditures: $300,000. *Unit head:* Dr. Shawn P. Curley, Director of Graduate Studies/Program Director, 612-624-6546, Fax: 612-624-8221, E-mail: curley@umn.edu. *Application contact:* Earlene K. Bronson, Assistant Director, 612-624-0875, Fax: 612-624-8221, E-mail: brons003@umn.edu.

University of Mississippi, Graduate School, School of Business Administration, Oxford, University, MS 38677. Offers business administration (MBA, PhD); systems management (MS); JD/MBA. *Accreditation:* AACSB. *Faculty:* 58 full-time (14 women), 7 part-time/adjunct (2 women). *Students:* 77 full-time (28 women), 54 part-time (5 women); includes 14 minority (8 African Americans, 1 American Indian/Alaska Native, 4 Asian Americans or Pacific Islanders, 1 Hispanic American), 13 international. In 2009, 47 master's, 4 doctorates awarded. *Degree requirements:* For doctorate, thesis/dissertation. *Entrance requirements:* For master's, GMAT, minimum GPA of 3.0; for doctorate, GMAT. Additional exam requirements/recommendations for international students: Required—TOEFL. *Application deadline:* For fall admission, 2/1 for domestic students; for spring admission, 10/1 for domestic students. Applications are processed on a rolling basis. Application fee: $25. Electronic applications accepted. *Financial support:* Fellowships, career-related internships or fieldwork, scholarships/grants, tuition waivers (full), and unspecified assistantships available. Financial award application deadline: 3/1; financial award applicants required to submit FAFSA. *Unit head:* Dr. Brian Reithel, Dean, 662-915-5820, Fax: 662-915-5821, E-mail: breithel@bus.olemiss.edu. *Application contact:* Dr. Christy M. Wyandt, Associate Dean, 662-915-7474, Fax: 662-915-7577, E-mail: cwyandt@olemiss.edu.

University of Missouri–St. Louis, College of Business Administration, Program in Information Systems, St. Louis, MO 63121. Offers information systems (MSIS, PhD); logistics and supply chain management (PhD). Part-time and evening/weekend programs available. *Faculty:* 8 full-time (0 women). *Students:* 5 full-time (4 women), 14 part-time (3 women); includes 5 minority (3 African Americans, 1 Asian American or Pacific Islander, 1 Hispanic American), 5 international. Average age 30. 24 applicants, 29% accepted, 3 enrolled. In 2009, 7 master's awarded. *Entrance requirements:* For master's, GMAT, 2 letters of recommendation; for doctorate, GMAT or GRE, 3 letters of recommendation. Additional exam requirements/recommendations for international students: Required—TOEFL (minimum score 550 paper-based; 213 computer-based). *Application deadline:* For fall admission, 7/1 priority date for domestic and international students; for spring admission, 12/1 priority date for domestic and international students. Applications are processed on a rolling basis. Application fee: $35 ($40 for international students). Electronic applications accepted. *Expenses:* Tuition, state resident: full-time $5377; part-time $297.70 per credit hour. Tuition, nonresident: full-time $13,882; part-time $771.20 per credit hour. Required fees: $220; $12.20 per credit hour. One-time fee: $12. Tuition and fees vary according to course level, campus/location and program. *Financial support:* Career-related internships or fieldwork, Federal Work-Study, and institutionally sponsored loans available. Support available to part-time students. Financial award application deadline: 4/1; financial award applicants required to submit FAFSA. *Faculty research:* International information systems, telecommunications, systems development, information systems sourcing. *Unit head:* Karl Kottemann, Assistant Director, 314-516-5885, Fax: 314-516-6420, E-mail: mba@umsl.edu. *Application contact:* 314-516-5458, Fax: 314-516-6996, E-mail: gradadm@umsl.edu.

University of Nebraska at Omaha, Graduate Studies, College of Information Science and Technology, Department of Information Systems and Quantitative Analysis, Omaha, NE 68182. Offers information systems and quantitative analysis (Certificate); information technology (PhD); management information systems (MS). Part-time and evening/weekend programs available. *Faculty:* 18 full-time (10 women). *Students:* 65 full-time (29 women), 100 part-time (31 women); includes 9 minority (4 African Americans, 4 Asian Americans or Pacific Islanders, 1 Hispanic American), 70 international. Average age 37. 173 applicants, 42% accepted, 39 enrolled. In 2009, 42 master's, 1 doctorate, 23 other advanced degrees awarded. *Degree requirements:* For master's, comprehensive exam, thesis (for some programs); for doctorate, comprehensive exam, thesis/dissertation. *Entrance requirements:* For master's, GMAT or GRE General Test; for doctorate, GMAT or GRE General Test, letters of recommendation. Additional exam requirements/recommendations for international students: Required—TOEFL (minimum score 575 paper-based; 230 computer-based; 89 iBT). *Application deadline:* For fall admission, 3/15 for domestic students; for spring admission, 10/1 for domestic students. Applications are processed on a rolling basis. Application fee: $45. Electronic applications accepted. *Financial support:* In 2009–10, 67 students received support; fellowships, research assistantships with tuition reimbursements available, teaching assistantships with tuition reimbursements available, career-related internships or fieldwork, Federal Work-Study, scholarships/grants, tuition waivers (partial), and unspecified assistantships available. Financial award application deadline: 3/1; financial award applicants required to submit FAFSA. *Unit head:* Dr. Ilze Zigurs, Chairperson, 402-554-3770. *Application contact:* Carla Frakes, Information Contact, 402-554-2423.

University of Nebraska–Lincoln, Graduate College, College of Agricultural Sciences and Natural Resources, Program in Mechanized Systems Management, Lincoln, NE 68588. Offers MS. *Degree requirements:* For master's, thesis optional. *Entrance requirements:* For master's, GRE General Test. Additional exam requirements/recommendations for international students: Required—TOEFL (minimum score 550 paper-based; 213 computer-based). Electronic applications accepted. *Faculty research:* Irrigation management, agricultural power and machinery systems, sensors and controls, food/industrial materials handling and processing systems.

University of Nevada, Las Vegas, Graduate College, College of Business, Department of Management Information Systems, Las Vegas, NV 89154-6034. Offers MS. *Faculty:* 7 full-time

Management Information Systems

University of Nevada, Las Vegas (continued)
(1 woman). *Students:* 11 full-time (7 women), 9 part-time (3 women); includes 7 minority (2 African Americans, 4 Asian Americans or Pacific Islanders, 1 Hispanic American), 7 international. Average age 31. 50 applicants, 88% accepted, 12 enrolled. In 2009, 14 master's awarded. *Entrance requirements:* For master's, GMAT or GRE. Additional exam requirements/recommendations for international students: Required—TOEFL (minimum score 550 paper-based; 213 computer-based; 80 iBT), IELTS (minimum score 7). *Application deadline:* For fall admission, 6/15 priority date for domestic students, 5/1 for international students; for spring admission, 11/15 priority date for domestic students, 10/1 for international students. Applications are processed on a rolling basis. Application fee: $60 ($95 for international students). Electronic applications accepted. *Financial support:* In 2009–10, 5 students received support, including 4 research assistantships with partial tuition reimbursements available (averaging $10,000 per year), 1 teaching assistantship with partial tuition reimbursement available (averaging $10,000 per year); institutionally sponsored loans, scholarships/grants, health care benefits, and unspecified assistantships also available. Financial award application deadline: 3/1. *Faculty research:* Methods of project evaluation, software piracy: behavior and policy, offshoring and outsourcing, diffusion of innovation, human-computer interaction. *Unit head:* Dr. Kenneth Peffers, Chair/ Associate Professor, 702-895-3796, Fax: 702-895-0802, E-mail: ken.peffers@unlv.edu. *Application contact:* Graduate College Admissions Evaluator, 702-895-3320, Fax: 702-895-4180, E-mail: gradcollege@unlv.edu.

University of Nevada, Reno, Graduate School, College of Business Administration, Department of Information Systems, Reno, NV 89557. Offers MS. *Degree requirements:* For master's, thesis optional. *Entrance requirements:* For master's, GRE or GMAT, minimum GPA of 2.75. Additional exam requirements/recommendations for international students: Required—TOEFL (minimum score 500 paper-based; 173 computer-based; 61 iBT), IELTS (minimum score 6). Electronic applications accepted.

University of New Mexico, Robert O. Anderson Graduate School of Management, Department of Marketing, Information and Decision Sciences, Albuquerque, NM 87131. Offers information assurance (MBA); management information systems (MBA); marketing management (MBA); operations management (MBA). Part-time and evening/weekend programs available. *Faculty:* 14 full-time (3 women), 5 part-time/adjunct (0 women). *Students:* 39 full-time (18 women), 37 part-time (19 women); includes 31 minority (3 African Americans, 1 American Indian/Alaska Native, 3 Asian Americans or Pacific Islanders, 24 Hispanic Americans), 4 international. Average age 28. 40 applicants, 100% accepted, 36 enrolled. In 2009, 39 master's awarded. *Entrance requirements:* For master's, GMAT or GRE (can be waived in some instances). Additional exam requirements/recommendations for international students: Required—TOEFL (minimum score 550 paper-based; 213 computer-based; 79 iBT). *Application deadline:* For fall admission, 4/1 priority date for domestic students, 5/1 for international students; for spring admission, 10/1 priority date for domestic students, 10/1 for international students. Applications are processed on a rolling basis. Application fee: $50. Electronic applications accepted. *Expenses:* Tuition, state resident: full-time $2099; part-time $233.20 per credit hour. Tuition, nonresident: full-time $6650. Required fees: $25 per semester. Tuition and fees vary according to course load, program and reciprocity agreements. *Financial support:* Fellowships, research assistantships, teaching assistantships, career-related internships or fieldwork, Federal Work-Study, scholarships/grants, and unspecified assistantships available. Support available to part-time students. Financial award application deadline: 6/1. *Faculty research:* Marketing, operations, information science. *Unit head:* Dr. Steve Yourstone, Chair, 505-277-6471, Fax: 505-277-7108. *Application contact:* Megan Conner, Academic Advisement Manager, 505-277-3290, Fax: 505-277-8436, E-mail: mconner@mgt.unm.edu.

The University of North Carolina at Chapel Hill, Kenan-Flagler Business School, Doctoral Program in Business Administration, Chapel Hill, NC 27599. Offers accounting (PhD); finance (PhD); marketing (PhD); operations management (PhD); organizational behavior (PhD); strategy (PhD). *Accreditation:* AACSB. *Degree requirements:* For doctorate, thesis/dissertation. *Entrance requirements:* For doctorate, GMAT or GRE General Test. Electronic applications accepted. *Expenses:* Contact institution.

The University of North Carolina at Greensboro, Graduate School, Bryan School of Business and Economics, Department of Information Systems and Operations Management, Greensboro, NC 27412-5001. Offers information systems (PhD); information technology (Certificate); information technology and management (MS); supply chain management (Certificate). *Entrance requirements:* For master's, GMAT, GRE General Test. Additional exam requirements/recommendations for international students: Required—TOEFL. Electronic applications accepted.

University of North Texas, Robert B. Toulouse School of Graduate Studies, College of Business Administration, Department of Information Technology and Decision Sciences, Denton, TX 76203-5017. Offers business computer information systems (PhD); decision technologies (MS); information technology (MS); management science (PhD). Part-time and evening/weekend programs available. *Degree requirements:* For doctorate, comprehensive exam, thesis/dissertation. *Entrance requirements:* For master's, GMAT; for doctorate, GMAT or GRE General Test. Additional exam requirements/recommendations for international students: Required—proof of English language proficiency required for non-native English speakers; Recommended—TOEFL (minimum score 550 paper-based; 213 computer-based; 79 iBT). *Application deadline:* Applications are processed on a rolling basis. Application fee: $50 ($75 for international students). Electronic applications accepted. *Expenses:* Tuition, state resident: full-time $4298; part-time $239 per contact hour. Tuition, nonresident: full-time $9878; part-time $549 per contact hour. Required fees: $265 per contact hour. *Financial support:* Fellowships, research assistantships, teaching assistantships, career-related internships or fieldwork and Federal Work-Study available. Financial award application deadline: 4/1; financial award applicants required to submit FAFSA. *Faculty research:* Large scale IS, business intelligence, security, applied statistics, quality and reliability management. *Unit head:* Chair. *Application contact:* Graduate Advisor, 940-565-4149, Fax: 940-565-4935, E-mail: itdsrecp@unt.edu.

University of Oklahoma, Graduate College, Gaylord College of Journalism and Mass Communication, Program in Journalism and Mass Communication, Norman, OK 73019-0390. Offers advertising and public relations (MA); information gathering and distribution (MA); mass communication management and policy (MA); professional writing (MA); telecommunication and new technology (MA). Part-time programs available. *Students:* 34 full-time (18 women), 43 part-time (23 women); includes 13 minority (4 African Americans, 5 American Indian/Alaska Native, 4 Hispanic Americans), 9 international. 45 applicants, 42% accepted, 9 enrolled. *Degree requirements:* For master's, thesis optional. *Entrance requirements:* For master's, GRE General Test, minimum GPA of 3.2, 9 hours of course work in journalism, course work in statistics. Additional exam requirements/recommendations for international students: Required—TOEFL (minimum score 600 paper-based; 250 computer-based), TWE (minimum score 5). *Application deadline:* For fall admission, 2/1 for domestic students, 4/1 for international students; for spring admission, 11/1 for domestic students, 9/1 for international students. Application fee: $40 ($90 for international students). Electronic applications accepted. *Expenses:* Tuition, state resident: full-time $3744; part-time $156 per credit hour. Tuition, nonresident: full-time $13,577; part-time $565.70 per credit hour. Required fees: $2415; $90.10 per credit hour. *Financial support:* In 2009–10, 43 students received support, including 4 fellowships (averaging $5,000 per year); career-related internships or fieldwork, scholarships/grants, health care benefits, and unspecified assistantships also available. *Faculty research:* Organizational management, rhetorical analysis, international public relations, digital production, normative theory. *Unit head:* Dr. Joe Foote, Dean, 405-325-2721, Fax: 405-325-7565, E-mail: jfoote@ou.edu. *Application contact:* Kelly Storm, Graduate Advisor, 405-325-2722, Fax: 405-325-7565, E-mail: kstorm@ou.edu.

University of Oklahoma, Graduate College, Michael F. Price College of Business, Division of Management Information Systems, Norman, OK 73019. Offers management (MS). Part-time programs available. *Faculty:* 9 full-time (3 women). *Students:* 6 full-time (2 women), 5 part-time (1 woman); includes 4 minority (3 Asian Americans or Pacific Islanders, 1 Hispanic American), 1 international. 14 applicants, 36% accepted, 4 enrolled. In 2009, 4 master's awarded. *Entrance requirements:* Additional exam requirements/recommendations for international students: Required—TOEFL (minimum score 550 paper-based; 213 computer-based). *Application deadline:* For fall admission, 2/1 for domestic students, 4/1 for international students; for spring admission, 11/1 for domestic students, 9/1 for international students. Applications are processed on a rolling basis. Application fee: $40 ($90 for international students). Electronic applications accepted. *Expenses:* Tuition, state resident: full-time $3744; part-time $156 per credit hour. Tuition, nonresident: full-time $13,577; part-time $565.70 per credit hour. Required fees: $2415; $90.10 per credit hour. *Financial support:* In 2009–10, 9 students received support, including 9 research assistantships with full tuition reimbursements available (averaging $12,042 per year), 3 teaching assistantships with full tuition reimbursements available (averaging $13,278 per year); scholarships/grants and unspecified assistantships also available. Financial award applicants required to submit FAFSA. *Faculty research:* IT enabled teams, business value of IT, knowledge management, technology adoption. Total annual research expenditures: $25,679. *Unit head:* Laku Chidambaram, Director, 405-325-5721, Fax: 405-325-2096, E-mail: laku@ou.edu. *Application contact:* Jim Smith, Senior Academic Counselor, 405-325-3744, Fax: 405-325-7753, E-mail: jlsmith@ou.edu.

University of Oregon, Graduate School, Interdisciplinary Program in Applied Information Management, Eugene, OR 97403. Offers MS. Part-time and evening/weekend programs available. *Degree requirements:* For master's, project. *Entrance requirements:* For master's, GMAT, GRE, or MAT. Additional exam requirements/recommendations for international students: Required—TOEFL. Electronic applications accepted. *Expenses:* Contact institution. *Faculty research:* Business management, information design.

University of Pennsylvania, Wharton School, Operations and Information Management Department, Philadelphia, PA 19104. Offers MBA, PhD. Terminal master's awarded for partial completion of doctoral program. *Degree requirements:* For master's, thesis, preliminary exams; for doctorate, thesis/dissertation, preliminary exams. *Entrance requirements:* For master's, GMAT, GRE; for doctorate, GRE. Electronic applications accepted. *Expenses:* Tuition: Full-time $25,660; part-time $4758 per course. Required fees: $2152; $270 per course. Tuition and fees vary according to course load, degree level and program. *Faculty research:* Supply chain management, operations research, economics of information systems, risk analysis, electronic commerce.

University of Phoenix, School of Business, College of Information Systems and Technology, Phoenix, AZ 85034-7209. Offers management (MIS). Evening/weekend programs available. *Faculty:* 8 full-time (4 women), 124 part-time/adjunct (38 women). *Students:* 2,693 full-time (937 women); includes 853 minority (539 African Americans, 16 American Indian/Alaska Native, 136 Asian Americans or Pacific Islanders, 162 Hispanic Americans), 187 international. Average age 38. In 2009, 1,104 master's awarded. *Degree requirements:* For master's, thesis (for some programs). *Entrance requirements:* For master's, 3 years of work experience, minimum undergraduate GPA of 3.0. Additional exam requirements/recommendations for international students: Required—TOEFL (minimum score 550 paper-based; 213 computer-based; 79 iBT). *Application deadline:* Applications are processed on a rolling basis. Application fee: $45. Electronic applications accepted. *Expenses:* Tuition: Full-time $13,272. Required fees: $660. Full-time tuition and fees vary according to course level, degree level and program. *Financial support:* Institutionally sponsored loans and scholarships/grants available. Financial award applicants required to submit FAFSA. *Unit head:* Dr. Blair Sith, Dean/Executive Director, 480-557-1241, Fax: 480-929-7164, E-mail: blair.smitha@phoenix.edu. *Application contact:* Chair, 680-766-0766.

University of Phoenix–Atlanta Campus, John Sperling School of Business, College of Information Systems and Technology, Sandy Springs, GA 30350-4153. Offers information systems (MIS); technology management (MBA). Evening/weekend programs available. *Degree requirements:* For master's, thesis (for some programs). *Entrance requirements:* For master's, 3 years of work experience, minimum undergraduate GPA of 3.0. Additional exam requirements/recommendations for international students: Required—TOEFL (minimum score 550 paper-based; 213 computer-based; 79 iBT). Electronic applications accepted.

University of Phoenix–Augusta Campus, College of Information Systems and Technology, Augusta, GA 30909-4583. Offers information systems (MIS); technology management (MBA).

University of Phoenix–Austin Campus, College of Information Systems and Technology, Austin, TX 78759. Offers information systems (MIS); technology management (MBA).

University of Phoenix–Bay Area Campus, John Sperling School of Business, College of Information Systems and Technology, Pleasanton, CA 94588-3677. Offers e-business (MBA); information systems (MIS); technology management (MBA). Evening/weekend programs available. *Degree requirements:* For master's, thesis (for some programs). *Entrance requirements:* For master's, minimum undergraduate GPA of 3.0, 3 years of work experience. Additional exam requirements/recommendations for international students: Required—TOEFL (minimum score 550 paper-based; 213 computer-based; 79 iBT). Electronic applications accepted.

University of Phoenix–Birmingham Campus, College of Information Systems and Technology, Birmingham, AL 35244. Offers information systems (MIS); technology management (MBA).

University of Phoenix–Boston Campus, John Sperling School of Business, College of Information Systems and Technology, Braintree, MA 02184-4949. Offers technology management (MBA). Evening/weekend programs available. *Degree requirements:* For master's, thesis (for some programs). *Entrance requirements:* For master's, minimum GPA of 3.0, 3 years of work experience. Additional exam requirements/recommendations for international students: Required—TOEFL (minimum score 550 paper-based; 213 computer-based; 79 iBT). Electronic applications accepted.

University of Phoenix–Central Florida Campus, John Sperling School of Business, College of Information Systems and Technology, Maitland, FL 32751-7057. Offers management (MIS); technology management (MBA). Evening/weekend programs available. *Degree requirements:* For master's, thesis (for some programs). *Entrance requirements:* For master's, minimum undergraduate GPA of 3.0, 3 years work experience. Additional exam requirements/recommendations for international students: Required—TOEFL (minimum score 550 paper-based; 213 computer-based; 79 iBT). Electronic applications accepted.

University of Phoenix–Central Valley Campus, College of Information Systems and Technology, Fresno, CA 93720-1562. Offers information systems (MIS); technology management (MBA).

University of Phoenix–Charlotte Campus, John Sperling School of Business, College of Information Systems and Technology, Charlotte, NC 28273-3409. Offers information systems (MIS); information systems management (MISM); technology management (MBA). Evening/weekend programs available. *Degree requirements:* For master's, thesis (for some programs). *Entrance requirements:* For master's, minimum undergraduate GPA of 3.0, 3 years work experience. Additional exam requirements/recommendations for international students: Required—TOEFL (minimum score 550 paper-based; 213 computer-based; 79 iBT). Electronic applications accepted.

University of Phoenix–Chattanooga Campus, College of Information Systems and Technology, Chattanooga, TN 37421-3707. Offers information systems (MIS); technology management (MBA). Postbaccalaureate distance learning degree programs offered.

University of Phoenix–Cheyenne Campus, College of Information Systems and Technology, Cheyenne, WY 82009. Offers information systems (MIS); technology management (MBA).

University of Phoenix–Chicago Campus, John Sperling School of Business, College of Information Systems and Technology, Schaumburg, IL 60173-4399. Offers e-business (MBA); information systems (MIS); management (MM); technology management (MBA). Evening/weekend programs available. *Degree requirements:* For master's, thesis (for some programs). *Entrance requirements:* For master's, 3 years of work experience, minimum undergraduate

GPA of 3.0. Additional exam requirements/recommendations for international students: Required—TOEFL (minimum score 550 paper-based; 213 computer-based; 79 iBT). Electronic applications accepted.

University of Phoenix–Cincinnati Campus, John Sperling School of Business, College of Information Systems and Technology, West Chester, OH 45069-4875. Offers electronic business (MBA); information systems (MIS); technology management (MBA). Evening/weekend programs available. Postbaccalaureate distance learning degree programs offered. *Degree requirements:* For master's, thesis (for some programs). *Entrance requirements:* For master's, minimum undergraduate GPA of 2.5, 3 years of work experience. Additional exam requirements/recommendations for international students: Required—TOEFL (minimum score 550 paper-based; 213 computer-based; 79 iBT). Electronic applications accepted.

University of Phoenix–Cleveland Campus, John Sperling School of Business, College of Information Systems and Technology, Independence, OH 44131-2194. Offers information management (MIS); technology management (MBA). Evening/weekend programs available. Postbaccalaureate distance learning degree programs offered (no on-campus study). *Degree requirements:* For master's, thesis (for some programs). *Entrance requirements:* For master's, minimum undergraduate GPA of 3.0, 3 years of work experience. Additional exam requirements/recommendations for international students: Required—TOEFL (minimum score 550 paper-based; 213 computer-based; 79 iBT). Electronic applications accepted.

University of Phoenix–Columbus Georgia Campus, John Sperling School of Business, College of Information Systems and Technology, Columbus, GA 31904-6321. Offers e-business (MBA); information systems (MIS); technology management (MBA). Evening/weekend programs available. Postbaccalaureate distance learning degree programs offered. *Degree requirements:* For master's, thesis (for some programs). *Entrance requirements:* For master's, minimum undergraduate GPA of 3.0, 3 years of work experience. Additional exam requirements/recommendations for international students: Required—TOEFL (minimum score 550 paper-based; 213 computer-based; 79 iBT). Electronic applications accepted.

University of Phoenix–Columbus Ohio Campus, John Sperling School of Business, College of Information Systems and Technology, Columbus, OH 43240-4032. Offers information systems (MIS); technology management (MBA). Postbaccalaureate distance learning degree programs offered.

University of Phoenix–Dallas Campus, John Sperling School of Business, College of Information Systems and Technology, Dallas, TX 75251-2009. Offers e-business (MBA); information systems (MIS); technology management (MBA). Evening/weekend programs available. *Degree requirements:* For master's, thesis (for some programs). *Entrance requirements:* For master's, minimum undergraduate GPA of 3.0, 3 years of work experience. Additional exam requirements/recommendations for international students: Required—TOEFL (minimum score 550 paper-based; 213 computer-based; 79 iBT). Electronic applications accepted.

University of Phoenix–Denver Campus, John Sperling School of Business, College of Information Systems and Technology, Lone Tree, CO 80124-5453. Offers e-business (MBA); management (MIS); technology management (MBA). Evening/weekend programs available. Postbaccalaureate distance learning degree programs offered. *Degree requirements:* For master's, thesis (for some programs). *Entrance requirements:* For master's, minimum undergraduate GPA of 3.0, 3 years of work experience. Additional exam requirements/recommendations for international students: Required—TOEFL (minimum score 550 paper-based; 213 computer-based; 79 iBT). Electronic applications accepted.

University of Phoenix–Des Moines Campus, College of Information Systems and Technology, Des Moines, IA 50266. Offers information systems (MIS); technology management (MBA). Postbaccalaureate distance learning degree programs offered.

University of Phoenix–Eastern Washington Campus, John Sperling School of Business, College of Information Systems and Technology, Spokane Valley, WA 99212-2531. Offers technology management (MBA).

University of Phoenix–Harrisburg Campus, College of Information Systems and Technology, Harrisburg, PA 17112. Offers information systems (MIS); technology management (MBA). Postbaccalaureate distance learning degree programs offered.

University of Phoenix–Hawaii Campus, John Sperling School of Business, College of Information Systems and Technology, Honolulu, HI 96813-4317. Offers information systems (MIS); technology management (MBA). Evening/weekend programs available. *Degree requirements:* For master's, thesis (for some programs). *Entrance requirements:* For master's, minimum undergraduate GPA of 3.0, 3 years of work experience. Additional exam requirements/recommendations for international students: Required—TOEFL (minimum score 550 paper-based; 213 computer-based; 79 iBT). Electronic applications accepted.

University of Phoenix–Houston Campus, John Sperling School of Business, College of Information Systems and Technology, Houston, TX 77079-2004. Offers e-business (MBA); information systems (MIS); technology management (MBA). Evening/weekend programs available. Postbaccalaureate distance learning degree programs offered. *Degree requirements:* For master's, comprehensive exam (for some programs), thesis. *Entrance requirements:* For master's, minimum undergraduate GPA of 3.0, 3 years of work experience. Additional exam requirements/recommendations for international students: Required—TOEFL (minimum score 550 paper-based; 213 computer-based; 79 iBT). Electronic applications accepted.

University of Phoenix–Idaho Campus, John Sperling School of Business, College of Information Systems and Technology, Meridian, ID 83642-3014. Offers information systems (MIS); technology management (MBA). Evening/weekend programs available. *Degree requirements:* For master's, thesis (for some programs). *Entrance requirements:* For master's, minimum undergraduate GPA of 3.0, 3 years of work experience. Additional exam requirements/recommendations for international students: Required—TOEFL (minimum score 550 paper-based; 213 computer-based). Electronic applications accepted.

University of Phoenix–Indianapolis Campus, John Sperling School of Business, College of Information Systems and Technology, Indianapolis, IN 46250-932. Offers information systems (MIS); technology management (MBA). Evening/weekend programs available. *Degree requirements:* For master's, thesis (for some programs). *Entrance requirements:* For master's, minimum undergraduate GPA of 3.0, 3 years of work experience. Additional exam requirements/recommendations for international students: Required—TOEFL (minimum score 550 paper-based; 213 computer-based). Electronic applications accepted.

University of Phoenix–Jersey City Campus, College of Information Systems and Technology, Jersey City, NJ 07310. Offers information systems (MIS); technology management (MBA). Postbaccalaureate distance learning degree programs offered.

University of Phoenix–Las Vegas Campus, John Sperling School of Business, College of Information Systems and Technology, Las Vegas, NV 89128. Offers information systems (MIS); technology management (MBA). Evening/weekend programs available. *Degree requirements:* For master's, thesis (for some programs). *Entrance requirements:* For master's, minimum undergraduate GPA of 3.0, 3 years of work experience. Additional exam requirements/recommendations for international students: Required—TOEFL (minimum score 550 paper-based; 213 computer-based; 79 iBT). Electronic applications accepted.

University of Phoenix–Louisiana Campus, John Sperling School of Business, College of Information Systems and Technology, Metairie, LA 70001-2082. Offers information systems/management (MIS); technology management (MBA). Evening/weekend programs available. *Degree requirements:* For master's, thesis (for some programs). *Entrance requirements:* For master's, minimum undergraduate GPA of 3.0, 3 years work experience. Additional exam requirements/recommendations for international students: Required—TOEFL (minimum score 550 paper-based; 213 computer-based). Electronic applications accepted.

University of Phoenix–Madison Campus, College of Information Systems and Technology, Madison, WI 53718-2416. Offers information systems (MIS); management (MIS); technology management (MBA).

University of Phoenix–Madison Campus, John Sperling School of Business, College of Information Systems and Technology, Madison, WI 53718-2416. Offers information systems (MIS); technology management (MBA). Evening/weekend programs available. *Degree requirements:* For master's, thesis (for some programs). *Entrance requirements:* For master's, 3 years of work experience, minimum undergraduate GPA of 3.0. Additional exam requirements/recommendations for international students: Required—TOEFL (minimum score 550 paper-based; 213 computer-based; 79 iBT). Electronic applications accepted.

University of Phoenix–Maryland Campus, John Sperling School of Business, College of Information Systems and Technology, Columbia, MD 21045-5424. Offers information systems (MIS); technology management (MBA). Evening/weekend programs available. *Degree requirements:* For master's, thesis (for some programs). *Entrance requirements:* For master's, minimum undergraduate GPA of 3.0, 3 years of work experience. Additional exam requirements/recommendations for international students: Required—TOEFL (minimum score 550 paper-based; 213 computer-based; 79 iBT). Electronic applications accepted.

University of Phoenix–Memphis Campus, College of Information Systems and Technology, Cordova, TN 38018. Offers information systems (MIS); technology management (MBA).

University of Phoenix–Metro Detroit Campus, School of Business, College of Information Systems and Technology, Troy, MI 48098-2623. Offers MIS. Evening/weekend programs available. *Faculty:* 1 full-time (0 women), 2 part-time/adjunct (1 woman). *Students:* 13 full-time (6 women); includes 4 minority (all African Americans). Average age 40. In 2009, 3 master's awarded. *Degree requirements:* For master's, thesis (for some programs). *Entrance requirements:* For master's, minimum undergraduate GPA of 3.0, 3 years work experience. Additional exam requirements/recommendations for international students: Required—TOEFL (minimum score 550 paper-based; 213 computer-based; 79 iBT). *Application deadline:* Applications are processed on a rolling basis. Application fee: $45. Electronic applications accepted. *Expenses:* Tuition: Full-time $14,136. Required fees: $660. *Financial support:* Institutionally sponsored loans and scholarships/grants available. Financial award applicants required to submit FAFSA. *Unit head:* Dr. Blair Smith, Dean/Executive Director, 480-557-1241, E-mail: adam.honea@phoenix.edu. *Application contact:* Chair, 800-834-2438, Fax: 248-267-0147.

University of Phoenix–Nashville Campus, John Sperling School of Business, College of Information Systems and Technology, Nashville, TN 37214-5048. Offers technology management (MBA). Evening/weekend programs available. *Degree requirements:* For master's, thesis (for some programs). *Entrance requirements:* For master's, 3 years of work experience, minimum undergraduate GPA of 3.0. Additional exam requirements/recommendations for international students: Required—TOEFL (minimum score 550 paper-based; 213 computer-based; 79 iBT). Electronic applications accepted.

University of Phoenix–New Mexico Campus, John Sperling School of Business, College of Information Systems and Technology, Albuquerque, NM 87113-1570. Offers e-business (MBA); information systems (MIS); technology management (MBA). Evening/weekend programs available. *Degree requirements:* For master's, thesis (for some programs). *Entrance requirements:* For master's, minimum undergraduate GPA of 3.0, 3 years of work experience. Additional exam requirements/recommendations for international students: Required—TOEFL (minimum score 550 paper-based; 213 computer-based; 79 iBT). Electronic applications accepted.

University of Phoenix–Northern Nevada Campus, College of Information Systems and Technology, Reno, NV 89521-5862. Offers information systems (MIS); technology management (MBA).

University of Phoenix–Northern Virginia Campus, College of Information Systems and Technology, Reston, VA 20190. Offers information systems and technology (MIS); management (MIS); technology management (MBA).

University of Phoenix–North Florida Campus, John Sperling School of Business, College of Information Systems and Technology, Jacksonville, FL 32216-0959. Offers information systems (MIS); management (MIS). Evening/weekend programs available. *Degree requirements:* For master's, thesis (for some programs). *Entrance requirements:* For master's, minimum undergraduate GPA of 3.0, 3 years work experience. Additional exam requirements/recommendations for international students: Required—TOEFL (minimum score 550 paper-based; 213 computer-based; 79 iBT). Electronic applications accepted.

University of Phoenix–Northwest Arkansas Campus, College of Information Systems and Technology, Rogers, AR 72756-9615. Offers information systems (MIS); technology management (MBA).

University of Phoenix–Oklahoma City Campus, John Sperling School of Business, College of Information Systems and Technology, Oklahoma City, OK 73116-8244. Offers e-business (MBA); technology management (MBA). Evening/weekend programs available. *Degree requirements:* For master's, thesis (for some programs). *Entrance requirements:* For master's, minimum undergraduate GPA of 3.0, 3 years of work experience. Additional exam requirements/recommendations for international students: Required—TOEFL (minimum score 550 paper-based; 213 computer-based; 79 iBT). Electronic applications accepted.

University of Phoenix–Omaha Campus, College of Information Systems and Technology, Omaha, NE 68154-5240. Offers information systems (MIS); technology management (MBA).

University of Phoenix–Oregon Campus, The John Sperling School of Business, College of Information Systems and Technology, Tigard, OR 97223. Offers information systems (MIS); technology management (MBA). Evening/weekend programs available. *Degree requirements:* For master's, thesis (for some programs). *Entrance requirements:* For master's, minimum undergraduate GPA of 2.5, 3 years work experience. Additional exam requirements/recommendations for international students: Required—TOEFL (minimum score 550 paper-based; 213 computer-based; 79 iBT). Electronic applications accepted.

University of Phoenix–Philadelphia Campus, The John Sperling School of Business, College of Information Systems and Technology, Wayne, PA 19087-2121. Offers information systems (MIS); technology management (MBA). Evening/weekend programs available. *Degree requirements:* For master's, thesis (for some programs). *Entrance requirements:* For master's, 3 years of work experience, minimum undergraduate GPA of 3.0. Additional exam requirements/recommendations for international students: Required—TOEFL (minimum score 550 paper-based; 213 computer-based; 79 iBT). Electronic applications accepted.

University of Phoenix–Pittsburgh Campus, John Sperling School of Business, College of Information Systems and Technology, Pittsburgh, PA 15276. Offers e-business (MBA); information systems (MIS); technology management (MBA). Evening/weekend programs available. *Degree requirements:* For master's, thesis (for some programs). *Entrance requirements:* For master's, minimum undergraduate GPA of 3.0, 3 years work experience. Additional exam requirements/recommendations for international students: Required—TOEFL (minimum score 550 paper-based; 213 computer-based; 79 iBT). Electronic applications accepted.

University of Phoenix–Raleigh Campus, College of Information Systems and Technology, Raleigh, NC 27606. Offers information systems and technology (MIS); management (MIS); technology management (MBA).

University of Phoenix–Richmond Campus, John Sperling School of Business, College of Information Systems and Technology, Richmond, VA 23230. Offers information systems (MIS); technology management (MBA). Evening/weekend programs available. *Degree requirements:* For master's, thesis (for some programs). *Entrance requirements:* For master's, minimum undergraduate GPA of 3.0, 3 years work experience. Additional exam requirements/

Management Information Systems

University of Phoenix–Richmond Campus (continued)
recommendations for international students: Required—TOEFL (minimum score 500 paper-based; 213 computer-based; 79 iBT). Electronic applications accepted.

University of Phoenix–Sacramento Valley Campus, John Sperling School of Business, College of Information Systems and Technology, Sacramento, CA 95833-3632. Offers management (MIS); technology management (MBA). Evening/weekend programs available. *Degree requirements:* For master's, thesis (for some programs). *Entrance requirements:* For master's, minimum undergraduate GPA of 3.0, 3 years work experience. Additional exam requirements/recommendations for international students: Required—TOEFL (minimum score 550 paper-based; 213 computer-based; 79 iBT). Electronic applications accepted.

University of Phoenix–St. Louis Campus, John Sperling School of Business, College of Information Systems and Technology, St. Louis, MO 63043-4828. Offers information systems (MIS); technology management (MBA). Evening/weekend programs available. *Degree requirements:* For master's, thesis (for some programs). *Entrance requirements:* For master's, minimum undergraduate GPA of 3.0, 3 years of work experience. Additional exam requirements/recommendations for international students: Required—TOEFL (minimum score 550 paper-based; 213 computer-based). Electronic applications accepted.

University of Phoenix–San Antonio Campus, College of Information Systems and Technology, San Antonio, TX 78230. Offers information systems (MIS); technology management (MBA).

University of Phoenix–San Diego Campus, John Sperling School of Business, College of Information Systems and Technology, San Diego, CA 92123. Offers management (MIS); technology management (MBA). Evening/weekend programs available. *Degree requirements:* For master's, thesis (for some programs). *Entrance requirements:* For master's, minimum undergraduate GPA of 3.0, 3 years work experience. Additional exam requirements/recommendations for international students: Required—TOEFL (minimum score 550 paper-based; 213 computer-based; 79 iBT). Electronic applications accepted.

University of Phoenix–Savannah Campus, College of Information Systems and Technology, Savannah, GA 31405-7400. Offers information systems and technology (MIS); technology management (MBA).

University of Phoenix–Southern Arizona Campus, John Sperling School of Business, College of Information Systems and Technology, Tucson, AZ 85711. Offers information systems (MIS); technology management (MBA). Evening/weekend programs available. *Degree requirements:* For master's, thesis (for some programs). *Entrance requirements:* For master's, minimum undergraduate GPA of 3.0, 3 years of work experience. Additional exam requirements/recommendations for international students: Required—TOEFL (minimum score 550 paper-based; 213 computer-based; 79 iBT). Electronic applications accepted.

University of Phoenix–Southern Colorado Campus, John Sperling School of Business, College of Information Systems and Technology, Colorado Springs, CO 80919-2335. Offers technology management (MBA). Evening/weekend programs available. *Degree requirements:* For master's, thesis (for some programs). *Entrance requirements:* For master's, minimum undergraduate GPA of 3.0, 3 years of work experience. Additional exam requirements/recommendations for international students: Required—TOEFL (minimum score 550 paper-based; 213 computer-based). Electronic applications accepted.

University of Phoenix–South Florida Campus, John Sperling School of Business, College of Information Systems and Technology, Fort Lauderdale, FL 33309. Offers management (MIS); technology management (MBA). Evening/weekend programs available. *Degree requirements:* For master's, thesis (for some programs). *Entrance requirements:* For master's, minimum undergraduate GPA of 3.0, 3 years of work experience. Additional exam requirements/recommendations for international students: Required—TOEFL (minimum score 550 paper-based; 213 computer-based; 79 iBT). Electronic applications accepted.

University of Phoenix–Springfield Campus, College of Information Systems and Technology, Springfield, MO 65804-7211. Offers information systems (MIS); technology management (MBA).

University of Phoenix–Tulsa Campus, John Sperling School of Business, College of Information Systems and Technology, Tulsa, OK 74134-1412. Offers information systems and technology (MIS); technology management (MBA).

University of Phoenix–Utah Campus, John Sperling School of Business, College of Information Systems and Technology, Salt Lake City, UT 84123-4617. Offers MIS. Evening/weekend programs available. *Degree requirements:* For master's, thesis (for some programs). *Entrance requirements:* For master's, minimum undergraduate GPA of 2.5, 3 years work experience. Additional exam requirements/recommendations for international students: Required—TOEFL (minimum score 550 paper-based; 213 computer-based; 79 iBT). Electronic applications accepted.

University of Phoenix–Vancouver Campus, John Sperling School of Business, College of Information Systems and Technology, Burnaby, BC V5C 6G9, Canada. Offers technology management (MBA). Evening/weekend programs available. *Degree requirements:* For master's, thesis (for some programs). *Entrance requirements:* For master's, minimum undergraduate GPA of 3.0, 3 years of work experience. Additional exam requirements/recommendations for international students: Required—TOEFL (minimum score 550 paper-based; 213 computer-based; 79 iBT). Electronic applications accepted.

University of Phoenix–Western Washington Campus, College of Information Systems and Technology, Tukwila, WA 98188. Offers information systems (MIS); technology management (MBA). Evening/weekend programs available. *Degree requirements:* For master's, thesis (for some programs). *Entrance requirements:* For master's, minimum undergraduate GPA of 3.0, 3 years of work experience. Additional exam requirements/recommendations for international students: Required—TOEFL (minimum score 550 paper-based; 213 computer-based; 79 iBT). Electronic applications accepted.

University of Phoenix–West Florida Campus, The John Sperling School of Business, College of Information Systems and Technology, Temple Terrace, FL 33637. Offers information systems (MIS); technology management (MBA). Evening/weekend programs available. *Degree requirements:* For master's, thesis (for some programs). *Entrance requirements:* For master's, minimum undergraduate GPA of 3.0, 3 years work experience. Additional exam requirements/recommendations for international students: Required—TOEFL (minimum score 550 paper-based; 213 computer-based; 79 iBT). Electronic applications accepted.

University of Pittsburgh, Katz Graduate School of Business, Doctoral Program in Business Administration, Pittsburgh, PA 15260. Offers accounting (PhD); finance (PhD); information systems (PhD); marketing (PhD); operations/decision sciences/artificial intelligence (PhD); organizational behavior and human resource management (PhD); strategic planning (PhD). *Accreditation:* AACSB. *Faculty:* 50 full-time (15 women). *Students:* 53 full-time (21 women); includes 8 minority (4 African Americans, 2 Asian Americans or Pacific Islanders, 2 Hispanic Americans), 22 international. 324 applicants, 4% accepted, 12 enrolled. In 2009, 11 doctorates awarded. *Degree requirements:* For doctorate, comprehensive exam, thesis/dissertation. *Entrance requirements:* For doctorate, GMAT or GRE, references, work experience relevant for individual program. Additional exam requirements/recommendations for international students: Required—TOEFL or IELTS. *Application deadline:* For fall admission, 2/1 priority date for domestic and international students. Applications are processed on a rolling basis. Application fee: $50. Electronic applications accepted. *Expenses:* Tuition, state resident: full-time $16,402; part-time $665 per credit. Tuition, nonresident: full-time $28,694; part-time $1175 per credit. Required fees: $690; $175 per term. Tuition and fees vary according to program. *Financial support:* In 2009–10, 36 students received support, including 31 research assistantships with full tuition reimbursements available (averaging $18,450 per year), 5 teaching assistantships with full tuition reimbursements available (averaging $23,511 per year); fellowships, Federal Work-Study, scholarships/grants, health care benefits, and unspecified assistantships also available. Financial award application deadline: 2/1. *Faculty research:* Accounting statements and reporting, incentives and governance; corporate finance, mergers and acquisitions; information systems processes, structures, OR, supply chain, and decision-making; organizational structure, knowledge management, and corporate strategy; consumer behavior and marketing models. Total annual research expenditures: $362,777. *Unit head:* Dr. John E. Hulland, Director, 412-648-1534, Fax: 412-624-3633, E-mail: jhulland@katz.pitt.edu. *Application contact:* Carrie Woods, Assistant Director, 412-648-1525, Fax: 412-624-3633, E-mail: cawoods@katz.pitt.edu.

University of Pittsburgh, Katz Graduate School of Business, Masters of Business Administration Programs, Pittsburgh, PA 15260. Offers accounting (MS); finance (MBA); general management (MBA); information systems (MBA, MSIS); marketing (MBA); organizational behavior and human resource management (MBA); organizational leadership (Certificate); six sigma (Certificate); strategy (MBA); technology, innovation and entrepreneurship (Certificate); MBA/JD; MBA/MIB; MBA/MPIA; MBA/MSE; MBA/MSIS. *Accreditation:* AACSB. Part-time and evening/weekend programs available. *Faculty:* 58 full-time (12 women), 23 part-time/adjunct (7 women). *Students:* 192 full-time (62 women), 506 part-time (179 women); includes 58 minority (29 African Americans, 1 American Indian/Alaska Native, 24 Asian Americans or Pacific Islanders, 4 Hispanic Americans), 101 international. Average age 29. 674 applicants, 52% accepted, 204 enrolled. In 2009, 263 master's awarded. *Entrance requirements:* For master's, GMAT, references, work experience relevant for individual programs. Additional exam requirements/recommendations for international students: Required—TOEFL (minimum score 600 paper-based; 250 computer-based; 100 iBT), or IELTS. *Application deadline:* For fall admission, 7/1 for domestic and international students; for winter admission, 11/1 for domestic and international students; for spring admission, 3/1 for domestic and international students. Applications are processed on a rolling basis. Application fee: $50. Electronic applications accepted. *Expenses:* Tuition, state resident: full-time $16,402; part-time $665 per credit. Tuition, nonresident: full-time $28,694; part-time $1175 per credit. Required fees: $690; $175 per term. Tuition and fees vary according to program. *Financial support:* In 2009–10, 75 students received support. Career-related internships or fieldwork and scholarships/grants available. Financial award application deadline: 6/1; financial award applicants required to submit FAFSA. *Faculty research:* Accounting statements and reporting, incentives and governance; corporate finance, mergers and acquisitions; information systems processes, structures, and decision-making; organizational structure, knowledge management, and corporate strategy; consumer behavior and marketing models. *Unit head:* William T. Valenta, Assistant Dean/MBA Program Director, 412-648-1610, Fax: 412-648-1659, E-mail: wtvalenta@katz.pitt.edu. *Application contact:* Cliff McCormick, Director of MBA Admissions, 412-648-1700, Fax: 412-648-1659, E-mail: mba@katz.pitt.edu.

University of Pittsburgh, Katz Graduate School of Business, MBA/MS in Management of Information Systems Dual Degree Program, Pittsburgh, PA 15260. Offers MBA/MS. Part-time and evening/weekend programs available. *Students:* 17 full-time (2 women), 14 part-time (1 woman); includes 4 minority (3 African Americans, 1 Hispanic American), 9 international. Average age 31. 35 applicants, 57% accepted, 11 enrolled. *Entrance requirements:* Additional exam requirements/recommendations for international students: Required—TOEFL (minimum score 600 paper-based; 250 computer-based; 100 iBT), or IELTS. *Application deadline:* For fall admission, 7/1 for domestic and international students; for winter admission, 11/1 for domestic and international students; for spring admission, 3/1 for domestic and international students. Applications are processed on a rolling basis. Application fee: $50. Electronic applications accepted. *Expenses:* Tuition, state resident: full-time $16,402; part-time $665 per credit. Tuition, nonresident: full-time $28,694; part-time $1175 per credit. Required fees: $690; $175 per term. Tuition and fees vary according to program. *Financial support:* In 2009–10, 6 students received support. Career-related internships or fieldwork and scholarships/grants available. Financial award application deadline: 6/1; financial award applicants required to submit FAFSA. *Faculty research:* Social media and their impacts on organizations, information technology adoption and diffusion, economics of information systems, software acquisition and implementation, human-computer interaction. *Unit head:* William T. Valenta, Assistant Dean/Director of MBA Programs, 412-648-1610, Fax: 412-648-1659, E-mail: wtvalenta@katz.pitt.edu. *Application contact:* Cliff McCormick, Director, MBA Admissions, 412-648-1700, Fax: 412-648-1659, E-mail: mba@katz.pitt.edu.

University of Redlands, School of Business, Redlands, CA 92373-0999. Offers business (MBA); information technology (MS); management (MA). Evening/weekend programs available. *Entrance requirements:* For master's, minimum GPA of 3.0, 2 letters of recommendation. *Expenses:* Tuition: Part-time $766 per unit. Required fees: $74 per semester. Part-time tuition and fees vary according to program. *Faculty research:* Human resources management, educational leadership, humanities, teacher education.

University of St. Thomas, Graduate Studies, Graduate Programs in Software, Saint Paul, MN 55105. Offers advanced studies in business analysis (Certificate); computer security (Certificate); information systems (Certificate); software design and development (Certificate); software engineering (MS); software management (MS); software systems (MSS); MS/MBA. Part-time and evening/weekend programs available. *Degree requirements:* For master's, thesis optional. *Entrance requirements:* Additional exam requirements/recommendations for international students: Required—TOEFL. *Application deadline:* For fall admission, 8/1 priority date for domestic students, 5/1 priority date for international students; for spring admission, 1/1 priority date for domestic students, 10/1 priority date for international students. Applications are processed on a rolling basis. Application fee: $30. *Expenses:* Contact institution. *Financial support:* Federal Work-Study, institutionally sponsored loans, and scholarships/grants available. Financial award application deadline: 4/1. *Faculty research:* Data mining, distributed databases, bioinformatics, computer security. *Unit head:* Dr. Bhabani Misra, Director, 651-962-5508, Fax: 651-962-5543, E-mail: bsmisra@stthomas.edu. *Application contact:* Douglas J. Stubeda, Assistant Director, 651-962-5503, Fax: 651-962-5543, E-mail: djstubeda@stthomas.edu.

University of San Francisco, School of Business and Professional Studies, Program in Information Systems, San Francisco, CA 94117-1080. Offers MS. Part-time and evening/weekend programs available. *Faculty:* 1 full-time (0 women), 12 part-time/adjunct (3 women). *Students:* 92 full-time (27 women), 1 (woman) part-time; includes 40 minority (6 African Americans, 1 American Indian/Alaska Native, 23 Asian Americans or Pacific Islanders, 10 Hispanic Americans), 10 international. Average age 38. 41 applicants, 68% accepted, 16 enrolled. In 2009, 51 master's awarded. *Degree requirements:* For master's, thesis. *Entrance requirements:* For master's, minimum GPA of 3.0. Application fee: $55 ($65 for international students). *Expenses:* Tuition: Full-time $19,710; part-time $1095 per unit. Part-time tuition and fees vary according to degree level, campus/location and program. *Financial support:* In 2009–10, 41 students received support. Application deadline: 3/2. *Unit head:* Dr. Moira Gunn, Director, 415-422-2592. *Application contact:* Advising Office, 415-422-6000, E-mail: graduate@usfca.edu.

The University of Scranton, College of Graduate and Continuing Education, Program in Business Administration, Scranton, PA 18510. Offers accounting (MBA); finance (MBA); general business administration (MBA); health care management (MBA); international business (MBA); management information systems (MBA); marketing (MBA); operations management (MBA). *Accreditation:* AACSB. Part-time and evening/weekend programs available. Postbaccalaureate distance learning degree programs offered (no on-campus study). *Faculty:* 34 full-time (8 women). *Students:* 92 full-time (38 women), 137 part-time (58 women); includes 27 minority (15 African Americans, 5 Asian Americans or Pacific Islanders, 7 Hispanic Americans), 21 international. Average age 31. 255 applicants, 79% accepted. In 2009, 33 master's awarded. *Degree requirements:* For master's, capstone experience. *Entrance requirements:* For master's, GMAT, minimum GPA of 2.75. Additional exam requirements/recommendations for international students: Required—TOEFL (minimum score 500 paper-based; 173 computer-based), IELTS (minimum score 5.5). *Application deadline:* Applications are processed on a rolling basis. Application fee: $0. *Financial support:* In 2009–10, 10 students received support, including 10 teaching assistantships with full and partial tuition reimbursements available (averaging $6,600 per year); fellowships, career-related internships or fieldwork, Federal Work-Study, and unspecified assistantships also available. Support available to part-time

students. Financial award application deadline: 3/1. *Faculty research:* Financial markets, strategic impact of total quality management, internal accounting controls, consumer preference, information systems and the Internet. *Unit head:* Dr. Murli Rajan, Director, 570-941-4043, Fax: 570-941-4342. *Application contact:* Joseph M. Roback, Director of Admissions, 570-941-4385, Fax: 570-941-5928, E-mail: robackj2@scranton.edu.

University of South Africa, College of Science, Engineering and Technology, Pretoria, South Africa. Offers chemical engineering (M Tech); information technology (M Tech).

University of South Alabama, Graduate School, School of Computer and Information Sciences, Mobile, AL 36688-0002. Offers computer science (MS); information systems (MS). Part-time and evening/weekend programs available. *Degree requirements:* For master's, thesis optional, project. *Entrance requirements:* For master's, GRE General Test. *Expenses:* Tuition, state resident: part-time $218 per contact hour. Required fees: $1102 per year. *Faculty research:* Numerical analysis, artificial intelligence, simulation, medical applications, software engineering.

University of Southern Mississippi, Graduate School, College of Business, School of Accountancy and Information Systems, Hattiesburg, MS 39406-0001. Offers accountancy (MPA). *Accreditation:* AACSB. Part-time and evening/weekend programs available. *Faculty:* 7 full-time (4 women), 2 part-time/adjunct (both women). *Students:* 15 full-time (10 women), 3 part-time (all women); includes 1 minority (African American). Average age 26. 15 applicants, 73% accepted, 11 enrolled. In 2009, 10 master's awarded. *Degree requirements:* For master's, comprehensive exam. *Entrance requirements:* For master's, GMAT. Additional exam requirements/recommendations for international students: Required—TOEFL. *Application deadline:* For fall admission, 7/15 priority date for domestic students, 7/15 for international students; for spring admission, 11/15 priority date for domestic students, 11/15 for international students. Applications are processed on a rolling basis. Application fee: $35. Electronic applications accepted. *Expenses:* Tuition, state resident: full-time $5096; part-time $284 per hour. Tuition, nonresident: full-time $13,052; part-time $726 per hour. Required fees: $402. Tuition and fees vary according to course level and course load. *Financial support:* In 2009–10, 7 research assistantships with full tuition reimbursements (averaging $6,000 per year) were awarded; Federal Work-Study and institutionally sponsored loans also available. Support available to part-time students. Financial award application deadline: 3/15; financial award applicants required to submit FAFSA. *Faculty research:* Bank liquidity, subchapter S corporations, internal auditing, governmental accounting, inflation accounting. *Unit head:* Dr. Stan Lewis, Director, 601-266-4322, Fax: 601-266-4639. *Application contact:* Dr. Francis Daniel, Graduate Coordinator, 601-266-4664, Fax: 601-266-5814.

University of South Florida, Graduate School, College of Business, Department of Business Administration, Tampa, FL 33620-9951. Offers accounting (PhD); entrepreneurship (MBA); finance (PhD); information systems (PhD); leadership and organizational effectiveness (MSM); management and organization (MBA); marketing (PhD). *Accreditation:* AACSB. Part-time and evening/weekend programs available. *Faculty:* 12 full-time (2 women). *Students:* 152 full-time (51 women), 201 part-time (65 women); includes 70 minority (14 African Americans, 30 Asian Americans or Pacific Islanders, 26 Hispanic Americans), 54 international. Average age 32. 460 applicants, 35% accepted, 93 enrolled. In 2009, 161 master's, 11 doctorates awarded. *Degree requirements:* For master's, comprehensive exam, thesis (for some programs); for doctorate, comprehensive exam, thesis/dissertation, 90 credit hours, minimum GPA of 3.0. *Entrance requirements:* For master's, GMAT, minimum GPA of 3.0 in last 60 hours of course work, 2 years of work experience, resume; for doctorate, GMAT, letters of recommendation, personal statement. Additional exam requirements/recommendations for international students: Required—TOEFL (minimum score 550 paper-based; 213 computer-based; 79 iBT). *Application deadline:* For fall admission, 6/1 for domestic students, 1/2 for international students; for spring admission, 10/15 for domestic students, 6/1 for international students. Application fee: $30. *Financial support:* Fellowships, research assistantships, teaching assistantships, scholarships/grants, health care benefits, and unspecified assistantships available. Financial award applicants required to submit FAFSA. *Unit head:* Irene Hurst, Program Director, 813-974-3335, Fax: 813-974-4518, E-mail: hurst@coba.usf.edu. *Application contact:* Wendy Baker, Assistant Director, Graduate Studies, 813-974-3335, Fax: 813-974-4518, E-mail: wbaker@usf.edu.

University of South Florida, Graduate School, College of Business, Information Systems and Decision Sciences Department, Tampa, FL 33620-9951. Offers business administration (PhD), including management information systems; management information systems (MS). Part-time programs available. *Faculty:* 14 full-time (2 women). *Students:* 41 full-time (17 women), 38 part-time (10 women); includes 18 minority (4 African Americans, 8 Asian Americans or Pacific Islanders, 6 Hispanic Americans), 28 international. Average age 32. 122 applicants, 61% accepted, 23 enrolled. In 2009, 47 master's awarded. Terminal master's awarded for partial completion of doctoral program. *Degree requirements:* For master's, thesis or alternative, 33 credit hours, minimum GPA of 3.0; for doctorate, comprehensive exam, thesis/dissertation. *Entrance requirements:* For master's, GMAT or GRE, minimum GPA of 3.0, industry experience (preferred); for doctorate, GMAT, letters of recommendation, personal statement. Additional exam requirements/recommendations for international students: Required—TOEFL (minimum score 550 paper-based; 213 computer-based; 79 iBT). *Application deadline:* For fall admission, 6/1 for domestic students, 1/2 for international students; for spring admission, 10/30 for domestic students, 6/1 for international students. Applications are processed on a rolling basis. Application fee: $30. Electronic applications accepted. *Financial support:* In 2009–10, teaching assistantships with tuition reimbursements (averaging $22,081 per year); scholarships/grants, health care benefits, and unspecified assistantships also available. Financial award applicants required to submit FAFSA. *Faculty research:* Business intelligence, software engineering, health informatics, information technology adoption, organizational impacts of IT. Total annual research expenditures: $200,892. *Unit head:* Dr. Kaushal Chari, Chairperson /Program Director, 813-974-5524, Fax: 813-974-6749, E-mail: kchari@usf.edu. *Application contact:* Mike Walters, Program Coordinator, 813-974-5524, Fax: 813-974-6749, E-mail: msmis@coba.usf.edu.

The University of Tampa, John H. Sykes College of Business, Tampa, FL 33606-1490. Offers accounting (MBA, MS); economics (MBA); entrepreneurship and innovation (MBA); finance (MBA, MS); information systems management (MBA); international business (MBA); management (MBA); marketing (MBA, MS); nonprofit management (MBA). *Accreditation:* AACSB. Part-time and evening/weekend programs available. *Faculty:* 62 full-time (22 women), 11 part-time/adjunct (4 women). *Students:* 240 full-time (101 women), 338 part-time (133 women); includes 95 minority (16 African Americans, 4 American Indian/Alaska Native, 24 Asian Americans or Pacific Islanders, 51 Hispanic Americans), 122 international. Average age 29. 564 applicants, 51% accepted, 186 enrolled. In 2009, 234 master's awarded. *Entrance requirements:* For master's, GMAT. Additional exam requirements/recommendations for international students: Required—TOEFL (minimum score 577 paper-based; 230 computer-based; 90 iBT), IELTS. *Application deadline:* For fall admission, 7/15 for domestic students, 6/1 for international students; for spring admission, 12/15 for domestic students, 11/1 for international students. Applications are processed on a rolling basis. Application fee: $40. Electronic applications accepted. *Expenses:* Tuition: Part-time $488 per credit hour. *Financial support:* In 2009–10, 332 students received support, including 71 research assistantships with full tuition reimbursements available (averaging $6,757 per year); career-related internships or fieldwork, scholarships/grants, and unspecified assistantships also available. Support available to part-time students. Financial award applicants required to submit FAFSA. *Faculty research:* Information systems, leadership, corporate governance, entrepreneurship, hedonic price estimation. *Unit head:* Dr. Don Morrill, Associate Dean, Graduate and Continuing Studies, 813-257-3557, E-mail: dmorrill@ut.edu. *Application contact:* Karen Full, Director of Admissions, Graduate and Continuing Studies, 813-257-3642, E-mail: kfull@ut.edu.

The University of Texas at Arlington, Graduate School, College of Business, Department of Information Systems and Management Science, Arlington, TX 76019. Offers information systems (MS). Part-time and evening/weekend programs available. *Students:* 46 full-time (16 women), 20 part-time (4 women); includes 23 minority (11 African Americans, 1 American Indian/Alaska Native, 6 Asian Americans or Pacific Islanders, 5 Hispanic Americans), 17 international. 64

applicants, 98% accepted, 3 enrolled. In 2009, 33 master's awarded. *Degree requirements:* For master's, thesis optional. *Entrance requirements:* For master's, GMAT, minimum GPA of 3.0. Additional exam requirements/recommendations for international students: Required—TOEFL (minimum score 550 paper-based; 213 computer-based; 79 iBT). *Application deadline:* For fall admission, 6/5 for domestic students, 4/1 for international students; for spring admission, 10/15 for domestic students, 9/1 for international students. Applications are processed on a rolling basis. Application fee: $35 ($50 for international students). *Financial support:* In 2009–10, fellowships (averaging $1,000 per year), research assistantships (averaging $6,000 per year), 10 teaching assistantships (averaging $13,000 per year) were awarded; career-related internships or fieldwork and scholarships/grants also available. Support available to part-time students. Financial award application deadline: 6/1; financial award applicants required to submit FAFSA. *Faculty research:* Database modeling, strategic issues in information systems, simulations, production operations management. *Unit head:* Dr. R. C. Baker, Chair, 817-272-3502, Fax: 817-272-5801, E-mail: rcbaker@uta.edu. *Application contact:* Dr. Carolyn Davis, Graduate Advisor, 817-272-7399, Fax: 817-272-5801, E-mail: carolynd@exchange.uta.edu.

The University of Texas at Arlington, Graduate School, College of Business, Program in Business Administration, Arlington, TX 76019. Offers accounting (PhD); business statistics (PhD); finance (MBA, PhD); information systems (MBA, PhD); management (MBA, PhD); management sciences (MBA); marketing (MBA, PhD); operations management (PhD); real estate (MBA). *Accreditation:* AACSB. Part-time and evening/weekend programs available. Postbaccalaureate distance learning degree programs offered (no on-campus study). *Students:* 587 full-time (188 women), 349 part-time (140 women); includes 188 minority (66 African Americans, 62 Asian Americans or Pacific Islanders, 60 Hispanic Americans), 371 international. 282 applicants, 96% accepted, 145 enrolled. In 2009, 431 master's awarded. Terminal master's awarded for partial completion of doctoral program. *Degree requirements:* For master's, thesis optional; for doctorate, comprehensive exam, thesis/dissertation. *Entrance requirements:* For master's, GMAT; for doctorate, GMAT, minimum GPA of 3.0 (undergraduate), 3.4 (graduate); 30 hours of graduate course work. Additional exam requirements/recommendations for international students: Required—TOEFL (minimum score 550 paper-based; 213 computer-based; 79 iBT). *Application deadline:* For fall admission, 6/5 for domestic students, 4/1 for international students; for spring admission, 10/15 for domestic students, 9/1 for international students. Applications are processed on a rolling basis. Application fee: $35 ($50 for international students). Electronic applications accepted. *Financial support:* In 2009–10, 1 fellowship (averaging $1,000 per year), 30 research assistantships (averaging $6,000 per year), 45 teaching assistantships (averaging $13,000 per year) were awarded; career-related internships or fieldwork, scholarships/grants, and unspecified assistantships also available. Financial award application deadline: 6/1; financial award applicants required to submit FAFSA. *Unit head:* Greg Frazier, Director PhD Programs, 817-272-3559, Fax: 817-272-5799, E-mail: frazier@exchange.uta.edu. *Application contact:* Melanie McGee, Director of MBA Program, 817-272-0658, Fax: 817-272-5799, E-mail: mwmcgee@uta.edu.

See Close-Up on page 273.

The University of Texas at Austin, Graduate School, McCombs School of Business, Department of Information, Risk, and Operations Management, Austin, TX 78712-1111. Offers information systems (PhD); risk analysis and decision making (PhD); supply chain and operations management (PhD). *Degree requirements:* For doctorate, thesis/dissertation. *Entrance requirements:* For doctorate, GMAT or GRE. Electronic applications accepted. *Faculty research:* Stochastic processing and queuing, discrete nonlinear and large-scale optimization simulation, quality assurance logistics, distributed artificial intelligence, organizational modeling.

The University of Texas at Dallas, School of Management, Program in Accounting and Information Management, Richardson, TX 75080. Offers assurance services (MS); financial planning and analysis (MS); information management (MS); international services (MS); management consulting (MS); software management (MS); taxation services (MS). *Accreditation:* AACSB. *Faculty:* 19 full-time (4 women), 10 part-time/adjunct (3 women). *Students:* 295 full-time (173 women), 275 part-time (156 women); includes 172 minority (29 African Americans, 3 American Indian/Alaska Native, 108 Asian Americans or Pacific Islanders, 32 Hispanic Americans), 171 international. Average age 29. 356 applicants, 74% accepted, 203 enrolled. In 2009, 254 master's awarded. *Entrance requirements:* For master's, GMAT. Additional exam requirements/recommendations for international students: Required—TOEFL (minimum score 550 paper-based; 213 computer-based). *Application deadline:* For fall admission, 7/15 for domestic students, 5/1 priority date for international students; for spring admission, 11/15 for domestic students, 9/1 priority date for international students. Applications are processed on a rolling basis. Application fee: $50 ($100 for international students). Electronic applications accepted. *Expenses:* Tuition, state resident: full-time $11,068; part-time $461 per credit hour. Tuition, nonresident: full-time $21,178; part-time $882 per credit hour. Tuition and fees vary according to course load. *Financial support:* In 2009–10, 3 research assistantships with full tuition reimbursements (averaging $10,072 per year), 4 teaching assistantships with full tuition reimbursements (averaging $10,050 per year) were awarded; fellowships, career-related internships or fieldwork, Federal Work-Study, institutionally sponsored loans, scholarships/grants, and unspecified assistantships also available. Support available to part-time students. Financial award application deadline: 4/30; financial award applicants required to submit FAFSA. *Faculty research:* Privatization and accounting/auditing, corporate performance and executive compensation, risk management, information technology in accounting. *Unit head:* Amy Troutman, Assistant Director, 972-883-6719, Fax: 972-883-6823, E-mail: amybass@utdallas.edu. *Application contact:* James Parker, Assistant Director of Graduate Recruitment, 972-883-5842, E-mail: jparker@utdallas.edu.

The University of Texas at Dallas, School of Management, Program in Information Systems and Operations Management, Richardson, TX 75080. Offers information technology management (MS), including enterprise systems, health care systems, information security; supply chain management (MS). Part-time and evening/weekend programs available. *Faculty:* 23 full-time (1 woman), 1 (woman) part-time/adjunct. *Students:* 153 full-time (54 women), 129 part-time (51 women); includes 36 minority (4 African Americans, 28 Asian Americans or Pacific Islanders, 4 Hispanic Americans), 212 international. Average age 27. 352 applicants, 74% accepted, 105 enrolled. In 2009, 67 master's awarded. *Degree requirements:* For master's, thesis optional. *Entrance requirements:* For master's, GMAT. Additional exam requirements/recommendations for international students: Required—TOEFL (minimum score 550 paper-based; 213 computer-based). *Application deadline:* For fall admission, 7/15 for domestic students, 5/1 priority date for international students; for spring admission, 11/15 for domestic students, 9/1 priority date for international students. Applications are processed on a rolling basis. Application fee: $50 ($100 for international students). Electronic applications accepted. *Expenses:* Tuition, state resident: full-time $11,068; part-time $461 per credit hour. Tuition, nonresident: full-time $21,178; part-time $882 per credit hour. Tuition and fees vary according to course load. *Financial support:* In 2009–10, 7 research assistantships with full tuition reimbursements (averaging $10,933 per year), 5 teaching assistantships with full tuition reimbursements (averaging $10,050 per year) were awarded; career-related internships or fieldwork, Federal Work-Study, institutionally sponsored loans, scholarships/grants, and unspecified assistantships also available. Support available to part-time students. Financial award application deadline: 4/30; financial award applicants required to submit FAFSA. *Faculty research:* Technology marketing, measuring information work productivity, electronic commerce, decision support systems, data quality. *Unit head:* Dr. Mark Thouin, Director, 972-883-4011, E-mail: mark.thouin@utdallas.edu. *Application contact:* James Parker, Assistant Director, 972-883-5842, E-mail: jparker@utdallas.edu.

The University of Texas at San Antonio, College of Business, Department of Information Systems and Technology Management, San Antonio, TX 78249-0617. Offers business administration-information technology (PhD); information systems (MBA); information technology (MSIT); management technology (MSMOT). *Faculty:* 10 full-time (3 women), 1 part-time/adjunct (0 women). *Students:* 16 full-time (5 women), 88 part-time (22 women); includes 33 minority (4 African Americans, 1 American Indian/Alaska Native, 6 Asian Americans or Pacific Islanders, 22 Hispanic Americans), 8 international. Average age 34. 51 applicants, 61%

Management Information Systems

The University of Texas at San Antonio (continued)
accepted, 22 enrolled. In 2009, 45 master's awarded. *Degree requirements:* For master's, comprehensive exam (for some programs), thesis (for some programs). *Entrance requirements:* For master's, GMAT, minimum GPA of 3.0. Additional exam requirements/recommendations for international students: Required—TOEFL (minimum score 500 paper-based; 173 computer-based; 61 iBT), IELTS (minimum score 5). *Application deadline:* For fall admission, 7/1 for domestic students, 4/1 for international students; for spring admission, 11/1 for domestic students, 9/1 for international students. Applications are processed on a rolling basis. Application fee: $45 ($80 for international students). Electronic applications accepted. *Expenses:* Tuition, state resident: full-time $3975; part-time $221 per contact hour. Tuition, nonresident: full-time $13,947; part-time $775 per contact hour. Required fees: $1853. *Financial support:* In 2009–10, 7 students received support, including 7 research assistantships (averaging $10,400 per year), 8 teaching assistantships (averaging $7,800 per year); scholarships/grants, tuition waivers (partial), and unspecified assistantships also available. Support available to part-time students. *Faculty research:* Infrastructure assurance, digitalforensics, management of technology, e-commerce, technology transfer. Total annual research expenditures: $162,886. *Unit head:* Dr. Glenn Dietrich, Chair, 210-458-5354, Fax: 210-458-6305, E-mail: gdietrich@utsa.edu. *Application contact:* Jan Clark, Graduate Advisor, 210-458-5244, E-mail: jan.clark@utsa.edu.

The University of Texas–Pan American, College of Business Administration, Program in International Business, Edinburg, TX 78539. Offers computer information systems (PhD); economics (PhD); finance (PhD); management (PhD); marketing (PhD). *Degree requirements:* For doctorate, comprehensive exam, thesis/dissertation. *Entrance requirements:* For doctorate, GMAT or GRE. Additional exam requirements/recommendations for international students: Required—TOEFL, IELTS. Electronic applications accepted. *Expenses:* Contact institution.

University of the Sacred Heart, Graduate Programs, Department of Business Administration, Program in Information Systems Management, San Juan, PR 00914-0383. Offers MBA. Part-time and evening/weekend programs available. *Degree requirements:* For master's, thesis. *Entrance requirements:* For master's, EXADEP, minimum undergraduate GPA of 2.75, interview.

University of the West, Department of Business Administration, Rosemead, CA 91770. Offers business administration (EMBA); finance (MBA); information technology and management (MBA); international business (MBA); nonprofit organization management (MBA). Part-time and evening/weekend programs available. *Entrance requirements:* Additional exam requirements/recommendations for international students: Required—TOEFL.

The University of Toledo, College of Graduate Studies, College of Business Administration, Department of Information Systems, Marketing, E-Commerce, and Sales, Program in Information Systems, Toledo, OH 43606-3390. Offers MBA. *Entrance requirements:* For master's, GMAT.

The University of Toledo, College of Graduate Studies, College of Business Administration, Department of Information Systems, Marketing, E-Commerce, and Sales, Program in Operations Management, Toledo, OH 43606-3390. Offers MBA. *Entrance requirements:* For master's, GMAT.

University of Tulsa, Graduate School, Collins College of Business, Master of Business Administration Program, Tulsa, OK 74104-3189. Offers accounting (MBA); business administration (MBA); energy management (MBA); finance (MBA); international business (MBA); management information systems (MBA); taxation (MBA); JD/MBA; MBA/MSCS; MBA/MSF. *Accreditation:* AACSB. Part-time and evening/weekend programs available. *Faculty:* 32 full-time (6 women). *Students:* 59 full-time (26 women), 45 part-time (18 women); includes 13 minority (4 African Americans, 4 American Indian/Alaska Native, 1 Asian American or Pacific Islander, 4 Hispanic Americans), 9 international. Average age 25. 78 applicants, 53% accepted, 30 enrolled. In 2009, 36 master's awarded. *Entrance requirements:* For master's, GMAT. Additional exam requirements/recommendations for international students: Required—TOEFL (minimum score 575 paper-based; 232 computer-based; 90 iBT), IELTS (minimum score 6.5). *Application deadline:* Applications are processed on a rolling basis. Application fee: $40. Electronic applications accepted. *Expenses:* Tuition: Full-time $16,182; part-time $899 per credit hour. Required fees: $4 per credit hour. Tuition and fees vary according to course load. *Financial support:* In 2009–10, 42 students received support, including 5 fellowships (averaging $11,894 per year), 2 research assistantships (averaging $9,322 per year), 35 teaching assistantships (averaging $8,112 per year); institutionally sponsored loans, scholarships/grants, health care benefits, tuition waivers (full and partial), and unspecified assistantships also available. Support available to part-time students. Financial award application deadline: 2/1; financial award applicants required to submit FAFSA. *Faculty research:* Accounting, energy management, finance, international business, management information systems, taxation. *Unit head:* Dr. Markham Collins, Associate Dean of the Collins College of Business, 918-631-2783, Fax: 918-631-2142, E-mail: markham-collins@utulsa.edu. *Application contact:* Dr. Markham Collins, Associate Dean of the Collins College of Business, 918-631-2783, Fax: 918-631-2142, E-mail: markham-collins@utulsa.edu.

University of Virginia, McIntire School of Commerce, Program in Management of Information Technology, Charlottesville, VA 22903. Offers MS. *Students:* 36 full-time (5 women), 38 part-time (7 women); includes 18 minority (2 African Americans, 13 Asian Americans or Pacific Islanders, 3 Hispanic Americans), 1 international. Average age 37. In 2009, 70 master's awarded. *Entrance requirements:* For master's, GMAT, 2 recommendations. Additional exam requirements/recommendations for international students: Required—TOEFL (minimum score 620 paper-based; 270 computer-based). *Application deadline:* For fall admission, 9/15 priority date for domestic students, 1/15 for international students. Applications are processed on a rolling basis. Application fee: $75. Electronic applications accepted. *Expenses:* Contact institution. *Financial support:* Fellowships, Federal Work-Study available. Financial award application deadline: 2/15; financial award applicants required to submit FAFSA. *Unit head:* Stefano Grazioli, Director, 434-982-2973, E-mail: grazioli@virginia.edu. *Application contact:* Matthew Miller, Assistant Director of Graduate Marketing and Admissions, 434-982-2245, Fax: 434-924-4511, E-mail: msmit@virginia.edu.

University of Wisconsin–Madison, Graduate School, Wisconsin School of Business, Doctoral Program in Accounting and Information Systems, Madison, WI 53706-1380. Offers PhD. *Accreditation:* AACSB. *Faculty:* 15 full-time (5 women), 1 part-time/adjunct (0 women). *Students:* 11 full-time (6 women), 2 international. Average age 33. 59 applicants, 15% accepted, 2 enrolled. *Degree requirements:* For doctorate, comprehensive exam, thesis/dissertation. *Entrance requirements:* For doctorate, GMAT or GRE. Additional exam requirements/recommendations for international students: Required—Pearson Test of English (minimum score 73, written 80); Recommended—TOEFL (minimum score 623 paper-based; 263 computer-based; 106 iBT), IELTS (minimum score 7.5). *Application deadline:* For fall admission, 12/15 priority date for domestic and international students. Application fee: $56. Electronic applications accepted. *Expenses:* Tuition, state resident: part-time $594 per credit. Tuition, nonresident: part-time $1504 per credit. Required fees: $65 per credit. Tuition and fees vary according to course load, program and reciprocity agreements. *Financial support:* In 2009–10, 11 students received support, including fellowships with full tuition reimbursements available (averaging $18,567 per year), research assistantships with full tuition reimbursements available (averaging $16,506 per year), 11 teaching assistantships with full tuition reimbursements available (averaging $14,088 per year); Federal Work-Study, institutionally sponsored loans, scholarships/grants, health care benefits, and unspecified assistantships also available. Financial award application deadline: 2/1. *Faculty research:* Auditing, financial reporting, economic theory, strategy, computer models. *Unit head:* Prof. Jon Davis, Chair, 608-263-4264. *Application contact:* Belle Heberling, Assistant Director for Research Programs, 608-262-3749, Fax: 608-890-0180, E-mail: phd@bus.wisc.edu.

University of Wisconsin–Madison, Graduate School, Wisconsin School of Business, Doctoral Program in Operations and Information Management, Madison, WI 53706-1380. Offers information systems (PhD); operations and information management (PhD). *Faculty:* 9 full-time (0 women), 2 part-time/adjunct (0 women). *Students:* 5 full-time (1 woman). Average age 34. 20 applicants, 5% accepted, 1 enrolled. *Degree requirements:* For doctorate, comprehensive

exam, thesis/dissertation. *Entrance requirements:* For doctorate, GMAT or GRE General Test. Additional exam requirements/recommendations for international students: Required—Pearson Test of English (minimum score 73, written 80); Recommended—TOEFL (minimum score 620 paper-based; 263 computer-based; 106 iBT), IELTS (minimum score 7.5). *Application deadline:* For fall admission, 12/15 priority date for domestic and international students. Application fee: $56. Electronic applications accepted. *Expenses:* Tuition, state resident: part-time $594 per credit. Tuition, nonresident: part-time $1504 per credit. Required fees: $65 per credit. Tuition and fees vary according to course load, program and reciprocity agreements. *Financial support:* In 2009–10, 4 students received support, including 2 fellowships with full tuition reimbursements available (averaging $18,567 per year), research assistantships with full tuition reimbursements available (averaging $16,506 per year), 2 teaching assistantships with full tuition reimbursements available (averaging $14,088 per year); Federal Work-Study, institutionally sponsored loans, scholarships/grants, health care benefits, and unspecified assistantships also available. Financial award application deadline: 2/1; financial award applicants required to submit FAFSA. *Faculty research:* Supply-chain management, reorganization of the factory, creating continuous innovation, transportation economics, organizational economics. *Unit head:* Prof. James G. Morris, Chair, 608-262-1284, E-mail: jmorris@bus.wisc.edu. *Application contact:* Belle Heberling, Assistant Director for Research Programs, 608-262-3749, Fax: 608-890-0180, E-mail: phd@bus.wisc.edu.

Utah State University, School of Graduate Studies, College of Business, Department of Business Information Systems, Logan, UT 84322. Offers business education (MS); business information systems (MS); business information systems and education (Ed D); education (PhD). Part-time programs available. Terminal master's awarded for partial completion of doctoral program. *Degree requirements:* For master's, thesis optional; for doctorate, thesis/dissertation. *Entrance requirements:* For master's, GMAT, minimum GPA of 3.2; for doctorate, GRE General Test, minimum GPA of 3.0. Additional exam requirements/recommendations for international students: Required—TOEFL. *Faculty research:* Oral and written communication, methods of teaching, CASE tools, object-oriented programming, decision support systems.

Valparaiso University, Graduate School, Program in Information Technology, Valparaiso, IN 46383. Offers MS. Part-time and evening/weekend programs available. *Faculty:* 6 part-time/adjunct (1 woman). *Students:* 16 full-time (3 women), 5 part-time (3 women), 16 international. Average age 28. In 2009, 1 master's awarded. *Entrance requirements:* For master's, minimum GPA of 3.0; minor or equivalent in computer science, information technology, or a related field. Additional exam requirements/recommendations for international students: Required—TOEFL (minimum score 550 paper-based; 213 computer-based; 80 iBT). *Application deadline:* Applications are processed on a rolling basis. Application fee: $30 ($50 for international students). Electronic applications accepted. *Financial support:* Available to part-time students. Applicants required to submit FAFSA. *Unit head:* Dr. David L. Rowland, Dean, Graduate Studies and Continuing Education/Associate Provost, 219-464-5313, Fax: 219-464-5381, E-mail: david.rowland@valpo.edu. *Application contact:* Jamie Haney, Coordinator of Graduate Admission, 219-464-5313, Fax: 219-464-5381, E-mail: jamie.haney@valpo.edu.

Villanova University, Villanova School of Business, MBA—Fast Track Program, Villanova, PA 19085. Offers finance (MBA); international business (MBA); management information systems (MBA); marketing (MBA). *Accreditation:* AACSB. Part-time and evening/weekend programs available. *Entrance requirements:* For master's, GMAT, minimum 4.5 years of professional work experience. Additional exam requirements/recommendations for international students: Required—TOEFL (minimum score 550 paper-based; 213 computer-based; 80 iBT). Electronic applications accepted. *Expenses:* Tuition: Part-time $630 per credit. Required fees: $60 per credit. Part-time tuition and fees vary according to degree level and program. *Faculty research:* Developing and leveraging technology, ethical business practices, managing for innovation and creativity, the global political economy, strategic marketing management.

Villanova University, Villanova School of Business, MBA—Flex Track Program, Villanova, PA 19085. Offers corporate management (general) (MBA); finance (MBA); international business (MBA); management information systems (MBA); marketing (MBA); JD/MBA. *Accreditation:* AACSB. Part-time and evening/weekend programs available. Postbaccalaureate distance learning degree programs offered (minimal on-campus study). *Entrance requirements:* For master's, GMAT, minimum 4.5 years work experience. Additional exam requirements/recommendations for international students: Required—TOEFL (minimum score 550 paper-based; 213 computer-based; 80 iBT). Electronic applications accepted. *Expenses:* Tuition: Part-time $630 per credit. Required fees: $60 per credit. Part-time tuition and fees vary according to degree level and program. *Faculty research:* Developing and leveraging technology, ethical business practices, managing for innovation and creativity, the global political economy, strategic marketing management.

Virginia Commonwealth University, Graduate School, School of Business, Program in Information Systems, Richmond, VA 23284-9005. Offers MS, PhD. *Degree requirements:* For doctorate, thesis/dissertation. *Entrance requirements:* For master's, GMAT.

Virginia International University, Computer Programs Department, Fairfax, VA 22030. Offers computer science (MS); information systems (MS). Part-time programs available. *Faculty:* 2 full-time (both women), 4 part-time/adjunct (0 women). *Students:* 62 full-time (30 women), all international. Average age 26. 175 applicants, 26% accepted, 9 enrolled. In 2009, 26 master's awarded. *Entrance requirements:* For master's, bachelor's degree. Additional exam requirements/recommendations for international students: Required—TOEFL (minimum score 550 paper-based; 213 computer-based; 80 iBT), IELTS. *Application deadline:* For fall admission, 7/31 for domestic students, 7/3 for international students; for spring admission, 12/18 for domestic students, 11/20 for international students. Applications are processed on a rolling basis. Application fee: $100. Electronic applications accepted. *Expenses:* Tuition: Full-time $10,044; part-time $569 per credit. One-time fee: $75. Tuition and fees vary according to degree level. *Financial support:* In 2009–10, 9 students received support. Scholarships/grants available. Financial award application deadline: 7/1. *Unit head:* Emilia Butu, Chair, 703-591-7042 Ext. 307, Fax: 703-591-7046, E-mail: emilia@viu.edu. *Application contact:* Emily L. Kraus, Director of Admissions, 703-591-7042 Ext. 309, Fax: 703-591-7048, E-mail: admissions@viu.edu.

Virginia Polytechnic Institute and State University, Graduate School, Intercollege, Program in Information Technology, Blacksburg, VA 24061. Offers MIT. *Students:* 17 full-time (4 women), 263 part-time (57 women); includes 88 minority (1 African American, 23 American Indian/Alaska Native, 27 Asian Americans or Pacific Islanders, 37 Hispanic Americans), 13 international. Average age 35. 108 applicants, 83% accepted, 71 enrolled. In 2009, 84 master's awarded. *Entrance requirements:* For master's, GRE, GMAT. Additional exam requirements/recommendations for international students: Required—TOEFL (minimum score 550 paper-based; 213 computer-based). *Application deadline:* For fall admission, 5/15 for international students; for spring admission, 10/15 for international students. Applications are processed on a rolling basis. Application fee: $65. Electronic applications accepted. *Expenses:* Tuition, area resident: Full-time $10,228; part-time $459 per credit hour. Tuition, nonresident: full-time $17,892; part-time $865 per credit hour. Required fees: $1966; $451 per semester. *Financial support:* Career-related internships or fieldwork, Federal Work-Study, scholarships/grants, and unspecified assistantships available. Financial award application deadline: 1/15. *Unit head:* Dr. Thomas T. Sheehan, Dean, 703-538-8361, Fax: 703-538-8415, E-mail: thsheeha@vt.edu. *Application contact:* Cindy Rubens, Information Contact, 703-818-8464, Fax: 703-538-8415, E-mail: crubens@vt.edu.

Virginia Polytechnic Institute and State University, Graduate School, Pamplin College of Business, Department of Business Information Technology, Blacksburg, VA 24061. Offers business administration (PhD); business information technology (PhD). *Faculty:* 22 full-time (6 women). *Students:* 4 full-time (0 women), 3 part-time (0 women); includes 3 minority (2 American Indian/Alaska Native, 1 Asian American or Pacific Islander). Average age 36. 8 applicants, 13% accepted. *Entrance requirements:* For doctorate, GRE, GMAT. Additional exam requirements/recommendations for international students: Required—TOEFL (minimum score 550 paper-based; 213 computer-based). *Application deadline:* For fall admission, 5/15 for international students; for spring admission, 10/15 for international students. Applications

are processed on a rolling basis. Application fee: $65. Electronic applications accepted. *Expenses:* Tuition, area resident: Full-time $10,228; part-time $459 per credit hour. Tuition, nonresident: full-time $17,892; part-time $865 per credit hour. Required fees: $1966; $451 per semester. *Financial support:* In 2009–10, 17 teaching assistantships with full tuition reimbursements (averaging $8,858 per year) were awarded; research assistantships, career-related internships or fieldwork, Federal Work-Study, scholarships/grants, and unspecified assistantships also available. Financial award application deadline: 1/15. *Faculty research:* Mathematical programming, computer simulation, decision support systems, production/operations research, information technology. Total annual research expenditures: $122,247. *Unit head:* Dr. Bernard W. Taylor, Dean, 540-231-6596, Fax: 540-231-7916, E-mail: betaylo3@vt.edu. *Application contact:* Cliff Ragsdale, Information Contact, 540-231-4697, Fax: 540-231-7916, E-mail: cragsdal@vt.edu.

Virginia Polytechnic Institute and State University, VT Online, Blacksburg, VA 24061. Offers aerospace engineering (MS); business information systems (Graduate Certificate); career and technical education (MS); computer engineering (M Eng, MS); decision support systems (Graduate Certificate); eLearning leadership (MA); electrical engineering (M Eng, MS); engineering administration (MEA); environmental politics and policy (Graduate Certificate); foundations of political analysis (Graduate Certificate); health product risk management (Graduate Certificate); information policy and society (Graduate Certificate); information security (Graduate Certificate); instructional technology (MA); liberal arts (Graduate Certificate); life sciences: health product risk management (MS); natural resources (MNR, Graduate Certificate); networking (Graduate Certificate); nonprofit and nongovernmental organization management (Graduate Certificate); ocean engineering (MS); political science (MA); security studies (Graduate Certificate); software development (Graduate Certificate). *Expenses:* Tuition, area resident: Full-time $10,228; part-time $459 per credit hour. Tuition, nonresident: full-time $17,892; part-time $865 per credit hour. Required fees: $1966; $451 per semester.

Walden University, Graduate Programs, School of Management, Minneapolis, MN 55401. Offers applied management and decision sciences (PhD), including accounting, engineering management, finance, general applied management and decision sciences, information systems management, knowledge management, leadership and organizational change, learning management, operations research, self-designed program in applied management and design sciences; business information management (MISM); enterprise information security (MISM); entrepreneurship (MBA, DBA); finance (MBA, DBA); global supply chain management (DBA); healthcare management (MBA); healthcare system improvement (MBA); human resource management (MBA); information systems management (DBA); international business (MBA, DBA); IT strategy and governance (MISM); leadership (MBA, MS, DBA), including entrepreneurship (MS), general management (MS), human resources leadership (MS), innovation and technology (MS), leader development (MS), project management (MS), self-designed (MS), sustainable futures (MS); managing global software and service supply chains (MISM); marketing (MBA, DBA); project management (MBA, MS); risk management (MBA); self-designed (MBA, DBA); social impact management (DBA); sustainable futures (MBA); technology (MBA); technology entrepreneurship (DBA). Part-time and evening/weekend programs available. Postbaccalaureate distance learning degree programs offered (minimal on-campus study). *Faculty:* 17 full-time, 211 part-time/adjunct. *Students:* 3,389 full-time (1,774 women), 815 part-time (482 women); includes 1,969 minority (1,640 African Americans, 36 American Indian/Alaska Native, 123 Asian Americans or Pacific Islanders, 170 Hispanic Americans), 95 international. Average age 41. In 2009, 699 master's, 42 doctorates awarded. *Degree requirements:* For doctorate, thesis/dissertation (for some programs), residency. *Entrance requirements:* For master's, bachelor's degree or equivalent in related field; minimum GPA of 2.5; official transcripts; goal statement; access to computer and Internet; for doctorate, master's degree or equivalent in related field; minimum GPA of 3.0; 3 years of related professional/academic experience (preferred). Additional exam requirements/recommendations for international students: Required—TOEFL (minimum score 550 paper-based; 213 computer-based), IELTS (minimum score 6.5), TOEFL, IELTS, or Michigan English Language Assessment Battery (minimum score 82). *Application deadline:* Applications are processed on a rolling basis. Application fee: $50. Electronic applications accepted. *Expenses:* Tuition: Full-time $13,665; part-time $560 per credit. Required fees: $1375. Tuition and fees vary according to course load, degree level and program. *Financial support:* In 2009–10, 466 students received support; fellowships, Federal Work-Study, scholarships/grants, unspecified assistantships, and family tuition reduction, active duty/veteran tuition reduction, group tuition reduction, interest-free payment plans available. Support available to part-time students. Financial award applicants required to submit FAFSA. *Unit head:* William Schulz, Interim Associate Dean, 800-925-3368. *Application contact:* Jennifer Hall, Director of Enrollment, 866-4-WALDEN, E-mail: info@waldenu.edu.

Walsh College of Accountancy and Business Administration, Graduate Programs, Program in Business Information Technology, Troy, MI 48007-7006. Offers MSBIT. *Faculty:* 2 full-time (1 woman), 8 part-time/adjunct (1 woman). *Students:* 14 full-time (6 women), 142 part-time (55 women); includes 38 minority (27 African Americans, 8 Asian Americans or Pacific Islanders, 3 Hispanic Americans), 3 international. 58 applicants, 81% accepted, 45 enrolled. *Application deadline:* For fall admission, 8/24 priority date for domestic students; for winter admission, 1/1 priority date for domestic students; for spring admission, 4/1 priority date for domestic students. Application fee: $25. *Expenses:* Tuition: Part-time $525 per credit. Required fees: $125 per semester. *Financial support:* Application deadline: 6/30. *Unit head:* Dr. Jeffrey Livermore, Chair, 248-823-1272, Fax: 248-689-0920. *Application contact:* Jeremy Guc, Director of Admissions and Academic Advising, 248-823-1610, Fax: 248-689-0938, E-mail: jguc@walshcollege.edu.

Washington State University, Graduate School, College of Business, Department of Accounting and Business Law, Pullman, WA 99164. Offers accounting and information systems (M Acc); accounting and taxation (M Acc). *Accreditation:* AACSB. *Faculty:* 9. *Students:* 36 full-time (16 women), 6 part-time (5 women); includes 5 minority (3 Asian Americans or Pacific Islanders, 2 Hispanic Americans), 11 international. Average age 27. 114 applicants, 42% accepted, 30 enrolled. In 2009, 25 master's awarded. *Degree requirements:* For master's, comprehensive exam (for some programs), thesis (for some programs), oral exam, research paper. *Entrance requirements:* For master's, GMAT (minimum score of 600), resume; statement of purpose identifying area of interest, experiences, and intended research focus; minimum GPA of 3.25. Additional exam requirements/recommendations for international students: Required—TOEFL (minimum score 580 paper-based; 237 computer-based), IELTS. *Application deadline:* For fall admission, 1/10 priority date for domestic students, 1/10 for international students. Applications are processed on a rolling basis. Application fee: $50. Electronic applications accepted. *Financial support:* In 2009–10, 19 students received support, including 1 fellowship (averaging $5,500 per year), research assistantships (averaging $13,917 per year), 8 teaching assistantships with tuition reimbursements available (averaging $13,056 per year); Federal Work-Study, institutionally sponsored loans, tuition waivers (partial), and teaching associateships also available. Financial award application deadline: 3/1. *Faculty research:* Ethics, taxation, auditing. *Unit head:* Dr. John Sweeney, Chair, 509-335-8541, Fax: 509-335-4275, E-mail: jtsweeney@wsu.edu. *Application contact:* Graduate School Admissions, 800-GRADWSU, Fax: 509-335-1949, E-mail: gradsch@wsu.edu.

Washington State University, Graduate School, College of Business, Graduate Programs in Business, Pullman, WA 99164. Offers accounting and business law (M Acc); business administration (MBA, PhD), including accounting (PhD), finance (PhD), management and operations (PhD), management information systems (PhD), marketing (PhD). *Accreditation:* AACSB. *Degree requirements:* For master's, comprehensive exam (for some programs), thesis (for some programs), final presentation; for doctorate, comprehensive exam, thesis/dissertation, oral and written exams. *Entrance requirements:* For master's and doctorate, GMAT, minimum GPA of 3.0, 3 letters of recommendation. Additional exam requirements/recommendations for international students: Required—TOEFL. Electronic applications accepted.

See Display on page 193.

Wayland Baptist University, Graduate Programs, Programs in Business Administration/Management, Plainview, TX 79072-6998. Offers general business (MBA); health care administration (MBA); human resource management (MBA); international management (MBA); management (MA, MBA), including health care administration (MA), human resource management (MA), organization management (MA); management information systems (MBA). Part-time and evening/weekend programs available. Postbaccalaureate distance learning degree programs offered (no on-campus study). *Faculty:* 10 full-time (3 women). *Students:* 6 full-time (1 woman), 55 part-time (31 women); includes 24 minority (9 African Americans, 1 American Indian/Alaska Native, 14 Hispanic Americans). Average age 34. 25 applicants, 76% accepted, 10 enrolled. In 2009, 8 master's awarded. *Degree requirements:* For master's, capstone course. *Entrance requirements:* For master's, GMAT, GRE or MAT. Additional exam requirements/recommendations for international students: Required—TOEFL (minimum score 500 paper-based; 173 computer-based; 61 iBT). *Application deadline:* Applications are processed on a rolling basis. Application fee: $50. Electronic applications accepted. *Expenses:* Tuition: Full-time $5796; part-time $322 per credit hour. Required fees: $782; $9 per credit hour. $60 per semester. Tuition and fees vary according to course load and campus/location. *Financial support:* Federal Work-Study, institutionally sponsored loans, and scholarships/grants available. Support available to part-time students. Financial award application deadline: 5/1; financial award applicants required to submit FAFSA. *Unit head:* Dr. Otto Schacht, Chairman, 806-291-1020, Fax: 806-291-1957. *Application contact:* Amanda Stanton, Graduate Studies, 806-291-3423, Fax: 806-291-1950, E-mail: stanton@wbu.edu.

Webster University, George Herbert Walker School of Business and Technology, Department of Business, St. Louis, MO 63119-3194. Offers business (MA); business and organizational security management (MBA); computer resources and information management (MBA); environmental management (MBA); finance (MA, MBA); health services management (MBA); human resources development (MBA); human resources management (MBA); international business (MA, MBA); management and leadership (MBA); marketing (MBA); procurement and acquisitions management (MBA); telecommunications management (MBA). *Accreditation:* ACBSP. Part-time and evening/weekend programs available. Postbaccalaureate distance learning degree programs offered (no on-campus study). *Faculty:* 9 full-time, 430 part-time/adjunct. *Students:* 1,190 full-time (543 women), 4,226 part-time (2,159 women). Average age 34. In 2009, 2,021 master's awarded. *Degree requirements:* For master's, comprehensive exam (for some programs), thesis (for some programs). *Entrance requirements:* Additional exam requirements/recommendations for international students: Required—TOEFL. *Application deadline:* Applications are processed on a rolling basis. Application fee: $35 ($50 for international students). *Expenses:* Tuition: Part-time $565 per credit hour. Tuition and fees vary according to degree level, campus/location and program. *Financial support:* Federal Work-Study available. Support available to part-time students. Financial award application deadline: 4/1; financial award applicants required to submit FAFSA. *Unit head:* Dr. Debbie Psihountas, Chair, 314-246-7553 Ext. 7017, Fax: 314-968-7077, E-mail: buschair@webster.edu. *Application contact:* Matt Nolan, Associate Vice President for Enrollment Management/Dean of Admissions, Fax: 314-968-7116, E-mail: gadmit@webster.edu.

Webster University, George Herbert Walker School of Business and Technology, Department of Management, St. Louis, MO 63119-3194. Offers business and organizational security management (MA); computer resources and information management (MA); environmental management (MS); government contracting (Certificate); health care management (MA); health services management (MA); human resources development (MA); human resources management (MA); management (DM); management and leadership (MA); marketing (MA); nonprofit management (Certificate); procurement and acquisitions management (MA); public administration (MA); quality management (MA); space systems operations management (MS); telecommunications management (MA). *Accreditation:* ACBSP. Part-time and evening/weekend programs available. Postbaccalaureate distance learning degree programs offered (no on-campus study). *Faculty:* 16 full-time, 781 part-time/adjunct. *Students:* 1,369 full-time (610 women), 5,182 part-time (3,047 women); includes 3,460 minority (2,835 African Americans, 38 American Indian/Alaska Native, 169 Asian Americans or Pacific Islanders, 418 Hispanic Americans), 80 international. Average age 37. In 2009, 2,491 master's, 13 doctorates, 68 other advanced degrees awarded. *Degree requirements:* For master's, thesis (for some programs); for doctorate, thesis/dissertation, written exam. *Entrance requirements:* For doctorate, GMAT, 3 years of work experience, MBA. Additional exam requirements/recommendations for international students: Required—TOEFL. *Application deadline:* Applications are processed on a rolling basis. Application fee: $25 ($50 for international students). *Expenses:* Tuition: Part-time $565 per credit hour. Tuition and fees vary according to degree level, campus/location and program. *Financial support:* Federal Work-Study available. Support available to part-time students. Financial award application deadline: 4/1; financial award applicants required to submit FAFSA. *Unit head:* Jim Brasfield, Chair, 314-961-2660 Ext. 7063, Fax: 314-968-7077, E-mail: mgtchair@webster.edu. *Application contact:* Matt Nolan, Associate Vice President for Enrollment Management/Dean of Admissions, Fax: 314-968-7116, E-mail: gadmit@webster.edu.

Webster University, George Herbert Walker School of Business and Technology, Department of Mathematics and Computer Science, St. Louis, MO 63119-3194. Offers computer science/distributed systems (MS, Certificate); decision support systems (Certificate); web services (Certificate). Part-time and evening/weekend programs available. Postbaccalaureate distance learning degree programs offered (no on-campus study). *Faculty:* 7 full-time, 8 part-time/adjunct. *Students:* 2 full-time (1 woman), 64 part-time (22 women); includes 20 minority (13 African Americans, 1 American Indian/Alaska Native, 5 Asian Americans or Pacific Islanders, 1 Hispanic American). Average age 39. In 2009, 4 master's, 6 other advanced degrees awarded. *Entrance requirements:* For master's, 36 hours of graduate course work. Additional exam requirements/recommendations for international students: Required—TOEFL. *Application deadline:* Applications are processed on a rolling basis. Application fee: $25 ($50 for international students). *Expenses:* Tuition: Part-time $565 per credit hour. Tuition and fees vary according to degree level, campus/location and program. *Financial support:* Federal Work-Study available. Support available to part-time students. Financial award application deadline: 4/1; financial award applicants required to submit FAFSA. *Faculty research:* Databases, computer information systems networks, operating systems, computer architecture. *Unit head:* Al Cawns, Chair, 314-968-7127, Fax: 314-963-6050, E-mail: cawnsae@webster.edu. *Application contact:* Matt Nolan, Associate Vice President for Enrollment Management/Dean of Admissions, Fax: 314-968-7116, E-mail: gadmit@webster.edu.

West Chester University of Pennsylvania, Office of Graduate Studies, College of Arts and Sciences, Department of Computer Science, West Chester, PA 19383. Offers computer science (MS, Certificate); computer security (Certificate); information systems (Certificate); Web technology (Certificate). Part-time and evening/weekend programs available. *Students:* 4 full-time (3 women), 15 part-time (5 women); includes 3 minority (1 African American, 2 Asian Americans or Pacific Islanders), 8 international. Average age 26. 20 applicants, 85% accepted, 9 enrolled. In 2009, 11 master's awarded. *Degree requirements:* For master's, thesis optional. *Entrance requirements:* For master's, GRE, three letters of recommendation; for Certificate, GRE General Test. Additional exam requirements/recommendations for international students: Required—TOEFL (minimum score 550 paper-based; 213 computer-based; 80 iBT). *Application deadline:* For fall admission, 4/15 priority date for domestic students, 3/15 for international students; for spring admission, 10/15 for domestic students, 9/1 for international students. Applications are processed on a rolling basis. Application fee: $35. Electronic applications accepted. *Expenses:* Tuition, state resident: full-time $6666; part-time $370 per credit. Tuition, nonresident: full-time $10,666; part-time $593 per credit. Required fees: $122.56 per credit. *Financial support:* In 2009–10, 6 research assistantships with full and partial tuition reimbursements (averaging $5,000 per year) were awarded; unspecified assistantships also available. Support available to part-time students. Financial award application deadline: 2/15; financial award applicants required to submit FAFSA. *Faculty research:* Automata theory, compilers, non well-founded sets. *Unit head:* Dr. James Fabrey, Chair, 610-436-2204, E-mail: jfabrey@wcupa.edu. *Application contact:* Dr. Afrand Agah, Graduate Coordinator, 610-436-4419, E-mail: aagah@wcupa.edu.

Western Governors University, Programs in Business, Salt Lake City, UT 84107. Offers information technology management (MBA); management and strategy (MBA); strategic

Management Information Systems

Western Governors University *(continued)*

leadership (MBA). Postbaccalaureate distance learning degree programs offered. Electronic applications accepted.

Western International University, Graduate Programs in Business, MBA Program in Information Technology, Phoenix, AZ 85021-2718. Offers MBA. Evening/weekend programs available. Postbaccalaureate distance learning degree programs offered (no on-campus study). *Faculty:* 208 part-time/adjunct (59 women). *Students:* 40 full-time (12 women); includes 7 minority (1 African American, 6 Asian Americans or Pacific Islanders), 8 international. Average age 33. In 2009, 14 master's awarded. *Degree requirements:* For master's, thesis. *Entrance requirements:* For master's, minimum GPA of 2.75. *Application deadline:* Applications are processed on a rolling basis. Application fee: $85 ($100 for international students). *Expenses:* Tuition: Full-time $12,600. One-time fee: $25 full-time. *Financial support:* Career-related internships or fieldwork, institutionally sponsored loans, and scholarships/grants available. Support available to part-time students. Financial award applicants required to submit FAFSA. *Unit head:* Craig Horrocks, Chair, 602-943-2311. *Application contact:* Karen Janitell, Director of Enrollment, 602-943-2311 Ext. 1063, Fax: 602-371-8637, E-mail: karen_janitell@apollogrp.edu.

Wilmington University, College of Business, New Castle, DE 19720-6491. Offers business administration (MBA); finance (MBA); health care administration (MBA, MS); homeland security (MBA, MS); human resource management (MS); management (MS); management information systems (MBA); organizational leadership (MS); public administration (MS); transportation and logistics (MBA, MS). Part-time and evening/weekend programs available. *Entrance requirements:* Additional exam requirements/recommendations for international students: Required—TOEFL (minimum score 500 paper-based; 173 computer-based). Electronic applications accepted.

Wilmington University, College of Technology, New Castle, DE 19720-6491. Offers corporate training (MS); information assurance (MS); information systems technologies (MS); Internet web design (MS); management information systems (MS). Part-time and evening/weekend programs available. *Entrance requirements:* Additional exam requirements/recommendations for international students: Required—TOEFL (minimum score 500 paper-based; 173 computer-based). Electronic applications accepted.

Winston-Salem State University, Program in Computer Science and Information Technology, Winston-Salem, NC 27110-0003. Offers MS. Part-time programs available. *Degree requirements:* For master's, thesis optional. *Entrance requirements:* For master's, GRE, resume. Electronic applications accepted. *Faculty research:* Artificial intelligence, network protocols, software engineering.

Worcester Polytechnic Institute, Graduate Studies and Research, Programs in Interdisciplinary Studies, Worcester, MA 01609-2280. Offers bioscience administration (MS); impact engineering (MS); manufacturing engineering management (MS); power systems management (MS); social science (PhD); systems modeling (MS). Part-time and evening/weekend programs available. *Faculty:* 1 part-time/adjunct (0 women). *Students:* 3 full-time (1 woman), 126 part-time (24 women). 184 applicants, 68% accepted, 100 enrolled. In 2009, 19 master's awarded. *Degree requirements:* For master's, thesis; for doctorate, comprehensive exam, thesis/dissertation. *Entrance requirements:* For master's and doctorate, 3 letters of recommendation. Additional exam requirements/recommendations for international students: Required—TOEFL (minimum score 550 paper-based; 213 computer-based; 79 iBT), IELTS (minimum score 6.5). *Application deadline:* For fall admission, 1/15 priority date for domestic students; for spring admission, 10/15 priority date for domestic students. Application fee: $70. *Financial support:* Institutionally sponsored loans, scholarships/grants, and unspecified assistantships available. Financial award application deadline: 1/15. *Unit head:* Dr. Fred J. Looft, Head, 508-831-5231, Fax: 508-831-

5491, E-mail: fjlooft@wpi.edu. *Application contact:* Lynne Dougherty, Administrative Assistant, 508-831-5301, Fax: 508-831-5717, E-mail: grad@wpi.edu.

Worcester Polytechnic Institute, Graduate Studies and Research, School of Business, Worcester, MA 01609-2280. Offers information technology (MS), including information security management; management (Graduate Certificate); marketing and technological innovation (MS); operations design and leadership (MS); technology (MBA). *Accreditation:* AACSB. Part-time and evening/weekend programs available. Postbaccalaureate distance learning degree programs offered (no on-campus study). *Faculty:* 25 full-time (12 women), 6 part-time/adjunct (2 women). *Students:* 89 full-time (44 women), 198 part-time (47 women). Average age 32. 229 applicants, 70% accepted, 71 enrolled. In 2009, 69 master's awarded. *Degree requirements:* For master's, thesis optional. *Entrance requirements:* For master's, GMAT (MBA), GMAT or GRE General Test (MS), resume; for Graduate Certificate, GMAT or GRE General Test, statement of purpose, 3 letters of recommendation. Additional exam requirements/recommendations for international students: Required—TOEFL (minimum score 550 paper-based; 213 computer-based; 79 iBT), IELTS (minimum score 6.5). *Application deadline:* For fall admission, 7/1 priority date for domestic students, 6/1 priority date for international students; for spring admission, 11/1 priority date for domestic students, 10/1 priority date for international students. Applications are processed on a rolling basis. Application fee: $70. Electronic applications accepted. *Financial support:* Career-related internships or fieldwork, institutionally sponsored loans, scholarships/grants, and unspecified assistantships available. Financial award application deadline: 6/1. *Faculty research:* Organizational aesthetics, resistance in organizations, dynamics of product innovation, economic approaches to productivity, corporate earnings forecasts and value relevance, ERP implementation, improving Web accessibility, information quality assessment, measuring strategic and transactional IT, website quality, service operations modeling, health care operations and performance analysis, loan process design. *Unit head:* Dr. Mark Rice, Dean, 508-831-5218, Fax: 508-831-5720, E-mail: rice@wpi.edu. *Application contact:* Norm Wilkinson, Director, Graduate Management Programs, 508-831-5957, Fax: 508-831-5720, E-mail: nwilkins@wpi.edu.

Wright State University, School of Graduate Studies, Raj Soin College of Business, Department of Information Systems and Operations Management, Information Systems Program, Dayton, OH 45435. Offers MIS.

Xavier University, Williams College of Business, Master of Business Administration Program, Cincinnati, OH 45207-3221. Offers business administration (Exec MBA, MBA); business intelligence (MBA); finance (MBA); international business (MBA); management information systems (MBA); marketing (MBA); MBA/MHSA; MSN/MBA. *Accreditation:* AACSB. Part-time and evening/weekend programs available. *Faculty:* 44 full-time (17 women), 9 part-time/adjunct (2 women). *Students:* 167 full-time (51 women), 862 part-time (283 women); includes 149 minority (60 African Americans, 62 Asian Americans or Pacific Islanders, 27 Hispanic Americans), 17 international. Average age 30. 355 applicants, 63% accepted, 187 enrolled. In 2009, 369 master's awarded. *Degree requirements:* For master's, capstone course. *Entrance requirements:* For master's, GMAT. Additional exam requirements/recommendations for international students: Required—TOEFL (minimum score 550 paper-based; 213 computer-based; 80 iBT). *Application deadline:* For fall admission, 8/1 priority date for domestic students, 5/1 for international students; for spring admission, 12/1 priority date for domestic students, 9/1 for international students. Applications are processed on a rolling basis. Application fee: $0. Electronic applications accepted. *Expenses:* Contact institution. *Financial support:* In 2009-10, 183 students received support. Scholarships/grants, tuition waivers (partial), and unspecified assistantships available. Financial award application deadline: 3/1; financial award applicants required to submit FAFSA. *Unit head:* Dr. Hema Krishnan, Associate Dean, 513-745-3206, Fax: 513-745-3455, E-mail: krishnan@xavier.edu. *Application contact:* Anna Marie Whelan, Assistant Director, MBA Programs, 513-745-3525, Fax: 513-745-2929, E-mail: whelana@xavier.edu.

HAWAI'I PACIFIC UNIVERSITY

Master of Science in Information Systems

Program of Study

The Master of Science in Information Systems (M.S.I.S.) program at Hawai'i Pacific University (HPU) is designed to create a generation of decision makers and experts in information technology, systems design, and problem solving with automated resources. The program uses an integrated approach of experimentation, testing, and analysis that leads to an understanding of the importance of well-crafted information and knowledge systems. A combination of rigorous course work and experiential learning enhanced by state-of-the-art technology, the full-time M.S.I.S. is designed to be completed in eighteen to twenty-four months. High-tech classroom facilities, online information databases, the Frear Technology Center, expert faculty members, and a dynamic campus environment provide students with an enriching and unique learning experience.

Students have the opportunity to work with professional faculty members on a one-on-one basis due to an average graduate class size of 14 students. As a result, students frequently develop strong mentoring relationships with faculty members. Since the program attracts Hawaii's leading professionals, participants can build a lifelong network of business contacts, thus gaining an enormous career advantage in today's competitive marketplace.

The 45-credit program provides the option to take three elective courses that match individual interests, or M.S.I.S. candidates may pursue concentrations in knowledge management, software engineering, telecommunication, or decision sciences. Students may also choose to complement their degree with a professional certificate in areas such as electronic commerce or organizational change.

Research Facilities

To support graduate studies, HPU's Meader and Atherton Libraries hold more than 110,000 bound volumes, 350,000 microfiche items, and periodical subscriptions to 1,500 print titles and 30,000 electronic journals. Databases of public and state university libraries, legislative information, and business-oriented statistical data are also available in the library or online. Students can access HPU's library databases, course information, their academic information, and an e-mail account through Pipeline, the University's internal Web site for students. The University's accessible on-campus computer center houses more than 100 computers with specialized software to support graduate academic programs. HPU also provides free Wi-Fi service so that students can wirelessly access Pipeline resources anywhere on campus using laptops. A significant number of online courses are available as well.

Financial Aid

The University participates in all federal financial aid programs designated for graduate students. These programs provide aid in the form of subsidized (need-based) and unsubsidized (non-need-based) Federal Stafford Student Loans. Through these loans, funds may be available to cover a student's entire cost of education. To apply for aid, students must submit the Free Application for Federal Student Aid (FAFSA) beginning January 1. Mailing of student award letters usually begins by the end of March. The University also offers several types of institutional graduate scholarships to new full-time, degree-seeking students. The Graduate Trustee Scholarship provides $6000 for two semesters, the Graduate Dean Scholarship provides $4000 for two semesters, and the Graduate Kokua Scholarship provides $2000 for two semesters. Priority consideration is given to those students who apply by the deadline.

Cost of Study

Tuition for graduate students enrolled in fall and spring semesters is determined on a per-credit basis; full-time status for a graduate student is 9 credits. Tuition for the optional winter and summer sessions is also determined on a per-credit basis. The estimated minimum funds needed for a nine-month academic year (September to May) based on 2010–11 school year expenses is $26,459. For the 2010–11 academic year, full-time tuition is $12,600 for most graduate degree programs, including the M.S.I.S. program. Books, supplies, and transportation cost $1885, and health insurance costs $880.

Living and Housing Costs

Most graduate students live in off-campus housing. The cost of living in off-campus apartments is approximately $11,094 for a double occupancy room.

Student Group

University enrollment currently stands at more than 8,200. HPU is one of the most culturally diverse universities in America with students from all 50 U.S. states and more than 100 countries.

Location

Hawai'i Pacific University combines the excitement of an urban, downtown campus with the serenity of a residential campus. The main campus is ideally located in downtown Honolulu, the business and financial center of the Pacific. The downtown campus comprises six buildings in the center of Honolulu's business district and is home to the College of Business Administration and the College of Humanities and Social Sciences. Eight miles away, situated on 135 acres in Kaneohe, the windward Hawai'i Loa campus is the site of the College of Nursing and Health Sciences and the College of Natural and Computational Sciences. HPU is affiliated with the Oceanic Institute, an applied aquaculture research facility located on a 56-acre site at Makapu'u Point on the windward coast of Oahu, Hawaii. Students can conveniently travel between the three sites using the HPU shuttle service. There are also eight military campus programs located at Pearl Harbor, Barbers Point, Hickam Air Force Base, Schofield Barracks, Fort Shafter, Tripler Army Medical Center, Kaneohe Marine Corps Air Station, and Camp Smith.

The University

Hawai'i Pacific University is a private, nonprofit university with approximately 8,200 students. Founded in 1965, HPU prides itself on maintaining strong academic programs, small class sizes, individual attention to students, and a diverse faculty and student population. HPU is recognized as a "Best in the West" college by Princeton Review and a "Best Buy" by *Barron's* business magazine. HPU offers more than fifty acclaimed undergraduate programs and thirteen distinguished graduate programs. The University has a faculty of more than 500, a student-faculty ratio of 15:1, and an average class size of less than 20. A wide range of counseling and other student support services are available. There are more than seventy student organizations on campus, including the Graduate Student Organization.

Applying

Students must have a baccalaureate degree from an accredited college or university in the United States or an equivalent degree from another country. Applicants should complete and forward a Graduate Admissions Application, send in the $50 nonrefundable application fee, have official transcripts sent from all colleges or universities previously attended, and forward two letters of recommendation. A personal statement about the applicant's academic and career goals is required; submitting a resume is optional. Applicants who have taken the Graduate Management Admission Test (GMAT) or the Graduate Record Examination (GRE) should have their scores sent directly to the Graduate Admissions Office. International students should submit scores from a recognized English proficiency test, such as the TOEFL. Admissions decisions are made on a rolling basis. Applicants are notified between one and two weeks after all documents have been submitted. Applicants are encouraged to submit their applications online.

Correspondence and Information

Graduate Admissions
Hawai'i Pacific University
1164 Bishop Street, Suite 911
Honolulu, Hawaii 96813
Phone: 808-544-1135
        866-GRAD-HPU (toll-free)
Fax: 808-544-0280
E-mail: graduate@hpu.edu
Web site: http://www.hpu.edu/hpumsis

Hawai'i Pacific University

THE FACULTY AND THEIR RESEARCH

Richard Chepkevich, Instructor in Computer Science/Information Systems; M.S.S.M., USC.
Cathrine Linnes, Assistant Professor of Information Systems; Ph.D., Nova Southeastern.
Kenneth Rossi, Assistant Professor of Information Systems; Ed.D., USC.
Lawrence Rowland, Assistant Professor of Information Systems; Ed.D., USC.
William A. Sodeman, Associate Professor of Information Systems; Ph.D., Georgia.
Edward Souza, Instructor of Information Systems; M.S. Hawai'i Pacific.

Section 13
Management Strategy and Policy

This section contains a directory of institutions offering graduate work in management strategy and policy. Additional information about programs listed in the directory may be obtained by writing directly to the dean of a graduate school or chair of a department at the address given in the directory.

For programs offering related work, see also in this book *Business Administration and Management*. In another guide in this series: ***Graduate Programs in the Humanities, Arts & Social Sciences*** See *Public, Regional, and Industrial Affairs (Public Administration and Public Policy)*

CONTENTS

Program Directories

Close-Ups

Management Strategy and Policy

Alliant International University–San Diego, Marshall Goldsmith School of Management, Business and Management Division, San Diego, CA 92131-1799. Offers business administration (MBA); information and technology management (DBA); international business (MIBA, DBA), including finance (DBA); marketing (DBA); strategic business (DBA); sustainable management (MBA); MBA/MA; MBA/PhD. Part-time and evening/weekend programs available. *Degree requirements:* For doctorate, thesis/dissertation. *Entrance requirements:* For master's, GMAT, minimum GPA of 3.0; for doctorate, GMAT, minimum GPA of 3.3. Additional exam requirements/recommendations for international students: Required—TOEFL (minimum score 550 paper-based; 213 computer-based), TWE (minimum score 5). Electronic applications accepted. *Faculty research:* Consumer behavior, international business, strategic management, information systems.

Azusa Pacific University, School of Business and Management, Azusa, CA 91702-7000. Offers business administration (MBA); human and organizational development (MA); international business (MBA); strategic management (MBA). Part-time and evening/weekend programs available. *Degree requirements:* For master's, thesis (for some programs), final project. *Entrance requirements:* For master's, GMAT, minimum GPA of 3.0. Additional exam requirements/recommendations for international students: Required—TOEFL (minimum score 600 paper-based). *Expenses:* Contact institution. *Faculty research:* Gender issues, financial risk, leadership and ethics, marketing strategy.

Bernard M. Baruch College of the City University of New York, Zicklin School of Business, Department of Management, New York, NY 10010-5585. Offers entrepreneurship (MBA); general management and policy (MBA); human resources management (MBA); management planning systems (PhD); management science (MBA); organization and policy studies (PhD); organizational behavior (MBA). Part-time and evening/weekend programs available. *Degree requirements:* For doctorate, comprehensive exam, thesis/dissertation. *Entrance requirements:* For master's, GMAT, 2 letters of recommendation, resume, 2 years of work experience; for doctorate, GMAT. Additional exam requirements/recommendations for international students: Required—TOEFL (minimum score 590 paper-based; 243 computer-based), TWE.

Black Hills State University, Graduate Studies, Program in Strategic Leadership, Spearfish, SD 57799. Offers MS. *Faculty:* 1 full-time (0 women), 4 part-time/adjunct (2 women). *Students:* 34 part-time (18 women); includes 2 minority (1 Asian American or Pacific Islander, 1 Hispanic American). Average age 35. 44 applicants, 100% accepted, 18 enrolled. *Entrance requirements:* Additional exam requirements/recommendations for international students: Required—TOEFL (minimum score 500 paper-based; 171 computer-based; 60 iBT). Application fee: $35. *Expenses:* Tuition, state resident: full-time $4170; part-time $139 per credit hour. Tuition, nonresident: full-time $8828; part-time $294 per credit. Required fees: $3476; $116 per credit hour. *Application contact:* Dr. George Earley, Director of Graduate Studies, 605-642-6270, Fax: 605-642-6273, E-mail: georgeearley@bhsu.edu.

Boston University, School of Management, Master of Business Administration Program, Boston, MA 02215. Offers entrepreneurship (MBA); finance (MBA); health sector management (MBA); international management (MBA); marketing (MBA); operations and technology management (MBA); public and nonprofit management (MBA); strategy and business analysis (MBA); JD/MBA; MBA/MA; MBA/MPH; MBA/MS; MBA/MSIS; MS/MBA. Part-time and evening/weekend programs available. *Faculty:* 119 full-time (31 women), 99 part-time/adjunct (30 women). *Students:* 326 full-time (138 women), 677 part-time (257 women); includes 149 minority (13 African Americans, 119 Asian Americans or Pacific Islanders, 17 Hispanic Americans), 149 international. Average age 30. 1,617 applicants, 38% accepted, 317 enrolled. In 2009, 284 master's awarded. *Entrance requirements:* For master's, GMAT, resume, 2 letters of recommendation. Additional exam requirements/recommendations for international students: Required—TOEFL or IELTS. *Application deadline:* For fall admission, 3/15 for domestic and international students; for spring admission, 11/15 for domestic students. Application fee: $125. Electronic applications accepted. *Expenses:* Tuition: Full-time $37,910; part-time $1184 per credit hour. Required fees: $386; $40 per semester. Part-time tuition and fees vary according to class time, course level, degree level and program. *Financial support:* Career-related internships or fieldwork, Federal Work-Study, institutionally sponsored loans, and scholarships/grants available. Support available to part-time students. Financial award applicants required to submit FAFSA. *Unit head:* Katherine Nolan, Assistant Dean, Graduate Programs, 617-353-4157, Fax: 617-353-5003, E-mail: mba@bu.edu. *Application contact:* Hayden Estrada, Assistant Dean, Admissions, 617-353-2670, Fax: 617-353-7368, E-mail: mba@bu.edu.

Case Western Reserve University, Weatherhead School of Management, Department of Marketing and Policy Studies, Cleveland, OH 44106. Offers labor and human resource policy (MBA); management policy (MBA); marketing (MBA). Part-time and evening/weekend programs available. *Entrance requirements:* For master's, GMAT. *Application deadline:* For fall admission, 4/15 priority date for domestic students. Applications are processed on a rolling basis. Application fee: $100. *Financial support:* Career-related internships or fieldwork, Federal Work-Study, institutionally sponsored loans, and tuition waivers (full and partial) available. Financial award application deadline: 5/1. *Unit head:* Sayan Chatterjee, Chairman, 216-368-5373. *Application contact:* Sayan Chatterjee, Chairman, 216-368-5373.

Claremont Graduate University, Graduate Programs, Peter F. Drucker and Masatoshi Ito Graduate School of Management, Program in Executive Management, Claremont, CA 91711-6160. Offers advanced management (MS); executive management (EMBA); leadership (Certificate); management (MA, PhD, Certificate); strategy (Certificate). *Accreditation:* AACSB. Part-time programs available. *Students:* 41 full-time (20 women), 85 part-time (39 women); includes 51 minority (12 African Americans, 17 Asian Americans or Pacific Islanders, 22 Hispanic Americans), 11 international. Average age 43. In 2009, 29 master's, 2 doctorates, 53 other advanced degrees awarded. *Entrance requirements:* Additional exam requirements/recommendations for international students: Required—TOEFL (minimum score 550 paper-based; 213 computer-based; 80 iBT). *Application deadline:* For fall admission, 2/15 priority date for domestic students. Applications are processed on a rolling basis. Application fee: $60. Electronic applications accepted. *Expenses:* Contact institution. *Financial support:* Federal Work-Study, institutionally sponsored loans, and scholarships/grants available. Support available to part-time students. Financial award application deadline: 2/15; financial award applicants required to submit FAFSA. *Faculty research:* Strategy and leadership, brand management, cost management and control, organizational transformation, general management. *Unit head:* Christina Wassenaar, Director, 909-607-7812, Fax: 909-607-9104, E-mail: christina.wassenaar@cgu.edu. *Application contact:* Albert Ramos, Admissions Coordinator, 909-621-8067, Fax: 909-621-8551, E-mail: albert.ramos@cgu.edu.

Davenport University, Sneden Graduate School, Grand Rapids, MI 49503. Offers accounting (MBA); business administration (EMBA); finance (MBA); health care management (MBA); human resources (MBA); information assurance (MS); public health (MPH); strategic management (MBA). Evening/weekend programs available. *Entrance requirements:* For master's, GMAT, minimum undergraduate GPA of 2.75. Additional exam requirements/recommendations for international students: Required—TOEFL. Electronic applications accepted. *Faculty research:* Leadership, management, marketing, organizational culture.

Davenport University, Sneden Graduate School, Dearborn, MI 48126-3799. Offers accounting (MBA); business administration (EMBA); finance (MBA); health care management (MBA); human resources management (MBA); information assurance (MS); marketing (MBA); public health (MPH); strategic management (MBA). Part-time and evening/weekend programs available. Postbaccalaureate distance learning degree programs offered (no on-campus study). *Entrance requirements:* For master's, minimum GPA of 2.7, previous course work in accounting and statistics. *Faculty research:* Accounting, international accounting, social and environmental accounting, finance.

Defiance College, Program in Business Administration, Defiance, OH 43512-1610. Offers criminal justice (MBA); health care (MBA); leadership (MBA). Part-time and evening/weekend programs available. *Degree requirements:* For master's, thesis. *Entrance requirements:* For master's, minimum GPA of 2.5.

DePaul University, Charles H. Kellstadt Graduate School of Business and College of Liberal Arts and Sciences, Department of Economics, Chicago, IL 60604-2287. Offers applied economics (MBA); business strategy (MBA); economics and policy analysis (MA); international business (MBA). Part-time and evening/weekend programs available. *Faculty:* 26 full-time (5 women), 21 part-time/adjunct (5 women). *Students:* 67 full-time (32 women), 28 part-time (16 women); includes 14 minority (3 African Americans, 6 Asian Americans or Pacific Islanders, 5 Hispanic Americans), 8 international. 47 applicants, 47 enrolled. In 2009, 7 master's awarded. *Degree requirements:* For master's, thesis optional. *Entrance requirements:* For master's, GMAT (MBA), GRE (MS). Additional exam requirements/recommendations for international students: Required—TOEFL. *Application deadline:* For fall admission, 7/1 for domestic students; for winter admission, 10/1 for domestic students; for spring admission, 2/1 for domestic students. Applications are processed on a rolling basis. Application fee: $40. Electronic applications accepted. *Expenses:* Tuition: Full-time $37,525; part-time $620 per credit hour. *Financial support:* In 2009–10, 3 students received support, including 2 research assistantships with partial tuition reimbursements available (averaging $9,999 per year). Support available to part-time students. *Faculty research:* Forensic economics, game theory sports, economics of education, banking in Poland and Thailand. *Unit head:* Dr. Thomas D. Donley, Chairperson, 312-362-8887, Fax: 312-362-5452, E-mail: tdonley@depaul.edu. *Application contact:* Gabriella Bucci, Director of Graduate Program in Economics, 773-362-6787, Fax: 312-362-5452, E-mail: gbucci@depaul.edu.

DePaul University, Charles H. Kellstadt Graduate School of Business, Department of Management, Chicago, IL 60604-2287. Offers entrepreneurship (MBA); health sector management (MBA); human resource management (MBA, MSHR); leadership/change management (MBA); management planning and strategy (MBA); operations management (MBA). Part-time and evening/weekend programs available. *Faculty:* 36 full-time (7 women), 35 part-time/adjunct (16 women). *Students:* 284 full-time (115 women), 147 part-time (69 women); includes 75 minority (20 African Americans, 1 American Indian/Alaska Native, 37 Asian Americans or Pacific Islanders, 17 Hispanic Americans), 18 international. In 2009, 112 master's awarded. *Entrance requirements:* For master's, GMAT, GRE (MSHR), 2 letters of recommendation, resume. Additional exam requirements/recommendations for international students: Required—TOEFL (minimum score 550 paper-based; 213 computer-based). *Application deadline:* For fall admission, 7/1 for domestic students; for winter admission, 10/1 for domestic students; for spring admission, 2/1 for domestic students. Applications are processed on a rolling basis. Application fee: $60. Electronic applications accepted. *Expenses:* Tuition: Full-time $37,525; part-time $620 per credit hour. *Financial support:* Research assistantships available. Financial award application deadline: 4/1. *Faculty research:* Growth management, creativity and innovation, quality management and business process design, entrepreneurship. *Application contact:* Christopher E. Kinsella, Director of Cohort MBA Programs, 312-362-8810, Fax: 312-362-6677, E-mail: kgsb@depaul.edu.

DePaul University, Charles H. Kellstadt Graduate School of Business, Department of Marketing, Chicago, IL 60604-2287. Offers brand management (MBA); customer relationship management (MBA); integrated marketing communication (MBA); marketing analysis (MSMA); marketing and management (MBA); marketing strategy and analysis (MBA); marketing strategy and planning (MBA); new product management (MBA); sales leadership (MBA). Part-time and evening/weekend programs available. *Faculty:* 23 full-time (4 women), 15 part-time/adjunct (6 women). *Students:* 190 full-time (95 women), 72 part-time (40 women); includes 24 minority (6 African Americans, 13 Asian Americans or Pacific Islanders, 5 Hispanic Americans), 22 international. In 2009, 88 master's awarded. *Entrance requirements:* For master's, GMAT, 2 letters of recommendation, resume. Additional exam requirements/recommendations for international students: Required—TOEFL (minimum score 550 paper-based; 213 computer-based). *Application deadline:* For fall admission, 7/1 for domestic students; for winter admission, 10/1 for domestic students; for spring admission, 2/1 for domestic students. Applications are processed on a rolling basis. Application fee: $60. Electronic applications accepted. *Expenses:* Tuition: Full-time $37,525; part-time $620 per credit hour. *Financial support:* In 2009–10, 6 research assistantships with partial tuition reimbursements (averaging $2,500 per year) were awarded. Financial award application deadline: 4/30. *Faculty research:* International and marketing role in developing economics, internet marketing, direct marketing, consumer behavior, new product development processes. Total annual research expenditures: $100,000. *Unit head:* Dr. Suzanne Louise Fogel, Chairperson/Associate Professor, 312-362-5150, Fax: 312-362-5647, E-mail: sfogel@depaul.edu. *Application contact:* Director of MBA Programs, 312-362-8810, Fax: 312-362-6677, E-mail: kgsb@depaul.edu.

Dominican University of California, Graduate Programs, School of Business and Leadership, Program in Strategic Leadership, San Rafael, CA 94901-2298. Offers MBA. Part-time and evening/weekend programs available. *Degree requirements:* For master's, thesis or alternative, practicum. *Entrance requirements:* For master's, minimum GPA of 3.0. Additional exam requirements/recommendations for international students: Required—TOEFL (minimum score 550 paper-based; 213 computer-based). Electronic applications accepted. *Expenses:* Contact institution.

Drexel University, LeBow College of Business, Program in Business Administration, Philadelphia, PA 19104-2875. Offers business administration (MBA, PhD, APC), including accounting (MBA, PhD); decision sciences (PhD); economics (MBA, PhD); finance (MBA, PhD); legal studies (MBA); management (MBA); marketing (MBA, PhD); organizational sciences (PhD); quantitative methods (MBA); strategic management (PhD). *Accreditation:* AACSB. Part-time and evening/weekend programs available. Postbaccalaureate distance learning degree programs offered (minimal on-campus study). Terminal master's awarded for partial completion of doctoral program. *Entrance requirements:* For master's, GMAT, minimum GPA of 2.75; for doctorate, GMAT. Additional exam requirements/recommendations for international students: Required—TOEFL. Electronic applications accepted. *Faculty research:* Decision support systems, individual and group behavior, operations research, techniques and strategy.

Duquesne University, School of Leadership and Professional Advancement, Pittsburgh, PA 15282-0001. Offers leadership (MS), including business ethics, community leadership, global leadership, information technology, leadership, liberal studies, professional administration, sports leadership. Part-time and evening/weekend programs available. Postbaccalaureate distance learning degree programs offered (no on-campus study). *Faculty:* 1 full-time (0 women), 70 part-time/adjunct (35 women). *Students:* 654 (307 women); includes 68 minority (57 African Americans, 1 American Indian/Alaska Native, 6 Asian Americans or Pacific Islanders, 4 Hispanic Americans). 161 applicants, 73% accepted, 103 enrolled. In 2009, 108 master's awarded. *Degree requirements:* For master's, capstone course. *Entrance requirements:* For master's, professional work experience, 500-word essay. Additional exam requirements/recommendations for international students: Required—TOEFL. *Application deadline:* Applications are processed on a rolling basis. Application fee: $0. Electronic applications accepted. *Expenses:* Tuition: Part-time $851 per credit. Required fees: $81 per credit. *Financial support:* Applicants required to submit FAFSA. *Unit head:* Dr. Dorothy Bassett, Dean, 412-396-2141, Fax: 412-396-4711, E-mail: bassettd@duq.edu. *Application contact:* Marianne Leister, Director of Student Services, 412-396-4933, Fax: 412-396-5072, E-mail: leister@duq.edu.

Florida State University, The Graduate School, College of Business, Tallahassee, FL 32306-1110. Offers accounting (M Acc), including accounting information services, assurance services, corporate accounting, taxation; business administration (MBA, PhD), including accounting (PhD), finance (PhD), management information systems (PhD), marketing (PhD), organizational behavior (PhD), risk management and insurance (PhD), strategic management (PhD);

finance (MS); insurance (MSM); management information systems (MS); JD/MBA; MSW/MBA. *Accreditation:* AACSB. Part-time programs available. Postbaccalaureate distance learning degree programs offered (no on-campus study). *Faculty:* 107 full-time (31 women), 2 part-time/adjunct (0 women). *Students:* 212 full-time (73 women), 345 part-time (107 women); includes 123 minority (37 African Americans, 2 American Indian/Alaska Native, 48 Asian Americans or Pacific Islanders, 36 Hispanic Americans). Average age 30. 908 applicants, 43% accepted, 307 enrolled. In 2009, 257 master's, 18 doctorates awarded. Terminal master's awarded for partial completion of doctoral program. *Degree requirements:* For doctorate, comprehensive exam, thesis/dissertation. *Entrance requirements:* For master's, GMAT, work experience (MBA, MS), minimum GPA of 3.0, letters of recommendation; for doctorate, GMAT, minimum graduate GPA of 3.5, letters of recommendation. Additional exam requirements/recommendations for international students: Required—TOEFL (minimum score 600 paper-based; 80 computer-based); Recommended—IELTS (minimum score 6.5). *Application deadline:* For fall admission, 6/1 for domestic students, 5/1 for international students; for spring admission, 10/1 for domestic students, 9/1 for international students. Applications are processed on a rolling basis. Application fee: $30. Electronic applications accepted. *Expenses:* Tuition, state resident: full-time $7413. Tuition, nonresident: full-time $22,567. *Financial support:* In 2009–10, 102 students received support, including 32 fellowships with full tuition reimbursements available (averaging $6,900 per year), 30 research assistantships with full tuition reimbursements available (averaging $4,500 per year), 40 teaching assistantships with full tuition reimbursements available (averaging $11,500 per year); career-related internships or fieldwork, scholarships/grants, health care benefits, tuition waivers (full and partial), and unspecified assistantships also available. Support available to part-time students. Financial award application deadline: 1/1. *Unit head:* Dr. Caryn Beck-Dudley, Dean, 850-644-3090, Fax: 850-644-0915. *Application contact:* Lisa Beverly, Director, Graduate Programs Admissions, 850-644-6458, Fax: 850-644-0588, E-mail: lbeverly@cob.fsu.edu.

Franklin Pierce University, Graduate Studies, Rindge, NH 03461-0060. Offers emerging network technology (Graduate Certificate); health practice management (MBA, Graduate Certificate); human resource management (MBA); human resources management (Graduate Certificate); information technology management (MS); leadership (MBA, DA), including transformational leadership (DA); nursing (MS); physical therapy (DPT); physician assistant (MPAS); sports facilities management (MS); teacher education (M Ed). *Accreditation:* APTA. Part-time programs available. Postbaccalaureate distance learning degree programs offered (no on-campus study). *Faculty:* 27 full-time (16 women), 18 part-time/adjunct (4 women). *Students:* 296 full-time (172 women), 249 part-time (165 women); includes 18 minority (5 African Americans, 7 Asian Americans or Pacific Islanders, 6 Hispanic Americans), 31 international. Average age 38. 227 applicants, 97% accepted, 185 enrolled. In 2009, 76 master's, 46 doctorates awarded. *Degree requirements:* For master's, concentrated original research projects; student teaching; fieldwork and/or internship; leadership project; for doctorate, concentrated original research projects, clinical fieldwork and/or internship, leadership project. *Entrance requirements:* For master's, minimum GPA of 2.5, 3 letters of recommendation; for doctorate, demonstrated success at previous academic institutions (minimum GPA of 2.5), 3 letters of recommendation, personal mission statement, interview; writing sample (for DA program). Additional exam requirements/recommendations for international students: Required—TOEFL (minimum score 550 paper-based; 195 computer-based). *Application deadline:* Applications are processed on a rolling basis. Application fee: $0. Electronic applications accepted. *Expenses:* Tuition: Part-time $1560 per course. Part-time tuition and fees vary according to degree level, campus/location and program. *Financial support:* In 2009–10, 36 students received support, including 22 teaching assistantships with full and partial tuition reimbursements available; career-related internships or fieldwork and unspecified assistantships also available. Support available to part-time students. Financial award applicants required to submit FAFSA. *Faculty research:* Evidence based practice in sports physical therapy, human resource management in economic crisis, leadership in nursing, innovation in sports facility management, differentiated learning and understanding by design. *Unit head:* Dr. Robert G. Goddard, Assistant Dean, 603-899-4361; Fax: 603-229-4580, E-mail: goddardr@franklinpierce.edu. *Application contact:* 800-325-1090, Fax: 603-898-0827, E-mail: gpsadmin@franklinpierce.edu.

Freed-Hardeman University, Program in Business Administration, Henderson, TN 38340-2399. Offers accounting (MBA); corporate responsibility (MBA); leadership (MBA). *Accreditation:* ACBSP. Part-time and evening/weekend programs available. Postbaccalaureate distance learning degree programs offered (no on-campus study). *Entrance requirements:* For master's, GMAT. Additional exam requirements/recommendations for international students: Required—TOEFL (minimum score 500 paper-based; 173 computer-based).

The George Washington University, School of Business, Department of Strategic Management and Public Policy, Washington, DC 20052. Offers MBA, PhD. Part-time and evening/weekend programs available. *Faculty:* 14 full-time (3 women), 3 part-time/adjunct (1 woman). *Students:* 199 full-time (89 women); includes 25 minority (7 African Americans, 1 American Indian/Alaska Native, 15 Asian Americans or Pacific Islanders, 2 Hispanic Americans), 55 international. Average age 28. 529 applicants, 53% accepted. In 2009, 110 master's awarded. *Degree requirements:* For doctorate, thesis/dissertation. *Entrance requirements:* For master's, GMAT; for doctorate, GMAT or GRE. Additional exam requirements/recommendations for international students: Required—TOEFL. *Application deadline:* For fall admission, 4/1 priority date for domestic students; for spring admission, 10/1 for domestic students. Applications are processed on a rolling basis. Application fee: $60. *Financial support:* In 2009–10, 1 student received support; fellowships, teaching assistantships, career-related internships or fieldwork, Federal Work-Study, and institutionally sponsored loans available. Financial award application deadline: 4/1. *Unit head:* Dr. Mark Starik, Chair, 202-994-6677, E-mail: starik@gwu.edu. *Application contact:* Kristin Williams, Assistant Vice President for Graduate and Special Enrollment Management, 202-994-0467, Fax: 202-994-0371, E-mail: ksw@gwu.edu.

Georgia Institute of Technology, Graduate Studies and Research, College of Management, Program in Business Administration, Atlanta, GA 30332-0001. Offers accounting (MBA); e-commerce (Certificate); engineering entrepreneurship (MBA); entrepreneurship (Certificate); finance (MBA); information technology management (MBA); international business (MBA, Certificate); management of technology (Certificate); marketing (MBA); operations management (MBA); organizational behavior (MBA); strategic management (MBA). *Accreditation:* AACSB.

Georgia Institute of Technology, Graduate Studies and Research, College of Management, Program in Management, Atlanta, GA 30332-0001. Offers accounting (PhD); finance (PhD); information technology management (PhD); marketing (PhD); operations management (PhD); organizational behavior (PhD); quantitative and computational finance (MS); strategic management (PhD). *Accreditation:* AACSB. *Degree requirements:* For doctorate, comprehensive exam, thesis/dissertation, oral exams. *Entrance requirements:* For master's and doctorate, GMAT. Additional exam requirements/recommendations for international students: Required—TOEFL. *Faculty research:* MIS, management of technology, international business, entrepreneurship, operations management.

Georgia State University, J. Mack Robinson College of Business, Department of Managerial Sciences, Atlanta, GA 30302-3083. Offers business analysis (MBA, MS); decision sciences (PhD); entrepreneurship (MBA); human resources management (MBA, MS); management (MBA, PhD); operations management (MBA, MS); organization change (MS); personnel employee relations (PhD); strategic management (PhD). Part-time and evening/weekend programs available. *Degree requirements:* For doctorate, thesis/dissertation. *Entrance requirements:* For master's and doctorate, GMAT. Additional exam requirements/recommendations for international students: Required—TOEFL (minimum score 610 paper-based; 255 computer-based; 101 iBT). Electronic applications accepted. *Faculty research:* Abusive supervision, entrepreneurship, time series and neural networks, organizational controls, inventory control systems.

Harvard University, Harvard Business School, Doctoral Programs in Management, Boston, MA 02163. Offers accounting and management (DBA); business economics (PhD); health policy management (PhD); management (DBA); marketing (DBA); organizational behavior

(PhD); science, technology and management (PhD); strategy (DBA); technology and operations management (DBA). *Degree requirements:* For doctorate, comprehensive exam (for some programs), thesis/dissertation. *Entrance requirements:* For doctorate, GRE General Test or GMAT. Additional exam requirements/recommendations for international students: Required—TOEFL. *Expenses:* Tuition: Full-time $33,696. Required fees: $1126. Full-time tuition and fees vary according to program.

HEC Montreal, School of Business Administration, Master of Science Programs in Administration, Program in Business Intelligence, Montréal, QC H3T 2A7, Canada. Offers M Sc. All courses are given in French. Part-time programs available. *Students:* 10 full-time (3 women), 8 part-time (1 woman). 14 applicants, 57% accepted, 4 enrolled. In 2009, 7 master's awarded. *Degree requirements:* For master's, one foreign language, thesis. *Application deadline:* For fall admission, 3/15 for domestic and international students; for winter admission, 9/15 for domestic and international students. Application fee: $77 Canadian dollars. Electronic applications accepted. Tuition and fees charges are reported in Canadian dollars. *Expenses:* Tuition, area resident: Part-time $65.60 Canadian dollars per credit. Tuition, state resident: full-time $2361.60 Canadian dollars; part-time $183.36 Canadian dollars per credit. Tuition, nonresident: full-time $6601 Canadian dollars; part-time $448.13 Canadian dollars per credit. International tuition: $16,132.68 Canadian dollars full-time. Required fees: $1254.15 Canadian dollars; $28.99 Canadian dollars per course. $91.68 Canadian dollars per term. Tuition and fees vary according to degree level and program. *Financial support:* Fellowships, research assistantships, teaching assistantships, scholarships/grants available. Financial award application deadline: 10/2. *Unit head:* Dr. Claude Laurin, Director, 514-340-6485, Fax: 514-340-5690, E-mail: claude.laurin@hec.ca. *Application contact:* Francine Blais, Administrative Director, 514-340-6112, Fax: 514-340-6411, E-mail: francine.blais@hec.ca.

Lamar University, College of Graduate Studies, College of Business, Beaumont, TX 77710. Offers accounting (MBA); experiential business and entrepreneurship (MBA); financial management (MBA); healthcare administration (MBA); information systems (MBA); management (MBA). *Accreditation:* AACSB. Part-time and evening/weekend programs available. *Faculty:* 18 full-time (4 women), 4 part-time/adjunct (0 women). *Students:* 62 full-time (27 women), 59 part-time (16 women); includes 19 minority (8 African Americans, 6 Asian Americans or Pacific Islanders, 5 Hispanic Americans), 19 international. Average age 29. 210 applicants, 34% accepted, 33 enrolled. In 2009, 41 master's awarded. *Degree requirements:* For master's, comprehensive exam (for some programs), thesis optional. *Entrance requirements:* For master's, GMAT. Additional exam requirements/recommendations for international students: Required—TOEFL (minimum score 525 paper-based; 197 computer-based). *Application deadline:* For fall admission, 3/15 priority date for domestic students; for spring admission, 10/1 priority date for domestic students. Applications are processed on a rolling basis. Application fee: $25 ($50 for international students). *Financial support:* In 2009–10, 12 students received support, including 4 research assistantships with partial tuition reimbursements available; fellowships with tuition reimbursements available, career-related internships or fieldwork, Federal Work-Study, institutionally sponsored loans, scholarships/grants, and tuition waivers (partial) also available. Support available to part-time students. Financial award application deadline: 4/1; financial award applicants required to submit FAFSA. *Faculty research:* Marketing, finance, quantitative methods, management information systems, legal, environmental. *Unit head:* Dr. Enrique R. Venta, Dean, 409-880-8604, Fax: 409-880-8088, E-mail: henry.venta@lamar.edu. *Application contact:* Dr. Brad Mayer, Professor and Associate Dean, 409-880-2383, Fax: 409-880-8605, E-mail: bradley.mayer@lamar.edu.

LeTourneau University, School of Graduate and Professional Studies, Longview, TX 75607-7001. Offers business administration (MBA); curriculum and instruction (M Ed); educational administration (M Ed); strategic leadership (MSL); teaching and learning (M Ed). Part-time and evening/weekend programs available. Postbaccalaureate distance learning degree programs offered (no on-campus study). *Faculty:* 8 full-time (1 woman), 19 part-time/adjunct (7 women). *Students:* 43 full-time (30 women), 245 part-time (164 women); includes 158 minority (130 African Americans, 2 American Indian/Alaska Native, 2 Asian Americans or Pacific Islanders, 24 Hispanic Americans). Average age 36. 1,717 applicants, 31% accepted, 288 enrolled. *Entrance requirements:* For master's, minimum GPA of 2.8. Additional exam requirements/recommendations for international students: Required—TOEFL. *Application deadline:* Applications are processed on a rolling basis. Electronic applications accepted. *Expenses:* Tuition: Full-time $10,710; part-time $595 per credit hour. *Financial support:* Applicants required to submit FAFSA. *Unit head:* Dr. Carol Green, Vice President, 903-233-3250, Fax: 903-233-3227, E-mail: carolgreen@letu.edu. *Application contact:* Chris Fontaine, Assistant Vice President for Enrollment Management and Market Research, 903-233-3250, Fax: 903-233-3227, E-mail: chrisfontaine@letu.edu.

Manhattanville College, Graduate Programs, Humanities and Social Sciences Programs, Program in Leadership and Strategic Management, Purchase, NY 10577-2132. Offers MS. Part-time and evening/weekend programs available. In 2009, 14 master's awarded. *Degree requirements:* For master's, thesis. *Entrance requirements:* For master's, 2 letters of recommendation, interview. Additional exam requirements/recommendations for international students: Required—TOEFL. *Application deadline:* Applications are processed on a rolling basis. Application fee: $70. *Financial support:* Career-related internships or fieldwork, Federal Work-Study, institutionally sponsored loans, and unspecified assistantships available. Financial award applicants required to submit FAFSA. *Unit head:* Donald Richards, Interim Dean, School of Graduate and Professional Studies, 914-323-5469, Fax: 914-694-3488, E-mail: gps@mville.edu. *Application contact:* Office of Admissions for Graduate and Professional Studies, 914-323-5418, E-mail: gps@mville.edu.

McGill University, Faculty of Graduate and Postdoctoral Studies, Desautels Faculty of Management, Montréal, QC H3A 2T5, Canada. Offers administration (PhD); entrepreneurial studies (MBA); finance (MBA); general management (Post Master's Certificate); information systems (MBA); international business (exchange program) (MBA); international Master's program in practicing management (MM); management (MBA); management for development (MBA); manufacturing management (MMM); marketing (MBA); operations management (MBA); public accountancy (Diploma); strategic management (MBA); MBA/LL B; MD/MBA.

Middle Tennessee State University, College of Graduate Studies, University College, Murfreesboro, TN 37132. Offers MPS. Part-time and evening/weekend programs available. Postbaccalaureate distance learning degree programs offered. *Students:* 1 (woman) full-time, 65 part-time (41 women); includes 13 minority (12 African Americans, 1 Hispanic American). 41 applicants, 78% accepted, 32 enrolled. In 2009, 4 master's awarded. *Entrance requirements:* Additional exam requirements/recommendations for international students: Required—TOEFL (minimum score 525 paper-based; 195 computer-based; 71 iBT) or IELTS (minimum score 6). *Application deadline:* For fall admission, 6/1 for domestic and international students. Applications are processed on a rolling basis. Application fee: $25 ($30 for international students). *Expenses:* Tuition, state resident: full-time $4404. Tuition, nonresident: full-time $10,956. *Financial support:* In 2009–10, 4 students received support. Application deadline: 5/1. *Unit head:* Dr. David Gotcher, Program Advisor, 615-904-8042, E-mail: dgotcher@mtsu.edu. *Application contact:* Dr. Michael Allen, Dean and Vice Provost for Research, 615-898-2840, Fax: 615-904-8020, E-mail: mallen@mtsu.edu.

Mountain State University, Graduate Studies, Program in Strategic Leadership, Beckley, WV 25802-9003. Offers MSSL. Part-time and evening/weekend programs available. Postbaccalaureate distance learning degree programs offered (no on-campus study). *Faculty:* 6 full-time (1 woman), 32 part-time/adjunct (10 women). *Students:* 388 full-time (193 women); includes 87 minority (59 African Americans, 1 American Indian/Alaska Native, 9 Asian Americans or Pacific Islanders, 18 Hispanic Americans), 33 international. Average age 38. 236 applicants, 90% accepted, 170 enrolled. In 2009, 263 master's awarded. *Degree requirements:* For master's, thesis or alternative. *Entrance requirements:* Additional exam requirements/recommendations for international students: Required—TOEFL (minimum score 550 paper-based; 213 computer-based); Recommended—IELTS (minimum score 6.5). *Application deadline:* For fall admission, 5/31 priority date for domestic and international students. Applications are

Management Strategy and Policy

Mountain State University (continued)

processed on a rolling basis. Application fee: $25 ($50 for international students). Electronic applications accepted. *Expenses:* Tuition: Full-time $6450. Tuition and fees vary according to program. *Financial support:* Federal Work-Study, scholarships/grants, and unspecified assistantships available. Support available to part-time students. Financial award applicants required to submit FAFSA. *Unit head:* Dr. William White, Dean, School of Leadership and Professional Development/Interim Dean, School of Graduate Studies, 304-929-1658, Fax: 304-929-1637, E-mail: wwhite@mountainstate.edu. *Application contact:* Kristen Stump, Online Recruiting Coordinator, 304-929-1702, Fax: 304-929-1710, E-mail: kmstump@mountainstate.edu.

Neumann University, Program in Strategic Leadership, Aston, PA 19014-1298. Offers MS. *Faculty:* 1 full-time (0 women), 6 part-time/adjunct (3 women). *Students:* 56 part-time (33 women). Average age 39. 40 applicants, 100% accepted, 35 enrolled. In 2009, 33 master's awarded. *Application deadline:* Applications are processed on a rolling basis. Application fee: $50. Electronic applications accepted. *Expenses:* Tuition: Full-time $10,260; part-time $570 per credit hour. *Financial support:* Available to part-time students. Application deadline: 3/15. *Unit head:* Dr. Fredenick Loomis, Coordinator, Division of Continuing Adult and Professional Studies, 610-361-5292, E-mail: loomisf@neumann.edu. *Application contact:* Kittie D. Pain, Associate Director of Admissions, Graduate and Adult Programs, 610-558-5613, Fax: 610-558-5652, E-mail: paink@neumann.edu.

New England College, Program in Management, Henniker, NH 03242-3293. Offers accounting (MSA); healthcare administration (MS); international relations (MA); marketing management (MS); nonprofit leadership (MS); project management (MS); strategic leadership (MS). Part-time and evening/weekend programs available. *Degree requirements:* For master's, independent research project. Electronic applications accepted.

New York University, Leonard N. Stern School of Business, Department of Management and Organizations, New York, NY 10012-1019. Offers management organizations (MBA); organization theory (PhD); organizational behavior (PhD); strategy (PhD). *Expenses:* Tuition: Full-time $30,528; part-time $1272 per credit. Required fees: $2177. *Faculty research:* Strategic management, managerial cognition, interpersonal processes, conflict and negotiation.

New York University, School of Continuing and Professional Studies, Division of Programs in Business, Graduate Programs in Management and Systems, New York, NY 10012-1019. Offers core business competencies (Advanced Certificate); database technologies (MS); enterprise and risk management (Advanced Certificate); enterprise risk management (MS); information technologies (Advanced Certificate); strategy and leadership (MS, Advanced Certificate); systems management (MS). Part-time and evening/weekend programs available. Postbaccalaureate distance learning degree programs offered (no on-campus study). *Faculty:* 2 full-time (0 women), 21 part-time/adjunct (6 women). *Students:* 32 full-time (18 women), 197 part-time (78 women). Average age 34. 168 applicants, 80% accepted, 69 enrolled. In 2009, 51 master's, 7 other advanced degrees awarded. *Degree requirements:* For master's, thesis, capstone project. *Entrance requirements:* For master's, GMAT or GRE General Test (for recent graduates), resume, 2 letters of recommendation, essay. Additional exam requirements/recommendations for international students: Required—TOEFL (minimum score 600 paper-based; 250 computer-based; 100 iBT), TWE. *Application deadline:* For fall admission, 2/1 priority date for domestic and international students; for spring admission, 10/15 priority date for domestic students, 8/15 priority date for international students. Applications are processed on a rolling basis. Application fee: $75. Electronic applications accepted. *Expenses:* Tuition: Full-time $30,528; part-time $1272 per credit. Required fees: $2177. *Financial support:* In 2009–10, 61 students received support, including 61 fellowships (averaging $2,300 per year); scholarships/grants also available. Support available to part-time students. Financial award application deadline: 3/1; financial award applicants required to submit FAFSA. *Unit head:* Israel Moskowitz, Director, 212-992-3600, Fax: 212-992-3650, E-mail: im36@nyu.edu. *Application contact:* Helen Sapp, Assistant Director, 212-992-3600, Fax: 212-992-3650, E-mail: helen.sapp@nyu.edu.

Northwestern University, The Graduate School, Kellogg School of Management, Program in Managerial Economics and Strategy, Evanston, IL 60208. Offers PhD. Admissions and degree offered through The Graduate School. *Degree requirements:* For doctorate, comprehensive exam, thesis/dissertation. *Entrance requirements:* For doctorate, GMAT or GRE General Test. Additional exam requirements/recommendations for international students: Required—TOEFL. Electronic applications accepted. *Faculty research:* Competitive strategy and organization, managerial economics, decision sciences, game theory, operations management.

Pace University, Lubin School of Business, Program in Management Science, New York, NY 10038. Offers management science (MBA); operations management (MBA). Part-time and evening/weekend programs available. *Entrance requirements:* For master's, GMAT. Additional exam requirements/recommendations for international students: Required—TOEFL. *Application deadline:* For fall admission, 7/31 priority date for domestic students; for spring admission, 11/30 for domestic students. Applications are processed on a rolling basis. Application fee: $70. Electronic applications accepted. *Expenses:* Tuition: Part-time $954 per credit. Tuition and fees vary according to course load, degree level and program. *Financial support:* Research assistantships, career-related internships or fieldwork available. Support available to part-time students. Financial award applicants required to submit FAFSA. *Unit head:* Dr. Christian Madu, Chairperson, 212-346-1919. *Application contact:* Susan Ford-Goldschein, Director of Admissions, 212-346-1652, Fax: 212-346-1585, E-mail: gradnyc@pace.edu.

Regent University, Graduate School, School of Global Leadership and Entrepreneurship, Virginia Beach, VA 23464-9800. Offers business administration (MBA); management (MA); organizational leadership (MA, PhD, Certificate); strategic foresight (MA); strategic leadership (DSL). Part-time and evening/weekend programs available. Postbaccalaureate distance learning degree programs offered (minimal on-campus study). *Faculty:* 15 full-time (3 women), 10 part-time/adjunct (3 women). *Students:* 14 full-time (4 women), 407 part-time (156 women); includes 123 minority (97 African Americans, 3 American Indian/Alaska Native, 6 Asian Americans or Pacific Islanders, 17 Hispanic Americans), 59 international. Average age 41. 153 applicants, 55% accepted, 31 enrolled. In 2009, 110 master's, 52 doctorates awarded. *Degree requirements:* For master's, thesis or alternative, 3 credit hour culminating experience; for doctorate, thesis/dissertation. *Entrance requirements:* For master's, GRE, GMAT, minimum undergraduate GPA of 2.75, computer literacy survey, 2 recommendations, resume, transcripts, essay; for doctorate, GRE, GMAT, sample of writing, minimum 3 years of relevant experience, computer literacy survey, 2 recommendations, resume, essay, transcripts; for Certificate, writing sample, resume, transcripts. Additional exam requirements/recommendations for international students: Required—TOEFL (minimum score 577 paper-based; 233 computer-based). *Application deadline:* For fall admission, 5/1 priority date for domestic students; for spring admission, 10/1 priority date for domestic students. Applications are processed on a rolling basis. Application fee: $50. Electronic applications accepted. *Expenses:* Contact institution. *Financial support:* In 2009–10, 258 students received support. Career-related internships or fieldwork, scholarships/grants, and tuition waivers (full and partial) available. Support available to part-time students. Financial award application deadline: 9/1. *Faculty research:* Servant leadership, ethics and values, telecommuting and family values, organizational communications, distance education. *Unit head:* Dr. Bruce Winston, Dean, 757-352-4306, Fax: 757-352-4634, E-mail: brucwin@regent.edu. *Application contact:* Matthew Chadwick, Director of Admissions, 800-373-5504, Fax: 757-352-4381, E-mail: admissions@regent.edu.

Roberts Wesleyan College, Division of Business, Rochester, NY 14624-1997. Offers nonprofit leadership (Certificate); strategic leadership (MS); strategic marketing (MS). Evening/weekend programs available. *Degree requirements:* For master's, thesis or alternative. *Entrance requirements:* For master's, GMAT, minimum GPA of 2.75, verifiable work experience. *Expenses:* Contact institution.

Rutgers, The State University of New Jersey, Newark, Rutgers Business School–Newark and New Brunswick, Department of Management and Global Business, Newark, NJ 07102. Offers customized concentration (MBA); global business (MBA); management and business strategy (MBA). *Entrance requirements:* For master's, GMAT. Additional exam requirements/recommendations for international students: Required—TOEFL.

Sage Graduate School, Graduate School, School of Management, Program in Business Administration, Troy, NY 12180-4115. Offers business strategy (MBA); finance (MBA); human resources (MBA); marketing (MBA); JD/MBA. Part-time and evening/weekend programs available. *Faculty:* 4 full-time (2 women), 6 part-time/adjunct (0 women). *Students:* 9 full-time (7 women), 68 part-time (44 women); includes 11 minority (5 African Americans, 2 Asian Americans or Pacific Islanders, 4 Hispanic Americans), 2 international. Average age 31. 50 applicants, 60% accepted, 17 enrolled. In 2009, 19 master's awarded. *Entrance requirements:* For master's, minimum GPA of 2.75, resume, 2 letters of recommendation. Additional exam requirements/recommendations for international students: Required—TOEFL (minimum score 550 paper-based; 213 computer-based). *Application deadline:* Applications are processed on a rolling basis. Application fee: $40. *Expenses:* Tuition: Full-time $10,620; part-time $590 per credit hour. *Financial support:* Fellowships, research assistantships, Federal Work-Study, scholarships/grants, and unspecified assistantships available. Support available to part-time students. Financial award application deadline: 3/1; financial award applicants required to submit FAFSA. *Unit head:* Daniel Robeson, Chair, Management Department, 518-292-1770, Fax: 518-292-5414, E-mail: robesd@sage.edu. *Application contact:* Wendy D. Diefendorf, Director of Graduate and Adult Admission, 518-244-2443, Fax: 518-244-6880, E-mail: diefew@sage.edu.

Saint Joseph's University, Erivan K. Haub School of Business, MS Program in Business Intelligence, Philadelphia, PA 19131-1395. Offers business intelligence (MS). Part-time and evening/weekend programs available. *Students:* 7 full-time (4 women), 69 part-time (14 women); includes 10 minority (5 African Americans, 3 Asian Americans or Pacific Islanders, 2 Hispanic Americans), 10 international. Average age 35. In 2009, 5 master's awarded. *Entrance requirements:* For master's, GMAT or GRE, 2 letters of recommendation, resume. Additional exam requirements/recommendations for international students: Required—TOEFL (minimum score 550 paper-based; 213 computer-based; 79 iBT) or IELTS (minimum score 6.5). *Application deadline:* For fall admission, 7/15 priority date for domestic students, 4/15 priority date for international students; for spring admission, 11/15 priority date for domestic students, 10/15 priority date for international students. Applications are processed on a rolling basis. Application fee: $35. Electronic applications accepted. *Expenses:* Tuition: Part-time $729 per credit hour. Tuition and fees vary according to degree level and program. *Financial support:* In 2009–10, teaching assistantships with partial tuition reimbursements (averaging $2,500 per year); unspecified assistantships also available. Financial award application deadline: 5/1. *Unit head:* Patricia Rafferty, Director, MS in Business Intelligence and MS in Human Resource Management Programs, 610-660-1318, Fax: 610-660-1229, E-mail: patricia.rafferty@sju.edu. *Application contact:* Patricia Rafferty, Director, MS in Business Intelligence and MS in Human Resource Management Programs, 610-660-1318, Fax: 610-660-1229, E-mail: patricia.rafferty@sju.edu.

Saint Mary-of-the-Woods College, Program in Leadership Development, Saint Mary-of-the-Woods, IN 47876. Offers MLD.

Southern Methodist University, Cox School of Business, MBA Program, Dallas, TX 75275. Offers accounting (MBA); finance (MBA); information technology and operations management (MBA); management (MBA); marketing (MBA); strategy and entrepreneurship (MBA). *Students:* 396 full-time (91 women), 401 part-time (109 women); includes 185 minority (34 African Americans, 5 American Indian/Alaska Native, 102 Asian Americans or Pacific Islanders, 44 Hispanic Americans), 76 international. Average age 31. In 2009, 363 master's awarded. *Unit head:* Dr. Albert W. Niemi, Dean, 214-768-3012, Fax: 214-768-3713, E-mail: aniemi@mail.cox.smu.edu. *Application contact:* Path Cudney, Director of MBA Admissions, 214-768-3001, Fax: 214-768-3956, E-mail: pcudney@mail.cox.smu.edu.

Stevens Institute of Technology, Graduate School, Wesley J. Howe School of Technology Management, Program in Management, Hoboken, NJ 07030. Offers general management (MS); global innovation management (MS); human resource management (MS); information management (MS); project management (MS); technology commercialization (MS); technology management (MS). Part-time programs available. *Degree requirements:* For master's, thesis optional. *Entrance requirements:* For master's, GMAT, GRE General Test. Additional exam requirements/recommendations for international students: Required—TOEFL. Electronic applications accepted. *Expenses:* Tuition: Full-time $9900; part-time $1100 per credit. Required fees: $286 per semester. *Faculty research:* Industrial economics.

Suffolk University, Sawyer Business School, Master of Business Administration Program, Boston, MA 02108-2770. Offers accounting (MBA); business administration (APC); corporate financial executive track (MBA); entrepreneurship (MBA); executive business administration (EMBA); finance (MBA); global business administration (GMBA); health administration (MBA); international business (MBA); marketing (MBA); organizational behavior (MBA); strategic management (MBA); taxation (MBA); JD/MBA; MBA/GDPA; MBA/MHA; MBA/MSA; MBA/MSF; MBA/MST. *Accreditation:* AACSB. Part-time and evening/weekend programs available. Postbaccalaureate distance learning degree programs offered (no on-campus study). *Faculty:* 103 full-time (30 women), 63 part-time/adjunct (19 women). *Students:* 173 full-time (68 women), 406 part-time (178 women); includes 51 minority (16 African Americans, 3 American Indian/Alaska Native, 22 Asian Americans or Pacific Islanders, 10 Hispanic Americans), 90 international. Average age 29. 460 applicants, 72% accepted, 157 enrolled. In 2009, 245 master's awarded. *Entrance requirements:* For master's, GMAT, minimum undergraduate GPA of 2.75 (MBA), 5 years of managerial experience (EMBA). Additional exam requirements/recommendations for international students: Required—TOEFL (minimum score 550 paper-based; 213 computer-based). *Application deadline:* For fall admission, 6/15 priority date for domestic students, 6/15 for international students; for spring admission, 11/1 priority date for domestic students, 11/1 for international students. Applications are processed on a rolling basis. Application fee: $50. Electronic applications accepted. *Expenses:* Tuition: Full-time $33,000; part-time $1100 per credit. Required fees: $20. Tuition and fees vary according to program. *Financial support:* In 2009–10, 284 students received support, including 99 fellowships with full and partial tuition reimbursements available (averaging $13,599 per year); career-related internships or fieldwork, Federal Work-Study, and institutionally sponsored loans also available. Support available to part-time students. Financial award application deadline: 4/1; financial award applicants required to submit FAFSA. *Faculty research:* Foreign investments; career strategies and boundaryless careers; corporate ethics codes; interest rates, inflation, and growth options; innovation and product development performance. *Unit head:* Lillian Hallberg, Assistant Dean of Graduate Programs/Director of MBA Programs, 617-573-8306, E-mail: lhallber@suffolk.edu. *Application contact:* Judith Reynolds, Director of Graduate Admissions, 617-573-8302, Fax: 617-305-1733, E-mail: grad.admission@suffolk.edu.

Syracuse University, Martin J. Whitman School of Management, PhD Program in Business Administration, Syracuse, NY 13244. Offers accounting (PhD); finance (PhD); management information systems (PhD); managerial statistics (PhD); marketing (PhD); operations management (PhD); organizational behavior (PhD); strategy and human resources (PhD); supply chain management (PhD). *Degree requirements:* For doctorate, comprehensive exam, thesis/dissertation, summer research paper. *Entrance requirements;* For doctorate, GMAT or GRE General Test, 3 recommendations. Additional exam requirements/recommendations for international students: Required—TOEFL (minimum score 600 paper-based; 250 computer-based; 100 iBT). Electronic applications accepted. *Expenses:* Tuition: Full-time $26,808; part-time $1117 per credit. Required fees: $1024. *Faculty research:* Marketing models, market microstructure, supply chain, auditing, corporate governance.

Taylor University, Master of Business Administration Program, Upland, IN 46989-1001. Offers emerging business strategies (MBA); global leadership (MBA). Part-time programs available. *Faculty:* 1 full-time (0 women), 9 part-time/adjunct (0 women). *Students:* 57 full-time (21 women), 4 part-time (1 woman); includes 3 African Americans, 1 Asian American or Pacific Islander, 2 Hispanic Americans. Average age 36. 55 applicants, 100% accepted, 52 enrolled. In 2009, 27 master's awarded. *Application deadline:* Applications are processed on a rolling

basis. Application fee: $100. *Expenses:* Tuition: Full-time $10,800. *Financial support:* In 2009–10, 2 students received support. Applicants required to submit FAFSA. *Unit head:* Dr. Larry Rottmeyer, Graduate Chair, 260-399-1622, E-mail: lrrottmeyer@taylor.edu. *Application contact:* Wendy Speakman, Program Director, 866-471-6062, Fax: 260-492-0452, E-mail: wnspeakman@taylor.edu.

See Display on page 162 and Close-Up on page 257.

Temple University, Graduate School, Fox School of Business, Doctoral Programs in Business, Philadelphia, PA 19122-6096. Offers accounting (PhD); entrepreneurship (PhD); finance (PhD); human resource administration (PhD); international business (PhD); management information systems (PhD); marketing (PhD); risk management and insurance (PhD); statistics (PhD); strategic management (PhD); tourism and sport (PhD). *Accreditation:* AACSB. *Degree requirements:* For doctorate, thesis/dissertation. *Entrance requirements:* For doctorate, GRE General Test, GMAT, minimum GPA of 3.0, master's degree. Additional exam requirements/recommendations for international students: Required—TOEFL (minimum score 600 paper-based; 250 computer-based; 100 iBT), IELTS (minimum score 7.5). Electronic applications accepted.

Tennessee Technological University, Graduate School, Program of Professional Studies, Cookeville, TN 38505. Offers human resources leadership (MPS); strategic leadership (MPS); training and development (MPS). *Students:* 4 full-time (2 women), 27 part-time (20 women); includes 5 minority (4 African Americans, 1 Hispanic American). 14 applicants, 57% accepted, 7 enrolled. In 2009, 1 master's awarded. *Degree requirements:* For master's, comprehensive exam, thesis or alternative. *Entrance requirements:* For master's, GRE. Additional exam requirements/recommendations for international students: Required—TOEFL (minimum score 550 paper-based; 79 iBT), IELTS (minimum score 5.5). *Application deadline:* For fall admission, 8/1 for domestic students, 5/1 for international students; for spring admission, 12/1 for domestic students, 10/1 for international students. Application fee: $25 ($30 for international students). Electronic applications accepted. *Expenses:* Tuition, state resident: full-time $7034; part-time $368 per credit hour. *Financial support:* Application deadline: 4/1. *Unit head:* Dr. Susan A. Elkins, Dean, School of Interdisciplinary Studies and Extended Education, 931-372-3394, Fax: 372-372-3499, E-mail: selkins@tntech.edu. *Application contact:* Shelia K. Kendrick, Coordinator of Graduate Studies, 931-372-3808, Fax: 931-372-3497, E-mail: skendrick@tntech.edu.

Towson University, College of Graduate Studies and Research, Program in Management and Leadership Development, Towson, MD 21252-0001. Offers Certificate. Part-time and evening/weekend programs available. *Entrance requirements:* For degree, minimum GPA 3.0, letter of intent.

Tufts University, Graduate School of Arts and Sciences, Graduate Certificate Programs, Program Evaluation Program, Medford, MA 02155. Offers Certificate. Part-time and evening/weekend programs available. Electronic applications accepted. *Expenses:* Contact institution.

United States International University, School of Business Administration, Nairobi, Kenya. Offers finance (MBA); information technology management (MBA); integrated studies (MBA); management and organizational development (MS); marketing (MBA); strategic management (MBA). Part-time and evening/weekend programs available. *Degree requirements:* For master's, thesis. *Entrance requirements:* For master's, GMAT, 2 letters of reference, resume. Additional exam requirements/recommendations for international students: Required—TOEFL (minimum score 550 paper-based; 213 computer-based). *Faculty research:* Marketing in small business enterprises, total quality management in Kenya.

Universidad del Este, Graduate School, Carolina, PR 00984. Offers accounting (MBA); adult education (M Ed); agribusiness (MBA); bilingual education (M Ed); criminal justice and criminology (MA); early education (M Ed); elementary education (M Ed); human resources (MBA); information security management (MBA); information technology and Web business development (MBA); management (MBA); public policy (MPA); social work (MA), including clinical social work; special education (M Ed); strategic leadership (MBA); teaching English (M Ed); teaching Spanish (M Ed).

The University of Arizona, Graduate College, Eller College of Management, Department of Management, Tucson, AZ 85721. Offers PhD. Evening/weekend programs available. *Faculty:* 16. *Students:* 94 full-time (32 women), 43 part-time (13 women); includes 5 minority (1 African American, 1 Asian American or Pacific Islander, 3 Hispanic Americans), 72 international. Average age 30. 373 applicants, 29% accepted, 47 enrolled. In 2009, 10 doctorates awarded. *Entrance requirements:* Additional exam requirements/recommendations for international students: Required—TOEFL (minimum score 550 paper-based; 213 computer-based; 79 iBT). *Application deadline:* For fall admission, 1/15 for domestic and international students. Applications are processed on a rolling basis. Application fee: $75. Electronic applications accepted. *Expenses:* Tuition, state resident: full-time $9028. Tuition, nonresident: full-time $24,890. *Financial support:* In 2009–10, 10 research assistantships with full tuition reimbursements (averaging $18,983 per year), 1 teaching assistantship with full tuition reimbursement (averaging $13,722 per year) were awarded; career-related internships or fieldwork, Federal Work-Study, institutionally sponsored loans, scholarships/grants, health care benefits, tuition waivers (partial), and unspecified assistantships also available. Financial award application deadline: 3/15. *Faculty research:* Organizational behavior, human resources, decision making, health economics and finance, immigration. Total annual research expenditures: $147,455. *Unit head:* Dr. Stephen Gilliland, Department Head, 520-621-9324, Fax: 520-621-4171, E-mail: sgill@eller.arizona.edu. *Application contact:* Information Contact, 520-621-1053, Fax: 520-621-4171.

The University of British Columbia, Sauder School of Business, Doctoral Program in Commerce and Business Administration, Vancouver, BC V6T 1Z1, Canada. Offers accounting (PhD); finance (PhD); international business (PhD); management information systems (PhD); management science (PhD); marketing (PhD); organizational behavior (PhD); strategy and business economics (PhD); transportation and logistics (PhD); urban land economics (PhD). *Degree requirements:* For doctorate, comprehensive exam, thesis/dissertation. *Entrance requirements:* For doctorate, GMAT or GRE. Additional exam requirements/recommendations for international students: Required—TOEFL (minimum score 600 paper-based; 250 computer-based; 100 iBT). Electronic applications accepted.

University of Calgary, Faculty of Graduate Studies, Centre for Military and Strategic Studies, Calgary, AB T2N 1N4, Canada. Offers MSS, PhD. PhD offered in special cases only. Part-time programs available. *Degree requirements:* For master's, thesis; for doctorate, comprehensive exam, thesis/dissertation. *Entrance requirements:* For master's, minimum GPA of 3.4. Additional exam requirements/recommendations for international students: Recommended—TOEFL (minimum score 550 paper-based). *Faculty research:* Military history, Israeli studies, strategic studies, int'l relations, Arctic security.

University of Central Missouri, The Graduate School, Harmon College of Business Administration, Warrensburg, MO 64093. Offers accountancy (MA); accounting (MBA); ethical strategic leadership (MBA); finance (MBA); general business (MBA); information systems (MBA); information technology (MS); marketing (MBA). Part-time programs available. Postbaccalaureate distance learning degree programs offered. *Faculty:* 31. *Students:* 87 full-time (34 women), 62 part-time (25 women); includes 10 minority (3 African Americans, 1 American Indian/Alaska Native, 5 Asian Americans or Pacific Islanders, 1 Hispanic American), 66 international. Average age 27. 55 applicants, 64% accepted, 27 enrolled. In 2009, 83 master's awarded. *Entrance requirements:* Additional exam requirements/recommendations for international students: Required—TOEFL (minimum score 550 paper-based; 79 computer-based). *Application deadline:* For fall admission, 6/1 priority date for domestic students, 5/1 for international students; for spring admission, 10/1 priority date for domestic students, 10/1 for international students. Applications are processed on a rolling basis. Application fee: $30 ($75 for international students). Electronic applications accepted. *Expenses:* Tuition, area resident: Part-time $245.80 per credit hour. Tuition, nonresident: part-time $491.60 per credit hour. Required fees: $24.20 per credit hour. Full-time tuition and fees vary according to course load, degree level, campus/location and reciprocity agreements. *Financial support:* Research assistantships with full and partial tuition reimbursements, teaching assistantships with full and partial tuition reimbursements, career-related internships or fieldwork, Federal Work-Study, scholarships/grants, and administrative and laboratory assistantships available. Support available to part-time students. Financial award application deadline: 3/1; financial award applicants required to submit FAFSA. *Unit head:* Dr. Roger Best, Dean, 660-543-4560, Fax: 660-543-8350, E-mail: best@ucmo.edu. *Application contact:* Laurie Delap, Admissions Coordinator, 660-543-4621, Fax: 660-543-4778, E-mail: gradinfo@ucmo.edu.

University of Dallas, Graduate School of Management, Irving, TX 75062-4736. Offers accounting (MBA, MM, MS); business management (MBA, MM); corporate finance (MBA, MM); financial services (MBA); global business (MBA, MM); health services management (MBA, MM); human resource management (MBA, MM); information assurance (MBA, MM, MS); information technology (MBA, MM, MS); information technology service management (MBA, MM, MS); marketing management (MBA, MM); organization development (MBA, MM); project management (MBA, MM); sports and entertainment management (MBA, MM); strategic leadership (MBA, MM); supply chain management (MBA); supply chain management and market logistics (MM). *Accreditation:* ACBSP. Part-time and evening/weekend programs available. Postbaccalaureate distance learning degree programs offered (no on-campus study). *Faculty:* 25 full-time (6 women), 31 part-time/adjunct (6 women). *Students:* 232 full-time (95 women), 923 part-time (365 women); includes 462 minority (184 African Americans, 14 American Indian/Alaska Native, 153 Asian Americans or Pacific Islanders, 111 Hispanic Americans), 184 international. Average age 34. 474 applicants, 85% accepted, 237 enrolled. In 2009, 399 master's awarded. *Entrance requirements:* Additional exam requirements/recommendations for international students: Required—TOEFL. *Application deadline:* Applications are processed on a rolling basis. Application fee: $50. Electronic applications accepted. *Expenses:* Contact institution. *Financial support:* In 2009–10, 399 students received support. Scholarships/grants and unspecified assistantships available. Financial award application deadline: 2/15; financial award applicants required to submit FAFSA. *Unit head:* Alounda Joseph, Director of Enrollment Processes, 972-721-5356, E-mail: admiss@gsm.udallas.edu. *Application contact:* Alounda Joseph, Director of Enrollment Processes, 972-721-5356, E-mail: admiss@gsm.udallas.edu.

University of Dayton, Graduate School, School of Business Administration, Dayton, OH 45469-1300. Offers accounting (MBA); business intelligence (MBA); entrepreneurship (MBA); finance (MBA); international business (MBA); marketing (MBA); MIS (MBA); operations management (MBA); technology-enhanced business/e-commerce (MBA); JD/MBA. *Accreditation:* AACSB. Part-time and evening/weekend programs available. *Faculty:* 29 full-time (8 women), 15 part-time/adjunct (2 women). *Students:* 134 full-time (48 women), 111 part-time (31 women); includes 14 minority (9 African Americans, 3 Asian Americans or Pacific Islanders, 2 Hispanic Americans), 29 international. Average age 29. 179 applicants, 63% accepted, 73 enrolled. In 2009, 102 master's awarded. *Entrance requirements:* For master's, GMAT. Additional exam requirements/recommendations for international students: Required—TOEFL (minimum score 550 paper-based; 213 computer-based; 79 iBT). *Application deadline:* For fall admission, 3/1 priority date for international students; for winter admission, 7/1 priority date for international students; for spring admission, 1/1 priority date for international students. Applications are processed on a rolling basis. Application fee: $0 ($50 for international students). Electronic applications accepted. *Expenses:* Contact institution. *Financial support:* In 2009–10, 13 fellowships with partial tuition reimbursements, 17 research assistantships with full and partial tuition reimbursements (averaging $7,020 per year) were awarded; career-related internships or fieldwork, institutionally sponsored loans, scholarships/grants, health care benefits, and unspecified assistantships also available. Support available to part-time students. Financial award application deadline: 3/15; financial award applicants required to submit FAFSA. *Faculty research:* Management information systems, economics, finance, entrepreneurship, marketing. *Unit head:* Janice M. Glynn, Director, MBA Program, 937-229-3733, Fax: 937-229-3882, E-mail: glynn@udayton.edu. *Application contact:* Jeffrey Carter, Assistant Director, MBA Program, 937-229-3733, Fax: 937-229-3882, E-mail: jeff.carter@notes.udayton.edu.

University of Denver, Daniels College of Business, Department of Statistics and Operations Technology, Denver, CO 80208. Offers business intelligence (MS); data mining (MS). *Faculty:* 7 full-time (2 women). *Students:* 6 full-time (0 women), 8 part-time (4 women); includes 1 minority (Hispanic American), 1 international. Average age 33. 23 applicants, 78% accepted, 11 enrolled. In 2009, 6 master's awarded. *Application deadline:* For fall admission, 1/15 priority date for domestic students. Applications are processed on a rolling basis. Application fee: $50. Electronic applications accepted. *Expenses:* Tuition: Full-time $34,596; part-time $961 per quarter hour. Required fees: $4 per quarter hour. Tuition and fees vary according to course load, campus/location and program. *Financial support:* Career-related internships or fieldwork, Federal Work-Study, institutionally sponsored loans, and scholarships/grants available. Support available to part-time students. Financial award application deadline: 2/15; financial award applicants required to submit FAFSA. *Unit head:* Dr. Anthony Hayter, Chair, 303-871-4341. *Application contact:* Information Contact, 303-871-3416, Fax: 303-871-4466, E-mail: daniels@du.edu.

University of Denver, University College, Denver, CO 80208. Offers applied communication (MAS, MPS, Certificate); computer information systems (MAS, Certificate); environmental policy and management (MAS, Certificate); geographic information systems (MAS, Certificate); human resource administration (MPS, Certificate); knowledge and information technologies (MAS); liberal studies (MLS, Certificate); modern languages (MLS, Certificate); organizational leadership (MPS, Certificate); security management (Certificate); technology management (MAS, Certificate), including 21st century strategic management (MAS), international markets (MAS), project management (MAS), research and development management (MAS); telecommunications (MAS, Certificate), including broadband (MAS), telecommunications management and policy (MAS), telecommunications technology (MAS), wireless networks (MAS). Part-time and evening/weekend programs available. Postbaccalaureate distance learning degree programs offered (no on-campus study). *Faculty:* 160 part-time/adjunct (64 women). *Students:* 53 full-time (25 women), 984 part-time (551 women); includes 171 minority (72 African Americans, 10 American Indian/Alaska Native, 33 Asian Americans or Pacific Islanders, 56 Hispanic Americans), 75 international. Average age 36. 537 applicants, 96% accepted, 494 enrolled. In 2009, 229 master's, 109 Certificates awarded. *Entrance requirements:* Additional exam requirements/recommendations for international students: Required—TOEFL (minimum score 550 paper-based; 213 computer-based). *Application deadline:* Applications are processed on a rolling basis. Application fee: $75. Electronic applications accepted. *Expenses:* Contact institution. *Financial support:* Applicants required to submit FAFSA. *Unit head:* Dr. James Davis, Dean, 303-871-2291, Fax: 303-871-4047, E-mail: jdavis@du.edu. *Application contact:* Information Contact, 303-871-3155.

University of Florida, Graduate School, Warrington College of Business Administration, Hough Graduate School of Business, Programs in Business Administration, Gainesville, FL 32611. Offers accounting (MBA); arts administration (MBA); business strategy and public policy (MBA); competitive strategy (MBA); decision and information sciences (MBA); electronic commerce (MBA); finance (MBA); general business (MBA); global management (MBA); Graham-Buffett security analysis (MBA); health administration (MBA); human resources management (MBA); international studies (MBA); Latin American business (MBA); management (MBA); marketing (MBA); sports administration (MBA); JD/MBA; MBA/MS; MBA/PhD; MBA/Pharm D; MD/MBA. *Accreditation:* AACSB. Part-time and evening/weekend programs available. Postbaccalaureate distance learning degree programs offered. *Entrance requirements:* For master's, GMAT, minimum GPA of 3.0, interview. Additional exam requirements/recommendations for international students: Required—TOEFL (minimum score 550 paper-based; 213 computer-based). Electronic applications accepted. *Faculty research:* Accounting, finance, insurance, management, real estate and urban analysis marketing.

University of Lethbridge, School of Graduate Studies, Lethbridge, AB T1K 3M4, Canada. Offers accounting (MScM); addictions counseling (M Sc); agricultural biotechnology (M Sc); agricultural studies (M Sc, MA); anthropology (MA); archaeology (MA); art (MA, MFA); biochemistry (M Sc); biological sciences (M Sc); biomolecular science (PhD); biosystems and biodiversity (PhD); Canadian studies (MA); chemistry (M Sc); computer science (M Sc); computer science and geographical information science (M Sc); counseling psychology (M Ed); dramatic

Management Strategy and Policy

University of Lethbridge (continued)

arts (MA); earth, space, and physical science (PhD); economics (MA); educational leadership (M Ed); English (MA); environmental science (M Sc); evolution and behavior (PhD); exercise science (M Sc); finance (MScM); French (MA); French/German (MA); French/Spanish (MA); general education (M Ed); general management (MScM); geography (M Sc, MA); German (MA); health science (M Sc); health sciences (MA); history (MA); human resource management and labour relations (MScM); individualized multidisciplinary (M Sc, MA); information systems (MScM); international management (MScM); kinesiology (M Sc, MA); management (M Sc, MA); marketing (MScM); mathematics (M Sc); music (M Mus, MA); Native American studies (MA); neuroscience (M Sc, PhD); new media (MA); nursing (M Sc); philosophy (MA); physics (M Sc); policy and strategy (MScM); political science (MA); psychology (M Sc, MA); religious studies (MA); social sciences (MA); sociology (MA); theatre and dramatic arts (MFA); theoretical and computational science (PhD); urban and regional studies (MA); women's studies (MA). Part-time and evening/weekend programs available. *Degree requirements:* For doctorate, comprehensive exam, thesis/dissertation. *Entrance requirements:* For master's, GMAT (M Sc in management), bachelor's degree in related field, minimum GPA of 3.0 during previous 20 graded semester courses, 2 years teaching or related experience (M Ed); for doctorate, master's degree, minimum graduate GPA of 3.5. Additional exam requirements/recommendations for international students: Required—TOEFL. *Faculty research:* Movement and brain plasticity, gibberellin physiology, photosynthesis, carbon cycling, molecular properties of main-group ring components.

University of Mary, Gary Tharaldson School of Business, Bismarck, ND 58504-9652. Offers health care (MBA); human resource management (MBA); management (MBA); project management (MPM); strategic leadership (MSSL). Part-time and evening/weekend programs available. *Degree requirements:* For master's, strategic planning seminar. *Entrance requirements:* For master's, minimum GPA of 2.5. Additional exam requirements/recommendations for international students: Required—TOEFL. *Expenses:* Tuition: Full-time $10,062; part-time $430 per credit. Tuition and fees vary according to course load, degree level, program and student level.

University of Minnesota, Twin Cities Campus, Carlson School of Management, Doctoral Program in Business Administration, Minneapolis, MN 55455-0213. Offers accounting (PhD); finance (PhD); information and decision sciences (PhD); marketing and logistics management (PhD); operations and management science (PhD); strategic management and organization (PhD). *Faculty:* 74 full-time (19 women). *Students:* 68 full-time (28 women); includes 7 minority (1 African American, 3 Asian Americans or Pacific Islanders, 3 Hispanic Americans), 46 international. Average age 29. 250 applicants, 5% accepted, 9 enrolled. In 2009, 11 doctorates awarded. *Degree requirements:* For doctorate, comprehensive exam, thesis/dissertation, written and oral preliminary exams, proposal defense. *Entrance requirements:* For doctorate, GMAT, GRE General Test. Additional exam requirements/recommendations for international students: Required—TOEFL (minimum score 600 paper-based; 250 computer-based; 100 iBT), IELTS (minimum score 7.5). *Application deadline:* For fall admission, 12/31 for domestic students, 12/31 priority date for international students. Applications are processed on a rolling basis. Application fee: $55 ($75 for international students). Electronic applications accepted. *Financial support:* In 2009–10, 68 fellowships with full tuition reimbursements (averaging $11,500 per year), 63 research assistantships with full tuition reimbursements (averaging $6,750 per year), 53 teaching assistantships with full tuition reimbursements (averaging $6,750 per year) were awarded; institutionally sponsored loans, scholarships/grants, health care benefits, and unspecified assistantships also available. Financial award application deadline: 12/31. *Faculty research:* Corporate strategy, finance, entrepreneurship, marketing, information and decision science, operations, accounting. Total annual research expenditures: $300,000. *Unit head:* Dr. Shawn P. Curley, Director of Graduate Studies/Program Director, 612-624-6546, Fax: 612-624-8221, E-mail: curley@umn.edu. *Application contact:* Earlene K. Bronson, Assistant Director, 612-624-0875, Fax: 612-624-8221, E-mail: brons003@umn.edu.

University of New Haven, Graduate School, School of Business, Program in Business Administration, West Haven, CT 06516-1916. Offers accounting (MBA, Certificate), including CPA (MBA); business management (Certificate); business policy and strategy (MBA); finance (MBA), including CFA; global marketing (MBA); human resource management (Certificate); human resources management (MBA); international business (Certificate); marketing (Certificate); sports management (MBA); telcommunications management (Certificate); MBA/MPA. Part-time and evening/weekend programs available. *Faculty:* 26 full-time (3 women), 23 part-time/adjunct (5 women). *Students:* 302 full-time (120 women), 194 part-time (101 women); includes 109 minority (56 African Americans, 3 American Indian/Alaska Native, 28 Asian Americans or Pacific Islanders, 22 Hispanic Americans), 110 international. Average age 31. 372 applicants, 83% accepted, 172 enrolled. In 2009, 194 master's, 31 other advanced degrees awarded. *Degree requirements:* For master's, thesis or alternative. *Entrance requirements:* For master's, GMAT. Additional exam requirements/recommendations for international students: Required—TOEFL (minimum score 520 paper-based; 190 computer-based; 70 iBT), IELTS (minimum score 5.5). *Application deadline:* For fall admission, 5/31 for international students; for winter admission, 10/15 for international students; for spring admission, 1/15 for international students. Applications are processed on a rolling basis. Application fee: $50. Electronic applications accepted. *Expenses:* Contact institution. *Financial support:* Research assistantships with partial tuition reimbursements, teaching assistantships with partial tuition reimbursements, Federal Work-Study, scholarships/grants, health care benefits, tuition waivers, and unspecified assistantships available. Support available to part-time students. Financial award applicants required to submit FAFSA. *Unit head:* Charles Coleman, Chairman, 203-932-7375. *Application contact:* Eloise Gormley, Director of Graduate Admissions, 203-932-7449, Fax: 203-932-7137, E-mail: gradinfo@newhaven.edu.

University of New Mexico, Robert O. Anderson Graduate School of Management, Department of Marketing, Information and Decision Sciences, Albuquerque, NM 87131. Offers information assurance (MBA); management information systems (MBA); marketing management (MBA); operations management (MBA). Part-time and evening/weekend programs available. *Faculty:* 14 full-time (3 women), 5 part-time/adjunct (0 women). *Students:* 39 full-time (18 women), 37 part-time (19 women); includes 31 minority (3 African Americans, 1 American Indian/Alaska Native, 3 Asian Americans or Pacific Islanders, 24 Hispanic Americans), 4 international. Average age 28. 40 applicants, 100% accepted, 36 enrolled. In 2009, 39 master's awarded. *Entrance requirements:* For master's, GMAT or GRE (can be waived in some instances). Additional exam requirements/recommendations for international students: Required—TOEFL (minimum score 550 paper-based; 213 computer-based; 79 iBT). *Application deadline:* For fall admission, 4/1 priority date for domestic students, 5/1 for international students; for spring admission, 10/1 priority date for domestic students, 10/1 for international students. Applications are processed on a rolling basis. Application fee: $50. Electronic applications accepted. *Expenses:* Tuition, state resident: full-time $2099; part-time $233.20 per credit hour. Tuition, nonresident: full-time $6650. Required fees: $25 per semester. Tuition and fees vary according to course load, program and reciprocity agreements. *Financial support:* Fellowships, research assistantships, teaching assistantships, career-related internships or fieldwork, Federal Work-Study, scholarships/grants, and unspecified assistantships available. Support available to part-time students. Financial award application deadline: 6/1. *Faculty research:* Marketing, operations, information science. *Unit head:* Dr. Steve Yourstone, Chair, 505-277-6471, Fax: 505-277-7108. *Application contact:* Megan Conner, Academic Advisement Manager, 505-277-3290, Fax: 505-277-8436, E-mail: mconner@mgt.unm.edu.

University of New Mexico, Robert O. Anderson Graduate School of Management, Department of Organizational Studies, Albuquerque, NM 87131. Offers human resources management (MBA); policy and planning (MBA). Part-time and evening/weekend programs available. *Faculty:* 14 full-time (10 women), 6 part-time/adjunct (2 women). *Students:* 25 full-time (23 women), 22 part-time (15 women); includes 25 minority (3 African Americans, 3 American Indian/Alaska Native, 2 Asian Americans or Pacific Islanders, 17 Hispanic Americans), 1 international. Average age 29. 28 applicants, 100% accepted, 28 enrolled. In 2009, 20 master's awarded. *Entrance requirements:* For master's, GMAT or GRE (can be waived in some instances). Additional exam requirements/recommendations for international students: Required—TOEFL (minimum score 550 paper-based; 213 computer-based; 79 iBT). *Application deadline:* For fall admission, 4/1 priority date for domestic students, 5/1 for international students; for spring admission, 10/1 priority date for domestic students, 10/1 for international students. Applications are processed on a rolling basis. Application fee: $50. Electronic applications accepted. *Expenses:* Tuition, state resident: full-time $2099; part-time $233.20 per credit hour. Tuition, nonresident: full-time $6650. Required fees: $25 per semester. Tuition and fees vary according to course load, program and reciprocity agreements. *Financial support:* Fellowships, research assistantships, teaching assistantships, career-related internships or fieldwork, Federal Work-Study, scholarships/grants, and unspecified assistantships available. Support available to part-time students. Financial award application deadline: 6/1. *Faculty research:* Business ethics and social corporate responsibility, diversity, human resources, organizational strategy, organizational behavior. *Unit head:* Dr. Jacqueline Hood, Chair, 505-277-6471, Fax: 505-277-7108. *Application contact:* Megan Conner, Academic Advisement Manager, 505-277-3290, Fax: 505-277-8436, E-mail: mconner@mgt.unm.edu.

The University of North Carolina at Chapel Hill, Kenan-Flagler Business School, Doctoral Program in Business Administration, Chapel Hill, NC 27599. Offers accounting (PhD); finance (PhD); marketing (PhD); operations management (PhD); organizational behavior (PhD); strategy (PhD). *Accreditation:* AACSB. *Degree requirements:* For doctorate, thesis/dissertation. *Entrance requirements:* For doctorate, GMAT or GRE General Test. Electronic applications accepted. *Expenses:* Contact institution.

University of Oklahoma, Graduate College, College of Liberal Studies, Norman, OK 73019-0390. Offers administrative leadership (MLS); integrated studies (MLS); interprofessional human and health services (MLS); museum studies (MLS). Part-time programs available. Post-baccalaureate distance learning degree programs offered (no on-campus study). *Faculty:* 15 full-time (8 women), 26 part-time/adjunct (16 women). *Students:* 17 full-time (11 women), 326 part-time (169 women); includes 71 minority (33 African Americans, 24 American Indian/Alaska Native, 4 Asian Americans or Pacific Islanders, 10 Hispanic Americans). 126 applicants, 90% accepted, 75 enrolled. In 2009, 94 master's awarded. *Degree requirements:* For master's, thesis, research project, internship. *Entrance requirements:* For master's, minimum GPA of 3.0 in last 60 hours, writing sample. Additional exam requirements/recommendations for international students: Required—TOEFL (minimum score 550 paper-based; 213 computer-based). *Application deadline:* For fall admission, 7/15 priority date for domestic students, 4/1 for international students; for spring admission, 12/1 for domestic students, 9/1 for international students. Applications are processed on a rolling basis. Application fee: $40 ($90 for international students). Electronic applications accepted. *Expenses:* Tuition, state resident: full-time $3744; part-time $156 per credit hour. Tuition, nonresident: full-time $13,577; part-time $565.70 per credit hour. Required fees: $2415; $90.10 per credit hour. *Financial support:* In 2009–10, 163 students received support. Career-related internships or fieldwork, scholarships/grants, and tuition waivers (partial) available. Support available to part-time students. Financial award applicants required to submit FAFSA. *Faculty research:* Distance education, adult learning processes, student satisfaction, administrative leadership, organizations, museum studies. *Unit head:* Dr. James Pappas, Dean and Vice President for University Outreach, 405-325-6361, Fax: 405-325-7196, E-mail: jpappas@ou.edu. *Application contact:* Dr. Julie Raadschelders, MA Program Coordinator, 405-325-1061, Fax: 405-325-9632, E-mail: jraadschelders@ou.edu.

University of Pittsburgh, Katz Graduate School of Business, Masters of Business Administration Programs, Pittsburgh, PA 15260. Offers accounting (MS); finance (MBA); general management (MBA); information systems (MBA, MSIS); marketing (MBA); organizational behavior and human resource management (MBA); organizational leadership (Certificate); six sigma (Certificate); strategy (MBA); technology, innovation and entrepreneurship (Certificate); MBA/JD; MBA/MIB; MBA/MPIA; MBA/MSE; MBA/MSIS. *Accreditation:* AACSB. Part-time and evening/weekend programs available. *Faculty:* 58 full-time (12 women), 23 part-time/adjunct (7 women). *Students:* 192 full-time (62 women), 506 part-time (179 women); includes 58 minority (29 African Americans, 1 American Indian/Alaska Native, 24 Asian Americans or Pacific Islanders, 4 Hispanic Americans), 101 international. Average age 29. 674 applicants, 52% accepted, 204 enrolled. In 2009, 263 master's awarded. *Entrance requirements:* For master's, GMAT, references, work experience relevant for individual programs. Additional exam requirements/recommendations for international students: Required—TOEFL (minimum score 600 paper-based; 250 computer-based; 100 iBT), or IELTS. *Application deadline:* For fall admission, 7/1 for domestic and international students; for winter admission, 11/1 for domestic and international students; for spring admission, 3/1 for domestic and international students. Applications are processed on a rolling basis. Application fee: $50. Electronic applications accepted. *Expenses:* Tuition, state resident: full-time $16,402; part-time $665 per credit. Tuition, nonresident: full-time $28,694; part-time $1175 per credit. Required fees: $690; $175 per term. Tuition and fees vary according to program. *Financial support:* In 2009–10, 75 students received support. Career-related internships or fieldwork and scholarships/grants available. Financial award application deadline: 6/1; financial award applicants required to submit FAFSA. *Faculty research:* Accounting statements and reporting, incentives and governance; corporate finance, mergers and acquisitions; information systems processes, structures, and decision-making; organizational structure, knowledge management, and corporate strategy; consumer behavior and marketing models. *Unit head:* William T. Valenta, Assistant Dean/MBA Program Director, 412-648-1610, Fax: 412-648-1659, E-mail: wtvalenta@katz.pitt.edu. *Application contact:* Cliff McCormick, Director of MBA Admissions, 412-648-1700, Fax: 412-648-1659, E-mail: mba@katz.pitt.edu.

The University of Western Ontario, Richard Ivey School of Business, London, ON N6A 3K7, Canada. Offers business (EMBA, PhD); corporate strategy and leadership elective (MBA); entrepreneurship elective (MBA); finance elective (MBA); health sector stream (MBA); international management elective (MBA); marketing elective (MBA); JD/MBA. *Faculty:* 61 full-time (13 women). *Students:* 164 full-time (50 women). Average age 29. In 2009, 167 master's awarded. *Degree requirements:* For master's, thesis (for some programs); for doctorate, thesis/dissertation. *Entrance requirements:* For master's, GMAT, 2 years of full-time work experience, interview. Additional exam requirements/recommendations for international students: Required—TOEFL (minimum score 100 computer-based; 100 iBT), IELTS (minimum score 6), IELTS or TOEFL. *Application deadline:* For fall admission, 10/12 for domestic students, 8/16 for international students; for winter admission, 12/16 for domestic students, 10/12 for international students; for spring admission, 1/10 priority date for domestic students, 12/16 for international students. Applications are processed on a rolling basis. Application fee: $150 Canadian dollars. Electronic applications accepted. *Financial support:* Scholarships/grants and health care benefits available. Financial award application deadline: 1/10. *Faculty research:* Strategy, organizational behavior, international business, finance, operations management. *Unit head:* Carol Stephenson, Dean, 519-661-3285, Fax: 519-661-4126, E-mail: cstephenson@ivey.ca. *Application contact:* Niki da Silva, Director, MBA Program Services, 519-661-3419, Fax: 519-661-3431, E-mail: ndasilva@ivey.ca.

University of West Florida, College of Professional Studies, Department of Professional and Community Leadership, Program in Administration, Pensacola, FL 32514-5750. Offers acquisition and contract administration (MSA); biomedical/pharmaceutical (MSA); criminal justice administration (MSA); database administration (MSA); education leadership (MSA); healthcare administration (MSA); human performance technology (MSA); leadership (MSA); nursing administration (MSA); public administration (MSA); software engineering administration (MSA). Part-time and evening/weekend programs available. Postbaccalaureate distance learning degree programs offered (no on-campus study). *Students:* 33 full-time (21 women), 168 part-time (97 women); includes 53 minority (32 African Americans, 2 American Indian/Alaska Native, 5 Asian Americans or Pacific Islanders, 14 Hispanic Americans), 1 international. Average age 34. 103 applicants, 74% accepted, 64 enrolled. In 2009, 47 master's awarded. *Entrance requirements:* For master's, GRE General Test, letter of intent, names of references. Additional exam requirements/recommendations for international students: Required—TOEFL (minimum score 550 paper-based; 213 computer-based). *Application deadline:* For fall admission, 6/1 for domestic students, 5/15 for international students; for spring admission, 11/1 for domestic

students, 10/1 for international students. Applications are processed on a rolling basis. Application fee: $30. *Expenses:* Tuition, state resident: full-time $4982; part-time $260 per credit hour. Tuition, nonresident: full-time $20,059; part-time $919 per credit hour. Required fees: $1247; $52 per credit hour. *Financial support:* Unspecified assistantships available. Financial award application deadline: 4/15; financial award applicants required to submit FAFSA. *Unit head:* Dr. Karen Rasmussen, Chairperson, 850-474-2301, Fax: 850-474-2804. *Application contact:* Terry McCray, Assistant Director of Graduate Admissions, 850-473-7718, Fax: 850-473-7714, E-mail: gradadmissions@uwf.edu.

University of Wisconsin–Madison, Graduate School, Wisconsin School of Business, Wisconsin Full-Time MBA Program, Madison, WI 53706-1380. Offers applied corporate finance (MBA); applied security analysis (MBA); arts administration (MBA); brand and product management (MBA); entrepreneurial management (MBA); marketing research (MBA); operations and technology management (MBA); real estate (MBA); risk management and insurance (MBA); strategic human resource management (MBA); strategic management in the life and engineering sciences (MBA); supply chain management (MBA). *Faculty:* 32 full-time (5 women). *Students:* 242 full-time (74 women); includes 47 minority (16 African Americans, 3 American Indian/Alaska Native, 16 Asian Americans or Pacific Islanders, 12 Hispanic Americans), 29 international. Average age 28. 526 applicants, 32% accepted, 117 enrolled. In 2009, 106 master's awarded. *Entrance requirements:* For master's, GMAT, bachelor's or equivalent degree, 2 years of work experience, letters of recommendation. Additional exam requirements/recommendations for international students: Required—TOEFL (minimum score 600 paper-based; 250 computer-based; 100 iBT), IELTS. *Application deadline:* For fall admission, 11/4 for domestic and international students; for winter admission, 2/5 for domestic and international students; for spring admission, 5/26 for domestic students, 4/5 for international students. Applications are processed on a rolling basis. Application fee: $56. Electronic applications accepted. *Expenses:* Tuition, state resident: part-time $594 per credit. Tuition, nonresident: part-time $1504 per credit. Required fees: $65 per credit. Tuition and fees vary according to course load, program and reciprocity agreements. *Financial support:* In 2009–10, 103 students received support, including 13 fellowships with full and partial tuition reimbursements available (averaging $15,000 per year), 53 research assistantships with full tuition reimbursements available (averaging $8,000 per year), 35 teaching assistantships with full tuition reimbursements available (averaging $11,000 per year); scholarships/grants, health care benefits, and unspecified assistantships also available. Financial award application deadline: 4/5; financial award applicants required to submit FAFSA. *Unit head:* Prof. Kenneth A. Kavajecz, Associate Dean, 608-265-3494, Fax: 608-265-4192, E-mail: kkavajecz@bus.wisc.edu. *Application contact:* Maria Reis, Assistant Director of MBA Marketing and Recruiting, 608-262-4000, Fax: 608-265-4192, E-mail: mreis@bus.wisc.edu.

Western Governors University, Programs in Business, Salt Lake City, UT 84107. Offers information technology management (MBA); management and strategy (MBA); strategic leadership (MBA). Postbaccalaureate distance learning degree programs offered. Electronic applications accepted.

Western International University, Graduate Programs in Business, Master of Arts Program in Innovative Leadership, Phoenix, AZ 85021-2718. Offers MA. Part-time and evening/weekend programs available. Postbaccalaureate distance learning degree programs offered (no on-campus study). *Faculty:* 44 part-time/adjunct (26 women). *Students:* 84 full-time (48 women); includes 22 minority (15 African Americans, 2 American Indian/Alaska Native, 1 Asian American or Pacific Islander, 4 Hispanic Americans), 1 international. Average age 39. In 2009, 10 master's awarded. *Entrance requirements:* For master's, minimum GPA of 2.75. Additional exam requirements/recommendations for international students: Required—TOEFL (minimum score 550 paper-based; 213 computer-based; 79 iBT), TWE (minimum score 5), or IELTS (minimum score 6.5). *Application deadline:* Applications are processed on a rolling basis. Application fee: $25. Electronic applications accepted. *Expenses:* Tuition: Full-time $12,600. One-time fee: $25 full-time. *Financial support:* Applicants required to submit FAFSA. *Unit head:* Dr. Deborah DeSimone, Chief Academic Officer, 602-429-1135, E-mail: deborah.desimone@west.edu. *Application contact:* Melissa Machuca, Director of Enrollment, 602-943-2311, Fax: 602-371-8637.

Xavier University, Williams College of Business, Master of Business Administration Program, Cincinnati, OH 45207-3221. Offers business administration (Exec MBA, MBA); business intelligence (MBA); finance (MBA); international business (MBA); management information systems (MBA); marketing (MBA); MBA/MHSA; MSN/MBA. *Accreditation:* AACSB. Part-time and evening/weekend programs available. *Faculty:* 44 full-time (17 women), 9 part-time/adjunct (2 women). *Students:* 167 full-time (51 women), 862 part-time (283 women); includes 149 minority (60 African Americans, 62 Asian Americans or Pacific Islanders, 27 Hispanic Americans), 17 international. Average age 30. 355 applicants, 63% accepted, 187 enrolled. In 2009, 369 master's awarded. *Degree requirements:* For master's, capstone course. *Entrance requirements:* For master's, GMAT. Additional exam requirements/recommendations for international students: Required—TOEFL (minimum score 550 paper-based; 213 computer-based; 80 iBT). *Application deadline:* For fall admission, 8/1 priority date for domestic students, 5/1 for international students; for spring admission, 12/1 priority date for domestic students, 9/1 for international students. Applications are processed on a rolling basis. Application fee: $0. Electronic applications accepted. *Expenses:* Contact institution. *Financial support:* In 2009–10, 183 students received support. Scholarships/grants, tuition waivers (partial), and unspecified assistantships available. Financial award application deadline: 3/1; financial award applicants required to submit FAFSA. *Unit head:* Dr. Hema Krishnan, Associate Dean, 513-745-3206, Fax: 513-745-3455, E-mail: krishnan@xavier.edu. *Application contact:* Anna Marie Whelan, Assistant Director, MBA Programs, 513-745-3525, Fax: 513-745-2929, E-mail: whelana@xavier.edu.

Sustainability Management

Alliant International University–San Diego, Marshall Goldsmith School of Management, Business and Management Division, San Diego, CA 92131-1799. Offers business administration (MBA); information and technology management (DBA); international business (MIBA, DBA), including finance (DBA), marketing (DBA); strategic business (DBA); sustainable management (MBA); MBA/MA; MBA/PhD. Part-time and evening/weekend programs available. *Degree requirements:* For doctorate, thesis/dissertation. *Entrance requirements:* For master's, GMAT, minimum GPA of 3.0; for doctorate, GMAT, minimum GPA of 3.3. Additional exam requirements/recommendations for international students: Required—TOEFL (minimum score 550 paper-based; 213 computer-based), TWE (minimum score 5). Electronic applications accepted. *Faculty research:* Consumer behavior, international business, strategic management, information systems.

Alliant International University–San Francisco, Marshall Goldsmith School of Management, Presidio School of Management, San Francisco, CA 94133-1221. Offers sustainable management (MBA).

Anaheim University, Programs in Business Administration, Anaheim, CA 92806-5150. Offers online global (MBA); online green (MBA); professional (MBA); sustainable management (Certificate, Diploma). Postbaccalaureate distance learning degree programs offered.

Antioch University New England, Graduate School, Department of Organization and Management, Program in Organizational and Environmental Sustainability (Green MBA), Keene, NH 03431-3552. Offers MBA. Part-time programs available. *Entrance requirements:* For master's, GRE, resume, 3 letters of recommendation. Additional exam requirements/recommendations for international students: Required—TOEFL (minimum score 600 paper-based; 250 computer-based).

Argosy University, Chicago, College of Business, Chicago, IL 60601. Offers accounting (DBA); customized professional concentration (MBA, DBA); finance (MBA); fraud examination (MBA); global business sustainability (DBA); healthcare administration (MBA); information systems (DBA); information systems management (MBA); international business (MBA, DBA); management (MBA, MSM, DBA); marketing (MBA, DBA); organizational leadership (Ed D); public administration (MBA); sustainable management (MBA). Postbaccalaureate distance learning degree programs offered (minimal on-campus study).

See Close-Up on page 199.

Argosy University, Dallas, College of Business, Farmers Branch, TX 75244. Offers accounting (DBA, AGC); corporate compliance (MBA, Graduate Certificate); customized professional concentration (MBA); finance (MBA, Graduate Certificate); fraud examination (MBA, Graduate Certificate); global business sustainability (DBA, AGC); healthcare administration (Graduate Certificate); healthcare management (MBA); information systems (MBA, DBA, AGC); information systems management (Graduate Certificate); international business (MBA, DBA, AGC, Graduate Certificate); management (MBA, DBA, AGC, Graduate Certificate); marketing (MBA, DBA, AGC, Graduate Certificate); public administration (MBA, Graduate Certificate); sustainable management (MBA, Graduate Certificate).

See Close-Up on page 201.

Argosy University, Denver, College of Business, Denver, CO 80231. Offers accounting (DBA); corporate compliance (MBA); customized professional concentration (MBA, DBA); finance (MBA); fraud examination (MBA); global business sustainability (DBA); healthcare administration (MBA); information systems (DBA); information systems management (MBA); international business (MBA, DBA); management (MBA, MSM, DBA); marketing (MBA, DBA); organizational leadership (Ed D); public administration (MBA); sustainable management (MBA).

See Close-Up on page 203.

Argosy University, Hawai'i, College of Business, Honolulu, HI 96813. Offers accounting (DBA); corporate compliance (MBA); customized professional concentration (MBA, DBA); finance (MBA, Certificate); fraud examination (MBA); global business sustainability (DBA); healthcare administration (MBA, Certificate); information systems (DBA); information systems management (MBA, Certificate); international business (MBA, DBA, Certificate); management (MBA, MSM, DBA); marketing (MBA, DBA, Certificate); organizational leadership (Ed D); public administration (MBA); sustainable management (MBA).

See Close-Up on page 205.

Argosy University, Inland Empire, College of Business, San Bernardino, CA 92408. Offers accounting (DBA); corporate compliance (MBA); customized professional concentration (MBA, DBA); finance (MBA); fraud examination (MBA); global business sustainability (DBA); healthcare administration (MBA); information systems (DBA); information systems management (MBA); international business (MBA, DBA); management (MBA, MSM, DBA); marketing (MBA, DBA); organizational leadership (Ed D); public administration (MBA); sustainable management (MBA).

See Close-Up on page 207.

Argosy University, Los Angeles, College of Business, Santa Monica, CA 90045. Offers accounting (DBA); corporate compliance (MBA); customized professional concentration (MBA, DBA); finance (MBA); fraud examination (MBA); global business sustainability (DBA); healthcare administration (MBA); information systems (DBA); information systems management (MBA); international business (MBA, DBA); management (MBA, MSM, DBA); marketing (MBA, DBA); organizational leadership (Ed D); public administration (MBA); sustainable management (MBA).

See Close-Up on page 209.

Argosy University, Orange County, College of Business, Orange, CA 92868. Offers accounting (DBA, Adv C); corporate compliance (MBA); customized professional concentration (MBA, DBA); finance (MBA, Certificate); fraud examination (MBA); global business sustainability (DBA); healthcare administration (MBA, Certificate); information systems (DBA, Adv C, Certificate); information systems management (MBA); international business (MBA, DBA, Adv C, Certificate); management (MBA, MSM, DBA, Adv C); marketing (MBA, DBA, Adv C, Certificate); organizational leadership (Ed D); public administration (MBA, Certificate); sustainable management (MBA).

See Close-Up on page 213.

Argosy University, Phoenix, College of Business, Phoenix, AZ 85021. Offers accounting (DBA); corporate compliance (MBA); customized professional concentration (MBA, DBA); finance (MBA); fraud examination (MBA); global business sustainability (DBA); healthcare administration (MBA); information systems (DBA); information systems management (MBA); international business (MBA, DBA); management (MBA, DBA); marketing (MBA, DBA); public administration (MBA); sustainable management (MBA).

See Close-Up on page 215.

Argosy University, Salt Lake City, College of Business, Draper, UT 84020. Offers accounting (DBA); corporate compliance (MBA); customized professional concentration (MBA, DBA); finance (MBA); fraud examination (MBA); global business sustainability (DBA); healthcare administration (MBA); information systems (DBA); information systems management (MBA); international business (MBA, DBA); management (MBA, DBA); marketing (MBA, DBA); public administration (MBA); sustainable management (MBA).

See Close-Up on page 217.

Argosy University, San Francisco Bay Area, College of Business, Alameda, CA 94501. Offers accounting (DBA); corporate compliance (MBA); customized professional concentration (MBA, DBA); finance (MBA); fraud examination (MBA); global business sustainability (DBA); healthcare administration (MBA); information systems (DBA); information systems management (MBA); international business (MBA, DBA); management (MBA, MSM, DBA); marketing (MBA, DBA); organizational leadership (Ed D); public administration (MBA); sustainable management (MBA).

See Close-Up on page 221.

Argosy University, Sarasota, College of Business, Sarasota, FL 34235. Offers accounting (DBA, Adv C); corporate compliance (MBA, DBA, Certificate); customized professional concentration (MBA, DBA); finance (MBA, Certificate); fraud examination (MBA, Certificate); global business sustainability (DBA, Adv C); healthcare administration (MBA, Certificate); information systems (DBA, Adv C, Certificate); information systems management (MBA); international business (MBA, DBA, Adv C, Certificate); management (MBA, MSM, DBA, Adv C, Certificate); marketing (MBA, DBA, Adv C, Certificate); organizational leadership (Ed D); public administration (MBA, Certificate); sustainable management (MBA, Certificate).

See Close-Up on page 223.

Argosy University, Schaumburg, College of Business, Schaumburg, IL 60173-5403. Offers accounting (DBA, Adv C); customized professional concentration (MBA, DBA); finance (MBA,

Sustainability Management

Argosy University, Schaumburg (continued)
Certificate); fraud examination (MBA); global business sustainability (DBA); healthcare administration (MBA, Certificate); information systems (DBA, Adv C, Certificate); information systems management (MBA); international business (MBA, DBA, Adv C, Certificate); management (MBA, MSM, DBA, Adv C, Certificate); marketing (MBA, DBA, Adv C, Certificate); organizational leadership (Ed D); public administration (MBA); sustainable management (MBA).

See Close-Up on page 225.

Argosy University, Seattle, College of Business, Seattle, WA 98121. Offers accounting (DBA); corporate compliance (MBA); customized professional concentration (MBA, DBA); finance (MBA); fraud examination (MBA); global business sustainability (DBA); healthcare administration (MBA); information systems (DBA); information systems management (MBA); international business (MBA, DBA); management (MBA, MSM, DBA); marketing (MBA, DBA); organizational leadership (Ed D); public administration (MBA); sustainable management (MBA).

See Close-Up on page 227.

Argosy University, Tampa, College of Business, Tampa, FL 33607. Offers accounting (DBA); corporate compliance (MBA); customized professional concentration (MBA, DBA); finance (MBA); fraud examination (MBA); global business sustainability (DBA); healthcare administration (MBA); information systems (DBA); information systems management (MBA); international business (MBA, DBA); management (MBA, MSM, DBA); marketing (MBA, DBA); organizational leadership (Ed D); public administration (MBA); sustainable management (MBA).

See Close-Up on page 229.

Argosy University, Twin Cities, College of Business, Eagan, MN 55121. Offers accounting (DBA); customized professional concentration (MBA, DBA); finance (MBA); fraud examination (MBA); global business sustainability (DBA); healthcare administration (MBA); information systems (DBA); information systems management (MBA); international business (MBA, DBA); management (MBA, MSM, DBA); marketing (MBA, DBA); organizational leadership (Ed D); public administration (MBA); sustainable management (MBA).

See Close-Up on page 231.

Argosy University, Washington DC, College of Business, Arlington, VA 22209. Offers accounting (DBA); customized professional concentration (MBA, DBA); finance (MBA); fraud examination (MBA); global business sustainability (DBA); healthcare administration (MBA); information systems (DBA); information systems management (MBA); international business (MBA, DBA, Certificate); management (MBA, MSM, DBA); marketing (MBA, DBA, Certificate); organizational leadership (Ed D); public administration (MBA); sustainable management (MBA).

See Close-Up on page 233.

City University of Seattle, Graduate Division, School of Management, Bellevue, WA 98005. Offers accounting (Certificate); change leadership (MBA, Certificate); financial management (MBA, Certificate); general management (MBA); general management-Europe (MBA); global leadership (Certificate); global marketing (MBA); individualized study (MBA); information security (MS); information systems (MBA); leadership (MA); marketing (MBA, Certificate); project management (MBA, MS, Certificate); sustainable business (Certificate); technology management (MBA, MS, Certificate). Part-time and evening/weekend programs available. Postbaccalaureate distance learning degree programs offered (no on-campus study). *Entrance requirements:* Additional exam requirements/recommendations for international students: Required—TOEFL (minimum score 540 paper-based; 207 computer-based); Recommended—IELTS. Electronic applications accepted. *Expenses:* Tuition: Full-time $14,760; part-time $615 per credit. Tuition and fees vary according to program.

Colorado State University, Graduate School, College of Business, Program in Global Social and Sustainable Enterprise, Fort Collins, CO 80523-1201. Offers MSBA. *Students:* 41 full-time (25 women), 2 part-time (1 woman); includes 7 minority (1 African American, 1 American Indian/Alaska Native, 3 Asian Americans or Pacific Islanders, 2 Hispanic Americans), 16 international. Average age 32. *Degree requirements:* For master's, variable foreign language requirement, comprehensive exam (for some programs), thesis, practicum. *Entrance requirements:* For master's, GMAT or GRE, 3 recommendations, current resume, minimum cumulative GPA of 3.0. Additional exam requirements/recommendations for international students: Required—TOEFL (minimum score 567 paper-based; 227 computer-based; 80 iBT); Recommended—IELTS (minimum score 6). *Application deadline:* For fall admission, 3/31 priority date for domestic students, 3/30 priority date for international students. Application fee: $50. *Expenses:* Tuition, state resident: full-time $6434; part-time $359.10 per credit. Tuition, nonresident: full-time $18,116; part-time $1006.45 per credit. Required fees: $1496; $83 per credit. *Financial support:* Fellowships with tuition reimbursements, research assistantships with tuition reimbursements, teaching assistantships, scholarships/grants and unspecified assistantships available. Financial award application deadline: 3/31; financial award applicants required to submit FAFSA. *Faculty research:* Entrepreneurial and collective decision making, entrepreneurship and sustainability, cooperative business analysis, organizational behavior, risk management. *Unit head:* Carl Hammerdorfer, Director, 970-491-8734, E-mail: carl.hammerdorfer@business.colostate.edu. *Application contact:* Sandy Dahlberg, Program Advisor, 970-491-6937, E-mail: sandy.dahlberg@colostate.edu.

Columbia University, School of Continuing Education, Program in Sustainability Management, New York, NY 10027. Offers MS. Program offered in collaboration with Columbia University's Earth Institute. Part-time programs available. *Faculty:* 47. *Application deadline:* For fall admission, 4/15 for domestic students. Applications are processed on a rolling basis. Application fee: $50. Electronic applications accepted. *Unit head:* Steven Cohen, Program Director, E-mail: sc32@columbia.edu. *Application contact:* Bryce Weinert, Admissions Adviser, 212-854-9666, E-mail: sce-apply@columbia.edu.

Dominican University of California, Graduate Programs, School of Business and Leadership, Green Business Administration Program, San Rafael, CA 94901-2298. Offers sustainable development (MBA). *Entrance requirements:* Additional exam requirements/recommendations for international students: Required—TOEFL (minimum score 550 paper-based; 213 computer-based).

Duquesne University, John F. Donahue Graduate School of Business, Pittsburgh, PA 15282-0001. Offers accountancy (MS); business administration (MBA); information systems management (MSISM); sustainability (MBA); JD/MBA; MBA/MA; MBA/MES; MBA/MHMS; MBA/MLLS; MBA/MS; MBA/MSN. *Accreditation:* AACSB. Part-time and evening/weekend programs available. *Faculty:* 52 full-time (12 women), 39 part-time/adjunct (7 women). *Students:* 122 full-time (56 women), 252 part-time (93 women); includes 14 minority (5 African Americans, 4 Asian Americans or Pacific Islanders, 5 Hispanic Americans), 30 international. Average age 31. 195 applicants, 95% accepted, 136 enrolled. In 2009, 97 master's awarded. *Entrance requirements:* For master's, GMAT, 2 letters of recommendation, current resume. Additional exam requirements/recommendations for international students: Required—TOEFL (minimum score 577 paper-based; 233 computer-based; 90 iBT); Recommended—TWE. *Application deadline:* For fall admission, 5/1 priority date for domestic students, 5/1 for international students; for spring admission, 10/1 for domestic and international students. Applications are processed on a rolling basis. Application fee: $0. Electronic applications accepted. *Expenses:* Tuition: Part-time $851 per credit. Required fees: $81 per credit. *Financial support:* In 2009–10, 46 students received support, including 14 fellowships with partial tuition reimbursements available, 32 research assistantships with partial tuition reimbursements available; career-related internships or fieldwork and unspecified assistantships also available. Support available to part-time students. Financial award application deadline: 7/1; financial award applicants required to submit FAFSA. *Faculty research:* International business, investment management, business ethics, technology management, supply chain management, business strategy, finance. *Unit head:* Alan R. Miciak, Dean, 412-396-5848, Fax: 412-396-5304, E-mail: miciaka@duq.edu. *Application contact:* Patricia Moore, Assistant Director, 412-396-6276, Fax: 412-396-1726, E-mail: moorep@duq.edu.

See Close-Up on page 239.

Fairleigh Dickinson University, College at Florham, Silberman College of Business, Certificate Program in Managing Sustainability, Madison, NJ 07940-1099. Offers Certificate. *Students:* 12 full-time (11 women). Average age 47. 17 applicants, 88% accepted, 12 enrolled.Application fee: $40. *Unit head:* Dan Twomey, Director, 973-443-8802, E-mail: daniel_twomey@fdu.edu. *Application contact:* Susan Brooman, University Director of Graduate Admissions.

Goddard College, Graduate Division, Master of Arts in Sustainable Business and Communities Program, Plainfield, VT 05667-9432. Offers MA. Postbaccalaureate distance learning degree programs offered (minimal on-campus study). *Faculty:* 7 part-time/adjunct (4 women). *Students:* 27 full-time. 21 applicants, 81% accepted, 14 enrolled. *Degree requirements:* For master's, thesis. *Entrance requirements:* For master's, 3 letters of recommendation, study plan and resource list, interview. Application fee: $40. *Expenses:* Tuition: Part-time $7223 per semester. Part-time tuition and fees vary according to program. *Financial support:* In 2009–10, 19 students received support. *Unit head:* Dr. Ann Driscoll, Director, 802-454-8311, Fax: 802-454-1029, E-mail: ann.driscoll@goddard.edu. *Application contact:* Jamie Kline, Admissions Counselor, 800-906-8312 Ext. 311, Fax: 802-454-1029, E-mail: jamie.kline@goddard.edu.

Illinois Institute of Technology, Stuart School of Business, Program in Business Administration, Chicago, IL 60616-3793. Offers financial management (MBA); innovation and emerging enterprises (MBA); management science (MBA); marketing (MBA); sustainability (MBA); JD/MBA; MBA/MS. *Accreditation:* AACSB. Part-time and evening/weekend programs available. *Faculty:* 14 full-time (2 women), 3 part-time/adjunct (all women). *Students:* 71 full-time (28 women), 45 part-time (18 women); includes 8 minority (4 African Americans, 4 Asian Americans or Pacific Islanders), 69 international. Average age 29. 274 applicants, 50% accepted, 33 enrolled. In 2009, 48 master's, 6 other advanced degrees awarded. *Entrance requirements:* For master's, GMAT. Additional exam requirements/recommendations for international students: Required—TOEFL (minimum score 600 paper-based; 250 computer-based; 90 iBT). *Application deadline:* For fall admission, 8/1 for domestic students, 5/1 for international students; for spring admission, 12/15 for domestic students, 10/15 for international students. Applications are processed on a rolling basis. Application fee: $75. Electronic applications accepted. *Expenses:* Contact institution. *Financial support:* Career-related internships or fieldwork, Federal Work-Study, institutionally sponsored loans, scholarships/grants, traineeships, health care benefits, and tuition waivers (partial) available. Support available to part-time students. Financial award applicants required to submit FAFSA. *Faculty research:* Global management and marketing strategy, technological innovation, management science, financial management, knowledge management. *Unit head:* M. Krishna Erramilli, Interim Director, 312-906-6573, Fax: 312-906-6549. *Application contact:* M. Krishna Erramilli, Interim Director, 312-906-6573, Fax: 312-906-6549.

Indiana University Bloomington, School of Public and Environmental Affairs, Public Affairs Programs, Bloomington, IN 47405-7000. Offers comparative and international affairs (MPA); economic development (MPA); environmental policy and natural resource management (MPA); information systems (MPA); local government management (MPA); nonprofit management (MPA); policy analysis (MPA); public affairs (PhD, Certificate); public financial administration (MPA); public management (MPA); sustainability and sustainable development (MPA); JD/MPA; MPA/MIS; MPA/MLS; MSES/MPA. *Accreditation:* NASPAA (one or more programs are accredited). Part-time programs available. *Faculty:* 75 full-time (22 women), 91 part-time/adjunct (24 women). *Students:* 389 full-time (222 women), 45 part-time (24 women); includes 38 minority (18 African Americans, 1 American Indian/Alaska Native, 12 Asian Americans or Pacific Islanders, 7 Hispanic Americans), 72 international. Average age 26. 474 applicants, 206 enrolled. In 2009, 190 master's, 11 doctorates, 3 other advanced degrees awarded. Terminal master's awarded for partial completion of doctoral program. *Degree requirements:* For master's, thesis optional; for doctorate, comprehensive exam, thesis/dissertation or alternative, A thesis is required for the Public Affairs and Public Policy degree. *Entrance requirements:* For master's, GRE, LSAT (if also applying for the Law School), 3 letters of recommendation, resume or curriculum vitae; for doctorate, GRE General Test. Additional exam requirements/recommendations for international students: Required—TOEFL (minimum score 590 paper-based; 243 computer-based; 96 iBT). *Application deadline:* For fall admission, 2/1 priority date for domestic students, 12/1 priority date for international students; for spring admission, 9/1 for international students. Application fee: $55 ($65 for international students). Electronic applications accepted. *Financial support:* Fellowships with full tuition reimbursements, research assistantships with partial tuition reimbursements, teaching assistantships with partial tuition reimbursements, career-related internships or fieldwork, Federal Work-Study, institutionally sponsored loans, unspecified assistantships, and Service Corps programs available. Financial award application deadline: 2/1; financial award applicants required to submit FAFSA. *Faculty research:* Comparative and international affairs, environmental policy and resource management, policy analysis, public finance, public management, urban management, nonprofit management. *Unit head:* Dean John Graham, Dean, School of Public and Environmental Affairs, 812-855-1432, E-mail: grahamjd@indiana.edu. *Application contact:* Jennifer Medlin, Assistant Director of Admissions and Financial Aid, 812-855-3784, Fax: 812-856-3665, E-mail: jlmedlin@indiana.edu.

Lipscomb University, MBA Program, Nashville, TN 37204-3951. Offers accounting (MBA); business administration (general) (MBA); conflict management (MBA); financial services (MBA); healthcare management (MBA); leadership (MBA); nonprofit management (MBA); sports administration (MBA); sustainable practice (MBA). *Accreditation:* ACBSP. Part-time and evening/weekend programs available. *Faculty:* 10 full-time (1 woman), 7 part-time/adjunct (2 women). *Students:* 43 full-time (23 women), 86 part-time (38 women); includes 23 minority (18 African Americans, 1 Asian American or Pacific Islander, 4 Hispanic Americans), 1 international. Average age 31. 95 applicants, 64% accepted, 35 enrolled. In 2009, 59 master's awarded. *Entrance requirements:* For master's, GMAT, interview, 2 references, resume. Additional exam requirements/recommendations for international students: Required—TOEFL (minimum score 570 paper-based; 230 computer-based). *Application deadline:* For fall admission, 2/1 for international students; for winter admission, 6/1 for international students. Applications are processed on a rolling basis. Application fee: $50 ($75 for international students). Electronic applications accepted. *Expenses:* Contact institution. *Financial support:* Career-related internships or fieldwork, Federal Work-Study, scholarships/grants, tuition waivers (partial), and unspecified assistantships available. Support available to part-time students. Financial award application deadline: 7/1; financial award applicants required to submit FAFSA. *Faculty research:* Impact of spirituality on organization commitment, leadership, psychological empowerment, training. *Unit head:* Dr. Mike Kendrick, Interim Chair of Graduate Business Studies, 615-966-1833, Fax: 615-966-1818, E-mail: mikekendrick@lipscomb.edu. *Application contact:* Emily Landsdell, 615-966-5284, E-mail: emily.lansdell@lipscomb.edu.

Maharishi University of Management, Graduate Studies, Program in Business Administration, Fairfield, IA 52557. Offers accounting (MBA); business administration (PhD); sustainability (MBA). Evening/weekend programs available. Postbaccalaureate distance learning degree programs offered (minimal on-campus study). *Degree requirements:* For doctorate, thesis/dissertation. *Entrance requirements:* For master's, GMAT, minimum GPA of 3.0; for doctorate, minimum GPA of 3.0. Additional exam requirements/recommendations for international students: Required—TOEFL. *Faculty research:* Leadership, effects of the group dynamics of consciousness on the economy, innovation, employee development, cooperative strategy.

Marlboro College, Graduate School, Program in Business Administration, Marlboro, VT 05344. Offers managing for sustainability (MBA). Part-time and evening/weekend programs available. Postbaccalaureate distance learning degree programs offered (minimal on-campus study). *Faculty:* 1 full-time (0 women), 15 part-time/adjunct (6 women). *Students:* 15 full-time (6 women), 6 part-time (3 women). Average age 41. *Degree requirements:* For master's, capstone project. *Entrance requirements:* For master's, 2 letters of recommendation. *Application deadline:* For winter admission, 10/30 priority date for domestic students. Application fee: $0. Electronic applications accepted. *Expenses:* Tuition: Full-time $9520; part-time $680 per credit. Tuition and fees vary according to course load and program. *Financial support:* Applicants required to submit FAFSA. *Unit head:* Ralph Meima, Program Director, 802-251-7690, Fax:

802-258-9201, E-mail: rmeima@marlboro.edu. *Application contact:* Joe Heslin, Associate Director of Admissions, 802-258-9209, Fax: 802-258-9201, E-mail: jheslin@gradcenter. marlboro.edu.

Michigan Technological University, Graduate School, Sustainable Futures Institute, Houghton, MI 49931. Offers sustainability (Certificate). Part-time programs available.

Rochester Institute of Technology, Graduate Enrollment Services, Golisano Institute for Sustainability, Rochester, NY 14623-5603. Offers PhD. *Students:* 12 full-time (8 women), 7 international. Average age 30. 28 applicants, 29% accepted, 7 enrolled. *Entrance requirements:* Additional exam requirements/recommendations for international students: Required—TOEFL (minimum score 600 paper-based; 250 computer-based; 100 iBT), or IELTS (minimum score 6.5). *Application deadline:* For fall admission, 1/15 priority date for domestic and international students. Application fee: $50. *Expenses:* Tuition: Full-time $31,533; part-time $876 per credit hour. Required fees: $210. *Financial support:* In 2009–10, 12 students received support. *Faculty research:* Remanufacturing and resource recovery, sustainable production, sustainable mobility, systems modernization and sustainment, pollution prevention. *Unit head:* Dr. Nabil Nasr, Assistant Provost and Director, 585-475-2602, E-mail: info@sustainability.rit.edu. *Application contact:* Diane Ellison, Assistant Vice President, Graduate Enrollment Services, 585-475-2229, Fax: 585-475-7164, E-mail: gradinfo@rit.edu.

South University, Graduate Programs, College of Business, Savannah, GA 31406. Offers corrections (MBA); entrepreneurship and small business (MBA); hospitality management (MBA); sustainability (MBA).

Syracuse University, Martin J. Whitman School of Management, Program in Sustainable Enterprise, Syracuse, NY 13244. Offers CAS. *Expenses:* Tuition: Full-time $26,808; part-time $1117 per credit. Required fees: $1024.

University of California, Berkeley, UC Berkeley Extension, Certificate Programs in Sustainability Studies, Berkeley, CA 94720-1500. Offers leadership in sustainability and environmental management (Professional Certificate); solar energy and green building (Professional Certificate); sustainable design (Professional Certificate). *Unit head:* Diana Wu, Dean, 510-642-4181. *Application contact:* Sustainability Studies, 510-642-4151, E-mail: course@unex. berkeley.edu.

University of Maine, Graduate School, College of Business, Public Policy and Health, The Maine Business School, Orono, ME 04469. Offers accounting (MS); business administration (MBA); business and sustainability (MBA). *Accreditation:* AACSB. Part-time and evening/weekend programs available. *Faculty:* 25 full-time (10 women), 1 (woman) part-time/adjunct. *Students:* 47 full-time (19 women), 14 part-time (6 women); includes 3 minority (2 American Indian/Alaska Native, 1 Hispanic American), 4 international. Average age 28. 56 applicants, 63% accepted, 25 enrolled. In 2009, 21 master's awarded. *Entrance requirements:* For master's, GMAT. Additional exam requirements/recommendations for international students: Required—TOEFL (minimum score 550 paper-based; 213 computer-based). *Application deadline:* For fall admission, 6/1 priority date for domestic and international students; for spring admission, 11/1 priority date for domestic and international students. Applications are processed on a rolling basis. Application fee: $65. Electronic applications accepted. *Expenses:* Contact institution. *Financial support:* In 2009–10, 16 students received support, including 4 teaching assistantships with tuition reimbursements available (averaging $12,790 per year); career-related internships or fieldwork, Federal Work-Study, institutionally sponsored loans, scholarships/

grants, tuition waivers (full and partial), and unspecified assistantships also available. Financial award application deadline: 3/1. *Faculty research:* Entrepreneurship, investment management, international markets, decision support systems, strategic planning. *Unit head:* Dr. Nory Jones, Director of Graduate Programs, 207-581-1971, Fax: 207-581-1930, E-mail: mba@maine.edu. *Application contact:* Scott G. Delcourt, Associate Dean of the Graduate School, 207-581-3291, Fax: 207-581-3232, E-mail: graduate@maine.edu.

University of Saskatchewan, College of Graduate Studies and Research, School of Environment and Sustainability, Saskatoon, SK S7N 5A2, Canada. Offers MES. Tuition and fees charges are reported in Canadian dollars. *Expenses:* Tuition, area resident: Full-time $3000 Canadian dollars; part-time $500 Canadian dollars per term. Required fees: $700 Canadian dollars; $100 Canadian dollars per term.

Walden University, Graduate Programs, School of Management, Minneapolis, MN 55401. Offers applied management and decision sciences (PhD), including accounting, engineering management, finance, general applied management and decision sciences, information systems management, knowledge management, leadership and organizational change, learning management, operations research, self-designed program in applied management and design sciences; business information management (MISM); enterprise information security (MISM); entrepreneurship (MBA, DBA); finance (MBA, DBA); global supply chain management (DBA); healthcare management (MBA); healthcare system improvement (MBA); human resource management (MBA); information systems management (DBA); international business (MBA, DBA); IT strategy and governance (MISM); leadership (MBA, MS, DBA), including entrepreneurship (MS), general management (MS), human resources leadership (MS), innovation and technology (MS), leader development (MS), project management (MS), self-designed (MS), sustainable futures (MS); managing global software and service supply chains (MISM); marketing (MBA, DBA); project management (MBA, MS); risk management (MBA); self-designed (MBA, DBA); social impact management (DBA); sustainable futures (MBA); technology (MBA); technology entrepreneurship (DBA). Part-time and evening/weekend programs available. Postbaccalaureate distance learning degree programs offered (minimal on-campus study). *Faculty:* 17 full-time, 211 part-time/adjunct. *Students:* 3,389 full-time (1,774 women), 815 part-time (482 women); includes 1,969 minority (1,640 African Americans, 36 American Indian/Alaska Native, 123 Asian Americans or Pacific Islanders, 170 Hispanic Americans), 95 international. Average age 41. In 2009, 699 master's, 42 doctorates awarded. *Degree requirements:* For doctorate, thesis/dissertation (for some programs), residency. *Entrance requirements:* For master's, bachelor's degree or equivalent in related field; minimum GPA of 2.5; official transcripts; goal statement; access to computer and Internet; for doctorate, master's degree or equivalent in related field; minimum GPA of 3.0; 3 years of related professional/academic experience (preferred). Additional exam requirements/recommendations for international students: Required—TOEFL (minimum score 550 paper-based; 213 computer-based), IELTS (minimum score 6.5), TOEFL, IELTS, or Michigan English Language Assessment Battery (minimum score 82). *Application deadline:* Applications are processed on a rolling basis. Application fee: $50. Electronic applications accepted. *Expenses:* Tuition: Full-time $13,665; part-time $560 per credit. Required fees: $1375. Tuition and fees vary according to course load, degree level and program. *Financial support:* In 2009–10, 466 students received support; fellowships, Federal Work-Study, scholarships/grants, unspecified assistantships, and family tuition reduction, active duty/veteran tuition reduction, group tuition reduction, interest-free payment plans available. Support available to part-time students. Financial award applicants required to submit FAFSA. *Unit head:* William Schulz, Interim Associate Dean, 800-925-3368. *Application contact:* Jennifer Hall, Director of Enrollment, 866-4-WALDEN, E-mail: info@waldenu.edu.

Section 14
Marketing

This section contains a directory of institutions offering graduate work in marketing. Additional information about programs listed in the directory may be obtained by writing directly to the dean of a graduate school or chair of a department at the address given in the directory.

For programs offering related work, see also in this book *Advertising and Public Relations, Business Administration and Management,* and *Hospitality Management.* In another guide in this series:

Graduate Programs in the Humanities, Arts & Social Sciences
See *Communication and Media* and *Public, Regional, and Industrial Affairs*

CONTENTS

Program Directories

Close-Ups

Marketing

Adelphi University, School of Business, MBA Program, Garden City, NY 11530-0701. Offers finance (MBA); management information systems (MBA); management/human resource management (MBA); marketing/e-commerce (MBA). *Accreditation:* AACSB. Part-time and evening/weekend programs available. *Students:* 77 full-time (30 women), 183 part-time (91 women); includes 56 minority (29 African Americans, 17 Asian Americans or Pacific Islanders, 10 Hispanic Americans), 81 international. Average age 30. In 2009, 64 master's awarded. *Degree requirements:* For master's, capstone course. *Entrance requirements:* For master's, GMAT, 2 letters of recommendation. Additional exam requirements/recommendations for international students: Required—TOEFL (minimum score 550 paper-based; 213 computer-based; 80 iBT). *Application deadline:* For fall admission, 4/1 for international students; for spring admission, 11/1 for international students. Applications are processed on a rolling basis. Application fee: $50. Electronic applications accepted. *Expenses:* Tuition: Full-time $28,340; part-time $830 per credit. Required fees: $600; $250 per credit. Full-time tuition and fees vary according to course load and program. *Financial support:* Research assistantships with full and partial tuition reimbursements, career-related internships or fieldwork, Federal Work-Study, institutionally sponsored loans, scholarships/grants, and unspecified assistantships available. Financial award application deadline: 3/1; financial award applicants required to submit FAFSA. *Faculty research:* Supply chain management, distribution channels, productivity benchmark analysis, data envelopment analysis, financial portfolio analysis. *Unit head:* Rakesh Gupta, 516-877-4670, Fax: 516-877-4607, E-mail: gradbusinquiries@adelphi.edu. *Application contact:* Christine Murphy, Director of Admissions, 516-877-3050, Fax: 516-877-3039, E-mail: graduateadmissions@adelphi.edu.

Alabama Agricultural and Mechanical University, School of Graduate Studies, School of Business, Department of Management and Marketing, Huntsville, AL 35811. Offers MBA. Part-time and evening/weekend programs available. *Degree requirements:* For master's, comprehensive exam, thesis optional. *Entrance requirements:* For master's, GMAT, minimum undergraduate GPA of 2.5. Additional exam requirements/recommendations for international students: Required—TOEFL (minimum score 500 paper-based; 173 computer-based; 61 iBT). Electronic applications accepted. *Faculty research:* Consumer behavior of blacks, small business marketing, economics of education, China in transition, international economics.

Alliant International University–San Diego, Marshall Goldsmith School of Management, Business and Management Division, San Diego, CA 92131-1799. Offers business administration (MBA); information and technology management (DBA); international business (MIBA, DBA), including finance (DBA), marketing (DBA); strategic business (DBA); sustainable management (MBA); MBA/MA; MBA/PhD. Part-time and evening/weekend programs available. *Degree requirements:* For doctorate, thesis/dissertation. *Entrance requirements:* For master's, GMAT, minimum GPA of 3.0; for doctorate, GMAT, minimum GPA of 3.3. Additional exam requirements/recommendations for international students: Required—TOEFL (minimum score 550 paper-based; 213 computer-based), TWE (minimum score 5). Electronic applications accepted. *Faculty research:* Consumer behavior, international business, strategic management, information systems.

American College of Thessaloniki, Department of Business Administration, Pylea, Greece. Offers banking and finance (MBA); entrepreneurship (MBA, Certificate); finance (Certificate); management (MBA, Certificate); marketing (MBA, Certificate). Part-time and evening/weekend programs available. *Faculty:* 6 full-time (1 woman), 10 part-time/adjunct (2 women). *Students:* 6 full-time (3 women), 44 part-time (30 women), 17 international. 25 applicants, 96% accepted, 24 enrolled. *Degree requirements:* For master's, thesis. *Entrance requirements:* For master's, bachelor's degree. *Application deadline:* For fall admission, 9/30 priority date for domestic students; for spring admission, 2/18 priority date for domestic students. Applications are processed on a rolling basis. Application fee: $70. Electronic applications accepted. *Unit head:* Dr. Nikolaos Kourkoumelis, Chair, Business Division, 30-310-398386, E-mail: nikolaos@act.edu. *Application contact:* Elli Konstantinou, Director of Student Recruitment, 30-310-398238, E-mail: elli@act.edu.

American InterContinental University Buckhead Campus, Program in Business Administration, Atlanta, GA 30326-1016. Offers accounting and finance (MBA); management (MBA); marketing (MBA). Evening/weekend programs available. Postbaccalaureate distance learning degree programs offered. *Entrance requirements:* For master's, minimum cumulative undergraduate GPA of 2.0. Additional exam requirements/recommendations for international students: Required—TOEFL (minimum score 530 paper-based; 230 computer-based). Electronic applications accepted. *Faculty research:* Leadership management, international advertising.

American InterContinental University Online, Program in Business Administration, Hoffman Estates, IL 60192. Offers accounting and finance (MBA); finance (MBA); healthcare management (MBA); human resource management (MBA); international business (MBA); management (MBA); marketing (MBA); operations management (MBA); organizational psychology and development (MBA); project management (MBA). Evening/weekend programs available. Postbaccalaureate distance learning degree programs offered (no on-campus study). *Entrance requirements:* Additional exam requirements/recommendations for international students: Required—TOEFL (minimum score 550 paper-based; 213 computer-based). Electronic applications accepted.

American InterContinental University South Florida, Program in International Business, Weston, FL 33326. Offers accounting and finance (MBA); human resource management (MBA); management (MBA); marketing (MBA). Part-time and evening/weekend programs available. Postbaccalaureate distance learning degree programs offered. Electronic applications accepted.

American International College, School of Business Administration, MBA Program, Springfield, MA 01109-3189. Offers accounting (MBA); corporate/public communication (MBA); finance (MBA); general business (MBA); hospitality, hotel and service management (MBA); international business (MBA); international business practice (MBA); management (MBA); management information systems (MBA); marketing (MBA). International business practice program developed in cooperation with the Mountbatten Institute. *Expenses:* Tuition: Full-time $12,510; part-time $695 per credit hour. Required fees: $35 per term.

American University, Kogod School of Business, Master of Business Administration Program, Washington, DC 20016-8044. Offers accounting (MBA); consulting (MBA), including information technology, international business, management; corporate finance: commercial banking (MBA); corporate finance: corporate financial management (MBA); corporate finance: investment banking (MBA), including corporate finance and private equity, trading and selling; entrepreneurship (MBA); global emerging markets (MBA), including business, finance, information technology; international trade and global supply chain management (MBA); leadership (MBA); marketing management (MBA); marketing research (MBA); real estate (MBA); MBA/JD; MBA/LL M. Part-time and evening/weekend programs available. *Faculty:* 14 full-time (6 women). *Students:* 133 full-time (56 women), 121 part-time (48 women); includes 54 minority (23 African Americans, 1 American Indian/Alaska Native, 16 Asian Americans or Pacific Islanders, 14 Hispanic Americans), 43 international. Average age 29. 539 applicants, 51% accepted, 86 enrolled. In 2009, 114 master's awarded. *Entrance requirements:* For master's, GMAT. Additional exam requirements/recommendations for international students: Required—TOEFL. *Application deadline:* For fall admission, 2/1 priority date for domestic students; for spring admission, 10/1 priority date for domestic students. Applications are processed on a rolling basis. Application fee: $100. *Expenses:* Contact institution. *Financial support:* In 2009–10, 19 students received support; fellowships, research assistantships with partial tuition reimbursements available, career-related internships or fieldwork, Federal Work-Study, and institutionally sponsored loans available. Support available to part-time students. Financial award application deadline: 2/1. *Faculty research:* Information technology, decision-aiding methodology, negotiation. *Unit head:* Dr. Stevan Holmberg, Chair, 202-885-6193, E-mail: sholmbe@american.edu. *Application*

contact: Shannon Demko, Associate Director of Graduate Admissions, 202-885-1994, Fax: 202-885-1108, E-mail: demko@american.edu.

The American University in Dubai, Master in Business Administration Program, Dubai, United Arab Emirates. Offers general (MBA); healthcare management (MBA); international finance (MBA); international marketing (MBA); management of construction enterprises (MBA). Part-time and evening/weekend programs available. *Degree requirements:* For master's, thesis optional. *Entrance requirements:* For master's, GMAT, Interview. Additional exam requirements/recommendations for international students: Required—TOEFL (minimum score 550 paper-based; 213 computer-based; 79 iBT). Electronic applications accepted.

Andrew Jackson University, Brian Tracy College of Business and Entrepreneurship, Birmingham, AL 35244. Offers entrepreneurship (MBA); finance (MBA); health services management (MBA); hospitality and tourism management (MBA); human resource management (MBA); international business (MBA); management (MBA); marketing (MBA). Part-time and evening/weekend programs available. Postbaccalaureate distance learning degree programs offered (no on-campus study). *Entrance requirements:* For master's, course work in calculus, statistics, macroeconomics. Additional exam requirements/recommendations for international students: Required—TOEFL (minimum score 550 paper-based; 213 computer-based). Electronic applications accepted.

Argosy University, Atlanta, College of Business, Atlanta, GA 30328. Offers accounting (DBA); corporate compliance (MBA); customized professional concentration (MBA, DBA); finance (MBA); healthcare administration (MBA); information systems (DBA); information systems management (MBA); international business (MBA, DBA); management (MBA, MSM, DBA); marketing (MBA, DBA).

See Close-Up on page 197.

Argosy University, Chicago, College of Business, Chicago, IL 60601. Offers accounting (DBA); customized professional concentration (MBA, DBA); finance (MBA); fraud examination (MBA); global business sustainability (DBA); healthcare administration (MBA); information systems (DBA); information systems management (MBA); international business (MBA, DBA); management (MBA, MSM, DBA); marketing (MBA, DBA); organizational leadership (Ed D); public administration (MBA); sustainable management (MBA). Postbaccalaureate distance learning degree programs offered (minimal on-campus study).

See Close-Up on page 199.

Argosy University, Dallas, College of Business, Farmers Branch, TX 75244. Offers accounting (DBA, AGC); corporate compliance (MBA, Graduate Certificate); customized professional concentration (MBA); finance (MBA, Graduate Certificate); fraud examination (MBA, Graduate Certificate); global business sustainability (DBA, AGC); healthcare administration (Graduate Certificate); healthcare management (MBA); information systems (MBA, DBA, AGC); information systems management (Graduate Certificate); international business (MBA, DBA, AGC, Graduate Certificate); management (MBA, DBA, AGC, Graduate Certificate); marketing (MBA, DBA, AGC, Graduate Certificate); public administration (MBA, Graduate Certificate); sustainable management (MBA, Graduate Certificate).

See Close-Up on page 201.

Argosy University, Denver, College of Business, Denver, CO 80231. Offers accounting (DBA); corporate compliance (MBA); customized professional concentration (MBA, DBA); finance (MBA); fraud examination (MBA); global business sustainability (DBA); healthcare administration (MBA); information systems (DBA); information systems management (MBA); international business (MBA, DBA); management (MBA, MSM, DBA); marketing (MBA, DBA); organizational leadership (Ed D); public administration (MBA); sustainable management (MBA).

See Close-Up on page 203.

Argosy University, Hawai'i, College of Business, Honolulu, HI 96813. Offers accounting (DBA); corporate compliance (MBA); customized professional concentration (MBA, DBA); finance (MBA, Certificate); fraud examination (MBA); global business sustainability (DBA); healthcare administration (MBA, Certificate); information systems (DBA); information systems management (MBA, Certificate); international business (MBA, DBA, Certificate); management (MBA, MSM, DBA); marketing (MBA, DBA, Certificate); organizational leadership (Ed D); public administration (MBA); sustainable management (MBA).

See Close-Up on page 205.

Argosy University, Inland Empire, College of Business, San Bernardino, CA 92408. Offers accounting (DBA); corporate compliance (MBA); customized professional concentration (MBA, DBA); finance (MBA); fraud examination (MBA); global business sustainability (DBA); healthcare administration (MBA); information systems (DBA); information systems management (MBA); international business (MBA, DBA); management (MBA, MSM, DBA); marketing (MBA, DBA); organizational leadership (Ed D); public administration (MBA); sustainable management (MBA).

See Close-Up on page 207.

Argosy University, Los Angeles, College of Business, Santa Monica, CA 90045. Offers accounting (DBA); corporate compliance (MBA); customized professional concentration (MBA, DBA); finance (MBA); fraud examination (MBA); global business sustainability (DBA); healthcare administration (MBA); information systems (DBA); information systems management (MBA); international business (MBA, DBA); management (MBA, MSM, DBA); marketing (MBA, DBA); organizational leadership (Ed D); public administration (MBA); sustainable management (MBA).

See Close-Up on page 209.

Argosy University, Nashville, College of Business, Nashville, TN 37214. Offers accounting (DBA); customized professional concentration (MBA, DBA); finance (MBA); healthcare administration (MBA); information systems (MBA, DBA); international business (MBA, DBA); management (MBA, MSM, DBA); marketing (MBA, DBA).

See Close-Up on page 211.

Argosy University, Orange County, College of Business, Orange, CA 92868. Offers accounting (DBA, Adv C); corporate compliance (MBA); customized professional concentration (MBA, DBA); finance (MBA, Certificate); fraud examination (MBA); global business sustainability (DBA); healthcare administration (MBA, Certificate); information systems (DBA, Adv C, Certificate); information systems management (MBA); international business (MBA, DBA, Adv C, Certificate); management (MBA, MSM, DBA, Adv C); marketing (MBA, DBA, Adv C, Certificate); organizational leadership (Ed D); public administration (MBA, Certificate); sustainable management (MBA).

See Close-Up on page 213.

Argosy University, Phoenix, College of Business, Phoenix, AZ 85021. Offers accounting (DBA); corporate compliance (MBA); customized professional concentration (MBA, DBA); finance (MBA); fraud examination (MBA); global business sustainability (DBA); healthcare administration (MBA); information systems (DBA); information systems management (MBA); international business (MBA, DBA); management (MBA, DBA); marketing (MBA, DBA); public administration (MBA); sustainable management (MBA).

See Close-Up on page 215.

Argosy University, Salt Lake City, College of Business, Draper, UT 84020. Offers accounting (DBA); corporate compliance (MBA); customized professional concentration (MBA, DBA); finance (MBA); fraud examination (MBA); global business sustainability (DBA); healthcare administration (MBA); information systems (DBA); information systems management (MBA); international business (MBA, DBA); management (MBA, DBA); marketing (MBA, DBA); public administration (MBA); sustainable management (MBA).

See Close-Up on page 217.

Marketing

Argosy University, San Diego, College of Business, San Diego, CA 92108. Offers accounting (DBA); corporate compliance (MBA); customized professional concentration (MBA, DBA); finance (MBA); fraud examination (MBA); global business sustainability (DBA); information systems (DBA); information systems management (MBA); international business (MBA, DBA); management (MBA, MSM, DBA); marketing (MBA, DBA); organizational leadership (Ed D); public administration (MBA).

See Close-Up on page 219.

Argosy University, San Francisco Bay Area, College of Business, Alameda, CA 94501. Offers accounting (DBA); corporate compliance (MBA); customized professional concentration (MBA, DBA); finance (MBA); fraud examination (MBA); global business sustainability (DBA); healthcare administration (MBA); information systems (DBA); information systems management (MBA); international business (MBA, DBA); management (MBA, MSM, DBA); marketing (MBA, DBA); organizational leadership (Ed D); public administration (MBA); sustainable management (MBA).

See Close-Up on page 221.

Argosy University, Sarasota, College of Business, Sarasota, FL 34235. Offers accounting (DBA, Adv C); corporate compliance (MBA, DBA, Certificate); customized professional concentration (MBA, DBA); finance (MBA, Certificate); fraud examination (MBA, Certificate); global business sustainability (DBA, Adv C); healthcare administration (MBA, Certificate); information systems (DBA, Adv C, Certificate); information systems management (MBA); international business (MBA, DBA, Adv C, Certificate); management (MBA, MSM, DBA, Adv C, Certificate); marketing (MBA, DBA, Adv C, Certificate); organizational leadership (Ed D); public administration (MBA, Certificate); sustainable management (MBA, Certificate).

See Close-Up on page 223.

Argosy University, Schaumburg, College of Business, Schaumburg, IL 60173-5403. Offers accounting (DBA, Adv C); customized professional concentration (MBA, DBA); finance (MBA, Certificate); fraud examination (MBA); global business sustainability (DBA); healthcare administration (MBA, Certificate); information systems (DBA, Adv C, Certificate); information systems management (MBA); international business (MBA, DBA, Adv C, Certificate); management (MBA, MSM, DBA, Adv C, Certificate); marketing (MBA, DBA, Adv C, Certificate); organizational leadership (Ed D); public administration (MBA); sustainable management (MBA).

See Close-Up on page 225.

Argosy University, Seattle, College of Business, Seattle, WA 98121. Offers accounting (DBA); corporate compliance (MBA); customized professional concentration (MBA, DBA); finance (MBA); fraud examination (MBA); global business sustainability (DBA); healthcare administration (MBA); information systems (DBA); information systems management (MBA); international business (MBA, DBA); management (MBA, MSM, DBA); marketing (MBA, DBA); organizational leadership (Ed D); public administration (MBA); sustainable management (MBA).

See Close-Up on page 227.

Argosy University, Tampa, College of Business, Tampa, FL 33607. Offers accounting (DBA); corporate compliance (MBA); customized professional concentration (MBA, DBA); finance (MBA); fraud examination (MBA); global business sustainability (DBA); healthcare administration (MBA); information systems (DBA); information systems management (MBA); international business (MBA, DBA); management (MBA, MSM, DBA); marketing (MBA, DBA); organizational leadership (Ed D); public administration (MBA); sustainable management (MBA).

See Close-Up on page 229.

Argosy University, Twin Cities, College of Business, Eagan, MN 55121. Offers accounting (DBA); customized professional concentration (MBA, DBA); finance (MBA); fraud examination (MBA); global business sustainability (DBA); healthcare administration (MBA); information systems (DBA); information systems management (MBA); international business (MBA, DBA); management (MBA, MSM, DBA); marketing (MBA, DBA); organizational leadership (Ed D); public administration (MBA); sustainable management (MBA).

See Close-Up on page 231.

Argosy University, Washington DC, College of Business, Arlington, VA 22209. Offers accounting (DBA); customized professional concentration (MBA, DBA); finance (MBA); fraud examination (MBA); global business sustainability (DBA); healthcare administration (MBA); information systems (DBA); information systems management (MBA); international business (MBA, DBA, Certificate); management (MBA, MSM, DBA); marketing (MBA, DBA, Certificate); organizational leadership (Ed D); public administration (MBA); sustainable management (MBA).

See Close-Up on page 233.

Arizona State University, Graduate College, W.P. Carey School of Business, Program in Business Administration, Tempe, AZ 85287. Offers agribusiness (PhD); business administration (MBA); finance (MBA, PhD); health sector management (MBA); information systems (PhD); management (MBA, PhD); marketing (MBA, PhD); supply chain management (MBA, PhD); JD/MBA; MBA/M Arch; MBA/MHSM. *Accreditation:* AACSB. *Degree requirements:* For master's, thesis optional; for doctorate, thesis/dissertation. *Entrance requirements:* For master's, GMAT.

Assumption College, Graduate School, Department of Business Studies, Worcester, MA 01609-1296. Offers accounting (MBA); business administration (CAGS); finance/economics (MBA); general business (MBA); human resources (MBA); international business (MBA); management (MBA); marketing (MBA); nonprofit leadership (MBA). Part-time and evening/weekend programs available. *Faculty:* 6 full-time (1 woman), 14 part-time/adjunct (2 women). *Students:* 19 full-time (11 women), 127 part-time (68 women); includes 22 minority (13 African Americans, 3 Asian Americans or Pacific Islanders, 6 Hispanic Americans). Average age 27. 88 applicants, 99% accepted. In 2009, 40 master's, 2 other advanced degrees awarded. *Entrance requirements:* For master's, 3 letters of recommendation, resume; for CAGS, 3 letters of recommendation, resume, essay. Additional exam requirements/recommendations for international students: Required—TOEFL (minimum score 540 paper-based; 200 computer-based; 76 iBT), IELTS (minimum score 6). *Application deadline:* For fall admission, 6/1 priority date for domestic students, 5/1 priority date for international students; for spring admission, 11/1 priority date for domestic students, 9/1 priority date for international students. Applications are processed on a rolling basis. Application fee: $30. Electronic applications accepted. *Expenses:* Tuition: Part-time $503 per credit. Required fees: $20 per semester. One-time fee: $100 part-time. Part-time tuition and fees vary according to campus/location. *Financial support:* In 2009–10, 47 students received support. Application deadline: 6/1. *Faculty research:* Workplace diversity, dynamics of team interaction, utilization of leased employees. *Unit head:* Michael Lewis, Director, 508-767-7372, Fax: 508-767-7252, E-mail: jhunter@assumption.edu. *Application contact:* Adrian O. Dumas, Director of Graduate Enrollment Management and Services, 508-767-7365, Fax: 508-767-7030, E-mail: adumas@assumption.edu.

Avila University, School of Business, Kansas City, MO 64145-1698. Offers accounting (MBA); finance (MBA); general management (MBA); health care administration (MBA); international business (MBA); management information systems (MBA); marketing (MBA). Part-time and evening/weekend programs available. *Faculty:* 9 full-time (3 women), 24 part-time/adjunct (5 women). *Students:* 148 full-time (71 women), 86 part-time (47 women); includes 56 minority (36 African Americans, 2 American Indian/Alaska Native, 13 Asian Americans or Pacific Islanders, 5 Hispanic Americans), 63 international. Average age 32. 53 applicants, 75% accepted, 40 enrolled. In 2009, 93 master's awarded. *Degree requirements:* For master's, comprehensive exam, capstone course. *Entrance requirements:* For master's, GMAT, minimum GPA of 3.0, interview. Additional exam requirements/recommendations for international students: Required—TOEFL (minimum score 550 paper-based). *Application deadline:* For fall admission, 7/30 priority date for domestic students, 7/30 for international students; for winter admission, 11/30 priority date for domestic students, 11/30 for international students; for spring admission, 2/28 priority date for domestic students, 2/28 for international students. Applications are processed on a rolling basis. Application fee: $0. Electronic applications accepted. *Expenses:* Contact institution. *Financial support:* In 2009–10, 102 students received support. Career-related internships or fieldwork available. Support available to part-time students. Financial award applicants required to submit FAFSA. *Faculty research:* Leadership characteristics, financial hedging, group dynamics. *Unit head:* Dr. Richard Woodall, Dean, 816-501-3720, Fax: 816-501-2463, E-mail: richard.woodall@avila.edu. *Application contact:* JoAnna Giffin, MBA Admissions Director, 816-501-3601, Fax: 816-501-2463, E-mail: joanna.giffin@avila.edu.

Baker College Center for Graduate Studies—Online, Graduate Programs—Online, Flint, MI 48507-9843. Offers accounting (MBA); business administration (DBA); finance (MBA); general business (MBA); health care management (MBA); human resources management (MBA); information management (MBA); leadership studies (MBA); management information systems (MSIS); marketing (MBA). Part-time and evening/weekend programs available. Postbaccalaureate distance learning degree programs offered. *Faculty:* 750. *Students:* 500 full-time, 500 part-time. Average age 37. *Degree requirements:* For master's, portfolio. *Entrance requirements:* For master's, 3 years of work experience, minimum undergraduate GPA of 2.5, writing sample, 3 letters of recommendation; for doctorate, MBA or acceptable related master's degree from accredited association, 5 years work experience, minimum graduate GPA of 3.25, writing sample, 3 professional references. Additional exam requirements/recommendations for international students: Required—TOEFL (minimum score 550 paper-based; 213 computer-based). *Application deadline:* For fall admission, 8/6 priority date for domestic students; for winter admission, 12/15 priority date for domestic students; for spring admission, 2/15 priority date for domestic students. Applications are processed on a rolling basis. Application fee: $25. Electronic applications accepted. *Expenses:* Tuition: Part-time $330 per credit hour. Tuition and fees vary according to degree level. *Financial support:* Scholarships/grants available. Support available to part-time students. Financial award applicants required to submit FAFSA. *Unit head:* Dr. Julia Teahen, President, 810-766-4023, Fax: 810-766-4399, E-mail: julia@baker.edu. *Application contact:* Chuck J. Gurden, Vice President for Graduate and Online Admissions, 800-469-3165, Fax: 810-766-4399, E-mail: adm-ol@baker.edu.

Barry University, Andreas School of Business, Graduate Certificate Programs, Miami Shores, FL 33161-6695. Offers finance (Certificate); health services administration (Certificate); international business (Certificate); management (Certificate); management information systems (Certificate); marketing (Certificate).

Bayamón Central University, Graduate Programs, Program in Business Administration, Bayamón, PR 00960-1725. Offers accounting (MBA); finance (MBA); general business (MBA); management (MBA); management of security and protection (MBA); marketing (MBA). Part-time and evening/weekend programs available. *Degree requirements:* For master's, comprehensive exam (for some programs). *Entrance requirements:* For master's, EXADEP, bachelor's degree in business or related field.

Benedictine University, Graduate Programs, Program in Business Administration, Lisle, IL 60532-0900. Offers accounting (MBA); entrepreneurship and managing innovation (MBA); financial management (MBA); health administration (MBA); human resource management (MBA); information systems security (MBA); international business (MBA); management consulting (MBA); management information systems (MBA); marketing management (MBA); operations management and logistics (MBA); organizational leadership (MBA); MBA/MPH; MBA/MS. Part-time and evening/weekend programs available. Postbaccalaureate distance learning degree programs offered (minimal on-campus study). *Faculty:* 4 full-time (2 women), 24 part-time/adjunct (3 women). *Students:* 247 full-time (141 women), 644 part-time (339 women); includes 223 minority (134 African Americans, 5 American Indian/Alaska Native, 44 Asian Americans or Pacific Islanders, 40 Hispanic Americans), 25 international. Average age 34. 287 applicants, 92% accepted, 229 enrolled. In 2009, 219 master's awarded. *Entrance requirements:* For master's, GMAT. Additional exam requirements/recommendations for international students: Required—TOEFL (minimum score 550 paper-based; 213 computer-based). *Application deadline:* For fall admission, 9/1 for domestic students; for winter admission, 12/1 for domestic students; for spring admission, 2/15 for domestic students. Applications are processed on a rolling basis. Application fee: $40. Electronic applications accepted. *Expenses:* Tuition: Part-time $750 per credit hour. Tuition and fees vary according to campus/location and program. *Financial support:* Career-related internships or fieldwork and health care benefits available. Support available to part-time students. *Faculty research:* Strategic leadership in professional organizations, sociology of professions, organizational change, social identity theory, applications to change management. *Unit head:* Dr. Sharon Borowicz, Director, 630-829-6219, E-mail: sborowicz@ben.edu. *Application contact:* Kari Gibbons, Director, Admissions, 630-829-6200, Fax: 630-829-6584, E-mail: kgibbons@ben.edu.

Bentley University, McCallum Graduate School of Business, Program in Marketing Analytics, Waltham, MA 02452-4705. Offers MSMA. Part-time and evening/weekend programs available. *Faculty:* 65 full-time (24 women), 16 part-time/adjunct (6 women). *Students:* 19 full-time (11 women), 22 part-time (15 women); includes 4 minority (1 Asian American or Pacific Islander, 3 Hispanic Americans), 21 international. Average age 26. 73 applicants, 66% accepted, 23 enrolled. *Entrance requirements:* For master's, GMAT. Additional exam requirements/recommendations for international students: Required—TOEFL (minimum score 600 paper-based; 250 computer-based; 100 iBT) or IELTS (minimum score 7). *Application deadline:* For fall admission, 12/1 priority date for domestic and international students; for spring admission, 10/1 priority date for domestic and international students. Application fee: $50. Electronic applications accepted. *Expenses:* Tuition: Full-time $26,208; part-time $1092 per credit. Required fees: $404. *Financial support:* Application deadline: 6/1. *Faculty research:* Marketing information processing, blogging and social media, customer loyalty and customer relationship management, measuring and improving productivity and online consumer behavior. *Unit head:* Dr. Paul Berger, Chair, 781-891-2746, E-mail: pberger@bentley.edu. *Application contact:* Sharon Hill, Director of Graduate Admissions, 781-891-2108, Fax: 781-891-2464, E-mail: bentleygraduateadmissions@bentley.edu.

Bernard M. Baruch College of the City University of New York, Zicklin School of Business, Department of Marketing, New York, NY 10010-5585. Offers MBA, MS, PhD. Part-time and evening/weekend programs available. *Degree requirements:* For doctorate, comprehensive exam, thesis/dissertation. *Entrance requirements:* For master's, GMAT, 2 letters of recommendation, resume, 2 years of work experience; for doctorate, GMAT. Additional exam requirements/recommendations for international students: Required—TOEFL (minimum score 590 paper-based; 243 computer-based), TWE (minimum score 5).

Boston University, School of Management, Doctorate in Business Administration Program, Boston, MA 02215. Offers accounting (PhD); information systems (PhD); marketing (PhD); operations and technology management (PhD); organizational behavior (PhD); strategy and innovation (PhD). *Students:* 31 full-time (18 women), 21 international. Average age 32. 158 applicants, 7% accepted, 6 enrolled. In 2009, 12 doctorates awarded. *Degree requirements:* For doctorate, comprehensive exam, thesis/dissertation, curriculum paper. *Entrance requirements:* For doctorate, GMAT or GRE General Test, resume, 3 letters of evaluation. Additional exam requirements/recommendations for international students: Required—TOEFL or IELTS. *Application deadline:* For fall admission, 1/5 for domestic and international students. Application fee: $125. *Expenses:* Tuition: Full-time $37,910; part-time $1184 per credit hour. Required fees: $386; $40 per semester. Part-time tuition and fees vary according to class time, course level, degree level and program. *Financial support:* Fellowships, research assistantships, teaching assistantships, career-related internships or fieldwork, Federal Work-Study, institutionally sponsored loans, scholarships/grants, and tuition waivers available. Support available to part-time students. Financial award applicants required to submit FAFSA. *Unit head:* Dr. Lloyd Baird, Director, 617-353-2670, E-mail: dba@bu.edu. *Application contact:* Hayden Estrada, Assistant Dean, Admissions, 617-353-2670, Fax: 617-353-7368, E-mail: dba@bu.edu.

Boston University, School of Management, Master of Business Administration Program, Boston, MA 02215. Offers entrepreneurship (MBA); finance (MBA); health sector management (MBA); international management (MBA); marketing (MBA); operations and technology management (MBA); public and nonprofit management (MBA); strategy and business analysis (MBA); JD/MBA; MBA/MA; MBA/MPH; MBA/MS; MBA/MSIS; MS/MBA. Part-time and evening/weekend programs available. *Faculty:* 119 full-time (31 women), 99 part-time/adjunct (30 women). *Students:* 326 full-time (138 women), 677 part-time (257 women); includes 149

Marketing

Boston University (continued)

minority (13 African Americans, 119 Asian Americans or Pacific Islanders, 17 Hispanic Americans), 149 international. Average age 30. 1,617 applicants, 38% accepted, 317 enrolled. In 2009, 284 master's awarded. *Entrance requirements:* For master's, GMAT, resume, 2 letters of recommendation. Additional exam requirements/recommendations for international students: Required—TOEFL or IELTS. *Application deadline:* For fall admission, 3/15 for domestic and international students; for spring admission, 11/15 for domestic students. Application fee: $125. Electronic applications accepted. *Expenses:* Tuition: Full-time $37,910; part-time $1184 per credit hour. Required fees: $386; $40 per semester. Part-time tuition and fees vary according to class time, course level, degree level and program. *Financial support:* Career-related internships or fieldwork, Federal Work-Study, institutionally sponsored loans, and scholarships/grants available. Support available to part-time students. Financial award applicants required to submit FAFSA. *Unit head:* Katherine Nolan, Assistant Dean, Graduate Programs, 617-353-4157, Fax: 617-353-5003, E-mail: mba@bu.edu. *Application contact:* Hayden Estrada, Assistant Dean, Admissions, 617-353-2670, Fax: 617-353-7368, E-mail: mba@bu.edu.

California Coast University, Programs in Business Administration, Santa Ana, CA 92701. Offers human resources management (MBA); management (MBA); marketing (MBA). Part-time and evening/weekend programs available. Postbaccalaureate distance learning degree programs offered (no on-campus study). Application fee: $75. Electronic applications accepted. *Application contact:* Christi Okuma, 714-547-9625, Fax: 714-547-5777, E-mail: ccu@calcoast.edu.

California Intercontinental University, School of Business, Diamond Bar, CA 91765. Offers banking and finance (MBA); entrepreneurship and business management (DBA); global business leadership (DBA); international management and marketing (MBA); organizational management and human resource management (MBA).

California Lutheran University, Graduate Studies, School of Business, Thousand Oaks, CA 91360-2787. Offers business (IMBA); entrepreneurship (MBA, Certificate); finance (MBA, Certificate); financial planning (MBA, Certificate); information systems and technology (MS); information technology management (MBA, Certificate); international business (MBA, Certificate); management and organization behavior (MBA); management and organizational behavior (Certificate); marketing (MBA, Certificate). Evening/weekend programs available. Post-baccalaureate distance learning degree programs offered. *Entrance requirements:* For master's, GMAT, interview, minimum GPA of 3.0. *Expenses:* Contact institution.

California State University, East Bay, Graduate Programs, College of Business and Economics, Department of Marketing, Option in Marketing Management, Hayward, CA 94542-3000. Offers MBA. Part-time and evening/weekend programs available. *Degree requirements:* For master's, comprehensive exam or thesis. *Entrance requirements:* For master's, GMAT, minimum GPA of 2.75. Additional exam requirements/recommendations for international students: Required—TOEFL (minimum score 550 paper-based; 213 computer-based). *Application deadline:* For fall admission, 6/30 for domestic and international students. Application fee: $55. Electronic applications accepted. *Financial support:* Fellowships, teaching assistantships, career-related internships or fieldwork, Federal Work-Study, institutionally sponsored loans, and scholarships/grants available. Support available to part-time students. Financial award application deadline: 3/1; financial award applicants required to submit FAFSA. *Unit head:* Dr. Nan Maxwell, Chair, 510-885-4336, E-mail: nan.maxwell.@csueastbay.edu. *Application contact:* Donna Wiley, Interim Associate Director, 510-885-2928, Fax: 510-885-4777, E-mail: donna.wiley@csueastbay.edu.

California State University, Fullerton, Graduate Studies, College of Business and Economics, Department of Marketing, Fullerton, CA 92834-9480. Offers marketing (MBA). Part-time programs available. *Students:* 18 full-time (9 women), 22 part-time (9 women); includes 5 minority (3 Asian Americans or Pacific Islanders, 2 Hispanic Americans), 14 international. Average age 27. 52 applicants, 58% accepted, 12 enrolled. In 2009, 16 master's awarded. *Degree requirements:* For master's, project or thesis. *Entrance requirements:* For master's, GMAT, minimum AACSB index of 950. Application fee: $55. *Expenses:* Tuition, nonresident: full-time $11,160; part-time $373 per credit. Required fees: $1440 per term. Tuition and fees vary according to course load, degree level and program. *Financial support:* Career-related internships or fieldwork, Federal Work-Study, institutionally sponsored loans, and scholarships/grants available. Support available to part-time students. Financial award application deadline: 3/1; financial award applicants required to submit FAFSA. *Unit head:* Dr. Irene Lange, Chair, 657-278-2223. *Application contact:* Admissions/Applications, 657-278-2371.

California State University, Los Angeles, Graduate Studies, College of Business and Economics, Department of Marketing, Los Angeles, CA 90032-8530. Offers international business (MBA, MS); marketing management (MBA, MS). Part-time and evening/weekend programs available. *Students:* 4 full-time (3 women), 10 part-time (6 women); includes 3 minority (1 African American, 1 Asian American or Pacific Islander, 1 Hispanic American), 10 international. Average age 28. 15 applicants, 100% accepted, 4 enrolled. In 2009, 18 master's awarded. *Degree requirements:* For master's, comprehensive exam (MBA), thesis (MS). *Entrance requirements:* For master's, GMAT, minimum GPA of 2.5 during previous 2 years of course work. Additional exam requirements/recommendations for international students: Required—TOEFL (minimum score 550 paper-based; 213 computer-based). *Application deadline:* For fall admission, 5/1 for domestic and international students. Applications are processed on a rolling basis. Application fee: $55. Electronic applications accepted. *Financial support:* Career-related internships or fieldwork and Federal Work-Study available. Support available to part-time students. Financial award application deadline: 3/1. *Unit head:* Dr. Paul Washburn, Acting Chair, 323-343-2960, Fax: 323-343-5462, E-mail: pwashbu@calstatela.edu. *Application contact:* Dr. Cheryl L. Ney, Associate Vice President for Academic Affairs and Dean of Graduate Studies, 323-343-3820, Fax: 323-343-5653, E-mail: cney@cslanet.calstatela.edu.

Canisius College, Graduate Division, Richard J. Wehle School of Business, Department of Management and Marketing, Buffalo, NY 14208-1098. Offers business administration (MBA). *Accreditation:* AACSB. Part-time and evening/weekend programs available. *Faculty:* 32 full-time (5 women), 3 part-time/adjunct (1 woman). *Students:* 89 full-time (37 women), 176 part-time (78 women); includes 22 minority (11 African Americans, 9 Asian Americans or Pacific Islanders, 2 Hispanic Americans), 8 international. Average age 28. 164 applicants, 73% accepted, 86 enrolled. In 2009, 96 master's awarded. *Entrance requirements:* For master's, GMAT. *Application deadline:* For fall admission, 7/1 priority date for domestic students; for spring admission, 11/1 priority date for domestic students. Applications are processed on a rolling basis. Application fee: $25. *Expenses:* Contact institution. *Financial support:* Research assistantships with partial tuition reimbursements, career-related internships or fieldwork, scholarships/grants, and unspecified assistantships available. Support available to part-time students. Financial award application deadline: 6/15; financial award applicants required to submit FAFSA. *Faculty research:* Risk aversion, information security, employee relations, urban finance, student expectations. *Unit head:* Dr. George Palumbo, Director, MBA Program, 716-888-2667, Fax: 716-888-3132, E-mail: palumbo@canisius.edu. *Application contact:* Laura McEwen, Director of Graduate Programs, 716-888-2140, Fax: 716-888-8211, E-mail: gradubus@canisius.edu.

Capella University, School of Business and Technology, Minneapolis, MN 55402. Offers accounting (MBA), including system design and programming; business (Certificate), including human resource management (MS, PhD, Certificate), information technology management (MS, PhD, Certificate), leadership (MBA, MS, PhD, Certificate); finance (MBA); general business (MBA); health care management (MBA); information technology (MS, Certificate), including general information technology (MS), information security, network architecture and design (MS), professional projects management (Certificate), project management and leadership (MS), system design and development (MS),); information technology management (MBA); marketing (MBA); organization and management (MBA, MS, PhD), including general business (PhD), general organization and management (MBA, MS), human resource management (MS, PhD, Certificate), information technology management (MS, PhD, Certificate), leadership (MBA, MS, PhD, Certificate); project management (MBA). Part-time and evening/weekend programs available. Postbaccalaureate distance learning degree programs offered (minimal

on-campus study). Terminal master's awarded for partial completion of doctoral program. *Degree requirements:* For master's, thesis optional, integrative project; for doctorate, comprehensive exam, thesis/dissertation. *Entrance requirements:* Additional exam requirements/recommendations for international students: Required—TOEFL (minimum score 550 paper-based; 213 computer-based), TWE (minimum score 4). Electronic applications accepted. *Faculty research:* Business policies: strategic, corporate, and financial management; interplay of technological, organizational and social change.

Carnegie Mellon University, Tepper School of Business, Program in Marketing, Pittsburgh, PA 15213-3891. Offers PhD. *Degree requirements:* For doctorate, thesis/dissertation.

Case Western Reserve University, Weatherhead School of Management, Department of Marketing and Policy Studies, Division of Marketing, Cleveland, OH 44106. Offers MBA. In 2009, 116 master's awarded. *Entrance requirements:* For master's, GMAT. *Financial support:* Application deadline: 5/1. *Faculty research:* Consumer decision making, global marketing, brand equity management, supply chain management, industrial and new technology marketing. *Unit head:* Stan Cort, Head, 216-368-2038, E-mail: mxr8@po.cwru.edu. *Application contact:* Stan Cort, Head, 216-368-2038, E-mail: mxr8@po.cwru.edu.

Case Western Reserve University, Weatherhead School of Management, Department of Operations, Cleveland, OH 44106. Offers management (MS, MSM), including finance (MS), information systems (MS), marketing (MS), operations research, quality management (MS), supply chain (MSM); management for liberal arts graduates (MSM); operations research (PhD); MBA/MSM. Part-time programs available. *Degree requirements:* For doctorate, thesis/dissertation. *Entrance requirements:* For master's, GRE General Test; for doctorate, GMAT, GRE General Test. *Application deadline:* Applications are processed on a rolling basis. Application fee: $100. *Financial support:* Tuition waivers (full and partial) available. Financial award application deadline: 5/1. *Faculty research:* Mathematical finance, mathematical programming, scheduling, stochastic optimization, environmental/energy models. *Unit head:* Kamlesh Mathur, Chairman, 216-368-3857, E-mail: kamlesh.mathur@case.edu. *Application contact:* Kamlesh Mathur, Chairman, 216-368-3857, E-mail: kamlesh.mathur@case.edu.

Central European University, CEU Business School, Budapest, Hungary. Offers finance (MBA); general management (MBA); information technology (M Sc); information technology management (MBA); management (EMBA); marketing (MBA); real estate management (MBA). Part-time and evening/weekend programs available. *Entrance requirements:* For master's, GMAT. Additional exam requirements/recommendations for international students: Required—TOEFL (minimum score 570 paper-based; 230 computer-based). Electronic applications accepted. *Faculty research:* Social and ethical business, marketing.

Central Michigan University, College of Graduate Studies, College of Business Administration, Department of Marketing and Hospitality Services Administration, Mount Pleasant, MI 48859. Offers marketing (MBA). Part-time and evening/weekend programs available. *Degree requirements:* For master's, thesis or alternative. *Entrance requirements:* For master's, GMAT. Electronic applications accepted. *Faculty research:* Consumer preferences and market assessment; marketing research and new product development; business economics and forecasting; SAP/marketing and logistics; services marketing and hospitality organizations.

City University of Seattle, Graduate Division, School of Management, Bellevue, WA 98005. Offers accounting (Certificate); change leadership (MBA, Certificate); financial management (MBA, Certificate); general management (MBA); general management-Europe (MBA); global leadership (Certificate); global marketing (MBA); individualized study (MBA); information security (MS); information systems (MBA); leadership (MA); marketing (MBA, Certificate); project management (MBA, MS, Certificate); sustainable business (Certificate); technology management (MBA, MS, Certificate). Part-time and evening/weekend programs available. Postbaccalaureate distance learning degree programs offered (no on-campus study). *Entrance requirements:* Additional exam requirements/recommendations for international students: Required—TOEFL (minimum score 540 paper-based; 207 computer-based); Recommended—IELTS. Electronic applications accepted. *Expenses:* Tuition: Full-time $14,760; part-time $615 per credit. Tuition and fees vary according to program.

Clark University, Graduate School, Graduate School of Management, Business Administration Program, Worcester, MA 01610-1477. Offers accounting (MBA); finance (MBA); global business (MBA); health care management (MBA); management (MBA); management of information technology (MBA); marketing (MBA). *Accreditation:* AACSB. Part-time and evening/weekend programs available. *Students:* 148 full-time (67 women), 120 part-time (52 women); includes 27 minority (12 African Americans, 2 American Indian/Alaska Native, 9 Asian Americans or Pacific Islanders, 4 Hispanic Americans), 108 international. Average age 29. 340 applicants, 57% accepted, 63 enrolled. In 2009, 118 master's awarded. *Degree requirements:* For master's, thesis optional. *Application deadline:* For fall admission, 6/1 priority date for domestic students; for spring admission, 12/1 priority date for domestic students. Applications are processed on a rolling basis. Application fee: $50. Electronic applications accepted. *Expenses:* Tuition: Full-time $34,900; part-time $4362.50 per course. *Financial support:* In 2009–10, research assistantships with partial tuition reimbursements (averaging $4,800 per year), teaching assistantships with partial tuition reimbursements (averaging $4,800 per year) were awarded; fellowships, career-related internships or fieldwork, Federal Work-Study, institutionally sponsored loans, and tuition waivers (partial) also available. Support available to part-time students. Financial award application deadline: 5/31. *Faculty research:* Organizational development, accounting, marketing, finance, human resource management. *Application contact:* Lynn Davis, Enrollment and Marketing Director, 508-793-7406, Fax: 508-793-8822, E-mail: clarkmba@clarku.edu.

Clemson University, Graduate School, College of Business and Behavioral Science, Department of Marketing, Clemson, SC 29634. Offers marketing (MS). *Faculty:* 15 full-time (3 women). *Students:* 12 full-time (11 women), 2 part-time (both women), 5 international. Average age 24. 58 applicants, 28% accepted, 11 enrolled. In 2009, 8 master's awarded. *Entrance requirements:* For master's, GMAT, minimum GPA of 3.0, letters of recommendation. Additional exam requirements/recommendations for international students: Required—TOEFL. *Application deadline:* Applications are processed on a rolling basis. Application fee: $70 ($80 for international students). Electronic applications accepted. *Expenses:* Tuition, state resident: full-time $8684; part-time $528 per credit hour. Tuition, nonresident: full-time $15,330; part-time $1078 per credit hour. Required fees: $736; $37 per semester. Part-time tuition and fees vary according to course load and program. *Financial support:* In 2009–10, 8 students received support; teaching assistantships with partial tuition reimbursements available, career-related internships or fieldwork, institutionally sponsored loans, scholarships/grants, health care benefits, and unspecified assistantships available. Support available to part-time students. Financial award applicants required to submit FAFSA. *Unit head:* Dr. Greg Pickett, Head, 864-656-5294, E-mail: pgregor@clemson.edu. *Application contact:* Dr. Thomas Baker, Program Contact, 864-656-2397, Fax: 864-656-0138, E-mail: tbaker2@clemson.edu.

Cleveland State University, College of Graduate Studies, Nance College of Business Administration, Department of Marketing, Cleveland, OH 44115. Offers global business (Graduate Certificate); marketing (MBA, DBA); marketing analytics (Graduate Certificate).

Cleveland State University, College of Graduate Studies, Nance College of Business Administration, Doctor of Business Administration (DBA) Program, Cleveland, OH 44115. Offers business administration (DBA); finance (DBA); information systems (DBA); marketing (DBA); operations management (DBA). *Accreditation:* AACSB. Part-time and evening/weekend programs available. *Degree requirements:* For doctorate, comprehensive exam, thesis/dissertation, oral dissertation defense. *Entrance requirements:* For doctorate, GMAT, MBA or equivalent. Additional exam requirements/recommendations for international students: Required—TOEFL (minimum score 550 paper-based; 213 computer-based; 79 iBT). Electronic applications accepted. *Faculty research:* Supply chain management, international business, strategic management, risk analysis.

Colorado Technical University Colorado Springs, Graduate Studies, Program in Management, Colorado Springs, CO 80907-3896. Offers accounting (MBA, MSA); business

administration (MBA); finance (MBA); human resources management (MBA); logistics/supply chain management (MBA); management (DM); marketing (MBA); mediation and dispute resolution (MBA); operations management (MBA); project management (MBA); technology management (MBA). Part-time and evening/weekend programs available. Postbaccalaureate distance learning degree programs offered. *Degree requirements:* For master's, thesis or alternative; for doctorate, thesis/dissertation. *Entrance requirements:* For doctorate, minimum graduate GPA of 3.0, 5 years of related work experience. *Faculty research:* Sexual harassment, performance evaluation, critical thinking.

Colorado Technical University Denver, Programs in Business Administration and Management, Greenwood Village, CO 80111. Offers accounting (MBA); business administration (MBA); business administration and management (EMBA); finance (MBA); human resource management (MBA); marketing (MBA); mediation and dispute resolution (MBA); operations management (MBA); project management (MBA); technology management (MBA). Part-time and evening/weekend programs available. *Degree requirements:* For master's, thesis or alternative. *Entrance requirements:* For master's, minimum undergraduate GPA of 3.0, resume.

Columbia Southern University, MBA Program, Orange Beach, AL 36561. Offers electronic business and technology (MBA); finance (MBA); general (MBA); healthcare management (MBA); hospitality and tourism (MBA); human resources management (MBA); international management (MBA); marketing (MBA); project management (MBA); public administration (MBA); sport management (MBA). Part-time and evening/weekend programs available. Postbaccalaureate distance learning degree programs offered (no on-campus study). *Entrance requirements:* For master's, bachelor's degree from accredited/approved institution. Additional exam requirements/recommendations for international students: Required—TOEFL. Electronic applications accepted.

Columbia University, Graduate School of Business, Doctoral Program in Business, New York, NY 10027. Offers business (PhD), including accounting, decision, risk, and operations, finance and economics, management, marketing. *Accreditation:* AACSB. *Faculty:* 149 full-time (23 women), 134 part-time/adjunct (16 women). *Students:* 91 full-time (37 women); includes 10 minority (8 Asian Americans or Pacific Islanders, 2 Hispanic Americans), 64 international. Average age 27. 758 applicants, 6% accepted, 20 enrolled. In 2009, 15 doctorates awarded. *Degree requirements:* For doctorate, comprehensive exam, thesis/dissertation, major field exam, research paper, thesis proposal. *Entrance requirements:* For doctorate, GMAT or GRE (finance), 2 letters of reference, resume. Additional exam requirements/recommendations for international students: Required—TOEFL. *Application deadline:* For fall admission, 1/1 for domestic and international students. Application fee: $75. Electronic applications accepted. *Expenses:* Contact institution. *Financial support:* In 2009–10, 91 students received support, including fellowships with full tuition reimbursements available (averaging $22,000 per year), research assistantships (averaging $4,000 per year); teaching assistantships, career-related internships or fieldwork, health care benefits, and tuition waivers (full) also available. *Faculty research:* Human decision making and behavioral research; real estate market and mortgage defaults; financial crisis and corporate governance; international business; security analysis and accounting. *Unit head:* Elizabeth Elam Chang, Administrative Director, 212-854-2836, Fax: 212-932-2359, E-mail: phdinfo@gsb.columbia.edu. *Application contact:* Elizabeth Elam Chang, Administrative Director, 212-854-2836, Fax: 212-932-2359, E-mail: phdinfo@gsb.columbia.edu.

Columbia University, Graduate School of Business, MBA Program, New York, NY 10027. Offers accounting (MBA); decision, risk, and operations (MBA); entrepreneurship (MBA); finance and economics (MBA); healthcare and pharmaceutical management (MBA); human resource management (MBA); international business (MBA); leadership and ethics (MBA); management (MBA); marketing (MBA); media (MBA); private equity (MBA); real estate (MBA); social enterprise (MBA); value investing (MBA); DDS/MBA; JD/MBA; MBA/MIA; MBA/MPH; MBA/MS; MD/MBA. *Faculty:* 149 full-time (23 women), 134 part-time/adjunct (16 women). *Students:* 1,293 full-time (435 women); includes 235 minority (65 African Americans, 4 American Indian/Alaska Native, 135 Asian Americans or Pacific Islanders, 31 Hispanic Americans), 417 international. Average age 28. 6,885 applicants, 15% accepted, 737 enrolled. In 2009, 696 master's awarded. *Entrance requirements:* For master's, GMAT, 2 letters of recommendation. Additional exam requirements/recommendations for international students: Required—TOEFL. *Application deadline:* For fall admission, 4/14 for domestic students, 3/3 for international students; for spring admission, 10/7 for domestic and international students. Applications are processed on a rolling basis. Application fee: $250. Electronic applications accepted. *Expenses:* Contact institution. *Financial support:* In 2009–10, 358 students received support, including 101 fellowships (averaging $23,250 per year); research assistantships, teaching assistantships, career-related internships or fieldwork, institutionally sponsored loans, and scholarships/grants also available. Financial award application deadline: 3/1; financial award applicants required to submit CSS PROFILE or FAFSA. *Faculty research:* Human decision making and behavioral research; real estate market and mortgage defaults; financial crisis and corporate governance; international business; security analysis and accounting. *Unit head:* Prof. Amir Ziv, Vice Dean of Students and the MBA Program, 212-854-3485, Fax: 212-932-0545, E-mail: az50@columbia.edu. *Application contact:* Mary J. Miller, Assistant Dean of Admissions, 212-854-1961, Fax: 212-662-6754, E-mail: apply@gsb.columbia.edu.

Concordia University Wisconsin, Graduate Programs, School of Business and Legal Studies, MBA Program, Mequon, WI 53097-2402. Offers finance (MBA); health care administration (MBA); human resource management (MBA); international business (MBA); international business-bilingual English/Chinese (MBA); management (MBA); management information systems (MBA); managerial communications (MBA); marketing (MBA); public administration (MBA); risk management (MBA). Postbaccalaureate distance learning degree programs offered (minimal on-campus study). *Degree requirements:* For master's, comprehensive exam, thesis or alternative. *Entrance requirements:* Additional exam requirements/recommendations for international students: Required—TOEFL. *Expenses:* Contact institution.

Cornell University, Graduate School, Graduate Field of Management, Ithaca, NY 14853-0001. Offers accounting (PhD); behavioral decision theory (PhD); finance (PhD); marketing (PhD); organizational behavior (PhD); production and operations management (PhD). *Accreditation:* AACSB. *Faculty:* 72 full-time (15 women). *Students:* 39 full-time (15 women); includes 2 minority (both Asian Americans or Pacific Islanders), 23 international. Average age 31. 388 applicants, 2% accepted, 4 enrolled. In 2009, 4 doctorates awarded. *Degree requirements:* For doctorate, comprehensive exam, thesis/dissertation. *Entrance requirements:* For doctorate, GMAT or GRE General Test. Additional exam requirements/recommendations for international students: Required—TOEFL (minimum score 600 paper-based; 250 computer-based; 77 iBT). *Application deadline:* For fall admission, 1/3 for domestic students. Application fee: $70. Electronic applications accepted. *Expenses:* Contact institution. *Financial support:* In 2009–10, 38 students received support, including 1 fellowship with full tuition reimbursement available, 3 research assistantships with full tuition reimbursements available; teaching assistantships with full tuition reimbursements available, institutionally sponsored loans, scholarships/grants, health care benefits, tuition waivers (full and partial), and unspecified assistantships also available. Financial award applicants required to submit FAFSA. *Faculty research:* Operations and manufacturing. *Unit head:* Director of Graduate Studies, 607-255-3669. *Application contact:* Graduate Field Assistant, 607-255-9431, E-mail: js_phd@cornell.edu.

Dallas Baptist University, College of Adult Education, Professional Development Program, Dallas, TX 75211-9299. Offers accounting (MA); church leadership (MA); counseling (MA); criminal justice (MA); English as a second language (MA); finance (MA); higher education (MA); leadership studies (MA); management (MA); management information systems (MA); marketing (MA); missions (MA). Part-time and evening/weekend programs available. *Entrance requirements:* For master's, minimum GPA of 3.0. Additional exam requirements/recommendations for international students: Required—TOEFL, IELTS. *Expenses:* Tuition: Full-time $10,674; part-time $593 per credit hour.

Dallas Baptist University, College of Business, Business Administration Program, Dallas, TX 75211-9299. Offers accounting (MBA); business communication (MBA); conflict resolution

management (MBA); e-business (MBA); entrepreneurship (MBA); finance (MBA); health care management (MBA); international business (MBA); leading the non-profit organization (MBA); management (MBA); management information systems (MBA); marketing (MBA); project management (MBA); technology and engineering management (MBA). *Accreditation:* ACBSP. Part-time and evening/weekend programs available. *Entrance requirements:* For master's, GMAT, minimum GPA of 3.0. Additional exam requirements/recommendations for international students: Required—TOEFL, IELTS. Electronic applications accepted. *Expenses:* Tuition: Full-time $10,674; part-time $593 per credit hour. *Faculty research:* Sports management, services marketing, retailing, strategic management, financial planning/investments.

Davenport University, Sneden Graduate School, Dearborn, MI 48126-3799. Offers accounting (MBA); business administration (EMBA); finance (MBA); health care management (MBA); human resources management (MBA); information assurance (MS); marketing (MBA); public health (MPH); strategic management (MBA). Part-time and evening/weekend programs available. Postbaccalaureate distance learning degree programs offered (no on-campus study). *Entrance requirements:* For master's, minimum GPA of 2.7, previous course work in accounting and statistics. *Faculty research:* Accounting, international accounting, social and environmental accounting, finance.

Delta State University, Graduate Programs, College of Business, Division of Management, Marketing, and Business Administration, Cleveland, MS 38733-0001. Offers management (MBA); marketing (MBA). *Accreditation:* ATS. Part-time and evening/weekend programs available. *Entrance requirements:* For master's, GMAT. *Expenses:* Tuition, state resident: full-time $4450; part-time $247 per credit hour. Tuition, nonresident: full-time $11,520; part-time $640 per credit hour.

DePaul University, Charles H. Kellstadt Graduate School of Business, Department of Marketing, Chicago, IL 60604-2287. Offers brand management (MBA); customer relationship management (MBA); integrated marketing communication (MBA); marketing analysis (MSMA); marketing and management (MBA); marketing strategy and analysis (MBA); marketing strategy and planning (MBA); new product management (MBA); sales leadership (MBA). Part-time and evening/weekend programs available. *Faculty:* 23 full-time (4 women), 15 part-time/adjunct (6 women). *Students:* 190 full-time (95 women), 72 part-time (40 women); includes 24 minority (6 African Americans, 13 Asian Americans or Pacific Islanders, 5 Hispanic Americans), 22 international. In 2009, 88 master's awarded. *Entrance requirements:* For master's, GMAT, 2 letters of recommendation, resume. Additional exam requirements/recommendations for international students: Required—TOEFL (minimum score 550 paper-based; 213 computer-based). *Application deadline:* For fall admission, 7/1 for domestic students; for winter admission, 10/1 for domestic students; for spring admission, 2/1 for domestic students. Applications are processed on a rolling basis. Application fee: $60. Electronic applications accepted. *Expenses:* Tuition: Full-time $37,525; part-time $620 per credit hour. *Financial support:* In 2009–10, 6 research assistantships with partial tuition reimbursements (averaging $2,500 per year) were awarded. Financial award application deadline: 4/30. *Faculty research:* International and marketing role in developing economics, internet marketing, direct marketing, consumer behavior, new product development processes. Total annual research expenditures: $100,000. *Unit head:* Dr. Suzanne Louise Fogel, Chairperson/Associate Professor, 312-362-5150, Fax: 312-362-5647, E-mail: sfogel@depaul.edu. *Application contact:* Director of MBA Programs, 312-362-8810, Fax: 312-362-6677, E-mail: kgsb@depaul.edu.

DeSales University, Graduate Division, Program in Business Administration, Center Valley, PA 18034-9568. Offers accounting (MBA); business administration (MBA); computer information systems (MBA); finance (MBA); health care systems management (MBA); management (MBA); marketing (MBA); project management (MBA); self-design (MBA); MSN/MBA. *Accreditation:* ACBSP. Part-time programs available. Postbaccalaureate distance learning degree programs offered (no on-campus study). *Students:* 433 part-time. In 2009, 218 master's awarded. *Entrance requirements:* For master's, minimum GPA of 3.0, 2 years of work experience. Additional exam requirements/recommendations for international students: Required—TOEFL. *Application deadline:* Applications are processed on a rolling basis. Application fee: $35. Electronic applications accepted. *Expenses:* Tuition: Full-time $17,500; part-time $665 per credit. Full-time tuition and fees vary according to program. Part-time tuition and fees vary according to course load. *Faculty research:* Quality improvement, executive development, productivity, cross-cultural managerial differences, leadership. *Unit head:* Dr. David Gilfoil, Director, 610-282-1100 Ext. 1828, Fax: 610-282-2869, E-mail: david.gilfoil@desales.edu. *Application contact:* Caryn Stopper, Director of Graduate Admissions, 610-282-1100 Ext. 1768, Fax: 610-282-0525, E-mail: caryn.stopper@desales.edu.

Dowling College, School of Business, Oakdale, NY 11769-1999. Offers aviation management (MBA, Certificate); banking and finance (MBA, Certificate); financial planning (Certificate); general management (MBA); health care management (MBA, Certificate); human resource management (Certificate); management and leadership (MBA); marketing (Certificate); project management (Certificate); public management (MBA, Certificate); total quality management (MBA, Certificate); JD/MBA. Part-time and evening/weekend programs available. *Faculty:* 14 full-time (5 women), 58 part-time/adjunct (5 women). *Students:* 324 full-time (142 women), 479 part-time (237 women); includes 238 minority (82 African Americans, 1 American Indian/Alaska Native, 117 Asian Americans or Pacific Islanders, 38 Hispanic Americans), 2 international. Average age 33. 457 applicants, 91% accepted, 153 enrolled. In 2009, 341 master's, 2 other advanced degrees awarded. *Degree requirements:* For master's, comprehensive exam, thesis optional. *Entrance requirements:* For master's, minimum GPA of 2.8, 2 letters of recommendation, courses in accounting and finance or seminar in accounting/finance, resume. Additional exam requirements/recommendations for international students: Required—TOEFL (minimum score 550 paper-based). *Application deadline:* For fall admission, 9/1 priority date for domestic students; for winter admission, 1/1 priority date for domestic students; for spring admission, 2/1 priority date for domestic students. Applications are processed on a rolling basis. Application fee: $50. Electronic applications accepted. *Expenses:* Tuition: Full-time $14,490; part-time $805 per credit. Required fees: $346 per term. *Financial support:* Career-related internships or fieldwork and Federal Work-Study available. Support available to part-time students. Financial award application deadline: 6/30; financial award applicants required to submit FAFSA. *Faculty research:* International finance, computer applications, labor relations, executive development. *Unit head:* Mathew Cordaro, Dean, 631-244-3162, Fax: 631-244-1018, E-mail: cordarom@dowling.edu. *Application contact:* Glenn M. Berman, Director of Admissions Operations, 631-244-3357, Fax: 631-244-1059, E-mail: glenn.berman@dowling.edu.

Drexel University, LeBow College of Business, Program in Business Administration, Philadelphia, PA 19104-2875. Offers business administration (MBA, PhD, APC), including accounting (MBA, PhD), decision sciences (PhD), economics (MBA, PhD), finance (MBA, PhD), legal studies (MBA), management (MBA), marketing (MBA, PhD), organizational sciences (PhD), quantitative methods (MBA), strategic management (PhD). *Accreditation:* AACSB. Part-time and evening/weekend programs available. Postbaccalaureate distance learning degree programs offered (minimal on-campus study). Terminal master's awarded for partial completion of doctoral program. *Entrance requirements:* For master's, GMAT, minimum GPA of 2.75; for doctorate, GMAT. Additional exam requirements/recommendations for international students: Required—TOEFL. Electronic applications accepted. *Faculty research:* Decision support systems, individual and group behavior, operations research, techniques and strategy.

Eastern Michigan University, Graduate School, Academic Affairs Division, Program in Integrated Marketing Communications, Ypsilanti, MI 48197. Offers MS. *Students:* 33 full-time (21 women), 47 part-time (33 women); includes 13 minority (10 African Americans, 1 American Indian/Alaska Native, 1 Asian American or Pacific Islander, 1 Hispanic American). Average age 33. In 2009, 138 master's awarded. Tuition and fees vary according to course level. *Unit head:* Dawn Gaymer, Assistant Dean, Graduate Business Programs, 734-487-4444, Fax: 734-487-1316, E-mail: dawn.malone@emich.edu. *Application contact:* K. Michelle Henry, Graduate Advisor, 734-487-4444, Fax: 734-487-1316, E-mail: michelle.henry@emich.edu.

Eastern Michigan University, Graduate School, College of Business, Programs in Business Administration, Ypsilanti, MI 48197. Offers business administration (MBA, Graduate Certificate);

Marketing

Eastern Michigan University (continued)

computer information systems (Graduate Certificate); e-business (MBA, Graduate Certificate); enterprise business intelligence (MBA); entrepreneurship (MBA, Graduate Certificate); finance (MBA, Graduate Certificate); human resources (MBA); human resources management (Graduate Certificate); information systems (MBA); internal auditing (MBA); international business (MBA, Graduate Certificate); marketing management (Graduate Certificate); nonprofit management (MBA); organizational development (Graduate Certificate); supply chain management (MBA, Graduate Certificate). *Accreditation:* AACSB. Part-time programs available. Postbaccalaureate distance learning degree programs offered (no on-campus study). *Students:* 166 full-time (80 women), 439 part-time (231 women); includes 150 minority (103 African Americans, 7 American Indian/Alaska Native, 31 Asian Americans or Pacific Islanders, 9 Hispanic Americans), 97 international. Average age 34. In 2009, 3 other advanced degrees awarded. *Entrance requirements:* For master's, GMAT (minimum score 450), minimum cumulative undergraduate GPA of 2.75. Additional exam requirements/recommendations for international students: Required—TOEFL. *Application deadline:* For fall admission, 5/15 for domestic students, 5/1 for international students; for winter admission, 10/15 for domestic students, 10/1 for international students; for spring admission, 3/15 for domestic students, 3/1 for international students. Applications are processed on a rolling basis. Application fee: $35. Tuition and fees vary according to course level. *Financial support:* Fellowships, research assistantships with full tuition reimbursements, teaching assistantships with full tuition reimbursements, career-related internships or fieldwork, Federal Work-Study, institutionally sponsored loans, scholarships/grants, tuition waivers (partial), and unspecified assistantships available. Support available to part-time students. Financial award applicants required to submit FAFSA. *Unit head:* K. Michelle Henry, Director of Academic Services, 734-487-4444, Fax: 734-483-1316, E-mail: cob.grad@emich.edu. *Application contact:* Beste Windes, Advisor, 734-487-4444, Fax: 734-483-1316, E-mail: cob.grad@emich.edu.

Emerson College, Graduate Studies, School of Communication, Department of Marketing Communication, Program in Integrated Marketing Communication, Boston, MA 02116-4624. Offers MA. Part-time and evening/weekend programs available. *Faculty:* 12 full-time (5 women), 17 part-time/adjunct (8 women). *Students:* 112 full-time (91 women), 18 part-time (12 women); includes 15 minority (9 African Americans, 2 Asian Americans or Pacific Islanders, 4 Hispanic Americans), 47 international. Average age 24. 246 applicants, 65% accepted, 64 enrolled. In 2009, 58 master's awarded. *Entrance requirements:* For master's, GMAT or GRE General Test. Additional exam requirements/recommendations for international students: Required—TOEFL (minimum score 550 paper-based; 213 computer-based; 80 iBT), IELTS (minimum score 6.5). *Application deadline:* For fall admission, 6/1 priority date for domestic students, 5/1 priority date for international students; for spring admission, 11/1 priority date for domestic students. Applications are processed on a rolling basis. Application fee: $60 ($75 for international students). Electronic applications accepted. *Expenses:* Tuition: Full-time $22,056; part-time $919 per credit. Required fees: $120. One-time fee: $170 full-time. *Financial support:* In 2009–10, 35 students received support, including 5 fellowships with partial tuition reimbursements available (averaging $14,000 per year), 19 research assistantships with partial tuition reimbursements available (averaging $10,000 per year); Federal Work-Study, scholarships/grants, and unspecified assistantships also available. Financial award application deadline: 3/1; financial award applicants required to submit FAFSA. *Faculty research:* Marketing, international business. *Unit head:* Prof. Cathy Waters, Graduate Program Director, 617-824-8492, E-mail: cathy_waters@emerson.edu. *Application contact:* Office of Graduate Admission, 617-824-8610, Fax: 617-824-8614, E-mail: gradapp@emerson.edu.

Emory University, Goizueta Business School, Doctoral Program in Business, Atlanta, GA 30322-1100. Offers accounting (PhD); finance (PhD); information systems (PhD); marketing (PhD); organization and management (PhD). *Faculty:* 57 full-time (11 women). *Students:* 37 full-time (14 women); includes 8 minority (3 African Americans, 4 Asian Americans or Pacific Islanders, 1 Hispanic American), 19 international. Average age 30. 218 applicants, 9% accepted, 9 enrolled. In 2009, 11 doctorates awarded. *Degree requirements:* For doctorate, comprehensive exam, thesis/dissertation. *Entrance requirements:* For doctorate, GMAT (strongly preferred) or GRE. Additional exam requirements/recommendations for international students: Required—TOEFL (minimum score 250 computer-based). *Application deadline:* For fall admission, 1/3 priority date for domestic and international students. Application fee: $50. Electronic applications accepted. *Unit head:* Dr. Lawrence Benveniste, Dean, 404-727-6377, Fax: 404-727-0868, E-mail: larry_benveniste@bus.emory.edu. *Application contact:* Allison Gilmore, Director of Admissions and Student Services, 404-727-6353, Fax: 404-727-5337, E-mail: phd@bus.emory.edu.

Fairfield University, Charles F. Dolan School of Business, Fairfield, CT 06824-5195. Offers accounting (MBA, MS, CAS); finance (MBA, MS, CAS); general management (MBA); human resource management (MBA, CAS); information systems and operations (MBA); information systems and operations management (CAS); international business (MBA, CAS); marketing (MBA, CAS); taxation (MBA, MS). *Accreditation:* AACSB. Part-time and evening/weekend programs available. *Degree requirements:* For master's, capstone course. *Entrance requirements:* For master's, GMAT (minimum score 500), 2 letters of reference, resume, minimum GPA of 3.0. Additional exam requirements/recommendations for international students: Required—TOEFL (minimum score 550 paper-based; 213 computer-based; 80 iBT). Electronic applications accepted. *Expenses:* Contact institution. *Faculty research:* Optimization strategies, international finance, consumer behavior, financial market volatility, Internet marketing, supply chain analysis, tax issues.

Fairleigh Dickinson University, College at Florham, Silberman College of Business, Department of Management, Marketing, and Entrepreneurial Studies, Program in Marketing, Madison, NJ 07940-1099. Offers MBA, Certificate. *Students:* 13 full-time (5 women), 28 part-time (15 women). Average age 29. 20 applicants, 60% accepted, 2 enrolled. In 2009, 12 master's awarded. *Entrance requirements:* For master's, GMAT. *Application deadline:* Applications are processed on a rolling basis. Application fee: $40.

Fairleigh Dickinson University, Metropolitan Campus, Silberman College of Business, Departments of Management, Marketing, and Entrepreneurial Studies, Program in Marketing, Teaneck, NJ 07666-1914. Offers MBA, Certificate. *Students:* 24 full-time (15 women), 9 part-time (4 women), 21 international. Average age 26. 33 applicants, 42% accepted, 7 enrolled. In 2009, 8 master's awarded. *Application deadline:* Applications are processed on a rolling basis. Application fee: $40. *Application contact:* Susan Brooman, University Director of Graduate Admissions, 201-692-2554, Fax: 201-692-2560, E-mail: globaleducation@fdu.edu.

Fashion Institute of Technology, School of Graduate Studies, Program in Cosmetics and Fragrance Marketing and Management, New York, NY 10001-5992. Offers MPS. *Degree requirements:* For master's, capstone seminar. *Entrance requirements:* Additional exam requirements/recommendations for international students: Required—TOEFL (minimum score 550 paper-based; 213 computer-based). Electronic applications accepted. *Expenses:* Tuition, state resident: full-time $8198; part-time $342 per credit. Tuition, nonresident: full-time $12,972; part-time $541 per credit. Required fees: $450.

Florida Agricultural and Mechanical University, Division of Graduate Studies, Research, and Continuing Education, School of Business and Industry, Tallahassee, FL 32307-3200. Offers accounting (MBA); finance (MBA); management information systems (MBA); marketing (MBA). *Faculty:* 42 full-time (28 women). *Students:* 71 full-time (45 women), 15 part-time (9 women); includes 80 minority (all African Americans), 4 international. In 2009, 90 master's awarded. *Degree requirements:* For master's, residency. *Entrance requirements:* For master's, GMAT, minimum GPA of 3.0. *Application deadline:* For fall admission, 5/18 for domestic students, 12/18 for international students; for spring admission, 11/12 for domestic students, 5/12 for international students. Application fee: $30. *Financial support:* Fellowships, Federal Work-Study and scholarships/grants available. *Unit head:* Dr. Amos Bradford, Interim Dean, 850-599-3565. *Application contact:* Dr. Amos Bradford, Interim Dean, 850-599-3565.

Florida Institute of Technology, Graduate Programs, College of Business, Online Programs, Melbourne, FL 32901-6975. Offers accounting and finance (MBA); healthcare management (MBA); information technology (MS); information technology management (MBA); management (MBA); marketing (MBA); project management (MBA). Part-time and evening/weekend programs available. Postbaccalaureate distance learning degree programs offered (no on-campus study). *Faculty:* 30 part-time/adjunct (6 women). *Students:* 6 full-time (2 women), 875 part-time (387 women); includes 290 minority (194 African Americans, 6 American Indian/Alaska Native, 44 Asian Americans or Pacific Islanders, 46 Hispanic Americans), 32 international. Average age 37. 329 applicants, 64% accepted, 177 enrolled. In 2009, 33 master's awarded. *Entrance requirements:* For master's, GMAT or resume showing 8 years of supervised experience, 2 letters of recommendation, resume, competency in math past college algebra. Additional exam requirements/recommendations for international students: Required—TOEFL (minimum score 550 paper-based; 213 computer-based; 79 iBT). *Application deadline:* For fall admission, 4/1 for international students; for spring admission, 9/30 for international students. Applications are processed on a rolling basis. Application fee: $50. Electronic applications accepted. *Expenses:* Tuition: Part-time $1015 per credit. Tuition and fees vary according to campus/location and program. *Financial support:* Available to part-time students. Application deadline: 3/1. *Unit head:* Dr. Mary S. Bonhomme, Dean, Florida Tech Online/Associate Provost for Online Learning, 321-674-8883, Fax: 321-674-8216, E-mail: bonhomme@fit.edu. *Application contact:* Carolyn Farrior, Director of Graduate Admissions Online Learning and Off Campus Programs, 321-674-7118, Fax: 321-674-8216, E-mail: cfarrior@fit.edu.

Florida State University, The Graduate School, College of Business, Tallahassee, FL 32306-1110. Offers accounting (M Acc), including accounting information services, assurance services, corporate accounting, taxation; business administration (MBA, PhD), including accounting (PhD), finance (PhD), management information systems (PhD), marketing (PhD), organizational behavior (PhD), risk management and insurance (PhD), strategic management (PhD); finance (MS); insurance (MSM); management information systems (MS); JD/MBA; MSW/MBA. *Accreditation:* AACSB. Part-time programs available. Postbaccalaureate distance learning degree programs offered (no on-campus study). *Faculty:* 107 full-time (31 women), 2 part-time/adjunct (0 women). *Students:* 212 full-time (73 women), 345 part-time (107 women); includes 123 minority (37 African Americans, 2 American Indian/Alaska Native, 48 Asian Americans or Pacific Islanders, 36 Hispanic Americans). Average age 30. 908 applicants, 43% accepted, 307 enrolled. In 2009, 257 master's, 18 doctorates awarded. Terminal master's awarded for partial completion of doctoral program. *Degree requirements:* For doctorate, comprehensive exam, thesis/dissertation. *Entrance requirements:* For master's, GMAT, work experience (MBA, MS), minimum GPA of 3.0, letters of recommendation; for doctorate, GMAT, minimum graduate GPA of 3.5, letters of recommendation. Additional exam requirements/recommendations for international students: Required—TOEFL (minimum score 600 paper-based; 80 computer-based); Recommended—IELTS (minimum score 6.5). *Application deadline:* For fall admission, 6/1 for domestic students, 5/1 for international students; for spring admission, 10/1 for domestic students, 9/1 for international students. Applications are processed on a rolling basis. Application fee: $30. Electronic applications accepted. *Expenses:* Tuition, state resident: full-time $7413. Tuition, nonresident: full-time $22,567. *Financial support:* In 2009–10, 102 students received support, including 32 fellowships with full tuition reimbursements available (averaging $6,900 per year), 30 research assistantships with full tuition reimbursements available (averaging $4,500 per year), 40 teaching assistantships with full tuition reimbursements available (averaging $11,500 per year); career-related internships or fieldwork, scholarships/grants, health care benefits, tuition waivers (full and partial), and unspecified assistantships also available. Support available to part-time students. Financial award application deadline: 1/1. *Unit head:* Dr. Caryn Beck-Dudley, Dean, 850-644-3090, Fax: 850-644-0915. *Application contact:* Lisa Beverly, Director, Graduate Programs Admissions, 850-644-6458, Fax: 850-644-0588, E-mail: lbeverly@cob.fsu.edu.

Florida State University, The Graduate School, College of Communication and Information, School of Communication, Tallahassee, FL 32306. Offers corporate and public communication (MA, MS); integrated marketing communication (MA, MS); mass communication (PhD); media and communication studies (MA, MS); speech communication (PhD). Part-time programs available. *Faculty:* 24 full-time (9 women), 6 part-time/adjunct (1 woman). *Students:* 153 full-time (110 women), 65 part-time (34 women); includes 62 minority (37 African Americans, 1 American Indian/Alaska Native, 24 Hispanic Americans). Average age 24. 230 applicants, 76% accepted, 85 enrolled. In 2009, 84 master's, 6 doctorates awarded. *Degree requirements:* For master's, thesis (for some programs); for doctorate, comprehensive exam, thesis/dissertation. *Entrance requirements:* For master's, GRE General Test, minimum GPA of 3.0; for doctorate, GRE General Test, minimum GPA of 3.3 in graduate course work. Additional exam requirements/recommendations for international students: Required—TOEFL (minimum score 600 paper-based; 250 computer-based; 100 iBT). *Application deadline:* For fall admission, 7/1 priority date for domestic students, 5/1 priority date for international students; for spring admission, 11/1 priority date for domestic and international students. Applications are processed on a rolling basis. Application fee: $30. Electronic applications accepted. *Expenses:* Tuition, state resident: full-time $7413. Tuition, nonresident: full-time $22,567. *Financial support:* In 2009–10, 52 students received support, including 1 fellowship with full tuition reimbursement available, 8 research assistantships with full tuition reimbursements available (averaging $14,000 per year), 40 teaching assistantships with full tuition reimbursements available (averaging $5,000 per year); career-related internships or fieldwork, Federal Work-Study, institutionally sponsored loans, scholarships/grants, tuition waivers (partial), and unspecified assistantships also available. Support available to part-time students. Financial award application deadline: 2/1; financial award applicants required to submit FAFSA. *Faculty research:* Communication technology and policy, marketing communication, communication content and effect, new communication/information technologies. Total annual research expenditures: $600,000. *Unit head:* Dr. Stephen D. McDowell, Director, 850-644-2276, Fax: 850-644-8642, E-mail: steve.mcdowell@cci.fsu.edu. *Application contact:* Natashia Hinson-Turner, Graduate Coordinator, 850-644-8746, Fax: 850-644-8642, E-mail: natashia.turner@cci.fsu.edu.

Fordham University, Graduate School of Business Administration, New York, NY 10023. Offers accounting (MBA); communications and media management (MBA); executive business administration (EMBA); finance (MBA, MS); information systems (MBA, MS); management systems (MBA); marketing (MBA); media management (MS); taxation (MS); taxation and accounting (MTA);); JD/MBA; MBA/MIM; MS/MBA. *Accreditation:* AACSB. Part-time and evening/weekend programs available. *Entrance requirements:* For master's, GMAT, 2 letters of recommendation, resume. Additional exam requirements/recommendations for international students: Required—TOEFL (minimum score 600 paper-based; 250 computer-based; 100 iBT). Electronic applications accepted. *Expenses:* Contact institution.

Franklin University, Marketing and Communications Program, Columbus, OH 43215-5399. Offers MS. Part-time and evening/weekend programs available. *Faculty:* 2 full-time (1 woman), 9 part-time/adjunct (7 women). *Students:* 74 full-time (50 women), 12 part-time (8 women); includes 18 minority (12 African Americans, 4 Asian Americans or Pacific Islanders, 2 Hispanic Americans), 3 international. Average age 34. 98 applicants. In 2009, 59 master's awarded. *Degree requirements:* For master's, thesis or alternative. *Entrance requirements:* For master's, minimum undergraduate GPA of 2.75, undergraduate course work in marketing and statistics. Additional exam requirements/recommendations for international students: Required—TOEFL (minimum score 600 paper-based; 232 computer-based). *Application deadline:* For fall admission, 8/15 priority date for domestic students; for winter admission, 12/20 priority date for domestic students; for spring admission, 4/4 priority date for domestic students. Applications are processed on a rolling basis. Application fee: $30. Electronic applications accepted. *Expenses:* Tuition: Full-time $5880; part-time $490 per credit hour. *Financial support:* Application deadline: 6/30. *Unit head:* Dr. Doug Ross, Program Chair, 614-947-6149. *Application contact:* Graduate Services Office, 614-797-4700, Fax: 614-224-7723, E-mail: gradschl@franklin.edu.

Full Sail University, Internet Marketing Master of Science Program—Online, Winter Park, FL 32792-7437. Offers MS. Postbaccalaureate distance learning degree programs offered.

Gannon University, School of Graduate Studies, College of Engineering and Business, School of Business, Program in Marketing, Erie, PA 16541-0001. Offers Certificate. Part-time

and evening/weekend programs available. *Entrance requirements:* For degree, GMAT. Additional exam requirements/recommendations for international students: Required—TOEFL (minimum score 79 iBT). *Application deadline:* Applications are processed on a rolling basis. Application fee: $25. Electronic applications accepted. *Expenses:* Tuition: Full-time $13,590; part-time $755 per credit. Required fees: $524; $17 per credit. Tuition and fees vary according to course load, degree level, campus/location and program. *Financial support:* Application deadline: 7/1. *Unit head:* Scott Miller, Associate Director, 814-871-7397, E-mail: miller032@gannon.edu. *Application contact:* Kara Morgan, Assistant Director of Graduate Admissions, 814-871-5831, Fax: 814-871-5827, E-mail: graduate@gannon.edu.

George Fox University, School of Business, Newberg, OR 97132-2697. Offers finance (MBA); management (DBA); management/general (MBA); marketing (DBA); organizational strategy (MBA); strategic human resource management (MBA). MBA offered in part-time and full-time formats. Also offered in Portland, OR and Boise, ID. Part-time and evening/weekend programs available. Postbaccalaureate distance learning degree programs offered (minimal on-campus study). *Faculty:* 15 full-time (5 women), 7 part-time/adjunct (0 women). *Students:* 14 full-time (3 women), 223 part-time (77 women); includes 28 minority (7 African Americans, 3 American Indian/Alaska Native, 9 Asian Americans or Pacific Islanders, 9 Hispanic Americans), 2 international. Average age 38. 88 applicants, 86% accepted, 63 enrolled. In 2009, 66 master's, 2 doctorates awarded. *Degree requirements:* For master's, capstone project; for doctorate, credit-applied research project. *Entrance requirements:* For master's, resume (5 years professional experience required); 3 professional references; interview; financial e-learning course; for doctorate, GRE or GMAT, resume; personal mission statement; academic research writing sample; official transcript from each college/university attended; three professional references. Additional exam requirements/recommendations for international students: Required—TOEFL (minimum score 577 paper-based; 233 computer-based; 90 iBT), or IELTS (minimum score 7). *Application deadline:* For fall admission, 8/1 for domestic and international students; for spring admission, 12/1 for domestic and international students. Applications are processed on a rolling basis. Application fee: $40. Electronic applications accepted. *Expenses:* Contact institution. *Financial support:* In 2009–10, 2 students received support. Applicants required to submit FAFSA. *Unit head:* Dr. Ken Armstrong, Professor of Management and Dean, School of Management, 800-631-0921. *Application contact:* Robin Halverson, Admissions Counselor, 800-493-4937, Fax: 503-554-6111, E-mail: mba@georgefox.edu.

The George Washington University, School of Business, Department of Marketing, Washington, DC 20052. Offers MBA, PhD. Part-time and evening/weekend programs available. *Degree requirements:* For doctorate, thesis/dissertation. *Entrance requirements:* For master's, GMAT; for doctorate, GMAT or GRE. Additional exam requirements/recommendations for international students: Required—TOEFL. *Faculty research:* Strategic marketing, marketing and public policy, marketing management.

Georgia Institute of Technology, Graduate Studies and Research, College of Management, Program in Business Administration, Atlanta, GA 30332-0001. Offers accounting (MBA); e-commerce (Certificate); engineering entrepreneurship (MBA); entrepreneurship (Certificate); finance (MBA); information technology management (MBA); international business (MBA, Certificate); management of technology (Certificate); marketing (MBA); operations management (MBA); organizational behavior (MBA); strategic management (MBA). *Accreditation:* AACSB.

Georgia Institute of Technology, Graduate Studies and Research, College of Management, Program in Management, Atlanta, GA 30332-0001. Offers accounting (PhD); finance (PhD); information technology management (PhD); marketing (PhD); operations management (PhD); organizational behavior (PhD); quantitative and computational finance (MS); strategic management (PhD). *Accreditation:* AACSB. *Degree requirements:* For doctorate, comprehensive exam, thesis/dissertation, oral exams. *Entrance requirements:* For master's and doctorate, GMAT. Additional exam requirements/recommendations for international students: Required—TOEFL. *Faculty research:* MIS, management of technology, international business, entrepreneurship, operations management.

Georgia State University, J. Mack Robinson College of Business, Department of Marketing, Atlanta, GA 30302-3083. Offers MBA, MS, PhD. Part-time and evening/weekend programs available. Terminal master's awarded for partial completion of doctoral program. *Degree requirements:* For doctorate, thesis/dissertation. *Entrance requirements:* For master's and doctorate, GMAT. Additional exam requirements/recommendations for international students: Required—TOEFL (minimum score 610 paper-based; 255 computer-based; 101 iBT). Electronic applications accepted. *Faculty research:* Business marketing; sales and sales management; international.

Golden Gate University, Ageno School of Business, San Francisco, CA 94105-2968. Offers accounting (MBA); business administration (EMBA, MBA, PMBA, DBA); finance (MBA, MS, Certificate); financial planning (MS, Certificate); human resource management (MBA, MS); human resources management (Certificate); information systems (MS); information technology (MBA); information technology management (Certificate); integrated marketing and communications (MS, Certificate); international business (MBA); management (MBA); marketing (MBA, MS, Certificate); operations management (Certificate); psychology (MA, Certificate); public relations (MS, Certificate); JD/MBA. Part-time and evening/weekend programs available. *Faculty:* 16 full-time (4 women), 241 part-time/adjunct (72 women). *Students:* 380 full-time (193 women), 750 part-time (414 women); includes 480 minority (98 African Americans, 2 American Indian/Alaska Native, 298 Asian Americans or Pacific Islanders, 82 Hispanic Americans), 166 international. Average age 33. 681 applicants, 78% accepted, 270 enrolled. In 2009, 550 master's, 13 doctorates awarded. *Degree requirements:* For doctorate, thesis/dissertation. *Entrance requirements:* For master's, GMAT (MBA), minimum GPA of 2.5 (MS). Additional exam requirements/recommendations for international students: Required—TOEFL. *Application deadline:* For fall admission, 5/15 for international students; for winter admission, 1/15 for international students; for spring admission, 9/15 for international students. Applications are processed on a rolling basis. Application fee: $70 ($110 for international students). Electronic applications accepted. *Expenses:* Contact institution. *Financial support:* Career-related internships or fieldwork, Federal Work-Study, institutionally sponsored loans, and scholarships/grants available. Support available to part-time students. Financial award applicants required to submit FAFSA. *Unit head:* Terry Connelly, Dean, 415-442-6519, Fax: 415-442-5369. *Application contact:* Angela Melero, Enrollment Services, 415-442-7800, Fax: 415-442-7807, E-mail: info@ggu.edu.

Goldey-Beacom College, Graduate Program, Wilmington, DE 19808-1999. Offers business administration (MBA); finance (MS); financial management (MBA); human resource management (MBA); information technology (MBA); international business management (MBA); management (MM); marketing management (MBA); taxation (MBA, MS). *Accreditation:* ACBSP. Part-time and evening/weekend programs available. *Faculty:* 20 full-time (8 women), 28 part-time/adjunct (10 women). *Students:* 38 full-time (18 women), 486 part-time (184 women); includes 350 minority (38 African Americans, 300 Asian Americans or Pacific Islanders, 12 Hispanic Americans). Average age 27. In 2009, 130 master's awarded. *Entrance requirements:* For master's, GMAT, MAT, GRE, minimum GPA of 3.0. Additional exam requirements/recommendations for international students: Required—TOEFL (minimum score 65 computer-based); Recommended—IELTS (minimum score 5). *Application deadline:* Applications are processed on a rolling basis. Electronic applications accepted. *Expenses:* Tuition: Full-time $14,166; part-time $787 per credit. Required fees: $180; $10 per credit. *Financial support:* In 2009–10, 486 students received support. Scholarships/grants available. Support available to part-time students. Financial award application deadline: 4/1; financial award applicants required to submit FAFSA. *Unit head:* Larry W. Eby, Director of Admissions, 302-225-6289, Fax: 302-996-5408, E-mail: ebylw@gbc.edu. *Application contact:* Ashley E. Mashington, Graduate Admissions Representative, 302-225-6259, Fax: 302-996-5408, E-mail: mashina@gbc.edu.

Grand Canyon University, College of Business, Phoenix, AZ 85017-1097. Offers accounting (MBA); executive fire service leadership (MS); finance (MBA); general management (MBA); health systems management (MBA); leadership (MBA, MS); management of information system (MBA); marketing (MBA); six sigma (MBA). *Accreditation:* ACBSP. Part-time and evening/weekend programs available. Postbaccalaureate distance learning degree programs offered (no on-campus study). *Entrance requirements:* For master's, equivalent of two years full-time professional work experience. Additional exam requirements/recommendations for international students: Required—TOEFL (minimum score 575 paper-based; 233 computer-based; 90 iBT), IELTS (minimum score 7). Electronic applications accepted.

Harvard University, Harvard Business School, Doctoral Programs in Management, Boston, MA 02163. Offers accounting and management (DBA); business economics (PhD); health policy management (PhD); management (DBA); marketing (DBA); organizational behavior (PhD); science, technology and management (PhD); strategy (DBA); technology and operations management (DBA). *Degree requirements:* For doctorate, comprehensive exam (for some programs), thesis/dissertation. *Entrance requirements:* For doctorate, GRE General Test or GMAT. Additional exam requirements/recommendations for international students: Required—TOEFL. *Expenses:* Tuition: Full-time $33,696. Required fees: $1126. Full-time tuition and fees vary according to program.

Hawai'i Pacific University, College of Business Administration, Honolulu, HI 96813. Offers accounting/CPA (MBA); e-business (MBA); economics (MBA); finance (MBA); human resource management (MA, MBA); information systems (MBA, MSIS), including knowledge management (MSIS), software engineering (MSIS), telecommunications security (MSIS); international business (MBA); management (MBA); marketing (MBA); organizational change (MA, MBA); travel industry management (MBA). Part-time and evening/weekend programs available. *Faculty:* 15 full-time (5 women), 11 part-time/adjunct (4 women). *Students:* 206 full-time (107 women), 197 part-time (105 women); includes 136 minority (18 African Americans, 3 American Indian/Alaska Native, 98 Asian Americans or Pacific Islanders, 17 Hispanic Americans), 151 international. Average age 30. 235 applicants, 90% accepted, 127 enrolled. In 2009, 141 master's awarded. *Degree requirements:* For master's, thesis. *Entrance requirements:* For master's, GMAT. Additional exam requirements/recommendations for international students: Recommended—TOEFL (minimum score 550 paper-based; 213 computer-based; 80 iBT), TWE (minimum score 5). *Application deadline:* For fall admission, 2/15 priority date for domestic students; for spring admission, 10/15 priority date for domestic students. Applications are processed on a rolling basis. Application fee: $50. Electronic applications accepted. *Expenses:* Tuition: Full-time $12,600; part-time $700 per credit hour. Tuition and fees vary according to program. *Financial support:* In 2009–10, 164 students received support; research assistantships, career-related internships or fieldwork, Federal Work-Study, scholarships/grants, and unspecified assistantships available. Support available to part-time students. Financial award application deadline: 3/1; financial award applicants required to submit FAFSA. *Faculty research:* Statistical control process as used by management, studies in comparative cross-cultural management styles, not-for-profit management. *Unit head:* Dr. Aytun Ozturk, Dean, 808-544-9301, Fax: 808-544-0283, E-mail: uozturk@hpu.edu. *Application contact:* Danny Lam, Assistant Director of Graduate Admissions, 808-544-1135, Fax: 808-544-0280, E-mail: graduate@hpu.edu.

See Close-Up on page 251.

HEC Montreal, School of Business Administration, Master of Science Programs in Administration, Program in Marketing, Montréal, QC H3T 2A7, Canada. Offers M Sc. All courses are given in French. Part-time programs available. *Students:* 70 full-time (41 women), 11 part-time (9 women). 83 applicants, 64% accepted, 24 enrolled. In 2009, 32 master's awarded. *Degree requirements:* For master's, one foreign language, thesis. *Application deadline:* For fall admission, 3/15 for domestic and international students; for winter admission, 9/15 for domestic and international students. Application fee: $77 Canadian dollars. Electronic applications accepted. Tuition and fees charges are reported in Canadian dollars. *Expenses:* Tuition, area resident: Part-time $65.60 Canadian dollars per credit. Tuition, state resident: full-time $2361.60 Canadian dollars; part-time $183.36 Canadian dollars per credit. Tuition, nonresident: full-time $6601 Canadian dollars; part-time $448.13 Canadian dollars per credit. International tuition: $16,132.68 Canadian dollars full-time. Required fees: $1254.15 Canadian dollars; $28.99 Canadian dollars per course. $91.68 Canadian dollars per term. Tuition and fees vary according to degree level and program. *Financial support:* Fellowships, research assistantships, teaching assistantships, scholarships/grants available. Financial award application deadline: 10/2. *Unit head:* Dr. Claude Laurin, Director, 514-340-6485, Fax: 514-340-5690, E-mail: claude.laurin@hec.ca. *Application contact:* Francine Blais, Administrative Director, 514-340-6112, Fax: 514-340-6411, E-mail: francine.blais@hec.ca.

Hofstra University, Frank G. Zarb School of Business, Department of Marketing and International Business, Hempstead, NY 11549. Offers business administration (MBA), including international business, marketing; marketing (MS); marketing research (MS). Part-time and evening/weekend programs available. *Faculty:* 9 full-time (0 women), 1 part-time/adjunct (0 women). *Students:* 52 full-time (28 women), 38 part-time (21 women); includes 9 minority (2 African Americans, 3 Asian Americans or Pacific Islanders, 4 Hispanic Americans), 40 international. Average age 27. 114 applicants, 71% accepted, 26 enrolled. In 2009, 29 master's awarded. *Degree requirements:* For master's, capstone course (MBA), thesis (MS). *Entrance requirements:* For master's, GMAT or GRE, 2 letters of recommendation, resume. Additional exam requirements/recommendations for international students: Required—TOEFL (minimum score 550 paper-based; 213 computer-based; 80 iBT); Recommended—IELTS (minimum score 6). *Application deadline:* Applications are processed on a rolling basis. Application fee: $60. Electronic applications accepted. *Expenses:* Contact institution. *Financial support:* In 2009–10, 24 students received support, including 21 fellowships with full and partial tuition reimbursements available (averaging $9,582 per year), 2 research assistantships with full and partial tuition reimbursements available (averaging $14,187 per year); career-related internships or fieldwork, Federal Work-Study, institutionally sponsored loans, scholarships/grants, tuition waivers (full and partial), and unspecified assistantships also available. Support available to part-time students. Financial award applicants required to submit FAFSA. *Faculty research:* Outsourcing, global alliances, retailing, web marketing, cross-cultural age research. *Unit head:* Dr. Benny Barak, Chairperson, 516-463-5707, Fax: 516-463-4834, E-mail: mktbzb@hofstra.edu. *Application contact:* Carol Drummer, Dean of Graduate Admissions, 516-463-4876, Fax: 516-463-4664, E-mail: gradstudent@hofstra.edu.

Holy Names University, Graduate Division, Department of Business, Oakland, CA 94619-1699. Offers energy and environment management (MBA); finance (MBA); management and leadership (MBA); marketing (MBA); sports management (MBA). Part-time and evening/weekend programs available. *Entrance requirements:* For master's, minimum undergraduate GPA of 2.6 overall, 3.0 in major. Additional exam requirements/recommendations for international students: Required—TOEFL (minimum score 550 paper-based; 213 computer-based; 80 iBT). *Faculty research:* Business ethics, sustainable economics, accounting models, cross-cultural management, diversity in organizations.

Hood College, Graduate School, Department of Economics and Management, Frederick, MD 21701-8575. Offers accounting (MBA); administration and management (MBA); finance (MBA); human resource management (MBA); information systems (MBA); marketing (MBA); public management (MBA). Part-time and evening/weekend programs available. *Faculty:* 5 full-time (1 woman), 9 part-time/adjunct (1 woman). *Students:* 21 full-time (16 women), 166 part-time (85 women); includes 33 minority (18 African Americans, 8 Asian Americans or Pacific Islanders, 7 Hispanic Americans), 15 international. Average age 32. 47 applicants, 87% accepted, 32 enrolled. In 2009, 31 master's awarded. *Degree requirements:* For master's, capstone/final research project. *Entrance requirements:* For master's, minimum GPA of 2.75, resume, letters of recommendation. *Application deadline:* For fall admission, 7/15 for domestic and international students; for spring admission, 12/15 for domestic and international students. Applications are processed on a rolling basis. Application fee: $35. Electronic applications accepted. *Expenses:* Tuition: Full-time $6480; part-time $360 per credit. Required fees: $100; $50 per term. *Financial support:* Applicants required to submit FAFSA. *Faculty research:* Corporate strategy and sustainable competitive advantages, business ethics, entrepreneurship, investments management, economic development. *Unit head:* Dr. Anita Jose, Program Director, 301-696-3691, Fax: 301-696-3597, E-mail: jose@hood.edu. *Application contact:* Dr. Allen P. Flora, Dean of Graduate School, 301-696-3811, Fax: 301-696-3597, E-mail: gofurther@hood.edu.

Marketing

Howard University, School of Business, Graduate Programs in Business, Washington, DC 20059-0002. Offers accounting (MBA); entrepreneurship (MBA); finance (MBA); general management (MBA); human resources management (MBA); information systems (MBA); international business (MBA); marketing (MBA); supply chain management (MBA); JD/MBA. *Accreditation:* AACSB. Part-time and evening/weekend programs available. Postbaccalaureate distance learning degree programs offered (no on-campus study). *Entrance requirements:* For master's, GMAT, minimum 1 year post undergraduate work experience, resume, 3 letters of recommendation, advanced college algebra. Additional exam requirements/recommendations for international students: Required—TOEFL. *Faculty research:* Marketing research in multi-ethnic populations, U.S. trade policies and international relations, risk management (finance).

Hult International Business School, Program in Business Administration—Hult London Campus, London, MA WC 1B 4JP, United Kingdom. Offers entrepreneurship (MBA); international business (MBA); international finance (MBA); marketing (MBA). Part-time programs available. *Degree requirements:* For master's, comprehensive exam, thesis, internship. *Entrance requirements:* Additional exam requirements/recommendations for international students: Required—TOEFL (minimum score 580 paper-based; 237 computer-based), TWE (minimum score 5). Electronic applications accepted.

Illinois Institute of Technology, Stuart School of Business, Program in Business Administration, Chicago, IL 60616-3793. Offers financial management (MBA); innovation and emerging enterprises (MBA); management science (MBA); marketing (MBA); sustainability (MBA); JD/MBA; MBA/MS. *Accreditation:* AACSB. Part-time and evening/weekend programs available. *Faculty:* 14 full-time (2 women), 3 part-time/adjunct (all women). *Students:* 71 full-time (28 women), 45 part-time (18 women); includes 8 minority (4 African Americans, 4 Asian Americans or Pacific Islanders), 69 international. Average age 29. 274 applicants, 50% accepted, 33 enrolled. In 2009, 48 master's, 6 other advanced degrees awarded. *Entrance requirements:* For master's, GMAT. Additional exam requirements/recommendations for international students: Required—TOEFL (minimum score 600 paper-based; 250 computer-based; 90 iBT). *Application deadline:* For fall admission, 8/1 for domestic students, 5/1 for international students; for spring admission, 12/15 for domestic students, 10/15 for international students. Applications are processed on a rolling basis. Application fee: $75. Electronic applications accepted. *Expenses:* Contact institution. *Financial support:* Career-related internships or fieldwork, Federal Work-Study, institutionally sponsored loans, scholarships/grants, traineeships, health care benefits, and tuition waivers (partial) available. Support available to part-time students. Financial award applicants required to submit FAFSA. *Faculty research:* Global management and marketing strategy, technological innovation, management science, financial management, knowledge management. *Unit head:* M. Krishna Erramilli, Interim Director, 312-906-6573, Fax: 312-906-6549. *Application contact:* M. Krishna Erramilli, Interim Director, 312-906-6573, Fax: 312-906-6549.

Illinois Institute of Technology, Stuart School of Business, Program in Marketing Communication, Chicago, IL 60616-3793. Offers MS, MBA/MS. Part-time and evening/weekend programs available. *Faculty:* 2 full-time (0 women), 5 part-time/adjunct (2 women). *Students:* 40 full-time (28 women), 9 part-time (6 women); includes 3 minority (1 Asian American or Pacific Islander, 2 Hispanic Americans), 42 international. Average age 24. 157 applicants, 69% accepted, 28 enrolled. In 2009, 17 master's awarded. *Entrance requirements:* For master's, GMAT or GRE General Test. Additional exam requirements/recommendations for international students: Required—TOEFL (minimum score 575 paper-based; 90 iBT). *Application deadline:* For fall admission, 8/1 for domestic students, 5/1 for international students; for spring admission, 12/15 for domestic students, 10/15 for international students. Applications are processed on a rolling basis. Application fee: $75. Electronic applications accepted. *Expenses:* Contact institution. *Financial support:* Career-related internships or fieldwork, Federal Work-Study, institutionally sponsored loans, scholarships/grants, traineeships, health care benefits, and tuition waivers (partial) available. Support available to part-time students. Financial award applicants required to submit FAFSA. *Unit head:* Thomas Anderson, Associate Dean, 312-906-6525, Fax: 312-906-6549, E-mail: anderson@stuart.iit.edu. *Application contact:* Thomas Anderson, Associate Dean, 312-906-6525, Fax: 312-906-6549, E-mail: anderson@stuart.iit.edu.

Indiana Tech, Program in Business Administration, Fort Wayne, IN 46803-1297. Offers accounting (MBA); health care administration (MBA); human resources (MBA); management (MBA); marketing (MBA). Part-time and evening/weekend programs available. Postbaccalaureate distance learning degree programs offered (no on-campus study). *Students:* 202 full-time (97 women), 37 part-time (18 women); includes 60 minority (45 African Americans, 2 American Indian/Alaska Native, 7 Asian Americans or Pacific Islanders, 6 Hispanic Americans), 5 international. Average age 38. *Entrance requirements:* For master's, GMAT, minimum undergraduate GPA of 2.5, 3 letters of recommendation. *Application deadline:* Applications are processed on a rolling basis. Application fee: $25. Electronic applications accepted. *Expenses:* Tuition: Full-time $5160; part-time $430 per credit hour. Tuition and fees vary according to degree level and program. *Financial support:* Applicants required to submit FAFSA. *Unit head:* Dr. Andrew Nwanne, Associate Dean of College of Professional Studies, 260-422-5561 Ext. 2214, E-mail: ainwanne@indianatech.edu. *Application contact:* Steve Herendeen, Manager of Campus Development and Support, 260-422-5561 Ext. 2121, E-mail: saherendeen@indianatech.edu.

Instituto Tecnologico de Santo Domingo, Graduate School, Santo Domingo, Dominican Republic. Offers applied linguistics (MA); construction administration (M Mgmt); corporate finance (M Mgmt); education (M Ed); engineering (M Eng), including data telecommunications, industrial engineering, logistics and supply chain, maintenance engineering, sanitary and environmental engineering, structural engineering; environmental science (M En S), including environmental education, environmental management, marine and coastal ecosystems, natural resources management; family therapy (MA); food science and technology (MS); human development (MA); human resources administration (M Mgmt); international business (M Mgmt); labor risks (M Mgmt); management (M Mgmt); marketing (M Mgmt); mathematics (MS); organizational development (M Mgmt); planning and taxation (M Mgmt); psychology (MA); social science (M Ed); upper management (M Mgmt). *Entrance requirements:* For master's, birth certificate, minimum GPA of 2.0.

Instituto Tecnológico y de Estudios Superiores de Monterrey, Campus Central de Veracruz, Graduate Programs, Córdoba, Mexico. Offers administration (MA); administration of information technologies (MTI); computer sciences (MCC); education (MEE); educational institution administration (MAD); educational technology (MTE); electronic commerce (MCE); finance (MAF); humanistic studies (MEH); international business for Latin America (MNL); marketing (MMT); science (MCP); technology management (MTT). Part-time and evening/weekend programs available. Postbaccalaureate distance learning degree programs offered (minimal on-campus study). *Degree requirements:* For master's, thesis (for some programs). *Entrance requirements:* For master's, PAEP College Board. Electronic applications accepted.

Instituto Tecnológico y de Estudios Superiores de Monterrey, Campus Ciudad Obregón, Program in Marketing Technology, Ciudad Obregón, Mexico. Offers MMT.

Instituto Tecnológico y de Estudios Superiores de Monterrey, Campus Cuernavaca, Programs in Business Administration, Temixco, Mexico. Offers finance (MA); human resources management (MA); international business (MA); marketing (MA).

Instituto Tecnológico y de Estudios Superiores de Monterrey, Campus Estado de México, Professional and Graduate Division, Estado de Mexico, Mexico. Offers administration of information technologies (MITA); architecture (M Arch); business administration (GMBA, MBA); computer sciences (MCS, PhD); education (M Ed); educational institution administration (MAD); educational technology and innovation (PhD); electronic commerce (MEC); environmental systems (MS); finance (MAF); humanistic studies (MHS); information sciences and knowledge management (MISKM); information systems (MS); manufacturing systems (MS); marketing (MEM); quality systems and productivity (MS); science and materials engineering (PhD); telecommunications management (MTM). Part-time programs available. Postbaccalaureate distance learning degree programs offered (minimal on-campus study). *Degree requirements:*

For master's, one foreign language, thesis (for some programs); for doctorate, one foreign language, thesis/dissertation. *Entrance requirements:* For master's, E-PAEP 500, interview; for doctorate, E-PAEP 500, research proposal. Additional exam requirements/recommendations for international students: Required—TOEFL (minimum score 550 paper-based). *Faculty research:* Surface treatments by plasmas, mechanical properties, robotics, graphical computing, mechatronics security protocols.

Instituto Tecnológico y de Estudios Superiores de Monterrey, Campus Monterrey, Graduate School of Business Administration and Leadership, Program in Business Administration, Monterrey, Mexico. Offers business administration (MA, MBA); finance (M Sc); international business (M Sc); marketing (M Sc). *Accreditation:* AACSB. Part-time programs available. *Degree requirements:* For master's, one foreign language, thesis. *Entrance requirements:* For master's, GMAT. Additional exam requirements/recommendations for international students: Required—TOEFL. *Faculty research:* Technology management, quality management, organizational theory and behavior.

Inter American University of Puerto Rico, Aguadilla Campus, Graduate School, Aguadilla, PR 00605. Offers accounting (MBA); business information systems (MBA); counseling psychology with an emphasis in family (MS); criminal justice (MA); educative management and leadership (MA); elementary education (MA); finance (MBA); human resources (MBA); industrial management (MBA); marketing (MBA). Part-time and evening/weekend programs available. *Degree requirements:* For master's, comprehensive exam. *Entrance requirements:* For master's, EXADEP, 2 letters of recommendation, minimum GPA of 2.5. Electronic applications accepted.

Inter American University of Puerto Rico, Metropolitan Campus, Graduate Programs, Program in Marketing, San Juan, PR 00919-1293. Offers MBA. *Degree requirements:* For master's, comprehensive exam. *Entrance requirements:* For master's, GRE or EXADEP, interview. Electronic applications accepted.

Inter American University of Puerto Rico, Ponce Campus, Graduate School, Mercedita, PR 00715-1602. Offers accounting (MBA); biology (M Ed); chemistry (M Ed); criminal justice (MA); elementary education (M Ed); English as a Second Language (M Ed); finance (MBA); history (M Ed); human resources (MBA); marketing (MBA); mathematics (M Ed); Spanish (M Ed). *Entrance requirements:* For master's, minimum GPA of 2.5.

Inter American University of Puerto Rico, San Germán Campus, Graduate Studies Center, Program in Business Administration, San Germán, PR 00683-5008. Offers accounting (MBA); finance (MBA); human resources (PhD); human resources management (MBA); industrial management (MBA); international business (PhD); management information systems (MBA); marketing management (MBA). Part-time and evening/weekend programs available. *Degree requirements:* For master's, comprehensive exam. *Entrance requirements:* For master's, GRE General Test or EXADEP, minimum GPA of 3.0.

International University in Geneva, Master of Arts in Media and Communication Program, Geneva, Switzerland. Offers luxury management (MA); marketing (MA). *Degree requirements:* For master's, comprehensive exam. *Entrance requirements:* Additional exam requirements/recommendations for international students: Required—TOEFL. Electronic applications accepted.

International University in Geneva, Master of Business Administration Program, Geneva, Switzerland. Offers finance (MBA); international business (MIB); investment management (MBA); luxury management (MBA); marketing (MBA); wealth management (MBA). *Accreditation:* ACBSP. Part-time and evening/weekend programs available. *Degree requirements:* For master's, comprehensive exam. *Entrance requirements:* For master's, GMAT. Additional exam requirements/recommendations for international students: Required—TOEFL. Electronic applications accepted.

The International University of Monaco, Graduate Programs, Monte Carlo, Monaco. Offers entrepreneurship (EMBA, MBA); financial engineering (M Sc); hedge fund and private equity (M Sc); international marketing (EMBA, MBA); international wealth management (M Sc); luxury goods and services (EMBA, M Sc, MBA); wealth and asset management (EMBA, MBA). Part-time programs available. *Degree requirements:* For master's, comprehensive exam (for some programs), applied research project. *Entrance requirements:* Additional exam requirements/recommendations for international students: Required—TOEFL (minimum score 550 paper-based; 213 computer-based), IELTS. Electronic applications accepted. *Faculty research:* Gaming, leadership, disintermediation.

Iona College, Hagan School of Business, Department of Marketing and International Business, New Rochelle, NY 10801-1890. Offers international business (PMC); marketing (MBA). Part-time and evening/weekend programs available. *Faculty:* 4 full-time (2 women), 3 part-time/adjunct (0 women). *Students:* 13 full-time (9 women), 41 part-time (26 women); includes 8 minority (4 African Americans, 1 Asian American or Pacific Islander, 3 Hispanic Americans), 1 international. Average age 29. 20 applicants, 90% accepted, 13 enrolled. In 2009, 14 master's, 38 other advanced degrees awarded. *Entrance requirements:* For master's, GMAT, 2 letters of recommendation; for PMC, GMAT. Additional exam requirements/recommendations for international students: Required—TOEFL (minimum score 550 paper-based; 213 computer-based). *Application deadline:* Applications are processed on a rolling basis. Application fee: $50. Electronic applications accepted. *Expenses:* Contact institution. *Financial support:* Scholarships/grants, tuition waivers (partial), and unspecified assistantships available. Support available to part-time students. Financial award application deadline: 4/15; financial award applicants required to submit FAFSA. *Faculty research:* Business ethics, international retailing, mega-marketing, consumer behavior and consumer confidence. *Unit head:* Dr. Frederica E. Rudell, Chair, 914-637-2748, E-mail: frudell@iona.edu. *Application contact:* Jude Fleurismond, Director of MBA Admissions, 914-633-2289, Fax: 914-637-2708, E-mail: jfleurismond@iona.edu.

The Johns Hopkins University, Carey Business School, Marketing Programs, Baltimore, MD 21218-2699. Offers MS. Part-time and evening/weekend programs available. *Faculty:* 29 full-time (6 women), 135 part-time/adjunct (29 women). *Students:* 53 full-time (43 women), 94 part-time (68 women); includes 30 minority (21 African Americans, 3 Asian Americans or Pacific Islanders, 6 Hispanic Americans), 47 international. Average age 30. 92 applicants, 55% accepted, 40 enrolled. In 2009, 30 master's awarded. *Degree requirements:* For master's, research project (MS). *Entrance requirements:* For master's, minimum GPA of 3.0, resume, work experience, two letters of recommendation. Additional exam requirements/recommendations for international students: Required—TOEFL (minimum score 600 paper-based; 250 computer-based; 100 iBT). *Application deadline:* For fall admission, 5/1 for international students; for spring admission, 10/15 for international students. Applications are processed on a rolling basis. Application fee: $100. Electronic applications accepted. *Financial support:* Scholarships/grants available. Support available to part-time students. Financial award application deadline: 4/1; financial award applicants required to submit FAFSA. *Faculty research:* Consumer behavior and advertising. *Unit head:* Dr. Dipankar Chakravarti, Vice Dean of Programs, 410-516-8561, Fax: 410-516-0233, E-mail: dipankar.chakravarti@jhu.edu. *Application contact:* Robin Greenberg, Admissions Coordinator, 410-516-4234, Fax: 410-516-0826, E-mail: carey.admissions@jhu.edu.

Johnson & Wales University, The Alan Shawn Feinstein Graduate School, MBA Program in Global Business Leadership, Providence, RI 02903-3703. Offers accounting (MBA); enhanced accounting (MBA); financial management (MBA); international trade (MBA); marketing (MBA); organizational leadership (MBA). Part-time programs available. *Faculty:* 13 full-time (3 women), 17 part-time/adjunct (4 women). *Students:* 523 full-time (272 women), 162 part-time (85 women); includes 29 minority (18 African Americans, 4 Asian Americans or Pacific Islanders, 7 Hispanic Americans), 385 international. Average age 27. 330 applicants, 82% accepted, 151 enrolled. In 2009, 274 master's awarded. *Entrance requirements:* For master's, minimum GPA of 2.75. Additional exam requirements/recommendations for international students: Required—TOEFL, TOEFL (minimum score 550 paper-based; 210 computer-based) or IELTS recommended; Recommended—TWE. *Application deadline:* For fall admission, 8/15 priority date for domestic students, 6/28 priority date for international students; for winter admission, 11/10 priority date for domestic students, 9/20 priority date for international students; for spring admission, 2/5 priority date for domestic students, 12/20 priority date for international students.

Applications are processed on a rolling basis. *Expenses:* Required fees: $340 per quarter hour. *Financial support:* Tuition waivers (partial) and unspecified assistantships available. Support available to part-time students. Financial award application deadline: 5/1. *Faculty research:* International banking, global economy, international trade, cultural differences. *Unit head:* Dr. Frank Pontarelli, Dean, 401-598-1333, Fax: 401-598-1125. *Application contact:* Dr. Allan G. Freedman, Director of Graduate Admissions, 401-598-1015, Fax: 401-598-1286, E-mail: gradadm@jwu.edu.

Johnson & Wales University, The Alan Shawn Feinstein Graduate School, MBA Program in Hospitality, Providence, RI 02903-3703. Offers event leadership (MBA); marketing (MBA). Part-time programs available. *Faculty:* 13 full-time (3 women), 17 part-time/adjunct (4 women). *Students:* 217 full-time (144 women), 25 part-time (15 women); includes 11 minority (7 African Americans, 1 Asian American or Pacific Islander, 3 Hispanic Americans), 186 international. Average age 25. 129 applicants, 80% accepted, 70 enrolled. In 2009, 48 master's awarded. *Entrance requirements:* For master's, minimum GPA of 2.85. Additional exam requirements/recommendations for international students: Required—TOEFL, TOEFL (minimum score 550 paper-based; 210 computer-based; 80 iBT) or IELTS (minimum score 6.5); Recommended—TWE. *Application deadline:* For fall admission, 8/15 priority date for domestic students, 6/28 priority date for international students; for winter admission, 11/10 priority date for domestic students, 9/20 priority date for international students; for spring admission, 2/15 priority date for domestic students, 12/20 priority date for international students. Applications are processed on a rolling basis. Application fee: $0. Electronic applications accepted. *Expenses:* Required fees: $340 per quarter hour. *Financial support:* Tuition waivers (partial) and unspecified assistantships available. Support available to part-time students. Financial award application deadline: 5/1. *Faculty research:* Trade and tourism, hotel marketing, personal budget assessments, international ventures. *Unit head:* Dr. Frank Pontarelli, Dean, 401-598-1333, Fax: 401-598-1125. *Application contact:* Dr. Allan G. Freedman, Director of Graduate Admissions, 401-598-1015, Fax: 401-598-1286, E-mail: gradadm@jwu.edu.

Kansas State University, Graduate School, College of Human Ecology, Department of Apparel, Textiles, and Interior Design, Manhattan, KS 66506. Offers design (MS); general apparel and textile (MS); marketing (MS); merchandising (MS); product development (MS). *Faculty:* 10 full-time (8 women), 1 (woman) part-time/adjunct. *Students:* 7 full-time (5 women), 15 part-time (12 women); includes 3 minority (1 African American, 1 Asian American or Pacific Islander, 1 Hispanic American). Average age 29. 13 applicants, 85% accepted, 7 enrolled. In 2009, 3 master's awarded. *Degree requirements:* For master's, thesis optional, residency. *Entrance requirements:* For master's, GRE General Test, minimum undergraduate GPA of 3.0. Additional exam requirements/recommendations for international students: Required—TOEFL (minimum score 600 paper-based; 250 computer-based). *Application deadline:* For fall admission, 2/1 priority date for domestic and international students; for spring admission, 8/1 priority date for domestic and international students. Applications are processed on a rolling basis. Application fee: $40 ($55 for international students). Electronic applications accepted. *Financial support:* In 2009–10, 3 research assistantships (averaging $14,460 per year), 5 teaching assistantships with full tuition reimbursements (averaging $10,590 per year) were awarded; career-related internships or fieldwork, Federal Work-Study, institutionally sponsored loans, and scholarships/grants also available. Support available to part-time students. Financial award application deadline: 3/1; financial award applicants required to submit FAFSA. *Faculty research:* Apparel marketing and consumer behavior, protective and functional clothing and textiles, social and environmental responsibility, apparel design, new product development. Total annual research expenditures: $40,303. *Unit head:* Jana Hawley, Head, 785-532-6993, Fax: 785-532-3796, E-mail: hawleyj@ksu.edu. *Application contact:* Gina Jackson, Application Contact, 785-532-6693, Fax: 785-532-3796, E-mail: gjackson@ksu.edu.

Kaplan University, Davenport Campus, School of Business, Davenport, IA 52807-2095. Offers business administration (MBA); change leadership (MS); entrepreneurship (MBA); finance (MBA); health care management (MBA, MS); human resource (MBA); international business (MBA); management (MS); marketing (MBA); project management (MBA, MS); supply chain management and logistics (MBA, MS). Part-time and evening/weekend programs available. Postbaccalaureate distance learning degree programs offered (no on-campus study). *Entrance requirements:* Additional exam requirements/recommendations for international students: Required—TOEFL (minimum score 550 paper-based; 218 computer-based; 80 iBT). Electronic applications accepted.

Keiser University, MBA, Master of Business Administration Program, Fort Lauderdale, FL 33309. Offers international business (MBA); leadership for managers (MBA); marketing (MBA). Part-time programs available. Postbaccalaureate distance learning degree programs offered (minimal on-campus study). *Faculty:* 8 full-time (3 women), 7 part-time/adjunct (2 women). *Students:* 18 full-time (14 women), 83 part-time (51 women); includes 51 minority (30 African Americans, 2 American Indian/Alaska Native, 2 Asian Americans or Pacific Islanders, 17 Hispanic Americans), 1 international. Average age 42. 30 applicants, 77% accepted, 18 enrolled. In 2009, 21 master's awarded. *Entrance requirements:* For master's, minimum GPA of 2.7 from an accredited institution. Additional exam requirements/recommendations for international students: Required—TOEFL. *Application deadline:* Applications are processed on a rolling basis. Application fee: $50. Electronic applications accepted. *Financial support:* In 2009–10, 95 students received support. Federal Work-Study available. Financial award applicants required to submit FAFSA. *Unit head:* Dr. Sara Malmstrom, Dean, 954-318-1620. *Application contact:* Manuel Christiansen, Associate Director of Admissions, 954-318-1620 Ext. 309, E-mail: mchristiansen@keiseruniversity.edu.

Kent State University, Graduate School of Management, Doctoral Program in Marketing, Kent, OH 44242-0001. Offers PhD. *Faculty:* 11 full-time (3 women). *Students:* 8 full-time (7 women); includes 1 minority (Asian American or Pacific Islander), 2 international. Average age 32. 7 applicants, 57% accepted, 3 enrolled. In 2009, 3 doctorates awarded. *Degree requirements:* For doctorate, comprehensive exam, thesis/dissertation, oral defense. *Entrance requirements:* For doctorate, GMAT. Additional exam requirements/recommendations for international students: Required—TOEFL (minimum score 600 paper-based; 250 computer-based; 100 iBT). *Application deadline:* For fall admission, 2/1 for domestic students, 1/1 for international students. Application fee: $30 ($60 for international students). Electronic applications accepted. *Financial support:* In 2009–10, 8 students received support, including 8 teaching assistantships with full tuition reimbursements available (averaging $15,000 per year); fellowships with full tuition reimbursements available, Federal Work-Study also available. Financial award application deadline: 2/1; financial award applicants required to submit FAFSA. *Faculty research:* Advertising effects, satisfaction, international marketing, high-tech marketing, personality and consumer behavior. *Unit head:* Dr. Pamela Grimm, Chair and Associate Professor, 330-672-2170, Fax: 330-672-5006, E-mail: pgrimm@kent.edu. *Application contact:* Felecia A. Urbanek, Coordinator, Graduate Programs, 330-672-2282, Fax: 330-672-7303, E-mail: gradbus@kent.edu.

Kentucky State University, College of Professional Studies, Frankfort, KY 40601. Offers business administration (MBA), including accounting, finance, management, marketing; public administration (MPA), including human resource management, international administration and development, management information systems, nonprofit management; special education (MA). Part-time and evening/weekend programs available. Postbaccalaureate distance learning degree programs offered (minimal on-campus study). *Faculty:* 11 full-time (3 women), 2 part-time/adjunct (both women). *Students:* 79 full-time (51 women), 66 part-time (34 women); includes 88 minority (85 African Americans, 2 Asian Americans or Pacific Islanders, 1 Hispanic American), 4 international. Average age 34. 92 applicants, 75% accepted, 52 enrolled. In 2009, 32 master's awarded. *Degree requirements:* For master's, comprehensive exam, thesis optional. *Entrance requirements:* For master's, GMAT, GRE. Additional exam requirements/recommendations for international students: Required—TOEFL (minimum score 525 paper-based; 173 computer-based). *Application deadline:* For fall admission, 7/1 priority date for domestic students, 4/15 priority date for international students; for spring admission, 11/15 priority date for domestic students, 8/1 priority date for international students. Applications are processed on a rolling basis. Application fee: $30 ($100 for international students). Electronic applications accepted. *Expenses:* Tuition, state resident: full-time $5634; part-time $313 per credit hour. Tuition, nonresident: full-time $14,598; part-time $811 per credit hour. Required fees: $450; $25 per credit hour. *Financial support:* In 2009–10, 113 students received support, including 4 research assistantships (averaging $14,035 per year); career-related internships or fieldwork, scholarships/grants, tuition waivers (partial), and unspecified assistantships also available. Financial award application deadline: 4/15; financial award applicants required to submit FAFSA. *Unit head:* Dr. Gashaw Lake, Dean, College of Professional Studies, 502-597-6105, Fax: 502-597-6715, E-mail: gashaw.lake@kysu.edu. *Application contact:* Cedric Cunningham, Administrative Assistant, Office of Graduate Studies, 502-597-6536, E-mail: cedric.cunningham@kysu.edu.

Lasell College, Graduate and Professional Studies in Communication, Newton, MA 02466-2709. Offers integrated marketing communication (MSC, Graduate Certificate); public relations (MSC, Graduate Certificate). Part-time and evening/weekend programs available. Postbaccalaureate distance learning degree programs offered (minimal on-campus study). *Faculty:* 3 full-time (all women), 1 part-time/adjunct (0 women). *Students:* 5 full-time (all women), 13 part-time (12 women); includes 3 minority (all African Americans). Average age 29. 19 applicants, 89% accepted, 11 enrolled. *Entrance requirements:* For master's and Graduate Certificate, bachelor's degree from an accredited institution. Additional exam requirements/recommendations for international students: Required—TOEFL (minimum score 550 paper-based; 213 computer-based; 75 iBT) or IELTS. *Application deadline:* For fall admission, 8/31 priority date for domestic students, 6/30 priority date for international students; for spring admission, 12/31 priority date for domestic students, 10/31 priority date for international students. Applications are processed on a rolling basis. Application fee: $40. Electronic applications accepted. *Expenses:* Tuition: Full-time $4890; part-time $525 per credit hour. Required fees: $55 per term. *Financial support:* Available to part-time students. Application deadline: 8/30. *Unit head:* Dr. Joan Dolamore, Dean of Graduate and Professional Studies, 617-243-2485, Fax: 617-243-2450, E-mail: gradinfo@lasell.edu. *Application contact:* Adrienne Franciosi, Director of Graduate Admission, 617-243-2214, Fax: 617-243-2450, E-mail: gradinfo@lasell.edu.

Lasell College, Graduate and Professional Studies in Management, Newton, MA 02466-2709. Offers elder care administration (MSM, Graduate Certificate); elder care marketing (MSM, Graduate Certificate); fundraising management (MSM, Graduate Certificate); human resource management (MSM, Graduate Certificate); management (MSM, Graduate Certificate); marketing (MSM, Graduate Certificate); non-profit management (MSM, Graduate Certificate); project management (MSM, Graduate Certificate). Part-time and evening/weekend programs available. Postbaccalaureate distance learning degree programs offered (no on-campus study). *Faculty:* 2 full-time (both women), 8 part-time/adjunct (6 women). *Students:* 26 full-time (18 women), 85 part-time (60 women); includes 10 African Americans, 4 Asian Americans or Pacific Islanders, 9 Hispanic Americans, 17 international. Average age 31. 55 applicants, 80% accepted, 31 enrolled. In 2009, 31 master's awarded. *Entrance requirements:* For master's and Graduate Certificate, bachelor's degree from an accredited institution. Additional exam requirements/recommendations for international students: Required—TOEFL (minimum score 550 paper-based; 213 computer-based; 75 iBT) or IELTS. *Application deadline:* For fall admission, 8/31 priority date for domestic students, 6/30 priority date for international students; for spring admission, 12/31 priority date for domestic students, 10/31 priority date for international students. Applications are processed on a rolling basis. Application fee: $40. Electronic applications accepted. *Expenses:* Tuition: Full-time $4890; part-time $525 per credit hour. Required fees: $55 per term. *Financial support:* Available to part-time students. Application deadline: 8/31. *Unit head:* Dr. Joan Dolamore, Dean of Graduate and Professional Studies, 617-243-2485, Fax: 617-243-2450, E-mail: gradinfo@lasell.edu. *Application contact:* Adrienne Franciosi, Director of Graduate Admission, 617-243-2214, Fax: 617-243-2450, E-mail: gradinfo@lasell.edu.

La Sierra University, School of Business and Management, Riverside, CA 92515. Offers accounting (MBA); finance (MBA); general management (MBA); human resources management (MBA); leadership, values, and ethics for business and management (Certificate); marketing (MBA). *Degree requirements:* For master's, research project. *Entrance requirements:* For master's, GMAT, minimum GPA of 3.0. Additional exam requirements/recommendations for international students: Required—TOEFL. *Faculty research:* Financial econometrics, institutional assessment and strategic planning, legal issues in management, behavioral finance, content of financial reports.

Lewis University, College of Business, Graduate School of Management, Program in Business Administration, Romeoville, IL 60446. Offers accounting (MBA); custom elective option (MBA); e-business (MBA); finance (MBA); healthcare management (MBA); human resources management (MBA); information security (MBA); international business (MBA); management information systems (MBA); marketing (MBA); project management (MBA); technology and operations management (MBA). Part-time and evening/weekend programs available. *Faculty:* 15 full-time (2 women), 18 part-time/adjunct (4 women). *Students:* 120 full-time (64 women), 222 part-time (103 women); includes 97 minority (62 African Americans, 4 Asian Americans or Pacific Islanders, 31 Hispanic Americans), 9 international. Average age 31. In 2009, 84 master's awarded. *Entrance requirements:* For master's, interview, bachelor's degree, resume, 2 recommendations. Additional exam requirements/recommendations for international students: Required—TOEFL (minimum score 550 paper-based; 213 computer-based). *Application deadline:* For fall admission, 8/15 priority date for domestic students, 5/1 priority date for international students; for spring admission, 11/15 priority date for international students. Applications are processed on a rolling basis. Application fee: $40. Electronic applications accepted. *Expenses:* Tuition: Full-time $6480; part-time $720 per credit. One-time fee: $40. Tuition and fees vary according to course load, degree level and program. *Financial support:* Career-related internships or fieldwork, Federal Work-Study, scholarships/grants, and unspecified assistantships available. Financial award application deadline: 5/1; financial award applicants required to submit FAFSA. *Unit head:* Dr. Maureen Culleeney, Academic Program Director, 815-838-0500 Ext. 5631, E-mail: culleema@lewisu.edu. *Application contact:* Michele King, Director of Admission, 815-838-0500 Ext. 5384, E-mail: gsm@lewisu.edu.

Lindenwood University, Graduate Programs, College of Individualized Education, St. Charles, MO 63301-1695. Offers administration (MSA); business administration (MBA); communications (MA); criminal justice and administration (MS); gerontology (MA); health management (MS); human resource management (MS); information technology (MBA, Certificate); management (MSA); managing information technology (MS); marketing (MSA); writing (MFA). Part-time and evening/weekend programs available. *Faculty:* 15 full-time (8 women), 128 part-time/adjunct (53 women). *Students:* 679 full-time (432 women), 90 part-time (57 women); includes 138 minority (121 African Americans, 2 American Indian/Alaska Native, 5 Asian Americans or Pacific Islanders, 10 Hispanic Americans), 18 international. Average age 34. 223 applicants, 44% accepted, 87 enrolled. In 2009, 478 master's awarded. *Degree requirements:* For master's, thesis (for some programs), 1 colloquium per term. *Entrance requirements:* For master's, interview, minimum GPA of 3.0. Additional exam requirements/recommendations for international students: Required—TOEFL (minimum score 550 paper-based; 213 computer-based; 80 iBT). *Application deadline:* For fall admission, 10/2 priority date for domestic and international students; for winter admission, 1/8 priority date for domestic and international students; for spring admission, 4/8 priority date for domestic and international students. Applications are processed on a rolling basis. Application fee: $30 ($100 for international students). *Expenses:* Tuition: Full-time $12,960; part-time $370 per credit hour. Required fees: $340. One-time fee: $30 full-time. Tuition and fees vary according to course level and course load. *Financial support:* In 2009–10, 631 students received support. Career-related internships or fieldwork, institutionally sponsored loans, tuition waivers (partial), and unspecified assistantships available. Financial award application deadline: 6/30; financial award applicants required to submit FAFSA. *Unit head:* Dan Kemper, Dean, 636-949-4501, Fax: 636-949-4505, E-mail: dkemper@lindenwood.edu. *Application contact:* Brett Barger, Dean of Evening Admissions and Extension Campuses, 636-949-4934, Fax: 636-949-4109, E-mail: adultadmissions@lindenwood.edu.

Lindenwood University, Graduate Programs, School of Business and Entrepreneurship, St. Charles, MO 63301-1695. Offers accounting (MBA, MS); business administration (MBA);

Marketing

Lindenwood University (continued)

entrepreneurial studies (MBA, MS); finance (MBA, MS); human resource management (MBA); human resources (MS); international business (MBA, MS); management (MBA, MS); management information systems (MBA, MS); marketing (MBA, MS); public management (MBA, MS); sport management (MA). *Accreditation:* ACBSP. Part-time and evening/weekend programs available. *Faculty:* 20 full-time (8 women), 17 part-time/adjunct (5 women). *Students:* 129 full-time (60 women), 138 part-time (61 women); includes 15 minority (11 African Americans, 2 Asian Americans or Pacific Islanders, 2 Hispanic Americans), 84 international. Average age 28. 149 applicants, 73 enrolled. In 2009, 142 master's awarded. *Degree requirements:* For master's, comprehensive exam (for some programs), thesis (for some programs). *Entrance requirements:* For master's, interview, minimum GPA of 3.0, letter of recommendation. Additional exam requirements/recommendations for international students: Required—TOEFL (minimum score 550 paper-based; 213 computer-based; 80 iBT). *Application deadline:* For fall admission, 7/30 priority date for domestic students, 9/16 priority date for international students; for winter admission, 12/19 priority date for domestic students, 12/17 priority date for international students; for spring admission, 2/25 priority date for domestic students, 2/11 priority date for international students. Applications are processed on a rolling basis. Application fee: $30 ($100 for international students). Electronic applications accepted. *Expenses:* Tuition: Full-time $12,960; part-time $370 per credit hour. Required fees: $340. One-time fee: $30 full-time. Tuition and fees vary according to course level and course load. *Financial support:* In 2009–10, 209 students received support. Career-related internships or fieldwork, Federal Work-Study, institutionally sponsored loans, and tuition waivers (partial) available. Financial award application deadline: 6/30; financial award applicants required to submit FAFSA. *Unit head:* Ed Morris, Dean of Management, 636-949-4832, E-mail: emorris@lindenwood.edu. *Application contact:* Brett Barger, Dean of Evening Admissions and Extension Campuses, 636-949-4934, Fax: 636-949-4109, E-mail: adultadmissions@lindenwood.edu.

Long Island University, C.W. Post Campus, College of Management, School of Business, Brookville, NY 11548-1300. Offers accounting and taxation (Certificate); business administration (Certificate); finance (MBA, Certificate); general business administration (MBA); international business (MBA, Certificate); management (MBA, Certificate); management information systems (MBA, Certificate); marketing (MBA, Certificate). *Accreditation:* AACSB. Part-time and evening/weekend programs available. *Entrance requirements:* For master's, GMAT, resume, minimum GPA of 3.0, 2 letters of recommendation. Additional exam requirements/recommendations for international students: Required—TOEFL (minimum score 527 paper-based; 197 computer-based). Electronic applications accepted. *Faculty research:* Financial markets, consumer behavior.

Louisiana State University and Agricultural and Mechanical College, Graduate School, E. J. Ourso College of Business, Department of Marketing, Baton Rouge, LA 70803. Offers business administration (PhD), including marketing. Part-time programs available. *Faculty:* 12 full-time (2 women). *Students:* 7 full-time (4 women), 4 part-time (2 women), 5 international. Average age 31. 14 applicants, 0% accepted, 0 enrolled. In 2009, 3 doctorates awarded. *Degree requirements:* For doctorate, thesis/dissertation. *Entrance requirements:* Additional exam requirements/recommendations for international students: Required—TOEFL (minimum score 550 paper-based; 213 computer-based; 79 iBT) or IELTS (minimum score 6.5). *Application deadline:* For fall admission, 1/25 priority date for domestic students, 5/15 for international students; for spring admission, 10/15 for international students. Applications are processed on a rolling basis. Application fee: $50 ($70 for international students). Electronic applications accepted. *Financial support:* In 2009–10, 10 students received support, including 7 teaching assistantships with full and partial tuition reimbursements available (averaging $16,328 per year); fellowships, research assistantships with partial tuition reimbursements available, career-related internships or fieldwork, Federal Work-Study, institutionally sponsored loans, scholarships/grants, health care benefits, and unspecified assistantships also available. Support available to part-time students. Financial award applicants required to submit FAFSA. *Faculty research:* Consumer behavior, marketing strategy, global marketing, e-commerce, branding/brand equity. Total annual research expenditures: $610. *Unit head:* Dr. Alvin C. Burns, Chair, 225-578-8786, Fax: 225-578-8616, E-mail: alburns@lsu.edu. *Application contact:* Dr. Ron Niedrich, Graduate Adviser, 225-578-9068, Fax: 225-578-8616, E-mail: niedrich@lsu.edu.

Louisiana Tech University, Graduate School, College of Business, Department of Marketing, Ruston, LA 71272. Offers MBA, DBA. Part-time programs available. *Degree requirements:* For doctorate, thesis/dissertation. *Entrance requirements:* For master's and doctorate, GMAT.

Loyola University Chicago, Graduate School of Business, Marketing Department, Chicago, IL 60660. Offers integrated marketing communications (MS); marketing (MSIMC). Part-time and evening/weekend programs available. *Entrance requirements:* For master's, GMAT, v. Additional exam requirements/recommendations for international students: Required—TOEFL (minimum score 550 paper-based; 213 computer-based; 80 iBT). Electronic applications accepted. *Expenses:* Contact institution. *Faculty research:* Web performance metrics, new venture marketing strategies over consumption, benefit segmentation strategies.

Loyola University Maryland, Graduate Programs, Sellinger School of Business and Management, Program in Business Administration, Baltimore, MD 21210-2699. Offers accounting (MBA); finance (MBA); general business (MBA); international business (MBA); management (MBA); management information systems (MBA); marketing (MBA). *Accreditation:* AACSB. Part-time and evening/weekend programs available. *Entrance requirements:* For master's, GMAT. Additional exam requirements/recommendations for international students: Required—TOEFL (minimum score 550 paper-based; 213 computer-based).

Lynn University, College of Business and Management, Boca Raton, FL 33431-5598. Offers aviation management (MBA); financial valuation and investment management (MBA); hospitality management (MBA); international business (MBA); marketing (MBA); mass communication and media management (MBA); sports and athletics administration (MBA). Part-time and evening/weekend programs available. Postbaccalaureate distance learning degree programs offered. *Degree requirements:* For master's, project. *Entrance requirements:* For master's, GMAT or GRE, minimum undergraduate GPA of 3.0, resume, 2 letters of recommendation. Additional exam requirements/recommendations for international students: Required—TOEFL (minimum score 550 paper-based; 213 computer-based). *Application deadline:* Applications are processed on a rolling basis. Application fee: $50. Electronic applications accepted. *Expenses:* Tuition: Part-time $580 per credit. One-time fee: $200 part-time. Part-time tuition and fees vary according to degree level. *Financial support:* Career-related internships or fieldwork, Federal Work-Study, institutionally sponsored loans, scholarships/grants, tuition waivers (full and partial), and unspecified assistantships available. Support available to part-time students. Financial award application deadline: 8/1; financial award applicants required to submit FAFSA. *Faculty research:* Labor relations, dynamic balance in leisure-time skills, ethics in athletics, hotel development. *Unit head:* Dr. Ralph Norcio, Associate Dean, 561-237-7010, Fax: 561-237-7014, E-mail: rnorcio@lynn.edu. *Application contact:* Dr. Larissa Baia, Assistant Director of Graduate Admissions, 561-237-7916, Fax: 561-237-7100, E-mail: admissionpm@lynn.edu.

Manhattanville College, Graduate Programs, Humanities and Social Sciences Programs, Program in Integrated Marketing Communications, Purchase, NY 10577-2132. Offers MS. Part-time and evening/weekend programs available. *Entrance requirements:* Additional exam requirements/recommendations for international students: Required—TOEFL. *Application deadline:* Applications are processed on a rolling basis. Application fee: $70. *Financial support:* Career-related internships or fieldwork, Federal Work-Study, institutionally sponsored loans, and unspecified assistantships available. Financial award applicants required to submit FAFSA. *Unit head:* Donald Richards, Dean, School of Graduate and Professional Studies, 914-323-5469, Fax: 914-694-3488, E-mail: gps@mville.edu. *Application contact:* Office of Admissions, Graduate and Professional Studies, 914-323-5418, E-mail: gps@mville.edu.

Marylhurst University, Department of Business Administration, Marylhurst, OR 97036-0261. Offers finance (MBA); general management (MBA); government policy and administration (MBA); green development (MBA); health care management (MBA); marketing (MBA); natural and organic resources (MBA); nonprofit management (MBA); organizational behavior (MBA); real estate (MBA); renewable energy (MBA); sustainable business (MBA). Part-time and evening/weekend programs available. Postbaccalaureate distance learning degree programs offered (no on-campus study). *Faculty:* 2 full-time (1 woman), 28 part-time/adjunct (5 women). *Students:* 30 full-time (12 women), 627 part-time (323 women); includes 79 minority (28 African Americans, 3 American Indian/Alaska Native, 17 Asian Americans or Pacific Islanders, 31 Hispanic Americans), 9 international. Average age 37. 299 applicants, 80% accepted, 209 enrolled. In 2009, 193 master's awarded. *Degree requirements:* For master's, comprehensive exam, capstone course. *Entrance requirements:* For master's, GMAT (if GPA less than 3.0 and fewer than 5 years of work experience), interview, resume, 2 letters of recommendation. Additional exam requirements/recommendations for international students: Recommended—TOEFL (minimum score 550 paper-based; 213 computer-based; 80 iBT). *Application deadline:* For fall admission, 9/11 priority date for domestic and international students; for winter admission, 12/15 priority date for domestic and international students; for spring admission, 3/17 priority date for domestic and international students. Applications are processed on a rolling basis. Application fee: $40 ($50 for international students). Electronic applications accepted. *Financial support:* Scholarships/grants available. Support available to part-time students. Financial award applicants required to submit FAFSA. *Unit head:* Bob Hanks, Director of Business and Real Estate Programs, 503-636-8141, Fax: 503-697-5597, E-mail: mba@marylhurst.edu. *Application contact:* Kathleen Schneff, Admissions Specialist, 800-634-9982 Ext. 3322, Fax: 503-635-6585, E-mail: admissions@marylhurst.edu.

Maryville University of Saint Louis, The John E. Simon School of Business, St. Louis, MO 63141-7299. Offers accounting (MBA, PGC); business studies (PGC); internet marketing (MBA, PGC); management (MBA, PGC); marketing (MBA, PGC). *Accreditation:* ACBSP. Part-time and evening/weekend programs available. *Students:* 17 full-time (9 women), 133 part-time (70 women); includes 14 minority (6 African Americans, 1 American Indian/Alaska Native, 3 Asian Americans or Pacific Islanders, 4 Hispanic Americans), 4 international. Average age 30. In 2009, 68 master's awarded. *Entrance requirements:* For master's, GMAT (unless applicant possesses undergraduate business degree with minimum cumulative GPA of 3.0, or has completed master's degree from accredited university, or has completed one early access course prior to undergraduate degree). Additional exam requirements/recommendations for international students: Required—TOEFL (minimum score 550 paper-based). *Application deadline:* Applications are processed on a rolling basis. Application fee: $40 ($60 for international students). Electronic applications accepted. *Expenses:* Tuition: Full-time $20,384; part-time $627.50 per credit hour. Required fees: $100 per semester. *Financial support:* Career-related internships or fieldwork, Federal Work-Study, tuition waivers (partial), and campus employment available. Financial award application deadline: 3/1; financial award applicants required to submit FAFSA. *Faculty research:* International business, e-marketing, strategic planning, interpersonal management skills, financial analysis. *Unit head:* Dr. Pamela Horwitz, Dean, 314-529-9418, Fax: 314-529-9975, E-mail: horwitz@maryville.edu. *Application contact:* Kathy Dougherty, Director of MBA Admissions and Enrollment, 314-529-9382, Fax: 314-529-9975, E-mail: business@maryville.edu.

McGill University, Faculty of Graduate and Postdoctoral Studies, Desautels Faculty of Management, Montréal, QC H3A 2T5, Canada. Offers administration (PhD); entrepreneurial studies (MBA); finance (MBA); general management (Post Master's Certificate); information systems (MBA); international business (exchange program) (MBA); international Master's program in practicing management (MM); management (MBA); management for development (MBA); manufacturing management (MMM); marketing (MBA); operations management (MBA); public accountancy (Diploma); strategic management (MBA); MBA/LL B; MD/MBA.

Meritus University, School of Business, Fredericton, NB E3C 2R2, Canada. Offers global management (MBA); health care management (MBA); human resources management (MBA); information technology management (MBA); marketing (MBA); technology management (MBA). Evening/weekend programs available. Postbaccalaureate distance learning degree programs offered (no on-campus study). *Faculty:* 5 full-time (1 woman), 50 part-time/adjunct (15 women). *Students:* 77 full-time (29 women). Average age 35. *Entrance requirements:* For master's, undergraduate degree or comparable equivalent with minimum cumulative GPA of 2.5; minimum equivalent of two years of full-time, post high-school work experience; current employment. Additional exam requirements/recommendations for international students: Required—TOEFL (minimum score 213 computer-based; 79 iBT), IELTS (minimum score 6.5), or TOEIC (minimum score 750) or Berlitz (minimum score 550). *Application deadline:* Applications are processed on a rolling basis. Application fee: $45. Electronic applications accepted. Tuition and fees charges are reported in Canadian dollars. *Expenses:* Tuition: Full-time $14,400 Canadian dollars. Required fees: $720 Canadian dollars. *Unit head:* Dr. Albert K. S. Wong, Program Chair, Business Administration, 604-657-5465, Fax: 602-643-4624, E-mail: albert.wong@staff.meritusu.ca. *Application contact:* Jeremy S. DeMerchant, Enrolment Manager, 506-443-8413, Fax: 602-759-3688, E-mail: jeremy.demerchant@staff.meritusu.ca.

Michigan State University, The Graduate School, Eli Broad Graduate School of Management, Department of Marketing, East Lansing, MI 48824. Offers MBA, PhD. *Faculty:* 16 full-time (5 women), 1 part-time/adjunct (0 women). *Students:* 20 applicants, 0% accepted. *Expenses:* Tuition, state resident: part-time $478.25 per credit hour. Tuition, nonresident: part-time $966.50 per credit hour. Part-time tuition and fees vary according to program. *Financial support:* In 2009–10, 2 research assistantships with tuition reimbursements (averaging $6,930 per year), 8 teaching assistantships with tuition reimbursements (averaging $7,799 per year) were awarded. Total annual research expenditures: $21,397. *Unit head:* Dr. Roger Calantone, Chairperson, 517-432-6400, Fax: 517-432-8048, E-mail: rogercal@msu.edu. *Application contact:* Kathy Waldie, Program Information Contact, 517-432-4321, Fax: 517-432-8048, E-mail: waldie@bus.msu.edu.

Middle Tennessee State University, College of Graduate Studies, Jennings A. Jones College of Business, Department of Management and Marketing, Murfreesboro, TN 37132. Offers MBA. *Accreditation:* AACSB. Part-time and evening/weekend programs available. Postbaccalaureate distance learning degree programs offered. *Faculty:* 18 full-time (4 women). *Students:* 69 full-time (25 women), 278 part-time (123 women); includes 88 minority (54 African Americans, 2 American Indian/Alaska Native, 23 Asian Americans or Pacific Islanders, 9 Hispanic Americans). Average age 27. 213 applicants, 66% accepted, 140 enrolled. In 2009, 121 master's awarded. *Degree requirements:* For master's, comprehensive exam. *Entrance requirements:* Additional exam requirements/recommendations for international students: Required—TOEFL (minimum score 525 paper-based; 195 computer-based; 71 iBT) or IELTS (minimum score 6). *Application deadline:* For fall admission, 6/1 for domestic and international students. Applications are processed on a rolling basis. Application fee: $25 ($30 for international students). Electronic applications accepted. *Expenses:* Tuition, state resident: full-time $4404. Tuition, nonresident: full-time $10,956. *Financial support:* In 2009–10, 8 students received support. Institutionally sponsored loans available. Support available to part-time students. Financial award application deadline: 5/1; financial award applicants required to submit FAFSA. *Faculty research:* International business, business strategy, organizational culture/leadership, consumer behavior, services marketing. *Unit head:* Dr. Jill Austin, Chair, 615-898-2736, Fax: 615-898-5308, E-mail: jaustin@mtsu.edu. *Application contact:* Dr. Michael Allen, Dean and Vice Provost for Research, 615-898-2840, Fax: 615-904-8020, E-mail: mallen@mtsu.edu.

Milwaukee School of Engineering, Rader School of Business, Program in Marketing and Export Management, Milwaukee, WI 53202-3109. Offers MS. *Faculty:* 1 full-time (0 women), 1 part-time/adjunct (0 women). *Students:* 2 full-time (1 woman), 7 part-time (3 women); includes 1 Asian American or Pacific Islander, 1 Hispanic American. Average age 28. 2 applicants, 100% accepted, 1 enrolled. *Degree requirements:* For master's, thesis optional, thesis defense or capstone project. *Entrance requirements:* For master's, GRE General Test or GMAT, 2 letters of recommendation. Additional exam requirements/recommendations for international students: Recommended—TOEFL (minimum score 550 paper-based; 213 computer-based; 79 iBT), IELTS. *Application deadline:* Applications are processed on a rolling basis. Application

fee: $30. Electronic applications accepted. *Expenses:* Tuition: Part-time $603 per credit. *Financial support:* In 2009–10, 6 students received support. Applicants required to submit FAFSA. *Unit head:* Dr. Bruce Thompson, Director, 414-277-7378, Fax: 414-277-7279, E-mail: thomson@msoe.com. *Application contact:* David E. Tietyen, Graduate Admissions Director, 800-332-6763, Fax: 414-277-7475, E-mail: wp@msoe.edu.

Mississippi State University, College of Business, Department of Marketing, Quantitative Analysis and Business Law, Mississippi State, MS 39762. Offers business administration (MBA, PhD), including marketing. Part-time and evening/weekend programs available. *Faculty:* 11 full-time (3 women). *Students:* 12 full-time (7 women), 1 (woman) part-time; includes 1 minority (African American), 3 international. Average age 31. 29 applicants, 10% accepted, 2 enrolled. In 2009, 2 doctorates awarded. *Degree requirements:* For doctorate, comprehensive exam, thesis/dissertation. *Entrance requirements:* For doctorate, GMAT, minimum GPA of 2.75 in last 60 undergraduate hours. Additional exam requirements/recommendations for international students: Required—TOEFL (minimum score 575 paper-based; 233 computer-based; 90 iBT); Recommended—IELTS (minimum score 6.5). *Application deadline:* For fall admission, 7/1 for domestic students, 5/1 for international students; for spring admission, 11/1 for domestic students, 9/1 for international students. Applications are processed on a rolling basis. Application fee: $40. Electronic applications accepted. *Expenses:* Tuition, state resident: full-time $2575.50; part-time $286.25 per credit hour. Tuition, nonresident: full-time $6510; part-time $723.50 per credit hour. Tuition and fees vary according to course load. *Financial support:* In 2009–10, 3 teaching assistantships (averaging $10,037 per year) were awarded; Federal Work-Study, institutionally sponsored loans, and scholarships/grants also available. Financial award application deadline: 4/1; financial award applicants required to submit FAFSA. *Unit head:* Dr. Brian Engelland, Professor and Department Head, 662-325-3163, Fax: 662-325-7012, E-mail: mqabl@cobilan.msstate.edu. *Application contact:* Dr. Barbara Spencer, Associate Dean for Research and Outreach, 662-325-1891, Fax: 662-325-8161, E-mail: gsbi@cobilan.msstate.edu.

Montclair State University, The Graduate School, School of Business, Department of Accounting, Law and Taxation, Montclair, NJ 07043-1624. Offers accounting (MBA, Certificate); finance (Certificate); management information systems (Certificate); marketing (Certificate). Part-time and evening/weekend programs available. *Faculty:* 15 full-time (5 women), 11 part-time/adjunct (9 women). *Students:* 44 full-time (23 women), 94 part-time (40 women). Average age 30. 81 applicants, 56% accepted, 29 enrolled. In 2009, 31 master's, 1 other advanced degree awarded. *Entrance requirements:* For master's, GMAT, 2 letters of recommendation, resume. Additional exam requirements/recommendations for international students: Required—TOEFL (minimum score 83 computer-based), or IELTS. *Application deadline:* For fall admission, 6/1 for international students; for spring admission, 10/1 for international students. Applications are processed on a rolling basis. Application fee: $60. Electronic applications accepted. *Expenses:* Tuition, area resident: Part-time $486.74 per credit. Tuition, state resident: part-time $486.74 per credit. Tuition, nonresident: part-time $751.34 per credit. Tuition and fees vary according to degree level and program. *Financial support:* In 2009–10, 2 research assistantships with full tuition reimbursements (averaging $7,000 per year) were awarded; Federal Work-Study and scholarships/grants also available. Support available to part-time students. Financial award application deadline: 3/1; financial award applicants required to submit FAFSA. *Unit head:* Prof. Frank Aquilino, Head, 973-655-4174. *Application contact:* Amy Aiello, Director of Graduate Admissions and Operations, 973-655-5147, Fax: 973-655-7869, E-mail: graduate.school@montclair.edu.

Montclair State University, The Graduate School, School of Business, Department of Marketing, Montclair, NJ 07043-1624. Offers MBA. Part-time and evening/weekend programs available. *Faculty:* 10 full-time (4 women), 7 part-time/adjunct (3 women). *Students:* 7 full-time (6 women), 34 part-time (23 women). Average age 27. 23 applicants, 52% accepted, 7 enrolled. In 2009, 10 master's awarded. *Entrance requirements:* For master's, GMAT, 2 letters of recommendation, resume. Additional exam requirements/recommendations for international students: Required—TOEFL (minimum score 83 computer-based), or IELTS. *Application deadline:* For fall admission, 6/1 for international students; for spring admission, 10/1 for international students. Applications are processed on a rolling basis. Application fee: $60. Electronic applications accepted. *Expenses:* Tuition, area resident: Part-time $486.74 per credit. Tuition, state resident: part-time $486.74 per credit. Tuition, nonresident: part-time $751.34 per credit. Tuition and fees vary according to degree level and program. *Financial support:* In 2009–10, 5 research assistantships with tuition reimbursements (averaging $7,000 per year) were awarded; Federal Work-Study, scholarships/grants, and unspecified assistantships also available. Support available to part-time students. Financial award application deadline: 3/1; financial award applicants required to submit FAFSA. *Unit head:* Dr. Avinandan Mukherjee, Chair, 973-655-5126. *Application contact:* Amy Aiello, Director of Graduate Admissions and Operations, 973-655-5147, Fax: 973-655-7869, E-mail: graduate.school@montclair.edu.

National University, Academic Affairs, School of Business and Management, Department of Leadership and Business Administration, La Jolla, CA 92037-1011. Offers alternative dispute resolution (MBA); e-business (MBA); financial management (MBA); human resource management (MBA); human resources management (MA); international business (MBA); knowledge management (MS); marketing (MBA); organizational leadership (MBA, MS); technology management (MBA). Part-time and evening/weekend programs available. Postbaccalaureate distance learning degree programs offered (no on-campus study). *Faculty:* 4 full-time (2 women), 22 part-time/adjunct (9 women). *Students:* 95 full-time (56 women), 228 part-time (129 women); includes 63 African Americans, 24 Asian Americans or Pacific Islanders, 61 Hispanic Americans, 6 international. Average age 38. 191 applicants, 100% accepted, 131 enrolled. In 2009, 62 master's awarded. *Degree requirements:* For master's, thesis. *Entrance requirements:* For master's, interview, minimum GPA of 2.5. Additional exam requirements/recommendations for international students: Required—TOEFL (minimum score 550 paper-based; 213 computer-based; 79 iBT), IELTS (minimum score 6). *Application deadline:* Applications are processed on a rolling basis. Application fee: $60 ($65 for international students). Electronic applications accepted. *Expenses:* Tuition: Part-time $338 per quarter hour. *Financial support:* Career-related internships or fieldwork, institutionally sponsored loans, scholarships/grants, and tuition waivers (partial) available. Support available to part-time students. Financial award application deadline: 6/30; financial award applicants required to submit FAFSA. *Unit head:* Dr. George Drops, Chair and Professor, 858-642-8438, Fax: 858-642-8406, E-mail: gdrops@nu.edu. *Application contact:* Dominick Giovanniello, Associate Regional Dean—San Diego, 800-NAT-UNIV, Fax: 858-541-7792, E-mail: dgiovann@nu.edu.

New England College, Program in Management, Henniker, NH 03242-3293. Offers accounting (MSA); healthcare administration (MS); international relations (MA); marketing management (MS); nonprofit leadership (MS); project management (MS); strategic leadership (MS). Part-time and evening/weekend programs available. *Degree requirements:* For master's, independent research project. Electronic applications accepted.

New Mexico State University, Graduate School, College of Business, Department of Marketing, Las Cruces, NM 88003-8001. Offers business administration (PhD), including marketing. *Faculty:* 6 full-time (2 women), 1 (woman) part-time/adjunct. *Students:* 8 full-time (3 women), 2 part-time (1 woman); includes 3 minority (all Hispanic Americans), 4 international. Average age 34. 24 applicants, 42% accepted, 7 enrolled. In 2009, 4 doctorates awarded. *Degree requirements:* For doctorate, comprehensive exam, thesis/dissertation. *Entrance requirements:* For doctorate, GMAT. Additional exam requirements/recommendations for international students: Required—TOEFL. *Application deadline:* For fall admission, 3/9 priority date for domestic and international students. *Expenses:* Tuition, state resident: full-time $4080; part-time $223 per credit. Tuition, nonresident: full-time $14,256; part-time $647 per credit. Required fees: $1278; $639 per semester. *Financial support:* In 2009–10, 8 teaching assistantships (averaging $20,727 per year) were awarded; research assistantships, health care benefits also available. *Unit head:* Dr. Elise Pookie Sautter, Head, 575-646-3341, Fax: 575-646-1498, E-mail: esautter@nmsu.edu. *Application contact:* Dr. Michael Hyman, Director, 575-646-5238, Fax: 575-646-1498, E-mail: mhyman@nmsu.edu.

New York Institute of Technology, Graduate Division, School of Management, Program in Business Administration, Old Westbury, NY 11568-8000. Offers accounting (Advanced Certificate); business administration (MBA); finance (Advanced Certificate); international business (Advanced Certificate); management of information systems (Advanced Certificate); marketing (Advanced Certificate). Part-time and evening/weekend programs available. *Students:* 599 full-time (262 women), 528 part-time (200 women); includes 51 minority (17 African Americans, 24 Asian Americans or Pacific Islanders, 10 Hispanic Americans), 324 international. Average age 29. In 2009, 691 master's, 7 other advanced degrees awarded. *Degree requirements:* For master's, thesis (for some programs). *Entrance requirements:* For master's, minimum QPA of 2.85. Additional exam requirements/recommendations for international students: Required—TOEFL (minimum score 550 paper-based; 213 computer-based). *Application deadline:* For fall admission, 7/1 priority date for domestic students; for spring admission, 12/1 priority date for domestic students. Applications are processed on a rolling basis. Application fee: $50. Electronic applications accepted. *Expenses:* Tuition: Part-time $825 per credit. *Financial support:* Fellowships, research assistantships with partial tuition reimbursements, institutionally sponsored loans, tuition waivers (full and partial), and unspecified assistantships available. Support available to part-time students. Financial award applicants required to submit FAFSA. *Faculty research:* Instructor performance appraisal; relationship between TOEFL, GMAT, GRE, and performance in foreign students. *Unit head:* Dr. Diamando Afxentiou, Acting Associate Dean, 516-686-3937, Fax: 516-686-7430, E-mail: dafxenti@nyit.edu. *Application contact:* Dr. Jacquelyn Nealon, Vice President for Enrollment Services, 516-686-7925, Fax: 516-686-7597, E-mail: jnealon@nyit.edu.

New York University, Leonard N. Stern School of Business, Department of Marketing, New York, NY 10012-1019. Offers entertainment, media and technology (MBA); general marketing (MBA); marketing (PhD); product management (MBA). *Expenses:* Tuition: Full-time $30,528; part-time $1272 per credit. Required fees: $2177.

New York University, School of Continuing and Professional Studies, Division of Programs in Business, Program in Interactive Marketing, New York, NY 10012-1019. Offers brand management (MS); digital marketing (MS); marketing analytics (MS). Part-time and evening/weekend programs available. *Faculty:* 1 (woman) full-time, 10 part-time/adjunct (2 women). *Students:* 52 full-time (39 women), 82 part-time (62 women); includes 32 minority (7 African Americans, 12 Asian Americans or Pacific Islanders, 13 Hispanic Americans). Average age 30. 235 applicants, 31% accepted, 38 enrolled. In 2009, 21 master's awarded. *Degree requirements:* For master's, comprehensive exam, thesis, capstone; writing of complete business plan. *Entrance requirements:* For master's, GRE General Test or GMAT (for recent graduates), resume, 2 letters of recommendation. Additional exam requirements/recommendations for international students: Required—TOEFL (minimum score 600 paper-based; 250 computer-based; 100 iBT), TWE. *Application deadline:* For fall admission, 2/1 priority date for domestic and international students; for spring admission, 10/15 priority date for domestic students, 8/15 priority date for international students. Applications are processed on a rolling basis. Application fee: $75. Electronic applications accepted. *Expenses:* Tuition: Full-time $30,528; part-time $1272 per credit. Required fees: $2177. *Financial support:* In 2009–10, 53 students received support, including 53 fellowships (averaging $2,461 per year); career-related internships or fieldwork, institutionally sponsored loans, and scholarships/grants also available. Support available to part-time students. Financial award application deadline: 3/1; financial award applicants required to submit FAFSA. *Faculty research:* Branding, digital marketing, Web analytics, consumer behavior, customer loyalty, campaign planning and management. *Unit head:* Dr. Marjorie Kalter, Director, 212-992-3207, Fax: 212-992-3676, E-mail: mk99@nyu.edu. *Application contact:* Fadia Saint-Juste, Assistant Director, 212-992-3249, Fax: 212-992-3676, E-mail: fs20@nyu.edu.

New York University, School of Continuing and Professional Studies, The Preston Robert Tisch Center for Hospitality, Tourism, and Sports Management, Program in Sports Business, New York, NY 10012-1019. Offers finance and development (MS); marketing and media (MS); sports business (Advanced Certificate). Part-time and evening/weekend programs available. *Faculty:* 13 full-time (5 women), 11 part-time/adjunct (2 women). *Students:* 43 full-time (10 women), 65 part-time (21 women); includes 10 minority (5 African Americans, 2 Asian Americans or Pacific Islanders, 3 Hispanic Americans). Average age 28. 140 applicants, 49% accepted, 42 enrolled. In 2009, 45 master's, 6 other advanced degrees awarded. *Degree requirements:* For master's, comprehensive exam (for some programs), thesis. *Entrance requirements:* For master's, GMAT or GRE General Test (for recent graduates), resume, 2 letters of recommendation, essay. Additional exam requirements/recommendations for international students: Required—TOEFL (minimum score 600 paper-based; 250 computer-based; 100 iBT), TWE. *Application deadline:* For fall admission, 2/1 priority date for domestic and international students; for spring admission, 10/15 priority date for domestic students, 8/15 priority date for international students. Applications are processed on a rolling basis. Application fee: $75. Electronic applications accepted. *Expenses:* Tuition: Full-time $30,528; part-time $1272 per credit. Required fees: $2177. *Financial support:* In 2009–10, 39 students received support, including 39 fellowships (averaging $3,408 per year); career-related internships or fieldwork, Federal Work-Study, institutionally sponsored loans, and scholarships/grants also available. Support available to part-time students. Financial award application deadline: 3/1; financial award applicants required to submit FAFSA. *Faculty research:* Implications of college football's bowl coalition series from a legal, economic, and academic perspective; social history of sports. *Unit head:* Lalia Rach, Divisional Dean, 212-998-9100, Fax: 212-995-4676, E-mail: lalia.rach@nyu.edu. *Application contact:* Sandra Dove-Lowther, Academic Services Director, 212-998-9106, Fax: 212-995-4676, E-mail: sd2@nyu.edu.

New York University, School of Continuing and Professional Studies, The Preston Robert Tisch Center for Hospitality, Tourism, and Sports Management, Program in Tourism and Travel Management, New York, NY 10012-1019. Offers customer relationship management (MS); strategic marketing (MS); tourism and travel management (Advanced Certificate); tourism development (MS); tourism planning and analysis (MS). Part-time and evening/weekend programs available. *Faculty:* 13 full-time (5 women), 11 part-time/adjunct (5 women). *Students:* 1 (woman) full-time, 6 part-time (4 women); includes 1 minority (Asian American or Pacific Islander). Average age 30. In 2009, 8 master's, 1 other advanced degree awarded. *Entrance requirements:* For master's, GMAT or GRE General Test (for recent graduates), resume, 2 letters of recommendation, essay. Additional exam requirements/recommendations for international students: Required—TOEFL (minimum score 600 paper-based; 250 computer-based; 100 iBT), TWE. *Application deadline:* For fall admission, 2/1 priority date for domestic and international students; for spring admission, 10/15 priority date for domestic students, 8/15 priority date for international students. Applications are processed on a rolling basis. Application fee: $75. Electronic applications accepted. *Expenses:* Tuition: Full-time $30,528; part-time $1272 per credit. Required fees: $2177. *Financial support:* In 2009–10, 4 students received support, including 4 fellowships (averaging $2,109 per year); research assistantships, career-related internships or fieldwork, Federal Work-Study, institutionally sponsored loans, and scholarships/grants also available. Support available to part-time students. Financial award application deadline: 3/1; financial award applicants required to submit FAFSA. *Faculty research:* Tourism planning for national parks and protected areas, leadership and organizational behavior issues. *Unit head:* Lalia Rach, 212-998-9100, Fax: 212-995-4676, E-mail: lalia.rach@nyu.edu. *Application contact:* Sandra Dove-Lowther, Office of Admissions, 212-998-9106, Fax: 212-995-4676, E-mail: sd2@nyu.edu.

Northeastern Illinois University, Graduate College, College of Business and Management, Chicago, IL 60625-4699. Offers accounting (MBA); finance (MBA); management (MBA); marketing (MBA). Part-time and evening/weekend programs available. *Degree requirements:* For master's, thesis optional. *Entrance requirements:* For master's, GMAT, minimum GPA of 2.75. Additional exam requirements/recommendations for international students: Required—TOEFL (minimum score 550 paper-based; 213 computer-based; 80 iBT). Electronic applications accepted. *Faculty research:* Perception of accountants and non-accountants toward future of the accounting industry, asynchronous learning outcomes, cost and efficiency of financial markets, impact of deregulation on airline industry, analysis of derivational instruments.

Marketing

Northern Kentucky University, Office of Graduate Programs, College of Business, Program in Business Administration, Highland Heights, KY 41099. Offers business administration (MBA); entrepreneurship (Certificate); finance (Certificate); international business (Certificate); marketing (Certificate); project management (Certificate); JD/MBA. *Accreditation:* AACSB. Part-time and evening/weekend programs available. *Students:* 33 full-time (16 women), 155 part-time (63 women); includes 16 minority (9 African Americans, 7 Asian Americans or Pacific Islanders), 7 international. Average age 30. 105 applicants, 65% accepted, 34 enrolled. In 2009, 42 master's, 31 other advanced degrees awarded. *Degree requirements:* For master's, thesis optional. *Entrance requirements:* For master's, GMAT (minimum score 450), minimum GPA of 2.5. Additional exam requirements/recommendations for international students: Required—TOEFL (minimum score 550 paper-based; 213 computer-based; 79 iBT); Recommended—IELTS (minimum score 6.5). *Application deadline:* For fall admission, 8/1 priority date for domestic students, 6/1 priority date for international students; for spring admission, 12/1 priority date for domestic students, 10/1 priority date for international students. Applications are processed on a rolling basis. Application fee: $40. Electronic applications accepted. *Expenses:* Tuition, state resident: full-time $6912; part-time $384 per credit hour. Tuition, nonresident: full-time $12,150; part-time $675 per credit hour. Tuition and fees vary according to course load, program and reciprocity agreements. *Financial support:* Unspecified assistantships available. Financial award applicants required to submit FAFSA. *Unit head:* James Bast, Director of MBA Programs, 859-572-7695, Fax: 859-572-7694, E-mail: mbusiness@nku.edu. *Application contact:* Dr. Peg Griffin, Director of Graduate Programs, 859-572-6934, Fax: 859-572-6670, E-mail: griffinp@nku.edu.

Northwestern University, The Graduate School, Kellogg School of Management, Department of Marketing, Evanston, IL 60208. Offers PhD. Admissions and degree offered through The Graduate School. *Degree requirements:* For doctorate, comprehensive exam, thesis/dissertation. *Entrance requirements:* For doctorate, GMAT or GRE General Test. Additional exam requirements/recommendations for international students: Required—TOEFL. Electronic applications accepted. *Faculty research:* Choice models, database and high-tech marketing, consumer information processing, ethnographic analysis of consumption, psychometric analysis of consumer behavior.

Northwestern University, Medill School of Journalism, Integrated Marketing Communications Program, Evanston, IL 60208. Offers advertising/sales promotion (MSIMC); direct database and e-commerce marketing (MSIMC); general studies (MSIMC); public relations (MSIMC). Part-time programs available. *Entrance requirements:* For master's, GRE General Test or GMAT, full-time work experience (preferred). Additional exam requirements/recommendations for international students: Required—TOEFL. Electronic applications accepted. *Faculty research:* Data mining, business to business marketing, values in advertising, political advertising.

Notre Dame de Namur University, Division of Academic Affairs, School of Business and Management, Department of Business Administration, Belmont, CA 94002-1908. Offers business administration (MBA); finance (MBA); human resource management (MBA); marketing (MBA). Part-time and evening/weekend programs available. *Faculty:* 7 full-time (1 woman), 6 part-time/adjunct (0 women). *Students:* 21 full-time (17 women), 87 part-time (49 women); includes 47 minority (3 African Americans, 4 American Indian/Alaska Native, 21 Asian Americans or Pacific Islanders, 19 Hispanic Americans), 9 international. Average age 34. 27 applicants, 100% accepted, 20 enrolled. In 2009, 43 master's awarded. *Entrance requirements:* For master's, minimum GPA of 2.5. Additional exam requirements/recommendations for international students: Required—TOEFL (minimum score 550 paper-based; 213 computer-based; 79 iBT). *Application deadline:* For fall admission, 8/1 priority date for domestic students; for spring admission, 12/1 priority date for domestic students. Applications are processed on a rolling basis. Application fee: $60. Electronic applications accepted. *Expenses:* Tuition: Part-time $720 per credit. Required fees: $35 per semester hour. *Financial support:* Career-related internships or fieldwork available. Support available to part-time students. Financial award applicants required to submit FAFSA. *Unit head:* Henry Roth, Director, 650-508-3721, E-mail: hroth@ndnu.edu. *Application contact:* Candace Hallmark, Associate Director of Admissions, 650-508-3592, Fax: 650-508-3426, E-mail: grad.admit@ndnu.edu.

Nova Southeastern University, H. Wayne Huizenga School of Business and Entrepreneurship, Doctoral Program in Business Administration, Fort Lauderdale, FL 33314-7796. Offers accounting (DBA); decision sciences (DBA); finance (DBA); human resource management (DBA); international business (DBA); management (DBA); marketing (DBA). Part-time and evening/weekend programs available. *Faculty:* 34 full-time (11 women), 2 part-time/adjunct (1 woman). *Students:* 6 full-time (1 woman), 129 part-time (41 women); includes 33 minority (17 African Americans, 6 Asian Americans or Pacific Islanders, 10 Hispanic Americans), 12 international. Average age 47. 58 applicants, 14% accepted, 5 enrolled. In 2009, 32 doctorates awarded. *Degree requirements:* For doctorate, comprehensive exam, thesis/dissertation. *Entrance requirements:* For doctorate, GMAT. Additional exam requirements/recommendations for international students: Required—TOEFL (minimum score 600 paper-based; 250 computer-based; 100 iBT), IELTS (minimum score 7). *Application deadline:* Applications are processed on a rolling basis. Application fee: $50. Electronic applications accepted. *Financial support:* Available to part-time students. Applicants required to submit FAFSA. *Faculty research:* Reputation management, call centers, international social capital, corporate earnings guidance, corporate governance. *Unit head:* Kristie Tetrault, Director of Program Administration, 954-262-5120, Fax: 954-262-3849, E-mail: kristie@huizenga.nova.edu. *Application contact:* Karen Goldberg, Associate Director of Recruitment and Special Events, 954-262-5039, Fax: 954-262-3822, E-mail: karen@huizenga.nova.edu.

Oakland University, Graduate Study and Lifelong Learning, School of Business Administration, Department of Management and Marketing, Rochester, MI 48309-4401. Offers business administration (MBA); entrepreneurship (Certificate); general management (Certificate); human resource management (Certificate); international business (Certificate); marketing (Certificate).

Oklahoma City University, Meinders School of Business, Program in Business Administration, Oklahoma City, OK 73106-1402. Offers finance (MBA); health administration (MBA); information technology (MBA); integrated marketing communications (MBA); international business (MBA); marketing (MBA); JD/MBA. *Accreditation:* ACBSP. Part-time and evening/weekend programs available. *Faculty:* 24 full-time (7 women), 11 part-time/adjunct (1 woman). *Students:* 268 full-time (91 women), 180 part-time (62 women); includes 51 minority (20 African Americans, 7 American Indian/Alaska Native, 11 Asian Americans or Pacific Islanders, 13 Hispanic Americans), 257 international. Average age 30. 158 applicants, 90% accepted, 35 enrolled. In 2009, 236 master's awarded. *Degree requirements:* For master's, comprehensive exam. *Entrance requirements:* Additional exam requirements/recommendations for international students: Required—TOEFL (minimum score 560 paper-based; 220 computer-based; 83 iBT). *Application deadline:* For fall admission, 8/20 for domestic students; for spring admission, 1/6 for domestic students. Applications are processed on a rolling basis. Application fee: $50 ($70 for international students). *Expenses:* Tuition: Full-time $15,930; part-time $885 per hour. *Financial support:* Fellowships with partial tuition reimbursements, career-related internships or fieldwork, Federal Work-Study, institutionally sponsored loans, and tuition waivers (partial) available. Support available to part-time students. Financial award application deadline: 8/1. *Faculty research:* Management information systems, international business strategies. *Unit head:* Dr. Mahmood Shandiz, Senior Associate Dean, 405-208-5130, Fax: 405-208-5098, E-mail: mshandiz@okcu.edu. *Application contact:* Michelle Lockhart, Director, Graduate Admissions, 800-633-7242, Fax: 405-208-5916, E-mail: gadmissions@okcu.edu.

Oklahoma State University, William S. Spears School of Business, Department of Marketing, Stillwater, OK 74078. Offers business administration (PhD), including marketing; marketing (MBA). Part-time programs available. *Faculty:* 17 full-time (3 women), 15 part-time/adjunct (6 women). *Students:* 10 full-time (1 woman), 3 part-time (0 women); includes 1 minority (Asian American or Pacific Islander), 6 international. Average age 34. In 2009, 4 doctorates awarded. *Degree requirements:* For master's, thesis or alternative; for doctorate, comprehensive exam, thesis/dissertation. *Entrance requirements:* For master's and doctorate, GRE or GMAT. Additional exam requirements/recommendations for international students: Required—TOEFL (minimum

score 550 paper-based; 79 iBT). *Application deadline:* For fall admission, 3/1 priority date for international students; for spring admission, 8/1 priority date for international students. Applications are processed on a rolling basis. Application fee: $40 ($75 for international students). Electronic applications accepted. *Expenses:* Tuition, state resident: full-time $3716; part-time $154.85 per credit hour. Tuition, nonresident: full-time $14,448; part-time $602 per credit hour. Required fees: $1772; $73.85 per credit hour. One-time fee: $50. Tuition and fees vary according to course load and campus/location. *Financial support:* In 2009–10, 7 research assistantships (averaging $16,872 per year), 4 teaching assistantships (averaging $16,611 per year) were awarded; career-related internships or fieldwork, Federal Work-Study, scholarships/grants, health care benefits, tuition waivers (partial), and unspecified assistantships also available. Support available to part-time students. Financial award application deadline: 3/1; financial award applicants required to submit FAFSA. *Faculty research:* Decision making (consumer, managerial, cross-functional), communication effects, services marketing, public policy and marketing, corporate image. *Unit head:* Dr. Joshua L. Wiener, Head, 405-744-5192, Fax: 405-744-5180. *Application contact:* Dr. Gordon Emslie, Dean, 405-744-6368, Fax: 405-744-0355, E-mail: grad-i@okstate.edu.

Old Dominion University, College of Business and Public Administration, Doctoral Program in Business Administration, Norfolk, VA 23529. Offers finance (PhD); information technology (PhD); marketing (PhD); strategic management (PhD). *Accreditation:* AACSB. *Faculty:* 21 full-time (2 women). *Students:* 28 full-time (12 women), 14 part-time (6 women); includes 5 minority (3 African Americans, 2 Asian Americans or Pacific Islanders), 25 international. Average age 35. 31 applicants, 65% accepted, 8 enrolled. In 2009, 6 doctorates awarded. *Degree requirements:* For doctorate, comprehensive exam, thesis/dissertation. *Entrance requirements:* For doctorate, GMAT. Additional exam requirements/recommendations for international students: Required—TOEFL (minimum score 550 paper-based; 213 computer-based; 79 iBT). *Application deadline:* For fall admission, 4/1 priority date for domestic and international students. Application fee: $50. Electronic applications accepted. *Expenses:* Tuition, state resident: full-time $8112; part-time $338 per credit. Tuition, nonresident: full-time $20,256; part-time $844 per credit. Required fees: $119 per semester. One-time fee: $50. *Financial support:* In 2009–10, 23 students received support, including 4 fellowships with full tuition reimbursements available (averaging $15,000 per year), 13 research assistantships with full tuition reimbursements available (averaging $15,000 per year), 6 teaching assistantships with full tuition reimbursements available (averaging $15,000 per year); career-related internships or fieldwork and scholarships/grants also available. Financial award application deadline: 4/1; financial award applicants required to submit FAFSA. *Faculty research:* International business, buyer behavior, financial markets, strategy, operations research. *Unit head:* Dr. Sylvia C. Hudgins, Graduate Program Director, 757-683-3551, Fax: 757-683-4076, E-mail: shudgins@odu.edu. *Application contact:* Dr. Sylvia C. Hudgins, Graduate Program Director, 757-683-3551, Fax: 757-683-4076, E-mail: shudgins@odu.edu.

Oral Roberts University, School of Business, Tulsa, OK 74171. Offers accounting (MBA); entrepreneurship (MBA); finance (MBA); international business (MBA); management (MBA); marketing (MBA); non-profit management (MBA); not for profit management (MNM). *Accreditation:* ACBSP. Part-time programs available. Postbaccalaureate distance learning degree programs offered (minimal on-campus study). *Faculty:* 7 full-time (0 women), 5 part-time/adjunct (4 women). *Students:* 68 full-time (30 women), 55 part-time (27 women); includes 54 minority (32 African Americans, 5 American Indian/Alaska Native, 8 Asian Americans or Pacific Islanders, 9 Hispanic Americans), 3 international. Average age 28. 71 applicants, 94% accepted, 56 enrolled. In 2009, 36 master's awarded. *Degree requirements:* For master's, thesis optional. *Entrance requirements:* For master's, minimum cumulative GPA of 3.0. Additional exam requirements/recommendations for international students: Required—TOEFL (minimum score 550 paper-based; 213 computer-based; 79 iBT). *Application deadline:* For fall admission, 7/1 priority date for domestic and international students; for spring admission, 12/1 priority date for domestic students, 10/15 priority date for international students. Applications are processed on a rolling basis. Application fee: $35. Electronic applications accepted. *Financial support:* In 2009–10, 39 students received support. Federal Work-Study, scholarships/grants, and unspecified assistantships available. Financial award application deadline: 6/1; financial award applicants required to submit FAFSA. *Faculty research:* Social media, international business and marketing. *Unit head:* Dr. Steven Greene, Dean, 918-495-7040, Fax: 918-495-7876, E-mail: businessdean@oru.edu. *Application contact:* Rebecca Gunn, Representative/Recruiter, 918-495-6117, Fax: 918-495-6500, E-mail: gradbusiness@oru.edu.

Ottawa University, Graduate Studies-Arizona, Programs in Business, Ottawa, KS 66067-3399. Offers business administration (MBA); finance (MBA); human resources (MA, MBA); leadership (MBA); marketing (MBA). Programs offered in Mesa, Phoenix, Tempe and West Valley, AZ. Part-time and evening/weekend programs available. Postbaccalaureate distance learning degree programs offered. *Degree requirements:* For master's, thesis or alternative. *Entrance requirements:* For master's, minimum undergraduate GPA of 3.0. Additional exam requirements/recommendations for international students: Required—TOEFL (minimum score 550 paper-based; 213 computer-based). Electronic applications accepted.

Pace University, Lubin School of Business, Marketing Program, New York, NY 10038. Offers marketing management (MBA); marketing research (MBA). Part-time and evening/weekend programs available. *Students:* 25 full-time (14 women), 67 part-time (33 women); includes 14 minority (6 African Americans, 1 American Indian/Alaska Native, 4 Asian Americans or Pacific Islanders, 3 Hispanic Americans), 35 international. Average age 27. 207 applicants, 62% accepted, 30 enrolled. In 2009, 33 master's awarded. *Entrance requirements:* For master's, GMAT. Additional exam requirements/recommendations for international students: Required—TOEFL. *Application deadline:* For fall admission, 7/31 priority date for domestic students; for spring admission, 11/30 for domestic students. Applications are processed on a rolling basis. Application fee: $70. Electronic applications accepted. *Expenses:* Tuition: Part-time $954 per credit. Tuition and fees vary according to course load, degree level and program. *Financial support:* Research assistantships, career-related internships or fieldwork and Federal Work-Study available. Support available to part-time students. Financial award applicants required to submit FAFSA. *Unit head:* Dr. Martin Topol, Chairperson, 212-346-1827. *Application contact:* Susan Ford-Goldschein, Director of Admissions, 212-346-1652, Fax: 212-346-1585, E-mail: gradnyc@pace.edu.

Philadelphia University, School of Business Administration, Program in Business Administration, Philadelphia, PA 19144. Offers business administration (MBA); finance (MBA); health care management (MBA); international business (MBA); marketing (MBA); MBA/MS. Part-time and evening/weekend programs available. Postbaccalaureate distance learning degree programs offered (no on-campus study). *Entrance requirements:* For master's, GMAT. Additional exam requirements/recommendations for international students: Required—TOEFL (minimum score 550 paper-based; 213 computer-based; 79 iBT).

Pontifical Catholic University of Puerto Rico, College of Business Administration, Program in Marketing, Ponce, PR 00717-0777. Offers MBA. Part-time and evening/weekend programs available. *Degree requirements:* For master's, thesis. *Entrance requirements:* For master's, GRE, interview, minimum GPA of 2.75.

Pontificia Universidad Catolica Madre y Maestra, Graduate School, Santiago, Dominican Republic. Offers administration (M Adm); architecture of interiors (M Arch); architecture of tourist lodgings (M Arch); banking and financial management (M Mgmt); civil law (LL M); construction administration (ME); corporate business law (LL M); criminal procedure law (LL M); environmental engineering (ME, MEE); finance (M Mgmt); history applied to education (M Ed); human resources (EMBA); insurance (M Mgmt); international business (M Mgmt); labor law and Social Security (LL M); logistics management (ME); marketing (M Mgmt); renewable energy (ME); strategic cost management (M Mgmt). *Entrance requirements:* For master's, curriculum vitae, interview.

Post University, Program in Business Administration, Waterbury, CT 06723-2540. Offers business administration (MBA); corporate innovation (MBA); entrepreneurship (MBA); finance (MBA); leadership (MBA); marketing (MBA). Postbaccalaureate distance learning degree programs offered.

Providence College, Graduate Studies, School of Business, Providence, RI 02918. Offers accountancy (MBA); economics (MBA); entrepreneurship (MBA); finance (MBA); international business (MBA); management (MBA); marketing (MBA); not-for-profit (MBA); quantitative (MBA). Part-time and evening/weekend programs available. *Faculty:* 14 full-time (8 women), 7 part-time/adjunct (3 women). *Students:* 63 full-time (18 women), 46 part-time (19 women); includes 4 minority (2 African Americans, 2 Asian Americans or Pacific Islanders), 7 international. Average age 26. 43 applicants, 88% accepted. In 2009, 40 master's awarded. *Degree requirements:* For master's, thesis optional. *Entrance requirements:* For master's, GMAT. Additional exam requirements/recommendations for international students: Required—TOEFL (minimum score 550 paper-based; 213 computer-based; 80 iBT). *Application deadline:* For fall admission, 8/1 priority date for domestic and international students; for spring admission, 12/1 priority date for domestic and international students. Applications are processed on a rolling basis. Application fee: $55. *Expenses:* Contact institution. *Financial support:* In 2009–10, 34 research assistantships with full tuition reimbursements (averaging $8,400 per year) were awarded; Federal Work-Study, institutionally sponsored loans, and unspecified assistantships also available. Support available to part-time students. Financial award application deadline: 8/1; financial award applicants required to submit FAFSA. *Unit head:* Dr. MaryJane Lenon, Director, MBA Program, 401-865-2566, Fax: 401-865-2978, E-mail: mjlenon@providence.edu. *Application contact:* Katherine A. Follett, Administrative Coordinator, 401-865-2333, Fax: 401-865-2978, E-mail: kfollett@providence.edu.

Queen's University at Kingston, Queens School of Business, Program in Business Administration, Kingston, ON K7L 3N6, Canada. Offers consulting and project management (MBA); finance (MBA); innovation and entrepreneurship (MBA); marketing (MBA). *Accreditation:* AACSB. *Degree requirements:* For master's, thesis optional, research project. *Entrance requirements:* For master's, GMAT, minimum B+ average. Additional exam requirements/recommendations for international students: Required—TOEFL. Electronic applications accepted. *Faculty research:* Management fundamentals, strategic thinking, global business, innovation and change, leadership.

Quinnipiac University, School of Business, Program in Business Administration, Hamden, CT 06518-1940. Offers chartered financial analyst (MBA); finance (MBA); healthcare management (MBA); information systems management (MBA); international business (MBA); management (MBA); marketing (MBA); JD/MBA. *Accreditation:* AACSB. Part-time and evening/weekend programs available. *Faculty:* 24 full-time (6 women), 12 part-time/adjunct (4 women). *Students:* 83 full-time (30 women), 106 part-time (36 women); includes 11 minority (2 African Americans, 1 American Indian/Alaska Native, 6 Asian Americans or Pacific Islanders, 2 Hispanic Americans), 13 international. Average age 29. 124 applicants, 79% accepted, 77 enrolled. In 2009, 63 master's awarded. *Entrance requirements:* For master's, GMAT, minimum GPA of 3.0. Additional exam requirements/recommendations for international students: Required—TOEFL (minimum score 575 paper-based; 233 computer-based; 90 iBT), IELTS (minimum score 6.5). *Application deadline:* For fall admission, 7/30 priority date for domestic students, 4/30 priority date for international students; for spring admission, 12/15 priority date for domestic students, 9/15 priority date for international students. Applications are processed on a rolling basis. Application fee: $45. Electronic applications accepted. *Expenses:* Tuition: Full-time $16,030; part-time $770 per credit. Required fees: $630; $35 per credit. *Financial support:* In 2009–10, 110 students received support. Federal Work-Study, tuition waivers (partial), and unspecified assistantships available. Support available to part-time students. Financial award application deadline: 4/15; financial award applicants required to submit FAFSA. *Faculty research:* Equity compensation, marketing relationships and public policy, corporate governance, international business, supply chain management. *Unit head:* Kimberly McKeage, MBA Program Director, 203-582-3676. *Application contact:* Jennifer Boutin, 800-462-1944, Fax: 203-582-3443, E-mail: jennifer.boutin@quinnipiac.edu.

Regent's American College London, Webster Graduate School, London, United Kingdom. Offers business (MBA); finance (MS); human resources (MA); information technology management (MA); international business (MA); international non-governmental organizations (MA); international relations (MA); management and leadership (MA); marketing (MA). Part-time programs available.

Regis University, College for Professional Studies, School of Management, Denver, CO 80221-1099. Offers accounting (MS); business administration (MBA); computer information technology (MSOL); executive internal management (Certificate); executive leadership (Certificate); finance (MBA); finance and accounting (MBA); human resource management (MSOL); international business (MBA); marketing (MBA); operations management (MBA); organization leadership (MS); organizational leadership (MSOL); project leadership and management (MSOL, Certificate); project management (Certificate); strategic business (Certificate); strategic human resource (Certificate); technical management (Certificate). Offered at Colorado Springs Campus, Northwest Denver Campus, Southeast Denver Campus, Fort Collins Campus, Broomfield Campus, Henderson (Nevada) Campus, and Summerlin (Nevada) Campus and online. Part-time and evening/weekend programs available. Postbaccalaureate distance learning degree programs offered (no on-campus study). *Degree requirements:* For master's, thesis optional, capstone project. *Entrance requirements:* For master's, GMAT or essays, interview, 2 years of full-time business work experience, resume; for Certificate, GMAT. Additional exam requirements/recommendations for international students: Required—TOEFL, TOEFL or university-based test; Recommended—TWE (minimum score 5). Electronic applications accepted. *Faculty research:* Impact of Info Technology on Small Business Regulation of Accounting, International Project financing, Mineral Development, Delivery of Healthcare to rural indigenos communities.

Roberts Wesleyan College, Division of Business, Rochester, NY 14624-1997. Offers nonprofit leadership (Certificate); strategic leadership (MS); strategic marketing (MS). Evening/weekend programs available. *Degree requirements:* For master's, thesis or alternative. *Entrance requirements:* For master's, GMAT, minimum GPA of 2.75, verifiable work experience. *Expenses:* Contact institution.

Rollins College, Crummer Graduate School of Business, Winter Park, FL 32789-4499. Offers entrepreneurship (MBA); finance (MBA); international business (MBA); management (MBA); marketing (MBA); operations and technology management (MBA). *Accreditation:* AACSB. Part-time and evening/weekend programs available. Postbaccalaureate distance learning degree programs offered (minimal on-campus study). *Faculty:* 25 full-time (3 women), 8 part-time/adjunct (2 women). *Students:* 277 full-time (105 women), 192 part-time (79 women); includes 95 minority (26 African Americans, 31 Asian Americans or Pacific Islanders, 38 Hispanic Americans), 48 international. Average age 29. 373 applicants, 53% accepted, 140 enrolled. In 2009, 220 master's awarded. *Entrance requirements:* For master's, GMAT. Additional exam requirements/recommendations for international students: Required—TOEFL. *Application deadline:* For fall admission, 6/1 priority date for domestic students; for spring admission, 12/1 for domestic students. Applications are processed on a rolling basis. Application fee: $50. Electronic applications accepted. *Expenses:* Contact institution. *Financial support:* In 2009–10, 95 students received support, including 95 fellowships, 56 research assistantships (averaging $2,400 per year); career-related internships or fieldwork, scholarships/grants, tuition waivers (full), and unspecified assistantships also available. *Faculty research:* Sustainability, world financial markets, international business, market research, strategic marketing. *Unit head:* Dr. Craig M. McAllaster, Dean, 407-646-2249, Fax: 407-646-1550, E-mail: cmcallaster@rollins.edu. *Application contact:* Linda Puritz, Student Admissions Office, 407-646-2405, Fax: 407-646-1550, E-mail: mbaadmissions@rollins.edu.

Rowan University, Graduate School, William G. Rohrer College of Business, Department of Marketing and Business Information Systems, Glassboro, NJ 08028-1701. Offers MBA. Part-time and evening/weekend programs available. *Faculty:* 2 full-time (1 woman), 2 part-time/adjunct (both women). *Students:* 1 (woman) full-time, 4 part-time (2 women). Average age 26. 4 applicants, 50% accepted, 1 enrolled. *Degree requirements:* For master's, comprehensive exam, thesis. *Entrance requirements:* For master's, GRE General Test. Additional exam requirements/recommendations for international students: Required—TOEFL. *Application*

deadline: Applications are processed on a rolling basis. Application fee: $50. Electronic applications accepted. *Expenses:* Tuition, state resident: full-time $10,624; part-time $590 per semester hour. Tuition, nonresident: full-time $10,624; part-time $590 per semester hour. Required fees: $2320; $125 per semester hour. *Unit head:* Dr. Mira Lalovic-Hand, Interim Associate Provost/Director of Graduate School, 856-256-5120, E-mail: lalovic-hand@rowan.edu. *Application contact:* Karen Haynes, Graduate Coordinator, 856-256-4052, E-mail: haynes@rowan.edu.

Rutgers, The State University of New Jersey, Newark, Graduate School, Program in Management, Newark, NJ 07102. Offers accounting (PhD); accounting information systems (PhD); computer information systems (PhD); finance (PhD); information technology (PhD); international business (PhD); management science (PhD); marketing (PhD); organization management (PhD). *Accreditation:* AACSB. *Degree requirements:* For doctorate, thesis/dissertation, cumulative exams. *Entrance requirements:* For doctorate, GMAT or GRE General Test, minimum undergraduate B average. Additional exam requirements/recommendations for international students: Required—TOEFL. Electronic applications accepted. *Faculty research:* Technology management, leadership and teams, consumer behavior, financial and markets, logistics.

Rutgers, The State University of New Jersey, Newark, Rutgers Business School–Newark and New Brunswick, Department of Marketing, Newark, NJ 07102. Offers MBA. *Entrance requirements:* For master's, GMAT. Additional exam requirements/recommendations for international students: Required—TOEFL.

Sacred Heart University, Graduate Programs, John F. Welch College of Business, Fairfield, CT 06825-1000. Offers accounting (MBA); finance (MBA); management (MBA); marketing (MBA). *Accreditation:* AACSB. Part-time and evening/weekend programs available. Post-baccalaureate distance learning degree programs offered. *Faculty:* 33 full-time, 15 part-time/adjunct. *Students:* 36 full-time (12 women), 124 part-time (64 women); includes 28 minority (10 African Americans, 8 Asian Americans or Pacific Islanders, 10 Hispanic Americans), 6 international. Average age 32. 63 applicants, 71% accepted, 37 enrolled. In 2009, 41 master's awarded. *Degree requirements:* For master's, thesis or alternative. *Entrance requirements:* For master's, GMAT (preferred) or GRE General Test. Additional exam requirements/recommendations for international students: Required—TOEFL (minimum score 550 paper-based; 213 computer-based; 75 iBT). *Application deadline:* Applications are processed on a rolling basis. Application fee: $50 ($100 for international students). Electronic applications accepted. *Expenses:* Contact institution. *Financial support:* Career-related internships or fieldwork, institutionally sponsored loans, and unspecified assistantships available. Support available to part-time students. Financial award applicants required to submit FAFSA. *Faculty research:* Management of organizations, international business management of technology. *Unit head:* Dr. John J. Petillo, Dean, 203-396-8084, E-mail: petilloj@sacredheart.edu. *Application contact:* Dean Alexis Haakonsen, Dean of Graduate Admissions, 203-365-7619, Fax: 203-365-4732, E-mail: gradstudies@sacredheart.edu.

Sage Graduate School, Graduate School, School of Management, Program in Business Administration, Troy, NY 12180-4115. Offers business strategy (MBA); finance (MBA); human resources (MBA); marketing (MBA); JD/MBA. Part-time and evening/weekend programs available. *Faculty:* 4 full-time (2 women), 6 part-time/adjunct (0 women). *Students:* 9 full-time (7 women), 68 part-time (44 women); includes 11 minority (5 African Americans, 2 Asian Americans or Pacific Islanders, 4 Hispanic Americans), 2 international. Average age 31. 50 applicants, 60% accepted, 17 enrolled. In 2009, 19 master's awarded. *Entrance requirements:* For master's, minimum GPA of 2.75, resume, 2 letters of recommendation. Additional exam requirements/recommendations for international students: Required—TOEFL (minimum score 550 paper-based; 213 computer-based). *Application deadline:* Applications are processed on a rolling basis. Application fee: $40. *Expenses:* Tuition: Full-time $10,620; part-time $590 per credit hour. *Financial support:* Fellowships, research assistantships, Federal Work-Study, scholarships/grants, and unspecified assistantships available. Support available to part-time students. Financial award application deadline: 3/1; financial award applicants required to submit FAFSA. *Unit head:* Daniel Robeson, Chair, Management Department, 518-292-1770, Fax: 518-292-5414, E-mail: robesd@sage.edu. *Application contact:* Wendy D. Diefendorf, Director of Graduate and Adult Admission, 518-244-2443, Fax: 518-244-6880, E-mail: diefew@sage.edu.

St. Edward's University, School of Management and Business, Area of Business Administration, Austin, TX 78704. Offers accounting (MBA); business management (MBA); corporate finance (MBA, Certificate); global entrepreneurship (MBA); human resource management (MBA, Certificate); management information systems (MBA, Certificate); marketing (MBA, Certificate); operations management (MBA, Certificate). Part-time and evening/weekend programs available. *Faculty:* 20 full-time (9 women), 13 part-time/adjunct (4 women). *Students:* 29 full-time (16 women), 307 part-time (152 women); includes 116 minority (27 African Americans, 1 American Indian/Alaska Native, 16 Asian Americans or Pacific Islanders, 72 Hispanic Americans), 9 international. Average age 33. 129 applicants, 75% accepted, 74 enrolled. In 2009, 108 master's awarded. *Degree requirements:* For master's, minimum of 24 resident hours. *Entrance requirements:* For master's, GMAT or GRE General Test, minimum GPA of 2.75 in last 60 hours of course work. Additional exam requirements/recommendations for international students: Required—TOEFL (minimum score 550 paper-based; 213 computer-based; 79 iBT) or IELTS (minimum score 6). *Application deadline:* For fall admission, 7/1 for domestic and international students; for spring admission, 11/1 for domestic and international students. Applications are processed on a rolling basis. Application fee: $45 ($50 for international students). Electronic applications accepted. *Expenses:* Tuition: Full-time $14,922; part-time $829 per credit hour. Required fees: $50 per trimester. Full-time tuition and fees vary according to course load and program. *Financial support:* In 2009–10, 14 students received support. Scholarships/grants available. *Faculty research:* Operations management, minority entrepreneurship, globalization, professional services marketing. *Unit head:* Dr. Dianne Hill, Director, 512-428-1295, Fax: 512-448-8492, E-mail: dianneh@stedwards.edu. *Application contact:* Kelly Luna, Graduate Admissions Coordinator, 512-233-1697, Fax: 512-428-1032, E-mail: kellyl@stedwards.edu.

St. John's University, The Peter J. Tobin College of Business, Department of Marketing, Queens, NY 11439. Offers MBA, Adv C. Part-time and evening/weekend programs available. *Students:* 50 full-time (32 women), 32 part-time (18 women); includes 15 minority (8 African Americans, 5 Asian Americans or Pacific Islanders, 2 Hispanic Americans), 26 international. Average age 26. 89 applicants, 69% accepted, 33 enrolled. In 2009, 33 master's awarded. *Degree requirements:* For master's, comprehensive exam (for some programs), thesis optional. *Entrance requirements:* For master's, GMAT, 2 letters of recommendation, resume; for Adv C, GMAT, 2 letters of recommendation, resume, undergraduate transcripts, essay. Additional exam requirements/recommendations for international students: Required—TOEFL (minimum score 500 paper-based; 173 computer-based; 61 iBT), IELTS (minimum score 5.5). *Application deadline:* For fall admission, 5/1 priority date for domestic and international students; for spring admission, 11/1 priority date for domestic and international students. Applications are processed on a rolling basis. Application fee: $70. Electronic applications accepted. *Expenses:* Contact institution. *Financial support:* Research assistantships, scholarships/grants available. Support available to part-time students. Financial award application deadline: 3/1; financial award applicants required to submit FAFSA. *Faculty research:* Global brand management, China's Stimulus Plan, measuring attitude, marketing in India, consumer decision making. *Unit head:* Dr. A. Noel Doherty, Acting Chair, 718-990-7370, Fax: 718-990-1868, E-mail: dohertya@stjohns.edu. *Application contact:* Nicole T. Bryan, Assistant Dean, 718-990-2599, Fax: 718-990-5242, E-mail: tcbgradadmissions@stjohns.edu.

Saint Joseph's University, Erivan K. Haub School of Business, Executive Master's in Food Marketing Program, Philadelphia, PA 19131-1395. Offers MBA, MS. Part-time programs available. *Students:* 70 part-time (35 women); includes 7 minority (3 African Americans, 2 Asian Americans or Pacific Islanders, 2 Hispanic Americans). Average age 36. In 2009, 14 master's awarded. *Entrance requirements:* For master's, 4 years of industry experience, interview or GMAT, 2 letters of recommendation, resume. Additional exam requirements/

Marketing

Saint Joseph's University (continued)
recommendations for international students: Required—TOEFL (minimum score 550 paper-based; 213 computer-based; 79 iBT) or IELTS (minimum score 6.5). *Application deadline:* For fall admission, 7/15 priority date for domestic students, 4/15 priority date for international students; for spring admission, 11/15 priority date for domestic students, 10/15 priority date for international students. Applications are processed on a rolling basis. Application fee: $0. Electronic applications accepted. *Expenses:* Contact institution. *Financial support:* In 2009–10, research assistantships with partial tuition reimbursements (averaging $4,000 per year), teaching assistantships (averaging $4,000 per year) were awarded; fellowships, institutionally sponsored loans, tuition waivers (partial), and unspecified assistantships also available. Financial award application deadline: 5/1; financial award applicants required to submit FAFSA. *Faculty research:* Marketing strategy, obesity, business ethics, bio-defense, international food marketing. *Unit head:* Christine Hartmann, Director, 610-660-1659, Fax: 610-660-3153, E-mail: chartman@sju.edu. *Application contact:* Amanda Basile, Program Administrator, Master's in Food Marketing Programs, 610-660-3151, Fax: 610-660-3153, E-mail: abasile@sju.edu.

Saint Joseph's University, Erivan K. Haub School of Business, Executive Pharmaceutical Marketing MBA Program, Philadelphia, PA 19131-1395. Offers executive pharmaceutical marketing (Post Master's Certificate); pharmaceutical marketing (MBA). Part-time and evening/weekend programs available. Postbaccalaureate distance learning degree programs offered (minimal on-campus study). *Students:* 12 full-time (4 women), 91 part-time (30 women); includes 14 minority (4 African Americans, 8 Asian Americans or Pacific Islanders, 2 Hispanic Americans). Average age 38. In 2009, 38 master's awarded. *Entrance requirements:* For master's, 4 years of industry experience, letter of recommendation, resume, interview; for Post Master's Certificate, MBA, 4 years of industry experience, resume. Additional exam requirements/recommendations for international students: Required—TOEFL (minimum score 550 paper-based; 213 computer-based; 79 iBT) or IELTS (minimum score 6.5). *Application deadline:* For fall admission, 7/15 priority date for domestic students, 4/15 priority date for international students; for spring admission, 11/15 priority date for domestic students, 10/15 priority date for international students. Applications are processed on a rolling basis. Electronic applications accepted. *Expenses:* Tuition: Part-time $729 per credit hour. Tuition and fees vary according to degree level and program. *Financial support:* Scholarships/grants available. Financial award applicants required to submit FAFSA. *Faculty research:* Pharmaceutical strategy, Internet and pharmaceuticals, pharmaceutical promotion. *Unit head:* Terese W. Waldron, Director, 610-660-3150, Fax: 610-660-5160, E-mail: twaldron@sju.edu. *Application contact:* Christine Anderson, Senior Manager, Executive Relations and Industry Outreach, 610-660-3157, Fax: 610-660-3160, E-mail: christine.anderson@sju.edu.

Saint Joseph's University, Erivan K. Haub School of Business, MS Program in International Marketing, Philadelphia, PA 19131. Offers MS. Part-time and evening/weekend programs available. *Students:* 33 full-time (27 women), 11 part-time (6 women); includes 3 minority (1 African American, 1 Asian American or Pacific Islander, 1 Hispanic American), 24 international. Average age 25. In 2009, 19 master's awarded. *Entrance requirements:* For master's, GMAT, 2 letters of recommendation, resume. Additional exam requirements/recommendations for international students: Required—TOEFL (minimum score 550 paper-based; 213 computer-based; 79 iBT) or IELTS (minimum score 6.5). *Application deadline:* For fall admission, 7/15 priority date for domestic students; for spring admission, 11/15 priority date for domestic students. Applications are processed on a rolling basis. Application fee: $35. Electronic applications accepted. *Expenses:* Tuition: Part-time $729 per credit hour. Tuition and fees vary according to degree level and program. *Financial support:* In 2009–10, 2 research assistantships with partial tuition reimbursements (averaging $8,000 per year) were awarded; unspecified assistantships also available. Financial award application deadline: 5/1; financial award applicants required to submit FAFSA. *Faculty research:* Export marketing, global marketing, international marketing research, new product development, emerging markets, international consumer behavior. *Unit head:* Christine Kaczmar-Russo, Director, 610-660-1238, Fax: 610-660-3239, E-mail: ckaczmar@sju.edu. *Application contact:* Christine Kaczmar-Russo, Director, 610-660-1238, Fax: 610-660-3239, E-mail: ckaczmar@sju.edu.

Saint Joseph's University, Erivan K. Haub School of Business, Professional MBA Program, Philadelphia, PA 19131-1395. Offers accounting (MBA); finance (MBA), including finance; general business (MBA); health and medical services administration (MBA); human resource management (MBA); international business (MBA); international marketing (MBA); management (MBA); marketing (MBA); DO/MBA. Part-time and evening/weekend programs available. *Students:* 51 full-time (24 women), 480 part-time (184 women); includes 71 minority (32 African Americans, 1 American Indian/Alaska Native, 30 Asian Americans or Pacific Islanders, 8 Hispanic Americans), 38 international. Average age 30. In 2009, 190 master's awarded. *Entrance requirements:* For master's, GMAT or GRE, 2 letters of recommendation, resume. Additional exam requirements/recommendations for international students: Required—TOEFL (minimum score 550 paper-based; 213 computer-based; 79 iBT) or IELTS (minimum score 6.5). *Application deadline:* For fall admission, 7/15 priority date for domestic students, 4/15 priority date for international students; for spring admission, 11/15 priority date for domestic students, 10/15 priority date for international students. Applications are processed on a rolling basis. Application fee: $35. Electronic applications accepted. *Expenses:* Tuition: Part-time $729 per credit hour. Tuition and fees vary according to degree level and program. *Financial support:* Scholarships/grants and unspecified assistantships available. Financial award application deadline: 5/1. *Unit head:* Adele C. Foley, Associate Dean/Director, Graduate Business Programs, 610-660-1691, Fax: 610-660-1599, E-mail: afoley@sju.edu. *Application contact:* Janine N. Guerra, Esq., Assistant Director, MBA Program, 610-660-1695, Fax: 610-660-1599, E-mail: jguerra@sju.edu.

Saint Leo University, Graduate Business Studies, Saint Leo, FL 33574-6665. Offers accounting (MBA); business (MBA); criminal justice (MBA); health services management (MBA); human resource administration (MBA); information security management (MBA); marketing (MBA); sport business (MBA). Part-time and evening/weekend programs available. Postbaccalaureate distance learning degree programs offered (no on-campus study). *Faculty:* 31 full-time (5 women), 48 part-time/adjunct (17 women). *Students:* 1,433 full-time (856 women), 3 part-time (1 woman); includes 601 minority (429 African Americans, 8 American Indian/Alaska Native, 75 Asian Americans or Pacific Islanders, 89 Hispanic Americans), 11 international. Average age 37. In 2009, 405 master's awarded. *Entrance requirements:* For master's, GMAT (minimum score 500 if applicant does not have 5 years of professional work experience), bachelor's degree from regionally-accredited college or university with minimum GPA of 3.0 in the last 60 hours of coursework; 5 years of professional work experience; resume; 2 letters of recommendation. Additional exam requirements/recommendations for international students: Required—TOEFL (minimum score 550 paper-based; 213 computer-based; 80 iBT). *Application deadline:* For fall admission, 7/1 priority date for domestic students; for spring admission, 11/12 priority date for domestic students. Applications are processed on a rolling basis. Application fee: $75. Electronic applications accepted. *Expenses:* Contact institution. *Financial support:* In 2009–10, 1 student received support. Career-related internships or fieldwork, Federal Work-Study, and health care benefits available. Financial award application deadline: 3/1; financial award applicants required to submit FAFSA. *Unit head:* Dr. Robert Robertson, Director, 352-588-7390, Fax: 352-588-8585, E-mail: mba@saintleo.edu. *Application contact:* Jared Welling, Director, Graduate/Weekend and Evening Admission, 800-707-8846, Fax: 352-588-7873, E-mail: grad.admissions@saintleo.edu.

Saint Peter's College, Graduate Business Programs, MBA Program, Jersey City, NJ 07306-5997. Offers finance (MBA); health care administration (MBA); international business (MBA); management (MBA); management information systems (MBA); marketing (MBA); MBA/MS. Part-time and evening/weekend programs available. *Entrance requirements:* Additional exam requirements/recommendations for international students: Required—TOEFL. *Application deadline:* Applications are processed on a rolling basis. Electronic applications accepted. *Expenses:* Tuition: Part-time $971 per credit. *Financial support:* Career-related internships or fieldwork, Federal Work-Study, and institutionally sponsored loans available. *Faculty research:* Finance, health care management, human resource management, international business, management, management information systems, marketing, risk management.

St. Thomas Aquinas College, Division of Business Administration, Sparkill, NY 10976. Offers business administration (MBA); finance (MBA); management (MBA); marketing (MBA). Part-time and evening/weekend programs available. *Entrance requirements:* For master's, GMAT. Additional exam requirements/recommendations for international students: Required—TOEFL. Electronic applications accepted.

Saint Xavier University, Graduate Studies, Graham School of Management, Chicago, IL 60655-3105. Offers e-commerce (MBA); employee health benefits (Certificate); finance (MBA, MS); financial analysis and investments (MBA); financial planning (MBA, Certificate); financial trading and practice (MBA, Certificate); generalist/administration (MBA); health administration (MBA, MS); managed care (Certificate); management (MBA, MS); marketing (MBA); public and non-profit management (MBA); public health (MPH); service management (MBA); training and performance management (MBA); MBA/MS. *Accreditation:* ACBSP. Part-time and evening/weekend programs available. *Entrance requirements:* For master's, GMAT, minimum GPA of 3.0, 2 years of work experience. Electronic applications accepted. *Expenses:* Contact institution.

San Diego State University, Graduate and Research Affairs, College of Business Administration, Department of Marketing, San Diego, CA 92182. Offers MS. Part-time and evening/weekend programs available. *Degree requirements:* For master's, thesis or alternative. *Entrance requirements:* For master's, GMAT, resume, letters of reference. Additional exam requirements/recommendations for international students: Required—TOEFL. Electronic applications accepted.

Santa Clara University, Leavey School of Business, Program in Business Administration, Santa Clara, CA 95053. Offers accounting (MBA); entrepreneurship (MBA); executive MBA (EMBA); finance (MBA); food and agribusiness (MBA); international business (MBA); leading people and organizations (MBA); managing technology and innovation (MBA); marketing management (MBA); supply chain management (MBA). *Accreditation:* AACSB. Part-time and evening/weekend programs available. *Students:* 228 full-time (88 women), 838 part-time (265 women); includes 388 minority (17 African Americans, 2 American Indian/Alaska Native, 326 Asian Americans or Pacific Islanders, 43 Hispanic Americans), 218 international. Average age 31. 486 applicants, 77% accepted, 263 enrolled. In 2009, 317 master's awarded. *Degree requirements:* For master's, thesis or alternative. *Entrance requirements:* For master's, GMAT, GRE. Additional exam requirements/recommendations for international students: Required—TOEFL (minimum score 600 paper-based; 250 computer-based; 100 iBT). *Application deadline:* For fall admission, 6/1 for domestic and international students; for spring admission, 1/19 for domestic students, 1/17 for international students. Applications are processed on a rolling basis. Application fee: $75 ($100 for international students). Electronic applications accepted. *Expenses:* Contact institution. *Financial support:* Fellowships with partial tuition reimbursements, research assistantships with partial tuition reimbursements, career-related internships or fieldwork, Federal Work-Study, institutionally sponsored loans, scholarships/grants, health care benefits, and unspecified assistantships available. Support available to part-time students. Financial award applicants required to submit FAFSA. *Unit head:* Elizabeth B. Ford, Senior Assistant Dean, 408-554-2752, Fax: 408-554-4571, E-mail: eford@scu.edu. *Application contact:* Jennifer W. Taylor, Senior Director, 408-554-4539, Fax: 408-554-4571, E-mail: mbaadmissions@scu.edu.

Seton Hall University, Stillman School of Business, Programs in Business Administration, South Orange, NJ 07079-2697. Offers accounting (MBA); finance (MBA); information technology management (MBA); international business (MBA); management (MBA); marketing (MBA); sport management (MBA). Part-time and evening/weekend programs available. *Faculty:* 57 full-time (13 women), 30 part-time/adjunct (3 women). *Students:* 69 full-time (26 women), 217 part-time (91 women); includes 53 minority (11 African Americans, 35 Asian Americans or Pacific Islanders, 7 Hispanic Americans), 38 international. Average age 29. 286 applicants, 70% accepted, 130 enrolled. In 2009, 110 master's awarded. *Degree requirements:* For master's, 20 hours of community service (Social Responsibility Project). *Entrance requirements:* For master's, GMAT, minimum GPA of 3.0. Additional exam requirements/recommendations for international students: Required—TOEFL (minimum score 607 paper-based; 254 computer-based; 102 iBT), or IELTS, or Pearson Test of English (PTE). *Application deadline:* For fall admission, 5/31 priority date for domestic students, 3/31 priority date for international students; for spring admission, 10/31 priority date for domestic students, 4/30 priority date for international students. Applications are processed on a rolling basis. Application fee: $75. Electronic applications accepted. *Financial support:* In 2009–10, research assistantships with full tuition reimbursements (averaging $34,404 per year); career-related internships or fieldwork, Federal Work-Study, scholarships/grants, and unspecified assistantships also available. Support available to part-time students. Financial award application deadline: 6/30; financial award applicants required to submit FAFSA. *Faculty research:* Financial, hedge funds, international business, legal issues, disclosure and branding. *Unit head:* Dr. Joyce A. Strawser, Associate Dean for Undergraduate and MBA Curricula, 973-761-9225, Fax: 973-761-9217, E-mail: strawsjo@shu.edu. *Application contact:* Catherine Bianchi, Director of Graduate Admissions, 973-761-9262, Fax: 973-761-9208, E-mail: catherine.bianchi@shu.edu.

Southern Adventist University, School of Business and Management, Collegedale, TN 37315-0370. Offers accounting (MBA); church administration (MSA); church and nonprofit leadership (MBA); financial management (MFM); healthcare administration (MBA); management (MBA); marketing management (MBA); outdoor education (MSA); MFM. Part-time and evening/weekend programs available. Postbaccalaureate distance learning degree programs offered (no on-campus study). *Faculty:* 2 full-time (0 women), 8 part-time/adjunct (1 woman). *Students:* 55 full-time (32 women), 30 part-time (22 women); includes 23 minority (14 African Americans, 1 American Indian/Alaska Native, 1 Asian American or Pacific Islander, 7 Hispanic Americans). Average age 35. In 2009, 20 master's awarded. *Entrance requirements:* For master's, GMAT. Additional exam requirements/recommendations for international students: Required—TOEFL (minimum score 600 paper-based; 250 computer-based; 100 iBT). *Application deadline:* For fall admission, 8/1 priority date for domestic students, 7/1 for international students; for winter admission, 12/1 priority date for domestic students, 11/1 for international students; for spring admission, 4/1 priority date for domestic students, 3/1 for international students. Applications are processed on a rolling basis. Application fee: $25. Electronic applications accepted. *Expenses:* Tuition: Full-time $13,149; part-time $487 per credit hour. *Financial support:* In 2009–10, 32 students received support. Scholarships/grants and unspecified assistantships available. Financial award application deadline: 9/1; financial award applicants required to submit FAFSA. *Unit head:* Dr. Don Van Ornam, Dean, 423-236-2750, Fax: 423-236-1527, E-mail: dvanorna@southern.edu. *Application contact:* Linda Wilhelm, Admissions Coordinator, 423-236-2751, Fax: 423-236-1527, E-mail: sbm@southern.edu.

Southern Methodist University, Cox School of Business, MBA Program, Dallas, TX 75275. Offers accounting (MBA); finance (MBA); information technology and operations management (MBA); management (MBA); marketing (MBA); strategy and entrepreneurship (MBA). *Students:* 396 full-time (91 women), 401 part-time (109 women); includes 185 minority (34 African Americans, 5 American Indian/Alaska Native, 102 Asian Americans or Pacific Islanders, 44 Hispanic Americans), 76 international. Average age 31. In 2009, 363 master's awarded. *Unit head:* Dr. Albert W. Niemi, Dean, 214-768-3012, Fax: 214-768-3713, E-mail: aniemi@mail.cox.smu.edu. *Application contact:* Path Cudney, Director of MBA Admissions, 214-768-3001, Fax: 214-768-3956, E-mail: pcudney@mail.cox.smu.edu.

Southern New Hampshire University, School of Business, Manchester, NH 03106-1045. Offers accounting (MS); business administration (MBA, Certificate), including accounting (Certificate), business administration (MBA), finance (Certificate), forensic accounting (Certificate), human resources management (Certificate), international business (Certificate), international sport management (Certificate), leadership of not for profit organizations (Certificate), marketing (Certificate), operations management (Certificate), sport management (Certificate), taxation (Certificate); finance (MS); hospitality and tourism leadership (Certificate); information technology (MS, Certificate); information technology/international business (Certificate); integrated marketing communications (Certificate); international business (MS,

DBA); marketing (MS); operations and project management (MS); organizational leadership (MS); project management (Certificate); sport management (MS); MBA/Certificate. *Accreditation:* ACBSP. Part-time and evening/weekend programs available. Postbaccalaureate distance learning degree programs offered (no on-campus study). Terminal master's awarded for partial completion of doctoral program. *Degree requirements:* For master's, one foreign language, comprehensive exam (for some programs), thesis or alternative; for doctorate, one foreign language, comprehensive exam, thesis/dissertation. *Entrance requirements:* For master's, minimum GPA of 2.5; for doctorate, GMAT. Additional exam requirements/recommendations for international students: Required—TOEFL (minimum score 500 paper-based). Electronic applications accepted.

Stephen F. Austin State University, Graduate School, College of Business, Program in Business Administration, Nacogdoches, TX 75962. Offers business (MBA); management and marketing (MBA). *Accreditation:* AACSB. Part-time and evening/weekend programs available. *Degree requirements:* For master's, comprehensive exam. *Entrance requirements:* For master's, GMAT, minimum AACSB index of 1000. Additional exam requirements/recommendations for international students: Required—TOEFL (minimum score 550 paper-based; 213 computer-based). *Faculty research:* Strategic implications, information search, multinational firms, philosophical guidance.

Stony Brook University, State University of New York, Graduate School, College of Business, Program in Business Administration, Stony Brook, NY 11794. Offers finance (MBA, Certificate); health care management (MBA, Certificate); human resource management (Certificate); human resources (MBA); information systems management (MBA, Certificate); management (MBA); marketing (MBA). *Faculty:* 17 full-time (2 women), 25 part-time/adjunct (5 women). *Students:* 134 full-time (64 women), 112 part-time (44 women); includes 54 minority (8 African Americans, 1 American Indian/Alaska Native, 35 Asian Americans or Pacific Islanders, 10 Hispanic Americans), 56 international. 222 applicants, 55% accepted. In 2009, 134 master's, 5 other advanced degrees awarded. Application fee: $60. *Expenses:* Tuition, state resident: full-time $8370; part-time $349 per credit. Tuition, nonresident: full-time $13,250; part-time $552 per credit. Required fees: $933. *Financial support:* In 2009–10, 2 teaching assistantships were awarded. *Unit head:* Joseph McDonnell, Interim Dean, 631-632-7180. *Application contact:* Dr. Aristotle Lekacos, Director, Graduate Program, 631-632-7171, E-mail: aristotle.lekacost@notes.cc.sunysb.edu.

Strayer University, Graduate Studies, Washington, DC 20005-2603. Offers accounting (MS); acquisition (MBA); business administration (MBA); communications technology (MS); educational management (M Ed); finance (MBA); health services administration (MHSA); hospitality and tourism management (MBA); human resource management (MBA); information systems (MS), including computer security management, decision support system management, enterprise resource management, network management, software engineering management, systems development management; management (MBA); management information systems (MS); marketing (MBA); professional accounting (MS), including accounting information systems, controllership, taxation; public administration (MPA); supply chain management (MBA); technology in education (M Ed). Programs also offered at campus locations in Birmingham, AL; Chamblee, GA; Cobb County, GA; Morrow, GA; White Marsh, MD; Charleston, SC; Columbia, SC; Greensboro, NC; Greenville, SC; Lexington, KY; Louisville, KY; Nashville, TN; North Raleigh, NC; Washington, DC. Part-time and evening/weekend programs available. Postbaccalaureate distance learning degree programs offered (minimal on-campus study). *Degree requirements:* For master's, thesis. *Entrance requirements:* For master's, GMAT, GRE General Test, bachelor's degree from an accredited college or university, minimum undergraduate GPA of 2.75. Electronic applications accepted.

Suffolk University, Sawyer Business School, Master of Business Administration Program, Boston, MA 02108-2770. Offers accounting (MBA); business administration (APC); corporate financial executive track (MBA); entrepreneurship (MBA); executive business administration (EMBA); finance (MBA); global business administration (GMBA); health administration (MBA); international business (MBA); marketing (MBA); organizational behavior (MBA); strategic management (MBA); taxation (MBA); JD/MBA; MBA/GDPA; MBA/MHA; MBA/MSA; MBA/MSF; MBA/MST. *Accreditation:* AACSB. Part-time and evening/weekend programs available. Post-baccalaureate distance learning degree programs offered (no on-campus study). *Faculty:* 103 full-time (30 women), 63 part-time/adjunct (19 women). *Students:* 173 full-time (68 women), 406 part-time (178 women); includes 51 minority (16 African Americans, 3 American Indian/Alaska Native, 22 Asian Americans or Pacific Islanders, 10 Hispanic Americans), 90 international. Average age 29. 460 applicants, 72% accepted, 157 enrolled. In 2009, 245 master's awarded. *Entrance requirements:* For master's, GMAT, minimum undergraduate GPA of 2.75 (MBA), 5 years of managerial experience (EMBA). Additional exam requirements/recommendations for international students: Required—TOEFL (minimum score 550 paper-based; 213 computer-based). *Application deadline:* For fall admission, 6/15 priority date for domestic students, 6/15 for international students; for spring admission, 11/1 priority date for domestic students, 11/1 for international students. Applications are processed on a rolling basis. Application fee: $50. Electronic applications accepted. *Expenses:* Tuition: Full-time $33,000; part-time $1100 per credit. Required fees: $20. Tuition and fees vary according to program. *Financial support:* In 2009–10, 284 students received support, including 99 fellowships with full and partial tuition reimbursements available (averaging $13,599 per year); career-related internships or fieldwork, Federal Work-Study, and institutionally sponsored loans also available. Support available to part-time students. Financial award application deadline: 4/1; financial award applicants required to submit FAFSA. *Faculty research:* Foreign investments; career strategies and boundaryless careers; corporate ethics codes; interest rates, inflation, and growth options; innovation and product development performance. *Unit head:* Lillian Hallberg, Assistant Dean of Graduate Programs/Director of MBA Programs, 617-573-8306, E-mail: lhallber@suffolk.edu. *Application contact:* Judith Reynolds, Director of Graduate Admissions, 617-573-8302, Fax: 617-305-1733, E-mail: grad.admission@suffolk.edu.

Syracuse University, Martin J. Whitman School of Management, PhD Program in Business Administration, Syracuse, NY 13244. Offers accounting (PhD); finance (PhD); management information systems (PhD); managerial statistics (PhD); marketing (PhD); operations management (PhD); organizational behavior (PhD); strategy and human resources (PhD); supply chain management (PhD). *Degree requirements:* For doctorate, comprehensive exam, thesis/dissertation, summer research paper. *Entrance requirements:* For doctorate, GMAT or GRE General Test, 3 recommendations. Additional exam requirements/recommendations for international students: Required—TOEFL (minimum score 600 paper-based; 250 computer-based; 100 iBT). Electronic applications accepted. *Expenses:* Tuition: Full-time $26,808; part-time $1117 per credit. Required fees: $1024. *Faculty research:* Marketing models, market microstructure, supply chain, auditing, corporate governance.

Syracuse University, Martin J. Whitman School of Management, Program in Business Administration, Syracuse, NY 13244. Offers accounting (MBA); entrepreneurship (MBA); finance (MBA); marketing (MBA); supply chain management (MBA). Postbaccalaureate distance learning degree programs offered (minimal on-campus study). *Entrance requirements:* For master's, GMAT, 2 letters of recommendation. Additional exam requirements/recommendations for international students: Required—TOEFL (minimum score 600 paper-based; 250 computer-based; 100 iBT). Electronic applications accepted. *Expenses:* Tuition: Full-time $26,808; part-time $1117 per credit. Required fees: $1024.

Temple University, Graduate School, Fox School of Business, Doctoral Programs in Business, Philadelphia, PA 19122-6096. Offers accounting (PhD); entrepreneurship (PhD); finance (PhD); human resource administration (PhD); international business (PhD); management information systems (PhD); marketing (PhD); risk management and insurance (PhD); statistics (PhD); strategic management (PhD); tourism and sport (PhD). *Accreditation:* AACSB. *Degree requirements:* For doctorate, thesis/dissertation. *Entrance requirements:* For doctorate, GRE General Test, GMAT, minimum GPA of 3.0, master's degree. Additional exam requirements/recommendations for international students: Required—TOEFL (minimum score 600 paper-based; 250 computer-based; 100 iBT), IELTS (minimum score 7.5). Electronic applications accepted.

Temple University, Graduate School, Fox School of Business, MBA Programs, Philadelphia, PA 19122-6096. Offers accounting (MBA); business management (MBA); financial management (MBA); healthcare and life sciences innovation (MBA); human resource management (MBA); international business (IMBA); IT management (MBA); marketing management (MBA); pharmaceutical management (MBA); strategic management (EMBA, MBA). EMBA offered in Philadelphia, PA and Tokyo, Japan. *Accreditation:* AACSB. Part-time and evening/weekend programs available. Postbaccalaureate distance learning degree programs offered (minimal on-campus study). *Entrance requirements:* For master's, GMAT, minimum undergraduate GPA of 3.0. Additional exam requirements/recommendations for international students: Required—TOEFL (minimum score 600 paper-based; 250 computer-based; 100 iBT), IELTS (minimum score 7.5).

Temple University, Graduate School, Fox School of Business, Specialized Master's Programs, Philadelphia, PA 19122-6096. Offers accounting and financial management (MS); actuarial science (MS); finance (MS); financial engineering (MS); healthcare financial management (MS); healthcare management (MHM); human resource management (MS); management information systems (MS); marketing (MS); statistics (MS). *Accreditation:* AACSB. Part-time programs available. *Entrance requirements:* For master's, GRE General Test or GMAT, minimum undergraduate GPA of 3.0. Additional exam requirements/recommendations for international students: Required—TOEFL (minimum score 600 paper-based; 250 computer-based; 100 iBT), IELTS (minimum score 7.5).

Texas A&M University, Mays Business School, Department of Marketing, College Station, TX 77843. Offers MS, PhD. Terminal master's awarded for partial completion of doctoral program. *Degree requirements:* For master's, comprehensive exam; for doctorate, thesis/dissertation. *Entrance requirements:* For master's, GMAT; for doctorate, GMAT or GRE General Test. Additional exam requirements/recommendations for international students: Required—TOEFL. *Expenses:* Tuition, state resident: full-time $3991; part-time $221.74 per credit hour. Tuition, nonresident: full-time $9049; part-time $502.74 per credit hour. *Faculty research:* Consumer behavior, innovation and product management, international marketing, marketing management and strategy, services marketing.

Texas Tech University, Jerry S. Rawls College of Business Administration, Area of Marketing and International Business, Lubbock, TX 79409. Offers marketing (PhD). Part-time programs available. *Faculty:* 12 full-time (3 women), 1 part-time/adjunct (0 women). *Students:* 7 full-time (2 women), 5 international. Average age 33. 18 applicants, 39% accepted, 5 enrolled. In 2009, 1 doctorate awarded. *Degree requirements:* For doctorate, thesis/dissertation, qualifying exams. *Entrance requirements:* For doctorate, GMAT, holistic profile of academic credentials. Additional exam requirements/recommendations for international students: Required—TOEFL (minimum score 550 paper-based; 213 computer-based; 79 iBT). *Application deadline:* For fall admission, 4/1 priority date for domestic students, 1/15 priority date for international students; for spring admission, 9/1 priority date for domestic students, 7/15 priority date for international students. Applications are processed on a rolling basis. Application fee: $50 ($75 for international students). Electronic applications accepted. *Expenses:* Tuition, state resident: full-time $5100; part-time $213 per credit hour. Tuition, nonresident: full-time $11,748; part-time $490 per credit hour. Required fees: $2298; $50 per credit hour. $555 per semester. *Financial support:* In 2009–10, 7 research assistantships (averaging $8,000 per year), 4 teaching assistantships (averaging $17,000 per year) were awarded; Federal Work-Study and scholarships/grants also available. *Faculty research:* Consumer behavior, macromarketing, marketing strategy and strategic planning. *Unit head:* Dr. Debra Laverie, Area Coordinator, 806-742-3953, Fax: 806-742-2199, E-mail: debbie.laveric@ttu.edu. *Application contact:* Cynthia D. Barnes, Director, Graduate Services Center, 806-742-3184, Fax: 806-742-3958, E-mail: ba_grad@ttu.edu.

Texas Tech University, Jerry S. Rawls College of Business Administration, Programs in Business Administration, Lubbock, TX 79409. Offers agricultural business (MBA); business administration (IMBA); entrepreneurship (MBA); finance (MBA); general business (MBA); health organization management (MBA); international business (MBA); management and leadership skills (MBA); management information systems (MBA); marketing (MBA); statistics (MBA); JD/MBA; MBA/M Arch; MBA/MA; MBA/MD; MBA/MS; MBA/Pharm D. Part-time and evening/weekend programs available. *Faculty:* 54 full-time (9 women), 5 part-time/adjunct (0 women). *Students:* 59 full-time (15 women), 487 part-time (148 women); includes 107 minority (24 African Americans, 4 American Indian/Alaska Native, 30 Asian Americans or Pacific Islanders, 49 Hispanic Americans), 51 international. Average age 30. 477 applicants, 81% accepted, 302 enrolled. In 2009, 185 degrees awarded. *Degree requirements:* For master's, capstone course. *Entrance requirements:* For master's, GMAT, holistic review of academic credentials. Additional exam requirements/recommendations for international students: Required—TOEFL (minimum score 550 paper-based; 213 computer-based; 79 iBT). *Application deadline:* For fall admission, 4/1 priority date for domestic students, 1/15 priority date for international students; for spring admission, 9/1 priority date for domestic students, 7/15 priority date for international students. Applications are processed on a rolling basis. Application fee: $50 ($75 for international students). Electronic applications accepted. *Expenses:* Tuition, state resident: full-time $5100; part-time $213 per credit hour. Tuition, nonresident: full-time $11,748; part-time $490 per credit hour. Required fees: $2298; $50 per credit hour. $555 per semester. *Financial support:* In 2009–10, 13 research assistantships (averaging $8,000 per year) were awarded; teaching assistantships, career-related internships or fieldwork, Federal Work-Study, scholarships/grants, health care benefits, and unspecified assistantships also available. Support available to part-time students. Financial award applicants required to submit FAFSA. *Unit head:* Dr. W. Jay Conover, Director, 806-742-1546, Fax: 806-742-3958, E-mail: jay.conover@ttu.edu. *Application contact:* Cynthia D. Barnes, Director, Graduate Services Center, 806-742-3184, Fax: 806-742-3958, E-mail: ba_grad@ttu.edu.

TUI University, College of Business Administration, Program in Business Administration, Cypress, CA 90630. Offers business administration (PhD); conflict and negotiation management (MBA); criminal justice administration (MBA); entrepreneurship (MBA); finance (MBA); general management (MBA); government accounting (MBA); human resource management (MBA); information security and digital assurance management (MBA); information technology management (MBA); international business (MBA); logistics management (MBA); marketing (MBA); project management (MBA); public management (MBA); quality management (MBA); strategic leadership (MBA). Part-time and evening/weekend programs available. Postbaccalaureate distance learning degree programs offered (no on-campus study). *Degree requirements:* For doctorate, comprehensive exam, thesis/dissertation, defense of dissertation. *Entrance requirements:* For master's, minimum GPA of 2.5 (students with GPA 3.0 or greater may transfer up to 30% of graduate level credits); for doctorate, minimum GPA of 3.4, curriculum vitae, course work in research methods or statistics. Additional exam requirements/recommendations for international students: Required—TOEFL. Electronic applications accepted.

United States International University, School of Business Administration, Nairobi, Kenya. Offers finance (MBA); information technology management (MBA); integrated studies (MBA); management and organizational development (MS); marketing (MBA); strategic management (MBA). Part-time and evening/weekend programs available. *Degree requirements:* For master's, thesis. *Entrance requirements:* For master's, GMAT, 2 letters of reference, resume. Additional exam requirements/recommendations for international students: Required—TOEFL (minimum score 550 paper-based; 213 computer-based). *Faculty research:* Marketing in small business enterprises, total quality management in Kenya.

Universidad del Turabo, Graduate Programs, School in Business Administration, Online Business Administration Program, Gurabo, PR 00778-3030. Offers human resources (MBA); management (MBA); marketing (MBA); materials management (MBA).

Universidad del Turabo, Graduate Programs, School in Business Administration, Program in Marketing, Gurabo, PR 00778-3030. Offers MBA. Part-time and evening/weekend programs available. *Students:* 29 full-time (24 women), 27 part-time (16 women); includes 51 Hispanic Americans. Average age 30. 26 applicants, 96% accepted, 19 enrolled. In 2009, 40 master's awarded. *Entrance requirements:* For master's, GRE, EXADEP, interview. *Application deadline:* For fall admission, 8/5 for domestic students. Application fee: $25. *Unit head:* Marcelino

Marketing

Universidad del Turabo *(continued)*
Rivera, Dean, 787-743-7979 Ext. 4117. *Application contact:* Virginia Gonzalez, Admissions Officer, 787-746-3009.

Universidad Iberoamericana, Graduate School, Santo Domingo D.N., Dominican Republic. Offers advertising management (MM); business (MBA); constitutional law (MA); dentistry (DMD); educational management (MA); integrated marketing communication (MA); psychopedagogical intervention (M Ed); strategic management of human talent (MM).

Universidad Metropolitana, School of Business Administration, Program in Marketing, San Juan, PR 00928-1150. Offers MBA. Part-time programs available. *Degree requirements:* For master's, thesis or alternative. *Entrance requirements:* For master's, GMAT, PAEG, interview. Electronic applications accepted.

Université de Sherbrooke, Faculty of Administration, Program in Marketing, Sherbrooke, QC J1K 2R1, Canada. Offers M Sc. *Entrance requirements:* For master's, bachelor's degree. Electronic applications accepted.

Université Laval, Faculty of Administrative Sciences, Programs in Business Administration, Québec, QC G1K 7P4, Canada. Offers accounting (MBA); agri-food management (MBA); electronic business (MBA, Diploma); factory management and logistics (MBA); finance (MBA); firm management (MBA); geomatic management (MBA); information technology management (MBA); international management (MBA); management (MBA); management accounting (MBA, Diploma); marketing (MBA); modeling and organizational decision (MBA); occupational health and safety management (MBA); pharmacy management (MBA); social and environmental responsibility (MBA); technological entrepreneurship (Diploma). *Accreditation:* AACSB. Part-time and evening/weekend programs available. Postbaccalaureate distance learning degree programs offered (no on-campus study). *Entrance requirements:* For master's and Diploma, knowledge of French and English. Electronic applications accepted.

University at Albany, State University of New York, School of Business, Department of Marketing, Albany, NY 12222-0001. Offers MBA. *Degree requirements:* For master's, field study project. *Entrance requirements:* For master's, GMAT. Additional exam requirements/recommendations for international students: Required—TOEFL (minimum score 550 paper-based; 213 computer-based). Electronic applications accepted. *Faculty research:* Sales management, buyer-seller interaction, family decision making, sociological influence on consumption, health promotion.

The University of Akron, Graduate School, College of Business Administration, Department of Marketing, Akron, OH 44325. Offers international business (MBA); international business for international executive (MBA); strategic marketing (MBA); JD/MBA. Part-time and evening/weekend programs available. *Faculty:* 9 full-time (2 women), 10 part-time/adjunct (2 women). *Students:* 20 full-time (7 women), 40 part-time (21 women); includes 2 minority (1 African American, 1 Asian American or Pacific Islander), 12 international. Average age 31. 40 applicants, 60% accepted, 16 enrolled. In 2009, 16 master's awarded. *Entrance requirements:* For master's, GMAT, minimum GPA of 2.75, letters of recommendation, resume. Additional exam requirements/recommendations for international students: Required—TOEFL (minimum score 550 paper-based; 213 computer-based; 79 iBT). *Application deadline:* For fall admission, 8/1 for domestic and international students; for spring admission, 12/1 for domestic and international students. Application fee: $30 ($40 for international students). Electronic applications accepted. *Expenses:* Tuition, state resident: full-time $6570; part-time $365 per credit hour. Tuition, nonresident: full-time $11,250; part-time $625 per credit hour. *Financial support:* In 2009–10, 7 research assistantships with full tuition reimbursements were awarded. *Faculty research:* Multi-channel marketing, direct interactive marketing, strategic retailing, marketing strategy and telemarketing. Total annual research expenditures: $38,705. *Unit head:* Dr. Douglas Hausknecht, Interim Chair, 330-972-5798, E-mail: hauskne@uakron.edu. *Application contact:* Dr. Susan Hanlon, Director of Graduate Business Programs, 330-972-7043, Fax: 330-972-6588, E-mail: shanlon@uakron.edu.

The University of Alabama, Graduate School, Manderson Graduate School of Business, Department of Management and Marketing, Program in Marketing, Tuscaloosa, AL 35487. Offers MS, PhD. *Accreditation:* AACSB. *Faculty:* 24 full-time (7 women). *Students:* 63 full-time (35 women), 6 part-time (4 women); includes 6 minority (1 African American, 1 American Indian/Alaska Native, 2 Asian Americans or Pacific Islanders, 2 Hispanic Americans), 22 international. Average age 25. 155 applicants, 33% accepted, 38 enrolled. In 2009, 34 master's, 2 doctorates awarded. Terminal master's awarded for partial completion of doctoral program. *Median time to degree:* Of those who began their doctoral program in fall 2001, 100% received their degree in 8 years or less. *Degree requirements:* For master's, internship; for doctorate, comprehensive exam, thesis/dissertation. *Entrance requirements:* For master's, GRE or GMAT; for doctorate, GRE or GMAT, minimum GPA of 3.0. Additional exam requirements/recommendations for international students: Required—TOEFL (minimum score 600 paper-based) or IELTS (minimum score 6.5). *Application deadline:* For fall admission, 4/1 priority date for domestic and international students; for spring admission, 2/1 priority date for domestic and international students. Applications are processed on a rolling basis. Application fee: $50 ($60 for international students). Electronic applications accepted. *Expenses:* Tuition, state resident: full-time $7000. Tuition, nonresident: full-time $19,200. *Financial support:* In 2009–10, 1 fellowship with full tuition reimbursement (averaging $15,000 per year), 5 research assistantships with full tuition reimbursements (averaging $25,000 per year), 5 teaching assistantships with full tuition reimbursements (averaging $25,000 per year) were awarded; scholarships/grants, health care benefits, and unspecified assistantships also available. *Faculty research:* Relationship marketing, consumer behavior, services marketing, professional selling, supply chain management. *Unit head:* Dr. Robert M. Morgan, Department Head, 205-348-6183, Fax: 205-348-6695, E-mail: rmorgan@cba.ua.edu. *Application contact:* Courtney Cox, Office Associate II, 205-348-6183, Fax: 205-348-6695, E-mail: crhodes@cba.ua.edu.

The University of Alabama in Huntsville, School of Graduate Studies, College of Business Administration, Department of Management and Marketing, Huntsville, AL 35899. Offers management (MBA), including acquisition management, finance, human resource management, logistics and supply chain management, marketing, project management. *Accreditation:* AACSB. Part-time and evening/weekend programs available. *Faculty:* 7 full-time (1 woman), 1 part-time/adjunct (0 women). *Students:* 41 full-time (19 women), 155 part-time (59 women); includes 30 minority (15 African Americans, 5 American Indian/Alaska Native, 7 Asian Americans or Pacific Islanders, 3 Hispanic Americans), 20 international. Average age 32. 138 applicants, 63% accepted, 68 enrolled. In 2009, 38 master's awarded. *Degree requirements:* For master's, comprehensive exam, thesis or alternative. *Entrance requirements:* For master's, GMAT (minimum score 500), minimum AACSB index of 1080. Additional exam requirements/recommendations for international students: Required—TOEFL (minimum score 550 paper-based; 213 computer-based; 62 iBT). *Application deadline:* For fall admission, 8/1 for domestic students, 4/1 for international students; for spring admission, 12/1 for domestic students, 9/1 for international students. Applications are processed on a rolling basis. Application fee: $40 ($50 for international students). Electronic applications accepted. *Expenses:* Tuition, state resident: part-time $355.75 per credit hour. Tuition, nonresident: part-time $847.10 per credit hour. Required fees: $210.80 per semester. Tuition and fees vary according to course load and program. *Financial support:* In 2009–10, 3 students received support, including 2 research assistantships with full tuition reimbursements available (averaging $14,400 per year), 1 teaching assistantship with full tuition reimbursement available (averaging $11,800 per year); career-related internships or fieldwork, Federal Work-Study, institutionally sponsored loans, scholarships/grants, health care benefits, and unspecified assistantships also available. Support available to part-time students. Financial award application deadline: 4/1; financial award applicants required to submit FAFSA. *Unit head:* Dr. Brent Wren, Chair, 256-824-6408, Fax: 256-824-6328, E-mail: wrenb@uah.edu. *Application contact:* Jennifer Pettitt, Director of Graduate Programs, 256-824-6681, Fax: 256-824-7571, E-mail: jennifer.pettitt@uah.edu.

University of Alberta, Faculty of Graduate Studies and Research, Doctoral Program in Business, Edmonton, AB T6G 2E1, Canada. Offers accounting (PhD); finance (PhD); human resources/industrial relations (PhD); management science (PhD); marketing (PhD); organizational analysis (PhD); MBA/PhD. *Accreditation:* AACSB. Part-time programs available. *Faculty:* 41 full-time (7 women), 1 part-time/adjunct (0 women). *Students:* 46 full-time (27 women), 5 part-time (3 women). Average age 34. 307 applicants, 7% accepted, 11 enrolled. In 2009, 2 doctorates awarded. *Degree requirements:* For doctorate, comprehensive exam, thesis/dissertation. *Entrance requirements:* For doctorate, GMAT. Additional exam requirements/recommendations for international students: Required—TOEFL (minimum score 550 paper-based; 213 computer-based). *Application deadline:* For fall admission, 6/1 priority date for domestic students; for winter admission, 5/1 for domestic students. Application fee: $0. Electronic applications accepted. Tuition and fees charges are reported in Canadian dollars. *Expenses:* Tuition, area resident: Full-time $4626 Canadian dollars; part-time $99.72 Canadian dollars per unit. International tuition: $8216 Canadian dollars full-time. Required fees: $3590 Canadian dollars; $99.72 Canadian dollars per unit. $215 Canadian dollars per term. *Financial support:* In 2009–10, 29 students received support, including 11 fellowships with full tuition reimbursements available (averaging $17,000 per year); scholarships/grants and tuition waivers (partial) also available. *Faculty research:* Accounting, capital markets and corporate finance, organizational change and human resource management, marketing, strategic management. Total annual research expenditures: $7.7 million. *Unit head:* Dr. Mike Percy, Director, 780-492-2361, Fax: 780-492-3325, E-mail: busphd@ualberta.ca. *Application contact:* Jeanette Gosine, Program Coordinator, 780-492-2361, Fax: 780-492-3325, E-mail: busphd@ualberta.ca.

The University of Arizona, Graduate College, Eller College of Management, Department of Marketing, Tucson, AZ 85721. Offers MS, PhD. *Faculty:* 12. *Degree requirements:* For doctorate, comprehensive exam, thesis/dissertation. *Entrance requirements:* For doctorate, GMAT (minimum score 600). Additional exam requirements/recommendations for international students: Required—TOEFL (minimum score 600 paper-based). *Application deadline:* For fall admission, 3/1 for domestic students, 12/1 for international students. Applications are processed on a rolling basis. Application fee: $75. Electronic applications accepted. *Expenses:* Tuition, state resident: full-time $9028. Tuition, nonresident: full-time $24,890. *Financial support:* In 2009–10, 1 research assistantship with full tuition reimbursement (averaging $18,175 per year), 8 teaching assistantships with full tuition reimbursements (averaging $17,838 per year) were awarded; career-related internships or fieldwork, Federal Work-Study, scholarships/grants, health care benefits, tuition waivers (partial), and unspecified assistantships also available. Financial award application deadline: 2/1. *Faculty research:* Consumer behavior, customer relationship management, research methods, brand strategy, public policy. *Unit head:* Dr. Robert F. Lusch, Head, 520-621-7480, Fax: 520-621-7483, E-mail: rlusch@eller.arizona.edu. *Application contact:* Audrey L. Hambleton, Graduate Secretary, 520-621-1321, Fax: 520-621-7483, E-mail: audrey@eller.arizona.edu.

University of Baltimore, Graduate School, Merrick School of Business, Department of Marketing, Baltimore, MD 21201-5779. Offers business/marketing and venturing (MS). Part-time and evening/weekend programs available. *Entrance requirements:* For master's, GMAT. Additional exam requirements/recommendations for international students: Required—TOEFL (minimum score 550 paper-based; 213 computer-based). Electronic applications accepted.

The University of British Columbia, Sauder School of Business, Doctoral Program in Commerce and Business Administration, Vancouver, BC V6T 1Z1, Canada. Offers accounting (PhD); finance (PhD); international business (PhD); management information systems (PhD); management science (PhD); marketing (PhD); organizational behavior (PhD); strategy and business economics (PhD); transportation and logistics (PhD); urban land economics (PhD). *Degree requirements:* For doctorate, comprehensive exam, thesis/dissertation. *Entrance requirements:* For doctorate, GMAT or GRE. Additional exam requirements/recommendations for international students: Required—TOEFL (minimum score 600 paper-based; 250 computer-based; 100 iBT). Electronic applications accepted.

University of California, Berkeley, Graduate Division, Haas School of Business, PhD in Business Administration Program, Berkeley, CA 94720-1500. Offers accounting (PhD); business and public policy (PhD); finance (PhD); management of organizations (PhD); marketing (PhD); operations management (PhD); real estate (PhD). *Accreditation:* AACSB. *Faculty:* 80 full-time (20 women), 130 part-time/adjunct (22 women). *Students:* 82 full-time (23 women); includes 22 minority (18 Asian Americans or Pacific Islanders, 4 Hispanic Americans), 29 international. Average age 30. 511 applicants, 5% accepted, 16 enrolled. In 2009, 8 doctorates awarded. *Degree requirements:* For doctorate, comprehensive exam, thesis/dissertation, oral exam, written preliminary exams. *Entrance requirements:* For doctorate, GMAT or GRE, minimum GPA of 3.0 in undergraduate and graduate coursework. Additional exam requirements/recommendations for international students: Required—TOEFL (minimum score 570 paper-based; 230 computer-based; 68 iBT), IELTS (minimum score 7). *Application deadline:* For fall admission, 12/10 for domestic and international students. Application fee: $70 ($90 for international students). Electronic applications accepted. *Financial support:* Fellowships with full and partial tuition reimbursements, research assistantships with full and partial tuition reimbursements, teaching assistantships with full and partial tuition reimbursements, career-related internships or fieldwork, Federal Work-Study, scholarships/grants, health care benefits, tuition waivers (full), unspecified assistantships, and transit pass, travel grants available. Financial award application deadline: 12/10; financial award applicants required to submit FAFSA. *Faculty research:* Accounting, business and public policy, finance, management of organizations, marketing, operations and information technology management, real estate. *Unit head:* Sunil Dutta, Director, 510-642-1229, Fax: 510-643-4255, E-mail: kimg@haas.berkeley.edu. *Application contact:* Kim Guilfoyle, Director, Student Affairs, 510-642-3944, Fax: 510-643-4255, E-mail: kimg@haas.berkeley.edu.

University of California, Berkeley, UC Berkeley Extension, Certificate Programs in Business, Berkeley, CA 94720-1500. Offers accounting (Certificate); business administration (Certificate); finance (Certificate); human resource management (Certificate); management (Certificate); marketing (Certificate); project management (Certificate). Postbaccalaureate distance learning degree programs offered. *Unit head:* Diana Wu, Dean, 510-642-4181. *Application contact:* Business, 510-642-4231, E-mail: business@unex.berkeley.edu.

University of California, Berkeley, UC Berkeley Extension, International Diploma Programs, Berkeley, CA 94720-1500. Offers business administration (Certificate); finance (Certificate); global business management (Certificate); marketing (Certificate); project management (Certificate). *Unit head:* Diana Wu, Dean, 510-642-4181. *Application contact:* International Diploma Programs, 510-642-2564, E-mail: diploma@unex.berkeley.edu.

University of Central Florida, College of Business Administration, Department of Marketing, Orlando, FL 32816. Offers PhD. *Expenses:* Tuition, state resident: part-time $306.31 per credit hour. Tuition, nonresident: part-time $1099.01 per credit hour. Part-time tuition and fees vary according to degree level and program. *Unit head:* Dr. Ronald E. Michaels, Chair, 407-823-2941, Fax: 407-823-6206, E-mail: rmichaels@bus.ucf.edu. *Application contact:* Judy Ryder, Director, Graduate Admissions, 407-823-2364, Fax: 407-823-0219, E-mail: judy.ryder@bus.ucf.edu.

University of Central Missouri, The Graduate School, Harmon College of Business Administration, Warrensburg, MO 64093. Offers accountancy (MA); accounting (MBA); ethical strategic leadership (MBA); finance (MBA); general business (MBA); information systems (MBA); information technology (MS); marketing (MBA). Part-time programs available. Postbaccalaureate distance learning degree programs offered. *Faculty:* 31. *Students:* 87 full-time (34 women), 62 part-time (25 women); includes 10 minority (3 African Americans, 1 American Indian/Alaska Native, 5 Asian Americans or Pacific Islanders, 1 Hispanic American), 66 international. Average age 27. 55 applicants, 64% accepted, 27 enrolled. In 2009, 83 master's awarded. *Entrance requirements:* Additional exam requirements/recommendations for international students: Required—TOEFL (minimum score 550 paper-based; 79 computer-based). *Application deadline:* For fall admission, 6/1 priority date for domestic students, 5/1 for international students; for spring admission, 10/1 priority date for domestic students, 10/1 for international students. Applications are processed on a rolling basis. Application fee: $30 ($75 for international students). Electronic applications accepted. *Expenses:* Tuition, area resident:

Part-time $245.80 per credit hour. Tuition, nonresident: part-time $491.60 per credit hour. Required fees: $24.20 per credit hour. Full-time tuition and fees vary according to course load, degree level, campus/location and reciprocity agreements. *Financial support:* Research assistantships with full and partial tuition reimbursements, teaching assistantships with full and partial tuition reimbursements, career-related internships or fieldwork, Federal Work-Study, scholarships/grants, and administrative and laboratory assistantships available. Support available to part-time students. Financial award application deadline: 3/1; financial award applicants required to submit FAFSA. *Unit head:* Dr. Roger Best, Dean, 660-543-4560, Fax: 660-543-8350, E-mail: best@ucmo.edu. *Application contact:* Laurie Delap, Admissions Coordinator, 660-543-4621, Fax: 660-543-4778, E-mail: gradinfo@ucmo.edu.

University of Cincinnati, Graduate School, College of Business, MS Program, Cincinnati, OH 45221. Offers accounting (MS); information systems (MS); marketing (MS); quantitative analysis (MS). Part-time and evening/weekend programs available. *Degree requirements:* For master's, thesis (for some programs). *Entrance requirements:* For master's, GMAT, GRE, resume, letters of recommendation. Additional exam requirements/recommendations for international students: Required—TOEFL (minimum score 600 paper-based; 250 computer-based; 100 iBT). Electronic applications accepted. *Expenses:* Contact institution.

University of Cincinnati, Graduate School, College of Business, PhD Program, Cincinnati, OH 45221. Offers accounting (PhD); finance (PhD); information systems (PhD); management (PhD); marketing (PhD); quantitative analysis and operations management (PhD). *Degree requirements:* For doctorate, comprehensive exam, thesis/dissertation. *Entrance requirements:* For doctorate, GMAT, GRE, resume, letters of recommendation. Additional exam requirements/recommendations for international students: Required—TOEFL (minimum score 600 paper-based; 250 computer-based; 100 iBT). Electronic applications accepted. *Expenses:* Contact institution.

University of Colorado at Boulder, Leeds School of Business, Division of Business Administration, Boulder, CO 80309. Offers accounting (MS, PhD); finance (PhD); information systems (PhD); marketing (PhD); operations (PhD); strategic, organizational, and entrepreneurial studies (PhD). Part-time and evening/weekend programs available. *Students:* 74 full-time (27 women), 15 part-time (8 women); includes 6 minority (1 African American, 3 Asian Americans or Pacific Islanders, 2 Hispanic Americans), 21 international. Average age 28. 271 applicants, 8% accepted, 19 enrolled. In 2009, 40 master's, 6 doctorates awarded. *Entrance requirements:* For master's, GMAT, minimum undergraduate GPA of 3.0. *Application deadline:* For fall admission, 3/31 for domestic and international students; for spring admission, 10/31 for domestic and international students. Application fee: $50 ($60 for international students). Electronic applications accepted. *Financial support:* In 2009–10, 16 fellowships (averaging $1,038 per year), 26 research assistantships (averaging $17,558 per year), 11 teaching assistantships (averaging $12,576 per year) were awarded; career-related internships or fieldwork, Federal Work-Study, scholarships/grants, and unspecified assistantships also available. Financial award applicants required to submit FAFSA.

University of Colorado Denver, Business School, Program in Marketing, Denver, CO 80217-3364. Offers MS. Part-time and evening/weekend programs available. *Students:* 8 full-time (5 women), 18 part-time (11 women); includes 2 minority (both Hispanic Americans), 6 international. 37 applicants, 54% accepted, 7 enrolled. In 2009, 13 master's awarded. *Entrance requirements:* For master's, GMAT. Additional exam requirements/recommendations for international students: Required—TOEFL (minimum score 525 paper-based; 197 computer-based). *Application deadline:* For fall admission, 6/1 priority date for domestic students, 3/15 for international students; for spring admission, 11/1 priority date for domestic students, 10/1 for international students. Applications are processed on a rolling basis. Application fee: $50 ($75 for international students). Electronic applications accepted. *Financial support:* Federal Work-Study, institutionally sponsored loans, and scholarships/grants available. Support available to part-time students. Financial award application deadline: 4/1; financial award applicants required to submit FAFSA. *Unit head:* Dr. David Forlani, Director, 303-556-6616, Fax: 303-556-5899, E-mail: david.forlani@ucdenver.edu. *Application contact:* Shelly Townley, Admissions Coordinator, 303-556-5956, Fax: 303-556-5904, E-mail: shelly.townley@ucdenver.edu.

University of Connecticut, Graduate School, School of Business, Storrs, CT 06269. Offers accounting (MS, PhD); business administration (Exec MBA, MBA, PhD); finance (PhD); health care management and insurance studies (MBA); management (PhD); management consulting (MBA); marketing (PhD); marketing intelligence (MBA); MA/MBA; MBA/MSW. *Accreditation:* AACSB. *Faculty:* 75 full-time (14 women). *Students:* 405 full-time (134 women), 999 part-time (364 women); includes 198 minority (43 African Americans, 3 American Indian/Alaska Native, 102 Asian Americans or Pacific Islanders, 50 Hispanic Americans), 136 international. Average age 31. 956 applicants, 20% accepted, 187 enrolled. In 2009, 413 master's, 6 doctorates awarded. *Degree requirements:* For master's, comprehensive exam; for doctorate, thesis/dissertation. *Entrance requirements:* For master's and doctorate, GMAT. Additional exam requirements/recommendations for international students: Required—TOEFL (minimum score 550 paper-based; 213 computer-based). *Application deadline:* For fall admission, 2/1 priority date for domestic and international students; for spring admission, 11/1 for domestic students, 10/1 for international students. Applications are processed on a rolling basis. Electronic applications accepted. *Expenses:* Tuition, state resident: full-time $4725; part-time $525 per credit. Tuition, nonresident: full-time $12,267; part-time $1363 per credit. Required fees: $346 per semester. Tuition and fees vary according to course load. *Financial support:* In 2009–10, 76 research assistantships with full tuition reimbursements, 41 teaching assistantships with full tuition reimbursements were awarded; fellowships, career-related internships or fieldwork, Federal Work-Study, scholarships/grants, health care benefits, and unspecified assistantships also available. Financial award application deadline: 2/1; financial award applicants required to submit FAFSA. *Unit head:* P. Christopher Earley, Dean, 860-486-2317, Fax: 860-846-0889, E-mail: paul.earley@uconn.edu. *Application contact:* Richard Dino, Admissions Chairperson, 860-486-4483, E-mail: rich.dino@uconn.edu.

See Close-Up on page 263.

University of Dallas, Graduate School of Management, Irving, TX 75062-4736. Offers accounting (MBA, MM, MS); business management (MBA, MM); corporate finance (MBA, MM); financial services (MBA); global business (MBA, MM); health services management (MBA, MM); human resource management (MBA, MM); information assurance (MBA, MM, MS); information technology (MBA, MM, MS); information technology service management (MBA, MM, MS); marketing management (MBA, MM); organization development (MBA, MM); project management (MBA, MM); sports and entertainment management (MBA, MM); strategic leadership (MBA, MM); supply chain management (MBA); supply chain management and market logistics (MM). *Accreditation:* ACBSP. Part-time and evening/weekend programs available. Postbaccalaureate distance learning degree programs offered (no on-campus study). *Faculty:* 25 full-time (6 women), 31 part-time/adjunct (6 women). *Students:* 232 full-time (95 women), 923 part-time (365 women); includes 462 minority (184 African Americans, 14 American Indian/Alaska Native, 153 Asian Americans or Pacific Islanders, 111 Hispanic Americans), 184 international. Average age 34. 474 applicants, 85% accepted, 237 enrolled. In 2009, 399 master's awarded. *Entrance requirements:* Additional exam requirements/recommendations for international students: Required—TOEFL. *Application deadline:* Applications are processed on a rolling basis. Application fee: $50. Electronic applications accepted. *Expenses:* Contact institution. *Financial support:* In 2009–10, 399 students received support. Scholarships/grants and unspecified assistantships available. Financial award application deadline: 2/15; financial award applicants required to submit FAFSA. *Unit head:* Alounda Joseph, Director of Enrollment Processes, 972-721-5356, E-mail: admiss@gsm.udallas.edu. *Application contact:* Alounda Joseph, Director of Enrollment Processes, 972-721-5356, E-mail: admiss@gsm.udallas.edu.

University of Dayton, Graduate School, School of Business Administration, Dayton, OH 45469-1300. Offers accounting (MBA); business intelligence (MBA); entrepreneurship (MBA); finance (MBA); international business (MBA); marketing (MBA); MIS (MBA); operations management (MBA); technology-enhanced business/e-commerce (MBA); JD/MBA. *Accreditation:* AACSB. Part-time and evening/weekend programs available. *Faculty:* 29 full-time (8 women), 15 part-time/adjunct (2 women). *Students:* 134 full-time (48 women), 111 part-time (31 women); includes 14 minority (9 African Americans, 3 Asian Americans or Pacific Islanders, 2 Hispanic Americans), 29 international. Average age 29. 179 applicants, 63% accepted, 73 enrolled. In 2009, 102 master's awarded. *Entrance requirements:* For master's, GMAT. Additional exam requirements/recommendations for international students: Required—TOEFL (minimum score 550 paper-based; 213 computer-based; 79 iBT). *Application deadline:* For fall admission, 3/1 priority date for international students; for winter admission, 7/1 priority date for international students; for spring admission, 1/1 priority date for international students. Applications are processed on a rolling basis. Application fee: $0 ($50 for international students). Electronic applications accepted. *Expenses:* Contact institution. *Financial support:* In 2009–10, 13 fellowships with partial tuition reimbursements, 17 research assistantships with full and partial tuition reimbursements (averaging $7,020 per year) were awarded; career-related internships or fieldwork, institutionally sponsored loans, scholarships/grants, health care benefits, and unspecified assistantships also available. Support available to part-time students. Financial award application deadline: 3/15; financial award applicants required to submit FAFSA. *Faculty research:* Management information systems, economics, finance, entrepreneurship, marketing. *Unit head:* Janice M. Glynn, Director, MBA Program, 937-229-3733, Fax: 937-229-3882, E-mail: glynn@udayton.edu. *Application contact:* Jeffrey Carter, Assistant Director, MBA Program, 937-229-3733, Fax: 937-229-3882, E-mail: jeff.carter@notes.udayton.edu.

University of Denver, Daniels College of Business, Department of Marketing, Denver, CO 80208. Offers IMBA, MBA, MS. Part-time and evening/weekend programs available. *Faculty:* 11 full-time (3 women), 6 part-time/adjunct (5 women). *Students:* 17 full-time (12 women), 27 part-time (17 women); includes 1 minority (Hispanic American), 23 international. Average age 26. 130 applicants, 60% accepted, 19 enrolled. In 2009, 26 master's awarded. *Entrance requirements:* For master's, GMAT. *Application deadline:* For fall admission, 1/15 priority date for domestic students. Applications are processed on a rolling basis. Application fee: $50. Electronic applications accepted. *Expenses:* Tuition: Full-time $34,596; part-time $961 per quarter hour. Required fees: $4 per quarter hour. Tuition and fees vary according to course load, campus/location and program. *Financial support:* In 2009–10, 30 students received support. Career-related internships or fieldwork, Federal Work-Study, institutionally sponsored loans, and scholarships/grants available. Support available to part-time students. Financial award application deadline: 2/15; financial award applicants required to submit FAFSA. *Faculty research:* Social policy issues in marketing, price bundling, marketing to the disabled, marketing to the elderly, international marketing and logistics. *Unit head:* Dr. Carol Johnson, Chair, 303-871-2276. *Application contact:* Information Contact, 303-871-3416, Fax: 303-871-4466, E-mail: daniels@du.edu.

The University of Findlay, Graduate and Professional Studies, College of Business, Findlay, OH 45840-3653. Offers financial management (MBA); human resource management (MBA); international management (MBA); management (MBA); marketing (MBA); public management (MBA). Part-time and evening/weekend programs available. Postbaccalaureate distance learning degree programs offered (no on-campus study). *Degree requirements:* For master's, thesis, cumulative project. *Entrance requirements:* For master's, GMAT, minimum undergraduate GPA of 3.0 in last 64 hours of course work. Additional exam requirements/recommendations for international students: Required—TOEFL (minimum score 550 paper-based; 213 computer-based; 80 iBT). Electronic applications accepted. *Expenses:* Contact institution. *Faculty research:* Health care management, operations and logistics management.

University of Florida, Graduate School, Warrington College of Business Administration, Hough Graduate School of Business, Department of Marketing, Gainesville, FL 32611. Offers MS, PhD. Terminal master's awarded for partial completion of doctoral program. *Degree requirements:* For master's, thesis optional; for doctorate, thesis/dissertation. *Entrance requirements:* For master's and doctorate, GMAT or GRE General Test, minimum GPA of 3.0. Additional exam requirements/recommendations for international students: Required—TOEFL (minimum score 550 paper-based; 213 computer-based). Electronic applications accepted. *Faculty research:* Consumer behavior, advertising and sales promotion, sales management, pricing and retailing, mathematical models of marketing phenomena.

University of Florida, Graduate School, Warrington College of Business Administration, Hough Graduate School of Business, Programs in Business Administration, Gainesville, FL 32611. Offers accounting (MBA); arts administration (MBA); business strategy and public policy (MBA); competitive strategy (MBA); decision and information sciences (MBA); electronic commerce (MBA); finance (MBA); general business (MBA); global management (MBA); Graham-Buffett security analysis (MBA); health administration (MBA); human resources management (MBA); international studies (MBA); Latin American business (MBA); management (MBA); marketing (MBA); sports administration (MBA); JD/MBA; MBA/MS; MBA/PhD; MBA/Pharm D; MD/MBA. *Accreditation:* AACSB. Part-time and evening/weekend programs available. Postbaccalaureate distance learning degree programs offered. *Entrance requirements:* For master's, GMAT, minimum GPA of 3.0, interview. Additional exam requirements/recommendations for international students: Required—TOEFL (minimum score 550 paper-based; 213 computer-based). Electronic applications accepted. *Faculty research:* Accounting, finance, insurance, management, real estate and urban analysis marketing.

University of Hawaii at Manoa, Graduate Division, Shidler College of Business, Program in Business Administration, Honolulu, HI 96822. Offers Asian business studies (MBA); Chinese business studies (MBA); decision sciences (MBA); entrepreneurship (MBA); finance (MBA); finance and banking (MBA); human resources management (MBA); information management (MBA); information technology (MBA); international business (MBA); Japanese business studies (MBA); marketing (MBA); organizational behavior (MBA); organizational management (MBA); real estate (MBA); student-designed track (MBA). *Accreditation:* AACSB. Part-time and evening/weekend programs available. *Faculty:* 46 full-time (8 women), 9 part-time/adjunct (4 women). *Students:* 259 full-time (90 women), 105 part-time (43 women); includes 123 minority (118 Asian Americans or Pacific Islanders, 5 Hispanic Americans), 119 international. Average age 32. 336 applicants, 52% accepted, 150 enrolled. In 2009, 113 master's awarded. *Degree requirements:* For master's, thesis optional. *Entrance requirements:* For master's, GMAT, minimum GPA of 3.0. Additional exam requirements/recommendations for international students: Required—TOEFL (minimum score 600 paper-based; 250 computer-based; 100 iBT), IELTS (minimum score 7). *Application deadline:* For fall admission, 5/1 for domestic students, 3/1 for international students. Application fee: $60. *Expenses:* Contact institution. *Financial support:* In 2009–10, 24 students received support, including 98 fellowships (averaging $3,481 per year), 3 research assistantships (averaging $16,626 per year). Total annual research expenditures: $427,000. *Application contact:* Tung Bui, Graduate Chair, 808-956-5565, Fax: 808-956-9889, E-mail: tung.bui@hawaii.edu.

University of Hawaii at Manoa, Graduate Division, Shidler College of Business, Program in International Management, Honolulu, HI 96822. Offers Asian finance (PhD); global information technology management (PhD); international accounting (PhD); international marketing (PhD); international organization and strategy (PhD). Part-time programs available. *Students:* 28 full-time (12 women), 5 part-time (0 women); includes 7 minority (all Asian Americans or Pacific Islanders), 17 international. Average age 33. 65 applicants, 18% accepted, 5 enrolled. In 2009, 1 doctorate awarded. *Degree requirements:* For doctorate, comprehensive exam, thesis/dissertation. *Entrance requirements:* For doctorate, GMAT or GRE General Test, minimum GPA of 3.0. Additional exam requirements/recommendations for international students: Required—TOEFL (minimum score 600 paper-based; 250 computer-based; 100 iBT), IELTS (minimum score 7). *Application deadline:* For fall admission, 3/1 for domestic and international students. Application fee: $60. *Expenses:* Contact institution. *Financial support:* In 2009–10, 2 fellowships (averaging $6,945 per year), 21 research assistantships (averaging $17,766 per year) were awarded. *Application contact:* Erica Okada, Graduate Chair, 808-956-6723, Fax: 808-956-6889, E-mail: emokada@hawaii.edu.

University of Houston, Bauer College of Business, Marketing Program, Houston, TX 77204. Offers MBA, PhD. Part-time and evening/weekend programs available. *Faculty:* 7 full-time (1 woman), 5 part-time/adjunct (0 women). *Degree requirements:* For doctorate, comprehensive

Marketing

University of Houston (continued)

exam, thesis/dissertation. *Entrance requirements:* For doctorate, GMAT or GRE. *Expenses:* Tuition, state resident: full-time $7676; part-time $320 per credit hour. Tuition, nonresident: full-time $14,324; part-time $597 per credit hour. Required fees: $3034. *Financial support:* In 2009–10, 12 teaching assistantships with full tuition reimbursements (averaging $7,100 per year) were awarded; career-related internships or fieldwork, Federal Work-Study, institutionally sponsored loans, scholarships/grants, health care benefits, and unspecified assistantships also available. Support available to part-time students. Financial award application deadline: 2/1; financial award applicants required to submit FAFSA. *Faculty research:* Accountancy and taxation, finance, international business, management. *Unit head:* Dr. Ed Blair, Chair, 713-743-4555, E-mail: blair@uh.edu. *Application contact:* 713-743-4900, Fax: 713-743-4942, E-mail: oss@uh.edu.

University of Houston–Victoria, School of Business Administration, Victoria, TX 77901-4450. Offers accounting (MBA); economic development and entrepreneurship (MS); finance (GMBA, MBA); general business (MBA); international business (MBA); management (GMBA, MBA); marketing (MBA). *Accreditation:* AACSB. Part-time and evening/weekend programs available. Postbaccalaureate distance learning degree programs offered (no on-campus study). *Entrance requirements:* For master's, GMAT. Additional exam requirements/recommendations for international students: Required—TOEFL (minimum score 550 paper-based; 213 computer-based). Electronic applications accepted. *Faculty research:* Economic development, marketing, finance.

The University of Iowa, Henry B. Tippie College of Business, Department of Marketing, Iowa City, IA 52242-1316. Offers business administration (PhD), including marketing. *Faculty:* 13 full-time (4 women), 5 part-time/adjunct (2 women). *Students:* 10 full-time (4 women); includes 2 minority (1 American Indian/Alaska Native, 1 Asian American or Pacific Islander), 8 international. Average age 30. 32 applicants, 13% accepted, 3 enrolled. In 2009, 2 doctorates awarded. *Degree requirements:* For doctorate, comprehensive exam, thesis/dissertation, thesis defense. *Entrance requirements:* For doctorate, GMAT or GRE, minimum undergraduate GPA of 2.7. Additional exam requirements/recommendations for international students: Required—TOEFL (minimum score 600 paper-based; 250 computer-based; 100 iBT). *Application deadline:* For fall admission, 1/15 for domestic and international students. Applications are processed on a rolling basis. Application fee: $60 ($85 for international students). Electronic applications accepted. *Financial support:* In 2009–10, 10 students received support, including 1 fellowship with full tuition reimbursement available (averaging $20,000 per year), 1 research assistantship with full tuition reimbursement available (averaging $16,575 per year), 8 teaching assistantships with full tuition reimbursements available (averaging $16,575 per year); institutionally sponsored loans, scholarships/grants, health care benefits, unspecified assistantships, and 10 partial fellowships ($1800 yearly average) also available. Financial award application deadline: 1/15. *Faculty research:* Judgments and decision making under certainty; consumer behavior: cognitive neuroscience, attitudes and evaluation; hierarchical bayesian estimation; marketing-finance interface; advertising effects. *Unit head:* Prof. Gary J. Russell, Department Executive Officer, 319-335-1013, Fax: 319-335-1956, E-mail: gary-j-russell@uiowa.edu. *Application contact:* Renea L. Jay, PhD Program Coordinator, 319-335-0830, Fax: 319-335-1956, E-mail: renea-jay@uiowa.edu.

The University of Iowa, Henry B. Tippie College of Business, Henry B. Tippie School of Management, Iowa City, IA 52242-1316. Offers corporate finance (MBA); investment management (MBA); marketing (MBA); process excellence (MBA); strategic innovation (MBA); JD/MBA; MBA/MA; MBA/MD; MBA/MHA; MBA/MSN. *Accreditation:* AACSB. Part-time and evening/weekend programs available. *Faculty:* 46 full-time (7 women), 12 part-time/adjunct (2 women). *Students:* 250 full-time (64 women), 794 part-time (277 women); includes 92 minority (17 African Americans, 2 American Indian/Alaska Native, 52 Asian Americans or Pacific Islanders, 21 Hispanic Americans), 146 international. Average age 32. 602 applicants, 60% accepted, 302 enrolled. In 2009, 348 master's awarded. *Entrance requirements:* For master's, GMAT, work experience, references. Additional exam requirements/recommendations for international students: Required—TOEFL (minimum score 600 paper-based; 250 computer-based; 100 iBT), IELTS (minimum score 7). *Application deadline:* For fall admission, 7/30 for domestic students, 4/15 for international students; for spring admission, 12/15 for domestic and international students. Applications are processed on a rolling basis. Application fee: $60 ($100 for international students). Electronic applications accepted. *Expenses:* Contact institution. *Financial support:* In 2009–10, 100 students received support, including 100 fellowships (averaging $6,819 per year), 92 research assistantships with partial tuition reimbursements available (averaging $10,388 per year); career-related internships or fieldwork, scholarships/grants, health care benefits, and unspecified assistantships also available. Financial award application deadline: 4/15; financial award applicants required to submit FAFSA. *Faculty research:* Capital markets, econometrics, optimization, investments and empirical corporate finance, Iowa electronic markets. *Unit head:* Prof. Jarjisu Sa-Aadu, Associate Dean, MBA Programs, 800-622-4692, Fax: 319-335-3604, E-mail: jsa-aadu@uiowa.edu. *Application contact:* Jodi Schafer, Director of Admissions and Financial Aid, 319-335-0864, Fax: 319-335-3604, E-mail: jodi-schafer@uiowa.edu.

University of La Verne, College of Business and Public Management, Graduate Programs in Business Administration, La Verne, CA 91750-4443. Offers accounting (MBA); executive management (MBA-EP); finance (MBA, MBA-EP); health services management (MBA); information technology (MBA, MBA-EP); international business (MBA, MBA-EP); leadership (MBA-EP); managed care (MBA); management (MBA, MBA-EP); marketing (MBA, MBA-EP). Part-time and evening/weekend programs available. *Faculty:* 22 full-time (11 women), 41 part-time/adjunct (8 women). *Students:* 409 full-time (213 women), 156 part-time (74 women); includes 371 minority (23 African Americans, 7 American Indian/Alaska Native, 259 Asian Americans or Pacific Islanders, 82 Hispanic Americans), 9 international. Average age 29. In 2009, 356 master's awarded. *Entrance requirements:* For master's, minimum undergraduate GPA of 3.0, 2 letters of recommendation, resume. Additional exam requirements/recommendations for international students: Required—TOEFL (minimum score 550 paper-based; 213 computer-based). *Application deadline:* Applications are processed on a rolling basis. Application fee: $50. *Expenses:* Contact institution. *Financial support:* Career-related internships or fieldwork, institutionally sponsored loans, and scholarships/grants available. Financial award application deadline: 3/2; financial award applicants required to submit FAFSA. *Unit head:* Dr. Abe Helou, Chairperson, 909-593-3511 Ext. 4211, Fax: 909-392-2704, E-mail: ihelou@laverne.edu. *Application contact:* Rina Lazarian, Program and Admission Specialist, 909-593-3511 Ext. 4819, Fax: 909-392-2704, E-mail: cbpm@ulv.edu.

University of La Verne, Regional Campus Administration, Graduate Programs, Inland Empire Campus, Rancho Cucamonga, CA 91730. Offers business (MBA-EP), including health services management, information technology, management, marketing; leadership and management (MS). *Faculty:* 2 full-time (both women), 12 part-time/adjunct (2 women). *Students:* 20 full-time (13 women), 61 part-time (41 women); includes 50 minority (10 African Americans, 11 Asian Americans or Pacific Islanders, 29 Hispanic Americans). Average age 37. In 2009, 24 master's awarded. *Entrance requirements:* For master's, 2 letters of recommendation, resume. *Application deadline:* Applications are processed on a rolling basis. Application fee: $50. *Expenses:* Contact institution. *Financial support:* Institutionally sponsored loans available. Financial award application deadline: 3/2; financial award applicants required to submit FAFSA. *Unit head:* Allan Stout, Director, 909-484-3858 Ext. 6002, Fax: 909-484-9469, E-mail: astout@laverne.edu. *Application contact:* Allan Stout, Director, 909-484-3858 Ext. 6002, Fax: 909-484-9469, E-mail: astout@laverne.edu.

University of Massachusetts Dartmouth, Graduate School, Charlton College of Business, Program in Business Administration, North Dartmouth, MA 02747-2300. Offers accounting (Postbaccalaureate Certificate); business administration (MBA); e-commerce (PMC); finance (PMC); general management (PMC); leadership (PMC); management (Postbaccalaureate Certificate); marketing (PMC); supply chain management (PMC). *Accreditation:* AACSB. Part-time programs available. *Faculty:* 42 full-time (13 women), 26 part-time/adjunct (6 women). *Students:* 93 full-time (41 women), 132 part-time (64 women); includes 22 minority (5 African Americans, 2 American Indian/Alaska Native, 6 Asian Americans or Pacific Islanders, 9 Hispanic Americans), 42 international. Average age 30. 186 applicants, 82% accepted, 94 enrolled. In 2009, 55 master's, 19 other advanced degrees awarded. *Entrance requirements:* For master's, GMAT, resume, letters of recommendation. Additional exam requirements/recommendations for international students: Required—TOEFL (minimum score 500 paper-based; 200 computer-based; 72 iBT). *Application deadline:* For fall admission, 6/1 for domestic students, 5/1 for international students; for spring admission, 10/1 for domestic students, 8/1 for international students. Application fee: $40 ($60 for international students). Electronic applications accepted. *Expenses:* Tuition, state resident: full-time $2071; part-time $86.29 per credit. Tuition, nonresident: full-time $8099; part-time $337.46 per credit. Required fees: $9446. Tuition and fees vary according to class time, course load and reciprocity agreements. *Financial support:* In 2009–10, 1 research assistantship with full tuition reimbursement (averaging $6,000 per year) was awarded; teaching assistantships, Federal Work-Study and unspecified assistantships also available. Support available to part-time students. Financial award application deadline: 3/1; financial award applicants required to submit FAFSA. *Faculty research:* Competitiveness of south coast enterprises, global sales, key performance indicators, agile manufacturing, green business. Total annual research expenditures: $19,000. *Unit head:* Dr. Norm Barber, Assistant Dean, 508-999-8543, E-mail: nbarber@umassd.edu. *Application contact:* Elan Turcotte-Shamski, Graduate Admissions Officer, 508-999-8604, Fax: 508-999-8183, E-mail: graduate@umassd.edu.

University of Memphis, Graduate School, Fogelman College of Business and Economics, Program in Business Administration, Memphis, TN 38152. Offers accounting (MBA, PhD); economics (MBA, PhD); executive business administration (MBA); finance (PhD); finance, insurance, and real estate (MBA, MS); international business administration (IMBA); management (MBA, MS, PhD); management information systems (MBA, MS, PhD); management science (MBA); marketing (MBA, MS); marketing and supply chain management (PhD); real estate development (MS); JD/MBA. *Accreditation:* AACSB. *Faculty:* 44 full-time (9 women), 5 part-time/adjunct (0 women). *Students:* 263 full-time (106 women), 181 part-time (66 women); includes 70 minority (46 African Americans, 3 American Indian/Alaska Native, 16 Asian Americans or Pacific Islanders, 5 Hispanic Americans), 109 international. Average age 31. 374 applicants, 73% accepted, 119 enrolled. In 2009, 140 master's, 17 doctorates awarded. *Degree requirements:* For master's, comprehensive exam; for doctorate, comprehensive exam, thesis/dissertation. *Entrance requirements:* For master's, GMAT, resume; for doctorate, GMAT, interview, minimum GPA of 3.4, resume, letter of recommendation. Additional exam requirements/recommendations for international students: Required—TOEFL (minimum score 550 paper-based; 220 computer-based). *Application deadline:* For fall admission, 8/1 for domestic students; for spring admission, 12/1 for domestic students. Application fee: $35 ($60 for international students). *Expenses:* Tuition, state resident: full-time $6246; part-time $347 per credit hour. Tuition, nonresident: full-time $15,894; part-time $883 per credit hour. Required fees: $1160. Full-time tuition and fees vary according to course load, degree level and program. *Financial support:* In 2009–10, 164 students received support; research assistantships with full tuition reimbursements available, teaching assistantships with full tuition reimbursements available, career-related internships or fieldwork, Federal Work-Study, scholarships/grants, and unspecified assistantships available. Financial award application deadline: 2/15; financial award applicants required to submit FAFSA. *Faculty research:* Competitive business strategy, finance microstructures, supply chain management innovations, health care economics, litigation risks and corporate audits. *Unit head:* Rajiv Grover, Dean, 901-678-3759, E-mail: rgrover@memphis.edu. *Application contact:* Dr. Carol V. Danehower, Associate Dean for Programs, 901-678-5402, Fax: 901-678-3579, E-mail: fcbegp@memphis.edu.

University of Miami, Graduate School, School of Business Administration, Program in Business Administration, Coral Gables, FL 33124. Offers accounting (MBA); computer information systems (MBA); executive and professional (MBA), including international business, management; finance (MBA); international business (MBA); management (MBA); management science (MBA); marketing (MBA); professional management (MSPM); JD/MBA; MBA/MSIE. *Accreditation:* AACSB. Evening/weekend programs available. *Degree requirements:* For master's, comprehensive exam. *Entrance requirements:* For master's, GMAT. Additional exam requirements/recommendations for international students: Required—TOEFL (minimum score 550 paper-based; 213 computer-based; 59 iBT). Electronic applications accepted. *Faculty research:* Leadership, e-commerce, supply chain management.

University of Michigan–Dearborn, School of Management, Dearborn, MI 48128-1491. Offers accounting (MBA, MS); finance (MBA, MS); information systems (MS); international business (MBA); management (MBA); management information systems (MBA); marketing (MBA); supply chain management (MBA); MBA/MHSA; MBA/MSE; MBA/MSF. *Accreditation:* AACSB. Part-time and evening/weekend programs available. Postbaccalaureate distance learning degree programs offered (no on-campus study). *Faculty:* 26 full-time (6 women), 8 part-time/adjunct (4 women). *Students:* 73 full-time (30 women), 412 part-time (134 women); includes 65 minority (20 African Americans, 1 American Indian/Alaska Native, 38 Asian Americans or Pacific Islanders, 6 Hispanic Americans), 76 international. Average age 30. 185 applicants, 56% accepted, 78 enrolled. In 2009, 151 master's awarded. *Entrance requirements:* For master's, GMAT, 2 years of work experience (MBA); course work in computer applications, statistics, and pre-calculus or finite mathematics; 18 credits of accounting course work beyond introductory courses (MS in accounting). Additional exam requirements/recommendations for international students: Required—TOEFL (minimum score 560 paper-based; 220 computer-based; 84 iBT). *Application deadline:* For fall admission, 8/1 priority date for domestic students, 6/1 for international students; for winter admission, 12/1 priority date for domestic students, 10/1 for international students; for spring admission, 4/1 priority date for domestic students, 2/1 for international students. Applications are processed on a rolling basis. Application fee: $60. Electronic applications accepted. *Expenses:* Contact institution. *Financial support:* Career-related internships or fieldwork, Federal Work-Study, and scholarships/grants available. Support available to part-time students. Financial award application deadline: 9/1; financial award applicants required to submit FAFSA. *Faculty research:* Cultural diversity, buyer-supplier relations, error detection in data, economic evolution. *Unit head:* Dr. Kim Schatzel, Dean, 313-593-5248, Fax: 313-271-9835, E-mail: schatzel@umd.umich.edu. *Application contact:* Joan Doherty, Academic Advisor/Counselor, 313-593-5460, Fax: 313-271-9838, E-mail: gradbusiness@umd.umich.edu.

University of Minnesota, Twin Cities Campus, Carlson School of Management, Carlson Full-Time MBA Program, Minneapolis, MN 55455. Offers finance (MBA); information technology (MBA); management (MBA); marketing (MBA); medical industry orientation (MBA); supply chain and operations (MBA); JD/MBA; MBA/MPP; MD/MBA; MHA/MBA; Pharm D/MBA. *Accreditation:* AACSB. *Faculty:* 60 full-time (11 women), 15 part-time/adjunct (7 women). *Students:* 217 full-time (78 women); includes 23 minority (6 African Americans, 1 American Indian/Alaska Native, 14 Asian Americans or Pacific Islanders, 2 Hispanic Americans), 41 international. Average age 28. 548 applicants, 41% accepted, 104 enrolled. In 2009, 91 master's awarded. *Entrance requirements:* For master's, GMAT. Additional exam requirements/recommendations for international students: Required—TOEFL (minimum score 580 paper-based; 240 computer-based; 82 iBT), or IELTS (minimum score 7), or Pearson Test of English (PTE). *Application deadline:* For fall admission, 4/1 for domestic students, 2/1 for international students. Application fee: $60 ($90 for international students). Electronic applications accepted. *Expenses:* Contact institution. *Financial support:* In 2009–10, 107 students received support, including 107 fellowships with full and partial tuition reimbursements available (averaging $22,174 per year); research assistantships with partial tuition reimbursements available, teaching assistantships with partial tuition reimbursements available, career-related internships or fieldwork, Federal Work-Study, institutionally sponsored loans, scholarships/grants, health care benefits, and unspecified assistantships also available. Financial award application deadline: 2/1; financial award applicants required to submit FAFSA. *Unit head:* Kathryn J. Carlson, Assistant Dean, MBA Programs and Graduate Business Career Center, 612-625-5555, Fax: 612-625-1012, E-mail: mba@umn.edu. *Application contact:* Tracy J. Keeling, Associate Director

of Admissions, Full-Time and Part-Time MBA Programs, 612-625-5555, Fax: 612-625-1012, E-mail: mba@umn.edu.

University of Minnesota, Twin Cities Campus, Carlson School of Management, Carlson Part-Time MBA Program, Minneapolis, MN 55455. Offers finance (MBA); information technology (MBA); management (MBA); marketing (MBA); supply chain and operations (MBA); JD/MBA; MBA/MPP; MD/MBA; MHA/MBA; Pharm D/MBA. Part-time and evening/weekend programs available. *Faculty:* 72 full-time (15 women), 26 part-time/adjunct (5 women). *Students:* 1,861 part-time (606 women); includes 188 minority (31 African Americans, 1 American Indian/Alaska Native, 132 Asian Americans or Pacific Islanders, 24 Hispanic Americans), 121 international. Average age 29. 387 applicants, 67% accepted, 238 enrolled. In 2009, 393 master's awarded. *Entrance requirements:* For master's, GMAT. Additional exam requirements/recommendations for international students: Required—TOEFL (minimum score 580 paper-based; 240 computer-based; 82 iBT), IELTS (minimum score 7) or Pearson Test of English (PTE) Academic. *Application deadline:* For fall admission, 5/1 priority date for domestic and international students; for spring admission, 10/1 priority date for domestic and international students. Application fee: $60 ($90 for international students). Electronic applications accepted. *Expenses:* Contact institution. *Financial support:* Applicants required to submit FAFSA. *Faculty research:* Strategy, IT, finance, marketing, operations, supply chain, entrepreneurship, quality management, accounting. *Unit head:* Kathryn J. Carlson, Assistant Dean, MBA Programs and Graduate Business Career Center, 612-624-2039, Fax: 612-625-1012, E-mail: mba@umn.edu. *Application contact:* Tracy J. Keeling, Associate Director of Admissions, Full-Time and Part-Time MBA Programs, 612-625-5555, Fax: 612-625-1012, E-mail: mba@umn.edu.

University of Minnesota, Twin Cities Campus, Carlson School of Management, Doctoral Program in Business Administration, Minneapolis, MN 55455-0213. Offers accounting (PhD); finance (PhD); information and decision sciences (PhD); marketing and logistics management (PhD); operations and management science (PhD); strategic management and organization (PhD). *Faculty:* 74 full-time (19 women). *Students:* 68 full-time (28 women); includes 7 minority (1 African American, 3 Asian Americans or Pacific Islanders, 3 Hispanic Americans), 46 international. Average age 29. 250 applicants, 5% accepted, 9 enrolled. In 2009, 11 doctorates awarded. *Degree requirements:* For doctorate, comprehensive exam, thesis/dissertation, written and oral preliminary exams, proposal defense. *Entrance requirements:* For doctorate, GMAT, GRE General Test. Additional exam requirements/recommendations for international students: Required—TOEFL (minimum score 600 paper-based; 250 computer-based; 100 iBT), IELTS (minimum score 7.5). *Application deadline:* For fall admission, 12/31 for domestic students, 12/31 priority date for international students. Applications are processed on a rolling basis. Application fee: $55 ($75 for international students). Electronic applications accepted. *Financial support:* In 2009–10, 68 fellowships with full tuition reimbursements (averaging $11,500 per year), 63 research assistantships with full tuition reimbursements (averaging $6,750 per year), 53 teaching assistantships with full tuition reimbursements (averaging $6,750 per year) were awarded; institutionally sponsored loans, scholarships/grants, health care benefits, and unspecified assistantships also available. Financial award application deadline: 12/31. *Faculty research:* Corporate strategy, finance, entrepreneurship, marketing, information and decision science, operations, accounting. Total annual research expenditures: $300,000. *Unit head:* Dr. Shawn P. Curley, Director of Graduate Studies/Program Director, 612-624-6546, Fax: 612-624-8221, E-mail: curley@umn.edu. *Application contact:* Earlene K. Bronson, Assistant Director, 612-624-0875, Fax: 612-624-8221, E-mail: brons003@umn.edu.

University of Missouri–St. Louis, College of Business Administration, Program in Business Administration, St. Louis, MO 63121. Offers accounting (MBA); business administration (Certificate); finance (MBA); human resource management (Certificate); logistics and supply chain management (MBA, Certificate); management (MBA); marketing (MBA); marketing management (Certificate); operations (MBA); quantitative management science (MBA). *Accreditation:* AACSB. Part-time and evening/weekend programs available. *Faculty:* 30 full-time (5 women), 11 part-time/adjunct (2 women). *Students:* 107 full-time (47 women), 310 part-time (120 women); includes 32 minority (17 African Americans, 6 Asian Americans or Pacific Islanders, 9 Hispanic Americans), 66 international. Average age 31. 285 applicants, 58% accepted, 130 enrolled. In 2009, 149 master's, 13 other advanced degrees awarded. *Entrance requirements:* For master's, GMAT, 2 letters of recommendation. Additional exam requirements/recommendations for international students: Required—TOEFL (minimum score 550 paper-based; 213 computer-based). *Application deadline:* For fall admission, 7/1 for domestic students; for spring admission, 11/1 for domestic students. Applications are processed on a rolling basis. Application fee: $35 ($40 for international students). Electronic applications accepted. *Expenses:* Tuition, state resident: full-time $5377; part-time $297.70 per credit hour. Tuition, nonresident: full-time $13,882; part-time $771.20 per credit hour. Required fees: $220; $12.20 per credit hour. One-time fee: $12. Tuition and fees vary according to course level, campus/location and program. *Financial support:* In 2009–10, 27 research assistantships with full and partial tuition reimbursements (averaging $8,525 per year), 6 teaching assistantships with full and partial tuition reimbursements (averaging $13,950 per year) were awarded; career-related internships or fieldwork, Federal Work-Study, and institutionally sponsored loans also available. Support available to part-time students. Financial award application deadline: 4/1; financial award applicants required to submit FAFSA. *Faculty research:* Human resources, strategic management, marketing strategy, consumer behavior product development, advertising. *Unit head:* Karl Kottemann, Assistant Director, 314-516-5885, Fax: 314-516-6420, E-mail: mba@umsl.edu. *Application contact:* 314-516-5458, Fax: 314-516-6996, E-mail: gradadm@umsl.edu.

University of Nebraska–Lincoln, Graduate College, College of Arts and Sciences, Department of Communication Studies, Lincoln, NE 68588. Offers instructional communication (MA, PhD); interpersonal communication (MA, PhD); marketing, communication studies, and advertising (MA, PhD); organizational communication (MA, PhD); rhetoric and culture (MA, PhD). *Degree requirements:* For master's, thesis optional; for doctorate, comprehensive exam, thesis/dissertation. *Entrance requirements:* For master's and doctorate, GRE General Test, writing sample. Additional exam requirements/recommendations for international students: Required—TOEFL (minimum score 600 paper-based; 250 computer-based). Electronic applications accepted. *Faculty research:* Message strategies, gender communication, political communication, organizational communication, instructional communication.

University of Nebraska–Lincoln, Graduate College, College of Business Administration, Interdepartmental Area of Business, Department of Marketing, Lincoln, NE 68588. Offers business (MA, PhD). *Degree requirements:* For doctorate, comprehensive exam, thesis/dissertation. *Entrance requirements:* For master's and doctorate, GMAT. Additional exam requirements/recommendations for international students: Required—TOEFL. Electronic applications accepted. *Faculty research:* Channel information, marketing research methodology, sales management, cross-cultural marketing, impact of new technology.

University of Nebraska–Lincoln, Graduate College, College of Journalism and Mass Communications, Lincoln, NE 68588. Offers marketing, communication and advertising (MA); professional journalism (MA). *Accreditation:* ACEJMC. Postbaccalaureate distance learning degree programs offered (no on-campus study). *Degree requirements:* For master's, thesis. *Entrance requirements:* For master's, samples of work. Additional exam requirements/recommendations for international students: Required—TOEFL (minimum score 600 paper-based; 250 computer-based). Electronic applications accepted. *Faculty research:* Interactive media and the Internet, community newspapers, children's radio, advertising involvement, telecommunications policy.

University of New Brunswick Fredericton, School of Graduate Studies, Faculty of Forestry and Environmental Management, Fredericton, NB E3B 5A3, Canada. Offers ecological foundations of forest management (PhD); environmental management (MEM); forest engineering (M Sc FE, MFE); forest products marketing (MBA); forest resources (M Sc F, MF, PhD). Part-time programs available. *Faculty:* 32 full-time (2 women). *Students:* 87 full-time (47 women), 11 part-time (4 women). In 2009, 10 master's, 5 doctorates awarded. *Degree requirements:* For master's, thesis; for doctorate, thesis/dissertation. *Entrance requirements:* For master's and doctorate, minimum GPA of 3.0. Additional exam requirements/recommendations for international students: Required—TOEFL (minimum score 580 paper-based), TWE (minimum score 4), or IELTS. *Application deadline:* For fall admission, 3/1 priority date for domestic students. Application fee: $50 Canadian dollars. Electronic applications accepted. Tuition and fees charges are reported in Canadian dollars. *Expenses:* Tuition, area resident: Full-time $5562 Canadian dollars; part-time $2781 Canadian dollars per year. Required fees: $49.75 Canadian dollars per term. *Financial support:* Research assistantships, teaching assistantships available. *Faculty research:* Forest management, forest ecology, wildlife ecology, wood tech, human dimensions in forestry. *Unit head:* Dr. John Kershaw, Director of Graduate Studies, 506-453-4933, Fax: 506-453-3538, E-mail: kershaw@unb.ca. *Application contact:* Faith Sharpe, Graduate Secretary, 506-458-7520, Fax: 506-453-3538, E-mail: fsharpe@unb.ca.

University of New Haven, Graduate School, School of Business, Program in Business Administration, West Haven, CT 06516-1916. Offers accounting (MBA, Certificate), including CPA (MBA); business management (Certificate); business policy and strategy (MBA); finance (MBA), including CFA; global marketing (MBA); human resource management (Certificate); human resources management (MBA); international business (Certificate); marketing (Certificate); sports management (MBA); telcommunications management (Certificate); MBA/MPA. Part-time and evening/weekend programs available. *Faculty:* 26 full-time (3 women), 23 part-time/adjunct (5 women). *Students:* 302 full-time (120 women), 194 part-time (101 women); includes 109 minority (56 African Americans, 3 American Indian/Alaska Native, 28 Asian Americans or Pacific Islanders, 22 Hispanic Americans), 110 international. Average age 31. 372 applicants, 83% accepted, 172 enrolled. In 2009, 194 master's, 31 other advanced degrees awarded. *Degree requirements:* For master's, thesis or alternative. *Entrance requirements:* For master's, GMAT. Additional exam requirements/recommendations for international students: Required—TOEFL (minimum score 520 paper-based; 190 computer-based; 70 iBT), IELTS (minimum score 5.5). *Application deadline:* For fall admission, 5/31 for international students; for winter admission, 10/15 for international students; for spring admission, 1/15 for international students. Applications are processed on a rolling basis. Application fee: $50. Electronic applications accepted. *Expenses:* Contact institution. *Financial support:* Research assistantships with partial tuition reimbursements, teaching assistantships with partial tuition reimbursements, Federal Work-Study, scholarships/grants, health care benefits, tuition waivers, and unspecified assistantships available. Support available to part-time students. Financial award applicants required to submit FAFSA. *Unit head:* Charles Coleman, Chairman, 203-932-7375. *Application contact:* Eloise Gormley, Director of Graduate Admissions, 203-932-7449, Fax: 203-932-7137, E-mail: gradinfo@newhaven.edu.

University of New Mexico, Robert O. Anderson Graduate School of Management, Department of Marketing, Information and Decision Sciences, Albuquerque, NM 87131. Offers information assurance (MBA); management information systems (MBA); marketing management (MBA); operations management (MBA). Part-time and evening/weekend programs available. *Faculty:* 14 full-time (3 women), 5 part-time/adjunct (0 women). *Students:* 39 full-time (18 women), 37 part-time (19 women); includes 31 minority (3 African Americans, 1 American Indian/Alaska Native, 3 Asian Americans or Pacific Islanders, 24 Hispanic Americans), 4 international. Average age 28. 40 applicants, 100% accepted, 36 enrolled. In 2009, 39 master's awarded. *Entrance requirements:* For master's, GMAT or GRE (can be waived in some instances). Additional exam requirements/recommendations for international students: Required—TOEFL (minimum score 550 paper-based; 213 computer-based; 79 iBT). *Application deadline:* For fall admission, 4/1 priority date for domestic students, 5/1 for international students; for spring admission, 10/1 priority date for domestic students, 10/1 for international students. Applications are processed on a rolling basis. Application fee: $50. Electronic applications accepted. *Expenses:* Tuition, state resident: full-time $2099; part-time $233.20 per credit hour. Tuition, nonresident: full-time $6650. Required fees: $25 per semester. Tuition and fees vary according to course load, program and reciprocity agreements. *Financial support:* Fellowships, research assistantships, teaching assistantships, career-related internships or fieldwork, Federal Work-Study, scholarships/grants, and unspecified assistantships available. Support available to part-time students. Financial award application deadline: 6/1. *Faculty research:* Marketing, operations, information science. *Unit head:* Dr. Steve Yourstone, Chair, 505-277-6471, Fax: 505-277-7108. *Application contact:* Megan Conner, Academic Advisement Manager, 505-277-3290, Fax: 505-277-8436, E-mail: mconner@mgt.unm.edu.

The University of North Carolina at Chapel Hill, Kenan-Flagler Business School, Doctoral Program in Business Administration, Chapel Hill, NC 27599. Offers accounting (PhD); finance (PhD); marketing (PhD); operations management (PhD); organizational behavior (PhD); strategy (PhD). *Accreditation:* AACSB. *Degree requirements:* For doctorate, thesis/dissertation. *Entrance requirements:* For doctorate, GMAT or GRE General Test. Electronic applications accepted. *Expenses:* Contact institution.

The University of North Carolina at Charlotte, Graduate School, Belk College of Business, Program in Sports Marketing Management, Charlotte, NC 28223-0001. Offers MBA. *Faculty:* 11 full-time (2 women), 1 part-time/adjunct (0 women). *Students:* 22 full-time (6 women), 1 part-time (0 women); includes 3 African Americans, 1 international. Average age 25. 51 applicants, 41% accepted, 14 enrolled. *Degree requirements:* For master's, thesis or alternative, internship. Application fee: $55. Total annual research expenditures: $2,699. *Unit head:* Dr. Linda Swayne, Director, 704-687-7663, Fax: 704-687-4014, E-mail: leswayne@uncc.edu. *Application contact:* Kathy B. Giddings, Director of Graduate Admissions, 704-687-5503, Fax: 704-687-3279, E-mail: gradadm@uncc.edu.

The University of North Carolina at Greensboro, Graduate School, School of Human Environmental Sciences, Department of Consumer, Apparel, and Retail Studies, Greensboro, NC 27412-5001. Offers MS, PhD. *Degree requirements:* For master's, one foreign language; for doctorate, one foreign language, thesis/dissertation. *Entrance requirements:* For master's and doctorate, GRE General Test. Additional exam requirements/recommendations for international students: Required—TOEFL. Electronic applications accepted. *Faculty research:* Impact of phosphate removal, protective clothing for pesticide workers, fabric hand: subjective and objective measurements.

University of North Texas, Robert B. Toulouse School of Graduate Studies, College of Business Administration, Department of Marketing and Logistics, Denton, TX 76203-5017. Offers PhD. Part-time programs available. *Faculty:* 2. *Degree requirements:* For doctorate, comprehensive exam, thesis/dissertation, referred publication. *Entrance requirements:* For doctorate, GMAT (minimum score: 550, 650 preferred). Additional exam requirements/recommendations for international students: Required—proof of English language proficiency required for non-native English speakers; Recommended—TOEFL (minimum score 550 paper-based; 213 computer-based; 79 iBT). *Application deadline:* Applications are processed on a rolling basis. Application fee: $50 ($75 for international students). *Expenses:* Tuition, state resident: full-time $4298; part-time $239 per contact hour. Tuition, nonresident: full-time $9878; part-time $549 per contact hour. Required fees: $265 per contact hour. *Financial support:* In 2009–10, teaching assistantships (averaging $6,000 per year); fellowships, career-related internships or fieldwork, Federal Work-Study, and institutionally sponsored loans also available. Financial award applicants required to submit FAFSA. *Faculty research:* Promotion, distribution channels, international distribution, sales management, consumer behavior, services marketing, NPD. *Application contact:* Graduate Advisor, 940-565-4419, Fax: 940-565-3837, E-mail: jeff.lewin@unt.edu.

University of Oregon, Graduate School, Charles H. Lundquist College of Business, Department of Marketing, Eugene, OR 97403. Offers PhD. Part-time programs available. *Degree requirements:* For doctorate, thesis/dissertation, 2 comprehensive exams. *Entrance requirements:* For doctorate, GMAT. Additional exam requirements/recommendations for international students: Required—TOEFL. *Faculty research:* Consumer behavior, marketing research, international marketing, marketing management, price quality.

University of Pennsylvania, Wharton School, Marketing Department, Philadelphia, PA 19104. Offers MBA, PhD. Terminal master's awarded for partial completion of doctoral program. *Degree requirements:* For master's, thesis optional; for doctorate, thesis/dissertation. *Entrance*

Marketing

University of Pennsylvania (continued)
requirements: For doctorate, GMAT or GRE. *Expenses:* Tuition: Full-time $25,660; part-time $4758 per course. Required fees: $2152; $270 per course. Tuition and fees vary according to course load, degree level and program. *Faculty research:* Scanner data, consumer preferences, decision-making theory, modeling for marketing and e-business.

University of Phoenix, School of Business, College of Graduate Business and Management, Phoenix, AZ 85034-7209. Offers accountancy (MSA); accounting (MBA); business administration (MBA); global management (MBA); human resources management (MBA, MM); management (MM); marketing (MBA); public administration (MBA, MM). *Accreditation:* ACBSP. Evening/weekend programs available. Postbaccalaureate distance learning degree programs offered. *Faculty:* 25 full-time (15 women), 4,861 part-time/adjunct (1,504 women). *Students:* 6,681 full-time (5,284 women); includes 2,558 minority (1,955 African Americans, 69 American Indian/Alaska Native, 90 Asian Americans or Pacific Islanders, 444 Hispanic Americans), 137 international. Average age 35. In 2009, 1,740 master's awarded. *Degree requirements:* For master's, thesis (for some programs). *Entrance requirements:* For master's, 3 years of work experience, minimum undergraduate GPA of 3.0. Additional exam requirements/recommendations for international students: Required—TOEFL (minimum score 550 paper-based; 213 computer-based; 79 iBT). *Application deadline:* Applications are processed on a rolling basis. Application fee: $45. Electronic applications accepted. *Expenses:* Tuition: Full-time $13,272. Required fees: $660. Full-time tuition and fees vary according to course level, degree level and program. *Financial support:* Institutionally sponsored loans and scholarships/grants available. Financial award applicants required to submit FAFSA. *Unit head:* Brian Lindquist, Dean/Executive Director and Associate Vice President, 480-557-1221, E-mail: brian.lindquist@phoenix.edu. *Application contact:* Chair, 602-387-7000, Fax: 602-387-6020.

University of Phoenix–Atlanta Campus, John Sperling School of Business, College of Graduate Business and Management, Sandy Springs, GA 30350-4153. Offers accounting (MBA); business administration (MBA); global management (MBA); human resources management (MBA, MM); management (MM); marketing (MBA); public administration (MM). Evening/weekend programs available. Postbaccalaureate distance learning degree programs offered. *Degree requirements:* For master's, thesis (for some programs). *Entrance requirements:* For master's, minimum undergraduate GPA of 3.0, 3 years of work experience. Additional exam requirements/recommendations for international students: Required—TOEFL (minimum score 550 paper-based; 213 computer-based; 79 iBT).

University of Phoenix–Augusta Campus, College of Graduate Business and Management, Augusta, GA 30909-4583. Offers accounting (MBA); business administration (MBA); business and management (MBA, MM); global management (MBA); human resources management (MBA, MM); management (MM); marketing (MBA); public administration (MBA, MM). Postbaccalaureate distance learning degree programs offered.

University of Phoenix–Austin Campus, College of Graduate Business and Management, Austin, TX 78759. Offers accounting (MBA); business administration (MBA); business and management (MBA); e-business (MBA); global management (MBA); human resources management (MBA, MM); management (MM); marketing (MBA); public administration (MBA). Postbaccalaureate distance learning degree programs offered.

University of Phoenix–Bay Area Campus, John Sperling School of Business, College of Graduate Business and Management, Pleasanton, CA 94588-3677. Offers accounting (MBA); business administration (MBA); global management (MBA); human resources management (MBA, MM); marketing (MBA); public administration (MBA, MM). Evening/weekend programs available. Postbaccalaureate distance learning degree programs offered (no on-campus study). *Degree requirements:* For master's, thesis (for some programs). *Entrance requirements:* For master's, minimum undergraduate GPA of 3.0, 3 years of work experience. Additional exam requirements/recommendations for international students: Required—TOEFL (minimum score 550 paper-based; 213 computer-based; 79 iBT). Electronic applications accepted.

University of Phoenix–Birmingham Campus, College of Graduate Business and Management, Birmingham, AL 35244. Offers accounting (MBA); business administration (MBA); global management (MBA); human resources management (MBA, MM); management (MM); marketing (MBA); public administration (MM).

University of Phoenix–Central Florida Campus, John Sperling School of Business, College of Graduate Business and Management, Maitland, FL 32751-7057. Offers accounting (MBA); business administration (MBA); business and management (MM); global management (MBA); human resources management (MBA, MM); management (MM); marketing (MBA); public administration (MBA, MM). Evening/weekend programs available. *Degree requirements:* For master's, thesis (for some programs). *Entrance requirements:* For master's, minimum undergraduate GPA of 3.0, 3 years work experience. Additional exam requirements/recommendations for international students: Required—TOEFL (minimum score 550 paper-based; 213 computer-based; 79 iBT). Electronic applications accepted.

University of Phoenix–Central Valley Campus, College of Graduate Business and Management, Fresno, CA 93720-1562. Offers accounting (MBA); business administration (MBA); global management (MBA); human resources management (MBA, MM); management (MM); marketing (MBA); public administration (MBA, MM).

University of Phoenix–Chattanooga Campus, College of Graduate Business and Management, Chattanooga, TN 37421-3707. Offers accounting (MBA); business administration (MBA); business and management (MBA); global management (MBA); human resources management (MBA, MM); management (MM); marketing (MBA); public administration (MBA, MM). Postbaccalaureate distance learning degree programs offered.

University of Phoenix–Cheyenne Campus, College of Graduate Business and Management, Cheyenne, WY 82009. Offers global management (MBA); human resources management (MBA, MM); management (MM); marketing (MBA); public administration (MBA, MM). Postbaccalaureate distance learning degree programs offered.

University of Phoenix–Cincinnati Campus, John Sperling School of Business, College of Graduate Business and Management, West Chester, OH 45069-4875. Offers accounting (MBA); business administration (MBA); global management (MBA); human resources management (MBA, MM); management (MM); marketing (MBA); public administration (MM). Evening/weekend programs available. *Degree requirements:* For master's, thesis (for some programs). *Entrance requirements:* For master's, minimum undergraduate GPA of 3.0, 3 years of work experience. Additional exam requirements/recommendations for international students: Required—TOEFL (minimum score 550 paper-based; 213 computer-based; 79 iBT). Electronic applications accepted.

University of Phoenix–Cleveland Campus, John Sperling School of Business, College of Graduate Business and Management, Independence, OH 44131-2194. Offers accounting (MBA); business administration (MBA); global management (MBA); human resources management (MBA, MM); management (MM); marketing (MBA); public administration (MBA, MM). Evening/weekend programs available. Postbaccalaureate distance learning degree programs offered (no on-campus study). *Degree requirements:* For master's, thesis (for some programs). *Entrance requirements:* For master's, minimum undergraduate GPA of 3.0, 3 years of work experience. Additional exam requirements/recommendations for international students: Required—TOEFL (minimum score 550 paper-based; 213 computer-based; 79 iBT). Electronic applications accepted.

University of Phoenix–Columbus Georgia Campus, John Sperling School of Business, College of Graduate Business and Management, Columbus, GA 31904-6321. Offers accounting (MBA); business administration (MBA); global management (MBA); human resources management (MBA, MM); management (MM); marketing (MBA); public administration (MBA). Evening/weekend programs available. *Degree requirements:* For master's, thesis (for some programs). *Entrance requirements:* For master's, minimum undergraduate GPA of 3.0, 3 years of work experience. Additional exam requirements/recommendations for international students: Required—TOEFL (minimum score 550 paper-based; 213 computer-based; 79 iBT). Electronic applications accepted.

University of Phoenix–Columbus Ohio Campus, John Sperling School of Business, College of Graduate Business and Management, Columbus, OH 43240-4032. Offers accounting (MBA); business administration (MBA); global management (MBA); human resources management (MBA, MM); management (MM); marketing (MBA); public administration (MM). Evening/weekend programs available. Postbaccalaureate distance learning degree programs offered. *Degree requirements:* For master's, thesis (for some programs). *Entrance requirements:* For master's, minimum undergraduate GPA of 3.0, 3 years of work experience. Additional exam requirements/recommendations for international students: Required—TOEFL (minimum score 550 paper-based; 213 computer-based; 79 iBT). Electronic applications accepted.

University of Phoenix–Dallas Campus, John Sperling School of Business, College of Graduate Business and Management, Dallas, TX 75251-2009. Offers accounting (MBA); business administration (MBA); global management (MBA); human resources management (MBA, MM); management (MM); marketing (MBA); public administration (MBA, MM). Evening/weekend programs available. Postbaccalaureate distance learning degree programs offered. *Degree requirements:* For master's, thesis (for some programs). *Entrance requirements:* For master's, 3 years of work experience, minimum undergraduate GPA of 3.0. Additional exam requirements/recommendations for international students: Required—TOEFL (minimum score 550 paper-based; 213 computer-based; 79 iBT). Electronic applications accepted.

University of Phoenix–Denver Campus, John Sperling School of Business, College of Graduate Business and Management, Lone Tree, CO 80124-5453. Offers accountancy (MSA); accounting (MBA); business administration (MBA); e-business (MBA); global management (MBA); human resources management (MBA, MM); management (MM); marketing (MBA); public administration (MBA, MM). Evening/weekend programs available. Postbaccalaureate distance learning degree programs offered. *Degree requirements:* For master's, thesis (for some programs). *Entrance requirements:* For master's, minimum undergraduate GPA of 3.0, 3 years work experience. Additional exam requirements/recommendations for international students: Required—TOEFL (minimum score 550 paper-based; 213 computer-based; 79 iBT). Electronic applications accepted.

University of Phoenix–Des Moines Campus, College of Graduate Business and Management, Des Moines, IA 50266. Offers accounting (MBA); business administration (MBA); global management (MBA); human resources management (MBA, MM); management (MM); marketing (MBA); public administration (MBA, MM). Postbaccalaureate distance learning degree programs offered.

University of Phoenix–Eastern Washington Campus, John Sperling School of Business, College of Graduate Business and Management, Spokane Valley, WA 99212-2531. Offers accounting (MBA); business administration (MBA); human resources management (MBA); marketing (MBA); public administration (MBA). Evening/weekend programs available. *Degree requirements:* For master's, thesis (for some programs). *Entrance requirements:* For master's, minimum undergraduate GPA of 3.0, 3 years of work experience. Additional exam requirements/recommendations for international students: Required—TOEFL (minimum score 550 paper-based; 213 computer-based; 79 iBT). Electronic applications accepted.

University of Phoenix–Harrisburg Campus, College of Graduate Business and Management, Harrisburg, PA 17112. Offers accounting (MBA); business administration (MBA); business and management (MBA); global management (MBA); human resources management (MBA, MM); management (MM); marketing (MBA); public administration (MBA, MM). Postbaccalaureate distance learning degree programs offered.

University of Phoenix–Hawaii Campus, John Sperling School of Business, College of Graduate Business and Management, Honolulu, HI 96813-4317. Offers accounting (MBA); business administration (MBA); global management (MBA); human resources management (MBA, MM); management (MM); marketing (MBA); public administration (MBA, MM). Evening/weekend programs available. *Degree requirements:* For master's, thesis (for some programs). *Entrance requirements:* For master's, minimum undergraduate GPA of 3.0, 3 years of work experience. Additional exam requirements/recommendations for international students: Required—TOEFL (minimum score 550 paper-based; 213 computer-based; 79 iBT). Electronic applications accepted.

University of Phoenix–Houston Campus, John Sperling School of Business, College of Graduate Business and Management, Houston, TX 77079-2004. Offers accounting (MBA); business administration (MBA); global management (MBA); human resources management (MBA, MM); management (MM); marketing (MBA); public administration (MBA, MM). Evening/weekend programs available. Postbaccalaureate distance learning degree programs offered. *Degree requirements:* For master's, thesis (for some programs). *Entrance requirements:* For master's, 3 years of work experience, minimum undergraduate GPA of 3.0. Additional exam requirements/recommendations for international students: Required—TOEFL (minimum score 550 paper-based; 213 computer-based; 79 iBT). Electronic applications accepted.

University of Phoenix–Idaho Campus, John Sperling School of Business, College of Graduate Business and Management, Meridian, ID 83642-3014. Offers accounting (MBA); administration (MBA); global management (MBA); human resources management (MBA, MM); management (MM); marketing (MBA); public administration (MM). Evening/weekend programs available. Postbaccalaureate distance learning degree programs offered. *Degree requirements:* For master's, thesis (for some programs). *Entrance requirements:* For master's, 3 years of work experience, minimum undergraduate GPA of 3.0. Additional exam requirements/recommendations for international students: Required—TOEFL (minimum score 550 paper-based; 213 computer-based). Electronic applications accepted.

University of Phoenix–Indianapolis Campus, John Sperling School of Business, College of Graduate Business and Management, Indianapolis, IN 46250-932. Offers accounting (MBA); business administration (MBA); global management (MBA); human resources management (MBA, MM); management (MM); marketing (MBA); public administration (MM). Evening/weekend programs available. *Degree requirements:* For master's, thesis (for some programs). *Entrance requirements:* For master's, minimum undergraduate GPA of 3.0, 3 years of work experience. Additional exam requirements/recommendations for international students: Required—TOEFL (minimum score 550 paper-based; 213 computer-based). Electronic applications accepted.

University of Phoenix–Jersey City Campus, College of Graduate Business and Management, Jersey City, NJ 07310. Offers accounting (MBA); business administration (MBA); global management (MBA); human resources management (MBA, MM); management (MM); marketing (MBA); public administration (MBA, MM).

University of Phoenix–Kansas City Campus, John Sperling School of Business, College of Graduate Business and Management, Kansas City, MO 64131-4517. Offers accounting (MBA); business administration (MBA); global management (MBA); human resources management (MBA, MM); management (MM); marketing (MBA); public administration (MBA, MM). Evening/weekend programs available. *Degree requirements:* For master's, thesis (for some programs). *Entrance requirements:* For master's, minimum undergraduate GPA of 3.0, 3 years of work experience. Additional exam requirements/recommendations for international students: Required—TOEFL (minimum score 550 paper-based; 213 computer-based). Electronic applications accepted.

University of Phoenix–Las Vegas Campus, John Sperling School of Business, College of Graduate Business and Management, Las Vegas, NV 89128. Offers accounting (MBA); business administration (MBA); global management (MBA); human resources management (MBA, MM); management (MM); marketing (MBA); public administration (MM). Evening/weekend programs available. Postbaccalaureate distance learning degree programs offered (no on-campus study). *Degree requirements:* For master's, thesis (for some programs). *Entrance requirements:* For master's, minimum undergraduate GPA of 3.0, 3 years of work experience.

Additional exam requirements/recommendations for international students: Required—TOEFL (minimum score 550 paper-based; 213 computer-based; 79 iBT). Electronic applications accepted.

University of Phoenix–Louisiana Campus, John Sperling School of Business, College of Graduate Business and Management, Metairie, LA 70001-2082. Offers accounting (MBA); business administration (MBA); global management (MBA); human resources management (MBA, MM); management (MM); marketing (MBA); public administration (MBA). Evening/weekend programs available. *Degree requirements:* For master's, thesis (for some programs). *Entrance requirements:* For master's, minimum undergraduate GPA of 3.0, 3 years work experience. Additional exam requirements/recommendations for international students: Required—TOEFL (minimum score 550 paper-based; 213 computer-based; 79 iBT). Electronic applications accepted.

University of Phoenix–Madison Campus, College of Graduate Business and Management, Madison, WI 53718-2416. Offers accounting (MBA); business and management (MBA); e-business (MBA); global management (MBA); human resources management (MBA, MM); management (MM); marketing (MBA); public administration (MBA).

University of Phoenix–Madison Campus, John Sperling School of Business, College of Graduate Business and Management, Madison, WI 53718-2416. Offers accounting (MBA); administration (MBA); global management (MBA); human resources management (MBA); management (MM); marketing (MBA); public administration (MBA). Evening/weekend programs available. *Degree requirements:* For master's, thesis (for some programs). *Entrance requirements:* For master's, 3 years of work experience, minimum undergraduate GPA of 3.0. Additional exam requirements/recommendations for international students: Required—TOEFL (minimum score 550 paper-based; 213 computer-based; 79 iBT). Electronic applications accepted.

University of Phoenix–Maryland Campus, John Sperling School of Business, College of Graduate Business and Management, Columbia, MD 21045-5424. Offers accounting (MBA); business administration (MBA); e-business (MBA); global management (MBA); human resources management (MBA, MM); management (MM); marketing (MBA); public administration (MBA, MM). Evening/weekend programs available. *Degree requirements:* For master's, thesis (for some programs). *Entrance requirements:* For master's, minimum undergraduate GPA of 3.0, 3 years of work experience. Additional exam requirements/recommendations for international students: Required—TOEFL (minimum score 550 paper-based; 213 computer-based; 79 iBT). Electronic applications accepted.

University of Phoenix–Memphis Campus, College of Graduate Business and Management, Cordova, TN 38018. Offers accounting (MBA); business and management (MBA); e-business (MBA); global management (MBA); human resources management (MBA, MM); management (MM); marketing (MBA); public administration (MBA, MM).

University of Phoenix–Metro Detroit Campus, School of Business, College of Graduate Business and Management, Troy, MI 48098-2623. Offers accountancy (MS); accounting (MBA); business administration (MBA); global management (MBA); human resources management (MBA, MM); management (MM); marketing (MBA). Evening/weekend programs available. *Degree requirements:* For master's, thesis (for some programs). *Entrance requirements:* For master's, minimum undergraduate GPA of 3.0, 3 years work experience. Additional exam requirements/recommendations for international students: Required—TOEFL (minimum score 550 paper-based; 213 computer-based; 79 iBT). Electronic applications accepted. *Expenses:* Tuition: Full-time $14,136. Required fees: $660.

University of Phoenix–Minneapolis/St. Louis Park Campus, College of Graduate Business and Management, St. Louis Park, MN 55426. Offers accounting (MBA); business administration (MBA); global management (MBA); human resources management (MBA); management (MM); marketing (MBA); public administration (MBA).

University of Phoenix–New Mexico Campus, John Sperling School of Business, College of Graduate Business and Management, Albuquerque, NM 87113-1570. Offers accounting (MBA); business administration (MBA); global management (MBA); human resource management (MBA); human resources management (MM); management (MM); marketing (MBA). Evening/weekend programs available. *Degree requirements:* For master's, thesis (for some programs). *Entrance requirements:* For master's, 3 years of work experience, minimum undergraduate GPA of 3.0. Additional exam requirements/recommendations for international students: Required—TOEFL (minimum score 550 paper-based; 213 computer-based; 79 iBT). Electronic applications accepted.

University of Phoenix–Northern Nevada Campus, College of Graduate Business and Management, Reno, NV 89521-5862. Offers accounting (MBA); business administration (MBA); global management (MBA); human resources management (MBA, MM); management (MM); marketing (MBA); public administration (MBA, MM).

University of Phoenix–Northern Virginia Campus, College of Graduate Business and Management, Reston, VA 20190. Offers accounting (MBA); business administration (MBA); e-business (MBA); global management (MBA); human resources management (MBA, MM); management (MM); marketing (MBA); public administration (MBA).

University of Phoenix–North Florida Campus, John Sperling School of Business, College of Graduate Business and Management, Jacksonville, FL 32216-0959. Offers accounting (MBA); business administration (MBA); global management (MBA); human resources management (MBA, MM); management (MM); marketing (MBA); public administration (MBA, MM). Evening/weekend programs available. *Degree requirements:* For master's, thesis (for some programs). *Entrance requirements:* For master's, minimum undergraduate GPA of 3.0, 3 years work experience. Additional exam requirements/recommendations for international students: Required—TOEFL (minimum score 550 paper-based; 213 computer-based; 79 iBT). Electronic applications accepted.

University of Phoenix–Northwest Arkansas Campus, College of Graduate Business and Management, Rogers, AR 72756-9615. Offers accounting (MBA); business and management (MBA); global management (MBA); human resources management (MBA, MM); management (MM); marketing (MBA); public administration (MBA, MM).

University of Phoenix–Oklahoma City Campus, John Sperling School of Business, College of Graduate Business and Management, Oklahoma City, OK 73116-8244. Offers accounting (MBA); business administration (MBA); global management (MBA); human resource management (MBA); management (MM); marketing (MBA). Evening/weekend programs available. *Degree requirements:* For master's, thesis (for some programs). *Entrance requirements:* For master's, minimum undergraduate GPA of 3.0, 3 years of work experience. Additional exam requirements/recommendations for international students: Required—TOEFL (minimum score 550 paper-based; 213 computer-based; 79 iBT). Electronic applications accepted.

University of Phoenix–Omaha Campus, College of Graduate Business and Management, Omaha, NE 68154-5240. Offers accounting (MBA); business and management (MBA); global management (MBA); human resources management (MBA, MM); management (MM); marketing (MBA); public administration (MBA, MM).

University of Phoenix–Oregon Campus, The John Sperling School of Business, College of Graduate Business and Management, Tigard, OR 97223. Offers accounting (MBA); business administration (MBA); global management (MBA); human resource management (MM); human resources management (MBA); management (MM); marketing (MBA); public administration (MM). Evening/weekend programs available. *Degree requirements:* For master's, thesis (for some programs). *Entrance requirements:* For master's, minimum undergraduate GPA of 3.0, 3 years of work experience. Additional exam requirements/recommendations for international students: Required—TOEFL (minimum score 550 paper-based; 213 computer-based; 79 iBT). Electronic applications accepted.

University of Phoenix–Philadelphia Campus, The John Sperling School of Business, College of Graduate Business and Management, Wayne, PA 19087-2121. Offers accounting (MBA); business administration (MBA); global management (MBA); human resources management (MBA, MM); management (MM); marketing (MBA); public administration (MM). Evening/weekend programs available. *Degree requirements:* For master's, thesis (for some programs). *Entrance requirements:* For master's, minimum undergraduate GPA of 3.0, 3 years work experience. Additional exam requirements/recommendations for international students: Required—TOEFL (minimum score 550 paper-based; 213 computer-based; 79 iBT). Electronic applications accepted.

University of Phoenix–Pittsburgh Campus, John Sperling School of Business, College of Graduate Business and Management, Pittsburgh, PA 15276. Offers accounting (MBA); business administration (MBA); global management (MBA); human resources management (MBA, MM); management (MM); marketing (MBA); public administration (MBA, MM). Evening/weekend programs available. *Degree requirements:* For master's, thesis (for some programs). *Entrance requirements:* For master's, minimum undergraduate GPA of 3.0, 3 years work experience. Additional exam requirements/recommendations for international students: Required—TOEFL (minimum score 550 paper-based; 213 computer-based; 79 iBT). Electronic applications accepted.

University of Phoenix–Puerto Rico Campus, John Sperling School of Business, College of Graduate Business and Management, Guaynabo, PR 00968. Offers accounting (MBA); business administration (MBA); global management (MBA); human resource management (MBA); marketing (MBA). Evening/weekend programs available. *Degree requirements:* For master's, thesis (for some programs). *Entrance requirements:* For master's, minimum undergraduate GPA of 3.0, 3 years work experience. Additional exam requirements/recommendations for international students: Required—TOEFL (minimum score 550 paper-based; 213 computer-based; 79 iBT). Electronic applications accepted.

University of Phoenix–Raleigh Campus, College of Graduate Business and Management, Raleigh, NC 27606. Offers accounting (MBA); business administration (MBA); e-business (MBA); global management (MBA); human resources management (MBA); marketing (MBA).

University of Phoenix–Richmond Campus, John Sperling School of Business, College of Graduate Business and Management, Richmond, VA 23230. Offers accounting (MBA); business administration (MBA); global management (MBA); human resources management (MBA, MM); management (MM); marketing (MBA); public administration (MBA, MM). Evening/weekend programs available. *Degree requirements:* For master's, thesis (for some programs). *Entrance requirements:* For master's, minimum undergraduate GPA of 3.0, 3 years work experience. Additional exam requirements/recommendations for international students: Required—TOEFL (minimum score 550 paper-based; 213 computer-based; 79 iBT). Electronic applications accepted.

University of Phoenix–Sacramento Valley Campus, John Sperling School of Business, College of Graduate Business and Management, Sacramento, CA 95833-3632. Offers accounting (MBA); business administration (MBA); global management (MBA); human resources management (MBA, MM); management (MM); marketing (MBA); public administration (MBA, MM). Evening/weekend programs available. *Degree requirements:* For master's, thesis (for some programs). *Entrance requirements:* For master's, minimum undergraduate GPA of 3.0, 3 years work experience. Additional exam requirements/recommendations for international students: Required—TOEFL (minimum score 550 paper-based; 213 computer-based; 79 iBT). Electronic applications accepted.

University of Phoenix–St. Louis Campus, John Sperling School of Business, College of Graduate Business and Management, St. Louis, MO 63043-4828. Offers accounting (MBA); business administration (MBA); global management (MBA); human resources management (MBA, MM); management (MM); marketing (MBA); public administration (MM). Evening/weekend programs available. *Degree requirements:* For master's, thesis (for some programs). *Entrance requirements:* For master's, 3 years of work experience, minimum undergraduate GPA of 3.0. Additional exam requirements/recommendations for international students: Required—TOEFL (minimum score 550 paper-based; 213 computer-based; 79 iBT). Electronic applications accepted.

University of Phoenix–San Antonio Campus, College of Graduate Business and Management, San Antonio, TX 78230. Offers accounting (MBA); business administration (MBA); e-business (MBA); global management (MBA); human resources management (MBA, MM); management (MM); marketing (MBA); public administration (MBA, MM).

University of Phoenix–San Diego Campus, John Sperling School of Business, College of Graduate Business and Management, San Diego, CA 92123. Offers accounting (MBA); business administration (MBA); global management (MBA); human resources management (MBA, MM); management (MM); marketing (MBA); public administration (MBA). Evening/weekend programs available. *Degree requirements:* For master's, thesis (for some programs). *Entrance requirements:* For master's, 3 years of work experience, minimum undergraduate GPA of 3.0. Additional exam requirements/recommendations for international students: Required—TOEFL (minimum score 550 paper-based; 213 computer-based; 79 iBT). Electronic applications accepted.

University of Phoenix–Savannah Campus, College of Graduate Business and Management, Savannah, GA 31405-7400. Offers accounting (MBA); business administration (MBA); global management (MBA); human resources management (MBA, MM); management (MM); marketing (MBA); public administration (MBA, MM).

University of Phoenix–Southern Arizona Campus, John Sperling School of Business, College of Graduate Business and Management, Tucson, AZ 85711. Offers accountancy (MS); accounting (MBA); business administration (MBA); global management (MBA); human resources management (MBA); management (MM); marketing (MBA). Evening/weekend programs available. *Degree requirements:* For master's, thesis (for some programs). *Entrance requirements:* For master's, minimum undergraduate GPA of 3.0, 3 years of work experience. Additional exam requirements/recommendations for international students: Required—TOEFL (minimum score 550 paper-based; 213 computer-based; 79 iBT). Electronic applications accepted.

University of Phoenix–Southern Colorado Campus, John Sperling School of Business, College of Graduate Business and Management, Colorado Springs, CO 80919-2335. Offers accounting (MBA); business administration (MBA); global management (MBA); human resources management (MBA, MM); management (MM); marketing (MBA); public administration (MM). Evening/weekend programs available. *Degree requirements:* For master's, thesis (for some programs). *Entrance requirements:* For master's, minimum undergraduate GPA of 3.0, 3 years of work experience. Additional exam requirements/recommendations for international students: Required—TOEFL (minimum score 550 paper-based; 213 computer-based; 79 iBT). Electronic applications accepted.

University of Phoenix–South Florida Campus, John Sperling School of Business, College of Graduate Business and Management, Fort Lauderdale, FL 33309. Offers accounting (MBA); business administration (MBA); global management (MBA); human resource management (MBA); human resources management (MM); management (MM); marketing (MBA); public administration (MBA, MM). Evening/weekend programs available. *Degree requirements:* For master's, thesis (for some programs). *Entrance requirements:* For master's, minimum undergraduate GPA of 3.0, 3 years work experience. Additional exam requirements/recommendations for international students: Required—TOEFL (minimum score 550 paper-based; 213 computer-based; 79 iBT). Electronic applications accepted.

University of Phoenix–Springfield Campus, College of Graduate Business and Management, Springfield, MO 65804-7211. Offers accounting (MBA); business administration (MBA); global management (MBA); human resources management (MBA, MM); management (MM); marketing (MBA); public administration (MBA, MM).

Marketing

University of Phoenix–Tulsa Campus, John Sperling School of Business, College of Graduate Business and Management, Tulsa, OK 74134-1412. Offers accounting (MBA); business (MM); business administration (MBA); global management (MBA); human resources management (MBA); marketing (MBA). Evening/weekend programs available. *Degree requirements:* For master's, thesis (for some programs). *Entrance requirements:* For master's, minimum undergraduate GPA of 3.0, 3 years work experience. Additional exam requirements/recommendations for international students: Required—TOEFL (minimum score 550 paper-based; 213 computer-based; 79 iBT).

University of Phoenix–Utah Campus, John Sperling School of Business, College of Graduate Business and Management, Salt Lake City, UT 84123-4617. Offers accounting (MBA); business administration (MBA); global management (MBA); human resource management (MBA, MM); management (MM); marketing (MBA); technology management (MBA). Evening/weekend programs available. *Degree requirements:* For master's, thesis (for some programs). *Entrance requirements:* For master's, minimum undergraduate GPA of 3.0, 3 years of work experience. Additional exam requirements/recommendations for international students: Required—TOEFL (minimum score 550 paper-based; 213 computer-based; 79 iBT). Electronic applications accepted.

University of Phoenix–Vancouver Campus, John Sperling School of Business, College of Graduate Business and Management, Burnaby, BC V5C 6G9, Canada. Offers accounting (MBA); business administration (MBA); global management (MBA); human resources management (MBA, MM); marketing (MBA). Evening/weekend programs available. *Degree requirements:* For master's, thesis (for some programs). *Entrance requirements:* For master's, minimum undergraduate GPA of 3.0, 3 years of work experience. Additional exam requirements/recommendations for international students: Required—TOEFL (minimum score 550 paper-based; 213 computer-based; 79 iBT). Electronic applications accepted.

University of Phoenix–Western Washington Campus, College of Graduate Business and Management, Tukwila, WA 98188. Offers accounting (MBA); business and management (MBA, MM); global management (MBA); human resources management (MBA, MM); marketing (MBA); public administration (MBA, MM). Evening/weekend programs available. *Degree requirements:* For master's, thesis (for some programs). *Entrance requirements:* For master's, minimum undergraduate GPA of 3.0, 3 years of work experience. Additional exam requirements/recommendations for international students: Required—TOEFL (minimum score 550 paper-based; 213 computer-based; 79 iBT). Electronic applications accepted.

University of Phoenix–West Florida Campus, The John Sperling School of Business, College of Graduate Business and Management, Temple Terrace, FL 33637. Offers accounting (MBA); business administration (MBA); global management (MBA); human resources management (MBA, MM); management (MM); marketing (MBA); public administration (MBA, MM). Evening/weekend programs available. *Degree requirements:* For master's, thesis (for some programs). *Entrance requirements:* For master's, 3 years of work experience, minimum undergraduate GPA of 3.0. Additional exam requirements/recommendations for international students: Required—TOEFL (minimum score 550 paper-based; 213 computer-based; 79 iBT). Electronic applications accepted.

University of Pittsburgh, Katz Graduate School of Business, Doctoral Program in Business Administration, Pittsburgh, PA 15260. Offers accounting (PhD); finance (PhD); information systems (PhD); marketing (PhD); operations/decision sciences/artificial intelligence (PhD); organizational behavior and human resource management (PhD); strategic planning (PhD). *Accreditation:* AACSB. *Faculty:* 50 full-time (15 women). *Students:* 53 full-time (21 women); includes 8 minority (4 African Americans, 2 Asian Americans or Pacific Islanders, 2 Hispanic Americans), 22 international. 324 applicants, 4% accepted, 12 enrolled. In 2009, 11 doctorates awarded. *Degree requirements:* For doctorate, comprehensive exam, thesis/dissertation. *Entrance requirements:* For doctorate, GMAT or GRE, references, work experience relevant for individual program. Additional exam requirements/recommendations for international students: Required—TOEFL or IELTS. *Application deadline:* For fall admission, 2/1 priority date for domestic and international students. Applications are processed on a rolling basis. Application fee: $50. Electronic applications accepted. *Expenses:* Tuition, state resident: full-time $16,402; part-time $665 per credit. Tuition, nonresident: full-time $28,694; part-time $1175 per credit. Required fees: $690; $175 per term. Tuition and fees vary according to program. *Financial support:* In 2009–10, 36 students received support, including 31 research assistantships with full tuition reimbursements available (averaging $18,450 per year), 5 teaching assistantships with full tuition reimbursements available (averaging $23,511 per year); fellowships, Federal Work-Study, scholarships/grants, health care benefits, and unspecified assistantships also available. Financial award application deadline: 2/1. *Faculty research:* Accounting statements and reporting, incentives and governance; corporate finance, mergers and acquisitions; information systems processes, structures, OR, supply chain, and decision-making; organizational structure, knowledge management, and corporate strategy; consumer behavior and marketing models. Total annual research expenditures: $362,777. *Unit head:* Dr. John E. Hulland, Director, 412-648-1534, Fax: 412-624-3633, E-mail: jhulland@katz.pitt.edu. *Application contact:* Carrie Woods, Assistant Director, 412-648-1525, Fax: 412-624-3633, E-mail: cawoods@katz.pitt.edu.

University of Pittsburgh, Katz Graduate School of Business, Masters of Business Administration Programs, Pittsburgh, PA 15260. Offers accounting (MS); finance (MBA); general management (MBA); information systems (MBA, MSIS); marketing (MBA); organizational behavior and human resource management (MBA); organizational leadership (Certificate); six sigma (Certificate); strategy (MBA); technology, innovation and entrepreneurship (Certificate); MBA/JD; MBA/MIB; MBA/MPIA; MBA/MSE; MBA/MSIS. *Accreditation:* AACSB. Part-time and evening/weekend programs available. *Faculty:* 58 full-time (12 women), 23 part-time/adjunct (7 women). *Students:* 192 full-time (62 women), 506 part-time (179 women); includes 58 minority (29 African Americans, 1 American Indian/Alaska Native, 24 Asian Americans or Pacific Islanders, 4 Hispanic Americans), 101 international. Average age 29. 674 applicants, 52% accepted, 204 enrolled. In 2009, 263 master's awarded. *Entrance requirements:* For master's, GMAT, references, work experience relevant for individual programs. Additional exam requirements/recommendations for international students: Required—TOEFL (minimum score 600 paper-based; 250 computer-based; 100 iBT), or IELTS. *Application deadline:* For fall admission, 7/1 for domestic and international students; for winter admission, 11/1 for domestic and international students; for spring admission, 3/1 for domestic and international students. Applications are processed on a rolling basis. Application fee: $50. Electronic applications accepted. *Expenses:* Tuition, state resident: full-time $16,402; part-time $665 per credit. Tuition, nonresident: full-time $28,694; part-time $1175 per credit. Required fees: $690; $175 per term. Tuition and fees vary according to program. *Financial support:* In 2009–10, 75 students received support. Career-related internships or fieldwork and scholarships/grants available. Financial award application deadline: 6/1; financial award applicants required to submit FAFSA. *Faculty research:* Accounting statements and reporting, incentives and governance; corporate finance, mergers and acquisitions; information systems processes, structures, and decision-making; organizational structure, knowledge management, and corporate strategy; consumer behavior and marketing models. *Unit head:* William T. Valenta, Assistant Dean/MBA Program Director, 412-648-1610, Fax: 412-648-1659, E-mail: wtvalenta@katz.pitt.edu. *Application contact:* Cliff McCormick, Director of MBA Admissions, 412-648-1700, Fax: 412-648-1659, E-mail: mba@katz.pitt.edu.

University of Puerto Rico, Río Piedras, College of Business Administration, San Juan, PR 00931-3300. Offers accounting (MBA); finance (MBA, PhD); general business (MBA); human resources management (MBA); international trade and business (MBA, PhD); marketing (MBA); operations management (MBA); quantitative methods (MBA). *Accreditation:* ACBSP. Part-time programs available. *Degree requirements:* For master's, comprehensive exam, thesis or alternative, research project. *Entrance requirements:* For master's, GMAT or PAEG, minimum GPA of 3.0, letter of recommendation; for doctorate, GMAT, PAEG, minimum GPA of 3.0, master degree. *Faculty research:* Management.

University of Rhode Island, Graduate School, College of Business Administration, Kingston, RI 02881. Offers accounting (MS); business administration (MBA, PhD), including finance and insurance (PhD), management (PhD), marketing (PhD), operations and supply chain management (MBA); finance (MBA); general business (MBA); management (MBA); marketing (MBA); supply chain management (MBA). *Accreditation:* AACSB. Part-time and evening/weekend programs available. *Faculty:* 54 full-time (15 women), 2 part-time/adjunct (1 woman). *Students:* 71 full-time (27 women), 157 part-time (56 women); includes 24 minority (6 African Americans, 10 Asian Americans or Pacific Islanders, 8 Hispanic Americans), 23 international. In 2009, 86 master's, 3 doctorates awarded. *Degree requirements:* For master's, comprehensive exam (for some programs), thesis optional; for doctorate, comprehensive exam, thesis/dissertation. *Entrance requirements:* For master's, GMAT or GRE, 2 letters of recommendation, resume; for doctorate, GMAT or GRE, 3 letters of recommendation, resume. Additional exam requirements/recommendations for international students: Required—TOEFL (minimum score 575 paper-based; 233 computer-based; 91 iBT). Application fee: $65. Electronic applications accepted. *Expenses:* Tuition, state resident: full-time $8828; part-time $490 per credit hour. Tuition, nonresident: full-time $22,100; part-time $1228 per credit hour. Required fees: $1118; $57 per semester. Tuition and fees vary according to program. *Financial support:* In 2009–10, 13 teaching assistantships with full and partial tuition reimbursements (averaging $13,095 per year) were awarded. Financial award applicants required to submit FAFSA. Total annual research expenditures: $245,746. *Unit head:* Dr. Mark Higgins, Dean, 401-874-4244, Fax: 401-874-4312, E-mail: markhiggins@uri.edu. *Application contact:* Lisa Lancellotta, Coordinator, MBA Programs, 401-874-4241, Fax: 401-874-4312, E-mail: mba@uri.edu.

University of San Francisco, School of Business and Professional Studies, Masagung Graduate School of Management, Program in Business Administration, San Francisco, CA 94117-1080. Offers business economics (MBA); e-business (MBA); entrepreneurship (MBA); finance (MBA); international business (MBA); management (MBA); marketing (MBA); telecommunications management and policy (MBA); JD/MBA; MSN/MBA. *Accreditation:* AACSB. *Faculty:* 17 full-time (4 women), 16 part-time/adjunct (7 women). *Students:* 278 full-time (140 women), 18 part-time (10 women); includes 94 minority (5 African Americans, 1 American Indian/Alaska Native, 69 Asian Americans or Pacific Islanders, 19 Hispanic Americans), 53 international. Average age 30. 410 applicants, 70% accepted, 133 enrolled. In 2009, 137 master's awarded. *Entrance requirements:* For master's, GMAT, minimum undergraduate GPA of 3.2. Additional exam requirements/recommendations for international students: Required—TOEFL. *Application deadline:* For fall admission, 7/1 priority date for domestic students; for spring admission, 11/30 for domestic students. Applications are processed on a rolling basis. Application fee: $55 ($65 for international students). *Expenses:* Tuition: Full-time $19,710; part-time $1095 per unit. Part-time tuition and fees vary according to degree level, campus/location and program. *Financial support:* In 2009–10, 155 students received support; fellowships available. Financial award application deadline: 3/2; financial award applicants required to submit FAFSA. *Faculty research:* International financial markets, technology transfer licensing, international marketing, strategic planning. Total annual research expenditures: $50,000. *Unit head:* Kelly Brookes, Director, 415-422-2221, Fax: 415-422-6315. *Application contact:* Director, MBA Program, 415-422-2221, Fax: 415-422-6315, E-mail: mba@usfca.edu.

University of Saskatchewan, College of Graduate Studies and Research, Edwards School of Business, Department of Management and Marketing, Saskatoon, SK S7N 5A2, Canada. Offers marketing (M Sc). Part-time programs available. *Degree requirements:* For master's, thesis. *Entrance requirements:* For master's, GMAT. Additional exam requirements/recommendations for international students: Required—TOEFL. Tuition and fees charges are reported in Canadian dollars. *Expenses:* Tuition, area resident: Full-time $3000 Canadian dollars; part-time $500 Canadian dollars per term. Required fees: $700 Canadian dollars; $100 Canadian dollars per term.

The University of Scranton, College of Graduate and Continuing Education, Program in Business Administration, Scranton, PA 18510. Offers accounting (MBA); finance (MBA); general business administration (MBA); health care management (MBA); international business (MBA); management information systems (MBA); marketing (MBA); operations management (MBA). *Accreditation:* AACSB. Part-time and evening/weekend programs available. Postbaccalaureate distance learning degree programs offered (no on-campus study). *Faculty:* 34 full-time (8 women). *Students:* 92 full-time (38 women), 137 part-time (58 women); includes 27 minority (15 African Americans, 5 Asian Americans or Pacific Islanders, 7 Hispanic Americans), 21 international. Average age 31. 255 applicants, 79% accepted. In 2009, 33 master's awarded. *Degree requirements:* For master's, capstone experience. *Entrance requirements:* For master's, GMAT, minimum GPA of 2.75. Additional exam requirements/recommendations for international students: Required—TOEFL (minimum score 500 paper-based; 173 computer-based), IELTS (minimum score 5.5). *Application deadline:* Applications are processed on a rolling basis. Application fee: $0. *Financial support:* In 2009–10, 10 students received support, including 10 teaching assistantships with full and partial tuition reimbursements available (averaging $6,600 per year); fellowships, career-related internships or fieldwork, Federal Work-Study, and unspecified assistantships also available. Support available to part-time students. Financial award application deadline: 3/1. *Faculty research:* Financial markets, strategic impact of total quality management, internal accounting controls, consumer preference, information systems and the Internet. *Unit head:* Dr. Murli Rajan, Director, 570-941-4043, Fax: 570-941-4342. *Application contact:* Joseph M. Roback, Director of Admissions, 570-941-4385, Fax: 570-941-5928, E-mail: robackj2@scranton.edu.

University of South Africa, College of Economic and Management Sciences, Pretoria, South Africa. Offers accounting (D Admin, D Com); accounting science (DA); auditing (D Admin, D Com); business administration (M Tech); business economics (D Admin); business leadership (DBL); business management (D Admin, D Com); economic management analysis (M Tech); economics (D Admin, D Com, PhD); human resource development (M Tech); industrial psychology (D Admin, D Com, PhD); logistics (D Com); marketing (M Tech); public administration (D Admin, D Com, DPA, PhD); public management (M Tech); quantitative management (D Admin, D Com); real estate (M Tech); statistics (D Admin, PhD); tourism management (D Admin, D Com); transport economics (D Admin, D Com).

University of South Florida, Graduate School, College of Business, Department of Business Administration, Tampa, FL 33620-9951. Offers accounting (PhD); entrepreneurship (MBA); finance (PhD); information systems (PhD); leadership and organizational effectiveness (MSM); management and organization (MBA); marketing (PhD). *Accreditation:* AACSB. Part-time and evening/weekend programs available. *Faculty:* 12 full-time (2 women). *Students:* 152 full-time (51 women), 201 part-time (65 women); includes 70 minority (14 African Americans, 30 Asian Americans or Pacific Islanders, 26 Hispanic Americans), 54 international. Average age 32. 460 applicants, 35% accepted, 93 enrolled. In 2009, 161 master's, 11 doctorates awarded. *Degree requirements:* For master's, comprehensive exam, thesis (for some programs); for doctorate, comprehensive exam, thesis/dissertation, 90 credit hours, minimum GPA of 3.0. *Entrance requirements:* For master's, GMAT, minimum GPA of 3.0 in last 60 hours of course work, 2 years of work experience, resume; for doctorate, GMAT, letters of recommendation, personal statement. Additional exam requirements/recommendations for international students: Required—TOEFL (minimum score 550 paper-based; 213 computer-based; 79 iBT). *Application deadline:* For fall admission, 6/1 for domestic students, 1/2 for international students; for spring admission, 10/15 for domestic students, 6/1 for international students. Application fee: $30. *Financial support:* Fellowships, research assistantships, teaching assistantships, scholarships/grants, health care benefits, and unspecified assistantships available. Financial award applicants required to submit FAFSA. *Unit head:* Irene Hurst, Program Director, 813-974-3335, Fax: 813-974-4518, E-mail: hurst@coba.usf.edu. *Application contact:* Wendy Baker, Assistant Director, Graduate Studies, 813-974-3335, Fax: 813-974-4518, E-mail: wbaker@usf.edu.

University of South Florida, Graduate School, College of Business, Department of Marketing, Tampa, FL 33620-9951. Offers business administration (PhD), including marketing. Part-time and evening/weekend programs available. *Faculty:* 8 full-time (0 women). *Students:* 13 full-time (10 women), 7 part-time (5 women); includes 5 minority (1 African American, 2 Asian Americans or Pacific Islanders, 2 Hispanic Americans), 1 international. 57 applicants, 35% accepted, 12

enrolled. In 2009, 3 master's awarded. Terminal master's awarded for partial completion of doctoral program. *Degree requirements:* For master's, thesis (for some programs); for doctorate, comprehensive exam, thesis/dissertation, 90 credit hours, minimum GPA of 3.0. *Entrance requirements:* For master's, GMAT, letter of recommendation, work experience (desirable); for doctorate, GMAT, letter of recommendation. Additional exam requirements/recommendations for international students: Required—TOEFL (minimum score 550 paper-based; 213 computer-based; 79 iBT). *Application deadline:* For fall admission, 6/1 for domestic students, 1/2 for international students; for spring admission, 10/15 for domestic students, 6/1 for international students. Applications are processed on a rolling basis. Application fee: $30. Electronic applications accepted. *Financial support:* In 2009–10, teaching assistantships (averaging $21,893 per year); health care benefits and unspecified assistantships also available. *Faculty research:* Consumer behavior, supply chain management, reverse logistics (product returns), pricing, branding. *Unit head:* Dr. Miriam Stamps, Chairperson, 813-974-6205, Fax: 813-974-6175, E-mail: mstamps@usf.edu. *Application contact:* Dr. Paul Solomon, Professor, 813-974-5995, Fax: 813-974-6175, E-mail: psolomon@usf.edu.

The University of Tampa, John H. Sykes College of Business, Tampa, FL 33606-1490. Offers accounting (MBA, MS); economics (MBA); entrepreneurship and innovation (MBA); finance (MBA, MS); information systems management (MBA); international business (MBA); management (MBA); marketing (MBA, MS); nonprofit management (MBA). *Accreditation:* AACSB. Part-time and evening/weekend programs available. *Faculty:* 62 full-time (22 women), 11 part-time/adjunct (4 women). *Students:* 240 full-time (101 women), 338 part-time (133 women); includes 95 minority (16 African Americans, 4 American Indian/Alaska Native, 24 Asian Americans or Pacific Islanders, 51 Hispanic Americans), 122 international. Average age 29. 564 applicants, 51% accepted, 186 enrolled. In 2009, 234 master's awarded. *Entrance requirements:* For master's, GMAT. Additional exam requirements/recommendations for international students: Required—TOEFL (minimum score 577 paper-based; 230 computer-based; 90 iBT), IELTS. *Application deadline:* For fall admission, 7/15 for domestic students, 6/1 for international students; for spring admission, 12/15 for domestic students, 11/1 for international students. Applications are processed on a rolling basis. Application fee: $40. Electronic applications accepted. *Expenses:* Tuition: Part-time $488 per credit hour. *Financial support:* In 2009–10, 332 students received support, including 71 research assistantships with full tuition reimbursements available (averaging $6,757 per year); career-related internships or fieldwork, scholarships/grants, and unspecified assistantships also available. Support available to part-time students. Financial award applicants required to submit FAFSA. *Faculty research:* Information systems, leadership, corporate governance, entrepreneurship, hedonic price estimation. *Unit head:* Dr. Don Morrill, Associate Dean, Graduate and Continuing Studies, 813-257-3557, E-mail: dmorrill@ut.edu. *Application contact:* Karen Full, Director of Admissions, Graduate and Continuing Studies, 813-257-3642, E-mail: kfull@ut.edu.

The University of Tennessee, Graduate School, College of Business Administration, Program in Business Administration, Knoxville, TN 37996. Offers accounting (PhD); finance (MBA, PhD); logistics and transportation (MBA, PhD); management (PhD); marketing (MBA, PhD); operations management (MBA); professional business administration (MBA); statistics (PhD); JD/MBA; MS/MBA. *Accreditation:* AACSB. Postbaccalaureate distance learning degree programs offered. *Degree requirements:* For master's, thesis or alternative; for doctorate, thesis/dissertation. *Entrance requirements:* For master's and doctorate, GMAT, minimum GPA of 2.7. Additional exam requirements/recommendations for international students: Required—TOEFL. Electronic applications accepted. *Expenses:* Tuition, state resident: full-time $6826; part-time $380 per semester hour. Tuition, nonresident: full-time $21,844; part-time $1147 per semester hour. Tuition and fees vary according to program.

The University of Texas at Arlington, Graduate School, College of Business, Program in Business Administration, Arlington, TX 76019. Offers accounting (PhD); business statistics (PhD); finance (MBA, PhD); information systems (MBA, PhD); management (MBA, PhD); management sciences (MBA); marketing (MBA, PhD); operations management (PhD); real estate (MBA). *Accreditation:* AACSB. Part-time and evening/weekend programs available. Postbaccalaureate distance learning degree programs offered (no on-campus study). *Students:* 587 full-time (188 women), 349 part-time (140 women); includes 188 minority (66 African Americans, 62 Asian Americans or Pacific Islanders, 60 Hispanic Americans), 371 international. 282 applicants, 96% accepted, 145 enrolled. In 2009, 431 master's awarded. Terminal master's awarded for partial completion of doctoral program. *Degree requirements:* For master's, thesis optional; for doctorate, comprehensive exam, thesis/dissertation. *Entrance requirements:* For master's, GMAT; for doctorate, GMAT, minimum GPA of 3.0 (undergraduate), 3.4 (graduate); 30 hours of graduate course work. Additional exam requirements/recommendations for international students: Required—TOEFL (minimum score 550 paper-based; 213 computer-based; 79 iBT). *Application deadline:* For fall admission, 6/5 for domestic students, 4/1 for international students; for spring admission, 10/15 for domestic students, 9/1 for international students. Applications are processed on a rolling basis. Application fee: $35 ($50 for international students). Electronic applications accepted. *Financial support:* In 2009–10, 1 fellowship (averaging $1,000 per year), 30 research assistantships (averaging $6,000 per year), 45 teaching assistantships (averaging $13,000 per year) were awarded; career-related internships or fieldwork, scholarships/grants, and unspecified assistantships also available. Financial award application deadline: 6/1; financial award applicants required to submit FAFSA. *Unit head:* Greg Frazier, Director PhD Programs, 817-272-3559, Fax: 817-272-5799, E-mail: frazier@exchange.uta.edu. *Application contact:* Melanie McGee, Director of MBA Program, 817-272-0658, Fax: 817-272-5799, E-mail: mwmcgee@uta.edu.

See Close-Up on page 273.

The University of Texas at Austin, Graduate School, McCombs School of Business, Department of Marketing, Austin, TX 78712-1111. Offers PhD. *Degree requirements:* For doctorate, comprehensive exam, thesis/dissertation. *Entrance requirements:* For doctorate, GMAT or GRE. Electronic applications accepted. *Faculty research:* Internet marketing, strategic marketing, buy behavior.

The University of Texas at Dallas, School of Management, Programs in Management Science, Richardson, TX 75080. Offers accounting (PhD); decision sciences (PhD); finance (PhD); management strategy and public policy (PhD); marketing (PhD); organizational behavior (PhD). *Accreditation:* AACSB. Part-time and evening/weekend programs available. *Faculty:* 12 full-time (3 women). *Students:* 72 full-time (23 women), 12 part-time (6 women); includes 10 minority (all Asian Americans or Pacific Islanders), 63 international. Average age 34. 173 applicants, 12% accepted, 7 enrolled. In 2009, 8 doctorates awarded. *Degree requirements:* For doctorate, thesis/dissertation. *Entrance requirements:* For doctorate, GMAT, minimum GPA of 3.0. Additional exam requirements/recommendations for international students: Required—TOEFL (minimum score 550 paper-based; 213 computer-based). *Application deadline:* For fall admission, 7/15 for domestic students, 5/1 priority date for international students; for spring admission, 11/15 for domestic students, 9/1 priority date for international students. Applications are processed on a rolling basis. Application fee: $50 ($100 for international students). Electronic applications accepted. *Expenses:* Tuition, state resident: full-time $11,068; part-time $461 per credit hour. Tuition, nonresident: full-time $21,178; part-time $882 per credit hour. Tuition and fees vary according to course load. *Financial support:* In 2009–10, 1 research assistantship with full tuition reimbursement (averaging $13,050 per year), 43 teaching assistantships with full tuition reimbursements (averaging $14,795 per year) were awarded; fellowships, career-related internships or fieldwork, Federal Work-Study, institutionally sponsored loans, scholarships/grants, and unspecified assistantships also available. Support available to part-time students. Financial award application deadline: 4/30; financial award applicants required to submit FAFSA. *Faculty research:* Empirical generalizations in marketing, diffusion of generations of technology, stochastic brand-choice theory, acceptance of trade deals by supermarkets, nonparametric estimations of market share response. *Unit head:* Dr. Sumit Sarkar, Program Director, 972-883-2745, Fax: 972-883-5977, E-mail: som-phd.@utdallas.edu. *Application contact:* James Parker, Assistant Director, 972-883-5842, E-mail: jparker@utdallas.edu.

The University of Texas at San Antonio, College of Business, Department of Marketing, San Antonio, TX 78249-0617. Offers business administration-marketing (PhD); marketing management (MBA). Part-time and evening/weekend programs available. *Faculty:* 7 full-time (1 woman), 2 part-time/adjunct (1 woman). *Students:* 3 full-time (1 woman), 6 part-time (2 women); includes 1 minority (American Indian/Alaska Native), 1 international. Average age 26. 2 applicants, 50% accepted, 0 enrolled. *Degree requirements:* For master's, comprehensive exam (for some programs), thesis (for some programs). *Entrance requirements:* For master's, GMAT, minimum GPA of 3.0. Additional exam requirements/recommendations for international students: Required—TOEFL (minimum score 500 paper-based; 173 computer-based; 61 iBT). *Application deadline:* For fall admission, 7/1 for domestic students, 4/1 for international students; for spring admission, 11/1 for domestic students, 9/1 for international students. Applications are processed on a rolling basis. Application fee: $45 ($80 for international students). Electronic applications accepted. *Expenses:* Tuition, state resident: full-time $3975; part-time $221 per contact hour. Tuition, nonresident: full-time $13,947; part-time $775 per contact hour. Required fees: $1853. *Financial support:* In 2009–10, 1 student received support, including 4 research assistantships (averaging $10,400 per year), 12 teaching assistantships (averaging $7,800 per year); career-related internships or fieldwork, Federal Work-Study, scholarships/grants, and unspecified assistantships also available. Support available to part-time students. *Faculty research:* Consumer behavior, cross-cultural research, psycholinguistics, pricing, mass media and materialism. Total annual research expenditures: $9,000. *Unit head:* Dr. Joel Saegert, Chair, 210-458-5375, Fax: 210-458-6335, E-mail: jsaegert@utsa.edu. *Application contact:* L. J. Shrum, Graduate Advisor, 210-458-5374, E-mail: lj.shrum@utsa.edu.

The University of Texas–Pan American, College of Business Administration, Program in International Business, Edinburg, TX 78539. Offers computer information systems (PhD); economics (PhD); finance (PhD); management (PhD); marketing (PhD). *Degree requirements:* For doctorate, comprehensive exam, thesis/dissertation. *Entrance requirements:* For doctorate, GMAT or GRE. Additional exam requirements/recommendations for international students: Required—TOEFL, IELTS. Electronic applications accepted. *Expenses:* Contact institution.

University of the Sacred Heart, Graduate Programs, Department of Business Administration, Program in International Marketing, San Juan, PR 00914-0383. Offers MBA. Part-time and evening/weekend programs available. *Degree requirements:* For master's, thesis. *Entrance requirements:* For master's, EXADEP, minimum undergraduate GPA of 2.75, interview.

The University of Toledo, College of Graduate Studies, College of Business Administration, Department of Marketing and International Business, Program in Marketing, Toledo, OH 43606-3390. Offers MBA. *Entrance requirements:* For master's, GMAT, minimum GPA of 2.7. Additional exam requirements/recommendations for international students: Required—TOEFL. Electronic applications accepted.

University of Virginia, McIntire School of Commerce, Program in Commerce, Charlottesville, VA 22903. Offers financial services (MSC); marketing and management (MSC). *Students:* 72 full-time (25 women); includes 9 minority (1 African American, 5 Asian Americans or Pacific Islanders, 3 Hispanic Americans), 14 international. Average age 22. 144 applicants, 70% accepted. *Entrance requirements:* For master's, GMAT, 2 letters of recommendation; prerequisite course work in financial accounting, microeconomics, and introduction to business. Additional exam requirements/recommendations for international students: Required—TOEFL (minimum score 600 paper-based; 250 computer-based; 100 iBT), IELTS (minimum score 7). *Application deadline:* For fall admission, 9/15 priority date for domestic students, 1/15 priority date for international students. Applications are processed on a rolling basis. Application fee: $75. Electronic applications accepted. *Expenses:* Contact institution. *Financial support:* Scholarships/grants available. Financial award application deadline: 3/1; financial award applicants required to submit CSS PROFILE or FAFSA. *Unit head:* Ira C. Harris, Head, 434-924-8816, Fax: 434-924-7074, E-mail: ich3x@comm.virginia.edu. *Application contact:* Emma Jean Candelier, Assistant Director, Commerce Graduate Marketing and Admissions, 434-243-4992, Fax: 434-924-7074, E-mail: mscommerce@virginia.edu.

The University of Western Ontario, Richard Ivey School of Business, London, ON N6A 3K7, Canada. Offers business (EMBA, PhD); corporate strategy and leadership elective (MBA); entrepreneurship elective (MBA); finance elective (MBA); health sector stream (MBA); international management elective (MBA); marketing elective (MBA); JD/MBA. *Faculty:* 61 full-time (13 women). *Students:* 164 full-time (50 women). Average age 29. In 2009, 167 master's awarded. *Degree requirements:* For master's, thesis (for some programs); for doctorate, thesis/dissertation. *Entrance requirements:* For master's, GMAT, 2 years of full-time work experience, interview. Additional exam requirements/recommendations for international students: Required—TOEFL (minimum score 100 computer-based; 100 iBT), IELTS (minimum score 6), IELTS or TOEFL. *Application deadline:* For fall admission, 10/12 for domestic students, 8/16 for international students; for winter admission, 12/16 for domestic students, 10/12 for international students; for spring admission, 1/10 priority date for domestic students, 12/16 for international students. Applications are processed on a rolling basis. Application fee: $150 Canadian dollars. Electronic applications accepted. *Financial support:* Scholarships/grants and health care benefits available. Financial award application deadline: 1/10. *Faculty research:* Strategy, organizational behavior, international business, finance, operations management. *Unit head:* Carol Stephenson, Dean, 519-661-3285, Fax: 519-661-4126, E-mail: cstephenson@ivey.ca. *Application contact:* Niki da Silva, Director, MBA Program Services, 519-661-3419, Fax: 519-661-3431, E-mail: ndasilva@ivey.ca.

University of Wisconsin–Madison, Graduate School, Wisconsin School of Business, Doctoral Program in Marketing, Madison, WI 53706-1380. Offers PhD. *Faculty:* 15 full-time (6 women), 3 part-time/adjunct (2 women). *Students:* 9 full-time (6 women), 6 international. Average age 31. 58 applicants, 7% accepted, 1 enrolled. In 2009, 1 doctorate awarded. *Degree requirements:* For doctorate, comprehensive exam, thesis/dissertation. *Entrance requirements:* For doctorate, GMAT or GRE. Additional exam requirements/recommendations for international students: Required—Pearson Test of English (minimum score 73, written 80); Recommended—TOEFL (minimum score 623 paper-based; 263 computer-based; 106 iBT), IELTS (minimum score 7.5). *Application deadline:* For fall admission, 12/15 priority date for domestic and international students. Application fee: $56. Electronic applications accepted. *Expenses:* Tuition, state resident: part-time $594 per credit. Tuition, nonresident: part-time $1504 per credit. Required fees: $65 per credit. Tuition and fees vary according to course load, program and reciprocity agreements. *Financial support:* In 2009–10, 9 students received support, including fellowships with full tuition reimbursements available (averaging $18,567 per year), research assistantships with full tuition reimbursements available (averaging $16,506 per year), 9 teaching assistantships with full tuition reimbursements available (averaging $14,088 per year); Federal Work-Study, institutionally sponsored loans, scholarships/grants, health care benefits, and unspecified assistantships also available. Financial award application deadline: 2/1; financial award applicants required to submit FAFSA. *Faculty research:* Marketing strategy, consumer behavior, channels of distribution, advertising, price promotions. *Unit head:* Prof. Jack Nevin, Chair, 608-262-8912, Fax: 608-262-0394, E-mail: jnevin@bus.wisc.edu. *Application contact:* Belle Heberling, Assistant Director for Research Programs, 608-262-3749, Fax: 608-890-0180, E-mail: phd@bus.wisc.edu.

University of Wisconsin–Whitewater, School of Graduate Studies, College of Business and Economics, Program in Business Administration, Whitewater, WI 53190-1790. Offers finance (MBA); human resource management (MBA); information technology management (MBA); international business (MBA); management (MBA); marketing (MBA); operations and supply chain management (MBA); technology and training (MBA). *Accreditation:* AACSB. Part-time and evening/weekend programs available. Postbaccalaureate distance learning degree programs offered (no on-campus study). *Degree requirements:* For master's, thesis or alternative. *Entrance requirements:* For master's, GMAT, minimum AACSB index of 1000, minimum GPA of 2.75. Additional exam requirements/recommendations for international students: Required—TOEFL (minimum score 550 paper-based; 213 computer-based). Electronic applications accepted. *Faculty research:* Interface between social institutions and individual behavior, technology and

Marketing

University of Wisconsin–Whitewater (continued)
innovation management, occupational mental health, workplace deviance and workplace romance.

See Display on page 190.

Villanova University, Villanova School of Business, MBA—Fast Track Program, Villanova, PA 19085. Offers finance (MBA); international business (MBA); management information systems (MBA); marketing (MBA). *Accreditation:* AACSB. Part-time and evening/weekend programs available. *Entrance requirements:* For master's, GMAT, minimum 4.5 years of professional work experience. Additional exam requirements/recommendations for international students: Required—TOEFL (minimum score 550 paper-based; 213 computer-based; 80 iBT). Electronic applications accepted. *Expenses:* Tuition: Part-time $630 per credit. Required fees: $60 per credit. Part-time tuition and fees vary according to degree level and program. *Faculty research:* Developing and leveraging technology, ethical business practices, managing for innovation and creativity, the global political economy, strategic marketing management.

Villanova University, Villanova School of Business, MBA—Flex Track Program, Villanova, PA 19085. Offers corporate management (general) (MBA); finance (MBA); international business (MBA); management information systems (MBA); marketing (MBA); JD/MBA. *Accreditation:* AACSB. Part-time and evening/weekend programs available. Postbaccalaureate distance learning degree programs offered (minimal on-campus study). *Entrance requirements:* For master's, GMAT, minimum 4.5 years work experience. Additional exam requirements/recommendations for international students: Required—TOEFL (minimum score 550 paper-based; 213 computer-based; 80 iBT). Electronic applications accepted. *Expenses:* Tuition: Part-time $630 per credit. Required fees: $60 per credit. Part-time tuition and fees vary according to degree level and program. *Faculty research:* Developing and leveraging technology, ethical business practices, managing for innovation and creativity, the global political economy, strategic marketing management.

Virginia Commonwealth University, Graduate School, School of Business, Program in Marketing and Business Law, Richmond, VA 23284-9005. Offers Certificate.

Virginia International University, Business Programs Department, Fairfax, VA 22030. Offers accounting (MBA); executive management (Graduate Certificate); global logistics (MBA); health care management (MBA); human resources management (MBA); international business management (MBA); international finance (MBA); marketing management (MBA). Part-time programs available. *Faculty:* 12 part-time/adjunct (1 woman). *Students:* 138 full-time (63 women), 7 part-time (5 women); includes 7 minority (1 African American, 5 Asian Americans or Pacific Islanders, 1 Hispanic American), 136 international. Average age 27. 331 applicants, 31% accepted, 40 enrolled. In 2009, 42 master's awarded. *Entrance requirements:* For master's and Graduate Certificate, bachelor's degree. Additional exam requirements/recommendations for international students: Required—TOEFL (minimum score 550 paper-based; 213 computer-based; 80 iBT), IELTS (minimum score 6). *Application deadline:* For fall admission, 7/31 for domestic students, 7/3 for international students; for spring admission, 12/18 for domestic students, 11/20 for international students. Applications are processed on a rolling basis. Application fee: $100. Electronic applications accepted. *Expenses:* Tuition: Full-time $10,044; part-time $569 per credit. One-time fee: $75. Tuition and fees vary according to degree level. *Financial support:* In 2009–10, 10 students received support. Scholarships/grants available. Financial award application deadline: 7/1. *Unit head:* Dr. Gail Whitaker, Chair, 703-591-7042 Ext. 346, Fax: 703-591-7046, E-mail: gwhitaker@viu.edu. *Application contact:* Emily L. Kraus, Director of Admissions, 703-591-7042 Ext. 309, Fax: 703-591-7048, E-mail: admissions@viu.edu.

Virginia Polytechnic Institute and State University, Graduate School, Pamplin College of Business, Department of Marketing, Blacksburg, VA 24061. Offers business administration (MS), including marketing; marketing (PhD). *Faculty:* 14 full-time (7 women). *Students:* 8 full-time (5 women); includes 3 minority (all American Indian/Alaska Native). Average age 28. 26 applicants, 15% accepted, 2 enrolled. *Entrance requirements:* For master's and doctorate, GRE, GMAT. Additional exam requirements/recommendations for international students: Required—TOEFL (minimum score 550 paper-based; 213 computer-based). *Application deadline:* For fall admission, 5/15 for international students; for spring admission, 10/15 for international students. Applications are processed on a rolling basis. Application fee: $65. Electronic applications accepted. *Expenses:* Tuition, area resident: Full-time $10,228; part-time $459 per credit hour. Tuition, nonresident: full-time $17,892; part-time $865 per credit hour. Required fees: $1966; $451 per semester. *Financial support:* In 2009–10, 9 teaching assistantships with full tuition reimbursements (averaging $11,455 per year) were awarded; career-related internships or fieldwork, Federal Work-Study, scholarships/grants, and unspecified assistantships also available. Financial award application deadline: 1/15. *Faculty research:* Consumer behavior, marketing research, channels of distribution, advertising, marketing strategy. Total annual research expenditures: $93,899. *Unit head:* Dr. Kent Nakamoto, Dean, 540-231-6949, Fax: 540-231-4487, E-mail: nakamoto@vt.edu. *Application contact:* David Brinberg, Information Contact, 540-231-7639, Fax: 540-231-4487, E-mail: dbrinber@vt.edu.

Wagner College, Division of Graduate Studies, Department of Business Administration, Program in Marketing, Staten Island, NY 10301-4495. Offers MBA. Part-time and evening/weekend programs available. *Degree requirements:* For master's, thesis optional. *Entrance requirements:* For master's, GMAT, minimum GPA of 2.6. Additional exam requirements/recommendations for international students: Required—TOEFL (minimum score 550 paper-based; 217 computer-based). *Expenses:* Tuition: Full-time $15,570; part-time $865 per credit. Required fees: $2.

Wake Forest University, Babcock Graduate School of Management, Full-time MBA Program, Winston-Salem, NC 27106. Offers consulting/general management (MBA); entrepreneurship (MBA); finance (MBA); health (MBA); marketing (MBA); operations management (MBA); JD/MBA; MSA/MBA; MD/MBA. *Accreditation:* AACSB. *Faculty:* 62 full-time (13 women), 36 part-time/adjunct (14 women). *Students:* 144 full-time (36 women); includes 17 minority (8 African Americans, 9 Asian Americans or Pacific Islanders), 22 international. Average age 28. In 2009, 81 master's awarded. *Entrance requirements:* For master's, GMAT or GRE, letters of recommendation, official transcripts, current resume or curriculum vitae, 2 years of work experience with the exception of joint-degree candidates. Additional exam requirements/recommendations for international students: Required—TOEFL (minimum score 600 paper-based; 250 computer-based; 100 iBT), Pearson Test of English (PTE). *Application deadline:* For fall admission, 6/1 for domestic and international students. Applications are processed on a rolling basis. Application fee: $75. Electronic applications accepted. *Expenses:* Contact institution. *Financial support:* In 2009–10, 95 students received support. Career-related internships or fieldwork, scholarships/grants, and unspecified assistantships available. Financial award application deadline: 3/1; financial award applicants required to submit FAFSA. *Faculty research:* The influence of personal relationships on business decision making and management of change; drivers of perceived value and consumer behavior; impact of accounting on auditing, financial, managerial, systems and taxation stakeholders; corporate governance and executive compensation; impact of operations strategies on competitiveness. *Unit head:* Sherry Moss, Director, Full-time MBA Program, 336-758-5422, Fax: 336-758-5830, E-mail: admissions@mba.wfu.edu. *Application contact:* LaKesha Alston, Administrative Assistant, 336-758-5422, Fax: 336-758-5830, E-mail: admissions@mba.wfu.edu.

Walden University, Graduate Programs, School of Management, Minneapolis, MN 55401. Offers applied management and decision sciences (PhD), including accounting, engineering management, finance, general applied management and decision sciences, information systems management, knowledge management, leadership and organizational change, learning management, operations research, self-designed program in applied management and design sciences; business information management (MISM); enterprise information security (MISM); entrepreneurship (MBA, DBA); finance (MBA, DBA); global supply chain management (DBA); healthcare management (MBA); healthcare system improvement (MBA); human resource management (MBA); information systems management (DBA); international business (MBA, DBA); IT strategy and governance (MISM); leadership (MBA, MS, DBA), including entrepreneurship (MS), general management (MS), human resources leadership (MS), innovation and technology (MS), leader development (MS), project management (MS), self-designed (MS), sustainable futures (MS); managing global software and service supply chains (MISM); marketing (MBA, DBA); project management (MBA, MS); risk management (MBA); self-designed (MBA, DBA); social impact management (DBA); sustainable futures (MBA); technology (MBA); technology entrepreneurship (DBA). Part-time and evening/weekend programs available. Postbaccalaureate distance learning degree programs offered (minimal on-campus study). *Faculty:* 17 full-time, 211 part-time/adjunct. *Students:* 3,389 full-time (1,774 women), 815 part-time (482 women); includes 1,969 minority (1,640 African Americans, 36 American Indian/Alaska Native, 123 Asian Americans or Pacific Islanders, 170 Hispanic Americans), 95 international. Average age 41. In 2009, 699 master's, 42 doctorates awarded. *Degree requirements:* For doctorate, thesis/dissertation (for some programs), residency. *Entrance requirements:* For master's, bachelor's degree or equivalent in related field; minimum GPA of 2.5; official transcripts; goal statement; access to computer and Internet; for doctorate, master's degree or equivalent in related field; minimum GPA of 3.0; 3 years of related professional/academic experience (preferred). Additional exam requirements/recommendations for international students: Required—TOEFL (minimum score 550 paper-based; 213 computer-based), IELTS (minimum score 6.5), TOEFL, IELTS, or Michigan English Language Assessment Battery (minimum score 82). *Application deadline:* Applications are processed on a rolling basis. Application fee: $50. Electronic applications accepted. *Expenses:* Tuition: Full-time $13,665; part-time $560 per credit. Required fees: $1375. Tuition and fees vary according to course load, degree level and program. *Financial support:* In 2009–10, 466 students received support; fellowships, Federal Work-Study, scholarships/grants, unspecified assistantships, and family tuition reduction, active duty/veteran tuition reduction, group tuition reduction, interest-free payment plans available. Support available to part-time students. Financial award applicants required to submit FAFSA. *Unit head:* William Schulz, Interim Associate Dean, 800-925-3368. *Application contact:* Jennifer Hall, Director of Enrollment, 866-4-WALDEN, E-mail: info@waldenu.edu.

Washington State University, Graduate School, College of Business, Graduate Programs in Business, Pullman, WA 99164. Offers accounting and business law (M Acc); business administration (MBA, PhD), including accounting (PhD), finance (PhD), management and operations (PhD), management information systems (PhD), marketing (PhD). *Accreditation:* AACSB. *Degree requirements:* For master's, comprehensive exam (for some programs), thesis (for some programs), final presentation; for doctorate, comprehensive exam, thesis/dissertation, oral and written exams. *Entrance requirements:* For master's and doctorate, GMAT, minimum GPA of 3.0, 3 letters of recommendation. Additional exam requirements/recommendations for international students: Required—TOEFL. Electronic applications accepted.

See Close-Up on page 0.

Webster University, George Herbert Walker School of Business and Technology, Department of Business, St. Louis, MO 63119-3194. Offers business (MA); business and organizational security management (MBA); computer resources and information management (MBA); environmental management (MBA); finance (MA, MBA); health services management (MBA); human resources development (MBA); human resources management (MBA); international business (MA, MBA); management and leadership (MBA); marketing (MBA); procurement and acquisitions management (MBA); telecommunications management (MBA). *Accreditation:* ACBSP. Part-time and evening/weekend programs available. Postbaccalaureate distance learning degree programs offered (no on-campus study). *Faculty:* 9 full-time, 430 part-time/adjunct. *Students:* 1,190 full-time (543 women), 4,226 part-time (2,159 women). Average age 34. In 2009, 2,021 master's awarded. *Degree requirements:* For master's, comprehensive exam (for some programs), thesis (for some programs). *Entrance requirements:* Additional exam requirements/recommendations for international students: Required—TOEFL. *Application deadline:* Applications are processed on a rolling basis. Application fee: $35 ($50 for international students). *Expenses:* Tuition: Part-time $565 per credit hour. Tuition and fees vary according to degree level, campus/location and program. *Financial support:* Federal Work-Study available. Support available to part-time students. Financial award application deadline: 4/1; financial award applicants required to submit FAFSA. *Unit head:* Dr. Debbie Psihountas, Chair, 314-246-7553 Ext. 7017, Fax: 314-968-7077, E-mail: buschair@webster.edu. *Application contact:* Matt Nolan, Associate Vice President for Enrollment Management/Dean of Admissions, Fax: 314-968-7116, E-mail: gadmit@webster.edu.

Webster University, George Herbert Walker School of Business and Technology, Department of Management, St. Louis, MO 63119-3194. Offers business and organizational security management (MA); computer resources and information management (MA); environmental management (MS); government contracting (Certificate); health care management (MA); health services management (MA); human resources development (MA); human resources management (MA); management (DM); management and leadership (MA); marketing (MA); nonprofit management (Certificate); procurement and acquisitions management (MA); public administration (MA); quality management (MA); space systems operations management (MS); telecommunications management (MA). *Accreditation:* ACBSP. Part-time and evening/weekend programs available. Postbaccalaureate distance learning degree programs offered (no on-campus study). *Faculty:* 16 full-time, 781 part-time/adjunct. *Students:* 1,369 full-time (610 women), 5,182 part-time (3,047 women); includes 3,460 minority (2,835 African Americans, 38 American Indian/Alaska Native, 169 Asian Americans or Pacific Islanders, 418 Hispanic Americans), 80 international. Average age 37. In 2009, 2,491 master's, 13 doctorates, 68 other advanced degrees awarded. *Degree requirements:* For master's, thesis (for some programs); for doctorate, thesis/dissertation, written exam. *Entrance requirements:* For doctorate, GMAT, 3 years of work experience, MBA. Additional exam requirements/recommendations for international students: Required—TOEFL. *Application deadline:* Applications are processed on a rolling basis. Application fee: $25 ($50 for international students). *Expenses:* Tuition: Part-time $565 per credit hour. Tuition and fees vary according to degree level, campus/location and program. *Financial support:* Federal Work-Study available. Support available to part-time students. Financial award application deadline: 4/1; financial award applicants required to submit FAFSA. *Unit head:* Jim Brasfield, Chair, 314-961-2660 Ext. 7063, Fax: 314-968-7077, E-mail: mgtchair@webster.edu. *Application contact:* Matt Nolan, Associate Vice President for Enrollment Management/Dean of Admissions, Fax: 314-968-7116, E-mail: gadmit@webster.edu.

West Chester University of Pennsylvania, Office of Graduate Studies, College of Business and Public Affairs, Department of Marketing, West Chester, PA 19383. Offers business administration: tech-electronic (MBA). Part-time and evening/weekend programs available. *Students:* 2 part-time (1 woman). Average age 44. 1 applicant, 100% accepted, 0 enrolled. In 2009, 2 master's awarded. *Entrance requirements:* For master's, GMAT, statement of professional goals, resume, two letters of reference. Additional exam requirements/recommendations for international students: Required—TOEFL (minimum score 550 paper-based; 213 computer-based; 80 iBT). *Application deadline:* For fall admission, 4/15 for domestic students, 3/15 for international students; for spring admission, 10/15 for domestic students, 9/1 for international students. Applications are processed on a rolling basis. Application fee: $35. Electronic applications accepted. *Expenses:* Tuition, state resident: full-time $6666; part-time $370 per credit. Tuition, nonresident: full-time $10,666; part-time $593 per credit. Required fees: $122.56 per credit. *Financial support:* In 2009–10, research assistantships with full and partial tuition reimbursements (averaging $5,000 per year); unspecified assistantships also available. Support available to part-time students. Financial award application deadline: 2/15; financial award applicants required to submit FAFSA. *Unit head:* Dr. Paul Christ, MBA Director and Graduate Coordinator, 610-425-5000, E-mail: pchrist@wcupa.edu. *Application contact:* Office of Graduate Studies, 610-436-2943, Fax: 610-436-2763, E-mail: gradstudy@wcupa.edu.

Western International University, Graduate Programs in Business, Master of Business Administration Program in Marketing, Phoenix, AZ 85021-2718. Offers MBA. Part-time and evening/weekend programs available. Postbaccalaureate distance learning degree programs offered (no on-campus study). *Faculty:* 23 part-time/adjunct (7 women). *Students:* 66 full-time (34 women); includes 21 minority (2 African Americans, 15 Asian Americans or Pacific Islanders, 4 Hispanic Americans), 8 international. Average age 32. In 2009, 26 master's awarded. *Entrance requirements:* For master's, minimum GPA of 2.75. Additional exam requirements/

recommendations for international students: Required—TOEFL (minimum score 550 paper-based; 213 computer-based; 79 iBT), TWE (minimum score 5), or IELTS (minimum score 6.5). *Application deadline:* Applications are processed on a rolling basis. Application fee: $25. Electronic applications accepted. *Expenses:* Tuition: Full-time $12,600. One-time fee: $25 full-time. *Financial support:* Applicants required to submit FAFSA. *Unit head:* Dr. Deborah DeSimone, Chief Academic Officer, 602-429-1135, E-mail: deborah.desimone@west.edu. *Application contact:* Melissa Machuca, Director of Enrollment, 602-943-2311, Fax: 602-371-8637.

West Virginia University, Perley Isaac Reed School of Journalism, Program in Integrated Marketing Communications, Morgantown, WV 26506. Offers MS. Part-time programs available. Postbaccalaureate distance learning degree programs offered (no on-campus study). *Entrance requirements:* For master's, GRE or GMAT. Additional exam requirements/recommendations for international students: Required—TOEFL.

Wilkes University, College of Graduate and Professional Studies, Jay S. Sidhu School of Business and Leadership, Wilkes-Barre, PA 18766-0002. Offers accounting (MBA); entrepreneurship (MBA); finance (MBA); human resource management (MBA); international business (MBA); management (MBA); marketing (MBA). *Accreditation:* ACBSP. Part-time and evening/weekend programs available. *Students:* 86 full-time (41 women), 118 part-time (59 women); includes 7 minority (4 African Americans, 1 Asian American or Pacific Islander, 2 Hispanic Americans), 48 international. Average age 29. In 2009, 59 master's awarded. *Entrance requirements:* For master's, GMAT. Additional exam requirements/recommendations for international students: Required—TOEFL (minimum score 500 paper-based; 173 computer-based; 79 iBT). *Application deadline:* Applications are processed on a rolling basis. Application fee: $45. *Expenses:* Contact institution. *Financial support:* Federal Work-Study and unspecified assistantships available. Financial award application deadline: 3/1; financial award applicants required to submit FAFSA. *Unit head:* Dr. Paul Browne, Dean, 570-408-4701, Fax: 570-408-7846, E-mail: paul.browne@wilkes.edu. *Application contact:* Kathleen Houlihan, Director of Graduate Studies, 570-408-3235, Fax: 570-408-7846, E-mail: kathleen.houlihan@wilkes.edu.

Worcester Polytechnic Institute, Graduate Studies and Research, School of Business, Worcester, MA 01609-2280. Offers information technology (MS), including information security management; management (Graduate Certificate); marketing and technological innovation (MS); operations design and leadership (MS); technology (MBA). *Accreditation:* AACSB. Part-time and evening/weekend programs available. Postbaccalaureate distance learning degree programs offered (no on-campus study). *Faculty:* 25 full-time (12 women), 6 part-time/adjunct (2 women). *Students:* 89 full-time (44 women), 198 part-time (47 women). Average age 32. 229 applicants, 70% accepted, 71 enrolled. In 2009, 69 master's awarded. *Degree requirements:* For master's, thesis optional. *Entrance requirements:* For master's, GMAT (MBA), GMAT or GRE General Test (MS), resume; for Graduate Certificate, GMAT or GRE General Test, statement of purpose, 3 letters of recommendation. Additional exam requirements/recommendations for international students: Required—TOEFL (minimum score 550 paper-based; 213 computer-based; 79 iBT), IELTS (minimum score 6.5). *Application deadline:* For fall admission, 7/1 priority date for domestic students, 6/1 priority date for international students; for spring admission, 11/1 priority date for domestic students, 10/1 priority date for international students. Applications are processed on a rolling basis. Application fee: $70. Electronic applications accepted. *Financial support:* Career-related internships or fieldwork, institutionally sponsored loans, scholarships/grants, and unspecified assistantships available. Financial award application deadline: 6/1. *Faculty research:* Organizational aesthetics, resistance in organizations, dynamics of product innovation, economic approaches to productivity, corporate earnings forecasts and value relevance, ERP implementation, improving Web accessibility, information quality assessment, measuring strategic and transactional IT, website quality, service operations modeling, health care operations and performance analysis, loan process design. *Unit head:* Dr. Mark Rice, Dean, 508-831-5218, Fax: 508-831-5720, E-mail: rice@wpi.edu. *Application*

contact: Norm Wilkinson, Director, Graduate Management Programs, 508-831-5957, Fax: 508-831-5720, E-mail: nwilkins@wpi.edu.

Wright State University, School of Graduate Studies, Raj Soin College of Business, Department of Marketing, Dayton, OH 45435. Offers MBA, MBA/MS. *Entrance requirements:* For master's, GMAT, minimum AACSB index of 1000. Additional exam requirements/recommendations for international students: Required—TOEFL.

Xavier University, Williams College of Business, Master of Business Administration Program, Cincinnati, OH 45207-3221. Offers business administration (Exec MBA, MBA); business intelligence (MBA); finance (MBA); international business (MBA); management information systems (MBA); marketing (MBA); MBA/MHSA; MSN/MBA. *Accreditation:* AACSB. Part-time and evening/weekend programs available. *Faculty:* 44 full-time (17 women), 9 part-time/adjunct (2 women). *Students:* 167 full-time (51 women), 862 part-time (283 women); includes 149 minority (60 African Americans, 62 Asian Americans or Pacific Islanders, 27 Hispanic Americans), 17 international. Average age 30. 355 applicants, 63% accepted, 187 enrolled. In 2009, 369 master's awarded. *Degree requirements:* For master's, capstone course. *Entrance requirements:* For master's, GMAT. Additional exam requirements/recommendations for international students: Required—TOEFL (minimum score 550 paper-based; 213 computer-based; 80 iBT). *Application deadline:* For fall admission, 8/1 priority date for domestic students, 5/1 for international students; for spring admission, 12/1 priority date for domestic students, 9/1 for international students. Applications are processed on a rolling basis. Application fee: $0. Electronic applications accepted. *Expenses:* Contact institution. *Financial support:* In 2009–10, 183 students received support. Scholarships/grants, tuition waivers (partial), and unspecified assistantships available. Financial award application deadline: 3/1; financial award applicants required to submit FAFSA. *Unit head:* Dr. Hema Krishnan, Associate Dean, 513-745-3206, Fax: 513-745-3455, E-mail: krishnan@xavier.edu. *Application contact:* Anna Marie Whelan, Assistant Director, MBA Programs, 513-745-3525, Fax: 513-745-2929, E-mail: whelana@xavier.edu.

Yale University, Yale School of Management and Graduate School of Arts and Sciences, Doctoral Program in Management, New Haven, CT 06520. Offers accounting (PhD); financial economics (PhD); marketing (PhD). *Accreditation:* AACSB. *Faculty:* 68 full-time (12 women). *Students:* 30 full-time (9 women), 13 international. Average age 28. 372 applicants, 7% accepted, 13 enrolled. In 2009, 5 doctorates awarded. *Degree requirements:* For doctorate, comprehensive exam, thesis/dissertation. *Entrance requirements:* For doctorate, GMAT or GRE General Test. Additional exam requirements/recommendations for international students: Required—TOEFL, IELTS. *Application deadline:* For fall admission, 1/2 for domestic and international students. Application fee: $85. Electronic applications accepted. *Expenses:* Contact institution. *Financial support:* In 2009–10, 29 students received support, including 29 fellowships with full tuition reimbursements available, 29 research assistantships with full tuition reimbursements available, 29 teaching assistantships with full tuition reimbursements available; institutionally sponsored loans, scholarships/grants, and health care benefits also available. Financial award application deadline: 1/2. *Faculty research:* Pricing of options and futures, term structure of interest rates, use of accounting numbers in debt contracts, product differentiation, e-commerce and marketing, behavioral finance. *Unit head:* Carla Mills, Registrar, 203-432-3955, Fax: 203-432-0342, E-mail: carla.mills@yale.edu. *Application contact:* Carla Mills, Registrar, 203-432-3955, Fax: 203-432-0342, E-mail: carla.mills@yale.edu.

See Close-Up on page 283.

Youngstown State University, Graduate School, Williamson College of Business Administration, Department of Marketing, Youngstown, OH 44555-0001. Offers MBA. Part-time and evening/weekend programs available. *Degree requirements:* For master's, thesis optional. *Entrance requirements:* For master's, GMAT, minimum GPA of 2.7. Additional exam requirements/recommendations for international students: Required—TOEFL. *Faculty research:* Media, international marketing, advanced marketing simulations, ethics in business.

Marketing Research

American University, Kogod School of Business, Master of Business Administration Program, Washington, DC 20016-8044. Offers accounting (MBA); consulting (MBA), including information technology, international business, management; corporate finance: commercial banking (MBA); corporate finance: corporate financial management (MBA); corporate finance: investment banking (MBA), including corporate finance and private equity, trading and selling; entrepreneurship (MBA); global emerging markets (MBA), including business, finance, information technology; international trade and global supply chain management (MBA); leadership (MBA); marketing management (MBA); marketing research (MBA); real estate (MBA); MBA/JD; MBA/LL M. Part-time and evening/weekend programs available. *Faculty:* 14 full-time (6 women). *Students:* 133 full-time (56 women), 121 part-time (48 women); includes 54 minority (23 African Americans, 1 American Indian/Alaska Native, 16 Asian Americans or Pacific Islanders, 14 Hispanic Americans), 43 international. Average age 29. 539 applicants, 51% accepted, 86 enrolled. In 2009, 114 master's awarded. *Entrance requirements:* For master's, GMAT. Additional exam requirements/recommendations for international students: Required—TOEFL. *Application deadline:* For fall admission, 2/1 priority date for domestic students; for spring admission, 10/1 priority date for domestic students. Applications are processed on a rolling basis. Application fee: $100. *Expenses:* Contact institution. *Financial support:* In 2009–10, 19 students received support; fellowships, research assistantships with partial tuition reimbursements available, career-related internships or fieldwork, Federal Work-Study, and institutionally sponsored loans available. Support available to part-time students. Financial award application deadline: 2/1. *Faculty research:* Information technology, decision-aiding methodology, negotiation. *Unit head:* Dr. Stevan Holmberg, Chair, 202-885-6193, E-mail: sholmbe@american.edu. *Application contact:* Shannon Demko, Associate Director of Graduate Admissions, 202-885-1994, Fax: 202-885-1108, E-mail: demko@american.edu.

Hofstra University, Frank G. Zarb School of Business, Department of Marketing and International Business, Hempstead, NY 11549. Offers business administration (MBA), including international business, marketing; marketing (MS); marketing research (MS). Part-time and evening/weekend programs available. *Faculty:* 9 full-time (0 women), 1 part-time/adjunct (0 women). *Students:* 52 full-time (28 women), 38 part-time (21 women); includes 9 minority (2 African Americans, 3 Asian Americans or Pacific Islanders, 4 Hispanic Americans), 40 international. Average age 27. 114 applicants, 71% accepted, 26 enrolled. In 2009, 29 master's awarded. *Degree requirements:* For master's, capstone course (MBA), thesis (MS). *Entrance requirements:* For master's, GMAT or GRE, 2 letters of recommendation, resume. Additional exam requirements/recommendations for international students: Required—TOEFL (minimum score 550 paper-based; 213 computer-based; 80 iBT); Recommended—IELTS (minimum score 6). *Application deadline:* Applications are processed on a rolling basis. Application fee: $60. Electronic applications accepted. *Expenses:* Contact institution. *Financial support:* In 2009–10, 24 students received support, including 21 fellowships with full and partial tuition reimbursements available (averaging $9,582 per year), 2 research assistantships with full and partial tuition reimbursements available (averaging $14,187 per year); career-related internships or fieldwork, Federal Work-Study, institutionally sponsored loans, scholarships/grants, tuition waivers (full and partial), and unspecified assistantships also available. Support available to part-time students. Financial award applicants required to submit FAFSA. *Faculty research:* Outsourcing, global alliances, retailing, web marketing, cross-cultural age research. *Unit head:* Dr. Benny Barak, Chairperson, 516-463-5707, Fax: 516-463-4834, E-mail: mktbzb@hofstra.edu.

Application contact: Carol Drummer, Dean of Graduate Admissions, 516-463-4876, Fax: 516-463-4664, E-mail: gradstudent@hofstra.edu.

Instituto Tecnológico y de Estudios Superiores de Monterrey, Campus Irapuato, Graduate Programs, Irapuato, Mexico. Offers administration (MBA); administration of information technology (MAIT); administration of telecommunications (MAT); architecture (M Arch); computer science (MCS); education (M Ed); educational administration (MEA); educational innovation and technology (DEIT); educational technology (MET); electronic commerce (MBA); environmental administration and planning (MEAP); environmental systems (MES); finances (MBA); humanistic studies (MHS); international management for Latin American executives (MIMLAE); library and information science (MLIS); manufacturing quality management (MMQM); marketing research (MBA).

Pace University, Lubin School of Business, Marketing Program, New York, NY 10038. Offers marketing management (MBA); marketing research (MBA). Part-time and evening/weekend programs available. *Students:* 25 full-time (14 women), 67 part-time (33 women); includes 14 minority (6 African Americans, 1 American Indian/Alaska Native, 4 Asian Americans or Pacific Islanders, 3 Hispanic Americans), 35 international. Average age 27. 207 applicants, 62% accepted, 30 enrolled. In 2009, 33 master's awarded. *Entrance requirements:* For master's, GMAT. Additional exam requirements/recommendations for international students: Required—TOEFL. *Application deadline:* For fall admission, 7/31 priority date for domestic students; for spring admission, 11/30 for domestic students. Applications are processed on a rolling basis. Application fee: $70. Electronic applications accepted. *Expenses:* Tuition: Part-time $954 per credit. Tuition and fees vary according to course load, degree level and program. *Financial support:* Research assistantships, career-related internships or fieldwork and Federal Work-Study available. Support available to part-time students. Financial award applicants required to submit FAFSA. *Unit head:* Dr. Martin Topol, Chairperson, 212-346-1827. *Application contact:* Susan Ford-Goldschein, Director of Admissions, 212-346-1652, Fax: 212-346-1585, E-mail: gradnyc@pace.edu.

Southern Illinois University Edwardsville, Graduate Studies and Research, School of Business, Department of Management and Marketing, Edwardsville, IL 62026-0001. Offers marketing research (MMR). Part-time and evening/weekend programs available. *Faculty:* 17 full-time (6 women). *Students:* 20 full-time (7 women), 9 part-time (5 women); includes 3 minority (1 African American, 2 Asian Americans or Pacific Islanders), 11 international. Average age 26. 38 applicants, 39% accepted. In 2009, 19 master's awarded. *Degree requirements:* For master's, thesis or alternative, final exam. *Entrance requirements:* For master's, GMAT. Additional exam requirements/recommendations for international students: Required—TOEFL (minimum score 550 paper-based; 213 computer-based; 79 iBT), IELTS (minimum score 6.5). *Application deadline:* For fall admission, 7/23 for domestic students, 6/1 for international students; for spring admission, 12/11 for domestic students, 10/1 for international students. Applications are processed on a rolling basis. Application fee: $30. Electronic applications accepted. *Expenses:* Tuition, state resident: part-time $1252.50 per semester. Tuition, nonresident: part-time $3131.25 per semester. Required fees: $586.85 per semester. Tuition and fees vary according to course load. *Financial support:* In 2009–10, 1 fellowship with full tuition reimbursement (averaging $8,364 per year), 18 research assistantships with full tuition reimbursements (averaging $8,064 per year), 8 teaching assistantships with full tuition reimbursements (averaging $8,064 per year) were awarded; career-related internships or fieldwork,

Marketing Research

Southern Illinois University Edwardsville *(continued)*
Federal Work-Study, institutionally sponsored loans, scholarships/grants, traineeships, and unspecified assistantships also available. Support available to part-time students. Financial award application deadline: 3/1; financial award applicants required to submit FAFSA. *Unit head:* Dr. Ralph Giacobbe, Chair, 618-650-2750, E-mail: rgiacob@siue.edu. *Application contact:* Dr. Madhav Segal, Program Director, 618-650-2601, E-mail: msegal@siue.edu.

Universidad Autonoma de Guadalajara, Graduate Programs, Guadalajara, Mexico. Offers administrative law and justice (LL M); advertising and corporate communications (MA); architecture (M Arch); business (MBA); computational science (MCC); education (Ed M, Ed D); English-Spanish translation (MA); fiscal law (MA); integrated management of digital animation (MA); international business (MIB); international corporate law (LL M); internet technologies (MS); labor health (MS); manufacturing systems (MMS); philosophy (MA, PhD); power electronics (MS); quality systems (MQS); renewable energy (MS); social evaluation of projects (MBA); strategic market research (MBA); teaching mathematics (MA).

Universidad de las Americas, A.C., Program in Business Administration, Mexico City, Mexico. Offers finance (MBA); marketing research (MBA); production and quality (MBA).

University of Georgia, Graduate School, Terry College of Business, Program in Marketing Research, Athens, GA 30602. Offers MMR. *Students:* 21 full-time (13 women); includes 2 minority (1 Asian American or Pacific Islander, 1 Hispanic American), 2 international. In 2009, 27 master's awarded. *Entrance requirements:* For master's, GMAT or GRE General Test. *Application deadline:* For fall admission, 7/1 priority date for domestic students; for spring admission, 11/15 for domestic students. Application fee: $50. Electronic applications accepted. *Expenses:* Tuition, state resident: full-time $6000; part-time $250 per credit hour. Tuition, nonresident: full-time $20,904; part-time $871 per credit hour. Required fees: $730 per semester. *Financial support:* Research assistantships available. *Unit head:* Dr. Charlotte Mason, Head, 706-542-3776, E-mail: cmason@terry.uga.edu. *Application contact:* Dr. Richard J. Fox, Graduate Coordinator, 706-542-3761, Fax: 706-542-3738, E-mail: rfox@terry.uga.edu.

The University of Texas at Arlington, Graduate School, College of Business, Department of Marketing, Arlington, TX 76019. Offers marketing research (MS). Part-time programs available. *Faculty:* 9 full-time (2 women). *Students:* 22 full-time (11 women), 14 part-time (5 women); includes 5 minority (1 American Indian/Alaska Native, 2 Asian Americans or Pacific Islanders, 2 Hispanic Americans), 17 international. 21 applicants, 86% accepted, 11 enrolled. In 2009, 9 master's awarded. *Degree requirements:* For master's, thesis optional. *Entrance requirements:* For master's, GMAT. Additional exam requirements/recommendations for international students: Required—TOEFL (minimum score 550 paper-based; 213 computer-based; 79 iBT). *Application deadline:* For fall admission, 6/5 for domestic students, 4/1 for international students; for spring admission, 10/15 for domestic students, 9/1 for international students. Applications are processed on a rolling basis. Application fee: $35 ($50 for international students). Electronic applications accepted. *Financial support:* In 2009–10, 39 fellowships (averaging $1,000 per year), research assistantships (averaging $6,000 per year), 8 teaching assistantships (averaging $13,000 per year) were awarded; career-related internships or fieldwork, scholarships/grants, and unspecified assistantships also available. Support available to part-time students. Financial award application deadline: 6/1; financial award applicants required to submit FAFSA. *Faculty research:* Marketing strategy, marketing research, international marketing. Total annual research expenditures: $30,000. *Unit head:* Dr. Larry Chonko, Chair, 817-272-0264, Fax: 817-272-2854, E-mail: chonko@uta.edu. *Application contact:* Dr. Robert Rogers, Program Director, 817-272-2340, Fax: 817-272-2854, E-mail: msmr@uta.edu.

University of Wisconsin–Madison, Graduate School, Wisconsin School of Business, Wisconsin Full-Time MBA Program, Madison, WI 53706-1380. Offers applied corporate finance (MBA); applied security analysis (MBA); arts administration (MBA); brand and product management (MBA); entrepreneurial management (MBA); marketing research (MBA); operations and technology management (MBA); real estate (MBA); risk management and insurance (MBA); strategic human resource management (MBA); strategic management in the life and engineering sciences (MBA); supply chain management (MBA). *Faculty:* 32 full-time (5 women). *Students:* 242 full-time (74 women); includes 47 minority (16 African Americans, 3 American Indian/ Alaska Native, 16 Asian Americans or Pacific Islanders, 12 Hispanic Americans), 29 international. Average age 28. 526 applicants, 32% accepted, 117 enrolled. In 2009, 106 master's awarded. *Entrance requirements:* For master's, GMAT, bachelor's or equivalent degree, 2 years of work experience, letters of recommendation. Additional exam requirements/recommendations for international students: Required—TOEFL (minimum score 600 paper-based; 250 computer-based; 100 iBT), IELTS. *Application deadline:* For fall admission, 11/4 for domestic and international students; for winter admission, 2/5 for domestic and international students; for spring admission, 5/26 for domestic students, 4/5 for international students. Applications are processed on a rolling basis. Application fee: $56. Electronic applications accepted. *Expenses:* Tuition, state resident: part-time $594 per credit. Tuition, nonresident: part-time $1504 per credit. Required fees: $65 per credit. Tuition and fees vary according to course load, program and reciprocity agreements. *Financial support:* In 2009–10, 103 students received support, including 13 fellowships with full and partial tuition reimbursements available (averaging $15,000 per year), 53 research assistantships with full tuition reimbursements available (averaging $8,000 per year), 35 teaching assistantships with full tuition reimbursements available (averaging $11,000 per year); scholarships/grants, health care benefits, and unspecified assistantships also available. Financial award application deadline: 4/5; financial award applicants required to submit FAFSA. *Unit head:* Prof. Kenneth A. Kavajecz, Associate Dean, 608-265-3494, Fax: 608-265-4192, E-mail: kkavajecz@bus.wisc.edu. *Application contact:* Maria Reis, Assistant Director of MBA Marketing and Recruiting, 608-262-4000, Fax: 608-265-4192, E-mail: mreis@bus.wisc.edu.

Section 15
Nonprofit Management

This section contains a directory of institutions offering graduate work in nonprofit management. Additional information about programs listed in the directory may be obtained by writing directly to the dean of a graduate school or chair of a department at the address given in the directory.

For programs offering related work, see also in this book *Accounting and Finance* and *Business Administration and Management*. In another guide in this series:

Graduate Programs in the Humanities, Arts & Social Sciences
See *Public, Regional, and Industrial Affairs*

CONTENTS

Program Directory

Nonprofit Management

American International College, School of Business Administration, Program in Nonprofit Management, Springfield, MA 01109-3189. Offers MS. Part-time programs available. *Entrance requirements:* Additional exam requirements/recommendations for international students: Required—TOEFL. Electronic applications accepted. *Expenses:* Tuition: Full-time $12,510; part-time $695 per credit hour. Required fees: $35 per term.

American Jewish University, Graduate School, David Lieber School of Graduate Studies, Program in Business Administration, Bel Air, CA 90077-1599. Offers general nonprofit administration (MBA); Jewish nonprofit administration (MBA). Part-time and evening/weekend programs available. *Degree requirements:* For master's, thesis, internship. *Entrance requirements:* For master's, GMAT or GRE General Test, interview, minimum undergraduate GPA of 3.0. Additional exam requirements/recommendations for international students: Required—TOEFL (minimum score 550 paper-based; 247 computer-based).

American University, School of Public Affairs, Department of Public Administration, Washington, DC 20016-8070. Offers advanced organization development (Certificate); fundamentals of organization development (Certificate); key executive leadership (MPA); leadership for organizational change (Certificate); non-profit management (Certificate); organization development (MSOD); organizational change (Certificate); public administration (MPA, PhD); public financial management (Certificate); public management (Certificate); public policy (MPP); public policy analysis (Certificate); LL M/MPA; MPA/JD; MPP/JD; MPP/LLM. Part-time and evening/weekend programs available. *Faculty:* 23 full-time (9 women), 13 part-time/adjunct (4 women). *Students:* 184 full-time (117 women), 252 part-time (165 women); includes 109 minority (68 African Americans, 3 American Indian/Alaska Native, 25 Asian Americans or Pacific Islanders, 13 Hispanic Americans), 23 international. Average age 31. 843 applicants, 71% accepted, 156 enrolled. In 2009, 172 master's, 4 doctorates awarded. *Degree requirements:* For master's, comprehensive exam; for doctorate, comprehensive exam, thesis/dissertation. *Entrance requirements:* For master's, GRE, statement of purpose; 2 recommendations; for doctorate, GRE, 3 recommendations; for Certificate, bachelor's degree. Additional exam requirements/recommendations for international students: Required—TOEFL. *Application deadline:* For fall admission, 2/1 for domestic students; for spring admission, 11/1 for domestic students. Application fee: $55. *Expenses:* Tuition: Full-time $22,266; part-time $1237 per credit hour. Required fees: $430. Tuition and fees vary according to program. *Financial support:* Fellowships, research assistantships, teaching assistantships, career-related internships or fieldwork, Federal Work-Study, and institutionally sponsored loans available. Financial award application deadline: 2/1. *Faculty research:* Urban management, conservation politics, state and local budgeting, tax policy. *Unit head:* Dr. Howard McCurdy, Chair, 202-885-6236, E-mail: mccurdy@american.edu. *Application contact:* Dr. Howard McCurdy, Chair, 202-885-6236, E-mail: mccurdy@american.edu.

Arizona State University, Graduate College, College of Public Programs, School of Community Resources and Development, Tempe, AZ 85287. Offers community resources and development (PhD); nonprofit studies (MNpS); recreation and tourism studies (MS). *Degree requirements:* For master's, thesis or alternative.

Assumption College, Graduate School, Department of Business Studies, Worcester, MA 01609-1296. Offers accounting (MBA); business administration (CAGS); finance/economics (MBA); general business (MBA); human resources (MBA); international business (MBA); management (MBA); marketing (MBA); nonprofit leadership (MBA). Part-time and evening/weekend programs available. *Faculty:* 6 full-time (1 woman), 14 part-time/adjunct (2 women). *Students:* 19 full-time (11 women), 127 part-time (68 women); includes 22 minority (13 African Americans, 3 Asian Americans or Pacific Islanders, 6 Hispanic Americans). Average age 27. 88 applicants, 99% accepted. In 2009, 40 master's, 2 other advanced degrees awarded. *Entrance requirements:* For master's, 3 letters of recommendation, resume; for CAGS, 3 letters of recommendation, resume, essay. Additional exam requirements/recommendations for international students: Required—TOEFL (minimum score 540 paper-based; 200 computer-based; 76 iBT), IELTS (minimum score 6). *Application deadline:* For fall admission, 6/1 priority date for domestic students, 5/1 priority date for international students; for spring admission, 11/1 priority date for domestic students, 9/1 priority date for international students. Applications are processed on a rolling basis. Application fee: $30. Electronic applications accepted. *Expenses:* Tuition: Part-time $503 per credit. Required fees: $20 per semester. One-time fee: $100 part-time. Part-time tuition and fees vary according to campus/location. *Financial support:* In 2009–10, 47 students received support. Application deadline: 6/1. *Faculty research:* Workplace diversity, dynamics of team interaction, utilization of leased employees. *Unit head:* Michael Lewis, Director, 508-767-7372, Fax: 508-767-7252, E-mail: jhunter@assumption.edu. *Application contact:* Adrian O. Dumas, Director of Graduate Enrollment Management and Services, 508-767-7365, Fax: 508-767-7030, E-mail: adumas@assumption.edu.

Avila University, Program in Organizational Development, Kansas City, MO 64145-1698. Offers management (MA), including fundraising, project management; organizational development (MS); project management (Graduate Certificate). Part-time and evening/weekend programs available. *Faculty:* 2 full-time (1 woman), 10 part-time/adjunct (7 women). *Students:* 50 full-time (41 women), 43 part-time (35 women); includes 28 minority (24 African Americans, 2 Asian Americans or Pacific Islanders, 2 Hispanic Americans), 2 international. Average age 36. 47 applicants, 64% accepted, 27 enrolled. In 2009, 16 master's awarded. *Degree requirements:* For master's, thesis optional. *Entrance requirements:* For master's, 2 letters of recommendation, minimum GPA of 3.25 during last 60 hours, resume. Additional exam requirements/recommendations for international students: Required—TOEFL. *Application deadline:* Applications are processed on a rolling basis. Application fee: $0. Electronic applications accepted. *Expenses:* Tuition: Full-time $8622; part-time $479 per credit hour. Required fees: $432; $24 per credit hour. Tuition and fees vary according to program. *Financial support:* In 2009–10, 69 students received support. Unspecified assistantships available. Support available to part-time students. Financial award applicants required to submit FAFSA. *Unit head:* Dr. Lacey Smith, Associate Dean, 816-501-3737, Fax: 816-941-4650, E-mail: advantage@avila.edu. *Application contact:* School of Professional Studies, 816-501-3737, Fax: 816-941-4650, E-mail: advantage@avila.edu.

Azusa Pacific University, Haggard School of Theology, Program in Non-Profit Leadership and Theology, Azusa, CA 91702-7000. Offers Christian non-profit leadership (MA).

Bay Path College, Program in Nonprofit Management and Philanthropy, Longmeadow, MA 01106-2292. Offers MS. Postbaccalaureate distance learning degree programs offered. *Degree requirements:* For master's, capstone project. *Entrance requirements:* For master's, current resume, 2 letters of recommendation.

Bay Path College, Program in Strategic Fundraising and Philanthropy, Longmeadow, MA 01106-2292. Offers MS. Postbaccalaureate distance learning degree programs offered. *Entrance requirements:* For master's, current resume, 2 letters of recommendation.

Bernard M. Baruch College of the City University of New York, School of Public Affairs, Program in Public Administration, New York, NY 10010-5585. Offers nonprofit administration (MPA); public management (MPA); MS/MPA. *Accreditation:* NASPAA. Part-time and evening/weekend programs available. *Degree requirements:* For master's, thesis, capstone. *Entrance requirements:* For master's, GRE General Test. Additional exam requirements/recommendations for international students: Required—TOEFL (minimum score 625 paper-based; 263 computer-based; 106 iBT). Electronic applications accepted. *Expenses:* Contact institution. *Faculty research:* Urbanization, population and poverty in the developing world, housing and community development, labor unions and housing, government-nongovernment relations, immigration policy, social network analysis, cross-sectoral governance, comparative healthcare systems, program evaluation, social welfare policy, health outcomes, educational policy and leadership, transnationalism, infant health, welfare reform, racial/ethnic disparities in health, urban politics, homelessness, race and ethnic relations.

Boston University, School of Management, Master of Business Administration Program, Boston, MA 02215. Offers entrepreneurship (MBA); finance (MBA); health sector management (MBA); international management (MBA); marketing (MBA); operations and technology management (MBA); public and nonprofit management (MBA); strategy and business analysis (MBA); JD/MBA; MBA/MA; MBA/MPH; MBA/MS; MBA/MSIS; MS/MBA. Part-time and evening/weekend programs available. *Faculty:* 119 full-time (31 women), 99 part-time/adjunct (30 women). *Students:* 326 full-time (138 women), 677 part-time (257 women); includes 149 minority (13 African Americans, 119 Asian Americans or Pacific Islanders, 17 Hispanic Americans), 149 international. Average age 30. 1,617 applicants, 38% accepted, 317 enrolled. In 2009, 284 master's awarded. *Entrance requirements:* For master's, GMAT, resume, 2 letters of recommendation. Additional exam requirements/recommendations for international students: Required—TOEFL or IELTS. *Application deadline:* For fall admission, 3/15 for domestic and international students; for spring admission, 11/15 for domestic students. Application fee: $125. Electronic applications accepted. *Expenses:* Tuition: Full-time $37,910; part-time $1184 per credit hour. Required fees: $386; $40 per semester. Part-time tuition and fees vary according to class time, course level, degree level and program. *Financial support:* Career-related internships or fieldwork, Federal Work-Study, institutionally sponsored loans, and scholarships/grants available. Support available to part-time students. Financial award applicants required to submit FAFSA. *Unit head:* Katherine Nolan, Assistant Dean, Graduate Programs, 617-353-4157, Fax: 617-353-5003, E-mail: mba@bu.edu. *Application contact:* Hayden Estrada, Assistant Dean, Admissions, 617-353-2670, Fax: 617-353-7368, E-mail: mba@bu.edu.

Brandeis University, The Heller School for Social Policy and Management, Program in Nonprofit Management, Waltham, MA 02454-9110. Offers aging services management (MBA); child, youth, and family management (MBA); health care management (MBA); social impact management (MBA); social policy and management (MBA); sustainable development (MBA); MBA/MA. *Accreditation:* AACSB. Part-time and evening/weekend programs available. *Degree requirements:* For master's, team consulting project. *Entrance requirements:* For master's, GMAT. Additional exam requirements/recommendations for international students: Required—TOEFL (minimum score 600 paper-based). Electronic applications accepted. *Expenses:* Contact institution. *Faculty research:* Health care, child and family, elder and disabled services, general human services.

Brigham Young University, Graduate Studies, Marriott School of Management, Master of Public Administration Program, Provo, UT 84602. Offers finance (MPA); human resources (MPA); local government (MPA); nonprofit management (MPA); JD/MPA. *Faculty:* 10 full-time (4 women), 18 part-time/adjunct (1 woman). *Students:* 128 full-time (54 women); includes 26 minority (3 African Americans, 13 Asian Americans or Pacific Islanders, 10 Hispanic Americans). Average age 27. 136 applicants, 66% accepted, 62 enrolled. In 2009, 53 master's awarded. *Entrance requirements:* For master's, GRE, GMAT, minimum GPA of 3.0. Additional exam requirements/recommendations for international students: Required—TOEFL (minimum score 580 paper-based; 85 iBT), IELTS (minimum score 7). *Application deadline:* For fall admission, 2/1 for domestic and international students. Application fee: $50. Electronic applications accepted. *Expenses:* Tuition: Full-time $5580; part-time $301 per credit hour. Tuition and fees vary according to student's religious affiliation. *Financial support:* In 2009–10, 96 students received support. Career-related internships or fieldwork and scholarships/grants available. Financial award application deadline: 4/15; financial award applicants required to submit FAFSA. *Faculty research:* Taxes, budgeting, nonprofit, ethics, decision modeling, work balance, organizational behavior. *Unit head:* Dr. David W. Hart, Director, 801-422-4221, Fax: 801-422-0311, E-mail: mpa@byu.edu. *Application contact:* Catherine Cooper, Director of Student Services, E-mail: mpa@byu.edu.

Cambridge College, School of Management, Cambridge, MA 02138-5304. Offers business negotiation and conflict resolution (M Mgt); general business (M Mgt); health care informatics (M Mgt); health care management (M Mgt); leadership in human and organizational dynamics (M Mgt); non-profit and public organization management (M Mgt); small business development (M Mgt); technology management (M Mgt). Part-time and evening/weekend programs available. *Faculty:* 4 full-time (3 women), 65 part-time/adjunct (32 women). *Students:* 297 full-time (178 women), 234 part-time (155 women); includes 217 minority (122 African Americans, 53 Asian Americans or Pacific Islanders, 42 Hispanic Americans), 135 international. Average age 39. In 2009, 259 master's awarded. *Degree requirements:* For master's, thesis, seminars. *Entrance requirements:* For master's, resume, 2 professional references. Additional exam requirements/recommendations for international students: Required—TOEFL (minimum score 550 paper-based; 213 computer-based; 79 iBT); Recommended—IELTS (minimum score 6). *Application deadline:* Applications are processed on a rolling basis. Application fee: $30. Electronic applications accepted. *Expenses:* Contact institution. *Financial support:* In 2009–10, 170 students received support. Career-related internships or fieldwork, Federal Work-Study, and scholarships/grants available. Financial award applicants required to submit FAFSA. *Faculty research:* Negotiation, mediation and conflict resolution; leadership; management of diverse organizations; case studies and simulation methodologies for management education, digital as a second language: social networking for digital immigrants. *Unit head:* Dr. Mary Ann Joseph, Acting Dean, 617-873-0227, E-mail: maryann.joseph@cambridgecollege.edu. *Application contact:* Stephen Lyons, Director of Enrollment, Graduate and N.I.T.E. Programs, 617-868-1000, Fax: 617-349-3561, E-mail: stephen.lyons@cambridgecollege.edu.

Capella University, School of Human Services, Minneapolis, MN 55402. Offers addictions counseling (Certificate); counseling studies (MS, PhD); criminal justice (MS, PhD, Certificate); diversity studies (Certificate); general human services (MS, PhD); health care administration (MS, PhD, Certificate); management of nonprofit agencies (MS, PhD, Certificate); marital, couple and family counseling/therapy (MS); marriage and family services (Certificate); mental health counseling (MS); professional counseling (Certificate); social and community services (MS, PhD, Certificate). Part-time and evening/weekend programs available. Postbaccalaureate distance learning degree programs offered (minimal on-campus study). Terminal master's awarded for partial completion of doctoral program. *Degree requirements:* For master's, thesis optional, integrative project; for doctorate, comprehensive exam, thesis/dissertation. *Entrance requirements:* Additional exam requirements/recommendations for international students: Required—TOEFL (minimum score 550 paper-based; 213 computer-based), TWE (minimum score 4). Electronic applications accepted. *Faculty research:* Compulsive and addictive behaviors, substance abuse, assessment of psychopathology and neuropsychology.

Capella University, School of Public Service Leadership, Minneapolis, MN 55402. Offers criminal justice (MS, PhD); emergency management (MS, PhD); general human services (MS, PhD); general public administration (MPA, DPA); gerontology (MS); health care administration (MS, PhD); health management and policy (MSPH); management of nonprofit agencies (MS, PhD); nurse educator (MS); public safety leadership (MS, PhD); social and community services (MS, PhD); social behavioral sciences (MSPH).

Carlos Albizu University, Miami Campus, Graduate Programs, Miami, FL 33172-2209. Offers clinical psychology (Psy D); entrepreneurship (MBA); exceptional student education (MS); industrial/organizational psychology (MS); marriage and family therapy (MS); mental health counseling (MS); nonprofit management (MBA); organizational management (MBA); psychology (MS); school counseling (MS); teaching English as a second language (MS). *Accreditation:* APA. Part-time and evening/weekend programs available. *Faculty:* 23 full-time (13 women), 41 part-time/adjunct (21 women). *Students:* 529 full-time (420 women), 171 part-time (139 women); includes 551 minority (55 African Americans, 1 American Indian/Alaska Native, 5 Asian Americans or Pacific Islanders, 490 Hispanic Americans). Average age 37. 278 applicants, 57% accepted, 142 enrolled. In 2009, 139 master's, 26 doctorates awarded. Terminal master's awarded for partial completion of doctoral program. *Degree requirements:* For master's, one foreign language, comprehensive exam, integrative project (MBA), research project (exceptional student education, teaching English as a second language); for doctorate, one foreign language, comprehensive exam, internship, project. *Entrance requirements:* For

master's, 3 letters of recommendation, interview, minimum GPA of 3.0, resume; for doctorate, 3 letters of recommendation, minimum GPA of 3.0, resume, interview. *Application deadline:* For fall admission, 8/1 priority date for domestic students; for spring admission, 11/30 priority date for domestic students. Applications are processed on a rolling basis. Application fee: $50. Electronic applications accepted. *Expenses:* Tuition: Full-time $9090; part-time $505 per credit hour. Required fees: $298 per term. Tuition and fees vary according to course load, degree level and program. *Financial support:* In 2009–10, 127 students received support. Federal Work-Study, scholarships/grants, and tuition discounts available. Financial award application deadline: 6/1; financial award applicants required to submit FAFSA. *Faculty research:* Psychotherapy, forensic psychology, neuropsychology, marketing strategy, entrepreneurship, special education. *Unit head:* Dr. Carmen S. Roca, Chancellor, 305-593-1223 Ext. 120, Fax: 305-629-8052, E-mail: croca@albizu.edu. *Application contact:* Annalye Alonso, Secretary, 305-593-1223 Ext. 137, Fax: 305-593-1854, E-mail: aalonso@albizu.edu.

Carlow University, School for Social Change, Pittsburgh, PA 15213-3165. Offers professional counseling (MS); professional counseling: school counseling (MS); professional leadership: management for nonprofit organizations (MS); professional leadership: organizational influence and policy (MS); professional leadership: training and development (MS). Part-time and evening/weekend programs available. *Entrance requirements:* Additional exam requirements/recommendations for international students: Required—TOEFL (minimum score 550 paper-based; 213 computer-based). Electronic applications accepted. *Expenses:* Tuition: Full-time $11,250; part-time $625 per credit. Tuition and fees vary according to course load, degree level and program. *Faculty research:* Gender and leadership, cross cultural communications and leadership, organizational culture.

Case Western Reserve University, Weatherhead School of Management, Mandel Center for Nonprofit Organizations, Cleveland, OH 44106. Offers MNO, CNM, JD/MNO, MNO/MSSA, MSSA/MNO. Part-time and evening/weekend programs available. *Students:* Average age 31. *Entrance requirements:* For master's and CNM, GMAT. Additional exam requirements/recommendations for international students: Required—TOEFL. *Application deadline:* For fall admission, 6/1 priority date for domestic students; for spring admission, 11/15 priority date for domestic students. Applications are processed on a rolling basis. Application fee: $25. *Expenses:* Contact institution. *Financial support:* In 2009–10, 39 students received support, including 1 fellowship with full and partial tuition reimbursement available; career-related internships or fieldwork, Federal Work-Study, and scholarships/grants also available. Financial award application deadline: 5/1; financial award applicants required to submit FAFSA. *Faculty research:* Leadership management of non-profit organizations, strategic alliances, economic analysis of non-profit organizations. *Unit head:* Wendy Jelinek, Director, 216-368-8566, Fax: 216-368-8592, E-mail: wendy.jelinek@case.edu. *Application contact:* Wendy Jelinek, Director, 216-368-8566, Fax: 216-368-8592, E-mail: wendy.jelinek@case.edu.

Cleary University, Online Program in Business Administration, Ann Arbor, MI 48105-2659. Offers accounting (MBA); financial planning (MBA); financial planning (Graduate Certificate); green business strategy (MBA); management (MBA); nonprofit management (MBA); organizational leadership (MBA). Part-time and evening/weekend programs available. Postbaccalaureate distance learning degree programs offered (no on-campus study). *Degree requirements:* For master's, thesis. *Entrance requirements:* For master's, bachelor's degree; minimum GPA of 2.5; professional resume indicating minimum 2 years management or related experience; undergraduate degree from an accredited college or university with at least 18 quarter hours (or 12 semester hours) of accounting study (for MBA in accounting). Additional exam requirements/recommendations for international students: Required—TOEFL (minimum score 550 paper-based; 213 computer-based; 79 iBT), Michigan English Language Assessment Battery (minimum score: 75). Electronic applications accepted.

Cleveland State University, College of Graduate Studies, Maxine Goodman Levin College of Urban Affairs, Program in Nonprofit Administration and Leadership, Cleveland, OH 44115. Offers geographic information systems (Certificate); local and urban management (Certificate); nonprofit administration and leadership (MNAL); nonprofit management (Certificate); urban economic development (Certificate). Part-time and evening/weekend programs available. *Degree requirements:* For master's, thesis or alternative, capstone course. *Entrance requirements:* For master's, GRE (minimum 40th percentile verbal and quantitative, 4.0 analytical writing), minimum GPA of 3.0. Additional exam requirements/recommendations for international students: Required—TOEFL (minimum score 525 paper-based; 197 computer-based; 65 iBT). Electronic applications accepted. *Faculty research:* Human resource management, volunteerism, performance measurement in nonprofits, government-nonprofit partnerships.

Cleveland State University, College of Graduate Studies, Maxine Goodman Levin College of Urban Affairs, Program in Public Administration, Cleveland, OH 44115. Offers geographic information systems (Certificate); local and urban management (Certificate); non-profit management (Certificate); public administration (MPA); urban real estate development (Certificate); JD/MPA. *Accreditation:* NASPAA. Part-time and evening/weekend programs available. *Degree requirements:* For master's, thesis or alternative, capstone course. *Entrance requirements:* For master's, GRE General Test (minimum 40th percentile verbal and quantitative, 4.0 writing), minimum GPA of 3.0. Additional exam requirements/recommendations for international students: Required—TOEFL (minimum score 525 paper-based; 197 computer-based; 65 iBT). Electronic applications accepted. *Faculty research:* Health care administration, public management, economic development, city management, nonprofit management.

Cleveland State University, College of Graduate Studies, Maxine Goodman Levin College of Urban Affairs, Program in Urban Studies, Cleveland, OH 44115. Offers geographic information systems (Certificate); local and urban management (Certificate); nonprofit management (Certificate); urban economic development (Certificate); urban real estate development and finance (Certificate); urban studies (MS); urban studies and public affairs (PhD). Part-time and evening/weekend programs available. *Degree requirements:* For master's, thesis or alternative, exit project, capstone course; for doctorate, comprehensive exam, thesis/dissertation. *Entrance requirements:* For master's, GRE General Test, minimum GPA of 3.0; for doctorate, GRE General Test, minimum GPA of 3.5. Additional exam requirements/recommendations for international students: Required—TOEFL (minimum score 525 paper-based; 197 computer-based; 65 iBT). Electronic applications accepted. *Faculty research:* Environmental issues, economic development, urban and public policy, public management.

The College at Brockport, State University of New York, School of Education and Human Services, Department of Public Administration, Brockport, NY 14420-2997. Offers arts administration (AGC); nonprofit management (AGC); public administration (MPA), including general public administration, health care management, nonprofit management, public safety. *Accreditation:* NASPAA. Part-time and evening/weekend programs available. *Students:* 25 full-time (18 women), 91 part-time (72 women); includes 18 minority (12 African Americans, 3 Asian Americans or Pacific Islanders, 3 Hispanic Americans). 42 applicants, 95% accepted, 33 enrolled. In 2009, 30 master's awarded. *Degree requirements:* For master's, thesis or alternative. *Entrance requirements:* For master's, GRE or minimum GPA of 3.0, letters of recommendation, statement of objectives. Additional exam requirements/recommendations for international students: Required—TOEFL (minimum score 550 paper-based; 213 computer-based; 79 iBT). *Application deadline:* For fall admission, 3/1 priority date for domestic and international students; for spring admission, 10/1 priority date for domestic and international students. Application fee: $50. Electronic applications accepted. *Expenses:* Tuition, state resident: full-time $8370; part-time $349 per credit. Tuition, nonresident: full-time $13,250; part-time $522 per credit. *Financial support:* In 2009–10, 1 fellowship with full tuition reimbursement (averaging $7,500 per year) was awarded; Federal Work-Study, scholarships/grants, and unspecified assistantships also available. Support available to part-time students. Financial award application deadline: 3/15; financial award applicants required to submit FAFSA. *Faculty research:* E-government, performance management, nonprofits and policy implementation, Medicaid and disabilities. *Unit head:* Dr. James Fatula, Chairperson, 585-395-2375, Fax: 585-395-2172, E-mail: jfatula@brockport.edu. *Application contact:* Dr. James Fatual, Chairperson, 585-395-2375, Fax: 585-395-2172, E-mail: jfatula@brockport.edu.

College of Notre Dame of Maryland, Graduate Studies, Program in Nonprofit Management, Baltimore, MD 21210-2476. Offers MA. Part-time and evening/weekend programs available. *Degree requirements:* For master's, thesis optional. *Entrance requirements:* For master's, minimum GPA of 3.0. Additional exam requirements/recommendations for international students: Required—TOEFL (minimum score 500 paper-based; 173 computer-based; 61 iBT). Electronic applications accepted.

The College of Saint Rose, Graduate Studies, School of Business, Department of Not-for-Profit Management, Albany, NY 12203-1419. Offers Certificate. Part-time and evening/weekend programs available. *Entrance requirements:* For degree, minimum undergraduate GPA of 3.0 or GMAT. Additional exam requirements/recommendations for international students: Required—TOEFL (minimum score 550 paper-based; 213 computer-based). Electronic applications accepted.

Columbia University, School of Continuing Education, Program in Fundraising Management, New York, NY 10027. Offers MS. Part-time and evening/weekend programs available. *Faculty:* 18 part-time/adjunct (6 women). *Students:* 60 part-time (48 women); includes 12 minority (6 African Americans, 4 Asian Americans or Pacific Islanders, 2 Hispanic Americans), 2 international. Average age 28. 39 applicants, 69% accepted, 17 enrolled. In 2009, 10 master's awarded. *Degree requirements:* For master's, internship. *Entrance requirements:* For master's, BA with minimum GPA of 3.0. Additional exam requirements/recommendations for international students: Required—American Language Program placement test. *Application deadline:* For fall admission, 6/15 priority date for domestic students. Application fee: $50. Electronic applications accepted. *Financial support:* Institutionally sponsored loans available. Financial award applicants required to submit FAFSA. *Faculty research:* Fundraising for annual campaigns, capital campaigns, nonprofit financial management, research for fundraising and planned giving. *Unit head:* Dr. Lucas G. Rubin, Director, 212-854-9699, E-mail: lr2008@columbia.edu. *Application contact:* Bryce Weinert, Admissions Adviser, 212-854-9666, E-mail: sce-apply@columbia.edu.

Corban University, Graduate School, The Corban MBA, Salem, OR 97301-9392. Offers management (MBA); non-profit management (MBA). Postbaccalaureate distance learning degree programs offered (no on-campus study).

Dallas Baptist University, College of Business, Business Administration Program, Dallas, TX 75211-9299. Offers accounting (MBA); business communication (MBA); conflict resolution management (MBA); e-business (MBA); entrepreneurship (MBA); finance (MBA); health care management (MBA); international business (MBA); leading the non-profit organization (MBA); management (MBA); management information systems (MBA); marketing (MBA); project management (MBA); technology and engineering management (MBA). *Accreditation:* ACBSP. Part-time and evening/weekend programs available. *Entrance requirements:* For master's, GMAT, minimum GPA of 3.0. Additional exam requirements/recommendations for international students: Required—TOEFL, IELTS. Electronic applications accepted. *Expenses:* Tuition: Full-time $10,674; part-time $593 per credit hour. *Faculty research:* Sports management, services marketing, retailing, strategic management, financial planning/investments.

DePaul University, School of Public Service, Chicago, IL 60604. Offers financial administration management (Certificate); health administration (Certificate); health law and policy (MS); international public services (MS); leadership and policy studies (MS); metropolitan planning (Certificate); public administration (MPA); public service management (MS), including association management, fundraising and philanthropy, healthcare administration, higher education administration, metropolitan planning; public services (Certificate); JD/MS. Part-time and evening/weekend programs available. Postbaccalaureate distance learning degree programs offered (minimal on-campus study). *Faculty:* 14 full-time (3 women), 43 part-time/adjunct (24 women). *Students:* 283 full-time (206 women), 298 part-time (208 women); includes 196 minority (112 African Americans, 1 American Indian/Alaska Native, 30 Asian Americans or Pacific Islanders, 53 Hispanic Americans), 18 international. Average age 26. 162 applicants, 100% accepted, 94 enrolled. In 2009, 108 master's awarded. *Degree requirements:* For master's, thesis or integrative seminar. *Entrance requirements:* For master's, minimum GPA of 2.7. Additional exam requirements/recommendations for international students: Required—TOEFL (minimum score 550 paper-based; 213 computer-based; 80 iBT), IELTS (minimum score 6.5). *Application deadline:* Applications are processed on a rolling basis. Application fee: $40. Electronic applications accepted. *Expenses:* Tuition: Full-time $37,525; part-time $620 per credit hour. *Financial support:* In 2009–10, 60 students received support, including 3 research assistantships with full tuition reimbursements available (averaging $7,000 per year); career-related internships or fieldwork, Federal Work-Study, institutionally sponsored loans, scholarships/grants, tuition waivers (partial), and unspecified assistantships also available. Support available to part-time students. Financial award application deadline: 7/1; financial award applicants required to submit FAFSA. *Faculty research:* Government financing, transportation, leadership, health care, volunteerism and organizational behavior, non-profit organizations. Total annual research expenditures: $20,000. *Unit head:* Dr. J. Patrick Murphy, Director, 312-362-5608, Fax: 312-362-5506, E-mail: jpmurphy@depaul.edu. *Application contact:* Megan B. Balderston, Director of Admissions and Marketing, 312-362-5565, Fax: 312-362-5506, E-mail: pubserv@depaul.edu.

Eastern Michigan University, Graduate School, College of Business, Programs in Business Administration, Ypsilanti, MI 48197. Offers business administration (MBA, Graduate Certificate); computer information systems (Graduate Certificate); e-business (MBA, Graduate Certificate); enterprise business intelligence (MBA); entrepreneurship (MBA, Graduate Certificate); finance (MBA, Graduate Certificate); human resources (MBA); human resources management (Graduate Certificate); information systems (MBA); internal auditing (MBA); international business (MBA, Graduate Certificate); marketing management (Graduate Certificate); nonprofit management (MBA); organizational development (Graduate Certificate); supply chain management (MBA, Graduate Certificate). *Accreditation:* AACSB. Part-time programs available. Postbaccalaureate distance learning degree programs offered (no on-campus study). *Students:* 166 full-time (80 women), 439 part-time (231 women); includes 150 minority (103 African Americans, 7 American Indian/Alaska Native, 31 Asian Americans or Pacific Islanders, 9 Hispanic Americans), 97 international. Average age 34. In 2009, 3 other advanced degrees awarded. *Entrance requirements:* For master's, GMAT (minimum score 450), minimum cumulative undergraduate GPA of 2.75. Additional exam requirements/recommendations for international students: Required—TOEFL. *Application deadline:* For fall admission, 5/15 for domestic students, 5/1 for international students; for winter admission, 10/15 for domestic students, 10/1 for international students; for spring admission, 3/15 for domestic students, 3/1 for international students. Applications are processed on a rolling basis. Application fee: $35. Tuition and fees vary according to course level. *Financial support:* Fellowships, research assistantships with full tuition reimbursements, teaching assistantships with full tuition reimbursements, career-related internships or fieldwork, Federal Work-Study, institutionally sponsored loans, scholarships/grants, tuition waivers (partial), and unspecified assistantships available. Support available to part-time students. Financial award applicants required to submit FAFSA. *Unit head:* K. Michelle Henry, Director of Academic Services, 734-487-4444, Fax: 734-483-1316, E-mail: cob.grad@emich.edu. *Application contact:* Beste Windes, Advisor, 734-487-4444, Fax: 734-483-1316, E-mail: cob.grad@emich.edu.

Eastern Michigan University, Graduate School, College of Health and Human Services, Interdisciplinary Program in Health and Human Services, Ypsilanti, MI 48197. Offers community building (Graduate Certificate); nonprofit management (Graduate Certificate). Part-time and evening/weekend programs available. In 2009, 1 other advanced degree awarded. *Entrance requirements:* Additional exam requirements/recommendations for international students: Required—TOEFL. Application fee: $35. Tuition and fees vary according to course level. *Unit head:* Dr. Marcia Bombyk, Program Coordinator, 734-487-4173, Fax: 734-487-8536, E-mail: marcia.bombyk@emich.edu. *Application contact:* Dr. Marcia Bombyk, Program Coordinator, 734-487-4173, Fax: 734-487-8536, E-mail: marcia.bombyk@emich.edu.

Eastern University, School of Leadership and Development, Program in Nonprofit Management, St. Davids, PA 19087-3696. Offers MS. *Entrance requirements:* For master's, GMAT (MBA), minimum GPA of 2.5.

Nonprofit Management

Fairleigh Dickinson University, Metropolitan Campus, Anthony J. Petrocelli College of Continuing Studies, Public Administration Institute, Teaneck, NJ 07666-1914. Offers public administration (MPA, Certificate); public non-profit management (Certificate). *Students:* 126 full-time (65 women), 139 part-time (77 women), 111 international. Average age 33. 222 applicants, 86% accepted, 68 enrolled. In 2009, 65 master's awarded. *Application deadline:* Applications are processed on a rolling basis. Application fee: $40. *Unit head:* Dr. William Roberts, Director, 201-692-2000. *Application contact:* Susan Brooman, University Director of Graduate Admissions, 201-692-2554, Fax: 201-692-2560, E-mail: globaleducation@fdu.edu.

Florida Atlantic University, College of Architecture, Urban and Public Affairs, School of Public Administration, Program in Nonprofit Management, Boca Raton, FL 33431-0991. Offers MNM. *Students:* 7 full-time (5 women), 18 part-time (15 women); includes 7 minority (4 African Americans, 3 Hispanic Americans). Average age 34. 31 applicants, 68% accepted, 7 enrolled. In 2009, 7 master's awarded. *Degree requirements:* For master's, thesis optional. *Entrance requirements:* For master's, GRE, minimum GPA of 3.0. Additional exam requirements/recommendations for international students: Required—TOEFL. *Application deadline:* For fall admission, 7/1 priority date for domestic students, 2/15 for international students; for spring admission, 11/1 priority date for domestic students, 7/15 for international students. Application fee: $30. *Expenses:* Tuition, state resident: full-time $7055; part-time $293.94 per credit hour. Tuition, nonresident: full-time $22,096; part-time $920.66 per credit hour. *Financial support:* Career-related internships or fieldwork and institutionally sponsored loans available. *Faculty research:* Governance, nonprofit management, resource development, public and private nonprofit enterprise, accounting for government. *Unit head:* Dr. Ron Nyhan, Coordinator, 954-762-5664, E-mail: rcnyhan@fau.edu. *Application contact:* Dr. Ron Nyhan, Coordinator, 954-762-5664, E-mail: rcnyhan@fau.edu.

George Mason University, College of Humanities and Social Sciences, Department of Public and International Affairs, Fairfax, VA 22030. Offers association management (Certificate); biodefense (MS, PhD); critical analysis and strategic responses to terrorism (Certificate); nonprofit management (Certificate); political science (MA, PhD); public administration (MPA); public management (Certificate). *Accreditation:* NASPAA (one or more programs are accredited). *Faculty:* 37 full-time (14 women), 34 part-time/adjunct (7 women). *Students:* 115 full-time (62 women), 323 part-time (182 women); includes 60 minority (29 African Americans, 1 American Indian/Alaska Native, 18 Asian Americans or Pacific Islanders, 12 Hispanic Americans), 21 international. Average age 31. 458 applicants, 60% accepted, 129 enrolled. In 2009, 147 master's, 2 doctorates, 6 other advanced degrees awarded. *Entrance requirements:* For master's, GRE General Test, minimum GPA of 3.0 in last 60 hours of course work. Additional exam requirements/recommendations for international students: Required—TOEFL. *Application deadline:* For fall admission, 3/1 priority date for domestic students; for spring admission, 10/15 for domestic students. Application fee: $75. Electronic applications accepted. *Expenses:* Tuition, state resident: full-time $7568; part-time $315.33 per credit hour. Tuition, nonresident: full-time $21,704; part-time $904.33 per credit hour. Required fees: $2184; $91 per credit hour. *Financial support:* In 2009–10, 27 students received support, including 3 fellowships with full tuition reimbursements available (averaging $18,000 per year), 10 research assistantships with full and partial tuition reimbursements available (averaging $11,033 per year), 14 teaching assistantships with full and partial tuition reimbursements available (averaging $9,213 per year); Federal Work-Study, scholarships/grants, unspecified assistantships, and health care benefits (full-time research or teaching assistantship recipients) also available. Support available to part-time students. Financial award application deadline: 3/1; financial award applicants required to submit FAFSA. *Faculty research:* The Rehnquist Court and economic liberties; intersection of economic development with high-tech industry, telecommunications, and entrepreneurism; political economy of development; violence, terrorism and U.S. foreign policy; international security issues. Total annual research expenditures: $429,868. *Unit head:* Dr. Robert Dudley, Chair, 703-993-1400, Fax: 703-993-1399, E-mail: rdudley@gmu.edu. *Application contact:* Peg Koback, Information Contact, 703-993-9466, E-mail: mkoback@gmu.edu.

The George Washington University, Columbian College of Arts and Sciences, Trachtenberg School of Public Policy and Public Administration, Programs in Public Administration, Washington, DC 20052. Offers budget and public finance (MPA); federal policy, politics, and management (MPA); international development management (MPA); managing public organizations (MPA); managing state and local governments (MPA); nonprofit management (MPA); policy analysis and evaluation (MPA); public administration (MPA); public-private policy and management (MPA). *Accreditation:* NASPAA. Part-time programs available. *Faculty:* 16 full-time (5 women), 4 part-time/adjunct (1 woman). *Students:* 58 full-time (39 women), 55 part-time (37 women); includes 18 minority (5 African Americans, 9 Asian Americans or Pacific Islanders, 4 Hispanic Americans), 7 international. Average age 28. 206 applicants, 66% accepted, 41 enrolled. In 2009, 55 master's awarded. *Entrance requirements:* For master's, GRE General Test. Additional exam requirements/recommendations for international students: Required—TOEFL (minimum score 600 paper-based; 250 computer-based; 100 iBT). *Application deadline:* For fall admission, 1/15 priority date for domestic students, 1/15 for international students; for spring admission, 10/1 for domestic students, 9/1 for international students. Applications are processed on a rolling basis. Application fee: $60. Electronic applications accepted. *Financial support:* In 2009–10, 28 students received support; fellowships, teaching assistantships, career-related internships or fieldwork, Federal Work-Study, and tuition waivers available. Financial award application deadline: 1/15. *Faculty research:* Regulatory reform, policy and program evaluation, ethics and public management, managing not-for-profits, policy-making in the White House and Congress. *Unit head:* Dr. Lori Brainard, Director, 202-994-6295, E-mail: brainard@gwu.edu. *Application contact:* Bethany Pope, 202-994-6662, E-mail: tspppa@gwu.edu.

Georgia State University, Andrew Young School of Policy Studies, Department of Public Management and Policy, Atlanta, GA 30303. Offers disaster management (Certificate); nonprofit management (Certificate); planning and economic development (Certificate); public administration (MPA), including criminal justice, management and finance, nonprofit management, planning and economic development, policy analysis and evaluation, public health; public policy (MPP, PhD), including disaster policy (MPP), nonprofit policy (MPP), planning and economic development policy (MPP), public finance policy (MPP), social policy (MPP); JD/MPA. *Accreditation:* NASPAA (one or more programs are accredited). Part-time and evening/weekend programs available. Terminal master's awarded for partial completion of doctoral program. *Degree requirements:* For master's, thesis optional; for doctorate, comprehensive exam, thesis/dissertation. *Entrance requirements:* For master's and doctorate, GRE General Test. Additional exam requirements/recommendations for international students: Required—TOEFL. Electronic applications accepted. *Faculty research:* Public management, policy analysis, public finance, planning and economic development, nonprofit leadership and policy.

Hamline University, School of Business, St. Paul, MN 55104-1284. Offers business (MBA); nonprofit management (MNM); public administration (MPA, DPA); JD/MANM; JD/MAPA; JD/MBA; LL M/MPA. Part-time and evening/weekend programs available. *Faculty:* 22 full-time (8 women), 39 part-time/adjunct (9 women). *Students:* 531 full-time (255 women), 154 part-time (87 women); includes 99 minority (55 African Americans, 6 American Indian/Alaska Native, 29 Asian Americans or Pacific Islanders, 9 Hispanic Americans), 76 international. Average age 33. 385 applicants, 72% accepted, 240 enrolled. In 2009, 228 master's, 1 doctorate awarded. *Degree requirements:* For master's, thesis (for some programs); for doctorate, comprehensive exam, thesis/dissertation. *Entrance requirements:* For master's, curriculum vitae, letters of recommendation, writing sample; for doctorate, personal statement, curriculum vitae, official transcripts, letters of recommendation, writing sample. Additional exam requirements/recommendations for international students: Required—TOEFL (minimum score 550 paper-based; 213 computer-based; 80 iBT). *Application deadline:* For fall admission, 8/15 priority date for domestic and international students; for spring admission, 1/15 for domestic students, 1/15 priority date for international students. Applications are processed on a rolling basis. Application fee: $0. Electronic applications accepted. *Expenses:* Tuition: Full-time $6816; part-time $426 per credit. Required fees: $6 per credit. One-time fee: $205. Tuition and fees vary according to degree level, campus/location and program. *Financial support:* In 2009–10, 14 students received support. Federal Work-Study and scholarships/grants available. Support available to part-time students. Financial award applicants required to submit FAFSA. *Faculty research:* Liberal arts based business programs, experiential learning, organizational process/politics, gender differences, social equity. *Unit head:* Dr. Julian Schuster, Dean, 651-523-2284, Fax: 651-523-3098, E-mail: jschuster01@hamline.edu. *Application contact:* Rae A. Lenway, Director, Graduate Recruitment and Admission, 651-523-2900, Fax: 651-523-3058, E-mail: rlenway@hamline.edu.

High Point University, Norcross Graduate School, High Point, NC 27262-3598. Offers business administration (MBA); educational leadership (M Ed); elementary education (M Ed); history (MA); nonprofit management (MA); special education (M Ed); sport studies (MS). *Accreditation:* ACBSP; NCATE. Part-time and evening/weekend programs available. *Degree requirements:* For master's, comprehensive exam (for some programs), thesis (for some programs). *Entrance requirements:* For master's, GMAT (MBA), GRE General Test, MAT, minimum GPA of 3.0. Additional exam requirements/recommendations for international students: Required—TOEFL (minimum score 550 paper-based). Electronic applications accepted.

Hope International University, School of Graduate and Professional Studies, Program in Business Administration, Fullerton, CA 92831-3138. Offers business administration (MBA); educational administration (MSM); international development (MBA, MSM); management (MBA); nonprofit management (MBA). Part-time programs available. Postbaccalaureate distance learning degree programs offered (no on-campus study). *Degree requirements:* For master's, comprehensive exam (for some programs), thesis (for some programs), project. *Entrance requirements:* For master's, minimum GPA of 3.0; 2 references. Additional exam requirements/recommendations for international students: Required—TOEFL (minimum score 550 paper-based; 213 computer-based; 86 iBT); Recommended—IELTS (minimum score 6.5). Electronic applications accepted. *Expenses:* Contact institution.

Husson University, School of Graduate and Professional Studies, Program in Business, Bangor, ME 04401-2999. Offers health care management (MSB); nonprofit management (MSB). Part-time and evening/weekend programs available. *Degree requirements:* For master's, thesis optional. *Entrance requirements:* For master's, GMAT, minimum GPA of 2.5.

Illinois Institute of Technology, Graduate College, College of Science and Letters, Department of Social Sciences, Chicago, IL 60616-3793. Offers nonprofit management (MPA); public administration (MPA); public safety and crisis management (MPA); JD/MPA; MBA/MPA. Part-time and evening/weekend programs available. *Faculty:* 10 full-time (2 women), 14 part-time/adjunct (2 women). *Students:* 69 full-time (31 women), 43 part-time (26 women); includes 15 minority (12 African Americans, 3 Hispanic Americans), 71 international. Average age 33. 160 applicants, 84% accepted, 66 enrolled. In 2009, 71 master's awarded. *Degree requirements:* For master's, comprehensive exam, capstone course (practicum). *Entrance requirements:* For master's, minimum undergraduate GPA of 3.0, 2 letters of recommendation. Additional exam requirements/recommendations for international students: Required—TOEFL (minimum score 523 paper-based; 70 iBT). *Application deadline:* For fall admission, 5/1 for domestic and international students; for spring admission, 10/15 for domestic and international students. Applications are processed on a rolling basis. Application fee: $50. Electronic applications accepted. *Expenses:* Tuition: Full-time $17,550; part-time $888 per credit hour. Required fees: $850; $7.50 per credit hour. One-time fee: $50 full-time. Full-time tuition and fees vary according to program. *Financial support:* Federal Work-Study, institutionally sponsored loans, scholarships/grants, and health care benefits available. Support available to part-time students. Financial award applicants required to submit FAFSA. *Faculty research:* Comparative public administration and policy, migration and ethnic politics, social dimension and impact of science and technology, urban politics, urban ethnography. *Unit head:* Dr. Patrick R. Ireland, Professor and Chairman, 312-567-5128, Fax: 312-567-6821, E-mail: socscience@iit.edu. *Application contact:* Lawerence Ruffolo, Assistant Director, Graduate Program in Public Administration, 312-906-5197, Fax: 312-906-5199, E-mail: lruffolo@kentlaw.edu.

Indiana University Bloomington, School of Public and Environmental Affairs, Public Affairs Programs, Bloomington, IN 47405-7000. Offers comparative and international affairs (MPA); economic development (MPA); environmental policy and natural resource management (MPA); information systems (MPA); local government management (MPA); nonprofit management (MPA); policy analysis (MPA); public affairs (PhD, Certificate); public financial administration (MPA); public management (MPA); sustainability and sustainable development (MPA); JD/MPA; MPA/MIS; MPA/MLS; MSES/MPA. *Accreditation:* NASPAA (one or more programs are accredited). Part-time programs available. *Faculty:* 75 full-time (22 women), 91 part-time/adjunct (24 women). *Students:* 389 full-time (222 women), 45 part-time (24 women); includes 38 minority (18 African Americans, 1 American Indian/Alaska Native, 12 Asian Americans or Pacific Islanders, 7 Hispanic Americans), 72 international. Average age 26. 474 applicants, 206 enrolled. In 2009, 190 master's, 11 doctorates, 3 other advanced degrees awarded. Terminal master's awarded for partial completion of doctoral program. *Degree requirements:* For master's, thesis optional; for doctorate, comprehensive exam, thesis/dissertation or alternative, A thesis is required for the Public Affairs and Public Policy degree. *Entrance requirements:* For master's, GRE, LSAT (if also applying for the Law School), 3 letters of recommendation, resume or curriculum vitae; for doctorate, GRE General Test. Additional exam requirements/recommendations for international students: Required—TOEFL (minimum score 590 paper-based; 243 computer-based; 96 iBT). *Application deadline:* For fall admission, 2/1 priority date for domestic students, 12/1 priority date for international students; for spring admission, 9/1 for international students. Application fee: $55 ($65 for international students). Electronic applications accepted. *Financial support:* Fellowships with full tuition reimbursements, research assistantships with partial tuition reimbursements, teaching assistantships with partial tuition reimbursements, career-related internships or fieldwork, Federal Work-Study, institutionally sponsored loans, unspecified assistantships, and Service Corps programs available. Financial award application deadline: 2/1; financial award applicants required to submit FAFSA. *Faculty research:* Comparative and international affairs, environmental policy and resource management, policy analysis, public finance, public management, urban management, nonprofit management. *Unit head:* Dean John Graham, Dean, School of Public and Environmental Affairs, 812-855-1432, E-mail: grahamjd@indiana.edu. *Application contact:* Jennifer Medlin, Assistant Director of Admissions and Financial Aid, 812-855-3784, Fax: 812-856-3665, E-mail: jlmedlin@indiana.edu.

Indiana University Northwest, School of Public and Environmental Affairs, Gary, IN 46408-1197. Offers criminal justice (MPA); environmental affairs (Graduate Certificate); health services administration (MPA); human services administration (MPA); nonprofit management (Graduate Certificate); public management (MPA, Graduate Certificate). *Accreditation:* NASPAA (one or more programs are accredited). Part-time programs available. *Faculty:* 5 full-time (3 women). *Students:* 19 full-time (14 women), 121 part-time (100 women); includes 100 minority (84 African Americans, 1 American Indian/Alaska Native, 1 Asian American or Pacific Islander, 14 Hispanic Americans). Average age 39. In 2009, 29 master's, 27 other advanced degrees awarded. *Entrance requirements:* For master's, GRE General Test or GMAT, letters of recommendation. *Application deadline:* For fall admission, 8/15 priority date for domestic students. Applications are processed on a rolling basis. Application fee: $25. *Financial support:* Career-related internships or fieldwork, Federal Work-Study, and tuition waivers (partial) available. Support available to part-time students. Financial award application deadline: 3/1. *Faculty research:* Employment in income security policies, evidence in criminal justice, equal employment law, social welfare policy and welfare reform, public finance in developing countries. *Unit head:* George Assibey-Mensah, Interim Dean/Division Director, 219-980-6695, Fax: 219-980-6737. *Application contact:* Sandra Hall Smith, Secretary, 219-980-6695, Fax: 219-980-6737, E-mail: shsmith@iun.edu.

Indiana University–Purdue University Indianapolis, School of Public and Environmental Affairs, Indianapolis, IN 46202-2896. Offers health administration (MHA); public affairs (MPA), including criminal justice, environmental management, nonprofit management, policy analysis, public management; JD/MHA; MBA/MHA; MLS/NMC; MLS/PMC; MSN/MHA. *Accreditation:* CAHME (one or more programs are accredited); NASPAA. Part-time and evening/weekend programs available. *Faculty:* 17 full-time (6 women). *Students:* 126 full-time (71 women), 283

part-time (164 women); includes 58 minority (29 African Americans, 1 American Indian/Alaska Native, 17 Asian Americans or Pacific Islanders, 11 Hispanic Americans), 20 international. Average age 33. 255 applicants, 77% accepted, 136 enrolled. In 2009, 77 master's awarded. *Entrance requirements:* For master's, GRE General Test, minimum GPA of 3.0 (preferred). Additional exam requirements/recommendations for international students: Required—TOEFL. *Application deadline:* For fall admission, 7/15 priority date for domestic students; for spring admission, 11/15 for domestic students. Applications are processed on a rolling basis. Application fee: $55 ($65 for international students). *Financial support:* In 2009–10, 11 fellowships with full and partial tuition reimbursements (averaging $5,890 per year), 10 teaching assistantships (averaging $9,900 per year) were awarded; research assistantships with full and partial tuition reimbursements, career-related internships or fieldwork, Federal Work-Study, institutionally sponsored loans, and scholarships/grants also available. Support available to part-time students. Financial award application deadline: 3/1. *Faculty research:* Economic development, water and air quality, ethics, financing, organization design and structure. Total annual research expenditures: $1.9 million. *Unit head:* Dr. Greg Lindsey, Associate Dean, 317-274-4656, Fax: 317-274-5153. *Application contact:* 317-274-4656, Fax: 317-274-5153, E-mail: speainfo@speanet.iupui.edu.

Indiana University South Bend, School of Public and Environmental Affairs, South Bend, IN 46634-7111. Offers health systems administration and policy (MPA); health systems management (Certificate); nonprofit management (Certificate); public and community services administration and policy (MPA); public management (Certificate); urban affairs (Certificate). *Accreditation:* NASPAA. Part-time and evening/weekend programs available. *Faculty:* 4 full-time (1 woman). *Students:* 18 part-time (13 women); includes 3 minority (2 African Americans, 1 Hispanic American). Average age 40. In 2009, 9 master's awarded. *Entrance requirements:* For master's, GRE General Test, minimum undergraduate GPA of 2.5. *Application deadline:* For fall admission, 7/1 priority date for domestic students; for spring admission, 11/1 for domestic students. Applications are processed on a rolling basis. Application fee: $46 ($58 for international students). *Financial support:* Fellowships, research assistantships, career-related internships or fieldwork, Federal Work-Study, and institutionally sponsored loans available. Support available to part-time students. Financial award application deadline: 3/1; financial award applicants required to submit FAFSA. *Unit head:* Leda M. Hall, Dean, 574-520-4803. *Application contact:* Leda M. Hall, Dean, 574-520-4803.

John Carroll University, Graduate School, Program in Nonprofit Administration, University Heights, OH 44118-4581. Offers MA. Part-time and evening/weekend programs available. *Degree requirements:* For master's, thesis optional. *Entrance requirements:* For master's, minimum GPA of 3.0, interview. Additional exam requirements/recommendations for international students: Required—TOEFL. Electronic applications accepted.

Kean University, College of Business and Public Administration, Program in Public Administration, Union, NJ 07083. Offers environmental management (MPA); health services administration (MPA); non-profit management (MPA); public administration (MPA). *Accreditation:* NASPAA. Part-time and evening/weekend programs available. *Faculty:* 8 full-time (4 women). *Students:* 48 full-time (33 women), 92 part-time (53 women); includes 85 minority (62 African Americans, 9 Asian Americans or Pacific Islanders, 14 Hispanic Americans), 9 international. Average age 31. 80 applicants, 74% accepted, 34 enrolled. In 2009, 49 master's awarded. *Degree requirements:* For master's, thesis, internship, research seminar. *Entrance requirements:* For master's, minimum GPA of 3.0, 2 letters of recommendation, interview. *Application deadline:* For fall admission, 5/1 for domestic students; for spring admission, 11/1 for domestic students. Application fee: $60 ($150 for international students). Electronic applications accepted. *Expenses:* Tuition, state resident: full-time $10,440; part-time $435 per credit. Tuition, nonresident: full-time $14,160; part-time $590 per credit. Required fees: $2642; $110 per credit. Part-time tuition and fees vary according to course load and degree level. *Financial support:* In 2009–10, 10 research assistantships with full tuition reimbursements (averaging $3,263 per year) were awarded; unspecified assistantships also available. *Unit head:* Dr. Patricia Moore, Program Coordinator, 908-737-4300, E-mail: pmoore@kean.edu. *Application contact:* Steven Koch, Pre-Admissions Coordinator, 908-737-5924, Fax: 908-737-5965, E-mail: skoch@kean.edu.

Kentucky State University, College of Professional Studies, Frankfort, KY 40601. Offers business administration (MBA), including accounting, finance, management, marketing; public administration (MPA), including human resource management, international administration and development, management information systems, nonprofit management; special education (MA). Part-time and evening/weekend programs available. Postbaccalaureate distance learning degree programs offered (minimal on-campus study). *Faculty:* 11 full-time (3 women), 2 part-time/adjunct (both women). *Students:* 79 full-time (51 women), 66 part-time (34 women); includes 88 minority (85 African Americans, 2 Asian Americans or Pacific Islanders, 1 Hispanic American), 4 international. Average age 34. 92 applicants, 75% accepted, 52 enrolled. In 2009, 32 master's awarded. *Degree requirements:* For master's, comprehensive exam, thesis optional. *Entrance requirements:* For master's, GMAT, GRE. Additional exam requirements/recommendations for international students: Required—TOEFL (minimum score 525 paper-based; 173 computer-based). *Application deadline:* For fall admission, 7/1 priority date for domestic students, 4/15 priority date for international students; for spring admission, 11/15 priority date for domestic students, 8/1 priority date for international students. Applications are processed on a rolling basis. Application fee: $30 ($100 for international students). Electronic applications accepted. *Expenses:* Tuition, state resident: full-time $5634; part-time $313 per credit hour. Tuition, nonresident: full-time $14,598; part-time $811 per credit hour. Required fees: $450; $25 per credit hour. *Financial support:* In 2009–10, 113 students received support, including 4 research assistantships (averaging $14,035 per year); career-related internships or fieldwork, scholarships/grants, tuition waivers (partial), and unspecified assistantships also available. Financial award application deadline: 4/15; financial award applicants required to submit FAFSA. *Unit head:* Dr. Gashaw Lake, Dean, College of Professional Studies, 502-597-6105, Fax: 502-597-6715, E-mail: gashaw.lake@kysu.edu. *Application contact:* Cedric Cunningham, Administrative Assistant, Office of Graduate Studies, 502-597-6536, E-mail: cedric.cunningham@kysu.edu.

Lasell College, Graduate and Professional Studies in Management, Newton, MA 02466-2709. Offers elder care administration (MSM, Graduate Certificate); elder care marketing (MSM, Graduate Certificate); fundraising management (MSM, Graduate Certificate); human resource management (MSM, Graduate Certificate); management (MSM, Graduate Certificate); marketing (MSM, Graduate Certificate); non-profit management (MSM, Graduate Certificate); project management (MSM, Graduate Certificate). Part-time and evening/weekend programs available. Postbaccalaureate distance learning degree programs offered (no on-campus study). *Faculty:* 2 full-time (both women), 8 part-time/adjunct (6 women). *Students:* 26 full-time (18 women), 85 part-time (60 women); includes 10 African Americans, 4 Asian Americans or Pacific Islanders, 9 Hispanic Americans, 17 international. Average age 31. 55 applicants, 80% accepted, 31 enrolled. In 2009, 31 master's awarded. *Entrance requirements:* For master's and Graduate Certificate, bachelor's degree from an accredited institution. Additional exam requirements/recommendations for international students: Required—TOEFL (minimum score 550 paper-based; 213 computer-based; 75 iBT) or IELTS. *Application deadline:* For fall admission, 8/31 priority date for domestic students, 6/30 priority date for international students; for spring admission, 12/31 priority date for domestic students, 10/31 priority date for international students. Applications are processed on a rolling basis. Application fee: $40. Electronic applications accepted. *Expenses:* Tuition: Full-time $4890; part-time $525 per credit hour. Required fees: $55 per term. *Financial support:* Available to part-time students. Application deadline: 8/31. *Unit head:* Dr. Joan Dolamore, Dean of Graduate and Professional Studies, 617-243-2485, Fax: 617-243-2450, E-mail: gradinfo@lasell.edu. *Application contact:* Adrienne Franciosi, Director of Graduate Admission, 617-243-2214, Fax: 617-243-2450, E-mail: gradinfo@lasell.edu.

Lasell College, Graduate and Professional Studies in Sport Management, Newton, MA 02466-2709. Offers sport hospitality management (MS, Graduate Certificate); sport leadership (MS, Graduate Certificate); sport non-profit management (MS, Graduate Certificate). Part-time programs available. Postbaccalaureate distance learning degree programs offered (no on-campus study). *Entrance requirements:* For master's and Graduate Certificate, bachelor's degree from an accredited institution. Additional exam requirements/recommendations for international students: Required—TOEFL (minimum score 550 paper-based; 213 computer-based; 75 iBT) or IELTS. *Application deadline:* For fall admission, 8/31 priority date for domestic students, 6/30 priority date for international students; for spring admission, 12/31 priority date for domestic students, 10/31 priority date for international students. Applications are processed on a rolling basis. Electronic applications accepted. *Expenses:* Tuition: Full-time $4890; part-time $525 per credit hour. Required fees: $55 per term. *Financial support:* Available to part-time students. Application deadline: 8/31. *Unit head:* Dr. Joan Dolamore, Dean of Graduate and Professional Studies, 617-243-2485, Fax: 617-243-2450, E-mail: gradinfo@lasell.edu. *Application contact:* Adrienne Franciosi, Director of Graduate Admission, 617-243-2214, Fax: 617-243-2450, E-mail: gradinfo@lasell.edu.

Lipscomb University, MBA Program, Nashville, TN 37204-3951. Offers accounting (MBA); business administration (general) (MBA); conflict management (MBA); financial services (MBA); healthcare management (MBA); leadership (MBA); nonprofit management (MBA); sports administration (MBA); sustainable practice (MBA). *Accreditation:* ACBSP. Part-time and evening/weekend programs available. *Faculty:* 10 full-time (1 woman), 7 part-time/adjunct (2 women). *Students:* 43 full-time (23 women), 86 part-time (38 women); includes 23 minority (18 African Americans, 1 Asian American or Pacific Islander, 4 Hispanic Americans), 1 international. Average age 31. 95 applicants, 64% accepted, 35 enrolled. In 2009, 59 master's awarded. *Entrance requirements:* For master's, GMAT, interview, 2 references, resume. Additional exam requirements/recommendations for international students: Required—TOEFL (minimum score 570 paper-based; 230 computer-based). *Application deadline:* For fall admission, 2/1 for international students; for winter admission, 6/1 for international students. Applications are processed on a rolling basis. Application fee: $50 ($75 for international students). Electronic applications accepted. *Expenses:* Contact institution. *Financial support:* Career-related internships or fieldwork, Federal Work-Study, scholarships/grants, tuition waivers (partial), and unspecified assistantships available. Support available to part-time students. Financial award application deadline: 7/1; financial award applicants required to submit FAFSA. *Faculty research:* Impact of spirituality on organization commitment, leadership, psychological empowerment, training. *Unit head:* Dr. Mike Kendrick, Interim Chair of Graduate Business Studies, 615-966-1833, Fax: 615-966-1818, E-mail: mikekendrick@lipscomb.edu. *Application contact:* Emily Landsdell, 615-966-5284, E-mail: emily.lansdell@lipscomb.edu.

Long Island University, C.W. Post Campus, College of Management, Department of Health Care and Public Administration, Brookville, NY 11548-1300. Offers gerontology (Certificate); health care administration (MPA); health care administration/gerontology (MPA); nonprofit management (MPA, Certificate); public administration (MPA). *Accreditation:* NASPAA (one or more programs are accredited). Part-time and evening/weekend programs available. *Degree requirements:* For master's, thesis. *Entrance requirements:* For master's, GMAT, minimum GPA of 2.5; for Certificate, minimum GPA of 2.5. Electronic applications accepted. *Faculty research:* Critical issues in sexuality, social work in religious communities, gerontological social work.

Marylhurst University, Department of Business Administration, Marylhurst, OR 97036-0261. Offers finance (MBA); general management (MBA); government policy and administration (MBA); green development (MBA); health care management (MBA); marketing (MBA); natural and organic resources (MBA); nonprofit management (MBA); organizational behavior (MBA); real estate (MBA); renewable energy (MBA); sustainable business (MBA). Part-time and evening/weekend programs available. Postbaccalaureate distance learning degree programs offered (no on-campus study). *Faculty:* 2 full-time (1 woman), 28 part-time/adjunct (5 women). *Students:* 30 full-time (12 women), 627 part-time (323 women); includes 79 minority (28 African Americans, 3 American Indian/Alaska Native, 17 Asian Americans or Pacific Islanders, 31 Hispanic Americans), 9 international. Average age 37. 299 applicants, 80% accepted, 209 enrolled. In 2009, 193 master's awarded. *Degree requirements:* For master's, comprehensive exam, capstone course. *Entrance requirements:* For master's, GMAT (if GPA less than 3.0 and fewer than 5 years of work experience), interview, resume, 2 letters of recommendation. Additional exam requirements/recommendations for international students: Recommended—TOEFL (minimum score 550 paper-based; 213 computer-based; 80 iBT). *Application deadline:* For fall admission, 9/11 priority date for domestic and international students; for winter admission, 12/15 priority date for domestic and international students; for spring admission, 3/17 priority date for domestic and international students. Applications are processed on a rolling basis. Application fee: $40 ($50 for international students). Electronic applications accepted. *Financial support:* Scholarships/grants available. Support available to part-time students. Financial award applicants required to submit FAFSA. *Unit head:* Bob Hanks, Director of Business and Real Estate Programs, 503-636-8141, Fax: 503-697-5597, E-mail: mba@marylhurst.edu. *Application contact:* Kathleen Schneff, Admissions Specialist, 800-634-9982 Ext. 3322, Fax: 503-635-6585, E-mail: admissions@marylhurst.edu.

Marywood University, Academic Affairs, College of Health and Human Services, Department of Nursing and Public Administration, Program in Public Administration, Scranton, PA 18509-1598. Offers nonprofit management (MPA). *Students:* 3 full-time (0 women), 13 part-time (9 women). Average age 30. In 2009, 9 master's awarded. *Entrance requirements:* Additional exam requirements/recommendations for international students: Required—TOEFL (minimum score 550 paper-based; 213 computer-based; 79 iBT). *Application deadline:* For fall admission, 4/1 priority date for domestic students, 3/31 priority date for international students; for spring admission, 11/1 priority date for domestic students, 8/31 priority date for international students. Applications are processed on a rolling basis. Application fee: $35. Electronic applications accepted. *Expenses:* Tuition: Part-time $715 per credit. Required fees: $270 per semester. Tuition and fees vary according to degree level, campus/location and program. *Financial support:* Career-related internships or fieldwork, scholarships/grants, and unspecified assistantships available. Support available to part-time students. Financial award application deadline: 6/30; financial award applicants required to submit FAFSA. *Unit head:* Dr. Katrina Maurer, Co-Chairperson, 570-348-6275, E-mail: maurer@marywood.edu. *Application contact:* Tammy Manka, Assistant Director of Graduate Admissions, 866-279-9663, E-mail: tmanka@marywood.edu.

Metropolitan State University, College of Management, St. Paul, MN 55106-5000. Offers business administration (MBA); information assurance security (Graduate Certificate); information management (MMIS); MIS generalist (Graduate Certificate); MIS systems analysis and design (Graduate Certificate); nonprofit management (MPNA); project management (Graduate Certificate); public administration (MPNA); systems management (MMIS). Part-time and evening/weekend programs available. *Degree requirements:* For master's, thesis optional, computer language (MMIS). *Entrance requirements:* For master's, GMAT (MBA), resume. Additional exam requirements/recommendations for international students: Required—TOEFL (minimum score 550 paper-based; 213 computer-based). *Expenses:* Tuition, state resident: full-time $5520; part-time $276 per credit hour. Tuition, nonresident: full-time $11,040; part-time $552 per credit hour. Required fees: $209; $10 per credit hour. Tuition and fees vary according to degree level. *Faculty research:* Yugoslav economic system, workers' cooperatives, participative management and job enrichment, global business systems.

MidAmerica Nazarene University, Graduate Studies in Management, Olathe, KS 66062-1899. Offers management (MBA); organizational administration (MA), including finance, international business, leadership, non-profit. Evening/weekend programs available. *Faculty:* 6 full-time (2 women), 18 part-time/adjunct (7 women). *Students:* 107 full-time (49 women), 7 part-time (3 women); includes 25 minority (18 African Americans, 1 Asian American or Pacific Islander, 6 Hispanic Americans). Average age 36. In 2009, 81 master's awarded. *Entrance requirements:* For master's, mathematical assessment, minimum undergraduate GPA of 3.0, letters of recommendation. Additional exam requirements/recommendations for international students: Required—TOEFL. *Application deadline:* For fall admission, 9/1 priority date for domestic students; for spring admission, 5/1 priority date for domestic students. Applications are processed on a rolling basis. Application fee: $100. Electronic applications accepted. *Financial support:* Application deadline: 5/1. *Faculty research:* Economic development, inter-

Nonprofit Management

MidAmerica Nazarene University (continued)
national finance, business development, employee evaluation. *Unit head:* Dr. Willadee Wehmeyer, Director, 913-971-3276, Fax: 913-791-3409, E-mail: wwehmeye@mnu.edu. *Application contact:* Melanie Sutherland, Administrative Assistant, 913-971-3276, Fax: 913-971-3409, E-mail: mba@mnu.edu.

New England College, Program in Management, Henniker, NH 03242-3293. Offers accounting (MSA); healthcare administration (MS); international relations (MA); marketing management (MS); nonprofit leadership (MS); project management (MS); strategic leadership (MS). Part-time and evening/weekend programs available. *Degree requirements:* For master's, independent research project. Electronic applications accepted.

New Mexico Highlands University, Graduate Studies, School of Business, Las Vegas, NM 87701. Offers business administration (MBA), including government nonprofit management, human resource management, international business, management, management information systems. *Accreditation:* ACBSP. *Degree requirements:* For master's, comprehensive exam, thesis or alternative. *Entrance requirements:* For master's, minimum undergraduate GPA of 3.0. Additional exam requirements/recommendations for international students: Required—TOEFL (minimum score 540 paper-based; 207 computer-based). *Faculty research:* Real estate valuation, studying expert judgments in complex accounting, decision environments, green marketing, environmentalism, marketing research methodology.

New Mexico Highlands University, Graduate Studies, School of Social Work, Las Vegas, NM 87701. Offers bilingual/bicultural social work practice (MSW); clinical practice (MSW); government non-profit management (MSW). *Accreditation:* CSWE. Part-time programs available. *Degree requirements:* For master's, comprehensive exam, thesis or alternative. *Entrance requirements:* For master's, minimum undergraduate GPA of 3.0. Additional exam requirements/recommendations for international students: Required—TOEFL (minimum score 540 paper-based; 207 computer-based). *Faculty research:* Treatment attrition among domestic violence batterers, children's health and mental health, Dejando Huellas: meeting the bilingual/bicultural needs of the Latino mental health patient, impact of culture on the therapeutic process, effects of generational gang involvement on adolescents' future.

The New School: A University, Milano The New School for Management and Urban Policy, Program in Nonprofit Management, New York, NY 10011. Offers MS. Part-time and evening/weekend programs available. *Faculty:* 9 full-time (3 women). *Students:* 85 full-time (71 women), 80 part-time (62 women); includes 41 minority (14 African Americans, 6 Asian Americans or Pacific Islanders, 21 Hispanic Americans), 11 international. Average age 29. 146 applicants, 84% accepted, 48 enrolled. In 2009, 49 master's awarded. *Degree requirements:* For master's, thesis. *Entrance requirements:* For master's, interview. Additional exam requirements/recommendations for international students: Required—TOEFL (minimum score 600 paper-based; 250 computer-based; 100 iBT). *Application deadline:* For fall admission, 3/1 priority date for domestic and international students; for spring admission, 10/1 priority date for domestic and international students. Applications are processed on a rolling basis. Application fee: $50. Electronic applications accepted. *Financial support:* Fellowships, Federal Work-Study, scholarships/grants, and tuition waivers (full and partial) available. Support available to part-time students. Financial award application deadline: 3/1; financial award applicants required to submit FAFSA. *Faculty research:* Management of nonprofit organizations, fundraising in minority nonprofit organizations. *Unit head:* Dr. Mary Watson, Chair, 212-229-5400 Ext. 1613, Fax: 212-229-5335, E-mail: watsonm@newschool.edu. *Application contact:* Merida Escandon, Director of Admissions, 212-229-5462 Ext. 1108, Fax: 212-229-5354, E-mail: milanoadmissions@newschool.edu.

New York University, Robert F. Wagner Graduate School of Public Service, Program in Public Administration, New York, NY 10012-1019. Offers public administration (PhD); public and nonprofit management and policy (MPA, Advanced Certificate), including developmental administration (Advanced Certificate), financial management and public finance, human resources management (Advanced Certificate), international administration (Advanced Certificate), management (MPA), management for public and nonprofit organizations (Advanced Certificate), public policy analysis, quantitative analysis and computer applications (Advanced Certificate), urban public policy (Advanced Certificate); JD/MPA; MBA/MPA; MPA/MA. *Accreditation:* NASPAA (one or more programs are accredited). Part-time and evening/weekend programs available. *Faculty:* 31 full-time (13 women), 33 part-time/adjunct (16 women). *Students:* 363 full-time (270 women), 228 part-time (171 women); includes 146 minority (46 African Americans, 64 Asian Americans or Pacific Islanders, 36 Hispanic Americans), 76 international. Average age 28. 1,117 applicants, 57% accepted, 225 enrolled. In 2009, 236 master's, 3 doctorates awarded. *Degree requirements:* For master's, thesis or alternative, capstone end event; for doctorate, one foreign language, thesis/dissertation. *Entrance requirements:* For master's, minimum undergraduate GPA of 3.0; for doctorate, GMAT or GRE General Test, minimum GPA of 3.5. Additional exam requirements/recommendations for international students: Required—TOEFL (minimum score 600 paper-based; 250 computer-based; 100 iBT), TWE (minimum score 4). *Application deadline:* For fall admission, 6/1 for domestic students, 1/15 for international students; for spring admission, 11/15 for domestic students, 10/1 for international students. Applications are processed on a rolling basis. Application fee: $80. Electronic applications accepted. *Expenses:* Contact institution. *Financial support:* In 2009–10, 155 students received support, including 150 fellowships (averaging $11,335 per year), 5 research assistantships with full tuition reimbursements available (averaging $22,440 per year); career-related internships or fieldwork, Federal Work-Study, institutionally sponsored loans, scholarships/grants, health care benefits, and unspecified assistantships also available. Support available to part-time students. Financial award application deadline: 12/1; financial award applicants required to submit FAFSA. *Unit head:* Katty Jones, Director, Program Services, 212-998-7411, Fax: 212-995-4164, E-mail: katty.jones@nyu.edu. *Application contact:* Christopher Alexander, Administrative Aide, Enrollment, 212-998-7414, Fax: 212-995-4611, E-mail: wagner.admissions@nyu.edu.

New York University, School of Continuing and Professional Studies, The George Heyman Jr. Center for Philanthropy and Fundraising, New York, NY 10012-1019. Offers fundraising (MS). Part-time and evening/weekend programs available. *Faculty:* 10 part-time/adjunct (6 women). *Students:* 11 full-time (10 women), 29 part-time (23 women); includes 6 minority (1 African American, 3 Asian Americans or Pacific Islanders, 2 Hispanic Americans). Average age 33. 22 applicants, 86% accepted, 13 enrolled. In 2009, 14 master's awarded. *Degree requirements:* For master's, capstone project. *Entrance requirements:* For master's, GRE General Test or GMAT (for recent graduates), 2 letters of recommendation, resume. Additional exam requirements/recommendations for international students: Required—TOEFL (minimum score 600 paper-based; 250 computer-based; 100 iBT), TWE. *Application deadline:* For fall admission, 2/1 priority date for domestic and international students; for spring admission, 10/15 priority date for domestic students, 8/15 priority date for international students. Applications are processed on a rolling basis. Application fee: $75. Electronic applications accepted. *Expenses:* Tuition: Full-time $30,528; part-time $1272 per credit. Required fees: $2177. *Financial support:* In 2009–10, 17 students received support, including 17 fellowships (averaging $2,482 per year); scholarships/grants also available. Financial award application deadline: 3/1; financial award applicants required to submit FAFSA. *Unit head:* Director. *Application contact:* Mayelly Moreno, 212-998-6777, Fax: 212-995-4784, E-mail: mm172@nyu.edu.

North Carolina State University, Graduate School, College of Humanities and Social Sciences, School of Public and International Affairs, Raleigh, NC 27695. Offers international studies (MIS); nonprofit management (Certificate); public administration (MPA, PhD). *Accreditation:* NASPAA (one or more programs are accredited). Part-time and evening/weekend programs available. *Entrance requirements:* For master's, GRE General Test, minimum GPA of 3.0 during previous 2 years. Electronic applications accepted. *Faculty research:* Public sector leadership and ethics, financial management, management systems evaluation, computer applications, service delivery.

North Central College, Graduate Programs, Department of Leadership Studies, Naperville, IL 60566-7063. Offers MLD. Part-time and evening/weekend programs available. *Degree requirements:* For master's, project. *Entrance requirements:* For master's, interview. *Expenses:* Contact institution.

Northern Kentucky University, Office of Graduate Programs, College of Arts and Sciences, Program in Public Administration, Highland Heights, KY 41099. Offers non-profit management (Certificate); public administration (MPA). *Accreditation:* NASPAA. Part-time and evening/weekend programs available. *Students:* 6 full-time (2 women), 87 part-time (46 women); includes 12 minority (9 African Americans, 3 Hispanic Americans), 1 international. Average age 35. 54 applicants, 67% accepted, 28 enrolled. In 2009, 21 master's, 10 other advanced degrees awarded. *Degree requirements:* For master's, capstone. *Entrance requirements:* For master's, GRE, GMAT or MAT, 2 letters of recommendation, writing sample, minimum GPA of 2.75, 2 supportive letters, resume, portfolio demonstrating professional activities. Additional exam requirements/recommendations for international students: Required—TOEFL (minimum score 550 paper-based; 213 computer-based; 79 iBT); Recommended—IELTS (minimum score 6.5). *Application deadline:* For fall admission, 7/1 priority date for domestic students, 6/1 for international students; for spring admission, 12/1 priority date for domestic students, 10/1 for international students. Applications are processed on a rolling basis. Application fee: $40. Electronic applications accepted. *Expenses:* Tuition, state resident: full-time $6912; part-time $384 per credit hour. Tuition, nonresident: full-time $12,150; part-time $675 per credit hour. Tuition and fees vary according to course load, program and reciprocity agreements. *Financial support:* Unspecified assistantships available. Financial award applicants required to submit FAFSA. *Faculty research:* Non-profit management, human resource management, local government, budgeting and finance, urban planning. *Unit head:* Dr. Shamima Ahmed, Director, 859-572-6402, Fax: 859-572-6184, E-mail: ahmed@nku.edu. *Application contact:* Beth Devantier, MPA Coordinator, 859-572-5326, Fax: 859-572-6184, E-mail: devantier@nku.edu.

Oklahoma City University, Petree College of Arts and Sciences, Division of Sociology and Justice Studies, Oklahoma City, OK 73106-1402. Offers applied sociology (MA), including nonprofit leadership; criminal justice (MCJ). Part-time and evening/weekend programs available. *Faculty:* 4 full-time (1 woman), 3 part-time/adjunct (2 women). *Students:* 11 full-time (8 women), 4 part-time (3 women); includes 3 minority (all African Americans), 1 international. Average age 31. 9 applicants, 89% accepted. In 2009, 7 master's awarded. *Degree requirements:* For master's, thesis optional. *Entrance requirements:* For master's, minimum GPA of 3.0, two letters of recommendation. Additional exam requirements/recommendations for international students: Required—TOEFL (minimum score 550 paper-based). *Application deadline:* For fall admission, 8/22 for domestic students; for spring admission, 1/15 for domestic students. Applications are processed on a rolling basis. Application fee: $30 ($70 for international students). *Expenses:* Contact institution. *Financial support:* Fellowships with partial tuition reimbursements, career-related internships or fieldwork available. Financial award application deadline: 8/1; financial award applicants required to submit FAFSA. *Faculty research:* Victims, police, corrections, security, women and crime. *Unit head:* Dr. Jody Horn, Director, 405-208-5247, Fax: 405-208-5447, E-mail: jhorn@okcu.edu. *Application contact:* Michelle Lockhart, Director, Admissions, 800-633-7242, Fax: 405-208-5916, E-mail: gadmissions@okcu.edu.

Oral Roberts University, School of Business, Tulsa, OK 74171. Offers accounting (MBA); entrepreneurship (MBA); finance (MBA); international business (MBA); management (MBA); marketing (MBA); non-profit management (MBA); not for profit management (MNM). *Accreditation:* ACBSP. Part-time programs available. Postbaccalaureate distance learning degree programs offered (minimal on-campus study). *Faculty:* 7 full-time (0 women), 5 part-time/adjunct (4 women). *Students:* 68 full-time (30 women), 55 part-time (27 women); includes 54 minority (32 African Americans, 5 American Indian/Alaska Native, 8 Asian Americans or Pacific Islanders, 9 Hispanic Americans), 3 international. Average age 28. 71 applicants, 94% accepted, 56 enrolled. In 2009, 36 master's awarded. *Degree requirements:* For master's, thesis optional. *Entrance requirements:* For master's, minimum cumulative GPA of 3.0. Additional exam requirements/recommendations for international students: Required—TOEFL (minimum score 550 paper-based; 213 computer-based; 79 iBT). *Application deadline:* For fall admission, 7/1 priority date for domestic and international students; for spring admission, 12/1 priority date for domestic students, 10/15 priority date for international students. Applications are processed on a rolling basis. Application fee: $35. Electronic applications accepted. *Financial support:* In 2009–10, 39 students received support. Federal Work-Study, scholarships/grants, and unspecified assistantships available. Financial award application deadline: 6/1; financial award applicants required to submit FAFSA. *Faculty research:* Social media, international business and marketing. *Unit head:* Dr. Steven Greene, Dean, 918-495-7040, Fax: 918-495-7876, E-mail: businessdean@oru.edu. *Application contact:* Rebecca Gunn, Representative/Recruiter, 918-495-6117, Fax: 918-495-6500, E-mail: gradbusiness@oru.edu.

Our Lady of the Lake University of San Antonio, School of Business and Leadership, Program in Nonprofit Management, San Antonio, TX 78207-4689. Offers MS. Part-time and evening/weekend programs available. Postbaccalaureate distance learning degree programs offered. *Students:* 28 part-time (22 women); includes 14 minority (2 African Americans, 12 Hispanic Americans). Average age 33. *Expenses:* Tuition: Full-time $12,330; part-time $685 per contact hour. Required fees: $139; $12 per contact hour. $57 per semester. Tuition and fees vary according to campus/location. *Unit head:* Dr. Robert Bisking, Dean, 210-434-6711, Fax: 210-434-0821. *Application contact:* Dr. Robert Bisking, Dean, 210-434-6711, Fax: 210-434-0821.

Pace University, Dyson College of Arts and Sciences, Department of Public Administration, New York, NY 10038. Offers environmental management (MPA); government management (MPA); health care administration (MPA); management for public safety and homeland security (MA); nonprofit management (MPA); JD/MPA. Offered at White Plains, NY location only. Part-time and evening/weekend programs available. *Faculty:* 4 full-time, 6 part-time/adjunct. *Students:* 52 full-time (31 women), 75 part-time (49 women); includes 47 minority (28 African Americans, 1 American Indian/Alaska Native, 1 Asian American or Pacific Islander, 17 Hispanic Americans), 8 international. Average age 30. 75 applicants, 100% accepted, 43 enrolled. In 2009, 38 master's awarded. *Degree requirements:* For master's, capstone project. *Entrance requirements:* For master's, GRE General Test. Additional exam requirements/recommendations for international students: Required—TOEFL. *Application deadline:* For fall admission, 8/1 priority date for domestic students; for spring admission, 12/1 priority date for domestic students. Applications are processed on a rolling basis. Application fee: $70. Electronic applications accepted. *Expenses:* Tuition: Part-time $954 per credit. Tuition and fees vary according to course load, degree level and program. *Financial support:* Research assistantships, career-related internships or fieldwork, Federal Work-Study, and tuition waivers (partial) available. Support available to part-time students. Financial award applicants required to submit FAFSA. *Unit head:* Dr. Farrokh Hormozi, Chairperson, 914-422-4285, E-mail: fhormozi@pace.edu. *Application contact:* Joanna Broda, Director of Admissions, 914-422-4283, Fax: 914-422-4287, E-mail: gradwp@pace.edu.

Park University, College of Graduate and Professional Studies, Kansas City, MO 54105. Offers adult education (M Ed); at-risk students (M Ed); disaster and emergency management (MPA); educational administration (M Ed); entrepreneurship (MBA); general business (MBA); general education (M Ed); government/business relations (MPA); healthcare/services management (MBA, MPA); international business (MBA); K-12 certification (MAT); management information systems (MBA); management of information systems (MPA); middle school certification (MAT); multi-cultural education (M Ed); nonprofit management (MPA); public management (MPA); school law (M Ed); secondary school certification (MAT); special education (M Ed). Part-time and evening/weekend programs available. Postbaccalaureate distance learning degree programs offered (no on-campus study). *Degree requirements:* For master's, comprehensive exam, thesis (for some programs). *Entrance requirements:* For master's, GRE, GMAT, teacher certification (M Ed). Additional exam requirements/recommendations for international students: Required—TOEFL (minimum score 550 paper-based). Electronic applications accepted. *Faculty research:* Literacy, leadership, brain based research, multicultural education, diversity.

Nonprofit Management

Providence College, Graduate Studies, School of Business, Providence, RI 02918. Offers accountancy (MBA); economics (MBA); entrepreneurship (MBA); finance (MBA); international business (MBA); management (MBA); marketing (MBA); not-for-profit (MBA); quantitative (MBA). Part-time and evening/weekend programs available. *Faculty:* 14 full-time (8 women), 7 part-time/adjunct (3 women). *Students:* 63 full-time (18 women), 46 part-time (19 women); includes 4 minority (2 African Americans, 2 Asian Americans or Pacific Islanders), 7 international. Average age 26. 43 applicants, 88% accepted. In 2009, 40 master's awarded. *Degree requirements:* For master's, thesis optional. *Entrance requirements:* For master's, GMAT. Additional exam requirements/recommendations for international students: Required—TOEFL (minimum score 550 paper-based; 213 computer-based; 80 iBT). *Application deadline:* For fall admission, 8/1 priority date for domestic and international students; for spring admission, 12/1 priority date for domestic and international students. Applications are processed on a rolling basis. Application fee: $55. *Expenses:* Contact institution. *Financial support:* In 2009–10, 34 research assistantships with full tuition reimbursements (averaging $8,400 per year) were awarded; Federal Work-Study, institutionally sponsored loans, and unspecified assistantships also available. Support available to part-time students. Financial award application deadline: 8/1; financial award applicants required to submit FAFSA. *Unit head:* Dr. MaryJane Lenon, Director, MBA Program, 401-865-2566, Fax: 401-865-2978, E-mail: mjlenon@providence.edu. *Application contact:* Katherine A. Follett, Administrative Coordinator, 401-865-2333, Fax: 401-865-2978, E-mail: kfollett@providence.edu.

Regis University, College for Professional Studies, Program in Nonprofit Management, Denver, CO 80221-1099. Offers leadership (Certificate); nonprofit management (MNM); program management (Certificate); resource development (Certificate). Offered at Northwest Denver Campus and Southeast Denver Campus. Part-time and evening/weekend programs available. Postbaccalaureate distance learning degree programs offered (no on-campus study). *Degree requirements:* For master's and Certificate, thesis optional, final research project. *Entrance requirements:* For master's, 2 years of significant paid or volunteer experience in a nonprofit organization or 400-hour practicum in nonprofit sector, resume, interview; for Certificate, 2 years of significant paid or volunteer experience in a nonprofit organization or 400-hour practicum in nonprofit sector; resumé. Additional exam requirements/recommendations for international students: Required—TOEFL (minimum score 213 computer-based), TWE (minimum score 5), TOEFL or university-based test. *Expenses:* Contact institution. *Faculty research:* International nonprofits, enterprise, grass roots nonprofits, leadership in non profit organizations.

Robert Morris University, Graduate Studies, School of Business, Moon Township, PA 15108-1189. Offers business administration and management (MBA); human resource management (MS); nonprofit management (MS); taxation (MS). *Accreditation:* AACSB. Part-time and evening/weekend programs available. *Faculty:* 29 full-time (11 women), 3 part-time/adjunct (0 women). *Students:* 209 part-time (97 women); includes 11 minority (9 African Americans, 1 Asian American or Pacific Islander, 1 Hispanic American), 4 international. Average age 31. 126 applicants, 70% accepted, 54 enrolled. In 2009, 85 master's awarded. *Entrance requirements:* For master's, GMAT, letters of recommendation. Additional exam requirements/recommendations for international students: Required—TOEFL (minimum score 550 paper-based; 213 computer-based; 79 iBT). *Application deadline:* For fall admission, 7/1 priority date for domestic and international students; for spring admission, 11/1 priority date for domestic and international students. Applications are processed on a rolling basis. Application fee: $35. Electronic applications accepted. *Expenses:* Tuition: Part-time $765 per credit. Required fees: $15 per credit. Full-time tuition and fees vary according to degree level. Part-time tuition and fees vary according to program. *Financial support:* Research assistantships with partial tuition reimbursements, Federal Work-Study, institutionally sponsored loans, and unspecified assistantships available. Support available to part-time students. Financial award application deadline: 5/1; financial award applicants required to submit FAFSA. *Unit head:* Dr. Derya A. Jacobs, Dean, 412-397-2191, Fax: 412-397-2585, E-mail: jacobs@rmu.edu. *Application contact:* Deborah Roach, Assistant Dean, Graduate Admissions, 412-397-5200, Fax: 412-397-2425, E-mail: graduateadmissions@rmu.edu.

Roberts Wesleyan College, Division of Business, Rochester, NY 14624-1997. Offers nonprofit leadership (Certificate); strategic leadership (MS); strategic marketing (MS). Evening/weekend programs available. *Degree requirements:* For master's, thesis or alternative. *Entrance requirements:* For master's, GMAT, minimum GPA of 2.75, verifiable work experience. *Expenses:* Contact institution.

St. Cloud State University, School of Graduate Studies, College of Social Sciences, Department of Economics, Program in Public and Nonprofit Institutions, St. Cloud, MN 56301-4498. Offers MS. Part-time programs available. *Faculty:* 20 full-time (5 women), 1 part-time/adjunct (0 women). *Students:* 4 full-time (2 women), 6 part-time (all women); includes 2 minority (both African Americans), 3 international. 6 applicants, 100% accepted. In 2009, 3 master's awarded. *Degree requirements:* For master's, thesis or alternative. *Entrance requirements:* For master's, GRE General Test, minimum GPA of 2.75. Additional exam requirements/recommendations for international students: Required—Michigan English Language Assessment Battery; Recommended—TOEFL (minimum score 550 paper-based; 213 computer-based), IELTS (minimum score 6.5). *Application deadline:* For fall admission, 6/1 priority date for domestic students, 6/1 for international students; for spring admission, 10/1 priority date for domestic students, 10/1 for international students. Applications are processed on a rolling basis. Application fee: $35. Electronic applications accepted. *Financial support:* Federal Work-Study, scholarships/grants, and unspecified assistantships available. Financial award application deadline: 3/1. *Unit head:* Dr. Patricia Hughes, Coordinator, 320-308-2076, E-mail: pahughes@stcloudstate.edu. *Application contact:* Linda Lou Krueger, School of Graduate Studies, 320-308-2113, Fax: 320-308-5371, E-mail: lekrueger@stcloudstate.edu.

Saint Xavier University, Graduate Studies, Graham School of Management, Chicago, IL 60655-3105. Offers e-commerce (MBA); employee health benefits (Certificate); finance (MBA, MS); financial analysis and investments (MBA); financial planning (MBA, Certificate); financial trading and practice (MBA, Certificate); generalist/administration (MBA); health administration (MBA, MS); managed care (Certificate); management (MBA, MS); marketing (MBA); public and non-profit management (MBA); public health (MPH); service management (MBA); training and performance management (MBA); MBA/MS. *Accreditation:* ACBSP. Part-time and evening/weekend programs available. *Entrance requirements:* For master's, GMAT, minimum GPA of 3.0, 2 years of work experience. Electronic applications accepted. *Expenses:* Contact institution.

San Francisco State University, Division of Graduate Studies, College of Behavioral and Social Sciences, Public Administration Program, San Francisco, CA 94132-1722. Offers integrated and collaborative services (MPA); nonprofit administration (MPA); policy analysis (MPA); public management (MPA); urban administration (MPA). *Accreditation:* NASPAA.

Seattle University, College of Arts and Sciences, The Center for Nonprofit and Social Enterprise Management, Seattle, WA 98122-1090. Offers MNPL. *Degree requirements:* For master's, thesis or alternative. *Entrance requirements:* For master's, interview, professional experience, minimum GPA of 3.0.

Seton Hall University, College of Arts and Sciences, Department of Public and Healthcare Administration, Program in Public Administration, South Orange, NJ 07079-2697. Offers nonprofit organization management (MPA). *Accreditation:* NASPAA. Part-time and evening/weekend programs available. *Faculty:* 5 full-time (3 women), 1 part-time/adjunct (0 women). *Students:* 29 full-time (22 women), 19 part-time (11 women); includes 18 minority (10 African Americans, 1 American Indian/Alaska Native, 6 Asian Americans or Pacific Islanders, 1 Hispanic American), 2 international. Average age 31. 44 applicants, 91% accepted, 19 enrolled. In 2009, 7 master's awarded. *Degree requirements:* For master's, thesis or alternative, internship or practicum. *Entrance requirements:* Additional exam requirements/recommendations for international students: Required—TOEFL. *Application deadline:* For fall admission, 7/1 priority date for domestic students; for spring admission, 11/1 priority date for domestic students. Applications are processed on a rolling basis. Application fee: $50. *Financial support:* Research assistantships, career-related internships or fieldwork, Federal Work-Study, scholarships/grants, and unspecified assistantships available. Financial award applicants required to submit FAFSA. *Unit head:* Dr. Matthew Hale, Chair, 973-761-9510, Fax: 973-275-2463, E-mail: halematt@shu.edu. *Application contact:* Dr. Matthew Hale, Chair, 973-761-9510, Fax: 973-275-2463, E-mail: halematt@shu.edu.

Southern Adventist University, School of Business and Management, Collegedale, TN 37315-0370. Offers accounting (MBA); church administration (MSA); church and nonprofit leadership (MBA); financial management (MFM); healthcare administration (MBA); management (MBA); marketing management (MBA); outdoor education (MSA); MFM. Part-time and evening/weekend programs available. Postbaccalaureate distance learning degree programs offered (no on-campus study). *Faculty:* 2 full-time (0 women), 8 part-time/adjunct (1 woman). *Students:* 55 full-time (32 women), 30 part-time (22 women); includes 23 minority (14 African Americans, 1 American Indian/Alaska Native, 1 Asian American or Pacific Islander, 7 Hispanic Americans). Average age 35. In 2009, 20 master's awarded. *Entrance requirements:* For master's, GMAT. Additional exam requirements/recommendations for international students: Required—TOEFL (minimum score 600 paper-based; 250 computer-based; 100 iBT). *Application deadline:* For fall admission, 8/1 priority date for domestic students, 7/1 for international students; for winter admission, 12/1 priority date for domestic students, 11/1 for international students; for spring admission, 4/1 priority date for domestic students, 3/1 for international students. Applications are processed on a rolling basis. Application fee: $25. Electronic applications accepted. *Expenses:* Tuition: Full-time $13,149; part-time $487 per credit hour. *Financial support:* In 2009–10, 32 students received support. Scholarships/grants and unspecified assistantships available. Financial award application deadline: 9/1; financial award applicants required to submit FAFSA. *Unit head:* Dr. Don Van Ornam, Dean, 423-236-2750, Fax: 423-236-1527, E-mail: dvanorna@southern.edu. *Application contact:* Linda Wilhelm, Admissions Coordinator, 423-236-2751, Fax: 423-236-1527, E-mail: sbm@southern.edu.

Southern New Hampshire University, School of Business, Manchester, NH 03106-1045. Offers accounting (MS); business administration (MBA, Certificate), including accounting (Certificate), business administration (MBA), finance (Certificate), forensic accounting (Certificate), human resources management (Certificate), international business (Certificate), international sport management (Certificate), leadership of not for profit organizations (Certificate), marketing (Certificate), operations management (Certificate), sport management (Certificate), taxation (Certificate); finance (MS); hospitality and tourism leadership (Certificate); information technology (MS, Certificate); information technology/international business (Certificate); integrated marketing communications (Certificate); international business (MS, DBA); marketing (MS); operations and project management (MS); organizational leadership (MS); project management (Certificate); sport management (MS); MBA/Certificate. *Accreditation:* ACBSP. Part-time and evening/weekend programs available. Postbaccalaureate distance learning degree programs offered (no on-campus study). Terminal master's awarded for partial completion of doctoral program. *Degree requirements:* For master's, one foreign language, comprehensive exam (for some programs), thesis or alternative; for doctorate, one foreign language, comprehensive exam, thesis/dissertation. *Entrance requirements:* For master's, minimum GPA of 2.5; for doctorate, GMAT. Additional exam requirements/recommendations for international students: Required—TOEFL (minimum score 500 paper-based). Electronic applications accepted.

Spertus Institute of Jewish Studies, Graduate Programs, Program in Nonprofit Management, Chicago, IL 60605-1901. Offers MSNM. Part-time and evening/weekend programs available. *Degree requirements:* For master's, one foreign language, thesis optional. *Entrance requirements:* For master's, interview, minimum GPA of 2.75, graduation from accredited undergraduate program. Electronic applications accepted.

Suffolk University, Sawyer Business School, Department of Public Administration, Boston, MA 02108-2770. Offers nonprofit management (MPA); public administration (CASPA); state and local government (MPA); JD/MPA; MPA/MS. *Accreditation:* NASPAA (one or more programs are accredited). Part-time and evening/weekend programs available. *Faculty:* 9 full-time (4 women), 9 part-time/adjunct (2 women). *Students:* 32 full-time (22 women), 106 part-time (65 women); includes 17 minority (9 African Americans, 1 American Indian/Alaska Native, 2 Asian Americans or Pacific Islanders, 5 Hispanic Americans), 9 international. Average age 31. 89 applicants, 83% accepted, 40 enrolled. In 2009, 57 master's awarded. *Entrance requirements:* Additional exam requirements/recommendations for international students: Required—TOEFL (minimum score 550 paper-based; 213 computer-based; 80 iBT). *Application deadline:* For fall admission, 6/15 priority date for domestic students, 6/15 for international students; for spring admission, 11/1 priority date for domestic students, 11/1 for international students. Applications are processed on a rolling basis. Application fee: $50. Electronic applications accepted. *Expenses:* Contact institution. *Financial support:* In 2009–10, 94 students received support, including 56 fellowships with full and partial tuition reimbursements available (averaging $8,017 per year); career-related internships or fieldwork and Federal Work-Study also available. Support available to part-time students. Financial award application deadline: 4/1; financial award applicants required to submit FAFSA. *Faculty research:* Local government, health care, federal policy, mental health, HIV/AIDS. *Unit head:* Dr. Doug Snow, Chair, 617-573-8330, Fax: 617-227-4618, E-mail: dsnow@suffolk.edu. *Application contact:* Judith Reynolds, Director of Graduate Admissions, 617-573-8302, Fax: 617-305-1733, E-mail: grad.admission@suffolk.edu.

Texas A&M University, George Bush School of Government and Public Service, College Station, TX 77843. Offers advanced international affairs (Certificate); homeland security (Certificate); international affairs (MPIA), including international economics and development, national security affairs; nonprofit management (Certificate); public service and administration (MPSA), including public management, public policy analysis. *Accreditation:* NASPAA. *Faculty:* 51. *Students:* 209 full-time (97 women), 93 part-time (43 women); includes 48 minority (15 African Americans, 5 Asian Americans or Pacific Islanders, 28 Hispanic Americans), 19 international. Average age 24. In 2009, 87 master's awarded. *Degree requirements:* For master's, summer internship. *Entrance requirements:* For master's, GRE (preferred) or GMAT. *Application deadline:* For fall admission, 1/24 for domestic and international students. Application fee: $50 ($75 for international students). Electronic applications accepted. *Expenses:* Tuition, state resident: full-time $3991; part-time $221.74 per credit hour. Tuition, nonresident: full-time $9049; part-time $502.74 per credit hour. *Financial support:* In 2009–10, fellowships (averaging $11,000 per year), research assistantships (averaging $11,250 per year) were awarded; career-related internships or fieldwork, Federal Work-Study, and institutionally sponsored loans also available. Financial award application deadline: 2/1; financial award applicants required to submit FAFSA. *Faculty research:* Public policy, presidential studies, public leadership, economic policy, social policy. *Unit head:* A. Benton Cocanougher, Interim Dean, 979-862-8842, E-mail: bushschool@tamu.edu. *Application contact:* Kathryn Meyer, Recruitment and Placement Officer, 979-458-4767, Fax: 979-845-4155, E-mail: admissions@bushschool.tamu.edu.

Trinity (Washington) University, School of Professional Studies, Washington, DC 20017-1094. Offers business administration (MBA); communication (MA); international security studies (MA); organizational management (MSA), including federal program management, human resource management, nonprofit management, organizational development, public and community health. Part-time and evening/weekend programs available. *Degree requirements:* For master's, thesis (for some programs), capstone project (MSA). *Entrance requirements:* For master's, minimum GPA of 2.5. Additional exam requirements/recommendations for international students: Required—TOEFL (minimum score 550 paper-based; 213 computer-based).

Trinity Western University, School of Graduate Studies, Program in Business Administration, Langley, BC V2Y 1Y1, Canada. Offers international business (MBA); managing the growing enterprise (MBA); non-profit and charitable organization management (MBA). Part-time programs available. Postbaccalaureate distance learning degree programs offered (minimal on-campus study). *Degree requirements:* For master's, thesis or alternative, applied project. *Entrance requirements:* For master's, GMAT (minimum score of 550 recommended). Additional exam requirements/recommendations for international students: Required—TOEFL (minimum score 600 paper-based; 250 computer-based; 100 iBT), IELTS. Electronic applications accepted.

Nonprofit Management

Trinity Western University, School of Graduate Studies, Program in Leadership, Langley, BC V2Y 1Y1, Canada. Offers business (MA, Certificate); Christian ministry (MA); education (MA, Certificate); healthcare (MA, Certificate); non-profit (MA, Certificate). Postbaccalaureate distance learning degree programs offered (minimal on-campus study). *Degree requirements:* For master's, major project. *Entrance requirements:* For master's, minimum GPA of 2.7. Additional exam requirements/recommendations for international students: Required—TOEFL (minimum score 620 paper-based; 260 computer-based; 105 iBT). Electronic applications accepted. *Expenses:* Contact institution. *Faculty research:* Servant leadership.

Troy University, Graduate School, College of Arts and Sciences, Program in Public Administration, Troy, AL 36082. Offers education (MPA); environmental management (MPA); government contracting (MPA); health care administration (MPA); justice administration (MPA); management information systems (MPA); national security affairs (MPA); nonprofit management (MPA); public human resources management (MPA); public management (MPA). *Accreditation:* NASPAA. Part-time and evening/weekend programs available. Postbaccalaureate distance learning degree programs offered (no on-campus study). *Students:* 239 full-time (161 women), 652 part-time (416 women); includes 596 minority (547 African Americans, 11 American Indian/Alaska Native, 6 Asian Americans or Pacific Islanders, 32 Hispanic Americans). Average age 34. 415 applicants, 80% accepted. In 2009, 247 master's awarded. *Degree requirements:* For master's, capstone course, research methodologies course. *Entrance requirements:* For master's, GRE, MAT or GMAT, minimum undergraduate GPA of 2.5, letter of recommendation. Additional exam requirements/recommendations for international students: Required—TOEFL (minimum score 523 paper-based; 193 computer-based; 70 iBT), IELTS (minimum score 6). *Application deadline:* Applications are processed on a rolling basis. Application fee: $50. Electronic applications accepted. *Financial support:* Available to part-time students. Applicants required to submit FAFSA. *Unit head:* Dr. Ellen Rosell, Chairman, 334-670-3758, Fax: 334-670-5647, E-mail: erosell@troy.edu. *Application contact:* Brenda K. Campbell, Director of Graduate Admissions, 334-670-3178, Fax: 334-670-3733, E-mail: bcamp@troy.edu.

Tufts University, Graduate School of Arts and Sciences, Graduate Certificate Programs, Management of Community Organizations Program, Medford, MA 02155. Offers Certificate. Part-time and evening/weekend programs available. Electronic applications accepted. *Expenses:* Contact institution.

University of Arkansas at Little Rock, Graduate School, College of Professional Studies, Program in Nonprofit Management, Little Rock, AR 72204-1099. Offers Graduate Certificate.

University of Central Florida, College of Health and Public Affairs, Department of Public Administration, Orlando, FL 32816. Offers emergency management and homeland security (Certificate); non-profit management (MNM, Certificate); public administration (MPA, Certificate); urban and regional planning (Certificate). *Accreditation:* NASPAA. Part-time and evening/weekend programs available. *Faculty:* 11 full-time (2 women), 6 part-time/adjunct (1 woman). *Students:* 68 full-time (45 women), 235 part-time (166 women); includes 105 minority (64 African Americans, 10 Asian Americans or Pacific Islanders, 31 Hispanic Americans), 7 international. Average age 31. 184 applicants, 75% accepted, 95 enrolled. In 2009, 80 master's, 36 other advanced degrees awarded. *Degree requirements:* For master's, comprehensive exam, thesis or alternative, research report. *Entrance requirements:* For master's, GRE General Test. *Application deadline:* For fall admission, 7/1 for domestic students; for spring admission, 12/1 for domestic students. Application fee: $30. Electronic applications accepted. *Expenses:* Tuition, state resident: part-time $306.31 per credit hour. Tuition, nonresident: part-time $1099.01 per credit hour. Part-time tuition and fees vary according to degree level and program. *Financial support:* In 2009–10, 8 students received support, including 4 fellowships with partial tuition reimbursements available (averaging $10,000 per year), 2 research assistantships with partial tuition reimbursements available (averaging $3,100 per year), 3 teaching assistantships with partial tuition reimbursements available (averaging $5,200 per year); career-related internships or fieldwork, Federal Work-Study, institutionally sponsored loans, tuition waivers (partial), and unspecified assistantships also available. Financial award application deadline: 3/1; financial award applicants required to submit FAFSA. *Unit head:* Dr. MaryAnn Feldheim, Chair, 407-823-3693, Fax: 407-823-5651. *Application contact:* Dr. MaryAnn Feldheim, Chair, 407-823-3693, Fax: 407-823-5651.

University of Connecticut, Graduate School, College of Liberal Arts and Sciences, Department of Public Policy, Field of Public Administration, Storrs, CT 06269. Offers nonprofit management (Graduate Certificate); public administration (MPA); public financial management (Graduate Certificate); JD/MPA; MPA/MSW. *Accreditation:* NASPAA. *Faculty:* 10 full-time (4 women). *Students:* 45 full-time (29 women), 37 part-time (11 women); includes 12 minority (4 African Americans, 1 Asian American or Pacific Islander, 7 Hispanic Americans), 5 international. Average age 31. 79 applicants, 38% accepted, 29 enrolled. In 2009, 31 master's, 21 other advanced degrees awarded. *Degree requirements:* For master's, comprehensive exam, internship. *Entrance requirements:* For master's, GRE General Test. Additional exam requirements/recommendations for international students: Required—TOEFL (minimum score 550 paper-based; 213 computer-based). *Application deadline:* For fall admission, 2/1 priority date for domestic and international students; for spring admission, 11/1 for domestic students, 10/1 for international students. Applications are processed on a rolling basis. Application fee: $55. Electronic applications accepted. *Expenses:* Tuition, state resident: full-time $4725; part-time $525 per credit. Tuition, nonresident: full-time $12,267; part-time $1363 per credit. Required fees: $346 per semester. Tuition and fees vary according to course load. *Financial support:* In 2009–10, 23 research assistantships with full tuition reimbursements, 1 teaching assistantship with full tuition reimbursement were awarded; career-related internships or fieldwork, Federal Work-Study, scholarships/grants, health care benefits, and unspecified assistantships also available. Financial award application deadline: 2/1; financial award applicants required to submit FAFSA. *Unit head:* William Simonsen, Chairperson, 860-570-9045, E-mail: william.simonsen@uconn.edu. *Application contact:* Valerie Rogers, Program Director, 860-570-9047, Fax: 860-570-9114, E-mail: valerie.rogers@uconn.edu.

University of Delaware, College of Human Services, Education and Public Policy, Center for Energy and Environmental Policy, Program in Urban Affairs and Public Policy, Newark, DE 19716. Offers community development and nonprofit leadership (MA); energy and environmental policy (MA); governance, planning and management (PhD); historic preservation (MA); social and urban policy (PhD); technology, environment and society (PhD). Part-time programs available. Terminal master's awarded for partial completion of doctoral program. *Degree requirements:* For master's, analytical paper or thesis; for doctorate, thesis/dissertation. *Entrance requirements:* For master's, GRE General Test, minimum GPA of 3.0; for doctorate, GRE General Test, minimum GPA of 3.5. Additional exam requirements/recommendations for international students: Required—TOEFL. Electronic applications accepted. *Faculty research:* Political economy; social policy analysis; technology and society; historic preservation; urban policy.

University of Georgia, Graduate School, School of Social Work, Institute for Non-Profit Organizations, Athens, GA 30602. Offers MA, Certificate. *Students:* 28 full-time (19 women), 4 part-time (2 women); includes 2 African Americans, 1 international. 25 applicants, 80% accepted, 17 enrolled. In 2009, 18 master's awarded. *Application deadline:* For fall admission, 7/1 priority date for domestic students; for spring admission, 11/15 for domestic students. Application fee: $50. *Expenses:* Tuition, state resident: full-time $6000; part-time $250 per credit hour. Tuition, nonresident: full-time $20,904; part-time $871 per credit hour. Required fees: $730 per semester. *Unit head:* Dr. Michelle Mohr Carney, Director, 706-542-5429, Fax: 706-542-3282, E-mail: mmcarney@uga.edu. *Application contact:* Dr. Brian Bride, Graduate Coordinator, 706-542-5425, Fax: 706-542-3282, E-mail: bbride@uga.edu.

University of La Verne, College of Business and Public Management, Program in Organizational Management and Leadership, La Verne, CA 91750-4443. Offers nonprofit management (Certificate); organizational leadership (Certificate); organizational management and leadership (MS). Part-time programs available. *Faculty:* 22 full-time (11 women), 41 part-time/adjunct (8 women). *Students:* 96 full-time (47 women), 60 part-time (34 women); includes 72 minority (17 African Americans, 24 Asian Americans or Pacific Islanders, 31 Hispanic Americans). Average age 33. In 2009, 68 master's awarded. *Degree requirements:* For master's, thesis or research

project. *Entrance requirements:* For master's, minimum undergraduate GPA of 2.75, 2 letters of recommendation, interview, resume. Additional exam requirements/recommendations for international students: Required—TOEFL (minimum score 550 paper-based; 213 computer-based). *Application deadline:* Applications are processed on a rolling basis. Application fee: $50. *Expenses:* Contact institution. *Financial support:* Institutionally sponsored loans available. Financial award application deadline: 3/2; financial award applicants required to submit FAFSA. *Unit head:* Dr. Kathy Duncan, Chairperson, 909-593-3511 Ext. 4415, E-mail: kduncan2@laverne.edu. *Application contact:* Program and Admissions Specialist, 909-593-3511 Ext. 4819, E-mail: cbpm@laverne.edu.

University of Louisville, Graduate School, College of Arts and Sciences, Department of Urban and Public Affairs, Louisville, KY 40208. Offers public administration (MPA), including human resources management, non-profit management, public policy and administration; urban and public affairs (PhD), including urban planning and development, urban policy and administration; urban planning (MUP), including administration of planning organizations, housing and community development, land use and environmental planning, spatial analysis. Part-time and evening/weekend programs available. *Faculty:* 22 full-time (7 women), 8 part-time/adjunct (1 woman). *Students:* 67 full-time (32 women), 35 part-time (20 women); includes 13 minority (10 African Americans, 1 Asian American or Pacific Islander, 2 Hispanic Americans), 6 international. Average age 31. 107 applicants, 57% accepted, 40 enrolled. In 2009, 25 master's, 5 doctorates awarded. Terminal master's awarded for partial completion of doctoral program. *Degree requirements:* For master's, internship; for doctorate, comprehensive exam, thesis/dissertation. *Entrance requirements:* For master's, GRE General Test, minimum GPA of 3.0; for doctorate, GRE General Test, master's degree in appropriate field. Additional exam requirements/recommendations for international students: Required—TOEFL (minimum score 550 paper-based; 213 computer-based; 79 iBT). *Application deadline:* For fall admission, 7/15 for domestic students; for spring admission, 11/15 for domestic students. Applications are processed on a rolling basis. Application fee: $50. Electronic applications accepted. *Financial support:* In 2009–10, 26 students received support; fellowships, research assistantships, health care benefits available. *Unit head:* Dr. David Simpson, Chair, 502-852-8019, Fax: 502-852-4558, E-mail: dave.simpson@louisville.edu. *Application contact:* Patty Sarley, Graduate Student Advisor, 502-852-7914, Fax: 502-852-4558, E-mail: plclea01@louisville.edu.

University of Maryland, Baltimore County, Graduate School, College of Arts, Humanities and Social Sciences, Department of Sociology and Anthropology, Baltimore, MD 21250. Offers applied sociology (MA, Postbaccalaureate Certificate), including applied sociology (MA), nonprofit sector (Postbaccalaureate Certificate). Part-time and evening/weekend programs available. *Faculty:* 16 full-time (9 women), 3 part-time/adjunct (all women). *Students:* 25 full-time (21 women), 39 part-time (29 women); includes 23 minority (15 African Americans, 1 American Indian/Alaska Native, 6 Asian Americans or Pacific Islanders, 1 Hispanic American), 1 international. Average age 32. 37 applicants, 78% accepted, 20 enrolled. In 2009, 26 master's awarded. *Degree requirements:* For master's, thesis or alternative. *Entrance requirements:* For master's, minimum GPA of 3.0, undergraduate statistics course. Additional exam requirements/recommendations for international students: Required—TOEFL. *Application deadline:* For fall admission, 7/15 for domestic students; for spring admission, 12/15 for domestic students. Applications are processed on a rolling basis. Application fee: $70. Electronic applications accepted. *Financial support:* In 2009–10, 11 students received support, including 7 research assistantships with full and partial tuition reimbursements available (averaging $12,500 per year), 4 teaching assistantships with full and partial tuition reimbursements available (averaging $12,500 per year); scholarships/grants, health care benefits, unspecified assistantships, and tuition remission also available. Financial award application deadline: 2/14; financial award applicants required to submit FAFSA. *Faculty research:* Sociology of aging, medical sociology, migration. *Unit head:* Dr. J. Kevin Eckert, Chairperson, 410-455-2076, Fax: 410-455-1154, E-mail: eckert@umbc.edu. *Application contact:* Dr. William G. Rothstein, Director, 410-455-2078, Fax: 410-455-1154, E-mail: rothstei@umbc.edu.

University of Memphis, Graduate School, College of Arts and Sciences, Division of Public and Nonprofit Administration, Memphis, TN 38152. Offers nonprofit administration (MPA); public management and policy (MPA); urban management and planning (MPA). *Accreditation:* NASPAA. Part-time and evening/weekend programs available. *Faculty:* 5 full-time (2 women), 1 (woman) part-time/adjunct. *Students:* 17 full-time (11 women), 39 part-time (28 women); includes 32 minority (31 African Americans, 1 Hispanic American), 1 international. Average age 34. 32 applicants, 88% accepted, 9 enrolled. In 2009, 17 master's awarded. *Degree requirements:* For master's, comprehensive exam, thesis or alternative, internship. *Entrance requirements:* For master's, GRE General Test, GMAT, or MAT, minimum GPA of 3.0. *Application deadline:* For fall admission, 8/1 for domestic students; for spring admission, 12/1 for domestic students. Applications are processed on a rolling basis. Application fee: $35 ($60 for international students). *Expenses:* Tuition, state resident: full-time $6246; part-time $347 per credit hour. Tuition, nonresident: full-time $15,894; part-time $883 per credit hour. Required fees: $1160. Full-time tuition and fees vary according to course load, degree level and program. *Financial support:* In 2009–10, 37 students received support; fellowships, research assistantships with full tuition reimbursements available, career-related internships or fieldwork, Federal Work-Study, scholarships/grants, and unspecified assistantships available. Support available to part-time students. Financial award application deadline: 2/15; financial award applicants required to submit FAFSA. *Faculty research:* Nonprofit organization governance, local government management, community collaboration, urban problems, accountability. *Unit head:* Dr. Dorothy Norris-Tirrell, Director, 901-678-3360, Fax: 901-678-2981, E-mail: dnrrstrr@memphis.edu. *Application contact:* Dr. Charles Menifield, Graduate Admissions Coordinator, 901-678-3360, Fax: 901-678-2981, E-mail: cmenifld@memphis.edu.

University of Michigan–Dearborn, College of Arts, Sciences, and Letters, Master of Public Administration Program, Dearborn, MI 48128. Offers assessment and evaluation (Certificate); nonprofit leadership (Certificate); public administration (MPA). Part-time and evening/weekend programs available. *Faculty:* 3 full-time (1 woman), 9 part-time/adjunct (2 women). *Students:* 13 full-time (10 women), 67 part-time (43 women); includes 20 minority (16 African Americans, 1 American Indian/Alaska Native, 2 Asian Americans or Pacific Islanders, 1 Hispanic American). Average age 35. 30 applicants, 90% accepted, 24 enrolled. In 2009, 36 master's awarded. *Degree requirements:* For master's, assessment seminar. *Entrance requirements:* For master's, GRE or minimum undergraduate GPA of 3.0, 3 letters of recommendation. Additional exam requirements/recommendations for international students: Required—TOEFL, TWE. *Application deadline:* For fall admission, 8/1 for domestic students, 4/1 for international students; for winter admission, 12/1 for domestic students, 11/1 for international students; for spring admission, 4/1 for domestic students, 3/1 for international students. Applications are processed on a rolling basis. Application fee: $60. *Expenses:* Tuition, state resident: part-time $504.10 per credit hour. Tuition, nonresident: part-time $957.90 per credit hour. *Financial support:* Career-related internships or fieldwork and Federal Work-Study available. Support available to part-time students. Financial award applicants required to submit FAFSA. *Faculty research:* Federal, state, and local agency management; independent sector management; educational administration. *Unit head:* Dr. Trevor Thrall, Director, 313-593-5282, Fax: 313-583-6700, E-mail: atthrall@umich.edu. *Application contact:* Carol Ligienza, Graduate Programs Coordinator, 313-593-1183, Fax: 313-583-6700, E-mail: caslgrad@umd.umich.edu.

University of Missouri–St. Louis, Graduate School, Program in Public Policy Administration, St. Louis, MO 63121. Offers health policy (MPPA); local government management (MPPA); managing human resources and organization (MPPA); nonprofit organization management (MPPA); nonprofit organization management and leadership (Certificate); policy research and analysis (MPPA). *Accreditation:* NASPAA. Part-time and evening/weekend programs available. *Faculty:* 7 full-time (4 women), 6 part-time/adjunct (1 woman). *Students:* 20 full-time (8 women), 69 part-time (45 women); includes 13 minority (11 African Americans, 2 Hispanic Americans), 8 international. Average age 31. 85 applicants, 58% accepted, 28 enrolled. In 2009, 12 master's, 34 Certificates awarded. *Degree requirements:* For master's, exit project. *Entrance requirements:* For master's, 3 letters of recommendation. Additional exam requirements/recommendations for international students: Required—TOEFL (minimum score 550 paper-

based; 213 computer-based). *Application deadline:* For fall admission, 7/1 priority date for domestic and international students; for spring admission, 12/1 priority date for domestic and international students. Applications are processed on a rolling basis. Application fee: $35 ($40 for international students). Electronic applications accepted. *Expenses:* Tuition, state resident: full-time $5377; part-time $297.70 per credit hour. Tuition, nonresident: full-time $13,882; part-time $771.20 per credit hour. Required fees: $220; $12.20 per credit hour. One-time fee: $12. Tuition and fees vary according to course level, campus/location and program. *Financial support:* In 2009–10, 2 research assistantships with full and partial tuition reimbursements (averaging $12,000 per year) were awarded; career-related internships or fieldwork also available. Financial award application deadline: 4/1; financial award applicants required to submit FAFSA. *Faculty research:* Urban policy, public finance, evaluation. *Unit head:* Dr. Brady Baybeck, Director, 314-516-5145, Fax: 314-516-5210, E-mail: baybeck@umsl.edu. *Application contact:* 314-516-5458, Fax: 314-516-6996, E-mail: gradadm@umsl.edu.

University of Nevada, Las Vegas, Graduate College, Greenspun College of Urban Affairs, Department of Environmental Studies, Las Vegas, NV 89154-4030. Offers crisis and emergency management (MS); environmental science (MS, PhD); non-profit management (Certificate); public administration (MPA); public affairs (PhD). Part-time programs available. *Faculty:* 6 full-time (2 women). *Students:* 39 full-time (18 women), 145 part-time (79 women); includes 47 minority (22 African Americans, 4 American Indian/Alaska Native, 3 Asian Americans or Pacific Islanders, 18 Hispanic Americans), 7 international. Average age 39. 16 applicants, 31% accepted, 2 enrolled. In 2009, 50 master's, 3 doctorates, 27 other advanced degrees awarded. *Degree requirements:* For master's, comprehensive exam (for some programs), thesis; for doctorate, comprehensive exam (for some programs), thesis/dissertation. *Entrance requirements:* Additional exam requirements/recommendations for international students: Required—TOEFL (minimum score 550 paper-based; 213 computer-based; 80 iBT), IELTS (minimum score 7). *Application deadline:* For fall admission, 6/1 priority date for domestic students, 2/15 priority date for international students; for spring admission, 11/15 priority date for domestic students, 10/1 for international students. Applications are processed on a rolling basis. Application fee: $60 ($95 for international students). Electronic applications accepted. *Financial support:* In 2009–10, 9 students received support, including 6 research assistantships with partial tuition reimbursements available (averaging $13,850 per year), 3 teaching assistantships with partial tuition reimbursements available (averaging $10,666 per year); institutionally sponsored loans, scholarships/grants, health care benefits, and unspecified assistantships also available. Financial award application deadline: 3/1. *Faculty research:* Environmental chemistry, environmental policy and management. *Unit head:* Dr. Ed Weber, Chair/ Associate Professor, 702-895-4440, Fax: 702-895-4436, E-mail: edward.weber@unlv.edu. *Application contact:* Graduate College Admissions Evaluator, 702-895-3320, Fax: 702-895-4180, E-mail: gradcollege@unlv.edu.

University of Nevada, Las Vegas, Graduate College, Greenspun College of Urban Affairs, Department of Public Administration, Las Vegas, NV 89154-6026. Offers crisis and emergency management (MS); non-profit management (Certificate); public administration (MPA); public affairs (PhD); public management (Certificate). *Accreditation:* NASPAA. Part-time and evening/weekend programs available. *Faculty:* 5 full-time (3 women), 2 part-time/adjunct (1 woman). *Students:* 30 full-time (12 women), 129 part-time (70 women); includes 39 minority (21 African Americans, 4 Asian Americans or Pacific Islanders, 14 Hispanic Americans), 3 international. Average age 38. 95 applicants, 76% accepted, 53 enrolled. In 2009, 48 master's, 28 other advanced degrees awarded. *Degree requirements:* For master's, comprehensive exam, professional paper. *Entrance requirements:* For master's, GRE General Test, GMAT or LSAT. Additional exam requirements/recommendations for international students: Required—TOEFL (minimum score 550 paper-based; 213 computer-based; 80 iBT), IELTS (minimum score 7). *Application deadline:* For fall admission, 6/1 priority date for domestic students, 5/1 for international students; for spring admission, 11/1 priority date for domestic students, 10/1 for international students. Applications are processed on a rolling basis. Application fee: $60 ($95 for international students). Electronic applications accepted. *Financial support:* In 2009–10, 8 students received support, including 6 research assistantships with partial tuition reimbursements available (averaging $12,333 per year), 2 teaching assistantships with partial tuition reimbursements available (averaging $12,000 per year); institutionally sponsored loans, scholarships/grants, health care benefits, and unspecified assistantships also available. Financial award application deadline: 3/1. *Faculty research:* Emergency and crisis management, homeland security, public and non-profit management, public policy, policy analysis and evaluation. *Unit head:* Dr. Anna Lukemeyer, Chair/ Associate Professor, 702-895-4828, Fax: 702-895-1813, E-mail: anna.lukemeyer@unlv.edu. *Application contact:* Graduate College Admissions Evaluator, 702-895-3320, Fax: 702-895-4180, E-mail: gradcollege@unlv.edu.

The University of North Carolina at Greensboro, Graduate School, College of Arts and Sciences, Department of Political Science, Greensboro, NC 27412-5001. Offers nonprofit management (Certificate); public affairs (MPA); urban and economic development (Certificate). *Accreditation:* NASPAA. *Degree requirements:* For master's, comprehensive exam. *Entrance requirements:* For master's, GRE General Test. Additional exam requirements/recommendations for international students: Required—TOEFL. Electronic applications accepted. *Faculty research:* U.S. Constitution, Canadian parliament, public management, ethical challenge of public service.

University of Northern Iowa, Graduate College, Program in Philanthropy and Nonprofit Development, Cedar Falls, IA 50614. Offers MA. *Students:* 3 full-time (all women), 7 part-time (all women); includes 1 minority (African American). 10 applicants. In 2009, 1 master's awarded. *Entrance requirements:* For master's, minimum GPA of 3.0; 3 letters of recommendation; experience in the philanthropy and/or nonprofit areas. Additional exam requirements/recommendations for international students: Required—TOEFL (minimum score 500 paper-based; 180 computer-based; 61 iBT). *Application deadline:* Applications are processed on a rolling basis. Application fee: $30 ($50 for international students). Electronic applications accepted. *Financial support:* Application deadline: 2/1. *Unit head:* Dr. Christopher R. Edginton, Director/Professor, 319-273-2840, Fax: 319-273-5958, E-mail: christopher.edginton@uni.edu. *Application contact:* Laurie S. Russell, Record Analyst, 319-273-2623, Fax: 319-273-6792, E-mail: laurie.russell@uni.edu.

University of Notre Dame, Mendoza College of Business, Program in Nonprofit Administration, Notre Dame, IN 46556. Offers MNA. *Accreditation:* AACSB. Part-time programs available. Postbaccalaureate distance learning degree programs offered (minimal on-campus study). *Faculty:* 10 full-time (0 women), 7 part-time/adjunct (5 women). *Students:* 4 full-time (2 women), 58 part-time (35 women); includes 4 minority (1 African American, 2 Asian Americans or Pacific Islanders, 1 Hispanic American), 1 international. Average age 30. 36 applicants, 92% accepted, 27 enrolled. In 2009, 20 master's awarded. *Degree requirements:* For master's, thesis. *Entrance requirements:* For master's, GRE General Test, work experience. Additional exam requirements/recommendations for international students: Required—TOEFL (minimum score 600 paper-based; 250 computer-based). *Application deadline:* For winter admission, 1/15 for domestic students; for spring admission, 3/31 for domestic students. Application fee: $50. Electronic applications accepted. *Expenses:* Contact institution. *Financial support:* In 2009–10, 17 students received support, including 33 fellowships (averaging $2,000 per year); institutionally sponsored loans and scholarships/grants also available. Support available to part-time students. *Unit head:* Thomas J. Harvey, Director, 574-631-7593, Fax: 574-631-6532, E-mail: harvey.18@nd.edu. *Application contact:* Kimberly M. Brennan, Program Manager, 574-631-3639, Fax: 574-631-6532, E-mail: brennan.53@nd.edu.

University of Pittsburgh, Graduate School of Public and International Affairs, Public Policy and Management Program for Mid-Career Professionals, Pittsburgh, PA 15260. Offers development planning (MPPM); international development (MPPM); international political economy (MPPM); international security studies (MPPM); management of non profit organizations (MPPM); metropolitan management and regional development (MPPM); policy analysis and evaluation (MPPM). Part-time programs available. *Faculty:* 28 full-time (8 women), 56 part-time/adjunct (20 women). *Students:* 3 full-time (0 women), 39 part-time (21 women); includes 2 minority (both African Americans), 1 international. Average age 38. 48 applicants, 75% accepted, 19 enrolled. In 2009, 17 master's awarded. *Degree requirements:* For master's, thesis optional, capstone seminar. *Entrance requirements:* For master's, 2 letters of recom-

mendation, resume, 5 years of supervisory or budgetary experience. Additional exam requirements/recommendations for international students: Required—TOEFL (minimum score 600 paper-based; 250 computer-based; 100 iBT), TWE (minimum score 4); Recommended—IELTS (minimum score 7). *Application deadline:* For fall admission, 6/1 priority date for domestic students, 2/15 for international students; for spring admission, 1/1 priority date for domestic students, 8/1 for international students. Applications are processed on a rolling basis. Application fee: $50. Electronic applications accepted. *Expenses:* Tuition, state resident: full-time $16,402; part-time $665 per credit. Tuition, nonresident: full-time $28,694; part-time $1175 per credit. Required fees: $690; $175 per term. Tuition and fees vary according to program. *Financial support:* In 2009–10, 10 students received support. Institutionally sponsored loans, scholarships/grants, and tuition waivers (partial) available. Support available to part-time students. Financial award application deadline: 2/1. *Faculty research:* Nonprofit management, urban and regional affairs, policy analysis and evaluation, security and intelligence studies, global political economy, nongovernmental organizations, civil society, development planning and environmental sustainability, human security. Total annual research expenditures: $357,117. *Unit head:* Dr. George Dougherty, Director, Executive Education, 412-648-7603, Fax: 412-648-2605, E-mail: gwdjr@pitt.edu. *Application contact:* Michael T. Rizzi, Associate Director of Student Services, 412-648-7640, Fax: 412-648-7641, E-mail: rizzim@pitt.edu.

University of San Diego, School of Leadership and Education Sciences, Department of Leadership Studies, San Diego, CA 92110-2492. Offers higher education leadership (MA); leadership studies (MA, PhD); nonprofit leadership and management (MA, Certificate). Part-time and evening/weekend programs available. *Faculty:* 8 full-time (5 women), 13 part-time/adjunct (9 women). *Students:* 23 full-time (12 women), 189 part-time (137 women); includes 63 minority (14 African Americans, 1 American Indian/Alaska Native, 17 Asian Americans or Pacific Islanders, 31 Hispanic Americans), 4 international. Average age 35. 186 applicants, 53% accepted, 72 enrolled. In 2009, 37 master's, 9 doctorates awarded. *Degree requirements:* For master's, thesis (for some programs), portfolio; for doctorate, comprehensive exam, thesis/dissertation. *Entrance requirements:* For master's, minimum GPA of 3.0, interview; for doctorate, GRE, master's degree, minimum GPA of 3.5 (recommended), interview, writing sample, resume. Additional exam requirements/recommendations for international students: Required—TOEFL (minimum score 580 paper-based; 237 computer-based; 83 iBT), TWE. *Application deadline:* For fall admission, 3/1 for domestic and international students. Application fee: $45. Electronic applications accepted. *Expenses:* Tuition: Full-time $21,042; part-time $1169 per unit. Required fees: $224. Full-time tuition and fees vary according to course load and degree level. *Financial support:* In 2009–10, 182 students received support. Career-related internships or fieldwork, Federal Work-Study, institutionally sponsored loans, unspecified assistantships, and stipends available. Support available to part-time students. Financial award application deadline: 4/1; financial award applicants required to submit FAFSA. *Faculty research:* Educational leadership, higher education policy and relations, leadership development, nonprofits and philanthropy, peace studies. *Unit head:* Dr. Cheryl Getz, Graduate Program Director, 619-260-4289, Fax: 619-260-6835, E-mail: cgetz@sandiego.edu. *Application contact:* Dr. John Mosby, Associate Director of Graduate Admissions, 619-260-4524, Fax: 619-260-4158, E-mail: grads@sandiego.edu.

University of San Francisco, School of Business and Professional Studies, Program in Nonprofit Administration, San Francisco, CA 94117-1080. Offers MNA. *Faculty:* 6 part-time/adjunct (5 women). *Students:* 63 full-time (48 women), 11 part-time (7 women); includes 14 minority (5 African Americans, 3 Asian Americans or Pacific Islanders, 6 Hispanic Americans), 4 international. Average age 36. 47 applicants, 77% accepted, 23 enrolled. In 2009, 28 master's awarded. *Degree requirements:* For master's, thesis optional. *Entrance requirements:* For master's, minimum GPA of 3.0. Application fee: $55 ($65 for international students). *Expenses:* Tuition: Full-time $19,710; part-time $1095 per unit. Part-time tuition and fees vary according to degree level, campus/location and program. *Financial support:* In 2009–10, 33 students received support. Application deadline: 3/2. *Faculty research:* Philanthropy in ethnic communities. *Unit head:* Dr. Kathleen Fletcher, Director, 415-422-5121. *Application contact:* 415-422-6000, E-mail: graduate@usfca.edu.

University of Southern Maine, Edmund S. Muskie School of Public Service, Program in Public Policy and Management, Portland, ME 04104-9300. Offers child and family policy (Certificate); non-profit management (Certificate); public policy and management (MPPM); JD/MPPM. *Accreditation:* NASPAA. Part-time and evening/weekend programs available. Postbaccalaureate distance learning degree programs offered (minimal on-campus study). *Degree requirements:* For master's, thesis, capstone project, field experience. *Entrance requirements:* For master's, GRE General Test or LSAT. Additional exam requirements/recommendations for international students: Required—TOEFL. Electronic applications accepted. *Faculty research:* Sustainable communities, juvenile justice, program management, nonprofit management.

The University of Tampa, John H. Sykes College of Business, Tampa, FL 33606-1490. Offers accounting (MBA, MS); economics (MBA); entrepreneurship and innovation (MBA); finance (MBA, MS); information systems management (MBA); international business (MBA); management (MBA); marketing (MBA, MS); nonprofit management (MBA). *Accreditation:* AACSB. Part-time and evening/weekend programs available. *Faculty:* 62 full-time (22 women), 11 part-time/adjunct (4 women). *Students:* 240 full-time (101 women), 338 part-time (133 women); includes 95 minority (16 African Americans, 4 American Indian/Alaska Native, 24 Asian Americans or Pacific Islanders, 51 Hispanic Americans), 122 international. Average age 29. 564 applicants, 51% accepted, 186 enrolled. In 2009, 234 master's awarded. *Entrance requirements:* For master's, GMAT. Additional exam requirements/recommendations for international students: Required—TOEFL (minimum score 577 paper-based; 230 computer-based; 90 iBT), IELTS. *Application deadline:* For fall admission, 7/15 for domestic students, 6/1 for international students; for spring admission, 12/15 for domestic students, 11/1 for international students. Applications are processed on a rolling basis. Application fee: $40. Electronic applications accepted. *Expenses:* Tuition: Part-time $488 per credit hour. *Financial support:* In 2009–10, 332 students received support, including 71 research assistantships with full tuition reimbursements available (averaging $6,757 per year); career-related internships or fieldwork, scholarships/grants, and unspecified assistantships also available. Support available to part-time students. Financial award applicants required to submit FAFSA. *Faculty research:* Information systems, leadership, corporate governance, entrepreneurship, hedonic price estimation. *Unit head:* Dr. Don Morrill, Associate Dean, Graduate and Continuing Studies, 813-257-3557, E-mail: dmorrill@ut.edu. *Application contact:* Karen Full, Director of Admissions, Graduate and Continuing Studies, 813-257-3642, E-mail: kfull@ut.edu.

The University of Tennessee at Chattanooga, Graduate School, College of Arts and Sciences, Department of Political Science, Chattanooga, TN 37403. Offers local government management (MPA); non profit management (MPA); public administration (MPA); public administration and non-profit management (Postbaccalaureate Certificate). Part-time and evening/weekend programs available. *Faculty:* 4 full-time (0 women). *Students:* 21 full-time (10 women), 23 part-time (12 women); includes 6 minority (3 African Americans, 2 Asian Americans or Pacific Islanders, 1 Hispanic American). Average age 29. 18 applicants, 89% accepted, 10 enrolled. In 2009, 13 master's awarded. *Degree requirements:* For master's, comprehensive exam, thesis or alternative, internship. *Entrance requirements:* For master's, GRE General Test. Additional exam requirements/recommendations for international students: Required—TOEFL (minimum score 550 paper-based; 213 computer-based; 79 iBT), IELTS (minimum score 6). *Application deadline:* For fall admission, 8/1 priority date for domestic students, 6/1 for international students; for spring admission, 12/1 priority date for domestic students, 10/1 for international students. Applications are processed on a rolling basis. Application fee: $35. Electronic applications accepted. *Expenses:* Tuition, state resident: full-time $5404; part-time $300 per credit hour. Tuition, nonresident: full-time $16,702; part-time $928 per credit hour. Required fees: $1150; $130 per credit hour. *Financial support:* In 2009–10, 6 research assistantships with full and partial tuition reimbursements (averaging $5,500 per year) were awarded; career-related internships or fieldwork, scholarships/grants, and unspecified assistantships also available. Support available to part-time students. *Faculty research:* Organizational cultures and renewal, management theory, public policy, policy analysis, nonprofit organization.

Nonprofit Management

The University of Tennessee at Chattanooga (continued)

Total annual research expenditures: $35,240. *Unit head:* Dr. Fouad M. Moughrabi, Head, 423-425-4281, Fax: 423-425-2373, E-mail: fouad-moughrabi@utc.edu. *Application contact:* Dr. Stephanie Bellar, Dean of Graduate Studies, 423-425-4666, Fax: 423-425-5223, E-mail: stephanie-bellar@utc.edu.

University of the Sacred Heart, Graduate Programs, Program in Nonprofit Organization Administration, San Juan, PR 00914-0383. Offers MS.

University of the West, Department of Business Administration, Rosemead, CA 91770. Offers business administration (EMBA); finance (MBA); information technology and management (MBA); international business (MBA); nonprofit organization management (MBA). Part-time and evening/weekend programs available. *Entrance requirements:* Additional exam requirements/recommendations for international students: Required—TOEFL.

University of Wisconsin–Milwaukee, Graduate School, School of Social Welfare, Department of Social Work, Milwaukee, WI 53201-0413. Offers applied gerontology (Certificate); marriage and family therapy (Certificate); non-profit management (Certificate); social work (MSW, PhD). *Accreditation:* CSWE. Part-time programs available. *Faculty:* 18 full-time (11 women). *Students:* 173 full-time (157 women), 101 part-time (92 women); includes 55 minority (38 African Americans, 2 American Indian/Alaska Native, 7 Asian Americans or Pacific Islanders, 8 Hispanic Americans). Average age 31. 303 applicants, 62% accepted, 93 enrolled. In 2009, 105 master's awarded. *Degree requirements:* For master's, thesis or alternative. *Entrance requirements:* For doctorate, GRE, bachelor's degree. Additional exam requirements/recommendations for international students: Required—TOEFL (minimum score 550 paper-based; 79 iBT), IELTS (minimum score 6.5). *Application deadline:* For fall admission, 1/1 priority date for domestic students; for spring admission, 9/1 for domestic students. Applications are processed on a rolling basis. Application fee: $45 ($75 for international students). *Expenses:* Tuition, state resident: full-time $8800. Tuition, nonresident: full-time $20,760. Tuition and fees vary according to program and reciprocity agreements. *Financial support:* In 2009–10, 3 fellowships, 4 teaching assistantships were awarded; research assistantships, career-related internships or fieldwork and unspecified assistantships also available. Support available to part-time students. Financial award application deadline: 4/15. Total annual research expenditures: $806,977. *Unit head:* Deborah Padgett, Representative, 414-229-4851, Fax: 414-229-5311, E-mail: dpadgett@uwm.edu. *Application contact:* Steve McMurtry, General Information Contact, 414-229-2249, Fax: 414-229-6967, E-mail: mcmurtry@uwm.edu.

University of Wisconsin–Milwaukee, Graduate School, Sheldon B. Lubar School of Business, Program in Nonprofit Management and Leadership, Milwaukee, WI 53201-0413. Offers MS, Certificate. *Faculty:* 11 full-time (6 women). *Students:* 13 full-time (9 women), 41 part-time (35 women); includes 10 minority (7 African Americans, 1 American Indian/Alaska Native, 2 Hispanic Americans). Average age 30. 19 applicants, 79% accepted, 6 enrolled. In 2009, 6 master's awarded. *Entrance requirements:* For master's, GRE/GMAT. Additional exam requirements/recommendations for international students: Required—TOEFL (minimum score 550 paper-based; 213 computer-based; 79 iBT), IELTS (minimum score 6.5). *Expenses:* Tuition, state resident: full-time $8800. Tuition, nonresident: full-time $20,760. Tuition and fees vary according to program and reciprocity agreements. *Financial support:* In 2009–10, 5 teaching assistantships were awarded. *Unit head:* Douglas Ihrke, Representative, 414-229-3176, E-mail: dihrke@uwm.edu. *Application contact:* Douglas Ihrke, Representative, 414-229-3176, E-mail: dihrke@uwm.edu.

Virginia Commonwealth University, Graduate School, College of Humanities and Sciences, Program in Nonprofit Management, Richmond, VA 23284-9005. Offers Graduate Certificate.

Virginia Polytechnic Institute and State University, VT Online, Blacksburg, VA 24061. Offers aerospace engineering (MS); business information systems (Graduate Certificate); career and technical education (MS); computer engineering (M Eng, MS); decision support systems (Graduate Certificate); eLearning leadership (MA); electrical engineering (M Eng, MS); engineering administration (MEA); environmental politics and policy (Graduate Certificate); foundations of political analysis (Graduate Certificate); health product risk management (Graduate Certificate); information policy and society (Graduate Certificate); information security (Graduate Certificate); instructional technology (MA); liberal arts (Graduate Certificate); life sciences: health product risk management (MS); natural resources (MNR, Graduate Certificate); networking (Graduate Certificate); nonprofit and nongovernmental organization management (Graduate Certificate); ocean engineering (MS); political science (MA); security studies (Graduate Certificate); software development (Graduate Certificate). *Expenses:* Tuition, area resident: Full-time $10,228; part-time $459 per credit hour. Tuition, nonresident: full-time $17,892; part-time $865 per credit hour. Required fees: $1966; $451 per semester.

Walden University, Graduate Programs, School of Counseling and Social Service, Minneapolis, MN 55401. Offers counselor education and supervision (PhD), including consultation, counseling and social change, forensic mental health counseling, general program, nonprofit management and leadership, trauma and crisis; human services (PhD), including clinical social work, counseling, criminal justice, family studies and intervention strategies, general program, human services administration, self-designed, social policy analysis and planning; marriage, couple, and family counseling (MS), including forensic counseling, trauma and crisis counseling; mental health counseling (MS), including forensic counseling. Part-time and evening/weekend programs available. Postbaccalaureate distance learning degree programs offered (minimal on-campus study). *Faculty:* 13 full-time, 78 part-time/adjunct. *Students:* 1,932 full-time (1,624 women), 210 part-time (181 women); includes 945 minority (817 African Americans, 24 American Indian/Alaska Native, 24 Asian Americans or Pacific Islanders, 80 Hispanic Americans), 34 international. Average age 39. In 2009, 55 master's, 5 doctorates awarded. *Degree requirements:* For master's, residency (for some programs); for doctorate, thesis/dissertation, residency. *Entrance requirements:* For master's, bachelor's degree or equivalent in related field, minimum GPA of 2.5; for doctorate, master's degree or equivalent in related field; minimum GPA of 3.0; official transcripts; three years' related professional/academic experience (preferred); access to computer and Internet. Additional exam requirements/recommendations for international students: Required—TOEFL (minimum score 550 paper-based; 213 computer-based), IELTS (minimum score 6.5), or Michigan English Language Assessment Battery (minimum score 82). *Application deadline:* Applications are processed on a rolling basis. Application fee: $50. Electronic applications accepted. *Expenses:* Tuition: Full-time $13,665; part-time $560 per credit. Required fees: $1375. Tuition and fees vary according to course load, degree level and program. *Financial support:* In 2009–10, 200 students received support; fellowships, Federal Work-Study, scholarships/grants, unspecified assistantships, and family tuition reduction, active duty/veteran tuition reduction, group tuition reduction, interest-free payment plans available. Support available to part-time students. Financial award applicants required to submit FAFSA. *Unit head:* Dr. Savitri Dixon-Saxon, Associate Dean, 800-925-3368. *Application contact:* Jennifer Hall, Director of Enrollment, 866-4-WALDEN, E-mail: info@waldenu.edu.

Walden University, Graduate Programs, School of Psychology, Minneapolis, MN 55401. Offers clinical child psychology (Post-Doctoral Certificate); clinical psychology (Post-Doctoral Certificate); counseling psychology (Post-Doctoral Certificate); forensic psychology (MS), including forensic psychology in the community, general program, mental health applications, program planning and evaluation in forensic settings, psychology and legal systems; general psychology (Post-Doctoral Certificate); health psychology (Post-Doctoral Certificate); organizational psychology (Post-Doctoral Certificate); organizational psychology and development (Postbaccalaureate Certificate); psychology (MS, PhD), including clinical psychology (PhD), counseling psychology (PhD), crisis management and response (MS), general program (MS), general psychology (PhD), health psychology, leadership development and coaching (MS), media psychology (MS), organizational psychology (PhD), organizational psychology and development (MS), organizational psychology and nonprofit management (MS), program evaluation and research (MS), psychology of culture (MS), psychology, public administration, and social change (MS), social psychology (MS), terrorism and security (MS); teaching online (Post-Master's Certificate). Part-time and evening/weekend programs available. Postbaccalaureate distance learning degree programs offered (minimal on-campus study). *Faculty:* 33 full-time, 222 part-time/adjunct. *Students:* 3,546 full-time (2,761 women), 1,133 part-time (908 women); includes 1,723 minority (1,319 African Americans, 56 American Indian/Alaska Native, 101 Asian Americans or Pacific Islanders, 247 Hispanic Americans), 80 international. Average age 41. In 2009, 495 master's, 70 doctorates, 2 other advanced degrees awarded. Terminal master's awarded for partial completion of doctoral program. *Degree requirements:* For master's, thesis optional; for doctorate, thesis/dissertation, residency. *Entrance requirements:* For master's, bachelor's degree or equivalent in related field; minimum GPA of 2.5; official transcripts; goal statement; access to computer and Internet; for doctorate, master's degree or equivalent in related field; minimum GPA of 3.0;3 years of related professional/academic experience (preferred). Additional exam requirements/recommendations for international students: Required—TOEFL (minimum score 550 paper-based; 213 computer-based), IELTS (minimum score 6.5), or Michigan English Language Assessment Battery (minimum score 82). *Application deadline:* Applications are processed on a rolling basis. Application fee: $50. Electronic applications accepted. *Expenses:* Tuition: Full-time $13,665; part-time $560 per credit. Required fees: $1375. Tuition and fees vary according to course load, degree level and program. *Financial support:* In 2009–10, 290 students received support; fellowships, Federal Work-Study, scholarships/grants, unspecified assistantships, and family tuition reduction, active duty/veteran tuition reduction, group tuition reduction, interest-free payment plans available. Support available to part-time students. Financial award applicants required to submit FAFSA. *Unit head:* Dr. Melanie Storms, Associate Dean, 800-925-3368. *Application contact:* Jennifer Hall, Director of Enrollment, 866-4-WALDEN, E-mail: info@waldenu.edu.

Walden University, Graduate Programs, School of Public Policy and Administration, Minneapolis, MN 55401. Offers government management (Postbaccalaureate Certificate); health policy (MPA); homeland security policy (MPA); interdisciplinary policy studies (MPA); law and public policy (MPA); local government management for sustainable communities (MPA); nonprofit management (Postbaccalaureate Certificate); nonprofit management and leadership (MPA, MS); policy analysis (MPA); public management and leadership (MPA); public policy and administration (MPA, PhD), including criminal justice (PhD), health services (PhD), homeland security policy and coordination (PhD), international nongovernmental organizations (PhD), law and public policy (PhD), local government management for sustainable communities (PhD), nonprofit management and leadership (PhD), public management and leadership (PhD), public policy (PhD), public safety management (PhD), terrorism, mediation, and peace (PhD); terrorism, mediation, and peace (MPA). Part-time and evening/weekend programs available. Postbaccalaureate distance learning degree programs offered (minimal on-campus study). *Faculty:* 7 full-time, 62 part-time/adjunct. *Students:* 1,468 full-time (941 women), 233 part-time (162 women); includes 852 minority (761 African Americans, 9 American Indian/Alaska Native, 19 Asian Americans or Pacific Islanders, 63 Hispanic Americans), 53 international. Average age 40. In 2009, 173 master's, 13 doctorates awarded. *Degree requirements:* For doctorate, thesis/dissertation, residency. *Entrance requirements:* For master's, bachelor's degree or equivalent in related field, minimum GPA of 2.5; for doctorate, master's degree or equivalent in related field; minimum GPA of 3.0; official transcripts; three years of related professional/academic experience (preferred); access to computer and Internet. Additional exam requirements/recommendations for international students: Required—TOEFL (minimum score 550 paper-based; 213 computer-based), IELTS (minimum score 6.5), or Michigan English Language Assessment Battery (minimum score 82). *Application deadline:* Applications are processed on a rolling basis. Application fee: $50. Electronic applications accepted. *Expenses:* Tuition: Full-time $13,665; part-time $560 per credit. Required fees: $1375. Tuition and fees vary according to course load, degree level and program. *Financial support:* In 2009–10, 207 students received support; fellowships with tuition reimbursements available, Federal Work-Study, scholarships/grants, unspecified assistantships, and family tuition reduction, active duty/veteran tuition reduction, group tuition reduction, interest-free payment plans available. Support available to part-time students. Financial award applicants required to submit FAFSA. *Unit head:* Dr. Mark Gordon, Associate Dean, 800-925-3368. *Application contact:* Jennifer Hall, Director of Enrollment, 866-4-WALDEN, E-mail: info@waldenu.edu.

Webster University, George Herbert Walker School of Business and Technology, Department of Management, St. Louis, MO 63119-3194. Offers business and organizational security management (MA); computer resources and information management (MA); environmental management (MS); government contracting (Certificate); health care management (MA); health services management (MA); human resources development (MA); human resources management (MA); management (DM); management and leadership (MA); marketing (MA); nonprofit management (Certificate); procurement and acquisitions management (MA); public administration (MA); quality management (MA); space systems operations management (MS); telecommunications management (MA). *Accreditation:* ACBSP. Part-time and evening/weekend programs available. Postbaccalaureate distance learning degree programs offered (no on-campus study). *Faculty:* 16 full-time, 781 part-time/adjunct. *Students:* 1,369 full-time (610 women), 5,182 part-time (3,047 women); includes 3,460 minority (2,835 African Americans, 38 American Indian/Alaska Native, 169 Asian Americans or Pacific Islanders, 418 Hispanic Americans), 80 international. Average age 37. In 2009, 2,491 master's, 13 doctorates, 68 other advanced degrees awarded. *Degree requirements:* For master's, thesis (for some programs); for doctorate, thesis/dissertation, written exam. *Entrance requirements:* For doctorate, GMAT, 3 years of work experience, MBA. Additional exam requirements/recommendations for international students: Required—TOEFL. *Application deadline:* Applications are processed on a rolling basis. Application fee: $25 ($50 for international students). *Expenses:* Tuition: Part-time $565 per credit hour. Tuition and fees vary according to degree level, campus/location and program. *Financial support:* Federal Work-Study available. Support available to part-time students. Financial award application deadline: 4/1; financial award applicants required to submit FAFSA. *Unit head:* Jim Brasfield, Chair, 314-961-2660 Ext. 7063, Fax: 314-968-7077, E-mail: mgtchair@webster.edu. *Application contact:* Matt Nolan, Associate Vice President for Enrollment Management/Dean of Admissions, Fax: 314-968-7116, E-mail: gadmit@webster.edu.

West Chester University of Pennsylvania, Office of Graduate Studies, College of Business and Public Affairs, Department of Political Science, West Chester, PA 19383. Offers administration (Certificate); human resource management (MSA, Certificate); individualized (MSA); non profit administration (Certificate); nonprofit administration (MSA); public administration (MSA); training and development (MSA). Part-time and evening/weekend programs available. *Students:* 3 full-time (2 women), 42 part-time (31 women); includes 8 minority (6 African Americans, 2 Hispanic Americans), 2 international. Average age 28. 28 applicants, 96% accepted, 11 enrolled. In 2009, 12 master's awarded. *Degree requirements:* For master's, comprehensive exam (for some programs). *Entrance requirements:* For master's, GMAT, GRE General Test, or MAT; for Certificate, GMAT, GRE General Test, or MAT, statement of professional goals, resume, two letters of reference. Additional exam requirements/recommendations for international students: Required—TOEFL (minimum score 550 paper-based; 213 computer-based; 80 iBT). *Application deadline:* For fall admission, 4/15 priority date for domestic students, 3/15 for international students; for spring admission, 10/15 for domestic students, 9/1 for international students. Applications are processed on a rolling basis. Application fee: $35. Electronic applications accepted. *Expenses:* Tuition, state resident: full-time $6666; part-time $370 per credit. Tuition, nonresident: full-time $10,666; part-time $593 per credit. Required fees: $122.56 per credit. *Financial support:* In 2009–10, 5 research assistantships with full and partial tuition reimbursements (averaging $5,000 per year) were awarded; unspecified assistantships also available. Support available to part-time students. Financial award application deadline: 2/15; financial award applicants required to submit FAFSA. *Unit head:* Dr. Christopher Fiorentino, Dean, College of Business and Public Affairs, 610-436-2930, E-mail: cfiorentino@wcupa.edu. *Application contact:* Dr. Lorraine Bernotsky, Graduate Coordinator, 610-738-0576, E-mail: lbernotsky@wcupa.edu.

Western Illinois University, School of Graduate Studies, College of Arts and Sciences, Department of Political Science, Macomb, IL 61455-1390. Offers political science (MA); public and non-profit management (Certificate). Part-time programs available. *Students:* 22 full-time (9 women), 3 part-time (1 woman); includes 4 minority (2 African Americans, 2 Hispanic

Americans), 6 international. Average age 26. 20 applicants, 70% accepted. In 2009, 10 master's, 1 other advanced degree awarded. *Degree requirements:* For master's, comprehensive exam, thesis or alternative. *Entrance requirements:* Additional exam requirements/recommendations for international students: Required—TOEFL (minimum score 550 paper-based; 213 computer-based; 80 iBT). *Application deadline:* Applications are processed on a rolling basis. Application fee: $30. Electronic applications accepted. *Expenses:* Tuition, state resident: full-time $4486; part-time $249.21 per credit hour. Tuition, nonresident: full-time $8972; part-time $498.42 per credit hour. Required fees: $72.62 per credit hour. *Financial support:* In 2009–10, 15 students received support, including 15 research assistantships with full tuition reimbursements available (averaging $7,280 per year). Financial award applicants required to submit FAFSA. *Unit head:* Dr. Richard Hardy, Chairperson, 309-298-1055. *Application contact:* Evelyn Hoing, Assistant Director of Graduate Studies, 309-298-1806, Fax: 309-298-2345, E-mail: grad-office@wiu.edu.

Western Michigan University, Graduate College, College of Arts and Sciences, School of Public Affairs and Administration, Kalamazoo, MI 49008. Offers health care administration (Graduate Certificate); nonprofit leadership and administration (Graduate Certificate); public administration (MPA, PhD): *Accreditation:* NASPAA (one or more programs are accredited). *Faculty:* 6 full-time (1 woman). *Students:* 100 full-time (57 women), 189 part-time (100 women); includes 59 minority (50 African Americans, 2 American Indian/Alaska Native, 5 Asian Americans or Pacific Islanders, 2 Hispanic Americans), 2 international. 85 applicants, 85% accepted, 30 enrolled. In 2009, 81 master's, 2 doctorates awarded. *Degree requirements:* For doctorate, thesis/dissertation, oral exams. *Entrance requirements:* For doctorate, GRE General Test. *Application deadline:* For fall admission, 2/15 priority date for domestic students. Application fee: $25. *Financial support:* Fellowships, research assistantships, teaching assistantships,

Federal Work-Study available. Financial award application deadline: 2/15; financial award applicants required to submit FAFSA. *Unit head:* Barbara S. Liggett, Interim Director, 269-387-8943. *Application contact:* Admissions and Orientation, 269-387-2000, Fax: 269-387-2355.

Worcester State College, Graduate Studies, Program in Non-Profit Management, Worcester, MA 01602-2597. Offers MS. Part-time and evening/weekend programs available. *Faculty:* 1 (woman) full-time, 2 part-time/adjunct (1 woman). *Students:* 5 full-time (4 women), 17 part-time (7 women); includes 4 minority (1 African American, 2 Asian Americans or Pacific Islanders, 1 Hispanic American), 2 international. Average age 35. 30 applicants, 53% accepted, 7 enrolled. In 2009, 9 master's awarded. *Degree requirements:* For master's, comprehensive exam (for some programs), thesis optional. *Entrance requirements:* For master's, GRE General Test or MAT. Additional exam requirements/recommendations for international students: Required—TOEFL (minimum score 550 paper-based; 213 computer-based; 79 iBT). *Application deadline:* Applications are processed on a rolling basis. Application fee: $30. *Expenses:* Tuition, area resident: Part-time $150 per credit. Tuition, state resident: part-time $150 per credit. Tuition, nonresident: part-time $150 per credit. Required fees: $85. *Financial support:* In 2009–10, 1 student received support, including 1 research assistantship with full tuition reimbursement available (averaging $4,800 per year); career-related internships or fieldwork, scholarships/grants, and unspecified assistantships also available. Financial award application deadline: 3/1; financial award applicants required to submit FAFSA. *Faculty research:* Politics of human services, models of supervision. *Unit head:* Dr. Shiko Gathuo, Coordinator, 508-929-8892, Fax: 508-929-8144, E-mail: agathuo@worcester.edu. *Application contact:* Nicole Brown, Assistant Dean of Continuing Education, 508-929-8787, Fax: 508-929-8100, E-mail: nbrown@worcester.edu.

Section 16
Organizational Studies

This section contains a directory of institutions offering graduate work in organizational studies, followed by an in-depth entry submitted by an institution that chose to prepare a detailed program description. Additional information about programs listed in the directory but not augmented by an in-depth entry may be obtained by writing directly to the dean of a graduate school or chair of a department at the address given in the directory.

For programs offering related work, see also in this book *Business Administration and Management, Human Resources,* and *Industrial and Manufacturing Management.* In another guide in this series: **Graduate Programs in the Humanities, Arts & Social Sciences** See *Communication and Media* and *Public, Regional, and Industrial Affairs*

CONTENTS

Program Directories

Close-Up

See also:

Organizational Behavior

Amridge University, Graduate and Professional Programs, Montgomery, AL 36117. Offers behavioral leadership and management (MA); biblical studies (MA, PhD); family therapy (D Min); leadership and management (MS); marriage and family therapy (M Div, MA, PhD); ministerial leadership (M Div, MS); pastoral counseling (M Div, MS); practical theology (MA); professional counseling (M Div, MA); theology (M Div, D Min). *Accreditation:* ATS. Part-time and evening/weekend programs available. Postbaccalaureate distance learning degree programs offered (no on-campus study). *Faculty:* 44 full-time (9 women), 18 part-time/adjunct (7 women). *Students:* 175 full-time (95 women), 192 part-time (93 women); includes 182 minority (172 African Americans, 1 American Indian/Alaska Native, 1 Asian American or Pacific Islander, 8 Hispanic Americans). Average age 35. *Degree requirements:* For master's, one foreign language, comprehensive exam (for some programs), thesis (for some programs); for doctorate, comprehensive exam (for some programs), thesis/dissertation; for M Div, comprehensive exam (for some programs). *Entrance requirements:* For M Div, master's, and doctorate, GRE General Test or MAT. Additional exam requirements/recommendations for international students: Required—TOEFL. *Application deadline:* For fall admission, 9/1 priority date for domestic students; for spring admission, 1/1 priority date for domestic students. Applications are processed on a rolling basis. Application fee: $75. Electronic applications accepted. *Expenses:* Tuition: Full-time $10,080; part-time $560 per semester hour. Required fees: $600 per term. *Financial support:* Federal Work-Study and scholarships/grants available. Support available to part-time students. Financial award applicants required to submit FAFSA. *Faculty research:* Homiletics, hermeneutics, ancient Near Eastern history. *Unit head:* Director of Enrollment Management, 800-351-4040 Ext. 7513, Fax: 334-387-3878. *Application contact:* Ora Davis, Admissions Officer, 334-387-3877 Ext. 7524, Fax: 334-387-3878, E-mail: admissions@amridgeuniversity.edu.

Argosy University, Chicago, College of Psychology and Behavioral Sciences, Doctoral Program in Clinical Psychology, Chicago, IL 60601. Offers child and adolescent psychology (Psy D); client-centered and experiential psychotherapies (Psy D); diversity and multicultural psychology (Psy D); family psychology (Psy D); forensic psychology (Psy D); health psychology (Psy D); neuropsychology (Psy D); organizational consulting (Psy D); psychoanalytic psychology (Psy D); psychology and spirituality (Psy D). *Accreditation:* APA.

Benedictine University, Graduate Programs, Program in Management and Organizational Behavior, Lisle, IL 60532-0900. Offers MS, MBA/MS, MPH/MS. Part-time and evening/weekend programs available. *Faculty:* 1 full-time (0 women), 15 part-time/adjunct (7 women). *Students:* 67 full-time (34 women), 117 part-time (74 women); includes 36 minority (25 African Americans, 5 Asian Americans or Pacific Islanders, 6 Hispanic Americans), 2 international. Average age 40. 90 applicants, 96% accepted, 72 enrolled. In 2009, 47 master's awarded. *Entrance requirements:* For master's, GMAT. Additional exam requirements/recommendations for international students: Required—TOEFL (minimum score 550 paper-based; 213 computer-based). *Application deadline:* For fall admission, 9/1 for domestic students; for winter admission, 12/1 for domestic students; for spring admission, 2/15 for domestic students. Applications are processed on a rolling basis. Application fee: $40. Electronic applications accepted. *Expenses:* Tuition: Part-time $750 per credit hour. Tuition and fees vary according to campus/location and program. *Financial support:* Career-related internships or fieldwork and health care benefits available. Support available to part-time students. *Faculty research:* Organizational change, transformation, development, learning organizations, career transitions for academics. *Unit head:* Dr. Peter F. Sorensen, Director, 630-829-6220, Fax: 630-960-1126, E-mail: psorensen@ben.edu. *Application contact:* Kari Gibbons, Director, Admissions, 630-829-6200, Fax: 630-829-6584, E-mail: kgibbons@ben.edu.

Bernard M. Baruch College of the City University of New York, Zicklin School of Business, Department of Management, New York, NY 10010-5585. Offers entrepreneurship (MBA); general management and policy (MBA); human resources management (MBA); management planning systems (PhD); management science (MBA); organization and policy studies (PhD); organizational behavior (MBA). Part-time and evening/weekend programs available. *Degree requirements:* For doctorate, comprehensive exam, thesis/dissertation. *Entrance requirements:* For master's, GMAT, 2 letters of recommendation, resume, 2 years of work experience; for doctorate, GMAT. Additional exam requirements/recommendations for international students: Required—TOEFL (minimum score 590 paper-based; 243 computer-based), TWE.

Boston College, Carroll School of Management, Department of Organization Studies, Chestnut Hill, MA 02467-3800. Offers PhD. *Faculty:* 11 full-time (4 women). *Students:* 24 full-time (15 women); includes 2 minority (1 African American, 1 Hispanic American), 8 international. Average age 32. 60 applicants, 12% accepted, 4 enrolled. In 2009, 8 doctorates awarded. *Degree requirements:* For doctorate, comprehensive exam, thesis/dissertation, teaching experience. *Entrance requirements:* For doctorate, GMAT or GRE, letters of recommendation, resume, transcripts. Additional exam requirements/recommendations for international students: Required—TOEFL. *Application deadline:* For spring admission, 2/1 for domestic and international students. Application fee: $50. *Financial support:* In 2009–10, 21 fellowships, 17 research assistantships with full tuition reimbursements were awarded. Financial award application deadline: 3/1; financial award applicants required to submit FAFSA. *Faculty research:* Organizational transformation, mergers and acquisitions, managerial effectiveness, organizational change, organizational structure. *Unit head:* Dr. Jeffrey L. Ringuest, Associate Dean, Graduate Programs, 617-552-9100, Fax: 617-552-0514, E-mail: gsomdean@bc.edu. *Application contact:* Shelley Burt, Director of Graduate Enrollment, 617-552-3920, Fax: 617-552-8078, E-mail: bcmba@bc.edu.

Boston University, School of Management, Doctorate in Business Administration Program, Boston, MA 02215. Offers accounting (PhD); information systems (PhD); marketing (PhD); operations and technology management (PhD); organizational behavior (PhD); strategy and innovation (PhD). *Students:* 31 full-time (18 women), 21 international. Average age 32. 158 applicants, 7% accepted, 6 enrolled. In 2009, 12 doctorates awarded. *Degree requirements:* For doctorate, comprehensive exam, thesis/dissertation, curriculum paper. *Entrance requirements:* For doctorate, GMAT or GRE General Test, resume, 3 letters of evaluation. Additional exam requirements/recommendations for international students: Required—TOEFL or IELTS. *Application deadline:* For fall admission, 1/5 for domestic and international students. Application fee: $125. *Expenses:* Tuition: Full-time $37,910; part-time $1184 per credit hour. Required fees: $386; $40 per semester. Part-time tuition and fees vary according to class time, course level, degree level and program. *Financial support:* Fellowships, research assistantships, teaching assistantships, career-related internships or fieldwork, Federal Work-Study, institutionally sponsored loans, scholarships/grants, and tuition waivers available. Support available to part-time students. Financial award applicants required to submit FAFSA. *Unit head:* Dr. Lloyd Baird, Director, 617-353-2670, E-mail: dba@bu.edu. *Application contact:* Hayden Estrada, Assistant Dean, Admissions, 617-353-2670, Fax: 617-353-7368, E-mail: dba@bu.edu.

Brooklyn College of the City University of New York, Division of Graduate Studies, Department of Psychology, Program in Industrial and Organizational Psychology, Brooklyn, NY 11210-2889. Offers human relations (MA); organizational behavior (MA). *Students:* 9 full-time (8 women), 96 part-time (73 women); includes 50 minority (33 African Americans, 7 Asian Americans or Pacific Islanders, 10 Hispanic Americans), 10 international. Average age 31. 123 applicants, 63% accepted, 44 enrolled. In 2009, 20 master's awarded. *Degree requirements:* For master's, comprehensive exam, thesis. *Entrance requirements:* For master's, 2 letters of recommendation. Additional exam requirements/recommendations for international students: Required—TOEFL (minimum score 520 paper-based; 190 computer-based; 69 iBT). *Application deadline:* For fall admission, 3/1 priority date for domestic students, 2/1 for international students. Applications are processed on a rolling basis. Electronic applications accepted. *Expenses:* Tuition, state resident: full-time $7360; part-time $310 per credit hour. Tuition, nonresident: full-time $13,800; part-time $575 per credit hour. Required fees: $140.10 per semester. *Unit head:* Benzion Chanowitz, Graduate Advisor, 718-951-5601, E-mail: bchanowitz@brooklyn.cuny.edu. *Application contact:* Hernan Sierra, Graduate Admissions Coordinator, 718-951-4536, Fax: 718-951-4506, E-mail: grads@brooklyn.cuny.edu.

California Lutheran University, Graduate Studies, School of Business, Thousand Oaks, CA 91360-2787. Offers business (IMBA); entrepreneurship (MBA, Certificate); finance (MBA, Certificate); financial planning (MBA, Certificate); information systems and technology (MS); information technology management (MBA, Certificate); international business (MBA, Certificate); management and organization behavior (MBA); management and organizational behavior (Certificate); marketing (MBA, Certificate). Evening/weekend programs available. Postbaccalaureate distance learning degree programs offered. *Entrance requirements:* For master's, GMAT, interview, minimum GPA of 3.0. *Expenses:* Contact institution.

Carnegie Mellon University, College of Humanities and Social Sciences, Department of Social and Decision Sciences, Pittsburgh, PA 15213-3891. Offers behavioral decision research (PhD); behavioral decision research and psychology (PhD); social and decision science (PhD); strategy, entrepeneurship, and technological change (PhD). Terminal master's awarded for partial completion of doctoral program. *Degree requirements:* For doctorate, comprehensive exam, thesis/dissertation, research paper. *Entrance requirements:* For doctorate, GRE General Test. Additional exam requirements/recommendations for international students: Required—TOEFL. Electronic applications accepted. *Faculty research:* Organization theory, political science, sociology, technology studies.

Carnegie Mellon University, Tepper School of Business, Organizational Behavior and Theory Program, Pittsburgh, PA 15213-3891. Offers PhD. *Degree requirements:* For doctorate, thesis/dissertation. *Entrance requirements:* For doctorate, GMAT or GRE General Test. Additional exam requirements/recommendations for international students: Required—TOEFL. *Faculty research:* Negotiation, organizational learning, interorganizational relations and strategy, group process and performance, communication process and electronic media, group goal setting, uncertainty in organizations, creation and effect of institutions and psychological contracts.

Case Western Reserve University, Weatherhead School of Management, Department of Organizational Behavior and Analysis, Cleveland, OH 44106. Offers MBA, MPOD, MS. Part-time and evening/weekend programs available. *Students:* Average age 28. *Entrance requirements:* For master's, GMAT. *Application deadline:* Applications are processed on a rolling basis. Application fee: $100. *Financial support:* Career-related internships or fieldwork, Federal Work-Study, institutionally sponsored loans, and tuition waivers (full and partial) available. Financial award application deadline: 5/1. *Faculty research:* Social innovation in global management, competency-based learning, life-long learning, organizational theory, organizational change. *Unit head:* David L. Cooperrider, Chairman, 216-368-2055, Fax: 216-368-4785, E-mail: david.cooperrider@case.edu. *Application contact:* Lila Robinson, Admissions Coordinator, 216-368-2055, Fax: 216-368-6228, E-mail: ler6@case.edu.

Columbia College, Graduate Programs, Department of Human Relations, Columbia, SC 29203-5998. Offers human behavior and conflict management (MA); interpersonal relations/conflict management (Certificate); organizational behavior/conflict management (Certificate). Part-time and evening/weekend programs available. Postbaccalaureate distance learning degree programs offered (minimal on-campus study). *Faculty:* 3 part-time/adjunct (2 women). *Students:* 21 part-time (17 women); includes 7 minority (all African Americans). Average age 29. 26 applicants, 100% accepted. In 2009, 12 master's awarded. *Degree requirements:* For master's, thesis, practicum. *Entrance requirements:* For master's, GRE General Test, MAT, 2 letters of recommendation, minimum GPA of 3.2. Additional exam requirements/recommendations for international students: Required—TOEFL. *Application deadline:* For fall admission, 7/15 priority date for domestic students, 7/15 for international students. Applications are processed on a rolling basis. Application fee: $50. Electronic applications accepted. *Expenses:* Contact institution. *Financial support:* Available to part-time students. Application deadline: 7/1. *Faculty research:* Envisioning and the resolution of conflict, environmental conflict resolution, crisis negotiation. *Unit head:* Dr. Elaine Ferraro, Chair, 803-786-3687, Fax: 803-786-3790, E-mail: eferraro@colacoll.edu. *Application contact:* Carolyn Emeneker, Director of Graduate School and Evening College Admissions, 803-786-3766, Fax: 803-786-3674, E-mail: emeneker@colacoll.edu.

Cornell University, Graduate School, Graduate Field of Management, Ithaca, NY 14853-0001. Offers accounting (PhD); behavioral decision theory (PhD); finance (PhD); marketing (PhD); organizational behavior (PhD); production and operations management (PhD). *Accreditation:* AACSB. *Faculty:* 72 full-time (15 women). *Students:* 39 full-time (15 women); includes 2 minority (both Asian Americans or Pacific Islanders), 23 international. Average age 31. 388 applicants, 2% accepted, 4 enrolled. In 2009, 4 doctorates awarded. *Degree requirements:* For doctorate, comprehensive exam, thesis/dissertation. *Entrance requirements:* For doctorate, GMAT or GRE General Test. Additional exam requirements/recommendations for international students: Required—TOEFL (minimum score 600 paper-based; 250 computer-based; 77 iBT). *Application deadline:* For fall admission, 1/3 for domestic students. Application fee: $70. Electronic applications accepted. *Expenses:* Contact institution. *Financial support:* In 2009–10, 38 students received support, including 1 fellowship with full tuition reimbursement available, 3 research assistantships with full tuition reimbursements available; teaching assistantships with full tuition reimbursements available, institutionally sponsored loans, scholarships/grants, health care benefits, tuition waivers (full and partial), and unspecified assistantships also available. Financial award applicants required to submit FAFSA. *Faculty research:* Operations and manufacturing. *Unit head:* Director of Graduate Studies, 607-255-3669. *Application contact:* Graduate Field Assistant, 607-255-9431, E-mail: js_phd@cornell.edu.

Cornell University, Graduate School, Graduate Fields of Industrial and Labor Relations, Ithaca, NY 14853-0001. Offers collective bargaining, labor law and labor history (MILR, MPS, MS, PhD); economic and social statistics (MILR); human resource studies (MILR, MPS, MS, PhD); industrial and labor relations problems (MILR, MPS, MS, PhD); international and comparative labor (MILR, MPS, MS, PhD); labor economics (MILR, MPS, MS, PhD); organizational behavior (MILR, MPS, MS, PhD). *Faculty:* 60 full-time (19 women). *Students:* 165 full-time (100 women); includes 35 minority (16 African Americans, 2 American Indian/Alaska Native, 11 Asian Americans or Pacific Islanders, 6 Hispanic Americans), 58 international. Average age 30. 271 applicants, 34% accepted, 69 enrolled. In 2009, 72 master's, 4 doctorates awarded. *Degree requirements:* For master's, thesis (MS); for doctorate, comprehensive exam, thesis/dissertation, teaching experience. *Entrance requirements:* For master's and doctorate, GMAT or GRE General Test, 2 academic recommendations. Additional exam requirements/recommendations for international students: Required—TOEFL (minimum score 550 paper-based; 213 computer-based; 77 iBT). Application fee: $70. Electronic applications accepted. *Expenses:* Contact institution. *Financial support:* In 2009–10, 73 students received support, including 7 fellowships with full tuition reimbursements available, 2 research assistantships with full tuition reimbursements available, 5 teaching assistantships with full tuition reimbursements available; institutionally sponsored loans, scholarships/grants, health care benefits, tuition waivers (full and partial), and unspecified assistantships also available. Financial award applicants required to submit FAFSA. *Unit head:* Director of Graduate Studies, 607-255-1522. *Application contact:* Graduate Field Assistant, 607-255-1522, E-mail: ilrgradapplicant@cornell.edu.

Drexel University, LeBow College of Business, Program in Business Administration, Philadelphia, PA 19104-2875. Offers business administration (MBA, PhD, APC), including accounting (MBA, PhD), decision sciences (PhD), economics (MBA, PhD), finance (MBA, PhD), legal studies (MBA), management (MBA), marketing (MBA, PhD), organizational sciences (PhD), quantitative methods (MBA), strategic management (PhD). *Accreditation:* AACSB. Part-time and evening/weekend programs available. Postbaccalaureate distance learning degree programs offered (minimal on-campus study). Terminal master's awarded for partial completion of doctoral program. *Entrance requirements:* For master's, GMAT, minimum GPA of 2.75; for doctorate, GMAT. Additional exam requirements/recommendations for international students: Required—TOEFL. Electronic applications accepted. *Faculty research:* Decision support systems, individual and group behavior, operations research, techniques and strategy.

Fairleigh Dickinson University, College at Florham, Maxwell Becton College of Arts and Sciences, Department of Psychology, Program in Organizational Behavior, Madison, NJ 07940-1099. Offers organizational behavior (MA); organizational leadership (Certificate). *Students:* 2 full-time (1 woman), 18 part-time (6 women). Average age 40. 6 applicants, 100% accepted, 5 enrolled. In 2009, 3 master's awarded. Application fee: $40. *Unit head:* Dr. Diane Wentworth, Chairperson, 973-443-8548. *Application contact:* Susan Brooman, University Director, Graduate Admissions, 973-443-8905, Fax: 973-443-8088, E-mail: grad@fdu.edu.

Florida Institute of Technology, Graduate Programs, College of Psychology and Liberal Arts, School of Psychology, Melbourne, FL 32901-6975. Offers applied behavior analysis (MS); applied behavior analysis and organizational behavior management (MS, PhD); clinical psychology (Psy D); industrial/organizational psychology (MS, PhD); organizational behavior management (MS). *Accreditation:* APA (one or more programs are accredited). Part-time programs available. *Faculty:* 24 full-time (11 women), 6 part-time/adjunct (1 woman). *Students:* 210 full-time (169 women), 4 part-time (2 women); includes 31 minority (8 African Americans, 6 Asian Americans or Pacific Islanders, 17 Hispanic Americans), 21 international. Average age 27. 195 applicants, 59% accepted, 55 enrolled. In 2009, 30 master's, 3 doctorates awarded. Terminal master's awarded for partial completion of doctoral program. *Degree requirements:* For master's, comprehensive exam (for some programs), thesis (for some programs), BCBA certification, final exam; for doctorate, comprehensive exam, thesis/dissertation, internship, full time resident of school for 4 years (8 semesters, 3 summers). *Entrance requirements:* For master's, GRE General Test, 3 letters of recommendation, minimum GPA of 3.0, resume; for doctorate, GRE General Test, GRE Subject Test (psychology), 3 letters of recommendation, minimum GPA of 3.2, resume, statement of objectives. Additional exam requirements/recommendations for international students: Required—TOEFL (minimum score 550 paper-based; 213 computer-based; 79 iBT). *Application deadline:* For fall admission, 1/15 for domestic and international students. Applications are processed on a rolling basis. Application fee: $50. Electronic applications accepted. *Expenses:* Tuition: Part-time $1015 per credit. Tuition and fees vary according to campus/location and program. *Financial support:* In 2009–10, 19 students received support, including 14 research assistantships with full and partial tuition reimbursements available (averaging $4,079 per year), 5 teaching assistantships with full and partial tuition reimbursements available (averaging $7,002 per year); fellowships with full and partial tuition reimbursements available, career-related internships or fieldwork, institutionally sponsored loans, tuition waivers (partial), unspecified assistantships, and tuition remissions also available. Support available to part-time students. Financial award application deadline: 3/1; financial award applicants required to submit FAFSA. *Faculty research:* Addictions, neuropsychology, child abuse, assessment, psychological trauma. Total annual research expenditures: $836,475. *Unit head:* Dr. Mary Beth Kenkel, Dean, 321-674-8142, Fax: 321-674-7105, E-mail: mkenkel@fit.edu. *Application contact:* Thomas M. Shea, Director of Graduate Admissions, 321-674-7577, Fax: 321-723-9468, E-mail: tshea@fit.edu.

Florida State University, The Graduate School, College of Business, Tallahassee, FL 32306-1110. Offers accounting (M Acc), including accounting information services, assurance services, corporate accounting, taxation; business administration (MBA, PhD), including accounting (PhD), finance (PhD), management information systems (PhD), marketing (PhD), organizational behavior (PhD), risk management and insurance (PhD), strategic management (PhD); finance (MS); insurance (MSM); management information systems (MS); JD/MBA; MSW/MBA. *Accreditation:* AACSB. Part-time programs available. Postbaccalaureate distance learning degree programs offered (no on-campus study). *Faculty:* 107 full-time (31 women), 2 part-time/adjunct (0 women). *Students:* 212 full-time (73 women), 345 part-time (107 women); includes 123 minority (37 African Americans, 2 American Indian/Alaska Native, 48 Asian Americans or Pacific Islanders, 36 Hispanic Americans). Average age 30. 908 applicants, 43% accepted, 307 enrolled. In 2009, 257 master's, 18 doctorates awarded. Terminal master's awarded for partial completion of doctoral program. *Degree requirements:* For doctorate, comprehensive exam, thesis/dissertation. *Entrance requirements:* For master's, GMAT, work experience (MBA, MS), minimum GPA of 3.0, letters of recommendation; for doctorate, GMAT, minimum graduate GPA of 3.5, letters of recommendation. Additional exam requirements/recommendations for international students: Required—TOEFL (minimum score 600 paper-based; 80 computer-based); Recommended—IELTS (minimum score 6.5). *Application deadline:* For fall admission, 6/1 for domestic students, 5/1 for international students; for spring admission, 10/1 for domestic students, 9/1 for international students. Applications are processed on a rolling basis. Application fee: $30. Electronic applications accepted. *Expenses:* Tuition, state resident: full-time $7413. Tuition, nonresident: full-time $22,567. *Financial support:* In 2009–10, 102 students received support, including 32 fellowships with full tuition reimbursements available (averaging $6,900 per year), 30 research assistantships with full tuition reimbursements available (averaging $4,500 per year), 40 teaching assistantships with full tuition reimbursements available (averaging $11,500 per year); career-related internships or fieldwork, scholarships/grants, health care benefits, tuition waivers (full and partial), and unspecified assistantships also available. Support available to part-time students. Financial award application deadline: 1/1. *Unit head:* Dr. Caryn Beck-Dudley, Dean, 850-644-3090, Fax: 850-644-0915. *Application contact:* Lisa Beverly, Director, Graduate Programs Admissions, 850-644-6458, Fax: 850-644-0588, E-mail: lbeverly@cob.fsu.edu.

Georgia Institute of Technology, Graduate Studies and Research, College of Management, Program in Business Administration, Atlanta, GA 30332-0001. Offers accounting (MBA); e-commerce (Certificate); engineering entrepreneurship (MBA); entrepreneurship (Certificate); finance (MBA); information technology management (MBA); international business (MBA, Certificate); management of technology (Certificate); marketing (MBA); operations management (MBA); organizational behavior (MBA); strategic management (MBA). *Accreditation:* AACSB.

Georgia Institute of Technology, Graduate Studies and Research, College of Management, Program in Management, Atlanta, GA 30332-0001. Offers accounting (PhD); finance (PhD); information technology management (PhD); marketing (PhD); operations management (PhD); organizational behavior (PhD); quantitative and computational finance (MS); strategic management (PhD). *Accreditation:* AACSB. *Degree requirements:* For doctorate, comprehensive exam, thesis/dissertation, oral exams. *Entrance requirements:* For master's and doctorate, GMAT. Additional exam requirements/recommendations for international students: Required—TOEFL. *Faculty research:* MIS, management of technology, international business, entrepreneurship, operations management.

Graduate School and University Center of the City University of New York, Graduate Studies, Program in Business, New York, NY 10016-4039. Offers accounting (PhD); behavioral science (PhD); finance (PhD); management planning systems (PhD). *Faculty:* 66 full-time (5 women). *Students:* 64 full-time (37 women); includes 7 minority (3 African Americans, 1 American Indian/Alaska Native, 2 Asian Americans or Pacific Islanders, 1 Hispanic American), 34 international. Average age 33. 89 applicants, 28% accepted, 18 enrolled. In 2009, 7 doctorates awarded. *Degree requirements:* For doctorate, thesis/dissertation. *Entrance requirements:* For doctorate, GMAT, writing sample (15 pages). Additional exam requirements/recommendations for international students: Required—TOEFL. *Application deadline:* For fall admission, 1/15 for domestic students. Application fee: $125. Electronic applications accepted. *Financial support:* In 2009–10, 50 students received support, including 54 fellowships, 5 teaching assistantships; research assistantships, career-related internships or fieldwork, Federal Work-Study, institutionally sponsored loans, and tuition waivers (full and partial) also available. Financial award application deadline: 2/1; financial award applicants required to submit FAFSA. *Unit head:* Dr. Joseph Weintrop, Executive Officer, 646-312-3092, Fax: 646-312-3031. *Application contact:* Les Gribben, Director of Admissions, 212-817-7470, Fax: 212-817-1624, E-mail: lgribben@gc.cuny.edu.

Harvard University, Graduate School of Arts and Sciences and Doctoral Programs in Management, Committee on Organizational Behavior, Cambridge, MA 02138. Offers PhD. *Entrance requirements:* For doctorate, GRE General Test or GMAT, major in psychology or sociology, course work in statistics or mathematics. Additional exam requirements/recommendations for international students: Required—TOEFL. *Expenses:* Tuition: Full-time $33,696. Required fees: $1126. Full-time tuition and fees vary according to program.

Harvard University, Harvard Business School, Doctoral Programs in Management, Boston, MA 02163. Offers accounting and management (DBA); business economics (PhD); health policy management (PhD); management (DBA); marketing (DBA); organizational behavior (PhD); science, technology and management (PhD); strategy (DBA); technology and operations management (DBA). *Degree requirements:* For doctorate, comprehensive exam (for some programs), thesis/dissertation. *Entrance requirements:* For doctorate, GRE General Test or GMAT. Additional exam requirements/recommendations for international students: Required—TOEFL. *Expenses:* Tuition: Full-time $33,696. Required fees: $1126. Full-time tuition and fees vary according to program.

John Jay College of Criminal Justice of the City University of New York, Graduate Studies, Programs in Criminal Justice, New York, NY 10019-1093. Offers criminal justice (MA, PhD); criminology and deviance (PhD); forensic psychology (PhD); forensic science (PhD); law and philosophy (PhD); organizational behavior (PhD); public policy (PhD). Part-time and evening/weekend programs available. Terminal master's awarded for partial completion of doctoral program. *Degree requirements:* For master's, thesis or alternative; for doctorate, one foreign language, thesis/dissertation. *Entrance requirements:* For master's, GRE General Test, minimum B average; for doctorate, GRE General Test. Additional exam requirements/recommendations for international students: Required—TOEFL (minimum score 500 paper-based; 173 computer-based).

Marylhurst University, Department of Business Administration, Marylhurst, OR 97036-0261. Offers finance (MBA); general management (MBA); government policy and administration (MBA); green development (MBA); health care management (MBA); marketing (MBA); natural and organic resources (MBA); nonprofit management (MBA); organizational behavior (MBA); real estate (MBA); renewable energy (MBA); sustainable business (MBA). Part-time and evening/weekend programs available. Postbaccalaureate distance learning degree programs offered (no on-campus study). *Faculty:* 2 full-time (1 woman), 28 part-time/adjunct (5 women). *Students:* 30 full-time (12 women), 627 part-time (323 women); includes 79 minority (28 African Americans, 3 American Indian/Alaska Native, 17 Asian Americans or Pacific Islanders, 31 Hispanic Americans), 9 international. Average age 37. 299 applicants, 80% accepted, 209 enrolled. In 2009, 193 master's awarded. *Degree requirements:* For master's, comprehensive exam, capstone course. *Entrance requirements:* For master's, GMAT (if GPA less than 3.0 and fewer than 5 years of work experience), interview, resume, 2 letters of recommendation. Additional exam requirements/recommendations for international students: Recommended—TOEFL (minimum score 550 paper-based; 213 computer-based; 80 iBT). *Application deadline:* For fall admission, 9/11 priority date for domestic and international students; for winter admission, 12/15 priority date for domestic and international students; for spring admission, 3/17 priority date for domestic and international students. Applications are processed on a rolling basis. Application fee: $40 ($50 for international students). Electronic applications accepted. *Financial support:* Scholarships/grants available. Support available to part-time students. Financial award applicants required to submit FAFSA. *Unit head:* Bob Hanks, Director of Business and Real Estate Programs, 503-636-8141, Fax: 503-697-5597, E-mail: mba@marylhurst.edu. *Application contact:* Kathleen Schneff, Admissions Specialist, 800-634-9982 Ext. 3322, Fax: 503-635-6585, E-mail: admissions@marylhurst.edu.

New York University, Leonard N. Stern School of Business, Department of Management and Organizations, New York, NY 10012-1019. Offers management organizations (MBA); organization theory (PhD); organizational behavior (PhD); strategy (PhD). *Expenses:* Tuition: Full-time $30,528; part-time $1272 per credit. Required fees: $2177. *Faculty research:* Strategic management, managerial cognition, interpersonal processes, conflict and negotiation.

Northwestern University, The Graduate School, Interdepartmental Programs and Kellogg School of Management, Program in Management and Organizations and Sociology, Evanston, IL 60208. Offers PhD. Program requires admission to both The Graduate School and the Kellogg Graduate School of Management. *Degree requirements:* For doctorate, comprehensive exam, thesis/dissertation. *Entrance requirements:* For doctorate, GRE General Test. Additional exam requirements/recommendations for international students: Required—TOEFL. Electronic applications accepted. *Faculty research:* Strategic alliances and organizational competitiveness, institutional change and the information of industries, social capital and the creation of financial capital, negotiation, organizational networks, diversity.

Northwestern University, The Graduate School, School of Education and Social Policy, Program in Learning and Organizational Change, Evanston, IL 60208. Offers MS. Part-time and evening/weekend programs available. Postbaccalaureate distance learning degree programs offered (minimal on-campus study). *Faculty:* 3 full-time (2 women), 26 part-time/adjunct (14 women). *Students:* 19 full-time (15 women), 59 part-time (46 women); includes 13 minority (4 African Americans, 8 Asian Americans or Pacific Islanders, 1 Hispanic American), 4 international. Average age 32. 40 applicants, 70% accepted, 20 enrolled. In 2009, 17 master's awarded. *Degree requirements:* For master's, thesis, practicum. *Entrance requirements:* For master's, GRE or GMAT (recommended), letters of recommendation. Additional exam requirements/recommendations for international students: Required—TOEFL (minimum score 600 paper-based; 250 computer-based; 100 iBT); Recommended—IELTS (minimum score 7). *Application deadline:* For fall admission, 6/23 for domestic students, 1/11 priority date for international students; for winter admission, 6/23 for domestic students; for spring admission, 1/12 priority date for domestic students. Applications are processed on a rolling basis. Application fee: $100. Electronic applications accepted. *Financial support:* Career-related internships or fieldwork, institutionally sponsored loans, and unspecified assistantships available. *Faculty research:* Strategic change, learning and performance, workplace learning, leadership development, cognitive design, knowledge management. *Unit head:* Dr. Kimberly S. Scott, Director, 847-467-3102. *Application contact:* Leslie L. Zimmerman, Program Coordinator, 847-491-7376, Fax: 847-491-3957, E-mail: l-zimmerman@northwestern.edu.

Phillips Graduate Institute, Program in Clinical Family Psychology and Organizational Consulting, Encino, CA 91316-1509. Offers clinical psychology (Psy D); organizational consulting (Psy D). Evening/weekend programs available. *Degree requirements:* For doctorate, thesis/dissertation. *Entrance requirements:* For doctorate, minimum GPA of 3.0, interview.

Phillips Graduate Institute, Programs in Marriage and Family Therapy, School Counseling and School Psychology, Encino, CA 91316-1509. Offers marital and family therapy (MA); organizational consulting (MA); school counseling (MA). Evening/weekend programs available. *Degree requirements:* For master's, comprehensive exam, thesis. *Entrance requirements:* For master's, minimum GPA of 2.5. *Faculty research:* Integration of interpersonal psychological theory, systems approach, firsthand experiential learning.

Polytechnic Institute of NYU, Department of Finance and Risk Engineering, Brooklyn, NY 11201-2990. Offers financial engineering (MS, Advanced Certificate), including capital markets (MS), computational finance (MS), financial technology (MS); financial technology management (Advanced Certificate); organizational behavior (Advanced Certificate); risk management (Advanced Certificate); technology management (Advanced Certificate). Part-time and evening/weekend programs available. *Faculty:* 6 full-time (1 woman), 20 part-time/adjunct (4 women). *Students:* 196 full-time (71 women), 79 part-time (15 women); includes 28 minority (5 African Americans, 23 Asian Americans or Pacific Islanders), 202 international. Average age 26. 497 applicants, 45% accepted, 85 enrolled. In 2009, 102 master's awarded. *Degree requirements:* For master's, comprehensive exam (for some programs), thesis (for some programs). *Entrance requirements:* For master's, GMAT, minimum B average in undergraduate course work. Additional exam requirements/recommendations for international students: Required—TOEFL (minimum score 550 paper-based; 213 computer-based; 80 iBT); Recommended—IELTS (minimum score 6.5). *Application deadline:* For fall admission, 7/31 priority date for domestic students, 4/30 priority date for international students; for spring admission, 12/31 priority date for domestic students, 11/30 priority date for international students. Applications are processed on a rolling basis. Application fee: $75. Electronic applications accepted. *Expenses:* Tuition: Full-time $21,492; part-time $1194 per credit hour. Required fees: $1160; $204 per course. *Financial support:* Institutionally sponsored loans, scholarships/grants, and unspecified assistantships available. Support available to part-time students. Financial award applicants required to

Organizational Behavior

Polytechnic Institute of NYU (continued)
submit FAFSA. *Unit head:* Prof. Charles S. Tapiero, Academic Director, 718-260-3653, Fax: 718-260-3874, E-mail: ctapiero@poly.edu. *Application contact:* JeanCarlo Bonilla, Director of Graduate Enrollment Management, 718-260-3182, Fax: 718-260-3624.

Polytechnic Institute of NYU, Department of Technology Management, Major in Organizational Behavior, Brooklyn, NY 11201-2990. Offers MS. Part-time and evening/weekend programs available. *Students:* 29 full-time (19 women), 25 part-time (20 women); includes 22 minority (13 African Americans, 5 Asian Americans or Pacific Islanders, 4 Hispanic Americans), 16 international. 54 applicants, 78% accepted, 20 enrolled. In 2009, 14 master's awarded. *Degree requirements:* For master's, comprehensive exam (for some programs), thesis (for some programs). *Entrance requirements:* For master's, GMAT, minimum B average in undergraduate course work. Additional exam requirements/recommendations for international students: Required—TOEFL (minimum score 550 paper-based; 213 computer-based; 80 iBT); Recommended—IELTS (minimum score 6.5). *Application deadline:* For fall admission, 7/31 priority date for domestic students, 4/30 priority date for international students; for spring admission, 12/31 priority date for domestic students, 11/30 priority date for international students. Applications are processed on a rolling basis. Application fee: $75. Electronic applications accepted. *Expenses:* Tuition: Full-time $21,492; part-time $1194 per credit hour. Required fees: $1160; $204 per course. *Financial support:* Applicants required to submit FAFSA. *Unit head:* Prof. Bharadwaj Rao, Head, 718-260-3617, Fax: 718-260-3874, E-mail: brao@poly.edu. *Application contact:* JeanCarlo Bonilla, Director of Graduate Enrollment Management, 718-260-3182, Fax: 718-260-3624.

Purdue University, Graduate School, Krannert School of Management, Doctoral Program in Organizational Behavior and Human Resource Management, West Lafayette, IN 47907-2056. Offers PhD. *Students:* 7 full-time (2 women); includes 1 African American, 2 American Indian/Alaska Native. Average age 34. 101 applicants, 4% accepted, 2 enrolled. In 2009, 2 doctorates awarded. *Degree requirements:* For doctorate, comprehensive exam, thesis/dissertation, dissertation proposal. *Entrance requirements:* For doctorate, GMAT or GRE, bachelor's degree, two semesters of calculus, one semester each of linear algebra and statistics. Additional exam requirements/recommendations for international students: Required—TOEFL (minimum score 575 paper-based; 233 computer-based); Recommended—TWE. *Application deadline:* For fall admission, 1/15 priority date for domestic and international students. Application fee: $55. *Financial support:* In 2009–10, fellowships with full tuition reimbursements (averaging $25,000 per year), research assistantships with partial tuition reimbursements (averaging $18,000 per year), teaching assistantships with partial tuition reimbursements (averaging $18,000 per year) were awarded; scholarships/grants, health care benefits, tuition waivers (full and partial), unspecified assistantships, and travel funds to present at a major conference also available. Support available to part-time students. Financial award application deadline: 1/15. *Faculty research:* Human research management, organizational behavior. *Unit head:* Dr. R. A. Cosier, Dean, 765-494-4366. *Application contact:* Krannert PhD Admissions, 765-494-4375, Fax: 765-494-0136, E-mail: krannertphd@purdue.edu.

Saybrook University, Graduate College of Psychology and Humanistic Studies, San Francisco, CA 94111-1920. Offers clinical psychology (Psy D); human science (MA, PhD), including consciousness and spirituality, humanistic and transpersonal psychology, integrative health studies, organizational systems, social transformation, transformative social change (MA); organizational systems (MA, PhD), including consciousness and spirituality, humanistic and transpersonal psychology, integrative health studies, leadership of sustainable systems (MA), organizational systems, social transformation; psychology (MA, PhD), including clinical psychology (PhD), consciousness and spirituality, creativity studies (MA), humanistic and transpersonal psychology, integrative health studies, Jungian studies, marriage and family therapy (MA), organizational systems, social transformation. Postbaccalaureate distance learning degree programs offered (minimal on-campus study). Terminal master's awarded for partial completion of doctoral program. *Degree requirements:* For master's, thesis or alternative; for doctorate, thesis/dissertation. Electronic applications accepted. *Faculty research:* Humanistic theory, health studies, organizational systems, consciousness and spirituality, social transformation.

Saybrook University, LIOS Graduate College, Leadership and Organization Development Track, San Francisco, CA 94111-1920. Offers MA. *Degree requirements:* For master's, thesis (for some programs), oral exams. *Entrance requirements:* For master's, bachelor's degree from an accredited college or university. *Faculty research:* Cross-functional work teams, communication, management authority, employee influence, systems theory.

Silver Lake College, Division of Graduate Studies, Program in Management and Organizational Behavior, Manitowoc, WI 54220-9319. Offers MS. Part-time and evening/weekend programs available. Postbaccalaureate distance learning degree programs offered (minimal on-campus study). *Faculty:* 21 part-time/adjunct (9 women). *Students:* 11 full-time (9 women), 50 part-time (33 women); includes 8 minority (1 African American, 6 American Indian/Alaska Native, 1 Asian American or Pacific Islander). Average age 34. 29 applicants, 62% accepted, 13 enrolled. In 2009, 47 master's awarded. *Degree requirements:* For master's, thesis optional. *Entrance requirements:* For master's, interview, minimum undergraduate GPA of 3.0, writing sample, three letters of recommendation, professional resume. Additional exam requirements/recommendations for international students: Required—TOEFL. *Application deadline:* For fall admission, 8/1 priority date for domestic students; for spring admission, 12/1 priority date for domestic students. Applications are processed on a rolling basis. Application fee: $50. Electronic applications accepted. *Expenses:* Tuition: Full-time $7380; part-time $410 per credit. Required fees: $10 per term. Part-time tuition and fees vary according to course load. *Financial support:* In 2009–10, 10 students received support. Career-related internships or fieldwork, Federal Work-Study, and scholarships/grants available. Support available to part-time students. Financial award application deadline: 6/30; financial award applicants required to submit FAFSA. *Unit head:* Suzanne M. Lawrence, Director, 920-686-6198, Fax: 920-684-7082, E-mail: law@silver.sl.edu. *Application contact:* Cindy St. John, Associate Director of Admissions, 800-236-4752 Ext. 350, Fax: 920-686-6350, E-mail: cstjohn@silver.sl.edu.

Suffolk University, Sawyer Business School, Master of Business Administration Program, Boston, MA 02108-2770. Offers accounting (MBA); business administration (APC); corporate financial executive track (MBA); entrepreneurship (MBA); executive business administration (EMBA); finance (MBA); global business administration (GMBA); health administration (MBA); international business (MBA); marketing (MBA); organizational behavior (MBA); strategic management (MBA); taxation (MBA); JD/MBA; MBA/GDPA; MBA/MHA; MBA/MSA; MBA/MSF; MBA/MST. *Accreditation:* AACSB. Part-time and evening/weekend programs available. Postbaccalaureate distance learning degree programs offered (no on-campus study). *Faculty:* 103 full-time (30 women), 63 part-time/adjunct (19 women). *Students:* 173 full-time (68 women), 406 part-time (178 women); includes 51 minority (16 African Americans, 3 American Indian/Alaska Native, 22 Asian Americans or Pacific Islanders, 10 Hispanic Americans), 90 international. Average age 29. 460 applicants, 72% accepted, 157 enrolled. In 2009, 245 master's awarded. *Entrance requirements:* For master's, GMAT, minimum undergraduate GPA of 2.75 (MBA), 5 years of managerial experience (EMBA). Additional exam requirements/recommendations for international students: Required—TOEFL (minimum score 550 paper-based; 213 computer-based). *Application deadline:* For fall admission, 6/15 priority date for domestic students, 6/15 for international students; for spring admission, 11/1 priority date for domestic students, 11/1 for international students. Applications are processed on a rolling basis. Application fee: $50. Electronic applications accepted. *Expenses:* Tuition: Full-time $33,000; part-time $1100 per credit. Required fees: $20. Tuition and fees vary according to program. *Financial support:* In 2009–10, 284 students received support, including 99 fellowships with full and partial tuition reimbursements available (averaging $13,599 per year); career-related internships or fieldwork, Federal Work-Study, and institutionally sponsored loans also available. Support available to part-time students. Financial award application deadline: 4/1; financial award applicants required to submit FAFSA. *Faculty research:* Foreign investments; career strategies and boundaryless careers; corporate ethics codes; interest rates, inflation, and growth options; innovation and product development performance. *Unit head:* Lillian Hallberg, Assistant Dean of Graduate Programs/Director of MBA Programs, 617-573-8306, E-mail: lhallber@suffolk.edu. *Application contact:* Judith Reynolds, Director of Graduate Admissions, 617-573-8302, Fax: 617-305-1733, E-mail: grad.admission@suffolk.edu.

Syracuse University, Martin J. Whitman School of Management, PhD Program in Business Administration, Syracuse, NY 13244. Offers accounting (PhD); finance (PhD); management information systems (PhD); managerial statistics (PhD); marketing (PhD); operations management (PhD); organizational behavior (PhD); strategy and human resources (PhD); supply chain management (PhD). *Degree requirements:* For doctorate, comprehensive exam, thesis/dissertation, summer research paper. *Entrance requirements:* For doctorate, GMAT or GRE General Test, 3 recommendations. Additional exam requirements/recommendations for international students: Required—TOEFL (minimum score 600 paper-based; 250 computer-based; 100 iBT). Electronic applications accepted. *Expenses:* Tuition: Full-time $26,808; part-time $1117 per credit. Required fees: $1024. *Faculty research:* Marketing models, market microstructure, supply chain, auditing, corporate governance.

Towson University, College of Graduate Studies and Research, Program in Organizational Change, Towson, MD 21252-0001. Offers CAS. *Entrance requirements:* For degree, GRE or MAT, 2 letters of recommendation, minimum GPA of 3.5. Additional exam requirements/recommendations for international students: Required—TOEFL (minimum score 550 paper-based; 213 computer-based). Electronic applications accepted. *Faculty research:* Leadership, school administration, change, social responsibility.

Universidad de las Americas, A.C., Program in International Organizations and Institutions, Mexico City, Mexico. Offers MA.

Université de Sherbrooke, Faculty of Administration, Program in Organizational Change and Intervention, Sherbrooke, QC J1K 2R1, Canada. Offers M Sc. *Entrance requirements:* For master's, bachelor's degree. Electronic applications accepted.

The University of British Columbia, Sauder School of Business, Doctoral Program in Commerce and Business Administration, Vancouver, BC V6T 1Z1, Canada. Offers accounting (PhD); finance (PhD); international business (PhD); management information systems (PhD); management science (PhD); marketing (PhD); organizational behavior (PhD); strategy and business economics (PhD); transportation and logistics (PhD); urban land economics (PhD). *Degree requirements:* For doctorate, comprehensive exam, thesis/dissertation. *Entrance requirements:* For doctorate, GMAT or GRE. Additional exam requirements/recommendations for international students: Required—TOEFL (minimum score 600 paper-based; 250 computer-based; 100 iBT). Electronic applications accepted.

University of California, Berkeley, Graduate Division, Haas School of Business, PhD in Business Administration Program, Berkeley, CA 94720-1500. Offers accounting (PhD); business and public policy (PhD); finance (PhD); management of organizations (PhD); marketing (PhD); operations management (PhD); real estate (PhD). *Accreditation:* AACSB. *Faculty:* 80 full-time (20 women), 130 part-time/adjunct (22 women). *Students:* 82 full-time (23 women); includes 22 minority (18 Asian Americans or Pacific Islanders, 4 Hispanic Americans), 29 international. Average age 30. 511 applicants, 5% accepted, 16 enrolled. In 2009, 8 doctorates awarded. *Degree requirements:* For doctorate, comprehensive exam, thesis/dissertation, oral exam, written preliminary exams. *Entrance requirements:* For doctorate, GMAT or GRE, minimum GPA of 3.0 in undergraduate and graduate coursework. Additional exam requirements/recommendations for international students: Required—TOEFL (minimum score 570 paper-based; 230 computer-based; 68 iBT), IELTS (minimum score 7). *Application deadline:* For fall admission, 12/10 for domestic and international students. Application fee: $70 ($90 for international students). Electronic applications accepted. *Financial support:* Fellowships with full and partial tuition reimbursements, research assistantships with full and partial tuition reimbursements, teaching assistantships with full and partial tuition reimbursements, career-related internships or fieldwork, Federal Work-Study, scholarships/grants, health care benefits, tuition waivers (full), unspecified assistantships, and transit pass, travel grants available. Financial award application deadline: 12/10; financial award applicants required to submit FAFSA. *Faculty research:* Accounting, business and public policy, finance, management of organizations, marketing, operations and information technology management, real estate. *Unit head:* Sunil Dutta, Director, 510-642-1229, Fax: 510-643-4255, E-mail: kimg@haas.berkeley.edu. *Application contact:* Kim Guilfoyle, Director, Student Affairs, 510-642-3944, Fax: 510-643-4255, E-mail: kimg@haas.berkeley.edu.

University of Hartford, College of Arts and Sciences, Department of Psychology, Program in Organizational Behavior, West Hartford, CT 06117-1599. Offers MS. Part-time and evening/weekend programs available. *Entrance requirements:* Additional exam requirements/recommendations for international students: Required—TOEFL (minimum score 550 paper-based; 213 computer-based). Electronic applications accepted.

University of Hawaii at Manoa, Graduate Division, Shidler College of Business, Program in Business Administration, Honolulu, HI 96822. Offers Asian business studies (MBA); Chinese business studies (MBA); decision sciences (MBA); entrepreneurship (MBA); finance (MBA); finance and banking (MBA); human resources management (MBA); information management (MBA); information technology (MBA); international business (MBA); Japanese business studies (MBA); marketing (MBA); organizational behavior (MBA); organizational management (MBA); real estate (MBA); student-designed track (MBA). *Accreditation:* AACSB. Part-time and evening/weekend programs available. *Faculty:* 46 full-time (8 women), 9 part-time/adjunct (4 women). *Students:* 259 full-time (90 women), 105 part-time (43 women); includes 123 minority (118 Asian Americans or Pacific Islanders, 5 Hispanic Americans), 119 international. Average age 32. 336 applicants, 52% accepted, 150 enrolled. In 2009, 113 master's awarded. *Degree requirements:* For master's, thesis optional. *Entrance requirements:* For master's, GMAT, minimum GPA of 3.0. Additional exam requirements/recommendations for international students: Required—TOEFL (minimum score 600 paper-based; 250 computer-based; 100 iBT), IELTS (minimum score 7). *Application deadline:* For fall admission, 5/1 for domestic students, 3/1 for international students. Application fee: $60. *Expenses:* Contact institution. *Financial support:* In 2009–10, 24 students received support, including 98 fellowships (averaging $3,481 per year), 3 research assistantships (averaging $16,626 per year). Total annual research expenditures: $427,000. *Application contact:* Tung Bui, Graduate Chair, 808-956-5565, Fax: 808-956-9889, E-mail: tung.bui@hawaii.edu.

The University of North Carolina at Chapel Hill, Kenan-Flagler Business School, Doctoral Program in Business Administration, Chapel Hill, NC 27599. Offers accounting (PhD); finance (PhD); marketing (PhD); operations management (PhD); organizational behavior (PhD); strategy (PhD). *Accreditation:* AACSB. *Degree requirements:* For doctorate, thesis/dissertation. *Entrance requirements:* For doctorate, GMAT or GRE General Test. Electronic applications accepted. *Expenses:* Contact institution.

University of Oklahoma, Graduate College, College of Arts and Sciences, Department of Psychology, Program in Organizational Dynamics, Tulsa, OK 74135. Offers MS. Part-time and evening/weekend programs available. *Students:* 3 full-time (1 woman), 26 part-time (16 women); includes 7 minority (2 African Americans, 3 American Indian/Alaska Native, 2 Hispanic Americans). 5 applicants, 100% accepted, 2 enrolled. In 2009, 8 master's awarded. *Entrance requirements:* For master's, minimum GPA of 3.0 in last 60 hours of undergraduate course work. Additional exam requirements/recommendations for international students: Required—TOEFL (minimum score 550 paper-based; 213 computer-based). *Application deadline:* For fall admission, 4/1 priority date for domestic students, 4/1 for international students; for spring admission, 11/1 for domestic students, 9/1 for international students. Applications are processed on a rolling basis. Application fee: $40 ($90 for international students). Electronic applications accepted. *Expenses:* Tuition, state resident: full-time $3744; part-time $156 per credit hour. Tuition, nonresident: full-time $13,577; part-time $565.70 per credit hour. Required fees: $2415; $90.10 per credit hour. *Financial support:* In 2009–10, 2 students received support. Health care benefits and unspecified assistantships available. Support available to part-time students. Financial award application deadline: 3/1; financial award applicants required to submit FAFSA. *Faculty research:* Academic integrity, meta-analysis, organizational citizenship

behavior, interdisciplinary teams, shared leadership. *Unit head:* Dr. Jorge Mendoza, Chair, 405-325-4511, Fax: 405-325-4737, E-mail: jmendoza@ou.edu. *Application contact:* Shanin Warren, Staff Assistant, 918-660-3489, Fax: 918-660-3490, E-mail: shaninwarren@ou.edu.

University of Pennsylvania, School of Arts and Sciences, Graduate Group in Organizational Dynamics, Philadelphia, PA 19104. Offers MS. Part-time and evening/weekend programs available. *Students:* 19 full-time (10 women), 151 part-time (88 women); includes 10 minority (7 African Americans, 3 Asian Americans or Pacific Islanders), 11 international. 49 applicants, 80% accepted, 31 enrolled. In 2009, 56 master's awarded. *Degree requirements:* For master's, thesis. *Application deadline:* For fall admission, 12/1 priority date for domestic students. Application fee: $70. Electronic applications accepted. *Expenses:* Tuition: Full-time $25,660; part-time $4758 per course. Required fees: $2152; $270 per course. Tuition and fees vary according to course load, degree level and program. *Financial support:* Scholarships/grants available. Support available to part-time students. Financial award application deadline: 12/15. *Unit head:* Director. *Application contact:* Director.

University of Pittsburgh, Katz Graduate School of Business, Doctoral Program in Business Administration, Pittsburgh, PA 15260. Offers accounting (PhD); finance (PhD); information systems (PhD); marketing (PhD); operations/decision sciences/artificial intelligence (PhD); organizational behavior and human resource management (PhD); strategic planning (PhD). *Accreditation:* AACSB. *Faculty:* 50 full-time (15 women). *Students:* 53 full-time (21 women); includes 8 minority (4 African Americans, 2 Asian Americans or Pacific Islanders, 2 Hispanic Americans), 22 international. 324 applicants, 4% accepted, 12 enrolled. In 2009, 11 doctorates awarded. *Degree requirements:* For doctorate, comprehensive exam, thesis/dissertation. *Entrance requirements:* For doctorate, GMAT or GRE, references, work experience relevant for individual program. Additional exam requirements/recommendations for international students: Required—TOEFL or IELTS. *Application deadline:* For fall admission, 2/1 priority date for domestic and international students. Applications are processed on a rolling basis. Application fee: $50. Electronic applications accepted. *Expenses:* Tuition, state resident: full-time $16,402; part-time $665 per credit. Tuition, nonresident: full-time $28,694; part-time $1175 per credit. Required fees: $690; $175 per term. Tuition and fees vary according to program. *Financial support:* In 2009–10, 36 students received support, including 31 research assistantships with full tuition reimbursements available (averaging $18,450 per year), 5 teaching assistantships with full tuition reimbursements available (averaging $23,511 per year); fellowships, Federal Work-Study, scholarships/grants, health care benefits, and unspecified assistantships also available. Financial award application deadline: 2/1. *Faculty research:* Accounting statements and reporting, incentives and governance; corporate finance, mergers and acquisitions; information systems processes, structures, OR, supply chain, and decision-making; organizational structure, knowledge management, and corporate strategy; consumer behavior and marketing models. Total annual research expenditures: $362,777. *Unit head:* Dr. John E. Hulland, Director, 412-648-1534, Fax: 412-624-3633, E-mail: jhulland@katz.pitt.edu. *Application contact:* Carrie Woods, Assistant Director, 412-648-1525, Fax: 412-624-3633, E-mail: cawoods@katz.pitt.edu.

University of Pittsburgh, Katz Graduate School of Business, Masters of Business Administration Programs, Pittsburgh, PA 15260. Offers accounting (MS); finance (MBA); general management (MBA); information systems (MBA, MSIS); marketing (MBA); organizational behavior and human resource management (MBA); organizational leadership (Certificate); six sigma (Certificate); strategy (MBA); technology, innovation and entrepreneurship (Certificate); MBA/JD; MBA/MIB; MBA/MPIA; MBA/MSE; MBA/MSIS. *Accreditation:* AACSB. Part-time and evening/weekend programs available. *Faculty:* 58 full-time (12 women), 23 part-time/adjunct (7 women). *Students:* 192 full-time (62 women), 506 part-time (179 women); includes 58 minority (29 African Americans, 1 American Indian/Alaska Native, 24 Asian Americans or Pacific Islanders, 4 Hispanic Americans), 101 international. Average age 29. 674 applicants, 52% accepted, 204 enrolled. In 2009, 263 master's awarded. *Entrance requirements:* For master's, GMAT, references, work experience relevant for individual programs. Additional exam requirements/recommendations for international students: Required—TOEFL (minimum score 600 paper-based; 250 computer-based; 100 iBT), or IELTS. *Application deadline:* For fall admission, 7/1 for domestic and international students; for winter admission, 11/1 for domestic and international students; for spring admission, 3/1 for domestic and international students. Applications are processed on a rolling basis. Application fee: $50. Electronic applications accepted. *Expenses:* Tuition, state resident: full-time $16,402; part-time $665 per credit.

Tuition, nonresident: full-time $28,694; part-time $1175 per credit. Required fees: $690; $175 per term. Tuition and fees vary according to program. *Financial support:* In 2009–10, 75 students received support. Career-related internships or fieldwork and scholarships/grants available. Financial award application deadline: 6/1; financial award applicants required to submit FAFSA. *Faculty research:* Accounting statements and reporting, incentives and governance; corporate finance, mergers and acquisitions; information systems processes, structures, and decision-making; organizational structure, knowledge management, and corporate strategy; consumer behavior and marketing models. *Unit head:* William T. Valenta, Assistant Dean/MBA Program Director, 412-648-1610, Fax: 412-648-1659, E-mail: wtvalenta@katz.pitt.edu. *Application contact:* Cliff McCormick, Director of MBA Admissions, 412-648-1700, Fax: 412-648-1659, E-mail: mba@katz.pitt.edu.

University of Saskatchewan, College of Graduate Studies and Research, Edwards School of Business, Department of Industrial Relations and Organizational Behavior, Saskatoon, SK S7N 5A2, Canada. Offers M Sc. Part-time programs available. *Degree requirements:* For master's, thesis. *Entrance requirements:* For master's, GMAT. Additional exam requirements/recommendations for international students: Required—TOEFL. Tuition and fees charges are reported in Canadian dollars. *Expenses:* Tuition, area resident: Full-time $3000 Canadian dollars; part-time $500 Canadian dollars per term. Required fees: $700 Canadian dollars; $100 Canadian dollars per term.

The University of Texas at Dallas, School of Management, Programs in Management Science, Richardson, TX 75080. Offers accounting (PhD); decision sciences (PhD); finance (PhD); management strategy and public policy (PhD); marketing (PhD); organizational behavior (PhD). *Accreditation:* AACSB. Part-time and evening/weekend programs available. *Faculty:* 12 full-time (3 women). *Students:* 72 full-time (23 women), 12 part-time (6 women); includes 10 minority (all Asian Americans or Pacific Islanders), 63 international. Average age 34. 173 applicants, 12% accepted, 7 enrolled. In 2009, 8 doctorates awarded. *Degree requirements:* For doctorate, thesis/dissertation. *Entrance requirements:* For doctorate, GMAT, minimum GPA of 3.0. Additional exam requirements/recommendations for international students: Required—TOEFL (minimum score 550 paper-based; 213 computer-based). *Application deadline:* For fall admission, 7/15 for domestic students, 5/1 priority date for international students; for spring admission, 11/15 for domestic students, 9/1 priority date for international students. Applications are processed on a rolling basis. Application fee: $50 ($100 for international students). Electronic applications accepted. *Expenses:* Tuition, state resident: full-time $11,068; part-time $461 per credit hour. Tuition, nonresident: full-time $21,178; part-time $882 per credit hour. Tuition and fees vary according to course load. *Financial support:* In 2009–10, 1 research assistantship with full tuition reimbursement (averaging $13,050 per year), 43 teaching assistantships with full tuition reimbursements (averaging $14,795 per year) were awarded; fellowships, career-related internships or fieldwork, Federal Work-Study, institutionally sponsored loans, scholarships/grants, and unspecified assistantships also available. Support available to part-time students. Financial award application deadline: 4/30; financial award applicants required to submit FAFSA. *Faculty research:* Empirical generalizations in marketing, diffusion of generations of technology, stochastic brand-choice theory, acceptance of trade deals by supermarkets, nonparametric estimations of market share response. *Unit head:* Dr. Sumit Sarkar, Program Director, 972-883-2745, Fax: 972-883-5977, E-mail: som-phd.@utdallas.edu. *Application contact:* James Parker, Assistant Director, 972-883-5842, E-mail: jparker@utdallas.edu.

Western International University, Graduate Programs in Business, Program in Human Dynamics, Phoenix, AZ 85021-2718. Offers MA. Evening/weekend programs available. Postbaccalaureate distance learning degree programs offered (no on-campus study). *Faculty:* 1 (woman) part-time/adjunct. *Students:* 21 full-time (15 women); includes 6 minority (4 African Americans, 1 Asian American or Pacific Islander, 1 Hispanic American), 1 international. Average age 37. *Entrance requirements:* Additional exam requirements/recommendations for international students: Required—TOEFL (minimum score 550 paper-based; 213 computer-based; 79 iBT). *Application deadline:* Applications are processed on a rolling basis. Application fee: $25. *Expenses:* Tuition: Full-time $12,600. One-time fee: $25 full-time. *Financial support:* Career-related internships or fieldwork and scholarships/grants available. Support available to part-time students. Financial award applicants required to submit FAFSA. *Unit head:* Dr. Deborah DeSimone, Chief Academic Officer, 602-429-1135, Fax: 602-749-0752, E-mail: deborah.desimone@apollogrp.edu. *Application contact:* Melissa Machuca, Director of Enrollment, 602-943-2311, Fax: 602-371-8637.

Organizational Management

Adler Graduate School, Program in Adlerian Studies, Richfield, MN 55423. Offers art therapy specialization (MA); clinical counseling track (MA); coaching and consulting in organizations (Certificate); management consulting and organizational leadership (MA); marriage and family track (MA); non-clinical Adlerian studies track (MA); personal and professional life coaching (Certificate); school counseling (MA). Part-time and evening/weekend programs available. *Degree requirements:* For master's, thesis or alternative, 500-700 hour internship (depending on license choice). *Entrance requirements:* For master's, minimum undergraduate GPA of 3.0, 12 credits of course work in psychology or related field.

Alvernia University, Graduate Studies, Program in Leadership, Reading, PA 19607-1799. Offers PhD. *Degree requirements:* For doctorate, comprehensive exam, thesis/dissertation (for some programs). *Entrance requirements:* For doctorate, GRE, GMAT, or MAT, minimum GPA of 3.3, 3 letters of recommendation, resume, interview.

The American College, Richard D. Irwin Graduate School, Bryn Mawr, PA 19010-2105. Offers financial services (MSFS); leadership (MSM). Part-time and evening/weekend programs available. Postbaccalaureate distance learning degree programs offered (minimal on-campus study). Electronic applications accepted. *Faculty research:* Retirement counseling, social security, aging, family composition, inflation.

American International College, School of Business Administration, Program in Organization Development, Springfield, MA 01109-3189. Offers MS. Part-time and evening/weekend programs available. *Degree requirements:* For master's, comprehensive exam (for some programs), thesis (for some programs), project or research report. *Entrance requirements:* Additional exam requirements/recommendations for international students: Required—TOEFL. Electronic applications accepted. *Expenses:* Tuition: Full-time $12,510; part-time $695 per credit hour. Required fees: $35 per term.

American University, School of Public Affairs, Department of Public Administration, Program in Organization Development, Washington, DC 20016-8070. Offers MSOD. *Students:* 1 (woman) full-time, 87 part-time (66 women); includes 26 minority (21 African Americans, 1 American Indian/Alaska Native, 2 Asian Americans or Pacific Islanders, 2 Hispanic Americans), 5 international. Average age 38. In 2009, 37 master's awarded. *Degree requirements:* For master's, comprehensive exam. *Entrance requirements:* For master's, GRE, 2 years of related professional experience, 2 recommendations. Additional exam requirements/recommendations for international students: Required—TOEFL. *Application deadline:* For fall admission, 2/1 for domestic students; for spring admission, 11/1 for domestic students. Application fee: $55. *Expenses:* Tuition: Full-time $22,266; part-time $1237 per credit hour. Required fees: $430. Tuition and fees vary according to program. *Financial support:* Application deadline: 2/1.

Amridge University, Graduate and Professional Programs, Montgomery, AL 36117. Offers behavioral leadership and management (MA); biblical studies (MA, PhD); family therapy

(D Min); leadership and management (MS); marriage and family therapy (M Div, MA, PhD); ministerial leadership (M Div, MS); pastoral counseling (M Div, MS); practical theology (MA); professional counseling (M Div, MA); theology (M Div, D Min). *Accreditation:* ATS. Part-time and evening/weekend programs available. Postbaccalaureate distance learning degree programs offered (no on-campus study). *Faculty:* 44 full-time (9 women), 18 part-time/adjunct (7 women). *Students:* 175 full-time (95 women), 192 part-time (93 women); includes 182 minority (172 African Americans, 1 American Indian/Alaska Native, 1 Asian American or Pacific Islander, 8 Hispanic Americans). Average age 35. *Degree requirements:* For master's, one foreign language, comprehensive exam (for some programs), thesis (for some programs); for doctorate, comprehensive exam (for some programs), thesis/dissertation; for M Div, comprehensive exam (for some programs). *Entrance requirements:* For M Div, master's, and doctorate, GRE General Test or MAT. Additional exam requirements/recommendations for international students: Required—TOEFL. *Application deadline:* For fall admission, 9/1 priority date for domestic students; for spring admission, 1/1 priority date for domestic students. Applications are processed on a rolling basis. Application fee: $75. Electronic applications accepted. *Expenses:* Tuition: Full-time $10,080; part-time $560 per semester hour. Required fees: $600 per term. *Financial support:* Federal Work-Study and scholarships/grants available. Support available to part-time students. Financial award applicants required to submit FAFSA. *Faculty research:* Homiletics, hermeneutics, ancient Near Eastern history. *Unit head:* Director of Enrollment Management, 800-351-4040 Ext. 7513, Fax: 334-387-3878. *Application contact:* Ora Davis, Admissions Officer, 334-387-3877 Ext. 7524, Fax: 334-387-3878, E-mail: admissions@amridgeuniversity.edu.

Antioch University Los Angeles, Graduate Programs, Program in Organizational Management, Culver City, CA 90230. Offers human resource development (MA); leadership (MA); organizational development (MA). Part-time and evening/weekend programs available. *Entrance requirements:* For master's, interview. Additional exam requirements/recommendations for international students: Required—TOEFL. *Faculty research:* Systems thinking and chaos theory, technology and organizational structure, nonprofit management, power and empowerment.

Antioch University New England, Graduate School, Department of Organization and Management, Program in Organizational Development, Keene, NH 03431-3552. Offers Certificate.

Antioch University New England, Graduate School, Department of Organization and Management, Program in Organizational Leadership and Management, Keene, NH 03431-3552. Offers MS. *Degree requirements:* For master's, practicum. *Entrance requirements:* For master's, previous course work and work experience in organization and management. Additional exam requirements/recommendations for international students: Required—TOEFL (minimum score 600 paper-based; 250 computer-based). Electronic applications accepted. *Expenses:* Contact institution. *Faculty research:* Developing a collaborative CEO performance evaluation process, search conference process as change mechanism, implementing workflow designs to increase organizational competitiveness.

Organizational Management

Antioch University Santa Barbara, Program in Organizational Management, Santa Barbara, CA 93101-1581. Offers MA. Part-time and evening/weekend programs available. Postbaccalaureate distance learning degree programs offered (minimal on-campus study). Electronic applications accepted. *Faculty research:* Multicultural communication, organizational change.

Antioch University Seattle, Graduate Programs, Center for Creative Change, Seattle, WA 98121-1814. Offers environment and community (MA); management (MS); organizational psychology (MA); strategic communications (MA); whole system design (MA). Evening/weekend programs available. Electronic applications accepted. *Expenses:* Contact institution.

Argosy University, Chicago, College of Business, Program in Organizational Leadership, Chicago, IL 60601. Offers Ed D.

See Close-Up on page 199.

Argosy University, Denver, College of Business, Denver, CO 80231. Offers accounting (DBA); corporate compliance (MBA); customized professional concentration (MBA, DBA); finance (MBA); fraud examination (MBA); global business sustainability (DBA); healthcare administration (MBA); information systems (DBA); information systems management (MBA); international business (MBA, DBA); management (MBA, MSM, DBA); marketing (MBA, DBA); organizational leadership (Ed D); public administration (MBA); sustainable management (MBA).

See Close-Up on page 203.

Argosy University, Hawai'i, College of Business, Program in Organizational Leadership, Honolulu, HI 96813. Offers Ed D.

See Close-Up on page 205.

Argosy University, Inland Empire, College of Business, San Bernardino, CA 92408. Offers accounting (DBA); corporate compliance (MBA); customized professional concentration (MBA, DBA); finance (MBA); fraud examination (MBA); global business sustainability (DBA); healthcare administration (MBA); information systems (DBA); information systems management (MBA); international business (MBA, DBA); management (MBA, MSM, DBA); marketing (MBA, DBA); organizational leadership (Ed D); public administration (MBA); sustainable management (MBA).

See Close-Up on page 207.

Argosy University, Los Angeles, College of Business, Santa Monica, CA 90045. Offers accounting (DBA); corporate compliance (MBA); customized professional concentration (MBA, DBA); finance (MBA); fraud examination (MBA); global business sustainability (DBA); healthcare administration (MBA); information systems (DBA); information systems management (MBA); international business (MBA, DBA); management (MBA, MSM, DBA); marketing (MBA, DBA); organizational leadership (Ed D); public administration (MBA); sustainable management (MBA).

See Close-Up on page 209.

Argosy University, Orange County, College of Business, Program in Organizational Leadership, Orange, CA 92868. Offers Ed D. *Unit head:* Dr. Gary Bruss, Dean, 800-716-9598, Fax: 714-437-1284, E-mail: gbruss@argosy.edu. *Application contact:* Mark Betz, Director of Admissions, 800-716-9598, Fax: 714-437-1697, E-mail: mbetz@argosy.edu.

See Close-Up on page 213.

Argosy University, San Diego, College of Business, San Diego, CA 92108. Offers accounting (DBA); corporate compliance (MBA); customized professional concentration (MBA, DBA); finance (MBA); fraud examination (MBA); global business sustainability (DBA); information systems (DBA); information systems management (MBA); international business (MBA, DBA); management (MBA, MSM, DBA); marketing (MBA, DBA); organizational leadership (Ed D); public administration (MBA).

See Close-Up on page 219.

Argosy University, San Francisco Bay Area, College of Business, Alameda, CA 94501. Offers accounting (DBA); corporate compliance (MBA); customized professional concentration (MBA, DBA); finance (MBA); fraud examination (MBA); global business sustainability (DBA); healthcare administration (MBA); information systems (DBA); information systems management (MBA); international business (MBA, DBA); management (MBA, MSM, DBA); marketing (MBA, DBA); organizational leadership (Ed D); public administration (MBA); sustainable management (MBA).

See Close-Up on page 221.

Argosy University, Sarasota, College of Business, Sarasota, FL 34235. Offers accounting (DBA, Adv C); corporate compliance (MBA, DBA, Certificate); customized professional concentration (MBA, DBA); finance (MBA, Certificate); fraud examination (MBA, Certificate); global business sustainability (DBA, Adv C); healthcare administration (MBA, Certificate); information systems (DBA, Adv C, Certificate); information systems management (MBA); international business (MBA, DBA, Adv C, Certificate); management (MBA, MSM, DBA, Adv C, Certificate); marketing (MBA, DBA, Adv C, Certificate); organizational leadership (Ed D); public administration (MBA, Certificate); sustainable management (MBA, Certificate).

See Close-Up on page 223.

Argosy University, Seattle, College of Business, Seattle, WA 98121. Offers accounting (DBA); corporate compliance (MBA); customized professional concentration (MBA, DBA); finance (MBA); fraud examination (MBA); global business sustainability (DBA); healthcare administration (MBA); information systems (DBA); information systems management (MBA); international business (MBA, DBA); management (MBA, MSM, DBA); marketing (MBA, DBA); organizational leadership (Ed D); public administration (MBA); sustainable management (MBA).

See Close-Up on page 227.

Argosy University, Tampa, College of Business, Tampa, FL 33607. Offers accounting (DBA); corporate compliance (MBA); customized professional concentration (MBA, DBA); finance (MBA); fraud examination (MBA); global business sustainability (DBA); healthcare administration (MBA); information systems (DBA); information systems management (MBA); international business (MBA, DBA); management (MBA, MSM, DBA); marketing (MBA, DBA); organizational leadership (Ed D); public administration (MBA); sustainable management (MBA).

See Close-Up on page 229.

Argosy University, Twin Cities, College of Business, Eagan, MN 55121. Offers accounting (DBA); customized professional concentration (MBA, DBA); finance (MBA); fraud examination (MBA); global business sustainability (DBA); healthcare administration (MBA); information systems (DBA); information systems management (MBA); international business (MBA, DBA); management (MBA, MSM, DBA); marketing (MBA, DBA); organizational leadership (Ed D); public administration (MBA); sustainable management (MBA).

See Close-Up on page 231.

Argosy University, Washington DC, College of Business, Arlington, VA 22209. Offers accounting (DBA); customized professional concentration (MBA, DBA); finance (MBA); fraud examination (MBA); global business sustainability (DBA); healthcare administration (MBA); information systems (DBA); information systems management (MBA); international business (MBA, DBA, Certificate); management (MBA, MSM, DBA); marketing (MBA, DBA, Certificate); organizational leadership (Ed D); public administration (MBA); sustainable management (MBA).

See Close-Up on page 233.

Athabasca University, Centre for Integrated Studies, Athabasca, AB T9S 3A3, Canada. Offers adult education (MA); community studies (MA); cultural studies (MA); educational studies (MA); global change (MA); work, organization, and leadership (MA). Part-time and evening/weekend programs available. Postbaccalaureate distance learning degree programs offered (no on-campus study). *Faculty:* 10 full-time (4 women), 12 part-time/adjunct (9 women). *Students:* 705 part-time. Average age 35. 195 applicants, 38 enrolled. In 2009, 52 master's awarded. *Degree requirements:* For master's, project. *Entrance requirements:* Additional exam requirements/recommendations for international students: Required—TOEFL (minimum score 560 paper-based; 220 computer-based). *Application deadline:* For fall admission, 3/1 for domestic and international students; for winter admission, 9/1 for domestic and international students. Application fee: $80. Electronic applications accepted. *Expenses:* Tuition: Part-time $16,500 per degree program. Required fees: $200 per year. One-time fee: $80 part-time. *Faculty research:* Women's history, literature and culture studies, sustainable development, labor and education. *Unit head:* Dr. Michael Gismondi, Program Director, 780-675-6218, Fax: 780-675-6921, E-mail: mikeg@athabascau.ca. *Application contact:* Derek Stovin, Program Administrator, 780-675-6236, Fax: 780-675-6921, E-mail: dereks@athabascau.ca.

Augsburg College, Program in Leadership, Minneapolis, MN 55454-1351. Offers MA. Part-time and evening/weekend programs available. *Degree requirements:* For master's, thesis or alternative. *Entrance requirements:* For master's, MAT, minimum GPA of 3.0. Additional exam requirements/recommendations for international students: Required—TOEFL (minimum score 600 paper-based; 250 computer-based). *Expenses:* Tuition: Full-time $16,713; part-time $1857 per course. Required fees: $450; $50 per course. Tuition and fees vary according to course load and program. *Faculty research:* Soviet leaders, artificial intelligence, homelessness.

Avila University, Program in Organizational Development, Kansas City, MO 64145-1698. Offers management (MA), including fundraising, project management; organizational development (MS); project management (Graduate Certificate). Part-time and evening/weekend programs available. *Faculty:* 2 full-time (1 woman), 10 part-time/adjunct (7 women). *Students:* 50 full-time (41 women), 43 part-time (35 women); includes 28 minority (24 African Americans, 2 Asian Americans or Pacific Islanders, 2 Hispanic Americans), 2 international. Average age 36. 47 applicants, 64% accepted, 27 enrolled. In 2009, 16 master's awarded. *Degree requirements:* For master's, thesis optional. *Entrance requirements:* For master's, 2 letters of recommendation, minimum GPA of 3.25 during last 60 hours, resume. Additional exam requirements/recommendations for international students: Required—TOEFL. *Application deadline:* Applications are processed on a rolling basis. Application fee: $0. Electronic applications accepted. *Expenses:* Tuition: Full-time $8622; part-time $479 per credit hour. Required fees: $432; $24 per credit hour. Tuition and fees vary according to program. *Financial support:* In 2009–10, 69 students received support. Unspecified assistantships available. Support available to part-time students. Financial award applicants required to submit FAFSA. *Unit head:* Dr. Lacey Smith, Associate Dean, 816-501-3737, Fax: 816-941-4650, E-mail: advantage@avila.edu. *Application contact:* School of Professional Studies, 816-501-3737, Fax: 816-941-4650, E-mail: advantage@avila.edu.

Azusa Pacific University, School of Behavioral and Applied Sciences, Department of Higher Education and Organizational Leadership, Program in Leadership and Organizational Studies, Azusa, CA 91702-7000. Offers MLOS.

Azusa Pacific University, School of Behavioral and Applied Sciences, Department of Higher Education and Organizational Leadership, Program in Organizational Leadership, Azusa, CA 91702-7000. Offers MA.

Benedictine University, Graduate Programs, Program in Business Administration, Lisle, IL 60532-0900. Offers accounting (MBA); entrepreneurship and managing innovation (MBA); financial management (MBA); health administration (MBA); human resource management (MBA); information systems security (MBA); international business (MBA); management consulting (MBA); management information systems (MBA); marketing management (MBA); operations management and logistics (MBA); organizational leadership (MBA); MBA/MPH; MBA/MS. Part-time and evening/weekend programs available. Postbaccalaureate distance learning degree programs offered (minimal on-campus study). *Faculty:* 4 full-time (2 women), 24 part-time/adjunct (3 women). *Students:* 247 full-time (141 women), 644 part-time (339 women); includes 223 minority (134 African Americans, 5 American Indian/Alaska Native, 44 Asian Americans or Pacific Islanders, 40 Hispanic Americans), 25 international. Average age 34. 287 applicants, 92% accepted, 229 enrolled. In 2009, 219 master's awarded. *Entrance requirements:* For master's, GMAT. Additional exam requirements/recommendations for international students: Required—TOEFL (minimum score 550 paper-based; 213 computer-based). *Application deadline:* For fall admission, 9/1 for domestic students; for winter admission, 12/1 for domestic students; for spring admission, 2/15 for domestic students. Applications are processed on a rolling basis. Application fee: $40. Electronic applications accepted. *Expenses:* Tuition: Part-time $750 per credit hour. Tuition and fees vary according to campus/location and program. *Financial support:* Career-related internships or fieldwork and health care benefits available. Support available to part-time students. *Faculty research:* Strategic leadership in professional organizations, sociology of professions, organizational change, social identity theory, applications to change management. *Unit head:* Dr. Sharon Borowicz, Director, 630-829-6219, E-mail: sborowicz@ben.edu. *Application contact:* Kari Gibbons, Director, Admissions, 630-829-6200, Fax: 630-829-6584, E-mail: kgibbons@ben.edu.

Benedictine University, Graduate Programs, Program in Organizational Development, Lisle, IL 60532-0900. Offers PhD. Evening/weekend programs available. *Faculty:* 2 full-time (0 women), 2 part-time/adjunct (1 woman). *Students:* 33 full-time (21 women), 7 part-time (4 women); includes 5 minority (4 African Americans, 1 Asian American or Pacific Islander), 8 international. Average age 44. In 2009, 16 doctorates awarded. *Degree requirements:* For doctorate, thesis/dissertation. *Entrance requirements:* Additional exam requirements/recommendations for international students: Required—TOEFL (minimum score 550 paper-based). *Application deadline:* For fall admission, 9/1 for domestic students; for winter admission, 12/1 for domestic students; for spring admission, 2/15 for domestic students. Application fee: $40. Electronic applications accepted. *Expenses:* Tuition: Part-time $750 per credit hour. Tuition and fees vary according to campus/location and program. *Financial support:* Career-related internships or fieldwork and health care benefits available. *Faculty research:* Change management, appreciative inquiry, innovation and organization design, global and international organization development, organization renewal. *Unit head:* Dr. Peter F. Sorensen, Director, 630-829-6220, Fax: 630-960-1126, E-mail: psorensen@ben.edu. *Application contact:* Kari Gibbons, Director, Admissions, 630-829-6200, Fax: 630-829-6584, E-mail: kgibbons@ben.edu.

Bernard M. Baruch College of the City University of New York, Zicklin School of Business, Department of Management, New York, NY 10010-5585. Offers entrepreneurship (MBA); general management and policy (MBA); human resources management (MBA); management planning systems (PhD); management science (MBA); organization and policy studies (PhD); organizational behavior (MBA). Part-time and evening/weekend programs available. *Degree requirements:* For doctorate, comprehensive exam, thesis/dissertation. *Entrance requirements:* For master's, GMAT, 2 letters of recommendation, resume, 2 years of work experience; for doctorate, GMAT. Additional exam requirements/recommendations for international students: Required—TOEFL (minimum score 590 paper-based; 243 computer-based), TWE.

Bethel University, Graduate School, Program in Organizational Leadership, St. Paul, MN 55112-6999. Offers MA. Evening/weekend programs available. *Faculty:* 4 full-time (2 women), 12 part-time/adjunct (6 women). *Students:* 66 full-time (39 women), 31 part-time (22 women); includes 12 minority (9 African Americans, 2 Asian Americans or Pacific Islanders, 1 Hispanic American), 3 international. Average age 36. 59 applicants, 86% accepted, 41 enrolled. In 2009, 34 master's awarded. *Degree requirements:* For master's, thesis. *Entrance requirements:* For master's, baccalaureate degree, interview, minimum GPA of 3.0, letters of reference, statement of purpose essay. Additional exam requirements/recommendations for international students: Required—TOEFL (minimum score 550 paper-based; 213 computer-based; 80 iBT). *Application deadline:* For fall admission, 6/15 priority date for domestic students; for winter admission, 12/1 priority date for domestic students. Applications are processed on a rolling basis. Application fee: $25. Electronic applications accepted. *Expenses:* Tuition: Full-time $7920; part-time $440 per credit. One-time fee: $25. Tuition and fees vary according to course load, degree level and program. *Financial support:* Applicants required to submit FAFSA. *Unit head:* Nikki Daniels, Assistant Dean, 651-635-8000, Fax: 651-635-8039, E-mail: n-daniels@bethel.edu. *Application contact:* Michael Price, Director of Admissions, 651-635-8000, Fax: 651-635-8004, E-mail: m-price@bethel.edu.

Organizational Management

Biola University, School of Professional Studies, La Mirada, CA 90639-0001. Offers Christian apologetics (MA); organizational leadership (MA). Part-time and evening/weekend programs available. *Entrance requirements:* For master's, minimum undergraduate GPA of 3.0. Additional exam requirements/recommendations for international students: Required—TOEFL (minimum score 550 paper-based; 213 computer-based).

Bluffton University, Programs in Business, Bluffton, OH 45817. Offers business administration (MBA); organizational management (MA). Evening/weekend programs available. *Entrance requirements:* Additional exam requirements/recommendations for international students: Required—TOEFL. Electronic applications accepted.

Boston College, Carroll School of Management, Department of Organization Studies, Chestnut Hill, MA 02467-3800. Offers PhD. *Faculty:* 11 full-time (4 women). *Students:* 24 full-time (15 women); includes 2 minority (1 African American, 1 Hispanic American), 8 international. Average age 32. 60 applicants, 12% accepted, 4 enrolled. In 2009, 8 doctorates awarded. *Degree requirements:* For doctorate, comprehensive exam, thesis/dissertation, teaching experience. *Entrance requirements:* For doctorate, GMAT or GRE, letters of recommendation, resume, transcripts. Additional exam requirements/recommendations for international students: Required—TOEFL. *Application deadline:* For spring admission, 2/1 for domestic and international students. Application fee: $50. *Financial support:* In 2009–10, 21 fellowships, 17 research assistantships with full tuition reimbursements were awarded. Financial award application deadline: 3/1; financial award applicants required to submit FAFSA. *Faculty research:* Organizational transformation, mergers and acquisitions, managerial effectiveness, organizational change, organizational structure. *Unit head:* Dr. Jeffrey L. Ringuest, Associate Dean, Graduate Programs, 617-552-9100, Fax: 617-552-0514, E-mail: gsomdean@bc.edu. *Application contact:* Shelley Burt, Director of Graduate Enrollment, 617-552-3920, Fax: 617-552-8078, E-mail: bcmba@bc.edu.

Bowling Green State University, Graduate College, College of Business Administration, Program in Organization Development, Bowling Green, OH 43403. Offers MOD. Part-time and evening/weekend programs available. *Degree requirements:* For master's, thesis or alternative, internship. *Entrance requirements:* For master's, GMAT or GRE General Test. Additional exam requirements/recommendations for international students: Required—TOEFL. Electronic applications accepted. *Faculty research:* Charismatic leadership, self-managing work teams, knowledge workers, stress, effects of change processes.

Brenau University, Graduate Programs, School of Business and Mass Communication, Gainesville, GA 30501. Offers accounting (MBA); business administration (MBA); healthcare management (MBA); organizational leadership (MS); project management (MBA). Part-time and evening/weekend programs available. Postbaccalaureate distance learning degree programs offered (no on-campus study). *Faculty:* 11 full-time (6 women), 22 part-time/adjunct (6 women). *Students:* 116 full-time (74 women), 256 part-time (181 women); includes 113 minority (98 African Americans, 6 Asian Americans or Pacific Islanders, 9 Hispanic Americans), 20 international. Average age 35. 278 applicants, 90% accepted, 185 enrolled. In 2009, 125 master's awarded. *Entrance requirements:* For master's, resume, minimum undergraduate GPA of 3.5. Additional exam requirements/recommendations for international students: Required—TOEFL (minimum score 500 paper-based). *Application deadline:* Applications are processed on a rolling basis. Electronic applications accepted. *Expenses:* Contact institution. *Financial support:* In 2009–10, 1 student received support. Application deadline: 7/15. *Unit head:* Dr. William S. Lightfoot, Dean, 770-538-5330, Fax: 770-537-4701, E-mail: wlightfoot@brenau.edu. *Application contact:* Christina White, Graduate Admissions Specialist, 770-718-5320, Fax: 770-718-5338, E-mail: cwhite@brenau.edu.

Briercrest Seminary, Graduate Programs, Program in Leadership and Management, Caronport, SK S0H 0S0, Canada. Offers organizational leadership (MA). Part-time programs available. *Degree requirements:* For master's, comprehensive exam, thesis optional. *Entrance requirements:* Additional exam requirements/recommendations for international students: Required—TOEFL (minimum score 550 paper-based; 213 computer-based).

Cabrini College, Graduate and Professional Studies, Radnor, PA 19087-3698. Offers education (M Ed); organization leadership (MS). Part-time and evening/weekend programs available. *Faculty:* 6 full-time (3 women), 135 part-time/adjunct (81 women). *Students:* 135 full-time (93 women), 1,825 part-time (1,430 women); includes 150 minority (112 African Americans, 1 American Indian/Alaska Native, 14 Asian Americans or Pacific Islanders, 23 Hispanic Americans). Average age 32. 714 applicants, 70% accepted, 460 enrolled. In 2009, 614 master's awarded. *Degree requirements:* For master's, thesis optional. *Entrance requirements:* For master's, GRE and/or MAT (in some cases), letter of recommendation, minimum GPA of 2.5. *Application deadline:* For fall admission, 7/29 priority date for domestic students; for spring admission, 12/9 for domestic students. Applications are processed on a rolling basis. Application fee: $50. Electronic applications accepted. *Expenses:* Tuition: Part-time $555 per credit. *Financial support:* Career-related internships or fieldwork and unspecified assistantships available. Support available to part-time students. Financial award applicants required to submit FAFSA. *Unit head:* Dr. Dennis R. Dougherty, Interim Dean for Graduate and Professional Studies, 610-902-8501, Fax: 610-902-8522, E-mail: dennis.dougherty@cabrini.edu. *Application contact:* Bruce D. Bryde, Director of Enrollment and Recruiting, 610-902-8291, Fax: 610-902-8522, E-mail: bruce.d.bryde@cabrini.edu.

California Coast University, Programs in Education, Santa Ana, CA 92701. Offers administration (M Ed); curriculum and instruction (M Ed); educational psychology (D Ed); organizational leadership (D Ed). Part-time and evening/weekend programs available. Postbaccalaureate distance learning degree programs offered (no on-campus study). Application fee: $75. *Application contact:* Christi Okuma, 714-547-9625, Fax: 714-547-5777, E-mail: ccu@calcoast.edu.

California College of the Arts, Graduate Programs, Program in Design Strategy, San Francisco, CA 94107. Offers MBA.

California Intercontinental University, School of Business, Diamond Bar, CA 91765. Offers banking and finance (MBA); entrepreneurship and business management (DBA); global business leadership (DBA); international management and marketing (MBA); organizational management and human resource management (MBA).

Cambridge College, School of Management, Cambridge, MA 02138-5304. Offers business negotiation and conflict resolution (M Mgt); general business (M Mgt); health care informatics (M Mgt); health care management (M Mgt); leadership in human and organizational dynamics (M Mgt); non-profit and public organization management (M Mgt); small business development (M Mgt); technology management (M Mgt). Part-time and evening/weekend programs available. *Faculty:* 4 full-time (3 women), 65 part-time/adjunct (32 women). *Students:* 297 full-time (178 women), 234 part-time (155 women); includes 217 minority (122 African Americans, 53 Asian Americans or Pacific Islanders, 42 Hispanic Americans), 135 international. Average age 39. In 2009, 259 master's awarded. *Degree requirements:* For master's, thesis, seminars. *Entrance requirements:* For master's, resume, 2 professional references. Additional exam requirements/recommendations for international students: Required—TOEFL (minimum score 550 paper-based; 213 computer-based; 79 iBT); Recommended—IELTS (minimum score 6). *Application deadline:* Applications are processed on a rolling basis. Application fee: $30. Electronic applications accepted. *Expenses:* Contact institution. *Financial support:* In 2009–10, 170 students received support. Career-related internships or fieldwork, Federal Work-Study, and scholarships/grants available. Financial award applicants required to submit FAFSA. *Faculty research:* Negotiation, mediation and conflict resolution; leadership; management of diverse organizations; case studies and simulation methodologies for management education, digital as a second language: social networking for digital immigrants. *Unit head:* Dr. Mary Ann Joseph, Acting Dean, 617-873-0227, E-mail: maryann.joseph@cambridgecollege.edu. *Application contact:* Stephen Lyons, Director of Enrollment, Graduate and N.I.T.E. Programs, 617-868-1000, Fax: 617-349-3561, E-mail: stephen.lyons@cambridgecollege.edu.

Capella University, Harold Abel School of Psychology, Minneapolis, MN 55402. Offers child and adolescent development (MS); clinical psychology (MS, Psy D); counseling psychology (MS); educational psychology (MS, PhD); evaluation, research, and measurement (MS); general psychology (MS, PhD); industrial/organizational psychology (MS, PhD); leadership coaching psychology (MS); organizational leader development (MS); school psychology (MS); sport psychology (MS). Part-time and evening/weekend programs available. Postbaccalaureate distance learning degree programs offered (minimal on-campus study). Terminal master's awarded for partial completion of doctoral program. *Degree requirements:* For master's, thesis optional, project; for doctorate, thesis/dissertation. *Entrance requirements:* For degree, master's degree in school psychology. Additional exam requirements/recommendations for international students: Required—TOEFL (minimum score 550 paper-based; 213 computer-based), TWE (minimum score 4); Recommended—IELTS. Electronic applications accepted.

Capella University, School of Business and Technology, Minneapolis, MN 55402. Offers accounting (MBA), including system design and programming; business (Certificate), including human resource management (MS, PhD, Certificate), information technology management (MS, PhD, Certificate), leadership (MBA, MS, PhD, Certificate); finance (MBA); general business (MBA); health care management (MBA); information technology (MS, Certificate), including general information technology (MS), information security, network architecture and design (MS), professional projects management (Certificate), project management and leadership (MS), system design and development (MS),); information technology management (MBA); marketing (MBA); organization and management (MBA, MS, PhD), including general business (PhD), general organization and management (MBA, MS), human resource management (MS, PhD, Certificate), information technology management (MS, PhD, Certificate), leadership (MBA, MS, PhD, Certificate); project management (MBA). Part-time and evening/weekend programs available. Postbaccalaureate distance learning degree programs offered (minimal on-campus study). Terminal master's awarded for partial completion of doctoral program. *Degree requirements:* For master's, thesis optional, integrative project; for doctorate, comprehensive exam, thesis/dissertation. *Entrance requirements:* Additional exam requirements/recommendations for international students: Required—TOEFL (minimum score 550 paper-based; 213 computer-based), TWE (minimum score 4). Electronic applications accepted. *Faculty research:* Business policies: strategic, corporate, and financial management; interplay of technological, organizational and social change.

Carlos Albizu University, Miami Campus, Graduate Programs, Miami, FL 33172-2209. Offers clinical psychology (Psy D); entrepreneurship (MBA); exceptional student education (MS); industrial/organizational psychology (MS); marriage and family therapy (MS); mental health counseling (MS); nonprofit management (MBA); organizational management (MBA); psychology (MS); school counseling (MS); teaching English as a second language (MS). *Accreditation:* APA. Part-time and evening/weekend programs available. *Faculty:* 23 full-time (13 women), 41 part-time/adjunct (21 women). *Students:* 529 full-time (420 women), 171 part-time (139 women); includes 551 minority (55 African Americans, 1 American Indian/Alaska Native, 5 Asian Americans or Pacific Islanders, 490 Hispanic Americans). Average age 37. 278 applicants, 57% accepted, 142 enrolled. In 2009, 139 master's, 26 doctorates awarded. Terminal master's awarded for partial completion of doctoral program. *Degree requirements:* For master's, one foreign language, comprehensive exam, integrative project (MBA), research project (exceptional student education, teaching English as a second language); for doctorate, one foreign language, comprehensive exam, internship, project. *Entrance requirements:* For master's, 3 letters of recommendation, interview, minimum GPA of 3.0, resume; for doctorate, 3 letters of recommendation, minimum GPA of 3.0, resume, interview. *Application deadline:* For fall admission, 8/1 priority date for domestic students; for spring admission, 11/30 priority date for domestic students. Applications are processed on a rolling basis. Application fee: $50. Electronic applications accepted. *Expenses:* Tuition: Full-time $9090; part-time $505 per credit hour. Required fees: $298 per term. Tuition and fees vary according to course load, degree level and program. *Financial support:* In 2009–10, 127 students received support. Federal Work-Study, scholarships/grants, and tuition discounts available. Financial award application deadline: 6/1; financial award applicants required to submit FAFSA. *Faculty research:* Psychotherapy, forensic psychology, neuropsychology, marketing strategy, entrepreneurship, special education. *Unit head:* Dr. Carmen S. Roca, Chancellor, 305-593-1223 Ext. 120, Fax: 305-629-8052, E-mail: croca@albizu.edu. *Application contact:* Annalye Alonso, Secretary, 305-593-1223 Ext. 137, Fax: 305-593-1854, E-mail: aalonso@albizu.edu.

Carlow University, School for Social Change, Pittsburgh, PA 15213-3165. Offers professional counseling (MS); professional counseling: school counseling (MS); professional leadership: management for nonprofit organizations (MS); professional leadership: organizational influence and policy (MS); professional leadership: training and development (MS). Part-time and evening/weekend programs available. *Entrance requirements:* Additional exam requirements/recommendations for international students: Required—TOEFL (minimum score 550 paper-based; 213 computer-based). Electronic applications accepted. *Expenses:* Tuition: Full-time $11,250; part-time $625 per credit. Tuition and fees vary according to course load, degree level and program. *Faculty research:* Gender and leadership, cross cultural communications and leadership, organizational culture.

Charleston Southern University, Program in Business, Charleston, SC 29423-8087. Offers accounting (MBA); finance (MBA); health care administration (MBA); information systems (MBA); organizational development (MBA). Part-time and evening/weekend programs available. *Faculty:* 14 full-time (1 woman), 6 part-time/adjunct (1 woman). *Students:* 316 part-time (157 women); includes 67 minority (53 African Americans, 1 American Indian/Alaska Native, 7 Asian Americans or Pacific Islanders, 6 Hispanic Americans), 7 international. Average age 32. 173 applicants, 85% accepted, 97 enrolled. In 2009, 69 master's awarded. *Degree requirements:* For master's, thesis optional. *Entrance requirements:* For master's, GMAT. Additional exam requirements/recommendations for international students: Required—TOEFL (minimum score 550 paper-based; 213 computer-based; 79 iBT). *Application deadline:* Applications are processed on a rolling basis. Application fee: $30. *Expenses:* Tuition: Part-time $350 per credit hour. Required fees: $40 per semester. Tuition and fees vary according to program. *Financial support:* Research assistantships with full tuition reimbursements available. Financial award application deadline: 4/15; financial award applicants required to submit FAFSA. *Unit head:* Dr. Scott Pearson, Director of the MBA Program, 843-863-7038, Fax: 843-863-7922, E-mail: spearson@csuniv.edu. *Application contact:* Alison Harrison, Graduate Enrollment Counselor, 843-863-7534, Fax: 843-863-7070, E-mail: aharrison@cusniv.edu.

City University of Seattle, Graduate Division, School of Management, Bellevue, WA 98005. Offers accounting (Certificate); change leadership (MBA, Certificate); financial management (MBA, Certificate); general management (MBA); general management-Europe (MBA); global leadership (Certificate); global marketing (MBA); individualized study (MBA); information security (MS); information systems (MBA); leadership (MA); marketing (MBA, Certificate); project management (MBA, MS, Certificate); sustainable business (Certificate); technology management (MBA, MS, Certificate). Part-time and evening/weekend programs available. Postbaccalaureate distance learning degree programs offered (no on-campus study). *Entrance requirements:* Additional exam requirements/recommendations for international students: Required—TOEFL (minimum score 540 paper-based; 207 computer-based); Recommended—IELTS. Electronic applications accepted. *Expenses:* Tuition: Full-time $14,760; part-time $615 per credit. Tuition and fees vary according to program.

Cleary University, Online Program in Business Administration, Ann Arbor, MI 48105-2659. Offers accounting (MBA); financial planning (MBA); financial planning (Graduate Certificate); green business strategy (MBA); management (MBA); nonprofit management (MBA); organizational leadership (MBA). Part-time and evening/weekend programs available. Postbaccalaureate distance learning degree programs offered (no on-campus study). *Degree requirements:* For master's, thesis. *Entrance requirements:* For master's, bachelor's degree; minimum GPA of 2.5; professional resume indicating minimum 2 years management or related experience; undergraduate degree from an accredited college or university with at least 18 quarter hours (or 12 semester hours) of accounting study (for MBA in accounting). Additional exam requirements/recommendations for international students: Required—TOEFL (minimum

Organizational Management

Cleary University (continued)

score 550 paper-based; 213 computer-based; 79 iBT), Michigan English Language Assessment Battery (minimum score: 75). Electronic applications accepted.

College of Mount St. Joseph, Master of Science in Organizational Leadership Program, Cincinnati, OH 45233-1670. Offers MS. Part-time and evening/weekend programs available. *Faculty:* 4 full-time (1 woman), 1 (woman) part-time/adjunct. *Students:* 1 (woman) full-time, 66 part-time (47 women); includes 12 minority (10 African Americans, 1 American Indian/Alaska Native, 1 Asian American or Pacific Islander). Average age 40. 25 applicants, 32% accepted, 7 enrolled. In 2009, 10 master's awarded. *Degree requirements:* For master's; integrative project. *Entrance requirements:* For master's, minimum GPA of 3.0, interview, 3 years of work experience, 3 letters of reference, resume. Additional exam requirements/recommendations for international students: Required—TOEFL (minimum score 560 paper-based; 220 computer-based; 83 iBT). *Application deadline:* Applications are processed on a rolling basis. Application fee: $50. Electronic applications accepted. *Expenses:* Contact institution. *Financial support:* In 2009–10, 2 students received support. Application deadline: 6/1. *Faculty research:* Gender and cultural effects on management education, group identity formation, leadership skill development, methods for improving instructional effectiveness, technology-based productivity improvement. *Unit head:* Daryl Smith, Chair of Organizational Leadership, 513-244-4920, Fax: 513-244-4270, E-mail: daryl_smith@mail.msj.edu. *Application contact:* Marilyn Hoskins, Assistant Director of Graduate Recruitment, 513-244-4723, Fax: 513-244-4629, E-mail: marilyn_hoskins@mail.msj.edu.

College of Saint Mary, Program in Organizational Leadership, Omaha, NE 68106. Offers MOL. Part-time and evening/weekend programs available. *Entrance requirements:* For master's, resume. Electronic applications accepted.

Colorado State University, Graduate School, College of Business, Program in Management Practice, Fort Collins, CO 80523-1201. Offers MMP. *Students:* 31 full-time (16 women), 5 part-time (3 women); includes 3 minority (1 Asian American or Pacific Islander, 2 Hispanic Americans), 3 international. Average age 25. 40 applicants, 93% accepted, 31 enrolled. In 2009, 10 master's awarded. *Entrance requirements:* For master's, GMAT or GRE, minimum cumulative GPA of 3.0, current resume, 3 recommendations. Additional exam requirements/recommendations for international students: Required—TOEFL or IELTS. Application fee: $50. *Expenses:* Tuition, state resident: full-time $6434; part-time $359.10 per credit. Tuition, nonresident: full-time $18,116; part-time $1006.45 per credit. Required fees: $1496; $83 per credit. *Financial support:* Unspecified assistantships available. Financial award application deadline: 4/1. *Faculty research:* Ethical behavior in the marketplace, sustainable entrepreneurship, corporate entrepreneurship, logistics in market orientation, organizational communication. *Unit head:* Tonja Rosales, Director, 970-491-4661, Fax: 970-491-0269, E-mail: tonja.rosales@colostate.edu. *Application contact:* Rachel Stoll, Admissions Coordinator, 970-491-3704, Fax: 970-491-3481, E-mail: rachel.stoll@colostate.edu.

Colorado Technical University Sioux Falls, Programs in Business Administration and Management, Sioux Falls, SD 57108. Offers business administration (MBA); business management (MSM); health science management (MSM); human resources management (MSM); information technology (MSM); organizational leadership (MSM); project management (MBA); technology management (MBA). Evening/weekend programs available. *Degree requirements:* For master's, thesis optional. *Entrance requirements:* For master's, minimum 2 years work experience, resume.

Concordia University, Graduate Programs, Ann Arbor, MI 48105-2797. Offers curriculum and instruction (MS); educational leadership (MS); organizational leadership and administration (MS). Part-time and evening/weekend programs available. *Faculty:* 3 full-time (2 women), 24 part-time/adjunct (10 women). *Students:* 179 full-time (117 women), 27 part-time (19 women). 84 applicants, 65% accepted, 43 enrolled. In 2009, 45 master's awarded. *Degree requirements:* For master's, thesis. *Entrance requirements:* Additional exam requirements/recommendations for international students: Required—TOEFL (minimum score 520 paper-based; 190 computer-based; 68 iBT); Recommended—IELTS, TWE. *Application deadline:* For fall admission, 9/1 priority date for domestic students, 8/1 priority date for international students; for winter admission, 1/5 priority date for domestic students, 12/1 priority date for international students; for spring admission, 5/12 priority date for domestic students, 4/1 priority date for international students. Applications are processed on a rolling basis. Application fee: $0 ($100 for international students). *Expenses:* Tuition: Full-time $7866; part-time $437 per credit hour. *Financial support:* Applicants required to submit FAFSA. *Unit head:* Dr. Dennis Genig, Vice President of Academics, 734-995-7383, Fax: 734-995-7448, E-mail: genigd@cuaa.edu. *Application contact:* Jean Christensen, Associate Director of Graduate Admission, 734-995-7521, Fax: 734-995-7530, E-mail: christj@cuaa.edu.

Concordia University, School of Graduate Studies, Faculty of Arts and Science, Department of Applied Human Sciences, Montréal, QC H3G 1M8, Canada. Offers human systems intervention (MA). *Degree requirements:* For master's, 2 week residential laboratory. *Entrance requirements:* For master's, 1 week residential laboratory, 2 full years of work experience. *Faculty research:* Health promotion, adult learning and transitions, applications of group development and small group leadership, adolescent development, generational issues in immigrant families.

Concordia University, St. Paul, College of Business and Organizational Leadership, St. Paul, MN 55104-5494. Offers business and organizational leadership (MBA); criminal justice leadership (MA); health care management (MBA); human resources management (MA); leadership and management (MA). *Accreditation:* ACBSP. Evening/weekend programs available. Postbaccalaureate distance learning degree programs offered (minimal on-campus study). *Faculty:* 10 full-time (5 women), 19 part-time/adjunct (4 women). *Students:* 295 full-time (169 women), 3 part-time (2 women); includes 30 minority (19 African Americans, 2 American Indian/Alaska Native, 5 Asian Americans or Pacific Islanders, 4 Hispanic Americans), 3 international. Average age 32. In 2009, 114 master's awarded. *Application deadline:* Applications are processed on a rolling basis. Application fee: $50. Electronic applications accepted. *Financial support:* Applicants required to submit FAFSA. *Unit head:* Dr. Bruce Corrie, Dean, 651-641-8226, Fax: 651-641-8807, E-mail: corrie@csp.edu. *Application contact:* Kimberly Craig, Director of Graduate and Cohort Admission, 651-603-6223, Fax: 651-603-6320, E-mail: craig@csp.edu.

Cumberland University, Program in Organizational Leadership and Human Relations Management, Lebanon, TN 37087. Offers MS. Part-time and evening/weekend programs available. *Degree requirements:* For master's, comprehensive exam. *Entrance requirements:* For master's, MAT, 3 letters of recommendation. Additional exam requirements/recommendations for international students: Required—TOEFL (minimum score 500 paper-based; 173 computer-based).

Dominican University, School of Leadership and Continuing Studies, River Forest, IL 60305-1099. Offers family ministry (MA); organizational leadership (MSOL). Part-time and evening/weekend programs available. *Faculty:* 12 part-time/adjunct (7 women). *Students:* 5 full-time (2 women), 59 part-time (38 women); includes 18 minority (14 African Americans, 1 American Indian/Alaska Native, 1 Asian American or Pacific Islander, 2 Hispanic Americans). Average age 42. In 2009, 15 master's awarded. *Entrance requirements:* Additional exam requirements/recommendations for international students: Required—TOEFL (minimum score 550 paper-based; 213 computer-based; 79 iBT). *Application deadline:* Applications are processed on a rolling basis. Application fee: $25. *Expenses:* Contact institution. *Unit head:* Dr. Bryan J. Watkins, Executive Director, 708-714-9001, E-mail: bwatkins@dom.edu. *Application contact:* Monica Halloran, Associate Director of Academic Advising, 708-714-9007, Fax: 708-714-9126, E-mail: mhallora@dom.edu.

Duquesne University, School of Leadership and Professional Advancement, Pittsburgh, PA 15282-0001. Offers leadership (MS), including business ethics, community leadership, global leadership, information technology, leadership, liberal studies, professional administration,

sports leadership. Part-time and evening/weekend programs available. Postbaccalaureate distance learning degree programs offered (no on-campus study). *Faculty:* 1 full-time (0 women), 70 part-time/adjunct (35 women). *Students:* 654 (307 women); includes 68 minority (57 African Americans, 1 American Indian/Alaska Native, 6 Asian Americans or Pacific Islanders, 4 Hispanic Americans). 161 applicants, 73% accepted, 103 enrolled. In 2009, 108 master's awarded. *Degree requirements:* For master's, capstone course. *Entrance requirements:* For master's, professional work experience, 500-word essay. Additional exam requirements/recommendations for international students: Required—TOEFL. *Application deadline:* Applications are processed on a rolling basis. Application fee: $0. Electronic applications accepted. *Expenses:* Tuition: Part-time $851 per credit. Required fees: $81 per credit. *Financial support:* Applicants required to submit FAFSA. *Unit head:* Dr. Dorothy Bassett, Dean, 412-396-2141, Fax: 412-396-4711, E-mail: bassettd@duq.edu. *Application contact:* Marianne Leister, Director of Student Services, 412-396-4933, Fax: 412-396-5072, E-mail: leister@duq.edu.

Eastern Connecticut State University, School of Education and Professional Studies/Graduate Division, Program in Organizational Management, Willimantic, CT 06226-2295. Offers MS. Part-time and evening/weekend programs available. *Degree requirements:* For master's, comprehensive exam or thesis. *Entrance requirements:* For master's, minimum GPA of 2.7. Additional exam requirements/recommendations for international students: Required—TOEFL (minimum score 550 paper-based; 213 computer-based).

Eastern Michigan University, Graduate School, College of Business, Department of Management, Program in Human Resources Management and Organizational Development, Ypsilanti, MI 48197. Offers MSHROD. Part-time and evening/weekend programs available. Postbaccalaureate distance learning degree programs offered (minimal on-campus study). *Students:* 23 full-time (11 women), 64 part-time (40 women); includes 12 minority (6 African Americans, 2 American Indian/Alaska Native, 1 Asian American or Pacific Islander, 3 Hispanic Americans), 44 international. Average age 30. In 2009, 54 master's awarded. *Degree requirements:* For master's, thesis optional. *Entrance requirements:* For master's, GMAT. Additional exam requirements/recommendations for international students: Required—TOEFL. *Application deadline:* Applications are processed on a rolling basis. Application fee: $35. Tuition and fees vary according to course level. *Financial support:* Fellowships, research assistantships with full tuition reimbursements, teaching assistantships with full tuition reimbursements, career-related internships or fieldwork, Federal Work-Study, institutionally sponsored loans, scholarships/grants, tuition waivers (partial), and unspecified assistantships available. Support available to part-time students. Financial award applicants required to submit FAFSA.

Eastern Michigan University, Graduate School, College of Business, Programs in Business Administration, Ypsilanti, MI 48197. Offers business administration (MBA, Graduate Certificate); computer information systems (Graduate Certificate); e-business (MBA, Graduate Certificate); enterprise business intelligence (MBA); entrepreneurship (MBA, Graduate Certificate); finance (MBA, Graduate Certificate); human resources (MBA); human resources management (Graduate Certificate); information systems (MBA); internal auditing (MBA); international business (MBA, Graduate Certificate); marketing management (Graduate Certificate); nonprofit management (MBA); organizational development (Graduate Certificate); supply chain management (MBA, Graduate Certificate). *Accreditation:* AACSB. Part-time programs available. Postbaccalaureate distance learning degree programs offered (no on-campus study). *Students:* 166 full-time (80 women), 439 part-time (231 women); includes 150 minority (103 African Americans, 7 American Indian/Alaska Native, 31 Asian Americans or Pacific Islanders, 9 Hispanic Americans), 97 international. Average age 34. In 2009, 3 other advanced degrees awarded. *Entrance requirements:* For master's, GMAT (minimum score 450), minimum cumulative undergraduate GPA of 2.75. Additional exam requirements/recommendations for international students: Required—TOEFL. *Application deadline:* For fall admission, 5/15 for domestic students, 5/1 for international students; for winter admission, 10/15 for domestic students, 10/1 for international students; for spring admission, 3/15 for domestic students, 3/1 for international students. Applications are processed on a rolling basis. Application fee: $35. Tuition and fees vary according to course level. *Financial support:* Fellowships, research assistantships with full tuition reimbursements, teaching assistantships with full tuition reimbursements, career-related internships or fieldwork, Federal Work-Study, institutionally sponsored loans, scholarships/grants, tuition waivers (partial), and unspecified assistantships available. Support available to part-time students. Financial award applicants required to submit FAFSA. *Unit head:* K. Michelle Henry, Director of Academic Services, 734-487-4444, Fax: 734-483-1316, E-mail: cob.grad@emich.edu. *Application contact:* Beste Windes, Advisor, 734-487-4444, Fax: 734-483-1316, E-mail: cob.grad@emich.edu.

Eastern University, Office of Interdisciplinary Programs, Program in Organizational Leadership, St. Davids, PA 19087-3696. Offers PhD.

Eastern University, School of Leadership and Development, St. Davids, PA 19087-3696. Offers economic development (MBA), including international development, urban development (MA, MBA); international development (MA), including global development, urban development (MA, MBA); nonprofit management (MS); organizational leadership (MA); M Div/MBA. Part-time and evening/weekend programs available. *Degree requirements:* For master's, thesis (for some programs). *Entrance requirements:* For master's, GMAT (MBA), minimum GPA of 2.5. *Expenses:* Contact institution. *Faculty research:* Micro-level economic development, China welfare and economic development, macroethics, micro- and macro-level economic development in transitional economics, organizational effectiveness.

Emory & Henry College, Graduate Programs, Emory, VA 24327-0947. Offers American history (MA Ed); organizational leadership (MOL); professional studies (M Ed); reading specialist (MA Ed). Part-time and evening/weekend programs available. *Entrance requirements:* For master's, GRE or PRAXIS I, recommendations, writing sample.

Emory University, Goizueta Business School, Doctoral Program in Business, Atlanta, GA 30322-1100. Offers accounting (PhD); finance (PhD); information systems (PhD); marketing (PhD); organization and management (PhD). *Faculty:* 57 full-time (11 women). *Students:* 37 full-time (14 women); includes 8 minority (3 African Americans, 4 Asian Americans or Pacific Islanders, 1 Hispanic American), 19 international. Average age 30. 218 applicants, 9% accepted, 9 enrolled. In 2009, 11 doctorates awarded. *Degree requirements:* For doctorate, comprehensive exam, thesis/dissertation. *Entrance requirements:* For doctorate, GMAT (strongly preferred) or GRE. Additional exam requirements/recommendations for international students: Required—TOEFL (minimum score 250 computer-based). *Application deadline:* For fall admission, 1/3 priority date for domestic and international students. Application fee: $50. Electronic applications accepted. *Unit head:* Dr. Lawrence Benveniste, Dean, 404-727-6377, Fax: 404-727-0868, E-mail: larry_benveniste@bus.emory.edu. *Application contact:* Allison Gilmore, Director of Admissions and Student Services, 404-727-6353, Fax: 404-727-5337, E-mail: phd@bus.emory.edu.

Endicott College, Apicius International School of Hospitality, Florence, MA 50122, Italy. Offers organizational management (M Ed). Program held entirely in Florence, Italy. *Entrance requirements:* For master's, MAT or GRE, 250-500 word essay explaining professional goals, official transcripts of all academic work, bachelor's degree, two letters of recommendation, personal interview. *Expenses:* Tuition: Part-time $389 per credit. One-time fee: $1350.

See Display on page 393.

Endicott College, Van Loan School of Graduate and Professional Studies, Program in Organizational Management, Beverly, MA 01915-2096. Offers M Ed. Part-time and evening/weekend programs available. *Faculty:* 3 full-time (1 woman), 5 part-time/adjunct (1 woman). *Students:* 46 full-time (21 women), 13 part-time (6 women). Average age 36. 30 applicants, 100% accepted, 30 enrolled. In 2009, 50 master's awarded. *Degree requirements:* For master's, thesis. *Entrance requirements:* For master's, GRE or MAT, letters of recommendation. Additional exam requirements/recommendations for international students: Required—TOEFL. *Application deadline:* Applications are processed on a rolling basis. Application fee: $50. *Expenses:* Contact institution. *Financial support:* Career-related internships or fieldwork, Federal Work-Study, institutionally sponsored loans, and tuition waivers (partial) available. *Unit head:* Richard

Benedetto, Associate Dean of Graduate School, 978-232-2744, Fax: 978-232-3000, E-mail: rbenedet@endicott.edu. *Application contact:* Richard Benedetto, Associate Dean of Graduate School, 978-232-2744, Fax: 978-232-3000, E-mail: rbenedet@endicott.edu.

Evangel University, Organizational Leadership Program, Springfield, MO 65802. Offers MOL. Part-time and evening/weekend programs available. Postbaccalaureate distance learning degree programs offered (minimal on-campus study). *Faculty:* 3 full-time (1 woman), 1 part-time/ adjunct (0 women). *Students:* 44 full-time (23 women), 3 part-time (1 woman); includes 2 minority (1 African American, 1 Asian American or Pacific Islander). Average age 37. 20 applicants, 60% accepted, 8 enrolled. In 2009, 8 master's awarded. *Degree requirements:* For master's, comprehensive exam, thesis, capstone project. *Entrance requirements:* For master's, GMAT or GRE. Additional exam requirements/recommendations for international students: Required—TOEFL (minimum score 550 paper-based; 213 computer-based). *Application deadline:* For fall admission, 7/15 priority date for domestic and international students; for spring admission, 11/15 priority date for domestic and international students. Applications are processed on a rolling basis. Application fee: $25. Electronic applications accepted. *Financial support:* In 2009–10, 9 students received support. Career-related internships or fieldwork and scholarships/grants available. Support available to part-time students. Financial award application deadline: 3/1; financial award applicants required to submit FAFSA. *Unit head:* Dr. Jeff Fulks, Director of Graduate Studies, 417-865-2815 Ext. 8260, Fax: 417-575-5484, E-mail: fulksj@ evangel.edu. *Application contact:* Charity H. Fahlstrom, Admissions Representative, Graduate and Professional Studies, 417-865-2815 Ext. 7227, Fax: 417-575-5484, E-mail: fahlstromc@ evangel.edu.

Fairleigh Dickinson University, College at Florham, Maxwell Becton College of Arts and Sciences, Department of Psychology, Program in Organizational Behavior, Madison, NJ 07940-1099. Offers organizational behavior (MA); organizational leadership (Certificate). *Students:* 2 full-time (1 woman), 18 part-time (6 women). Average age 40. 6 applicants, 100% accepted, 5 enrolled. In 2009, 3 master's awarded. Application fee: $40. *Unit head:* Dr. Diane Wentworth, Chairperson, 973-443-8548. *Application contact:* Susan Brooman, University Director, Graduate Admissions, 973-443-8905, Fax: 973-443-8088, E-mail: grad@fdu.edu.

Fielding Graduate University, Graduate Programs, School of Human and Organization Development, Santa Barbara, CA 93105-3538. Offers evidence-based coaching (Certificate); human and organizational systems (PhD); human development (PhD); integral studies (Certificate); organization management and development (MA, Certificate). Postbaccalaureate distance learning degree programs offered (minimal on-campus study). *Faculty:* 29 full-time (15 women), 20 part-time/adjunct (7 women). *Students:* 453 full-time (317 women), 161 part-time (111 women); includes 119 minority (63 African Americans, 5 American Indian/Alaska Native, 23 Asian Americans or Pacific Islanders, 28 Hispanic Americans), 46 international. Average age 48. 198 applicants, 95% accepted, 126 enrolled. In 2009, 42 master's, 45 doctorates, 90 other advanced degrees awarded. Terminal master's awarded for partial completion of doctoral program. *Degree requirements:* For master's, thesis or alternative; for doctorate, comprehensive exam, thesis/dissertation. *Entrance requirements:* For master's, minimum GPA of 2.5, letter of recommendation; for doctorate, 2 letters of recommendation, writing sample, resume, self-assessment statement. *Application deadline:* For fall admission, 3/1 for domestic and international students; for spring admission, 9/1 for domestic and international students. Application fee: $75. Electronic applications accepted. *Expenses:* Contact institution. *Financial support:* In 2009–10, 267 students received support. Scholarships/grants and health care benefits available. Support available to part-time students. Financial award application deadline: 5/15; financial award applicants required to submit FAFSA. *Unit head:* Dr. Charles McClintock, Dean, 805-898-2930, Fax: 805-687-4590, E-mail: cmcclintock@fielding.edu. *Application contact:* Carmen Kuchera, Admission Counselor, 800-340-1099, Fax: 805-687-9793, E-mail: ckuchera@fielding.edu.

Gannon University, School of Graduate Studies, College of Humanities, Education, and Social Sciences, School of Humanities, Program in Organizational Learning and Leadership, Erie, PA 16541-0001. Offers PhD. Part-time and evening/weekend programs available. *Students:* 4 full-time (1 woman), 45 part-time (26 women); includes 4 minority (all African Americans), 1 international. Average age 41. 30 applicants, 80% accepted, 18 enrolled. *Degree requirements:* For doctorate, thesis/dissertation. *Entrance requirements:* For doctorate, GRE (verbal, quantitative and written sections taken within the last 3 years), minimum graduate GPA of 3.5, 2 years post-baccalaureate work experience. Additional exam requirements/recommendations for international students: Required—TOEFL (minimum score 79 iBT). *Application deadline:* For spring admission, 2/1 for domestic students. Application fee: $50. Electronic applications accepted. *Expenses:* Tuition: Full-time $13,590; part-time $755 per credit. Required fees: $524; $17 per credit. Tuition and fees vary according to course load, degree level, campus/ location and program. *Financial support:* Scholarships/grants and unspecified assistantships available. Financial award applicants required to submit FAFSA. *Unit head:* Dr. David B. Barker, Director, 814-871-7700, E-mail: barker002@gannon.edu. *Application contact:* Kara Morgan, Director of Graduate Recruitment, 814-871-5831, Fax: 814-871-5827, E-mail: graduate@gannon.edu.

Geneva College, Program in Organizational Leadership, Beaver Falls, PA 15010-3599. Offers MS. Evening/weekend programs available. *Faculty:* 3 full-time (2 women), 10 part-time/adjunct (3 women). *Students:* 97 full-time (56 women); includes 23 minority (all African Americans). 15 applicants, 100% accepted, 15 enrolled. In 2009, 18 master's awarded. *Degree requirements:* For master's, thesis. *Entrance requirements:* For master's, 3-5 years of professional experience, minimum GPA of 3.0 (preferred), resume, writing sample, interview. Additional exam requirements/recommendations for international students: Required—TOEFL. *Application deadline:* Applications are processed on a rolling basis. Application fee: $15. Electronic applications accepted. *Expenses:* Contact institution. *Financial support:* Applicants required to submit FAFSA. *Faculty research:* Servant leadership. *Unit head:* Dr. James K. Dittmar, Chair, 724-847-6853, Fax: 724-847-4198, E-mail: jkd@geneva.edu. *Application contact:* Linda Roundtree, Enrollment Counselor, 724-847-6856, Fax: 724-847-4198, E-mail: lroundtr@ geneva.edu.

George Fox University, School of Business, Newberg, OR 97132-2697. Offers finance (MBA); management (DBA); management/general (MBA); marketing (DBA); organizational strategy (MBA); strategic human resource management (MBA). MBA offered in part-time and full-time formats. Also offered in Portland, OR and Boise, ID. Part-time and evening/weekend programs available. Postbaccalaureate distance learning degree programs offered (minimal on-campus study). *Faculty:* 15 full-time (5 women), 7 part-time/adjunct (0 women). *Students:* 14 full-time (3 women), 223 part-time (77 women); includes 28 minority (7 African Americans, 3 American Indian/Alaska Native, 9 Asian Americans or Pacific Islanders, 9 Hispanic Americans), 2 international. Average age 38. 88 applicants, 86% accepted, 63 enrolled. In 2009, 66 master's, 2 doctorates awarded. *Degree requirements:* For master's, capstone project; for doctorate, credit-applied research project. *Entrance requirements:* For master's, resume (5 years professional experience required); 3 professional references; interview; financial e-learning course; for doctorate, GRE or GMAT, resume; personal mission statement; academic research writing sample; official transcript from each college/university attended; three professional references. Additional exam requirements/recommendations for international students: Required—TOEFL (minimum score 577 paper-based; 233 computer-based; 90 iBT), or IELTS (minimum score 7). *Application deadline:* For fall admission, 8/1 for domestic and international students; for spring admission, 12/1 for domestic and international students. Applications are processed on a rolling basis. Application fee: $40. Electronic applications accepted. *Expenses:* Contact institution. *Financial support:* In 2009–10, 2 students received support. Applicants required to submit FAFSA. *Unit head:* Dr. Ken Armstrong, Professor of Management and Dean, School of Management, 800-631-0921. *Application contact:* Robin Halverson, Admissions Counselor, 800-493-4937, Fax: 503-554-6111, E-mail: mba@georgefox.edu.

George Mason University, School of Public Policy, Program in Organization Development and Knowledge Management, Arlington, VA 22201. Offers MS. Evening/weekend programs available. *Faculty:* 61 full-time (14 women), 30 part-time/adjunct (4 women). *Students:* 73 full-time (50 women), 10 part-time (7 women); includes 13 minority (6 African Americans, 1 Asian American or Pacific Islander, 6 Hispanic Americans), 4 international. 60 applicants, 75% accepted, 33 enrolled. In 2009, 31 master's awarded. *Degree requirements:* For master's, thesis or alternative. *Entrance requirements:* For master's, GRE (for students seeking merit-based scholarships), minimum GPA of 3.0, 2 letters of recommendation, resume. Additional exam requirements/recommendations for international students: Required—TOEFL (minimum score 575 paper-based; 230 computer-based; 88 iBT). *Application deadline:* For fall admission, 6/1 priority date for domestic students, 5/1 priority date for international students. Applications are processed on a rolling basis. Application fee: $60. Electronic applications accepted. *Expenses:* Contact institution. *Financial support:* Career-related internships or fieldwork, Federal Work-Study, scholarships/grants, tuition waivers (partial), and unspecified assistantships available. Support available to part-time students. Financial award application deadline: 3/1; financial award applicants required to submit FAFSA. *Unit head:* Dr. Ann Baker, Director, 703-993-8099, E-mail: spp@gmu.edu. *Application contact:* Leslie Metzger Levin, Assistant Dean of Graduate Admissions and Marketing, 703-993-8099, Fax: 703-993-4876, E-mail: lmetzger@gmu.edu.

The George Washington University, Columbian College of Arts and Sciences, Department of Organizational Sciences and Communication, Washington, DC 20052. Offers human resources management (MA); industrial/organizational psychology (PhD); organizational management (MA). Part-time and evening/weekend programs available. *Faculty:* 10 full-time (6 women), 18 part-time/adjunct (15 women). *Students:* 23 full-time (13 women), 41 part-time (34 women); includes 15 minority (7 African Americans, 2 Asian Americans or Pacific Islanders, 6 Hispanic Americans), 8 international. Average age 29. 74 applicants, 84% accepted, 32 enrolled. In 2009, 28 master's awarded. *Degree requirements:* For master's, comprehensive exam. *Entrance requirements:* For master's, GRE General Test, minimum GPA of 3.0. Additional exam requirements/recommendations for international students: Required—TOEFL (minimum score 500 paper-based; 213 computer-based; 80 iBT). *Application deadline:* For fall admission, 1/15 priority date for domestic and international students; for spring admission, 10/1 priority date for domestic students, 9/1 priority date for international students. Applications are processed on a rolling basis. Application fee: $60. Electronic applications accepted. *Financial support:* Federal Work-Study and institutionally sponsored loans available. *Unit head:* Dr. David Costanza, Acting Director, 202-994-1875, Fax: 202-994-1881, E-mail: dconstanz@gwu.edu. *Application contact:* Information Contact, 202-994-1880, Fax: 202-994-1881.

Georgia State University, J. Mack Robinson College of Business, Department of Managerial Sciences, Atlanta, GA 30302-3083. Offers business analysis (MBA, MS); decision sciences (PhD); entrepreneurship (MBA); human resources management (MBA, MS); management (MBA, PhD); operations management (MBA, MS); organization change (MS); personnel employee relations (PhD); strategic management (PhD). Part-time and evening/weekend programs available. *Degree requirements:* For doctorate, thesis/dissertation. *Entrance requirements:* For master's and doctorate, GMAT. Additional exam requirements/recommendations for international students: Required—TOEFL (minimum score 610 paper-based; 255 computer-based; 101 iBT). Electronic applications accepted. *Faculty research:* Abusive supervision, entrepreneurship, time series and neural networks, organizational controls, inventory control systems.

Gonzaga University, School of Professional Studies, Program in Organizational Leadership, Spokane, WA 99258. Offers MOL. Postbaccalaureate distance learning degree programs offered. *Faculty:* 10 full-time (3 women), 13 part-time/adjunct (5 women). *Students:* 68 full-time (37 women), 632 part-time (308 women); includes 115 minority (49 African Americans, 12 American Indian/Alaska Native, 19 Asian Americans or Pacific Islanders, 35 Hispanic Americans), 1 international. Average age 36. In 2009, 205 master's awarded. *Entrance requirements:* For master's, GRE General Test or MAT, minimum B average in undergraduate course work. Additional exam requirements/recommendations for international students: Required—TOEFL. *Application deadline:* For fall admission, 7/20 priority date for domestic students; for spring admission, 11/1 for domestic students. Applications are processed on a rolling basis. Application fee: $50. Tuition and fees vary according to course level, course load, degree level, campus/ location and program. *Financial support:* Application deadline: 3/1. *Unit head:* Dr. Joseph Albert, Head, 509-328-4220 Ext. 3564. *Application contact:* Dr. Joseph Albert, Head, 509-328-4220 Ext. 3564.

Grand Canyon University, College of Education, Phoenix, AZ 85017-1097. Offers curriculum and instruction (M Ed); education administration (M Ed); elementary education (M Ed); organizational leadership (Ed D); secondary education (M Ed); special education (M Ed); teaching (MA). Part-time and evening/weekend programs available. Postbaccalaureate distance learning degree programs offered (no on-campus study). *Degree requirements:* For master's, publishable research paper (M Ed), e-portfolio. *Entrance requirements:* Additional exam requirements/ recommendations for international students: Required—TOEFL (minimum score 550 paper-based; 213 computer-based; 79 iBT), IELTS (minimum score 6). Electronic applications accepted.

Grand View University, Program in Innovative Leadership, Des Moines, IA 50316-1599. Offers business (MS); education (MS); nursing (MS). *Entrance requirements:* For master's, GRE or GMAT, minimum undergraduate GPA of 3.0, professional resume, 3 letters of recommendation, interview. Additional exam requirements/recommendations for international students: Required—TOEFL (minimum score 550 paper-based; 210 computer-based). Electronic applications accepted.

Grantham University, College of Arts and Sciences, Kansas City, MO 64153. Offers case management (MSN); health systems management (MS); healthcare administration (MHA); nursing (MSN); nursing education (MSN); nursing informatics (MSN); nursing management and organizational leadership (MSN). Part-time and evening/weekend programs available. Postbaccalaureate distance learning degree programs offered (no on-campus study). In 2009, 48 master's awarded. *Degree requirements:* For master's, thesis (for some programs), capstone project. *Entrance requirements:* For master's, bachelor's degree from accredited degree-granting institution. Additional exam requirements/recommendations for international students: Required—TOEFL (minimum score 500 paper-based; 213 computer-based; 61 iBT). *Application deadline:* Applications are processed on a rolling basis. Electronic applications accepted. *Expenses:* Tuition: Part-time $265 per credit hour. One-time fee: $30 part-time. *Financial support:* Institutionally sponsored loans and scholarships/grants available. *Unit head:* Dr. Kim Humerickhouse, Dean, 800-955-2527, Fax: 816-595-5757, E-mail: admissions@grantham.edu. *Application contact:* Matthew Hawes, Vice President of Enrollment Management, 800-955-2527, Fax: 816-595-5757, E-mail: admissions@grantham.edu.

Harding University, College of Business Administration, Searcy, AR 72149-0001. Offers accounting (MBA); health care management (MBA); information technology management (MBA); international business (MBA); leadership and organizational management (MBA). *Accreditation:* ACBSP. Part-time and evening/weekend programs available. Postbaccalaureate distance learning degree programs offered (no on-campus study). *Faculty:* 27 part-time/ adjunct (6 women). *Students:* 105 full-time (46 women), 140 part-time (66 women); includes 31 minority (18 African Americans, 3 American Indian/Alaska Native, 6 Asian Americans or Pacific Islanders, 4 Hispanic Americans), 43 international. Average age 31. 82 applicants, 96% accepted, 66 enrolled. In 2009, 130 master's awarded. *Degree requirements:* For master's, portfolio. *Entrance requirements:* For master's, minimum GPA of 3.0, 2 letters of recommendation, resume. Additional exam requirements/recommendations for international students: Required—TOEFL (minimum score 550 paper-based; 213 computer-based; 80 iBT). *Application deadline:* For fall admission, 8/1 priority date for domestic and international students; for spring admission, 12/1 priority date for domestic and international students. Applications are processed on a rolling basis. Application fee: $35. *Expenses:* Tuition: Full-time $9720; part-time $540 per credit hour. Required fees: $22 per credit hour. Tuition and fees vary according to course load and program. *Financial support:* In 2009–10, 27 students received support. Unspecified assistantships available. Financial award application deadline: 7/30; financial award applicants required to submit FAFSA. *Unit head:* Glen Metheny, Director of Graduate Studies, 501-279-5851, Fax:

Organizational Management

Harding University (continued)
501-279-4805, E-mail: gmetheny@harding.edu. *Application contact:* Melanie Kiihnl, Recruiting Manager/Director of Marketing, 501-279-4523, Fax: 501-279-4805, E-mail: mba@harding.edu.

Hawai'i Pacific University, College of Business Administration, Program in Organizational Change, Honolulu, HI 96813. Offers MA. *Faculty:* 3 full-time (0 women), 1 (woman) part-time/adjunct. *Students:* 28 full-time (17 women), 30 part-time (22 women); includes 5 African Americans, 10 Asian Americans or Pacific Islanders, 2 Hispanic Americans, 17 international. Average age 34. 24 applicants, 96% accepted, 19 enrolled. In 2009, 17 master's awarded. *Expenses:* Tuition: Full-time $12,600; part-time $700 per credit hour. Tuition and fees vary according to program. *Unit head:* Dr. Gordon Jones, Dean, 808-544-1181, Fax: 808-544-0247, E-mail: gjones@hpu.edu. *Application contact:* Danny Lam, Assistant Director of Graduate Admissions, 808-544-1135, Fax: 808-544-0280, E-mail: graduate@hpu.edu.

See Close-Up on page 565.

HEC Montreal, School of Business Administration, Master of Science Programs in Administration, Program in Organizational Development, Montréal, QC H3T 2A7, Canada. Offers M Sc. Part-time programs available. *Students:* 19 full-time (12 women), 2 part-time (both women). 39 applicants, 62% accepted, 13 enrolled. *Degree requirements:* For master's, one foreign language, thesis. *Application deadline:* For fall admission, 3/15 for domestic and international students; for winter admission, 9/15 for domestic and international students. Application fee: $77. Electronic applications accepted. Tuition and fees charges are reported in Canadian dollars. *Expenses:* Tuition, area resident: Part-time $65.60 Canadian dollars per credit. Tuition, state resident: full-time $2361.60 Canadian dollars; part-time $183.36 Canadian dollars per credit. Tuition, nonresident: full-time $6601 Canadian dollars; part-time $448.13 Canadian dollars per credit. International tuition: $16,132.68 Canadian dollars full-time. Required fees: $1254.15 Canadian dollars; $28.99 Canadian dollars per course. $91.68 Canadian dollars per term. Tuition and fees vary according to degree level and program. *Financial support:* Research assistantships, teaching assistantships, scholarships/grants available. *Unit head:* Claude Laurin, Director, 514-340-6485, Fax: 514-340-5690, E-mail: claude.laurin@hec.ca. *Application contact:* Francine Blais, Administrative Director, 514-340-6112, Fax: 514-340-6411, E-mail: francine.blais@hec.ca.

HEC Montreal, School of Business Administration, Master of Science Programs in Administration, Program in Organizational Studies, Montréal, QC H3T 2A7, Canada. Offers M Sc. Part-time programs available. *Students:* 4 applicants, 100% accepted, 1 enrolled. *Degree requirements:* For master's, one foreign language, thesis. *Application deadline:* For fall admission, 3/15 for domestic and international students; for winter admission, 9/15 for domestic and international students. Application fee: $77. Tuition and fees charges are reported in Canadian dollars. *Expenses:* Tuition, area resident: Part-time $65.60 Canadian dollars per credit. Tuition, state resident: full-time $2361.60 Canadian dollars; part-time $183.36 Canadian dollars per credit. Tuition, nonresident: full-time $6601 Canadian dollars; part-time $448.13 Canadian dollars per credit. International tuition: $16,132.68 Canadian dollars full-time. Required fees: $1254.15 Canadian dollars; $28.99 Canadian dollars per course. $91.68 Canadian dollars per term. Tuition and fees vary according to degree level and program. *Financial support:* Research assistantships, teaching assistantships, scholarships/grants available. Financial award application deadline: 10/2. *Unit head:* Claude Laurin, Director, 514-340-6485, Fax: 514-340-5690, E-mail: claude.laurin@hec.ca. *Application contact:* Francine Blais, Administrative Director, 514-340-6112, Fax: 514-340-6411, E-mail: francine.blais@hec.ca.

Immaculata University, College of Graduate Studies, Program in Organization Studies, Immaculata, PA 19345. Offers MA. Part-time and evening/weekend programs available. *Degree requirements:* For master's, comprehensive exam, thesis optional. *Entrance requirements:* For master's, GMAT, GRE General Test, MAT, minimum GPA of 3.0. Additional exam requirements/recommendations for international students: Required—TOEFL, IELTS. Electronic applications accepted.

Indiana Tech, Program in Organizational Leadership, Fort Wayne, IN 46803-1297. Offers MS. Part-time and evening/weekend programs available. Postbaccalaureate distance learning degree programs offered (minimal on-campus study). *Students:* 33 full-time (16 women), 5 part-time (2 women); includes 18 minority (16 African Americans, 1 Asian American or Pacific Islander, 1 Hispanic American). Average age 38. *Entrance requirements:* For master's, 3 years work experience with an increasing level of supervisory responsibilities, bachelor's degree transcript from accredited institution with minimum cumulative GPA of 2.5, 3 letters of recommendation, essay, current resume. *Application deadline:* Applications are processed on a rolling basis. Application fee: $25. Electronic applications accepted. *Expenses:* Tuition: Full-time $5160; part-time $430 per credit hour. Tuition and fees vary according to degree level and program. *Financial support:* Applicants required to submit FAFSA. *Unit head:* Dr. Barbara Perry, Dean of General Studies, 260-422-5561 Ext. 2120. *Application contact:* Steve Herendeen, Associate Vice President of College of Professional Studies Admissions, 260-422-5561 Ext. 2121, Fax: 260-422-1518, E-mail: saherendeen@indianatech.edu.

Indiana University–Purdue University Fort Wayne, College of Engineering, Technology, and Computer Science, Department of Organizational Leadership and Supervision, Fort Wayne, IN 46805-1499. Offers human resources (MS); leadership (MS); organizational leadership and supervision (Certificate). Part-time programs available. *Faculty:* 3 full-time (1 woman). *Students:* 6 full-time (5 women), 28 part-time (17 women); includes 7 minority (6 African Americans, 1 Asian American or Pacific Islander), 3 international. Average age 36. 19 applicants, 74% accepted, 12 enrolled. In 2009, 4 master's awarded. *Entrance requirements:* For master's, GRE or GMAT (if undergraduate GPA is below 3.0), current resume, 2 recent letters of recommendation, essay. Additional exam requirements/recommendations for international students: Required—TOEFL (minimum score 550 paper-based; 213 computer-based; 77 iBT); Recommended—TWE. *Application deadline:* For fall admission, 8/1 for domestic students, 5/15 for international students; for spring admission, 12/1 for domestic students, 10/15 for international students. Applications are processed on a rolling basis. Application fee: $55 ($60 for international students). Electronic applications accepted. *Expenses:* Tuition, state resident: full-time $4595; part-time $255 per credit. Tuition, nonresident: full-time $10,963; part-time $609 per credit. Required fees: $528; $29.35 per credit. Tuition and fees vary according to course load. *Financial support:* In 2009–10, 1 teaching assistantship with partial tuition reimbursement (averaging $12,740 per year) was awarded; scholarships/grants also available. Support available to part-time students. Financial award application deadline: 3/1; financial award applicants required to submit FAFSA. *Faculty research:* Career-conducive organizations, career development, human resources development. Total annual research expenditures: $3,394. *Unit head:* Dr. Kimberly McDonald, Chair, 260-481-6418, Fax: 260-481-6417, E-mail: mcdonalk@ipfw.edu. *Application contact:* Dr. Linda Hite, Director of Graduate Studies, 260-481-6416, Fax: 260-481-6417, E-mail: hitel@ipfw.edu.

Indiana Wesleyan University, College of Graduate Studies, Department of Graduate Studies in Leadership, Marion, IN 46953. Offers organizational leadership (Ed D). Part-time programs available. Postbaccalaureate distance learning degree programs offered (minimal on-campus study). *Degree requirements:* For doctorate, comprehensive exam, thesis/dissertation, applied field project. *Entrance requirements:* For doctorate, GRE, GMAT. Additional exam requirements/recommendations for international students: Required—TOEFL. *Expenses:* Tuition: Full-time $7380; part-time $410 per credit. One-time fee: $85. Tuition and fees vary according to campus/location. *Faculty research:* Organizational leadership as a new structural model for research and teaching, wisdom and its application for leaders, stewardship and its application for leaders, followership and its application for leaders, the importance of a world view in establishing authenticity for leaders.

Instituto Tecnologico de Santo Domingo, Graduate School, Santo Domingo, Dominican Republic. Offers applied linguistics (MA); construction administration (M Mgmt); corporate finance (M Mgmt); education (M Ed); engineering (M Eng), including data telecommunications, industrial engineering, logistics and supply chain, maintenance engineering, sanitary and environmental engineering, structural engineering; environmental science (M En S), including environmental education, environmental management, marine and coastal ecosystems, natural resources management; family therapy (MA); food science and technology (MS); human development (MA); human resources administration (M Mgmt); international business (M Mgmt); labor risks (M Mgmt); management (M Mgmt); marketing (M Mgmt); mathematics (MS); organizational development (M Mgmt); planning and taxation (M Mgmt); psychology (MA); social science (M Ed); upper management (M Mgmt). *Entrance requirements:* For master's, birth certificate, minimum GPA of 2.0.

John F. Kennedy University, School of Management, Program in Business Administration, Pleasant Hill, CA 94523-4817. Offers business administration (MBA); organizational leadership (Certificate). Part-time and evening/weekend programs available. *Degree requirements:* For master's, thesis or alternative. *Entrance requirements:* For master's, interview. Additional exam requirements/recommendations for international students: Required—TOEFL.

Johnson & Wales University, The Alan Shawn Feinstein Graduate School, MBA Program in Global Business Leadership, Providence, RI 02903-3703. Offers accounting (MBA); enhanced accounting (MBA); financial management (MBA); international trade (MBA); marketing (MBA); organizational leadership (MBA). Part-time programs available. *Faculty:* 13 full-time (3 women), 17 part-time/adjunct (4 women). *Students:* 523 full-time (272 women), 162 part-time (85 women); includes 29 minority (18 African Americans, 4 Asian Americans or Pacific Islanders, 7 Hispanic Americans), 385 international. Average age 27. 330 applicants, 82% accepted, 151 enrolled. In 2009, 274 master's awarded. *Entrance requirements:* For master's, minimum GPA of 2.75. Additional exam requirements/recommendations for international students: Required—TOEFL, TOEFL (minimum score 550 paper-based; 210 computer-based) or IELTS recommended; Recommended—TWE. *Application deadline:* For fall admission, 8/15 priority date for domestic students, 6/28 priority date for international students; for winter admission, 11/10 priority date for domestic students, 9/20 priority date for international students; for spring admission, 2/5 priority date for domestic students, 12/20 priority date for international students. Applications are processed on a rolling basis. *Expenses:* Required fees: $340 per quarter hour. *Financial support:* Tuition waivers (partial) and unspecified assistantships available. Support available to part-time students. Financial award application deadline: 5/1. *Faculty research:* International banking, global economy, international trade, cultural differences. *Unit head:* Dr. Frank Pontarelli, Dean, 401-598-1333, Fax: 401-598-1125. *Application contact:* Dr. Allan G. Freedman, Director of Graduate Admissions, 401-598-1015, Fax: 401-598-1286, E-mail: gradadm@jwu.edu.

Jones International University, Graduate School of Education, Centennial, CO 80112. Offers adult education (M Ed); corporate training and knowledge management (M Ed); curriculum and instruction (M Ed), including elementary teacher licensure, secondary teacher licensure; e-learning technology and design (M Ed); educational leadership and administration (M Ed); educational leadership and administration: principal and administrator licensure (M Ed); elementary curriculum instruction and assessment (M Ed); higher education leadership and administration (M Ed); K-12 instructional technology (M Ed); K-12 instructional technology: teacher licensure (M Ed); secondary curriculum instruction and assessment (M Ed); technology and design (M Ed). Part-time and evening/weekend programs available. Postbaccalaureate distance learning degree programs offered (no on-campus study). *Entrance requirements:* For master's, minimum cumulative GPA of 2.5. Additional exam requirements/recommendations for international students: Recommended—TOEFL (minimum score 550 paper-based; 213 computer-based). Electronic applications accepted.

Judson University, Graduate Programs, Elgin, IL 60123-1498. Offers architecture (M Arch); literacy (M Ed); organizational leadership (MA); teaching (M Ed). Part-time and evening/weekend programs available. Postbaccalaureate distance learning degree programs offered (no on-campus study). *Degree requirements:* For master's, comprehensive exam (for some programs), thesis. *Entrance requirements:* For master's, interviews.

Kaplan University, Davenport Campus, School of Business, Davenport, IA 52807-2095. Offers business administration (MBA); change leadership (MS); entrepreneurship (MBA); finance (MBA); health care management (MBA, MS); human resource (MBA); international business (MBA); management (MS); marketing (MBA); project management (MBA, MS); supply chain management and logistics (MBA, MS). Part-time and evening/weekend programs available. Postbaccalaureate distance learning degree programs offered (no on-campus study). *Entrance requirements:* Additional exam requirements/recommendations for international students: Required—TOEFL (minimum score 550 paper-based; 218 computer-based; 80 iBT). Electronic applications accepted.

LaGrange College, Graduate Programs, Program in Organizational Leadership, LaGrange, GA 30240-2999. Offers MA. Program is held on Albany campus. Evening/weekend programs available. *Entrance requirements:* For master's, GRE or MAT, minimum GPA of 2.5, 3 letters of reference. Additional exam requirements/recommendations for international students: Required—TOEFL (minimum score 500 paper-based; 173 computer-based; 61 iBT). Electronic applications accepted.

Lewis University, College of Arts and Sciences, Program in Organizational Leadership, Romeoville, IL 60446. Offers higher education/student services (MA); organizational management (MA); public administration (MA); training and development (MA). Part-time and evening/weekend programs available. *Faculty:* 2 full-time (0 women), 9 part-time/adjunct (2 women). *Students:* 24 full-time (11 women), 111 part-time (91 women); includes 42 minority (33 African Americans, 1 American Indian/Alaska Native, 1 Asian American or Pacific Islander, 7 Hispanic Americans), 1 international. Average age 38. In 2009, 41 master's awarded. *Entrance requirements:* For master's, bachelor's degree, at least 25 years of age, minimum of 3 years of work experience, minimum GPA of 3.0, letter of recommendation, interview. Additional exam requirements/recommendations for international students: Required—TOEFL (minimum score 550 paper-based; 213 computer-based). *Application deadline:* For fall admission, 5/1 priority date for international students; for spring admission, 11/15 priority date for international students. Applications are processed on a rolling basis. Application fee: $40. Electronic applications accepted. *Expenses:* Tuition: Full-time $6480; part-time $720 per credit. One-time fee: $40. Tuition and fees vary according to course load, degree level and program. *Financial support:* Federal Work-Study, scholarships/grants, tuition waivers, and unspecified assistantships available. Financial award application deadline: 5/1; financial award applicants required to submit FAFSA. *Unit head:* Dr. Rich Walsh, Director, 815-838-0500, E-mail: walshri@lewisu.edu. *Application contact:* Bernadette Valderrama, Information Contact, 815-838-0500 Ext. 5629.

Lourdes College, School of Graduate and Professional Studies, Program in Organizational Leadership, Sylvania, OH 43560-2898. Offers MOL. Evening/weekend programs available. *Entrance requirements:* Additional exam requirements/recommendations for international students: Required—TOEFL.

Manhattanville College, Graduate Programs, Humanities and Social Sciences Programs, Program in Organizational Management and Human Resource Development, Purchase, NY 10577-2132. Offers MS. Part-time and evening/weekend programs available. In 2009, 25 master's awarded. *Degree requirements:* For master's, thesis. *Entrance requirements:* For master's, interview, 2 letters of recommendation. Additional exam requirements/recommendations for international students: Required—TOEFL. *Application deadline:* Applications are processed on a rolling basis. Application fee: $70. *Financial support:* Career-related internships or fieldwork, Federal Work-Study, institutionally sponsored loans, and unspecified assistantships available. Financial award application deadline: 3/1; financial award applicants required to submit FAFSA. *Unit head:* Dr. Don Richards, Interim Dean, School of Graduate and Professional Studies, 914-323-5469, Fax: 914-694-3488, E-mail: gps@mville.edu. *Application contact:* Office of Admissions for Graduate and Professional Studies, 914-323-5418, E-mail: gps@mville.edu.

Mansfield University of Pennsylvania, Graduate Studies, Program in Organizational Leadership, Mansfield, PA 16933. Offers MA. Postbaccalaureate distance learning degree programs offered. *Expenses:* Tuition, state resident: full-time $6666; part-time $370 per credit. Tuition, nonresident: full-time $10,666; part-time $593 per credit. Required fees: $1388. *Unit head:* Dr. Peter Chiaramonte, Director, 570-662-4344, E-mail: pchiaram@mansfield.edu.

Application contact: Christina Hale, Assistant Director of Enrollment Management/Graduate Admissions, 570-662-4812, Fax: 570-662-4121, E-mail: chale@mansfield.edu.

Marian University, Business Division, Fond du Lac, WI 54935-4699. Offers organizational leadership and quality (MS). Part-time and evening/weekend programs available. *Faculty:* 10 part-time/adjunct (2 women). *Students:* 7 full-time (5 women), 86 part-time (62 women); includes 10 minority (5 African Americans, 3 Asian Americans or Pacific Islanders, 2 Hispanic Americans). Average age 38. 48 applicants, 79% accepted, 38 enrolled. In 2009, 49 master's awarded. *Degree requirements:* For master's, comprehensive group project. *Entrance requirements:* For master's, 3 years of managerial experience, minimum GPA of 2.75, letters of professional reference. *Application deadline:* Applications are processed on a rolling basis. Application fee: $25. Electronic applications accepted. *Expenses:* Contact institution. *Financial support:* In 2009–10, 25 students received support. Institutionally sponsored loans available. Support available to part-time students. Financial award application deadline: 3/1; financial award applicants required to submit FAFSA. *Faculty research:* Organizational values, statistical decision making, learning organization, quality planning, customer research. *Unit head:* Donna Innes, Assistant Provost and Dean of PACE, 920-923-8760, Fax: 920-923-7167, E-mail: dinnes@marianuniversity.edu. *Application contact:* Tracy Qualman, Director of Marketing and Admission, 920-923-7159, Fax: 920-923-7167, E-mail: tqualmann@marianuniversity.edu.

Marymount University, Educational Partnerships Program, Arlington, VA 22207-4299. Offers business administration (MBA); health care management (MS); management studies (Certificate); organization development (Certificate). Part-time and evening/weekend programs available. *Students:* 25 part-time (17 women); includes 12 minority (11 African Americans, 1 Asian American or Pacific Islander), 1 international. Average age 43. *Entrance requirements:* For master's, GRE or GMAT, resume; for Certificate, resume. Additional exam requirements/recommendations for international students: Required—TOEFL (minimum score 600 paper-based; 250 computer-based; 96 iBT), IELTS (minimum score 6.5). *Application deadline:* For fall admission, 7/1 for international students; for spring admission, 10/15 for international students. Applications are processed on a rolling basis. Application fee: $40. Electronic applications accepted. *Expenses:* Tuition: Full-time $13,050; part-time $725 per credit hour. Required fees: $135; $7.50 per credit hour. *Financial support:* Career-related internships or fieldwork, Federal Work-Study, scholarships/grants, and unspecified assistantships available. Support available to part-time students. Financial award applicants required to submit FAFSA. *Unit head:* Dr. Sherri Hughes, Vice President for Academic Affairs and Provost, 703-284-1550, E-mail: sherri.hughes@marymount.edu. *Application contact:* Francesca Reed, Director, Graduate Admissions, 703-284-5901, Fax: 703-527-3815, E-mail: grad.admissions@marymount.edu.

Medaille College, Program in Business Administration—Amherst, Amherst, NY 14221. Offers business administration (MBA); organizational leadership (MA). Evening/weekend programs available. *Faculty:* 6 full-time (2 women), 23 part-time/adjunct (4 women). *Students:* 211 full-time (126 women); includes 34 minority (29 African Americans, 1 Asian American or Pacific Islander, 4 Hispanic Americans). Average age 31. 107 applicants, 62% accepted, 66 enrolled. In 2009, 89 master's awarded. *Degree requirements:* For master's, thesis or alternative. *Entrance requirements:* For master's, GMAT, minimum undergraduate GPA of 2.7, 3 years of work experience. Additional exam requirements/recommendations for international students: Required—TOEFL (minimum score 550 paper-based; 213 computer-based). *Application deadline:* Applications are processed on a rolling basis. Application fee: $100. *Expenses:* Contact institution. *Financial support:* In 2009–10, 180 students received support. Federal Work-Study available. Financial award applicants required to submit FAFSA. *Unit head:* Jennifer Bavifard, Associate Dean for Special Programs, 716-631-1061 Ext. 150, Fax: 716-631-1380, E-mail: jbavifar@medaille.edu. *Application contact:* Jacqueline Matheny, Executive Director of Marketing and Enrollment, 716-932-2541, Fax: 716-632-1811, E-mail: jmatheny@medaille.edu.

Medaille College, Program in Business Administration—Rochester, Rochester, NY 14623. Offers business administration (MBA); organizational leadership (MA). Evening/weekend programs available. *Degree requirements:* For master's, thesis or alternative. *Entrance requirements:* For master's, GMAT, 3 years of work experience, minimum undergraduate GPA of 2.7. Additional exam requirements/recommendations for international students: Required—TOEFL (minimum score 550 paper-based; 213 computer-based). *Expenses:* Contact institution.

Mercy College, School of Business, Program in Organizational Leadership, Dobbs Ferry, NY 10522-1189. Offers MS. Part-time and evening/weekend programs available. Postbaccalaureate distance learning degree programs offered (no on-campus study). *Students:* 84 full-time (61 women), 7 part-time (5 women); includes 47 African Americans, 2 Asian Americans or Pacific Islanders, 19 Hispanic Americans. Average age 36. 103 applicants, 58% accepted, 51 enrolled. In 2009, 80 master's awarded. *Entrance requirements:* For master's, assessment by program director, resume, 2 letters of reference, interview. Additional exam requirements/recommendations for international students: Required—TOEFL (minimum score 600 paper-based; 250 computer-based; 100 iBT). *Application deadline:* For fall admission, 8/1 for international students. Applications are processed on a rolling basis. Application fee: $40. Electronic applications accepted. *Expenses:* Contact institution. *Financial support:* Career-related internships or fieldwork, Federal Work-Study, scholarships/grants, and unspecified assistantships available. Support available to part-time students. Financial award applicants required to submit FAFSA. *Faculty research:* Organizational behavior, strategic management, collaborative relationship. *Unit head:* Benjamin Manyindo, Program Director, 212-615-3330, E-mail: bmanyindo@mercy.edu. *Application contact:* Carolyn Bow, Assistant Director, 914-674-7285, E-mail: cbow@mercy.edu.

Mercyhurst College, Graduate Program, Program in Organizational Leadership, Erie, PA 16546. Offers MS, Certificate. Part-time and evening/weekend programs available. *Degree requirements:* For master's, thesis. *Entrance requirements:* For master's, GRE General Test or MAT, interview. Additional exam requirements/recommendations for international students: Required—TOEFL. Electronic applications accepted. *Faculty research:* Leadership training, organizational communication, leadership pedagogy.

Mid-America Christian University, Program in Leadership, Oklahoma City, OK 73170-4504. Offers MA. *Entrance requirements:* For master's, bachelor's degree from a regionally accredited college or university, minimum overall cumulative GPA of 2.75 of bachelor course work. Additional exam requirements/recommendations for international students: Required—TOEFL (minimum score 550 paper-based; 213 computer-based).

MidAmerica Nazarene University, Graduate Studies in Management, Olathe, KS 66062-1899. Offers management (MBA); organizational administration (MA), including finance, international business, leadership, non-profit. Evening/weekend programs available. *Faculty:* 6 full-time (2 women), 18 part-time/adjunct (7 women). *Students:* 107 full-time (49 women), 7 part-time (3 women); includes 25 minority (18 African Americans, 1 Asian American or Pacific Islander, 6 Hispanic Americans). Average age 36. In 2009, 81 master's awarded. *Entrance requirements:* For master's, mathematical assessment, minimum undergraduate GPA of 3.0, letters of recommendation. Additional exam requirements/recommendations for international students: Required—TOEFL. *Application deadline:* For fall admission, 9/1 priority date for domestic students; for spring admission, 5/1 priority date for domestic students. Applications are processed on a rolling basis. Application fee: $100. Electronic applications accepted. *Financial support:* Application deadline: 5/1. *Faculty research:* Economic development, international finance, business development, employee evaluation. *Unit head:* Dr. Willadee Wehmeyer, Director, 913-971-3276, Fax: 913-791-3409, E-mail: wwehmeye@mnu.edu. *Application contact:* Melanie Sutherland, Administrative Assistant, 913-971-3276, Fax: 913-971-3409, E-mail: mba@mnu.edu.

Midway College, Leadership MBA Program, Midway, KY 40347-1120. Offers MBA. *Degree requirements:* For master's, capstone course. *Entrance requirements:* For master's, GMAT, bachelor's degree, minimum GPA of 3.0, 3 years of professional work experience, interview. Additional exam requirements/recommendations for international students: Required—TOEFL (minimum score 550 paper-based; 213 computer-based; 80 iBT). *Expenses:* Tuition: Part-time $500 per credit hour. One-time fee: $100 part-time.

Misericordia University, College of Professional Studies and Social Sciences, Program in Organizational Management, Dallas, PA 18612-1098. Offers MS. Part-time and evening/weekend programs available. *Faculty:* 1 full-time (0 women), 7 part-time/adjunct (3 women). *Students:* 75 part-time (44 women); includes 1 minority (African American). Average age 36. In 2009, 31 master's awarded. *Degree requirements:* For master's, thesis or alternative, practicum. *Entrance requirements:* For master's, GRE General Test or MAT, minimum GPA of 2.8. *Application deadline:* For fall admission, 8/1 priority date for domestic students. Applications are processed on a rolling basis. Application fee: $25. Electronic applications accepted. *Expenses:* Contact institution. *Financial support:* In 2009–10, 40 students received support. Career-related internships or fieldwork and scholarships/grants available. Support available to part-time students. Financial award application deadline: 6/30; financial award applicants required to submit FAFSA. *Unit head:* Dr. Corina Mihai, Director of Business Graduate Programs, 570-674-8022, E-mail: cmihai@misericordia.edu. *Application contact:* Larree Brown, Coordinator of Part-Time Undergraduate and Graduate Programs, 570-674-6451, Fax: 570-674-6232, E-mail: lbrown@misericordia.edu.

Mountain State University, Graduate Studies, Program in Executive Leadership, Beckley, WV 25802-9003. Offers DEL. *Expenses:* Tuition: Full-time $6450. Tuition and fees vary according to program. *Unit head:* Dr. William White, Dean, School of Leadership and Professional Development/Interim Dean, School of Graduate Studies, 304-929-1658, E-mail: wwhite@mountainstate.edu. *Application contact:* Anita Diaz, Enrollment Coordinator of Graduate Studies, 304-461-3213, Fax: 304-929-1637, E-mail: adiaz@mountainstate.edu.

National University, Academic Affairs, College of Letters and Sciences, Department of Professional Studies, La Jolla, CA 92037-1011. Offers forensic science (MFS), including criminalistics and investigation; public administration (MPA), including alternative dispute resolution, human resource management, organizational leadership, public finance. Part-time and evening/weekend programs available. Postbaccalaureate distance learning degree programs offered (no on-campus study). *Faculty:* 5 full-time (3 women), 27 part-time/adjunct (7 women). *Students:* 167 full-time (95 women), 246 part-time (133 women); includes 188 minority (71 African Americans, 2 American Indian/Alaska Native, 41 Asian Americans or Pacific Islanders, 74 Hispanic Americans). Average age 38. 284 applicants, 100% accepted, 206 enrolled. In 2009, 104 master's awarded. *Degree requirements:* For master's, thesis. *Entrance requirements:* For master's, interview, minimum GPA of 2.5. Additional exam requirements/recommendations for international students: Required—TOEFL (minimum score 550 paper-based; 213 computer-based; 79 iBT), IELTS (minimum score 6). *Application deadline:* Applications are processed on a rolling basis. Application fee: $60 ($65 for international students). Electronic applications accepted. *Expenses:* Tuition: Part-time $338 per quarter hour. *Financial support:* Career-related internships or fieldwork, institutionally sponsored loans, scholarships/grants, and tuition waivers (partial) available. Support available to part-time students. Financial award application deadline: 6/30; financial award applicants required to submit FAFSA. *Unit head:* Chandrika M. Kelso, Associate Professor and Chair, 858-642-8433, Fax: 858-642-8715, E-mail: ckelso@nu.edu. *Application contact:* Dominick Giovanniello, Associate Regional Dean—San Diego, 800-NAT-UNIV, Fax: 858-541-7792, E-mail: dgiovann@nu.edu.

National University, Academic Affairs, School of Business and Management, Department of Leadership and Business Administration, La Jolla, CA 92037-1011. Offers alternative dispute resolution (MBA); e-business (MBA); financial management (MBA); human resource management (MBA); human resources management (MA); international business (MBA); knowledge management (MS); marketing (MBA); organizational leadership (MBA, MS); technology management (MBA). Part-time and evening/weekend programs available. Postbaccalaureate distance learning degree programs offered (no on-campus study). *Faculty:* 4 full-time (2 women), 22 part-time/adjunct (9 women). *Students:* 95 full-time (56 women), 228 part-time (129 women); includes 63 African Americans, 24 Asian Americans or Pacific Islanders, 61 Hispanic Americans, 6 international. Average age 38. 191 applicants, 100% accepted, 131 enrolled. In 2009, 62 master's awarded. *Degree requirements:* For master's, thesis. *Entrance requirements:* For master's, interview, minimum GPA of 2.5. Additional exam requirements/recommendations for international students: Required—TOEFL (minimum score 550 paper-based; 213 computer-based; 79 iBT), IELTS (minimum score 6). *Application deadline:* Applications are processed on a rolling basis. Application fee: $60 ($65 for international students). Electronic applications accepted. *Expenses:* Tuition: Part-time $338 per quarter hour. *Financial support:* Career-related internships or fieldwork, institutionally sponsored loans, scholarships/grants, and tuition waivers (partial) available. Support available to part-time students. Financial award application deadline: 6/30; financial award applicants required to submit FAFSA. *Unit head:* Dr. George Drops, Chair and Professor, 858-642-8438, Fax: 858-642-8406, E-mail: gdrops@nu.edu. *Application contact:* Dominick Giovanniello, Associate Regional Dean—San Diego, 800-NAT-UNIV, Fax: 858-541-7792, E-mail: dgiovann@nu.edu.

National University, Academic Affairs, School of Business and Management, Department of Management and Marketing, La Jolla, CA 92037-1011. Offers e-business (MS); knowledge management (MS); management (MA); organizational leadership (MS). Part-time and evening/weekend programs available. Postbaccalaureate distance learning degree programs offered (no on-campus study). *Faculty:* 18 full-time (3 women), 37 part-time/adjunct (8 women). *Students:* 465 full-time (230 women), 702 part-time (319 women). Average age 34. 654 applicants, 100% accepted, 423 enrolled. In 2009, 308 master's awarded. *Degree requirements:* For master's, thesis. *Entrance requirements:* For master's, interview, minimum GPA of 2.5. Additional exam requirements/recommendations for international students: Required—TOEFL (minimum score 550 paper-based; 213 computer-based; 79 iBT), IELTS (minimum score 6). *Application deadline:* Applications are processed on a rolling basis. Application fee: $60 ($65 for international students). Electronic applications accepted. *Expenses:* Tuition: Part-time $338 per quarter hour. *Financial support:* Career-related internships or fieldwork, institutionally sponsored loans, scholarships/grants, and tuition waivers (partial) available. Support available to part-time students. Financial award application deadline: 6/30; financial award applicants required to submit FAFSA. *Unit head:* Dr. Brian Simpson, Chair and Professor, 858-642-8431, Fax: 858-642-8406, E-mail: bsimpson@nu.edu. *Application contact:* Dominick Giovanniello, Associate Regional Dean—San Diego, 800-NAT-UNIV, Fax: 858-541-7792, E-mail: dgiovann@nu.edu.

Newman University, School of Business, Wichita, KS 67213-2097. Offers finance (MBA); international business (MBA); leadership (MBA); management (MBA); technology (MBA). Part-time programs available. *Faculty:* 5 full-time (1 woman), 8 part-time/adjunct (2 women). *Students:* 29 full-time (13 women), 105 part-time (52 women); includes 30 minority (9 African Americans, 1 American Indian/Alaska Native, 10 Asian Americans or Pacific Islanders, 10 Hispanic Americans), 23 international. Average age 32. 80 applicants, 76% accepted, 47 enrolled. In 2009, 76 master's awarded. *Degree requirements:* For master's, thesis optional. *Entrance requirements:* For master's, interview; minimum GPA of 3.0; 3 letters of recommendation; course work in algebra, statistics, macroeconomics, and financial accounting. Additional exam requirements/recommendations for international students: Required—TOEFL (minimum score 600 paper-based; 250 computer-based; 100 iBT). *Application deadline:* For fall admission, 8/1 priority date for domestic students, 7/15 priority date for international students; for winter admission, 1/1 priority date for domestic students; for spring admission, 1/1 priority date for domestic students, 11/15 priority date for international students. Applications are processed on a rolling basis. Application fee: $25 ($40 for international students). Electronic applications accepted. *Expenses:* Contact institution. *Financial support:* In 2009–10, 3 students received support. Federal Work-Study available. Financial award application deadline: 8/15; financial award applicants required to submit FAFSA. *Unit head:* Dr. Joe Goetz, Dean of the College of Professional Studies/Director, 316-942-4291 Ext. 2111, Fax: 316-942-4486, E-mail: goetzj@newmanu.edu. *Application contact:* Linda Kay Sabala, Director of Graduate Admissions, 316-942-4291 Ext. 2230, Fax: 316-942-4483, E-mail: sabalal@newmanu.edu.

The New School: A University, Milano The New School for Management and Urban Policy, Program in Organizational Change Management, New York, NY 10011. Offers MS. Part-time

Organizational Management

The New School: A University (continued)

and evening/weekend programs available. *Faculty:* 9 full-time (3 women). *Students:* 29 full-time (26 women), 62 part-time (41 women); includes 31 minority (17 African Americans, 1 American Indian/Alaska Native, 6 Asian Americans or Pacific Islanders, 7 Hispanic Americans), 8 international. Average age 34. 41 applicants, 78% accepted, 23 enrolled. In 2009, 20 master's awarded. *Degree requirements:* For master's, thesis. *Entrance requirements:* For master's, 3 years of work experience, interview. Additional exam requirements/recommendations for international students: Required—TOEFL (minimum score 600 paper-based; 250 computer-based; 100 iBT). *Application deadline:* For fall admission, 3/1 priority date for domestic and international students; for spring admission, 10/1 priority date for domestic and international students. Applications are processed on a rolling basis. Application fee: $50. Electronic applications accepted. *Financial support:* Fellowships, Federal Work-Study, scholarships/grants, and tuition waivers (full and partial) available. Support available to part-time students. Financial award application deadline: 3/1; financial award applicants required to submit FAFSA. *Unit head:* Dr. Mary Watson, Chair, 212-229-5400 Ext. 1613, Fax: 212-229-5335, E-mail: watsonm@newschool.edu. *Application contact:* Merida Escandon, Director of Admissions, 212-229-5462 Ext. 1108, Fax: 212-229-5354, E-mail: milanoadmissions@newschool.edu.

New York University, Leonard N. Stern School of Business, Department of Management and Organizations, New York, NY 10012-1019. Offers management organizations (MBA); organization theory (PhD); organizational behavior (PhD); strategy (PhD). *Expenses:* Tuition: Full-time $30,528; part-time $1272 per credit. Required fees: $2177. *Faculty research:* Strategic management, managerial cognition, interpersonal processes, conflict and negotiation.

North Carolina Agricultural and Technical State University, Graduate School, School of Education, Department of Human Development and Services, Greensboro, NC 27411. Offers adult education (MS); counselor education (MS); human resources-agency counseling (MS); human resources-rehabilitation counseling (MS); leadership studies (PhD); school administration (MS). *Accreditation:* ACA. Part-time and evening/weekend programs available. *Degree requirements:* For master's, comprehensive exam, thesis, qualifying exam. *Entrance requirements:* For master's, GRE General Test, minimum GPA of 3.0.

Northern Kentucky University, Office of Graduate Programs, College of Business, Program in Executive Leadership and Organizational Change, Highland Heights, KY 41099. Offers MS. Part-time and evening/weekend programs available. *Students:* 44 part-time (21 women); includes 6 minority (4 African Americans, 1 Asian American or Pacific Islander, 1 Hispanic American). Average age 41. 51 applicants, 55% accepted, 24 enrolled. In 2009, 25 master's awarded. *Degree requirements:* For master's, field research project. *Entrance requirements:* For master's, minimum GPA of 2.5; essay on professional career objective; 3 letters of recommendation, 1 from a current organization; 3 years of professional or managerial work experience. Additional exam requirements/recommendations for international students: Required—TOEFL (minimum score 600 paper-based; 213 computer-based; 79 iBT); Recommended—IELTS (minimum score 6.5). *Application deadline:* For fall admission, 6/15 priority date for domestic students, 6/1 priority date for international students. Application fee: $40. Electronic applications accepted. *Expenses:* Tuition, state resident: full-time $6912; part-time $384 per credit hour. Tuition, nonresident: full-time $12,150; part-time $675 per credit hour. Tuition and fees vary according to course load, program and reciprocity agreements. *Financial support:* Unspecified assistantships available. Financial award applicants required to submit FAFSA. *Faculty research:* Leadership and development, organizational change, field research, team and conflict management, strategy development and systems thinking. *Unit head:* Dr. Kenneth Rhee, Program Director, 859-572-6310, Fax: 859-572-7694, E-mail: rhee@nku.edu. *Application contact:* Amberly Hurst-Nutini, Coordinator, 859-572-5947, Fax: 859-572-7694, E-mail: hurstam@nku.edu.

Northwestern University, The Graduate School, Kellogg School of Management, Department of Management and Organizations, Evanston, IL 60208. Offers PhD. Admissions and degree offered through The Graduate School. *Degree requirements:* For doctorate, comprehensive exam, thesis/dissertation. *Entrance requirements:* For doctorate, GMAT or GRE General Test. Additional exam requirements/recommendations for international students: Required—TOEFL. Electronic applications accepted. *Faculty research:* Bargaining and negotiation, organizational design, decision making, organizational change, strategic alliances.

Northwestern University, The Graduate School, School of Education and Social Policy, Program in Learning and Organizational Change, Evanston, IL 60208. Offers MS. Part-time and evening/weekend programs available. Postbaccalaureate distance learning degree programs offered (minimal on-campus study). *Faculty:* 3 full-time (2 women), 26 part-time/adjunct (14 women). *Students:* 19 full-time (15 women), 59 part-time (46 women); includes 13 minority (4 African Americans, 8 Asian Americans or Pacific Islanders, 1 Hispanic American), 4 international. Average age 32. 40 applicants, 70% accepted, 20 enrolled. In 2009, 17 master's awarded. *Degree requirements:* For master's, thesis, practicum. *Entrance requirements:* For master's, GRE or GMAT (recommended), letters of recommendation. Additional exam requirements/recommendations for international students: Required—TOEFL (minimum score 600 paper-based; 250 computer-based; 100 iBT); Recommended—IELTS (minimum score 7). *Application deadline:* For fall admission, 6/23 for domestic students, 1/11 priority date for international students; for winter admission, 6/23 for domestic students; for spring admission, 1/12 priority date for domestic students. Applications are processed on a rolling basis. Application fee: $100. Electronic applications accepted. *Financial support:* Career-related internships or fieldwork, institutionally sponsored loans, and unspecified assistantships available. *Faculty research:* Strategic change, learning and performance, workplace learning, leadership development, cognitive design, knowledge management. *Unit head:* Dr. Kimberly S. Scott, Director, 847-467-3102. *Application contact:* Leslie L. Zimmerman, Program Coordinator, 847-491-7376, Fax: 847-491-3957, E-mail: l-zimmerman@northwestern.edu.

Northwest University, School of Business and Management, Kirkland, WA 98033. Offers business administration (MBA); social entrepreneurship (MA). Evening/weekend programs available. *Faculty:* 9 full-time (1 woman), 6 part-time/adjunct (4 women). *Students:* 25 full-time (9 women), 4 part-time (1 woman); includes 6 minority (4 African Americans, 2 Asian Americans or Pacific Islanders), 4 international. Average age 34. 31 applicants, 90% accepted, 16 enrolled. In 2009, 11 master's awarded. *Degree requirements:* For master's, formalized research. *Entrance requirements:* For master's, GMAT, 4 foundation courses. Additional exam requirements/recommendations for international students: Required—TOEFL (minimum score 550 paper-based). *Application deadline:* For fall admission, 8/1 for domestic and international students; for spring admission, 12/1 for domestic and international students. Applications are processed on a rolling basis. Application fee: $75. Electronic applications accepted. *Financial support:* Federal Work-Study, scholarships/grants, health care benefits, and tuition waivers (full) available. Financial award applicants required to submit FAFSA. *Unit head:* Dr. Teresa Gillespie, Dean, 425-889-5290, E-mail: teresa.gillespie@northwestu.edu. *Application contact:* Roy Rowland, Director of Graduate and Professional Studies Enrollment, 425-889-5213, Fax: 425-803-3059, E-mail: roy.rowland@northwestu.edu.

Norwich University, School of Graduate and Continuing Studies, Program in Organizational Leadership, Northfield, VT 05663. Offers MSOL. Evening/weekend programs available. *Faculty:* 9 part-time/adjunct (4 women). *Students:* 138 full-time (65 women), 5 part-time (0 women); includes 16 minority (9 African Americans, 3 Asian Americans or Pacific Islanders, 4 Hispanic Americans). Average age 43. 198 applicants, 76% accepted, 143 enrolled. In 2009, 138 master's awarded. *Entrance requirements:* Additional exam requirements/recommendations for international students: Required—TOEFL (minimum score 550 paper-based; 212 computer-based; 83 iBT). *Application deadline:* For fall admission, 8/10 for domestic and international students; for winter admission, 11/7 for domestic and international students; for spring admission, 2/6 for domestic and international students. Application fee: $50. Full-time tuition and fees vary according to course level and course load. *Financial support:* Applicants required to submit FAFSA. *Unit head:* Diane Ravenscroft, Program Director, 802-485-2567, Fax: 802-485-2533, E-mail: dravensc@norwich.edu. *Application contact:* Alec Adams, Administrative Director, 802-485-2567, E-mail: aadams@norwich.edu.

Nova Southeastern University, Fischler School of Education and Human Services, Program in Education, Fort Lauderdale, FL 33314-7796. Offers educational leadership (Ed D); health care education (Ed D); higher education leadership (Ed D); human services administration (Ed D); instructional leadership (Ed D); instructional technology and distance education (Ed D); organizational leadership (Ed D); special education (Ed D); speech language pathology (Ed D). Part-time and evening/weekend programs available. Postbaccalaureate distance learning degree programs offered (minimal on-campus study). *Faculty:* 88 full-time (46 women), 132 part-time/adjunct (63 women). *Students:* 2,805 full-time (2,128 women), 1,411 part-time (1,081 women); includes 2,629 minority (2,034 African Americans, 19 American Indian/Alaska Native, 62 Asian Americans or Pacific Islanders, 514 Hispanic Americans), 30 international. Average age 41. 964 applicants, 69% accepted, 513 enrolled. In 2009, 445 doctorates awarded. *Degree requirements:* For doctorate, thesis/dissertation. *Entrance requirements:* For doctorate, MAT or GRE, master's degree, 2 letters of recommendation, work experience. Additional exam requirements/recommendations for international students: Required—TSE (recommended, minimum score 50); Recommended—TOEFL (minimum score 550 paper-based; 213 computer-based; 80 iBT), IELTS (minimum score 6). *Application deadline:* For fall admission, 8/20 priority date for domestic and international students; for winter admission, 12/19 priority date for domestic and international students; for spring admission, 4/26 priority date for domestic students, 4/25 priority date for international students. Applications are processed on a rolling basis. Application fee: $50. Electronic applications accepted. *Financial support:* In 2009–10, 2 fellowships with full tuition reimbursements (averaging $30,000 per year) were awarded; scholarships/grants and tuition waivers (full) also available. Support available to part-time students. Financial award application deadline: 4/15; financial award applicants required to submit FAFSA. *Unit head:* Dr. Ronald Kern, Dean of Academic Affairs, 800-986-3223 Ext. 7809, Fax: 954-262-3606, E-mail: rk429@nsu.nova.edu. *Application contact:* Dr. Jennifer Quinones Nottingham, Dean of Student Affairs, 800-986-3223 Ext. 1546.

Nova Southeastern University, Fischler School of Education and Human Services, Program in Organizational Leadership, Fort Lauderdale, FL 33314-7796. Offers Ed D. Part-time and evening/weekend programs available. Postbaccalaureate distance learning degree programs offered (minimal on-campus study). *Faculty:* 1 full-time (0 women), 8 part-time/adjunct (2 women). *Students:* 246 full-time (180 women), 5 part-time (3 women); includes 160 minority (133 African Americans, 1 American Indian/Alaska Native, 7 Asian Americans or Pacific Islanders, 19 Hispanic Americans), 1 international. 3 applicants, 67% accepted, 2 enrolled. In 2009, 92 doctorates awarded. *Degree requirements:* For doctorate, thesis/dissertation. *Entrance requirements:* For doctorate, MAT or GRE, master's degree, minimum GPA of 3.0, letter of recommendation. Additional exam requirements/recommendations for international students: Required—TSE (recommended, minimum score 50); Recommended—TOEFL (minimum score 550 paper-based; 213 computer-based; 80 iBT), IELTS (minimum score 6). *Application deadline:* For fall admission, 8/11 priority date for domestic and international students; for winter admission, 12/28 priority date for domestic and international students; for spring admission, 4/22 priority date for domestic and international students. Applications are processed on a rolling basis. Application fee: $50. Electronic applications accepted. *Financial support:* Tuition waivers (full) available. Financial award application deadline: 1/7; financial award applicants required to submit FAFSA. *Unit head:* Dr. Karen D. Bowser, Associate Dean of Doctoral Programs, 954-262-8677, Fax: 954-262-3606, E-mail: bowserk@nova.edu. *Application contact:* Dr. Jennifer Quinones Nottingham, Dean of Student Affairs, 800-986-3223 Ext. 8624, Fax: 954-262-3883, E-mail: jlquinon@nova.edu.

Nyack College, School of Adult and Distance Education, Nyack, NY 10960-3698. Offers organizational leadership (MS). *Degree requirements:* For master's, thesis.

Olivet Nazarene University, Program in Organizational Leadership, Bourbonnais, IL 60914. Offers MOL.

Our Lady of the Lake University of San Antonio, School of Business and Leadership, Program in Leadership Studies, San Antonio, TX 78207-4689. Offers PhD. *Faculty:* 5 full-time (1 woman), 5 part-time/adjunct (1 woman). *Students:* 8 full-time (4 women), 151 part-time (95 women); includes 111 minority (15 African Americans, 4 Asian Americans or Pacific Islanders, 92 Hispanic Americans), 1 international. Average age 41. In 2009, 23 doctorates awarded. *Degree requirements:* For doctorate, thesis/dissertation, internship, qualifying exam. *Entrance requirements:* For doctorate, GRE General Test or MAT, interview. *Application deadline:* For fall admission, 3/1 for domestic students. Application fee: $25 ($50 for international students). *Expenses:* Tuition: Full-time $12,330; part-time $685 per contact hour. Required fees: $139; $12 per contact hour. $57 per semester. Tuition and fees vary according to campus/location. *Unit head:* Dr. Robert Bisking, Chair, 210-434-6711, E-mail: biskr@lake.ollusa.edu. *Application contact:* Dr. Robert Bisking, Chair, 210-434-6711, E-mail: biskr@lake.ollusa.edu.

Our Lady of the Lake University of San Antonio, School of Business and Leadership, Program in Organizational Leadership, San Antonio, TX 78207-4689. Offers MS. *Students:* 1 (woman) full-time, 50 part-time (35 women); includes 4 African Americans, 2 Asian Americans or Pacific Islanders, 26 Hispanic Americans. Average age 37. In 2009, 7 master's awarded. *Expenses:* Tuition: Full-time $12,330; part-time $685 per contact hour. Required fees: $139; $12 per contact hour. $57 per semester. Tuition and fees vary according to campus/location. *Unit head:* Dr. Robert Bisking, Dean, 210-434-6711 Ext. 2281, Fax: 210-434-0821, E-mail: rbisking@ollusa.edu. *Application contact:* Dr. Robert Bisking, Dean, 210-434-6711 Ext. 2281, Fax: 210-434-0821, E-mail: rbisking@ollusa.edu.

Oxford Graduate School, Graduate Programs, Dayton, TN 37321-6736. Offers family life education (M Litt); organizational leadership in nonprofits (M Litt); religion and society (D Phil).

Palm Beach Atlantic University, MacArthur School of Leadership, West Palm Beach, FL 33416-4708. Offers organizational leadership (MS). Part-time and evening/weekend programs available. *Faculty:* 3 full-time (1 woman), 4 part-time/adjunct (1 woman). *Students:* 1 (woman) full-time, 91 part-time (52 women); includes 40 minority (30 African Americans, 1 American Indian/Alaska Native, 1 Asian American or Pacific Islander, 8 Hispanic Americans), 2 international. Average age 38. 61 applicants, 66% accepted, 34 enrolled. In 2009, 10 master's awarded. *Entrance requirements:* For master's, GRE, minimum GPA of 3.0. Additional exam requirements/recommendations for international students: Required—TOEFL (minimum score 550 paper-based; 213 computer-based). *Application deadline:* For fall admission, 7/15 priority date for domestic students; for spring admission, 11/15 priority date for domestic students. Applications are processed on a rolling basis. Application fee: $45. Electronic applications accepted. *Expenses:* Tuition: Full-time $8010; part-time $445 per credit hour. Required fees: $99 per semester. Tuition and fees vary according to course load and degree level. *Financial support:* Tuition waivers (partial) available. Financial award applicants required to submit FAFSA. *Unit head:* Dr. Jim Laub, Dean, 561-803-2318, Fax: 561-803-2306, E-mail: jim_laub@pba.edu. *Application contact:* Graduate Admissions, 888-468-6722, Fax: 561-803-2115, E-mail: grad@pba.edu.

Pepperdine University, Graziadio School of Business and Management, Malibu, CA 90263. Offers applied finance (MS); business administration (MBA); fully-employed (MBA); international business administration (IMBA); management and leadership (MS); organizational development (MSOD); presidential and key executive business administration (Exec MBA). *Accreditation:* AACSB. Part-time and evening/weekend programs available. *Faculty:* 86 full-time (18 women), 49 part-time/adjunct (12 women). *Students:* 872 full-time (343 women), 804 part-time (357 women); includes 530 minority (76 African Americans, 7 American Indian/Alaska Native, 306 Asian Americans or Pacific Islanders, 141 Hispanic Americans), 162 international. *Entrance requirements:* For master's, GMAT or MAT. Additional exam requirements/recommendations for international students: Required—TOEFL (minimum score 550 paper-based). *Application deadline:* For fall admission, 6/28 for domestic students. Applications are processed on a rolling basis. Application fee: $45. *Expenses:* Contact institution. *Financial support:* Career-related internships or fieldwork, institutionally sponsored loans, scholarships/grants, and unspecified assistantships available. Support available to part-time students. Financial award applicants required to submit FAFSA. *Unit head:* Dr. Linda A. Livingstone, Dean, 310-568-5689, Fax: 310-568-5766, E-mail: linda.livingstone@pepperdine.edu. *Application*

contact: Darrell Eriksen, Director of Admission and Student Accounts, 310-568-5525, E-mail: darrell.eriksen@pepperdine.edu.

Peru State College, Graduate Programs, Program in Organizational Management, Peru, NE 68421. Offers MS. *Program offered online only. Part-time programs available. Degree requirements:* For master's, thesis (for some programs). *Expenses:* Contact institution. *Faculty research:* Emotional intelligence.

Pfeiffer University, Program in Business Administration, Misenheimer, NC 28109-0960. Offers business administration (MBA); organizational management (MS); MBA/MHA; MBA/MS. Part-time and evening/weekend programs available. Postbaccalaureate distance learning degree programs offered (minimal on-campus study). *Entrance requirements:* For master's, GMAT, minimum GPA of 3.0.

Pfeiffer University, Program in Organizational Change and Leadership, Misenheimer, NC 28109-0960. Offers MS, MBA/MS. *Entrance requirements:* For master's, GRE or GMAT.

Philadelphia Biblical University, School of Business and Leadership, Langhorne, PA 19047-2990. Offers organizational leadership (MSOL). Part-time and evening/weekend programs available. *Faculty:* 2 full-time (0 women), 3 part-time/adjunct (0 women). *Students:* 6 full-time (3 women), 24 part-time (13 women); includes 8 minority (all African Americans), 3 international. Average age 41. 12 applicants, 33% accepted, 4 enrolled. In 2009, 6 master's awarded. *Entrance requirements:* Additional exam requirements/recommendations for international students: Required—TOEFL (minimum score 550 paper-based; 213 computer-based). *Application deadline:* Applications are processed on a rolling basis. Application fee: $25. Electronic applications accepted. *Expenses:* Tuition: Full-time $10,350; part-time $575 per credit. Required fees: $10; $10 per year. Tuition and fees vary according to program. *Financial support:* In 2009–10, 6 students received support. Scholarships/grants available. Support available to part-time students. Financial award applicants required to submit FAFSA. *Unit head:* Dr. William Bowles, Chair, Graduate Programs in Business and Leadership, 215-702-4871, Fax: 215-702-4248, E-mail: wbowles@pbu.edu. *Application contact:* Timothy Nessler, Assistant Director, Graduate Admissions, 800-572-2472, Fax: 215-702-4248, E-mail: tnessler@pbu.edu.

Point Park University, School of Business, Pittsburgh, PA 15222-1984. Offers business (MBA); organizational leadership (MA). Part-time and evening/weekend programs available. *Faculty:* 13 full-time, 18 part-time/adjunct. *Students:* 151 full-time (84 women), 236 part-time (118 women); includes 102 minority (92 African Americans, 2 American Indian/Alaska Native, 6 Asian Americans or Pacific Islanders, 2 Hispanic Americans), 29 international. Average age 33. 416 applicants, 67% accepted, 194 enrolled. In 2009, 186 master's awarded. *Degree requirements:* For master's, comprehensive exam (for some programs), thesis or alternative. *Entrance requirements:* For master's, minimum QPA of 2.75; 2 letters of recommendation; resume (MA). Additional exam requirements/recommendations for international students: Required—TOEFL (minimum score 550 paper-based; 79 iBT). *Application deadline:* Applications are processed on a rolling basis. Application fee: $30. Electronic applications accepted. *Expenses:* Tuition: Full-time $11,880; part-time $660 per credit. Required fees: $486; $27 per credit. *Financial support:* In 2009–10, 122 students received support, including 6 research assistantships with full tuition reimbursements available (averaging $6,400 per year); scholarships/grants also available. Financial award application deadline: 4/15; financial award applicants required to submit FAFSA. *Faculty research:* Technology issues, foreign direct investment, multinational corporate issues, cross-cultural international organizations/administrations, regional integration issues. *Unit head:* Dr. Angela Isaac, Dean, 412-392-8011, Fax: 412-392-8048, E-mail: aisaac@pointpark.edu. *Application contact:* Marty M. Paonessa, Associate Director, Graduate and Adult Enrollment, 412-392-3915, Fax: 412-392-6164, E-mail: mpaonessa@pointpark.edu.

Quinnipiac University, School of Business, Program in Organizational Leadership, Hamden, CT 06518-1940. Offers MS. *Students:* 4 full-time (3 women), 102 part-time (66 women); includes 9 minority (6 African Americans, 1 Asian American or Pacific Islander, 2 Hispanic Americans). 61 applicants, 75% accepted, 31 enrolled. In 2009, 38 master's awarded. *Entrance requirements:* Additional exam requirements/recommendations for international students: Required—TOEFL (minimum score 575 paper-based; 233 computer-based; 90 iBT), IELTS (minimum score 6.5). *Application deadline:* Applications are processed on a rolling basis. Application fee: $45. Electronic applications accepted. *Expenses:* Tuition: Full-time $16,030; part-time $770 per credit. Required fees: $630; $35 per credit. *Unit head:* Dr. Kimberly McKeage, MBA Director, 203-582-3676, Fax: 203-582-8664, E-mail: kim.mckeage@quinnipiac.edu. *Application contact:* Valerie Schlesinger, Associate Director of Admissions, QU Online, 203-582-8949, Fax: 203-582-3443, E-mail: valerie.schlesinger@quinnipiac.edu.

Regent University, Graduate School, School of Global Leadership and Entrepreneurship, Virginia Beach, VA 23464-9800. Offers business administration (MBA); management (MA); organizational leadership (MA, PhD, Certificate); strategic foresight (MA); strategic leadership (DSL). Part-time and evening/weekend programs available. Postbaccalaureate distance learning degree programs offered (minimal on-campus study). *Faculty:* 15 full-time (3 women), 10 part-time/adjunct (3 women). *Students:* 14 full-time (4 women), 407 part-time (156 women); includes 123 minority (97 African Americans, 3 American Indian/Alaska Native, 6 Asian Americans or Pacific Islanders, 17 Hispanic Americans), 59 international. Average age 41. 153 applicants, 55% accepted, 31 enrolled. In 2009, 110 master's, 52 doctorates awarded. *Degree requirements:* For master's, thesis or alternative, 3 credit hour culminating experience; for doctorate, thesis/dissertation. *Entrance requirements:* For master's, GRE, GMAT, minimum undergraduate GPA of 2.75, computer literacy survey, 2 recommendations, resume, transcripts, essay; for doctorate, GRE, GMAT, sample of writing, minimum 3 years of relevant experience, computer literacy survey, 2 recommendations, resume, essay, transcripts; for Certificate, writing sample, resume, transcripts. Additional exam requirements/recommendations for international students: Required—TOEFL (minimum score 577 paper-based; 233 computer-based). *Application deadline:* For fall admission, 5/1 priority date for domestic students; for spring admission, 10/1 priority date for domestic students. Applications are processed on a rolling basis. Application fee: $50. Electronic applications accepted. *Expenses:* Contact institution. *Financial support:* In 2009–10, 258 students received support. Career-related internships or fieldwork, scholarships/grants, and tuition waivers (full and partial) available. Support available to part-time students. Financial award application deadline: 9/1. *Faculty research:* Servant leadership, ethics and values, telecommuting and family values, organizational communications, distance education. *Unit head:* Dr. Bruce Winston, Dean, 757-352-4306, Fax: 757-352-4634, E-mail: brucwin@regent.edu. *Application contact:* Matthew Chadwick, Director of Admissions, 800-373-5504, Fax: 757-352-4381, E-mail: admissions@regent.edu.

Regis University, College for Professional Studies, School of Management, Denver, CO 80221-1099. Offers accounting (MS); business administration (MBA); computer information technology (MSOL); executive internal management (Certificate); executive leadership (Certificate); finance (MBA); finance and accounting (MBA); human resource management (MSOL); international business (MBA); marketing (MBA); operations management (MBA); organization leadership (MS); organizational leadership (MSOL); project leadership and management (MSOL, Certificate); project management (Certificate); strategic business (Certificate); strategic human resource (Certificate); technical management (Certificate). Offered at Colorado Springs Campus, Northwest Denver Campus, Southeast Denver Campus, Fort Collins Campus, Broomfield Campus, Henderson (Nevada) Campus, and Summerlin (Nevada) Campus and online. Part-time and evening/weekend programs available. Postbaccalaureate distance learning degree programs offered (no on-campus study). *Degree requirements:* For master's, thesis optional, capstone project. *Entrance requirements:* For master's, GMAT or essays, interview, 2 years of full-time business work experience, resume; for Certificate, GMAT. Additional exam requirements/recommendations for international students: Required—TOEFL, TOEFL or university-based test; Recommended—TWE (minimum score 5). Electronic applications accepted. *Faculty research:* Impact of Info Technology on Small Business Regulation of Accounting, International Project financing, Mineral Development, Delivery of Healthcare to rural indigenos communities.

Rider University, Department of Graduate Education, Leadership and Counseling, Program in Organizational Leadership, Lawrenceville, NJ 08648-3001. Offers MA. *Entrance requirements:* For master's, resume.

Robert Morris University, Graduate Studies, School of Communications and Information Systems, Moon Township, PA 15108-1189. Offers communication and information systems (MS); competitive intelligence systems (MS); information security and assurance (MS); information systems and communications (D Sc); information systems management (MS); information technology project management (MS); Internet information systems (MS); organizational studies (MS). Part-time and evening/weekend programs available. *Faculty:* 28 full-time (9 women), 9 part-time/adjunct (3 women). *Students:* 257 part-time (76 women); includes 41 minority (31 African Americans, 8 Asian Americans or Pacific Islanders, 2 Hispanic Americans), 16 international. Average age 33. 106 applicants, 100% accepted, 106 enrolled. In 2009, 84 master's, 8 doctorates awarded. *Degree requirements:* For doctorate, thesis/dissertation. *Entrance requirements:* For doctorate, employer letter of endorsement, interview. Additional exam requirements/recommendations for international students: Required—TOEFL (minimum score 550 paper-based; 213 computer-based; 79 iBT). *Application deadline:* For fall admission, 7/1 priority date for domestic and international students; for spring admission, 11/1 priority date for domestic and international students. Applications are processed on a rolling basis. Application fee: $35. Electronic applications accepted. *Expenses:* Contact institution. *Financial support:* Research assistantships with partial tuition reimbursements, institutionally sponsored loans and unspecified assistantships available. Support available to part-time students. Financial award application deadline: 5/1. *Unit head:* Dr. Barbara J. Levine, Dean, 412-397-2591, Fax: 412-397-2481, E-mail: levine@rmu.edu. *Application contact:* Deborah Roach, Assistant Dean, Graduate Admissions, 412-397-5200, Fax: 412-397-2425, E-mail: graduateadmissions@rmu.edu.

Roosevelt University, Graduate Division, College of Education, Program in Educational Leadership, Chicago, IL 60605. Offers MA, Ed D.

Rutgers, The State University of New Jersey, Newark, Rutgers Business School–Newark and New Brunswick, Doctoral Programs in Business, Newark, NJ 07102. Offers accounting (PhD); accounting information systems (PhD); finance (PhD); individualized study (PhD); information technology (PhD); international business (PhD); management science (PhD); organizational management (PhD); supply chain management (PhD).

Sage Graduate School, Graduate School, School of Management, Troy, NY 12180-4115. Offers business administration (MBA), including business strategy, finance, human resources, marketing; health services administration (MS, Certificate), including dietetic internship (Certificate), gerontology (MS); organizational management (MS), including public administration; JD/MBA. Part-time and evening/weekend programs available. *Faculty:* 4 full-time (2 women), 6 part-time/adjunct (0 women). *Students:* 23 full-time (20 women), 136 part-time (94 women); includes 25 minority (13 African Americans, 2 Asian Americans or Pacific Islanders, 10 Hispanic Americans), 2 international. Average age 31. 101 applicants, 59% accepted, 44 enrolled. In 2009, 39 master's awarded. *Entrance requirements:* For master's, minimum GPA of 2.75. Additional exam requirements/recommendations for international students: Required—TOEFL (minimum score 550 paper-based; 213 computer-based). *Application deadline:* Applications are processed on a rolling basis. Application fee: $40. *Expenses:* Tuition: Full-time $10,620; part-time $590 per credit hour. *Financial support:* Fellowships, research assistantships, Federal Work-Study, scholarships/grants, and unspecified assistantships available. Support available to part-time students. Financial award application deadline: 3/1; financial award applicants required to submit FAFSA. *Unit head:* Daniel Robeson, Chair, Management Department, 518-292-1770, Fax: 518-292-5414, E-mail: robesd@sage.edu. *Application contact:* Wendy D. Diefendorf, Director of Graduate and Adult Admission, 518-244-2443, Fax: 518-244-6880, E-mail: diefew@sage.edu.

St. Ambrose University, College of Business, Program in Organizational Leadership, Davenport, IA 52801. Offers MOL. Part-time and evening/weekend programs available. *Faculty:* 5 full-time (0 women), 5 part-time/adjunct (2 women). *Students:* 19 full-time (15 women), 102 part-time (68 women); includes 14 minority (10 African Americans, 1 American Indian/Alaska Native, 3 Hispanic Americans). Average age 36. 62 applicants, 79% accepted, 48 enrolled. In 2009, 33 master's awarded. *Degree requirements:* For master's, comprehensive exam (for some programs), thesis or alternative, integration projects. *Entrance requirements:* Additional exam requirements/recommendations for international students: Required—TOEFL. *Application deadline:* For fall admission, 8/15 priority date for domestic students; for winter admission, 12/15 priority date for domestic students; for spring admission, 1/1 priority date for domestic students. Applications are processed on a rolling basis. Application fee: $25. Electronic applications accepted. *Expenses:* Contact institution. *Financial support:* In 2009–10, 51 students received support, including 10 research assistantships (averaging $3,343 per year); scholarships/grants, tuition waivers (partial), and unspecified assistantships also available. Financial award application deadline: 3/15; financial award applicants required to submit FAFSA. *Unit head:* Dr. Ron O. Wastyn, Director, 563-322-1014, Fax: 563-324-0842, E-mail: wastynronaldo@sau.edu. *Application contact:* Megan M. Gisi, Program Coordinator, 563-322-1051, Fax: 563-324-0842, E-mail: gisimeganm@sau.edu.

St. Catherine University, Graduate Programs, Program in Organizational Leadership, St. Paul, MN 55105. Offers MA. Part-time and evening/weekend programs available. *Faculty:* 5 full-time (4 women). *Students:* 11 full-time (10 women), 164 part-time (159 women); includes 15 minority (7 African Americans, 5 Asian Americans or Pacific Islanders, 3 Hispanic Americans), 1 international. Average age 40. 55 applicants, 75% accepted, 37 enrolled. In 2009, 35 master's awarded. *Degree requirements:* For master's, thesis. *Entrance requirements:* For master's, GMAT, GRE General Test or MAT, 2 years of work experience, minimum GPA of 3.0. Additional exam requirements/recommendations for international students: Required—TOEFL (minimum score 600 paper-based; 250 computer-based; 100 iBT). *Application deadline:* For fall admission, 8/1 priority date for domestic students; for winter admission, 12/1 priority date for domestic students; for spring admission, 3/1 priority date for domestic students. Applications are processed on a rolling basis. Application fee: $35. Tuition and fees vary according to program. *Financial support:* In 2009–10, 72 students received support; research assistantships, career-related internships or fieldwork and institutionally sponsored loans available. Support available to part-time students. Financial award application deadline: 4/1; financial award applicants required to submit FAFSA. *Faculty research:* Ethics. *Unit head:* Rebecca Hawthorne, Director, 651-690-6420, Fax: 651-690-6024. *Application contact:* 651-690-6933, Fax: 651-690-6064.

St. Edward's University, School of Management and Business, Program in Organizational Leadership and Ethics, Austin, TX 78704. Offers MS. Part-time and evening/weekend programs available. *Students:* 45 part-time (34 women); includes 17 minority (4 African Americans, 13 Hispanic Americans). Average age 38. 24 applicants, 88% accepted, 20 enrolled. In 2009, 20 master's awarded. *Degree requirements:* For master's, minimum of 24 hours in residence. *Entrance requirements:* For master's, GMAT or GRE General Test, minimum GPA of 2.75 in last 60 hours of course work. Additional exam requirements/recommendations for international students: Required—TOEFL (minimum score 550 paper-based; 213 computer-based; 79 iBT) or IELTS (minimum score 6). *Application deadline:* For fall admission, 7/1 for domestic and international students; for spring admission, 11/1 for domestic and international students. Applications are processed on a rolling basis. Application fee: $45 ($50 for international students). Electronic applications accepted. *Expenses:* Tuition: Full-time $14,922; part-time $829 per credit hour. Required fees: $50 per trimester. Full-time tuition and fees vary according to course load and program. *Financial support:* Scholarships/grants available. *Faculty research:* Business ethics. *Unit head:* Dr. Tom Sechrest, Director, 512-637-1954, Fax: 512-448-8492, E-mail: thomasl@stedwards.edu. *Application contact:* Benjamin Jimenez, Graduate Admissions Coordinator, 512-233-1694, Fax: 512-428-1032, E-mail: benjij@stedwards.edu.

St. Joseph's College, Long Island Campus, Program in Management, Patchogue, NY 11772-2399. Offers health care (AC); health care management (MS); human resource management (AC); human resources management (MS); organizational management (MS).

Organizational Management

Saint Joseph's University, College of Arts and Sciences, Department of Education, Philadelphia, PA 19131-1395. Offers educational leadership (Ed D); elementary education (MS); instructional technology (MS); organizational development and leadership (MS); professional education (MS); reading specialist (MS); secondary education (MS); special education (MS). Part-time and evening/weekend programs available. *Students:* 5 full-time (3 women), 750 part-time (561 women); includes 100 minority (76 African Americans, 1 American Indian/Alaska Native, 11 Asian Americans or Pacific Islanders, 12 Hispanic Americans), 3 international. Average age 33. In 2009, 210 master's, 14 doctorates awarded. *Entrance requirements:* For master's, 2 letters of recommendation, minimum GPA of 3.0, application, official transcripts, personal statement; for doctorate, GRE, master's degree from accredited institution, minimum graduate GPA of 3.5, computer competence, commitment to participate in cohort, interview with program director. Additional exam requirements/recommendations for international students: Required—TOEFL (minimum score 550 paper-based; 213 computer-based; 79 iBT). *Application deadline:* For fall admission, 7/15 priority date for domestic students, 4/15 for international students; for winter admission, 11/15 for domestic students, 1/15 for international students; for spring admission, 11/15 priority date for domestic students, 11/15 for international students. Applications are processed on a rolling basis. Application fee: $35. Electronic applications accepted. *Expenses:* Contact institution. *Financial support:* Unspecified assistantships available. Financial award applicants required to submit FAFSA. *Faculty research:* Early childhood course design, public education professional development. Total annual research expenditures: $91,900. *Unit head:* Dr. Teri Sosa, Director of Graduate Education, 610-660-3162, E-mail: tsosa@sju.edu. *Application contact:* Kate McConnell, Director, Graduate College of Arts and Sciences Admissions and Retention, 610-660-3184, Fax: 610-660-3230, E-mail: kate.mcconnell@sju.edu.

Saint Joseph's University, College of Arts and Sciences, Organization Development and Leadership Programs, Philadelphia, PA 19131-1395. Offers adult learning and training (MS, Certificate); organization dynamics and leadership (MS, Certificate); organizational psychology and development (MS, Certificate). Part-time and evening/weekend programs available. Postbaccalaureate distance learning degree programs offered (no on-campus study). *Students:* 9 full-time (6 women), 75 part-time (50 women); includes 23 minority (20 African Americans, 1 Asian American or Pacific Islander, 2 Hispanic Americans), 10 international. Average age 37. In 2009, 29 master's awarded. *Entrance requirements:* For master's, GRE (if GPA less than 2.7), minimum GPA of 2.7, 2 letters of recommendation, resume. Additional exam requirements/recommendations for international students: Required—TOEFL (minimum score 550 paper-based; 213 computer-based; 79 iBT). *Application deadline:* For fall admission, 7/15 priority date for domestic students, 4/15 for international students; for winter admission, 1/15 for international students; for spring admission, 11/15 priority date for domestic students, 10/15 for international students. Applications are processed on a rolling basis. Application fee: $35. Electronic applications accepted. *Expenses:* Tuition: Part-time $729 per credit hour. Tuition and fees vary according to degree level and program. *Financial support:* Applicants required to submit FAFSA. *Unit head:* Dr. Felice Tilin, Director, 610-660-1575, E-mail: ftilin@sju.edu. *Application contact:* Kate McConnell, Director, Graduate College of Arts and Sciences Admissions and Retention, 610-660-3184, Fax: 610-660-3230, E-mail: kate.mcconnell@sju.edu.

Saint Louis University, Graduate School, College of Education and Public Service and Graduate School, Department of Public Policy Studies, St. Louis, MO 63103-2097. Offers geographic information systems (Certificate); organizational development (Certificate); public administration (MAPA); public policy analysis (PhD); urban affairs (MAUA); urban planning and real estate development (MUPRED). *Accreditation:* NASPAA. Part-time programs available. *Degree requirements:* For master's, comprehensive exam (for some programs), thesis (for some programs); for doctorate, comprehensive exam, thesis/dissertation, preliminary exams. *Entrance requirements:* For master's, GMAT, GRE General Test, or LSAT, letters of recommendation, resume; for doctorate, GMAT, GRE General Test, or LSAT, letters of recommendation, resumé, interview, transcripts, goal statement. Additional exam requirements/recommendations for international students: Required—TOEFL (minimum score 525 paper-based; 194 computer-based). Electronic applications accepted. *Faculty research:* Urban politics, brown fields, e-government, and administration, evaluation research, community development, electronic government and governance.

Saint Mary's University of Minnesota, Schools of Graduate and Professional Programs, Graduate School of Business and Technology, Organizational Leadership Program, Winona, MN 55987-1399. Offers MA. *Unit head:* Viki Kimsal, Director, 507-238-4510, E-mail: vkimsal@smumn.edu. *Application contact:* Yasin Alsaidi, Director of Admissions for Graduate and Professional Programs, 612-728-5207, Fax: 612-728-5121, E-mail: yalsaidi@smumn.edu.

Santa Clara University, Leavey School of Business, Program in Business Administration, Santa Clara, CA 95053. Offers accounting (MBA); entrepreneurship (MBA); executive MBA (EMBA); finance (MBA); food and agribusiness (MBA); international business (MBA); leading people and organizations (MBA); managing technology and innovation (MBA); marketing management (MBA); supply chain management (MBA). *Accreditation:* AACSB. Part-time and evening/weekend programs available. *Students:* 228 full-time (88 women), 838 part-time (265 women); includes 388 minority (17 African Americans, 2 American Indian/Alaska Native, 326 Asian Americans or Pacific Islanders, 43 Hispanic Americans), 218 international. Average age 31. 486 applicants, 77% accepted, 263 enrolled. In 2009, 317 master's awarded. *Degree requirements:* For master's, thesis or alternative. *Entrance requirements:* For master's, GMAT, GRE. Additional exam requirements/recommendations for international students: Required—TOEFL (minimum score 600 paper-based; 250 computer-based; 100 iBT). *Application deadline:* For fall admission, 6/1 for domestic and international students; for spring admission, 1/19 for domestic students, 1/17 for international students. Applications are processed on a rolling basis. Application fee: $75 ($100 for international students). Electronic applications accepted. *Expenses:* Contact institution. *Financial support:* Fellowships with partial tuition reimbursements, research assistantships with partial tuition reimbursements, career-related internships or fieldwork, Federal Work-Study, institutionally sponsored loans, scholarships/grants, health care benefits, and unspecified assistantships available. Support available to part-time students. Financial award applicants required to submit FAFSA. *Unit head:* Elizabeth B. Ford, Senior Assistant Dean, 408-554-2752, Fax: 408-554-4571, E-mail: eford@scu.edu. *Application contact:* Jennifer W. Taylor, Senior Director, 408-554-4539, Fax: 408-554-4571, E-mail: mbaadmissions@scu.edu.

Saybrook University, Graduate College of Psychology and Humanistic Studies, San Francisco, CA 94111-1920. Offers clinical psychology (Psy D); human science (MA, PhD), including consciousness and spirituality, humanistic and transpersonal psychology, integrative health studies, organizational systems, social transformation, transformative social change (MA); organizational systems (MA, PhD), including consciousness and spirituality, humanistic and transpersonal psychology, integrative health studies, leadership of sustainable systems (MA), organizational systems, social transformation; psychology (MA, PhD), including clinical psychology (PhD), consciousness and spirituality, creativity studies (MA), humanistic and transpersonal psychology, integrative health studies, Jungian studies, marriage and family therapy (MA), organizational systems, social transformation. Postbaccalaureate distance learning degree programs offered (minimal on-campus study). Terminal master's awarded for partial completion of doctoral program. *Degree requirements:* For master's, thesis or alternative; for doctorate, thesis/dissertation. Electronic applications accepted. *Faculty research:* Humanistic theory, health studies, organizational systems, consciousness and spirituality, social transformation.

Saybrook University, LIOS Graduate College, Leadership and Organization Development Track, San Francisco, CA 94111-1920. Offers MA. *Degree requirements:* For master's, thesis (for some programs), oral exams. *Entrance requirements:* For master's, bachelor's degree from an accredited college or university. *Faculty research:* Cross-functional work teams, communication, management authority, employee influence, systems theory.

Seattle University, Albers School of Business and Economics, Center for Leadership Formation, Seattle, WA 98122-1090. Offers EMBA, Certificate.

Shippensburg University of Pennsylvania, School of Graduate Studies, College of Arts and Sciences, Department of Sociology and Anthropology, Shippensburg, PA 17257-2299. Offers organizational development and leadership (MS), including business, communications, education, environmental management, higher education, historical administration, individual and organizational development, public organizations, social structures and organizations. Part-time and evening/weekend programs available. *Degree requirements:* For master's, capstone experience. *Entrance requirements:* For master's, interview (if GPA less than 2.75), resume. Additional exam requirements/recommendations for international students: Required—TOEFL (minimum score 560 paper-based; 220 computer-based); Recommended—IELTS (minimum score 6). Electronic applications accepted.

SIT Graduate Institute, Graduate Programs, Master's Programs in Intercultural Service, Leadership, and Management, Program in Management, Brattleboro, VT 05302-0676. Offers MS.

SIT Graduate Institute, Graduate Programs, Program in Global Management (Oman), Brattleboro, VT 05302-0676. Offers MGM. Program offered in the Sultanate of Oman. Part-time programs available. *Degree requirements:* For master's, capstone project. *Entrance requirements:* Additional exam requirements/recommendations for international students: Required—TOEFL (minimum score of 550 paper-based, 213 computer-based, 79 iBT) or IELTS (minimum score of 6.0).

Southern New Hampshire University, School of Business, Manchester, NH 03106-1045. Offers accounting (MS); business administration (MBA, Certificate), including accounting (Certificate), business administration (MBA), finance (Certificate), forensic accounting (Certificate), human resources management (Certificate), international business (Certificate), international sport management (Certificate), leadership of not for profit organizations (Certificate), marketing (Certificate), operations management (Certificate), sport management (Certificate), taxation (Certificate); finance (MS); hospitality and tourism leadership (Certificate); information technology (MS, Certificate); information technology/international business (Certificate); integrated marketing communications (Certificate); international business (MS, DBA); marketing (MS); operations and project management (MS); organizational leadership (MS); project management (Certificate); sport management (MS); MBA/Certificate. *Accreditation:* ACBSP. Part-time and evening/weekend programs available. Postbaccalaureate distance learning degree programs offered (no on-campus study). Terminal master's awarded for partial completion of doctoral program. *Degree requirements:* For master's, one foreign language, comprehensive exam (for some programs), thesis or alternative; for doctorate, one foreign language, comprehensive exam, thesis/dissertation. *Entrance requirements:* For master's, minimum GPA of 2.5; for doctorate, GMAT. Additional exam requirements/recommendations for international students: Required—TOEFL (minimum score 500 paper-based). Electronic applications accepted.

Southwestern College, Fifth-Year Graduate Programs, Winfield, KS 67156-2499. Offers leadership (MS); management (MBA). Part-time programs available. *Faculty:* 4 full-time (2 women), 6 part-time/adjunct (3 women). *Students:* 21 full-time (9 women), 4 part-time (1 woman); includes 5 minority (3 African Americans, 1 American Indian/Alaska Native, 1 Hispanic American), 4 international. Average age 24. 22 applicants, 86% accepted, 16 enrolled. In 2009, 17 master's awarded. *Entrance requirements:* For master's, baccalaureate degree, minimum GPA of 3.0. Additional exam requirements/recommendations for international students: Required—TOEFL (minimum score 550 paper-based; 213 computer-based). *Application deadline:* For fall admission, 4/1 priority date for domestic students; for spring admission, 12/1 priority date for domestic students. Applications are processed on a rolling basis. Application fee: $25. Electronic applications accepted. *Financial support:* In 2009–10, 20 students received support. Federal Work-Study, tuition waivers (partial), and unspecified assistantships available. Financial award application deadline: 4/1; financial award applicants required to submit FAFSA. *Unit head:* Dr. James Sheppard, Vice President for Academic Affairs, 620-229-6227, Fax: 620-229-6224, E-mail: james.sheppard@sckans.edu. *Application contact:* Marla Sexson, Director of Admissions, 800-846-1543 Ext. 6364, Fax: 620-229-6344, E-mail: marla.sexson@sckans.edu.

Spring Arbor University, School of Graduate and Professional Studies, Spring Arbor, MI 49283-9799. Offers counseling (MAC); family studies (MAFS); nursing (MSN); organizational management (MAOM). Part-time and evening/weekend programs available. Postbaccalaureate distance learning degree programs offered (no on-campus study). *Faculty:* 8 full-time (3 women), 99 part-time/adjunct (45 women). *Students:* 412 full-time (327 women), 420 part-time (351 women); includes 215 minority (182 African Americans, 2 American Indian/Alaska Native, 10 Asian Americans or Pacific Islanders, 21 Hispanic Americans), 3 international. Average age 40. In 2009, 257 master's awarded. *Entrance requirements:* For master's, minimum GPA of 3.0, interview, writing sample, 2 professional references. Additional exam requirements/recommendations for international students: Required—TOEFL (minimum score 550 paper-based; 220 computer-based). *Application deadline:* Applications are processed on a rolling basis. Application fee: $40. Electronic applications accepted. *Expenses:* Tuition: Full-time $5400; part-time $450 per credit hour. Required fees: $240; $150 per year. Tuition and fees vary according to course load and program. *Financial support:* Scholarships/grants available. Support available to part-time students. Financial award applicants required to submit FAFSA. *Unit head:* Dr. Robert Hamill, Dean of Graduate and Professional Studies, 517-750-1200 Ext. 1343, Fax: 517-750-6602, E-mail: rhamill@arbor.edu. *Application contact:* Greg Bentle, Coordinator of Graduate Recruitment, 517-750-6763, Fax: 517-750-6624, E-mail: gbentle@arbor.edu.

Springfield College, Graduate Programs, Program in Human Services, Springfield, MA 01109-3797. Offers human services (MS), including community counseling psychology, mental health counseling, organizational management and leadership. Part-time programs available. *Degree requirements:* For master's, comprehensive exam, thesis (for some programs), research project. *Entrance requirements:* For master's, GRE. Additional exam requirements/recommendations for international students: Required—TOEFL (minimum score 550 paper-based; 213 computer-based). Electronic applications accepted. *Expenses:* Contact institution.

State University of New York at Plattsburgh, School of Business and Economics, Program in Leadership, Plattsburgh, NY 12901-2681. Offers MS. Part-time and evening/weekend programs available. *Faculty:* 4 full-time (1 woman), 3 part-time/adjunct (0 women). *Students:* 6 full-time (5 women), 15 part-time (9 women); includes 2 minority (both Asian Americans or Pacific Islanders), 3 international. Average age 32. 19 applicants, 89% accepted, 12 enrolled. *Degree requirements:* For master's, thesis. *Entrance requirements:* For master's, GRE, GMAT, or MAT. Additional exam requirements/recommendations for international students: Required—TOEFL (minimum score 550 paper-based; 213 computer-based; 79 iBT). *Application deadline:* For fall admission, 2/15 priority date for domestic students; for spring admission, 10/15 priority date for domestic students. Applications are processed on a rolling basis. Application fee: $75. *Expenses:* Tuition, state resident: full-time $8370; part-time $349 per credit hour. Tuition, nonresident: full-time $13,250; part-time $552 per credit hour. Required fees: $1130. *Financial support:* Application deadline: 4/15. *Unit head:* Dr. Suzanne Catana, Coordinator, 518-696-2710, E-mail: catanasl@plattsburgh.edu. *Application contact:* Marguerite Adelman, Assistant Director, Graduate Admissions, 518-564-4723, Fax: 518-564-4722, E-mail: adelmaml@plattsburgh.edu.

State University of New York College at Potsdam, School of Education and Professional Studies, Program in Information and Communication Technology, Potsdam, NY 13676. Offers educational technology specialist (MS Ed); human performance technology (MS Ed); information technology (MS Ed); organizational leadership (MS Ed); technology educator (MS Ed). Part-time and evening/weekend programs available. Postbaccalaureate distance learning degree programs offered. *Faculty:* 4 full-time (1 woman), 2 part-time/adjunct (1 woman). *Students:* 22 full-time (12 women), 28 part-time (17 women); includes 4 minority (3 African Americans, 1 Asian American or Pacific Islander), 7 international. 28 applicants, 100% accepted, 20 enrolled. In 2009, 21 master's awarded. *Degree requirements:* For master's, thesis optional, culminating experience. *Entrance requirements:* For master's, minimum GPA of 2.75 in last 60 hours of course work. Additional exam requirements/recommendations for international students:

Required—TOEFL (minimum score 550 paper-based; 213 computer-based; 80 iBT), IELTS (minimum score 6). *Application deadline:* For fall admission, 4/1 priority date for domestic and international students; for spring admission, 10/15 priority date for domestic and international students. Applications are processed on a rolling basis. Application fee: $50. *Expenses:* Tuition, state resident: full-time $8370; part-time $349 per credit hour. Tuition, nonresident: full-time $13,250; part-time $552 per credit hour. Required fees: $942; $38.70 per credit hour. *Financial support:* In 2009–10, 1 student received support; fellowships, teaching assistantships, career-related internships or fieldwork, Federal Work-Study, scholarships/grants, and unspecified assistantships available. Support available to part-time students. Financial award application deadline: 3/1; financial award applicants required to submit FAFSA. *Unit head:* Dr. Anthony Betrus, Chairperson, 315-267-2535, Fax: 315-267-4802, E-mail: betrusak@potsdam.edu. *Application contact:* Peter Cutler, Graduate Admissions Counselor, 315-267-3154, Fax: 315-267-4802, E-mail: cutlerpj@potsdam.edu.

Suffolk University, College of Arts and Sciences, Department of Education and Human Services, Programs in Human Resource, Learning and Performance, Boston, MA 02108-2770. Offers global human resources (Graduate Certificate); human resources (MS, Graduate Certificate); organizational development (CAGS, Graduate Certificate); organizational learning and development (MS, Graduate Certificate); MS/Certificate. Part-time and evening/weekend programs available. *Entrance requirements:* For master's, GRE General Test or MAT, 2 letters of recommendation, resume. *Application deadline:* For fall admission, 6/15 priority date for domestic students, 6/15 for international students; for spring admission, 11/15 priority date for domestic students, 11/15 for international students. Applications are processed on a rolling basis. Application fee: $50. *Expenses:* Tuition: Full-time $33,000; part-time $1100 per credit. Required fees: $20. Tuition and fees vary according to program. *Financial support:* Fellowships available. Financial award application deadline: 4/1. *Faculty research:* Adult training methods, adult learning theory, instructional design, learning and teaching styles, systems thinking. *Unit head:* Christine M. Westphal, Graduate Program Director, 617-994-6455, Fax: 617-305-1743, E-mail: cwestpha@suffolk.edu. *Application contact:* Judith Reynolds, Director of Graduate Admissions, 617-573-8302, Fax: 617-305-1733, E-mail: grad.admission@suffolk.edu.

Thomas Edison State College, School of Business and Management, Program in Organizational Leadership, Trenton, NJ 08608-1176. Offers Graduate Certificate. Part-time programs available. Postbaccalaureate distance learning degree programs offered (no on-campus study). *Students:* 29 part-time (12 women); includes 5 minority (all African Americans), 2 international. Average age 42. In 2009, 2 Graduate Certificates awarded. *Entrance requirements:* Additional exam requirements/recommendations for international students: Required—TOEFL (minimum score 550 paper-based; 213 computer-based; 79 iBT). *Application deadline:* For fall admission, 8/15 priority date for domestic and international students; for winter admission, 11/15 priority date for domestic and international students; for spring admission, 2/15 priority date for domestic and international students. Applications are processed on a rolling basis. Application fee: $75. Electronic applications accepted. *Expenses:* Tuition, area resident: Part-time $479 per credit. Tuition, state resident: part-time $479 per credit. Tuition, nonresident: part-time $479 per credit. *Financial support:* Applicants required to submit FAFSA. *Unit head:* Dr. Joseph Santora, Dean, School of Business and Management, 609-984-1130, Fax: 609-984-3898, E-mail: infor@tesc.edu. *Application contact:* David Hoftiezer, Director of Admissions, 888-442-8372, Fax: 609-984-8447, E-mail: admissions@tesc.edu.

Trevecca Nazarene University, Graduate Division, Graduate Business Programs, Major in Management, Nashville, TN 37210-2877. Offers MSM. Evening/weekend programs available. *Students:* 107 full-time (53 women); includes 25 minority (24 African Americans, 1 Asian American or Pacific Islander). In 2009, 17 master's awarded. *Entrance requirements:* For master's, GMAT, proficiency exam (quantitative skills), minimum GPA of 2.5, resume, 2 letters of recommendation, employer letter of recommendation, written business analysis. Additional exam requirements/recommendations for international students: Required—TOEFL (minimum score 550 paper-based; 213 computer-based). *Application deadline:* Applications are processed on a rolling basis. Application fee: $25. *Expenses:* Contact institution. *Financial support:* Applicants required to submit FAFSA. *Unit head:* Dr. Jon Burch, Director of Graduate Management Program, 615-248-1529, E-mail: management@trevecca.edu. *Application contact:* Marcus Lackey, Admissions Counselor, 615-248-1529, E-mail: management@trevecca.edu.

Trinity (Washington) University, School of Professional Studies, Washington, DC 20017-1094. Offers business administration (MBA); communication (MA); international security studies (MA); organizational management (MSA), including federal program management, human resource management, nonprofit management, organizational development, public and community health. Part-time and evening/weekend programs available. *Degree requirements:* For master's, thesis (for some programs), capstone project (MSA). *Entrance requirements:* For master's, minimum GPA of 2.5. Additional exam requirements/recommendations for international students: Required—TOEFL (minimum score 550 paper-based; 213 computer-based).

Trinity Western University, School of Graduate Studies, Program in Leadership, Langley, BC V2Y 1Y1, Canada. Offers business (MA, Certificate); Christian ministry (MA); education (MA, Certificate); healthcare (MA, Certificate); non-profit (MA, Certificate). Postbaccalaureate distance learning degree programs offered (minimal on-campus study). *Degree requirements:* For master's, major project. *Entrance requirements:* For master's, minimum GPA of 2.7. Additional exam requirements/recommendations for international students: Required—TOEFL (minimum score 620 paper-based; 260 computer-based; 105 iBT). Electronic applications accepted. *Expenses:* Contact institution. *Faculty research:* Servant leadership.

Troy University, Graduate School, College of Business, Program in Management, Troy, AL 36082. Offers healthcare management (MSM); human resources management (MSM); information systems (MSM); international hospitality management (MSM); international management (MSM); leadership and organizational effectiveness (MSM); public management (MS, MSM). *Accreditation:* ACBSP. Evening/weekend programs available. *Students:* 193 full-time (130 women), 575 part-time (374 women); includes 473 minority (417 African Americans, 12 American Indian/Alaska Native, 20 Asian Americans or Pacific Islanders, 24 Hispanic Americans). Average age 35. 275 applicants, 91% accepted. In 2009, 332 master's awarded. *Degree requirements:* For master's, thesis or alternative. *Entrance requirements:* For master's, GMAT (minimum score 500) or GRE General Test (minimum score 900), minimum GPA of 2.5; letter of recommendation. Additional exam requirements/recommendations for international students: Required—TOEFL (minimum score 523 paper-based; 193 computer-based; 70 iBT), IELTS, or ACT Compass ESL (minimum score 270 on Listening, Reading, and Grammar with no individual score below 85 and a minimum score of 8 out of 12 on writing test). *Application deadline:* Applications are processed on a rolling basis. Application fee: $50. Electronic applications accepted. *Expenses:* Contact institution. *Unit head:* Dr. Henry M. Findley, Interim Chair/Professor, 334-670-3271, Fax: 334-670-3599, E-mail: hfindley@troy.edu. *Application contact:* Brenda K. Campbell, Director of Graduate Admissions, 334-670-3178, Fax: 334-670-3733, E-mail: bcamp@troy.edu.

Tusculum College, Graduate School, Program in Organizational Management, Greeneville, TN 37743-9997. Offers MAOM. *Degree requirements:* For master's, thesis or alternative. *Entrance requirements:* For master's, GMAT, GRE Subject Test, MAT, 3 years of work experience, minimum GPA of 2.75.

Université Laval, Faculty of Administrative Sciences, Programs in Business Administration, Québec, QC G1K 7P4, Canada. Offers accounting (MBA); agri-food management (MBA); electronic business (MBA, Diploma); factory management and logistics (MBA); finance (MBA); firm management (MBA); geomatic management (MBA); information technology management (MBA); international management (MBA); management (MBA); management accounting (MBA, Diploma); marketing (MBA); modeling and organizational decision (MBA); occupational health and safety management (MBA); pharmacy management (MBA); social and environmental responsibility (MBA); technological entrepreneurship (Diploma). *Accreditation:* AACSB. Part-time and evening/weekend programs available. Postbaccalaureate distance learning degree programs offered (no on-campus study). *Entrance requirements:* For master's and Diploma, knowledge of French and English. Electronic applications accepted.

University of Alberta, Faculty of Graduate Studies and Research, Doctoral Program in Business, Edmonton, AB T6G 2E1, Canada. Offers accounting (PhD); finance (PhD); human resources/industrial relations (PhD); management science (PhD); marketing (PhD); organizational analysis (PhD); MBA/PhD. *Accreditation:* AACSB. Part-time programs available. *Faculty:* 41 full-time (7 women), 1 part-time/adjunct (0 women). *Students:* 46 full-time (27 women), 5 part-time (3 women). Average age 34. 307 applicants, 7% accepted, 11 enrolled. In 2009, 2 doctorates awarded. *Degree requirements:* For doctorate, comprehensive exam, thesis/dissertation. *Entrance requirements:* For doctorate, GMAT. Additional exam requirements/recommendations for international students: Required—TOEFL (minimum score 550 paper-based; 213 computer-based). *Application deadline:* For fall admission, 6/1 priority date for domestic students; for winter admission, 5/1 for domestic students. Application fee: $0. Electronic applications accepted. Tuition and fee charges are reported in Canadian dollars. *Expenses:* Tuition, area resident: Full-time $4626 Canadian dollars; part-time $99.72 Canadian dollars per unit. International tuition: $8216 Canadian dollars full-time. Required fees: $3590 Canadian dollars; $99.72 Canadian dollars per unit. $215 Canadian dollars per term. *Financial support:* In 2009–10, 29 students received support, including 11 fellowships with full tuition reimbursements available (averaging $17,000 per year); scholarships/grants and tuition waivers (partial) also available. *Faculty research:* Accounting, capital markets and corporate finance, organizational change and human resource management, marketing, strategic management. Total annual research expenditures: $7.7 million. *Unit head:* Dr. Mike Percy, Director, 780-492-2361, Fax: 780-492-3325, E-mail: busphd@ualberta.ca. *Application contact:* Jeanette Gosine, Program Coordinator, 780-492-2361, Fax: 780-492-3325, E-mail: busphd@ualberta.ca.

University of Cincinnati, Graduate School, McMicken College of Arts and Sciences, Center for Organizational Leadership, Cincinnati, OH 45221. Offers MALER. Part-time and evening/weekend programs available. *Entrance requirements:* For master's, GRE or GMAT. Additional exam requirements/recommendations for international students: Required—TOEFL (minimum score 520 paper-based; 190 computer-based; 68 iBT). Electronic applications accepted. *Faculty research:* Leadership and diversity.

University of Colorado at Boulder, Leeds School of Business, Division of Business Administration, Boulder, CO 80309. Offers accounting (MS, PhD); finance (PhD); information systems (PhD); marketing (PhD); operations (PhD); strategic, organizational, and entrepreneurial studies (PhD). Part-time and evening/weekend programs available. *Students:* 74 full-time (27 women), 15 part-time (8 women); includes 6 minority (1 African American, 3 Asian Americans or Pacific Islanders, 2 Hispanic Americans), 21 international. Average age 28. 271 applicants, 8% accepted, 19 enrolled. In 2009, 40 master's, 6 doctorates awarded. *Entrance requirements:* For master's, GMAT, minimum undergraduate GPA of 3.0. *Application deadline:* For fall admission, 3/31 for domestic and international students; for spring admission, 10/31 for domestic and international students. Application fee: $50 ($60 for international students). Electronic applications accepted. *Financial support:* In 2009–10, 16 fellowships (averaging $1,038 per year), 26 research assistantships (averaging $17,558 per year), 11 teaching assistantships (averaging $12,576 per year) were awarded; career-related internships or fieldwork, Federal Work-Study, scholarships/grants, and unspecified assistantships also available. Financial award applicants required to submit FAFSA.

University of Dallas, Graduate School of Management, Irving, TX 75062-4736. Offers accounting (MBA, MM, MS); business management (MBA, MM); corporate finance (MBA, MM); financial services (MBA); global business (MBA, MM); health services management (MBA, MM); human resource management (MBA, MM); information assurance (MBA, MM, MS); information technology (MBA, MM, MS); information technology service management (MBA, MM, MS); marketing management (MBA, MM); organization development (MBA, MM); project management (MBA, MM); sports and entertainment management (MBA, MM); strategic leadership (MBA, MM); supply chain management (MBA); supply chain management and market logistics (MM). *Accreditation:* ACBSP. Part-time and evening/weekend programs available. Postbaccalaureate distance learning degree programs offered (no on-campus study). *Faculty:* 25 full-time (6 women), 31 part-time/adjunct (6 women). *Students:* 232 full-time (95 women), 923 part-time (365 women); includes 462 minority (184 African Americans, 14 American Indian/Alaska Native, 153 Asian Americans or Pacific Islanders, 111 Hispanic Americans), 184 international. Average age 34. 474 applicants, 85% accepted, 237 enrolled. In 2009, 399 master's awarded. *Entrance requirements:* Additional exam requirements/recommendations for international students: Required—TOEFL. *Application deadline:* Applications are processed on a rolling basis. Application fee: $50. Electronic applications accepted. *Expenses:* Contact institution. *Financial support:* In 2009–10, 399 students received support. Scholarships/grants and unspecified assistantships available. Financial award application deadline: 2/15; financial award applicants required to submit FAFSA. *Unit head:* Alounda Joseph, Director of Enrollment Processes, 972-721-5356, E-mail: admiss@gsm.udallas.edu. *Application contact:* Alounda Joseph, Director of Enrollment Processes, 972-721-5356, E-mail: admiss@gsm.udallas.edu.

University of Denver, University College, Denver, CO 80208. Offers applied communication (MAS, MPS, Certificate); computer information systems (MAS, Certificate); environmental policy and management (MAS, Certificate); geographic information systems (MAS, Certificate); human resource administration (MPS, Certificate); knowledge and information technologies (MAS); liberal studies (MLS, Certificate); modern languages (MLS, Certificate); organizational leadership (MPS, Certificate); security management (Certificate); technology management (MAS, Certificate), including 21st century strategic management (MAS), international markets (MAS), project management (MAS), research and development management (MAS); telecommunications (MAS, Certificate), including broadband (MAS), telecommunications management and policy (MAS), telecommunications technology (MAS), wireless networks (MAS). Part-time and evening/weekend programs available. Postbaccalaureate distance learning degree programs offered (no on-campus study). *Faculty:* 160 part-time/adjunct (64 women). *Students:* 53 full-time (25 women), 984 part-time (551 women); includes 171 minority (72 African Americans, 10 American Indian/Alaska Native, 33 Asian Americans or Pacific Islanders, 56 Hispanic Americans), 75 international. Average age 36. 537 applicants, 96% accepted, 494 enrolled. In 2009, 229 master's, 109 Certificates awarded. *Entrance requirements:* Additional exam requirements/recommendations for international students: Required—TOEFL (minimum score 550 paper-based; 213 computer-based). *Application deadline:* Applications are processed on a rolling basis. Application fee: $75. Electronic applications accepted. *Expenses:* Contact institution. *Financial support:* Applicants required to submit FAFSA. *Unit head:* Dr. James Davis, Dean, 303-871-2291, Fax: 303-871-4047, E-mail: jdavis@du.edu. *Application contact:* Information Contact, 303-871-3155.

University of Guelph, Graduate Program Services, College of Management and Economics, MA (Leadership) Program, Guelph, ON N1G 2W1, Canada. Offers MA. Part-time and evening/weekend programs available. Postbaccalaureate distance learning degree programs offered (minimal on-campus study). *Entrance requirements:* For master's, minimum B-average, minimum 5 years of relevant work experience. Additional exam requirements/recommendations for international students: Required—TOEFL (minimum score 550 paper-based; 213 computer-based). Electronic applications accepted. *Faculty research:* Theories of leadership, organizational change, ethics in leadership, decision making, politics of organizations.

University of Hawaii at Manoa, Graduate Division, Shidler College of Business, Program in Business Administration, Honolulu, HI 96822. Offers Asian business studies (MBA); Chinese business studies (MBA); decision sciences (MBA); entrepreneurship (MBA); finance (MBA); finance and banking (MBA); human resources management (MBA); information management (MBA); information technology (MBA); international business (MBA); Japanese business studies (MBA); marketing (MBA); organizational behavior (MBA); organizational management (MBA); real estate (MBA); student-designed track (MBA). *Accreditation:* AACSB. Part-time and evening/weekend programs available. *Faculty:* 46 full-time (8 women), 9 part-time/adjunct (4 women). *Students:* 259 full-time (90 women), 105 part-time (43 women); includes 123 minority (118 Asian Americans or Pacific Islanders, 5 Hispanic Americans), 119 international. Average age

Organizational Management

University of Hawaii at Manoa (continued)
32. 336 applicants, 52% accepted, 150 enrolled. In 2009, 113 master's awarded. *Degree requirements:* For master's, thesis optional. *Entrance requirements:* For master's, GMAT, minimum GPA of 3.0. Additional exam requirements/recommendations for international students: Required—TOEFL (minimum score 600 paper-based; 250 computer-based; 100 iBT), IELTS (minimum score 7). *Application deadline:* For fall admission, 5/1 for domestic students, 3/1 for international students. Application fee: $60. *Expenses:* Contact institution. *Financial support:* In 2009–10, 24 students received support, including 98 fellowships (averaging $3,481 per year), 3 research assistantships (averaging $16,626 per year). Total annual research expenditures: $427,000. *Application contact:* Tung Bui, Graduate Chair, 808-956-5565, Fax: 808-956-9889, E-mail: tung.bui@hawaii.edu.

University of Hawaii at Manoa, Graduate Division, Shidler College of Business, Program in International Management, Honolulu, HI 96822. Offers Asian finance (PhD); global information technology management (PhD); international accounting (PhD); international marketing (PhD); international organization and strategy (PhD). Part-time programs available. *Students:* 28 full-time (12 women), 5 part-time (0 women); includes 7 minority (all Asian Americans or Pacific Islanders), 17 international. Average age 33. 65 applicants, 18% accepted, 5 enrolled. In 2009, 1 doctorate awarded. *Degree requirements:* For doctorate, comprehensive exam, thesis/dissertation. *Entrance requirements:* For doctorate, GMAT or GRE General Test, minimum GPA of 3.0. Additional exam requirements/recommendations for international students: Required—TOEFL (minimum score 600 paper-based; 250 computer-based; 100 iBT), IELTS (minimum score 7). *Application deadline:* For fall admission, 3/1 for domestic and international students. Application fee: $60. *Expenses:* Contact institution. *Financial support:* In 2009–10, 2 fellowships (averaging $6,945 per year), 21 research assistantships (averaging $17,766 per year) were awarded. *Application contact:* Erica Okada, Graduate Chair, 808-956-6723, Fax: 808-956-6889, E-mail: emokada@hawaii.edu.

The University of Kansas, University of Kansas Medical Center, School of Nursing, Kansas City, KS 66160. Offers clinical research management (PMC); family nurse practitioner (PMC); health care informatics (PMC); health professions educator (PMC); nurse midwife (PMC); nursing (MS, DNP, PhD); organizational leadership (PMC); psychiatric/mental health nurse practitioner (PMC); public health nursing (PMC). *Accreditation:* AACN; ACNM/DOA. Part-time programs available. Postbaccalaureate distance learning degree programs offered (minimal on-campus study). *Faculty:* 65. *Students:* 59 full-time (56 women), 309 part-time (285 women); includes 37 minority (17 African Americans, 4 American Indian/Alaska Native, 7 Asian Americans or Pacific Islanders, 9 Hispanic Americans), 10 international. Average age 38. 138 applicants, 59% accepted, 82 enrolled. In 2009, 78 master's, 3 doctorates awarded. Terminal master's awarded for partial completion of doctoral program. *Degree requirements:* For master's, thesis optional, general oral exam; for doctorate, one foreign language, thesis/dissertation, comprehensive oral and written exam. *Entrance requirements:* For master's, bachelor's degree in nursing, minimum GPA of 3.0, RN license, 1 year of clinical experience; for doctorate, GRE General Test, master's degree in nursing, minimum GPA of 3.5. Additional exam requirements/recommendations for international students: Required—TOEFL. *Application deadline:* For fall admission, 4/1 for domestic students; for spring admission, 9/1 for domestic students. Application fee: $60. Electronic applications accepted. *Expenses:* Tuition, state resident: full-time $6492; part-time $270.50 per credit hour. Tuition, nonresident: full-time $15,510; part-time $646.25 per credit hour. Required fees: $847; $70.56 per credit hour. Tuition and fees vary according to course load and program. *Financial support:* In 2009–10, 93 students received support, including 7 research assistantships (averaging $24,000 per year), 23 teaching assistantships with full and partial tuition reimbursements available (averaging $24,000 per year); traineeships also available. Financial award application deadline: 2/14; financial award applicants required to submit FAFSA. *Faculty research:* Breastfeeding practices of teen mothers, national database of nursing quality indicators, caregiving of families of patients using technology in the home, self care talk intervention partnership between caregivers of stroke survivors and nurses, smoking cessation. Total annual research expenditures: $5 million. *Unit head:* Dr. Karen L. Miller, Dean, 913-588-1601, Fax: 913-588-1660, E-mail: kmiller@kumc.edu. *Application contact:* Dr. Rita K. Clifford, Associate Dean, Student Affairs, 913-588-1619, Fax: 913-588-1615, E-mail: rcliffor@kumc.edu.

University of La Verne, College of Business and Public Management, Program in Organizational Management and Leadership, La Verne, CA 91750-4443. Offers nonprofit management (Certificate); organizational leadership (Certificate); organizational management and leadership (MS). Part-time programs available. *Faculty:* 22 full-time (11 women), 41 part-time/adjunct (8 women). *Students:* 96 full-time (47 women), 60 part-time (34 women); includes 72 minority (17 African Americans, 24 Asian Americans or Pacific Islanders, 31 Hispanic Americans). Average age 33. In 2009, 68 master's awarded. *Degree requirements:* For master's, thesis or research project. *Entrance requirements:* For master's, minimum undergraduate GPA of 2.75, 2 letters of recommendation, interview, resume. Additional exam requirements/recommendations for international students: Required—TOEFL (minimum score 550 paper-based; 213 computer-based). *Application deadline:* Applications are processed on a rolling basis. Application fee: $50. *Expenses:* Contact institution. *Financial support:* Institutionally sponsored loans available. Financial award application deadline: 3/2; financial award applicants required to submit FAFSA. *Unit head:* Dr. Kathy Duncan, Chairperson, 909-593-3511 Ext. 4415, E-mail: kduncan2@laverne.edu. *Application contact:* Program and Admissions Specialist, 909-593-3511 Ext. 4819, E-mail: cbpm@laverne.edu.

University of La Verne, Regional Campus Administration, Graduate Programs, Central Coast/Vandenberg Air Force Base Campuses, La Verne, CA 91750-4443. Offers business (MBA-EP), including health services management, information technology; health administration (MHA); leadership and management (MS). *Faculty:* 18 part-time/adjunct (6 women). *Students:* 19 full-time (12 women), 35 part-time (14 women); includes 20 minority (7 African Americans, 2 American Indian/Alaska Native, 2 Asian Americans or Pacific Islanders, 9 Hispanic Americans). Average age 36. In 2009, 20 master's awarded. *Entrance requirements:* For master's, 2 letters of recommendation, resume. *Application deadline:* Applications are processed on a rolling basis. Application fee: $50. *Expenses:* Contact institution. *Financial support:* Institutionally sponsored loans available. Financial award application deadline: 3/2; financial award applicants required to submit FAFSA. *Unit head:* Kitt Vincent, Director, Central Coast Campus, 805-542-9690 Ext. 6043, Fax: 805-542-9735, E-mail: kvincent@laverne.edu. *Application contact:* Kitt Vincent, Director, Central Coast Campus, 805-542-9690 Ext. 6043, Fax: 805-542-9735, E-mail: kvincent@laverne.edu.

University of La Verne, Regional Campus Administration, Graduate Programs, Inland Empire Campus, Rancho Cucamonga, CA 91730. Offers business (MBA-EP), including health services management, information technology, management, marketing; leadership and management (MS). *Faculty:* 2 full-time (both women), 12 part-time/adjunct (2 women). *Students:* 20 full-time (13 women), 61 part-time (41 women); includes 50 minority (10 African Americans, 11 Asian Americans or Pacific Islanders, 29 Hispanic Americans). Average age 37. In 2009, 24 master's awarded. *Entrance requirements:* For master's, 2 letters of recommendation, resume. *Application deadline:* Applications are processed on a rolling basis. Application fee: $50. *Expenses:* Contact institution. *Financial support:* Institutionally sponsored loans available. Financial award application deadline: 3/2; financial award applicants required to submit FAFSA. *Unit head:* Allan Stout, Director, 909-484-3858 Ext. 6002, Fax: 909-484-9469, E-mail: astout@laverne.edu. *Application contact:* Allan Stout, Director, 909-484-3858 Ext. 6002, Fax: 909-484-9469, E-mail: astout@laverne.edu.

University of La Verne, Regional Campus Administration, Graduate Programs, Kern County Campus, Bakersfield, CA 93301. Offers business (MBA-EP); health administration (MHA); leadership and management (MS). *Faculty:* 1 part-time/adjunct (0 women). *Students:* 10 part-time (5 women); includes 5 minority (2 Asian Americans or Pacific Islanders, 3 Hispanic Americans). Average age 32. In 2009, 2 master's awarded. *Entrance requirements:* For master's, 2 letters of recommendation, resume. *Application deadline:* Applications are processed on a rolling basis. Application fee: $50. *Expenses:* Contact institution. *Financial support:* Institutionally sponsored loans available. Financial award application deadline: 3/2; financial award applicants required to submit FAFSA. *Unit head:* Nora Dominguez, Interim Director, 661-328-1430 Ext. 6024, E-mail: ndominguez@laverne.edu. *Application contact:* Nora Dominguez, Interim Director, 661-328-1430 Ext. 6024, E-mail: ndominguez@laverne.edu.

University of Maryland Eastern Shore, Graduate Programs, Program in Organizational Leadership, Princess Anne, MD 21853-1299. Offers PhD. Evening/weekend programs available. *Degree requirements:* For doctorate, comprehensive exam, thesis/dissertation, internship. *Entrance requirements:* For doctorate, interview, writing sample, successful record of employment or career in organization/profession. Additional exam requirements/recommendations for international students: Required—TOEFL (minimum score 213 computer-based; 80 iBT). Electronic applications accepted.

University of Massachusetts Dartmouth, Graduate School, Charlton College of Business, Program in Business Administration, North Dartmouth, MA 02747-2300. Offers accounting (Postbaccalaureate Certificate); business administration (MBA); e-commerce (PMC); finance (PMC); general management (PMC); leadership (PMC); management (Postbaccalaureate Certificate); marketing (PMC); supply chain management (PMC). *Accreditation:* AACSB. Part-time programs available. *Faculty:* 42 full-time (13 women), 26 part-time/adjunct (6 women). *Students:* 93 full-time (41 women), 132 part-time (64 women); includes 22 minority (5 African Americans, 2 American Indian/Alaska Native, 6 Asian Americans or Pacific Islanders, 9 Hispanic Americans), 42 international. Average age 30. 186 applicants, 82% accepted, 94 enrolled. In 2009, 55 master's, 19 other advanced degrees awarded. *Entrance requirements:* For master's, GMAT, resume, letters of recommendation. Additional exam requirements/recommendations for international students: Required—TOEFL (minimum score 500 paper-based; 200 computer-based; 72 iBT). *Application deadline:* For fall admission, 6/1 for domestic students, 5/1 for international students; for spring admission, 10/1 for domestic students, 8/1 for international students. Application fee: $40 ($60 for international students). Electronic applications accepted. *Expenses:* Tuition, state resident: full-time $2071; part-time $86.29 per credit. Tuition, nonresident: full-time $8099; part-time $337.46 per credit. Required fees: $9446. Tuition and fees vary according to class time, course load and reciprocity agreements. *Financial support:* In 2009–10, 1 research assistantship with full tuition reimbursement (averaging $6,000 per year) was awarded; teaching assistantships, Federal Work-Study and unspecified assistantships also available. Support available to part-time students. Financial award application deadline: 3/1; financial award applicants required to submit FAFSA. *Faculty research:* Competitiveness of south coast enterprises, global sales, key performance indicators, agile manufacturing, green business. Total annual research expenditures: $19,000. *Unit head:* Dr. Norm Barber, Assistant Dean, 508-999-8543, E-mail: nbarber@umassd.edu. *Application contact:* Elan Turcotte-Shamski, Graduate Admissions Officer, 508-999-8604, Fax: 508-999-8183, E-mail: graduate@umassd.edu.

University of New Haven, Graduate School, College of Arts and Sciences, Program in Industrial and Organizational Psychology, West Haven, CT 06516-1916. Offers conflict management (MA); human resource management (MA); industrial organizational psychology (MA); organizational development (MA); psychology of conflict management (Certificate). Part-time and evening/weekend programs available. *Faculty:* 5 full-time (3 women), 10 part-time/adjunct (5 women). *Students:* 97 full-time (59 women), 34 part-time (26 women); includes 20 minority (9 African Americans, 2 American Indian/Alaska Native, 2 Asian Americans or Pacific Islanders, 7 Hispanic Americans), 11 international. Average age 28. 85 applicants, 98% accepted, 48 enrolled. In 2009, 71 master's awarded. *Degree requirements:* For master's, thesis or alternative. *Entrance requirements:* Additional exam requirements/recommendations for international students: Required—TOEFL (minimum score 520 paper-based; 190 computer-based; 70 iBT); Recommended—IELTS (minimum score 5.5). *Application deadline:* For fall admission, 5/31 for international students; for winter admission, 10/15 for international students; for spring admission, 1/15 for international students. Applications are processed on a rolling basis. Application fee: $50. Electronic applications accepted. *Expenses:* Contact institution. *Financial support:* Research assistantships with partial tuition reimbursements, teaching assistantships with partial tuition reimbursements, career-related internships or fieldwork, Federal Work-Study, scholarships/grants, tuition waivers, and unspecified assistantships available. Support available to part-time students. Financial award applicants required to submit FAFSA. *Unit head:* Dr. Stuart D. Sidle, Coordinator, 203-932-7341. *Application contact:* Eloise Gormley, Information Contact, 203-932-7449.

University of New Mexico, Robert O. Anderson Graduate School of Management, Department of Organizational Studies, Albuquerque, NM 87131. Offers human resources management (MBA); policy and planning (MBA). Part-time and evening/weekend programs available. *Faculty:* 14 full-time (10 women), 6 part-time/adjunct (2 women). *Students:* 25 full-time (23 women), 22 part-time (15 women); includes 25 minority (3 African Americans, 3 American Indian/Alaska Native, 2 Asian Americans or Pacific Islanders, 17 Hispanic Americans), 1 international. Average age 29. 28 applicants, 100% accepted, 28 enrolled. In 2009, 20 master's awarded. *Entrance requirements:* For master's, GMAT or GRE (can be waived in some instances). Additional exam requirements/recommendations for international students: Required—TOEFL (minimum score 550 paper-based; 213 computer-based; 79 iBT). *Application deadline:* For fall admission, 4/1 priority date for domestic students, 5/1 for international students; for spring admission, 10/1 priority date for domestic students, 10/1 for international students. Applications are processed on a rolling basis. Application fee: $50. Electronic applications accepted. *Expenses:* Tuition, state resident: full-time $2099; part-time $233.20 per credit hour. Tuition, nonresident: full-time $6650. Required fees: $25 per semester. Tuition and fees vary according to course load, program and reciprocity agreements. *Financial support:* Fellowships, research assistantships, teaching assistantships, career-related internships or fieldwork, Federal Work-Study, scholarships/grants, and unspecified assistantships available. Support available to part-time students. Financial award application deadline: 6/1. *Faculty research:* Business ethics and social corporate responsibility, diversity, human resources, organizational strategy, organizational behavior. *Unit head:* Dr. Jacqueline Hood, Chair, 505-277-6471, Fax: 505-277-7108. *Application contact:* Megan Conner, Academic Advisement Manager, 505-277-3290, Fax: 505-277-8436, E-mail: mconner@mgt.unm.edu.

University of Oklahoma—Tulsa, Program in Organizational Dynamics, Tulsa, OK 74135-2512. Offers MA.

University of Pennsylvania, School of Arts and Sciences, Graduate Group in Organizational Dynamics, Philadelphia, PA 19104. Offers MS. Part-time and evening/weekend programs available. *Students:* 19 full-time (10 women), 151 part-time (88 women); includes 10 minority (7 African Americans, 3 Asian Americans or Pacific Islanders), 11 international. 49 applicants, 80% accepted, 31 enrolled. In 2009, 56 master's awarded. *Degree requirements:* For master's, thesis. *Application deadline:* For fall admission, 12/1 priority date for domestic students. Application fee: $70. Electronic applications accepted. *Expenses:* Tuition: Full-time $25,660; part-time $4758 per course. Required fees: $2152; $270 per course. Tuition and fees vary according to course load, degree level and program. *Financial support:* Scholarships/grants available. Support available to part-time students. Financial award application deadline: 12/15. *Unit head:* Director. *Application contact:* Director.

University of Phoenix, School of Advanced Studies, Phoenix, AZ 85034-7209. Offers business administration (DBA); education (Ed D); educational leadership (Ed D), including curriculum and instruction, educational leadership, educational technology; health administration (DHA); higher education administration (PhD); industrial/organizational psychology (PhD); nursing (PhD); organizational leadership (DM), including information systems and technology, organizational leadership. Evening/weekend programs available. *Faculty:* 83 full-time (47 women), 540 part-time/adjunct (264 women). *Students:* 7,749 full-time (5,032 women); includes 3,180 minority (2,473 African Americans, 61 American Indian/Alaska Native, 221 Asian Americans or Pacific Islanders, 425 Hispanic Americans), 490 international. Average age 44. In 2009, 467 doctorates awarded. *Degree requirements:* For doctorate, thesis/dissertation. *Entrance requirements:* For doctorate, 3 letters of recommendation, minimum master's GPA of 3.0, 3 years professional work experience. Additional exam requirements/recommendations for inter-

national students: Required—TOEFL (minimum score 550 paper-based; 213 computer-based; 79 iBT). *Application deadline:* Applications are processed on a rolling basis. Application fee: $45. Electronic applications accepted. *Expenses:* Tuition: Full-time $13,272. Required fees: $660. Full-time tuition and fees vary according to course level, degree level and program. *Financial support:* Institutionally sponsored loans and scholarships/grants available. Financial award applicants required to submit FAFSA. *Unit head:* Dr. Jeremy Moreland, Dean/Executive Director, 480-557-3231, E-mail: jeremy.moreland@phoenix.edu. *Application contact:* Information Contact, 800-697-8223.

University of St. Thomas, Graduate Studies, School of Education, Program in Organization Learning and Development, St. Paul, MN 55105-1096. Offers career development (Certificate); e-learning (Certificate); human resource management (Certificate); human resources and change leadership (MA); learning technology (Certificate); learning technology for learning development and change (MA); organization development (Ed D, Certificate). Part-time and evening/weekend programs available. Postbaccalaureate distance learning degree programs offered (minimal on-campus study). *Faculty:* 5 full-time (4 women), 6 part-time/adjunct (2 women). *Students:* 6 full-time (5 women), 161 part-time (130 women); includes 24 minority (13 African Americans, 7 Asian Americans or Pacific Islanders, 4 Hispanic Americans), 1 international. Average age 37. 115 applicants, 75% accepted, 85 enrolled. In 2009, 29 master's, 7 doctorates, 18 other advanced degrees awarded. *Degree requirements:* For doctorate, comprehensive exam, thesis/dissertation. *Entrance requirements:* For master's, minimum GPA of 3.0, 2 letters of reference, personal statement; for doctorate, minimum GPA of 3.5, interview; for Certificate, minimum graduate GPA of 3.25. Additional exam requirements/recommendations for international students: Required—TOEFL (minimum score 550 paper-based; 213 computer-based). *Application deadline:* For fall admission, 8/1 priority date for domestic and international students; for winter admission, 12/1 priority date for domestic students, 12/1 for international students; for spring admission, 12/1 priority date for domestic and international students. Applications are processed on a rolling basis. Application fee: $50. *Expenses:* Contact institution. *Financial support:* Fellowships, research assistantships, institutionally sponsored loans and scholarships/grants available. Support available to part-time students. Financial award applicants required to submit FAFSA. *Faculty research:* Workplace conflict, physician leaders, entrepreneurship education, mentoring. *Unit head:* Dr. Christopher S. Vye, Acting Department Chair, 651-962-4666, Fax: 651-962-4169, E-mail: csvye@stthomas.edu. *Application contact:* Liz G. Knight, Department Coordinator, 651-962-4459, Fax: 651-962-4169, E-mail: egknight@stthomas.edu.

University of San Francisco, School of Business and Professional Studies, Program in Organization Development, San Francisco, CA 94117-1080. Offers MS. Part-time and evening/weekend programs available. *Faculty:* 4 full-time (1 woman), 10 part-time/adjunct (3 women). *Students:* 162 full-time (118 women), 1 (woman) part-time; includes 66 minority (15 African Americans, 3 American Indian/Alaska Native, 27 Asian Americans or Pacific Islanders, 21 Hispanic Americans), 5 international. Average age 38. 61 applicants, 95% accepted, 45 enrolled. In 2009, 58 master's awarded. *Degree requirements:* For master's, thesis. *Entrance requirements:* For master's, minimum GPA of 3.0. Application fee: $55 ($65 for international students). *Expenses:* Tuition: Full-time $19,710; part-time $1095 per unit. Part-time tuition and fees vary according to degree level, campus/location and program. *Financial support:* In 2009–10, 78 students received support. Application deadline: 3/2. *Unit head:* Dr. Sharon Wagner, Head, 415-422-6886. *Application contact:* 415-422-6000, E-mail: graduate@usfca.edu.

The University of Scranton, College of Graduate and Continuing Education, Department of Health Administration and Human Resources, Program in Human Resources Administration, Scranton, PA 18510. Offers human resources (MS); human resources development (MS); organizational leadership (MS). Part-time and evening/weekend programs available. *Students:* 10 full-time (6 women), 8 part-time (5 women); includes 2 minority (1 African American, 1 Hispanic American), 8 international. Average age 34. 1 applicant, 0% accepted. In 2009, 21 master's awarded. *Degree requirements:* For master's, capstone experience. *Entrance requirements:* For master's, minimum GPA of 2.75. Additional exam requirements/recommendations for international students: Required—TOEFL (minimum score 500 paper-based; 173 computer-based), IELTS (minimum score 5.5). *Application deadline:* Applications are processed on a rolling basis. Application fee: $0. *Financial support:* Fellowships, teaching assistantships, career-related internships or fieldwork, Federal Work-Study, and unspecified assistantships available. Support available to part-time students. Financial award application deadline: 3/1. *Unit head:* Dr. Daniel West, Director, 570-941-6218, E-mail: westd1@scranton.edu. *Application contact:* Joseph M. Roback, Director of Admissions, 570-941-4385, Fax: 570-941-5928, E-mail: roback_j2@scranton.edu.

University of Southern California, Graduate School, School of Policy, Planning, and Development, Executive Master of Leadership Program, Los Angeles, CA 90089. Offers EML. Part-time programs available. *Faculty:* 51 full-time (12 women), 74 part-time/adjunct (26 women). *Students:* 17 full-time (5 women), 46 part-time (16 women); includes 41 minority (12 African Americans, 1 American Indian/Alaska Native, 8 Asian Americans or Pacific Islanders, 20 Hispanic Americans). 52 applicants, 73% accepted, 36 enrolled. In 2009, 23 master's awarded. *Entrance requirements:* Additional exam requirements/recommendations for international students: Required—TOEFL (minimum score 600 paper-based; 250 computer-based; 100 iBT). *Application deadline:* For fall admission, 2/1 for domestic and international students. Application fee: $85. Electronic applications accepted. *Expenses:* Contact institution. *Financial support:* In 2009–10, 2 students received support. Scholarships/grants and tuition waivers (partial) available. Financial award application deadline: 2/1. *Faculty research:* Strategic planning, organizational transformation, srategic management, leadership. Total annual research expenditures: $5 million. *Unit head:* Dr. Richard Callahan, Director, 916-442-6911 Ext. 25, Fax: 916-444-7712, E-mail: rcallaha@usc.edu. *Application contact:* Marisol R. Gonzalez, Director of Recruitment and Admission, 213-740-0550, Fax: 213-740-7573, E-mail: marisolr@usc.edu.

The University of Texas at Dallas, School of Management, Program in Management and Administrative Sciences, Richardson, TX 75080. Offers e-commerce (MS); health care management (MS); innovation and entrepreneurship (MS); organizations and strategy (MS). *Accreditation:* AACSB. Part-time and evening/weekend programs available. *Faculty:* 12 full-time (3 women), 13 part-time/adjunct (3 women). *Students:* 46 full-time (29 women), 103 part-time (47 women); includes 53 minority (12 African Americans, 34 Asian Americans or Pacific Islanders, 7 Hispanic Americans), 32 international. Average age 33. 156 applicants, 66% accepted, 47 enrolled. In 2009, 83 master's awarded. *Degree requirements:* For master's, thesis optional. *Entrance requirements:* For master's, GMAT. Additional exam requirements/recommendations for international students: Required—TOEFL (minimum score 550 paper-based; 213 computer-based). *Application deadline:* For fall admission, 7/15 for domestic students, 5/1 priority date for international students; for spring admission, 11/15 for domestic students, 9/1 priority date for international students. Applications are processed on a rolling basis. Application fee: $50 ($100 for international students). Electronic applications accepted. *Expenses:* Tuition, state resident: full-time $11,068; part-time $461 per credit hour. Tuition, nonresident: full-time $21,178; part-time $882 per credit hour. Tuition and fees vary according to course load. *Financial support:* In 2009–10, 25 teaching assistantships with full tuition reimbursements (averaging $14,400 per year) were awarded; fellowships, research assistantships, career-related internships or fieldwork, Federal Work-Study, institutionally sponsored loans, scholarships/grants, and unspecified assistantships also available. Support available to part-time students. Financial award application deadline: 4/30; financial award applicants required to submit FAFSA. *Faculty research:* Integrated and detailed knowledge of functional areas of management, analytical tools for effective appraisal and decision making. *Unit head:* Dr. Doug Eckel, Assistant Dean, 972-883-5923, E-mail: dogb.eckel@utdallas.edu. *Application contact:* James Parker, Assistant Director, 972-883-5842, E-mail: jparker@utdallas.edu.

The University of Texas at San Antonio, College of Business, Department of Management, San Antonio, TX 78249-0617. Offers business administration-organizational management (PhD); international business (MBA); management science (MBA). *Accreditation:* AACSB. Part-time and evening/weekend programs available. *Faculty:* 12 full-time (4 women), 4 part-time/adjunct (2 women). *Students:* 3 full-time (1 woman), 6 part-time (2 women); includes 3 minority (1 African American, 1 Asian American or Pacific Islander, 1 Hispanic American). Average age 34. 29 applicants, 59% accepted. In 2009, 1 master's awarded. *Degree requirements:* For master's, comprehensive exam (for some programs), thesis (for some programs). *Entrance requirements:* For master's, GMAT, minimum GPA of 3.0. Additional exam requirements/recommendations for international students: Required—TOEFL (minimum score 500 paper-based; 173 computer-based; 61 iBT), IELTS (minimum score 5). *Application deadline:* For fall admission, 7/1 for domestic students, 4/1 for international students; for spring admission, 11/1 for domestic students, 9/1 for international students. Applications are processed on a rolling basis. Application fee: $45 ($80 for international students). Electronic applications accepted. *Expenses:* Tuition, state resident: full-time $3975; part-time $221 per contact hour. Tuition, nonresident: full-time $13,947; part-time $775 per contact hour. Required fees: $1853. *Financial support:* In 2009–10, 2 research assistantships (averaging $15,600 per year), 8 teaching assistantships (averaging $7,800 per year) were awarded; career-related internships or fieldwork, Federal Work-Study, scholarships/grants, and unspecified assistantships also available. Support available to part-time students. *Faculty research:* Business ethics, entrepreneurship, human resource management, knowledge management, international management. *Unit head:* Dr. Robert L. Cardy, Chair, 210-458-7480, Fax: 210-458-6335, E-mail: robert.cardy@utsa.edu. *Application contact:* Cynthia Lengnick-Hall, Graduate Advisor, 210-458-5387, E-mail: cynthia.lengnickhall@utsa.edu.

University of the Incarnate Word, School of Graduate Studies and Research, Dreeben School of Education, Programs in Education, San Antonio, TX 78209-6397. Offers adult education (M Ed, MA); cross-cultural education (M Ed, MA); early childhood literacy (M Ed, MA); general education (M Ed, MA); Higher Education (PhD); instructional technology (M Ed, MA); international education and entrepreneurship (PhD); kinesiology (M Ed, MA); literacy (M Ed, MA); organizational leadership (PhD); organizational learning and learning (M Ed, MA); reading (M Ed, MA); special education (M Ed, MA); teacher leadership (M Ed, MA). Part-time and evening/weekend programs available. *Students:* 20 full-time (11 women), 201 part-time (122 women); includes 113 minority (29 African Americans, 2 American Indian/Alaska Native, 2 Asian Americans or Pacific Islanders, 80 Hispanic Americans), 30 international. Average age 41. In 2009, 26 master's, 19 doctorates awarded. *Degree requirements:* For master's, capstone; for doctorate, thesis/dissertation, qualifying exam. *Entrance requirements:* For master's, baccalaureate degree; minimum foundation GPA of 2.5; interview; for doctorate, master's degree; interview; supervised writing sample. Additional exam requirements/recommendations for international students: Required—TOEFL (minimum score 560 paper-based; 220 computer-based; 83 iBT). *Application deadline:* Applications are processed on a rolling basis. Application fee: $20. Electronic applications accepted. *Expenses:* Tuition: Full-time $12,150; part-time $675 per credit hour. Required fees: $83 per credit hour. *Financial support:* Federal Work-Study and scholarships/grants available. Financial award applicants required to submit FAFSA. *Unit head:* Dr. Denise Staudt, Dean, Dreeben School of Education, 210-829-2762, E-mail: staudt@uiwtx.edu. *Application contact:* Andrea Cyterski-Acosta, Dean of Enrollment, 210-829-6005, Fax: 210-829-3921, E-mail: admis@uiwtx.edu.

University of the Incarnate Word, School of Graduate Studies and Research, H-E-B School of Business and Administration, Programs in Administration, San Antonio, TX 78209-6397. Offers adult education (MAA); applied administration (MAA); communication arts (MAA); healthcare administration (MAA); instructional technology (MAA); international business (Certificate); nutrition (MAA); organizational development (MAA, Certificate); project management (Certificate); sports management (MAA). Part-time and evening/weekend programs available. Postbaccalaureate distance learning degree programs offered (no on-campus study). *Students:* 30 full-time (17 women), 163 part-time (114 women); includes 128 minority (18 African Americans, 3 Asian Americans or Pacific Islanders, 107 Hispanic Americans), 8 international. Average age 35. In 2009, 68 master's awarded. *Degree requirements:* For master's, capstone. *Entrance requirements:* For master's, GRE, GMAT, undergraduate degree, minimum GPA of 2.5. Additional exam requirements/recommendations for international students: Required—TOEFL (minimum score 560 paper-based; 220 computer-based; 83 iBT). *Application deadline:* Applications are processed on a rolling basis. Application fee: $20. Electronic applications accepted. *Expenses:* Tuition: Full-time $12,150; part-time $675 per credit hour. Required fees: $83 per credit hour. *Financial support:* Federal Work-Study and scholarships/grants available. Financial award applicants required to submit FAFSA. *Unit head:* Dr. Daniel Dominguez, MAA Director, 210-829-3180, Fax: 210-805-3564, E-mail: domingue@uiwtx.edu. *Application contact:* Andrea Cyterski-Acosta, Dean of Enrollment, 210-829-6005, Fax: 210-829-3921, E-mail: admis@uiwtx.edu.

Upper Iowa University, Online Master's Programs, Fayette, IA 52142-1857. Offers accounting (MBA); corporate financial management (MBA); global business (MBA); health and human services (MPA); higher education administration (MHEA); homeland security (MPA); human resources management (MBA); justice administration (MPA); organizational development (MBA); public personnel management (MPA); quality management (MBA). MBA also available at Madison, WI campus. Part-time programs available. Postbaccalaureate distance learning degree programs offered (no on-campus study). *Faculty:* 3 full-time (0 women), 66 part-time/adjunct (27 women). *Students:* 723 full-time (442 women). *Degree requirements:* For master's, research project. *Entrance requirements:* For master's, GMAT, GRE, or minimum GPA of 2.7 during last 60 hours. Additional exam requirements/recommendations for international students: Required—TOEFL (minimum score 570 paper-based; 230 computer-based). *Application deadline:* Applications are processed on a rolling basis. Application fee: $50. Electronic applications accepted. *Expenses:* Tuition: Full-time $6948; part-time $386 per credit hour. *Financial support:* Available to part-time students. Applicants required to submit FAFSA. *Faculty research:* Total quality management, CQI, teams, organization culture and climate, management. *Application contact:* David Hannum, Admissions Advisor, 800-603-3756, E-mail: hannumd@uiu.edu.

Vanderbilt University, Peabody College, Department of Leadership, Policy, and Organizations, Nashville, TN 37240-1001. Offers education policy (MPP); educational leadership and policy (Ed D); higher education (M Ed); higher education, leadership and policy (Ed D); human resource development (M Ed); international education policy and management (M Ed); organizational leadership (M Ed). Part-time and evening/weekend programs available. *Faculty:* 28 full-time (13 women), 8 part-time/adjunct (3 women). *Students:* 155 full-time (111 women), 95 part-time (52 women); includes 36 minority (27 African Americans, 6 Asian Americans or Pacific Islanders, 3 Hispanic Americans), 21 international. Average age 31. 298 applicants, 76% accepted, 94 enrolled. In 2009, 65 master's, 21 doctorates awarded. *Degree requirements:* For master's, comprehensive exam, thesis optional; for doctorate, thesis/dissertation, qualifying exams, residency. *Entrance requirements:* For master's and doctorate, GRE General Test. Additional exam requirements/recommendations for international students: Required—TOEFL (minimum score 550 paper-based; 213 computer-based). *Application deadline:* For fall admission, 12/31 priority date for domestic and international students; for spring admission, 11/1 priority date for domestic and international students. Applications are processed on a rolling basis. Application fee: $0. Electronic applications accepted. *Financial support:* In 2009–10, 155 students received support, including 3 fellowships with full and partial tuition reimbursements available, 61 research assistantships with full and partial tuition reimbursements available, 1 teaching assistantship with full and partial tuition reimbursement available; Federal Work-Study, institutionally sponsored loans, scholarships/grants, tuition waivers (partial), and unspecified assistantships also available. Support available to part-time students. Financial award application deadline: 2/1; financial award applicants required to submit FAFSA. *Faculty research:* Education and leadership policy, education finances/economics of education, higher education leadership and policy, educator pay for performance and school choice, international and comparative education and policy management. *Unit head:* Dr. Ellen B. Goldring, Chair, 615-322-8000, Fax: 615-343-7094, E-mail: ellen.b.goldring@vanderbilt.edu. *Application contact:* Rosie Moody, Educational Coordinator, 615-322-8019, Fax: 615-343-7094, E-mail: rosie.moody@vanderbilt.edu.

Walden University, Graduate Programs, School of Management, Minneapolis, MN 55401. Offers applied management and decision sciences (PhD), including accounting, engineering management, finance, general applied management and decision sciences, information systems

Organizational Management

Walden University (continued)

management, knowledge management, leadership and organizational change, learning management, operations research, self-designed program in applied management and design sciences; business information management (MISM); enterprise information security (MISM); entrepreneurship (MBA, DBA); finance (MBA, DBA); global supply chain management (DBA); healthcare management (MBA); healthcare system improvement (MBA); human resource management (MBA); information systems management (DBA); international business (MBA, DBA); IT strategy and governance (MISM); leadership (MBA, MS, DBA), including entrepreneurship (MS), general management (MS), human resources leadership (MS), innovation and technology (MS), leader development (MS); project management (MS), self-designed (MS); sustainable futures (MS); managing global software and service supply chains (MISM); marketing (MBA, DBA); project management (MBA, MS); risk management (MBA); self-designed (MBA, DBA); social impact management (DBA); sustainable futures (MBA); technology (MBA); technology entrepreneurship (DBA). Part-time and evening/weekend programs available. Postbaccalaureate distance learning degree programs offered (minimal on-campus study). *Faculty:* 17 full-time, 211 part-time/adjunct. *Students:* 3,389 full-time (1,774 women), 815 part-time (482 women); includes 1,969 minority (1,640 African Americans, 36 American Indian/Alaska Native, 123 Asian Americans or Pacific Islanders, 170 Hispanic Americans), 95 international. Average age 41. In 2009, 699 master's, 42 doctorates awarded. *Degree requirements:* For doctorate, thesis/dissertation (for some programs), residency. *Entrance requirements:* For master's, bachelor's degree or equivalent in related field; minimum GPA of 2.5; official transcripts; goal statement; access to computer and Internet; for doctorate, master's degree or equivalent in related field; minimum GPA of 3.0; 3 years of related professional/academic experience (preferred). Additional exam requirements/recommendations for international students: Required—TOEFL (minimum score 550 paper-based; 213 computer-based), IELTS (minimum score 6.5), TOEFL, IELTS, or Michigan English Language Assessment Battery (minimum score 82). *Application deadline:* Applications are processed on a rolling basis. Application fee: $50. Electronic applications accepted. *Expenses:* Tuition: Full-time $13,665; part-time $560 per credit. Required fees: $1375. Tuition and fees vary according to course load, degree level and program. *Financial support:* In 2009–10, 466 students received support; fellowships, Federal Work-Study, scholarships/grants, unspecified assistantships, and family tuition reduction, active duty/veteran tuition reduction, group tuition reduction, interest-free payment plans available. Support available to part-time students. Financial award applicants required to submit FAFSA. *Unit head:* William Schulz, Interim Associate Dean, 800-925-3368. *Application contact:* Jennifer Hall, Director of Enrollment, 866-4-WALDEN, E-mail: info@waldenu.edu.

Walden University, Graduate Programs, School of Public Policy and Administration, Minneapolis, MN 55401. Offers government management (Postbaccalaureate Certificate); health policy (MPA); homeland security policy (MPA); interdisciplinary policy studies (MPA); law and public policy (MPA); local government management for sustainable communities (MPA); nonprofit management (Postbaccalaureate Certificate); nonprofit management and leadership (MPA, MS); policy analysis (MPA); public management and leadership (MPA); public policy and administration (MPA, PhD), including criminal justice (PhD), health services (PhD), homeland security policy and coordination (PhD), international nongovernmental organizations (PhD), law and public policy (PhD), local government management for sustainable communities (PhD), nonprofit management and leadership (PhD), public management and leadership (PhD), public policy (PhD), public safety management (PhD), terrorism, mediation, and peace (PhD); terrorism, mediation, and peace (MPA). Part-time and evening/weekend programs available. Postbaccalaureate distance learning degree programs offered (minimal on-campus study). *Faculty:* 7 full-time, 62 part-time/adjunct. *Students:* 1,468 full-time (941 women), 233 part-time (162 women); includes 852 minority (761 African Americans, 9 American Indian/Alaska Native, 19 Asian Americans or Pacific Islanders, 63 Hispanic Americans), 53 international. Average age 40. In 2009, 173 master's, 13 doctorates awarded. *Degree requirements:* For doctorate, thesis/dissertation, residency. *Entrance requirements:* For master's, bachelor's degree or equivalent in related field, minimum GPA of 2.5; for doctorate, master's degree or equivalent in related field; minimum GPA of 3.0; official transcripts; three years of related professional/academic experience (preferred); access to computer and Internet. Additional exam requirements/recommendations for international students: Required—TOEFL (minimum score 550 paper-based; 213 computer-based), IELTS (minimum score 6.5), or Michigan English Language Assessment Battery (minimum score 82). *Application deadline:* Applications are processed on a rolling basis. Application fee: $50. Electronic applications accepted. *Expenses:* Tuition: Full-time $13,665; part-time $560 per credit. Required fees: $1375. Tuition and fees vary according to course load, degree level and program. *Financial support:* In 2009–10, 207 students received support; fellowships with tuition reimbursements available, Federal Work-Study, scholarships/grants, unspecified assistantships, and family tuition reduction, active duty/veteran tuition reduction, group tuition reduction, interest-free payment plans available. Support available to part-time students. Financial award applicants required to submit FAFSA. *Unit head:* Dr. Mark Gordon, Associate Dean, 800-925-3368. *Application contact:* Jennifer Hall, Director of Enrollment, 866-4-WALDEN, E-mail: info@waldenu.edu.

Warner Pacific College, Graduate Programs, Portland, OR 97215-4099. Offers biblical and theological studies (MA); biblical studies (M Rel); education (M Ed); management/organizational leadership (MS); pastoral ministries (M Rel); religion and ethics (M Rel); teaching (MA); theology (M Rel). Part-time programs available. *Degree requirements:* For master's, thesis or alternative, presentation of defense. *Entrance requirements:* For master's, interview, minimum GPA of 2.5; letters of recommendations. *Faculty research:* New Testament studies, nineteenth-century Wesleyan theology, preaching and church growth, Christian ethics.

Wayland Baptist University, Graduate Programs, Programs in Business Administration/Management, Plainview, TX 79072-6998. Offers general business (MBA); health care administration (MBA); human resource management (MBA); international management (MBA); management (MA, MBA), including health care administration (MA), human resource management (MA), organization management (MA); management information systems (MBA). Part-time and evening/weekend programs available. Postbaccalaureate distance learning degree programs offered (no on-campus study). *Faculty:* 10 full-time (3 women). *Students:* 6 full-time (1 woman), 55 part-time (31 women); includes 24 minority (9 African Americans, 1 American Indian/Alaska Native, 14 Hispanic Americans). Average age 34. 25 applicants, 76% accepted, 10 enrolled. In 2009, 8 master's awarded. *Degree requirements:* For master's, capstone course. *Entrance requirements:* For master's, GMAT, GRE or MAT. Additional exam requirements/recommendations for international students: Required—TOEFL (minimum score 500 paper-based; 173 computer-based; 61 iBT). *Application deadline:* Applications are processed on a rolling basis. Application fee: $50. Electronic applications accepted. *Expenses:* Tuition: Full-time $5796; part-time $322 per credit hour. Required fees: $782; $9 per credit hour. $60 per semester. Tuition and fees vary according to course load and campus/location. *Financial support:* Federal Work-Study, institutionally sponsored loans, and scholarships/grants available. Support available to part-time students. Financial award application deadline: 5/1; financial award applicants required to submit FAFSA. *Unit head:* Dr. Otto Schacht, Chairman, 806-291-1020, Fax: 806-291-1957. *Application contact:* Amanda Stanton, Graduate Studies, 806-291-3423, Fax: 806-291-1950, E-mail: stanton@wbu.edu.

Waynesburg University, Graduate and Professional Studies, Waynesburg, PA 15370-1222. Offers business (MBA), including finance, health systems, human resources, leadership, market development; counseling (MA), including addictions counseling, clinical mental health; education (MAT); nursing (MSN), including administration, education, informatics, palliative care; nursing practice (DNP); special education (M Ed); technology (M Ed); MSN/MBA. *Accreditation:* AACN. Part-time and evening/weekend programs available. *Faculty:* 11 full-time (5 women), 136 part-time/adjunct (80 women). *Students:* 116 full-time (85 women), 984 part-time (682 women). 711 applicants, 80% accepted, 485 enrolled. In 2009, 320 master's, 41 doctorates awarded. *Degree requirements:* For doctorate, thesis/dissertation. *Entrance requirements:* Additional exam requirements/recommendations for international students:

Required—TOEFL. *Application deadline:* For fall admission, 8/1 priority date for domestic students. Applications are processed on a rolling basis. Electronic applications accepted. *Expenses:* Tuition: Part-time $520 per credit. *Financial support:* Available to part-time students. Application deadline: 5/1. *Unit head:* David Mariner, Dean, 724-743-4420, Fax: 724-743-4425, E-mail: dmariner@waynesburg.edu. *Application contact:* Michael Bednarski, Director of Admissions, 724-743-4420, Fax: 724-743-4425, E-mail: mbednars@waynesburg.edu.

Wayne State College, Department of Health, Human Performance and Sport, Wayne, NE 68787. Offers exercise science (MSE); organizational management (MS), including sport management. Part-time and evening/weekend programs available. *Degree requirements:* For master's, comprehensive exam, thesis optional. *Entrance requirements:* For master's, GRE General Test, minimum GPA of 3.0. Additional exam requirements/recommendations for international students: Required—TOEFL (minimum score 550 paper-based; 213 computer-based). Electronic applications accepted.

Webster University, College of Arts and Sciences, Department of History, Politics and International Relations, Program in International Nongovernmental Organizations, St. Louis, MO 63119-3194. Offers MA. *Expenses:* Tuition: Part-time $565 per credit hour. Tuition and fees vary according to degree level, campus/location and program.

Western International University, Graduate Programs in Business, Program in Organization Development, Phoenix, AZ 85021-2718. Offers MBA. *Faculty:* 204. *Students:* 3 full-time (2 women). *Entrance requirements:* For master's, minimum GPA of 2.75. *Application deadline:* Applications are processed on a rolling basis. Application fee: $85 ($100 for international students). *Expenses:* Tuition: Full-time $12,600. One-time fee: $25 full-time. *Unit head:* Dr. Deborah DeSimone, Chief Academic Officer, 602-943-2311 Ext. 1135, Fax: 602-749-0752, E-mail: deborah.desimone@apollogrp.edu. *Application contact:* Karen Janitell, Director of Enrollment, 602-943-2311 Ext. 1063, Fax: 602-371-8637, E-mail: karen_janitell@apollogrp.edu.

Wheeling Jesuit University, Center for Professional and Graduate Studies, Wheeling, WV 26003-6295. Offers MSOL. Part-time and evening/weekend programs available. *Faculty:* 6 full-time (2 women), 11 part-time/adjunct (2 women). *Students:* 31 part-time (12 women); includes 1 minority (African American), 1 international. Average age 35. 13 applicants, 92% accepted, 11 enrolled. In 2009, 9 master's awarded. *Degree requirements:* For master's, thesis. *Entrance requirements:* For master's, MAT, minimum GPA of 2.75. Additional exam requirements/recommendations for international students: Required—TOEFL. *Application deadline:* Applications are processed on a rolling basis. Application fee: $25. Electronic applications accepted. *Expenses:* Tuition: Full-time $9000; part-time $500 per credit hour. Required fees: $195 per semester. One-time fee: $375. Tuition and fees vary according to program. *Financial support:* In 2009–10, 18 students received support. Unspecified assistantships available. Financial award application deadline: 8/1; financial award applicants required to submit FAFSA. *Unit head:* John E. Mansuy, Dean of Professional and Graduate Studies, 304-243-2250, Fax: 304-243-4441, E-mail: johnm@wju.edu. *Application contact:* Melissa Rataiczak, Director of Business Development, 304-243-2250, Fax: 304-243-4441, E-mail: mrataiczak@wju.edu.

Wilmington University, College of Business, New Castle, DE 19720-6491. Offers business administration (MBA); finance (MBA); health care administration (MBA, MS); homeland security (MBA, MS); human resource management (MS); management (MS); management information systems (MBA); organizational leadership (MS); public administration (MS); transportation and logistics (MBA, MS). Part-time and evening/weekend programs available. *Entrance requirements:* Additional exam requirements/recommendations for international students: Required—TOEFL (minimum score 500 paper-based; 173 computer-based). Electronic applications accepted.

Woodbury University, School of Business and Management, Program in Organizational Leadership, Burbank, CA 91504-1099. Offers MA. Evening/weekend programs available. *Faculty:* 1 (woman) full-time, 9 part-time/adjunct (5 women). *Students:* 82 full-time (51 women); includes 4 African Americans, 6 Asian Americans or Pacific Islanders, 21 Hispanic Americans, 3 international. Average age 37. In 2009, 60 master's awarded. *Entrance requirements:* For master's, GRE General Test (if GPA less than 2.5), 12 month cohort. *Application deadline:* For fall admission, 8/1 priority date for domestic students; for spring admission, 12/1 priority date for domestic students. Applications are processed on a rolling basis. Application fee: $35. *Expenses:* Tuition: Full-time $9576; part-time $798 per unit. Required fees: $100; $8 per unit. $50 per year. *Financial support:* Application deadline: 7/15. *Unit head:* Paul Decker, Director of the Institute for Excellence in Teaching and Learning, 818-252-5267, E-mail: paul.decker@woodbury.edu. *Application contact:* Ruth Lorzenana, Director of Admissions, 800-784-9663, Fax: 818-767-7520, E-mail: admissions@woodbury.edu.

Worcester Polytechnic Institute, Graduate Studies and Research, School of Business, Worcester, MA 01609-2280. Offers information technology (MS), including information security management; management (Graduate Certificate); marketing and technological innovation (MS); operations design and leadership (MS); technology (MBA). *Accreditation:* AACSB. Part-time and evening/weekend programs available. Postbaccalaureate distance learning degree programs offered (no on-campus study). *Faculty:* 25 full-time (12 women), 6 part-time/adjunct (2 women). *Students:* 89 full-time (44 women), 198 part-time (47 women). Average age 32. 229 applicants, 70% accepted, 71 enrolled. In 2009, 69 master's awarded. *Degree requirements:* For master's, thesis optional. *Entrance requirements:* For master's, GMAT (MBA), GMAT or GRE General Test (MS), resume; for Graduate Certificate, GMAT or GRE General Test, statement of purpose, 3 letters of recommendation. Additional exam requirements/recommendations for international students: Required—TOEFL (minimum score 550 paper-based; 213 computer-based; 79 iBT), IELTS (minimum score 6.5). *Application deadline:* For fall admission, 7/1 priority date for domestic students, 6/1 priority date for international students; for spring admission, 11/1 priority date for domestic students, 10/1 priority date for international students. Applications are processed on a rolling basis. Application fee: $70. Electronic applications accepted. *Financial support:* Career-related internships or fieldwork, institutionally sponsored loans, scholarships/grants, and unspecified assistantships available. Financial award application deadline: 6/1. *Faculty research:* Organizational aesthetics, resistance in organizations, dynamics of product innovation, economic approaches to productivity, corporate earnings forecasts and value relevance, ERP implementation, improving Web accessibility, information quality assessment, measuring strategic and transactional IT, website quality, service operations modeling, health care operations and performance analysis, loan process design. *Unit head:* Dr. Mark Rice, Dean, 508-831-5218, Fax: 508-831-5720, E-mail: rice@wpi.edu. *Application contact:* Norm Wilkinson, Director, Graduate Management Programs, 508-831-5957, Fax: 508-831-5720, E-mail: nwilkins@wpi.edu.

Worcester State College, Graduate Studies, Program in Management, Worcester, MA 01602-2597. Offers accounting (MS); organizational leadership (MS). *Faculty:* 4 full-time (3 women), 1 part-time/adjunct (0 women). *Students:* 2 full-time (0 women), 12 part-time (5 women); includes 1 minority (African American), 2 international. Average age 28. 17 applicants, 59% accepted, 1 enrolled. In 2009, 7 master's awarded. *Degree requirements:* For master's, comprehensive exam (for some programs), thesis optional. *Entrance requirements:* Additional exam requirements/recommendations for international students: Required—TOEFL (minimum score 550 paper-based; 213 computer-based; 79 iBT). *Application deadline:* Applications are processed on a rolling basis. Application fee: $30. *Expenses:* Tuition, area resident: Part-time $150 per credit. Tuition, state resident: part-time $150 per credit. Tuition, nonresident: part-time $150 per credit. Required fees: $85. *Financial support:* In 2009–10, 3 students received support, including 3 research assistantships with full tuition reimbursements available (averaging $4,800 per year); career-related internships or fieldwork, scholarships/grants, and unspecified assistantships also available. Financial award application deadline: 3/1; financial award applicants required to submit FAFSA. *Unit head:* Dr. Elizabeth Wark, Coordinator, 508-929-8743, Fax: 508-929-8048, E-mail: ewark@worcester.edu. *Application contact:* Nicole Brown, Assistant Dean of Continuing Education, 508-929-8787, Fax: 508-929-8100, E-mail: nbrown@worcester.edu.

HAWAI'I PACIFIC UNIVERSITY

Master of Arts in Organizational Change

Programs of Study

Hawai'i Pacific University's Master of Arts in Organizational Change (MA/OC) prepares professionals to lead and implement the change needed in today's fast-paced business environment. The MA/OC program takes a multidisciplinary perspective, using concepts and methods from such fields as organizational development, management, sociology, anthropology, communication, information systems, psychology, and comparative economics.

The Master of Arts in Organizational Change program emphasizes the management, design, implementation, and application of such change methods as continuous improvement and performance management. Students learn how to design innovations for organizational culture change, as well as how to implement an actual program of change in an organization. The program is accredited by the Accrediting Commission for Senior Colleges of the Western Association of Schools and Colleges (WASC).

The Master of Arts in Organizational Change program requires a minimum of 42 semester credits of graduate work. The 42 semester hours are divided into 36 semester hours of core courses and 6 semester hours of capstone courses. The program may be completed online from any location in the world.

The learning objectives of the MA/OC online program are the same as for the on-campus program. Students attain a solid foundation in the theory and practice of organizational design and behavior; achieve competency in recognizing and reconciling cultural differences effecting change and development; understand change and development theories and practices from a systemic, holistic perspective; are able to critically evaluate the effectiveness of various change and development models and methods in both global and local contexts; understand the dynamics of change—in particular, innovation diffusion, change leadership, knowledge management, problem solving, and technology transfer; understand the global-wide change and development profession, including the roles of consultants, change agents, educators, political leaders, nonprofit administrators, and corporate executives; and are able to work with various stakeholders to design and implement effective and sustainable change and development initiatives.

Students who complete the MA/OC program at Hawai'i Pacific University are given priority in the application process for a Ph.D. in Organizational Change and Development at Southern Cross University.

The joint master's degree program in organizational change and corporate communication (MAOC/MACOM) is designed for students who wish to develop skills in change leadership and organizational development, while acquiring a broad and thorough understanding of communication.

Research Facilities

To support graduate studies, HPU's Meader and Atherton Libraries offer more than 110,000 bound volumes, 350,000 microfiche items, and periodical subscriptions to 1,500 print titles and 30,000 electronic journals. Databases of public and state university libraries, legislative information, and business-oriented statistical data are also available in the library or online. Students can access HPU's library databases, course information, their academic information, and an e-mail account through Pipeline, the university's internal Web site for students. The University's accessible on-campus computer center houses more than 100 computers with specialized software to support graduate academic programs. HPU also provides free Wi-Fi so students can have wireless access to Pipeline resources anywhere on campus using laptops. A significant number of online courses are available.

Financial Aid

The University participates in all federal financial aid programs designated for graduate students. These programs provide aid in the form of subsidized (need-based) and unsubsidized (non-need-based) Federal Stafford Student Loans. Through these loans, funds may be available to cover the student's entire cost of education. To apply for aid, students must submit the Free Application for Federal Student Aid (FAFSA) beginning January 1. Mailing of student award letters usually begins by the end of March. The University also offers several institutional scholarships to new full-time, degree-seeking students. The Graduate Trustee Scholarship provides $6000 for two semesters; the Graduate Dean Scholarship provides $4000 for two semesters; and the Graduate Kokua Scholarship provides $2000 for two semesters. Priority consideration is given to those students who apply by the deadline.

Cost of Study

Tuition for graduate students enrolled in fall and spring semesters is determined on a per-credit basis; full-time status for a graduate student is 9 credits. Tuition for the optional winter and summer sessions is also determined on a per-credit basis. The estimated minimum funds needed for a nine-month academic year (September to May) based on 2010–11 school-year expenses is $26,459. For the 2010–11 academic year, full-time tuition is $12,600 for most graduate degree programs, including the MA/OC program. Books, supplies, and transportation cost $1885, and health insurance costs $880.

Living and Housing Costs

Most graduate students live in off-campus housing. The cost of living in off-campus apartments is approximately $11,094 for a double-occupancy room.

Student Group

University enrollment currently stands at more than 8,200. HPU is one of the most culturally diverse universities in America with students from all fifty U.S. states and more than 100 countries.

Location

Hawai'i Pacific University combines the excitement of an urban, downtown campus with the serenity of a residential campus. The main campus is ideally located in downtown Honolulu, the business and financial center of the Pacific. The downtown campus comprises six buildings in the center of Honolulu's business district and is home to the College of Business Administration and the College of Humanities & Social Sciences. Eight miles away, situated on 135 acres in Kaneohe, the windward Hawai'i Loa campus is the site of the College of Nursing & Health Sciences and the College of Natural & Computational Sciences. HPU is affiliated with the Oceanic Institute, an applied aquaculture research facility located on a 56-acre site at Makapu'u Point on the windward coast of Oahu, Hawaii. Students can conveniently travel between the three sites using the HPU shuttle service. There are also eight military campus programs located at Pearl Harbor, Barbers Point, Hickam Air Force Base, Schofield Barracks, Fort Shafter, Tripler Army Medical Center, Kaneohe Marine Corps Air Station, and Camp Smith.

The University

HPU is a private, nonprofit university with approximately 8,200 students. Founded in 1965, HPU prides itself on maintaining strong academic programs, small class sizes, individual attention to students, and a diverse faculty and student population. HPU is recognized as a "Best in the West" college by the *Princeton Review* and a "Best Buy" by *Barron's* business magazine. HPU offers more than fifty acclaimed undergraduate programs and thirteen distinguished graduate programs. The University has a faculty of more than 500, a student-faculty ratio of 15:1, and an average class size of less than 20. A wide range of counseling and other student support services are available. There are more than seventy student organizations on campus, including the Graduate Student Organization.

Applying

Students must have a baccalaureate degree from an accredited college or university in the United States or an equivalent degree from another country. Applicants should complete and forward a graduate admissions application, send in the $50 nonrefundable application fee, have official transcripts sent from all colleges or universities previously attended, and forward two letters of recommendation. A personal statement about the applicant's academic and career goals is required; submitting a resume is optional. Applicants who have taken the Graduate Record Examination (GRE) should have their scores sent directly to the Graduate Admissions Office. International students should submit scores of a recognized English proficiency test such as TOEFL. Admissions decisions are made on a rolling basis, and applicants are notified between one and two weeks after all documents have been submitted. Applicants are encouraged to submit their applications online.

Correspondence and Information

Graduate Admissions
Hawai'i Pacific University
1164 Bishop Street, Suite 911
Honolulu, Hawai'i 96813
Phone: 808-544-1135
          800-500-5565 (toll-free)
Fax: 808-544-0280
E-mail: graduate@hpu.edu
Web site: http://www.hpu.edu/hpumatesl

Hawai'i Pacific University

THE FACULTY AND THEIR RESEARCH

Hawai'i Pacific University's faculty members are known not only as outstanding teachers, but also as scholars in their respective fields. Faculty members in the Master of Arts in Organizational Change program have conducted extensive research in such areas as government, military, health care, and corporate networks. With stellar academic backgrounds and wide-ranging experiences in public service, HPU's faculty members bring a balance of theory and practical insight to the classroom. With an emphasis on meaningful faculty-student interaction, most courses are taught in a seminar format, where faculty members work one-on-one with graduate students.

Gui Albieri, Instructor and Associate Director of International Admissions; M.A., Hawai'i Pacific; Ph.D. candidate, Fielding Graduate University. Sustainable development.

W. Gerald Glover, Professor and Program Chair of Organizational Change; Ph.D., Florida. Economic and community development in the Bahamas, change initiatives in business and government organizations.

Stewart Hase, Associate Professor; Ph.D. Organizational change, organizational development and learning.

Gordon Jones, Professor of Computer Science and Information Systems and Dean of the College of Professional Studies; Ph.D., New Mexico. Impact of technology on the culture, structures and functions of multinational corporations.

Brian Mace, Adjunct Faculty; M.B.A., Hawai'i Pacific. Information Management Officer for U.S. Marine Corps Forces, Pacific.

Margo Poole, Adjunct Faculty; Ph.D., Newcastle (Australia). Environmental psychology, diffusion of innovations, knowledge diffusion, emotion, personal values and personality.

Richard Ward, Associate Professor; Ed.D., USC. Management experience includes internal change agent, human resources manager, operations and training manager, aircraft maintenance manager, logistics manager, safety manager, airport manager, and management engineer.

Arthur Whatley, Professor; Ph.D., North Texas State. Management and organizational effectiveness.

Wes Woodruff, Assistant Professor; M.A., Hawai'i Pacific; Ph.D. candidate, Southern Cross. Training and simulation.

Larry Zimmerman, Assistant Professor; Ph.D. (educational leadership and higher education), Nebraska–Lincoln. National cultural identity of international students.

Section 17
Project Management

This section contains a directory of institutions offering graduate work in project management. Additional information about programs listed in the directory may be obtained by writing directly to the dean of a graduate school or chair of a department at the address given in the directory.

For programs offering related work, see also in this book *Business Administration and Management.*

CONTENTS

Program Directory

Project Management

American Graduate University, Program in Project Management, Covina, CA 91724. Offers MPM, Certificate. Part-time programs available. Postbaccalaureate distance learning degree programs offered (no on-campus study). *Faculty:* 2 full-time (1 woman), 15 part-time/adjunct (2 women). *Students:* 129 part-time. In 2009, 71 master's awarded. *Entrance requirements:* For master's, 2 letters of recommendation, proctor designation. Additional exam requirements/recommendations for international students: Required—TOEFL. *Application deadline:* Applications are processed on a rolling basis. Application fee: $50. Electronic applications accepted. *Expenses:* Tuition: Part-time $275 per credit. *Unit head:* Paul McDonald, President, 626-966-4576 Ext. 1006, E-mail: paulmcdonald@agu.edu. *Application contact:* Marie Sirney, Director of Admissions, 626-966-4576 Ext. 1003, Fax: 626-915-1709, E-mail: mariesirney@agu.edu.

American InterContinental University Online, Program in Business Administration, Hoffman Estates, IL 60192. Offers accounting and finance (MBA); finance (MBA); healthcare management (MBA); human resource management (MBA); international business (MBA); management (MBA); marketing (MBA); operations management (MBA); organizational psychology and development (MBA); project management (MBA). Evening/weekend programs available. Postbaccalaureate distance learning degree programs offered (no on-campus study). *Entrance requirements:* Additional exam requirements/recommendations for international students: Required—TOEFL (minimum score 550 paper-based; 213 computer-based). Electronic applications accepted.

American InterContinental University Online, Program in Information Technology, Hoffman Estates, IL 60192. Offers Internet security (MIT); IT project management (MIT). Evening/weekend programs available. Postbaccalaureate distance learning degree programs offered (no on-campus study). *Entrance requirements:* Additional exam requirements/recommendations for international students: Required—TOEFL (minimum score 550 paper-based; 213 computer-based). Electronic applications accepted.

Aspen University, Program in Business Administration, Denver, CO 80246. Offers business administration (MBA); finance (MBA); information management (MBA); project management (MBA, Certificate). Part-time and evening/weekend programs available. Postbaccalaureate distance learning degree programs offered (no on-campus study). *Entrance requirements:* Additional exam requirements/recommendations for international students: Required—TOEFL (minimum score 530 paper-based; 71 computer-based). Electronic applications accepted.

Athabasca University, Centre for Innovative Management, St. Albert, AB T8N 1B4, Canada. Offers business administration (MBA); information technology management (MBA), including policing concentration; management (GDM); project management (MBA, GDM). Part-time and evening/weekend programs available. Postbaccalaureate distance learning degree programs offered (no on-campus study). *Faculty:* 9 full-time (6 women), 2 part-time/adjunct (0 women). *Students:* 898 part-time. Average age 36. 297 applicants, 33 enrolled. In 2009, 179 master's, 180 other advanced degrees awarded. *Degree requirements:* For master's, thesis or alternative, applied project. *Entrance requirements:* For master's, 3-8 years of managerial experience, 3 years with undergraduate degree, 5 years managerial experience with professional designation, 8-10 years management experience (on exception). *Application deadline:* For fall admission, 6/15 for domestic and international students; for winter admission, 10/15 for domestic and international students; for spring admission, 2/15 for domestic and international students. Applications are processed on a rolling basis. Application fee: $200. Electronic applications accepted. *Expenses:* Contact institution. *Financial support:* Scholarships/grants available. *Faculty research:* Human resources, project management, operations research, information technology management, corporate stewardship, energy management. *Unit head:* Dr. Alexander Kondra, Dean, 780-418-6582, E-mail: alexk@athabascau.ca. *Application contact:* Shannon Oscroft, Receptionist and Customer Service Representative, 780-459-1144, E-mail: shannono@athabascau.ca.

Avila University, Program in Organizational Development, Kansas City, MO 64145-1698. Offers management (MA), including fundraising, project management; organizational development (MS); project management (Graduate Certificate). Part-time and evening/weekend programs available. *Faculty:* 2 full-time (1 woman), 10 part-time/adjunct (7 women). *Students:* 50 full-time (41 women), 43 part-time (35 women); includes 28 minority (24 African Americans, 2 Asian Americans or Pacific Islanders, 2 Hispanic Americans), 2 international. Average age 36. 47 applicants, 64% accepted, 27 enrolled. In 2009, 16 master's awarded. *Degree requirements:* For master's, thesis optional. *Entrance requirements:* For master's, 2 letters of recommendation, minimum GPA of 3.25 during last 60 hours, resume. Additional exam requirements/recommendations for international students: Required—TOEFL. *Application deadline:* Applications are processed on a rolling basis. Application fee: $0. Electronic applications accepted. *Expenses:* Tuition: Full-time $8622; part-time $479 per credit hour. Required fees: $432; $24 per credit hour. Tuition and fees vary according to program. *Financial support:* In 2009-10, 69 students received support. Unspecified assistantships available. Support available to part-time students. Financial award applicants required to submit FAFSA. *Unit head:* Dr. Lacey Smith, Associate Dean, 816-501-3737, Fax: 816-941-4650, E-mail: advantage@avila.edu. *Application contact:* School of Professional Studies, 816-501-3737, Fax: 816-941-4650, E-mail: advantage@avila.edu.

Boston University, Metropolitan College, Department of Administrative Sciences, Boston, MA 02215. Offers banking and financial management (MSM); business continuity in emergency management (MSM); economics development and tourism management (MSAS); electronic commerce, systems, and technology (MSAS); financial economics (MSAS); human resource management (MSM); innovation and technology (MSAS); insurance management (MSM); international market management (MSM); multinational commerce (MSAS); project management (MSM). *Accreditation:* AACSB. Part-time and evening/weekend programs available. Postbaccalaureate distance learning degree programs offered (no on-campus study). *Students:* 123 full-time (48 women), 204 part-time (92 women); includes 31 minority (10 African Americans, 1 American Indian/Alaska Native, 11 Asian Americans or Pacific Islanders, 9 Hispanic Americans), 146 international. Average age 30. In 2009, 154 master's awarded. *Degree requirements:* For master's, thesis optional. *Entrance requirements:* For master's, 1 year of work experience, minimum GPA of 3.0. Additional exam requirements/recommendations for international students: Required—TOEFL (minimum score 560 paper-based; 220 computer-based; 84 iBT). *Application deadline:* Applications are processed on a rolling basis. Application fee: $70. Electronic applications accepted. *Expenses:* Tuition: Full-time $37,910; part-time $1184 per credit hour. Required fees: $386; $40 per semester. Part-time tuition and fees vary according to class time, course level, degree level and program. *Financial support:* In 2009-10, 15 students received support, including 8 research assistantships (averaging $10,000 per year); career-related internships or fieldwork and Federal Work-Study also available. *Faculty research:* International business, innovative process. *Unit head:* Dr. Kip Becker, Chairman, 617-353-3016, E-mail: adminsc@bu.edu. *Application contact:* Lucille Dicker, Administrative Sciences Department, 617-353-3016, E-mail: adminsc@bu.edu.

Brandeis University, Rabb School of Continuing Studies, Division of Graduate Professional Studies, Program in Management of Projects and Programs, Waltham, MA 02454-9110. Offers MS, Graduate Certificate. Part-time and evening/weekend programs available. Postbaccalaureate distance learning degree programs offered (no on-campus study). *Faculty:* 2 full-time (both women), 32 part-time/adjunct (8 women). *Students:* 59 part-time (25 women); includes 7 minority (3 African Americans, 4 Asian Americans or Pacific Islanders). Average age 35. 11 applicants, 100% accepted, 11 enrolled. In 2009, 12 master's, 5 other advanced degrees awarded. *Degree requirements:* For master's, thesis. *Entrance requirements:* For master's, resume, letter of recommendation; for Graduate Certificate, resume, official transcripts, recommendations. Additional exam requirements/recommendations for international students: Recommended—TOEFL (minimum score 600 paper-based; 250 computer-based; 100 iBT). *Application deadline:* For fall admission, 6/15 priority date for domestic students; for winter admission, 10/15 priority date for domestic students; for spring admission, 2/15 priority date for

domestic students. Applications are processed on a rolling basis. Application fee: $50. Electronic applications accepted. *Unit head:* Thomas Carter, Program Chair, 781-736-8787, Fax: 781-736-34320, E-mail: twcarter@brandeis.edu. *Application contact:* Frances Stearns, Associate Director of Admissions and Student Services, 781-736-8785, Fax: 781-736-3420, E-mail: fstearns@brandeis.edu.

Brandeis University, Rabb School of Continuing Studies, Division of Graduate Professional Studies, Virtual Team Management and Communication Program, Waltham, MA 02454-9110. Offers MS, Graduate Certificate. Part-time and evening/weekend programs available. Postbaccalaureate distance learning degree programs offered (no on-campus study). *Faculty:* 2 full-time (both women), 32 part-time/adjunct (8 women). *Students:* 1 part-time (0 women). Average age 35. *Entrance requirements:* For master's, statement of goals, resume, official transcripts, recommendations; for Graduate Certificate, resume, recommendations. Additional exam requirements/recommendations for international students: Recommended—TOEFL (minimum score 600 paper-based; 250 computer-based; 100 iBT). *Application deadline:* For fall admission, 6/15 priority date for domestic students; for winter admission, 10/15 priority date for domestic students; for spring admission, 2/15 priority date for domestic students. Applications are processed on a rolling basis. Application fee: $50. Electronic applications accepted. *Unit head:* Dr. Aline Yurik, Program Chair, 781-736-8787, Fax: 781-736-3420, E-mail: ayurik@brandeis.edu. *Application contact:* Frances Stearns, Associate Director of Admissions and Student Services, 781-736-8785, Fax: 781-736-3420, E-mail: fstearns@brandeis.edu.

Brenau University, Graduate Programs, School of Business and Mass Communication, Gainesville, GA 30501. Offers accounting (MBA); business administration (MBA); healthcare management (MBA); organizational leadership (MS); project management (MBA). Part-time and evening/weekend programs available. Postbaccalaureate distance learning degree programs offered (no on-campus study). *Faculty:* 11 full-time (6 women), 22 part-time/adjunct (6 women). *Students:* 116 full-time (74 women), 256 part-time (181 women); includes 113 minority (98 African Americans, 6 Asian Americans or Pacific Islanders, 9 Hispanic Americans), 20 international. Average age 35. 278 applicants, 90% accepted, 185 enrolled. In 2009, 125 master's awarded. *Entrance requirements:* For master's, resume, minimum undergraduate GPA of 3.5. Additional exam requirements/recommendations for international students: Required—TOEFL (minimum score 500 paper-based). *Application deadline:* Applications are processed on a rolling basis. Electronic applications accepted. *Expenses:* Contact institution. *Financial support:* In 2009-10, 1 student received support. Application deadline: 7/15. *Unit head:* Dr. William S. Lightfoot, Dean, 770-538-5330, Fax: 770-537-4701, E-mail: wlightfoot@brenau.edu. *Application contact:* Christina White, Graduate Admissions Specialist, 770-718-5320, Fax: 770-718-5338, E-mail: cwhite@brenau.edu.

California Intercontinental University, School of Information Technology, Diamond Bar, CA 91765. Offers information systems and enterprise resource management (DBA); information systems and knowledge management (MBA); project and quality management (MBA).

Capella University, School of Business and Technology, Minneapolis, MN 55402. Offers accounting (MBA), including system design and programming; business (Certificate), including human resource management (MS, PhD, Certificate), information technology management (MS, PhD, Certificate), leadership (MBA, MS, PhD, Certificate); finance (MBA); general business (MBA); health care management (MBA); information technology (MS, Certificate), including general information technology (MS), information security, network architecture and design (MS), professional projects management (Certificate), project management and leadership (MS), system design and development (MS),); information technology management (MBA); marketing (MBA); organization and management (MBA, MS, PhD), including general business (PhD), general organization and management (MBA, MS), human resource management (MS, PhD, Certificate), information technology management (MS, PhD, Certificate), leadership (MBA, MS, PhD, Certificate); project management (MBA). Part-time and evening/weekend programs available. Postbaccalaureate distance learning degree programs offered (minimal on-campus study). Terminal master's awarded for partial completion of doctoral program. *Degree requirements:* For master's, thesis optional, integrative project; for doctorate, comprehensive exam, thesis/dissertation. *Entrance requirements:* Additional exam requirements/recommendations for international students: Required—TOEFL (minimum score 550 paper-based; 213 computer-based), TWE (minimum score 4). Electronic applications accepted. *Faculty research:* Business policies: strategic, corporate, and financial management; interplay of technological, organizational and social change.

Christian Brothers University, School of Business, Memphis, TN 38104-5581. Offers business (MBA); financial planning (Certificate); project management (Certificate). Part-time and evening/weekend programs available. *Faculty:* 4 full-time (1 woman), 4 part-time/adjunct (1 woman). *Students:* 5 full-time (all women), 169 part-time (69 women); includes 64 minority (51 African Americans, 9 Asian Americans or Pacific Islanders, 4 Hispanic Americans), 3 international. Average age 35. In 2009, 59 master's awarded. *Entrance requirements:* For master's, GMAT, GRE. Additional exam requirements/recommendations for international students: Required—TOEFL. *Application deadline:* Applications are processed on a rolling basis. Application fee: $50. *Financial support:* Institutionally sponsored loans available. Support available to part-time students. *Unit head:* Dr. Scott Lawyer, Dean, 901-321-3104, Fax: 901-321-3566, E-mail: mlawyer@cbu.edu. *Application contact:* Dr. Scott Lawyer, Director, Graduate Business Programs, 901-321-3104, Fax: 901-321-3566, E-mail: mlawyer@cbu.edu.

City University of Seattle, Graduate Division, School of Management, Bellevue, WA 98005. Offers accounting (Certificate); change leadership (MBA, Certificate); financial management (MBA, Certificate); general management (MBA); general management-Europe (MBA); global leadership (Certificate); global marketing (MBA); individualized study (MBA); information security (MS); information systems (MBA); leadership (MA); marketing (MBA, Certificate); project management (MBA, MS, Certificate); sustainable business (Certificate); technology management (MBA, MS, Certificate). Part-time and evening/weekend programs available. Postbaccalaureate distance learning degree programs offered (no on-campus study). *Entrance requirements:* Additional exam requirements/recommendations for international students: Required—TOEFL (minimum score 540 paper-based; 207 computer-based); Recommended—IELTS. Electronic applications accepted. *Expenses:* Tuition: Full-time $14,760; part-time $615 per credit. Tuition and fees vary according to program.

Colorado Technical University Colorado Springs, Graduate Studies, Program in Management, Colorado Springs, CO 80907-3896. Offers accounting (MBA, MSA); business administration (MBA); finance (MBA); human resources management (MBA); logistics/supply chain management (MBA); management (DM); marketing (MBA); mediation and dispute resolution (MBA); operations management (MBA); project management (MBA); technology management (MBA). Part-time and evening/weekend programs available. Postbaccalaureate distance learning degree programs offered. *Degree requirements:* For master's, thesis or alternative; for doctorate, thesis/dissertation. *Entrance requirements:* For doctorate, minimum graduate GPA of 3.0, 5 years of related work experience. *Faculty research:* Sexual harassment, performance evaluation, critical thinking.

Colorado Technical University Denver, Programs in Business Administration and Management, Greenwood Village, CO 80111. Offers accounting (MBA); business administration (MBA); business administration and management (EMBA); finance (MBA); human resource management (MBA); marketing (MBA); mediation and dispute resolution (MBA); operations management (MBA); project management (MBA); technology management (MBA). Part-time and evening/weekend programs available. *Degree requirements:* For master's, thesis or alternative. *Entrance requirements:* For master's, minimum undergraduate GPA of 3.0, resume.

Colorado Technical University Sioux Falls, Programs in Business Administration and Management, Sioux Falls, SD 57108. Offers business administration (MBA); business management (MSM); health science management (MSM); human resources management (MSM); information

technology (MSM); organizational leadership (MSM); project management (MBA); technology management (MBA). Evening/weekend programs available. *Degree requirements:* For master's, thesis optional. *Entrance requirements:* For master's, minimum 2 years work experience, resume.

Dallas Baptist University, College of Business, Business Administration Program, Dallas, TX 75211-9299. Offers accounting (MBA); business communication (MBA); conflict resolution management (MBA); e-business (MBA); entrepreneurship (MBA); finance (MBA); health care management (MBA); international business (MBA); leading the non-profit organization (MBA); management (MBA); management information systems (MBA); marketing (MBA); project management (MBA); technology and engineering management (MBA). *Accreditation:* ACBSP. Part-time and evening/weekend programs available. *Entrance requirements:* For master's, GMAT, minimum GPA of 3.0. Additional exam requirements/recommendations for international students: Required—TOEFL, IELTS. Electronic applications accepted. *Expenses:* Tuition: Full-time $10,674; part-time $593 per credit hour. *Faculty research:* Sports management, services marketing, retailing, strategic management, financial planning/investments.

DePaul University, College of Computing and Digital Media, Chicago, IL 60604. Offers business information technology (MS); computational finance (MS); computer and information sciences (PhD); computer game development (MS); computer graphics and motion technology (MS); computer science (MS); computer, information and network security (MS), including applied technology; digital cinema (MFA, MS), including information technology project management (MS); e-commerce technology (MS); human-computer interaction (MS); information systems (MS); information technology (MA); information technology project management (MS); software engineering (MS); telecommunications systems (MS); JD/MS. Part-time and evening/weekend programs available. Postbaccalaureate distance learning degree programs offered (no on-campus study). *Faculty:* 78 full-time (16 women), 191 part-time/adjunct (51 women). *Students:* 922 full-time (239 women), 887 part-time (209 women); includes 466 minority (193 African Americans, 3 American Indian/Alaska Native, 162 Asian Americans or Pacific Islanders, 108 Hispanic Americans), 276 international. Average age 31. 853 applicants, 67% accepted, 294 enrolled. In 2009, 444 master's, 4 doctorates awarded. *Degree requirements:* For master's, thesis (for some programs); for doctorate, comprehensive exam, thesis/dissertation. *Entrance requirements:* For master's, GRE or GMAT (MS in computational finance only), bachelor's degree; for doctorate, GRE, master's degree in computer science. Additional exam requirements/recommendations for international students: Required—TOEFL (minimum score 550 paper-based; 213 computer-based), IELTS (minimum score 6.5), Pearson Test of English (minimum score 53). *Application deadline:* For fall admission, 8/15 priority date for domestic students, 6/1 priority date for international students; for winter admission, 12/15 priority date for domestic students, 9/15 priority date for international students; for spring admission, 3/1 priority date for domestic students, 12/15 priority date for international students. Applications are processed on a rolling basis. Application fee: $25. Electronic applications accepted. *Expenses:* Contact institution. *Financial support:* In 2009–10, 69 students received support, including 6 fellowships with full tuition reimbursements available (averaging $25,858 per year), 75 teaching assistantships with full and partial tuition reimbursements available (averaging $5,780 per year); research assistantships, Federal Work-Study, scholarships/grants, tuition waivers (full and partial), and unspecified assistantships also available. Support available to part-time students. Financial award application deadline: 4/30; financial award applicants required to submit FAFSA. *Faculty research:* Bioinformatics, visual computing, graphics and animation, high performance and scientific computing, databases. Total annual research expenditures: $790,000. *Unit head:* Dr. David Miller, Dean, 312-362-8381, Fax: 312-362-5185. *Application contact:* Dr. Liz Friedman, Assistant Dean of Student Services, 312-362-5384, Fax: 312-362-5327, E-mail: efriedm2@cdm.depaul.edu.

DeSales University, Graduate Division, Program in Business Administration, Center Valley, PA 18034-9568. Offers accounting (MBA); business administration (MBA); computer information systems (MBA); finance (MBA); health care systems management (MBA); management (MBA); marketing (MBA); project management (MBA); self-design (MBA); MSN/MBA. *Accreditation:* ACBSP. Part-time programs available. Postbaccalaureate distance learning degree programs offered (no on-campus study). *Students:* 433 part-time. In 2009, 218 master's awarded. *Entrance requirements:* For master's, minimum GPA of 3.0, 2 years of work experience. Additional exam requirements/recommendations for international students: Required—TOEFL. *Application deadline:* Applications are processed on a rolling basis. Application fee: $35. Electronic applications accepted. *Expenses:* Tuition: Full-time $17,500; part-time $665 per credit. Full-time tuition and fees vary according to program. Part-time tuition and fees vary according to course load. *Faculty research:* Quality improvement, executive development, productivity, cross-cultural managerial differences, leadership. *Unit head:* Dr. David Gilfoil, Director, 610-282-1100 Ext. 1828, Fax: 610-282-2869, E-mail: david.gilfoil@desales.edu. *Application contact:* Caryn Stopper, Director of Graduate Admissions, 610-282-1100 Ext. 1768, Fax: 610-282-0525, E-mail: caryn.stopper@desales.edu.

DeVry University, Keller Graduate School of Management, Downers Grove, IL 60515. Offers accounting and financial management (MAFM); business administration (MBA); human resources management (MHRM); information systems management (MISM); network and communications management (MNCM); project management (MPM); public administration (MPA).

Dowling College, School of Business, Oakdale, NY 11769-1999. Offers aviation management (MBA, Certificate); banking and finance (MBA, Certificate); financial planning (Certificate); general management (MBA); health care management (MBA, Certificate); human resource management (Certificate); management and leadership (MBA); marketing (Certificate); project management (Certificate); public management (MBA, Certificate); total quality management (MBA, Certificate); JD/MBA. Part-time and evening/weekend programs available. *Faculty:* 14 full-time (5 women), 58 part-time/adjunct (5 women). *Students:* 324 full-time (142 women), 479 part-time (237 women); includes 238 minority (82 African Americans, 1 American Indian/Alaska Native, 117 Asian Americans or Pacific Islanders, 38 Hispanic Americans), 2 international. Average age 33. 457 applicants, 91% accepted, 153 enrolled. In 2009, 341 master's, 2 other advanced degrees awarded. *Degree requirements:* For master's, comprehensive exam, thesis optional. *Entrance requirements:* For master's, minimum GPA of 2.8, 2 letters of recommendation, courses in accounting and finance or seminar in accounting/finance, resume. Additional exam requirements/recommendations for international students: Required—TOEFL (minimum score 550 paper-based). *Application deadline:* For fall admission, 9/1 priority date for domestic students; for winter admission, 1/1 priority date for domestic students; for spring admission, 2/1 priority date for domestic students. Applications are processed on a rolling basis. Application fee: $50. Electronic applications accepted. *Expenses:* Tuition: Full-time $14,490; part-time $805 per credit. Required fees: $346 per term. *Financial support:* Career-related internships or fieldwork and Federal Work-Study available. Support available to part-time students. Financial award application deadline: 6/30; financial award applicants required to submit FAFSA. *Faculty research:* International finance, computer applications, labor relations, executive development. *Unit head:* Mathew Cordaro, Dean, 631-244-3162, Fax: 631-244-1018, E-mail: cordarom@dowling.edu. *Application contact:* Glenn M. Berman, Director of Admissions Operations, 631-244-3357, Fax: 631-244-1059, E-mail: glenn.berman@dowling.edu.

Drexel University, School of Technology and Professional Studies, Philadelphia, PA 19104-2875. Offers construction management (MS); engineering technology (MS); food science (MS); hospitality management (MS); professional studies: creativity studies (MS); professional studies: e-learning leadership (MS); professional studies: homeland security management (MS); project management (MS); property management (MS); sport management (MS). Postbaccalaureate distance learning degree programs offered.

Embry-Riddle Aeronautical University Worldwide, Worldwide Headquarters, Program in Project Management, Daytona Beach, FL 32114-3900. Offers MSPM. Part-time and evening/weekend programs available. Postbaccalaureate distance learning degree programs offered. *Faculty:* 16 full-time (2 women), 28 part-time/adjunct (9 women). *Students:* 95 full-time (32 women), 83 part-time (16 women); includes 40 minority (21 African Americans, 7 Asian Americans or Pacific Islanders, 12 Hispanic Americans). Average age 39. 143 applicants, 85% accepted, 87 enrolled. In 2009, 4 master's awarded. *Degree requirements:* For master's, thesis (for some programs). *Application deadline:* Applications are processed on a rolling basis. Application fee: $50. Electronic applications accepted. *Financial support:* In 2009–10, 14 students received support. *Unit head:* Dr. Kees Rietsema, Chair, 602-750-0685, E-mail: rietsd37@erau.edu. *Application contact:* Linda Dammer, Director of Admissions, 386-226-6910, Fax: 386-226-6984, E-mail: ecinfo@erau.edu.

Florida Institute of Technology, Graduate Programs, College of Business, Extended Studies Division, Melbourne, FL 32901-6975. Offers acquisition and contract management (PMBA); business administration (PMBA); computer information systems (MS); e-business (PMBA); human resource management (PMBA); human resources management (MS); logistics management (MS), including humanitarian and disaster relief logistics; management (MS), including acquisition and contract management, e-business, human resource management, information systems, logistics management, management, transportation management; material acquisition management (MS); project management (MS), including information systems, operations research; public administration (MPA); quality management (MS); space management (MS); space systems (MS); systems management (MS), including information systems, operations research, systems management. Part-time and evening/weekend programs available. Postbaccalaureate distance learning degree programs offered (no on-campus study). *Faculty:* 12 full-time (3 women), 117 part-time/adjunct (20 women). *Students:* 74 full-time (32 women), 1,041 part-time (484 women); includes 343 minority (240 African Americans, 12 American Indian/Alaska Native, 44 Asian Americans or Pacific Islanders, 47 Hispanic Americans), 22 international. Average age 35. 520 applicants, 72% accepted, 279 enrolled. In 2009, 509 master's awarded. *Degree requirements:* For master's, capstone course. *Entrance requirements:* For master's, GMAT or resume showing 8 years of supervised experience, minimum GPA of 3.0, 2 letters of recommendation, resume. Additional exam requirements/recommendations for international students: Required—TOEFL (minimum score 550 paper-based; 213 computer-based; 79 iBT). *Application deadline:* For fall admission, 4/1 for international students; for spring admission, 9/30 for international students. Applications are processed on a rolling basis. Application fee: $50. Electronic applications accepted. *Expenses:* Tuition: Part-time $1015 per credit. Tuition and fees vary according to campus/location and program. *Financial support:* Application deadline: 3/1. *Unit head:* Dr. Clifford Bragdon, Dean, 321-674-8821, Fax: 321-674-7597, E-mail: cbragdon@fit.edu. *Application contact:* Carolyn Farrior, Director of Graduate Admissions Online Learning and Off Campus Programs, 321-674-7118, Fax: 321-674-8216, E-mail: cfarrior@fit.edu.

Florida Institute of Technology, Graduate Programs, College of Business, Online Programs, Melbourne, FL 32901-6975. Offers accounting and finance (MBA); healthcare management (MBA); information technology (MS); information technology management (MBA); management (MBA); marketing (MBA); project management (MBA). Part-time and evening/weekend programs available. Postbaccalaureate distance learning degree programs offered (no on-campus study). *Faculty:* 30 part-time/adjunct (6 women). *Students:* 6 full-time (2 women), 875 part-time (387 women); includes 290 minority (194 African Americans, 6 American Indian/Alaska Native, 44 Asian Americans or Pacific Islanders, 46 Hispanic Americans), 32 international. Average age 37. 329 applicants, 64% accepted, 177 enrolled. In 2009, 33 master's awarded. *Entrance requirements:* For master's, GMAT or resume showing 8 years of supervised experience, 2 letters of recommendation, resume, competency in math past college algebra. Additional exam requirements/recommendations for international students: Required—TOEFL (minimum score 550 paper-based; 213 computer-based; 79 iBT). *Application deadline:* For fall admission, 4/1 for international students; for spring admission, 9/30 for international students. Applications are processed on a rolling basis. Application fee: $50. Electronic applications accepted. *Expenses:* Tuition: Part-time $1015 per credit. Tuition and fees vary according to campus/location and program. *Financial support:* Available to part-time students. Application deadline: 3/1. *Unit head:* Dr. Mary S. Bonhomme, Dean, Florida Tech Online/Associate Provost for Online Learning, 321-674-8883, Fax: 321-674-8216, E-mail: bonhomme@fit.edu. *Application contact:* Carolyn Farrior, Director of Graduate Admissions Online Learning and Off Campus Programs, 321-674-7118, Fax: 321-674-8216, E-mail: cfarrior@fit.edu.

The George Washington University, School of Business, Department of Decision Sciences, Washington, DC 20052. Offers project management (MS). *Faculty:* 15 full-time (1 woman), 6 part-time/adjunct (0 women). *Students:* 21 full-time (6 women), 230 part-time (108 women); includes 75 minority (42 African Americans, 2 American Indian/Alaska Native, 18 Asian Americans or Pacific Islanders, 13 Hispanic Americans), 32 international. Average age 38. 98 applicants, 88% accepted. In 2009, 78 master's awarded. *Financial support:* Tuition waivers available. *Unit head:* Srinivas Prasad, Chair, 202-994-2078, Fax: 202-994-6382, E-mail: prasad@gwu.edu. *Application contact:* Kristin Williams, Assistant Vice President for Graduate and Special Enrollment Management, 202-994-0467, Fax: 202-994-0371, E-mail: ksw@gwu.edu.

The George Washington University, School of Business, Department of Information Systems and Technology Management, Washington, DC 20052. Offers information and decision systems (PhD); information systems (MSIST); information systems development (MSIST); information systems management (MBA); information systems project management (MSIST); management information systems (MSIST); management of science, technology, and innovation (MBA, PhD). Programs also offered in Ashburn and Arlington, VA. Part-time and evening/weekend programs available. *Faculty:* 13 full-time (4 women), 3 part-time/adjunct (1 woman). *Students:* 76 full-time (27 women), 160 part-time (50 women); includes 83 minority (30 African Americans, 1 American Indian/Alaska Native, 39 Asian Americans or Pacific Islanders, 13 Hispanic Americans), 35 international. Average age 33. 217 applicants, 72% accepted, 77 enrolled. In 2009, 117 master's, 7 doctorates awarded. *Entrance requirements:* For master's, GMAT. Additional exam requirements/recommendations for international students: Required—TOEFL. *Application deadline:* For fall admission, 4/1 priority date for domestic students; for spring admission, 10/1 for domestic students. Applications are processed on a rolling basis. Application fee: $60. *Financial support:* In 2009–10, 35 students received support; fellowships, teaching assistantships, career-related internships or fieldwork, Federal Work-Study, institutionally sponsored loans, and tuition waivers available. Financial award application deadline: 4/1. *Faculty research:* Expert systems, decision support systems. *Unit head:* Richard G. Donnelly, Chair, 202-994-4364, E-mail: rgd@gwu.edu. *Application contact:* Kristin Williams, Assistant Vice President for Graduate and Special Enrollment Management, 202-994-0467, Fax: 202-994-0371, E-mail: ksw@gwu.edu.

Grantham University, Mark Skousen School of Business, Kansas City, MO 64153. Offers business administration (MBA); information management (MBA); information technology (MS); project management (MBA, MSIM). Part-time and evening/weekend programs available. Postbaccalaureate distance learning degree programs offered (no on-campus study). In 2009, 48 master's awarded. *Degree requirements:* For master's, capstone project. *Entrance requirements:* For master's, bachelor's degree from accredited degree-granting institution. Additional exam requirements/recommendations for international students: Required—TOEFL (minimum score 500 paper-based; 213 computer-based; 61 iBT). *Application deadline:* Applications are processed on a rolling basis. Application fee: $0. Electronic applications accepted. *Expenses:* Tuition: Part-time $265 per credit hour. One-time fee: $30 part-time. *Financial support:* Institutionally sponsored loans and scholarships/grants available. *Unit head:* Rhonda Corwin, Dean, 800-955-2527, Fax: 816-595-5757, E-mail: admissions@grantham.edu. *Application contact:* Matthew Hawes, Vice President of Enrollment Management, 800-955-2527, Fax: 816-595-5757, E-mail: admissions@grantham.edu.

Harrisburg University of Science and Technology, Program in Project Management, Harrisburg, PA 17101. Offers construction services specialization (MS); governmental services specialization (MS); information technology specialization (MS). Part-time and evening/weekend programs available. *Faculty:* 1 full-time (0 women), 3 part-time/adjunct (0 women). *Students:* 1 full-time (0 women), 21 part-time (4 women); includes 5 minority (2 African Americans, 3 Asian Americans or Pacific Islanders), 2 international. Average age 30. 26 applicants, 92% accepted, 22 enrolled. In 2009, 3 master's awarded. *Entrance requirements:* For master's, BS, BBA. Additional exam requirements/recommendations for international

Project Management

Harrisburg University of Science and Technology (continued)
students: Required—TOEFL (minimum score 520 paper-based; 200 computer-based; 80 iBT). *Application deadline:* For fall admission, 8/1 priority date for domestic students, 7/1 priority date for international students. Applications are processed on a rolling basis. Application fee: $0. Electronic applications accepted. *Expenses:* Tuition: Full-time $18,000; part-time $650 per semester hour. *Financial support:* In 2009–10, 7 students received support. Scholarships/grants available. Financial award applicants required to submit FAFSA. *Unit head:* Dr. Amjad Umar, Director and Professor, 717-901-5141, Fax: 717-901-3141, E-mail: aumar@harrisburgu.edu. *Application contact:* Julie Cullings, Information Contact, 717-901-5163, Fax: 717-901-3163, E-mail: admissions@harrisburgu.edu.

Jones International University, School of Business, Centennial, CO 80112. Offers accounting (MBA); business communication (MABC); entrepreneurship (MABC, MBA); finance (MBA); global enterprise management (MBA); health care management (MBA); information security management (MBA); information technology management (MBA); leadership and influence (MABC); leading the customer-driven organization (MABC); negotiation and conflict management (MBA); project management (MABC, MBA). Program only offered online. Part-time and evening/weekend programs available. Postbaccalaureate distance learning degree programs offered (no on-campus study). *Degree requirements:* For master's, capstone project. *Entrance requirements:* For master's, minimum cumulative GPA of 2.5. Additional exam requirements/recommendations for international students: Recommended—TOEFL (minimum score 550 paper-based; 213 computer-based). Electronic applications accepted.

Kaplan University, Davenport Campus, School of Business, Davenport, IA 52807-2095. Offers business administration (MBA); change leadership (MS); entrepreneurship (MBA); finance (MBA); health care management (MBA, MS); human resource (MBA); international business (MBA); management (MS); marketing (MBA); project management (MBA, MS); supply chain management and logistics (MBA, MS). Part-time and evening/weekend programs available. Postbaccalaureate distance learning degree programs offered (no on-campus study). *Entrance requirements:* Additional exam requirements/recommendations for international students: Required—TOEFL (minimum score 550 paper-based; 218 computer-based; 80 iBT). Electronic applications accepted.

Lakeland College, Graduate Studies Division, Program in Business Administration, Sheboygan, WI 53082-0359. Offers accounting (MBA); finance (MBA); healthcare management (MBA); project management (MBA). *Entrance requirements:* For master's, GMAT. *Expenses:* Contact institution.

Lasell College, Graduate and Professional Studies in Management, Newton, MA 02466-2709. Offers elder care administration (MSM, Graduate Certificate); elder care marketing (MSM, Graduate Certificate); fundraising management (MSM, Graduate Certificate); human resource management (MSM, Graduate Certificate); management (MSM, Graduate Certificate); marketing (MSM, Graduate Certificate); non-profit management (MSM, Graduate Certificate); project management (MSM, Graduate Certificate). Part-time and evening/weekend programs available. Postbaccalaureate distance learning degree programs offered (no on-campus study). *Faculty:* 2 full-time (both women), 8 part-time/adjunct (6 women). *Students:* 26 full-time (18 women), 85 part-time (60 women); includes 10 African Americans, 4 Asian Americans or Pacific Islanders, 9 Hispanic Americans, 17 international. Average age 31. 55 applicants, 80% accepted, 31 enrolled. In 2009, 31 master's awarded. *Entrance requirements:* For master's and Graduate Certificate, bachelor's degree from an accredited institution. Additional exam requirements/recommendations for international students: Required—TOEFL (minimum score 550 paper-based; 213 computer-based; 75 iBT) or IELTS. *Application deadline:* For fall admission, 8/31 priority date for domestic students, 6/30 priority date for international students; for spring admission, 12/31 priority date for domestic students, 10/31 priority date for international students. Applications are processed on a rolling basis. Application fee: $40. Electronic applications accepted. *Expenses:* Tuition: Full-time $4890; part-time $525 per credit hour. Required fees: $55 per term. *Financial support:* Available to part-time students. Application deadline: 8/31. *Unit head:* Dr. Joan Dolamore, Dean of Graduate and Professional Studies, 617-243-2485, Fax: 617-243-2450, E-mail: gradinfo@lasell.edu. *Application contact:* Adrienne Franciosi, Director of Graduate Admission, 617-243-2214, Fax: 617-243-2450, E-mail: gradinfo@lasell.edu.

Lehigh University, College of Business and Economics, Bethlehem, PA 18015. Offers accounting (MS), including accounting and information analysis; business administration (MBA); economics (MS, PhD), including economics, health and bio-pharmaceutical economics (MS); entrepreneurship (Certificate); finance (MS), including analytical finance; project management (Certificate); supply chain management (Certificate); MBA/E; MBA/M Ed. *Accreditation:* AACSB. Part-time and evening/weekend programs available. Postbaccalaureate distance learning degree programs offered (minimal on-campus study). *Faculty:* 42 full-time (11 women), 12 part-time/adjunct (2 women). *Students:* 145 full-time (64 women), 264 part-time (82 women); includes 28 minority (6 African Americans, 19 Asian Americans or Pacific Islanders, 3 Hispanic Americans), 111 international. Average age 30. 624 applicants, 47% accepted, 114 enrolled. In 2009, 111 master's, 2 doctorates awarded. Terminal master's awarded for partial completion of doctoral program. *Degree requirements:* For master's, thesis optional; for doctorate, comprehensive exam, thesis/dissertation, proposal defense. *Entrance requirements:* For master's, GMAT, GRE General Test; MCAT, DAT (health and biopharmaceutical economics); for doctorate, GMAT or GRE General Test. Additional exam requirements/recommendations for international students: Required—TOEFL (minimum score 600 paper-based; 250 computer-based; 94 iBT). *Application deadline:* For fall admission, 7/15 for domestic students, 5/1 for international students; for spring admission, 12/1 for domestic and international students. Applications are processed on a rolling basis. Application fee: $100. Electronic applications accepted. *Expenses:* Contact institution. *Financial support:* In 2009–10, 2 fellowships with full tuition reimbursements (averaging $13,200 per year), 10 research assistantships with full and partial tuition reimbursements (averaging $2,800 per year), 17 teaching assistantships with full tuition reimbursements (averaging $13,840 per year) were awarded; career-related internships or fieldwork, scholarships/grants, health care benefits, tuition waivers (full and partial), and unspecified assistantships also available. Support available to part-time students. Financial award application deadline: 1/15. *Faculty research:* Public finance, energy, investments, activity-based costing, management information systems. *Unit head:* Martin K. Saffer, Graduate Business Programs, 610-758-4450, Fax: 610-758-5283, E-mail: mks207@lehigh.edu. *Application contact:* Corinn McBride, Director of Recruitment and Admissions, 610-758-3418, Fax: 610-758-5283, E-mail: com207@lehigh.edu.

Lewis University, College of Business, Graduate School of Management, Program in Business Administration, Romeoville, IL 60446. Offers accounting (MBA); custom elective option (MBA); e-business (MBA); finance (MBA); healthcare management (MBA); human resources management (MBA); information security (MBA); international business (MBA); management information systems (MBA); marketing (MBA); project management (MBA); technology and operations management (MBA). Part-time and evening/weekend programs available. *Faculty:* 15 full-time (2 women), 18 part-time/adjunct (4 women). *Students:* 120 full-time (64 women), 222 part-time (103 women); includes 97 minority (62 African Americans, 4 Asian Americans or Pacific Islanders, 31 Hispanic Americans), 9 international. Average age 31. In 2009, 84 master's awarded. *Entrance requirements:* For master's, interview, bachelor's degree, resume, 2 recommendations. Additional exam requirements/recommendations for international students: Required—TOEFL (minimum score 550 paper-based; 213 computer-based). *Application deadline:* For fall admission, 8/15 priority date for domestic students, 5/1 priority date for international students; for spring admission, 11/15 priority date for international students. Applications are processed on a rolling basis. Application fee: $40. Electronic applications accepted. *Expenses:* Tuition: Full-time $6480; part-time $720 per credit. One-time fee: $40. Tuition and fees vary according to course load, degree level and program. *Financial support:* Career-related internships or fieldwork, Federal Work-Study, scholarships/grants, and unspecified assistantships available. Financial award application deadline: 5/1; financial award applicants required to submit FAFSA. *Unit head:* Dr. Maureen Culleeney, Academic Program Director, 815-838-0500 Ext. 5631, E-mail: culleema@lewisu.edu. *Application contact:* Michele King, Director of Admission, 815-838-0500 Ext. 5384, E-mail: gsm@lewisu.edu.

Marymount University, School of Business Administration, Program in Information Technology, Arlington, VA 22207-4299. Offers computer security and information assurance (Certificate); health care informatics (Certificate); information technology (MS, Certificate); information technology project management: technology leadership (Certificate). Part-time and evening/weekend programs available. *Faculty:* 6 full-time (3 women), 4 part-time/adjunct (0 women). *Students:* 28 full-time (11 women), 23 part-time (6 women); includes 15 minority (9 African Americans, 1 American Indian/Alaska Native, 4 Asian Americans or Pacific Islanders, 1 Hispanic American), 21 international. Average age 31. 45 applicants, 100% accepted, 26 enrolled. In 2009, 19 master's, 1 other advanced degree awarded. *Degree requirements:* For master's, thesis or alternative. *Entrance requirements:* For master's, GMAT or GRE General Test, interview, resume, bachelor's degree in computer-related field or degree in another subject with a post-baccalaureate certificate in a computer-related field; for Certificate, resume. Additional exam requirements/recommendations for international students: Required—TOEFL (minimum score 600 paper-based; 250 computer-based; 96 iBT), IELTS (minimum score 6.5). *Application deadline:* For fall admission, 7/15 for domestic students, 7/1 for international students; for spring admission, 11/15 for domestic students, 10/15 for international students. Applications are processed on a rolling basis. Application fee: $40. Electronic applications accepted. *Expenses:* Tuition: Full-time $13,050; part-time $725 per credit hour. Required fees: $135; $7.50 per credit hour. *Financial support:* In 2009–10, 5 students received support; research assistantships with full tuition reimbursements available, career-related internships or fieldwork, Federal Work-Study, scholarships/grants, and unspecified assistantships available. Support available to part-time students. Financial award applicants required to submit FAFSA. *Unit head:* Dr. Diane Murphy, Chair, 703-284-5958, Fax: 703-527-3830, E-mail: diane.murphy@marymount.edu. *Application contact:* Francesca Reed, Director, Graduate Admissions, 703-284-5901, Fax: 703-527-3815, E-mail: grad.admissions@marymount.edu.

Marymount University, School of Business Administration, Program in Management, Arlington, VA 22207-4299. Offers leadership (Certificate); management (MS); project management (Certificate). Part-time and evening/weekend programs available. *Faculty:* 11 full-time (7 women), 11 part-time/adjunct (4 women). *Students:* 1 (woman) full-time, 25 part-time (17 women); includes 10 minority (7 African Americans, 1 Asian American or Pacific Islander, 2 Hispanic Americans), 1 international. Average age 40. 12 applicants, 83% accepted, 8 enrolled. In 2009, 11 master's, 2 other advanced degrees awarded. *Entrance requirements:* For master's, GMAT or GRE General Test, resume, at least 3 years of managerial experience, essay; for Certificate, resume, at least 3 years of managerial experience. Additional exam requirements/recommendations for international students: Required—TOEFL (minimum score 600 paper-based; 250 computer-based; 96 iBT), IELTS (minimum score 6.5). *Application deadline:* For fall admission, 7/15 for domestic students, 7/1 for international students; for spring admission, 11/15 for domestic students, 10/15 for international students. Applications are processed on a rolling basis. Application fee: $40. Electronic applications accepted. *Expenses:* Tuition: Full-time $13,050; part-time $725 per credit hour. Required fees: $135; $7.50 per credit hour. *Financial support:* In 2009–10, 4 students received support; research assistantships with full tuition reimbursements available, career-related internships or fieldwork, Federal Work-Study, scholarships/grants, and unspecified assistantships available. Support available to part-time students. Financial award applicants required to submit FAFSA. *Unit head:* Dr. Lorri Cooper, Director, Master's in Management, 703-284-5950, Fax: 703-527-3830, E-mail: lorri.cooper@marymount.edu. *Application contact:* Francesca Reed, Director, Graduate Admissions, 703-284-5901, Fax: 703-527-3815, E-mail: grad.admissions@marymount.edu.

Metropolitan State University, College of Management, St. Paul, MN 55106-5000. Offers business administration (MBA); information assurance security (Graduate Certificate); information management (MMIS); MIS generalist (Graduate Certificate); MIS systems analysis and design (Graduate Certificate); nonprofit management (MPNA); project management (Graduate Certificate); public administration (MPNA); systems management (MMIS). Part-time and evening/weekend programs available. *Degree requirements:* For master's, thesis optional, computer language (MMIS). *Entrance requirements:* For master's, GMAT (MBA), resume. Additional exam requirements/recommendations for international students: Required—TOEFL (minimum score 550 paper-based; 213 computer-based). *Expenses:* Tuition, state resident: full-time $5520; part-time $276 per credit hour. Tuition, nonresident: full-time $11,040; part-time $552 per credit hour. Required fees: $209; $10 per credit hour. Tuition and fees vary according to degree level. *Faculty research:* Yugoslav economic system, workers' cooperatives, participative management and job enrichment, global business systems.

Mississippi State University, College of Business, Graduate Studies in Business, MS State, MS 39762. Offers business administration (MBA); project management (MBA). *Accreditation:* AACSB. Part-time and evening/weekend programs available. Postbaccalaureate distance learning degree programs offered (no on-campus study). *Students:* 114 full-time (38 women), 207 part-time (54 women); includes 27 minority (12 African Americans, 9 Asian Americans or Pacific Islanders, 6 Hispanic Americans), 20 international. Average age 29. 215 applicants, 70% accepted, 113 enrolled. In 2009, 148 master's awarded. Terminal master's awarded for partial completion of doctoral program. *Degree requirements:* For master's, comprehensive exam (for some programs), thesis optional. *Entrance requirements:* For master's, GMAT, minimum GPA of 3.0 in last 60 hours of course work. Additional exam requirements/recommendations for international students: Required—TOEFL (minimum score 575 paper-based; 233 computer-based; 90 iBT); Recommended—IELTS (minimum score 6.5). *Application deadline:* For fall admission, 7/1 for domestic students, 5/1 for international students; for spring admission, 11/1 for domestic students, 9/1 for international students. Applications are processed on a rolling basis. Application fee: $40. Electronic applications accepted. *Expenses:* Tuition, state resident: full-time $2575.50; part-time $286.25 per credit hour. Tuition, nonresident: full-time $6510; part-time $723.50 per credit hour. Tuition and fees vary according to course load. *Financial support:* In 2009–10, 27 research assistantships with full tuition reimbursements (averaging $8,462 per year), 16 teaching assistantships with full tuition reimbursements (averaging $10,037 per year) were awarded; Federal Work-Study, institutionally sponsored loans, scholarships/grants, and unspecified assistantships also available. Financial award application deadline: 4/1; financial award applicants required to submit FAFSA. *Unit head:* Dr. Barbara Spencer, Director, 662-325-1891, Fax: 662-325-8161, E-mail: gsbi@cobilan.msstate.edu. *Application contact:* Dr. Barbara Spencer, Director, 662-325-1891, Fax: 662-325-8161, E-mail: gsbi@cobilan.msstate.edu.

Missouri State University, Graduate College, Interdisciplinary Program in Administrative Studies, Springfield, MO 65897. Offers applied communication (MS); criminal justice (MS); environmental management (MS); project management (MS); sports management (MS). Part-time and evening/weekend programs available. Postbaccalaureate distance learning degree programs offered (no on-campus study). *Students:* 17 full-time (11 women), 60 part-time (26 women); includes 6 minority (4 African Americans, 1 Asian American or Pacific Islander, 1 Hispanic American), 2 international. Average age 35. 24 applicants, 100% accepted, 19 enrolled. In 2009, 16 master's awarded. *Degree requirements:* For master's, comprehensive exam, thesis or alternative. *Entrance requirements:* For master's, GRE, GMAT, 3 years of work experience. Additional exam requirements/recommendations for international students: Required—TOEFL (minimum score 550 paper-based; 213 computer-based; 79 iBT). *Application deadline:* For fall admission, 7/20 priority date for domestic students; for spring admission, 12/20 priority date for domestic students. Applications are processed on a rolling basis. Application fee: $35 ($50 for international students). Electronic applications accepted. *Expenses:* Tuition, state resident: full-time $3852; part-time $214 per credit hour. Tuition, nonresident: full-time $7524; part-time $418 per credit hour. Required fees: $696; $172 per semester. Tuition and fees vary according to course level, course load, degree level and program. *Financial support:* In 2009–10, 1 teaching assistantship with full tuition reimbursement (averaging $7,340 per year) was awarded; career-related internships or fieldwork, Federal Work-Study, institutionally sponsored loans, scholarships/grants, and unspecified assistantships also available. Support available to part-time students. Financial award application deadline: 3/31; financial

award applicants required to submit FAFSA. *Unit head:* John Bourhis, Director, 417-836-6390, E-mail: johnbourhis@missouristate.edu. *Application contact:* Eric Eckert, Coordinator of Graduate Admissions and Recruitment, 417-836-5331, Fax: 417-836-6200, E-mail: ericeckert@missouristate.edu.

Montana Tech of The University of Montana, Graduate School, Project Engineering and Management Program, Butte, MT 59701-8997. Offers MPEM. Part-time and evening/weekend programs available. Postbaccalaureate distance learning degree programs offered (no on-campus study). *Faculty:* 1 full-time (0 women), 7 part-time/adjunct (1 woman). *Students:* 15 part-time (6 women); includes 2 minority (both American Indian/Alaska Native). 10 applicants, 50% accepted, 3 enrolled. In 2009, 3 master's awarded. *Degree requirements:* For master's, comprehensive exam, final project presentation. *Entrance requirements:* For master's, minimum GPA of 3.0. Additional exam requirements/recommendations for international students: Required—TOEFL (minimum score 550 paper-based; 213 computer-based; 71 iBT). *Application deadline:* For fall admission, 4/1 priority date for domestic students, 3/1 priority date for international students; for spring admission, 10/1 priority date for domestic students, 7/1 priority date for international students. Applications are processed on a rolling basis. Application fee: $30. Electronic applications accepted. *Expenses:* Tuition, state resident: full-time $5068; part-time $319 per credit. Tuition, nonresident: full-time $14,815; part-time $875 per credit. Tuition and fees vary according to course load and campus/location. *Financial support:* Application deadline: 4/1. *Unit head:* Dr. Kumar Ganesan, Director, 406-496-4239, Fax: 406-496-4650, E-mail: kganesan@mtech.edu. *Application contact:* Cindy Dunstan, Administrator, Graduate School, 406-496-4304, Fax: 406-496-4710, E-mail: cdunstan@mtech.edu.

New England College, Program in Management, Henniker, NH 03242-3293. Offers accounting (MSA); healthcare administration (MS); international relations (MA); marketing management (MS); nonprofit leadership (MS); project management (MS); strategic leadership (MS). Part-time and evening/weekend programs available. *Degree requirements:* For master's, independent research project. Electronic applications accepted.

Northern Kentucky University, Office of Graduate Programs, College of Business, Program in Business Administration, Highland Heights, KY 41099. Offers business administration (MBA); entrepreneurship (Certificate); finance (Certificate); international business (Certificate); marketing (Certificate); project management (Certificate); JD/MBA. *Accreditation:* AACSB. Part-time and evening/weekend programs available. *Students:* 33 full-time (16 women), 155 part-time (63 women); includes 16 minority (9 African Americans, 7 Asian Americans or Pacific Islanders), 7 international. Average age 30. 105 applicants, 65% accepted, 34 enrolled. In 2009, 42 master's, 31 other advanced degrees awarded. *Degree requirements:* For master's, thesis optional. *Entrance requirements:* For master's, GMAT (minimum score 450), minimum GPA of 2.5. Additional exam requirements/recommendations for international students: Required—TOEFL (minimum score 550 paper-based; 213 computer-based; 79 iBT); Recommended—IELTS (minimum score 6.5). *Application deadline:* For fall admission, 8/1 priority date for domestic students, 6/1 priority date for international students; for spring admission, 12/1 priority date for domestic students, 10/1 priority date for international students. Applications are processed on a rolling basis. Application fee: $40. Electronic applications accepted. *Expenses:* Tuition, state resident: full-time $6912; part-time $384 per credit hour. Tuition, nonresident: full-time $12,150; part-time $675 per credit hour. Tuition and fees vary according to course load, program and reciprocity agreements. *Financial support:* Unspecified assistantships available. Financial award applicants required to submit FAFSA. *Unit head:* James Bast, Director of MBA Programs, 859-572-7695, Fax: 859-572-7694, E-mail: mbusiness@nku.edu. *Application contact:* Dr. Peg Griffin, Director of Graduate Programs, 859-572-6934, Fax: 859-572-6670, E-mail: griffinp@nku.edu.

Northwestern University, McCormick School of Engineering and Applied Science, Department of Civil and Environmental Engineering, Program in Project Management, Evanston, IL 60208. Offers MS. Part-time programs available. *Faculty:* 2 full-time (0 women), 22 part-time/adjunct (5 women). *Students:* 35 full-time (9 women), 17 part-time (2 women); includes 9 minority (3 African Americans, 4 Asian Americans or Pacific Islanders, 2 Hispanic Americans), 8 international. 55 applicants, 87% accepted, 30 enrolled. In 2009, 23 master's awarded. *Degree requirements:* For master's, capstone report. *Entrance requirements:* Additional exam requirements/recommendations for international students: Required—TOEFL (minimum score 560 paper-based; 220 computer-based). *Application deadline:* For fall admission, 8/15 for domestic students, 6/15 for international students; for winter admission, 11/15 for domestic students, 9/15 for international students; for spring admission, 2/15 for domestic students, 12/15 for international students. Applications are processed on a rolling basis. Application fee: $50. Electronic applications accepted. *Faculty research:* Construction management, environmental management, infrastructure management. *Unit head:* Prof. Raymond J. Krizek, Director, 847-491-4040, Fax: 847-491-4011, E-mail: rjkrizek@northwestern.edu. *Application contact:* Prof. Ahmad Hadavi, Associate Director, 847-467-3219, Fax: 847-491-4011, E-mail: a-hadavi@northwestern.edu.

Northwestern University, School of Continuing Studies, Program in Information Systems, Evanston, IL 60208. Offers database and Internet technologies (MS); information systems management (MS); information systems security (MS); software project management and development (MS).

Polytechnic Institute of NYU, Department of Technology Management, Brooklyn, NY 11201-2990. Offers construction management (Advanced Certificate); electronic business management (Advanced Certificate); entrepreneurship (Advanced Certificate); human resources management (Advanced Certificate); information management (Advanced Certificate); management (MS); management of technology (MS); organizational behavior (MS, Advanced Certificate); project management (Advanced Certificate); technology management (MBA, PhD, Advanced Certificate); telecommunications and information management (MS); telecommunications management (Advanced Certificate). Part-time and evening/weekend programs available. *Faculty:* 5 full-time (1 woman), 26 part-time/adjunct (3 women). *Students:* 272 full-time (111 women), 103 part-time (41 women); includes 64 minority (20 African Americans, 1 American Indian/Alaska Native, 34 Asian Americans or Pacific Islanders, 9 Hispanic Americans), 193 international. Average age 30. 518 applicants, 57% accepted, 135 enrolled. In 2009, 148 master's awarded. *Degree requirements:* For master's, comprehensive exam (for some programs), thesis (for some programs); for doctorate, comprehensive exam, thesis/dissertation. *Entrance requirements:* For master's, GMAT, minimum B average in undergraduate course work. Additional exam requirements/recommendations for international students: Required—TOEFL (minimum score 550 paper-based; 213 computer-based; 80 iBT); Recommended—IELTS (minimum score 6.5). *Application deadline:* For fall admission, 7/31 priority date for domestic students, 4/30 priority date for international students; for spring admission, 12/31 priority date for domestic students, 11/30 priority date for international students. Applications are processed on a rolling basis. Application fee: $75. Electronic applications accepted. *Expenses:* Tuition: Full-time $21,492; part-time $1194 per credit hour. Required fees: $1160; $204 per course. *Financial support:* In 2009–10, 1 fellowship (averaging $26,400 per year) was awarded; research assistantships, teaching assistantships, institutionally sponsored loans, scholarships/grants, and unspecified assistantships also available. Support available to part-time students. *Unit head:* Prof. Bharadwaj Rao, Head, 718-260-3617, Fax: 718-260-3874, E-mail: brao@poly.edu. *Application contact:* JeanCarlo Bonilla, Director of Graduate Enrollment Management, 718-260-3182, Fax: 718-260-3624, E-mail: gradinfo@poly.edu.

Queen's University at Kingston, Queens School of Business, Program in Business Administration, Kingston, ON K7L 3N6, Canada. Offers consulting and project management (MBA); finance (MBA); innovation and entrepreneurship (MBA); marketing (MBA). *Accreditation:* AACSB. *Degree requirements:* For master's, thesis optional, research project. *Entrance requirements:* For master's, GMAT, minimum B+ average. Additional exam requirements/recommendations for international students: Required—TOEFL. Electronic applications accepted. *Faculty research:* Management fundamentals, strategic thinking, global business, innovation and change, leadership.

Regis University, College for Professional Studies, School of Management, Denver, CO 80221-1099. Offers accounting (MS); business administration (MBA); computer information technology (MSOL); executive internal management (Certificate); executive leadership (Certificate); finance (MBA); finance and accounting (MBA); human resource management (MSOL); international business (MBA); marketing (MBA); operations management (MBA); organization leadership (MS); organizational leadership (MSOL); project leadership and management (MSOL, Certificate); project management (Certificate); strategic business (Certificate); strategic human resource (Certificate); technical management (Certificate). Offered at Colorado Springs Campus, Northwest Denver Campus, Southeast Denver Campus, Fort Collins Campus, Broomfield Campus, Henderson (Nevada) Campus, and Summerlin (Nevada) Campus and online. Part-time and evening/weekend programs available. Postbaccalaureate distance learning degree programs offered (no on-campus study). *Degree requirements:* For master's, thesis optional, capstone project. *Entrance requirements:* For master's, GMAT or essays, interview, 2 years of full-time business work experience, resume; for Certificate, GMAT. Additional exam requirements/recommendations for international students: Required—TOEFL, TOEFL or university-based test; Recommended—TWE (minimum score 5). Electronic applications accepted. *Faculty research:* Impact of Info Technology on Small Business Regulation of Accounting, International Project financing, Mineral Development, Delivery of Healthcare to rural indigenos communities.

Robert Morris University, Graduate Studies, School of Communications and Information Systems, Moon Township, PA 15108-1189. Offers communication and information systems (MS); competitive intelligence systems (MS); information security and assurance (MS); information systems and communications (D Sc); information systems management (MS); information technology project management (MS); Internet information systems (MS); organizational studies (MS). Part-time and evening/weekend programs available. *Faculty:* 28 full-time (9 women), 9 part-time/adjunct (3 women). *Students:* 257 part-time (76 women); includes 41 minority (31 African Americans, 8 Asian Americans or Pacific Islanders, 2 Hispanic Americans), 16 international. Average age 33. 106 applicants, 100% accepted, 106 enrolled. In 2009, 84 master's, 8 doctorates awarded. *Degree requirements:* For doctorate, thesis/dissertation. *Entrance requirements:* For doctorate, employer letter of endorsement, interview. Additional exam requirements/recommendations for international students: Required—TOEFL (minimum score 550 paper-based; 213 computer-based; 79 iBT). *Application deadline:* For fall admission, 7/1 priority date for domestic and international students; for spring admission, 11/1 priority date for domestic and international students. Applications are processed on a rolling basis. Application fee: $35. Electronic applications accepted. *Expenses:* Contact institution. *Financial support:* Research assistantships with partial tuition reimbursements, institutionally sponsored loans and unspecified assistantships available. Support available to part-time students. Financial award application deadline: 5/1. *Unit head:* Dr. Barbara J. Levine, Dean, 412-397-2591, Fax: 412-397-2481, E-mail: levine@rmu.edu. *Application contact:* Deborah Roach, Assistant Dean, Graduate Admissions, 412-397-5200, Fax: 412-397-2425, E-mail: graduateadmissions@rmu.edu.

Rowan University, Graduate School, College of Engineering, Department of Civil and Environmental Engineering, Program in Project Management, Glassboro, NJ 08028-1701. Offers MS. *Students:* 50 part-time (14 women); includes 7 minority (1 African American, 4 Asian Americans or Pacific Islanders, 2 Hispanic Americans). Average age 28. 15 applicants, 100% accepted, 12 enrolled. *Entrance requirements:* For master's, GRE General Test. Additional exam requirements/recommendations for international students: Required—TOEFL. *Application deadline:* Applications are processed on a rolling basis. Application fee: $50. Electronic applications accepted. *Expenses:* Tuition, state resident: full-time $10,624; part-time $590 per semester hour. Tuition, nonresident: full-time $10,624; part-time $590 per semester hour. Required fees: $2320; $125 per semester hour. *Unit head:* Kauser Jahan, Chair, 856-256-5323, E-mail: jahan@rowan.edu. *Application contact:* Dr. Ralph Dusseau, Program Adviser, 856-256-5332.

Royal Roads University, Graduate Studies, Applied Leadership and Management Program, Victoria, BC V9B 5Y2, Canada. Offers executive coaching (Graduate Certificate); health systems leadership (Graduate Certificate); project management (Graduate Certificate); public relations management (Graduate Certificate); strategic human resources management (Graduate Certificate).

St. Edward's University, School of Management and Business, Program in Project Management, Austin, TX 78704. Offers MS. Part-time and evening/weekend programs available. *Students:* 30 part-time (12 women); includes 16 minority (4 African Americans, 2 Asian Americans or Pacific Islanders, 10 Hispanic Americans). Average age 37. 17 applicants, 71% accepted, 9 enrolled. In 2009, 10 master's awarded. *Degree requirements:* For master's, minimum of 24 resident hours. *Entrance requirements:* For master's, GMAT or GRE General Test, minimum GPA of 2.75 in last 60 hours of course work. Additional exam requirements/recommendations for international students: Required—TOEFL (minimum score 550 paper-based; 213 computer-based; 79 iBT) or IELTS (minimum score 6). *Application deadline:* For fall admission, 7/1 for domestic and international students; for spring admission, 11/1 for domestic and international students. Applications are processed on a rolling basis. Application fee: $45 ($50 for international students). Electronic applications accepted. *Expenses:* Tuition: Full-time $14,922; part-time $829 per credit hour. Required fees: $50 per trimester. Full-time tuition and fees vary according to course load and program. *Financial support:* Scholarships/grants available. *Unit head:* Dr. John S. Loucks, Director, 512-448-8630, Fax: 512-448-8492, E-mail: johnsl@stedwards.edu. *Application contact:* Benjamin Jimenez, Graduate Admissions Coordinator, 512-233-1694, Fax: 512-428-1032, E-mail: benjij@stedwards.edu.

Saint Mary's University of Minnesota, Schools of Graduate and Professional Programs, Graduate School of Business and Technology, Project Management Program, Winona, MN 55987-1399. Offers MS, Certificate. *Unit head:* Dr. Gerald Ellis, Director, 612-728-5178, E-mail: gellis@smumn.edu. *Application contact:* Yasin Alsaidi, Director of Admissions for Graduate and Professional Programs, 612-728-5207, Fax: 612-728-5121, E-mail: yalsaidi@smumn.edu.

Southern Illinois University Edwardsville, Graduate Studies and Research, School of Business, Program in Business Administration, Edwardsville, IL 62026-0001. Offers management information systems (MBA); project management (MBA). *Accreditation:* AACSB. Part-time and evening/weekend programs available. *Students:* 27 full-time (16 women), 120 part-time (45 women); includes 7 minority (all African Americans), 7 international. Average age 26. 124 applicants, 43% accepted. In 2009, 95 master's awarded. *Degree requirements:* For master's, thesis or alternative, final exam. *Entrance requirements:* For master's, GMAT. Additional exam requirements/recommendations for international students: Required—TOEFL (minimum score 550 paper-based; 213 computer-based; 79 iBT), IELTS (minimum score 6.5). *Application deadline:* For fall admission, 7/23 for domestic students, 6/1 for international students; for spring admission, 12/11 for domestic students, 10/1 for international students. Applications are processed on a rolling basis. Application fee: $30. Electronic applications accepted. *Expenses:* Tuition, state resident: part-time $1252.50 per semester. Tuition, nonresident: part-time $3131.25 per semester. Required fees: $586.85 per semester. Tuition and fees vary according to course load. *Financial support:* In 2009–10, 15 teaching assistantships with full tuition reimbursements (averaging $8,064 per year) were awarded; fellowships with full tuition reimbursements, research assistantships with full tuition reimbursements, career-related internships or fieldwork, Federal Work-Study, institutionally sponsored loans, scholarships/grants, traineeships, and unspecified assistantships also available. Support available to part-time students. Financial award application deadline: 3/1; financial award applicants required to submit FAFSA. *Unit head:* Dr. Janice Joplin, Director, 618-650-2485, E-mail: jjoplin@siue.edu. *Application contact:* Dr. Janice Joplin, Director, 618-650-2485, E-mail: jjoplin@siue.edu.

Southern New Hampshire University, School of Business, Manchester, NH 03106-1045. Offers accounting (MS); business administration (MBA, Certificate), including accounting (Certificate), business administration (MBA), finance (Certificate), forensic accounting (Certificate), human resources management (Certificate), international business (Certificate), international sport management (Certificate), leadership of not for profit organizations

Project Management

Southern New Hampshire University (continued)
(Certificate), marketing (Certificate), operations management (Certificate), sport management (Certificate), taxation (Certificate); finance (MS); hospitality and tourism leadership (Certificate); information technology (MS, Certificate); information technology/international business (Certificate); integrated marketing communications (Certificate); international business (MS, DBA); marketing (MS); operations and project management (MS); organizational leadership (MS); project management (Certificate); sport management (MS); MBA/Certificate. *Accreditation:* ACBSP. Part-time and evening/weekend programs available. Postbaccalaureate distance learning degree programs offered (no on-campus study). Terminal master's awarded for partial completion of doctoral program. *Degree requirements:* For master's, one foreign language, comprehensive exam (for some programs), thesis or alternative; for doctorate, one foreign language, comprehensive exam, thesis/dissertation. *Entrance requirements:* For master's, minimum GPA of 2.5; for doctorate, GMAT. Additional exam requirements/recommendations for international students: Required—TOEFL (minimum score 500 paper-based). Electronic applications accepted.

Stevens Institute of Technology, Graduate School, Wesley J. Howe School of Technology Management, Program in Business Administration, Hoboken, NJ 07030. Offers engineering management (MBA); financial engineering (MBA); information management (MBA); information technology in financial services (MBA); information technology in the pharmaceutical industry (MBA); information technology outsourcing (MBA); pharmaceutical management (MBA); project management (MBA); technology management (MBA); telecommunications management (MBA). *Expenses:* Tuition: Full-time $9900; part-time $1100 per credit. Required fees: $286 per semester.

Stevens Institute of Technology, Graduate School, Wesley J. Howe School of Technology Management, Program in Information Systems, Hoboken, NJ 07030. Offers computer science (MS); e-commerce (MS); enterprise systems (MS); entrepreneurial information technology (MS); information architecture (MS); information management (MS, Certificate); information security (MS); information technology in financial services industry (MS); information technology in the pharmaceutical industry (MS); information technology outsourcing management (MS); project management (MS, Certificate); software engineering (MS); telecommunications (MS). *Degree requirements:* For master's, thesis optional. *Entrance requirements:* For master's, GMAT, GRE General Test. Additional exam requirements/recommendations for international students: Required—TOEFL. Electronic applications accepted. *Expenses:* Tuition: Full-time $9900; part-time $1100 per credit. Required fees: $286 per semester.

Stevens Institute of Technology, Graduate School, Wesley J. Howe School of Technology Management, Program in Management, Hoboken, NJ 07030. Offers general management (MS); global innovation management (MS); human resource management (MS); information management (MS); project management (MS); technology commercialization (MS); technology management (MS). Part-time programs available. *Degree requirements:* For master's, thesis optional. *Entrance requirements:* For master's, GMAT, GRE General Test. Additional exam requirements/recommendations for international students: Required—TOEFL. Electronic applications accepted. *Expenses:* Tuition: Full-time $9900; part-time $1100 per credit. Required fees: $286 per semester. *Faculty research:* Industrial economics.

TUI University, College of Business Administration, Program in Business Administration, Cypress, CA 90630. Offers business administration (PhD); conflict and negotiation management (MBA); criminal justice administration (MBA); entrepreneurship (MBA); finance (MBA); general management (MBA); government accounting (MBA); human resource management (MBA); information security and digital assurance management (MBA); information technology management (MBA); international business (MBA); logistics management (MBA); marketing (MBA); project management (MBA); public management (MBA); quality management (MBA); strategic leadership (MBA). Part-time and evening/weekend programs available. Postbaccalaureate distance learning degree programs offered (no on-campus study). *Degree requirements:* For doctorate, comprehensive exam, thesis/dissertation, defense of dissertation. *Entrance requirements:* For master's, minimum GPA of 2.5 (students with GPA 3.0 or greater may transfer up to 30% of graduate level credits); for doctorate, minimum GPA of 3.4, curriculum vitae, course work in research methods or statistics. Additional exam requirements/recommendations for international students: Required—TOEFL. Electronic applications accepted.

Universidad del Turabo, Graduate Programs, School in Business Administration, Program in Project Management, Gurabo, PR 00778-3030. Offers MBA. *Students:* 39 full-time (17 women), 33 part-time (12 women); includes 67 Hispanic Americans. Average age 33. 33 applicants, 100% accepted, 27 enrolled. In 2009, 22 master's awarded. *Unit head:* Marcelino Rivera, Dean, 787-743-7979 Ext. 4117. *Application contact:* Virginia Gonzalez, Admissions Officer, 787-746-3009.

Universidad Nacional Pedro Henriquez Urena, Graduate School, Santo Domingo, Dominican Republic. Offers administrative sciences (PhD); business administration (MBA); environmental engineering (MEE); project management (M Man, MPM); sanitation engineering (ME); veterinary medicine (DVM).

Université du Québec à Chicoutimi, Graduate Programs, Program in Project Management, Chicoutimi, QC G7H 2B1, Canada. Offers M Sc. Part-time programs available. *Entrance requirements:* For master's, appropriate bachelor's degree, proficiency in French.

Université du Québec à Montréal, Graduate Programs, Program in Project Management, Montréal, QC H3C 3P8, Canada. Offers MGP, Diploma. Part-time programs available. *Entrance requirements:* For master's and Diploma, appropriate bachelor's degree or equivalent, proficiency in French.

Université du Québec à Rimouski, Graduate Programs, Program in Project Management, Rimouski, QC G5L 3A1, Canada. Offers M Sc, Diploma. Part-time programs available. *Entrance requirements:* For master's, proficiency in French, appropriate bachelor's degree.

Université du Québec en Abitibi-Témiscamingue, Graduate Programs, Program in Project Management, Rouyn-Noranda, QC J9X 5E4, Canada. Offers M Sc, DESS. Part-time programs available. *Entrance requirements:* For master's, appropriate bachelor's degree, proficiency in French.

Université du Québec en Outaouais, Graduate Programs, Program in Project Management, Gatineau, QC J8X 3X7, Canada. Offers M Sc, MA, Diploma. Part-time programs available. *Entrance requirements:* For master's, appropriate bachelor's degree, proficiency in French.

The University of Alabama in Huntsville, School of Graduate Studies, College of Business Administration, Department of Management and Marketing, Huntsville, AL 35899. Offers management (MBA), including acquisition management, finance, human resource management, logistics and supply chain management, marketing, project management. *Accreditation:* AACSB. Part-time and evening/weekend programs available. *Faculty:* 7 full-time (1 woman), 1 part-time/adjunct (0 women). *Students:* 41 full-time (19 women), 155 part-time (59 women); includes 30 minority (15 African Americans, 5 American Indian/Alaska Native, 7 Asian Americans or Pacific Islanders, 3 Hispanic Americans), 20 international. Average age 32. 138 applicants, 63% accepted, 68 enrolled. In 2009, 38 master's awarded. *Degree requirements:* For master's, comprehensive exam, thesis or alternative. *Entrance requirements:* For master's, GMAT (minimum score 500), minimum AACSB index of 1080. Additional exam requirements/recommendations for international students: Required—TOEFL (minimum score 550 paper-based; 213 computer-based; 62 iBT). *Application deadline:* For fall admission, 8/1 for domestic students, 4/1 for international students; for spring admission, 12/1 for domestic students, 9/1 for international students. Applications are processed on a rolling basis. Application fee: $40 ($50 for international students). Electronic applications accepted. *Expenses:* Tuition, state resident: part-time $355.75 per credit hour. Tuition, nonresident: part-time $847.10 per credit hour. Required fees: $210.80 per semester. Tuition and fees vary according to course load and program. *Financial support:* In 2009–10, 3 students received support, including 2 research assistantships with full tuition reimbursements available (averaging $14,400 per year), 1 teaching assistantship with full tuition reimbursement available (averaging $11,800 per year); career-related internships or fieldwork, Federal Work-Study, institutionally sponsored loans, scholarships/grants, health care benefits, and unspecified assistantships also available. Support available to part-time students. Financial award application deadline: 4/1; financial award applicants required to submit FAFSA. *Unit head:* Dr. Brent Wren, Chair, 256-824-6408, Fax: 256-824-6328, E-mail: wrenb@uah.edu. *Application contact:* Jennifer Pettitt, Director of Graduate Programs, 256-824-6681, Fax: 256-824-7571, E-mail: jennifer.pettitt@uah.edu.

University of Alaska Anchorage, School of Engineering, Program in Project Management, Anchorage, AK 99508. Offers MS. Part-time and evening/weekend programs available. Postbaccalaureate distance learning degree programs offered (no on-campus study). *Degree requirements:* For master's, thesis or alternative, case study and research project. *Entrance requirements:* For master's, two years of project management experience. Additional exam requirements/recommendations for international students: Required—TOEFL (minimum score 550 paper-based; 213 computer-based). *Expenses:* Contact institution.

University of Atlanta, Graduate Programs, Atlanta, GA 30360. Offers business (MS); business administration (Exec MBA, MBA); computer science (MS); educational leadership (MS, Ed D); healthcare administration (MS, D Sc, Graduate Certificate); information technology for management (Graduate Certificate); international project management (Graduate Certificate); law (JD); managerial science (DBA); project management (Graduate Certificate); social science (MS). Postbaccalaureate distance learning degree programs offered. *Faculty:* 54 part-time/adjunct (10 women). *Students:* 251 full-time. *Entrance requirements:* For master's, minimum cumulative GPA of 2.5. *Expenses:* Tuition: Part-time $1000 per course. Part-time tuition and fees vary according to course load and degree level.

University of California, Berkeley, UC Berkeley Extension, Certificate Programs in Business, Berkeley, CA 94720-1500. Offers accounting (Certificate); business administration (Certificate); finance (Certificate); human resource management (Certificate); management (Certificate); marketing (Certificate); project management (Certificate). Postbaccalaureate distance learning degree programs offered. *Unit head:* Diana Wu, Dean, 510-642-4181. *Application contact:* Business, 510-642-4231, E-mail: business@unex.berkeley.edu.

University of California, Berkeley, UC Berkeley Extension, International Diploma Programs, Berkeley, CA 94720-1500. Offers business administration (Certificate); finance (Certificate); global business management (Certificate); marketing (Certificate); project management (Certificate). *Unit head:* Diana Wu, Dean, 510-642-4181. *Application contact:* International Diploma Programs, 510-642-2564, E-mail: diploma@unex.berkeley.edu.

University of Dallas, Graduate School of Management, Irving, TX 75062-4736. Offers accounting (MBA, MM, MS); business management (MBA, MM); corporate finance (MBA, MM); financial services (MBA); global business (MBA, MM); health services management (MBA, MM); human resource management (MBA, MM); information assurance (MBA, MM, MS); information technology (MBA, MM, MS); information technology service management (MBA, MM, MS); marketing management (MBA, MM); organization development (MBA, MM); project management (MBA, MM); sports and entertainment management (MBA, MM); strategic leadership (MBA, MM); supply chain management (MBA); supply chain management and market logistics (MM). *Accreditation:* ACBSP. Part-time and evening/weekend programs available. Postbaccalaureate distance learning degree programs offered (no on-campus study). *Faculty:* 25 full-time (6 women), 31 part-time/adjunct (6 women). *Students:* 232 full-time (95 women), 923 part-time (365 women); includes 462 minority (184 African Americans, 14 American Indian/Alaska Native, 153 Asian Americans or Pacific Islanders, 111 Hispanic Americans), 184 international. Average age 34. 474 applicants, 85% accepted, 237 enrolled. In 2009, 399 master's awarded. *Entrance requirements:* Additional exam requirements/recommendations for international students: Required—TOEFL. *Application deadline:* Applications are processed on a rolling basis. Application fee: $50. Electronic applications accepted. *Expenses:* Contact institution. *Financial support:* In 2009–10, 399 students received support. Scholarships/grants and unspecified assistantships available. Financial award application deadline: 2/15; financial award applicants required to submit FAFSA. *Unit head:* Alounda Joseph, Director of Enrollment Processes, 972-721-5356, E-mail: admiss@gsm.udallas.edu. *Application contact:* Alounda Joseph, Director of Enrollment Processes, 972-721-5356, E-mail: admiss@gsm.udallas.edu.

University of Denver, University College, Denver, CO 80208. Offers applied communication (MAS, MPS, Certificate); computer information systems (MAS, Certificate); environmental policy and management (MAS, Certificate); geographic information systems (MAS, Certificate); human resource administration (MPS, Certificate); knowledge and information technologies (MAS); liberal studies (MLS, Certificate); modern languages (MLS, Certificate); organizational leadership (MPS, Certificate); security management (Certificate); technology management (MAS, Certificate), including 21st century strategic management (MAS), international markets (MAS), project management (MAS), research and development management (MAS); telecommunications (MAS, Certificate), including broadband (MAS), telecommunications management and policy (MAS), telecommunications technology (MAS), wireless networks (MAS). Part-time and evening/weekend programs available. Postbaccalaureate distance learning degree programs offered (no on-campus study). *Faculty:* 160 part-time/adjunct (64 women). *Students:* 53 full-time (25 women), 984 part-time (551 women); includes 171 minority (72 African Americans, 10 American Indian/Alaska Native, 33 Asian Americans or Pacific Islanders, 56 Hispanic Americans), 75 international. Average age 36. 537 applicants, 96% accepted, 494 enrolled. In 2009, 229 master's, 109 Certificates awarded. *Entrance requirements:* Additional exam requirements/recommendations for international students: Required—TOEFL (minimum score 550 paper-based; 213 computer-based). *Application deadline:* Applications are processed on a rolling basis. Application fee: $75. Electronic applications accepted. *Expenses:* Contact institution. *Financial support:* Applicants required to submit FAFSA. *Unit head:* Dr. James Davis, Dean, 303-871-2291, Fax: 303-871-4047, E-mail: jdavis@du.edu. *Application contact:* Information Contact, 303-871-3155.

University of Houston, College of Technology, Department of Information and Logistics Technology, Houston, TX 77204. Offers technology project management (MS), including information systems security, logistics. Part-time and evening/weekend programs available. *Faculty:* 6 full-time (3 women), 6 part-time/adjunct (2 women). *Students:* 59 full-time (18 women), 47 part-time (15 women); includes 18 minority (6 African Americans, 5 Asian Americans or Pacific Islanders, 7 Hispanic Americans), 58 international. Average age 29. 69 applicants, 87% accepted, 33 enrolled. In 2009, 25 master's awarded. *Degree requirements:* For master's, project or thesis (most programs). *Entrance requirements:* For master's, GMAT. Additional exam requirements/recommendations for international students: Required—TOEFL (minimum score 550 paper-based; 79 iBT). *Application deadline:* For fall admission, 7/1 for domestic students, 4/1 for international students; for spring admission, 12/1 for domestic students, 10/1 for international students. Applications are processed on a rolling basis. Application fee: $75 ($150 for international students). Electronic applications accepted. *Expenses:* Tuition, state resident: full-time $7676; part-time $320 per credit hour. Tuition, nonresident: full-time $14,324; part-time $597 per credit hour. Required fees: $3034. *Financial support:* In 2009–10, 11 fellowships with full tuition reimbursements (averaging $10,500 per year), 1 research assistantship with full tuition reimbursement (averaging $10,500 per year), 4 teaching assistantships with full tuition reimbursements (averaging $10,500 per year) were awarded. *Unit head:* Michael Gibson, Chairperson, 713-743-5116, E-mail: mlgibson@uh.edu. *Application contact:* Tiffany Roosa, Graduate Advisor, 713-743-2987, Fax: 713-743-4151, E-mail: troosa@uh.edu.

University of Management and Technology, Program in Business Administration, Arlington, VA 22209. Offers acquisition management (DBA); general management (MBA, DBA); project management (MBA, DBA). Part-time and evening/weekend programs available. Postbaccalaureate distance learning degree programs offered (no on-campus study). *Degree requirements:* For master's, comprehensive exam. *Entrance requirements:* For master's, 3 recommendations, resume. Additional exam requirements/recommendations for international students: Required—TOEFL (minimum score 550 paper-based; 213 computer-based). Electronic applications accepted.

University of Management and Technology, Program in Computer Science and Information Technology, Arlington, VA 22209. Offers computer science (MS); information technology (AC); information technology project management (MS); management information systems (MS); project management (AC); software engineering (MS). Part-time and evening/weekend programs available. Postbaccalaureate distance learning degree programs offered (no on-campus study). *Entrance requirements:* For master's, 3 recommendations, resume. Additional exam requirements/recommendations for international students: Required—TOEFL (minimum score 550 paper-based; 213 computer-based). Electronic applications accepted.

University of Management and Technology, Program in Management, Arlington, VA 22209. Offers acquisition management (MS, AC); general management (MS); project management (MS, AC); public administration (MPA, MS, AC). Part-time and evening/weekend programs available. Postbaccalaureate distance learning degree programs offered (no on-campus study). *Entrance requirements:* For master's, 3 recommendations, resume. Additional exam requirements/recommendations for international students: Required—TOEFL (minimum score 550 paper-based; 213 computer-based). Electronic applications accepted.

University of Mary, Gary Tharaldson School of Business, Bismarck, ND 58504-9652. Offers health care (MBA); human resource management (MBA); management (MBA); project management (MPM); strategic leadership (MSSL). Part-time and evening/weekend programs available. *Degree requirements:* For master's, strategic planning seminar. *Entrance requirements:* For master's, minimum GPA of 2.5. Additional exam requirements/recommendations for international students: Required—TOEFL. *Expenses:* Tuition: Full-time $10,062; part-time $430 per credit. Tuition and fees vary according to course load, degree level, program and student level.

University of Ottawa, Faculty of Graduate and Postdoctoral Studies, Faculty of Engineering, Engineering Management Program, Ottawa, ON K1N 6N5, Canada. Offers engineering management (M Eng); information technology (Certificate); project management (Certificate). *Degree requirements:* For master's, thesis or alternative. *Entrance requirements:* For master's and Certificate, honors degree or equivalent, minimum B average. Electronic applications accepted.

University of San Francisco, School of Business and Professional Studies, Program in Project Management, San Francisco, CA 94117-1080. Offers MS. *Faculty:* 1 (woman) full-time, 5 part-time/adjunct (3 women). *Students:* 44 full-time (23 women); includes 20 minority (5 African Americans, 1 American Indian/Alaska Native, 9 Asian Americans or Pacific Islanders, 5 Hispanic Americans), 2 international. Average age 37. 48 applicants, 77% accepted, 27 enrolled. In 2009, 26 master's awarded. *Expenses:* Tuition: Full-time $19,710; part-time $1095 per unit. Part-time tuition and fees vary according to degree level, campus/location and program. *Financial support:* In 2009–10, 27 students received support. *Unit head:* Dr. Linda Henderson, Director, 415-422-2592. *Application contact:* Dr. Linda Henderson, Director, 415-422-2592.

The University of Tennessee at Chattanooga, Graduate School, College of Engineering and Computer Science, Program in Engineering Management, Chattanooga, TN 37403. Offers engineering management (MS); fundamentals of engineering management (Graduate Certificate); power systems management (Graduate Certificate); project and value management (Graduate Certificate); quality management (Graduate Certificate). Postbaccalaureate distance learning degree programs offered (no on-campus study). *Faculty:* 4 full-time (1 woman). *Students:* 22 full-time (7 women), 69 part-time (11 women); includes 25 minority (12 African Americans, 9 Asian Americans or Pacific Islanders, 4 Hispanic Americans), 12 international. Average age 33. 46 applicants, 67% accepted, 24 enrolled. In 2009, 25 master's, 8 other advanced degrees awarded. *Degree requirements:* For master's, thesis. *Entrance requirements:* For master's, GRE General Test, letters of recommendation; minimum undergraduate GPA of 2.5 overall or 3.0 in senior year. Additional exam requirements/recommendations for international students: Required—TOEFL (minimum score 550 paper-based; 213 computer-based; 79 iBT), IELTS (minimum score 6). *Application deadline:* For fall admission, 8/1 priority date for domestic students, 6/1 for international students; for spring admission, 12/1 priority date for domestic students, 10/1 for international students. Applications are processed on a rolling basis. Application fee: $35. Electronic applications accepted. *Expenses:* Tuition, state resident: full-time $5404; part-time $300 per credit hour. Tuition, nonresident: full-time $16,702; part-time $928 per credit hour. Required fees: $1150; $130 per credit hour. *Financial support:* In 2009–10, 5 research assistantships with full and partial tuition reimbursements (averaging $5,500 per year) were awarded; career-related internships or fieldwork, scholarships/grants, and unspecified assistantships also available. Support available to part-time students. *Faculty research:* Plant layout design, lean manufacturing, six sigma, value management, product development. *Unit head:* Dr. Neslihan Alp, Director, 423-425-4032, Fax: 423-425-5229, E-mail: neslihan-alp@utc.edu. *Application contact:* Dr. Stephanie Bellar, Dean of Graduate Studies, 423-425-4666, Fax: 423-425-5223, E-mail: stephanie-bellar@utc.edu.

The University of Texas at Dallas, School of Management, Program in Business Administration, Richardson, TX 75080. Offers cohort (MBA); executive business administration (EMBA); global leadership (EMBA); global online (MBA); healthcare management (EMBA); professional business administration (MBA); project management (EMBA). *Accreditation:* AACSB. Part-time and evening/weekend programs available. Postbaccalaureate distance learning degree programs offered. *Faculty:* 79 full-time (13 women), 29 part-time/adjunct (9 women). *Students:* 314 full-time (104 women), 857 part-time (244 women); includes 377 minority (52 African Americans, 5 American Indian/Alaska Native, 231 Asian Americans or Pacific Islanders, 89 Hispanic Americans), 211 international. Average age 32. 712 applicants, 48% accepted, 317 enrolled. In 2009, 409 master's awarded. *Degree requirements:* For master's, thesis optional. *Entrance requirements:* For master's, GMAT, 10 years of business experience (EMBA), minimum GPA of 3.0. Additional exam requirements/recommendations for international students: Required—TOEFL (minimum score 550 paper-based; 213 computer-based). *Application deadline:* For fall admission, 7/15 for domestic students, 5/1 priority date for international students; for spring admission, 11/15 for domestic students, 9/1 priority date for international students. Applications are processed on a rolling basis. Application fee: $50 ($100 for international students). Electronic applications accepted. *Expenses:* Contact institution. *Financial support:* In 2009–10, 5 research assistantships with full tuition reimbursements (averaging $10,692 per year), 23 teaching assistantships with full tuition reimbursements (averaging $10,050 per year) were awarded; fellowships, career-related internships or fieldwork, Federal Work-Study, institutionally sponsored loans, scholarships/grants, and unspecified assistantships also available. Support available to part-time students. Financial award application deadline: 4/30; financial award applicants required to submit FAFSA. *Faculty research:* Production scheduling, trade and finance, organizational decision making, life/work planning. *Unit head:* Lisa Shatz, Director, 972-883-6191, E-mail: mba@utdallas.edu. *Application contact:* James Parker, Assistant Director, 972-883-5842, E-mail: jparker@utdallas.edu.

University of the Incarnate Word, School of Graduate Studies and Research, H-E-B School of Business and Administration, Programs in Administration, San Antonio, TX 78209-6397. Offers adult education (MAA); applied administration (MAA); communication arts (MAA); healthcare administration (MAA); instructional technology (MAA); international business (Certificate); nutrition (MAA); organizational development (MAA, Certificate); project management (Certificate); sports management (MAA). Part-time and evening/weekend programs available. Postbaccalaureate distance learning degree programs offered (no on-campus study). *Students:* 30 full-time (17 women), 163 part-time (114 women); includes 128 minority (18 African Americans, 3 Asian Americans or Pacific Islanders, 107 Hispanic Americans), 8 international. Average age 35. In 2009, 68 master's awarded. *Degree requirements:* For master's, capstone. *Entrance requirements:* For master's, GRE, GMAT, undergraduate degree, minimum GPA of 2.5. Additional exam requirements/recommendations for international students: Required—TOEFL (minimum score 560 paper-based; 220 computer-based; 83 iBT). *Application deadline:* Applications are processed on a rolling basis. Application fee: $20. Electronic applications accepted. *Expenses:* Tuition: Full-time $12,150; part-time $675 per credit hour. Required fees: $83 per credit hour. *Financial support:* Federal Work-Study and scholarships/grants available. Financial award applicants required to submit FAFSA. *Unit head:* Dr. Daniel Dominguez, MAA Director, 210-829-3180, Fax: 210-805-3564, E-mail: domingue@uiwtx.edu. *Application contact:* Andrea Cyterski-Acosta, Dean of Enrollment, 210-829-6005, Fax: 210-829-3921, E-mail: admis@uiwtx.edu.

University of Wisconsin–Platteville, School of Graduate Studies, Distance Learning Center, Online Master of Science in Project Management Program, Platteville, WI 53818-3099. Offers MS. Part-time and evening/weekend programs available. Postbaccalaureate distance learning degree programs offered (no on-campus study). *Students:* 8 full-time (1 woman), 187 part-time (60 women); includes 19 minority (10 African Americans, 1 American Indian/Alaska Native, 3 Asian Americans or Pacific Islanders, 5 Hispanic Americans), 27 international. 43 applicants, 100% accepted, 43 enrolled. In 2009, 50 master's awarded. *Degree requirements:* For master's, thesis or alternative. *Entrance requirements:* Additional exam requirements/recommendations for international students: Required—TOEFL (minimum score 500 paper-based; 173 computer-based; 61 iBT). *Application deadline:* For fall admission, 7/1 priority date for domestic students; for spring admission, 11/1 priority date for domestic students. Applications are processed on a rolling basis. Application fee: $56. Electronic applications accepted. *Expenses:* Tuition, state resident: full-time $6706. Tuition, nonresident: full-time $16,772. *Unit head:* William Haskins, Coordinator, 608-342-1961, Fax: 608-342-1466, E-mail: haskinsd@uwplatt.edu. *Application contact:* William Haskins, Coordinator, 608-342-1961, Fax: 608-342-1466, E-mail: haskinsd@uwplatt.edu.

Walden University, Graduate Programs, NTU School of Engineering and Applied Science, Minneapolis, MN 55401. Offers competitive product management (Postbaccalaureate Certificate); engineering management (Postbaccalaureate Certificate); software engineering (MS); software project management (Postbaccalaureate Certificate); software testing (Postbaccalaureate Certificate); systems engineering (MS, Postbaccalaureate Certificate); technical project management (Postbaccalaureate Certificate). Part-time and evening/weekend programs available. Postbaccalaureate distance learning degree programs offered (no on-campus study). *Faculty:* 31 part-time/adjunct. *Students:* 22 full-time (6 women), 120 part-time (14 women); includes 26 minority (19 African Americans, 7 Asian Americans or Pacific Islanders). Average age 38. In 2009, 41 master's awarded. *Degree requirements:* For master's, thesis optional. *Entrance requirements:* For master's, bachelor's degree or equivalent in related field, minimum GPA of 2.5. Additional exam requirements/recommendations for international students: Required—TOEFL (minimum score 550 paper-based; 213 computer-based), IELTS (minimum score 6.5), or Michigan English Language Assessment Battery (minimum score 82). *Application deadline:* Applications are processed on a rolling basis. Application fee: $50. Electronic applications accepted. *Expenses:* Tuition: Full-time $13,665; part-time $560 per credit. Required fees: $1375. Tuition and fees vary according to course load, degree level and program. *Financial support:* Fellowships, Federal Work-Study, scholarships/grants, unspecified assistantships, and family tuition reduction, active duty/veteran tuition reduction, group tuition reduction, interest-free payment plans available. Support available to part-time students. Financial award applicants required to submit FAFSA. *Unit head:* Colin Wightman, Interim Associate Dean, 800-925-3368. *Application contact:* Jennifer Hall, Director of Enrollment, 866-4-WALDEN, E-mail: info@walden.edu.

Walden University, Graduate Programs, School of Management, Minneapolis, MN 55401. Offers applied management and decision sciences (PhD), including accounting, engineering management, finance, general applied management and decision sciences, information systems management, knowledge management, leadership and organizational change, learning management, operations research, self-designed program in applied management and design sciences; business information management (MISM); enterprise information security (MISM); entrepreneurship (MBA, DBA); finance (MBA, DBA); global supply chain management (DBA); healthcare management (MBA); healthcare system improvement (MBA); human resource management (MBA); information systems management (DBA); international business (MBA, DBA); IT strategy and governance (MISM); leadership (MBA, MS, DBA), including entrepreneurship (MS), general management (MS), human resources leadership (MS), innovation and technology (MS), leader development (MS), project management (MS), self-designed (MS), sustainable futures (MS); managing global software and service supply chains (MISM); marketing (MBA, DBA); project management (MBA, MS); risk management (MBA); self-designed (MBA, DBA); social impact management (DBA); sustainable futures (MBA); technology (MBA); technology entrepreneurship (DBA). Part-time and evening/weekend programs available. Postbaccalaureate distance learning degree programs offered (minimal on-campus study). *Faculty:* 17 full-time, 211 part-time/adjunct. *Students:* 3,389 full-time (1,774 women), 815 part-time (482 women); includes 1,969 minority (1,640 African Americans, 36 American Indian/Alaska Native, 123 Asian Americans or Pacific Islanders, 170 Hispanic Americans), 95 international. Average age 41. In 2009, 699 master's, 42 doctorates awarded. *Degree requirements:* For doctorate, thesis/dissertation (for some programs), residency. *Entrance requirements:* For master's, bachelor's degree or equivalent in related field; minimum GPA of 2.5; official transcripts; goal statement; access to computer and Internet; for doctorate, master's degree or equivalent in related field; minimum GPA of 3.0; 3 years of related professional/academic experience (preferred). Additional exam requirements/recommendations for international students: Required—TOEFL (minimum score 550 paper-based; 213 computer-based), IELTS (minimum score 6.5), TOEFL, IELTS, or Michigan English Language Assessment Battery (minimum score 82). *Application deadline:* Applications are processed on a rolling basis. Application fee: $50. Electronic applications accepted. *Expenses:* Tuition: Full-time $13,665; part-time $560 per credit. Required fees: $1375. Tuition and fees vary according to course load, degree level and program. *Financial support:* In 2009–10, 466 students received support; fellowships, Federal Work-Study, scholarships/grants, unspecified assistantships, and family tuition reduction, active duty/veteran tuition reduction, group tuition reduction, interest-free payment plans available. Support available to part-time students. Financial award applicants required to submit FAFSA. *Unit head:* William Schulz, Interim Associate Dean, 800-925-3368. *Application contact:* Jennifer Hall, Director of Enrollment, 866-4-WALDEN, E-mail: info@waldenu.edu.

Western Carolina University, Graduate School, College of Business, Program in Project Management, Cullowhee, NC 28723. Offers MPM. Part-time and evening/weekend programs available. Postbaccalaureate distance learning degree programs offered (no on-campus study). *Students:* 2 full-time (both women), 97 part-time (32 women). Average age 40. 48 applicants, 77% accepted, 32 enrolled. In 2009, 41 master's awarded. *Entrance requirements:* For master's, GMAT or GRE, work experience in project management, appropriate undergraduate degree with minimum GPA of 3.0, employer recommendation, resume. Additional exam requirements/recommendations for international students: Required—TOEFL (minimum score 550 paper-based; 270 computer-based; 79 iBT). *Application deadline:* For fall admission, 5/1 priority date for domestic students; for spring admission, 9/1 priority date for domestic students. Applications are processed on a rolling basis. Application fee: $45. *Financial support:* Fellowships, research assistantships with full and partial tuition reimbursements, teaching assistantships with full and partial tuition reimbursements, institutionally sponsored loans, scholarships/grants, and unspecified assistantships available. Financial award application deadline: 3/31; financial award applicants required to submit FAFSA. *Unit head:* Dr. Jeanne Dorle, Director, 828-227-3603, Fax: 828-227-7414, E-mail: jdorle@email.wcu.edu. *Application contact:* Admissions Specialist for Project Management, 828-227-7398, Fax: 828-227-7480, E-mail: gradsch@email.wcu.edu.

Winthrop University, College of Business Administration, Program in Software Project Management, Rock Hill, SC 29733. Offers software development (MS); software project management (Certificate). *Entrance requirements:* For master's, GMAT.

Wright State University, School of Graduate Studies, Raj Soin College of Business, Department of Management, Dayton, OH 45435. Offers flexible business (MBA); health care management (MBA); international business (MBA); management, innovation and change (MBA); project management (MBA); supply chain management (MBA); MBA/MS. *Entrance requirements:* For master's, GMAT, minimum AACSB index of 1000. Additional exam requirements/recommendations for international students: Required—TOEFL.

Section 18
Quality Management

This section contains a directory of institutions offering graduate work in quality management. Additional information about programs listed in the directory may be obtained by writing directly to the dean of a graduate school or chair of a department at the address given in the directory.

For programs offering related work, see also in this book *Business Administration and Management.*

CONTENTS

Program Directory

Quality Management

California Intercontinental University, School of Information Technology, Diamond Bar, CA 91765. Offers information systems and enterprise resource management (DBA); information systems and knowledge management (MBA); project and quality management (MBA).

California State University, Dominguez Hills, College of Extended and International Education, Program in Quality Assurance, Carson, CA 90747-0001. Offers MS. Part-time and evening/weekend programs available. Postbaccalaureate distance learning degree programs offered (no on-campus study). *Faculty:* 11 part-time/adjunct (1 woman). *Students:* 8 full-time (5 women), 212 part-time (106 women); includes 85 minority (17 African Americans, 3 American Indian/Alaska Native, 44 Asian Americans or Pacific Islanders, 21 Hispanic Americans). Average age 41. 131 applicants, 79% accepted, 41 enrolled. In 2009, 25 master's awarded. *Degree requirements:* For master's, thesis. *Entrance requirements:* For master's, minimum GPA of 2.75. Additional exam requirements/recommendations for international students: Required—TOEFL. *Application deadline:* For fall admission, 10/1 priority date for domestic and international students; for spring admission, 8/1 priority date for domestic and international students. Application fee: $55. Electronic applications accepted. *Expenses:* Contact institution. *Faculty research:* Six sigma, lean thinking, risk management, quality management. *Unit head:* Dr. Milton Krivokuca, Coordinator, 310-243-3880, Fax: 310-516-4423, E-mail: mkrivokuca@csudh.edu. *Application contact:* Rodger Hamrick, Program Assistant, 310-243-3880, E-mail: rhamrick@csudh.edu.

Calumet College of Saint Joseph, Program in Quality Assurance, Whiting, IN 46394-2195. Offers MS.

Case Western Reserve University, Weatherhead School of Management, Department of Operations, Cleveland, OH 44106. Offers management (MS, MSM), including finance (MS), information systems (MS), marketing (MS), operations research, quality management (MS), supply chain (MSM); management for liberal arts graduates (MSM); operations research (PhD); MBA/MSM. Part-time programs available. *Degree requirements:* For doctorate, thesis/dissertation. *Entrance requirements:* For master's, GRE General Test; for doctorate, GMAT, GRE General Test. *Application deadline:* Applications are processed on a rolling basis. Application fee: $100. *Financial support:* Tuition waivers (full and partial) available. Financial award application deadline: 5/1. *Faculty research:* Mathematical finance, mathematical programming, scheduling, stochastic optimization, environmental/energy models. *Unit head:* Kamlesh Mathur, Chairman, 216-368-3857, E-mail: kamlesh.mathur@case.edu. *Application contact:* Kamlesh Mathur, Chairman, 216-368-3857, E-mail: kamlesh.mathur@case.edu.

Dowling College, School of Business, Oakdale, NY 11769-1999. Offers aviation management (MBA, Certificate); banking and finance (MBA, Certificate); financial planning (Certificate); general management (MBA); health care management (MBA, Certificate); human resource management (Certificate); management and leadership (MBA); marketing (Certificate); project management (Certificate); public management (MBA, Certificate); total quality management (MBA, Certificate); JD/MBA. Part-time and evening/weekend programs available. *Faculty:* 14 full-time (5 women), 58 part-time/adjunct (5 women). *Students:* 324 full-time (142 women), 479 part-time (237 women); includes 238 minority (82 African Americans, 1 American Indian/Alaska Native, 117 Asian Americans or Pacific Islanders, 38 Hispanic Americans), 2 international. Average age 33. 457 applicants, 91% accepted, 153 enrolled. In 2009, 341 master's, 2 other advanced degrees awarded. *Degree requirements:* For master's, comprehensive exam, thesis optional. *Entrance requirements:* For master's, minimum GPA of 2.8, 2 letters of recommendation, courses in accounting and finance or seminar in accounting/finance, resume. Additional exam requirements/recommendations for international students: Required—TOEFL (minimum score 550 paper-based). *Application deadline:* For fall admission, 9/1 priority date for domestic students; for winter admission, 1/1 priority date for domestic students; for spring admission, 2/1 priority date for domestic students. Applications are processed on a rolling basis. Application fee: $50. Electronic applications accepted. *Expenses:* Tuition: Full-time $14,490; part-time $805 per credit. Required fees: $346 per term. *Financial support:* Career-related internships or fieldwork and Federal Work-Study available. Support available to part-time students. Financial award application deadline: 6/30; financial award applicants required to submit FAFSA. *Faculty research:* International finance, computer applications, labor relations, executive development. *Unit head:* Mathew Cordaro, Dean, 631-244-3162, Fax: 631-244-1018, E-mail: cordarom@dowling.edu. *Application contact:* Glenn M. Berman, Director of Admissions Operations, 631-244-3357, Fax: 631-244-1059, E-mail: glenn.berman@dowling.edu.

Eastern Michigan University, Graduate School, College of Technology, School of Engineering Technology, Program in Quality Management, Ypsilanti, MI 48197. Offers quality (MS, Graduate Certificate); quality management (MS). Part-time and evening/weekend programs available. Postbaccalaureate distance learning degree programs offered (minimal on-campus study). *Students:* 2 full-time (0 women), 79 part-time (28 women); includes 13 minority (9 African Americans, 4 Asian Americans or Pacific Islanders), 6 international. Average age 41. In 2009, 12 master's, 2 other advanced degrees awarded. *Entrance requirements:* Additional exam requirements/recommendations for international students: Required—TOEFL. *Application deadline:* Applications are processed on a rolling basis. Application fee: $35. Tuition and fees vary according to course level. *Financial support:* Fellowships, research assistantships with full tuition reimbursements, teaching assistantships with full tuition reimbursements, career-related internships or fieldwork, Federal Work-Study, institutionally sponsored loans, scholarships/grants, tuition waivers (partial), and unspecified assistantships available. Support available to part-time students. Financial award applicants required to submit FAFSA. *Unit head:* Dr. Walter Tucker, Program Coordinator, 734-487-2040, Fax: 734-487-8755, E-mail: walter.tucker@emich.edu. *Application contact:* Dr. Walter Tucker, Program Coordinator, 734-487-2040, Fax: 734-487-8755, E-mail: walter.tucker@emich.edu.

Ferris State University, College of Business, Big Rapids, MI 49307. Offers application development (MSISM); business intelligence and infomatics (MBA); database administration (MSISM); design and innovation management process (MBA); e-business (MSISM); networking (MSISM); quality management (MBA); security (MSISM). *Accreditation:* ACBSP. Part-time and evening/weekend programs available. *Faculty:* 10 full-time (3 women), 2 part-time/adjunct (both women). *Students:* 33 full-time (6 women), 134 part-time (65 women); includes 13 minority (8 African Americans, 2 American Indian/Alaska Native, 2 Asian Americans or Pacific Islanders, 1 Hispanic American), 33 international. Average age 30. 120 applicants, 31% accepted, 26 enrolled. In 2009, 66 master's awarded. *Entrance requirements:* For master's, GRE or GMAT (waived if GPA is 3.5 or better), minimum GPA of 3.0 in CIS and business core, 2.75 overall; writing sample; 3 letters of reference; resume. Additional exam requirements/recommendations for international students: Required—TOEFL (minimum score 500 paper-based; 173 computer-based; 64 iBT). *Application deadline:* For fall admission, 7/1 priority date for domestic students, 6/15 for international students; for winter admission, 11/1 priority date for domestic students, 10/15 for international students; for spring admission, 3/1 priority date for domestic students, 2/15 for international students. Applications are processed on a rolling basis. Application fee: $30 for international students. Electronic applications accepted. *Financial support:* In 2009–10, 14 teaching assistantships were awarded; career-related internships or fieldwork, Federal Work-Study, and unspecified assistantships also available. Support available to part-time students. Financial award applicants required to submit FAFSA. *Faculty research:* Quality improvement, client/server end-user computing, information management and policy, security, digital forensics. *Unit head:* Dr. David Steenstra, Department Chair, 231-591-2168, Fax: 231-591-2973, E-mail: yosts@ferris.edu. *Application contact:* Shannon Yost, Department Secretary, 231-591-2168, Fax: 231-591-2973, E-mail: yosts@ferris.edu.

Florida Institute of Technology, Graduate Programs, College of Business, Extended Studies Division, Melbourne, FL 32901-6975. Offers acquisition and contract management (PMBA); business administration (PMBA); computer information systems (MS); e-business (PMBA); human resource management (PMBA); human resources management (MS); logistics management (MS), including humanitarian and disaster relief logistics; management (MS), including acquisition and contract management, e-business, human resource management, information systems, logistics management, management, transportation management; material acquisition management (MS); project management (MS), including information systems, operations research; public administration (MPA); quality management (MS); space management (MS); space systems (MS); systems management (MS), including information systems, operations research, systems management. Part-time and evening/weekend programs available. Postbaccalaureate distance learning degree programs offered (no on-campus study). *Faculty:* 12 full-time (3 women), 117 part-time/adjunct (20 women). *Students:* 74 full-time (32 women), 1,041 part-time (484 women); includes 343 minority (240 African Americans, 12 American Indian/Alaska Native, 44 Asian Americans or Pacific Islanders, 47 Hispanic Americans), 22 international. Average age 35. 520 applicants, 72% accepted, 279 enrolled. In 2009, 509 master's awarded. *Degree requirements:* For master's, capstone course. *Entrance requirements:* For master's, GMAT or resume showing 8 years of supervised experience, minimum GPA of 3.0, 2 letters of recommendation, resume. Additional exam requirements/recommendations for international students: Required—TOEFL (minimum score 550 paper-based; 213 computer-based; 79 iBT). *Application deadline:* For fall admission, 4/1 for international students; for spring admission, 9/30 for international students. Applications are processed on a rolling basis. Application fee: $50. Electronic applications accepted. *Expenses:* Tuition: Part-time $1015 per credit. Tuition and fees vary according to campus/location and program. *Financial support:* Application deadline: 3/1. *Unit head:* Dr. Clifford Bragdon, Dean, 321-674-8821, Fax: 321-674-7597, E-mail: cbragdon@fit.edu. *Application contact:* Carolyn Farrior, Director of Graduate Admissions Online Learning and Off Campus Programs, 321-674-7118, Fax: 321-674-8216, E-mail: cfarrior@fit.edu.

Hofstra University, Frank G. Zarb School of Business, Department of Information Technology and Quantitative Methods, Hempstead, NY 11549. Offers business administration (MBA), including information technology, quality management; information technology (MS). Part-time and evening/weekend programs available. *Faculty:* 10 full-time (2 women), 1 part-time/adjunct (0 women). *Students:* 8 full-time (2 women), 16 part-time (4 women); includes 5 minority (1 African American, 3 Asian Americans or Pacific Islanders, 1 Hispanic American), 2 international. Average age 30. 22 applicants, 64% accepted, 9 enrolled. In 2009, 9 master's awarded. *Degree requirements:* For master's, capstone course (MBA), thesis (MS). *Entrance requirements:* For master's, GMAT or GRE, 2 letters of recommendation, resume. Additional exam requirements/recommendations for international students: Required—TOEFL (minimum score 550 paper-based; 213 computer-based; 80 iBT); Recommended—IELTS (minimum score 6). *Application deadline:* Applications are processed on a rolling basis. Application fee: $60. Electronic applications accepted. *Expenses:* Contact institution. *Financial support:* In 2009–10, 3 students received support, including 3 fellowships with full and partial tuition reimbursements available (averaging $14,483 per year); research assistantships with full and partial tuition reimbursements available, career-related internships or fieldwork, Federal Work-Study, institutionally sponsored loans, scholarships/grants, tuition waivers (full and partial), and unspecified assistantships also available. Support available to part-time students. Financial award applicants required to submit FAFSA. *Faculty research:* IT outsourcing: IT strategy; SAP and enterprise systems; data mining/electronic medical records; IT and crisis management; inventory theory and modeling, forecasting. *Unit head:* Dr. Mohammed H. Tafti, Chairperson, 516-463-5720, E-mail: acsmht@hofstra.edu. *Application contact:* Carol Drummer, Dean of Graduate Admissions, 516-463-4876, Fax: 516-463-4664, E-mail: gradstudent@hofstra.edu.

Instituto Tecnológico y de Estudios Superiores de Monterrey, Campus Ciudad de México, Virtual University Division, Ciudad de Mexico, Mexico. Offers administration of information technologies (MA); computer sciences (MA); education (MA, PhD); educational technology (MA); environmental engineering (MA); environmental systems (MA); humanistic studies (MA); industrial engineering (MA); international business for Latin America (MA); quality systems (MA); quality systems and productivity (MA). Part-time and evening/weekend programs available. Postbaccalaureate distance learning degree programs offered (minimal on-campus study). *Entrance requirements:* For master's and doctorate, Instituto entrance exam. Additional exam requirements/recommendations for international students: Required—TOEFL.

Instituto Tecnológico y de Estudios Superiores de Monterrey, Campus Ciudad Juárez, Program in Quality Management, Ciudad Juárez, Mexico. Offers MQM.

Instituto Tecnológico y de Estudios Superiores de Monterrey, Campus Estado de México, Professional and Graduate Division, Estado de Mexico, Mexico. Offers administration of information technologies (MITA); architecture (M Arch); business administration (GMBA, MBA); computer sciences (MCS, PhD); education (M Ed); educational institution administration (MAD); educational technology and innovation (PhD); electronic commerce (MEC); environmental systems (MS); finance (MAF); humanistic studies (MHS); information sciences and knowledge management (MISKM); information systems (MS); manufacturing systems (MS); marketing (MEM); quality systems and productivity (MS); science and materials engineering (PhD); telecommunications management (MTM). Part-time programs available. Postbaccalaureate distance learning degree programs offered (minimal on-campus study). *Degree requirements:* For master's, one foreign language, thesis (for some programs); for doctorate, one foreign language, thesis/dissertation. *Entrance requirements:* For master's, E-PAEP 500, interview; for doctorate, E-PAEP 500, research proposal. Additional exam requirements/recommendations for international students: Required—TOEFL (minimum score 550 paper-based). *Faculty research:* Surface treatments by plasmas, mechanical properties, robotics, graphical computing, mechatronics security protocols.

Instituto Tecnológico y de Estudios Superiores de Monterrey, Campus Irapuato, Graduate Programs, Irapuato, Mexico. Offers administration (MBA); administration of information technology (MAIT); administration of telecommunications (MAT); architecture (M Arch); computer science (MCS); education (M Ed); educational administration (MEA); educational innovation and technology (DEIT); educational technology (MET); electronic commerce (MBA); environmental administration and planning (MEAP); environmental systems (MES); finances (MBA); humanistic studies (MHS); international management for Latin American executives (MIMLAE); library and information science (MLIS); manufacturing quality management (MMQM); marketing research (MBA).

Madonna University, School of Business, Livonia, MI 48150-1173. Offers business administration (MBA); international business (MSBA); leadership studies (MSBA); leadership studies in criminal justice (MSBA); quality and operations management (MSBA). Part-time and evening/weekend programs available. Postbaccalaureate distance learning degree programs offered (minimal on-campus study). *Degree requirements:* For master's, thesis (for some programs), foreign language proficiency (international business). *Entrance requirements:* For master's, GMAT, GRE General Test, minimum GPA of 3.0. Electronic applications accepted. *Faculty research:* Management, women in management, future studies.

Marian University, Business Division, Fond du Lac, WI 54935-4699. Offers organizational leadership and quality (MS). Part-time and evening/weekend programs available. *Faculty:* 10 part-time/adjunct (2 women). *Students:* 7 full-time (5 women), 86 part-time (62 women); includes 10 minority (5 African Americans, 3 Asian Americans or Pacific Islanders, 2 Hispanic Americans). Average age 38. 48 applicants, 79% accepted, 38 enrolled. In 2009, 49 master's awarded. *Degree requirements:* For master's, comprehensive group project. *Entrance requirements:* For master's, 3 years of managerial experience, minimum GPA of 2.75, letters of professional reference. *Application deadline:* Applications are processed on a rolling basis. Application fee: $25. Electronic applications accepted. *Expenses:* Contact institution. *Financial support:* In 2009–10, 25 students received support. Institutionally sponsored loans available. Support available to part-time students. Financial award application deadline: 3/1; financial award applicants required to submit FAFSA. *Faculty research:* Organizational values, statistical decision making, learning organization, quality planning, customer research. *Unit head:* Donna Innes, Assistant Provost and Dean of PACE, 920-923-8760, Fax: 920-923-7167, E-mail:

dinnes@marianuniversity.edu. *Application contact:* Tracy Qualman, Director of Marketing and Admission, 920-923-7159, Fax: 920-923-7167, E-mail: tqualmann@marianuniversity.edu.

The National Graduate School of Quality Management, Program in Quality Systems Management, Falmouth, MA 02541. Offers e-commerce (MS); management (MS); six sigma (MS).

Northwestern University, School of Continuing Studies, Program in Quality Assurance and Regulatory Science, Evanston, IL 60208. Offers MS.

Northwest Missouri State University, Graduate School, Melvin and Valorie Booth College of Business and Professional Studies, Program in Quality, Maryville, MO 64468-6001. Offers quality (MBA, MS); quality management (Certificate). *Faculty:* 16 full-time (2 women). *Students:* 1 full-time (0 women), 1 part-time (0 women). 2 applicants, 50% accepted, 1 enrolled. In 2009, 2 master's awarded. *Entrance requirements:* For master's, GRE, GMAT. Additional exam requirements/recommendations for international students: Required—TOEFL. *Expenses:* Tuition, state resident: part-time $296.34 per credit hour. Tuition, nonresident: part-time $510.43 per credit hour. *Financial support:* Application deadline: 4/1. *Unit head:* Dr. Chi-Lo Lim, Director, 660-562-1758. *Application contact:* Dr. Gregory Haddock, Dean of Graduate School, 660-562-1145, Fax: 660-562-1096, E-mail: gradsch@nwmissouri.edu.

Penn State University Park, Graduate School, Intercollege Graduate Programs, Intercollege Program in Quality and Manufacturing Management, State College, University Park, PA 16802-1503. Offers MMM. *Unit head:* Dr. Jose A. Ventura, Co-Director, 814-865-5802, Fax: 814-863-4745, E-mail: jav1@psu.edu. *Application contact:* Cynthia E. Nicosia, Director, Graduate Enrollment Services, 814-865-1795, Fax: 814-865-4627, E-mail: cey1@psu.edu.

Regis College, Department of Health Product Regulation and Clinical Research, Weston, MA 02493. Offers MS. Part-time and evening/weekend programs available. *Faculty:* 1 full-time (0 women), 7 part-time/adjunct (2 women). *Students:* 1 (woman) full-time, 26 part-time (21 women); includes 2 minority (both Asian Americans or Pacific Islanders). Average age 37. 10 applicants, 100% accepted, 8 enrolled. In 2009, 15 master's awarded. *Degree requirements:* For master's, thesis optional, internship. *Entrance requirements:* For master's, GRE or MAT. Additional exam requirements/recommendations for international students: Required—TOEFL (minimum score 550 paper-based; 213 computer-based). *Application deadline:* Applications are processed on a rolling basis. Application fee: $50. *Expenses:* Contact institution. *Financial support:* In 2009–10, 7 students received support. Career-related internships or fieldwork and scholarships/grants available. Financial award applicants required to submit FAFSA. *Faculty research:* FDA regulatory affairs medical device. *Unit head:* Charles Burr, Director, 781-768-7008, E-mail: charles.burr@regiscollege.edu. *Application contact:* Christine Petherick, Administrative Coordinator, Graduate Admission, 866-438-7344, Fax: 781-768-7071, E-mail: christine.petherick@regiscollege.edu.

Rutgers, The State University of New Jersey, New Brunswick, Graduate School-New Brunswick, Program in Statistics, Piscataway, NJ 08854-8097. Offers applied statistics (MS); biostatistics (MS); data mining (MS); quality and productivity management (MS); statistics (MS, PhD). Part-time programs available. Terminal master's awarded for partial completion of doctoral program. *Degree requirements:* For master's, comprehensive exam, essay, exam, non-thesis essay paper; for doctorate, one foreign language, thesis/dissertation, qualifying oral and written exams. *Entrance requirements:* For master's, GRE General Test; for doctorate, GRE General Test, GRE Subject Test (recommended). Additional exam requirements/recommendations for international students: Required—TOEFL (minimum score 550 paper-based; 213 computer-based). Electronic applications accepted. *Faculty research:* Probability, decision theory, linear models, multivariate statistics, statistical computing.

Saint Joseph's College of Maine, Program in Business Administration, Standish, ME 04084. Offers quality leadership (MBA). Part-time programs available. *Entrance requirements:* For master's, 2 years work experience.

San Jose State University, Graduate Studies and Research, Charles W. Davidson College of Engineering, Department of Aviation and Technology, San Jose, CA 95192-0001. Offers quality assurance (MS). *Students:* 3 full-time (all women), 9 part-time (4 women); includes 5 minority (4 Asian Americans or Pacific Islanders, 1 Hispanic American), 4 international. Average age 32. 13 applicants, 54% accepted, 4 enrolled. In 2009, 3 master's awarded. *Entrance requirements:* For master's, GRE. *Application deadline:* For fall admission, 6/29 for domestic students; for spring admission, 11/30 for domestic students. Applications are processed on a rolling basis. Application fee: $59. Electronic applications accepted. *Financial support:* Applicants required to submit FAFSA. *Unit head:* Seth P. Bates, Chair, 408-924-3227, Fax: 408-924-3198, E-mail: seth.bates@sjsu.edu. *Application contact:* Ali M. Zargar, Graduate Advisor, 408-924-3194, E-mail: ali.zargar@sjsu.edu.

Southern Polytechnic State University, School of Engineering Technology and Management, Department of Industrial Engineering Technology, Marietta, GA 30060-2896. Offers quality assurance (MS, Graduate Certificate). Part-time and evening/weekend programs available. Postbaccalaureate distance learning degree programs offered (minimal on-campus study). *Faculty:* 3 full-time (2 women), 4 part-time/adjunct (3 women). *Students:* 4 full-time (1 woman), 80 part-time (23 women); includes 15 African Americans, 5 Asian Americans or Pacific Islanders, 3 Hispanic Americans, 6 international. Average age 42. 30 applicants, 97% accepted, 18 enrolled. In 2009, 29 master's awarded. *Degree requirements:* For master's and Graduate Certificate, comprehensive exam (for some programs). *Entrance requirements:* For master's, 2 years full-time work experience in industrial engineering field, 3 reference forms, minimum GPA of 2.7; for Graduate Certificate, 2 years full-time work experience, minimum GPA of 2.7. Additional exam requirements/recommendations for international students: Required—TOEFL (minimum score 550 paper-based; 213 computer-based; 79 iBT), IELTS (minimum score 6.5). *Application deadline:* For fall admission, 7/1 priority date for domestic students, 5/1 priority date for international students; for spring admission, 11/1 priority date for domestic students, 9/1 priority date for international students. Applications are processed on a rolling basis. Application fee: $20. Electronic applications accepted. *Expenses:* Tuition, state resident: full-time $2896; part-time $181 per credit hour. Tuition, nonresident: full-time $11,552; part-time $722 per credit hour. Required fees: $1096. *Financial support:* In 2009–10, 1 research assistantship with partial tuition reimbursement (averaging $1,500 per year) was awarded; career-related internships or fieldwork, scholarships/grants, and unspecified assistantships also available. Support available to part-time students. Financial award application deadline: 5/1; financial award applicants required to submit FAFSA. *Faculty research:* Application on industrial engineering to public sector, investigation of the response model method in robust design, effectiveness of on-line education, learning community, physical and mechanical properties of shape-wear garments to their functional performance, the advantage of tablet computer technology in a distance learning format, NSF grant for research in the field of Health Care, BRIGE: Optimization Models for Public Health Policy. *Unit head:* Tom Ball, Chair, 678-915-7162, Fax: 678-915-4991, E-mail: tball@spsu.edu. *Application contact:* Nikki Palamiotis, Director of Graduate Studies, 678-915-4276, Fax: 678-915-7292, E-mail: npalamio@spsu.edu.

Stevens Institute of Technology, Graduate School, Charles V. Schaefer Jr. School of Engineering, Department of Civil, Environmental, and Ocean Engineering, Program in Construction Management, Hoboken, NJ 07030. Offers construction accounting/estimating (Certificate); construction engineering (Certificate); construction law/disputes (Certificate); construction management (MS); construction/quality management (Certificate). *Degree requirements:* For master's, thesis optional. *Entrance requirements:* For master's, GMAT, GRE General Test. Additional exam requirements/recommendations for international students: Required—TOEFL. Electronic applications accepted. *Expenses:* Tuition: Full-time $9900; part-time $1100 per credit. Required fees: $286 per semester.

TUI University, College of Business Administration, Program in Business Administration, Cypress, CA 90630. Offers business administration (PhD); conflict and negotiation management (MBA); criminal justice administration (MBA); entrepreneurship (MBA); finance (MBA); general management (MBA); government accounting (MBA); human resource management (MBA); information security and digital assurance management (MBA); information technology management (MBA); international business (MBA); logistics management (MBA); marketing (MBA); project management (MBA); public management (MBA); quality management (MBA); strategic leadership (MBA). Part-time and evening/weekend programs available. Postbaccalaureate distance learning degree programs offered (no on-campus study). *Degree requirements:* For doctorate, comprehensive exam, thesis/dissertation, defense of dissertation. *Entrance requirements:* For master's, minimum GPA of 2.5 (students with GPA 3.0 or greater may transfer up to 30% of graduate level credits); for doctorate, minimum GPA of 3.4, curriculum vitae, course work in research methods or statistics. Additional exam requirements/recommendations for international students: Required—TOEFL. Electronic applications accepted.

TUI University, College of Health Sciences, Program in Health Sciences, Cypress, CA 90630. Offers clinical research administration (MS, Certificate); emergency and disaster management (MS, Certificate); environmental health science (Certificate); health care administration (PhD); health care management (MS), including health informatics; health education (MS, Certificate); health informatics (Certificate); health sciences (PhD); international health (MS); international health: educator or researcher option (PhD); international health: practitioner option (PhD); law and expert witness studies (MS, Certificate); public health (MS); quality assurance (Certificate). Part-time and evening/weekend programs available. Postbaccalaureate distance learning degree programs offered (no on-campus study). *Degree requirements:* For doctorate, comprehensive exam, thesis/dissertation, defense of dissertation. *Entrance requirements:* For master's, minimum GPA of 2.5 (students with GPA 3.0 or greater may transfer up to 30% of graduate level credits); for doctorate, minimum GPA of 3.4, curriculum vitae, course work in research methods or statistics. Additional exam requirements/recommendations for international students: Required—TOEFL. Electronic applications accepted.

Universidad de las Americas, A.C., Program in Business Administration, Mexico City, Mexico. Offers finance (MBA); marketing research (MBA); production and quality (MBA).

Universidad del Turabo, Graduate Programs, School in Business Administration, Program in Quality Management, Gurabo, PR 00778-3030. Offers MBA. *Students:* 32 full-time (24 women), 41 part-time (29 women); includes 69 Hispanic Americans. Average age 33. 37 applicants, 81% accepted, 20 enrolled. In 2009, 34 master's awarded. *Unit head:* Marcelino Rivera, Dean, 787-743-7979 Ext. 4117. *Application contact:* Virginia Gonzalez, Admissions Officer, 787-746-3009.

The University of Alabama, Graduate School, College of Human Environmental Sciences, Program in Human Environmental Science, Tuscaloosa, AL 35487. Offers family financial planning and counseling (MS); interactive technology (MS); quality management (MS); restaurant and meeting management (MS); rural community health (MS); sport management (MS). *Students:* 70 full-time (40 women), 99 part-time (45 women); includes 44 minority (42 African Americans, 2 Hispanic Americans), 1 international. Average age 33. 124 applicants, 71% accepted, 71 enrolled. In 2009, 70 degrees awarded. *Degree requirements:* For master's, comprehensive exam. *Entrance requirements:* For master's, GRE (for some specializations), minimum GPA of 3.0. Additional exam requirements/recommendations for international students: Required—TOEFL. *Application deadline:* Applications are processed on a rolling basis. Application fee: $50 ($60 for international students). Electronic applications accepted. *Expenses:* Tuition, state resident: full-time $7000. Tuition, nonresident: full-time $19,200. *Faculty research:* Hospitality management, sports medicine education, technology and education. *Unit head:* Dr. Milla D. Boschung, Dean, 205-348-6250, Fax: 205-348-1786, E-mail: mboschun@ches.ua.edu. *Application contact:* Dr. Stuart Usdan, Associate Dean, 205-348-6150, Fax: 205-348-3789, E-mail: susdan@ches.ua.edu.

The University of Tennessee at Chattanooga, Graduate School, College of Engineering and Computer Science, Program in Engineering Management, Chattanooga, TN 37403. Offers engineering management (MS); fundamentals of engineering management (Graduate Certificate); power systems management (Graduate Certificate); project and value management (Graduate Certificate); quality management (Graduate Certificate). Postbaccalaureate distance learning degree programs offered (no on-campus study). *Faculty:* 4 full-time (1 woman). *Students:* 22 full-time (7 women), 69 part-time (11 women); includes 25 minority (12 African Americans, 9 Asian Americans or Pacific Islanders, 4 Hispanic Americans), 12 international. Average age 33. 46 applicants, 67% accepted, 24 enrolled. In 2009, 25 master's, 8 other advanced degrees awarded. *Degree requirements:* For master's, thesis. *Entrance requirements:* For master's, GRE General Test, letters of recommendation; minimum undergraduate GPA of 2.5 overall or 3.0 in senior year. Additional exam requirements/recommendations for international students: Required—TOEFL (minimum score 550 paper-based; 213 computer-based; 79 iBT), IELTS (minimum score 6). *Application deadline:* For fall admission, 8/1 priority date for domestic students, 6/1 for international students; for spring admission, 12/1 priority date for domestic students, 10/1 for international students. Applications are processed on a rolling basis. Application fee: $35. Electronic applications accepted. *Expenses:* Tuition, state resident: full-time $5404; part-time $300 per credit hour. Tuition, nonresident: full-time $16,702; part-time $928 per credit hour. Required fees: $1150; $130 per credit hour. *Financial support:* In 2009–10, 5 research assistantships with full and partial tuition reimbursements (averaging $5,500 per year) were awarded; career-related internships or fieldwork, scholarships/grants, and unspecified assistantships also available. Support available to part-time students. *Faculty research:* Plant layout design, lean manufacturing, six sigma, value management, product development. *Unit head:* Dr. Neslihan Alp, Director, 423-425-4032, Fax: 423-425-5229, E-mail: neslihan-alp@utc.edu. *Application contact:* Dr. Stephanie Bellar, Dean of Graduate Studies, 423-425-4666, Fax: 423-425-5223, E-mail: stephanie-bellar@utc.edu.

Upper Iowa University, Online Master's Programs, Fayette, IA 52142-1857. Offers accounting (MBA); corporate financial management (MBA); global business (MBA); health and human services (MPA); higher education administration (MHEA); homeland security (MPA); human resources management (MBA); justice administration (MPA); organizational development (MBA); public personnel management (MPA); quality management (MBA). MBA also available at Madison, WI campus. Part-time programs available. Postbaccalaureate distance learning degree programs offered (no on-campus study). *Faculty:* 3 full-time (0 women), 66 part-time/adjunct (27 women). *Students:* 723 full-time (442 women). *Degree requirements:* For master's, research project. *Entrance requirements:* For master's, GMAT, GRE, or minimum GPA of 2.7 during last 60 hours. Additional exam requirements/recommendations for international students: Required—TOEFL (minimum score 570 paper-based; 230 computer-based). *Application deadline:* Applications are processed on a rolling basis. Application fee: $50. Electronic applications accepted. *Expenses:* Tuition: Full-time $6948; part-time $386 per credit hour. *Financial support:* Available to part-time students. Applicants required to submit FAFSA. *Faculty research:* Total quality management, CQI, teams, organization culture and climate, management. *Application contact:* David Hannum, Admissions Advisor, 800-603-3756, E-mail: hannumd@uiu.edu.

Webster University, George Herbert Walker School of Business and Technology, Department of Management, St. Louis, MO 63119-3194. Offers business and organizational security management (MA); computer resources and information management (MA); environmental management (MS); government contracting (Certificate); health care management (MA); health services management (MA); human resources development (MA); human resources management (MA); management (DM); management and leadership (MA); marketing (MA); nonprofit management (Certificate); procurement and acquisitions management (MA); public administration (MA); quality management (MA); space systems operations management (MS); telecommunications management (MA). *Accreditation:* ACBSP. Part-time and evening/weekend programs available. Postbaccalaureate distance learning degree programs offered (no on-campus study). *Faculty:* 16 full-time, 781 part-time/adjunct. *Students:* 1,369 full-time (610 women), 5,182 part-time (3,047 women); includes 3,460 minority (2,835 African Americans, 38 American Indian/Alaska Native, 169 Asian Americans or Pacific Islanders, 418 Hispanic Americans), 80 international. Average age 37. In 2009, 2,491 master's, 13 doctorates, 68 other advanced degrees awarded. *Degree requirements:* For master's, thesis (for some programs); for doctorate, thesis/dissertation, written exam. *Entrance requirements:* For doctorate, GMAT, 3 years of work experience, MBA. Additional exam requirements/recommendations for international

Quality Management

Webster University *(continued)*
students: Required—TOEFL. *Application deadline:* Applications are processed on a rolling basis. Application fee: $25 ($50 for international students). *Expenses:* Tuition: Part-time $565 per credit hour. Tuition and fees vary according to degree level, campus/location and program. *Financial support:* Federal Work-Study available. Support available to part-time students.

Financial award application deadline: 4/1; financial award applicants required to submit FAFSA. *Unit head:* Jim Brasfield, Chair, 314-961-2660 Ext. 7063, Fax: 314-968-7077, E-mail: mgtchair@webster.edu. *Application contact:* Matt Nolan, Associate Vice President for Enrollment Management/Dean of Admissions, Fax: 314-968-7116, E-mail: gadmit@webster.edu.

Section 19
Quantitative Analysis

This section contains a directory of institutions offering graduate work in quantitative analysis. Additional information about programs listed in the directory may be obtained by writing directly to the dean of a graduate school or chair of a department at the address given in the directory.

For programs offering related work, see also in this book *Business Administration and Management*

CONTENTS

Program Directory

Close-Up

See:

Quantitative Analysis

Bernard M. Baruch College of the City University of New York, Zicklin School of Business, Department of Statistics and Computer Information Systems, Program in Decision Sciences, New York, NY 10010-5585. Offers MBA, MS. Part-time and evening/weekend programs available. *Entrance requirements:* For master's, GMAT, 2 letters of recommendation, resume, 2 years of work experience. Additional exam requirements/recommendations for international students: Required—TOEFL (minimum score 590 paper-based; 243 computer-based), TWE (minimum score 5).

Drexel University, LeBow College of Business, Program in Business Administration, Philadelphia, PA 19104-2875. Offers business administration (MBA, PhD, APC), including accounting (MBA, PhD), decision sciences (PhD), economics (MBA, PhD), finance (MBA, PhD), legal studies (MBA), management (MBA), marketing (MBA, PhD), organizational sciences (PhD), quantitative methods (MBA), strategic management (PhD). *Accreditation:* AACSB. Part-time and evening/weekend programs available. Postbaccalaureate distance learning degree programs offered (minimal on-campus study). Terminal master's awarded for partial completion of doctoral program. *Entrance requirements:* For master's, GMAT, minimum GPA of 2.75; for doctorate, GMAT. Additional exam requirements/recommendations for international students: Required—TOEFL. Electronic applications accepted. *Faculty research:* Decision support systems, individual and group behavior, operations research, techniques and strategy.

Georgia State University, J. Mack Robinson College of Business, Department of Managerial Sciences, Atlanta, GA 30302-3083. Offers business analysis (MBA, MS); decision sciences (PhD); entrepreneurship (MBA); human resources management (MBA, MS); management (MBA, PhD); operations management (MBA, MS); organization change (MS); personnel employee relations (PhD); strategic management (PhD). Part-time and evening/weekend programs available. *Degree requirements:* For doctorate, thesis/dissertation. *Entrance requirements:* For master's and doctorate, GMAT. Additional exam requirements/ recommendations for international students: Required—TOEFL (minimum score 610 paper-based; 255 computer-based; 101 iBT). Electronic applications accepted. *Faculty research:* Abusive supervision, entrepreneurship, time series and neural networks, organizational controls, inventory control systems.

Lehigh University, College of Business and Economics, Department of Finance, Bethlehem, PA 18015. Offers analytical finance (MS). *Faculty:* 8 full-time (2 women). *Students:* 42 full-time (25 women), 29 part-time (11 women); includes 3 minority (2 African Americans, 1 Asian American or Pacific Islander), 42 international. Average age 27. 162 applicants, 38% accepted, 30 enrolled. In 2009, 27 master's awarded. *Degree requirements:* For master's, capstone project. *Entrance requirements:* For master's, GMAT or GRE, bachelor's degree from a mathematically rigorous program, minimum GPA of 3.0. Additional exam requirements/ recommendations for international students: Required—TOEFL (minimum score 600 paper-based; 250 computer-based; 94 iBT). *Application deadline:* For fall admission, 7/15 for domestic students, 5/1 for international students. Applications are processed on a rolling basis. Application fee: $100. Electronic applications accepted. *Expenses:* Contact institution. Total annual research expenditures: $169,555. *Unit head:* Richard Kish, Co-Director, 610-758-4205, E-mail: rjk7@ lehigh.edu. *Application contact:* Corinn McBride, Director of Recruitment and Admissions, 610-758-3418, Fax: 610-758-5283, E-mail: com207@lehigh.edu.

New York University, Robert F. Wagner Graduate School of Public Service, Program in Public Administration, New York, NY 10012-1019. Offers public administration (PhD); public and nonprofit management and policy (MPA, Advanced Certificate), including developmental administration (Advanced Certificate), financial management and public finance, human resources management (Advanced Certificate), international administration (Advanced Certificate), management (MPA), management for public and nonprofit organizations (Advanced Certificate), public policy analysis, quantitative analysis and computer applications (Advanced Certificate), urban public policy (Advanced Certificate); JD/MPA; MBA/MPA; MPA/MA. *Accreditation:* NASPAA (one or more programs are accredited). Part-time and evening/ weekend programs available. *Faculty:* 31 full-time (13 women), 33 part-time/adjunct (16 women). *Students:* 363 full-time (270 women), 228 part-time (171 women); includes 146 minority (46 African Americans, 64 Asian Americans or Pacific Islanders, 36 Hispanic Americans), 76 international. Average age 28. 1,117 applicants, 57% accepted, 225 enrolled. In 2009, 236 master's, 3 doctorates awarded. *Degree requirements:* For master's, thesis or alternative, capstone end event; for doctorate, one foreign language, thesis/dissertation. *Entrance requirements:* For master's, minimum undergraduate GPA of 3.0; for doctorate, GMAT or GRE General Test, minimum GPA of 3.5. Additional exam requirements/recommendations for international students: Required—TOEFL (minimum score 600 paper-based; 250 computer-based; 100 iBT), TWE (minimum score 4). *Application deadline:* For fall admission, 6/1 for domestic students, 1/15 for international students; for spring admission, 11/15 for domestic students, 10/1 for international students. Applications are processed on a rolling basis. Application fee: $80. Electronic applications accepted. *Expenses:* Contact institution. *Financial support:* In 2009–10, 155 students received support, including 150 fellowships (averaging $11,335 per year), 5 research assistantships with full tuition reimbursements available (averaging $22,440 per year); career-related internships or fieldwork, Federal Work-Study, institutionally sponsored loans, scholarships/grants, health care benefits, and unspecified assistantships also available. Support available to part-time students. Financial award application deadline: 12/1; financial award applicants required to submit FAFSA. *Unit head:* Katty Jones, Director, Program Services, 212-998-7411, Fax: 212-995-4164, E-mail: katty.jones@nyu.edu. *Application contact:* Christopher Alexander, Administrative Aide, Enrollment, 212-998-7414, Fax: 212-995-4611, E-mail: wagner. admissions@nyu.edu.

Oklahoma State University, William S. Spears School of Business, Department of Finance, Stillwater, OK 74078. Offers finance (PhD); quantitative financial economics (MS). Part-time programs available. *Faculty:* 14 full-time (2 women), 5 part-time/adjunct (0 women). *Students:* 21 full-time (9 women), 8 part-time (1 woman), 12 international. Average age 30. 60 applicants, 35% accepted, 6 enrolled. In 2009, 9 master's, 1 doctorate awarded. *Degree requirements:* For master's, thesis or alternative; for doctorate, comprehensive exam, thesis/dissertation. *Entrance requirements:* For master's and doctorate, GRE or GMAT. Additional exam requirements/recommendations for international students: Required—TOEFL (minimum score 550 paper-based; 79 iBT). *Application deadline:* For fall admission, 3/1 priority date for international students; for spring admission, 8/1 priority date for international students. Applications are processed on a rolling basis. Application fee: $40 ($75 for international students). Electronic applications accepted. *Expenses:* Tuition, state resident: full-time $3716; part-time $154.85 per credit hour. Tuition, nonresident: full-time $14,448; part-time $602 per credit hour. Required fees: $1772; $73.85 per credit hour. One-time fee: $50. Tuition and fees vary according to course load and campus/location. *Financial support:* In 2009–10, 14 research assistantships (averaging $9,552 per year), 3 teaching assistantships (averaging $32,656 per year) were awarded; career-related internships or fieldwork, Federal Work-Study, scholarships/ grants, health care benefits, tuition waivers (partial), and unspecified assistantships also available. Support available to part-time students. Financial award application deadline: 3/1; financial award applicants required to submit FAFSA. *Faculty research:* Corporate risk management, derivatives banking, investments and securities issuance, corporate governance, banking. *Unit head:* Dr. John Polonchek, Head, 405-744-5199, Fax: 405-744-5180. *Application contact:* Dr. Gordon Emslie, Dean, 405-744-6368, Fax: 405-744-0355, E-mail: grad-i@ okstate.edu.

Providence College, Graduate Studies, School of Business, Providence, RI 02918. Offers accountancy (MBA); economics (MBA); entrepreneurship (MBA); finance (MBA); international business (MBA); management (MBA); marketing (MBA); not-for-profit (MBA); quantitative (MBA). Part-time and evening/weekend programs available. *Faculty:* 14 full-time (8 women), 7 part-time/adjunct (3 women). *Students:* 63 full-time (18 women), 46 part-time (19 women); includes 4 minority (2 African Americans, 2 Asian Americans or Pacific Islanders), 7 international. Average age 26. 43 applicants, 88% accepted. In 2009, 40 master's awarded. *Degree*

requirements: For master's, thesis optional. *Entrance requirements:* For master's, GMAT. Additional exam requirements/recommendations for international students: Required—TOEFL (minimum score 550 paper-based; 213 computer-based; 80 iBT). *Application deadline:* For fall admission, 8/1 priority date for domestic and international students; for spring admission, 12/1 priority date for domestic and international students. Applications are processed on a rolling basis. Application fee: $55. *Expenses:* Contact institution. *Financial support:* In 2009–10, 34 research assistantships with full tuition reimbursements (averaging $8,400 per year) were awarded; Federal Work-Study, institutionally sponsored loans, and unspecified assistantships also available. Support available to part-time students. Financial award application deadline: 8/1; financial award applicants required to submit FAFSA. *Unit head:* Dr. MaryJane Lenon, Director, MBA Program, 401-865-2566, Fax: 401-865-2978, E-mail: mjlenon@providence.edu. *Application contact:* Katherine A. Follett, Administrative Coordinator, 401-865-2333, Fax: 401-865-2978, E-mail: kfollett@providence.edu.

St. John's University, The Peter J. Tobin College of Business, Department of Computer Information Systems and Decision Sciences, Queens, NY 11439. Offers MBA, Adv C. Part-time and evening/weekend programs available. *Students:* 9 full-time (4 women), 2 part-time (0 women); includes 2 minority (both Asian Americans or Pacific Islanders), 6 international. Average age 26. 8 applicants, 75% accepted, 3 enrolled. In 2009, 5 master's awarded. *Degree requirements:* For master's, comprehensive exam (for some programs), thesis optional. *Entrance requirements:* For master's, GMAT, 2 letters of recommendation, resume; for Adv C, GMAT, 2 letters of recommendation, resume, undergraduate transcripts, essay. Additional exam requirements/recommendations for international students: Required—TOEFL (minimum score 500 paper-based; 173 computer-based; 61 iBT), IELTS (minimum score 5.5). *Application deadline:* For fall admission, 5/1 priority date for domestic and international students; for spring admission, 11/1 priority date for domestic and international students. Applications are processed on a rolling basis. Application fee: $70. Electronic applications accepted. *Expenses:* Contact institution. *Financial support:* Research assistantships, scholarships/grants available. Support available to part-time students. Financial award application deadline: 3/1; financial award applicants required to submit FAFSA. *Unit head:* Dr. Victor Lu, Chair, 718-990-6392, Fax: 718-990-1868, E-mail: luf@stjohns.edu. *Application contact:* Nicole T. Bryan, Assistant Dean, 718-990-2599, Fax: 718-990-5242, E-mail: tcbgradadmissions@stjohns.edu.

Syracuse University, Martin J. Whitman School of Management, PhD Program in Business Administration, Syracuse, NY 13244. Offers accounting (PhD); finance (PhD); management information systems (PhD); managerial statistics (PhD); marketing (PhD); operations management (PhD); organizational behavior (PhD); strategy and human resources (PhD); supply chain management (PhD). *Degree requirements:* For doctorate, comprehensive exam, thesis/dissertation, summer research paper. *Entrance requirements:* For doctorate, GMAT or GRE General Test, 3 recommendations. Additional exam requirements/recommendations for international students: Required—TOEFL (minimum score 600 paper-based; 250 computer-based; 100 iBT). Electronic applications accepted. *Expenses:* Tuition: Full-time $26,808; part-time $1117 per credit. Required fees: $1024. *Faculty research:* Marketing models, market microstructure, supply chain, auditing, corporate governance.

Texas Tech University, Jerry S. Rawls College of Business Administration, Area of Information Systems and Quantitative Sciences, Lubbock, TX 79409. Offers business statistics (MS, PhD); healthcare management (MS); management information systems (MS, PhD); production and operations management (MS, PhD); risk management (MS). Part-time programs available. *Faculty:* 14 full-time (0 women). *Students:* 61 full-time (14 women), 5 part-time (1 woman); includes 2 minority (1 African American, 1 Asian American or Pacific Islander), 52 international. Average age 27. 94 applicants, 84% accepted, 35 enrolled. In 2009, 6 master's, 6 doctorates awarded. Terminal master's awarded for partial completion of doctoral program. *Degree requirements:* For master's, comprehensive exam or capstone course; for doctorate, thesis/ dissertation, qualifying exams. *Entrance requirements:* For master's and doctorate, GMAT, holistic profile of academic credentials. Additional exam requirements/recommendations for international students: Required—TOEFL (minimum score 550 paper-based; 213 computer-based; 79 iBT). *Application deadline:* For fall admission, 4/1 priority date for domestic students, 1/15 priority date for international students; for spring admission, 9/1 priority date for domestic students, 7/15 priority date for international students. Applications are processed on a rolling basis. Application fee: $50 ($75 for international students). Electronic applications accepted. *Expenses:* Tuition, state resident: full-time $5100; part-time $213 per credit hour. Tuition, nonresident: full-time $11,748; part-time $490 per credit hour. Required fees: $2298; $50 per credit hour. $555 per semester. *Financial support:* In 2009–10, 4 research assistantships (averaging $8,000 per year), 8 teaching assistantships (averaging $17,000 per year) were awarded; Federal Work-Study, scholarships/grants, and unspecified assistantships also available. *Faculty research:* Database management systems, systems management and engineering, expert systems and adaptive knowledge-based sciences, statistical analysis and design. *Unit head:* Dr. Bradley Ewing, Area Coordinator, 806-742-3939, Fax: 806-742-3193, E-mail: bradley. ewing@ttu.edu. *Application contact:* Cynthia D. Barnes, Director, Graduate Services Center, 806-742-3184, Fax: 806-742-3958, E-mail: ba_grad@ttu.edu.

The University of British Columbia, Faculty of Arts and Faculty of Graduate Studies, Department of Psychology, Vancouver, BC V6T 1Z4, Canada. Offers behavioral neuroscience (MA, PhD); clinical psychology (MA, PhD); cognitive science (MA, PhD); developmental psychology (MA, PhD); health psychology (MA, PhD); quantitative methods (MA, PhD); social/ personality psychology (MA, PhD). *Accreditation:* APA (one or more programs are accredited). Terminal master's awarded for partial completion of doctoral program. *Degree requirements:* For master's, thesis; for doctorate, comprehensive exam, thesis/dissertation. *Entrance requirements:* For master's and doctorate, GRE General Test. Additional exam requirements/ recommendations for international students: Required—TOEFL (minimum score 550 paper-based; 230 computer-based; 80 iBT). Electronic applications accepted. *Faculty research:* Clinical, developmental, social/personality, cognition, behavioral neuroscience.

University of California, Santa Barbara, Graduate Division, College of Letters and Sciences, Division of Mathematics, Life, and Physical Sciences, Department of Geography, Santa Barbara, CA 93106-4060. Offers cognitive science (PhD); geography (MA); quantitative methods in the social sciences (PhD); transportation (PhD); MA/PhD. *Students:* 67 full-time (33 women). Average age 30. 92 applicants, 28% accepted, 15 enrolled. In 2009, 3 master's, 13 doctorates awarded. *Degree requirements:* For master's, comprehensive exam (for some programs), thesis; for doctorate, comprehensive exam, thesis/dissertation. *Entrance requirements:* For master's, GRE General Test, 3 letters of recommendation, resume/curriculum vitae; for doctorate, GRE General Test, 3 letters of recommendation, statement of purpose, personal achievements/ contributions statement, resume/curriculum vitae, transcripts for post-secondary institutions attended. Additional exam requirements/recommendations for international students: Required— TOEFL (minimum score 550 paper-based; 213 computer-based; 80 iBT) or IELTS (minimum score 7). *Application deadline:* For fall admission, 2/1 for domestic and international students. Application fee: $70 ($90 for international students). Electronic applications accepted. *Financial support:* In 2009–10, 59 students received support, including 36 fellowships with full and partial tuition reimbursements available (averaging $10,700 per year), 29 research assistantships with full and partial tuition reimbursements available (averaging $8,600 per year), 31 teaching assistantships with partial tuition reimbursements available (averaging $8,000 per year); Federal Work-Study, institutionally sponsored loans, scholarships/grants, health care benefits, and unspecified assistantships also available. Financial award applicants required to submit FAFSA. *Faculty research:* Earth system science, human environment relations, modeling, measurement and computation, quantitative methods in social sciences. *Unit head:* Dr. Oliver Chadwick, Chair, 805-893-4223, E-mail: oac@geog.ucsb.edu. *Application contact:* Graduate Program Assistant, 805-893-3663, Fax: 805-893-3146, E-mail: grad_assistant@geog.ucsb.edu.

University of California, Santa Barbara, Graduate Division, College of Letters and Sciences, Division of Mathematics, Life, and Physical Sciences, Department of Statistics and Applied

Probability, Santa Barbara, CA 93106-3110. Offers financial mathematics and statistics (PhD); quantitative methods in the social sciences (PhD); statistics (MA), including applied statistics, mathematical statistics; statistics and applied probability (PhD); MA/PhD. *Faculty:* 12 full-time (3 women), 4 part-time/adjunct (1 woman). *Students:* 42 full-time (12 women). Average age 28. 218 applicants, 39% accepted, 14 enrolled. In 2009, 20 master's, 1 doctorate awarded. Terminal master's awarded for partial completion of doctoral program. *Degree requirements:* For master's, comprehensive exam, thesis or alternative; for doctorate, comprehensive exam, thesis/dissertation. *Entrance requirements:* For master's, GRE General Test, 3 letters of recommendation, resume/curriculum vitae; for doctorate, GRE General Test, 3 letters of recommendation, statement of purpose, personal achievements/contributions statement, resume/curriculum vitae, transcripts for post-secondary institutions attended. Additional exam requirements/recommendations for international students: Required—TOEFL (minimum score 550 paper-based; 213 computer-based; 80 iBT), or IELTS (minimum score 7). *Application deadline:* For fall admission, 1/1 for domestic and international students; for winter admission, 11/1 for domestic and international students; for spring admission, 2/1 for domestic and international students. Application fee: $70 ($90 for international students). Electronic applications accepted. *Financial support:* In 2009–10, 29 students received support, including 5 fellowships with full and partial tuition reimbursements available (averaging $7,400 per year), 28 teaching assistantships with partial tuition reimbursements available (averaging $10,300 per year); Federal Work-Study, institutionally sponsored loans, scholarships/grants, health care benefits, and unspecified assistantships also available. Financial award application deadline: 1/1; financial award applicants required to submit FAFSA. *Faculty research:* Bayesian inference, financial mathematics, stochastic processes, environmental statistics, biostatistical modeling. *Unit head:* Dr. Yuedong Wang, Chair, 805-893-4870, Fax: 805-893-2334, E-mail: yeudong@pstat.ucsb.edu. *Application contact:* Rickie R. Lazzerini, Graduate Program Assistant, 805-893-4857, Fax: 805-893-2334, E-mail: gradinfo@pstat.ucsb.edu.

University of Cincinnati, Graduate School, College of Business, MS Program, Cincinnati, OH 45221. Offers accounting (MS); information systems (MS); marketing (MS); quantitative analysis (MS). Part-time and evening/weekend programs available. *Degree requirements:* For master's, thesis (for some programs). *Entrance requirements:* For master's, GMAT, GRE, resume, letters of recommendation. Additional exam requirements/recommendations for international students: Required—TOEFL (minimum score 600 paper-based; 250 computer-based; 100 iBT). Electronic applications accepted. *Expenses:* Contact institution.

University of Cincinnati, Graduate School, College of Business, PhD Program, Cincinnati, OH 45221. Offers accounting (PhD); finance (PhD); information systems (PhD); management (PhD); marketing (PhD); quantitative analysis and operations management (PhD). *Degree requirements:* For doctorate, comprehensive exam, thesis/dissertation. *Entrance requirements:* For doctorate, GMAT, GRE, resume, letters of recommendation. Additional exam requirements/recommendations for international students: Required—TOEFL (minimum score 600 paper-based; 250 computer-based; 100 iBT). Electronic applications accepted. *Expenses:* Contact institution.

University of Connecticut, Graduate School, College of Liberal Arts and Sciences, Department of Public Policy, Field of Survey Research, Storrs, CT 06269. Offers quantitative research methods (Graduate Certificate); survey research (MA). *Faculty:* 1 full-time (0 women). *Students:* 11 full-time (9 women), 8 part-time (7 women); includes 2 minority (1 African American, 1 Asian American or Pacific Islander), 1 international. Average age 31. 4 applicants, 25% accepted, 1 enrolled. In 2009, 3 master's, 7 other advanced degrees awarded. *Degree requirements:* For master's, comprehensive exam. *Entrance requirements:* For master's, GRE General Test. Additional exam requirements/recommendations for international students: Required—TOEFL (minimum score 550 paper-based; 213 computer-based). *Application deadline:* For fall admission, 2/1 priority date for domestic and international students; for spring admission, 11/1 for domestic students, 10/1 for international students. Applications are processed on a rolling basis. Application fee: $55. Electronic applications accepted. *Expenses:* Tuition, state resident: full-time $4725; part-time $525 per credit. Tuition, nonresident: full-time $12,267; part-time $1363 per credit. Required fees: $346 per semester. Tuition and fees vary according to course load. *Financial support:* In 2009–10, 6 research assistantships with full tuition reimbursements, 5 teaching assistantships with full tuition reimbursements were awarded; Federal Work-Study, scholarships/grants, health care benefits, and unspecified assistantships also available. Financial award application deadline: 2/1; financial award applicants required to submit FAFSA. *Unit head:* Jennifer Dineen, Chairperson, 860-486-2000, E-mail: jennifer.dineen@uconn.edu. *Application contact:* Valerie Rogers, Program Director, 860-570-9047, Fax: 860-570-9114, E-mail: valerie.rogers@uconn.edu.

University of Florida, Graduate School, Warrington College of Business Administration, Hough Graduate School of Business, Programs in Business Administration, Gainesville, FL 32611. Offers accounting (MBA); arts administration (MBA); business strategy and public policy (MBA); competitive strategy (MBA); decision and information sciences (MBA); electronic commerce (MBA); finance (MBA); general business (MBA); global management (MBA); Graham-Buffett security analysis (MBA); health administration (MBA); human resources management (MBA); international studies (MBA); Latin American business (MBA); management (MBA); marketing (MBA); sports administration (MBA); JD/MBA; MBA/MS; MBA/PhD; MBA/Pharm D; MD/MBA. *Accreditation:* AACSB. Part-time and evening/weekend programs available. Postbaccalaureate distance learning degree programs offered. *Entrance requirements:* For master's, GMAT, minimum GPA of 3.0, interview. Additional exam requirements/recommendations for international students: Required—TOEFL (minimum score 550 paper-based; 213 computer-based). Electronic applications accepted. *Faculty research:* Accounting, finance, insurance, management, real estate and urban analysis marketing.

University of Illinois at Chicago, Graduate College, School of Public Health, Biostatistics Section, Chicago, IL 60607-7128. Offers biostatistics (MS, PhD); quantitative methods (MPH). Part-time programs available. Terminal master's awarded for partial completion of doctoral program. *Degree requirements:* For master's, thesis, field practicum; for doctorate, thesis/dissertation, independent research, internship. *Entrance requirements:* For master's and doctorate, GRE General Test, minimum GPA of 2.75. Additional exam requirements/recommendations for international students: Required—TOEFL. Electronic applications accepted.

University of Missouri–St. Louis, College of Business Administration, Program in Business Administration, St. Louis, MO 63121. Offers accounting (MBA); business administration (Certificate); finance (MBA); human resource management (Certificate); logistics and supply chain management (MBA, Certificate); management (MBA); marketing (MBA); marketing management (Certificate); operations (MBA); quantitative management science (MBA). *Accreditation:* AACSB. Part-time and evening/weekend programs available. *Faculty:* 30 full-time (5 women), 11 part-time/adjunct (2 women). *Students:* 107 full-time (47 women), 310 part-time (120 women); includes 32 minority (17 African Americans, 6 Asian Americans or Pacific Islanders, 9 Hispanic Americans), 66 international. Average age 31. 285 applicants, 58% accepted, 130 enrolled. In 2009, 149 master's, 13 other advanced degrees awarded. *Entrance requirements:* For master's, GMAT, 2 letters of recommendation. Additional exam requirements/recommendations for international students: Required—TOEFL (minimum score 550 paper-based; 213 computer-based). *Application deadline:* For fall admission, 7/1 for domestic students; for spring admission, 11/1 for domestic students. Applications are processed on a rolling basis. Application fee: $35 ($40 for international students). Electronic applications accepted. *Expenses:* Tuition, state resident: full-time $5377; part-time $297.70 per credit hour. Tuition, nonresident: full-time $13,882; part-time $771.20 per credit hour. Required fees: $220; $12.20 per credit hour. One-time fee: $12. Tuition and fees vary according to course level, campus/location and program. *Financial support:* In 2009–10, 27 research assistantships with full and partial tuition reimbursements (averaging $8,525 per year), 6 teaching assistantships with full and partial tuition reimbursements (averaging $13,950 per year) were awarded; career-related internships or fieldwork, Federal Work-Study, and institutionally sponsored loans also available. Support available to part-time students. Financial award application deadline: 4/1; financial award applicants required to submit FAFSA. *Faculty research:* Human resources, strategic management, marketing strategy, consumer behavior product development, advertising. *Unit head:* Karl Kottemann, Assistant Director, 314-516-5885, Fax: 314-516-6420, E-mail: mba@umsl.edu. *Application contact:* 314-516-5458, Fax: 314-516-6996, E-mail: gradadm@umsl.edu.

University of North Texas, Robert B. Toulouse School of Graduate Studies, College of Business Administration, Department of Information Technology and Decision Sciences, Denton, TX 76203-5017. Offers business computer information systems (PhD); decision technologies (MS); information technology (MS); management science (PhD). Part-time and evening/weekend programs available. *Degree requirements:* For doctorate, comprehensive exam, thesis/dissertation. *Entrance requirements:* For master's, GMAT; for doctorate, GMAT or GRE General Test. Additional exam requirements/recommendations for international students: Required—proof of English language proficiency required for non-native English speakers; Recommended—TOEFL (minimum score 550 paper-based; 213 computer-based; 79 iBT). *Application deadline:* Applications are processed on a rolling basis. Application fee: $50 ($75 for international students). Electronic applications accepted. *Expenses:* Tuition, state resident: full-time $4298; part-time $239 per contact hour. Tuition, nonresident: full-time $9878; part-time $549 per contact hour. Required fees: $265 per contact hour. *Financial support:* Fellowships, research assistantships, teaching assistantships, career-related internships or fieldwork and Federal Work-Study available. Financial award application deadline: 4/1; financial award applicants required to submit FAFSA. *Faculty research:* Large scale IS, business intelligence, security, applied statistics, quality and reliability management. *Unit head:* Chair. *Application contact:* Graduate Advisor, 940-565-4149, Fax: 940-565-4935, E-mail: itdsrecp@unt.edu.

University of Oregon, Graduate School, Charles H. Lundquist College of Business, Department of Decision Sciences, Eugene, OR 97403. Offers MA, MS. *Entrance requirements:* For master's, GMAT. *Faculty research:* Time-series analysis, production scheduling, nonparametric methods, decision theory.

University of Pittsburgh, Katz Graduate School of Business, Doctoral Program in Business Administration, Pittsburgh, PA 15260. Offers accounting (PhD); finance (PhD); information systems (PhD); marketing (PhD); operations/decision sciences/artificial intelligence (PhD); organizational behavior and human resource management (PhD); strategic planning (PhD). *Accreditation:* AACSB. *Faculty:* 50 full-time (15 women). *Students:* 53 full-time (21 women); includes 8 minority (4 African Americans, 2 Asian Americans or Pacific Islanders, 2 Hispanic Americans), 22 international. 324 applicants, 4% accepted, 12 enrolled. In 2009, 11 doctorates awarded. *Degree requirements:* For doctorate, comprehensive exam, thesis/dissertation. *Entrance requirements:* For doctorate, GMAT or GRE, references, work experience relevant for individual program. Additional exam requirements/recommendations for international students: Required—TOEFL or IELTS. *Application deadline:* For fall admission, 2/1 priority date for domestic and international students. Applications are processed on a rolling basis. Application fee: $50. Electronic applications accepted. *Expenses:* Tuition, state resident: full-time $16,402; part-time $665 per credit. Tuition, nonresident: full-time $28,694; part-time $1175 per credit. Required fees: $690; $175 per term. Tuition and fees vary according to program. *Financial support:* In 2009–10, 36 students received support, including 31 research assistantships with full tuition reimbursements available (averaging $18,450 per year), 5 teaching assistantships with full tuition reimbursements available (averaging $23,511 per year); fellowships, Federal Work-Study, scholarships/grants, health care benefits, and unspecified assistantships also available. Financial award application deadline: 2/1. *Faculty research:* Accounting statements and reporting, incentives and governance; corporate finance, mergers and acquisitions; information systems processes, structures, OR, supply chain, and decision-making; organizational structure, knowledge management, and corporate strategy; consumer behavior and marketing models. Total annual research expenditures: $362,777. *Unit head:* Dr. John E. Hulland, Director, 412-648-1534, Fax: 412-624-3633, E-mail: jhulland@katz.pitt.edu. *Application contact:* Carrie Woods, Assistant Director, 412-648-1525, Fax: 412-624-3633, E-mail: cawoods@katz.pitt.edu.

University of Puerto Rico, Río Piedras, College of Business Administration, San Juan, PR 00931-3300. Offers accounting (MBA); finance (MBA, PhD); general business (MBA); human resources management (MBA); international trade and business (MBA, PhD); marketing (MBA); operations management (MBA); quantitative methods (MBA). *Accreditation:* ACBSP. Part-time programs available. *Degree requirements:* For master's, comprehensive exam, thesis or alternative, research project. *Entrance requirements:* For master's, GMAT or PAEG, minimum GPA of 3.0, letter of recommendation; for doctorate, GMAT, PAEG, minimum GPA of 3.0, master degree. *Faculty research:* Management.

University of South Africa, College of Economic and Management Sciences, Pretoria, South Africa. Offers accounting (D Admin, D Com); accounting science (DA); auditing (D Admin, D Com); business administration (M Tech); business economics (D Admin); business leadership (DBL); business management (D Admin, D Com); economic management analysis (M Tech); economics (D Admin, D Com, PhD); human resource development (M Tech); industrial psychology (D Admin, D Com, PhD); logistics (D Com); marketing (M Tech); public administration (D Admin, D Com, DPA, PhD); public management (M Tech); quantitative management (D Admin, D Com); real estate (M Tech); statistics (D Admin, PhD); tourism management (D Admin, D Com); transport economics (D Admin, D Com).

University of Southern California, Graduate School, College of Letters, Arts and Sciences, Department of Psychology, Los Angeles, CA 90089. Offers brain and cognitive science (PhD); clinical science (PhD); developmental psychology (PhD); human behavior (MHB); psychology (MA); quantitative methods (PhD); social psychology (PhD); PhD/MPH. *Accreditation:* APA. *Faculty:* 34 full-time (10 women), 17 part-time/adjunct (7 women). *Students:* 107 full-time (73 women); includes 38 minority (6 African Americans, 21 Asian Americans or Pacific Islanders, 11 Hispanic Americans), 19 international. 430 applicants, 6% accepted, 13 enrolled. In 2009, 17 master's, 12 doctorates awarded. *Degree requirements:* For doctorate, comprehensive exam, thesis/dissertation, one-year internship (for clinical science students). *Entrance requirements:* For doctorate, GRE. Additional exam requirements/recommendations for international students: Recommended—TOEFL (minimum score 600 paper-based; 250 computer-based; 100 iBT). *Application deadline:* For fall admission, 12/1 for domestic and international students. Application fee: $95. Electronic applications accepted. *Expenses:* Tuition: Full-time $25,980; part-time $1315 per unit. Required fees: $554. One-time fee: $35 full-time. Full-time tuition and fees vary according to degree level and program. *Financial support:* In 2009–10, 80 students received support, including 16 fellowships with full tuition reimbursements available (averaging $22,500 per year), 22 research assistantships with full tuition reimbursements available (averaging $19,000 per year), 38 teaching assistantships with full tuition reimbursements available (averaging $19,000 per year); career-related internships or fieldwork, scholarships/grants, traineeships, and health care benefits also available. *Faculty research:* Affective neuroscience; children and families; vision, culture and ethnicity; intergroup relations; aggression and violence; language and reading development; substance abuse. *Unit head:* Dr. Margaret Gatz, Chair and Professor, 213-740-2203, Fax: 213-746-9028, E-mail: gatz@usc.edu. *Application contact:* Irene Takaragawa, Graduate Advisor, 213-740-2205, E-mail: itakarag@usc.edu.

The University of Texas at Arlington, Graduate School, College of Business, Department of Finance and Real Estate, Arlington, TX 76019. Offers quantitative finance (MS); real estate (MS). Part-time and evening/weekend programs available. *Faculty:* 7 full-time (1 woman). *Students:* 39 full-time (7 women), 36 part-time (9 women); includes 15 minority (4 African Americans, 11 Asian Americans or Pacific Islanders), 28 international. In 2009, 14 master's awarded. *Degree requirements:* For master's, thesis optional. *Entrance requirements:* For master's, GMAT, minimum GPA of 3.0. Additional exam requirements/recommendations for international students: Required—TOEFL (minimum score 550 paper-based; 213 computer-based; 79 iBT). *Application deadline:* For fall admission, 6/5 priority date for domestic students, 4/1 for international students; for spring admission, 10/15 for domestic students, 9/1 for international students. Applications are processed on a rolling basis. Application fee: $35 ($50 for international students). *Financial support:* In 2009–10, 3 fellowships (averaging $1,000 per year), research assistantships (averaging $6,000 per year), 14 teaching assistantships (averaging $13,000 per year) were awarded; career-related internships or fieldwork, Federal Work-Study,

Quantitative Analysis

The University of Texas at Arlington (continued)

and institutionally sponsored loans also available. Financial award application deadline: 6/1; financial award applicants required to submit FAFSA. *Unit head:* Dr. David Diltz, Chair, 817-272-3705, Fax: 817-272-2252, E-mail: diltz@uta.edu. *Application contact:* Dr. Andy Hansz, Graduate Advisor, 817-272-3705, Fax: 817-272-2252, E-mail: realestate@uta.edu.

The University of Texas at Arlington, Graduate School, College of Business, Program in Business Administration, Arlington, TX 76019. Offers accounting (PhD); business statistics (PhD); finance (MBA, PhD); information systems (MBA, PhD); management (MBA, PhD); management sciences (MBA); marketing (MBA, PhD); operations management (PhD); real estate (MBA). *Accreditation:* AACSB. Part-time and evening/weekend programs available. Postbaccalaureate distance learning degree programs offered (no on-campus study). *Students:* 587 full-time (188 women), 349 part-time (140 women); includes 188 minority (66 African Americans, 62 Asian Americans or Pacific Islanders, 60 Hispanic Americans), 371 international. 282 applicants, 96% accepted, 145 enrolled. In 2009, 431 master's awarded. Terminal master's awarded for partial completion of doctoral program. *Degree requirements:* For master's, thesis optional; for doctorate, comprehensive exam, thesis/dissertation. *Entrance requirements:* For master's, GMAT; for doctorate, GMAT, minimum GPA of 3.0 (undergraduate), 3.4 (graduate); 30 hours of graduate course work. Additional exam requirements/recommendations for international students: Required—TOEFL (minimum score 550 paper-based; 213 computer-based; 79 iBT). *Application deadline:* For fall admission, 6/5 for domestic students, 4/1 for international students; for spring admission, 10/15 for domestic students, 9/1 for international students. Applications are processed on a rolling basis. Application fee: $35 ($50 for international students). Electronic applications accepted. *Financial support:* In 2009–10, 1 fellowship (averaging $1,000 per year), 30 research assistantships (averaging $6,000 per year), 45 teaching assistantships (averaging $13,000 per year) were awarded; career-related internships or fieldwork, scholarships/grants, and unspecified assistantships also available. Financial award application deadline: 6/1; financial award applicants required to submit FAFSA. *Unit head:* Greg Frazier, Director PhD Programs, 817-272-3559, Fax: 817-272-5799, E-mail: frazier@exchange.uta.edu. *Application contact:* Melanie McGee, Director of MBA Program, 817-272-0658, Fax: 817-272-5799, E-mail: mwmcgee@uta.edu.

See Close-Up on page 273.

The University of Texas at Dallas, School of Management, Programs in Management Science, Richardson, TX 75080. Offers accounting (PhD); decision sciences (PhD); finance (PhD); management strategy and public policy (PhD); marketing (PhD); organizational behavior (PhD). *Accreditation:* AACSB. Part-time and evening/weekend programs available. *Faculty:* 12 full-time (3 women). *Students:* 72 full-time (23 women), 12 part-time (6 women); includes 10 minority (all Asian Americans or Pacific Islanders), 63 international. Average age 34. 173 applicants, 12% accepted, 7 enrolled. In 2009, 8 doctorates awarded. *Degree requirements:* For doctorate, thesis/dissertation. *Entrance requirements:* For doctorate, GMAT, minimum GPA of 3.0. Additional exam requirements/recommendations for international students: Required—TOEFL (minimum score 550 paper-based; 213 computer-based). *Application deadline:* For fall admission, 7/15 for domestic students, 5/1 priority date for international students; for spring admission, 11/15 for domestic students, 9/1 priority date for international students. Applications are processed on a rolling basis. Application fee: $50 ($100 for international students). Electronic applications accepted. *Expenses:* Tuition, state resident: full-time $11,068; part-time $461 per credit hour. Tuition, nonresident: full-time $21,178; part-time $882 per credit hour. Tuition and fees vary according to course load. *Financial support:* In 2009–10, 1 research assistantship with full tuition reimbursement (averaging $13,050 per year), 43 teaching assistantships with full tuition reimbursements (averaging $14,795 per year) were awarded; fellowships, career-related internships or fieldwork, Federal Work-Study, institutionally sponsored loans, scholarships/grants, and unspecified assistantships also available. Support available to part-time students. Financial award application deadline: 4/30; financial award applicants required to submit FAFSA. *Faculty research:* Empirical generalizations in marketing, diffusion of generations of technology, stochastic brand-choice theory, acceptance of trade deals by supermarkets, nonparametric estimations of market share response. *Unit head:* Dr. Sumit Sarkar, Program Director, 972-883-2745, Fax: 972-883-5977, E-mail: som-phd.@

utdallas.edu. *Application contact:* James Parker, Assistant Director, 972-883-5842, E-mail: jparker@utdallas.edu.

Virginia Commonwealth University, Graduate School, School of Business, Program in Decision Sciences, Richmond, VA 23284-9005. Offers MBA. *Entrance requirements:* For master's, GMAT.

Virginia Polytechnic Institute and State University, VT Online, Blacksburg, VA 24061. Offers aerospace engineering (MS); business information systems (Graduate Certificate); career and technical education (MS); computer engineering (M Eng, MS); decision support systems (Graduate Certificate); eLearning leadership (MA); electrical engineering (M Eng, MS); engineering administration (MEA); environmental politics and policy (Graduate Certificate); foundations of political analysis (Graduate Certificate); health product risk management (Graduate Certificate); information policy and society (Graduate Certificate); information security (Graduate Certificate); instructional technology (MA); liberal arts (Graduate Certificate); life sciences: health product risk management (MS); natural resources (MNR, Graduate Certificate); networking (Graduate Certificate); nonprofit and nongovernmental organization management (Graduate Certificate); ocean engineering (MS); political science (MA); security studies (Graduate Certificate); software development (Graduate Certificate). *Expenses:* Tuition, area resident: Full-time $10,228; part-time $459 per credit hour. Tuition, nonresident: full-time $17,892; part-time $865 per credit hour. Required fees: $1966; $451 per semester.

Walden University, Graduate Programs, School of Management, Minneapolis, MN 55401. Offers applied management and decision sciences (PhD), including accounting, engineering management, finance, general applied management and decision sciences, information systems management, knowledge management, leadership and organizational change, learning management, operations research, self-designed program in applied management and design sciences; business information management (MISM); enterprise information security (MISM); entrepreneurship (MBA, DBA); finance (MBA, DBA); global supply chain management (DBA); healthcare management (MBA); healthcare system improvement (MBA); human resource management (MBA); information systems management (DBA); international business (MBA, DBA); IT strategy and governance (MISM); leadership (MBA, MS, DBA), including entrepreneurship (MS), general management (MS), human resources leadership (MS), innovation and technology (MS), leader development (MS), project management (MS), self-designed (MS), sustainable futures (MS); managing global software and service supply chains (MISM); marketing (MBA, DBA); project management (MBA, MS); risk management (MBA, DBA); self-designed (MBA, DBA); social impact management (DBA); sustainable futures (MBA); technology (MBA); technology entrepreneurship (DBA). Part-time and evening/weekend programs available. Postbaccalaureate distance learning degree programs offered (minimal on-campus study). *Faculty:* 17 full-time, 211 part-time/adjunct. *Students:* 3,389 full-time (1,774 women), 815 part-time (482 women); includes 1,969 minority (1,640 African Americans, 36 American Indian/Alaska Native, 123 Asian Americans or Pacific Islanders, 170 Hispanic Americans), 95 international. Average age 41. In 2009, 699 master's, 42 doctorates awarded. *Degree requirements:* For doctorate, thesis/dissertation (for some programs), residency. *Entrance requirements:* For master's, bachelor's degree or equivalent in related field; minimum GPA of 2.5; official transcripts; goal statement; access to computer and Internet; for doctorate, master's degree or equivalent in related field; minimum GPA of 3.0; 3 years of related professional/academic experience (preferred). Additional exam requirements/recommendations for international students: Required—TOEFL (minimum score 550 paper-based; 213 computer-based), IELTS (minimum 6.5), TOEFL, IELTS, or Michigan English Language Assessment Battery (minimum score 82). *Application deadline:* Applications are processed on a rolling basis. Application fee: $50. Electronic applications accepted. *Expenses:* Tuition: Full-time $13,665; part-time $560 per credit. Required fees: $1375. Tuition and fees vary according to course load, degree level and program. *Financial support:* In 2009–10, 466 students received support; fellowships, Federal Work-Study, scholarships/grants, unspecified assistantships, and family tuition reduction, active duty/veteran tuition reduction, group tuition reduction, interest-free payment plans available. Support available to part-time students. Financial award applicants required to submit FAFSA. *Unit head:* William Schulz, Interim Associate Dean, 800-925-3368. *Application contact:* Jennifer Hall, Director of Enrollment, 866-4-WALDEN, E-mail: info@waldenu.edu.

Section 20
Real Estate

This section contains a directory of institutions offering graduate work in real estate. Additional information about programs listed in the directory may be obtained by writing directly to the dean of a graduate school or chair of a department at the address given in the directory.

For programs offering related work, see also in this book *Business Administration and Management.*

CONTENTS

Program Directory

Real Estate

American University, Kogod School of Business, Department of Finance, Program in Real Estate, Washington, DC 20016-8044. Offers MS. Part-time and evening/weekend programs available. *Students:* 6 full-time (0 women), 4 part-time (1 woman); includes 2 minority (both African Americans), 2 international. Average age 29. *Entrance requirements:* For master's, GMAT. Additional exam requirements/recommendations for international students: Required—TOEFL. *Application deadline:* For fall admission, 2/1 priority date for domestic students; for spring admission, 10/1 priority date for domestic students. Applications are processed on a rolling basis. Application fee: $100. *Expenses:* Tuition: Full-time $22,266; part-time $1237 per credit hour. Required fees: $430. Tuition and fees vary according to program. *Financial support:* Fellowships, career-related internships or fieldwork, Federal Work-Study, and institutionally sponsored loans available. Support available to part-time students. Financial award application deadline: 2/1.

American University, Kogod School of Business, Master of Business Administration Program, Washington, DC 20016-8044. Offers accounting (MBA); consulting (MBA), including information technology, international business, management; corporate finance: commercial banking (MBA); corporate finance: corporate financial management (MBA); corporate finance: investment banking (MBA), including corporate finance and private equity, trading and selling; entrepreneurship (MBA); global emerging markets (MBA), including business, finance, information technology; international trade and global supply chain management (MBA); leadership (MBA); marketing management (MBA); marketing research (MBA); real estate (MBA); MBA/JD; MBA/LL M. Part-time and evening/weekend programs available. *Faculty:* 14 full-time (6 women). *Students:* 133 full-time (56 women), 121 part-time (48 women); includes 54 minority (23 African Americans, 1 American Indian/Alaska Native, 16 Asian Americans or Pacific Islanders, 14 Hispanic Americans), 43 international. Average age 29. 539 applicants, 51% accepted, 86 enrolled. In 2009, 114 master's awarded. *Entrance requirements:* For master's, GMAT. Additional exam requirements/recommendations for international students: Required—TOEFL. *Application deadline:* For fall admission, 2/1 priority date for domestic students; for spring admission, 10/1 priority date for domestic students. Applications are processed on a rolling basis. Application fee: $100. *Expenses:* Contact institution. *Financial support:* In 2009–10, 19 students received support; fellowships, research assistantships with partial tuition reimbursements available, career-related internships or fieldwork, Federal Work-Study, and institutionally sponsored loans available. Support available to part-time students. Financial award application deadline: 2/1. *Faculty research:* Information technology, decision-aiding methodology, negotiation. *Unit head:* Dr. Stevan Holmberg, Chair, 202-885-6193, E-mail: sholmbe@american.edu. *Application contact:* Shannon Demko, Associate Director of Graduate Admissions, 202-885-1994, Fax: 202-885-1108, E-mail: demko@american.edu.

California State University, Sacramento, Graduate Studies, College of Business Administration, Sacramento, CA 95819. Offers accountancy (MS); business administration (MBA); human resources (MBA); management information science (MS); urban land development (MBA). *Accreditation:* AACSB. Part-time and evening/weekend programs available. *Degree requirements:* For master's, thesis or alternative, writing proficiency exam. *Entrance requirements:* For master's, GMAT. Additional exam requirements/recommendations for international students: Required—TOEFL. Electronic applications accepted.

Central European University, CEU Business School, Budapest, Hungary. Offers finance (MBA); general management (MBA); information technology (M Sc); information technology management (MBA); management (EMBA); marketing (MBA); real estate management (MBA). Part-time and evening/weekend programs available. *Entrance requirements:* For master's, GMAT. Additional exam requirements/recommendations for international students: Required—TOEFL (minimum score 570 paper-based; 230 computer-based). Electronic applications accepted. *Faculty research:* Social and ethical business, marketing.

Clemson University, Graduate School, College of Architecture, Arts, and Humanities, Department of Planning and Landscape Architecture and College of Business and Behavioral Science, Program in Real Estate Development, Clemson, SC 29634. Offers MRED. *Students:* 40 full-time (7 women). Average age 26. 54 applicants, 43% accepted, 20 enrolled. In 2009, 19 master's awarded. *Entrance requirements:* For master's, GRE or GMAT, 3 letters of recommendation. Additional exam requirements/recommendations for international students: Required—TOEFL (minimum score 600 paper-based). *Application deadline:* For fall admission, 2/1 priority date for domestic and international students. Applications are processed on a rolling basis. Application fee: $70 ($80 for international students). Electronic applications accepted. *Expenses:* Tuition, state resident: full-time $8684; part-time $528 per credit hour. Tuition, nonresident: full-time $15,330; part-time $1078 per credit hour. Required fees: $736; $37 per semester. Part-time tuition and fees vary according to course load and program. *Financial support:* In 2009–10, 2 students received support, including 2 fellowships with full and partial tuition reimbursements available (averaging $5,000 per year); research assistantships with partial tuition reimbursements available, teaching assistantships with partial tuition reimbursements available, career-related internships or fieldwork, institutionally sponsored loans, scholarships/grants, health care benefits, and unspecified assistantships also available. Support available to part-time students. *Unit head:* Dr. Elaine M. Worzala, Director, Center for Real Estate Development, 864-656-3657, Fax: 864-656-7519, E-mail: eworzal@clemson.edu. *Application contact:* Dr. Terry Farris, Program Director, 864-656-3903, Fax: 864-656-7519.

Cleveland State University, College of Graduate Studies, Maxine Goodman Levin College of Urban Affairs, Program in Environmental Studies, Cleveland, OH 44115. Offers environmental studies (MAES); geographic information systems (Certificate); urban real estate development and finance (Certificate); JD/MAES. Part-time and evening/weekend programs available. *Degree requirements:* For master's, thesis or alternative, exit project. *Entrance requirements:* For master's, GRE General Test (minimum score: verbal and quantitative 40th percentile, analytical writing 4.0), minimum GPA of 3.0. Additional exam requirements/recommendations for international students: Required—TOEFL (minimum score 525 paper-based; 197 computer-based; 65 iBT). Electronic applications accepted. *Faculty research:* Environmental policy and administration, environmental planning, geographic information systems (GIS), nonprofit management.

Cleveland State University, College of Graduate Studies, Maxine Goodman Levin College of Urban Affairs, Program in Public Administration, Cleveland, OH 44115. Offers geographic information systems (Certificate); local and urban management (Certificate); non-profit management (Certificate); public administration (MPA); urban real estate development (Certificate); JD/MPA. *Accreditation:* NASPAA. Part-time and evening/weekend programs available. *Degree requirements:* For master's, thesis or alternative, capstone course. *Entrance requirements:* For master's, GRE General Test (minimum 40th percentile verbal and quantitative, 4.0 writing), minimum GPA of 3.0. Additional exam requirements/recommendations for international students: Required—TOEFL (minimum score 525 paper-based; 197 computer-based; 65 iBT). Electronic applications accepted. *Faculty research:* Health care administration, public management, economic development, city management, nonprofit management.

Cleveland State University, College of Graduate Studies, Maxine Goodman Levin College of Urban Affairs, Program in Urban Planning, Design, and Development, Cleveland, OH 44115. Offers geographic information systems (Certificate); local and urban management (Certificate); urban economic development (Certificate); urban planning, design, and development (MUPDD); urban real estate development and finance (Certificate); JD/MUPDD. *Accreditation:* ACSP. Part-time and evening/weekend programs available. *Degree requirements:* For master's, project or thesis. *Entrance requirements:* For master's, GRE General Test (minimum 50th percentile verbal and quantitative, 4.0 analytical writing), minimum GPA of 3.0. Additional exam requirements/recommendations for international students: Required—TOEFL (minimum score 525 paper-based; 197 computer-based; 65 iBT). Electronic applications accepted. *Faculty research:* Housing and neighborhood development, urban housing policy, environmental sustainability, economic development.

Cleveland State University, College of Graduate Studies, Maxine Goodman Levin College of Urban Affairs, Program in Urban Studies, Cleveland, OH 44115. Offers geographic information systems (Certificate); local and urban management (Certificate); nonprofit management (Certificate); urban economic development (Certificate); urban real estate development and finance (Certificate); urban studies (MS); urban studies and public affairs (PhD). Part-time and evening/weekend programs available. *Degree requirements:* For master's, thesis or alternative, exit project, capstone course; for doctorate, comprehensive exam, thesis/dissertation. *Entrance requirements:* For master's, GRE General Test, minimum GPA of 3.0; for doctorate, GRE General Test, minimum GPA of 3.5. Additional exam requirements/recommendations for international students: Required—TOEFL (minimum score 525 paper-based; 197 computer-based; 65 iBT). Electronic applications accepted. *Faculty research:* Environmental issues, economic development, urban and public policy, public management.

Columbia University, Graduate School of Architecture, Planning, and Preservation, Program in Real Estate Development, New York, NY 10027. Offers MS. *Degree requirements:* For master's, thesis. *Entrance requirements:* For master's, GRE General Test.

Columbia University, Graduate School of Business, MBA Program, New York, NY 10027. Offers accounting (MBA); decision, risk, and operations (MBA); entrepreneurship (MBA); finance and economics (MBA); healthcare and pharmaceutical management (MBA); human resource management (MBA); international business (MBA); leadership and ethics (MBA); management (MBA); marketing (MBA); media (MBA); private equity (MBA); real estate (MBA); social enterprise (MBA); value investing (MBA); DDS/MBA; JD/MBA; MBA/MIA; MBA/MPH; MBA/MS; MD/MBA. *Faculty:* 149 full-time (23 women), 134 part-time/adjunct (16 women). *Students:* 1,293 full-time (435 women); includes 235 minority (65 African Americans, 4 American Indian/Alaska Native, 135 Asian Americans or Pacific Islanders, 31 Hispanic Americans), 417 international. Average age 28. 6,885 applicants, 15% accepted, 737 enrolled. In 2009, 696 master's awarded. *Entrance requirements:* For master's, GMAT, 2 letters of recommendation. Additional exam requirements/recommendations for international students: Required—TOEFL. *Application deadline:* For fall admission, 4/14 for domestic students, 3/3 for international students; for spring admission, 10/7 for domestic and international students. Applications are processed on a rolling basis. Application fee: $250. Electronic applications accepted. *Expenses:* Contact institution. *Financial support:* In 2009–10, 358 students received support, including 101 fellowships (averaging $23,250 per year); research assistantships, teaching assistantships, career-related internships or fieldwork, institutionally sponsored loans, and scholarships/grants also available. Financial award application deadline: 3/1; financial award applicants required to submit CSS PROFILE or FAFSA. *Faculty research:* Human decision making and behavioral research; real estate market and mortgage defaults; financial crisis and corporate governance; international business; security analysis and accounting. *Unit head:* Prof. Amir Ziv, Vice Dean of Students and the MBA Program, 212-854-3485, Fax: 212-932-0545, E-mail: az50@columbia.edu. *Application contact:* Mary J. Miller, Assistant Dean of Admissions, 212-854-1961, Fax: 212-662-6754, E-mail: apply@gsb.columbia.edu.

Cornell University, Graduate School, Graduate Fields of Architecture, Art and Planning, Field of Real Estate, Ithaca, NY 14853-0001. Offers MPSRE. *Faculty:* 25 full-time (2 women). *Students:* 44 full-time (8 women); includes 7 minority (2 African Americans, 2 Asian Americans or Pacific Islanders, 3 Hispanic Americans), 8 international. Average age 30. 142 applicants, 21% accepted, 23 enrolled. In 2009, 24 master's awarded. *Degree requirements:* For master's, project paper. *Entrance requirements:* For master's, GMAT, 2 letters of recommendation, resume. Additional exam requirements/recommendations for international students: Required—TOEFL (minimum score 600 paper-based; 250 computer-based; 77 iBT). *Application deadline:* For fall admission, 1/15 for domestic students. Application fee: $70. Electronic applications accepted. *Expenses:* Tuition: Full-time $29,500. Required fees: $70. Full-time tuition and fees vary according to degree level, program and student level. *Financial support:* In 2009–10, 3 students received support, including 1 fellowship with full tuition reimbursement available; research assistantships with full tuition reimbursements available, teaching assistantships with full tuition reimbursements available, institutionally sponsored loans, scholarships/grants, health care benefits, and unspecified assistantships also available. Financial award applicants required to submit FAFSA. *Faculty research:* Smart growth, economic development, urban redevelopment, development financing, securitization of real estate. *Unit head:* Director of Graduate Studies, 607-255-7110, Fax: 607-255-0242. *Application contact:* Graduate Field Assistant, 607-255-7110, Fax: 607-255-0242, E-mail: real_estate@cornell.edu.

DePaul University, Charles H. Kellstadt Graduate School of Business, Department of Finance, Chicago, IL 60604-2287. Offers behavioral finance (MBA); computational finance (MS); finance (MBA, MSF); financial analysis (MBA); financial management and control (MBA); international marketing and finance (MBA); managerial finance (MBA); real estate (MS); real estate finance and investment (MBA); strategy, execution and valuation (MBA). Part-time and evening/weekend programs available. *Faculty:* 26 full-time (5 women), 23 part-time/adjunct (2 women). *Students:* 432 full-time (120 women), 197 part-time (47 women); includes 94 minority (13 African Americans, 1 American Indian/Alaska Native, 55 Asian Americans or Pacific Islanders, 25 Hispanic Americans), 82 international. In 2009, 239 master's awarded. *Entrance requirements:* For master's, GMAT, 2 letters of recommendation, resume. Additional exam requirements/recommendations for international students: Required—TOEFL (minimum score 550 paper-based; 213 computer-based; 80 iBT). *Application deadline:* For fall admission, 7/1 for domestic students, 6/1 for international students; for winter admission, 10/1 for domestic students, 9/1 for international students; for spring admission, 2/1 for domestic students, 1/1 for international students. Applications are processed on a rolling basis. Application fee: $60. Electronic applications accepted. *Expenses:* Tuition: Full-time $37,525; part-time $620 per credit hour. *Financial support:* In 2009–10, 8 students received support, including 6 research assistantships with partial tuition reimbursements available (averaging $4,340 per year); scholarships/grants and unspecified assistantships also available. Financial award application deadline: 4/1; financial award applicants required to submit FAFSA. *Faculty research:* Derivatives, valuation, international finance, real estate, corporate finance. *Unit head:* Ali M. Fatemi, Professor and Chair, 312-362-8826, Fax: 312-362-6566, E-mail: afatemi@depaul.edu. *Application contact:* Christopher E. Kinsella, Director of Cohort MBA Programs, 312-362-8810, Fax: 312-362-6677, E-mail: kgsb@depaul.edu.

DePaul University, Charles H. Kellstadt Graduate School of Business, Department of Real Estate, Chicago, IL 60604-2287. Offers real estate (MS); real estate finance and investment (MBA). *Students:* 70 full-time (17 women), 44 part-time (12 women); includes 11 minority (2 African Americans, 1 American Indian/Alaska Native, 7 Asian Americans or Pacific Islanders, 1 Hispanic American), 3 international. *Expenses:* Tuition: Full-time $37,525; part-time $620 per credit hour. *Unit head:* Susanne Cannon, Chairman/Director. *Application contact:* Dustin Carnwell, Director of Recruiting and Admission, 312-362-8810, Fax: 312-362-6677, E-mail: kgsb@depaul.edu.

Drexel University, School of Technology and Professional Studies, Philadelphia, PA 19104-2875. Offers construction management (MS); engineering technology (MS); food science (MS); hospitality management (MS); professional studies: creativity studies (MS); professional studies: e-learning leadership (MS); professional studies: homeland security management (MS); project management (MS); property management (MS); sport management (MS). Post-baccalaureate distance learning degree programs offered.

Florida International University, Alvah H. Chapman, Jr. Graduate School of Business, Department of Finance and Real Estate, Miami, FL 33199. Offers finance (MSF); international real estate (MS); real estate (MS). Part-time and evening/weekend programs available. *Faculty:* 17 full-time (3 women). *Students:* 94 full-time (24 women), 12 part-time (5 women); includes 55 minority (15 African Americans, 5 Asian Americans or Pacific Islanders, 35 Hispanic Americans), 28 international. Average age 30. 184 applicants, 32% accepted, 51 enrolled. In 2009, 109 master's awarded. *Entrance requirements:* For master's, GMAT or GRE, minimum GPA of 3.0

(upper-level coursework); letter of intent; resume. Additional exam requirements/recommendations for international students: Required—TOEFL (minimum score 550 paper-based; 213 computer-based; 80 iBT), or IELTS (minimum score 6.5). *Application deadline:* For fall admission, 6/1 for domestic students, 4/1 for international students; for spring admission, 10/1 for domestic students, 9/1 for international students. Applications are processed on a rolling basis. Application fee: $30. Electronic applications accepted. *Expenses:* Contact institution. *Financial support:* Institutionally sponsored loans and scholarships/grants available. Financial award application deadline: 3/1; financial award applicants required to submit FAFSA. *Faculty research:* Investment; corporate and international finance; commercial real estate. *Unit head:* Dr. Chun-Hao Chang, Chair, 305-348-2680, Fax: 305-348-4245, E-mail: chun-hao.chang@fiu.edu. *Application contact:* Isabel Lopez, Assistant Director, Finance and Real Estate Graduate Programs, 305-348-4198, E-mail: lopezi@fiu.edu.

Florida International University, Alvah H. Chapman, Jr. Graduate School of Business, Program in Real Estate, Miami, FL 33199. Offers international real estate (MS); real estate (MS). Part-time and evening/weekend programs available. *Entrance requirements:* For master's, GMAT or GRE, letter of intent; resume. Additional exam requirements/recommendations for international students: Required—TOEFL (minimum score 550 paper-based; 213 computer-based; 80 iBT), or IELTS (minimum score 6.5). *Application deadline:* For fall admission, 4/1 for domestic and international students. Application fee: $30. Electronic applications accepted. *Expenses:* Contact institution. *Financial support:* Institutionally sponsored loans and scholarships/grants available. Financial award application deadline: 3/1; financial award applicants required to submit FAFSA. *Faculty research:* International real estate, real estate investments, commercial real estate. *Unit head:* Dr. Chun-Hao Chang, Chair, Finance and Real Estate Department, 305-348-2680, Fax: 305-348-4245, E-mail: chun-hao.chang@fiu.edu. *Application contact:* Isabel Lopez, Assistant Director, Finance and Real Estate Graduate Programs, 305-348-4198, E-mail: lopezi@fiu.edu.

George Mason University, School of Management, Fairfax, VA 22030. Offers accounting (MS); business administration (MBA); executive business administration (EMBA); real estate development (MS); taxation (MS); technology management (MS). Part-time and evening/weekend programs available. *Faculty:* 80 full-time (26 women), 57 part-time/adjunct (13 women). *Students:* 162 full-time (72 women), 336 part-time (120 women); includes 55 minority (12 African Americans, 1 American Indian/Alaska Native, 29 Asian Americans or Pacific Islanders, 13 Hispanic Americans), 39 international. Average age 31. 371 applicants, 61% accepted, 145 enrolled. In 2009, 168 master's awarded. *Entrance requirements:* For master's, GMAT. Additional exam requirements/recommendations for international students: Required—TOEFL. *Application deadline:* Applications are processed on a rolling basis. Application fee: $75. Electronic applications accepted. *Expenses:* Tuition, state resident: full-time $7568; part-time $315.33 per credit hour. Tuition, nonresident: full-time $21,704; part-time $904.33 per credit hour. Required fees: $2184; $91 per credit hour. *Financial support:* In 2009–10, 13 students received support, including 10 research assistantships with full and partial tuition reimbursements available (averaging $3,372 per year), 4 teaching assistantships with full and partial tuition reimbursements available (averaging $3,511 per year); fellowships, career-related internships or fieldwork, Federal Work-Study, unspecified assistantships, and health care benefits (full-time research or teaching assistantship recipients) also available. Support available to part-time students. Financial award application deadline: 3/1; financial award applicants required to submit FAFSA. *Faculty research:* Current leading global issues: offshore outsourcing, international financial risk, comparative systems of innovation. Total annual research expenditures: $346,607. *Unit head:* Jorge Haddock, Dean, 703-993-1875, E-mail: jhaddock@gmu.edu. *Application contact:* Melanie Pflugshaupt, Administrative Coordinator to Dean's Office, 703-993-3638, E-mail: mpflugsh@gmu.edu.

Georgetown University, Graduate School of Arts and Sciences, School of Continuing Studies, Washington, DC 20057. Offers American studies (MALS); Catholic studies (MALS); classical civilizations (MALS); ethics and the professions (MALS); human resources management (MPS); humanities (MALS); individualized study (MALS); international affairs (MALS); Islam and Muslim-Christian relations (MALS); journalism (MPS); liberal studies (DLS); literature and society (MALS); medieval and early modern European studies (MALS); public relations (MPS); real estate (MPS); religious studies (MALS); social and public policy (MALS); sports industry management (MPS); the theory and practice of American democracy (MALS); visual culture (MALS). *Entrance requirements:* Additional exam requirements/recommendations for international students: Required—TOEFL.

The George Washington University, School of Business, Department of Finance, Washington, DC 20052. Offers finance (MSF, PhD); finance and investments (MBA); real estate and urban development (MBA). Part-time and evening/weekend programs available. *Faculty:* 17 full-time (3 women), 10 part-time/adjunct (2 women). *Students:* 74 full-time (26 women), 40 part-time (13 women); includes 15 minority (4 African Americans, 8 Asian Americans or Pacific Islanders, 3 Hispanic Americans), 74 international. Average age 30. 211 applicants, 58% accepted, 59 enrolled. In 2009, 61 master's awarded. *Degree requirements:* For doctorate, thesis/dissertation. *Entrance requirements:* For master's, GMAT; for doctorate, GMAT or GRE. Additional exam requirements/recommendations for international students: Required—TOEFL. *Application deadline:* For fall admission, 4/1 priority date for domestic students; for spring admission, 10/1 for domestic students. Applications are processed on a rolling basis. Application fee: $60. *Financial support:* In 2009–10, 38 students received support; fellowships, teaching assistantships, career-related internships or fieldwork, Federal Work-Study, and institutionally sponsored loans available. Financial award application deadline: 4/1. *Unit head:* Mark S. Klock, Chair, 202-994-5996, E-mail: klock@gwu.edu. *Application contact:* Kristin Williams, Assistant Vice President for Graduate and Special Enrollment Management, 202-994-0467, Fax: 202-994-0371, E-mail: ksw@gwu.edu.

Georgia State University, J. Mack Robinson College of Business, Department of Real Estate, Atlanta, GA 30302-3083. Offers MBA, MSRE, PhD, Certificate. Part-time and evening/weekend programs available. Terminal master's awarded for partial completion of doctoral program. *Degree requirements:* For doctorate, comprehensive exam, thesis/dissertation. *Entrance requirements:* For master's and doctorate, GMAT. Additional exam requirements/recommendations for international students: Required—TOEFL (minimum score 610 paper-based; 255 computer-based; 101 iBT). Electronic applications accepted.

Hofstra University, Frank G. Zarb School of Business, Department of Finance, Hempstead, NY 11549. Offers business administration (MBA), including finance, real estate; finance (MS); quantitative finance (MS). Part-time and evening/weekend programs available. *Faculty:* 10 full-time (2 women), 3 part-time/adjunct (0 women). *Students:* 122 full-time (36 women), 93 part-time (30 women); includes 24 minority (7 African Americans, 11 Asian Americans or Pacific Islanders, 6 Hispanic Americans), 73 international. Average age 27. 223 applicants, 76% accepted, 67 enrolled. In 2009, 70 master's awarded. *Degree requirements:* For master's, capstone course (MBA), thesis (MS). *Entrance requirements:* For master's, GMAT or GRE, 2 letters of recommendation, resume. Additional exam requirements/recommendations for international students: Required—TOEFL (minimum score 550 paper-based; 213 computer-based; 80 iBT); Recommended—IELTS (minimum score 6). *Application deadline:* Applications are processed on a rolling basis. Application fee: $60. Electronic applications accepted. *Expenses:* Contact institution. *Financial support:* In 2009–10, 44 students received support, including 38 fellowships with full and partial tuition reimbursements available (averaging $9,548 per year), 1 research assistantship with full and partial tuition reimbursement available (averaging $14,532 per year); Federal Work-Study, institutionally sponsored loans, scholarships/grants, and tuition waivers (full and partial) also available. Support available to part-time students. Financial award applicants required to submit FAFSA. *Faculty research:* Corporate finance, investments, banking, real estate, derivatives. *Unit head:* Dr. Nancy W. White, Chairperson, 516-463-5699, Fax: 516-463-4834, E-mail: finnwh@hofstra.edu. *Application contact:* Carol Drummer, Dean of Graduate Admissions, 516-463-4876, Fax: 516-463-4664, E-mail: gradstudent@hofstra.edu.

John Marshall Law School, Graduate and Professional Programs, Chicago, IL 60604-3968. Offers comparative legal studies (LL M); employee benefits (LL M, MS); information technology

(LL M, MS); intellectual property (LL M); international business and trade (LL M); law (JD); real estate (LL M, MS); taxation (LL M, MS); JD/LL M; JD/MA; JD/MBA; JD/MPA. *Accreditation:* ABA. Part-time and evening/weekend programs available. *Faculty:* 73 full-time (26 women), 110 part-time/adjunct (33 women). *Students:* 1,139 full-time (505 women), 407 part-time (204 women); includes 353 minority (130 African Americans, 15 American Indian/Alaska Native, 91 Asian Americans or Pacific Islanders, 117 Hispanic Americans), 43 international. Average age 27. 3,027 applicants, 44% accepted, 385 enrolled. In 2009, 401 first professional degrees, 16 master's awarded. *Degree requirements:* For JD, 90 credits. *Entrance requirements:* For JD, LSAT; for master's, JD. Additional exam requirements/recommendations for international students: Required—TOEFL. *Application deadline:* For fall admission, 3/1 priority date for domestic and international students; for spring admission, 10/15 priority date for domestic and international students. Applications are processed on a rolling basis. Application fee: $60. Electronic applications accepted. *Expenses:* Contact institution. *Financial support:* In 2009–10, 1,350 students received support. Scholarships/grants and tuition waivers (full and partial) available. Support available to part-time students. Financial award application deadline: 6/1; financial award applicants required to submit FAFSA. *Unit head:* John Corkery, Dean, 312-427-2737. *Application contact:* William B. Powers, Associate Dean of Admission and Student Affairs, 800-537-4280, Fax: 312-427-5136, E-mail: admission@jmls.edu.

The Johns Hopkins University, Carey Business School, The Edward St. John Department of Real Estate, Baltimore, MD 21218-2699. Offers MS. Part-time and evening/weekend programs available. *Faculty:* 29 full-time (6 women), 135 part-time/adjunct (29 women). *Students:* 36 full-time (4 women), 130 part-time (36 women); includes 17 minority (10 African Americans, 4 Asian Americans or Pacific Islanders, 3 Hispanic Americans), 7 international. Average age 31. 108 applicants, 54% accepted, 45 enrolled. In 2009, 70 master's awarded. *Degree requirements:* For master's, 36 credits including final project. *Entrance requirements:* For master's, GMAT, GRE, or LSAT (full-time only), minimum GPA of 3.0, resume, work experience, two letters of recommendation. Additional exam requirements/recommendations for international students: Required—TOEFL (minimum score 600 paper-based; 250 computer-based; 100 iBT). *Application deadline:* For fall admission, 5/1 for international students; for spring admission, 10/15 for international students. Applications are processed on a rolling basis. Application fee: $100. Electronic applications accepted. *Financial support:* Scholarships/grants available. Support available to part-time students. Financial award application deadline: 4/1; financial award applicants required to submit FAFSA. *Unit head:* Dr. Dipankar Chakravarti, Vice Dean of Programs, 410-516-8561, E-mail: dipankar.chakravarti@jhu.edu. *Application contact:* Robin Greenberg, Admissions Coordinator, 410-516-4234, Fax: 410-516-0826, E-mail: carey.admissions@jhu.edu.

Marylhurst University, Department of Business Administration, Marylhurst, OR 97036-0261. Offers finance (MBA); general management (MBA); government policy and administration (MBA); green development (MBA); health care management (MBA); marketing (MBA); natural and organic resources (MBA); nonprofit management (MBA); organizational behavior (MBA); real estate (MBA); renewable energy (MBA); sustainable business (MBA). Part-time and evening/weekend programs available. Postbaccalaureate distance learning degree programs offered (no on-campus study). *Faculty:* 2 full-time (1 woman), 28 part-time/adjunct (5 women). *Students:* 30 full-time (12 women), 627 part-time (323 women); includes 79 minority (28 African Americans, 3 American Indian/Alaska Native, 17 Asian Americans or Pacific Islanders, 31 Hispanic Americans), 9 international. Average age 37. 299 applicants, 80% accepted, 209 enrolled. In 2009, 193 master's awarded. *Degree requirements:* For master's, comprehensive exam, capstone course. *Entrance requirements:* For master's, GMAT (if GPA less than 3.0 and fewer than 5 years of work experience), interview, resume, 2 letters of recommendation. Additional exam requirements/recommendations for international students: Recommended—TOEFL (minimum score 550 paper-based; 213 computer-based; 80 iBT). *Application deadline:* For fall admission, 9/11 priority date for domestic and international students; for winter admission, 12/15 priority date for domestic and international students; for spring admission, 3/17 priority date for domestic and international students. Applications are processed on a rolling basis. Application fee: $40 ($50 for international students). Electronic applications accepted. *Financial support:* Scholarships/grants available. Support available to part-time students. Financial award applicants required to submit FAFSA. *Unit head:* Bob Hanks, Director of Business and Real Estate Programs, 503-636-8141, Fax: 503-697-5597, E-mail: mba@marylhurst.edu. *Application contact:* Kathleen Schneff, Admissions Specialist, 800-634-9982 Ext. 3322, Fax: 503-635-6585, E-mail: admissions@marylhurst.edu.

Massachusetts Institute of Technology, School of Architecture and Planning, Center for Real Estate, Cambridge, MA 02139-4307. Offers MSRED. *Faculty:* 4 full-time (0 women), 4 part-time/adjunct (1 woman). *Students:* 13 full-time (1 woman); includes 1 minority (Asian American or Pacific Islander), 6 international. Average age 31. 121 applicants, 24% accepted. In 2009, 40 degrees awarded. *Degree requirements:* For master's, thesis. *Entrance requirements:* For master's, GMAT. Additional exam requirements/recommendations for international students: Required—TOEFL (minimum score 600 paper-based; 250 computer-based), IELTS (minimum score 7.5). *Application deadline:* For fall admission, 1/5 for domestic students. Application fee: $75. Electronic applications accepted. *Expenses:* Tuition: Full-time $37,510; part-time $585 per unit. Required fees: $272. *Financial support:* In 2009–10, 5 students received support. Health care benefits available. *Faculty research:* Real estate finance and investment, housing, urban design, real estate development, planning, project management, infrastructure delivery methods, urban economics, entrepreneurship, strategic planning, leadership development. Total annual research expenditures: $89,000. *Unit head:* Prof. Brian A. Ciochetti, Director, 617-253-4373, Fax: 617-258-6991, E-mail: mit-cre@mit.edu. *Application contact:* Maria Vieira, Associate Director of Education, 617-253-4373.

New York University, School of Continuing and Professional Studies, Schack Institute of Real Estate, New York, NY 10012-1019. Offers construction management (MS, Advanced Certificate), including construction management (Advanced Certificate), construction management for the development process (MS), project management (MS); real estate (MS, Advanced Certificate), including development (MS), finance and investment (MS), real estate (Advanced Certificate), strategic real estate management (MS). Part-time and evening/weekend programs available. *Faculty:* 12 full-time (2 women), 87 part-time/adjunct (10 women). *Students:* 129 full-time (20 women), 494 part-time (117 women); includes 99 minority (23 African Americans, 60 Asian Americans or Pacific Islanders, 16 Hispanic Americans). Average age 31. 353 applicants, 70% accepted, 142 enrolled. In 2009, 320 master's, 131 other advanced degrees awarded. *Degree requirements:* For master's, comprehensive exam (for some programs), thesis. *Entrance requirements:* For master's, GRE General Test or GMAT (for recent graduates), resume, 2 letters of recommendation. Additional exam requirements/recommendations for international students: Required—TOEFL (minimum score 600 paper-based; 250 computer-based; 100 iBT), TWE. *Application deadline:* For fall admission, 2/1 priority date for domestic and international students; for spring admission, 10/15 priority date for domestic students, 8/15 priority date for international students. Applications are processed on a rolling basis. Application fee: $75. Electronic applications accepted. *Expenses:* Tuition: Full-time $30,528; part-time $1272 per credit. Required fees: $2177. *Financial support:* In 2009–10, 168 students received support, including 168 fellowships (averaging $2,394 per year); scholarships/grants also available. Support available to part-time students. Financial award application deadline: 3/1; financial award applicants required to submit FAFSA. *Faculty research:* Project financial management, sustainable design, impact of large-scale development projects, economics and market cycles, international property rights, comparative metropolitan economies, current market trends. *Unit head:* James Stuckey, Divisional Dean, 212-992-3335, Fax: 212-992-3686, E-mail: james.stuckey@nyu.edu. *Application contact:* Jennifer Monahan, Director of Administration and Student Services, 212-992-3335, Fax: 212-992-3686, E-mail: jm189@nyu.edu.

Nova Southeastern University, H. Wayne Huizenga School of Business and Entrepreneurship, Program in Real Estate Development, Fort Lauderdale, FL 33314-7796. Offers MS. Evening/weekend programs available. *Faculty:* 1 full-time (0 women), 4 part-time/adjunct (0 women). *Students:* 1 full-time (0 women), 14 part-time (4 women); includes 5 minority (3 African Americans, 2 Hispanic Americans), 2 international. Average age 33. 29 applicants, 45%

Real Estate

Nova Southeastern University *(continued)*
accepted, 6 enrolled. *Entrance requirements:* Additional exam requirements/recommendations for international students: Required—TOEFL (minimum score 550 paper-based; 213 computer-based; 79 iBT), IELTS (minimum score 6). *Application deadline:* For fall admission, 7/1 for domestic and international students; for winter admission, 10/1 for domestic and international students; for spring admission, 1/1 for domestic and international students. Applications are processed on a rolling basis. Application fee: $50. Electronic applications accepted. *Financial support:* Federal Work-Study and scholarships/grants available. Support available to part-time students. Financial award applicants required to submit FAFSA. *Unit head:* Steve Harvey, Assistant Dean of Program Administration, 954-262-5047, Fax: 954-262-3829, E-mail: harvey@nsu.nova.edu. *Application contact:* Karen Goldberg, Associate Director of Recruitment and Special Events, 954-262-5039, Fax: 954-262-3822, E-mail: karen@nova.edu.

Pacific States University, College of Business, Los Angeles, CA 90006. Offers accounting (MBA); business administration (DBA); finance (MBA); international business (MBA); management of information technology (MBA); real estate management (MBA). Part-time and evening/weekend programs available. Postbaccalaureate distance learning degree programs offered (no on-campus study). *Entrance requirements:* For master's, minimum undergraduate GPA of 2.5 during last 90 hours of course work. Additional exam requirements/recommendations for international students: Required—TOEFL (minimum score 133 computer-based).

Roosevelt University, Graduate Division, Walter E. Heller College of Business Administration, School of Finance and Real Estate, Chicago, IL 60605. Offers commercial real estate development (Certificate); real estate (MBA, MS).

Texas A&M University, Mays Business School, Real Estate Program, College Station, TX 77843. Offers MLERE. *Entrance requirements:* For master's, GMAT or GRE. Additional exam requirements/recommendations for international students: Required—TOEFL. Electronic applications accepted. *Expenses:* Tuition, state resident: full-time $3991; part-time $221.74 per credit hour. Tuition, nonresident: full-time $9049; part-time $502.74 per credit hour.

University of California, Berkeley, Graduate Division, Haas School of Business, PhD in Business Administration Program, Berkeley, CA 94720-1500. Offers accounting (PhD); business and public policy (PhD); finance (PhD); management of organizations (PhD); marketing (PhD); operations management (PhD); real estate (PhD). *Accreditation:* AACSB. *Faculty:* 80 full-time (20 women), 130 part-time/adjunct (22 women). *Students:* 82 full-time (23 women); includes 22 minority (18 Asian Americans or Pacific Islanders, 4 Hispanic Americans), 29 international. Average age 30. 511 applicants, 5% accepted, 16 enrolled. In 2009, 8 doctorates awarded. *Degree requirements:* For doctorate, comprehensive exam, thesis/dissertation, oral exam, written preliminary exams. *Entrance requirements:* For doctorate, GMAT or GRE, minimum GPA of 3.0 in undergraduate and graduate coursework. Additional exam requirements/recommendations for international students: Required—TOEFL (minimum score 570 paper-based; 230 computer-based; 68 iBT), IELTS (minimum score 7). *Application deadline:* For fall admission, 12/10 for domestic and international students. Application fee: $70 ($90 for international students). Electronic applications accepted. *Financial support:* Fellowships with full and partial tuition reimbursements, research assistantships with full and partial tuition reimbursements, teaching assistantships with full and partial tuition reimbursements, career-related internships or fieldwork, Federal Work-Study, scholarships/grants, health care benefits, tuition waivers (full), unspecified assistantships, and transit pass, travel grants available. Financial award application deadline: 12/10; financial award applicants required to submit FAFSA. *Faculty research:* Accounting, business and public policy, finance, management of organizations, marketing, operations and information technology management, real estate. *Unit head:* Sunil Dutta, Director, 510-642-1229, Fax: 510-643-4255, E-mail: kimg@haas.berkeley.edu. *Application contact:* Kim Guilfoyle, Director, Student Affairs, 510-642-3944, Fax: 510-643-4255, E-mail: kimg@haas.berkeley.edu.

University of Central Florida, College of Business Administration, Dr. P. Phillips School of Real Estate, Orlando, FL 32816. Offers MS. Part-time programs available. *Expenses:* Tuition, state resident: part-time $306.31 per credit hour. Tuition, nonresident: part-time $1099.01 per credit hour. Part-time tuition and fees vary according to degree level and program. *Unit head:* Dr. Thomas L. Keon, Dean, 407-823-2183, E-mail: thomas.keon@bus.ucf.edu. *Application contact:* Judy Ryder, Director, Graduate Admissions, 407-823-2364, Fax: 407-823-0219, E-mail: jryder@bus.ucf.edu.

University of Central Florida, College of Business Administration, Program in Real Estate, Orlando, FL 32816. Offers MSRE. *Expenses:* Tuition, state resident: part-time $306.31 per credit hour. Tuition, nonresident: part-time $1099.01 per credit hour. Part-time tuition and fees vary according to degree level and program.

University of Denver, Daniels College of Business, School of Real Estate and Construction Management, Denver, CO 80208. Offers construction management (IMBA, MS); real estate (IMBA, MBA, MS). Part-time programs available. *Faculty:* 7 full-time (0 women), 3 part-time/adjunct (1 woman). *Students:* 32 full-time (5 women), 70 part-time (11 women); includes 9 minority (4 African Americans, 1 American Indian/Alaska Native, 2 Asian Americans or Pacific Islanders, 2 Hispanic Americans), 6 international. Average age 32. 88 applicants, 76% accepted, 41 enrolled. In 2009, 91 master's awarded. *Entrance requirements:* For master's, GMAT. *Application deadline:* For fall admission, 1/15 priority date for domestic students. Applications are processed on a rolling basis. Application fee: $50. Electronic applications accepted. *Expenses:* Tuition: Full-time $34,596; part-time $961 per quarter hour. Required fees: $4 per quarter hour. Tuition and fees vary according to course load, campus/location and program. *Financial support:* In 2009–10, 70 students received support. Career-related internships or fieldwork, Federal Work-Study, institutionally sponsored loans, and scholarships/grants available. Support available to part-time students. Financial award application deadline: 2/15; financial award applicants required to submit FAFSA. *Unit head:* Dr. Mark Levine, Director, 303-871-2142. *Application contact:* Information Contact, 303-871-3416, Fax: 303-871-4466, E-mail: daniels@du.edu.

University of Florida, Graduate School, Warrington College of Business Administration, Hough Graduate School of Business, Department of Finance, Insurance and Real Estate, Gainesville, FL 32611. Offers business administration (MS), including entrepreneurship, insurance, real estate and urban analysis, retailing; finance (PhD); financial services (Certificate); insurance (PhD); real estate and urban analysis (PhD); JD/MS. Terminal master's awarded for partial completion of doctoral program. *Degree requirements:* For doctorate, thesis/dissertation. *Entrance requirements:* For master's, GMAT or GRE General Test, minimum GPA of 3.0 for last 60 hours of undergraduate degree, work experience (preferred); for doctorate, GMAT or GRE General Test, minimum GPA of 3.0. Additional exam requirements/recommendations for international students: Required—TOEFL (minimum score 550 paper-based; 213 computer-based). Electronic applications accepted. *Faculty research:* Financial management, financial markets and institutions, investments, risk and insurance, real estate development.

University of Hawaii at Manoa, Graduate Division, Shidler College of Business, Program in Business Administration, Honolulu, HI 96822. Offers Asian business studies (MBA); Chinese business studies (MBA); decision sciences (MBA); entrepreneurship (MBA); finance (MBA); finance and banking (MBA); human resources management (MBA); information management (MBA); information technology (MBA); international business (MBA); Japanese business studies (MBA); marketing (MBA); organizational behavior (MBA); organizational management (MBA); real estate (MBA); student-designed track (MBA). *Accreditation:* AACSB. Part-time and evening/weekend programs available. *Faculty:* 46 full-time (8 women), 9 part-time/adjunct (4 women). *Students:* 259 full-time (90 women), 105 part-time (43 women); includes 123 minority (118 Asian Americans or Pacific Islanders, 5 Hispanic Americans), 119 international. Average age 32. 336 applicants, 52% accepted, 150 enrolled. In 2009, 113 master's awarded. *Degree requirements:* For master's, thesis optional. *Entrance requirements:* For master's, GMAT, minimum GPA of 3.0. Additional exam requirements/recommendations for international students: Required—TOEFL (minimum score 600 paper-based; 250 computer-based; 100 iBT), IELTS (minimum score 7). *Application deadline:* For fall admission, 5/1 for domestic students, 3/1 for

international students. Application fee: $60. *Expenses:* Contact institution. *Financial support:* In 2009–10, 24 students received support, including 98 fellowships (averaging $3,481 per year), 3 research assistantships (averaging $16,626 per year). Total annual research expenditures: $427,000. *Application contact:* Tung Bui, Graduate Chair, 808-956-5565, Fax: 808-956-9889, E-mail: tung.bui@hawaii.edu.

University of Illinois at Chicago, Graduate College, Liautaud Graduate School of Business, Center for Urban Real Estate, Chicago, IL 60607-7128. Offers real estate (MA).

University of Maryland, College Park, Academic Affairs, School of Architecture, Planning and Preservation, Program in Real Estate Development, College Park, MD 20742. Offers MRED. *Students:* 29 full-time (6 women), 54 part-time (14 women); includes 23 minority (15 African Americans, 1 American Indian/Alaska Native, 4 Asian Americans or Pacific Islanders, 3 Hispanic Americans), 9 international. 92 applicants, 46% accepted, 21 enrolled. In 2009, 26 master's awarded. *Application deadline:* For fall admission, 3/15 for domestic students, 2/1 for international students; for spring admission, 10/1 for domestic students, 7/15 for international students. *Expenses:* Tuition, area resident: Part-time $471 per credit hour. Tuition, state resident: part-time $471 per credit hour. Tuition, nonresident: part-time $1016 per credit hour. Required fees: $337.04 per term. *Financial support:* In 2009–10, 5 teaching assistantships (averaging $14,871 per year) were awarded; fellowships also available. *Unit head:* Dr. Margaret McFarland, Director, 301-405-6709, E-mail: mmcf@umd.edu. *Application contact:* Dean of Graduate School, 301-405-0358.

University of Memphis, Graduate School, Fogelman College of Business and Economics, Program in Business Administration, Memphis, TN 38152. Offers accounting (MBA, PhD); economics (MBA, PhD); executive business administration (MBA); finance (PhD); finance, insurance, and real estate (MBA, MS); international business administration (IMBA); management (MBA, MS, PhD); management information systems (MBA, MS, PhD); management science (MBA); marketing (MBA, MS); marketing and supply chain management (PhD); real estate development (MS); JD/MBA. *Accreditation:* AACSB. *Faculty:* 44 full-time (9 women), 5 part-time/adjunct (0 women). *Students:* 263 full-time (106 women), 181 part-time (66 women); includes 70 minority (46 African Americans, 3 American Indian/Alaska Native, 16 Asian Americans or Pacific Islanders, 5 Hispanic Americans), 109 international. Average age 31. 374 applicants, 73% accepted, 119 enrolled. In 2009, 140 master's, 17 doctorates awarded. *Degree requirements:* For master's, comprehensive exam; for doctorate, comprehensive exam, thesis/dissertation. *Entrance requirements:* For master's, GMAT, resume; for doctorate, GMAT, interview, minimum GPA of 3.4, resume, letter of recommendation. Additional exam requirements/recommendations for international students: Required—TOEFL (minimum score 550 paper-based; 220 computer-based). *Application deadline:* For fall admission, 8/1 for domestic students; for spring admission, 12/1 for domestic students. Application fee: $35 ($60 for international students). *Expenses:* Tuition, state resident: full-time $6246; part-time $347 per credit hour. Tuition, nonresident: full-time $15,894; part-time $883 per credit hour. Required fees: $1160. Full-time tuition and fees vary according to course load, degree level and program. *Financial support:* In 2009–10, 164 students received support; research assistantships with full tuition reimbursements available, teaching assistantships with full tuition reimbursements available, career-related internships or fieldwork, Federal Work-Study, scholarships/grants, and unspecified assistantships available. Financial award application deadline: 2/15; financial award applicants required to submit FAFSA. *Faculty research:* Competitive business strategy, finance microstructures, supply chain management innovations, health care economics, litigation risks and corporate audits. *Unit head:* Rajiv Grover, Dean, 901-678-3759, E-mail: rgrover@memphis.edu. *Application contact:* Dr. Carol V. Danehower, Associate Dean for Programs, 901-678-5402, Fax: 901-678-3579, E-mail: fcbegp@memphis.edu.

University of Michigan, Taubman College of Architecture and Urban Planning, Urban and Regional Planning Program, Ann Arbor, MI 48109. Offers real estate development (Certificate); urban planning (MUP); JD/MUP; M Arch/MUP; MBA/MUP; MLA/MUP; MPP/MUP. Offered through the Horace H. Rackham School of Graduate Studies; students in the Certificate program must either be currently enrolled in a graduate program or have earned a master's or PhD degree within the last five years. *Accreditation:* ACSP (one or more programs are accredited). Part-time programs available. *Degree requirements:* For master's, thesis or alternative, professional project, capstone studio. *Entrance requirements:* For master's, GRE General Test, LSAT or GMAT. Additional exam requirements/recommendations for international students: Required—TOEFL (minimum score 600 paper-based; 250 computer-based; 100 iBT). Electronic applications accepted. *Expenses:* Tuition, state resident: full-time $17,286; part-time $1099 per credit hour. Tuition, nonresident: full-time $34,944; part-time $2080 per credit hour. Required fees: $95 per semester. Tuition and fees vary according to course load, degree level and program. *Faculty research:* Housing community and economic development; transportation planning; physical planning and urban design; planning in developing countries; land use and environmental planning.

University of North Texas, Robert B. Toulouse School of Graduate Studies, College of Business Administration, Department of Finance, Insurance, Real Estate, and Law, Denton, TX 76203. Offers finance (PhD); finance, insurance, real estate, and law (MS); real estate (MS). Part-time programs available. *Degree requirements:* For master's, thesis optional; for doctorate, comprehensive exam, thesis/dissertation. *Entrance requirements:* For master's, GMAT; for doctorate, GMAT or GRE General Test. Additional exam requirements/recommendations for international students: Recommended—TOEFL (minimum score 550 paper-based; 213 computer-based; 79 iBT). Application fee: $50 ($75 for international students). *Expenses:* Tuition, state resident: full-time $4298; part-time $239 per contact hour. Tuition, nonresident: full-time $9878; part-time $549 per contact hour. Required fees: $265 per contact hour. *Financial support:* Fellowships, research assistantships, teaching assistantships, career-related internships or fieldwork and tuition waivers (partial) available. Financial award application deadline: 4/1; financial award applicants required to submit FAFSA. *Faculty research:* Financial impact of regulation, risk management, taxes and valuation, bankruptcy, real financial options. *Application contact:* PhD Advisor, 940-565-2511, Fax: 940-565-4234, E-mail: john.kensinger@unt.edu.

University of Pennsylvania, Wharton School, Real Estate Department, Philadelphia, PA 19104. Offers MBA, PhD. Terminal master's awarded for partial completion of doctoral program. *Degree requirements:* For doctorate, thesis/dissertation. *Entrance requirements:* For master's, GMAT; for doctorate, GRE General Test. *Expenses:* Tuition: Full-time $25,660; part-time $4758 per course. Required fees: $2152; $270 per course. Tuition and fees vary according to course load, degree level and program. *Faculty research:* Public economics and taxation economics and finance of real estate markets, economics of housing markets, real estate development.

University of St. Thomas, Graduate Studies, Opus College of Business, Master of Science in Real Estate Program, Minneapolis, MN 55403. Offers MS. Part-time and evening/weekend programs available. *Students:* 20 part-time (8 women); includes 2 minority (1 African American, 1 Asian American or Pacific Islander). Average age 29. 3 applicants, 100% accepted, 3 enrolled. In 2009, 2 master's awarded. *Entrance requirements:* For master's, GMAT. Additional exam requirements/recommendations for international students: Required—TOEFL, IELTS or Michigan English Language Assessment Battery. *Application deadline:* For fall admission, 6/1 for domestic students, 4/15 for international students; for spring admission, 11/1 for domestic students, 10/1 for international students. Applications are processed on a rolling basis. Application fee: $40. Electronic applications accepted. *Financial support:* Fellowships, research assistantships, institutionally sponsored loans and scholarships/grants available. Financial award application deadline: 7/1; financial award applicants required to submit FAFSA. *Unit head:* Herb Tousley, Director, 651-962-4289, E-mail: msrealestate@stthomas.edu. *Application contact:* Susan Eckstein, Program Manager, 651-962-4289, Fax: 651-962-4410, E-mail: msrealestate@stthomas.edu.

University of South Africa, College of Economic and Management Sciences, Pretoria, South Africa. Offers accounting (D Admin, D Com); accounting science (DA); auditing (D Admin, D Com); business administration (M Tech); business economics (D Admin); business leadership

(DBL); business management (D Admin, D Com); economic management analysis (M Tech); economics (D Admin, D Com, PhD); human resource development (M Tech); industrial psychology (D Admin, D Com, PhD); logistics (D Com); marketing (M Tech); public administration (D Admin, D Com, DPA, PhD); public management (M Tech); quantitative management (D Admin, D Com); real estate (M Tech); statistics (D Admin, PhD); tourism management (D Admin, D Com); transport economics (D Admin, D Com).

University of Southern California, Graduate School, School of Policy, Planning, and Development, Master of Real Estate Development Program, Los Angeles, CA 90089. Offers MRED, M Pl/MRED, JD/MRED, MBA/MRED. Part-time programs available. *Faculty:* 51 full-time (12 women), 74 part-time/adjunct (26 women). *Students:* 53 full-time (6 women), 15 part-time (4 women); includes 10 minority (1 African American, 4 Asian Americans or Pacific Islanders, 5 Hispanic Americans), 7 international. 202 applicants, 52% accepted, 56 enrolled. In 2009, 53 master's awarded. *Degree requirements:* For master's, comprehensive exam. *Entrance requirements:* For master's, GRE or GMAT. Additional exam requirements/recommendations for international students: Required—TOEFL (minimum score 600 paper-based; 250 computer-based; 100 iBT). *Application deadline:* For fall admission, 2/1 for domestic and international students. Application fee: $85. Electronic applications accepted. *Expenses:* Contact institution. *Financial support:* In 2009–10, 7 students received support. Scholarships/grants and tuition waivers (partial) available. Financial award application deadline: 2/1. *Faculty research:* Urban development, urban economics, real estate finance, housing markets. Total annual research expenditures: $5 million. *Unit head:* Dr. Christian Redfearn, Director, Graduate Programs in Real Estate Development, 213-821-1364, Fax: 213-740-0001, E-mail: redfearn@usc.edu. *Application contact:* Marisol R. Gonzalez, Director of Recruitment and Admission, 213-740-0550, Fax: 213-740-7573, E-mail: marisolr@usc.edu.

University of South Florida, Graduate School, College of Business, Department of Finance, Tampa, FL 33620-9951. Offers business (PhD), including finance; finance (MS); real estate (MS). Part-time and evening/weekend programs available. *Faculty:* 12 full-time (2 women). *Students:* 10 full-time (3 women), 12 part-time (3 women); includes 6 minority (4 African Americans, 2 Hispanic Americans), 4 international. Average age 32. 86 applicants, 38% accepted, 7 enrolled. In 2009, 8 master's awarded. Terminal master's awarded for partial completion of doctoral program. *Degree requirements:* For master's, thesis or alternative, 30 credits, minimum GPA of 3.0; for doctorate, comprehensive exam, thesis/dissertation. *Entrance requirements:* For master's, GMAT, minimum GPA of 3.0; for doctorate, GMAT, letters of recommendation, personal statement. Additional exam requirements/recommendations for international students: Required—TOEFL (minimum score 550 paper-based; 213 computer-based; 79 iBT). *Application deadline:* For fall admission, 6/1 for domestic students, 1/2 for international students; for spring admission, 10/15 for domestic students, 6/1 for international students. Application fee: $30. Electronic applications accepted. *Financial support:* In 2009–10, teaching assistantships with tuition reimbursements (averaging $22,083 per year); scholarships/grants, health care benefits, and unspecified assistantships also available. Financial award application deadline: 6/30. *Faculty research:* Corporate governance, international finance, asset pricing models, risk management, market efficiency. Total annual research expenditures: $75,865. *Unit head:* Dr. Scott Besley, Chairperson, 813-974-2081, Fax: 813-974-3084, E-mail: sbesley@coba.usf.edu. *Application contact:* Dr. Scott Besley, Chairperson, 813-974-2081, Fax: 813-974-3084, E-mail: sbesley@coba.usf.edu.

The University of Texas at Arlington, Graduate School, College of Business, Department of Finance and Real Estate, Arlington, TX 76019. Offers quantitative finance (MS); real estate (MS). Part-time and evening/weekend programs available. *Faculty:* 7 full-time (1 woman). *Students:* 39 full-time (7 women), 36 part-time (9 women); includes 15 minority (4 African Americans, 11 Asian Americans or Pacific Islanders), 28 international. In 2009, 14 master's awarded. *Degree requirements:* For master's, thesis optional. *Entrance requirements:* For master's, GMAT, minimum GPA of 3.0. Additional exam requirements/recommendations for international students: Required—TOEFL (minimum score 550 paper-based; 213 computer-based; 79 iBT). *Application deadline:* For fall admission, 6/5 priority date for domestic students, 4/1 for international students; for spring admission, 10/15 for domestic students, 9/1 for international students. Applications are processed on a rolling basis. Application fee: $35 ($50 for international students). *Financial support:* In 2009–10, 3 fellowships (averaging $1,000 per year), research assistantships (averaging $6,000 per year), 14 teaching assistantships (averaging $13,000 per year) were awarded; career-related internships or fieldwork, Federal Work-Study, and institutionally sponsored loans also available. Financial award application deadline: 6/1; financial award applicants required to submit FAFSA. *Unit head:* Dr. David Diltz, Chair, 817-272-3705, Fax: 817-272-2252, E-mail: diltz@uta.edu. *Application contact:* Dr. Andy Hansz, Graduate Advisor, 817-272-3705, Fax: 817-272-2252, E-mail: realestate@uta.edu.

The University of Texas at Arlington, Graduate School, College of Business, Program in Business Administration, Arlington, TX 76019. Offers accounting (PhD); business statistics (PhD); finance (MBA, PhD); information systems (MBA, PhD); management (MBA, PhD); management sciences (MBA); marketing (MBA, PhD); operations management (PhD); real estate (MBA). *Accreditation:* AACSB. Part-time and evening/weekend programs available. Postbaccalaureate distance learning degree programs offered (no on-campus study). *Students:* 587 full-time (188 women), 349 part-time (140 women); includes 188 minority (66 African Americans, 62 Asian Americans or Pacific Islanders, 60 Hispanic Americans), 371 international. 282 applicants, 96% accepted, 145 enrolled. In 2009, 431 master's awarded. Terminal master's awarded for partial completion of doctoral program. *Degree requirements:* For master's, thesis optional; for doctorate, comprehensive exam, thesis/dissertation. *Entrance requirements:* For master's, GMAT; for doctorate, GMAT, minimum GPA of 3.0 (undergraduate), 3.4 (graduate); 30 hours of graduate course work. Additional exam requirements/recommendations for international students: Required—TOEFL (minimum score 550 paper-based; 213 computer-based; 79 iBT). *Application deadline:* For fall admission, 6/5 for domestic students, 4/1 for international students; for spring admission, 10/15 for domestic students, 9/1 for international students. Applications are processed on a rolling basis. Application fee: $35 ($50 for international students). Electronic applications accepted. *Financial support:* In 2009–10, 1 fellowship (averaging $1,000 per year), 30 research assistantships (averaging $6,000 per year), 45 teaching assistantships (averaging $13,000 per year) were awarded; career-related internships or fieldwork, scholarships/grants, and unspecified assistantships also available. Financial award application deadline: 6/1; financial award applicants required to submit FAFSA. *Unit head:* Greg Frazier, Director PhD Programs, 817-272-3559, Fax: 817-272-5799, E-mail: frazier@exchange.uta.edu. *Application contact:* Melanie McGee, Director of MBA Program, 817-272-0658, Fax: 817-272-5799, E-mail: mwmcgee@uta.edu.

See Close-Up on page 273.

University of Utah, Graduate School, David Eccles School of Business, Program in Real Estate Development, Salt Lake City, UT 84112-1107. Offers MRED. *Students:* 27 applicants, 96% accepted. *Entrance requirements:* For master's, GMAT or GRE, minimum undergraduate GPA of 3.0. Additional exam requirements/recommendations for international students: Required—TOEFL (minimum score 600 paper-based; 250 computer-based; 100 iBT), IELTS (minimum score 7). *Application deadline:* For fall admission, 4/1 priority date for domestic and international students. Applications are processed on a rolling basis. Application fee: $55 ($65 for international students). Electronic applications accepted. *Expenses:* Tuition, state resident: full-time $4004; part-time $1674 per semester. Tuition, nonresident: full-time $14,134; part-time $5915 per semester. Required fees: $324 per semester. Tuition and fees vary according to course load, degree level and program. *Financial support:* Scholarships/grants and unspecified assistantships available. *Unit head:* Buzz Welch, Program Director, 801-581-7463, E-mail: buzz.welch@utah.edu. *Application contact:* Andrea Chmelik, Admissions Coordinator, 801-585-1719, Fax: 801-581-3666, E-mail: andrea.chmelik@business.utah.edu.

University of Wisconsin–Madison, Graduate School, Wisconsin School of Business, Doctoral Program in Real Estate and Urban Land Economics, Madison, WI 53706-1380. Offers PhD. *Faculty:* 4 full-time (0 women). *Students:* 5 full-time (all women), all international. Average age 26. 16 applicants, 13% accepted, 1 enrolled. *Degree requirements:* For doctorate, comprehensive exam, thesis/dissertation. *Entrance requirements:* For doctorate, GMAT or GRE. Additional exam requirements/recommendations for international students: Required—TOEFL (minimum score 600 paper-based; 250 computer-based; 100 iBT). *Application deadline:* For fall admission, 12/15 priority date for domestic and international students. Application fee: $56. Electronic applications accepted. *Expenses:* Tuition, state resident: part-time $594 per credit. Tuition, nonresident: part-time $1504 per credit. Required fees: $65 per credit. Tuition and fees vary according to course load, program and reciprocity agreements. *Financial support:* In 2009–10, 5 students received support, including fellowships with full tuition reimbursements available (averaging $18,567 per year), research assistantships with full tuition reimbursements available (averaging $16,506 per year), 5 teaching assistantships with full tuition reimbursements available (averaging $14,088 per year); career-related internships or fieldwork, Federal Work-Study, institutionally sponsored loans, scholarships/grants, health care benefits, and unspecified assistantships also available. Financial award application deadline: 2/1; financial award applicants required to submit FAFSA. *Faculty research:* Real estate finance, real estate equity investments, zoning restructurings, home ownership, international real estate and public policy. *Unit head:* Prof. Francois Ortalo-Magne, Chair, 608-262-7867, Fax: 608-265-2738, E-mail: fom@bus.wisc.edu. *Application contact:* Belle Heberling, Assistant Director for Research Programs, 608-262-3749, Fax: 608-890-0180, E-mail: phd@bus.wisc.edu.

University of Wisconsin–Madison, Graduate School, Wisconsin School of Business, Wisconsin Full-Time MBA Program, Madison, WI 53706-1380. Offers applied corporate finance (MBA); applied security analysis (MBA); arts administration (MBA); brand and product management (MBA); entrepreneurial management (MBA); marketing research (MBA); operations and technology management (MBA); real estate (MBA); risk management and insurance (MBA); strategic human resource management (MBA); strategic management in the life and engineering sciences (MBA); supply chain management (MBA). *Faculty:* 32 full-time (5 women). *Students:* 242 full-time (74 women); includes 47 minority (16 African Americans, 3 American Indian/Alaska Native, 16 Asian Americans or Pacific Islanders, 12 Hispanic Americans), 29 international. Average age 28. 526 applicants, 32% accepted, 117 enrolled. In 2009, 106 master's awarded. *Entrance requirements:* For master's, GMAT, bachelor's or equivalent degree, 2 years of work experience, letters of recommendation. Additional exam requirements/recommendations for international students: Required—TOEFL (minimum score 600 paper-based; 250 computer-based; 100 iBT), IELTS. *Application deadline:* For fall admission, 11/4 for domestic and international students; for winter admission, 2/5 for domestic and international students; for spring admission, 5/26 for domestic students, 4/5 for international students. Applications are processed on a rolling basis. Application fee: $56. Electronic applications accepted. *Expenses:* Tuition, state resident: part-time $594 per credit. Tuition, nonresident: part-time $1504 per credit. Required fees: $65 per credit. Tuition and fees vary according to course load, program and reciprocity agreements. *Financial support:* In 2009–10, 103 students received support, including 13 fellowships with full and partial tuition reimbursements available (averaging $15,000 per year), 53 research assistantships with full tuition reimbursements available (averaging $8,000 per year), 35 teaching assistantships with full tuition reimbursements available (averaging $11,000 per year); scholarships/grants, health care benefits, and unspecified assistantships also available. Financial award application deadline: 4/5; financial award applicants required to submit FAFSA. *Unit head:* Prof. Kenneth A. Kavajecz, Associate Dean, 608-265-3494, Fax: 608-265-4192, E-mail: kkavajecz@bus.wisc.edu. *Application contact:* Maria Reis, Assistant Director of MBA Marketing and Recruiting, 608-262-4000, Fax: 608-265-4192, E-mail: mreis@bus.wisc.edu.

University of Wisconsin–Milwaukee, Graduate School, School of Architecture and Urban Planning, Department of Urban Planning, Milwaukee, WI 53201-0413. Offers geographic information systems (Certificate); real estate development (Certificate); urban planning (MUP); M Arch/MUP; MPA/MUP; MUP/MS. *Accreditation:* ACSP. Part-time programs available. *Faculty:* 4 full-time (1 woman). *Students:* 29 full-time (11 women), 5 part-time (3 women), 2 international. Average age 28. 52 applicants, 71% accepted, 13 enrolled. In 2009, 22 master's awarded. *Degree requirements:* For master's, comprehensive exam, thesis or alternative. *Entrance requirements:* For master's, GRE General Test. Additional exam requirements/recommendations for international students: Required—TOEFL (minimum score 550 paper-based; 213 computer-based; 79 iBT), IELTS (minimum score 6.5). *Application deadline:* For fall admission, 1/1 priority date for domestic students; for spring admission, 9/1 for domestic students. Applications are processed on a rolling basis. Application fee: $45 ($75 for international students). *Expenses:* Tuition, state resident: full-time $8800. Tuition, nonresident: full-time $20,760. Tuition and fees vary according to program and reciprocity agreements. *Financial support:* In 2009–10, 3 teaching assistantships were awarded; career-related internships or fieldwork and unspecified assistantships also available. Support available to part-time students. Financial award application deadline: 4/15. Total annual research expenditures: $4,667. *Unit head:* Joan Simuncak, Representative, 414-229-4015, Fax: 414-229-6976, E-mail: joanarch@uwm.edu. *Application contact:* General Information Contact, 414-229-4982, Fax: 414-229-6967, E-mail: gradschool@uwm.edu.

Virginia Commonwealth University, Graduate School, School of Business, Program in Finance, Insurance, and Real Estate, Richmond, VA 23284-9005. Offers MS. *Entrance requirements:* For master's, GMAT.

Virginia Commonwealth University, Graduate School, School of Business, Program in Real Estate and Urban Land Development, Richmond, VA 23284-9005. Offers Certificate.

Washington State University, Graduate School, College of Business, Department of Finance, Insurance and Real Estate, Pullman, WA 99164. Offers PhD.

Woodbury University, School of Architecture, Burbank, CA 91504-1099. Offers architecture (M Arch); real estate development (M Arch). *Faculty:* 2 full-time (1 woman), 4 part-time/adjunct (1 woman). *Students:* 22 full-time (5 women); includes 7 minority (2 African Americans, 4 Asian Americans or Pacific Islanders, 1 Hispanic American), 4 international. Average age 31. In 2009, 8 master's awarded. *Degree requirements:* For master's, thesis. *Entrance requirements:* For master's, 3 letters of recommendation, portfolio. Additional exam requirements/recommendations for international students: Required—TOEFL (minimum score 550 paper-based; 213 computer-based), IELTS (minimum score 7). *Application deadline:* For fall admission, 3/1 priority date for domestic and international students. Application fee: $60. *Expenses:* Contact institution. *Unit head:* Norman Millar, Chair, 318-767-0888 Ext. 130, Fax: 318-504-9320, E-mail: norman.millar@woodbury.edu. *Application contact:* Debra Abel, Administrative Director, 619-235-2900, Fax: 619-235-2901, E-mail: debra.abel@woodbury.edu.

Section 21
Transportation Management, Logistics, and Supply Chain Management

This section contains a directory of institutions offering graduate work in transportation management, logistics, and supply chain management. Additional information about programs listed in the directory may be obtained by writing directly to the dean of a graduate school or chair of a department at the address given in the directory.

For programs offering related work, see also in this book *Business Administration and Management*.

CONTENTS

Program Directories

Display

Aviation Management

Concordia University, School of Graduate Studies, John Molson School of Business, Montréal, QC H3G 1M8, Canada. Offers administration (M Sc, Diploma); aviation management (Certificate, Diploma); business administration (MBA, UA Undergraduate Associate, PhD), including international aviation (UA Undergraduate Associate); chartered accountancy (Diploma); community organizational development (Certificate); event management and fundraising (Certificate); executive business administration (EMBA); investment management (Diploma); investment management option (MBA); management accounting (Certificate); management of healthcare organizations (Certificate); sport administration (Diploma). *Accreditation:* AACSB. Part-time and evening/weekend programs available. *Degree requirements:* For master's, one foreign language, thesis (for some programs), research project; for doctorate, one foreign language, thesis/dissertation; for other advanced degree, one foreign language. *Entrance requirements:* For master's and doctorate, GMAT. Additional exam requirements/recommendations for international students: Required—TOEFL. *Expenses:* Contact institution. *Faculty research:* General business, capital markets, international business.

Daniel Webster College, MBA Program for Aviation Professionals, Nashua, NH 03063-1300. Offers MBA. Part-time and evening/weekend programs available. *Degree requirements:* For master's, capstone research project. *Entrance requirements:* Additional exam requirements/recommendations for international students: Required—TOEFL (minimum score 550 paper-based; 213 computer-based; 79 iBT). Electronic applications accepted.

Delta State University, Graduate Programs, College of Business, Department of Commercial Aviation, Cleveland, MS 38733-0001. Offers MCA. Part-time and evening/weekend programs available. Postbaccalaureate distance learning degree programs offered (minimal on-campus study). *Degree requirements:* For master's, thesis or alternative. *Entrance requirements:* For master's, GMAT. *Expenses:* Tuition, state resident: full-time $4450; part-time $247 per credit hour. Tuition, nonresident: full-time $11,520; part-time $640 per credit hour.

Dowling College, School of Business, Oakdale, NY 11769-1999. Offers aviation management (MBA, Certificate); banking and finance (MBA, Certificate); financial planning (Certificate); general management (MBA); health care management (MBA, Certificate); human resource management (Certificate); management and leadership (MBA); marketing (Certificate); project management (Certificate); public management (MBA, Certificate); total quality management (MBA, Certificate); JD/MBA. Part-time and evening/weekend programs available. *Faculty:* 14 full-time (5 women), 58 part-time/adjunct (5 women). *Students:* 324 full-time (142 women), 479 part-time (237 women); includes 238 minority (82 African Americans, 1 American Indian/Alaska Native, 117 Asian Americans or Pacific Islanders, 38 Hispanic Americans), 2 international. Average age 33. 457 applicants, 91% accepted, 153 enrolled. In 2009, 341 master's, 2 other advanced degrees awarded. *Degree requirements:* For master's, comprehensive exam, thesis optional. *Entrance requirements:* For master's, minimum GPA of 2.8, 2 letters of recommendation, courses in accounting and finance or seminar in accounting/finance, resume. Additional exam requirements/recommendations for international students: Required—TOEFL (minimum score 550 paper-based). *Application deadline:* For fall admission, 9/1 priority date for domestic students; for winter admission, 1/1 priority date for domestic students; for spring admission, 2/1 priority date for domestic students. Applications are processed on a rolling basis. Application fee: $50. Electronic applications accepted. *Expenses:* Tuition: Full-time $14,490; part-time $805 per credit. Required fees: $346 per term. *Financial support:* Career-related internships or fieldwork and Federal Work-Study available. Support available to part-time students. Financial award application deadline: 6/30; financial award applicants required to submit FAFSA. *Faculty research:* International finance, computer applications, labor relations, executive development. *Unit head:* Mathew Cordaro, Dean, 631-244-3162, Fax: 631-244-1018, E-mail: cordarom@dowling.edu. *Application contact:* Glenn M. Berman, Director of Admissions Operations, 631-244-3357, Fax: 631-244-1059, E-mail: glenn.berman@dowling.edu.

Embry-Riddle Aeronautical University, Daytona Beach Campus Graduate Program, Department of Business Administration, Daytona Beach, FL 32114-3900. Offers business administration in aviation (MBAA). *Accreditation:* ACBSP. Part-time and evening/weekend programs available. Postbaccalaureate distance learning degree programs offered (minimal on-campus study). *Faculty:* 1 part-time/adjunct (0 women). *Students:* 95 full-time (21 women), 71 part-time (26 women); includes 30 minority (16 African Americans, 7 Asian Americans or Pacific Islanders, 7 Hispanic Americans), 49 international. Average age 30. 96 applicants, 57% accepted, 42 enrolled. In 2009, 52 master's awarded. *Degree requirements:* For master's, thesis or alternative. *Entrance requirements:* For master's, minimum GPA of 2.5. Additional exam requirements/recommendations for international students: Required—TOEFL (minimum score 550 paper-based; 213 computer-based; 79 iBT). *Application deadline:* For fall admission, 8/1 priority date for domestic students; for spring admission, 12/1 priority date for domestic students. Applications are processed on a rolling basis. Application fee: $50. *Expenses:* Tuition: Full-time $13,740; part-time $1145 per credit hour. *Financial support:* In 2009–10, 39 students received support, including 21 research assistantships with partial tuition reimbursements available (averaging $4,492 per year), 3 teaching assistantships (averaging $4,492 per year); career-related internships or fieldwork, Federal Work-Study, and unspecified assistantships also available. Support available to part-time students. Financial award application deadline: 4/15; financial award applicants required to submit FAFSA. *Faculty research:* Aircraft safety operations analysis, energy consumption analysis, statistical analysis of general aviation accidents, airport funding strategies, industry assessment and marketing analysis for ENAER aerospace. Total annual research expenditures: $120,079. *Unit head:* Dr. Blaise Waguespack, Program Coordinator, 386-226-7235, Fax: 386-226-6696, E-mail: waguespb@erau.edu. *Application contact:* Keith Deaton, Director, International and Graduate Admissions, 800-388-3728, Fax: 386-226-7070, E-mail: graduate.admissions@erau.edu.

Embry-Riddle Aeronautical University Worldwide, Worldwide Headquarters, Program in Management, Daytona Beach, FL 32114-3900. Offers MSM, MSM/MBAA. Part-time and evening/weekend programs available. Postbaccalaureate distance learning degree programs offered. *Faculty:* 16 full-time (2 women), 28 part-time/adjunct (9 women). *Students:* 216 full-time (49 women), 337 part-time (93 women); includes 148 minority (78 African Americans, 2 American Indian/Alaska Native, 22 Asian Americans or Pacific Islanders, 46 Hispanic Americans), 7 international. Average age 37. 223 applicants, 87% accepted, 148 enrolled. In 2009, 102 master's awarded. *Degree requirements:* For master's, thesis optional. *Entrance requirements:* For master's, GMAT. *Application deadline:* Applications are processed on a rolling basis. Application fee: $50. Electronic applications accepted. *Financial support:* In 2009–10, 22 students received support. Applicants required to submit FAFSA. *Unit head:* Dr. Kees Rietsema, Chair, 602-750-0685, E-mail: rietsd37@erau.edu. *Application contact:* Linda Dammer, Director of Admissions, 386-226-6910, Fax: 386-226-6984, E-mail: ecinfo@erau.edu.

Lewis University, College of Arts and Sciences, Program in Aviation and Transportation, Romeoville, IL 60446. Offers administration (MS); safety and security (MS). Part-time and evening/weekend programs available. *Faculty:* 2 full-time (0 women), 1 part-time/adjunct (0 women). *Students:* 2 full-time (0 women), 10 part-time (1 woman); includes 2 minority (1 African American, 1 Hispanic American). Average age 37. In 2009, 2 master's awarded. *Entrance requirements:* For master's, bachelor's degree, minimum GPA of 3.0, personal statement, 3 letters of recommendation. Additional exam requirements/recommendations for international students: Required—TOEFL (minimum score 550 paper-based; 213 computer-based). *Application deadline:* For fall admission, 5/1 priority date for international students; for spring admission, 11/15 priority date for international students. Applications are processed on a rolling basis. Application fee: $40. Electronic applications accepted. *Expenses:* Tuition: Full-time $6480; part-time $720 per credit. One-time fee: $40. Tuition and fees vary according to course load, degree level and program. *Financial support:* Application deadline: 5/1. *Unit head:* Dr. Randal DeMik, Head, 815-838-0500 Ext. 5559, E-mail: demikra@lewisu.edu. *Application contact:* Diane Blazevich, Information Contact, 815-838-0500 Ext. 5434, E-mail: blazevdi@lewisu.edu.

Lynn University, College of Business and Management, Boca Raton, FL 33431-5598. Offers aviation management (MBA); financial valuation and investment management (MBA); hospitality management (MBA); international business (MBA); marketing (MBA); mass communication and media management (MBA); sports and athletics administration (MBA). Part-time and evening/weekend programs available. Postbaccalaureate distance learning degree programs offered. *Degree requirements:* For master's, project. *Entrance requirements:* For master's, GMAT or GRE, minimum undergraduate GPA of 3.0, resume, 2 letters of recommendation. Additional exam requirements/recommendations for international students: Required—TOEFL (minimum score 550 paper-based; 213 computer-based). *Application deadline:* Applications are processed on a rolling basis. Application fee: $50. Electronic applications accepted. *Expenses:* Tuition: Part-time $580 per credit. One-time fee: $200 part-time. Part-time tuition and fees vary according to degree level. *Financial support:* Career-related internships or fieldwork, Federal Work-Study, institutionally sponsored loans, scholarships/grants, tuition waivers (full and partial), and unspecified assistantships available. Support available to part-time students. Financial award application deadline: 8/1; financial award applicants required to submit FAFSA. *Faculty research:* Labor relations, dynamic balance in leisure-time skills, ethics in athletics, hotel development. *Unit head:* Dr. Ralph Norcio, Associate Dean, 561-237-7010, Fax: 561-237-7014, E-mail: rnorcio@lynn.edu. *Application contact:* Dr. Larissa Baia, Assistant Director of Graduate Admissions, 561-237-7916, Fax: 561-237-7100, E-mail: admissionpm@lynn.edu.

Middle Tennessee State University, College of Graduate Studies, College of Basic and Applied Sciences, Department of Aerospace, Program in Aviation Administration, Murfreesboro, TN 37132. Offers MS. Part-time and evening/weekend programs available. Postbaccalaureate distance learning degree programs offered. *Students:* 9 full-time (3 women), 13 part-time (3 women); includes 8 minority (6 African Americans, 2 Asian Americans or Pacific Islanders). 8 applicants, 75% accepted, 6 enrolled. *Degree requirements:* For master's, one foreign language, comprehensive exam. *Entrance requirements:* For master's, GRE or MAT. Additional exam requirements/recommendations for international students: Required—TOEFL (minimum score 525 paper-based; 195 computer-based; 71 iBT) or IELTS (minimum score 6). *Application deadline:* For fall admission, 6/1 for domestic and international students. Applications are processed on a rolling basis. Application fee: $25 ($30 for international students). *Expenses:* Tuition, state resident: full-time $4404. Tuition, nonresident: full-time $10,956. *Financial support:* Institutionally sponsored loans available. Support available to part-time students. Financial award application deadline: 5/1. *Unit head:* Dr. Wayne Dornan, Chair, 615-898-2788, E-mail: wdornan@mtsu.edu. *Application contact:* Dr. Wayne Dornan, Chair, 615-898-2788, E-mail: wdornan@mtsu.edu.

Southeastern Oklahoma State University, Department of Aviation Science, Durant, OK 74701-0609. Offers aerospace administration and logistics (MS). Part-time and evening/weekend programs available. *Students:* 33 full-time (4 women), 53 part-time (13 women); includes 16 minority (5 African Americans, 2 American Indian/Alaska Native, 3 Asian Americans or Pacific Islanders, 6 Hispanic Americans), 1 international. Average age 30. 86 applicants, 100% accepted, 86 enrolled. *Entrance requirements:* For master's, minimum GPA of 3.0 in last 60 hours or 2.75 overall. Additional exam requirements/recommendations for international students: Required—TOEFL (minimum score 550 paper-based; 213 computer-based). *Application deadline:* For fall admission, 8/1 for domestic students, 6/1 for international students; for spring admission, 1/5 for domestic students, 11/1 for international students. Application fee: $20 ($55 for international students). Electronic applications accepted. *Financial support:* Federal Work-Study and institutionally sponsored loans available. Support available to part-time students. Financial award application deadline: 6/15. *Unit head:* Dr. David Conway, Director, 580-745-3240, Fax: 580-924-0741, E-mail: dconway@se.edu. *Application contact:* Carrie Williamson, Administrative Assistant-Graduate Office, 580-745-2200, Fax: 580-745-7474, E-mail: cwilliamson@se.edu.

Vaughn College of Aeronautics and Technology, Graduate Programs, Flushing, NY 11369. Offers airport management (MS). *Degree requirements:* For master's, project or thesis.

Logistics

Air Force Institute of Technology, Graduate School of Engineering and Management, Department of Operational Sciences, Dayton, OH 45433-7765. Offers logistics management (MS); operations research (MS, PhD); space operations (MS). Part-time programs available. *Degree requirements:* For master's, thesis; for doctorate, thesis/dissertation. *Entrance requirements:* For doctorate, GRE General Test, minimum GPA of 3.0, U.S. citizenship. *Faculty research:* Optimization, simulation, combat modeling and analysis, reliability and maintainability, resource scheduling.

American Public University System, AMU/APU Graduate Programs, Charles Town, WV 25414. Offers air warfare (MA Military Studies); American Revolution (MA Military Studies); business administration (MBA); Civil War (MA Military Studies); criminal justice (MA); defense management (MA Military Studies); emergency and disaster management (MA); environmental policy and management (MS); fire science management (MA); global engagement (MA); history (MA); homeland security (MA); humanities (MA); intelligence (MA Military Studies, MA Strategic Intelligence); international peace and conflict resolution (MA); international relations and conflict resolution (MA); joint warfare (MA Military Studies); land warfare international perspective (MA Military Studies); management (MA); military history (MA); military leadership (MA Military Studies); national security studies (MA); naval warfare international (MA Military Studies); naval warfare US (MA Military Studies); political science (MA); public administration (MA); public health (MA); security management (MA); space studies (MS); special ops/LIC (MA Military Studies); sports management (MA); transportation and logistics management (MA); transportation management (MA); unconventional warfare (MA Military Studies); World War II (MA Military Studies). Programs offered via distance learning only. Part-time and evening/weekend programs available. Postbaccalaureate distance learning degree programs offered (no on-campus study). *Students:* 788 full-time (330 women), 6,916 part-time (2,050 women); includes 1,767 minority (908 African Americans, 70 American Indian/Alaska Native, 223 Asian Americans or Pacific Islanders, 566 Hispanic Americans), 77 international. Average age 35. *Degree requirements:* For master's, comprehensive exam or practicum. *Entrance requirements:* For master's, bachelor's degree or equivalent, minimum GPA of 2.7 in last 60 hours of course work. *Application deadline:* Applications are processed on a rolling basis. Application fee: $0. Electronic applications accepted. *Financial support:* Applicants required to submit FAFSA. *Faculty research:* Military history, criminal justice, management performance, national security.

Unit head: Dr. Frank McCluskey, Provost, 877-468-6268, Fax: 304-724-3780. *Application contact:* Terry Grant, Director of Enrollment Management, 877-468-6268, Fax: 304-724-3780, E-mail: info@apus.edu.

Benedictine University, Graduate Programs, Program in Business Administration, Lisle, IL 60532-0900. Offers accounting (MBA); entrepreneurship and managing innovation (MBA); financial management (MBA); health administration (MBA); human resource management (MBA); information systems security (MBA); international business (MBA); management consulting (MBA); management information systems (MBA); marketing management (MBA); operations management and logistics (MBA); organizational leadership (MBA); MBA/MPH; MBA/MS. Part-time and evening/weekend programs available. Postbaccalaureate distance learning degree programs offered (minimal on-campus study). *Faculty:* 4 full-time (2 women), 24 part-time/adjunct (3 women). *Students:* 247 full-time (141 women), 644 part-time (339 women); includes 223 minority (134 African Americans, 5 American Indian/Alaska Native, 44 Asian Americans or Pacific Islanders, 40 Hispanic Americans), 25 international. Average age 34. 287 applicants, 92% accepted, 229 enrolled. In 2009, 219 master's awarded. *Entrance requirements:* For master's, GMAT. Additional exam requirements/recommendations for international students: Required—TOEFL (minimum score 550 paper-based; 213 computer-based). *Application deadline:* For fall admission, 9/1 for domestic students; for winter admission, 12/1 for domestic students; for spring admission, 2/15 for domestic students. Applications are processed on a rolling basis. Application fee: $40. Electronic applications accepted. *Expenses:* Tuition: Part-time $750 per credit hour. Tuition and fees vary according to campus/location and program. *Financial support:* Career-related internships or fieldwork and health care benefits available. Support available to part-time students. *Faculty research:* Strategic leadership in professional organizations, sociology of professions, organizational change, social identity theory, applications to change management. *Unit head:* Dr. Sharon Borowicz, Director, 630-829-6219, E-mail: sborowicz@ben.edu. *Application contact:* Kari Gibbons, Director, Admissions, 630-829-6200, Fax: 630-829-6584, E-mail: kgibbons@ben.edu.

California State University, Long Beach, Graduate Studies, College of Liberal Arts, Department of Economics, Long Beach, CA 90840. Offers economics (MA); global logistics (MA). Part-time programs available. *Faculty:* 2 full-time (1 woman). *Students:* 15 full-time (5 women), 20 part-time (10 women); includes 11 minority (3 African Americans, 1 American Indian/Alaska Native, 4 Asian Americans or Pacific Islanders, 3 Hispanic Americans), 10 international. Average age 29. 78 applicants, 71% accepted, 17 enrolled. *Degree requirements:* For master's, comprehensive exam or thesis. *Entrance requirements:* For master's, GRE General Test, GRE Subject Test, minimum GPA of 3.0. *Application deadline:* For fall admission, 4/1 for domestic students. Applications are processed on a rolling basis. Application fee: $55. Electronic applications accepted. *Expenses:* Required fees: $1802 per semester. Part-time tuition and fees vary according to course load. *Financial support:* Federal Work-Study, institutionally sponsored loans, and scholarships/grants available. Financial award application deadline: 3/2. *Faculty research:* Trade and development, economic forecasting, resource economics. *Unit head:* Dr. Joseph P. Magaddino, Chair, 562-985-5061, Fax: 562-985-5804, E-mail: magaddin@csulb.edu. *Application contact:* Dr. Alejandra C. Edwards, Graduate Advisor, 562-985-5969, Fax: 562-985-5804, E-mail: acoxedwa@csulb.edu.

Case Western Reserve University, School of Graduate Studies, Case School of Engineering, Department of Electrical Engineering and Computer Science, Cleveland, OH 44106. Offers computer engineering (MS, PhD); computing and information sciences (MS, PhD); electrical engineering (MS, PhD); systems and control engineering (MS, PhD). Part-time and evening/weekend programs available. Postbaccalaureate distance learning degree programs offered (minimal on-campus study). *Faculty:* 32 full-time (2 women). *Students:* 175 full-time (26 women), 28 part-time (6 women); includes 9 minority (3 African Americans, 6 Asian Americans or Pacific Islanders), 107 international. In 2009, 29 master's, 15 doctorates awarded. Terminal master's awarded for partial completion of doctoral program. *Degree requirements:* For master's, thesis; for doctorate, thesis/dissertation, qualifying exam, teaching experience. *Entrance requirements:* For master's and doctorate, GRE General Test. Additional exam requirements/recommendations for international students: Required—TOEFL. *Application deadline:* For fall admission, 2/1 for domestic students; for spring admission, 11/1 for domestic students. Applications are processed on a rolling basis. Application fee: $50. *Financial support:* Fellowships with full and partial tuition reimbursements, research assistantships with full and partial tuition reimbursements, teaching assistantships, career-related internships or fieldwork, Federal Work-Study, and institutionally sponsored loans available. Support available to part-time students. Financial award application deadline: 3/1; financial award applicants required to submit FAFSA. *Faculty research:* Applied artificial intelligence, automation, computer-aided design and testing of digital systems. Total annual research expenditures: $5.5 million. *Unit head:* Dwight Davy, Department Chair, 216-368-2802, E-mail: dtd@case.edu. *Application contact:* David Easler, Student Affairs Coordinator, 216-368-4080, Fax: 216-368-2801, E-mail: david.easler@case.edu.

Central Connecticut State University, School of Graduate Studies, School of Technology, Department of Manufacturing and Construction Management, New Britain, CT 06050-4010. Offers construction management (MS, Certificate); lean manufacturing and six sigma (Certificate); supply chain and logistics (Certificate); technology management (MS). Part-time and evening/weekend programs available. *Faculty:* 17 full-time (5 women), 25 part-time/adjunct (1 woman). *Students:* 13 full-time (4 women), 66 part-time (9 women); includes 11 minority (4 African Americans, 4 Asian Americans or Pacific Islanders, 3 Hispanic Americans), 4 international. Average age 33. 46 applicants, 50% accepted, 17 enrolled. In 2009, 27 master's, 1 other advanced degree awarded. *Degree requirements:* For master's, comprehensive exam, thesis or alternative; for Certificate, qualifying exam. *Entrance requirements:* For master's, minimum undergraduate GPA of 2.7. Additional exam requirements/recommendations for international students: Required—TOEFL. *Application deadline:* For fall admission, 7/1 for domestic students; for spring admission, 12/1 for domestic students. Applications are processed on a rolling basis. Application fee: $50. Electronic applications accepted. *Expenses:* Tuition, area resident: Full-time $4662; part-time $440 per credit. Tuition, state resident: full-time $6994; part-time $440 per credit. Tuition, nonresident: full-time $12,988; part-time $440 per credit. Required fees: $3606. One-time fee: $62 part-time. *Financial support:* In 2009–10, 5 students received support, including 3 research assistantships; career-related internships or fieldwork, Federal Work-Study, scholarships/grants, and unspecified assistantships also available. Support available to part-time students. Financial award application deadline: 3/1; financial award applicants required to submit FAFSA. *Faculty research:* All aspects of middle management, technical supervision in the workplace. *Unit head:* Dr. Jacob Kovel, Chair, 860-832-1830. *Application contact:* Dr. Jacob Kovel, Chair, 860-832-1830.

Central Michigan University, Central Michigan University Off-Campus Programs, Program in Business Administration, Mount Pleasant, MI 48859. Offers logistics management (MBA, Certificate); SAP (MBA); value-driven organization (MBA). Part-time and evening/weekend programs available. *Entrance requirements:* For master's, GMAT. *Financial support:* Scholarships/grants available. Support available to part-time students. *Unit head:* Dr. Monica Holmes, Associate Dean, 989-774-3337, E-mail: holme1mc@cmich.edu. *Application contact:* Off-Campus Programs Call Center, 877-268-4636.

Colorado Technical University Colorado Springs, Graduate Studies, Program in Management, Colorado Springs, CO 80907-3896. Offers accounting (MBA, MSA); business administration (MBA); finance (MBA); human resources management (MBA); logistics/supply chain management (MBA); management (DM); marketing (MBA); mediation and dispute resolution (MBA); operations management (MBA); project management (MBA); technology management (MBA). Part-time and evening/weekend programs available. Postbaccalaureate distance learning degree programs offered. *Degree requirements:* For master's, thesis or alternative; for doctorate, thesis/dissertation. *Entrance requirements:* For doctorate, minimum graduate GPA of 3.0, 5 years of related work experience. *Faculty research:* Sexual harassment, performance evaluation, critical thinking.

East Carolina University, Graduate School, College of Technology and Computer Science, Department of Technology Systems, Greenville, NC 27858-4353. Offers computer network

professional (Certificate); industrial technology (MS), including computer networking management, digital communications, industrial distribution and logistics, information security, manufacturing, performance improvement, planning; information assurance (Certificate); occupational safety (MS); technology management (PhD); Website developer (Certificate). *Entrance requirements:* For master's and Certificate, GRE General Test or MAT, minimum GPA of 2.5; for doctorate, GRE General Test, related work experience.

Embry-Riddle Aeronautical University Worldwide, Worldwide Headquarters, Program in Logistics and Supply Chain Management, Daytona Beach, FL 32114-3900. Offers MSLSCM. *Faculty:* 16 full-time (2 women), 28 part-time/adjunct (9 women). *Students:* 8 full-time (2 women), 12 part-time (3 women); includes 8 minority (3 African Americans, 4 Asian Americans or Pacific Islanders, 1 Hispanic American). Average age 39. 53 applicants, 75% accepted. *Degree requirements:* For master's, thesis (for some programs). Application fee: $50. *Financial support:* In 2009–10, 2 students received support. *Unit head:* Dr. Kees Rietsema, Chair, 602-750-0685, E-mail: rietsd37@erau.edu. *Application contact:* Linda Dammer, Director of Admissions, 386-226-6910, Fax: 386-226-6984, E-mail: ecinfo@erau.edu.

Florida Institute of Technology, Graduate Programs, College of Business, Extended Studies Division, Melbourne, FL 32901-6975. Offers acquisition and contract management (PMBA); business administration (PMBA); computer information systems (MS); e-business (PMBA); human resource management (PMBA); human resources management (MS); logistics management (MS), including humanitarian and disaster relief logistics; management (MS), including acquisition and contract management, e-business, human resource management, information systems, logistics management, management, transportation management; material acquisition management (MS); project management (MS), including information systems, operations research; public administration (MPA); quality management (MS); space management (MS); space systems (MS); systems management (MS), including information systems, operations research, systems management. Part-time and evening/weekend programs available. Postbaccalaureate distance learning degree programs offered (no on-campus study). *Faculty:* 12 full-time (3 women), 117 part-time/adjunct (20 women). *Students:* 74 full-time (32 women), 1,041 part-time (484 women); includes 343 minority (240 African Americans, 12 American Indian/Alaska Native, 44 Asian Americans or Pacific Islanders, 47 Hispanic Americans), 22 international. Average age 35. 520 applicants, 72% accepted, 279 enrolled. In 2009, 509 master's awarded. *Degree requirements:* For master's, capstone course. *Entrance requirements:* For master's, GMAT or resume showing 8 years of supervised experience, minimum GPA of 3.0, 2 letters of recommendation, resume. Additional exam requirements/recommendations for international students: Required—TOEFL (minimum score 550 paper-based; 213 computer-based; 79 iBT). *Application deadline:* For fall admission, 4/1 for international students; for spring admission, 9/30 for international students. Applications are processed on a rolling basis. Application fee: $50. Electronic applications accepted. *Expenses:* Tuition: Part-time $1015 per credit. Tuition and fees vary according to campus/location and program. *Financial support:* Application deadline: 3/1. *Unit head:* Dr. Clifford Bragdon, Dean, 321-674-8821, Fax: 321-674-7597, E-mail: cbragdon@fit.edu. *Application contact:* Carolyn Farrior, Director of Graduate Admissions Online Learning and Off Campus Programs, 321-674-7118, Fax: 321-674-8216, E-mail: cfarrior@fit.edu.

George Mason University, School of Public Policy, Program in Transportation Policy, Operations and Logistics, Arlington, VA 22201. Offers MA. Part-time programs available. Postbaccalaureate distance learning degree programs offered (no on-campus study). *Faculty:* 61 full-time (14 women), 30 part-time/adjunct (4 women). *Students:* 9 full-time (2 women), 29 part-time (8 women); includes 2 minority (both African Americans), 5 international. Average age 31. 27 applicants, 59% accepted, 10 enrolled. In 2009, 21 master's awarded. *Degree requirements:* For master's, thesis or alternative. *Entrance requirements:* For master's, GRE (for students seeking merit-based scholarships), minimum undergraduate GPA of 3.0, resume, 2 letters of recommendation. Additional exam requirements/recommendations for international students: Required—TOEFL (minimum score 575 paper-based; 230 computer-based; 88 iBT). *Application deadline:* For fall admission, 6/1 priority date for domestic students, 5/1 priority date for international students; for spring admission, 12/1 priority date for domestic students, 11/1 priority date for international students. Applications are processed on a rolling basis. Application fee: $60. Electronic applications accepted. *Expenses:* Contact institution. *Financial support:* Career-related internships or fieldwork, Federal Work-Study, scholarships/grants, and tuition waivers (partial) available. Support available to part-time students. Financial award application deadline: 3/1; financial award applicants required to submit FAFSA. *Unit head:* Dr. Jonathan Gifford, Director, 703-993-8099, E-mail: spp@gmu.edu. *Application contact:* Leslie Metzger Levin, Assistant Dean of Graduate Admissions and Marketing, 703-993-8099, Fax: 703-993-4876, E-mail: lmetzger@gmu.edu.

Georgia College & State University, Graduate School, College of Arts and Sciences, Department of Government and Sociology, Logistics Education Center, Milledgeville, GA 31061. Offers logistics management (MSA). Part-time and evening/weekend programs available. *Students:* 5 full-time (2 women), 70 part-time (30 women); includes 22 minority (14 African Americans, 3 Asian Americans or Pacific Islanders, 5 Hispanic Americans). Average age 35. 41 applicants, 93% accepted, 26 enrolled. In 2009, 24 master's awarded. *Entrance requirements:* For master's, MAT, GRE, GMAT. Additional exam requirements/recommendations for international students: Recommended—TOEFL (minimum score 550 paper-based; 213 computer-based; 79 iBT). *Application deadline:* For fall admission, 7/1 priority date for domestic students, 4/1 for international students; for spring admission, 11/15 for domestic students, 9/1 for international students. Applications are processed on a rolling basis. Application fee: $40. Electronic applications accepted. *Expenses:* Tuition, area resident: Part-time $241 per credit hour. Tuition, state resident: full-time $4338. Tuition, nonresident: full-time $17,352; part-time $964 per credit hour. Required fees: $609 per semester. Tuition and fees vary according to course load and campus/location. *Financial support:* Application deadline: 3/1. *Unit head:* Glenn Easterly, Director of Robins Center/Coordinator of Logistics Program, 478-327-7376, Fax: 478-926-2468, E-mail: glenn.easterly@gcsu.edu. *Application contact:* Glenn Easterly, Director of Robins Center/Coordinator of Logistics Program, 478-327-7376, Fax: 478-926-2468, E-mail: glenn.easterly@gcsu.edu.

HEC Montreal, School of Business Administration, Master of Science Programs in Administration, Program in Logistics, Montréal, QC H3T 2A7, Canada. Offers M Sc. All courses are given in French. Part-time programs available. *Students:* 14 full-time (6 women), 4 part-time (2 women). 22 applicants, 64% accepted, 7 enrolled. In 2009, 4 master's awarded. *Degree requirements:* For master's, one foreign language, thesis. *Application deadline:* For fall admission, 3/15 for domestic and international students; for winter admission, 9/15 for domestic and international students. Application fee: $77 Canadian dollars. Electronic applications accepted. Tuition and fees charges are reported in Canadian dollars. *Expenses:* Tuition, area resident: Part-time $65.60 Canadian dollars per credit. Tuition, state resident: full-time $2361.60 Canadian dollars; part-time $183.36 Canadian dollars per credit. Tuition, nonresident: full-time $6601 Canadian dollars; part-time $448.13 Canadian dollars per credit. International tuition: $16,132.68 Canadian dollars full-time. Required fees: $1254.15 Canadian dollars; $28.99 Canadian dollars per course. $91.68 Canadian dollars per term. Tuition and fees vary according to degree level and program. *Financial support:* Fellowships, research assistantships, teaching assistantships, scholarships/grants available. Financial award application deadline: 10/2. *Unit head:* Dr. Claude Laurin, Director, 514-340-6485, Fax: 514-340-5690, E-mail: claude.laurin@hec.ca. *Application contact:* Francine Blais, Administrative Director, 514-340-6112, Fax: 514-340-6411, E-mail: francine.blais@hec.ca.

Kaplan University, Davenport Campus, School of Business, Davenport, IA 52807-2095. Offers business administration (MBA); change leadership (MS); entrepreneurship (MBA); finance (MBA); health care management (MBA, MS); human resource (MBA); international business (MBA); management (MS); marketing (MBA); project management (MBA, MS); supply chain management and logistics (MBA, MS). Part-time and evening/weekend programs available. Postbaccalaureate distance learning degree programs offered (no on-campus study). *Entrance requirements:* Additional exam requirements/recommendations for international

Logistics

Kaplan University, Davenport Campus (continued)
students: Required—TOEFL (minimum score 550 paper-based; 218 computer-based; 80 iBT). Electronic applications accepted.

Maine Maritime Academy, Department of Graduate Studies, Program in Maritime Management, Castine, ME 04420. Offers MS, Certificate, Diploma. Part-time programs available. *Degree requirements:* For master's, thesis optional, capstone course. *Entrance requirements:* For master's, GMAT or GRE General Test, letters of recommendation. Additional exam requirements/recommendations for international students: Required—TOEFL. *Faculty research:* Human resources in maritime environment, management of organization change, economic analysis and maritime law.

Massachusetts Institute of Technology, School of Engineering, Engineering Systems Division, Cambridge, MA 02139-4307. Offers engineering and management (SM); engineering systems (SM, PhD); logistics (M Eng); technology and policy (SM); technology, management and policy (PhD); SM/MBA. *Faculty:* 8 full-time (0 women). *Students:* 285 full-time (72 women), 1 part-time (0 women); includes 36 minority (8 African Americans, 19 Asian Americans or Pacific Islanders, 9 Hispanic Americans), 116 international. Average age 31. 874 applicants, 28% accepted, 188 enrolled. In 2009, 143 master's, 11 doctorates awarded. *Degree requirements:* For master's, thesis; for doctorate, comprehensive exam, thesis/dissertation. *Entrance requirements:* For master's and doctorate, GRE General Test or GMAT (for some programs). Additional exam requirements/recommendations for international students: Required—IELTS (minimum score 7.5); Recommended—TOEFL (minimum score 610 paper-based; 255 computer-based; 103 iBT). Application fee: $75. *Expenses:* Contact institution. *Financial support:* In 2009–10, 224 students received support, including 41 fellowships with tuition reimbursements available (averaging $26,522 per year), 95 research assistantships with tuition reimbursements available (averaging $26,506 per year), 17 teaching assistantships with tuition reimbursements available (averaging $21,300 per year); career-related internships or fieldwork, Federal Work-Study, institutionally sponsored loans, scholarships/grants, health care benefits, and unspecified assistantships also available. *Faculty research:* Critical infrastructures, extended enterprises, energy and sustainability, health care delivery, humans and technology, uncertainty and dynamics, design and implementation, networks and flows, policy and standards. Total annual research expenditures: $10.7 million. *Unit head:* Prof. Yossi Sheffi, Director, 617-253-1764, E-mail: esdinquiries@mit.edu. *Application contact:* Graduate Admissions, 617-253-1182, E-mail: esdgrad@mit.edu.

North Dakota State University, College of Graduate and Interdisciplinary Studies, College of Engineering and Architecture, Department of Civil Engineering, Fargo, ND 58108. Offers civil engineering (MS, PhD); environmental engineering (MS, PhD); transportation and logistics (PhD). PhD in transportation and logistics offered jointly with Upper Great Plains Transportation Institute. Part-time programs available. Postbaccalaureate distance learning degree programs offered (minimal on-campus study). *Students:* 20 full-time (4 women), 12 part-time (0 women); includes 2 minority (both Asian Americans or Pacific Islanders), 21 international. In 2009, 7 master's, 1 doctorate awarded. *Degree requirements:* For master's, thesis; for doctorate, comprehensive exam, thesis/dissertation. *Entrance requirements:* Additional exam requirements/recommendations for international students: Required—TOEFL (minimum score 525 paper-based; 197 computer-based; 71 iBT). *Application deadline:* For fall admission, 7/1 priority date for domestic students, 1/15 priority date for international students; for spring admission, 5/1 priority date for international students. Applications are processed on a rolling basis. Application fee: $45 ($60 for international students). *Financial support:* Fellowships with full tuition reimbursements, research assistantships with full tuition reimbursements, teaching assistantships with full tuition reimbursements, career-related internships or fieldwork, Federal Work-Study, and institutionally sponsored loans available. Support available to part-time students. Financial award application deadline: 1/15. *Faculty research:* Wastewater, solid waste, composites, nanotechnology. Total annual research expenditures: $800,000. *Unit head:* Dr. Dinesh R. Katti, Chair, 701-231-7244, Fax: 701-231-6185, E-mail: dinesh.katti@ndsu.edu. *Application contact:* Dr. Kalpana Katti, Associate Professor and Associate Graduate Program Coordinator, 701-231-9504, Fax: 701-231-6185, E-mail: kalpana.katti@ndsu.edu.

North Dakota State University, College of Graduate and Interdisciplinary Studies, Interdisciplinary Program in Transportation and Logistics, Fargo, ND 58108. Offers PhD. *Students:* 14 full-time (4 women), 10 part-time (2 women); includes 2 African Americans, 1 Asian American or Pacific Islander, 8 international. In 2009, 2 doctorates awarded. *Entrance requirements:* For doctorate, 1 year of calculus, statistics and probability, minimum GPA of 3.0. Additional exam requirements/recommendations for international students: Required—TOEFL (minimum score 550 paper-based; 213 computer-based; 79 iBT). *Application deadline:* For fall admission, 5/1 priority date for domestic students. Applications are processed on a rolling basis. Application fee: $45 ($60 for international students). *Financial support:* Research assistantships with full tuition reimbursements available. *Faculty research:* Supply chain optimization, spatial analysis of transportation networks, advanced traffic analysis, transportation demand, railroad/intermodal freight. *Unit head:* Dr. Denver Tolliver, Director, 701-231-7190, Fax: 701-231-1945, E-mail: denver.tolliver@ndsu.nodak.edu. *Application contact:* Dr. Denver Tolliver, Director, 701-231-7190, Fax: 701-231-1945, E-mail: denver.tolliver@ndsu.nodak.edu.

The Ohio State University, Graduate School, Max M. Fisher College of Business, Program in Business Logistics Engineering, Columbus, OH 43210. Offers MBLE. *Students:* 32 full-time (15 women), 15 part-time (8 women); includes 1 minority (Asian American or Pacific Islander), 40 international. Average age 26. In 2009, 16 master's awarded. *Entrance requirements:* For master's, GRE or GMAT. Additional exam requirements/recommendations for international students: Required—TOEFL. *Application deadline:* Applications are processed on a rolling basis. Application fee: $40 ($50 for international students). Electronic applications accepted. *Expenses:* Tuition, state resident: full-time $10,683. Tuition, nonresident: full-time $25,923. Tuition and fees vary according to course load and program. *Unit head:* Walter Zinn, Graduate Studies Committee Chair, 416-292-0797, Fax: 416-292-9006, E-mail: zinn.13@osu.edu. *Application contact:* Graduate Admissions, 614-292-9444, Fax: 614-292-3895, E-mail: domestic.grad@osu.edu.

Pontificia Universidad Catolica Madre y Maestra, Graduate School, Santiago, Dominican Republic. Offers administration (M Adm); architecture of interiors (M Arch); architecture of tourist lodgings (M Arch); banking and financial management (M Mgmt); civil law (LL M); construction administration (ME); corporate business law (LL M); criminal procedure law (LL M); environmental engineering (ME, MEE); finance (M Mgmt); history applied to education (M Ed); human resources (EMBA); insurance (M Mgmt); international business (M Mgmt); labor law and Social Security (LL M); logistics management (ME); marketing (M Mgmt); renewable energy (ME); strategic cost management (M Mgmt). *Entrance requirements:* For master's, curriculum vitae, interview.

Stevens Institute of Technology, Graduate School, School of Systems and Enterprises, Program in Systems Design and Operational Effectiveness, Hoboken, NJ 07030. Offers M Eng. *Expenses:* Tuition: Full-time $9900; part-time $1100 per credit. Required fees: $286 per semester.

Stevens Institute of Technology, Graduate School, School of Systems and Enterprises, Program in Systems Engineering, Hoboken, NJ 07030. Offers agile systems and enterprises (Certificate); systems and supportability engineering (Certificate); systems engineering (M Eng, PhD); systems engineering management (Certificate). *Expenses:* Tuition: Full-time $9900; part-time $1100 per credit. Required fees: $286 per semester.

TUI University, College of Business Administration, Program in Business Administration, Cypress, CA 90630. Offers business administration (PhD); conflict and negotiation management (MBA); criminal justice administration (MBA); entrepreneurship (MBA); finance (MBA); general management (MBA); government accounting (MBA); human resource management (MBA); information security and digital assurance management (MBA); information technology management (MBA); international business (MBA); logistics management (MBA); marketing (MBA); project management (MBA); public management (MBA); quality management (MBA); strategic leadership (MBA). Part-time and evening/weekend programs available. Postbaccalaureate distance learning degree programs offered (no on-campus study). *Degree requirements:* For doctorate, comprehensive exam, thesis/dissertation, defense of dissertation. *Entrance requirements:* For master's, minimum GPA of 2.5 (students with GPA 3.0 or greater may transfer up to 30% of graduate level credits); for doctorate, minimum GPA of 3.4, curriculum vitae, course work in research methods or statistics. Additional exam requirements/recommendations for international students: Required—TOEFL. Electronic applications accepted.

Universidad del Turabo, Graduate Programs, School in Business Administration, Online Business Administration Program, Gurabo, PR 00778-3030. Offers human resources (MBA); management (MBA); marketing (MBA); materials management (MBA).

Universidad del Turabo, Graduate Programs, School in Business Administration, Program in Logistics and Materials Management, Gurabo, PR 00778-3030. Offers MBA. Part-time and evening/weekend programs available. *Faculty:* 4 full-time (2 women), 21 part-time/adjunct (3 women). *Students:* 21 full-time (10 women), 33 part-time (16 women); includes 44 Hispanic Americans. Average age 33. 36 applicants, 92% accepted, 22 enrolled. In 2009, 30 master's awarded. *Entrance requirements:* For master's, GRE, EXADEP, interview. *Application deadline:* For fall admission, 8/5 for domestic students. Application fee: $25. *Unit head:* Marcelino Rivera, Dean, 787-743-7979 Ext. 4117. *Application contact:* Virginia Gonzalez, Admissions Officer, 787-746-3009.

University at Buffalo, the State University of New York, Graduate School, School of Management, Buffalo, NY 14260. Offers accounting (MS); business administration (EMBA, MBA, PMBA); finance (MS), including financial engineering, financial management; information assurance (Certificate); management (PhD); management information systems (MS); supply chains and operations management (MS); Au D/MBA; JD/MBA; M Arch/MBA; MA/MBA; MD/MBA; MPH/MBA; MSW/MBA; Pharm D/MBA. *Accreditation:* AACSB. Part-time and evening/weekend programs available. *Faculty:* 66 full-time (19 women), 21 part-time/adjunct (4 women). *Students:* 502 full-time (176 women), 199 part-time (54 women); includes 29 minority (10 African Americans, 16 Asian Americans or Pacific Islanders, 3 Hispanic Americans), 306 international. Average age 27. 1,944 applicants, 31% accepted, 324 enrolled. In 2009, 363 master's, 7 doctorates, 3 other advanced degrees awarded. *Degree requirements:* For master's, thesis (for some programs); for doctorate, comprehensive exam, thesis/dissertation. *Entrance requirements:* For master's, GMAT (MBA, MS in accounting), GRE General Test (for all other MS concentrations); for doctorate, GMAT or GRE. Additional exam requirements/recommendations for international students: Required—TOEFL (minimum score 230 computer-based; 95 iBT). *Application deadline:* For fall admission, 6/2 priority date for domestic students, 3/1 priority date for international students. Applications are processed on a rolling basis. Application fee: $100. Electronic applications accepted. *Expenses:* Contact institution. *Financial support:* In 2009–10, 91 students received support, including 5 fellowships with full and partial tuition reimbursements available (averaging $4,000 per year), 41 research assistantships with full and partial tuition reimbursements available (averaging $16,000 per year), 28 teaching assistantships with full and partial tuition reimbursements available (averaging $15,000 per year); career-related internships or fieldwork, Federal Work-Study, institutionally sponsored loans, scholarships/grants, health care benefits, and unspecified assistantships also available. Financial award application deadline: 2/15; financial award applicants required to submit FAFSA. *Faculty research:* Earnings management and electronic information assurance, supply chains and operations management, corporate financing and asset pricing, consumer behavior and quantitative modeling of marketing behavior, leadership and politics in organizations. Total annual research expenditures: $230,000. *Unit head:* David W. Frasier, Assistant Dean, 716-645-3204, Fax: 716-645-2341, E-mail: davidf@buffalo.edu. *Application contact:* David W. Frasier, Assistant Dean, 716-645-3204, Fax: 716-645-2341, E-mail: davidf@buffalo.edu.

The University of Alabama in Huntsville, School of Graduate Studies, College of Business Administration, Department of Management and Marketing, Huntsville, AL 35899. Offers management (MBA), including acquisition management, finance, human resource management, logistics and supply chain management, marketing, project management. *Accreditation:* AACSB. Part-time and evening/weekend programs available. *Faculty:* 7 full-time (1 woman), 1 part-time/adjunct (0 women). *Students:* 41 full-time (19 women), 155 part-time (59 women); includes 30 minority (15 African Americans, 5 American Indian/Alaska Native, 7 Asian Americans or Pacific Islanders, 3 Hispanic Americans), 20 international. Average age 32. 138 applicants, 63% accepted, 68 enrolled. In 2009, 38 master's awarded. *Degree requirements:* For master's, comprehensive exam, thesis or alternative. *Entrance requirements:* For master's, GMAT (minimum score 500), minimum AACSB index of 1080. Additional exam requirements/recommendations for international students: Required—TOEFL (minimum score 550 paper-based; 213 computer-based; 62 iBT). *Application deadline:* For fall admission, 8/1 for domestic students, 4/1 for international students; for spring admission, 12/1 for domestic students, 9/1 for international students. Applications are processed on a rolling basis. Application fee: $40 ($50 for international students). Electronic applications accepted. *Expenses:* Tuition, state resident: part-time $355.75 per credit hour. Tuition, nonresident: part-time $847.10 per credit hour. Required fees: $210.80 per semester. Tuition and fees vary according to course load and program. *Financial support:* In 2009–10, 3 students received support, including 2 research assistantships with full tuition reimbursements available (averaging $14,400 per year), 1 teaching assistantship with full tuition reimbursement available (averaging $11,800 per year); career-related internships or fieldwork, Federal Work-Study, institutionally sponsored loans, scholarships/grants, health care benefits, and unspecified assistantships also available. Support available to part-time students. Financial award application deadline: 4/1; financial award applicants required to submit FAFSA. *Unit head:* Dr. Brent Wren, Chair, 256-824-6408, Fax: 256-824-6328, E-mail: wrenb@uah.edu. *Application contact:* Jennifer Pettitt, Director of Graduate Programs, 256-824-6681, Fax: 256-824-7571, E-mail: jennifer.pettitt@uah.edu.

University of Alaska Anchorage, College of Business and Public Policy, Program in Logistics, Anchorage, AK 99508. Offers global supply chain management (MS); supply chain management (Certificate). Part-time and evening/weekend programs available. Postbaccalaureate distance learning degree programs offered (no on-campus study). *Degree requirements:* For master's, thesis or alternative, research project. *Entrance requirements:* Additional exam requirements/recommendations for international students: Required—TOEFL (minimum score 550 paper-based; 213 computer-based).

University of Dallas, Graduate School of Management, Irving, TX 75062-4736. Offers accounting (MBA, MM, MS); business management (MBA, MM); corporate finance (MBA, MM); financial services (MBA); global business (MBA, MM); health services management (MBA, MM); human resource management (MBA, MM); information assurance (MBA, MM, MS); information technology (MBA, MM, MS); information technology service management (MBA, MM, MS); marketing management (MBA, MM); organization development (MBA, MM); project management (MBA, MM); sports and entertainment management (MBA, MM); strategic leadership (MBA, MM); supply chain management (MBA); supply chain management and market logistics (MM). *Accreditation:* ACBSP. Part-time and evening/weekend programs available. Postbaccalaureate distance learning degree programs offered (no on-campus study). *Faculty:* 25 full-time (6 women), 31 part-time/adjunct (6 women). *Students:* 232 full-time (95 women), 923 part-time (365 women); includes 462 minority (184 African Americans, 14 American Indian/Alaska Native, 153 Asian Americans or Pacific Islanders, 111 Hispanic Americans), 184 international. Average age 34. 474 applicants, 85% accepted, 237 enrolled. In 2009, 399 master's awarded. *Entrance requirements:* Additional exam requirements/recommendations for international students: Required—TOEFL. *Application deadline:* Applications are processed on a rolling basis. Application fee: $50. Electronic applications accepted. *Expenses:* Contact institution. *Financial support:* In 2009–10, 399 students received support. Scholarships/grants and unspecified assistantships available. Financial award application deadline: 2/15; financial award applicants required to submit FAFSA. *Unit head:* Alounda Joseph, Director of Enrollment Processes, 972-721-5356, E-mail: admiss@gsm.udallas.edu. *Application contact:* Alounda Joseph, Director of Enrollment Processes, 972-721-5356, E-mail: admiss@gsm.udallas.edu.

University of Houston, College of Technology, Department of Information and Logistics Technology, Houston, TX 77204. Offers technology project management (MS), including

information systems security, logistics. Part-time and evening/weekend programs available. *Faculty:* 6 full-time (3 women), 6 part-time/adjunct (2 women). *Students:* 59 full-time (18 women), 47 part-time (15 women); includes 18 minority (6 African Americans, 5 Asian Americans or Pacific Islanders, 7 Hispanic Americans), 58 international. Average age 29. 69 applicants, 87% accepted, 33 enrolled. In 2009, 25 master's awarded. *Degree requirements:* For master's, project or thesis (most programs). *Entrance requirements:* For master's, GMAT. Additional exam requirements/recommendations for international students: Required—TOEFL (minimum score 550 paper-based; 79 iBT). *Application deadline:* For fall admission, 7/1 for domestic students, 4/1 for international students; for spring admission, 12/1 for domestic students, 10/1 for international students. Applications are processed on a rolling basis. Application fee: $75 ($150 for international students). Electronic applications accepted. *Expenses:* Tuition, state resident: full-time $7676; part-time $320 per credit hour. Tuition, nonresident: full-time $14,324; part-time $597 per credit hour. Required fees: $3034. *Financial support:* In 2009–10, 11 fellowships with full tuition reimbursements (averaging $10,500 per year), 1 research assistantship with full tuition reimbursement (averaging $10,500 per year), 4 teaching assistantships with full tuition reimbursements (averaging $10,500 per year) were awarded. *Unit head:* Michael Gibson, Chairperson, 713-743-5116, E-mail: mlgibson@uh.edu. *Application contact:* Tiffany Roosa, Graduate Advisor, 713-743-2987, Fax: 713-743-4151, E-mail: troosa@uh.edu.

University of Louisville, J.B. Speed School of Engineering, Department of Industrial Engineering, Louisville, KY 40292-0001. Offers engineering management (M Eng); industrial engineering (M Eng, MS, PhD); logistics and distribution (Certificate). *Accreditation:* ABET (one or more programs are accredited). Part-time programs available. *Faculty:* 9 full-time (1 woman). *Students:* 37 full-time (13 women), 35 part-time (7 women); includes 11 minority (6 African Americans, 5 Asian Americans or Pacific Islanders), 19 international. Average age 29. 62 applicants, 61% accepted, 23 enrolled. In 2009, 27 master's, 2 doctorates awarded. Terminal master's awarded for partial completion of doctoral program. *Degree requirements:* For master's, comprehensive exam (for some programs), thesis or alternative; for doctorate, comprehensive exam, thesis/dissertation, minimum GPA of 3.0. *Entrance requirements:* For master's and doctorate, GRE General Test. Additional exam requirements/recommendations for international students: Required—TOEFL (minimum score 550 paper-based; 213 computer-based; 80 iBT). *Application deadline:* For fall admission, 7/12 priority date for domestic and international students; for winter admission, 11/29 priority date for domestic and international students; for spring admission, 3/28 priority date for domestic and international students. Applications are processed on a rolling basis. Application fee: $50. Electronic applications accepted. *Financial support:* In 2009–10, 16 students received support, including 8 fellowships with full tuition reimbursements available (averaging $20,000 per year), 1 research assistantship with full tuition reimbursement available (averaging $20,000 per year), 6 teaching assistantships with full tuition reimbursements available (averaging $20,000 per year). Financial award application deadline: 1/25; financial award applicants required to submit FAFSA. *Faculty research:* Optimization,computer simulation, logistics and distribution, ergonomics and human factors, advanced manufacturing process. Total annual research expenditures: $359,000. *Unit head:* Dr. John S. Usher, Chair, 502-852-6342, Fax: 502-852-5633, E-mail: usher@louisville.edu. *Application contact:* Dr. Michael Day, Associate Dean, 502-852-6195, Fax: 502-852-7294, E-mail: day@louisville.edu.

University of Minnesota, Twin Cities Campus, Carlson School of Management, Doctoral Program in Business Administration, Minneapolis, MN 55455-0213. Offers accounting (PhD); finance (PhD); information and decision sciences (PhD); marketing and logistics management (PhD); operations and management science (PhD); strategic management and organization (PhD). *Faculty:* 74 full-time (19 women). *Students:* 68 full-time (28 women); includes 7 minority (1 African American, 3 Asian Americans or Pacific Islanders, 3 Hispanic Americans), 46 international. Average age 29. 250 applicants, 5% accepted, 9 enrolled. In 2009, 11 doctorates awarded. *Degree requirements:* For doctorate, comprehensive exam, thesis/dissertation, written and oral preliminary exams, proposal defense. *Entrance requirements:* For doctorate, GMAT, GRE General Test. Additional exam requirements/recommendations for international students: Required—TOEFL (minimum score 600 paper-based; 250 computer-based; 100 iBT), IELTS (minimum score 7.5). *Application deadline:* For fall admission, 12/31 for domestic students, 12/31 priority date for international students. Applications are processed on a rolling basis. Application fee: $55 ($75 for international students). Electronic applications accepted. *Financial support:* In 2009–10, 68 fellowships with full tuition reimbursements (averaging $11,500 per year), 63 research assistantships with full tuition reimbursements (averaging $6,750 per year), 53 teaching assistantships with full tuition reimbursements (averaging $6,750 per year) were awarded; institutionally sponsored loans, scholarships/grants, health care benefits, and unspecified assistantships also available. Financial award application deadline: 12/31. *Faculty research:* Corporate strategy, finance, entrepreneurship, marketing, information and decision science, operations, accounting. Total annual research expenditures: $300,000. *Unit head:* Dr. Shawn P. Curley, Director of Graduate Studies/Program Director, 612-624-6546, Fax: 612-624-8221, E-mail: curley@umn.edu. *Application contact:* Earlene K. Bronson, Assistant Director, 612-624-0875, Fax: 612-624-8221, E-mail: brons003@umn.edu.

University of Missouri–St. Louis, College of Business Administration, Program in Business Administration, St. Louis, MO 63121. Offers accounting (MBA); business administration (Certificate); finance (MBA); human resource management (Certificate); logistics and supply chain management (MBA, Certificate); management (MBA); marketing (MBA); marketing management (Certificate); operations (MBA); quantitative management science (MBA). *Accreditation:* AACSB. Part-time and evening/weekend programs available. *Faculty:* 30 full-time (5 women), 11 part-time/adjunct (2 women). *Students:* 107 full-time (47 women), 310 part-time (120 women); includes 32 minority (17 African Americans, 6 Asian Americans or Pacific Islanders, 9 Hispanic Americans), 66 international. Average age 31. 285 applicants, 58% accepted, 130 enrolled. In 2009, 149 master's, 13 other advanced degrees awarded. *Entrance requirements:* For master's, GMAT, 2 letters of recommendation. Additional exam requirements/recommendations for international students: Required—TOEFL (minimum score 550 paper-based; 213 computer-based). *Application deadline:* For fall admission, 7/1 for domestic students; for spring admission, 11/1 for domestic students. Applications are processed on a rolling basis. Application fee: $35 ($40 for international students). Electronic applications accepted. *Expenses:* Tuition, state resident: full-time $5377; part-time $297.70 per credit hour. Tuition, nonresident: full-time $13,882; part-time $771.20 per credit hour. Required fees: $220; $12.20 per credit hour. One-time fee: $12. Tuition and fees vary according to course level, campus/location and program. *Financial support:* In 2009–10, 27 research assistantships with full and partial tuition reimbursements (averaging $8,525 per year), 6 teaching assistantships with full and partial tuition reimbursements (averaging $13,950 per year) were awarded; career-related internships or fieldwork, Federal Work-Study, and institutionally sponsored loans also available. Support available to part-time students. Financial award application deadline: 4/1; financial award applicants required to submit FAFSA. *Faculty research:* Human resources, strategic management, marketing strategy, consumer behavior product development, advertising. *Unit head:* Karl Kottemann, Assistant Director, 314-516-5885, Fax: 314-516-6420, E-mail: mba@umsl.edu. *Application contact:* 314-516-5458, Fax: 314-516-6996, E-mail: gradadm@umsl.edu.

University of Missouri–St. Louis, College of Business Administration, Program in Information Systems, St. Louis, MO 63121. Offers information systems (MSIS, PhD); logistics and supply chain management (PhD). Part-time and evening/weekend programs available. *Faculty:* 8 full-time (0 women). *Students:* 5 full-time (4 women), 14 part-time (3 women); includes 5 minority (3 African Americans, 1 Asian American or Pacific Islander, 1 Hispanic American), 5 international. Average age 30. 24 applicants, 29% accepted, 3 enrolled. In 2009, 7 master's awarded. *Entrance requirements:* For master's, GMAT, 2 letters of recommendation; for doctorate, GMAT or GRE, 3 letters of recommendation. Additional exam requirements/recommendations for international students: Required—TOEFL (minimum score 550 paper-based; 213 computer-based). *Application deadline:* For fall admission, 7/1 priority date for domestic and international students; for spring admission, 12/1 priority date for domestic and international students. Applications are processed on a rolling basis. Application fee: $35 ($40 for international students). Electronic applications accepted. *Expenses:* Tuition, state resident: full-time $5377; part-time $297.70 per credit hour. Tuition, nonresident: full-time $13,882;

part-time $771.20 per credit hour. Required fees: $220; $12.20 per credit hour. One-time fee: $12. Tuition and fees vary according to course level, campus/location and program. *Financial support:* Career-related internships or fieldwork, Federal Work-Study, and institutionally sponsored loans available. Support available to part-time students. Financial award application deadline: 4/1; financial award applicants required to submit FAFSA. *Faculty research:* International information systems, telecommunications, systems development, information systems sourcing. *Unit head:* Karl Kottemann, Assistant Director, 314-516-5885, Fax: 314-516-6420, E-mail: mba@umsl.edu. *Application contact:* 314-516-5458, Fax: 314-516-6996, E-mail: gradadm@umsl.edu.

University of New Hampshire, Graduate School, College of Engineering and Physical Sciences, Department of Mechanical Engineering, Durham, NH 03824. Offers mechanical engineering (MS, PhD); systems design (PhD). Part-time programs available. *Faculty:* 14 full-time (1 woman). *Students:* 26 full-time (6 women), 25 part-time (3 women), 16 international. Average age 29. 35 applicants, 71% accepted, 16 enrolled. In 2009, 3 master's, 2 doctorates awarded. *Degree requirements:* For master's, thesis or alternative; for doctorate, thesis/dissertation. *Entrance requirements:* For master's and doctorate, GRE. Additional exam requirements/recommendations for international students: Required—TOEFL (minimum score 550 paper-based; 213 computer-based; 80 iBT). *Application deadline:* For fall admission, 4/1 priority date for domestic students, 4/1 for international students; for spring admission, 12/1 for domestic students. Applications are processed on a rolling basis. Application fee: $25. Electronic applications accepted. *Expenses:* Tuition, state resident: full-time $10,380; part-time $577 per credit hour. Tuition, nonresident: full-time $24,350; part-time $1002 per credit hour. Required fees: $1550; $387.50 per semester. Tuition and fees vary according to course load and program. *Financial support:* In 2009–10, 32 students received support, including 1 fellowship, 17 research assistantships, 12 teaching assistantships; Federal Work-Study, scholarships/grants, and tuition waivers (full and partial) also available. Support available to part-time students. Financial award application deadline: 2/15. *Faculty research:* Solid mechanics, dynamics, materials science, dynamic systems, automatic control. *Unit head:* Dr. Todd Gross, Chairperson, 603-862-2445. *Application contact:* Tracey Harvey, Administrative Assistant, 603-862-1353, E-mail: mechanical.engineering@unh.edu.

University of South Africa, College of Economic and Management Sciences, Pretoria, South Africa. Offers accounting (D Admin, D Com); accounting science (DA); auditing (D Admin, D Com); business administration (M Tech); business economics (D Admin); business leadership (DBL); business management (D Admin, D Com); economic management analysis (M Tech); economics (D Admin, D Com, PhD); human resource development (M Tech); industrial psychology (D Admin, D Com, PhD); logistics (D Com); marketing (M Tech); public administration (D Admin, D Com, DPA, PhD); public management (M Tech); quantitative management (D Admin, D Com); real estate (M Tech); statistics (D Admin, PhD); tourism management (D Admin, D Com); transport economics (D Admin, D Com).

The University of Tennessee, Graduate School, College of Business Administration, Program in Business Administration, Knoxville, TN 37996. Offers accounting (PhD); finance (MBA, PhD); logistics and transportation (MBA, PhD); management (PhD); marketing (MBA, PhD); operations management (MBA); professional business administration (MBA); statistics (PhD); JD/MBA; MS/MBA. *Accreditation:* AACSB. Postbaccalaureate distance learning degree programs offered. *Degree requirements:* For master's, thesis or alternative; for doctorate, thesis/dissertation. *Entrance requirements:* For master's and doctorate, GMAT, minimum GPA of 2.7. Additional exam requirements/recommendations for international students: Required—TOEFL. Electronic applications accepted. *Expenses:* Tuition, state resident: full-time $6826; part-time $380 per semester hour. Tuition, nonresident: full-time $21,844; part-time $1147 per semester hour. Tuition and fees vary according to program.

The University of Texas at Arlington, Graduate School, College of Engineering, Department of Industrial and Manufacturing Systems Engineering, Program in Logistics, Arlington, TX 76019. Offers MS. *Students:* 7 full-time (1 woman), 7 part-time (3 women); includes 3 minority (1 Asian American or Pacific Islander, 2 Hispanic Americans), 9 international. 13 applicants, 92% accepted, 2 enrolled. *Degree requirements:* For master's, comprehensive exam, thesis optional. *Entrance requirements:* For master's, GRE, GMAT, minimum GPA of 3.0. Additional exam requirements/recommendations for international students: Required—TOEFL (minimum score 550 paper-based; 213 computer-based). *Application deadline:* For fall admission, 6/6 for domestic students, 4/4 for international students; for spring admission, 10/17 for domestic students, 9/5 for international students. Application fee: $35 ($50 for international students). *Financial support:* Fellowships, research assistantships, teaching assistantships, career-related internships or fieldwork, Federal Work-Study, institutionally sponsored loans, scholarships/grants, and unspecified assistantships available. Financial award application deadline: 6/1; financial award applicants required to submit FAFSA. *Unit head:* Dr. Donald H. Liles, Chair, 817-272-3092, Fax: 817-272-3406, E-mail: dliles@uta.edu. *Application contact:* Dr. Jamie Rogers, Graduate Advisor, 817-272-2495, Fax: 817-272-3406, E-mail: jrogers@uta.edu.

University of Washington, Graduate School, Interdisciplinary Program in Global Trade, Transportation and Logistics Studies, Seattle, WA 98195. Offers Certificate.

Virginia International University, Business Programs Department, Fairfax, VA 22030. Offers accounting (MBA); executive management (Graduate Certificate); global logistics (MBA); health care management (MBA); human resources management (MBA); international business management (MBA); international finance (MBA); marketing management (MBA). Part-time programs available. *Faculty:* 12 part-time/adjunct (1 woman). *Students:* 138 full-time (63 women), 7 part-time (5 women); includes 7 minority (1 African American, 5 Asian Americans or Pacific Islanders, 1 Hispanic American), 136 international. Average age 27. 331 applicants, 31% accepted, 40 enrolled. In 2009, 42 master's awarded. *Entrance requirements:* For master's and Graduate Certificate, bachelor's degree. Additional exam requirements/recommendations for international students: Required—TOEFL (minimum score 550 paper-based; 213 computer-based; 80 iBT), IELTS (minimum score 6). *Application deadline:* For fall admission, 7/31 for domestic students, 7/3 for international students; for spring admission, 12/18 for domestic students, 11/20 for international students. Applications are processed on a rolling basis. Application fee: $100. Electronic applications accepted. *Expenses:* Tuition: Full-time $10,044; part-time $569 per credit. One-time fee: $75. Tuition and fees vary according to degree level. *Financial support:* In 2009–10, 10 students received support. Scholarships/grants available. Financial award application deadline: 7/1. *Unit head:* Dr. Gail Whitaker, Chair, 703-591-7042 Ext. 346, Fax: 703-591-7046, E-mail: gwhitaker@viu.edu. *Application contact:* Emily L. Kraus, Director of Admissions, 703-591-7042 Ext. 309, Fax: 703-591-7048, E-mail: admissions@viu.edu.

Virginia Polytechnic Institute and State University, Graduate School, College of Engineering, Department of Electrical and Computer Engineering, Blacksburg, VA 24061. Offers computer engineering (M Eng, MS, PhD); electrical engineering (M Eng, MS, PhD). *Faculty:* 71 full-time (6 women). *Students:* 404 full-time (71 women), 139 part-time (26 women); includes 371 minority (338 American Indian/Alaska Native, 9 Asian Americans or Pacific Islanders, 24 Hispanic Americans), 10 international. Average age 28. 1,506 applicants, 14% accepted, 136 enrolled. In 2009, 59 master's, 31 doctorates awarded. *Entrance requirements:* For master's and doctorate, GRE, GMAT. Additional exam requirements/recommendations for international students: Required—TOEFL (minimum score 590 paper-based; 213 computer-based). *Application deadline:* For fall admission, 5/15 for international students; for spring admission, 10/15 for international students. Applications are processed on a rolling basis. Application fee: $65. Electronic applications accepted. *Expenses:* Tuition, area resident: Full-time $10,228; part-time $459 per credit hour. Tuition, nonresident: full-time $17,892; part-time $865 per credit hour. Required fees: $1966; $451 per semester. *Financial support:* In 2009–10, 10 fellowships with full tuition reimbursements (averaging $2,295 per year), 179 research assistantships with full tuition reimbursements (averaging $21,523 per year), 38 teaching assistantships with full tuition reimbursements (averaging $14,162 per year) were awarded; career-related internships or fieldwork, Federal Work-Study, scholarships/grants, and unspecified assistantships also available. Financial award application deadline: 1/15. *Faculty research:* Electromagnetics,

Logistics

Virginia Polytechnic Institute and State University *(continued)*
controls, electronics, power, communications. *Unit head:* Dr. James S. Thorp, Dean, 540-231-7494, Fax: 540-231-3362, E-mail: jsthorp@vt.edu. *Application contact:* Paul Plassmann, Information Contact, 540-231-5379, Fax: 540-231-3362, E-mail: plassmann@vt.edu.

Wilmington University, College of Business, New Castle, DE 19720-6491. Offers business administration (MBA); finance (MBA); health care administration (MBA, MS); homeland security (MBA, MS); human resource management (MS); management (MS); management information

systems (MBA); organizational leadership (MS); public administration (MS); transportation and logistics (MBA, MS). Part-time and evening/weekend programs available. *Entrance requirements:* Additional exam requirements/recommendations for international students: Required—TOEFL (minimum score 500 paper-based; 173 computer-based). Electronic applications accepted.

Wright State University, School of Graduate Studies, Raj Soin College of Business, Department of Information Systems and Operations Management, Logistics and Supply Chain Management Program, Dayton, OH 45435. Offers MS.

Supply Chain Management

American University, Kogod School of Business, Master of Business Administration Program, Washington, DC 20016-8044. Offers accounting (MBA); consulting (MBA), including information technology, international business, management; corporate finance: commercial banking (MBA); corporate finance: corporate financial management (MBA); corporate finance: investment banking (MBA), including corporate finance and private equity, trading and selling; entrepreneurship (MBA); global emerging markets (MBA), including business, finance, information technology; international trade and global supply chain management (MBA); leadership (MBA); marketing management (MBA); marketing research (MBA); real estate (MBA); MBA/JD; MBA/LL M. Part-time and evening/weekend programs available. *Faculty:* 14 full-time (6 women). *Students:* 133 full-time (56 women), 121 part-time (48 women); includes 54 minority (23 African Americans, 1 American Indian/Alaska Native, 16 Asian Americans or Pacific Islanders, 14 Hispanic Americans), 43 international. Average age 29. 539 applicants, 51% accepted, 86 enrolled. In 2009, 114 master's awarded. *Entrance requirements:* For master's, GMAT. Additional exam requirements/recommendations for international students: Required—TOEFL. *Application deadline:* For fall admission, 2/1 priority date for domestic students; for spring admission, 10/1 priority date for domestic students. Applications are processed on a rolling basis. Application fee: $100. *Expenses:* Contact institution. *Financial support:* In 2009–10, 19 students received support; fellowships, research assistantships with partial tuition reimbursements available, career-related internships or fieldwork, Federal Work-Study, and institutionally sponsored loans available. Support available to part-time students. Financial award application deadline: 2/1. *Faculty research:* Information technology, decision-aiding methodology, negotiation. *Unit head:* Dr. Stevan Holmberg, Chair, 202-885-6193, E-mail: sholmbe@american.edu. *Application contact:* Shannon Demko, Associate Director of Graduate Admissions, 202-885-1994, Fax: 202-885-1108, E-mail: demko@american.edu.

Arizona State University, Graduate College, W.P. Carey School of Business, Program in Business Administration, Tempe, AZ 85287. Offers agribusiness (PhD); business administration (MBA); finance (MBA, PhD); health sector management (MBA); information systems (PhD); management (MBA, PhD); marketing (MBA, PhD); supply chain management (MBA, PhD); JD/MBA; MBA/M Arch; MBA/MHSM. *Accreditation:* AACSB. *Degree requirements:* For master's, thesis optional; for doctorate, thesis/dissertation. *Entrance requirements:* For master's, GMAT.

Case Western Reserve University, Weatherhead School of Management, Department of Operations, Management Program, Cleveland, OH 44106. Offers operations research (MSM); supply chain (MSM); MBA/MSM. *Accreditation:* AACSB. Part-time and evening/weekend programs available. *Students:* Average age 28. *Entrance requirements:* For master's, GMAT or GRE, 3 letters of recommendation, resume. Additional exam requirements/recommendations for international students: Required—TOEFL (minimum score 600 paper-based; 250 computer-based). Application fee: $100. *Financial support:* Career-related internships or fieldwork, institutionally sponsored loans, scholarships/grants, tuition waivers (partial), and unspecified assistantships available. Financial award application deadline: 3/1. *Faculty research:* Supply chain management, operations management, operations/finance interface optimization, scheduling. *Unit head:* Kamlesh Mathur, Chairman, 216-368-3857, E-mail: kamlesh.mathur@case.edu. *Application contact:* Olivia Seifert, Program Manager, 216-368-2031, Fax: 216-368-5548, E-mail: deborah.bibb@case.edu.

Central Connecticut State University, School of Graduate Studies, School of Technology, Department of Manufacturing and Construction Management, New Britain, CT 06050-4010. Offers construction management (MS, Certificate); lean manufacturing and six sigma (Certificate); supply chain and logistics (Certificate); technology management (MS). Part-time and evening/weekend programs available. *Faculty:* 17 full-time (5 women), 25 part-time/adjunct (1 woman). *Students:* 13 full-time (4 women), 66 part-time (9 women); includes 11 minority (4 African Americans, 4 Asian Americans or Pacific Islanders, 3 Hispanic Americans), 4 international. Average age 33. 46 applicants, 50% accepted, 17 enrolled. In 2009, 27 master's, 1 other advanced degree awarded. *Degree requirements:* For master's, comprehensive exam, thesis or alternative; for Certificate, qualifying exam. *Entrance requirements:* For master's, minimum undergraduate GPA of 2.7. Additional exam requirements/recommendations for international students: Required—TOEFL. *Application deadline:* For fall admission, 7/1 for domestic students; for spring admission, 12/1 for domestic students. Applications are processed on a rolling basis. Application fee: $50. Electronic applications accepted. *Expenses:* Tuition, area resident: Full-time $4662; part-time $440 per credit. Tuition, state resident: full-time $6994; part-time $440 per credit. Tuition, nonresident: full-time $12,988; part-time $440 per credit. Required fees: $3606. One-time fee: $62 part-time. *Financial support:* In 2009–10, 5 students received support, including 3 research assistantships; career-related internships or fieldwork, Federal Work-Study, scholarships/grants, and unspecified assistantships also available. Support available to part-time students. Financial award application deadline: 3/1; financial award applicants required to submit FAFSA. *Faculty research:* All aspects of middle management, technical supervision in the workplace. *Unit head:* Dr. Jacob Kovel, Chair, 860-832-1830. *Application contact:* Dr. Jacob Kovel, Chair, 860-832-1830.

Eastern Michigan University, Graduate School, College of Business, Programs in Business Administration, Ypsilanti, MI 48197. Offers business administration (MBA, Graduate Certificate); computer information systems (Graduate Certificate); e-business (MBA, Graduate Certificate); enterprise business intelligence (MBA); entrepreneurship (MBA, Graduate Certificate); finance (MBA, Graduate Certificate); human resources (MBA); human resources management (Graduate Certificate); information systems (MBA); internal auditing (MBA); international business (MBA, Graduate Certificate); marketing management (Graduate Certificate); nonprofit management (MBA); organizational development (Graduate Certificate); supply chain management (MBA, Graduate Certificate). *Accreditation:* AACSB. Part-time programs available. Postbaccalaureate distance learning degree programs offered (no on-campus study). *Students:* 166 full-time (80 women), 439 part-time (231 women); includes 150 minority (103 African Americans, 7 American Indian/Alaska Native, 31 Asian Americans or Pacific Islanders, 9 Hispanic Americans), 97 international. Average age 34. In 2009, 3 other advanced degrees awarded. *Entrance requirements:* For master's, GMAT (minimum score 450), minimum cumulative undergraduate GPA of 2.75. Additional exam requirements/recommendations for international students: Required—TOEFL. *Application deadline:* For fall admission, 5/15 for domestic students, 5/1 for international students; for winter admission, 10/15 for domestic students, 10/1 for international students; for spring admission, 3/15 for domestic students, 3/1 for international students. Applications are processed on a rolling basis. Application fee: $35. Tuition and fees vary according to course level. *Financial support:* Fellowships, research assistantships with full tuition reimbursements, teaching assistantships with full tuition reimbursements, career-related internships or fieldwork, Federal Work-Study, institutionally sponsored loans, scholarships/grants, tuition waivers (partial), and unspecified assistantships available. Support available to part-time students. Financial award applicants required to submit FAFSA. *Unit head:* K.

Michelle Henry, Director of Academic Services, 734-487-4444, Fax: 734-483-1316, E-mail: cob.grad@emich.edu. *Application contact:* Beste Windes, Advisor, 734-487-4444, Fax: 734-483-1316, E-mail: cob.grad@emich.edu.

Elmhurst College, Graduate Programs, Program in Supply Chain Management, Elmhurst, IL 60126-3296. Offers MS. Part-time and evening/weekend programs available. *Faculty:* 2 full-time (0 women), 3 part-time/adjunct (0 women). *Students:* 39 part-time (12 women); includes 11 minority (7 African Americans, 1 Asian American or Pacific Islander, 3 Hispanic Americans), 2 international. Average age 35. 35 applicants, 69% accepted, 19 enrolled. In 2009, 17 master's awarded. *Entrance requirements:* For master's, 3 recommendations. Additional exam requirements/recommendations for international students: Required—TOEFL (minimum score 550 paper-based; 213 computer-based). *Application deadline:* Applications are processed on a rolling basis. Application fee: $25. Electronic applications accepted. *Expenses:* Contact institution. *Financial support:* In 2009–10, 5 students received support. Federal Work-Study and scholarships/grants available. Support available to part-time students. Financial award application deadline: 6/1; financial award applicants required to submit FAFSA. *Unit head:* Dr. Ted Lerud, Associate Dean of the Faculty, 630-617-3661, Fax: 630-617-6415, E-mail: gradadm@elmhurst.edu. *Application contact:* Elizabeth D. Kuebler, Director of Adult and Graduate Admission, 630-617-3069, Fax: 630-617-5501, E-mail: betsyk@elmhurst.edu.

Embry-Riddle Aeronautical University Worldwide, Worldwide Headquarters, Program in Logistics and Supply Chain Management, Daytona Beach, FL 32114-3900. Offers MSLSCM. *Faculty:* 16 full-time (2 women), 28 part-time/adjunct (9 women). *Students:* 8 full-time (2 women), 12 part-time (3 women); includes 8 minority (3 African Americans, 4 Asian Americans or Pacific Islanders, 1 Hispanic American). Average age 39. 53 applicants, 75% accepted. *Degree requirements:* For master's, thesis (for some programs). Application fee: $50. *Financial support:* In 2009–10, 2 students received support. *Unit head:* Dr. Kees Rietsema, Chair, 602-750-0685, E-mail: rietsd37@erau.edu. *Application contact:* Linda Dammer, Director of Admissions, 386-226-6910, Fax: 386-226-6984, E-mail: ecinfo@erau.edu.

Florida Institute of Technology, Graduate Programs, College of Business, Extended Studies Division, Melbourne, FL 32901-6975. Offers acquisition and contract management (PMBA); business administration (PMBA); computer information systems (MS); e-business (PMBA); human resource management (PMBA); human resources management (MS); logistics management (MS), including humanitarian and disaster relief logistics; management (MS), including acquisition and contract management, e-business, human resource management, information systems, logistics management, management, transportation management; material acquisition management (MS); project management (MS), including information systems, operations research; public administration (MPA); quality management (MS); space management (MS); space systems (MS); systems management (MS), including information systems, operations research, systems management. Part-time and evening/weekend programs available. Postbaccalaureate distance learning degree programs offered (no on-campus study). *Faculty:* 12 full-time (3 women), 117 part-time/adjunct (20 women). *Students:* 74 full-time (32 women), 1,041 part-time (484 women); includes 343 minority (240 African Americans, 12 American Indian/Alaska Native, 44 Asian Americans or Pacific Islanders, 47 Hispanic Americans), 22 international. Average age 35. 520 applicants, 72% accepted, 279 enrolled. In 2009, 509 master's awarded. *Degree requirements:* For master's, capstone course. *Entrance requirements:* For master's, GMAT or resume showing 8 years of supervised experience, minimum GPA of 3.0, 2 letters of recommendation, resume. Additional exam requirements/recommendations for international students: Required—TOEFL (minimum score 550 paper-based; 213 computer-based; 79 iBT). *Application deadline:* For fall admission, 4/1 for international students; for spring admission, 9/30 for international students. Applications are processed on a rolling basis. Application fee: $50. Electronic applications accepted. *Expenses:* Tuition: Part-time $1015 per credit. Tuition and fees vary according to campus/location and program. *Financial support:* Application deadline: 3/1. *Unit head:* Dr. Clifford Bragdon, Dean, 321-674-8821, Fax: 321-674-7597, E-mail: cbragdon@fit.edu. *Application contact:* Carolyn Farrior, Director of Graduate Admissions Online Learning and Off Campus Programs, 321-674-7118, Fax: 321-674-8216, E-mail: cfarrior@fit.edu.

HEC Montreal, School of Business Administration, Diploma Programs in Administration, Program in Supply Chain Management, Montréal, QC H3T 2A7, Canada. Offers Diploma. Part-time programs available. *Students:* 24 full-time (6 women), 90 part-time (30 women). 71 applicants, 76% accepted, 42 enrolled. In 2009, 30 Diplomas awarded. *Degree requirements:* For Diploma, one foreign language. *Entrance requirements:* For degree, 2 years of working experience, letters of recommendation. *Application deadline:* For fall admission, 4/15 for domestic and international students; for winter admission, 10/1 for domestic and international students. Application fee: $77 Canadian dollars. Tuition and fees charges are reported in Canadian dollars. *Expenses:* Tuition, area resident: Part-time $65.60 Canadian dollars per credit. Tuition, state resident: full-time $2361.60 Canadian dollars; part-time $183.36 Canadian dollars per credit. Tuition, nonresident: full-time $6601 Canadian dollars; part-time $448.13 Canadian dollars per credit. International tuition: $16,132.68 Canadian dollars full-time. Required fees: $1254.15 Canadian dollars; $28.99 Canadian dollars per course. $91.68 Canadian dollars per term. Tuition and fees vary according to degree level and program. *Financial support:* Research assistantships, teaching assistantships available. Financial award application deadline: 10/2. *Unit head:* Louise Cote, Director, 514-340-6205, Fax: 514-340-5640, E-mail: louise.cote@hec.ca. *Application contact:* Marie Deshaies, Senior Student Advisor, 514-340-6135, Fax: 514-340-6411, E-mail: marie.deshaies@hec.ca.

Howard University, School of Business, Graduate Programs in Business, Washington, DC 20059-0002. Offers accounting (MBA); entrepreneurship (MBA); finance (MBA); general management (MBA); human resources management (MBA); information systems (MBA); international business (MBA); marketing (MBA); supply chain management (MBA); JD/MBA. *Accreditation:* AACSB. Part-time and evening/weekend programs available. Postbaccalaureate distance learning degree programs offered (no on-campus study). *Entrance requirements:* For master's, GMAT, minimum 1 year post undergraduate work experience, resume, 3 letters of recommendation, advanced college algebra. Additional exam requirements/recommendations for international students: Required—TOEFL. *Faculty research:* Marketing research in multi-ethnic populations, U.S. trade policies and international relations, risk management (finance).

Instituto Tecnologico de Santo Domingo, Graduate School, Santo Domingo, Dominican Republic. Offers applied linguistics (MA); construction administration (M Mgmt); corporate finance (M Mgmt); education (M Ed); engineering (M Eng), including data telecommunications, industrial engineering, logistics and supply chain, maintenance engineering, sanitary and environmental engineering, structural engineering; environmental science (M En S), including environmental education, environmental management, marine and coastal ecosystems, natural

resources management; family therapy (MA); food science and technology (MS); human development (MA); human resources administration (M Mgmt); international business (M Mgmt); labor risks (M Mgmt); management (M Mgmt); marketing (M Mgmt); mathematics (MS); organizational development (M Mgmt); planning and taxation (M Mgmt); psychology (MA); social science (M Ed); upper management (M Mgmt). *Entrance requirements:* For master's, birth certificate, minimum GPA of 2.0.

Kaplan University, Davenport Campus, School of Business, Davenport, IA 52807-2095. Offers business administration (MBA); change leadership (MS); entrepreneurship (MBA); finance (MBA); health care management (MBA, MS); human resource (MBA); international business (MBA); management (MS); marketing (MBA); project management (MBA, MS); supply chain management and logistics (MBA, MS). Part-time and evening/weekend programs available. Postbaccalaureate distance learning degree programs offered (no on-campus study). *Entrance requirements:* Additional exam requirements/recommendations for international students: Required—TOEFL (minimum score 550 paper-based; 218 computer-based; 80 iBT). Electronic applications accepted.

Lehigh University, College of Business and Economics, Bethlehem, PA 18015. Offers accounting (MS), including accounting and information analysis; business administration (MBA); economics (MS, PhD), including economics, health and bio-pharmaceutical economics (MS); entrepreneurship (Certificate); finance (MS), including analytical finance; project management (Certificate); supply chain management (Certificate); MBA/E; MBA/M Ed. *Accreditation:* AACSB. Part-time and evening/weekend programs available. Postbaccalaureate distance learning degree programs offered (minimal on-campus study). *Faculty:* 42 full-time (11 women), 12 part-time/adjunct (2 women). *Students:* 145 full-time (64 women), 264 part-time (82 women); includes 28 minority (6 African Americans, 19 Asian Americans or Pacific Islanders, 3 Hispanic Americans), 111 international. Average age 30. 624 applicants, 47% accepted, 114 enrolled. In 2009, 111 master's, 2 doctorates awarded. Terminal master's awarded for partial completion of doctoral program. *Degree requirements:* For master's, thesis optional; for doctorate, comprehensive exam, thesis/dissertation, proposal defense. *Entrance requirements:* For master's, GMAT, GRE General Test; MCAT, DAT (health and biopharmaceutical economics); for doctorate, GMAT or GRE General Test. Additional exam requirements/recommendations for international students: Required—TOEFL (minimum score 600 paper-based; 250 computer-based; 94 iBT). *Application deadline:* For fall admission, 7/15 for domestic students, 5/1 for international students; for spring admission, 12/1 for domestic and international students. Applications are processed on a rolling basis. Application fee: $100. Electronic applications accepted. *Expenses:* Contact institution. *Financial support:* In 2009–10, 2 fellowships with full tuition reimbursements (averaging $13,200 per year), 10 research assistantships with full and partial tuition reimbursements (averaging $2,800 per year), 17 teaching assistantships with full tuition reimbursements (averaging $13,840 per year) were awarded; career-related internships or fieldwork, scholarships/grants, health care benefits, tuition waivers (full and partial), and unspecified assistantships also available. Support available to part-time students. Financial award application deadline: 1/15. *Faculty research:* Public finance, energy, investments, activity-based costing, management information systems. *Unit head:* Martin K. Saffer, Graduate Business Programs, 610-758-4450, Fax: 610-758-5283, E-mail: mks207@lehigh.edu. *Application contact:* Corinn McBride, Director of Recruitment and Admissions, 610-758-3418, Fax: 610-758-5283, E-mail: com207@lehigh.edu.

Maine Maritime Academy, Department of Graduate Studies, Program in Global Supply Chain Management, Castine, ME 04420. Offers MS, Certificate, Diploma. Part-time programs available. *Degree requirements:* For master's, capstone course. *Entrance requirements:* For master's, GMAT or GRE, letters of recommendation. Additional exam requirements/recommendations for international students: Required—TOEFL.

Michigan State University, The Graduate School, Eli Broad Graduate School of Management, Department of Supply Chain Management, East Lansing, MI 48824. Offers business administration (PhD); supply chain management (MS). Part-time programs available. *Faculty:* 17 full-time (3 women). *Students:* 22 full-time (7 women), 36 part-time (8 women); includes 11 minority (6 African Americans, 1 Asian American or Pacific Islander, 4 Hispanic Americans), 12 international. Average age 33. 51 applicants, 6% accepted. In 2009, 23 master's, 1 doctorate awarded. *Degree requirements:* For master's, field study, research project; for doctorate, comprehensive exam, thesis/dissertation, oral defense of dissertation proposal and dissertation. *Entrance requirements:* For master's, GMAT, bachelor's degree in related field, letters of recommendation, 2-3 years of work experience, minimum GPA of 3.0 in last 2 years of undergraduate course work; for doctorate, GMAT or GRE, letters of recommendation. Additional exam requirements/recommendations for international students: Required—TOEFL. Electronic applications accepted. *Expenses:* Contact institution. *Financial support:* In 2009–10, 8 research assistantships with tuition reimbursements (averaging $7,799 per year) were awarded. Total annual research expenditures: $244,341. *Unit head:* Dr. David J. Closs, Chairperson, 517-432-6406, Fax: 517-432-8048, E-mail: closs@msu.edu. *Application contact:* Cheryl Lundeen, Program Information, 517-432-6335, Fax: 517-432-8048, E-mail: lundeenc@bus.msu.edu.

Moravian College, Moravian College Comenius Center, Business and Management Programs, Bethlehem, PA 18018-6650. Offers general management (MBA); health care management (MBA); leadership (MSHRM); learning and performance management (MSHRM); supply chain management (MBA). Part-time and evening/weekend programs available. *Faculty:* 6 full-time (2 women), 10 part-time/adjunct (3 women). *Students:* 59 part-time (30 women). Average age 29. 27 applicants, 74% accepted, 10 enrolled. In 2009, 20 master's awarded. *Entrance requirements:* For master's, GMAT. Additional exam requirements/recommendations for international students: Required—TOEFL (minimum score 550 paper-based; 260 computer-based; 90 iBT). *Application deadline:* Applications are processed on a rolling basis. Application fee: $40. *Expenses:* Contact institution. *Financial support:* In 2009–10, 1 fellowship with full tuition reimbursement was awarded. *Faculty research:* Leadership, change management, human resources. *Unit head:* Dr. William A. Kleintop, Associate Dean for Business and Management Programs, 610-507-1400, Fax: 610-861-1400, E-mail: comenius@moravian.edu. *Application contact:* Linda J. Doyle, Information Contact, 610-861-1400, Fax: 610-861-1466, E-mail: mba@moravian.edu.

North Carolina State University, Graduate School, College of Management, Program in Business Administration, Raleigh, NC 27695. Offers biosciences management (MBA); entrepreneurship and technology commercialization (MBA); financial management (MBA); innovation management (MBA); marketing management (MBA); services management and consulting (MBA); supply chain management (MBA). *Accreditation:* AACSB. Part-time programs available. *Degree requirements:* For master's, thesis optional. *Entrance requirements:* For master's, GMAT, interview, 3 letters of recommendation. Additional exam requirements/recommendations for international students: Required—TOEFL (minimum score 600 paper-based; 250 computer-based; 100 iBT). Electronic applications accepted. *Faculty research:* Manufacturing strategy, information systems, technology commercialization, managing research and development, historical stock returns.

Quinnipiac University, School of Business, Program in Business Administration, Supply Chain Management Track, Hamden, CT 06518-1940. Offers MBA. *Expenses:* Tuition: Full-time $16,030; part-time $770 per credit. Required fees: $630; $35 per credit.

Rutgers, The State University of New Jersey, Newark, Rutgers Business School–Newark and New Brunswick, Doctoral Programs in Business, Newark, NJ 07102. Offers accounting (PhD); accounting information systems (PhD); finance (PhD); individualized study (PhD); information technology (PhD); international business (PhD); management science (PhD); organizational management (PhD); supply chain management (PhD).

Santa Clara University, Leavey School of Business, Program in Business Administration, Santa Clara, CA 95053. Offers accounting (MBA); entrepreneurship (MBA); executive MBA (EMBA); finance (MBA); food and agribusiness (MBA); international business (MBA); leading people and organizations (MBA); managing technology and innovation (MBA); marketing management (MBA); supply chain management (MBA). *Accreditation:* AACSB. Part-time and evening/weekend programs available. *Students:* 228 full-time (88 women), 838 part-time (265 women); includes 388 minority (17 African Americans, 2 American Indian/Alaska Native, 326 Asian Americans or Pacific Islanders, 43 Hispanic Americans), 218 international. Average age 31. 486 applicants, 77% accepted, 263 enrolled. In 2009, 317 master's awarded. *Degree requirements:* For master's, thesis or alternative. *Entrance requirements:* For master's, GMAT, GRE. Additional exam requirements/recommendations for international students: Required—TOEFL (minimum score 600 paper-based; 250 computer-based; 100 iBT). *Application deadline:* For fall admission, 6/1 for domestic and international students; for spring admission, 1/19 for domestic students, 1/17 for international students. Applications are processed on a rolling basis. Application fee: $75 ($100 for international students). Electronic applications accepted. *Expenses:* Contact institution. *Financial support:* Fellowships with partial tuition reimbursements, research assistantships with partial tuition reimbursements, career-related internships or fieldwork, Federal Work-Study, institutionally sponsored loans, scholarships/grants, health care benefits, and unspecified assistantships available. Support available to part-time students. Financial award applicants required to submit FAFSA. *Unit head:* Elizabeth B. Ford, Senior Assistant Dean, 408-554-2752, Fax: 408-554-4571, E-mail: eford@scu.edu. *Application contact:* Jennifer W. Taylor, Senior Director, 408-554-4539, Fax: 408-554-4571, E-mail: mbaadmissions@scu.edu.

Strayer University, Graduate Studies, Washington, DC 20005-2603. Offers accounting (MS); acquisition (MBA); business administration (MBA); communications technology (MS); educational management (M Ed); finance (MBA); health services administration (MHSA); hospitality and tourism management (MBA); human resource management (MBA); information systems (MS), including computer security management, decision support system management, enterprise resource management, network management, software engineering management, systems development management; management (MBA); management information systems (MS); marketing (MBA); professional accounting (MS), including accounting information systems, controllership, taxation; public administration (MPA); supply chain management (MBA); technology in education (M Ed). Programs also offered at campus locations in Birmingham, AL; Chamblee, GA; Cobb County, GA; Morrow, GA; White Marsh, MD; Charleston, SC; Columbia, SC; Greensboro, NC; Greenville, SC; Lexington, KY; Louisville, KY; Nashville, TN; North Raleigh, NC; Washington, DC. Part-time and evening/weekend programs available. Postbaccalaureate distance learning degree programs offered (minimal on-campus study). *Degree requirements:* For master's, thesis. *Entrance requirements:* For master's, GMAT, GRE General Test, bachelor's degree from an accredited college or university, minimum undergraduate GPA of 2.75. Electronic applications accepted.

Syracuse University, Martin J. Whitman School of Management, PhD Program in Business Administration, Syracuse, NY 13244. Offers accounting (PhD); finance (PhD); management information systems (PhD); managerial statistics (PhD); marketing (PhD); operations management (PhD); organizational behavior (PhD); strategy and human resources (PhD); supply chain management (PhD). *Degree requirements:* For doctorate, comprehensive exam, thesis/dissertation, summer research paper. *Entrance requirements:* For doctorate, GMAT or GRE General Test, 3 recommendations. Additional exam requirements/recommendations for international students: Required—TOEFL (minimum score 600 paper-based; 250 computer-based; 100 iBT). Electronic applications accepted. *Expenses:* Tuition: Full-time $26,808; part-time $1117 per credit. Required fees: $1024. *Faculty research:* Marketing models, market microstructure, supply chain, auditing, corporate governance.

Syracuse University, Martin J. Whitman School of Management, Program in Business Administration, Syracuse, NY 13244. Offers accounting (MBA); entrepreneurship (MBA); finance (MBA); marketing (MBA); supply chain management (MBA). Postbaccalaureate distance learning degree programs offered (minimal on-campus study). *Entrance requirements:* For master's, GMAT, 2 letters of recommendation. Additional exam requirements/recommendations for international students: Required—TOEFL (minimum score 600 paper-based; 250 computer-based; 100 iBT). Electronic applications accepted. *Expenses:* Tuition: Full-time $26,808; part-time $1117 per credit. Required fees: $1024.

Syracuse University, Martin J. Whitman School of Management, Program in Supply Chain Management, Syracuse, NY 13244. Offers MBA, PhD. *Expenses:* Tuition: Full-time $26,808; part-time $1117 per credit. Required fees: $1024.

The University of Akron, Graduate School, College of Business Administration, Department of Management, Program in Management-Supply Chain Management, Akron, OH 44325. Offers MSM. *Students:* 6 full-time (2 women), 11 part-time (3 women); includes 1 minority (Asian American or Pacific Islander), 2 international. Average age 36. 5 applicants, 80% accepted, 4 enrolled. In 2009, 6 master's awarded. *Entrance requirements:* For master's, GMAT, minimum GPA of 2.75, letters of recommendation, resume. Additional exam requirements/recommendations for international students: Required—TOEFL (minimum score 550 paper-based; 213 computer-based; 79 iBT). *Application deadline:* For fall admission, 8/1 for domestic and international students; for spring admission, 12/1 for domestic and international students. Application fee: $30 ($40 for international students). Electronic applications accepted. *Expenses:* Tuition, state resident: full-time $6570; part-time $365 per credit hour. Tuition, nonresident: full-time $11,250; part-time $625 per credit hour. *Unit head:* Dr. Ravi Krovi, Chair, 330-972-8108, Fax: 330-972-6588, E-mail: krovi@uakron.edu. *Application contact:* Dr. Susan Hanlon, Director of Graduate Business Programs, 330-972-7043, Fax: 330-972-6588, E-mail: shanlon@uakron.edu.

The University of Alabama in Huntsville, School of Graduate Studies, College of Business Administration, Department of Management and Marketing, Huntsville, AL 35899. Offers management (MBA), including acquisition management, finance, human resource management, logistics and supply chain management, marketing, project management. *Accreditation:* AACSB. Part-time and evening/weekend programs available. *Faculty:* 7 full-time (1 woman), 1 part-time/adjunct (0 women). *Students:* 41 full-time (19 women), 155 part-time (59 women); includes 30 minority (15 African Americans, 5 American Indian/Alaska Native, 7 Asian Americans or Pacific Islanders, 3 Hispanic Americans), 20 international. Average age 32. 138 applicants, 63% accepted, 68 enrolled. In 2009, 38 master's awarded. *Degree requirements:* For master's, comprehensive exam, thesis or alternative. *Entrance requirements:* For master's, GMAT (minimum score 500), minimum AACSB index of 1080. Additional exam requirements/recommendations for international students: Required—TOEFL (minimum score 550 paper-based; 213 computer-based; 62 iBT). *Application deadline:* For fall admission, 8/1 for domestic students, 4/1 for international students; for spring admission, 12/1 for domestic students, 9/1 for international students. Applications are processed on a rolling basis. Application fee: $40 ($50 for international students). Electronic applications accepted. *Expenses:* Tuition, state resident: part-time $355.75 per credit hour. Tuition, nonresident: part-time $847.10 per credit hour. Required fees: $210.80 per semester. Tuition and fees vary according to course load and program. *Financial support:* In 2009–10, 3 students received support, including 2 research assistantships with full tuition reimbursements available (averaging $14,400 per year), 1 teaching assistantship with full tuition reimbursement available (averaging $11,800 per year); career-related internships or fieldwork, Federal Work-Study, institutionally sponsored loans, scholarships/grants, health care benefits, and unspecified assistantships also available. Support available to part-time students. Financial award application deadline: 4/1; financial award applicants required to submit FAFSA. *Unit head:* Dr. Brent Wren, Chair, 256-824-6408, Fax: 256-824-6328, E-mail: wrenb@uah.edu. *Application contact:* Jennifer Pettitt, Director of Graduate Programs, 256-824-6681, Fax: 256-824-7571, E-mail: jennifer.pettitt@uah.edu.

University of Dallas, Graduate School of Management, Irving, TX 75062-4736. Offers accounting (MBA, MM, MS); business management (MBA, MM); corporate finance (MBA, MM); financial services (MBA); global business (MBA, MM); health services management (MBA, MM); human resource management (MBA, MM); information assurance (MBA, MM, MS); information technology (MBA, MM, MS); information technology service management (MBA, MM, MS); marketing management (MBA, MM); organization development (MBA, MM); project management (MBA, MM); sports and entertainment management (MBA, MM); strategic leadership (MBA, MM); supply chain management (MBA); supply chain management and

Supply Chain Management

University of Dallas (continued)
market logistics (MM). *Accreditation:* ACBSP. Part-time and evening/weekend programs available. Postbaccalaureate distance learning degree programs offered (no on-campus study). *Faculty:* 25 full-time (6 women), 31 part-time/adjunct (6 women). *Students:* 232 full-time (95 women), 923 part-time (365 women); includes 462 minority (184 African Americans, 14 American Indian/Alaska Native, 153 Asian Americans or Pacific Islanders, 111 Hispanic Americans), 184 international. Average age 34. 474 applicants, 85% accepted, 237 enrolled. In 2009, 399 master's awarded. *Entrance requirements:* Additional exam requirements/recommendations for international students: Required—TOEFL. *Application deadline:* Applications are processed on a rolling basis. Application fee: $50. Electronic applications accepted. *Expenses:* Contact institution. *Financial support:* In 2009–10, 399 students received support. Scholarships/grants and unspecified assistantships available. Financial award application deadline: 2/15; financial award applicants required to submit FAFSA. *Unit head:* Alounda Joseph, Director of Enrollment Processes, 972-721-5356, E-mail: admiss@gsm.udallas.edu. *Application contact:* Alounda Joseph, Director of Enrollment Processes, 972-721-5356, E-mail: admiss@gsm.udallas.edu.

University of Florida, Graduate School, Warrington College of Business Administration, Hough Graduate School of Business, Department of Information Systems and Operations Management, Gainesville, FL 32611. Offers decision and information sciences (MS, PhD); supply chain management (MS). Terminal master's awarded for partial completion of doctoral program. *Degree requirements:* For doctorate, thesis/dissertation. *Entrance requirements:* For master's and doctorate, GMAT or GRE General Test, minimum GPA of 3.0. Additional exam requirements/recommendations for international students: Required—TOEFL (minimum score 550 paper-based; 213 computer-based). *Faculty research:* Expert systems, nonconvex optimization, manufacturing management, production and operation management, telecommunication.

University of Louisville, J.B. Speed School of Engineering, Department of Industrial Engineering, Louisville, KY 40292-0001. Offers engineering management (M Eng); industrial engineering (M Eng, MS, PhD); logistics and distribution (Certificate). *Accreditation:* ABET (one or more programs are accredited). Part-time programs available. *Faculty:* 9 full-time (1 woman). *Students:* 37 full-time (13 women), 35 part-time (7 women); includes 11 minority (6 African Americans, 5 Asian Americans or Pacific Islanders), 19 international. Average age 29. 62 applicants, 61% accepted, 23 enrolled. In 2009, 27 master's, 2 doctorates awarded. Terminal master's awarded for partial completion of doctoral program. *Degree requirements:* For master's, comprehensive exam (for some programs), thesis or alternative; for doctorate, comprehensive exam, thesis/dissertation, minimum GPA of 3.0. *Entrance requirements:* For master's and doctorate, GRE General Test. Additional exam requirements/recommendations for international students: Required—TOEFL (minimum score 550 paper-based; 213 computer-based; 80 iBT). *Application deadline:* For fall admission, 7/12 priority date for domestic and international students; for winter admission, 11/29 priority date for domestic and international students; for spring admission, 3/28 priority date for domestic and international students. Applications are processed on a rolling basis. Application fee: $50. Electronic applications accepted. *Financial support:* In 2009–10, 16 students received support, including 8 fellowships with full tuition reimbursements available (averaging $20,000 per year), 1 research assistantship with full tuition reimbursement available (averaging $20,000 per year), 6 teaching assistantships with full tuition reimbursements available (averaging $20,000 per year). Financial award application deadline: 1/25; financial award applicants required to submit FAFSA. *Faculty research:* Optimization,computer simulation, logistics and distribution, ergonomics and human factors, advanced manufacturing process. Total annual research expenditures: $359,000. *Unit head:* Dr. John S. Usher, Chair, 502-852-6342, Fax: 502-852-5633, E-mail: usher@louisville.edu. *Application contact:* Dr. Michael Day, Associate Dean, 502-852-6195, Fax: 502-852-7294, E-mail: day@louisville.edu.

University of Massachusetts Dartmouth, Graduate School, Charlton College of Business, Program in Business Administration, North Dartmouth, MA 02747-2300. Offers accounting (Postbaccalaureate Certificate); business administration (MBA); e-commerce (PMC); finance (PMC); general management (PMC); leadership (PMC); management (Postbaccalaureate Certificate); marketing (PMC); supply chain management (PMC). *Accreditation:* AACSB. Part-time programs available. *Faculty:* 42 full-time (13 women), 26 part-time/adjunct (6 women). *Students:* 93 full-time (41 women), 132 part-time (64 women); includes 22 minority (5 African Americans, 2 American Indian/Alaska Native, 6 Asian Americans or Pacific Islanders, 9 Hispanic Americans), 42 international. Average age 30. 186 applicants, 82% accepted, 94 enrolled. In 2009, 55 master's, 19 other advanced degrees awarded. *Entrance requirements:* For master's, GMAT, resume, letters of recommendation. Additional exam requirements/recommendations for international students: Required—TOEFL (minimum score 500 paper-based; 200 computer-based; 72 iBT). *Application deadline:* For fall admission, 6/1 for domestic students, 5/1 for international students; for spring admission, 10/1 for domestic students, 8/1 for international students. Application fee: $40 ($60 for international students). Electronic applications accepted. *Expenses:* Tuition, state resident: full-time $2071; part-time $86.29 per credit. Tuition, nonresident: full-time $8099; part-time $337.46 per credit. Required fees: $9446. Tuition and fees vary according to class time, course load and reciprocity agreements. *Financial support:* In 2009–10, 1 research assistantship with full tuition reimbursement (averaging $6,000 per year) was awarded; teaching assistantships, Federal Work-Study and unspecified assistantships also available. Support available to part-time students. Financial award application deadline: 3/1; financial award applicants required to submit FAFSA. *Faculty research:* Competitiveness of south coast enterprises, global sales, key performance indicators, agile manufacturing, green business. Total annual research expenditures: $19,000. *Unit head:* Dr. Norm Barber, Assistant Dean, 508-999-8543, E-mail: nbarber@umassd.edu. *Application contact:* Elan Turcotte-Shamski, Graduate Admissions Officer, 508-999-8604, Fax: 508-999-8183, E-mail: graduate@umassd.edu.

University of Memphis, Graduate School, Fogelman College of Business and Economics, Program in Business Administration, Memphis, TN 38152. Offers accounting (MBA, PhD); economics (MBA, PhD); executive business administration (MBA); finance (PhD); finance, insurance, and real estate (MBA, MS); international business administration (IMBA); management (MBA, MS, PhD); management information systems (MBA, MS, PhD); management science (MBA); marketing (MBA, MS); marketing and supply chain management (PhD); real estate development (MS); JD/MBA. *Accreditation:* AACSB. *Faculty:* 44 full-time (9 women), 5 part-time/adjunct (0 women). *Students:* 263 full-time (106 women), 181 part-time (66 women); includes 70 minority (46 African Americans, 3 American Indian/Alaska Native, 16 Asian Americans or Pacific Islanders, 5 Hispanic Americans), 109 international. Average age 31. 374 applicants, 73% accepted, 119 enrolled. In 2009, 140 master's, 17 doctorates awarded. *Degree requirements:* For master's, comprehensive exam; for doctorate, comprehensive exam, thesis/dissertation. *Entrance requirements:* For master's, GMAT, resume; for doctorate, GMAT, interview, minimum GPA of 3.4, resume, letter of recommendation. Additional exam requirements/recommendations for international students: Required—TOEFL (minimum score 550 paper-based; 220 computer-based). *Application deadline:* For fall admission, 8/1 for domestic students; for spring admission, 12/1 for domestic students. Application fee: $35 ($60 for international students). *Expenses:* Tuition, state resident: full-time $6246; part-time $347 per credit hour. Tuition, nonresident: full-time $15,894; part-time $883 per credit hour. Required fees: $1160. Full-time tuition and fees vary according to course load, degree level and program. *Financial support:* In 2009–10, 164 students received support; research assistantships with full tuition reimbursements available, teaching assistantships with full tuition reimbursements available, career-related internships or fieldwork, Federal Work-Study, scholarships/grants, and unspecified assistantships available. Financial award application deadline: 2/15; financial award applicants required to submit FAFSA. *Faculty research:* Competitive business strategy, finance microstructures, supply chain management innovations, health care economics, litigation risks and corporate audits. *Unit head:* Rajiv Grover, Dean, 901-678-3759, E-mail: rgrover@memphis.edu. *Application contact:* Dr. Carol V. Danehower, Associate Dean for Programs, 901-678-5402, Fax: 901-678-3579, E-mail: fcbegp@memphis.edu.

University of Michigan–Dearborn, School of Management, Dearborn, MI 48128-1491. Offers accounting (MBA, MS); finance (MBA, MS); information systems (MS); international business (MBA); management (MBA); management information systems (MBA); marketing (MBA); supply chain management (MBA); MBA/MHSA; MBA/MSE; MBA/MSF. *Accreditation:* AACSB. Part-time and evening/weekend programs available. Postbaccalaureate distance learning degree programs offered (no on-campus study). *Faculty:* 26 full-time (6 women), 8 part-time/adjunct (4 women). *Students:* 73 full-time (30 women), 412 part-time (134 women); includes 65 minority (20 African Americans, 1 American Indian/Alaska Native, 38 Asian Americans or Pacific Islanders, 6 Hispanic Americans), 76 international. Average age 30. 185 applicants, 56% accepted, 78 enrolled. In 2009, 151 master's awarded. *Entrance requirements:* For master's, GMAT, 2 years of work experience (MBA); course work in computer applications, statistics, and pre-calculus or finite mathematics; 18 credits of accounting course work beyond introductory courses (MS in accounting). Additional exam requirements/recommendations for international students: Required—TOEFL (minimum score 560 paper-based; 220 computer-based; 84 iBT). *Application deadline:* For fall admission, 8/1 priority date for domestic students, 6/1 for international students; for winter admission, 12/1 priority date for domestic students, 10/1 for international students; for spring admission, 4/1 priority date for domestic students, 2/1 for international students. Applications are processed on a rolling basis. Application fee: $60. Electronic applications accepted. *Expenses:* Contact institution. *Financial support:* Career-related internships or fieldwork, Federal Work-Study, and scholarships/grants available. Support available to part-time students. Financial award application deadline: 9/1; financial award applicants required to submit FAFSA. *Faculty research:* Cultural diversity, buyer-supplier relations, error detection in data, economic evolution. *Unit head:* Dr. Kim Schatzel, Dean, 313-593-5248, Fax: 313-271-9835, E-mail: schatzel@umd.umich.edu. *Application contact:* Joan Doherty, Academic Advisor/Counselor, 313-593-5460, Fax: 313-271-9838, E-mail: gradbusiness@umd.umich.edu.

University of Minnesota, Twin Cities Campus, Carlson School of Management, Carlson Full-Time MBA Program, Minneapolis, MN 55455. Offers finance (MBA); information technology (MBA); management (MBA); marketing (MBA); medical industry orientation (MBA); supply chain and operations (MBA); JD/MBA; MBA/MPP; MD/MBA; MHA/MBA; Pharm D/MBA. *Accreditation:* AACSB. *Faculty:* 60 full-time (11 women), 15 part-time/adjunct (7 women). *Students:* 217 full-time (78 women); includes 23 minority (6 African Americans, 1 American Indian/Alaska Native, 14 Asian Americans or Pacific Islanders, 2 Hispanic Americans), 41 international. Average age 28. 548 applicants, 41% accepted, 104 enrolled. In 2009, 91 master's awarded. *Entrance requirements:* For master's, GMAT. Additional exam requirements/recommendations for international students: Required—TOEFL (minimum score 580 paper-based; 240 computer-based; 82 iBT), or IELTS (minimum score 7), or Pearson Test of English (PTE). *Application deadline:* For fall admission, 4/1 for domestic students, 2/1 for international students. Application fee: $60 ($90 for international students). Electronic applications accepted. *Expenses:* Contact institution. *Financial support:* In 2009–10, 107 students received support, including 107 fellowships with full and partial tuition reimbursements available (averaging $22,174 per year); research assistantships with partial tuition reimbursements available, teaching assistantships with partial tuition reimbursements available, career-related internships or fieldwork, Federal Work-Study, institutionally sponsored loans, scholarships/grants, health care benefits, and unspecified assistantships also available. Financial award application deadline: 2/1; financial award applicants required to submit FAFSA. *Unit head:* Kathryn J. Carlson, Assistant Dean, MBA Programs and Graduate Business Career Center, 612-625-5555, Fax: 612-625-1012, E-mail: mba@umn.edu. *Application contact:* Tracy J. Keeling, Associate Director of Admissions, Full-Time and Part-Time MBA Programs, 612-625-5555, Fax: 612-625-1012, E-mail: mba@umn.edu.

University of Minnesota, Twin Cities Campus, Carlson School of Management, Carlson Part-Time MBA Program, Minneapolis, MN 55455. Offers finance (MBA); information technology (MBA); management (MBA); marketing (MBA); supply chain and operations (MBA); JD/MBA; MBA/MPP; MD/MBA; MHA/MBA; Pharm D/MBA. Part-time and evening/weekend programs available. *Faculty:* 72 full-time (15 women), 26 part-time/adjunct (5 women). *Students:* 1,861 part-time (606 women); includes 188 minority (31 African Americans, 1 American Indian/Alaska Native, 132 Asian Americans or Pacific Islanders, 24 Hispanic Americans), 121 international. Average age 29. 387 applicants, 67% accepted, 238 enrolled. In 2009, 393 master's awarded. *Entrance requirements:* For master's, GMAT. Additional exam requirements/recommendations for international students: Required—TOEFL (minimum score 580 paper-based; 240 computer-based; 82 iBT), IELTS (minimum score 7) or Pearson Test of English (PTE) Academic. *Application deadline:* For fall admission, 5/1 priority date for domestic and international students; for spring admission, 10/1 priority date for domestic and international students. Application fee: $60 ($90 for international students). Electronic applications accepted. *Expenses:* Contact institution. *Financial support:* Applicants required to submit FAFSA. *Faculty research:* Strategy, IT, finance, marketing, operations, supply chain, entrepreneurship, quality management, accounting. *Unit head:* Kathryn J. Carlson, Assistant Dean, MBA Programs and Graduate Business Career Center, 612-624-2039, Fax: 612-625-1012, E-mail: mba@umn.edu. *Application contact:* Tracy J. Keeling, Associate Director of Admissions, Full-Time and Part-Time MBA Programs, 612-625-5555, Fax: 612-625-1012, E-mail: mba@umn.edu.

University of Missouri–St. Louis, College of Business Administration, Program in Business Administration, St. Louis, MO 63121. Offers accounting (MBA); business administration (Certificate); finance (MBA); human resource management (Certificate); logistics and supply chain management (MBA, Certificate); management (MBA); marketing (MBA); marketing management (Certificate); operations (MBA); quantitative management science (MBA). *Accreditation:* AACSB. Part-time and evening/weekend programs available. *Faculty:* 30 full-time (5 women), 11 part-time/adjunct (2 women). *Students:* 107 full-time (47 women), 310 part-time (120 women); includes 32 minority (17 African Americans, 6 Asian Americans or Pacific Islanders, 9 Hispanic Americans), 66 international. Average age 31. 285 applicants, 58% accepted, 130 enrolled. In 2009, 149 master's, 13 other advanced degrees awarded. *Entrance requirements:* For master's, GMAT, 2 letters of recommendation. Additional exam requirements/recommendations for international students: Required—TOEFL (minimum score 550 paper-based; 213 computer-based). *Application deadline:* For fall admission, 7/1 for domestic students; for spring admission, 11/1 for domestic students. Applications are processed on a rolling basis. Application fee: $35 ($40 for international students). Electronic applications accepted. *Expenses:* Tuition, state resident: full-time $5377; part-time $297.70 per credit hour. Tuition, nonresident: full-time $13,882; part-time $771.20 per credit hour. Required fees: $220; $12.20 per credit hour. One-time fee: $12. Tuition and fees vary according to course level, campus/location and program. *Financial support:* In 2009–10, 27 research assistantships with full and partial tuition reimbursements (averaging $8,525 per year), 6 teaching assistantships with full and partial tuition reimbursements (averaging $13,950 per year) were awarded; career-related internships or fieldwork, Federal Work-Study, and institutionally sponsored loans also available. Support available to part-time students. Financial award application deadline: 4/1; financial award applicants required to submit FAFSA. *Faculty research:* Human resources, strategic management, marketing strategy, consumer behavior product development, advertising. *Unit head:* Karl Kottemann, Assistant Director, 314-516-5885, Fax: 314-516-6420, E-mail: mba@umsl.edu. *Application contact:* 314-516-5458, Fax: 314-516-6996, E-mail: gradadm@umsl.edu.

University of Missouri–St. Louis, College of Business Administration, Program in Information Systems, St. Louis, MO 63121. Offers information systems (MSIS, PhD); logistics and supply chain management (PhD). Part-time and evening/weekend programs available. *Faculty:* 8 full-time (0 women). *Students:* 5 full-time (4 women), 14 part-time (3 women); includes 5 minority (3 African Americans, 1 Asian American or Pacific Islander, 1 Hispanic American), 5 international. Average age 30. 24 applicants, 29% accepted, 3 enrolled. In 2009, 7 master's awarded. *Entrance requirements:* For master's, GMAT, 2 letters of recommendation; for doctorate, GMAT or GRE, 3 letters of recommendation. Additional exam requirements/recommendations for international students: Required—TOEFL (minimum score 550 paper-based; 213 computer-based). *Application deadline:* For fall admission, 7/1 priority date for domestic and international students; for spring admission, 12/1 priority date for domestic and international students. Applications are processed on a rolling basis. Application fee: $35 ($40 for international students). Electronic applications accepted. *Expenses:* Tuition, state resident: full-time $5377; part-time $297.70 per credit hour. Tuition, nonresident: full-time $13,882;

part-time $771.20 per credit hour. Required fees: $220; $12.20 per credit hour. One-time fee: $12. Tuition and fees vary according to course level, campus/location and program. *Financial support:* Career-related internships or fieldwork, Federal Work-Study, and institutionally sponsored loans available. Support available to part-time students. Financial award application deadline: 4/1; financial award applicants required to submit FAFSA. *Faculty research:* International information systems, telecommunications, systems development, information systems sourcing. *Unit head:* Karl Kottemann, Assistant Director, 314-516-5885, Fax: 314-516-6420, E-mail: mba@umsl.edu. *Application contact:* 314-516-5458, Fax: 314-516-6996, E-mail: gradadm@umsl.edu.

The University of North Carolina at Greensboro, Graduate School, Bryan School of Business and Economics, Department of Information Systems and Operations Management, Greensboro, NC 27412-5001. Offers information systems (PhD); information technology (Certificate); information technology and management (MS); supply chain management (Certificate). *Entrance requirements:* For master's, GMAT, GRE General Test. Additional exam requirements/recommendations for international students: Required—TOEFL. Electronic applications accepted.

University of Rhode Island, Graduate School, College of Business Administration, Kingston, RI 02881. Offers accounting (MS); business administration (MBA, PhD), including finance and insurance (PhD), management (PhD), marketing (PhD), operations and supply chain management (MBA); finance (MBA); general business (MBA); management (MBA); marketing (MBA); supply chain management (MBA). *Accreditation:* AACSB. Part-time and evening/weekend programs available. *Faculty:* 54 full-time (15 women), 2 part-time/adjunct (1 woman). *Students:* 71 full-time (27 women), 157 part-time (56 women); includes 24 minority (6 African Americans, 10 Asian Americans or Pacific Islanders, 8 Hispanic Americans), 23 international. In 2009, 86 master's, 3 doctorates awarded. *Degree requirements:* For master's, comprehensive exam (for some programs), thesis optional; for doctorate, comprehensive exam, thesis/dissertation. *Entrance requirements:* For master's, GMAT or GRE, 2 letters of recommendation, resume; for doctorate, GMAT or GRE, 3 letters of recommendation, resume. Additional exam requirements/recommendations for international students: Required—TOEFL (minimum score 575 paper-based; 233 computer-based; 91 iBT). Application fee: $65. Electronic applications accepted. *Expenses:* Tuition, state resident: full-time $8828; part-time $490 per credit hour. Tuition, nonresident: full-time $22,100; part-time $1228 per credit hour. Required fees: $1118; $57 per semester. Tuition and fees vary according to program. *Financial support:* In 2009–10, 13 teaching assistantships with full and partial tuition reimbursements (averaging $13,095 per year) were awarded. Financial award applicants required to submit FAFSA. Total annual research expenditures: $245,746. *Unit head:* Dr. Mark Higgins, Dean, 401-874-4244, Fax: 401-874-4312, E-mail: markhiggins@uri.edu. *Application contact:* Lisa Lancellotta, Coordinator, MBA Programs, 401-874-4241, Fax: 401-874-4312, E-mail: mba@uri.edu.

University of San Diego, School of Business Administration, San Diego, CA 92110-2492. Offers accountancy (MS); business administration (MBA); executive leadership (MSEL); global leadership (MSGL); international business administration (IMBA); real estate (MSRE); supply chain management (MS, Certificate); taxation (MS); JD/IMBA; JD/MBA. *Accreditation:* AACSB. Part-time and evening/weekend programs available. *Faculty:* 36 full-time (11 women), 18 part-time/adjunct (4 women). *Students:* 173 full-time (53 women), 259 part-time (91 women); includes 61 minority (9 African Americans, 4 American Indian/Alaska Native, 29 Asian Americans or Pacific Islanders, 19 Hispanic Americans), 32 international. Average age 31. 555 applicants, 61% accepted, 191 enrolled. In 2009, 248 master's awarded. *Degree requirements:* For master's, variable foreign language requirement, community service, capstone project. *Entrance requirements:* For master's, GMAT (MBA, IMBA, MSRE), minimum GPA of 3.0, minimum 2 years of full-time work experience. Additional exam requirements/recommendations for international students: Required—TOEFL (minimum score 580 paper-based; 237 computer-based; 92 iBT), TWE. Application fee: $80. Electronic applications accepted. *Expenses:* Tuition: Full-time $21,042; part-time $1169 per unit. Required fees: $224. Full-time tuition and fees vary according to course load and degree level. *Financial support:* In 2009–10, 312 students received support. Career-related internships or fieldwork, Federal Work-Study, institutionally sponsored loans, scholarships/grants, and unspecified assistantships available. Support available to part-time students. Financial award application deadline: 4/1; financial award applicants required to submit FAFSA. *Faculty research:* Exchange rate forecasting, corporate governance, performance of private equity funds, economic geography, food banking. *Unit head:* Dr. David Pyke, Interim Dean, 619-260-4886, E-mail: sbadean@sandiego.edu. *Application contact:* Dr. John Mosby, Associate Director of Graduate Admissions, 619-260-4524, Fax: 619-260-4158, E-mail: grads@sandiego.edu.

University of Southern California, Graduate School, Viterbi School of Engineering, Department of Industrial and Systems Engineering, Los Angeles, CA 90089. Offers digital supply chain management (MS); engineering management (MS); engineering technology communication (Graduate Certificate); health systems operations (Graduate Certificate); industrial and systems engineering (MS, PhD, Engr); manufacturing engineering (MS); operations research engineering (MS); optimization and supply chain management (Graduate Certificate); product development engineering (MS); safety systems and security (MS); systems architecting and engineering (MS, Graduate Certificate); systems safety and security (Graduate Certificate); transportation systems (Graduate Certificate); MS/MBA. Part-time programs available. Postbaccalaureate distance learning degree programs offered (minimal on-campus study). *Faculty:* 11 full-time (2 women), 39 part-time/adjunct (7 women). *Students:* 250 full-time (71 women), 145 part-time (37 women); includes 67 minority (6 African Americans, 2 American Indian/Alaska Native, 39 Asian Americans or Pacific Islanders, 20 Hispanic Americans), 253 international. 679 applicants, 58% accepted, 206 enrolled. In 2009, 98 master's, 7 doctorates awarded. *Degree requirements:* For doctorate, thesis/dissertation; for other advanced degree, comprehensive exam. *Entrance requirements:* For master's, doctorate, and other advanced degree, GRE General Test. *Application deadline:* For fall admission, 3/1 priority date for domestic and international students; for spring admission, 10/1 for domestic students, 10/1 priority date for international students. Applications are processed on a rolling basis. Application fee: $85. Electronic applications accepted. *Expenses:* Tuition: Full-time $25,980; part-time $1315 per unit. Required fees: $554. One-time fee: $35 full-time. Full-time tuition and fees vary according to degree level and program. *Financial support:* In 2009–10, fellowships with full tuition reimbursements (averaging $30,000 per year), research assistantships with full tuition reimbursements (averaging $19,250 per year), teaching assistantships with full tuition reimbursements (averaging $19,250 per year) were awarded; career-related internships or fieldwork, scholarships/grants, health care benefits, and unspecified assistantships also available. Financial award application deadline: 12/1; financial award applicants required to submit CSS PROFILE or FAFSA. *Faculty research:* Health systems, music cognition and retrieval, transportation andlogistics, manufacturing and automation, engineering systems design, risk and economic analysis. Total annual research expenditures: $1.2 million. *Unit head:* Dr. James E. Moore, Chair, 213-740-4885, Fax: 213-740-1120, E-mail: jmoore@usc.edu. *Application contact:* Mary Ordaz, Student Service Advisor, 213-740-4886, Fax: 213-740-1120, E-mail: isedept@usc.edu.

The University of Texas at Austin, Graduate School, McCombs School of Business, Department of Information, Risk, and Operations Management, Austin, TX 78712-1111. Offers information systems (PhD); risk analysis and decision making (PhD); supply chain and operations management (PhD). *Degree requirements:* For doctorate, thesis/dissertation. *Entrance requirements:* For doctorate, GMAT or GRE. Electronic applications accepted. *Faculty research:* Stochastic processing and queuing, discrete nonlinear and large-scale optimization simulation, quality assurance logistics, distributed artificial intelligence, organizational modeling.

The University of Texas at Dallas, School of Management, Program in Information Systems and Operations Management, Richardson, TX 75080. Offers information technology management (MS), including enterprise systems, health care systems, information security; supply chain management (MS). Part-time and evening/weekend programs available. *Faculty:* 23 full-time (1 woman), 1 (woman) part-time/adjunct. *Students:* 153 full-time (54 women), 129 part-time (51 women); includes 36 minority (4 African Americans, 28 Asian Americans or Pacific Islanders, 4 Hispanic Americans), 212 international. Average age 27. 352 applicants, 74% accepted, 105 enrolled. In 2009, 67 master's awarded. *Degree requirements:* For master's, thesis optional. *Entrance requirements:* For master's, GMAT. Additional exam requirements/recommendations for international students: Required—TOEFL (minimum score 550 paper-based; 213 computer-based). *Application deadline:* For fall admission, 7/15 for domestic students, 5/1 priority date for international students; for spring admission, 11/15 for domestic students, 9/1 priority date for international students. Applications are processed on a rolling basis. Application fee: $50 ($100 for international students). Electronic applications accepted. *Expenses:* Tuition, state resident: full-time $11,068; part-time $461 per credit hour. Tuition, nonresident: full-time $21,178; part-time $882 per credit hour. Tuition and fees vary according to course load. *Financial support:* In 2009–10, 7 research assistantships with full tuition reimbursements (averaging $10,933 per year), 5 teaching assistantships with full tuition reimbursements (averaging $10,050 per year) were awarded; career-related internships or fieldwork, Federal Work-Study, institutionally sponsored loans, scholarships/grants, and unspecified assistantships also available. Support available to part-time students. Financial award application deadline: 4/30; financial award applicants required to submit FAFSA. *Faculty research:* Technology marketing, measuring information work productivity, electronic commerce, decision support systems, data quality. *Unit head:* Dr. Mark Thouin, Director, 972-883-4011, E-mail: mark.thouin@utdallas.edu. *Application contact:* James Parker, Assistant Director, 972-883-5842, E-mail: jparker@utdallas.edu.

University of Wisconsin–Madison, Graduate School, Wisconsin School of Business, Wisconsin Full-Time MBA Program, Madison, WI 53706-1380. Offers applied corporate finance (MBA); applied security analysis (MBA); arts administration (MBA); brand and product management (MBA); entrepreneurial management (MBA); marketing research (MBA); operations and technology management (MBA); real estate (MBA); risk management and insurance (MBA); strategic human resource management (MBA); strategic management in the life and engineering sciences (MBA); supply chain management (MBA). *Faculty:* 32 full-time (5 women). *Students:* 242 full-time (74 women); includes 47 minority (16 African Americans, 3 American Indian/Alaska Native, 16 Asian Americans or Pacific Islanders, 12 Hispanic Americans), 29 international. Average age 28. 526 applicants, 32% accepted, 117 enrolled. In 2009, 106 master's awarded. *Entrance requirements:* For master's, GMAT, bachelor's or equivalent degree, 2 years of work experience, letters of recommendation. Additional exam requirements/recommendations for international students: Required—TOEFL (minimum score 600 paper-based; 250 computer-based; 100 iBT), IELTS. *Application deadline:* For fall admission, 11/4 for domestic and international students; for winter admission, 2/5 for domestic and international students; for spring admission, 5/26 for domestic students, 4/5 for international students. Applications are processed on a rolling basis. Application fee: $56. Electronic applications accepted. *Expenses:* Tuition, state resident: part-time $594 per credit. Tuition, nonresident: part-time $1504 per credit. Required fees: $65 per credit. Tuition and fees vary according to course load, program and reciprocity agreements. *Financial support:* In 2009–10, 103 students received support, including 13 fellowships with full and partial tuition reimbursements available (averaging $15,000 per year), 53 research assistantships with full tuition reimbursements available (averaging $8,000 per year), 35 teaching assistantships with full tuition reimbursements available (averaging $11,000 per year); scholarships/grants, health care benefits, and unspecified assistantships also available. Financial award application deadline: 4/5; financial award applicants required to submit FAFSA. *Unit head:* Prof. Kenneth A. Kavajecz, Associate Dean, 608-265-3494, Fax: 608-265-4192, E-mail: kkavajecz@bus.wisc.edu. *Application contact:* Maria Reis, Assistant Director of MBA Marketing and Recruiting, 608-262-4000, Fax: 608-265-4192, E-mail: mreis@bus.wisc.edu.

University of Wisconsin–Whitewater, School of Graduate Studies, College of Business and Economics, Program in Business Administration, Whitewater, WI 53190-1790. Offers finance (MBA); human resource management (MBA); information technology management (MBA); international business (MBA); management (MBA); marketing (MBA); operations and supply chain management (MBA); technology and training (MBA). *Accreditation:* AACSB. Part-time and evening/weekend programs available. Postbaccalaureate distance learning degree programs offered (no on-campus study). *Degree requirements:* For master's, thesis or alternative. *Entrance requirements:* For master's, GMAT, minimum AACSB index of 1000, minimum GPA of 2.75. Additional exam requirements/recommendations for international students: Required—TOEFL (minimum score 550 paper-based; 213 computer-based). Electronic applications accepted. *Faculty research:* Interface between social institutions and individual behavior, technology and innovation management, occupational mental health, workplace deviance and workplace romance.

See Display on page 190.

Walden University, Graduate Programs, School of Management, Minneapolis, MN 55401. Offers applied management and decision sciences (PhD), including accounting, engineering management, finance, general applied management and decision sciences, information systems management, knowledge management, leadership and organizational change, learning management, operations research, self-designed program in applied management and design sciences; business information management (MISM); enterprise information security (MISM); entrepreneurship (MBA, DBA); finance (MBA, DBA); global supply chain management (DBA); healthcare management (MBA); healthcare system improvement (MBA); human resource management (MBA); information systems management (DBA); international business (MBA, DBA); IT strategy and governance (MISM); leadership (MBA, MS, DBA), including entrepreneurship (MS), general management (MS), human resources leadership (MS), innovation and technology (MS), leader development (MS), project management (MS), self-designed (MS), sustainable futures (MS); managing global software and service supply chains (MISM); marketing (MBA, DBA); project management (MBA, MS); risk management (MBA); self-designed (MBA, DBA); social impact management (DBA); sustainable futures (MBA); technology (MBA); technology entrepreneurship (DBA). Part-time and evening/weekend programs available. Postbaccalaureate distance learning degree programs offered (minimal on-campus study). *Faculty:* 17 full-time, 211 part-time/adjunct. *Students:* 3,389 full-time (1,774 women), 815 part-time (482 women); includes 1,969 minority (1,640 African Americans, 36 American Indian/Alaska Native, 123 Asian Americans or Pacific Islanders, 170 Hispanic Americans), 95 international. Average age 41. In 2009, 699 master's, 42 doctorates awarded. *Degree requirements:* For doctorate, thesis/dissertation (for some programs), residency. *Entrance requirements:* For master's, bachelor's degree or equivalent in related field; minimum GPA of 2.5; official transcripts; goal statement; access to computer and Internet; for doctorate, master's degree or equivalent in related field; minimum GPA of 3.0; 3 years of related professional/academic experience (preferred). Additional exam requirements/recommendations for international students: Required—TOEFL (minimum score 550 paper-based; 213 computer-based), IELTS (minimum score 6.5), TOEFL, IELTS, or Michigan English Language Assessment Battery (minimum score 82). *Application deadline:* Applications are processed on a rolling basis. Application fee: $50. Electronic applications accepted. *Expenses:* Tuition: Full-time $13,665; part-time $560 per credit. Required fees: $1375. Tuition and fees vary according to course load, degree level and program. *Financial support:* In 2009–10, 466 students received support; fellowships, Federal Work-Study, scholarships/grants, unspecified assistantships, and family tuition reduction, active duty/veteran tuition reduction, group tuition reduction, interest-free payment plans available. Support available to part-time students. Financial award applicants required to submit FAFSA. *Unit head:* William Schulz, Interim Associate Dean, 800-925-3368. *Application contact:* Jennifer Hall, Director of Enrollment, 866-4-WALDEN, E-mail: info@waldenu.edu.

Washington University in St. Louis, Olin Business School, Program in Supply Chain Management, St. Louis, MO 63130-4899. Offers MS. Part-time programs available. *Faculty:* 73 full-time (14 women), 45 part-time/adjunct (7 women). *Students:* 5 full-time (2 women), 1 (woman) part-time, 2 international. *Entrance requirements:* For master's, GMAT or GRE. Additional exam requirements/recommendations for international students: Required—TOEFL. *Application deadline:* For fall admission, 11/2 for domestic and international students; for winter admission, 2/1 for domestic and international students; for spring admission, 3/1 for domestic students. Application fee: $100. Electronic applications accepted. *Financial support:* Applicants required to submit FAFSA. *Unit head:* Joseph Peter Fox, Associate Dean and Director of MBA Programs, 314-935-6322, Fax: 314-935-4464, E-mail: fox@wustl.edu.

Supply Chain Management

Washington University in St. Louis *(continued)*
Application contact: Dr. Gary Hochberg, Director, Specialized Master's Programs, 314-935-6380, Fax: 314-935-4464, E-mail: hochberg@wustl.edu.

Wright State University, School of Graduate Studies, Raj Soin College of Business, Department of Information Systems and Operations Management, Logistics and Supply Chain Management Program, Dayton, OH 45435. Offers MS.

Wright State University, School of Graduate Studies, Raj Soin College of Business, Department of Management, Dayton, OH 45435. Offers flexible business (MBA); health care management (MBA); international business (MBA); management, innovation and change (MBA); project management (MBA); supply chain management (MBA); MBA/MS. *Entrance requirements:* For master's, GMAT, minimum AACSB index of 1000. Additional exam requirements/recommendations for international students: Required—TOEFL.

Transportation Management

American Public University System, AMU/APU Graduate Programs, Charles Town, WV 25414. Offers air warfare (MA Military Studies); American Revolution (MA Military Studies); business administration (MBA); Civil War (MA Military Studies); criminal justice (MA); defense management (MA Military Studies); emergency and disaster management (MA); environmental policy and management (MS); fire science management (MA); global engagement (MA); history (MA); homeland security (MA); humanities (MA); intelligence (MA Military Studies, MA Strategic Intelligence); international peace and conflict resolution (MA); international relations and conflict resolution (MA); joint warfare (MA Military Studies); land warfare international perspective (MA Military Studies); management (MA); military history (MA); military leadership (MA Military Studies); national security studies (MA); naval warfare international (MA Military Studies); naval warfare US (MA Military Studies); political science (MA); public administration (MA); public health (MA); security management (MA); space studies (MS); special ops/LIC (MA Military Studies); sports management (MA); transportation and logistics management (MA); transportation management (MA); unconventional warfare (MA Military Studies); World War II (MA Military Studies). Programs offered via distance learning only. Part-time and evening/weekend programs available. Postbaccalaureate distance learning degree programs offered (no on-campus study). *Students:* 788 full-time (330 women), 6,916 part-time (2,050 women); includes 1,767 minority (908 African Americans, 70 American Indian/Alaska Native, 223 Asian Americans or Pacific Islanders, 566 Hispanic Americans), 77 international. Average age 35. *Degree requirements:* For master's, comprehensive exam or practicum. *Entrance requirements:* For master's, bachelor's degree or equivalent, minimum GPA of 2.7 in last 60 hours of course work. *Application deadline:* Applications are processed on a rolling basis. Application fee: $0. Electronic applications accepted. *Financial support:* Applicants required to submit FAFSA. *Faculty research:* Military history, criminal justice, management performance, national security. *Unit head:* Dr. Frank McCluskey, Provost, 877-468-6268, Fax: 304-724-3780. *Application contact:* Terry Grant, Director of Enrollment Management, 877-468-6268, Fax: 304-724-3780, E-mail: info@apus.edu.

Arizona State University, Graduate College, College of Design, Interdisciplinary Program in Transportation Systems, Tempe, AZ 85287. Offers Certificate. Students must be enrolled in an appropriate degree program.

Arizona State University, Graduate College, College of Technology and Innovation, Department of Aeronautical Management Technology, Tempe, AZ 85287. Offers MS. Part-time and evening/weekend programs available. *Degree requirements:* For master's, thesis or applied project and oral defense. *Entrance requirements:* For master's, minimum GPA of 3.0, 30 semester hours in technology or equivalent, 16 hours of physical science and mathematics. Additional exam requirements/recommendations for international students: Required—TOEFL (minimum score 550 paper-based; 213 computer-based; 83 iBT); Recommended—TWE. Electronic applications accepted. *Faculty research:* Aviation training and education, human factors, aviation psychology, high altitude flight physiology, women in aviation, safety, aerospace medicine, metacognition, self regulation, learning strategies of pilots, aviation law, airline management.

Concordia University, School of Graduate Studies, John Molson School of Business, Montréal, QC H3G 1M8, Canada. Offers administration (M Sc, Diploma); aviation management (Certificate, Diploma); business administration (MBA, UA Undergraduate Associate, PhD), including international aviation (UA Undergraduate Associate); chartered accountancy (Diploma); community organizational development (Certificate); event management and fundraising (Certificate); executive business administration (EMBA); investment management (Diploma); investment management option (MBA); management accounting (Certificate); management of healthcare organizations (Certificate); sport administration (Diploma). *Accreditation:* AACSB. Part-time and evening/weekend programs available. *Degree requirements:* For master's, one foreign language, thesis (for some programs), research project; for doctorate, one foreign language, thesis/dissertation; for other advanced degree, one foreign language. *Entrance requirements:* For master's and doctorate, GMAT. Additional exam requirements/recommendations for international students: Required—TOEFL. *Expenses:* Contact institution. *Faculty research:* General business, capital markets, international business.

Florida Institute of Technology, Graduate Programs, College of Business, Extended Studies Division, Melbourne, FL 32901-6975. Offers acquisition and contract management (PMBA); business administration (PMBA); computer information systems (MS); e-business (PMBA); human resource management (PMBA); human resources management (MS); logistics management (MS), including humanitarian and disaster relief logistics; management (MS), including acquisition and contract management, e-business, human resource management, information systems, logistics management, management, transportation management; material acquisition management (MS); project management (MS), including information systems, operations research; public administration (MPA); quality management (MS); space management (MS); space systems (MS); systems management (MS), including information systems, operations research, systems management. Part-time and evening/weekend programs available. Postbaccalaureate distance learning degree programs offered (no on-campus study). *Faculty:* 12 full-time (3 women), 117 part-time/adjunct (20 women). *Students:* 74 full-time (32 women), 1,041 part-time (484 women); includes 343 minority (240 African Americans, 12 American Indian/Alaska Native, 44 Asian Americans or Pacific Islanders, 47 Hispanic Americans), 22 international. Average age 35. 520 applicants, 72% accepted, 279 enrolled. In 2009, 509 master's awarded. *Degree requirements:* For master's, capstone course. *Entrance requirements:* For master's, GMAT or resume showing 8 years of supervised experience, minimum GPA of 3.0, 2 letters of recommendation, resume. Additional exam requirements/recommendations for international students: Required—TOEFL (minimum score 550 paper-based; 213 computer-based; 79 iBT). *Application deadline:* For fall admission, 4/1 for international students; for spring admission, 9/30 for international students. Applications are processed on a rolling basis. Application fee: $50. Electronic applications accepted. *Expenses:* Tuition: Part-time $1015 per credit. Tuition and fees vary according to campus/location and program. *Financial support:* Application deadline: 3/1. *Unit head:* Dr. Clifford Bragdon, Dean, 321-674-8821, Fax: 321-674-7597, E-mail: cbragdon@fit.edu. *Application contact:* Carolyn Farrior, Director of Graduate Admissions Online Learning and Off Campus Programs, 321-674-7118, Fax: 321-674-8216, E-mail: cfarrior@fit.edu.

George Mason University, School of Public Policy, Program in Transportation Policy, Operations and Logistics, Arlington, VA 22201. Offers MA. Part-time programs available. Postbaccalaureate distance learning degree programs offered (no on-campus study). *Faculty:* 61 full-time (14 women), 30 part-time/adjunct (4 women). *Students:* 9 full-time (2 women), 29 part-time (8 women); includes 2 minority (both African Americans), 5 international. Average age 31. 27 applicants, 59% accepted, 10 enrolled. In 2009, 21 master's awarded. *Degree requirements:* For master's, thesis or alternative. *Entrance requirements:* For master's, GRE

(for students seeking merit-based scholarships), minimum undergraduate GPA of 3.0, resume, 2 letters of recommendation. Additional exam requirements/recommendations for international students: Required—TOEFL (minimum score 575 paper-based; 230 computer-based; 88 iBT). *Application deadline:* For fall admission, 6/1 priority date for domestic students, 5/1 priority date for international students; for spring admission, 12/1 priority date for domestic students, 11/1 priority date for international students. Applications are processed on a rolling basis. Application fee: $60. Electronic applications accepted. *Expenses:* Contact institution. *Financial support:* Career-related internships or fieldwork, Federal Work-Study, scholarships/grants, and tuition waivers (partial) available. Support available to part-time students. Financial award application deadline: 3/1; financial award applicants required to submit FAFSA. *Unit head:* Dr. Jonathan Gifford, Director, 703-993-8099, E-mail: spp@gmu.edu. *Application contact:* Leslie Metzger Levin, Assistant Dean of Graduate Admissions and Marketing, 703-993-8099, Fax: 703-993-4876, E-mail: lmetzger@gmu.edu.

Iowa State University of Science and Technology, Graduate College, College of Design, Department of Community and Regional Planning, Ames, IA 50011. Offers community and regional planning (MCRP); transportation (MS); M Arch/MCRP; MBA/MCRP; MCRP/MLA; MCRP/MPA. *Accreditation:* ACSP (one or more programs are accredited). Part-time programs available. *Faculty:* 11 full-time (3 women), 1 part-time/adjunct (0 women). *Students:* 21 full-time (11 women), 13 part-time (7 women); includes 2 minority (both African Americans), 6 international. Average age 31. 34 applicants, 71% accepted, 14 enrolled. In 2009, 10 master's awarded. *Degree requirements:* For master's, thesis or alternative. *Entrance requirements:* For master's, GRE General Test. Additional exam requirements/recommendations for international students: Required—TOEFL (minimum score 550 paper-based; 213 computer-based; 79 iBT) or IELTS (minimum score 6.5). *Application deadline:* For fall admission, 1/1 priority date for domestic and international students. Applications are processed on a rolling basis. Application fee: $40 ($90 for international students). Electronic applications accepted. *Expenses:* Tuition, state resident: full-time $6716. Tuition, nonresident: full-time $8908. Tuition and fees vary according to course level, course load, program and student level. *Financial support:* In 2009–10, 11 teaching assistantships with full and partial tuition reimbursements (averaging $7,210 per year) were awarded; research assistantships with full and partial tuition reimbursements, career-related internships or fieldwork, institutionally sponsored loans, tuition waivers (partial), and unspecified assistantships also available. Support available to part-time students. Financial award application deadline: 2/1; financial award applicants required to submit FAFSA. *Faculty research:* Economic development, housing, land use, geographic information systems planning in developing nations, regional and community revitalization, transportation planning in developing countries. *Unit head:* Dr. Douglas Johnston, Chair, 515-294-8958, Fax: 515-294-2348, E-mail: landarch@iastate.edu. *Application contact:* Dr. Francis Owusu, Director of Graduate Education, 515-294-7769, E-mail: crp@iastate.edu.

Iowa State University of Science and Technology, Graduate College, Interdisciplinary Programs, Program in Transportation, Ames, IA 50011. Offers MS. *Students:* 3 full-time (2 women), 1 part-time (0 women), 2 international. In 2009, 2 master's awarded. *Degree requirements:* For master's, thesis. *Entrance requirements:* For master's, GMAT or GRE General Test. Additional exam requirements/recommendations for international students: Required—TOEFL (minimum score 550 paper-based; 82 iBT) or IELTS (minimum score 6.5). *Application deadline:* For fall admission, 7/15 priority date for domestic students, 2/15 priority date for international students. Application fee: $40 ($90 for international students). Electronic applications accepted. *Expenses:* Tuition, state resident: full-time $6716. Tuition, nonresident: full-time $8908. Tuition and fees vary according to course level, course load, program and student level. *Financial support:* In 2009–10, 2 research assistantships with full and partial tuition reimbursements (averaging $8,000 per year) were awarded; teaching assistantships, scholarships/grants, health care benefits, and unspecified assistantships also available. *Unit head:* Dr. Nadia Gkritza, Supervisory Committee Chair, 515-294-2343, Fax: 515-294-0467. *Application contact:* Information Contact, 515-294-5836, Fax: 515-294-2592, E-mail: grad_admissions@iastate.edu.

Maine Maritime Academy, Department of Graduate Studies, Program in Maritime Management, Castine, ME 04420. Offers MS, Certificate, Diploma. Part-time programs available. *Degree requirements:* For master's, thesis optional, capstone course. *Entrance requirements:* For master's, GMAT or GRE General Test, letters of recommendation. Additional exam requirements/recommendations for international students: Required—TOEFL. *Faculty research:* Human resources in maritime environment, management of organization change, economic analysis and maritime law.

McGill University, Faculty of Graduate and Postdoctoral Studies, Faculty of Engineering, School of Urban Planning, Montréal, QC H3A 2T5, Canada. Offers environmental planning (MUP); housing (MUP); transportation (MUP); urban design (MUP); urban planning, policy and design (PhD).

Morgan State University, School of Graduate Studies, Clarence M. Mitchell, Jr. School of Engineering, Department of Transportation, Baltimore, MD 21251. Offers MS. Part-time and evening/weekend programs available. *Degree requirements:* For master's, thesis optional, comprehensive exam or equivalent. *Entrance requirements:* For master's, minimum undergraduate GPA of 2.5. Additional exam requirements/recommendations for international students: Required—TOEFL (minimum score 550 paper-based; 213 computer-based). *Faculty research:* Distributional impacts of congestion, pricing education and training for intelligent vehicle highway systems.

New Jersey Institute of Technology, Office of Graduate Studies, Newark College of Engineering, Interdisciplinary Program in Transportation, Newark, NJ 07102. Offers MS, PhD. Part-time and evening/weekend programs available. Terminal master's awarded for partial completion of doctoral program. *Degree requirements:* For master's, thesis or alternative; for doctorate, thesis/dissertation, residency. *Entrance requirements:* For master's, GRE General Test; for doctorate, GRE General Test, minimum graduate GPA of 3.5. Additional exam requirements/recommendations for international students: Required—TOEFL (minimum score 550 paper-based; 213 computer-based; 79 iBT). Electronic applications accepted. *Faculty research:* Transportation planning, administration, and policy; intelligent vehicle highway systems; bridge maintenance.

North Dakota State University, College of Graduate and Interdisciplinary Studies, College of Engineering and Architecture, Department of Civil Engineering, Fargo, ND 58108. Offers civil engineering (MS, PhD); environmental engineering (MS, PhD); transportation and logistics (PhD). PhD in transportation and logistics offered jointly with Upper Great Plains Transportation Institute. Part-time programs available. Postbaccalaureate distance learning degree programs offered (minimal on-campus study). *Students:* 20 full-time (4 women), 12 part-time (0 women);

includes 2 minority (both Asian Americans or Pacific Islanders), 21 international. In 2009, 7 master's, 1 doctorate awarded. *Degree requirements:* For master's, thesis; for doctorate, comprehensive exam, thesis/dissertation. *Entrance requirements:* Additional exam requirements/recommendations for international students: Required—TOEFL (minimum score 525 paper-based; 197 computer-based; 71 iBT). *Application deadline:* For fall admission, 7/1 priority date for domestic students, 1/15 priority date for international students; for spring admission, 5/1 priority date for international students. Applications are processed on a rolling basis. Application fee: $45 ($60 for international students). *Financial support:* Fellowships with full tuition reimbursements, research assistantships with full tuition reimbursements, teaching assistantships with full tuition reimbursements, career-related internships or fieldwork, Federal Work-Study, and institutionally sponsored loans available. Support available to part-time students. Financial award application deadline: 1/15. *Faculty research:* Wastewater, solid waste, composites, nanotechnology. Total annual research expenditures: $800,000. *Unit head:* Dr. Dinesh R. Katti, Chair, 701-231-7244, Fax: 701-231-6185, E-mail: dinesh.katti@ndsu.edu. *Application contact:* Dr. Kalpana Katti, Associate Professor and Graduate Program Coordinator, 701-231-9504, Fax: 701-231-6185, E-mail: kalpana.katti@ndsu.edu.

North Dakota State University, College of Graduate and Interdisciplinary Studies, Interdisciplinary Program in Transportation and Logistics, Fargo, ND 58108. Offers PhD. *Students:* 14 full-time (4 women), 10 part-time (2 women); includes 2 African Americans, 1 Asian American or Pacific Islander, 8 international. In 2009, 2 doctorates awarded. *Entrance requirements:* For doctorate, 1 year of calculus, statistics and probability, minimum GPA of 3.0. Additional exam requirements/recommendations for international students: Required—TOEFL (minimum score 550 paper-based; 213 computer-based; 79 iBT). *Application deadline:* For fall admission, 5/1 priority date for domestic students. Applications are processed on a rolling basis. Application fee: $45 ($60 for international students). *Financial support:* Research assistantships with full tuition reimbursements available. *Faculty research:* Supply chain optimization, spatial analysis of transportation networks, advanced traffic analysis, transportation demand, railroad/intermodal freight. *Unit head:* Dr. Denver Tolliver, Director, 701-231-7190, Fax: 701-231-1945, E-mail: denver.tolliver@ndsu.nodak.edu. *Application contact:* Dr. Denver Tolliver, Director, 701-231-7190, Fax: 701-231-1945, E-mail: denver.tolliver@ndsu.nodak.edu.

Polytechnic Institute of NYU, Department of Civil Engineering, Major in Transportation Management, Brooklyn, NY 11201-2990. Offers MS. Part-time and evening/weekend programs available. *Students:* 1 full-time (0 women), 22 part-time (6 women); includes 12 minority (10 African Americans, 1 American Indian/Alaska Native, 1 Asian American or Pacific Islander). 17 applicants, 53% accepted, 5 enrolled. In 2009, 3 master's awarded. *Degree requirements:* For master's, comprehensive exam (for some programs), thesis (for some programs). *Entrance requirements:* Additional exam requirements/recommendations for international students: Required—TOEFL (minimum score 550 paper-based; 213 computer-based; 80 iBT); Recommended—IELTS (minimum score 6.5). *Application deadline:* For fall admission, 7/31 priority date for domestic students, 4/30 priority date for international students; for spring admission, 12/31 priority date for domestic students, 10/30 priority date for international students. Applications are processed on a rolling basis. Application fee: $75. Electronic applications accepted. *Expenses:* Tuition: Full-time $21,492; part-time $1194 per credit hour. Required fees: $1160; $204 per course. *Financial support:* Fellowships, research assistantships, teaching assistantships, institutionally sponsored loans, scholarships/grants, and unspecified assistantships available. Support available to part-time students. Financial award applicants required to submit FAFSA. *Unit head:* Dr. Lawrence Chiarelli, Head, 718-260-4040, Fax: 718-260-3433, E-mail: lchiarel@poly.edu. *Application contact:* JeanCarlo Bonilla, Director of Graduate Enrollment Management, 718-260-3182, Fax: 718-260-3624, E-mail: gradinfo@poly.edu.

San Jose State University, Graduate Studies and Research, Lucas Graduate School of Business, Program in Transportation Management, San Jose, CA 95192-0001. Offers MS. Part-time and evening/weekend programs available. Postbaccalaureate distance learning degree programs offered (minimal on-campus study). *Degree requirements:* For master's, comprehensive exam, thesis or alternative. *Entrance requirements:* For master's, GMAT, minimum GPA of 3.0. *Application deadline:* For fall admission, 6/29 priority date for domestic students; for spring admission, 11/30 for domestic students. Applications are processed on a rolling basis. Application fee: $59. Electronic applications accepted. *Financial support:* Applicants required to submit FAFSA. *Faculty research:* Surface intermodal transportation, economics, security. Total annual research expenditures: $100,000. *Unit head:* Dr. Peter J. Haas, Education Director, 408-924-5691, Fax: 408-924-3555. *Application contact:* Dr. Peter J. Haas, Education Director, 408-924-5691, Fax: 408-924-3555.

State University of New York Maritime College, Program in International Transportation Management, Throggs Neck, NY 10465-4198. Offers MS. Part-time and evening/weekend programs available. *Degree requirements:* For master's, thesis. *Entrance requirements:* For master's, minimum GPA of 2.5. Additional exam requirements/recommendations for international students: Required—TOEFL. *Faculty research:* Ports, intermodal, shipping, logistics, port tax.

Texas Southern University, School of Science and Technology, Program in Transportation, Planning and Management, Houston, TX 77004-4584. Offers MS. Part-time and evening/weekend programs available. *Faculty:* 3 full-time (1 woman), 1 (woman) part-time/adjunct. *Students:* 27 full-time (15 women), 18 part-time (8 women); includes 39 minority (16 African Americans, 21 Asian Americans or Pacific Islanders, 2 Hispanic Americans), 2 international. Average age 30. 16 applicants, 100% accepted, 15 enrolled. In 2009, 8 master's awarded. *Degree requirements:* For master's, comprehensive exam, thesis optional. *Entrance requirements:* For master's, GRE General Test, minimum GPA of 2.5. Additional exam requirements/

recommendations for international students: Required—TOEFL. *Application deadline:* For fall admission, 7/1 for domestic and international students; for spring admission, 11/1 for domestic and international students. Applications are processed on a rolling basis. Application fee: $50 ($75 for international students). Electronic applications accepted. *Expenses:* Tuition, state resident: full-time $1805; part-time $100 per credit hour. Tuition, nonresident: full-time $6470; part-time $343 per credit hour. Tuition and fees vary according to course level, course load and degree level. *Financial support:* In 2009–10, 23 research assistantships (averaging $7,485 per year), 2 teaching assistantships (averaging $2,525 per year) were awarded; fellowships with partial tuition reimbursements, career-related internships or fieldwork, scholarships/grants, and unspecified assistantships also available. Financial award application deadline: 5/1. *Faculty research:* Highway traffic operations, transportation and policy planning, air quality in transportation, transportation modeling. Total annual research expenditures: $500,000. *Unit head:* Dr. Lei Yu, Chair, 713-313-7282, Fax: 713-313-1856, E-mail: yu_lx@tsu.edu. *Application contact:* Paula Eakins, Administrative Assistant, 713-313-1841, E-mail: eakins_pl@tsu.edu.

The University of British Columbia, Sauder School of Business, Doctoral Program in Commerce and Business Administration, Vancouver, BC V6T 1Z1, Canada. Offers accounting (PhD); finance (PhD); international business (PhD); management information systems (PhD); management science (PhD); marketing (PhD); organizational behavior (PhD); strategy and business economics (PhD); transportation and logistics (PhD); urban land economics (PhD). *Degree requirements:* For doctorate, comprehensive exam, thesis/dissertation. *Entrance requirements:* For doctorate, GMAT or GRE. Additional exam requirements/recommendations for international students: Required—TOEFL (minimum score 600 paper-based; 250 computer-based; 100 iBT). Electronic applications accepted.

University of California, Davis, College of Engineering, Graduate Group in Transportation Technology and Policy, Davis, CA 95616. Offers MS, PhD. Terminal master's awarded for partial completion of doctoral program. *Degree requirements:* For master's, comprehensive exam (for some programs), thesis (for some programs); for doctorate, thesis/dissertation. *Entrance requirements:* For master's, GRE General Test, minimum GPA of 3.0; for doctorate, GRE General Test, minimum GPA of 3.5. Additional exam requirements/recommendations for international students: Required—TOEFL (minimum score 550 paper-based; 213 computer-based). Electronic applications accepted.

University of California, Santa Barbara, Graduate Division, College of Letters and Sciences, Division of Mathematics, Life, and Physical Sciences, Department of Geography, Santa Barbara, CA 93106-4060. Offers cognitive science (PhD); geography (MA); quantitative methods in the social sciences (PhD); transportation (PhD); MA/PhD. *Students:* 67 full-time (33 women). Average age 30. 92 applicants, 28% accepted, 15 enrolled. In 2009, 3 master's, 13 doctorates awarded. *Degree requirements:* For master's, comprehensive exam (for some programs), thesis; for doctorate, comprehensive exam, thesis/dissertation. *Entrance requirements:* For master's, GRE General Test, 3 letters of recommendation, resume/curriculum vitae; for doctorate, GRE General Test, 3 letters of recommendation, statement of purpose, personal achievements/contributions statement, resume/curriculum vitae, transcripts for post-secondary institutions attended. Additional exam requirements/recommendations for international students: Required—TOEFL (minimum score 550 paper-based; 213 computer-based; 80 iBT) or IELTS (minimum score 7). *Application deadline:* For fall admission, 2/1 for domestic and international students. Application fee: $70 ($90 for international students). Electronic applications accepted. *Financial support:* In 2009–10, 59 students received support, including 36 fellowships with full and partial tuition reimbursements available (averaging $10,700 per year), 29 research assistantships with full and partial tuition reimbursements available (averaging $8,600 per year), 31 teaching assistantships with partial tuition reimbursements available (averaging $8,000 per year); Federal Work-Study, institutionally sponsored loans, scholarships/grants, health care benefits, and unspecified assistantships also available. Financial award applicants required to submit FAFSA. *Faculty research:* Earth system science, human environment relations, modeling, measurement and computation, quantitative methods in social sciences. *Unit head:* Dr. Oliver Chadwick, Chair, 805-893-4223, E-mail: oac@geog.ucsb.edu. *Application contact:* Graduate Program Assistant, 805-893-3663, Fax: 805-893-3146, E-mail: grad_assistant@geog.ucsb.edu.

The University of Tennessee, Graduate School, College of Business Administration, Program in Business Administration, Knoxville, TN 37996. Offers accounting (PhD); finance (MBA, PhD); logistics and transportation (MBA, PhD); management (PhD); marketing (MBA, PhD); operations management (MBA); professional business administration (MBA); statistics (PhD); JD/MBA; MS/MBA. *Accreditation:* AACSB. Postbaccalaureate distance learning degree programs offered. *Degree requirements:* For master's, thesis or alternative; for doctorate, thesis/dissertation. *Entrance requirements:* For master's and doctorate, GMAT, minimum GPA of 2.7. Additional exam requirements/recommendations for international students: Required—TOEFL. Electronic applications accepted. *Expenses:* Tuition, state resident: full-time $6826; part-time $380 per semester hour. Tuition, nonresident: full-time $21,844; part-time $1147 per semester hour. Tuition and fees vary according to program.

University of Washington, Graduate School, Interdisciplinary Program in Global Trade, Transportation and Logistics Studies, Seattle, WA 98195. Offers Certificate.

Wilmington University, College of Business, New Castle, DE 19720-6491. Offers business administration (MBA); finance (MBA); health care administration (MBA, MS); homeland security (MBA, MS); human resource management (MS); management (MS); management information systems (MBA); organizational leadership (MS); public administration (MS); transportation and logistics (MBA, MS). Part-time and evening/weekend programs available. *Entrance requirements:* Additional exam requirements/recommendations for international students: Required—TOEFL (minimum score 500 paper-based; 173 computer-based). Electronic applications accepted.

ACADEMIC AND PROFESSIONAL PROGRAMS IN EDUCATION

Section 22
Education

This section contains a directory of institutions offering graduate work in education, followed by in-depth entries submitted by institutions that chose to prepare detailed program descriptions. Additional information about programs listed in the directory but not augmented by an in-depth entry may be obtained by writing directly to the dean of a graduate school or chair of a department at the address given in the directory.

For programs offering related work, see also in this book *Administration, Instruction, and Theory; Health-Related Professions; Instructional Levels; Leisure Studies and Recreation; Physical Education and Kinesiology; Special Focus;* and *Subject Areas.* In another guide in this series:

Graduate Programs in the Humanities, Arts & Social Sciences
See *Psychology and Counseling (School Psychology)*

CONTENTS

Program Directory

Close-Ups and Display

Education—General

Abilene Christian University, Graduate School, College of Education and Human Services, Abilene, TX 79699-9100. Offers M Ed, MS, MSSW. *Faculty:* 20 part-time/adjunct (12 women). *Students:* 89 full-time (68 women), 229 part-time (168 women); includes 38 minority (23 African Americans, 2 Asian Americans or Pacific Islanders, 13 Hispanic Americans), 9 international. 235 applicants, 51% accepted, 114 enrolled. In 2009, 39 master's awarded. *Degree requirements:* For master's, comprehensive exam. *Application deadline:* For fall admission, 4/1 priority date for domestic students; for spring admission, 11/1 for domestic students. Applications are processed on a rolling basis. Application fee: $40. Electronic applications accepted. *Expenses:* Tuition: Full-time $11,520; part-time $640 per hour. Required fees: $1090; $53.50 per hour. $10 per term. Tuition and fees vary according to program. *Financial support:* In 2009–10, 236 students received support. Application deadline: 4/1. *Unit head:* Dr. Malesa Breeding, Dean, 325-674-2700. *Application contact:* William Horn, Graduate Admissions Counselor, 325-674-2656, Fax: 325-674-6717, E-mail: gradinfo@acu.edu.

Acadia University, Faculty of Professional Studies, School of Education, Wolfville, NS B4P 2R6, Canada. Offers counseling (M Ed); curriculum studies (M Ed), including cultural and media studies, learning and technology, science, math and technology; inclusive education (M Ed); leadership (M Ed); learning and technology (M Ed). Part-time and evening/weekend programs available. *Faculty:* 20 full-time (10 women). *Students:* 33 full-time (26 women), 223 part-time (173 women). 314 applicants, 75% accepted, 166 enrolled. In 2009, 145 master's awarded. *Degree requirements:* For master's, thesis optional. *Entrance requirements:* For master's, B Ed or the equivalent, 2 years of teaching or related experience. Additional exam requirements/recommendations for international students: Required—TOEFL (minimum score 580 paper-based; 237 computer-based; 93 iBT), IELTS (minimum score 6.5). *Application deadline:* Applications are processed on a rolling basis. Application fee: $50. *Financial support:* Research assistantships, teaching assistantships, unspecified assistantships available. Financial award application deadline: 2/1. *Unit head:* Ann Vibert, Director, E-mail: ann.vibert@acadiau.ca. *Application contact:* Sheila Langille, Secretary, 902-585-1229, Fax: 902-585-1071, E-mail: sheila.langille@acadiau.ca.

Adams State College, The Graduate School, Department of Teacher Education, Alamosa, CO 81102. Offers education (MA); special education (MA). *Accreditation:* Teacher Education Accreditation Council. Part-time programs available. Postbaccalaureate distance learning degree programs offered. *Degree requirements:* For master's, qualifying exam. *Entrance requirements:* For master's, GRE General Test or MAT, minimum undergraduate GPA of 3.0.

Adelphi University, School of Education, Garden City, NY 11530-0701. Offers MA, MS, DA, Certificate. *Accreditation:* NCATE. Part-time and evening/weekend programs available. *Faculty:* 69 full-time (47 women), 146 part-time/adjunct (106 women). *Students:* 467 full-time (401 women), 754 part-time (584 women); includes 206 minority (100 African Americans, 1 American Indian/Alaska Native, 25 Asian Americans or Pacific Islanders, 80 Hispanic Americans), 15 international. Average age 29. 1,214 applicants, 56% accepted, 413 enrolled. In 2009, 572 master's awarded. *Degree requirements:* For doctorate, one foreign language, comprehensive exam, thesis/dissertation. *Entrance requirements:* For master's, resume, letters of recommendation, minimum cumulative GPA of 2.75; for doctorate, GRE General Test, 3 letters of recommendation, interview. Additional exam requirements/recommendations for international students: Required—TOEFL (minimum score 550 paper-based; 213 computer-based; 80 iBT). *Application deadline:* For fall admission, 4/1 for international students; for spring admission, 11/1 for international students. Applications are processed on a rolling basis. Application fee: $50. Electronic applications accepted. *Expenses:* Tuition: Full-time $28,340; part-time $830 per credit. Required fees: $600; $250 per credit. Full-time tuition and fees vary according to course load and program. *Financial support:* In 2009–10, 116 teaching assistantships (averaging $4,898 per year) were awarded; career-related internships or fieldwork, Federal Work-Study, institutionally sponsored loans, tuition waivers (full), and unspecified assistantships also available. Support available to part-time students. Financial award application deadline: 2/15; financial award applicants required to submit FAFSA. *Faculty research:* Multicultural and gender issues, psychometric assessment, quantitative research methods. *Unit head:* Dr. Jane Ashdown, Dean, 516-877-4065, E-mail: jashdown@adelphi.edu. *Application contact:* Christine Murphy, Director of Admissions, 516-877-3050, Fax: 516-877-3039, E-mail: graduateadmissions@adelphi.edu.

Alabama Agricultural and Mechanical University, School of Graduate Studies, School of Education, Huntsville, AL 35811. Offers M Ed, MS, MS Ed, Ed S. *Accreditation:* NCATE. Part-time and evening/weekend programs available. *Degree requirements:* For master's, comprehensive exam. *Entrance requirements:* For master's, GRE General Test. Additional exam requirements/recommendations for international students: Required—TOEFL (minimum score 500 paper-based; 173 computer-based; 61 iBT). Electronic applications accepted. *Faculty research:* Speech defects, aging, blindness, multicultural education, learning styles.

Alabama State University, School of Graduate Studies, College of Education, Montgomery, AL 36101-0271. Offers M Ed, MS, Ed D, Ed S. *Accreditation:* NCATE. Part-time programs available. *Degree requirements:* For master's, comprehensive exam; for Ed S, comprehensive exam, thesis. *Entrance requirements:* For master's, GRE General Test, MAT, graduate writing competency test; for Ed S, graduate writing competency test, GRE, MAT. Additional exam requirements/recommendations for international students: Required—TOEFL (minimum score 500 paper-based; 173 computer-based). *Faculty research:* Whole language instruction, African-American children's literature.

Alaska Pacific University, Graduate Programs, Education Department, Program in Teaching, Anchorage, AK 99508-4672. Offers teaching (K-8) (MAT). *Degree requirements:* For master's, research project. *Entrance requirements:* For master's, GRE or MAT, PRAXIS, minimum GPA of 3.0.

Albany State University, College of Education, Albany, GA 31705-2717. Offers M Ed, Certificate, Ed S. *Accreditation:* NCATE. Part-time programs available. *Faculty:* 17 full-time (8 women), 8 part-time/adjunct (7 women). *Students:* 97 full-time (77 women), 150 part-time (123 women); includes 199 minority (197 African Americans, 2 Asian Americans or Pacific Islanders). Average age 34. 40 applicants, 95% accepted, 32 enrolled. In 2009, 72 master's, 43 Certificates awarded. *Degree requirements:* For master's, comprehensive exam, GACE II. *Entrance requirements:* For master's, GRE General Test or MAT, GACE I. Additional exam requirements/recommendations for international students: Required—TOEFL. *Application deadline:* For fall admission, 11/16 for domestic students, 2/16 for international students; for spring admission, 4/19 for domestic students, 9/19 for international students. Applications are processed on a rolling basis. Application fee: $20. Electronic applications accepted. *Expenses:* Tuition, state resident: full-time $2970; part-time $162 per credit hour. Tuition, nonresident: full-time $12,168; part-time $676 per credit hour. Required fees: $962; $75 per credit hour. *Financial support:* Fellowships, research assistantships, teaching assistantships, career-related internships or fieldwork, Federal Work-Study, and scholarships/grants available. Support available to part-time students. Financial award application deadline: 4/1; financial award applicants required to submit CSS PROFILE or FAFSA. *Faculty research:* Teaching and learning reading, children in inclusive classrooms, teaching children science and mathematics, training teachers to meet the learning styles of children, increasing scholarship in professional development. *Unit head:* Dr. Kimberly King-Jupiter, Dean, 229-430-4715, Fax: 229-430-4993, E-mail: wilburn.campbell@asurams.edu. *Application contact:* Dr. Rani George, Interim Dean of Graduate School, 229-430-5118, Fax: 229-430-6398, E-mail: rani.george@asurams.edu.

Albright College, Department of Education—Graduate Division, Reading, PA 19612-5234. Offers early childhood education (MS); elementary education (MS); English as a second language (MA); general education (MA); special education (MS). Part-time and evening/weekend programs available. *Degree requirements:* For master's, thesis. *Entrance requirements:* For master's, GRE General Test or MAT, minimum undergraduate GPA of 3.0, 2 letters of recommendation, interview. Additional exam requirements/recommendations for international

students: Recommended—TOEFL (minimum score 525 paper-based; 197 computer-based). Electronic applications accepted.

Alcorn State University, School of Graduate Studies, School of Psychology and Education, Alcorn State, MS 39096-7500. Offers agricultural education (MS Ed); elementary education (MS Ed, Ed S); guidance and counseling (MS Ed); industrial education (MS Ed); secondary education (MS Ed), including health and physical education; special education (MS Ed). *Accreditation:* NCATE. *Degree requirements:* For master's, thesis optional.

Alfred University, Graduate School, Division of Education, Alfred, NY 14802-1205. Offers literacy teacher (MS Ed); numeracy (MS). *Accreditation:* Teacher Education Accreditation Council. Part-time programs available. *Entrance requirements:* For master's, LAST, Assessment of Teaching Skills (written), Content Specialty Test. Additional exam requirements/recommendations for international students: Required—TOEFL (minimum score 590 paper-based; 243 computer-based; 90 iBT), IELTS (minimum score 6.5). Electronic applications accepted. *Expenses:* Tuition: Full-time $33,296; part-time $708 per credit hour. Required fees: $880; $144 per year. Full-time tuition and fees vary according to program. *Faculty research:* Whole language, ethics in counseling and psychotherapy.

Alliant International University–Fresno, Graduate School of Education, TeachersCHOICE Preparation Programs, Fresno, CA 93727. Offers MA. Part-time programs available. *Entrance requirements:* For master's, CBEST, CSET, interview; offer of employment as a teacher of record in a California school; minimum GPA of 3.0, 2 letters of recommendation.

Alliant International University–Irvine, Graduate School of Education, Teacher Education Programs, Irvine, CA 92612. Offers auditory oral education (Certificate); CLAD (Certificate); preliminary multiple subject (Credential); preliminary multiple subject with BCLAD (Credential); preliminary single subject (Credential); professional clear multiple subject (Credential); professional clear single subject (Credential); teaching (MA, Credential); technology and learning (MA). Part-time and evening/weekend programs available. *Entrance requirements:* For degree, California Basic Educational Skills Test, minimum GPA of 2.5. Additional exam requirements/recommendations for international students: Required—TOEFL (minimum score 550 paper-based; 213 computer-based), TWE. Electronic applications accepted.

Alliant International University–Los Angeles, Graduate School of Education, TeachersCHOICE Preparation Programs, Alhambra, CA 91803-1360. Offers MA. Part-time programs available. *Entrance requirements:* For master's, CBEST, CSET, interview; offer of employment as a teacher of record in a California school; minimum GPA of 3.0, 2 letters of recommendation.

Alliant International University–México City, Graduate School of Education, Mexico City, Mexico. Offers teaching (MA). Part-time and evening/weekend programs available. Postbaccalaureate distance learning degree programs offered (no on-campus study). *Entrance requirements:* For master's, minimum GPA of 3.0, letters of recommendation, interview. Additional exam requirements/recommendations for international students: Required—TOEFL (minimum score 550 paper-based; 213 computer-based), TWE (minimum score 5).

Alliant International University–Sacramento, Graduate School of Education, TeachersCHOICE Preparation Programs, Sacramento, CA 95825. Offers MA. *Entrance requirements:* For master's, CBEST, CSET, interview; offer of employment as a teacher of record in a California school; minimum GPA of 3.0; 2 letters of recommendation.

Alliant International University–San Diego, Graduate School of Education, Teacher Education Programs, San Diego, CA 92131-1799. Offers preliminary single subject (Credential); professional clear multiple subject (Credential); professional clear single subject (Credential); teacher education (MA). Part-time and evening/weekend programs available. *Entrance requirements:* For degree, California Basic Educational Skills Test, minimum GPA of 2.5. Additional exam requirements/recommendations for international students: Required—TOEFL (minimum score 550 paper-based; 213 computer-based), TWE. Electronic applications accepted. *Faculty research:* Curriculum and instructional planning.

Alliant International University–San Francisco, Graduate School of Education, Teacher Education Programs, San Francisco, CA 94133-1221. Offers auditory oral education (Certificate); CLAD (Certificate); preliminary multiple subject (Credential); preliminary multiple subject with BCLAD (Credential); preliminary single subject (Credential); professional clear multiple subject (Credential); professional clear single subject (Credential); teaching (MA). Part-time and evening/weekend programs available. *Entrance requirements:* For degree, California Basic Educational Skills Test, minimum GPA of 2.5. Additional exam requirements/recommendations for international students: Required—TOEFL (minimum score 550 paper-based; 213 computer-based), TWE.

Alvernia University, Graduate Studies, Program in Education, Reading, PA 19607-1799. Offers urban education (M Ed). Part-time and evening/weekend programs available. *Degree requirements:* For master's, thesis optional. *Entrance requirements:* For master's, GRE or MAT (alumni excluded). Electronic applications accepted.

Alverno College, School of Education, Milwaukee, WI 53234-3922. Offers adaptive education (MA); administrative leadership (MA); adult education and organizational development (MA); adult educational and instructional design (MA); adult educational and instructional technology (MA); global connections in the humanities (MA); instructional leadership (MA); instructional technology for K-12 settings (MA); professional development (MA); reading education (MA); reading education with adaptive education (MA); science education (MA); teaching in alternative schools (MA). *Accreditation:* NCATE. Part-time and evening/weekend programs available. *Faculty:* 10 full-time (all women), 17 part-time/adjunct (15 women). *Students:* 65 full-time (59 women), 82 part-time (75 women); includes 31 minority (24 African Americans, 1 American Indian/Alaska Native, 1 Asian American or Pacific Islander, 5 Hispanic Americans), 2 international. Average age 38. 113 applicants, 64% accepted, 61 enrolled. In 2009, 56 master's awarded. *Degree requirements:* For master's, presentation/defense of proposal, conference presentation of inquiry projects. *Entrance requirements:* For master's, bachelor's degree in related field, communication samples from work setting, 3 letters of recommendation. Additional exam requirements/recommendations for international students: Required—TOEFL. *Application deadline:* For fall admission, 7/15 priority date for domestic and international students; for spring admission, 12/15 priority date for domestic and international students. Applications are processed on a rolling basis. Application fee: $50. Electronic applications accepted. *Financial support:* In 2009–10, 92 students received support. Federal Work-Study available. Support available to part-time students. Financial award application deadline: 4/15; financial award applicants required to submit FAFSA. *Faculty research:* Student self-assessment, self-reflection, integration of curriculum, identifying needs of students in strategic situations and designing appropriate classroom strategies. *Unit head:* Dr. Mary Diez, Graduate Dean, 414-382-6214, Fax: 414-382-6332, E-mail: mary.diez@alverno.edu. *Application contact:* Angela Peterson-Adams, Graduate Recruiter, 414-382-6104, Fax: 414-382-6354, E-mail: angela.peterson-adams@alverno.edu.

American InterContinental University Online, Program in Education, Hoffman Estates, IL 60192. Offers curriculum and instruction (M Ed); educational assessment and evaluation (M Ed); instructional technology (M Ed); leadership of educational organizations (M Ed). Evening/weekend programs available. Postbaccalaureate distance learning degree programs offered (no on-campus study). *Entrance requirements:* Additional exam requirements/recommendations for international students: Required—TOEFL (minimum score 550 paper-based; 213 computer-based). Electronic applications accepted.

American International College, School of Arts, Education and Sciences, Department of Education, Springfield, MA 01109-3189. Offers early childhood education (M Ed, CAGS); educational leadership and supervision (Ed D); elementary education (M Ed, CAGS); middle/secondary education (M Ed, CAGS); moderate disabilities (M Ed, CAGS); reading (M Ed,

CAGS); school adjustment counseling (MA, CAGS); school administration (M Ed, CAGS); school guidance counseling (MA, CAGS); teaching (MA, MS); teaching and learning (Ed D). Part-time and evening/weekend programs available. Terminal master's awarded for partial completion of doctoral program. *Degree requirements:* For master's, comprehensive exam (for some programs), thesis (for some programs), practicum; for doctorate, comprehensive exam (for some programs), thesis/dissertation; for CAGS, practicum. *Entrance requirements:* For master's, minimum B- average in undergraduate course work; for doctorate, GRE General Test, interview. Additional exam requirements/recommendations for international students: Required—TOEFL. Electronic applications accepted. *Expenses:* Tuition: Full-time $12,510; part-time $695 per credit hour. Required fees: $35 per term.

American Jewish University, Graduate School, Fingerhut School of Education, Program in Education, Bel Air, CA 90077-1599. Offers MA Ed. *Degree requirements:* For master's, one foreign language. *Entrance requirements:* For master's, GRE General Test, interview, minimum GPA of 3.0. Additional exam requirements/recommendations for international students: Required—TOEFL. *Faculty research:* Philosophy of education, curriculum development, teacher training.

American Jewish University, Graduate School, Fingerhut School of Education, Program in Education for Working Professionals, Bel Air, CA 90077-1599. Offers MA Ed. *Degree requirements:* For master's, comprehensive exam, internships. *Entrance requirements:* For master's, GRE General Test, interview. Additional exam requirements/recommendations for international students: Required—TOEFL.

American University, College of Arts and Sciences, School of Education, Teaching, and Health, Washington, DC 20016-8030. Offers curriculum and instruction (M Ed, Certificate); early childhood education (MAT, Certificate); elementary education (MAT); English for speakers of other languages (MAT, Certificate); health promotion management (MS); international training and development (MAT); international training and education (MA); nutrition education (Certificate); secondary teaching (MAT, Certificate); special education (MA), including special education: learning disabilities; MAT/MA. *Accreditation:* NCATE. Part-time and evening/weekend programs available. *Faculty:* 15 full-time (9 women), 68 part-time/adjunct (45 women). *Students:* 74 full-time (56 women), 392 part-time (293 women); includes 110 minority (71 African Americans, 9 American Indian/Alaska Native, 11 Asian Americans or Pacific Islanders, 19 Hispanic Americans), 3 international. Average age 27. 354 applicants, 87% accepted, 218 enrolled. In 2009, 196 master's awarded. *Degree requirements:* For master's, comprehensive exam, thesis or alternative, PRAXIS II. *Entrance requirements:* For master's, GRE General Test, minimum GPA of 3.0; for Certificate, bachelor's degree. Additional exam requirements/recommendations for international students: Required—TOEFL. *Application deadline:* For fall admission, 2/1 priority date for domestic students; for spring admission, 10/1 priority date for domestic students. Applications are processed on a rolling basis. Application fee: $80. *Expenses:* Tuition: Full-time $22,266; part-time $1237 per credit hour. Required fees: $430. Tuition and fees vary according to program. *Financial support:* Fellowships, research assistantships with full and partial tuition reimbursements, teaching assistantships with full and partial tuition reimbursements, career-related internships or fieldwork, Federal Work-Study, and institutionally sponsored loans available. Support available to part-time students. Financial award application deadline: 2/1; financial award applicants required to submit FAFSA. *Faculty research:* Gender equity, socioeconomic technology, learning disabilities, gifted and talented education. *Unit head:* Dr. Sarah Irvine-Belson, Dean, 202-885-3714, Fax: 202-885-1187, E-mail: educate@american.edu. *Application contact:* Kathleen Clowery, Director, Graduate Admissions, 202-885-3621, Fax: 202-885-1505.

American University of Beirut, Graduate Programs, Faculty of Arts and Sciences, Beirut, Lebanon. Offers anthropology (MA); Arabic language and literature (MA); archaeology (MA); biology (MS); chemistry (MS); computer science (MS); economics (MA); education (MA); English language (MA); English literature (MA); environmental policy planning (MSES); financial economics (MAFE); geology (MS); history (MA); mathematics (MA, MS); Middle Eastern studies (MA); philosophy (MA); physics (MS); political studies (MA); psychology (MA); public administration (MA); sociology (MA); statistics (MA, MS). Part-time programs available. *Degree requirements:* For master's, one foreign language, comprehensive exam, thesis (for some programs). *Entrance requirements:* For master's, GRE, letter of recommendation. Additional exam requirements/recommendations for international students: Required—TOEFL (minimum score 600 paper-based; 250 computer-based; 100 iBT), IELTS (minimum score 7.5). *Faculty research:* String theory and supergravity; computer graphics; algebra and number theory; popular Arabic literature; marine and freshwater biology; integrating science, math and technology.

American University of Puerto Rico, Program in Education, Bayamón, PR 00960-2037. Offers art history (M Ed); elementary education (4-6) (M Ed); elementary education (k-3) (M Ed); general science education (M Ed); physical education (k-12) (M Ed); special education at secondary level (transition) (M Ed). *Faculty:* 1 full-time (0 women), 22 part-time/adjunct (6 women). *Students:* 121 full-time (98 women), 64 part-time (50 women); includes all Hispanic Americans. Average age 30. 250 applicants, 80% accepted, 185 enrolled. *Entrance requirements:* For master's, EXADEP or GRE or MAT, 2 letters of recommendation, minimum GPA of 2.5. *Application deadline:* For fall admission, 8/4 for domestic students; for winter admission, 10/18 for domestic students; for spring admission, 3/22 for domestic students. Applications are processed on a rolling basis. Application fee: $50. *Application contact:* Information Contact, E-mail: oficnaadmisiones@aupr.edu.

Anderson University, College of Education, Anderson, SC 29621-4035. Offers M Ed. *Accreditation:* NCATE.

Anderson University, School of Education, Anderson, IN 46012-3495. Offers M Ed. *Accreditation:* NCATE.

Andrews University, School of Graduate Studies, School of Education, Berrien Springs, MI 49104. Offers MA, MAT, MS, Ed D, PhD, Ed S. *Accreditation:* NCATE. Part-time programs available. *Faculty:* 22 full-time (8 women), 1 (woman) part-time/adjunct. *Students:* 77 full-time (50 women), 211 part-time (112 women); includes 104 minority (64 African Americans, 3 American Indian/Alaska Native, 7 Asian Americans or Pacific Islanders, 30 Hispanic Americans), 47 international. Average age 42. 157 applicants, 52% accepted, 47 enrolled. In 2009, 28 master's, 13 doctorates, 8 other advanced degrees awarded. Terminal master's awarded for partial completion of doctoral program. *Degree requirements:* For doctorate, thesis/dissertation. *Entrance requirements:* For master's, GRE Subject Test. Additional exam requirements/recommendations for international students: Required—TOEFL (minimum score 550 paper-based). *Application deadline:* Applications are processed on a rolling basis. Application fee: $40. *Financial support:* Fellowships, research assistantships, teaching assistantships, career-related internships or fieldwork, Federal Work-Study, institutionally sponsored loans, and tuition waivers (partial) available. Support available to part-time students. *Unit head:* Dr. James R. Jeffery, Dean, 269-471-3464. *Application contact:* Carolyn Hurst, Supervisor of Graduate Admission, 800-253-2874, Fax: 269-471-6321, E-mail: graduate@andrews.edu.

Angelo State University, College of Graduate Studies, College of Education, Department of Teacher Education, San Angelo, TX 76909. Offers educational diagnostics (M Ed); reading specialist (M Ed). *Faculty:* 17 full-time (12 women). *Students:* 5 full-time (all women), 17 part-time (all women); includes 4 minority (all Hispanic Americans). Average age 39. 9 applicants, 100% accepted, 9 enrolled. In 2009, 29 master's awarded. *Application deadline:* For fall admission, 7/15 priority date for domestic students, 6/10 for international students; for spring admission, 12/1 priority date for domestic students, 11/1 for international students. *Expenses:* Tuition, state resident: full-time $3396; part-time $142 per credit hour. Tuition, nonresident: full-time $10,152; part-time $423 per credit hour. Required fees: $1786; $36.25 per credit hour. $494 per semester. Full-time tuition and fees vary according to course load, degree level and program. *Unit head:* Dr. Linda Lucksinger, Department Head, 325-942-2052 Ext. 266, E-mail: linda.lucksinger@angelo.edu. *Application contact:* Theresa Fortin, Graduate Admissions Assistant, 325-942-2169, Fax: 325-942-2194, E-mail: theresa.fortin@angelo.edu.

Anna Maria College, Graduate Division, Program in Education, Paxton, MA 01612. Offers early childhood education (M Ed); education (CAGS); elementary education (M Ed); English language arts (M Ed); visual arts (M Ed). Part-time and evening/weekend programs available. *Entrance requirements:* For master's, bachelor's degree in liberal arts or sciences, minimum GPA of 3.0. Additional exam requirements/recommendations for international students: Required—TOEFL (minimum score 500 paper-based). Electronic applications accepted.

Antioch University Los Angeles, Graduate Programs, Program in Education, Culver City, CA 90230. Offers MA. Evening/weekend programs available. *Entrance requirements:* Additional exam requirements/recommendations for international students: Required—TOEFL.

Antioch University Midwest, Graduate Programs, Individualized Liberal and Professional Studies Program, Yellow Springs, OH 45387-1609. Offers liberal and professional studies (MA), including counseling, creative writing, education, film studies, liberal studies, management, modern literature, psychology, theatre, visual arts. Part-time and evening/weekend programs available. Postbaccalaureate distance learning degree programs offered (minimal on-campus study). *Faculty:* 1 full-time (0 women), 2 part-time/adjunct (1 woman). *Students:* 23 full-time (13 women), 41 part-time (30 women); includes 13 minority (11 African Americans, 2 Hispanic Americans). Average age 40. 21 applicants, 76% accepted, 15 enrolled. In 2009, 24 master's awarded. *Degree requirements:* For master's, thesis or alternative. *Entrance requirements:* For master's, resume, 2 letters of reference. *Application deadline:* For fall admission, 8/1 for domestic students; for winter admission, 12/1 for domestic students; for spring admission, 3/10 for domestic students. Applications are processed on a rolling basis. Application fee: $50. Electronic applications accepted. *Expenses:* Contact institution. *Financial support:* Federal Work-Study available. Financial award applicants required to submit FAFSA. *Unit head:* Dr. Jon Saari, Chair, 937-769-1879, Fax: 937-769-1807, E-mail: jsaari@antioch.edu. *Application contact:* Seth Gordon, Assistant Director of Admissions, 937-769-1800 Ext. 1825, Fax: 937-769-1804, E-mail: sgordon@antioch.edu.

Antioch University Midwest, Graduate Programs, School of Education, Yellow Springs, OH 45387-1609. Offers M Ed. *Accreditation:* NCATE. Part-time and evening/weekend programs available. *Faculty:* 12 full-time (8 women), 7 part-time/adjunct (4 women). *Students:* 282 full-time (187 women), 82 part-time (60 women); includes 110 minority (100 African Americans, 4 American Indian/Alaska Native, 3 Asian Americans or Pacific Islanders, 3 Hispanic Americans). Average age 31. 228 applicants, 86% accepted, 183 enrolled. In 2009, 137 master's awarded. *Degree requirements:* For master's, thesis or alternative. *Entrance requirements:* For master's, resume, 2 letters of reference. *Application deadline:* For fall admission, 9/7 for domestic students; for winter admission, 12/10 for domestic students; for spring admission, 3/8 for domestic students. Applications are processed on a rolling basis. Application fee: $50. Electronic applications accepted. *Expenses:* Contact institution. *Financial support:* Federal Work-Study available. Financial award applicants required to submit FAFSA. *Unit head:* Dr. Zak Shariff, Director, 937-769-1880, Fax: 937-769-1805, E-mail: zsharif@antioch.edu. *Application contact:* Oscar Robinson, Director of Admissions, 937-769-1823, Fax: 937-769-1804, E-mail: orobinson@antioch.edu.

Antioch University New England, Graduate School, Department of Education, Keene, NH 03431-3552. Offers experienced educators (M Ed); integrated learning (M Ed), including early childhood education, elementary education; Waldorf teacher training (M Ed). *Degree requirements:* For master's, thesis (for some programs), internship. *Entrance requirements:* Additional exam requirements/recommendations for international students: Required—TOEFL (minimum score 600 paper-based; 250 computer-based). *Expenses:* Contact institution. *Faculty research:* Classroom and school restructuring, problem-based learning, Waldorf collaborative leadership, ecological literacy.

Antioch University Santa Barbara, Program in Education/Teacher Credentialing, Santa Barbara, CA 93101-1581. Offers MA. Part-time programs available. *Entrance requirements:* Additional exam requirements/recommendations for international students: Required—TOEFL (minimum score 550 paper-based; 213 computer-based). Electronic applications accepted.

Antioch University Seattle, Graduate Programs, Program in Education, Seattle, WA 98121-1814. Offers MA. Part-time and evening/weekend programs available. *Expenses:* Contact institution. *Faculty research:* Transformative learning, intercultural studies, gay and lesbian studies.

Aquinas College, School of Education, Grand Rapids, MI 49506-1799. Offers MAT, ME, MS. Part-time and evening/weekend programs available. *Faculty:* 16 full-time (12 women), 16 part-time/adjunct (13 women). *Students:* 27 full-time (23 women), 156 part-time (125 women); includes 12 minority (3 African Americans, 1 American Indian/Alaska Native, 8 Hispanic Americans). Average age 36. In 2009, 101 master's awarded. *Degree requirements:* For master's, teaching project. *Entrance requirements:* For master's, Michigan Basic Skills Test, minimum undergraduate GPA of 3.0, teaching certificate. Additional exam requirements/recommendations for international students: Required—TOEFL (minimum score 550 paper-based; 213 computer-based). *Application deadline:* Applications are processed on a rolling basis. Application fee: $0. *Expenses:* Contact institution. *Financial support:* In 2009–10, 141 students received support. Scholarships/grants available. Support available to part-time students. Financial award application deadline: 3/15; financial award applicants required to submit FAFSA. *Unit head:* Nanette Clatterbuck, Dean, 616-632-2973, Fax: 616-732-4465, E-mail: clattnan@aquinas.edu. *Application contact:* Michele Polega, Coordinator of Graduate Education Programs, 616-632-2440, E-mail: pciegmic@aquinas.edu.

Arcadia University, Graduate Studies, Department of Education, Glenside, PA 19038-3295. Offers art education (M Ed, MA Ed); biology education (MA Ed); chemistry education (MA Ed); child development (CAS); computer education (M Ed, CAS); computer education 7–12 (MA Ed); early childhood education (M Ed, CAS), including individualized (M Ed), master teacher (M Ed), research in child development (M Ed); educational leadership (M Ed, CAS); educational psychology (CAS); elementary education (M Ed, CAS); English education (MA Ed); environmental education (MA Ed, CAS); history education (MA Ed); language arts (M Ed, CAS); mathematics education (M Ed, MA Ed, CAS); music education (MA Ed); psychology (MA Ed); pupil personnel services (CAS); reading (M Ed, CAS); school library science (M Ed); science education (M Ed, CAS); secondary education (M Ed, CAS); special education (M Ed, Ed D, CAS); theater arts (MA Ed); written communication (MA Ed). *Accreditation:* NASAD. Part-time and evening/weekend programs available. Postbaccalaureate distance learning degree programs offered (minimal on-campus study). *Faculty:* 12 full-time (8 women), 38 part-time/adjunct (26 women). *Students:* 89 full-time (74 women), 622 part-time (487 women); includes 112 minority (94 African Americans, 9 Asian Americans or Pacific Islanders, 9 Hispanic Americans), 2 international. Average age 32. In 2009, 257 master's, 4 doctorates awarded. *Application deadline:* Applications are processed on a rolling basis. Application fee: $40. Electronic applications accepted. *Expenses:* Tuition: Full-time $30,450; part-time $620 per credit hour. Required fees: $165. Tuition and fees vary according to program. *Financial support:* Career-related internships or fieldwork, tuition waivers (partial), and unspecified assistantships available. *Unit head:* Dr. Steven P. Gulkus. *Application contact:* 215-572-2925, Fax: 215-572-2126, E-mail: grad@arcadia.edu.

Argosy University, Atlanta, College of Education, Atlanta, GA 30328. Offers educational leadership (MAEd, Ed D, Ed S), including higher education administration (Ed D), K-12 education (Ed D); teaching and learning (MAEd, Ed D, Ed S), including education technology (Ed D), higher education (Ed D), K-12 education (Ed D).

See Close-Up on page 887.

Argosy University, Chicago, College of Education, Chicago, IL 60601. Offers adult education and training (MA Ed); community college executive leadership (Ed D); educational leadership (MA Ed, Ed D, Ed S), including district leadership (Ed D), higher education administration (Ed D), K-12 education (Ed D); instructional leadership (Ed D, Ed S), including higher education (Ed D), K-12 education (Ed D). Postbaccalaureate distance learning degree programs offered (minimal on-campus study).

See Close-Up on page 675.

Education—General

Argosy University, Dallas, College of Education, Farmers Branch, TX 75244. Offers educational administration (MA Ed); educational leadership (Ed D); higher and postsecondary education (MA Ed); instructional leadership (MA Ed); school psychology (MA).

See Close-Up on page 677.

Argosy University, Denver, College of Education, Denver, CO 80231. Offers community college executive leadership (Ed D); educational leadership (MA Ed, Ed D), including higher education (Ed D), K-12 education (Ed D); instructional leadership (MA Ed, Ed D), including higher education administration (Ed D), K-12 education (Ed D).

See Close-Up on page 679.

Argosy University, Hawai'i, College of Education, Honolulu, HI 96813. Offers adult education and training (MAEd); educational leadership (Ed D), including higher education administration, K-12 education; instructional leadership (Ed D), including higher education, K-12 education; school psychology (MA).

See Close-Up on page 681.

Argosy University, Inland Empire, College of Education, San Bernardino, CA 92408. Offers community college executive leadership (Ed D); educational leadership (MA Ed, Ed D), including higher education administration (Ed D), K-12 education (Ed D); instructional leadership (MA Ed, Ed D), including higher education (Ed D), K-12 education (Ed D), multiple subject teacher preparation (MA Ed), single subject teacher preparation (MA Ed).

See Close-Up on page 889.

Argosy University, Los Angeles, College of Education, Santa Monica, CA 90045. Offers community college executive leadership (Ed D); educational leadership (MA Ed, Ed D), including higher education administration (Ed D), K-12 education (Ed D); instructional leadership (MA Ed, Ed D), including higher education (Ed D), K-12 education (Ed D), multiple subject teacher preparation (MA Ed), single subject teacher preparation (MA Ed).

See Close-Up on page 683.

Argosy University, Nashville, College of Education, Nashville, TN 37214. Offers MA Ed, Ed D, Ed S.

See Close-Up on page 891.

Argosy University, Orange County, College of Education, Orange, CA 92868. Offers community college executive leadership (Ed D); educational leadership (MA Ed, Ed D), including higher education administration (Ed D), K-12 education (Ed D); instructional leadership (MA Ed, Ed D), including education technology (Ed D), higher education (Ed D), K-12 education (Ed D), multiple subject teacher preparation (MA Ed), single subject teacher preparation (MA Ed).

See Close-Up on page 685.

Argosy University, Phoenix, College of Education, Phoenix, AZ 85021. Offers adult education and training (MA Ed); advanced educational administration (Ed D, Ed S); community college executive leadership (Ed D); educational administration (MA Ed); educational leadership (MA Ed, Ed D, Ed S), including education technology (Ed D), higher education administration (Ed D), K-12 education (Ed D); higher and postsecondary education (MA Ed); initial educational administration (Ed D, Ed S); school psychology (MA); teaching and learning (MA Ed, Ed D, Ed S), including education technology (Ed D), higher education (Ed D), K-12 education (Ed D).

See Close-Up on page 687.

Argosy University, Salt Lake City, College of Education, Draper, UT 84020. Offers educational leadership (MA Ed, Ed D).

See Close-Up on page 689.

Argosy University, San Diego, College of Education, San Diego, CA 92108. Offers community college executive leadership (Ed D); educational leadership (MA Ed, Ed D), including higher education administration (Ed D), K-12 education (Ed D); instructional leadership (MA Ed, Ed D), including higher education (Ed D), K-12 education (Ed D).

See Close-Up on page 691.

Argosy University, San Francisco Bay Area, College of Education, Alameda, CA 94501. Offers community college executive leadership (Ed D); educational leadership (MA Ed, Ed D), including education technology (Ed D), higher education administration (Ed D), K-12 education (Ed D); instructional leadership (MA Ed, Ed D), including education technology (Ed D), higher education (Ed D), K-12 education (Ed D), multiple subject teacher preparation (MA Ed), single subject teacher preparation (MA Ed).

See Close-Up on page 693.

Argosy University, Sarasota, College of Education, Sarasota, FL 34235. Offers community college executive leadership (Ed D); educational leadership (MA Ed, Ed D, Ed S), including higher education administration (Ed D), K-12 education (Ed D); school counseling (MA, Ed S); school psychology (MA); teaching and learning (MA Ed, Ed D, Ed S), including education technology (Ed D), higher education (Ed D), K-12 education (Ed D).

See Close-Up on page 695.

Argosy University, Schaumburg, College of Education, Schaumburg, IL 60173-5403. Offers community college executive leadership (Ed D); educational leadership (MA Ed, Ed D, Ed S), including district leadership (Ed D), higher education administration (Ed D), K-12 education (Ed D); instructional leadership (Ed D, Ed S), including higher education (Ed D), K-12 education (Ed D).

See Close-Up on page 697.

Argosy University, Seattle, College of Education, Seattle, WA 98121. Offers adult education and training (MA Ed); community college executive leadership (Ed D); educational leadership (MA Ed, Ed D), including higher education administration (Ed D), K-12 education (Ed D); higher and postsecondary education (MA Ed); instructional leadership (MA Ed, Ed D), including education technology (Ed D), higher education (Ed D), K-12 education (Ed D).

See Close-Up on page 699.

Argosy University, Tampa, College of Education, Tampa, FL 33607. Offers community college executive leadership (Ed D); educational leadership (MA Ed, Ed D, Ed S), including higher education administration (Ed D), K-12 education (Ed D); school counseling (MA); teaching and learning (MA Ed, Ed D, Ed S), including higher education (Ed D), K-12 education (Ed D).

See Close-Up on page 701.

Argosy University, Twin Cities, College of Education, Eagan, MN 55121. Offers advanced educational administration (Ed D, Ed S); educational leadership (MA Ed, Ed D, Ed S), including higher education administration (Ed D), K-12 education (Ed D); higher and postsecondary education (MA Ed); initial educational administration (Ed D, Ed S); instructional leadership (MA Ed, Ed D, Ed S), including education technology (Ed D), higher education (Ed D), K-12 education (Ed D).

See Close-Up on page 703.

Argosy University, Washington DC, College of Education, Arlington, VA 22209. Offers community college executive leadership (Ed D); educational leadership (MA Ed, Ed D, Ed S), including higher education administration (Ed D), K-12 education (Ed D); instructional leadership (MA Ed, Ed D, Ed S), including higher education (Ed D), K-12 education (Ed D).

See Close-Up on page 705.

Arizona State University, Graduate College, College of Teacher Education and Leadership, Tempe, AZ 85287. Offers educational administration and supervision (M Ed); elementary education (M Ed, Certificate); leadership/innovation (administration) (Ed D); leadership/innovation (teaching) (Ed D); physical education (MPE); secondary education (M Ed, Certificate); special education (M Ed). Part-time and evening/weekend programs available. *Degree requirements:* For master's, applied project or comprehensive exam; for doctorate, comprehensive exam, thesis/dissertation. *Entrance requirements:* For master's, 3 letters of recommendation, minimum undergraduate GPA of 3.0, resume; for doctorate, master's degree in education or related field, 3 professional references, resumé, graduate GPA of 3.0, 3 letters of recommendation. Additional exam requirements/recommendations for international students: Required—TOEFL (minimum score 550 paper-based; 213 computer-based; 83 iBT), IELTS (minimum score 6.5). Electronic applications accepted. *Expenses:* Contact institution. *Faculty research:* Self-regulated learning in students, collaboration and consultation skills for educators, school reform and restructuring, hands-on science and mathematics programs, educational technology.

Arizona State University, Graduate College, Mary Lou Fulton College of Education, Tempe, AZ 85287. Offers M Ed, MA, MC, Ed D, PhD. Part-time programs available. *Degree requirements:* For doctorate, thesis/dissertation. *Entrance requirements:* For master's and doctorate, GRE General Test or MAT.

Arkansas State University—Jonesboro, Graduate School, College of Education, Jonesboro, State University, AR 72467. Offers MRC, MS, MSE, Ed D, Certificate, Ed S, SCCT. *Accreditation:* NCATE. Part-time programs available. Postbaccalaureate distance learning degree programs offered (no on-campus study). *Faculty:* 37 full-time (17 women), 29 part-time/adjunct (16 women). *Students:* 84 full-time (65 women), 935 part-time (778 women); includes 186 minority (168 African Americans, 6 American Indian/Alaska Native, 4 Asian Americans or Pacific Islanders, 8 Hispanic Americans), 11 international. Average age 36. 1,033 applicants, 70% accepted, 321 enrolled. In 2009, 138 master's, 6 doctorates, 26 other advanced degrees awarded. *Degree requirements:* For master's and other advanced degree, comprehensive exam, thesis or alternative; for doctorate, comprehensive exam, thesis/dissertation. *Entrance requirements:* For master's, GRE General Test or MAT, appropriate bachelor's degree, interview, letters of reference; for doctorate, GRE General Test or MAT, interview, master's degree, letters of reference, official transcript, personal statement, immunization records, writing sample; for other advanced degree, GRE General Test, MAT, interview, master's degree, letters of reference, official transcript, 3 years teaching experience, mentor, teaching license, immunization records. Additional exam requirements/recommendations for international students: Required—TOEFL (minimum score 550 paper-based; 213 computer-based; 79 iBT), IELTS (minimum score 6). *Application deadline:* Applications are processed on a rolling basis. Application fee: $50. Electronic applications accepted. *Expenses:* Tuition, state resident: full-time $3744; part-time $208 per credit hour. Tuition, nonresident: full-time $9540; part-time $530 per credit hour. Required fees: $896; $47 per credit hour. $25 per term. One-time fee: $50. Tuition and fees vary according to course load and program. *Financial support:* In 2009–10, 69 students received support; fellowships, teaching assistantships, career-related internships or fieldwork, scholarships/grants, and unspecified assistantships available. Financial award application deadline: 7/1; financial award applicants required to submit FAFSA. *Unit head:* Dr. Don Maness, Dean, 870-972-3057, Fax: 870-972-3828, E-mail: dmaness@astate.edu. *Application contact:* Dr. Andrew Sustich, Dean of the Graduate School, 870-972-3029, Fax: 870-972-3857, E-mail: sustich@astate.edu.

Arkansas Tech University, Graduate College, College of Arts and Humanities, Russellville, AR 72801. Offers communication (MLA); English (M Ed, MA); fine arts (MLA); history (MA); multi-media journalism (MA); psychology (MS); social science (MLA); Spanish (MA, MLA); teaching English as a second language (MA, MLA). Part-time programs available. *Students:* 39 full-time (30 women), 80 part-time (63 women); includes 11 minority (3 African Americans, 1 American Indian/Alaska Native, 1 Asian American or Pacific Islander, 6 Hispanic Americans), 23 international. Average age 33. In 2009, 70 master's awarded. *Degree requirements:* For master's, comprehensive exam (for some programs), thesis (for some programs), project. *Entrance requirements:* For master's, GRE General Test or MAT. Additional exam requirements/recommendations for international students: Required—TOEFL (minimum score 550 paper-based; 213 computer-based; 79 iBT), IELTS (minimum score 6). *Application deadline:* For fall admission, 3/1 priority date for domestic students, 5/1 priority date for international students; for spring admission, 10/1 priority date for domestic and international students. Applications are processed on a rolling basis. Application fee: $0 ($50 for international students). Electronic applications accepted. *Expenses:* Tuition, state resident: full-time $3438; part-time $191 per hour. Tuition, nonresident: full-time $6876; part-time $382 per hour. Required fees: $482; $9 per credit hour. $140 per semester. Tuition and fees vary according to course load. *Financial support:* In 2009–10, teaching assistantships with full tuition reimbursements (averaging $4,000 per year); research assistantships, career-related internships or fieldwork, Federal Work-Study, scholarships/grants, health care benefits, and unspecified assistantships also available. Support available to part-time students. Financial award application deadline: 4/15; financial award applicants required to submit FAFSA. *Unit head:* Dr. Micheal Tarver, Dean, 479-968-0274, Fax: 479-964-0812, E-mail: mtarver@atu.edu. *Application contact:* Dr. Mary B. Gunter, Dean of Graduate College, 479-968-0398, Fax: 479-964-0542, E-mail: graduate.school@atu.edu.

Arkansas Tech University, Graduate College, College of Education, Russellville, AR 72801. Offers college student personnel (MS); educational leadership (M Ed, Ed S); English education (M Ed); instructional improvement (M Ed); secondary education (M Ed); teaching, learning and leadership (M Ed). *Accreditation:* NCATE. Part-time and evening/weekend programs available. Postbaccalaureate distance learning degree programs offered (no on-campus study). *Students:* 39 full-time (26 women), 246 part-time (179 women); includes 27 minority (18 African Americans, 4 American Indian/Alaska Native, 5 Hispanic Americans), 4 international. Average age 33. In 2009, 92 master's, 11 other advanced degrees awarded. *Degree requirements:* For master's, comprehensive exam, thesis optional, action research project. *Entrance requirements:* For master's, GRE General Test or MAT. Additional exam requirements/recommendations for international students: Required—TOEFL (minimum score 550 paper-based; 213 computer-based; 79 iBT), IELTS (minimum score 6). *Application deadline:* For fall admission, 3/1 priority date for domestic students, 5/1 priority date for international students; for spring admission, 10/1 priority date for domestic and international students. Applications are processed on a rolling basis. Application fee: $0 ($50 for international students). Electronic applications accepted. *Expenses:* Tuition, state resident: full-time $3438; part-time $191 per hour. Tuition, nonresident: full-time $6876; part-time $382 per hour. Required fees: $482; $9 per credit hour. $140 per semester. Tuition and fees vary according to course load. *Financial support:* In 2009–10, teaching assistantships with full tuition reimbursements (averaging $4,000 per year); research assistantships, career-related internships or fieldwork, Federal Work-Study, scholarships/grants, health care benefits, and unspecified assistantships also available. Support available to part-time students. Financial award application deadline: 4/15; financial award applicants required to submit FAFSA. *Unit head:* Dr. Eldon G. Clary, Dean, 479-968-0350, Fax: 479-968-0350, E-mail: eclary@atu.edu. *Application contact:* Dr. Mary B. Gunter, Dean of Graduate College, 479-968-0398, Fax: 479-964-0542, E-mail: graduate.school@atu.edu.

Armstrong Atlantic State University, School of Graduate Studies, Program in Education, Savannah, GA 31419-1997. Offers adult education (M Ed); curriculum and instruction (M Ed); early childhood education (M Ed); education (M Ed); elementary education (M Ed); middle grades education (M Ed); secondary education (M Ed), including business education, English education, mathematics education, science education, social science education; special education (M Ed), including behavioral disorders, learning disabilities, speech-language pathology. *Accreditation:* NCATE. Part-time and evening/weekend programs available. Postbaccalaureate distance learning degree programs offered (minimal on-campus study). *Degree requirements:* For master's, comprehensive exam, portfolio. *Entrance requirements:* For master's, GRE General Test or MAT, minimum GPA of 2.5, letters of recommendation. Additional exam requirements/recommendations for international students: Required—TOEFL (minimum score 523 paper-based; 193 computer-based). Electronic applications accepted.

Ashland University, Dwight Schar College of Education, Ashland, OH 44805-3702. Offers M Ed, Ed D. *Accreditation:* NCATE. Part-time and evening/weekend programs available. *Faculty:* 53 full-time (36 women), 176 part-time/adjunct (98 women). *Students:* 377 full-time (281 women), 856 part-time (637 women); includes 91 minority (69 African Americans, 3 American Indian/Alaska Native, 4 Asian Americans or Pacific Islanders, 15 Hispanic Americans), 15 international. Average age 33. 467 applicants, 98% accepted, 428 enrolled. In 2009, 603

master's, 16 doctorates awarded. *Degree requirements:* For master's, thesis optional, capstone project; for doctorate, comprehensive exam, thesis/dissertation. *Entrance requirements:* For master's, GRE General Test or MAT, teaching certificate, minimum GPA of 2.75; for doctorate, GRE, master's degree, minimum GPA of 3.3, writing sample, letters of recommendation. Additional exam requirements/recommendations for international students: Required—TOEFL. *Application deadline:* For fall admission, 8/27 for domestic students; for spring admission, 1/14 for domestic students. Applications are processed on a rolling basis. Application fee: $30. *Financial support:* In 2009–10, 474 students received support; teaching assistantships with partial tuition reimbursements available, scholarships/grants available. Financial award application deadline: 4/15. *Faculty research:* Teacher performance, administrative performance, collaborative learning groups, talent development, environmental education. Total annual research expenditures: $180,000. *Unit head:* Dr. James P. Van Keuren, Dean, 419-289-5377, E-mail: jvankeu1@ashland.edu. *Application contact:* Dr. Linda Billman, Director and Chair, Graduate Studies in Education/Associate Dean, 419-289-5369, Fax: 419-289-5331, E-mail: lbillman@ashland.edu.

Athabasca University, Centre for Distance Education, Athabasca, AB T9S 3A3, Canada. Offers distance education (MDE); distance education technology (Advanced Diploma). Part-time programs available. Postbaccalaureate distance learning degree programs offered (no on-campus study). *Faculty:* 11 full-time (4 women), 1 (woman) part-time/adjunct. *Students:* 311 part-time. Average age 36. 135 applicants, 14 enrolled. In 2009, 46 master's, 10 other advanced degrees awarded. *Degree requirements:* For master's, thesis optional. *Entrance requirements:* For master's, 3 or 4 year baccalaureate degree. *Application deadline:* For fall admission, 3/1 for domestic and international students. Application fee: $80. Electronic applications accepted. *Expenses:* Contact institution. *Faculty research:* Role development, interaction, educational technology, and communities of practice in distance education; instructional design. *Unit head:* Dr. Mohamed Ally, Director, 866-916-8650, E-mail: mohameda@athabascau.ca. *Application contact:* Centre for Distance Education, 800-788-9041 Ext. 6179, Fax: 780-675-6170, E-mail: mde@athabascau.ca.

Athabasca University, Centre for Integrated Studies, Athabasca, AB T9S 3A3, Canada. Offers adult education (MA); community studies (MA); cultural studies (MA); educational studies (MA); global change (MA); work, organization, and leadership (MA). Part-time and evening/weekend programs available. Postbaccalaureate distance learning degree programs offered (no on-campus study). *Faculty:* 10 full-time (4 women), 12 part-time/adjunct (9 women). *Students:* 705 part-time. Average age 35. 195 applicants, 38 enrolled. In 2009, 52 master's awarded. *Degree requirements:* For master's, project. *Entrance requirements:* Additional exam requirements/recommendations for international students: Required—TOEFL (minimum score 560 paper-based; 220 computer-based). *Application deadline:* For fall admission, 3/1 for domestic and international students; for winter admission, 9/1 for domestic and international students. Application fee: $80. Electronic applications accepted. *Expenses:* Tuition: Part-time $16,500 per degree program. Required fees: $200 per year. One-time fee: $80 part-time. *Faculty research:* Women's history, literature and culture studies, sustainable development, labor and education. *Unit head:* Dr. Michael Gismondi, Program Director, 780-675-6218, Fax: 780-675-6921, E-mail: mikeg@athabascau.ca. *Application contact:* Derek Stovin, Program Administrator, 780-675-6236, Fax: 780-675-6921, E-mail: dereks@athabascau.ca.

Atlantic Union College, Graduate Education Program, South Lancaster, MA 01561-1000. Offers M Ed. Offered during summer only. Part-time programs available. Postbaccalaureate distance learning degree programs offered (minimal on-campus study). *Degree requirements:* For master's, thesis. *Entrance requirements:* For master's, GRE, minimum GPA of 3.0.

Auburn University, Graduate School, College of Education, Auburn University, AL 36849. Offers M Ed, MS, Ed D, PhD, Ed S. *Accreditation:* NCATE. Part-time programs available. *Faculty:* 85 full-time (52 women), 23 part-time/adjunct (15 women). *Students:* 363 full-time (258 women), 476 part-time (328 women); includes 203 minority (177 African Americans, 2 American Indian/Alaska Native, 9 Asian Americans or Pacific Islanders, 15 Hispanic Americans), 26 international. Average age 33. 699 applicants, 61% accepted, 303 enrolled. In 2009, 207 master's, 50 doctorates, 8 other advanced degrees awarded. *Degree requirements:* For master's, thesis (for some programs); for doctorate, thesis/dissertation. *Entrance requirements:* For master's, doctorate, and Ed S, GRE General Test. Application fee: $50 ($60 for international students). Electronic applications accepted. *Expenses:* Tuition, state resident: full-time $6240. Tuition, nonresident: full-time $18,720. International tuition: $18,938 full-time. Required fees: $492. Tuition and fees vary according to course load, program and reciprocity agreements. *Financial support:* Fellowships, research assistantships, teaching assistantships, career-related internships or fieldwork and Federal Work-Study available. Support available to part-time students. Financial award application deadline: 3/15; financial award applicants required to submit FAFSA. *Faculty research:* Dropout phenomena, high school students and substance use and abuse. *Unit head:* Dr. Frances Kochan, Dean, 334-844-4446. *Application contact:* Dr. George Flowers, Dean of the Graduate School, 334-844-2125.

Auburn University Montgomery, School of Education, Montgomery, AL 36124-4023. Offers M Ed, Ed S. *Accreditation:* NCATE. Part-time and evening/weekend programs available. *Faculty:* 25 full-time (19 women), 5 part-time/adjunct (3 women). *Students:* 144 full-time (124 women), 233 part-time (187 women); includes 167 minority (161 African Americans, 2 American Indian/Alaska Native, 2 Asian Americans or Pacific Islanders, 2 Hispanic Americans), 3 international. Average age 33. In 2009, 90 master's awarded. *Degree requirements:* For master's and Ed S, comprehensive exam. *Entrance requirements:* For master's, GRE General Test or MAT, BS in teaching, certification; for Ed S, GRE General Test or MAT, certification. *Application deadline:* Applications are processed on a rolling basis. Electronic applications accepted. *Expenses:* Tuition, state resident: full-time $2841; part-time $225 per credit hour. Tuition, nonresident: full-time $8241; part-time $675 per credit hour. Required fees: $282; $8 per hour. $45 per term. *Financial support:* In 2009–10, 2 teaching assistantships were awarded; career-related internships or fieldwork and scholarships/grants also available. Support available to part-time students. Financial award application deadline: 3/1; financial award applicants required to submit FAFSA. *Unit head:* Dr. Jennifer A. Brown, Dean, 334-244-3413, Fax: 334-244-3835, E-mail: jbrown@mail.aum.edu. *Application contact:* Dr. Sam Flynt, Associate Graduate Coordinator, 334-244-3270, Fax: 334-244-3835, E-mail: sflynt@mail.aum.edu.

Augsburg College, Program in Education, Minneapolis, MN 55454-1351. Offers MAE. *Accreditation:* NCATE. Part-time and evening/weekend programs available. *Degree requirements:* For master's, comprehensive exam, final project. *Entrance requirements:* For master's, minimum GPA of 3.0. Additional exam requirements/recommendations for international students: Required—TOEFL (minimum score 600 paper-based; 250 computer-based). Electronic applications accepted. *Expenses:* Tuition: Full-time $16,713; part-time $1857 per course. Required fees: $450; $50 per course. Tuition and fees vary according to course load and program.

Augusta State University, Graduate Studies, College of Education, Augusta, GA 30904-2200. Offers M Ed, MAT, Ed S. *Accreditation:* NCATE. Part-time and evening/weekend programs available. *Entrance requirements:* For master's, GRE, MAT, minimum GPA of 2.5.

Aurora University, College of Education, Aurora, IL 60506-4892. Offers curriculum and instruction (Ed D); education (MAT); education and administration (Ed D); educational leadership (MEL); reading instruction (MA). *Accreditation:* NCATE. Part-time and evening/weekend programs available. *Degree requirements:* For doctorate, thesis/dissertation. *Entrance requirements:* For master's, 2 years of teaching experience, valid teaching certificate. Additional exam requirements/recommendations for international students: Required—TOEFL (minimum score 550 paper-based; 213 computer-based). Electronic applications accepted. *Expenses:* Contact institution.

Austin College, Program in Education, Sherman, TX 75090-4400. Offers art education (MA); elementary education (MA); middle school education (MA); music education (MA); physical education and coaching (MA); secondary education (MA); theatre education (MA). Part-time programs available. *Faculty:* 5 full-time (3 women), 1 (woman) part-time/adjunct. *Students:* 29 full-time (21 women); includes 3 minority (1 Asian American or Pacific Islander, 2 Hispanic

Americans). Average age 23. In 2009, 23 master's awarded. *Degree requirements:* For master's, one foreign language, thesis or alternative. *Entrance requirements:* For master's, Texas Academic Skills Program Test. *Application deadline:* For fall admission, 5/1 priority date for domestic students; for spring admission, 1/15 priority date for domestic students. Applications are processed on a rolling basis. Application fee: $35. Electronic applications accepted. *Expenses:* Tuition: Full-time $31,575. Required fees: $160. *Financial support:* Career-related internships or fieldwork, Federal Work-Study, scholarships/grants, and unspecified assistantships available. Support available to part-time students. Financial award application deadline: 4/1; financial award applicants required to submit FAFSA. *Unit head:* Dr. Barbara Sylvester, Director of Teaching Program, 903-813-2327, Fax: 903-813-2326, E-mail: bsylvester@austincollege.edu. *Application contact:* Dr. Barbara Sylvester, Director of Teaching Program, 903-813-2327, Fax: 903-813-2326, E-mail: bsylvester@austincollege.edu.

Austin Peay State University, College of Graduate Studies, College of Education, Clarksville, TN 37044. Offers MA Ed, MAT, Ed S. *Accreditation:* NCATE. Part-time and evening/weekend programs available. Postbaccalaureate distance learning degree programs offered. *Faculty:* 16 full-time (11 women), 7 part-time/adjunct (6 women). *Students:* 108 full-time (85 women), 180 part-time (143 women); includes 42 minority (24 African Americans, 1 American Indian/Alaska Native, 2 Asian Americans or Pacific Islanders, 15 Hispanic Americans), 1 international. Average age 34. 203 applicants, 96% accepted, 120 enrolled. In 2009, 108 master's, 4 other advanced degrees awarded. *Degree requirements:* For master's, comprehensive exam, thesis optional. *Entrance requirements:* For master's, GRE General Test, 3 letters of recommendation, minimum undergraduate GPA of 2.75; for Ed S, GRE General Test, master's degree, minimum graduate GPA of 3.0, 3 letters of recommendation. Additional exam requirements/recommendations for international students: Required—TOEFL (minimum score 500 paper-based; 173 computer-based). *Application deadline:* For fall admission, 7/27 priority date for domestic students; for spring admission, 12/17 priority date for domestic students. Applications are processed on a rolling basis. Application fee: $25. Electronic applications accepted. *Expenses:* Tuition, state resident: full-time $6160; part-time $608 per credit hour. Tuition, nonresident: full-time $17,080; part-time $854 per credit hour. Required fees: $1224; $61.20 per credit hour. *Financial support:* In 2009–10, 8 students received support, including 8 research assistantships with full tuition reimbursements available (averaging $5,184 per year); career-related internships or fieldwork, Federal Work-Study, institutionally sponsored loans, scholarships/grants, and unspecified assistantships also available. Support available to part-time students. Financial award application deadline: 3/1; financial award applicants required to submit FAFSA. *Unit head:* Dr. Carlette Hardin, Interim Director, 931-221-7696, Fax: 931-221-1292, E-mail: forbusl@apsu.edu. *Application contact:* Dr. Dixie Dennis, Dean, College of Graduate Studies, 931-221-7662, Fax: 931-221-7641, E-mail: dennisdi@apsu.edu.

Averett University, Master in Education Program, Danville, VA 24541-3692. Offers art education (M Ed); biology (M Ed); biology education (M Ed); chemistry (M Ed); chemistry education (M Ed); curriculum and instruction (M Ed); elementary education (M Ed); English (M Ed); English education (M Ed); health and physical education (M Ed); history and social studies education (M Ed); math (M Ed); mathematics education (M Ed); physical science (M Ed); reading specialization (M Ed); special education (learning disabilities specialization PK-12) (M Ed). Program also offered at Richmond, VA regional campus location. Part-time and evening/weekend programs available. *Faculty:* 4 full-time (3 women), 36 part-time/adjunct (22 women). *Students:* 182 full-time (160 women), 110 part-time (94 women); includes 113 minority (94 African Americans, 1 American Indian/Alaska Native, 7 Asian Americans or Pacific Islanders, 11 Hispanic Americans). Average age 37. 119 applicants, 99% accepted, 98 enrolled. In 2009, 92 master's awarded. *Degree requirements:* For master's, comprehensive exam, thesis optional. *Entrance requirements:* For master's, PRAXIS, GRE General Test, MAT or NTE, writing proficiency exam, 3 letters of recommendation, current teacher's licensure or eligibility for licensure, minimum undergraduate GPA of 3.0 in previous 2 years. Additional exam requirements/recommendations for international students: Required—TOEFL (minimum score 600 paper-based; 200 computer-based). *Application deadline:* Applications are processed on a rolling basis. *Expenses:* Contact institution. *Financial support:* Career-related internships or fieldwork, Federal Work-Study, and scholarships/grants available. Financial award application deadline: 4/1; financial award applicants required to submit FAFSA. *Faculty research:* Literary assessment-PreK-6, handwriting instruction and assessment-PreK-6, written language instruction and assessment-PreK-6 and special needs students learning styles, curriculum and instruction processes. *Unit head:* Dr. Lynn H. Wolf, Chair/Associate Professor/Director, 434-793-3995, Fax: 434-791-4392, E-mail: lynn.wolf@averett.edu. *Application contact:* Dr. Lynn H. Wolf, Chair/Associate Professor/Director, 434-793-3995, Fax: 434-791-4392, E-mail: lynn.wolf@averett.edu.

Avila University, School of Education, Kansas City, MO 64145-1698. Offers education (MA); English for speakers of other languages (Advanced Certificate). Part-time and evening/weekend programs available. *Faculty:* 6 full-time (4 women), 12 part-time/adjunct (9 women). *Students:* 195 full-time (148 women), 52 part-time (40 women); includes 27 minority (19 African Americans, 3 American Indian/Alaska Native, 1 Asian American or Pacific Islander, 4 Hispanic Americans). Average age 34. 289 applicants, 74% accepted, 154 enrolled. In 2009, 52 master's awarded. *Entrance requirements:* For master's, minimum GPA of 3.0, writing sample, recommendation, interview; for Advanced Certificate, foreign language. Additional exam requirements/recommendations for international students: Required—TOEFL (minimum score 580 paper-based; 237 computer-based; 92 iBT). *Application deadline:* Applications are processed on a rolling basis. Application fee: $0. Electronic applications accepted. *Expenses:* Contact institution. *Financial support:* In 2009–10, 64 students received support, including 1 research assistantship; career-related internships or fieldwork also available. Support available to part-time students. Financial award applicants required to submit FAFSA. *Unit head:* Deana Angotti, Director of Graduate Education, 816-501-2446, Fax: 816-501-2915, E-mail: deana.augotti@avila.edu. *Application contact:* Deana Angotti, Director of Graduate Education, 816-501-2446, Fax: 816-501-2915, E-mail: deana.augotti@avila.edu.

Azusa Pacific University, School of Education, Department of Advanced Studies, Azusa, CA 91702-7000. Offers curriculum and instruction in a multicultural setting (MA); educational technology (M Ed); physical education (M Ed); school librarianship (MA); teaching (MA). *Faculty research:* Social/cultural issues, literacy and technology in K–12 and higher education school settings, ethics and organizational leadership, teacher expectation/school reform, community education.

Azusa Pacific University, School of Education, Department of Education, Azusa, CA 91702-7000. Offers educational leadership (Ed D); language development (MA); pupil personnel services (MA). *Accreditation:* NCATE. Part-time and evening/weekend programs available. *Degree requirements:* For master's, core exams, oral presentation; for doctorate, oral defense of dissertation, qualifying exam. *Entrance requirements:* For master's, minimum GPA of 3.0; for doctorate, GRE General Test or MAT, 5 years of experience, writing sample. Additional exam requirements/recommendations for international students: Required—TOEFL.

Baker University, School of Education, Baldwin City, KS 66006-0065. Offers MA Ed, MASL, MSSE, MST, Ed D. Master's-level programs also offered in Wichita, KS. *Accreditation:* NCATE. Part-time and evening/weekend programs available. *Degree requirements:* For master's, portfolio of learning; for doctorate, thesis/dissertation, portfolio of learning. *Entrance requirements:* For master's, 2 years full-time work experience, teaching certificate; for doctorate, admission interview. Additional exam requirements/recommendations for international students: Required—TOEFL (minimum score 600 paper-based; 250 computer-based).

Baldwin-Wallace College, Graduate Programs, Division of Education, Berea, OH 44017-2088. Offers educational technology (MA Ed); leadership in higher education (MA Ed); literacy (MA Ed); mild/moderate educational needs (MA Ed); school leadership (MA Ed); teaching and learning (MA Ed). *Accreditation:* NCATE. Part-time and evening/weekend programs available. *Faculty:* 10 full-time (5 women), 6 part-time/adjunct (4 women). *Students:* 118 full-time (97 women), 101 part-time (81 women); includes 16 minority (14 African Americans, 1 Asian American or Pacific Islander, 1 Hispanic American). Average age 31. 155 applicants, 68%

Education—General

Baldwin-Wallace College (continued)

accepted, 49 enrolled. In 2009, 100 master's awarded. *Degree requirements:* For master's, comprehensive exam. *Entrance requirements:* For master's, bachelor's degree in field, MAT or minimum GPA of 2.75. Additional exam requirements/recommendations for international students: Required—TOEFL (minimum score 523 paper-based; 193 computer-based; 70 iBT). *Application deadline:* For fall admission, 8/15 priority date for domestic students; for spring admission, 12/15 priority date for domestic students. Applications are processed on a rolling basis. Application fee: $25. Electronic applications accepted. *Expenses:* Tuition: Full-time $14,174; part-time $682 per credit. Tuition and fees vary according to program. *Financial support:* In 2009–10, 63 students received support. Career-related internships or fieldwork available. Support available to part-time students. Financial award application deadline: 5/1; financial award applicants required to submit FAFSA. *Faculty research:* Literacy; technology and literacy; diversity in education; assessment; special education. *Unit head:* Karen Kaye, Chair, 440-826-2168, Fax: 440-826-3779, E-mail: kkaye@bw.edu. *Application contact:* Winifred W. Gerhardt, Director of Admission for the Evening and Weekend College, 440-826-2222, Fax: 440-826-3830, E-mail: admission@bw.edu.

Ball State University, Graduate School, Teachers College, Muncie, IN 47306-1099. Offers MA, MAE, Ed D, PhD, Ed S, Graduate Certificate. *Accreditation:* NCATE. Part-time and evening/weekend programs available. Postbaccalaureate distance learning degree programs offered (no on-campus study). Terminal master's awarded for partial completion of doctoral program. *Degree requirements:* For doctorate, comprehensive exam, thesis/dissertation; for other advanced degree, comprehensive exam, thesis. *Entrance requirements:* For master's, minimum undergraduate GPA of 2.75 (for most programs); for doctorate, GRE General Test, minimum graduate GPA of 3.2; for other advanced degree, GRE General Test. Additional exam requirements/recommendations for international students: Required—TOEFL (minimum score 550 paper-based; 213 computer-based), IELTS (minimum score 6.5).

Bank Street College of Education, Graduate School, New York, NY 10025. Offers Ed M, MS, MS Ed. *Faculty:* 67 full-time (58 women), 66 part-time/adjunct (53 women). *Students:* 372 full-time (325 women), 585 part-time (519 women); includes 215 minority (78 African Americans, 3 American Indian/Alaska Native, 43 Asian Americans or Pacific Islanders, 91 Hispanic Americans), 9 international. Average age 31. 644 applicants, 81% accepted, 395 enrolled. In 2009, 335 master's awarded. *Degree requirements:* For master's, thesis. *Entrance requirements:* For master's, interview. Additional exam requirements/recommendations for international students: Required—TOEFL (minimum score 600 paper-based; 250 computer-based; 100 iBT), IELTS (minimum score 7). *Application deadline:* For fall admission, 3/1 priority date for domestic and international students; for spring admission, 11/1 priority date for domestic and international students. Applications are processed on a rolling basis. Application fee: $65. Electronic applications accepted. *Expenses:* Tuition: Part-time $1120 per credit. *Financial support:* In 2009–10, 695 students received support. Career-related internships or fieldwork, Federal Work-Study, scholarships/grants, and unspecified assistantships available. Support available to part-time students. Financial award application deadline: 4/15; financial award applicants required to submit FAFSA. *Faculty research:* Understanding developmental variations in inclusive classrooms, urban teacher education and technology, learner-centered education, improving teacher preparation. *Unit head:* Dr. Virginia Casper, Dean, 212-875-4703, Fax: 212-875-4753, E-mail: vcasper@bankstreet.edu. *Application contact:* Ann Morgan, Director of Graduate Admissions, 212-875-4403, Fax: 212-875-4678, E-mail: amorgan@bankstreet.edu.

See Close-Up on page 707.

Bard College, Master of Arts in Teaching Program, Annandale-on-Hudson, NY 12504. Offers MAT. *Degree requirements:* For master's, 2 research projects, field work. *Entrance requirements:* For master's, resume, 3 letters of recommendation. Additional exam requirements/recommendations for international students: Required—TOEFL. Electronic applications accepted.

Barry University, School of Education, Miami Shores, FL 33161-6695. Offers MS, Ed D, PhD, Certificate, Ed S. Part-time and evening/weekend programs available. Postbaccalaureate distance learning degree programs offered. *Degree requirements:* For master's, comprehensive exam; for doctorate, thesis/dissertation. *Entrance requirements:* For master's, GRE General Test or MAT, minimum GPA of 3.0; for doctorate, GRE General Test, minimum GPA of 3.25; for other advanced degree, GRE General Test, minimum GPA of 3.0. Additional exam requirements/recommendations for international students: Required—TOEFL (minimum score 550 paper-based; 213 computer-based). Electronic applications accepted.

Bayamón Central University, Graduate Programs, Program in Education, Bayamón, PR 00960-1725. Offers administration and supervision (MA Ed); commercial education (MA Ed); education of the autistic (MA Ed); elementary education (K–3) (MA Ed); elementary education (K–6) (MA Ed); guidance and counseling (MA Ed); organizational psychology (MA); pre-elementary teacher (MA Ed); rehabilitation counseling (MA Ed); special education (MA Ed), including attention deficit disorder, learning disabilities. Part-time and evening/weekend programs available. *Degree requirements:* For master's, comprehensive exam. *Entrance requirements:* For master's, EXADEP, bachelor's degree in education or related field.

Baylor University, Graduate School, School of Education, Waco, TX 76798. Offers MA, MS Ed, Ed D, PhD, Ed S. *Accreditation:* NCATE. Part-time programs available. Postbaccalaureate distance learning degree programs offered (minimal on-campus study). *Students:* 170 full-time (117 women), 96 part-time (59 women); includes 51 minority (20 African Americans, 8 Asian Americans or Pacific Islanders, 23 Hispanic Americans), 14 international. In 2009, 92 master's, 8 doctorates, 4 other advanced degrees awarded. *Degree requirements:* For doctorate, thesis/dissertation. *Application deadline:* Applications are processed on a rolling basis. Application fee: $25. Electronic applications accepted. *Financial support:* Research assistantships, teaching assistantships, career-related internships or fieldwork, Federal Work-Study, institutionally sponsored loans, scholarships/grants, and tuition waivers (partial) available. *Unit head:* Interim Dean, 254-710-3111, Fax: 254-710-3987. *Application contact:* Julie Baker, Administrative Assistant, 254-710-3050, Fax: 254-710-3870, E-mail: julie_baker@baylor.edu.

Belhaven University, School of Education, Jackson, MS 39202-1789. Offers elementary education (M Ed, MAT); secondary education (M Ed, MAT). Part-time and evening/weekend programs available. *Faculty:* 4 full-time (all women), 19 part-time/adjunct (10 women). *Students:* 159 full-time (132 women), 51 part-time (42 women); includes 108 African Americans, 1 American Indian/Alaska Native, 7 Hispanic Americans. Average age 34. 392 applicants, 70% accepted, 140 enrolled. In 2009, 44 master's awarded. *Degree requirements:* For master's, comprehensive exam, portfolio. *Entrance requirements:* For master's, PRAXIS I, PRAXIS II, minimum GPA of 2.8. *Application deadline:* Applications are processed on a rolling basis. Application fee: $25. Electronic applications accepted. *Expenses:* Tuition: Full-time $8730; part-time $485 per credit hour. Required fees: $1260; $70 per credit hour. Tuition and fees vary according to campus/location. *Financial support:* Federal Work-Study, scholarships/grants, tuition waivers (full), and unspecified assistantships available. Support available to part-time students. Financial award applicants required to submit FAFSA. *Unit head:* Dr. Sandra L. Rasberry, Dean, 601-968-8703, Fax: 601-974-6461, E-mail: srasberry@belhaven.edu. *Application contact:* Jenny Mixon, Director of Graduate and Online Admission, 601-968-8947, Fax: 601-968-5953, E-mail: gradadmission@belhaven.edu.

Bellarmine University, Annsley Frazier Thornton School of Education, Louisville, KY 40205-0671. Offers early elementary education (MA, MAT); instructional leadership and school administration/school principal (MA); learning and behavior disorders (MA); middle school education (MA, MAT); reading and writing endorsement (MA); secondary school education (MAT); Waldorf inspired curriculum (MA). *Accreditation:* NCATE. Part-time and evening/weekend programs available. *Faculty:* 16 full-time (11 women), 20 part-time/adjunct (13 women). *Students:* 67 full-time (47 women), 140 part-time (111 women); includes 14 minority (10 African Americans, 1 American Indian/Alaska Native, 3 Asian Americans or Pacific Islanders), 1 international. Average age 33. In 2009, 106 degrees awarded. *Degree requirements:* For master's, comprehensive exam, thesis (for some programs). *Entrance requirements:* For master's, GRE, baccalaureate degree from an accredited institution; minimum overall GPA of 2.75, 3.0 in major; letters of recommendation; valid Kentucky provisional or professional certificate. Additional exam requirements/recommendations for international students: Required—TOEFL (minimum score 550 paper-based; 213 computer-based; 80 iBT). *Application deadline:* Applications are processed on a rolling basis. Application fee: $25. *Expenses:* Contact institution. *Financial support:* Scholarships/grants available. Financial award applicants required to submit FAFSA. *Faculty research:* Literacy, service learning, dispositions, educational technology, special education. *Unit head:* Dr. Cindy Gnadinger, Dean, 502-452-8191, Fax: 502-452-8189, E-mail: cgnadinger@bellarmine.edu. *Application contact:* Theresa Klapheke, Administrative Director of Graduate Programs, 502-452-8271, Fax: 502-452-8002, E-mail: tklapheke@bellarmine.edu.

Belmont University, College of Arts and Sciences, School of Education, Nashville, TN 37212-3757. Offers education (M Ed); elementary education (MAT), including early childhood education, elementary education, language arts education; English (MAT); history (MAT); mathematics (MAT); middle grade education (MAT); science (MAT); secondary education (MAT); special education (MAT); sports administration (MSA). *Accreditation:* NCATE. Part-time and evening/weekend programs available. *Degree requirements:* For master's, comprehensive exam, thesis, culminating portfolio. *Entrance requirements:* For master's, MAT or GRE and/or LSAT or GMAT, minimum GPA of 2.75. Additional exam requirements/recommendations for international students: Required—TOEFL. *Expenses:* Contact institution. *Faculty research:* Improving secondary literacy, Montessori, classroom management strategies, teacher residency programs, online professional development, mentoring, leadership, sociological issues in sport, faculty development, coaching.

Bemidji State University, School of Graduate Studies, College of Professional Studies, Program in Education, Bemidji, MN 56601-2699. Offers M Ed, MS. Part-time programs available. *Degree requirements:* For master's, thesis. *Entrance requirements:* For master's, letters of recommendation. Additional exam requirements/recommendations for international students: Required—TOEFL. Electronic applications accepted.

Benedictine University, Graduate Programs, Program in Education, Lisle, IL 60532-0900. Offers curriculum and instruction and collaborative teaching (M Ed); elementary education (MA Ed); leadership and administration (M Ed); reading and literacy (M Ed); secondary education (MA Ed); special education (MA Ed). Part-time and evening/weekend programs available. *Faculty:* 4 full-time (2 women), 52 part-time/adjunct (30 women). *Students:* 286 full-time (252 women), 443 part-time (349 women); includes 61 minority (22 African Americans, 11 Asian Americans or Pacific Islanders, 28 Hispanic Americans), 5 international. Average age 33. 341 applicants, 90% accepted, 264 enrolled. In 2009, 299 master's awarded. *Degree requirements:* For master's, comprehensive exam, thesis (for some programs). *Entrance requirements:* For master's, GRE or MAT. Additional exam requirements/recommendations for international students: Required—TOEFL (minimum score 550 paper-based; 213 computer-based). *Application deadline:* For fall admission, 9/1 for domestic students; for winter admission, 12/1 for domestic students; for spring admission, 2/15 for domestic students. Applications are processed on a rolling basis. Application fee: $40. Electronic applications accepted. *Expenses:* Contact institution. *Financial support:* Career-related internships or fieldwork and health care benefits available. Support available to part-time students. *Unit head:* Dr. Richard Campbell, Director, 630-829-6242, Fax: 630-960-1126, E-mail: rcampbell@ben.edu. *Application contact:* Kari Gibbons, Director, Admissions, 630-829-6200, Fax: 630-829-6584, E-mail: kgibbons@ben.edu.

Bennington College, Graduate Programs, MA in Teaching a Second Language Program, Bennington, VT 05201. Offers education (MATSL); foreign language education (MATSL); French (MATSL); Spanish (MATSL). Part-time programs available. *Faculty:* 1 full-time (0 women), 3 part-time/adjunct (2 women). *Students:* 16 part-time (14 women); includes 3 minority (1 African American, 2 Hispanic Americans). Average age 37. 16 applicants, 63% accepted, 9 enrolled. In 2009, 6 master's awarded. *Degree requirements:* For master's, one foreign language, 2 major projects and presentations. *Entrance requirements:* For master's, Oral Proficiency Interview (OPI). Additional exam requirements/recommendations for international students: Required—TOEFL (minimum score 577 paper-based; 233 computer-based; 91 iBT). *Application deadline:* For spring admission, 4/1 priority date for domestic and international students. Applications are processed on a rolling basis. Application fee: $60. *Expenses:* Contact institution. *Financial support:* In 2009–10, 1 student received support. Scholarships/grants available. Financial award application deadline: 4/1; financial award applicants required to submit FAFSA. *Faculty research:* Acquisition, evaluation, assessment, conceptual teaching and learning content-driven communication, applied linguistics. *Unit head:* Carol Meyer, Director, 802-440-4375, E-mail: cmeyer@bennington.edu. *Application contact:* Nancy Pearlman, Assistant Director, 802-440-4710, E-mail: matsl@bennington.edu.

Bennington College, Graduate Programs, MA in Teaching Program, Bennington, VT 05201. Offers art education (MAT); early childhood (MAT); elementary education (MAT); English education (MAT); foreign language education (MAT); k-12 education (MAT); mathematics education (MAT); music education (MAT); science education (MAT); secondary education (MAT); social studies education (MAT); theater arts (MAT). *Faculty:* 5 part-time/adjunct (3 women). *Students:* 8 full-time (5 women), 1 part-time (0 women). Average age 28. 11 applicants, 27% accepted, 1 enrolled. In 2009, 4 master's awarded. *Degree requirements:* For master's, comprehensive exam, 1 year teaching practicum, professional portfolio. *Entrance requirements:* For master's, interview. *Application deadline:* For fall admission, 3/1 for domestic students. Application fee: $60. *Expenses:* Contact institution. *Financial support:* In 2009–10, 6 students received support, including 4 fellowships (averaging $10,475 per year); scholarships/grants and unspecified assistantships also available. Financial award application deadline: 4/1; financial award applicants required to submit FAFSA. *Unit head:* Carol Meyer, Director of Programs in Teacher Education, 802-440-4375, E-mail: cmeyer@bennington.edu. *Application contact:* Nancy Pearlman, Assistant Director of Programs in Teacher Education, 802-440-4710, Fax: 802-440-4383, E-mail: npearlman@bennington.edu.

Berry College, Graduate Programs, Graduate Programs in Education, Mount Berry, GA 30149-0159. Offers early childhood education (M Ed); leadership in curriculum and instruction (Ed S), including curriculum and instruction, educational leadership; middle-grades education and reading (M Ed); secondary education (M Ed). *Accreditation:* NCATE. Part-time programs available. *Faculty:* 15 part-time/adjunct (8 women). *Students:* 4 full-time (2 women), 109 part-time (85 women); includes 8 minority (4 African Americans, 4 Hispanic Americans). Average age 32. In 2009, 24 master's, 5 Ed Ss awarded. *Degree requirements:* For master's, thesis optional, oral exams; for Ed S, thesis, portfolio, oral exams. *Entrance requirements:* For master's, GRE General Test, MAT, or NTE, minimum GPA of 2.5; for Ed S, M Ed from NCATE accredited school, minimum GPA of 3.25. Additional exam requirements/recommendations for international students: Required—TOEFL (minimum score 550 paper-based; 213 computer-based). *Application deadline:* For fall admission, 5/1 for domestic and international students; for spring admission, 10/1 for domestic and international students. Applications are processed on a rolling basis. Application fee: $25 ($30 for international students). *Expenses:* Contact institution. *Financial support:* In 2009–10, 38 students received support, including 11 research assistantships with full tuition reimbursements available (averaging $3,511 per year); scholarships/grants, tuition waivers (partial), and unspecified assistantships also available. Support available to part-time students. Financial award application deadline: 4/1; financial award applicants required to submit FAFSA. *Faculty research:* Curriculum development, teaching strategies, teacher training, math education. *Unit head:* Dr. Jacqueline McDowell, Dean, Charter School of Education and Human Sciences, 706-236-1717, Fax: 706-238-5827, E-mail: jmcdowell@berry.edu. *Application contact:* Brett Kennedy, Director of Admissions, 706-236-2215, Fax: 706-290-2178, E-mail: admissions@berry.edu.

Bethany University, Program in Teacher Education, Scotts Valley, CA 95066-2820. Offers education (MA); educational leadership (MA). Part-time and evening/weekend programs available. *Degree requirements:* For master's, thesis. *Entrance requirements:* For master's, GRE General Test.

Bethel College, Division of Graduate Studies, Program in Education, Mishawaka, IN 46545-5591. Offers M Ed, MAT. *Accreditation:* NCATE. Part-time programs available. *Faculty:* 1 full-time (0 women), 13 part-time/adjunct (10 women). *Students:* 30 full-time (18 women), 63 part-time (37 women); includes 13 minority (10 African Americans, 3 Hispanic Americans), 1 international. 95 applicants, 81% accepted, 69 enrolled. In 2009, 13 master's awarded. *Entrance requirements:* Additional exam requirements/recommendations for international students: Required—TOEFL (minimum score 540 paper-based; 207 computer-based). *Application deadline:* For fall admission, 5/1 for international students; for spring admission, 10/1 for international students. Application fee: $25. Electronic applications accepted. *Financial support:* Career-related internships or fieldwork available. Financial award applicants required to submit FAFSA. *Unit head:* Dr. Ralph Stutzman, Director, 574-257-3493, E-mail: stutzmr@bethelcollege.edu. *Application contact:* Dr. Ralph Stutzman, Director, 574-257-3493, E-mail: stutzmr@bethelcollege.edu.

Bethel University, Graduate School, Department of Education, St. Paul, MN 55112-6999. Offers education K-12 (MA), including autism spectrum disorders, coordinator of work-based learning, differentiation, international baccalaureate, literacy, special education; educational administration (Ed D), including director of special education, K-12 principal license, superintendent license; literacy (Certificate); literacy education (MA); special education (MA), including autism spectrum disorders; teaching (MA). *Accreditation:* Teacher Education Accreditation Council. Evening/weekend programs available. Postbaccalaureate distance learning degree programs offered (minimal on-campus study). *Faculty:* 17 full-time (11 women), 37 part-time/adjunct (17 women). *Students:* 182 full-time (119 women), 172 part-time (120 women); includes 18 minority (2 African Americans, 1 American Indian/Alaska Native, 6 Asian Americans or Pacific Islanders, 9 Hispanic Americans), 1 international. Average age 35. 236 applicants, 79% accepted, 173 enrolled. In 2009, 51 master's, 5 doctorates awarded. *Degree requirements:* For master's, thesis, practicum; for doctorate, comprehensive exam, thesis/dissertation, internship. *Entrance requirements:* For master's, baccalaureate degree, statement of purpose essay, interview, current teaching license (if applicable), minimum GPA of 3.0, teaching experience (if applicable), letters of reference; for doctorate, MAT or GRE, minimum GPA of 3.0, letters of reference, statement of purpose essay, pre-assessment of prior experience and preparation, current license (if applicable), master's degree, interview, work experience in education. Additional exam requirements/recommendations for international students: Required—TOEFL (minimum score 550 paper-based; 213 computer-based; 80 iBT). *Application deadline:* For fall admission, 8/1 priority date for domestic students; for winter admission, 12/5 priority date for domestic students; for spring admission, 5/1 priority date for domestic students. Applications are processed on a rolling basis. Application fee: $25. Electronic applications accepted. *Expenses:* Contact institution. *Financial support:* Applicants required to submit FAFSA. *Unit head:* Dr. Judi Landrum, Assistant Dean, 651-635-8000, Fax: 651-638-8004, E-mail: j-landrum@bethel.edu. *Application contact:* Michael Price, Director of Admissions, 651-635-8000, Fax: 651-635-8004, E-mail: m-price@bethel.edu.

Bethel University, Program in Education, McKenzie, TN 38201. Offers administration and supervision (MA Ed); biology education K8-12 (MAT); elementary education (MAT); English education K8-12 (MAT); history education K8-12 (MAT); physical education K8-12 (MAT); special education K8-12 (MAT). Part-time and evening/weekend programs available. *Degree requirements:* For master's, thesis (for some programs). *Entrance requirements:* For master's, GRE General Test or MAT, minimum undergraduate GPA of 2.5.

Biola University, School of Arts and Sciences, La Mirada, CA 90639-0001. Offers MA Ed. Part-time and evening/weekend programs available. *Degree requirements:* For master's, thesis or alternative. *Entrance requirements:* For master's, California Basic Educational Skills Test, PRAXIS or MSAT, minimum GPA of 3.0. Additional exam requirements/recommendations for international students: Required—TOEFL (minimum score 550 paper-based; 213 computer-based).

Bishop's University, School of Education, Sherbrooke, QC J1M 0C8, Canada. Offers advanced studies in education (Diploma); education (M Ed, MA); teaching English as a second language (Certificate). Part-time programs available. Postbaccalaureate distance learning degree programs offered (minimal on-campus study). *Degree requirements:* For master's, thesis (for some programs). *Entrance requirements:* For master's, teaching license, 2 years of teaching experience. *Faculty research:* Integration of special needs students, multigrade classes/small schools, leadership in organizational development, second language acquisition.

Bloomsburg University of Pennsylvania, School of Graduate Studies, College of Professional Studies, School of Education, Bloomsburg, PA 17815-1301. Offers M Ed, MS. *Accreditation:* NCATE. *Entrance requirements:* For master's, minimum QPA of 3.0. Additional exam requirements/recommendations for international students: Required—TOEFL. Electronic applications accepted.

Bluffton University, Program in Education, Bluffton, OH 45817. Offers MA Ed. *Accreditation:* NCATE. Part-time programs available. *Degree requirements:* For master's, action research project, public presentation. *Entrance requirements:* Additional exam requirements/recommendations for international students: Required—TOEFL. Electronic applications accepted. *Faculty research:* Mentoring.

Boise State University, Graduate College, College of Education, Boise, ID 83725-0399. Offers M Ed, MA, MET, MPE, MS, MS Ed, Ed D. *Accreditation:* NCATE. Part-time programs available. *Degree requirements:* For doctorate, thesis/dissertation. *Entrance requirements:* For master's, minimum GPA of 3.0; for doctorate, GRE General Test, minimum GPA of 3.0. Electronic applications accepted. *Expenses:* Tuition, state resident: full-time $3106; part-time $209 per credit. Tuition, nonresident: part-time $284 per credit.

Boston College, Lynch Graduate School of Education, Chestnut Hill, MA 02467-3800. Offers M Ed, MA, MAT, MST, Ed D, PhD, CAES, JD/M Ed, JD/MA, M Ed/MA, MA/MA, MBA/MA. *Accreditation:* Teacher Education Accreditation Council. Part-time and evening/weekend programs available. *Faculty:* 54 full-time (28 women), 40 part-time/adjunct (29 women). *Students:* 655 full-time (483 women), 250 part-time (172 women); includes 144 minority (53 African Americans, 2 American Indian/Alaska Native, 47 Asian Americans or Pacific Islanders, 42 Hispanic Americans), 88 international. 1,911 applicants, 52% accepted, 398 enrolled. In 2009, 281 master's, 63 doctorates, 8 other advanced degrees awarded. Terminal master's awarded for partial completion of doctoral program. *Degree requirements:* For master's and CAES, comprehensive exam; for doctorate, comprehensive exam, thesis/dissertation. *Entrance requirements:* For master's and CAES, GRE General Test or MAT; for doctorate, GRE General Test. Additional exam requirements/recommendations for international students: Required—TOEFL. Application fee: $60. Electronic applications accepted. *Financial support:* In 2009–10, 924 fellowships with full and partial tuition reimbursements, 324 research assistantships with full and partial tuition reimbursements, 110 teaching assistantships with full and partial tuition reimbursements were awarded; career-related internships or fieldwork, Federal Work-Study, institutionally sponsored loans, scholarships/grants, traineeships, health care benefits, tuition waivers (full and partial), and unspecified assistantships also available. Support available to part-time students. Financial award applicants required to submit FAFSA. *Faculty research:* Assessment, evaluation and public policy; counseling and developmental psychology; higher education leadership; curriculum and instruction; Catholic education. Total annual research expenditures: $12.8 million. *Unit head:* Rev. Joseph O'Keefe, Dean, 617-552-8426, Fax: 617-552-0812, E-mail: okeefejo@bc.edu. *Application contact:* Adam Poluzzi, Director, Graduate Admission and Financial Aid, 617-552-4214, Fax: 617-552-0398, E-mail: poluzzi@bc.edu.

Boston University, School of Education, Boston, MA 02215. Offers Ed M, MAT, Ed D, CAGS, MSW/Ed D, MSW/Ed M. Part-time programs available. Terminal master's awarded for partial completion of doctoral program. *Degree requirements:* For master's, thesis optional; for doctorate, comprehensive exam, thesis/dissertation; for CAGS, comprehensive exam. *Entrance requirements:* For master's, doctorate, and CAGS, GRE General Test or MAT. Additional exam requirements/recommendations for international students: Required—TOEFL. Electronic applications accepted. *Expenses:* Tuition: Full-time $37,910; part-time $1184 per credit hour. Required fees: $386; $40 per semester. Part-time tuition and fees vary according to class time, course level, degree level and program. *Faculty research:* Moral development, language development in young children, mathematics curriculum development, educational reform and standards, science curriculum development.

Bowie State University, Graduate Programs, Program in Teaching, Bowie, MD 20715-9465. Offers MAT. *Accreditation:* NCATE. Part-time and evening/weekend programs available. *Entrance requirements:* For master's, PRAXIS I. Electronic applications accepted.

Bradley University, Graduate School, College of Education and Health Sciences, Peoria, IL 61625-0002. Offers MA, MSN, DPT, Certificate. *Accreditation:* NCATE. Part-time and evening/weekend programs available. *Degree requirements:* For master's, comprehensive exam, thesis optional. *Entrance requirements:* For master's, GRE General Test or MAT, letters of recommendation; for doctorate, GRE, letters of recommendation. Additional exam requirements/recommendations for international students: Required—TOEFL (minimum score 550 paper-based; 213 computer-based; 79 iBT). *Faculty research:* Health care, professional nurse traineeship, gifted education.

Brandon University, Faculty of Education, Brandon, MB R7A 6A9, Canada. Offers curriculum and instruction (M Ed, Diploma); educational administration (M Ed, Diploma); guidance and counseling (M Ed, Diploma); special education (M Ed, Diploma). *Degree requirements:* For master's, thesis. *Entrance requirements:* For master's, minimum GPA of 3.0, teaching certificate or equivalent. Additional exam requirements/recommendations for international students: Required—TOEFL. *Faculty research:* Comparative education, environmental studies, parent/school council.

Brenau University, Graduate Programs, School of Education, Gainesville, GA 30501. Offers early childhood (Ed S); early childhood education (M Ed, MAT); middle grades (Ed S); middle grades education (M Ed, MAT); secondary education (MAT); special education (M Ed, MAT). *Accreditation:* NCATE. Part-time and evening/weekend programs available. Postbaccalaureate distance learning degree programs offered (no on-campus study). *Faculty:* 12 full-time (7 women), 25 part-time/adjunct (21 women). *Students:* 161 full-time (146 women), 143 part-time (122 women); includes 43 minority (30 African Americans, 5 Asian Americans or Pacific Islanders, 8 Hispanic Americans), 1 international. Average age 35. 163 applicants, 34% accepted, 47 enrolled. In 2009, 154 master's, 20 other advanced degrees awarded. *Degree requirements:* For master's, thesis optional, comprehensive exam or applied research project, effective portfolio; for Ed S, applied research project. *Entrance requirements:* For master's, GRE, MAT, interview, minimum GPA of 3.0, 3 references, writing samples; for Ed S, GRE, MAT, master's degree, minimum GPA of 3.0, writing sample, letters of reference. Additional exam requirements/recommendations for international students: Required—TOEFL (minimum score 500 paper-based). *Application deadline:* Applications are processed on a rolling basis. Application fee: $35. Electronic applications accepted. *Expenses:* Contact institution. *Financial support:* In 2009–10, 2 students received support. Scholarships/grants available. Support available to part-time students. Financial award application deadline: 7/15; financial award applicants required to submit FAFSA. *Unit head:* Dr. Lora Bailey, Dean, 770-534-6220, Fax: 770-534-6221, E-mail: lbailey@brenau.edu. *Application contact:* Christina White, Dean of Admissions, 770-718-5320, Fax: 770-718-5337, E-mail: cwhite@brenau.edu.

Briar Cliff University, Program in Education, Sioux City, IA 51104-0100. Offers MA. Program offered during the summer only. Postbaccalaureate distance learning degree programs offered (minimal on-campus study). *Faculty:* 3 full-time (1 woman), 5 part-time/adjunct (2 women). *Students:* 38 applicants, 16% accepted. *Entrance requirements:* For master's, 2 letters of recommendation, writing sample. *Application deadline:* For spring admission, 4/15 priority date for domestic students. Applications are processed on a rolling basis. Application fee: $25. Electronic applications accepted. *Expenses:* Tuition: Full-time $8856; part-time $492 per credit hour. Required fees: $23 per credit hour. *Financial support:* Application deadline: 5/1. *Unit head:* Dr. Ruth Schock, Director, 712-279-5556, Fax: 712-279-1698, E-mail: ruth.schock@briarcliff.edu. *Application contact:* Cheryl Olson, Continuing Studies Admission Representative, 712-279-1777, Fax: 712-279-1632, E-mail: cheryl.olson@briarcliff.edu.

Bridgewater State University, School of Graduate Studies, School of Education and Allied Science, Bridgewater, MA 02325-0001. Offers M Ed, MAT, MS, CAGS. *Accreditation:* NCATE. Part-time and evening/weekend programs available. *Degree requirements:* For CAGS, comprehensive exam. *Entrance requirements:* For master's, GRE General Test or Massachusetts Test for Educator Licensure; for CAGS, master's degree. Additional exam requirements/recommendations for international students: Required—TOEFL (minimum score 215 computer-based).

Brigham Young University, Graduate Studies, David O. McKay School of Education, Provo, UT 84602. Offers M Ed, MA, MS, PhD, Ed S. *Accreditation:* NCATE; Teacher Education Accreditation Council. Part-time programs available. *Faculty:* 64 full-time (27 women), 28 part-time/adjunct (10 women). *Students:* 150 full-time (92 women), 204 part-time (133 women); includes 33 minority (2 African Americans, 13 American Indian/Alaska Native, 6 Asian Americans or Pacific Islanders, 12 Hispanic Americans), 22 international. Average age 32. 247 applicants, 52% accepted, 105 enrolled. In 2009, 66 master's, 13 doctorates, 10 other advanced degrees awarded. *Degree requirements:* For master's, comprehensive exam, thesis; for doctorate, comprehensive exam, thesis/dissertation; for Ed S, comprehensive exam (for some programs). *Entrance requirements:* For master's, GRE General Test, minimum GPA of 3.25, minimum 1 year of teaching experience, letters of recommendation; for doctorate, GRE General Test, minimum GPA of 3.0 in last 60 hours of undergraduate coursework. Additional exam requirements/recommendations for international students: Required—TOEFL (minimum score 580 paper-based; 237 computer-based). *Application deadline:* For fall admission, 2/1 for domestic and international students; for winter admission, 2/1 for domestic and international students; for spring admission, 2/15 for domestic and international students. Application fee: $50. Electronic applications accepted. *Expenses:* Tuition: Full-time $5580; part-time $301 per credit hour. Tuition and fees vary according to student's religious affiliation. *Financial support:* In 2009–10, 200 students received support, including 75 research assistantships with full and partial tuition reimbursements available (averaging $10,107 per year), 35 teaching assistantships with full and partial tuition reimbursements available (averaging $5,414 per year); fellowships, career-related internships or fieldwork, institutionally sponsored loans, scholarships/grants, tuition waivers (partial), and unspecified assistantships also available. Support available to part-time students. Financial award applicants required to submit FAFSA. *Faculty research:* Reading, learning, teacher education, assessment and evaluation, speech-language pathology. *Unit head:* Dr. K. Richard Young, Dean, 801-422-3695, Fax: 801-422-0200, E-mail: richard_young@byu.edu. *Application contact:* Jay Oliver, Director, Education Student Services, 801-422-1202, Fax: 801-422-0195, E-mail: jay_oliver@byu.edu.

Brock University, Faculty of Graduate Studies, Faculty of Education, St. Catharines, ON L2S 3A1, Canada. Offers M Ed, PhD. Part-time and evening/weekend programs available. *Degree requirements:* For master's, thesis optional; for doctorate, thesis/dissertation. *Entrance requirements:* For master's, 1 year of teaching experience, honors degree; for doctorate, master's degree. Additional exam requirements/recommendations for international students: Required—TOEFL (minimum score 550 paper-based; 213 computer-based; 80 iBT), IELTS (minimum score 6.5), TWE (minimum score 4). Electronic applications accepted. *Expenses:* Contact institution. *Faculty research:* International and comparative education, early childhood education, educational leadership, adult education.

Brooklyn College of the City University of New York, Division of Graduate Studies, School of Education, Brooklyn, NY 11210-2889. Offers MA, MAT, MS Ed, CAS. *Accreditation:* NCATE. Part-time and evening/weekend programs available. *Students:* 239 full-time (195 women), 1,500 part-time (1,120 women); includes 757 minority (481 African Americans, 4 American Indian/Alaska Native, 88 Asian Americans or Pacific Islanders, 184 Hispanic Americans), 38 international. Average age 31. 1,117 applicants, 77% accepted, 609 enrolled. In 2009, 669 master's, 46 other advanced degrees awarded. *Entrance requirements:* For master's, LAST, 2 letters of recommendation, essay, resume, state teaching certificate; for CAS, master's degree.

Education—General

Brooklyn College of the City University of New York (continued)
Additional exam requirements/recommendations for international students: Required—TOEFL (minimum score 500 paper-based; 173 computer-based; 61 iBT). *Application deadline:* For fall admission, 3/1 priority date for domestic students, 2/1 priority date for international students; for spring admission, 11/1 priority date for domestic students, 10/1 priority date for international students. Applications are processed on a rolling basis. Application fee: $125. Electronic applications accepted. *Expenses:* Tuition, state resident: full-time $7360; part-time $310 per credit hour. Tuition, nonresident: full-time $13,800; part-time $575 per credit hour. Required fees: $140.10 per semester. *Financial support:* Fellowships, career-related internships or fieldwork, Federal Work-Study, institutionally sponsored loans, scholarships/grants, and tuition waivers (full and partial) available. Support available to part-time students. Financial award application deadline: 5/1; financial award applicants required to submit FAFSA. *Unit head:* Dr. Deborah Shanley, Dean, 718-951-5214, Fax: 718-951-4816, E-mail: dshanley@brooklyn.cuny.edu. *Application contact:* Hernan Sierra, Graduate Admissions Coordinator, 718-951-4536, Fax: 718-951-4506, E-mail: grads@brooklyn.cuny.edu.

Brown University, Graduate School, Department of Education, Providence, RI 02912. Offers teaching (MAT), including biology, elementary education, English, history/social studies; urban education policy (AM). *Degree requirements:* For master's, student teaching, portfolio. *Entrance requirements:* For master's, GRE General Test, letters of recommendation, interview. Electronic applications accepted.

Bucknell University, Graduate Studies, College of Arts and Sciences, Department of Education, Lewisburg, PA 17837. Offers classroom teaching (MS Ed); educational research (MS Ed); elementary and secondary counseling (MA, MS Ed); elementary and secondary principalship (MA, MS Ed); reading (MA, MS Ed); school psychology (MS Ed); supervision of curriculum and instruction (MA, MS Ed). Part-time programs available. *Degree requirements:* For master's, thesis or alternative. *Entrance requirements:* For master's, GRE General Test, minimum GPA of 2.8. Additional exam requirements/recommendations for international students: Required—TOEFL.

Buena Vista University, School of Education, Storm Lake, IA 50588. Offers curriculum and instruction (M Ed), including effective teaching, TESL; school guidance and counseling (MS Ed). Program offered in summer only. Part-time and evening/weekend programs available. Postbaccalaureate distance learning degree programs offered (minimal on-campus study). *Degree requirements:* For master's, thesis, fieldwork/practicum, capstone portfolio. *Entrance requirements:* For master's, Analytical Writing Assessment (in-house), minimum undergraduate GPA of 2.75. Electronic applications accepted. *Faculty research:* Reading, curriculum, educational psychology, special education.

Butler University, College of Education, Indianapolis, IN 46208-3485. Offers administration (MS); elementary education (MS); reading (MS); school counseling (MS); secondary education (MS); special education (MS). *Accreditation:* ACA; NCATE. Part-time and evening/weekend programs available. *Faculty:* 9 full-time (7 women), 7 part-time/adjunct (6 women). *Students:* 18 full-time (11 women), 137 part-time (111 women); includes 17 minority (14 African Americans, 1 American Indian/Alaska Native, 2 Asian Americans or Pacific Islanders), 9 international. Average age 31. 57 applicants, 77% accepted, 24 enrolled. In 2009, 61 master's awarded. *Entrance requirements:* For master's, GRE General Test, MAT, interview. *Application deadline:* For fall admission, 8/15 priority date for domestic students. Applications are processed on a rolling basis. Application fee: $35. Electronic applications accepted. *Financial support:* Institutionally sponsored loans available. Support available to part-time students. Financial award application deadline: 7/15; financial award applicants required to submit FAFSA. *Faculty research:* Ethics in cybercounseling, history of sports for disabled, effect of fetal alcohol syndrome on perceptual learning, reading recovery's theoretical framework in teacher education. *Unit head:* Dr. Ena Shelley, Dean, 317-940-9752, Fax: 317-940-6481. *Application contact:* Karen Farrell, Department Secretary, 317-940-9220, E-mail: kfarrell@butler.edu.

Cabrini College, Graduate and Professional Studies, Radnor, PA 19087-3698. Offers education (M Ed); organization leadership (MS). Part-time and evening/weekend programs available. *Faculty:* 6 full-time (3 women), 135 part-time/adjunct (81 women). *Students:* 135 full-time (93 women), 1,825 part-time (1,430 women); includes 150 minority (112 African Americans, 1 American Indian/Alaska Native, 14 Asian Americans or Pacific Islanders, 23 Hispanic Americans). Average age 32. 714 applicants, 70% accepted, 460 enrolled. In 2009, 614 master's awarded. *Degree requirements:* For master's, thesis optional. *Entrance requirements:* For master's, GRE and/or MAT (in some cases), letter of recommendation, minimum GPA of 2.5. *Application deadline:* For fall admission, 7/29 priority date for domestic students; for spring admission, 12/9 for domestic students. Applications are processed on a rolling basis. Application fee: $50. Electronic applications accepted. *Expenses:* Tuition: Part-time $555 per credit. *Financial support:* Career-related internships or fieldwork and unspecified assistantships available. Support available to part-time students. Financial award applicants required to submit FAFSA. *Unit head:* Dr. Dennis R. Dougherty, Interim Dean for Graduate and Professional Studies, 610-902-8501, Fax: 610-902-8522, E-mail: dennis.dougherty@cabrini.edu. *Application contact:* Bruce D. Bryde, Director of Enrollment and Recruiting, 610-902-8291, Fax: 610-902-8522, E-mail: bruce.d.bryde@cabrini.edu.

California Baptist University, Program in Education, Riverside, CA 92504-3206. Offers cross-cultural language and academic development (MA); educational leadership (MS); educational leadership and faith-based instruction (MS); educational technology (MS); instructional computer applications (MS); reading (MS); school counseling (MS); school psychology (MS); special education (MS); special education in mild/moderate disabilities (MS); special education in moderate/severe disabilities (MS); teaching (MS); teaching and learning (MS Ed). Part-time programs available. *Faculty:* 16 full-time (9 women), 10 part-time/adjunct (all women). *Students:* 73 full-time (60 women), 368 part-time (298 women); includes 170 minority (34 African Americans, 4 American Indian/Alaska Native, 18 Asian Americans or Pacific Islanders, 114 Hispanic Americans). 266 applicants, 72% accepted, 169 enrolled. In 2009, 120 master's awarded. *Degree requirements:* For master's, comprehensive exam (for some programs), thesis optional. *Entrance requirements:* For master's, minimum undergraduate GPA of 2.75, 12 semester hours of pre-requisite course work in education. Additional exam requirements/recommendations for international students: Required—TOEFL (minimum score 575 paper-based; 230 computer-based; 89 iBT). *Application deadline:* For fall admission, 8/1 priority date for domestic students, 7/1 for international students; for spring admission, 12/1 priority date for domestic students, 10/15 priority date for international students. Applications are processed on a rolling basis. Application fee: $45. Electronic applications accepted. *Expenses:* Tuition: Full-time $8352; part-time $464 per semester hour. Required fees: $125 per semester. Tuition and fees vary according to course load, campus/location and program. *Financial support:* Career-related internships or fieldwork, Federal Work-Study, and scholarships/grants available. Support available to part-time students. Financial award applicants required to submit FAFSA. *Unit head:* Dr. Mary Crist, Dean, School of Education, 951-343-4313, Fax: 951-343-4516, E-mail: mcrist@calbaptist.edu. *Application contact:* Gail Ronveaux, Dean of Graduate Enrollment, 951-343-5045, Fax: 951-343-5095, E-mail: graduateadmissions@calbaptist.edu.

California Coast University, Programs in Education, Santa Ana, CA 92701. Offers administration (M Ed); curriculum and instruction (M Ed); educational psychology (D Ed); organizational leadership (D Ed). Part-time and evening/weekend programs available. Postbaccalaureate distance learning degree programs offered (no on-campus study). Application fee: $75. *Application contact:* Christi Okuma, 714-547-9625, Fax: 714-547-5777, E-mail: ccu@calcoast.edu.

California Lutheran University, Graduate Studies, School of Education, Thousand Oaks, CA 91360-2787. Offers counseling and guidance (MS); curriculum and instruction (MA), including reading education; educational leadership (MA, Ed D), including educational leadership (MA), educational leadership (k-12) (Ed D), higher education leadership (Ed D); special education (MS); teaching (M Ed). *Accreditation:* NCATE. Part-time and evening/weekend programs available. *Entrance requirements:* For master's, GRE General Test, interview, minimum GPA of 3.0.

California Polytechnic State University, San Luis Obispo, College of Science and Mathematics, School of Education, San Luis Obispo, CA 93407. Offers MA. Part-time and evening/weekend programs available. *Faculty:* 7 full-time (2 women), 6 part-time/adjunct (all women). *Students:* 57 full-time (49 women), 13 part-time (10 women); includes 16 minority (1 African American, 1 American Indian/Alaska Native, 3 Asian Americans or Pacific Islanders, 11 Hispanic Americans). Average age 29. 135 applicants, 41% accepted, 45 enrolled. In 2009, 84 master's awarded. *Degree requirements:* For master's, comprehensive exam (for some programs), thesis (for some programs). *Entrance requirements:* For master's, minimum GPA of 3.0 in last 90 quarter units, letters of recommendation. Additional exam requirements/recommendations for international students: Required—TOEFL (minimum score 550 paper-based; 213 computer-based), or IELTS (minimum score 6). *Application deadline:* For fall admission, 2/1 priority date for domestic students, 11/30 for international students. Application fee: $55. *Expenses:* Tuition, nonresident: full-time $11,160; part-time $248 per unit. Required fees: $7134; $1553 per quarter. *Financial support:* Research assistantships, career-related internships or fieldwork, Federal Work-Study, and institutionally sponsored loans available. Support available to part-time students. Financial award application deadline: 3/2; financial award applicants required to submit FAFSA. *Faculty research:* Rural school counseling, partner school effectiveness, college student affairs, special education, educational leadership and administration. *Unit head:* Dr. Patricia Mulligan, Director, 805-756-1505, Fax: 805-756-7430, E-mail: pmulliga@calpoly.edu. *Application contact:* Dr. James Maraviglia, Assistant Vice President for Admissions, Recruitment, and Financial Aid, 805-756-2311, Fax: 805-756-5400, E-mail: admissions@calpoly.edu.

California State Polytechnic University, Pomona, Academic Affairs, College of Education and Integrative Studies, Pomona, CA 91768-2557. Offers MA. Part-time programs available. *Faculty:* 44 full-time (30 women), 30 part-time/adjunct (19 women). *Students:* 85 full-time (59 women), 220 part-time (151 women); includes 163 minority (21 African Americans, 1 American Indian/Alaska Native, 41 Asian Americans or Pacific Islanders, 100 Hispanic Americans), 1 international. Average age 36. 83 applicants, 87% accepted, 44 enrolled. In 2009, 133 master's awarded. *Degree requirements:* For master's, thesis or alternative. *Application deadline:* For fall admission, 5/1 priority date for domestic students; for winter admission, 10/15 priority date for domestic students; for spring admission, 1/20 priority date for domestic students. Applications are processed on a rolling basis. Application fee: $55. Electronic applications accepted. *Expenses:* Tuition, nonresident: full-time $6696; part-time $248 per credit. Required fees: $5487; $3237 per term. Tuition and fees vary according to course load, degree level and program. *Financial support:* Career-related internships or fieldwork, Federal Work-Study, and institutionally sponsored loans available. Support available to part-time students. Financial award application deadline: 3/2; financial award applicants required to submit FAFSA. *Faculty research:* Cognitive style, human factors, learning-handicapped children, teaching and learning, severely handicapped children. *Unit head:* Dr. Peggy Kelly, Dean, 909-869-2307, E-mail: pkelly@csupomona.edu. *Application contact:* Dr. Dorothy MacNevin, Co-Chair, Graduate Education Department, 909-869-2311, Fax: 909-869-4822, E-mail: dmacnevin@csupomona.edu.

California State University, Bakersfield, Division of Graduate Studies, School of Education, Bakersfield, CA 93311. Offers MA, MA Ed, MS, Certificate. *Accreditation:* NCATE. *Degree requirements:* For master's, thesis or alternative, culminating projects.

California State University, Chico, Graduate School, College of Communication and Education, Department of Education, Program in Education, Chico, CA 95929-0722. Offers MA. *Accreditation:* NCATE. *Students:* 31 full-time (24 women), 74 part-time (47 women); includes 19 minority (3 African Americans, 6 Asian Americans or Pacific Islanders, 10 Hispanic Americans), 1 international. Average age 39. 44 applicants, 70% accepted, 21 enrolled. In 2009, 36 master's awarded. *Entrance requirements:* Additional exam requirements/recommendations for international students: Required—TOEFL (minimum score 550 paper-based; 213 computer-based; 80 iBT), IELTS (minimum score 6.5). *Application deadline:* For fall admission, 3/1 priority date for domestic students, 3/1 for international students; for spring admission, 9/15 priority date for domestic students, 9/15 for international students. Applications are processed on a rolling basis. Application fee: $55. Electronic applications accepted. *Unit head:* Dr. Cris Guenter, Graduate Coordinator, 530-898-6157. *Application contact:* School of Graduate, International, and Interdisciplinary Studies, 530-898-6880, Fax: 530-898-6889, E-mail: grin@csuchico.edu.

California State University, Dominguez Hills, College of Professional Studies, School of Education, Division of Graduate Education, Carson, CA 90747-0001. Offers counseling (MA); curriculum and instruction (MA); educational administration (MA); individualized education (MA); multicultural education (MA); technology-based education (MA, Certificate). Part-time and evening/weekend programs available. *Faculty:* 15 full-time (9 women), 14 part-time/adjunct (8 women). *Students:* 311 full-time (231 women), 281 part-time (201 women); includes 407 minority (117 African Americans, 3 American Indian/Alaska Native, 62 Asian Americans or Pacific Islanders, 225 Hispanic Americans), 5 international. Average age 36. 381 applicants, 74% accepted, 181 enrolled. In 2009, 285 master's awarded. *Entrance requirements:* For master's, minimum GPA of 2.75. *Application deadline:* For fall admission, 6/1 for domestic students. Application fee: $55. *Expenses:* Tuition, nonresident: full-time $6696; part-time $372 per unit. Required fees: $5946; $1752 per semester. *Unit head:* Dr. Farah Fisher, Chairperson, 310-243-3926, E-mail: ffisher@csudh.edu. *Application contact:* Admissions Office, 310-243-3530.

California State University, East Bay, Graduate Programs, College of Education and Allied Studies, Department of Teacher Education, Hayward, CA 94542-3000. Offers education (MS), including curriculum, early childhood education, educational technology leadership, reading instruction. *Faculty:* 18 full-time (10 women), 4 part-time/adjunct (3 women). *Students:* Average age 37. In 2009, 135 master's awarded. *Degree requirements:* For master's, project or thesis. *Entrance requirements:* For master's, minimum GPA of 3.0 in field, 2.5 overall; teaching experience. Additional exam requirements/recommendations for international students: Required—TOEFL (minimum score 550 paper-based; 213 computer-based). *Application deadline:* For fall admission, 6/30 for domestic and international students. Application fee: $55. Electronic applications accepted. *Financial support:* Career-related internships or fieldwork, Federal Work-Study, and institutionally sponsored loans available. Support available to part-time students. Financial award application deadline: 3/1; financial award applicants required to submit FAFSA. *Unit head:* Dr. Jeanette Bicais, Chair, 510-885-3027, E-mail: jeanette.bicais@csueastbay.edu. *Application contact:* Donna Wiley, Interim Associate Director, 510-885-2928, Fax: 510-885-4777, E-mail: donna.wiley@csueastbay.edu.

California State University, Fresno, Division of Graduate Studies, School of Education and Human Development, Fresno, CA 93740-8027. Offers MA, MS, Ed D. *Accreditation:* NCATE. Part-time and evening/weekend programs available. *Degree requirements:* For master's, thesis or alternative; for doctorate, thesis/dissertation. *Entrance requirements:* For master's, GRE General Test, MAT; for doctorate, GRE or MAT, minimum GPA of 3.2, master's degree. Additional exam requirements/recommendations for international students: Required—TOEFL. Electronic applications accepted. *Faculty research:* Adult community education, parenting, gifted and talented curriculum and instruction, peer mediation and conflict resolution.

California State University, Long Beach, Graduate Studies, College of Education, Long Beach, CA 90840. Offers MA, MS, Ed D. *Accreditation:* NCATE. Part-time and evening/weekend programs available. *Faculty:* 67 full-time (40 women), 15 part-time/adjunct (7 women). *Students:* 266 full-time (201 women), 546 part-time (440 women); includes 447 minority (84 African Americans, 6 American Indian/Alaska Native, 127 Asian Americans or Pacific Islanders, 230 Hispanic Americans), 17 international. Average age 33. 918 applicants, 38% accepted, 283 enrolled. *Entrance requirements:* For master's, GRE General Test, minimum GPA of 2.75. *Application deadline:* For fall admission, 3/1 for domestic students. Applications are processed on a rolling basis. Application fee: $55. Electronic applications accepted. *Expenses:* Required

fees: $1802 per semester. Part-time tuition and fees vary according to course load. *Financial support:* Federal Work-Study, institutionally sponsored loans, and scholarships/grants available. Financial award application deadline: 3/2. *Faculty research:* K-16 educational reform and partnership, gender issues related to teaching and learning, urban education (poverty, diversity, language), assessment and standards-based education. *Unit head:* Dr. Marquita Grenot-Scheyer, Dean, 562-985-1609, Fax: 562-985-4951, E-mail: cedinfo@csulb.edu. *Application contact:* Nancy L. McGlothin, Coordinator for Graduate Studies and Research, 562-985-8476, Fax: 562-985-4951, E-mail: nmcgloth@csulb.edu.

California State University, Los Angeles, Graduate Studies, Charter College of Education, Los Angeles, CA 90032-8530. Offers MA, MS, PhD. *Accreditation:* NCATE. Part-time and evening/weekend programs available. *Faculty:* 41 full-time (27 women), 36 part-time/adjunct (22 women). *Students:* 824 full-time (606 women), 837 part-time (617 women); includes 1,008 minority (89 African Americans, 201 Asian Americans or Pacific Islanders, 718 Hispanic Americans), 78 international. Average age 34. 416 applicants, 99% accepted, 263 enrolled. In 2009, 396 master's awarded. *Degree requirements:* For doctorate, thesis/dissertation. *Entrance requirements:* For master's, minimum GPA of 2.75 in last 90 units of course work, teaching certificate; for doctorate, GRE General Test, master's degree; minimum undergraduate GPA of 3.0, graduate 3.5. Additional exam requirements/recommendations for international students: Required—TOEFL (minimum score 500 paper-based; 173 computer-based). *Application deadline:* For fall admission, 5/1 for domestic and international students. Applications are processed on a rolling basis. Application fee: $55. Electronic applications accepted. *Financial support:* Career-related internships or fieldwork and Federal Work-Study available. Support available to part-time students. Financial award application deadline: 3/1. *Unit head:* Dr. Mary Falvey, Dean, 323-343-4300, Fax: 323-343-4318, E-mail: mfalvey@calstatela.edu. *Application contact:* Dr. Cheryl L. Ney, Dean of Graduate Studies, 323-343-3820, Fax: 323-343-5653, E-mail: cney@cslanet.calstatela.edu.

California State University, Monterey Bay, College of Professional Studies, Institute for Advanced Studies in Education, Seaside, CA 93955-8001. Offers MA. *Accreditation:* NCATE. Part-time and evening/weekend programs available. *Degree requirements:* For master's, one foreign language, thesis, 2 years of teaching experience. *Entrance requirements:* For master's, recommendations, verification of U. S. Constitution requirement. Additional exam requirements/recommendations for international students: Required—TOEFL (minimum score 550 paper-based; 213 computer-based; 71 iBT). Electronic applications accepted. *Faculty research:* Multicultural education, linguistic diversity, behavior analysis.

California State University, Northridge, Graduate Studies, College of Education, Northridge, CA 91330. Offers MA, MA Ed, MS, Ed D. *Accreditation:* NCATE. Part-time and evening/weekend programs available. *Faculty:* 82 full-time (52 women), 182 part-time/adjunct (113 women). *Students:* 621 full-time (497 women), 694 part-time (532 women); includes 558 minority (78 African Americans, 6 American Indian/Alaska Native, 102 Asian Americans or Pacific Islanders, 372 Hispanic Americans), 27 international. Average age 34. 1,011 applicants, 58% accepted, 448 enrolled. In 2009, 645 master's awarded. *Entrance requirements:* Additional exam requirements/recommendations for international students: Required—TOEFL. *Application deadline:* For fall admission, 11/30 for domestic students. Application fee: $55. *Financial support:* Fellowships, career-related internships or fieldwork, Federal Work-Study, institutionally sponsored loans, scholarships/grants, and tuition waivers (partial) available. Support available to part-time students. Financial award application deadline: 3/1. *Faculty research:* Federal teacher center support, bilingual teacher training. *Unit head:* Dr. Michael E. Spagna, Dean, 818-677-2590. *Application contact:* Dr. Michael E. Spagna, Dean, 818-677-2590.

California State University, Sacramento, Graduate Studies, College of Education, Sacramento, CA 95819. Offers MA, MS. Part-time programs available. *Degree requirements:* For master's, thesis or alternative, writing proficiency exam. *Entrance requirements:* Additional exam requirements/recommendations for international students: Required—TOEFL. Electronic applications accepted.

California State University, San Bernardino, Graduate Studies, College of Education, San Bernardino, CA 92407-2397. Offers bilingual/cross-cultural education (MA); curriculum and instruction (MA); educational administration (MA); educational leadership and curriculum (Ed D); educational psychology and counseling (MA, MS), including correctional and alternative education (MA), counseling and guidance (MS), rehabilitation counseling (MA); elementary education (MA); English as a second language (MA); environmental education (MA); general education (MA); history and English for secondary teachers (MA); instructional technology (MA); reading (MA); secondary education (MA); special education and rehabilitation counseling (MA), including rehabilitation counseling, special education; teaching of science (MA); vocational and career education (MA). *Accreditation:* NCATE. Part-time and evening/weekend programs available. *Faculty:* 35 full-time (15 women), 24 part-time/adjunct (15 women). *Students:* 921 full-time (710 women), 716 part-time (490 women); includes 751 minority (137 African Americans, 12 American Indian/Alaska Native, 73 Asian Americans or Pacific Islanders, 529 Hispanic Americans), 18 international. Average age 36. 493 applicants, 86% accepted, 243 enrolled. In 2009, 370 master's awarded. *Degree requirements:* For master's, comprehensive exam (for some programs), thesis (for some programs), advancement to candidacy. *Entrance requirements:* For master's, minimum GPA of 3.0 in education. *Application deadline:* For fall admission, 8/31 priority date for domestic students. Application fee: $55. *Financial support:* Career-related internships or fieldwork and Federal Work-Study available. Support available to part-time students. *Faculty research:* Multicultural education, brain-based learning, science education, social studies/global education. *Unit head:* Dr. Patricia Arlin, Dean, 909-537-5600, Fax: 909-537-7011, E-mail: parlin@csusb.edu. *Application contact:* Olivia Rosas, Director of Admissions, 909-537-7577, Fax: 909-537-7034, E-mail: orosas@csusb.edu.

California State University, San Marcos, College of Education, San Marcos, CA 92096-0001. Offers MA. *Accreditation:* NCATE. Part-time and evening/weekend programs available. *Degree requirements:* For master's, thesis. *Entrance requirements:* For master's, minimum GPA of 3.0, teaching credentials, 1 year of teaching experience. *Faculty research:* Multicultural literature, art as knowledge, poetry and second language acquisition, restructuring K–12 education and improving the training of K–8 science teachers.

California State University, Stanislaus, College of Education, Turlock, CA 95382. Offers MA, Ed D, Graduate Certificate. *Accreditation:* NCATE. Part-time and evening/weekend programs available. *Degree requirements:* For master's, thesis. *Entrance requirements:* For master's, MAT, minimum GPA of 3.0. Additional exam requirements/recommendations for international students: Required—TOEFL (minimum score 550 paper-based; 213 computer-based).

California University of Pennsylvania, School of Graduate Studies and Research, School of Education, California, PA 15419-1394. Offers M Ed, MAT, MS, MSW. *Accreditation:* NCATE. Part-time and evening/weekend programs available. Postbaccalaureate distance learning degree programs offered (minimal on-campus study). *Degree requirements:* For master's, comprehensive exam, thesis optional. *Entrance requirements:* For master's, PRAXIS, MAT, minimum QPA of 3.0. Additional exam requirements/recommendations for international students: Required—TOEFL (minimum score 550 paper-based; 213 computer-based; 80 iBT). Electronic applications accepted. *Faculty research:* Autism counseling, injury and education, early childhood education, National Board certification.

Calvin College, Graduate Programs in Education, Grand Rapids, MI 49546-4388. Offers curriculum and instruction (M Ed); educational leadership (M Ed); learning disabilities (M Ed); literacy (M Ed). Part-time programs available. *Faculty:* 3 full-time (2 women), 4 part-time/adjunct (1 woman). *Students:* 7 full-time (6 women), 113 part-time (79 women); includes 9 minority (2 African Americans, 5 Asian Americans or Pacific Islanders, 2 Hispanic Americans). Average age 29. In 2009, 27 master's awarded. *Degree requirements:* For master's, thesis or seminar. *Entrance requirements:* For master's, teaching certificate. Additional exam requirements/recommendations for international students: Required—TOEFL (minimum score 550 paper-based; 213 computer-based). *Application deadline:* For fall admission, 8/1 priority date for domestic students, 6/1 priority date for international students; for spring admission, 1/1 priority date for domestic students, 2/1 priority date for international students. Applications are processed on a rolling basis. Application fee: $0. Electronic applications accepted. *Expenses:* Tuition: Full-time $10,080. *Financial support:* Federal Work-Study, scholarships/grants, and tuition waivers (full and partial) available. Support available to part-time students. Financial award application deadline: 4/3. *Faculty research:* Literacy, racialized gender and gendered identity, teacher learning, learning disabilities identification. *Unit head:* Dr. Debra Buursma, Graduate Program Director, 616-526-6231, Fax: 616-526-6505, E-mail: dbuursma@calvin.edu. *Application contact:* Cindi Hoekstra, Program Coordinator, 616-526-6158, Fax: 616-526-6505, E-mail: choekstr@calvin.edu.

Cambridge College, School of Education, Cambridge, MA 02138-5304. Offers autism specialist (M Ed); autism/behavior analyst (M Ed); behavior analyst (Post-Master's Certificate); behavioral management (M Ed); early childhood teacher (M Ed); education specialist in curriculum and instruction (CAGS); educational leadership (Ed D); elementary teacher (M Ed); English as a second language (M Ed, Certificate); general science (M Ed); health education, health promotion (Post-Master's Certificate); health/family and consumer sciences (M Ed); history (M Ed); individualized degree (M Ed); information technology literacy (M Ed); instructional technology (M Ed); interdisciplinary studies (M Ed); library teacher (M Ed); literacy education (M Ed); mathematics (M Ed); mathematics specialist (Certificate); middle school mathematics and science (M Ed); school administration (M Ed, CAGS); school guidance counselor (M Ed); school nurse education (M Ed); school social worker/school adjustment counselor (M Ed); special education administrator (CAGS); special education/moderate disabilities (M Ed); teaching skills and methodologies (M Ed). Part-time and evening/weekend programs available. Postbaccalaureate distance learning degree programs offered (minimal on-campus study). *Faculty:* 10 full-time (3 women), 283 part-time/adjunct (187 women). *Students:* 974 full-time (755 women), 1,071 part-time (835 women); includes 940 minority (762 African Americans, 4 American Indian/Alaska Native, 22 Asian Americans or Pacific Islanders, 152 Hispanic Americans), 28 international. Average age 39. In 2009, 866 master's, 4 doctorates, 209 CAGSs awarded. *Degree requirements:* For master's, thesis, internship/practicum (licensure program only); for doctorate, thesis/dissertation; for other advanced degree, thesis. *Entrance requirements:* For master's, interview, resume, documentation of licensure, 2 professional references; for doctorate, official transcripts, interview, resume, documentation of licensure (if any), written personal statement/essay, portfolio of scholarly and professional work, qualifying assessment, 2 professional references, health insurance, immunizations form; for other advanced degree, official transcripts, interview, resume, documentation of licensure (if any), written personal statement/essay, 2 professional references, health insurance, immunizations form. Additional exam requirements/recommendations for international students: Required—TOEFL (minimum score 550 paper-based; 213 computer-based; 79 iBT); Recommended—IELTS (minimum score 6). *Application deadline:* Applications are processed on a rolling basis. Application fee: $30. Electronic applications accepted. *Expenses:* Contact institution. *Financial support:* In 2009–10, 1,373 students received support. Career-related internships or fieldwork, Federal Work-Study, and scholarships/grants available. Financial award applicants required to submit FAFSA. *Faculty research:* Adult education, accelerated learning, mathematics education, brain compatible learning, special education and law. *Unit head:* Dr. N. Alan Sheppard, Interim Associate Dean, 617-873-0619, E-mail: alan.sheppard@cambridgecollege.edu. *Application contact:* Stephen Lyons, Director of Enrollment, Graduate and N.I.T.E. Programs, 617-868-1000, Fax: 617-349-3561, E-mail: stephen.lyons@cambridgecollege.edu.

Cameron University, Office of Graduate Studies, Program in Education, Lawton, OK 73505-6377. Offers M Ed. *Accreditation:* NCATE. Part-time and evening/weekend programs available. *Degree requirements:* For master's, portfolio. *Entrance requirements:* Additional exam requirements/recommendations for international students: Required—TOEFL (minimum score 550 paper-based; 213 computer-based). Electronic applications accepted. *Faculty research:* Motivation, computer learning, special education mathematics, inquiry-based learning.

Cameron University, Office of Graduate Studies, Program in Teaching, Lawton, OK 73505-6377. Offers MAT. *Accreditation:* NCATE. *Degree requirements:* For master's, portfolio. *Entrance requirements:* Additional exam requirements/recommendations for international students: Required—TOEFL (minimum score 550 paper-based; 213 computer-based). Electronic applications accepted. *Faculty research:* Teacher retention/attrition, teacher education.

Campbellsville University, School of Education, Campbellsville, KY 42718-2799. Offers curriculum and instruction (MAE); special education (MASE). *Accreditation:* NCATE. Part-time and evening/weekend programs available. Postbaccalaureate distance learning degree programs offered (minimal on-campus study). *Degree requirements:* For master's, thesis, research paper. *Entrance requirements:* For master's, GRE or PRAXIS, minimum undergraduate GPA of 2.75, teaching certificate, professional growth plan, letters of recommendation, disposition assessment, entrance interview. Electronic applications accepted. *Expenses:* Tuition: Full-time $6750; part-time $375 per credit hour. *Faculty research:* Professional development, curriculum development, school governance, assessment, special education.

Campbell University, Graduate and Professional Programs, School of Education, Buies Creek, NC 27506. Offers administration (MSA); community counseling (MA); elementary education (M Ed); English education (M Ed); interdisciplinary studies (M Ed); mathematics education (M Ed); middle grades education (M Ed); physical education (M Ed); school counseling (M Ed); secondary education (M Ed); social science education (M Ed). *Accreditation:* NCATE. Part-time and evening/weekend programs available. *Degree requirements:* For master's, comprehensive exam. *Entrance requirements:* For master's, GRE General Test, minimum GPA of 2.7. *Faculty research:* Spiritual values and wellness issues in counseling, stress and professional burnout among counselors, thinking strategies, leadership, adaptive technology.

Canisius College, Graduate Division, School of Education and Human Services, Department of Graduate Education, Buffalo, NY 14208-1098. Offers adolescence education (grades 7-12) (MS); childhood education (grades 1-6) (MS); college student personnel administration (MS); deaf education (MS); differentiated instruction (MS Ed); educational administration and supervision (MS); general education (MS Ed); initial teacher certification (elementary education) (MS); initial teacher certification (secondary education) (MS); literacy (MS Ed); special education (MS). *Accreditation:* NCATE. Part-time and evening/weekend programs available. *Faculty:* 22 full-time (14 women), 84 part-time/adjunct (54 women). *Students:* 409 full-time (288 women), 261 part-time (187 women); includes 29 minority (24 African Americans, 5 Hispanic Americans), 156 international. Average age 30. 518 applicants, 74% accepted, 240 enrolled. In 2009, 346 master's awarded. Application fee: $25. *Financial support:* Research assistantships with full tuition reimbursements, career-related internships or fieldwork, institutionally sponsored loans, scholarships/grants, health care benefits, tuition waivers (full and partial), and unspecified assistantships available. *Faculty research:* Autism, Asperger's disease, private higher education, reading strategies. *Unit head:* Rev. Paul Nochelski, Chair of Graduate Education and Leadership, 716-888-3297, Fax: 716-888-3299. *Application contact:* James D. Bagwell, Director of Graduate Recruitment and Admissions, 716-888-2544, Fax: 716-888-3290, E-mail: bagwellj@canisius.edu.

Cape Breton University, School of Education, Health, and Wellness, Sydney, NS B1P 6L2, Canada. Offers educational counseling (Diploma); educational curriculum (Diploma); educational studies in arts education (Certificate); educational technology (Diploma). Part-time and evening/weekend programs available. Postbaccalaureate distance learning degree programs offered (no on-campus study). *Faculty:* 15 part-time/adjunct (5 women). *Students:* 171 part-time (103 women). Average age 30. *Application deadline:* For fall admission, 8/1 priority date for domestic students. Applications are processed on a rolling basis. Application fee: $50. Electronic applications accepted. *Unit head:* Susan Basso, Coordinator of the Education Program, 902-563-1651, Fax: 902-563-1861. *Application contact:* Terry MacDonald, Coordinator, Teacher Education Program, 902-563-1647, Fax: 902-563-1449, E-mail: terry_macdonald@cbu.ca.

Capella University, School of Education, Minneapolis, MN 55402. Offers college teaching (Certificate); curriculum and instruction (MS, PhD); education (MS); enrollment management (MS); instructional design for online learning (MS, PhD); k-12 studies in education (MS, PhD); leadership for higher education (MS, PhD); leadership in education administration (Certificate); leadership in educational administration (MS, PhD); postsecondary and adult education (MS,

Education—General

Capella University (continued)

PhD); professional studies in education (MS, PhD); reading and literacy (MS); training and performance improvement (MS, PhD). Part-time and evening/weekend programs available. Postbaccalaureate distance learning degree programs offered (minimal on-campus study). Terminal master's awarded for partial completion of doctoral program. *Degree requirements:* For master's, thesis optional, integrative project; for doctorate, comprehensive exam, thesis/dissertation. *Entrance requirements:* Additional exam requirements/recommendations for international students: Required—TOEFL (minimum score 550 paper-based; 213 computer-based), TWE (minimum score 4). Electronic applications accepted. *Faculty research:* Higher education administration, distance learning, adult education, training and curriculum design.

Cardinal Stritch University, College of Education, Milwaukee, WI 53217-3985. Offers MA, MAT, ME, MS, Ed D, PhD. *Accreditation:* NCATE. Part-time and evening/weekend programs available. *Degree requirements:* For master's, comprehensive exam, thesis (for some programs); for doctorate, thesis/dissertation, practica/field experience. *Entrance requirements:* For doctorate, minimum GPA of 3.5 in master's coursework, portfolio, interview, letters of recommendation (3).

Caribbean University, Graduate School, Bayamón, PR 00960-0493. Offers administration and supervision (MA Ed); criminal justice (MA); curriculum and instruction (MA Ed), including elementary education, English education, history education, mathematics education, primary education, science education, Spanish education; education (PhD); gerontology (MSN); human resources (MBA); museology, archiving and art history (MA Ed); neonatal pediatrics (MSN); physical education (MA Ed); special education (MA Ed). *Entrance requirements:* For master's, interview, minimum GPA of 2.5.

Carlow University, School of Education, Program in Educational Praxis, Pittsburgh, PA 15213-3165. Offers MA. Part-time and evening/weekend programs available. *Entrance requirements:* Additional exam requirements/recommendations for international students: Required—TOEFL. Electronic applications accepted. *Expenses:* Tuition: Full-time $11,250; part-time $625 per credit. Tuition and fees vary according to course load, degree level and program.

Carnegie Mellon University, College of Humanities and Social Sciences, Center for Innovation in Learning, Pittsburgh, PA 15213-3891. Offers instructional science (PhD). *Faculty research:* Improvement of undergraduate education, teaching and learning at the college level.

Carroll University, Graduate Program in Education, Waukesha, WI 53186-5593. Offers education (M Ed); learning and teaching (M Ed). Part-time and evening/weekend programs available. *Faculty:* 8 full-time (7 women), 11 part-time/adjunct (10 women). *Students:* 53 full-time (40 women), 196 part-time (150 women); includes 12 minority (3 African Americans, 4 American Indian/Alaska Native, 2 Asian Americans or Pacific Islanders, 3 Hispanic Americans), 1 international. Average age 34. 141 applicants, 54% accepted, 67 enrolled. In 2009, 71 master's awarded. *Degree requirements:* For master's, thesis. *Entrance requirements:* For master's, minimum undergraduate GPA of 2.5 in related field. Additional exam requirements/recommendations for international students: Required—TOEFL. *Application deadline:* For fall admission, 8/15 priority date for domestic students. Applications are processed on a rolling basis. Application fee: $0. Electronic applications accepted. *Expenses:* Tuition: Part-time $505 per credit. *Financial support:* Available to part-time students. Application deadline: 3/15. *Faculty research:* Qualitative research methods, whole language approaches to teaching, the writing process, multicultural education, gifted/talented learners. *Unit head:* Dr. Bruce Strom, Chair, 262-524-7130, Fax: 262-524-7139, E-mail: bstrom@carrollu.edu. *Application contact:* Tami Bartunek, Graduate Admission Counselor, 262-524-7643, E-mail: tbartune@carrollu.edu.

Carson-Newman College, Graduate Program in Education, Jefferson City, TN 37760. Offers curriculum and instruction (M Ed); educational leadership (M Ed); elementary education (MAT); school counseling (MS); secondary education (MAT); teaching English as a second language (MATESL). *Accreditation:* NCATE. Part-time and evening/weekend programs available. *Faculty:* 5 full-time (2 women), 10 part-time/adjunct (3 women). *Students:* 112 full-time (84 women), 84 part-time (52 women); includes 5 African Americans, 17 international. Average age 32. 86 applicants, 98% accepted. In 2009, 55 master's awarded. *Degree requirements:* For master's, thesis or alternative. *Entrance requirements:* For master's, NTE, minimum GPA of 3.0 in major, 2.5 overall. *Application deadline:* For fall admission, 7/15 priority date for domestic students. Applications are processed on a rolling basis. Application fee: $25 ($50 for international students). *Expenses:* Tuition: Full-time $5490; part-time $305 per semester hour. Required fees: $200. *Financial support:* In 2009–10, 41 students received support. Federal Work-Study and unspecified assistantships available. Financial award application deadline: 4/1; financial award applicants required to submit FAFSA. *Unit head:* Dr. Sharon Teets, Chair, 865-471-3461. *Application contact:* Graduate Admissions and Services Adviser, 865-471-3460, Fax: 865-471-3875.

Carthage College, Division of Teacher Education, Kenosha, WI 53140. Offers classroom guidance and counseling (M Ed); creative arts (M Ed); gifted and talented children (M Ed); language arts (M Ed); modern language (M Ed); natural sciences (M Ed); reading (M Ed, Certificate); social sciences (M Ed); teacher leadership (M Ed). Part-time and evening/weekend programs available. *Degree requirements:* For master's, thesis optional. *Entrance requirements:* For master's, MAT, minimum B average, letters of reference.

Castleton State College, Division of Graduate Studies, Department of Education, Castleton, VT 05735. Offers curriculum and instruction (MA Ed); educational leadership (MA Ed, CAGS); language arts and reading (MA Ed, CAGS); special education (MA Ed, CAGS). Part-time and evening/weekend programs available. *Degree requirements:* For master's, thesis or alternative; for CAGS, publishable paper. *Entrance requirements:* For master's, GRE General Test, MAT, interview, minimum undergraduate GPA of 3.0; for CAGS, educational research, master's degree, minimum undergraduate GPA of 3.0. *Expenses:* Tuition, state resident: full-time $10,290; part-time $429 per credit. Tuition, nonresident: full-time $15,420; part-time $643 per credit. One-time fee: $200 full-time. *Faculty research:* Assessment, narrative.

Catawba College, Program in Education, Salisbury, NC 28144-2488. Offers elementary education (M Ed). *Accreditation:* NCATE. Part-time and evening/weekend programs available. *Faculty:* 4 full-time (3 women). *Students:* 39 part-time (all women). *Degree requirements:* For master's, portfolio. *Entrance requirements:* For master's, NTE, PRAXIS II, minimum undergraduate GPA of 3.0, valid teaching license, official transcripts, 3 references, essay, interview. *Application deadline:* Applications are processed on a rolling basis. Application fee: $25. *Expenses:* Tuition: Part-time $160 per credit hour. *Financial support:* Scholarships/grants available. Financial award applicants required to submit FAFSA. *Faculty research:* Integrated arts in elementary schools, professional development schools. *Unit head:* Dr. Rhonda Truitt, Chair, Department of Teacher Education, 704-637-4468, Fax: 704-637-4732, E-mail: rltruitt@catawba.edu. *Application contact:* Dr. Lou W. Kasias, Director, Graduate Program, 704-637-4462, Fax: 704-637-4732, E-mail: lakasias@catawba.edu.

The Catholic University of America, School of Arts and Sciences, Department of Education, Washington, DC 20064. Offers Catholic educational leadership (PhD); education (Certificate); educational psychology (PhD); learning and instruction (MA); secondary education (MA); special education (MA). *Accreditation:* NCATE. Part-time programs available. *Faculty:* 11 full-time (8 women), 3 part-time/adjunct (0 women). *Students:* 6 full-time (5 women), 56 part-time (39 women); includes 9 minority (5 African Americans, 2 Asian Americans or Pacific Islanders, 2 Hispanic Americans), 2 international. Average age 38. 54 applicants, 59% accepted, 14 enrolled. In 2009, 14 master's, 6 doctorates, 1 other advanced degree awarded. *Degree requirements:* For master's, comprehensive exam, thesis or alternative; for doctorate, comprehensive exam, thesis/dissertation. *Entrance requirements:* For master's and doctorate, GRE General Test or MAT, statement of purpose, official copies of academic transcripts, three letters of recommendation. Additional exam requirements/recommendations for international students: Required—TOEFL (minimum score 580 paper-based; 237 computer-based). *Application deadline:* For fall admission, 8/1 priority date for domestic students, 7/15 for international students; for spring admission, 12/1 priority date for domestic students, 10/15 for international students. Applications are processed on a rolling basis. Application fee: $55. Electronic applications accepted. *Expenses:* Tuition: Full-time $31,740; part-time $1245 per credit hour. Required fees: $50; $25 per semester hour. One-time fee: $425. *Financial support:* Fellowships, research assistantships, teaching assistantships, Federal Work-Study, scholarships/grants, tuition waivers (full and partial), and unspecified assistantships available. Financial award application deadline: 2/1; financial award applicants required to submit FAFSA. *Faculty research:* Catholic school issues, reflective teaching, cognitive psychology, urban education. Total annual research expenditures: $68,905. *Unit head:* Dr. Merylann J. Schuttloffel, Chair, 202-319-5805, Fax: 202-319-5815, E-mail: schuttloffel@cua.edu. *Application contact:* Julie Schwing, Director of Graduate Admissions, 202-319-5057, Fax: 202-319-6533, E-mail: cua-admissions@cua.edu.

Cedar Crest College, Department of Education, Allentown, PA 18104-6196. Offers M Ed. Part-time and evening/weekend programs available. *Entrance requirements:* Additional exam requirements/recommendations for international students: Required—TOEFL. *Faculty research:* Science education, reading, history of PA, math education.

Cedarville University, Graduate Programs, Cedarville, OH 45314-0601. Offers M Ed. Part-time and evening/weekend programs available. *Degree requirements:* For master's, thesis. *Entrance requirements:* For master's, GRE, 2 professional recommendations. Additional exam requirements/recommendations for international students: Required—TOEFL (minimum score 550 paper-based; 213 computer-based). Electronic applications accepted.

Centenary College, Program in Education, Hackettstown, NJ 07840-2100. Offers instructional leadership (MA); special education (MA). *Accreditation:* Teacher Education Accreditation Council. Part-time and evening/weekend programs available. Postbaccalaureate distance learning degree programs offered (minimal on-campus study). *Degree requirements:* For master's, thesis. *Entrance requirements:* For master's, interview, minimum undergraduate GPA of 2.8.

Centenary College of Louisiana, Graduate Programs, Department of Education, Shreveport, LA 71104. Offers administration (M Ed); elementary education (MAT); secondary education (MAT); supervision of instruction (M Ed). Part-time and evening/weekend programs available. *Degree requirements:* For master's, comprehensive exam. *Entrance requirements:* For master's, GRE General Test (M Ed), PRAXIS I and PRAXIS II (MAT), teacher certification (M Ed), minimum GPA of 2.5. *Expenses:* Contact institution. *Faculty research:* Teachers as advocates for teachers, portfolio assessment, disabled readers.

Central Connecticut State University, School of Graduate Studies, School of Education and Professional Studies, New Britain, CT 06050-4010. Offers MAT, MS, Ed D, Certificate, Sixth Year Certificate. *Accreditation:* NCATE. Part-time and evening/weekend programs available. *Faculty:* 66 full-time (34 women), 92 part-time/adjunct (51 women). *Students:* 247 full-time (194 women), 931 part-time (720 women); includes 116 minority (58 African Americans, 4 American Indian/Alaska Native, 7 Asian Americans or Pacific Islanders, 47 Hispanic Americans), 11 international. Average age 33. 622 applicants, 52% accepted, 267 enrolled. In 2009, 283 master's, 10 doctorates, 97 other advanced degrees awarded. *Degree requirements:* For master's, comprehensive exam, thesis or alternative; for doctorate, thesis/dissertation; for other advanced degree, qualifying exam. *Entrance requirements:* For master's, minimum undergraduate GPA of 2.7; for doctorate, GRE. Additional exam requirements/recommendations for international students: Required—TOEFL. *Application deadline:* For fall admission, 7/1 for domestic students, 5/1 for international students; for spring admission, 12/1 for domestic students, 11/1 for international students. Applications are processed on a rolling basis. Application fee: $50. Electronic applications accepted. *Expenses:* Tuition, area resident: Full-time $4662; part-time $440 per credit. Tuition, state resident: full-time $6994; part-time $440 per credit. Tuition, nonresident: full-time $12,988; part-time $440 per credit. Required fees: $3606. One-time fee: $62 part-time. *Financial support:* In 2009–10, 78 students received support, including 35 research assistantships; career-related internships or fieldwork, Federal Work-Study, scholarships/grants, and unspecified assistantships also available. Support available to part-time students. Financial award application deadline: 3/1; financial award applicants required to submit FAFSA. *Unit head:* Dr. Mitchell Sakofs, Dean, 860-832-2100, E-mail: sakofsm@ccsu.edu. *Application contact:* Dr. Mitchell Sakofs, Dean, 860-832-2100, E-mail: sakofsm@ccsu.edu.

Central Methodist University, College of Graduate and Extended Studies, Fayette, MO 65248-1198. Offers clinical counseling (MS); clinical nurse leader (MSN); education (M Ed). Part-time and evening/weekend programs available. Postbaccalaureate distance learning degree programs offered (no on-campus study). *Degree requirements:* For master's, thesis. *Entrance requirements:* For master's, GRE General Test, minimum GPA of 2.75. Electronic applications accepted.

Central Michigan University, Central Michigan University Off-Campus Programs, Program in Education, Mount Pleasant, MI 48859. Offers adult education (MA); community college (MA); education (MA); guidance and development (MA); instructional (MA); reading and literacy K-12 (MA). Part-time and evening/weekend programs available. *Entrance requirements:* For master's, minimum GPA of 2.7 in major. Additional exam requirements/recommendations for international students: Required—TOEFL. *Application deadline:* Applications are processed on a rolling basis. Application fee: $50. Electronic applications accepted. *Financial support:* Scholarships/grants available. Support available to part-time students. *Unit head:* Jennifer Cochran, Director, 989-774-2584, E-mail: jennifer.cochran@cmich.edu. *Application contact:* 877-268-4636, E-mail: cmuoffcampus@cmich.edu.

Central Michigan University, College of Graduate Studies, College of Education and Human Services, Mount Pleasant, MI 48859. Offers MA, MS, Ed D, Ed S, Graduate Certificate. Part-time and evening/weekend programs available. *Degree requirements:* For master's and other advanced degree, thesis or alternative; for doctorate, thesis/dissertation. *Entrance requirements:* For doctorate, GRE or MAT, master's degree, minimum GPA of 3.5, 3 years of professional education experience. Electronic applications accepted.

Central State University, Program in Education, Wilberforce, OH 45384. Offers M Ed. *Accreditation:* NCATE. Part-time and evening/weekend programs available. *Degree requirements:* For master's, thesis or alternative. *Entrance requirements:* For master's, GRE.

Central Washington University, Graduate Studies and Research, College of Education and Professional Studies, Department of Education, Ellensburg, WA 98926. Offers master teacher (M Ed); reading education (M Ed); special education (M Ed). Part-time programs available. *Faculty:* 37 full-time (16 women). *Students:* 10 full-time (7 women), 57 part-time (39 women); includes 5 minority (2 American Indian/Alaska Native, 3 Hispanic Americans). In 2009, 39 master's awarded. *Degree requirements:* For master's, thesis or alternative. *Entrance requirements:* For master's, minimum GPA of 3.0. Additional exam requirements/recommendations for international students: Required—TOEFL (minimum score 550 paper-based; 213 computer-based; 79 iBT). *Application deadline:* For fall admission, 2/1 priority date for domestic students; for winter admission, 10/1 for domestic students; for spring admission, 1/1 for domestic students. Applications are processed on a rolling basis. Application fee: $50. Electronic applications accepted. *Expenses:* Tuition, state resident: full-time $7353; part-time $245 per credit. Tuition, nonresident: full-time $16,383; part-time $546 per credit. Required fees: $882. Tuition and fees vary according to degree level. *Financial support:* In 2009–10, 6 teaching assistantships with partial tuition reimbursements (averaging $9,145 per year) were awarded; Federal Work-Study, health care benefits, and unspecified assistantships also available. Financial award application deadline: 3/1; financial award applicants required to submit FAFSA. *Unit head:* Dr. Connie Lambert, Dean, 509-963-1411, Fax: 509-963-1049. *Application contact:* Justine Eason, Admissions Program Coordinator, 509-963-3103, Fax: 509-963-1799, E-mail: masters@cwu.edu.

Chadron State College, School of Professional and Graduate Studies, Department of Education, Chadron, NE 69337. Offers business (MA Ed); community counseling (MA Ed); educational administration (MS Ed, Sp Ed); elementary education (MS Ed); history (MA Ed); language and literature (MA Ed); secondary administration (MS Ed); secondary education (MS Ed).

Accreditation: NCATE. Part-time and evening/weekend programs available. Postbaccalaureate distance learning degree programs offered. *Degree requirements:* For master's, thesis optional. *Entrance requirements:* For master's, GRE General Test, GRE Writing Test, minimum GPA of 2.75 or 12 graduate hours at CSC with minimum GPA of 3.25. Additional exam requirements/recommendations for international students: Required—TOEFL. Electronic applications accepted. *Faculty research:* Rural education, technology, mental health.

Chaminade University of Honolulu, Graduate Services, Program in Education, Honolulu, HI 96816-1578. Offers social science via peace education (M Ed). Part-time and evening/weekend programs available. Postbaccalaureate distance learning degree programs offered (minimal on-campus study). *Degree requirements:* For master's, thesis or alternative. *Entrance requirements:* For master's, minimum GPA of 2.75, 3 letters of recommendation. Additional exam requirements/recommendations for international students: Required—TOEFL (minimum score 550 paper-based). *Faculty research:* Peace and curriculum education.

Chapman University, Graduate Studies, College of Educational Studies, Orange, CA 92866. Offers MA, MS, PhD, Credential, Ed S. Part-time and evening/weekend programs available. *Faculty:* 24 full-time (15 women), 25 part-time/adjunct (16 women). *Students:* 229 full-time (197 women), 231 part-time (186 women); includes 167 minority (7 African Americans, 2 American Indian/Alaska Native, 63 Asian Americans or Pacific Islanders, 95 Hispanic Americans), 2 international. Average age 30. 336 applicants, 58% accepted, 141 enrolled. In 2009, 142 master's awarded. *Degree requirements:* For master's, comprehensive exam (for some programs), thesis optional. *Entrance requirements:* For master's, GRE General Test, California Basic Educational Skills Test, minimum undergraduate GPA of 2.5. Additional exam requirements/recommendations for international students: Required—TOEFL (minimum score 550 paper-based; 213 computer-based; 80 iBT). *Application deadline:* Applications are processed on a rolling basis. Application fee: $55. Electronic applications accepted. Tuition and fees vary according to course load, degree level and program. *Financial support:* Fellowships, Federal Work-Study and scholarships/grants available. Financial award application deadline: 6/30; financial award applicants required to submit FAFSA. *Unit head:* Dr. Don Cardinal, Dean, 714-997-6781, E-mail: cardinal@chapman.edu. *Application contact:* Brianna Keitel, Admissions Coordinator, 714-997-6714, E-mail: keitel@chapman.edu.

Charleston Southern University, School of Education, Charleston, SC 29423-8087. Offers administration and supervision (M Ed), including elementary, secondary; elementary education (M Ed); secondary education (M Ed). *Accreditation:* NCATE. Part-time and evening/weekend programs available. *Faculty:* 4 full-time (2 women). *Students:* 70 part-time (57 women); includes 17 minority (all African Americans). Average age 34. 48 applicants, 79% accepted, 22 enrolled. In 2009, 27 master's awarded. *Degree requirements:* For master's, thesis optional. *Entrance requirements:* For master's, GRE or MAT. Additional exam requirements/recommendations for international students: Required—TOEFL (minimum score 550 paper-based; 213 computer-based; 79 iBT). *Application deadline:* Applications are processed on a rolling basis. Application fee: $30. *Expenses:* Contact institution. *Financial support:* Research assistantships with full tuition reimbursements, career-related internships or fieldwork and Federal Work-Study available. Financial award application deadline: 4/15; financial award applicants required to submit FAFSA. *Unit head:* Dr. Norma Harper, Dean, 843-863-7765, Fax: 843-863-7085, E-mail: nharper@csuniv.edu. *Application contact:* Alison Harrison, Graduate Enrollment Counselor, 843-863-7534, Fax: 843-863-7070, E-mail: aharrison@cwuniv.edu.

Chatham University, Program in Education, Pittsburgh, PA 15232-2826. Offers early childhood education (MAT); elementary education (MAT); English—secondary (MAT); environmental education (K-12) (MAT); secondary art (MAT); secondary biology education (MAT); secondary chemistry education (MAT); secondary English education (MAT); secondary math education (MAT); secondary physics education (MAT); secondary social studies education (MAT); special education (MAT). *Students:* 52 full-time (41 women), 20 part-time (16 women). Average age 30. 39 applicants, 79% accepted, 26 enrolled. In 2009, 37 master's awarded. *Degree requirements:* For master's, thesis, teaching experience. *Entrance requirements:* For master's, PRAXIS I, minimum GPA of 3.0, sample of written work, recommendation letters. Additional exam requirements/recommendations for international students: Required—TOEFL (minimum score 600 paper-based; 250 computer-based; 100 iBT), IELTS (minimum score 6.5), TWE. *Application deadline:* For fall admission, 5/1 priority date for domestic and international students; for spring admission, 10/15 priority date for domestic and international students. Applications are processed on a rolling basis. Application fee: $45. Electronic applications accepted. *Financial support:* Career-related internships or fieldwork available. Financial award applicants required to submit FAFSA. *Faculty research:* Gifted education, environmental education, technology in education, writing as learning, class size and achievement. *Unit head:* Dr. Barbara Biglan, Interim Director, 412-365-1170, E-mail: biglan@chatham.edu. *Application contact:* Dory Perry, Associate Director of Graduate Admissions, 412-365-2758, Fax: 412-365-1609, E-mail: gradadmissions@chatham.edu.

Chestnut Hill College, School of Graduate Studies, Department of Education, Philadelphia, PA 19118-2693. Offers early childhood education (M Ed); educational leadership (M Ed); elementary education (M Ed); secondary education (M Ed). Part-time and evening/weekend programs available. *Degree requirements:* For master's, thesis optional. *Entrance requirements:* For master's, PRAXIS I or proof of teaching certification, letters of recommendation, writing sample, 6 graduate credits with minimum B grade if undergraduate GPA less than 3.0. Additional exam requirements/recommendations for international students: Required—TOEFL (minimum score 500 paper-based; 213 computer-based). *Faculty research:* Culturally responsive pedagogy, gender issues, autism, inclusive education, mentoring and induction programs.

Cheyney University of Pennsylvania, School of Education and Professional Studies, Cheyney, PA 19319. Offers M Ed, MAT, MPA, MS, Certificate. *Accreditation:* NCATE. Part-time and evening/weekend programs available. *Degree requirements:* For master's and Certificate, thesis or alternative. *Entrance requirements:* For master's and Certificate, GRE General Test, MAT, minimum GPA of 2.75. Electronic applications accepted. *Faculty research:* Teacher motivation, critical thinking.

Chicago State University, School of Graduate and Professional Studies, College of Education, Chicago, IL 60628. Offers M Ed, MA, MAT, MS Ed, Ed D. *Accreditation:* NCATE. Part-time programs available. *Degree requirements:* For master's, thesis optional. *Entrance requirements:* For master's, minimum GPA of 2.75.

Christian Brothers University, School of Arts, Memphis, TN 38104-5581. Offers Catholic studies (MACS); curriculum and instruction (M Ed); educational leadership (MSEL); teacher-leadership (M Ed); teaching (MAT). Part-time and evening/weekend programs available. *Faculty:* 7 full-time (4 women), 10 part-time/adjunct (7 women). *Students:* 62 full-time (49 women), 175 part-time (125 women); includes 70 minority (60 African Americans, 5 Asian Americans or Pacific Islanders, 5 Hispanic Americans). Average age 32. In 2009, 92 master's awarded. *Entrance requirements:* For master's, GRE, GMAT, PRAXIS II. *Application deadline:* Applications are processed on a rolling basis. Application fee: $35. *Expenses:* Contact institution. *Financial support:* Institutionally sponsored loans available. Support available to part-time students. *Unit head:* Dr. Marius Carriere, Dean, 901-321-3366, Fax: 901-321-4340, E-mail: mcarrier@cbu.edu. *Application contact:* Dr. Talana L. Vogel, Director, 901-321-4101, Fax: 901-321-3408, E-mail: tvogel@cbu.edu.

Christopher Newport University, Graduate Studies, Department of Teacher Preparation, Newport News, VA 23606-2998. Offers art (PK-12) (MAT); biology (6-12) (MAT); computer science (6-12) (MAT); elementary (PK-6) (MAT); English (6-12) (MAT); French (PK-12) (MAT); history and social science (6-12) (MAT); mathematics (6-12) (MAT); music (PK-12) (MAT), including choral, instrumental; physics (6-12) (MAT); Spanish (PK-12) (MAT). Part-time and evening/weekend programs available. *Faculty:* 24 full-time (13 women), 4 part-time/adjunct (2 women). *Students:* 76 full-time (66 women), 12 part-time (10 women); includes 3 minority (2 African Americans, 1 Hispanic American). Average age 24. 3 applicants, 100% accepted, 2 enrolled. In 2009, 58 master's awarded. *Degree requirements:* For master's, comprehensive exam, thesis or alternative. *Entrance requirements:* For master's, PRAXIS I, minimum GPA of

3.0. Additional exam requirements/recommendations for international students: Required—TOEFL (minimum score 580 paper-based; 237 computer-based; 92 iBT). *Application deadline:* For fall admission, 8/15 for domestic students, 4/1 for international students; for spring admission, 10/15 for domestic students, 10/1 for international students. Applications are processed on a rolling basis. Application fee: $45. Electronic applications accepted. *Expenses:* Tuition, area resident: part-time $384 per credit hour. Tuition, state resident: part-time $384 per credit hour. Tuition, nonresident: part-time $701 per credit hour. *Financial support:* In 2009–10, 3 research assistantships with full and partial tuition reimbursements (averaging $2,000 per year) were awarded; career-related internships or fieldwork, Federal Work-Study, and unspecified assistantships also available. Support available to part-time students. Financial award application deadline: 3/1; financial award applicants required to submit FAFSA. *Faculty research:* Early literacy development, instructional innovations, professional teaching standards, multicultural issues, aesthetic education. *Unit head:* Dr. Marsha Sprague, Director, 757-594-7388, Fax: 757-594-7803, E-mail: msprague@cnu.edu. *Application contact:* Lyn Sawyer, Associate Director, Graduate Admissions, 757-594-7544, Fax: 757-594-7649, E-mail: gradstdy@cnu.edu.

The Citadel, The Military College of South Carolina, Citadel Graduate College, School of Education, Charleston, SC 29409. Offers M Ed, MAT, Ed S. *Accreditation:* NCATE. Part-time and evening/weekend programs available. *Faculty:* 12 full-time (7 women), 8 part-time/adjunct (5 women). *Students:* 44 full-time (34 women), 212 part-time (160 women); includes 43 minority (35 African Americans, 2 Asian Americans or Pacific Islanders, 6 Hispanic Americans). Average age 30. In 2009, 132 master's, 7 other advanced degrees awarded. *Degree requirements:* For master's and Ed S, comprehensive exam (for some programs), thesis (for some programs), internship. *Entrance requirements:* For master's, GRE (minimum score 900) or MAT (minimum score 396), minimum undergraduate GPA of 2.5, 2.7 for last 60 undergraduate semester hours; for Ed S, GRE (minimum 900) or MAT (minimum 396), minimum GPA of 3.5; SC State Professional Certificate with school administrator endorsement and two years in an administrative position equivalent to assistant principal or higher in education. Additional exam requirements/recommendations for international students: Required—TOEFL (minimum score 550 paper-based; 213 computer-based; 79 iBT). *Application deadline:* Applications are processed on a rolling basis. Application fee: $30. Electronic applications accepted. *Expenses:* Tuition, state resident: part-time $400 per credit hour. Tuition, nonresident: part-time $657 per credit hour. Required fees: $40 per term. *Financial support:* Fellowships, career-related internships or fieldwork, health care benefits, and unspecified assistantships available. Support available to part-time students. Financial award application deadline: 7/1; financial award applicants required to submit FAFSA. *Unit head:* Dr. Tony W. Johnson, Dean, 843-953-5871, Fax: 843-953-7258, E-mail: tony.johnson@citadel.edu. *Application contact:* Dr. Steve A. Nida, Associate Provost, The Citadel Graduate College, 843-953-5089, Fax: 843-953-7630, E-mail: cgc@citadel.edu.

City College of the City University of New York, Graduate School, School of Education, New York, NY 10031-9198. Offers MA, MS, AC. *Accreditation:* NCATE. Part-time and evening/weekend programs available. *Students:* 24 full-time (20 women), 349 part-time (247 women); includes 322 minority (121 African Americans, 58 Asian Americans or Pacific Islanders, 143 Hispanic Americans), 9 international. 227 applicants, 84% accepted. In 2009, 376 master's awarded. *Entrance requirements:* For master's, Liberal Arts and Sciences Test (LAST), Content Specialty Test (CST). Additional exam requirements/recommendations for international students: Required—TOEFL. *Application deadline:* For fall admission, 3/15 for domestic students; for spring admission, 10/15 for domestic students. Application fee: $125. *Expenses:* Tuition, state resident: part-time $310 per credit. Tuition, nonresident: part-time $575 per credit. Tuition and fees vary according to course load and program. *Financial support:* Fellowships, research assistantships, teaching assistantships, career-related internships or fieldwork, Federal Work-Study, and tuition waivers (full and partial) available. Support available to part-time students. *Unit head:* Doris Cintron, Dean, 212-650-5302. *Application contact:* Stacia Pusey, Graduate Admissions Adviser-Education, 212-650-5345, E-mail: spusey@ccny.cuny.edu.

City University of Seattle, Graduate Division, Gordon Albright School of Education, Bellevue, WA 98005. Offers curriculum and instruction (M Ed); educational leadership (M Ed); educational leadership: administrator certification (Certificate); executive leadership: superintendent certification (Certificate); guidance and counseling (M Ed); leadership (M Ed); leadership and school counseling (M Ed); professional certification for teachers (Certificate); reading and literacy (M Ed); reading and literacy in education (M Ed); teacher certification (elementary K-8) (MIT); teacher certification (special education K-12) (MIT); technology, curriculum, and instruction (M Ed). Part-time and evening/weekend programs available. Postbaccalaureate distance learning degree programs offered (no on-campus study). *Entrance requirements:* Additional exam requirements/recommendations for international students: Required—TOEFL (minimum score 540 paper-based; 207 computer-based); Recommended—IELTS. Electronic applications accepted. *Expenses:* Contact institution.

Claflin University, Graduate Programs, Orangeburg, SC 29115. Offers biotechnology (MS); business administration (MBA); educational studies (M Ed). Part-time programs available. *Entrance requirements:* For master's, GRE, GMAT, baccalaureate degree, 3 letters of recommendation. Additional exam requirements/recommendations for international students: Recommended—TOEFL (minimum score 550 paper-based; 213 computer-based).

Claremont Graduate University, Graduate Programs, School of Educational Studies, Claremont, CA 91711-6160. Offers Africana education (Certificate); education and policy (MA, PhD); higher education/student affairs (MA, PhD); human development (MA, PhD); public school administration (MA, PhD); quantitative evaluation (MA, PhD); special education (MA, PhD); teacher education (MA); teaching and learning (MA, PhD); urban leadership (PhD); MBA/PhD. Part-time programs available. *Faculty:* 18 full-time (12 women), 1 part-time/adjunct (0 women). *Students:* 279 full-time (190 women), 174 part-time (122 women); includes 196 minority (50 African Americans, 1 American Indian/Alaska Native, 37 Asian Americans or Pacific Islanders, 108 Hispanic Americans), 10 international. Average age 37. In 2009, 84 master's, 23 doctorates awarded. Terminal master's awarded for partial completion of doctoral program. *Entrance requirements:* For master's and doctorate, GRE General Test. Additional exam requirements/recommendations for international students: Required—TOEFL (minimum score 550 paper-based; 213 computer-based; 80 iBT). *Application deadline:* For fall admission, 2/1 priority date for domestic students. Applications are processed on a rolling basis. Application fee: $60. Electronic applications accepted. *Expenses:* Tuition: Full-time $35,046; part-time $1524 per credit. Required fees: $161 per semester. *Financial support:* Fellowships, research assistantships, Federal Work-Study, institutionally sponsored loans, and scholarships/grants available. Support available to part-time students. Financial award application deadline: 2/15; financial award applicants required to submit FAFSA. *Faculty research:* Education administration, K-12 and higher education, multicultural education, education policy, diversity in higher education, faculty issues. *Unit head:* Margaret Grogan, Dean, 909-621-8075, Fax: 909-621-8734, E-mail: margaret.grogan@cgu.edu.

Clarion University of Pennsylvania, Office of Research and Graduate Studies, College of Education and Human Services, Clarion, PA 16214. Offers M Ed, MS, MSLS, CAS. *Accreditation:* NCATE. Part-time programs available. *Degree requirements:* For master's, thesis or alternative. *Entrance requirements:* For master's, minimum QPA of 3.0.

Clark Atlanta University, School of Education, Atlanta, GA 30314. Offers MA, MAT, Ed D, Ed S. *Accreditation:* NCATE. Part-time and evening/weekend programs available. *Faculty:* 17 full-time (10 women), 8 part-time/adjunct (4 women). *Students:* 56 full-time (37 women), 118 part-time (75 women); includes 165 minority (160 African Americans, 1 American Indian/Alaska Native, 1 Asian American or Pacific Islander, 3 Hispanic Americans), 1 international. Average age 33. 92 applicants, 75% accepted, 32 enrolled. In 2009, 28 master's, 16 doctorates, 1 other advanced degree awarded. *Degree requirements:* For master's, comprehensive exam; for doctorate, comprehensive exam, thesis/dissertation. *Entrance requirements:* For master's, GRE General Test, minimum undergraduate GPA of 2.6; for doctorate, GRE General Test, minimum graduate GPA of 3.0. Additional exam requirements/recommendations for international students: Required—TOEFL (minimum score 500 paper-based; 173 computer-

Education—General

Clark Atlanta University (continued)

based). *Application deadline:* For fall admission, 4/1 for domestic and international students; for spring admission, 11/1 for domestic and international students. Applications are processed on a rolling basis. Application fee: $40 ($55 for international students). Electronic applications accepted. *Expenses:* Tuition: Full-time $12,240; part-time $680 per credit hour. Required fees: $710; $355 per semester. *Financial support:* Career-related internships or fieldwork, Federal Work-Study, scholarships/grants, and unspecified assistantships available. Support available to part-time students. Financial award application deadline: 4/30; financial award applicants required to submit FAFSA. *Unit head:* Dr. Sean Warner, Interim Dean, 404-880-8504, E-mail: swarner@cau.edu. *Application contact:* Michelle Clark-Davis, Graduate Program Admissions, 404-880-6605, E-mail: cauadmissions@cau.edu.

Clarke College, Program in Education, Dubuque, IA 52001-3198. Offers early childhood/special education (MAE); educational administration: elementary and secondary (MAE); educational media: elementary and secondary (MAE); multi-categorical resource k-12 (MAE); multidisciplinary studies (MAE); reading: elementary (MAE); technology in education (MAE). Part-time and evening/weekend programs available. Postbaccalaureate distance learning degree programs offered (minimal on-campus study). *Faculty:* 5 full-time (all women). *Students:* 1 (woman) full-time, 45 part-time (40 women). Average age 31. 19 applicants, 74% accepted, 13 enrolled. In 2009, 11 master's awarded. *Degree requirements:* For master's, comprehensive exam, thesis optional. *Entrance requirements:* For master's, GRE General Test or MAT, minimum GPA of 2.75. *Application deadline:* Applications are processed on a rolling basis. Application fee: $25. Electronic applications accepted. *Expenses:* Tuition: Full-time $10,836; part-time $602 per credit hour. Required fees: $30 per credit hour. *Financial support:* Career-related internships or fieldwork available. Financial award applicants required to submit FAFSA. *Unit head:* Dr. Larry Bice, Chair, 319-588-6397, Fax: 319-584-8604. *Application contact:* Joan Coates, Information Contact, 563-588-6354, Fax: 563-588-6789, E-mail: graduate@clarke.edu.

Clark University, Graduate School, Department of Education, Worcester, MA 01610-1477. Offers MAT. *Faculty:* 10 full-time (8 women), 2 part-time/adjunct (1 woman). *Students:* 39 full-time (27 women), 7 part-time (2 women); includes 2 minority (1 Asian American or Pacific Islander, 1 Hispanic American). Average age 26. 48 applicants, 100% accepted, 41 enrolled. In 2009, 28 master's awarded. *Degree requirements:* For master's, thesis or alternative, oral exam. *Entrance requirements:* For master's, GRE General Test, minimum GPA of 3.0, professional experience. Additional exam requirements/recommendations for international students: Required—TOEFL. *Application deadline:* For fall admission, 2/1 priority date for domestic students. Applications are processed on a rolling basis. Application fee: $50. *Expenses:* Tuition: Full-time $34,900; part-time $4362.50 per course. *Financial support:* Fellowships with full and partial tuition reimbursements, research assistantships with full and partial tuition reimbursements, teaching assistantships with full and partial tuition reimbursements, institutionally sponsored loans and tuition waivers (partial) available. Financial award application deadline: 5/1. *Faculty research:* Developmental learning, instructional theory, educational program management, special education, urban education. Total annual research expenditures: $810,000. *Unit head:* Dr. Thomas DelPrete, Chair, 508-793-7222. *Application contact:* Marlene Shepard, Program Coordinator, 508-793-7222, Fax: 508-793-8864, E-mail: education@clarku.edu.

Clayton State University, School of Graduate Studies, Program in Education, Morrow, GA 30260-0285. Offers English (MAT); mathematics (MAT). *Accreditation:* NCATE. *Students:* 6 full-time (3 women), 2 part-time (1 woman); includes 2 African Americans, 1 international. Average age 24. 16 applicants, 56% accepted, 7 enrolled. *Application deadline:* For fall admission, 7/15 for domestic students, 5/1 for international students; for spring admission, 4/15 for domestic students, 2/1 for international students. Application fee: $50. *Unit head:* Dr. Ruth Caillouet, Program Coordinator, Master of Arts in Teaching English, 678-466-4735, Fax: 678-466-4899, E-mail: ruthcaillouet@clayton.edu. *Application contact:* Melanie Nolan, Administrative Assistant, Master of Arts in Teaching English, 678-466-4735, Fax: 678-466-4899, E-mail: melanienolan@clayton.edu.

Clemson University, Graduate School, College of Health, Education, and Human Development, School of Education, Clemson, SC 29634. Offers administration and supervision (M Ed, Ed S); counselor education (M Ed), including clinical mental health counseling, community counseling, school counseling, student affairs; curriculum and instruction (PhD); early childhood education (M Ed); educational leadership (PhD); elementary education (M Ed); human resource development (MHRD); middle grades education (MAT); reading (M Ed); secondary education (M Ed), including English, mathematics, natural sciences, social studies; secondary math and science (MAT); special education (M Ed). Part-time programs available. *Faculty:* 64 full-time (39 women), 8 part-time/adjunct (4 women). *Students:* 224 full-time (166 women), 356 part-time (240 women); includes 66 minority (52 African Americans, 1 American Indian/Alaska Native, 5 Asian Americans or Pacific Islanders, 8 Hispanic Americans), 7 international. Average age 33. 435 applicants, 67% accepted, 165 enrolled. In 2009, 188 master's, 27 doctorates, 1 other advanced degree awarded. *Degree requirements:* For doctorate, thesis/dissertation. *Entrance requirements:* For master's and doctorate, GRE General Test; for Ed S, GRE General Test, PRAXIS II, 1 year of teaching experience. Additional exam requirements/recommendations for international students: Required—TOEFL. *Application deadline:* Applications are processed on a rolling basis. Application fee: $70 ($80 for international students). Electronic applications accepted. *Expenses:* Contact institution. *Financial support:* In 2009–10, 112 students received support, including 18 fellowships with full and partial tuition reimbursements available (averaging $4,444 per year), 27 research assistantships with partial tuition reimbursements available (averaging $14,286 per year), 14 teaching assistantships with partial tuition reimbursements available (averaging $14,676 per year); career-related internships or fieldwork, institutionally sponsored loans, scholarships/grants, health care benefits, tuition waivers (full), and unspecified assistantships also available. Support available to part-time students. Financial award application deadline: 6/1; financial award applicants required to submit FAFSA. Total annual research expenditures: $1.7 million. *Unit head:* Dr. Michael J. Padilla, Director/Associate Dean, 864-656-4444, Fax: 864-656-0311, E-mail: padilla@clemson.edu. *Application contact:* Dr. David Fleming, Graduate Programs Coordinator, 864-656-1881, Fax: 864-656-0311, E-mail: dflemin@clemson.edu.

Cleveland State University, College of Graduate Studies, College of Education and Human Services, Cleveland, OH 44115. Offers M Ed, MPH, MSN, PhD, Certificate, Ed S, MSN/MBA. *Accreditation:* NCATE. Part-time and evening/weekend programs available. Postbaccalaureate distance learning degree programs offered (minimal on-campus study). *Degree requirements:* For master's, comprehensive exam (for some programs), thesis optional; for doctorate, one foreign language, comprehensive exam, thesis/dissertation; for other advanced degree, comprehensive exam (for some programs), thesis optional, internship. *Entrance requirements:* For master's, GRE General Test or MAT, minimum undergraduate GPA of 2.75, 3.0 if undergraduate degree is 6 or more years old; for doctorate, GRE General Test, master's degree, minimum graduate GPA of 3.25; for other advanced degree, GRE General Test or MAT, master's degree, minimum graduate GPA of 3.0. Additional exam requirements/recommendations for international students: Required—TOEFL (minimum score 525 paper-based; 197 computer-based; 65 iBT). Electronic applications accepted. *Faculty research:* Adult learning and development, counseling theory and practice, equity issues in education (race, ethnicity, gender, socioeconomics), health care and health education, population nursing, urban educational leadership, curriculum and instruction.

Coastal Carolina University, Spadoni College of Education, Conway, SC 29528-6054. Offers education (MAT); educational leadership (M Ed); learning and teaching (M Ed); secondary education (M Ed). *Accreditation:* NCATE. Part-time and evening/weekend programs available. *Faculty:* 12 full-time (4 women), 3 part-time/adjunct (1 woman). *Students:* 66 full-time (41 women), 138 part-time (105 women); includes 29 minority (24 African Americans, 1 American Indian/Alaska Native, 2 Asian Americans or Pacific Islanders, 2 Hispanic Americans), 3 international. Average age 33. 242 applicants, 88% accepted, 150 enrolled. In 2009, 76 master's awarded. *Degree requirements:* For master's, comprehensive exam. *Entrance requirements:* For master's, GRE General Test, MAT, 2 letters of recommendation, copy of teaching credential. Additional exam requirements/recommendations for international students: Required—TOEFL (minimum score 550 paper-based; 213 computer-based; 79 iBT). *Application deadline:* For fall admission, 7/1 priority date for domestic and international students; for spring admission, 11/15 priority date for domestic and international students. Applications are processed on a rolling basis. Application fee: $45. Electronic applications accepted. *Expenses:* Tuition, state resident: full-time $9600; part-time $400 per credit hour. Tuition, nonresident: full-time $11,880; part-time $495 per credit hour. Required fees: $80; $40 per term. *Financial support:* Fellowships, research assistantships, unspecified assistantships available. Support available to part-time students. Financial award application deadline: 3/1; financial award applicants required to submit FAFSA. *Unit head:* Dr. Diane L. Mark, Dean, 843-349-2629, Fax: 843-349-2106, E-mail: dmark@coastal.edu. *Application contact:* Dr. Richard L. Johnson, Director of Graduate Studies, 843-349-2192, Fax: 843-349-6444, E-mail: rjohnson@coastal.edu.

Coe College, Department of Education, Cedar Rapids, IA 52402-5092. Offers MAT. Part-time programs available. *Entrance requirements:* For master's, minimum undergraduate GPA of 2.75, letters of reference. *Faculty research:* Math education, international and multicultural education.

The College at Brockport, State University of New York, School of Education and Human Services, Department of Education and Human Development, Brockport, NY 14420-2997. Offers adolescence education (MS Ed), including adolescence biology education, adolescence chemistry education, adolescence earth science education, adolescence English education, adolescence mathematics education, adolescence physics education, adolescence social studies education; alternate adolescence inclusive education (MS Ed), including alternate adolescence English inclusive education, alternate adolescence mathematics inclusive education, alternate adolescence science inclusive education, alternate adolescence social studies inclusive education; bilingual education (MS Ed, AGC), including bilingual education, Spanish (AGC); childhood curriculum specialist (MS Ed); childhood literacy (MS Ed). *Accreditation:* NCATE. *Students:* 49 full-time (29 women), 245 part-time (182 women); includes 12 minority (4 African Americans, 3 Asian Americans or Pacific Islanders, 5 Hispanic Americans). 109 applicants, 54% accepted, 53 enrolled. In 2009, 92 master's awarded. *Degree requirements:* For master's, thesis or alternative. *Entrance requirements:* For master's, minimum GPA of 3.0, letters of recommendation, interview (for some programs). Additional exam requirements/recommendations for international students: Required—TOEFL (minimum score 550 paper-based; 213 computer-based; 79 iBT). *Application deadline:* For fall admission, 2/15 priority date for domestic and international students; for spring admission, 9/15 priority date for domestic and international students. Application fee: $80. Electronic applications accepted. *Expenses:* Tuition, state resident: full-time $8370; part-time $349 per credit. Tuition, nonresident: full-time $13,250; part-time $522 per credit. *Financial support:* In 2009–10, 1 teaching assistantship with full tuition reimbursement (averaging $6,000 per year) was awarded; Federal Work-Study, scholarships/grants, and unspecified assistantships also available. Support available to part-time students. Financial award application deadline: 3/15; financial award applicants required to submit FAFSA. *Faculty research:* Educational assessment, literacy education, inclusive education, teacher preparation, qualitative methodology. *Unit head:* Dr. Sue Novinger, Chairperson, 585-395-2205, Fax: 585-395-2172, E-mail: snovinge@brockport.edu. *Application contact:* Dr. Sue Novinger, Chairperson, 585-395-2205, Fax: 585-395-2172, E-mail: snovinge@brockport.edu.

College of Charleston, Graduate School, School of Education, Health, and Human Performance, Charleston, SC 29424-0001. Offers M Ed, MAT, Certificate. *Accreditation:* NCATE. Part-time and evening/weekend programs available. *Faculty:* 31 full-time (26 women), 11 part-time/adjunct (10 women). *Students:* 116 full-time (95 women), 59 part-time (54 women); includes 18 minority (12 African Americans, 2 American Indian/Alaska Native, 4 Hispanic Americans), 5 international. Average age 30. 69 applicants, 64% accepted, 39 enrolled. In 2009, 30 master's awarded. *Degree requirements:* For master's, thesis or alternative, written qualifying exam, student teaching experience (MAT). *Entrance requirements:* For master's, teaching certificate (M Ed). Additional exam requirements/recommendations for international students: Required—TOEFL. *Application deadline:* Applications are processed on a rolling basis. Application fee: $45. Electronic applications accepted. *Financial support:* In 2009–10, research assistantships (averaging $19,000 per year), teaching assistantships (averaging $13,300 per year) were awarded; career-related internships or fieldwork, Federal Work-Study, scholarships/grants, and unspecified assistantships also available. Support available to part-time students. Financial award application deadline: 4/1; financial award applicants required to submit FAFSA. *Faculty research:* Computer-assisted instruction, higher education, faculty development, teaching study skills to college students. *Unit head:* Dr. Frances Welch, Dean, 843-953-5613, Fax: 843-953-5407, E-mail: welchf@cofc.edu. *Application contact:* Susan Hallatt, Director of Graduate Admissions, 843-953-5614, Fax: 843-953-1434, E-mail: hallatts@cofc.edu.

The College of Idaho, Program in Teacher Education, Caldwell, ID 83605. Offers MAT. *Degree requirements:* For master's, thesis. *Entrance requirements:* For master's, GRE, portfolio, minimum undergraduate GPA of 3.0, interview. *Faculty research:* Discourse analysis, at-risk youth, children's literature, research design, program evaluation.

College of Mount St. Joseph, Graduate Education Program, Cincinnati, OH 45233-1670. Offers adolescent young adult education (MA); art (MA); inclusive early childhood education (MA); instructional leadership (MA); middle childhood education (MA); multi-age education (MA); multicultural special education (MA); music (MA); reading (MA). *Accreditation:* Teacher Education Accreditation Council. Part-time and evening/weekend programs available. *Faculty:* 15 full-time (11 women), 9 part-time/adjunct (6 women). *Students:* 93 full-time (75 women), 99 part-time (66 women); includes 19 minority (18 African Americans, 1 American Indian/Alaska Native). Average age 34. 116 applicants, 97% accepted, 94 enrolled. In 2009, 51 master's awarded. *Degree requirements:* For master's, research project, student teaching, clinical and field-based experiences. *Entrance requirements:* For master's, GRE, PRAXIS II in teaching content area (math or science), 2 letters of recommendation, interview, resume. Additional exam requirements/recommendations for international students: Required—TOEFL (minimum score 560 paper-based; 220 computer-based; 83 iBT). *Application deadline:* Applications are processed on a rolling basis. Application fee: $50. Electronic applications accepted. *Expenses:* Tuition: Part-time $500 per hour. Required fees: $200 per year. Tuition and fees vary according to degree level and program. *Financial support:* In 2009–10, 51 students received support. Scholarships/grants available. Financial award applicants required to submit FAFSA. *Faculty research:* Foreign and second language learning problems/reading disabilities/hyperlexia, multicultural/bilingual special education, alternative educator licensure, science education, pedagogical content knowledge. *Unit head:* Dr. Mary West, Chair of Graduate Education, 513-244-3263, Fax: 513-244-4867, E-mail: mary_west@mail.msj.edu. *Application contact:* Marilyn Hoskins, Assistant Director of Graduate Recruitment, 513-244-4723, Fax: 513-244-4629, E-mail: marilyn_hoskins@mail.msj.edu.

College of Mount Saint Vincent, School of Professional and Continuing Studies, Department of Teacher Education, Riverdale, NY 10471-1093. Offers instructional technology and global perspectives (Certificate); middle level education (Certificate); multicultural studies (Certificate); urban and multicultural education (MS Ed). *Accreditation:* Teacher Education Accreditation Council. Part-time programs available. *Degree requirements:* For master's, comprehensive exam. *Entrance requirements:* For master's, interview, New York teaching certificate. Additional exam requirements/recommendations for international students: Required—TOEFL.

The College of New Jersey, Graduate Division, School of Education, Ewing, NJ 08628. Offers M Ed, MA, MAT, Certificate, Ed S. *Accreditation:* NCATE. Part-time and evening/weekend programs available. *Students:* 214 full-time (166 women), 345 part-time (284 women); includes 75 minority (28 African Americans, 22 Asian Americans or Pacific Islanders, 25 Hispanic Americans), 8 international. 885 applicants, 70% accepted. In 2009, 310 master's, 24 other advanced degrees awarded. *Degree requirements:* For master's, comprehensive exam. *Entrance requirements:* For master's, GRE, minimum GPA of 3.0 in field or 2.75 overall; for other advanced degree, previous master's degree or higher. Additional exam requirements/

recommendations for international students: Required—TOEFL. *Application deadline:* For fall admission, 2/1 priority date for domestic students; for spring admission, 10/1 priority date for domestic students. Application fee: $70. Electronic applications accepted. *Expenses:* Tuition, state resident: part-time $573.70 per credit. Tuition, nonresident: part-time $887.75 per credit. Required fees: $140.85 per credit. One-time fee: $10 part-time. *Financial support:* Tuition waivers (partial) and unspecified assistantships available. Financial award application deadline: 5/1; financial award applicants required to submit FAFSA. *Unit head:* Dr. William Behre, Dean, 609-771-2100. *Application contact:* Susan L. Hydro, Assistant Dean, Office of Graduate Studies, 609-771-2300, Fax: 609-637-5105, E-mail: graduate@tcnj.edu.

The College of New Rochelle, Graduate School, Division of Education, New Rochelle, NY 10805-2308. Offers creative teaching and learning (MS Ed, Certificate); elementary education/early childhood education (MS Ed); literacy education (MS Ed); school administration and supervision (MS, Advanced Certificate, Advanced Diploma), including dual certification: school building leader/school district leader (MS); school building leader (MS, Advanced Certificate), school district leader (MS, Advanced Diploma); special education (MS Ed); teaching English as a second language and multilingual/multicultural education (MS Ed, Certificate), including bilingual education (Certificate), teaching English as a second language (MS Ed). Part-time and evening/weekend programs available. *Degree requirements:* For master's, comprehensive exam (for some programs), thesis (for some programs). *Entrance requirements:* For master's, interview, minimum GPA of 3.0 in field, 2.7 overall.

College of Notre Dame of Maryland, Graduate Studies, Program in Teaching, Baltimore, MD 21210-2476. Offers MA. *Accreditation:* NCATE. *Entrance requirements:* For master's, Watson-Glaser Critical Thinking Appraisal, writing test, grammar test, interview. Additional exam requirements/recommendations for international students: Required—TOEFL (minimum score 500 paper-based; 173 computer-based; 61 iBT). Electronic applications accepted.

College of Saint Elizabeth, Department of Education, Morristown, NJ 07960-6989. Offers accelerated certification for teachers (Certificate); assistive technology (Certificate); education: human services leadership (MA); educational leadership (MA, Ed D); educational technology (MA). Part-time and evening/weekend programs available. *Faculty:* 10 full-time (3 women), 20 part-time/adjunct (11 women). *Students:* 119 full-time (88 women), 332 part-time (292 women); includes 63 minority (35 African Americans, 3 Asian Americans or Pacific Islanders, 25 Hispanic Americans), 1 international. Average age 37. 201 applicants, 82% accepted, 146 enrolled. In 2009, 140 master's, 81 other advanced degrees awarded. *Degree requirements:* For master's, thesis or alternative, portfolio. *Entrance requirements:* For master's, interview, minimum undergraduate GPA of 3.0. *Application deadline:* For fall admission, 6/30 priority date for domestic students; for spring admission, 11/30 for domestic students. Applications are processed on a rolling basis. Application fee: $35. Electronic applications accepted. *Expenses:* Tuition: Part-time $797 per credit hour. Required fees: $65 per credit hour. *Financial support:* Career-related internships or fieldwork, tuition waivers (partial), and unspecified assistantships available. Support available to part-time students. Financial award application deadline: 3/15; financial award applicants required to submit FAFSA. *Faculty research:* Developmental stages for teaching and human services professionals, effectiveness of humanities core curriculum. *Unit head:* Dr. Alan H. Markowitz, Director of Graduate Education Programs, 973-290-4374, Fax: 973-290-4389, E-mail: amarkowitz@cse.edu. *Application contact:* Donna Tatarka, Dean of Admission, 973-290-4705, Fax: 973-290-4710, E-mail: dtatarka@cse.edu.

College of St. Joseph, Graduate Programs, Division of Education, Rutland, VT 05701-3899. Offers elementary education (M Ed); general education (M Ed); reading (M Ed); secondary education (M Ed), including English, social studies; special education (M Ed). Part-time and evening/weekend programs available. *Degree requirements:* For master's, comprehensive exam. *Entrance requirements:* For master's, 2 letters of reference, interview. Electronic applications accepted. *Expenses:* Tuition: Full-time $13,500; part-time $350 per credit. Required fees: $45 per term. One-time fee: $445. Tuition and fees vary according to program.

College of Saint Mary, Program in Teaching, Omaha, NE 68106. Offers MAT. Evening/weekend programs available. *Entrance requirements:* For master's, Pre-Professional Skills Tests (PPST), minimum cumulative GPA of 2.5, background check.

The College of Saint Rose, Graduate Studies, School of Education, Albany, NY 12203-1419. Offers MS, MS Ed, Certificate. *Accreditation:* NCATE. Part-time and evening/weekend programs available. *Degree requirements:* For master's, thesis or alternative. *Entrance requirements:* For master's, minimum undergraduate GPA of 3.0. Additional exam requirements/recommendations for international students: Required—TOEFL (minimum score 550 paper-based; 213 computer-based). Electronic applications accepted.

The College of St. Scholastica, Graduate Studies, Program in Teaching, Duluth, MN 55811-4199. Offers M Ed, Certificate. *Accreditation:* Teacher Education Accreditation Council. Part-time programs available. Postbaccalaureate distance learning degree programs offered (minimal on-campus study). *Entrance requirements:* Additional exam requirements/recommendations for international students: Required—TOEFL (minimum score 550 paper-based; 213 computer-based; 79 iBT). Electronic applications accepted.

College of Santa Fe, Department of Education, Santa Fe, NM 87505-7634. Offers at-risk youth (MA), including bilingual/multicultural education, classroom teaching, community counseling, educational administration, leadership, school counseling, self-designed program, TESOL/Multicultural; curriculum and instruction (MA); multicultural special education (MA). Part-time and evening/weekend programs available. *Entrance requirements:* For master's, minimum GPA of 3.0. *Faculty research:* Integrated curriculum, child development, brain research, learning styles, systemic issues in education.

College of Staten Island of the City University of New York, Graduate Programs, Department of Education, Staten Island, NY 10314-6600. Offers adolescence education (MS Ed); childhood education (MS Ed); leadership in education (6th Year Certificate); special education (MS Ed); special education middle childhood generalist (5-9) (MS Ed). *Accreditation:* NCATE. *Students:* 63 full-time (53 women), 543 part-time (447 women); includes 91 minority (19 African Americans, 25 Asian Americans or Pacific Islanders, 47 Hispanic Americans), 3 international. Average age 30. 303 applicants, 74% accepted, 188 enrolled. In 2009, 165 master's, 15 6th Year Certificates awarded. Application fee: $125. *Expenses:* Tuition, state resident: full-time $7360; part-time $310 per credit. Tuition, nonresident: part-time $575 per credit. Required fees: $378; $113 per semester. *Financial support:* In 2009–10, 2 students received support. Federal Work-Study available. Support available to part-time students. Financial award applicants required to submit FAFSA. Total annual research expenditures: $14,940. *Unit head:* Dr. Kenneth Gold, Chairperson, 718-982-3737, Fax: 718-982-3743, E-mail: educationmasters@mail.csi.cuny.edu. *Application contact:* Sasha Spence, Assistant Director of Graduate Recruitment and Admissions, 718-982-2699, Fax: 718-982-2500, E-mail: sasha.spence@.csi.cuny.edu.

College of the Humanities and Sciences, Harrison Middleton University, Graduate Program, Tempe, AZ 85282. Offers education (MA, Ed D); humanities (MA); imaginative literature (MA); interdisciplinary studies (DA); jurisprudence (MA); natural science (MA); philosophy and religion (MA); social science (MA). Part-time and evening/weekend programs available. Postbaccalaureate distance learning degree programs offered (no on-campus study). *Faculty:* 17 full-time (7 women), 14 part-time/adjunct (6 women). *Students:* 49 full-time (18 women). In 2009, 4 master's awarded. *Application deadline:* Applications are processed on a rolling basis. Application fee: $50. Electronic applications accepted. *Application contact:* Deborah Deacon, Dean of Graduate Studies, 877-248-6724, Fax: 800-762-1622, E-mail: ddeacon@chumsci.edu.

The College of William and Mary, School of Education, Williamsburg, VA 23187-8795. Offers M Ed, MA Ed, Ed D, PhD, Ed S. *Accreditation:* NCATE. Part-time and evening/weekend programs available. *Faculty:* 40 full-time (22 women), 28 part-time/adjunct (24 women). *Students:* 178 full-time (139 women), 164 part-time (120 women); includes 57 minority (50 African Americans, 1 American Indian/Alaska Native, 6 Asian Americans or Pacific Islanders), 5 international. Average age 33. 439 applicants, 58% accepted, 172 enrolled. In 2009, 129 master's, 28 doctorates, 12 other advanced degrees awarded. *Degree requirements:* For

master's, project; for doctorate, comprehensive exam, thesis/dissertation. *Entrance requirements:* For master's, GRE or MAT, minimum GPA of 2.5; for doctorate, GRE or MAT, minimum GPA of 3.5; for Ed S, GRE, minimum GPA of 3.0. Additional exam requirements/recommendations for international students: Required—TOEFL. *Application deadline:* For fall admission, 1/15 for domestic and international students; for spring admission, 10/1 for domestic and international students. Application fee: $45. Electronic applications accepted. *Expenses:* Tuition, state resident: full-time $6400; part-time $315 per credit hour. Tuition, nonresident: full-time $19,720; part-time $840 per credit hour. Required fees: $4114. *Financial support:* In 2009–10, 180 students received support, including 1 fellowship with full tuition reimbursement available (averaging $20,000 per year), 99 research assistantships with full and partial tuition reimbursements available (averaging $11,000 per year); career-related internships or fieldwork, Federal Work-Study, institutionally sponsored loans, scholarships/grants, and unspecified assistantships also available. Financial award application deadline: 1/15; financial award applicants required to submit FAFSA. *Faculty research:* Writing, gifted education, curriculum and instruction, special education, leadership, faculty development, cultural diversity. Total annual research expenditures: $5.7 million. *Unit head:* Dr. Virginia McLaughlin, Dean, 757-221-2317, E-mail: vamcla@wm.edu. *Application contact:* Dorothy Smith Osborne, Director of Admissions, 757-221-2317, Fax: 757-221-2293, E-mail: dsosbo@wm.edu.

Collège universitaire de Saint-Boniface, Department of Education, Saint-Boniface, MB R2H 0H7, Canada. Offers M Ed.

Colorado Christian University, Program in Curriculum and Instruction, Lakewood, CO 80226. Offers MA. Part-time and evening/weekend programs available. *Degree requirements:* For master's, thesis optional, practicum. *Entrance requirements:* For master's, interviews, letters of recommendation. Additional exam requirements/recommendations for international students: Required—TOEFL. Electronic applications accepted. *Expenses:* Contact institution.

The Colorado College, Department of Education, Colorado Springs, CO 80903-3294. Offers elementary education (MAT), including elementary school teaching; secondary education (MAT), including art teaching (K-12), English teaching, foreign language teaching, mathematics teaching, music teaching, science teaching, social studies teaching. *Faculty:* 3 full-time (2 women), 12 part-time/adjunct (9 women). *Students:* 25 full-time (14 women); includes 1 minority (Asian American or Pacific Islander). Average age 27. 43 applicants, 84% accepted, 25 enrolled. In 2009, 23 master's awarded. *Degree requirements:* For master's, thesis, internship. *Entrance requirements:* For master's, PRAXIS II or PLACE Exam. *Application deadline:* For fall admission, 12/1 priority date for domestic and international students. Applications are processed on a rolling basis. Application fee: $50. *Expenses:* Tuition: Part-time $2545 per credit. *Financial support:* In 2009–10, 25 students received support, including 15 teaching assistantships (averaging $16,000 per year); career-related internships or fieldwork, institutionally sponsored loans, health care benefits, and tuition waivers (partial) also available. Financial award application deadline: 2/15; financial award applicants required to submit FAFSA. *Unit head:* Paul Kuerbis, Chair, 719-389-6726, Fax: 719-389-6473, E-mail: pkuerbis@coloradocollege.edu. *Application contact:* Debra Yazulla Mortenson, Education Services Manager, 719-389-6472, Fax: 719-389-6473, E-mail: debra.mortenson@coloradocollege.edu.

Colorado State University, Graduate School, College of Applied Human Sciences, School of Education, Fort Collins, CO 80523-1588. Offers adult education and training (M Ed); community college leadership (PhD); counseling and career development (M Ed); education and human resource studies (M Ed, PhD); educational leadership (M Ed, PhD); interdisciplinary studies (PhD); organizational performance and change (M Ed, PhD); student affairs in higher education (MS). *Accreditation:* ACA; Teacher Education Accreditation Council. Part-time and evening/weekend programs available. *Faculty:* 21 full-time (10 women). *Students:* 195 full-time (132 women), 469 part-time (292 women); includes 114 minority (31 African Americans, 12 American Indian/Alaska Native, 22 Asian Americans or Pacific Islanders, 49 Hispanic Americans), 24 international. Average age 38. 451 applicants, 41% accepted, 141 enrolled. In 2009, 175 master's, 54 doctorates awarded. *Degree requirements:* For master's, comprehensive exam (for some programs), thesis optional; for doctorate, comprehensive exam, thesis/dissertation, minimum of 60 credits. *Entrance requirements:* For master's, GRE, minimum undergraduate GPA of 3.0, 3 letters of recommendation, curriculum vitae/resume; for doctorate, minimum GPA of 3.0, 3 letters of recommendation, curriculum vitae. Additional exam requirements/recommendations for international students: Required—TOEFL (minimum score 550 paper-based; 213 computer-based). *Application deadline:* For fall admission, 3/15 for domestic and international students; for spring admission, 11/1 for domestic students, 10/1 for international students. Applications are processed on a rolling basis. Application fee: $50. Electronic applications accepted. *Expenses:* Tuition, state resident: full-time $6434; part-time $359.10 per credit. Tuition, nonresident: full-time $18,116; part-time $1006.45 per credit. Required fees: $1496; $83 per credit. *Financial support:* In 2009–10, 8 students received support, including 3 research assistantships with full tuition reimbursements available (averaging $13,790 per year), 5 teaching assistantships with full tuition reimbursements available (averaging $10,253 per year); fellowships, Federal Work-Study, scholarships/grants, and unspecified assistantships also available. Financial award applicants required to submit FAFSA. *Faculty research:* Innovative instruction, diverse learners, transition, scientifically-based evaluation methods, leadership and organizational development. Total annual research expenditures: $655,700. *Unit head:* Dr. Carole Makela, Interim Director, 970-491-6317, Fax: 970-491-1317, E-mail: carole.makela@colostate.edu. *Application contact:* Dr. Sharon Anderson, Director of Graduate Programs, 970-491-6861, Fax: 970-491-1317, E-mail: sharon.anderson@colostate.edu.

Colorado State University–Pueblo, College of Education, Engineering and Professional Studies, Education Program, Pueblo, CO 81001-4901. Offers art education (M Ed); foreign language education (M Ed); health and physical education (M Ed); instructional technology (M Ed); linguistically diverse education (M Ed); music education (M Ed); special education (M Ed). *Accreditation:* Teacher Education Accreditation Council. Part-time programs available. *Degree requirements:* For master's, portfolio. *Entrance requirements:* For master's, 3 recommendations, teaching license. Additional exam requirements/recommendations for international students: Required—TOEFL (minimum score 500 paper-based; 173 computer-based). Electronic applications accepted. *Faculty research:* Portfolio assessment, math education, science education.

Columbia College, Graduate Programs, Department of Education, Columbia, SC 29203-5998. Offers divergent learning (M Ed). *Accreditation:* NCATE. Part-time and evening/weekend programs available. Postbaccalaureate distance learning degree programs offered (minimal on-campus study). *Faculty:* 3 full-time (1 woman), 18 part-time/adjunct (10 women). *Students:* 175 full-time (158 women), 60 part-time (37 women); includes 59 minority (57 African Americans, 2 Asian Americans or Pacific Islanders), 1 international. Average age 27. 152 applicants, 98% accepted, 135 enrolled. In 2009, 143 master's awarded. *Degree requirements:* For master's, thesis. *Entrance requirements:* For master's, GRE General Test, MAT, 2 recommendations, current South Carolina teaching certificate, minimum GPA of 3.2. *Expenses:* Contact institution. *Financial support:* Available to part-time students. Application deadline: 7/1. *Unit head:* Dr. Mary Steppling, Chair, 803-786-3782, Fax: 803-786-3034, E-mail: msteppling@colacoll.edu. *Application contact:* Carolyn Emeneker, Director of Graduate School and Evening College Admissions, 803-786-3766, Fax: 803-786-3674, E-mail: emeneker@colacoll.edu.

Columbia College, Master of Arts in Teaching Program, Columbia, MO 65216-0002. Offers MAT. Evening/weekend programs available. Postbaccalaureate distance learning degree programs offered (no on-campus study). *Faculty:* 4 full-time (3 women), 4 part-time/adjunct (3 women). *Students:* 119 full-time (103 women), 51 part-time (43 women); includes 9 minority (7 African Americans, 2 Hispanic Americans), 1 international. Average age 34. 70 applicants, 69% accepted, 23 enrolled. In 2009, 33 master's awarded. *Degree requirements:* For master's, culminating experience. *Entrance requirements:* For master's, 3 letters of recommendation, minimum cumulative undergraduate GPA of 3.0, resume. Additional exam requirements/recommendations for international students: Required—TOEFL (minimum score 550 paper-based; 213 computer-based; 79 iBT). *Application deadline:* For fall admission, 8/9 priority date

Education—General

Columbia College (continued)
for domestic and international students; for spring admission, 12/27 priority date for domestic and international students. Applications are processed on a rolling basis. Application fee: $55. Electronic applications accepted. *Expenses:* Tuition: Full-time $3588; part-time $299 per credit hour. Tuition and fees vary according to course load. *Financial support:* In 2009–10, 69 students received support. Career-related internships or fieldwork, Federal Work-Study, and scholarships/grants available. Financial award application deadline: 3/15; financial award applicants required to submit FAFSA. *Unit head:* Dr. Kristina Miller, Graduate Program Coordinator, 573-875-7590, Fax: 573-876-4493, E-mail: kmiller@ccis.edu. *Application contact:* Samantha White, Director of Admissions, 573-875-7352, Fax: 573-875-7506, E-mail: sjwhite@ccis.edu.

Columbia College Chicago, Graduate School, Department of Educational Studies, Chicago, IL 60605-1996. Offers elementary education (MAT); English (MAT); interdisciplinary arts (MAT); multicultural education (MA); urban teaching (MA). Part-time and evening/weekend programs available. *Degree requirements:* For master's, thesis, student teaching experience, 100 pre-clinical hours. *Entrance requirements:* For master's, supplemental recommendation form. Additional exam requirements/recommendations for international students: Required—TOEFL (minimum score 550 paper-based; 213 computer-based). Electronic applications accepted. *Expenses:* Tuition: Part-time $651 per credit hour. Required fees: $205 per semester. One-time fee: $285 part-time. Tuition and fees vary according to program.

Columbia International University, Columbia Graduate School, Columbia, SC 29230-3122. Offers Bible teaching (MABT); Christian higher education leadership (Ed D); Christian school educational leadership (Ed D); counseling (MACN); curriculum and instruction (M Ed), including Christian school guidance, English as a second language, learning disabilities, school technology; early childhood and elementary education (MAT); educational administration (M Ed); teaching English as a foreign language (Certificate); teaching English as a foreign language and intercultural studies (MATF). Part-time and evening/weekend programs available. *Degree requirements:* For master's, internships, professional project. *Entrance requirements:* For master's, Minnesota Multiphasic Personality Inventory, MAT, minimum GPA of 2.7. Additional exam requirements/recommendations for international students: Required—TOEFL. Electronic applications accepted.

Columbus State University, Graduate Studies, College of Education and Health Professions, Columbus, GA 31907-5645. Offers M Ed, MAT, MPA, MS, Ed D, Ed S. *Accreditation:* ACA (one or more programs are accredited); NCATE. Part-time and evening/weekend programs available. Postbaccalaureate distance learning degree programs offered (minimal on-campus study). *Faculty:* 29 full-time (18 women), 21 part-time/adjunct (13 women). *Students:* 239 full-time (179 women), 425 part-time (352 women); includes 211 minority (183 African Americans, 2 American Indian/Alaska Native, 9 Asian Americans or Pacific Islanders, 17 Hispanic Americans), 3 international. Average age 35. 385 applicants, 64% accepted, 175 enrolled. In 2009, 140 master's, 56 other advanced degrees awarded. *Degree requirements:* For master's, thesis, exit exam; for Ed S, thesis or alternative. *Entrance requirements:* For master's, GRE General Test, minimum GPA of 2.75; for Ed S, GRE General Test. Additional exam requirements/recommendations for international students: Required—TOEFL (minimum score 550 paper-based; 213 computer-based; 79 iBT). *Application deadline:* For fall admission, 5/1 priority date for domestic students, 5/1 for international students; for spring admission, 11/11 for domestic students, 11/1 for international students. Applications are processed on a rolling basis. Application fee: $30. Electronic applications accepted. *Financial support:* In 2009–10, 417 students received support, including 43 research assistantships with partial tuition reimbursements available (averaging $3,000 per year); career-related internships or fieldwork, Federal Work-Study, institutionally sponsored loans, scholarships/grants, tuition waivers (partial), and unspecified assistantships also available. Support available to part-time students. Financial award application deadline: 5/1; financial award applicants required to submit FAFSA. *Unit head:* Dr. David Rock, Dean, 706-568-2212, Fax: 706-569-3134, E-mail: rock_david@colstate.edu. *Application contact:* Katie Thornton, Graduate Admissions Specialist, 706-568-2035, Fax: 706-568-2462, E-mail: thornton_katie@colstate.edu.

Concordia College, Program in Education, Moorhead, MN 56562. Offers world language instruction (M Ed). *Degree requirements:* For master's, thesis/seminar. *Entrance requirements:* For master's, 2 professional references, 1 personal reference.

Concordia University, College of Education, Portland, OR 97211-6099. Offers curriculum and instruction (elementary) (M Ed); educational administration (M Ed); elementary education (MAT); secondary education (MAT). Part-time programs available. Postbaccalaureate distance learning degree programs offered (no on-campus study). *Degree requirements:* For master's, comprehensive exam, work samples/portfolio. *Entrance requirements:* For master's, California Basic Educational Skills Test or PRAXIS I, minimum undergraduate GPA of 2.8, graduate 3.0; 2 letters of recommendation. Additional exam requirements/recommendations for international students: Required—TOEFL (minimum score 525 paper-based; 195 computer-based). Electronic applications accepted. *Faculty research:* Learner centered classroom, brain-based learning future of on-line learning.

Concordia University, School of Education, Irvine, CA 92612-3299. Offers curriculum and instruction (MA); education and preliminary teaching credential (M Ed); educational administration and preliminary administrative services credential (MA). Part-time and evening/weekend programs available. Postbaccalaureate distance learning degree programs offered. *Faculty:* 18 full-time (9 women), 53 part-time/adjunct (25 women). *Students:* 569 full-time (439 women), 81 part-time (55 women); includes 160 minority (28 African Americans, 2 American Indian/Alaska Native, 38 Asian Americans or Pacific Islanders, 92 Hispanic Americans), 1 international. Average age 39. 263 applicants, 94% accepted, 203 enrolled. In 2009, 308 master's awarded. *Degree requirements:* For master's, action research project. *Entrance requirements:* For master's, California Basic Educational Skills Test, California Subject Examinations for Teachers, 2 references, copy of credential. Additional exam requirements/recommendations for international students: Required—TOEFL. *Application deadline:* For fall admission, 7/15 priority date for domestic students, 6/1 for international students; for spring admission, 11/30 priority date for domestic students, 10/1 for international students. Applications are processed on a rolling basis. Application fee: $50 ($125 for international students). Electronic applications accepted. *Expenses:* Contact institution. *Financial support:* In 2009–10, 478 students received support. Scholarships/grants available. Financial award applicants required to submit FAFSA. *Unit head:* Dr. Janice Nelson, Dean, 949-854-8002 Ext. 1249, E-mail: janice.nelson@cui.edu. *Application contact:* Narleen Narciso, Assistant Director of School of Education Admissions, 949-854-8002 Ext. 1132, Fax: 949-854-6894, E-mail: narleen.narciso@cui.edu.

Concordia University, School of Graduate Studies, Faculty of Arts and Science, Department of Education, Montréal, QC H3G 1M8, Canada. Offers adult education (Diploma); applied linguistics (MA); child study (MA); educational studies (MA); educational technology (MA, PhD); instructional technology (Diploma); teaching English as a second language (Certificate). *Degree requirements:* For master's, one foreign language, thesis optional; for doctorate, comprehensive exam, thesis/dissertation. *Entrance requirements:* For doctorate, MA in educational technology or equivalent.

Concordia University Chicago, College of Education, Program in Teaching, River Forest, IL 60305-1499. Offers early childhood education (MAT); elementary education (MAT); secondary education (MAT). *Degree requirements:* For master's, thesis or alternative. *Entrance requirements:* For master's, minimum GPA of 2.9. Additional exam requirements/recommendations for international students: Required—TOEFL (minimum score 550 paper-based; 195 computer-based). Electronic applications accepted.

Concordia University, Nebraska, Graduate Programs in Education, Seward, NE 68434-1599. Offers M Ed, MPE, MS. *Accreditation:* NCATE. Part-time and evening/weekend programs available. *Degree requirements:* For master's, comprehensive exam, thesis or alternative. *Entrance requirements:* For master's, GRE, MAT, or NTE, minimum GPA of 3.0, BS in education or equivalent. Additional exam requirements/recommendations for international students: Required—TOEFL. Electronic applications accepted.

Concordia University, St. Paul, College of Education, St. Paul, MN 55104-5494. Offers curriculum and instruction (MA Ed), including K-12 reading endorsement; differentiated instruction (MA Ed); early childhood education (MA Ed); educational leadership (MA Ed); family life education (MA); K-12 reading endorsement (Certificate); special education (Certificate); sports management (MA). *Accreditation:* NCATE. Evening/weekend programs available. Postbaccalaureate distance learning degree programs offered (minimal on-campus study). *Faculty:* 12 full-time (8 women), 59 part-time/adjunct (47 women). *Students:* 697 full-time (571 women), 13 part-time (12 women); includes 64 minority (31 African Americans, 1 American Indian/Alaska Native, 21 Asian Americans or Pacific Islanders, 11 Hispanic Americans), 1 international. Average age 34. In 2009, 402 master's, 29 other advanced degrees awarded. *Application deadline:* Applications are processed on a rolling basis. Application fee: $50. Electronic applications accepted. *Financial support:* Applicants required to submit FAFSA. *Unit head:* Dr. Donald Helmstetter, Dean, 651-641-8227, Fax: 651-641-8807, E-mail: helmstetter@csp.edu. *Application contact:* Kimberly Craig, Director of Graduate and Cohort Admission, 651-603-6223, Fax: 651-603-6320, E-mail: craig@csp.edu.

Concordia University Texas, College of Education, Austin, TX 78726. Offers M Ed. Part-time and evening/weekend programs available. *Degree requirements:* For master's, thesis (for some programs), portfolio presentation.

Concordia University Wisconsin, Graduate Programs, Department of Education, Mequon, WI 53097-2402. Offers art education (MS Ed); curriculum and instruction (MS Ed); early childhood (MS Ed); educational administration (MS Ed); environmental education (MS Ed); family studies (MS Ed); reading (MS Ed); school counseling (MS Ed); special education (MS Ed). Part-time and evening/weekend programs available. Postbaccalaureate distance learning degree programs offered (minimal on-campus study). *Degree requirements:* For master's, comprehensive exam, thesis or alternative. *Entrance requirements:* For master's, minimum GPA of 3.0, teaching license. Additional exam requirements/recommendations for international students: Required—TOEFL. *Faculty research:* Motivation, developmental learning, learning styles.

Converse College, School of Education and Graduate Studies, Spartanburg, SC 29302-0006. Offers art education (M Ed); early childhood education (MAT); education (Ed S), including administration and supervision, curriculum and instruction, marriage and family therapy; elementary education (M Ed, MAT); gifted education (M Ed); leadership (M Ed); liberal arts (MLA), including English (M Ed, MAT, MLA), history, political science; secondary education (M Ed, MAT), including biology (MAT), chemistry (MAT), English (M Ed, MAT, MLA), mathematics, natural sciences (M Ed), social sciences; special education (M Ed, MAT), including learning disabilities (MAT), mental disabilities (MAT), special education (M Ed). *Accreditation:* NCATE. Part-time and evening/weekend programs available. *Entrance requirements:* For master's, PRAXIS II (M Ed), minimum GPA of 2.75; for Ed S, GRE or MAT, minimum GPA of 3.0. Electronic applications accepted. *Faculty research:* Motivation, classroom management, predictors of success in classroom teaching, sex equity in public education, gifted research.

Coppin State University, Division of Graduate Studies, Division of Education, Department of Curriculum and Instruction, Program in Teaching, Baltimore, MD 21216-3698. Offers teacher education (MAT). Part-time and evening/weekend programs available. Postbaccalaureate distance learning degree programs offered. *Degree requirements:* For master's, thesis, exit portfolio. *Entrance requirements:* For master's, GRE, resume, references.

Corban University, Graduate School, Education Program, Salem, OR 97301-9392. Offers MS Ed.

Cornell University, Graduate School, Graduate Fields of Agriculture and Life Sciences, Field of Education, Ithaca, NY 14853-0001. Offers agricultural education (MAT); biology (7-12) (MAT); chemistry (7-12) (MAT); curriculum and instruction (MPS, MS, PhD); earth science (7-12) (MAT); extension and adult education (MPS, MS, PhD); mathematics (7-12) (MAT); physics (7-12) (MAT). *Faculty:* 26 full-time (9 women). *Students:* 65 full-time (50 women); includes 15 minority (4 African Americans, 7 Asian Americans or Pacific Islanders, 4 Hispanic Americans), 2 international. Average age 34. 96 applicants, 33% accepted, 21 enrolled. In 2009, 27 master's, 2 doctorates awarded. Terminal master's awarded for partial completion of doctoral program. *Degree requirements:* For master's, thesis (MS); for doctorate, comprehensive exam, thesis/dissertation. *Entrance requirements:* For master's and doctorate, GRE General Test, sample of written work (recommended), 2 letters of recommendation. Additional exam requirements/recommendations for international students: Required—TOEFL (minimum score 550 paper-based; 213 computer-based; 77 iBT). *Application deadline:* For fall admission, 2/15 for domestic students. Application fee: $70. Electronic applications accepted. *Expenses:* Tuition: Full-time $29,500. Required fees: $70. Full-time tuition and fees vary according to degree level, program and student level. *Financial support:* In 2009–10, 33 students received support, including 3 fellowships with full tuition reimbursements available, 5 teaching assistantships with full tuition reimbursements available; research assistantships with full tuition reimbursements available, institutionally sponsored loans, scholarships/grants, health care benefits, tuition waivers (full and partial), and unspecified assistantships also available. Financial award applicants required to submit FAFSA. *Faculty research:* Moral development and professional ethics; public issues education and community development; socio/political issues in public education; teacher education and curriculum in agricultural science, and mathematics; extension research. *Unit head:* Director of Graduate Studies, 607-255-4278, Fax: 607-255-7905. *Application contact:* Graduate Field Assistant, 607-255-4278, Fax: 607-255-7905, E-mail: rh22@cornell.edu.

Cornerstone University, Graduate Programs, Grand Rapids, MI 49525-5897. Offers business administration (MBA); education (MA Ed); management (MSM); teaching English to speakers of other languages (MA, Graduate Certificate). Programs also offered at Holland, Kalamazoo, and Troy, MI campuses. Part-time programs available. Postbaccalaureate distance learning degree programs offered. *Degree requirements:* For master's, comprehensive exam (for some programs), thesis (for some programs). *Entrance requirements:* For master's, minimum GPA of 2.5, 2 letters of reference. Additional exam requirements/recommendations for international students: Required—TOEFL (minimum score 575 paper-based; 235 computer-based). Electronic applications accepted.

Covenant College, Program in Education, Lookout Mountain, GA 30750. Offers M Ed. Part-time programs available. *Degree requirements:* For master's, comprehensive exam, special project. *Entrance requirements:* For master's, GRE General Test, 2 professional recommendations, minimum GPA of 3.0, writing sample.

Creighton University, Graduate School, College of Arts and Sciences, Department of Education, Omaha, NE 68178-0001. Offers counselor education (MS), including college student affairs, community counseling, elementary school guidance, secondary school guidance; educational leadership (MS), including elementary school administration, secondary school administration, teacher leadership; special populations in education (MS); teaching (M Ed), including elementary teaching, secondary teaching. *Accreditation:* NCATE. Part-time and evening/weekend programs available. *Faculty:* 14 full-time (8 women). *Students:* 16 full-time (11 women), 112 part-time (78 women); includes 12 minority (3 African Americans, 2 American Indian/Alaska Native, 3 Asian Americans or Pacific Islanders, 4 Hispanic Americans), 5 international. Average age 31. 23 applicants, 70% accepted, 16 enrolled. In 2009, 45 master's awarded. *Degree requirements:* For master's, portfolio. *Entrance requirements:* For master's, GRE General Test, PPST, 3 letters of recommendation; writing samples, resume. Additional exam requirements/recommendations for international students: Required—TOEFL (minimum score 550 paper-based; 213 computer-based; 80 iBT). *Application deadline:* For fall admission, 7/1 priority date for domestic students, 3/1 priority date for international students; for winter admission, 12/1 for domestic students, 7/1 for international students; for spring admission, 4/1 for domestic students, 10/1 for international students. Applications are processed on a rolling basis. Application fee: $50. Electronic applications accepted. *Expenses:* Tuition: Full-time $11,700; part-time $650 per credit hour. Required fees: $126 per semester. *Financial support:* Teaching assistantships, scholarships/grants and tuition waivers (partial) available. Support available to part-time

students. Financial award applicants required to submit FAFSA. *Unit head:* Dr. Sharon Ishii-Jordan, Chair, 402-280-2553, E-mail: sharonishii-jordan@creighton.edu. *Application contact:* Taunya Plater, Senior Program Coordinator, 402-280-2870, Fax: 402-280-2899, E-mail: taunyaplater@creighton.edu.

Cumberland University, Program in Education, Lebanon, TN 37087. Offers MAE. Part-time and evening/weekend programs available. Postbaccalaureate distance learning degree programs offered (no on-campus study). *Degree requirements:* For master's, comprehensive exam. *Entrance requirements:* For master's, GRE General Test, MAT, or NTE, 3 letters of recommendation. Additional exam requirements/recommendations for international students: Required—TOEFL (minimum score 500 paper-based; 173 computer-based).

Curry College, Graduate Studies, Program in Education, Milton, MA 02186-9984. Offers educational administration (M Ed); educational diagnostic assessment (Certificate); educational therapy (Certificate); elementary education (M Ed); foundations (non-license) (M Ed); learning disabilities across the lifespan (Certificate); reading (M Ed, Certificate); special education (M Ed). Part-time and evening/weekend programs available. *Faculty:* 6 full-time (4 women), 12 part-time/adjunct (9 women). *Students:* 101 part-time (82 women). Average age 37. In 2009, 25 master's awarded. *Degree requirements:* For master's, project or thesis. *Entrance requirements:* For master's, MAT or GRE, interview, recommendations, resume, written statement. Additional exam requirements/recommendations for international students: Required—TOEFL (minimum score 550 paper-based; 213 computer-based; 80 iBT). *Application deadline:* For fall admission, 8/1 priority date for domestic students, 6/1 for international students; for winter admission, 10/1 for international students; for spring admission, 1/1 for domestic students, 1/28 for international students. Applications are processed on a rolling basis. Application fee: $50. *Expenses:* Contact institution. *Financial support:* Career-related internships or fieldwork and tuition waivers (partial) available. *Faculty research:* Classroom trauma, therapeutic writing, inclusionary practices. *Unit head:* Dr. Donald Gratz, Director and Associate Professor, 617-333-2243, E-mail: dgratz0703@curry.edu. *Application contact:* John Bresnahan, Director of Graduate Enrollment and Student Services, 617-333-2243, Fax: 617-979-3535, E-mail: jbresnah0104@curry.edu.

Daemen College, Education Department, Amherst, NY 14226-3592. Offers adolescence education (MS); childhood education (MS); childhood special education (MS); childhood special-alternative certification (MS); early childhood special-alternative certification (MS). Part-time programs available. *Faculty:* 14 full-time (11 women), 42 part-time/adjunct (36 women). *Students:* 320 full-time (292 women), 225 part-time (202 women); includes 5 minority (3 African Americans, 1 American Indian/Alaska Native, 1 Hispanic American), 135 international. Average age 25. 331 applicants, 82% accepted, 220 enrolled. In 2009, 302 master's awarded. *Degree requirements:* For master's, comprehensive exam, thesis optional, completion of degree within 5 years. *Entrance requirements:* For master's, 2 letters of recommendation, proof of initial certificate of licensure for professional programs, resume, minimum undergraduate GPA of 3.0. Additional exam requirements/recommendations for international students: Required—TOEFL (minimum score 500 paper-based; 173 computer-based; 61 iBT). *Application deadline:* For fall admission, 3/1 priority date for domestic and international students; for spring admission, 10/1 priority date for domestic and international students. Applications are processed on a rolling basis. Application fee: $25. Electronic applications accepted. *Expenses:* Tuition: Part-time $770 per credit hour. Tuition and fees vary according to course load, program and reciprocity agreements. *Financial support:* In 2009–10, 16 students received support. Institutionally sponsored loans, scholarships/grants, and some discounted programs available. Financial award application deadline: 2/15; financial award applicants required to submit FAFSA. *Faculty research:* Transition for students with disabilities, early childhood special education, traumatic brain injury (TBI), reading assessment. *Unit head:* Dr. Mary H. Fox, Chair, 716-839-8530, Fax: 716-839-8516, E-mail: mfox@daemen.edu. *Application contact:* Scott Rowe, Associate Director of Graduate Admissions, 716-839-8225, Fax: 716-839-8229, E-mail: srowe@daemen.edu.

Dakota State University, College of Education, Madison, SD 57042-1799. Offers instructional technology (MSET). *Accreditation:* NCATE. Part-time programs available. Postbaccalaureate distance learning degree programs offered (minimal on-campus study). *Faculty:* 7 full-time (3 women), 3 part-time/adjunct (0 women). *Students:* 1 full-time (0 women), 31 part-time (18 women), 1 international. Average age 34. 12 applicants, 92% accepted, 10 enrolled. In 2009, 22 master's awarded. *Degree requirements:* For master's, thesis, electronic portfolio. *Entrance requirements:* For master's, GRE General Test, demonstration of technology skills, minimum GPA of 2.7. Additional exam requirements/recommendations for international students: Required—TOEFL. *Application deadline:* For fall admission, 8/1 for domestic students, 6/1 for international students. Applications are processed on a rolling basis. Application fee: $35 ($85 for international students). Electronic applications accepted. *Financial support:* In 2009–10, 15 students received support; research assistantships, teaching assistantships, Federal Work-Study, scholarships/grants, tuition waivers (partial), and administrative assistantships available. Support available to part-time students. Financial award applicants required to submit FAFSA. *Faculty research:* Educational technology evaluation, computer supported collaborative learning, cognitive theory and visual representation of the effects of ambiguitous wireless computing on student learning and productivity. *Unit head:* Dr. Judy Dittman, Dean, 605-256-5177, Fax: 605-256-7300, E-mail: judy.dittman@dsu.edu. *Application contact:* Annette Miller, Secretary, Office of Graduate Studies and Research, 605-256-5799, Fax: 605-256-5093, E-mail: annette.miller@dsu.edu.

Dakota Wesleyan University, Program in Education, Mitchell, SD 57301-4398. Offers curriculum and instruction (MA Ed); education (MA); educational policy and administration (MA Ed); pre K-12 principal with certification (MA Ed); secondary with certification (MA Ed). Part-time and evening/weekend programs available. *Faculty:* 12 part-time/adjunct (7 women). *Students:* 31 part-time (15 women); includes 4 African Americans. Average age 30. 9 applicants, 100% accepted, 9 enrolled. In 2009, 14 master's awarded. *Degree requirements:* For master's, comprehensive exam, thesis optional, electronic portfolio. *Entrance requirements:* For master's, minimum GPA of 2.7, elementary statistics course. Additional exam requirements/recommendations for international students: Required—TOEFL (minimum score 500 paper-based; 71 computer-based), IELTS (minimum score 6.5). *Application deadline:* For fall admission, 8/1 priority date for domestic and international students; for winter admission, 12/1 priority date for domestic students; for spring admission, 4/1 priority date for domestic students, 12/1 priority date for international students. Applications are processed on a rolling basis. Application fee: $50. Electronic applications accepted. *Expenses:* Tuition: Full-time $5400; part-time $300 per credit hour. *Faculty research:* Math, political policy, technology in the classroom. *Unit head:* Dr. Ruth Haidle, Director of Graduate Studies, 605-995-2630, Fax: 605-995-2609, E-mail: ruhaidle@dwv.edu. *Application contact:* Coordinator of Graduate Admissions, 800-333-8506, Fax: 605-995-2699, E-mail: admissions@dwv.edu.

Dallas Baptist University, Dorothy M. Bush College of Education, Teaching Program, Dallas, TX 75211-9299. Offers elementary (MAT); English as a second language (MAT); hi-level (MAT); secondary (MAT). Part-time and evening/weekend programs available. *Entrance requirements:* For master's, GRE General Test, minimum GPA of 3.0. Additional exam requirements/recommendations for international students: Required—TOEFL, IELTS. Electronic applications accepted. *Expenses:* Tuition: Full-time $10,674; part-time $593 per credit hour.

Defiance College, Program in Education, Defiance, OH 43512-1610. Offers adolescent and young adult (MA); mild and moderate intervention specialist (MA); sport science (MA). Part-time programs available. *Degree requirements:* For master's, thesis (for some programs). *Entrance requirements:* For master's, teaching certificate.

Delaware State University, Graduate Programs, College of Education, Dover, DE 19901-2277. Offers MA, Ed D. *Accreditation:* NCATE. Part-time and evening/weekend programs available. *Degree requirements:* For master's, comprehensive exam, thesis optional. *Entrance requirements:* For master's, GRE General Test, minimum GPA of 3.0 in major, 2.75 overall. Additional exam requirements/recommendations for international students: Required—TOEFL (minimum score 500 paper-based). Electronic applications accepted.

Delta State University, Graduate Programs, College of Education, Cleveland, MS 38733-0001. Offers M Ed, MAT, Ed D, Ed S. *Accreditation:* NCATE. Part-time and evening/weekend programs available. *Degree requirements:* For master's, thesis optional; for doctorate, thesis/dissertation. *Entrance requirements:* For doctorate, GRE General Test; for Ed S, master's degree, teaching certificate. *Expenses:* Tuition, state resident: full-time $4450; part-time $247 per credit hour. Tuition, nonresident: full-time $11,520; part-time $640 per credit hour.

DePaul University, School for New Learning, Chicago, IL 60604. Offers applied technology (MS); educating adults (MA); integrated professional studies (MA). Part-time and evening/weekend programs available. *Faculty:* 8 full-time (2 women), 9 part-time/adjunct (5 women). *Students:* 12 full-time (7 women), 107 part-time (78 women); includes 62 minority (50 African Americans, 1 Asian American or Pacific Islander, 11 Hispanic Americans). Average age 42. 30 applicants, 80% accepted. In 2009, 20 master's awarded. *Degree requirements:* For master's, thesis or alternative. *Entrance requirements:* For master's, 3 years of work experience, current related employment. *Application deadline:* For fall admission, 9/1 priority date for domestic students; for spring admission, 3/1 priority date for domestic students. Applications are processed on a rolling basis. Application fee: $25. Electronic applications accepted. *Expenses:* Tuition: Full-time $37,525; part-time $620 per credit hour. *Financial support:* In 2009–10, 7 students received support. Scholarships/grants and tuition waivers (partial) available. Financial award applicants required to submit FAFSA. *Faculty research:* Interactive problem-based learning, liberal learning and professional competence, effective instructional practice. *Unit head:* Dr. Russ Rogers, Program Director, 312-362-8512, Fax: 312-362-8809, E-mail: rrogers@depaul.edu. *Application contact:* Sarah Hellstrom, Assistant Director, 312-362-5744, Fax: 312-362-8809, E-mail: shellstr@depaul.edu.

DePaul University, School of Education, Chicago, IL 60106. Offers bilingual and bicultural education (M Ed, MA); curriculum studies (M Ed, MA, Ed D); educational leadership (M Ed, MA, Ed D), including administration and supervision (M Ed, MA), Catholic school leadership (M Ed, MA), physical education (M Ed, MA); human development and learning (MA); human services and counseling (M Ed, MA), including agencies, family concerns, and higher education, elementary schools, human services management, secondary schools; reading and learning disabilities (M Ed, MA); social culture studies in education and development (M Ed, MA), including curriculum studies/development; teaching and learning (early childhood, elementary and secondary) (M Ed), including elementary education (M Ed, MA), secondary education (M Ed, MA); teaching and learning (early childhood, elementary, and secondary) (MA), including elementary education (M Ed, MA), secondary education (M Ed, MA). *Accreditation:* NCATE. Part-time and evening/weekend programs available. *Faculty:* 61 full-time (40 women), 66 part-time/adjunct (41 women). *Students:* 799 full-time (779 women), 470 part-time (365 women); includes 319 minority (153 African Americans, 3 American Indian/Alaska Native, 48 Asian Americans or Pacific Islanders, 115 Hispanic Americans), 15 international. Average age 30. 635 applicants, 74% accepted, 318 enrolled. In 2009, 604 master's, 5 doctorates awarded. *Degree requirements:* For doctorate, thesis/dissertation. *Entrance requirements:* For master's, interview, minimum GPA of 2.75, 2 letters of recommendation; for doctorate, interview, master's degree, writing sample, 3 letters of recommendation. Additional exam requirements/recommendations for international students: Required—TOEFL (minimum score 550 paper-based; 213 computer-based; 80 iBT). *Application deadline:* Applications are processed on a rolling basis. Application fee: $40. Electronic applications accepted. *Expenses:* Tuition: Full-time $37,525; part-time $620 per credit hour. *Financial support:* In 2009–10, 14 research assistantships with tuition reimbursements (averaging $5,800 per year) were awarded; career-related internships or fieldwork also available. *Faculty research:* Reflective teaching, children at risk, loss, ethnicity, urban education. Total annual research expenditures: $1.6 million. *Unit head:* Dr. Marie Donovan, Dean, 773-325-7581, Fax: 773-325-7713, E-mail: mdonovan@depaul.edu. *Application contact:* Brandon Washington, Data Project Manager, 773-325-1152, Fax: 773-325-2270, E-mail: bwashin3@depaul.edu.

DeSales University, Graduate Division, Program in Education, Center Valley, PA 18034-9568. Offers elementary education (M Ed); instructional technology for K-12 (M Ed); interdisciplinary (M Ed); mathematics (M Ed); special education (M Ed); TESOL/ESL (M Ed). Part-time and evening/weekend programs available. Postbaccalaureate distance learning degree programs offered (no on-campus study). *Students:* 218 part-time. *Degree requirements:* For master's, thesis project. *Entrance requirements:* For master's, teaching certificate. Additional exam requirements/recommendations for international students: Required—TOEFL. *Application deadline:* Applications are processed on a rolling basis. Application fee: $35. Electronic applications accepted. *Expenses:* Tuition: Full-time $17,500; part-time $665 per credit. Full-time tuition and fees vary according to program. Part-time tuition and fees vary according to course load. *Financial support:* Application deadline: 5/1. *Faculty research:* Effective teaching, computer interfacing in chemistry labs, computer applications to teaching, history of philosophy, aesthetics multidrug-resistant cancer. *Unit head:* Dr. Lujean Baab, Director, 610-282-1100 Ext. 1739, Fax: 610-282-3734, E-mail: lujean.baab@desales.edu. *Application contact:* Caryn Stopper, Director of Graduate Admissions, 610-282-1100 Ext. 1768, Fax: 610-282-0525, E-mail: caryn.stopper@desales.edu.

Doane College, Program in Education, Crete, NE 68333-2430. Offers curriculum and instruction (M Ed); educational leadership (M Ed). *Accreditation:* NCATE. Part-time and evening/weekend programs available. *Students:* 156 full-time (123 women), 495 part-time (383 women); includes 20 minority (7 African Americans, 1 American Indian/Alaska Native, 4 Asian Americans or Pacific Islanders, 8 Hispanic Americans). Average age 33. In 2009, 274 master's awarded. *Degree requirements:* For master's, thesis. *Entrance requirements:* For master's, minimum GPA of 2.5. *Application deadline:* Applications are processed on a rolling basis. Application fee: $25. Electronic applications accepted. *Expenses:* Contact institution. *Financial support:* Applicants required to submit FAFSA. *Unit head:* Lyn C. Forester, Dean, 402-826-8604, Fax: 402-826-8278. *Application contact:* Wilma Daddario, Assistant Dean, 402-464-1223, Fax: 402-466-4228, E-mail: wdaddario@doane.edu.

Dominican College, Division of Teacher Education, Department of Teacher Education, Orangeburg, NY 10962-1210. Offers childhood education (MS Ed); teacher of students with disabilities (MS Ed); teacher of visually impaired (MS Ed). *Accreditation:* Teacher Education Accreditation Council. Part-time and evening/weekend programs available. Postbaccalaureate distance learning degree programs offered (minimal on-campus study). *Faculty:* 2 full-time (both women), 6 part-time/adjunct (all women). *Students:* 50 part-time (42 women); includes 2 minority (both Hispanic Americans). Average age 39. In 2009, 10 master's awarded. *Degree requirements:* For master's, practicum, research project. *Entrance requirements:* For master's, interview, 3 letters of recommendation, minimum undergraduate GPA of 3.0. Additional exam requirements/recommendations for international students: Required—TOEFL (minimum score 550 paper-based; 213 computer-based). *Application deadline:* Applications are processed on a rolling basis. Application fee: $50. *Financial support:* Applicants required to submit FAFSA. *Unit head:* Dr. Rona Shaw, Program Director, 845-848-4081, Fax: 845-359-7802, E-mail: rona.shaw@dc.edu. *Application contact:* Director of Admissions, 845-848-7900, Fax: 845-365-3150, E-mail: admissions@dc.edu.

Dominican University, School of Education, River Forest, IL 60305-1099. Offers curriculum and instruction (MA Ed); early childhood education (MS); education (MAT); educational administration (MA); elementary (online) (MS); English as a second language (online) (MS); reading (online) (MS); special education (MS). Part-time and evening/weekend programs available. Postbaccalaureate distance learning degree programs offered. *Faculty:* 16 full-time (12 women), 59 part-time/adjunct (46 women). *Students:* 236 full-time (182 women), 622 part-time (509 women); includes 180 minority (54 African Americans, 3 American Indian/Alaska Native, 36 Asian Americans or Pacific Islanders, 87 Hispanic Americans), 2 international. Average age 32. In 2009, 199 master's awarded. *Entrance requirements:* For master's, Illinois certification test of basic skills. Additional exam requirements/recommendations for international students: Required—TOEFL (minimum score 550 paper-based; 213 computer-based; 79 iBT). *Application deadline:* Applications are processed on a rolling basis. Application fee: $25. *Expenses:* Contact institution. *Financial support:* Career-related internships or fieldwork, scholarships/grants, and tuition waivers (partial) available. Support available to part-time

Education—General

Dominican University (continued)
students. Financial award application deadline: 8/15; financial award applicants required to submit FAFSA. *Faculty research:* Governance of private education institutions, reading and language arts, inclusion, organizational planning, leadership and vision. *Unit head:* Dr. Colleen Reardon, Dean, 718-524-6643, Fax: 708-524-6665, E-mail: creardon@dom.edu. *Application contact:* Keven Hansen, Coordinator of Recruitment and Admissions, 708-524-6921, Fax: 708-524-6665, E-mail: educate@dom.edu.

Dominican University of California, Graduate Programs, School of Education and Counseling Psychology, Multiple Subject Credential Program, San Rafael, CA 94901-2298. Offers Credential. Program also offered in Ukiah, CA. *Entrance requirements:* For degree, California Basic Educational Skills Test, PRAXIS, 48 units of course work in education, bachelor'ss degree in area other than education, minimum GPA of 2.7. Additional exam requirements/recommendations for international students: Required—TOEFL (minimum score 550 paper-based; 213 computer-based). Electronic applications accepted.

Dominican University of California, Graduate Programs, School of Education and Counseling Psychology, Program in Education, San Rafael, CA 94901-2298. Offers MS. *Entrance requirements:* For master's, minimum GPA of 3.0, research project. Additional exam requirements/recommendations for international students: Required—TOEFL (minimum score 550 paper-based; 213 computer-based). Electronic applications accepted.

Dominican University of California, Graduate Programs, School of Education and Counseling Psychology, Single Subject Credential Program, San Rafael, CA 94901-2298. Offers Credential. *Entrance requirements:* For degree, California Basic Educational Skills Test, PRAXIS, minimum GPA of 2.7, bachelor's degree in area other than education, 48 units of course work in education. Additional exam requirements/recommendations for international students: Required—TOEFL (minimum score 550 paper-based; 213 computer-based). Electronic applications accepted.

Dordt College, Program in Education, Sioux Center, IA 51250-1697. Offers M Ed. Part-time programs available. Postbaccalaureate distance learning degree programs offered (minimal on-campus study). *Degree requirements:* For master's, comprehensive exam, thesis. *Entrance requirements:* For master's, GRE or MAT. Additional exam requirements/recommendations for international students: Required—TOEFL. Electronic applications accepted.

Dowling College, Graduate Programs in Education, Oakdale, NY 11769-1999. Offers adolescence education (MS Ed), including educational administration; advanced certificate in gifted education (AC); childhood and early childhood education (MS Ed); childhood education (MS Ed); educational administration (AC, PD), including computers in education (PD), school administration and supervision (PD), school district administration (PD); educational technology specialist (AC); literacy (MS Ed); literacy/special education (MS Ed); secondary education (MS Ed); special education (MS Ed). *Accreditation:* NCATE. Part-time and evening/weekend programs available. Postbaccalaureate distance learning degree programs offered. *Faculty:* 32 full-time (18 women), 98 part-time/adjunct (59 women). *Students:* 563 full-time (393 women), 885 part-time (668 women); includes 133 minority (47 African Americans, 2 American Indian/Alaska Native, 10 Asian Americans or Pacific Islanders, 74 Hispanic Americans). Average age 32. 363 applicants, 89% accepted, 213 enrolled. In 2009, 459 master's, 85 ACs awarded. *Degree requirements:* For master's and other advanced degree, comprehensive exam. *Entrance requirements:* For master's, minimum GPA of 3.0; for other advanced degree, teaching certificate. Additional exam requirements/recommendations for international students: Required—TOEFL (minimum score 550 paper-based). *Application deadline:* For fall admission, 9/1 priority date for domestic students; for winter admission, 1/1 priority date for domestic students; for spring admission, 2/1 priority date for domestic students. Applications are processed on a rolling basis. Application fee: $50. Electronic applications accepted. *Expenses:* Tuition: Full-time $14,490; part-time $805 per credit. Required fees: $346 per term. *Financial support:* Career-related internships or fieldwork and Federal Work-Study available. Support available to part-time students. Financial award application deadline: 6/30; financial award applicants required to submit FAFSA. *Faculty research:* Natural readers, Korean styles and learning strategies, mothers of children with disabilities, computers in instruction, cultural background and organizational roadblocks to problem solving. *Unit head:* Dr. Clyde Payne, Dean of the School of Education, 631-244-3404, Fax: 631-589-6644, E-mail: paynec@dowling.edu. *Application contact:* Glenn M. Berman, Assistant Vice President for Enrollment Services/Dean of Admissions, 631-244-3357, Fax: 631-244-1059, E-mail: glenn.berman@dowling.edu.

Drake University, School of Education, Des Moines, IA 50311-4516. Offers MAT, MS, MSE, MST, Ed D, Ed S. Part-time and evening/weekend programs available. *Faculty:* 21 full-time (12 women), 38 part-time/adjunct (25 women). *Students:* 95 full-time (76 women), 630 part-time (467 women); includes 19 African Americans, 6 Asian Americans or Pacific Islanders, 14 Hispanic Americans, 7 international. Average age 34. 363 applicants, 63% accepted, 213 enrolled. In 2009, 206 master's, 10 doctorates, 24 other advanced degrees awarded. *Degree requirements:* For master's and Ed S, comprehensive exam, internships (for some programs); for doctorate, comprehensive exam, thesis/dissertation, internships (for some programs). *Entrance requirements:* For master's, GRE General Test, MAT, or Drake Writing Assessment, resume, 2 letters of recommendation; for doctorate, GRE General Test or MAT, master's degree, 3 letters of recommendation; for Ed S, GRE General Test or MAT. Additional exam requirements/recommendations for international students: Required—TOEFL (minimum score 550 paper-based; 213 computer-based). *Application deadline:* For fall admission, 7/1 priority date for domestic students, 6/1 priority date for international students; for spring admission, 11/1 priority date for domestic students, 10/1 priority date for international students. Applications are processed on a rolling basis. Application fee: $25. Electronic applications accepted. *Expenses:* Contact institution. *Financial support:* In 2009–10, 14 research assistantships were awarded; career-related internships or fieldwork and unspecified assistantships also available. Support available to part-time students. *Faculty research:* Counseling and rehabilitation, behavioral supports, inquiry-based science methods, teacher quality enhancement. Total annual research expenditures: $1.5 million. *Unit head:* Dr. Janet McMahill, Dean, 515-271-3829, E-mail: janet.mcmahill@drake.edu. *Application contact:* Ann J. Martin, Graduate Coordinator, 515-271-2034, Fax: 515-271-2831, E-mail: ann.martin@drake.edu.

Drew University, Caspersen School of Graduate Studies, Program in Education, Madison, NJ 07940-1493. Offers biology (MAT); chemistry (MAT); English (MAT); French (MAT); Italian (MAT); math (MAT); physics (MAT); social studies (MAT); Spanish (MAT); theatre arts (MAT). Part-time programs available. *Students:* 21 full-time (10 women), 6 part-time (2 women); includes 1 minority (Hispanic American). Average age 24. 40 applicants, 90% accepted, 27 enrolled. In 2009, 13 master's awarded. *Entrance requirements:* For master's, transcripts, personal statement, recommendations. Additional exam requirements/recommendations for international students: Required—TOEFL, TWE. *Application deadline:* For fall admission, 2/1 priority date for domestic students. Applications are processed on a rolling basis. Application fee: $35. *Expenses:* Contact institution. *Financial support:* In 2009–10, 22 students received support. Federal Work-Study, scholarships/grants, and tuition waivers (partial) available. Support available to part-time students. Financial award application deadline: 2/15; financial award applicants required to submit FAFSA. *Unit head:* Dr. Ross Danis. *Application contact:* Carla J. Burns, Director of Graduate Admissions, 973-408-3110, Fax: 973-408-3242, E-mail: gradm@drew.edu.

Drexel University, School of Education, Philadelphia, PA 19104-2875. Offers educational administration and collaborative learning (MS); educational leadership and learning technology (PhD); global and international education (MS); graduate intern teaching (Certificate); higher education (MS); instructional technology (Spt); post-bachelor's teaching (Certificate); school principal (Certificate); school superintendent (Certificate); science of instruction (MS); teaching English as a second language (Certificate); teaching, learning and curriculum (MS). Part-time and evening/weekend programs available. Postbaccalaureate distance learning degree programs offered. *Degree requirements:* For doctorate, thesis/dissertation. Electronic applications accepted. *Expenses:* Contact institution.

Drury University, Graduate Programs in Education, Springfield, MO 65802. Offers elementary education (M Ed); gifted education (M Ed); human services (M Ed); instructional mathematics K-8 (M Ed); instructional technology (M Ed); middle school teaching (M Ed); secondary education (M Ed); special education (M Ed); special reading (M Ed). *Accreditation:* NCATE. Part-time and evening/weekend programs available. *Degree requirements:* For master's, thesis. *Entrance requirements:* For master's, GRE or MAT, minimum GPA of 2.75. Additional exam requirements/recommendations for international students: Required—TOEFL. Electronic applications accepted. *Faculty research:* Cultural enrichment, research skills, parental involvement relating to reading skills, reading strategies for mainstreaming children.

Duke University, Graduate School, Program in Teaching, Durham, NC 27708. Offers MAT, MAT/MEM. *Accreditation:* NCATE. *Students:* 13 full-time (6 women). 48 applicants, 46% accepted, 13 enrolled. In 2009, 9 master's awarded. *Entrance requirements:* For master's, GRE General Test. Additional exam requirements/recommendations for international students: Required—TOEFL (minimum score 550 paper-based; 213 computer-based; 83 iBT), IELTS (minimum score 7). *Application deadline:* For fall admission, 12/8 priority date for domestic students; for spring admission, 11/1 for domestic students. Application fee: $75. Electronic applications accepted. *Financial support:* Application deadline: 12/31. *Unit head:* Ginny Buckner, Director, 919-684-4353, Fax: 919-684-4483, E-mail: fns@duke.edu. *Application contact:* Cynthia Robertson, Associate Dean for Enrollment Services, 919-684-3913, E-mail: grad-admissions@duke.edu.

Duquesne University, School of Education, Pittsburgh, PA 15282-0001. Offers MS Ed, Ed D, PhD, CAGS, Post-Master's Certificate. *Accreditation:* NCATE. Part-time and evening/weekend programs available. *Faculty:* 43 full-time (25 women), 26 part-time/adjunct (12 women). *Students:* 530 full-time (415 women), 182 part-time (129 women); includes 58 minority (40 African Americans, 11 Asian Americans or Pacific Islanders, 7 Hispanic Americans), 17 international. Average age 34. 577 applicants, 55% accepted, 190 enrolled. In 2009, 205 master's, 55 doctorates awarded. *Degree requirements:* For master's, thesis optional; for doctorate, thesis/dissertation. *Entrance requirements:* For master's, MAT, minimum GPA of 3.0; for doctorate, GRE General Test, MAT, minimum GPA of 3.25; for other advanced degree, MAT, GRE, interview. Additional exam requirements/recommendations for international students: Required—TOEFL (minimum score 550 paper-based; 80 computer-based). *Application deadline:* For fall admission, 8/1 for domestic and international students; for spring admission, 12/1 for domestic and international students. Applications are processed on a rolling basis. Application fee: $0. Electronic applications accepted. *Expenses:* Tuition: Part-time $851 per credit. Required fees: $81 per credit. *Financial support:* Research assistantships, teaching assistantships with tuition reimbursements, career-related internships or fieldwork, Federal Work-Study, institutionally sponsored loans, and tuition waivers available. Support available to part-time students. Total annual research expenditures: $40,000. *Unit head:* Dr. Olga Welch, Dean, 412-396-6102, Fax: 412-396-5585. *Application contact:* Michael Dolinger, Director of Student and Academic Services, 412-396-6647, Fax: 412-396-5585, E-mail: mcelligott@duq.edu.

D'Youville College, Department of Education, Buffalo, NY 14201-1084. Offers elementary education (MS Ed, Teaching Certificate); secondary education (MS Ed, Teaching Certificate); special education (MS Ed). Part-time and evening/weekend programs available. *Degree requirements:* For master's, one foreign language, comprehensive exam, project or thesis. *Entrance requirements:* For master's, GRE (if GPA less than 2.75), minimum GPA of 3.0. Additional exam requirements/recommendations for international students: Required—TOEFL (minimum score 500 paper-based; 173 computer-based). Electronic applications accepted. *Faculty research:* Developmental disabilities, multiculturalism, early childhood education.

Earlham College, Graduate Programs, Richmond, IN 47374-4095. Offers M Ed, MAT. *Entrance requirements:* For master's, GRE, PRAXIS I, PRAXIS II.

East Carolina University, Graduate School, College of Education, Greenville, NC 27858-4353. Offers MA, MA Ed, MLS, MS, MSA, Ed D, CAS, Ed S. *Accreditation:* NCATE. Part-time and evening/weekend programs available. Postbaccalaureate distance learning degree programs offered (no on-campus study). *Degree requirements:* For master's, comprehensive exam, thesis optional; for doctorate, thesis/dissertation. *Entrance requirements:* For master's, GRE or MAT, bachelor's degree in related field, minimum GPA of 2.5; for doctorate, GRE or MAT, interview, minimum GPA of 3.5. Additional exam requirements/recommendations for international students: Required—TOEFL.

East Central University, School of Graduate Studies, Department of Education, Ada, OK 74820-6899. Offers M Ed. *Accreditation:* NCATE. Part-time and evening/weekend programs available. *Entrance requirements:* For master's, minimum GPA of 2.5. Electronic applications accepted.

Eastern Connecticut State University, School of Education and Professional Studies/Graduate Division, Willimantic, CT 06226-2295. Offers MS. *Accreditation:* NCATE. Part-time and evening/weekend programs available. *Degree requirements:* For master's, comprehensive exam, thesis optional. *Entrance requirements:* For master's, minimum GPA of 2.7. Additional exam requirements/recommendations for international students: Required—TOEFL (minimum score 550 paper-based; 213 computer-based).

Eastern Illinois University, Graduate School, College of Education and Professional Studies, Charleston, IL 61920-3099. Offers MS, MS Ed, Ed S. *Accreditation:* NCATE. Part-time and evening/weekend programs available. *Faculty:* 38 full-time (20 women). In 2009, 294 master's, 45 other advanced degrees awarded. *Degree requirements:* For Ed S, thesis. *Application deadline:* For fall admission, 3/31 priority date for domestic students. Applications are processed on a rolling basis. Application fee: $30. *Expenses:* Tuition, state resident: full-time $9434; part-time $239 per credit hour. Tuition, nonresident: full-time $23,774; part-time $717 per credit hour. Required fees: $802.63. *Financial support:* In 2009–10, 12 research assistantships with tuition reimbursements (averaging $8,100 per year), 13 teaching assistantships with tuition reimbursements (averaging $8,100 per year) were awarded; career-related internships or fieldwork and Federal Work-Study also available. Support available to part-time students. *Unit head:* Dr. Diane Jackman, Dean, 217-581-2524, Fax: 217-581-2518, E-mail: dhjackman@eiu.edu. *Application contact:* Bill Elliott, Director of Graduate Admissions, 217-581-7489, Fax: 217-581-6020, E-mail: wjelliott@eiu.edu.

Eastern Kentucky University, The Graduate School, College of Education, Richmond, KY 40475-3102. Offers MA, MA Ed, MAT. *Accreditation:* NCATE. Part-time programs available. Postbaccalaureate distance learning degree programs offered (minimal on-campus study). *Entrance requirements:* For master's, GRE General Test, minimum GPA of 2.5. *Faculty research:* Dispositions to teach, technology in education, distance learning.

Eastern Mennonite University, Program in Education, Harrisonburg, VA 22802-2462. Offers MA. *Accreditation:* NCATE. Part-time programs available. *Faculty:* 5 full-time (4 women), 3 part-time/adjunct (1 woman). *Students:* 4 full-time (all women), 177 part-time (156 women); includes 10 minority (5 African Americans, 2 Asian Americans or Pacific Islanders, 3 Hispanic Americans), 3 international. Average age 34. In 2009, 43 master's awarded. *Degree requirements:* For master's, portfolio, research projects. *Entrance requirements:* For master's, 1 year of teaching experience, interview, minimum undergraduate GPA of 2.75. Additional exam requirements/recommendations for international students: Required—TOEFL (minimum score 550 paper-based; 213 computer-based). *Application deadline:* Applications are processed on a rolling basis. Application fee: $25. *Expenses:* Contact institution. *Financial support:* Federal Work-Study and scholarships/grants available. Financial award application deadline: 6/30; financial award applicants required to submit FAFSA. *Faculty research:* Effective literacy instruction for middle school English language learners, beginning teacher's emotional experiences, constructivist learning environments, restorative discipline. *Unit head:* Dr. Donovan D. Steiner, Director, 540-432-4144, Fax: 540-432-4071, E-mail: steinerd@emu.edu. *Application contact:* Yvonne Martin, Education Secretary, 540-432-4350, Fax: 540-432-4071, E-mail: yvonne.martin@emu.edu.

Eastern Michigan University, Graduate School, College of Education, Ypsilanti, MI 48197. Offers MA, Ed D, PhD, Graduate Certificate, Post Master's Certificate, SPA. *Accreditation:* NCATE. Part-time and evening/weekend programs available. Postbaccalaureate distance learning degree programs offered (minimal on-campus study). *Faculty:* 91 full-time (66 women). *Students:* 190 full-time (143 women), 1,144 part-time (899 women); includes 240 minority (179 African Americans, 17 American Indian/Alaska Native, 19 Asian Americans or Pacific Islanders, 25 Hispanic Americans), 13 international. Average age 35. 762 applicants, 63% accepted, 329 enrolled. In 2009, 327 master's, 8 doctorates, 25 other advanced degrees awarded. *Degree requirements:* For doctorate, thesis/dissertation. *Entrance requirements:* For master's, GRE; for doctorate, GRE General Test. Additional exam requirements/recommendations for international students: Required—TOEFL. *Application deadline:* Applications are processed on a rolling basis. Application fee: $35. Tuition and fees vary according to course level. *Financial support:* Fellowships, research assistantships with full tuition reimbursements, teaching assistantships with full tuition reimbursements, career-related internships or fieldwork, Federal Work-Study, institutionally sponsored loans, scholarships/grants, tuition waivers (partial), and unspecified assistantships available. Support available to part-time students. Financial award applicants required to submit FAFSA. *Unit head:* Dr. Michael Bretting, Interim Dean and Associate Dean, 734-487-1414, Fax: 734-484-6471, E-mail: mbretting@emich.edu. *Application contact:* Graduate Admissions, 734-487-3400, Fax: 734-487-6559, E-mail: graduate.admissions@emich.edu.

Eastern Nazarene College, Adult and Graduate Studies, Division of Education, Quincy, MA 02170. Offers early childhood education (M Ed, Certificate); elementary education (M Ed, Certificate); English as a second language (M Ed, Certificate); instructional enrichment and development (M Ed, Certificate); middle school education (M Ed, Certificate); moderate special needs education (M Ed, Certificate); principal (Certificate); program development and supervision (M Ed, Certificate); secondary education (M Ed, Certificate); special education administrator (Certificate); supervisor (Certificate); teacher of reading (M Ed, Certificate). M Ed and Certificate also available through weekend program for administration, special needs, and reading only. Part-time and evening/weekend programs available. *Entrance requirements:* Additional exam requirements/recommendations for international students: Required—TOEFL (minimum score 550 paper-based).

Eastern New Mexico University, Graduate School, College of Education and Technology, Department of Curriculum and Instruction, Portales, NM 88130. Offers education (M Ed). Part-time programs available. *Faculty:* 14 full-time (8 women), 3 part-time/adjunct (0 women). *Students:* 14 full-time (10 women), 215 part-time (161 women); includes 73 minority (4 African Americans, 6 American Indian/Alaska Native, 63 Hispanic Americans). Average age 38. 119 applicants, 83% accepted, 44 enrolled. In 2009, 46 master's awarded. *Degree requirements:* For master's, comprehensive exam, thesis optional. *Entrance requirements:* For master's, minimum GPA of 2.8, letters of recommendation, photocopy of teaching license, writing assessment. Additional exam requirements/recommendations for international students: Required—TOEFL (minimum score 550 paper-based; 213 computer-based; 79 iBT), IELTS (minimum score 6). *Application deadline:* For fall admission, 7/20 priority date for domestic students, 6/20 priority date for international students. Applications are processed on a rolling basis. Application fee: $10. Electronic applications accepted. *Expenses:* Tuition, state resident: full-time $2922; part-time $121.75 per credit hour. Tuition, nonresident: full-time $8454; part-time $352.25 per credit hour. Required fees: $1038; $43.25 per credit hour. *Financial support:* In 2009–10, 9 research assistantships with partial tuition reimbursements (averaging $8,500 per year), 1 teaching assistantship with partial tuition reimbursement (averaging $4,250 per year) were awarded; fellowships, tuition waivers (partial) and unspecified assistantships also available. Support available to part-time students. Financial award applicants required to submit FAFSA. *Unit head:* Dr. Romelia Hurtado de Vivas, Graduate Coordinator, 575-562-2977, E-mail: romelia.hurtadodevivas@enmu.edu. *Application contact:* Dr. Romelia Hurtado de Vivas, Graduate Coordinator, 575-562-2977, E-mail: romelia.hurtadodevivas@enmu.edu.

Eastern New Mexico University, Graduate School, College of Education and Technology, Department of Educational Studies, Portales, NM 88130. Offers counseling (MA); education (M Ed); school counseling (M Ed); special education (M Ed, M Sp Ed). *Accreditation:* NCATE. Part-time and evening/weekend programs available. *Faculty:* 5 full-time (3 women). *Students:* 5 full-time (1 woman), 85 part-time (73 women); includes 27 minority (6 African Americans, 1 American Indian/Alaska Native, 1 Asian American or Pacific Islander, 19 Hispanic Americans). Average age 35. 33 applicants, 82% accepted, 25 enrolled. In 2009, 19 master's awarded. *Degree requirements:* For master's, comprehensive exam, thesis optional. *Entrance requirements:* For master's, minimum GPA of 2.8, letter of recommendation, photocopy of teaching license, writing assessment. Additional exam requirements/recommendations for international students: Required—TOEFL (minimum score 550 paper-based; 213 computer-based; 79 iBT), IELTS (minimum score 6). *Application deadline:* For fall admission, 7/20 priority date for domestic students, 6/20 priority date for international students. Applications are processed on a rolling basis. Application fee: $10. Electronic applications accepted. *Expenses:* Tuition, state resident: full-time $2922; part-time $121.75 per credit hour. Tuition, nonresident: full-time $8454; part-time $352.25 per credit hour. Required fees: $1038; $43.25 per credit hour. *Financial support:* In 2009–10, 5 research assistantships with tuition reimbursements (averaging $4,250 per year) were awarded; fellowships, teaching assistantships, career-related internships or fieldwork and unspecified assistantships also available. Support available to part-time students. Financial award applicants required to submit FAFSA. *Unit head:* Dr. Thomas Toglia, Graduate Coordinator, 575-562-2526, E-mail: thomas.toglia@enmu.edu. *Application contact:* Dr. Thomas Toglia, Graduate Coordinator, 575-562-2526, E-mail: thomas.toglia@enmu.edu.

Eastern Oregon University, School of Education and Business, Master of Science Program, La Grande, OR 97850-2899. Offers MS. Part-time programs available. Postbaccalaureate distance learning degree programs offered (no on-campus study). *Degree requirements:* For master's, thesis. *Entrance requirements:* For master's, GRE General Test.

Eastern University, Graduate Education Programs, St. Davids, PA 19087-3696. Offers multicultural education (M Ed); school health services (M Ed); school nurse (Certificate). Part-time programs available. *Entrance requirements:* For master's, minimum GPA of 2.5. Additional exam requirements/recommendations for international students: Required—TOEFL.

Eastern Washington University, Graduate Studies, College of Education and Human Development, Department of Education, Cheney, WA 99004-2431. Offers adult education (M Ed); curriculum development (M Ed); early childhood education (M Ed); educational leadership (M Ed); elementary teaching (M Ed); foundations of education (M Ed); instructional media and technology (M Ed); literacy (M Ed). *Accreditation:* NCATE. Part-time programs available. *Degree requirements:* For master's, comprehensive exam. *Entrance requirements:* For master's, minimum GPA of 3.0. *Expenses:* Tuition, state resident: full-time $7476; part-time $249 per quarter hour. Tuition, nonresident: full-time $18,030; part-time $601 per quarter hour. Required fees: $3.50 per quarter hour. $142 per quarter.

East Stroudsburg University of Pennsylvania, Graduate School, College of Education, East Stroudsburg, PA 18301-2999. Offers M Ed. Part-time and evening/weekend programs available. *Faculty:* 30 full-time (18 women), 11 part-time/adjunct (7 women). *Students:* 131 full-time (94 women), 478 part-time (380 women); includes 44 minority (14 African Americans, 1 American Indian/Alaska Native, 7 Asian Americans or Pacific Islanders, 22 Hispanic Americans), 3 international. Average age 34. In 2009, 146 master's awarded. *Degree requirements:* For master's, comprehensive exam, thesis (for some programs). *Entrance requirements:* Additional exam requirements/recommendations for international students: Required—TOEFL (minimum score 560 paper-based; 220 computer-based; 83 iBT). *Application deadline:* For fall admission, 7/31 priority date for domestic students, 5/1 priority date for international students; for spring admission, 11/30 for domestic students, 10/1 for international students. Applications are processed on a rolling basis. Application fee: $50. *Expenses:* Tuition, state resident: full-time $9942; part-time $387 per credit. Tuition, nonresident: full-time $14,240; part-time $619 per credit. *Financial support:* In 2009–10, 63 research assistantships with full and partial tuition reimbursements (averaging $2,113 per year) were awarded; career-related internships or fieldwork, Federal Work-Study, and institutionally sponsored loans also available. Financial award application deadline: 3/1; financial award applicants required to submit FAFSA. *Unit head:* Dr. Pamela Kramer, Dean, 570-422-3377, Fax: 570-422-3506, E-mail: pkramer@po-box.esu.edu. *Application contact:* Kevin Quintero, Graduate Admissions Coordinator, 570-422-3890, Fax: 570-422-3711, E-mail: kquintero@po-box.esu.edu.

East Tennessee State University, School of Graduate Studies, College of Education, Johnson City, TN 37614. Offers M Ed, MA, MAT, Ed D, Ed S. *Accreditation:* NCATE. Part-time and evening/weekend programs available. Terminal master's awarded for partial completion of doctoral program. *Degree requirements:* For doctorate, thesis/dissertation, oral and written exams; for Ed S, internship, practicum. *Entrance requirements:* For master's, GRE; for doctorate, GRE General Test, GRE Subject Test; for Ed S, GRE General Test, teacher certification. Additional exam requirements/recommendations for international students: Required—TOEFL (minimum score 550 paper-based; 213 computer-based).

Edgewood College, Program in Education, Madison, WI 53711-1997. Offers director of instruction (Certificate); director of special education and pupil services (Certificate); education (MA Ed); educational administration (MA); educational leadership (Ed D); program coordinator (Certificate); school business administration (Certificate); school principalship K-12 (Certificate). *Accreditation:* NCATE (one or more programs are accredited). Part-time and evening/weekend programs available. *Students:* 36 full-time (21 women), 232 part-time (141 women); includes 39 minority (10 African Americans, 3 American Indian/Alaska Native, 9 Asian Americans or Pacific Islanders, 17 Hispanic Americans), 1 international. Average age 37. In 2009, 30 master's, 23 doctorates awarded. *Degree requirements:* For master's, practicum, research project. *Entrance requirements:* For master's, minimum GPA of 2.75, 2 letters of recommendation, personal statement; for doctorate, resume, 2 letters of recommendation, interview. Additional exam requirements/recommendations for international students: Required—TOEFL (minimum score 525 paper-based; 197 computer-based; 72 iBT). *Application deadline:* For fall admission, 8/24 for domestic students, 8/1 for international students; for spring admission, 1/10 for domestic students, 10/1 for international students. Applications are processed on a rolling basis. Application fee: $25. Electronic applications accepted. *Expenses:* Tuition: Part-time $688 per credit hour. *Unit head:* Dr. Jane Belmore, Interim Dean, 608-663-8336, Fax: 608-663-3291, E-mail: jbelmore@edgewood.edu. *Application contact:* Joann Eastman, Admissions Counselor, 608-663-3250, Fax: 608-663-2214, E-mail: gps@edgewood.edu.

Edinboro University of Pennsylvania, School of Graduate Studies and Research, School of Education, Edinboro, PA 16444. Offers M Ed, MA, Certificate. Certificates issued by a state agency. *Accreditation:* NCATE. Part-time and evening/weekend programs available. *Faculty:* 39 full-time (28 women), 20 part-time/adjunct (12 women). *Students:* 279 full-time (191 women), 1,079 part-time (829 women); includes 42 minority (28 African Americans, 3 American Indian/Alaska Native, 3 Asian Americans or Pacific Islanders, 8 Hispanic Americans). Average age 32. In 2009, 293 master's, 74 other advanced degrees awarded. *Degree requirements:* For master's and Certificate, competency exam. *Entrance requirements:* For master's and Certificate, GRE or MAT, minimum QPA of 2.5. *Application deadline:* Applications are processed on a rolling basis. Application fee: $30. Electronic applications accepted. *Expenses:* Tuition, state resident: full-time $6666; part-time $370 per credit. Tuition, nonresident: full-time $10,666; part-time $593 per credit. Required fees: $2206.28. One-time fee: $204 part-time. *Financial support:* In 2009–10, 78 research assistantships with full and partial tuition reimbursements (averaging $4,050 per year) were awarded; career-related internships or fieldwork, Federal Work-Study, institutionally sponsored loans, scholarships/grants, and unspecified assistantships also available. Support available to part-time students. Financial award application deadline: 2/15; financial award applicants required to submit FAFSA. *Unit head:* Dr. James Bolton, Interim Dean, 814-732-2752, Fax: 814-732-2268, E-mail: jbolton@edinboro.edu. *Application contact:* Dr. R. Scott Baldwin, Dean, 814-732-2752, Fax: 814-732-2268, E-mail: sbaldwin@edinboro.edu.

Elizabeth City State University, School of Education and Psychology, Elizabeth City, NC 27909-7806. Offers M Ed, MSA. Part-time and evening/weekend programs available. *Degree requirements:* For master's, comprehensive exam (for some programs), thesis. Electronic applications accepted.

Elms College, Division of Education, Chicopee, MA 01013-2839. Offers early childhood education (MAT); education (M Ed, CAGS); elementary education (MAT); English as a second language (MAT); reading (MAT); secondary education (MAT), including biology education, English education, Spanish education; special education (MAT). Part-time and evening/weekend programs available. *Faculty:* 12 full-time (8 women), 4 part-time/adjunct (2 women). *Students:* 17 full-time (14 women), 153 part-time (136 women); includes 5 minority (1 American Indian/Alaska Native, 4 Hispanic Americans). Average age 36. 43 applicants, 88% accepted, 37 enrolled. In 2009, 23 master's, 8 other advanced degrees awarded. *Degree requirements:* For master's, thesis (for some programs). *Entrance requirements:* For master's, Massachusetts Educators Certification Test, minimum GPA of 3.0; for CAGS, master's degree in education. Additional exam requirements/recommendations for international students: Required—TOEFL. *Application deadline:* For fall admission, 7/1 priority date for domestic students; for spring admission, 11/1 priority date for domestic students. Applications are processed on a rolling basis. Application fee: $30. *Financial support:* In 2009–10, 2 teaching assistantships with partial tuition reimbursements were awarded; tuition waivers (partial) also available. Support available to part-time students. Financial award applicants required to submit FAFSA. *Unit head:* Dr. Mary Janeczek, Director, 413-594-2761, Fax: 413-592-4871, E-mail: janeczeke@elms.edu. *Application contact:* Dana Malone, Associate Director for Graduate Studies and Continuing Education, 413-265-2445, Fax: 413-265-2459, E-mail: maloned@elms.edu.

Elon University, Program in Education, Elon, NC 27244-2010. Offers elementary education (M Ed); gifted education (M Ed); special education (M Ed). *Accreditation:* NCATE. Part-time programs available. *Faculty:* 15 full-time (11 women). *Students:* 1 (woman) full-time, 79 part-time (65 women); includes 15 minority (13 African Americans, 1 Asian American or Pacific Islander, 1 Hispanic American), 1 international. Average age 30. 57 applicants, 84% accepted, 39 enrolled. In 2009, 45 master's awarded. *Entrance requirements:* For master's, GRE, MAT. Additional exam requirements/recommendations for international students: Required—TOEFL (minimum score 550 paper-based; 213 computer-based; 79 iBT). *Application deadline:* For winter admission, 6/1 priority date for domestic students. Applications are processed on a rolling basis. Application fee: $50. Electronic applications accepted. *Expenses:* Contact institution. *Financial support:* In 2009–10, 4 students received support. Federal Work-Study and scholarships/grants available. Support available to part-time students. Financial award application deadline: 6/1; financial award applicants required to submit FAFSA. *Faculty research:* Teaching reading to low-achieving second and third graders, pre- and post-student teaching attitudes toward teaching, children's writing, whole language methodology, critical creative thinking. *Unit head:* Dr. Judith B. Howard, Director, 336-278-5885, Fax: 336-278-5919, E-mail: howardj@elon.edu. *Application contact:* Art Fadde, Director of Graduate Admissions, 800-334-8448 Ext. 3, Fax: 336-278-7699, E-mail: afadde@elon.edu.

Embry-Riddle Aeronautical University Worldwide, Worldwide Headquarters, Program in Space Education, Daytona Beach, FL 32114-3900. Offers MSSE. *Faculty:* 1 full-time (0 women). *Students:* 8 part-time (5 women); includes 2 minority (both Asian Americans or Pacific Islanders). Average age 38. 3 applicants, 67% accepted, 1 enrolled. In 2009, 11 master's awarded. *Degree requirements:* For master's, thesis (for some programs). Application fee: $50. *Financial support:* In 2009–10, 1 student received support. *Unit head:* Dr. Kees Rietsema, Chair, 602-750-0685, E-mail: rietsd37@erau.edu. *Application contact:* Linda Dammer, Director of Admissions, 386-226-6910, Fax: 386-226-6984, E-mail: ecinfo@erau.edu.

Emmanuel College, Graduate Programs, Programs in Education, Boston, MA 02115. Offers educational leadership (CAGS); elementary education (MAT); school administration (M Ed); secondary education (MAT). Part-time and evening/weekend programs available. *Faculty:* 6 part-time/adjunct (2 women). *Students:* 6 full-time (5 women), 46 part-time (33 women); includes 8 minority (4 African Americans, 4 Hispanic Americans). Average age 33. 16 applicants, 56% accepted, 9 enrolled. In 2009, 23 master's awarded. *Entrance requirements:* For master's,

Education—General

Emmanuel College (continued)
interview, resume, 2 letters of recommendation, essay, bachelor's degree; for CAGS, interview, leadership statement, resume, 2 letters of recommendation. Additional exam requirements/recommendations for international students: Required—TOEFL (minimum score 600 paper-based; 250 computer-based). *Application deadline:* For fall admission, 8/15 priority date for domestic students; for spring admission, 12/8 priority date for domestic students. Applications are processed on a rolling basis. Application fee: $50. Electronic applications accepted. *Expenses:* Tuition: Part-time $665 per credit. *Faculty research:* Literature/reading, history of education, multicultural education, special education. *Unit head:* Dr. Judith Marley, Dean, Graduate and Professional Programs, 617-735-9700, Fax: 617-507-0434, E-mail: gpp@emmanuel.edu. *Application contact:* Enrollment Counselor, 617-735-9700, Fax: 617-507-0434, E-mail: gpp@emmanuel.edu.

Emory & Henry College, Graduate Programs, Emory, VA 24327-0947. Offers American history (MA Ed); organizational leadership (MOL); professional studies (M Ed); reading specialist (MA Ed). Part-time and evening/weekend programs available. *Entrance requirements:* For master's, GRE or PRAXIS I, recommendations, writing sample.

Emory University, Graduate School of Arts and Sciences, Division of Educational Studies, Atlanta, GA 30322-1100. Offers educational studies (MA, PhD, DAST); middle grades teaching (M Ed, MAT); secondary teaching (M Ed, MAT). *Accreditation:* NCATE. Terminal master's awarded for partial completion of doctoral program. *Degree requirements:* For master's, thesis; for doctorate, comprehensive exam, thesis/dissertation. *Entrance requirements:* For master's and doctorate, GRE General Test, minimum GPA of 3.0. Additional exam requirements/recommendations for international students: Required—TOEFL. Electronic applications accepted. *Faculty research:* Educational policy, educational measurement, urban and multicultural education, mathematics and science education, comparative education.

Emporia State University, School of Graduate Studies, The Teachers College, Emporia, KS 66801-5087. Offers MS, Ed S. *Accreditation:* NCATE. Part-time programs available. Postbaccalaureate distance learning degree programs offered (no on-campus study). *Faculty:* 81 full-time (50 women), 5 part-time/adjunct (3 women). *Students:* 160 full-time (123 women), 976 part-time (675 women); includes 58 minority (20 African Americans, 7 American Indian/Alaska Native, 9 Asian Americans or Pacific Islanders, 22 Hispanic Americans), 27 international. 217 applicants, 95% accepted, 188 enrolled. In 2009, 403 master's, 10 other advanced degrees awarded. *Degree requirements:* For master's, comprehensive exam or thesis; for Ed S, comprehensive exam, thesis or alternative, internship. *Entrance requirements:* For master's, appropriate bachelor's degree; for Ed S, GRE, graduate essay exam, letters of recommendation, teacher certification. *Application deadline:* Applications are processed on a rolling basis. Application fee: $30 ($75 for international students). Electronic applications accepted. *Expenses:* Tuition, state resident: full-time $4154; part-time $173 per credit hour. Tuition, nonresident: full-time $12,864; part-time $536 per credit hour. Required fees: $948; $58 per credit hour. Tuition and fees vary according to campus/location. *Financial support:* In 2009–10, 2 research assistantships (averaging $7,412 per year), 24 teaching assistantships with full tuition reimbursements (averaging $6,159 per year) were awarded; career-related internships or fieldwork, Federal Work-Study, institutionally sponsored loans, health care benefits, and unspecified assistantships also available. Financial award application deadline: 3/15; financial award applicants required to submit FAFSA. *Unit head:* Dr. J. Phillip Bennett, Dean, 620-341-5367, Fax: 620-341-5785, E-mail: pbennett@emporia.edu. *Application contact:* Mary Sewell, Admissions Coordinator, 800-950-GRAD, Fax: 620-341-5909, E-mail: msewell@emporia.edu.

Evangel University, Department of Education, Springfield, MO 65802. Offers educational leadership (M Ed); reading education (M Ed); secondary teaching (M Ed); teaching (MA). *Accreditation:* NCATE. Part-time and evening/weekend programs available. *Faculty:* 4 full-time (2 women), 5 part-time/adjunct (3 women). *Students:* 10 full-time (6 women), 40 part-time (31 women). Average age 33. 14 applicants, 86% accepted, 11 enrolled. In 2009, 23 master's awarded. *Degree requirements:* For master's, comprehensive exam, thesis optional. *Entrance requirements:* For master's, PRAXIS II (preferred) or GRE. Additional exam requirements/recommendations for international students: Required—TOEFL (minimum score 550 paper-based; 213 computer-based). *Application deadline:* For fall admission, 7/15 priority date for domestic students; for spring admission, 11/15 priority date for domestic students. Applications are processed on a rolling basis. Application fee: $25. *Financial support:* In 2009–10, 3 students received support. Career-related internships or fieldwork, institutionally sponsored loans, and scholarships/grants available. Support available to part-time students. Financial award application deadline: 3/1; financial award applicants required to submit FAFSA. *Unit head:* Dr. Colleen Hardy, Program Coordinator, 417-865-2815 Ext. 8553, E-mail: hardyc@evangel.edu. *Application contact:* Charity H. Fahlstrom, Admissions Representative, Graduate and Professional Studies, 417-865-2811 Ext. 7227, Fax: 417-865-9599.

The Evergreen State College, Graduate Programs, Program in Curriculum and Instruction, Olympia, WA 98505. Offers English as a second language (M Ed); mathematics (M Ed). *Faculty:* 2 full-time (both women). *Students:* 40 part-time (30 women); includes 5 minority (1 African American, 1 American Indian/Alaska Native, 2 Asian Americans or Pacific Islanders, 1 Hispanic American). Average age 42. 23 applicants, 100% accepted, 17 enrolled. *Degree requirements:* For master's, research paper and presentation, passing score on WEST-E (math or ELL). *Entrance requirements:* For master's, bachelor's degree with 4-quarter/3-semester credits in child/adolescent development, lifespan development or another human development course covering the cognitive, affective, and psychological components of individuals; minimum GPA of 3.0 in last 90 quarter/60 semester credits; 1 year classroom teaching experience (preferred). *Application deadline:* For fall admission, 3/29 priority date for domestic and international students. Applications are processed on a rolling basis. Application fee: $50. Electronic applications accepted. *Expenses:* Contact institution. *Financial support:* In 2009–10, 1 student received support, including 1 fellowship (averaging $2,250 per year); scholarships/grants and tuition waivers (partial) also available. Financial award application deadline: 3/15; financial award applicants required to submit FAFSA. *Faculty research:* Multicultural education, bilingual education, ELL, qualitative research methodologies, critical theory, education leadership policy, math and science education. *Unit head:* Sherry Walton, Director, 360-867-6856, Fax: 360-867-6575, E-mail: adairl@evergreen.edu. *Application contact:* Lynne Adair, Program Coordinator, 360-867-6639, Fax: 360-867-6575, E-mail: adairl@evergreen.edu.

The Evergreen State College, Graduate Programs, Program in Teaching, Olympia, WA 98505. Offers MIT. *Faculty:* 6 full-time (4 women). *Students:* 73 full-time (46 women); includes 8 minority (2 African Americans, 2 American Indian/Alaska Native, 2 Asian Americans or Pacific Islanders, 2 Hispanic Americans). Average age 30. 60 applicants, 92% accepted, 43 enrolled. In 2009, 34 master's awarded. *Degree requirements:* For master's, thesis, 20 week teaching internship. *Entrance requirements:* For master's, Washington Educator Skills Test-Basic, Washington Educator Skills Test-Endorsements/PRAXIS II, minimum undergraduate GPA of 3.0 for last 90 quarter hours, resume, endorsement worksheets, 3 letters of recommendation. Additional exam requirements/recommendations for international students: Required—TOEFL (minimum score 600 paper-based; 250 computer-based; 100 iBT). *Application deadline:* For fall admission, 5/3 priority date for domestic and international students. Applications are processed on a rolling basis. Application fee: $50. Electronic applications accepted. *Expenses:* Contact institution. *Financial support:* In 2009–10, 13 students received support, including 13 fellowships (averaging $3,250 per year); career-related internships or fieldwork, Federal Work-Study, scholarships/grants, and tuition waivers (partial) also available. Financial award application deadline: 3/15; financial award applicants required to submit FAFSA. *Faculty research:* Assessment, literacy/multicultural/special education, math/science instruction, social justice, research methodology/design, theories of learning. *Unit head:* Dr. Sherry Walton, MIT Director, 360-867-6753, E-mail: waltonsl@evergreen.edu. *Application contact:* Maggie Foran, Associate Director, 360-867-6559, Fax: 360-867-5430, E-mail: foranm@evergreen.edu.

Fairfield University, Graduate School of Education and Allied Professions, Fairfield, CT 06824-5195. Offers MA, CAS. *Accreditation:* NCATE. Part-time and evening/weekend programs available. *Degree requirements:* For master's, comprehensive exam. *Entrance requirements:* For master's, minimum QPA of 3.0, 2 recommendations, resume. Additional exam requirements/recommendations for international students: Required—TOEFL (minimum score 550 paper-based; 213 computer-based; 80 iBT). Electronic applications accepted. *Faculty research:* Literacy, adolescence psychology, special education, early childhood education, teaching development.

Fairleigh Dickinson University, College at Florham, University College: Arts, Sciences, and Professional Studies, Peter Sammartino School of Education, Madison, NJ 07940-1099. Offers education for certified teachers (MA, Certificate); educational leadership (MA); instructional technology (Certificate); literacy/reading (Certificate); teaching (MAT). *Students:* 66 full-time (53 women), 49 part-time (25 women). Average age 27. 91 applicants, 87% accepted, 68 enrolled. In 2009, 74 master's awarded. *Application deadline:* Applications are processed on a rolling basis. Application fee: $40. *Application contact:* Susan Brooman, University Director, Graduate Admissions, 973-443-8905, Fax: 973-443-8088, E-mail: grad@fdu.edu.

Fairleigh Dickinson University, Metropolitan Campus, University College: Arts, Sciences, and Professional Studies, Peter Sammartino School of Education, Teaneck, NJ 07666-1914. Offers dyslexia specialist (Certificate); education for certified teachers (MA); educational leadership (MA); instructional technology (Certificate); learning disabilities (MA); literacy/reading (Certificate); multilingual education (MA); teacher of the handicapped (Certificate); teaching (MAT). *Accreditation:* Teacher Education Accreditation Council. Part-time programs available. *Students:* 61 full-time (56 women), 530 part-time (464 women), 10 international. Average age 36. 283 applicants, 93% accepted, 231 enrolled. In 2009, 152 master's awarded. *Degree requirements:* For master's, research project (MAT). *Application deadline:* Applications are processed on a rolling basis. Application fee: $40. *Unit head:* Dr. Vicki Cohen, Director, 201-692-2525, Fax: 201-692-2603, E-mail: vicki_cohen@fdu.edu. *Application contact:* Susan Brooman, University Director of Graduate Admissions, 201-692-2554, Fax: 201-692-2560, E-mail: globaleducation@fdu.edu.

Fairmont State University, Graduate Studies, Programs in Education, Fairmont, WV 26554. Offers education (MAT); leadership studies (M Ed); online learning (M Ed); professional studies (M Ed); reading (M Ed); special education (M Ed). *Accreditation:* NCATE.

Felician College, Program in Education, Lodi, NJ 07644-2117. Offers education (MA); educational supervision (MA, PMC); elementary education (MA); principal (PMC); principal/supervision dual certification (MA); school nurse/health (MA); school nurse/health educator (Certificate); special education (MA). *Accreditation:* Teacher Education Accreditation Council. Part-time and evening/weekend programs available. *Students:* 12 full-time (9 women), 93 part-time (83 women); includes 5 African Americans, 1 Asian American or Pacific Islander, 9 Hispanic Americans, 3 international. Average age 37. 18 applicants, 50% accepted, 9 enrolled. *Degree requirements:* For master's, project. *Entrance requirements:* For master's, MAT, minimum GPA of 3.0, 3 letters of recommendation. Additional exam requirements/recommendations for international students: Recommended—TOEFL (minimum score 550 paper-based; 213 computer-based). *Application deadline:* Applications are processed on a rolling basis. Application fee: $40. *Financial support:* Federal Work-Study available. *Unit head:* Dr. Rosemarie Liebmann, Associate Dean, 201-559-3537, E-mail: liebmannr@felician.edu. *Application contact:* Dr. Wendy Lin-Cook, Director of Adult and Graduate Admission, 201-559-6077, Fax: 201-559-6138, E-mail: adultandgraduate@felician.edu.

See Close-Up on page 709.

Ferris State University, College of Education and Human Services, School of Education, Big Rapids, MI 49307. Offers administration (MSCTE); curriculum and instruction (M Ed), including administration, elementary education, experiential education, philanthropic education, reading, secondary education, special education, subject matter option; education technology (MSCTE); instructor (MSCTE); post-secondary administration (MSCTE); training and development (MSCTE). Part-time and evening/weekend programs available. Postbaccalaureate distance learning degree programs offered. *Faculty:* 12 full-time (8 women), 11 part-time/adjunct (5 women). *Students:* 19 full-time (13 women), 185 part-time (122 women); includes 24 minority (20 African Americans, 1 Asian American or Pacific Islander, 3 Hispanic Americans), 1 international. Average age 36. 37 applicants, 32% accepted, 11 enrolled. In 2009, 73 master's awarded. *Degree requirements:* For master's, thesis, research paper. *Entrance requirements:* For master's, 2 years of work experience for vocational setting, minimum GPA of 2.75. Additional exam requirements/recommendations for international students: Recommended—TOEFL (minimum score 500 paper-based; 173 computer-based; 61 iBT). *Application deadline:* For fall admission, 7/1 priority date for domestic students; for spring admission, 11/1 priority date for domestic students. Applications are processed on a rolling basis. Application fee: $30. *Financial support:* Career-related internships or fieldwork and scholarships/grants available. Support available to part-time students. Financial award applicants required to submit FAFSA. *Faculty research:* Suicide prevention, reading, women in education, special needs, administration. *Unit head:* Dr. Liza Ing, Director, 231-591-5362, Fax: 231-591-2041. *Application contact:* Kimisue Worrall, Secretary, 231-591-5361, Fax: 231-591-2043.

Florida Agricultural and Mechanical University, Division of Graduate Studies, Research, and Continuing Education, College of Education, Tallahassee, FL 32307-3200. Offers M Ed, MBE, MS Ed, PhD. *Accreditation:* NCATE. Part-time and evening/weekend programs available. *Faculty:* 47 full-time (33 women). *Students:* 105 full-time (63 women), 81 part-time (64 women); includes 176 minority (174 African Americans, 1 Asian American or Pacific Islander, 1 Hispanic American), 5 international. In 2009, 37 master's, 5 doctorates awarded. *Degree requirements:* For master's, thesis (for some programs); for doctorate, thesis/dissertation. *Entrance requirements:* For master's, GRE General Test, minimum GPA of 3.0. Additional exam requirements/recommendations for international students: Required—TOEFL. *Application deadline:* For fall admission, 5/18 for domestic students, 12/18 for international students; for spring admission, 11/12 for domestic students, 5/12 for international students. Application fee: $30. *Financial support:* Fellowships, teaching assistantships, Federal Work-Study and institutionally sponsored loans available. *Unit head:* Dr. Robert Lemons, Dean, 850-599-3482, Fax: 850-561-2211. *Application contact:* Dr. Chanta M. Haywood, Dean of Graduate Studies, Research, and Continuing Education, 850-599-3315, Fax: 850-599-3727.

Florida Atlantic University, College of Education, Boca Raton, FL 33431-0991. Offers M Ed, MS, Ed D, PhD, Ed S. *Accreditation:* NCATE. Part-time and evening/weekend programs available. *Faculty:* 104 full-time (66 women), 196 part-time/adjunct (140 women). *Students:* 347 full-time (256 women), 669 part-time (547 women); includes 282 minority (134 African Americans, 25 Asian Americans or Pacific Islanders, 123 Hispanic Americans), 11 international. Average age 34. 800 applicants, 58% accepted, 242 enrolled. In 2009, 299 master's, 31 doctorates awarded. *Degree requirements:* For doctorate, comprehensive exam, thesis/dissertation; for Ed S, departmental qualifying exam. *Entrance requirements:* For master's, doctorate, and Ed S, GRE General Test. *Application deadline:* Applications are processed on a rolling basis. Application fee: $30. Electronic applications accepted. *Expenses:* Tuition, state resident: full-time $7055; part-time $293.94 per credit hour. Tuition, nonresident: full-time $22,096; part-time $920.66 per credit hour. *Financial support:* Fellowships with partial tuition reimbursements, research assistantships with partial tuition reimbursements, teaching assistantships with partial tuition reimbursements, career-related internships or fieldwork, Federal Work-Study, and unspecified assistantships available. *Faculty research:* Marriage and family counseling, multicultural education, self-directed learning, assessment, reading. *Unit head:* Dr. Valerie J. Bristor, Dean, 561-297-3564, E-mail: bristor@fau.edu. *Application contact:* Dr. Eliah Watlington, Associate Dean, 561-296-8520, Fax: 261-297-2991, E-mail: ewatling@fau.edu.

Florida Gulf Coast University, College of Education, Fort Myers, FL 33965-6565. Offers M Ed, MA. Part-time and evening/weekend programs available. Postbaccalaureate distance learning degree programs offered (minimal on-campus study). *Faculty:* 31 full-time (23 women), 41 part-time/adjunct (29 women). *Students:* 221 full-time (189 women), 84 part-time (69 women); includes 48 minority (15 African Americans, 6 American Indian/Alaska Native, 2 Asian Americans or Pacific Islanders, 25 Hispanic Americans), 1 international. Average age 33. 182 applicants, 77% accepted, 48 enrolled. In 2009, 91 master's awarded. *Entrance requirements:* For master's, GRE General Test, MAT, minimum GPA of 3.0. Additional exam requirements/

recommendations for international students: Required—TOEFL (minimum score 550 paper-based; 213 computer-based). *Application deadline:* For fall admission, 7/1 priority date for domestic students; for spring admission, 10/15 for domestic students. Applications are processed on a rolling basis. Application fee: $30. Electronic applications accepted. *Faculty research:* Inclusion, emergent literacy, pre-service and in-service teacher education, education policy. Total annual research expenditures: $3.7 million. *Unit head:* Dr. Marci Greene, Dean, 239-590-7781, Fax: 239-590-7801, E-mail: mgreene@fgcu.edu. *Application contact:* Edward Beckett, Adviser/Counselor, 239-590-7759, Fax: 239-590-7801, E-mail: ebeckett@fgcu.edu.

Florida International University, College of Education, Miami, FL 33199. Offers MA, MAT, MS, Ed D, PhD, Certificate, Ed S. *Accreditation:* NCATE. Part-time and evening/weekend programs available. *Degree requirements:* For doctorate, comprehensive exam, thesis/dissertation. *Entrance requirements:* For master's and other advanced degree, GRE General Test (some programs); for doctorate, GRE General Test. Additional exam requirements/recommendations for international students: Required—TOEFL (minimum score 550 paper-based; 213 computer-based; 80 iBT), IELTS (minimum score 6.3). Electronic applications accepted. *Expenses:* Tuition, state resident: full-time $8008; part-time $4004 per year. Tuition, nonresident: full-time $20,104; part-time $10,052 per year. Required fees: $298; $149 per term. *Faculty research:* School improvement, cognitive processes, international development, urban education, multicultural/multilingual education.

Florida Memorial University, School of Education, Miami-Dade, FL 33054. Offers elementary education (MS); exceptional student education (MS); reading (MS). *Degree requirements:* For master's, comprehensive exam or thesis, field and clinical experiences, exit exam. *Entrance requirements:* For master's, GRE, CLAST, PRAXIS I, baccalaureate or graduate degree with minimum GPA of 3.0 in last 60 hours, 3 recommendations.

Florida Southern College, Programs in Teaching, Lakeland, FL 33801-5698. Offers teaching (MAT); teaching and learning (M Ed). Part-time and evening/weekend programs available. *Degree requirements:* For master's, FICE General Knowledge test and professional education exam (MAT), eligibility for the Florida Professional Teacher Certificate (M Ed). *Entrance requirements:* For master's, Florida Teacher Certification exam (MAT). Additional exam requirements/recommendations for international students: Required—TOEFL (minimum score 550 paper-based).

Florida State University, The Graduate School, College of Education, Tallahassee, FL 32306. Offers MS, Ed D, PhD, Ed S, MS/Ed S. *Accreditation:* NCATE. Part-time and evening/weekend programs available. Postbaccalaureate distance learning degree programs offered. *Faculty:* 213 full-time (146 women), 50 part-time/adjunct (33 women). *Students:* 640 full-time (412 women), 514 part-time (361 women); includes 249 minority (134 African Americans, 8 American Indian/Alaska Native, 40 Asian Americans or Pacific Islanders, 67 Hispanic Americans), 124 international. 705 applicants, 60% accepted, 242 enrolled. In 2009, 355 master's, 45 doctorates, 32 other advanced degrees awarded. Terminal master's awarded for partial completion of doctoral program. *Degree requirements:* For master's and Ed S, comprehensive exam, thesis optional; for doctorate, comprehensive exam, thesis/dissertation, preliminary exam, prospectus defense. *Entrance requirements:* For master's, doctorate, and Ed S, GRE General Test, minimum GPA of 3.0. Additional exam requirements/recommendations for international students: Required—TOEFL (minimum score 550 paper-based; 213 computer-based; 80 iBT). *Application deadline:* For fall admission, 6/1 priority date for domestic and international students; for spring admission, 10/1 for domestic and international students. Applications are processed on a rolling basis. Application fee: $30. Electronic applications accepted. *Expenses:* Tuition, state resident: full-time $7413. Tuition, nonresident: full-time $22,567. *Financial support:* In 2009–10, 17 fellowships with full and partial tuition reimbursements, 154 research assistantships with full and partial tuition reimbursements, 292 teaching assistantships with full and partial tuition reimbursements were awarded; career-related internships or fieldwork, scholarships/grants, and traineeships also available. Financial award applicants required to submit FAFSA. *Faculty research:* Educational policy, higher education, sport administration, reading research, preparing school leaders. Total annual research expenditures: $12.5 million. *Unit head:* Dr. Marcy P. Driscoll, Dean, 850-644-6885, Fax: 850-644-2725, E-mail: driscoll@coe.fsu.edu. *Application contact:* Dr. Pamela S. Carroll, Academic Dean, 850-644-0372, Fax: 850-644-1258, E-mail: pcarroll@fsu.edu.

Fontbonne University, Graduate Programs, Department of Education, St. Louis, MO 63105-3098. Offers MA. *Accreditation:* NCATE. Part-time and evening/weekend programs available. Postbaccalaureate distance learning degree programs offered (minimal on-campus study). *Faculty:* 3 full-time (2 women), 18 part-time/adjunct (15 women). *Students:* 73 full-time (67 women), 201 part-time (171 women); includes 89 minority (86 African Americans, 1 American Indian/Alaska Native, 1 Asian American or Pacific Islander, 1 Hispanic American). Average age 36. In 2009, 74 master's awarded. *Entrance requirements:* For master's, minimum GPA of 3.0. *Application deadline:* For fall admission, 8/1 priority date for domestic students, 8/1 for international students. Applications are processed on a rolling basis. Application fee: $25 ($30 for international students). *Expenses:* Tuition: Part-time $562 per credit hour. *Financial support:* Available to part-time students. *Application deadline:* 4/1. *Unit head:* Dr. William Freeman, Dean, 314-719-3022, Fax: 314-889-1451, E-mail: wfreeman@fontbonne.edu. *Application contact:* Dr. James Muskopf, Director, 314-889-4536, Fax: 314-719-8002, E-mail: jmuskopf@fontbonne.edu.

Fordham University, Graduate School of Education, New York, NY 10023. Offers MAT, MS, MSE, MST, Ed D, PhD, Adv C. *Accreditation:* NCATE. Part-time and evening/weekend programs available. *Degree requirements:* For master's and Adv C, comprehensive exam (for some programs); for doctorate, thesis/dissertation. *Entrance requirements:* For master's and Adv C, minimum GPA of 3.0; for doctorate, GRE or MAT. *Expenses:* Contact institution.

Fort Hays State University, Graduate School, College of Education and Technology, Hays, KS 67601-4099. Offers MS, MSE, Ed S. *Accreditation:* NCATE. Part-time programs available. *Degree requirements:* For master's, comprehensive exam, thesis or alternative. *Entrance requirements:* Additional exam requirements/recommendations for international students: Required—TOEFL (minimum score 550 paper-based; 213 computer-based). Electronic applications accepted.

Franciscan University of Steubenville, Graduate Programs, Department of Education, Steubenville, OH 43952-1763. Offers administration (MS Ed); teaching (MS Ed). Part-time and evening/weekend programs available. *Degree requirements:* For master's, project. *Entrance requirements:* For master's, minimum undergraduate GPA of 2.5 or written exam. *Expenses:* Contact institution.

Francis Marion University, Graduate Programs, School of Education, Florence, SC 29502-0547. Offers early childhood education (M Ed); elementary education (M Ed); learning disabilities (M Ed, MAT); remedial education (M Ed); secondary education (M Ed). *Accreditation:* NCATE. Part-time programs available. *Faculty:* 20 full-time (15 women). *Students:* 8 full-time (7 women), 107 part-time (90 women); includes 33 minority (all African Americans), 1 international. Average age 34. 221 applicants, 94% accepted, 94 enrolled. In 2009, 57 degrees awarded. *Degree requirements:* For master's, comprehensive exam. *Entrance requirements:* For master's, GRE General Test, MAT, NTE, or PRAXIS II. *Application deadline:* For fall admission, 3/15 priority date for domestic students; for spring admission, 10/15 priority date for domestic students. Applications are processed on a rolling basis. Application fee: $30. *Expenses:* Tuition, state resident: full-time $8345; part-time $417.25 per semester hour. Tuition, nonresident: full-time $16,690; part-time $814.50 per semester hour. Required fees: $335; $12.25 per semester hour. $30 per semester. *Financial support:* In 2009–10, 4 research assistantships (averaging $6,000 per year) were awarded; unspecified assistantships also available. Support available to part-time students. Financial award application deadline: 3/1; financial award applicants required to submit FAFSA. *Faculty research:* Identification and alternate assessment of at-risk students. *Unit head:* Dr. James R. Faulkenberry, Dean, 843-661-1460, Fax: 843-661-4647. *Application contact:* Dr. James R. Faulkenberry, Dean, 843-661-1460, Fax: 843-661-4647.

Franklin Pierce University, Graduate Studies, Rindge, NH 03461-0060. Offers emerging network technology (Graduate Certificate); health practice management (MBA, Graduate Certificate); human resource management (MBA); human resources management (Graduate Certificate); information technology management (MS); leadership (MBA, DA), including transformational leadership (DA); nursing (MS); physical therapy (DPT); physician assistant (MPAS); sports facilities management (MS); teacher education (M Ed). *Accreditation:* APTA. Part-time programs available. Postbaccalaureate distance learning degree programs offered (no on-campus study). *Faculty:* 27 full-time (16 women), 18 part-time/adjunct (4 women). *Students:* 296 full-time (172 women), 249 part-time (165 women); includes 18 minority (5 African Americans, 7 Asian Americans or Pacific Islanders, 6 Hispanic Americans), 31 international. Average age 38. 227 applicants, 97% accepted, 185 enrolled. In 2009, 76 master's, 46 doctorates awarded. *Degree requirements:* For master's, concentrated original research projects; student teaching; fieldwork and/or internship; leadership project; for doctorate, concentrated original research projects, clinical fieldwork and/or internship, leadership project. *Entrance requirements:* For master's, minimum GPA of 2.5, 3 letters of recommendation; for doctorate, demonstrated success at previous academic institutions (minimum GPA of 2.5), 3 letters of recommendation, personal mission statement, interview; writing sample (for DA program). Additional exam requirements/recommendations for international students: Required—TOEFL (minimum score 550 paper-based; 195 computer-based). *Application deadline:* Applications are processed on a rolling basis. Application fee: $0. Electronic applications accepted. *Expenses:* Tuition: Part-time $1560 per course. Part-time tuition and fees vary according to degree level, campus/location and program. *Financial support:* In 2009–10, 36 students received support, including 22 teaching assistantships with full and partial tuition reimbursements available; career-related internships or fieldwork and unspecified assistantships also available. Support available to part-time students. Financial award applicants required to submit FAFSA. *Faculty research:* Evidence based practice in sports physical therapy, human resource management in economic crisis, leadership in nursing, innovation in sports facility management, differentiated learning and understanding by design. *Unit head:* Dr. Robert G. Goddard, Assistant Dean, 603-899-4361, Fax: 603-229-4580, E-mail: goddardr@franklinpierce.edu. *Application contact:* 800-325-1090, Fax: 603-898-0827, E-mail: gpsadmin@franklinpierce.edu.

Freed-Hardeman University, Program in Education, Henderson, TN 38340-2399. Offers curriculum and instruction (M Ed); school counseling (M Ed), including administration and supervision, special education; school leadership (Ed S). *Accreditation:* NCATE. Part-time and evening/weekend programs available. *Degree requirements:* For master's, comprehensive exam, thesis optional; for Ed S, thesis. *Entrance requirements:* For master's, GRE General Test or NTE; for Ed S, 3 years of teaching experience. Additional exam requirements/recommendations for international students: Required—TOEFL (minimum score 500 paper-based; 173 computer-based).

Fresno Pacific University, Graduate Programs, School of Education, Fresno, CA 93702-4709. Offers administration (MA Ed), including administrative services; foundations, curriculum and teaching (MA Ed), including curriculum and teaching, school library and information technology; language, literacy, and culture (MA Ed), including bilingual/cross-cultural education, language development, multilingual contexts, reading; mathematics/science/computer education (MA Ed), including educational technology, integrated mathematics/science education, mathematics education; pupil personnel services (MA Ed), including school counseling, school psychology; special education (MA Ed), including mild/moderate, moderate/severe, physical and health impairments. Part-time and evening/weekend programs available. *Degree requirements:* For master's, thesis (for some programs). *Entrance requirements:* For master's, interview; GMAT, GRE, MAT, or 6 units of course work with a faculty recommendation. Additional exam requirements/recommendations for international students: Required—TOEFL (minimum score 550 paper-based; 213 computer-based). Electronic applications accepted.

Friends University, Graduate School, Division of Science, Arts, and Education, Program in Teaching, Wichita, KS 67213. Offers elementary education (MAT); secondary education (MAT). *Accreditation:* NCATE. Evening/weekend programs available. Postbaccalaureate distance learning degree programs offered (minimal on-campus study). *Entrance requirements:* Additional exam requirements/recommendations for international students: Required—TOEFL (minimum score 560 paper-based; 220 computer-based; 83 iBT), IELTS (minimum score 6). Electronic applications accepted.

Frostburg State University, Graduate School, College of Education, Frostburg, MD 21532-1099. Offers M Ed, MAT, MS. *Accreditation:* NCATE. Part-time and evening/weekend programs available. *Faculty:* 29 full-time (12 women), 14 part-time/adjunct (11 women). *Students:* 142 full-time (105 women), 270 part-time (206 women); includes 16 minority (10 African Americans, 2 American Indian/Alaska Native, 1 Asian American or Pacific Islander, 3 Hispanic Americans), 3 international. Average age 31. 234 applicants, 70% accepted, 145 enrolled. In 2009, 139 master's awarded. *Entrance requirements:* Additional exam requirements/recommendations for international students: Required—TOEFL. *Application deadline:* For fall admission, 7/15 priority date for domestic students. Applications are processed on a rolling basis. Application fee: $30. Electronic applications accepted. *Expenses:* Tuition, state resident: full-time $5706; part-time $317 per credit hour. Tuition, nonresident: full-time $6948; part-time $386 per credit hour. Required fees: $1476; $82 per credit hour. $11 per term. One-time fee: $30 full-time. *Financial support:* In 2009–10, 29 research assistantships with full tuition reimbursements (averaging $5,000 per year) were awarded; career-related internships or fieldwork and Federal Work-Study also available. Financial award application deadline: 4/1; financial award applicants required to submit FAFSA. *Unit head:* Dr. Kenneth Witmer, Dean, 301-687-4759, E-mail: kwitmer@frostburg.edu. *Application contact:* Vickie Mazer, Director, Graduate Services, 301-687-7053, Fax: 301-687-4597, E-mail: vmmazer@frostburg.edu.

Furman University, Graduate Division, Department of Education, Greenville, SC 29613. Offers curriculum and instruction (MA); early childhood education (MA); English as a second language (MA); literacy (MA); school leadership (MA); special education (MA). *Accreditation:* NCATE. Part-time programs available. Postbaccalaureate distance learning degree programs offered (minimal on-campus study). *Faculty:* 14 full-time (8 women), 10 part-time/adjunct (6 women). *Students:* 114 part-time (93 women); includes 13 minority (10 African Americans, 3 Asian Americans or Pacific Islanders). Average age 29. 24 applicants, 100% accepted, 23 enrolled. In 2009, 71 master's awarded. *Degree requirements:* For master's, comprehensive exam (for some programs), thesis or alternative. *Entrance requirements:* For master's, PRAXIS II. *Application deadline:* For fall admission, 8/1 priority date for domestic students, 7/15 priority date for international students; for spring admission, 12/1 priority date for domestic and international students. Applications are processed on a rolling basis. Application fee: $50. *Financial support:* In 2009–10, 43 students received support; fellowships, scholarships/grants available. Financial award application deadline: 5/15; financial award applicants required to submit FAFSA. *Faculty research:* Literacy, pedagogy and practice, social justice, advanced leadership, achievement in high poverty schools. *Unit head:* Dr. Nelly Hecker, Head, 864-294-3385. *Application contact:* Helen Reynolds, Department Assistant, 864-294-2213, Fax: 864-294-3579, E-mail: helen.reynolds@furman.edu.

Gannon University, School of Graduate Studies, College of Humanities, Education, and Social Sciences, School of Education, Erie, PA 16541-0001. Offers M Ed, MS, PhD, Certificate. Part-time and evening/weekend programs available. Postbaccalaureate distance learning degree programs offered (no on-campus study). *Faculty:* 9 full-time (4 women), 46 part-time/adjunct (21 women). *Students:* 28 full-time (23 women), 430 part-time (307 women); includes 9 minority (6 African Americans, 1 Asian American or Pacific Islander, 2 Hispanic Americans). Average age 32. 207 applicants, 91% accepted, 99 enrolled. In 2009, 265 master's, 1 other advanced degree awarded. *Degree requirements:* For master's, thesis (for some programs), portfolio project. *Entrance requirements:* For master's, bachelor's degree, minimum QPA of 3.0. Additional exam requirements/recommendations for international students: Required—TOEFL (minimum score 79 iBT). *Application deadline:* Applications are processed on a rolling basis. Application fee: $25. Electronic applications accepted. *Expenses:* Contact institution. *Financial support:* In 2009–10, 4 fellowships (averaging $5,355 per year) were awarded; career-related internships or fieldwork, scholarships/grants, and unspecified assistantships

Education—General

Gannon University (continued)
also available. Financial award application deadline: 7/1; financial award applicants required to submit FAFSA. *Unit head:* Dr. Francis S. Grandinetti, Director, 814-871-7533, E-mail: grandine002@gannon.edu. *Application contact:* Kara Morgan, Assistant Director of Graduate Admissions, 814-871-5831, Fax: 814-871-5827, E-mail: graduate@gannon.edu.

Gardner-Webb University, Graduate School, School of Education, Boiling Springs, NC 28017. Offers curriculum and instruction (Ed D); educational leadership (Ed D); elementary education (MA); middle grades education (MA); school administration (MA). *Accreditation:* NCATE. Part-time and evening/weekend programs available. *Faculty:* 7 full-time (3 women), 11 part-time/adjunct (2 women). *Students:* 9 full-time (5 women), 387 part-time (259 women); includes 118 minority (109 African Americans, 1 American Indian/Alaska Native, 2 Asian Americans or Pacific Islanders, 6 Hispanic Americans). Average age 37. In 2009, 133 master's, 15 doctorates awarded. *Degree requirements:* For master's, comprehensive exam. *Entrance requirements:* For master's, GRE General Test or NTE, PRAXIS, minimum GPA of 2.5. *Application deadline:* For fall admission, 8/1 priority date for domestic students. Applications are processed on a rolling basis. Application fee: $25. Electronic applications accepted. *Expenses:* Tuition: Part-time $305 per credit hour. *Financial support:* Unspecified assistantships available. *Unit head:* Dr. Carrol Smith, Chair, 704-406-3913, Fax: 704-406-3921, E-mail: dsimmons@gardner-webb.edu. *Application contact:* Dr. Franki Burch, Dean, Graduate School, 704-406-4422, Fax: 704-406-4329, E-mail: gradschool@gardner-webb.edu.

Geneva College, Program in Higher Education, Beaver Falls, PA 15010-3599. Offers campus ministry (MA); college teaching (MA); educational leadership (MA); student affairs administration (MA). Part-time and evening/weekend programs available. Postbaccalaureate distance learning degree programs offered (minimal on-campus study). *Faculty:* 2 full-time (0 women), 4 part-time/adjunct (0 women). *Students:* 28 full-time (13 women), 37 part-time (21 women); includes 2 minority (1 African American, 1 Asian American or Pacific Islander). Average age 25. 41 applicants, 98% accepted, 19 enrolled. In 2009, 29 master's awarded. *Degree requirements:* For master's, research seminar. *Entrance requirements:* For master's, minimum GPA of 3.0, writing sample, 3 letters of recommendation. Additional exam requirements/recommendations for international students: Required—TOEFL. *Application deadline:* For fall admission, 9/1 priority date for domestic students; for winter admission, 1/2 priority date for domestic students; for spring admission, 3/11 priority date for domestic students. Applications are processed on a rolling basis. Electronic applications accepted. *Expenses:* Tuition: Full-time $11,250; part-time $625 per credit. Tuition and fees vary according to program. *Financial support:* In 2009–10, 1 research assistantship with partial tuition reimbursement (averaging $4,500 per year), 1 teaching assistantship with partial tuition reimbursement (averaging $4,500 per year) were awarded; career-related internships or fieldwork and unspecified assistantships also available. Support available to part-time students. Financial award application deadline: 9/1; financial award applicants required to submit FAFSA. *Faculty research:* Student development, learning theories, church-related higher education, assessment, organizational culture. *Unit head:* Dr. Donald Opitz, Director, 724-847-6883, Fax: 724-847-6107, E-mail: hed@geneva.edu. *Application contact:* Jerryn S. Carson, Coordinator, 724-847-6510, Fax: 724-847-6696, E-mail: hed@geneva.edu.

George Fox University, School of Education, Newberg, OR 97132-2697. Offers M Ed, MA, MAT, MS, Ed D, Certificate, Ed S. Tuition and fees vary according to course level and course load.

George Mason University, College of Education and Human Development, Fairfax, VA 22030. Offers M Ed, MA, MS, PhD, Certificate. *Accreditation:* NCATE. Part-time and evening/weekend programs available. Postbaccalaureate distance learning degree programs offered (minimal on-campus study). *Faculty:* 114 full-time (74 women), 170 part-time/adjunct (122 women). *Students:* 354 full-time (286 women), 2,336 part-time (1,873 women); includes 311 minority (124 African Americans, 1 American Indian/Alaska Native, 68 Asian Americans or Pacific Islanders, 118 Hispanic Americans), 76 international. Average age 33. 1,594 applicants, 74% accepted, 924 enrolled. In 2009, 884 master's, 27 doctorates, 157 other advanced degrees awarded. *Degree requirements:* For doctorate, comprehensive exam, final project, internship. *Entrance requirements:* For master's, PRAXIS I, minimum GPA of 3.0 in last 60 hours of course work, goals statement and/or interview; for doctorate, GRE or MAT, appropriate master's degree, interview. Additional exam requirements/recommendations for international students: Required—TOEFL (minimum score 575 paper-based; 230 computer-based). Application fee: $75. Electronic applications accepted. *Expenses:* Tuition, state resident: full-time $7568; part-time $315.33 per credit hour. Tuition, nonresident: full-time $21,704; part-time $904.33 per credit hour. Required fees: $2184; $91 per credit hour. *Financial support:* In 2009–10, 84 students received support, including 3 fellowships with full tuition reimbursements available (averaging $18,000 per year), 68 research assistantships with full and partial tuition reimbursements available (averaging $7,892 per year), 22 teaching assistantships with full and partial tuition reimbursements available (averaging $2,494 per year); career-related internships or fieldwork, Federal Work-Study, scholarships/grants, unspecified assistantships, and health care benefits (full-time research or teaching assistantship recipients) also available. Support available to part-time students. Financial award application deadline: 3/1; financial award applicants required to submit FAFSA. *Faculty research:* Special education/human disabilities, mathematics/science/technology education, education leadership, school/community/agency/higher education, counseling and administration. Total annual research expenditures: $8.8 million. *Unit head:* Martin Ford, Acting Dean, 703-993-2004, E-mail: mford@gmu.edu.

Georgetown College, Department of Education, Georgetown, KY 40324-1696. Offers reading and writing (MA Ed); special education (MA Ed); teaching (MA Ed). *Accreditation:* NCATE. Part-time programs available. *Degree requirements:* For master's, portfolio. *Entrance requirements:* For master's, teaching certificate, minimum GPA of 2.7 or GRE General Test.

The George Washington University, Graduate School of Education and Human Development, Washington, DC 20052. Offers M Ed, MA Ed, MAT, Ed D, PhD, Certificate, Ed S, Graduate Certificate. *Accreditation:* NCATE. Part-time and evening/weekend programs available. Postbaccalaureate distance learning degree programs offered (no on-campus study). *Faculty:* 77 full-time (46 women), 79 part-time/adjunct (61 women). *Students:* 473 full-time (372 women), 1,415 part-time (1,038 women); includes 564 minority (387 African Americans, 20 American Indian/Alaska Native, 82 Asian Americans or Pacific Islanders, 75 Hispanic Americans), 75 international. Average age 36. 1,452 applicants, 92% accepted, 752 enrolled. In 2009, 575 master's, 69 doctorates, 226 other advanced degrees awarded. *Degree requirements:* For master's and other advanced degree, comprehensive exam; for doctorate, comprehensive exam, thesis/dissertation. *Entrance requirements:* For master's, GRE General Test or MAT, minimum GPA of 2.75; for doctorate, GRE General Test or MAT, interview, minimum GPA of 3.3; for other advanced degree, GRE General Test or MAT, minimum GPA of 3.3. *Application deadline:* For fall admission, 1/15 priority date for domestic students; for spring admission, 10/1 for domestic students. Applications are processed on a rolling basis. Application fee: $60. Electronic applications accepted. *Financial support:* In 2009–10, 279 students received support; fellowships with tuition reimbursements available, research assistantships with tuition reimbursements available, teaching assistantships with tuition reimbursements available, career-related internships or fieldwork, Federal Work-Study, and tuition waivers (full and partial) available. Support available to part-time students. Financial award application deadline: 1/15. *Faculty research:* Policy, special education, bilingual education, counseling, human resource development. Total annual research expenditures: $4.6 million. *Unit head:* Dr. Mary Hatwood Futrell, Dean, 202-994-6161, Fax: 202-994-7207, E-mail: mfutrell@gwu.edu. *Application contact:* Sarah Lang, Director of Graduate Admissions, 202-994-1447, Fax: 202-994-7207, E-mail: slang@gwu.edu.

Georgia College & State University, Graduate School, The John H. Lounsbury College of Education, Milledgeville, GA 31061. Offers M Ed, MAT, Ed S. *Accreditation:* NCATE. Part-time programs available. *Faculty:* 46 full-time (32 women). *Students:* 194 full-time (129 women), 167 part-time (147 women); includes 74 minority (66 African Americans, 8 Hispanic Americans), 1 international. Average age 33. 214 applicants, 96% accepted, 142 enrolled. In 2009, 175 master's, 114 other advanced degrees awarded. *Degree requirements:* For master's, comprehensive exam; for Ed S, comprehensive exam, minimum GPA of 3.0. *Entrance requirements:* For master's, on-site writing assessment, 2 professional recommendations, level 4 teaching certificate; for Ed S, on-site writing assessment, master's degree, 2 years of teaching experience, 2 professional recommendations, level 5 GA teacher certification. Additional exam requirements/recommendations for international students: Recommended—TOEFL (minimum score 550 paper-based; 213 computer-based; 79 iBT). *Application deadline:* For fall admission, 7/1 priority date for domestic students. Applications are processed on a rolling basis. Application fee: $40. Electronic applications accepted. *Expenses:* Tuition, area resident: Part-time $241 per credit hour. Tuition, state resident: full-time $4338. Tuition, nonresident: full-time $17,352; part-time $964 per credit hour. Required fees: $609 per semester. Tuition and fees vary according to course load and campus/location. *Financial support:* In 2009–10, 16 research assistantships were awarded; career-related internships or fieldwork, Federal Work-Study, and unspecified assistantships also available. Support available to part-time students. Financial award application deadline: 3/1; financial award applicants required to submit FAFSA. *Unit head:* Dr. Linda Irwin-Devitis, Dean, 478-445-4546, E-mail: linda.irwin-devitis@gcsu.edu. *Application contact:* Shanda Brand, Graduate Coordinator, 478-445-1383, Fax: 478-445-6582, E-mail: shanda.brand@gcsu.edu.

Georgian Court University, School of Education, Lakewood, NJ 08701-2697. Offers administration and leadership (MA); education (MA). *Accreditation:* Teacher Education Accreditation Council. Part-time and evening/weekend programs available. *Faculty:* 27 full-time (15 women), 45 part-time/adjunct (30 women). *Students:* 184 full-time (155 women), 525 part-time (444 women); includes 64 minority (15 African Americans, 2 American Indian/Alaska Native, 7 Asian Americans or Pacific Islanders, 40 Hispanic Americans), 1 international. Average age 32. 612 applicants, 77% accepted, 267 enrolled. In 2009, 91 master's awarded. *Degree requirements:* For master's, comprehensive exam (for some programs), thesis (for some programs). *Entrance requirements:* For master's, GRE, MAT or NTE/PRAXIS, 3 letters of recommendation. Additional exam requirements/recommendations for international students: Required—TOEFL (minimum score 550 paper-based; 213 computer-based). *Application deadline:* For fall admission, 8/1 priority date for domestic students, 4/1 for international students; for spring admission, 1/1 priority date for domestic students, 7/1 for international students. Applications are processed on a rolling basis. Application fee: $40. Electronic applications accepted. *Expenses:* Tuition: Full-time $12,510; part-time $695 per credit. Required fees: $416 per year. Tuition and fees vary according to campus/location. *Financial support:* In 2009–10, 183 students received support. Scholarships/grants, health care benefits, and unspecified assistantships available. Financial award application deadline: 4/15; financial award applicants required to submit FAFSA. *Unit head:* Dr. Jacqueline Kress, Dean, 732-987-2525. *Application contact:* Eugene Soltys, Director of Graduate Admissions, 732-987-2770, Fax: 732-987-2084, E-mail: graduateadmissions@georgian.edu.

Georgia Southern University, Jack N. Averitt College of Graduate Studies, College of Education, Statesboro, GA 30460. Offers M Ed, MAT, Ed D, Ed S. *Accreditation:* NCATE. Part-time and evening/weekend programs available. Postbaccalaureate distance learning degree programs offered (no on-campus study). *Faculty:* 66 full-time (47 women), 8 part-time/adjunct (6 women). *Students:* 339 full-time (271 women), 1,075 part-time (856 women); includes 371 minority (334 African Americans, 3 American Indian/Alaska Native, 8 Asian Americans or Pacific Islanders, 26 Hispanic Americans), 10 international. Average age 36. 409 applicants, 86% accepted, 190 enrolled. In 2009, 188 master's, 69 doctorates, 58 other advanced degrees awarded. *Degree requirements:* For master's, comprehensive exam (for some programs), portfolio or assessments; for doctorate, comprehensive exam, thesis/dissertation, exams; for Ed S, assessments. *Entrance requirements:* For master's, GRE General Test or MAT, minimum GPA of 2.5; for doctorate, GRE General Test or MAT, minimum GPA of 3.5, letters of reference, writing sample; for Ed S, GRE General Test or MAT, minimum graduate GPA of 3.25. Additional exam requirements/recommendations for international students: Required—TOEFL (minimum score 550 paper-based; 213 computer-based; 80 iBT). *Application deadline:* For fall admission, 3/1 priority date for domestic and international students; for spring admission, 10/1 priority date for domestic students, 10/1 for international students. Applications are processed on a rolling basis. Application fee: $50. Electronic applications accepted. *Expenses:* Tuition, state resident: full-time $5040; part-time $210 per credit hour. Tuition, nonresident: full-time $20,136; part-time $839 per credit hour. Required fees: $1644. *Financial support:* In 2009–10, 817 students received support, including 26 research assistantships with partial tuition reimbursements available (averaging $7,200 per year), teaching assistantships with partial tuition reimbursements available (averaging $7,200 per year); career-related internships or fieldwork, Federal Work-Study, scholarships/grants, tuition waivers (partial), unspecified assistantships, and doctoral stipends also available. Support available to part-time students. Financial award application deadline: 4/15; financial award applicants required to submit FAFSA. *Faculty research:* Teacher preparation, curriculum improvement. Total annual research expenditures: $2.4 million. *Unit head:* Dr. Stephanie Kenney, Interim Dean, 912-478-5648, Fax: 912-478-5093, E-mail: skenney@georgiasouthern.edu. *Application contact:* Dr. Charles Ziglar, Coordinator of Graduate Student Recruitment, 912-478-5635, Fax: 912-478-0740, E-mail: gradadmissions@georgiasouthern.edu.

Georgia Southwestern State University, Graduate Studies, School of Education, Americus, GA 31709-4693. Offers early childhood education (M Ed, Ed S); health and physical education (M Ed); middle grades education (M Ed, Ed S); reading (M Ed); secondary education (M Ed); special education (M Ed). *Accreditation:* NCATE. *Degree requirements:* For master's, comprehensive exam. *Entrance requirements:* For master's, GRE General Test or MAT, minimum GPA of 2.5; for Ed S, GRE General Test or MAT, minimum graduate GPA of 3.25, M Ed from accredited college or university, 3 years teaching experience. Electronic applications accepted.

Georgia State University, College of Education, Atlanta, GA 30302-3083. Offers M Ed, MAT, MLM, MS, PhD, Ed S. *Accreditation:* NCATE. Part-time and evening/weekend programs available. Postbaccalaureate distance learning degree programs offered (no on-campus study). *Degree requirements:* For master's, comprehensive exam, portfolio (for some programs); for doctorate, comprehensive exam, thesis/dissertation; for Ed S, portfolio. *Entrance requirements:* For master's, GRE General Test; for doctorate and Ed S, GRE General Test, MAT. Additional exam requirements/recommendations for international students: Required—TOEFL (minimum score 550 paper-based; 213 computer-based). Electronic applications accepted. *Faculty research:* Evaluation and test development; teacher/school administration effectiveness; curriculum strategies and interventions; school safety, climate, and classroom management; policies and best practices in urban education.

Goddard College, Graduate Division, Master of Arts in Education and Licensure Program, Plainfield, VT 05667-9432. Offers community education (MA); teacher licensure (MA). Part-time programs available. Postbaccalaureate distance learning degree programs offered (minimal on-campus study). *Faculty:* 1 full-time (0 women), 9 part-time/adjunct (7 women). *Students:* 39 full-time, 5 part-time. Average age 33. 29 applicants, 83% accepted, 20 enrolled. *Degree requirements:* For master's, thesis. *Entrance requirements:* For master's, 3 letters of recommendation, interview. *Application deadline:* Applications are processed on a rolling basis. Application fee: $40. Electronic applications accepted. *Expenses:* Tuition: Part-time $7223 per semester. Part-time tuition and fees vary according to program. *Financial support:* In 2009–10, 37 students received support. Applicants required to submit FAFSA. *Faculty research:* Democratic curriculum leadership, service learning and academic achievement, middle grades curriculum, community education. *Unit head:* Dr. Susan Fleming, Director, 802-454-8311 Ext. 259, Fax: 802-454-7835, E-mail: susan.fleming@goddard.edu. *Application contact:* Jamie Kline, Admissions Counselor, 800-906-8312 Ext. 311, Fax: 802-454-1029, E-mail: jamie.kline@goddard.edu.

Gonzaga University, School of Education, Spokane, WA 99258. Offers M Anesth Ed, M Ed, MA Ed Ad, MAA, MAC, MAP, MASPAA, MAT, MES, MIT. *Accreditation:* NCATE. Part-time and evening/weekend programs available. *Faculty:* 28 full-time (12 women), 28 part-time/adjunct (14 women). *Students:* 74 full-time (55 women), 461 part-time (299 women); includes 24

minority (1 African American, 7 American Indian/Alaska Native, 6 Asian Americans or Pacific Islanders, 10 Hispanic Americans), 1 international. Average age 36. In 2009, 312 master's awarded. *Degree requirements:* For master's, comprehensive exam. *Entrance requirements:* Additional exam requirements/recommendations for international students: Required—TOEFL. Application fee: $50. Tuition and fees vary according to course level, course load, degree level, campus/location and program. *Financial support:* Teaching assistantships, Federal Work-Study and tuition waivers (full and partial) available. Support available to part-time students. Financial award application deadline: 3/1. *Unit head:* Dr. John Sunderland, Dean, 509-328-4220 Ext. 3503, Fax: 509-324-5812, E-mail: sunderland@gonzaga.edu. *Application contact:* Julie McCulloh, Dean of Admissions, 509-313-6592, Fax: 509-313-5780, E-mail: mcculloh@gu.gonzaga.edu.

Gordon College, Graduate Education, Wenham, MA 01984-1899. Offers education (M Ed, MAT); music education (MME). *Accreditation:* NASM. Part-time and evening/weekend programs available. *Entrance requirements:* For master's, GRE or MAT, references. Additional exam requirements/recommendations for international students: Required—TOEFL (minimum score 550 paper-based; 213 computer-based). *Faculty research:* Reading, early childhood development, ELL (English Language Learners).

Goucher College, Programs in Education, Baltimore, MD 21204-2794. Offers M Ed, MAT. Part-time and evening/weekend programs available. *Degree requirements:* For master's, thesis (M Ed), final presentation (MAT). *Entrance requirements:* For master's, minimum GPA of 3.0. Additional exam requirements/recommendations for international students: Required—TOEFL (minimum score 560 paper-based). *Faculty research:* Urban education, middle school, school improvement, teacher education, at-risk student achievement.

Governors State University, College of Education, Program in Education, University Park, IL 60466-0975. Offers MA. Part-time and evening/weekend programs available. *Degree requirements:* For master's, comprehensive exam, thesis or alternative, practicum. *Entrance requirements:* For master's, minimum GPA of 2.75 in last 60 hours of undergraduate course work, minimum graduate GPA of 3.0. *Faculty research:* Teaching problem-solving microcomputer use in special education, science, and mathematics.

Graceland University, Gleazer School of Education, Lamoni, IA 50140. Offers collaborative learning and teaching (M Ed); differentiated instruction (M Ed); instructional leadership (M Ed); mild/moderate special education (M Ed); quality schools (M Ed); technology integration (M Ed). *Accreditation:* NCATE. Part-time and evening/weekend programs available. Postbaccalaureate distance learning degree programs offered (no on-campus study). *Faculty:* 8 full-time (7 women), 25 part-time/adjunct (14 women). *Students:* 505 full-time (406 women); includes 18 minority (6 African Americans, 3 American Indian/Alaska Native, 4 Asian Americans or Pacific Islanders, 5 Hispanic Americans), 7 international. Average age 36. 167 applicants, 100% accepted, 160 enrolled. In 2009, 277 master's awarded. *Degree requirements:* For master's, action research project. *Entrance requirements:* For master's, minimum GPA of 3.0, teaching certificate, current teaching contract. *Application deadline:* For fall admission, 7/15 for domestic students; for winter admission, 10/15 for domestic students; for spring admission, 1/15 priority date for domestic students. Application fee: $50. Electronic applications accepted. *Expenses:* Tuition: Full-time $7110; part-time $395 per semester hour. Required fees: $1110; $185 per course. *Financial support:* In 2009–10, 437 students received support. Institutionally sponsored loans and scholarships/grants available. Financial award application deadline: 12/15; financial award applicants required to submit FAFSA. *Unit head:* Dr. Nancy Halferty, Dean, 641-784-5000 Ext. 5251, E-mail: halferty@graceland.edu. *Application contact:* Cathy Porter, Program Consultant, 816-833-0524 Ext. 4516, E-mail: cgporter@graceland.edu.

Grambling State University, School of Graduate Studies and Research, College of Education, Grambling, LA 71245. Offers MS, Ed D. *Accreditation:* NCATE. Part-time and evening/weekend programs available. *Faculty:* 22 full-time (13 women). *Students:* 69 full-time (37 women), 89 part-time (65 women); includes 129 minority (127 African Americans, 1 American Indian/Alaska Native, 1 Asian American or Pacific Islander), 6 international. Average age 35. 92 applicants, 77% accepted, 51 enrolled. In 2009, 20 master's, 9 doctorates awarded. *Degree requirements:* For master's, comprehensive exam, thesis (for some programs); for doctorate, comprehensive exam, thesis/dissertation. *Entrance requirements:* For master's, GRE; for doctorate, GRE (minimum 1000, 500 on Verbal), master's degree, minimum GPA of 3.0 on last degree. Additional exam requirements/recommendations for international students: Required—TOEFL (minimum score 500 paper-based; 173 computer-based; 61 iBT). *Application deadline:* For fall admission, 7/1 for domestic and international students; for spring admission, 12/1 for domestic and international students. Applications are processed on a rolling basis. Application fee: $20 ($30 for international students). Electronic applications accepted. *Expenses:* Tuition, state resident: full-time $2610. Tuition, nonresident: full-time $2610. *Financial support:* In 2009–10, 13 research assistantships (averaging $9,547 per year) were awarded; career-related internships or fieldwork, health care benefits, tuition waivers (full), and unspecified assistantships also available. Financial award application deadline: 5/31. *Unit head:* Dr. Sean Warner, Dean, 318-274-3235, Fax: 318-274-2799, E-mail: warners@gram.edu. *Application contact:* Laketha Richards, Administrative Assistant III, 318-274-6105, Fax: 318-274-6249, E-mail: richardsl@gram.edu.

Grand Canyon University, College of Education, Phoenix, AZ 85017-1097. Offers curriculum and instruction (M Ed); education administration (M Ed); elementary education (M Ed); organizational leadership (Ed D); secondary education (M Ed); special education (M Ed); teaching (MA). Part-time and evening/weekend programs available. Postbaccalaureate distance learning degree programs offered (no on-campus study). *Degree requirements:* For master's, publishable research paper (M Ed), e-portfolio. *Entrance requirements:* Additional exam requirements/recommendations for international students: Required—TOEFL (minimum score 550 paper-based; 213 computer-based; 79 iBT), IELTS (minimum score 6). Electronic applications accepted.

Grand Valley State University, College of Education, Programs in General Education, Allendale, MI 49401-9403. Offers adult and higher education (M Ed); early childhood education (M Ed); educational differentiation (M Ed); educational leadership (M Ed); educational technology integration (M Ed); elementary education (M Ed); middle level education (M Ed); school library media services (M Ed); secondary level education (M Ed); teaching English to speakers of other languages (M Ed). Part-time and evening/weekend programs available. Postbaccalaureate distance learning degree programs offered (minimal on-campus study). *Faculty:* 82 full-time (42 women), 43 part-time/adjunct (25 women). *Students:* 100 full-time (53 women), 723 part-time (478 women); includes 59 minority (25 African Americans, 4 American Indian/Alaska Native, 13 Asian Americans or Pacific Islanders, 17 Hispanic Americans), 10 international. Average age 33. 237 applicants, 96% accepted, 117 enrolled. In 2009, 291 master's awarded. *Degree requirements:* For master's, thesis. *Entrance requirements:* For master's, GRE General Test or minimum GPA of 3.0. Additional exam requirements/recommendations for international students: Required—TOEFL. *Application deadline:* Applications are processed on a rolling basis. Application fee: $30. Electronic applications accepted. *Expenses:* Tuition, state resident: part-time $471 per credit hour. Tuition, nonresident: part-time $646 per credit hour. Tuition and fees vary according to course level. *Financial support:* In 2009–10, 73 students received support, including 55 fellowships (averaging $2,273 per year), 19 research assistantships with full and partial tuition reimbursements available (averaging $8,000 per year); career-related internships or fieldwork, Federal Work-Study, scholarships/grants, and unspecified assistantships also available. *Faculty research:* Effectiveness of technology in education, parental involvement, effective teaching, effective schools research. *Unit head:* Dr. Linda McCrea, Director, 616-331-2080, E-mail: mccreal@gvsu.edu. *Application contact:* Thomas Owens, Student Information and Services Center, 616-331-6282, Fax: 616-331-2000, E-mail: owenst@gvsu.edu.

Grand View University, Program in Innovative Leadership, Des Moines, IA 50316-1599. Offers business (MS); education (MS); nursing (MS). *Entrance requirements:* For master's, GRE or GMAT, minimum undergraduate GPA of 3.0, professional resume, 3 letters of recommendation, interview. Additional exam requirements/recommendations for international students: Required—TOEFL (minimum score 550 paper-based; 210 computer-based). Electronic applications accepted.

Gratz College, Graduate Programs, Program in Education, Melrose Park, PA 19027. Offers MA. Part-time programs available. *Degree requirements:* For master's, one foreign language, project. *Entrance requirements:* For master's, teaching certificate.

Greensboro College, Program in Education, Greensboro, NC 27401-1875. Offers elementary education (M Ed); special education (M Ed). Part-time and evening/weekend programs available. *Degree requirements:* For master's, thesis. *Entrance requirements:* For master's, GRE, teacher license, 2 years of teaching experience, 2 letters of recommendation. Additional exam requirements/recommendations for international students: Required—TOEFL (minimum score 550 paper-based; 213 computer-based). Electronic applications accepted.

Greenville College, Program in Education, Greenville, IL 62246-0159. Offers education (MAT); elementary education (MAE); secondary education (MAE). *Degree requirements:* For master's, thesis (for some programs). *Entrance requirements:* For master's, GRE, Illinois Basic Skills Test, teacher certification. Electronic applications accepted.

Gwynedd-Mercy College, School of Education, Gwynedd Valley, PA 19437-0901. Offers educational administration (MS); master teacher (MS); reading (MS); school counseling (MS); special education (MS). Part-time and evening/weekend programs available. *Degree requirements:* For master's, thesis, internship, practicum. *Entrance requirements:* For master's, GRE or MAT; PRAXIS I Test, minimum GPA of 3.0. *Faculty research:* Learning and the brain, reading literacy, ethics and moral judgment, leadership, teaching and multicultural education.

Hamline University, School of Education, St. Paul, MN 55104-1284. Offers education (MA Ed, Ed D); English as a second language (MAESL); literacy education (MALED); natural science and environmental education (MA Ed); teaching (MAT). *Accreditation:* NCATE (one or more programs are accredited). Part-time and evening/weekend programs available. *Faculty:* 27 full-time (18 women), 128 part-time/adjunct (100 women). *Students:* 324 full-time (242 women), 1,049 part-time (780 women); includes 116 minority (36 African Americans, 4 American Indian/Alaska Native, 42 Asian Americans or Pacific Islanders, 34 Hispanic Americans), 25 international. Average age 33. 501 applicants, 79% accepted, 311 enrolled. In 2009, 196 master's, 9 doctorates awarded. *Degree requirements:* For master's, thesis; for doctorate, comprehensive exam, thesis/dissertation. *Entrance requirements:* For doctorate, personal statement, master's degree, 3 years experience, letters of recommendation, writing sample, interview. Additional exam requirements/recommendations for international students: Required—TOEFL (minimum score 550 paper-based; 213 computer-based; 79 iBT), TWE (minimum score 5). *Application deadline:* Applications are processed on a rolling basis. Application fee: $0. Electronic applications accepted. *Expenses:* Tuition: Full-time $6816; part-time $426 per credit. Required fees: $6 per credit. One-time fee: $205. Tuition and fees vary according to degree level, campus/location and program. *Financial support:* In 2009–10, 8 students received support. Federal Work-Study and scholarships/grants available. Support available to part-time students. Financial award applicants required to submit FAFSA. *Faculty research:* Adult basic education, service learning, teacher dispositions, diversity, technology. *Unit head:* Dr. Sheila Wright, Dean, 651-523-2600, Fax: 651-523-2489, E-mail: swright04@hamline.edu. *Application contact:* Rae A. Lenway, Director, Graduate Recruitment and Admission, 651-523-2900, Fax: 651-523-3058, E-mail: rlenway@hamline.edu.

Hampton University, Graduate College, Department of Education, Hampton, VA 23668. Offers counseling (MA), including college student development, community agency counseling, pastoral counseling, school counseling; elementary education (MA); special education (MA); teaching (MT), including early childhood education, middle school education, music education, secondary education, special education. *Accreditation:* NCATE. Part-time and evening/weekend programs available. *Entrance requirements:* For master's, GRE General Test.

Hannibal-LaGrange College, Program in Education, Hannibal, MO 63401-1999. Offers literacy (MS Ed); teaching and learning (MS Ed). Part-time and evening/weekend programs available. *Entrance requirements:* For master's, copy of current teaching certificate.

Harding University, College of Education, Searcy, AR 72149-0001. Offers advanced studies in teaching and learning (M Ed); art (MSE); behavioral science (MSE); counseling (MS, Ed S); early childhood special education (M Ed, MSE); education (MSE); educational leadership (M Ed, Ed S); elementary education (M Ed); English (MSE); family and consumer science (MSE); French (MSE); history/social science (MSE); kinesiology (MSE); math (MSE); physical science (MSE); reading (M Ed); secondary education (M Ed); Spanish (MSE); special education licensure (M Ed); teaching (MAT); teaching English as a second language (M Ed). *Accreditation:* NCATE. Part-time and evening/weekend programs available. *Faculty:* 11 full-time (4 women), 49 part-time/adjunct (26 women). *Students:* 104 full-time (85 women), 392 part-time (282 women); includes 77 minority (67 African Americans, 5 American Indian/Alaska Native, 1 Asian American or Pacific Islander, 4 Hispanic Americans), 5 international. Average age 36. 153 applicants, 92% accepted, 131 enrolled. In 2009, 153 master's, 6 other advanced degrees awarded. *Degree requirements:* For master's, comprehensive exam (for some programs), thesis optional, portfolio(s); for Ed S, comprehensive exam, portfolio, specialist project. *Entrance requirements:* For master's, GRE, MAT, PRAXIS; for Ed S, MAT or GRE. Additional exam requirements/recommendations for international students: Required—TOEFL (minimum score 550 paper-based; 79 iBT). *Application deadline:* For fall admission, 8/1 for domestic and international students; for spring admission, 1/1 for domestic and international students. Applications are processed on a rolling basis. Application fee: $35. *Expenses:* Tuition: Full-time $9720; part-time $540 per credit hour. Required fees: $22 per credit hour. Tuition and fees vary according to course load and program. *Financial support:* In 2009–10, 30 students received support. Unspecified assistantships available. *Faculty research:* Reading, comprehension, school violence, educational technology, behavior, college choice, differentiated instruction, brain-based teaching. *Unit head:* Dr. Clara Carroll, Chair, 501-279-4501, Fax: 501-279-4083, E-mail: ccarroll@harding.edu. *Application contact:* Information Contact, 501-279-4315, E-mail: gradstudiesedu@harding.edu.

Hardin-Simmons University, Graduate School, Irvin School of Education, Abilene, TX 79698-0001. Offers M Ed. Part-time programs available. *Faculty:* 12 full-time (7 women), 7 part-time/adjunct (5 women). *Students:* 38 full-time (23 women), 58 part-time (42 women); includes 21 minority (6 African Americans, 15 Hispanic Americans), 1 international. Average age 29. 40 applicants, 93% accepted, 27 enrolled. In 2009, 55 master's awarded. *Degree requirements:* For master's, comprehensive exam. *Entrance requirements:* For master's, minimum undergraduate GPA of 3.0 in major, 2.7 overall. Additional exam requirements/recommendations for international students: Required—TOEFL (minimum score 550 paper-based; 213 computer-based; 75 iBT). *Application deadline:* For fall admission, 8/15 priority date for domestic students, 4/1 for international students; for spring admission, 1/5 priority date for domestic students, 9/1 for international students. Applications are processed on a rolling basis. Application fee: $50. *Expenses:* Tuition: Full-time $11,430; part-time $635 per credit hour. Required fees: $650; $110 per semester. Tuition and fees vary according to degree level. *Financial support:* In 2009–10, 47 students received support, including 23 fellowships (averaging $1,217 per year); career-related internships or fieldwork, scholarships/grants, and coaching assistantships also available. Support available to part-time students. Financial award application deadline: 6/30; financial award applicants required to submit FAFSA. *Unit head:* Dr. Pam Williford, Dean, 325-670-1352, Fax: 325-670-5859, E-mail: pwilliford@hsutx.edu. *Application contact:* Dr. Gary Stanlake, Dean of Graduate Studies, 325-670-1298, Fax: 325-670-1564, E-mail: gradoff@hsutx.edu.

Harvard University, Graduate School of Education, Cambridge, MA 02138. Offers Ed M, Ed D. Part-time programs available. *Faculty:* 70 full-time (33 women), 36 part-time/adjunct (20 women). *Students:* 893 full-time (646 women), 99 part-time (71 women); includes 235 minority (80 African Americans, 6 American Indian/Alaska Native, 92 Asian Americans or Pacific Islanders, 57 Hispanic Americans), 136 international. Average age 29. 2,125 applicants, 45% accepted, 679 enrolled. In 2009, 556 master's, 41 doctorates awarded. Terminal master's

Education—General

Harvard University (continued)

awarded for partial completion of doctoral program. *Degree requirements:* For doctorate, thesis/dissertation. *Entrance requirements:* For master's, GRE General Test, 3 letters of recommendation; for doctorate, GRE General Test, 3 letters of recommendation, official transcripts, statement of purpose. Additional exam requirements/recommendations for international students: Required—TOEFL (minimum score 600 paper-based; 250 computer-based; 100 iBT), TWE (minimum score 5). *Application deadline:* For fall admission, 1/4 for domestic and international students. Application fee: $85. Electronic applications accepted. *Expenses:* Contact institution. *Financial support:* In 2009–10, 689 students received support, including 154 fellowships with full and partial tuition reimbursements available (averaging $11,882 per year), 41 research assistantships (averaging $11,990 per year), 173 teaching assistantships (averaging $9,174 per year); career-related internships or fieldwork, Federal Work-Study, institutionally sponsored loans, scholarships/grants, health care benefits, tuition waivers (full and partial), and unspecified assistantships also available. Support available to part-time students. Financial award application deadline: 2/1; financial award applicants required to submit FAFSA. *Faculty research:* Learning and development, educational leadership and organizations, education policy analysis. Total annual research expenditures: $18.1 million. *Unit head:* Dr. Kathleen McCartney, Dean, 617-495-3401. *Application contact:* Information Contact, 617-495-3414, Fax: 617-496-3577, E-mail: gseadmissions@harvard.edu.

Hastings College, Department of Teacher Education, Hastings, NE 68901-7696. Offers MAT. *Accreditation:* NCATE. Part-time programs available. *Degree requirements:* For master's, comprehensive exam, thesis, or oral teaching presentation; digital portfolio. *Entrance requirements:* For master's, minimum GPA of 2.5, 2 letters of reference, interview. Additional exam requirements/recommendations for international students: Required—TOEFL. Electronic applications accepted. *Faculty research:* Assessments, performance competencies.

Hebrew College, Shoolman Graduate School of Education, Newton Centre, MA 02459. Offers early childhood Jewish education (Certificate); Jewish day school education (Certificate); Jewish education (MJ Ed); Jewish family education (Certificate); Jewish special education (Certificate); Jewish youth education, informal education and camping (Certificate). Part-time and evening/weekend programs available. Postbaccalaureate distance learning degree programs offered. *Degree requirements:* For master's, one foreign language. *Entrance requirements:* For master's, GRE, interview. Additional exam requirements/recommendations for international students: Required—TOEFL.

Hebrew Union College–Jewish Institute of Religion, Rhea Hirsch School of Education, Los Angeles, CA 90007-3796. Offers day school teaching: California state teaching credential (Certificate); Jewish education (MAJE, PhD); MAJCS/MAJE. Terminal master's awarded for partial completion of doctoral program. *Degree requirements:* For master's, one foreign language, thesis or alternative, Hebrew; for doctorate, one foreign language, thesis/dissertation, Hebrew. *Entrance requirements:* For master's, GRE General Test, Hebrew, interview, minimum undergraduate GPA of 3.0; for doctorate, GRE General Test, interview, knowledge of Hebrew, minimum GPA of 3.0. Additional exam requirements/recommendations for international students: Required—TOEFL (minimum score 550 paper-based). Electronic applications accepted.

Hebrew Union College–Jewish Institute of Religion, School of Education, New York, NY 10012-1186. Offers MARE. Part-time programs available. *Degree requirements:* For master's, one foreign language, thesis. *Entrance requirements:* For master's, GRE, minimum 2 years of college-level Hebrew.

Heidelberg University, Program in Education, Tiffin, OH 44883-2462. Offers MA. Part-time and evening/weekend programs available. *Faculty:* 6 full-time (3 women), 4 part-time/adjunct (3 women). *Students:* 55 part-time (35 women); includes 10 minority (4 African Americans, 5 Asian Americans or Pacific Islanders, 1 Hispanic American). Average age 35. 110 applicants, 83% accepted. In 2009, 22 master's awarded. *Degree requirements:* For master's, thesis or alternative, internship, practicum. *Entrance requirements:* For master's, minimum GPA of 2.5, 3 letters of reference. Additional exam requirements/recommendations for international students: Required—TOEFL (minimum score 550 paper-based). *Application deadline:* Applications are processed on a rolling basis. Application fee: $25. *Expenses:* Tuition: Part-time $415 per credit hour. *Financial support:* In 2009–10, 20 students received support. Federal Work-Study available. Support available to part-time students. Financial award applicants required to submit FAFSA. *Unit head:* Dr. Diane Armstrong, Director of Graduate Studies, 419-448-2175, Fax: 419-448-2072, E-mail: darmstro@heidelberg.edu. *Application contact:* Melissa Nye, Graduate Studies Office, 419-448-2288, Fax: 419-448-2072, E-mail: mnye@heidelberg.edu.

Henderson State University, Graduate Studies, School of Education, Arkadelphia, AR 71999-0001. Offers MAT, MS, MSE, Ed S, Graduate Certificate. *Accreditation:* NCATE. Part-time programs available. *Faculty:* 28 full-time (14 women), 5 part-time/adjunct (2 women). *Students:* 61 full-time (35 women), 255 part-time (199 women); includes 58 minority (48 African Americans, 1 American Indian/Alaska Native, 1 Asian American or Pacific Islander, 8 Hispanic Americans), 6 international. Average age 34. 59 applicants, 100% accepted, 59 enrolled. In 2009, 114 master's, 5 other advanced degrees awarded. *Entrance requirements:* For master's, GRE General Test or MAT, minimum GPA of 2.7, teacher certification. Additional exam requirements/recommendations for international students: Required—TOEFL (minimum score 550 paper-based; 213 computer-based); Recommended—IELTS (minimum score 6). *Application deadline:* For fall admission, 8/1 priority date for domestic students, 6/30 priority date for international students; for spring admission, 1/1 priority date for domestic students, 11/30 priority date for international students. Application fee: $25 ($75 for international students). Electronic applications accepted. *Expenses:* Tuition, state resident: full-time $3798; part-time $211 per credit hour. Tuition, nonresident: full-time $7596; part-time $422 per credit hour. Required fees: $903. *Financial support:* Teaching assistantships with tuition reimbursements available. *Unit head:* Dr. Judy Harrison, Dean, 870-230-5358, Fax: 870-230-5455, E-mail: harrisj@hsu.edu. *Application contact:* Dr. Marck L. Beggs, Graduate Dean, 870-230-5126, Fax: 870-230-5479, E-mail: beggsm@hsu.edu.

Heritage University, Graduate Programs in Education, Toppenish, WA 98948-9599. Offers counseling (M Ed); educational administration (M Ed); professional studies (M Ed), including bilingual education/ESL, biology, English and literature, reading/literacy, special education; teaching (MIT). Part-time and evening/weekend programs available. *Degree requirements:* For master's, comprehensive exam, thesis (for some programs). *Entrance requirements:* For master's, interview, letters of recommendation, teaching certificate. Additional exam requirements/recommendations for international students: Recommended—TOEFL (minimum score 550 paper-based; 213 computer-based).

Hodges University, Graduate Programs, Naples, FL 34119. Offers business administration (MBA); computer information technology (MS); criminal justice (MCJ); education (MPS); information systems management (MIS); interdisciplinary (MPS); law (MPS); management (MSM); professional studies (MPS); psychology (MPS); public administration (MPA). Part-time and evening/weekend programs available. Postbaccalaureate distance learning degree programs offered (no on-campus study). *Faculty:* 14 full-time (4 women), 4 part-time/adjunct (3 women). *Students:* 37 full-time (28 women), 217 part-time (142 women); includes 76 minority (35 African Americans, 5 Asian Americans or Pacific Islanders, 36 Hispanic Americans). Average age 36. 92 applicants, 91% accepted, 81 enrolled. In 2009, 92 master's awarded. *Degree requirements:* For master's, comprehensive exam (for some programs), thesis (for some programs). *Entrance requirements:* For master's, in-house entrance exam. *Application deadline:* Applications are processed on a rolling basis. Application fee: $50. Electronic applications accepted. *Expenses:* Tuition: Full-time $16,605; part-time $615 per credit hour. Required fees: $570. *Financial support:* In 2009–10, 200 students received support. Federal Work-Study and scholarships/grants available. Financial award application deadline: 7/9; financial award applicants required to submit FAFSA. *Unit head:* Terry McMahan, President, 239-513-1122, Fax: 239-598-6253, E-mail: tmcmahan@hodges.edu. *Application contact:* Rita Lampus, Vice President of Student Enrollment Management, 239-513-1122, Fax: 239-598-6253, E-mail: rlampus@hodges.edu.

Hofstra University, School of Education, Health, and Human Services, Hempstead, NY 11549. Offers MA, MHA, MS, MS Ed, Ed D, PhD, Advanced Certificate, CAS, PD. *Accreditation:* Teacher Education Accreditation Council. Part-time and evening/weekend programs available. Postbaccalaureate distance learning degree programs offered (minimal on-campus study). *Faculty:* 74 full-time (50 women), 103 part-time/adjunct (65 women). *Students:* 797 full-time (600 women), 809 part-time (644 women); includes 299 minority (161 African Americans, 4 American Indian/Alaska Native, 37 Asian Americans or Pacific Islanders, 97 Hispanic Americans), 26 international. Average age 30. 1,111 applicants, 81% accepted, 572 enrolled. In 2009, 559 master's, 9 doctorates, 43 other advanced degrees awarded. Terminal master's awarded for partial completion of doctoral program. *Degree requirements:* For master's, variable foreign language requirement, comprehensive exam (for some programs), thesis (for some programs), capstone, electronic portfolio, student teaching, practicum, internship, seminars, field work, curriculum project, clinical hours; for doctorate, variable foreign language requirement, comprehensive exam (for some programs), thesis/dissertation, qualifying hearing; for other advanced degree, comprehensive exam (for some programs), thesis optional, electronic portfolio, fieldwork, internship, state exams, exit project. *Entrance requirements:* For master's, GRE, letters of recommendation, interview, portfolio, resume, certification; for doctorate, GRE, 3 letters of recommendation, essay, interview, 2 years full-time teaching. Additional exam requirements/recommendations for international students: Required—TOEFL (minimum score 550 paper-based; 213 computer-based; 80 iBT). *Application deadline:* Applications are processed on a rolling basis. Application fee: $60. Electronic applications accepted. *Expenses:* Tuition: Full-time $16,200; part-time $900 per credit hour. Required fees: $970; $145 per term. Tuition and fees vary according to program. *Financial support:* In 2009–10, 717 students received support, including 178 fellowships with full and partial tuition reimbursements available (averaging $3,585 per year), 28 research assistantships with full and partial tuition reimbursements available (averaging $12,653 per year); career-related internships or fieldwork, Federal Work-Study, institutionally sponsored loans, traineeships, health care benefits, tuition waivers (full and partial), unspecified assistantships, and partial scholarships also available. Support available to part-time students. Financial award applicants required to submit FAFSA. *Faculty research:* Inclusive schooling; reflective practice; health care policy; childhood obesity; constructive pedagogy. Total annual research expenditures: $274,500. *Unit head:* Dr. David Foulk, Dean, 516-463-5740, Fax: 516-463-6461, E-mail: soedff@hofstra.edu. *Application contact:* Carol Drummer, Dean of Graduate Admissions, 516-463-4876, Fax: 516-463-4664, E-mail: gradstudent@hofstra.edu.

Hollins University, Graduate Programs, Program in Teaching, Roanoke, VA 24020-1603. Offers MAT. *Accreditation:* Teacher Education Accreditation Council. Part-time and evening/weekend programs available. *Faculty:* 3 full-time (all women), 6 part-time/adjunct (2 women). *Students:* 17 full-time (16 women), 38 part-time (32 women); includes 2 minority (1 African American, 1 Hispanic American). Average age 29. 15 applicants, 67% accepted, 10 enrolled. In 2009, 17 master's awarded. *Degree requirements:* For master's, thesis. *Entrance requirements:* For master's, PRAXIS I, letters of recommendation, writing sample. Additional exam requirements/recommendations for international students: Required—TOEFL (minimum score 550 paper-based; 213 computer-based; 79 iBT). *Application deadline:* For fall admission, 7/1 for domestic and international students; for spring admission, 12/1 for domestic and international students. Applications are processed on a rolling basis. Application fee: $40. Electronic applications accepted. *Expenses:* Tuition: Full-time $27,780; part-time $295 per contact hour. Required fees: $280; $70 per unit. Part-time tuition and fees vary according to course load and program. *Financial support:* In 2009–10, 36 students received support, including 6 fellowships (averaging $3,540 per year); Federal Work-Study and scholarships/grants also available. Support available to part-time students. Financial award application deadline: 7/15; financial award applicants required to submit FAFSA. *Faculty research:* Television violence and its effect on the developing brain, phonological/phonemic awareness, technology in the classroom. *Unit head:* Dr. Kristi Fowler, Director, 540-362-7460, Fax: 540-362-6288, E-mail: kfowler@hollins.edu. *Application contact:* Donna Martin, Secretary of Education, 540-362-7460, Fax: 540-362-6288, E-mail: dmartin@hollins.edu.

Holy Family University, Graduate School, School of Education, Philadelphia, PA 19114. Offers education (M Ed); education leadership (M Ed); elementary education (M Ed); reading specialist (M Ed); secondary education (M Ed); special education (M Ed). Part-time and evening/weekend programs available. *Faculty:* 14 full-time (10 women), 42 part-time/adjunct (23 women). *Students:* 63 full-time (48 women), 608 part-time (487 women); includes 45 minority (23 African Americans, 7 Asian Americans or Pacific Islanders, 15 Hispanic Americans), 1 international. Average age 31. 202 applicants, 86% accepted, 146 enrolled. In 2009, 248 master's awarded. *Degree requirements:* For master's, thesis optional. *Entrance requirements:* For master's, GRE or MAT, interview. *Application deadline:* For fall admission, 7/1 priority date for domestic students; for winter admission, 11/1 priority date for domestic students. Applications are processed on a rolling basis. Application fee: $25. *Expenses:* Tuition: Part-time $600 per credit. Required fees: $58 per semester. *Financial support:* Research assistantships, Federal Work-Study available. Support available to part-time students. Financial award application deadline: 2/15; financial award applicants required to submit FAFSA. *Faculty research:* Cognition, developmental issues, sociological issues in education. *Unit head:* Dr. Leonard Soroka, Dean, 267-341-3565, Fax: 215-824-2438, E-mail: lsoroka@holyfanily.edu. *Application contact:* Gidget Marie Montelibano, Graduate Admissions Counselor, 267-341-3558, Fax: 215-637-1478, E-mail: gmontelibano@holyfamily.edu.

Holy Names University, Graduate Division, Department of Education, Oakland, CA 94619-1699. Offers educational therapy (Certificate); level 1 education specialist mild/moderate disabilities (Credential); level 2 education specialist mild/moderate disabilities (Credential); multiple subject teaching credential (Credential); single subject teaching credential (Credential); teaching English as a second language (TESL) (M Ed); urban education: educational therapy (M Ed); urban education: K-12 education (M Ed); urban education: special education (M Ed). Part-time programs available. *Degree requirements:* For master's, comprehensive exam, research paper, thesis or project. *Entrance requirements:* For master's, minimum undergraduate GPA of 2.6 overall, 3.0 in major. Additional exam requirements/recommendations for international students: Required—TOEFL (minimum score 550 paper-based; 213 computer-based; 80 iBT). *Faculty research:* Cognitive development, language development, learning handicaps.

Hood College, Graduate School, Department of Education, Frederick, MD 21701-8575. Offers curriculum and instruction (MS), including early childhood education, elementary education, elementary school science and mathematics, secondary education, special education; educational leadership (MS, Certificate); reading specialization (MS). Part-time and evening/weekend programs available. *Faculty:* 4 full-time (all women), 39 part-time/adjunct (21 women). *Students:* 2 full-time (both women), 397 part-time (326 women); includes 41 minority (29 African Americans, 5 Asian Americans or Pacific Islanders, 7 Hispanic Americans). Average age 33. 100 applicants, 92% accepted, 84 enrolled. In 2009, 73 master's, 65 other advanced degrees awarded. *Degree requirements:* For master's, action research project, portfolio (reading). *Entrance requirements:* For master's, minimum GPA of 2.75, teaching certification. *Application deadline:* For fall admission, 7/15 for domestic and international students; for spring admission, 12/15 for domestic and international students. Applications are processed on a rolling basis. Application fee: $35. Electronic applications accepted. *Expenses:* Tuition: Full-time $6480; part-time $360 per credit. Required fees: $100; $50 per term. *Financial support:* Applicants required to submit FAFSA. *Faculty research:* Leadership, action research, brain research, learning styles. *Unit head:* Dr. John George, Chairperson, 301-696-3471, Fax: 301-696-3597, E-mail: george@hood.edu. *Application contact:* Dr. Allen P. Flora, Dean of Graduate School, 301-696-3811, Fax: 301-696-3597, E-mail: gofurther@hood.edu.

Hope International University, School of Graduate and Professional Studies, Program in Education, Fullerton, CA 92831-3138. Offers ME. Part-time and evening/weekend programs available. *Degree requirements:* For master's, comprehensive exam (for some programs), thesis. *Entrance requirements:* For master's, minimum GPA of 3.0, 2 references. Additional exam requirements/recommendations for international students: Required—TOEFL (minimum score 550 paper-based; 213 computer-based; 86 iBT); Recommended—IELTS (minimum

score 6.5). Electronic applications accepted. *Expenses:* Contact institution. *Faculty research:* Distance education.

Houston Baptist University, College of Education and Behavioral Sciences, Programs in Education, Houston, TX 77074-3298. Offers bilingual education (M Ed); counselor education (M Ed); curriculum and instruction (M Ed); educational administration (M Ed); educational diagnostician (M Ed); reading education (M Ed). Part-time programs available. *Entrance requirements:* For master's, GRE General Test or MAT. Additional exam requirements/recommendations for international students: Required—TOEFL (minimum score 550 paper-based; 213 computer-based).

Howard University, School of Education, Washington, DC 20059. Offers M Ed, MA, MAT, MS, Ed D, PhD, CAGS. *Accreditation:* NCATE. Part-time and evening/weekend programs available. *Faculty:* 29 full-time (19 women), 12 part-time/adjunct (9 women). *Students:* 132 full-time (96 women), 87 part-time (61 women); includes 178 minority (170 African Americans, 3 Asian Americans or Pacific Islanders, 5 Hispanic Americans), 9 international. Average age 32. 160 applicants, 69% accepted, 81 enrolled. In 2009, 48 master's, 9 doctorates, 2 other advanced degrees awarded. *Degree requirements:* For master's, comprehensive exam, expository writing exam; for doctorate, one foreign language, comprehensive exam, thesis/dissertation, expository writing exam, internship. *Entrance requirements:* For master's, minimum GPA of 2.7; for doctorate, GRE General Test, minimum GPA of 3.4. Additional exam requirements/recommendations for international students: Required—TOEFL (minimum score 550 paper-based; 213 computer-based). *Application deadline:* For fall admission, 2/15 priority date for domestic students; for spring admission, 11/1 for domestic students. Applications are processed on a rolling basis. Application fee: $45. Electronic applications accepted. *Financial support:* In 2009–10, 60 students received support, including 11 fellowships with full tuition reimbursements available (averaging $15,000 per year), 46 research assistantships with full tuition reimbursements available (averaging $6,000 per year); career-related internships or fieldwork, Federal Work-Study, institutionally sponsored loans, scholarships/grants, tuition waivers (full and partial), and unspecified assistantships also available. Financial award application deadline: 2/15; financial award applicants required to submit FAFSA. *Faculty research:* Policy affecting education for African-Americans; information technology use in underserved school populations; increasing literacy skills for public school students; violence intervention and prevention; successes, problems, and needs of disabled African-Americans. Total annual research expenditures: $3.8 million. *Unit head:* Dr. Leslie T. Fenwick, Head, 202-806-7334, Fax: 202-806-5302, E-mail: lfenwick@howard.edu. *Application contact:* Dr. Melanie Carter, Associate Dean for Academic Programs and Student Affairs, 202-806-7340, Fax: 202-806-5302, E-mail: melcarter@howard.edu.

Humboldt State University, Graduate Studies, College of Professional Studies, School of Education, Arcata, CA 95521-8299. Offers MA. Part-time and evening/weekend programs available. *Students:* 9 full-time (6 women), 24 part-time (19 women); includes 4 minority (3 American Indian/Alaska Native, 1 Hispanic American). Average age 35. 32 applicants, 53% accepted, 13 enrolled. In 2009, 4 master's awarded. *Degree requirements:* For master's, thesis or alternative. *Entrance requirements:* For master's, minimum GPA of 3.0, 3 letters of recommendation. Additional exam requirements/recommendations for international students: Required—TOEFL (minimum score 500 paper-based; 173 computer-based). *Application deadline:* For fall admission, 2/1 for domestic and international students. Application fee: $55. *Expenses:* Tuition, nonresident: full-time $8928. Required fees: $6102. Tuition and fees vary according to program. *Financial support:* Application deadline: 3/1. *Unit head:* Dr. David Ellerd, Chair, 707-826-3726, Fax: 707-826-5868, E-mail: dae11@humboldt.edu. *Application contact:* Dr. Keri Gelenian, Coordinator, 707-826-3738, E-mail: kg5@humboldt.edu.

Hunter College of the City University of New York, Graduate School, School of Education, New York, NY 10021-5085. Offers MA, MS, MS Ed, AC. *Accreditation:* NCATE. *Faculty:* 59 full-time (50 women), 77 part-time/adjunct (52 women). *Students:* 253 full-time (221 women), 1,381 part-time (1,115 women); includes 256 minority (77 African Americans, 2 American Indian/Alaska Native, 63 Asian Americans or Pacific Islanders, 114 Hispanic Americans). Average age 31. 1,225 applicants, 56% accepted, 456 enrolled. In 2009, 583 master's, 4 other advanced degrees awarded. *Degree requirements:* For master's, thesis; for AC, portfolio review. *Entrance requirements:* For degree, minimum B average in graduate course work, teaching certificate, minimum 3 years of full-time teaching experience, interview, 2 letters of support. Additional exam requirements/recommendations for international students: Required—TOEFL. *Application deadline:* For fall admission, 4/1 for domestic students, 2/1 for international students; for spring admission, 11/1 for domestic students, 9/1 for international students. Applications are processed on a rolling basis. Application fee: $125. *Expenses:* Tuition, state resident: full-time $7360; part-time $310 per credit. Required fees: $250 per semester. *Financial support:* Fellowships, career-related internships or fieldwork, Federal Work-Study, institutionally sponsored loans, and tuition waivers (full and partial) available. Support available to part-time students. *Faculty research:* Multicultural and multiracial urban education; mentoring new teachers; mathematics and science education; bilingual, bicultural, and special education. *Unit head:* Dr. David Steiner, Dean, 212-772-4622, E-mail: david.steiner@hunter.cuny.edu. *Application contact:* Milena Solo, Director for Graduate Admissions, 212-772-4482, Fax: 212-650-3336, E-mail: milena.solo@hunter.cuny.edu.

Huntington University, Graduate School, Huntington, IN 46750-1299. Offers counseling (MA), including licensed mental health counselor; education (M Ed); youth ministry leadership (MA). Part-time programs available. Postbaccalaureate distance learning degree programs offered (minimal on-campus study). *Faculty:* 2 full-time (0 women), 36 part-time/adjunct (12 women). *Students:* 57 full-time (31 women), 87 part-time (58 women); includes 9 minority (8 African Americans, 1 Hispanic American), 1 international. Average age 33. 50 applicants, 92% accepted, 27 enrolled. In 2009, 4 master's awarded. *Degree requirements:* For master's, thesis. *Entrance requirements:* For master's, GRE (for counseling and education students only). Additional exam requirements/recommendations for international students: Required—TOEFL. *Application deadline:* For fall admission, 7/1 priority date for domestic students, 5/1 priority date for international students; for winter admission, 10/1 priority date for domestic students, 9/1 priority date for international students; for spring admission, 11/30 priority date for domestic students, 10/30 priority date for international students. Applications are processed on a rolling basis. Application fee: $20. Electronic applications accepted. *Expenses:* Tuition: Part-time $370 per credit hour. Part-time tuition and fees vary according to program. *Financial support:* In 2009–10, 53 students received support. Scholarships/grants and unspecified assistantships available. Support available to part-time students. Financial award application deadline: 8/1; financial award applicants required to submit FAFSA. *Faculty research:* Leadership, educational technology trends, evangelism, youth ministry, mental health. *Unit head:* Dr. Steven Holtrop, Associate Dean for Graduate and Adult Studies, 260-359-4166, Fax: 260-359-4126, E-mail: sholtrop@huntington.edu. *Application contact:* Lori Garde, Program Coordinator, 260-359-4039, Fax: 260-359-4126, E-mail: lgarde@huntington.edu.

Idaho State University, Office of Graduate Studies, College of Education, Pocatello, ID 83209-8059. Offers M Ed, MPE, Ed D, PhD, 5th Year Certificate, 6th Year Certificate, Ed S. *Accreditation:* NCATE. Part-time programs available. *Faculty:* 24 full-time (11 women), 1 (woman) part-time/adjunct. *Students:* 70 full-time (39 women), 268 part-time (127 women); includes 20 minority (6 African Americans, 6 American Indian/Alaska Native, 3 Asian Americans or Pacific Islanders, 5 Hispanic Americans), 15 international. Average age 38. 57 applicants, 61% accepted, 8 enrolled. In 2009, 59 master's, 8 doctorates, 26 other advanced degrees awarded. *Degree requirements:* For master's, comprehensive exam, thesis optional, oral exam, written exam; for doctorate, comprehensive exam, thesis/dissertation, written exam; for other advanced degree, comprehensive exam, oral exam, written exam, practicum or field project. *Entrance requirements:* For master's, GRE General Test or MAT, minimum undergraduate GPA of 3.0, interview, bachelor's degree or equivalent; for doctorate, GRE General Test or MAT, minimum undergraduate GPA of 3.0, 3.5 graduate; departmental interview; current curriculum vitae, computer skill competency checklist; for other advanced degree, GRE General Test, minimum graduate GPA of 3.0, master's degree, letter from supervisor attesting to school administration potential. Additional exam requirements/recommendations for international students: Required—TOEFL (minimum score 550 paper-based; 213 computer-based; 80 iBT). *Application deadline:* For fall admission, 7/1 for domestic students, 6/1 for international students; for spring admission, 12/1 for domestic students, 11/1 for international students. Applications are processed on a rolling basis. Application fee: $55. Electronic applications accepted. *Expenses:* Tuition, state resident: full-time $3318; part-time $297 per credit hour. Tuition, nonresident: full-time $13,120; part-time $437 per credit hour. Required fees: $2530. Tuition and fees vary according to program. *Financial support:* In 2009–10, 21 teaching assistantships with full and partial tuition reimbursements (averaging $10,841 per year) were awarded; research assistantships with full and partial tuition reimbursements, career-related internships or fieldwork, Federal Work-Study, institutionally sponsored loans, scholarships/grants, health care benefits, tuition waivers (full and partial), and unspecified assistantships also available. Support available to part-time students. Financial award application deadline: 1/1; financial award applicants required to submit FAFSA. *Faculty research:* School reform, inclusion, students at risk, teacher education standards, teaching cases, education leadership. Total annual research expenditures: $327,219. *Unit head:* Dr. Deborah Hedeen, Dean, 208-282-3259, Fax: 208-282-4697, E-mail: hededebo@isu.edu. *Application contact:* Dr. Peter Denner, Director, Office of Standards and Assessment, 208-282-2783, Fax: 208-282-4697, E-mail: dennpete@isu.edu.

Illinois State University, Graduate School, College of Education, Normal, IL 61790-2200. Offers MS, MS Ed, Ed D, PhD. *Accreditation:* NCATE. Part-time programs available. *Degree requirements:* For doctorate, thesis/dissertation, 2 terms of residency. *Entrance requirements:* For master's and doctorate, GRE General Test.

Indiana State University, School of Graduate Studies, College of Education, Terre Haute, IN 47809. Offers M Ed, MS, PhD, Ed S, MA/MS. *Accreditation:* NCATE. Part-time and evening/weekend programs available. *Degree requirements:* For doctorate, thesis/dissertation. *Entrance requirements:* For master's, minimum undergraduate GPA of 2.5; for doctorate, GRE General Test; for Ed S, GRE General Test, minimum graduate GPA of 3.25. Electronic applications accepted.

Indiana University Bloomington, School of Education, Bloomington, IN 47405-7000. Offers MS, Ed D, PhD, Ed S. *Accreditation:* NCATE. Part-time programs available. Postbaccalaureate distance learning degree programs offered. *Faculty:* 102 full-time (43 women), 112 part-time/adjunct (45 women). *Students:* 842 full-time (578 women), 292 part-time (197 women); includes 187 minority (87 African Americans, 7 American Indian/Alaska Native, 41 Asian Americans or Pacific Islanders, 52 Hispanic Americans), 220 international. Average age 33. 911 applicants, 61% accepted, 213 enrolled. In 2009, 235 master's, 82 doctorates, 27 other advanced degrees awarded. Terminal master's awarded for partial completion of doctoral program. *Degree requirements:* For master's, thesis optional; for doctorate, comprehensive exam, thesis/dissertation; for Ed S, comprehensive exam (for some programs), thesis (for some programs), comprehensive exam or project. *Entrance requirements:* For master's and Ed S, GRE General Test, minimum GPA of 3.0 (recommended), 3 letters of recommendation; for doctorate, GRE General Test, minimum GPA of 3.0, 3 letters of recommendation. Additional exam requirements/recommendations for international students: Required—TOEFL (minimum score 550 paper-based; 213 computer-based; 79 iBT). *Application deadline:* For fall admission, 1/15 priority date for domestic students, 12/1 priority date for international students; for spring admission, 11/1 priority date for domestic students, 9/1 priority date for international students. Applications are processed on a rolling basis. Application fee: $55 ($65 for international students). Electronic applications accepted. *Financial support:* Fellowships with full and partial tuition reimbursements, research assistantships with tuition reimbursements, teaching assistantships with tuition reimbursements, Federal Work-Study, scholarships/grants, tuition waivers (full and partial), and unspecified assistantships available. Financial award application deadline: 3/1. Total annual research expenditures: $5.6 million. *Unit head:* Dr. Gerardo Gonzalez, Dean, 812-856-8001, Fax: 812-856-8088, E-mail: gonzalez@indiana.edu. *Application contact:* Elizabeth Tilghman, Admissions Coordinator, 812-856-8552, Fax: 812-856-8505, E-mail: etilghma@indiana.edu.

Indiana University East, School of Education, Richmond, IN 47374-1289. Offers MS Ed. *Accreditation:* NCATE. *Entrance requirements:* For master's, 3 letters of recommendation, interview.

Indiana University Kokomo, Division of Education, Kokomo, IN 46904-9003. Offers elementary education (MS Ed). *Accreditation:* NCATE. Part-time and evening/weekend programs available. *Faculty:* 1 full-time (0 women). *Students:* 17 part-time (13 women). Average age 34. In 2009, 6 master's awarded. *Degree requirements:* For master's, thesis optional, research project. *Entrance requirements:* For master's, GRE General Test, minimum GPA of 2.5. *Application deadline:* For fall admission, 8/1 for domestic students; for spring admission, 12/1 for domestic students. Applications are processed on a rolling basis. Application fee: $40 ($50 for international students). *Financial support:* In 2009–10, 2 fellowships (averaging $375 per year) were awarded; minority teacher scholarships also available. *Faculty research:* Reading, teaching effectiveness, portfolio, curriculum development. *Unit head:* D. Antonio Cantu, Dean, 765-455-9441, Fax: 765-455-9503. *Application contact:* Charlotte Miller, Coordinator, Educational and Student Resources, 765-455-9367, Fax: 765-455-9503, E-mail: cmiller@iuk.edu.

Indiana University Northwest, School of Education, Gary, IN 46408-1197. Offers elementary education (MS Ed); secondary education (MS Ed). *Accreditation:* NCATE. Part-time and evening/weekend programs available. *Faculty:* 5 full-time (2 women). *Students:* 35 full-time (29 women), 150 part-time (115 women); includes 83 minority (69 African Americans, 1 American Indian/Alaska Native, 13 Hispanic Americans). Average age 37. In 2009, 33 master's awarded. *Entrance requirements:* For master's, GRE General Test or MAT, minimum GPA of 3.0. *Application deadline:* For fall admission, 7/15 priority date for domestic students; for spring admission, 11/15 for domestic students. Application fee: $25. *Unit head:* Dr. Stanley E. Wigle, Dean, 219-980-6510, Fax: 219-981-4208, E-mail: amsanche@iun.edu. *Application contact:* Dr. Stanley E. Wigle, Dean, 219-980-6510, Fax: 219-981-4208, E-mail: amsanche@iun.edu.

Indiana University of Pennsylvania, School of Graduate Studies and Research, College of Education and Educational Technology, Indiana, PA 15705-1087. Offers M Ed, MA, MS, D Ed, PhD, Certificate. *Accreditation:* NCATE. Part-time and evening/weekend programs available. *Faculty:* 65 full-time (37 women), 6 part-time/adjunct (4 women). *Students:* 253 full-time (190 women), 509 part-time (376 women); includes 48 minority (39 African Americans, 1 American Indian/Alaska Native, 5 Asian Americans or Pacific Islanders, 3 Hispanic Americans), 14 international. Average age 32. 961 applicants, 48% accepted, 281 enrolled. In 2009, 248 master's, 41 doctorates, 17 other advanced degrees awarded. Terminal master's awarded for partial completion of doctoral program. *Degree requirements:* For master's, thesis optional; for doctorate, comprehensive exam, thesis/dissertation. *Entrance requirements:* For master's and doctorate, 2 letters of recommendation. Additional exam requirements/recommendations for international students: Required—TOEFL. *Application deadline:* Applications are processed on a rolling basis. Application fee: $40. *Expenses:* Tuition, state resident: full-time $6666; part-time $370 per credit hour. Tuition, nonresident: full-time $10,666; part-time $593 per credit hour. Required fees: $813 per semester. *Financial support:* In 2009–10, 17 fellowships (averaging $1,324 per year), 116 research assistantships (averaging $4,802 per year), 9 teaching assistantships with partial tuition reimbursements (averaging $14,956 per year) were awarded; career-related internships or fieldwork and Federal Work-Study also available. Support available to part-time students. Financial award application deadline: 3/15; financial award applicants required to submit FAFSA. *Unit head:* Dr. Mary Ann Rafoth, Dean, 724-357-2480, Fax: 724-357-5595. *Application contact:* Dr. Edward Nardi, Associate Dean, 724-357-2480, Fax: 724-357-5595, E-mail: ewnardi@iup.edu.

Indiana University–Purdue University Fort Wayne, College of Arts and Sciences, Department of Mathematical Sciences, Fort Wayne, IN 46805-1499. Offers applied mathematics (MS); applied statistics (Certificate); mathematics (MS); operations research (MS); teaching (MAT). Part-time and evening/weekend programs available. *Faculty:* 17 full-time (4 women), 2 part-time/adjunct (1 woman). *Students:* 2 full-time (0 women), 15 part-time (6 women); includes 2 minority (1 American Indian/Alaska Native, 1 Asian American or Pacific Islander), 1 international.

Education—General

Indiana University–Purdue University Fort Wayne (continued)

Average age 35. 5 applicants, 60% accepted, 3 enrolled. In 2009, 2 master's, 2 other advanced degrees awarded. *Entrance requirements:* For master's, minimum GPA of 3.0, major or minor in mathematics, three letters of recommendation. Additional exam requirements/recommendations for international students: Required—TOEFL (minimum score 550 paper-based; 213 computer-based; 77 iBT); Recommended—TWE. *Application deadline:* For fall admission, 8/1 priority date for domestic students, 7/1 priority date for international students; for spring admission, 12/1 for domestic students, 10/1 for international students. Applications are processed on a rolling basis. Application fee: $55 ($60 for international students). Electronic applications accepted. *Expenses:* Tuition, state resident: full-time $4595; part-time $255 per credit. Tuition, nonresident: full-time $10,963; part-time $609 per credit. Required fees: $528; $29.35 per credit. Tuition and fees vary according to course load. *Financial support:* In 2009–10, 1 research assistantship with partial tuition reimbursement (averaging $12,740 per year), 6 teaching assistantships with partial tuition reimbursements (averaging $12,740 per year) were awarded; scholarships/grants and unspecified assistantships also available. Support available to part-time students. Financial award application deadline: 3/1; financial award applicants required to submit FAFSA. *Faculty research:* Target value, toroidal queen's graph, holomorphic maps. *Unit head:* Dr. David A. Legg, Chair, 260-481-6222, Fax: 260-481-0155, E-mail: legg@ipfw.edu. *Application contact:* Dr. W. Douglas Weakley, Director of Graduate Studies, 260-481-6233, Fax: 260-481-0155, E-mail: weakley@ipfw.edu.

Indiana University–Purdue University Fort Wayne, School of Education, Fort Wayne, IN 46805-1499. Offers MS Ed, Certificate. *Accreditation:* NCATE. Part-time programs available. *Faculty:* 25 full-time (14 women). *Students:* 4 full-time (3 women), 207 part-time (160 women); includes 27 minority (16 African Americans, 2 Asian Americans or Pacific Islanders, 9 Hispanic Americans). Average age 35. 69 applicants, 99% accepted, 60 enrolled. In 2009, 86 master's awarded. *Entrance requirements:* For master's, minimum GPA of 2.5, 3 professional letters of recommendation. Additional exam requirements/recommendations for international students: Required—TOEFL (minimum score 550 paper-based; 213 computer-based; 77 iBT). *Application deadline:* For fall admission, 4/1 priority date for domestic and international students. Applications are processed on a rolling basis. Application fee: $55. *Expenses:* Tuition, state resident: full-time $4595; part-time $255 per credit. Tuition, nonresident: full-time $10,963; part-time $609 per credit. Required fees: $528; $29.35 per credit. Tuition and fees vary according to course load. *Financial support:* In 2009–10, 2 teaching assistantships with partial tuition reimbursements (averaging $12,740 per year) were awarded; scholarships/grants also available. Support available to part-time students. Financial award application deadline: 3/1; financial award applicants required to submit FAFSA. *Faculty research:* Korea education, public education, Irish immigration, consolidation of Indiana government schools. Total annual research expenditures: $130,816. *Unit head:* Dr. Barry Kanpol, Dean, 260-481-6456, Fax: 260-481-5408, E-mail: kanpolb@ipfw.edu. *Application contact:* Vicky L. Schmidt, Graduate Recorder, 260-481-6450, Fax: 260-481-5408, E-mail: schmidt@ipfw.edu.

Indiana University–Purdue University Indianapolis, School of Education, Indianapolis, IN 46202-2896. Offers computer education (Certificate); curriculum and instruction (MS); early childhood (MS); educational leadership (MS, Certificate); English as a second language (Certificate); higher education and student affairs (MS); kindergarten (Certificate); language education (MS); reading (Certificate); school counseling (MS); special education (MS, Certificate). Part-time and evening/weekend programs available. *Faculty:* 41 full-time, 80 part-time/adjunct. *Students:* 72 full-time (60 women), 427 part-time (325 women); includes 57 minority (42 African Americans, 1 American Indian/Alaska Native, 4 Asian Americans or Pacific Islanders, 10 Hispanic Americans), 5 international. Average age 32. 181 applicants, 78% accepted, 112 enrolled. In 2009, 162 master's awarded. *Degree requirements:* For master's, thesis optional. *Entrance requirements:* For master's, GRE General Test, minimum GPA of 3.0. Additional exam requirements/recommendations for international students: Required—TOEFL. *Application deadline:* For fall admission, 5/1 priority date for domestic students; for spring admission, 11/1 for domestic students. Application fee: $55 ($65 for international students). *Financial support:* In 2009–10, 2 fellowships (averaging $780 per year), 18 teaching assistantships (averaging $9,756 per year) were awarded; research assistantships with partial tuition reimbursements, Federal Work-Study, institutionally sponsored loans, scholarships/grants, and tuition waivers (partial) also available. Support available to part-time students. *Faculty research:* Teachers in the process of change, learning cycles, children's concepts of science. Total annual research expenditures: $614,458. *Unit head:* Dr. Chris Leland, Interim Executive Associate Dean, 317-274-6801, Fax: 317-274-6864. *Application contact:* Sarah Brandenburg, Graduate Advisor, 317-274-6801, Fax: 317-274-6864, E-mail: edugrad@iupui.edu.

Indiana University South Bend, School of Education, South Bend, IN 46634-7111. Offers counseling and human services (MS Ed); elementary education (MS Ed); secondary education (MS Ed); special education (MS Ed). *Accreditation:* NCATE. Part-time and evening/weekend programs available. *Faculty:* 21 full-time (11 women), 9 part-time/adjunct (3 women). *Students:* 72 full-time (48 women), 256 part-time (202 women); includes 36 minority (24 African Americans, 2 American Indian/Alaska Native, 1 Asian American or Pacific Islander, 9 Hispanic Americans), 9 international. Average age 36. In 2009, 103 master's awarded. *Degree requirements:* For master's, thesis or alternative, exit project. *Entrance requirements:* For master's, letters of recommendation, GRE or minimum GPA of 3.0. Additional exam requirements/recommendations for international students: Required—TOEFL. *Application deadline:* For fall admission, 7/1 for domestic students; for spring admission, 11/1 for domestic students. Applications are processed on a rolling basis. Application fee: $46 ($58 for international students). Electronic applications accepted. *Financial support:* Career-related internships or fieldwork available. Support available to part-time students. Financial award application deadline: 3/1; financial award applicants required to submit FAFSA. *Faculty research:* Professional dispositions, early childhood literacy, online learning, program assessments, problem-based learning. *Unit head:* Dr. Michael Horvath, Professor/Dean, 574-520-4339, Fax: 574-520-4550. *Application contact:* Dr. Todd Norris, Director of Education Student Services, 574-520-4845, E-mail: toanorri@iusb.edu.

Indiana University Southeast, School of Education, New Albany, IN 47150-6405. Offers counselor education (MS Ed); elementary education (MS Ed); secondary education (MS Ed). *Accreditation:* NCATE. Part-time and evening/weekend programs available. *Students:* 7 full-time (all women), 366 part-time (305 women); includes 31 minority (27 African Americans, 3 American Indian/Alaska Native, 1 Asian American or Pacific Islander), 1 international. Average age 32. In 2009, 138 master's awarded. *Entrance requirements:* For master's, minimum undergraduate GPA of 2.5, graduate 3.0. *Application deadline:* Applications are processed on a rolling basis. Application fee: $35. *Financial support:* In 2009–10, 29 students received support. Career-related internships or fieldwork, Federal Work-Study, and institutionally sponsored loans available. Support available to part-time students. Financial award applicants required to submit FAFSA. *Faculty research:* Learning styles, technology, constructivism, group process, innovative math strategies. *Unit head:* Dr. Gloria Murray, Dean, 812-941-2169, Fax: 812-941-2667, E-mail: soeinfo@ius.edu. *Application contact:* Dr. Gloria Murray, Dean, 812-941-2169, Fax: 812-941-2667, E-mail: soeinfo@ius.edu.

Indiana Wesleyan University, College of Adult and Professional Studies, Department of Master's Studies in Education, Marion, IN 46953. Offers curriculum and instruction (M Ed). *Accreditation:* NCATE. Part-time and evening/weekend programs available. Postbaccalaureate distance learning degree programs offered (no on-campus study). *Degree requirements:* For master's, portfolio. *Entrance requirements:* For master's, minimum GPA of 2.75, teaching experience, teaching license. Additional exam requirements/recommendations for international students: Required—TOEFL (minimum score 550 paper-based; 213 computer-based). Electronic applications accepted. *Expenses:* Tuition: Full-time $7380; part-time $410 per credit. One-time fee: $85. Tuition and fees vary according to course/location. *Faculty research:* Mentoring, performance-based assessments, faith integration, integration of technology, program assessment.

Institute for Christian Studies, Graduate Programs, Toronto, ON M5T 1R4, Canada. Offers education (M Phil F, PhD); history of philosophy (M Phil F, PhD); philosophical aesthetics (M Phil F, PhD); philosophy of religion (M Phil F, PhD); political theory (M Phil F, PhD); systematic philosophy (M Phil F, PhD); theology (M Phil F, PhD); worldview studies (MWS). Part-time programs available. Postbaccalaureate distance learning degree programs offered (minimal on-campus study). *Degree requirements:* For master's, one foreign language, thesis; for doctorate, 2 foreign languages, thesis/dissertation. *Entrance requirements:* For master's and doctorate, philosophy background. Additional exam requirements/recommendations for international students: Required—TOEFL (minimum score 600 paper-based; 250 computer-based). *Faculty research:* Human rights, anthropology of self, medieval discourse, gender and body, post-modern thought; biblical hermeneutics, creational aesthetics, ecumenism, epistemology, political theory and public policy, relational psychotherapy.

Instituto Tecnologico de Santo Domingo, Graduate School, Santo Domingo, Dominican Republic. Offers applied linguistics (MA); construction administration (M Mgmt); corporate finance (M Mgmt); education (M Ed); engineering (M Eng), including data telecommunications, industrial engineering, logistics and supply chain, maintenance engineering, sanitary and environmental engineering, structural engineering; environmental science (M En S), including environmental education, environmental management, marine and coastal ecosystems, natural resources management; family therapy (MA); food science and technology (MS); human development (MA); human resources administration (M Mgmt); international business (M Mgmt); labor risks (M Mgmt); management (M Mgmt); marketing (M Mgmt); mathematics (MS); organizational development (M Mgmt); planning and taxation (M Mgmt); psychology (MA); social science (M Ed); upper management (M Mgmt). *Entrance requirements:* For master's, birth certificate, minimum GPA of 2.0.

Instituto Tecnológico y de Estudios Superiores de Monterrey, Campus Central de Veracruz, Graduate Programs, Córdoba, Mexico. Offers administration (MA); administration of information technologies (MTI); computer sciences (MCC); education (MEE); educational institution administration (MAD); educational technology (MTE); electronic commerce (MCE); finance (MAF); humanistic studies (MEH); international business for Latin America (MNL); marketing (MMT); science (MCP); technology management (MTT). Part-time and evening/weekend programs available. Postbaccalaureate distance learning degree programs offered (minimal on-campus study). *Degree requirements:* For master's, thesis (for some programs). *Entrance requirements:* For master's, PAEP College Board. Electronic applications accepted.

Instituto Tecnológico y de Estudios Superiores de Monterrey, Campus Ciudad de México, Virtual University Division, Ciudad de Mexico, Mexico. Offers administration of information technologies (MA); computer sciences (MA); education (MA, PhD); educational technology (MA); environmental engineering (MA); environmental systems (MA); humanistic studies (MA); industrial engineering (MA); international business for Latin America (MA); quality systems (MA); quality systems and productivity (MA). Part-time and evening/weekend programs available. Postbaccalaureate distance learning degree programs offered (minimal on-campus study). *Entrance requirements:* For master's and doctorate, Instituto entrance exam. Additional exam requirements/recommendations for international students: Required—TOEFL.

Instituto Tecnológico y de Estudios Superiores de Monterrey, Campus Ciudad Juárez, Program in Education, Ciudad Juárez, Mexico. Offers M Ed.

Instituto Tecnológico y de Estudios Superiores de Monterrey, Campus Ciudad Obregón, Programs in Education, Ciudad Obregón, Mexico. Offers cognitive development (ME); communications (ME); mathematics (ME).

Instituto Tecnológico y de Estudios Superiores de Monterrey, Campus Estado de México, Professional and Graduate Division, Estado de Mexico, Mexico. Offers administration of information technologies (MITA); architecture (M Arch); business administration (GMBA, MBA); computer sciences (MCS, PhD); education (M Ed); educational institution administration (MAD); educational technology and innovation (PhD); electronic commerce (MEC); environmental systems (MS); finance (MAF); humanistic studies (MHS); information sciences and knowledge management (MISKM); information systems (MS); manufacturing systems (MS); marketing (MEM); quality systems and productivity (MS); science and materials engineering (PhD); telecommunications management (MTM). Part-time programs available. Postbaccalaureate distance learning degree programs offered (minimal on-campus study). *Degree requirements:* For master's, one foreign language, thesis (for some programs); for doctorate, one foreign language, thesis/dissertation. *Entrance requirements:* For master's, E-PAEP 500, interview; for doctorate, E-PAEP 500, research proposal. Additional exam requirements/recommendations for international students: Required—TOEFL (minimum score 550 paper-based). *Faculty research:* Surface treatments by plasmas, mechanical properties, robotics, graphical computing, mechatronics security protocols.

Instituto Tecnológico y de Estudios Superiores de Monterrey, Campus Irapuato, Graduate Programs, Irapuato, Mexico. Offers administration (MBA); administration of information technology (MAIT); administration of telecommunications (MAT); architecture (M Arch); computer science (MCS); education (M Ed); educational administration (MEA); educational innovation and technology (DEIT); educational technology (MET); electronic commerce (MBA); environmental administration and planning (MEAP); environmental systems (MES); finances (MBA); humanistic studies (MHS); international management for Latin American executives (MIMLAE); library and information science (MLIS); manufacturing quality management (MMQM); marketing research (MBA).

Instituto Tecnológico y de Estudios Superiores de Monterrey, Campus Sonora Norte, Program in Education, Hermosillo, Mexico. Offers MA. *Entrance requirements:* For master's, MAT.

Inter American University of Puerto Rico, Arecibo Campus, Programs in Education, Arecibo, PR 00614-4050. Offers administration and educational supervision (MA Ed); counseling and guidance (MA Ed); curriculum and teaching (MA Ed), including biology education, English as a second language, history education, math education, Spanish; elementary education (MA Ed). *Degree requirements:* For master's, comprehensive exam, thesis optional. *Entrance requirements:* For master's, GRE, EXADEP, bachelor's degree in education or teaching license (administration and supervision) or courses in education and psychology (counseling and guidance), minimum GPA of 2.5 in last 60 credits.

Inter American University of Puerto Rico, Barranquitas Campus, Program in Education, Barranquitas, PR 00794. Offers curriculum and teaching (M Ed); educational administration and supervision (MA); elementary education (M Ed); information and library service technology (M Ed). *Degree requirements:* For master's, comprehensive exam, thesis optional. *Entrance requirements:* For master's, EXADEP, letter of recommendation. Electronic applications accepted.

Inter American University of Puerto Rico, Metropolitan Campus, Graduate Programs, Program in Education, San Juan, PR 00919-1293. Offers curriculum and instruction (Ed D); educational administration (Ed D); guidance and counseling (MA, Ed D); special education administration (Ed D). *Degree requirements:* For doctorate, comprehensive exam, thesis/dissertation. *Entrance requirements:* For doctorate, GRE, MAT, or EXADEP. Electronic applications accepted.

International Baptist College, Program in Education, Chandler, AZ 85286. Offers M Ed. *Degree requirements:* For master's, research paper/thesis. *Entrance requirements:* For master's, letter of recommendation.

Iona College, School of Arts and Science, Program in Education, New Rochelle, NY 10801-1890. Offers biology education (MS Ed, MST); educational leadership (MS Ed); English education (MS Ed, MST); literacy education (MS Ed); mathematics education (MS Ed, MST); social studies education (MS Ed, MST); Spanish education (MS Ed, MST); teaching in childhood education (MST). *Accreditation:* NCATE. Part-time and evening/weekend programs available. *Faculty:* 24 full-time (13 women), 16 part-time/adjunct (10 women). *Students:* 41 full-time (35 women), 118 part-time (87 women); includes 15 minority (5 African Americans, 1 Asian American or Pacific Islander, 9 Hispanic Americans). Average age 28. 91 applicants, 67% accepted, 41 enrolled. In 2009, 61 master's awarded. *Degree requirements:* For master's,

thesis or alternative. *Entrance requirements:* For master's, minimum GPA of 2.5 (MST), New York teaching certificate (MS Ed). Additional exam requirements/recommendations for international students: Required—TOEFL (minimum score 550 paper-based; 213 computer-based). *Application deadline:* Applications are processed on a rolling basis. Application fee: $50. Electronic applications accepted. *Expenses:* Tuition: Part-time $830 per credit. *Financial support:* Unspecified assistantships available. Support available to part-time students. Financial award application deadline: 4/15; financial award applicants required to submit FAFSA. *Faculty research:* Reading/writing, educational technology, administration, early literacy assessment, literacy development. *Unit head:* Dr. Catherine O'Callaghan, Chair, 914-633-2210, Fax: 914-633-2608, E-mail: cocallaghan@iona.edu. *Application contact:* Veronica Jarek-Prinz, Director of Graduate Admissions, 914-633-2420, Fax: 914-633-2277, E-mail: vjarekprinz@iona.edu.

Jackson State University, Graduate School, School of Education, Jackson, MS 39217. Offers MS, MS Ed, Ed D, PhD, Ed S. *Accreditation:* NCATE. Part-time and evening/weekend programs available. Terminal master's awarded for partial completion of doctoral program. *Degree requirements:* For master's, comprehensive exam; for doctorate, comprehensive exam, thesis/dissertation. *Entrance requirements:* For master's, GRE General Test; for doctorate, MAT, teaching experience. Additional exam requirements/recommendations for international students: Required—TOEFL.

Jacksonville State University, College of Graduate Studies and Continuing Education, College of Education and Professional Studies, Jacksonville, AL 36265-1602. Offers MS, MS Ed, Ed S. *Accreditation:* NCATE. Part-time and evening/weekend programs available. *Degree requirements:* For master's, comprehensive exam, thesis (for some programs). *Entrance requirements:* For master's, GRE General Test or MAT. Additional exam requirements/recommendations for international students: Required—TOEFL (minimum score 500 paper-based; 173 computer-based; 61 iBT). Electronic applications accepted.

Jacksonville University, College of Arts and Sciences, School of Education, Jacksonville, FL 32211. Offers computer sciences (MAT); early childhood education (Certificate); elementary education (MAT); integrated learning with educational technology (MAT); mathematics education (MAT); music education (MAT); reading education (MAT); second careers as a teacher (Certificate). Part-time and evening/weekend programs available. *Degree requirements:* For master's, comprehensive exam. *Entrance requirements:* For master's, GRE General Test, minimum GPA of 3.0. Additional exam requirements/recommendations for international students: Required—TOEFL (minimum score 550 paper-based), TWE. *Expenses:* Contact institution.

John Carroll University, Graduate School, Department of Education and Allied Studies, University Heights, OH 44118-4581. Offers administration (M Ed, MA); educational and school psychology (M Ed, MA); professional teacher education (M Ed, MA); school based adolescent-young adult education (M Ed); school based early childhood education (M Ed); school based middle childhood education (M Ed); school based multi-age education (M Ed); school counseling (M Ed, MA). *Accreditation:* NCATE. Part-time and evening/weekend programs available. *Degree requirements:* For master's, comprehensive exam, research essay or thesis (MA only). *Entrance requirements:* For master's, GRE General Test or MAT, minimum GPA of 2.75. *Faculty research:* Children's literacy, diversity issues, teaching development, impact of technology.

John F. Kennedy University, School of Education and Liberal Arts, Department of Education, Pleasant Hill, CA 94523-4817. Offers MAT. Part-time and evening/weekend programs available. *Degree requirements:* For master's, thesis. *Entrance requirements:* For master's, California Basic Educational Skills Test, NTE, interview. Additional exam requirements/recommendations for international students: Required—TOEFL.

The Johns Hopkins University, School of Education, Department of Interdisciplinary Studies in Education, Baltimore, MD 21218. Offers earth/space science (Certificate); education (MS), including educational studies; mind, brain, and teaching (Certificate); teaching the adult learner (Certificate); urban education (Certificate). Part-time and evening/weekend programs available. Postbaccalaureate distance learning degree programs offered (minimal on-campus study). *Faculty:* 2 full-time (1 woman), 6 part-time/adjunct (5 women). *Students:* 8 full-time (7 women), 171 part-time (150 women); includes 44 minority (29 African Americans, 1 American Indian/Alaska Native, 11 Asian Americans or Pacific Islanders, 3 Hispanic Americans), 7 international. Average age 34. 77 applicants, 68% accepted, 39 enrolled. In 2009, 69 master's, 17 other advanced degrees awarded. *Degree requirements:* For master's, capstone course. *Entrance requirements:* For master's and Certificate, minimum undergraduate GPA of 3.0. Additional exam requirements/recommendations for international students: Required—TOEFL (minimum score 600 paper-based; 250 computer-based; 100 iBT). *Application deadline:* For fall admission, 5/1 for international students; for spring admission, 10/15 for international students. Applications are processed on a rolling basis. Application fee: $80. Electronic applications accepted. *Financial support:* Scholarships/grants available. Support available to part-time students. Financial award application deadline: 6/1; financial award applicants required to submit FAFSA. *Faculty research:* Neuro-education; urban school reform; leadership development; teacher leadership; charter schools; techniques for teaching reading to adolescents with delayed reading skills; school culture. *Unit head:* Dr. Mariale Hardiman, Assistant Dean and Chair, 410-516-8225, Fax: 410-516-3939, E-mail: mclean@jhu.edu. *Application contact:* Jennifer Shaffer, Director of Admissions, 410-516-9797, Fax: 410-516-9799, E-mail: educationinfo@jhu.edu.

The Johns Hopkins University, School of Education, Department of Teacher Development and Leadership, Baltimore, MD 21218-2699. Offers adolescent literacy education (Certificate); data-based decision making and organizational improvement (Certificate); education (MS), including reading, school administration and supervision, technology for educators; educational leadership for independent schools (Certificate); effective teaching of reading (Certificate); emergent literacy education (Certificate); English as a second language instruction (Certificate); gifted education (Certificate); leadership for school, family, and community collaboration (Certificate); leadership in technology integration (Certificate); school administration and supervision (Certificate); teacher development and leadership (Ed D); teacher leadership (Certificate); technology for educators (MS). Part-time and evening/weekend programs available. Postbaccalaureate distance learning degree programs offered (minimal on-campus study). *Faculty:* 8 full-time (2 women), 53 part-time/adjunct (36 women). *Students:* 17 full-time (16 women), 462 part-time (358 women); includes 117 minority (77 African Americans, 25 Asian Americans or Pacific Islanders, 15 Hispanic Americans), 11 international. Average age 33. 217 applicants, 62% accepted, 107 enrolled. In 2009, 85 master's, 2 doctorates, 181 other advanced degrees awarded. *Degree requirements:* For master's and Certificate, portfolio; for doctorate, comprehensive exam (for some programs), thesis/dissertation, portfolio or comprehensive exam. *Entrance requirements:* For master's and Certificate, bachelor's degree; minimum undergraduate GPA of 3.0; essay/statement of goals; for doctorate, GRE, essay/statement of goals; three letters of recommendation; curriculum vitae/resume; K-12 professional experience; interview; writing assessment. Additional exam requirements/recommendations for international students: Required—TOEFL (minimum score 600 paper-based; 250 computer-based; 100 iBT). *Application deadline:* For fall admission, 5/1 for international students; for spring admission, 10/15 for international students. Applications are processed on a rolling basis. Application fee: $80. Electronic applications accepted. *Financial support:* In 2009–10, 5 research assistantships, 1 teaching assistantship were awarded; scholarships/grants also available. Support available to part-time students. Financial award application deadline: 6/1; financial award applicants required to submit FAFSA. *Faculty research:* Application of psychoanalytic concepts to teaching, schools, and education reform; adolescent literacies; use of emerging technologies for teaching, learning, and school leadership; quantitative analyses of the social contexts of education; school, family, and community collaboration; program evaluation methodologies. *Unit head:* Dr. Edward Pajak, Chair, 410-516-9755, Fax: 410-516-9770, E-mail: mbuckingham@jhu.edu. *Application contact:* Jennifer Shaffer, Director of Admissions, 410-516-9797, Fax: 410-516-9799, E-mail: educationinfo@jhu.edu.

The Johns Hopkins University, School of Education, Department of Teacher Preparation, Baltimore, MD 21218. Offers education (MS), including educational studies; elementary education (MAT); English for speakers of other languages (MAT); K-8 mathematics lead-teacher

(Certificate); K-8 science lead-teacher (Certificate); secondary education (MAT), including biology, chemistry, earth/space/environmental science, English, French, mathematics, physics, social studies, Spanish. Part-time and evening/weekend programs available. *Faculty:* 13 full-time (11 women), 35 part-time/adjunct (21 women). *Students:* 162 full-time (119 women), 347 part-time (256 women); includes 138 minority (80 African Americans, 3 American Indian/Alaska Native, 38 Asian Americans or Pacific Islanders, 17 Hispanic Americans), 3 international. Average age 27. 89 applicants, 37% accepted, 24 enrolled. In 2009, 177 master's awarded. *Degree requirements:* For master's, portfolio, PRAXIS II, internship. *Entrance requirements:* For master's, PRAXIS I, SAT, ACT, or GRE (MAT), minimum undergraduate GPA of 3.0, interview, 1 letter of recommendation, curriculum vitae/resume; for Certificate, bachelor's degree, minimum undergraduate GPA of 3.0, essay/statement of goals, interview. Additional exam requirements/recommendations for international students: Required—TOEFL (minimum score 600 paper-based; 250 computer-based; 100 iBT). *Application deadline:* For fall admission, 5/1 for international students; for spring admission, 10/15 for international students. Applications are processed on a rolling basis. Application fee: $80. Electronic applications accepted. *Financial support:* Scholarships/grants available. Support available to part-time students. Financial award application deadline: 6/1; financial award applicants required to submit FAFSA. *Faculty research:* Teacher retention; STEM education reform; alternative certification programs; school-university partnerships; urban education; action research/data-informed instruction; family engagement. *Unit head:* Dr. Francis Masci, Chair, 410-516-9774, Fax: 410-516-9770, E-mail: matjhu@jhu.edu. *Application contact:* Jennifer Shaffer, Director of Admissions, 410-516-9797, Fax: 410-516-9799, E-mail: educationinfo@jhu.edu.

Johnson & Wales University, The Alan Shawn Feinstein Graduate School, MAT Program in Teacher Education, Providence, RI 02903-3703. Offers business education and secondary special education (MAT); elementary education and elementary special education (MAT); elementary education and elementary/secondary special education (MAT); elementary education and secondary special education (MAT); food service education and secondary special education (MAT). Part-time and evening/weekend programs available. *Faculty:* 7 full-time (3 women), 3 part-time/adjunct (2 women). *Students:* 105 full-time (77 women), 1 international. Average age 31. 73 applicants, 89% accepted, 56 enrolled. In 2009, 55 master's awarded. *Entrance requirements:* For master's, MAT, minimum GPA of 2.75. Additional exam requirements/recommendations for international students: Required—TOEFL (minimum score 550 paper-based; 210 computer-based) or IELTS recommended. *Application deadline:* For fall admission, 8/21 priority date for domestic students, 6/15 priority date for international students; for winter admission, 11/15 priority date for domestic students, 10/1 priority date for international students. Applications are processed on a rolling basis. Application fee: $0. *Expenses:* Required fees: $340 per quarter hour. *Financial support:* Unspecified assistantships available. Financial award application deadline: 5/1. *Faculty research:* Secondary education, student teaching, educational reform, evaluation procedures. *Unit head:* Dr. Robert Gable, Director, 401-598-4738, Fax: 401-598-1162, E-mail: rgable@jwu.edu. *Application contact:* Dr. Allan G. Freedman, Director of Graduate Admissions, 401-598-1015, Fax: 401-598-1286, E-mail: gradadm@jwu.edu.

Johnson & Wales University, The Alan Shawn Feinstein Graduate School, M Ed Program in Teaching and Learning, Providence, RI 02903-3703. Offers M Ed. Evening/weekend programs available. *Faculty:* 7 full-time (3 women), 3 part-time/adjunct (2 women). *Students:* 21 full-time (16 women); includes 1 minority (Hispanic American). Average age 40. 13 applicants, 100% accepted, 12 enrolled. In 2009, 9 master's awarded. *Entrance requirements:* For master's, bachelor's degree with minimum GPA of 2.75 from accredited institution of higher education, valid teaching license. *Expenses:* Required fees: $340 per quarter hour. *Unit head:* Dr. Frank Pontarelli, Dean, 401-598-1333, Fax: 401-598-1125. *Application contact:* Dr. Allan G. Freedman, Director of Graduate Admissions, 401-598-1015, Fax: 401-598-1286, E-mail: gradadm@jwu.edu.

Johnson Bible College, Teacher Education Program, Knoxville, TN 37998-1001. Offers Bible and educational technology (MA); holistic education (MA). Part-time programs available. *Degree requirements:* For master's, multimedia action research presentation. *Entrance requirements:* For master's, interview, minimum GPA of 3.0, portfolio, teaching license. Additional exam requirements/recommendations for international students: Required—TOEFL. *Faculty research:* Instructional technology.

Johnson State College, Graduate Program in Education, Johnson, VT 05656. Offers applied behavior analysis (MA Ed), including children's mental health; curriculum and instruction (MA Ed); gifted and talented (MA Ed); literacy (MA Ed); science education (MA Ed); secondary education (MA Ed, CAGS); special education (MA Ed). Part-time programs available. *Degree requirements:* For master's, comprehensive exam, thesis or alternative. *Entrance requirements:* For master's, interview. Additional exam requirements/recommendations for international students: Required—TOEFL. *Expenses:* Tuition, area resident: Part-time $416 per credit. Tuition, state resident: part-time $416 per credit. Tuition, nonresident: part-time $899 per credit.

Jones International University, Graduate School of Education, Centennial, CO 80112. Offers adult education (M Ed); corporate training and knowledge management (M Ed); curriculum and instruction (M Ed), including elementary teacher licensure, secondary teacher licensure; e-learning technology and design (M Ed); educational leadership and administration (M Ed); educational leadership and administration: principal and administrator licensure (M Ed); elementary curriculum instruction and assessment (M Ed); higher education leadership and administration (M Ed); K-12 instructional technology (M Ed); K-12 instructional technology: teacher licensure (M Ed); secondary curriculum instruction and assessment (M Ed); technology and design (M Ed). Part-time and evening/weekend programs available. Postbaccalaureate distance learning degree programs offered (no on-campus study). *Entrance requirements:* For master's, minimum cumulative GPA of 2.5. Additional exam requirements/recommendations for international students: Recommended—TOEFL (minimum score 550 paper-based; 213 computer-based). Electronic applications accepted.

Judson University, Graduate Programs, Elgin, IL 60123-1498. Offers architecture (M Arch); literacy (M Ed); organizational leadership (MA); teaching (M Ed). Part-time and evening/weekend programs available. Postbaccalaureate distance learning degree programs offered (no on-campus study). *Degree requirements:* For master's, comprehensive exam (for some programs), thesis. *Entrance requirements:* For master's, interviews.

Kansas State University, Graduate School, College of Education, Manhattan, KS 66506. Offers MS, Ed D, PhD. *Accreditation:* NCATE. Part-time and evening/weekend programs available. Postbaccalaureate distance learning degree programs offered. *Faculty:* 56 full-time (26 women), 34 part-time/adjunct (9 women). *Students:* 134 full-time (87 women), 487 part-time (373 women); includes 37 minority (19 African Americans, 1 American Indian/Alaska Native, 7 Asian Americans or Pacific Islanders, 10 Hispanic Americans), 7 international. Average age 38. 152 applicants, 95% accepted, 123 enrolled. In 2009, 121 master's, 23 doctorates awarded. Terminal master's awarded for partial completion of doctoral program. *Degree requirements:* For master's, thesis or alternative, oral or comprehensive exam; for doctorate, thesis/dissertation, residency. *Entrance requirements:* For master's and doctorate, GRE or MAT. Additional exam requirements/recommendations for international students: Required—GRE General Test or TOEFL. *Application deadline:* For fall admission, 2/1 priority date for domestic and international students; for spring admission, 8/1 priority date for domestic and international students. Applications are processed on a rolling basis. Application fee: $40 ($55 for international students). Electronic applications accepted. *Financial support:* In 2009–10, 2 research assistantships (averaging $14,735 per year), 7 teaching assistantships with full tuition reimbursements (averaging $13,145 per year) were awarded; career-related internships or fieldwork, Federal Work-Study, institutionally sponsored loans, and scholarships/grants also available. Support available to part-time students. Financial award application deadline: 3/1; financial award applicants required to submit FAFSA. *Faculty research:* Teacher preparation, program evaluation, science education, ESL-bilingual education, rural issues in education. Total annual research expenditures: $534,778. *Unit head:* Michael Holen, Dean, 785-532-5525, Fax: 785-532-7304, E-mail: mholen@ksu.edu. *Application contact:* Paul R. Burden, Assistant Dean, 785-532-5595, Fax: 785-532-7304, E-mail: burden@ksu.edu.

Education—General

Kaplan University, Davenport Campus, School of Teacher Education, Davenport, IA 52807-2095. Offers education (M Ed); secondary education (M Ed); teaching and learning (MA); teaching literacy and language: grades 6-12 (MA); teaching literacy and language: grades K-6 (MA); teaching mathematics: grades 6-8 (MA); teaching mathematics: grades 9-12 (MA); teaching mathematics: grades K-5 (MA); teaching science: grades 6-12 (MA); teaching science: grades K-6 (MA); teaching students with special needs (MA); teaching with technology (MA). Part-time and evening/weekend programs available. Postbaccalaureate distance learning degree programs offered (no on-campus study). *Entrance requirements:* Additional exam requirements/recommendations for international students: Required—TOEFL (minimum score 550 paper-based; 218 computer-based; 80 iBT).

Kean University, College of Education, Union, NJ 07083. Offers MA, MS. *Accreditation:* NCATE. Part-time programs available. *Faculty:* 67 full-time (45 women). *Students:* 233 full-time (204 women), 854 part-time (723 women); includes 276 minority (115 African Americans, 1 American Indian/Alaska Native, 34 Asian Americans or Pacific Islanders, 126 Hispanic Americans), 9 international. Average age 33. 690 applicants, 76% accepted, 336 enrolled. In 2009, 272 master's awarded. *Degree requirements:* For master's, comprehensive exam, thesis, practicum, portfolio, field experience. *Entrance requirements:* For master's, GRE General Test, MAT, PRAXIS, minimum GPA of 3.0, teaching certificate, letters of recommendation, interview, official transcripts from all institutions. *Application deadline:* For fall admission, 5/1 for domestic students; for spring admission, 11/1 for domestic students. Application fee: $60 ($150 for international students). Electronic applications accepted. *Expenses:* Tuition, state resident: full-time $10,440; part-time $435 per credit. Tuition, nonresident: full-time $14,160; part-time $590 per credit. Required fees: $2642; $110 per credit. Part-time tuition and fees vary according to course load and degree level. *Financial support:* In 2009–10, 19 research assistantships with full tuition reimbursements (averaging $3,263 per year) were awarded; unspecified assistantships also available. *Unit head:* Dr. Susan Polirstok, Dean, 908-737-3750, Fax: 908-737-3760, E-mail: fpolirsts@kean.edu. *Application contact:* Ann-Marie Kay, Assistant Director of Graduate Admissions, 908-737-4723, Fax: 908-737-5965, E-mail: grad-adm@kean.edu.

Keene State College, School of Professional and Graduate Studies, Keene, NH 03435. Offers curriculum and instruction (M Ed); education leadership (PMC); educational leadership (M Ed); school counselor (M Ed, PMC); special education (M Ed); teacher certification (Post-baccalaureate Certificate). *Accreditation:* NCATE. Part-time and evening/weekend programs available. *Faculty:* 21 full-time (13 women), 14 part-time/adjunct (13 women). *Students:* 8 full-time (5 women), 80 part-time (56 women); includes 1 Asian American or Pacific Islander, 1 Hispanic American, 1 international. Average age 34. 94 applicants, 80% accepted, 62 enrolled. In 2009, 55 master's, 10 other advanced degrees awarded. *Entrance requirements:* For master's, PRAXIS I, resume; minimum GPA of 2.5. Additional exam requirements/recommendations for international students: Required—TOEFL (minimum score 550 paper-based; 173 computer-based; 61 iBT). *Application deadline:* For fall admission, 4/1 for domestic students; for spring admission, 12/1 for domestic students. Application fee: $40. *Expenses:* Tuition, state resident: part-time $320 per credit. Tuition, nonresident: part-time $350 per credit. Required fees: $92 per credit. $10 per term. Tuition and fees vary according to course load. *Financial support:* Research assistantships, career-related internships or fieldwork, Federal Work-Study, institutionally sponsored loans, and unspecified assistantships available. Support available to part-time students. Financial award application deadline: 3/1; financial award applicants required to submit FAFSA. *Unit head:* Dr. Melinda Treadwell, Dean, 603-358-2220. *Application contact:* Peggy Richmond, Director of Admissions, 603-358-2276, Fax: 603-358-2767, E-mail: admissions@keene.edu.

Keiser University, Master of Science in Education Program, Fort Lauderdale, FL 33309. Offers college administration (MS); leadership (MS); teaching and learning (MS). Part-time programs available. Postbaccalaureate distance learning degree programs offered (no on-campus study). *Faculty:* 2 full-time (both women), 3 part-time/adjunct (2 women). *Students:* 9 full-time (7 women), 13 part-time (11 women); includes 17 minority (14 African Americans, 1 American Indian/Alaska Native, 2 Hispanic Americans). Average age 35. 16 applicants, 88% accepted, 11 enrolled. *Entrance requirements:* For master's, minimum GPA of 2.7 from an accredited institution. Additional exam requirements/recommendations for international students: Required—TOEFL. *Application deadline:* Applications are processed on a rolling basis. Application fee: $50. Electronic applications accepted. *Financial support:* In 2009–10, 10 students received support. Federal Work-Study available. Financial award applicants required to submit FAFSA. *Unit head:* Dr. Sara Malmstrom, Dean, Graduate School, 954-318-1620. *Application contact:* Manuel Christiansen, Associate Director of Admissions, 954-318-1620 Ext. 309, E-mail: mchristiansen@keiseruniversity.edu.

Kennesaw State University, Leland and Clarice C. Bagwell College of Education, Kennesaw, GA 30144-5591. Offers M Ed, MAT, Ed D, Ed S. *Accreditation:* NCATE. Part-time programs available. *Students:* 266 full-time (215 women), 207 part-time (157 women); includes 82 minority (55 African Americans, 1 American Indian/Alaska Native, 7 Asian Americans or Pacific Islanders, 19 Hispanic Americans), 6 international. Average age 34. 113 applicants, 83% accepted, 69 enrolled. In 2009, 282 master's, 14 other advanced degrees awarded. *Degree requirements:* For master's, thesis or alternative. *Entrance requirements:* For master's, GRE General Test, minimum GPA of 2.75, renewable teaching certificate. Additional exam requirements/recommendations for international students: Required—TOEFL (minimum score 550 paper-based; 213 computer-based; 80 iBT), IELTS (minimum score 6). *Application deadline:* For fall admission, 7/1 for domestic and international students; for spring admission, 10/1 for domestic and international students. Application fee: $60. Electronic applications accepted. *Expenses:* Tuition, state resident: full-time $2341; part-time $196 per credit hour. Tuition, nonresident: full-time $9396; part-time $783 per credit hour. Required fees: $573 per semester. *Financial support:* Federal Work-Study available. Support available to part-time students. Financial award application deadline: 6/15; financial award applicants required to submit FAFSA. *Unit head:* Dr. Arlinda Eaton, Dean, 770-423-6117, Fax: 770-423-6567. *Application contact:* Alisha Bello, Administrative Coordinator, 770-423-6043, Fax: 770-420-4435, E-mail: abello2@kennesaw.edu.

Kent State University, Graduate School of Education, Health, and Human Services, Kent, OH 44242-0001. Offers M Ed, MA, MAT, MPH, MS, Au D, PhD, Ed S. *Accreditation:* NCATE. Part-time and evening/weekend programs available. Postbaccalaureate distance learning degree programs offered. *Faculty:* 235 full-time (148 women), 166 part-time/adjunct (120 women). *Students:* 896 full-time (711 women), 806 part-time (638 women); includes 200 minority (145 African Americans, 1 American Indian/Alaska Native, 31 Asian Americans or Pacific Islanders, 23 Hispanic Americans), 29 international. 1,138 applicants, 45% accepted. In 2009, 534 master's, 35 doctorates, 28 other advanced degrees awarded. *Degree requirements:* For master's, thesis (for some programs); for doctorate, comprehensive exam, thesis/dissertation. *Entrance requirements:* For doctorate and Ed S, GRE General Test. Additional exam requirements/recommendations for international students: Required—TOEFL (minimum score 525 paper-based; 197 computer-based). *Application deadline:* Applications are processed on a rolling basis. Application fee: $30 ($60 for international students). Electronic applications accepted. *Financial support:* In 2009–10, 28 fellowships with full tuition reimbursements (averaging $11,889 per year), 85 research assistantships with full tuition reimbursements (averaging $8,429 per year), 26 teaching assistantships with full tuition reimbursements (averaging $11,889 per year) were awarded; Federal Work-Study, scholarships/grants, and unspecified assistantships also available. Financial award application deadline: 4/1; financial award applicants required to submit FAFSA. *Unit head:* Dr. Daniel Mahony, Dean, 330-672-2202, Fax: 330-672-3407, E-mail: dmahony@kent.edu. *Application contact:* Nancy Miller, Academic Program Coordinator, Office of Graduate Student Services, 330-672-2576, Fax: 330-672-9162, E-mail: nmiller1@kent.edu.

Kutztown University of Pennsylvania, College of Education, Kutztown, PA 19530-0730. Offers M Ed, MA, MLS, Certificate. *Accreditation:* NCATE. Part-time and evening/weekend programs available. *Faculty:* 33 full-time (21 women), 2 part-time/adjunct (both women). *Students:* 214 full-time (144 women), 395 part-time (319 women); includes 28 minority (13 African Americans, 1 American Indian/Alaska Native, 3 Asian Americans or Pacific Islanders, 11 Hispanic Americans), 4 international. Average age 29. 380 applicants, 75% accepted, 97 enrolled. In 2009, 130 master's awarded. *Degree requirements:* For master's, comprehensive exam. *Entrance requirements:* For master's, GRE. Additional exam requirements/recommendations for international students: Required—TOEFL. *Application deadline:* For fall admission, 8/15 priority date for domestic and international students; for spring admission, 12/15 priority date for domestic and international students. Applications are processed on a rolling basis. Application fee: $35. Electronic applications accepted. *Expenses:* Tuition, state resident: full-time $6666; part-time $370 per credit. Tuition, nonresident: full-time $10,666; part-time $593 per credit. Required fees: $62 per credit. $60 per semester. *Financial support:* Career-related internships or fieldwork, Federal Work-Study, scholarships/grants, and unspecified assistantships available. Financial award application deadline: 3/1; financial award applicants required to submit FAFSA. *Unit head:* Dr. Darrell Garber, Dean, 610-683-4253, Fax: 610-683-4255, E-mail: garber@kutztown.edu. *Application contact:* Kelly D. Burr, Associate Director, Graduate Admissions, 610-683-4200, Fax: 610-683-1393, E-mail: graduate@kutztown.edu.

LaGrange College, Graduate Programs, Department of Education, LaGrange, GA 30240-2999. Offers curriculum and instruction (M Ed); middle grades (MAT); secondary education (MAT). Part-time and evening/weekend programs available. *Degree requirements:* For master's, comprehensive exam. *Entrance requirements:* For master's, GRE, MAT, minimum GPA of 2.5. Additional exam requirements/recommendations for international students: Required—TOEFL (minimum score 550 paper-based).

Lake Erie College, Division of Education, Painesville, OH 44077-3389. Offers curriculum and instruction (MS Ed); education (MS Ed); educational leadership (MS Ed); reading (MS Ed). Part-time and evening/weekend programs available. *Degree requirements:* For master's, comprehensive exam (for some programs), thesis optional, applied research project. *Entrance requirements:* For master's, GRE General Test or minimum GPA of 3.0. Additional exam requirements/recommendations for international students: Required—TOEFL (minimum score 590 paper-based). Electronic applications accepted. *Expenses:* Contact institution. *Faculty research:* Cooperative learning, portfolio assessment, education systems abroad, Web-based instruction.

Lakehead University, Graduate Studies, Faculty of Education, Thunder Bay, ON P7B 5E1, Canada. Offers educational studies (PhD); gerontology (M Ed); women's studies (M Ed). Part-time and evening/weekend programs available. *Degree requirements:* For master's, project or thesis. *Entrance requirements:* For master's, minimum B average. Additional exam requirements/recommendations for international students: Required—TOEFL. *Faculty research:* Art education, AIDS education, language arts education, gerontology, women's studies.

Lakeland College, Graduate Studies Division, Program in Education, Sheboygan, WI 53082-0359. Offers M Ed. *Accreditation:* Teacher Education Accreditation Council. *Degree requirements:* For master's, thesis. *Expenses:* Contact institution.

Lamar University, College of Graduate Studies, College of Education and Human Development, Beaumont, TX 77710. Offers M Ed, MS, DE, Ed D, Certificate. *Accreditation:* NCATE. Part-time and evening/weekend programs available. Postbaccalaureate distance learning degree programs offered. *Faculty:* 36 full-time (25 women), 8 part-time/adjunct (3 women). *Students:* 58 full-time (37 women), 3,343 part-time (2,439 women); includes 956 minority (412 African Americans, 24 American Indian/Alaska Native, 45 Asian Americans or Pacific Islanders, 475 Hispanic Americans), 11 international. Average age 39. 2,998 applicants, 74% accepted, 406 enrolled. In 2009, 230 master's, 21 doctorates awarded. *Degree requirements:* For master's, comprehensive exam, thesis optional; for doctorate, comprehensive exam, thesis/dissertation. *Entrance requirements:* For master's, GRE General Test, minimum GPA of 2.5; for doctorate, GRE, interview. Additional exam requirements/recommendations for international students: Required—TOEFL. *Application deadline:* For fall admission, 8/1 for domestic students; for spring admission, 12/1 for domestic students. Applications are processed on a rolling basis. Application fee: $25 ($50 for international students). *Financial support:* Fellowships, research assistantships, teaching assistantships, career-related internships or fieldwork, Federal Work-Study, institutionally sponsored loans, and scholarships/grants available. Support available to part-time students. Financial award application deadline: 4/1. *Faculty research:* School dropouts, suicide prevention in public school students, school climate and gifted performance, teacher evaluation. *Unit head:* Dr. H. Lowery-Moore, Dean, 409-880-8661. *Application contact:* Dr. Lula Henry, Director of Professional Service, 409-880-8218.

Lander University, School of Education, Greenwood, SC 29649-2099. Offers elementary education (M Ed); teaching (MAT). *Accreditation:* NCATE. Part-time programs available. *Degree requirements:* For master's, comprehensive exam, thesis or alternative. *Entrance requirements:* For master's, GRE General Test. Additional exam requirements/recommendations for international students: Required—TOEFL (minimum score 550 paper-based; 213 computer-based). Electronic applications accepted.

Langston University, School of Education and Behavioral Sciences, Langston, OK 73050. Offers bilingual/multicultural (M Ed); elementary education (M Ed); English as a second language (M Ed); rehabilitation counseling (M Sc); urban education (M Ed). *Accreditation:* CORE; NCATE (one or more programs are accredited). Part-time programs available. *Degree requirements:* For master's, comprehensive exam, thesis optional. *Entrance requirements:* For master's, GRE, writing skills test, minimum GPA of 2.5, 3 letters of recommendation. Additional exam requirements/recommendations for international students: Required—TOEFL, TWE. *Faculty research:* Bilingual/multicultural education, financing post-secondary education.

La Salle University, School of Arts and Sciences, Program in Education, Philadelphia, PA 19141-1199. Offers MA. Part-time and evening/weekend programs available. *Degree requirements:* For master's, comprehensive exam. *Entrance requirements:* For master's, MAT. *Expenses:* Contact institution. *Faculty research:* Educational reform and social realities, adult development, curriculum design for special needs children, developmentally-based schooling.

La Sierra University, School of Education, Riverside, CA 92515. Offers MA, MAT, Ed D, Ed S. Part-time and evening/weekend programs available. Terminal master's awarded for partial completion of doctoral program. *Degree requirements:* For doctorate, thesis/dissertation; for Ed S, thesis optional. *Entrance requirements:* For master's, minimum GPA of 3.0; for doctorate, GRE General Test, GRE Subject Test, minimum GPA of 3.3; for Ed S, minimum GPA of 3.3.

Lee University, Program in Education, Cleveland, TN 37320-3450. Offers classroom teaching (M Ed, Ed S); educational leadership (M Ed, Ed S); elementary/secondary education (MAT); secondary education (MAT); special education (elementary) (M Ed); special education (secondary) (M Ed, MAT); special education (severe disabilities) (M Ed). Part-time programs available. *Faculty:* 11 full-time (4 women), 3 part-time/adjunct (2 women). *Students:* 65 full-time (45 women), 140 part-time (80 women); includes 8 minority (5 African Americans, 1 American Indian/Alaska Native, 2 Hispanic Americans), 6 international. Average age 31. 4 applicants, 100% accepted, 2 enrolled. In 2009, 75 master's, 7 other advanced degrees awarded. *Degree requirements:* For master's, variable foreign language requirement, comprehensive exam, thesis, internship. *Entrance requirements:* For master's, MAT or GRE General Test, minimum GPA of 2.75, 3 letters of recommendation, interview, writing sample. Additional exam requirements/recommendations for international students: Required—TOEFL (minimum score 450 paper-based; 45 computer-based). *Application deadline:* For fall admission, 4/1 priority date for domestic students; for spring admission, 10/1 priority date for domestic students. Applications are processed on a rolling basis. Application fee: $25. *Expenses:* Tuition: Full-time $11,100; part-time $463 per credit. Required fees: $305. *Financial support:* Career-related internships or fieldwork, Federal Work-Study, institutionally sponsored loans, scholarships/grants, and unspecified assistantships available. Financial award application deadline: 3/1; financial award applicants required to submit FAFSA. *Unit head:* Dr. Gary Riggins, Director, 423-614-8193. *Application contact:* Vicki Glasscock, Graduate Admissions Director, 423-614-8059, E-mail: vglasscock@leeuniversity.edu.

Lehigh University, College of Education, Bethlehem, PA 18015. Offers M Ed, MA, MS, Ed D, PhD, Certificate, Ed S, Graduate Certificate, MBA/M Ed. Part-time and evening/weekend programs available. Postbaccalaureate distance learning degree programs offered (minimal on-campus study). *Faculty:* 32 full-time (19 women), 45 part-time/adjunct (25 women). *Students:* 158 full-time (126 women), 393 part-time (285 women); includes 46 minority (22 African Americans, 1 American Indian/Alaska Native, 12 Asian Americans or Pacific Islanders, 11 Hispanic Americans), 43 international. Average age 32. 525 applicants, 44% accepted, 130 enrolled. In 2009, 171 master's, 15 doctorates awarded. Terminal master's awarded for partial completion of doctoral program. *Degree requirements:* For master's, thesis (for some programs), internship; for doctorate, comprehensive exam, thesis/dissertation, internship. *Entrance requirements:* Additional exam requirements/recommendations for international students: Required—TOEFL (minimum score 600 paper-based; 250 computer-based; 93 iBT). *Application deadline:* For fall admission, 1/1 for domestic and international students; for spring admission, 11/1 for domestic and international students. Applications are processed on a rolling basis. Application fee: $65. Electronic applications accepted. *Expenses:* Contact institution. *Financial support:* In 2009–10, 112 students received support, including 4 fellowships with full and partial tuition reimbursements available (averaging $20,000 per year), 39 research assistantships with full and partial tuition reimbursements available (averaging $14,700 per year); teaching assistantships with full and partial tuition reimbursements available, career-related internships or fieldwork, Federal Work-Study, institutionally sponsored loans, scholarships/grants, tuition waivers (full and partial), and unspecified assistantships also available. Financial award application deadline: 3/1; financial award applicants required to submit FAFSA. *Unit head:* Dr. Gary M. Sasso, Dean, 610-758-3221, Fax: 610-758-6223, E-mail: gary.sasso@lehigh.edu. *Application contact:* Donna M. Johnson, Coordinator, 610-758-3231, Fax: 610-758-6223, E-mail: dmj4@lehigh.edu.

Lehman College of the City University of New York, Division of Education, Bronx, NY 10468-1589. Offers MA, MS Ed. *Accreditation:* NCATE. Part-time and evening/weekend programs available.

Le Moyne College, Department of Education, Syracuse, NY 13214. Offers adolescent education (MS Ed, MST); adolescent education/special education (MS Ed, MST); adolescent English (grades 7-12) (MST); adolescent history (grades 7-12) (MST); childhood education (MS Ed); childhood education/special education (MS Ed); elementary education (MS Ed); general professional education (MS Ed); inclusive childhood education (MST); middle child specialist/special education (MS Ed); middle childhood specialist (MS Ed); school building leadership (MS Ed, CAS); school district business leader (MS Ed, CAS); school district leadership (MS Ed, CAS); secondary education (MS Ed); special education (MS Ed). *Accreditation:* Teacher Education Accreditation Council. Part-time and evening/weekend programs available. *Faculty:* 15 full-time (8 women), 61 part-time/adjunct (33 women). *Students:* 40 full-time (30 women), 260 part-time (180 women); includes 25 minority (11 African Americans, 3 American Indian/Alaska Native, 3 Asian Americans or Pacific Islanders, 8 Hispanic Americans). Average age 31. 168 applicants, 89% accepted, 140 enrolled. In 2009, 180 master's awarded. *Degree requirements:* For master's, thesis. *Entrance requirements:* For master's, GRE General Test, 2 letters of recommendation. Additional exam requirements/recommendations for international students: Required—TOEFL (minimum score 550 paper-based; 213 computer-based; 79 iBT). *Application deadline:* For fall admission, 4/1 priority date for domestic and international students; for spring admission, 10/1 priority date for domestic and international students. Applications are processed on a rolling basis. Application fee: $50. *Expenses:* Contact institution. *Financial support:* In 2009–10, 28 students received support. Career-related internships or fieldwork and health care benefits available. Support available to part-time students. Financial award applicants required to submit FAFSA. *Faculty research:* Recruitment/retention strategies, minority teachers, special education, multiculturalism, literacy, technology, video games learning, autism, school district organization. *Unit head:* Dr. Norbert J. Henry, Interim Chair/Director, 315-445-4376, Fax: 315-445-4744, E-mail: henry@lemoyne.edu. *Application contact:* Kristen P. Trapasso, Director of Graduate Admission, 315-445-4265, Fax: 315-445-6027, E-mail: trapaskp@lemoyne.edu.

Lenoir-Rhyne University, Graduate Programs, School of Education, Hickory, NC 28601. Offers MA. *Accreditation:* NCATE. Part-time and evening/weekend programs available. *Degree requirements:* For master's, comprehensive exam, thesis optional. *Entrance requirements:* For master's, GRE General Test or MAT, minimum undergraduate GPA of 2.7, graduate 3.0. Additional exam requirements/recommendations for international students: Required—TOEFL (minimum score 600 paper-based). Electronic applications accepted.

Lesley University, School of Education, Cambridge, MA 02138-2790. Offers curriculum and instruction (M Ed, CAGS); early childhood education (M Ed); educational studies (PhD); elementary education (M Ed); individually designed (M Ed); middle school education (M Ed); moderate special needs (M Ed); reading (M Ed, CAGS); science in education (M Ed); severe special needs (M Ed); special needs (CAGS); technology in education (M Ed, CAGS). *Accreditation:* Teacher Education Accreditation Council. Part-time and evening/weekend programs available. Postbaccalaureate distance learning degree programs offered (no on-campus study). *Degree requirements:* For master's, practicum; for doctorate, thesis/dissertation. *Entrance requirements:* For doctorate, GRE General Test or MAT, interview, master's degree, resume; for CAGS, interview, master's degree. Additional exam requirements/recommendations for international students: Required—TOEFL (minimum score 550 paper-based; 213 computer-based; 80 iBT). Electronic applications accepted. *Faculty research:* Assessment in literacy, mathematics and science; autism spectrum disorders; instructional technology and online learning; multicultural education and ELL.

LeTourneau University, School of Graduate and Professional Studies, Longview, TX 75607-7001. Offers business administration (MBA); curriculum and instruction (M Ed); educational administration (M Ed); strategic leadership (MSL); teaching and learning (M Ed). Part-time and evening/weekend programs available. Postbaccalaureate distance learning degree programs offered (no on-campus study). *Faculty:* 8 full-time (1 woman), 19 part-time/adjunct (7 women). *Students:* 43 full-time (30 women), 245 part-time (164 women); includes 158 minority (130 African Americans, 2 American Indian/Alaska Native, 2 Asian Americans or Pacific Islanders, 24 Hispanic Americans). Average age 36. 1,717 applicants, 31% accepted, 288 enrolled. *Entrance requirements:* For master's, minimum GPA of 2.8. Additional exam requirements/recommendations for international students: Required—TOEFL. *Application deadline:* Applications are processed on a rolling basis. Electronic applications accepted. *Expenses:* Tuition: Full-time $10,710; part-time $595 per credit hour. *Financial support:* Applicants required to submit FAFSA. *Unit head:* Dr. Carol Green, Vice President, 903-233-3250, Fax: 903-233-3227, E-mail: carolgreen@letu.edu. *Application contact:* Chris Fontaine, Assistant Vice President for Enrollment Management and Market Research, 903-233-3250, Fax: 903-233-3227, E-mail: chrisfontaine@letu.edu.

Lewis & Clark College, Graduate School of Education and Counseling, Department of Teacher Education, Inservice Program, Portland, OR 97219-7899. Offers MAT. Part-time and evening/weekend programs available. *Entrance requirements:* Additional exam requirements/recommendations for international students: Required—TOEFL (minimum score 575 paper-based; 232 computer-based; 91 iBT). Electronic applications accepted. *Expenses:* Tuition: Part-time $713 per semester hour. Tuition and fees vary according to course level and campus/location.

Lewis University, College of Education, Romeoville, IL 60446. Offers advanced study in education (CAS), including general administrative, superintendent endorsement; curriculum and instruction: instructional technology (M Ed); curriculum and teacher leadership (M Ed); educational leadership (M Ed, MA); educational leadership for teaching and learning (Ed D); elementary education (MA); English as a second language (M Ed); instructional technology (M Ed); reading and literacy (M Ed, MA); secondary education (MA), including biology, chemistry, English, history, math, physics, psychology and social science; special education (MA). *Accreditation:* NCATE. Part-time and evening/weekend programs available. *Faculty:* 24 full-time (15 women), 47 part-time/adjunct (26 women). *Students:* 105 full-time (75 women), 333 part-time (264 women); includes 58 minority (35 African Americans, 6 Asian Americans or Pacific Islanders, 17 Hispanic Americans), 2 international. Average age 32. In 2009, 133 master's awarded. *Degree requirements:* For master's, thesis optional; for doctorate, thesis/dissertation. *Entrance requirements:* For master's, departmental qualifying exam, writing exam, minimum GPA of 2.75, 3 letters of recommendation, interview. Additional exam requirements/recommendations for international students: Required—TOEFL (minimum score 550 paper-based; 213 computer-based). *Application deadline:* For fall admission, 5/1 priority date for international students; for spring admission, 11/15 priority date for international students. Applications are processed on a rolling basis. Application fee: $40. Electronic applications accepted. *Expenses:* Tuition: Full-time $6480; part-time $720 per credit. One-time fee: $40. Tuition and fees vary according to course load, degree level and program. *Financial support:* Federal Work-Study, scholarships/grants, tuition waivers (partial), and unspecified assistantships available. Financial award application deadline: 5/1; financial award applicants required to submit FAFSA. *Unit head:* Dr. Jeanette Mines, Dean, 815-838-0500 Ext. 5316, Fax: 815-836-5879, E-mail: minesje@lewisu.edu. *Application contact:* Julie Nickel, Assistant Director, Graduate and Adult Admission, 815-838-0500 Ext. 5610, E-mail: grad@lewisu.edu.

Liberty University, School of Education, Lynchburg, VA 24502. Offers administration and supervision (M Ed); curriculum and instruction (M Ed); early childhood education (M Ed); education specialist (Ed S); educational leadership (Ed D); elementary education (M Ed); gifted education (M Ed); reading specialist (M Ed); school counseling (M Ed); secondary education (M Ed); special education (M Ed). *Accreditation:* NCATE. Part-time programs available. Postbaccalaureate distance learning degree programs offered (minimal on-campus study). *Degree requirements:* For doctorate, comprehensive exam, thesis/dissertation. *Entrance requirements:* For master's, GRE General Test or MAT (aken in or before 1999), 2 letters of recommendation, minimum undergraduate GPA of 3.0, curriculum vitae; for doctorate, GRE General Test or MAT (if taken before 1999), minimum master's GPA of 3.0, 3 years of teacher experience; for Ed S, GRE General Test or MAT (if taken before 1999), minimum master's GPA of 3.0, 3 years of teaching experience. Additional exam requirements/recommendations for international students: Required—TOEFL (minimum score 600 paper-based; 250 computer-based). Electronic applications accepted. *Expenses:* Contact institution. *Faculty research:* Self-determination, character education, bibliotherapy, learning styles, distance education.

Lincoln Memorial University, Carter and Moyers School of Education, Harrogate, TN 37752-1901. Offers administration and supervision (M Ed, Ed S); counseling and guidance (M Ed); curriculum and instruction (M Ed, Ed S); English (M Ed). Part-time and evening/weekend programs available. Postbaccalaureate distance learning degree programs offered. *Faculty:* 31 full-time (13 women), 22 part-time/adjunct (11 women). *Students:* 190 full-time (151 women), 1,299 part-time (959 women); includes 144 minority (128 African Americans, 1 American Indian/Alaska Native, 5 Asian Americans or Pacific Islanders, 10 Hispanic Americans), 4 international. 1,562 applicants, 96% accepted, 1489 enrolled. In 2009, 173 master's, 901 Ed Ss awarded. *Degree requirements:* For master's, comprehensive exam, thesis optional; for Ed S, comprehensive exam. *Entrance requirements:* For master's, PRAXIS, NTE, GRE, MAT, letters of recommendation; for Ed S, graduate transcripts. *Application deadline:* For fall admission, 8/10 for domestic and international students; for spring admission, 1/10 for domestic and international students. Application fee: $25. *Expenses:* Tuition: Full-time $11,700; part-time $390 per hour. *Financial support:* In 2009–10, 973 students received support. Career-related internships or fieldwork, health care benefits, and unspecified assistantships available. Support available to part-time students. Financial award application deadline: 4/1; financial award applicants required to submit FAFSA. *Faculty research:* Brain compatible teaching and learning; poverty in Appalachia; leadership for change; ethics, moral responsibility and social justice; human and organizational learning. *Unit head:* Dr. David Hand, Dean, 423-869-6259, Fax: 423-869-6261, E-mail: david.hand@lmunet.edu. *Application contact:* Terri Knuckles, Office Manager, Graduate Education, 423-869-6223, Fax: 423-869-6261, E-mail: terri.knuckles@lmunet.edu.

Lindenwood University, Graduate Programs, School of Education, St. Charles, MO 63301-1695. Offers education (MA); educational administration (MA, Ed D, Ed S); instructional leadership (Ed D, Ed S); library media (MA); professional and school counseling (MA); professional counseling (MA); school administration (Ed S); school counseling (MA); teaching (MA). Part-time and evening/weekend programs available. *Faculty:* 33 full-time (13 women), 176 part-time/adjunct (83 women). *Students:* 558 full-time (415 women), 1,957 part-time (1,516 women); includes 580 minority (549 African Americans, 6 American Indian/Alaska Native, 16 Asian Americans or Pacific Islanders, 9 Hispanic Americans), 13 international. Average age 35. 248 applicants, 120 enrolled. In 2009, 730 master's, 62 doctorates, 67 other advanced degrees awarded. *Degree requirements:* For master's, thesis (for some programs); for doctorate, thesis/dissertation, minimum GPA of 3.0; for Ed S, comprehensive exam, specialist project, minimum GPA of 3.0. *Entrance requirements:* For master's, interview, minimum GPA of 3.0, writing sample, letter of recommendation; for doctorate, GRE, minimum graduate GPA of 3.4, resume, interview, writing sample, 4 letters of recommendation; for Ed S, master's degree in education, relevant work experience. Additional exam requirements/recommendations for international students: Required—TOEFL (minimum score 550 paper-based; 213 computer-based; 80 iBT). *Application deadline:* For fall admission, 8/27 priority date for domestic and international students; for spring admission, 1/28 priority date for domestic and international students. Applications are processed on a rolling basis. Application fee: $30 ($100 for international students). Electronic applications accepted. *Expenses:* Tuition: Full-time $12,960; part-time $370 per credit hour. Required fees: $340. One-time fee: $30 full-time. Tuition and fees vary according to course level and course load. *Financial support:* In 2009–10, 1,591 students received support. Career-related internships or fieldwork, institutionally sponsored loans, tuition waivers (partial), and unspecified assistantships available. Financial award application deadline: 6/30; financial award applicants required to submit FAFSA. *Unit head:* Dr. Cynthia Bice, Dean, 636-949-4618, Fax: 636-949-4197, E-mail: cbice@lindenwood.edu. *Application contact:* Brett Barger, Dean of Evening Admissions and Extension Campuses, 636-949-4934, Fax: 636-949-4109, E-mail: adultadmissions@lindenwood.edu.

Lipscomb University, Program in Education, Nashville, TN 37204-3951. Offers English language learners (MAT); instructional leadership (M Ed); instructional technology (M Ed); learning and teaching (MALT); math specialty (M Ed); school administration and supervision (M Ed); special education instruction, K-12 (MASE). *Accreditation:* NCATE. Part-time and evening/weekend programs available. *Faculty:* 4 full-time (1 woman), 12 part-time/adjunct (8 women). *Students:* 140 full-time (103 women), 200 part-time (144 women); includes 32 minority (29 African Americans, 3 Hispanic Americans). Average age 31. 206 applicants, 75% accepted. In 2009, 131 master's awarded. *Entrance requirements:* For master's, MAT or GRE General Test, 2 reference letters. Additional exam requirements/recommendations for international students: Required—TOEFL (minimum score 570 paper-based; 230 computer-based). *Application deadline:* For fall admission, 8/29 priority date for domestic students; for spring admission, 1/16 priority date for domestic students. Applications are processed on a rolling basis. Application fee: $50. *Expenses:* Tuition: Full-time $16,002; part-time $889 per credit hour. Tuition and fees vary according to program. *Financial support:* In 2009–10, 67 students received support. Federal Work-Study, tuition waivers (full), and unspecified assistantships available. Support available to part-time students. Financial award applicants required to submit FAFSA. *Faculty research:* Facilitative learning styles, leadership, student assessment, interactive multimedia inclusion. *Unit head:* Dr. Deborah Boyd, Director of M Ed Program, 615-966-6263. *Application contact:* Kristin Green, Administrative Assistant, 615-966-7628 Ext. 6081, Fax: 615-966-7628, E-mail: kristin.green@lipscomb.edu.

Lock Haven University of Pennsylvania, Department of Education, Lock Haven, PA 17745-2390. Offers alternative education (M Ed); teaching and learning (M Ed). *Accreditation:* NCATE. Part-time and evening/weekend programs available. Postbaccalaureate distance learning degree programs offered. *Degree requirements:* For master's, thesis. *Entrance requirements:* For master's, minimum undergraduate GPA of 3.0. Additional exam requirements/recommendations for international students: Required—TOEFL. Electronic applications accepted. *Expenses:* Tuition, state resident: full-time $6666; part-time $370 per credit hour. Tuition, nonresident:

Education—General

Lock Haven University of Pennsylvania (continued)
full-time $10,666; part-time $593 per credit hour. Required fees: $1988; $112 per credit hour. One-time fee: $25. Tuition and fees vary according to course load, campus/location and program.

Long Island University at Riverhead, Education Division, Riverhead, NY 11901. Offers applied behavior analysis (Advanced Certificate); childhood education (MS Ed), including childhood education, elementary education; literacy education (MS Ed); teaching students with disabilities (MS Ed). *Accreditation:* Teacher Education Accreditation Council. Part-time and evening/weekend programs available. *Faculty:* 1 full-time (0 women), 11 part-time/adjunct (7 women). *Students:* 29 full-time (25 women), 90 part-time (82 women). Average age 30. 48 applicants, 69% accepted, 33 enrolled. In 2009, 38 master's awarded. *Degree requirements:* For master's, thesis (for some programs); for Advanced Certificate, comprehensive exam (for some programs). *Entrance requirements:* For master's, minimum GPA of 2.75, writing sample, letter of reference, interview, official college transcripts. Additional exam requirements/recommendations for international students: Required—TOEFL (minimum score 550 paper-based; 250 computer-based). *Application deadline:* Applications are processed on a rolling basis. Electronic applications accepted. *Financial support:* In 2009–10, 105 students received support. Scholarships/grants and tuition waivers (partial) available. Support available to part-time students. Financial award applicants required to submit FAFSA. *Unit head:* Dr. R. Lawrence McCann, Director, 631-287-8211, E-mail: admissions@southampton.liu.edu. *Application contact:* Andrea Borra, Director of Graduate Admissions and Program Administration, 631-287-8010 Ext. 8326, Fax: 631-287-8253, E-mail: andrea.borra@liu.edu.

Long Island University, Brentwood Campus, School of Education, Brentwood, NY 11717. Offers childhood education (MS); early childhood education (MS); literacy (MS); mental health counseling (MS); school counseling (MS); special education (MS). Part-time and evening/weekend programs available.

Long Island University, Brooklyn Campus, School of Education, Brooklyn, NY 11201-8423. Offers MS, MS Ed, Certificate. *Accreditation:* Teacher Education Accreditation Council. Part-time and evening/weekend programs available. *Degree requirements:* For master's, thesis optional. *Entrance requirements:* For master's, 2 letters of recommendation. Additional exam requirements/recommendations for international students: Required—TOEFL (minimum score 500 paper-based; 173 computer-based). Electronic applications accepted.

Long Island University, C.W. Post Campus, School of Education, Brookville, NY 11548-1300. Offers MA, MS, MS Ed, Ed D, AC. *Accreditation:* Teacher Education Accreditation Council. Part-time and evening/weekend programs available. *Degree requirements:* For AC, internship. Electronic applications accepted.

Long Island University, Westchester Graduate Campus, Programs in Education-Teaching, Purchase, NY 10577. Offers early childhood education (MS Ed, Advanced Certificate); elementary education (MS Ed, Advanced Certificate); literacy education (MS Ed, Advanced Certificate); second language, TESOL, bilingual education (MS Ed, Advanced Certificate); special education and secondary education (MS Ed, Advanced Certificate). *Accreditation:* Teacher Education Accreditation Council. Part-time and evening/weekend programs available. *Degree requirements:* For master's, comprehensive exam.

Longwood University, Office of Graduate Studies, College of Education and Human Services, Farmville, VA 23909. Offers communication sciences and disorders (MS); community and college counseling (MS); curriculum and instruction specialist-elementary (MS), including mild disabilities, modern languages; curriculum and instruction specialist-secondary (MS), including English, mild disabilities, modern languages; educational leadership (MS); guidance and counseling (MS); literacy and culture (MS); school library media (MS). *Accreditation:* NCATE. Part-time and evening/weekend programs available. *Degree requirements:* For master's, comprehensive exam, thesis optional. *Entrance requirements:* For master's, GRE (communication sciences and disorders), minimum GPA of 2.75. Additional exam requirements/recommendations for international students: Required—TOEFL (minimum score 550 paper-based; 213 computer-based).

Louisiana State University and Agricultural and Mechanical College, Graduate School, College of Education, Baton Rouge, LA 70803. Offers M Ed, MA, MS, PhD, Ed S. *Accreditation:* NCATE. Part-time and evening/weekend programs available. *Students:* 239 full-time (166 women), 190 part-time (140 women); includes 88 minority (74 African Americans, 5 Asian Americans or Pacific Islanders, 9 Hispanic Americans), 19 international. Average age 31. 202 applicants, 61% accepted, 86 enrolled. In 2009, 158 master's, 20 doctorates, 15 other advanced degrees awarded. Terminal master's awarded for partial completion of doctoral program. *Degree requirements:* For doctorate, thesis/dissertation; for Ed S, thesis optional. *Entrance requirements:* For master's and doctorate, GRE General Test, minimum GPA of 3.0. Additional exam requirements/recommendations for international students: Required—TOEFL (minimum score 550 paper-based; 213 computer-based; 79 iBT) or IELTS (minimum score 6.5). *Application deadline:* For fall admission, 1/25 priority date for domestic students, 5/15 for international students; for spring admission, 10/15 for international students. Applications are processed on a rolling basis. Application fee: $50 ($70 for international students). Electronic applications accepted. *Financial support:* In 2009–10, 251 students received support, including 6 fellowships (averaging $23,435 per year), 27 research assistantships with partial tuition reimbursements available (averaging $10,143 per year), 56 teaching assistantships with partial tuition reimbursements available (averaging $11,637 per year); career-related internships or fieldwork, Federal Work-Study, institutionally sponsored loans, health care benefits, tuition waivers (partial), and unspecified assistantships also available. Support available to part-time students. Financial award applicants required to submit FAFSA. *Faculty research:* Instructional learning, educational administration, exercise physiology, sports psychology, literacy education curriculum and instruction. Total annual research expenditures: $22.1 million. *Unit head:* Dr. Jayne Fleener, Dean, 225-578-1258, Fax: 225-578-2267, E-mail: fleener@lsu.edu. *Application contact:* Dr. Patricia Exner, Associate Dean, 225-578-2208, Fax: 225-578-2267, E-mail: pexner@lsu.edu.

Louisiana State University in Shreveport, College of Education and Human Development, Program in Education, Shreveport, LA 71115-2399. Offers education (M Ed); education curriculum and instruction (M Ed); educational leadership (M Ed). Part-time programs available. *Students:* 3 full-time (all women), 43 part-time (32 women); includes 4 minority (all African Americans), 2 international. Average age 35. 22 applicants, 95% accepted, 10 enrolled. In 2009, 26 master's awarded. *Degree requirements:* For master's, orally presented project, 200-hour internship (educational leadership). *Entrance requirements:* For master's, GRE, minimum GPA of 2.5; teacher certification; recommendations and interview (for educational leadership). Additional exam requirements/recommendations for international students: Required—TOEFL (minimum score 500 paper-based; 173 computer-based; 61 iBT). *Application deadline:* For fall admission, 6/30 for domestic and international students; for spring admission, 11/30 for domestic and international students. Applications are processed on a rolling basis. Application fee: $10 ($20 for international students). *Financial support:* In 2009–10, 4 research assistantships with partial tuition reimbursements (averaging $10,000 per year) were awarded. *Unit head:* Dr. Julie Bergeron, Coordinator of Graduate Programs in Education, 318-797-5033, Fax: 318-798-4144, E-mail: julie.bergeron@lsus.edu. *Application contact:* Dr. Julie Bergeron, Coordinator of Graduate Programs in Education, 318-797-5033, Fax: 318-798-4144, E-mail: julie.bergeron@lsus.edu.

Louisiana Tech University, Graduate School, College of Education, Ruston, LA 71272. Offers M Ed, MA, MS, Ed D, PhD. *Accreditation:* NCATE. Part-time programs available. *Degree requirements:* For doctorate, thesis/dissertation. *Entrance requirements:* For master's and doctorate, GRE General Test.

Lourdes College, School of Graduate and Professional Studies, Program in Education, Sylvania, OH 43560-2898. Offers endorsement in computer technology (M Ed). *Accreditation:* Teacher Education Accreditation Council. Evening/weekend programs available. *Entrance requirements:* Additional exam requirements/recommendations for international students: Required—TOEFL.

Loyola Marymount University, School of Education, Los Angeles, CA 90045-2659. Offers MA, Ed D. *Accreditation:* NCATE. Part-time and evening/weekend programs available. *Degree requirements:* For master's, comprehensive exam. Application fee: $50. Electronic applications accepted. *Financial support:* Research assistantships, Federal Work-Study and scholarships/grants available. Support available to part-time students. Financial award application deadline: 6/1; financial award applicants required to submit FAFSA. *Unit head:* Dr. Shane Martin, Dean, 310-338-2863, Fax: 310-338-1976, E-mail: smartin@lmu.edu. *Application contact:* Chake H. Kouyoumjian, Director, Graduate Admissions, 310-338-2721, Fax: 310-338-6086, E-mail: ckouyoum@lmu.edu.

Loyola University Chicago, School of Education, Chicago, IL 60660. Offers M Ed, MA, Ed D, PhD, Certificate, Ed S. *Accreditation:* NCATE. Part-time and evening/weekend programs available. *Faculty:* 47 full-time (32 women), 53 part-time/adjunct (37 women). *Students:* 539 full-time (383 women), 300 part-time (217 women); includes 188 minority (102 African Americans, 4 American Indian/Alaska Native, 25 Asian Americans or Pacific Islanders, 57 Hispanic Americans), 29 international. Average age 36. 757 applicants, 56% accepted, 191 enrolled. In 2009, 209 master's, 58 doctorates, 20 other advanced degrees awarded. *Degree requirements:* For master's, comprehensive exam (for some programs), thesis (for some programs); for doctorate, comprehensive exam, thesis/dissertation; for other advanced degree, comprehensive exam. *Entrance requirements:* For master's, minimum GPA of 3.0, 3 letters of recommendation, resume, transcripts; for doctorate, GRE, interview, minimum GPA of 3.0, 3 letters of recommendation, resume; for other advanced degree, GRE, interview, minimum GPA of 3.0, letters of recommendation, resume, transcripts. Additional exam requirements/recommendations for international students: Required—TOEFL (minimum score 550 paper-based; 213 computer-based; 79 iBT). *Application deadline:* For fall admission, 7/1 for domestic and international students; for spring admission, 11/1 for domestic and international students. Application fee: $50. Electronic applications accepted. *Expenses:* Tuition: Full-time $14,220; part-time $790 per credit hour. Required fees: $60 per semester hour. Tuition and fees vary according to program. *Financial support:* In 2009–10, 55 fellowships with full tuition reimbursements (averaging $11,000 per year), 59 research assistantships with full tuition reimbursements (averaging $11,000 per year), 20 teaching assistantships (averaging $2,000 per year) were awarded; career-related internships or fieldwork, Federal Work-Study, institutionally sponsored loans, scholarships/grants, tuition waivers (partial), and unspecified assistantships also available. Support available to part-time students. Financial award application deadline: 2/15; financial award applicants required to submit FAFSA. *Faculty research:* Policy studies, historical foundations, teacher education, research methodologies, comparative education. Total annual research expenditures: $2.1 million. *Unit head:* Dr. David Prasse, Dean, 312-915-6992, Fax: 312-915-6980, E-mail: dprasse@luc.edu. *Application contact:* Marie Rosin-Dittmar, Information Contact, 312-915-6800, E-mail: schleduc@luc.edu.

Loyola University Maryland, Graduate Programs, College of Arts and Sciences, Department of Education, Baltimore, MD 21210-2699. Offers administration and supervision (M Ed, MA, CAS); curriculum and instruction (M Ed, MA, CAS); educational technology (M Ed); Montessori education (M Ed, CAS); reading (M Ed, CAS); school counseling (M Ed, CAS); special education (M Ed, CAS). *Accreditation:* NCATE. Part-time and evening/weekend programs available. *Entrance requirements:* For master's and CAS, GRE General Test, GRE Subject Test (recommended). Additional exam requirements/recommendations for international students: Required—TOEFL (minimum score 550 paper-based; 213 computer-based).

Lynchburg College, Graduate Studies, School of Education and Human Development, Lynchburg, VA 24501-3199. Offers community counseling (M Ed); counselor education (M Ed), including community counseling; curriculum and instruction (M Ed); educational leadership (M Ed); English education (M Ed); reading (M Ed); school counseling (M Ed); science education (M Ed); special education (M Ed), including autism spectrum disorder, early childhood special education, mental retardation, teaching children with learning disabilities, teaching the emotionally disturbed. Part-time and evening/weekend programs available. *Degree requirements:* For master's, comprehensive exam. *Entrance requirements:* For master's, GRE, minimum undergraduate GPA of 3.0. Additional exam requirements/recommendations for international students: Required—TOEFL. *Expenses:* Tuition: Full-time $7020; part-time $390 per credit hour.

Lyndon State College, Graduate Programs in Education, Lyndonville, VT 05851-0919. Offers education (M Ed), including curriculum and instruction, reading specialist, special education, teaching and counseling; natural sciences (MST), including science education. Part-time and evening/weekend programs available. *Degree requirements:* For master's, exam or major field project. *Entrance requirements:* Additional exam requirements/recommendations for international students: Recommended—TOEFL (minimum score 500 paper-based; 173 computer-based). *Faculty research:* Impaired reading, cognitive style, counseling relationship.

Lynn University, Donald and Helen Ross College of Education, Boca Raton, FL 33431-5598. Offers educational leadership (M Ed, PhD); exceptional student education (M Ed); teacher preparation (PhD). Part-time and evening/weekend programs available. *Degree requirements:* For master's, thesis (for some programs); for doctorate, thesis/dissertation, qualifying paper. *Entrance requirements:* For master's, GRE, minimum undergraduate GPA of 3.0, resume, 2 letters of recommendation; for doctorate, GRE or GMAT, minimum GPA of 3.25, resume, 2 letters of recommendation. Additional exam requirements/recommendations for international students: Required—TOEFL (minimum score 550 paper-based; 213 computer-based). *Application deadline:* Applications are processed on a rolling basis. Application fee: $50. Electronic applications accepted. *Expenses:* Tuition: Part-time $580 per credit. One-time fee: $200 part-time. Part-time tuition and fees vary according to degree level. *Financial support:* Career-related internships or fieldwork, Federal Work-Study, institutionally sponsored loans, scholarships/grants, tuition waivers (partial), and unspecified assistantships available. Support available to part-time students. Financial award application deadline: 8/1; financial award applicants required to submit FAFSA. *Faculty research:* Non-traditional education, innovative curricula, multicultural education, simulation games. *Application contact:* Dr. Larissa Baia, Assistant Director of Graduate Admissions, 561-237-7916, Fax: 561-237-7100, E-mail: lbaia@lynn.edu.

Madonna University, Programs in Education, Livonia, MI 48150-1173. Offers Catholic school leadership (MSA); educational leadership (MSA); learning disabilities (MAT); literacy education (MAT); teaching and learning (MAT). *Accreditation:* NCATE. Part-time and evening/weekend programs available. *Degree requirements:* For master's, thesis or alternative. Electronic applications accepted.

Maharishi University of Management, Graduate Studies, Department of Education, Fairfield, IA 52557. Offers teaching elementary education (MA); teaching secondary education (MA). *Degree requirements:* For master's, thesis or alternative. *Entrance requirements:* For master's, GRE, minimum GPA of 3.0. Additional exam requirements/recommendations for international students: Required—TOEFL. *Faculty research:* Unified field-based approach to education, moral climate, scientific study of teaching.

Malone University, Graduate Program in Education, Canton, OH 44709. Offers curriculum and instruction (MA); curriculum, instruction, and professional development (MA); instructional technology (MA); intervention specialist (MA); reading (MA). Part-time and evening/weekend programs available. *Faculty:* 7 full-time (4 women), 7 part-time/adjunct (5 women). *Students:* 2 full-time (1 woman), 64 part-time (55 women); includes 1 minority (African American). Average age 34. In 2009, 27 master's awarded. *Degree requirements:* For master's, research project. *Entrance requirements:* For master's, minimum GPA of 3.0, teaching license. Additional exam requirements/recommendations for international students: Required—TOEFL (minimum score 550 paper-based; 213 computer-based; 79 iBT). *Application deadline:* Applications are processed on a rolling basis. Application fee: $25. *Expenses:* Tuition: Part-time $450 per semester hour. *Financial support:* Tuition waivers (partial) available. Support available to part-time students.

Financial award application deadline: 6/30. *Faculty research:* The Bible as children's literature, special needs students and literacy development, middle level education, school/university partnerships and professional development, child/adolescent literature and popular culture. *Unit head:* Dr. Alice E. Christie, Director, 330-478-8541, Fax: 330-471-8563, E-mail: achristie@malone.edu. *Application contact:* David L. Kleffman, Assistant Director of Enrollment, 330-471-8447, Fax: 330-471-8343, E-mail: dkleffman@malone.edu.

Manhattan College, Graduate Division, School of Education, Riverdale, NY 10471. Offers counseling (MA, Diploma), including counseling (Diploma), mental health counseling (MA), school counseling (MA); school building leadership (MS Ed, Diploma); special education (MS Ed), including 5 year dual childhood/special education, dual childhood/special education, special education. *Accreditation:* Teacher Education Accreditation Council. Part-time and evening/weekend programs available. *Degree requirements:* For master's, thesis, internship. *Entrance requirements:* For master's, minimum GPA of 3.0. *Faculty research:* Adapted physical education, cross-training of preschool regular and special education teachers.

Manhattanville College, Graduate Programs, School of Education, Purchase, NY 10577-2132. Offers M Ed, MAT, MPS. *Accreditation:* NCATE. Part-time and evening/weekend programs available. *Students:* 321 full-time (225 women), 590 part-time (429 women); includes 76 minority (26 African Americans, 9 Asian Americans or Pacific Islanders, 41 Hispanic Americans), 5 international. In 2009, 295 master's awarded. *Entrance requirements:* For master's, minimum undergraduate GPA of 3.0, 2 letters of recommendation. Additional exam requirements/recommendations for international students: Required—TOEFL (minimum score 550 paper-based; 213 computer-based). *Application deadline:* Applications are processed on a rolling basis. Application fee: $70. Electronic applications accepted. *Financial support:* Career-related internships or fieldwork, Federal Work-Study, institutionally sponsored loans, and unspecified assistantships available. Financial award application deadline: 3/1; financial award applicants required to submit FAFSA. *Unit head:* Dr. Shelley Wepner, Dean, 914-323-5192, Fax: 914-694-2386, E-mail: wepners@mville.edu. *Application contact:* Jeanine Pardey-Levine, Director of Admissions, 914-323-3208, Fax: 914-694-1732, E-mail: edschool@mville.edu.

Mansfield University of Pennsylvania, Graduate Studies, Department of Education and Special Education, Mansfield, PA 16933. Offers elementary education (M Ed); secondary education (MS). *Accreditation:* NCATE (one or more programs are accredited). Part-time and evening/weekend programs available. Postbaccalaureate distance learning degree programs offered (no on-campus study). *Faculty:* 9 full-time (6 women). *Students:* 52 full-time (40 women), 56 part-time (41 women); includes 4 minority (1 African American, 1 Asian American or Pacific Islander, 2 Hispanic Americans), 2 international. Average age 29. In 2009, 56 master's awarded. *Degree requirements:* For master's, comprehensive exam, thesis optional. *Entrance requirements:* For master's, minimum GPA of 3.0. Additional exam requirements/recommendations for international students: Required—TOEFL (minimum score 550 paper-based; 220 computer-based). *Application deadline:* For fall admission, 8/1 priority date for domestic students, 8/1 for international students; for spring admission, 11/1 priority date for domestic students, 9/1 for international students. Applications are processed on a rolling basis. Application fee: $25. Electronic applications accepted. *Expenses:* Tuition, state resident: full-time $6666; part-time $370 per credit. Tuition, nonresident: full-time $10,666; part-time $593 per credit. Required fees: $1388. *Financial support:* Career-related internships or fieldwork and unspecified assistantships available. Support available to part-time students. Financial award application deadline: 5/1; financial award applicants required to submit FAFSA. *Unit head:* Dr. Jesus Lucero, Chairperson, 570-662-4791, E-mail: jlucero@mansfield.edu. *Application contact:* Christina Hale, Assistant Director of Enrollment Services/Graduate Admissions, 570-662-4812, Fax: 570-662-4121, E-mail: chale@mansfield.edu.

Marian University, School of Education, Indianapolis, IN 46222-1997. Offers MAT. *Accreditation:* NCATE. Part-time and evening/weekend programs available. *Faculty:* 13 full-time (11 women), 10 part-time/adjunct (all women). *Students:* 26 full-time (21 women), 192 part-time (118 women); includes 32 minority (21 African Americans, 4 Asian Americans or Pacific Islanders, 7 Hispanic Americans). Average age 29. In 2009, 47 master's awarded. *Entrance requirements:* For master's, PRAXIS I and/or PRAXIS II. *Application deadline:* For fall admission, 2/1 priority date for domestic students. Applications are processed on a rolling basis. Application fee: $0. *Expenses:* Tuition: Full-time $9400; part-time $350 per credit hour. *Financial support:* In 2009–10, 58 students received support. Applicants required to submit FAFSA. *Unit head:* Dr. Lindan Hill, Dean, 317-955-6089, Fax: 317-955-6448, E-mail: lhill@marian.edu. *Application contact:* Dr. Cheryl Hertzer, Chair, 317-955-6087, Fax: 317-955-6448, E-mail: chertzer@marian.edu.

Marian University, School of Education, Fond du Lac, WI 54935-4699. Offers educational leadership (MAE, PhD); teacher development (MAE). *Accreditation:* NCATE. Part-time programs available. *Faculty:* 16 full-time (8 women), 52 part-time/adjunct (37 women). *Students:* 31 full-time (19 women), 618 part-time (387 women); includes 35 minority (13 African Americans, 4 American Indian/Alaska Native, 8 Asian Americans or Pacific Islanders, 10 Hispanic Americans), 2 international. Average age 36. 105 applicants, 80% accepted, 84 enrolled. In 2009, 290 master's, 2 doctorates awarded. *Degree requirements:* For master's, exam, field-based experience project, portfolio; for doctorate, comprehensive exam, thesis/dissertation, field-based experience. *Entrance requirements:* For master's, minimum GPA of 3.0, BA in education or related field, teaching license; for doctorate, GRE, MAT, resume, 2 writing samples, interview. *Application deadline:* Applications are processed on a rolling basis. Application fee: $50. *Expenses:* Tuition: Part-time $380 per credit hour. Part-time tuition and fees vary according to course level and program. *Financial support:* In 2009–10, 200 students received support. Federal Work-Study and institutionally sponsored loans available. Support available to part-time students. Financial award application deadline: 3/1; financial award applicants required to submit FAFSA. *Faculty research:* At-risk youth, multicultural issues, values in education, teaching/learning strategies. *Unit head:* Sue Stoddart, Dean, 920-923-8099, Fax: 920-923-7663, E-mail: sstoddart@marianuniversity.edu. *Application contact:* Robert Bohnsack, Graduate Education Admissions, 920-923-8100, Fax: 920-923-7154, E-mail: bbohnsack@marianuniversity.edu.

Marietta College, Program in Education, Marietta, OH 45750-4000. Offers MA. *Accreditation:* NCATE. Part-time and evening/weekend programs available. *Degree requirements:* For master's, writing portfolio. *Entrance requirements:* For master's, MAT. *Faculty research:* Teaching of reading.

Marist College, Graduate Programs, School of Social and Behavioral Sciences, Poughkeepsie, NY 12601-1387. Offers counseling psychology (MA); education (M Ed); education psychology (MA); school psychology (MA, Adv C). Part-time and evening/weekend programs available. *Degree requirements:* For master's, thesis optional. *Entrance requirements:* For master's, GRE General Test, letters of recommendation, minimum undergraduate GPA of 3.0, interview. Additional exam requirements/recommendations for international students: Required—TOEFL (minimum score 550 paper-based; 213 computer-based; 80 iBT); Recommended—IELTS (minimum score 6.5). Electronic applications accepted. *Expenses:* Tuition: Full-time $12,510; part-time $695 per credit hour. *Faculty research:* AIDS prevention, educational intervention, humanistic counseling research, aging and development, neuroimaging.

Marlboro College, Graduate School, Program in Teaching with Technology, Marlboro, VT 05344. Offers MAT. Part-time and evening/weekend programs available. Postbaccalaureate distance learning degree programs offered (minimal on-campus study). *Faculty:* 7 part-time/adjunct (5 women). *Students:* 6 full-time (3 women), 4 part-time (2 women). Average age 38. 5 applicants, 100% accepted, 5 enrolled. In 2009, 4 master's awarded. *Degree requirements:* For master's, capstone project. *Entrance requirements:* For master's, 2 letters of recommendation. *Application deadline:* Applications are processed on a rolling basis. Application fee: $0. Electronic applications accepted. *Expenses:* Tuition: Full-time $9520; part-time $680 per credit. Tuition and fees vary according to course load and program. *Financial support:* Available to part-time students. Applicants required to submit FAFSA. *Application contact:* Joe Heslin, Associate Director of Admissions, 802-258-9209, Fax: 802-258-9201, E-mail: jheslin@gradcenter.marlboro.edu.

Marquette University, Graduate School, College of Education, Milwaukee, WI 53201-1881. Offers MA, Ed D, PhD, Spec. *Accreditation:* NCATE. Part-time programs available. *Faculty:* 23 full-time (14 women), 23 part-time/adjunct (14 women). *Students:* 87 full-time (67 women), 183 part-time (124 women); includes 29 minority (18 African Americans, 7 Asian Americans or Pacific Islanders, 4 Hispanic Americans), 3 international. Average age 32. 293 applicants, 47% accepted, 88 enrolled. In 2009, 63 master's, 10 doctorates awarded. Terminal master's awarded for partial completion of doctoral program. *Degree requirements:* For master's, comprehensive exam, thesis; for doctorate, thesis/dissertation, qualifying exam. *Entrance requirements:* For master's, GRE General Test or MAT; for doctorate, GRE General Test, MAT, sample of written work; for Spec, GRE General Test or MAT, master's degree. Additional exam requirements/recommendations for international students: Required—TOEFL. Application fee: $40. *Expenses:* Contact institution. *Financial support:* In 2009–10, 5 research assistantships, 5 teaching assistantships were awarded; Federal Work-Study, institutionally sponsored loans, scholarships/grants, and tuition waivers (full and partial) also available. Support available to part-time students. Financial award application deadline: 2/15. *Faculty research:* Parenting, psychology of motivation, reading assessment, socialization of educational administrators, education philosophy of Cardinal Newman. *Unit head:* Dr. Bill Henk, Dean, 414-288-7376. *Application contact:* Dr. Joan Whipp, Assistant Dean, 414-288-1421, Fax: 414-288-5333.

Marshall University, Academic Affairs Division, College of Education and Human Services, Huntington, WV 25755. Offers MA, MAT, MS. *Accreditation:* NCATE. Evening/weekend programs available. *Faculty:* 45 full-time (24 women), 40 part-time/adjunct (24 women). *Students:* 577 full-time (415 women), 1,091 part-time (858 women); includes 78 minority (57 African Americans, 4 American Indian/Alaska Native, 9 Asian Americans or Pacific Islanders, 8 Hispanic Americans), 48 international. Average age 30. In 2009, 414 master's awarded. *Degree requirements:* For master's, thesis optional, comprehensive assessment. *Entrance requirements:* Additional exam requirements/recommendations for international students: Required—TOEFL (minimum score 550 paper-based). *Application deadline:* Applications are processed on a rolling basis. Application fee: $40 ($100 for international students). *Financial support:* Career-related internships or fieldwork, Federal Work-Study, tuition waivers (full and partial), and unspecified assistantships available. Support available to part-time students. *Unit head:* Dr. Rosalyn Anstine Templeton, Executive Dean, 304-696-3131, E-mail: templetonr@marshall.edu. *Application contact:* Graduate Admissions, 304-746-1900, Fax: 304-746-1902, E-mail: services@marshall.edu.

Martin Luther College, Graduate Studies, New Ulm, MN 56073. Offers instruction (MS Ed); leadership (MS Ed); special education (MS Ed). Part-time programs available. Postbaccalaureate distance learning degree programs offered. *Degree requirements:* For master's, capstone project or comprehensive exam. *Entrance requirements:* For master's, undergraduate degree in education from an accredited college or university, minimum undergraduate GPA of 3.0. Electronic applications accepted.

Mary Baldwin College, Graduate Studies, Program in Teaching, Staunton, VA 24401-3610. Offers elementary education (MAT); middle grades education (MAT). *Accreditation:* Teacher Education Accreditation Council.

Marygrove College, Graduate Division, Program in the Art of Teaching, Detroit, MI 48221-2599. Offers MAT. Postbaccalaureate distance learning degree programs offered (no on-campus study). *Degree requirements:* For master's, portfolio. *Entrance requirements:* For master's, MAT, interview, minimum undergraduate GPA of 3.0, teaching certificate.

Marylhurst University, Department of Education, Marylhurst, OR 97036-0261. Offers M Ed, MA. Part-time programs available. *Faculty:* 4 full-time (2 women), 30 part-time/adjunct (26 women). *Students:* 71 full-time (47 women), 68 part-time (53 women); includes 6 minority (2 African Americans, 3 Asian Americans or Pacific Islanders, 1 Hispanic American), 1 international. Average age 35. 60 applicants, 100% accepted, 51 enrolled. In 2009, 29 master's awarded. *Degree requirements:* For master's, comprehensive exam. *Entrance requirements:* For master's, PRAXIS I or CBEST, resume, writing sample, letter of introduction, fingerprint verification. Additional exam requirements/recommendations for international students: Required—TOEFL (minimum score 550 paper-based; 213 computer-based; 80 iBT). *Application deadline:* For fall admission, 3/1 priority date for domestic and international students. Applications are processed on a rolling basis. Application fee: $40 ($50 for international students). *Financial support:* Federal Work-Study and scholarships/grants available. Support available to part-time students. Financial award applicants required to submit FAFSA. *Unit head:* Dr. Thomas Ruhl, Chair, 503-636-8141, Fax: 503-636-9526, E-mail: truhl@marylhurst.edu. *Application contact:* Kathleen Schneff, Admissions Specialist, 800-634-9982 Ext. 3322, Fax: 503-635-6585, E-mail: admissions@marylhurst.edu.

Marymount University, School of Education and Human Services, Program in Education, Arlington, VA 22207-4299. Offers elementary education (M Ed); English as a second language (M Ed); professional studies (M Ed); secondary education (M Ed); special education, general curriculum (M Ed). *Accreditation:* NCATE. Part-time and evening/weekend programs available. *Faculty:* 9 full-time (6 women), 9 part-time/adjunct (8 women). *Students:* 55 full-time (46 women), 117 part-time (100 women); includes 13 minority (1 African American, 4 Asian Americans or Pacific Islanders, 8 Hispanic Americans), 7 international. Average age 31. 73 applicants, 93% accepted, 55 enrolled. In 2009, 62 master's awarded. *Degree requirements:* For master's, thesis or alternative. *Entrance requirements:* For master's, GRE or MAT and PRAXIS I or SAT/ACT, 2 letters of recommendation, interview. Additional exam requirements/recommendations for international students: Required—TOEFL (minimum score 600 paper-based; 250 computer-based; 96 iBT), IELTS (minimum score 6.5). *Application deadline:* For fall admission, 7/1 for international students; for spring admission, 10/15 for international students. Applications are processed on a rolling basis. Application fee: $40. Electronic applications accepted. *Expenses:* Tuition: Full-time $13,050; part-time $725 per credit hour. Required fees: $135; $7.50 per credit hour. *Financial support:* In 2009–10, 48 students received support; research assistantships with full tuition reimbursements available, career-related internships or fieldwork, Federal Work-Study, scholarships/grants, and unspecified assistantships available. Support available to part-time students. Financial award applicants required to submit FAFSA. *Unit head:* Dr. Shelly Haser, Chair, 703-526-6855, Fax: 703-284-1631, E-mail: shelly.haser@marymount.edu. *Application contact:* Francesca Reed, Director, Graduate Admissions, 703-284-5901, Fax: 703-527-3815, E-mail: grad.admissions@marymount.edu.

Maryville University of Saint Louis, School of Education, St. Louis, MO 63141-7299. Offers art education (MA Ed); early childhood education (MA Ed); educational leadership (Ed D); educational leadership: principal certification (MA Ed); elementary education (MA Ed); elementary education/English (MA Ed); elementary education/psychology (MA Ed); environmental education (MA Ed); gifted education (MA Ed); literacy specialist (MA Ed); middle grades education (MA Ed); secondary teaching and inquiry (MA Ed); teacher as leader (MA Ed). *Accreditation:* NASAD; NCATE. Part-time and evening/weekend programs available. *Students:* 25 full-time (18 women), 198 part-time (145 women); includes 33 minority (27 African Americans, 2 American Indian/Alaska Native, 1 Asian American or Pacific Islander, 3 Hispanic Americans). Average age 36. In 2009, 61 master's, 45 doctorates awarded. *Degree requirements:* For master's, thesis, project. *Entrance requirements:* For master's and doctorate, minimum GPA of 3.0, 3 professional recommendations. Additional exam requirements/recommendations for international students: Required—TOEFL (minimum score 550 paper-based). *Application deadline:* Applications are processed on a rolling basis. Application fee: $40 ($60 for international students). Electronic applications accepted. *Expenses:* Tuition: Full-time $20,384; part-time $627.50 per credit hour. Required fees: $100 per semester. *Financial support:* Career-related internships or fieldwork, Federal Work-Study, tuition waivers (partial), and professional educator discounts available. Financial award application deadline: 3/1; financial award applicants required to submit FAFSA. *Faculty research:* Collaboration with public schools, pre-service program development, mathematics, diversity, literacy. *Unit head:* Dr. Sam Hausfather, Dean, 314-529-9466, Fax: 314-529-9921, E-mail: shausfather@maryville.edu. *Application contact:* Holly Stanwich, Graduate Admissions Coordinator, 314-529-9542, Fax: 314-529-9921, E-mail: teachered@maryville.edu.

Education—General

Marywood University, Academic Affairs, Reap College of Education and Human Development, Department of Education, Scranton, PA 18509-1598. Offers early childhood intervention (MS); elementary education (MAT); higher education administration (MS); instructional leadership (M Ed); reading education (MS); school leadership (MS); secondary/k-12 education (MAT). *Accreditation:* NCATE. *Students:* 36 full-time (24 women), 85 part-time (75 women); includes 5 minority (1 African American, 1 American Indian/Alaska Native, 1 Asian American or Pacific Islander, 2 Hispanic Americans). Average age 31. In 2009, 36 master's awarded. *Entrance requirements:* Additional exam requirements/recommendations for international students: Required—TOEFL (minimum score 550 paper-based; 213 computer-based; 79 iBT). Application fee: $35. Electronic applications accepted. *Expenses:* Tuition: Part-time $715 per credit. Required fees: $270 per semester. Tuition and fees vary according to degree level, campus/location and program. *Financial support:* Career-related internships or fieldwork, scholarships/grants, and unspecified assistantships available. Support available to part-time students. Financial award application deadline: 6/30; financial award applicants required to submit FAFSA. *Faculty research:* Catholic identity in higher education, school reading programs, teacher practice enhancement, cooperative learning, institutional and instructional leadership. *Unit head:* Sr. Ann Jablonski, Chair, 570-348-6211, E-mail: jablonski@marywood.edu. *Application contact:* Tammy Manka, Assistant Director of Graduate Admissions, 866-279-9663, E-mail: tmanka@marywood.edu.

Massachusetts College of Art and Design, Graduate Programs, Program in Teaching, Boston, MA 02115-5882. Offers MA. *Students:* 5 full-time (all women), 2 part-time (both women). Average age 24. *Degree requirements:* For master's, comprehensive exam, thesis (for some programs). *Entrance requirements:* For master's, portfolio, resume, college transcripts, statement of purpose, letters of reference, interview. Additional exam requirements/recommendations for international students: Required—TOEFL (minimum score 563 paper-based; 223 computer-based; 85 iBT); Recommended—IELTS (minimum score 6.5). *Application deadline:* For fall admission, 1/15 for domestic and international students. Applications are processed on a rolling basis. Application fee: $75. Electronic applications accepted. *Expenses:* Tuition, state resident: full-time $18,450; part-time $615 per credit. Tuition, nonresident: full-time $18,450; part-time $615 per credit. Tuition and fees vary according to program. *Unit head:* George Creamer, Director, 617-879-7163, Fax: 617-879-7171, E-mail: creamer@massart.edu. *Application contact:* George Creamer, Director, 617-879-7163, Fax: 617-879-7171, E-mail: creamer@massart.edu.

Massachusetts College of Liberal Arts, Program in Education, North Adams, MA 01247-4100. Offers curriculum (M Ed); educational administration (M Ed); reading (M Ed); special education (M Ed). Part-time and evening/weekend programs available. *Degree requirements:* For master's, thesis. *Entrance requirements:* For master's, writing sample. *Faculty research:* Anxiety, methodology, mainstreaming.

McGill University, Faculty of Graduate and Postdoctoral Studies, Faculty of Education, Department of Integrated Studies in Education, Montréal, QC H3A 2T5, Canada. Offers culture and values in education (MA, PhD); curriculum studies (MA); educational leadership (MA, Certificate); educational studies (PhD); integrated studies in education (M Ed); second language education (MA, PhD).

McKendree University, Graduate Programs, Master of Arts in Education Program, Lebanon, IL 62254-1299. Offers certification (MA Ed); educational administration and leadership (MA Ed); educational studies (MA Ed); higher education administrative services (MA Ed); music education (MA Ed); special education (MA Ed); teacher leadership (MA Ed); transition to teaching (MA Ed). *Accreditation:* NCATE. Part-time and evening/weekend programs available. Postbaccalaureate distance learning degree programs offered (no on-campus study). *Faculty:* 18 full-time (7 women), 56 part-time/adjunct (34 women). *Students:* 107 full-time (83 women), 445 part-time (325 women); includes 41 minority (32 African Americans, 3 Asian Americans or Pacific Islanders, 6 Hispanic Americans). Average age 35. 225 applicants, 77% accepted, 129 enrolled. In 2009, 200 master's awarded. *Entrance requirements:* For master's, official transcripts from institutions attended, minimum GPA of 3.0, resume, references. Additional exam requirements/recommendations for international students: Required—TOEFL. *Application deadline:* Applications are processed on a rolling basis. Application fee: $0. Electronic applications accepted. *Expenses:* Tuition: Full-time $6300; part-time $350 per credit hour. One-time fee: $125. *Financial support:* In 2009–10, 1 student received support. Application deadline: 6/30. *Unit head:* Dr. Joseph J. Cipfl, Interim Chair of the School of Education, 618-537-6462, Fax: 618-537-6417, E-mail: jjcipfl@mckendree.edu. *Application contact:* Sabrina Storner, Director of Graduate Admission, 618-537-6477, Fax: 618-537-6410, E-mail: skstorner@mckendree.edu.

McNeese State University, Doré School of Graduate Studies, Burton College of Education, Department of Teacher Education, Lake Charles, LA 70609. Offers curriculum and instruction (M Ed), including early childhood education, elementary education, secondary education; school counseling (M Ed); special education mild/moderate grades 1-12 (M Ed); teaching (MAT), including elementary education grades 1-5, secondary education grades 6-12, special education—mild/moderate grades 1-12. *Accreditation:* NCATE. Evening/weekend programs available. *Faculty:* 14 full-time (8 women). *Students:* 55 full-time (48 women), 159 part-time (143 women); includes 43 minority (34 African Americans, 1 American Indian/Alaska Native, 2 Asian Americans or Pacific Islanders, 6 Hispanic Americans), 1 international. In 2009, 52 master's awarded. *Entrance requirements:* For master's, GRE, teaching certificate. *Application deadline:* For fall admission, 5/15 priority date for domestic and international students; for spring admission, 10/15 priority date for domestic and international students. Applications are processed on a rolling basis. Application fee: $20 ($30 for international students). *Expenses:* Tuition, area resident: Full-time $2556. Tuition, state resident: full-time $2556. Required fees: $1031. Tuition and fees vary according to course load. *Financial support:* Application deadline: 5/1. *Unit head:* Dr. Royce Zant, Head, 337-475-5404, Fax: 337-475-5398, E-mail: rzant@mcneese.edu. *Application contact:* Dr. George F. Mead, Interim Dean of Dore' School of Graduate Studies, 337-475-5396, Fax: 337-475-5397, E-mail: admissions@mcneese.edu.

Medaille College, Program in Education, Buffalo, NY 14214-2695. Offers adolescent education (MS Ed); curriculum and instruction (MS Ed); education preparation (MS Ed); literacy (MS Ed); special education (MS). *Accreditation:* Teacher Education Accreditation Council. Part-time and evening/weekend programs available. *Faculty:* 22 full-time (16 women), 47 part-time/adjunct (36 women). *Students:* 721 full-time (596 women), 2 part-time (both women); includes 34 minority (16 African Americans, 1 American Indian/Alaska Native, 14 Asian Americans or Pacific Islanders, 3 Hispanic Americans). Average age 26. 621 applicants, 46% accepted, 288 enrolled. In 2009, 608 master's awarded. *Degree requirements:* For master's, thesis or alternative. *Entrance requirements:* For master's, minimum undergraduate GPA of 2.7. Additional exam requirements/recommendations for international students: Required—TOEFL (minimum score 550 paper-based; 213 computer-based). *Application deadline:* For fall admission, 8/15 priority date for domestic students; for spring admission, 1/15 priority date for domestic students. Applications are processed on a rolling basis. Application fee: $35. Electronic applications accepted. *Financial support:* In 2009–10, 501 students received support. Federal Work-Study available. Financial award applicants required to submit FAFSA. *Faculty research:* Curriculum planning, truancy, tracking minority students, curriculum design, mentoring students. *Unit head:* Dr. Robert DiSibio, Director of Graduate Programs, 716-932-2548, Fax: 716-631-1380, E-mail: rdisibio@medaille.edu. *Application contact:* Jacqueline Matheny, Executive Director of Marketing and Enrollment, 716-932-2541, Fax: 716-632-1811, E-mail: jmatheny@medaille.edu.

Memorial University of Newfoundland, School of Graduate Studies, Faculty of Education, St. John's, NL A1C 5S7, Canada. Offers counseling psychology (M Ed); curriculum, teaching, and learning studies (M Ed); education (PhD); educational leadership studies (M Ed); information technology (M Ed); post-secondary studies (M Ed, Diploma), including health professional education (Diploma). Part-time programs available. *Degree requirements:* For master's, thesis optional, internship, paper folio, project; for doctorate, comprehensive exam, thesis/dissertation, thesis seminar, oral defense of thesis. *Entrance requirements:* For master's, undergraduate degree with at least 2nd class standing, 1-2 years work experience; for doctorate, minimum A

average in graduate course work, MA in education, 2 years professional experience; for Diploma, 2nd class degree, 2 years of work experience with adult learners, appropriate academic qualifications and work experience in a health-related field. Electronic applications accepted. *Faculty research:* Critical thinking, literacy, cognitive studies and counseling, educational change, technology in instruction.

Mercer University, Graduate Studies, Cecil B. Day Campus, Tift College of Education (Atlanta), Macon, GA 31207-0003. Offers curriculum and instruction (PhD); early childhood education (M Ed, MAT); educational leadership (PhD, Ed S); middle grades education (M Ed, MAT); reading education (M Ed); secondary education (M Ed, MAT); teacher leadership (Ed S). *Accreditation:* NCATE. Part-time and evening/weekend programs available. *Faculty:* 27 full-time (14 women), 6 part-time/adjunct (3 women). *Students:* 302 full-time (251 women), 543 part-time (430 women); includes 334 minority (311 African Americans, 1 American Indian/Alaska Native, 21 Asian Americans or Pacific Islanders, 1 Hispanic American), 7 international. Average age 34. In 2009, 195 master's, 20 doctorates awarded. *Degree requirements:* For master's and Ed S, research project; for doctorate, thesis/dissertation. *Entrance requirements:* For master's, GRE or MAT, minimum undergraduate GPA of 2.75; for doctorate, GRE; for Ed S, GRE or MAT, minimum GPA of 3.25, 3 years of teaching experience. Additional exam requirements/recommendations for international students: Required—TOEFL. *Application deadline:* For fall admission, 8/1 for domestic and international students; for spring admission, 12/1 for domestic and international students. Applications are processed on a rolling basis. Application fee: $25. *Expenses:* Contact institution. *Financial support:* Federal Work-Study available. Support available to part-time students. Financial award application deadline: 5/1. *Faculty research:* Educational computing, content area reading, concept learning, importance of play for young children, multicultural literature. *Unit head:* Dr. Carl R. Martray, Dean, 478-301-5397, Fax: 478-301-2280, E-mail: martray_cr@mercer.edu. *Application contact:* Dr. Allison Gilmore, Associate Dean for Graduate Teacher Education, 678-547-6330, Fax: 678-547-6055, E-mail: gilmore_a@mercer.edu.

Mercer University, Graduate Studies, Macon Campus, Tift College of Education (Macon), Macon, GA 31207-0003. Offers collaborative education (M Ed); curriculum and instruction (PhD); educational leadership (PhD, Ed S). *Accreditation:* NCATE. Part-time and evening/weekend programs available. *Faculty:* 14 full-time (8 women), 2 part-time/adjunct (1 woman). *Students:* 85 full-time (78 women), 86 part-time (66 women); includes 51 minority (49 African Americans, 1 Asian American or Pacific Islander, 1 Hispanic American). Average age 33. In 2009, 57 master's, 12 doctorates, 6 other advanced degrees awarded. *Degree requirements:* For master's, research project report; for doctorate, thesis/dissertation. *Entrance requirements:* For master's, GRE or MAT, minimum GPA of 2.75; for doctorate, GRE. Additional exam requirements/recommendations for international students: Required—TOEFL. *Application deadline:* For fall admission, 8/1 for domestic students; for spring admission, 12/1 for domestic students. Applications are processed on a rolling basis. Application fee: $25. *Expenses:* Contact institution. *Financial support:* Federal Work-Study and institutionally sponsored loans available. Support available to part-time students. Financial award application deadline: 5/1. *Faculty research:* Teacher effectiveness, specific learning disabilities, inclusion. *Unit head:* Dr. Carl R. Martray, Dean, 478-301-5397, Fax: 478-301-2280, E-mail: martray_cr@mercer.edu. *Application contact:* Dr. Penny Elkins, Associate Dean, 678-547-6556, Fax: 678-547-6389, E-mail: elkins_pl@mercer.edu.

Mercy College, School of Education, Dobbs Ferry, NY 10522-1189. Offers adolescence education, grades 7-12 (MS); applied behavior analysis (Post Master's Certificate); bilingual education (MS); childhood education, grade 1-6 (MS); early childhood education, birth-grade 2 (MS); early childhood education/students with disabilities (MS); individualized certification plan for teachers (ICPT) (MS); middle childhood education, grades 5-9 (MS); school building leadership (MS, Advanced Certificate); teaching English to speakers of other languages (TESOL) (MS); teaching literacy (MS); teaching literacy, birth-6 (MS); teaching literacy/birth-grade 12 (MS); teaching literacy/grades 5-12 (MS); urban education (MS). *Faculty:* 55 full-time (37 women), 78 part-time/adjunct (47 women). *Students:* 538 full-time (455 women), 1,298 part-time (1,029 women); includes 699 minority (336 African Americans, 3 American Indian/Alaska Native, 30 Asian Americans or Pacific Islanders, 330 Hispanic Americans), 4 international. Average age 33. 779 applicants, 73% accepted, 465 enrolled. In 2009, 870 master's, 5 other advanced degrees awarded. *Degree requirements:* For master's, thesis. *Entrance requirements:* For master's, interview, resume, minimum undergraduate GPA of 3.0. Additional exam requirements/recommendations for international students: Required—TOEFL (minimum score 600 paper-based; 250 computer-based; 100 iBT). *Application deadline:* For fall admission, 8/1 for international students. Applications are processed on a rolling basis. Application fee: $40. Electronic applications accepted. *Expenses:* Contact institution. *Financial support:* In 2009–10, 161 students received support. Career-related internships or fieldwork, Federal Work-Study, scholarships/grants, and unspecified assistantships available. Support available to part-time students. Financial award applicants required to submit FAFSA. *Faculty research:* Teaching, literacy, educational evaluation. *Unit head:* Dr. Andrew Peiser, Interim Dean for the School of Education, 914-674-7489, E-mail: apeiser@mercy.edu. *Application contact:* Mary Ellen Hoffman, Interim Associate Dean, 914-674-7334, E-mail: mehoffman@mercy.edu.

Meredith College, John E. Weems Graduate School, School of Education, Raleigh, NC 27607-5298. Offers M Ed, MAT. *Accreditation:* NCATE. Part-time and evening/weekend programs available. *Faculty:* 7 full-time (all women), 8 part-time/adjunct (7 women). *Students:* 41 full-time (38 women), 93 part-time (90 women); includes 19 minority (10 African Americans, 7 Asian Americans or Pacific Islanders, 2 Hispanic Americans). Average age 33. 106 applicants, 62% accepted, 66 enrolled. In 2009, 8 master's awarded. *Degree requirements:* For master's, thesis optional. *Entrance requirements:* For master's, GRE General Test or MAT, minimum GPA of 2.5, teaching license, recommendations. Additional exam requirements/recommendations for international students: Required—TOEFL. *Application deadline:* For fall admission, 7/1 priority date for domestic students; for spring admission, 11/1 priority date for domestic students. Applications are processed on a rolling basis. Application fee: $50. Electronic applications accepted. *Expenses:* Contact institution. *Financial support:* Career-related internships or fieldwork, institutionally sponsored loans, and tuition waivers (partial) available. Support available to part-time students. Financial award application deadline: 2/15; financial award applicants required to submit FAFSA. *Unit head:* Erin Barrow, Graduate Program Manager, 919-760-8316, Fax: 919-760-2303, E-mail: barrower@meredith.edu. *Application contact:* Dr. Ellen Graden, Coordinator, 919-760-8077, Fax: 919-760-2303, E-mail: gradene@meredith.edu.

Merrimack College, Department of Education, North Andover, MA 01845-5800. Offers M Ed. Part-time and evening/weekend programs available. *Degree requirements:* For master's, research project, practicum or clinical experience. *Entrance requirements:* For master's, GRE General Test or MAT, Massachusetts Test for Educator License (communication and literacy), teaching license for professional options. *Faculty research:* Educational technology, teaching mathematics, leadership, teaching multi-cultural education, reading.

Mesa State College, Center for Teacher Education, Grand Junction, CO 81501-3122. Offers educational leadership (MAEd); ESOL (MAEd). *Accreditation:* NCATE. Part-time and evening/weekend programs available. Postbaccalaureate distance learning degree programs offered (minimal on-campus study). *Faculty:* 6 full-time (3 women), 8 part-time/adjunct (3 women). *Students:* 1 (woman) full-time, 71 part-time (50 women); includes 3 Hispanic Americans. Average age 37. 11 applicants, 27% accepted, 3 enrolled. In 2009, 29 master's awarded. *Degree requirements:* For master's, capstone course. *Entrance requirements:* For master's, GRE, 2 professional letters of recommendation. Additional exam requirements/recommendations for international students: Required—TOEFL (minimum score 550 paper-based; 207 computer-based). *Application deadline:* For fall admission, 4/1 for domestic students; for spring admission, 3/31 for domestic students. Applications are processed on a rolling basis. Application fee: $50. Electronic applications accepted. *Expenses:* Tuition, state resident: full-time $5400; part-time $300 per credit hour. Tuition, nonresident: full-time $16,200; part-time $900 per credit hour. Required fees: $460; $25 per credit hour. Tuition and fees vary according to program. *Financial support:* Applicants required to submit FAFSA. *Unit head:* Valerie Dobbs, Director of Teacher Education, 970-248-1953, Fax: 970-248-1112, E-mail: vdobbs@mesastate.edu. *Application*

contact: Mary Kienietz, Administrative Assistant, 970-248-1785, Fax: 970-248-1112, E-mail: mkieniet@mesastate.edu.

Miami University, Graduate School, School of Education and Allied Professions, Oxford, OH 45056. Offers M Ed, MA, MAT, MS, Ed D, PhD, Ed S. *Accreditation:* NCATE. Part-time programs available. *Students:* 224 full-time (156 women), 199 part-time (158 women); includes 60 minority (43 African Americans, 1 American Indian/Alaska Native, 7 Asian Americans or Pacific Islanders, 9 Hispanic Americans), 22 international. *Entrance requirements:* For master's, minimum undergraduate GPA of 3.0 during previous 2 years or 2.75 overall; for doctorate, minimum undergraduate GPA of 2.75, graduate 3.0. Application fee: $50. *Expenses:* Tuition, state resident: full-time $11,280. Tuition, nonresident: full-time $24,912. Required fees: $516. *Financial support:* Fellowships with full tuition reimbursements, research assistantships with full tuition reimbursements, teaching assistantships with full tuition reimbursements, career-related internships or fieldwork, Federal Work-Study, health care benefits, tuition waivers (full), and unspecified assistantships available. Financial award application deadline: 3/1; financial award applicants required to submit FAFSA. *Unit head:* Dr. Carine M. Feyten, Dean, 513-529-6317, Fax: 513-529-7270. *Application contact:* Graduate Admission Coordinator, 513-529-3734, Fax: 513-529-3762, E-mail: gradschool@muohio.edu.

Michigan State University, The Graduate School, College of Education, East Lansing, MI 48824. Offers MA, MS, PhD, Ed S. *Accreditation:* Teacher Education Accreditation Council. *Faculty:* 120 full-time (68 women). *Students:* 630 full-time (416 women), 677 part-time (473 women); includes 162 minority (88 African Americans, 8 American Indian/Alaska Native, 37 Asian Americans or Pacific Islanders, 29 Hispanic Americans), 185 international. Average age 32. 877 applicants, 51% accepted. In 2009, 407 master's, 95 doctorates awarded. *Entrance requirements:* Additional exam requirements/recommendations for international students: Required—TOEFL. Electronic applications accepted. *Expenses:* Tuition, state resident: part-time $478.25 per credit hour. Tuition, nonresident: part-time $966.50 per credit hour. Part-time tuition and fees vary according to program. *Financial support:* In 2009–10, 218 research assistantships with tuition reimbursements (averaging $6,854 per year), 202 teaching assistantships with tuition reimbursements (averaging $6,855 per year) were awarded. Total annual research expenditures: $9.3 million. *Unit head:* Dr. Carole Ames, Dean, 517-355-1734, Fax: 517-353-6393, E-mail: cames@msu.edu. *Application contact:* Dr. Carole Ames, Dean, 517-355-1734, Fax: 517-353-6393, E-mail: cames@msu.edu.

MidAmerica Nazarene University, Graduate Studies in Education, Olathe, KS 66062-1899. Offers ESOL (M Ed); professional teaching (M Ed); special education (MA); technology enhanced teaching (M Ed). *Accreditation:* NCATE. Part-time and evening/weekend programs available. Postbaccalaureate distance learning degree programs offered (no on-campus study). *Faculty:* 6 full-time (2 women), 14 part-time/adjunct (8 women). *Students:* 2 full-time (1 woman), 148 part-time (120 women); includes 15 minority (7 African Americans, 3 American Indian/Alaska Native, 1 Asian American or Pacific Islander, 4 Hispanic Americans). Average age 36. In 2009, 72 master's awarded. *Degree requirements:* For master's, thesis or alternative, creative project, technology leadership practicum. *Entrance requirements:* For master's, minimum undergraduate GPA of 2.8, 2 years of teaching experience. *Application deadline:* Applications are processed on a rolling basis. Application fee: $25. *Expenses:* Contact institution. *Financial support:* Applicants required to submit FAFSA. *Unit head:* Dr. Martin Dunlap, Director, 913-971-3292, Fax: 913-971-3407, E-mail: mhdunlap@mnu.edu. *Application contact:* Glenna Murray, Administrative Assistant, 913-971-3292, Fax: 913-971-3407, E-mail: gkmurray@mnu.edu.

Middle Tennessee State University, College of Graduate Studies, College of Education and Behavioral Science, Murfreesboro, TN 37132. Offers M Ed, MA, MCJ, MS, PhD, Ed S, Graduate Certificate. *Accreditation:* NCATE. Part-time and evening/weekend programs available. Postbaccalaureate distance learning degree programs offered. *Faculty:* 109 full-time (56 women), 7 part-time/adjunct (2 women). *Students:* 88 full-time (61 women), 1,081 part-time (885 women); includes 197 minority (163 African Americans, 1 American Indian/Alaska Native, 24 Asian Americans or Pacific Islanders, 9 Hispanic Americans). Average age 31. 715 applicants. In 2009, 338 master's, 11 doctorates, 94 other advanced degrees awarded. *Degree requirements:* For master's, variable foreign language requirement, comprehensive exam (for some programs), thesis (for some programs); for doctorate, comprehensive exam, thesis/dissertation; for other advanced degree, thesis (for some programs). *Entrance requirements:* Additional exam requirements/recommendations for international students: Required—TOEFL (minimum score 525 paper-based; 195 computer-based; 71 iBT) or IELTS (minimum score 6). *Application deadline:* For fall admission, 6/1 for domestic and international students. Applications are processed on a rolling basis. Application fee: $25 ($30 for international students). Electronic applications accepted. *Expenses:* Tuition, state resident: full-time $4404. Tuition, nonresident: full-time $10,956. *Financial support:* In 2009–10, 79 students received support. Career-related internships or fieldwork and institutionally sponsored loans available. Support available to part-time students. Financial award application deadline: 5/1; financial award applicants required to submit FAFSA. *Unit head:* Dr. Lana Seivers, Dean, 615-898-2874, Fax: 615-898-2530. *Application contact:* Dr. Michael Allen, Dean and Vice Provost for Research, 615-898-2840, Fax: 615-904-8020, E-mail: mallen@mtsu.edu.

Midwestern State University, Graduate Studies, College of Education, Wichita Falls, TX 76308. Offers M Ed, MA, ME. Part-time and evening/weekend programs available. *Degree requirements:* For master's, comprehensive exam, thesis (for some programs). *Entrance requirements:* For master's, GRE General Test or MAT. Additional exam requirements/recommendations for international students: Required—TOEFL (minimum score 550 paper-based; 213 computer-based). Electronic applications accepted. *Expenses:* Tuition, state resident: full-time $1620; part-time $90 per credit hour. Tuition, nonresident: full-time $2160; part-time $120 per credit hour. International tuition: $7506 full-time. Required fees: $3068.80; $145.60 per credit hour. $179 per semester.

Millersville University of Pennsylvania, College of Graduate and Professional Studies, School of Education, Millersville, PA 17551-0302. Offers M Ed, MS. *Accreditation:* NCATE. Part-time and evening/weekend programs available. *Faculty:* 86 full-time (45 women), 44 part-time/adjunct (21 women). *Students:* 80 full-time (62 women), 294 part-time (231 women); includes 12 minority (5 African Americans, 3 Asian Americans or Pacific Islanders, 4 Hispanic Americans), 1 international. Average age 30. 138 applicants, 66% accepted, 64 enrolled. In 2009, 137 master's awarded. *Degree requirements:* For master's, comprehensive exam (for some programs), thesis optional, graded portfolio (educational foundations). *Entrance requirements:* For master's, GRE or MAT, 3 letters of recommendation. Additional exam requirements/recommendations for international students: Required—TOEFL (minimum score 500 paper-based; 183 computer-based; 65 iBT) or IELTS (minimum score 6). *Application deadline:* For fall admission, 1/15 priority date for domestic and international students; for winter admission, 10/1 priority date for domestic and international students; for spring admission, 10/1 priority date for domestic and international students. Applications are processed on a rolling basis. Application fee: $40 ($50 for international students). Electronic applications accepted. *Expenses:* Tuition, state resident: full-time $6666; part-time $370 per credit. Tuition, nonresident: full-time $10,666; part-time $593 per credit. Required fees: $1578.50; $76.25 per credit. One-time fee: $60 part-time. Tuition and fees vary according to course load. *Financial support:* In 2009–10, 76 students received support, including 76 research assistantships with full and partial tuition reimbursements available (averaging $4,190 per year); institutionally sponsored loans and unspecified assistantships also available. Support available to part-time students. Financial award application deadline: 3/15; financial award applicants required to submit FAFSA. *Unit head:* Dr. Jane S. Bray, Dean, 717-872-3379, Fax: 717-872-3856, E-mail: jane.bray@millersville.edu. *Application contact:* Dr. Victor S. DeSantis, Dean of Graduate and Professional Studies, 717-872-3099, Fax: 717-872-3453, E-mail: victor.desantis@millersville.edu.

Milligan College, Area of Teacher Education, Milligan College, TN 37682. Offers M Ed. *Accreditation:* NCATE. Part-time programs available. *Faculty:* 6 full-time (5 women), 8 part-time/adjunct (5 women). *Students:* 37 full-time (22 women), 27 part-time (21 women); includes 3 minority (2 African Americans, 1 Hispanic American). 9 applicants, 100% accepted, 9 enrolled. In 2009, 39 master's awarded. *Degree requirements:* For master's, thesis, portfolio, research project. *Entrance requirements:* For master's, MAT or GRE General Test, interview. *Application deadline:* For fall admission, 8/1 priority date for domestic students; for winter admission, 11/15 priority date for domestic students; for spring admission, 4/1 priority date for domestic students. Applications are processed on a rolling basis. Application fee: $30. Electronic applications accepted. *Expenses:* Contact institution. *Financial support:* Career-related internships or fieldwork, institutionally sponsored loans, and scholarships/grants available. Financial award application deadline: 4/15; financial award applicants required to submit FAFSA. *Faculty research:* Teacher education evaluation, professional development centers, internship, early childhood, technology. *Unit head:* Dr. Lyn C. Howell, Director of Teacher Education, 423-461-8484, Fax: 423-461-3103, E-mail: lchowell@milligan.edu. *Application contact:* Jan Loveday, Graduate Admissions Specialist, 423-461-8306, Fax: 423-461-8982, E-mail: jloveday@milligan.edu.

Mills College, Graduate Studies, School of Education, Oakland, CA 94613-1000. Offers child life in hospitals (MA); early childhood education (MA); education (MA), including art education, curriculum and instruction, elementary education, English education, foreign language education, mathematics education, science education, secondary education, social studies education, teaching; educational leadership (MA, Ed D); infant mental health (MA). Part-time and evening/weekend programs available. *Faculty:* 11 full-time (9 women), 16 part-time/adjunct (14 women). *Students:* 138 full-time (119 women), 55 part-time (48 women); includes 71 minority (34 African Americans, 19 Asian Americans or Pacific Islanders, 18 Hispanic Americans), 3 international. Average age 34. 210 applicants, 82% accepted, 93 enrolled. In 2009, 54 master's, 15 doctorates awarded. Terminal master's awarded for partial completion of doctoral program. *Degree requirements:* For master's, comprehensive exam. *Entrance requirements:* For doctorate, GRE General Test. Additional exam requirements/recommendations for international students: Required—TOEFL. *Application deadline:* For fall admission, 2/1 for domestic and international students; for spring admission, 11/1 for domestic and international students. Applications are processed on a rolling basis. Application fee: $50. Electronic applications accepted. *Expenses:* Tuition: Full-time $26,326; part-time $6584 per course. Required fees: $896. One-time fee: $896 part-time. Tuition and fees vary according to program. *Financial support:* In 2009–10, 188 students received support, including 186 fellowships (averaging $6,499 per year), 28 teaching assistantships with partial tuition reimbursements available (averaging $3,187 per year); career-related internships or fieldwork and scholarships/grants also available. Support available to part-time students. Financial award application deadline: 2/1; financial award applicants required to submit FAFSA. *Faculty research:* Child development, gender and education, public policy, cross-cultural development, development of literacy. Total annual research expenditures: $1.2 million. *Unit head:* Joseph Kahne, Chairperson, 510-430-3190, Fax: 510-430-3314, E-mail: grad-studies@mills.edu. *Application contact:* Jessica King, Graduate Admission Specialist, 510-430-3305, Fax: 510-430-2159, E-mail: grad-studies@mills.edu.

Minnesota State University Mankato, College of Graduate Studies, College of Education, Mankato, MN 56001. Offers MAT, MS, Ed D, Certificate, SP. *Accreditation:* NCATE. Part-time and evening/weekend programs available. *Students:* 147 full-time (110 women), 477 part-time (335 women). In 2009, 46 other advanced degrees awarded. *Degree requirements:* For master's, comprehensive exam, thesis or alternative; for other advanced degree, thesis. *Entrance requirements:* For master's, GRE or MAT, minimum GPA of 3.0 during previous 2 years; for other advanced degree, minimum GPA of 3.0. Additional exam requirements/recommendations for international students: Required—TOEFL. *Application deadline:* Applications are processed on a rolling basis. Application fee: $40. Electronic applications accepted. *Expenses:* Tuition, state resident: full-time $5364. Tuition, nonresident: full-time $8314. *Financial support:* Fellowships with partial tuition reimbursements, research assistantships with full tuition reimbursements, teaching assistantships with full tuition reimbursements, career-related internships or fieldwork, Federal Work-Study, institutionally sponsored loans, and unspecified assistantships available. Support available to part-time students. Financial award application deadline: 3/15; financial award applicants required to submit FAFSA. *Faculty research:* Longitudinal studies of alternative education graduates, student achievement scores. *Unit head:* Dr. Jean Haar, Interim Dean, 507-389-5445. *Application contact:* 507-389-2321, E-mail: grad@mnsu.edu.

Minnesota State University Moorhead, Graduate Studies, College of Education and Human Services, Moorhead, MN 56563-0002. Offers counseling and student affairs (MS); curriculum and instruction (MS); educational leadership (MS, Ed S); nursing (MS); reading (MS); special education (MS); speech-language pathology (MS). *Accreditation:* NCATE. Part-time and evening/weekend programs available. *Degree requirements:* For master's, comprehensive exam, final oral exam, project or thesis. *Entrance requirements:* Additional exam requirements/recommendations for international students: Required—TOEFL. Electronic applications accepted.

Misericordia University, College of Professional Studies and Social Sciences, Program in Education/Curriculum, Dallas, PA 18612-1098. Offers MS. Part-time and evening/weekend programs available. Postbaccalaureate distance learning degree programs offered. *Faculty:* 4 full-time (3 women), 9 part-time/adjunct (4 women). *Students:* 48 part-time (37 women); includes 2 minority (1 Asian American or Pacific Islander, 1 Hispanic American). Average age 32. In 2009, 9 master's awarded. *Degree requirements:* For master's, thesis or alternative. *Entrance requirements:* For master's, GRE General Test or MAT, minimum GPA of 3.0. *Application deadline:* For fall admission, 8/1 priority date for domestic students. Applications are processed on a rolling basis. Application fee: $25. Electronic applications accepted. *Financial support:* In 2009–10, 12 students received support. Scholarships/grants available. Support available to part-time students. Financial award application deadline: 6/30; financial award applicants required to submit FAFSA. *Unit head:* Dr. Catherine Kosenak, Director of Graduate Education Programs, 570-674-8058, E-mail: ckosenak@misericordia.edu. *Application contact:* Larree Brown, Coordinator of Part-Time Undergraduate and Graduate Programs, 570-674-6451, Fax: 570-674-6232, E-mail: lbrown@misericordia.edu.

Mississippi College, Graduate School, School of Education, Clinton, MS 39058. Offers M Ed, MS, Ed D, Ed S. *Accreditation:* NCATE. Part-time and evening/weekend programs available. Postbaccalaureate distance learning degree programs offered (no on-campus study). *Faculty:* 19 full-time (10 women), 23 part-time/adjunct (10 women). *Students:* 101 full-time (81 women), 396 part-time (327 women); includes 228 minority (224 African Americans, 3 American Indian/Alaska Native, 1 Asian American or Pacific Islander), 8 international. Average age 30. In 2009, 193 master's awarded. *Degree requirements:* For master's, comprehensive exam, thesis optional. *Entrance requirements:* For master's, GRE or NTE, minimum GPA of 2.5, Class A Certificate (for some programs); for Ed S, NTE, minimum GPA of 3.0. Additional exam requirements/recommendations for international students: Recommended—IELTS. Application fee: $30. Electronic applications accepted. *Expenses:* Tuition: Part-time $452 per credit hour. Required fees: $101 per semester. Tuition and fees vary according to degree level, campus/location, program and student level. *Financial support:* Teaching assistantships, career-related internships or fieldwork, Federal Work-Study, scholarships/grants, and unspecified assistantships available. Support available to part-time students. Financial award application deadline: 4/1; financial award applicants required to submit FAFSA. *Unit head:* Dr. Don Locke, Dean, 601-925-3250, E-mail: locke@mc.edu. *Application contact:* Elnora Lewis, Secretary, 601-925-3225, Fax: 601-925-3889, E-mail: lewis09@mc.edu.

Mississippi State University, College of Education, Mississippi State, MS 39762. Offers MAT, MS, MSIT, Ed D, PhD, Ed S. *Accreditation:* NCATE. Part-time and evening/weekend programs available. Postbaccalaureate distance learning degree programs offered (minimal on-campus study). *Faculty:* 54 full-time (33 women), 1 (woman) part-time/adjunct. *Students:* 300 full-time (200 women), 547 part-time (429 women); includes 353 minority (342 African Americans, 4 American Indian/Alaska Native, 3 Asian Americans or Pacific Islanders, 4 Hispanic Americans), 11 international. Average age 35. 423 applicants, 65% accepted, 217 enrolled. In 2009, 197 master's, 64 doctorates, 42 other advanced degrees awarded. Terminal master's awarded for partial completion of doctoral program. *Degree requirements:* For master's, thesis optional, comprehensive oral or written exam; for doctorate, thesis/dissertation; for Ed S, thesis or alternative, final written or oral exam. *Entrance requirements:* For master's, doctorate, and Ed S, GRE. Additional exam requirements/recommendations for international students:

Education—General

Mississippi State University (continued)

Required—TOEFL (minimum score 550 paper-based; 213 computer-based; 79 iBT); Recommended—IELTS (minimum score 6.5). *Application deadline:* For fall admission, 7/1 for domestic students, 5/1 for international students; for spring admission, 11/1 for domestic students, 9/1 for international students. Applications are processed on a rolling basis. Application fee: $40. Electronic applications accepted. *Expenses:* Tuition, state resident: full-time $2575.50; part-time $286.25 per credit hour. Tuition, nonresident: full-time $6510; part-time $723.50 per credit hour. Tuition and fees vary according to course load. *Financial support:* In 2009–10, 8 research assistantships (averaging $8,794 per year), 19 teaching assistantships (averaging $9,344 per year) were awarded; career-related internships or fieldwork, Federal Work-Study, institutionally sponsored loans, scholarships/grants, and unspecified assistantships also available. Financial award applicants required to submit FAFSA. *Faculty research:* Leadership behavior, creativity measures, early childhood education, employability of the blind, quality indicators of professional educators. *Unit head:* Dr. Richard Blackbourn, Dean, 662-325-3717, Fax: 662-325-8784, E-mail: rlb277@msstate.edu. *Application contact:* Dr. Sue Minchew, Associate Dean and Professor, 662-325-3717, Fax: 662-325-8784, E-mail: sminshew@colled.msstate.edu.

Mississippi University for Women, Graduate School, College of Education and Human Sciences, Columbus, MS 39701-9998. Offers differentiated instruction (M Ed); gifted studies (M Ed); teaching (MAT). *Accreditation:* ASHA; NCATE. Part-time programs available. *Degree requirements:* For master's, comprehensive exam, thesis optional. *Entrance requirements:* For master's, GRE General Test or NTE (M Ed in gifted education or MS in speech/language pathology), MAT (M Ed in instructional management), minimum QPA of 3.0.

Mississippi Valley State University, Department of Education, Itta Bena, MS 38941-1400. Offers education (MAT); elementary education (MA). *Accreditation:* NCATE.

Missouri Baptist University, Graduate Programs, St. Louis, MO 63141-8660. Offers business administration (MBA); Christian ministries (MACM); counseling (MAC); education (MSE); education administration (MEA); educational leadership (MSE, Ed S); teaching (MAT).

Missouri Southern State University, Program in Teaching, Joplin, MO 64801-1595. Offers MAT. *Accreditation:* NCATE.

Molloy College, Graduate Education Program, Rockville Centre, NY 11571-5002. Offers MS Ed, Certificate. *Accreditation:* NCATE. *Faculty:* 20 full-time (15 women), 24 part-time/adjunct (15 women). *Students:* 120 full-time (91 women), 225 part-time (178 women); includes 16 African Americans, 6 Asian Americans or Pacific Islanders, 24 Hispanic Americans. Average age 30. In 2009, 128 master's awarded. *Application deadline:* Applications are processed on a rolling basis. *Expenses:* Tuition: Part-time $765 per credit. Required fees: $340 per semester. *Unit head:* Sr. Bernadette Donovan, Associate Dean and Director of Graduate Programs, 516-678-5000 Ext. 6280. *Application contact:* Alina Haitz, Assistant Director of Graduate Admissions, 516-678-5000 Ext. 6399, Fax: 516-256-2247, E-mail: ahaitz@molloy.edu.

Monmouth University, Graduate School, School of Education, West Long Branch, NJ 07764-1898. Offers education (M Ed); initial certification (MAT), including elementary level, K-12, secondary level; learning disabilities-teacher consultant (Certificate); principal (MS Ed); principal/school administrator (MS Ed); reading specialist (MS Ed, Certificate); school counseling (MS Ed); special education (MS Ed), including autism, learning disabilities teacher consultant, teacher of students with disabilities, teaching in inclusive settings; supervisor (Certificate); teacher of the handicapped (Certificate); teaching english to speakers of other languages (TESOL) (Certificate). *Accreditation:* NCATE. Part-time and evening/weekend programs available. *Faculty:* 20 full-time (13 women), 32 part-time/adjunct (22 women). *Students:* 182 full-time (146 women), 353 part-time (286 women); includes 40 minority (15 African Americans, 3 American Indian/Alaska Native, 5 Asian Americans or Pacific Islanders, 17 Hispanic Americans), 1 international. Average age 29. 361 applicants, 96% accepted, 176 enrolled. In 2009, 178 master's awarded. *Entrance requirements:* For master's, minimum GPA of 3.0 in major, 2.75 overall; 2 letters of recommendation (for some programs). Additional exam requirements/recommendations for international students: Required—TOEFL (minimum score 550 paper-based; 213 computer-based; 79 iBT), IELTS (minimum score 5), Michigan English Language Assessment Battery (minimum score 77), Cambridge A, B, C. *Application deadline:* For fall admission, 7/15 priority date for domestic students, 7/1 for international students; for spring admission, 11/15 priority date for domestic students, 11/1 for international students. Applications are processed on a rolling basis. Application fee: $50. Electronic applications accepted. *Expenses:* Tuition: Part-time $773 per credit. Required fees: $157 per semester. *Financial support:* In 2009–10, 326 students received support, including 211 fellowships (averaging $1,824 per year), 23 research assistantships (averaging $7,943 per year); career-related internships or fieldwork, scholarships/grants, and unspecified assistantships also available. Support available to part-time students. Financial award applicants required to submit FAFSA. *Faculty research:* Multicultural literacy, science and mathematics teaching strategies, teacher as reflective practitioner, children with disabilities, varied contexts of learning. *Unit head:* Dr. Terri Rothman, Associate Dean, 732-571-7507, Fax: 732-263-5277, E-mail: trothman@monmouth.edu. *Application contact:* Kevin Roane, Director, Office of Graduate Admission, 732-571-3452, Fax: 732-263-5123, E-mail: gradadm@monmouth.edu.

Montana State University, College of Graduate Studies, College of Education, Health, and Human Development, Department of Education, Bozeman, MT 59717. Offers adult and higher education (Ed D); curriculum and instruction (Ed D, Ed S); education (M Ed), including adult and higher education, curriculum and instruction, educational leadership, school counseling; educational leadership (Ed D, Ed S). Part-time programs available. Postbaccalaureate distance learning degree programs offered (minimal on-campus study). *Faculty:* 22 full-time (13 women), 18 part-time/adjunct (14 women). *Students:* 15 full-time (8 women), 210 part-time (126 women); includes 29 minority (27 American Indian/Alaska Native, 1 Asian American or Pacific Islander, 1 Hispanic American), 2 international. Average age 37. 52 applicants. In 2009, 62 master's, 9 doctorates awarded. *Degree requirements:* For master's, comprehensive exam; for doctorate, comprehensive exam, thesis/dissertation. *Entrance requirements:* For master's and doctorate, GRE General Test. Additional exam requirements/recommendations for international students: Required—TOEFL (minimum score 550 paper-based; 213 computer-based). *Application deadline:* For fall admission, 7/15 priority date for domestic students, 5/15 priority date for international students; for spring admission, 12/1 priority date for domestic students, 10/1 priority date for international students. Applications are processed on a rolling basis. Application fee: $30. Electronic applications accepted. *Expenses:* Tuition, state resident: full-time $5635; part-time $3492 per year. Tuition, nonresident: full-time $17,212; part-time $7865.10 per year. Required fees: $1441; $153.15 per credit. Tuition and fees vary according to course load and program. *Financial support:* In 2009–10, 45 students received support, including 5 teaching assistantships with tuition reimbursements available (averaging $9,000 per year); traineeships, tuition waivers (full and partial), and unspecified assistantships also available. Financial award application deadline: 3/1; financial award applicants required to submit FAFSA. *Faculty research:* Online teaching and learning, statistical strategies to course and student assessment, environmental education, copyright issues/web-based resources, multicultural education, curriculum design, preparation for North American teachers to be administrators, NCES data sets, relational trust in public school administration. Total annual research expenditures: $1.2 million. *Unit head:* Dr. Joanne Erickson, Interim Department Head, 406-994-6670, Fax: 406-994-3261, E-mail: jle@montana.edu. *Application contact:* Dr. Carl A. Fox, Vice Provost for Graduate Education, 406-994-4145, Fax: 406-994-7433, E-mail: gradstudy@montana.edu.

Montana State University Billings, College of Education, Billings, MT 59101-0298. Offers M Ed, MS Sp Ed, Certificate. *Accreditation:* NCATE. Part-time programs available. Postbaccalaureate distance learning degree programs offered (minimal on-campus study). *Degree requirements:* For master's, thesis optional. *Entrance requirements:* For master's, GRE General Test. *Faculty research:* Social studies education, science education.

Montana State University–Northern, College of Education and Graduate Programs, Havre, MT 59501-7751. Offers counselor education (M Ed); learning development (M Ed). Part-time and evening/weekend programs available. Postbaccalaureate distance learning degree programs offered (minimal on-campus study). *Degree requirements:* For master's, comprehensive exam, oral exams or thesis. *Entrance requirements:* For master's, GRE General Test or MAT, minimum GPA of 3.0. Electronic applications accepted.

Montclair State University, The Graduate School, College of Education and Human Services, Montclair, NJ 07043-1624. Offers M Ed, MA, MAT, MPH, MS, Ed D, PhD, Certificate. *Accreditation:* NCATE. Part-time and evening/weekend programs available. *Faculty:* 107 full-time (76 women), 233 part-time/adjunct (161 women). *Students:* 463 full-time (334 women), 1,010 part-time (807 women). Average age 32. 633 applicants, 60% accepted, 299 enrolled. In 2009, 427 master's, 2 doctorates, 19 other advanced degrees awarded. *Degree requirements:* For master's, comprehensive exam (for some programs), thesis (for some programs); for doctorate, comprehensive exam, thesis/dissertation. *Entrance requirements:* For master's, GRE, GMAT, MAT, 2 letters of recommendation; for doctorate, GRE General Test, 3 letters of recommendation. Additional exam requirements/recommendations for international students: Required—TOEFL (minimum score 83 computer-based), or IELTS. *Application deadline:* For fall admission, 6/1 for international students; for spring admission, 10/1 for international students. Applications are processed on a rolling basis. Application fee: $60. Electronic applications accepted. *Expenses:* Tuition, area resident: Part-time $486.74 per credit. Tuition, state resident: part-time $486.74 per credit. Tuition, nonresident: part-time $751.34 per credit. Tuition and fees vary according to degree level and program. *Financial support:* In 2009–10, 70 research assistantships with full tuition reimbursements (averaging $7,000 per year), 6 teaching assistantships with full tuition reimbursements were awarded; Federal Work-Study, scholarships/grants, and unspecified assistantships also available. Support available to part-time students. Financial award application deadline: 3/1; financial award applicants required to submit FAFSA. *Faculty research:* Elementary and high school education, data collection, adolescent physical/activity. *Unit head:* Dr. Ada Beth Cutler, Dean, 973-655-5167, E-mail: cutler@mail.montclair.edu. *Application contact:* Amy Aiello, Director of Graduate Admissions and Operations, E-mail: graduate.school@montclair.edu.

Montreat College, School of Professional and Adult Studies, Montreat, NC 28757-1267. Offers business administration (MBA); K-6 education (MA Ed). Evening/weekend programs available. Postbaccalaureate distance learning degree programs offered. *Entrance requirements:* Additional exam requirements/recommendations for international students: Required—TOEFL (minimum score 500 paper-based; 190 computer-based).

Morehead State University, Graduate Programs, College of Education, Morehead, KY 40351. Offers MA, MA Ed, MAT, Ed S. *Accreditation:* NCATE. Part-time and evening/weekend programs available. *Faculty:* 42 full-time (25 women), 10 part-time/adjunct (4 women). *Students:* 102 full-time (70 women), 616 part-time (448 women); includes 23 minority (15 African Americans, 2 American Indian/Alaska Native, 1 Asian American or Pacific Islander, 5 Hispanic Americans). Average age 34. 423 applicants, 71% accepted, 157 enrolled. In 2009, 253 master's, 5 other advanced degrees awarded. *Degree requirements:* For master's, comprehensive exam, thesis or alternative; for Ed S, thesis. *Entrance requirements:* For master's, GRE General Test or PRAXIS, minimum overall undergraduate GPA of 2.5; for Ed S, GRE General Test, interview, master's degree, minimum GPA of 3.5, work experience. Additional exam requirements/recommendations for international students: Required—TOEFL (minimum score 500 paper-based; 173 computer-based). *Application deadline:* For fall admission, 8/1 priority date for domestic and international students; for spring admission, 12/1 priority date for domestic and international students. Applications are processed on a rolling basis. Application fee: $30. Electronic applications accepted. *Expenses:* Tuition, state resident: full-time $6318; part-time $351 per credit hour. Tuition, nonresident: full-time $15,804; part-time $878 per credit hour. *Financial support:* In 2009–10, 3 research assistantships (averaging $10,000 per year), 4 teaching assistantships (averaging $10,000 per year) were awarded; career-related internships or fieldwork, Federal Work-Study, and unspecified assistantships also available. Financial award application deadline: 3/15; financial award applicants required to submit FAFSA. *Faculty research:* Regional economic development, computer applications for school administrators, effectiveness of teacher interns, perceptual processes, alcoholism. *Unit head:* Dr. Cathy Gunn, Dean, 606-783-2162, Fax: 606-783-5029, E-mail: c.gunn@moreheadstate.edu. *Application contact:* Michelle Barber, Graduate Recruitment and Retention Assistant Director, 606-783-5127, Fax: 606-783-5061, E-mail: m.barber@moreheadstate.edu.

Morgan State University, School of Graduate Studies, School of Education and Urban Studies, Baltimore, MD 21251. Offers MAT, MS, MSW, Ed D, PhD. Part-time programs available. *Degree requirements:* For master's, comprehensive exam; for doctorate, comprehensive exam, thesis/dissertation. *Entrance requirements:* For doctorate, GRE General Test or MAT. Additional exam requirements/recommendations for international students: Required—TOEFL (minimum score 550 paper-based; 213 computer-based). *Faculty research:* Multicultural education, cooperative learning, psychology of cognition.

Morningside College, Graduate Division, Department of Education, Sioux City, IA 51106. Offers professional educator (MAT); special education: instructional strategist I: mild/moderate elementary (K-6) (MAT); special education: instructional strategist II-mild/moderate secondary (7-12) (MAT); special education: K-12 instructional strategist II-behavior disorders/learning disabilities (MAT); special education: K-12 instructional strategist II-mental disabilities (MAT). Part-time and evening/weekend programs available. *Entrance requirements:* For master's, MAT, writing sample.

Mount Aloysius College, Program in Education, Cresson, PA 16630-1999. Offers MS. Part-time programs available.

Mount Mary College, Graduate Programs, Programs in Education, Milwaukee, WI 53222-4597. Offers education (MA); professional development (MA). Part-time and evening/weekend programs available. *Faculty:* 5 full-time (all women), 10 part-time/adjunct (7 women). *Students:* 34 full-time (27 women), 39 part-time (37 women); includes 9 minority (5 African Americans, 4 Hispanic Americans). Average age 37. 23 applicants, 83% accepted, 18 enrolled. In 2009, 24 master's awarded. *Degree requirements:* For master's, action research project. *Entrance requirements:* For master's, minimum GPA of 2.75, teaching license. Additional exam requirements/recommendations for international students: Required—TOEFL (minimum score 500 paper-based; 173 computer-based). *Application deadline:* For fall admission, 8/29 priority date for domestic and international students; for spring admission, 1/20 for domestic and international students. Applications are processed on a rolling basis. Application fee: $35 ($100 for international students). *Expenses:* Tuition: Part-time $595 per credit. Tuition and fees vary according to program. *Financial support:* In 2009–10, 1 student received support. Federal Work-Study available. Support available to part-time students. Financial award application deadline: 5/1; financial award applicants required to submit FAFSA. *Faculty research:* Staff development, writing across the curriculum, effective schools, critical thinking skills, mathematics education. *Unit head:* Dr. Deb Dosemagen, Director, 414-256-1214, E-mail: dosemagd@mtmary.edu. *Application contact:* Dr. Deb Dosemagen, Director, 414-256-1214, E-mail: dosemagd@mtmary.edu.

Mount Mercy College, Program in Education, Cedar Rapids, IA 52402-4797. Offers reading (MA Ed); special education (MA Ed). *Entrance requirements:* For master's, minimum cumulative GPA of 3.0, 2 letters of recommendation, resume, valid teaching license. Additional exam requirements/recommendations for international students: Required—TOEFL (minimum score 570 paper-based; 88 iBT). Electronic applications accepted.

Mount Saint Mary College, Division of Education, Newburgh, NY 12550-3494. Offers adolescence and special education (MS Ed); adolescence education (MS Ed); childhood and special education (MS Ed); childhood education (MS Ed); literacy (5-12) (Advanced Certificate); literacy (birth-6) (Advanced Certificate); literacy and special education (MS Ed); literacy/childhood (MS Ed); middle school (5-6) (MS Ed); middle school (7-9) (MS Ed); special education (1-6) (MS Ed); special education (7-12) (MS Ed). *Accreditation:* NCATE. Part-time and evening/weekend programs available. *Faculty:* 15 full-time (13 women), 16 part-time/adjunct (10 women). *Students:* 76 full-time (63 women), 226 part-time (188 women); includes 27 minority (7 African Americans, 3 Asian Americans or Pacific Islanders, 17 Hispanic Americans). Average age 30. 141 applicants, 56% accepted, 44 enrolled. In 2009, 142 master's awarded. *Application*

deadline: Applications are processed on a rolling basis. Application fee: $45. *Expenses:* Tuition: Full-time $13,356; part-time $742 per credit. Required fees: $50 per semester. *Financial support:* In 2009–10, 106 students received support. Unspecified assistantships available. Financial award application deadline: 4/15; financial award applicants required to submit FAFSA. *Faculty research:* Learning and teaching styles, computers in special education, language development. *Unit head:* Dr. Theresa Lewis, Coordinator, 845-569-3149, Fax: 845-569-3535, E-mail: tlewis@msmc.edu. *Application contact:* Dr. Theresa Lewis, Coordinator, 845-569-3149, Fax: 845-569-3535, E-mail: tlewis@msmc.edu.

Mount St. Mary's College, Graduate Division, Department of Education, Los Angeles, CA 90049-1599. Offers administrative services (MS); elementary education (MS); instructional leadership (MS); secondary education (MS); special education (MS). Part-time and evening/weekend programs available. *Faculty:* 7 full-time (all women), 14 part-time/adjunct (12 women). *Students:* 90 full-time (68 women), 53 part-time (41 women); includes 69 minority (12 African Americans, 8 Asian Americans or Pacific Islanders, 49 Hispanic Americans). Average age 36. In 2009, 35 master's awarded. *Degree requirements:* For master's, thesis, research project. *Entrance requirements:* For master's, minimum GPA of 2.5. Additional exam requirements/recommendations for international students: Required—TOEFL (minimum score 550 iBT). *Application deadline:* For fall admission, 7/15 priority date for domestic students; for spring admission, 11/15 priority date for domestic students. *Expenses:* Tuition: Part-time $730 per unit. Part-time tuition and fees vary according to degree level and program. *Financial support:* Career-related internships or fieldwork, institutionally sponsored loans, and tuition waivers (full and partial) available. Support available to part-time students. Financial award application deadline: 3/15; financial award applicants required to submit FAFSA. *Unit head:* Dr. Shelly Tochluk, Chair, 213-477-2623, E-mail: stochluk@msmc.la.edu. *Application contact:* Director of Graduate Admission.

Mount St. Mary's University, Program in Education, Emmitsburg, MD 21727-7799. Offers M Ed, MAT. *Accreditation:* NCATE. Part-time and evening/weekend programs available. *Faculty:* 6 full-time (5 women), 5 part-time/adjunct (4 women). *Students:* 34 full-time (26 women), 81 part-time (67 women); includes 7 minority (3 African Americans, 1 Asian American or Pacific Islander, 3 Hispanic Americans), 1 international. Average age 33. 53 applicants, 75% accepted, 23 enrolled. In 2009, 24 master's awarded. *Degree requirements:* For master's, thesis (for some programs), exit portfolio/presentation. *Entrance requirements:* For master's, PRAXIS I, PRAXIS II. Additional exam requirements/recommendations for international students: Required—TOEFL (minimum score 550 paper-based; 213 computer-based). *Application deadline:* For fall admission, 8/15 for domestic and international students. Applications are processed on a rolling basis. Application fee: $35. *Expenses:* Contact institution. *Financial support:* In 2009–10, 50 students received support. Career-related internships or fieldwork and unspecified assistantships available. Financial award applicants required to submit FAFSA. *Faculty research:* Paraprofessionals/instructional assistants in the general and special education classrooms, professional development schools, nature of pre-service teacher's reflections, use of '"language of possibility' in teacher-student interactions in public and Catholic high schools, teacher development. *Unit head:* Laura Frazier, Director, 301-447-5371, Fax: 301-447-5250, E-mail: frazier@msmary.edu. *Application contact:* Laura Frazier, Director, 301-447-5371, Fax: 301-447-5250, E-mail: frazier@msmary.edu.

Mount Saint Vincent University, Graduate Programs, Faculty of Education, Halifax, NS B3M 2J6, Canada. Offers adult education (M Ed, MA Ed, MA-R); curriculum studies (M Ed, MA Ed, MA-R), including education of young adolescents, general studies, teaching English as a second language; educational foundations (M Ed, MA Ed, MA-R); educational psychology (M Ed, MA Ed, MA-R), including education of the blind or visually impaired (M Ed, MA Ed), education of the deaf or hard of hearing (M Ed, MA Ed), educational psychology (MA-R), human relations (M Ed, MA Ed); elementary education (M Ed, MA Ed, MA-R); literacy education (M Ed, MA Ed, MA-R); school psychology (MASP). Part-time and evening/weekend programs available. Postbaccalaureate distance learning degree programs offered (minimal on-campus study). *Degree requirements:* For master's, thesis (for some programs), practicum. *Entrance requirements:* For master's, bachelor's degree in related field. Electronic applications accepted.

Mount Vernon Nazarene University, Department of Education, Mount Vernon, OH 43050-9500. Offers education (MA Ed); professional educator's license (MA Ed). *Accreditation:* NCATE. Part-time and evening/weekend programs available. *Degree requirements:* For master's, project.

Multnomah University, Multnomah Bible College Graduate Degree Programs, Portland, OR 97220-5898. Offers counseling (MA); teaching (MA); TESOL (MA). *Faculty:* 3 full-time (all women), 26 part-time/adjunct (16 women). *Students:* 45 full-time (30 women), 22 part-time (13 women); includes 10 minority (1 African American, 1 American Indian/Alaska Native, 5 Asian Americans or Pacific Islanders, 3 Hispanic Americans), 1 international. Average age 35. 56 applicants, 42 enrolled. *Degree requirements:* For master's, thesis optional. *Entrance requirements:* Additional exam requirements/recommendations for international students: Required—TOEFL (minimum score 550 paper-based; 213 computer-based). *Application deadline:* For fall admission, 7/15 for domestic and international students; for spring admission, 11/15 for domestic and international students. *Expenses:* Tuition: Full-time $10,464; part-time $436 per credit hour. *Financial support:* In 2009–10, 61 students received support. Career-related internships or fieldwork and scholarships/grants available. Support available to part-time students. Financial award application deadline: 7/1; financial award applicants required to submit FAFSA. *Unit head:* Dr. Wayne Strickland, Academic Dean, 503-251-6401. *Application contact:* Penny Rader, Seminary Admissions Counselor, 503-251-6485, Fax: 503-254-1268, E-mail: admiss@multnomah.edu.

Murray State University, College of Education, Murray, KY 42071. Offers MA Ed, MS, Ed D, PhD, Ed S. *Accreditation:* NCATE. Part-time programs available.

Muskingum University, Graduate Programs in Education, New Concord, OH 43762. Offers MAE, MAT. *Accreditation:* NCATE. Part-time programs available. *Entrance requirements:* For master's, minimum GPA of 2.7, teaching license. *Faculty research:* Brain behavior relationships, school partnerships, staff development, school law, proficiency testing, multi-age groupings.

Naropa University, Graduate Programs, Program in Contemplative Education, Boulder, CO 80302-6697. Offers MA. Part-time and evening/weekend programs available. Postbaccalaureate distance learning degree programs offered (minimal on-campus study). *Degree requirements:* For master's, thesis. *Entrance requirements:* For master's, interview (by phone or in person), 3 letters of recommendation, resume. Additional exam requirements/recommendations for international students: Required—TOEFL (minimum score 600 paper-based; 250 computer-based). Electronic applications accepted.

National-Louis University, National College of Education, Chicago, IL 60603. Offers M Ed, MAT, MS Ed, Ed D, CAS, Ed S. *Accreditation:* NCATE. Part-time and evening/weekend programs available. *Faculty:* 170 full-time (120 women), 179 part-time/adjunct (144 women). *Students:* 695 full-time (552 women), 2,853 part-time (2,153 women); includes 768 minority (433 African Americans, 5 American Indian/Alaska Native, 108 Asian Americans or Pacific Islanders, 222 Hispanic Americans). Average age 34. 631 applicants, 63% accepted, 378 enrolled. In 2009, 1,662 master's, 22 doctorates, 160 other advanced degrees awarded. *Degree requirements:* For doctorate, comprehensive exam, thesis/dissertation. *Entrance requirements:* For master's, MAT or GRE, minimum GPA of 3.0; for doctorate, GRE General Test, minimum GPA of 3.25, interview, resume, writing sample, 4 recommendations. Additional exam requirements/recommendations for international students: Required—TOEFL (minimum score 550 paper-based; 213 computer-based; 79 iBT). *Application deadline:* Applications are processed on a rolling basis. Application fee: $40. *Expenses:* Tuition: Full-time $17,160; part-time $715 per semester hour. Tuition and fees vary according to course load, degree level, campus/location and program. *Financial support:* Fellowships, research assistantships, teaching assistantships, career-related internships or fieldwork, Federal Work-Study, institutionally sponsored loans, and scholarships/grants available. Support available to part-time students. Financial award applicants required to submit FAFSA. *Unit head:* Dr. Alison Hilsabeck, Dean, 312-361-3580, Fax: 312-261-2580, E-mail: ahilsabeck@nl.edu. *Application contact:* Dr. George Valcourt, Vice President of Enrollment and Student Services, 312-261-3550, Fax: 312-261-3550, E-mail: george.valcourt@nl.edu.

National University, Academic Affairs, School of Education, La Jolla, CA 92037-1011. Offers M Ed, MA, MS. Part-time and evening/weekend programs available. Postbaccalaureate distance learning degree programs offered (no on-campus study). *Faculty:* 91 full-time (52 women), 563 part-time/adjunct (346 women). *Students:* 4,587 full-time (3,257 women), 8,352 part-time (5,636 women); includes 4,156 minority (1,040 African Americans, 81 American Indian/Alaska Native, 697 Asian Americans or Pacific Islanders, 2,338 Hispanic Americans), 14 international. Average age 36. 6,628 applicants, 100% accepted, 5075 enrolled. In 2009, 2,329 master's awarded. *Degree requirements:* For master's, thesis (for some programs). *Entrance requirements:* For master's, interview, minimum GPA of 2.5. Additional exam requirements/recommendations for international students: Required—TOEFL (minimum score 550 paper-based; 213 computer-based; 79 iBT), IELTS (minimum score 6). *Application deadline:* Applications are processed on a rolling basis. Application fee: $60 ($65 for international students). Electronic applications accepted. *Expenses:* Tuition: Part-time $338 per quarter hour. *Financial support:* Career-related internships or fieldwork, institutionally sponsored loans, scholarships/grants, and tuition waivers (partial) available. Support available to part-time students. Financial award application deadline: 6/30. *Faculty research:* Teacher education, special education, educational effectiveness, teaching abroad, school counseling. *Unit head:* Dr. Carl Kalani Beyer, Interim Dean, 858-642-8320, Fax: 858-642-8724, E-mail: cbeyer@nu.edu. *Application contact:* Dominick Giovanniello, Associate Regional Dean—San Diego, 800-NAT-UNIV, Fax: 858-541-7792, E-mail: dgiovann@nu.edu.

Nazareth College of Rochester, Graduate Studies, Department of Education, Rochester, NY 14618-3790. Offers educational technology/computer education (MS Ed); inclusive education-adolescence level (MS Ed); inclusive education-childhood level (MS Ed); inclusive education-early childhood level (MS Ed); literacy education (MS Ed); teaching English to speakers of other languages (MS Ed). *Accreditation:* Teacher Education Accreditation Council. Part-time and evening/weekend programs available. *Entrance requirements:* For master's, minimum GPA of 3.0.

Neumann University, Program in Education, Aston, PA 19014-1298. Offers MS. Part-time programs available. *Faculty:* 2 full-time (1 woman), 31 part-time/adjunct (15 women). *Students:* 44 full-time (32 women), 220 part-time (166 women); includes 19 minority (16 African Americans, 1 Asian American or Pacific Islander, 2 Hispanic Americans). Average age 34. 100 applicants, 100% accepted, 75 enrolled. In 2009, 60 master's awarded. *Entrance requirements:* For master's, GRE, MAT, or PRAXIS. Additional exam requirements/recommendations for international students: Required—TOEFL. *Application deadline:* Applications are processed on a rolling basis. Application fee: $50. *Expenses:* Tuition: Full-time $10,260; part-time $570 per credit hour. *Financial support:* Available to part-time students. Application deadline: 3/15. *Unit head:* Dr. Andrew DeSanto, Coordinator, Division of Education and Human Services, 610-558-5404, Fax: 610-459-1370, E-mail: desantoa@neumann.edu. *Application contact:* Kittie D. Pain, Associate Director of Admissions, Graduate and Adult Programs, 610-558-5613, Fax: 610-558-5652, E-mail: paink@neumann.edu.

Neumann University, Programs in Education, Aston, PA 19014-1298. Offers Ed D. *Degree requirements:* For doctorate, comprehensive exam, thesis/dissertation. *Entrance requirements:* For doctorate, PRAXIS, GRE. *Expenses:* Contact institution.

New England College, Program in Education, Henniker, NH 03242-3293. Offers higher education administration (MS); literacy and language arts (M Ed); meeting the needs of all learners/special education (M Ed); teacher leadership/school reform (M Ed). Part-time and evening/weekend programs available.

Newman University, School of Education, Wichita, KS 67213-2097. Offers building leadership (MS Ed); curriculum and instruction (MS Ed), including accountability, English as a second language. *Accreditation:* NCATE. Part-time programs available. Postbaccalaureate distance learning degree programs offered (no on-campus study). *Faculty:* 3 full-time (0 women), 22 part-time/adjunct (all women). *Students:* 12 full-time (8 women), 329 part-time (263 women); includes 29 minority (5 African Americans, 2 American Indian/Alaska Native, 5 Asian Americans or Pacific Islanders, 17 Hispanic Americans), 4 international. Average age 37. 41 applicants, 76% accepted, 24 enrolled. In 2009, 57 master's awarded. *Degree requirements:* For master's, thesis optional. *Entrance requirements:* For master's, interview, minimum GPA of 3.0, writing sample, 3 letters of recommendation. Additional exam requirements/recommendations for international students: Required—TOEFL (minimum score 600 paper-based; 250 computer-based; 100 iBT). *Application deadline:* For fall admission, 8/15 priority date for domestic students, 7/15 priority date for international students; for spring admission, 1/10 priority date for domestic students, 11/15 priority date for international students. Applications are processed on a rolling basis. Application fee: $25 ($40 for international students). Electronic applications accepted. *Expenses:* Contact institution. *Financial support:* In 2009–10, 8 students received support. Federal Work-Study available. Financial award application deadline: 8/15; financial award applicants required to submit FAFSA. *Unit head:* Dr. Guy Glidden, Director, 316-942-4291 Ext. 2331, Fax: 316-942-4483, E-mail: gliddeng@newmanu.edu. *Application contact:* Linda Kay Sabala, Director of Graduate Admissions, 316-942-4291 Ext. 2230, Fax: 316-942-4483, E-mail: sabalal@newmanu.edu.

New Mexico Highlands University, Graduate Studies, School of Education, Las Vegas, NM 87701. Offers curriculum and instruction (MA); education (MA), including counseling, school counseling; educational leadership (MA); exercise and sport sciences (MA), including human performance and sport, sports administration, teacher education; guidance and counseling (MA), including professional counseling, rehabilitation counseling, school counseling; special education (MA), including . Part-time programs available. *Degree requirements:* For master's, comprehensive exam, thesis or alternative. *Entrance requirements:* For master's, minimum undergraduate GPA of 3.0. Additional exam requirements/recommendations for international students: Required—TOEFL (minimum score 540 paper-based; 207 computer-based). *Faculty research:* Teaching the United States Constitution, middle school curriculum, integrated computer applications for pre-service classroom teachers, adolescent literacy, narrative cognitive modes in NM multicultural setting.

New Mexico State University, Graduate School, College of Education, Las Cruces, NM 88003-8001. Offers MA, MAT, Ed D, PhD, Ed S. *Accreditation:* NCATE. Part-time and evening/weekend programs available. Postbaccalaureate distance learning degree programs offered (minimal on-campus study). *Faculty:* 68 full-time (42 women), 27 part-time/adjunct (19 women). *Students:* 325 full-time (261 women), 568 part-time (424 women); includes 437 minority (27 African Americans, 29 American Indian/Alaska Native, 15 Asian Americans or Pacific Islanders, 366 Hispanic Americans), 37 international. Average age 37. 599 applicants, 85% accepted, 288 enrolled. In 2009, 222 master's, 19 doctorates, 6 other advanced degrees awarded. *Degree requirements:* For doctorate, thesis/dissertation. *Application deadline:* Applications are processed on a rolling basis. Application fee: $30 ($50 for international students). Electronic applications accepted. *Expenses:* Tuition, state resident: full-time $4080; part-time $223 per credit. Tuition, nonresident: full-time $14,256; part-time $647 per credit. Required fees: $1278; $639 per semester. *Financial support:* In 2009–10, 24 research assistantships (averaging $10,150 per year), 87 teaching assistantships (averaging $10,234 per year) were awarded; fellowships, career-related internships or fieldwork, Federal Work-Study, and health care benefits also available. Support available to part-time students. Financial award application deadline: 3/1. *Faculty research:* Bilingual special education, early childhood education/Head Start, leadership in border settings, exercise physiology, school-based mental health. *Unit head:* Dr. Michael Morehead, Interim Dean, 575-646-3404, Fax: 575-646-6032, E-mail: mmorehea@nmsu.edu. *Application contact:* Dr. Michael Morehead, Interim Dean, 575-646-3404, Fax: 575-646-6032, E-mail: mmorehea@nmsu.edu.

New York Institute of Technology, Graduate Division, School of Education, Old Westbury, NY 11568-8000. Offers MS, Advanced Certificate, Professional Diploma. *Accreditation:* NCATE.

Education—General

New York Institute of Technology (continued)

Part-time and evening/weekend programs available. Postbaccalaureate distance learning degree programs offered. *Students:* 40 full-time (23 women), 428 part-time (265 women); includes 80 minority (36 African Americans, 18 Asian Americans or Pacific Islanders, 26 Hispanic Americans), 11 international. Average age 34. In 2009, 118 master's, 2 other advanced degrees awarded. *Entrance requirements:* For master's, minimum QPA of 3.0. Additional exam requirements/recommendations for international students: Required—TOEFL (minimum score 550 paper-based; 213 computer-based). *Application deadline:* For fall admission, 7/1 priority date for domestic students; for spring admission, 12/1 priority date for domestic students. Applications are processed on a rolling basis. Application fee: $50. Electronic applications accepted. *Expenses:* Tuition: Part-time $825 per credit. *Financial support:* Research assistantships with partial tuition reimbursements, career-related internships or fieldwork, institutionally sponsored loans, and tuition waivers (full and partial) available. Support available to part-time students. Financial award applicants required to submit FAFSA. *Faculty research:* Distance learning, instructional uses of the World Wide Web, telecommunication technologies, emotional intelligence. *Unit head:* Dr. Michael Uttendorfer, Dean, 516-686-7706, Fax: 516-686-7655, E-mail: muttendo@nyit.edu. *Application contact:* Dr. Jacquelyn Nealon, Vice President for Enrollment Services, 516-686-7925, Fax: 516-686-7597, E-mail: jnealon@nyit.edu.

New York University, Steinhardt School of Culture, Education, and Human Development, New York, NY 10003. Offers MA, MFA, MM, MPH, MS, DPS, DPT, Ed D, PhD, Advanced Certificate, MM/Advanced Certificate, MPA/MA. *Accreditation:* Teacher Education Accreditation Council. Part-time programs available. *Faculty:* 259 full-time (151 women), 898 part-time/adjunct (488 women). *Students:* 2,357 full-time (1,841 women), 1,414 part-time (1,098 women); includes 820 minority (242 African Americans, 7 American Indian/Alaska Native, 289 Asian Americans or Pacific Islanders, 282 Hispanic Americans), 552 international. Average age 30. 6,436 applicants, 47% accepted, 1308 enrolled. In 2009, 1,286 master's, 122 doctorates, 18 other advanced degrees awarded. *Degree requirements:* For master's, thesis (for some programs); for doctorate, comprehensive exam (for some programs), thesis/dissertation. *Entrance requirements:* For doctorate, GRE General Test, interview. Additional exam requirements/recommendations for international students: Required—TOEFL. *Application deadline:* For fall admission, 12/15 priority date for domestic students, 12/15 for international students; for spring admission, 1/1 for domestic and international students. Applications are processed on a rolling basis. Application fee: $75. Electronic applications accepted. *Expenses:* Contact institution. *Financial support:* Fellowships with full and partial tuition reimbursements, research assistantships with full and partial tuition reimbursements, teaching assistantships with full and partial tuition reimbursements, career-related internships or fieldwork, Federal Work-Study, institutionally sponsored loans, scholarships/grants, traineeships, tuition waivers (partial), and unspecified assistantships available. Support available to part-time students. Financial award application deadline: 2/1; financial award applicants required to submit FAFSA. *Faculty research:* Equity, urban adolescents, arts in education, globalization, community and public health. Total annual research expenditures: $22.8 million. *Unit head:* Dr. Mary Brabeck, Dean, 212-998-5000. *Application contact:* John Myers, Director of Enrollment Management, 212-998-5030, Fax: 212-995-4328, E-mail: steinhardt.gradadmissions@nyu.edu.

Niagara University, Graduate Division of Education, Niagara Falls, Niagara University, NY 14109. Offers educational leadership (MS Ed, Certificate), including administration/supervision (Certificate), educational administration/supervision (MS Ed), educational leadership school district building (MS Ed), school business administration (Certificate), school business leadership (MS Ed), school district administration (Certificate); foundations of teaching (MA, MS Ed); literacy instruction (MS Ed); mental health counseling (MS, Certificate); school counseling (MS Ed, Certificate); school psychology (MS, Certificate); teacher education (Certificate), including early childhood and childhood education, middle and adolescence education, special education (grades 1-12). *Accreditation:* NCATE (one or more programs are accredited). Part-time and evening/weekend programs available. *Entrance requirements:* For master's, GRE General Test or MAT. *Expenses:* Contact institution. *Faculty research:* Instructional supervision, appraisal and evaluation, career opportunities.

Nicholls State University, Graduate Studies, College of Education, Department of Teacher Education, Thibodaux, LA 70310. Offers administration and supervision (M Ed); counselor education (M Ed); curriculum and instruction (M Ed). *Accreditation:* NCATE. Part-time and evening/weekend programs available. *Degree requirements:* For master's, comprehensive exam, portfolio. *Entrance requirements:* For master's, GRE General Test, teaching license. Electronic applications accepted.

Nipissing University, Faculty of Education, North Bay, ON P1B 8L7, Canada. Offers M Ed, Certificate. Part-time and evening/weekend programs available. *Degree requirements:* For master's, comprehensive exam (for some programs), thesis (for some programs). *Entrance requirements:* For master's, 1 year of experience, letters of recommendation, minimum undergraduate GPA of 3.0. Additional exam requirements/recommendations for international students: Required—TOEFL (minimum score 600 paper-based; 250 computer-based), IELTS (minimum score 7), TWE (minimum score 5).

Norfolk State University, School of Graduate Studies, School of Education, Norfolk, VA 23504. Offers MA, MAT. *Accreditation:* NCATE. Part-time programs available. *Degree requirements:* For master's, comprehensive exam. *Entrance requirements:* For master's, PRAXIS, GRE/GMAT, interview, teacher license. *Faculty research:* Urban, pre-elementary, and special education.

North Carolina Agricultural and Technical State University, Graduate School, School of Education, Greensboro, NC 27411. Offers MA Ed, MAT, MS. *Accreditation:* NCATE. Part-time and evening/weekend programs available. *Degree requirements:* For master's, comprehensive exam, qualifying exam. *Entrance requirements:* For master's, GRE General Test.

North Carolina Central University, Division of Academic Affairs, School of Education, Durham, NC 27707-3129. Offers M Ed, MA, MAT, MSA. *Accreditation:* NCATE. Part-time and evening/weekend programs available. *Degree requirements:* For master's, comprehensive exam, thesis or alternative. *Entrance requirements:* For master's, minimum GPA of 3.0 in major, 2.5 overall. Additional exam requirements/recommendations for international students: Required—TOEFL.

North Carolina State University, Graduate School, College of Education, Raleigh, NC 27695. Offers M Ed, MS, MS Ed, MSA, Ed D, PhD, Certificate. *Accreditation:* NCATE. Part-time programs available. *Degree requirements:* For doctorate, thesis/dissertation. *Entrance requirements:* For master's, doctorate, and Certificate, GRE General Test or MAT, minimum GPA of 3.0 in major. Electronic applications accepted. *Faculty research:* Moral/ethical development, financial policy analysis, middle years education, adult education.

North Central College, Graduate Programs, Department of Education, Naperville, IL 60566-7063. Offers curriculum and instruction (MA Ed); leadership and administration (MA Ed). Part-time and evening/weekend programs available. *Degree requirements:* For master's, clinical practicum, project. *Entrance requirements:* For master's, interview. *Expenses:* Contact institution.

Northcentral University, Graduate Studies, Prescott Valley, AZ 86314. Offers business (MBA, DBA, PhD, CAGS); education (M Ed, Ed D, PhD, CAGS); marriage and family therapy (MA, PhD); psychology (MA, PhD, CAGS). Evening/weekend programs available. Postbaccalaureate distance learning degree programs offered (no on-campus study). *Students:* 8,148 full-time (4,063 women); includes 984 minority (646 African Americans, 54 American Indian/Alaska Native, 125 Asian Americans or Pacific Islanders, 159 Hispanic Americans). Average age 43. In 2009, 271 master's, 189 doctorates, 13 other advanced degrees awarded. *Entrance requirements:* For master's, bachelor's degree from regionally-accredited institution, current resume; for doctorate and CAGS, master's degree from regionally-accredited university. Additional exam requirements/recommendations for international students: Required—TOEFL (minimum score 95 computer-based), IELTS (minimum score 7), Pearson Test of English (minimum score 65). *Application deadline:* Applications are processed on a rolling basis. Application fee: $75. *Expenses:* Tuition: Part-time $560 per credit. Part-time tuition and fees

vary according to degree level and program. *Financial support:* Scholarships/grants available. *Unit head:* Dr. Barnaby Barratt, Provost and Professor of Psychology, 888-327-2877, Fax: 928-759-6381, E-mail: bbarratt@ncu.edu. *Application contact:* Kevin Lustig, Director of Admissions, 480-478-7490, Fax: 928-759-6285, E-mail: klustig@ncu.edu.

North Dakota State University, College of Graduate and Interdisciplinary Studies, College of Human Development and Education, School of Education, Fargo, ND 58108. Offers agricultural education (M Ed, MS), including agricultural education, agricultural extension education (MS); counseling (M Ed, MS, PhD); curriculum and instruction (M Ed, MS), including pedagogy, physical education and athletic administration; education (PhD); educational leadership (M Ed, MS, Ed S); family and consumer sciences education (M Ed, MS); history education (M Ed, MS); institutional analysis (Ed D); mathematics education (M Ed, MS); music education (M Ed, MS); occupational and adult education (Ed D); science education (M Ed, MS). *Accreditation:* NCATE. Part-time and evening/weekend programs available. Postbaccalaureate distance learning degree programs offered (minimal on-campus study). *Faculty:* 25 full-time (9 women), 3 part-time/adjunct (1 woman). *Students:* 29 full-time (25 women), 207 part-time (132 women); includes 15 minority (4 African Americans, 6 American Indian/Alaska Native, 3 Asian Americans or Pacific Islanders, 2 Hispanic Americans), 4 international. 88 applicants, 67% accepted, 56 enrolled. In 2009, 44 master's, 5 doctorates awarded. *Degree requirements:* For master's, comprehensive exam; for doctorate, thesis/dissertation; for Ed S, thesis. *Entrance requirements:* For degree, GRE General Test, master's degree, minimum GPA of 3.25. Additional exam requirements/recommendations for international students: Required—TOEFL. *Application deadline:* Applications are processed on a rolling basis. Application fee: $45 ($60 for international students). *Financial support:* Research assistantships, teaching assistantships, career-related internships or fieldwork, Federal Work-Study, institutionally sponsored loans, and tuition waivers (full) available. Financial award application deadline: 4/15. *Unit head:* Dr. William Martin, Chair, 701-231-7202, Fax: 701-231-7416, E-mail: william.martin@ndsu.edu. *Application contact:* Dr. William Martin, Chair, 701-231-7202, Fax: 701-231-7416, E-mail: william.martin@ndsu.edu.

Northeastern Illinois University, Graduate College, College of Education, Chicago, IL 60625-4699. Offers MA, MAT, MSI. Part-time and evening/weekend programs available. *Degree requirements:* For master's, comprehensive exam (for some programs), thesis (for some programs). *Entrance requirements:* For master's, minimum GPA of 2.75. Additional exam requirements/recommendations for international students: Required—TOEFL (minimum score 550 paper-based; 213 computer-based; 80 iBT). Electronic applications accepted. *Faculty research:* Leadership, problem-based learning strategies, school improvement, bilingual education, use of technology.

Northeastern State University, Graduate College, College of Education, Tahlequah, OK 74464-2399. Offers M Ed, MS, MS Ed. *Accreditation:* NCATE. Part-time and evening/weekend programs available. *Degree requirements:* For master's, thesis. *Entrance requirements:* For master's, GRE or MAT. Additional exam requirements/recommendations for international students: Required—TOEFL (minimum score 213 computer-based). Electronic applications accepted.

Northern Arizona University, Graduate College, College of Education, Flagstaff, AZ 86011. Offers M Ed, MA, Ed D, PhD, Certificate. *Accreditation:* NCATE. Part-time and evening/weekend programs available. *Faculty:* 118 full-time (76 women). *Students:* 1,166 full-time (875 women), 2,712 part-time (2,010 women); includes 960 minority (139 African Americans, 215 American Indian/Alaska Native, 57 Asian Americans or Pacific Islanders, 549 Hispanic Americans), 16 international. Average age 36. 1,463 applicants, 77% accepted. In 2009, 1,634 master's, 23 doctorates awarded. *Degree requirements:* For master's, comprehensive exam, thesis (for some programs); for doctorate, comprehensive exam, thesis/dissertation. *Entrance requirements:* For master's, minimum GPA of 3.0; for doctorate, GRE or MAT. Additional exam requirements/recommendations for international students: Required—TOEFL (minimum score 550 paper-based; 213 computer-based; 80 iBT), IELTS (minimum score 7), or a bachelor's degree from an English-speaking university and demonstrated proficiency. *Application deadline:* For fall admission, 2/1 for domestic students, 9/1 for international students. Applications are processed on a rolling basis. Application fee: $65. Electronic applications accepted. *Financial support:* In 2009–10, 4 research assistantships with partial tuition reimbursements (averaging $10,000 per year), 28 teaching assistantships with partial tuition reimbursements (averaging $10,000 per year) were awarded; career-related internships or fieldwork, Federal Work-Study, health care benefits, tuition waivers (full and partial), and unspecified assistantships also available. Financial award application deadline: 3/30; financial award applicants required to submit FAFSA. *Unit head:* Dr. Daniel Kain, Dean, 928-523-7113. *Application contact:* Dr. Patricia Baron, Director of Graduate Admissions, 928-523-4348, Fax: 928-523-8950, E-mail: graduate.college@nau.edu.

Northern Illinois University, Graduate School, College of Education, De Kalb, IL 60115-2854. Offers MS, MS Ed, Ed D, Ed S. *Accreditation:* NCATE. Part-time and evening/weekend programs available. Postbaccalaureate distance learning degree programs offered (minimal on-campus study). *Faculty:* 110 full-time (66 women), 5 part-time/adjunct (3 women). *Students:* 292 full-time (182 women), 1,529 part-time (1,074 women); includes 374 minority (178 African Americans, 8 American Indian/Alaska Native, 43 Asian Americans or Pacific Islanders, 145 Hispanic Americans), 56 international. Average age 36. 545 applicants, 58% accepted, 221 enrolled. In 2009, 473 master's, 58 doctorates, 26 other advanced degrees awarded. Terminal master's awarded for partial completion of doctoral program. *Degree requirements:* For master's and Ed S, comprehensive exam, thesis optional; for doctorate, thesis/dissertation, candidacy exam, dissertation defense. *Entrance requirements:* For master's, GRE General Test or MAT, minimum GPA of 2.75; for doctorate, GRE General Test or MAT, minimum GPA of 2.75 (undergraduate), 3.2 (graduate); for Ed S, GRE General Test, master's degree; minimum undergraduate GPA of 2.75, graduate 3.2. Additional exam requirements/recommendations for international students: Required—TOEFL (minimum score 550 paper-based; 213 computer-based). *Application deadline:* For fall admission, 6/1 for domestic students, 5/1 for international students; for spring admission, 11/1 for domestic students, 10/1 for international students. Applications are processed on a rolling basis. Application fee: $30. Electronic applications accepted. *Expenses:* Tuition, state resident: full-time $6576; part-time $274 per credit hour. Tuition, nonresident: full-time $13,152; part-time $548 per credit hour. Required fees: $1813; $75.53 per credit hour. Part-time tuition and fees vary according to course load. *Financial support:* Fellowships with full tuition reimbursements, research assistantships with full tuition reimbursements, teaching assistantships with full tuition reimbursements, career-related internships or fieldwork, Federal Work-Study, scholarships/grants, tuition waivers (full), and staff assistantships available. Support available to part-time students. Financial award applicants required to submit FAFSA. *Unit head:* Dr. Lemuel W. Watson, Dean, 815-753-9055, Fax: 851-753-2100, E-mail: watson@niu.edu. *Application contact:* Graduate School Office, 815-753-0395, E-mail: gradsch@niu.edu.

Northern Kentucky University, Office of Graduate Programs, College of Education and Human Services, Highland Heights, KY 41099. Offers community counseling (MS, Certificate), including college student development administration (Certificate), community counseling; education (MA), including teacher as a leader; educational leadership (Ed D); instructional leadership (MA); school counseling (MA, Certificate), including school counseling (MA), temporary school counseling provision (Certificate); teaching (MA, Certificate), including school superintendent (MA), special education (MA), teaching (MA). *Accreditation:* NCATE. Part-time and evening/weekend programs available. *Students:* 51 full-time (42 women), 410 part-time (309 women); includes 24 minority (10 African Americans, 1 American Indian/Alaska Native, 6 Asian Americans or Pacific Islanders, 7 Hispanic Americans), 2 international. Average age 32. 327 applicants, 50% accepted, 148 enrolled. In 2009, 245 master's, 2 other advanced degrees awarded. *Entrance requirements:* For master's, GRE. Additional exam requirements/recommendations for international students: Required—TOEFL (minimum score 550 paper-based; 213 computer-based; 79 iBT); Recommended—IELTS (minimum score 6.5). *Application deadline:* For fall admission, 8/1 priority date for domestic students, 6/1 for international students; for spring admission, 12/1 priority date for domestic students, 10/1 for international

students. Applications are processed on a rolling basis. Application fee: $40. Electronic applications accepted. *Expenses:* Tuition, state resident: full-time $6912; part-time $384 per credit hour. Tuition, nonresident: full-time $12,150; part-time $675 per credit hour. Tuition and fees vary according to course load, program and reciprocity agreements. *Financial support:* Unspecified assistantships available. Financial award applicants required to submit FAFSA. *Unit head:* Dr. Mark Wasicsko, Dean, 859-572-5229, Fax: 859-572-6623, E-mail: wasicskom1@nku.edu. *Application contact:* Dr. Peg Griffin, Director of Graduate Programs, 859-572-6934, Fax: 859-572-6670, E-mail: griffinp@nku.edu.

Northern Michigan University, College of Graduate Studies, College of Professional Studies, School of Education, Marquette, MI 49855-5301. Offers administration and supervision (MA Ed, Ed S); elementary education (MA Ed); learning disabilities (MA Ed); reading education (MA Ed, Ed S), including literacy leadership (Ed S), reading (MA Ed), reading specialist (MA Ed); school guidance counseling (MA Ed); science education (MS); secondary education (MA Ed). *Accreditation:* Teacher Education Accreditation Council. Part-time programs available. *Degree requirements:* For master's, thesis or alternative. *Entrance requirements:* For master's, minimum GPA of 3.0.

Northern State University, Division of Graduate Studies in Education, Aberdeen, SD 57401-7198. Offers MS, MS Ed. *Accreditation:* NCATE. Part-time and evening/weekend programs available. *Faculty:* 84 full-time (21 women). *Students:* 47 full-time (29 women), 96 part-time (62 women); includes 9 minority (2 African Americans, 3 American Indian/Alaska Native, 3 Asian Americans or Pacific Islanders, 1 Hispanic American). Average age 32. In 2009, 85 master's awarded. *Degree requirements:* For master's, thesis optional. *Entrance requirements:* For master's, minimum GPA of 2.75. Additional exam requirements/recommendations for international students: Required—TOEFL (minimum score 550 paper-based; 213 computer-based; 78 iBT). *Application deadline:* For fall admission, 8/15 priority date for domestic students; for spring admission, 12/15 for domestic students. Applications are processed on a rolling basis. Application fee: $35. Electronic applications accepted. *Financial support:* In 2009–10, 51 students received support, including 31 teaching assistantships with partial tuition reimbursements available (averaging $5,314 per year); career-related internships or fieldwork, Federal Work-Study, institutionally sponsored loans, scholarships/grants, and unspecified assistantships also available. Support available to part-time students. Financial award application deadline: 3/1; financial award applicants required to submit FAFSA. *Unit head:* Dr. Constance Geier, Interim Director of Graduate Studies, 605-626-2558, Fax: 605-626-7190, E-mail: geierc@northern.edu. *Application contact:* Tammy K. Griffith, Program Assistant, 605-626-2558, Fax: 605-626-7190, E-mail: griffith@northern.edu.

North Georgia College & State University, Graduate Studies, Program in Teacher Education, Dahlonega, GA 30597. Offers early childhood education (M Ed); educational leadership (Ed S); middle grades education (M Ed); secondary education (M Ed), including art education, biology education, chemistry education, English education, history education, mathematics education, physical education, science education; special education (M Ed), including interrelated special education, learning disabilities. *Accreditation:* NCATE. Part-time and evening/weekend programs available. Postbaccalaureate distance learning degree programs offered (minimal on-campus study). *Degree requirements:* For master's, comprehensive exam, thesis optional. *Entrance requirements:* For master's, GRE General Test or MAT, minimum GPA of 2.75; for Ed S, GRE General Test or MAT, 3 years of teaching experience, master's degree, minimum graduate GPA of 3.25. Electronic applications accepted. *Faculty research:* Computers and teachers' attitudes, rural versus urban teacher attitudes, teacher leadership roles, minority recruitment in teaching force.

North Park University, School of Education, Chicago, IL 60625-4895. Offers MA. *Degree requirements:* For master's, thesis. *Entrance requirements:* For master's, GRE General Test. *Faculty research:* Teacher leadership, research design, teacher education.

Northwest Christian University, School of Education and Counseling, Eugene, OR 97401-3745. Offers community counseling (MA); education (M Ed); school counseling (MA). Part-time and evening/weekend programs available. *Faculty:* 6 full-time (3 women). *Students:* 68 full-time, 14 part-time. 68 applicants, 78% accepted, 43 enrolled. *Entrance requirements:* For master's, MAT, interview, minimum GPA of 3.0. *Application deadline:* For fall admission, 3/15 priority date for domestic students. Applications are processed on a rolling basis. Application fee: $50. Electronic applications accepted. *Expenses:* Tuition: Full-time $9900; part-time $550 per credit hour. Tuition and fees vary according to program. *Financial support:* Scholarships/grants available. *Unit head:* Jim Howard, Dean, 541-684-7262, Fax: 541-684-7310, E-mail: jhoward@northwestchristian.edu. *Application contact:* Kathy Wilson, Assistant Director of Admission, Graduate and Professional Studies, 541-684-7326, Fax: 541-684-7333, E-mail: kwilson@northwestchristian.edu.

Northwestern Oklahoma State University, School of Professional Studies, Alva, OK 73717-2799. Offers counseling psychology (MCP); elementary education (M Ed); reading specialist (M Ed); school counseling (M Ed); secondary education (M Ed). *Accreditation:* NCATE (one or more programs are accredited). Part-time programs available. *Faculty:* 48 full-time (25 women), 24 part-time/adjunct (17 women). *Students:* 69 full-time (50 women), 172 part-time (120 women); includes 22 minority (5 African Americans, 11 American Indian/Alaska Native, 6 Hispanic Americans), 2 international. Average age 31. 156 applicants, 100% accepted. In 2009, 65 master's awarded. *Degree requirements:* For master's, comprehensive exam (for some programs), thesis optional, portfolio. *Entrance requirements:* For master's, GRE General Test or MAT, minimum GPA of 2.75. *Application deadline:* Applications are processed on a rolling basis. Application fee: $15. *Financial support:* Federal Work-Study available. Support available to part-time students. Financial award application deadline: 5/1; financial award applicants required to submit FAFSA. *Unit head:* Dr. Sue Diel, Chair, 580-327-8451. *Application contact:* Leah Haines, Coordinator of Graduate Studies, 580-327-8410, E-mail: ldhaines@nwosu.edu.

Northwestern State University of Louisiana, Graduate Studies and Research, College of Education, Natchitoches, LA 71497. Offers M Ed, MA, MAT, Ed S. *Accreditation:* ACA (one or more programs are accredited); NCATE. *Degree requirements:* For master's, comprehensive exam, thesis (for some programs); for Ed S, comprehensive exam, thesis. *Entrance requirements:* For master's, GRE General Test, GRE Subject Test, minimum undergraduate GPA of 2.5; for Ed S, GRE General Test.

Northwestern University, The Graduate School, School of Education and Social Policy, Evanston, IL 60208. Offers education and social policy (MS), including advanced teaching, elementary education and policy, higher education administration, secondary teaching; human development and social policy (PhD); learning and organizational change (MS); learning sciences (MA, PhD). MA and PhD admissions and degrees offered through The Graduate School. Part-time and evening/weekend programs available. *Faculty:* 43 full-time (15 women), 64 part-time/adjunct (34 women). *Students:* 156 full-time (122 women), 152 part-time (115 women); includes 60 minority (24 African Americans, 2 American Indian/Alaska Native, 26 Asian Americans or Pacific Islanders, 8 Hispanic Americans), 9 international. Average age 29. In 2009, 109 master's, 15 doctorates awarded. *Degree requirements:* For doctorate, comprehensive exam, thesis/dissertation. *Entrance requirements:* For master's and doctorate, GRE General Test. Electronic applications accepted. *Expenses:* Contact institution. *Financial support:* In 2009–10, 33 fellowships with full tuition reimbursements (averaging $25,800 per year), 24 research assistantships with full tuition reimbursements (averaging $25,800 per year), 15 teaching assistantships with full tuition reimbursements (averaging $25,800 per year) were awarded; career-related internships or fieldwork, Federal Work-Study, institutionally sponsored loans, scholarships/grants, traineeships, and tuition waivers (partial) also available. Financial award application deadline: 1/15; financial award applicants required to submit FAFSA. *Faculty research:* Technology, curriculum design, welfare, education reform, learning. *Unit head:* Mark P. Hoffman, Graduate Student Administrative Liaison, 847-491-3790, Fax: 847-491-4664, E-mail: markhoffman@northwestern.edu. *Application contact:* 847-491-3790, Fax: 847-491-4664, E-mail: sesp@northwestern.edu.

See Close-Up on page 711.

Northwest Missouri State University, Graduate School, College of Education and Human Services, Maryville, MO 64468-6001. Offers MS, MS Ed, Certificate, Ed S. *Accreditation:* NCATE. Part-time programs available. *Faculty:* 46 full-time (29 women). *Students:* 116 full-time (65 women), 322 part-time (241 women); includes 29 minority (20 African Americans, 1 American Indian/Alaska Native, 2 Asian Americans or Pacific Islanders, 6 Hispanic Americans), 4 international. 117 applicants, 81% accepted, 71 enrolled. In 2009, 181 master's, 15 other advanced degrees awarded. *Degree requirements:* For master's, comprehensive exam; for other advanced degree, comprehensive exam, thesis. *Entrance requirements:* For master's, GRE General Test, writing sample; for other advanced degree, minimum graduate GPA of 3.25. Additional exam requirements/recommendations for international students: Required—TOEFL (minimum score 550 paper-based; 213 computer-based). *Application deadline:* For fall admission, 7/1 for domestic and international students; for spring admission, 11/15 for domestic and international students. Application fee: $0 ($50 for international students). Electronic applications accepted. *Expenses:* Tuition, state resident: part-time $296.34 per credit hour. Tuition, nonresident: part-time $510.43 per credit hour. *Financial support:* In 2009–10, 16 research assistantships with full tuition reimbursements (averaging $6,000 per year), 36 teaching assistantships with full tuition reimbursements (averaging $6,000 per year) were awarded; unspecified assistantships also available. Financial award application deadline: 4/1; financial award applicants required to submit FAFSA. *Faculty research:* Great books of educational administration. *Unit head:* Dr. Max Ruhl, Dean, 660-562-1778. *Application contact:* Dr. Gregory Haddock, Dean of Graduate School, 660-562-1145, Fax: 660-562-1096, E-mail: gradsch@nwmissouri.edu.

Northwest Nazarene University, Graduate Studies, Program in Teacher Education, Nampa, ID 83686-5897. Offers curriculum and instruction (M Ed); educational leadership (M Ed); exceptional child (M Ed); reading education (M Ed); school counseling (M Ed). *Accreditation:* ACA; NCATE. Part-time programs available. *Degree requirements:* For master's, comprehensive exam (for some programs), action research project. *Entrance requirements:* For master's, minimum undergraduate GPA of 2.8 overall or 3.0 during final 30 semester credits. *Faculty research:* Action research, cooperative learning, accountability, institutional accreditation.

Northwest University, School of Education, Kirkland, WA 98033. Offers education (M Ed); teaching (MIT). Part-time and evening/weekend programs available. *Faculty:* 6 full-time (3 women), 6 part-time/adjunct (3 women). *Students:* 32 full-time (26 women), 19 part-time (16 women); includes 8 minority (1 African American, 4 Asian Americans or Pacific Islanders, 3 Hispanic Americans). 77 applicants, 83% accepted, 47 enrolled. In 2009, 41 master's awarded. *Degree requirements:* For master's, action research project. *Entrance requirements:* For master's, Washington Educator Skills Test-Basic, Washington Educator Skills Test-Endorsements, minimum GPA of 3.3. *Application deadline:* For fall admission, 3/1 priority date for domestic students. Applications are processed on a rolling basis. Application fee: $75. *Expenses:* Contact institution. *Financial support:* Federal Work-Study and health care benefits available. *Unit head:* Dr. Gary Newbill, Dean, 425-889-5272, E-mail: gary.newbill@northwestu.edu. *Application contact:* Pam Skolrud, Coordinator/Certification Specialist, 425-889-5299, Fax: 425-889-6332, E-mail: pam.skolrud@northwestu.edu.

Notre Dame College, Graduate Studies, South Euclid, OH 44121-4293. Offers accounting (Certificate); creative critical thinking (M Ed); financial services management (Certificate); information systems (Certificate); learning disabilities (M Ed); management (Certificate); paralegal (Certificate); pastoral ministry (Certificate); reading (M Ed); teacher education (Certificate). Part-time and evening/weekend programs available. *Degree requirements:* For master's, thesis. *Entrance requirements:* For master's, GRE General Test, MAT, minimum GPA of 2.75, valid teaching certificate. *Faculty research:* Cognitive psychology, teaching critical thinking in the classroom.

Notre Dame de Namur University, Division of Academic Affairs, School of Education and Leadership, Program in Teacher Education, Belmont, CA 94002-1908. Offers education (MA); multiple subject teaching credential (Certificate); single subject teaching credential (Certificate). Part-time programs available. In 2009, 25 master's awarded. *Entrance requirements:* Additional exam requirements/recommendations for international students: Required—TOEFL (minimum score 550 paper-based; 213 computer-based; 79 iBT). Application fee: $60. *Expenses:* Tuition: Part-time $720 per credit. Required fees: $35 per semester hour. *Financial support:* Career-related internships or fieldwork available. Support available to part-time students. Financial award applicants required to submit FAFSA. *Unit head:* Dr. Kim Tolley, Director, 650-508-3464, E-mail: ktolley@ndnu.edu. *Application contact:* Candace Hallmark, Associate Director of Admissions, 650-508-3592, Fax: 650-508-3426, E-mail: grad.admit@ndnu.edu.

Nova Southeastern University, Fischler School of Education and Human Services, Fort Lauderdale, FL 33314-7796. Offers MA, MHS, MS, Ed D, SLPD, Ed S. Part-time and evening/weekend programs available. *Faculty:* 105 full-time (55 women), 438 part-time/adjunct (266 women). *Students:* 4,193 full-time (3,320 women), 5,384 part-time (4,481 women); includes 5,324 minority (3,835 African Americans, 36 American Indian/Alaska Native, 133 Asian Americans or Pacific Islanders, 1,320 Hispanic Americans), 59 international. Average age 38. 4,354 applicants, 65% accepted, 2078 enrolled. In 2009, 2,203 master's, 445 doctorates, 836 other advanced degrees awarded. *Degree requirements:* For master's, practicum, internship; for doctorate, thesis/dissertation; for Ed S, thesis, practicum, internship. *Entrance requirements:* For master's, MAT or GRE (for some programs), CLAST, PRAXIS I, CBEST, General Knowledge Test, teaching certification, minimum GPA of 2.5, verification of teaching, BS; for doctorate, MAT or GRE, master's degree, minimum cumulative GPA of 3.0; for Ed S, MAT or GRE, master's degree, teaching certificate; minimum GPA of 3.0. Additional exam requirements/recommendations for international students: Required—TSE (recommended, minimum score 50); Recommended—TOEFL (minimum score 550 paper-based; 213 computer-based; 80 iBT), IELTS (minimum score 6). *Application deadline:* Applications are processed on a rolling basis. Application fee: $50. Electronic applications accepted. *Financial support:* In 2009–10, 6,903 students received support, including 2 fellowships with full tuition reimbursements available (averaging $30,000 per year); career-related internships or fieldwork, Federal Work-Study, and tuition waivers (full) also available. Support available to part-time students. Financial award application deadline: 4/15; financial award applicants required to submit FAFSA. *Unit head:* Dr. H. Wells Singleton, Provost/Dean, 954-262-8730, Fax: 954-262-3894, E-mail: singlew@nova.edu. *Application contact:* Dr. Jennifer Quinones Nottingham, Dean of Student Affairs, 800-986-3223 Ext. 8500, E-mail: jlquinon@nova.edu.

Nyack College, School of Education, Nyack, NY 10960-3698. Offers childhood education (MS); childhood special education (MS); inclusive education (MS). Part-time and evening/weekend programs available. *Degree requirements:* For master's, comprehensive exam (for some programs), thesis (for some programs), field experience. *Entrance requirements:* For master's, GRE, baccalaureate degree with minimum GPA of 3.0, evidence of initial/provisional teaching certification. Additional exam requirements/recommendations for international students: Required—TOEFL (minimum score 500 paper-based), TWE (minimum score 4). *Expenses:* Contact institution.

Oakland City University, School of Education and Technology, Oakland City, IN 47660-1099. Offers educational leadership (Ed D); teaching (MA). *Accreditation:* NCATE. Terminal master's awarded for partial completion of doctoral program. *Degree requirements:* For master's, thesis; for doctorate, comprehensive exam, thesis/dissertation. *Entrance requirements:* For master's, MAT, minimum GPA of 3.0, interview, resume, letters of recommendation; for doctorate, MAT, GRE, minimum GPA of 3.2, interview, resumé, letters of recommendation. *Expenses:* Contact institution. *Faculty research:* Assessment, cultural diversity, teacher education, education leadership.

Oakland University, Graduate Study and Lifelong Learning, School of Education and Human Services, Rochester, MI 48309-4401. Offers M Ed, MA, MAT, MTD, PhD, Certificate, Ed S. *Accreditation:* Teacher Education Accreditation Council. Part-time and evening/weekend programs available. *Degree requirements:* For doctorate, thesis/dissertation. *Entrance requirements:* For master's and doctorate, minimum GPA of 3.0 for unconditional admission. Additional exam requirements/recommendations for international students: Required—TOEFL

Education—General

Oakland University (continued)
(minimum score 550 paper-based; 213 computer-based). Electronic applications accepted. *Faculty research:* Earth science for middle and high school teachers.

Oberlin College, Graduate Teacher Education Program, Oberlin, OH 44074. Offers early childhood education (M Ed); middle childhood education (M Ed). *Degree requirements:* For master's, comprehensive exam, portfolio. *Entrance requirements:* For master's, GRE General Test, PRAXIS II. *Faculty research:* Literacy learning, teacher education reform, program development.

Occidental College, Graduate Studies, Department of Education, Los Angeles, CA 90041-3314. Offers elementary education (MAT), including liberal studies; secondary education (MAT), including English and comparative literary studies, history, life science, mathematics, physical science, social science, Spanish. Part-time programs available. *Degree requirements:* For master's, comprehensive exam, graduate synthesis paper. *Entrance requirements:* For master's, GRE General Test, minimum GPA of 3.0. Additional exam requirements/recommendations for international students: Required—TOEFL (minimum score 625 paper-based; 263 computer-based). *Expenses:* Contact institution. *Faculty research:* Preparing teacher-leaders, curriculum development.

Oglethorpe University, Division of Education, Atlanta, GA 30319-2797. Offers early childhood education (MAT). Part-time programs available. *Degree requirements:* For master's, comprehensive exam. *Entrance requirements:* For master's, GRE General Test, PRAXIS, minimum GPA of 2.8, 3 recommendations.

Ohio Dominican University, Graduate Programs, Division of Education, Columbus, OH 43219-2099. Offers M Ed. *Accreditation:* NCATE. Part-time and evening/weekend programs available. *Students:* 280 full-time (236 women), 45 part-time (38 women); includes 37 minority (33 African Americans, 4 Hispanic Americans). Average age 35. In 2009, 45 master's awarded. *Degree requirements:* For master's, thesis or alternative. *Entrance requirements:* For master's, minimum undergraduate GPA of 3.0, teaching certificate, teaching experience, 3 letters of recommendation. Additional exam requirements/recommendations for international students: Required—TOEFL (minimum score 550 paper-based; 213 computer-based). *Application deadline:* For fall admission, 7/15 priority date for domestic and international students; for spring admission, 12/15 priority date for domestic and international students. Applications are processed on a rolling basis. Application fee: $25. *Financial support:* Applicants required to submit FAFSA. *Unit head:* Dr. Bonnie Beach, Dean, 614-251-4625, E-mail: beachb@ohiodominican.edu. *Application contact:* Jill M. Westerfeld, Graduate Admissions Recruiter, 614-251-4725, Fax: 614-251-4634, E-mail: westerfj@ohiodominican.edu.

The Ohio State University, Graduate School, College of Education and Human Ecology, Columbus, OH 43210. Offers M Ed, MA, MS, PhD. *Accreditation:* NCATE. *Faculty:* 178. *Students:* 623 full-time (451 women), 719 part-time (549 women); includes 190 minority (126 African Americans, 8 American Indian/Alaska Native, 25 Asian Americans or Pacific Islanders, 31 Hispanic Americans), 197 international. Average age 33. In 2009, 539 master's, 85 doctorates awarded. Terminal master's awarded for partial completion of doctoral program. *Degree requirements:* For master's, comprehensive exam (for some programs), thesis optional; for doctorate, comprehensive exam, thesis/dissertation. *Entrance requirements:* For doctorate, GRE. Additional exam requirements/recommendations for international students: Required—TOEFL (minimum score 600 paper-based; 250 computer-based). *Application deadline:* For fall admission, 8/15 priority date for domestic students, 7/1 priority date for international students; for winter admission, 12/1 priority date for domestic students, 11/1 priority date for international students; for spring admission, 3/1 priority date for domestic students, 2/1 priority date for international students. Applications are processed on a rolling basis. Application fee: $40 ($50 for international students). Electronic applications accepted. *Expenses:* Tuition, state resident: full-time $10,683. Tuition, nonresident: full-time $25,923. Tuition and fees vary according to course load and program. *Financial support:* Fellowships with tuition reimbursements, research assistantships with tuition reimbursements, teaching assistantships with tuition reimbursements, career-related internships or fieldwork, Federal Work-Study, institutionally sponsored loans, scholarships/grants, traineeships, health care benefits, and unspecified assistantships available. Support available to part-time students. *Faculty research:* Math and science education; teach professional development; issues related to urban education; health, well-being, and sports; literacy education. Total annual research expenditures: $19 million. *Unit head:* Cheryl Achterberg, Dean, 614-292-2461, Fax: 614-292-8052, E-mail: cachterberg@ehe.osu.edu. *Application contact:* 614-292-9444, Fax: 614-292-3895, E-mail: domestic.grad@osu.edu.

The Ohio State University at Lima, Graduate Programs, Lima, OH 45804. Offers early childhood education (M Ed); education (MA); middle childhood education (M Ed); social work (MSW). *Students:* 23 full-time (18 women), 83 part-time (72 women); includes 1 minority (African American). Average age 34. *Degree requirements:* For master's, comprehensive exam (for some programs), thesis (for some programs). *Entrance requirements:* For master's, GRE, minimum GPA of 3.0. Additional exam requirements/recommendations for international students: Required—TOEFL, IELTS or Michigan English Language Assessment Battery. *Application deadline:* For fall admission, 8/15 priority date for domestic students, 7/1 priority date for international students; for winter admission, 12/1 priority date for domestic students, 11/1 priority date for international students; for spring admission, 3/1 priority date for domestic students, 2/1 priority date for international students. Applications are processed on a rolling basis. Application fee: $40 ($50 for international students). Electronic applications accepted. *Expenses:* Tuition, state resident: full-time $10,155. Tuition, nonresident: full-time $25,395. Tuition and fees vary according to course load. *Unit head:* Dr. John Snyder, Dean/Director, 419-995-8481, E-mail: snyder.4@osu.edu. *Application contact:* Graduate Admissions, 614-292-9444, Fax: 614-292-3895, E-mail: domestic.grad@osu.edu.

The Ohio State University at Marion, Graduate Programs, Marion, OH 43302-5695. Offers early childhood education (pre-K to grade 3) (M Ed); integrated teaching and learning (MA); middle childhood education (grades 4-9) (M Ed); nursing (MS, PhD); social work (MSW); MS/PhD. Part-time programs available. *Students:* 49 full-time (38 women), 34 part-time (25 women); includes 2 minority (both African Americans). Average age 31. *Degree requirements:* For master's, comprehensive exam (for some programs), thesis (for some programs). *Entrance requirements:* For master's and doctorate, GRE, minimum undergraduate GPA of 3.0. Additional exam requirements/recommendations for international students: Required—TOEFL, IELTS or Michigan English Language Assessment Battery. *Application deadline:* For fall admission, 8/15 priority date for domestic students, 7/1 priority date for international students; for winter admission, 12/1 priority date for domestic students, 11/1 priority date for international students; for spring admission, 3/1 priority date for domestic students, 2/1 priority date for international students. Applications are processed on a rolling basis. Application fee: $40 ($50 for international students). Electronic applications accepted. *Expenses:* Tuition, state resident: full-time $10,155. Tuition, nonresident: full-time $25,395. Tuition and fees vary according to course load. *Unit head:* Gregory S. Rose, Dean/Director, 740-389-6786 Ext. 6218, E-mail: rose.9@osu.edu. *Application contact:* Graduate Admissions, 614-292-9444, Fax: 614-292-3895, E-mail: domestic.grad@osu.edu.

The Ohio State University–Newark Campus, Graduate Programs, Newark, OH 43055-1797. Offers early/middle childhood education (M Ed); integrated teaching and learning (MA); social work (MSW). *Students:* 40 full-time (36 women), 64 part-time (59 women); includes 5 minority (4 African Americans, 1 Asian American or Pacific Islander), 1 international. Average age 31. *Degree requirements:* For master's, comprehensive exam (for some programs), thesis (for some programs). *Entrance requirements:* For master's, GRE, minimum GPA of 3.0. Additional exam requirements/recommendations for international students: Required—TOEFL, IELTS or Michigan English Language Assessment Battery. *Application deadline:* For fall admission, 8/15 priority date for domestic students, 7/1 priority date for international students; for winter admission, 12/1 priority date for domestic students, 11/1 priority date for international students; for spring admission, 3/1 priority date for domestic students, 2/1 priority date for international students. Applications are processed on a rolling basis. Application fee: $40 ($50 for international students). Electronic applications accepted. *Expenses:* Tuition, state resident: full-time $10,155. Tuition, nonresident: full-time $25,395. Tuition and fees vary according to course load. *Unit head:* Dr. William L. MacDonald, Dean/Director, 740-366-9333 Ext. 330, E-mail: macdonald.24@osu.edu. *Application contact:* Graduate Admissions, 614-292-9444, Fax: 614-292-3985, E-mail: domestic.grad@osu.edu.

Ohio University, Graduate College, College of Education, Athens, OH 45701-2979. Offers M Ed, Ed D, PhD. *Accreditation:* NCATE. Part-time and evening/weekend programs available. *Faculty:* 42 full-time (25 women), 23 part-time/adjunct (8 women). *Students:* 420 full-time (290 women), 376 part-time (296 women); includes 69 minority (51 African Americans, 7 American Indian/Alaska Native, 5 Asian Americans or Pacific Islanders, 6 Hispanic Americans), 69 international. 468 applicants, 70% accepted, 195 enrolled. In 2009, 144 master's, 46 doctorates awarded. *Degree requirements:* For master's, comprehensive exam (for some programs), thesis or alternative; for doctorate, comprehensive exam, thesis/dissertation. *Entrance requirements:* For master's, GRE General Test or MAT; for doctorate, GRE General Test, MAT, master's degree. Additional exam requirements/recommendations for international students: Required—TOEFL (minimum score 550 paper-based; 80 iBT) or IELTS Academic (minimum score 6.5). *Application deadline:* Applications are processed on a rolling basis. Application fee: $50 ($55 for international students). Electronic applications accepted. *Expenses:* Tuition, state resident: full-time $7839; part-time $323 per quarter hour. Tuition, nonresident: full-time $15,831; part-time $654 per quarter hour. Required fees: $2931. *Financial support:* Research assistantships with full and partial tuition reimbursements, teaching assistantships with full and partial tuition reimbursements, Federal Work-Study, institutionally sponsored loans, tuition waivers (full and partial), and unspecified assistantships available. Financial award application deadline: 3/15. *Faculty research:* School improvement, partnerships, literacy, rural education. Total annual research expenditures: $2.2 million. *Unit head:* Dr. Renee A. Middleton, Dean, 740-593-4403, E-mail: middletonr@ohio.edu. *Application contact:* Floyd J. Doney, Director of Student Affairs, 740-593-4400, Fax: 740-593-9310, E-mail: doney@ohio.edu.

Ohio Valley University, School of Graduate Education, Vienna, WV 26105-8000. Offers M Ed. Postbaccalaureate distance learning degree programs offered. *Entrance requirements:* For master's, bachelor's degree or higher from an accredited institution, 2 letters of recommendation.

Oklahoma City University, Petree College of Arts and Sciences, Division of Education and Kinesiology Exercise Studies, Oklahoma City, OK 73106-1402. Offers M Ed. Part-time and evening/weekend programs available. *Faculty:* 5 full-time (3 women), 14 part-time/adjunct (9 women). *Students:* 17 full-time (14 women), 26 part-time (23 women); includes 3 minority (2 African Americans, 1 American Indian/Alaska Native), 7 international. Average age 33. 19 applicants, 100% accepted, 12 enrolled. *Degree requirements:* For master's, comprehensive exam, thesis optional. *Entrance requirements:* For master's, minimum GPA of 3.0. Additional exam requirements/recommendations for international students: Required—TOEFL (minimum score 550 paper-based; 213 computer-based; 79 iBT). *Application deadline:* For fall admission, 8/20 for domestic students; for spring admission, 1/6 for domestic students. Applications are processed on a rolling basis. Application fee: $50 ($70 for international students). *Expenses:* Tuition: Full-time $15,930; part-time $885 per hour. *Financial support:* Fellowships with partial tuition reimbursements, career-related internships or fieldwork, Federal Work-Study, tuition waivers (full and partial), and unspecified assistantships available. Support available to part-time students. Financial award application deadline: 8/1; financial award applicants required to submit FAFSA. *Unit head:* Dr. Terry Conley, Interim Chair/Associate Dean, 405-208-5446, Fax: 405-208-5447, E-mail: tconley@okcu.edu. *Application contact:* Michelle Lockhart, Director, Admissions, 800-633-7242, Fax: 405-208-5916, E-mail: gadmissions@okcu.edu.

Oklahoma State University, College of Education, Stillwater, OK 74078. Offers MS, Ed D, PhD, Ed S. *Accreditation:* NCATE. Part-time programs available. Postbaccalaureate distance learning degree programs offered. *Faculty:* 102 full-time (59 women), 62 part-time/adjunct (40 women). *Students:* 279 full-time (197 women), 587 part-time (421 women); includes 150 minority (51 African Americans, 68 American Indian/Alaska Native, 12 Asian Americans or Pacific Islanders, 19 Hispanic Americans), 49 international. Average age 36. 466 applicants, 41% accepted, 125 enrolled. In 2009, 156 master's, 78 doctorates awarded. *Degree requirements:* For master's, thesis or alternative; for doctorate, comprehensive exam, thesis/dissertation. *Entrance requirements:* For master's and doctorate, GRE or GMAT. Additional exam requirements/recommendations for international students: Required—TOEFL (minimum score 550 paper-based; 79 iBT). *Application deadline:* For fall admission, 3/1 priority date for international students; for spring admission, 8/1 priority date for international students. Applications are processed on a rolling basis. Application fee: $40 ($75 for international students). Electronic applications accepted. *Expenses:* Tuition, state resident: full-time $3716; part-time $154.85 per credit hour. Tuition, nonresident: full-time $14,448; part-time $602 per credit hour. Required fees: $1772; $73.85 per credit hour. One-time fee: $50. Tuition and fees vary according to course load and campus/location. *Financial support:* In 2009–10, 64 research assistantships (averaging $7,416 per year), 92 teaching assistantships (averaging $8,693 per year) were awarded; career-related internships or fieldwork, Federal Work-Study, scholarships/grants, health care benefits, tuition waivers (partial), and unspecified assistantships also available. Support available to part-time students. Financial award application deadline: 3/1; financial award applicants required to submit FAFSA. *Unit head:* Dr. Pamela Fry, Dean, 405-744-3373, Fax: 405-744-6399. *Application contact:* Dr. Gordon Emslie, Dean, 405-744-6368, Fax: 405-744-0355, E-mail: grad-i@okstate.edu.

Old Dominion University, Darden College of Education, Norfolk, VA 23529. Offers MS, MS Ed, PhD, Ed S. *Accreditation:* NCATE. Part-time and evening/weekend programs available. Postbaccalaureate distance learning degree programs offered (no on-campus study). *Faculty:* 94 full-time (55 women), 62 part-time/adjunct (40 women). *Students:* 596 full-time (475 women), 928 part-time (718 women); includes 291 minority (211 African Americans, 11 American Indian/Alaska Native, 38 Asian Americans or Pacific Islanders, 31 Hispanic Americans), 27 international. Average age 33. 1,125 applicants, 72% accepted. In 2009, 569 master's, 27 doctorates, 22 other advanced degrees awarded. *Degree requirements:* For master's, thesis (for some programs), exam; for doctorate, comprehensive exam, thesis/dissertation; for Ed S, comprehensive exam. *Entrance requirements:* For doctorate, GRE General Test, master's degree, minimum GPA of 3.25; for Ed S, GRE General Test or MAT. Additional exam requirements/recommendations for international students: Required—TOEFL (minimum score 550 paper-based). *Application deadline:* For fall admission, 6/1 priority date for domestic and international students; for spring admission, 11/1 priority date for domestic and international students. Applications are processed on a rolling basis. Application fee: $40. Electronic applications accepted. *Expenses:* Tuition, state resident: full-time $8112; part-time $338 per credit. Tuition, nonresident: full-time $20,256; part-time $844 per credit. Required fees: $119 per semester. One-time fee: $50. *Financial support:* In 2009–10, 141 students received support, including 9 fellowships with full and partial tuition reimbursements available (averaging $15,000 per year), 60 research assistantships with full and partial tuition reimbursements available (averaging $15,000 per year), 72 teaching assistantships with full and partial tuition reimbursements available (averaging $15,000 per year); career-related internships or fieldwork, Federal Work-Study, institutionally sponsored loans, scholarships/grants, tuition waivers (partial), and unspecified assistantships also available. Support available to part-time students. Financial award application deadline: 2/15; financial award applicants required to submit CSS PROFILE or FAFSA. *Faculty research:* Effective urban teaching practices, curriculum theory, clinical practices, special education, instructional technology. Total annual research expenditures: $8.1 million. *Unit head:* Dr. William H. Graves, Dean, 757-683-3938, Fax: 757-683-5083, E-mail: wgraves@odu.edu. *Application contact:* Alice McAdory, Director of Admissions, 757-683-3685, Fax: 757-683-3255, E-mail: gradadmit@odu.edu.

Olivet College, Program in Education, Olivet, MI 49076-9701. Offers MAT. *Degree requirements:* For master's, portfolio. *Entrance requirements:* For master's, current K-12 teacher certification. Electronic applications accepted.

Olivet Nazarene University, Graduate School, Division of Education, Bourbonnais, IL 60914. Offers curriculum and instruction (MAE); elementary education (MAT); library information

specialist (MAE); reading specialist (MAE); school leadership (MAE); secondary education (MAT). *Accreditation:* NCATE. Evening/weekend programs available. *Degree requirements:* For master's, thesis or alternative.

Oral Roberts University, School of Education, Tulsa, OK 74171. Offers Christian school administration (K-12) (MA Ed, Ed D); Christian school curriculum development (MA Ed); college and higher education administration (Ed D); public school administration (K-12) (MA Ed, Ed D); public school teaching (MA Ed). *Accreditation:* NCATE. Part-time programs available. Post-baccalaureate distance learning degree programs offered (minimal on-campus study). *Faculty:* 7 full-time (2 women), 6 part-time/adjunct (2 women). *Students:* 344 full-time (223 women); includes 117 minority (93 African Americans, 7 American Indian/Alaska Native, 11 Asian Americans or Pacific Islanders, 6 Hispanic Americans). 80 applicants, 94% accepted, 65 enrolled. In 2009, 14 master's, 4 doctorates awarded. *Degree requirements:* For master's, comprehensive exam, thesis optional; for doctorate, comprehensive exam, thesis/dissertation. *Entrance requirements:* For master's, GRE General Test or MAT, minimum GPA of 3.0; for doctorate, minimum GPA of 3.0. Additional exam requirements/recommendations for international students: Required—TOEFL (minimum score 500 paper-based; 173 computer-based). *Application deadline:* For fall admission, 1/1 for domestic and international students; for spring admission, 1/1 priority date for domestic students, 1/1 for international students. Applications are processed on a rolling basis. *Expenses:* Contact institution. *Financial support:* In 2009–10, 4 research assistantships (averaging $5,000 per year) were awarded; scholarships/grants and unspecified assistantships also available. Financial award application deadline: 6/1; financial award applicants required to submit FAFSA. *Faculty research:* Teacher effectiveness, college success in high achieving African-Americans, professional development practices. *Unit head:* Dr. Kim Boyd, Dean, 918-495-7108, E-mail: kboyd@oru.edu. *Application contact:* Lance Miller, Graduate Admissions, 918-495-6553, Fax: 918-495-6222, E-mail: gradeducation@oru.edu.

Oregon State University, Graduate School, College of Education, Program in General Education, Corvallis, OR 97331. Offers Ed M, MAIS, MS, Ed D, PhD. Part-time programs available. *Students:* 7 full-time (5 women), 122 part-time (80 women); includes 21 minority (4 African Americans, 6 American Indian/Alaska Native, 3 Asian Americans or Pacific Islanders, 8 Hispanic Americans), 4 international. Average age 43. In 2009, 19 master's, 11 doctorates awarded. Terminal master's awarded for partial completion of doctoral program. *Degree requirements:* For master's, variable foreign language requirement, thesis (for some programs); for doctorate, variable foreign language requirement, thesis/dissertation. *Entrance requirements:* For master's, California Basic Educational Skills Test, NTE, minimum GPA of 3.0 in last 90 hours of course work; for doctorate, GRE or MAT, master's degree, minimum GPA of 3.0 in last 90 hours of course work. Additional exam requirements/recommendations for international students: Required—TOEFL. *Application deadline:* For fall admission, 3/1 priority date for domestic students. Applications are processed on a rolling basis. Application fee: $50. *Expenses:* Tuition, state resident: full-time $9774; part-time $362 per credit. Tuition, nonresident: full-time $15,849; part-time $587 per credit. Required fees: $1639. Full-time tuition and fees vary according to course load and program. *Financial support:* Fellowships, research assistantships, teaching assistantships, career-related internships or fieldwork, Federal Work-Study, and institutionally sponsored loans available. Support available to part-time students. Financial award application deadline: 2/1. *Faculty research:* School administration, educational foundations, research methodology, education policy development, higher education administration. *Unit head:* Dr. Kenneth J. Winograd, Chair, 541-737-5988, Fax: 541-737-2040, E-mail: winograk@oregonstate.edu. *Application contact:* Dr. Kenneth J. Winograd, Chair, 541-737-5988, Fax: 541-737-2040, E-mail: winograk@oregonstate.edu.

Oregon State University–Cascades, Program in Education, Bend, OR 97701. Offers MAT.

Ottawa University, Graduate Studies-Arizona, Program in Education, Ottawa, KS 66067-3399. Offers community college counseling (MA); curriculum and instruction (MA); early childhood (MA); education intervention (MA); education leadership (MA); education technology (MA); Montessori early childhood education (MA); Montessori elementary education (MA); professional development (MA); school guidance counseling (MA); special education—cross categorical (MA). Programs offered in Mesa, Phoenix, Tempe and West Valley, AZ. *Accreditation:* NCATE. Part-time programs available. *Degree requirements:* For master's, thesis or alternative. *Entrance requirements:* For master's, minimum undergraduate GPA of 3.0, copy of current state certification or teaching license. Additional exam requirements/recommendations for international students: Required—TOEFL (minimum score 550 paper-based; 213 computer-based). Electronic applications accepted. *Expenses:* Contact institution.

Otterbein University, Department of Education, Westerville, OH 43081. Offers MAE, MAT. *Accreditation:* NCATE. *Degree requirements:* For master's, capstone project. *Entrance requirements:* For master's, 2 reference forms. Additional exam requirements/recommendations for international students: Required—TOEFL (minimum score 550 paper-based; 213 computer-based; 79 iBT). *Faculty research:* Computer technology middle level education, assessment, teacher leadership, multicultural education.

Our Lady of Holy Cross College, Program in Education and Counseling, New Orleans, LA 70131-7399. Offers administration and supervision (M Ed); curriculum and instruction (M Ed); marriage and family counseling (MA); school counseling (M Ed, MA). *Accreditation:* ACA; NCATE. Part-time and evening/weekend programs available. *Degree requirements:* For master's, thesis. *Entrance requirements:* For master's, GRE General Test, minimum GPA of 2.7.

Our Lady of the Lake University of San Antonio, School of Professional Studies, San Antonio, TX 78207-4689. Offers communication and learning disorders (MA); curriculum and instruction (M Ed), including bilingual, early childhood education, English as a second language, integrated math teaching, integrated science teaching, master reading teacher, master technology teacher, reading specialist; early elementary education (M Ed); generic special education (M Ed), including elementary education; human sciences (MA); intermediate education (M Ed), including math/science education, professional studies; learning resources specialist (M Ed); principal (M Ed); psychology (MS, Psy D), including counseling psychology, marriage and family therapy (MS), school psychology (MS); school counseling (M Ed); secondary education (M Ed). Part-time and evening/weekend programs available. *Students:* 186 full-time (158 women), 314 part-time (273 women); includes 309 minority (43 African Americans, 2 American Indian/Alaska Native, 7 Asian Americans or Pacific Islanders, 257 Hispanic Americans), 6 international. Average age 36. In 2009, 157 master's, 3 doctorates awarded. *Degree requirements:* For master's, comprehensive exam; for doctorate, thesis/dissertation, internship, qualifying exam. *Entrance requirements:* For master's, GRE General Test or MAT; for doctorate, GRE General Test or MAT, interview. Additional exam requirements/recommendations for international students: Required—TOEFL. *Application deadline:* Applications are processed on a rolling basis. Application fee: $25 ($50 for international students). Electronic applications accepted. *Expenses:* Tuition: Full-time $12,330; part-time $685 per contact hour. Required fees: $139; $12 per contact hour. $57 per semester. Tuition and fees vary according to campus/location. *Financial support:* Research assistantships, teaching assistantships, career-related internships or fieldwork, Federal Work-Study, institutionally sponsored loans, scholarships/grants, and tuition waivers (partial) available. Support available to part-time students. *Unit head:* Dr. Teresita Aguilar, Dean, 210-434-6711 Ext. 2291, Fax: 210-431-3927, E-mail: secs@lake.ollusa.edu. *Application contact:* 210-434-6711 Ext. 2314, Fax: 210-431-4036, E-mail: gradadm@lake.ollusa.edu.

Pace University, School of Education, New York, NY 10038. Offers administration and supervision (MS Ed); adolescent education (MST); childhood education (MST); curriculum and instruction (MS); education (MST); literacy (MSE); school business management (Certificate); teaching students with disabilities (MSE); teaching visual arts (MST). *Accreditation:* NCATE. Part-time and evening/weekend programs available. *Students:* 235 full-time (177 women), 766 part-time (515 women); includes 158 minority (58 African Americans, 1 American Indian/Alaska Native, 37 Asian Americans or Pacific Islanders, 62 Hispanic Americans), 7 international. Average age 30. 332 applicants, 83% accepted, 165 enrolled. In 2009, 669 master's, 34 other advanced degrees awarded. *Degree requirements:* For master's, internship. *Entrance requirements:* For master's, interview, teaching certificate. Additional exam requirements/recommendations for international students: Required—TOEFL. *Application deadline:* For fall admission, 7/31 priority date for domestic students; for spring admission, 11/30 for domestic students. Applications are processed on a rolling basis. Application fee: $70. Electronic applications accepted. *Expenses:* Contact institution. *Financial support:* Research assistantships, career-related internships or fieldwork and Federal Work-Study available. Support available to part-time students. Financial award applicants required to submit FAFSA. *Unit head:* Dr. Harriet Feldman, Interim Dean, 212-346-1512. *Application contact:* Susan Ford-Goldschein, Director of Admissions, 212-346-1652, Fax: 212-346-1585, E-mail: gradnyc@pace.edu.

Pacific Lutheran University, Division of Graduate Studies, School of Education, Tacoma, WA 98447. Offers MAE. *Accreditation:* NCATE. Part-time and evening/weekend programs available. *Degree requirements:* For master's, comprehensive exam, thesis optional. *Entrance requirements:* For master's, GRE General Test or MAT, interview. Additional exam requirements/recommendations for international students: Required—TOEFL (minimum score 550 paper-based; 213 computer-based). *Expenses:* Contact institution.

Pacific Union College, Education Department, Angwin, CA 94508-9707. Offers education (M Ed). Program runs during summer only. Part-time programs available. *Faculty:* 3 full-time (1 woman). *Students:* 16 part-time (12 women); includes 2 minority (both Asian Americans or Pacific Islanders). Average age 30. In 2009, 2 master's awarded. *Degree requirements:* For master's, thesis, action research project, field experiences. *Entrance requirements:* For master's, GRE, interview, teaching credential, letters of recommendation. *Application deadline:* Applications are processed on a rolling basis. Application fee: $0. *Expenses:* Tuition: Part-time $350 per quarter hour. Tuition and fees vary according to student's religious affiliation. *Financial support:* Available to part-time students. *Unit head:* Dr. Jim Roy, Chair/Professor, 707-965-6644, Fax: 707-965-6645, E-mail: jroy@puc.edu. *Application contact:* Marsha Crow, Credential Analyst/Associate Professor, 707-965-6643, Fax: 707-965-6645, E-mail: mcrow@puc.edu.

Pacific University, College of Education, Forest Grove, OR 97116-1797. Offers early childhood education (MAT); education (MAE); elementary education (MAT); high school education (MAT); middle school education (MAT); special education (MAT); visual function in learning (M Ed). *Accreditation:* NCATE. Part-time and evening/weekend programs available. *Degree requirements:* For master's, research project. *Entrance requirements:* For master's, California Basic Educational Skills Test, PRAXIS II, minimum undergraduate GPA of 2.75, 3.0 graduate. Additional exam requirements/recommendations for international students: Required—TOEFL. Electronic applications accepted. *Expenses:* Contact institution. *Faculty research:* Defining a culturally competent classroom, technology in the k-12 classroom, Socratic seminars, social studies education.

Palm Beach Atlantic University, School of Education and Behavioral Studies, West Palm Beach, FL 33416-4708. Offers counseling psychology (MSCP), including addictions/mental health, marriage and family therapy, mental health counseling, school guidance counseling. Part-time and evening/weekend programs available. *Faculty:* 16 full-time (8 women), 2 part-time/adjunct (0 women). *Students:* 230 full-time (193 women), 74 part-time (63 women); includes 109 minority (70 African Americans, 1 Asian American or Pacific Islander, 38 Hispanic Americans), 8 international. Average age 35. 136 applicants, 70% accepted, 88 enrolled. In 2009, 86 master's awarded. *Entrance requirements:* For master's, GRE, minimum GPA of 3.0. Additional exam requirements/recommendations for international students: Required—TOEFL (minimum score 550 paper-based; 213 computer-based). *Application deadline:* For fall admission, 7/15 priority date for domestic students; for spring admission, 11/15 priority date for domestic students. Applications are processed on a rolling basis. Application fee: $45. Electronic applications accepted. *Expenses:* Tuition: Full-time $8010; part-time $445 per credit hour. Required fees: $99 per semester. Tuition and fees vary according to course load and degree level. *Financial support:* Applicants required to submit FAFSA. *Unit head:* Dr. Lisa Stubbs, Program Director, 561-803-2286. *Application contact:* Graduate Admissions, 888-468-6722, Fax: 561-803-2115, E-mail: grad@pba.edu.

Park University, College of Graduate and Professional Studies, Kansas City, MO 54105. Offers adult education (M Ed); at-risk students (M Ed); disaster and emergency management (MPA); educational administration (M Ed); entrepreneurship (MBA); general business (MBA); general education (M Ed); government/business relations (MPA); healthcare/services management (MBA, MPA); international business (MBA); K-12 certification (MAT); management information systems (MBA); management of information systems (MPA); middle school certification (MAT); multi-cultural education (M Ed); nonprofit management (MPA); public management (MPA); school law (M Ed); secondary school certification (MAT); special education (M Ed). Part-time and evening/weekend programs available. Postbaccalaureate distance learning degree programs offered (no on-campus study). *Degree requirements:* For master's, comprehensive exam, thesis (for some programs). *Entrance requirements:* For master's, GRE, GMAT, teacher certification (M Ed). Additional exam requirements/recommendations for international students: Required—TOEFL (minimum score 550 paper-based). Electronic applications accepted. *Faculty research:* Literacy, leadership, brain based research, multicultural education, diversity.

Penn State Great Valley, Graduate Studies, Education Division, Malvern, PA 19355-1488. Offers M Ed, MS. *Unit head:* Dr. Roy Clariana, Division Head, 610-648-3253, Fax: 610-725-5253, E-mail: rbc4@psu.edu. *Application contact:* Dr. Roy Clariana, Division Head, 610-648-3253, Fax: 610-725-5253, E-mail: rbc4@psu.edu.

Penn State Harrisburg, Graduate School, School of Behavioral Sciences and Education, Middletown, PA 17057-4898. Offers M Ed, MA, D Ed. Part-time and evening/weekend programs available. *Financial support:* Career-related internships or fieldwork available. *Unit head:* Dr. William D. Milheim, Director, 717-948-6205, Fax: 717-948-6209, E-mail: wdm2@psu.edu. *Application contact:* Dr. Robert W. Coffman, Director of Admissions, 717-948-6214, E-mail: rwc11@psu.edu.

Penn State University Park, Graduate School, College of Education, State College, University Park, PA 16802-1503. Offers M Ed, MA, MS, D Ed, PhD. *Accreditation:* NCATE. *Students:* 478 full-time (337 women), 275 part-time (167 women). Average age 35. 655 applicants, 48% accepted, 233 enrolled. In 2009, 176 master's, 74 doctorates awarded. *Entrance requirements:* Additional exam requirements/recommendations for international students: Required—TOEFL (minimum score 550 paper-based; 213 computer-based; 80 iBT). *Application deadline:* Applications are processed on a rolling basis. Application fee: $65. Electronic applications accepted. *Financial support:* Fellowships, research assistantships, teaching assistantships available. Financial award applicants required to submit FAFSA. *Unit head:* Dr. David H. Monk, Dean, 814-865-2526, Fax: 814-865-0555, E-mail: dhm6@psu.edu. *Application contact:* Cynthia E. Nicosia, Director, Graduate Enrollment Services, 814-865-1834, E-mail: cey1@psu.edu.

Pepperdine University, Graduate School of Education and Psychology, Division of Education, Malibu, CA 90263. Offers administration and preliminary administrative services credential (MS); education (MA); educational leadership, administration, and policy (Ed D); learning technologies (MA, Ed D); organization change (Ed D); organizational leadership (Ed D). Part-time and evening/weekend programs available. Postbaccalaureate distance learning degree programs offered (minimal on-campus study). *Faculty:* 25 full-time (15 women), 11 part-time/adjunct (4 women). *Students:* 267 full-time (203 women), 439 part-time (281 women); includes 264 minority (104 African Americans, 7 American Indian/Alaska Native, 64 Asian Americans or Pacific Islanders, 89 Hispanic Americans), 17 international. In 2009, 330 master's, 68 doctorates awarded. *Degree requirements:* For doctorate, thesis/dissertation. *Entrance requirements:* For master's, GRE General Test; for doctorate, GRE General Test, MAT. Additional exam requirements/recommendations for international students: Required—TOEFL. *Application deadline:* Applications are processed on a rolling basis. Application fee: $45. *Expenses:* Contact institution. *Financial support:* Research assistantships, teaching assistantships, career-related internships or fieldwork, institutionally sponsored loans, and scholarships/grants available. Support available to part-time students. Financial award application deadline: 7/1; financial award applicants required to submit FAFSA. *Unit head:* Dr. Chester McCall, Associate Dean, 310-568-2323, E-mail: chester.mccall@pepperdine.edu. *Application contact:* Brenden Wysocki, Admissions Manager, 310-568-5786.

Education—General

Peru State College, Graduate Programs, Program in Education, Peru, NE 68421. Offers curriculum and instruction (MS Ed). *Accreditation:* NCATE. Part-time programs available. *Degree requirements:* For master's, comprehensive exam (for some programs), thesis optional.

Pfeiffer University, School of Education, Misenheimer, NC 28109-0960. Offers elementary education (MS); teaching (MAT). *Accreditation:* NCATE. *Entrance requirements:* For master's, GRE, MAT, minimum GPA of 2.75.

Philadelphia Biblical University, School of Education, Langhorne, PA 19047-2990. Offers educational leadership and administration (MS El); teacher education (MS Ed). Part-time and evening/weekend programs available. *Faculty:* 5 full-time (3 women), 2 part-time/adjunct (both women). *Students:* 14 full-time (9 women), 61 part-time (45 women); includes 11 minority (10 African Americans, 1 Asian American or Pacific Islander), 7 international. Average age 34. 45 applicants, 62% accepted, 23 enrolled. In 2009, 39 master's awarded. *Entrance requirements:* Additional exam requirements/recommendations for international students: Required—TOEFL (minimum score 550 paper-based; 213 computer-based). *Application deadline:* Applications are processed on a rolling basis. Application fee: $25. Electronic applications accepted. *Expenses:* Tuition: Full-time $10,350; part-time $575 per credit. Required fees: $10; $10 per year. Tuition and fees vary according to program. *Financial support:* In 2009–10, 14 students received support. Scholarships/grants available. Support available to part-time students. Financial award applicants required to submit FAFSA. *Unit head:* Dr. Martha MacCullough, Dean, 215-702-4387, E-mail: teacher.ed@pbu.edu. *Application contact:* Katerina Penkova, Enrollment Counselor, Graduate Education, 800-572-2472, Fax: 215-702-4248, E-mail: kpenkova@pbu.edu.

Piedmont College, School of Education, Demorest, GA 30535-0010. Offers early childhood education (MA, MAT); instruction (Ed S); secondary education (MA, MAT). Part-time and evening/weekend programs available. *Degree requirements:* For master's, thesis, field experience in the teaching classroom. *Entrance requirements:* For master's, GRE General Test, MAT, minimum undergraduate GPA of 2.5; for Ed S, minimum graduate GPA of 3.5, valid teaching certificate. Additional exam requirements/recommendations for international students: Required—TOEFL (minimum score 550 paper-based; 213 computer-based).

Pittsburg State University, Graduate School, College of Education, Pittsburg, KS 66762. Offers MAT, MS, Ed S. *Accreditation:* NCATE. *Degree requirements:* For master's, thesis or alternative. *Expenses:* Tuition: state resident: full-time $4212; part-time $176 per credit. Tuition, nonresident: full-time $11,530; part-time $480 per credit. Required fees: $940; $43 per credit. Tuition and fees vary according to course level, course load, degree level, campus/location, reciprocity agreements and student level.

Plymouth State University, College of Graduate Studies, Graduate Studies in Education, Program in Certificate of Advanced Graduate Studies, Plymouth, NH 03264-1595. Offers CAGS. Part-time and evening/weekend programs available.

Point Loma Nazarene University, Program in Education, San Diego, CA 92106-2899. Offers MA, MAT, Ed S. Part-time and evening/weekend programs available. *Students:* 590 full-time (433 women), 321 part-time (238 women); includes 333 minority (42 African Americans, 6 American Indian/Alaska Native, 39 Asian Americans or Pacific Islanders, 246 Hispanic Americans). Average age 34. In 2009, 306 master's awarded. *Degree requirements:* For master's, thesis optional. *Entrance requirements:* For master's, GRE General Test or MAT, portfolio, letters of recommendation; for Ed S, GRE General Test or MAT, portfolio. *Application deadline:* For fall admission, 5/15 priority date for domestic students; for spring admission, 11/1 for domestic students. Applications are processed on a rolling basis. Application fee: $35. *Financial support:* Career-related internships or fieldwork available. Financial award application deadline: 4/10. *Unit head:* Dr. Kerry Fulcher, Acting Provost, 619-849-2284, Fax: 619-849-2579, E-mail: kerryfulcher@pointloma.edu. *Application contact:* Dejon DAvis, Director of Graduate Admission, 619-563-2856, E-mail: dejondavis@pointloma.edu.

Point Park University, School of Arts and Sciences, Department of Education, Pittsburgh, PA 15222-1984. Offers curriculum and instruction (MA); educational administration (MA); teaching and leadership (M Ed). Part-time and evening/weekend programs available. *Faculty:* 2 full-time, 5 part-time/adjunct. *Students:* 9 full-time (7 women), 51 part-time (36 women); includes 11 minority (9 African Americans, 2 Asian Americans or Pacific Islanders), 1 international. Average age 36. 41 applicants, 68% accepted, 25 enrolled. In 2009, 12 master's awarded. *Degree requirements:* For master's, comprehensive exam (for some programs), thesis or alternative. *Entrance requirements:* For master's, minimum GPA of 3.0, resume, 2 letters of recommendation. Additional exam requirements/recommendations for international students: Required—TOEFL. *Application deadline:* Applications are processed on a rolling basis. Application fee: $30. Electronic applications accepted. *Expenses:* Tuition: Full-time $11,880; part-time $660 per credit. Required fees: $486; $27 per credit. *Financial support:* In 2009–10, 19 students received support, including 1 research assistantship with full tuition reimbursement available (averaging $6,400 per year); scholarships/grants also available. Financial award application deadline: 4/15; financial award applicants required to submit FAFSA. *Unit head:* Dr. Darlene Marnich, Chair, 412-392-3474, Fax: 412-392-3927, E-mail: dmarnich@pointpark.edu. *Application contact:* Lynn C. Ribar, Associate Director, Graduate and Adult Enrollment, 412-392-3908, Fax: 412-392-6164, E-mail: lribar@pointpark.edu.

Pontifical Catholic University of Puerto Rico, College of Education, Ponce, PR 00717-0777. Offers M Ed, MA Ed, MRE, PhD. Part-time and evening/weekend programs available. *Degree requirements:* For master's, comprehensive exam, thesis (for some programs). *Entrance requirements:* For master's, GRE General Test, 2 letters of recommendation, interview, minimum GPA of 2.75; for doctorate, EXADEP, GRE or MAT, 3 letters of recommendation. *Faculty research:* Teaching English as a second language, learning styles, leadership styles.

Portland State University, Graduate Studies, School of Education, Portland, OR 97207-0751. Offers M Ed, MA, MAT, MS, MST, Ed D. *Accreditation:* NCATE. Part-time and evening/weekend programs available. *Degree requirements:* For doctorate, thesis/dissertation. *Entrance requirements:* For master's, minimum GPA of 3.0 in upper-division course work or 2.75 overall. Additional exam requirements/recommendations for international students: Required—TOEFL (minimum score 550 paper-based; 213 computer-based).

Post University, Program in Education, Waterbury, CT 06723-2540. Offers education (M Ed); instructional design and technology (M Ed); teaching and learning (M Ed). Postbaccalaureate distance learning degree programs offered.

Prairie View A&M University, College of Education, Prairie View, TX 77446-0519. Offers M Ed, MA, MS, MS Ed, PhD. *Accreditation:* NCATE. Part-time and evening/weekend programs available. Postbaccalaureate distance learning degree programs offered (no on-campus study). *Faculty:* 31 full-time (12 women), 33 part-time/adjunct (14 women). *Students:* 85 full-time (64 women), 1,234 part-time (955 women); includes 1,164 minority (1,118 African Americans, 3 Asian Americans or Pacific Islanders, 43 Hispanic Americans), 9 international. Average age 35. 1,093 applicants, 95% accepted, 1003 enrolled. In 2009, 490 master's, 17 doctorates awarded. *Degree requirements:* For master's, thesis optional, minimum GPA of 3.0; for doctorate, comprehensive exam, thesis/dissertation. *Entrance requirements:* For master's, 3 letters of reference, minimum undergraduate GPA of 2.5; for doctorate, GRE General Test, 3 letters of reference, minimum undergraduate GPA of 3.0, essay. Additional exam requirements/recommendations for international students: Required—TOEFL (minimum score 550 paper-based). *Application deadline:* For fall admission, 7/1 priority date for domestic students, 6/1 for international students; for spring admission, 11/1 priority date for domestic students, 10/1 for international students. Applications are processed on a rolling basis. Application fee: $50. Electronic applications accepted. *Expenses:* Tuition: state resident: full-time $2200. Tuition, nonresident: full-time $5600. Required fees: $1720. Tuition and fees vary according to course load. *Financial support:* In 2009–10, 1,050 students received support, including 7 research assistantships with tuition reimbursements available (averaging $24,000 per year); fellowships with tuition reimbursements available, teaching assistantships, career-related internships or fieldwork, institutionally sponsored loans, scholarships/grants, and unspecified assistantships

also available. Support available to part-time students. Financial award application deadline: 4/1; financial award applicants required to submit FAFSA. *Faculty research:* Mentoring, assessment, humanistic education, diversity, literacy education, recruitment, student retention, school collaboration, leadership skills, structural equations. *Unit head:* Dr. Lucian Yates, Dean, 936-261-3600, Fax: 936-261-2911, E-mail: luyates@pvamu.edu.

Prescott College, Graduate Programs, Program in Education, Prescott, AZ 86301. Offers early childhood education (MA); early childhood special education (MA); education (MA); elementary education (MA); environmental education leadership and administration (MA); equine-assisted experiential learning (MA); school guidance counseling (MA); secondary education (MA); special education, learning disability (MA); special education, mental retardation (MA); special education, serious emotional disability (MA); student-directed independent study (MA); sustainability education (PhD). Part-time programs available. Postbaccalaureate distance learning degree programs offered (minimal on-campus study). *Faculty:* 3 full-time (1 woman), 79 part-time/adjunct (41 women). *Students:* 75 full-time (44 women), 46 part-time (36 women); includes 18 minority (3 African Americans, 3 American Indian/Alaska Native, 4 Asian Americans or Pacific Islanders, 8 Hispanic Americans), 2 international. Average age 39. 66 applicants, 67% accepted, 31 enrolled. In 2009, 22 master's, 4 doctorates awarded. *Degree requirements:* For master's, thesis, fieldwork or internship, practicum; for doctorate, thesis/dissertation. *Entrance requirements:* For master's, 2 letters of recommendation, resume; for doctorate, 3 letters of recommendation, resume, official transcripts, personal statement, program proposal. Additional exam requirements/recommendations for international students: Required—TOEFL (minimum score 500 paper-based; 173 computer-based). *Application deadline:* For fall admission, 4/15 priority date for domestic and international students; for spring admission, 9/15 priority date for domestic and international students. Applications are processed on a rolling basis. Application fee: $40. Electronic applications accepted. *Expenses:* Tuition: Full-time $14,712; part-time $613 per credit. Required fees: $50 per term. One-time fee: $150. Tuition and fees vary according to course load and degree level. *Financial support:* Career-related internships or fieldwork and Federal Work-Study available. Financial award applicants required to submit FAFSA. *Unit head:* Noel Caniglia, Chair, 928-358-3201, Fax: 928-776-5151, E-mail: ncaniglia@prescott.edu. *Application contact:* Kerstin Alicki, Admissions Counselor, 877-412-8705, Fax: 928-277-4695, E-mail: admissions@prescott.edu.

Providence College, Graduate Studies, Department of Education, Providence, RI 02918. Offers administration (M Ed), including elementary administration, secondary administration; counseling (M Ed); literacy (M Ed); secondary teacher (M Ed), including secondary education; special education (M Ed), including elementary special education, secondary special education. Part-time and evening/weekend programs available. *Faculty:* 4 full-time (3 women), 39 part-time/adjunct (22 women). *Students:* 78 full-time (59 women), 172 part-time (124 women); includes 5 minority (2 African Americans, 1 American Indian/Alaska Native, 2 Hispanic Americans), 2 international. Average age 32. 119 applicants, 56% accepted. In 2009, 129 master's awarded. *Degree requirements:* For master's, comprehensive exam. *Entrance requirements:* For master's, GRE General Test. Additional exam requirements/recommendations for international students: Required—TOEFL (minimum score 550 paper-based; 213 computer-based; 80 iBT). *Application deadline:* For fall admission, 8/1 priority date for domestic and international students; for spring admission, 12/1 for domestic students, 12/1 priority date for international students. Applications are processed on a rolling basis. Application fee: $55. *Expenses:* Tuition: Full-time $9909; part-time $367 per credit. One-time fee: $200. Tuition and fees vary according to course load and program. *Financial support:* In 2009–10, 14 research assistantships with full tuition reimbursements (averaging $8,400 per year) were awarded; career-related internships or fieldwork, institutionally sponsored loans, and unspecified assistantships also available. Support available to part-time students. Financial award application deadline: 8/1; financial award applicants required to submit FAFSA. *Unit head:* Dr. Brian M. McCadden, Dean, School of Professional Studies, 401-865-2247, Fax: 401-865-1147, E-mail: bmccadde@providence.edu. *Application contact:* Carol A. Daniels, Coordinator of Graduate Faculty and Administrative Services, 401-865-2247, Fax: 401-865-1147, E-mail: daniels@providence.edu.

Purdue University, Graduate School, School of Education, West Lafayette, IN 47907. Offers MS, MS Ed, PhD, Ed S. *Accreditation:* NCATE. Part-time and evening/weekend programs available. *Degree requirements:* For master's, thesis optional; for doctorate, thesis/dissertation, oral and written exams; for Ed S, oral presentation, project. *Entrance requirements:* For master's, minimum B average; for doctorate, GRE General Test; for Ed S, GRE, minimum B average. Additional exam requirements/recommendations for international students: Required—TOEFL. Electronic applications accepted.

Purdue University Calumet, Graduate School, School of Education, Hammond, IN 46323-2094. Offers counseling (MS Ed), including human services, mental health counseling, school counseling; educational administration (MS Ed); instructional technology (MS Ed); special education (MS Ed). *Accreditation:* NCATE. *Entrance requirements:* Additional exam requirements/recommendations for international students: Required—TOEFL.

Purdue University North Central, Program in Education, Westville, IN 46391-9542. Offers elementary education (MS Ed). *Accreditation:* NCATE. Part-time and evening/weekend programs available. *Degree requirements:* For master's, one foreign language. *Entrance requirements:* For master's, GRE, minimum GPA of 3.0. Electronic applications accepted. *Faculty research:* Diversity, integration.

Queens College of the City University of New York, Division of Graduate Studies, Division of Education, Flushing, NY 11367-1597. Offers MA, MS Ed, AC. *Accreditation:* NCATE. Part-time and evening/weekend programs available. *Faculty:* 73 full-time (50 women). *Students:* 255 full-time (197 women), 2,108 part-time (1,600 women). 1,603 applicants, 58% accepted, 709 enrolled. In 2009, 638 master's, 124 other advanced degrees awarded. *Degree requirements:* For master's, research project; for AC, thesis optional. *Entrance requirements:* For master's, minimum GPA of 3.0. Additional exam requirements/recommendations for international students: Required—TOEFL. *Application deadline:* For fall admission, 4/1 for domestic students; for spring admission, 11/1 for domestic students. Applications are processed on a rolling basis. Application fee: $125. *Expenses:* Tuition, state resident: full-time $7360; part-time $310 per credit. Tuition, nonresident: part-time $575 per credit. One-time fee: $195 full-time; $145.25 part-time. *Financial support:* Career-related internships or fieldwork, Federal Work-Study, institutionally sponsored loans, and tuition waivers (partial) available. Support available to part-time students. Financial award application deadline: 4/1; financial award applicants required to submit FAFSA. *Unit head:* Dr. Penny Hammrich, Dean, 718-997-5220. *Application contact:* Mario Caruso, Director of Graduate Admissions, 718-997-5200, Fax: 718-997-5193, E-mail: graduate_admissions@qc.edu.

Queen's University at Kingston, School of Graduate Studies and Research, Faculty of Education, Kingston, ON K7L 3N6, Canada. Offers M Ed, PhD. Part-time programs available. *Degree requirements:* For master's, thesis optional; for doctorate, comprehensive exam, thesis/dissertation. *Entrance requirements:* Additional exam requirements/recommendations for international students: Required—TOEFL (minimum score 580 paper-based; 237 computer-based); Recommended—TWE (minimum score 4). *Faculty research:* Literacy, assessment and evaluation, special needs, mathematics, science and technology education.

Queens University of Charlotte, Wayland H. Cato, Jr. School of Education, Charlotte, NC 28274-0002. Offers education in literacy (M Ed); elementary education (MAT); school administration (MSA). *Accreditation:* NCATE. Part-time and evening/weekend programs available. *Degree requirements:* For master's, comprehensive exam. *Entrance requirements:* For master's, GRE General Test. *Expenses:* Contact institution.

Quincy University, Program in Education, Quincy, IL 62301-2699: Offers curriculum and instruction (MS Ed); leadership (MRS); reading education (MS Ed); school administration (MS Ed); special education (MS Ed); teaching certification (MS Ed). Part-time programs available. Postbaccalaureate distance learning degree programs offered. *Faculty:* 3 full-time (2 women), 19 part-time/adjunct (16 women). *Students:* 328 full-time (222 women), 88 part-time (57

women); includes 60 African Americans, 9 Asian Americans or Pacific Islanders, 69 Hispanic Americans. In 2009, 10 master's awarded. *Degree requirements:* For master's, thesis. *Entrance requirements:* For master's, MAT or GRE. Additional exam requirements/recommendations for international students: Required—TOEFL. *Application deadline:* Applications are processed on a rolling basis. Application fee: $25. Electronic applications accepted. *Expenses:* Tuition: Full-time $8400; part-time $350 per credit hour. Required fees: $360; $15 per credit hour. Tuition and fees vary according to course load, campus/location and program. *Financial support:* Available to part-time students. Applicants required to submit FAFSA. *Unit head:* Dot Nelson, Director, 217-228-5432 Ext. 3111, E-mail: nelsodo@quincy.edu. *Application contact:* Jennifer O'Donnell, Coordinator of Adult Studies, 217-228-5404, Fax: 217-228-5479, E-mail: admissions@quincy.edu.

Quinnipiac University, Division of Education, Hamden, CT 06518-1940. Offers MAT. *Accreditation:* NCATE. *Faculty:* 8 full-time, 28 part-time/adjunct. *Students:* 157 full-time (126 women), 40 part-time (25 women); includes 11 minority (3 African Americans, 4 Asian Americans or Pacific Islanders, 4 Hispanic Americans). Average age 24. 183 applicants, 92% accepted, 149 enrolled. In 2009, 91 master's awarded. *Entrance requirements:* For master's, PRAXIS I, minimum GPA of 2.67, interview. Additional exam requirements/recommendations for international students: Required—TOEFL (minimum score 575 paper-based; 233 computer-based; 90 iBT), IELTS (minimum score 6.5). *Application deadline:* For fall admission, 3/31 priority date for domestic students, 3/31 for international students. Applications are processed on a rolling basis. Application fee: $45. Electronic applications accepted. *Expenses:* Tuition: Full-time $16,030; part-time $770 per credit. Required fees: $630; $35 per credit. *Financial support:* Career-related internships or fieldwork, Federal Work-Study, scholarships/grants, tuition waivers (partial), and unspecified assistantships available. Financial award application deadline: 4/30; financial award applicants required to submit FAFSA. *Faculty research:* Equity and excellence in education. *Unit head:* Dr. Cynthia Dubea, Dean, 203-582-8730, Fax: 203-582-8709, E-mail: cynthia.dubea@quinnipiac.edu. *Application contact:* Jennifer Boutin, Associate Director of Graduate Admissions, 800-462-1944, Fax: 203-582-3443, E-mail: jennifer.boutin@quinnipiac.edu.

Radford University, College of Graduate and Professional Studies, College of Education and Human Development, Radford, VA 24142. Offers MS. *Accreditation:* NCATE. Part-time programs available. *Faculty:* 35 full-time (25 women), 56 part-time/adjunct (36 women). *Students:* 148 full-time (113 women), 297 part-time (231 women); includes 34 minority (26 African Americans, 1 American Indian/Alaska Native, 4 Asian Americans or Pacific Islanders, 3 Hispanic Americans), 3 international. Average age 31. 272 applicants, 92% accepted, 187 enrolled. In 2009, 182 master's awarded. *Degree requirements:* For master's, comprehensive exam, thesis optional. *Entrance requirements:* For master's, GRE or MAT, minimum GPA of 2.75; 2 letters of reference. Additional exam requirements/recommendations for international students: Required—TOEFL (minimum score 550 paper-based; 213 computer-based; 79 iBT). *Application deadline:* For fall admission, 4/15 priority date for domestic students, 12/1 for international students; for spring admission, 7/1 for international students. Applications are processed on a rolling basis. Application fee: $50. Electronic applications accepted. *Expenses:* Tuition, state resident: full-time $5086; part-time $211 per credit hour. Tuition, nonresident: full-time $12,608; part-time $525 per credit hour. Required fees: $2508; $105 per credit hour. *Financial support:* In 2009–10, 237 students received support, including 29 research assistantships with partial tuition reimbursements available (averaging $8,000 per year), 9 teaching assistantships with partial tuition reimbursements available (averaging $8,700 per year); career-related internships or fieldwork, Federal Work-Study, institutionally sponsored loans, scholarships/grants, and unspecified assistantships also available. Financial award application deadline: 3/1; financial award applicants required to submit FAFSA. *Unit head:* Dr. Patricia Shoemaker, Dean, 540-831-5439, Fax: 540-831-5440, E-mail: pshoemak@radford.edu. *Application contact:* Graduate Admissions, 540-831-5431, Fax: 540-831-6061, E-mail: gradcollege@radford.edu.

Radford University, College of Graduate and Professional Studies, College of Education and Human Development, School of Teacher Education and Leadership, Program in Education, Radford, VA 24142. Offers content area studies (MS); curriculum and instruction (MS); early childhood education (MS); educational technology (MS); library media (MS). *Accreditation:* NCATE. Part-time and evening/weekend programs available. *Faculty:* 14 full-time (11 women), 12 part-time/adjunct (8 women). *Students:* 54 full-time (37 women), 84 part-time (69 women); includes 8 minority (6 African Americans, 2 Asian Americans or Pacific Islanders), 3 international. Average age 30. 83 applicants, 92% accepted, 65 enrolled. In 2009, 34 master's awarded. *Degree requirements:* For master's, comprehensive exam. *Entrance requirements:* For master's, GRE or MAT, minimum GPA of 3.0, 2 letters of professional reference. Additional exam requirements/recommendations for international students: Required—TOEFL (minimum score 550 paper-based; 213 computer-based; 79 iBT). *Application deadline:* For fall admission, 12/1 for international students; for spring admission, 7/1 for international students. Applications are processed on a rolling basis. Application fee: $50. Electronic applications accepted. *Expenses:* Tuition, state resident: full-time $5086; part-time $211 per credit hour. Tuition, nonresident: full-time $12,608; part-time $525 per credit hour. Required fees: $2508; $105 per credit hour. *Financial support:* In 2009–10, 22 students received support, including 14 research assistantships with partial tuition reimbursements available (averaging $8,000 per year); career-related internships or fieldwork, Federal Work-Study, institutionally sponsored loans, scholarships/grants, and unspecified assistantships also available. Financial award application deadline: 3/1; financial award applicants required to submit FAFSA. *Unit head:* Dr. Elizabeth Dore, Coordinator, 540-831-5843, Fax: 540-831-5059, E-mail: edore@radford.edu. *Application contact:* Graduate Admissions, 540-831-5431, Fax: 540-831-6061, E-mail: gradcollege@radford.edu.

Randolph College, Programs in Education, Lynchburg, VA 24503. Offers curriculum and instruction (MAT); special education-learning disabilities (M Ed, MAT). *Accreditation:* Teacher Education Accreditation Council. *Entrance requirements:* For master's, minimum GPA of 3.0 in prerequisite education coursework, 2.7 in major or field of interest (MAT); teaching license (M Ed); 2 recommendations; interview.

Regent University, Graduate School, School of Education, Virginia Beach, VA 23464-9800. Offers career switcher (M Ed); Christian school program (M Ed); cross-categorical special education (M Ed); education (M Ed, Ed D); education licensure (M Ed); educational leadership (M Ed); elementary education (M Ed); individualized degree plan (M Ed); leadership in character education (M Ed); master teacher (M Ed); mathematics education (M Ed); special education leadership (Ed S); student affairs (M Ed); TESOL (M Ed). *Accreditation:* Teacher Education Accreditation Council. Part-time and evening/weekend programs available. Postbaccalaureate distance learning degree programs offered (minimal on-campus study). *Faculty:* 26 full-time (13 women), 104 part-time/adjunct (78 women). *Students:* 141 full-time (116 women), 622 part-time (488 women); includes 218 minority (186 African Americans, 1 American Indian/Alaska Native, 10 Asian Americans or Pacific Islanders, 21 Hispanic Americans), 8 international. Average age 39. 509 applicants, 60% accepted, 176 enrolled. In 2009, 212 master's, 15 doctorates awarded. *Degree requirements:* For master's, thesis or alternative; for doctorate, comprehensive exam, thesis/dissertation. *Entrance requirements:* For master's, MAT, minimum undergraduate GPA of 2.75, writing sample, resume, recommendations, interview; for doctorate, GRE, writing sample, 3 years of relevant professional experience, master's-level paper, copies of published work, resume, transcripts, interview, recommendations. Additional exam requirements/recommendations for international students: Required—TOEFL (minimum score 577 paper-based; 233 computer-based). *Application deadline:* For fall admission, 4/1 priority date for domestic students; for spring admission, 10/15 priority date for domestic students. Applications are processed on a rolling basis. Application fee: $50. Electronic applications accepted. *Expenses:* Contact institution. *Financial support:* In 2009–10, 480 students received support; fellowships, career-related internships or fieldwork, scholarships/grants, tuition waivers (full and partial), and unspecified assistantships available. Support available to part-time students. Financial award application deadline: 4/1; financial award applicants required to submit FAFSA. *Faculty research:* Character development and discipline for children, education leadership development, diversity in schools, classroom management, technology in education settings. *Unit head:* Dr. Alan A. Arroyo, Dean, 757-352-4261, Fax: 757-352-4318, E-mail: alanarr@regent.edu. *Application contact:* Matthew Chadwick, Director of Admissions, 800-373-5504, Fax: 757-352-4381, E-mail: admissions@regent.edu.

Regis College, Department of Education, Weston, MA 02493. Offers elementary teacher (MAT); reading (MAT); special education (MAT). Part-time and evening/weekend programs available. *Faculty:* 2 full-time (both women), 5 part-time/adjunct (all women). *Students:* 2 full-time (both women), 49 part-time (42 women); includes 1 minority (Asian American or Pacific Islander). Average age 36. 8 applicants, 88% accepted, 4 enrolled. In 2009, 11 master's awarded. *Degree requirements:* For master's, thesis. *Entrance requirements:* For master's, GRE or MAT. Additional exam requirements/recommendations for international students: Required—TOEFL. *Application deadline:* Applications are processed on a rolling basis. Application fee: $50. Electronic applications accepted. *Expenses:* Tuition: Full-time $29,000; part-time $800 per credit. Tuition and fees vary according to course load, degree level and program. *Financial support:* In 2009–10, 1 student received support, including 1 fellowship with full tuition reimbursement available (averaging $11,970 per year); Federal Work-Study and scholarships/grants also available. Financial award applicants required to submit FAFSA. *Faculty research:* Reflective teaching, gender-based education, integrated teaching. *Unit head:* Dr. Leona McCaughey-Oreszak, Program Director, 781-768-7421, Fax: 781-768-7159, E-mail: leona.mccaughey-oreszak@regiscollege.edu. *Application contact:* Christine Petherick, Administrative Coordinator, Graduate Admission, 866-438-7344, Fax: 781-768-7071, E-mail: christine.petherick@regiscollege.edu.

Regis University, College for Professional Studies, Program in Teacher Education, Denver, CO 80221-1099. Offers adult learning, training, and development (M Ed); curriculum, instruction, and assessment (M Ed); early childhood (M Ed); educational technology (Certificate); elementary (M Ed); ESL (M Ed); fine arts (M Ed), including arts, music; instructional technology (M Ed); professional leadership (M Ed); reading (M Ed); secondary (M Ed); self-designed (M Ed); space studies (M Ed); special education (M Ed); teacher licensure (M Ed). Program also offered in Henderson and Las Vegas (Summerlin), NV. *Accreditation:* Teacher Education Accreditation Council. Part-time and evening/weekend programs available. Postbaccalaureate distance learning degree programs offered (no on-campus study). *Degree requirements:* For master's, thesis. *Entrance requirements:* For master's, resumé, minimum GPA of 2.75, criminal background check. Additional exam requirements/recommendations for international students: Required—TOEFL (minimum score 213 computer-based), TWE (minimum score 5). Electronic applications accepted. *Faculty research:* Issues of equity in the middle school classroom, professional learning communities, school reform, socialinguistic and discursive obstacles to student integration, inclusive language arts curriculum.

Regis University, Regis College, Denver, CO 80221-1099. Offers education (MA). Offered at Northwest Denver Campus. *Accreditation:* Teacher Education Accreditation Council. Part-time and evening/weekend programs available. *Degree requirements:* For master's, capstone presentation. *Entrance requirements:* For master's, 1 year of teaching experience, Colorado teaching certificate, videotape sample of teaching. *Expenses:* Contact institution.

Reinhardt University, Program in Early Childhood Education, Waleska, GA 30183-2981. Offers MAT. Part-time and evening/weekend programs available. Postbaccalaureate distance learning degree programs offered. *Faculty:* 3 full-time (all women), 1 (woman) part-time/adjunct. *Students:* 43 full-time (39 women), 1 (woman) part-time; includes 5 minority (4 African Americans, 1 Hispanic American). Average age 31. 54 applicants, 87% accepted. *Degree requirements:* For master's, comprehensive exam. *Entrance requirements:* For master's, GACE, background check. Additional exam requirements/recommendations for international students: Required—TOEFL. *Application deadline:* For fall admission, 5/7 for domestic and international students. Applications are processed on a rolling basis. Application fee: $25. Electronic applications accepted. *Expenses:* Tuition: Full-time $16,500; part-time $325 per credit hour. One-time fee: $100. Tuition and fees vary according to course load and program. *Financial support:* Application deadline: 5/1. *Unit head:* Nancy Carter, Coordinator, 770-720-5948, Fax: 770-720-9173, E-mail: ntc@reinhardt.edu. *Application contact:* Ray Schumacher, Admissions Counselor, 770-993-6971, Fax: 770-475-0263, E-mail: res@reinhardt.edu.

Rhode Island College, School of Graduate Studies, Feinstein School of Education and Human Development, Program in Education, Providence, RI 02908-1991. Offers PhD. *Accreditation:* NCATE. Part-time and evening/weekend programs available. *Faculty:* 10 part-time/adjunct (6 women). *Students:* 50 part-time (38 women); includes 6 minority (1 African American, 1 American Indian/Alaska Native, 3 Asian Americans or Pacific Islanders, 1 Hispanic American). Average age 41. In 2009, 3 doctorates awarded. *Degree requirements:* For doctorate, comprehensive exam, thesis/dissertation. *Entrance requirements:* For doctorate, GRE or MAT, minimum 3 years of successful teaching; 3 letters of recommendation, including one from principal; interview. Additional exam requirements/recommendations for international students: Recommended—TOEFL (minimum score 550 paper-based; 213 computer-based; 79 iBT). *Application deadline:* For fall admission, 3/15 for domestic students; for spring admission, 11/1 for domestic students. Applications are processed on a rolling basis. Application fee: $50. *Expenses:* Tuition, state resident: full-time $7440; part-time $310 per credit hour. Tuition, nonresident: full-time $14,784; part-time $616 per credit hour. Required fees: $552; $20 per credit. $70 per term. *Financial support:* Health care benefits available. Support available to part-time students. Financial award application deadline: 5/15; financial award applicants required to submit FAFSA. *Unit head:* Karen Castagno, Co-Director, 401-456-8594. *Application contact:* Graduate Studies, 401-456-8700.

Rice University, Graduate Programs, Programs in Education Certification, Houston, TX 77251-1892. Offers MAT. *Entrance requirements:* For master's, GRE General Test, minimum GPA of 3.0. Additional exam requirements/recommendations for international students: Required—TOEFL (minimum score 600 paper-based; 250 computer-based; 90 iBT). Electronic applications accepted. *Faculty research:* Assessment, integration of math and science.

The Richard Stockton College of New Jersey, School of Graduate and Continuing Education, Program in Education, Pomona, NJ 08240-0195. Offers MA. Part-time and evening/weekend programs available. *Degree requirements:* For master's, comprehensive exam (for some programs), project. *Entrance requirements:* For master's, GRE, minimum GPA of 2.75, teaching certificate. Additional exam requirements/recommendations for international students: Required—TOEFL. *Expenses:* Tuition, state resident: part-time $497.36 per credit hour. Tuition, nonresident: part-time $765.61 per credit hour. Required fees: $129.12 per credit hour. Tuition and fees vary according to degree level. *Faculty research:* Curriculum instruction, math, science, special education, language arts, literacy.

Rider University, Department of Graduate Education, Leadership and Counseling, Lawrenceville, NJ 08648-3001. Offers counseling services (MA, Certificate, Ed S), including counseling services (MA, Ed S), director of school counseling (Certificate), school counseling services (Certificate); curriculum, instruction and supervision (MA, Certificate), including curriculum, instruction and supervision (MA), supervisor (Certificate); educational administration (MA, Certificate), including educational administration (MA), principal (Certificate), school administrator (Certificate); organizational leadership (MA); reading/language arts (MA, Certificate), including reading specialist (Certificate), reading/language arts (MA); school psychology (Certificate, Ed S); special education (MA, Certificate), including alternative route in special education (Certificate), special education (MA), teacher of students with disabilities (Certificate), teacher of the handicapped (Certificate); teacher certification (Certificate), including business education, elementary education, English as a second language, English education, mathematics education, preschool to grade 3, science education, social studies education, world languages; teaching (MA). *Accreditation:* NCATE. Part-time and evening/weekend programs available. *Degree requirements:* For master's, comprehensive exam (for some programs), thesis or alternative, internship, portfolios; for other advanced degree, internship, professional portfolio. *Entrance requirements:* For master's, GRE (counseling, school psychology), MAT, interview, resume, letters of recommendation; for other advanced degree, PRAXIS. Additional exam requirements/recommendations for international students: Required—TOEFL (minimum score 550 paper-based; 213 computer-based). Electronic applications

Education—General

Rider University (continued)

accepted. *Faculty research:* Gifted students, self-esteem, hope and mental health, conflicts in group work, cultural diversity and counseling assessment of special needs in children.

Rivier College, School of Graduate Studies, Department of Education, Nashua, NH 03060. Offers curriculum and instruction (M Ed); early childhood education (M Ed); educational administration (M Ed); educational studies (M Ed); elementary education (M Ed); elementary education and general special education (M Ed); emotional and behavioral disorders (M Ed); general social education (M Ed); leadership and learning (Ed D, CAGS); learning disabilities (M Ed); learning disabilities and reading (M Ed); mental health counseling (MA); reading (M Ed); school counseling (M Ed). Part-time and evening/weekend programs available. *Faculty:* 13 full-time (9 women), 38 part-time/adjunct (25 women). *Students:* 87 full-time (78 women), 293 part-time (246 women); includes 10 minority (3 African Americans, 4 Asian Americans or Pacific Islanders, 3 Hispanic Americans). Average age 38. 182 applicants, 82% accepted, 72 enrolled. In 2009, 110 master's, 18 other advanced degrees awarded. *Degree requirements:* For master's, comprehensive exam (for some programs), internships. *Entrance requirements:* For master's, GRE General Test or MAT. *Application deadline:* Applications are processed on a rolling basis. Application fee: $25. *Expenses:* Tuition: Part-time $447 per credit. *Financial support:* Available to part-time students. Application deadline: 2/1. *Unit head:* Dr. Patricia Howson, Chairman, 603-897-8562, E-mail: phowson@rivier.edu. *Application contact:* Mathew Kittredge, Director of Graduate Admissions, 603-897-8129, Fax: 603-897-8810, E-mail: mkittredge@rivier.edu.

Robert Morris University, Graduate Studies, School of Education and Social Sciences, Moon Township, PA 15108-1189. Offers business education (MS); education (Postbaccalaureate Certificate); instructional leadership (MS); instructional management and leadership (PhD). *Accreditation:* Teacher Education Accreditation Council. Part-time and evening/weekend programs available. *Faculty:* 14 full-time (3 women), 11 part-time/adjunct (6 women). *Students:* 353 part-time (229 women); includes 24 minority (21 African Americans, 1 Asian American or Pacific Islander, 2 Hispanic Americans), 1 international. Average age 31. 117 applicants, 96% accepted, 79 enrolled. In 2009, 79 master's, 14 doctorates, 97 other advanced degrees awarded. *Degree requirements:* For doctorate, thesis/dissertation. *Entrance requirements:* Additional exam requirements/recommendations for international students: Required—TOEFL (minimum score 550 paper-based; 213 computer-based; 79 iBT). *Application deadline:* For fall admission, 7/1 priority date for domestic and international students; for spring admission, 11/1 priority date for domestic and international students. Applications are processed on a rolling basis. Application fee: $35. Electronic applications accepted. *Expenses:* Contact institution. *Unit head:* Dr. John E. Graham, Dean, 412-397-3228, Fax: 412-397-2524, E-mail: graham@rmu.edu. *Application contact:* Debra Roach, Assistant Dean, Graduate Admissions, 412-397-5200, Fax: 412-397-2425, E-mail: graduateadmissions@rmu.edu.

Roberts Wesleyan College, Division of Teacher Education, Rochester, NY 14624-1997. Offers adolescence education (M Ed); childhood and special education (M Ed); literacy education (M Ed); urban education (M Ed). Part-time and evening/weekend programs available. *Degree requirements:* For master's, thesis.

Rockford College, Graduate Studies, Department of Education, Rockford, IL 61108-2393. Offers education (MAT); elementary education (MAT); instructional strategies (MAT); reading (MAT); secondary education (MAT); special education (MAT). Master's students may work towards initial certification in elementary, K-12, or secondary education. Students in the Special Education Program may earn a Learning Behavior Specialist I (LBSI) certificate. Part-time and evening/weekend programs available. *Degree requirements:* For master's, thesis optional, professional portfolio (instructional strategies program). *Entrance requirements:* For master's, GRE General Test, basic skills test (for students seeking certification), 3 letters of recommendation. Additional exam requirements/recommendations for international students: Required—TOEFL (minimum score 550 paper-based; 213 computer-based; 79 iBT). Electronic applications accepted.

Rockhurst University, School of Graduate and Professional Studies, Program in Education, Kansas City, MO 64110-2561. Offers M Ed. *Accreditation:* Teacher Education Accreditation Council. Part-time and evening/weekend programs available. *Faculty:* 9 full-time (6 women), 4 part-time/adjunct (3 women). *Students:* 98 full-time (65 women), 146 part-time (100 women); includes 34 minority (18 African Americans, 1 American Indian/Alaska Native, 5 Asian Americans or Pacific Islanders, 10 Hispanic Americans), 1 international. Average age 31. 164 applicants, 57% accepted, 66 enrolled. In 2009, 72 master's awarded. *Entrance requirements:* For master's, minimum GPA of 2.5, 2 letters of recommendation. Additional exam requirements/recommendations for international students: Required—TOEFL (minimum score 550 paper-based; 213 computer-based; 79 iBT). *Application deadline:* Applications are processed on a rolling basis. Application fee: $25. Electronic applications accepted. *Expenses:* Contact institution. *Financial support:* Applicants required to submit FAFSA. *Faculty research:* English language learners: urban literacy, on-line discussions, character education, teaching K-12 students about math and literacy. *Unit head:* Dr. Patricia Lucido, Chair of Education Department, 816-501-4208, E-mail: patricia.lucido@rockhurst.edu. *Application contact:* Cheryl Hooper, Director of Graduate Recruitment Admission, 816-501-4097, Fax: 816-501-4241, E-mail: cheryl.hooper@rockhurst.edu.

Roger Williams University, School of Education, Bristol, RI 02809. Offers MA, MAT. Part-time and evening/weekend programs available. *Entrance requirements:* For master's, resume, 3 letters of recommendation. Additional exam requirements/recommendations for international students: Recommended—IELTS. Electronic applications accepted. *Expenses:* Contact institution.

Rollins College, Hamilton Holt School, Program in Education, Winter Park, FL 32789-4499. Offers elementary education (M Ed, MAT); secondary education (MAT), including English, mathematics, music. Part-time and evening/weekend programs available. *Faculty:* 5 full-time (3 women), 3 part-time/adjunct (2 women). *Students:* 14 full-time (11 women), 26 part-time (25 women); includes 7 minority (4 African Americans, 3 Hispanic Americans). Average age 31. 27 applicants, 100% accepted, 27 enrolled. In 2009, 10 master's awarded. *Degree requirements:* For master's, comprehensive exam. *Entrance requirements:* For master's, GRE or MAT, interview. Additional exam requirements/recommendations for international students: Required—TOEFL. *Application deadline:* For fall admission, 7/16 for domestic students; for winter admission, 12/3 for domestic students; for spring admission, 4/22 for domestic students. Applications are processed on a rolling basis. Application fee: $50. *Expenses:* Contact institution. *Financial support:* Teaching assistantships, scholarships/grants available. Support available to part-time students. *Unit head:* Dr. J. Scott Hewit, Director, 407-646-2300, E-mail: jhewit@rollins.edu. *Application contact:* Rebecca Cordray, Coordinator of Records and Registration, 407-646-1568, Fax: 407-975-6430, E-mail: rcordray@rollins.edu.

Roosevelt University, Graduate Division, College of Education, Chicago, IL 60605. Offers MA, Ed D. *Accreditation:* ACA; NCATE. Part-time and evening/weekend programs available. *Degree requirements:* For doctorate, thesis/dissertation. *Entrance requirements:* For doctorate, GRE or MAT.

Rowan University, Graduate School, College of Education, Glassboro, NJ 08028-1701. Offers M Ed, MA, MST, MST, Ed D, Ed S. *Accreditation:* NCATE. Part-time and evening/weekend programs available. *Faculty:* 30 full-time (22 women), 51 part-time/adjunct (29 women). *Students:* 180 full-time (147 women), 550 part-time (424 women); includes 127 minority (97 African Americans, 1 American Indian/Alaska Native, 7 Asian Americans or Pacific Islanders, 22 Hispanic Americans). Average age 34. 242 applicants, 94% accepted, 183 enrolled. In 2009, 198 master's, 28 doctorates awarded. *Degree requirements:* For master's, comprehensive exam, thesis; for doctorate, thesis/dissertation. *Entrance requirements:* For master's, GRE General Test, PRAXIS I, PRAXIS II; for doctorate, GRE, master's degree. Additional exam requirements/recommendations for international students: Required—TOEFL. *Application deadline:* Applications are processed on a rolling basis. Application fee: $50. Electronic applications accepted. *Expenses:* Tuition, state resident: full-time $10,624; part-time $590 per

semester hour. Tuition, nonresident: full-time $10,624; part-time $590 per semester hour. Required fees: $2320; $125 per semester hour. *Financial support:* Career-related internships or fieldwork, Federal Work-Study, scholarships/grants, health care benefits, and unspecified assistantships available. Support available to part-time students. *Unit head:* Dr. Mira Lalovic-Hand, Interim Associate Provost/Director of Graduate School, 856-256-5120. *Application contact:* Karen Haynes, Graduate Coordinator, 856-256-4052, Fax: 856-256-4436, E-mail: haynes@rowan.edu.

Rutgers, The State University of New Jersey, New Brunswick, Graduate School of Education, Piscataway, NJ 08854-8097. Offers Ed M, Ed D, PhD. *Accreditation:* Teacher Education Accreditation Council. Part-time and evening/weekend programs available. Terminal master's awarded for partial completion of doctoral program. *Degree requirements:* For master's, comprehensive exam (for some programs); for doctorate, thesis/dissertation. *Entrance requirements:* For master's and doctorate, GRE General Test. Additional exam requirements/recommendations for international students: Required—TOEFL (minimum score 575 paper-based; 233 computer-based; 83 iBT). Electronic applications accepted.

Sacred Heart University, Graduate Programs, College of Education and Health Professions, Isabelle Farrington School of Education, Fairfield, CT 06825-1000. Offers administration (CAS); educational technology (MAT); elementary education (MAT); reading (CAS); secondary education (MAT); teaching (CAS). Part-time and evening/weekend programs available. Postbaccalaureate distance learning degree programs offered (minimal on-campus study). *Faculty:* 23 full-time (10 women). *Students:* 377 full-time (291 women), 691 part-time (495 women); includes 63 minority (31 African Americans, 2 American Indian/Alaska Native, 8 Asian Americans or Pacific Islanders, 22 Hispanic Americans), 2 international. Average age 34. 429 applicants, 90% accepted, 338 enrolled. In 2009, 409 master's, 66 other advanced degrees awarded. *Degree requirements:* For master's, thesis or alternative. *Entrance requirements:* For master's, PRAXIS (teacher certification/MAT); for CAS, PRAXIS I. Additional exam requirements/recommendations for international students: Required—TOEFL (minimum score 550 paper-based; 213 computer-based). *Application deadline:* Applications are processed on a rolling basis. Application fee: $50 ($100 for international students). Electronic applications accepted. *Expenses:* Contact institution. *Financial support:* Teaching assistantships with partial tuition reimbursements, career-related internships or fieldwork, institutionally sponsored loans, traineeships, tuition waivers (partial), and unspecified assistantships available. Support available to part-time students. Financial award applicants required to submit FAFSA. *Faculty research:* Reading education, learning theory, teacher preparation, education of underachievers. *Unit head:* Dr. Edward Malin, Director, 203-371-7800, Fax: 203-365-7513. *Application contact:* Kathy Dilks, Assistant Dean of Graduate Admissions, 203-365-7619, Fax: 203-365-4732, E-mail: gradstudies@sacredheart.edu.

Sage Graduate School, Graduate School, School of Education, Troy, NY 12180-4115. Offers applied behavior analysis and autism (MS); childhood education (MS Ed); childhood education/literacy (MS); childhood special education (MS Ed); community health education (MS); educational leadership (Ed D); guidance and counseling (MS, Post Master's Certificate); literacy (MS Ed); literacy/childhood special education (MS Ed); school health education (MS); teaching (MAT), including art education, English, mathematics, social studies. *Accreditation:* NCATE. Part-time and evening/weekend programs available. *Faculty:* 15 full-time (9 women), 19 part-time/adjunct (16 women). *Students:* 144 full-time (114 women), 294 part-time (225 women); includes 29 minority (6 African Americans, 1 American Indian/Alaska Native, 8 Asian Americans or Pacific Islanders, 14 Hispanic Americans). Average age 28. 408 applicants, 51% accepted, 154 enrolled. In 2009, 157 master's awarded. *Entrance requirements:* Additional exam requirements/recommendations for international students: Required—TOEFL (minimum score 550 paper-based; 213 computer-based). *Application deadline:* Applications are processed on a rolling basis. Application fee: $40. *Expenses:* Tuition: Full-time $10,620; part-time $590 per credit hour. *Financial support:* Fellowships, research assistantships, Federal Work-Study, scholarships/grants, tuition waivers (partial), and unspecified assistantships available. Support available to part-time students. Financial award application deadline: 3/1; financial award applicants required to submit FAFSA. *Faculty research:* Literacy development in at-risk children, effective behavior strategies for class instruction. *Unit head:* Dr. Nancy A. DeKorp, Interim Dean, Education, 518-244-2496, Fax: 518-244-2334, E-mail: dekorn@sage.edu. *Application contact:* Wendy D. Diefendorf, Director of Graduate and Adult Admission, 518-244-2443, Fax: 518-244-6880, E-mail: diefew@sage.edu.

Saginaw Valley State University, College of Education, University Center, MI 48710. Offers M Ed, MA, MAT, Ed S. *Accreditation:* NCATE. Part-time and evening/weekend programs available. *Faculty:* 94 full-time (69 women), 53 part-time/adjunct (36 women). *Students:* 60 full-time (48 women), 935 part-time (755 women); includes 42 minority (20 African Americans, 4 American Indian/Alaska Native, 1 Asian American or Pacific Islander, 17 Hispanic Americans), 12 international. Average age 34. 180 applicants, 99% accepted, 124 enrolled. In 2009, 358 master's, 37 other advanced degrees awarded. *Entrance requirements:* For master's, minimum GPA of 3.0, teaching certificate. Additional exam requirements/recommendations for international students: Required—TOEFL (minimum score 525 paper-based; 197 computer-based; 71 iBT). *Application deadline:* Applications are processed on a rolling basis. Application fee: $25. Electronic applications accepted. *Financial support:* Federal Work-Study and scholarships/grants available. Support available to part-time students. Financial award applicants required to submit FAFSA. *Unit head:* Dr. Steve P. Barbus, Dean, 989-964-6067, Fax: 989-790-4385, E-mail: barbus@svsu.edu. *Application contact:* Kathy Lopez, Certification Officer, 989-964-4661, Fax: 989-964-4385, E-mail: klopez@svsu.edu.

St. Ambrose University, College of Education and Health Sciences, Program in Education, Davenport, IA 52803-2898. Offers special education (M Ed); teaching (M Ed). *Accreditation:* Teacher Education Accreditation Council. Part-time and evening/weekend programs available. Postbaccalaureate distance learning degree programs offered (no on-campus study). *Faculty:* 3 full-time (0 women), 4 part-time/adjunct (3 women). *Students:* 7 full-time (6 women), 35 part-time (29 women); includes 1 minority (Hispanic American). Average age 39. 20 applicants, 100% accepted, 20 enrolled. In 2009, 24 master's awarded. *Degree requirements:* For master's, comprehensive exam. *Entrance requirements:* For master's, GRE General Test or MAT, minimum GPA of 2.75. Additional exam requirements/recommendations for international students: Required—TOEFL. *Application deadline:* For fall admission, 8/15 priority date for domestic students; for spring admission, 11/1 for domestic students. Applications are processed on a rolling basis. Application fee: $25. Electronic applications accepted. *Expenses:* Tuition: Part-time $702 per credit hour. Tuition and fees vary according to degree level, program and reciprocity agreements. *Financial support:* In 2009–10, 23 students received support, including 1 research assistantship with partial tuition reimbursement available (averaging $3,600 per year); career-related internships or fieldwork, scholarships/grants, tuition waivers (full and partial), and unspecified assistantships also available. Financial award application deadline: 3/15; financial award applicants required to submit FAFSA. *Faculty research:* Disabilities and postsecondary career avenues, self-determination. *Unit head:* Marguerite K. Woods, Head, 563-388-7653, Fax: 563-388-7662, E-mail: woodsmargueritek@sau.edu. *Application contact:* Penny L. McCulloch, Administrative Assistant, 563-322-1034, Fax: 563-388-7662, E-mail: mccullochpennyl@sau.edu.

St. Bonaventure University, School of Graduate Studies, School of Education, St. Bonaventure, NY 14778-2284. Offers MS Ed, Adv C. *Accreditation:* NCATE. Part-time and evening/weekend programs available. *Faculty:* 14 full-time (5 women), 12 part-time/adjunct (6 women). *Students:* 156 full-time (129 women), 108 part-time (77 women); includes 11 minority (4 African Americans, 2 American Indian/Alaska Native, 5 Hispanic Americans), 1 international. Average age 31. 220 applicants, 74% accepted, 121 enrolled. In 2009, 113 master's, 5 Adv Cs awarded. *Application deadline:* For fall admission, 8/1 for domestic students; for spring admission, 10/15 priority date for domestic students. Applications are processed on a rolling basis. Application fee: $30. *Expenses:* Tuition: Full-time $11,700; part-time $650 per credit. *Financial support:* Research assistantships, career-related internships or fieldwork and Federal Work-Study available. Support available to part-time students. *Faculty research:* Learning disabilities, self-concept, reading diagnosis, professional development schools. *Unit head:* Dr. Peggy Yehl Burke, Dean, 716-

375-2394, E-mail: pyburke@sbu.edu. *Application contact:* Dr. Peggy Yehl Burke, Dean, 716-375-2394, E-mail: pyburke@sbu.edu.

St. Catherine University, Graduate Programs, Program in Education–Curriculum and Instruction, St. Paul, MN 55105. Offers MA. Part-time and evening/weekend programs available. Postbaccalaureate distance learning degree programs offered (minimal on-campus study). *Faculty:* 14 full-time (11 women). *Students:* 104 full-time (85 women); includes 2 minority (both Asian Americans or Pacific Islanders). Average age 35. 53 applicants, 83% accepted, 38 enrolled. In 2009, 70 master's awarded. *Degree requirements:* For master's, thesis. *Entrance requirements:* For master's, current teaching license, classroom experience, minimum GPA of 3.0. Additional exam requirements/recommendations for international students: Required—Michigan English Language Assessment Battery or TOEFL (minimum score 600 paper-based; 250 computer-based; 100 iBT). *Application deadline:* For fall admission, 6/1 priority date for domestic students; for winter admission, 1/1 priority date for domestic students; for spring admission, 5/1 priority date for domestic students. Applications are processed on a rolling basis. Application fee: $35. *Expenses:* Contact institution. *Financial support:* In 2009–10, 50 students received support. Application deadline: 4/1. *Unit head:* Dr. Linda Distad, Associate Dean of Education, 651-690-6798, Fax: 651-690-8651. *Application contact:* 651-690-6933, Fax: 651-690-6064.

St. Cloud State University, School of Graduate Studies, College of Education, St. Cloud, MN 56301-4498. Offers MS, Ed D, Spt. *Accreditation:* NCATE. Part-time and evening/weekend programs available. Postbaccalaureate distance learning degree programs offered (no on-campus study). *Faculty:* 96 full-time (52 women), 18 part-time/adjunct (14 women). *Students:* 297 full-time (226 women), 560 part-time (409 women); includes 78 minority (28 African Americans, 8 American Indian/Alaska Native, 35 Asian Americans or Pacific Islanders, 7 Hispanic Americans), 50 international. 293 applicants, 74% accepted. In 2009, 128 master's awarded. *Degree requirements:* For master's, comprehensive exam (for some programs), thesis or alternative; for doctorate, comprehensive exam, thesis/dissertation; for Spt, thesis, field study. *Entrance requirements:* For master's, GRE General Test, minimum GPA of 2.75; for Spt, GRE General Test, minimum GPA of 3.25. Additional exam requirements/recommendations for international students: Required—Michigan English Language Assessment Battery; Recommended—TOEFL (minimum score 550 paper-based; 213 computer-based), IELTS (minimum score 6.5). *Application deadline:* Applications are processed on a rolling basis. Application fee: $35. *Financial support:* Career-related internships or fieldwork, Federal Work-Study, scholarships/grants, and unspecified assistantships available. Financial award application deadline: 3/1. *Unit head:* Dr. Glen Palm, Interim Dean, 320-308-3023, Fax: 320-308-4237, E-mail: gfpalm@stcloudstate.edu. *Application contact:* Linda Lou Krueger, School of Graduate Studies, 320-308-2113, Fax: 320-308-5371, E-mail: lekrueger@stcloudstate.edu.

St. Edward's University, School of Education, Austin, TX 78704. Offers MA, Certificate. Part-time and evening/weekend programs available. *Students:* 5 full-time (4 women), 36 part-time (26 women); includes 10 minority (1 African American, 9 Hispanic Americans). Average age 30. 23 applicants, 70% accepted, 12 enrolled. In 2009, 9 master's awarded. *Degree requirements:* For master's, minimum of 24 resident hours. *Entrance requirements:* For master's, GRE General Test, minimum GPA of 3.0 in last 60 hours or 2.75 overall. Additional exam requirements/recommendations for international students: Required—TOEFL (minimum score 550 paper-based; 213 computer-based; 79 iBT) or IELTS (minimum score 6). *Application deadline:* For fall admission, 7/1 for domestic and international students; for spring admission, 11/1 for domestic and international students. Applications are processed on a rolling basis. Application fee: $45 ($50 for international students). Electronic applications accepted. *Expenses:* Tuition: Full-time $14,922; part-time $829 per credit hour. Required fees: $50 per trimester. Full-time tuition and fees vary according to course load and program. *Financial support:* In 2009–10, 3 students received support. Scholarships/grants available. *Unit head:* Dr. Judy Leavell, Interim Dean, 512-637-5674, Fax: 512-428-1372, E-mail: judyl@stedwards.edu. *Application contact:* Kay L. Arnold, Assistant Director of Admissions, 512-233-1636, Fax: 512-428-1032, E-mail: kayla@stedwards.edu.

Saint Francis University, Graduate Education Program, Loretto, PA 15940-0600. Offers education (M Ed); leadership (M Ed); reading (M Ed). Part-time and evening/weekend programs available. *Faculty:* 29 part-time/adjunct (7 women). *Students:* 150 part-time (100 women); includes 3 minority (2 African Americans, 1 Hispanic American). Average age 30. 20 applicants, 100% accepted, 20 enrolled. In 2009, 50 master's awarded. *Degree requirements:* For master's, comprehensive exam, thesis optional. *Entrance requirements:* For master's, GRE or MAT (if undergraduate GPA less than 2.8), minimum undergraduate QPA of 2.5. *Application deadline:* Applications are processed on a rolling basis. Application fee: $30. *Expenses:* Contact institution. *Financial support:* Applicants required to submit FAFSA. *Unit head:* Dr. Janette D. Kelly, Director, Graduate Education, 814-472-3068, Fax: 814-472-3864, E-mail: jkelly@francis.edu. *Application contact:* Sherri L. Toth, Coordinator, 814-472-3058, Fax: 814-472-3864, E-mail: stoth@francis.edu.

St. Francis Xavier University, Graduate Studies, Graduate Studies in Education, Antigonish, NS B2G 2W5, Canada. Offers curriculum and instruction (M Ed); educational administration and leadership (M Ed). Part-time programs available. Postbaccalaureate distance learning degree programs offered (minimal on-campus study). *Degree requirements:* For master's, thesis. *Entrance requirements:* For master's, minimum undergraduate B average, 2 years of teaching experience. *Faculty research:* Inclusive education, qualitative research.

St. John Fisher College, Ralph C. Wilson Jr. School of Education, Rochester, NY 14618-3597. Offers MS, MS Ed, Ed D, Certificate. *Accreditation:* NCATE. Part-time and evening/weekend programs available. *Faculty:* 25 full-time (13 women), 23 part-time/adjunct (17 women). *Students:* 209 full-time (153 women), 215 part-time (170 women); includes 81 minority (64 African Americans, 2 American Indian/Alaska Native, 1 Asian American or Pacific Islander, 14 Hispanic Americans). Average age 32. 368 applicants, 83% accepted, 207 enrolled. In 2009, 201 master's, 25 doctorates awarded. *Entrance requirements:* For master's, 2 letters of recommendation, current resume, official transcripts. Additional exam requirements/recommendations for international students: Required—TOEFL (minimum score 575 paper-based; 233 computer-based; 80 iBT). *Application deadline:* Applications are processed on a rolling basis. Application fee: $30. Electronic applications accepted. *Expenses:* Tuition: Part-time $680 per credit hour. Required fees: $25 per semester. Tuition and fees vary according to degree level and program. *Financial support:* In 2009–10, 350 students received support. Federal Work-Study and scholarships/grants available. Financial award applicants required to submit FAFSA. *Unit head:* Dr. Wendy A. Paterson, Dean, 585-385-3813, E-mail: jadams@sjfc.edu. *Application contact:* Jose Perales, Director of Graduate Admissions, 585-385-8067, E-mail: jperales@sjfc.edu.

St. John's University, The School of Education, Queens, NY 11439. Offers MS Ed, Ed D, PhD, PD. *Accreditation:* Teacher Education Accreditation Council. Part-time and evening/weekend programs available. Postbaccalaureate distance learning degree programs offered (no on-campus study). *Faculty:* 46 full-time (29 women), 99 part-time/adjunct (49 women). *Students:* 386 full-time (313 women), 1,266 part-time (981 women); includes 470 minority (185 African Americans, 67 Asian Americans or Pacific Islanders, 218 Hispanic Americans), 38 international. Average age 32. 1,002 applicants, 78% accepted, 485 enrolled. In 2009, 424 master's, 34 doctorates, 34 other advanced degrees awarded. *Degree requirements:* For master's, minimum GPA of 3.0; for doctorate, comprehensive exam, thesis/dissertation. *Entrance requirements:* For master's, 2 letters of recommendation, official transcript, minimum GPA of 3.0, personal statement; for doctorate, GRE General Test, MAT (PhD in literacy), interview, writing sample, 2 years of teaching experience, resume (PhD in literacy only). Additional exam requirements/recommendations for international students: Required—TOEFL (minimum score 500 paper-based; 173 computer-based; 61 iBT), IELTS (minimum score 5.5). *Application deadline:* For fall admission, 4/1 priority date for domestic students, 6/1 for international students; for spring admission, 11/1 priority date for domestic and international students. Applications are processed on a rolling basis. Application fee: $70. Electronic applications accepted. *Expenses:* Tuition: Full-time $16,290; part-time $905 per credit. Required fees: $300; $150 per semester. Tuition and fees vary according to program. *Financial support:* In 2009–10, 1,061 students received support, including 96 fellowships with full and partial tuition reimbursements available (averaging $14,714 per year), 2 research assistantships with full and partial tuition reimbursements available (averaging $12,218 per year), 3 teaching assistantships with full and partial tuition reimbursements available (averaging $13,575 per year); career-related internships or fieldwork, scholarships/grants, and unspecified assistantships also available. Support available to part-time students. Financial award application deadline: 3/1; financial award applicants required to submit FAFSA. *Faculty research:* Results of school partnerships, effective means of working with recent immigrant populations, results of graduates who participated in programs leading to alternative certification routes, resolution of issues surrounding middle schools, identifying means of supporting children at both ends of the academic continuum. Total annual research expenditures: $4.7 million. *Unit head:* Dr. Jerrold Ross, Dean, 718-990-1305, Fax: 718-990-6096, E-mail: rossj@stjohns.edu. *Application contact:* Dr. Kelly K. Ronayne, Associate Dean for Graduate Admissions, 718-990-2303, Fax: 718-990-2343, E-mail: graded@stjohns.edu.

Saint Joseph College, Department of Education, West Hartford, CT 06117-2700. Offers education (MA); special education (MA). Part-time and evening/weekend programs available. *Students:* 72 full-time (67 women), 299 part-time (267 women); includes 25 minority (14 African Americans, 6 Asian Americans or Pacific Islanders, 5 Hispanic Americans), 1 international. *Degree requirements:* For master's, comprehensive exam, thesis or alternative. *Entrance requirements:* For master's, 2 letters of recommendation. *Application deadline:* Applications are processed on a rolling basis. Application fee: $50. Electronic applications accepted. *Expenses:* Tuition: Part-time $595 per credit. Required fees: $30 per credit. Tuition and fees vary according to program. *Financial support:* Career-related internships or fieldwork and unspecified assistantships available. Support available to part-time students. Financial award applicants required to submit FAFSA. *Application contact:* Graduate Admissions Office, 860-231-5261, E-mail: graduate@sjc.edu.

St. Joseph's College, New York, Graduate Programs, Program in Education, Brooklyn, NY 11205-3688. Offers infant/toddler early childhood special education (MA); literacy and cognition (MA); special education (MA), including severe and multiple disabilities.

See Close-Up on page 713.

Saint Joseph's College of Maine, Program in Teacher Education, Standish, ME 04084. Offers MS. Program available by correspondence. Part-time programs available. Postbaccalaureate distance learning degree programs offered (minimal on-campus study). *Degree requirements:* For master's, summer residency. Electronic applications accepted.

Saint Joseph's University, College of Arts and Sciences, Department of Education, Philadelphia, PA 19131-1395. Offers educational leadership (Ed D); elementary education (MS); instructional technology (MS); organizational development and leadership (MS); professional education (MS); reading specialist (MS); secondary education (MS); special education (MS). Part-time and evening/weekend programs available. *Students:* 5 full-time (3 women), 750 part-time (561 women); includes 100 minority (76 African Americans, 1 American Indian/Alaska Native, 11 Asian Americans or Pacific Islanders, 12 Hispanic Americans), 3 international. Average age 33. In 2009, 210 master's, 14 doctorates awarded. *Entrance requirements:* For master's, 2 letters of recommendation, minimum GPA of 3.0, application, official transcripts, personal statement; for doctorate, GRE, master's degree from accredited institution, minimum graduate GPA of 3.5, computer competence, commitment to participate in cohort, interview with program director. Additional exam requirements/recommendations for international students: Required—TOEFL (minimum score 550 paper-based; 213 computer-based; 79 iBT). *Application deadline:* For fall admission, 7/15 priority date for domestic students, 4/15 for international students; for winter admission, 11/15 for domestic students, 1/15 for international students; for spring admission, 11/15 priority date for domestic students, 10/15 for international students. Applications are processed on a rolling basis. Application fee: $35. Electronic applications accepted. *Expenses:* Contact institution. *Financial support:* Unspecified assistantships available. Financial award applicants required to submit FAFSA. *Faculty research:* Early childhood course design, public education professional development. Total annual research expenditures: $91,900. *Unit head:* Dr. Teri Sosa, Director of Graduate Education, 610-660-3162, E-mail: tsosa@sju.edu. *Application contact:* Kate McConnell, Director, Graduate College of Arts and Sciences Admissions and Retention, 610-660-3184, Fax: 610-660-3230, E-mail: kate.mcconnell@sju.edu.

St. Lawrence University, Department of Education, Canton, NY 13617-1455. Offers counseling and human development (M Ed, MS, CAS), including mental health counseling (MS), school counseling (M Ed, CAS); educational leadership (M Ed, CAS), including combined school building leadership/school district leadership (CAS), educational leadership (M Ed), school building leadership (M Ed), school district leadership (CAS); general studies in education (M Ed). *Accreditation:* Teacher Education Accreditation Council. Part-time and evening/weekend programs available. *Degree requirements:* For master's, thesis optional. *Entrance requirements:* For master's, GRE General Test. *Faculty research:* Defense mechanisms, conflict negotiations and mediation, teacher education policy.

Saint Leo University, Graduate Studies in Education, Saint Leo, FL 33574-6665. Offers educational leadership (M Ed, Ed S); exceptional student education (M Ed); higher education leadership (Ed S); instructional design (MS); instructional leadership (M Ed); reading (M Ed). Part-time and evening/weekend programs available. Postbaccalaureate distance learning degree programs offered (minimal on-campus study). *Faculty:* 13 full-time (10 women), 12 part-time/adjunct (9 women). *Students:* 432 full-time (355 women), 35 part-time (24 women); includes 56 minority (40 African Americans, 2 American Indian/Alaska Native, 2 Asian Americans or Pacific Islanders, 12 Hispanic Americans), 1 international. Average age 37. In 2009, 131 master's awarded. *Degree requirements:* For master's, comprehensive exam, appropriate State of Florida Certification Tests. *Entrance requirements:* For master's, GRE (minimum score of 1000) or MAT (minimum score of 410) if undergraduate GPA for last 60 hours of coursework was below 3.0 (for M Ed), bachelor's degree from regionally-accredited college or university with minimum GPA of 3.0 for last 60 hours of coursework, 2 recommendations, resume, statement of professional goals, copy of valid teaching certificate (for M Ed); for Ed S, GRE (minimum score 1000) or MAT (minimum score 410) if undergraduate GPA for last 60 hours of coursework less than 3.0, bachelor's degree from regionally-accredited college or university with minimum GPA of 3.0 for last 60 hours of coursework, 2 recommendations, resume, valid teaching certificate. Additional exam requirements/recommendations for international students: Required—TOEFL (minimum score 550 paper-based; 213 computer-based; 80 iBT). *Application deadline:* For fall admission, 7/1 priority date for domestic students; for spring admission, 11/12 priority date for domestic students. Applications are processed on a rolling basis. Application fee: $75. Electronic applications accepted. *Expenses:* Tuition: Part-time $1767 per course. Required fees: $115 per course. *Financial support:* Career-related internships or fieldwork, Federal Work-Study, and health care benefits available. Financial award application deadline: 3/1; financial award applicants required to submit FAFSA. *Faculty research:* The role of the school leader in data analysis of student achievement, teacher recruitment, and teacher effectiveness. *Unit head:* Dr. John Smith, Director, 352-588-8309, Fax: 352-588-8861, E-mail: med@saintleo.edu. *Application contact:* Jared Welling, Director, Graduate/Weekend and Evening Admission, 800-707-8846, Fax: 352-588-7873, E-mail: grad.admissions@saintleo.edu.

Saint Louis University, Graduate School, College of Education and Public Service and Graduate School, Department of Educational Studies, St. Louis, MO 63103-2097. Offers curriculum and instruction (MA, Ed D, PhD); educational foundations (MA, Ed D, PhD); special education (MA); teaching (MAT). *Accreditation:* NCATE. Part-time programs available. *Degree requirements:* For master's, comprehensive exam; for doctorate, comprehensive exam, thesis/dissertation, preliminary oral and written exams. *Entrance requirements:* For master's, GRE General Test or MAT, letters of recommendation, resume; for doctorate, GRE General Test, letters of recommendation, resumé, goal statement, transcripts. Additional exam requirements/recommendations for international students: Required—TOEFL (minimum score 525 paper-

Education—General

Saint Louis University (continued)
based; 194 computer-based). Electronic applications accepted. *Faculty research:* Teacher preparation, multicultural issues, children with special needs, qualitative research in education, inclusion.

Saint Martin's University, Graduate Programs, College of Education, Lacey, WA 98503. Offers administration (M Ed); English as a second language (M Ed); guidance and counseling (M Ed); reading (M Ed); special education (M Ed); teaching (MIT); technology in education (M Ed). *Accreditation:* Teacher Education Accreditation Council. Part-time and evening/weekend programs available. *Faculty:* 13 full-time (9 women), 11 part-time/adjunct (7 women). *Students:* 61 full-time (42 women), 23 part-time (17 women); includes 7 minority (2 African Americans, 1 American Indian/Alaska Native, 3 Asian Americans or Pacific Islanders, 1 Hispanic American), 1 international. Average age 35. 26 applicants, 92% accepted, 22 enrolled. In 2009, 12 master's awarded. *Degree requirements:* For master's, comprehensive exam (for some programs), thesis or alternative, project or comprehensives. *Entrance requirements:* For master's, GRE General Test or MAT, resume. Additional exam requirements/recommendations for international students: Required—TOEFL (minimum score 560 paper-based; 220 computer-based; 83 iBT). *Application deadline:* For fall admission, 6/1 priority date for domestic and international students; for spring admission, 10/1 priority date for domestic and international students. Applications are processed on a rolling basis. Application fee: $35. *Expenses:* Tuition: Full-time $12,440; part-time $827 per credit hour. *Financial support:* In 2009–10, 62 students received support. Career-related internships or fieldwork, Federal Work-Study, institutionally sponsored loans, and unspecified assistantships available. Support available to part-time students. Financial award application deadline: 3/1; financial award applicants required to submit FAFSA. *Faculty research:* Reader's theatre and reader/writer workshops, curriculum and assessment integration, gender and equity, classroom evaluations, organizational leadership. *Unit head:* Dr. Joyce Westgard, Director, 360-438-4509, Fax: 360-438-4486, E-mail: westgard@stmartin.edu. *Application contact:* Ryan M. Smith, Administrative Assistant, 360-438-4333, Fax: 360-438-4486, E-mail: ryan.smith@stmartin.edu.

Saint Mary's College of California, Kalmanovitz School of Education, Moraga, CA 94556. Offers M Ed, MA, MAT. Part-time and evening/weekend programs available. *Faculty:* 28 full-time (25 women), 45 part-time/adjunct (38 women). *Students:* 198 full-time (158 women), 364 part-time (290 women); includes 113 minority (32 African Americans, 3 American Indian/Alaska Native, 31 Asian Americans or Pacific Islanders, 47 Hispanic Americans), 14 international. Average age 29. In 2009, 125 master's awarded. *Degree requirements:* For master's, thesis or alternative. *Entrance requirements:* For master's, interview, minimum GPA of 3.0. *Application deadline:* Applications are processed on a rolling basis. Application fee: $50. *Expenses:* Contact institution. *Financial support:* In 2009–10, 44 students received support. Career-related internships or fieldwork and tuition waivers (partial) available. Support available to part-time students. Financial award application deadline: 2/15; financial award applicants required to submit FAFSA. *Faculty research:* Teacher effectiveness, school-based management, multicultural teaching, language and literacy development. *Unit head:* Dr. Nancy L. Sorenson, Dean, 925-631-4309, Fax: 925-376-8379, E-mail: nsorenso@stmarys-ca.edu. *Application contact:* Jane Joyce, Coordinator, Recruitment and Admissions, 925-631-4700, Fax: 925-376-8379, E-mail: soereq@stmarys-ca.edu.

St. Mary's College of Maryland, Department of Educational Studies, St. Mary's City, MD 20686-3001. Offers MAT. *Faculty:* 8 full-time (7 women). *Students:* 42 full-time (35 women). In 2009, 26 master's awarded. *Degree requirements:* For master's, internship, electronic portfolio, research projects, PRAXIS II. *Entrance requirements:* For master's, SAT, ACT, GRE or PRAXIS I, 2 letters of recommendation. Additional exam requirements/recommendations for international students: Required—TOEFL. *Application deadline:* For fall admission, 10/1 for domestic students. Application fee: $50. *Expenses:* Tuition, state resident: full-time $17,365. Tuition, nonresident: full-time $17,365. *Financial support:* Application deadline: 3/1. *Faculty research:* Supporting English language learners across the curriculum; supporting women and minorities in math and science; instructional technology; multicultural young adult literature; educating teachers to be advocates for equity and social justice. *Unit head:* Dr. Lois Thomas Stover, Chair, 240-895-2187, E-mail: itstover@smcm.edu. *Application contact:* Dr. Lois Thomas Stover, Chair, 240-895-2187, E-mail: itstover@smcm.edu.

St. Mary's University, Graduate School, Department of Teacher Education, San Antonio, TX 78228-8507. Offers Catholic principalship (Certificate); Catholic school leadership (MA, Certificate), including Catholic school administrators (Certificate), Catholic school leadership (MA), Catholic school teachers (Certificate); educational leadership (MA, Certificate), including educational leadership (MA), principalship (mid-management) (Certificate); reading (MA). Part-time and evening/weekend programs available. *Degree requirements:* For master's, comprehensive exam. *Entrance requirements:* For master's, GRE General Test. Additional exam requirements/recommendations for international students: Required—TOEFL (minimum score 550 paper-based; 213 computer-based; 80 iBT). Electronic applications accepted. *Expenses:* Tuition: Full-time $8004. Required fees: $536. One-time fee: $5 full-time. Full-time tuition and fees vary according to program.

Saint Mary's University of Minnesota, Schools of Graduate and Professional Programs, Graduate School of Education, Education Program, Winona, MN 55987-1399. Offers education (MA); gifted and talented instruction (Certificate). *Unit head:* Claudia Risnes, Director, 612-728-5179, Fax: 612-728-5121, E-mail: crisnes@smumn.edu. *Application contact:* Yasin Alsaidi, Director of Admissions for Graduate and Professional Programs, 612-728-5207, Fax: 612-728-5121, E-mail: yalsaidi@smumn.edu.

Saint Mary's University of Minnesota, Schools of Graduate and Professional Programs, Graduate School of Education, Education-Wisconsin Program, Winona, MN 55987-1399. Offers MA. *Application contact:* Yasin Alsaidi, Director of Admissions for Graduate and Professional Programs, 612-728-5207, Fax: 612-728-5121, E-mail: yalsaidi@smumn.edu.

Saint Mary's University of Minnesota, Schools of Graduate and Professional Programs, Graduate School of Education, Teaching and Learning Program, Winona, MN 55987-1399. Offers M Ed. *Unit head:* Suzanne Peterson, Director, 952-891-3792, E-mail: speterso@smumn.edu. *Application contact:* Jana Korder, Director of Admissions for Graduate and Professional Programs, 507-457-6615, E-mail: jkorder@smumn.edu.

Saint Michael's College, Graduate Programs, Program in Education, Colchester, VT 05439. Offers administration (M Ed, CAGS); arts in education (CAGS); curriculum and instruction (M Ed, CAGS); information technology (CAGS); reading (M Ed); special education (M Ed, CAGS); technology (M Ed). Part-time and evening/weekend programs available. *Degree requirements:* For master's, thesis. *Entrance requirements:* For master's, minimum GPA of 3.0. Electronic applications accepted. *Faculty research:* Integrative curriculum, moral and spiritual dimensions of education, learning styles, multiple intelligences, integrating technology into the curriculum.

St. Norbert College, Program in Education, De Pere, WI 54115-2099. Offers MS. Part-time and evening/weekend programs available. *Faculty:* 7 part-time/adjunct (4 women). *Students:* 17 part-time (14 women); includes 3 minority (1 African American, 2 American Indian/Alaska Native). 17 applicants, 100% accepted, 17 enrolled. *Degree requirements:* For master's, advocacy project. *Entrance requirements:* For master's, minimum undergraduate GPA of 3.0, graduate 3.25; 2 years of teaching experience; state teacher certification or proof of teaching experience. Application fee: $35. Electronic applications accepted. *Expenses:* Tuition: Part-time $390 per credit hour. *Faculty research:* Literacy, portfolios, integrated curriculum, technology. *Unit head:* Dr. Susan M. Landt, Director/Professor, 920-403-1328, Fax: 920-403-4078, E-mail: susan.landt@snc.edu. *Application contact:* Karen L. Cleereman, Office Manager, Fax: 920-403-4044, E-mail: karen.cleereman@snc.edu.

Saint Peter's College, Graduate Programs in Education, Jersey City, NJ 07306-5997. Offers administration and supervision (MA), including educational leadership; educational leadership (Ed D); reading specialist (MA), including reading; special education (MA), including special education; teaching (MA, Certificate), including elementary teacher (Certificate), supervisor of instruction (Certificate), teaching (MA). *Accreditation:* Teacher Education Accreditation Council. Part-time and evening/weekend programs available. *Degree requirements:* For master's, comprehensive exam. *Entrance requirements:* For master's, GRE or MAT. Additional exam requirements/recommendations for international students: Required—TOEFL. *Application deadline:* Applications are processed on a rolling basis. Electronic applications accepted. *Expenses:* Tuition: Part-time $971 per credit. *Financial support:* Career-related internships or fieldwork, Federal Work-Study, and institutionally sponsored loans available. *Unit head:* Dr. Anthony Sciarrillo, Chairperson, 201-761-6473, Fax: 201-435-5270. *Application contact:* Dr. Anthony Sciarrillo, Chairperson, 201-761-6473, Fax: 201-435-5270.

St. Thomas Aquinas College, Division of Teacher Education, Sparkill, NY 10976. Offers adolescence education (MST); childhood and special education (MST); childhood education (MST); educational leadership (MS Ed); reading (MS Ed, PMC); special education (MS Ed, PMC); teaching (MS Ed), including elementary education, middle school education, secondary education. *Accreditation:* NCATE. Part-time and evening/weekend programs available. *Degree requirements:* For master's, comprehensive exam, comprehensive professional portfolio; for PMC, action research project. *Entrance requirements:* For master's, New York State Qualifying Exam, GRE General Test or minimum GPA of 3.0, teaching certificate; for PMC, GRE General Test or minimum GPA of 3.0. Electronic applications accepted. *Faculty research:* Computer applications in education, adolescent special education students, literacy development, inclusive practices for special education students.

St. Thomas University, School of Leadership Studies, Institute for Education, Miami Gardens, FL 33054-6459. Offers earth/space science (Certificate); educational administration (MS, Certificate); educational leadership (Ed D); elementary education (MS); ESOL (Certificate); gifted education (Certificate); instructional technology (MS, Certificate); professional/studies (Certificate); reading (MS, Certificate); special education (MS). Part-time and evening/weekend programs available. *Degree requirements:* For master's, comprehensive exam; for doctorate, comprehensive exam, thesis/dissertation. *Entrance requirements:* For master's, interview, minimum GPA of 3.0 or GRE; for doctorate, GRE or MAT. Additional exam requirements/recommendations for international students: Required—TOEFL (minimum score 550 paper-based; 213 computer-based; 79 iBT). Electronic applications accepted.

Saint Vincent College, Program in Education, Latrobe, PA 15650-2690. Offers curriculum and instruction (MS); environmental education (MS); library media management (MS); school administration (MS); special education (MS). Part-time and evening/weekend programs available. *Degree requirements:* For master's, comprehensive exam. *Entrance requirements:* For master's, GRE (if undergraduate GPA less than 3.0). Additional exam requirements/recommendations for international students: Required—TOEFL (minimum score 550 paper-based; 213 computer-based). *Faculty research:* Assessment and instructional technology.

Saint Xavier University, Graduate Studies, School of Education, Chicago, IL 60655-3105. Offers counseling (MA); counselor education (MA); curriculum and instruction (MA); early childhood education (MA); education (CAS); educational administration (MA); elementary education (MA); field-based education (MA); general educational studies (MA); individualized program (MA); learning disabilities (MA); reading (MA); secondary education (MA). *Accreditation:* NCATE. Part-time and evening/weekend programs available. *Degree requirements:* For master's, thesis or project. *Entrance requirements:* For master's, minimum GPA of 3.0. *Expenses:* Contact institution.

Salem College, Department of Education, Winston-Salem, NC 27101. Offers early education and leadership (MAT); elementary education (MAT); English as a second language (MAT); language and literacy (M Ed); middle school education (MAT); secondary education (MAT); special education (MAT). *Accreditation:* NCATE. Part-time and evening/weekend programs available. *Degree requirements:* For master's, comprehensive exam, practicum (MAT), project (M Ed), oral and written comprehensive exams. *Entrance requirements:* For master's, GRE, minimum GPA of 2.5. *Faculty research:* Content area reading strategies, literacy development, brain compatible instruction.

Salem International University, School of Education, Salem, WV 26426-0500. Offers curriculum and instruction (M Ed); educational leadership (M Ed). Part-time and evening/weekend programs available. Postbaccalaureate distance learning degree programs offered. *Degree requirements:* For master's, comprehensive exam (for some programs), thesis (for some programs). *Entrance requirements:* For master's, GRE, MAT, NTE, 3 letters of recommendation. Additional exam requirements/recommendations for international students: Required—TOEFL (minimum score 550 paper-based; 213 computer-based). Electronic applications accepted. *Expenses:* Contact institution. *Faculty research:* Improved classroom effectiveness.

Salisbury University, Graduate Division, Department of Education, Salisbury, MD 21801-6837. Offers educational leadership (M Ed); general (M Ed); reading specialist (M Ed); teaching (MAT). *Accreditation:* NCATE. Part-time and evening/weekend programs available. *Faculty:* 23 full-time (14 women), 9 part-time/adjunct (8 women). *Students:* 33 full-time (18 women), 129 part-time (100 women); includes 14 minority (12 African Americans, 1 Asian American or Pacific Islander, 1 Hispanic American), 1 international. Average age 31. 71 applicants, 54% accepted, 12 enrolled. In 2009, 70 master's awarded. *Degree requirements:* For master's, comprehensive exam (for some programs). *Entrance requirements:* For master's, minimum GPA of 2.75. Additional exam requirements/recommendations for international students: Required—TOEFL (minimum score 550 paper-based; 213 computer-based). *Application deadline:* For fall admission, 3/3 for domestic students; for spring admission, 10/1 for domestic students. Applications are processed on a rolling basis. Application fee: $45. Electronic applications accepted. *Expenses:* Tuition, area resident: Part-time $278 per credit hour. Tuition, state resident: part-time $278 per credit hour. Tuition, nonresident: part-time $574 per credit hour. Required fees: $57 per credit hour. *Financial support:* In 2009–10, 30 students received support. Career-related internships or fieldwork and scholarships/grants available. Support available to part-time students. Financial award applicants required to submit FAFSA. *Unit head:* Dr. Laura Marasco, Program Coordinator, 410-546-6012, E-mail: llmarasco@salisbury.edu. *Application contact:* Tina Melczarek, Administrative Assistant I, 410-543-6281, Fax: 410-548-2593, E-mail: tmmelczarek@salisbury.edu.

Samford University, Orlean Bullard Beeson School of Education and Professional Studies, Birmingham, AL 35229. Offers early childhood education (Ed S); early childhood/elementary education (MS Ed); educational administration (Ed S); educational leadership (Ed D); elementary education (Ed S); gifted education (MS Ed); instructional leadership (MS Ed); secondary collaboration (MS Ed); M Div/MS Ed. *Accreditation:* NCATE. Part-time programs available. *Faculty:* 11 full-time (8 women), 9 part-time/adjunct (5 women). *Students:* 16 full-time (13 women), 173 part-time (131 women); includes 47 minority (46 African Americans, 1 American Indian/Alaska Native), 1 international. Average age 40. 15 applicants, 100% accepted, 15 enrolled. In 2009, 52 master's, 11 doctorates, 27 other advanced degrees awarded. *Degree requirements:* For master's, comprehensive exam; for doctorate, comprehensive exam, thesis/dissertation. *Entrance requirements:* For master's, GRE or MAT, minimum GPA of 3.0; for doctorate, minimum GPA of 3.7; for Ed S, GRE, master's degree, teaching certificate, minimum GPA of 3.25. Additional exam requirements/recommendations for international students: Required—TOEFL (minimum score 550 paper-based; 213 computer-based). *Application deadline:* Applications are processed on a rolling basis. Application fee: $25. *Expenses:* Tuition: Full-time $26,660; part-time $595 per credit hour. Required fees: $110 per semester. *Financial support:* In 2009–10, 127 students received support; research assistantships, career-related internships or fieldwork, Federal Work-Study, scholarships/grants, and tuition waivers (partial) available. Support available to part-time students. Financial award applicants required to submit FAFSA. *Faculty research:* School law, the characteristics of beginning teachers, the nature of school reform, school culture, quality improvement in education, K-12 student achievement. *Unit head:* Dr. Jean Ann Box, Dean, 205-726-2559, E-mail: jabox@samford.edu. *Application contact:* Dr. Maurice Persall, Director, Graduate Office, 205-726-2019, E-mail: jmpersal@samford.edu.

Sam Houston State University, College of Education and Applied Science, Huntsville, TX 77341. Offers M Ed, MA, MLS, Ed D, PhD. *Accreditation:* NCATE. Part-time and evening/weekend programs available. *Faculty:* 70 full-time (46 women), 12 part-time/adjunct (10 women). *Students:* 144 full-time (109 women), 1,079 part-time (887 women); includes 373 minority (158 African Americans, 3 American Indian/Alaska Native, 15 Asian Americans or Pacific Islanders, 197 Hispanic Americans), 16 international. Average age 35. 494 applicants, 94% accepted, 353 enrolled. In 2009, 466 master's, 17 doctorates awarded. *Entrance requirements:* For master's, GRE General Test. Additional exam requirements/recommendations for international students: Required—TOEFL (minimum score 550 paper-based; 213 computer-based; 79 iBT). *Application deadline:* For fall admission, 8/1 for domestic students; for spring admission, 12/1 for domestic students. Application fee: $20. *Expenses:* Tuition, state resident: full-time $3690; part-time $205 per credit hour. Tuition, nonresident: full-time $8676; part-time $482 per credit hour. Required fees: $1474. Tuition and fees vary according to course load and campus/location. *Financial support:* Research assistantships, teaching assistantships, career-related internships or fieldwork, Federal Work-Study, institutionally sponsored loans, and tuition waivers (partial) available. Support available to part-time students. Financial award application deadline: 5/31; financial award applicants required to submit FAFSA. *Unit head:* Dr. Genevieve Brown, Dean, 936-294-1101, Fax: 936-294-1102, E-mail: edu_gxb@shsu.edu. *Application contact:* Molly Doughtie, Advisor, 936-294-1105, E-mail: edu_mxd@shsu.edu.

San Diego State University, Graduate and Research Affairs, College of Education, San Diego, CA 92182. Offers MA, MS, Ed D, PhD. *Accreditation:* NCATE. Part-time and evening/weekend programs available. *Degree requirements:* For master's, thesis optional; for doctorate, thesis/dissertation. *Entrance requirements:* For master's, GRE General Test, letters of reference; for doctorate, GRE General Test, 3 letters of reference, resumé. Additional exam requirements/recommendations for international students: Required—TOEFL. Electronic applications accepted. *Faculty research:* Special education, rehabilitation counseling, educational psychology.

San Francisco State University, Division of Graduate Studies, College of Education, San Francisco, CA 94132-1722. Offers MA, MA Ed, MS, PhD, AC. *Accreditation:* NCATE.

San Jose State University, Graduate Studies and Research, Connie L. Lurie College of Education, San Jose, CA 95192-0001. Offers MA, Certificate. *Accreditation:* NCATE. Evening/weekend programs available. *Students:* 1,035 full-time (811 women), 535 part-time (424 women); includes 590 minority (48 African Americans, 2 American Indian/Alaska Native, 258 Asian Americans or Pacific Islanders, 282 Hispanic Americans), 22 international. Average age 38. 1,177 applicants, 53% accepted, 525 enrolled. In 2009, 441 master's awarded. *Application deadline:* For fall admission, 6/29 for domestic students; for spring admission, 11/30 for domestic students. Applications are processed on a rolling basis. Application fee: $59. Electronic applications accepted. *Financial support:* Career-related internships or fieldwork available. Financial award applicants required to submit FAFSA. *Unit head:* Elaine Chin, Dean, 408-924-3600, Fax: 408-924-3713. *Application contact:* Elaine Chin, Dean, 408-924-3600, Fax: 408-924-3713.

Santa Clara University, School of Education and Counseling Psychology, Department of Education, Santa Clara, CA 95053. Offers alternative and correctional education (Certificate); educational administration (MA), including educational administration; interdisciplinary education (MA), including interdisciplinary education; reading (Certificate); special education (MA, Certificate), including early childhood special education (Certificate), special education (MA); teacher education (Certificate), including multiple subject teaching, single subject teaching. Part-time and evening/weekend programs available. *Students:* 73 full-time (57 women), 218 part-time (169 women); includes 78 minority (7 African Americans, 39 Asian Americans or Pacific Islanders, 32 Hispanic Americans), 10 international. Average age 33. In 2009, 68 master's, 72 other advanced degrees awarded. *Degree requirements:* For master's, comprehensive exam (for some programs), thesis (for some programs); for Certificate, comprehensive exam. *Entrance requirements:* For master's, GRE or MAT. Additional exam requirements/recommendations for international students: Required—TOEFL (minimum score 550 paper-based; 213 computer-based; 80 iBT). *Application deadline:* For fall admission, 6/15 for domestic and international students; for winter admission, 10/15 for domestic and international students; for spring admission, 1/31 for domestic and international students. Applications are processed on a rolling basis. Application fee: $50. Electronic applications accepted. *Expenses:* Contact institution. *Financial support:* Fellowships, Federal Work-Study, institutionally sponsored loans, and scholarships/grants available. Support available to part-time students. Financial award application deadline: 5/15; financial award applicants required to submit FAFSA. *Unit head:* Dr. Atom Yee, Interim Dean, 408-554-4455, Fax: 408-554-5038, E-mail: ayee@scu.edu. *Application contact:* Paul Somoff, Admissions and Financial Aid Coordinator, 408-554-7884, Fax: 408-554-4367, E-mail: psomoff@scu.edu.

Sarah Lawrence College, Graduate Studies, Program in Art of Teaching, Bronxville, NY 10708-5999. Offers MS Ed. Part-time programs available. *Faculty:* 8 part-time/adjunct (7 women). *Students:* 21 full-time (18 women), 10 part-time (9 women); includes 10 minority (4 African Americans, 1 Asian American or Pacific Islander, 5 Hispanic Americans), 1 international. Average age 28. 26 applicants, 85% accepted, 10 enrolled. In 2009, 17 master's awarded. *Degree requirements:* For master's, thesis, fieldwork, oral presentation. *Entrance requirements:* For master's, minimum B average in undergraduate coursework. Additional exam requirements/recommendations for international students: Required—TOEFL (minimum score 600 paper-based). *Application deadline:* For fall admission, 3/1 priority date for domestic and international students. Applications are processed on a rolling basis. Application fee: $60. *Expenses:* Contact institution. *Financial support:* In 2009–10, 17 students received support, including 17 fellowships (averaging $9,248 per year); career-related internships or fieldwork, scholarships/grants, and unspecified assistantships also available. Support available to part-time students. Financial award application deadline: 3/1; financial award applicants required to submit CSS PROFILE or FAFSA. *Unit head:* Sara Wilford, Director, 914-395-2371. *Application contact:* Emanual Lomax, Dean of Graduate Studies, 914-395-2371, E-mail: elomax@sarahlawrence.edu.

Savannah College of Art and Design, Graduate School, Program in Professional Education, Savannah, GA 31402-3146. Offers MA. *Degree requirements:* For master's, comprehensive exam, student teaching. *Entrance requirements:* Additional exam requirements/recommendations for international students: Required—TOEFL (minimum score 450 paper-based; 133 computer-based). Electronic applications accepted. *Expenses:* Tuition: Full-time $28,515; part-time $627 per credit hour. One-time fee: $500. Tuition and fees vary according to course load.

Schreiner University, Department of Education, Kerrville, TX 78028-5697. Offers M Ed, MET. Evening/weekend programs available. *Faculty:* 3 full-time (2 women), 1 (woman) part-time/adjunct. *Students:* 21 full-time (20 women); includes 4 minority (all Hispanic Americans). Average age 40. In 2009, 10 degrees awarded. *Degree requirements:* For master's, exam (MET), thesis (M Ed). *Entrance requirements:* For master's, GRE General Test, minimum GPA of 3.0, interview. *Application deadline:* For fall admission, 7/1 priority date for domestic students. Applications are processed on a rolling basis. Application fee: $25. Electronic applications accepted. *Expenses:* Tuition: Full-time $15,300. Required fees: $300. *Financial support:* In 2009–10, 21 students received support. Institutionally sponsored loans available. Financial award application deadline: 8/1; financial award applicants required to submit FAFSA. *Faculty research:* Gang behaviors, gifted and talented education, varied intelligences, reading, classroom management. *Unit head:* Dr. Carole Diane Errett, Director, Teacher Education and Graduate Studies, 830-792-7445, Fax: 830-792-7382, E-mail: cderrett@schreiner.edu. *Application contact:* Betty Lavonne Miller, Administrative Assistant, 830-792-7455, Fax: 830-792-7382, E-mail: lmiller@schreiner.edu.

Seattle University, College of Education, Seattle, WA 98122-1090. Offers M Ed, MA, MIT, Ed D, Certificate, Ed S, Post-Master's Certificate. *Accreditation:* NCATE. Part-time and evening/weekend programs available. *Degree requirements:* For master's and other advanced degree, comprehensive exam; for doctorate, comprehensive exam, thesis/dissertation. *Entrance requirements:* For doctorate, GRE General Test, MAT, interview, MA, minimum GPA of 3.5, 3 years of related experience. Additional exam requirements/recommendations for international students: Required—TOEFL. *Expenses:* Contact institution. *Faculty research:* Service learning, learning and technology, assessment models of professional education, alternative delivery systems.

Seton Hall University, College of Education and Human Services, South Orange, NJ 07079-2697. Offers MA, MS, Ed D, Exec Ed D, PhD, Ed S. *Accreditation:* NCATE. Part-time and evening/weekend programs available. *Faculty:* 39 full-time (21 women), 116 part-time/adjunct (32 women). *Students:* 232 full-time (153 women), 798 part-time (519 women); includes 221 minority (134 African Americans, 1 American Indian/Alaska Native, 19 Asian Americans or Pacific Islanders, 67 Hispanic Americans), 22 international. Average age 35. 432 applicants, 66% accepted, 199 enrolled. In 2009, 302 master's, 51 doctorates, 51 other advanced degrees awarded. *Degree requirements:* For master's, comprehensive exam; for doctorate, comprehensive exam, thesis/dissertation, internship. *Entrance requirements:* For doctorate, interview. *Application deadline:* Applications are processed on a rolling basis. Application fee: $50. Electronic applications accepted. *Financial support:* In 2009–10, 13 students received support; fellowships, research assistantships, career-related internships or fieldwork, institutionally sponsored loans, and unspecified assistantships available. Financial award application deadline: 2/1. *Faculty research:* Information technology and classrooms, adult development including career family systems, therapy effectiveness, management systems, principal effectiveness. Total annual research expenditures: $30,000. *Unit head:* Dr. Joseph V. De Pierro, Dean, 973-761-9025. *Application contact:* Dr. Manina Urgolo Huckvale, Associate Dean, 973-761-9668, Fax: 973-275-2187, E-mail: manina.Urgolo-Huckvale@shu.edu.

Seton Hill University, Program in Inclusive Education, Greensburg, PA 15601. Offers MA. *Accreditation:* Teacher Education Accreditation Council. Part-time and evening/weekend programs available. Postbaccalaureate distance learning degree programs offered (no on-campus study). *Faculty:* 5 full-time (2 women), 5 part-time/adjunct (4 women). *Students:* 10 full-time (all women), 14 part-time (11 women); includes 1 African American. Average age 38. 17 applicants, 100% accepted, 16 enrolled. In 2009, 1 master's awarded. *Degree requirements:* For master's, thesis optional. *Entrance requirements:* For master's, minimum GPA of 3.0. Additional exam requirements/recommendations for international students: Required—TOEFL (minimum score 600 paper-based; 250 computer-based), IELTS (minimum score 6.5). Application fee: $35. *Expenses:* Tuition: Full-time $12,780; part-time $710 per credit. Required fees: $300; $150 per semester. Tuition and fees vary according to course load and program. *Financial support:* Scholarships/grants, tuition waivers (partial), and unspecified assistantships available. Support available to part-time students. Financial award application deadline: 8/15; financial award applicants required to submit FAFSA. *Unit head:* Dr. Sondra Lettrich, Director, 724-830-1010, Fax: 724-830-1294, E-mail: lettrich@setonhill.edu. *Application contact:* Laurel Pellis, Advisor, 724-838-4209, Fax: 724-830-1891, E-mail: lpellis@setonhill.edu.

Shawnee State University, Program in Curriculum and Instruction, Portsmouth, OH 45662-4344. Offers M Ed. *Accreditation:* NCATE.

Shenandoah University, School of Education and Human Development, Winchester, VA 22601-5195. Offers administrative leadership (D Ed); advanced professional teaching English to speakers of other languages (Certificate); education (MSE); elementary education (Certificate); middle school education (Certificate); organizational leadership (MS); professional studies (Certificate); professional studies (for initial teacher licensure) (Certificate); professional studies (for special education teacher licensure) (Certificate); professional studies (for VA licensure reading specialists) (Certificate); professional studies (for VA licensure) (Certificate); professional teaching English to speakers of other languages (Certificate); public management (Certificate); school reform (Certificate); secondary education (Certificate). *Accreditation:* Teacher Education Accreditation Council. Part-time and evening/weekend programs available. Postbaccalaureate distance learning degree programs offered (minimal on-campus study). *Faculty:* 13 full-time (7 women), 27 part-time/adjunct (20 women). *Students:* 11 full-time (8 women), 382 part-time (276 women); includes 35 minority (17 African Americans, 1 American Indian/Alaska Native, 6 Asian Americans or Pacific Islanders, 11 Hispanic Americans), 4 international. Average age 39. 272 applicants, 95% accepted, 218 enrolled. In 2009, 103 master's, 2 doctorates awarded. *Degree requirements:* For master's, comprehensive exam (for some programs), thesis (for some programs), internship; for doctorate, comprehensive exam, thesis/dissertation; for Certificate, full time teaching in area for 1 year. *Entrance requirements:* For master's, minimum GPA of 3.0 or satisfactory GRE, 3 letters of recommendation, valid teaching license, essay; for doctorate, minimum graduate GPA of 3.5, 3 years of teaching experience, 3 letters of recommendation, writing samples; for Certificate, minimum undergraduate GPA of 3.0, essay, 3 letters of recommendation. Additional exam requirements/recommendations for international students: Required—TOEFL (minimum score 550 paper-based; 213 computer-based; 79 iBT), IELTS (minimum score 6.5). *Application deadline:* For fall admission, 7/1 for domestic and international students; for spring admission, 10/15 for domestic and international students. Application fee: $30. Electronic applications accepted. *Expenses:* Tuition: Full-time $11,925; part-time $695 per credit. Required fees: $400 per semester. *Financial support:* Application deadline: 3/15. *Unit head:* Dr. Steven E. Humphries, Dean, 540-535-3574, E-mail: shumphri@su.edu. *Application contact:* David Anthony, Dean of Admissions, 540-665-4581, Fax: 540-665-4627, E-mail: admit@su.edu.

Shippensburg University of Pennsylvania, School of Graduate Studies, College of Arts and Sciences, Department of Sociology and Anthropology, Shippensburg, PA 17257-2299. Offers organizational development and leadership (MS), including business, communications, education, environmental management, higher education, historical administration, individual and organizational development, public organizations, social structures and organizations. Part-time and evening/weekend programs available. *Degree requirements:* For master's, capstone experience. *Entrance requirements:* For master's, interview (if GPA less than 2.75), resume. Additional exam requirements/recommendations for international students: Required—TOEFL (minimum score 560 paper-based; 220 computer-based); Recommended—IELTS (minimum score 6). Electronic applications accepted.

Shippensburg University of Pennsylvania, School of Graduate Studies, College of Education and Human Services, Shippensburg, PA 17257-2299. Offers M Ed, MS, MSW, Certificate. *Accreditation:* NCATE. Part-time and evening/weekend programs available. *Entrance requirements:* Additional exam requirements/recommendations for international students: Required—TOEFL (minimum score 560 paper-based; 220 computer-based); Recommended—IELTS (minimum score 6). Electronic applications accepted.

Siena Heights University, Graduate College, Program in Teacher Education, Adrian, MI 49221-1796. Offers early childhood education (MA), including Montessori education; elementary education (MA), including elementary education/reading; mathematics education (MA); middle school education (MA); secondary education (MA), including secondary education/reading. Part-time programs available. *Degree requirements:* For master's, thesis, presentation. *Entrance requirements:* For master's, minimum GPA of 3.0, interview. *Faculty research:* Teaching/learning styles, outcomes-based teaching, multiple intelligences, assessment.

Sierra Nevada College, Teacher Education Program, Incline Village, NV 89451. Offers elementary education (MAT); secondary education (MAT). Part-time and evening/weekend programs available. *Degree requirements:* For master's, comprehensive exam, thesis, PRAXIS I and II. *Entrance requirements:* For master's, 2 letters of recommendation, minimum GPA of 3.0.

Silver Lake College, Division of Graduate Studies, Program in Education, Manitowoc, WI 54220-9319. Offers administrative leadership (MA Ed); teacher leadership (MA Ed). Part-time and evening/weekend programs available. Postbaccalaureate distance learning degree programs offered (no on-campus study). *Faculty:* 1 (woman) full-time, 12 part-time/adjunct (10 women). *Students:* 43 part-time (28 women); includes 4 minority (2 African Americans, 2 Hispanic Americans). Average age 36. 22 applicants, 73% accepted, 15 enrolled. In 2009, 20 master's awarded. *Degree requirements:* For master's, comprehensive exam, thesis or alternative, public presentation of culminating project. *Entrance requirements:* For master's, interview, minimum undergraduate GPA of 3.0, writing sample, 3 letters of recommendation. Additional

Education—General

Silver Lake College (continued)
exam requirements/recommendations for international students: Required—TOEFL. *Application deadline:* For fall admission, 8/1 for domestic and international students; for spring admission, 12/1 for domestic and international students. Applications are processed on a rolling basis. Application fee: $50. Electronic applications accepted. *Expenses:* Tuition: Full-time $7380; part-time $410 per credit. Required fees: $10 per term. Part-time tuition and fees vary according to course load. *Financial support:* Scholarships/grants available. Support available to part-time students. Financial award applicants required to submit FAFSA. *Unit head:* Dr. Julie A. Mayrose, Director, 800-236-4752 Ext. 370, Fax: 920-684-7082, E-mail: mayrose@siler.sl.edu. *Application contact:* Jamie Grant, Associate Director of Admissions, 800-236-4752 Ext. 186, Fax: 920-686-6322, E-mail: jgrant@silver.sl.edu.

Simmons College, College of Arts and Sciences Graduate Studies, Department of Education, Boston, MA 02115. Offers educational leadership (MS Ed, PhD, CAGS); special education (MS Ed, PhD, Ed S), including applied behavior analysis (PhD), assistive technology (MS Ed, Ed S), behavioral education (MS Ed, Ed S), health professions education (PhD), language and literacy (MS Ed, Ed S), moderate disabilities (Ed S), moderate special needs (MS Ed), severe disabilities (Ed S), severe special needs (MS Ed), special education administration; teacher preparation (MAT, MS, MS Ed, CAGS), including educational leadership (MS Ed), elementary education (MAT), general education (CAGS), general purposes (MS), middle school education (MAT), professional license (CAGS), professional license: elementary (MS Ed), professional license: middle/high (MS Ed), secondary education (MAT), urban education (MS Ed, CAGS); teaching English as a second language (MAT); MA/MA; MAT/MA. *Entrance requirements:* Additional exam requirements/recommendations for international students: Required—TOEFL (minimum score 600 paper-based; 250 computer-based; 100 iBT). *Application deadline:* For fall admission, 8/1 priority date for domestic and international students; for spring admission, 12/15 priority date for domestic and international students. Applications are processed on a rolling basis. Application fee: $35. Electronic applications accepted. *Expenses:* Tuition: Part-time $925 per credit hour. Part-time tuition and fees vary according to program. *Financial support:* Scholarships/grants and tuition waivers (partial) available. Financial award application deadline: 3/1; financial award applicants required to submit FAFSA. *Application contact:* Kristen Haack, Director, Graduate Studies Admission, 617-521-2917, Fax: 617-521-3058, E-mail: gsa@simmons.edu.

Simon Fraser University, Graduate Studies, Faculty of Education, Burnaby, BC V5A 1S6, Canada. Offers M Ed, M Sc, MA, Ed D, PhD. *Degree requirements:* For master's, project or thesis; for doctorate, thesis/dissertation. *Entrance requirements:* For master's, minimum GPA of 3.0; for doctorate, GRE, master's degree or exceptional record in a bachelor's degree, minimum GPA of 3.5. Additional exam requirements/recommendations for international students: Required—TOEFL or IELTS. *Faculty research:* Drama education, gender equity, children's literature, theory and curriculum development, counseling psychology.

Simpson College, Department of Education, Indianola, IA 50125-1297. Offers secondary education (MAT). *Degree requirements:* For master's, PRAXIS II, electronic portfolio. *Entrance requirements:* For master's, bachelor's degree; minimum cumulative GPA of 2.75, 3.0 in major; 3 letters of recommendation.

Simpson University, School of Education, Redding, CA 96003-8606. Offers education (MA); education and preliminary administrative services (MA); education and preliminary teaching (MA); teaching (MA). Part-time and evening/weekend programs available. *Faculty:* 6 full-time (3 women), 5 part-time/adjunct (1 woman). *Students:* 45 full-time (31 women), 90 part-time (62 women); includes 9 minority (1 African American, 4 Asian Americans or Pacific Islanders, 4 Hispanic Americans). In 2009, 42 master's awarded. *Degree requirements:* For master's, thesis optional. *Entrance requirements:* For master's, California Basic Educational Skills Test, CSET, 2 letters of reference. Additional exam requirements/recommendations for international students: Required—TOEFL (minimum score 550 paper-based; 180 computer-based). *Application deadline:* Applications are processed on a rolling basis. Application fee: $25. Electronic applications accepted. *Financial support:* Scholarships/grants available. Financial award applicants required to submit FAFSA. *Unit head:* Dr. Glee Brooks, Dean, 530-226-4606, Fax: 530-226-4861, E-mail: edadmissions@simpsonu.edu. *Application contact:* Marie Moe, Director of Continuing and Graduate Admissions, 530-226-4784, Fax: 530-226-4861, E-mail: edadmissions@simpsonu.edu.

Sinte Gleska University, Graduate Education Program, Mission, SD 57555. Offers elementary education (M Ed). Part-time and evening/weekend programs available. *Degree requirements:* For master's, thesis. *Entrance requirements:* For master's, 2 years of experience in elementary education, minimum GPA of 2.5, South Dakota elementary education certification. *Faculty research:* American Indian graduate education, teaching of Native American students.

SIT Graduate Institute, Graduate Programs, Programs in Language Teacher Education, Brattleboro, VT 05302-0676. Offers English for speakers of other languages (MAT); French (MAT); Spanish (MAT). *Degree requirements:* For master's, one foreign language, thesis, teaching practice. *Entrance requirements:* For master's, 4 letters of reference. Additional exam requirements/recommendations for international students: Required—TOEFL.

Slippery Rock University of Pennsylvania, Graduate Studies (Recruitment), College of Education, Slippery Rock, PA 16057-1383. Offers M Ed, MA, MS. *Accreditation:* NCATE. Part-time and evening/weekend programs available. *Degree requirements:* For master's, comprehensive exam. *Entrance requirements:* For master's, GRE General Test, MAT, minimum GPA of 2.75 (3.0 for initial certification programs). Additional exam requirements/recommendations for international students: Required—TOEFL (minimum score 550 paper-based; 213 computer-based). *Application deadline:* For fall admission, 3/1 priority date for domestic students, 5/1 priority date for international students; for spring admission, 11/1 priority date for domestic students, 9/1 priority date for international students. Applications are processed on a rolling basis. Application fee: $25 ($30 for international students). Electronic applications accepted. *Expenses:* Tuition, state resident: full-time $6666; part-time $370 per credit. Tuition, nonresident: full-time $10,666; part-time $593 per credit. Required fees: $2184; $182 per credit. *Financial support:* Career-related internships or fieldwork, Federal Work-Study, scholarships/grants, and unspecified assistantships available. Support available to part-time students. Financial award application deadline: 5/1; financial award applicants required to submit FAFSA. *Unit head:* Dr. Kathleen Strickland, Interim Dean, 724-738-2007, Fax: 724-738-2880, E-mail: kathleen.strickland@sru.edu. *Application contact:* Angela Piverotto, Director of Graduate Admissions, 724-738-2051, Fax: 724-738-2146, E-mail: graduate.admissions@sru.edu.

Smith College, Graduate and Special Programs, Department of Education and Child Study, Northampton, MA 01063. Offers education of the deaf (MED); elementary education (MAT); middle school education (MAT); secondary education (MAT), including biological sciences education, chemistry education, English education, French education, geology education, government education, history education, mathematics education, physics education, Spanish education. Part-time programs available. *Faculty:* 6 full-time (4 women), 3 part-time/adjunct (2 women). *Students:* 20 full-time (14 women), 5 part-time (3 women); includes 2 minority (1 African American, 1 Asian American or Pacific Islander), 1 international. Average age 30. 41 applicants, 88% accepted, 22 enrolled. In 2009, 19 master's awarded. *Entrance requirements:* Additional exam requirements/recommendations for international students: Required—TOEFL. *Application deadline:* For fall admission, 4/1 for domestic students, 1/15 for international students; for spring admission, 12/1 for domestic students. Application fee: $60. *Financial support:* In 2009–10, 20 students received support, including 6 teaching assistantships with full tuition reimbursements available (averaging $11,910 per year); career-related internships or fieldwork, institutionally sponsored loans, and scholarships/grants also available. Support available to part-time students. Financial award application deadline: 1/15; financial award applicants required to submit CSS PROFILE or FAFSA. *Unit head:* Alan Rudnitsky, Chair, 413-585-3261, Fax: 413-585-3268, E-mail: arudnits@smith.edu. *Application contact:* Ruth Morgan, Administrative Assistant, 413-585-3050, Fax: 413-585-3054, E-mail: gradstdy@smith.edu.

Sonoma State University, School of Education, Rohnert Park, CA 94928. Offers MA. *Accreditation:* NCATE. Part-time and evening/weekend programs available. *Faculty:* 19 full-time (14 women), 3 part-time/adjunct (2 women). *Students:* 14 full-time (all women), 134 part-time (109 women); includes 16 minority (2 African Americans, 2 Asian Americans or Pacific Islanders, 12 Hispanic Americans), 4 international. Average age 38. 106 applicants, 71% accepted, 5 enrolled. In 2009, 70 master's awarded. *Degree requirements:* For master's, thesis or alternative. *Entrance requirements:* For master's, minimum GPA of 2.5. Additional exam requirements/recommendations for international students: Required—TOEFL (minimum score 500 paper-based; 173 computer-based). Application fee: $55. *Expenses:* Tuition, nonresident: full-time $11,160. Required fees: $6226. Full-time tuition and fees vary according to course load. *Financial support:* Fellowships, career-related internships or fieldwork and Federal Work-Study available. Support available to part-time students. Financial award application deadline: 3/2; financial award applicants required to submit FAFSA. *Unit head:* Dr. Mary Gendernalik-Cooper, Dean, 707-664-2132, E-mail: gendernm@sonoma.edu. *Application contact:* Elaine Sundberg, Associate Vice Provost, Academic Programs/Graduate Studies, 707-664-2215, Fax: 707-664-4060, E-mail: elaine.sundberg@sonoma.edu.

South Carolina State University, School of Graduate Studies, Department of Education, Orangeburg, SC 29117-0001. Offers early childhood and special education (M Ed); early childhood education (MAT); elementary education (M Ed, MAT); engineering (MAT); general science (MAT); mathematics (MAT); secondary education (M Ed), including biology education, business education, counselor education, English education, home economics education, industrial education, mathematics education, science education, social studies education; special education (M Ed), including emotionally handicapped, learning disabilities, mentally handicapped. *Accreditation:* NCATE. Part-time and evening/weekend programs available. *Degree requirements:* For master's, thesis optional, departmental qualifying exam. *Entrance requirements:* For master's, GRE General Test, NTE, interview, teaching certificate. Electronic applications accepted. *Expenses:* Tuition, state resident: part-time $470 per credit hour. Tuition, nonresident: part-time $924 per credit hour. *Faculty research:* Critical thinking, child abuse, stress, test-taking skills, conflict resolution, mainstreaming.

South Dakota State University, Graduate School, College of Education and Human Sciences, Brookings, SD 57007. Offers M Ed, MFCS, MS, PhD. *Degree requirements:* For master's, thesis, oral exam. *Entrance requirements:* Additional exam requirements/recommendations for international students: Required—TOEFL.

Southeastern Louisiana University, College of Education and Human Development, Hammond, LA 70402. Offers M Ed, MAT, Ed D. *Accreditation:* NCATE. Part-time programs available. *Faculty:* 39 full-time (25 women), 1 (woman) part-time/adjunct. *Students:* 101 full-time (92 women), 376 part-time (317 women); includes 93 minority (79 African Americans, 1 American Indian/Alaska Native, 3 Asian Americans or Pacific Islanders, 10 Hispanic Americans), 2 international. Average age 35. 153 applicants, 56% accepted, 64 enrolled. In 2009, 136 master's awarded. *Degree requirements:* For master's, comprehensive exam (for some programs), thesis optional; for doctorate, thesis/dissertation. *Entrance requirements:* For master's, GRE; for doctorate, GRE (minimum combined score for verbal and quantitative sections of 900), master's degree from an accredited university; minimum GPA of 3.0 on the last 60 undergraduate hours, 3.25 on all graduate-level course work. Additional exam requirements/recommendations for international students: Required—TOEFL (minimum score 500 paper-based; 173 computer-based; 61 iBT). *Application deadline:* For fall admission, 7/15 priority date for domestic students, 6/1 priority date for international students; for spring admission, 12/1 priority date for domestic students, 10/1 priority date for international students. Applications are processed on a rolling basis. Application fee: $20 ($30 for international students). Electronic applications accepted. *Expenses:* Tuition, state resident: full-time $3086; part-time $225 per credit hour. Tuition, nonresident: part-time $529 per credit hour. Required fees: $1195. Tuition and fees vary according to course level and course load. *Financial support:* In 2009–10, 27 students received support. Career-related internships or fieldwork, Federal Work-Study, institutionally sponsored loans, scholarships/grants, and administrative assistantships available. Support available to part-time students. Financial award application deadline: 5/1; financial award applicants required to submit FAFSA. *Faculty research:* School counseling, marriage counseling, using the Web and professional development in technology integration, legal and ethical issues in education, reading. Total annual research expenditures: $548,506. *Unit head:* Dr. Bill Neal, Interim Dean, 985-549-2217, Fax: 985-549-2070, E-mail: bill.neal@selu.edu. *Application contact:* Sandra Meyers, Graduate Admissions Analyst, 985-549-5620, Fax: 985-549-5632, E-mail: admissions@selu.edu.

Southeastern Oklahoma State University, School of Education, Durant, OK 74701-0609. Offers math specialist (M Ed); reading specialist (M Ed); school administration (M Ed); school counseling (M Ed). *Accreditation:* NCATE. Part-time and evening/weekend programs available. *Faculty:* 52 full-time (19 women), 1 (woman) part-time/adjunct. *Students:* 14 full-time (11 women), 73 part-time (58 women); includes 22 minority (4 African Americans, 17 American Indian/Alaska Native, 1 Hispanic American). Average age 32. 18 applicants, 100% accepted, 18 enrolled. *Degree requirements:* For master's, comprehensive exam, thesis optional, portfolio (M Ed). *Entrance requirements:* For master's, GRE General Test (MBS), minimum GPA of 3.0 in last 60 hours or 2.75 overall. Additional exam requirements/recommendations for international students: Required—TOEFL (minimum score 550 paper-based; 213 computer-based). *Application deadline:* For fall admission, 8/1 for domestic students, 6/1 for international students; for spring admission, 1/5 for domestic students, 11/1 for international students. Application fee: $20 ($55 for international students). Electronic applications accepted. *Financial support:* In 2009–10, 1 teaching assistantship with full tuition reimbursement (averaging $5,000 per year) was awarded; Federal Work-Study, institutionally sponsored loans, and tuition waivers (partial) also available. Support available to part-time students. Financial award application deadline: 6/15; financial award applicants required to submit FAFSA. *Unit head:* Dr. Melanie Price, Chair, 580-745-2602, Fax: 580-745-7474, E-mail: mprice@se.edu. *Application contact:* Carrie Williamson, Graduate Secretary, 580-745-2200, Fax: 580-745-7474, E-mail: cwilliamson@se.edu.

Southeastern University, College of Education, Lakeland, FL 33801-6099. Offers educational leadership (M Ed); elementary education (M Ed); teaching and learning (M Ed).

Southern Adventist University, School of Education and Psychology, Collegedale, TN 37315-0370. Offers clinical mental health counseling (MS); inclusive education (MS Ed); instructional leadership (MS Ed); literacy education (MS Ed); outdoor teacher education (MS Ed); school counseling (MS). *Accreditation:* NCATE. Part-time and evening/weekend programs available. *Faculty:* 4 full-time (2 women), 8 part-time/adjunct (5 women). *Students:* 33 full-time (15 women), 17 part-time (13 women); includes 16 minority (7 African Americans, 9 Hispanic Americans). Average age 30. In 2009, 23 master's awarded. *Degree requirements:* For master's, comprehensive exam (for some programs), thesis optional, position paper (MS), portfolio (MS Ed in outdoor teacher education). *Entrance requirements:* For master's, interview (MS); 9 semester hours of upper division course work in psychology or related field, including 1 course in psychology research or statistics; 9 semester hours of education (MS Ed). Additional exam requirements/recommendations for international students: Required—TOEFL (minimum score 600 paper-based; 250 computer-based; 100 iBT). *Application deadline:* For fall admission, 7/1 priority date for domestic students, 6/1 priority date for international students; for winter admission, 11/1 priority date for domestic students, 10/1 priority date for international students; for spring admission, 4/1 priority date for domestic students, 3/1 priority date for international students. Applications are processed on a rolling basis. Application fee: $25. Electronic applications accepted. *Expenses:* Tuition: Full-time $13,149; part-time $487 per credit hour. *Financial support:* In 2009–10, 7 students received support, including 1 research assistantship with full tuition reimbursement available (averaging $15,000 per year), 5 teaching assistantships with full tuition reimbursements available (averaging $15,000 per year); career-related internships or fieldwork, scholarships/grants, tuition waivers (partial), and unspecified assistantships also available. Support available to part-time students. Financial award application deadline: 4/1; financial award applicants required to submit FAFSA. *Unit head:* Dr. Wesley

Taylor, Dean, 423-236-2444, Fax: 423-236-1765, E-mail: jwtv@southern.edu. *Application contact:* Mikhaile Spence, Information Contact, 423-236-2496, Fax: 423-236-1765, E-mail: maspence@southern.edu.

Southern Arkansas University–Magnolia, Graduate Programs, Magnolia, AR 71753. Offers agriculture (MS); business administration (MBA); computer and information sciences (MS); counseling (MS); education (M Ed), including counseling and development, curriculum and instruction emphasis, educational administration and supervision, elementary education, middle level emphasis, reading emphasis, secondary education, TESOL emphasis; kinesiology (MS); library media and information specialist (M Ed); mental health and clinical counseling (MS); public administration (EMPA); school counseling (M Ed); teaching (MAT). *Accreditation:* NCATE. Part-time and evening/weekend programs available. *Faculty:* 43 full-time (24 women), 12 part-time/adjunct (7 women). *Students:* 116 full-time (78 women), 333 part-time (255 women); includes 105 minority (98 African Americans, 3 American Indian/Alaska Native, 3 Asian Americans or Pacific Islanders, 1 Hispanic American), 11 international. Average age 33. In 2009, 88 master's awarded. *Degree requirements:* For master's, comprehensive exam, thesis optional. *Entrance requirements:* For master's, GRE, MAT or GMAT, minimum GPA of 2.75. *Application deadline:* For fall admission, 8/15 for domestic students; for winter admission, 1/8 for domestic students; for spring admission, 1/8 for domestic students. Applications are processed on a rolling basis. Application fee: $0. *Expenses:* Tuition, state resident: full-time $3798; part-time $211 per hour. Tuition, nonresident: full-time $5580; part-time $310 per hour. Required fees: $584. *Financial support:* Career-related internships or fieldwork, Federal Work-Study, scholarships/grants, tuition waivers (full), and unspecified assistantships available. Financial award applicants required to submit FAFSA. *Faculty research:* Alternative certification for teachers, supervision of instruction, instructional leadership, counseling. *Unit head:* Dr. Kim Bloss, Dean, Graduate Studies, 870-235-4150, Fax: 870-235-5227, E-mail: kkbloss@saumag.edu. *Application contact:* Dr. Kim Bloss, Dean, Graduate Studies, 870-235-4150, Fax: 870-235-5227, E-mail: kkbloss@saumag.edu.

Southern Connecticut State University, School of Graduate Studies, School of Education, New Haven, CT 06515-1355. Offers MS, MS Ed, Ed D, Diploma. *Accreditation:* NCATE. Part-time programs available. *Faculty:* 52 full-time, 37 part-time/adjunct. *Students:* 1,507. 561 applicants, 71% accepted, 326 enrolled. In 2009, 363 master's, 151 other advanced degrees awarded. *Degree requirements:* For doctorate, comprehensive exam, thesis/dissertation. *Entrance requirements:* For degree, master's degree. Application fee: $50. Electronic applications accepted. Tuition and fees vary according to program. *Financial support:* Research assistantships, teaching assistantships, career-related internships or fieldwork available. *Unit head:* Dr. Sharon Misasi, Interim Dean, 203-392-5900, E-mail: misasis1@southernct.edu. *Application contact:* Lisa Galvin, Assistant Dean of Graduate Studies, 203-392-5240, Fax: 203-392-5235, E-mail: galvinl1@southernct.edu.

Southern Illinois University Carbondale, Graduate School, College of Education, Carbondale, IL 62901-4701. Offers MPH, MS, MS Ed, MSW, PhD, Rh D, JD/MSW. *Accreditation:* NCATE. Part-time programs available. Terminal master's awarded for partial completion of doctoral program. *Degree requirements:* For doctorate, thesis/dissertation. *Entrance requirements:* For master's, minimum GPA of 2.7. Additional exam requirements/recommendations for international students: Required—TOEFL. *Faculty research:* Safety education, community health, curriculum development, gifted, effective schools.

Southern Illinois University Edwardsville, Graduate Studies and Research, School of Education, Edwardsville, IL 62026-0001. Offers MA, MAT, MS, MS Ed, Ed S, Post-Master's Certificate, Postbaccalaureate Certificate, SD. *Accreditation:* NCATE. Part-time programs available. *Faculty:* 80 full-time (43 women). *Students:* 169 full-time (142 women), 561 part-time (419 women); includes 63 minority (48 African Americans, 1 American Indian/Alaska Native, 4 Asian Americans or Pacific Islanders, 10 Hispanic Americans), 7 international. Average age 26. 581 applicants, 42% accepted. In 2009, 225 master's, 21 other advanced degrees awarded. *Degree requirements:* For master's, thesis (for some programs), final exam, portfolio. *Entrance requirements:* For master's, GRE. Additional exam requirements/recommendations for international students: Required—TOEFL (minimum score 550 paper-based; 213 computer-based; 79 iBT), IELTS (minimum score 6.5). *Application deadline:* For fall admission, 7/23 for domestic students, 6/1 for international students; for spring admission, 12/11 for domestic students, 10/1 for international students. Applications are processed on a rolling basis. Application fee: $30. Electronic applications accepted. *Expenses:* Tuition, state resident: part-time $1252.50 per semester. Tuition, nonresident: part-time $3131.25 per semester. Required fees: $586.85 per semester. Tuition and fees vary according to course load. *Financial support:* In 2009–10, 2 fellowships with full tuition reimbursements (averaging $8,370 per year), 5 research assistantships with full tuition reimbursements (averaging $8,064 per year), 87 teaching assistantships with full tuition reimbursements (averaging $8,064 per year) were awarded; career-related internships or fieldwork, Federal Work-Study, institutionally sponsored loans, scholarships/grants, traineeships, and unspecified assistantships also available. Support available to part-time students. Financial award application deadline: 3/1; financial award applicants required to submit FAFSA. *Unit head:* Dr. Bette Bergeron, Interim Dean, 618-650-3350, E-mail: bberger@siue.edu. *Application contact:* Dr. Mary Weishaar, Associate Dean, 618-650-3491, E-mail: mweisha@siue.edu.

Southern Methodist University, Annette Caldwell Simmons School of Education and Human Development, Department of Teaching and Learning, Dallas, TX 75275. Offers bilingual/ESL education (MBE); education (M Ed, PhD); educational preparation (Certificate); gifted and talented focus (MBE); learning therapist (Certificate). Part-time and evening/weekend programs available. *Faculty:* 16 full-time (12 women), 31 part-time/adjunct (26 women). *Students:* 28 full-time (23 women), 413 part-time (335 women); includes 125 minority (40 African Americans, 4 American Indian/Alaska Native, 14 Asian Americans or Pacific Islanders, 67 Hispanic Americans), 16 international. Average age 36. 36 applicants, 92% accepted, 29 enrolled. In 2009, 85 master's, 28 other advanced degrees awarded. Terminal master's awarded for partial completion of doctoral program. *Degree requirements:* For master's, comprehensive exam, minimum GPA of 3.0; for doctorate, thesis/dissertation, qualifying exams, major area paper, evidence of teaching competency, dissemination of research (e.g., conference presentation), professional portfolio. *Entrance requirements:* For master's, minimum GPA of 3.0 or GRE, 3 letters of recommendation; for doctorate, GRE, minimum GPA of 3.3, 3 years of full-time teaching, 3 letters of recommendation, interview. Additional exam requirements/recommendations for international students: Required—TOEFL. Application fee: $75. Electronic applications accepted. *Financial support:* In 2009–10, 31 students received support; teaching assistantships, scholarships/grants and tuition waivers available. Financial award application deadline: 5/1. *Faculty research:* Reading intervention, mathematics intervention, bilingual education, new literacies. Total annual research expenditures: $2.7 million. *Unit head:* Prof. Jill H. Allor, Associate Professor and Chair, 214-768-2346, Fax: 214-768-8700, E-mail: jallor@smu.edu. *Application contact:* Dr. Deborah Diffily, Administrative Assistant, 214-768-2346, E-mail: ddiffily@smu.edu.

Southern Nazarene University, Graduate College, School of Education, Bethany, OK 73008. Offers curriculum and instruction (MA); educational leadership (MA). *Accreditation:* NCATE. Part-time and evening/weekend programs available. *Degree requirements:* For master's, thesis optional. *Entrance requirements:* For master's, MAT, English proficiency exam, minimum GPA of 3.0 in last 60 hours/major, 2.7 overall.

Southern New Hampshire University, School of Education, Manchester, NH 03106-1045. Offers business education (MS); child development (M Ed); computer technology education (Certificate); curriculum and instruction (M Ed); education (M Ed, CAS); elementary education (M Ed); general special education (Certificate); school business administrator (Certificate); secondary education (M Ed); training and development (Certificate). Part-time and evening/weekend programs available. Postbaccalaureate distance learning degree programs offered (no on-campus study). *Degree requirements:* For master's, comprehensive exam (for some programs), thesis or alternative. *Entrance requirements:* For master's, PRAXIS I, minimum GPA of 2.75. Additional exam requirements/recommendations for international students: Required—TOEFL (minimum score 550 paper-based; 213 computer-based). Electronic applications accepted. *Expenses:* Contact institution.

Southern Oregon University, Graduate Studies, School of Education, Ashland, OR 97520. Offers elementary education (MA Ed, MS Ed), including classroom teacher, early childhood, handicapped learner, reading, supervision; secondary education (MA Ed, MS Ed), including classroom teacher, handicapped learner, reading, supervision; teaching (MAT). *Degree requirements:* For master's, thesis optional. *Entrance requirements:* For master's, GRE General Test, minimum GPA of 3.0. Electronic applications accepted.

Southern University and Agricultural and Mechanical College, Graduate School, College of Education, Baton Rouge, LA 70813. Offers M Ed, MA, MS, PhD. *Accreditation:* NCATE. *Degree requirements:* For master's, comprehensive exam, thesis optional. *Entrance requirements:* For master's and doctorate, GRE General Test. Additional exam requirements/recommendations for international students: Required—TOEFL (minimum score 525 paper-based; 193 computer-based).

Southern Utah University, College of Education, Program in Education, Cedar City, UT 84720-2498. Offers M Ed. *Accreditation:* Teacher Education Accreditation Council. *Faculty:* 10 full-time (3 women), 3 part-time/adjunct (2 women). *Students:* 13 full-time (7 women), 524 part-time (382 women); includes 27 minority (17 African Americans, 10 Hispanic Americans). 51 applicants, 82% accepted, 42 enrolled. In 2009, 200 master's awarded. *Application deadline:* Applications are processed on a rolling basis. Application fee: $50 ($65 for international students). Electronic applications accepted. *Financial support:* In 2009–10, 21 teaching assistantships (averaging $715 per year) were awarded. *Unit head:* Dr. Prent Klag, Dean, 435-586-7803, Fax: 435-865-8485, E-mail: klag@suu.edu. *Application contact:* Bobbie Jensen, Administrative Assistant, 435-865-8383, Fax: 435-865-8485, E-mail: jensenb@suu.edu.

Southern Wesleyan University, Program in Education, Central, SC 29630-1020. Offers M Ed. Program also offered at Greenville, SC site. *Accreditation:* NCATE. Evening/weekend programs available. *Entrance requirements:* For master's, 3 years teaching experience including current teacher status, minimum GPA of 2.7, teacher certification.

Southwest Baptist University, Program in Education, Bolivar, MO 65613-2597. Offers education (MS); educational administration (MS, Ed S). Part-time programs available. *Degree requirements:* For master's, comprehensive exam, thesis optional, 6 hour residency; for Ed S, comprehensive exam, 5 hour residency. *Entrance requirements:* For master's, GRE or PRAXIS II, interviews, minimum GPA of 2.75; for Ed S, master's degree. Additional exam requirements/recommendations for international students: Required—TOEFL (minimum score 550 paper-based; 213 computer-based). *Faculty research:* At-risk programs, principal retention, mentoring beginning principals.

Southwestern Adventist University, Education Department, Graduate Program, Keene, TX 76059. Offers curriculum and instruction with reading emphasis (M Ed); educational leadership (M Ed). Part-time and evening/weekend programs available. *Degree requirements:* For master's, thesis or alternative, professional paper. *Entrance requirements:* For master's, GRE General Test.

Southwestern Assemblies of God University, Thomas F. Harrison School of Graduate Studies, Program in Education, Waxahachie, TX 75165-5735. Offers Christian school administration (MS); curriculum development (MS); early education administration (M Ed); middle and secondary education (M Ed). *Degree requirements:* For master's, comprehensive written and oral exams. *Entrance requirements:* For master's, GRE General Test, minimum GPA of 2.5. Electronic applications accepted.

Southwestern College, Education Programs, Winfield, KS 67156-2499. Offers curriculum and instruction (M Ed); special education (M Ed); teaching (MA). *Accreditation:* NCATE. Part-time and evening/weekend programs available. Postbaccalaureate distance learning degree programs offered (minimal on-campus study). *Faculty:* 2 full-time (1 woman), 14 part-time/adjunct (12 women). *Students:* 1 (woman) full-time, 112 part-time (88 women); includes 9 minority (2 African Americans, 1 American Indian/Alaska Native, 3 Asian Americans or Pacific Islanders, 3 Hispanic Americans), 2 international. Average age 37. 50 applicants, 98% accepted, 46 enrolled. In 2009, 18 master's awarded. *Degree requirements:* For master's, practicum, portfolio. *Entrance requirements:* For master's, baccalaureate degree, minimum GPA of 2.5, valid teaching certificate (for special education). Additional exam requirements/recommendations for international students: Required—TOEFL (minimum score 550 paper-based; 213 computer-based). *Application deadline:* For fall admission, 8/1 for domestic students; for spring admission, 12/1 for domestic students. Applications are processed on a rolling basis. Application fee: $0. Electronic applications accepted. *Expenses:* Contact institution. *Financial support:* In 2009–10, 77 students received support. Federal Work-Study, tuition waivers (partial), and unspecified assistantships available. Financial award application deadline: 4/1; financial award applicants required to submit FAFSA. *Unit head:* Dr. David Hofmeister, Director of Teacher Education, 800-846-1543 Ext. 6115, Fax: 620-229-6341, E-mail: david.hofmeister@sckans.edu. *Application contact:* Lindy Kralicek, Education Program Representative, 888-684-5335 Ext. 130, Fax: 316-688-5218, E-mail: lindy.kralicek@sckans.edu.

Southwestern Oklahoma State University, College of Professional and Graduate Studies, School of Behavioral Sciences and Education, Weatherford, OK 73096-3098. Offers community counseling (M Ed); early childhood education (M Ed); educational administration (M Ed); elementary education (M Ed); health sciences and microbiology (M Ed); kinesiology (M Ed); parks and recreation management (M Ed); school counseling (M Ed); school psychology (MS); school psychometry (M Ed); secondary education (M Ed); special education (M Ed). *Accreditation:* NCATE. Part-time and evening/weekend programs available. Postbaccalaureate distance learning degree programs offered (minimal on-campus study). *Degree requirements:* For master's, exam. *Entrance requirements:* For master's, GRE General Test or minimum undergraduate GPA of 3.0. Additional exam requirements/recommendations for international students: Required—TOEFL.

Southwest Minnesota State University, Department of Education, Marshall, MN 56258. Offers education (MS); special education (MS). Part-time and evening/weekend programs available. Postbaccalaureate distance learning degree programs offered (no on-campus study). *Faculty:* 12 full-time (8 women), 11 part-time/adjunct (5 women). *Students:* 317 full-time (233 women), 95 part-time (71 women); includes 11 minority (4 African Americans, 2 Asian Americans or Pacific Islanders, 5 Hispanic Americans), 2 international. Average age 30. In 2009, 101 master's awarded. *Entrance requirements:* Additional exam requirements/recommendations for international students: Required—TOEFL or IELTS. *Application deadline:* For fall admission, 8/28 for domestic students, 6/15 for international students; for spring admission, 1/15 for domestic students, 12/15 for international students. Applications are processed on a rolling basis. Application fee: $20. *Expenses:* Tuition, state resident: full-time $5487; part-time $304.85 per credit. Tuition, nonresident: full-time $5487; part-time $304.85 per credit. Required fees: $680; $37.76 per credit. Tuition and fees vary according to course load and reciprocity agreements. *Financial support:* Institutionally sponsored loans and unspecified assistantships available. Support available to part-time students. Financial award application deadline: 3/1; financial award applicants required to submit FAFSA. *Unit head:* Dr. Donna Burgraff, Dean of Business, Education and Professional Studies, 507-537-6218, E-mail: donna.burgraff@smsu.edu. *Application contact:* CoriAnn Dahlager, Graduate Office Coordinator, 507-537-6819, E-mail: coriann.dahlager@smsu.edu.

Spalding University, Graduate Studies, College of Education, Louisville, KY 40203-2188. Offers MA, MAT, Ed D. *Accreditation:* NCATE. Part-time and evening/weekend programs available. *Faculty:* 10 full-time (6 women), 40 part-time/adjunct (26 women). *Students:* 150 full-time (112 women), 134 part-time (86 women); includes 73 minority (69 African Americans, 2 American Indian/Alaska Native, 1 Asian American or Pacific Islander, 1 Hispanic American), 29 international. Average age 37. 79 applicants, 78% accepted, 57 enrolled. In 2009, 56 master's, 15 doctorates awarded. *Degree requirements:* For master's, portfolio, final project, clinical experience; for doctorate, comprehensive exam, thesis/dissertation. *Entrance*

Education—General

Spalding University (continued)
requirements: For master's and doctorate, GRE General Test or MAT, interview, resume, recommendations. Additional exam requirements/recommendations for international students: Required—TOEFL (minimum score 535 paper-based; 203 computer-based). *Application deadline:* Applications are processed on a rolling basis. Application fee: $30. Electronic applications accepted. *Expenses:* Tuition: Full-time $11,340; part-time $630 per credit hour. Tuition and fees vary according to program. *Financial support:* In 2009–10, 121 students received support, including 4 research assistantships with partial tuition reimbursements available (averaging $3,638 per year); scholarships/grants, traineeships, and unspecified assistantships also available. Financial award application deadline: 3/15; financial award applicants required to submit FAFSA. *Faculty research:* School leadership, assessment of student learning, classroom management. *Unit head:* Dr. Beverly Keepers, Dean, 502-588-7121, Fax: 502-585-7123, E-mail: bkeepers@spalding.edu. *Application contact:* Admissions Office, 502-585-7111, E-mail: admissions@spalding.edu.

Spring Arbor University, School of Education, Spring Arbor, MI 49283-9799. Offers education (MAE); special education (MSE). *Accreditation:* NCATE. Part-time programs available. *Faculty:* 8 full-time (5 women), 4 part-time/adjunct (1 woman). *Students:* 28 full-time (all women), 129 part-time (109 women); includes 12 minority (7 African Americans, 2 Asian Americans or Pacific Islanders, 3 Hispanic Americans), 1 international. Average age 38. In 2009, 69 master's awarded. *Degree requirements:* For master's, thesis. *Entrance requirements:* For master's, GRE if GPA is below 2.5, writing sample, 2 professional letters of recommendation. Additional exam requirements/recommendations for international students: Required—TOEFL (minimum score 550 paper-based; 220 computer-based). *Application deadline:* For fall admission, 9/1 priority date for domestic students; for winter admission, 2/1 priority date for domestic students; for spring admission, 2/1 priority date for domestic students. Applications are processed on a rolling basis. Application fee: $40. Electronic applications accepted. *Expenses:* Tuition: Full-time $5400; part-time $450 per credit hour. Required fees: $240; $150 per year. Tuition and fees vary according to course load and program. *Financial support:* Applicants required to submit FAFSA. *Unit head:* Dr. Linda Sherrill, Dean, 517-750-1200 Ext. 1562, Fax: 517-750-6629, E-mail: lsherril@arbor.edu. *Application contact:* Terri Reeves, Coordinator of Graduate Recruitment, 517-750-6554, Fax: 517-750-6629, E-mail: treeves@arbor.edu.

Springfield College, Graduate Programs, Program in Education, Springfield, MA 01109-3797. Offers counseling and secondary education (M Ed, MS); early childhood education (M Ed, MS); education (M Ed, MS); educational administration (M Ed, MS); educational studies (M Ed, MS); elementary education (M Ed, MS); secondary education (M Ed, MS); special education (M Ed, MS). Part-time and evening/weekend programs available. *Entrance requirements:* Additional exam requirements/recommendations for international students: Required—TOEFL (minimum score 550 paper-based; 213 computer-based). Electronic applications accepted. *Expenses:* Tuition: Full-time $19,800; part-time $825 per credit hour. Required fees: $150.

Spring Hill College, Graduate Programs, Program in Education, Mobile, AL 36608-1791. Offers early childhood education (MAT, MS Ed); educational theory (MS Ed); elementary education (MAT, MS Ed); secondary education (MAT, MS Ed). Part-time programs available. *Faculty:* 3 full-time (all women), 3 part-time/adjunct (2 women). *Students:* 9 full-time (7 women), 26 part-time (21 women); includes 6 minority (5 African Americans, 1 Asian American or Pacific Islander). Average age 31. 33 applicants, 48% accepted, 9 enrolled. In 2009, 14 master's awarded. *Degree requirements:* For master's, comprehensive exam, completion of program within 6 calendar years of entrance into graduate studies at Spring Hill. *Entrance requirements:* For master's, GRE, MAT, NTE, or PRAXIS, bachelor's degree. Additional exam requirements/recommendations for international students: Required—TOEFL (minimum score 550 paper-based; 213 computer-based; 80 iBT), IELTS (minimum score 6.5). *Application deadline:* For fall admission, 8/1 priority date for domestic and international students; for spring admission, 12/1 priority date for domestic and international students. Applications are processed on a rolling basis. Application fee: $25 ($35 for international students). Electronic applications accepted. *Expenses:* Contact institution. *Financial support:* In 2009–10, 24 students received support. Career-related internships or fieldwork, institutionally sponsored loans, and scholarships/grants available. Support available to part-time students. Financial award applicants required to submit FAFSA. *Unit head:* Dr. Ann A. Adams, Chair of Teacher Education, 251-380-3479, Fax: 251-460-2184, E-mail: aadams@shc.edu. *Application contact:* Donna B. Tarasavage, Director of Marketing and Recruiting, Graduate and Continuing Studies, 251-380-3067, Fax: 251-460-2190, E-mail: dtarasavage@shc.edu.

Stanford University, School of Education, Stanford, CA 94305-9991. Offers MA, Ed D, PhD. *Accreditation:* NCATE. *Degree requirements:* For doctorate, thesis/dissertation. *Entrance requirements:* For master's and doctorate, GRE General Test. Electronic applications accepted. *Expenses:* Tuition: Full-time $37,380; part-time $2760 per quarter. Required fees: $501.

State University of New York at Binghamton, Graduate School, School of Education, Binghamton, NY 13902-6000. Offers MAT, MS Ed, MST, Ed D. *Accreditation:* Teacher Education Accreditation Council. Part-time and evening/weekend programs available. *Faculty:* 23 full-time (14 women), 18 part-time/adjunct (13 women). *Students:* 165 full-time (100 women), 149 part-time (109 women); includes 15 minority (3 African Americans, 1 American Indian/Alaska Native, 4 Asian Americans or Pacific Islanders, 7 Hispanic Americans), 7 international. Average age 31. 162 applicants, 75% accepted, 102 enrolled. In 2009, 100 master's, 1 doctorate awarded. *Degree requirements:* For doctorate, thesis/dissertation. *Entrance requirements:* For master's, GRE General Test; for doctorate, GRE General Test, writing sample. Additional exam requirements/recommendations for international students: Required—TOEFL (minimum score 550 paper-based; 213 computer-based; 80 iBT). *Application deadline:* For fall admission, 2/1 priority date for domestic and international students; for spring admission, 10/15 priority date for domestic and international students. Applications are processed on a rolling basis. Application fee: $60. Electronic applications accepted. *Financial support:* In 2009–10, 35 students received support, including 7 fellowships with full tuition reimbursements available (averaging $12,000 per year), 17 teaching assistantships with full tuition reimbursements available (averaging $12,000 per year); research assistantships, career-related internships or fieldwork, Federal Work-Study, institutionally sponsored loans, scholarships/grants, health care benefits, tuition waivers (full and partial), and unspecified assistantships also available. Financial award application deadline: 2/15; financial award applicants required to submit FAFSA. *Unit head:* Dr. S. G. Grant, Dean, 607-777-7329, E-mail: ssgrant@binghamton.edu. *Application contact:* Victoria Williams, Recruiting and Admissions Coordinator, 607-777-2151, Fax: 607-777-2501, E-mail: vwilliam@binghamton.edu.

State University of New York at Fredonia, Graduate Studies, College of Education, Fredonia, NY 14063-1136. Offers educational administration (CAS); elementary education (MS Ed); literacy (MS Ed); secondary education (MS Ed); teaching English to speakers of other languages (MS Ed). *Accreditation:* NCATE. Part-time and evening/weekend programs available. *Degree requirements:* For master's, thesis optional; for CAS, thesis or alternative. *Expenses:* Tuition, state resident: full-time $8370; part-time $349 per credit. Tuition, nonresident: full-time $13,250; part-time $552 per credit. Required fees: $1289; $53.55 per credit.

State University of New York at New Paltz, Graduate School, School of Education, New Paltz, NY 12561. Offers MAT, MPS, MS Ed, MST, CAS. *Accreditation:* NCATE. Part-time and evening/weekend programs available. *Faculty:* 33 full-time (22 women), 22 part-time/adjunct (18 women). *Students:* 197 full-time (146 women), 490 part-time (374 women); includes 63 minority (15 African Americans, 7 American Indian/Alaska Native, 10 Asian Americans or Pacific Islanders, 31 Hispanic Americans), 2 international. Average age 32. 350 applicants, 59% accepted, 169 enrolled. In 2009, 311 master's, 85 other advanced degrees awarded. *Degree requirements:* For master's, comprehensive exam (for some programs), portfolio; for CAS, internship. *Entrance requirements:* For master's, GRE, MAT, minimum GPA of 3.0, New York State Teaching Certificate; for CAS, minimum GPA of 3.0. Additional exam requirements/recommendations for international students: Required—TOEFL (minimum score 550 paper-based; 213 computer-based; 80 iBT), IELTS (minimum score 6.5). *Application deadline:* For fall admission, 3/1 priority date for domestic and international students; for spring admission, 10/1 priority date for domestic and international students. Applications are processed on a rolling basis. Application fee: $50. Electronic applications accepted. *Financial support:* In 2009–10, 12 students received support, including 3 fellowships (averaging $9,000 per year); career-related internships or fieldwork, Federal Work-Study, institutionally sponsored loans, scholarships/grants, and tuition waivers (full) also available. Financial award application deadline: 8/1; financial award applicants required to submit FAFSA. *Faculty research:* Kindergarten readiness, translation learning experiences, assessment in mathematics education, long- and short-term outcomes of delayed school entry, parental involvement in children's education. *Unit head:* Dr. Robert Michael, Dean, 845-257-2800, E-mail: michaelr@newpaltz.edu. *Application contact:* Caroline Murphy, Graduate Admissions Advisor, 845-257-3285, Fax: 845-257-3284, E-mail: gradschool@newpaltz.edu.

State University of New York at Oswego, Graduate Studies, School of Education, Oswego, NY 13126. Offers MAT, MS, MS Ed, CAS, MS Ed/CAS, MS/CAS. *Accreditation:* NCATE. Part-time programs available. *Entrance requirements:* For degree, GRE General Test, interview, MA or MS, minimum GPA of 3.0. Additional exam requirements/recommendations for international students: Required—TOEFL (minimum score 560 paper-based; 220 computer-based).

State University of New York College at Cortland, Graduate Studies, School of Education, Cortland, NY 13045. Offers childhood/early child education (MS Ed, MST); educational leadership (CAS); literacy (MS Ed); teaching students with disabilities (MS Ed). *Accreditation:* NCATE. Part-time and evening/weekend programs available. *Entrance requirements:* Additional exam requirements/recommendations for international students: Required—TOEFL.

State University of New York College at Geneseo, Graduate Studies, School of Education, Geneseo, NY 14454-1401. Offers childhood multicultural education (1-6) (MS Ed); early childhood education (MS Ed); elementary education (MS Ed); reading (MS Ed); secondary education (MS Ed). *Accreditation:* NCATE. Part-time and evening/weekend programs available. *Faculty:* 31 full-time (18 women), 3 part-time/adjunct (0 women). *Students:* 26 full-time (24 women), 79 part-time (67 women); includes 3 minority (1 African American, 2 Asian Americans or Pacific Islanders). Average age 26. 73 applicants, 100% accepted, 59 enrolled. In 2009, 46 master's awarded. *Degree requirements:* For master's, thesis optional. *Application deadline:* For fall admission, 3/1 priority date for domestic students; for spring admission, 10/1 for domestic students. Application fee: $50. *Expenses:* Tuition, state resident: full-time $8370; part-time $349 per credit hour. Tuition, nonresident: full-time $13,250; part-time $552 per credit hour. Required fees: $700.52; $29 per credit hour. *Financial support:* In 2009–10, 6 students received support. Scholarships/grants, health care benefits, tuition waivers (full), and unspecified assistantships available. Support available to part-time students. Financial award application deadline: 4/1; financial award applicants required to submit FAFSA. *Unit head:* Dr. Osman Alawiye, Dean/Chairperson, 585-245-5560, Fax: 585-245-5220, E-mail: alawiyeo@geneseo.edu. *Application contact:* Dr. Susan Salmon, Assistant to the Dean/Graduate Liaison, 585-245-5560, Fax: 585-245-5220, E-mail: salmon@geneseo.edu.

State University of New York College at Oneonta, Graduate Education, Division of Education, Oneonta, NY 13820-4015. Offers educational psychology and counseling (MS Ed, CAS), including school counselor K-12; educational technology specialist (MS Ed); elementary education and reading (MS Ed), including childhood education, literacy education; secondary education (MS Ed), including adolescence education, family and consumer science education; special education (MS Ed), including adolescence, childhood. *Accreditation:* NCATE. Part-time and evening/weekend programs available. *Students:* 16 full-time (10 women), 66 part-time (39 women). Average age 25. 80 applicants, 94% accepted, 75 enrolled. In 2009, 18 master's awarded. *Entrance requirements:* For master's, GRE General Test. *Application deadline:* For fall admission, 3/25 priority date for domestic students; for spring admission, 10/1 priority date for domestic students. Applications are processed on a rolling basis. Application fee: $50. *Expenses:* Tuition, state resident: part-time $349 per credit hour. Tuition, nonresident: full-time $12,870; part-time $552 per credit hour. Required fees: $1280; $15.85 per credit hour. *Unit head:* Dr. Joanne Curran, Associate Dean, 607-436-2541, Fax: 607-436-2554, E-mail: curranjm@oneonta.edu. *Application contact:* Dean, 607-436-2523, Fax: 607-436-3084, E-mail: gradoffice@oneonta.edu.

State University of New York Empire State College, Graduate Studies, Program in Teaching, Saratoga Springs, NY 12866-4391. Offers MA.

Stephen F. Austin State University, Graduate School, College of Education, Nacogdoches, TX 75962. Offers M Ed, MA, MS, Ed D. *Accreditation:* NCATE. Part-time and evening/weekend programs available. *Degree requirements:* For master's, comprehensive exam; for doctorate, thesis/dissertation. *Entrance requirements:* For master's, GRE General Test; for doctorate, GRE General Test, interview, writing sample. Additional exam requirements/recommendations for international students: Required—TOEFL.

Stetson University, College of Arts and Sciences, Division of Education, DeLand, FL 32723. Offers M Ed, MS. *Accreditation:* NCATE (one or more programs are accredited). Part-time and evening/weekend programs available. *Students:* 99 full-time (82 women), 51 part-time (48 women); includes 38 minority (16 African Americans, 3 American Indian/Alaska Native, 19 Hispanic Americans), 2 international. Average age 33. In 2009, 101 master's awarded. *Entrance requirements:* For master's, GRE General Test or MAT. *Application deadline:* For fall admission, 3/1 priority date for domestic students; for spring admission, 11/1 for domestic students. Applications are processed on a rolling basis. Application fee: $25. Tuition and fees vary according to course load, campus/location and program. *Financial support:* Career-related internships or fieldwork, institutionally sponsored loans, scholarships/grants, and tuition waivers (partial) available. Support available to part-time students. *Faculty research:* Values, cultural diversity, cooperative learning, reading. *Application contact:* Diana Belian, Office of Graduate Studies, 386-822-7075, Fax: 386-822-7388, E-mail: dbelian@stetson.edu.

Strayer University, Graduate Studies, Washington, DC 20005-2603. Offers accounting (MS); acquisition (MBA); business administration (MBA); communications technology (MS); educational management (M Ed); finance (MBA); health services administration (MHSA); hospitality and tourism management (MBA); human resource management (MBA); information systems (MS), including computer security management, decision support system management, enterprise resource management, network management, software engineering management, systems development management; management (MBA); management information systems (MS); marketing (MBA); professional accounting (MS), including accounting information systems, controllership, taxation; public administration (MPA); supply chain management (MBA); technology in education (M Ed). Programs also offered at campus locations in Birmingham, AL; Chamblee, GA; Cobb County, GA; Morrow, GA; White Marsh, MD; Charleston, SC; Columbia, SC; Greensboro, NC; Greenville, SC; Lexington, KY; Louisville, KY; Nashville, TN; North Raleigh, NC; Washington, DC. Part-time and evening/weekend programs available. Postbaccalaureate distance learning degree programs offered (minimal on-campus study). *Degree requirements:* For master's, thesis. *Entrance requirements:* For master's, GMAT, GRE General Test, bachelor's degree from an accredited college or university, minimum undergraduate GPA of 2.75. Electronic applications accepted.

Suffolk University, College of Arts and Sciences, Department of Education and Human Services, Boston, MA 02108-2770. Offers administration of higher education (M Ed, CAGS), including administration of higher education (M Ed), leadership (CAGS); human resource, learning and performance (MS, CAGS, Graduate Certificate), including global human resources (Graduate Certificate), human resources (MS, Graduate Certificate), organizational development (CAGS, Graduate Certificate), organizational learning and development (MS, Graduate Certificate); mental health counseling (MS, CAGS); school counseling (M Ed, CAGS); school teaching (M Ed, CAGS), including foundations of education (M Ed), middle school teaching (M Ed), secondary school teaching (M Ed); MPA/MSMHC; MS/Certificate. Part-time and evening/weekend programs available. *Faculty:* 19 full-time (11 women), 13 part-time/adjunct (6 women). *Students:* 50 full-time (38 women), 146 part-time (109 women); includes 14 minority (8 African Americans, 1 American Indian/Alaska Native, 3 Asian Americans or Pacific Islanders, 2 Hispanic

Americans), 9 international. Average age 28. 175 applicants, 78% accepted, 70 enrolled. In 2009, 75 master's, 4 other advanced degrees awarded. *Entrance requirements:* For master's, GRE General Test or MAT, 2 letters of recommendation, resume. Additional exam requirements/recommendations for international students: Required—TOEFL (minimum score 550 paper-based; 213 computer-based; 80 iBT). *Application deadline:* For fall admission, 6/15 priority date for domestic students, 6/15 for international students; for spring admission, 11/1 priority date for domestic students, 11/1 for international students. Applications are processed on a rolling basis. Application fee: $50. Electronic applications accepted. *Expenses:* Contact institution. *Financial support:* In 2009–10, 106 students received support, including 31 fellowships with full and partial tuition reimbursements available (averaging $10,803 per year); career-related internships or fieldwork, Federal Work-Study, and institutionally sponsored loans also available. Support available to part-time students. Financial award application deadline: 4/1; financial award applicants required to submit FAFSA. *Faculty research:* Predicting competent Head Start preschools, cultural differences. *Unit head:* Dr. Glen Eskedal, Chairperson, 617-573-8264 Ext. 8261, Fax: 617-305-1743, E-mail: geskedal@suffolk.edu. *Application contact:* Judith Reynolds, Director of Graduate Admissions, 617-573-8302, Fax: 617-305-1733, E-mail: grad.admission@suffolk.edu.

Sul Ross State University, Rio Grande College of Sul Ross State University, Alpine, TX 79832. Offers business administration (MBA); teacher education (M Ed), including bilingual education, counseling, educational diagnostics, elementary education, general education, reading, school administration, secondary education. Part-time and evening/weekend programs available. *Degree requirements:* For master's, thesis optional. *Entrance requirements:* For master's, GMAT or GRE General Test, minimum GPA of 2.5 in last 60 hours of undergraduate work. *Faculty research:* Drug and substance abuse counseling, U.S.-Mexico border economic development.

Sul Ross State University, School of Professional Studies, Department of Teacher Education, Alpine, TX 79832. Offers bilingual education (M Ed); counseling (M Ed); educational diagnostics (M Ed); elementary education (M Ed); reading specialist (M Ed); school administration (M Ed); secondary education (M Ed); supervision (M Ed). Part-time and evening/weekend programs available. *Degree requirements:* For master's, thesis optional. *Entrance requirements:* For master's, GMAT or GRE General Test, minimum GPA of 2.5 in last 60 hours of undergraduate work. *Faculty research:* Critical thinking skills, adolescent eating disorders, reading-based study skills, cross-cultural adaptations, educational leadership.

Sweet Briar College, Department of Education, Sweet Briar, VA 24595. Offers M Ed, MAT. Part-time programs available. *Degree requirements:* For master's, comprehensive exam (for some programs), thesis. *Entrance requirements:* For master's, PRAXIS I and II, Virginia Communication and Literacy Assessment (MAT), GRE (M Ed), Virginia Reading Assessment (MAT), current teaching license (M Ed). Electronic applications accepted. *Faculty research:* Differentiation K-12 student achievement, mentoring and teacher retention, teaching science by inquiry.

Syracuse University, School of Education, Syracuse, NY 13244. Offers M Mus, MS, Ed D, PhD, CAS, Ed D/PhD. *Accreditation:* NCATE. Part-time programs available. *Faculty:* 51 full-time (32 women), 46 part-time/adjunct (32 women). *Students:* 351 full-time (254 women), 290 part-time (210 women); includes 74 minority (39 African Americans, 6 American Indian/Alaska Native, 19 Asian Americans or Pacific Islanders, 10 Hispanic Americans), 61 international. Average age 33. 436 applicants, 74% accepted, 162 enrolled. In 2009, 174 master's, 21 doctorates, 21 other advanced degrees awarded. *Degree requirements:* For master's, thesis or alternative; for doctorate, thesis/dissertation; for CAS, thesis. *Entrance requirements:* For master's, GRE (for some programs); for doctorate and CAS, GRE. Additional exam requirements/recommendations for international students: Required—TOEFL (minimum score 100 iBT). *Application deadline:* For fall admission, 2/1 priority date for domestic and international students; for spring admission, 10/15 priority date for domestic and international students. Applications are processed on a rolling basis. Application fee: $75. Electronic applications accepted. *Expenses:* Tuition: Full-time $26,808; part-time $1117 per credit. Required fees: $1024. *Financial support:* Fellowships with full and partial tuition reimbursements, research assistantships with full and partial tuition reimbursements, teaching assistantships with full and partial tuition reimbursements, career-related internships or fieldwork, institutionally sponsored loans, scholarships/grants, health care benefits, tuition waivers (partial), and unspecified assistantships available. Support available to part-time students. Financial award application deadline: 1/1; financial award applicants required to submit FAFSA. *Faculty research:* Teaching and curriculum, reading and language arts, literacy, inclusive education, communication sciences and disorders. *Unit head:* Dr. Douglas Biklen, Dean, 315-443-4751. *Application contact:* Liza Rochelson, Graduate Recruiter, School of Education, 315-443-2505, E-mail: e-gradrcrt@syr.edu.

Tarleton State University, College of Graduate Studies, College of Education, Stephenville, TX 76402. Offers M Ed, Ed D, Certificate. Part-time and evening/weekend programs available. Postbaccalaureate distance learning degree programs offered (minimal on-campus study). *Degree requirements:* For master's, comprehensive exam, thesis (for some programs); for doctorate, thesis/dissertation. *Entrance requirements:* For master's, GRE General Test, minimum GPA of 3.0; for doctorate, GRE, 4 letters of reference, leadership portfolio. Additional exam requirements/recommendations for international students: Required—TOEFL (minimum score 550 paper-based; 213 computer-based; 80 iBT). Electronic applications accepted.

Teachers College, Columbia University, Graduate Faculty of Education, New York, NY 10027-6696. Offers Ed M, MA, MS, Ed D, Ed DCT, PhD, Certificate, MBA/Ed D. *Accreditation:* NCATE. Part-time and evening/weekend programs available. *Faculty:* 152 full-time (90 women). *Students:* 1,776 full-time (1,394 women), 3,326 part-time (2,524 women); includes 1,404 minority (469 African Americans, 609 Asian Americans or Pacific Islanders, 326 Hispanic Americans), 544 international. Average age 31. 4,901 applicants, 59% accepted, 1319 enrolled. In 2009, 1,774 master's, 220 doctorates awarded. *Degree requirements:* For doctorate, comprehensive exam, thesis/dissertation. Application fee: $65. Electronic applications accepted. *Financial support:* Fellowships, research assistantships, teaching assistantships, career-related internships or fieldwork, Federal Work-Study, institutionally sponsored loans, traineeships, tuition waivers (full and partial), and unspecified assistantships available. Support available to part-time students. Financial award application deadline: 2/1. *Faculty research:* Education and the economy, postsecondary governance and finance, career success, dropout prevention evaluation, education across the lifespan. *Unit head:* Susan Furhman, President, 212-678-3050. *Application contact:* Thomas Rock, Director of Admissions, 212-678-3083, Fax: 212-678-4171, E-mail: rock@tc.edu.

Temple University, Graduate School, College of Education, Philadelphia, PA 19122-6096. Offers Ed M, MS Ed, Ed D, PhD. *Accreditation:* Teacher Education Accreditation Council. Part-time and evening/weekend programs available. Terminal master's awarded for partial completion of doctoral program. *Degree requirements:* For doctorate, thesis/dissertation. *Entrance requirements:* For master's, GRE General Test or MAT, minimum GPA of 3.0. Additional exam requirements/recommendations for international students: Required—TOEFL (minimum score 550 paper-based; 213 computer-based; 79 iBT). Electronic applications accepted. *Faculty research:* School improvement in city schools, teaching strategies, student motivation, individual differences in learning, educational leadership and policy studies.

Tennessee State University, The School of Graduate Studies and Research, College of Education, Nashville, TN 37209-1561. Offers M Ed, MA Ed, MS, Ed D, PhD, Ed S. *Accreditation:* NCATE. Part-time and evening/weekend programs available. *Degree requirements:* For doctorate, thesis/dissertation. *Entrance requirements:* For doctorate, minimum GPA of 3.25. *Faculty research:* Class size, biobehavioral research, equity, dropout rate, K–12 teachers: first 5 years of employment.

Tennessee Technological University, Graduate School, College of Education, Cookeville, TN 38505. Offers M Ed, MA, PhD, Ed S. *Accreditation:* NCATE. Part-time and evening/weekend programs available. *Faculty:* 58 full-time (16 women). *Students:* 428 full-time (314 women), 747 part-time (571 women); includes 76 minority (55 African Americans, 5 American Indian/Alaska Native, 4 Asian Americans or Pacific Islanders, 12 Hispanic Americans). Average age 27. 951 applicants, 88% accepted, 599 enrolled. In 2009, 305 master's, 5 doctorates, 249 other advanced degrees awarded. *Degree requirements:* For master's and Ed S, comprehensive exam, thesis or alternative; for doctorate, comprehensive exam, thesis/dissertation. *Entrance requirements:* For master's, GRE or MAT; for doctorate, GRE; for Ed S, MAT or GRE. Additional exam requirements/recommendations for international students: Required—TOEFL (minimum score 550 paper-based; 79 iBT), IELTS (minimum score 5.5). *Application deadline:* For fall admission, 8/1 for domestic students, 5/1 for international students; for spring admission, 12/1 for domestic students, 10/1 for international students. Application fee: $25 ($30 for international students). Electronic applications accepted. *Expenses:* Tuition, state resident: full-time $7034; part-time $368 per credit hour. *Financial support:* In 2009–10, 42 fellowships (averaging $8,000 per year), 33 research assistantships (averaging $4,000 per year), 26 teaching assistantships (averaging $4,000 per year) were awarded; career-related internships or fieldwork also available. Support available to part-time students. Financial award application deadline: 4/1. *Faculty research:* Teacher evaluation. *Unit head:* Dr. Larry Peach, Interim Dean, 931-372-3124, Fax: 931-372-6319, E-mail: lpeach@tntech.edu. *Application contact:* Shelia K. Kendrick, Coordinator of Graduate Studies, 931-372-3808, Fax: 931-372-3497, E-mail: skendrick@tntech.edu.

Tennessee Temple University, Graduate Studies in Education, Chattanooga, TN 37404. Offers M Ed. Part-time programs available. *Degree requirements:* For master's, comprehensive exam, thesis or alternative. *Entrance requirements:* For master's, GRE, minimum GPA of 3.0.

Texas A&M International University, Office of Graduate Studies and Research, College of Education, Laredo, TX 78041-1900. Offers MS, MS Ed, PhD. Part-time and evening/weekend programs available. *Faculty:* 17 full-time (6 women), 3 part-time/adjunct (2 women). *Students:* 31 full-time (18 women), 401 part-time (322 women); includes 411 minority (1 African American, 1 American Indian/Alaska Native, 409 Hispanic Americans), 2 international. Average age 34. 235 applicants, 78% accepted, 119 enrolled. In 2009, 108 master's awarded. *Degree requirements:* For master's, thesis (for some programs). *Entrance requirements:* For master's, GRE General Test. Additional exam requirements/recommendations for international students: Required—TOEFL (minimum score 550 paper-based; 213 computer-based). *Application deadline:* For fall admission, 4/30 priority date for domestic students; for spring admission, 11/30 for domestic students. Applications are processed on a rolling basis. Application fee: $25. *Financial support:* In 2009–10, 101 students received support, including 5 fellowships, 10 research assistantships; Federal Work-Study and institutionally sponsored loans also available. Support available to part-time students. Financial award application deadline: 11/1; financial award applicants required to submit FAFSA. *Unit head:* Dr. Humberto Gonzalez, Dean, 956-326-2420, E-mail: hgonzalez@tamiu.edu. *Application contact:* Rosie Espinoza-Dickinson, Director of Admissions, 956-326-2200, Fax: 956-326-2199, E-mail: enroll@tamiu.edu.

Texas A&M University, College of Education and Human Development, College Station, TX 77843. Offers M Ed, MS, Ed D, PhD. Part-time and evening/weekend programs available. Postbaccalaureate distance learning degree programs offered (no on-campus study). *Faculty:* 141. *Students:* 569 full-time (386 women), 762 part-time (544 women); includes 400 minority (164 African Americans, 8 American Indian/Alaska Native, 33 Asian Americans or Pacific Islanders, 195 Hispanic Americans), 148 international. Average age 36. In 2009, 263 master's, 86 doctorates awarded. *Degree requirements:* For doctorate, thesis/dissertation. *Entrance requirements:* For master's and doctorate, GRE General Test. Additional exam requirements/recommendations for international students: Required—TOEFL. Application fee: $50 ($75 for international students). Electronic applications accepted. *Expenses:* Tuition, state resident: full-time $3991; part-time $221.74 per credit hour. Tuition, nonresident: full-time $9049; part-time $502.74 per credit hour. *Financial support:* In 2009–10, fellowships with partial tuition reimbursements (averaging $12,000 per year), research assistantships with partial tuition reimbursements (averaging $10,000 per year), teaching assistantships with partial tuition reimbursements (averaging $10,000 per year) were awarded; career-related internships or fieldwork, Federal Work-Study, institutionally sponsored loans, scholarships/grants, tuition waivers (partial), and unspecified assistantships also available. Financial award applicants required to submit FAFSA. *Unit head:* Doug Palmer, Dean, 979-845-5311, E-mail: dpalmer@tamu.edu. *Application contact:* Becky Carr, Assistant Dean, 979-845-5311, Fax: 979-845-6129, E-mail: bcarr@tamu.edu.

Texas A&M University–Commerce, Graduate School, College of Education and Human Services, Commerce, TX 75429-3011. Offers M Ed, MA, MS, MSW, Ed D, PhD. Part-time programs available. Terminal master's awarded for partial completion of doctoral program. *Degree requirements:* For master's, comprehensive exam; for doctorate, thesis/dissertation, departmental qualifying exam. *Entrance requirements:* For master's and doctorate, GRE General Test. Electronic applications accepted. *Faculty research:* Reading, early childhood, deviance, migration, physical fitness.

Texas A&M University–Corpus Christi, Graduate Studies and Research, College of Education, Corpus Christi, TX 78412-5503. Offers counseling (MS, PhD), including counseling (MS), counselor education (PhD); curriculum and instruction (MS, Ed D); early childhood education (MS); educational administration (MS); educational leadership (Ed D); educational technology (MS); elementary education (MS); kinesiology (MS); reading (MS); secondary education (MS); special education (MS). Part-time and evening/weekend programs available. *Degree requirements:* For master's, comprehensive exam, thesis (for some programs); for doctorate, comprehensive exam, thesis/dissertation. *Entrance requirements:* For master's, GRE General Test. Additional exam requirements/recommendations for international students: Required—TOEFL. Electronic applications accepted.

Texas A&M University–Kingsville, College of Graduate Studies, College of Education, Kingsville, TX 78363. Offers M Ed, MA, MS, Ed D, PhD. Part-time and evening/weekend programs available. *Degree requirements:* For master's, comprehensive exam; for doctorate, one foreign language, comprehensive exam, thesis/dissertation. *Entrance requirements:* For master's, GRE General Test, minimum GPA of 3.0; for doctorate, GRE General Test, MAT, minimum GPA of 3.25. *Faculty research:* Rural schools, facilities planning, linguistics.

Texas A&M University–Texarkana, Graduate Studies and Research, College of Education and Liberal Arts, Texarkana, TX 75505-5518. Offers adult education (MS); curriculum and instruction (M Ed); education (MS); educational administration (M Ed); English (MA); instructional technology (MS); interdisciplinary studies (MA, MS); special education (MS). Part-time and evening/weekend programs available. *Degree requirements:* For master's, comprehensive exam (for some programs), thesis optional. *Entrance requirements:* For master's, minimum GPA of 2.5 on last 60 hours of bachelor's degree. Additional exam requirements/recommendations for international students: Required—TOEFL. Electronic applications accepted.

Texas Christian University, College of Education, Fort Worth, TX 76129-0002. Offers M Ed, Ed D, PhD, Certificate, MBA/Ed D. Part-time and evening/weekend programs available. *Degree requirements:* For master's, oral exams; for doctorate, capstone project. *Entrance requirements:* For doctorate, GRE or MAT. Additional exam requirements/recommendations for international students: Required—TOEFL (minimum score 550 paper-based; 213 computer-based; 80 iBT). *Application deadline:* For fall admission, 7/15 for domestic and international students; for spring admission, 11/15 for domestic and international students. Applications are processed on a rolling basis. Application fee: $50. *Expenses:* Tuition: Full-time $17,640; part-time $980 per credit hour. Tuition and fees vary according to program. *Financial support:* Teaching assistantships with full tuition reimbursements, career-related internships or fieldwork and unspecified assistantships available. Financial award application deadline: 3/15; financial award applicants required to submit FAFSA. *Unit head:* Dr. Kay B. Stevens, Dean, 817-257-7661, E-mail: k.stevens2@tcu.edu. *Application contact:* Robyn P. Shepheard, Academic Program Specialist, 817-257-7661, E-mail: r.shepheard@tcu.edu.

Texas Southern University, College of Education, Houston, TX 77004-4584. Offers M Ed, MS, Ed D. Part-time and evening/weekend programs available. *Faculty:* 24 full-time (12 women), 3 part-time/adjunct (0 women). *Students:* 125 full-time (97 women), 225 part-time (181 women);

Education—General

Texas Southern University (continued)
includes 310 minority (294 African Americans, 3 Asian Americans or Pacific Islanders, 13 Hispanic Americans), 3 international. Average age 36. 132 applicants, 95% accepted, 98 enrolled. In 2009, 68 master's, 13 doctorates awarded. *Degree requirements:* For master's, comprehensive exam; for doctorate, comprehensive exam, thesis/dissertation. *Entrance requirements:* For master's, GRE General Test, minimum GPA of 2.5; for doctorate, GRE General Test or MAT, master's degree, minimum B+ average. Additional exam requirements/recommendations for international students: Required—TOEFL. *Application deadline:* For fall admission, 7/1 for domestic and international students; for spring admission, 11/1 for domestic and international students. Applications are processed on a rolling basis. Application fee: $50 ($75 for international students). Electronic applications accepted. *Expenses:* Tuition, state resident: full-time $1805; part-time $100 per credit hour. Tuition, nonresident: full-time $6470; part-time $343 per credit hour. Tuition and fees vary according to course level, course load and degree level. *Financial support:* In 2009–10, 2 research assistantships (averaging $6,500 per year), 5 teaching assistantships (averaging $5,525 per year) were awarded; fellowships, scholarships/grants and unspecified assistantships also available. Support available to part-time students. Financial award application deadline: 5/1. *Unit head:* Dr. Jay Cummings, Dean, E-mail: cummings_jr@tsu.edu. *Application contact:* Dr. Gregory Maddox, Dean of the Graduate School, 713-313-7011 Ext. 4410, Fax: 713-639-1876, E-mail: maddox_gh@tsu.edu.

Texas State University–San Marcos, Graduate School, College of Education, San Marcos, TX 78666. Offers M Ed, MA, MSRLS, PhD, SSP. Part-time and evening/weekend programs available. *Faculty:* 89 full-time (53 women), 34 part-time/adjunct (26 women). *Students:* 504 full-time (368 women), 886 part-time (708 women); includes 414 minority (83 African Americans, 5 American Indian/Alaska Native, 29 Asian Americans or Pacific Islanders, 297 Hispanic Americans), 12 international. Average age 32. 659 applicants, 76% accepted, 355 enrolled. In 2009, 356 master's, 8 doctorates awarded. *Degree requirements:* For master's, comprehensive exam, thesis (for some programs). *Entrance requirements:* For master's, GRE (for some programs). Additional exam requirements/recommendations for international students: Required—TOEFL (minimum score 550 paper-based; 213 computer-based). *Application deadline:* For fall admission, 6/15 priority date for domestic students; for spring admission, 10/15 priority date for domestic students. Applications are processed on a rolling basis. Application fee: $40 ($90 for international students). Electronic applications accepted. *Expenses:* Tuition, state resident: full-time $5784; part-time $241 per credit hour. Tuition, nonresident: full-time $13,224; part-time $551 per credit hour. Required fees: $1728; $48 per credit hour. $306. Tuition and fees vary according to course load. *Financial support:* In 2009–10, 982 students received support, including 75 research assistantships (averaging $5,648 per year), 58 teaching assistantships (averaging $5,162 per year); fellowships, career-related internships or fieldwork, Federal Work-Study, and institutionally sponsored loans also available. Support available to part-time students. Financial award application deadline: 4/1; financial award applicants required to submit FAFSA. *Faculty research:* Texas Family Literacy Resource Center, Adult Education Credential project. Total annual research expenditures: $1.9 million. *Unit head:* Dr. Rosalinda Barrera, Dean, 512-245-2150, Fax: 512-245-8345, E-mail: rb43@txstate.edu. *Application contact:* Dr. J. Michael Willoughby, Dean of Graduate School, 512-245-2581, Fax: 512-245-8365, E-mail: gradcollege@txstate.edu.

Texas Tech University, Graduate School, College of Education, Lubbock, TX 79409. Offers M Ed, Ed D, PhD. *Accreditation:* NCATE. Part-time programs available. *Faculty:* 61 full-time (39 women), 6 part-time/adjunct (5 women). *Students:* 332 full-time (238 women), 595 part-time (436 women); includes 208 minority (51 African Americans, 7 American Indian/Alaska Native, 9 Asian Americans or Pacific Islanders, 141 Hispanic Americans), 51 international. Average age 35. 976 applicants, 65% accepted, 266 enrolled. In 2009, 172 master's, 23 doctorates awarded. *Degree requirements:* For master's, thesis or alternative; for doctorate, thesis/dissertation. *Entrance requirements:* For master's and doctorate, GRE General Test. Additional exam requirements/recommendations for international students: Required—TOEFL (minimum score 550 paper-based; 213 computer-based). *Application deadline:* For fall admission, 3/1 priority date for international students; for spring admission, 11/1 priority date for international students. Applications are processed on a rolling basis. Application fee: $50 ($75 for international students). Electronic applications accepted. *Expenses:* Contact institution. *Financial support:* In 2009–10, 4 research assistantships with partial tuition reimbursements (averaging $19,389 per year), 1 teaching assistantship with partial tuition reimbursement (averaging $10,800 per year) were awarded; career-related internships or fieldwork, Federal Work-Study, and institutionally sponsored loans also available. Support available to part-time students. Financial award application deadline: 4/15; financial award applicants required to submit FAFSA. *Faculty research:* Multicultural foundations of education, teacher education, psychological processes of teaching and learning, teaching populations with special needs, institutional technology. Total annual research expenditures: $907,242. *Unit head:* Dr. Charles Ruch, Interim Dean, 806-742-1998 Ext. 450, Fax: 806-742-2179, E-mail: charles.ruch@ttu.edu. *Application contact:* Stephenie Allyn McDaniel, Administrative Assistant, 806-742-1988 Ext. 434, Fax: 806-742-2179, E-mail: stephenie.mcdaniel@ttu.edu.

Texas Wesleyan University, Graduate Programs, Programs in Education, Fort Worth, TX 76105-1536. Offers education (M Ed, Ed D); marriage and family therapy (MSMFT); professional counseling (MA); school counseling (MS). Part-time and evening/weekend programs available. Postbaccalaureate distance learning degree programs offered (no on-campus study). *Faculty:* 11 full-time (7 women), 3 part-time/adjunct (2 women). *Students:* 56 full-time (47 women), 208 part-time (174 women); includes 102 minority (54 African Americans, 2 American Indian/Alaska Native, 3 Asian Americans or Pacific Islanders, 43 Hispanic Americans), 4 international. Average age 36. 102 applicants, 77% accepted, 66 enrolled. In 2009, 179 master's awarded. *Entrance requirements:* For master's, GRE General Test, minimum GPA of 3.0 in final 60 hours of undergraduate course work, interview. *Application deadline:* For fall admission, 6/15 priority date for domestic students; for spring admission, 10/15 priority date for domestic students. Applications are processed on a rolling basis. Application fee: $40 ($50 for international students). Tuition and fees vary according to degree level. *Financial support:* Career-related internships or fieldwork, Federal Work-Study, scholarships/grants, and tuition waivers (full and partial) available. Support available to part-time students. Financial award application deadline: 3/15; financial award applicants required to submit FAFSA. *Faculty research:* Teacher effectiveness, bilingual education, analytic teaching. *Unit head:* Dr. Carlos Martinez, Dean, School of Education, 817-531-4940, Fax: 817-531-4943. *Application contact:* DeTrae Warren, Graduate Admission Recruiter, 817-531-4931, Fax: 817-531-4935, E-mail: dwarren@txwes.edu.

Texas Woman's University, Graduate School, College of Professional Education, Denton, TX 76201. Offers M Ed, MA, MAT, MLS, MS, Ed D, PhD. Part-time and evening/weekend programs available. *Faculty:* 70 full-time (56 women), 18 part-time/adjunct (15 women). *Students:* 281 full-time (252 women), 1,154 part-time (1,067 women); includes 424 minority (198 African Americans, 11 American Indian/Alaska Native, 34 Asian Americans or Pacific Islanders, 181 Hispanic Americans), 36 international. Average age 36. 511 applicants, 84% accepted, 255 enrolled. In 2009, 490 master's, 26 doctorates awarded. Terminal master's awarded for partial completion of doctoral program. *Degree requirements:* For master's, comprehensive exam (for some programs), thesis (for some programs); for doctorate, comprehensive exam, thesis/dissertation. *Entrance requirements:* For master's and doctorate, minimum GPA of 3.0. Additional exam requirements/recommendations for international students: Required—TOEFL (minimum score 550 paper-based; 213 computer-based; 79 iBT). *Application deadline:* For fall admission, 7/1 priority date for domestic students, 3/1 for international students; for spring admission, 12/1 priority date for domestic students, 7/1 for international students. Applications are processed on a rolling basis. Application fee: $50. Electronic applications accepted. *Expenses:* Tuition, state resident: full-time $3564; part-time $198 per credit hour. Tuition, nonresident: full-time $8550; part-time $475 per credit hour. Required fees: $69.26 per credit hour. Tuition and fees vary according to course load. *Financial support:* In 2009–10, 270 students received support, including 39 research assistantships (averaging $11,198 per year), 8 teaching assistantships (averaging $10,886 per year); career-related internships or fieldwork, Federal Work-Study, institutionally sponsored loans, scholarships/grants, traineeships, health care benefits, and unspecified assistantships also available. Support available to part-time students. Financial award application deadline: 3/1; financial award applicants required to submit FAFSA. *Unit head:* Dr. Nan L. Restine, Dean, 940-898-2202, Fax: 940-898-2209, E-mail: cope@twu.edu. *Application contact:* Samuel Wheeler, Assistant Director of Admissions, 940-898-3188, Fax: 940-898-3081, E-mail: wheelersr@twu.edu.

Thomas More College, Program in Teaching, Crestview Hills, KY 41017-3495. Offers MAT. *Faculty:* 4 full-time (3 women), 4 part-time/adjunct (all women). *Students:* 1 (woman) full-time, 30 part-time (15 women). Average age 31. 25 applicants, 88% accepted, 18 enrolled. In 2009, 18 master's awarded. *Degree requirements:* For master's, comprehensive exam. *Entrance requirements:* For master's, GRE (minimum combined score of 1200 if GPA less than 2.7), PRAXIS II in content area, minimum undergraduate content GPA of 2.7, interview. Additional exam requirements/recommendations for international students: Required—TOEFL (minimum score 600 paper-based; 250 computer-based; 100 iBT). *Application deadline:* For fall admission, 6/1 for domestic students. Applications are processed on a rolling basis. Application fee: $0. Electronic applications accepted. *Expenses:* Tuition: Full-time $11,242.50; part-time $527 per credit. Tuition and fees vary according to program. *Financial support:* In 2009–10, 5 students received support. Federal Work-Study, institutionally sponsored loans, and scholarships/grants available. Financial award application deadline: 3/15; financial award applicants required to submit FAFSA. *Unit head:* Joyce Hamberg, Director, 859-344-3404, Fax: 859-344-3345, E-mail: joyce.hamberg@thomasmore.edu. *Application contact:* Joyce Hamberg, 859-344-3404, Fax: 859-344-3345, E-mail: joyce.hamberg@thomasmore.edu.

Thomas University, Department of Education, Thomasville, GA 31792-7499. Offers M Ed. Part-time programs available. *Entrance requirements:* For master's, resume, 3 academic/professional references. Additional exam requirements/recommendations for international students: Required—TOEFL (minimum score 600 paper-based; 250 computer-based). Electronic applications accepted.

Thompson Rivers University, Program in Education, Kamloops, BC V2C 5N3, Canada. Offers M Ed. Part-time programs available. *Entrance requirements:* For master's, 2 letters of reference, minimum GPA of 3.0 in final 2 years of undergraduate degree.

Touro University, Graduate Programs, Vallejo, CA 94592. Offers education (MA); osteopathic medicine (DO); pharmacy (Pharm D); physical therapy (DPT); physician assistant studies (MS); public health (MPH). *Accreditation:* AOsA; ARC-PA. Part-time and evening/weekend programs available. *Faculty:* 91 full-time (52 women), 51 part-time/adjunct (28 women). *Students:* 1,439 full-time (891 women). 6,914 applicants, 12% accepted, 503 enrolled. In 2009, 229 first professional degrees, 103 master's awarded. *Degree requirements:* For master's, comprehensive exam, thesis; for first professional degree, comprehensive exam. *Entrance requirements:* BS/BA. *Application deadline:* For fall admission, 3/15 for domestic students; for winter admission, 12/1 for domestic students. Applications are processed on a rolling basis. Application fee: $100. Electronic applications accepted. *Financial support:* In 2009–10, 1,236 students received support, including 119 fellowships (averaging $1,535 per year), 24 research assistantships (averaging $3,686 per year), 13 teaching assistantships (averaging $4,058 per year); Federal Work-Study and scholarships/grants also available. Support available to part-time students. Financial award applicants required to submit FAFSA. *Faculty research:* Cancer, heart disease. *Application contact:* Steve Davis, Associate Director of Admissions, 707-638-5270, Fax: 707-638-5250, E-mail: steven.davis@tu.edu.

Towson University, College of Graduate Studies and Research, Program in Teaching, Towson, MD 21252-0001. Offers MAT. *Degree requirements:* For master's, portfolio. *Entrance requirements:* For master's, PRAXIS I, 2 letters of reference, resume. Additional exam requirements/recommendations for international students: Required—TOEFL (minimum score 550 paper-based). Electronic applications accepted. *Faculty research:* Professional development.

Trevecca Nazarene University, Graduate Division, School of Education, Nashville, TN 37210-2877. Offers educational leadership (M Ed); English language learners (PreK-12) (M Ed); instructional effectiveness (M Ed); instructional technology (M Ed); leadership and professional practice (Ed D); library and information science (MLI Sc); reading PreK-12 (M Ed); teaching (MAT), including teaching 7-12, teaching K-6. *Accreditation:* NCATE. Part-time and evening/weekend programs available. *Faculty:* 13 full-time (9 women), 22 part-time/adjunct (13 women). *Students:* 546 full-time (408 women), 75 part-time (53 women); includes 132 minority (118 African Americans, 1 American Indian/Alaska Native, 4 Asian Americans or Pacific Islanders, 9 Hispanic Americans), 2 international. Average age 36. In 2009, 275 master's, 23 doctorates awarded. *Degree requirements:* For master's, exit assessment; for doctorate, thesis/dissertation, proposal study, symposium presentation. *Entrance requirements:* For master's, GRE General Test, MAT, minimum GPA of 2.7, 2 reference forms; for doctorate, GMAT, GRE, MAT, or NTE, minimum GPA of 3.4, resume, writing sample, interview, reference forms. Additional exam requirements/recommendations for international students: Required—TOEFL (minimum score 550 paper-based; 213 computer-based). *Application deadline:* Applications are processed on a rolling basis. Application fee: $50. *Expenses:* Contact institution. *Financial support:* Applicants required to submit FAFSA. *Unit head:* Dr. Esther Swink, Dean/Director of Graduate Education Programs, 615-248-1201, Fax: 615-248-1597, E-mail: eswink@trevecca.edu. *Application contact:* Admissions Office, 615-248-1201, Fax: 615-248-1597, E-mail: admissions_ged@trevecca.edu.

Trinity Baptist College, Graduate Programs, Jacksonville, FL 32221. Offers Bible (M Ed); Christian school administration (M Ed); classroom practices (M Ed); ministry (M Min); special education (M Ed). Postbaccalaureate distance learning degree programs offered. *Entrance requirements:* For master's, GRE (M Ed), 2 letters of recommendation; minimum GPA of 2.5 (M Min) or 3.0 (M Ed); computer proficiency.

Trinity International University, Trinity Graduate School, Deerfield, IL 60015-1284. Offers bioethics (MA); communication and culture (MA); counseling psychology (MA); instructional leadership (M Ed); teaching (MA). Part-time and evening/weekend programs available. Postbaccalaureate distance learning degree programs offered (minimal on-campus study). *Degree requirements:* For master's, comprehensive exam. *Entrance requirements:* For master's, GRE General Test or MAT, minimum undergraduate GPA of 3.0. Additional exam requirements/recommendations for international students: Required—TOEFL (minimum score 580 paper-based; 237 computer-based), TWE (minimum score 4). Electronic applications accepted.

Trinity University, Department of Education, San Antonio, TX 78212-7200. Offers school administration (M Ed); school psychology (MA); teacher education (MAT). *Accreditation:* NCATE. Part-time and evening/weekend programs available. *Entrance requirements:* For master's, GRE General Test, minimum GPA of 3.0, interview.

Trinity (Washington) University, School of Education, Washington, DC 20017-1094. Offers counseling (MA); early childhood education (MAT); educating for change (M Ed); educational administration (MSA); elementary education (MAT); school counseling (MA); secondary education (MAT), including English, social studies; special education (MAT); teaching English as a second language (MAT); teaching English to speakers of other languages (M Ed); the teaching of reading (M Ed). *Accreditation:* NCATE. Part-time and evening/weekend programs available. *Degree requirements:* For master's, thesis (for some programs), capstone project(s). *Entrance requirements:* For master's, PRAXIS I, minimum GPA of 2.8. Additional exam requirements/recommendations for international students: Required—TOEFL (minimum score 550 paper-based; 213 computer-based). *Faculty research:* Technology, literacy, special education, organizations, inclusion models.

Troy University, Graduate School, College of Arts and Sciences, Program in Public Administration, Troy, AL 36082. Offers education (MPA); environmental management (MPA); government contracting (MPA); health care administration (MPA); justice administration (MPA); management information systems (MPA); national security affairs (MPA); nonprofit management (MPA); public human resources management (MPA); public management (MPA). *Accreditation:* NASPAA. Part-time and evening/weekend programs available. Postbaccalaureate distance

learning degree programs offered (no on-campus study). *Students:* 239 full-time (161 women), 652 part-time (416 women); includes 596 minority (547 African Americans, 11 American Indian/Alaska Native, 6 Asian Americans or Pacific Islanders, 32 Hispanic Americans). Average age 34. 415 applicants, 80% accepted. In 2009, 247 master's awarded. *Degree requirements:* For master's, capstone course, research methodologies course. *Entrance requirements:* For master's, GRE, MAT or GMAT, minimum undergraduate GPA of 2.5, letter of recommendation. Additional exam requirements/recommendations for international students: Required—TOEFL (minimum score 523 paper-based; 193 computer-based; 70 iBT), IELTS (minimum score 6). *Application deadline:* Applications are processed on a rolling basis. Application fee: $50. Electronic applications accepted. *Financial support:* Available to part-time students. Applicants required to submit FAFSA. *Unit head:* Dr. Ellen Rosell, Chairman, 334-670-3758, Fax: 334-670-5647, E-mail: erosell@troy.edu. *Application contact:* Brenda K. Campbell, Director of Graduate Admissions, 334-670-3178, Fax: 334-670-3733, E-mail: bcamp@troy.edu.

Troy University, Graduate School, College of Education, Troy, AL 36082. Offers M Ed, MS, Ed S. *Accreditation:* NCATE. Part-time and evening/weekend programs available. *Students:* 855 full-time (677 women), 1,339 part-time (1,278 women). Average age 33. 1,124 applicants, 91% accepted. In 2009, 860 master's, 244 other advanced degrees awarded. *Degree requirements:* For master's, comprehensive exam, thesis. *Entrance requirements:* For master's, GRE General Test, MAT or GMAT, minimum GPA of 2.5; for Ed S, GRE General Test, MAT or GMAT, Alabama Class A certificate or equivalent, minimum graduate GPA of 3.0. Additional exam requirements/recommendations for international students: Required—TOEFL (minimum score 523 paper-based; 193 computer-based; 70 iBT), IELTS (minimum score 6). *Application deadline:* For fall admission, 6/1 for international students; for spring admission, 10/15 for international students. Applications are processed on a rolling basis. Application fee: $50. Electronic applications accepted. *Financial support:* Career-related internships or fieldwork available. Support available to part-time students. Financial award applicants required to submit FAFSA. *Unit head:* Dr. Lance Tatum, Interim Dean, 334-670-3365, Fax: 334-670-3474, E-mail: ltatum@troy.edu. *Application contact:* Brenda K. Campbell, Director of Graduate Admissions, 334-670-3178, Fax: 334-670-3733, E-mail: bcamp@troy.edu.

Truman State University, Graduate School, School of Health Sciences and Education, Program in Education, Kirksville, MO 63501-4221. Offers MAE. *Accreditation:* NCATE. *Degree requirements:* For master's, comprehensive exam, thesis or alternative. *Entrance requirements:* For master's, GRE, minimum GPA of 2.75. Additional exam requirements/recommendations for international students: Required—TOEFL (minimum score 550 paper-based; 213 computer-based). Electronic applications accepted. *Expenses:* Tuition, state resident: part-time $291 per credit. Tuition, nonresident: part-time $499 per credit hour. Tuition and fees vary according to course load.

Tufts University, Graduate School of Arts and Sciences, Department of Education, Medford, MA 02155. Offers education (MA, MAT, MS, PhD), including education (MS, PhD), middle and secondary education (MA, MAT), secondary education (MA); school psychology (MA, Ed S). *Faculty:* 13 full-time, 9 part-time/adjunct. *Students:* 163 (122 women); includes 26 minority (9 African Americans, 2 American Indian/Alaska Native, 6 Asian Americans or Pacific Islanders, 9 Hispanic Americans), 4 international. Average age 27. 249 applicants, 74% accepted, 94 enrolled. In 2009, 90 master's, 5 doctorates, 16 other advanced degrees awarded. *Degree requirements:* For doctorate, thesis/dissertation. *Entrance requirements:* For master's and doctorate, GRE General Test. Additional exam requirements/recommendations for international students: Required—TOEFL (minimum score 550 paper-based; 213 computer-based; 80 iBT). *Application deadline:* For fall admission, 2/1 for domestic students, 12/15 for international students; for spring admission, 10/15 for domestic students, 9/15 for international students. Applications are processed on a rolling basis. Application fee: $75. Electronic applications accepted. *Expenses:* Tuition: Full-time $38,096; part-time $3962 per credit. Required fees: $686; $40 per year. Tuition and fees vary according to course level, course load, degree level, program and student level. *Financial support:* Teaching assistantships with full and partial tuition reimbursements, Federal Work-Study, scholarships/grants, and tuition waivers (partial) available. Support available to part-time students. Financial award application deadline: 2/1; financial award applicants required to submit FAFSA. *Unit head:* Barbara Brizuela, Chair, 617-627-3244, Fax: 617-627-3901. *Application contact:* Patricia Romeo, Department Administrator, 617-627-3244.

TUI University, College of Education, Cypress, CA 90630. Offers MA Ed, PhD. Part-time and evening/weekend programs available. Postbaccalaureate distance learning degree programs offered (no on-campus study). *Degree requirements:* For doctorate, comprehensive exam, thesis/dissertation, defense of dissertation. *Entrance requirements:* For master's, minimum GPA of 2.5 (students with GPA 3.0 or greater may transfer up to 30% of graduate level credits); for doctorate, minimum GPA of 3.4, curriculum vitae, course work in research methods or statistics. Additional exam requirements/recommendations for international students: Required—TOEFL (minimum score 525 paper-based). Electronic applications accepted.

Tusculum College, Graduate School, Program in Education, Greeneville, TN 37743-9997. Offers adult education (MA Ed); K–12 (MA Ed). Evening/weekend programs available. *Degree requirements:* For master's, thesis or alternative. *Entrance requirements:* For master's, 3 years of work experience, minimum GPA of 2.75.

Union College, Graduate Programs, Department of Education, Barbourville, KY 40906-1499. Offers elementary education (MA); health and physical education (MA); middle grades (MA); music education (MA); principalship (MA); reading specialist (MA); secondary education (MA); special education (MA). *Degree requirements:* For master's, thesis optional. *Entrance requirements:* For master's, GRE General Test, NTE.

Union Graduate College, School of Education, Schenectady, NY 12308-3107. Offers biology (MAT, MS); chemistry (MAT); Chinese (MAT); earth science (MAT); English (MAT); French (MAT); general science (MAT); German (MAT); Greek (MAT); languages (MAT); Latin (MAT); mathematics (MAT); mathematics and technology (MS); mentoring and teacher leadership (AC); middle childhood extension (AC); national board certificate and teacher leadership (AC); physical science (MS); physics (MAT); social studies (MAT); Spanish (MAT). *Accreditation:* Teacher Education Accreditation Council. *Faculty:* 3 full-time (1 woman), 39 part-time/adjunct (19 women). *Students:* 46 full-time (27 women), 45 part-time (39 women); includes 5 minority (1 Asian American or Pacific Islander, 4 Hispanic Americans), 2 international. Average age 33. 66 applicants, 73% accepted, 39 enrolled. In 2009, 44 master's awarded. *Degree requirements:* For master's, thesis or project. *Entrance requirements:* For master's, minimum GPA of 3.0, letters of recommendation. Additional exam requirements/recommendations for international students: Required—TOEFL (minimum score 550 paper-based; 213 computer-based). *Application deadline:* Applications are processed on a rolling basis. Application fee: $60. Electronic applications accepted. *Expenses:* Contact institution. *Financial support:* In 2009–10, 12 research assistantships with tuition reimbursements (averaging $3,000 per year) were awarded; Federal Work-Study, scholarships/grants, health care benefits, and tuition waivers (partial) also available. Support available to part-time students. Financial award applicants required to submit FAFSA. *Faculty research:* Transformative learning, science education, National Board Certification, teacher leadership, teacher quality. *Unit head:* Dr. Patrick Allen, Dean, 518-631-9870, Fax: 518-631-9901. *Application contact:* Christine Angley, Assistant, 518-631-9871, Fax: 518-631-9903, E-mail: angleyc@uniongraduatecollege.edu.

Union Institute & University, Doctor of Education Program, Cincinnati, OH 45206-1925. Offers educational leadership (Ed D); higher education (Ed D). Postbaccalaureate distance learning degree programs offered (minimal on-campus study). *Faculty:* 2 full-time (0 women), 7 part-time/adjunct (3 women). *Students:* 19 full-time (13 women); includes 5 minority (3 African Americans, 2 Hispanic Americans). Average age 49. *Application deadline:* Applications are processed on a rolling basis. Tuition and fees vary according to course load, degree level, campus/location and program. *Financial support:* Federal Work-Study and scholarships/grants available. *Unit head:* Dr. Arlene Sacks, Dean, 305-653-6713, E-mail: arlene.sacks@myunion.edu. *Application contact:* Michelle Flick, Admissions Counselor, 513-861-6400 Ext. 1225, E-mail: admissions@tui.edu.

Union Institute & University, Education Programs–Florida Center, North Miami Beach, FL 33162. Offers educational leadership (M Ed, Ed S); exceptional student education (M Ed, Ed S); guidance and counseling (M Ed, Ed S); reading (M Ed, Ed S). *Faculty:* 3 full-time (1 woman), 23 part-time/adjunct (19 women). *Students:* 32 full-time (21 women); includes 23 minority (21 African Americans, 2 Hispanic Americans). Average age 37. In 2009, 8 master's, 3 Ed Ss awarded. *Degree requirements:* For master's, thesis or alternative, portfolio. *Entrance requirements:* For master's, letters of recommendation. *Application deadline:* Applications are processed on a rolling basis. Application fee: $50. *Expenses:* Contact institution. *Financial support:* Federal Work-Study, scholarships/grants, and tuition waivers (partial) available. Financial award applicants required to submit FAFSA. *Unit head:* Dr. Arlene Sacks, Dean, 305-653-6713 Ext. 2152, E-mail: arlene.sacks@myunion.edu. *Application contact:* Josefina Rosario, Admissions Counselor, 305-653-6713 Ext. 2172, E-mail: admissions@tui.edu.

Union Institute & University, Master of Arts Program–Online, Montpelier, VT 05602. Offers creativity studies (MA); education (MA); health and wellness (MA); history and culture (MA); leadership, public policy, and social issues (MA); literature and writing (MA); psychology (MA). Part-time programs available. Postbaccalaureate distance learning degree programs offered (no on-campus study). *Faculty:* 3 full-time (1 woman), 16 part-time/adjunct (11 women). *Students:* 27 full-time (23 women), 113 part-time (84 women); includes 30 minority (22 African Americans, 2 American Indian/Alaska Native, 1 Asian American or Pacific Islander, 5 Hispanic Americans). Average age 40. In 2009, 26 master's awarded. *Degree requirements:* For master's, thesis. *Application deadline:* Applications are processed on a rolling basis. Application fee: $50. Electronic applications accepted. *Expenses:* Contact institution. *Financial support:* Career-related internships or fieldwork and tuition waivers available. Financial award applicants required to submit FAFSA. *Unit head:* Dr. Brian Webb, Program Director, 802-828-8777, E-mail: brian.webb@tui.edu. *Application contact:* Kathleen Murphy, Interim Director of Admissions—Montpelier, 888-828-8575, E-mail: admissions@myunion.edu.

Union Institute & University, M Ed Program–Online, Cincinnati, OH 45206-1925. Offers M Ed. Postbaccalaureate distance learning degree programs offered (no on-campus study). *Faculty:* 3 full-time (1 woman), 23 part-time/adjunct (19 women). *Students:* 2 full-time (0 women); includes 1 African American. *Degree requirements:* For master's, electronic portfolio. *Application deadline:* Applications are processed on a rolling basis. Tuition and fees vary according to course load, degree level, campus/location and program. *Financial support:* Federal Work-Study and scholarships/grants available. Financial award applicants required to submit FAFSA. *Unit head:* Dr. Arlene Sacks, Dean, 305-653-6713. *Application contact:* Michelle Flick, Admissions Counselor, 513-861-6400 Ext. 1225, E-mail: cinti-admissions@tui.edu.

Union Institute & University, M Ed Program–Vermont Campus, Montpelier, VT 05602. Offers school administration (M Ed), including principalship; school counseling (M Ed); teaching (M Ed), including art, early childhood, elementary, English, math, middle schools, science, social studies, special education. *Faculty:* 3 full-time (1 woman), 23 part-time/adjunct (19 women). *Students:* 41 part-time (29 women). Average age 38. In 2009, 15 master's awarded. *Degree requirements:* For master's, thesis. *Entrance requirements:* For master's, 3 letters of reference. *Application deadline:* Applications are processed on a rolling basis. Application fee: $50. *Expenses:* Contact institution. *Financial support:* Federal Work-Study, scholarships/grants, and tuition waivers available. Financial award applicants required to submit FAFSA. *Unit head:* Dr. Arlene Sacks, Dean, Graduate Programs in Education, 305-653-6713 Ext. 2152, E-mail: arlene.sacks@myunion.edu. *Application contact:* Dr. Arlene Sacks, Dean, Graduate Programs in Education, 305-653-6713 Ext. 2152, E-mail: arlene.sacks@myunion.edu.

Union University, School of Education, Jackson, TN 38305-3697. Offers education (M Ed, MA Ed); education administration generalist (Ed S); educational leadership (Ed D); educational supervision (Ed S); higher education (Ed D). M Ed also available at Germantown campus. *Accreditation:* NCATE. Part-time and evening/weekend programs available. *Degree requirements:* For master's, thesis (for some programs), capstone research course; for doctorate, comprehensive exam, thesis/dissertation; for Ed S, thesis or alternative. *Entrance requirements:* For master's, MAT, PRAXIS II or GRE, minimum GPA of 3.0, teaching license, writing sample; for doctorate, GRE, minimum graduate GPA of 3.2, writing sample; for Ed S, PRAXIS II, minimum graduate GPA of 3.2, writing sample. *Faculty research:* Mathematics education, direct instruction, language disorders and special education, brain compatible learning, empathy and school leadership.

Universidad Adventista de las Antillas, EGECED Department, Mayagüez, PR 00681-0118. Offers curriculum and instruction (MA), including secondary biology, secondary history, secondary Spanish; education (MA), including ESL (elementary school level), ESL (high school level), school administration and supervision. *Degree requirements:* For master's, comprehensive exam (for some programs), thesis (for some programs). *Entrance requirements:* For master's, EXADEP or GRE General Test, recommendations. Application fee: $175. Electronic applications accepted. *Expenses:* Tuition: Full-time $3990; part-time $190 per credit. Required fees: $570; $190 per credit. $1375 per summer. *Financial support:* Fellowships, Federal Work-Study available. *Unit head:* Dr. Zilma Sepulveda, Director, 787-834-9595 Ext. 2282, Fax: 787-834-9595, E-mail: zsantiago@uaa.edu. *Application contact:* Prof. Evelyn del Valle, Admissions Department Director, 787-834-9595 Ext. 2261, Fax: 787-834-9597, E-mail: admissions@uaa.edu.

Universidad Autonoma de Guadalajara, Graduate Programs, Guadalajara, Mexico. Offers administrative law and justice (LL M); advertising and corporate communications (MA); architecture (M Arch); business (MBA); computational science (MCC); education (Ed M, Ed D); English-Spanish translation (MA); fiscal law (MA); integrated management of digital animation (MA); international business (MIB); international corporate law (LL M); internet technologies (MS); labor health (MS); manufacturing systems (MMS); philosophy (MA, PhD); power electronics (MS); quality systems (MQS); renewable energy (MS); social evaluation of projects (MBA); strategic market research (MBA); teaching mathematics (MA).

Universidad de las Americas, A.C., Program in Education, Mexico City, Mexico. Offers M Ed. *Entrance requirements:* For master's, 2 years of professional experience; undergraduate degree in early childhood education, human communication, psychology, science of education, special education or related fields.

Universidad de las Américas–Puebla, Division of Graduate Studies, School of Social Sciences, Program in Education, Puebla, Mexico. Offers MA. Part-time and evening/weekend programs available. *Degree requirements:* For master's, one foreign language, thesis. *Faculty research:* Curriculum development, curriculum evaluation, instructional technology, critical thinking.

Universidad del Turabo, Graduate Programs, Programs in Education, Gurabo, PR 00778-3030. Offers administration of school libraries (Certificate); athletic training (MPHE); coaching (MPHE); curriculum and instruction and appropriate environment (D Ed); curriculum and teaching (M Ed); educational administration (M Ed); educational leadership (D Ed); guidance counseling (M Ed); library service and information technology (M Ed); special education (M Ed); teaching at primary level (M Ed); teaching English as a second language (M Ed); teaching of fine arts (M Ed); wellness (MPHE). Part-time and evening/weekend programs available. *Students:* 408 full-time (306 women), 559 part-time (448 women); includes 804 Hispanic Americans. Average age 36. 475 applicants, 93% accepted, 344 enrolled. In 2009, 463 master's, 5 doctorates awarded. *Entrance requirements:* For master's, GRE, EXADEP, interview. *Application deadline:* For fall admission, 8/5 for domestic students. Application fee: $25. *Financial support:* Institutionally sponsored loans available. *Unit head:* Angela Candelario, Dean, 787-743-7979 Ext. 4126. *Application contact:* Virginia Gonzalez, Admissions Officer, 787-746-3009.

Universidad FLET, Department of Graduate Studies, Miami, FL 33186. Offers education (M Ed); theological studies (MTS). *Degree requirements:* For master's, thesis or project. *Entrance requirements:* For master's, letter of recommendation.

Universidad Metropolitana, Graduate Programs in Education, San Juan, PR 00928-1150. Offers administration and supervision (M Ed); curriculum and teaching (M Ed); educational

Education—General

Universidad Metropolitana (continued)
administration and supervision (M Ed); environmental education (M Ed); fitness management (M Ed); managing leisure services (M Ed); pre-school centers administration (M Ed); pre-school education (M Ed); special education (M Ed); teaching of physical education (M Ed). Part-time and evening/weekend programs available. *Degree requirements:* For master's, thesis or alternative. Electronic applications accepted.

Université de Moncton, Faculty of Education, Graduate Studies in Education, Moncton, NB E1A 3E9, Canada. Offers educational psychology (M Ed, MA Ed); guidance (M Ed, MA Ed); school administration (M Ed, MA Ed); teaching (M Ed, MA Ed). Part-time programs available. *Degree requirements:* For master's, proficiency in English and French. *Entrance requirements:* For master's, minimum GPA of 3.0. *Faculty research:* Guidance, ethnolinguistic vitality, children's rights, ecological education, entrepreneurship.

Université de Montréal, Faculty of Education, Montréal, QC H3C 3J7, Canada. Offers M Ed, MA, PhD, DESS. Part-time and evening/weekend programs available. *Faculty:* 71 full-time (39 women), 19 part-time/adjunct (9 women). *Students:* 325 full-time (196 women), 911 part-time (652 women). 819 applicants, 60% accepted, 375 enrolled. In 2009, 97 master's, 13 doctorates, 144 other advanced degrees awarded. *Degree requirements:* For doctorate, thesis/dissertation, general exam. *Application deadline:* For fall admission, 2/1 priority date for domestic students; for winter admission, 11/1 priority date for domestic students; for spring admission, 2/1 priority date for domestic students. Application fee: $100. Electronic applications accepted. *Financial support:* Fellowships, research assistantships, teaching assistantships available. *Unit head:* Louise Poirier, Dean, 514-343-6658, Fax: 514-343-7276, E-mail: louise.poirier.2@umontreal.ca. *Application contact:* Francois Bowen, Graduate Chairman and Vice Dean, 514-343-7491, Fax: 514-343-7276, E-mail: francois.bowen@umontreal.ca.

Université de Sherbrooke, Faculty of Education, Sherbrooke, QC J1K 2R1, Canada. Offers M Ed, MA, Diploma. Part-time and evening/weekend programs available. *Degree requirements:* For master's, thesis. *Faculty research:* Career education, teaching, professional instruction.

Université du Québec à Chicoutimi, Graduate Programs, Program in Education, Chicoutimi, QC G7H 2B1, Canada. Offers M Ed, MA, PhD. Part-time programs available. *Degree requirements:* For doctorate, thesis/dissertation. *Entrance requirements:* For master's, appropriate bachelor's degree, proficiency in French; for doctorate, appropriate master's degree, proficiency in French.

Université du Québec à Montréal, Graduate Programs, Program in Education, Montréal, QC H3C 3P8, Canada. Offers education (M Ed, MA, PhD); education of the environmental sciences (Diploma). Part-time programs available. *Degree requirements:* For master's, thesis (for some programs); for doctorate, thesis/dissertation. *Entrance requirements:* For master's and Diploma, appropriate bachelor's degree or equivalent, proficiency in French; for doctorate, appropriate master's degree or equivalent, proficiency in French.

Université du Québec à Rimouski, Graduate Programs, Program in Education, Rimouski, QC G5L 3A1, Canada. Offers M Ed, MA, PhD, Diploma. Part-time programs available. *Degree requirements:* For master's, thesis optional; for doctorate, thesis/dissertation. *Entrance requirements:* For master's, appropriate bachelor's degree, proficiency in French; for doctorate, appropriate master's degree, proficiency in French.

Université du Québec à Trois-Rivières, Graduate Programs, Program in Education, Trois-Rivières, QC G9A 5H7, Canada. Offers M Ed, PhD. Part-time programs available. *Degree requirements:* For master's, research report. *Entrance requirements:* For master's, appropriate bachelor's degree, proficiency in French.

Université du Québec en Abitibi-Témiscamingue, Graduate Programs, Program in Education, Rouyn-Noranda, QC J9X 5E4, Canada. Offers M Ed, MA, PhD, DESS. Part-time programs available. *Degree requirements:* For master's, thesis optional; for doctorate, thesis/dissertation. *Entrance requirements:* For master's, appropriate bachelor's degree, proficiency in French; for doctorate, appropriate master's degree, proficiency in French.

Université du Québec en Outaouais, Graduate Programs, Program in Education, Gatineau, QC J8X 3X7, Canada. Offers M Ed, MA, PhD, Diploma. Part-time programs available. *Degree requirements:* For master's, thesis optional; for doctorate, thesis/dissertation. *Entrance requirements:* For master's, appropriate bachelor's degree, proficiency in French; for doctorate, appropriate master's degree, proficiency in French.

Université Laval, Faculty of Education, Québec, QC G1K 7P4, Canada. Offers MA, PhD, Diploma. Part-time programs available. *Degree requirements:* For doctorate, comprehensive exam, thesis/dissertation. Electronic applications accepted.

University at Albany, State University of New York, School of Education, Albany, NY 12222-0001. Offers MA, MS, Ed D, PhD, Psy D, CAS. *Accreditation:* Teacher Education Accreditation Council. Part-time and evening/weekend programs available. *Degree requirements:* For doctorate, thesis/dissertation. *Entrance requirements:* For doctorate, GRE General Test. Additional exam requirements/recommendations for international students: Required—TOEFL (minimum score 550 paper-based; 213 computer-based). Electronic applications accepted.

University at Buffalo, the State University of New York, Graduate School, Graduate School of Education, Buffalo, NY 14260. Offers Ed M, MA, MLS, MS, Ed D, PhD, Certificate, Certificate/Ed M. *Accreditation:* Teacher Education Accreditation Council. Part-time programs available. Postbaccalaureate distance learning degree programs offered (minimal on-campus study). Terminal master's awarded for partial completion of doctoral program. *Degree requirements:* For doctorate, thesis/dissertation. *Entrance requirements:* For master's, GRE General Test. Additional exam requirements/recommendations for international students: Required—TOEFL (minimum score 79 iBT). Electronic applications accepted. *Faculty research:* Early childhood mathematics education, finance and management of higher education, curricular policy, practice and reform, student behavior in small classes, psychological measurement and assessment.

The University of Akron, Graduate School, College of Education, Akron, OH 44325. Offers MA, MS, Ed D, PhD. *Accreditation:* NCATE. Part-time programs available. *Faculty:* 60 full-time (39 women), 139 part-time/adjunct (90 women). *Students:* 504 full-time (357 women), 963 part-time (708 women); includes 149 minority (118 African Americans, 1 American Indian/Alaska Native, 19 Asian Americans or Pacific Islanders, 11 Hispanic Americans), 24 international. Average age 36. 564 applicants, 68% accepted, 277 enrolled. In 2009, 339 master's, 18 doctorates awarded. *Degree requirements:* For doctorate, one foreign language, comprehensive exam, thesis/dissertation, written and oral exams. *Entrance requirements:* For master's, letters of recommendation, resume, supplemental forms, statement of purpose; for doctorate, GRE or MAT, minimum GPA of 3.25, writing sample, interview, letters of recommendation, curriculum vitae/resume. Additional exam requirements/recommendations for international students: Required—TOEFL (minimum score 550 paper-based; 213 computer-based; 79 iBT). *Application deadline:* Applications are processed on a rolling basis. Application fee: $30 ($40 for international students). Electronic applications accepted. *Expenses:* Tuition, state resident: full-time $6570; part-time $365 per credit hour. Tuition, nonresident: full-time $11,250; part-time $625 per credit hour. *Financial support:* In 2009–10, 59 research assistantships with full tuition reimbursements, 56 teaching assistantships with full tuition reimbursements were awarded. *Faculty research:* History, philosophy of education, ethnographic research in education, case study methodology in education, multiple linear regression. Total annual research expenditures: $4.8 million. *Unit head:* Dr. Mark Shermis, Dean, 330-972-7680, E-mail: shermis@uakron.edu. *Application contact:* Dr. Mark Shermis, Dean, 330-972-7680, E-mail: shermis@uakron.edu.

The University of Alabama at Birmingham, College of Arts and Sciences, School of Education, Birmingham, AL 35294. Offers MA, MA Ed, Ed D, PhD, Ed S. *Accreditation:* NCATE. Part-time and evening/weekend programs available. *Degree requirements:* For master's, thesis optional; for doctorate, thesis/dissertation; for Ed S, comprehensive exam, thesis optional. *Entrance requirements:* For master's, GRE General Test, MAT, or NTE, minimum GPA of 3.0; for doctorate, GRE General Test, MAT, minimum GPA of 3.25; for Ed S, GRE General Test, MAT, minimum GPA of 3.0, master's degree. Electronic applications accepted.

University of Alaska Anchorage, College of Education, Anchorage, AK 99508. Offers M Ed, MAT, Certificate. *Accreditation:* NCATE. Part-time programs available. *Degree requirements:* For master's, comprehensive exam, thesis or alternative, portfolio. *Entrance requirements:* For master's, interview, minimum GPA of 3.0. Additional exam requirements/recommendations for international students: Required—TOEFL (minimum score 550 paper-based; 213 computer-based).

University of Alaska Fairbanks, School of Education, Fairbanks, AK 99775. Offers counseling (M Ed), including counseling; education (M Ed, PhD), including cross-cultural education (M Ed), curriculum and instruction (M Ed), education (M Ed), elementary education (M Ed), interdisciplinary (PhD), language and literacy (M Ed), reading (M Ed), secondary education (M Ed); guidance and counseling (M Ed). *Accreditation:* NCATE. Postbaccalaureate distance learning degree programs offered. *Faculty:* 23 full-time (15 women), 10 part-time/adjunct (9 women). *Students:* 54 full-time (38 women), 103 part-time (79 women); includes 23 minority (2 African Americans, 15 American Indian/Alaska Native, 2 Asian Americans or Pacific Islanders, 4 Hispanic Americans), 1 international. Average age 37. 126 applicants, 63% accepted, 59 enrolled. In 2009, 40 master's, 18 other advanced degrees awarded. *Degree requirements:* For master's, comprehensive exam, thesis or alternative, student teaching. *Entrance requirements:* For master's, GRE General Test, PRAXIS I, PRAXIS II, writing sample, evidence of technology competence, criminal background check. Additional exam requirements/recommendations for international students: Required—TOEFL (minimum score 550 paper-based; 213 computer-based; 80 iBT). *Application deadline:* For fall admission, 3/1 for domestic and international students; for spring admission, 10/15 for domestic students, 9/1 for international students. Application fee: $60. Electronic applications accepted. *Expenses:* Tuition, state resident: full-time $7584; part-time $316 per credit. Tuition, nonresident: full-time $15,504; part-time $646 per credit. Required fees: $23 per credit. $135 per semester. Tuition and fees vary according to course level, course load and reciprocity agreements. *Financial support:* In 2009–10, 1 research assistantship (averaging $13,330 per year), 5 teaching assistantships (averaging $10,376 per year) were awarded; fellowships, career-related internships or fieldwork, Federal Work-Study, scholarships/grants, health care benefits, and unspecified assistantships also available. Support available to part-time students. Financial award application deadline: 2/15; financial award applicants required to submit FAFSA. *Faculty research:* Native ways of knowing, classroom research in methods of literacy instruction, multiple intelligence theory, geometry concept development, mathematics and science curriculum development. *Unit head:* Dr. Eric C. Madsen, Dean, 907-474-7341, Fax: 907-474-5451, E-mail: fysoed@uaf.edu. *Application contact:* Dr. Eric C. Madsen, Dean, 907-474-7341, Fax: 907-474-5451, E-mail: fysoed@uaf.edu.

University of Alaska Southeast, Graduate Programs, Program in Education, Juneau, AK 99801. Offers early childhood education (M Ed, MAT); educational technology (M Ed); elementary education (MAT); reading (M Ed); secondary education (MAT). *Accreditation:* NCATE. Part-time and evening/weekend programs available. Postbaccalaureate distance learning degree programs offered (minimal on-campus study). *Degree requirements:* For master's, comprehensive exam or project, portfolio. *Entrance requirements:* For master's, PRAXIS, minimum GPA of 3.0, writing sample, letters of recommendation. Electronic applications accepted. *Faculty research:* Applied classroom research, culturally responsive practices, action research, teaching effectiveness.

The University of Arizona, Graduate College, College of Education, Tucson, AZ 85721. Offers M Ed, MA, MS, Ed D, PhD, Ed S. Part-time programs available. Postbaccalaureate distance learning degree programs offered (no on-campus study). *Faculty:* 49. *Students:* 521 full-time (324 women), 504 part-time (197 women); includes 107 minority (17 African Americans, 19 American Indian/Alaska Native, 10 Asian Americans or Pacific Islanders, 61 Hispanic Americans), 76 international. Average age 35. 428 applicants, 57% accepted, 161 enrolled. In 2009, 150 master's, 60 doctorates awarded. Terminal master's awarded for partial completion of doctoral program. *Degree requirements:* For master's, comprehensive exam, thesis (for some programs); for doctorate, comprehensive exam, thesis/dissertation. *Entrance requirements:* For doctorate, GRE. Additional exam requirements/recommendations for international students: Required—TOEFL (minimum score 550 paper-based; 213 computer-based; 79 iBT). *Application deadline:* For fall admission, 2/1 priority date for domestic and international students; for spring admission, 10/1 priority date for domestic students, 9/1 priority date for international students. Applications are processed on a rolling basis. Application fee: $75. Electronic applications accepted. *Expenses:* Tuition, state resident: full-time $9028. Tuition, nonresident: full-time $24,890. *Financial support:* In 2009–10, 33 research assistantships with full tuition reimbursements (averaging $13,353 per year), 29 teaching assistantships with full tuition reimbursements (averaging $12,261 per year) were awarded; career-related internships or fieldwork, Federal Work-Study, institutionally sponsored loans, scholarships/grants, health care benefits, tuition waivers (full and partial), and unspecified assistantships also available. Support available to part-time students. Financial award application deadline: 3/1. *Faculty research:* Teacher effectiveness, pupil achievement, learning skills, program evaluation, instructional method effects. Total annual research expenditures: $4.7 million. *Unit head:* Dr. Ronald Marx, Dean, 520-621-1081, Fax: 520-621-9271, E-mail: ronmarx@email.arizona.edu. *Application contact:* General Information, 520-621-3471, Fax: 520-621-4101, E-mail: gradadm@grad.arizona.edu.

University of Arkansas, Graduate School, College of Education and Health Professions, Fayetteville, AR 72701-1201. Offers M Ed, MAT, MS, MSN, Ed D, PhD, Ed S. *Accreditation:* NCATE. *Students:* 415 full-time (304 women), 560 part-time (399 women); includes 155 minority (105 African Americans, 19 American Indian/Alaska Native, 15 Asian Americans or Pacific Islanders, 16 Hispanic Americans), 35 international. 461 applicants, 43% accepted. In 2009, 275 master's, 34 doctorates awarded. *Degree requirements:* For doctorate, thesis/dissertation. Application fee: $40 ($50 for international students). *Expenses:* Tuition, state resident: full-time $7355; part-time $356.58 per hour. Tuition, nonresident: full-time $17,401; part-time $775.17 per hour. Required fees: $1203. *Financial support:* In 2009–10, 27 fellowships with tuition reimbursements, 70 research assistantships, 22 teaching assistantships were awarded; career-related internships or fieldwork and Federal Work-Study also available. Support available to part-time students. Financial award application deadline: 4/1; financial award applicants required to submit FAFSA. *Unit head:* Dr. Thomas E. Smith, Dean, 479-575-3208, Fax: 479-575-3119, E-mail: tecsmith@uark.edu. *Application contact:* Graduate Admissions, 479-575-6246, Fax: 479-575-5908, E-mail: gradinfo@uark.edu.

University of Arkansas at Little Rock, Graduate School, College of Education, Little Rock, AR 72204-1099. Offers M Ed, MA, Ed D, Ed S, Graduate Certificate. *Accreditation:* CORE; NCATE (one or more programs are accredited). Part-time and evening/weekend programs available. *Degree requirements:* For doctorate, comprehensive exam, oral defense of dissertation, residency; for other advanced degree, comprehensive exam. *Entrance requirements:* For master's, minimum GPA of 2.75; for doctorate, GRE General Test or MAT, minimum graduate GPA of 3.0, teaching certificate, work experience; for other advanced degree, GRE General Test or MAT, teaching certificate.

University of Arkansas at Monticello, School of Education, Monticello, AR 71656. Offers education (M Ed, MAT); educational leadership (M Ed). *Accreditation:* NCATE. Part-time and evening/weekend programs available. Postbaccalaureate distance learning degree programs offered (minimal on-campus study). *Degree requirements:* For master's, comprehensive exam. *Entrance requirements:* For master's, minimum GPA of 3.0. Additional exam requirements/recommendations for international students: Required—TOEFL (minimum score 550 paper-based; 213 computer-based). Electronic applications accepted.

University of Arkansas at Pine Bluff, Program in Education, Pine Bluff, AR 71601-2799. Offers elementary education (M Ed); secondary education (M Ed), including general science, physical education, social studies. *Accreditation:* NCATE. Part-time and evening/weekend programs available. *Degree requirements:* For master's, comprehensive exam. *Entrance requirements:* For master's, GRE, minimum GPA of 2.75, NTE or Standard Arkansas Teaching

Certificate. *Faculty research:* Teacher certification, accreditation, assessment, standards, portfolio development, rehabilitation, technology.

University of Bridgeport, School of Education and Human Resources, Division of Education, Bridgeport, CT 06604. Offers education (MS); educational management (Ed D, Diploma), including intermediate administrator or supervisor (Diploma), leadership (Ed D); elementary education (MS, Diploma), including early childhood education, elementary education; secondary education (MS, Diploma), including computer specialist (Diploma), international education (Diploma), reading specialist, secondary education. Part-time and evening/weekend programs available. *Degree requirements:* For master's, final exam, final project, or thesis; for doctorate, comprehensive exam, thesis/dissertation; for Diploma, thesis or alternative, final project. *Entrance requirements:* For master's, minimum undergraduate QPA of 2.67; for doctorate, GRE, MAT; for Diploma, GRE General Test or MAT, minimum graduate QPA of 3.0. Additional exam requirements/recommendations for international students: Recommended—TOEFL (minimum score 550 paper-based; 213 computer-based; 80 iBT), IELTS (minimum score 6.5). Electronic applications accepted. *Faculty research:* Self-concept, internship assessment, stress and situational development, follow-up of graduation, trend analysis.

The University of British Columbia, Faculty of Education, Vancouver, BC V6T1Z4, Canada. Offers M Ed, M Sc, MA, MET, MHK, Ed D, PhD, Diploma. Part-time and evening/weekend programs available. Postbaccalaureate distance learning degree programs offered (no on-campus study). Terminal master's awarded for partial completion of doctoral program. *Degree requirements:* For master's, thesis (for some programs); for doctorate, comprehensive exam, thesis/dissertation. *Entrance requirements:* Additional exam requirements/recommendations for international students: Required—TOEFL. Electronic applications accepted. *Expenses:* Contact institution. *Faculty research:* Curriculum and pedagogy; school counseling psychology; educational administration; human kinetics; language and literacy education.

University of California, Berkeley, Graduate Division, School of Education, Berkeley, CA 94720-1500. Offers MA, PhD, MA/Credential, Ph D/Credential, PhD/MA. *Students:* 423 full-time (308 women); includes 166 minority (49 African Americans, 10 American Indian/Alaska Native, 64 Asian Americans or Pacific Islanders, 43 Hispanic Americans), 31 international. Average age 34. 706 applicants, 119 enrolled. In 2009, 120 master's, 33 doctorates awarded. Terminal master's awarded for partial completion of doctoral program. *Degree requirements:* For master's, exam or thesis; for doctorate, thesis/dissertation, oral qualifying exam (PhD). *Entrance requirements:* For master's and doctorate, GRE General Test, minimum undergraduate GPA of 3.0 during last 2 years, 3 letters of recommendation. *Application deadline:* For fall admission, 12/1 for domestic students. Application fee: $70 ($90 for international students). *Financial support:* Fellowships, research assistantships, teaching assistantships, career-related internships or fieldwork and unspecified assistantships available. *Faculty research:* Cognition and development; language, literacy and culture. *Unit head:* Dr. P. David Pearson, Dean, 510-642-3726, E-mail: gsedeansoffice@lists.berkeley.edu. *Application contact:* Rochelle Fraga, Admissions Assistant, 510-642-0841, Fax: 510-642-4808, E-mail: gse_info@berkeley.edu.

University of California, Berkeley, UC Berkeley Extension, Certificate Programs in Education, Berkeley, CA 94720-1500. Offers college admissions and career planning (Certificate); teaching English as a second language (Certificate). *Unit head:* Diana Wu, Dean, 510-642-4181. *Application contact:* Education, 510-642-1171, E-mail: askeducation@unex.berkeley.edu.

University of California, Davis, Graduate Studies, Graduate Group in Education, Davis, CA 95616. Offers education (MA, Ed D); instructional studies (PhD); psychological studies (PhD); sociocultural studies (PhD). Terminal master's awarded for partial completion of doctoral program. *Degree requirements:* For master's, comprehensive exam (for some programs), thesis (for some programs); for doctorate, thesis/dissertation. *Entrance requirements:* For master's and doctorate, GRE. Additional exam requirements/recommendations for international students: Required—TOEFL (minimum score 550 paper-based; 213 computer-based). Electronic applications accepted. *Faculty research:* Language and literacy, mathematics education, science education, teacher development, school psychology.

University of California, Irvine, Office of Graduate Studies, Department of Education, Irvine, CA 92697. Offers educational administration (Ed D); educational administration and leadership (Ed D); elementary and secondary education (MAT). Part-time and evening/weekend programs available. *Students:* 292 full-time (210 women), 11 part-time (9 women); includes 114 minority (7 African Americans, 2 American Indian/Alaska Native, 64 Asian Americans or Pacific Islanders, 41 Hispanic Americans), 6 international. Average age 28. 523 applicants, 75% accepted, 233 enrolled. In 2009, 164 master's, 20 doctorates awarded. *Degree requirements:* For doctorate, thesis/dissertation. *Entrance requirements:* For master's, GRE, minimum GPA of 3.0; for doctorate, GRE General Test, minimum GPA of 3.0. Additional exam requirements/recommendations for international students: Required—TOEFL (minimum score 550 paper-based; 213 computer-based). *Application deadline:* For fall admission, 1/4 priority date for domestic students, 1/4 for international students. Application fee: $70 ($90 for international students). Electronic applications accepted. *Financial support:* Fellowships, research assistantships with full tuition reimbursements, institutionally sponsored loans, traineeships, health care benefits, and unspecified assistantships available. Financial award application deadline: 3/1; financial award applicants required to submit FAFSA. *Faculty research:* Education technology, learning theory, social theory, cultural diversity, postmodernism. *Unit head:* David Brant, Interim Chair, 949-824-7840, E-mail: dbrant@uci.edu. *Application contact:* Sarah K. Singh, Student Affairs Officer, 949-824-7832, Fax: 949-824-2965, E-mail: sksingh@uci.edu.

University of California, Los Angeles, Graduate Division, Graduate School of Education and Information Studies, Department of Education, Los Angeles, CA 90095. Offers M Ed, MA, Ed D, PhD. Evening/weekend programs available. *Degree requirements:* For master's, comprehensive exam; for doctorate, thesis/dissertation, oral and written qualifying exams. *Entrance requirements:* For master's, GRE General Test, minimum GPA of 3.0; for doctorate, GRE General Test, minimum undergraduate GPA of 3.0. Additional exam requirements/recommendations for international students: Required—TOEFL (minimum score 560 paper-based; 220 computer-based; 87 iBT). Electronic applications accepted.

University of California, Riverside, Graduate Division, Graduate School of Education, Riverside, CA 92521-0102. Offers autism (M Ed); curriculum and instruction (MA, PhD); diversity and equity (M Ed); educational leadership and policy (MA, PhD); educational psychology (MA, PhD); general education (M Ed); higher education administration and policy (M Ed, PhD); leadership (M Ed); reading (M Ed); school psychology (PhD); special education (M Ed, MA, PhD). *Faculty:* 23 full-time (12 women), 12 part-time/adjunct (8 women). *Students:* 230 full-time (183 women), 6 part-time (3 women); includes 75 minority (12 African Americans, 1 American Indian/Alaska Native, 21 Asian Americans or Pacific Islanders, 41 Hispanic Americans), 6 international. Average age 32. 288 applicants, 60% accepted, 118 enrolled. In 2009, 68 master's, 13 doctorates awarded. Terminal master's awarded for partial completion of doctoral program. *Degree requirements:* For master's, comprehensive exam (for some programs), comprehensive exams or thesis (MA), case study or analytical report (M Ed); for doctorate, thesis/dissertation, written and oral qualifying exams, college teaching practicum. *Entrance requirements:* For master's, GRE General Test, GRE Subject Test, CBEST, CSET, minimum GPA of 3.2; for doctorate, GRE General Test, GRE Subject Test, master's degree (desirable), minimum GPA of 3.2. Additional exam requirements/recommendations for international students: Required—TOEFL (minimum score 550 paper-based; 213 computer-based; 80 iBT). *Application deadline:* For fall admission, 9/1 for domestic students, 4/1 for international students; for winter admission, 12/1 for domestic students, 9/1 for international students; for spring admission, 3/1 for domestic students, 10/1 for international students. Applications are processed on a rolling basis. Application fee: $70 ($85 for international students). Electronic applications accepted. *Financial support:* In 2009–10, 55 students received support, including 13 fellowships with full and partial tuition reimbursements available (averaging $26,809 per year), 21 research assistantships with full and partial tuition reimbursements available (averaging $14,238 per year), 1 teaching assistantship with full and partial tuition reimbursement available (averaging $16,638 per year); career-related internships or fieldwork, Federal Work-Study, institutionally sponsored loans, scholarships/grants, and unspecified assistantships also available. Financial award application deadline: 1/5; financial award applicants required to submit FAFSA. *Faculty research:* Responsiveness to intervention, faculty core, response to intervention of English language learners, advanced modeling techniques, study on social capital, trust, and motivation. Total annual research expenditures: $5.6 million. *Unit head:* Dr. Steven T. Bossert, Dean, 951-827-5802, Fax: 951-827-3942, E-mail: steven.bossert@ucr.edu. *Application contact:* Dr. John Wills, Graduate Advisor for Admission, 951-827-6362, Fax: 951-827-3942, E-mail: edgrad@ucr.edu.

University of California, San Diego, Office of Graduate Studies, Program in Teacher Education, La Jolla, CA 92093. Offers bilingual education (MA); curriculum design (MA); teacher education (M Ed); teaching and learning (Ed D). *Entrance requirements:* For master's, GRE General Test. Electronic applications accepted.

University of California, Santa Barbara, Graduate Division, Gevirtz Graduate School of Education, Santa Barbara, CA 93106-9490. Offers counseling, clinical and school psychology (PhD), including clinical psychology, counseling psychology, school psychology; education (M Ed, MA, PhD), including child and adolescent development (MA, PhD), cultural perspectives and comparative education (MA, PhD), educational leadership and organizations (MA, PhD), research methodology (MA, PhD), special education disabilities and risk studies (MA), special education, disabilities and risk studies (PhD), teaching (M Ed), teaching and learning (MA, PhD); educational leadership (Ed D); school psychology (M Ed); MA/PhD. *Accreditation:* APA (one or more programs are accredited). Postbaccalaureate distance learning degree programs offered (minimal on-campus study). *Faculty:* 42 full-time (20 women), 10 part-time/adjunct (4 women). *Students:* 390 full-time (303 women); includes 149 minority (14 African Americans, 3 American Indian/Alaska Native, 57 Asian Americans or Pacific Islanders, 75 Hispanic Americans), 16 international. Average age 31. 717 applicants, 40% accepted, 170 enrolled. In 2009, 140 master's, 46 doctorates awarded. Terminal master's awarded for partial completion of doctoral program. *Degree requirements:* For master's, comprehensive exam (for some programs), thesis (for some programs); for doctorate, comprehensive exam (for some programs), thesis/dissertation, qualifying exam. *Entrance requirements:* For master's, GRE, 3 letters of recommendation, resume/curriculum vitae; for doctorate, GRE, 3 letters of recommendation, statement of purpose, personal achievements/contributions statement, resume/curriculum vitae, transcripts for post-secondary institutions attended. Additional exam requirements/recommendations for international students: Required—TOEFL (minimum score 550 paper-based; 213 computer-based; 80 iBT) or IELTS (minimum score 7). Application fee: $70 ($90 for international students). Electronic applications accepted. *Financial support:* In 2009–10, 253 students received support, including 206 fellowships with full and partial tuition reimbursements available (averaging $5,000 per year), 62 research assistantships with full and partial tuition reimbursements available (averaging $6,200 per year), 87 teaching assistantships with partial tuition reimbursements available (averaging $6,500 per year); career-related internships or fieldwork, Federal Work-Study, institutionally sponsored loans, scholarships/grants, traineeships, health care benefits, and unspecified assistantships also available. Financial award applicants required to submit FAFSA. *Faculty research:* Professional development, early childhood development, school violence, literacy, science/math initiative. Total annual research expenditures: $4.4 million. *Unit head:* Dr. Jane Conoley, Chair, 805-893-2185, E-mail: jane-conoley@education.ucsb.edu. *Application contact:* Kathryn Marie Tucciarone, Student Affairs Officer, 805-893-2137, E-mail: katiet@education.ucsb.edu.

University of California, Santa Cruz, Division of Graduate Studies, Division of Social Sciences, Department of Education, Santa Cruz, CA 95064. Offers education (MA); language and literacy studies (PhD); mathematics and science education (PhD); social context and policy studies of education (PhD). Terminal master's awarded for partial completion of doctoral program. *Degree requirements:* For master's, thesis; for doctorate, thesis/dissertation. *Faculty research:* Bilingual/multicultural education, special education, curriculum and instruction, child development.

University of Central Arkansas, Graduate School, College of Education, Conway, AR 72035-0001. Offers MAT, MS, MSE, Ed S. *Accreditation:* NCATE. Part-time programs available. *Faculty:* 28 full-time (16 women), 1 (woman) part-time/adjunct. *Students:* 90 full-time (65 women), 504 part-time (424 women); includes 83 minority (67 African Americans, 10 American Indian/Alaska Native, 4 Asian Americans or Pacific Islanders, 2 Hispanic Americans), 4 international. Average age 33. 277 applicants, 87% accepted, 242 enrolled. In 2009, 102 master's awarded. Terminal master's awarded for partial completion of doctoral program. *Degree requirements:* For master's, comprehensive exam, thesis optional. *Entrance requirements:* For master's, GRE General Test, minimum GPA of 2.7. Additional exam requirements/recommendations for international students: Required—TOEFL (minimum score 550 paper-based; 213 computer-based). *Application deadline:* For fall admission, 3/1 priority date for domestic and international students; for spring admission, 10/1 priority date for domestic and international students. Applications are processed on a rolling basis. Application fee: $25 ($50 for international students). *Expenses:* Tuition, state resident: full-time $5136; part-time $214 per credit hour. Required fees: $379.50; $127 per term. Tuition and fees vary according to course level, course load and campus/location. *Financial support:* Career-related internships or fieldwork, Federal Work-Study, scholarships/grants, tuition waivers (partial), and unspecified assistantships available. Financial award application deadline: 2/15; financial award applicants required to submit FAFSA. *Unit head:* Dr. Patricia Phelps, Interim Dean, 501-450-5401, Fax: 501-450-5424, E-mail: pattyp@uca.edu. *Application contact:* Brenda Herring, Admissions Assistant, 501-450-5065, Fax: 501-450-5678, E-mail: bherring@uca.edu.

University of Central Arkansas, Graduate School, College of Education, Department of Teaching, Learning, and Technology, Graduate Program in Teaching, Conway, AR 72035-0001. Offers MAT. Part-time programs available. Postbaccalaureate distance learning degree programs offered (minimal on-campus study). *Students:* 43 full-time (35 women), 216 part-time (171 women); includes 37 minority (28 African Americans, 5 American Indian/Alaska Native, 2 Asian Americans or Pacific Islanders, 2 Hispanic Americans), 1 international. Average age 31. 88 applicants, 97% accepted, 67 enrolled. In 2009, 69 master's awarded. *Degree requirements:* For master's, comprehensive exam, thesis optional. *Entrance requirements:* For master's, GRE General Test, minimum GPA of 2.7. Additional exam requirements/recommendations for international students: Required—TOEFL (minimum score 550 paper-based; 213 computer-based). *Application deadline:* For fall admission, 3/1 priority date for domestic and international students; for spring admission, 10/1 priority date for domestic and international students. Applications are processed on a rolling basis. Application fee: $25 ($50 for international students). *Expenses:* Tuition, state resident: full-time $5136; part-time $214 per credit hour. Required fees: $379.50; $127 per term. Tuition and fees vary according to course level, course load and campus/location. *Financial support:* Federal Work-Study, scholarships/grants, and unspecified assistantships available. Financial award application deadline: 2/15; financial award applicants required to submit FAFSA. *Unit head:* Tammy Benson, Unit Head, 501-450-5462. *Application contact:* Brenda Herring, Admissions Assistant, 501-450-5065, Fax: 501-450-5678, E-mail: bherring@uca.edu.

University of Central Arkansas, Graduate School, College of Education, Department of Teaching, Learning, and Technology, Program in Advanced Studies of Teaching and Learning, Conway, AR 72035-0001. Offers MSE. *Students:* 1 (woman) full-time, 25 part-time (24 women); includes 2 minority (both African Americans). Average age 36. 6 applicants, 100% accepted, 2 enrolled. In 2009, 14 master's awarded. *Entrance requirements:* For master's, GRE General Test, minimum GPA of 2.7. Additional exam requirements/recommendations for international students: Required—TOEFL (minimum score 550 paper-based; 213 computer-based). *Application deadline:* For fall admission, 3/1 priority date for domestic and international students; for spring admission, 10/1 priority date for domestic and international students. Applications are processed on a rolling basis. Application fee: $25 ($50 for international students). *Expenses:* Tuition, state resident: full-time $5136; part-time $214 per credit hour. Required fees: $379.50; $127 per term. Tuition and fees vary according to course level, course load and campus/location. *Financial support:* Federal Work-Study, scholarships/grants, and unspecified assistantships available. Financial award application deadline: 2/15; financial award applicants required to submit FAFSA. *Application contact:* Brenda Herring, Admissions Assistant, 501-450-5065, Fax: 501-450-5678, E-mail: bherring@uca.edu.

Education—General

University of Central Florida, College of Education, Department of Educational Studies, Orlando, FL 32816. Offers applied learning and instruction (MA); community college education (Certificate); curriculum and instruction (Ed S); education (Ed D, PhD, Ed S); gifted education (Certificate); global and comparative education (Certificate); initial teacher professional preparation (Certificate); teacher leadership (M Ed); urban education (Certificate). *Accreditation:* NCATE. Part-time and evening/weekend programs available. *Faculty:* 18 full-time (10 women), 16 part-time/adjunct (10 women). *Students:* 155 full-time (106 women), 156 part-time (131 women); includes 80 minority (37 African Americans, 5 Asian Americans or Pacific Islanders, 38 Hispanic Americans), 22 international. Average age 36. 200 applicants, 57% accepted, 77 enrolled. In 2009, 9 master's, 34 doctorates, 17 other advanced degrees awarded. *Degree requirements:* For other advanced degree, thesis or alternative, final exam. *Entrance requirements:* For degree, GRE General Test, minimum GPA of 3.0, resume. Additional exam requirements/recommendations for international students: Required—TOEFL. *Application deadline:* For fall admission, 2/20 for domestic students; for spring admission, 9/20 for domestic students. Application fee: $30. Electronic applications accepted. *Expenses:* Tuition, state resident: part-time $306.31 per credit hour. Tuition, nonresident: part-time $1099.01 per credit hour. Part-time tuition and fees vary according to degree level and program. *Financial support:* In 2009–10, 82 students received support, including 55 fellowships with partial tuition reimbursements available (averaging $8,300 per year), 29 research assistantships with partial tuition reimbursements available (averaging $7,000 per year), 43 teaching assistantships with partial tuition reimbursements available (averaging $8,000 per year); career-related internships or fieldwork, Federal Work-Study, institutionally sponsored loans, and unspecified assistantships also available. Financial award application deadline: 3/1; financial award applicants required to submit FAFSA. *Unit head:* Dr. Karen Biraimah, Chair, 407-823-2428, E-mail: biraimah@mail.ucf.edu. *Application contact:* Dr. Karen Biraimah, Chair, 407-823-2428, E-mail: biraimah@mail.ucf.edu.

University of Central Missouri, The Graduate School, College of Education, Warrensburg, MO 64093. Offers career and technical education administration (MS); career and technical education industry training (MS); career and technical education leadership/teaching (MS); college student personnel administration (MS); counseling (MS); curriculum and instruction (Ed S); educational leadership (Ed D); educational technology (MS); elementary education/educational foundations and literacy (MSE); elementary school administration (MSE); elementary school principalship (Ed S); human services/learning resources (Ed S); human services/professional counseling (Ed S); human services/special education (Ed S); human services/technology and occupational education (Ed S); K-12 education/educational foundations and literacy (MSE); K-12 special education (MSE); library science and information services (MS); literacy education (MSE); secondary education/educational foundations & literacy (MSE); secondary school administration (MSE); secondary school principalship (Ed S); superintendency (Ed S); teaching (MAT). Part-time programs available. Postbaccalaureate distance learning degree programs offered. *Faculty:* 42. *Students:* 123 full-time (82 women), 721 part-time (552 women); includes 58 minority (38 African Americans, 3 American Indian/Alaska Native, 6 Asian Americans or Pacific Islanders, 11 Hispanic Americans), 6 international. Average age 34. 229 applicants, 88% accepted, 190 enrolled. In 2009, 212 master's, 47 other advanced degrees awarded. *Entrance requirements:* Additional exam requirements/recommendations for international students: Required—TOEFL (minimum score 550 paper-based; 79 computer-based). *Application deadline:* For fall admission, 6/1 priority date for domestic students, 5/1 for international students; for spring admission, 10/1 priority date for domestic students, 10/1 for international students. Applications are processed on a rolling basis. Application fee: $30 ($75 for international students). Electronic applications accepted. *Expenses:* Tuition, area resident: Part-time $245.80 per credit hour. Tuition, nonresident: part-time $491.60 per credit hour. Required fees: $24.20 per credit hour. Full-time tuition and fees vary according to course load, degree level, campus/location and reciprocity agreements. *Financial support:* Research assistantships with full and partial tuition reimbursements, teaching assistantships with full and partial tuition reimbursements, career-related internships or fieldwork, Federal Work-Study, scholarships/grants, and administrative and laboratory assistantships available. Support available to part-time students. Financial award application deadline: 3/1; financial award applicants required to submit FAFSA. *Unit head:* Dr. Michael Wright, Dean, 660-543-4272, Fax: 660-543-8753, E-mail: mwright@ucmo.edu. *Application contact:* Laurie Delap, Admissions Coordinator, 660-543-4621, Fax: 660-543-4778, E-mail: gradinfo@ucmo.edu.

University of Central Oklahoma, College of Graduate Studies and Research, College of Education, Edmond, OK 73034-5209. Offers M Ed, MA, MS. *Accreditation:* NCATE. Part-time programs available. *Faculty:* 73 full-time (46 women), 32 part-time/adjunct (19 women). *Students:* 329 full-time (270 women), 706 part-time (575 women); includes 177 minority (90 African Americans, 36 American Indian/Alaska Native, 17 Asian Americans or Pacific Islanders, 34 Hispanic Americans), 57 international. Average age 34. 255 applicants, 99% accepted. In 2009, 287 master's awarded. *Entrance requirements:* For master's, GRE General Test. Additional exam requirements/recommendations for international students: Required—TOEFL (minimum score 550 paper-based; 213 computer-based). *Application deadline:* For fall admission, 7/1 for international students; for spring admission, 11/1 for international students. Applications are processed on a rolling basis. Application fee: $25. Electronic applications accepted. *Expenses:* Tuition, state resident: full-time $4128; part-time $172 per credit hour. Tuition, nonresident: full-time $10,373; part-time $432.20 per credit hour. Required fees: $433.20; $18.05 per credit hour. *Financial support:* Career-related internships or fieldwork and unspecified assistantships available. Financial award application deadline: 3/31; financial award applicants required to submit FAFSA. *Unit head:* Dr. James Machell, Dean, 405-974-5701, Fax: 405-974-3851. *Application contact:* Dr. Richard Bernard, Dean, Graduate College, 405-974-3493, Fax: 405-974-3852, E-mail: gradcoll@uco.edu.

University of Cincinnati, Graduate School, College of Education, Criminal Justice, and Human Services, Cincinnati, OH 45221. Offers M Ed, MA, MS, Ed D, PhD, CAGS, Certificate, Ed S. *Accreditation:* NCATE. Part-time programs available. Postbaccalaureate distance learning degree programs offered (no on-campus study). *Degree requirements:* For master's, comprehensive exam (for some programs), thesis (for some programs); for doctorate, comprehensive exam, thesis/dissertation. *Entrance requirements:* For master's and doctorate, GRE. Additional exam requirements/recommendations for international students: Required—TOEFL (minimum score 550 paper-based), OEPT 3. Electronic applications accepted. *Faculty research:* Alcohol and drug prevention, family-based prevention, criminal justice, literacy, urban education.

University of Colorado at Boulder, Graduate School, School of Education, Boulder, CO 80309. Offers MA, PhD. *Accreditation:* NCATE. Part-time programs available. *Faculty:* 30 full-time (17 women). *Students:* 165 full-time (116 women), 283 part-time (238 women); includes 81 minority (2 African Americans, 3 American Indian/Alaska Native, 21 Asian Americans or Pacific Islanders, 55 Hispanic Americans), 6 international. Average age 33. 388 applicants, 44% accepted, 91 enrolled. In 2009, 123 master's, 9 doctorates awarded. *Degree requirements:* For master's, comprehensive exam, thesis or alternative; for doctorate, one foreign language, comprehensive exam, thesis/dissertation. *Entrance requirements:* For master's, GRE General Test or MAT, minimum undergraduate GPA of 2.75; for doctorate, GRE General Test. *Application deadline:* For fall admission, 2/1 priority date for domestic students, 12/1 for international students; for spring admission, 9/1 for domestic students, 12/1 for international students. Application fee: $50 ($60 for international students). *Financial support:* In 2009–10, 82 fellowships (averaging $3,279 per year), 50 research assistantships (averaging $12,516 per year) were awarded; career-related internships or fieldwork, Federal Work-Study, scholarships/grants, and tuition waivers (full and partial) also available. Support available to part-time students. Total annual research expenditures: $5.1 million.

University of Colorado at Colorado Springs, Graduate School, College of Education, Colorado Springs, CO 80933-7150. Offers counseling and human services (MA); curriculum and instruction (MA); educational administration (MA); educational leadership (MA, PhD); special education (MA). *Accreditation:* ACA; NCATE. Part-time and evening/weekend programs available. Postbaccalaureate distance learning degree programs offered (minimal on-campus study). *Faculty:* 23 full-time (15 women), 11 part-time/adjunct (8 women). *Students:* 317 full-time (243 women), 160 part-time (132 women); includes 81 minority (23 African Americans, 3 American Indian/Alaska Native, 13 Asian Americans or Pacific Islanders, 42 Hispanic Americans), 2 international. Average age 36. 375 applicants, 94% accepted, 254 enrolled. In 2009, 203 master's awarded. *Degree requirements:* For master's, comprehensive exam, thesis or alternative, microcomputer proficiency; for doctorate, comprehensive exam, research lab. *Entrance requirements:* For master's, GRE General Test, MAT. *Application deadline:* For fall admission, 6/15 for domestic students; for spring admission, 10/15 for domestic students. Applications are processed on a rolling basis. Application fee: $60 ($75 for international students). *Expenses:* Tuition, state resident: full-time $8922; part-time $639 per credit hour. Tuition, nonresident: full-time $19,372; part-time $1154 per credit hour. Tuition and fees vary according to course level, course load, degree level, program, reciprocity agreements and student level. *Financial support:* Fellowships, career-related internships or fieldwork, Federal Work-Study, and scholarships/grants available. Support available to part-time students. Financial award application deadline: 3/1; financial award applicants required to submit FAFSA. *Faculty research:* Job training for special populations, materials development for classroom. Total annual research expenditures: $1.4 million. *Unit head:* Dr. LaVonne Neal, Dean, 719-255-4111, Fax: 719-262-4110, E-mail: lneal@uccs.edu. *Application contact:* Melissa Schecter, Student Services Manager, 719-255-4526, Fax: 719-255-4110, E-mail: mschedte@uccs.edu.

University of Colorado Denver, School of Education and Human Development, Denver, CO 80217-3364. Offers MA, PhD, Ed S. *Accreditation:* NCATE. Part-time and evening/weekend programs available. *Faculty:* 67 full-time (51 women), 101 part-time/adjunct (83 women). *Students:* 504 full-time (398 women), 759 part-time (635 women); includes 138 minority (23 African Americans, 4 American Indian/Alaska Native, 30 Asian Americans or Pacific Islanders, 81 Hispanic Americans), 23 international. Average age 33. 507 applicants, 71% accepted, 254 enrolled. In 2009, 445 master's, 11 doctorates, 27 other advanced degrees awarded. *Degree requirements:* For doctorate, one foreign language, comprehensive exam, thesis/dissertation. *Entrance requirements:* For master's, minimum GPA of 2.75; for doctorate, GRE (LSAT, MCAT, or GMAT scores may be considered in place). Additional exam requirements/recommendations for international students: Required—TOEFL (minimum score 525 paper-based; 197 computer-based). *Application deadline:* For fall admission, 4/15 for domestic students; for spring admission, 9/15 for domestic students. Applications are processed on a rolling basis. Application fee: $50 ($75 for international students). Electronic applications accepted. *Expenses:* Contact institution. *Financial support:* Fellowships, research assistantships, teaching assistantships, Federal Work-Study, institutionally sponsored loans, and scholarships/grants available. Support available to part-time students. Financial award application deadline: 4/1; financial award applicants required to submit FAFSA. Total annual research expenditures: $4.5 million. *Unit head:* Lynn K. Rhodes, Dean, 303-315-6345, E-mail: lynn.rhodes@ucdenver.edu. *Application contact:* Lori Sisneros, Student Services Coordinator, 303-315-4979, Fax: 303-315-6311, E-mail: lori.sisneros@ucdenver.edu.

University of Connecticut, Graduate School, Neag School of Education, Storrs, CT 06269. Offers MA, DPT, Ed D, PhD, Post-Master's Certificate. *Accreditation:* NCATE. *Faculty:* 86 full-time (43 women). *Students:* 509 full-time (365 women), 338 part-time (236 women); includes 118 minority (38 African Americans, 1 American Indian/Alaska Native, 27 Asian Americans or Pacific Islanders, 52 Hispanic Americans), 36 international. Average age 32. 1,121 applicants, 21% accepted, 139 enrolled. In 2009, 316 master's, 33 doctorates, 83 other advanced degrees awarded. Terminal master's awarded for partial completion of doctoral program. *Degree requirements:* For master's, comprehensive exam, thesis or alternative; for doctorate, thesis/dissertation. *Entrance requirements:* For doctorate, GRE General Test. Additional exam requirements/recommendations for international students: Required—TOEFL (minimum score 550 paper-based; 213 computer-based). *Application deadline:* For fall admission, 2/1 priority date for domestic and international students; for spring admission, 11/1 for domestic students, 10/1 for international students. Applications are processed on a rolling basis. Application fee: $55. Electronic applications accepted. *Expenses:* Tuition, state resident: full-time $4725; part-time $525 per credit. Tuition, nonresident: full-time $12,267; part-time $1363 per credit. Required fees: $346 per semester. Tuition and fees vary according to course load. *Financial support:* In 2009–10, 189 research assistantships with full tuition reimbursements, 24 teaching assistantships with full tuition reimbursements were awarded; fellowships, Federal Work-Study, scholarships/grants, health care benefits, and unspecified assistantships also available. Financial award application deadline: 2/1; financial award applicants required to submit FAFSA. *Unit head:* Richard L. Schwab, Dean, 860-486-3815, Fax: 860-486-0210, E-mail: richard.schwab@uconn.edu. *Application contact:* Thomas DeFranco, Chairperson, 860-486-3815, Fax: 860-486-0210, E-mail: thomas.defranco@uconn.edu.

University of Dayton, Graduate School, School of Education and Allied Professions, Dayton, OH 45469-1300. Offers MS Ed, DPT, PhD, Ed S. *Accreditation:* NCATE. Part-time and evening/weekend programs available. Postbaccalaureate distance learning degree programs offered (no on-campus study). *Faculty:* 57 full-time (30 women), 86 part-time/adjunct (55 women). *Students:* 691 full-time (492 women), 660 part-time (508 women); includes 158 minority (128 African Americans, 13 Asian Americans or Pacific Islanders, 17 Hispanic Americans), 22 international. Average age 32. 1,015 applicants, 50% accepted, 446 enrolled. In 2009, 444 master's, 5 doctorates, 11 other advanced degrees awarded. *Degree requirements:* For doctorate, comprehensive exam, thesis/dissertation, residency; for Ed S, thesis or alternative. *Entrance requirements:* For master's, GRE or MAT (if GPA less than 2.75); for doctorate, GRE General Test or MAT, administrative experience, master's degree, minimum GPA of 3.5. Additional exam requirements/recommendations for international students: Required—TOEFL (minimum score 550 paper-based; 213 computer-based; 80 iBT). *Application deadline:* For fall admission, 3/15 priority date for domestic students, 3/1 priority date for international students; for winter admission, 7/1 priority date for international students; for spring admission, 1/1 priority date for international students. Applications are processed on a rolling basis. Application fee: $0 ($50 for international students). Electronic applications accepted. *Expenses:* Contact institution. *Financial support:* In 2009–10, 32 research assistantships with full tuition reimbursements (averaging $9,378 per year), 2 teaching assistantships with full tuition reimbursements (averaging $9,378 per year) were awarded. Financial award applicants required to submit FAFSA. *Faculty research:* Charter schools. *Unit head:* Dr. Thomas J. Lasley, Dean, 937-229-3146, Fax: 937-229-3199, E-mail: thomas.lasley@notes.udayton.edu. *Application contact:* Graduate Admissions, 937-229-4411, Fax: 937-229-4729, E-mail: gradadmission@udayton.edu.

University of Delaware, College of Human Services, Education and Public Policy, School of Education, Newark, DE 19716. Offers education (PhD); educational leadership (Ed D); higher education (M Ed); instruction (MI); reading (M Ed); school leadership (M Ed); school psychology (MA, Ed S); teaching English as a second language (TESL) (MA). *Accreditation:* NCATE. Part-time and evening/weekend programs available. Terminal master's awarded for partial completion of doctoral program. *Degree requirements:* For master's, comprehensive exam (for some programs), thesis (for some programs); for doctorate, comprehensive exam (for some programs), thesis/dissertation. *Entrance requirements:* For master's and doctorate, GRE, 3 letters of recommendation. Additional exam requirements/recommendations for international students: Required—TOEFL (minimum score 600 paper-based; 250 computer-based). Electronic applications accepted. *Faculty research:* Teacher education; curriculum theory and development; community based education models, educational leadership.

University of Denver, College of Education, Denver, CO 80208. Offers counseling psychology (MA, PhD); curriculum and instruction (MA, PhD, Certificate), including curriculum leadership (MA, PhD); educational administration and policy studies (Certificate); educational psychology (MA, PhD, Ed S), including child and family studies (MA, PhD), quantitative research methods (MA, PhD), school psychology (PhD, Ed S); higher education and adult studies (MA, PhD); library and information science (MLIS); library and information sciences (Certificate); school administration (PhD). *Accreditation:* ALA; APA (one or more programs are accredited). Part-time and evening/weekend programs available. Postbaccalaureate distance learning degree programs offered (no on-campus study). *Faculty:* 33 full-time (24 women), 62 part-time/adjunct (41 women). *Students:* 384 full-time (305 women), 453 part-time (336 women); includes 164

minority (47 African Americans, 8 American Indian/Alaska Native, 14 Asian Americans or Pacific Islanders, 95 Hispanic Americans), 20 international. Average age 34. 1,065 applicants, 59% accepted, 433 enrolled. In 2009, 206 master's, 38 doctorates, 117 other advanced degrees awarded. Terminal master's awarded for partial completion of doctoral program. *Degree requirements:* For master's, comprehensive exam; for doctorate, 2 foreign languages, comprehensive exam, thesis/dissertation. *Entrance requirements:* For master's and doctorate, GRE General Test or MAT. *Application deadline:* Applications are processed on a rolling basis. Application fee: $50. Electronic applications accepted. *Expenses:* Tuition: Full-time $34,596; part-time $961 per quarter hour. Required fees: $4 per quarter hour. Tuition and fees vary according to course load, campus/location and program. *Financial support:* In 2009–10, 78 teaching assistantships with full and partial tuition reimbursements (averaging $11,700 per year) were awarded; career-related internships or fieldwork, Federal Work-Study, institutionally sponsored loans, and scholarships/grants also available. Support available to part-time students. Financial award application deadline: 3/1; financial award applicants required to submit FAFSA. *Faculty research:* Parkinson's disease, personnel training, development and assessments, gifted education, service-learning, transportation, public schools. Total annual research expenditures: $340,000. *Unit head:* Dr. Gregory M. Anderson, Dean, 303-871-3665. *Application contact:* Janet Erickson, Director of Graduate Admission, 303-871-2485, E-mail: edinfo@du.edu.

University of Detroit Mercy, College of Liberal Arts and Education, Department of Education, Detroit, MI 48221. Offers curriculum and instruction (MA); educational administration (MA); special education (MA), including emotionally impaired, learning disabilities. Part-time and evening/weekend programs available.

University of Evansville, College of Education and Health Sciences, Evansville, IN 47722. Offers MS, DPT. *Accreditation:* APTA; NCATE. *Faculty:* 10 full-time (6 women), 7 part-time/adjunct (4 women). *Students:* 80 full-time (60 women), 6 part-time (4 women), 10 international. Average age 25. 86 applicants, 66% accepted, 42 enrolled. In 2009, 10 master's, 28 doctorates awarded. *Degree requirements:* For doctorate, case study, 30 weeks of full-time clinical internships (20 credit hours). *Entrance requirements:* For master's, GRE or GMAT, 2 letters of reference, interview; for doctorate, bachelor's degree, science and math prerequisite courses, minimum GPA of 2.75, interview, recommendations. Additional exam requirements/recommendations for international students: Required—TOEFL. *Application deadline:* Applications are processed on a rolling basis. *Expenses:* Contact institution. *Financial support:* In 2009–10, 74 students received support. Scholarships/grants available. Financial award applicants required to submit FAFSA. *Faculty research:* Selective functional movement screen, pediatric services, school based physical therapy services, functional movement analysis, gait, interventions for lower extremity injuries, low back pain, lumbar multifidus, typical motor development, cultural competence, international health systems, healthcare ethics, health care marketing. *Unit head:* Dr. Lynn Penland, Dean, 812-488-2360, Fax: 812-488-1146, E-mail: lp22@evansville.edu. *Application contact:* Dr. Lynn Penland, Dean, 812-488-2360, Fax: 812-488-1146, E-mail: lp22@evansville.edu.

The University of Findlay, Graduate and Professional Studies, College of Education, Findlay, OH 45840-3653. Offers administration (MA Ed); early childhood (MA Ed); elementary education (MA Ed); human resource development (MA Ed); leadership (MA Ed); special education (MA Ed); technology (MA Ed); web instruction (MA Ed). *Accreditation:* NCATE. Part-time and evening/weekend programs available. *Degree requirements:* For master's, thesis, cumulative project. *Entrance requirements:* For master's, minimum undergraduate GPA of 2.75 in last 62 hours of course work. Additional exam requirements/recommendations for international students: Required—TOEFL (minimum score 550 paper-based; 213 computer-based; 80 iBT). Electronic applications accepted. *Expenses:* Contact institution. *Faculty research:* Children's literature, books and artwork, educational technology, professional development.

University of Florida, Graduate School, College of Education, Gainesville, FL 32611. Offers M Ed, MAE, Ed D, PhD, Ed S, PhD/JD. *Accreditation:* NCATE. Part-time programs available. Terminal master's awarded for partial completion of doctoral program. *Degree requirements:* For doctorate, thesis/dissertation. *Entrance requirements:* For master's and doctorate, GRE General Test, minimum GPA of 3.0; for Ed S, GRE General Test. Additional exam requirements/recommendations for international students: Required—TOEFL (minimum score 550 paper-based; 213 computer-based). Electronic applications accepted.

University of Georgia, Graduate School, College of Education, Athens, GA 30602. Offers M Ed, MA, MA Ed, MAT, MM Ed, MS, Ed D, PhD, Ed S. *Accreditation:* NCATE. *Faculty:* 177 full-time (90 women), 1 (woman) part-time/adjunct. *Students:* 943 full-time (665 women), 907 part-time (646 women); includes 324 minority (225 African Americans, 7 American Indian/Alaska Native, 45 Asian Americans or Pacific Islanders, 47 Hispanic Americans), 152 international. 1,715 applicants, 52% accepted, 548 enrolled. In 2009, 394 master's, 110 doctorates, 84 other advanced degrees awarded. *Degree requirements:* For doctorate, thesis/dissertation. *Entrance requirements:* For doctorate, GRE General Test. *Application deadline:* For fall admission, 7/1 priority date for domestic students; for spring admission, 11/15 for domestic students. Application fee: $50. Electronic applications accepted. *Expenses:* Tuition, state resident: full-time $6000; part-time $250 per credit hour. Tuition, nonresident: full-time $20,904; part-time $871 per credit hour. Required fees: $730 per semester. *Financial support:* Fellowships, research assistantships, teaching assistantships, unspecified assistantships available. *Unit head:* Dr. Arthur M. Horne, Interim Dean, 706-542-6446, Fax: 706-542-0360, E-mail: ahorne@uga.edu. *Application contact:* Krista Haynes, Director of Enrolled Student Services, 706-425-1789, Fax: 706-425-3094, E-mail: gradoff@uga.edu.

University of Great Falls, Graduate Studies, Programs in Education, Great Falls, MT 59405. Offers M Ed. Part-time and evening/weekend programs available. *Degree requirements:* For master's, thesis, extensive portfolio. *Entrance requirements:* For master's, GRE General Test or MAT, 3 letters of recommendation. Additional exam requirements/recommendations for international students: Required—TOEFL (minimum score 500 paper-based; 205 computer-based). Electronic applications accepted. *Faculty research:* Native American attitudinal research.

University of Guam, Office of Graduate Studies, School of Education, Mangilao, GU 96923. Offers M Ed, MA. *Accreditation:* NCATE. Part-time programs available. *Degree requirements:* For master's, comprehensive oral and written exams. *Entrance requirements:* For master's, GRE General Test. Additional exam requirements/recommendations for international students: Required—TOEFL. *Faculty research:* Multicultural issues, computerized student advising.

University of Hartford, College of Education, Nursing, and Health Professions, West Hartford, CT 06117-1599. Offers M Ed, MS, MSN, MSPT, DPT, Ed D, CAGS, Sixth Year Certificate. *Accreditation:* NCATE. Part-time and evening/weekend programs available. *Degree requirements:* For doctorate, thesis/dissertation; for other advanced degree, comprehensive exam or research project. *Entrance requirements:* For doctorate, MAT. Additional exam requirements/recommendations for international students: Required—TOEFL (minimum score 550 paper-based; 213 computer-based). Electronic applications accepted. *Expenses:* Contact institution.

University of Hawaii at Hilo, Program in Education, Hilo, HI 96720-4091. Offers M Ed. Part-time and evening/weekend programs available. Electronic applications accepted.

University of Hawaii at Manoa, Graduate Division, College of Education, Honolulu, HI 96822. Offers M Ed, M Ed T, MS, PhD, Graduate Certificate. *Accreditation:* NCATE. Part-time and evening/weekend programs available. *Entrance requirements:* Additional exam requirements/recommendations for international students: Required—TOEFL or IELTS. *Expenses:* Tuition, state resident: full-time $8900; part-time $372 per credit. Tuition, nonresident: full-time $21,400; part-time $898 per credit. Required fees: $207 per semester.

University of Houston, College of Education, Houston, TX 77204. Offers M Ed, MS, Ed D, PhD. *Accreditation:* NCATE. Part-time and evening/weekend programs available. *Faculty:* 60 full-time (28 women), 42 part-time/adjunct (28 women). *Students:* 344 full-time (252 women), 470 part-time (351 women); includes 296 minority (122 African Americans, 4 American Indian/Alaska Native, 71 Asian Americans or Pacific Islanders, 99 Hispanic Americans), 58 international. Average age 33. 469 applicants, 69% accepted, 184 enrolled. In 2009, 165 master's, 57 doctorates awarded. *Degree requirements:* For master's, comprehensive exam or thesis; for doctorate, comprehensive exam, thesis/dissertation. *Entrance requirements:* For master's, GRE General Test or MAT; for doctorate, GRE General Test, interview. *Application deadline:* Applications are processed on a rolling basis. Application fee: $75 for international students. Electronic applications accepted. *Expenses:* Tuition, state resident: full-time $7676; part-time $320 per credit hour. Tuition, nonresident: full-time $14,324; part-time $597 per credit hour. Required fees: $3034. *Financial support:* In 2009–10, 10 fellowships with full tuition reimbursements (averaging $9,500 per year), 14 research assistantships with full tuition reimbursements (averaging $9,500 per year), 91 teaching assistantships with full tuition reimbursements (averaging $9,500 per year) were awarded; career-related internships or fieldwork, Federal Work-Study, institutionally sponsored loans, scholarships/grants, health care benefits, and unspecified assistantships also available. Support available to part-time students. Financial award application deadline: 2/1; financial award applicants required to submit FAFSA. *Unit head:* Robert K. Wimpelberg, Dean, 713-743-5008, Fax: 713-743-5013, E-mail: rwimpelberg@uh.edu. *Application contact:* Robert K. Wimpelberg, Dean, 713-743-5008, Fax: 713-743-5013, E-mail: rwimpelberg@uh.edu.

University of Houston–Clear Lake, School of Education, Houston, TX 77058-1098. Offers MS, Ed D. *Accreditation:* NCATE. Part-time and evening/weekend programs available. *Degree requirements:* For master's, thesis optional; for doctorate, comprehensive exam, thesis/dissertation. *Entrance requirements:* For master's, GRE or minimum GPA of 3.0 in last 60 hours; for doctorate, GRE, master's degree, letters of reference. Additional exam requirements/recommendations for international students: Required—TOEFL (minimum score 550 paper-based; 213 computer-based). Electronic applications accepted.

University of Houston–Victoria, School of Education and Human Development, Victoria, TX 77901-4450. Offers administration and supervision (M Ed); counseling (M Ed); curriculum and instruction (M Ed); special education (M Ed). Part-time and evening/weekend programs available. Postbaccalaureate distance learning degree programs offered. *Degree requirements:* For master's, comprehensive exam, project or thesis. *Entrance requirements:* For master's, GRE General Test. Additional exam requirements/recommendations for international students: Required—TOEFL. Electronic applications accepted. *Faculty research:* Reading and language arts education, evaluation and diagnosis of special children's abilities.

University of Idaho, College of Graduate Studies, College of Education, Moscow, ID 83844-2282. Offers M Ed, MS, Ed D, PhD, Ed S, Ed Sp PTE. *Accreditation:* NCATE. *Faculty:* 56 full-time (33 women), 42 part-time/adjunct (8 women). *Students:* 125 full-time (83 women), 454 part-time (277 women). In 2009, 123 master's, 34 doctorates, 53 other advanced degrees awarded. *Degree requirements:* For doctorate, thesis/dissertation. *Entrance requirements:* For master's, minimum GPA of 2.8; for doctorate, minimum undergraduate GPA of 2.8, 3.0 graduate. *Application deadline:* For fall admission, 8/1 for domestic students; for spring admission, 12/15 for domestic students. Application fee: $55 ($60 for international students). *Expenses:* Tuition, state resident: full-time $6120. Tuition, nonresident: full-time $17,712. *Financial support:* Teaching assistantships, Federal Work-Study available. Support available to part-time students. Financial award application deadline: 2/15. *Faculty research:* Technology integration, curricular development for cooperative environments, increasing science literacy, best practices for online pedagogy. *Unit head:* Dr. Jerry McMurtry, Interim Dean, 208-885-6773. *Application contact:* Dr. Jerry McMurtry, Interim Dean, 208-885-6773.

University of Illinois at Chicago, Graduate College, College of Education, Chicago, IL 60607-7128. Offers M Ed, Ed D, PhD. Part-time and evening/weekend programs available. Terminal master's awarded for partial completion of doctoral program. *Degree requirements:* For doctorate, thesis/dissertation. *Entrance requirements:* For master's, minimum GPA of 2.75; for doctorate, GRE General Test, minimum GPA of 2.75. Additional exam requirements/recommendations for international students: Required—TOEFL. Electronic applications accepted. *Faculty research:* Teaching and learning, program design, school and classroom organization with emphasis on urban settings.

University of Illinois at Springfield, Graduate Programs, College of Education and Human Services, Springfield, IL 62703-5407. Offers MA. Part-time and evening/weekend programs available. Postbaccalaureate distance learning degree programs offered (no on-campus study). *Faculty:* 18 full-time (7 women), 14 part-time/adjunct (7 women). *Students:* 69 full-time (59 women), 430 part-time (319 women); includes 61 minority (50 African Americans, 3 American Indian/Alaska Native, 3 Asian Americans or Pacific Islanders, 5 Hispanic Americans), 2 international. Average age 35. 213 applicants, 59% accepted, 87 enrolled. In 2009, 161 master's awarded. *Entrance requirements:* Additional exam requirements/recommendations for international students: Required—TOEFL (minimum score 500 paper-based; 176 computer-based; 61 iBT). Application fee: $50 ($60 for international students). Electronic applications accepted. *Expenses:* Tuition, state resident: full-time $6390; part-time $266.25 per credit hour. Tuition, nonresident: full-time $14,226; part-time $592.75 per credit hour. Required fees: $2044; $14.36 per credit hour. $722.50 per term. *Financial support:* In 2009–10, research assistantships with full tuition reimbursements (averaging $8,109 per year), teaching assistantships with full tuition reimbursements (averaging $8,109 per year) were awarded; career-related internships or fieldwork, Federal Work-Study, scholarships/grants, health care benefits, and unspecified assistantships also available. Support available to part-time students. Financial award application deadline: 11/15; financial award applicants required to submit FAFSA. *Unit head:* Dr. Larry Stonecipher, Dean, 217-206-7815, Fax: 217-206-6775, E-mail: stonecipher.larry@uis.edu. *Application contact:* Dr. Lynn Pardie, Office of Graduate Studies, 800-252-8533, Fax: 217-206-7623, E-mail: pardie.lynn@uis.edu.

University of Illinois at Urbana–Champaign, Graduate College, College of Education, Champaign, IL 61820. Offers Ed M, MA, MS, Ed D, PhD, CAS, MBA/M Ed. *Faculty:* 91 full-time (50 women), 3 part-time/adjunct (all women). *Students:* 437 full-time (295 women), 651 part-time (457 women); includes 266 minority (137 African Americans, 6 American Indian/Alaska Native, 52 Asian Americans or Pacific Islanders, 71 Hispanic Americans), 168 international. 829 applicants, 45% accepted, 212 enrolled. In 2009, 262 master's, 74 doctorates, 5 other advanced degrees awarded. *Application deadline:* Applications are processed on a rolling basis. Application fee: $60 ($75 for international students). Electronic applications accepted. *Financial support:* In 2009–10, 93 fellowships, 156 research assistantships, 160 teaching assistantships were awarded; tuition waivers (full and partial) also available. *Unit head:* Mary A. Kalantzis, Dean, 217-333-0960, Fax: 217-333-5847, E-mail: kalantzi@illinois.edu. *Application contact:* Mary A. Kalantzis, Dean, 217-333-0960, Fax: 217-333-5847, E-mail: kalantzi@illinois.edu.

University of Indianapolis, Graduate Programs, School of Education, Indianapolis, IN 46227-3697. Offers art education (MAT); biology (MAT); chemistry (MAT); curriculum and instruction (MA); earth sciences (MAT); education (MA, MAT); educational leadership (MA); elementary education (MA); English (MAT); French (MAT); math (MAT); physical education (MAT); physics (MAT); secondary education (MA), including art education, education, English education, social studies education; social studies (MAT); Spanish (MAT). *Accreditation:* NCATE. Part-time and evening/weekend programs available. *Faculty:* 4 full-time (3 women), 3 part-time/adjunct (2 women). *Students:* 52 full-time (28 women), 110 part-time (67 women); includes 3 minority (all African Americans), 2 international. Average age 33. *Entrance requirements:* For master's, GRE Subject Test, PRAXIS I, minimum GPA of 2.5, 3 letters of recommendation, interview, writing exercise. Additional exam requirements/recommendations for international students: Required—TOEFL (minimum score 550 paper-based; 213 computer-based). *Application deadline:* Applications are processed on a rolling basis. Application fee: $50. *Financial support:* Federal Work-Study available. Financial award application deadline: 5/1; financial award applicants required to submit FAFSA. *Faculty research:* Assessment of teacher education, perceptions of prospective teachers by parents. *Unit head:* Dr. Kathy Moran, Dean, 317-788-3285, Fax: 317-788-3300, E-mail: kmoran@uindy.edu. *Application contact:* Chemain Slater, 317-788-2051, E-mail: slaterc@uindy.edu.

The University of Iowa, Graduate College, College of Education, Iowa City, IA 52242-1316. Offers MA, MAT, PhD, Ed S, JD/PhD. *Degree requirements:* For master's and Ed S, exam; for

Education—General

The University of Iowa (continued)

doctorate, comprehensive exam, thesis/dissertation. *Entrance requirements:* For master's, doctorate, and Ed S, GRE General Test, minimum GPA of 3.0. Additional exam requirements/recommendations for international students: Required—TOEFL (minimum score 550 paper-based; 213 computer-based; 81 iBT). Electronic applications accepted. *Faculty research:* Computer-assisted instrumentation, testing and measurement, instructional design.

The University of Kansas, Graduate Studies, School of Education, Lawrence, KS 66045-3101. Offers MA, MS, MS Ed, Ed D, PhD, Ed S. *Accreditation:* NCATE. Part-time programs available. *Students:* 714 full-time (499 women), 431 part-time (319 women); includes 119 minority (37 African Americans, 13 American Indian/Alaska Native, 33 Asian Americans or Pacific Islanders, 36 Hispanic Americans), 129 international. Average age 32. 788 applicants, 62% accepted, 363 enrolled. In 2009, 274 master's, 46 doctorates, 10 other advanced degrees awarded. *Degree requirements:* For doctorate, thesis/dissertation. *Entrance requirements:* For master's and Ed S, minimum GPA of 3.0; for doctorate, GRE General Test. Additional exam requirements/recommendations for international students: Required—TOEFL. Application fee: $45 ($55 for international students). Electronic applications accepted. *Expenses:* Tuition, state resident: full-time $6492; part-time $270.50 per credit hour. Tuition, nonresident: full-time $15,510; part-time $646.25 per credit hour. Required fees: $847; $70.56 per credit hour. Tuition and fees vary according to course load and program. *Financial support:* Fellowships, research assistantships with partial tuition reimbursements, teaching assistantships with full and partial tuition reimbursements, career-related internships or fieldwork, scholarships/grants, and unspecified assistantships available. Financial award application deadline: 2/1. *Unit head:* Dr. Rick Ginsberg, Dean, 785-864-4297. *Application contact:* Mary Ann Williams, Graduate Admissions Coordinator, 785-864-4510, E-mail: mwilliams@ku.edu.

University of Kentucky, Graduate School, College of Education, Lexington, KY 40506-0032. Offers M Ed, MA Ed, MRC, MS, MS Ed, Ed D, PhD, Ed S. *Accreditation:* NCATE. Part-time and evening/weekend programs available. Terminal master's awarded for partial completion of doctoral program. *Degree requirements:* For master's and Ed S, comprehensive exam; for doctorate, comprehensive exam, thesis/dissertation. *Entrance requirements:* For master's, GRE General Test, minimum undergraduate GPA of 2.75; for doctorate, GRE General Test, minimum graduate GPA of 3.0; for Ed S, GRE General Test. Additional exam requirements/recommendations for international students: Required—TOEFL (minimum score 550 paper-based; 213 computer-based). Electronic applications accepted.

University of La Verne, College of Education and Organizational Leadership, Credential Program in Teacher Education, La Verne, CA 91750-4443. Offers multiple subject (Credential); single subject (Credential). Part-time programs available. *Faculty:* 19 full-time (14 women), 35 part-time/adjunct (27 women). *Students:* 40 full-time (29 women), 176 part-time (127 women); includes 88 minority (8 African Americans, 1 American Indian/Alaska Native, 7 Asian Americans or Pacific Islanders, 72 Hispanic Americans). Average age 32. *Entrance requirements:* For degree, California Basic Educational Skills Test, minimum GPA of 3.0, interview, writing sample. Additional exam requirements/recommendations for international students: Required—TOEFL (minimum score 550 paper-based; 213 computer-based). *Application deadline:* Applications are processed on a rolling basis. Application fee: $50. *Expenses:* Contact institution. *Financial support:* Institutionally sponsored loans, scholarships/grants, and unspecified assistantships available. Financial award application deadline: 3/2; financial award applicants required to submit FAFSA. *Unit head:* Dr. Anita Flemington, Chairperson, 909-593-3511 Ext. 4623, E-mail: aflemington@laverne.edu. *Application contact:* Christy Ranells, Program and Admission Specialist, 909-593-3511 Ext. 4644, Fax: 909-392-2761, E-mail: cranells@laverne.edu.

University of La Verne, College of Education and Organizational Leadership, Master's Program in Education, La Verne, CA 91750-4443. Offers advanced teaching skills (M Ed); education (special emphasis) (M Ed). Part-time programs available. *Faculty:* 19 full-time (14 women), 35 part-time/adjunct (27 women). *Students:* 28 full-time (22 women), 133 part-time (106 women); includes 78 minority (11 African Americans, 4 American Indian/Alaska Native, 5 Asian Americans or Pacific Islanders, 58 Hispanic Americans). Average age 32. In 2009, 49 master's awarded. *Degree requirements:* For master's, thesis optional. *Entrance requirements:* For master's, California Basic Educational Skills Test, interview, writing sample, minimum GPA of 3.0, 3 letters of recommendation. Additional exam requirements/recommendations for international students: Required—TOEFL (minimum score 550 paper-based; 213 computer-based). *Application deadline:* Applications are processed on a rolling basis. Application fee: $50. *Expenses:* Contact institution. *Financial support:* Institutionally sponsored loans and unspecified assistantships available. Financial award application deadline: 3/2; financial award applicants required to submit FAFSA. *Unit head:* Valerie Beltran, Chair, 909-593-3511 Ext. 4659, E-mail: vbeltran@laverne.edu. *Application contact:* Christy Ranells, Program and Admission Specialist, 909-593-3511 Ext. 4644, Fax: 909-392-2761, E-mail: cranells@ulv.edu.

University of La Verne, Regional Campus Administration, Graduate Credential Program in Education, California Statewide Campus, La Verne, CA 91750-4443. Offers cross cultural language and academic development (Credential); multiple subject (Credential); single subject (Credential). *Faculty:* 2 full-time (1 woman), 1 (woman) part-time/adjunct. *Students:* 101 full-time (70 women), 50 part-time (40 women); includes 45 minority (5 African Americans, 3 American Indian/Alaska Native, 5 Asian Americans or Pacific Islanders, 32 Hispanic Americans). Average age 33. *Entrance requirements:* For degree, California Basic Educational Skills Test, minimum undergraduate GPA of 2.75, 3 letters of recommendation, interview. *Application deadline:* Applications are processed on a rolling basis. Application fee: $50. *Expenses:* Contact institution. *Financial support:* Institutionally sponsored loans available. Financial award application deadline: 3/2; financial award applicants required to submit FAFSA. *Unit head:* Juline Behrens, Director, 800-695-4858 Ext. 5400, Fax: 909-981-8695, E-mail: jbehrens@laverne.edu. *Application contact:* Juline Behrens, Director, 800-695-4858 Ext. 5400, Fax: 909-981-8695, E-mail: jbehrens@laverne.edu.

University of La Verne, Regional Campus Administration, Master's Programs in Education, California Statewide Campus, La Verne, CA 91750-4443. Offers educational management (M Ed), including preliminary administrative services credential; multiple or single subject teaching credential (M Ed); school counseling (MS), including public personnel services credential. *Faculty:* 3 full-time (1 woman), 97 part-time/adjunct (58 women). *Students:* 145 full-time (117 women), 174 part-time (139 women); includes 165 minority (31 African Americans, 2 American Indian/Alaska Native, 12 Asian Americans or Pacific Islanders, 120 Hispanic Americans). Average age 34. In 2009, 208 master's awarded. *Entrance requirements:* For master's, California Basic Educational Skills Test, 3 letters of recommendation, teaching credential. *Application deadline:* Applications are processed on a rolling basis. Application fee: $50. *Expenses:* Contact institution. *Financial support:* Fellowships, institutionally sponsored loans available. Financial award application deadline: 3/2; financial award applicants required to submit FAFSA. *Unit head:* Juline Behrens, Director, 800-695-4858 Ext. 5400, Fax: 909-981-8695, E-mail: jbehrens@laverne.edu. *Application contact:* Juline Behrens, Director, 800-695-4858 Ext. 5400, Fax: 909-981-8695, E-mail: jbehrens@laverne.edu.

University of Lethbridge, School of Graduate Studies, Lethbridge, AB T1K 3M4, Canada. Offers accounting (MScM); addictions counseling (M Sc); agricultural biotechnology (M Sc); agricultural studies (M Sc, MA); anthropology (MA); archaeology (MA); art (MA, MFA); biochemistry (M Sc); biological sciences (M Sc); biomolecular science (PhD); biosystems and biodiversity (PhD); Canadian studies (MA); chemistry (M Sc); computer science (M Sc); computer science and geographical information science (M Sc); counseling psychology (M Ed); dramatic arts (MA); earth, space, and physical science (PhD); economics (MA); educational leadership (M Ed); English (MA); environmental science (M Sc); evolution and behavior (PhD); exercise science (M Sc); finance (MScM); French (MA); French/German (MA); French/Spanish (MA); general education (M Ed); general management (MScM); geography (M Sc, MA); German (MA); health science (M Sc); health sciences (MA); history (MA); human resource management and labour relations (MScM); individualized multidisciplinary (M Sc, MA); information systems (MScM); international management (MScM); kinesiology (M Sc, MA); management (M Sc, MA); marketing (MScM); mathematics (M Sc); music (M Mus, MA); Native American studies (MA); neuroscience (M Sc, PhD); new media (MA); nursing (M Sc); philosophy (MA); physics (M Sc); policy and strategy (MScM); political science (MA); psychology (M Sc, MA); religious studies (MA); social sciences (MA); sociology (MA); theatre and dramatic arts (MFA); theoretical and computational science (PhD); urban and regional studies (MA); women's studies (MA). Part-time and evening/weekend programs available. *Degree requirements:* For doctorate, comprehensive exam, thesis/dissertation. *Entrance requirements:* For master's, GMAT (M Sc in management), bachelor's degree in related field, minimum GPA of 3.0 during previous 20 graded semester courses, 2 years teaching or related experience (M Ed); for doctorate, master's degree, minimum graduate GPA of 3.5. Additional exam requirements/recommendations for international students: Required—TOEFL. *Faculty research:* Movement and brain plasticity, gibberellin physiology, photosynthesis, carbon cycling, molecular properties of main-group ring components.

University of Louisiana at Lafayette, College of Education, Lafayette, LA 70504. Offers M Ed, Ed D. *Accreditation:* NCATE. Part-time programs available. *Degree requirements:* For master's, thesis or alternative. *Entrance requirements:* For master's, GRE General Test, teaching certificate. Additional exam requirements/recommendations for international students: Required—TOEFL (minimum score 550 paper-based; 213 computer-based). Electronic applications accepted.

University of Louisiana at Monroe, Graduate School, College of Education and Human Development, Monroe, LA 71209-0001. Offers M Ed, MA, MAT, MS, Ed D, PhD, SSP. *Accreditation:* NCATE. Part-time and evening/weekend programs available. Postbaccalaureate distance learning degree programs offered. *Faculty:* 78 full-time (53 women), 8 part-time/adjunct (4 women). *Students:* 172 full-time (129 women), 304 part-time (243 women); includes 129 minority (121 African Americans, 4 American Indian/Alaska Native, 4 Hispanic Americans), 5 international. Average age 34. In 2009, 140 master's, 10 doctorates, 2 other advanced degrees awarded. *Degree requirements:* For master's, thesis; for doctorate, thesis/dissertation. *Entrance requirements:* For master's, GRE General Test, minimum cumulative GPA of 2.75; for doctorate, GRE General Test (minimum score of 1000 Verbal and Quantitative or 1500 Verbal, Quantitative and Analytic), minimum cumulative GPA of 2.75; for SSP, GRE General Test, minimum cumulative GPA of 3.0. Additional exam requirements/recommendations for international students: Required—TOEFL (minimum score 500 paper-based; 173 computer-based; 61 iBT). *Application deadline:* For fall admission, 8/24 priority date for domestic students, 7/1 for international students; for winter admission, 12/14 priority date for domestic students; for spring admission, 1/19 priority date for domestic students, 11/1 for international students. Applications are processed on a rolling basis. Application fee: $20 ($30 for international students). Electronic applications accepted. *Expenses:* Tuition, state resident: part-time $159 per credit hour. Tuition, nonresident: part-time $159 per credit hour. Required fees: $1300 per year. Tuition and fees vary according to course load. *Financial support:* In 2009–10, 31 research assistantships (averaging $2,944 per year), 3 teaching assistantships (averaging $3,333 per year) were awarded; career-related internships or fieldwork, Federal Work-Study, institutionally sponsored loans, and unspecified assistantships also available. Financial award application deadline: 4/1; financial award applicants required to submit FAFSA. *Unit head:* Dr. Sandra M. Lemoine, Dean, 318-342-1235, Fax: 318-342-1240, E-mail: slemoine@ulm.edu. *Application contact:* Dr. Jack Palmer, Director of Graduate Studies, 318-342-1250, Fax: 318-342-1240, E-mail: palmer@ulm.edu.

University of Louisville, Graduate School, College of Education and Human Development, Louisville, KY 40292-0001. Offers M Ed, MA, MAT, MS, Ed D, PhD, Ed S. *Accreditation:* NCATE. Part-time and evening/weekend programs available. Postbaccalaureate distance learning degree programs offered. *Faculty:* 96 full-time (60 women), 62 part-time/adjunct (45 women). *Students:* 521 full-time (355 women), 732 part-time (531 women); includes 167 minority (131 African Americans, 2 American Indian/Alaska Native, 21 Asian Americans or Pacific Islanders, 13 Hispanic Americans), 21 international. Average age 33. 714 applicants, 58% accepted, 303 enrolled. In 2009, 404 master's, 42 doctorates, 22 other advanced degrees awarded. Terminal master's awarded for partial completion of doctoral program. *Entrance requirements:* For master's, doctorate, and Ed S, GRE General Test. Additional exam requirements/recommendations for international students: Required—TOEFL (minimum score 560 paper-based; 210 computer-based; 83 iBT). Application fee: $50. Electronic applications accepted. *Financial support:* In 2009–10, 272 students received support, including 7 fellowships with full tuition reimbursements available (averaging $18,000 per year), 26 research assistantships with full tuition reimbursements available (averaging $18,000 per year), 13 teaching assistantships with full tuition reimbursements available (averaging $18,000 per year); career-related internships or fieldwork, Federal Work-Study, and scholarships/grants also available. Financial award application deadline: 6/1. *Faculty research:* Mathematics and science education, early childhood development, literacy acquisition and development, culturally responsive education, instructional technology development, health promotion, sports administration, exercise physiology, prevention science, counseling psychology, mental health counseling, school counseling, college student personnel, art therapy, educational leadership, school reform, evaluation, P-12 and higher education administration, organizational development. Total annual research expenditures: $8 million. *Unit head:* Dr. Blake Haselton, Interim Dean, 502-852-6411, Fax: 502-852-1464, E-mail: blake.haselton@louisville.edu. *Application contact:* Libby Leggett, Director, Graduate Admissions, 502-852-3101, Fax: 502-852-6536, E-mail: gradadm@louisville.edu.

University of Maine, Graduate School, College of Education and Human Development, Interdisciplinary Program in Teaching, Orono, ME 04469. Offers MST. *Students:* 14 full-time (12 women), 33 part-time (25 women); includes 3 minority (1 African American, 1 American Indian/Alaska Native, 1 Asian American or Pacific Islander), 1 international. Average age 41. 12 applicants, 67% accepted, 7 enrolled. In 2009, 10 master's awarded. *Entrance requirements:* For master's, GRE General Test, MAT. Application fee: $65. *Unit head:* Dr. Susan McKay, Director, 207-581-1016. *Application contact:* Scott G. Delcourt, Associate Dean of the Graduate School, 207-581-3219, Fax: 207-581-3232, E-mail: graduate@maine.edu.

University of Maine at Farmington, Program in Education, Farmington, ME 04938-1990. Offers administration (MS Ed); educational technology (MS Ed); studies in literature and literacy (MS Ed). *Accreditation:* NCATE. *Entrance requirements:* For master's, teaching certificate, 2 years' teaching experience.

University of Manitoba, Faculty of Graduate Studies, College Universitaire de Saint Boniface, Education ProgramûSaint-Boniface, Winnipeg, MB R3T 2N2, Canada. Offers M Ed.

University of Manitoba, Faculty of Graduate Studies, Faculty of Education, Winnipeg, MB R3T 2N2, Canada. Offers M Ed, PhD. *Degree requirements:* For master's, thesis or alternative.

University of Mary, Program in Education, Bismarck, ND 58504-9652. Offers college teaching (M Ed); curriculum, instruction and assessment (M Ed); early childhood education (M Ed); early childhood special education (M Ed); elementary education administration (M Ed); emotional disorders (M Ed); learning disabilities (M Ed); reading (M Ed); secondary education administration (M Ed); special education (M Ed); special education strategist (M Ed). Part-time programs available. *Degree requirements:* For master's, portfolio or thesis. *Entrance requirements:* For master's, interview, letters of reference. Additional exam requirements/recommendations for international students: Required—TOEFL (minimum score 550 paper-based). *Expenses:* Tuition: Full-time $10,062; part-time $430 per credit. Tuition and fees vary according to course load, degree level, program and student level. *Faculty research:* Innovative pedagogy in higher education, technology in education, content standards, children of poverty, children with diverse learning needs.

University of Mary Hardin-Baylor, Graduate Studies in Education, Belton, TX 76513. Offers educational administration (M Ed, Ed D); educational psychology (M Ed); exercise and sport science (M Ed); general studies (M Ed); reading education (M Ed). Part-time and evening/weekend programs available. *Degree requirements:* For master's, comprehensive exam; for doctorate, thesis/dissertation. *Entrance requirements:* For master's, GRE General Test, minimum GPA of 2.75, Texas teaching certificate. Electronic applications accepted.

University of Maryland, Baltimore County, Graduate School, College of Arts, Humanities and Social Sciences, Department of Education, Baltimore, MD 21250. Offers computer/web-based instruction (Postbaccalaureate Certificate); distance education (Postbaccalaureate Certificate); education (MA), including mathematics education, science education, STEM education; elementary/middle science education (Postbaccalaureate Certificate); instructional systems development: training systems (MA, Graduate Certificate), including distance education (Graduate Certificate), e-learning in instructional design (Graduate Certificate), instructional systems development, instructional technology (Graduate Certificate); language, literacy, culture (PhD); math education (Postbaccalaureate Certificate); STEM education (Postbaccalaureate Certificate); teaching (MAT), including early childhood education, elementary education, secondary education; teaching English to speakers of other languages (MA, Postbaccalaureate Certificate). *Accreditation:* NCATE. Part-time and evening/weekend programs available. Postbaccalaureate distance learning degree programs offered (no on-campus study). *Faculty:* 24 full-time (18 women), 25 part-time/adjunct (19 women). *Students:* 90 full-time (79 women), 320 part-time (264 women); includes 64 minority (36 African Americans, 2 American Indian/Alaska Native, 16 Asian Americans or Pacific Islanders, 10 Hispanic Americans), 21 international. Average age 34. 209 applicants, 63% accepted, 98 enrolled. In 2009, 106 master's, 3 doctorates awarded. *Degree requirements:* For master's, comprehensive exam (for some programs), thesis (for some programs); for doctorate, comprehensive exam, thesis/dissertation. *Entrance requirements:* For master's, GRE General Test, GRE Subject Test (MA), PRAXIS I (MAT), minimum GPA of 3.0. Additional exam requirements/recommendations for international students: Required—TOEFL. *Application deadline:* For fall admission, 6/1 for domestic students; for spring admission, 11/1 for domestic students. Applications are processed on a rolling basis. Application fee: $50. Electronic applications accepted. *Financial support:* In 2009–10, 12 students received support, including research assistantships with full tuition reimbursements available (averaging $12,000 per year); fellowships, teaching assistantships, career-related internships or fieldwork, Federal Work-Study, scholarships/grants, tuition waivers (partial), and unspecified assistantships also available. Financial award application deadline: 3/1. *Faculty research:* Teacher leadership; STEM education; ESOL/bilingual education; early childhood education; language, literacy and culture. Total annual research expenditures: $1.3 million. *Unit head:* Dr. Eugene Schaffer, Department Chair, 410-455-2465, Fax: 410-455-3986, E-mail: schaffer@umbc.edu. *Application contact:* Dr. Susan M. Blunck, Director, 410-455-2869, Fax: 410-455-3986, E-mail: blunck@umbc.edu.

University of Maryland, College Park, Academic Affairs, College of Education, College Park, MD 20742. Offers M Ed, MA, Ed D, PhD, AGSC, CAGS. *Accreditation:* NCATE. Part-time and evening/weekend programs available. Postbaccalaureate distance learning degree programs offered. *Faculty:* 188 full-time (130 women), 90 part-time/adjunct (72 women). *Students:* 808 full-time (628 women), 390 part-time (304 women); includes 329 minority (178 African Americans, 7 American Indian/Alaska Native, 86 Asian Americans or Pacific Islanders, 58 Hispanic Americans), 129 international. 1,145 applicants, 33% accepted, 253 enrolled. In 2009, 273 master's, 67 doctorates, 5 other advanced degrees awarded. *Degree requirements:* For doctorate, thesis/dissertation. *Entrance requirements:* For master's, GRE General Test or MAT, minimum GPA of 3.0. *Application deadline:* For fall admission, 12/15 for domestic students, 2/1 for international students; for spring admission, 6/1 for international students. Applications are processed on a rolling basis. Application fee: $60. Electronic applications accepted. *Expenses:* Tuition, area resident: Part-time $471 per credit hour. Tuition, state resident: part-time $471 per credit hour. Tuition, nonresident: part-time $1016 per credit hour. Required fees: $337.04 per term. *Financial support:* In 2009–10, 56 fellowships with full and partial tuition reimbursements (averaging $17,736 per year), 44 research assistantships with tuition reimbursements (averaging $17,235 per year), 282 teaching assistantships with tuition reimbursements (averaging $16,475 per year) were awarded; career-related internships or fieldwork, Federal Work-Study, and scholarships/grants also available. Support available to part-time students. Financial award applicants required to submit FAFSA. Total annual research expenditures: $13.4 million. *Unit head:* Donna L. Wiseman, Dean, 301-405-2336, Fax: 301-314-9890, E-mail: dlwise@umd.edu. *Application contact:* Dean of Graduate School, 301-405-0376, Fax: 301-314-9305.

See Close-Up on page 715.

University of Maryland Eastern Shore, Graduate Programs, Department of Education, Program in Teaching, Princess Anne, MD 21853-1299. Offers MAT. *Accreditation:* NCATE. *Degree requirements:* For master's, comprehensive exam, internship, seminar paper, PRAXIS II. *Entrance requirements:* For master's, PRAXIS I, interview, minimum GPA of 3.0, writing sample. Additional exam requirements/recommendations for international students: Required—TOEFL (minimum score 213 computer-based; 80 iBT). Electronic applications accepted.

University of Maryland University College, Graduate School of Management and Technology, Master of Arts in Teaching Program, Adelphi, MD 20783. Offers MAT. *Students:* 45 part-time (35 women); includes 12 minority (7 African Americans, 3 Asian Americans or Pacific Islanders, 2 Hispanic Americans). Average age 32. 302 applicants, 100% accepted, 43 enrolled. *Degree requirements:* For master's, comprehensive exam, thesis or alternative. *Application deadline:* Applications are processed on a rolling basis. Application fee: $50. Electronic applications accepted. *Expenses:* Tuition, state resident: full-time $7704; part-time $428 per credit hour. Tuition, nonresident: full-time $11,862; part-time $659 per credit hour. *Financial support:* Application deadline: 6/1. *Unit head:* Dr. Barbara Schwartz-Bechet, Director, 240-684-2400, Fax: 240-684-2401, E-mail: bschwartz-bechet@umuc.edu. *Application contact:* Coordinator, Graduate Admissions, 800-888-UMUC, Fax: 240-684-2151, E-mail: newgrad@umuc.edu.

University of Maryland University College, Graduate School of Management and Technology, Program in Education, Adelphi, MD 20783. Offers M Ed. Part-time and evening/weekend programs available. Postbaccalaureate distance learning degree programs offered (no on-campus study). *Students:* 5 full-time (all women), 290 part-time (221 women); includes 101 minority (77 African Americans, 2 American Indian/Alaska Native, 12 Asian Americans or Pacific Islanders, 10 Hispanic Americans), 3 international. Average age 36. 153 applicants, 100% accepted, 63 enrolled. In 2009, 33 master's awarded. *Degree requirements:* For master's, thesis or alternative. *Application deadline:* Applications are processed on a rolling basis. Application fee: $50. Electronic applications accepted. *Expenses:* Tuition, state resident: full-time $7704; part-time $428 per credit hour. Tuition, nonresident: full-time $11,862; part-time $659 per credit hour. *Financial support:* Federal Work-Study and scholarships/grants available. Support available to part-time students. Financial award application deadline: 6/1; financial award applicants required to submit FAFSA. *Unit head:* Dr. Gail Viamonte, Director, 240-684-2400, Fax: 240-684-2401, E-mail: gviamonte@umuc.edu. *Application contact:* Coordinator, Graduate Admissions, 800-888-UMUC, Fax: 240-684-2151, E-mail: newgrad@umuc.edu.

University of Mary Washington, College of Graduate and Professional Studies, Fredericksburg, VA 22406-7239. Offers business administration (MBA); education (M Ed); management information systems (MSMIS). Part-time and evening/weekend programs available. *Entrance requirements:* For master's, GMAT (MBA), PRAXIS I (M Ed), minimum GPA of 3.0. Additional exam requirements/recommendations for international students: Required—TOEFL (minimum score 600 paper-based; 250 computer-based; 100 iBT).

University of Massachusetts Amherst, Graduate School, School of Education, Amherst, MA 01003. Offers M Ed, Ed D, PhD, CAGS. *Accreditation:* NCATE. Part-time programs available. Postbaccalaureate distance learning degree programs offered (minimal on-campus study). *Faculty:* 74 full-time (41 women). *Students:* 396 full-time (284 women), 351 part-time (236 women); includes 117 minority (60 African Americans, 2 American Indian/Alaska Native, 17 Asian Americans or Pacific Islanders, 38 Hispanic Americans), 109 international. Average age 34. 760 applicants, 64% accepted, 269 enrolled. In 2009, 183 master's, 22 doctorates awarded. Terminal master's awarded for partial completion of doctoral program. *Degree requirements:* For master's, thesis or alternative; for doctorate, comprehensive exam, thesis/dissertation. *Entrance requirements:* Additional exam requirements/recommendations for international students: Required—TOEFL (minimum score 550 paper-based; 213 computer-based; 80 iBT), IELTS (minimum score 6.5). *Application deadline:* For fall admission, 1/15 for domestic and international students. Applications are processed on a rolling basis. Application fee: $50 ($65

for international students). Electronic applications accepted. *Expenses:* Tuition, state resident: full-time $2640; part-time $110 per credit. Tuition, nonresident: full-time $9936; part-time $414 per credit. Tuition and fees vary according to course load. *Financial support:* In 2009–10, 1 fellowship with full tuition reimbursement (averaging $8,036 per year), research assistantships with full tuition reimbursements (averaging $8,555 per year), 83 teaching assistantships with full tuition reimbursements (averaging $4,661 per year) were awarded; career-related internships or fieldwork, Federal Work-Study, scholarships/grants, traineeships, health care benefits, tuition waivers (full), and unspecified assistantships also available. Support available to part-time students. Financial award application deadline: 1/15. *Unit head:* Dr. Christine B. McCormick, Dean, 413-545-6984, Fax: 413-545-4240. *Application contact:* Jean M. Ames, Supervisor of Admissions, 413-545-0722, Fax: 413-577-0010, E-mail: gradadm@grad.umass.edu.

University of Massachusetts Boston, Office of Graduate Studies, Graduate College of Education, Boston, MA 02125-3393. Offers M Ed, MA, Ed D, CAGS, Certificate. Part-time and evening/weekend programs available. *Degree requirements:* For master's, comprehensive exam; for doctorate, comprehensive exam, thesis/dissertation. *Entrance requirements:* For master's, GRE General Test or MAT; for doctorate, GRE General Test or MAT, minimum GPA of 2.75; for other advanced degree, minimum GPA of 2.75. *Faculty research:* Effects of ethnicity on applied psychology and education, enhancing equity and excellence in public schools, diversity and change in higher education, improving the functioning of individuals with disabilities.

University of Massachusetts Dartmouth, Graduate School, School of Education, Public Policy, and Civic Engagement, Department of Teaching and Learning, North Dartmouth, MA 02747-2300. Offers elementary education (MAT, Postbaccalaureate Certificate); middle school education (MAT); principal initial licensure (Postbaccalaureate Certificate); secondary school education (MAT). *Faculty:* 7 full-time (4 women), 6 part-time/adjunct (3 women). *Students:* 53 full-time (33 women), 183 part-time (118 women); includes 16 minority (6 African Americans, 1 American Indian/Alaska Native, 2 Asian Americans or Pacific Islanders, 7 Hispanic Americans). Average age 35. 188 applicants, 75% accepted, 109 enrolled. In 2009, 34 master's, 4 other advanced degrees awarded. *Degree requirements:* For master's, thesis or alternative. *Entrance requirements:* For master's, MAT or GRE, GMAT, minimum undergraduate GPA of 2.7, teacher certification, 3 letters of recommendation. Additional exam requirements/recommendations for international students: Required—TOEFL (minimum score 500 paper-based). *Application deadline:* For fall admission, 4/20 priority date for domestic students, 2/20 for international students; for spring admission, 11/15 priority date for domestic students, 9/15 for international students. Applications are processed on a rolling basis. Application fee: $40 ($60 for international students). *Expenses:* Tuition, state resident: full-time $2071; part-time $86.29 per credit. Tuition, nonresident: full-time $8099; part-time $337.46 per credit. Required fees: $9446. Tuition and fees vary according to class time, course load and reciprocity agreements. *Financial support:* Federal Work-Study available. Financial award application deadline: 3/1. Total annual research expenditures: $1.3 million. *Unit head:* Dr. Gerard Koot, Director, 508-999-8305, Fax: 508-999-9125, E-mail: gkoot@umassd.edu. *Application contact:* Elan Turcotte-Shamski, Graduate Admissions Officer, 508-999-8604, Fax: 508-999-8183, E-mail: graduate@umassd.edu.

University of Massachusetts Lowell, Graduate School of Education, Lowell, MA 01854-2881. Offers administration, planning, and policy (CAGS); curriculum and instruction (M Ed, CAGS); educational administration (M Ed); language arts and literacy (Ed D); leadership in schooling (Ed D); math and science education (Ed D); reading and language (M Ed, CAGS). *Accreditation:* NCATE. Part-time and evening/weekend programs available. Postbaccalaureate distance learning degree programs offered (no on-campus study). Terminal master's awarded for partial completion of doctoral program. *Degree requirements:* For doctorate, thesis/dissertation. *Entrance requirements:* For master's, doctorate, and CAGS, GRE General Test. Additional exam requirements/recommendations for international students: Required—TOEFL. Electronic applications accepted.

University of Memphis, Graduate School, College of Education, Memphis, TN 38152. Offers M Ed, MAT, MS, Ed D, PhD, Graduate Certificate. *Accreditation:* NCATE. Part-time and evening/weekend programs available. *Faculty:* 94 full-time (55 women), 41 part-time/adjunct (23 women). *Students:* 316 full-time (223 women), 906 part-time (693 women); includes 530 minority (503 African Americans, 5 American Indian/Alaska Native, 6 Asian Americans or Pacific Islanders, 16 Hispanic Americans), 17 international. Average age 34. 489 applicants, 73% accepted, 121 enrolled. In 2009, 230 master's, 37 doctorates, 17 other advanced degrees awarded. Terminal master's awarded for partial completion of doctoral program. *Degree requirements:* For master's, comprehensive exam; for doctorate, comprehensive exam, thesis/dissertation. *Entrance requirements:* For master's, GRE General Test or MAT; for doctorate, GRE General Test. *Application deadline:* Applications are processed on a rolling basis. Application fee: $35 ($60 for international students). *Expenses:* Tuition, state resident: full-time $6246; part-time $347 per credit hour. Tuition, nonresident: full-time $15,894; part-time $883 per credit hour. Required fees: $1160. Full-time tuition and fees vary according to course load, degree level and program. *Financial support:* In 2009–10, 921 students received support; research assistantships with full tuition reimbursements available, teaching assistantships with full tuition reimbursements available, career-related internships or fieldwork, Federal Work-Study, scholarships/grants, tuition waivers (partial), and unspecified assistantships available. Financial award application deadline: 2/15; financial award applicants required to submit FAFSA. *Faculty research:* Urban school effectiveness, literacy development, teacher effectiveness, exercise physiology, crisis counseling. Total annual research expenditures: $3.3 million. *Unit head:* Dr. Donald J. Wagner, Dean, 901-678-4265, Fax: 901-678-4778, E-mail: djwagner@memphis.edu. *Application contact:* Dr. Ernest A. Rakow, Associate Dean of Administration and Graduate Programs, 901-678-2363, Fax: 901-678-4778, E-mail: erakow@memphis.edu.

University of Miami, Graduate School, School of Education, Coral Gables, FL 33124. Offers MS Ed, Ed D, PhD, Certificate, Ed S. *Faculty:* 32 full-time (14 women), 1 part-time/adjunct (0 women). *Students:* 189 full-time (140 women), 46 part-time (31 women); includes 91 minority (22 African Americans, 1 American Indian/Alaska Native, 2 Asian Americans or Pacific Islanders, 66 Hispanic Americans), 23 international. Average age 30. 359 applicants, 46% accepted, 92 enrolled. In 2009, 94 master's, 14 doctorates, 5 other advanced degrees awarded. Terminal master's awarded for partial completion of doctoral program. *Degree requirements:* For master's, comprehensive exam (for some programs), thesis optional, electronic portfolio, special project, personal growth experience; for doctorate, thesis/dissertation, qualifying exam. *Entrance requirements:* For master's and doctorate, GRE General Test. Additional exam requirements/recommendations for international students: Required—TOEFL (minimum score 550 paper-based; 80 iBT); Recommended—IELTS (minimum score 6.5). *Application deadline:* For fall admission, 10/15 for international students. Application fee: $65. *Financial support:* In 2009–10, 153 students received support, including 3 fellowships with full tuition reimbursements available (averaging $18,900 per year), 40 research assistantships with full and partial tuition reimbursements available (averaging $18,900 per year), 10 teaching assistantships with full and partial tuition reimbursements available (averaging $18,900 per year); career-related internships or fieldwork, institutionally sponsored loans, scholarships/grants, traineeships, health care benefits, tuition waivers (full and partial), and unspecified assistantships also available. Support available to part-time students. Financial award application deadline: 3/1; financial award applicants required to submit FAFSA. *Faculty research:* Social skills and learning disabilities, planning for mainstreamed pupils, alcohol and drug abuse, restructuring education for all learners. Total annual research expenditures: $4.8 million. *Unit head:* Dr. Walter Secada, Senior Associate Dean, 305-284-2102, Fax: 305-284-6998, E-mail: wsecada@miami.edu. *Application contact:* SOE Directory, 305-284-3711, Fax: 305-284-3003, E-mail: soe@miami.edu.

See Display on page 658 and Close-Up on page 717.

University of Michigan, Horace H. Rackham School of Graduate Studies, Combined Program in Education and Psychology, Ann Arbor, MI 48109. Offers PhD. *Faculty:* 20 part-time/adjunct (9 women). *Students:* 30 full-time (21 women); includes 14 minority (8 African Americans, 2 Asian Americans or Pacific Islanders, 4 Hispanic Americans), 5 international. Average age 28. 47 applicants, 19% accepted, 7 enrolled. In 2009, 3 doctorates awarded. *Degree requirements:*

UNIVERSITY OF MIAMI

Graduate Programs in
EDUCATION

The School of Education of the University of Miami (UM) offers curricula leading to the degrees of Master of Science in Education and Doctor of Philosophy in Education.

Master's level programs (all M.S.Ed.)

- **Enrollment Management**
- **Early Childhood Special Education**
- **Counseling and Research**
- **Exercise Physiology**
- **Marriage and Family Therapy**
- **Mental Health Counseling**
- **Research, Measurement, and Evaluation**
- **Sport Administration**

Doctoral level programs

- **Counseling Psychology (Ph.D.)**
- **Exercise Physiology (Ph.D.)**
- **Higher Education Leadership (Ed.D.)**
- **Language and Literacy Learning in Multilingual Settings (Ph.D.)**
- **Math and Science Education (Ph.D.)**
- **Research, Measurement, and Evaluation (Ph.D.)**
- **Special Education (Ph.D.)**

For more information visit our website:

http://www.education.miami.edu

For doctorate, thesis/dissertation, independent research project, preliminary exam, oral defense of dissertation. *Entrance requirements:* For doctorate, GRE General Test with Analytical Writing Test. Additional exam requirements/recommendations for international students: Required—TOEFL (minimum score 600 paper-based; 250 computer-based; 100 iBT). *Application deadline:* For fall admission, 12/5 for domestic and international students. Application fee: $60 ($75 for international students). Electronic applications accepted. *Expenses:* Tuition, state resident: full-time $17,286; part-time $1099 per credit hour. Tuition, nonresident: full-time $34,944; part-time $2080 per credit hour. Required fees: $95 per semester. Tuition and fees vary according to course load, degree level and program. *Financial support:* In 2009–10, 28 students received support, including 15 fellowships with full tuition reimbursements available (averaging $26,304 per year), 8 research assistantships with full tuition reimbursements available (averaging $25,189 per year), 8 teaching assistantships with full tuition reimbursements available (averaging $27,303 per year); institutionally sponsored loans, scholarships/grants, traineeships, tuition waivers, and unspecified assistantships also available. Financial award application deadline: 12/5. *Faculty research:* Human development in context of schools, families, communities; cognitive and learning sciences; motivation and self-regulated learning; culture, ethnicity, social and class influences on learning and motivation. *Unit head:* Tabbye M. Chavous, Director, 734-647-0626, Fax: 734-647-2164, E-mail: tchavous@umich.edu. *Application contact:* Janie Knieper, Administrative Specialist, 734-647-0626, Fax: 734-615-2164, E-mail: cpep@umich.edu.

University of Michigan, Horace H. Rackham School of Graduate Studies, School of Education, Ann Arbor, MI 48109-1259. Offers AM, MA, MS, PhD, MA/Certification, MBA/MA, MPP/MA, PhD/MA. *Faculty:* 52 full-time (30 women). *Students:* 451 full-time (323 women), 42 part-time (37 women); includes 119 minority (47 African Americans, 2 American Indian/Alaska Native, 36 Asian Americans or Pacific Islanders, 34 Hispanic Americans), 51 international. 639 applicants, 62% accepted, 206 enrolled. In 2009, 143 master's, 37 doctorates awarded. Terminal master's awarded for partial completion of doctoral program. *Degree requirements:* For master's, thesis optional; for doctorate, comprehensive exam, thesis/dissertation. *Entrance requirements:* For master's and doctorate, GRE General Test. Additional exam requirements/recommendations for international students: Required—TOEFL (minimum score 600 paper-based; 250 computer-based). *Application deadline:* For fall admission, 12/1 priority date for domestic students, 12/1 for international students. Application fee: $60 ($75 for international students). Electronic applications accepted. *Expenses:* Tuition, state resident: full-time $17,286; part-time $1099 per credit hour. Tuition, nonresident: full-time $34,944; part-time $2080 per credit hour. Required fees: $95 per semester. Tuition and fees vary according to course load, degree level and program. *Financial support:* In 2009–10, 301 students received support, including 627 fellowships (averaging $4,839 per year), 162 research assistantships with full tuition reimbursements available (averaging $16,627 per year), 73 teaching assistantships with full tuition reimbursements available (averaging $16,694 per year); career-related internships or fieldwork, Federal Work-Study, institutionally sponsored loans, scholarships/grants, health care benefits, tuition waivers, and unspecified assistantships also available. Support available to part-time students. Financial award application deadline: 12/1; financial award applicants required to submit FAFSA. *Faculty research:* Teaching, learning, policy, leadership; technology. Total annual research expenditures: $17.5 million. *Unit head:* Dr. Deborah Loewenberg Ball, Dean, 734-615-4415, Fax: 734-764-3473, E-mail: dball@umich.edu. *Application contact:* Laura Mayers, Student Services Assistant, 734-764-7563, Fax: 734-763-1495, E-mail: ed.grad.admit@umich.edu.

University of Michigan–Dearborn, School of Education, Doctoral Program in Education, Dearborn, MI 48126. Offers curriculum and practice (Ed D); educational leadership (Ed D); educational psychology/special education (Ed D); metropolitan education (Ed D). Part-time and evening/weekend programs available. *Faculty:* 7 full-time (4 women). *Students:* 1 (woman) full-time, 17 part-time (9 women); includes 5 minority (3 African Americans, 1 Asian American or Pacific Islander, 1 Hispanic American). Average age 46. 62 applicants, 31% accepted, 18 enrolled. *Degree requirements:* For doctorate, comprehensive exam, thesis/dissertation. *Entrance requirements:* For doctorate, GRE (taken within the last 5 years), master's degree with minimum GPA of 3.3, 3 letters of recommendation (1 from faculty), 3 years professional and/or teaching experience. Additional exam requirements/recommendations for international students: Required—TOEFL (minimum score 550 paper-based), Test of Spoken English (TES). *Application deadline:* For fall admission, 3/1 for domestic and international students. Application fee: $60. *Expenses:* Tuition, state resident: part-time $504.10 per credit hour. Tuition, nonresident: part-time $957.90 per credit hour. *Faculty research:* Educational leadership, metropolitan education, curriculum and practice, educational psychology, special education, assessment. *Unit head:* Gail Luera, Associate Dean/Interim Coordinator, 313-593-5098, E-mail: grl@umich.edu. *Application contact:* Catherine Parkins, Customer Service Assistant, 313-583-6349, Fax: 313-593-4748, E-mail: cparkins@umd.umich.edu.

University of Michigan–Dearborn, School of Education, Program in Education, Dearborn, MI 48126-2638. Offers MA. Part-time and evening/weekend programs available. Postbaccalaureate distance learning degree programs offered (minimal on-campus study). *Faculty:* 14 full-time (8 women), 37 part-time/adjunct (all women). *Students:* 5 full-time (all women), 145 part-time (129 women); includes 11 minority (3 African Americans, 4 Asian Americans or Pacific Islanders, 4 Hispanic Americans). Average age 34. 39 applicants, 100% accepted, 39 enrolled. In 2009, 68 master's awarded. *Entrance requirements:* For master's, minimum GPA of 3.0, writing sample, teaching certificate, 3 letters of recommendation. *Application deadline:* For fall admission, 9/5 for domestic students; for winter admission, 12/22 for domestic students; for spring admission, 5/6 for domestic students. Applications are processed on a rolling basis. Application fee: $60. *Expenses:* Tuition, state resident: part-time $504.10 per credit hour. Tuition, nonresident: part-time $957.90 per credit hour. *Financial support:* Career-related internships or fieldwork available. Support available to part-time students. Financial award application deadline: 4/1; financial award applicants required to submit FAFSA. *Unit head:* Dr. Ray Kettel, Head, 313-593-5091, E-mail: rpkettel@umd.umich.edu. *Application contact:* Pat Parker, Customer Service Assistant, 313-593-5091, Fax: 313-593-4748, E-mail: paparker@umd.umich.edu.

University of Michigan–Dearborn, School of Education, Program in Teaching, Dearborn, MI 48126-2638. Offers MAT. Part-time and evening/weekend programs available. *Faculty:* 10 full-time (6 women), 30 part-time/adjunct (all women). *Students:* 27 full-time (16 women), 19 part-time (14 women); includes 7 minority (5 African Americans, 2 Asian Americans or Pacific Islanders). Average age 34. 13 applicants, 100% accepted, 13 enrolled. In 2009, 29 master's awarded. *Entrance requirements:* For master's, Michigan Test for Teacher Certification (Basic Skills Test and Subject Area Test in teaching), minimum cumulative GPA of 3.0, interview, 3 letters of recommendation. *Application deadline:* For fall admission, 9/5 for domestic students; for winter admission, 12/22 for domestic students; for spring admission, 5/5 for domestic students. Applications are processed on a rolling basis. Application fee: $30. Electronic applications accepted. *Expenses:* Tuition, state resident: part-time $504.10 per credit hour. Tuition, nonresident: part-time $957.90 per credit hour. *Financial support:* Career-related internships or fieldwork available. Support available to part-time students. Financial award application deadline: 4/1; financial award applicants required to submit FAFSA. *Unit head:* Dr. Paul R. Fossum, Coordinator, 313-593-0982, Fax: 313-593-9961, E-mail: pfossum@umich.edu. *Application contact:* Pat Parker, Customer Service Assistant, 313-593-5091, Fax: 313-593-4748, E-mail: paparker@umd.umich.edu.

University of Michigan–Flint, School of Education and Human Services, Flint, MI 48502-1950. Offers MA. Part-time programs available. *Faculty:* 17 full-time (14 women), 10 part-time/adjunct (5 women). *Students:* 32 full-time (29 women), 223 part-time (193 women); includes 23 minority (21 African Americans, 2 American Indian/Alaska Native). Average age 35. 63 applicants, 86% accepted, 43 enrolled. In 2009, 91 master's awarded. *Entrance requirements:* For master's, BS with minimum GPA of 3.0. Additional exam requirements/recommendations for international students: Required—TOEFL (minimum score 560 paper-based; 220 computer-based; 84 iBT), IELTS (minimum score 6.5). *Application deadline:* For fall admission, 8/1 priority date for domestic students, 5/1 priority date for international students; for winter admission, 11/15 priority date for domestic students, 9/15 priority date for international students;

for spring admission, 3/15 priority date for domestic students, 1/15 priority date for international students. Applications are processed on a rolling basis. Application fee: $55. *Expenses:* Contact institution. *Financial support:* Federal Work-Study, scholarships/grants, and unspecified assistantships available. Support available to part-time students. Financial award application deadline: 6/1; financial award applicants required to submit FAFSA. *Unit head:* Dr. Susanne Chandler, Dean, 810-766-6878, Fax: 810-766-6891, E-mail: chandes@umflint.edu. *Application contact:* Beulah Alexander, Executive Secretary, 810-766-6879, Fax: 810-766-6891, E-mail: beulaha@umflint.edu.

University of Minnesota, Duluth, Graduate School, College of Education and Human Service Professions, Department of Education, Duluth, MN 55812-2496. Offers Ed D. Part-time and evening/weekend programs available. *Degree requirements:* For doctorate, comprehensive exam. *Entrance requirements:* For doctorate, GRE, MA (preferred) minimum GPA of 3.0, 3 letters of recommendation, 3 work samples. Additional exam requirements/recommendations for international students: Required—TOEFL (minimum score 550 paper-based; 213 computer-based).

University of Minnesota, Twin Cities Campus, Graduate School, College of Education and Human Development, Minneapolis, MN 55455-0213. Offers M Ed, MA, MSW, Ed D, PhD, Certificate, Ed S. *Accreditation:* NCATE. Part-time programs available. *Faculty:* 160 full-time (80 women). *Students:* 1,617 full-time (1,180 women), 1,108 part-time (769 women); includes 350 minority (146 African Americans, 29 American Indian/Alaska Native, 119 Asian Americans or Pacific Islanders, 56 Hispanic Americans), 237 international. Average age 33. 2,355 applicants, 56% accepted, 1086 enrolled. In 2009, 983 master's, 122 doctorates, 176 other advanced degrees awarded. Application fee: $55. *Financial support:* In 2009–10, 61 fellowships (averaging $26,073 per year), 315 research assistantships with full tuition reimbursements (averaging $26,085 per year), 219 teaching assistantships with full tuition reimbursements (averaging $27,876 per year) were awarded; scholarships/grants and tuition waivers (partial) also available. Financial award applicants required to submit FAFSA. *Faculty research:* Learning technologies, literacy, violence prevention, exercise science and movement, assessment and accountability, aging, science and mathematics education, curriculum-based measurement and student assessment. Total annual research expenditures: $28.6 million. *Unit head:* Dr. Jean K. Quam, Dean, 612-626-9252, Fax: 612-626-7496, E-mail: jquam@umn.edu. *Application contact:* Dr. Mary Trettin, Associate Dean, 612-625-6501, Fax: 612-626-1580, E-mail: mtrettin@umn.edu.

University of Mississippi, Graduate School, School of Education, Oxford, University, MS 38677. Offers M Ed, MA, Ed D, PhD, Ed S, Specialist. *Accreditation:* NCATE. *Faculty:* 55 full-time (41 women), 24 part-time/adjunct (14 women). *Students:* 177 full-time (145 women), 526 part-time (412 women); includes 227 minority (220 African Americans, 1 American Indian/Alaska Native, 2 Asian Americans or Pacific Islanders, 4 Hispanic Americans), 10 international. In 2009, 175 master's, 21 doctorates, 27 other advanced degrees awarded. *Degree requirements:* For doctorate, thesis/dissertation. *Entrance requirements:* For master's, GRE General Test, minimum GPA of 3.0; for doctorate, GRE General Test. Additional exam requirements/recommendations for international students: Required—TOEFL. *Application deadline:* For fall admission, 4/1 for domestic students; for spring admission, 10/1 for domestic students. Applications are processed on a rolling basis. Application fee: $25. Electronic applications accepted. *Financial support:* Scholarships/grants available. Financial award application deadline: 3/1; financial award applicants required to submit FAFSA. *Unit head:* Dr. Linda Chitwood, Interim Dean, 662-915-7063, Fax: 662-915-7249, E-mail: soe@olemiss.edu. *Application contact:* Dr. Christy M. Wyandt, Associate Dean, 662-915-7474, Fax: 662-915-7577, E-mail: cwyandt@olemiss.edu.

University of Missouri, Graduate School, College of Education, Columbia, MO 65211. Offers M Ed, MA, Ed D, PhD, Ed S. Part-time and evening/weekend programs available. *Faculty:* 111 full-time (66 women), 98 part-time/adjunct (80 women). *Students:* 507 full-time (379 women), 1,167 part-time (837 women); includes 131 minority (66 African Americans, 7 American Indian/Alaska Native, 27 Asian Americans or Pacific Islanders, 31 Hispanic Americans), 108 international. Average age 34. 1,019 applicants, 63% accepted, 458 enrolled. In 2009, 235 master's, 29 doctorates awarded. Terminal master's awarded for partial completion of doctoral program. *Degree requirements:* For master's, variable foreign language requirement, thesis (for some programs); for doctorate, variable foreign language requirement, comprehensive exam (for some programs), thesis/dissertation. *Entrance requirements:* For master's, minimum GPA of 3.0; for doctorate, GRE General Test. *Application deadline:* Applications are processed on a rolling basis. Application fee: $45 ($60 for international students). *Financial support:* Fellowships, research assistantships, teaching assistantships, institutionally sponsored loans and scholarships/grants available. *Unit head:* Dr. Rose Porter, Interim Dean, 573-882-8524, E-mail: porterr@missouri.edu. *Application contact:* Adrienne Vaughn, Recruitment Coordinator, E-mail: alvhcd@mizzou.edu.

University of Missouri–Kansas City, School of Education, Kansas City, MO 64110-2499. Offers administration (Ed D); counseling and guidance (MA, Ed S); counseling psychology (PhD); curriculum and instruction (MA, Ed S); education (PhD); educational administration (Ed S); reading education (MA, Ed S); special education (MA). PhD with concentration in education (interdisciplinary) is offered through the School of Graduate Studies. *Accreditation:* NCATE. Part-time and evening/weekend programs available. *Faculty:* 62 full-time (52 women), 45 part-time/adjunct (34 women). *Students:* 207 full-time (154 women), 401 part-time (290 women); includes 142 minority (107 African Americans, 14 Asian Americans or Pacific Islanders, 21 Hispanic Americans), 18 international. Average age 34. 294 applicants, 61% accepted, 150 enrolled. In 2009, 184 master's, 9 doctorates, 49 other advanced degrees awarded. *Degree requirements:* For doctorate, thesis/dissertation, internship, practicum. *Entrance requirements:* For master's, GRE, minimum GPA of 2.75, 2 letters of reference, written statement of purpose; for doctorate, GRE, minimum GPA of 3.0; for Ed S, minimum GPA of 3.0. Additional exam requirements/recommendations for international students: Required—TOEFL (minimum score 550 paper-based; 213 computer-based; 80 iBT). *Application deadline:* For fall admission, 4/1 priority date for domestic and international students; for spring admission, 11/1 priority date for domestic and international students. Applications are processed on a rolling basis. Application fee: $45 ($50 for international students). *Expenses:* Tuition, state resident: full-time $5378; part-time $299 per credit hour. Tuition, nonresident: full-time $13,881; part-time $771 per credit hour. Required fees: $641; $71 per credit hour. Tuition and fees vary according to course load and program. *Financial support:* In 2009–10, 19 research assistantships with partial tuition reimbursements (averaging $9,821 per year) were awarded; career-related internships or fieldwork, Federal Work-Study, institutionally sponsored loans, and tuition waivers (full and partial) also available. Support available to part-time students. Financial award application deadline: 3/1; financial award applicants required to submit FAFSA. *Faculty research:* Urban education, inquiry-based field study, theories of counseling and psychotherapy, school literacy, educational technology. Total annual research expenditures: $2.9 million. *Unit head:* Dr. Wanda Blanchett, Dean, 816-235-2234, Fax: 816-235-5270, E-mail: education@umkc.edu. *Application contact:* Erica Hernandez-Scott, Student Recruiter, 816-235-1295, Fax: 816-235-5270, E-mail: hernandeze@umkc.edu.

University of Missouri–St. Louis, College of Education, St. Louis, MO 63121. Offers M Ed, Ed D, PhD, Certificate, Ed S. *Accreditation:* NCATE. Part-time and evening/weekend programs available. *Faculty:* 71 full-time (33 women), 81 part-time/adjunct (51 women). *Students:* 245 full-time (178 women), 1,178 part-time (876 women); includes 330 minority (284 African Americans, 7 American Indian/Alaska Native, 20 Asian Americans or Pacific Islanders, 19 Hispanic Americans), 28 international. Average age 34. In 2009, 329 master's, 14 doctorates, 3 other advanced degrees awarded. *Degree requirements:* For master's, comprehensive exam, thesis optional; for doctorate, thesis/dissertation. *Entrance requirements:* For doctorate, GRE General Test, 3 letters of recommendation. Additional exam requirements/recommendations for international students: Recommended—TOEFL (minimum score 550 paper-based; 213 computer-based). *Application deadline:* For fall admission, 7/1 priority date for domestic and international students; for spring admission, 12/1 priority date for domestic and international students. Applications are processed on a rolling basis. Application fee: $35 ($40 for international students). Electronic applications accepted. *Expenses:* Tuition, state resident: full-time

$5377; part-time $297.70 per credit hour. Tuition, nonresident: full-time $13,882; part-time $771.20 per credit hour. Required fees: $220; $12.20 per credit hour. One-time fee: $12. Tuition and fees vary according to course level, campus/location and program. *Financial support:* In 2009–10, 32 research assistantships with full and partial tuition reimbursements (averaging $10,700 per year), 8 teaching assistantships with full and partial tuition reimbursements (averaging $12,400 per year) were awarded. Financial award application deadline: 4/1; financial award applicants required to submit FAFSA. *Faculty research:* Remedial reading, literacy, educational policy and research, science education. *Unit head:* Dr. Kathleen Haywood, Director of Graduate Studies, 314-516-5483, Fax: 314-516-5227, E-mail: kathleen_haywood@umsl.edu. *Application contact:* 314-516-5458, Fax: 314-516-6996, E-mail: gradadm@umsl.edu.

University of Mobile, Graduate Programs, Program in Education, Mobile, AL 36613. Offers MA. Part-time programs available. *Faculty:* 6 full-time (3 women), 2 part-time/adjunct (both women). *Students:* 16 full-time (15 women), 40 part-time (all women); includes 33 minority (32 African Americans, 1 American Indian/Alaska Native). Average age 36. 13 applicants, 100% accepted, 13 enrolled. In 2009, 19 master's awarded. *Degree requirements:* For master's, comprehensive exam, thesis optional. *Entrance requirements:* For master's, GRE, Alabama teaching certificate. Additional exam requirements/recommendations for international students: Required—TOEFL (minimum score 550 paper-based; 213 computer-based; 80 iBT). *Application deadline:* For fall admission, 8/3 priority date for domestic students; for spring admission, 12/23 for domestic students. Applications are processed on a rolling basis. Application fee: $40 ($50 for international students). *Financial support:* Application deadline: 8/1. *Faculty research:* Retention, writing across the curriculum. *Unit head:* Dr. Peter Kingsford, Dean, School of Education, 251-442-2355, Fax: 251-442-2523, E-mail: pkingsford@mail.umobile.edu. *Application contact:* Tammy C. Eubanks, Administrative Assistant to Dean of Graduate Programs, 251-442-2270, Fax: 251-442-2523, E-mail: teubanks@umobile.edu.

The University of Montana, Graduate School, School of Education, Missoula, MT 59812-0002. Offers M Ed, MA, MS, Ed D, Ed S. *Accreditation:* NCATE. Part-time programs available. *Degree requirements:* For Ed S, thesis. *Entrance requirements:* For master's, GRE General Test, minimum GPA of 3.0; for Ed S, GRE General Test. Additional exam requirements/recommendations for international students: Required—TOEFL. *Faculty research:* Cooperative learning, administrative styles.

The University of Montana, Graduate School, School of Fine Arts, Department of Art, Missoula, MT 59812-0002. Offers fine arts (MA, MFA), including art (MA), art history (MA), ceramics (MFA), integrated arts and education (MA), media arts (MFA), painting and drawing (MFA), photography (MFA), printmaking (MFA), sculpture (MFA). *Accreditation:* NASAD (one or more programs are accredited). *Degree requirements:* For master's, thesis exhibit. *Entrance requirements:* For master's, GRE General Test, portfolio.

The University of Montana, Graduate School, School of Fine Arts, Department of Drama/Dance, Missoula, MT 59812-0002. Offers fine arts (MA, MFA), including acting (MFA), design/technology (MFA), directing (MFA), drama (MA), integrated arts and education (MA), media arts (MFA). *Accreditation:* NAST (one or more programs are accredited). *Degree requirements:* For master's, thesis or alternative. *Entrance requirements:* For master's, GRE General Test, audition, portfolio, production notebook.

University of Montevallo, College of Education, Montevallo, AL 35115. Offers M Ed, Ed S. *Accreditation:* NCATE. Part-time and evening/weekend programs available. *Students:* 168 full-time (138 women), 224 part-time (170 women); includes 72 minority (50 African Americans, 1 American Indian/Alaska Native, 19 Asian Americans or Pacific Islanders, 2 Hispanic Americans), 2 international. In 2009, 127 master's, 10 Ed Ss awarded. *Degree requirements:* For master's, comprehensive exam. *Entrance requirements:* For master's, GRE General Test, MAT, minimum undergraduate GPA of 2.5. Additional exam requirements/recommendations for international students: Required—TOEFL (minimum score 550 paper-based). *Application deadline:* For fall admission, 7/15 for domestic students; for spring admission, 11/15 for domestic students. Application fee: $25. *Expenses:* Tuition, state resident: full-time $5592; part-time $233 per credit. Tuition, nonresident: full-time $11,184; part-time $466 per credit hour. Required fees: $482; $241 per semester. One-time fee: $25 part-time. *Financial support:* Federal Work-Study, scholarships/grants, and unspecified assistantships available. *Unit head:* Dean. *Application contact:* Rebecca Hartley, Assistant Director, 205-665-6350, E-mail: hartleyrs@montevallo.edu.

University of Nebraska at Kearney, College of Graduate Study, College of Education, Kearney, NE 68849-0001. Offers MA Ed, MS Ed, Ed S. *Accreditation:* NCATE. Part-time and evening/weekend programs available. *Degree requirements:* For master's, thesis optional. *Entrance requirements:* For degree, GRE General Test. Electronic applications accepted.

University of Nebraska at Omaha, Graduate Studies, College of Education, Omaha, NE 68182. Offers MA, MS, Ed D, Certificate, Ed S. *Accreditation:* NCATE. Part-time and evening/weekend programs available. *Faculty:* 58 full-time (28 women). *Students:* 136 full-time (103 women), 736 part-time (568 women); includes 59 minority (38 African Americans, 2 American Indian/Alaska Native, 4 Asian Americans or Pacific Islanders, 15 Hispanic Americans), 17 international. Average age 33. 328 applicants, 55% accepted, 116 enrolled. In 2009, 255 master's, 12 doctorates, 7 other advanced degrees awarded. *Degree requirements:* For master's, comprehensive exam, thesis (for some programs); for doctorate, comprehensive exam, thesis/dissertation. *Entrance requirements:* For master's, minimum GPA of 3.0; for doctorate, GRE General Test, resume, 3 samples of research/written work. Additional exam requirements/recommendations for international students: Required—TOEFL. *Application deadline:* For fall admission, 3/1 priority date for domestic students; for spring admission, 10/1 priority date for domestic students. Applications are processed on a rolling basis. Application fee: $45. *Financial support:* In 2009–10, 350 students received support; fellowships, research assistantships with tuition reimbursements available, teaching assistantships with tuition reimbursements available, career-related internships or fieldwork, Federal Work-Study, institutionally sponsored loans, scholarships/grants, tuition waivers (full), and unspecified assistantships available. Support available to part-time students. Financial award application deadline: 3/1; financial award applicants required to submit FAFSA. *Unit head:* Dr. John Langan, Chairperson, 402-554-2212. *Application contact:* Penny Harmoney, Director, Graduate Studies, 402-554-2341, Fax: 402-554-3143, E-mail: graduate@unomaha.edu.

University of Nevada, Las Vegas, Graduate College, College of Education, Las Vegas, NV 89154-3001. Offers M Ed, MS, Ed D, Exec Ed D, PhD, Advanced Certificate, Ed S. *Accreditation:* NCATE. Part-time and evening/weekend programs available. *Faculty:* 108 full-time (58 women), 55 part-time/adjunct (40 women). *Students:* 525 full-time (393 women), 856 part-time (617 women); includes 278 minority (90 African Americans, 8 American Indian/Alaska Native, 70 Asian Americans or Pacific Islanders, 110 Hispanic Americans), 29 international. Average age 36. 682 applicants, 82% accepted, 430 enrolled. In 2009, 534 master's, 32 doctorates, 14 other advanced degrees awarded. *Degree requirements:* For master's, comprehensive exam (for some programs), thesis optional; for doctorate, comprehensive exam, thesis/dissertation. *Entrance requirements:* Additional exam requirements/recommendations for international students: Required—TOEFL (minimum score 550 paper-based; 213 computer-based; 80 iBT), IELTS (minimum score 7). *Application deadline:* For fall admission, 8/1 for domestic students, 5/1 for international students; for spring admission, 12/1 for domestic and international students. Applications are processed on a rolling basis. Application fee: $60 ($95 for international students). Electronic applications accepted. *Financial support:* In 2009–10, 115 students received support, including 1 fellowship with full tuition reimbursement available (averaging $14,000 per year), 49 research assistantships with partial tuition reimbursements available (averaging $10,781 per year), 65 teaching assistantships with partial tuition reimbursements available (averaging $9,396 per year); institutionally sponsored loans, scholarships/grants, health care benefits, and unspecified assistantships also available. Financial award application deadline: 3/1. *Faculty research:* Preparing professionals for changing educational contexts, improving capacity to create conditions for learning, collaborating and improving stakeholder and constituent initiatives, developing programs and offerings for new populations and global markets, examining factors impacting professional practice and public policy. Total annual research expenditures: $5.3 million. *Unit head:* Dr. William Speer, Interim Dean, 702-895-3375, Fax: 702-895-4068,

Education—General

University of Nevada, Las Vegas (continued)
E-mail: william.speer@unlv.edu. *Application contact:* Graduate College Admissions Evaluator, 702-895-3320, Fax: 702-895-4180, E-mail: gradcollege@unlv.edu.

University of Nevada, Reno, Graduate School, College of Education, Reno, NV 89557. Offers M Ed, MA, MS, Ed D, PhD, Ed S. *Accreditation:* NCATE. Terminal master's awarded for partial completion of doctoral program. *Degree requirements:* For master's, thesis optional; for doctorate, thesis/dissertation. *Entrance requirements:* For master's, GRE, minimum GPA of 2.75; for doctorate, GRE, minimum GPA of 3.0. Additional exam requirements/recommendations for international students: Required—TOEFL (minimum score 500 paper-based; 173 computer-based; 61 iBT), IELTS (minimum score 6). Electronic applications accepted.

University of New Brunswick Fredericton, School of Graduate Studies, Faculty of Education, Fredericton, NB E3B 5A3, Canada. Offers M Ed, PhD. Part-time programs available. Post-baccalaureate distance learning degree programs offered. *Faculty:* 34 full-time (21 women), 17 part-time/adjunct (9 women). *Students:* 71 full-time (51 women), 309 part-time (237 women). In 2009, 140 master's, 2 doctorates awarded. *Degree requirements:* For master's, variable foreign language requirement, thesis optional; for doctorate, variable foreign language requirement, comprehensive exam, thesis/dissertation. *Entrance requirements:* For master's, minimum GPA of 3.0. Additional exam requirements/recommendations for international students: Required—TOEFL (minimum score 650 paper-based; 280 computer-based); Recommended—TWE (minimum score 5.5). *Application deadline:* 1/31 priority date for domestic and international students. Application fee: $50 Canadian dollars. Electronic applications accepted. Tuition and fees charges are reported in Canadian dollars. *Expenses:* Tuition, area resident: Full-time $5562 Canadian dollars; part-time $2781 Canadian dollars per year. Required fees: $49.75 Canadian dollars per term. *Financial support:* In 2009–10, 20 research assistantships (averaging $2,600 per year), 18 teaching assistantships (averaging $3,777 per year) were awarded; tuition waivers also available. *Faculty research:* Second language research; health and education research; social policy; youth, science, teaching and learning; early childhood. *Unit head:* Dr. Ellen Carusetta, Director of Graduate Studies, 506-453-3544, Fax: 506-453-3569, E-mail: carusett@unb.ca. *Application contact:* Carolyn King, Graduate Secretary, 506-458-7147, Fax: 506-453-3569, E-mail: kingc@unb.ca.

University of New England, College of Arts and Sciences, Program in Education, Biddeford, ME 04005-9526. Offers curriculm and instruction strategy (MS Ed); educational leadership (MS Ed); general studies (MS Ed); literacy (MS Ed); teaching methodologies (MS Ed). Part-time programs available. Postbaccalaureate distance learning degree programs offered (minimal on-campus study). *Faculty:* 2 full-time (1 woman), 25 part-time/adjunct (15 women). *Students:* 473 full-time (362 women), 177 part-time (133 women); includes 29 African Americans, 12 Asian Americans or Pacific Islanders, 16 Hispanic Americans. In 2009, 319 master's awarded. *Degree requirements:* For master's, collaborative action research project, integrative seminar portfolio. *Entrance requirements:* For master's, teaching certificate, 2 years of teaching experience. Additional exam requirements/recommendations for international students: Required—TOEFL. *Application deadline:* For fall admission, 9/15 for domestic students; for spring admission, 1/15 for domestic students. Applications are processed on a rolling basis. Application fee: $40. Electronic applications accepted. *Expenses:* Contact institution. *Financial support:* Application deadline: 5/1. *Faculty research:* Distance learning, effective teaching, transition planning, adult learning. *Unit head:* Dr. Doug Lynch, Chair of Education Department, 207-283-0171 Ext. 2888, E-mail: dlynch@une.edu. *Application contact:* Stacy Gato, Assistant Director of Graduate Admissions, 207-221-4225, Fax: 207-221-4898, E-mail: gradadmissions@une.edu.

University of New Hampshire, Center for Graduate and Professional Studies, Manchester, NH 03101. Offers business administration (MBA); counseling (M Ed); education (M Ed, MAT); educational administration and supervision (M Ed, CAGS); industrial statistics (Certificate); public administration (MPA); public health (MPH, Certificate); social work (MSW). Part-time and evening/weekend programs available. *Students:* 86 full-time (57 women), 150 part-time (87 women); includes 13 minority (3 African Americans, 6 Asian Americans or Pacific Islanders, 4 Hispanic Americans), 7 international. 127 applicants, 73% accepted, 60 enrolled. In 2009, 81 master's, 5 other advanced degrees awarded. *Degree requirements:* For master's, thesis or alternative. *Entrance requirements:* Additional exam requirements/recommendations for international students: Required—TOEFL (minimum score 550 paper-based; 213 computer-based; 80 iBT), TOEIC, TSE. *Application deadline:* For fall admission, 6/1 for domestic students, 4/1 for international students; for spring admission, 12/1 for domestic students. Applications are processed on a rolling basis. Application fee: $65. Electronic applications accepted. *Expenses:* Tuition, state resident: full-time $10,380; part-time $577 per credit hour. Tuition, nonresident: full-time $24,350; part-time $1002 per credit hour. Required fees: $1550; $387.50 per semester. Tuition and fees vary according to course load and program. *Financial support:* In 2009–10, 20 students received support, including 1 fellowship, 1 teaching assistantship; research assistantships, Federal Work-Study, scholarships/grants, health care benefits, and unspecified assistantships also available. Support available to part-time students. Financial award application deadline: 3/1; financial award applicants required to submit FAFSA. *Unit head:* Kate Ferreira, Director, 603-641-4313, E-mail: unhm.gradcenter@unh.edu. *Application contact:* Graduate Admissions Office, 603-862-3000, Fax: 603-862-0275, E-mail: grad.school@unh.edu.

University of New Hampshire, Graduate School, College of Liberal Arts, Department of Education, Durham, NH 03824. Offers counseling (M Ed, MA); early childhood education (M Ed), including early childhood education, special needs; education (PhD); educational administration (M Ed, Ed S); elementary education (M Ed, MAT); reading (M Ed); secondary education (M Ed, MAT); special education (M Ed, Postbaccalaureate Certificate); teacher leadership (M Ed, Postbaccalaureate Certificate). *Accreditation:* Teacher Education Accreditation Council. Part-time programs available. *Faculty:* 29 full-time (19 women). *Students:* 171 full-time (127 women), 236 part-time (167 women); includes 10 minority (3 African Americans, 3 Asian Americans or Pacific Islanders, 4 Hispanic Americans), 4 international. Average age 36. 178 applicants, 72% accepted, 87 enrolled. In 2009, 208 master's, 4 doctorates, 19 other advanced degrees awarded. *Degree requirements:* For doctorate, thesis/dissertation. *Entrance requirements:* For master's, doctorate, and other advanced degree, GRE General Test. Additional exam requirements/recommendations for international students: Required—TOEFL (minimum score 550 paper-based; 213 computer-based; 80 iBT). *Application deadline:* For fall admission, 4/1 priority date for domestic students, 4/1 for international students; for spring admission, 12/1 priority date for domestic students. Applications are processed on a rolling basis. Application fee: $65. Electronic applications accepted. *Expenses:* Tuition, state resident: full-time $10,380; part-time $577 per credit hour. Tuition, nonresident: full-time $24,350; part-time $1002 per credit hour. Required fees: $1550; $387.50 per semester. Tuition and fees vary according to course load and program. *Financial support:* In 2009–10, 59 students received support, including 18 teaching assistantships; fellowships, research assistantships, career-related internships or fieldwork, Federal Work-Study, scholarships/grants, and tuition waivers (full and partial) also available. Support available to part-time students. Financial award application deadline: 2/15. *Unit head:* Dr. Todd Demitchell, Chairperson, 603-862-5043, E-mail: education.department@unh.edu. *Application contact:* Lisa Wilder, Graduate Coordinator, 603-862-2310, E-mail: education.department@unh.edu.

University of New Haven, Graduate School, College of Arts and Sciences, Programs in Education, West Haven, CT 06516-1916. Offers professional education (MS); teacher certification (MS). Part-time and evening/weekend programs available. *Faculty:* 7 full-time (5 women), 23 part-time/adjunct (12 women). *Students:* 172 full-time (128 women), 109 part-time (79 women); includes 18 minority (8 African Americans, 1 American Indian/Alaska Native, 3 Asian Americans or Pacific Islanders, 6 Hispanic Americans). Average age 28. 193 applicants, 85% accepted, 127 enrolled. In 2009, 136 master's awarded. *Entrance requirements:* For master's, PRAXIS I. Additional exam requirements/recommendations for international students: Required—TOEFL (minimum score 520 paper-based; 190 computer-based; 70 iBT); Recommended—IELTS (minimum score 5.5). *Application deadline:* For fall admission, 5/31 for international students; for winter admission, 10/15 for international students; for spring admission, 1/15 for international students. Applications are processed on a rolling basis. Application fee: $50. Electronic applications accepted. *Expenses:* Tuition: Part-time $700 per credit. Required fees: $45 per term. One-time fee: $390 part-time. *Financial support:* Research assistantships with partial tuition reimbursements, teaching assistantships with partial tuition reimbursements, career-related internships or fieldwork, Federal Work-Study, scholarships/grants, tuition waivers, and unspecified assistantships available. Financial award applicants required to submit FAFSA. *Unit head:* Dr. Paulette Pepin, Director, 203-932-7039. *Application contact:* Eloise Gormley, Director of Graduate Admissions, 203-932-7449, Fax: 203-932-7137, E-mail: gradinfo@newhaven.edu.

University of New Mexico, Graduate School, College of Education, Department of Teacher Education, Albuquerque, NM 87131-2039. Offers elementary education (MA); secondary education (MA). Part-time and evening/weekend programs available. *Faculty:* 25 full-time (21 women), 8 part-time/adjunct (7 women). *Students:* 137 full-time (93 women), 214 part-time (172 women); includes 111 minority (9 African Americans, 19 American Indian/Alaska Native, 6 Asian Americans or Pacific Islanders, 77 Hispanic Americans), 12 international. Average age 36. 98 applicants, 67% accepted, 53 enrolled. In 2009, 103 master's awarded. *Degree requirements:* For master's, comprehensive exam, thesis optional. *Entrance requirements:* For master's, minimum overall GPA of 3.0, some experience working with students. Additional exam requirements/recommendations for international students: Required—TOEFL (minimum score 550 paper-based; 213 computer-based). *Application deadline:* For fall admission, 3/1 for domestic students; for spring admission, 10/1 for domestic students. Applications are processed on a rolling basis. Application fee: $50. Electronic applications accepted. *Expenses:* Tuition, state resident: full-time $2099; part-time $233.20 per credit hour. Tuition, nonresident: full-time $6650. Required fees: $25 per semester. Tuition and fees vary according to course load, program and reciprocity agreements. *Financial support:* In 2009–10, 4 teaching assistantships with partial tuition reimbursements (averaging $11,641 per year) were awarded; career-related internships or fieldwork, scholarships/grants, and unspecified assistantships also available. Financial award applicants required to submit FAFSA. Total annual research expenditures: $15,147. *Unit head:* Dr. Rosalita Mitchell, Department Chair, 505-277-9611, Fax: 505-277-0455, E-mail: ted@unm.edu. *Application contact:* Sarah Valles, Administrator, 505-277-0504, Fax: 505-277-0455, E-mail: ted@unm.edu.

University of New Orleans, Graduate School, College of Education and Human Development, New Orleans, LA 70148. Offers M Ed, MAT, PhD, GCE. *Accreditation:* NCATE. Part-time programs available. Postbaccalaureate distance learning degree programs offered. *Degree requirements:* For master's, comprehensive exam, thesis optional; for doctorate, comprehensive exam, thesis/dissertation. *Entrance requirements:* For master's and doctorate, GRE General Test. Additional exam requirements/recommendations for international students: Required—TOEFL (minimum score 550 paper-based; 213 computer-based; 79 iBT). Electronic applications accepted. *Faculty research:* Special education and habilitation, educational administration, exercise physiology, wellness, effective school instruction.

University of North Alabama, College of Education, Florence, AL 35632-0001. Offers MA, MA Ed, Ed S. *Accreditation:* NCATE. Part-time and evening/weekend programs available. *Faculty:* 7 full-time (all women), 19 part-time/adjunct (10 women). *Students:* 92 full-time (64 women), 195 part-time (146 women); includes 26 minority (18 African Americans, 5 American Indian/Alaska Native, 1 Asian American or Pacific Islander, 2 Hispanic Americans). Average age 30. In 2009, 96 master's, 6 other advanced degrees awarded. *Degree requirements:* For master's, comprehensive exam. *Entrance requirements:* For master's, GRE, MAT, or NTE, minimum GPA of 2.5, Alabama Class B Certificate or equivalent, teaching experience. *Application deadline:* For fall admission, 7/1 priority date for domestic students; for spring admission, 12/1 for domestic students. Applications are processed on a rolling basis. Application fee: $25. Electronic applications accepted. *Expenses:* Tuition, state resident: full-time $5040; part-time $210 per credit hour. Tuition, nonresident: full-time $10,080; part-time $420 per credit hour. Required fees: $906. *Financial support:* Federal Work-Study available. Support available to part-time students. Financial award application deadline: 4/1. *Unit head:* Dr. Donna Jacobs, Dean, 256-765-4252, Fax: 256-765-4664, E-mail: dpjacobs@una.edu. *Application contact:* Kim Mauldin, Director of Admissions, 256-765-4608, Fax: 256-765-4960, E-mail: komauldin@una.edu.

The University of North Carolina at Chapel Hill, Graduate School, School of Education, Chapel Hill, NC 27514-3500. Offers M Ed, MA, MAT, MSA, Ed D, PhD. *Accreditation:* NCATE. Part-time programs available. *Faculty:* 50 full-time (33 women), 34 part-time/adjunct (17 women). *Students:* 307 full-time (238 women), 249 part-time (199 women); includes 135 minority (102 African Americans, 7 American Indian/Alaska Native, 14 Asian Americans or Pacific Islanders, 12 Hispanic Americans), 21 international. Average age 33. 665 applicants, 57% accepted, 235 enrolled. In 2009, 165 master's, 28 doctorates awarded. *Degree requirements:* For master's, comprehensive exam, thesis (for some programs); for doctorate, comprehensive exam, thesis/dissertation. *Entrance requirements:* For master's and doctorate, GRE General Test, minimum GPA of 3.0 during last 2 years of undergraduate course work. Additional exam requirements/recommendations for international students: Required—TOEFL (minimum score 550 paper-based; 79 computer-based). *Application deadline:* For fall admission, 12/15 priority date for domestic and international students; for spring admission, 11/1 priority date for domestic and international students. Applications are processed on a rolling basis. Application fee: $77. Electronic applications accepted. *Financial support:* Fellowships with full and partial tuition reimbursements, research assistantships with full and partial tuition reimbursements, teaching assistantships with full tuition reimbursements, Federal Work-Study, scholarships/grants, traineeships, health care benefits, and unspecified assistantships available. Financial award application deadline: 3/1; financial award applicants required to submit FAFSA. *Faculty research:* Curriculum development; school success and intervention; professional development, recruitment and retention; service-learning; evaluation. Total annual research expenditures: $6.4 million. *Unit head:* Dr. Bill McDiarmid, Dean, 919-966-7000, Fax: 919-962-1533. *Application contact:* Amy Butler, Student Services Assistant, 919-966-1346, Fax: 919-962-1533, E-mail: abutler@email.unc.edu.

The University of North Carolina at Charlotte, Graduate School, College of Education, Program in Teacher Education, Charlotte, NC 28223-0001. Offers art education (K-12) (MAT); dance education (K-12) (MAT); elementary education (K-6) (MAT); English as a second language (K-12) (MAT); foreign language education (K-12) (MAT); general teacher education (MAT); middle grades education (6-9) (MAT); music education (K-12) (MAT); secondary education (9-12) (MAT); special education (K-12) (MAT); theatre education (K-12) (MAT). *Faculty:* 108 full-time (64 women), 16 part-time/adjunct (12 women). *Students:* 29 full-time (20 women), 229 part-time (189 women); includes 32 minority (22 African Americans, 2 American Indian/Alaska Native, 3 Asian Americans or Pacific Islanders, 5 Hispanic Americans). Average age 32. 108 applicants, 92% accepted, 85 enrolled. In 2009, 59 master's awarded. *Entrance requirements:* For master's, GRE or MAT. Additional exam requirements/recommendations for international students: Required—TOEFL (minimum score 557 paper-based; 220 computer-based; 83 iBT). *Application deadline:* For fall admission, 7/1 for domestic students, 5/1 for international students; for spring admission, 11/1 for domestic students, 10/1 for international students. Applications are processed on a rolling basis. Application fee: $55. Electronic applications accepted. *Financial support:* In 2009–10, 5 students received support, including 1 research assistantship (averaging $18,000 per year), 3 teaching assistantships (averaging $12,183 per year); career-related internships or fieldwork, Federal Work-Study, institutionally sponsored loans, scholarships/grants, and administrative assistantship also available. Support available to part-time students. Financial award application deadline: 4/1; financial award applicants required to submit FAFSA. Total annual research expenditures: $5.1 million. *Unit head:* Dr. Kimberly J. Hartman, Coordinator, 704-687-8883, Fax: 704-687-6430, E-mail: khartman@uncc.edu. *Application contact:* Kathy B. Giddings, Director of Graduate Admissions, 704-687-5503, Fax: 704-687-3279, E-mail: gradadmn@uncc.edu.

The University of North Carolina at Greensboro, Graduate School, School of Education, Greensboro, NC 27412-5001. Offers M Ed, MLIS, MS, MSA, Ed D, PhD, Certificate, Ed S, PMC, MS/Ed S, MS/PhD. *Accreditation:* NCATE. Part-time and evening/weekend programs

available. *Degree requirements:* For doctorate, thesis/dissertation. *Entrance requirements:* For master's, doctorate, and other advanced degree, GRE General Test. Additional exam requirements/recommendations for international students: Required—TOEFL. Electronic applications accepted. *Faculty research:* Effects of homogeneous grouping, women in higher education, assessment of student achievement.

The University of North Carolina at Pembroke, Graduate Studies, School of Education, Pembroke, NC 28372-1510. Offers elementary education (MA Ed); middle grades education (MA Ed, MAT); reading education (MA Ed); school administration (MSA); school counseling (MA Ed). *Accreditation:* NCATE. Part-time and evening/weekend programs available. *Degree requirements:* For master's, comprehensive exam (for some programs), thesis optional. *Entrance requirements:* For master's, GRE General Test or MAT, minimum GPA of 3.0 in major, 2.5 overall. Additional exam requirements/recommendations for international students: Required—TOEFL.

The University of North Carolina Wilmington, School of Education, Wilmington, NC 28403-3297. Offers M Ed, MAT, MS, MSA, Ed D. *Accreditation:* NCATE. Part-time and evening/weekend programs available. *Degree requirements:* For master's, comprehensive exam, thesis (for some programs); for doctorate, comprehensive exam, thesis/dissertation. *Entrance requirements:* For master's, GRE General Test, MAT, minimum B average in upper-division undergraduate course work. Additional exam requirements/recommendations for international students: Required—TOEFL (minimum score 550 paper-based; 217 computer-based; 79 iBT), IELTS (minimum score 6.5).

University of North Dakota, Graduate School, College of Education and Human Development, Grand Forks, ND 58202. Offers M Ed, MA, MS, MSW, Ed D, PhD, Specialist. *Accreditation:* NCATE. Part-time and evening/weekend programs available. Postbaccalaureate distance learning degree programs offered (minimal on-campus study). *Degree requirements:* For master's, comprehensive exam, thesis or alternative; for doctorate, comprehensive exam, thesis/dissertation; for Specialist, comprehensive exam (for some programs), thesis (for some programs). *Entrance requirements:* For master's, GRE General Test, MAT, GRE Subject Test, minimum GPA of 3.0; for doctorate, GRE Subject Test, minimum GPA of 3.5. Additional exam requirements/recommendations for international students: Required—TOEFL (minimum score 550 paper-based; 213 computer-based; 79 iBT), IELTS (minimum score 6.5). Electronic applications accepted.

University of Northern British Columbia, Office of Graduate Studies, Prince George, BC V2N 4Z9, Canada. Offers business administration (Diploma); community health science (M Sc); disability management (MA); education (M Ed); first nations studies (MA); gender studies (MA); history (MA); interdisciplinary studies (MA); international studies (MA); mathematical, computer and physical sciences (M Sc); natural resources and environmental studies (M Sc, MA, MNRES, PhD); political science (MA); psychology (M Sc, PhD); social work (MSW). Part-time and evening/weekend programs available. Postbaccalaureate distance learning degree programs offered (no on-campus study). *Degree requirements:* For master's, thesis; for doctorate, thesis/dissertation. *Entrance requirements:* For master's, GRE, minimum B average in undergraduate course work; for doctorate, candidacy exam, minimum A average in graduate course work.

University of Northern Colorado, Graduate School, College of Education and Behavioral Sciences, Greeley, CO 80639. Offers MA, MAT, MS, Ed D, PhD, Psy D, Ed S. *Accreditation:* NCATE. Part-time programs available. Postbaccalaureate distance learning degree programs offered. *Faculty:* 80 full-time (42 women). *Students:* 335 full-time (251 women), 456 part-time (352 women); includes 71 minority (11 African Americans, 3 American Indian/Alaska Native, 11 Asian Americans or Pacific Islanders, 46 Hispanic Americans), 54 international. Average age 35. 520 applicants, 77% accepted, 188 enrolled. In 2009, 274 master's, 39 doctorates, 24 other advanced degrees awarded. *Degree requirements:* For master's, comprehensive exam, thesis optional; for doctorate, comprehensive exam, thesis/dissertation; for Ed S, comprehensive exam, thesis. *Entrance requirements:* For doctorate, GRE General Test. *Application deadline:* Applications are processed on a rolling basis. Application fee: $50 ($60 for international students). *Expenses:* Tuition, state resident: full-time $5770; part-time $320.55 per credit hour. Tuition, nonresident: full-time $13,847; part-time $769.27 per credit hour. Required fees: $948.78; $52.72 per credit. *Financial support:* In 2009–10, 32 research assistantships (averaging $5,527 per year), 23 teaching assistantships (averaging $5,951 per year) were awarded; fellowships, unspecified assistantships also available. Financial award application deadline: 3/1; financial award applicants required to submit FAFSA. *Unit head:* Dr. Eugene P. Sheehan, Dean, 970-351-2817, Fax: 970-351-2312, E-mail: coeinfo@unco.edu. *Application contact:* Linda Sisson, Graduate Student Admission Coordinator, 970-351-1807, Fax: 970-351-2371, E-mail: linda.sisson@unco.edu.

University of Northern Iowa, Graduate College, College of Education, Cedar Falls, IA 50614. Offers MA, MAE, Ed D, Ed S. Part-time and evening/weekend programs available. *Students:* 200 full-time (140 women), 386 part-time (264 women); includes 54 minority (35 African Americans, 6 Asian Americans or Pacific Islanders, 13 Hispanic Americans), 23 international. 356 applicants, 61% accepted, 166 enrolled. In 2009, 168 master's, 7 doctorates, 6 other advanced degrees awarded. *Degree requirements:* For Ed S, thesis or alternative. *Entrance requirements:* For master's, minimum GPA of 3.0; for doctorate, GRE, master's degree, minimum GPA of 3.5; for Ed S, GRE General Test, GRE Subject Test. Additional exam requirements/recommendations for international students: Required—TOEFL (minimum score 500 paper-based; 180 computer-based; 61 iBT). *Application deadline:* For fall admission, 8/1 priority date for domestic students. Applications are processed on a rolling basis. Application fee: $30 ($50 for international students). Electronic applications accepted. *Financial support:* Career-related internships or fieldwork, Federal Work-Study, institutionally sponsored loans, scholarships/grants, and tuition waivers (full and partial) available. Support available to part-time students. Financial award application deadline: 2/1. *Unit head:* Dr. William Callahan, Dean, 319-273-2167, Fax: 319-273-5886, E-mail: bill.callahan@uni.edu. *Application contact:* Laurie S. Russell, Record Analyst, 319-273-2623, Fax: 319-273-6792, E-mail: laurie.russell@uni.edu.

University of North Florida, College of Education and Human Services, Jacksonville, FL 32224. Offers M Ed, Ed D. *Accreditation:* NCATE. Part-time and evening/weekend programs available. *Faculty:* 53 full-time (34 women). *Students:* 102 full-time (84 women), 297 part-time (222 women); includes 82 minority (53 African Americans, 3 American Indian/Alaska Native, 9 Asian Americans or Pacific Islanders, 17 Hispanic Americans), 1 international. Average age 35. 121 applicants, 45% accepted, 31 enrolled. In 2009, 152 master's, 15 doctorates awarded. Terminal master's awarded for partial completion of doctoral program. *Degree requirements:* For doctorate, thesis/dissertation. *Entrance requirements:* For master's, GRE General Test, minimum GPA of 3.0 in last 60 hours, interview, 3 letters of recommendation; for doctorate, GRE General Test, master's degree, interview, writing sample, 3 letters of recommendation. Additional exam requirements/recommendations for international students: Required—TOEFL (minimum score 500 paper-based; 173 computer-based). *Application deadline:* For fall admission, 7/1 priority date for domestic students, 5/1 for international students; for spring admission, 11/1 priority date for domestic students, 10/1 for international students. Applications are processed on a rolling basis. Application fee: $30. Electronic applications accepted. *Expenses:* Tuition, state resident: full-time $6649.20; part-time $277.05 per credit hour. Tuition, nonresident: full-time $22,970; part-time $957.08 per credit hour. Required fees: $985; $41.03 per credit hour. *Financial support:* In 2009–10, 110 students received support, including 4 research assistantships (averaging $2,870 per year), 1 teaching assistantship (averaging $5,700 per year); career-related internships or fieldwork, Federal Work-Study, scholarships/grants, and tuition waivers (partial) also available. Support available to part-time students. Financial award application deadline: 4/1; financial award applicants required to submit FAFSA. *Faculty research:* Effective instruction, technology education, exceptional student education, multiculturalism. Total annual research expenditures: $1.7 million. *Unit head:* Dr. Larry Daniel, Dean, 904-620-2520, E-mail: ldaniel@unf.edu. *Application contact:* Dr. John Kemppainen, Director, Office of Student Services, 904-620-2530, Fax: 904-620-1135, E-mail: jkemppai@unf.edu.

University of North Texas, Robert B. Toulouse School of Graduate Studies, College of Education, Denton, TX 76203-5017. Offers M Ed, MS, Ed D, PhD, Certificate. *Accreditation:* NCATE. Part-time and evening/weekend programs available. Terminal master's awarded for partial completion of doctoral program. *Degree requirements:* For master's, thesis or alternative; for doctorate, thesis/dissertation. *Entrance requirements:* For master's and doctorate, GRE General Test. Additional exam requirements/recommendations for international students: Required—proof of English language proficiency required for non-native English speakers; Recommended—TOEFL (minimum score 550 paper-based; 213 computer-based). Application fee: $50 ($75 for international students). *Expenses:* Tuition, state resident: full-time $4298; part-time $239 per contact hour. Tuition, nonresident: full-time $9878; part-time $549 per contact hour. Required fees: $265 per contact hour. *Financial support:* Fellowships, research assistantships, teaching assistantships, career-related internships or fieldwork, Federal Work-Study, institutionally sponsored loans, and tuition waivers (partial) available. Support available to part-time students. Financial award application deadline: 4/15; financial award applicants required to submit FAFSA. *Faculty research:* Teacher competency, educational measurement, higher education, biological and chemical bases of learning, technology in the classroom. *Application contact:* Associate Dean, 940-565-2383, Fax: 940-565-2141.

University of Notre Dame, Graduate School, College of Arts and Letters, Division of Social Science, Institute for Educational Initiatives, Notre Dame, IN 46556. Offers M Ed, MA. Enrollment restricted to participants in the Alliance for Catholic Education (ACE) program. *Entrance requirements:* For master's, GRE General Test, acceptance into the Alliance for Catholic Education program. Electronic applications accepted. *Faculty research:* Effective teaching, motivation, social and ethical development, literacy.

University of Oklahoma, Graduate College, College of Education, Norman, OK 73019-0390. Offers M Ed, Ed D, PhD, Certificate. *Accreditation:* NCATE. Evening/weekend programs available. Postbaccalaureate distance learning degree programs offered (no on-campus study). *Faculty:* 76 full-time (45 women), 4 part-time/adjunct (0 women). *Students:* 324 full-time (206 women), 437 part-time (313 women); includes 182 minority (74 African Americans, 64 American Indian/Alaska Native, 19 Asian Americans or Pacific Islanders, 25 Hispanic Americans), 27 international. 317 applicants, 73% accepted, 162 enrolled. In 2009, 159 master's, 34 doctorates awarded. *Degree requirements:* For doctorate, thesis/dissertation. *Entrance requirements:* For master's, minimum GPA of 3.0 in last 60 hours of undergraduate course work, BS in education; for doctorate, GRE General Test, master's degree. Additional exam requirements/recommendations for international students: Required—TOEFL (minimum score 550 paper-based; 213 computer-based). *Application deadline:* For fall admission, 6/1 for domestic students, 4/1 for international students; for spring admission, 11/1 for domestic students, 9/1 for international students. Applications are processed on a rolling basis. Application fee: $40 ($90 for international students). Electronic applications accepted. *Expenses:* Tuition, state resident: full-time $3744; part-time $156 per credit hour. Tuition, nonresident: full-time $13,577; part-time $565.70 per credit hour. Required fees: $2415; $90.10 per credit hour. *Financial support:* In 2009–10, 403 students received support, including 8 fellowships with full tuition reimbursements available (averaging $5,000 per year), 107 research assistantships with partial tuition reimbursements available (averaging $11,765 per year), 21 teaching assistantships with partial tuition reimbursements available (averaging $11,522 per year); career-related internships or fieldwork, Federal Work-Study, institutionally sponsored loans, scholarships/grants, tuition waivers (full and partial), and unspecified assistantships also available. Support available to part-time students. Financial award applicants required to submit FAFSA. Total annual research expenditures: $5.6 million. *Unit head:* Dr. Joan Karen Smith, Dean, 405-325-1081, Fax: 405-325-7390, E-mail: jksmith@ou.edu. *Application contact:* Dr. Joan Karen Smith, Dean, 405-325-1081, Fax: 405-325-7390, E-mail: jksmith@ou.edu.

University of Oregon, Graduate School, College of Education, Eugene, OR 97403. Offers M Ed, MA, MS, D Ed, PhD. Part-time programs available. Terminal master's awarded for partial completion of doctoral program. *Degree requirements:* For master's, exam, paper, or project; for doctorate, comprehensive exam, thesis/dissertation. *Entrance requirements:* Additional exam requirements/recommendations for international students: Required—TOEFL. *Faculty research:* Basic and applied research in teaching, learning and habilitation in all settings, schooling effectiveness.

University of Ottawa, Faculty of Graduate and Postdoctoral Studies, Faculty of Education, Ottawa, ON K1N 6N5, Canada. Offers M Ed, MA Ed, PhD, Certificate. Postbaccalaureate distance learning degree programs offered (minimal on-campus study). *Degree requirements:* For master's, thesis or alternative; for doctorate, comprehensive exam, thesis/dissertation, seminar. *Entrance requirements:* For master's, honors degree or equivalent, minimum B average; for doctorate, master's degree, minimum B+ average. Electronic applications accepted. *Faculty research:* Teaching, learning and evaluation; second language education; organizational studies in education; society, culture and literacies; educational counseling.

University of Pennsylvania, Graduate School of Education, Philadelphia, PA 19104. Offers M Phil, MS Ed, Ed D, PhD, DMD/MS Ed. Part-time programs available. *Faculty:* 59 full-time (26 women), 27 part-time/adjunct (9 women). *Students:* 1,002 full-time (715 women), 321 part-time (228 women); includes 177 minority (102 African Americans, 5 American Indian/Alaska Native, 46 Asian Americans or Pacific Islanders, 24 Hispanic Americans), 154 international. 1,860 applicants, 56% accepted, 623 enrolled. In 2009, 388 master's, 85 doctorates awarded. Terminal master's awarded for partial completion of doctoral program. *Degree requirements:* For master's, exam; for doctorate, thesis/dissertation, exam. *Entrance requirements:* For master's, GRE. *Application deadline:* For fall admission, 12/15 priority date for domestic students. Applications are processed on a rolling basis. Application fee: $70. Electronic applications accepted. *Expenses:* Contact institution. *Financial support:* In 2009–10, 101 students received support; fellowships, research assistantships, teaching assistantships, institutionally sponsored loans, scholarships/grants, traineeships, health care benefits, and unspecified assistantships available. Financial award application deadline: 12/15. *Unit head:* Dr. Andrew Porter, Graduate Dean, 215-898-7014. *Application contact:* Alyssa D'Alconzo, Associate Director, Admissions, 215-898-6415, Fax: 215-746-6884, E-mail: admissions@gse.upenn.edu.

University of Phoenix, College of Natural Sciences, College of Education, Phoenix, AZ 85034-7209. Offers administration and supervision (MAEd); adult education and training (MAEd); curriculum and instruction (MAEd); curriculum and instruction-adult education (MAEd); curriculum and instruction-computer education (MAEd); curriculum and instruction-English and language arts education (MAEd); curriculum and instruction-English as a second language (MAEd); curriculum and instruction-mathematics education (MAEd); curriculum education (MAEd); early childhood (MAEd); elementary teacher education (MAEd); secondary teacher education (MAEd); special education (MAEd); teacher leadership (MAEd). *Accreditation:* Teacher Education Accreditation Council. Evening/weekend programs available. Postbaccalaureate distance learning degree programs offered (no on-campus study). *Faculty:* 47 full-time (34 women), 844 part-time/adjunct (636 women). *Students:* 13,657 full-time (10,698 women); includes 4,000 minority (3,063 African Americans, 74 American Indian/Alaska Native, 241 Asian Americans or Pacific Islanders, 622 Hispanic Americans), 307 international. Average age 36. In 2009, 17,246 master's awarded. *Degree requirements:* For master's, thesis (for some programs). *Entrance requirements:* For master's, 3 years of work experience, minimum GPA of 2.5. Additional exam requirements/recommendations for international students: Required—TOEFL (minimum score 550 paper-based; 213 computer-based; 79 iBT). *Application deadline:* Applications are processed on a rolling basis. Application fee: $45. Electronic applications accepted. *Expenses:* Tuition: Full-time $13,272. Required fees: $660. Full-time tuition and fees vary according to course level, degree level and program. *Financial support:* Institutionally sponsored loans and scholarships/grants available. Financial award applicants required to submit FAFSA. *Unit head:* Dr. Meredith Curley, Dean/Executive Director, 480-557-1217, Fax: 480-557-1588, E-mail: meredith.curley@phoenix.edu. *Application contact:* Chair, 602-387-7000, Fax: 602-387-6020.

University of Phoenix, School of Advanced Studies, Phoenix, AZ 85034-7209. Offers business administration (DBA); education (Ed D); educational leadership (Ed D), including curriculum

Education—General

University of Phoenix (continued)
and instruction, educational leadership, educational technology; health administration (DHA); higher education administration (PhD); industrial/organizational psychology (PhD); nursing (PhD); organizational leadership (DM), including information systems and technology, organizational leadership. Evening/weekend programs available. *Faculty:* 83 full-time (47 women), 540 part-time/adjunct (264 women). *Students:* 7,749 full-time (5,032 women); includes 3,180 minority (2,473 African Americans, 61 American Indian/Alaska Native, 221 Asian Americans or Pacific Islanders, 425 Hispanic Americans), 490 international. Average age 44. In 2009, 467 doctorates awarded. *Degree requirements:* For doctorate, thesis/dissertation. *Entrance requirements:* For doctorate, 3 letters of recommendation, minimum master's GPA of 3.0, 3 years professional work experience. Additional exam requirements/recommendations for international students: Required—TOEFL (minimum score 550 paper-based; 213 computer-based; 79 iBT). *Application deadline:* Applications are processed on a rolling basis. Application fee: $45. Electronic applications accepted. *Expenses:* Tuition: Full-time $13,272. Required fees: $660. Full-time tuition and fees vary according to course level, degree level and program. *Financial support:* Institutionally sponsored loans and scholarships/grants available. Financial award applicants required to submit FAFSA. *Unit head:* Dr. Jeremy Moreland, Dean/Executive Director, 480-557-3231, E-mail: jeremy.moreland@phoenix.edu. *Application contact:* Information Contact, 800-697-8223.

University of Phoenix–Austin Campus, College of Education, Austin, TX 78759. Offers curriculum and instruction (MA Ed).

University of Phoenix–Bay Area Campus, The Artemis School, College of Education, Pleasanton, CA 94588-3677. Offers curriculum instruction (MA Ed); curriculum instruction—adult education (MA Ed); elementary teacher education (MA Ed); secondary teacher education (MA Ed). Evening/weekend programs available. Postbaccalaureate distance learning degree programs offered (no on-campus study). *Degree requirements:* For master's, thesis (for some programs). *Entrance requirements:* For master's, minimum undergraduate GPA of 2.5, 3 years of work experience. Additional exam requirements/recommendations for international students: Required—TOEFL (minimum score 550 paper-based; 213 computer-based; 79 iBT). Electronic applications accepted.

University of Phoenix–Central Florida Campus, The Artemis School, College of Education, Maitland, FL 32751-7057. Offers administration and supervision (MA Ed); curriculum and instruction (MA Ed); curriculum and instruction-computer education (MA Ed); curriculum and instruction-mathematics education (MA Ed); early childhood education (MA Ed); elementary teacher education (MA Ed); secondary teacher education (MA Ed). Evening/weekend programs available. *Degree requirements:* For master's, thesis (for some programs). *Entrance requirements:* For master's, 3 years of work experience, minimum undergraduate GPA of 2.5. Additional exam requirements/recommendations for international students: Required—TOEFL (minimum score 550 paper-based; 213 computer-based; 79 iBT). Electronic applications accepted.

University of Phoenix–Central Massachusetts Campus, The Artemis School, College of Education, Westborough, MA 01581-3906. Offers MA Ed. Evening/weekend programs available. *Degree requirements:* For master's, thesis (for some programs). *Entrance requirements:* For master's, minimum undergraduate GPA of 2.5, 3 years of work experience. Additional exam requirements/recommendations for international students: Required—TOEFL (minimum score 550 paper-based; 213 computer-based; 79 iBT). Electronic applications accepted.

University of Phoenix–Central Valley Campus, College of Education, Fresno, CA 93720-1562. Offers curriculum and instruction (MA Ed); curriculum and instruction-computer education (MA Ed); elementary teacher education (MA Ed); secondary teacher education (MA Ed).

University of Phoenix–Chattanooga Campus, College of Education, Chattanooga, TN 37421-3707. Offers administration and supervision (MA Ed); curriculum and instruction (MA Ed); elementary teacher education (MA Ed); secondary teacher education (MA Ed).

University of Phoenix–Dallas Campus, The Artemis School, College of Education, Dallas, TX 75251-2009. Offers curriculum and instruction (MA Ed).

University of Phoenix–Denver Campus, The Artemis School, College of Education, Lone Tree, CO 80124-5453. Offers administration and supervision (MAEd); curriculum instruction (MAEd); elementary teacher education (MAEd); school counseling (MSC); secondary teacher education (MAEd). Evening/weekend programs available. *Degree requirements:* For master's, thesis (for some programs). *Entrance requirements:* For master's, minimum undergraduate GPA of 2.5, 3 years work experience. Additional exam requirements/recommendations for international students: Required—TOEFL (minimum score 550 paper-based; 213 computer-based; 79 iBT). Electronic applications accepted.

University of Phoenix–Hawaii Campus, The Artemis School, College of Education, Honolulu, HI 96813-4317. Offers administration and supervision (MA Ed); curriculum and instruction (MA Ed); elementary education (MA Ed); secondary education (MA Ed); special education (MA Ed); teacher education for elementary licensure (MA Ed). Evening/weekend programs available. *Degree requirements:* For master's, thesis (for some programs). *Entrance requirements:* For master's, minimum undergraduate GPA of 2.5, 3 years of work experience. Additional exam requirements/recommendations for international students: Required—TOEFL (minimum score 550 paper-based; 213 computer-based; 79 iBT). Electronic applications accepted.

University of Phoenix–Houston Campus, The Artemis School, College of Education, Houston, TX 77079-2004. Offers curriculum and instruction (MA Ed).

University of Phoenix–Idaho Campus, The Artemis School, College of Education, Meridian, ID 83642-3014. Offers administration and supervision (MA Ed); curriculum and instruction (MA Ed); elementary teacher education (MA Ed); secondary teacher education (MA Ed). Evening/weekend programs available. *Degree requirements:* For master's, thesis (for some programs). *Entrance requirements:* For master's, minimum undergraduate GPA of 2.5, 3 years of work experience. Additional exam requirements/recommendations for international students: Required—TOEFL (minimum score 550 paper-based; 213 computer-based). Electronic applications accepted.

University of Phoenix–Indianapolis Campus, The Artemis School, College of Education, Indianapolis, IN 46250-932. Offers elementary teacher education (MA Ed); secondary teacher education (MA Ed).

University of Phoenix–Kansas City Campus, The Artemis School, College of Education, Kansas City, MO 64131-4517. Offers administration and supervision (MA Ed). Postbaccalaureate distance learning degree programs offered.

University of Phoenix–Las Vegas Campus, The Artemis School, College of Education, Las Vegas, NV 89128. Offers administration and supervision (MA Ed); curriculum and instruction (MA Ed); school counseling (MSC); teacher education-elementary licensure (MA Ed). Evening/weekend programs available. *Degree requirements:* For master's, thesis (for some programs). *Entrance requirements:* For master's, minimum undergraduate GPA of 2.5, 3 years of work experience. Additional exam requirements/recommendations for international students: Required—TOEFL (minimum score 550 paper-based; 213 computer-based; 79 iBT). Electronic applications accepted.

University of Phoenix–Louisiana Campus, The Artemis School, College of Education, Metairie, LA 70001-2082. Offers curriculum and instruction (MA Ed); early childhood education (MA Ed). Postbaccalaureate distance learning degree programs offered. *Degree requirements:* For master's, thesis. *Entrance requirements:* For master's, minimum undergraduate GPA of 2.5, 3 years work experience. Additional exam requirements/recommendations for international students: Required—TOEFL (minimum score 550 paper-based; 213 computer-based; 79 iBT).

University of Phoenix–Memphis Campus, College of Education, Cordova, TN 38018. Offers administration and supervision (MA Ed); curriculum and instruction (MA Ed); elementary teacher education (MA Ed); secondary teacher education (MA Ed).

University of Phoenix–Metro Detroit Campus, College of Education, Troy, MI 48098-2623. Offers administration and supervision (MA Ed); elementary teacher education (MA Ed); secondary teacher education (MA Ed); special education (MA Ed). Evening/weekend programs available. *Faculty:* 3 full-time (1 woman), 2 part-time/adjunct (both women). *Students:* 34 full-time (30 women); includes 23 minority (all African Americans). Average age 44. In 2009, 44 master's awarded. *Degree requirements:* For master's, thesis (for some programs). *Entrance requirements:* For master's, 3 years of work experience, minimum undergraduate GPA of 2.5. Additional exam requirements/recommendations for international students: Required—TOEFL (minimum score 550 paper-based; 213 computer-based; 79 iBT). *Application deadline:* Applications are processed on a rolling basis. Application fee: $45. Electronic applications accepted. *Expenses:* Tuition: Full-time $14,136. Required fees: $660. *Financial support:* Institutionally sponsored loans and scholarships/grants available. Financial award applicants required to submit FAFSA. *Unit head:* Dr. Meredith Curley, Dean/Executive Director, 480-557-1217, E-mail: meredith.curley@phoenix.edu. *Application contact:* Chair, 800-834-2438, Fax: 248-267-0147.

University of Phoenix–Nashville Campus, The Artemis School, College of Education, Nashville, TN 37214-5048. Offers administration and supervision (MA Ed); curriculum and instruction (MA Ed); elementary teacher education (MA Ed); secondary teacher education (MA Ed). Evening/weekend programs available. *Degree requirements:* For master's, thesis (for some programs). *Entrance requirements:* For master's, minimum undergraduate GPA of 2.5, 3 years work experience. Additional exam requirements/recommendations for international students: Required—TOEFL (minimum score 500 paper-based; 213 computer-based; 79 iBT). Electronic applications accepted.

University of Phoenix–New Mexico Campus, The Artemis School, College of Education, Albuquerque, NM 87113-1570. Offers administration and supervision (MAEd); curriculum and instruction (MAEd); elementary teacher education (MAEd); school counseling (MSC); secondary teacher education (MAEd). Evening/weekend programs available. *Degree requirements:* For master's, thesis (for some programs). *Entrance requirements:* For master's, minimum undergraduate GPA of 2.5, 3 years of work experience. Additional exam requirements/recommendations for international students: Required—TOEFL (minimum score 550 paper-based; 213 computer-based; 79 iBT). Electronic applications accepted.

University of Phoenix–Northern Nevada Campus, College of Education, Reno, NV 89521-5862. Offers administration and supervision (MA Ed); curriculum and instruction (MA Ed); elementary teacher education (MA Ed); secondary teacher education (MA Ed).

University of Phoenix–Northern Virginia Campus, College of Education, Reston, VA 20190. Offers administration and supervision (MA Ed).

University of Phoenix–North Florida Campus, The Artemis School, College of Education, Jacksonville, FL 32216-0959. Offers administration and supervision (MA Ed); curriculum and instruction (MA Ed), including computer education, mathematics education; early childhood education (MA Ed); elementary teacher education (MA Ed); secondary teacher education (MA Ed). Evening/weekend programs available. *Degree requirements:* For master's, thesis (for some programs). *Entrance requirements:* For master's, 3 years of work experience, minimum undergraduate GPA of 2.5. Additional exam requirements/recommendations for international students: Required—TOEFL (minimum score 550 paper-based; 213 computer-based; 49 iBT). Electronic applications accepted.

University of Phoenix–Omaha Campus, College of Education, Omaha, NE 68154-5240. Offers administration and supervision (MA Ed); curriculum and instruction (MA Ed), including adult education, computer education, curriculum and instruction, English and language arts education, English as a second language, mathematics education; elementary teacher education (MA Ed); secondary teacher education (MA Ed); special education (MA Ed).

University of Phoenix–Oregon Campus, The Artemis School, College of Education, Tigard, OR 97223. Offers curriculum and instruction (MA Ed); early childhood education (MA Ed); elementary education (MA Ed), including early childhood specialization, middle level specialization; secondary education (MA Ed), including middle level specialization. Evening/weekend programs available. *Degree requirements:* For master's, thesis (for some programs). *Entrance requirements:* For master's, minimum undergraduate GPA of 2.5, 3 years work experience. Additional exam requirements/recommendations for international students: Required—TOEFL (minimum score 550 paper-based; 213 computer-based; 79 iBT). Electronic applications accepted.

University of Phoenix–Phoenix Campus, College of Social Sciences, College of Education, Phoenix, AZ 85040-1958. Offers administration and supervision (MA Ed); elementary teacher education (MA Ed); secondary teacher education (MA Ed); special education (MA Ed). Evening/weekend programs available. *Faculty:* 39 full-time (23 women), 422 part-time/adjunct (255 women). *Students:* 443 full-time (297 women); includes 79 minority (32 African Americans, 8 American Indian/Alaska Native, 8 Asian Americans or Pacific Islanders, 31 Hispanic Americans), 6 international. Average age 35. In 2009, 199 master's awarded. *Degree requirements:* For master's, thesis (for some programs). *Entrance requirements:* For master's, 3 years of work experience, minimum undergraduate GPA of 2.5. Additional exam requirements/recommendations for international students: Required—TOEFL (minimum score 550 paper-based; 213 computer-based; 79 iBT). *Application deadline:* Applications are processed on a rolling basis. Application fee: $45. Electronic applications accepted. *Expenses:* Tuition: Full-time $10,272. Required fees: $760. *Financial support:* Institutionally sponsored loans and scholarships/grants available. Financial award applicants required to submit FAFSA. *Unit head:* Dr. Meredith Curley, Dean/Executive Director, 480-557-1217, Fax: 480-557-1588, E-mail: meredith.curley@phoenix.edu. *Application contact:* College Chair, 480-804-2000.

University of Phoenix–Puerto Rico Campus, The Artemis School, College of Education, Guaynabo, PR 00968. Offers administration and supervision (MA Ed); early childhood education (MA Ed); school counselor (MSC). Evening/weekend programs available. *Degree requirements:* For master's, thesis (for some programs). *Entrance requirements:* For master's, minimum undergraduate GPA of 2.5, 3 years work experience. Additional exam requirements/recommendations for international students: Required—TOEFL (minimum score 550 paper-based; 213 computer-based; 79 iBT). Electronic applications accepted.

University of Phoenix–Sacramento Valley Campus, The Artemis School, College of Education, Sacramento, CA 95833-3632. Offers adult education (MA Ed); curriculum instruction (MA Ed); elementary teacher education (MA Ed); secondary teacher education (MA Ed); teacher education (Certificate). Evening/weekend programs available. *Degree requirements:* For master's, thesis (for some programs). *Entrance requirements:* For master's, 3 years of work experience, minimum undergraduate GPA of 2.5. Additional exam requirements/recommendations for international students: Required—TOEFL (minimum score 550 paper-based; 213 computer-based; 79 iBT). Electronic applications accepted.

University of Phoenix–San Diego Campus, The Artemis School, College of Education, San Diego, CA 92123. Offers curriculum and instruction (MA Ed), including computer education, curriculum and instruction, English as a second language; elementary teacher education (MA Ed); secondary teacher education (MA Ed). Evening/weekend programs available. *Degree requirements:* For master's, thesis (for some programs). *Entrance requirements:* For master's, 3 years of work experience, minimum undergraduate GPA of 3.0. Additional exam requirements/recommendations for international students: Required—TOEFL (minimum score 550 paper-based; 213 computer-based; 79 iBT). Electronic applications accepted.

University of Phoenix–Southern Arizona Campus, The Artemis School, College of Education, Tucson, AZ 85711. Offers administration and supervision (MA Ed); adult education and training (MA Ed); curriculum instruction (MA Ed); educational counseling (MA Ed); elementary teacher education (MA Ed); school counseling (MSC); secondary teacher education (MA Ed); special

education (MA Ed, Certificate). Evening/weekend programs available. *Degree requirements:* For master's, thesis (for some programs). *Entrance requirements:* For master's, minimum undergraduate GPA of 2.5, 3 years of work experience. Additional exam requirements/recommendations for international students: Required—TOEFL (minimum score 550 paper-based; 213 computer-based; 79 iBT). Electronic applications accepted.

University of Phoenix–Southern California Campus, College of Education, Costa Mesa, CA 92626. Offers administration and supervision (MA Ed); adult education and training (MA Ed); curriculum and instruction (MA Ed), including computer education, curriculum and instruction, English and language arts, English as a second language, mathematics education; early childhood education (MA Ed); special education (MA Ed); teacher leadership (MA Ed). Evening/weekend programs available. *Faculty:* 47 full-time (34 women), 844 part-time/adjunct (636 women). *Students:* 558 full-time (391 women); includes 222 minority (60 African Americans, 4 American Indian/Alaska Native, 26 Asian Americans or Pacific Islanders, 132 Hispanic Americans), 9 international. Average age 34. In 2009, 303 master's awarded. *Degree requirements:* For master's, thesis (for some programs). *Entrance requirements:* For master's, minimum undergraduate GPA of 2.5, 3 years work experience. Additional exam requirements/recommendations for international students: Required—TOEFL (minimum score 550 paper-based; 213 computer-based; 79 iBT). *Application deadline:* Applications are processed on a rolling basis. Application fee: $45. Electronic applications accepted. *Expenses:* Tuition: Full-time $15,120. Required fees: $660. *Financial support:* Institutionally sponsored loans and scholarships/grants available. Financial award applicants required to submit FAFSA. *Unit head:* Dr. Meredith Curley, Dean/Executive Director, 480-557-1217, Fax: 480-557-1588, E-mail: meredith.curley@phoenix.edu. *Application contact:* Campus College Chair, 714-378-1878, Fax: 714-378-5875.

University of Phoenix–Southern Colorado Campus, The Artemis School, College of Education, Colorado Springs, CO 80919-2335. Offers administration and supervision (MA Ed); curriculum and instruction (MA Ed); elementary teacher education (MA Ed); principal licensure certification (Certificate); school counseling (MSC); secondary teacher education (MA Ed). Evening/weekend programs available. *Degree requirements:* For master's, thesis (for some programs). *Entrance requirements:* For master's, minimum undergraduate GPA of 2.5, 3 years of work experience. Additional exam requirements/recommendations for international students: Required—TOEFL (minimum score 550 paper-based; 213 computer-based; 79 iBT). Electronic applications accepted.

University of Phoenix–South Florida Campus, The Artemis School, College of Education, Fort Lauderdale, FL 33309. Offers administration and supervision (MA Ed); curriculum and instruction (MA Ed), including computer education, curriculum and instruction, mathematics education; early childhood education (MA Ed); elementary teacher education (MA Ed); secondary teacher education (MA Ed). Evening/weekend programs available. *Degree requirements:* For master's, thesis (for some programs). *Entrance requirements:* For master's, 3 years of work experience, minimum undergraduate GPA of 2.5. Additional exam requirements/recommendations for international students: Required—TOEFL (minimum score 550 paper-based; 213 computer-based; 79 iBT). Electronic applications accepted.

University of Phoenix–Springfield Campus, College of Education, Springfield, MO 65804-7211. Offers administration and supervision (MA Ed); curriculum and instruction (MA Ed), including computer education, curriculum and instruction, English and language arts education, English as a second language, mathematics education; English and language arts education (MA Ed).

University of Phoenix–Utah Campus, The Artemis School, College of Education, Salt Lake City, UT 84123-4617. Offers administration and supervision (MA Ed); curriculum and instruction (MA Ed); elementary teacher education (MA Ed); school counseling (MSC); secondary teacher education (MA Ed); special education (MA Ed). Evening/weekend programs available. *Degree requirements:* For master's, thesis (for some programs). *Entrance requirements:* For master's, minimum undergraduate GPA of 2.5, 3 years work experience. Additional exam requirements/recommendations for international students: Required—TOEFL (minimum score 550 paper-based; 213 computer-based; 79 iBT). Electronic applications accepted.

University of Phoenix–Vancouver Campus, The Artemis School, College of Education, Burnaby, BC V5C 6G9, Canada. Offers administration and supervision (MA Ed); curriculum and instruction (MA Ed), including computer education, curriculum and instruction. Evening/weekend programs available. *Degree requirements:* For master's, thesis (for some programs). *Entrance requirements:* For master's, minimum undergraduate GPA of 2.5, 3 years work experience. Additional exam requirements/recommendations for international students: Required—TOEFL (minimum score 550 paper-based; 213 computer-based; 79 iBT). Electronic applications accepted.

University of Phoenix–West Florida Campus, The Artemis School, College of Education, Temple Terrace, FL 33637. Offers administration and supervision (MA Ed); curriculum and instruction (MA Ed), including computer education, curriculum and instruction, mathematics education; curriculum and technology (MA Ed); early childhood education (MA Ed); elementary teacher education (MA Ed); secondary teacher education (MA Ed). Evening/weekend programs available. *Degree requirements:* For master's, thesis (for some programs). *Entrance requirements:* For master's, 3 years of work experience, minimum undergraduate GPA of 2.5. Additional exam requirements/recommendations for international students: Required—TOEFL (minimum score 550 paper-based; 213 computer-based; 79 iBT).

University of Pittsburgh, School of Education, Pittsburgh, PA 15260. Offers M Ed, MA, MAT, MS, Ed D, PhD. Part-time and evening/weekend programs available. Postbaccalaureate distance learning degree programs offered (minimal on-campus study). *Faculty:* 98 full-time (55 women), 115 part-time/adjunct (74 women). *Students:* 566 full-time (408 women), 584 part-time (431 women); includes 110 minority (83 African Americans, 2 American Indian/Alaska Native, 16 Asian Americans or Pacific Islanders, 9 Hispanic Americans), 68 international. Average age 31. 905 applicants, 75% accepted, 535 enrolled. In 2009, 343 master's, 35 doctorates awarded. Terminal master's awarded for partial completion of doctoral program. *Degree requirements:* For master's, comprehensive exam, thesis (for some programs); for doctorate, comprehensive exam, thesis/dissertation. *Entrance requirements:* For doctorate, GRE. Additional exam requirements/recommendations for international students: Required—TOEFL (minimum score 550 paper-based; 213 computer-based; 80 iBT). *Application deadline:* For fall admission, 2/1 priority date for domestic students, 2/1 for international students; for spring admission, 11/15 priority date for domestic students, 7/1 for international students. Applications are processed on a rolling basis. Application fee: $50. Electronic applications accepted. *Expenses:* Tuition, state resident: full-time $16,402; part-time $665 per credit. Tuition, nonresident: full-time $28,694; part-time $1175 per credit. Required fees: $690; $175 per term. Tuition and fees vary according to program. *Financial support:* In 2009–10, 18 fellowships with full and partial tuition reimbursements (averaging $14,485 per year), 50 research assistantships with full and partial tuition reimbursements (averaging $14,000 per year), 86 teaching assistantships with full and partial tuition reimbursements (averaging $13,987 per year) were awarded; career-related internships or fieldwork, Federal Work-Study, institutionally sponsored loans, scholarships/grants, traineeships, tuition waivers (partial), and unspecified assistantships also available. Support available to part-time students. Financial award applicants required to submit FAFSA. Total annual research expenditures: $15.3 million. *Unit head:* Dr. Alan Lesgold, Dean, 412-648-1773, Fax: 412-648-1825, E-mail: al@pitt.edu. *Application contact:* Marianne L. Budziszewski, Director of Admissions and Enrollment Services, 412-648-7056, Fax: 412-648-1899, E-mail: soeinfo@pitt.edu.

University of Portland, School of Education, Portland, OR 97203-5798. Offers M Ed, MA, MAT. M Ed also available through the Graduate Outreach Program for teachers residing in the Oregon and Washington State areas. *Accreditation:* NCATE. Part-time and evening/weekend programs available. *Faculty:* 19 full-time (8 women), 10 part-time/adjunct (5 women). *Students:* 64 full-time (47 women), 188 part-time (130 women); includes 28 minority (22 Asian Americans or Pacific Islanders, 6 Hispanic Americans), 80 international. Average age 35. In 2009, 127

master's awarded. *Entrance requirements:* For master's, minimum GPA of 3.0, teaching certificate, letters of recommendation, resume, statement of goals, official transcripts. Additional exam requirements/recommendations for international students: Required—TOEFL (minimum score 550 paper-based; 80 iBT), IELTS (minimum score 7). *Application deadline:* For fall admission, 7/15 priority date for domestic and international students; for spring admission, 12/15 priority date for domestic and international students. Applications are processed on a rolling basis. Application fee: $50. *Expenses:* Tuition: Part-time $860 per semester hour. *Financial support:* Federal Work-Study and scholarships/grants available. Support available to part-time students. Financial award application deadline: 3/1; financial award applicants required to submit FAFSA. *Faculty research:* Multicultural education, supervision/leadership. *Unit head:* Dr. Thomas Greene, Dean, 503-943-7135, Fax: 503-943-8042, E-mail: ciriello@up.edu. *Application contact:* Dr. Bruce Weitzel, Associate Dean, 503-943-7135, E-mail: weitzel@up.edu.

University of Prince Edward Island, Faculty of Education, Charlottetown, PE C1A 4P3, Canada. Offers leadership and learning (M Ed). Part-time programs available. *Degree requirements:* For master's, thesis. *Entrance requirements:* For master's, 2 years of professional experience, bachelor of education, professional certificate. Additional exam requirements/recommendations for international students: Required—TOEFL (minimum score 550 paper-based; 213 computer-based; 80 iBT), Canadian Academic English Language Assessment, Michigan English Language Assessment Battery, Canadian Test of English for Scholars and Trainees. *Faculty research:* Distance learning, aboriginal communities and education leadership development, international development, immersion language learning.

University of Puerto Rico, Río Piedras, College of Education, San Juan, PR 00931-3300. Offers M Ed, MS, Ed D. *Accreditation:* NCATE. Part-time programs available. *Degree requirements:* For master's, thesis; for doctorate, thesis/dissertation, internship. *Entrance requirements:* For master's, GRE or PAEG, minimum GPA of 3.0, letter of recommendation; for doctorate, GRE or PAEG, master's degree, minimum GPA of 3.0, letter of recommendation (2), interview. *Faculty research:* Curriculum, math teaching.

University of Puget Sound, Graduate Studies, School of Education, Tacoma, WA 98416. Offers M Ed, MAT. *Accreditation:* NCATE. *Faculty:* 10 full-time (6 women), 1 (woman) part-time/adjunct. *Students:* 46 full-time (27 women), 26 part-time (20 women); includes 13 minority (5 African Americans, 4 Asian Americans or Pacific Islanders, 4 Hispanic Americans). Average age 28. 95 applicants, 77% accepted, 56 enrolled. In 2009, 51 master's awarded. *Degree requirements:* For master's, capstone course. *Entrance requirements:* For master's, GRE General Test, minimum GPA of 3.0. Additional exam requirements/recommendations for international students: Required—TOEFL (minimum score 550 paper-based; 213 computer-based; 80 iBT). *Application deadline:* For fall admission, 3/1 priority date for domestic and international students. Applications are processed on a rolling basis. Application fee: $60. Electronic applications accepted. Tuition and fees vary according to course load, degree level and program. *Financial support:* In 2009–10, 18 students received support; teaching assistantships, career-related internships or fieldwork and scholarships/grants available. Financial award application deadline: 3/31; financial award applicants required to submit FAFSA. *Unit head:* Dr. John Woodward, Dean, 253-879-3375, E-mail: woodward@pugetsound.edu. *Application contact:* Dr. George H. Mills, Vice President for Enrollment, 253-879-3211, Fax: 253-879-3993, E-mail: admission@pugetsound.edu.

University of Redlands, School of Education, Redlands, CA 92373-0999. Offers MA, Ed D, Certificate. Part-time and evening/weekend programs available. *Entrance requirements:* For master's, minimum undergraduate GPA of 3.0, 2 letters of recommendation. Additional exam requirements/recommendations for international students: Required—TOEFL (minimum score 550 paper-based; 213 computer-based). *Expenses:* Contact institution.

University of Regina, Faculty of Graduate Studies and Research, Faculty of Education, Regina, SK S4S 0A2, Canada. Offers M Ad Ed, M Ed, MHRD, PhD. Part-time programs available. *Faculty:* 42 full-time (20 women), 4 part-time/adjunct (3 women). *Students:* 88 full-time (63 women), 186 part-time (138 women). 153 applicants, 77% accepted. In 2009, 101 master's, 2 doctorates awarded. *Degree requirements:* For master's, practicum, project, or thesis; for doctorate, thesis/dissertation. *Entrance requirements:* Additional exam requirements/recommendations for international students: Required—TOEFL (minimum score 580 paper-based; 237 computer-based; 80 iBT). *Application deadline:* For fall admission, 2/15 for domestic students; for winter admission, 2/15 for domestic students; for spring admission, 2/15 for domestic students. Application fee: $90 ($100 for international students). Electronic applications accepted. *Expenses:* Contact institution. *Financial support:* In 2009–10, 13 fellowships (averaging $19,000 per year), 6 research assistantships (averaging $16,910 per year), 18 teaching assistantships (averaging $6,650 per year) were awarded; career-related internships or fieldwork and scholarships/grants also available. Financial award application deadline: 6/15. *Faculty research:* Curriculum and instruction, administration, educational psychology, human resource development. *Unit head:* Dr. Warren Wessel, Associate Dean, Graduate Program and Research, 306-585-4555, Fax: 306-585-5387, E-mail: warren.wessel@uregina.ca. *Application contact:* Tania Gates, Graduate Program Coordinator, 306-585-4506, Fax: 306-585-4506, E-mail: edgrad@uregina.ca.

University of Rhode Island, Graduate School, College of Human Science and Services, School of Education, Kingston, RI 02881. Offers adult education (MA); education (PhD); elementary education (MA); music education (MM); reading education (MA); secondary education (MA); special education (MA); MS/PhD. *Accreditation:* NCATE. Part-time and evening/weekend programs available. *Faculty:* 19 full-time (12 women), 5 part-time/adjunct (1 woman). *Students:* 44 full-time (33 women), 128 part-time (101 women); includes 14 minority (8 African Americans, 2 American Indian/Alaska Native, 2 Asian Americans or Pacific Islanders, 2 Hispanic Americans), 3 international. In 2009, 44 master's, 7 doctorates awarded. *Degree requirements:* For master's, comprehensive exam (for some programs), thesis optional; for doctorate, comprehensive exam, thesis/dissertation. *Entrance requirements:* For master's, 2 letters of recommendation; interview (for special education applicants); for doctorate, GRE, 3 letters of recommendation, resume. Additional exam requirements/recommendations for international students: Required—TOEFL (minimum score 600 paper-based; 250 computer-based; 100 iBT). *Application deadline:* For fall admission, 1/31 for international students. Application fee: $65. Electronic applications accepted. *Expenses:* Tuition, state resident: full-time $8828; part-time $490 per credit hour. Tuition, nonresident: full-time $22,100; part-time $1228 per credit hour. Required fees: $1118; $57 per semester. Tuition and fees vary according to program. *Financial support:* In 2009–10, 5 research assistantships with full and partial tuition reimbursements (averaging $11,518 per year), 3 teaching assistantships with full and partial tuition reimbursements (averaging $10,421 per year) were awarded; career-related internships or fieldwork also available. Financial award applicants required to submit FAFSA. Total annual research expenditures: $3.4 million. *Unit head:* Dr. David Byrd, Director, 401-874-5484, Fax: 401-874-5471, E-mail: dbyrd@uri.edu. *Application contact:* Dr. John Boulmetis, Coordinator of Graduate Studies, 401-874-4159, Fax: 401-874-7610, E-mail: johnb@uri.edu.

University of Rio Grande, Graduate School, Rio Grande, OH 45674. Offers classroom teaching (M Ed), including fine arts, learning disabilities, mathematics, reading education. *Accreditation:* NCATE. Part-time and evening/weekend programs available. *Degree requirements:* For master's, final research project, portfolio. *Entrance requirements:* For master's, minimum GPA of 2.7 in major, 2.5 overall. Additional exam requirements/recommendations for international students: Required—TOEFL. *Faculty research:* Interagency collaboration, reading and mathematics, learning styles, college access, literacy.

University of Rochester, Margaret Warner Graduate School of Education and Human Development, Rochester, NY 14627. Offers MAT, MS, Ed D, PhD, MS/PhD. *Accreditation:* ACA (one or more programs are accredited); NCATE. Part-time and evening/weekend programs available. Terminal master's awarded for partial completion of doctoral program. *Degree requirements:* For master's, thesis (for some programs); for doctorate, thesis/dissertation, qualifying exam.

Education—General

University of St. Francis, College of Education, Joliet, IL 60435-6169. Offers educational leadership (MS), including reading; elementary education certification (M Ed); reading (MS); secondary education certification (M Ed), including English education, math education, science education, social studies education; special education (M Ed); teaching and learning (MS), including character education, curriculum and instruction, differentiated instruction, technology. *Accreditation:* NCATE. Part-time and evening/weekend programs available. *Faculty:* 10 full-time (8 women), 26 part-time/adjunct (18 women). *Students:* 60 full-time (45 women), 349 part-time (283 women); includes 36 minority (10 African Americans, 2 Asian Americans or Pacific Islanders, 24 Hispanic Americans). Average age 33. 211 applicants, 65% accepted, 102 enrolled. In 2009, 174 master's awarded. *Entrance requirements:* For master's, Illinois Basic Skills Test (M Ed), teaching certificate (MS), minimum undergraduate GPA of 2.75, 2 letters of recommendation, computer competency. Additional exam requirements/recommendations for international students: Required—TOEFL (minimum score 550 paper-based; 213 computer-based). *Application deadline:* Applications are processed on a rolling basis. Application fee: $30. Electronic applications accepted. *Expenses:* Contact institution. *Financial support:* In 2009–10, 254 students received support. Federal Work-Study, scholarships/grants, tuition waivers (partial), and unspecified assistantships available. Support available to part-time students. Financial award applicants required to submit FAFSA. *Unit head:* Dr. John Gambro, Dean, 815-740-3332, Fax: 815-740-2264, E-mail: jgambro@stfrancis.edu. *Application contact:* Sandra Sloka, Director of Admissions for Graduate and Degree Completion Programs, 800-735-7500, Fax: 815-740-5032, E-mail: ssloka@stfrancis.edu.

University of Saint Francis, Graduate School, Department of Education, Fort Wayne, IN 46808-3994. Offers special education (MS Ed). *Accreditation:* NCATE. Part-time and evening/weekend programs available. *Entrance requirements:* For master's, MAT, minimum GPA of 2.5.

University of Saint Mary, Graduate Programs, Program in Education, Leavenworth, KS 66048-5082. Offers curriculum and instruction (MAT). *Accreditation:* NCATE. Part-time and evening/weekend programs available. Postbaccalaureate distance learning degree programs offered (no on-campus study). *Degree requirements:* For master's, thesis, oral presentation. *Entrance requirements:* For master's, minimum undergraduate GPA of 2.75. *Faculty research:* Curriculum and instruction.

University of Saint Mary, Graduate Programs, Program in Teaching, Leavenworth, KS 66048-5082. Offers education (MA). Part-time and evening/weekend programs available. *Degree requirements:* For master's, thesis. *Entrance requirements:* For master's, minimum undergraduate GPA of 2.75.

University of St. Thomas, Graduate Studies, School of Education, St. Paul, MN 55105-1096. Offers MA, MAT, Ed D, Certificate, Ed S. Part-time and evening/weekend programs available. *Faculty:* 34 full-time (21 women), 61 part-time/adjunct (39 women). *Students:* 98 full-time (82 women), 954 part-time (654 women); includes 103 minority (54 African Americans, 1 American Indian/Alaska Native, 31 Asian Americans or Pacific Islanders, 17 Hispanic Americans), 12 international. Average age 35. 1,419 applicants, 76% accepted, 902 enrolled. In 2009, 292 master's, 24 doctorates, 145 other advanced degrees awarded. *Entrance requirements:* For master's, minimum GPA of 3.0 or MAT. Additional exam requirements/recommendations for international students: Required—TOEFL (minimum score 550 paper-based; 213 computer-based; 80 iBT). *Application deadline:* For fall admission, 6/1 priority date for domestic students; for spring admission, 11/1 priority date for domestic students. Applications are processed on a rolling basis. Application fee: $50. *Expenses:* Contact institution. *Financial support:* Fellowships, research assistantships, career-related internships or fieldwork, institutionally sponsored loans, and scholarships/grants available. Support available to part-time students. Financial award applicants required to submit FAFSA. *Unit head:* Dr. Bruce H. Kramer, Dean, 651-962-4435, Fax: 651-962-4169, E-mail: bhkramer@stthomas.edu. *Application contact:* Vicky L. Rasmusson, Admissions Coordinator, 651-962-4430, Fax: 651-962-4169, E-mail: vlrasmusson@stthomas.edu.

University of St. Thomas, School of Education, Houston, TX 77006-4696. Offers M Ed. Part-time and evening/weekend programs available. *Faculty:* 11 full-time (6 women), 13 part-time/adjunct (8 women). *Students:* 9 full-time (all women), 227 part-time (168 women); includes 92 minority (35 African Americans, 2 American Indian/Alaska Native, 8 Asian Americans or Pacific Islanders, 47 Hispanic Americans), 20 international. Average age 34. 99 applicants, 98% accepted, 89 enrolled. In 2009, 115 master's awarded. *Degree requirements:* For master's, comprehensive exam. *Entrance requirements:* For master's, GRE General Test (minimum score 900), Texas teaching certificate or Texas Academic Skills Program Test, minimum GPA of 3.0 in last 60 hours of course work. Additional exam requirements/recommendations for international students: Required—TOEFL (minimum score 550 paper-based; 213 computer-based). *Application deadline:* Applications are processed on a rolling basis. Application fee: $35. Electronic applications accepted. *Expenses:* Contact institution. *Financial support:* In 2009–10, 8 students received support. Federal Work-Study and scholarships/grants available. Support available to part-time students. Financial award application deadline: 3/1; financial award applicants required to submit FAFSA. *Unit head:* Dr. Robert M. LeBlanc, Dean, 713-525-3548, Fax: 713-525-3871, E-mail: leblancr@stthom.edu. *Application contact:* Paula C. Hollis, Administrative Assistant, 713-525-3541, Fax: 713-525-3871, E-mail: hollisp@stthom.edu.

University of San Diego, School of Leadership and Education Sciences, San Diego, CA 92110-2492. Offers M Ed, MA, MAT, PhD, Certificate. *Accreditation:* NCATE. Part-time and evening/weekend programs available. *Faculty:* 31 full-time (18 women), 53 part-time/adjunct (40 women). *Students:* 238 full-time (199 women), 308 part-time (233 women); includes 167 minority (31 African Americans, 2 American Indian/Alaska Native, 47 Asian Americans or Pacific Islanders, 87 Hispanic Americans), 13 international. Average age 31. 574 applicants, 62% accepted, 212 enrolled. In 2009, 170 master's, 15 doctorates awarded. *Degree requirements:* For doctorate, comprehensive exam (for some programs), thesis/dissertation (for some programs). *Entrance requirements:* For doctorate, GRE General Test, master's degree. Additional exam requirements/recommendations for international students: Required—TOEFL (minimum score 580 paper-based; 237 computer-based; 83 iBT), TWE. Application fee: $45. *Expenses:* Tuition: Full-time $21,042; part-time $1169 per unit. Required fees: $224. Full-time tuition and fees vary according to course load and degree level. *Financial support:* In 2009–10, 446 students received support. Career-related internships or fieldwork, Federal Work-Study, institutionally sponsored loans, unspecified assistantships, and stipends available. Support available to part-time students. Financial award application deadline: 4/1; financial award applicants required to submit FAFSA. *Unit head:* Dr. Paula A. Cordeiro, Dean, 619-260-4540, Fax: 619-260-6835, E-mail: cordeiro@sandiego.edu. *Application contact:* Dr. John Mosby, Associate Director of Graduate Admissions, 619-260-4524, Fax: 619-260-4158, E-mail: grads@sandiego.edu.

University of San Francisco, School of Education, San Francisco, CA 94117-1080. Offers MA, Ed D. Part-time and evening/weekend programs available. *Faculty:* 22 full-time (15 women), 97 part-time/adjunct (62 women). *Students:* 695 full-time (526 women), 196 part-time (133 women); includes 279 minority (66 African Americans, 10 American Indian/Alaska Native, 95 Asian Americans or Pacific Islanders, 108 Hispanic Americans), 50 international. Average age 34. 890 applicants, 67% accepted, 325 enrolled. In 2009, 303 master's, 48 doctorates awarded. *Degree requirements:* For doctorate, thesis/dissertation. Application fee: $55 ($65 for international students). *Expenses:* Tuition: Full-time $19,710; part-time $1095 per unit. Part-time tuition and fees vary according to degree level, campus/location and program. *Financial support:* In 2009–10, 546 students received support; fellowships, research assistantships, teaching assistantships available. Financial award application deadline: 3/2; financial award applicants required to submit FAFSA. *Unit head:* Dr. Walter Gmelch, Dean, 415-422-6525. *Application contact:* Beth Teabue, Associate Director of Graduate Outreach, 415-422-5467, E-mail: schoolofeducation@usfca.edu.

University of Saskatchewan, College of Graduate Studies and Research, College of Education, Saskatoon, SK S7N 5A2, Canada. Offers M Ed, MC Ed, PhD, Diploma. Part-time programs available. *Faculty:* 75. *Students:* 454. In 2009, 111 master's, 6 doctorates awarded. *Degree requirements:* For master's, thesis (for some programs); for doctorate, comprehensive exam (for some programs), thesis/dissertation. *Entrance requirements:* Additional exam requirements/recommendations for international students: Required—TOEFL (minimum score 80 iBT); Recommended—IELTS (minimum score 6.5). *Application deadline:* For fall admission, 7/1 priority date for domestic students. Applications are processed on a rolling basis. Application fee: $75. Electronic applications accepted. Tuition and fees charges are reported in Canadian dollars. *Expenses:* Tuition, area resident: Full-time $3000 Canadian dollars; part-time $500 Canadian dollars per term. Required fees: $700 Canadian dollars; $100 Canadian dollars per term. *Financial support:* Fellowships, research assistantships, teaching assistantships available. Financial award application deadline: 1/31. *Unit head:* Dr. Cecilia Reynolds, Dean, 306-966-7647, Fax: 306-966-7624, E-mail: cecilia.reynolds@usask.ca. *Application contact:* Dr. Cecilia Reynolds, Dean, 306-966-7647, Fax: 306-966-7624, E-mail: cecilia.reynolds@usask.ca.

The University of Scranton, College of Graduate and Continuing Education, Department of Education, Scranton, PA 18510. Offers curriculum and instruction (MA, MS); early childhood education (MA, MS); educational administration (MS); elementary education (MS); English as a second language (MS); reading education (MS); secondary education (MS); special education (MS). *Accreditation:* NCATE. Part-time and evening/weekend programs available. Postbaccalaureate distance learning degree programs offered (no on-campus study). *Faculty:* 17 full-time (11 women), 47 part-time/adjunct (18 women). *Students:* 350 full-time (254 women), 434 part-time (299 women); includes 87 minority (47 African Americans, 4 American Indian/Alaska Native, 7 Asian Americans or Pacific Islanders, 29 Hispanic Americans), 10 international. Average age 33. 235 applicants, 94% accepted. In 2009, 407 master's awarded. *Degree requirements:* For master's, comprehensive exam, thesis (for some programs), capstone experience. *Entrance requirements:* For master's, minimum GPA of 2.75. Additional exam requirements/recommendations for international students: Required—TOEFL (minimum score 500 paper-based; 173 computer-based), IELTS (minimum score 5.5). *Application deadline:* Applications are processed on a rolling basis. Application fee: $0. *Financial support:* In 2009–10, 15 students received support, including 15 teaching assistantships with full and partial tuition reimbursements available (averaging $7,040 per year); fellowships, career-related internships or fieldwork, Federal Work-Study, and unspecified assistantships also available. Support available to part-time students. Financial award application deadline: 3/1. *Faculty research:* Meta-analysis as a research tool, family involvement in school activities, effect of curriculum integration on student learning and attitude, the effects of inclusion on students, development of emotional intelligence of young children. *Unit head:* Dr. Art Chambers, Chair, 570-941-4668, Fax: 570-941-5515, E-mail: lchambersa2@scranton.edu. *Application contact:* Joseph M. Roback, Director of Admissions, 570-941-4385, Fax: 570-941-5928, E-mail: roback j2@scranton.edu.

University of Sioux Falls, Fredrikson School of Education, Sioux Falls, SD 57105-1699. Offers leadership (M Ed); reading (M Ed); superintendent (Ed S); teaching (M Ed); technology (M Ed). Summer admission only. *Accreditation:* NCATE. Part-time and evening/weekend programs available. *Degree requirements:* For master's, comprehensive exam (for some programs), research application project; for Ed S, comprehensive exam, portfolio. *Entrance requirements:* For master's, minimum GPA of 3.0, 1 year of teaching experience; for Ed S, minimum 3 years of teaching experience, minimum cumulative GPA of 3.5, 1 year of administrative experience. Additional exam requirements/recommendations for international students: Required—TOEFL. *Faculty research:* Reading, literacy, leadership.

University of South Africa, College of Human Sciences, Pretoria, South Africa. Offers adult education (M Ed); African languages (MA, PhD); African politics (MA, PhD); Afrikaans (MA, PhD); ancient history (MA, PhD); ancient Near Eastern studies (MA, PhD); anthropology (MA, PhD); applied linguistics (MA); Arabic (MA, PhD); archaeology (MA); art history (MA); Biblical archaeology (MA); Biblical studies (M Th, D Th, PhD); Christian spirituality (M Th, D Th); church history (M Th, D Th); classical studies (MA, PhD); clinical psychology (MA); communication (MA, PhD); comparative education (M Ed, Ed D); consulting psychology (D Admin, D Com, PhD); curriculum studies (M Ed, Ed D); development studies (M Admin, MA, D Admin, PhD); didactics (M Ed, Ed D); education (M Tech); education management (M Ed, Ed D); educational psychology (M Ed); English (MA); environmental education (M Ed); French (MA, PhD); German (MA, PhD); Greek (MA); guidance and counseling (M Ed); health studies (MA, PhD), including health sciences education (MA), health services management (MA), medical and surgical nursing science (critical care general) (MA), midwifery and neonatal nursing science (MA), trauma and emergency care (MA); history (MA, PhD); history of education (Ed D); inclusive education (M Ed, Ed D); information and communications technology policy and regulation (MA); information science (MA, MIS, PhD); international politics (MA, PhD); Islamic studies (MA, PhD); Italian (MA, PhD); Judaica (MA, PhD); linguistics (MA, PhD); mathematical education (M Ed); mathematics education (MA); missiology (M Th, D Th); modern Hebrew (MA, PhD); musicology (MA, MMus, D Mus, PhD); natural science education (M Ed); New Testament (M Th, D Th); Old Testament (D Th); pastoral therapy (M Th, D Th); philosophy (MA); philosophy of education (M Ed, Ed D); politics (MA, PhD); Portuguese (MA, PhD); practical theology (M Th, D Th); psychology (MA, MS, PhD); psychology of education (M Ed, Ed D); public health (MA); religious studies (MA, D Th, PhD); Romance languages (MA); Russian (MA, PhD); Semitic languages (MA, PhD); social behavior studies in HIV/AIDS (MA); social science (mental health) (MA); social science in development studies (MA); social science in psychology (MA); social science in social work (MA); social science in sociology (MA); social work (MSW, DSW, PhD); socio-education (M Ed, Ed D); sociolinguistics (MA); sociology (MA, PhD); Spanish (MA, PhD); systematic theology (M Th, D Th); TESOL (teaching English to speakers of other languages) (MA); theological ethics (M Th, D Th); theory of literature (MA, PhD); urban ministries (D Th); urban ministry (M Th).

University of South Alabama, Graduate School, College of Education, Mobile, AL 36688-0002. Offers M Ed, MS, PhD, Ed S. *Accreditation:* NCATE. Part-time programs available. *Degree requirements:* For master's, comprehensive exam; for doctorate, comprehensive exam, thesis/dissertation. *Entrance requirements:* For master's, GRE General Test or MAT. *Expenses:* Tuition, state resident: part-time $218 per contact hour. Required fees: $1102 per year.

University of South Carolina, The Graduate School, College of Education, Columbia, SC 29208. Offers IMA, M Ed, MAT, MS, MT, Ed D, PhD, Certificate, Ed S. *Accreditation:* NCATE. Part-time and evening/weekend programs available. Postbaccalaureate distance learning degree programs offered (minimal on-campus study). *Degree requirements:* For master's, comprehensive exam, thesis (for some programs), foreign language (MA); for doctorate, one foreign language, comprehensive exam, thesis/dissertation. *Entrance requirements:* For master's, GRE General Test or Miller Analogies Test, official transcripts, letters of recommendation and letter of intent; for doctorate, GRE General Test, or Miller Analogies Test/qualifying exams, etters of recommendation, letters of intent, interview. Electronic applications accepted. *Faculty research:* Inquiry learning, assessment of student learning, equity issues in education, multicultural education, cultural diversity.

University of South Carolina Aiken, School of Education, Aiken, SC 29801-6309. Offers M Ed. Part-time and evening/weekend programs available. *Entrance requirements:* For master's, GRE or MAT. Electronic applications accepted.

University of South Carolina Upstate, Graduate Programs, Spartanburg, SC 29303-4999. Offers early childhood education (M Ed); elementary education (M Ed); special education: visual impairment (M Ed). *Accreditation:* NCATE. Part-time and evening/weekend programs available. *Faculty:* 8 full-time (7 women), 4 part-time/adjunct (2 women). *Students:* 5 full-time (all women), 107 part-time (102 women). Average age 34. *Degree requirements:* For master's, professional portfolio. *Entrance requirements:* For master's, GRE General Test or MAT, interview, minimum undergraduate GPA of 2.5, teaching certificate, 2 letters of recommendation. *Application deadline:* Applications are processed on a rolling basis. Application fee: $40. *Expenses:* Tuition, state resident: full-time $9436; part-time $467 per credit hour. Tuition, nonresident: full-time $20,336; part-time $992 per credit hour. Required fees: $500. Tuition and fees vary according to course load. *Financial support:* Institutionally sponsored loans and institutional work-study available. Financial award application deadline: 7/15; financial award applicants

required to submit FAFSA. *Faculty research:* Rough and tumble play, social justice education, American Indian literatures and cultures, diversity and multicultural education, science teaching strategy. *Unit head:* Dr. Rebecca L. Stevens, Director of Graduate Programs, 864-503-5521, Fax: 864-503-5574, E-mail: rstevens@uscupstate.edu. *Application contact:* Donette Stewart, Associate Vice Chancellor for Enrollment Services, 864-503-5280, E-mail: dstewart@uscupstate.edu.

The University of South Dakota, Graduate School, School of Education, Vermillion, SD 57069-2390. Offers MA, MS, Ed D, PhD, Ed S. *Accreditation:* NCATE. Part-time and evening/weekend programs available. Postbaccalaureate distance learning degree programs offered (no on-campus study). *Degree requirements:* For master's and Ed S, comprehensive exam, thesis or alternative; for doctorate, comprehensive exam, thesis/dissertation. *Entrance requirements:* For master's and doctorate, GRE General Test or Miller Analogies Test, minimum GPA of 2.7. Additional exam requirements/recommendations for international students: Required—TOEFL (minimum score 550 paper-based; 213 computer-based; 79 iBT). Electronic applications accepted.

University of Southern California, Graduate School, Rossier School of Education, Los Angeles, CA 90089. Offers MAT, ME, MMFT, MS, Ed D, PhD. *Faculty:* 96 full-time (51 women), 27 part-time/adjunct (15 women). *Students:* 1,169 full-time (833 women), 97 part-time (62 women); includes 653 minority (126 African Americans, 15 American Indian/Alaska Native, 242 Asian Americans or Pacific Islanders, 270 Hispanic Americans), 76 international. 950 applicants, 70% accepted, 407 enrolled. In 2009, 226 master's, 157 doctorates awarded. *Degree requirements:* For master's, thesis optional; for doctorate, thesis/dissertation. *Entrance requirements:* For master's and doctorate, GRE. Additional exam requirements/recommendations for international students: Required—TOEFL (minimum score 250 computer-based; 100 iBT). Application fee: $85. Electronic applications accepted. *Expenses:* Tuition: Full-time $25,980; part-time $1315 per unit. Required fees: $554. One-time fee: $35 full-time. Full-time tuition and fees vary according to degree level and program. *Financial support:* In 2009–10, 385 students received support; research assistantships with full and partial tuition reimbursements available, teaching assistantships with tuition reimbursements available, career-related internships or fieldwork, Federal Work-Study, scholarships/grants, health care benefits, and unspecified assistantships available. Support available to part-time students. Financial award applicants required to submit FAFSA. *Faculty research:* Data-driven decision-making in K-12 schools and districts; examination of college and university leadership and management in U. S. and Asia; studies in facilitating student learning; organizational change and the role of leaders; leadership, diversity, learning and accountability. Total annual research expenditures: $14.2 million. *Unit head:* Karen Gallagher. *Application contact:* Karen Gallagher.

University of Southern Indiana, Graduate Studies, College of Education and Human Services, Department of Teacher Education, Evansville, IN 47712-3590. Offers elementary education (MS); secondary education (MS). *Accreditation:* NCATE. Part-time and evening/weekend programs available. *Faculty:* 7 full-time (3 women), 1 (woman) part-time/adjunct. *Students:* 3 full-time (1 woman), 126 part-time (101 women); includes 6 minority (5 African Americans, 1 Asian American or Pacific Islander), 2 international. Average age 33. 57 applicants, 100% accepted, 37 enrolled. In 2009, 38 master's awarded. *Entrance requirements:* For master's, GRE General Test, NTE or PRAXIS I, minimum GPA of 3.0, teaching license. Additional exam requirements/recommendations for international students: Required—TOEFL (minimum score 550 paper-based; 213 computer-based; 79 iBT), IELTS (minimum score 6). *Application deadline:* For fall admission, 7/1 priority date for domestic students, 1/1 priority date for international students. Applications are processed on a rolling basis. Application fee: $25. Electronic applications accepted. *Expenses:* Tuition, state resident: full-time $4592; part-time $255 per credit hour. Tuition, nonresident: full-time $9060; part-time $503 per credit hour. Required fees: $220; $22.75 per term. Tuition and fees vary according to course load and reciprocity agreements. *Financial support:* In 2009–10, 38 students received support. Federal Work-Study, scholarships/grants, tuition waivers (full and partial), and unspecified assistantships available. Financial award application deadline: 3/1; financial award applicants required to submit FAFSA. *Unit head:* Dr. Vella Goebel, Director, 812-461-5306, E-mail: vgoebel@usi.edu. *Application contact:* Dr. Vella Goebel, Director, 812-461-5306, E-mail: vgoebel@usi.edu.

University of Southern Maine, College of Education and Human Development, Gorham, ME 04038. Offers MS, MS Ed, Psy D, CAS, Certificate. *Accreditation:* Teacher Education Accreditation Council. Part-time and evening/weekend programs available. Postbaccalaureate distance learning degree programs offered (minimal on-campus study). *Faculty:* 34 full-time (17 women), 26 part-time/adjunct (15 women). *Students:* 286 full-time (200 women), 303 part-time (231 women); includes 14 minority (2 African Americans, 4 American Indian/Alaska Native, 8 Hispanic Americans). 373 applicants, 76% accepted, 221 enrolled. In 2009, 206 master's, 3 doctorates, 22 other advanced degrees awarded. Terminal master's awarded for partial completion of doctoral program. *Degree requirements:* For master's, comprehensive exam (for some programs), thesis or alternative; for doctorate, thesis/dissertation; for other advanced degree, thesis or alternative. *Entrance requirements:* For master's, GRE General Test or MAT, PRAXIS (extended teacher education), proof of teacher certification; for doctorate, GRE; for other advanced degree, master's degree. Additional exam requirements/recommendations for international students: Required—TOEFL (minimum score 550 paper-based; 213 computer-based; 79 iBT). Application fee: $50. Electronic applications accepted. *Financial support:* In 2009–10, 58 students received support, including 18 research assistantships (averaging $4,500 per year); career-related internships or fieldwork, Federal Work-Study, institutionally sponsored loans, scholarships/grants, and unspecified assistantships also available. Support available to part-time students. Financial award application deadline: 3/1; financial award applicants required to submit FAFSA. *Faculty research:* Teacher development, library technology outreach, literacy through literature, college-bound, multicultural education, school psychology, education policy and evaluation. Total annual research expenditures: $3 million. *Unit head:* Betty Lou Whitford, Dean, 207-780-5371, Fax: 207-780-5315. *Application contact:* Mary Sloan, Director of Graduate Admissions, 207-780-4386, Fax: 207-780-4969, E-mail: msloan@usm.maine.edu.

University of Southern Mississippi, Graduate School, College of Education and Psychology, Hattiesburg, MS 39406-0001. Offers M Ed, MA, MAT, MLIS, MS, Ed D, PhD, Ed S, Graduate Certificate, SLS. *Accreditation:* NCATE. Part-time programs available. *Faculty:* 98 full-time (51 women), 13 part-time/adjunct (4 women). *Students:* 293 full-time (223 women), 608 part-time (480 women); includes 205 minority (184 African Americans, 1 American Indian/Alaska Native, 4 Asian Americans or Pacific Islanders, 16 Hispanic Americans), 15 international. Average age 36. 541 applicants, 42% accepted, 200 enrolled. In 2009, 243 master's, 52 doctorates, 40 other advanced degrees awarded. Terminal master's awarded for partial completion of doctoral program. *Degree requirements:* For master's, comprehensive exam, thesis (for some programs); for doctorate, comprehensive exam, thesis/dissertation; for other advanced degree, comprehensive exam, thesis. *Entrance requirements:* For master's, GRE General Test, MAT; for doctorate and other advanced degree, GRE General Test. Additional exam requirements/recommendations for international students: Required—TOEFL. *Application deadline:* For fall admission, 3/1 for domestic and international students; for spring admission, 11/1 for domestic and international students. Applications are processed on a rolling basis. Application fee: $35. Electronic applications accepted. *Expenses:* Tuition, state resident: full-time $5096; part-time $284 per hour. Tuition, nonresident: full-time $13,052; part-time $726 per hour. Required fees: $402. Tuition and fees vary according to course level and course load. *Financial support:* In 2009–10, 80 research assistantships with full tuition reimbursements (averaging $9,586 per year), 53 teaching assistantships with full tuition reimbursements (averaging $7,775 per year) were awarded; career-related internships or fieldwork, Federal Work-Study, and institutionally sponsored loans also available. Financial award application deadline: 3/15; financial award applicants required to submit FAFSA. *Faculty research:* Reading, sleep, animal cognition. *Unit head:* Dr. Wanda Maulding, Interim Chair, 601-266-4568, Fax: 601-266-4175. *Application contact:* Shonna Breland, Manager of Graduate Admissions, 601-266-6563, Fax: 601-266-5138.

University of South Florida, Graduate School, College of Education–Main Campus, Tampa, FL 33620-9951. Offers M Ed, MA, MAT, Ed D, PhD, Ed S. *Accreditation:* NCATE. Part-time and evening/weekend programs available. Postbaccalaureate distance learning degree programs offered (no on-campus study). *Faculty:* 134 full-time (82 women), 36 part-time/adjunct (21 women). *Students:* 610 full-time (450 women), 1,133 part-time (844 women); includes 409 minority (203 African Americans, 10 American Indian/Alaska Native, 45 Asian Americans or Pacific Islanders, 151 Hispanic Americans), 58 international. Average age 30. 1,030 applicants, 63% accepted, 533 enrolled. In 2009, 433 master's, 49 doctorates, 8 other advanced degrees awarded. *Degree requirements:* For master's, comprehensive exam, thesis (for some programs); for doctorate, comprehensive exam, thesis/dissertation, 2 tools of research in foreign language, statistics, and/or computers. *Entrance requirements:* For master's, GRE General Test, minimum GPA of 3.5 in last 60 hours of course work; for doctorate, GRE General Test, minimum GPA of 3.5; for Ed S, GRE General Test. Additional exam requirements/recommendations for international students: Required—TOEFL (minimum score 550 paper-based; 213 computer-based). *Application deadline:* For fall admission, 2/15 for domestic students, 1/2 for international students; for spring admission, 10/15 for domestic students, 6/1 for international students. Application fee: $30. Electronic applications accepted. *Financial support:* Career-related internships or fieldwork, Federal Work-Study, institutionally sponsored loans, scholarships/grants, health care benefits, and unspecified assistantships available. Support available to part-time students. Financial award applicants required to submit FAFSA. Total annual research expenditures: $22 million. *Unit head:* Dr. Colleen S. Kennedy, Dean, 813-974-3400, Fax: 813-974-3826. *Application contact:* Dr. Diane Briscoe, Coordinator of Graduate Studies, 813-974-1804, Fax: 813-974-3391, E-mail: briscoe@usf.edu.

See Close-Up on page 719.

The University of Tampa, Program in Teaching, Tampa, FL 33606-1490. Offers curriculum and instruction (M Ed); math education (MAT); science education (MAT); social science education (MAT). Part-time and evening/weekend programs available. *Faculty:* 9 full-time (6 women), 5 part-time/adjunct (4 women). *Students:* 1 full-time (0 women), 68 part-time (51 women); includes 11 minority (3 African Americans, 1 Asian American or Pacific Islander, 7 Hispanic Americans), 1 international. Average age 30. 119 applicants, 71% accepted, 69 enrolled. In 2009, 36 master's awarded. *Degree requirements:* For master's, comprehensive exam, thesis. *Entrance requirements:* For master's, General Knowledge Test, GRE General Test, SAE Subject Area Exam, bachelor's degree in education or professional teaching certificate. Additional exam requirements/recommendations for international students: Required—TOEFL (minimum score 577 paper-based; 230 computer-based; 90 iBT), IELTS (minimum score 7). *Application deadline:* For fall admission, 5/1 for domestic students. Application fee: $40. *Expenses:* Tuition: Part-time $488 per credit hour. *Financial support:* In 2009–10, 67 students received support. Applicants required to submit FAFSA. *Unit head:* Dr. Martha Harrison, Associate Professor of Education, 813-253-3333 Ext. 3373, E-mail: mharrison@ut.edu. *Application contact:* Karen Full, Director of Admissions for Graduate and Continuing Studies, 813-257-3642, E-mail: kfull@ut.edu.

The University of Tennessee, Graduate School, College of Education, Health and Human Sciences, Knoxville, TN 37996. Offers MPH, MS, Ed D, PhD, Ed S, MS/MPH. *Accreditation:* NCATE. Part-time and evening/weekend programs available. Postbaccalaureate distance learning degree programs offered (no on-campus study). Terminal master's awarded for partial completion of doctoral program. *Degree requirements:* For master's and Ed S, thesis optional; for doctorate, thesis/dissertation. *Entrance requirements:* For master's, minimum GPA of 2.7; for doctorate and Ed S, GRE General Test, minimum GPA of 2.7. Additional exam requirements/recommendations for international students: Required—TOEFL. Electronic applications accepted. *Expenses:* Tuition, state resident: full-time $6826; part-time $380 per semester hour. Tuition, nonresident: full-time $21,844; part-time $1147 per semester hour. Tuition and fees vary according to program.

The University of Tennessee at Chattanooga, Graduate School, College of Health, Education and Professional Studies, Graduate Studies Division of Education, Chattanooga, TN 37403. Offers counseling (M Ed), including community counseling, school counseling; education (M Ed, Post-Master's Certificate), including elementary education (M Ed), school leadership, secondary education (M Ed), special education (M Ed); educational specialist (Ed S), including educational technology, school psychology; learning and leadership (Ed D), including educational leadership. *Accreditation:* ACA; NCATE. Part-time and evening/weekend programs available. Postbaccalaureate distance learning degree programs offered (no on-campus study). *Faculty:* 23 full-time (14 women), 7 part-time/adjunct (3 women). *Students:* 183 full-time (133 women), 325 part-time (229 women); includes 69 minority (53 African Americans, 3 American Indian/Alaska Native, 3 Asian Americans or Pacific Islanders, 10 Hispanic Americans), 2 international. Average age 35. 193 applicants, 85% accepted, 111 enrolled. In 2009, 107 master's, 1 doctorate, 31 other advanced degrees awarded. *Degree requirements:* For master's, comprehensive exam, thesis optional, culminating experience; for doctorate, comprehensive exam, thesis/dissertation; for other advanced degree, internship. *Entrance requirements:* For master's, GRE General Test, PPST 1, teaching certificate; for doctorate, GRE General Test, master's degree, two years of practical work experience in organizational environment; for other advanced degree, GRE General Test, letters of reference. Additional exam requirements/recommendations for international students: Required—TOEFL (minimum score 550 paper-based; 213 computer-based; 79 iBT), IELTS (minimum score 6). *Application deadline:* For fall admission, 8/1 for domestic students, 6/1 for international students; for spring admission, 12/1 for domestic students, 10/1 for international students. Applications are processed on a rolling basis. Application fee: $35. Electronic applications accepted. *Expenses:* Tuition, state resident: full-time $5404; part-time $300 per credit hour. Tuition, nonresident: full-time $16,702; part-time $928 per credit hour. Required fees: $1150; $130 per credit hour. *Financial support:* In 2009–10, 22 research assistantships with full and partial tuition reimbursements (averaging $5,500 per year) were awarded; career-related internships or fieldwork, institutionally sponsored loans, scholarships/grants, and unspecified assistantships also available. Support available to part-time students. *Faculty research:* School counseling, community counseling, elementary and secondary education, school leadership and administration. *Unit head:* Dr. John Freeman, Head, 423-425-4133, Fax: 423-425-5380, E-mail: john-freeman@utc.edu. *Application contact:* Dr. Stephanie Bellar, Dean of Graduate Studies, 423-425-4666, Fax: 423-425-5223, E-mail: stephanie-bellar@utc.edu.

The University of Tennessee at Martin, Graduate Programs, College of Education and Behavioral Sciences, Martin, TN 38238-1000. Offers MS Ed. *Accreditation:* NCATE. Part-time programs available. Postbaccalaureate distance learning degree programs offered (minimal on-campus study). *Faculty:* 52. *Students:* 286 (217 women). 234 applicants, 61% accepted, 100 enrolled. In 2009, 78 master's awarded. *Degree requirements:* For master's, comprehensive exam. *Entrance requirements:* For master's, GRE General Test, minimum GPA of 2.5. Additional exam requirements/recommendations for international students: Required—TOEFL (minimum score 525 paper-based; 197 computer-based; 71 iBT). *Application deadline:* For fall admission, 8/1 priority date for domestic students, 7/15 priority date for international students; for spring admission, 12/15 priority date for domestic students, 12/1 priority date for international students. Applications are processed on a rolling basis. Application fee: $30 ($130 for international students). Electronic applications accepted. *Expenses:* Tuition, state resident: full-time $6660; part-time $372 per hour. Tuition, nonresident: full-time $18,000; part-time $1005 per hour. *Financial support:* In 2009–10, 18 students received support, including 14 research assistantships with full tuition reimbursements available (averaging $7,070 per year), 4 teaching assistantships with full tuition reimbursements available (averaging $6,597 per year); scholarships/grants and unspecified assistantships also available. Support available to part-time students. Financial award application deadline: 1/15; financial award applicants required to submit FAFSA. *Faculty research:* Environmental education, self-concept, science education, attention deficit disorder, special education. Total annual research expenditures: $1 million. *Unit head:* Dr. Mary Lee Hall, Dean, 731-881-7127, Fax: 731-881-7975, E-mail: mlhall@utm.edu. *Application contact:* Linda S. Arant, Student Services Specialist, 731-881-7012, Fax: 731-881-7499, E-mail: larant@utm.edu.

The University of Texas at Arlington, Graduate School, College of Education, Arlington, TX 76019. Offers curriculum and instruction (M Ed); educational leadership and policy studies

Education—General

The University of Texas at Arlington (continued)

(M Ed); K-16 educational, leadership and policy studies (PhD); physiology of exercise (MS); teaching (M Ed T). *Accreditation:* NCATE. Part-time and evening/weekend programs available. *Faculty:* 35 full-time (22 women), 4 part-time/adjunct (2 women). *Students:* 125 full-time (83 women), 586 part-time (479 women); includes 283 minority (125 African Americans, 4 American Indian/Alaska Native, 19 Asian Americans or Pacific Islanders, 135 Hispanic Americans), 15 international. Average age 35. 601 applicants, 99% accepted, 238 enrolled. In 2009, 161 degrees awarded. *Degree requirements:* For master's, comprehensive exam (for some programs), thesis (for some programs), comprehensive activity, research project; for doctorate, comprehensive exam, thesis/dissertation. *Entrance requirements:* For master's, GRE General Test, minimum undergraduate GPA of 3.0 in last 60 hours of course work, writing sample, 3 letters of recommendation; for doctorate, GRE General Test, interview, minimum GPA of 3.5, master's degree in education or other appropriate field, 3 years of documented experience in an education related work environment. Additional exam requirements/recommendations for international students: Required—TOEFL (minimum score 550 paper-based; 213 computer-based). *Application deadline:* For fall admission, 6/5 priority date for domestic students, 4/3 priority date for international students; for spring admission, 10/17 priority date for domestic students, 9/5 priority date for international students. Applications are processed on a rolling basis. Application fee: $35 ($50 for international students). Electronic applications accepted. *Financial support:* In 2009–10, 9 fellowships (averaging $1,000 per year), 6 research assistantships (averaging $6,250 per year), 10 teaching assistantships with full tuition reimbursements (averaging $5,200 per year) were awarded; career-related internships or fieldwork, Federal Work-Study, scholarships/grants, and unspecified assistantships also available. Financial award application deadline: 6/1; financial award applicants required to submit FAFSA. *Unit head:* Dr. Jeanne M. Gerlach, Dean, 817-272-2591, Fax: 817-272-2530, E-mail: coedadvising@uta.edu. *Application contact:* Kas McConnell, Graduate Advisor, 817-272-7489, Fax: 817-272-7624, E-mail: coedadvising@uta.edu.

The University of Texas at Austin, Graduate School, College of Education, Austin, TX 78712-1111. Offers M Ed, MA, Ed D, PhD. Part-time programs available. *Entrance requirements:* For master's and doctorate, GRE General Test. Electronic applications accepted.

The University of Texas at Brownsville, Graduate Studies, School of Education, Brownsville, TX 78520-4991. Offers bilingual education (M Ed); counseling and guidance (M Ed); curriculum and instruction (M Ed); early childhood education (M Ed); educational administration (M Ed); educational technology (M Ed); English as a second language (M Ed); reading specialist (M Ed); special education/educational diagnostician (M Ed). Part-time and evening/weekend programs available. Postbaccalaureate distance learning degree programs offered (minimal on-campus study). *Degree requirements:* For master's, thesis optional. *Entrance requirements:* For master's, GRE General Test. Additional exam requirements/recommendations for international students: Required—TOEFL.

The University of Texas at El Paso, Graduate School, College of Education, El Paso, TX 79968-0001. Offers M Ed, MA, Ed D, PhD. Part-time and evening/weekend programs available. Postbaccalaureate distance learning degree programs offered. *Students:* 1,399 (1,012 women); includes 1,118 minority (37 African Americans, 15 Asian Americans or Pacific Islanders, 1,066 Hispanic Americans), 51 international. Average age 34. 589 applicants, 79% accepted. In 2009, 263 master's, 9 doctorates awarded. *Degree requirements:* For master's, thesis optional; for doctorate, thesis/dissertation. *Entrance requirements:* For master's, minimum graduate GPA of 3.0, letter of intent, resume, letters of recommendation, copy of teaching certificate, district service record; for doctorate, GRE, resume, letters of recommendation, scholarly paper. Additional exam requirements/recommendations for international students: Required—TOEFL; Recommended—IELTS. *Application deadline:* For fall admission, 8/1 for domestic students, 3/1 for international students; for spring admission, 11/1 priority date for domestic students, 9/1 for international students. Applications are processed on a rolling basis. Application fee: $45 ($80 for international students). Electronic applications accepted. *Financial support:* In 2009–10, research assistantships with partial tuition reimbursements (averaging $16,642 per year), teaching assistantships with partial tuition reimbursements (averaging $13,314 per year) were awarded; fellowships with partial tuition reimbursements, institutionally sponsored loans, scholarships/grants, health care benefits, tuition waivers (partial), and unspecified assistantships also available. Support available to part-time students. Financial award application deadline: 3/15; financial award applicants required to submit FAFSA. *Unit head:* Dr. Josie V. Tinajero, Dean, 915-747-5572, Fax: 915-747-5755, E-mail: tinajero@utep.edu. *Application contact:* Dr. Patricia D. Witherspoon, Dean of the Graduate School, 915-747-5491, Fax: 915-747-5788, E-mail: withersp@utep.edu.

The University of Texas of the Permian Basin, Office of Graduate Studies, School of Education, Odessa, TX 79762-0001. Offers MA. *Accreditation:* NCATE. *Entrance requirements:* For master's, GRE General Test. Additional exam requirements/recommendations for international students: Required—TOEFL (minimum score 550 paper-based; 213 computer-based).

The University of Texas–Pan American, College of Education, Edinburg, TX 78539. Offers M Ed, MA, MS, Ed D. Part-time and evening/weekend programs available. *Degree requirements:* For master's, thesis optional. *Entrance requirements:* For master's, GRE General Test. *Expenses:* Tuition, state resident: full-time $3630.60; part-time $201.70 per credit hour. Tuition, nonresident: full-time $8617; part-time $478.70 per credit hour. Required fees: $806.50. *Faculty research:* Literacy development, bilingual education, brain mapping.

University of the Cumberlands, Graduate Programs in Education, Williamsburg, KY 40769-1372. Offers early childhood education (MA Ed); elementary education (MA Ed, MAT), including elementary (P-5), middle school (5-9); elementary/secondary principalship (MA Ed, Certificate); middle school education (MA Ed, MAT); principalship (Ed S); reading and writing specialist (MA Ed); secondary education (MA Ed, MAT); special education (MA Ed, MAT); specialization in supervision of instruction/superintendency (Ed S). Part-time and evening/weekend programs available. *Degree requirements:* For master's, comprehensive exam. *Entrance requirements:* For master's, GRE or NTE, Kentucky teaching certificate; for other advanced degree, master's degree, 3 years of teaching experience.

University of the District of Columbia, College of Arts and Sciences, Department of Education, Washington, DC 20008-1175. Offers early childhood education (MA); special education (MA). *Accreditation:* NCATE. Part-time programs available. *Students:* 4 full-time (3 women), 2 part-time (1 woman); all minorities (5 African Americans, 1 Asian American or Pacific Islander). Average age 33. 16 applicants. In 2009, 30 master's awarded. *Degree requirements:* For master's, comprehensive exam, research paper. *Entrance requirements:* For master's, GRE General Test, writing proficiency exam. *Application deadline:* For fall admission, 6/15 priority date for domestic students; for spring admission, 11/1 for domestic students. Applications are processed on a rolling basis. Application fee: $20. *Expenses:* Tuition, state resident: full-time $7580. Tuition, nonresident: full-time $14,580. Required fees: $620. *Financial support:* Fellowships, research assistantships available. *Unit head:* Dr. Patricia Myers, Chair, 202-274-7401. *Application contact:* Ann Marie Waterman, Associate Vice President for Admission, Recruitment and Financial Aid, 202-274-6069.

University of the Incarnate Word, School of Graduate Studies and Research, Dreeben School of Education, Program in Teaching, San Antonio, TX 78209-6397. Offers all-level teaching (MAT); elementary teaching (MAT); secondary teaching (MAT). Part-time and evening/weekend programs available. *Students:* 45 part-time (38 women); includes 27 minority (7 African Americans, 20 Hispanic Americans). Average age 33. In 2009, 37 master's awarded. *Degree requirements:* For master's, internship. *Entrance requirements:* For master's, GRE, Texas Higher Education Assessment test (THEA), interview. Additional exam requirements/recommendations for international students: Required—TOEFL (minimum score 560 paper-based; 220 computer-based; 83 iBT). *Application deadline:* Applications are processed on a rolling basis. Application fee: $20. Electronic applications accepted. *Expenses:* Tuition: Full-time $12,150; part-time $675 per credit hour. Required fees: $83 per credit hour. *Financial support:* Federal Work-Study and scholarships/grants available. Financial award applicants required to submit FAFSA. *Unit head:* Dr. Elda Martinez, Director of Teacher Education, 210-832-3297, Fax: 210-829-3134, E-mail: eemartin@uiwtx.edu. *Application contact:* Andrea Cyterski-Acosta, Dean of Enrollment, 210-829-6005, Fax: 210-829-3921, E-mail: admis@uiwtx.edu.

University of the Incarnate Word, School of Graduate Studies and Research, Dreeben School of Education, Programs in Education, San Antonio, TX 78209-6397. Offers adult education (M Ed, MA); cross-cultural education (M Ed, MA); early childhood literacy (M Ed, MA); general education (M Ed, MA); Higher Education (PhD); instructional technology (M Ed, MA); international education and entrepreneurship (PhD); kinesiology (M Ed, MA); literacy (M Ed, MA); organizational leadership (PhD); organizational learning and learning (M Ed, MA); reading (M Ed, MA); special education (M Ed, MA); teacher leadership (M Ed, MA). Part-time and evening/weekend programs available. *Students:* 20 full-time (11 women), 201 part-time (122 women); includes 113 minority (29 African Americans, 2 American Indian/Alaska Native, 2 Asian Americans or Pacific Islanders, 80 Hispanic Americans), 30 international. Average age 41. In 2009, 26 master's, 19 doctorates awarded. *Degree requirements:* For master's, capstone; for doctorate, thesis/dissertation, qualifying exam. *Entrance requirements:* For master's, baccalaureate degree; minimum foundation GPA of 2.5; interview; for doctorate, master's degree; interview; supervised writing sample. Additional exam requirements/recommendations for international students: Required—TOEFL (minimum score 560 paper-based; 220 computer-based; 83 iBT). *Application deadline:* Applications are processed on a rolling basis. Application fee: $20. Electronic applications accepted. *Expenses:* Tuition: Full-time $12,150; part-time $675 per credit hour. Required fees: $83 per credit hour. *Financial support:* Federal Work-Study and scholarships/grants available. Financial award applicants required to submit FAFSA. *Unit head:* Dr. Denise Staudt, Dean, Dreeben School of Education, 210-829-2762, E-mail: staudt@uiwtx.edu. *Application contact:* Andrea Cyterski-Acosta, Dean of Enrollment, 210-829-6005, Fax: 210-829-3921, E-mail: admis@uiwtx.edu.

University of the Pacific, School of Education, Stockton, CA 95211-0197. Offers M Ed, MA, Ed D, Ed S. *Accreditation:* NCATE. *Faculty:* 20 full-time (12 women), 3 part-time/adjunct (2 women). *Students:* 89 full-time (59 women), 199 part-time (138 women); includes 104 minority (28 African Americans, 1 American Indian/Alaska Native, 46 Asian Americans or Pacific Islanders, 29 Hispanic Americans), 4 international. Average age 35. 146 applicants, 86% accepted, 87 enrolled. In 2009, 57 master's, 20 doctorates awarded. *Degree requirements:* For doctorate, thesis/dissertation. *Entrance requirements:* For master's, GRE General Test; for doctorate, GRE General Test, GRE Subject Test. Additional exam requirements/recommendations for international students: Required—TOEFL (minimum score 475 paper-based; 150 computer-based). *Application deadline:* For fall admission, 3/1 priority date for domestic students; for spring admission, 10/15 for domestic students. Applications are processed on a rolling basis. Application fee: $75. *Financial support:* In 2009–10, 13 teaching assistantships were awarded; institutionally sponsored loans also available. Support available to part-time students. Financial award application deadline: 3/1; financial award applicants required to submit FAFSA. *Unit head:* Dr. Lynn Beck, Dean, 209-946-2683, E-mail: lbeck@pacific.edu. *Application contact:* Office of Graduate Admissions, 209-946-2344.

University of the Sacred Heart, Graduate Programs, Department of Education, San Juan, PR 00914-0383. Offers early childhood education (M Ed); information technology and multimedia (Certificate); instruction systems and education technology (M Ed), including English, information technology and multimedia, instructional design, mathematics, Spanish. Part-time and evening/weekend programs available. *Degree requirements:* For master's, thesis. *Entrance requirements:* For master's, EXADEP, minimum undergraduate GPA of 2.75, interview.

University of the Southwest, Graduate Programs, Hobbs, NM 88240-9129. Offers business administration (MBA); curriculum and instruction (MSE); curriculum and instruction: bilingual (MSE); curriculum and instruction: reading (MSE); curriculum and instruction: TESOL (MSE); early childhood education (MSE); educational diagnostician (MSE); mental health counseling (MSE); school business administration (MSE); school counseling (MSE); special education (MSE). Part-time and evening/weekend programs available. Postbaccalaureate distance learning degree programs offered (no on-campus study). *Faculty:* 10 full-time (6 women), 10 part-time/adjunct (4 women). *Students:* 112 full-time (93 women), 99 part-time (72 women). Average age 35. 94 applicants, 47% accepted, 39 enrolled. In 2009, 32 master's awarded. *Degree requirements:* For master's, comprehensive exam. *Application deadline:* For fall admission, 3/1 priority date for domestic students; for spring admission, 10/1 for domestic students. Applications are processed on a rolling basis. Application fee: $25. Electronic applications accepted. *Expenses:* Tuition: Part-time $512 per hour. Tuition and fees vary according to course load. *Financial support:* In 2009–10, 196 students received support; research assistantships with partial tuition reimbursements available, Federal Work-Study, scholarships/grants, and tuition waivers (partial) available. Support available to part-time students. Financial award application deadline: 4/1; financial award applicants required to submit FAFSA. *Unit head:* Dr. Mary Harris, Dean of Education, 575-392-6561 Ext. 1056, Fax: 575-392-6006, E-mail: mharris@usw.edu. *Application contact:* Ryanne Evans, Assistant Registrar, 575-392-6561 Ext. 1031, Fax: 575-392-6006, E-mail: revans@usw.edu.

University of the Virgin Islands, Graduate Programs, Division of Education, Saint Thomas, VI 00802-9990. Offers MAE. Part-time and evening/weekend programs available. *Degree requirements:* For master's, comprehensive exam, thesis or alternative. *Entrance requirements:* For master's, minimum GPA of 2.5, BA degree from accredited institution. Additional exam requirements/recommendations for international students: Required—TOEFL (minimum score 550 paper-based; 213 computer-based). *Faculty research:* Student self-concept and sense of futility.

The University of Toledo, College of Graduate Studies, College of Education, Toledo, OH 43606-3390. Offers MAE, ME, MES, MME, DE, PhD, Ed S. *Accreditation:* NCATE. Part-time and evening/weekend programs available. Terminal master's awarded for partial completion of doctoral program. *Degree requirements:* For doctorate, comprehensive exam, thesis/dissertation; for Ed S, thesis optional. *Entrance requirements:* For doctorate, GRE. Electronic applications accepted. *Faculty research:* Cognitive studies, learning and memory, learning resources, whole language, administration of professional development schools.

University of Toronto, School of Graduate Studies, Social Sciences Division, Faculty of Education, Toronto, ON M5S 1A1, Canada. Offers M Ed, MA, MT, Ed D, PhD. Part-time and evening/weekend programs available. *Degree requirements:* For master's, thesis (for some programs); for doctorate, thesis/dissertation. *Entrance requirements:* For master's, minimum B average in final year, 1 year of professional experience in field (MA, M Ed); for doctorate, minimum B+ average, professional experience in education or a relevant field (Ed D). *Expenses:* Contact institution.

University of Tulsa, Graduate School, College of Arts and Sciences, School of Education, Tulsa, OK 74104-3189. Offers education (M Ed, MA), including education (MA), elementary certification (M Ed), secondary certification (M Ed); mathematics and science education (MSMSE); teaching arts (MTA). *Accreditation:* Teacher Education Accreditation Council. Part-time programs available. *Faculty:* 6 full-time (2 women), 1 (woman) part-time/adjunct. *Students:* 8 full-time (6 women), 8 part-time (6 women); includes 3 minority (1 African American, 2 American Indian/Alaska Native), 2 international. Average age 33. 18 applicants, 72% accepted, 9 enrolled. In 2009, 4 master's awarded. *Degree requirements:* For master's, thesis optional. *Entrance requirements:* For master's, GRE General Test. Additional exam requirements/recommendations for international students: Required—TOEFL (minimum score 575 paper-based; 231 computer-based), IELTS (minimum score 6.5). *Application deadline:* For fall admission, 2/1 priority date for domestic students. Applications are processed on a rolling basis. Application fee: $40. Electronic applications accepted. *Expenses:* Tuition: Full-time $16,182; part-time $899 per credit hour. Required fees: $4 per credit hour. Tuition and fees vary according to course load. *Financial support:* In 2009–10, 7 students received support, including 1 fellowship with full and partial tuition reimbursement available (averaging $11,594 per year), 6 teaching assistantships with full and partial tuition reimbursements available (averaging $10,627 per year); research assistantships with full and partial tuition reimbursements available, Federal Work-Study,

scholarships/grants, tuition waivers (full and partial), and unspecified assistantships also available. Support available to part-time students. Financial award application deadline: 2/1; financial award applicants required to submit FAFSA. *Faculty research:* Elementary/secondary certification, math/science education, educational policy studies, language and discourse. Total annual research expenditures: $5.1 million. *Unit head:* Dr. Thomas Benediktson, Dean, 918-631-2541, Fax: 918-631-3721, E-mail: dale-benediktson@utulsa.edu. *Application contact:* Dr. David Brown, Advisor, 918-631-2719, Fax: 918-631-2133, E-mail: david-brown@utulsa.edu.

University of Utah, Graduate School, College of Education, Salt Lake City, UT 84112. Offers M Ed, M Phil, M Stat, MA, MAT, MS, Ed D, PhD, MPA/Ed D, MPA/PhD. Part-time and evening/weekend programs available. *Faculty:* 63 full-time (38 women), 25 part-time/adjunct (20 women). *Students:* 262 full-time (190 women), 249 part-time (155 women); includes 85 minority (13 African Americans, 8 American Indian/Alaska Native, 18 Asian Americans or Pacific Islanders, 46 Hispanic Americans), 13 international. Average age 35. 353 applicants, 42% accepted, 115 enrolled. In 2009, 156 master's, 28 doctorates awarded. *Entrance requirements:* For master's, minimum undergraduate GPA of 3.0. Additional exam requirements/recommendations for international students: Required—TOEFL (minimum score 500 paper-based; 173 computer-based). *Application deadline:* For fall admission, 4/1 for domestic and international students; for spring admission, 11/1 for domestic and international students. Applications are processed on a rolling basis. Application fee: $55 ($65 for international students). Electronic applications accepted. *Expenses:* Contact institution. *Financial support:* Fellowships with full tuition reimbursements, research assistantships with full tuition reimbursements, teaching assistantships with full and partial tuition reimbursements, career-related internships or fieldwork, Federal Work-Study, institutionally sponsored loans, scholarships/grants, tuition waivers (full and partial), and unspecified assistantships available. Support available to part-time students. Financial award application deadline: 2/1; financial award applicants required to submit FAFSA. *Faculty research:* Leadership, autism, reading instruction, mental retardation, diagnosis. Total annual research expenditures: $276,891. *Unit head:* Michael Hardman, Dean, 801-581-8121, Fax: 801-585-6476, E-mail: michael.hardman@utah.edu. *Application contact:* Mindy Jones, Executive Secretary, 801-581-8222, Fax: 801-581-5223, E-mail: mindy.jones@utah.edu.

University of Vermont, Graduate College, College of Education and Social Services, Burlington, VT 05405. Offers M Ed, MAT, MS, MSW, Ed D. *Accreditation:* NCATE. Part-time programs available. *Students:* 437 (325 women); includes 43 minority (16 African Americans, 2 American Indian/Alaska Native, 15 Asian Americans or Pacific Islanders, 10 Hispanic Americans), 6 international. 562 applicants, 60% accepted, 155 enrolled. In 2009, 139 master's, 18 doctorates awarded. *Degree requirements:* For doctorate, thesis/dissertation. *Entrance requirements:* Additional exam requirements/recommendations for international students: Required—TOEFL (minimum score 550 paper-based; 213 computer-based; 80 iBT). Application fee: $40. Electronic applications accepted. *Expenses:* Tuition, state resident: part-time $508 per credit hour. Tuition, nonresident: part-time $1281 per credit hour. *Financial support:* Fellowships, research assistantships, teaching assistantships, career-related internships or fieldwork and Federal Work-Study available. *Unit head:* Dr. Fayneese Miller, Dean, 802-656-3424. *Application contact:* Dr. Fayneese Miller, Dean, 802-656-3424.

University of Vermont, Graduate College, College of Education and Social Services, Department of Education, Program in Educational Studies, Burlington, VT 05405. Offers M Ed. *Students:* 3. 4 applicants, 25% accepted, 1 enrolled. *Degree requirements:* For master's, thesis or alternative. *Entrance requirements:* Additional exam requirements/recommendations for international students: Required—TOEFL (minimum score 550 paper-based; 213 computer-based; 80 iBT). *Application deadline:* For fall admission, 8/1 priority date for domestic students. Applications are processed on a rolling basis. Application fee: $40. Electronic applications accepted. *Expenses:* Tuition, state resident: part-time $508 per credit hour. Tuition, nonresident: part-time $1281 per credit hour. *Financial support:* Fellowships, research assistantships, teaching assistantships available. Financial award application deadline: 3/1. *Unit head:* Dr. D. Shiman, Coordinator, 802-656-3356. *Application contact:* Dr. D. Shiman, Coordinator, 802-656-3356.

University of Victoria, Faculty of Graduate Studies, Faculty of Education, Victoria, BC V8W 2Y2, Canada. Offers M Ed, M Sc, MA, PhD.

University of Virginia, Curry School of Education, Charlottesville, VA 22903. Offers M Ed, MT, Ed D, PhD, Ed S. *Accreditation:* Teacher Education Accreditation Council. *Faculty:* 87 full-time (49 women), 8 part-time/adjunct (6 women). *Students:* 534 full-time (404 women), 254 part-time (179 women); includes 78 minority (36 African Americans, 2 American Indian/Alaska Native, 26 Asian Americans or Pacific Islanders, 14 Hispanic Americans), 66 international. Average age 28. 659 applicants, 47% accepted, 175 enrolled. In 2009, 586 master's, 131 doctorates, 68 other advanced degrees awarded. *Degree requirements:* For master's, comprehensive exam (for some programs), thesis (for some programs); for doctorate, comprehensive exam (for some programs), thesis/dissertation. *Entrance requirements:* For master's, doctorate, and Ed S, GRE General Test, letters of recommendation. Additional exam requirements/recommendations for international students: Required—TOEFL (minimum score 600 paper-based; 250 computer-based; 90 iBT), IELTS (minimum score 7). *Application deadline:* Applications are processed on a rolling basis. Application fee: $60. Electronic applications accepted. *Financial support:* Fellowships, research assistantships, teaching assistantships, Federal Work-Study available. Financial award application deadline: 1/5; financial award applicants required to submit FAFSA. *Unit head:* Robert C. Pianta, Dean, 434-924-3334. *Application contact:* Joanne McNergney, Assistant Dean for Admissions and Student Services, E-mail: curry-admissions@virginia.edu.

University of Washington, Graduate School, College of Education, Seattle, WA 98195. Offers curriculum and instruction (M Ed, Ed D, PhD), including educational technology, general curriculum (Ed D, PhD), language, literacy, and culture, mathematics education, multicultural education, reading and language arts education (Ed D), science education, social studies education, teaching and curriculum (M Ed); educational leadership and policy studies (M Ed, Ed D, PhD), including administration (Ed D), educational policy, organization, and leadership (M Ed, PhD), higher education, leadership for learning (Ed D), social and cultural foundations of education (M Ed, PhD); educational psychology (M Ed, PhD), including educational psychology (PhD), human development and cognition (M Ed), learning sciences, measurement, statistics and research design (M Ed), school psychology (M Ed); instructional leadership (M Ed); intercollegiate athletic leadership (M Ed); special education (M Ed, Ed D, PhD), including early childhood special education (M Ed), emotional and behavioral disabilities (M Ed), learning disabilities (M Ed), low-incidence disabilities (M Ed), severe disabilities (M Ed), special education (Ed D, PhD); teacher education (MIT). *Accreditation:* APA. Part-time and evening/weekend programs available. *Degree requirements:* For master's, thesis optional; for doctorate, thesis/dissertation. *Entrance requirements:* For master's and doctorate, GRE General Test, minimum GPA of 3.0. Additional exam requirements/recommendations for international students: Required—TOEFL. Electronic applications accepted. *Faculty research:* School restructuring/effective schools, special education interventions, literacy and writing, technology, school partnerships, teacher preparation.

University of Washington, Graduate School, Education Programs, Bothell Campus, Seattle, WA 98195. Offers M Ed. Part-time and evening/weekend programs available. *Degree requirements:* For master's, thesis or alternative. *Entrance requirements:* For master's, GRE, MAT. Electronic applications accepted.

University of Washington, Graduate School, Education Programs, Tacoma Campus, Seattle, WA 98195. Offers education (M Ed, Professional Certificate). Part-time and evening/weekend programs available. *Degree requirements:* For master's, final project. *Entrance requirements:* For master's, GRE General Test; for Professional Certificate, Washington Educator Skills Test—Basic. Electronic applications accepted. *Faculty research:* Special education, technology, literacy, children's literature, science.

University of Washington, Bothell, Program in Education, Bothell, WA 98011-8246. Offers leadership development for educators (M Ed); secondary/middle level endorsement (M Ed). Part-time and evening/weekend programs available. *Faculty:* 9 full-time (7 women), 1 (woman) part-time/adjunct. *Students:* 25 full-time (15 women), 118 part-time (91 women); includes 17 minority (6 African Americans, 6 Asian Americans or Pacific Islanders, 5 Hispanic Americans). Average age 34. 78 applicants, 76% accepted, 55 enrolled. In 2009, 47 master's awarded. *Degree requirements:* For master's, thesis. *Entrance requirements:* Additional exam requirements/recommendations for international students: Required—TOEFL. *Application deadline:* For fall admission, 8/14 priority date for domestic and international students; for spring admission, 2/12 priority date for domestic and international students. Applications are processed on a rolling basis. Application fee: $65. Electronic applications accepted. *Expenses:* Tuition, state resident: full-time $10,160; part-time $484 per credit hour. Tuition, nonresident: full-time $23,500; part-time $1120 per credit hour. Required fees: $567; $21.50 per credit hour. Tuition and fees vary according to course load and program. *Financial support:* Federal Work-Study and unspecified assistantships available. *Faculty research:* Multicultural education in citizenship education, intercultural education, knowledge and practice in the principalship, educational public policy, national board certification for teachers, teacher learning in literacy, technology and its impact on teaching and learning of mathematics, reading assessments, professional development in literacy education and mobility, digital media, education and class. *Unit head:* Dr. Bradley S. Portin, Director and Professor, 425-352-3482, Fax: 425-352-5234, E-mail: bportin@uwb.edu. *Application contact:* Amelia Bowers, Education Program Advisor, 425-352-5274, Fax: 425-352-5434, E-mail: abowers@uwb.edu.

University of Washington, Tacoma, Graduate Programs, Program in Education, Tacoma, WA 98402-3100. Offers educational administrator (M Ed); K-8 teacher education (M Ed); professional certification (M Ed); secondary science (M Ed); special education (M Ed). Part-time and evening/weekend programs available. *Faculty:* 13 full-time (8 women), 9 part-time/adjunct (8 women). *Students:* 85 full-time (66 women), 118 part-time (99 women); includes 24 minority (4 African Americans, 9 Asian Americans or Pacific Islanders, 11 Hispanic Americans). Average age 33. 36 applicants, 75% accepted, 23 enrolled. In 2009, 68 master's awarded. *Entrance requirements:* For master's, official sealed transcript from every college/university attended, personal goal statement, letters of recommendation, copy of valid teaching certificate. *Application deadline:* For fall admission, 8/1 for domestic students; for winter admission, 11/1 priority date for domestic students; for spring admission, 2/1 priority date for domestic students. Applications are processed on a rolling basis. Application fee: $65. Electronic applications accepted. *Expenses:* Tuition, state resident: full-time $10,660; part-time $484 per credit. Tuition, nonresident: full-time $24,000; part-time $1119 per credit. Required fees: $150 per term. Tuition and fees vary according to course load and program. *Faculty research:* Global learning communities for English/Chinese languages, evaluation of mathematics and reading intervention programs, response to intervention, school wide behavioral and emotional support, mathematics education and culturally responsive mathematics education. *Unit head:* Dr. Karen Landenburger, Chancellor, 253-692-4430, Fax: 253-692-5612, E-mail: uwted@u.washington.edu. *Application contact:* Dr. Carla Van Rossum, Recruiter/Advisor, 253-692-4430, Fax: 253-692-5612, E-mail: uwted@u.washington.edu.

The University of West Alabama, School of Graduate Studies, College of Education, Livingston, AL 35470. Offers M Ed, MAT, MSCE. *Accreditation:* NCATE. Part-time and evening/weekend programs available. *Entrance requirements:* For master's, GRE General Test, MAT, minimum GPA of 2.75.

The University of Western Ontario, Faculty of Graduate Studies, Social Sciences Division, Faculty of Education, London, ON N6A 5B8, Canada. Offers M Ed. Part-time programs available. *Entrance requirements:* For master's, minimum B average.

University of West Georgia, Graduate School, College of Education, Carrollton, GA 30118. Offers M Ed, Ed D, Certificate, Ed S. *Accreditation:* NCATE. Part-time and evening/weekend programs available. *Faculty:* 63 full-time (42 women), 18 part-time/adjunct (14 women). *Students:* 331 full-time (274 women), 1,041 part-time (852 women); includes 336 minority (310 African Americans, 4 American Indian/Alaska Native, 2 Asian Americans or Pacific Islanders, 20 Hispanic Americans), 3 international. Average age 35. 514 applicants, 63% accepted, 132 enrolled. In 2009, 248 master's, 8 doctorates, 142 Certificates awarded. *Degree requirements:* For doctorate, thesis/dissertation, research paper; for other advanced degree, research paper. *Entrance requirements:* For master's, GRE, minimum GPA of 2.5; for doctorate, GRE, minimum GPA of 3.0; for other advanced degree, GRE, master's degree, minimum graduate GPA of 3.0. *Application deadline:* For fall admission, 7/17 for domestic students; for spring admission, 11/20 for domestic students. Applications are processed on a rolling basis. Application fee: $30. Electronic applications accepted. *Expenses:* Tuition, state resident: full-time $2952; part-time $164 per semester hour. Tuition, nonresident: full-time $11,808; part-time $656 per semester hour. Required fees: $42.90 per semester hour. $307 per semester. Tuition and fees vary according to course load. *Financial support:* In 2009–10, 46 research assistantships with partial tuition reimbursements (averaging $6,000 per year) were awarded; career-related internships or fieldwork and unspecified assistantships also available. Support available to part-time students. Financial award applicants required to submit FAFSA. *Faculty research:* Language and culture via distance education, speech pathology, staff development, mathematics/science instruction, alternative track: certification of noneducational degree. *Unit head:* Dr. Kim Metcalf, Dean, 678-839-6570, Fax: 678-839-6098, E-mail: kmetcalf@westga.edu. *Application contact:* Dr. Charles W. Clark, Dean, 678-839-6508, E-mail: cclark@westga.edu.

University of Windsor, Faculty of Graduate Studies, Faculty of Education, Windsor, ON N9B 3P4, Canada. Offers education (M Ed); educational studies (PhD). Part-time and evening/weekend programs available. *Degree requirements:* For master's, thesis or alternative; for doctorate, comprehensive exam, thesis/dissertation. *Entrance requirements:* For master's, minimum B average, teaching certificate; for doctorate, M Ed or MA in education, minimum A average, evidence of research competencies. Additional exam requirements/recommendations for international students: Required—TOEFL (minimum score 600 paper-based; 250 computer-based). Electronic applications accepted. *Faculty research:* School structures, teacher morale, cognitive deficits, new technologies in art education, internal and external factors that affect learning and teaching.

University of Wisconsin–Eau Claire, College of Education and Human Sciences, Eau Claire, WI 54702-4004. Offers MEPD, MS, MSE, MST. *Faculty:* 35 full-time (20 women). *Students:* 34 full-time (33 women), 40 part-time (33 women); includes 5 minority (1 African American, 1 American Indian/Alaska Native, 3 Asian Americans or Pacific Islanders), 1 international. Average age 29. 155 applicants, 17% accepted, 23 enrolled. In 2009, 47 master's awarded. *Degree requirements:* For master's, comprehensive exam. *Entrance requirements:* For master's, GRE (MAT, MST, MSE, MS), pre-professional skills test (MAT), minimum undergraduate GPA of 2.75 or 2.9 in the last half of undergraduate work. Additional exam requirements/recommendations for international students: Required—TOEFL (minimum score 550 paper-based; 213 computer-based; 79 iBT). *Application deadline:* For fall admission, 7/1 priority date for domestic students, 6/1 priority date for international students; for spring admission, 12/1 priority date for domestic students, 11/1 priority date for international students. Applications are processed on a rolling basis. Application fee: $56. Electronic applications accepted. *Expenses:* Tuition, state resident: full-time $6705.90; part-time $372.55 per credit. Tuition, nonresident: full-time $16,771; part-time $931.74 per credit. Required fees: $925.50; $51.19 per credit. One-time fee: $56. *Financial support:* In 2009–10, 45 students received support. Application deadline: 3/1. *Unit head:* Dr. Gail Scukanec, Dean, 715-836-3264, Fax: 715-836-3245, E-mail: scukangp@uwec.edu. *Application contact:* Kristina Anderson, Director of Admissions, 715-836-5415, Fax: 715-836-2409, E-mail: admissions@uwec.edu.

University of Wisconsin–Green Bay, Graduate Studies, Program in Applied Leadership for Teaching and Learning, Green Bay, WI 54311-7001. Offers MS Ed. Part-time and evening/weekend programs available. *Faculty:* 4 full-time (3 women), 1 (woman) part-time/adjunct. *Students:* 3 full-time (all women), 23 part-time (19 women); includes 4 minority (3 American Indian/Alaska Native, 1 Asian American or Pacific Islander). Average age 34. 7 applicants, 86% accepted, 6 enrolled. In 2009, 10 master's awarded. *Degree requirements:* For master's, thesis or alternative. *Entrance requirements:* For master's, minimum GPA of 3.0. *Application deadline:* For fall admission, 8/1 for domestic students; for spring admission, 11/1 for domestic

Education—General

University of Wisconsin–Green Bay *(continued)*
students. Applications are processed on a rolling basis. Application fee: $56. Electronic applications accepted. *Expenses:* Tuition, state resident: full-time $6706; part-time $373 per credit. Tuition, nonresident: full-time $16,722; part-time $932 per credit. Required fees: $1250; $52 per credit. Tuition and fees vary according to degree level and reciprocity agreements. *Financial support:* Application deadline: 7/15. *Faculty research:* Curriculum design, assessment. *Unit head:* Dr. Tim Kaufman, Director, 920-465-2964, E-mail: kaufmant@uwgb.edu. *Application contact:* Pam Harvey-Jacobs, Director of Admissions, 920-465-2111, Fax: 920-465-5754, E-mail: uwgb@uwgb.edu.

University of Wisconsin–La Crosse, Office of University Graduate Studies, College of Liberal Studies, Department of Educational Studies, La Crosse, WI 54601-3742. Offers college student development and administration (MS Ed); professional development (MEPD), including elementary education, K–12, professional development, secondary education; special education (MS Ed), including emotional disturbance, learning disabilities. Part-time programs available. *Faculty:* 27 full-time (19 women), 18 part-time/adjunct (13 women). *Students:* 17 full-time (11 women), 350 part-time (280 women); includes 8 minority (3 Asian Americans or Pacific Islanders, 5 Hispanic Americans), 6 international. Average age 33. 136 applicants, 89% accepted, 78 enrolled. In 2009, 247 master's awarded. *Degree requirements:* For master's, thesis optional. *Entrance requirements:* For master's, minimum GPA of 2.85. Additional exam requirements/recommendations for international students: Required—TOEFL (minimum score 550 paper-based; 213 computer-based; 79 iBT). *Application deadline:* Applications are processed on a rolling basis. Application fee: $56. Electronic applications accepted. *Financial support:* In 2009–10, 4 research assistantships with partial tuition reimbursements (averaging $6,648 per year) were awarded; career-related internships or fieldwork, Federal Work-Study, institutionally sponsored loans, health care benefits, unspecified assistantships, and grant-funded positions also available. Support available to part-time students. Financial award application deadline: 3/15; financial award applicants required to submit FAFSA. *Unit head:* Dr. Dan Duquette, Acting Chair, 608-785-8132, E-mail: duquette.rode@uwlax.edu. *Application contact:* Kathryn Kiefer, Director of Admissions, 608-785-8939, E-mail: admissions@uwlax.edu.

University of Wisconsin–Madison, Graduate School, School of Education, Madison, WI 53706-1380. Offers MA, MFA, MS, PhD, Certificate. *Faculty:* 147 full-time (66 women). *Students:* 715 full-time (484 women), 384 part-time (260 women). In 2009, 203 master's, 86 doctorates awarded. *Degree requirements:* For doctorate, thesis/dissertation. *Entrance requirements:* Additional exam requirements/recommendations for international students: Required—TOEFL (minimum score 580 paper-based; 237 computer-based; 92 iBT), IELTS (minimum score 7). Application fee: $56. *Expenses:* Tuition, state resident: part-time $594 per credit. Tuition, nonresident: part-time $1504 per credit. Required fees: $65 per credit. Tuition and fees vary according to course load, program and reciprocity agreements. *Financial support:* In 2009–10, 54 fellowships with full tuition reimbursements, 19 research assistantships with full tuition reimbursements, 166 teaching assistantships with full tuition reimbursements were awarded; traineeships and project assistantships also available. Total annual research expenditures: $25.7 million. *Unit head:* Dr. Julie K. Underwood, Dean, 608-262-1763. *Application contact:* Dr. Julie K. Underwood, Dean, 608-262-1763.

University of Wisconsin–Milwaukee, Graduate School, School of Education, Milwaukee, WI 53201. Offers MS, PhD, Certificate, Ed S. Part-time programs available. *Faculty:* 72 full-time (50 women). *Students:* 345 full-time (260 women), 350 part-time (286 women); includes 150 minority (83 African Americans, 4 American Indian/Alaska Native, 25 Asian Americans or Pacific Islanders, 38 Hispanic Americans), 15 international. Average age 33. 454 applicants, 56% accepted, 99 enrolled. In 2009, 159 master's, 34 doctorates awarded. *Degree requirements:* For doctorate, thesis/dissertation. *Entrance requirements:* For doctorate, GRE General Test. *Application deadline:* For fall admission, 1/1 priority date for domestic students; for spring admission, 9/1 for domestic students. Applications are processed on a rolling basis. Application fee: $45 ($75 for international students). *Expenses:* Tuition, state resident: full-time $8800. Tuition, nonresident: full-time $20,760. Tuition and fees vary according to program and reciprocity agreements. *Financial support:* In 2009–10, 9 teaching assistantships were awarded; career-related internships or fieldwork, Federal Work-Study, and unspecified assistantships also available. Support available to part-time students. Financial award application deadline: 4/15. Total annual research expenditures: $5.8 million. *Unit head:* Alfonzo Thurman, Dean, 414-229-4181, E-mail: athurman@uwm.edu. *Application contact:* General Information Contact, 414-229-4982, Fax: 414-229-6967, E-mail: gradschool@uwm.edu.

University of Wisconsin–Oshkosh, The Office of Graduate Studies, College of Education and Human Services, Oshkosh, WI 54901. Offers MS, MSE. Part-time and evening/weekend programs available. *Degree requirements:* For master's, comprehensive exam (for some programs), thesis or alternative, field report, PPST, PRAXIS II. *Entrance requirements:* For master's, PPST, PRAXIS II, teaching license, letters of recommendation, interview. Additional exam requirements/recommendations for international students: Required—TOEFL (minimum score 550 paper-based; 213 computer-based; 79 iBT). Electronic applications accepted.

University of Wisconsin–Platteville, School of Graduate Studies, College of Liberal Arts and Education, School of Education, Platteville, WI 53818-3099. Offers adult education (MSE); elementary education (MSE); English education (MSE); middle school education (MSE); secondary education (MSE); vocational and technical education (MSE). *Accreditation:* NCATE. Part-time programs available. *Faculty:* 8 part-time/adjunct (3 women). *Students:* 16 full-time (12 women), 183 part-time (137 women); includes 35 minority (27 African Americans, 1 American Indian/Alaska Native, 1 Asian American or Pacific Islander, 6 Hispanic Americans), 63 international. 23 applicants, 100% accepted, 23 enrolled. In 2009, 85 master's awarded. *Degree requirements:* For master's, comprehensive exam, thesis or alternative. *Entrance requirements:* Additional exam requirements/recommendations for international students: Required—TOEFL (minimum score 500 paper-based; 173 computer-based; 61 iBT). *Application deadline:* For fall admission, 7/1 priority date for domestic students; for spring admission, 11/1 for domestic students. Applications are processed on a rolling basis. Application fee: $56. Electronic applications accepted. *Expenses:* Tuition, state resident: full-time $6706. Tuition, nonresident: full-time $16,772. *Financial support:* Research assistantships with partial tuition reimbursements, career-related internships or fieldwork, Federal Work-Study, institutionally sponsored loans, scholarships/grants, and unspecified assistantships available. Support available to part-time students. *Unit head:* Dr. Karen Stinson, Director, 608-342-1131, Fax: 608-342-1133. *Application contact:* Lisa Popp, School of Graduate Studies, 608-342-1322, Fax: 608-342-1389, E-mail: poppl@uwplatt.edu.

University of Wisconsin–River Falls, Outreach and Graduate Studies, College of Education and Professional Studies, Department of Teacher Education, River Falls, WI 54022. Offers elementary education (MSE); professional development shared inquiry communities (MSE); reading (MSE). Part-time programs available. *Degree requirements:* For master's, comprehensive exam, thesis or alternative. *Entrance requirements:* For master's, minimum GPA of 2.75. Additional exam requirements/recommendations for international students: Required—TOEFL (minimum score 500 paper-based; 65 iBT), IELTS (minimum score 5.5). Electronic applications accepted.

University of Wisconsin–Stevens Point, College of Professional Studies, School of Education, Stevens Point, WI 54481-3897. Offers education—general/reading (MSE); education—general/special (MSE); educational administration (MSE); elementary education (MSE); guidance and counseling (MSE). Part-time programs available. *Students:* 3 full-time (2 women), 35 part-time (21 women); includes 1 minority (Asian American or Pacific Islander). *Degree requirements:* For master's, comprehensive exam, thesis or alternative. *Entrance requirements:* For master's, teacher certification, minimum undergraduate GPA of 3.0, 2 years of teaching experience, letters of recommendation. Additional exam requirements/recommendations for international students: Required—TOEFL (minimum score 523 paper-based; 193 computer-based). *Application deadline:* For fall admission, 5/1 priority date for domestic students. Applications are processed on a rolling basis. Application fee: $45. *Expenses:* Tuition, state resident: full-time $7740; part-time $430 per credit hour. Tuition, nonresident: full-time $17,804; part-time

$989 per credit hour. Tuition and fees vary according to course load and reciprocity agreements. *Financial support:* In 2009–10, 8 research assistantships with partial tuition reimbursements were awarded; teaching assistantships, Federal Work-Study, tuition waivers (partial), and unspecified assistantships also available. Support available to part-time students. Financial award application deadline: 5/1; financial award applicants required to submit FAFSA. *Faculty research:* Gifted education early childhood, special education curriculum and instruction, standards-based education. *Unit head:* Dr. JoAnne Katzmarek, Associate Dean, 715-346-4802, Fax: 715-346-4846, E-mail: jkatzmar@uwsp.edu. *Application contact:* Dr. Patricia Caro, Director of Graduate Advising, 715-346-3248, Fax: 715-346-4846, E-mail: pcaro@uwsp.edu.

University of Wisconsin–Stout, Graduate School, School of Education, Menomonie, WI 54751. Offers MS, MS Ed, Ed S. *Accreditation:* NCATE. Part-time programs available. Postbaccalaureate distance learning degree programs offered (no on-campus study). *Degree requirements:* For master's and Ed S, thesis. *Entrance requirements:* For degree, minimum GPA of 3.25. Additional exam requirements/recommendations for international students: Required—TOEFL (minimum score 500 paper-based; 173 computer-based; 61 iBT). Electronic applications accepted.

University of Wisconsin–Superior, Graduate Division, Department of Teacher Education, Superior, WI 54880-4500. Offers instruction (MSE); special education (MSE), including emotional/behavior disabilities, learning disabilities; teaching reading (MSE). Part-time and evening/weekend programs available. Postbaccalaureate distance learning degree programs offered (minimal on-campus study). *Faculty:* 7 full-time (6 women). *Students:* 13 full-time (9 women), 97 part-time (70 women); includes 3 minority (all American Indian/Alaska Native). Average age 34. 18 applicants, 100% accepted. In 2009, 27 master's awarded. *Degree requirements:* For master's, research project. *Entrance requirements:* For master's, minimum GPA of 2.75, teaching certificate. *Application deadline:* For fall admission, 4/1 priority date for domestic students; for spring admission, 10/15 priority date for domestic students. Applications are processed on a rolling basis. Application fee: $45. *Financial support:* Career-related internships or fieldwork, Federal Work-Study, institutionally sponsored loans, scholarships/grants, and tuition waivers (partial) available. Support available to part-time students. Financial award application deadline: 4/15; financial award applicants required to submit FAFSA. *Faculty research:* Science teaching. *Unit head:* Terri Kronzer, Chairperson, 715-394-8506, E-mail: tkronzer@uwsuper.edu. *Application contact:* Sandy Wallgren, Program Assistant/Status Examiner, 715-394-8295, Fax: 715-394-8146, E-mail: gradstudy@uwsuper.edu.

University of Wisconsin–Whitewater, School of Graduate Studies, College of Education, Whitewater, WI 53190-1790. Offers MS, MS Ed. *Accreditation:* NCATE. Part-time and evening/weekend programs available. Postbaccalaureate distance learning degree programs offered (no on-campus study). *Entrance requirements:* Additional exam requirements/recommendations for international students: Required—TOEFL (minimum score 550 paper-based; 213 computer-based). Electronic applications accepted.

Urbana University, College of Education and Sports Studies, Urbana, OH 43078-2091. Offers classroom education (M Ed). Part-time and evening/weekend programs available. *Faculty:* 8 full-time (3 women). *Students:* 4 full-time (3 women), 55 part-time (38 women); includes 6 minority (5 African Americans, 1 Asian American or Pacific Islander), 1 international. Average age 31. 20 applicants, 100% accepted. In 2009, 19 master's awarded. *Degree requirements:* For master's, comprehensive oral exam, capstone research project. *Entrance requirements:* For master's, minimum GPA of 2.7, teaching license. Additional exam requirements/recommendations for international students: Required—TOEFL (minimum score 550 paper-based; 213 computer-based). *Application deadline:* For fall admission, 8/16 priority date for domestic students, 8/16 for international students; for winter admission, 1/3 priority date for domestic students, 1/3 for international students; for spring admission, 6/1 priority date for domestic students, 6/1 for international students. Applications are processed on a rolling basis. Application fee: $25. *Expenses:* Tuition: Full-time $8550; part-time $475 per semester hour. Required fees: $950; $475 per semester. One-time fee: $25. *Financial support:* In 2009–10, 3 students received support. Institutionally sponsored loans, tuition waivers (partial), and unspecified assistantships available. Support available to part-time students. Financial award application deadline: 6/1; financial award applicants required to submit FAFSA. *Faculty research:* Best professional practices, reading/special education, classroom management, teaching models, school finance. *Unit head:* Dr. Denise A. Boldman, Dean, 937-484-1243, Fax: 937-484-1365, E-mail: dboldman@urbana.edu. *Application contact:* Brian Kesse, Director of Admissions, 937-484-1370, Fax: 937-484-1389, E-mail: bkesse@urbana.edu.

Ursuline College, School of Graduate Studies, Program for Advanced Study in Education (PASE), Pepper Pike, OH 44124-4398. Offers MA. Part-time programs available. *Faculty:* 1 (woman) full-time, 5 part-time/adjunct (4 women). *Students:* 55 part-time (47 women); includes 13 minority (11 African Americans, 2 Hispanic Americans). Average age 34. 28 applicants, 100% accepted, 28 enrolled. In 2009, 5 master's awarded. *Degree requirements:* For master's, comprehensive exam (for some programs), thesis (for some programs). *Entrance requirements:* Additional exam requirements/recommendations for international students: Required—TOEFL (minimum score 500 paper-based; 173 computer-based). *Application deadline:* Applications are processed on a rolling basis. Application fee: $25. Electronic applications accepted. *Expenses:* Tuition: Full-time $14,544; part-time $808 per credit hour. Required fees: $230; $75 per semester. *Financial support:* Applicants required to submit FAFSA. *Unit head:* Edna West, Director, 440-684-6034. *Application contact:* Melanie Steele, Secretary, 440-646-8199, Fax: 440-684-6138, E-mail: gradsch@ursuline.edu.

Ursuline College, School of Graduate Studies, Program in Education, Pepper Pike, OH 44124-4398. Offers art education (MA); early childhood education (MA); language arts education (MA); life science education (MA); math education (MA); middle school education (MA); social studies education (MA); special education (MA). *Accreditation:* NCATE. *Faculty:* 1 (woman) full-time, 10 part-time/adjunct (8 women). *Students:* 53 full-time (40 women), 3 part-time (all women); includes 8 minority (7 African Americans, 1 Hispanic American). Average age 34. In 2009, 11 master's awarded. *Degree requirements:* For master's, comprehensive exam. *Entrance requirements:* For master's, minimum undergraduate GPA of 3.0. Additional exam requirements/recommendations for international students: Required—TOEFL (minimum score 500 paper-based; 173 computer-based). *Application deadline:* For fall admission, 8/1 priority date for domestic students. Applications are processed on a rolling basis. Application fee: $25. *Expenses:* Contact institution. *Financial support:* Federal Work-Study available. Financial award application deadline: 3/1. *Unit head:* Karen Godenschwager Nelson, Director, 440-684-8338, Fax: 440-684-6088, E-mail: kgodenschwager@ursuline.edu. *Application contact:* Melanie Steele, Secretary, 440-646-8199, Fax: 440-684-6138, E-mail: gradsch@ursuline.edu.

Utah State University, School of Graduate Studies, College of Education and Human Services, Logan, UT 84322. Offers M Ed, MA, MFHD, MRC, MS, Au D, Ed D, PhD, Ed S. Part-time and evening/weekend programs available. Postbaccalaureate distance learning degree programs offered (no on-campus study). *Degree requirements:* For doctorate, comprehensive exam, thesis/dissertation. *Entrance requirements:* For master's, GRE General Test, minimum GPA of 3.0; for doctorate, GRE General Test, master's degree; for Ed S, GRE General Test, GRE Subject Test. Additional exam requirements/recommendations for international students: Required—TOEFL (minimum score 550 paper-based; 213 computer-based). *Faculty research:* Literacy instruction, design and delivery of instruction, children at-risk and their families, hearing assessment and management, language and literacy development.

Utah Valley University, Program in Education, Orem, UT 84058-5999. Offers M Ed. *Accreditation:* Teacher Education Accreditation Council. Part-time programs available. *Faculty:* 4 full-time (all women). *Students:* 1 (woman) full-time, 41 part-time (30 women); includes 6 minority (3 Asian Americans or Pacific Islanders, 3 Hispanic Americans). Average age 34. 35 applicants, 97% accepted, 34 enrolled. *Entrance requirements:* For master's, GRE, minimum GPA of 3.2, 3 letters of recommendation. Additional exam requirements/recommendations for international students: Required—TOEFL (minimum score 83 iBT). *Application deadline:* For fall admission, 3/15 for domestic and international students. Application fee: $45 ($100 for international students). Electronic applications accepted. *Expenses:* Tuition, state resident:

full-time $5805; part-time $325 per credit. Tuition, nonresident: full-time $18,792; part-time $1044 per credit. Required fees: $292 per semester. Tuition and fees vary according to course load and program. *Financial support:* Application deadline: 5/1. *Unit head:* Mohammed El-Saidi, Interim Vice President for Academic Affairs, 801-863-8517, E-mail: mohammed.el-saidi@uvu.edu. *Application contact:* Paula Nye, Administrative Assistant, 801-863-8270.

Utica College, Teacher Education Programs, Utica, NY 13502-4892. Offers MS, MS Ed, CAS. *Accreditation:* Teacher Education Accreditation Council. *Faculty:* 10 full-time (7 women). *Students:* 34 full-time (27 women), 119 part-time (81 women); includes 8 minority (4 African Americans, 1 American Indian/Alaska Native, 1 Asian American or Pacific Islander, 2 Hispanic Americans). Average age 29. In 2009, 46 master's awarded. *Degree requirements:* For master's, comprehensive exam or thesis. *Entrance requirements:* For master's, CST, LAST, minimum GPA of 3.0. Additional exam requirements/recommendations for international students: Required—TOEFL (minimum score 525 paper-based; 195 computer-based). *Application deadline:* Applications are processed on a rolling basis. Application fee: $50. Electronic applications accepted. *Expenses:* Contact institution. *Financial support:* Career-related internships or fieldwork, scholarships/grants, tuition waivers (partial), and unspecified assistantships available. Support available to part-time students. Financial award application deadline: 3/15; financial award applicants required to submit FAFSA. *Unit head:* Dr. Lois Fisch, Director, Institute for Excellence in Education, 315-792-3815, E-mail: lfisch@utica.edu. *Application contact:* John D. Rowe, Director of Graduate Admissions, 315-792-3824, Fax: 315-792-3003, E-mail: jrowe@utica.edu.

Valley City State University, School of Education and Graduate Studies, Valley City, ND 58072. Offers English language learners (ELL) (M Ed); library and information technologies (M Ed); teaching and technology (M Ed); technology education (M Ed). *Accreditation:* NCATE. Part-time and evening/weekend programs available. Postbaccalaureate distance learning degree programs offered (no on-campus study). *Faculty:* 19 full-time (13 women), 4 part-time/adjunct (3 women). *Students:* 7 full-time (4 women), 115 part-time (73 women); includes 4 minority (1 African American, 1 American Indian/Alaska Native, 1 Asian American or Pacific Islander, 1 Hispanic American). Average age 36. 33 applicants, 97% accepted, 22 enrolled. In 2009, 22 master's awarded. *Degree requirements:* For master's, action research report, comprehensive portfolio. *Entrance requirements:* For master's, GRE, MAT, PRAXIS II or National Teaching Board for Professional Standards (if GPAless than 3.0). Additional exam requirements/recommendations for international students: Required—TOEFL (minimum score 525 paper-based; 193 computer-based). *Application deadline:* For fall admission, 5/24 priority date for domestic and international students; for winter admission, 12/11 priority date for domestic and international students; for spring admission, 4/24 priority date for domestic and international students. Applications are processed on a rolling basis. Application fee: $35. Electronic applications accepted. *Expenses:* Tuition, state resident: full-time $4266; part-time $237.40 per credit hour. Tuition, nonresident: full-time $4266; part-time $237.40 per credit hour. Required fees: $237.40 per credit hour. One-time fee: $35. *Financial support:* In 2009–10, 30 students received support. Applicants required to submit FAFSA. *Faculty research:* Academically at-risk students in higher education, communication pedagogy and technology, gender communication, computer mediated communication, creativity in music. Total annual research expenditures: $26,000. *Unit head:* Dr. Gary Thompson, Dean, 701-845-7197, E-mail: gary.thompson@vcsu.edu. *Application contact:* Misty Lindgren, 701-845-7303, Fax: 701-845-7305, E-mail: misty.lindgren@vcsu.edu.

Valparaiso University, Graduate School, Department of Education, Valparaiso, IN 46383. Offers initial licensure (M Ed); teaching and learning (M Ed); M Ed/Ed S. *Accreditation:* NCATE. Part-time and evening/weekend programs available. *Faculty:* 12 part-time/adjunct (9 women). *Students:* 34 full-time (25 women), 27 part-time (21 women); includes 3 minority (1 African American, 2 Hispanic Americans), 3 international. Average age 29. In 2009, 23 master's awarded. *Entrance requirements:* For master's, GRE General Test, Pre-Professional Skills Test (PPST), minimum GPA of 3.0. Additional exam requirements/recommendations for international students: Required—TOEFL (minimum score 550 paper-based; 213 computer-based; 80 iBT). *Application deadline:* Applications are processed on a rolling basis. Application fee: $30 ($50 for international students). Electronic applications accepted. *Financial support:* Scholarships/grants, traineeships, and unspecified assistantships available. Support available to part-time students. Financial award applicants required to submit FAFSA. *Unit head:* Dr. Jan Westrick, Chair, Department of Education, 219-464-5077, Fax: 219-464-6720, E-mail: jan.westrick@valpo.edu. *Application contact:* Jamie Haney, Coordinator of Graduate Admission, 219-464-5313, Fax: 219-464-5381, E-mail: jamie.haney@valpo.edu.

Vanderbilt University, Graduate School, Program in Learning, Teaching and Diversity, Nashville, TN 37240-1001. Offers MS, PhD. *Faculty:* 25 full-time (15 women). *Students:* 45 full-time (27 women), 1 (woman) part-time; includes 4 minority (2 African Americans, 2 Asian Americans or Pacific Islanders), 4 international. Average age 34. 99 applicants, 14% accepted, 8 enrolled. In 2009, 5 doctorates awarded. *Degree requirements:* For doctorate, comprehensive exam, thesis/dissertation. *Entrance requirements:* For doctorate, GRE General Test. Additional exam requirements/recommendations for international students: Required—TOEFL (minimum score 570 paper-based; 230 computer-based; 88 iBT). *Application deadline:* For fall admission, 12/31 for domestic and international students. Application fee: $0. Electronic applications accepted. *Financial support:* Fellowships with full and partial tuition reimbursements, research assistantships with full tuition reimbursements, teaching assistantships with full tuition reimbursements, Federal Work-Study, institutionally sponsored loans, scholarships/grants, traineeships, and health care benefits available. Financial award application deadline: 1/15; financial award applicants required to submit CSS PROFILE or FAFSA. *Faculty research:* New pedagogies for math, science, and language; the support of English language learners; the uses of new technology and media in the classroom; middle school mathematics and the institutional setting of teaching. *Unit head:* David Dickinson, Interim Chair, 615-322-8100, Fax: 615-322-8999, E-mail: david.dickinson@vanderbilt.edu. *Application contact:* Rogers P. Hall, Director of Graduate Studies, 615-322-8092, Fax: 615-322-8999, E-mail: r.hall@vanderbilt.edu.

Vanderbilt University, Peabody College, Nashville, TN 37240-1001. Offers M Ed, MPP, Ed D. *Accreditation:* APA (one or more programs are accredited); NCATE. Part-time programs available. *Faculty:* 146 full-time (80 women), 67 part-time/adjunct (48 women). *Students:* 423 full-time (361 women), 146 part-time (86 women); includes 73 minority (48 African Americans, 13 Asian Americans or Pacific Islanders, 12 Hispanic Americans), 32 international. Average age 28. 713 applicants, 69% accepted, 261 enrolled. In 2009, 229 master's, 22 doctorates awarded. *Degree requirements:* For master's, comprehensive exam, thesis optional; for doctorate, thesis/dissertation, qualifying examinations, residency. *Entrance requirements:* For master's, GRE General Test, MAT; for doctorate, GRE General Test. Additional exam requirements/recommendations for international students: Required—TOEFL (minimum score 550 paper-based; 213 computer-based). *Application deadline:* For fall admission, 12/31 priority date for domestic and international students; for spring admission, 11/1 priority date for domestic and international students. Applications are processed on a rolling basis. Application fee: $0. Electronic applications accepted. *Expenses:* Contact institution. *Financial support:* In 2009–10, 449 students received support, including 3 fellowships with full and partial tuition reimbursements available, 194 research assistantships with full and partial tuition reimbursements available, 22 teaching assistantships with full and partial tuition reimbursements available; career-related internships or fieldwork, Federal Work-Study, institutionally sponsored loans, scholarships/grants, traineeships, tuition waivers (partial), and unspecified assistantships also available. Support available to part-time students. Financial award application deadline: 2/1; financial award applicants required to submit FAFSA. Total annual research expenditures: $35.4 million. *Unit head:* Dr. Camilla P. Benbow, Dean, 615-322-8407, Fax: 615-322-8501, E-mail: camilla.benbow@vanderbilt.edu. *Application contact:* Kimberly Brazil-Tanner, Recruitment Coordinator, 615-332-8410, Fax: 615-343-3474, E-mail: kim.brazil@vanderbilt.edu.

See Close-Up on page 721.

Vanguard University of Southern California, Graduate Programs in Education, Costa Mesa, CA 92626-9601. Offers MA. Evening/weekend programs available. *Faculty:* 5 full-time (4 women), 11 part-time/adjunct (all women). *Students:* 44 full-time (29 women), 70 part-time (56 women); includes 17 minority (1 African American, 1 American Indian/Alaska Native, 5 Asian Americans or Pacific Islanders, 10 Hispanic Americans). Average age 29. 66 applicants, 77% accepted, 49 enrolled. In 2009, 30 master's awarded. *Degree requirements:* For master's, thesis or alternative. *Entrance requirements:* For master's, California Basic Educational Skills Test, California Subject Examinations for Teachers, minimum GPA of 3.0. Additional exam requirements/recommendations for international students: Required—TOEFL (minimum score 550 paper-based; 213 computer-based; 79 iBT). *Application deadline:* For fall admission, 4/1 priority date for domestic and international students; for spring admission, 10/1 priority date for domestic and international students. Applications are processed on a rolling basis. Application fee: $45. Electronic applications accepted. *Expenses:* Contact institution. *Financial support:* In 2009–10, 114 students received support; teaching assistantships, scholarships/grants available. Support available to part-time students. Financial award application deadline: 3/2; financial award applicants required to submit FAFSA. *Faculty research:* Reading, educational administration. *Unit head:* Dr. Doug Grove, Dean, 714-556-3610 Ext. 3309, Fax: 714-966-5495, E-mail: dgrove@vanguard.edu. *Application contact:* Michelle Romo, Graduate Education Coordinator, 714-556-3610 Ext. 3302, Fax: 714-966-5495, E-mail: mromo@vanguard.edu.

Villanova University, Graduate School of Liberal Arts and Sciences, Department of Education and Human Services, Villanova, PA 19085-1699. Offers community counseling (MS), including counseling and human relations; educational leadership (MA); elementary school counseling (MS), including counseling and human relations; elementary teacher education (MA); higher education (MA); secondary school counseling (MS), including counseling and human relations; secondary teacher education (MA). Part-time and evening/weekend programs available. *Faculty:* 12 full-time (6 women), 10 part-time/adjunct (5 women). *Students:* 70 full-time (61 women), 86 part-time (61 women); includes 13 minority (3 African Americans, 4 Asian Americans or Pacific Islanders, 6 Hispanic Americans). Average age 29. 85 applicants, 96% accepted, 44 enrolled. In 2009, 75 master's awarded. *Degree requirements:* For master's, comprehensive exam. *Entrance requirements:* For master's, GRE or MAT, minimum GPA of 3.0. Additional exam requirements/recommendations for international students: Required—TOEFL. *Application deadline:* For fall admission, 3/1 for domestic and international students; for spring admission, 11/15 for domestic and international students. Applications are processed on a rolling basis. Application fee: $50. Electronic applications accepted. *Expenses:* Tuition: Part-time $630 per credit. Required fees: $60 per credit. Part-time tuition and fees vary according to degree level and program. *Financial support:* Research assistantships, career-related internships or fieldwork and Federal Work-Study available. Financial award applicants required to submit FAFSA. *Unit head:* Dr. Connie Titone, Chairperson, 610-519-4620. *Application contact:* Dr. Connie Titone, Chairperson, 610-519-4620.

See Close-Up on page 723.

Virginia Commonwealth University, Graduate School, School of Education, Richmond, VA 23284-9005. Offers M Ed, MS, MSAT, MT, PhD, Certificate. *Accreditation:* NCATE. Part-time programs available. *Degree requirements:* For doctorate, thesis/dissertation. *Entrance requirements:* For master's, GRE General Test or MAT; for doctorate, GRE, interview, master's degree.

Virginia State University, School of Graduate Studies, Research, and Outreach, School of Liberal Arts and Education, Petersburg, VA 23806-0001. Offers M Ed, MA, MS, CAGS. *Accreditation:* NCATE. Part-time and evening/weekend programs available.

Viterbo University, Graduate Program in Education, La Crosse, WI 54601-4797. Offers MA. Courses held on weekends and during summer. *Accreditation:* NCATE. Part-time and evening/weekend programs available. *Degree requirements:* For master's, thesis. *Entrance requirements:* For master's, MAT, teaching certificate, 2 years of teaching experience.

Wagner College, Division of Graduate Studies, Department of Education, Staten Island, NY 10301-4495. Offers adolescent education (MS Ed); childhood education (MS Ed); early childhood education (birth-grade 2) (MS Ed); educational leadership (Certificate), including school building leader, school district leader; literacy (B-6) (MS Ed); middle level education (5-9) (MS Ed). *Accreditation:* NCATE. Part-time and evening/weekend programs available. *Degree requirements:* For master's, thesis (for some programs). *Entrance requirements:* For master's, Liberal Arts and Sciences Test (LAST), New York State Teacher Certification Examinations (NYSTCE), minimum GPA of 2.75. Additional exam requirements/recommendations for international students: Required—TOEFL (minimum score 550 paper-based; 217 computer-based). *Expenses:* Tuition: Full-time $15,570; part-time $865 per credit. Required fees: $2.

Wake Forest University, Graduate School of Arts and Sciences, Department of Education, Winston-Salem, NC 27109. Offers secondary education (MA Ed). *Accreditation:* ACA; NCATE. Part-time programs available. *Faculty:* 11 full-time (7 women), 8 part-time/adjunct (6 women). *Students:* 23 full-time (16 women), 26 part-time (21 women); includes 25 minority (11 African Americans, 2 Asian Americans or Pacific Islanders, 12 Hispanic Americans). Average age 28. 61 applicants, 52% accepted, 27 enrolled. In 2009, 32 master's awarded. *Degree requirements:* For master's, thesis optional. *Entrance requirements:* For master's, GRE General Test. Additional exam requirements/recommendations for international students: Required—TOEFL (minimum score 550 paper-based; 213 computer-based). *Application deadline:* For fall admission, 1/15 for domestic students, 1/15 priority date for international students. Application fee: $45 ($55 for international students). Electronic applications accepted. *Expenses:* Contact institution. *Financial support:* In 2009–10, 23 students received support, including 23 fellowships with full tuition reimbursements available (averaging $6,000 per year); teaching assistantships with full tuition reimbursements available, scholarships/grants and tuition waivers (full) also available. Support available to part-time students. Financial award application deadline: 2/15. *Faculty research:* Teaching and learning. *Unit head:* Dr. MaryLynn Redmond, Chair, 336-758-5341, Fax: 336-758-4591, E-mail: redmond@wfu.edu. *Application contact:* Dr. Leah McCoy, Program Director, 336-758-5998, Fax: 336-758-4591, E-mail: mccoy@wfu.edu.

Walden University, Graduate Programs, Richard W. Riley College of Education and Leadership, Minneapolis, MN 55401. Offers administrator leadership for teaching and learning (Ed D, Ed S); curriculum, instruction, and professional development (Ed S); early childhood education (birth-grade 3) (MAT); education (MS, PhD), including adolescent literacy and technology (grades 6-12) (MS), adult education leadership (PhD), community college leadership (PhD), curriculum, instruction, and assessment, early childhood education (PhD), educational leadership (MS), educational technology (PhD), elementary reading and literacy (MS), elementary reading and mathematics (MS), emotional/behavioral disorders (K-12) (MS), general program, higher education (PhD), integrating technology in the classroom (MS), K-12 educational leadership (PhD), learning disabilities (K-12) (MS), literacy and learning in the content areas (MS), mathematics (grades 6-8) (MS), mathematics (grades K-5) (MS), middle level education (grades 5-8) (MS), professional development (MS), science (grades K-8) (MS), self-designed (PhD), special education (PhD), special education (non-licensure) (MS), teacher leadership (grades K-12) (MS); educational leadership and administration (principal preparation) (Ed S); educational technology (Ed S); higher education and adult learning (Ed D); instructional design (Postbaccalaureate Certificate); instructional design and technology (MS), including general program (MS, PhD), online learning, training and performance improvement; special education: emotional/behavioral disorders (K-12) (MAT); special education: learning disabilities (K-12) (MAT); teacher leadership (Ed D, Ed S). Part-time and evening/weekend programs available. Postbaccalaureate distance learning degree programs offered (minimal on-campus study). *Faculty:* 54 full-time, 835 part-time/adjunct. *Students:* 13,940 full-time (11,339 women), 1,940 part-time (1,637 women); includes 4,626 minority (3,795 African Americans, 111 American Indian/Alaska Native, 199 Asian Americans or Pacific Islanders, 521 Hispanic Americans), 124 international. Average age 38. In 2009, 4,688 master's, 190 doctorates awarded. *Degree requirements:* For doctorate, thesis/dissertation (for some programs), residency; for other advanced degree, residency (for some programs). *Entrance requirements:* For master's, bachelor's degree or equivalent in related field; minimum GPA of 2.5; official transcripts; goal statement; access to computer and Internet; for doctorate, master's degree or equivalent in related field; minimum GPA of 3.0; official transcripts; three years' related professional/academic experience (preferred); access to computer and Internet; for other advanced degree,

Education—General

Walden University (continued)

master's degree or equivalent in related field; minimum GPA of 3.0; 3 years related professional/ academic experience (preferred); access to computer and Internet (Ed S). Additional exam requirements/recommendations for international students: Required—TOEFL (minimum score 550 paper-based; 213 computer-based), IELTS (minimum score 6.5), or Michigan English Language Assessment Battery (minimum score 82). *Application deadline:* Applications are processed on a rolling basis. Application fee: $50. Electronic applications accepted. *Expenses:* Tuition: Full-time $13,665; part-time $560 per credit. Required fees: $1375. Tuition and fees vary according to course load, degree level and program. *Financial support:* In 2009–10, 2,418 students received support; fellowships, Federal Work-Study, scholarships/grants, unspecified assistantships, and family tuition reduction, active duty/veteran tuition reduction, group tuition reduction, interest-free payment plans available. Support available to part-time students. Financial award applicants required to submit FAFSA. *Unit head:* Dr. Kate Steffens, Dean, 800-925-3368. *Application contact:* Jennifer Hall, Director of Enrollment, 866-4-WALDEN, E-mail: info@waldenu.edu.

Walla Walla University, Graduate School, School of Education and Psychology, College Place, WA 99324-1198. Offers counseling psychology (MA); curriculum and instruction (M Ed, MA, MAT); educational leadership (M Ed, MA, MAT); literacy instruction (M Ed, MA, MAT); students at risk (M Ed, MA, MAT); teaching (MAT). Part-time programs available. *Faculty:* 7 full-time (3 women), 1 part-time/adjunct (0 women). *Students:* 32 full-time (14 women), 9 part-time (7 women); includes 5 minority (1 African American, 1 American Indian/Alaska Native, 2 Asian Americans or Pacific Islanders, 1 Hispanic American). Average age 30. 41 applicants, 80% accepted, 21 enrolled. In 2009, 29 master's awarded. *Entrance requirements:* For master's, GRE General Test, minimum GPA of 2.75. Additional exam requirements/ recommendations for international students: Required—TOEFL (minimum score 550 paper-based; 213 computer-based; 79 iBT). *Application deadline:* For fall admission, 4/1 priority date for domestic students. Applications are processed on a rolling basis. Application fee: $50. Electronic applications accepted. *Expenses:* Tuition: Full-time $19,929. *Financial support:* In 2009–10, 29 students received support; research assistantships, teaching assistantships, Federal Work-Study and tuition waivers (partial) available. Support available to part-time students. Financial award application deadline: 4/1; financial award applicants required to submit FAFSA. *Faculty research:* Admissions/retention, instructional psychology, moral development, teaching of reading. *Unit head:* Dr. Julian Melgosa, Dean, 509-527-2272, Fax: 509-527-2248, E-mail: julian.melgosa@wallawalla.edu. *Application contact:* Dr. Joe G. Galusha, Dean of Graduate Studies, 509-527-2421, Fax: 509-527-2237, E-mail: joe.galusha@wallawalla.edu.

Walsh University, Graduate Studies, Program in Education, North Canton, OH 44720-3396. Offers MA. *Accreditation:* NCATE. Part-time and evening/weekend programs available. *Faculty:* 5 full-time (3 women), 11 part-time/adjunct (5 women). *Students:* 24 full-time (16 women), 67 part-time (53 women); includes 5 minority (4 African Americans, 1 Hispanic American), 3 international. Average age 34. 13 applicants, 92% accepted, 9 enrolled. In 2009, 36 master's awarded. *Degree requirements:* For master's, comprehensive exam, thesis optional, teaching skills laboratory. *Entrance requirements:* For master's, MAT or GRE, interview, minimum GPA of 3.0, writing sample, 3 recommendation forms, moral affidavit. Additional exam requirements/ recommendations for international students: Required—TOEFL (minimum score 500 paper-based; 173 computer-based; 61 iBT). *Application deadline:* For fall admission, 7/15 priority date for domestic students. Applications are processed on a rolling basis. Application fee: $25. Electronic applications accepted. *Expenses:* Tuition: Full-time $9630; part-time $535 per credit hour. Tuition and fees vary according to course load and program. *Financial support:* In 2009–10, 76 students received support, including 10 research assistantships (averaging $5,178 per year); tuition waivers (partial), unspecified assistantships, and tuition discounts also available. Financial award application deadline: 12/31. *Faculty research:* Technology in education, strategies for working with children with special needs, reading literacy. *Unit head:* Dr. Gary Jacobs, Director of Graduate Education Studies, 330-490-7336, Fax: 330-490-7326, E-mail: gjacobs@walsh.edu. *Application contact:* Stephanie Wheeler, Director of Graduate and Transfer Admissions, 330-490-7181, Fax: 330-490-7182, E-mail: swheeler@walsh.edu.

Warner Pacific College, Graduate Programs, Portland, OR 97215-4099. Offers biblical and theological studies (MA); biblical studies (M Rel); education (M Ed); management/organizational leadership (MS); pastoral ministries (M Rel); religion and ethics (M Rel); teaching (MA); theology (M Rel). Part-time programs available. *Degree requirements:* For master's, thesis or alternative, presentation of defense. *Entrance requirements:* For master's, interview, minimum GPA of 2.5, letters of recommendations. *Faculty research:* New Testament studies, nineteenth-century Wesleyan theology, preaching and church growth, Christian ethics.

Warner University, Teacher Education Department, Lake Wales, FL 33859. Offers MAEd. Part-time and evening/weekend programs available. *Degree requirements:* For master's, thesis, accomplished practices portfolio. *Entrance requirements:* For master's, GRE or MAT, minimum GPA of 3.0 in last 60 hours of undergraduate coursework; documented teacher education certification; 2 letters of recommendation. Additional exam requirements/recommendations for international students: Required—TOEFL (minimum score 550 paper-based). Electronic applications accepted.

Washburn University, College of Arts and Sciences, Department of Education, Topeka, KS 66621. Offers curriculum and instruction (M Ed); educational leadership (M Ed); reading (M Ed); special education (M Ed). *Accreditation:* NCATE. Part-time programs available. *Degree requirements:* For master's, comprehensive exam, thesis or alternative, portfolio. *Entrance requirements:* For master's, GRE General Test, MAT, minimum GPA of 3.0 during previous 2 years. Additional exam requirements/recommendations for international students: Required—TOEFL (minimum score 523 paper-based; 193 computer-based). Electronic applications accepted. *Faculty research:* Teachers in math, working with educators in special education.

Washington State University, Graduate School, College of Education, Pullman, WA 99164. Offers Ed M, M Ed, MA, MIT, MS, Ed D, PhD, Certificate. *Accreditation:* NCATE. *Faculty:* 88. *Students:* 231 full-time (156 women), 378 part-time (276 women); includes 80 minority (12 African Americans, 4 American Indian/Alaska Native, 20 Asian Americans or Pacific Islanders, 44 Hispanic Americans), 29 international. Average age 34. 670 applicants, 40% accepted, 143 enrolled. In 2009, 166 master's, 30 doctorates awarded. Terminal master's awarded for partial completion of doctoral program. *Degree requirements:* For master's, comprehensive exam (for some programs), thesis (for some programs), oral and written exams; for doctorate, comprehensive exam, thesis/dissertation, oral and written exams. *Entrance requirements:* For master's, GRE General Test, current resume, three letters of recommendation, transcripts of all past academic work; for doctorate, GRE General Test or MAT, current resume, three letters of recommendation, transcripts of all past academic work. Additional exam requirements/ recommendations for international students: Required—TOEFL (minimum score 550 paper-based; 213 computer-based), IELTS. *Application deadline:* For fall admission, 1/10 for domestic and international students. Application fee: $50. Electronic applications accepted. *Financial support:* In 2009–10, 12 fellowships (averaging $2,844 per year), 58 research assistantships with partial tuition reimbursements (averaging $13,917 per year), 39 teaching assistantships with partial tuition reimbursements (averaging $13,056 per year) were awarded; career-related internships or fieldwork, Federal Work-Study, institutionally sponsored loans, scholarships/ grants, tuition waivers (partial), and staff assistantships, teaching associateships also available. Financial award application deadline: 2/15; financial award applicants required to submit FAFSA. *Faculty research:* At-risk; bilingual/multicultural, mathematics, special, and cross-cultural education. Total annual research expenditures: $1.3 million. *Unit head:* Graduate Coordinator, 509-335-9195, Fax: 509-335-2097, E-mail: gradstudies@wsu.edu. *Application contact:* Graduate School Admissions, 800-GRADWSU, Fax: 509-335-1949, E-mail: gradsch@wsu.edu.

Washington State University Spokane, Graduate Programs, Program in Education, Spokane, WA 99210. Offers educational leadership (Ed M, MA); principal (Certificate); professional certification for teachers (Certificate); program administrator (Certificate); school psychologist (Certificate); superintendent (Certificate); teaching (MIT). *Faculty:* 24. *Students:* 18 full-time (8 women), 38 part-time (25 women); includes 1 minority (Hispanic American). 22 applicants, 73% accepted, 8 enrolled. *Degree requirements:* For master's, comprehensive exam (for some programs), thesis (for some programs). *Entrance requirements:* For master's, GRE or GMAT, minimum GPA of 3.0, 3 letters of recommendation, resume. Additional exam requirements/recommendations for international students: Required—TOEFL (minimum score 550 paper-based; 213 computer-based). *Application deadline:* For fall admission, 1/10 priority date for domestic students, 1/10 for international students; for spring admission, 7/1 priority date for domestic students, 7/1 for international students. Application fee: $50. *Expenses:* Tuition, state resident: part-time $423 per credit. Tuition, nonresident: part-time $1032 per credit. *Financial support:* In 2009–10, 33 students received support, including research assistantships (averaging $14,634 per year), teaching assistantships (averaging $13,383 per year). Total annual research expenditures: $16,557. *Unit head:* Dr. Joan Kingrey, Director, 509-358-7939, Fax: 509-358-7900, E-mail: kingrey@wsu.edu. *Application contact:* Graduate School Admissions, 800-GRADWSU, Fax: 509-335-1949, E-mail: gradsch@wsu.edu.

Washington State University Tri-Cities, Graduate Programs, Program in Education, Richland, WA 99354. Offers counseling (Ed M); educational leadership (Ed M, Ed D); literacy (Ed M); secondary certification (Ed M); teaching (MIT). Part-time programs available. *Faculty:* 24. *Students:* 11 full-time (8 women), 97 part-time (80 women); includes 17 minority (1 African American, 3 Asian Americans or Pacific Islanders, 13 Hispanic Americans). Average age 36. In 2009, 39 master's awarded. *Degree requirements:* For master's, comprehensive exam, thesis or alternative; for doctorate, comprehensive exam, thesis/dissertation. *Entrance requirements:* For master's, GRE, minimum GPA of 3.0, Working with Youth form, Character and Fitness form, 3 letters of recommendation. Additional exam requirements/recommendations for international students: Required—TOEFL. *Application deadline:* For fall admission, 1/10 priority date for domestic students, 1/10 for international students; for spring admission, 7/1 priority date for domestic students, 7/1 for international students. Applications are processed on a rolling basis. Application fee: $50. Electronic applications accepted. *Expenses:* Tuition, state resident: part-time $423 per credit. Tuition, nonresident: part-time $1032 per credit. *Financial support:* In 2009–10, 59 students received support, including research assistantships (averaging $14,634 per year), teaching assistantships (averaging $13,383 per year); Federal Work-Study, scholarships/grants, and unspecified assistantships also available. Financial award application deadline: 2/15. *Faculty research:* Multicultural counseling, socio-cultural influences in schools, diverse learners, teacher education, K-12 educational leadership. *Unit head:* Dr. Elizabeth Nagel, Director, 509-372-7398, E-mail: elizabeth_nagel@tricity.wsu.edu. *Application contact:* Helen Berry, Academic Coordinator, 800-GRADWSU, Fax: 509-372-3796, E-mail: hberry@tricity.wsu.edu.

Washington State University Vancouver, Graduate Programs, Program in Education, Vancouver, WA 98686. Offers Ed M, MIT, Ed D. Part-time programs available. *Faculty:* 30. *Students:* 48 full-time (31 women), 132 part-time (93 women); includes 8 minority (1 American Indian/Alaska Native, 4 Asian Americans or Pacific Islanders, 3 Hispanic Americans). Average age 35. In 2009, 57 master's, 3 doctorates awarded. *Degree requirements:* For master's, comprehensive exam, thesis (for some programs); for doctorate, comprehensive exam, thesis/ dissertation. *Entrance requirements:* For master's, WEST-B, PRAXIS II (MIT), minimum GPA of 3.0, 3 letters of recommendation. Additional exam requirements/recommendations for international students: Required—TOEFL (minimum score 550 paper-based; 213 computer-based). *Application deadline:* For fall admission, 1/10 priority date for domestic students, 1/10 for international students; for spring admission, 7/1 priority date for domestic students, 7/1 for international students. Application fee: $50. *Expenses:* Tuition, state resident: full-time $4228; part-time $423 per credit. Tuition, nonresident: full-time $10,322; part-time $1032 per credit. *Financial support:* In 2009–10, research assistantships (averaging $14,634 per year), teaching assistantships (averaging $13,383 per year) were awarded; Federal Work-Study, scholarships/ grants, and unspecified assistantships also available. Financial award application deadline: 2/15. *Faculty research:* Language literacy and culture, developing learning community, developing teacher-mentors. Total annual research expenditures: $493,391. *Unit head:* Dr. June Canty, Academic Director, 360-546-9108, E-mail: canty@vancouver.wsu.edu. *Application contact:* Jillane Homme, Graduate Academic Coordinator, 360-546-9075, Fax: 360-546-9040, E-mail: jhomme22@vancouver.wsu.edu.

Washington University in St. Louis, Graduate School of Arts and Sciences, Department of Education, St. Louis, MO 63130-4899. Offers educational research (PhD); elementary education (MA Ed); secondary education (MA Ed, MAT). *Degree requirements:* For master's, thesis or alternative; for doctorate, thesis/dissertation. *Entrance requirements:* For master's, GRE General Test or MAT; for doctorate, GRE General Test. Electronic applications accepted.

Wayland Baptist University, Graduate Programs, Program in Education, Plainview, TX 79072-6998. Offers education administration (M Ed); higher education administration (M Ed); instructional leadership (M Ed); instructional technology (M Ed); special education (M Ed). Part-time and evening/weekend programs available. Postbaccalaureate distance learning degree programs offered (no on-campus study). *Faculty:* 6 full-time (4 women). *Students:* 4 full-time (2 women), 45 part-time (26 women); includes 6 minority (3 African Americans, 3 Hispanic Americans). Average age 30. 26 applicants, 77% accepted, 9 enrolled. In 2009, 4 master's awarded. *Degree requirements:* For master's, comprehensive exam, capstone course. *Entrance requirements:* For master's, GRE, GMAT or MAT. Additional exam requirements/ recommendations for international students: Required—TOEFL (minimum score 500 paper-based; 173 computer-based; 61 iBT). *Application deadline:* Applications are processed on a rolling basis. Application fee: $50. Electronic applications accepted. *Expenses:* Tuition: Full-time $5796; part-time $322 per credit hour. Required fees: $782; $9 per credit hour. $60 per semester. Tuition and fees vary according to course load and campus/location. *Financial support:* Federal Work-Study, institutionally sponsored loans, and scholarships/grants available. Support available to part-time students. Financial award application deadline: 5/1; financial award applicants required to submit FAFSA. *Unit head:* Dr. Jim Todd, Chairman, 806-291-1045, Fax: 806-291-1951. *Application contact:* Amanda Stanton, Graduate Studies, 806-291-3423, Fax: 806-291-1950, E-mail: stanton@wbu.edu.

Waynesburg University, Graduate and Professional Studies, Waynesburg, PA 15370-1222. Offers business (MBA), including finance, health systems, human resources, leadership, market development; counseling (MA), including addictions counseling, clinical mental health; education (MAT); nursing (MSN), including administration, education, informatics, palliative care; nursing practice (DNP); special education (M Ed); technology (M Ed); MSN/MBA. *Accreditation:* AACN. Part-time and evening/weekend programs available. *Faculty:* 11 full-time (5 women), 136 part-time/adjunct (80 women). *Students:* 116 full-time (85 women), 984 part-time (682 women). 711 applicants, 80% accepted, 485 enrolled. In 2009, 320 master's, 41 doctorates awarded. *Degree requirements:* For doctorate, thesis/dissertation. *Entrance requirements:* Additional exam requirements/recommendations for international students: Required—TOEFL. *Application deadline:* For fall admission, 8/1 priority date for domestic students. Applications are processed on a rolling basis. Electronic applications accepted. *Expenses:* Tuition: Part-time $520 per credit. *Financial support:* Available to part-time students. Application deadline: 5/1. *Unit head:* David Mariner, Dean, 724-743-4420, Fax: 724-743-4425, E-mail: dmariner@waynesburg.edu. *Application contact:* Michael Bednarski, Director of Admissions, 724-743-4420, Fax: 724-743-4425, E-mail: mbednars@waynesburg.edu.

Wayne State College, School of Education and Counseling, Wayne, NE 68787. Offers MSE, Ed S. *Accreditation:* NCATE. Part-time and evening/weekend programs available. *Degree requirements:* For master's, comprehensive exam, thesis (for some programs). *Entrance requirements:* For master's, GRE General Test, minimum cumulative GPA of 3.0; for Ed S, GRE General Test, minimum GPA of 3.2 in all program coursework. Additional exam requirements/recommendations for international students: Required—TOEFL (minimum score 550 paper-based; 213 computer-based).

Wayne State University, College of Education, Detroit, MI 48202. Offers M Ed, MA, MAT, Ed D, PhD, Certificate, Ed S. Evening/weekend programs available. Terminal master's awarded

for partial completion of doctoral program. *Degree requirements:* For doctorate, thesis/dissertation. *Entrance requirements:* Additional exam requirements/recommendations for international students: Required—TOEFL (minimum score 550 paper-based; 213 computer-based); Recommended—TWE (minimum score 6). Electronic applications accepted. *Faculty research:* Alternative routes to teacher certification; innovations in science, mathematics and technology education; literacy; k-12 school reform, including special education and self-determination for special populations; adult workplace learning.

See Close-Up on page 725.

Weber State University, Jerry and Vickie Moyes College of Education, Ogden, UT 84408-1001. Offers M Ed, MSAT. *Accreditation:* NCATE. Part-time and evening/weekend programs available. *Degree requirements:* For master's, project presentation and exam. *Entrance requirements:* Additional exam requirements/recommendations for international students: Required—TOEFL (minimum score 550 paper-based; 213 computer-based), American Council on the Teaching of Foreign Languages test.

Webster University, School of Education, St. Louis, MO 63119-3194. Offers MAT, Ed S. *Accreditation:* NCATE. Part-time programs available. Postbaccalaureate distance learning degree programs offered (no on-campus study). *Faculty:* 21 full-time, 73 part-time/adjunct. *Students:* 159 full-time (122 women), 726 part-time (595 women); includes 209 minority (187 African Americans, 4 American Indian/Alaska Native, 8 Asian Americans or Pacific Islanders, 10 Hispanic Americans), 2 international. Average age 35. 183 applicants, 100% accepted, 132 enrolled. In 2009, 345 master's, 12 other advanced degrees awarded. *Degree requirements:* For master's, thesis (for some programs). *Entrance requirements:* For master's, minimum GPA of 2.5. Additional exam requirements/recommendations for international students: Required—TOEFL. *Application deadline:* Applications are processed on a rolling basis. Application fee: $35 ($50 for international students). *Expenses:* Tuition: Part-time $565 per credit hour. Tuition and fees vary according to degree level, campus/location and program. *Financial support:* Career-related internships or fieldwork and Federal Work-Study available. Support available to part-time students. Financial award application deadline: 4/1; financial award applicants required to submit FAFSA. *Unit head:* Dr. Brenda Fyfe, Dean, 314-968-6913, Fax: 314-968-7118, E-mail: fyfebv@webster.edu. *Application contact:* Matt Nolan, Associate Vice President for Enrollment Management/Dean of Admissions, Fax: 314-968-7116, E-mail: gadmit@webster.edu.

Wesleyan College, Department of Education, Macon, GA 31210-4462. Offers early childhood education (MA). Part-time programs available. *Degree requirements:* For master's, thesis or alternative, practicum, professional portfolio. *Entrance requirements:* For master's, GRE or MAT, interview, teaching certificate, 3 letters of recommendation. Additional exam requirements/recommendations for international students: Required—TOEFL. *Faculty research:* Neuroscience, gender bias in science and mathematics.

Wesley College, Education Program, Dover, DE 19901-3875. Offers M Ed, MA Ed, MAT. *Accreditation:* NCATE. Part-time and evening/weekend programs available. *Degree requirements:* For master's, thesis optional. *Entrance requirements:* For master's, GRE. *Faculty research:* Learning styles, community-higher education partnerships, curriculum models, science learning and teaching, literacy development in early elementary.

West Chester University of Pennsylvania, Office of Graduate Studies, College of Education, West Chester, PA 19383. Offers M Ed, MS, Certificate, Teaching Certificate. *Accreditation:* NCATE. Part-time and evening/weekend programs available. *Students:* 85 full-time (74 women), 649 part-time (575 women); includes 62 minority (38 African Americans, 1 American Indian/Alaska Native, 10 Asian Americans or Pacific Islanders, 13 Hispanic Americans), 2 international. Average age 29. 406 applicants, 96% accepted, 241 enrolled. In 2009, 233 master's, 23 other advanced degrees awarded. *Entrance requirements:* Additional exam requirements/recommendations for international students: Required—TOEFL (minimum score 550 paper-based; 213 computer-based; 80 iBT). *Application deadline:* For fall admission, 4/15 priority date for domestic students, 3/15 for international students; for spring admission, 10/15 for domestic students, 9/1 for international students. Applications are processed on a rolling basis. Application fee: $35. Electronic applications accepted. *Expenses:* Tuition, state resident: full-time $6666; part-time $370 per credit. Tuition, nonresident: full-time $10,666; part-time $593 per credit. Required fees: $122.56 per credit. *Financial support:* In 2009–10, 30 research assistantships with full and partial tuition reimbursements (averaging $5,000 per year) were awarded; unspecified assistantships also available. Support available to part-time students. Financial award application deadline: 2/15; financial award applicants required to submit FAFSA. *Unit head:* Dr. Joseph Malak, Dean, 610-436-2428, E-mail: jmalak@wcupa.edu. *Application contact:* Office of Graduate Studies, 610-436-2943, Fax: 610-436-2763, E-mail: gradstudy@wcupa.edu.

Western Carolina University, Graduate School, College of Education and Allied Professions, Cullowhee, NC 28723. Offers M Ed, MA, MA Ed, MAT, MS, MSA, Ed D, Ed S, PMC. *Accreditation:* NCATE. Part-time and evening/weekend programs available. Postbaccalaureate distance learning degree programs offered. *Students:* 201 full-time (151 women), 606 part-time (440 women). Average age 35. 456 applicants, 71% accepted, 244 enrolled. In 2009, 142 master's, 13 doctorates, 5 other advanced degrees awarded. *Degree requirements:* For master's, comprehensive exam, thesis; for doctorate, comprehensive exam, thesis/dissertation. *Entrance requirements:* For master's, GRE, appropriate undergraduate degree with minimum GPA of 3.0, 3 recommendations, writing sample, resume, interview; for doctorate, GRE General Test, minimum graduate GPA of 3.5, appropriate master's degree; for other advanced degree, GRE General Test, minimum graduate GPA of 3.5, work experience, appropriate master's degree. Additional exam requirements/recommendations for international students: Required—TOEFL (minimum score 550 paper-based; 270 computer-based; 79 iBT). *Application deadline:* For fall admission, 2/1 for domestic students; for spring admission, 9/1 priority date for domestic students. Applications are processed on a rolling basis. Application fee: $45. *Financial support:* In 2009–10, 102 students received support, including 2 fellowships (averaging $6,000 per year), 46 research assistantships with full and partial tuition reimbursements available (averaging $7,246 per year), 54 teaching assistantships with full and partial tuition reimbursements available (averaging $7,037 per year); career-related internships or fieldwork, institutionally sponsored loans, scholarships/grants, and unspecified assistantships also available. Financial award application deadline: 3/31; financial award applicants required to submit FAFSA. *Faculty research:* Evolutionary psychology, marital and family development, program evaluation, rural education, special education, educational leadership, employee recruitment/retention. *Unit head:* Dr. A. Michael Dougherty, Dean, 828-227-7311, Fax: 828-227-7388, E-mail: dougherty@email.wcu.edu. *Application contact:* Admissions Specialist for Education and Allied Professions, 828-227-7398, Fax: 828-227-7480, E-mail: gradsch@email.wcu.edu.

Western Connecticut State University, Division of Graduate Studies, School of Professional Studies, Department of Education and Educational Psychology, Danbury, CT 06810-6885. Offers community counseling (MS); counselor education (MS), including guidance and counseling; curriculum (MS); English education (MS); guidance and counseling (MS); instructional leadership (Ed D); instructional technology (MS); mathematics education (MS); reading (MS); school counseling (MS); secondary education (MAT), including biology option, mathematics option; special education (MS). *Accreditation:* NCATE. Part-time programs available. *Faculty:* 11 full-time (7 women), 13 part-time/adjunct (7 women). *Students:* 54 full-time (41 women), 290 part-time (224 women); includes 14 minority (4 African Americans, 3 American Indian/Alaska Native, 1 Asian American or Pacific Islander, 6 Hispanic Americans). Average age 34. 90 applicants, 100% accepted, 90 enrolled. In 2009, 94 master's, 2 doctorates awarded. *Degree requirements:* For master's, thesis or alternative, completion of program in 6 years. *Entrance requirements:* For master's, MAT (if GPA is below 2.8), valid teaching certificate, letters of reference; for doctorate, GRE or MAT, resume, three recommendations (one in a supervisory capacity in an educational setting), satisfactory interview with WCSU representatives from the EdD Admissions Committee. Additional exam requirements/recommendations for international students: Recommended—TOEFL (minimum score 550 paper-based; 213 computer-based; 79 iBT), IELTS (minimum score 6). *Application deadline:* For fall admission, 8/5 priority date for domestic students; for spring admission, 1/5 for domestic students. Applications are processed on a rolling basis. Application fee: $50. *Expenses:* Contact institution. *Financial support:* In 2009–10, 3 students received support. Scholarships/grants available. Financial award application deadline: 5/1; financial award applicants required to submit FAFSA. *Unit head:* Dr. Theresa Canada, Chairperson, Department of Education and Educational Psychology, 203-837-8509, Fax: 203-837-8413, E-mail: canadat@wcsu.edu. *Application contact:* Chris Shankle, Associate Director of Graduate Studies, 203-837-9005, Fax: 203-837-8326, E-mail: shanklec@wcsu.edu.

Western Governors University, Teachers College, Salt Lake City, UT 84107. Offers English language learning (K-12) (MA); learning and technology (M Ed, MA); management and innovation (M Ed); mathematics education (5-12) (MA); mathematics education (5-9) (MA); mathematics education (K-6) (MA); measurement and evaluation (M Ed); science (5-12) (MA), including biology, geology; science education (5-9) (MA); teaching (MAT); technology for principals (Post-Graduate Certificate). *Accreditation:* NCATE. Part-time and evening/weekend programs available. Postbaccalaureate distance learning degree programs offered (no on-campus study). *Degree requirements:* For master's, comprehensive exam. *Entrance requirements:* Additional exam requirements/recommendations for international students: Required—TOEFL (minimum score 450 paper-based). Electronic applications accepted. *Expenses:* Contact institution.

Western Illinois University, School of Graduate Studies, College of Education and Human Services, Macomb, IL 61455-1390. Offers MA, MS, MS Ed, Ed D, Certificate, Ed S. *Accreditation:* NCATE. Part-time and evening/weekend programs available. Postbaccalaureate distance learning degree programs offered (no on-campus study). *Students:* 297 full-time (166 women), 758 part-time (539 women); includes 81 minority (42 African Americans, 3 American Indian/Alaska Native, 8 Asian Americans or Pacific Islanders, 28 Hispanic Americans), 34 international. Average age 32. 394 applicants, 56% accepted. In 2009, 337 master's, 6 doctorates, 20 other advanced degrees awarded. *Degree requirements:* For master's, comprehensive exam (for some programs), thesis or alternative; for doctorate, comprehensive exam, thesis/dissertation, electronic portfolio. *Entrance requirements:* For master's, GRE and MAT (for selected programs); for doctorate, GRE. Additional exam requirements/recommendations for international students: Required—TOEFL. *Application deadline:* Applications are processed on a rolling basis. Application fee: $30. Electronic applications accepted. *Expenses:* Tuition, state resident: full-time $4486; part-time $249.21 per credit hour. Tuition, nonresident: full-time $8972; part-time $498.42 per credit hour. Required fees: $72.62 per credit hour. *Financial support:* In 2009–10, 173 students received support, including 157 research assistantships with full tuition reimbursements available (averaging $7,280 per year), 16 teaching assistantships with full tuition reimbursements available (averaging $8,400 per year). Financial award applicants required to submit FAFSA. *Unit head:* Dr. Bernard N. DiGrino, Interim Dean, 309-298-1690. *Application contact:* Evelyn Hoing, Assistant Director of Graduate Studies, 309-298-1806, Fax: 309-298-2345, E-mail: grad-office@wiu.edu.

Western New Mexico University, Graduate Division, School of Education, Silver City, NM 88062-0680. Offers bilingual education (MAT); counseling (MA); educational leadership (MA); elementary education (MAT); reading (MAT); school psychology (MA); secondary education (MAT); special education (MAT); TESOL (teaching English to speakers of other languages) (MAT). *Accreditation:* NCATE. *Degree requirements:* For master's, comprehensive exam. *Entrance requirements:* For master's, GRE General Test, GRE Subject Test, minimum GPA of 3.2 in last 64 hours of undergraduate study. Additional exam requirements/recommendations for international students: Required—TOEFL (minimum score 550 paper-based; 213 computer-based). Electronic applications accepted.

Western Oregon University, Graduate Programs, College of Education, Monmouth, OR 97361-1394. Offers MAT, MS, MS Ed. *Accreditation:* NCATE. Part-time and evening/weekend programs available. Postbaccalaureate distance learning degree programs offered (minimal on-campus study). *Degree requirements:* For master's, comprehensive exam (for some programs), thesis optional, written exam. *Entrance requirements:* For master's, minimum GPA of 3.0. Additional exam requirements/recommendations for international students: Required—TOEFL (minimum score 550 paper-based; 213 computer-based; 79 iBT), IELTS (minimum score 6.5). *Faculty research:* Effectiveness of work, sample methodology, documentation of learning gains, appropriateness of advanced proficiency.

Western Washington University, Graduate School, Woodring College of Education, Bellingham, WA 98225-5996. Offers M Ed, MA, MIT. *Accreditation:* NCATE. Part-time programs available. Postbaccalaureate distance learning degree programs offered (minimal on-campus study). *Degree requirements:* For master's, comprehensive exam, thesis optional. *Entrance requirements:* For master's, GRE General Test or MAT, minimum GPA of 3.0 in last 60 semester hours or last 90 quarter hours. Additional exam requirements/recommendations for international students: Required—TOEFL (minimum score 567 paper-based; 227 computer-based). Electronic applications accepted.

Westfield State College, Division of Graduate and Continuing Education, Department of Education, Westfield, MA 01086. Offers early childhood education (M Ed); elementary education (M Ed); occupational education (M Ed, CAGS); reading (M Ed); school administration (M Ed, CAGS); secondary education (M Ed); special education (M Ed); technology for educators (M Ed). *Accreditation:* NCATE. Part-time and evening/weekend programs available. *Degree requirements:* For master's, comprehensive exam; for CAGS, research-based field internship. *Entrance requirements:* For master's, GRE General Test or MAT, minimum undergraduate GPA of 2.7; for CAGS, master's degree. *Faculty research:* Collaborative teacher education, developmental early childhood education.

West Liberty University, School of Education, West Liberty, WV 26074. Offers MA Ed. *Accreditation:* NCATE. *Degree requirements:* For master's, capstone experience. *Entrance requirements:* For master's, GRE or MAT, minimum GPA of 2.5, teaching license, interview. Electronic applications accepted.

Westminster College, Programs in Education, New Wilmington, PA 16172-0001. Offers administration (M Ed, Certificate); general education (M Ed); guidance and counseling (M Ed, Certificate); reading (M Ed, Certificate). Part-time and evening/weekend programs available. *Degree requirements:* For master's, comprehensive exam, portfolio. *Entrance requirements:* For master's, GRE or MAT, minimum GPA of 3.0.

Westminster College, School of Education, Salt Lake City, UT 84105-3697. Offers community leadership (MA); education (M Ed); teaching (MAT). *Accreditation:* Teacher Education Accreditation Council. Part-time and evening/weekend programs available. *Faculty:* 12 full-time (10 women), 36 part-time/adjunct (26 women). *Students:* 96 full-time (71 women), 46 part-time (32 women); includes 7 minority (1 African American, 2 Asian Americans or Pacific Islanders, 4 Hispanic Americans), 1 international. Average age 32. 137 applicants, 72% accepted, 88 enrolled. In 2009, 28 master's awarded. *Degree requirements:* For master's, project or thesis. *Entrance requirements:* For master's, personal resume, 2 professional recommendations, minimum GPA of 3.0, copy of current teaching certificate. Additional exam requirements/recommendations for international students: Required—TOEFL (minimum score 600 paper-based). *Application deadline:* Applications are processed on a rolling basis. Application fee: $40. Electronic applications accepted. *Expenses:* Contact institution. *Financial support:* In 2009–10, 56 students received support. Career-related internships or fieldwork and tuition reimbursement, tuition remission available. Support available to part-time students. Financial award applicants required to submit FAFSA. *Faculty research:* Early childhood literacy, English as a Second Language instruction, special education, instruction in teacher education, e-portfolios as assessment tools, funds of knowledge. *Unit head:* Robert Shaw, Interim Dean, 801-832-2470, Fax: 801-832-3105. *Application contact:* Joel Bauman, Vice President of Enrollment Services, 801-832-2200, Fax: 801-832-3101, E-mail: admission@westminstercollege.edu.

West Texas A&M University, College of Education and Social Sciences, Division of Education, Canyon, TX 79016-0001. Offers administration (M Ed); counseling education (M Ed); curriculum and instruction (M Ed); educational diagnostician (M Ed); educational technology (M Ed); professional counseling (MA); reading (M Ed); special education (M Ed). Part-time and evening/

Education—General

West Texas A&M University (continued)

weekend programs available. Postbaccalaureate distance learning degree programs offered (minimal on-campus study). *Degree requirements:* For master's, comprehensive exam, thesis optional. *Entrance requirements:* For master's, GRE General Test. Additional exam requirements/recommendations for international students: Required—TOEFL (minimum score 550 paper-based). Electronic applications accepted. *Faculty research:* Modified internship for novice teachers, effective instructional strategies, cognitive-relational group, community college, recruitment/retention.

West Virginia University, College of Human Resources and Education, Morgantown, WV 26506. Offers MA, MS, Au D, Ed D, PhD. *Accreditation:* NCATE. Part-time and evening/weekend programs available. Postbaccalaureate distance learning degree programs offered (no on-campus study). *Degree requirements:* For master's, content exams; for doctorate, comprehensive exam, thesis/dissertation. *Entrance requirements:* Additional exam requirements/recommendations for international students: Required—TOEFL. Electronic applications accepted. *Faculty research:* Internet training and integration for teachers, rural education, teacher preparation, organization of schools, evaluation of personnel.

West Virginia Wesleyan College, Department of Education, Buckhannon, WV 26201. Offers M Ed. *Accreditation:* NCATE. *Expenses:* Tuition: Part-time $360 per credit hour.

Wheaton College, Graduate School, Department of Education, Wheaton, IL 60187-5593. Offers elementary level (MAT); secondary level (MAT). *Accreditation:* NCATE. *Degree requirements:* For master's, thesis or alternative. *Entrance requirements:* For master's, GRE General Test. Electronic applications accepted.

Wheelock College, Graduate Programs, Boston, MA 02215-4176. Offers MS, MSW. *Accreditation:* NCATE (one or more programs are accredited). Part-time and evening/weekend programs available. Postbaccalaureate distance learning degree programs offered (minimal on-campus study). *Entrance requirements:* For master's, interview. Additional exam requirements/recommendations for international students: Required—TOEFL (minimum score 550 paper-based; 260 computer-based). *Faculty research:* Teacher development and leadership, national standards science education, high academic achievement for students of color, cultural influences on development, media literacy.

Whittier College, Graduate Programs, Department of Education and Child Development, Whittier, CA 90608-0634. Offers educational administration (MA Ed); elementary education (MA Ed); secondary education (MA Ed). Part-time and evening/weekend programs available. *Degree requirements:* For master's, thesis. *Entrance requirements:* For master's, GRE General Test, MAT, minimum GPA of 3.5, academic writing sample.

Whitworth University, School of Education, Graduate Studies in Education, Spokane, WA 99251-0001. Offers administration (M Ed); counseling (M Ed), including school counselors, social agency/church setting; elementary education (M Ed); gifted and talented (MAT); secondary education (M Ed); special education (MAT); teaching (MIT). *Accreditation:* NCATE. Part-time and evening/weekend programs available. *Degree requirements:* For master's, comprehensive exam, thesis (for some programs). *Entrance requirements:* For master's, GRE General Test, MAT. Additional exam requirements/recommendations for international students: Required—TOEFL. Tuition and fees vary according to program. *Faculty research:* Rural program development, mainstreaming, special needs learners.

Wichita State University, Graduate School, College of Education, Wichita, KS 67260. Offers M Ed, MAT, Ed D, Ed S. *Accreditation:* NCATE. Part-time and evening/weekend programs available. *Expenses:* Tuition, state resident: full-time $4247; part-time $235.95 per credit hour. Tuition, nonresident: full-time $11,171; part-time $620.60 per credit hour. Required fees: $34; $3.60 per credit hour. $17 per term. Tuition and fees vary according to campus/location and program. *Unit head:* Dr. Pearl Sharon Iorio, Dean, 316-978-3301, Fax: 316-978-3302, E-mail: sharon.iorio@wichita.edu. *Application contact:* Dr. Pearl Sharon Iorio, Dean, 316-978-3301, Fax: 316-978-3302, E-mail: sharon.iorio@wichita.edu.

Widener University, School of Human Service Professions, Center for Education, Chester, PA 19013-5792. Offers adult education (M Ed); counseling in higher education (M Ed); counselor education (M Ed); early childhood education (M Ed); educational foundations (M Ed); educational leadership (M Ed); educational psychology (M Ed); elementary education (M Ed); English and language arts (M Ed); health education (M Ed); higher education leadership (Ed D); home and school visitor (M Ed); human sexuality (M Ed); mathematics education (M Ed); middle school education (M Ed); principalship (M Ed); reading and language arts (Ed D); reading education (M Ed); school administration (Ed D); science education (M Ed); social studies education (M Ed); special education (M Ed); technology education (M Ed). *Accreditation:* NCATE. Part-time and evening/weekend programs available. *Faculty:* 34 full-time (22 women), 37 part-time/adjunct (14 women). *Students:* 203 full-time (154 women), 415 part-time (298 women); includes 50 minority (34 African Americans, 1 American Indian/Alaska Native, 5 Asian Americans or Pacific Islanders, 10 Hispanic Americans), 3 international. Average age 39. 139 applicants, 88% accepted. In 2009, 168 master's, 31 doctorates awarded. Terminal master's awarded for partial completion of doctoral program. *Degree requirements:* For doctorate, thesis/dissertation. *Entrance requirements:* For master's, minimum GPA of 2.5; for doctorate, GRE or MAT, minimum GPA of 2.0 (undergraduate), 3.5 (graduate). *Application deadline:* Applications are processed on a rolling basis. Application fee: $25 ($300 for international students). Electronic applications accepted. *Expenses:* Contact institution. *Financial support:* Career-related internships or fieldwork, tuition waivers (full and partial), and unspecified assistantships available. Support available to part-time students. Financial award application deadline: 5/1. *Faculty research:* Reading and cognition, adult education, technology education, educational leadership, special education. *Unit head:* Dr. Michael W. LeDoux, Associate Dean, 610-499-4294, Fax: 610-499-4623, E-mail: mwledoux@widener.edu. *Application contact:* Dr. Roberta D. Nolan, Director of Graduate Admissions, 610-499-4125, E-mail: rdnolan@widener.edu.

Wilkes University, College of Graduate and Professional Studies, School of Education, Wilkes-Barre, PA 18766-0002. Offers classroom technology (MS Ed); educational computing (MS Ed); educational development and strategies (MS Ed); educational leadership (MS Ed); educational technology (Ed D); elementary education (MS Ed); higher education administration (Ed D); instructional technology (MS Ed); K-12 administration (Ed D); online teaching (MS Ed); school business leadership (MS Ed); secondary education (MS Ed), including biology, chemistry, English, history; special education (MS Ed). Part-time and evening/weekend programs available. Postbaccalaureate distance learning degree programs offered (minimal on-campus study). *Students:* 89 full-time (60 women), 2,849 part-time (2,058 women); includes 52 minority (10 African Americans, 2 American Indian/Alaska Native, 13 Asian Americans or Pacific Islanders, 27 Hispanic Americans), 6 international. Average age 33. In 2009, 947 master's awarded. *Entrance requirements:* Additional exam requirements/recommendations for international students: Required—TOEFL (minimum score 500 paper-based; 173 computer-based; 79 iBT). *Application deadline:* Applications are processed on a rolling basis. Application fee: $45. *Expenses:* Contact institution. *Financial support:* Federal Work-Study and unspecified assistantships available. Financial award application deadline: 3/1; financial award applicants required to submit FAFSA. *Unit head:* Dr. Michael Speziale, Dean, 570-408-4679, Fax: 570-408-4905, E-mail: michael.speziale@wilkes.edu. *Application contact:* Kathleen Houlihan, Director of Graduate Studies, 570-408-3235, Fax: 570-408-7846, E-mail: kathleen.houlihan@wilkes.edu.

Willamette University, School of Education, Salem, OR 97301-3931. Offers teaching (MAT). *Accreditation:* NCATE. Evening/weekend programs available. *Degree requirements:* For master's, leadership project (action research). *Entrance requirements:* For master's, California Basic Educational Skills Test, Multiple Subject Assessment for Teachers, PRAXIS, minimum GPA of 3.0, classroom experience, 2 letters of reference. Electronic applications accepted. *Expenses:* Contact institution. *Faculty research:* Educational leadership, multicultural education, middle school education, clinical supervision, educational technology.

William Carey University, School of Education, Hattiesburg, MS 39401-5499. Offers art education (M Ed); art of teaching (M Ed); elementary education (M Ed, Ed S); English education

(M Ed); gifted education (M Ed); history and social science (M Ed); mild/moderate disabilities (M Ed); secondary education (M Ed). Part-time programs available. *Degree requirements:* For master's, comprehensive exam. *Entrance requirements:* For master's, GRE, MAT, minimum GPA of 2.5, Class A teacher's license. Additional exam requirements/recommendations for international students: Required—TOEFL (minimum score 550 paper-based; 213 computer-based).

William Howard Taft University, Graduate Programs, The Boyer Graduate School of Education, Santa Ana, CA 92704. Offers M Ed.

William Paterson University of New Jersey, College of Education, Wayne, NJ 07470-8420. Offers curriculum and learning (M Ed); educational leadership (M Ed); reading (M Ed); special education and counseling services (M Ed), including counseling services, special education; teaching (MAT). *Accreditation:* NCATE. Part-time and evening/weekend programs available. *Students:* 119 full-time (100 women), 662 part-time (550 women); includes 111 minority (25 African Americans, 1 American Indian/Alaska Native, 9 Asian Americans or Pacific Islanders, 76 Hispanic Americans), 2 international. *Degree requirements:* For master's, comprehensive exam. *Entrance requirements:* For master's, GRE General Test, MAT, minimum GPA of 2.75, teaching certificate. *Application deadline:* Applications are processed on a rolling basis. Application fee: $50. Electronic applications accepted. *Financial support:* Research assistantships with full tuition reimbursements, career-related internships or fieldwork, Federal Work-Study, and unspecified assistantships available. Support available to part-time students. Financial award application deadline: 4/1; financial award applicants required to submit FAFSA. *Faculty research:* Urban community service. *Unit head:* Dr. Candace Burns, Dean, 973-720-2137, Fax: 973-720-2955, E-mail: burnsc@wpunj.edu. *Application contact:* Liana Fornarotto, Assistant Director, Graduate Admissions, 973-720-3578, Fax: 973-720-2035, E-mail: fornarottol@wpunj.edu.

Wilmington College, Department of Education, Wilmington, OH 45177. Offers reading (M Ed); special education (M Ed). Part-time programs available. *Degree requirements:* For master's, comprehensive exam. *Entrance requirements:* For master's, GRE or MAT, minimum GPA of 3.0, 2 letters of recommendation. Additional exam requirements/recommendations for international students: Required—TOEFL. *Faculty research:* Reading instruction, special education practices, conflict resolution in the schools, models of higher education for teachers.

Wilmington University, College of Education, New Castle, DE 19720-6491. Offers applied education technology (M Ed); career and technical education (M Ed); elementary and secondary school counseling (M Ed); elementary special education (M Ed); elementary studies (M Ed); instruction: gifted and talented (M Ed); instruction: teaching and learning (M Ed); literacy (M Ed); reading (M Ed); school leadership (M Ed); secondary teaching (MAT). *Accreditation:* NCATE. Part-time and evening/weekend programs available. *Entrance requirements:* For master's, 2 letters of recommendation, interview. Additional exam requirements/recommendations for international students: Required—TOEFL (minimum score 500 paper-based; 173 computer-based). Electronic applications accepted.

Wilson College, Program in Education, Chambersburg, PA 17201-1285. Offers M Ed. Evening/weekend programs available. *Degree requirements:* For master's, project. *Entrance requirements:* For master's, PRAXIS, minimum undergraduate cumulative GPA of 3.0, 2 letters of recommendation, current certification for eligibility to teach in grades K-12, resume, personal interview. Electronic applications accepted.

Wingate University, Program in Education, Wingate, NC 28174-0159. Offers educational leadership (MA Ed); elementary education (MA Ed, MAT); physical education (MA Ed); sport administration (MA Ed). *Accreditation:* NCATE. Part-time and evening/weekend programs available. *Degree requirements:* For master's, portfolio. *Entrance requirements:* For master's, GRE General Test or MAT, teaching certificate (MA Ed).

Winona State University, College of Education, Department of Education, Winona, MN 55987-5838. Offers MS. *Accreditation:* NCATE. Part-time and evening/weekend programs available. *Degree requirements:* For master's, comprehensive exam, thesis (for some programs). *Entrance requirements:* For master's, minimum GPA of 2.75/teaching license.

Winthrop University, College of Education, Rock Hill, SC 29733. Offers M Ed, MAT, MS. *Accreditation:* NCATE. Part-time programs available. *Entrance requirements:* Additional exam requirements/recommendations for international students: Required—TOEFL (minimum paper-based score of 520, computer-based 190, iBT 68) or IELTS (minimum score of 6). Electronic applications accepted.

Wittenberg University, Graduate Program, Springfield, OH 45501-0720. Offers education (MA). *Accreditation:* NCATE.

Worcester State College, Graduate Studies, Department of Education, Worcester, MA 01602-2597. Offers early childhood education (M Ed); elementary education (M Ed); leadership and administration (M Ed, CAGS); middle school education (M Ed); moderate special needs (M Ed); reading (M Ed, CAGS); school psychology (M Ed, CAGS); secondary education (M Ed). Part-time and evening/weekend programs available. *Faculty:* 9 full-time (7 women), 19 part-time/adjunct (7 women). *Students:* 30 full-time (25 women), 237 part-time (180 women); includes 14 minority (3 African Americans, 2 Asian Americans or Pacific Islanders, 9 Hispanic Americans), 2 international. Average age 34. 302 applicants, 75% accepted, 77 enrolled. In 2009, 109 master's, 189 CAGSs awarded. *Degree requirements:* For master's, comprehensive exam (for some programs), thesis optional. *Entrance requirements:* For master's, GRE General Test, MAT or GMAT, teaching certificate. Additional exam requirements/recommendations for international students: Required—TOEFL (minimum score 550 paper-based; 213 computer-based; 79 iBT). *Application deadline:* Applications are processed on a rolling basis. Application fee: $30. *Expenses:* Tuition, area resident: Part-time $150 per credit. Tuition, state resident: part-time $150 per credit. Tuition, nonresident: part-time $150 per credit. Required fees: $85. *Financial support:* In 2009–10, 8 students received support, including 8 research assistantships with full tuition reimbursements available (averaging $4,800 per year); career-related internships or fieldwork, scholarships/grants, and unspecified assistantships also available. Financial award application deadline: 3/1; financial award applicants required to submit FAFSA. *Unit head:* Dr. Elaine Tateronis, Coordinator, 508-929-8823, Fax: 508-929-8164, E-mail: etateronis@worcester.edu. *Application contact:* Nicole Brown, Assistant Dean of Graduate and Continuing Education, 508-929-8787, Fax: 508-929-8100, E-mail: nbrown@worcester.edu.

Wright State University, School of Graduate Studies, College of Education and Human Services, Dayton, OH 45435. Offers M Ed, MA, MRC, MS, MST, Ed S. *Accreditation:* NCATE. Part-time and evening/weekend programs available. *Degree requirements:* For Ed S, thesis. *Entrance requirements:* For master's, GRE General Test, MAT, PRAXIS II; for Ed S, GRE General Test, MAT. Additional exam requirements/recommendations for international students: Required—TOEFL.

Xavier University, College of Social Sciences, Health and Education, School of Education, Cincinnati, OH 45207. Offers M Ed, MA, MS. *Accreditation:* Teacher Education Accreditation Council. *Faculty:* 22 full-time (11 women), 73 part-time/adjunct (39 women). *Students:* 298 full-time (218 women), 557 part-time (430 women); includes 93 minority (70 African Americans, 1 American Indian/Alaska Native, 7 Asian Americans or Pacific Islanders, 15 Hispanic Americans), 6 international. Average age 33. 247 applicants, 91% accepted, 165 enrolled. In 2009, 361 master's awarded. *Entrance requirements:* Additional exam requirements/recommendations for international students: Required—TOEFL (minimum score 550 paper-based; 213 computer-based; 79 iBT). *Application deadline:* Applications are processed on a rolling basis. Application fee: $35. Electronic applications accepted. *Expenses:* Contact institution. *Financial support:* In 2009–10, 518 students received support. Applicants required to submit FAFSA. *Unit head:* Dr. Jennifer Fager, Associate Dean, 513-745-3495, Fax: 513-745-1052, E-mail: fagerj@xavier.edu. *Application contact:* Dr. Jennifer Fager, Associate Dean, 513-745-3495, Fax: 513-745-1052, E-mail: fagerj@xavier.edu.

Xavier University of Louisiana, Graduate School, Programs in Education, New Orleans, LA 70125-1098. Offers curriculum and instruction (MA); education administration and supervision (MA); guidance and counseling (MA). *Accreditation:* NCATE. Part-time and evening/weekend programs available. *Degree requirements:* For master's, comprehensive exam, thesis or alternative. *Entrance requirements:* For master's, GRE General Test, MAT, minimum GPA of 2.5. Additional exam requirements/recommendations for international students: Required—TOEFL.

York College of Pennsylvania, Department of Education, York, PA 17405-7199. Offers M Ed. Part-time and evening/weekend programs available. *Faculty:* 3 full-time (2 women), 6 part-time/adjunct (4 women). *Students:* 1 (woman) full-time, 84 part-time (67 women); includes 1 minority (African American). Average age 31. 21 applicants, 67% accepted, 11 enrolled. In 2009, 30 master's awarded. *Degree requirements:* For master's, thesis optional, portfolio. *Entrance requirements:* For master's, GRE, MAT or PRAXIS, letters of recommendation, portfolio. Additional exam requirements/recommendations for international students: Required—TOEFL (minimum score 530 paper-based; 200 computer-based; 72 iBT). *Application deadline:* For fall admission, 7/15 priority date for domestic students, 4/1 priority date for international students; for spring admission, 11/15 priority date for domestic students, 10/1 priority date for international students. Applications are processed on a rolling basis. Application fee: $60.

Electronic applications accepted. *Expenses:* Tuition: Full-time $10,980; part-time $610 per credit hour. Required fees: $320 per semester. *Financial support:* Federal Work-Study available. *Faculty research:* Mentoring, principal development, principal retention. *Unit head:* Dr. Stacey Dammann, Director, 717-815-6476, E-mail: sdammann@ycp.edu. *Application contact:* Nancy Spataro, Director of Admissions, 717-815-1600, Fax: 717-849-1607, E-mail: admissions@ycp.edu.

York University, Faculty of Graduate Studies, Faculty of Education, Toronto, ON M3J 1P3, Canada. Offers M Ed, PhD. Part-time programs available. *Degree requirements:* For master's, thesis or alternative; for doctorate, comprehensive exam, thesis/dissertation. Electronic applications accepted.

Youngstown State University, Graduate School, Beeghly College of Education, Youngstown, OH 44555-0001. Offers MS Ed, Ed D. *Accreditation:* NCATE. Part-time and evening/weekend programs available. *Degree requirements:* For master's, comprehensive exam; for doctorate, comprehensive exam, thesis/dissertation. *Entrance requirements:* For master's, minimum GPA of 2.7; for doctorate, GRE General Test, GRE Subject Test, interview, minimum GPA of 3.5. Additional exam requirements/recommendations for international students: Required—TOEFL. *Faculty research:* Euthanasia, psychometrics, ethical issues, community relations, educational law.

ARGOSY UNIVERSITY.

ARGOSY UNIVERSITY, CHICAGO

College of Education

Programs of Study	Argosy University, Chicago, offers the Master of Arts in Education (M.A.Ed.) degree in adult education and training, and educational leadership; the Education Specialist (Ed.S.) degree in educational leadership and instructional leadership; and the Doctor of Education (Ed.D.) degree in educational leadership, instructional leadership, and community college executive leadership.
	The M.A.Ed. in educational leadership program is designed to instill key philosophies, theories, and values that impact education. It prepares students to improve policies and practices within organizations through the motivation and supervision of others. Students develop skills needed to design, implement, and evaluate educational programs and curricula. Courses include educational law, educational finance, organizational communication, human resource management, instruction supervision, and organizational management. The program now offers principal/general administrative certification, also known as Type 75 certification. The M.A.Ed. in educational leadership noncertification program is designed to prepare graduates for roles as effective leaders in the field of education.
	The Ed.S. in educational leadership program concentrates on applied organizational theory within the context of educational organizations. This specialized program develops the competencies required to secure educational administrator positions at the elementary or secondary school level. The program now offers superintendent certification.
	The Ed.S. in instructional leadership program enables experienced teachers to become more effective practitioners and educational leaders with a focus on instruction. Course work is designed to satisfy the requirements of students seeking career advancement and those who are working toward a doctoral degree.
	The Ed.D. in community college executive leadership program offers an accelerated course of study intended to meet the needs of community college administrators who are looking to move into senior administrative positions (such as president, vice president, dean, and director) in community colleges.
	The Ed.D. in educational leadership program is designed to enhance educational leadership strengths. Students learn innovative and collaborative techniques used to manage and govern educational institutions. The program prepares students for administrative leadership positions at the district, regional, state, or national level. Students must choose a concentration in district leadership, higher education administration, or K–12 education.
	The Ed.D. in instructional leadership program draws upon educational theories and practices to help students discover new learning techniques for diverse audiences. Students enrolled in this program master teaching methodologies, hone classroom skills, and gain the knowledge required to become curriculum administrators or educational leaders with a focus on instruction. Students must choose a concentration in higher education or K–12 education.
	Note: The M.A.Ed. in educational leadership–Illinois Type 75 principal preparation/general administrative track and the Certificate of Advanced Studies (CAS) in educational leadership/Illinois Type 75 principal preparation/general administrative certification can lead to State of Illinois Type 75 General Administrative Certificate. The Ed.S. in educational leadership/Illinois Type 75 certification–superintendent preparation track, Certificate of Advanced Studies in educational leadership/Illinois Type 75 certification–superintendent preparation track, and the Ed.D. in educational leadership–superintendent preparation track can lead to State of Illinois Type 75 Superintendent's Endorsement. All other programs offered through the College of Education do not lead to teacher or administrator certification, licensure, or endorsement in any state in the United States. The programs offered through Argosy University online programs do not lead to teacher or administrator certification, licensure, or endorsement in any state in the United States regardless of the state in which the student resides.
Research Facilities	Argosy University libraries provide curriculum support and educational resources, including current text materials, diagnostic training documents, reference materials and databases, journals and dissertations, and major and current titles in program areas. There is an online public-access catalog of library resources available throughout the Argosy University system. Students have remote access to the campus library database, enabling them to study and conduct research at home. Academic databases offer dissertation abstracts, academic journals, and professional periodicals. All library computers are Internet accessible. Software applications include Word, Excel, PowerPoint, SPSS, and various test-scoring programs.
Financial Aid	Financial aid is available to those who qualify. Argosy University, Chicago, offers access to federal and state aid programs, merit-based awards, grants, loans, and a work-study program. As a first step, students should complete the Free Application for Federal Student Aid (FAFSA). Prospective students can apply electronically at http://www.fafsa.ed.gov or at the campus.
Cost of Study	Tuition varies by program. Students should contact Argosy University, Chicago, for tuition information.
Living and Housing Costs	Students typically live in apartments in the metropolitan Chicago area. Living expenses vary according to each student's preferred standard of living, housing, and transportation. The University does not offer or operate student housing. Most of the students are full-time working professionals who live within driving distance of the campus. Several nearby hotels offer special rates for those who commute from long distances. The Admissions Department also maintains a list of housing options, including contact information for University students who wish to share housing. For more information, students should contact the Admissions Department.
Student Group	Admission to Argosy University, Chicago, is selective to ensure a dynamic and engaged student body. It encourages diversity in academic and employment backgrounds and promotes integration of the student body into professional life through established connections with local and national professional associations. Argosy University offers a professionally oriented education with rich opportunities to gain practical experience in class, field placements, and internships. Full-time students and working professionals gain the extensive knowledge and range of skills necessary for effective performance in their chosen fields.
Student Outcomes	Students can register with the University's online career-services system and use select services from a distance, such as degree-specific career e-mail lists, national job posts, and virtual job fairs. Students should contact the University for more information.
Location	Chicago is a city of world-class status and beauty, drawing visitors from around the globe. Argosy University, Chicago, sits in the heart of The Loop, the city's business and entertainment center. Located on the shores of Lake Michigan, Chicago is home to world-champion sports teams, an internationally acclaimed symphony orchestra, renowned architecture, and a variety of history and art museums. Recreational opportunities include hiking and cycling on miles of lakefront trails, golfing, and shopping.
	Many educational institutions and agencies in the area provide excellent opportunities for student training. Chicago's business environment includes a broad array of companies, including Boeing and Pepsi America. The commercial banking headquarters of JPMorgan Chase is also located in Chicago.
The University	Argosy University is a private institution with nineteen locations across the nation. Argosy University, Chicago, provides a career resources office, an academic resources center, and extensive information access for research. It offers the resources of a large university, plus the friendliness and personal attention of a small campus. Argosy University, Chicago, is closely associated with the University's Schaumburg, Illinois campus, located 45 minutes from downtown Chicago.
	The innovative programs feature dynamic, relevant, and practical curricula delivered in flexible class formats. Students enjoy scheduling options that make it easier to fit school into their busy lives, choosing from day and evening courses, on campus or online. Many students find a combination of class formats to be an ideal way of continuing their education while meeting family and professional demands.
	Argosy University is accredited by the Higher Learning Commission and a member of the North Central Association (30 North LaSalle Street, Suite 2400, Chicago, Illinois 60602; 800-621-7440 (toll-free); http://www.ncahlc.org).
Applying	Argosy University, Chicago, accepts students year-round on a rolling admissions basis, depending on availability of required courses. Applications for admission are available online or by contacting the campus.
Correspondence and Information	Argosy University, Chicago 225 North Michigan Avenue, Suite 1300 Chicago, Illinois 60601 Phone: 312-777-7600 800-626-4123 (toll-free) Fax: 312-777-7748 E-mail: auadmissions@argosy.edu Web site: http://www.argosy.edu/chicago

Argosy University, Chicago

THE FACULTY

The Argosy University faculty comprises working professionals who are eager to help students succeed. Members bring real-world experience and the latest practice innovations to the academic setting. The diverse faculty members of the College of Education are widely recognized for contributions to the field. Most hold doctoral degrees. They provide a substantive education that combines comprehensive knowledge with critical skills and practical workplace relevance. Above all, faculty members are committed to their students' personal and professional development.

ARGOSY UNIVERSITY.

ARGOSY UNIVERSITY, DALLAS

College of Education

Programs of Study

Argosy University, Dallas offers the Master of Arts in Education (M.A.Ed.) degree in educational leadership and instructional leadership and the Doctor of Education (Ed.D.) degree in educational leadership.

The M.A.Ed. in educational leadership program is designed to instill key philosophies, theories, and values that impact education. It prepares students to improve policies and practices within organizations through the motivation and supervision of others. Students develop skills needed to design, implement, and evaluate educational programs and curricula. Courses include educational law, educational finance, organizational communication, human resource management, instruction supervision, and organizational management.

The M.A.Ed. in instructional leadership program examines the challenges and problems encountered in today's educational environment. Course work encompasses the historical, philosophical, psychological, social, technical, and theoretical aspects of education. Students develop skills in analysis, oral and written communication, problem solving, critical thinking, team building, and computer technology. The program is designed for those who wish to develop or enhance classroom skills, become curriculum supervisors, or become educational leaders with a focus on instruction. Upon completion of the program, students may choose to complete their principal certification.

The Ed.D. in educational leadership noncertification program is designed for those students preparing for or advancing their careers as educational leaders in professional positions as school district, regional, state, or national administrators. The Ed.D. in educational leadership noncertification program requires concentrations in higher education administration or K–12 education.

Note: The M.A.Ed. in educational leadership, principal certification can lead to Texas Education Agency Principal Certificate. All other programs offered through the College of Education do not lead to teacher or administrator certification, licensure, or endorsement in any state in the United States. The programs offered through Argosy University online programs do not lead to teacher or administrator certification, licensure, or endorsement in any state in the United States regardless of the state in which the student resides.

Research Facilities

Argosy University libraries provide curriculum support and educational resources, including current text materials, diagnostic training documents, reference materials and databases, journals and dissertations, and major and current titles in program areas. There is an online public-access catalog of library resources available throughout the Argosy University system. Students have remote access to the campus library database, enabling them to study and conduct research at home. Academic databases offer dissertation abstracts, academic journals, and professional periodicals. All library computers are Internet accessible. Software applications include Word, Excel, PowerPoint, SPSS, and various test-scoring programs.

Financial Aid

Financial aid is available to those who qualify. Argosy University, Dallas, offers access to federal and state aid programs, merit-based awards, grants, loans, and a work-study program. As a first step, students should complete the Free Application for Federal Student Aid (FAFSA). Prospective students can apply electronically at http://www.fafsa.ed.gov or at the campus.

Cost of Study

Tuition varies by program. Students should contact Argosy University, Dallas, for tuition information.

Living and Housing Costs

Students typically live in apartments in the metropolitan Dallas area. Living expenses vary according to each student's preferred standard of living, housing, and transportation. The University does not offer or operate student housing. Most of the students are full-time working professionals who live within driving distance of the campus. Several nearby hotels offer special rates for those who commute from long distances. The Admissions Department also maintains a list of housing options, including contact information for University students who wish to share housing. For more information, students should contact the Admissions Department.

Student Group

Admission to Argosy University, Dallas, is selective to ensure a dynamic and engaged student body. It encourages diversity in academic and employment backgrounds and promotes integration of the student body into professional life through established connections with local and national professional associations. Argosy University offers a professionally oriented education with rich opportunities to gain practical experience in class, field placements, and internships. Full-time students and working professionals gain the extensive knowledge and range of skills necessary for effective performance in their chosen fields.

Student Outcomes

Students can register with the University's online career-services system and use select services from a distance, such as degree-specific career e-mail lists, national job posts, and virtual job fairs. Students should contact the University for more information.

Location

Argosy University, Dallas, offers a north-central location in Dallas, with easy access to freeways, libraries, shops, restaurants, theaters, art museums, and other tourist attractions. Many educational institutions and agencies in the area provide excellent opportunities for student training. The business environment in the Dallas/Ft. Worth metropolitan area includes a broad array of companies, including Lockheed Martin Corporation, Baylor University Medical System, and Southwest Airlines.

The University

Argosy University is a private institution with nineteen locations across the nation. Argosy University, Dallas, provides students with a network of resources found at larger universities and the friendliness and personal attention of a small campus.

The innovative programs feature dynamic, relevant, and practical curricula delivered in flexible class formats. Students enjoy scheduling options that make it easier to fit school into their busy lives, choosing from day and evening courses, on campus or online. Many students find a combination of class formats to be an ideal way of continuing their education while meeting family and professional demands.

Argosy University is accredited by the Higher Learning Commission and a member of the North Central Association (30 North LaSalle Street, Suite 2400, Chicago, Illinois 60602; 800-621-7440 (toll-free); http://www.ncahlc.org).

Applying

Argosy University, Dallas, accepts students year-round on a rolling admissions basis, depending on availability of required courses. Applications for admission are available online or by contacting the campus.

Correspondence and Information

Argosy University, Dallas
5001 Lyndon B. Johnson Freeway
Heritage Square
Farmers Branch, Texas 75244
Phone: 214-890-9900
          866-954-9900 (toll-free)
Fax: 214-378-8555
E-mail: auadmissions@argosy.edu
Web site: http://www.argosy.edu/dallas

Argosy University, Dallas

THE FACULTY

The Argosy University faculty comprises working professionals who are eager to help students succeed. Members bring real-world experience and the latest practice innovations to the academic setting. The diverse faculty members of the College of Education are widely recognized for contributions to the field. Most hold doctoral degrees. They provide a substantive education that combines comprehensive knowledge with critical skills and practical workplace relevance. Above all, faculty members are committed to their students' personal and professional development.

ARGOSY UNIVERSITY, DENVER

College of Education

ARGOSY UNIVERSITY

Program of Study	Argosy University, Denver, offers the Master of Arts in Education (M.A.Ed.) degree in educational leadership, instructional leadership, instructional specialist in English language learners/English second language (ELL/ESL), instruction specialist in reading (elementary), and instructional specialist in reading (middle/secondary); and the Doctor of Education (Ed.D.) degree in educational leadership, instructional leadership, and community college executive leadership.
	The M.A.Ed. in educational leadership program is designed to instill key philosophies, theories, and values that impact education. It prepares students to improve policies and practices within organizations through the motivation and supervision of others. Students develop skills needed to design, implement, and evaluate educational programs and curricula. Courses include educational law, educational finance, organizational communication, human resource management, instruction supervision, and organizational management.
	The M.A.Ed. in instructional leadership program examines the challenges and problems encountered in today's educational environment. Course work encompasses the historical, philosophical, psychological, social, technical, and theoretical aspects of education. Students develop skills in analysis, oral and written communication, problem solving, critical thinking, team building, and computer technology. The program is designed for those who wish to develop or enhance classroom skills, become curriculum supervisors, or become educational leaders with a focus on instruction.
	The M.A.Ed. instructional specialist in ELL/ESL program prepares teachers to work with ELL/ESL students. Upon completion of the program, teachers are equipped to effectively support the learning of such students.
	The M.A.Ed. instructional specialist in reading (elementary) program prepares teachers to work with beginning and developing readers. As a result of this program, teachers are prepared to integrate reading across the curriculum and increase students' vocabulary and reading fluency.
	The M.A.Ed. instructional specialist in reading (middle/secondary) program prepares teachers to work with beginning and developing readers. As a result of this program, teachers are prepared to integrate reading across the curriculum and increase students' vocabulary and reading fluency.
	The Ed.D. in community college executive leadership program offers an accelerated course of study intended to meet the needs of community college administrators who are looking to move into senior administrative positions (such as president, vice president, dean, and director) in community colleges.
	The Ed.D. in educational leadership program is designed to enhance educational leadership strengths. Students learn innovative and collaborative techniques used to manage and govern educational institutions. The program prepares students for administrative leadership positions at the district, regional, state, or national level. Students must choose a concentration in higher education administration or K–12 education.
	The Ed.D. in instructional leadership program draws upon educational theories and practices to help students discover new learning techniques for diverse audiences. Students enrolled in this program master teaching methodologies, hone classroom skills, and gain the knowledge required to become curriculum administrators or educational leaders with a focus on instruction. Students must choose a concentration in higher education or K–12 education.
	Note: These programs do not lead to teacher or administrator certification, licensure, or endorsement in any state in the United States.
Research Facilities	Argosy University libraries provide curriculum support and educational resources, including current text materials, diagnostic training documents, reference materials and databases, journals and dissertations, and major and current titles in program areas. There is an online public access catalog of library resources available throughout the Argosy University system. Students have remote access to the campus library database, enabling them to study and conduct research at home. Academic databases offer dissertation abstracts, academic journals, and professional periodicals. All library computers are Internet accessible. Software applications include Word, Excel, PowerPoint, SPSS, and various test-scoring programs.
Financial Aid	Financial aid is available to those who qualify. Argosy University, Denver, offers access to federal and state aid programs, merit-based awards, grants, loans, and a work-study program. As a first step, students should complete the Free Application for Federal Student Aid (FAFSA). Prospective students can apply electronically at http://www.fafsa.ed.gov or at the campus.
Cost of Study	Tuition varies by program. Students should contact Argosy University, Denver, for tuition information.
Living and Housing Costs	Students typically live in apartments in the metropolitan Denver area. Living expenses vary according to each student's preferred standard of living, housing, and transportation. The University does not offer or operate student housing. Most of the students are full-time working professionals who live within driving distance of the campus. Several nearby hotels offer special rates for those who commute from long distances. The Admissions Department also maintains a list of housing options, including contact information for University students who wish to share housing. For more information, students should contact the Admissions Department.
Student Group	Admission to Argosy University, Denver, is selective to ensure a dynamic and engaged student body. The University encourages diversity in academic and employment backgrounds and promotes integration of the student body into professional life through established connections with local and national professional associations. Argosy University offers a professionally oriented education with rich opportunities to gain practical experience in class, field placements, and internships. Full-time students and working professionals gain the extensive knowledge and range of skills necessary for effective performance in their chosen fields.
Student Outcomes	Students can register with the University's online career-services system and use select services from a distance, such as degree-specific career e-mail lists, national job posts, and virtual job fairs. Students should contact the University for more information.
Location	Argosy University, Denver, is conveniently located at 7600 East Eastman Avenue in Denver, Colorado. The campus is close to a variety of local libraries, shops, restaurants, theaters, and art museums. Denver's thriving professional organizations, major corporations, high-tech companies, hospitals, schools, clinics, and social service agencies can also provide varied training opportunities for students.
The University	Argosy University is a private institution with nineteen locations across the nation. Argosy University, Denver, provides students with a network of resources found at larger universities and the friendliness and personal attention of a small campus.
	The innovative programs feature dynamic, relevant, and practical curricula delivered in flexible class formats. Students enjoy scheduling options that make it easier to fit school into their busy lives, choosing from day and evening courses, on campus or online. Many students find a combination of class formats to be an ideal way of continuing their education while meeting family and professional demands.
	Argosy University is accredited by the Higher Learning Commission and a member of the North Central Association (30 North LaSalle Street, Suite 2400, Chicago, Illinois 60602; 800-621-7440 (toll-free); http://www.ncahlc.org).
Applying	Argosy University, Denver, accepts students year-round on a rolling admissions basis, depending on availability of required courses. Applications for admission are available online or by contacting the campus.
Correspondence and Information	Argosy University, Denver 7600 East Eastman Avenue Denver, Colorado 80231 Phone: 303-248-2700 866-431-5981 (toll-free) Fax: 303-248-2800 E-mail: auadmissions@argosy.edu Web site: http://www.argosy.edu/denver

Argosy University, Denver

THE FACULTY

The Argosy University faculty comprises working professionals who are eager to help students succeed. Members bring real-world experience and the latest practice innovations to the academic setting. The diverse faculty members of the College of Education are widely recognized for contributions to the field. Most hold doctoral degrees. They provide a substantive education that combines comprehensive knowledge with critical skills and practical workplace relevance. Above all, faculty members are committed to their students' personal and professional development.

ARGOSY UNIVERSITY, HAWAI'I

College of Education

Program of Study

Argosy University, Hawai'i, offers the Master of Arts in Education (M.A.Ed.) in adult education and training, instructional specialist in English language learners/English second language (ELL/ESL), instructional specialist in reading (elementary), and instructional specialist in reading (middle/secondary); and the Doctor of Education (Ed.D.) degree in educational leadership and in instructional leadership.

The M.A.Ed. in adult education and training program is designed for the working professional associated with adult learning, training, or staff development in business, government, and or other private or public organizations. The goal of the program is to enhance the knowledge and skills in the area of adult learning for employment and other organizational settings.

The M.A.Ed. instructional specialist in ELL/ESL program prepares teachers to work with ELL/ESL students. Upon completion of the program, teachers are equipped to effectively support the learning of such students.

The M.A.Ed. instructional specialist in reading (elementary) program prepares teachers to work with beginning and developing readers. As a result of this program, teachers are prepared to integrate reading across the curriculum and increase students' vocabulary and reading fluency.

The M.A.Ed. instructional specialist in reading (middle/secondary) program prepares teachers to work with beginning and developing readers. As a result of this program, teachers are prepared to integrate reading across the curriculum and increase students' vocabulary and reading fluency.

The Ed.D. in educational leadership program is designed to enhance educational leadership strengths. Students learn innovative and collaborative techniques used to manage and govern educational institutions. The program prepares students for administrative leadership positions at the district, regional, state, or national level. Students must choose a concentration in higher education administration or K–12 education.

The Ed.D. in instructional leadership program draws upon educational theories and practices to help students discover new learning techniques for diverse audiences. Students enrolled in this program master teaching methodologies, hone classroom skills, and gain the knowledge required to become curriculum administrators or educational leaders with a focus on instruction. Students must choose a concentration in higher education or K–12 education.

Note: These programs do not lead to teacher or administrator certification, licensure, or endorsement in any state in the United States.

Research Facilities

Argosy University libraries provide curriculum support and educational resources, including current text materials, diagnostic training documents, reference materials and databases, journals and dissertations, and major and current titles in program areas. There is an online public-access catalog of library resources available throughout the Argosy University system. Students have remote access to the campus library database, enabling them to study and conduct research at home. Academic databases offer dissertation abstracts, academic journals, and professional periodicals. All library computers are Internet accessible. Software applications include Word, Excel, PowerPoint, SPSS, and various test-scoring programs.

Financial Aid

Financial aid is available to those who qualify. Argosy University, Hawai'i, offers access to federal and state aid programs, merit-based awards, grants, loans, and a work-study program. As a first step, students should complete the Free Application for Federal Student Aid (FAFSA). Prospective students can apply electronically at http://www.fafsa.ed.gov or at the campus.

Cost of Study

Tuition varies by program. Students should contact Argosy University, Hawai'i, for tuition information.

Living and Housing Costs

Students typically live in apartments in the metropolitan Honolulu area. Living expenses vary according to each student's preferred standard of living, housing, and transportation. The University does not offer or operate student housing. Most of the students are full-time working professionals who live within driving distance of the campus. Several nearby hotels offer special rates for those who commute from long distances. The Admissions Department also maintains a list of housing options, including contact information for University students who wish to share housing. For more information, students should contact the Admissions Department.

Student Group

Admission to Argosy University, Hawai'i, is selective to ensure a dynamic and engaged student body. The University encourages diversity in academic and employment backgrounds and promotes integration of the student body into professional life through established connections with local and national professional associations. Argosy University offers a professionally oriented education with rich opportunities to gain practical experience in class, field placements, and internships. Full-time students and working professionals gain the extensive knowledge and range of skills necessary for effective performance in their chosen fields.

Student Outcomes

Students can register with the University's online career-services system and use select services from a distance, such as degree-specific career e-mail lists, national job posts, and virtual job fairs. Students should contact the University for more information.

Location

Argosy University, Hawai'i, is located in downtown Honolulu on Oahu. Additional satellite locations on Maui and in Hilo on the island of Hawaii offer programs to communities on the neighbor islands. These locations connect the campus to Hawaii and to the local and native communities of the Pacific Islands and the Pacific Rim. Students enjoy the cultural and recreational opportunities that these locations provide. University faculty and staff members often work in cooperation with the Hawaiian community to create an educational focus on social issues, human diversity, and programs that make a difference to underserved populations.

Many educational institutions and agencies in the area provide excellent opportunities for student training. Honolulu's business environment includes a broad array of companies. The area's largest employers include Bank of Hawaii, Queens Medical Center, and the U.S. government.

The University

Argosy University is a private institution with nineteen locations across the nation. Argosy University, Hawai'i, provides students with a career resources office, an academic resources center, and extensive information access for research. It offers the resources of a large university, plus the friendliness and personal attention of a small campus.

The innovative programs feature dynamic, relevant, and practical curricula delivered in flexible class formats. Students enjoy scheduling options that make it easier to fit school into their busy lives, choosing from day and evening courses, on campus or online. Many students find a combination of class formats to be an ideal way of continuing their education while meeting family and professional demands.

Argosy University is accredited by the Higher Learning Commission and a member of the North Central Association (30 North LaSalle Street, Suite 2400, Chicago, Illinois 60602; 800-621-7440 (toll-free); http://www.ncahlc.org).

Applying

Argosy University, Hawai'i, accepts students year-round on a rolling admissions basis, depending on availability of required courses. Applications for admission are available online or by contacting the campus.

Correspondence and Information

Argosy University, Hawai'i
400 ASB Tower
1001 Bishop Street
Honolulu, Hawaii 96813
Phone: 808-536-5555
      888-323-2777 (toll-free)
Fax: 808-536-5505
E-mail: auadmissions@argosy.edu
Web site: http://www.argosy.edu/hawaii

Argosy University, Hawai'i

THE FACULTY

The Argosy University faculty comprises working professionals who are eager to help students succeed. Members bring real-world experience and the latest practice innovations to the academic setting. The diverse faculty members of the College of Education are widely recognized for contributions to the field. Most hold doctoral degrees. They provide a substantive education that combines comprehensive knowledge with critical skills and practical workplace relevance. Above all, faculty members are committed to their students' personal and professional development.

ARGOSY UNIVERSITY

ARGOSY UNIVERSITY, LOS ANGELES

College of Education

Programs of Study

Argosy University, Los Angeles, offers the Master of Arts in Education (M.A.Ed.) degree in educational leadership, instructional leadership, instructional specialist in English language learners/English second language (ELL/ESL), instructional specialist in reading (elementary), and instructional specialist in reading (middle/secondary); and the Doctor of Education (Ed.D.) degree in community college executive leadership, educational leadership, and instructional leadership.

The M.A.Ed. in educational leadership program is designed to instill key philosophies, theories, and values that impact education. It prepares students to improve policies and practices within organizations through the motivation and supervision of others. Students develop skills needed to design, implement, and evaluate educational programs and curricula. Courses include educational law, educational finance, organizational communication, human resource management, instruction supervision, and organizational management.

The M.A.Ed. in instructional leadership program examines the challenges and problems encountered in today's educational environment. Course work encompasses the historical, philosophical, psychological, social, technical, and theoretical aspects of education. Students develop skills in analysis, oral and written communication, problem solving, critical thinking, team building, and computer technology. The program is designed for those who wish to develop or enhance classroom skills, become instructional supervisors, or become educational leaders with a focus on instruction. Students may choose optional concentrations in single- or multiple-subject teacher credential preparation.

The M.A.Ed. instructional specialist in ELL/ESL program prepares teachers to work with ELL/ESL students. Upon completion of the program, teachers are equipped to effectively support the learning of such students.

The M.A.Ed. instructional specialist in reading (elementary) program prepares teachers to work with beginning and developing readers. As a result of this program, teachers are prepared to integrate reading across the curriculum and increase students' vocabulary and reading fluency.

The M.A.Ed. instructional specialist in reading (middle/secondary) program prepares teachers to work with beginning and developing readers. As a result of this program, teachers are prepared to integrate reading across the curriculum and increase students' vocabulary and reading fluency.

The Ed.D. in community college executive leadership program offers an accelerated course of study intended to meet the needs of community college administrators who are looking to move into senior administrative positions (such as president, vice president, dean, and director) in community colleges.

The Ed.D. in educational leadership program is designed to enhance educational leadership strengths. Students learn innovative and collaborative techniques used to manage and govern educational institutions. The program prepares students for administrative leadership positions at the district, regional, state, or national level. Students must choose a concentration in higher education administration or K–12 education.

The Ed.D. in instructional leadership program draws on educational theories and practices to help students discover new learning techniques for diverse audiences. Students enrolled in this program master teaching methodologies, hone classroom skills, and gain the knowledge required to become curriculum administrators or educational leaders with a focus on instruction. Students must choose a concentration in higher education or K–12 education.

Note: The M.A.Ed. in instructional leadership (multiple subject teacher credential prep) and the M.A.Ed. in instructional leadership (single subject teacher credential prep) programs can lead to multiple subject teaching credential or single subject teaching credential depending on the program concentration selected. All other programs offered through the College of Education do not lead to teacher or administrator certification, licensure, or endorsement in any state in the United States. The programs offered through Argosy University online programs do not lead to teacher or administrator certification, licensure, or endorsement in any state in the United States regardless of the state in which the student resides.

Research Facilities

Argosy University libraries provide curriculum support and educational resources, including current text materials, diagnostic training documents, reference materials and databases, journals and dissertations, and major and current titles in program areas. There is an online public-access catalog of library resources available throughout the Argosy University system. Students have remote access to the campus library database, enabling them to study and conduct research at home. Academic databases offer dissertation abstracts, academic journals, and professional periodicals. All library computers are Internet accessible. Software applications include Word, Excel, PowerPoint, SPSS, and various test-scoring programs.

Financial Aid

Financial aid is available to those who qualify. Argosy University, Los Angeles, offers access to federal and state aid programs, merit-based awards, grants, loans, and a work-study program. As a first step, students should complete the Free Application for Federal Student Aid (FAFSA). Prospective students can apply electronically at http://www.fafsa.ed.gov or at the campus.

Cost of Study

Tuition varies by program. Students should contact Argosy University, Los Angeles, for tuition information.

Living and Housing Costs

Students typically live in apartments in the metropolitan Santa Monica area. Living expenses vary according to each student's preferred standard of living, housing, and transportation. The University does not offer or operate student housing. Most of the students are full-time working professionals who live within driving distance of the campus. Several nearby hotels offer special rates for those who commute from long distances. The Admissions Department also maintains a list of housing options, including contact information for University students who wish to share housing. For more information, students should contact the Admissions Department.

Student Group

Admission to Argosy University, Los Angeles, is selective to ensure a dynamic and engaged student body. It encourages diversity in academic and employment backgrounds and promotes integration of the student body into professional life through established connections with local and national professional associations. Argosy University offers a professionally oriented education with rich opportunities to gain practical experience in class, field placements, and internships. Full-time students and working professionals gain the extensive knowledge and range of skills necessary for effective performance in their chosen fields.

Student Outcomes

Students can register with the University's online career-services system and use select services from a distance, such as degree-specific career e-mail lists, national job posts, and virtual job fairs. Students should contact the University for more information.

Location

Argosy University, Los Angeles, is conveniently located near the interchange between I-405 and I-105, just minutes from Los Angeles International Airport and the Pacific coast. The business environment in the Los Angeles metropolitan area features a broad array of companies, including a proliferation of entertainment, technology, and software firms. Among the principal employers in the area are Yahoo!, MTV Networks, RAND Corporation, and Symantec Corporation. The many businesses in the area provide varied opportunities for student training.

The University

Argosy University is a private institution with nineteen locations across the nation. Argosy University, Los Angeles, provides students with a career resources office, an academic resources center, and extensive information access for research. It offers the resources of a large university plus the friendliness and personal attention of a small campus.

The innovative programs feature dynamic, relevant, and practical curricula delivered in flexible class formats. Students enjoy scheduling options that make it easier to fit school into their busy lives, choosing from day and evening courses, on campus or online. Many students find a combination of class formats to be an ideal way of continuing their education while meeting family and professional demands.

Argosy University is accredited by the Higher Learning Commission and a member of the North Central Association (30 North LaSalle Street, Suite 2400, Chicago, Illinois 60602; 800-621-7440 (toll-free); http://www.ncahlc.org).

Applying

Argosy University, Los Angeles, accepts students year-round on a rolling admissions basis, depending on availability of required courses. Applications for admission are available online or by contacting the campus.

Correspondence and Information

Argosy University, Los Angeles
5230 Pacific Concourse
Los Angeles, California 90045
Phone: 310-866-4000
866-505-0332 (toll-free)
Fax: 310-399-1804
E-mail: auadmissions@argosy.edu
Web site: http://www.argosy.edu/losangeles

Argosy University, Los Angeles

THE FACULTY

The Argosy University faculty comprises working professionals who are eager to help students succeed. Members bring real-world experience and the latest-practice innovations to the academic setting. The diverse faculty members of the College of Education are widely recognized for contributions to the field. Most hold doctoral degrees. They provide a substantive education that combines comprehensive knowledge with critical skills and practical workplace relevance. Above all, faculty members are committed to their students' personal and professional development.

ARGOSY UNIVERSITY.

ARGOSY UNIVERSITY, ORANGE COUNTY

College of Education

Programs of Study	Argosy University, Orange County, offers the Master of Arts in Education (M.A.Ed.) degree in educational leadership, instructional leadership, instructional specialist in English language learners/English second language (ELL/ESL), instructional specialist in reading (elementary), and instructional specialist in reading (middle/secondary); and the Doctor of Education (Ed.D.) degree in community college executive leadership, educational leadership, and instructional leadership.

The M.A.Ed. in educational leadership program is designed to instill key philosophies, theories, and values that impact education. It prepares students to improve policies and practices within organizations through the motivation and supervision of others. Students develop skills needed to design, implement, and evaluate educational programs and curricula. Courses include educational law, educational finance, organizational communication, human resource management, instruction supervision, and organizational management.

The M.A.Ed. in instructional leadership program examines the challenges and problems encountered in today's educational environment. Course work encompasses the historical, philosophical, psychological, social, technical, and theoretical aspects of education. Students develop skills in analysis, oral and written communication, problem solving, critical thinking, team building, and computer technology. The program is designed for those who wish to develop or enhance classroom skills, become curriculum supervisors, or become educational leaders with a focus on instruction. Students may choose optional concentrations in single or multiple subject teacher credential preparation.

The M.A.Ed. instructional specialist in ELL/ESL program prepares teachers to work with ELL/ESL students. Upon completion of the program, teachers are equipped to effectively support the learning of such students.

The M.A.Ed. instructional specialist in reading (elementary) program prepares teachers to work with beginning and developing readers. As a result of this program, teachers are prepared to integrate reading across the curriculum and increase students' vocabulary and reading fluency.

The M.A.Ed. instructional specialist in reading (middle/secondary) program prepares teachers to work with beginning and developing readers. As a result of this program, teachers are prepared to integrate reading across the curriculum and increase students' vocabulary and reading fluency.

The Ed.D. in community college executive leadership program offers an accelerated course of study intended to meet the needs of community college administrators who are looking to move into senior administrative positions (such as president, vice president, dean, and director) in community colleges.

The Ed.D. in educational leadership program is designed to enhance educational leadership strengths. Students learn innovative and collaborative techniques used to manage and govern educational institutions. The program prepares students for administrative leadership positions at the district, regional, state, or national level. Students must choose a concentration in higher education administration or K–12 education.

The Ed.D. in instructional leadership program draws upon educational theories and practices to help students discover new learning techniques for diverse audiences. Students enrolled in this program master teaching methodologies, hone classroom skills, and gain the knowledge required to become curriculum administrators or educational leaders with a focus on instruction. Students must choose a concentration in education technology, higher education, or K–12 education.

Note: The M.A.Ed. in instructional leadership (multiple subject teacher credential prep) and the M.A.Ed. in instructional leadership (single subject teacher credential prep) programs can lead to multiple subject teaching credential or single subject teaching credential depending on the program concentration selected. All other programs offered through the College of Education do not lead to teacher or administrator certification, licensure, or endorsement in any state in the United States. The programs offered through Argosy University online programs do not lead to teacher or administrator certification, licensure, or endorsement in any state in the United States regardless of the state in which the student resides.

Research Facilities	Argosy University libraries provide curriculum support and educational resources, including current text materials, diagnostic training documents, reference materials and databases, journals and dissertations, and major and current titles in program areas. There is an online public-access catalog of library resources available throughout the Argosy University system. Students have remote access to the campus library database, enabling them to study and conduct research at home. Academic databases offer dissertation abstracts, academic journals, and professional periodicals. All library computers are Internet accessible. Software applications include Word, Excel, PowerPoint, SPSS, and various test-scoring programs.
Financial Aid	Financial aid is available to those who qualify. Argosy University, Orange County, offers access to federal and state aid programs, merit-based awards, grants, loans, and a work-study program. As a first step, students should complete the Free Application for Federal Student Aid (FAFSA). Prospective students can apply electronically at http://www.fafsa.ed.gov or at the campus.
Cost of Study	Tuition varies by program. Students should contact Argosy University, Orange County, for tuition information.
Living and Housing Costs	Students typically live in apartments in the metropolitan area. Living expenses vary according to each student's preferred standard of living, housing, and transportation. The University does not offer or operate student housing. Most of the students are full-time working professionals who live within driving distance of the campus. Several nearby hotels offer special rates for those who commute from long distances. The Admissions Department also maintains a list of housing options, including contact information for University students who wish to share housing. For more information, students should contact the Admissions Department.
Student Group	Admission to Argosy University, Orange County, is selective to ensure a dynamic and engaged student body. It encourages diversity in academic and employment backgrounds and promotes integration of the student body into professional life through established connections with local and national professional associations. Argosy University offers a professionally oriented education with rich opportunities to gain practical experience in class, field placements, and internships. Full-time students and working professionals gain the extensive knowledge and range of skills necessary for effective performance in their chosen fields.
Student Outcomes	Students can register with the University's online career-services system and use select services from a distance, such as degree-specific career e-mail lists, national job posts, and virtual job fairs. Students should contact the University for more information.
Location	Argosy University, Orange County, attracts students from Southern California, as well as from around the country and the world. Orange County features a temperate climate, sunny beaches, and a host of cultural and entertainment options. The campus is located approximately 30 miles south of downtown Los Angeles, 90 miles north of San Diego, and just minutes from one of the many freeways that connect the Southern California basin. Regional parks and preserved lands provide opportunities for hiking, biking, riding, and other recreational activities. Whether it's ultrachic Newport Beach, artsy Laguna Beach, or unspoiled Catalina Island, Orange County's ocean-side personalities are as varied as the people who visit the area.

Many educational institutions and agencies in the area provide varied opportunities for student training. Orange County's business environment includes an array of companies. The area's largest employers include Ingram Micro Inc., Orange County Register, ITT Industries, and OneSource.

The University	Argosy University is a private institution with nineteen locations across the nation. Argosy University, Orange County, provides students with a career resources office, an academic resources center, and extensive information access for research. It offers the resources of a large university, plus the friendliness and personal attention of a small campus.

The innovative programs feature dynamic, relevant, and practical curricula delivered in flexible class formats. Students enjoy scheduling options that make it easier to fit school into their busy lives, choosing from day and evening courses, on campus or online. Many students find a combination of class formats to be an ideal way of continuing their education while meeting family and professional demands.

Argosy University is accredited by the Higher Learning Commission and a member of the North Central Association (30 North LaSalle Street, Suite 2400, Chicago, Illinois 60602; 800-621-7440 (toll-free); http://www.ncahlc.org).

Applying	Argosy University, Orange County, accepts students year-round on a rolling admissions basis, depending on availability of required courses. Applications for admission are available online or by contacting the campus.
Correspondence and Information	Argosy University, Orange County 601 South Lewis Street Orange, California 92868 Phone: 714-620-3700 800-716-9598 (toll-free) Fax: 714-620-3800 E-mail: auadmissions@argosy.edu Web site: http://www.argosy.edu/orangecounty/

Argosy University, Orange County

THE FACULTY

The Argosy University faculty comprises working professionals who are eager to help students succeed. Members bring real-world experience and the latest practice innovations to the academic setting. The diverse faculty members of the College of Education are widely recognized for contributions to the field. Most hold doctoral degrees. They provide a substantive education that combines comprehensive knowledge with critical skills and practical workplace relevance. Above all, faculty members are committed to their students' personal and professional development.

ARGOSY UNIVERSITY, PHOENIX

College of Education

ARGOSY UNIVERSITY

Programs of Study	Argosy University, Phoenix, offers the Master of Arts in Education (M.A.Ed.) degree in adult education and training, educational leadership, and instructional leadership; the Education Specialist (Ed.S.) degree in educational leadership and instructional leadership; and the Doctor of Education (Ed.D.) degree in community college executive leadership, educational leadership, and instructional leadership.
	The M.A.Ed. in educational leadership program is designed to instill key philosophies, theories, and values that impact education. It prepares students to improve policies and practices within organizations through the motivation and supervision of others. Students develop skills needed to design, implement, and evaluate educational programs and curricula. Courses include educational law, educational finance, organizational communication, human resource management, instruction supervision, and organizational management. The M.A.Ed. in educational leadership non-certification program is designed to prepare graduates for roles as effective leaders in the field of education.
	The M.A.Ed. in instructional leadership program examines the challenges and problems encountered in today's educational environment. Course work encompasses the historical, philosophical, psychological, social, technical, and theoretical aspects of education. Students develop skills in analysis, oral and written communication, problem solving, critical thinking, team building, and computer technology. The program is designed for those who wish to develop or enhance classroom skills, become curriculum supervisors, or become educational leaders with a focus on instruction.
	The Ed.S. in educational leadership program concentrates on applied organizational theory within the context of educational organizations. This specialized program develops the competencies required to secure educational administrator positions at the elementary or secondary school level.
	The Ed.S. in instructional leadership program enables experienced teachers to become more effective practitioners and educational leaders with a focus on instruction. Course work is designed to satisfy the requirements of students seeking career advancement and those who are working toward a doctoral degree.
	The Ed.D. in community college executive leadership program offers an accelerated course of study intended to meet the needs of community college administrators who are looking to move into senior administrative positions (such as president, vice president, dean, and director) in community colleges.
	The Ed.D. in educational leadership program is designed to enhance educational leadership strengths. Students learn innovative and collaborative techniques used to manage and govern educational institutions. The program prepares students for administrative leadership positions at the district, regional, state, or national level. Students must choose a concentration in higher education administration or K–12 education.
	The Ed.D. in instructional leadership program draws upon educational theories and practices to help students discover new learning techniques for diverse audiences. Students enrolled in this program master teaching methodologies, hone classroom skills, and gain the knowledge required to become curriculum administrators or educational leaders with a focus on instruction. Students must choose a concentration in higher education or K–12 education.
	Note: The M.A.Ed. in educational leadership, principal certification program can lead to the Arizona Department of Education Principal Certificate. All other programs offered through the College of Education do not lead to teacher or administrator certification, licensure, or endorsement in any state in the United States. The programs offered through Argosy University online programs do not lead to teacher or administrator certification, licensure, or endorsement in any state in the United States regardless of the state in which the student resides.
Research Facilities	Argosy University libraries provide curriculum support and educational resources, including current text materials, diagnostic training documents, reference materials and databases, journals and dissertations, and major and current titles in program areas. There is an online public-access catalog of library resources available throughout the Argosy University system. Students have remote access to the campus library database, enabling them to study and conduct research at home. Academic databases offer dissertation abstracts, academic journals, and professional periodicals. All library computers are Internet accessible. Software applications include Word, Excel, PowerPoint, SPSS, and various test-scoring programs.
Financial Aid	Financial aid is available to those who qualify. Argosy University, Phoenix, offers access to federal and state aid programs, merit-based awards, grants, loans, and a work-study program. As a first step, students should complete the Free Application for Federal Student Aid (FAFSA). Prospective students can apply electronically at http://www.fafsa.ed.gov or at the campus.
Cost of Study	Tuition varies by program. Students should contact Argosy University, Phoenix, for tuition information.
Living and Housing Costs	Students typically live in apartments in the metropolitan Phoenix area. Living expenses vary according to each student's preferred standard of living, housing, and transportation. The University does not offer or operate student housing. Most of the students are full-time working professionals who live within driving distance of the campus. Several nearby hotels offer special rates for those who commute from long distances. The Admissions Department also maintains a list of housing options, including contact information for University students who wish to share housing. For more information, students should contact the Admissions Department.
Student Group	Admission to Argosy University, Phoenix, is selective to ensure a dynamic and engaged student body. It encourages diversity in academic and employment backgrounds and promotes integration of the student body into professional life through established connections with local and national professional associations. Argosy University offers a professionally oriented education with rich opportunities to gain practical experience in class, field placements, and internships. Full-time students and working professionals gain the extensive knowledge and range of skills necessary for effective performance in their chosen fields.
Student Outcomes	Students can register with the University's online career-services system and use select services from a distance, such as degree-specific career e-mail lists, national job posts, and virtual job fairs. Students should contact the University for more information.
Location	Argosy University, Phoenix, offers a high-quality education in an intimate, small-group setting. The campus is located near I-17, close to shops, restaurants, and recreational areas. Phoenix is home to several major-league sports teams, and the city offers an array of cultural activities ranging from opera and theater to science museums. The multicultural environment of Arizona, coupled with Argosy University's professional training affiliations throughout the state, creates an exciting opportunity for students to work with urban, rural, and culturally diverse populations.
	The business environment in Phoenix includes a variety of companies, such as Intel and Go Daddy Group, an Internet company. Wells Fargo, Home Depot, Lowe's, and Wal-Mart also represent some of the area's largest employers.
The University	Argosy University is a private institution with nineteen locations across the nation. Argosy University, Phoenix, provides students with a career resources office, an academic resources center, and extensive information access for research. It offers the resources of a large university, plus the friendliness and personal attention of a small campus.
	The innovative programs feature dynamic, relevant, and practical curricula delivered in flexible class formats. Students enjoy scheduling options that make it easier to fit school into their busy lives, choosing from day and evening courses, on campus or online. Many students find a combination of class formats to be an ideal way of continuing their education while meeting family and professional demands.
	Argosy University is accredited by the Higher Learning Commission and a member of the North Central Association (30 North LaSalle Street, Suite 2400, Chicago, Illinois 60602; 800-621-7440 (toll-free); http://www.ncahlc.org).
Applying	Argosy University, Phoenix, accepts students year-round on a rolling admissions basis, depending on availability of required courses. Applications for admission are available online or by contacting the campus.
Correspondence and Information	Argosy University, Phoenix 2233 West Dunlap Avenue Phoenix, Arizona 85021 Phone: 602-216-2600 866-216-2777 (toll-free) Fax: 602-216-2601 E-mail: auadmissions@argosy.edu Web site: http://argosy.edu/phoenix/

Argosy University, Phoenix

THE FACULTY

The Argosy University faculty comprises working professionals who are eager to help students succeed. Members bring real-world experience and the latest practice innovations to the academic setting. The diverse faculty members of the College of Education are widely recognized for contributions to the field. Most hold doctoral degrees. They provide a substantive education that combines comprehensive knowledge with critical skills and practical workplace relevance. Above all, faculty members are committed to their students' personal and professional development.

ARGOSY UNIVERSITY

ARGOSY UNIVERSITY, SALT LAKE CITY

College of Education

Programs of Study	Argosy University, Salt Lake City, offers the Master of Arts in Education (M.A.Ed.) degree in educational leadership and the Doctor of Education (Ed.D.) degree in educational leadership.
	The M.A.Ed. in educational leadership program is designed to instill key philosophies, theories, and values that impact education. It prepares students to improve policies and practices within organizations through the motivation and supervision of others. Students develop skills needed to design, implement, and evaluate educational programs and curricula. Courses include educational law, educational finance, organizational communication, human resource management, instruction supervision, and organizational management.
	The Ed.D. in educational leadership program is designed to enhance educational leadership strengths. Students learn innovative and collaborative techniques used to manage and govern educational institutions. The program prepares students for administrative leadership positions at the district, regional, state, or national level.
	Note: These programs do not lead to teacher or administrator certification, licensure, or endorsement in any state in the United States.
Research Facilities	Argosy University libraries provide curriculum support and educational resources, including current text materials, diagnostic training documents, reference materials and databases, journals and dissertations, and major and current titles in program areas. There is an online public access catalog of library resources available throughout the Argosy University system. Students have remote access to the campus library database, enabling them to study and conduct research at home. Academic databases offer dissertation abstracts, academic journals, and professional periodicals. All library computers are Internet accessible. Software applications include Word, Excel, PowerPoint, SPSS, and various test-scoring programs.
Financial Aid	Financial aid is available to those who qualify. Argosy University, Salt Lake City, offers access to federal and state aid programs, merit-based awards, grants, loans, and a work-study program. As a first step, students should complete the Free Application for Federal Student Aid (FAFSA). Prospective students can apply electronically at http://www.fafsa.ed.gov or at the campus.
Cost of Study	Tuition varies by program. Students should contact Argosy University, Salt Lake City, for tuition information.
Living and Housing Costs	Students typically live in apartments in the metropolitan Salt Lake City area. Living expenses vary according to each student's preferred standard of living, housing, and transportation. The University does not offer or operate student housing. Most of the students are full-time working professionals who live within driving distance of the campus. Several nearby hotels offer special rates for those who commute from long distances. The Admissions Department also maintains a list of housing options, including contact information for University students who wish to share housing. For more information, students should contact the Admissions Department.
Student Group	Admission to Argosy University, Salt Lake City, is selective to ensure a dynamic and engaged student body. It encourages diversity in academic and employment backgrounds and promotes integration of the student body into professional life through established connections with local and national professional associations. Argosy University offers a professionally oriented education with rich opportunities to gain practical experience in class, field placements, and internships. Full-time students and working professionals gain the extensive knowledge and range of skills necessary for effective performance in their chosen fields.
Student Outcomes	Students can register with the University's online career-services system and use select services from a distance, such as degree-specific career e-mail lists, national job posts, and virtual job fairs. Students should contact the University for more information.
Location	Argosy University, Salt Lake City, offers a high-quality education in an intimate, small-group setting. Argosy University, Salt Lake City, is conveniently located in Draper, Utah, nestled in the Wasatch Mountains about 20 miles south of Salt Lake City. The area's business climate and numerous hospitals, schools, clinics, and social service agencies can provide many exciting training opportunities for students.
The University	Argosy University is a private institution with nineteen locations across the nation. Argosy University, Salt Lake City, provides students with a career resources office, an academic resources center, and extensive information access for research. It offers the resources of a large university, plus the friendliness and personal attention of a small campus.
	The innovative programs feature dynamic, relevant, and practical curricula delivered in flexible class formats. Students enjoy scheduling options that make it easier to fit school into their busy lives, choosing from day and evening courses, on campus or online. Many students find a combination of class formats to be an ideal way of continuing their education while meeting family and professional demands.
	Argosy University is accredited by the Higher Learning Commission and a member of the North Central Association (30 North LaSalle Street, Suite 2400, Chicago, Illinois 60602; 800-621-7440 (toll-free); http://www.ncahlc.org).
Applying	Argosy University, Salt Lake City, accepts students year-round on a rolling admissions basis, depending on availability of required courses. Applications for admission are available online or by contacting the campus.
Correspondence and Information	Argosy University, Salt Lake City 121 Election Road, Suite 300 Draper, Utah 84020 Phone: 801-601-5000 888-639-4756 (toll-free) Fax: 801-601-4990 E-mail: auadmissions@argosy.edu Web site: http://www.argosy.edu/saltlakecity

Argosy University, Salt Lake City

THE FACULTY

The Argosy University faculty comprises working professionals who are eager to help students succeed. Members bring real-world experience and the latest practice innovations to the academic setting. The diverse faculty members of the College of Education are widely recognized for contributions to their field. Most hold doctoral degrees. They provide a substantive education that combines comprehensive knowledge with critical skills and practical workplace relevance. Above all, faculty members are committed to their students' personal and professional development.

ARGOSY UNIVERSITY, SAN DIEGO

ARGOSY UNIVERSITY.

College of Education

Programs of Study
Argosy University, San Diego, offers the Master of Arts in Education (M.A.Ed.) degree in educational leadership, instructional leadership, instructional specialist in English language learners/English second language (ELL/ESL), instructional specialist in reading (elementary), and instructional specialist in reading (middle/secondary); and the Doctor of Education (Ed.D.) degree in community college executive leadership, educational leadership, and instructional leadership.

The M.A.Ed. in educational leadership program is designed to instill key philosophies, theories, and values that impact education. It prepares students to improve policies and practices within organizations through the motivation and supervision of others. Students develop skills needed to design, implement, and evaluate educational programs and curricula. Courses include educational law, educational finance, organizational communication, human resource management, instruction supervision, and organizational management.

The M.A.Ed. in instructional leadership program examines the challenges and problems encountered in today's educational environment. Course work encompasses the historical, philosophical, psychological, social, technical, and theoretical aspects of education. Students develop skills in analysis, oral and written communication, problem solving, critical thinking, team building, and computer technology. The program is designed for those who wish to develop or enhance classroom skills, become curriculum supervisors, or become educational leaders with a focus on instruction. Students may choose optional concentrations in single- or multiple-subject teacher credential preparation.

The M.A.Ed. instructional specialist in ELL/ESL program prepares teachers to work with ELL/ESL students. Upon completion of the program, teachers are equipped to effectively support the learning of such students.

The M.A.Ed. instructional specialist in reading (elementary) program prepares teachers to work with beginning and developing readers. As a result of this program, teachers are prepared to integrate reading across the curriculum and increase students' vocabulary and reading fluency.

The M.A.Ed. instructional specialist in reading (middle/secondary) program prepares teachers to work with beginning and developing readers. As a result of this program, teachers are prepared to integrate reading across the curriculum and increase students' vocabulary and reading fluency.

The Ed.D. in community college executive leadership program offers an accelerated course of study intended to meet the needs of community college administrators who are looking to move into senior administrative positions (such as president, vice president, dean, and director) in community colleges.

The Ed.D. in educational leadership program is designed to enhance educational leadership strengths. Students learn innovative and collaborative techniques used to manage and govern educational institutions. The program prepares students for administrative leadership positions at the district, regional, state, or national level. Students must choose a concentration in higher education administration or K–12 education.

The Ed.D. in instructional leadership program draws upon educational theories and practices to help students discover new learning techniques for diverse audiences. Students enrolled in this program master teaching methodologies, hone classroom skills, and gain the knowledge required to become curriculum administrators or educational leaders with a focus on instruction. Students must choose a concentration in higher education or K–12 education.

Note: The M.A.Ed. in instructional leadership (multiple subject teacher credential prep) and the M.A.Ed. in instructional leadership (single-subject teacher credential prep) can lead to Multiple Subject Teaching Credential or Single Subject Teaching Credential depending on the program concentration selected. All other programs offered through the College of Education do not lead to teacher or administrator certification, licensure, or endorsement in any state in the United States. The programs offered through Argosy University online programs do not lead to teacher or administrator certification, licensure, or endorsement in any state in the United States regardless of the state in which the student resides.

Research Facilities
Argosy University libraries provide curriculum support and educational resources, including current text materials, diagnostic training documents, reference materials and databases, journals and dissertations, and major and current titles in program areas. There is an online public access catalog of library resources available throughout the Argosy University system. Students have remote access to the campus library database, enabling them to study and conduct research at home. Academic databases offer dissertation abstracts, academic journals, and professional periodicals. All library computers are Internet accessible. Software applications include Word, Excel, PowerPoint, SPSS, and various test-scoring programs.

Financial Aid
Financial aid is available to those who qualify. Argosy University, San Diego, offers access to federal and state aid programs, merit-based awards, grants, loans, and a work-study program. As a first step, students should complete the Free Application for Federal Student Aid (FAFSA). Prospective students can apply electronically at http://www.fafsa.ed.gov or at the campus.

Cost of Study
Tuition varies by program. Students should contact Argosy University, San Diego, for tuition information.

Living and Housing Costs
Students typically live in apartments in the metropolitan San Diego area. Living expenses vary according to each student's preferred standard of living, housing, and transportation. The University does not offer or operate student housing. Most of the students are full-time working professionals who live within driving distance of the campus. Several nearby hotels offer special rates for those who commute from long distances. The Admissions Department also maintains a list of housing options, including contact information for University students who wish to share housing. For more information, students should contact the Admissions Department.

Student Group
Admission to Argosy University, San Diego, is selective to ensure a dynamic and engaged student body. It encourages diversity in academic and employment backgrounds and promotes integration of the student body into professional life through established connections with local and national professional associations. Argosy University offers a professionally oriented education with rich opportunities to gain practical experience in class, field placements, and internships. Full-time students and working professionals gain the extensive knowledge and range of skills necessary for effective performance in their chosen fields.

Student Outcomes
Students can register with the University's online career-services system and use select services from a distance, such as degree-specific career e-mail lists, national job posts, and virtual job fairs. Students should contact the University for more information.

Location
San Diego, southern California's second-largest city, offers an ideal climate year-round, 70 miles of beautiful beaches, colorful neighborhoods, and a dynamic downtown district. Argosy University, San Diego, offers classrooms, a library resource center, student lounge, staff and faculty offices, and other amenities. The area offers numerous attractions, including Sea World and the famous San Diego Zoo and Wild Animal Park. San Diego's business environment includes several Fortune 500 companies such as QUALCOMM and Pfizer, Inc., and a concentration of high-tech companies. Many educational institutions and agencies in the area provide varied opportunities for student training.

The University
Argosy University is a private institution with nineteen locations across the nation. Argosy University, San Diego, provides a career resources office, an academic resources center, and extensive information access for research. It offers the resources of a large university plus the friendliness and personal attention of a small campus.

The innovative programs feature dynamic, relevant, and practical curricula delivered in flexible class formats. Students enjoy scheduling options that make it easier to fit school into their busy lives, choosing from day and evening courses, on campus or online. Many students find a combination of class formats to be an ideal way of continuing their education while meeting family and professional demands.

Argosy University is accredited by the Higher Learning Commission and a member of the North Central Association (30 North LaSalle Street, Suite 2400, Chicago, Illinois 60602; 800-621-7440 (toll-free); http://www.ncahlc.org).

Applying
Argosy University, San Diego, accepts students year-round on a rolling admissions basis, depending on availability of required courses. Applications for admission are available online or by contacting the campus.

Correspondence and Information
Argosy University, San Diego
1615 Murray Canyon Road
San Diego, California 92108
Phone: 619-321-3000
866-505-0333 (toll-free)
Fax: 619-321-3005
E-mail: auadmissions@argosy.edu
Web site: http://argosy.edu/sandiego/

Argosy University, San Diego

THE FACULTY

The Argosy University faculty comprises working professionals who are eager to help students succeed. Members bring real-world experience and the latest practice innovations to the academic setting. The diverse faculty members of the College of Education are widely recognized for contributions to their field. Many are published scholars, and most hold doctoral degrees. They provide a substantive education that combines comprehensive knowledge with critical skills and practical workplace relevance. Above all, faculty members are committed to their students' personal and professional development.

ARGOSY UNIVERSITY.

ARGOSY UNIVERSITY, SAN FRANCISCO BAY AREA

College of Education

Programs of Study	Argosy University, San Francisco Bay Area, offers the Master of Arts in Education (M.A.Ed.) degree in educational leadership, instructional leadership, instructional specialist in English language learners/English second language (ELL/ESL), instructional specialist in reading (elementary), and instructional specialist in reading (middle/secondary); and the Doctor of Education (Ed.D.) degree in community college executive leadership, educational leadership, and instructional leadership.

The M.A.Ed. in educational leadership program is designed to instill key philosophies, theories, and values that impact education. It prepares students to improve policies and practices within organizations through the motivation and supervision of others. Students develop skills needed to design, implement, and evaluate educational programs and curricula. Courses include educational law, educational finance, organizational communication, human resource management, instruction supervision, and organizational management.

The M.A.Ed. in instructional leadership program examines the challenges and problems encountered in today's educational environment. Course work encompasses the historical, philosophical, psychological, social, technical, and theoretical aspects of education. Students develop skills in analysis, oral and written communication, problem solving, critical thinking, team building, and computer technology. The program is designed for those who wish to develop or enhance classroom skills, become curriculum supervisors, or become educational leaders with a focus on instruction. Students may choose optional concentrations in single- or multiple-subject teacher credential preparation.

The M.A.Ed. instructional specialist in ELL/ESL program prepares teachers to work with ELL/ESL students. Upon completion of the program, teachers are equipped to effectively support the learning of such students.

The M.A.Ed. instructional specialist in reading (elementary) program prepares teachers to work with beginning and developing readers. As a result of this program, teachers are prepared to integrate reading across the curriculum and increase students' vocabulary and reading fluency.

The M.A.Ed. instructional specialist in reading (middle/secondary) program prepares teachers to work with beginning and developing readers. As a result of this program, teachers are prepared to integrate reading across the curriculum and increase students' vocabulary and reading fluency.

The Ed.D. in community college executive leadership program offers an accelerated course of study intended to meet the needs of community college administrators who are looking to move into senior administrative positions (such as president, vice president, dean, and director) in community colleges.

The Ed.D. in educational leadership program is designed to enhance educational leadership strengths. Students learn innovative and collaborative techniques used to manage and govern educational institutions. The program prepares students for administrative leadership positions at the district, regional, state, or national level. Students must choose a concentration in higher education administration or K–12 education.

The Ed.D. in instructional leadership program draws on educational theories and practices to help students discover new learning techniques for diverse audiences. Students enrolled in this program master teaching methodologies, hone classroom skills, and gain the knowledge required to become curriculum administrators or educational leaders with a focus on instruction. Students must choose a concentration in higher education or K–12 education.

Note: The M.A.Ed. in instructional leadership (multiple subject teacher credential prep) and the M.A.Ed. in instructional leadership (single subject teacher credential prep) programs can lead to multiple subject teaching credential or single subject teaching credential depending on the program concentration selected. All other programs offered through the College of Education do not lead to teacher or administrator certification, licensure, or endorsement in any state in the United States. The programs offered through Argosy University online programs do not lead to teacher or administrator certification, licensure, or endorsement in any state in the United States regardless of the state in which the student resides.

Research Facilities	Argosy University libraries provide curriculum support and educational resources, including current text materials, diagnostic training documents, reference materials and databases, journals and dissertations, and major and current titles in program areas. There is an online public-access catalog of library resources available throughout the Argosy University system. Students have remote access to the campus library database, enabling them to study and conduct research at home. Academic databases offer dissertation abstracts, academic journals, and professional periodicals. All library computers are Internet accessible. Software applications include Word, Excel, PowerPoint, SPSS, and various test-scoring programs.
Financial Aid	Financial aid is available to those who qualify. Argosy University, San Francisco Bay Area, offers access to federal and state aid programs, merit-based awards, grants, loans, and a work-study program. As a first step, students should complete the Free Application for Federal Student Aid (FAFSA). Prospective students can apply electronically at http://www.fafsa.ed.gov or at the campus.
Cost of Study	Tuition varies by program. Students should contact Argosy University, San Francisco Bay Area, for tuition information.
Living and Housing Costs	Students typically live in apartments in the metropolitan area. Living expenses vary according to each student's preferred standard of living, housing, and transportation. The University does not offer or operate student housing. Most of the students are full-time working professionals who live within driving distance of the campus. Several nearby hotels offer special rates for those who commute from long distances. The Admissions Department also maintains a list of housing options, including contact information for University students who wish to share housing. For more information, students should contact the Admissions Department.
Student Group	Admission to Argosy University, San Francisco Bay Area, is selective to ensure a dynamic and engaged student body. It encourages diversity in academic and employment backgrounds and promotes integration of the student body into professional life through established connections with local and national professional associations. Argosy University offers a professionally oriented education with rich opportunities to gain practical experience in class, field placements, and internships. Full-time students and working professionals gain the extensive knowledge and range of skills necessary for effective performance in their chosen fields.
Student Outcomes	Students can register with the University's online career-services system and use select services from a distance, such as degree-specific career e-mail lists, national job posts, and virtual job fairs. Students should contact the University for more information.
Location	Located in northern California, Argosy University, San Francisco Bay Area, attracts students from the immediate area as well as from around the country and the world. The energy in San Francisco is contagious. Numerous surveys rank San Francisco as one of the most wired cities in the world, thanks to its high concentration of computer-savvy citizens and businesses.

Many educational institutions and agencies in the area provide varied opportunities for student training. The Bay Area and nearby Silicon Valley are home to leading new media companies such as Pixar, ILM, and Sega. A who's who of technology companies call the Bay Area home, including Apple, Cisco, Hewlett-Packard, Intel, Oracle, and Sun Microsystems. The Bay Area also is the home of traditional companies such as BankAmerica, Chevron, Levi-Strauss, Safeway, and Wells Fargo.

The University	Argosy University is a private institution with nineteen locations across the nation. Argosy University, San Francisco Bay Area, provides students with a career resources office, an academic resources center, and extensive information access for research. It offers the resources of a large university plus the friendliness and personal attention of a small campus. The innovative programs feature dynamic, relevant, and practical curricula delivered in flexible class formats. Students enjoy scheduling options that make it easier to fit school into their busy lives, choosing from day and evening courses, on campus or online. Many students find a combination of class formats to be an ideal way of continuing their education while meeting family and professional demands.

Argosy University is accredited by the Higher Learning Commission and a member of the North Central Association (30 North LaSalle Street, Suite 2400, Chicago, Illinois 60602; 800-621-7440 (toll-free); http://www.ncahlc.org).

Applying	Argosy University, San Francisco Bay Area, accepts students year-round on a rolling admissions basis, depending on availability of required courses. Applications for admission are available online or by contacting the campus.
Correspondence and Information	Argosy University, San Francisco Bay Area 1005 Atlantic Avenue Alameda, California 94501 Phone: 510-215-0277 866-215-2777 (toll free) Fax: 510-215-0299 E-mail: auadmissions@argosy.edu Web site: http://www.argosy.edu/sanfrancisco

Argosy University, San Francisco Bay Area

THE FACULTY

The Argosy University faculty comprises working professionals who are eager to help students succeed. Members bring real-world experience and the latest practice innovations to the academic setting. The diverse faculty members of the College of Education are widely recognized for contributions to the field. Most hold doctoral degrees. They provide a substantive education that combines comprehensive knowledge with critical skills and practical workplace relevance. Above all, faculty members are committed to their students' personal and professional development.

ARGOSY UNIVERSITY.

ARGOSY UNIVERSITY, SARASOTA

College of Education

Programs of Study	Argosy University, Sarasota, offers the Master of Arts in Education (M.A.Ed.) degree in educational leadership and instructional leadership; and the Education Specialist (Ed.S.) degree in educational leadership and instructional leadership; and the Doctor of Education (Ed.D.) degree in community college executive leadership, educational leadership, and instructional leadership.
	The M.A.Ed. in educational leadership program is designed to instill key philosophies, theories, and values that impact education. It prepares students to improve policies and practices within organizations through the motivation and supervision of others. Students develop skills needed to design, implement, and evaluate educational programs and curricula. Courses include educational law, educational finance, organizational communication, human resource management, instruction supervision, and organizational management.
	The M.A.Ed. in instructional leadership program examines the challenges and problems encountered in today's educational environment. Course work encompasses the historical, philosophical, psychological, social, technical, and theoretical aspects of education. Students develop skills in analysis, oral and written communication, problem solving, critical thinking, team building, and computer technology. The program is designed for those who wish to develop or enhance classroom skills, become curriculum supervisors, or become educational leaders with a focus on instruction.
	The Ed.S. in educational leadership program concentrates on applied organizational theory within the context of educational organizations. This specialized program develops the competencies required to secure educational administrator positions at the elementary or secondary school level.
	The Ed.S. in instructional leadership program enables experienced teachers to become more effective practitioners and educational leaders with a focus on instruction. Course work is designed to satisfy the requirements of students seeking career advancement and those who are working toward a doctoral degree.
	The Ed.D. in community college executive leadership program offers an accelerated course of study intended to meet the needs of community college administrators who are looking to move into senior administrative positions (such as president, vice president, dean, and director) in community colleges.
	The Ed.D. in educational leadership program is designed to enhance educational leadership strengths. Students learn innovative and collaborative techniques used to manage and govern educational institutions. The program prepares students for administrative leadership positions at the district, regional, state, or national level. Students must choose a concentration in higher education administration or K–12 education.
	The Ed.D. in instructional leadership program draws upon educational theories and practices to help students discover new learning techniques for diverse audiences. Students enrolled in this program master teaching methodologies, hone classroom skills, and gain the knowledge required to become curriculum administrators or educational leaders with a focus on instruction. Students must choose a concentration in education technology, higher education, or K–12 education.
	Note: These programs do not lead to teacher or administrator certification, licensure, or endorsement in any state in the United States.
Research Facilities	Argosy University libraries provide curriculum support and educational resources, including current text materials, diagnostic training documents, reference materials and databases, journals and dissertations, and major and current titles in program areas. There is an online public-access catalog of library resources available throughout the Argosy University system. Students have remote access to the campus library database, enabling them to study and conduct research at home. Academic databases offer dissertation abstracts, academic journals, and professional periodicals. All library computers are Internet accessible. Software applications include Word, Excel, PowerPoint, SPSS, and various test-scoring programs.
Financial Aid	Financial aid is available to those who qualify. Argosy University, Sarasota, offers access to federal and state aid programs, merit-based awards, grants, loans, and a work-study program. As a first step, students should complete the Free Application for Federal Student Aid (FAFSA). Prospective students can apply electronically at http://www.fafsa.ed.gov or at the campus.
Cost of Study	Tuition varies by program. Students should contact Argosy University, Sarasota, for tuition information.
Living and Housing Costs	Students typically live in apartments in the metropolitan Sarasota area. Living expenses vary according to each student's preferred standard of living, housing, and transportation. The University does not offer or operate student housing. Most of the students are full-time working professionals who live within driving distance of the campus. Several nearby hotels offer special rates for students when they attend one-week in-residence intersessions. The Admissions Department also maintains a list of housing options, including contact information for University students who wish to share housing. For more information, students should contact the Admissions Department.
Student Group	Admission to Argosy University, Sarasota, is selective to ensure a dynamic and engaged student body. It encourages diversity in academic and employment backgrounds and promotes integration of the student body into professional life through established connections with local and national professional associations. Argosy University offers a professionally oriented education with rich opportunities to gain practical experience in class, field placements, and internships. Full-time students and working professionals gain the extensive knowledge and range of skills necessary for effective performance in their chosen fields.
Student Outcomes	Students can register with the University's online career-services system and use select services from a distance, such as degree-specific career e-mail lists, national job posts, and virtual job fairs. Students should contact the University for more information.
Location	Located in northeast Sarasota, the campus is specifically designed for postsecondary and graduate-level instruction through a unique combination of in-residence course work, tutorials, and online study courses. Several of the programs are off-site tutorials and intensive one-week classroom sessions. Students may also complete up to 49 percent of the work of some degree programs via online courses that allow interaction with faculty members and classmates from any Internet connection.
	Sarasota is recognized as Florida's cultural center and is home to a professional symphony, ballet, and opera as well as dozens of theaters and art galleries. Well-known vacation attractions such as Disney World, Busch Gardens–Tampa, and the city of Miami are within a few hours' drive. The area enjoys mild winters and endless summer beauty.
	The business sector in the Gulf Coast community helps make it one of the top 20 places to live and work. ASO Corporation, Nelson Publishing, and Select Technology Group are among the numerous companies headquartered in Sarasota County. The area's top employers include Sarasota Memorial Hospital and Publix Supermarkets. Many educational institutions and agencies in the area provide varied opportunities for student training.
The University	Argosy University is a private institution with nineteen locations across the nation. Argosy University, Sarasota, provides students with a career resources office, an academic resources center, and extensive information access for research. It offers the resources of a large university plus the friendliness and personal attention of a small campus.
	The innovative programs feature dynamic, relevant, and practical curricula delivered in flexible class formats. Students enjoy scheduling options that make it easier to fit school into their busy lives, choosing from day and evening courses, on campus or online. Many students find a combination of class formats to be an ideal way of continuing their education while meeting family and professional demands.
	Argosy University is accredited by the Higher Learning Commission and a member of the North Central Association (30 North LaSalle Street, Suite 2400, Chicago, Illinois 60602; 800-621-7440 (toll-free); http://www.ncahlc.org).
Applying	Argosy University, Sarasota, accepts students year-round on a rolling admissions basis, depending on availability of required courses. Applications for admission are available online or by contacting the campus.
Correspondence and Information	Argosy University, Sarasota 5250 17th Street Sarasota, Florida 34235 Phone: 941-379-0404 800-331-5995 (toll-free) Fax: 941-371-8910 E-mail: auadmissions@argosy.edu Web site: http://www.argosy.edu/sarasota

Argosy University, Sarasota

THE FACULTY

The Argosy University faculty comprises working professionals who are eager to help students succeed. Members bring real-world experience and the latest practice innovations to the academic setting. The diverse faculty members of the College of Education are widely recognized for contributions to their field. Most hold doctoral degrees. They provide a substantive education that combines comprehensive knowledge with critical skills and practical workplace relevance. Above all, faculty members are committed to their students' personal and professional development.

ARGOSY UNIVERSITY

ARGOSY UNIVERSITY, SCHAUMBURG

College of Education

Programs of Study	Argosy University, Schaumburg, offers the Master of Arts in Education (M.A.Ed.) in educational leadership; the Education Specialist (Ed.S.) degree in educational leadership and instructional leadership; and the Doctor of Education (Ed.D.) degree in community college executive leadership, educational leadership, and instructional leadership.

The M.A.Ed. in educational leadership program is designed to instill key philosophies, theories, and values that impact education. It prepares students to improve policies and practices within organizations through the motivation and supervision of others. Students develop skills needed to design, implement, and evaluate educational programs and curricula. Courses include educational law, educational finance, organizational communication, human resource management, instruction supervision, and organizational management. The program now offers principal/general administrative certification, also known as Type 75 certification.

The Ed.S. in educational leadership program concentrates on applied organizational theory within the context of educational organizations. This specialized program develops the competencies required to secure educational administrator positions at the elementary or secondary school level. The program now offers superintendent certification.

The Ed.S. in instructional leadership program enables experienced teachers to become more effective practitioners and educational leaders with a focus on instruction. Course work is designed to satisfy the requirements of students seeking career advancement and those who are working toward a doctoral degree.

The Ed.D. in community college executive leadership program offers an accelerated course of study intended to meet the needs of community college administrators who are looking to move into senior administrative positions (such as president, vice president, dean, and director) in community colleges.

The Ed.D. in educational leadership program is designed to enhance educational leadership strengths. Students learn innovative and collaborative techniques used to manage and govern educational institutions. The program prepares students for administrative leadership positions at the district, regional, state, or national level. Students must choose a concentration in higher education administration or K–12 education. The program now offers an optional concentration in district leadership.

The Ed.D. in instructional leadership program draws upon educational theories and practices to help students discover new learning techniques for diverse audiences. Students enrolled in this program master teaching methodologies, hone classroom skills, and gain the knowledge required to become curriculum administrators or educational leaders with a focus on instruction. Students must choose a concentration in education technology, higher education, or K–12 education.

Note: The M.A.Ed. in educational leadership–Illinois Type 75 principal preparation/general administrative track and the certificate of advanced studies (CAS) in educational leadership–Illinois Type 75 principal preparation/general administrative certification can lead to State of Illinois Type 75 general administrative certificate. The Ed.S. in educational leadership–Illinois Type 75 certification/superintendent preparation track, certification of advanced studies in educational leadership–Illinois Type 75 certification/superintendent preparation track, and the Ed.D. in educational leadership–superintendent preparation track can lead to State of Illinois Type 75 superintendent's endorsement. All other programs offered through the College of Education do not lead to teacher or administrator certification, licensure, or endorsement in any state in the United States. The programs offered through Argosy University online programs do not lead to teacher or administrator certification, licensure, or endorsement in any state in the United States regardless of the state in which the student resides. |
Research Facilities	Argosy University libraries provide curriculum support and educational resources, including current text materials, diagnostic training documents, reference materials and databases, journals and dissertations, and major and current titles in program areas. There is an online public access catalog of library resources available throughout the Argosy University system. Students have remote access to the campus library database, enabling them to study and conduct research at home. Academic databases offer dissertation abstracts, academic journals, and professional periodicals. All library computers are Internet accessible. Software applications include Word, Excel, PowerPoint, SPSS, and various test-scoring programs.
Financial Aid	Financial aid is available to those who qualify. Argosy University, Schaumburg, offers access to federal and state aid programs, merit-based awards, grants, loans, and a work-study program. As a first step, students should complete the Free Application for Federal Student Aid (FAFSA). Prospective students can apply electronically at http://www.fafsa.ed.gov or at the campus.
Cost of Study	Tuition varies by program. Students should contact Argosy University, Schaumburg, for tuition information.
Living and Housing Costs	Students typically live in apartments in the metropolitan Schaumburg area. Living expenses vary according to each student's preferred standard of living, housing, and transportation. The University does not offer or operate student housing. Most of the students are full-time working professionals who live within driving distance of the campus. Several nearby hotels offer special rates for those who commute from long distances. The Admissions Department also maintains a list of housing options, including contact information for University students who wish to share housing. For more information, students should contact the Admissions Department.
Student Group	Admission to Argosy University, Schaumburg, is selective to ensure a dynamic and engaged student body. It encourages diversity in academic and employment backgrounds and promotes integration of the student body into professional life through established connections with local and national professional associations. Argosy University offers a professionally oriented education with rich opportunities to gain practical experience in class, field placements, and internships. Full-time students and working professionals gain the extensive knowledge and range of skills necessary for effective performance in their chosen fields.
Student Outcomes	Students can register with the University's online career-services system and use select services from a distance, such as degree-specific career e-mail lists, national job posts, and virtual job fairs. Students should contact the University for more information.
Location	Argosy University, Schaumburg, is conveniently located in the northwest suburban area, approximately 45 minutes from downtown Chicago. The University's small size offers a highly personal atmosphere and flexible programs tailored to students' needs. Visitors to Chicago experience a range of attractions to stimulate both intellectual and recreational pursuits. Located on the shores of Lake Michigan in the Midwest, Chicago is home to world-champion sports teams, an internationally acclaimed symphony orchestra, renowned architecture, and nearly 3 million residents. Among the variety of history and art museums in the city, the Chicago Cultural Center offers more than 600 art programs and exhibits each year. Recreational opportunities include hiking and cycling on miles of lakefront trails, golfing, and shopping.

Many educational institutions and agencies in the area provide varied opportunities for student training. Schaumburg's business environment includes 5,000 businesses that employ 80,000 people. The area's largest employers are Motorola, Experian, Cingular, and IBM. |
| **The University** | Argosy University is a private institution with nineteen locations across the nation. Argosy University, Schaumburg, provides students with a career resources office, an academic resources center, and extensive information access for research. It offers the resources of a large university, plus the friendliness and personal attention of a small campus.

The innovative programs feature dynamic, relevant, and practical curricula delivered in flexible class formats. Students enjoy scheduling options that make it easier to fit school into their busy lives, choosing from day and evening courses, on campus or online. Many students find a combination of class formats to be an ideal way of continuing their education while meeting family and professional demands.

Argosy University is accredited by the Higher Learning Commission and a member of the North Central Association (30 North LaSalle Street, Suite 2400, Chicago, Illinois 60602; 800-621-7440 (toll-free); http://www.ncahlc.org). |
| **Applying** | Argosy University, Schaumburg, accepts students year-round on a rolling admissions basis, depending on availability of required courses. Applications for admission are available online or by contacting the campus. |
| **Correspondence and Information** | Argosy University, Schaumburg
999 North Plaza Drive, Suite 111
Schaumburg, Illinois 60173-5403

Phone: 847-969-4900
     866-290-2777 (toll-free)
Fax: 847-969-4998
E-mail: auadmissions@argosy.edu
Web site: http://www.argosy.edu/schaumburg |

Argosy University, Schaumburg

THE FACULTY

The Argosy University faculty comprises working professionals who are eager to help students succeed. Members bring real-world experience and the latest practice innovations to the academic setting. The diverse faculty members of the College of Education are widely recognized for contributions to the field. Most hold doctoral degrees. They provide a substantive education that combines comprehensive knowledge with critical skills and practical workplace relevance. Above all, faculty members are committed to their students' personal and professional development.

ARGOSY UNIVERSITY, SEATTLE

ARGOSY UNIVERSITY

College of Education

Programs of Study	Argosy University, Seattle, offers the Master of Arts in Education (M.A.Ed.) degree in educational leadership and instructional leadership and the Doctor of Education (Ed.D.) degree in community college executive leadership, educational leadership, and instructional leadership.
	The M.A.Ed. in educational leadership program is designed to instill key philosophies, theories, and values that impact education. It prepares students to improve policies and practices within organizations through the motivation and supervision of others. Students develop skills needed to design, implement, and evaluate educational programs and curricula. Courses include educational law, educational finance, organizational communication, human resource management, instruction supervision, and organizational management.
	The M.A.Ed. in instructional leadership program examines the challenges and problems encountered in today's educational environment. Course work encompasses the historical, philosophical, psychological, social, technical, and theoretical aspects of education. Students develop skills in analysis, oral and written communication, problem solving, critical thinking, team building, and computer technology. The program is designed for those who wish to develop or enhance classroom skills, become curriculum supervisors, or become educational leaders with a focus on instruction.
	The Ed.D. in community college executive leadership program offers an accelerated course of study intended to meet the needs of community college administrators who are looking to move into senior administrative positions (such as president, vice president, dean, and director) in community colleges.
	The Ed.D. in educational leadership program is designed to enhance educational leadership strengths. Students learn innovative and collaborative techniques used to manage and govern educational institutions. The program prepares students for administrative leadership positions at the district, regional, state, or national level. Students must choose a concentration in district leadership, higher education administration, or K–12 education.
	The Ed.D. in instructional leadership program draws on educational theories and practices to help students discover new learning techniques for diverse audiences. Students enrolled in this program master teaching methodologies, hone classroom skills, and gain the knowledge required to become curriculum administrators or educational leaders with a focus on instruction. Students must choose a concentration in education technology, higher education, or K–12 education.
	Note: These programs do not lead to teacher or administrator certification, licensure, or endorsement in any state in the United States.
Research Facilities	Argosy University libraries provide curriculum support and educational resources, including current text materials, diagnostic training documents, reference materials and databases, journals and dissertations, and major and current titles in program areas. There is an online public-access catalog of library resources available throughout the Argosy University system. Students have remote access to the campus library database, enabling them to study and conduct research at home. Academic databases offer dissertation abstracts, academic journals, and professional periodicals. All library computers are Internet accessible. Software applications include Word, Excel, PowerPoint, SPSS, and various test-scoring programs.
Financial Aid	Financial aid is available to those who qualify. Argosy University, Seattle, offers access to federal and state aid programs, merit-based awards, grants, loans, and a work-study program. As a first step, students should complete the Free Application for Federal Student Aid (FAFSA). Prospective students can apply electronically at http://www.fafsa.ed.gov or at the campus.
Cost of Study	Tuition varies by program. Students should contact Argosy University, Seattle, for tuition information.
Living and Housing Costs	Students typically live in apartments in the Seattle metropolitan area. Living expenses vary according to each student's preferred standard of living, housing, and transportation. The University does not offer or operate student housing. Most of the students are full-time working professionals who live within driving distance of the campus. Several nearby hotels offer special rates for those who commute from long distances. The Admissions Department also maintains a list of housing options, including contact information for University students who wish to share housing. For more information, students should contact the Admissions Department.
Student Group	Admission to Argosy University, Seattle, is selective to ensure a dynamic and engaged student body. It encourages diversity in academic and employment backgrounds and promotes integration of the student body into professional life through established connections with local and national professional associations. Argosy University offers a professionally oriented education with rich opportunities to gain practical experience in class, field placements, and internships. Full-time students and working professionals gain the extensive knowledge and range of skills necessary for effective performance in their chosen fields.
Student Outcomes	Students can register with the University's online career-services system and use select services from a distance, such as degree-specific career e-mail lists, national job posts, and virtual job fairs. Students should contact the University for more information.
Location	Argosy University, Seattle, aspires to provide a supportive, collaborative, engaging, yet challenging learning environment. Easily reached through the King County Public Transportation System, the campus offers convenient access to local libraries, shops, restaurants, theaters, and art museums. Seattle offers numerous historical and multicultural museums, a symphony, the ballet, and many theater companies. The city is home to several major-league sports teams and offers myriad outdoor recreational opportunities, such as camping, hiking, fishing, skiing, and rock-climbing.
	Many educational institutions and agencies in the area provide varied opportunities for student training. Seattle's business environment encompasses a wide range of industries and features such giants as Microsoft, Boeing, and Alaska Air Group. The Port of Seattle and the University of Washington are also among the area's largest employers.
The University	Argosy University is a private institution with nineteen locations across the nation. Argosy University, Seattle, provides students with a career resources office, an academic resources center, and extensive information access for research. It offers the resources of a large university plus the friendliness and personal attention of a small campus. The innovative programs feature dynamic, relevant, and practical curricula delivered in flexible class formats. Students enjoy scheduling options that make it easier to fit school into their busy lives, choosing from day and evening courses, on campus or online. Many students find a combination of class formats to be an ideal way of continuing their education while meeting family and professional demands.
	Argosy University is accredited by the Higher Learning Commission and a member of the North Central Association (30 North LaSalle Street, Suite 2400, Chicago, Illinois 60602; 800-621-7440 (toll-free); http://www.ncahlc.org).
Applying	Argosy University, Seattle, accepts students year-round on a rolling admissions basis, depending on availability of required courses. Applications for admission are available online or by contacting the campus.
Correspondence and Information	Argosy University, Seattle 2601-A Elliott Avenue Seattle, Washington 98121 Phone: 206-283-4500 866-283-2777 (toll-free) Fax: 206-283-5777 E-mail: auadmissions@argosy.edu Web site: http://www.argosy.edu/seattle

Argosy University, Seattle

THE FACULTY

The Argosy University faculty comprises working professionals who are eager to help students succeed. Members bring real-world experience and the latest practice innovations to the academic setting. The diverse faculty members of the College of Education are widely recognized for contributions to the field. Most hold doctoral degrees. They provide a substantive education that combines comprehensive knowledge with critical skills and practical workplace relevance. Above all, faculty members of the College of Education are committed to their students' personal and professional development.

ARGOSY UNIVERSITY

ARGOSY UNIVERSITY, TAMPA

College of Education

Programs of Study	Argosy University, Tampa, offers the Master of Arts in Education (M.A.Ed.) in educational leadership and instructional leadership; the Education Specialist (Ed.S.) degree in educational leadership and instructional leadership; and the Doctor of Education (Ed.D.) degree in community college executive leadership, educational leadership, and instructional leadership. The M.A.Ed. in educational leadership program is designed to instill key philosophies, theories, and values that impact education. It prepares students to improve policies and practices within organizations through the motivation and supervision of others. Students develop skills needed to design, implement, and evaluate educational programs and curricula. Courses include educational law, educational finance, organizational communication, human resource management, instruction supervision, and organizational management. The M.A.Ed. in instructional leadership program examines the challenges and problems encountered in today's educational environment. Course work encompasses the historical, philosophical, psychological, social, technical, and theoretical aspects of education. Students develop skills in analysis, oral and written communication, problem solving, critical thinking, team building, and computer technology. The program is designed for those who wish to develop or enhance classroom skills, become curriculum supervisors, or become educational leaders with a focus on instruction. The Ed.S. in educational leadership program concentrates on applied organizational theory within the context of educational organizations. This specialized program develops the competencies required to secure educational administrator positions at the elementary or secondary school level. The Ed.S. in instructional leadership program enables experienced teachers to become more effective practitioners and educational leaders with a focus on instruction. Course work is designed to satisfy the requirements of students seeking career advancement and those who are working toward a doctoral degree. The Ed.D. in community college executive leadership program offers an accelerated course of study intended to meet the needs of community college administrators who are looking to move into senior administrative positions (such as president, vice president, dean, and director) in community colleges. The Ed.D. in educational leadership program is designed to enhance educational leadership strengths. Students learn innovative and collaborative techniques used to manage and govern educational institutions. The program prepares students for administrative leadership positions at the district, regional, state, or national level. Students must choose a concentration in higher education administration or K–12 education. The Ed.D. in instructional leadership program draws upon educational theories and practices to help students discover new learning techniques for diverse audiences. Students enrolled in this program master teaching methodologies, hone classroom skills, and gain the knowledge required to become curriculum administrators or educational leaders with a focus on instruction. Students must choose a concentration in higher education or K–12 education. Note: These programs do not lead to teacher or administrator certification, licensure, or endorsement in any state in the United States.
Research Facilities	Argosy University libraries provide curriculum support and educational resources, including current text materials, diagnostic training documents, reference materials and databases, journals and dissertations, and major and current titles in program areas. There is an online public-access catalog of library resources available throughout the Argosy University system. Students have remote access to the campus library database, enabling them to study and conduct research at home. Academic databases offer dissertation abstracts, academic journals, and professional periodicals. All library computers are Internet accessible. Software applications include Word, Excel, PowerPoint, SPSS, and various test-scoring programs.
Financial Aid	Financial aid is available to those who qualify. Argosy University, Tampa, offers access to federal and state aid programs, merit-based awards, grants, loans, and a work-study program. As a first step, students should complete the Free Application for Federal Student Aid (FAFSA). Prospective students can apply electronically at http://www.fafsa.ed.gov or at the campus.
Cost of Study	Tuition varies by program. Students should contact Argosy University, Tampa, for tuition information.
Living and Housing Costs	Students typically live in apartments in the metropolitan Tampa area. Living expenses vary according to each student's preferred standard of living, housing, and transportation. The University does not offer or operate student housing. Most of the students are full-time working professionals who live within driving distance of the campus. Several nearby hotels offer special rates for those who commute from long distances. The Admissions Department also maintains a list of housing options, including contact information, for University students who wish to share housing. For more information, students should contact the Admissions Department.
Student Group	Admission to Argosy University, Tampa, is selective to ensure a dynamic and engaged student body. It encourages diversity in academic and employment backgrounds and promotes integration of the student body into professional life through established connections with local and national professional associations. Argosy University offers a professionally oriented education with rich opportunities to gain practical experience in class, field placements, and internships. Full-time students and working professionals gain the extensive knowledge and range of skills necessary for effective performance in their chosen fields.
Student Outcomes	Students can register with the University's online career-services system and use select services from a distance, such as degree-specific career e-mail lists, national job posts, and virtual job fairs. Students should contact the University for more information.
Location	Located in sunny Florida, Argosy University, Tampa, attracts a diverse student population from throughout the United States, the Caribbean, Europe, Africa, and Asia. The school offers rigorous programs of study in a supportive, collaborative environment. The campus sits within an hour's drive of some of the most popular tourist destinations in the world, including the Disney theme parks, Busch Gardens, and the Florida Gulf Coast beaches. Major-league sporting events, concerts, theaters, world-renowned restaurants, recreational facilities, and a cosmopolitan social scene are all within easy reach. Tampa combines the opportunities of a large city with the friendliness of a small town with a strong sense of community. Many educational institutions and agencies in the area provide varied opportunities for student training. The Tampa-St. Petersburg-Clearwater metropolitan area offers a diversified economic base fueled by an array of companies, including Verizon Communications and JP Morgan Chase.
The University	Argosy University is a private institution with nineteen locations across the nation. Argosy University, Tampa, provides students with a career resources office, an academic resources center, and extensive information access for research. It offers the resources of a large university, plus the friendliness and personal attention of a small campus. The innovative programs feature dynamic, relevant, and practical curricula delivered in flexible class formats. Students enjoy scheduling options that make it easier to fit school into their busy lives, choosing from day and evening courses, on campus or online. Many students find a combination of class formats to be an ideal way of continuing their education while meeting family and professional demands. Argosy University is accredited by the Higher Learning Commission and a member of the North Central Association (30 North LaSalle Street, Suite 2400, Chicago, Illinois 60602; 800-621-7440 (toll-free); http://www.ncahlc.org).
Applying	Argosy University, Tampa, accepts students year-round on a rolling admissions basis, depending on availability of required courses. Applications for admission are available online or by contacting the campus.
Correspondence and Information	Argosy University, Tampa 1403 North Howard Avenue Tampa, Florida 33607 Phone: 813-393-5290 800-850-6488 (toll-free) Fax: 813-874-1989 E-mail: auadmissions@argosy.edu Web site: http://www.argosy.edu/tampa

Argosy University, Tampa

THE FACULTY

The Argosy University faculty comprises working professionals who are eager to help students succeed. Members bring real-world experience and the latest practice innovations to the academic setting. The diverse faculty members of the College of Education are widely recognized for contributions to the field. Most hold doctoral degrees. They provide a substantive education that combines comprehensive knowledge with critical skills and practical workplace relevance. Above all, faculty members are committed to their students' personal and professional development.

ARGOSY UNIVERSITY

ARGOSY UNIVERSITY, TWIN CITIES

College of Education

Programs of Study	Argosy University, Twin Cities, offers the Master of Arts in Education (M.A.Ed.) degrees in educational leadership and instructional leadership; the Education Specialist (Ed.S.) degree in educational leadership and instructional leadership; and the Doctor of Education (Ed.D.) degree in educational leadership and instructional leadership.

The M.A.Ed. in educational leadership program is designed to instill key philosophies, theories, and values that impact education. It prepares students to improve policies and practices within organizations through the motivation and supervision of others. Students develop skills needed to design, implement, and evaluate educational programs and curricula. Courses include educational law, educational finance, organizational communication, human resource management, instruction supervision, and organizational management.

The M.A.Ed. in instructional leadership program examines the challenges and problems encountered in today's educational environment. Course work encompasses the historical, philosophical, psychological, social, technical, and theoretical aspects of education. Students develop skills in analysis, oral and written communication, problem solving, critical thinking, team building, and computer technology. The program is designed for those who wish to develop or enhance classroom skills, become curriculum supervisors, or become educational leaders with a focus on instruction.

The Ed.S. in educational leadership program concentrates on applied organizational theory within the context of educational organizations. This specialized program develops the competencies required to secure educational administrator positions at the elementary or secondary school level.

The Ed.S. in instructional leadership program enables experienced teachers to become more effective practitioners and educational leaders with a focus on instruction. Course work is designed to satisfy the requirements of students seeking career advancement and those who are working toward a doctoral degree.

The Ed.D. in educational leadership program is designed to enhance educational leadership strengths. Students learn innovative and collaborative techniques used to manage and govern educational institutions. The program prepares students for administrative leadership positions at the district, regional, state, or national level. Students must choose a concentration in higher education administration or K–12 education.

The Ed.D. in instructional leadership program draws upon educational theories and practices to help students discover new learning techniques for diverse audiences. Students enrolled in this program master teaching methodologies, hone classroom skills, and gain the knowledge required to become curriculum administrators or educational leaders with a focus on instruction. Students must choose a concentration in educational technology, higher education, or K–12 education.

Note: These programs do not lead to teacher or administrator certification, licensure, or endorsement in any state in the United States.

Research Facilities Argosy University libraries provide curriculum support and educational resources including current text materials, diagnostic training documents, reference materials and databases, journals and dissertations, and major and current titles in program areas. There is an online public-access catalog of library resources available throughout the Argosy University system. Students have remote access to the campus library database, enabling them to study and conduct research at home. Academic databases offer dissertation abstracts, academic journals, and professional periodicals. All library computers are Internet accessible. Software applications include Word, Excel, PowerPoint, SPSS, and various test-scoring programs.

Financial Aid Financial aid is available to those who qualify. Argosy University, Twin Cities, offers access to federal and state aid programs, merit-based awards, grants, loans, and a work-study program. As a first step, students should complete the Free Application for Federal Student Aid (FAFSA). Prospective students can apply electronically at http://www.fafsa.ed.gov or at the campus.

Cost of Study Tuition varies by program. Students should contact Argosy University, Twin Cities, for tuition information.

Living and Housing Costs Students typically live in apartments in the metropolitan area. Living expenses vary according to each student's preferred standard of living, housing, and transportation. The University does not offer or operate student housing. Most of the students are full-time working professionals who live within driving distance of the campus. Several nearby hotels offer special rates for those who commute from long distances. The Admissions Department also maintains a list of housing options, including contact information for University students who wish to share housing. For more information, students should contact the Admissions Department.

Student Group Admission to Argosy University, Twin Cities, is selective to ensure a dynamic and engaged student body. The University encourages diversity in academic and employment backgrounds and promotes integration of the student body into professional life through established connections with local and national professional associations. Argosy University offers a professionally oriented education with rich opportunities to gain practical experience in class, field placements, and internships. Full-time students and working professionals gain the extensive knowledge and range of skills necessary for effective performance in their chosen fields.

Student Outcomes Students can register with the University's online career-services system and use select services from a distance, such as degree-specific career e-mail lists, national job posts, and virtual job fairs. Students should contact the University for more information.

Location Argosy University, Twin Cities, offers rigorous academics in a supportive environment. The campus is nestled in a parklike suburban setting within 10 miles of the airport and the Mall of America. Students enjoy the convenience of nearby shops, restaurants, and housing and easy freeway access. The neighboring Eagan Community Center offers many amenities, including walking paths, a fitness center, meeting rooms, and an outdoor amphitheater. The Twin Cities of Minneapolis and St. Paul have been rated by popular magazines as one of the most livable metropolitan areas in the country. With a population of 2.5 million, the area offers an abundance of recreational activities. Year-round outdoor activities, nationally acclaimed venues for theater art and music, and professional sports teams attract residents and visitors alike.

Many educational institutions and agencies in the area provide varied opportunities for student training. The Minneapolis-St. Paul metropolitan area offers a diversified economic base fueled by an array of companies. Among the numerous publicly traded companies headquartered in the area are Target, UnitedHealth Group, 3M, General Mills, and U.S. Bancorp.

The University Argosy University is a private institution with nineteen locations across the nation. Argosy University, Twin Cities, provides students with a career resources office, an academic resources center and extensive information access for research. It offers the resources of a large university plus the friendliness and personal attention of a small campus. The innovative programs feature dynamic, relevant, and practical curricula delivered in flexible class formats. Students enjoy scheduling options that make it easier to fit school into their busy lives, choosing from day and evening courses, on campus or online. Many students find a combination of class formats to be an ideal way of continuing their education while meeting family and professional demands.

Argosy University is accredited by the Higher Learning Commission and a member of the North Central Association (30 North LaSalle Street, Suite 2400, Chicago, Illinois 60602; 800-621-7440 (toll-free); http://www.ncahlc.org).

Applying Argosy University, Twin Cities, accepts students year-round on a rolling admissions basis, depending on the availability of required courses. Applications for admission are available online or by contacting the campus.

Correspondence and Information
Argosy University, Twin Cities
1515 Central Parkway
Eagan, Minnesota 55121
Phone: 651-846-2882
        888-844-2004 (toll-free)
Fax: 651-994-7956
E-mail: auadmissions@argosy.edu
Web site: http://www.argosy.edu/twincities

Argosy University, Twin Cities

THE FACULTY

The Argosy University faculty comprises working professionals who are eager to help students succeed. Members bring real-world experience and the latest practice innovations to the academic setting. The diverse faculty members of the College of Education are widely recognized for contributions to the field. Most hold doctoral degrees. They provide a substantive education that combines comprehensive knowledge with critical skills and practical workplace relevance. Above all, faculty members are committed to their students' personal and professional development.

ARGOSY UNIVERSITY, WASHINGTON DC

College of Education

Programs of Study	Argosy University, Washington DC, offers the Master of Arts in Education (M.A.Ed.) degree in educational leadership and instructional leadership; the Education Specialist (Ed.S.) degree in educational leadership and instructional leadership; and the Doctor of Education (Ed.D.) degree in educational leadership, instructional leadership, and community college executive leadership.
	The M.A.Ed. in educational leadership program is designed to instill key philosophies, theories, and values that impact education. It prepares students to improve policies and practices within organizations through the motivation and supervision of others. Students develop skills needed to design, implement, and evaluate educational programs and curricula. Courses include educational law, educational finance, organizational communication, human resource management, instruction supervision, and organizational management.
	The M.A.Ed. in instructional leadership program examines the challenges and problems encountered in today's educational environment. Course work encompasses the historical, philosophical, psychological, social, technical, and theoretical aspects of education. Students develop skills in analysis, oral and written communication, problem solving, critical thinking, team building, and computer technology. The program is designed for those who wish to develop or enhance classroom skills, become curriculum supervisors, or become educational leaders with a focus on instruction.
	The Ed.S. in educational leadership program concentrates on applied organizational theory within the context of educational organizations. This specialized program develops the competencies required to secure educational administrator positions at the elementary or secondary school level.
	The Ed.S. in instructional leadership program enables experienced teachers to become more effective practitioners and educational leaders with a focus on instruction. Course work was designed by faculty members to satisfy the requirements of students seeking career advancement and those working toward a doctoral degree.
	The Ed.D. in community college executive leadership program offers an accelerated course of study intended to meet the needs of community college administrators who are looking to move into senior administrative positions (such as president, vice president, dean, and director) in community colleges.
	The Ed.D. in educational leadership program is designed to enhance educational leadership strengths. Students learn innovative and collaborative techniques used to manage and govern educational institutions. The program prepares students for administrative leadership positions at the district, regional, state, or national level. Students must choose a concentration in higher education administration or K–12 education.
	The Ed.D. in instructional leadership program draws upon educational theories and practices to help students discover new learning techniques for diverse audiences. Students enrolled in this program master teaching methodologies, hone classroom skills, and gain the knowledge required to become curriculum administrators or educational leaders with a focus on instruction. Students must choose a concentration in higher education or K–12 education.
	Note: These programs do not lead to teacher or administrator certification, licensure, or endorsement in any state in the United States.
Research Facilities	Argosy University libraries provide curriculum support and educational resources, including current text materials, diagnostic training documents, reference materials and databases, journals and dissertations, and major and current titles in program areas. There is an online public-access catalog of library resources available throughout the Argosy University system. Students have remote access to the campus library database, enabling them to study and conduct research at home. Academic databases offer dissertation abstracts, academic journals, and professional periodicals. All library computers are Internet accessible. Software applications include Word, Excel, PowerPoint, SPSS, and various test-scoring programs.
Financial Aid	Financial aid is available to those who qualify. Argosy University, Washington DC, offers access to federal and state aid programs, merit-based awards, grants, loans, and a work-study program. As a first step, students should complete the Free Application for Federal Student Aid (FAFSA). Prospective students can apply electronically at http://www.fafsa.ed.gov or at the campus.
Cost of Study	Tuition varies by program. Students should contact Argosy University, Washington DC, for tuition information.
Living and Housing Costs	Students typically live in apartments in the metropolitan Washington, D.C., area. Living expenses vary according to each student's preferred standard of living, housing, and transportation. The University does not offer or operate student housing. Most of the students are full-time working professionals who live within driving distance of the campus. Several nearby hotels offer special rates for those who commute from long distances. The Admissions Department also maintains a list of housing options, including contact information for university students who wish to share housing. For more information, students should contact the Admissions Department.
Student Group	Admission to Argosy University, Washington DC, is selective to ensure a dynamic and engaged student body. It encourages diversity in academic and employment backgrounds and promotes integration of the student body into professional life through established connections with local and national professional associations. Argosy University offers a professionally oriented education with rich opportunities to gain practical experience in class, field placements, and internships. Full-time students and working professionals gain the extensive knowledge and range of skills necessary for effective performance in their chosen fields.
Student Outcomes	Students can register with the University's online career-services system and use select services from a distance, such as degree-specific career e-mail lists, national job posts, and virtual job fairs. Students should contact the University for more information.
Location	Argosy University, Washington DC, is located in suburban Arlington, Virginia. The University is conveniently situated to provide access to most major highways in the area and is easily accessible by public transportation. In proximity to Georgetown, students enjoy access to the many diverse attractions of the D.C. area. Additional campus space is located at The Art Institute of Washington Building (1820 Fort Myer Drive). The University houses administrative offices and seven classrooms at this location. Perhaps best known as the home of the Pentagon and Arlington National Cemetery, Arlington, Virginia, is one of the most highly educated areas in the nation. It is also one of the most diverse. Many educational institutions and agencies in the area provide varied opportunities for student training. Major employers in the region include MCI Telecommunications Corporation, Bell Atlantic Network Services, and Gannett/USA Today Company, Inc.
The University	Argosy University is a private institution with nineteen locations across the nation. Argosy University, Washington DC, provides students with a career resources office, an academic resources center, and extensive information access for research. It offers the resources of a large university, plus the friendliness and personal attention of a small campus. The innovative programs feature dynamic, relevant, and practical curricula delivered in flexible class formats. Students enjoy scheduling options that make it easier to fit school into their busy lives, choosing from day and evening courses, on campus or online. Many students find a combination of class formats to be an ideal way of continuing their education while meeting family and professional demands.
	Argosy University is accredited by the Higher Learning Commission and a member of the North Central Association (30 North LaSalle Street, Suite 2400, Chicago, Illinois 60602; 800-621-7440 (toll-free); http://www.ncahlc.org).
Applying	Argosy University, Washington DC, accepts students year-round on a rolling admissions basis, depending on availability of required courses. Applications for admission are available online or by contacting the campus.
Correspondence and Information	Argosy University, Washington DC 1550 Wilson Boulevard, Suite 600 Arlington, Virginia 22209 Phone: 703-526-5800 866-703-2777 (toll-free) Fax: 703-243-8973 E-mail: auadmissions@argosy.edu Web site: http://www.argosy.edu/washingtondc

Argosy University, Washington DC

THE FACULTY

The Argosy University faculty comprises working professionals who are eager to help students succeed. Members bring real-world experience and the latest practice innovations to the academic setting. The diverse faculty members of the College of Education are widely recognized for contributions to the field. Most hold doctoral degrees. They provide a substantive education that combines comprehensive knowledge with critical skills and practical workplace relevance. Above all, faculty members are committed to their students' personal and professional development.

Bank Street

BANK STREET COLLEGE OF EDUCATION

Graduate School

Programs of Study
Bank Street College Graduate School of Education is committed to providing outstanding master's degree programs for graduate students through small classes combined with extensive supervised fieldwork and advisement. The programs integrate direct experience with children, teachers, and families with theoretical material and with observation and reflection. Bank Street's creative approach to teaching and learning prepares educators to facilitate learning rather than dictating information and recognizes that children learn best when they are actively engaged with materials, ideas, and people. The Graduate School prepares individuals who will encourage learners to engage fully in the process of discovery and of creating understanding.

Recognized for its innovative leadership in the field of education, Bank Street College grants the degree of Master of Science in Education, with specializations in curriculum and instruction, dual certification programs in special and general education, dual language/bilingual education, early childhood education, educational leadership in the arts, elementary education, infant and family development, leadership in early childhood, leadership in mathematics education, leadership in museum education, leadership for educational change, middle school education, museum education, reading and literacy, studies in education, and teaching students with disabilities. The College also grants the degree of Master of Science, with a specialization in child life. The College offers an advanced Master of Education (M.Ed.) degree in advanced literacy specialization, special education, or educational leadership for qualified students who already hold a master's degree in education.

The faculty's primary commitment is to the professional growth and development of the graduate students. The Graduate School is accredited by the Regents Accreditation of Teacher Education (RATE) and by the Middle States Association of Colleges and Schools.

All programs include extensive fieldwork during which students put into practice what they are learning in their courses. Faculty advisers at Bank Street work closely with graduate students to promote and support each student's professional growth and development. Advisers mentor their students in appropriate settings in the field and meet with their advisees individually and in small conference groups where students learn collaboratively and engage in thoughtful reflection about their development in their chosen field.

Research Facilities
The Bank Street library is a resource for research, graduate study, and professional development. It contains a wide range of books, journals, online databases, Graduate School theses and portfolios, and an extraordinary children's book collection. Bank Street also houses a nationally known demonstration school for children ages 3 to 13, the School for Children. Graduate students have opportunities for study, research, and observation with children, experienced teachers, and parents both in this setting and in the many public and independent schools with which Bank Street College is associated.

Financial Aid
Bank Street's financial aid program makes it possible for full- and part-time students to receive partial support to finance their graduate study. Financial aid may be in the form of tuition scholarships and low-interest loans. Scholarships and grants are awarded based on financial need. Work-study opportunities are available. Students apply for aid using the Free Application for Federal Student Aid. Students should contact the Office of Financial Aid at 212-875-4408.

Cost of Study
Tuition for each credit was $1175 for 2010–11.

Living and Housing Costs
Applicants may contact the Office of Financial Aid for information on estimating the cost of living. Students may contact the Office of Graduate Admissions to gain information about housing at International House, a private graduate residence, or in local apartments.

Student Group
The College enrolls about 950 graduate students. These students usually have undergraduate degrees in the liberal arts and sciences or in education. Often students come to Bank Street to pursue education as a change of career. Others may be recent college graduates or they may be seasoned teachers seeking their master's degree while continuing to work in the classroom. Approximately 30 percent of the students are members of minority groups.

Location
Located on Manhattan's Upper West Side and close to the parks along the Hudson River, Bank Street College is in a residential and academic community convenient to New York City's museums, restaurants, parks, theaters, and public transportation.

The College
For nearly a century, Bank Street has been a leader in exemplary teacher education and a powerful force for innovation and best practices in teaching and in educational leadership. Bank Street's pioneering ideas have profoundly influenced successful teaching and learning approaches in school classrooms, museums, and other learning environments in communities across the nation. Bank Street College consists of the Graduate School of Education, the School for Children, and the Division of Continuing Education.

Applying
Applicants may apply at any time throughout the year. The priority deadline for the fall semester is February 15. The priority deadline for the spring semester is November 1. Applications are available by mail or online at http://www.bankstreet.edu/gs. Applicants must submit transcripts, three letters of reference, and a reflective autobiography. The College seeks students who have an undergraduate average of B or better, strong motivation for professional development, and a commitment to learner-centered education. Applicants to the middle school programs need to have completed an undergraduate major in a subject that is taught at the middle school level.

Correspondence and Information
Ann Morgan, Director of Admissions
Graduate School
Bank Street College of Education
610 West 112th Street
New York, New York 10025
Phone: 212-875-4404
Fax: 212-875-4678
E-mail: gradcourses@bankstreet.edu
Web site: http://www.bankstreet.edu

Bank Street College of Education

THE FACULTY AND THEIR RESEARCH

Bilingual Education:
Director: Francisco Najera, Ph.D., CUNY Graduate Center. Practitioner background: elementary school teacher in bilingual and monolingual classrooms, public school leadership and administration. Academic interests: second-language acquisition and its impact on literacy development, language development and disorders, bilingualism, dual language and bilingual education, the preparation of teachers. (212-875-4530; fnajera@bankstreet.edu)

The bilingual education programs prepare teachers to provide effective bilingual education and dual-language immersion experiences for children. The programs integrate courses for the bilingual extension with the core programs in general education or in special and general education. Applicants must be fluent in English and in Spanish.

Child Life
Director: Troy Pinkney-Ragsdale, M.A., Ohio State. Practitioner background: director of therapeutic recreation for skilled and assisted living facilities, director of child life for pediatric facilities within various major hospitals. Academic interests: diversity issues as they relate to health care and education, literacy initiatives, the preparation of child life professionals, health care, especially in pediatrics. (212-875-4473; tpinkney-ragsdale@bankstreet.edu)

The master's degree program in child life is for those who wish to work with and advocate for ill children in child life departments in hospital and clinical settings. Graduates earn certification as child life specialists through the Child Life Council.

Early Childhood Education
Chair: Adrianne Kamsler, Ed.M., Lesley. Practitioner background: director of staff development program; staff developer; public school teacher, prekindergarten to grade 6, general and special education. Academic interests: teacher development, children's literature, the structure of schools. (212-875-4571; akamsler@bankstreet.edu)

All of the early childhood education master's degree programs lead to certification to work with children ages birth through grade 2. The programs include early childhood general education, early childhood and childhood general education dual certification in general education birth through grade 6 (Stan Chu, 212-875-4499), and early childhood special and general education (Sue Carbary, 212-875-4509).

Elementary Education
Director: Michele Morales, M.S.Ed., Bank Street College of Education. Practitioner background: New York City public school teacher; mathematics staff developer; N–6 methods instructor to teachers in the U.S., Switzerland, and Belgium. Academic interests: the teacher learning process, mathematics education, leadership and systems change (212-875-4588; mmorales@bankstreet.edu)

These programs in elementary education prepare individuals to work with children in grades 1 through 6. Included are programs in elementary general education; early childhood and elementary education dual certification in general education leading to certification to work with children birth through grade 6 (Michele Morales, 212-875-4588); elementary special and general education dual certification (Diane Newman, 212-875-4547); museum education (Nina Jensen, 212-875-4491), and elementary education and reading dual certification (Susan Goetz-Haver, 212-875-4692).

Infant and Family Development
Director: Sue Carbary, M.S.Ed., Ed.M., Bank Street College of Education. Practitioner background: early childhood special education, program director of home/community-based special education and early intervention program. Academic interests: child development with a focus on birth to age 3, parent support and parent education, best practices in infant, toddler, and early childhood child-care settings. (212-875-4509; scarbary@bankstreet.edu)

These master's degree programs emphasize early childhood development and early intervention and include both certification and noncertification versions. The programs are for those who wish to focus on working with children ages birth through age three and with their families. Graduate students may choose dual certification in early childhood special and general education with an emphasis on early intervention with infants and toddlers.

Leadership in the Arts
Director: Cathleen Wiggins, M.S.Ed., Bank Street College of Education. Practitioner background: public school teacher, community garden and arts program worker, facilitator of SEED (Seeking Educational Equity and Diversity). Academic interests: cultural diversity and the arts, diversity training, school leadership preparation. (212-875-4529; cathleenh@bankstreet.edu)

This is a collaborative master's degree program with two pathways. One pathway is for art educators, focuses on leadership in the visual arts, and is a cooperative program between Bank Street College and Parsons School of Design in leadership for art educators. The other pathway focuses on leadership in creative writing and is a cooperative program between Bank Street College and Sarah Lawrence College. The program leads to certification as a school building leader for those who have been teaching for at least three years. In this two-year program, courses are taken during July for three summers.

Leadership in Community-Based Learning
Director: Rima Shore, Ph.D. Columbia. Practitioner background: Twenty-five years of experience documenting and supporting the work of community-based organizations, advocacy organizations, and early childhood programs.

The master's degree program is for individuals in community-based programs such as after-school programs who seek a strong foundation in human development, curriculum, working with communities, and leadership.

Leadership in Early Childhood
Director: Denise Prince, M.S.Ed., Bank Street College of Education. Practitioner background: teacher and director of early childhood programs, program planner in New York City early intervention program. Academic interests: early childhood education, professional development of teachers, school reform, parent involvement, inclusive education. (212-875-4585; dprince@bankstreet.edu)

The master's degree program in early childhood leadership is for early childhood professionals who wish to move into management and supervisory positions. The program leads to certification as a school building leader. In this two-year program, courses are taken during July for three summers.

Leadership for Educational Change
Director: Gil Schmerler, Ed.D., Columbia Teachers College. Practitioner background: high school English teacher, director of an alternative public high school, principal of independent middle school and independent high school. Academic interests: small schools, middle schools, teacher leadership, service learning, team building in schools. (212-875-4709; ace@bankstreet.edu)

The leadership for educational change program is open to teachers who wish to prepare for positions of leadership and staff development, leading to certification as a school building leader. Students may also choose to become certified as a school district leader.

Leadership in Mathematics Education
Director: Barbara Dubitsky, Ed.D., Columbia Teachers College. Practitioner background: middle school math teacher and math coordinator, mathematics consultant to schools and school districts, public school teacher (grades 4–6). Academic interests: mathematics education in elementary and middle schools, preparing teachers to engage children in mathematical thinking and problem solving. (212-875-4712; dubitsky@bankstreet.edu)

This program is for teachers in elementary education or in middle schools who wish to enhance their curriculum in mathematics or to become staff developers in their schools. The master's degree program in leadership in mathematics education leads to certification as a school building leader. Courses are taken during July for three summers.

Leadership in Museum Education
Director: Leslie Bedford, M.A.T., Harvard. Practitioner background: high school teacher, museum educator, exhibit developer, senior museum administrator and consultant, professional development for arts organizations. Academic interests: museum studies with a focus on museum exhibitions and the creative power of imagination. (212-875-4704; Lbedford@bankstreet.edu)

This program is for professionals working in museum settings or other cultural and community organizations who wish to move into management and supervisory positions. It is a two-year program, with courses given one weekend each month.

Middle School Education
Director: Sue Ruskin-Mayher, Ph.D., NYU. Practitioner background: junior high language arts teacher. Academic interests: middle school education, reading and literacy, urban education, social studies education in the middle school. (212-875-4780; sruskin-mayher@bankstreet.edu)

The master's degree programs in middle school education are for individuals preparing to teach all subjects across the curriculum as well as specialize in a subject area in grades 5 through 9. Students may apply to a program in middle school general education or in middle school special and general education dual certification. Those seeking information about programs in middle school special education should see Special Education, below. Students should also see Museum Education, below.

Museum Education
Director: Nina Jensen, M.Ph., CUNY Graduate Center. Practitioner background: museum educator. Academic interests: visitor experiences and learning in museums, community access to museums. (212-875-4491; ninajensen@bankstreet.edu)

This master's degree program is for individuals preparing to work in museum education and/or in schools. The program focuses on the educational role and mission of museums in a pluralistic society. Graduate students may choose programs combining museum education with certification in elementary education or in middle school education.

Reading and Literacy
Director: Susan Goetz-Haver, Ph.D., NYU. Practitioner background: New York City classroom teacher (general and special education), literacy specialist, staff developer, poet. Academic interests: reading and literacy, supporting teachers in urban schools, curriculum development, children and poetry. (212-875-4692; sgoetz-haver@bankstreet.edu)

The master's degree programs in teaching literacy view reading, writing, and language development as integrated processes. Graduate students may choose a dual certification program in teaching literacy and elementary education leading to certification as a reading and literacy specialist and as a classroom teacher, first grade through sixth grade. Graduate students with a prior classroom certification may choose a single certification program leading to certification as a literacy specialist.

Special Education
Chair: Olga Romero, Ph.D., CUNY Graduate Center. Practitioner background: elementary and middle school teacher in bilingual and monolingual classrooms, bilingual speech and language pathologist, bilingual speech and language evaluator. Academic interests: language development and disorders, preparation of teachers. (212-875-4468; olgar@bankstreet.edu).

These single and dual certification programs in special education are for individuals preparing to work with children who have learning disabilities, behavioral problems, and emotional disturbances. Applicants with prior certification in general education may apply to single-certification programs for teaching children with disabilities. The programs in special education are at three age levels: early childhood (Sue Carbary, 212-875-4509), elementary education (Diane Newman, 212-875-4547), and middle school, grades 5 through 9 (Valentine Burr, 212-875-4791). Applicants may also choose programs leading to dual certification in general education and special education and in social work with Columbia University School of Social Work. Applicants to the dual degree in special education and social work program with Columbia University School of Social Work need to apply to each institution. Candidates may also choose to incorporate an annotation to work with multiply handicapped students, including children with autism.

Studies in Education
Director: Lia Gelb, M.S.Ed., Bank Street College of Education. Practitioner background: early childhood classroom teacher. Academic interests: early childhood curriculum, professional development, educational development and practice in nontraditional settings. (212-875-4489; liag@bankstreet.edu)

This program is an individually structured, noncertification master's degree program in education.

FELICIAN COLLEGE

Programs in Education

Programs of Study	Felician College is a coeducational liberal arts institution deeply rooted in the Catholic/Franciscan tradition. Felician College is dedicated to providing an academic environment that encourages its students to reach their highest potential while preparing them to meet the challenges of the twenty-first century with an informed mind and an understanding heart.
	Felician College offers two master's degree programs in education, a Master of Arts in education and a Master of Arts in educational leadership. Master's and certificate programs in school nurse/teacher of health education are also available.
	The Master of Arts in education is for certified teachers looking to earn a master's degree and advance their career or for students and career changers who seek to become certified teachers and want the advantage of a master's degree. The Master of Arts in education program offers the following tracks/endorsements: elementary education (K–5) or elementary education (K–5) and teacher of students with disabilities (K–12). For those seeking certification in elementary education (K–5), 37 credits are required for completion of the program. For teachers who already hold certification, this track requires the successful completion of 33 credits. For those seeking certification in elementary education (K–5) and teacher of students with disabilities (K–12), 46 credits are required for completion of the program. For teachers who already hold certification, 42 credits are required.
	The Master of Arts in educational leadership offers experienced teachers the opportunity to earn a master's degree with principal and/or supervision endorsements. It is designed for those who aspire to a leadership position in public or private schools and who want both the academic theory and hands-on, practical experience of educational leadership. Those who seek the master's in educational leadership with principal and supervision endorsement are required to complete 36 credits, including 6 credits in an internship. Applicants to this program are required to have five years of educational experience under valid certification. Those who seek the master's in educational leadership with supervision endorsement only are required to complete 33 credits. Three years of educational experience under valid certification is required of applicants to this program track.
	The Master of Arts in education for school nursing and/or heath education program prepares registered nurses with a baccalaureate degree to obtain dual licensure in school nurse and teacher of health education, or for licensed school nurses to obtain a master's degree.
	The school nurse and/or teacher of health education certificate program prepares registered nurses with a baccalaureate degree to provide nursing service and health education in the K–12 school setting. The program is approved by the State of New Jersey Department of Education and consists of 19 credits (seven courses). The certificate can be completed in either two or four semesters.
Research Facilities	The College Library is a two-story building that serves the needs of students, faculty and staff members, and alumni with more than 110,000 books and over 800 periodical subscriptions. This collection is enhanced by large holdings of materials in microform, which can be used on the library's reader/printer equipment. With its computers linked to information services such as Dialog and OCLC, and as a member of the New Jersey Library Network and VALE, the library locates and obtains information, journal articles, and books not available in its collection from sources all over the country. Computerized databases can also be accessed directly by users through the online FirstSearch workstation, where up-to-date information on 40 million books and an index of 15,000 periodicals is available. The library is also connected to the Internet and has several CD-ROM workstations. Through EBSCOhost, Bell & Howell's ProQuest, CINAHL, and other services, students and faculty and staff members have access to numerous online journal indexes—as well as articles from thousands of periodicals—from anywhere on the campus computer network or from their home computers. An experienced staff of professional librarians is available to assist users.
	The College's computer facilities include an academic and administrative network, four computerized labs, a computerized learning center, and two computer centers that are available for students, with a total of about 200 computers available for student/faculty member use. All classrooms, offices, and facilities are wired for Internet and e-mail.
Financial Aid	To qualify for financial aid, a student must complete the Free Application for Federal Student Aid (FAFSA).
Cost of Study	In 2010–11, graduate tuition is $825 per credit. Fees are additional.
Living and Housing Costs	Students are housed in two dormitories on the Rutherford campus, Milton and Elliott Halls. Both buildings have housing organized around student suites containing semiprivate baths. On-campus room and board is approximately $10,150 per year. On-campus housing is not available to married students.
Student Group	Felician College enrolls approximately 2,300 students. In fall 2009, there were approximately 350 students enrolled in graduate programs.
Location	Felician College's Lodi campus is located on the banks of the Saddle River on a beautifully landscaped campus of 27 acres and offers a collegiate setting in suburban Bergen County, within easy driving distance of New York City. The Felician College Rutherford Campus is set on 10.5 beautifully landscaped acres in the heart of the historic community of Rutherford, New Jersey. Only 15 minutes from the Lodi campus, the Rutherford complex contains student residences, classroom buildings, a student center, and a gymnasium. The campus is a short distance from downtown Rutherford, where there are many shops and businesses of interest to students. Regular shuttle bus service between the two campuses is a quick 10-minute ride that turns two campuses into a one-campus home for the students.
The College	Felician College, a coeducational liberal arts college, is a Catholic, private, independent institution for students representing diverse religious, racial, and ethnic backgrounds. The College operates on two campuses in Lodi and Rutherford, New Jersey. The College is one of the institutions of higher learning conducted by the Felician Sisters in the United States. Its mission is to provide a values-oriented education based in the liberal arts while it prepares students for meaningful lives and careers in contemporary society. To meet the needs of students and to provide personal enrichment courses to matriculated and nonmatriculated students, Felician College offers day, evening, and weekend programs. The College is accredited by the Middle States Association of Colleges and Schools and carries program accreditation from the Commission on Collegiate Nursing Education, the International Assembly for Collegiate Business Education, and the Teacher Education Accreditation Council.
Applying	Applicants should complete the application for adult and graduate admission and submit it along with the $40 application fee; transcript(s) from all undergraduate and/or graduate institutions previously attended; a copy of New Jersey teacher certification, if currently certified; three letters of reference (one personal and two professional); and a personal statement. An interview and additional information may be required.
Correspondence and Information	Programs in Education Felician College 262 South Main Street Lodi, New Jersey 07644-2117
	Phone: 201-559-6077 Fax: 201-559-6138 E-mail: adultandgraduate@felician.edu Web site: http://www.felician.edu/

Felician College

THE FACULTY

Donna Barron, Associate Professor and Dean of Teacher Education; Ph.D., Dayton.

Robert Brown, Instructor of Teacher Education; M.A., William Paterson; M.B.A., Fairleigh Dickinson.

Rosemarie Crownover, Instructor of Teacher Education; M.S., Fordham.

Anne DeGroot, Instructor of Teacher Education; M.Ed., William Paterson.

Kathleen DeNoble, Assistant Professor of Teacher Education; Ed.D., Nova Southeastern.

Lillian Garcia, Assistant Professor of Special Education; Psy.D., Yeshiva.

Deborah Herman, Instructor of Teacher Education; M.S., Fordham.

Willard Kobuskie, Instructor of Teacher Education; M.A., Columbia.

Rosemarie Liebmann, Assistant Professor of Teacher Education; Ed.D., Seton Hall.

Annette Rycharski, Instructor of Teacher Education and Director, Placement and Certification; M.S., St. John's (New York).

Mary Anne Witowski, Assistant Professor of Teacher Education and Chair of Elementary Education; M.A., St. John's (New York).

NORTHWESTERN UNIVERSITY

School of Education and Social Policy

Programs of Study	The School of Education and Social Policy offers programs leading to the M.S., M.A., and Ph.D. degrees. There are four program areas: Education (M.S.), Learning and Organizational Change (M.S.), Learning Sciences (M.A. and Ph.D.), and Human Development and Social Policy (Ph.D.).
	The Learning Sciences M.A. and Ph.D. programs are dedicated to the preparation of researchers, developers, and practitioners qualified to advance the scientific understanding and practice of teaching and learning. Both programs in the learning sciences are interdisciplinary, offering a synthesis of computational, educational, and social science research; linguistics; computer science; anthropology; and cognitive science.
	The Human Development and Social Policy Ph.D. program prepares students to bridge human development, social science, and social policy. Graduates of this program assume positions as professors, researchers, and policy makers who can bring multidisciplinary knowledge about human development directly to bear upon policy.
	Concentrations in the M.S. in Education program include public and private school teaching, advanced teaching, and higher education administration. Students enrolled full-time typically complete the program in twelve months, provided they matriculate with no course deficiencies; opportunities for part-time study toward a master's degree are also available.
Research Facilities	Research libraries contain more than 4.9 million volumes, 4.6 million microfilm units, and 98,844 current periodical and serial publications. Research and teaching activities are supported by a state-of-the-art multimedia computing network with full Internet access. The School is actively involved with the Institute for Policy Research, a University-wide research center that promotes interdisciplinary urban policy research and training. Specialized research and service resources within the School include the Center for Talent Development, a nationally prominent center that identifies and provides programming for academically talented youth, their parents, and the professionals who work with them. The Tarry Center for Collaborative Teaching and Learning provides state-of-the-art facilities for innovative teaching with technology.
Financial Aid	Several forms of aid are available, including fellowships and scholarships. In addition, there are teaching assistantships awarded to doctoral students who work with the School's undergraduate programs. Special opportunities for research assistantships and other employment also exist within the School's and the University's many research centers. Arrangements for loans are also possible.
Cost of Study	Tuition for full-time study in the M.S. in Education program in 2010–11 is $39,990; part-time enrollment is possible at $2666 per course. Tuition for full-time study in the M.S. in Learning and Organizational Change program is $53,685; part-time enrollment is $3579 per course. Tuition for full-time study (three courses per quarter) in pursuit of the M.A. or Ph.D. in 2010–11 is $39,840 for the academic year or $13,280 per quarter.
Living and Housing Costs	The University operates a residence in Evanston for the use of graduate students. For those Northwestern students interested in securing off-campus housing near the University, information and assistance are also available.
Student Group	Graduate study occurs within the context of individualized instruction, and enrollments are selective. Currently, 208 students are enrolled in master's programs, and 71 are enrolled in Ph.D. programs. Since an interdisciplinary perspective is valued, students with preparation in a wide range of disciplinary areas are encouraged to apply.
Student Outcomes	Graduates teach and conduct research in academic and nonacademic settings; occupy strategic policy positions in government, corporations, and institutions; and assume positions of responsibility in a wide range of service organizations. Potential professional settings for learning sciences graduates include University research and teaching as well as business, industry, or school system-based careers studying, designing, and/or implementing learning environments. Graduates of the Ph.D. in Human Development and Social Policy program assume positions as teachers, researchers, or policy makers who can bring multidisciplinary knowledge about human development directly to bear upon policy. Graduates of the Learning Sciences M.A. program are practitioners in the vanguard of teaching and learning systems development and instructional resource development. Most students in the M.S. in Education program gain on-site experience through supervised internships for future careers as professional educators.
Location	The campus is located on Lake Michigan, 12 miles north of Chicago. The beautiful lakefront campus offers a rich cultural environment through a wealth of theatrical, musical, and athletic events. The extensive cultural resources of Chicago are readily accessible via public transportation.
The University and The School	Established in 1851, Northwestern has grown to become one of the most distinguished private universities in the country. The School of Education and Social Policy has developed from its origins as a department of pedagogy by continually broadening its scope to encompass those educative, learning, and socializing experiences that take place throughout the life span in families, schools, communities, and the workplace.
Applying	Applications for admission are reviewed and acted upon as they are received. Students should consult program brochures for specific application deadlines. Applicants planning to seek financial aid must meet early submission deadlines.
Correspondence and Information	School of Education and Social Policy Northwestern University 2120 Campus Drive Evanston, Illinois 60208-2610 Phone: 847-491-3790 (Office of Student Affairs) 847-467-1458 (M.S. in Education) 847-491-7494 (Learning Sciences Ph.D.) 847-491-4329 (Human Development and Social Policy Ph.D.) 847-491-7376 (Learning and Organizational Change M.S.) 847-491-7494 (Learning Sciences M.A.) Web site: http://www.sesp.northwestern.edu

Northwestern University

THE FACULTY AND THEIR RESEARCH

Emma Adam, Ph.D., Minnesota. Parent, child, and adolescent stress and emotion; attachment; health policy.

Lawrence A. Birnbaum, Ph.D., Yale. Natural language understanding, opportunistic planning systems, machine learning.

Justine Cassell, Ph.D., Chicago. Designing technological tools to understand and enhance human communication, embodied conversational agents.

Lindsay Chase-Lansdale, Ph.D., Michigan. Child and adolescent development, family functioning, public policy, multidisciplinary research, poverty and welfare reform, family structure, risk and resilience.

Jeannette Colyvas, Ph.D., Stanford. Organizations and entrepreneurship; comparing public, private, and nonprofit forms of organizing; the study of networks.

Fay L. Cook, Ph.D., Chicago. Social welfare policy, public attitudes, policy issues in aging, family support systems.

Thomas D. Cook, Ph.D., Stanford. Social-psychological processes, measurement of attitudes, evaluation of social programs.

Solomon Cytrynbaum, Ph.D., Michigan. Evaluation of school reform, gender and authority in groups and organizations, organizational consultation, application of group and systems theory and research to school change.

David Figlio, Ph.D., Wisconsin–Madison. Accountability policy, economics of education, teacher quality, teacher labor markets, anti-poverty policy, intergenerational transmission of human capital, evaluation design.

Kenneth D. Forbus, Ph.D., MIT. Qualitative physics, cognitive simulation of analogy, intelligence tutoring systems and learning environments for science and engineering.

Dedre Gentner, Ph.D., Berkeley. Learning, reasoning, and conceptual change in adults and children; mental models; acquisition of meaning.

Kristian Hammond, Ph.D., Yale. Building computer systems designed around human needs and abilities.

Sophie Haroutunian-Gordon, Ph.D., Chicago. Philosophy of education, philosophy of psychology, inquiry, interpretive discussion, teacher preparation.

Larry Hedges, Ph.D., Stanford. Statistical methods for research in education, social sciences, and policy studies; social distribution of test scores.

Barton J. Hirsch, Ph.D., Oregon. Community psychology, social networks, ecology of adolescent development, after-school programs.

Michael Horn, Ph.D., Tufts. Human-computer interaction, emerging technology in learning settings.

Kemi Jona, Ph.D., Northwestern. Online learning, virtual schools, technologies to support online learning and collaboration, online laboratory science course design, corporate e-learning strategy and design.

John Kretzmann, Ph.D., Northwestern. Sociology, community development.

Eva Lam, Ph.D., Berkeley. Second language and literacy development, literacy and technology, language and identity, language socialization, globalization and English learning, multilingualism and cultural diversity in education.

Carol D. Lee, Ph.D., Chicago. Cultural contexts affecting learning broadly and literacy specifically, teacher preparation and development, classroom discourse, urban education.

Dan A. Lewis, Ph.D., California, Santa Cruz. Policy analysis, urban social problems, community organization, urban school reform.

Regina Logan, Ph.D., Northwestern. Teaching and learning processes.

Jelani Mandara, Ph.D., California, Riverside. Effects of parenting, fathers, and other home factors on child and adolescent academic and social development, achievement gap, and person-centered research methods.

Dan P. McAdams, Ph.D., Harvard. Personality development, identity and life stories, intimacy, adult development.

Steven McGee, Ph.D., Northwestern. High school transformation, science curriculum development.

Ann McKenna, Ph.D., Berkeley. Examining effective teaching and learning methods in biomedical engineering education.

Douglas L. Medin, Ph.D., South Dakota. Theories of learning, memory and induction, computational models of cognition, concepts and classification of learning, models of similarity.

Brad Olson, Ph.D., Iowa. Health care–based approaches to alcohol and substance abuse problems, personality, social psychology.

Paula M. Olszewski-Kubilius, Ph.D., Northwestern. Gifted education, child development, minority gifted child development.

Andrew Ortony, Ph.D., London. Knowledge representation and figurative language comprehension; models of cognition, motivation, and emotion.

Penelope L. Peterson, Ph.D., Stanford. Learning and teaching in schools and classrooms, particularly in mathematics and literacy; teacher learning in reform contexts; relations among educational research, policy, and practice.

Carla Pugh, Ph.D., Stanford; M.D., Howard. Technology and medical education.

David Rapp, Ph.D., SUNY at Stony Brook. Experimental psychology, comprehension of texts, psychology of learning.

Michelle Reininger, Ph.D., Stanford. Economics of education, teacher labor markets; teacher quality; educational policy.

Brian J. Reiser, Ph.D., Yale. Intelligent tutoring systems, interactive learning environments for science and technology, scientific inquiry skills.

Christopher K. Riesbeck, Ph.D., Stanford. Natural language and analyzers, case-based reasoners, intelligent computational media.

James E. Rosenbaum, Ph.D., Harvard. Adolescent and adult development, organizational careers.

Kimberly Scott, Ph.D., Ohio State. Organizational effectiveness and change, organizational learning, job satisfaction.

Bruce Sherin, Ph.D., Berkeley. Science education, instructional technology, external representations in science and mathematical learning.

Miriam Sherin, Ph.D., Berkeley. Mathematics teaching and learning, teacher cognition, teacher education.

Sylvia Smith-Demuth, Ph.D., Chicago. Mathematics achievement, mathematics teaching, learning and cognition, social context of education, opportunity to learn.

Bruce D. Spencer, Ph.D., Yale. Social and educational measurement, statistics for policy analysis, demography, decision theory.

James P. Spillane, Ph.D., Michigan State. Educational policy, intergovernmental relations, school reform, relations between policy and local practice.

Reed Stevens, Ph.D., Berkeley. Curriculum design, learning in atypical settings.

Edd Taylor, Ph.D., Berkeley. Early childhood education, elementary education, mathematics education.

Lois Trautvetter, Ph.D., Michigan. Higher education, gender issues and females in science.

David H. Uttal, Ph.D., Michigan. Mental representation, cognitive development, spatial cognition, early symbolization.

Sandra R. Waxman, Ph.D., Pennsylvania. Language and conceptual development, early cognitive development, language and thought.

Uri Wilensky, Ph.D., MIT. Science and mathematics learning and technology.

ST. JOSEPH'S COLLEGE, NEW YORK

Programs in Education

Programs of Study

St. Joseph's College (SJC) offers graduate education that balances in-depth research and theoretical study with hands-on professional training. This unique educational experience enables students to enter the workplace extremely well prepared and able to apply their knowledge with confidence born from experience.

The newest program is the Master of Arts in mathematics education, a 30-credit degree that can be earned in two years of part-time study. The purpose of the program is to prepare students to become accomplished mathematics teachers. It aims to extend the depth and breadth of mathematical skills previously learned on the undergraduate level and to enable teaching professionals to use these expanded skills to motivate and engage a diverse population of students with varying cognitive skills and learning styles. Completion of the program will satisfy the degree requirements for professional certification in New York State.

The Master of Arts program in special education with annotation in severe and multiple disabilities provides students with basic core classes (12 credits) and courses that link special education to the New York State Learning Standards in the area of special education as well as severe and multiple disabilities. The 36-credit program includes a strong research component, which is characteristic of the integration of theory and practice.

The Master of Arts in literacy and cognition responds to the No Child Left Behind Act, providing students with basic core classes that link literacy instruction to the New York State Learning Standards. The program addresses the challenges teachers face in the area of literacy as they work with students and families of diverse cultures. The M.A. in literacy and cognition program grants certifications in literacy and cognition from birth through grade 6.

The Master of Arts in infant/toddler early childhood special education was introduced in 1995 as the Master of Arts in Therapeutic Education and underwent a name change in 2003. The courses offered are appropriate for teachers who wish to augment their expertise in teaching by acquiring the knowledge and developing competencies working with infants, toddlers, and young children and their families. The M.A. in infant/toddler early childhood special education program grants certifications in early childhood and early childhood special education, from birth to grade 2.

Research Facilities

The Dillon Child Study Center offers toddler, preschool, and kindergarten programs based on the child development approach to the education of young children. Located on SJC's Brooklyn campus, the center is historically one of the first college preschools on the East Coast.

The Callahan Library at the Long Island Campus is a modern, 25,000-square-foot, freestanding facility with seating for more than 300 readers. A curriculum library, seminar rooms, administrative offices, and two classrooms are housed in this building. Holdings include more than 105,000 volumes and 307 periodical titles, and they are supplemented by videos and other instructional aids. Patrons have access to the Internet and to several online academic databases. A fully automated library system, Endeavor, ensures the efficient retrieval and management of all library resources. Other resources include the library at St. Joseph's Brooklyn Campus, with more than 109,000 volumes, and membership in the Long Island Library Resources Council, which facilitates cooperative associations with the academic and special libraries on Long Island. Internet access, subscriptions to several online full-text databases, and membership in the international bibliographic utility, OCLC, allow almost limitless access to available information.

McEntegart Hall is a fully air-conditioned five-level structure. Three spacious reading areas with a capacity for 300 readers, including individual study carrels and shelf space for 200,000 volumes, provide an excellent environment for research. In addition, McEntegart Hall houses the college archives, a curriculum library, three computer laboratories, a nursing education laboratory, and a videoconference room. There are eight classrooms, a chapel, cafeteria, and faculty and student lounges.

A high-speed fiber-optic intracampus network connects all offices, instructional facilities, computer laboratories, and libraries on both the Brooklyn and Long Island campuses. The network provides Internet access to all students and faculty and staff members. An integrated online library system enables students to search for and check out books at either campus. Online databases and other electronic resources are available to students from either campus or from their home computers. Two wireless laptop classrooms with "smart classroom" features provide flexible instruction spaces with the latest technologies. Videoconferencing facilities connect the two campuses, allowing for real-time distance learning in a small-group setting.

Financial Aid

Financial aid is available in the form of federal and private loans. Students should contact the Financial Aid Office for more information (Brooklyn Campus, telephone: 718-940-5700; Long Island Campus, telephone: 631-687-2600).

Cost of Study

The 2010–11 tuition is $650 per credit. Per semester, the college and technology fees for 12 or more credits totaled $200.

Living and Housing Costs

On-campus housing is not available. The St. George Hotel, New York's number-one resource for student housing, and St. Joseph's College have partnered to offer off-campus housing. Accommodations include cable TV, high-speed access, a completely furnished bedroom, a full bath, a closet, a kitchen on each floor, and 24-hour security. Housing applications are available online.

Student Group

The total enrollment for all graduate programs on both campuses is 678.

Location

St. Joseph's College has two campuses—the main campus in the residential Clinton Hill section of Brooklyn and the campus in Patchogue, New York. The main campus offers easy access to all transit lines; to the Long Island Expressway; to all bridges in Brooklyn, Manhattan, and Queens; and to the Verrazano-Narrows Bridge to Staten Island. Within the space of half an hour, students leaving St. Joseph's College may find themselves in the Metropolitan Museum of Art, the 42nd Street Library, Carnegie Hall and Lincoln Center, the Broadway theater district, Madison Square Garden, or Shea Stadium. The College itself stands in the center of one of the nation's most diversified academic communities, consisting of six colleges and universities within a 2-mile radius of each other. The 27-acre Long Island campus, adjacent to Great Patchogue Lake, is an ideal setting for studying, socializing, and partaking in extracurricular activities. Just off Sunrise Highway, the College is easily accessible from all parts of Long Island.

The College

St. Joseph's College is a fully accredited institution that has been dedicated to providing a diverse population of students in the New York metropolitan area with an affordable education rooted in the liberal arts tradition since 1916. Independent and coeducational, the College provides a strong academic and value-oriented education at the undergraduate and graduate levels. For the eighth year in a row, the 2010 ranking of America's Best Colleges by *U.S. News & World Report* placed St. Joseph's College in the top tier of the Northern Comprehensive Colleges–Bachelor's category.

Building on the strength of the St. Joseph's College long-renowned teacher education program, the master's programs in infant/toddler early childhood special education and in literacy/cognition are designed to produce innovative teachers in the fields of early childhood, childhood, and special education and in literacy and English language arts.

Applying

Students should have a bachelor's degree from an accredited institution, with a minimum GPA of 3.0. Applicants must submit the completed application, the application fee, official transcripts, a current resume, copies of all teaching certificates, and two letters of recommendation. An interview is required.

Correspondence and Information

Brooklyn Campus
St. Joseph's College
245 Clinton Avenue
Brooklyn, New York 11205

Phone: 718-940-5800
E-mail: brooklynap@sjcny.edu
Web site: http://www.sjcny.edu/ Academics/Graduate-Programs/
260

Long Island Campus
St. Joseph's College
155 West Roe Boulevard
Patchogue, New York 11772

Phone: 631-687-4500
E-mail: suffolkap@sjcny.edu

St. Joseph's College, New York

THE FACULTY

Esther Berkowitz, Assistant Professor of Child Study and Director of the M.A. in Literacy and Cognition; Ph.D., Fordham.
S. Elizabeth Calfapietra, Associate Professor of Child Study; Ed.D., Columbia.
S. Frances Carmody, Professor of Child Study Development; Ph.D., Syracuse.
Susan Straut Collard, Professor of Child Study, Co-Director of Child Study Department, and Director of Dillon Child Study Center; Ph.D., Columbia.
S. Miriam Honora Corr, Chairperson of the Child Study Department; Ed.D., Columbia.
Barry Friedman, Assistant Professor of Child Study; Ph.D., Hofstra.
Wendy P. Hope, Associate Professor of Child Study; Ph.D., NYU.
S. Helen Kearney, Assistant Professor of Child Study; Ph.D., NYU.
Claire Lenz, Assistant Professor of Child Study and Director of the Master of Arts in Literacy and Cognition, Suffolk Program; Ed.D., St. John's (New York).
Karen Russo, Assistant Professor of Child Study; St. John's (New York).

UNIVERSITY OF MARYLAND, COLLEGE PARK

College of Education

Programs of Study

The University of Maryland, College Park is the flagship campus of the University System of Maryland. The College of Education offers an array of graduate concentrations leading to the degrees of the Doctor of Philosophy (Ph.D.), the Doctor of Education (Ed.D.), the Master of Arts (M.A.), and the Master of Education (M.Ed.). Some departments offer the advanced graduate specialist (AGS) certificate.

The Department of Counseling and Personnel Services (http://www.education.umd.edu/edcp) offers master's degree programs in college student personnel, rehabilitation counseling, and school counseling. An AGS certificate is offered in psychiatric vocational rehabilitation. Doctoral programs are offered in college student personnel administration, counselor education, counseling psychology, and school psychology.

The Department of Curriculum and Instruction (http://www.education.umd.edu/edci) offers a rich and diverse academic experience grounded in rigorous scholarship through its undergraduate, graduate certification, master's, and doctoral degree programs. The department is comprised of nine interrelated program areas that span the following educational disciplines and are available across most degree options: art education, elementary education, English/literacy/speech communication/theater education, mathematics education, minority and urban education, music education, reading education, science education, second language/TESOL, social studies education, and teacher education/professional development.

The Department of Education Leadership, Higher Education and International Education (http://www.education.umd.edu/edhi) offers graduate degree programs to prepare students for leadership positions as scholars, researchers, and administrators in higher education, international agencies, and organizational leadership. Master's and doctoral programs are offered in three areas of specialization: organizational leadership and policy studies (Ph.D., Ed.D., and M.A.), higher education (Ph.D. and M.A.), and international education policy (Ph.D. and M.A.).

The Department of Education Policy Studies (http://www.education.umd.edu/edps) concentrates on the preparation of scholars and researchers capable of applying the disciplines of economics, history, philosophy, political science, anthropology, sociology, and cultural studies to the study of education policy and practice. It offers master's and doctoral degree programs in three areas of specialization: curriculum theory and development (Ph.D., Ed.D., and M.A., with a concentration available in Jewish studies), sociocultural foundations of education, and education policy (Ph.D. and M.A.).

The Department of Human Development/Institute for Child Study (http://www.education.umd.edu/edhd) offers graduate degrees to develop competencies in the scientific knowledge of human development. Programs prepare students for careers in research, teaching, and the application of knowledge in human development and learning. Master's degrees are offered in human development and a concentration in early childhood. The Ph.D. degree offered is in human development, with areas of concentration in educational psychology, early childhood, and developmental science. At the doctoral level, the educational psychology specialty focuses on research-based training in the application of psychological theory and research; the early childhood concentration offers comprehensive training in the study of development and education of young children; and the developmental sciences specialty (jointly administered with the psychology department) focuses on research training linking the psychophysiological, social, emotional, and cognitive aspects of development. The department operates the Center for Young Children in support of graduate studies and research, and houses the Center for Children, Relationships, and Culture, a research center devoted to these topics.

The Department of Measurement, Statistics, and Evaluation (http://www.education.umd.edu/edms) offers programs at the master's (M.A.) and doctoral (Ph.D.) levels in the areas of program evaluation, measurement, and statistics. Ample opportunity exists to engage in research with faculty members and to present research results in areas such as computer-based testing, design of experiments, construction and evaluation of measuring instruments, generalizability theory, measurement theory, multidimensional scaling, multivariate analysis, program evaluation, latent class analysis, structured equations modeling, and research methodology.

The Department of Special Education (http://www.education.umd.edu/edsp) offers graduate programs at the master's (including a teacher certification program) and doctoral levels with areas of concentration in policy studies, behavioral disorders and learning disabilities, infancy and early childhood special education, elementary special education, secondary/transition special education, learning disabilities, and severe disabilities. Graduate degrees emphasize research, instruction, and policy studies.

Research Facilities

The College of Education is home to thirteen research-based centers and institutes. The campus libraries contain more than 2.3 million volumes and subscribe to some 26,000 periodicals and newspapers. Additional collections of research materials are available in electronic formats, on microfilm, microfiche, phonograph records, tapes, and films. Maryland's libraries system has eight branches and houses an extensive collection of books, periodicals, reserves, and other materials. More information on library resources and services is available by calling 301-405-0800 or visiting the Web site at http://www.lib.umd.edu.

Financial Aid

A limited number of teaching and research assistantships are available through the departments within the College of Education. Other types of financial assistance are offered through the Graduate School. Financial aid applications should be submitted with the application for graduate study. For more information, students should call the Office of Student Financial Aid at 301-314-9000, or visit http://www.financialaid.umd.edu. Graduate assistantships are listed by employment services (301-405-5679).

Cost of Study

Tuition for the 2009–10 academic year was as follows: Maryland residents paid $471 per credit hour; nonresidents paid $1016 per credit hour. All students admitted to the Graduate School must pay graduate tuition, whether or not the credit will be used to satisfy program requirements. Graduate students are charged for tuition at the graduate rate, regardless of the level of courses for which they register. Mandatory fees, such as registration, shuttle bus, and health, are assessed each semester.

Living and Housing Costs

Housing costs vary on and off campus. Current information on housing for graduate students is available from Off-Campus Housing Services (telephone: 301-314-3645; Web site: http://www.och.umd.edu).

Student Group

The College enrolls 2,039 students, of whom 1,198 are graduate students. Of the total graduate enrollment, 932 are women; 329 are members of minority groups (178 African Americans, 86 Asian Americans or Pacific Islanders, 58 Hispanic Americans, and 7 Native Americans); and 129 are international students.

Location

Nestled on 1,300 acres in suburban College Park, the University is located in the thriving Baltimore-Washington corridor. The University's location—just 9 miles from downtown Washington, D.C., and approximately 30 miles from both Baltimore and Annapolis—enhances the research opportunities of its faculty members and students by providing access to some of the finest libraries and research centers in the country.

The University and The College

With more than 3,000 faculty members, the University of Maryland is an internationally recognized premier research institution offering master's degrees in 108 areas and doctoral degrees in eighty-five. Programs within each of the College's seven departments rank in the top twenty-five nationwide; *U.S. News & World Report 2010* ranks Counseling and Personnel Services first in the nation.

Applying

Information, application forms, and the latest electronic edition of the Graduate Catalog can be obtained from the University of Maryland Graduate School Web site at http://www.gradschool.umd.edu. Application can also be made online through the College of Education Web site at http://www.education.umd.edu/studentinfo. Each graduate program maintains its own deadlines for application. For the fall semester, these deadlines usually run from December 1 of the previous year to mid-February. Spring applications—if the program accepts them—are usually taken in September and October. Please contact the graduate program directly for specific information on deadlines. International applicants should apply at least six months before the program deadlines.

Correspondence and Information

College of Education, Office of Student Services
1204 Benjamin Building
University of Maryland
College Park, Maryland 20742-1121

Phone: 301-405-2364
Fax: 301-314-5887
Web site: http://www.education.umd.edu/studentinfo

University of Maryland, College Park

THE FACULTY AND THEIR RESEARCH

Department of Counseling and Personnel Services

Julia A. Bryan, Ph.D. Counseling and counselor education of reading skill and impairment, how children learn the meaning of words. Ellen S. Fabian, Ph.D. Support systems for adults with disabilities, school-to-work transition for special needs young adults. Paul B. Gold, Ph.D. Rehabilitation counseling and counselor education. Gary D. Gottfredson, Ph.D. Organization and program development, multicultural education. Mary Ann Hoffman, Ph.D. Psychosocial aspects of health and wellness, counselor training and supervision. Cheryl Holcomb-McCoy, Ph.D. Multicultural counseling competence, impact of racial identity in school counseling programs. Karen Kurotsuchi Inkelas, Ph.D. Living-learning programs, Asian American students. Dennis M. Kivlighan Jr., Ph.D., Chair. Process and outcome of group and individual counseling and psychotherapy, counseling interventions in influencing achievement goal. Susan Komives, Ed.D. Student leadership, leadership identity development, generational cohorts. Courtland C. Lee, Ph.D. Psychosocial development of African American males, evaluation of culturally specific counseling interventions in schools. Robert W. Lent, Ph.D. Social cognitive career theory, psychological adjustment processes. Margaretha Lucas, Ph.D. Career and identity development, evaluation of clinical services. Kim MacDonald-Wilson, Ph.D. Rehabilitation counseling, psychiatric rehabilitation. Matthew J. Miller, Ph.D. Counseling psychology. Pepper Phillips, Ph.D. Homophobia in schools, gay-, lesbian-, bisexual-headed family coping strategies. Stephen J. Quaye, Ph.D. Gains and outcomes associated with inclusive racial climates, crossracial interactions, and color-conscious pedagogical approaches. Sylvia A. Rosenfield, Ph.D. School consultation services, instructional consultation, urban education. William E. Sedlacek, Ph.D. Student and faculty research, multicultural issues. William O. Strein, Ed.D. Children's self-perceptions of competence, affective correlations of learning/schooling. Hedwig Teglasi-Golubcow, Ph.D. Temperament and personality assessment, integration of cognitive processes in personality development.

Department of Curriculum and Instruction

Peter P. Afflerbach, Ph.D. Reading assessment, development of reading strategies, think-aloud protocol. Andrew Brantlinger, Ph.D. Teacher education/professional development. Patricia F. Campbell, Ph.D. Enhancing instructional practice, increasing mathematics achievement in urban schools. Daniel Chazan, Ed.D. Teaching with technology, student-centered mathematics teaching. Joseph Cirrincione, Ph.D. Social studies and geography education. Lawrence Clark, Ph.D. Educational studies and mathematics instructional practices. Janet E. Coffey, Ph.D. Assessment in science education, science education reform. Mariam J. Dreher, Ph.D. Effective reading instruction, reading motivation in elementary school. Ann Ryu Edwards, Ph.D. Mathematics teacher learning and development, social/interactional processes of mathematical cognition and learning, equity in mathematics education. David M. Hammer, Ph.D. Teacher thinking and physics education. William G. Holliday, Ph.D. Science education, motivation and literacy in science. Sherick Hughes, Ph.D. Culture, curriculum, and change program, School of Education. Maria Hyler, Ph.D. Teacher education/professional development, minority and urban education. Stephen M. Koziol, Ph.D., Interim Associate Dean. Teacher education program design, English teaching methodology, secondary literacy. Victoria M. MacDonald, Ed.D. History of American education. Melinda Martin-Beltran, Ph.D. Second-language learning, bilingualism and classroom interaction, cultural and linguistic diversity. Joseph L. McCaleb, Ph.D. Literacy education, storytelling, literacy and community. James R. McGinnis, Ph.D. Science teacher education, equity in science teaching and learning. Chauncey Monte-Sano, Ph.D. Learning to write and reason with evidence in history classrooms, effective history/social studies teaching. Connie E. North, Ph.D. Teacher education/professional development. John F. O'Flahavan, Ph.D. Early literacy, teacher professional development. Rebecca L. Oxford, Ph.D. Language learning styles, strategies and motivation. Megan Madigan Peercy, Ph.D. Second-language learning, bilingualism and classroom interaction, cultural and linguistic diversity. Olivia N. Saracho, Ph.D. Emergent literacy, teacher preparation, cognitive style. Wayne H. Slater, Ph.D. Written communication, reading comprehension, teacher education. Denis F. Sullivan, Ph.D. Computers in education, history of technical education. Jennifer Danridge Turner, Ph.D. Cultural diversity issues in early literacy teaching and learning, urban education. Linda R. Valli, Ph.D., Interim Chair. Teacher learning, cultural diversity, school improvement. Bruce A. VanSledright, Ph.D. American history in diverse classrooms, citizenship education. Thomas D. Weible, Ph.D., Senior Associate Dean and Interim Chair, EDHI. Certification standards in social studies, history instruction. Donna L. Wiseman, Ph.D., Dean. Teacher education program development, school-university partnerships.

Department of Education Leadership, Higher Education and International Education

Alberto Cabrera, Ph.D. Research methodologies, college choice, minorities in higher education, economics of education. Thomas Davis, Ph.D. Organizational leadership, school finance and school facilities. Noah Drezner, Ph.D. Higher education, philanthropy and fundraising. Sharon Fries-Britt, Ph.D. Experiences of high-achieving black collegians, recruitment and retention of minority faculty. Steven J. Klees, Ph.D. Comparative and international education, political economy and education. Jing Lin, Ed.D. Comparative education, gender and peace education. Hanne B. Mawhinney, Ph.D. Institutional dynamics of leadership and policy change, accountability, critical feminist theory. Kerry Ann O'Meara, Ph.D. Systems that recruit, support and retain faculty in higher education. Carol S. Parham, Ed.D. Personnel administration, educational leadership, labor negotiations. Patricia K. Richardson, Ph.D. Public school administration, school improvement. Nelly Penaloza Stromquist, Ph.D. International education policy, issues related to comparative education and gender. Marvin Titus, Ph.D. Economics of higher education and higher education financing strategies re: college student access, persistence and labor market outcomes.

Department of Education Policy Studies

Robert G. Croninger, Ph.D. Policy analysis, sociology, equity, quantitative research. Barbara J. Finkelstein, Ed.D. History, transcultural educational policy and practice, biographical studies. Dennis Herschbach, Ph.D. Vocational and technical education, education in developing countries. Francine H. Hultgren, Ph.D., Interim Chair. Hermeneutic phenomenological inquiry, curriculum theory and development. Betty Malen, Ph.D. Education policy and politics, theories of political behavior, politics of education reforms. Jennifer King Rice, Ph.D. Education policy, education reform for at-risk students. Steven Selden, Ed.D. Critical curriculum theory, eugenics, comparative curriculum.

Department of Human Development

Patricia A. Alexander, Ph.D. Cognition, strategic processing, domain knowledge development. Donald J. Bolger, Ph.D. Cognitive and neural mechanisms involved in acquiring reading skill and the underlying developmental disorders leading to reading failure. Natasha J. Cabrera, Ph.D. Paternal involvement, low-income families. Nathan A. Fox, Ph.D. Attachment, emotion regulation, developmental psychophysiology. Nathan C. Hall, Ph.D. Psychosocial determinants of optimal development in academic achievement settings. Brenda Jones-Harden, Ph.D. Development and mental health of foster and at-risk children. Melanie A. Killen, Ph.D. Social cognition, moral reasoning, exclusion and prejudice. Elisa L. Klein, Ph.D. Early childhood education, social policy and children. Robert F. Marcus, Ph.D. Family relationships, social skills, delinquency and violence. Geetha B. Ramani, Ph.D. Cognitive and social development of young children. Elizabeth Robertson-Tchabo, Ph.D. Cognitive development and aging. Kenneth H. Rubin, Ph.D. Socioemotional and personality development, parent-child relationships. Judith Torney-Purta, Ph.D. Social/political cognition, worldwide civic education. Min Wang, Ph.D. Language and reading acquisition, second-language/bilingual literacy development. Kathryn R. Wentzel, Ph.D. Motivation, social relationships, academic achievement. Allan L. Wigfield, Ph.D., Chair. Motivation and self-concept in children and adolescents.

Department of Measurement, Statistics and Evaluation

Gregory R. Hancock, Ph.D., Chair. Structural equation modeling, multiple comparisons procedures. Jeffrey R. Harring, Ph.D. Modeling of longitudinal data. Hong Jiao, Ph.D. Measurement and statistics. Robert W. Lissitz, Ph.D. Psychometrics, educational assessment, program evaluation. George B. Macready, Ph.D. Latent class models, assessment of model fit, adaptive testing. Robert J. Mislevy, Ph.D. Educational assessment, statistical methods. Andre A. Rupp, Ph.D. High-stakes testing evaluation.

Department of Special Education

Paula J. Beckman, Ph.D. Infancy and early childhood special education, working with families. Philip J. Burke, Ph.D., Chair. Policy studies, teacher education. Susan De La Paz, Ph.D. Learning disabilities and writing strategy instruction. William Drakeford, Ph.D. Behavioral and emotional disorders, literacy, adolescent education. Andrew L. Egel, Ph.D. Autism and other severe disabilities. Frances L. Kohl, Ph.D. Severe and multiple disabilities, inclusion in school and community. Peter E. Leone, Ph.D. Emotional and behavioral disorders of children and adolescents, juvenile justice. Joan A. Lieber, Ph.D. Early childhood social interaction, inclusion of preschoolers with disabilities. Paula Maccini, Ph.D. Mathematics intervention for secondary students with learning disabilities. Margaret J. McLaughlin, Ph.D., Interim Associate Dean. Policy studies and inclusion. M. Sherril Moon, Ed.D. School-to-work transition and community integration of students with severe disabilities. Debra Ann Neubert, Ph.D. School-to-adult-life transition, transition assessment. Rebecca Silverman, Ed.D. Early prevention and intervention for children at risk for experiencing reading difficulties. Deborah L. Speece, Ph.D. Educational handicaps, learning disabilities, identifying learning disabilities.

UNIVERSITY OF MIAMI

School of Education

Programs of Study

The University of Miami (UM) School of Education offers curricula leading to the degrees of Master of Science in Education (M.S.Ed.), Specialist in Education (Ed.S.), Doctor of Education (Ed.D.), and Doctor of Philosophy (Ph.D.).

At the master's level, programs are available in community and social change; higher education administration with concentrations in enrollment management and student life and development; early childhood special education; counseling and research; exercise physiology and exercise physiology with a concentration in strength and conditioning; marriage and family therapy; mental health counseling; research, measurement, and evaluation; sport administration; and sports medicine with a concentration in athletic training.

Doctoral degrees are offered in counseling psychology; exercise physiology; higher education leadership; language and literacy learning in multilingual settings; mathematics and science education; research, measurement, and evaluation; and special education.

The counseling psychology doctoral program is accredited by the American Psychological Association (APA).

Research Facilities

All students may use the University library. In addition, a special computer laboratory administered by the School of Education is available. The School also operates an exercise physiology laboratory and a training clinic for counseling students.

Financial Aid

Graduate assistantships are available to doctoral program applicants. Full-time teachers under contract and teachers on official leave or sabbatical may be eligible for the teacher tuition discount scholarships. Other tuition assistance may be available through grants.

Cost of Study

Tuition is $1538 per credit for graduate course work in fall 2010.

Living and Housing Costs

Residential colleges are not open to graduate students; however, the Department of Residence Halls does provide off-campus housing resources for students, including an online search engine with area listings.

Student Group

Approximately 250 students are enrolled in the School of Education for study in programs leading to graduate degrees. These include students from a variety of states and many countries.

Location

The suburb of Coral Gables is one of the municipalities that make up metropolitan Miami. This subtropical area, which stretches from Fort Lauderdale to the Florida Keys, is an exciting, multicultural cosmopolitan community that offers substantial cultural and recreational attractions. For those interested in outdoor recreation, the Florida Keys, Biscayne Bay, and Everglades National Park are nearby.

The University

The University, founded in Coral Gables in 1925, is an independent, nonprofit, nonsectarian institution open to all qualified men and women. Its schools, colleges, and research institutes now occupy four campuses. The main campus is in Coral Gables, the medical campus is in Miami, the marine sciences campus is on Virginia Key, and the south campus—primarily a research campus—is in south Dade County. The University supports a full calendar of significant events during the year. Almost all departments and schools sponsor weekly seminars open to graduate students.

The University is a member of a number of consortia established for teaching or research purposes with other universities in the United States and with universities in Latin America and the Caribbean.

Applying

Applications for admission to graduate study must be received through the UM Graduate School Web site. All applicants must submit an online application with fee, a statement of personal goals, a current resume, transcripts from all institutions attended, three recommendation letters, and Graduate Record Examinations (GRE) General Test scores. Teachers with at least three years of full-time teaching experience may be eligible to apply for a GRE waiver when applying to the master's program offered by the Department of Teaching and Learning. The Ph.D. program application deadline is December 10 for counseling psychology; February 1 for research, measurement and evaluation; February 15 for teaching and learning; and April 1 for exercise physiology. Admission to most other graduate programs is on a rolling basis. If the student is applying to a graduate program, additional application materials should be sent to the Graduate Admissions Office.

Correspondence and Information

Graduate Admissions Office
School of Education
University of Miami
P.O. Box 248065
Coral Gables, Florida 33124-2040

Phone: 305-284-3711
E-mail: soe@miami.edu
Web site: http://www.education.miami.edu

University of Miami

THE FACULTY AND THEIR RESEARCH

Soyeon Ahn, Assistant Professor; Ph.D., Michigan State, 2008. Measurement and quantitative methods.

Etiony Aldarondo, Associate Dean of Research; Ph.D., Massachusetts Amherst, 1992. Family violence, multicultural counseling.

Brian Arwari, Lecturer; Ph.D., Rome, 2006. Psychophysiology and cognitive psychology.

Mary Avalos, Research Assistant Professor; Ph.D., California, Riverside, 1999. Curriculum and instruction, TESOL and reading.

Ann Bessell, Research Associate Professor; Miami (Florida), 1999. Special education, classroom and behavior management.

William Blanton, Professor; Ed.D., Georgia, 1970. Reading education.

Kent Burnett, Associate Professor; Ph.D., Stanford, 1984. Health psychology, behavioral medicine, assessment, computer applications in psychology.

Maria Carlo, Associate Professor; Ph.D., Massachusetts, 1994. Bilingual education, literacy.

Wendy Cavendish, Assistant Professor; Ph.D., Miami (Florida), 2006. Special education.

Arlene Clachar, Associate Professor; Ph.D., Columbia, 1987. Sociolinguistics, applied linguistics.

Joshua Diem, Instructor; Ph.D., North Carolina at Chapel Hill, 2004. Culture, curriculum, and change.

Batya Elbaum, Associate Professor and Associate Department Chair; Ph.D., Utah, 1994. Special education research and policy.

Scotney Evans, Assistant Professor; Ph.D., Vanderbilt (Peabody), 2005. Community research and action.

Blaine Fowers, Professor and Department Chair; Ph.D., Texas at Austin, 1987. Marriage and family therapy, research with couples, philosophy of psychology.

Mileidis Gort, Assistant Professor; Ed.D., Boston University, 2001. Literacy, language, and culture.

Kysha Harriell, Director of Clinical Education; Ph.D., Miami (Florida), 2010. Educational research, exercise physiology.

Beth Harry, Professor and Department Chair; Ph.D., Syracuse, 1989. Family and multicultural issues.

Kevin A. Jacobs, Assistant Professor; Ph.D., Ohio State, 2000. Exercise biochemistry, metabolism, cardiovascular physiology.

Laura Kohn-Wood, Associate Professor; Ph.D., Virginia, 1996. Clinical psychology.

Debbiesiu Lee, Assistant Professor; Ph.D., Arizona State, 2005. Counseling psychology.

Okhee Lee-Salwen, Professor; Ph.D., Michigan State, 1989. Science education, educational psychology.

Brian Lewis, Clinical Associate Professor; Ph.D., Florida, 1984. Health psychology, stress and wellness, clinical training, therapy, outcomes assessment.

Robert McMahon, Professor; Ph.D., Wisconsin–Madison, 1973. Substance-abuse disorders; HIV/AIDS; psychological assessment; stress, coping, and social support.

Anita Meinbach, Clinical Assistant Professor; Ed.D., Miami (Florida), 1982. Elementary education.

Marjorie Montague, Professor; Ph.D., Arizona, 1984. Learning disabilities and behavior disorders.

Robert Moore, Associate Professor and Associate Department Chair; Ed.D., Indiana, 1969. Learning and behavior problems.

Susan Mullane, Clinical Associate Professor; Ph.D., Miami (Florida), 1995. Leadership, ethics, sport administration.

Nicholas D. Myers, Assistant Professor; Ph.D., Michigan State, 2005. Measurement and quantitative methods.

Marilyn Neff, Clinical Assistant Professor and Associate Dean of Planning, Communications, and External Relations; Ed.D., Miami (Florida), 1986. Educational leadership.

Guerda Nicolas, Associate Professor and Department Chair; Ph.D., Boston University, 1997. Clinical psychology.

Randall D. Penfield, Associate Professor; Ph.D., Toronto, 2000. Statistics, measurement, and psychometrics.

Arlette Perry, Professor and Department Chair; Ph.D., NYU, 1981. Cardiovascular physiology, obesity, women's health, pediatric physiology.

Carol-Anne Phekoo, Clinical Assistant Professor; Ph.D., Miami (Florida), 1999. Higher education/enrollment management.

Shawn Post-Klauber, Associate Professor and Associate Dean of Undergraduate Studies; Ph.D., Miami (Florida), 1977. Reading and learning disabilities.

Isaac Prilleltensky, Professor and Dean; Ph.D., Manitoba, 1989. Psychology.

Ora Prilleltensky, Assistant Clinical Professor; Ed.D., Toronto, 1998. Counseling psychology, disability studies.

Eugene Provenzo Jr., Professor; Ph.D., Washington (St. Louis), 1976. Foundations of education.

Bobby Robertson, Professor; Ed.D., Oregon, 1972. Anatomy and kinesiology, athletic sports injury, gross anatomy.

Stephanie Schmitz, Lecturer; Ph.D., North Carolina at Chapel Hill, 1987. Clinical psychology, family and human services.

Jeanne Schumm, Professor; Ph.D., Miami (Florida), 1984. Reading.

Walter G. Secada, Professor and Senior Associate Dean of Graduate Studies; Ph.D., Northwestern, 1985. Mathematics education.

Joseph Signorile, Professor; Ph.D., Texas A&M, 1990. Exercise physiology, muscle physiology, power training, aging.

Wesley Smith, Clinical Assistant Professor; Ph.D., Miami (Florida), 2007. Exercise physiology.

Warren Whisenant, Associate Professor and Associate Department Chair; Ph.D., Florida State, 1998. Sport management, sport finance.

UNIVERSITY OF SOUTH FLORIDA

College of Education

Programs of Study

The University of South Florida (USF) College of Education is committed to excellence in teaching, research, and service. It offers a variety of graduate programs that lead to the Doctor of Philosophy (Ph.D.), Doctor of Education (Ed.D.), Education Specialist (Ed.S.), Master of Education (M.Ed.), Master of Arts (M.A.), and Master of Arts in Teaching (M.A.T.) degrees. Doctoral degrees are designed to prepare graduates to conduct research, teach in a college or university setting, and hold administrative or leadership positions in educational institutions, school systems, and other public or private agencies. The master's and education specialist programs are designed to prepare educational practitioners in advanced studies in their field.

The Ph.D. degree is offered in school psychology, second language acquisition/instructional technology, and curriculum and instruction, with specializations in the areas of adult education, career and workforce education, counselor education, elementary education, English education, higher education, instructional technology, interdisciplinary education, mathematics education, measurement and evaluation, reading education, science education, secondary education (including social science), special education, and teaching and learning in the content area (general education). The Ed.D is offered in educational leadership (K–12), community college leadership, and educational program development with concentrations in adult education and elementary education. The Ed.S., M.Ed., and M.A. degrees are offered in most of the areas listed above, plus the areas of college student affairs. M.A. degrees are offered in the areas noted as well as in career and technical education, college teaching, counselor education, early childhood education, exercise science, foreign language education/ESOL, gifted education, physical education, and social science education. The M.A.T. degree is offered in elementary education/ESOL, English education/ESOL, exceptional student education varying exceptionalities/ESOL, foreign language education/ESOL, mathematics education, science education, and social science education.

The doctoral programs require completion of core courses and courses in the specialization area, satisfactory performance on a qualifying examination, and completion of a dissertation. The Ph.D. program requires two semesters of full-time residency on the Tampa campus. The Ed.S. programs require a minimum of 36 credit hours, including completion of a thesis and a written comprehensive examination. The master's programs require a minimum of 30 to 33 credit hours and a comprehensive examination.

A number of programs are fully online, including master's degree programs in career and technical education, gifted education, instructional technology (plus the Ed.S. degree program), and physical education. Several programs are partially online, including master's degrees in adult education, early childhood, educational leadership, elementary education, measurement and evaluation, reading, varying exceptionalities, and the doctorate in workforce and career education.

Research Facilities

The USF Library System is among the finest in the Florida State University System. It houses more than 2 million volumes, 31,685 journals and periodicals, and an extensive collection of electronic resources, including 20,697 e-journal subscriptions, 628 abstracting and indexing databases, 215,890 e-books, and 826,000 digital images. In addition, it has a Special Collections Department with more than 1 million items and a Government Documents Collection. College of Education students have access to a number of research centers and institutes that are housed within the College and in the broader USF community. The College's state-of-the-art technology system serves to enhance teaching and research and links faculty members and graduate students to national and international networks. Laboratories for exercise physiology and biomechanics provide students with opportunities for research.

Financial Aid

Financial aid is available to qualified graduate students in the form of graduate assistantships, fellowships, scholarships, and loan programs. For the 2009–10 academic year, graduate assistantship stipends ranged from $7800 (master's students) to $15,000 (doctoral students) for 20 hours of work per week for two semesters (fall and spring); additional summer employment is available. Students on graduate assistantships and some fellowships are granted tuition waivers. Inquiries about fellowships, grants, and scholarships should be directed to the USF Graduate School or the College of Education's Office of Graduate Studies.

Cost of Study

For the 2009–10 academic year, graduate tuition was $331.79 per credit hour for Florida residents and $818.66 per credit hour for nonresidents.

Living and Housing Costs

On-campus and off-campus housing is available to graduate students, although on-campus housing is limited. The University operates an apartment village that provides housing for graduate students at monthly rates ranging from $550 to $850 (single occupancy, including utilities, local phone service, Internet access, and cable). Most graduate students live off campus, selecting from a variety of housing options available in the area. The average cost of apartment rentals in the USF area is $520–$600 per month for a one-bedroom and $490–$520 per person per month if 2 people share a two-bedroom unit.

Student Group

The University's total enrollment for fall 2009 was more than 40,000, with a graduate enrollment of approximately 8,500 students. Graduate enrollment (including full-time and part-time students) in the College of Education was approximately 1,750 for fall 2009—accounting for 21 percent of USF's graduate enrollment. Full-time graduate students account for 35 percent of the College's graduate enrollment. Approximately 74 percent of the graduate students are women, 23 percent are members of minority groups, and 3.3 percent are international students.

Student Outcomes

Graduates of the College of Education are employed in a variety of settings, including universities, four- and two-year colleges, K–12 schools and school systems, central offices of school systems, business, and industry. Many alumni of the College are recipients of outstanding teaching and leadership awards.

Location

The USF College of Education is located in Tampa, in the vibrant Tampa Bay area on the west coast of Florida. One of the fastest-growing metropolitan areas of the nation, it is easily accessible to the waters of the Gulf of Mexico and Tampa Bay and within a 90-minute drive of the Orlando area. The region thrives with its variety of cultural and sports activities.

The University and The College

The University of South Florida, founded in 1956, is a multicampus, comprehensive research university and is strongly committed to the balanced pursuit of teaching, research, and service. The ninth-largest university in the nation, it comprises ten colleges on three campuses and is home to a medical school, a major mental health research institute, and three public broadcasting stations. The College of Education is one of the largest urban colleges of education in the country, with a current student enrollment of approximately 3,900 (declared majors only), and is accredited by the National Council for Accreditation of Teacher Education (NCATE).

Applying

A completed graduate application form, GRE General Test scores, and official transcripts from all institutions of higher education attended are required. Individual departments may have additional requirements. The GRE may be waived at the discretion of individual graduate programs. Applicants whose native language is not English are required to submit scores from the Test of English as a Foreign Language (TOEFL). Application forms may be obtained from the Office of Graduate Admissions. Completed applications are due no later than June 1 (for the fall semester), October 15 (for the spring semester), and March 2 (for the summer semester). Some programs may have earlier application deadlines and may admit only for the fall semester. Applications for graduate assistantships should be made directly to the department in which the student's program is housed.

Correspondence and Information

Coordinator of Graduate Studies
Office of Student Academic Services, EDU 106
University of South Florida
Tampa, Florida 33620-5650

Phone: 813-974-3406
Fax: 813-974-3391
E-mail: briscoe@usf.edu
Web site: http://www.coedu.usf.edu/main/sas/

Office of Graduate Admissions
University of South Florida
4202 Fowler Avenue—BEH304
Tampa, Florida 33620

University of South Florida

THE FACULTY

Adult, Career, and Higher Education
Rosemary Closson, Assistant Professor; Ph.D., Florida State, 1994.
Donald A. Dellow, Associate Professor; Ed.D., Florida, 1971.
James Eison, Professor; Ph.D., Tennessee, 1979.
Edward Fletcher, Assistant Professor, Ph.D., Ohio State, 2009.
Victor Hernandez-Gantes, Associate Professor; Ph.D., Virginia Tech, 1993.
Waynne B. James, Professor; Ed.D., Tennessee, 1976.
Kathleen King, Ed.D., Widener, 1997
Lahja-Johann Lasonen, Ph.D., Virginia Tech, 1990.
Derek Mulenga, Instructor; Ed.D., Northern Illinois, 1999.
W. Robert Sullins, Associate Professor; Ed.D., Florida, 1968.
William Young, Professor; Ed.D., Penn State, 1976.

Childhood Education and Literacy Studies
Ilene Berson, Professor; Ph.D., Toledo, 1997.
Jolyn Blank, Assistant Professor; Ph.D., Illinois at Urbana-Champaign, 2006.
Roger Brindley, Professor; Ed.D., Georgia, 1996.
Danielle Dennis, Assistant Professor; Ph.D., Tennessee, Knoxville, 2007.
Beatrice Green, M.A., Miami (Ohio), 1979.
Ann Hall, Instructor; Ph.D., Georgia, 1979.
Sophia Han, Assistant Professor; Ph.D., Florida, 2009.
James R. King, Professor; Ed.D., West Virginia, 1980.
Charlie Lippincott, Instructor; Ed.D., Arkansas, 1980.
Marcia Mann, Professor; Ph.D., Nebraska, 1970.
John Manning, Assistant Professor; Ed.D., Massachusetts Amherst, 1998.
Audra Parker, Assistant Professor; Ph.D., Georgia, 2005.
Janet Richards, Professor; Ph.D., New Orleans, 1985.
Jenifer J. Schneider, Associate Professor; Ph.D., Ohio State, 1996.
Donna Stewart, Instructor; M.A., California State Polytechnic, 1970, Ohio State, 1973.
Nancy Lynn Williams, Associate Professor; Ph.D., LSU, 1989.
Diane Yendol-Hoppey, Ph.D., Penn State, 1999.

Educational Leadership and Policy Studies
Vonzell Agosto, Assistant Professor; Ph.D., Wisconsin, 2009.
William R. Black, Assistant Professor; Ph.D., Texas at Austin, 2004.
Darlene Bruner, Associate Professor; Ed.D., South Florida, 1997.
Leonard Burrello, Professor; Ed.D., Syracuse, 1969.
Bobbie Greenlee, Assistant Professor; Ed.D., South Florida, 1997.
Valerie Janesick, Professor; Ph.D., Michigan State, 1977.
Zorka Karanxha, Assistant Professor; Ed.D., Lehigh, 2004.
Anthony Rolle, Professor and Chair; Ph.D., Indiana, 2000.

Educational Measurement and Research
Yi-Hsin Chen, Assistant Professor; Ph.D., Arizona State, 2006.
Robert F. Dedrick, Professor; Ph.D., Michigan, 1988.
Chris DeLuca, Assistant Professor; Ph.D., Queen's at Kingston, 2009.
John M. Ferron, Professor; Ph.D., North Carolina at Chapel Hill, 1993.
Jeffrey D. Kromrey, Professor; Ph.D., South Florida, 1989.
Liliana Rodriguez-Campos, Associate Professor; Ph.D., Western Michigan, 2002.

School of Physical Education & Exercise Science
Candi D. Ashley, Associate Professor; Ph.D., Alabama, 1995.
Bill Campbell, Assistant Professor; Ph.D., Baylor, 2007.
Joann Eickhoff-Shemek, Professor; Ph.D., Nebraska, 1995.
Nell Faucette, Professor; Ed.D., Georgia, 1984.
Sara Flory, Assistant Professor; Ph.D., Wayne State (Michigan), 2010.
Lisa Hansen, Assistant Professor; Ph.D., South Florida, 2009.
Marcus Kilpatrick, Associate Professor; Ph.D., Texas at Austin, 1999.
Stephen Sanders, Professor; Ed.D., Virginia Tech, 1993.
Michael Stewart, Professor; Ph.D., Ohio State, 1977.
Haichun Sun, Assistant Professor; Ph.D., Maryland, 2007.
Ralph C. Wilcox, Professor; Ph.D., Alberta, 1982.

Psychological and Social Foundations
George M. Batsche Jr., Professor; Ed.D., Ball State, 1978.
Kathy L. Bradley-Klug, Associate Professor; Ph.D., Lehigh, 1996.
Deirdre L. Cobb-Roberts, Associate Professor; Ph.D., Illinois at Urbana-Champaign, 1998.
Darlene DeMarie, Associate Professor; Ph.D., Florida, 1988.

Sherman J. Dorn, Professor; Ph.D., Pennsylvania, 1992.
Herbert A. Exum, Professor; Ph.D., Minnesota, 1978.
Wilma Henry, Associate Professor; Ed.D., East Texas State, 1980.
Erwin V. Johanningmeier, Professor; Ph.D., Illinois, 1967.
Harold Keller, Professor; Ph.D., Florida State, 1968.
Sarah Kiefer, Assistant Professor; Ph.D., Illinois at Urbana-Champaign, 2007.
Lisa Lopez, Assistant Professor; Ph.D., Miami (Florida), 2001.
Kofi Marfo, Professor; Ph.D., Alberta, 1985.
Thomas E. Miller, Associate Professor, Ed.D., Indiana, 1979.
Michelle Mitcham, Assistant Professor; Ph.D., Central Florida, 2005.
Julia A. Ogg, Assistant Professor; Ph.D., Michigan State, 2008.
Debra Osborn, Associate Professor; Ph.D., Florida State, 1998.
Linda M. Raffaele-Mendez, Associate Professor; Ph.D., Texas at Austin, 1993.
Barbara Shircliffe, Associate Professor; Ph.D., SUNY at Buffalo, 1997.
Marian S. Street, Associate Professor; Ph.D., Florida, 1980.
Shannon Suldo, Associate Professor; Ph.D., South Carolina, 2004.
Tony X. Tan, Associate Professor; Ed.D., Harvard, 2004.
Kim M. Vaz, Associate Professor; Ph.D., Indiana Bloomington, 1990.
Carlos Zalaquett, Associate Professor; Ph.D., Texas, 1993.

Secondary Education
Jane Applegate, Professor; Ph.D., Ohio State, 1978.
Richard A. Austin, Associate Professor; Ph.D., Florida, 1983.
Ann Barron, Professor; Ed.D., Central Florida, 1991.
Michael J. Berson, Professor; Ph.D., Toledo, 1993.
Barbara C. Cruz, Professor; Ed.D., Florida International, 1990.
Steven E. Downey, Assistant Professor; Ph.D., Illinois at Urbana-Champaign, 2000.
James A. Duplass, Professor; Ph.D., Saint Louis, 1974.
Cheryl Ellerbrock, Assistant Professor; Ph.D., Florida, 2007.
Linda Evans, Assistant Professor; Ph.D., South Florida, 1997.
Allan Feldman, Professor; Ph.D., Stanford, 1993.
Helen Gerretson, Assistant Professor; Ph.D., Florida, 1998.
Benjamin Herman, Assistant Professor; Ph.D., Iowa State, 2010.
Tina Hohlfeld, Assistant Professor; Ph.D., South Florida, 2008.
J. Howard Johnston, Professor; Ph.D., Wyoming, 1974.
Patricia L. Jones, Associate Professor; Ph.D., Oklahoma, 1991.
Joan F. Kaywell, Professor; Ph.D., Florida, 1987.
Colleen S. Kennedy, Professor; Ph.D., Washington, 1976.
Gladis Kersaint, Associate Professor; Ph.D., Illinois State, 1998.
Deoksoon Kim, Assistant Professor; Ph.D., New Mexico, 2005.
Dick J. Puglisi, Professor; Ph.D., Georgia State, 1973.
Adam Schwartz, Assistant Professor; Ph.D., Arizona, 2009.
Glenn G. Smith, Assistant Professor; Ph.D., Arizona State, 1998.
Philip Smith, Instructor; Ph.D., South Florida, 2005.
Barbara Spector, Professor; Ph.D., Syracuse, 1977.
Denisse R. Thompson, Professor; Ph.D., Chicago, 1992.
Stephen J. Thornton, Professor; Ph.D., Stanford 1985.
Marcela van Olphen, Assistant Professor; Ph.D., Purdue, 2002.
Eugenia Vomvoridi-Ivanovic, Assistant Professor; Ph.D., Illinois at Chicago, 2009.
Dana L. Zeidler, Professor; Ph.D., Syracuse, 1982.

Special Education
David Allsopp, Professor; Ph.D., Florida, 1995.
Michael Churton, Professor; Ed.D., Southern Mississippi, 1979.
Karen L. Colucci, Instructor; Ph.D., South Florida, 1994.
Ann M. Cranston-Gingras, Professor; Ph.D., South Florida, 1987.
Elizabeth M. Doone, Instructor; Ph.D., South Florida, 1998.
David Hoppey, Assistant Professor; Ph.D., Florida, 2006.
Bruce Anthony Jones, Professor; Ph.D., Columbia, 1989.
Phyllis Jones, Associate Professor; Ph.D., Northumbria, 2002.
Patricia Jeannie Kleinhammer-Tramill, Professor; Ph.D., Kansas, 1981.
Patricia Alvarez McHatton, Associate Professor; Ph.D., South Florida, 2004.
Elizabeth Shaunessy, Associate Professor; Ph.D., Southern Mississippi, 2003.
Daphne D. Thomas, Associate Professor; Ph.D., North Carolina at Chapel Hill, 1989.
Brenda L. Townsend Walker, Professor; Ph.D., Kansas, 1991; J.F., Stetson, 2006.

VANDERBILT UNIVERSITY

Peabody College

Programs of Study	Vanderbilt University's Peabody College of Education and Human Development offers programs leading to the Master of Education (M.Ed.), Master of Public Policy (M.P.P.), and Doctor of Education (Ed.D.) degrees. The Vanderbilt Graduate School, through Peabody departments, offers the Doctor of Philosophy degree. Peabody is committed to preparing students to become research scholars or innovative practitioners in the field of education and human development. Students may attend full- or part-time. Weekend courses are offered in several programs for working professionals who want to earn an advanced degree.

Students may pursue the Master of Education (M.Ed.) in child studies; community development and action; elementary education; English language learners; higher education administration (including specializations in administration, student life, institutional advancement, and service learning); human development counseling (with specializations in school or community counseling); human resource development; international education policy and management; learning, diversity, and urban studies; learning and instruction (including specializations in teaching and learning; digital literacies; language, culture, and international studies; science and mathematics; or an individualized program); organizational leadership; reading education; secondary education; and special education (including specializations in applied behavior analysis, early childhood, high-incidence disabilities, and low-incidence disabilities). A Master of Public Policy is available in education policy. Vanderbilt also offers a joint M.P.P./J.D. program.

Students interested in doctoral study may enroll in educational leadership and policy (Ed.D.); higher education leadership and policy (Ed.D.); community research and action (Ph.D.); leadership and policy studies (Ph.D., with specializations in educational leadership and policy, higher education leadership and policy, and international education policy and management); learning, teaching, and diversity (Ph.D., with specializations in development, learning, and diversity; language, literacy, and culture; and mathematics and science); psychological sciences (Ph.D., with specializations in clinical science, cognitive science, developmental science, and quantitative methods and evaluation); and special education (Ph.D., with specializations in early childhood, high-incidence disabilities, and severe disabilities).

Peabody's teacher education and advanced certification programs are approved by the National Council for Accreditation of Teacher Education (NCATE). Programs in psychology and counseling are accredited by the American Psychological Association and the Council on Accreditation of Counseling and Related Educational Programs (CACREP), respectively.

Research Opportunities	In addition to the Vanderbilt University Library System, which has more than 2.6 million volumes, excellent research facilities and opportunities to conduct research are available through the Vanderbilt Kennedy Center for Research on Human Development, the Learning Sciences Institute, the Peabody Research Institute, the Susan Gray School, the National Center on School Choice, the National Center on Performance Initiatives, and the Center for Community Studies. The many local field sites available for research include hospitals, Metropolitan Nashville Public Schools, private schools, rehabilitation centers, schools for people with disabilities, government agencies, corporations, and nonprofit organizations.
Financial Aid	More than 60 percent of new students at Peabody receive financial aid. The College sponsors several substantial scholarship programs with offerings that range from partial to full tuition, including several scholarships designated for outstanding students from minority groups. In addition, assistantships, traineeships, loans, and part-time employment are available. Awards are made annually, and every attempt is made to meet a student's financial need. Application for financial aid does not affect the admission decision.
Cost of Study	Tuition for study at Peabody College for the 2009–10 academic year was $1125 per semester credit hour for the M.Ed., M.P.P., and Ed.D. programs, and $1568 per semester credit hour for programs offered through the Graduate School.
Living and Housing Costs	Vanderbilt's location in Nashville offers students the advantage of a wide range of living choices. Costs for housing, food, and other living expenses are moderate when compared with other metropolitan areas nationwide.
Student Group	Vanderbilt has a diverse student body of about 12,000. Peabody has an enrollment of approximately 1,800 students, of whom about 700 are graduate students. Women make up about 65 percent of Peabody's graduate students, while students from minority groups make up about 20 percent. Students have a broad range of academic backgrounds and include recent graduates of baccalaureate programs as well as men and women who have many years of professional experience. The median age of current students is 27.
Student Outcomes	Graduates who earn a master's or doctoral degree from Peabody are prepared to work for educational, corporate, government, and service organizations in a variety of roles. More than 10,000 alumni are practicing teachers, more than 175 are school superintendents, and more than 50 are current or former college or university presidents.
Location	Nashville, the capital of Tennessee, is a cosmopolitan city with a metropolitan area population of 1.23 million. Vanderbilt University is one of more than a dozen institutions of higher learning located in Nashville and the surrounding area, leading Nashville to be called the "Athens of the South."

Nashville offers residents and visitors much in the way of music, art, and recreation. More than 100 local venues provide a wide variety of music, while classical and contemporary music is performed by the Nashville Symphony Orchestra and the Nashville Chamber Orchestra. The Tennessee Performing Arts Center (TPAC) is home to two theater companies, a ballet company, and an opera company. Vanderbilt's own Great Performances series frequently brings the best in chamber music, new music, theater, and all forms of dance to the Vanderbilt campus. Outstanding exhibitions of fine art can be seen at the Frist Center for the Visual Arts and at Cheekwood Botanical Garden and Museum of Art. There are more than 6,000 acres of public parks in the city, and the surrounding region of rolling hills and lakes is dotted with state parks and recreation areas.

Nashville has been named one of the 15 best U.S. cities for work and family by *Fortune* magazine, was ranked as the number 1 most popular U.S. city for corporate relocations by *Expansion Management* magazine, and was named by *Forbes* magazine as one of the 25 cities most likely to have the country's highest job growth over the coming five years. More information on Nashville can be found online at http://www.vanderbilt.edu/nashville.

The University and The College	Vanderbilt University, founded in 1873, is a private nondenominational institution with a strong tradition of graduate and professional education. Peabody, recognized for more than a century as one of the nation's foremost independent colleges of education, merged with Vanderbilt University in 1979. The College is currently ranked the number one graduate school of education in the nation by *U.S. News & World Report*. Peabody seeks to create knowledge through research, to prepare leaders, to support practitioners, and to strengthen communities at all levels.
Applying	Admission to professional degree programs is based on an evaluation of the applicant's potential for academic success and professional service, with consideration given to transcripts of previous course work, GRE General Test or MAT scores, letters of reference, and a letter outlining personal goals. Additional supporting credentials, such as a sample of the applicant's scholarly writing or a personal interview, may also be required.

The application fee is waived for applicants who apply online at http://www.peabody.vanderbilt.edu/gradadmissions. A nonrefundable $40 fee must accompany each paper application. Applicants who apply after the December 31 deadline should know that admission and financial assistance depend upon the availability of space and funds in the department in which they seek to study.

Correspondence and Information	Graduate Admissions Peabody College of Vanderbilt University Peabody Station, Box 327 Nashville, Tennessee 37203

Phone: 615-322-8410
Fax: 615-343-3474
E-mail: peabody.admissions@vanderbilt.edu
Web site: http://peabody.vanderbilt.edu

Vanderbilt University

THE FACULTY

Department of Human and Organizational Development
Sandra Barnes, Professor; Ph.D., Georgia State.
Kimberly D. Bess, Assistant Professor; Ph.D., Vanderbilt.
Vera Chatman, Professor of the Practice; Ph.D., George Peabody.
Joseph Cunningham, Associate Professor; Ed.D., Illinois.
Victoria J. Davis, Clinical Assistant Professor; Ed.D., Vanderbilt.
Paul R. Dokecki, Professor; Ph.D., George Peabody.
James C. Fraser, Associate Professor; Ph.D., Georgia State.
Gina Frieden, Assistant Professor of the Practice; Ph.D., Memphis State.
Susan K. Friedman, Lecturer; M.B.A., Arizona State.
Brian Griffith, Assistant Clinical Professor; Ph.D., South Carolina.
Craig Anne Heflinger, Professor; Ph.D., Vanderbilt.
Robert B. Innes, Associate Professor; Ph.D., Michigan.
Linda Isaacs, Lecturer; Ed.D., Vanderbilt.
Torin Monahan, Associate Professor; Ph.D., Rensselaer.
Velma McBride Murry, Professor; Ph.D., Missouri–Columbia.
Maury Nation, Associate Professor; Ph.D., South Carolina.
Douglas Perkins, Associate Professor; Ph.D., NYU.
Susan Saegert, Professor; Ph.D., Michigan.
Sharon Shields, Professor of the Practice; Ph.D., George Peabody.
Marybeth Shinn, Professor; Ph.D., Michigan.
Heather Smith, Assistant Professor of the Practice; Ph.D., Central Florida.
Paul Speer, Associate Professor; Ph.D., Missouri–Kansas City.
William L. Turner, Professor; Ph.D., Virginia Tech.
Andrew Van Schaack, Assistant Professor; Ph.D., Utah State.

Department of Leadership, Policy, and Organizations
Robert Dale Ballou, Associate Professor; Ph.D., Yale.
Leonard Bradley, Lecturer; M.A., Tennessee.
John Braxton, Professor; D.Ed., Penn State.
Timothy Caboni, Lecturer; Ph.D., Vanderbilt.
Mark D. Cannon, Associate Professor; Ph.D., Harvard.
Robert L. Crowson, Professor; Ph.D., Chicago.
Corbette Doyle, Lecturer; M.B.A., Vanderbilt.
William R. Doyle, Assistant Professor; Ph.D., Stanford.
Mimi Engel, Assistant Professor; Ph.D., Northwestern.
Janet Eyler, Professor of the Practice; Ph.D., Indiana.
Stella M. Flores, Assistant Professor; Ed.D., Harvard.
Constance Bumgarner Gee, Associate Professor; Ph.D., Penn State.
Ellen Goldring, Professor; Ph.D., Chicago.
Stephen P. Heyneman, Professor; Ph.D., Chicago.
Catherine Gavin Loss, Lecturer; Ph.D., Virginia.
Christopher P. Loss, Assistant Professor; Ph.D., Virginia.
Michael McLendon, Associate Professor; Ph.D., Michigan.
Joseph Murphy, Professor; Ph.D., Ohio State.
Christina R. Neimann, Lecturer; M.A., New Mexico.
Jane Robbins, Senior Lecturer; Ph.D., Pennsylvania.
Pearl Sims, Lecturer; Ed.D., Vanderbilt.
Thomas M. Smith, Associate Professor; Ph.D., Penn State.
Claire Smrekar, Associate Professor; Ph.D., Stanford.
Thomas Ward, Lecturer; M.Ed., Middle Tennessee State.

Department of Psychology and Human Development
Camilla P. Benbow, Professor; Ed.D., Johns Hopkins.
Leonard Bickman, Professor; Ph.D., CUNY.
Sun-Joo Cho, Assistant Professor; Ph.D., Georgia.
David A. Cole, Professor; Ph.D., Houston.
Bruce E. Compas, Professor; Ph.D., UCLA.
David Cordray, Professor; Ph.D., Claremont.
Elizabeth May Dykens, Professor; Ph.D., Kansas.
Judy Garber, Associate Professor; Ph.D., Minnesota, Twin Cities.
James H. Hogge, Professor; Ph.D., Texas.

Kathleen Hoover-Dempsey, Associate Professor; Ph.D., Michigan State.
Daniel T. Levin, Associate Professor; Ph.D., Cornell.
David Lubinski, Professor; Ph.D., Minnesota.
Bruce McCandliss, Professor; Ph.D., Oregon.
Joseph McLaughlin, Associate Professor; Ph.D., Vanderbilt.
Amy Needham, Professor; Ph.D., Illinois.
Laura R. Novick, Associate Professor; Ph.D., Stanford.
John R. Rieser, Professor; Ph.D., Minnesota, Twin Cities.
Bethany Rittle-Johnson, Assistant Professor; Ph.D., Carnegie Mellon.
Howard M. Sandler, Professor; Ph.D., Northwestern.
Megan M. Saylor, Assistant Professor; Ph.D., Oregon.
Craig A. Smith, Associate Professor; Ph.D., Stanford.
James Steiger, Professor; Ph.D., Purdue.
Georgene Troseth, Associate Professor; Ph.D., Illinois at Urbana-Champaign.
Tedra Ann Walden, Professor; Ph.D., Florida.
Bahr Weiss, Associate Professor; Ph.D., North Carolina at Chapel Hill.

Department of Special Education
Andrea Capizzi, Assistant Professor of the Practice; Ph.D., Vanderbilt.
Laurie Cutting, Associate Professor; Ph.D., Northwestern.
Alex da Fonte, Assistant Professor; M.S., Purdue.
Stephen N. Elliott, Professor; Ph.D., Arizona State.
Donna Y. Ford, Professor; Ph.D., Cleveland State.
Steve Graham, Professor; Ed.D., Kansas.
Deborah D. Hatton, Associate Professor; Ph.D., North Carolina.
Robert Hodapp, Professor; Ph.D., Boston University.
Carolyn Hughes, Professor; Ph.D., Illinois.
Ann Kaiser, Professor; Ph.D., Kansas.
Craig Kennedy, Professor; Ph.D., California, Santa Barbara.
Kathleen L. Lane, Associate Professor; Ph.D., California, Riverside.
Kim Paulsen, Associate Professor of the Practice; Ed.D., Nevada, Las Vegas.
Dan Reschly, Professor; Ph.D., Oregon.
Joseph H. Wehby, Associate Professor; Ph.D., Vanderbilt.
Mark Wolery, Professor; Ph.D., Washington (Seattle).
Ruth Wolery, Assistant Professor of the Practice; Ph.D., Pittsburgh.
Paul J. Yoder, Professor; Ph.D., North Carolina.

Department of Teaching and Learning
Paul A. Cobb, Professor; Ph.D., Georgia.
Douglas Clark, Associate Professor; Ph.D., Berkeley.
Bridget Dalton, Assistant Professor; Ed.D., Harvard.
David Dickinson, Professor; Ed.D., Harvard.
Dale C. Farran, Professor; Ph.D., Bryn Mawr.
Clifford A. Hofwolt, Associate Professor; Ed.D., Northern Colorado.
Ilana Horn, Associate Professor; Ph.D., Berkeley.
Robert T. Jimenez, Professor; Ph.D., Illinois at Urbana-Champaign.
Kevin Leander, Associate Professor; Ph.D., Ilinois.
Richard Lehrer, Professor; Ph.D., Chicago.
Henry Richard Milner, Associate Professor; M.A., Ohio State.
Ann M. Neely, Associate Professor of the Practice; Ed.D., Georgia.
Caron Neitzel, Assistant Professor; B.A., Indiana.
Karon Jean Nicol-LeCompte, Assistant Clinical Professor; Ph.D., M.S., Sam Houston State.
Amy Palmeri, Assistant Professor of the Practice; Ph.D., Indiana Bloomington.
Lisa Pray, Associate Professor of the Practice; Ph.D., Arizona State.
Victoria J. Risko, Professor; Ed.D., West Virginia.
Deborah W. Rowe, Associate Professor; Ph.D., Indiana.
Leona Schauble, Professor; Ph.D., Columbia.
Pratim Sengupta, Assistant Professor; Ph. D., Northwestern.
Marcy Singer-Gabella, Professor of the Practice; Ph.D., Stanford.

VILLANOVA UNIVERSITY

Department of Education and Human Services
Graduate Programs in Education

Programs of Study

The Department of Education and Human Services at Villanova University offers a Master of Arts degree (M.A.) in three areas: graduate teacher education (GTE), educational leadership, and a master's degree with Pennsylvania Instructional I certification. In addition, Villanova offers a 15-hour post-master's certificate in teacher leadership. The curriculum of each program explores educational theory and pedagogy through a historical perspective, providing instruction in assessment and educational research. The programs prepare graduates for successful positions in educational settings.

To satisfy the requirements for a master's degree in GTE, students move through a 30-credit program, with a core curriculum of statistics, research, philosophy, and curriculum and instruction courses. In addition, students may enroll in courses in their specific content area and must attend three workshops. Following the completion of mandated courses, students have the freedom to select from a number of electives pertaining to various educational areas. Students must also pass a comprehensive examination (administered three times a year) before a degree is awarded.

Those enrolled in the Educational Leadership Program may select from the following options: 33-credit Master of Arts in educational leadership (focus on K–12 schooling); 33-credit Master of Arts in educational leadership (concentration in higher education); and post-master's principal certification (minimum of 12 credits; required credits depend on previous coursework). Villanova's Educational Leadership Program is unique in its interdisciplinary emphasis. Besides a core of requirements in education, students also take coursework in public administration, ethics, and communication. Students may also select from a range of electives or decide to complete a thesis. Before the degree is awarded, students must pass a comprehensive examination.

The Master of Arts in Education plus Teacher Certification Program requires the completion of 36 credits, which includes student teaching. The curriculum explores educational theory and pedagogy through a historical perspective, providing instruction in assessment and educational research. Upon completion, those enrolled receive an M.A. in education plus their Pennsylvania Instructional I certification. This course of study can be completed full-time in a twelve-month period or part-time over a two-year period.

The Teacher Leadership Certificate (TLC) is designed for professionals who already possess M.Ed., M.A.T., M.A., or M.S. degrees in education or other fields. The TLC is a 15-credit program designed for individuals who wish to develop their leadership ability for use in the classroom, or in such expanded roles as lead teacher, team leader, curriculum developer, department chairperson, new teacher mentor, or special project leader. The TLC is intended for teachers who want to apply their knowledge and skills to the larger school community, yet may not want to leave their classrooms to do so.

Research Facilities

The Falvey Memorial Library at Villanova University houses about 600,000 volumes and an excellent collection of more than 3,000 periodicals. An interlibrary loan system operates with the efficiency of e-mail. The library is located in the middle of the campus and includes numerous public-use computer stations that are equipped with sophisticated search engines and data retrieval mechanisms.

Financial Aid

Applicants may compete for full financial awards, including tuition remission and a yearly stipend, which are renewable for a second year. Tuition scholarships (tuition remission without a stipend) are also offered and are renewable for the second year. The work these awards require ranges from assisting individual faculty members with research materials to aiding with instruction and related activities. Tuition reduction is also available for current teachers.

Cost of Study

Fees and expenses for graduate students in 2010–11 are $50 for the application fee, $650 per credit for tuition, and $60 per semester for general University fees. Currently, a tuition-relief agenda is offered, granting a 20 percent tuition reduction for educators in non-Catholic schools and a 40 percent tuition reduction for Catholic school educators. Prospective students should contact the Department of Education and Human Services for details at 610-519-4620.

Living and Housing Costs

A variety of affordable housing possibilities are available near the Villanova University campus. Housing costs vary in accordance with the option chosen. Room and board for a single graduate student may average about $8000 for a twelve-month period. Villanova does not provide on-campus housing for graduate students; however, some serve as resident heads and assistants in the dormitories.

Student Group

Many students enter the program as a career-changing opportunity, while others wish to take on administrative roles or simply continue their education. Therefore, the majority of the student body is employed full-time.

Student Outcomes

Students find that their degree offers a multitude of opportunities to further their career and publish academic material, and many have continued on to doctoral studies in highly regarded universities throughout the world.

Location

Villanova University is situated on the historic Main Line, in a safe, western suburb of Philadelphia. The campus is on Lancaster Avenue (Route 30), 2 minutes from the Blue Route (Route 476) and 15 minutes from the Pennsylvania Turnpike, the Schuylkill Expressway, and Route 202. With ample parking and mass transit stops right on campus grounds, students can travel easily to and from the campus by car, bus, train, or light rail.

The University

Villanova University is an institution that is rich in history and tradition. From its modest beginnings on the country estate of a Revolutionary War officer, the University has seen significant growth in its student population and in its position as a leading coeducational institution of higher learning. Among the highly respected graduate programs that the College of Liberal Arts and Sciences features, the Ph.D. program in Continental philosophy and the M.A. programs in history, psychology, and political science offer special resources of collateral interest for the education programs.

Applying

Applications are welcome from all students who are interested in advanced educational study, and Villanova's graduates are increasingly earning both admission to and financial aid from distinguished Ph.D. programs. Applications for admission must include complete undergraduate transcripts (from all institutions attended), three letters of recommendation, and a one-page, typed statement outlining the applicant's objectives.

Correspondence and Information

Director of Graduate Studies
Department of Education and Human Services
Villanova University
Villanova, Pennsylvania 19085
Phone: 610-519-4620
Fax: 610-519-4623
E-mail: eduhs@villanova.edu
Web site: http://education.villanova.edu

Villanova University

THE FACULTY

John H. Durnin, Associate Professor and Acting Chair; Ph.D., Pennsylvania, 1971.

Victor D. Brooks, Professor; Ed.D., Pennsylvania, 1974.
Jerusha O. Conner, Assistant Professor; Ph.D., Stanford, 2007.
Edward Garcia Fierros, Associate Professor; Ph.D., Boston College, 1999.
Wm. Ray Heitzmann, Professor; Ph.D., Delaware, 1974.
Richard M. Jacobs, O.S.A., Professor; M.Div., Ph.D., Tulsa, 1990.
Robert J. Murray, O.S.A., Assistant Professor; Ph.D., Temple, 1995.
Ernest E. Ramirez, Assistant Professor; Ph.D., Oklahoma, 1981.
Deborah L. Schussler, Associate Professor; Ed.D., Vanderbilt, 2002.
Connie Titone, Professor and Chairperson; Ed.D., Harvard, 1995.
Teresa G. Wojcik, Assistant Professor; Ph.D., Pennsylvania, 2005.

WAYNE STATE UNIVERSITY

College of Education

Programs of Study	Programs of study lead to the following degrees: M.A., M.A.T., M.Ed., Ed.D., and Ph.D. and the Education Specialist Certificate. Programs are offered in elementary, secondary, and K–12 education. Initial certification specializations include English education, foreign language education, mathematics education, science education, social studies education, and career and technical education. K–12 areas include special education, reading language and literacy, art education, and kinesiology.

In addition to the above-mentioned areas, graduate degrees are also offered in bilingual-bicultural education, early childhood education, educational leadership and policy studies, instructional technology, administration and supervision, counseling, marriage and family psychology, art therapy, educational psychology, school and community psychology, evaluation and research, rehabilitation and community inclusion, health education, and sports administration.

Graduate programs are designed to prepare leaders in teaching, administration, curriculum, and research at all levels, extending beyond schools and universities to corporations seeking to expand education and training programs. College faculty members are making significant contributions toward infusing instructional technology into the full range of instructional programs. |
| **Research Facilities** | Students have access not only to the vast library collections at Wayne State but also to the collections of Michigan's two other research institutions through the interlibrary loan system that utilizes a state-of-the-art online cataloging system.

The College has three classrooms equipped with more than 100 networked Macintosh and IBM computers for instructional purposes. In addition, the College maintains an instructional technology laboratory, a video production studio, a distance education room, an adolescent research laboratory, and a counseling laboratory and houses a research support laboratory, all of which contain some of the most advanced hardware and software available.

The College also operates a full-day early childhood center (toddlers to 4-year-olds) as part of the teacher education program, which offers a wide range of training and research opportunities. |
Financial Aid	The University provides a range of graduate scholarships and fellowships to outstanding students. Some of these, such as the Rumble Fellowship, cover tuition, books, and housing, with an additional stipend for living expenses. The College also provides several graduate tuition scholarships annually.
Cost of Study	The in-state tuition for the 2009–10 academic year ranged from $1731.70 for 3 hours to $6362.65 for a full 12-hour course load. Comparable expenses for a nonresident were $3467.80 and $13307.05, respectively.
Living and Housing Costs	The cost of living in metropolitan Detroit is moderate in comparison to the living expenses in metropolitan areas of the eastern or western parts of the nation. The University Housing Office can provide housing information and assist students in locating housing on campus.
Student Group	The College of Education has the largest number of graduate students of any college in the University. The majority of students work as faculty members and administrators in schools and colleges throughout southeast Michigan. Graduates of the College have assumed leadership positions both inside and outside education throughout the country.
Location	The main campus is located in the center of Detroit's expanding cultural center. In addition to its own Hilberry and Bonstelle theaters, the University is in proximity to the Fisher Theater, the Detroit Institute of Arts, the Charles H. Wright Museum of African-American History, the Detroit Historical Museum, the Detroit Main Library, and the Detroit Medical Center.
The University	As one of the fifty-six public universities classified as a major research university by the Carnegie Commission on Higher Education, Wayne State has schools and colleges of medicine, law, engineering, education, liberal arts and science, business administration, nursing, social work, fine performing and communication arts, and pharmacy and health sciences.

The College of Education is located in the heart of the main campus and within walking distance of the central offices of the Detroit Public Schools. The College has a long history of working cooperatively with Detroit and suburban teachers and administrators in joint research and teaching initiatives. |
| **Applying** | Students who have not been formally admitted to the Graduate School should file their initial applications with the University Admissions Office, Welcome Center. Students may apply online at http://gradadmissions.wayne.edu. |
| **Correspondence and Information** | Dr. Janice W. Green
Assistant Dean, Academic Services
489 Education Building
Wayne State University
Detroit, Michigan 48202-3489
Phone: 313-577-1605
E-mail: askcoe@wayne.edu
Web site: http://www.wayne.edu/ |

Wayne State University

THE FACULTY

Administrative and Organizational Studies (AOS)
R. Craig Roney, Interim Assistant Dean; Ph.D., Colorado, 241 Education.

Michael Addonizio, Ph.D., Michigan State.
Michael Barbour, Ph.D., Georgia.
Sharon Field, Ed.D., Washington (Seattle).
Marytza Gawlik, Ph.D., Berkeley.
Ingrid Guerra, Ph.D., Florida State.
William Hill, Ph.D., Wayne State.
Frances LaPlante-Sosnowsky, Ed.D., Wayne State.
Thomas McLennan, Ed.D., Wayne State.
James Moseley, Ed.D., Wayne State.
Michael Owens, Ph.D., Utah.
Monte Piliawsky, Ph.D., Tulane.
Ben Pogodzinski, Ph.D., Michigan State.
Timothy Spannaus, Ph.D., Wayne State.
Karen Tonso, Ph.D., Colorado at Boulder.
Monica Tracey, Ph.D., Wayne State.
Ke Zhang, Ph.D., Penn State.

Kinesiology, Health, and Sports Studies (KHSS)
Sarah J. Erbaugh, Assistant Dean, Ph.D., Wisconsin–Madison, 261 Matthaei.

Judith S. Anderson, M.A., Wayne State.
Yun-Seok Choi, Ph.D., New Mexico.
Suzanna Dillon, Ph.D., Texas Woman's.
Hermann-Josef Engels, Ph.D., Florida State.
Mariane Fahlman, Ph.D., Toledo.
Randall Gretebeck, Ph.D., Wisconsin–Madison.
Noel Kulik, M.A., North Carolina.
Qin Lai, Ph.D., Texas A&M.
Jeffrey J. Martin, Ph.D., North Carolina at Greensboro.
Nathan McCaughtry, Ph.D., Wisconsin.
Anne Murphy, Ph.D., Michigan State.
Megan Rickard, M.S., Florida.
Peter A. Roberts, M.A., Michigan State.
Bo Shen, Ph.D., Maryland.
Steven Singleton, Ph.D., Michigan.
Laurel Whalen, M.A., Wayne State.
John C. Wirth, Ph.D., Illinois.

Teacher Education (TED)
R. Craig Roney, Assistant Dean, Ph.D., Colorado, 241 Education.

Oscar Abbott, Ph.D., Wayne State.
Kathleen Arkles, M.A., Norwich.
Poonam Arya, Ph.D., NYU.
Elsie Babcock, M.A., Wayne State.
Navaz Bhavnagri, Ph.D., Illinois.
Viveka Borun, Ph.D., Columbia.
Mary Brady, Ph.D., Wayne State.
James F. G. Brown, Ph.D., Union University.
Kristy Brugar, M.A., Michigan State.
John S. Camp, Ph.D., Columbia.
Sherry Cormier-Kuhn, Ed.D., Wayne State.
Kathleen Crawford-McKinney, Ph.D., Arizona.

Gina DeBlase, Ph.D., SUNY at Buffalo.
Hal Dittenber, M.A., Eastern Michigan.
Jazlin Ebenezer, Ph.D., British Columbia.
Thomas Edwards, Ph.D., Ohio State.
Sharon L. Elliott, Ed.D., Wayne State.
Karen Feathers, Ed.D., Indiana.
Holly Feen-Calligan, Ph.D., Wright State.
Maria Ferreira, Ph.D., Indiana.
David Grueber, Ph.D., Michigan State.
Janice E. Hale, Ph.D., Georgia State.
Steven Ilmer, Ph.D., Michigan.
Justine Kane, Ph.D., Illinois.
Mark Larson, Ed.D., Washington (Seattle).
Jennifer Lewis, Ph.D., Michigan.
Margarita Machado-Casas, Ph.D., North Carolina.
Anna Miller, M.A., Wayne State.
Gerald Oglan, Ph.D., Windsor.
Julie Osburn, M.Ed., Wayne State.
S. Asli Ozgun-Koca, Ph.D., Ohio.
J. Michael Peterson, Ph.D., North Texas State.
Robert Pettapiece, Ed.D., Wayne State.
Kathryn Roberts, Ph.D., Michigan State.
Sally Roberts, Ed.D., Wayne State.
R. Craig Roney, Ph.D., Colorado.
Marc Rosa, Ed.D., Wayne State.
Sharon Sellers-Clark, Ph.D., Wayne State.
Gary R. Smith, Ph.D., Northwestern.
Jo-Ann Snyder, Ed.D., Wayne State.
Geralyn Stephens, Ed.D., Wayne State.
Ebony Thomas, Ph.D., Michigan.
Jacqueline Tilles, Ph.D., Michigan.
David Whitin, Ed.D., Indiana.
Phyllis Whitin, Ph.D., South Carolina.
Anne W. Williamson, M.S.L.S., Wayne State.
Paula C. Wood, Ph.D., Michigan State.
Ava Zeineddin, Ph.D., Illinois at Urbana-Champaign.
Marshall F. Zumberg, Ph.D., Michigan State.
Gregory Zyric, Ph.D., South Carolina.

Theoretical and Behavioral Foundations (TBF)
R. Craig Roney, Interim Assistant Dean, Ph.D., Colorado, 241 Education.

Arnold B. Coven, Ed.D., Arizona.
Gail Fahoome, Ph.D., Wayne State.
Stephen B. Hillman, Ph.D., Indiana.
Alan M. Hoffman, Ed.D., Penn State.
Stuart Itzkowitz, Ph.D., Wayne State.
Benjamin Kelcey, Ph.D., Michigan.
Barry S. Markman, Ph.D., Emory.
Delila Owens, Ph.D., Michigan State.
George Parris, Ph.D., Michigan State.
Francesca Pernice-Duca, Ph.D., Michigan State.
John J. Pietrofesa, Ed.D., Miami (Florida).
Shlomo Sawilowsky, Ph.D., South Florida.
Cheryl Somers, Ph.D., Ball State.
Tami Wright, Ph.D., Wayne State.
Jina Yoon, Ph.D., Texas A&M.

Section 23
Administration, Instruction, and Theory

This section contains a directory of institutions offering graduate work in administration, instruction, and theory, followed by in-depth entries submitted by institutions that chose to prepare detailed program descriptions. Additional information about programs listed in the directory but not augmented by an in-depth entry may be obtained by writing directly to the dean of a graduate school or chair of a department at the address given in the directory.

For programs offering related work, see also in this book *Education, Health-Related Professions, Instructional Levels, Leisure Studies and Recreation, Physical Education and Kinesiology, Special Focus,* and *Subject Areas.* In another guide in this series:
Graduate Programs in the Humanities, Arts & Social Sciences
See *Psychology and Counseling (School Psychology)*

CONTENTS

Program Directories

Close-Ups

See also:

Curriculum and Instruction

Abilene Christian University, Graduate School, College of Education and Human Services, Graduate Studies in Education, Curriculum and Instruction Program, Abilene, TX 79699-9100. Offers M Ed. Part-time programs available. Postbaccalaureate distance learning degree programs offered (no on-campus study). *Students:* 10 full-time (7 women), 55 part-time (49 women); includes 3 minority (2 African Americans, 1 Hispanic American), 2 international. 64 applicants, 52% accepted, 26 enrolled. *Degree requirements:* For master's, comprehensive exam. *Application deadline:* For fall admission, 4/1 priority date for domestic students; for spring admission, 11/1 for domestic students. Applications are processed on a rolling basis. Application fee: $40. Electronic applications accepted. *Expenses:* Tuition: Full-time $11,520; part-time $640 per hour. Required fees: $1090; $53.50 per hour. $10 per term. Tuition and fees vary according to program. *Financial support:* In 2009–10, 51 students received support. Career-related internships or fieldwork and Federal Work-Study available. Support available to part-time students. Financial award application deadline: 4/1; financial award applicants required to submit FAFSA. *Unit head:* Dr. Donnie Snider, Graduate Advisor, 325-674-2974, Fax: 325-674-2123, E-mail: donnie.snider@acu.edu. *Application contact:* William Horn, Graduate Admissions Counselor, 325-674-2656, Fax: 325-674-6717, E-mail: gradinfo@acu.edu.

Acadia University, Faculty of Professional Studies, School of Education, Program in Curriculum Studies, Wolfville, NS B4P 2R6, Canada. Offers cultural and media studies (M Ed); learning and technology (M Ed); science, math and technology (M Ed). Evening/weekend programs available. *Faculty:* 12 full-time (5 women). *Students:* 7 full-time (all women), 49 part-time (33 women). 61 applicants, 80% accepted. In 2009, 32 master's awarded. *Degree requirements:* For master's, thesis optional. *Entrance requirements:* For master's, B Ed or the equivalent, minimum B average in undergraduate course work, 2 years of teaching experience. Additional exam requirements/recommendations for international students: Required—TOEFL (minimum score 580 paper-based; 237 computer-based; 93 iBT), IELTS (minimum score 6.5). *Application deadline:* For fall admission, 3/15 priority date for domestic and international students. Applications are processed on a rolling basis. Application fee: $50. *Financial support:* Teaching assistantships available. Financial award application deadline: 3/15. *Faculty research:* Literacy development, postmodern philosophy and curriculum theory, historiography, philosophy of education, learning and technology. *Unit head:* Ann Vibert, Director, E-mail: ann.vibert@acadiau.ca. *Application contact:* Sheila Langille, Secretary, 902-585-1229, Fax: 902-585-1071, E-mail: sheila.langille@acadiau.ca.

American InterContinental University Online, Program in Education, Hoffman Estates, IL 60192. Offers curriculum and instruction (M Ed); educational assessment and evaluation (M Ed); instructional technology (M Ed); leadership of educational organizations (M Ed). Evening/weekend programs available. Postbaccalaureate distance learning degree programs offered (no on-campus study). *Entrance requirements:* Additional exam requirements/recommendations for international students: Required—TOEFL (minimum score 550 paper-based; 213 computer-based). Electronic applications accepted.

American University, College of Arts and Sciences, School of Education, Teaching, and Health, Program in Curriculum and Instruction, Washington, DC 20016-8001. Offers M Ed, Certificate. *Students:* 3 full-time (2 women), 4 part-time (all women); includes 1 minority (African American), 1 international. Average age 30. 7 applicants, 100% accepted, 3 enrolled. *Degree requirements:* For master's, comprehensive exam, PRAXIS II. *Entrance requirements:* For master's, GRE, prior teaching experience (preferred). Application fee: $80. *Expenses:* Tuition: Full-time $22,266; part-time $1237 per credit hour. Required fees: $430. Tuition and fees vary according to program. *Unit head:* Dr. Sarah Irvine-Belson, Dean, 202-885-3714, Fax: 202-885-1187, E-mail: educate@american.edu. *Application contact:* Kathleen Clowery, Director, Graduate Admissions, 202-885-3621, Fax: 202-885-1505.

Andrews University, School of Graduate Studies, School of Education, Department of Teaching, Learning, and Curriculum, Program in Curriculum and Instruction, Berrien Springs, MI 49104. Offers MA, Ed D, PhD, Ed S. *Faculty:* 5 full-time (1 woman). *Students:* 5 full-time (3 women), 15 part-time (12 women); includes 9 minority (8 African Americans, 1 Hispanic American), 6 international. Average age 49. 10 applicants, 50% accepted, 1 enrolled. In 2009, 2 master's, 4 doctorates, 1 other advanced degree awarded. *Degree requirements:* For master's, thesis optional; for doctorate, thesis/dissertation. *Entrance requirements:* For master's, GRE Subject Test. Additional exam requirements/recommendations for international students: Required—TOEFL (minimum score 550 paper-based). *Application deadline:* Applications are processed on a rolling basis. Application fee: $40. *Financial support:* Fellowships, research assistantships, teaching assistantships, career-related internships or fieldwork, Federal Work-Study, institutionally sponsored loans, and tuition waivers (partial) available. Support available to part-time students. *Unit head:* Dr. Larry D. Burton, Coordinator, 269-971-6674. *Application contact:* Carolyn Hurst, Supervisor of Graduate Admission, 800-253-2874, Fax: 269-471-6321, E-mail: graduate@andrews.edu.

Angelo State University, College of Graduate Studies, College of Education, Department of Curriculum and Instruction, Program in Curriculum and Instruction, San Angelo, TX 76909. Offers MA. Part-time and evening/weekend programs available. *Faculty:* 17 full-time (12 women). *Students:* 16 full-time (13 women), 34 part-time (26 women); includes 12 minority (1 African American, 1 American Indian/Alaska Native, 1 Asian American or Pacific Islander, 9 Hispanic Americans). Average age 36. 15 applicants, 100% accepted, 12 enrolled. In 2009, 6 master's awarded. *Degree requirements:* For master's, comprehensive exam. *Entrance requirements:* For master's, GRE General Test. Additional exam requirements/recommendations for international students: Required—TOEFL or IELTS. *Application deadline:* For fall admission, 7/15 priority date for domestic students, 6/10 for international students; for spring admission, 12/1 priority date for domestic students, 11/1 for international students. Applications are processed on a rolling basis. Application fee: $40 ($50 for international students). Electronic applications accepted. *Expenses:* Tuition, state resident: full-time $3396; part-time $142 per credit hour. Tuition, nonresident: full-time $10,152; part-time $423 per credit hour. Required fees: $1786; $36.25 per credit hour. $494 per semester. Full-time tuition and fees vary according to course load, degree level and program. *Financial support:* In 2009–10, 6 students received support. Career-related internships or fieldwork, Federal Work-Study, scholarships/grants, and unspecified assistantships available. Support available to part-time students. Financial award application deadline: 3/1; financial award applicants required to submit FAFSA. *Unit head:* Dr. Kim Livengood, Graduate Advisor, 325-942-2647 Ext. 478, E-mail: kim.livengood@angelo.edu. *Application contact:* Theresa Fortin, Graduate Admissions Assistant, 325-942-2169, Fax: 325-942-2039, E-mail: theresa.fortin@angelo.edu.

Appalachian State University, Cratis D. Williams Graduate School, Department of Curriculum and Instruction, Boone, NC 28608. Offers curriculum specialist (MA); educational media (MA); elementary education (MA); middle grades education (MA), including language arts, mathematics, science, social studies. *Accreditation:* NCATE. Part-time and evening/weekend programs available. Postbaccalaureate distance learning degree programs offered (no on-campus study). *Faculty:* 32 full-time (22 women), 9 part-time/adjunct (3 women). *Students:* 16 full-time (12 women), 168 part-time (140 women); includes 2 minority (both African Americans), 1 international. 97 applicants, 99% accepted, 77 enrolled. In 2009, 78 master's awarded. *Degree requirements:* For master's, comprehensive exam, thesis or alternative. *Entrance requirements:* For master's, GRE General Test or MAT, 3 letters of recommendation. Additional exam requirements/recommendations for international students: Required—TOEFL (minimum score 570 paper-based; 230 computer-based; 79 iBT), IELTS (minimum score 6.5). *Application deadline:* For fall admission, 7/1 for domestic students, 2/1 for international students; for spring admission, 11/1 for domestic students, 7/1 for international students. Applications are processed on a rolling basis. Application fee: $50. Electronic applications accepted. *Expenses:* Tuition, state resident: full-time $2960. Tuition, nonresident: full-time $14,051. Required fees: $2320. *Financial support:* In 2009–10, 8 teaching assistantships (averaging $8,000 per year) were awarded; fellowships, research assistantships, career-related internships or fieldwork, Federal Work-Study, scholarships/grants, and unspecified assistantships also available. Financial award application deadline: 4/1; financial award applicants required to submit FAFSA. *Faculty research:* Media literacy, elementary teaching, curriculum development, online learning environments. Total annual research expenditures: $690,000. *Unit head:* Dr. Michael Jacobson, Chairperson, 828-262-2224. *Application contact:* Sandy Krause, Director of Admissions and Recruiting, 828-262-2130, Fax: 828-262-2709, E-mail: krausesl@appstate.edu.

Arizona State University, Graduate College, Mary Lou Fulton College of Education, Division of Curriculum and Instruction, Interdisciplinary PhD Program in Curriculum and Instruction, Tempe, AZ 85287. Offers PhD. *Degree requirements:* For doctorate, thesis/dissertation.

Arizona State University, Graduate College, Mary Lou Fulton College of Education, Division of Curriculum and Instruction, Program in Curriculum and Instruction, Tempe, AZ 85287. Offers M Ed, MA, Ed D. *Degree requirements:* For doctorate, thesis/dissertation. *Entrance requirements:* For master's and doctorate, GRE General Test or MAT. *Faculty research:* Early childhood, media and computers, elementary education, English education, exercise and wellness education.

Arkansas State University—Jonesboro, Graduate School, College of Education, Department of Educational Leadership, Curriculum, and Special Education, Jonesboro, State University, AR 72467. Offers community college administration education (SCCT); curriculum and instruction (MSE); education theory and practice (MSE); educational leadership (MSE, Ed D, Ed S), including curriculum and instruction (MSE, Ed S); special education (MSE), including gifted and talented and creative, instructional specialist 4-12, instructional specialist P-4. *Accreditation:* NCATE. Part-time programs available. Postbaccalaureate distance learning degree programs offered (no on-campus study). *Faculty:* 15 full-time (6 women), 19 part-time/adjunct (11 women). *Students:* 16 full-time (11 women), 734 part-time (606 women); includes 111 minority (96 African Americans, 4 American Indian/Alaska Native, 4 Asian Americans or Pacific Islanders, 7 Hispanic Americans), 2 international. Average age 38. 882 applicants, 70% accepted, 240 enrolled. In 2009, 80 master's, 6 doctorates, 15 other advanced degrees awarded. *Degree requirements:* For master's, comprehensive exam, thesis or alternative; for doctorate, comprehensive exam, thesis/dissertation; for other advanced degree, comprehensive exam. *Entrance requirements:* For master's, GRE General Test or MAT, appropriate bachelor's degree, letters of reference, interview; for doctorate, GRE General Test or MAT, interview, master's degree, letters of reference, official transcript, personal statement, writing sample, immunization records; for other advanced degree, GRE General Test or MAT, interview, master's degree, letters of reference, official transcript, 3 years teaching experience, mentor, teaching license, immunization records. Additional exam requirements/recommendations for international students: Required—TOEFL (minimum score 550 paper-based; 213 computer-based; 79 iBT), IELTS (minimum score 6). *Application deadline:* Applications are processed on a rolling basis. Application fee: $50. Electronic applications accepted. *Expenses:* Tuition, state resident: full-time $3744; part-time $208 per credit hour. Tuition, nonresident: full-time $9540; part-time $530 per credit hour. Required fees: $896; $47 per credit hour. $25 per term. One-time fee: $50. Tuition and fees vary according to course load and program. *Financial support:* In 2009–10, 16 students received support; fellowships, teaching assistantships, career-related internships or fieldwork, scholarships/grants, and unspecified assistantships available. Financial award application deadline: 7/1; financial award applicants required to submit FAFSA. *Unit head:* Dr. Mitchell Holifield, Chair, 870-972-3062, Fax: 870-680-8130, E-mail: hfield@astate.edu. *Application contact:* Dr. Andrew Sustich, Dean of the Graduate School, 870-972-3029, Fax: 870-972-3857, E-mail: sustich@astate.edu.

Arkansas Tech University, Graduate College, College of Education, Russellville, AR 72801. Offers college student personnel (MS); educational leadership (M Ed, Ed S); English education (M Ed); instructional improvement (M Ed); secondary education (M Ed); teaching, learning and leadership (M Ed). *Accreditation:* NCATE. Part-time and evening/weekend programs available. Postbaccalaureate distance learning degree programs offered (no on-campus study). *Students:* 39 full-time (26 women), 246 part-time (179 women); includes 27 minority (18 African Americans, 4 American Indian/Alaska Native, 5 Hispanic Americans), 4 international. Average age 33. In 2009, 92 master's, 11 other advanced degrees awarded. *Degree requirements:* For master's, comprehensive exam, thesis optional, action research project. *Entrance requirements:* For master's, GRE General Test or MAT. Additional exam requirements/recommendations for international students: Required—TOEFL (minimum score 550 paper-based; 213 computer-based; 79 iBT), IELTS (minimum score 6). *Application deadline:* For fall admission, 3/1 priority date for domestic students, 5/1 priority date for international students; for spring admission, 10/1 priority date for domestic and international students. Applications are processed on a rolling basis. Application fee: $0 ($50 for international students). Electronic applications accepted. *Expenses:* Tuition, state resident: full-time $3438; part-time $191 per hour. Tuition, nonresident: full-time $6876; part-time $382 per hour. Required fees: $482; $9 per credit hour. $140 per semester. Tuition and fees vary according to course load. *Financial support:* In 2009–10, teaching assistantships with full tuition reimbursements (averaging $4,000 per year); research assistantships, career-related internships or fieldwork, Federal Work-Study, scholarships/grants, health care benefits, and unspecified assistantships also available. Support available to part-time students. Financial award application deadline: 4/15; financial award applicants required to submit FAFSA. *Unit head:* Dr. Eldon G. Clary, Dean, 479-968-0350, Fax: 479-968-0350, E-mail: eclary@atu.edu. *Application contact:* Dr. Mary B. Gunter, Dean of Graduate College, 479-968-0398, Fax: 479-964-0542, E-mail: graduate.school@atu.edu.

Armstrong Atlantic State University, School of Graduate Studies, Program in Education, Savannah, GA 31419-1997. Offers adult education (M Ed); curriculum and instruction (M Ed); early childhood education (M Ed); education (M Ed); elementary education (M Ed); middle grades education (M Ed); secondary education (M Ed), including business education, English education, mathematics education, science education, social science education; special education (M Ed), including behavioral disorders, learning disabilities, speech-language pathology. *Accreditation:* NCATE. Part-time and evening/weekend programs available. Postbaccalaureate distance learning degree programs offered (minimal on-campus study). *Degree requirements:* For master's, comprehensive exam, portfolio. *Entrance requirements:* For master's, GRE General Test or MAT, minimum GPA of 2.5, letters of recommendation. Additional exam requirements/recommendations for international students: Required—TOEFL (minimum score 523 paper-based; 193 computer-based). Electronic applications accepted.

Ashland University, Dwight Schar College of Education, Department of Educational Administration, Ashland, OH 44805-3702. Offers curriculum specialist (M Ed); principalship (M Ed); pupil services (M Ed). Part-time programs available. *Faculty:* 6 full-time (3 women), 31 part-time/adjunct (12 women). *Students:* 118 full-time (70 women), 239 part-time (135 women); includes 37 minority (29 African Americans, 1 American Indian/Alaska Native, 2 Asian Americans or Pacific Islanders, 5 Hispanic Americans), 2 international. Average age 33. 129 applicants, 98% accepted, 114 enrolled. In 2009, 166 master's awarded. *Degree requirements:* For master's, thesis or alternative, internship. *Entrance requirements:* For master's, teaching certificate or license, bachelor's degree, minimum cumulative GPA of 2.75. Additional exam requirements/recommendations for international students: Required—TOEFL. *Application deadline:* Applications are processed on a rolling basis. Application fee: $30. Electronic applications accepted. *Financial support:* Institutionally sponsored loans and scholarships/grants available. Financial award application deadline: 4/15. *Faculty research:* Gender and religious considerations in employment, ISLLC standards, adjunct faculty training, politics of school finance, ethnicity and employment. *Unit head:* Dr. Larry Cook, Chair, 419-289-5396, Fax: 419-208-5702, E-mail: lcook@ashland.edu. *Application contact:* Dr. Larry Cook, Chair, 419-289-5396, Fax: 419-208-5702, E-mail: lcook@ashland.edu.

Ashland University, Dwight Schar College of Education, Department of Educational Foundations, Ashland, OH 44805-3702. Offers curriculum and instruction (M Ed), including classroom instruction. Part-time and evening/weekend programs available. *Faculty:* 13 full-time (9 women),

60 part-time/adjunct (31 women). *Students:* 92 full-time (83 women), 242 part-time (194 women); includes 20 minority (13 African Americans, 2 Asian Americans or Pacific Islanders, 5 Hispanic Americans), 7 international. Average age 34. 161 applicants, 99% accepted, 146 enrolled. In 2009, 166 master's awarded. *Degree requirements:* For master's, inquiry seminar, internship, or thesis. *Entrance requirements:* For master's, teaching certificate or license, bachelor's degree, minimum cumulative GPA of 2.75. Additional exam requirements/recommendations for international students: Required—TOEFL. *Application deadline:* Applications are processed on a rolling basis. Application fee: $30. Electronic applications accepted. *Financial support:* In 2009–10, 229 students received support. Application deadline: 4/15. *Faculty research:* Character education, teacher reflection, religion and education, professional education, environmental education. *Unit head:* Dr. Louise Fleming, Chair, 419-289-5347, E-mail: lfleming@ashland.edu. *Application contact:* Dr. Louise Fleming, Chair, 419-289-5347, E-mail: lfleming@ashland.edu.

Auburn University, Graduate School, College of Education, Department of Educational Foundations, Leadership, and Technology, Auburn University, AL 36849. Offers adult education (M Ed, MS, Ed D); curriculum and instruction (M Ed, MS, Ed D, Ed S); curriculum supervision (M Ed, MS, Ed D, Ed S); educational psychology (PhD); higher education administration (M Ed, MS, Ed D, Ed S); media instructional design (MS); media specialist (M Ed); school administration (M Ed, MS, Ed D, Ed S). *Accreditation:* NCATE. Part-time programs available. *Faculty:* 21 full-time (11 women), 6 part-time/adjunct (4 women). *Students:* 68 full-time (40 women), 175 part-time (103 women); includes 87 minority (84 African Americans, 1 Asian American or Pacific Islander, 2 Hispanic Americans), 8 international. Average age 37. 112 applicants, 65% accepted, 53 enrolled. In 2009, 31 master's, 12 doctorates, 1 other advanced degree awarded. *Degree requirements:* For master's, thesis (for some programs); for doctorate, thesis/dissertation; for Ed S, field project. *Entrance requirements:* For master's, doctorate, and Ed S, GRE General Test. *Application deadline:* For fall admission, 7/7 for domestic students; for spring admission, 11/24 for domestic students. Applications are processed on a rolling basis. Application fee: $50 ($60 for international students). Electronic applications accepted. *Expenses:* Tuition, state resident: full-time $6240. Tuition, nonresident: full-time $18,720. International tuition: $18,938 full-time. Required fees: $492. Tuition and fees vary according to course load, program and reciprocity agreements. *Financial support:* Teaching assistantships, Federal Work-Study available. Support available to part-time students. Financial award application deadline: 3/15; financial award applicants required to submit FAFSA. *Unit head:* Dr. Jose Llanes, Head, 334-844-4460. *Application contact:* Dr. George Flowers, Dean of the Graduate School, 334-844-4700.

Augusta State University, Graduate Studies, College of Education, Program in Curriculum/Instruction, Augusta, GA 30904-2200. Offers M Ed. *Degree requirements:* For master's, thesis, portfolio. *Entrance requirements:* For master's, GRE, MAT, minimum GPA of 2.5.

Aurora University, College of Education, Aurora, IL 60506-4892. Offers curriculum and instruction (Ed D); education (MAT); education and administration (Ed D); educational leadership (MEL); reading instruction (MA). *Accreditation:* NCATE. Part-time and evening/weekend programs available. *Degree requirements:* For doctorate, thesis/dissertation. *Entrance requirements:* For master's, 2 years of teaching experience, valid teaching certificate. Additional exam requirements/recommendations for international students: Required—TOEFL (minimum score 550 paper-based; 213 computer-based). Electronic applications accepted. *Expenses:* Contact institution.

Austin Peay State University, College of Graduate Studies, College of Education, Department of Educational Specialties, Clarksville, TN 37044. Offers administration and supervision (Ed S); curriculum and instruction (MA Ed); education leadership (MA Ed); elementary education (Ed S); secondary education (Ed S); special education (MA Ed). Part-time and evening/weekend programs available. Postbaccalaureate distance learning degree programs offered. *Faculty:* 7 full-time (4 women), 4 part-time/adjunct (3 women). *Students:* 17 full-time (11 women), 96 part-time (76 women); includes 20 minority (12 African Americans, 1 American Indian/Alaska Native, 7 Hispanic Americans). Average age 36. 81 applicants, 99% accepted, 45 enrolled. In 2009, 47 master's awarded. *Degree requirements:* For master's, comprehensive exam, thesis optional. *Entrance requirements:* For master's, GRE General Test, 3 letters of recommendation, minimum undergraduate GPA of 2.75. Additional exam requirements/recommendations for international students: Required—TOEFL (minimum score 500 paper-based; 173 computer-based). *Application deadline:* For fall admission, 7/27 priority date for domestic students; for spring admission, 12/17 priority date for domestic students. Applications are processed on a rolling basis. Application fee: $25. Electronic applications accepted. *Expenses:* Tuition, state resident: full-time $6160; part-time $608 per credit hour. Tuition, nonresident: full-time $17,080; part-time $854 per credit hour. Required fees: $1224; $61.20 per credit hour. *Financial support:* Career-related internships or fieldwork, Federal Work-Study, institutionally sponsored loans, scholarships/grants, and unspecified assistantships available. Support available to part-time students. Financial award application deadline: 3/1; financial award applicants required to submit FAFSA. *Unit head:* Dr. Moniqueka Gold, Chair, 931-221-7696, Fax: 931-221-1292, E-mail: goldm@apsu.edu. *Application contact:* Dr. Dixie Dennis, Dean, College of Graduate Studies, 931-221-7662, Fax: 931-221-7641, E-mail: dennisdi@apsu.edu.

Austin Peay State University, College of Graduate Studies, College of Education, Department of Teaching and Learning, Clarksville, TN 37044. Offers elementary education K-6 (MAT); reading (MA Ed); secondary education 7-12 (MAT); special education K-12 (MAT). Part-time and evening/weekend programs available. Postbaccalaureate distance learning degree programs offered. *Faculty:* 8 full-time (6 women), 3 part-time/adjunct (all women). *Students:* 91 full-time (74 women), 84 part-time (67 women); includes 14 minority (12 African Americans, 2 Asian Americans or Pacific Islanders), 1 international. Average age 32. 122 applicants, 94% accepted, 75 enrolled. In 2009, 61 master's awarded. *Degree requirements:* For master's, comprehensive exam, thesis optional. *Entrance requirements:* For master's, GRE General Test, 3 letters of recommendation, minimum undergraduate GPA of 2.75. Additional exam requirements/recommendations for international students: Required—TOEFL (minimum score 500 paper-based; 173 computer-based). *Application deadline:* For fall admission, 7/27 priority date for domestic students; for spring admission, 12/17 priority date for domestic students. Applications are processed on a rolling basis. Application fee: $25. Electronic applications accepted. *Expenses:* Tuition, state resident: full-time $6160; part-time $608 per credit hour. Tuition, nonresident: full-time $17,080; part-time $854 per credit hour. Required fees: $1224; $61.20 per credit hour. *Financial support:* Career-related internships or fieldwork, Federal Work-Study, institutionally sponsored loans, scholarships/grants, and unspecified assistantships available. Support available to part-time students. Financial award application deadline: 3/1; financial award applicants required to submit FAFSA. *Unit head:* Dr. Rebecca McMahan, Interim Chair, 931-221-7513, Fax: 931-221-1292, E-mail: mcmahanb@apsu.edu. *Application contact:* Dr. Dixie Dennis, Dean, College of Graduate Studies, 931-221-7662, Fax: 931-221-7641, E-mail: dennisdi@apsu.edu.

Averett University, Master in Education Program, Danville, VA 24541-3692. Offers art education (M Ed); biology (M Ed); biology education (M Ed); chemistry (M Ed); chemistry education (M Ed); curriculum and instruction (M Ed); elementary education (M Ed); English (M Ed); English education (M Ed); health and physical education (M Ed); history and social studies education (M Ed); math (M Ed); mathematics education (M Ed); physical science (M Ed); reading specialization (M Ed); special education (learning disabilities specialization PK-12) (M Ed). Program also offered at Richmond, VA regional campus location. Part-time and evening/weekend programs available. *Faculty:* 4 full-time (3 women), 36 part-time/adjunct (22 women). *Students:* 182 full-time (160 women), 110 part-time (94 women); includes 113 minority (94 African Americans, 1 American Indian/Alaska Native, 7 Asian Americans or Pacific Islanders, 11 Hispanic Americans). Average age 37. 119 applicants, 99% accepted, 98 enrolled. In 2009, 92 master's awarded. *Degree requirements:* For master's, comprehensive exam, thesis optional. *Entrance requirements:* For master's, PRAXIS, GRE General Test, MAT or NTE, writing proficiency exam, 3 letters of recommendation, current teacher's licensure or eligibility for licensure, minimum undergraduate GPA of 3.0 in previous 2 years. Additional exam requirements/recommendations for international students: Required—TOEFL (minimum score 600 paper-based; 200 computer-based). *Application deadline:* Applications are processed on a rolling basis. *Expenses:* Contact institution. *Financial support:* Career-related internships or fieldwork, Federal Work-Study, and scholarships/grants available. Financial award application deadline: 4/1; financial award applicants required to submit FAFSA. *Faculty research:* Literary assessment-PreK-6, handwriting instruction and assessment-PreK-6, written language instruction and assessment-PreK-6 and special needs students learning styles, curriculum and instruction processes. *Unit head:* Dr. Lynn H. Wolf, Chair/Associate Professor/Director, 434-793-3995, Fax: 434-791-4392, E-mail: lynn.wolf@averett.edu. *Application contact:* Dr. Lynn H. Wolf, Chair/Associate Professor/Director, 434-793-3995, Fax: 434-791-4392, E-mail: lynn.wolf@averett.edu.

Azusa Pacific University, School of Education, Department of Advanced Studies, Program in Curriculum and Instruction in a Multicultural Setting, Azusa, CA 91702-7000. Offers MA. *Accreditation:* NCATE. Part-time and evening/weekend programs available. *Degree requirements:* For master's, core exams, oral presentation. *Entrance requirements:* For master's, 12 units of course work in education, minimum GPA of 3.0. *Faculty research:* Diversity in teacher education programs, teacher morale, student perception of school, case study instruction.

Azusa Pacific University, School of Education, Department of Advanced Studies, Program in Teaching, Azusa, CA 91702-7000. Offers MA.

Ball State University, Graduate School, Teachers College, Department of Educational Studies, Program in Curriculum and Instruction, Muncie, IN 47306-1099. Offers curriculum (MAE, Ed S). *Accreditation:* NCATE. *Degree requirements:* For Ed S, thesis. *Entrance requirements:* For degree, GRE General Test, interview.

Barry University, School of Education, Program in Curriculum and Instruction, Miami Shores, FL 33161-6695. Offers accomplished teacher (Ed S); culture, language and literacy (TESOL) (PhD); curriculum evaluation and research (PhD); early childhood (Ed S); early childhood education (PhD); elementary (Ed S); elementary education (PhD); ESOL (Ed S); gifted (Ed S); Montessori (Ed S); PKP/elementary (Ed S); reading (Ed S); reading, language and cognition (PhD). *Entrance requirements:* For doctorate, GRE, minimum GPA of 3.25.

Baylor University, Graduate School, School of Education, Department of Curriculum and Instruction, Waco, TX 76798. Offers MA, MS Ed, Ed D, Ed S. *Accreditation:* NCATE. Postbaccalaureate distance learning degree programs offered (minimal on-campus study). *Faculty:* 11 full-time (5 women), 2 part-time/adjunct (1 woman). *Students:* 35 full-time (28 women), 33 part-time (22 women); includes 13 minority (3 African Americans, 4 Asian Americans or Pacific Islanders, 6 Hispanic Americans), 6 international. Average age 30. 19 applicants, 79% accepted. In 2009, 24 master's, 2 doctorates awarded. *Degree requirements:* For doctorate, thesis/dissertation. *Entrance requirements:* For master's and doctorate, GRE General Test or GMAT. *Application deadline:* For fall admission, 7/30 priority date for domestic students; for spring admission, 12/1 for domestic students. Applications are processed on a rolling basis. Application fee: $25. *Financial support:* Research assistantships, teaching assistantships, Federal Work-Study and institutionally sponsored loans available. *Faculty research:* Teacher education, language and literacy. *Unit head:* Dr. Betty Conaway, Graduate Program Director, 254-710-6115, Fax: 254-710-3987, E-mail: betty_conaway@baylor.edu. *Application contact:* Amy Williams, Administrative Assistant, 254-710-4481, Fax: 254-710-3870, E-mail: amy_williams1@baylor.edu.

Benedictine University, Graduate Programs, Program in Education, Lisle, IL 60532-0900. Offers curriculum and instruction and collaborative teaching (M Ed); elementary education (MA Ed); leadership and administration (M Ed); reading and literacy (M Ed); secondary education (MA Ed); special education (MA Ed). Part-time and evening/weekend programs available. *Faculty:* 4 full-time (2 women), 52 part-time/adjunct (30 women). *Students:* 286 full-time (252 women), 443 part-time (349 women); includes 61 minority (22 African Americans, 11 Asian Americans or Pacific Islanders, 28 Hispanic Americans), 5 international. Average age 33. 341 applicants, 90% accepted, 264 enrolled. In 2009, 299 master's awarded. *Degree requirements:* For master's, comprehensive exam, thesis (for some programs). *Entrance requirements:* For master's, GRE or MAT. Additional exam requirements/recommendations for international students: Required—TOEFL (minimum score 550 paper-based; 213 computer-based). *Application deadline:* For fall admission, 9/1 for domestic students; for winter admission, 12/1 for domestic students; for spring admission, 2/15 for domestic students. Applications are processed on a rolling basis. Application fee: $40. Electronic applications accepted. *Expenses:* Contact institution. *Financial support:* Career-related internships or fieldwork and health care benefits available. Support available to part-time students. *Unit head:* Dr. Richard Campbell, Director, 630-829-6242, Fax: 630-960-1126, E-mail: rcampbell@ben.edu. *Application contact:* Kari Gibbons, Director, Admissions, 630-829-6200, Fax: 630-829-6584, E-mail: kgibbons@ben.edu.

Berry College, Graduate Programs, Graduate Programs in Education, Program in Leadership in Curriculum and Instruction, Mount Berry, GA 30149-0159. Offers curriculum and instruction (Ed S); educational leadership (Ed S). *Accreditation:* NCATE. *Faculty:* 4 part-time/adjunct (1 woman). *Students:* 11 part-time (10 women); includes 1 minority (African American). Average age 37. In 2009, 5 Ed Ss awarded. *Degree requirements:* For Ed S, thesis, portfolio, oral exams. *Entrance requirements:* For degree, M Ed from NCATE accredited school, minimum GPA of 3.25. Additional exam requirements/recommendations for international students: Required—TOEFL (minimum score 550 paper-based; 213 computer-based). *Application deadline:* For fall admission, 5/1 for domestic and international students; for spring admission, 10/1 for domestic and international students. Applications are processed on a rolling basis. Application fee: $25 ($30 for international students). *Expenses:* Contact institution. *Financial support:* In 2009–10, 5 students received support. Scholarships/grants available. Support available to part-time students. Financial award application deadline: 4/1; financial award applicants required to submit FAFSA. *Faculty research:* Curriculum development, teacher training, pedagogy. *Unit head:* Dr. Jacqueline McDowell, 706-236-1717, Fax: 706-238-5827, E-mail: jmcdowell@berry.edu. *Application contact:* Brett Kennedy, Director of Admissions, 706-236-2215, Fax: 706-290-2178, E-mail: admissions@berry.edu.

Black Hills State University, Graduate Studies, Program in Curriculum and Instruction, Spearfish, SD 57799. Offers MS. Part-time programs available. *Faculty:* 7 full-time (6 women), 2 part-time/adjunct (both women). *Students:* 3 full-time (all women), 103 part-time (89 women); includes 2 minority (1 African American, 1 American Indian/Alaska Native). Average age 38. 74 applicants, 97% accepted, 48 enrolled. In 2009, 51 master's awarded. *Entrance requirements:* Additional exam requirements/recommendations for international students: Required—TOEFL (minimum score 500 paper-based; 171 computer-based; 60 iBT). *Application deadline:* Applications are processed on a rolling basis. Application fee: $35. *Expenses:* Tuition, state resident: full-time $4170; part-time $139 per credit hour. Tuition, nonresident: full-time $8828; part-time $294 per credit. Required fees: $3476; $116 per credit hour. *Unit head:* Dr. Kristi Pearce, Director of Graduate Studies, 800-225-2478. *Application contact:* Dr. Patricia Simpson, Director of Graduate Studies, 605-642-6270, E-mail: patricia.simpson@bhsu.edu.

Bloomsburg University of Pennsylvania, School of Graduate Studies, College of Professional Studies, School of Education, Department of Educational Studies and Secondary Education, Program in Curriculum and Instruction, Bloomsburg, PA 17815-1301. Offers M Ed. *Accreditation:* NCATE. *Degree requirements:* For master's, thesis. *Entrance requirements:* For master's, MAT or PRAXIS, minimum QPA of 3.0. Additional exam requirements/recommendations for international students: Required—TOEFL (minimum score 550 paper-based; 213 computer-based; 79 iBT). Electronic applications accepted. *Faculty research:* Administration.

Bob Jones University, Graduate Programs, Greenville, SC 29614. Offers accountancy (MS); Bible (MA); Bible translation (MA); Biblical studies (Certificate); broadcast management (MS); business administration (MBA); church history (MA, PhD); church ministries (MA); church music (MM); cinema and video production (MA); counseling (MS); curriculum and instruction (Ed D); divinity (M Div); dramatic production (MA); educational leadership (MS, Ed D, Ed S); elementary education (M Ed, MAT); English (M Ed, MA, MAT); fine arts (MA); graphic design

Curriculum and Instruction

Bob Jones University *(continued)*
(MA); history (M Ed, MA); illustration (MA); interpretative speech (MA); mathematics (M Ed, MAT); medical missions (Certificate); ministry (MM, D Min); multi-categorical special education (M Ed, MAT); music (M Ed); New Testament interpretation (PhD); Old Testament interpretation (PhD); orchestral instrument performance (MM); organ performance (MM); pastoral studies (MA); personnel services (MS, Ed S); piano pedagogy (MM); piano performance (MM); platform arts (MA); radio and television broadcasting (MS); rhetoric and public address (MA); secondary education (M Ed); studio art (MA); teaching Bible (MA); theology (MA, PhD); voice performance (MM); youth ministries (MA); M Div/MM.

Boise State University, Graduate College, College of Education, Department of Curriculum, Instruction and Foundational Studies, Doctoral Program in Curriculum and Instruction, Boise, ID 83725-0399. Offers Ed D. *Accreditation:* NCATE. Part-time programs available. *Degree requirements:* For doctorate, thesis/dissertation. *Entrance requirements:* For doctorate, GRE General Test, minimum GPA of 3.0. Electronic applications accepted. *Expenses:* Tuition, state resident: full-time $3106; part-time $209 per credit. Tuition, nonresident: part-time $284 per credit.

Boston College, Lynch Graduate School of Education, Department of Teacher Education/ Special Education and Curriculum and Instruction, Curriculum and Instruction Specialization, Chestnut Hill, MA 02467-3800. Offers M Ed, PhD, CAES, JD/M Ed. Part-time and evening/weekend programs available. *Students:* 33 full-time (23 women), 109 part-time (84 women); includes 15 minority (6 African Americans, 1 American Indian/Alaska Native, 4 Asian Americans or Pacific Islanders, 4 Hispanic Americans), 19 international. 205 applicants, 62% accepted, 50 enrolled. In 2009, 35 master's, 16 doctorates, 1 other advanced degree awarded. Terminal master's awarded for partial completion of doctoral program. *Degree requirements:* For master's and CAES, comprehensive exam; for doctorate, comprehensive exam, thesis/dissertation. *Entrance requirements:* For master's and CAES, GRE General Test or MAT; for doctorate, GRE General Test. Additional exam requirements/recommendations for international students: Required—TOEFL (minimum score 550 paper-based; 213 computer-based; 81 iBT). Application fee: $60. Electronic applications accepted. *Financial support:* Fellowships with full and partial tuition reimbursements, research assistantships with full and partial tuition reimbursements, teaching assistantships with full and partial tuition reimbursements, career-related internships or fieldwork, Federal Work-Study, scholarships/grants, traineeships, health care benefits, tuition waivers (full and partial), and unspecified assistantships available. Support available to part-time students. Financial award applicants required to submit FAFSA. *Faculty research:* Literacy; bilingualism; urban education; technology and education; diversity and social justice in education. *Unit head:* Dr. Maria E. Brisk, Chairperson, 617-552-4216, Fax: 617-552-0812, E-mail: brisk@bc.edu. *Application contact:* Adam Poluzzi, Director, Graduate Admission and Financial Aid, 617-552-4214, Fax: 617-552-0398, E-mail: poluzzi@bc.edu.

Boston University, School of Education, Department of Curriculum and Teaching, Program in Curriculum and Teaching, Boston, MA 02215. Offers Ed M, MAT, Ed D, CAGS. *Degree requirements:* For master's, thesis optional; for doctorate, comprehensive exam, thesis/dissertation. *Entrance requirements:* For doctorate, GRE General Test or MAT. Additional exam requirements/recommendations for international students: Required—TOEFL. Electronic applications accepted. *Expenses:* Tuition: Full-time $37,910; part-time $1184 per credit hour. Required fees: $386; $40 per semester. Part-time tuition and fees vary according to class time, course level, degree level and program.

Bowling Green State University, Graduate College, College of Education and Human Development, School of Education and Intervention Services, Teaching and Learning Division, Program in Curriculum and Teaching, Bowling Green, OH 43403. Offers curriculum (M Ed); master teaching (M Ed). Part-time and evening/weekend programs available. *Degree requirements:* For master's, thesis or alternative. *Entrance requirements:* For master's, GRE General Test or PRAXIS. Additional exam requirements/recommendations for international students: Required—TOEFL. Electronic applications accepted. *Faculty research:* Cognitive development in cultural context, sociocultural and activity theory, philosophy in education, performance assessment.

Bradley University, Graduate School, College of Education and Health Sciences, Department of Curriculum and Instruction, Peoria, IL 61625-0002. Offers MA, Certificate. *Accreditation:* NCATE. Part-time and evening/weekend programs available. *Degree requirements:* For master's, comprehensive exam, thesis optional. *Entrance requirements:* For master's, GRE General Test or MAT, 2 letters of recommendation. Additional exam requirements/recommendations for international students: Required—TOEFL (minimum score 550 paper-based; 213 computer-based; 79 iBT).

Brandon University, Faculty of Education, Brandon, MB R7A 6A9, Canada. Offers curriculum and instruction (M Ed, Diploma); educational administration (M Ed, Diploma); guidance and counseling (M Ed, Diploma); special education (M Ed, Diploma). *Degree requirements:* For master's, thesis. *Entrance requirements:* For master's, minimum GPA of 3.0, teaching certificate or equivalent. Additional exam requirements/recommendations for international students: Required—TOEFL. *Faculty research:* Comparative education, environmental studies, parent/school council.

Brescia University, Program in Curriculum and Instruction, Owensboro, KY 42301-3023. Offers MSCI. Part-time and evening/weekend programs available. *Faculty:* 3 full-time (2 women). *Students:* 28 part-time (26 women); includes 3 minority (1 American Indian/Alaska Native, 2 Asian Americans or Pacific Islanders). Average age 36. 1 applicant, 100% accepted, 1 enrolled. In 2009, 5 master's awarded. *Degree requirements:* For master's, action research project, portfolio. *Entrance requirements:* For master's, PRAXIS II, interview, minimum GPA of 2.5. *Application deadline:* Applications are processed on a rolling basis. Application fee: $50. Electronic applications accepted. *Expenses:* Tuition: Full-time $7200; part-time $400 per credit hour. *Financial support:* In 2009–10, 5 students received support. Institutionally sponsored loans available. Support available to part-time students. Financial award application deadline: 3/1; financial award applicants required to submit FAFSA. *Unit head:* Dr. Patricia Akojie, Coordinator, 270-686-4200, Fax: 270-686-4230. *Application contact:* Christopher Houk, Director of Admissions, 270-686-4241, Fax: 270-686-4201, E-mail: admissions@brescia.edu.

Bucknell University, Graduate Studies, College of Arts and Sciences, Department of Education, Specialization in Supervision of Curriculum and Instruction, Lewisburg, PA 17837. Offers MA, MS Ed. *Degree requirements:* For master's, thesis or alternative. *Entrance requirements:* For master's, GRE General Test, minimum GPA of 2.8. Additional exam requirements/recommendations for international students: Required—TOEFL.

Buena Vista University, School of Education, Storm Lake, IA 50588. Offers curriculum and instruction (M Ed), including effective teaching, TESL; school guidance and counseling (MS Ed). Program offered in summer only. Part-time and evening/weekend programs available. Post-baccalaureate distance learning degree programs offered (minimal on-campus study). *Degree requirements:* For master's, thesis, fieldwork/practicum, capstone portfolio. *Entrance requirements:* For master's, Analytical Writing Assessment (in-house), minimum undergraduate GPA of 2.75. Electronic applications accepted. *Faculty research:* Reading, curriculum, educational psychology, special education.

Caldwell College, Graduate Studies, Program in Curriculum and Instruction, Caldwell, NJ 07006-6195. Offers MA. Part-time and evening/weekend programs available. *Degree requirements:* For master's, thesis, research paper. *Entrance requirements:* For master's, GRE General Test, MAT, interview, minimum GPA of 2.75, teaching certificate, writing sample. Additional exam requirements/recommendations for international students: Required—TOEFL (minimum score 580 paper-based; 237 computer-based). Electronic applications accepted. *Faculty research:* Early childhood, information technology, educational leadership.

California Baptist University, Program in Education, Riverside, CA 92504-3206. Offers cross-cultural language and academic development (MA); educational leadership (MS); educational leadership and faith-based instruction (MS); educational technology (MS); instructional computer applications (MS); reading (MS); school counseling (MS); school psychology (MS); special education (MS); special education in mild/moderate disabilities (MS); special education in moderate/severe disabilities (MS); teaching (MS); teaching and learning (MS Ed). Part-time programs available. *Faculty:* 16 full-time (9 women), 10 part-time/adjunct (all women). *Students:* 73 full-time (60 women), 368 part-time (298 women); includes 170 minority (34 African Americans, 4 American Indian/Alaska Native, 18 Asian Americans or Pacific Islanders, 114 Hispanic Americans). 266 applicants, 72% accepted, 169 enrolled. In 2009, 120 master's awarded. *Degree requirements:* For master's, comprehensive exam (for some programs), thesis optional. *Entrance requirements:* For master's, minimum undergraduate GPA of 2.75, 12 semester hours of pre-requisite course work in education. Additional exam requirements/recommendations for international students: Required—TOEFL (minimum score 575 paper-based; 230 computer-based; 89 iBT). *Application deadline:* For fall admission, 8/1 priority date for domestic students, 7/1 for international students; for spring admission, 12/1 priority date for domestic students, 10/15 priority date for international students. Applications are processed on a rolling basis. Application fee: $45. Electronic applications accepted. *Expenses:* Tuition: Full-time $8352; part-time $464 per semester hour. Required fees: $125 per semester. Tuition and fees vary according to course load, campus/location and program. *Financial support:* Career-related internships or fieldwork, Federal Work-Study, and scholarships/grants available. Support available to part-time students. Financial award applicants required to submit FAFSA. *Unit head:* Dr. Mary Crist, Dean, School of Education, 951-343-4313, Fax: 951-343-4516, E-mail: mcrist@calbaptist.edu. *Application contact:* Gail Ronveaux, Dean of Graduate Enrollment, 951-343-5045, Fax: 951-343-5095, E-mail: graduateadmissions@calbaptist.edu.

California Coast University, Programs in Education, Santa Ana, CA 92701. Offers administration (M Ed); curriculum and instruction (M Ed); educational psychology (D Ed); organizational leadership (D Ed). Part-time and evening/weekend programs available. Post-baccalaureate distance learning degree programs offered (no on-campus study). Application fee: $75. *Application contact:* Christi Okuma, 714-547-9625, Fax: 714-547-5777, E-mail: ccu@calcoast.edu.

California State University, Bakersfield, Division of Graduate Studies, School of Education, Program in Curriculum and Instruction, Bakersfield, CA 93311. Offers curriculum and instruction (MA Ed); educational technology (MA Ed). *Accreditation:* NCATE. Postbaccalaureate distance learning degree programs offered. *Degree requirements:* For master's, thesis or alternative, culminating projects. *Entrance requirements:* For master's, CBEST, copy of current teaching credential, minimum GPA of 3.0 for last 90 units, 3 letters of recommendation.

California State University, Chico, Graduate School, College of Communication and Education, Department of Education, Option in Curriculum and Instruction, Chico, CA 95929-0722. Offers MA.

California State University, Dominguez Hills, College of Professional Studies, School of Education, Division of Graduate Education, Program in Curriculum and Instruction, Carson, CA 90747-0001. Offers MA. Part-time and evening/weekend programs available. *Faculty:* 5 full-time (3 women), 1 (woman) part-time/adjunct. *Students:* 20 full-time (19 women), 76 part-time (59 women); includes 61 minority (24 African Americans, 1 American Indian/Alaska Native, 11 Asian Americans or Pacific Islanders, 25 Hispanic Americans). Average age 35. 50 applicants, 64% accepted, 21 enrolled. In 2009, 53 master's awarded. *Degree requirements:* For master's, comprehensive exam. *Entrance requirements:* For master's, minimum GPA of 2.75. Additional exam requirements/recommendations for international students: Required—TOEFL. *Application deadline:* For fall admission, 6/1 for domestic students. Applications are processed on a rolling basis. Application fee: $55. *Expenses:* Tuition, nonresident: full-time $6696; part-time $372 per unit. Required fees: $5946; $1752 per semester. *Faculty research:* Cooperative learning, student engagement. *Unit head:* Dr. James L. Cooper, Professor, 310-243-3961, E-mail: jcooper@csudh.edu. *Application contact:* Admissions Office, 310-243-3530.

California State University, Fresno, Division of Graduate Studies, School of Education and Human Development, Department of Curriculum and Instruction, Fresno, CA 93740-8027. Offers education (MA), including curriculum and instruction. *Accreditation:* NCATE. Part-time and evening/weekend programs available. *Degree requirements:* For master's, thesis or alternative. *Entrance requirements:* For master's, GRE General Test, MAT, minimum GPA of 2.75. Additional exam requirements/recommendations for international students: Required—TOEFL. Electronic applications accepted. *Faculty research:* Teacher excellence, teacher quality improvement, online assessment.

California State University, Northridge, Graduate Studies, College of Education, Department of Elementary Education, Northridge, CA 91330. Offers curriculum and instruction (MA); language and literacy (MA); multilingual/multicultural education (MA); teaching and learning (MA). *Accreditation:* NCATE. Part-time and evening/weekend programs available. *Faculty:* 18 full-time (14 women), 32 part-time/adjunct (24 women). *Students:* 29 full-time (all women), 61 part-time (57 women); includes 38 minority (1 African American, 10 Asian Americans or Pacific Islanders, 27 Hispanic Americans), 1 international. Average age 31. 64 applicants, 64% accepted, 28 enrolled. *Degree requirements:* For master's, comprehensive exam. *Entrance requirements:* For master's, GRE General Test or minimum GPA of 3.0. Additional exam requirements/recommendations for international students: Required—TOEFL. *Application deadline:* For fall admission, 11/30 for domestic students. Application fee: $55. *Financial support:* Federal Work-Study available. Financial award application deadline: 3/1. *Unit head:* Dr. David Kretschmer, Chair, 818-677-2621. *Application contact:* Joyce Burstein, Graduate Coordinator, 818-677-2621 Ext. 6850, E-mail: joyce.burstein@csun.edu.

California State University, Sacramento, Graduate Studies, College of Education, Department of Teacher Education, Sacramento, CA 95819. Offers curriculum and instruction (MA); early childhood education (MA); reading education (MA). Part-time programs available. *Degree requirements:* For master's, thesis or alternative, writing proficiency exam. *Entrance requirements:* Additional exam requirements/recommendations for international students: Required—TOEFL. Electronic applications accepted.

California State University, San Bernardino, Graduate Studies, College of Education, Program in Curriculum and Instruction, San Bernardino, CA 92407-2397. Offers MA. *Faculty:* 1 full-time (0 women), 1 part-time/adjunct (0 women). *Students:* 32 full-time (28 women), 19 part-time (14 women); includes 19 minority (5 African Americans, 4 Asian Americans or Pacific Islanders, 10 Hispanic Americans). Average age 34. 42 applicants, 93% accepted, 21 enrolled. In 2009, 31 master's awarded. *Degree requirements:* For master's, comprehensive exam (for some programs), thesis (for some programs). Application fee: $55. *Unit head:* Dr. Jay Fiene, Department Chair, 909-537-7621, Fax: 909-537-7510, E-mail: jfiene@csusb.edu. *Application contact:* Olivia Rosas, Director of Admissions, 909-537-7577, Fax: 909-537-7034, E-mail: orosas@csusb.edu.

California State University, Stanislaus, College of Education, Department of Teacher Education, Turlock, CA 95382. Offers curriculum and instruction (MA), including elementary education, multilingual education, reading, secondary education; education (MA); middle/junior high studies (Graduate Certificate). Part-time and evening/weekend programs available. *Degree requirements:* For master's, thesis. *Entrance requirements:* For master's, MAT or GRE, 3 letters of recommendation. Additional exam requirements/recommendations for international students: Required—TOEFL (minimum score 550 paper-based; 213 computer-based). Electronic applications accepted. *Faculty research:* Children's perspectives on historical events, method elementary schools dual language education, K-12 reading and CYRM programs.

Calvin College, Graduate Programs in Education, Grand Rapids, MI 49546-4388. Offers curriculum and instruction (M Ed); educational leadership (M Ed); learning disabilities (M Ed); literacy (M Ed). Part-time programs available. *Faculty:* 3 full-time (2 women), 4 part-time/adjunct (1 woman). *Students:* 7 full-time (6 women), 113 part-time (79 women); includes 9 minority (2 African Americans, 5 Asian Americans or Pacific Islanders, 2 Hispanic Americans). Average age 29. In 2009, 27 master's awarded. *Degree requirements:* For master's, thesis or seminar. *Entrance requirements:* For master's, teaching certificate. Additional exam requirements/

recommendations for international students: Required—TOEFL (minimum score 550 paper-based; 213 computer-based). *Application deadline:* For fall admission, 8/1 priority date for domestic students, 6/1 priority date for international students; for spring admission, 1/1 priority date for domestic students, 2/1 priority date for international students. Applications are processed on a rolling basis. Application fee: $0. Electronic applications accepted. *Expenses:* Tuition: Full-time $10,080. *Financial support:* Federal Work-Study, scholarships/grants, and tuition waivers (full and partial) available. Support available to part-time students. Financial award application deadline: 4/3. *Faculty research:* Literacy, racialized gender and gendered identity, teacher learning, learning disabilities identification. *Unit head:* Dr. Debra Buursma, Graduate Program Director, 616-526-6231, Fax: 616-526-6505, E-mail: dbuursma@calvin.edu. *Application contact:* Cindi Hoekstra, Program Coordinator, 616-526-6158, Fax: 616-526-6505, E-mail: choekstr@calvin.edu.

Cambridge College, School of Education, Cambridge, MA 02138-5304. Offers autism specialist (M Ed); autism/behavior analyst (M Ed); behavior analyst (Post-Master's Certificate); behavioral management (M Ed); early childhood teacher (M Ed); education specialist in curriculum and instruction (CAGS); educational leadership (Ed D); elementary teacher (M Ed); English as a second language (M Ed, Certificate); general science (M Ed); health education, health promotion (Post-Master's Certificate); health/family and consumer sciences (M Ed); history (M Ed); individualized degree (M Ed); information technology literacy (M Ed); instructional technology (M Ed); interdisciplinary studies (M Ed); library teacher (M Ed); literacy education (M Ed); mathematics (M Ed); mathematics specialist (Certificate); middle school mathematics and science (M Ed); school administration (M Ed, CAGS); school guidance counselor (M Ed); school nurse education (M Ed); school social worker/school adjustment counselor (M Ed); special education administrator (CAGS); special education/moderate disabilities (M Ed); teaching skills and methodologies (M Ed). Part-time and evening/weekend programs available. Post-baccalaureate distance learning degree programs offered (minimal on-campus study). *Faculty:* 10 full-time (3 women), 283 part-time/adjunct (187 women). *Students:* 974 full-time (755 women), 1,071 part-time (835 women); includes 940 minority (762 African Americans, 4 American Indian/Alaska Native, 22 Asian Americans or Pacific Islanders, 152 Hispanic Americans), 28 international. Average age 39. In 2009, 866 master's, 4 doctorates, 209 CAGSs awarded. *Degree requirements:* For master's, thesis, internship/practicum (licensure program only); for doctorate, thesis/dissertation; for other advanced degree, thesis. *Entrance requirements:* For master's, interview, resume, documentation of licensure, 2 professional references; for doctorate, official transcripts, interview, resume, documentation of licensure (if any), written personal statement/essay, portfolio of scholarly and professional work, qualifying assessment, 2 professional references, health insurance, immunizations form; for other advanced degree, official transcripts, interview, resume, documentation of licensure (if any), written personal statement/essay, 2 professional references, health insurance, immunizations form. Additional exam requirements/recommendations for international students: Required—TOEFL (minimum score 550 paper-based; 213 computer-based; 79 iBT); Recommended—IELTS (minimum score 6). *Application deadline:* Applications are processed on a rolling basis. Application fee: $30. Electronic applications accepted. *Expenses:* Contact institution. *Financial support:* In 2009–10, 1,373 students received support. Career-related internships or fieldwork, Federal Work-Study, and scholarships/grants available. Financial award applicants required to submit FAFSA. *Faculty research:* Adult education, accelerated learning, mathematics education, brain compatible learning, special education and law. *Unit head:* Dr. N. Alan Sheppard, Interim Associate Dean, 617-873-0619, E-mail: alan.sheppard@cambridgecollege.edu. *Application contact:* Stephen Lyons, Director of Enrollment, Graduate and N.I.T.E. Programs, 617-868-1000, Fax: 617-349-3561, E-mail: stephen.lyons@cambridgecollege.edu.

Campbellsville University, School of Education, Campbellsville, KY 42718-2799. Offers curriculum and instruction (MAE); special education (MASE). *Accreditation:* NCATE. Part-time and evening/weekend programs available. Postbaccalaureate distance learning degree programs offered (minimal on-campus study). *Degree requirements:* For master's, thesis, research paper. *Entrance requirements:* For master's, GRE or PRAXIS, minimum undergraduate GPA of 2.75, teaching certificate, professional growth plan, letters of recommendation, disposition assessment, entrance interview. Electronic applications accepted. *Expenses:* Tuition: Full-time $6750; part-time $375 per credit hour. *Faculty research:* Professional development, curriculum development, school governance, assessment, special education.

Cape Breton University, School of Education, Health, and Wellness, Sydney, NS B1P 6L2, Canada. Offers educational counseling (Diploma); educational curriculum (Diploma); educational studies in arts education (Certificate); educational technology (Diploma). Part-time and evening/weekend programs available. Postbaccalaureate distance learning degree programs offered (no on-campus study). *Faculty:* 15 part-time/adjunct (5 women). *Students:* 171 part-time (103 women). Average age 30. *Application deadline:* For fall admission, 8/1 priority date for domestic students. Applications are processed on a rolling basis. Application fee: $50. Electronic applications accepted. *Unit head:* Susan Basso, Coordinator of the Education Program, 902-563-1651, Fax: 902-563-1861. *Application contact:* Terry MacDonald, Coordinator, Teacher Education Program, 902-563-1647, Fax: 902-563-1449, E-mail: terry_macdonald@cbu.ca.

Capella University, School of Education, Minneapolis, MN 55402. Offers college teaching (Certificate); curriculum and instruction (MS, PhD); education (MS); enrollment management (MS); instructional design for online learning (MS, PhD); k-12 studies in education (MS, PhD); leadership for higher education (MS, PhD); leadership in education administration (Certificate); leadership in educational administration (MS, PhD); postsecondary and adult education (MS, PhD); professional studies in education (MS, PhD); reading and literacy (MS); training and performance improvement (MS, PhD). Part-time and evening/weekend programs available. Postbaccalaureate distance learning degree programs offered (minimal on-campus study). Terminal master's awarded for partial completion of doctoral program. *Degree requirements:* For master's, thesis optional, integrative project; for doctorate, comprehensive exam, thesis/dissertation. *Entrance requirements:* Additional exam requirements/recommendations for international students: Required—TOEFL (minimum score 550 paper-based; 213 computer-based), TWE (minimum score 4). Electronic applications accepted. *Faculty research:* Higher education administration, distance learning, adult education, training and curriculum design.

Caribbean University, Graduate School, Bayamón, PR 00960-0493. Offers administration and supervision (MA Ed); criminal justice (MA); curriculum and instruction (MA Ed), including elementary education, English education, history education, mathematics education, primary education, science education, Spanish education; education (PhD); gerontology (MSN); human resources (MBA); museology, archiving and art history (MA Ed); neonatal pediatrics (MSN); physical education (MA Ed); special education (MA Ed). *Entrance requirements:* For master's, interview, minimum GPA of 2.5.

Carson-Newman College, Graduate Program in Education, Jefferson City, TN 37760. Offers curriculum and instruction (M Ed); educational leadership (M Ed); elementary education (MAT); school counseling (MS); secondary education (MAT); teaching English as a second language (MATESL). *Accreditation:* NCATE. Part-time and evening/weekend programs available. *Faculty:* 5 full-time (2 women), 10 part-time/adjunct (3 women). *Students:* 112 full-time (84 women), 84 part-time (52 women); includes 5 African Americans, 17 international. Average age 32. 86 applicants, 98% accepted. In 2009, 55 master's awarded. *Degree requirements:* For master's, thesis or alternative. *Entrance requirements:* For master's, NTE, minimum GPA of 3.0 in major, 2.5 overall. *Application deadline:* For fall admission, 7/15 priority date for domestic students. Applications are processed on a rolling basis. Application fee: $25 ($50 for international students). *Expenses:* Tuition: Full-time $5490; part-time $305 per semester hour. Required fees: $200. *Financial support:* In 2009–10, 41 students received support. Federal Work-Study and unspecified assistantships available. Financial award application deadline: 4/1; financial award applicants required to submit FAFSA. *Unit head:* Dr. Sharon Teets, Chair, 865-471-3461. *Application contact:* Graduate Admissions and Services Adviser, 865-471-3460, Fax: 865-471-3875.

Castleton State College, Division of Graduate Studies, Department of Education, Program in Curriculum and Instruction, Castleton, VT 05735. Offers MA Ed. Part-time and evening/weekend programs available. *Degree requirements:* For master's, thesis or alternative. *Entrance requirements:* For master's, GRE General Test, MAT, interview, minimum undergraduate GPA of 3.0. *Expenses:* Tuition, state resident: full-time $10,290; part-time $429 per credit. Tuition, nonresident: full-time $15,420; part-time $643 per credit. One-time fee: $200 full-time.

The Catholic University of America, School of Arts and Sciences, Department of Education, Washington, DC 20064. Offers Catholic educational leadership (PhD); education (Certificate); educational psychology (PhD); learning and instruction (MA); secondary education (MA); special education (MA). *Accreditation:* NCATE. Part-time programs available. *Faculty:* 11 full-time (8 women), 3 part-time/adjunct (0 women). *Students:* 6 full-time (5 women), 56 part-time (39 women); includes 9 minority (5 African Americans, 2 Asian Americans or Pacific Islanders, 2 Hispanic Americans), 2 international. Average age 38. 54 applicants, 59% accepted, 14 enrolled. In 2009, 14 master's, 6 doctorates, 1 other advanced degree awarded. *Degree requirements:* For master's, comprehensive exam, thesis or alternative; for doctorate, comprehensive exam, thesis/dissertation. *Entrance requirements:* For master's and doctorate, GRE General Test or MAT, statement of purpose, official copies of academic transcripts, three letters of recommendation. Additional exam requirements/recommendations for international students: Required—TOEFL (minimum score 580 paper-based; 237 computer-based). *Application deadline:* For fall admission, 8/1 priority date for domestic students, 7/15 for international students; for spring admission, 12/1 priority date for domestic students, 10/15 for international students. Applications are processed on a rolling basis. Application fee: $55. Electronic applications accepted. *Expenses:* Tuition: Full-time $31,740; part-time $1245 per credit hour. Required fees: $50; $25 per semester hour. One-time fee: $425. *Financial support:* Fellowships, research assistantships, teaching assistantships, Federal Work-Study, scholarships/grants, tuition waivers (full and partial), and unspecified assistantships available. Financial award application deadline: 2/1; financial award applicants required to submit FAFSA. *Faculty research:* Catholic school issues, reflective teaching, cognitive psychology, urban education. Total annual research expenditures: $68,905. *Unit head:* Dr. Merylann J. Schuttloffel, Chair, 202-319-5805, Fax: 202-319-5815, E-mail: schuttloffel@cua.edu. *Application contact:* Julie Schwing, Director of Graduate Admissions, 202-319-5057, Fax: 202-319-6533, E-mail: cua-admissions@cua.edu.

Centenary College of Louisiana, Graduate Programs, Department of Education, Shreveport, LA 71104. Offers administration (M Ed); elementary education (MAT); secondary education (MAT); supervision of instruction (M Ed). Part-time and evening/weekend programs available. *Degree requirements:* For master's, comprehensive exam. *Entrance requirements:* For master's, GRE General Test (M Ed), PRAXIS I and PRAXIS II (MAT), teacher certification (M Ed), minimum GPA of 2.5. *Expenses:* Contact institution. *Faculty research:* Teachers as advocates for teachers, portfolio assessment, disabled readers.

Central Michigan University, College of Graduate Studies, College of Education and Human Services, Department of Educational Leadership, Mount Pleasant, MI 48859. Offers educational leadership (MA, Ed D), including charter school leadership (Ed D), educational technology (Ed D), general educational leadership, higher education administration (Ed D), higher education leadership (Ed D), K-12 curriculum (Ed D), K-12 leadership (Ed D), student affairs administration (Ed D); general educational administration (Ed S); school principalship (MA). Part-time and evening/weekend programs available. *Degree requirements:* For master's and Ed S, thesis or alternative; for doctorate, thesis/dissertation. *Entrance requirements:* For doctorate, GRE or MAT, master's degree, minimum GPA of 3.5, 3 years of professional education experience. Electronic applications accepted. *Faculty research:* Elementary administration, secondary administration, student achievement, in-service training, internships in administration.

Chapman University, Graduate Studies, College of Educational Studies, Program in Education, Orange, CA 92866. Offers curriculum and foundations (MA); educational leadership and administration (MA); reading and literacy (MA). Part-time and evening/weekend programs available. *Faculty:* 24 full-time (15 women), 25 part-time/adjunct (16 women). *Students:* 7 full-time (all women), 35 part-time (25 women); includes 20 minority (1 African American, 8 Asian Americans or Pacific Islanders, 11 Hispanic Americans). Average age 32. 18 applicants, 89% accepted, 9 enrolled. In 2009, 32 master's awarded. *Degree requirements:* For master's, comprehensive exam, thesis optional. *Entrance requirements:* For master's, GRE General Test, MAT, or California Subject Examinations for Teachers, minimum undergraduate GPA of 2.5. Additional exam requirements/recommendations for international students: Required—TOEFL (minimum score 550 paper-based). *Application deadline:* Applications are processed on a rolling basis. Application fee: $55. Electronic applications accepted. *Expenses:* Contact institution. *Financial support:* Fellowships, Federal Work-Study and scholarships/grants available. Financial award application deadline: 6/30; financial award applicants required to submit FAFSA. *Unit head:* Dr. Barbara Tye, Coordinator, 714-997-6781. *Application contact:* Rika Judd, Information Contact, 714-997-6786, Fax: 714-997-6713, E-mail: rjudd@chapman.edu.

Chapman University, Graduate Studies, College of Educational Studies, Program in Education: Cultural and Curricular Studies, Orange, CA 92866. Offers PhD. Part-time and evening/weekend programs available. *Faculty:* 24 full-time (15 women), 25 part-time/adjunct (16 women). *Students:* 23 part-time (18 women); includes 9 minority (2 African Americans, 1 Asian American or Pacific Islander, 6 Hispanic Americans). Average age 37. 23 applicants, 70% accepted, 10 enrolled. *Degree requirements:* For doctorate, thesis/dissertation. Tuition and fees vary according to course load, degree level and program. *Financial support:* Fellowships, Federal Work-Study and scholarships/grants available. *Unit head:* Dr. Joel Colbert, Director, 714-744-7076. *Application contact:* Rika Judd, Graduate Admission Counselor, 714-997-6786, Fax: 714-997-6713, E-mail: rjudd@chapman.edu.

Christian Brothers University, School of Arts, Memphis, TN 38104-5581. Offers Catholic studies (MACS); curriculum and instruction (M Ed); educational leadership (MSEL); teacher-leadership (M Ed); teaching (MAT). Part-time and evening/weekend programs available. *Faculty:* 7 full-time (4 women), 10 part-time/adjunct (7 women). *Students:* 62 full-time (49 women), 175 part-time (125 women); includes 70 minority (60 African Americans, 5 Asian Americans or Pacific Islanders, 5 Hispanic Americans). Average age 32. In 2009, 92 master's awarded. *Entrance requirements:* For master's, GRE, GMAT, PRAXIS II. *Application deadline:* Applications are processed on a rolling basis. Application fee: $35. *Expenses:* Contact institution. *Financial support:* Institutionally sponsored loans available. Support available to part-time students. *Unit head:* Dr. Marius Carriere, Dean, 901-321-3366, Fax: 901-321-4340, E-mail: mcarrier@cbu.edu. *Application contact:* Dr. Talana L. Vogel, Director, 901-321-4101, Fax: 901-321-3408, E-mail: tvogel@cbu.edu.

City University of Seattle, Graduate Division, Gordon Albright School of Education, Bellevue, WA 98005. Offers curriculum and instruction (M Ed); educational leadership (M Ed); educational leadership: administrator certification (Certificate); executive leadership: superintendent certification (Certificate); guidance and counseling (M Ed); leadership (M Ed); leadership and school counseling (M Ed); professional certification for teachers (Certificate); reading and literacy (M Ed); reading and literacy in education (M Ed); teacher certification (elementary K-8) (MIT); teacher certification (special education K-12) (MIT); technology, curriculum, and instruction (M Ed). Part-time and evening/weekend programs available. Postbaccalaureate distance learning degree programs offered (no on-campus study). *Entrance requirements:* Additional exam requirements/recommendations for international students: Required—TOEFL (minimum score 540 paper-based; 207 computer-based); Recommended—IELTS. Electronic applications accepted. *Expenses:* Contact institution.

Clarion University of Pennsylvania, Office of Research and Graduate Studies, College of Education and Human Services, Department of Education, Program in Education, Clarion, PA 16214. Offers curriculum and instruction (M Ed); early childhood (M Ed); English (M Ed); history (M Ed); literacy (M Ed); science (M Ed); technology (M Ed). *Accreditation:* NCATE. Part-time programs available. *Degree requirements:* For master's, comprehensive exam, thesis or alternative. *Entrance requirements:* For master's, minimum QPA of 3.0, teacher certification. Additional exam requirements/recommendations for international students: Required—TOEFL (minimum score 550 paper-based; 213 computer-based; 80 iBT). Electronic applications accepted.

Curriculum and Instruction

Clark Atlanta University, School of Education, Department of Curriculum, Atlanta, GA 30314. Offers MA, MAT. Part-time programs available. *Faculty:* 7 full-time (5 women), 5 part-time/adjunct (4 women). *Students:* 21 full-time (12 women), 18 part-time (12 women); all minorities (all African Americans). Average age 32. 30 applicants, 57% accepted, 5 enrolled. In 2009, 12 master's awarded. *Degree requirements:* For master's, one foreign language, comprehensive exam. *Entrance requirements:* For master's, GRE General Test, minimum undergraduate GPA of 2.6. Additional exam requirements/recommendations for international students: Required—TOEFL (minimum score 500 paper-based; 173 computer-based). *Application deadline:* For fall admission, 4/1 for domestic and international students; for spring admission, 11/1 for domestic and international students. Applications are processed on a rolling basis. Application fee: $40 ($55 for international students). *Expenses:* Tuition: Full-time $12,240; part-time $680 per credit hour. Required fees: $710; $355 per semester. *Financial support:* Career-related internships or fieldwork, Federal Work-Study, scholarships/grants, and unspecified assistantships available. Support available to part-time students. Financial award application deadline: 4/30; financial award applicants required to submit FAFSA. *Unit head:* Dr. Doris Terrell, Chairperson, 404-880-6336, E-mail: dterrell@cau.edu. *Application contact:* Michelle Clark-Davis, Graduate Program Admissions, 404-880-6605, E-mail: cauadmissions@cau.edu.

Clemson University, Graduate School, College of Health, Education, and Human Development, School of Education, Program in Curriculum and Instruction, Clemson, SC 29634. Offers PhD. *Accreditation:* NCATE. *Students:* 29 full-time (23 women), 24 part-time (21 women); includes 4 minority (3 African Americans, 1 Hispanic American), 1 international. Average age 39. 46 applicants, 59% accepted, 15 enrolled. In 2009, 8 doctorates awarded. *Degree requirements:* For doctorate, thesis/dissertation. *Entrance requirements:* For doctorate, GRE General Test, teaching certificate. Additional exam requirements/recommendations for international students: Required—TOEFL. *Application deadline:* Applications are processed on a rolling basis. Application fee: $70 ($80 for international students). Electronic applications accepted. *Expenses:* Contact institution. *Financial support:* In 2009–10, 23 students received support, including 5 fellowships with full and partial tuition reimbursements available (averaging $8,000 per year), 10 research assistantships with partial tuition reimbursements available (averaging $15,875 per year), 8 teaching assistantships with partial tuition reimbursements available (averaging $17,591 per year); career-related internships or fieldwork, institutionally sponsored loans, scholarships/grants, health care benefits, and unspecified assistantships also available. Support available to part-time students. Financial award application deadline: 6/1; financial award applicants required to submit FAFSA. *Unit head:* Dr. Michael J. Padilla, Director/Associate Dean, 864-656-4444, Fax: 864-656-0311, E-mail: padilla@clemson.edu. *Application contact:* Dr. David S. Fleming, Graduate Coordinator, 864-656-1881, Fax: 864-656-0311, E-mail: dflemin@clemson.edu.

The College at Brockport, State University of New York, School of Education and Human Services, Department of Education and Human Development, Program in Childhood Curriculum Specialist, Brockport, NY 14420-2997. Offers MS Ed. *Accreditation:* NCATE. Part-time programs available. *Students:* 14 full-time (13 women), 49 part-time (37 women); includes 10 minority (2 African Americans, 3 Asian Americans or Pacific Islanders, 5 Hispanic Americans). 15 applicants, 87% accepted, 13 enrolled. In 2009, 27 master's awarded. *Degree requirements:* For master's, thesis or alternative. *Entrance requirements:* For master's, minimum GPA of 3.0, letters of recommendation. Additional exam requirements/recommendations for international students: Required—TOEFL (minimum score 550 paper-based; 213 computer-based; 79 iBT). *Application deadline:* For fall admission, 2/15 priority date for domestic and international students; for spring admission, 9/15 priority date for domestic and international students. Application fee: $80. Electronic applications accepted. *Expenses:* Tuition, state resident: full-time $8370; part-time $349 per credit. Tuition, nonresident: full-time $13,250; part-time $522 per credit. *Financial support:* Federal Work-Study, scholarships/grants, and unspecified assistantships available. Support available to part-time students. Financial award application deadline: 3/15; financial award applicants required to submit FAFSA. *Unit head:* Dr. Sue Novinger, Chairperson, 585-395-2205, Fax: 585-395-2172, E-mail: snovinge@brockport.edu. *Application contact:* Coordinator of Certification and Graduate Advisement.

The College of Saint Rose, Graduate Studies, School of Education, Teacher Education Department, Albany, NY 12203-1419. Offers business and marketing (MS Ed); childhood education (MS Ed); curriculum and instruction (MS Ed); early childhood education (MS Ed); elementary education (K-6) (MS Ed); secondary education (MS Ed, Certificate); teacher education (MS Ed, Certificate), including bilingual pupil personnel services (Certificate), teacher education (MS Ed). Part-time and evening/weekend programs available. *Entrance requirements:* For master's, minimum undergraduate GPA of 3.0. Additional exam requirements/recommendations for international students: Required—TOEFL (minimum score 550 paper-based; 213 computer-based). Electronic applications accepted.

College of Santa Fe, Department of Education, Santa Fe, NM 87505-7634. Offers at-risk youth (MA), including bilingual/multicultural education, classroom teaching, community counseling, educational administration, leadership, school counseling, self-designed program, TESOL/Multicultural; curriculum and instruction (MA); multicultural special education (MA). Part-time and evening/weekend programs available. *Entrance requirements:* For master's, minimum GPA of 3.0. *Faculty research:* Integrated curriculum, child development, brain research, learning styles, systemic issues in education.

The College of William and Mary, School of Education, Program in Curriculum and Instruction, Williamsburg, VA 23187-8795. Offers elementary education (MA Ed); gifted education (MA Ed); math specialist (MA Ed); reading education (MA Ed); secondary education (MA Ed), including English education, mathematics education, modern foreign languages education, science education, social studies education; special education (MA Ed), including general curriculum, resource collaborating teaching. *Accreditation:* NCATE. Part-time programs available. *Faculty:* 18 full-time (12 women), 17 part-time/adjunct (15 women). *Students:* 54 full-time (45 women), 12 part-time (all women); includes 3 minority (2 African Americans, 1 Asian American or Pacific Islander), 2 international. Average age 27. 120 applicants, 75% accepted. In 2009, 70 master's awarded. *Degree requirements:* For master's, project. *Entrance requirements:* For master's, GRE or MAT, minimum GPA of 2.5. Additional exam requirements/recommendations for international students: Required—TOEFL. *Application deadline:* For fall admission, 1/15 for domestic and international students; for spring admission, 10/1 for domestic and international students. Application fee: $45. Electronic applications accepted. *Expenses:* Tuition, state resident: full-time $6400; part-time $315 per credit hour. Tuition, nonresident: full-time $19,720; part-time $840 per credit hour. Required fees: $4114. *Financial support:* In 2009–10, 30 students received support, including 10 research assistantships with full and partial tuition reimbursements available (averaging $5,500 per year); career-related internships or fieldwork, Federal Work-Study, institutionally sponsored loans, scholarships/grants, and unspecified assistantships also available. Financial award application deadline: 1/15; financial award applicants required to submit FAFSA. *Faculty research:* National Council of Teachers of Mathematics Standards, counseling, self-concept and self-esteem, special education, curriculum development. *Unit head:* Dr. C. Denise Johnson, Area Coordinator, 757-221-1528, E-mail: cdjohn@wm.edu. *Application contact:* Dorothy Smith Osborne, Director of Admissions, 757-221-2317, Fax: 757-221-2293, E-mail: dsosbo@wm.edu.

The College of William and Mary, School of Education, Program in Education Policy, Planning, and Leadership, Williamsburg, VA 23187-8795. Offers curriculum and educational technology (Ed D, PhD); curriculum leadership (Ed D, PhD); educational leadership (M Ed), including higher education administration (M Ed, Ed D, PhD), K-12 administration and supervision; educational policy, planning, and leadership (Ed D, PhD), including general education administration, gifted education administration, higher education administration (M Ed, Ed D, PhD), special education administration; gifted education administration (M Ed). *Accreditation:* NCATE. Part-time and evening/weekend programs available. *Faculty:* 12 full-time (6 women), 3 part-time/adjunct (1 woman). *Students:* 41 full-time (26 women), 134 part-time (93 women); includes 35 minority (32 African Americans, 3 Asian Americans or Pacific Islanders), 2 international. Average age 38. 108 applicants, 57% accepted, 44 enrolled. In 2009, 20 master's, 22 doctorates awarded. *Degree requirements:* For doctorate, comprehensive exam, thesis/dissertation. *Entrance requirements:* For master's, GRE or MAT, minimum GPA of 2.5; for doctorate, GRE or MAT, minimum GPA of 3.0. Additional exam requirements/recommendations for international students: Required—TOEFL. *Application deadline:* For fall admission, 1/15 for domestic and international students. Application fee: $45. Electronic applications accepted. *Expenses:* Tuition, state resident: full-time $6400; part-time $315 per credit hour. Tuition, nonresident: full-time $19,720; part-time $840 per credit hour. Required fees: $4114. *Financial support:* In 2009–10, 56 students received support, including 32 research assistantships with full and partial tuition reimbursements available (averaging $13,000 per year); career-related internships or fieldwork, Federal Work-Study, institutionally sponsored loans, scholarships/grants, and unspecified assistantships also available. Support available to part-time students. Financial award application deadline: 1/15; financial award applicants required to submit FAFSA. *Faculty research:* Higher education policy, faculty incentives, history of adversity, resilience, leadership. *Unit head:* Dr. Megan Tschannen-Moran, Area Coordinator, 757-221-2187, E-mail: mxtsch@wm.edu. *Application contact:* Dorothy Smith Osborne, Director of Admissions, 757-221-2317, Fax: 757-221-2293, E-mail: dsosbo@wm.edu.

Colorado Christian University, Program in Curriculum and Instruction, Lakewood, CO 80226. Offers MA. Part-time and evening/weekend programs available. *Degree requirements:* For master's, thesis optional, practicum. *Entrance requirements:* For master's, interviews, letters of recommendation. Additional exam requirements/recommendations for international students: Required—TOEFL. Electronic applications accepted. *Expenses:* Contact institution.

Columbia International University, Columbia Graduate School, Columbia, SC 29230-3122. Offers Bible teaching (MABT); Christian higher education leadership (Ed D); Christian school educational leadership (Ed D); counseling (MACN); curriculum and instruction (M Ed), including Christian school guidance, English as a second language, learning disabilities, school technology; early childhood and elementary education (MAT); educational administration (M Ed); teaching English as a foreign language (Certificate); teaching English as a foreign language and intercultural studies (MATF). Part-time and evening/weekend programs available. *Degree requirements:* For master's, internships, professional project. *Entrance requirements:* For master's, Minnesota Multiphasic Personality Inventory, MAT, minimum GPA of 2.7. Additional exam requirements/recommendations for international students: Required—TOEFL. Electronic applications accepted.

Columbus State University, Graduate Studies, College of Education and Health Professions, Department of Counseling, Foundations, and Leadership, Columbus, GA 31907-5645. Offers community counseling (MS); curriculum and leadership (Ed D); educational leadership (M Ed, Ed S); school counseling (M Ed). *Accreditation:* ACA; NCATE. Part-time and evening/weekend programs available. Postbaccalaureate distance learning degree programs offered (minimal on-campus study). *Faculty:* 11 full-time (3 women), 7 part-time/adjunct (3 women). *Students:* 92 full-time (65 women), 110 part-time (88 women); includes 68 minority (62 African Americans, 1 American Indian/Alaska Native, 1 Asian American or Pacific Islander, 4 Hispanic Americans), 1 international. Average age 35. 134 applicants, 65% accepted, 61 enrolled. In 2009, 32 master's, 34 other advanced degrees awarded. *Degree requirements:* For master's, thesis, exit exam; for Ed S, thesis or alternative. *Entrance requirements:* For master's, GRE General Test, minimum GPA of 2.75; for doctorate, minimum graduate GPA of 3.5, four years of professional service; for Ed S, GRE General Test. Additional exam requirements/recommendations for international students: Required—TOEFL (minimum score 550 paper-based; 213 computer-based; 79 iBT). *Application deadline:* For fall admission, 5/1 priority date for domestic students, 5/1 for international students; for spring admission, 11/1 for domestic and international students. Applications are processed on a rolling basis. Application fee: $30. Electronic applications accepted. *Financial support:* In 2009–10, 110 students received support, including 7 research assistantships with partial tuition reimbursements available (averaging $3,000 per year); career-related internships or fieldwork, Federal Work-Study, institutionally sponsored loans, scholarships/grants, tuition waivers (partial), and unspecified assistantships also available. Support available to part-time students. Financial award application deadline: 5/1; financial award applicants required to submit FAFSA. *Unit head:* Dr. Paul Tom Hackett, Chair, 706-568-5061, Fax: 706-569-3134, E-mail: hackett_paul@colstate.edu. *Application contact:* Katie Thornton, Graduate Admissions Specialist, 706-568-2035, Fax: 706-568-2462, E-mail: thornton_katie@colstate.edu.

Concordia University, College of Education, Portland, OR 97211-6099. Offers curriculum and instruction (elementary) (M Ed); educational administration (M Ed); elementary education (MAT); secondary education (MAT). Part-time programs available. Postbaccalaureate distance learning degree programs offered (no on-campus study). *Degree requirements:* For master's, comprehensive exam, work samples/portfolio. *Entrance requirements:* For master's, California Basic Educational Skills Test or PRAXIS I, minimum undergraduate GPA of 2.8, graduate 3.0; 2 letters of recommendation. Additional exam requirements/recommendations for international students: Required—TOEFL (minimum score 525 paper-based; 195 computer-based). Electronic applications accepted. *Faculty research:* Learner centered classroom, brain-based learning future of on-line learning.

Concordia University, Graduate Programs, Ann Arbor, MI 48105-2797. Offers curriculum and instruction (MS); educational leadership (MS); organizational leadership and administration (MS). Part-time and evening/weekend programs available. *Faculty:* 3 full-time (2 women), 24 part-time/adjunct (10 women). *Students:* 179 full-time (117 women), 27 part-time (19 women). 84 applicants, 65% accepted, 43 enrolled. In 2009, 45 master's awarded. *Degree requirements:* For master's, thesis. *Entrance requirements:* Additional exam requirements/recommendations for international students: Required—TOEFL (minimum score 520 paper-based; 190 computer-based; 68 iBT); Recommended—IELTS, TWE. *Application deadline:* For fall admission, 9/1 priority date for domestic students, 8/1 priority date for international students; for winter admission, 1/5 priority date for domestic students, 12/1 priority date for international students; for spring admission, 5/12 priority date for domestic students, 4/1 priority date for international students. Applications are processed on a rolling basis. Application fee: $0 ($100 for international students). *Expenses:* Tuition: Full-time $7866; part-time $437 per credit hour. *Financial support:* Applicants required to submit FAFSA. *Unit head:* Dr. Dennis Genig, Vice President of Academics, 734-995-7383, Fax: 734-995-7448, E-mail: genigd@cuaa.edu. *Application contact:* Jean Christensen, Associate Director of Graduate Admission, 734-995-7521, Fax: 734-995-7530, E-mail: christj@cuaa.edu.

Concordia University, School of Education, Irvine, CA 92612-3299. Offers curriculum and instruction (MA); education and preliminary teaching credential (M Ed); educational administration and preliminary administrative services credential (MA). Part-time and evening/weekend programs available. Postbaccalaureate distance learning degree programs offered. *Faculty:* 18 full-time (9 women), 53 part-time/adjunct (25 women). *Students:* 569 full-time (439 women), 81 part-time (55 women); includes 160 minority (28 African Americans, 2 American Indian/Alaska Native, 38 Asian Americans or Pacific Islanders, 92 Hispanic Americans), 1 international. Average age 39. 263 applicants, 94% accepted, 203 enrolled. In 2009, 308 master's awarded. *Degree requirements:* For master's, action research project. *Entrance requirements:* For master's, California Basic Educational Skills Test, California Subject Examinations for Teachers, 2 references, copy of credential. Additional exam requirements/recommendations for international students: Required—TOEFL. *Application deadline:* For fall admission, 7/15 priority date for domestic students, 6/1 for international students; for spring admission, 11/30 priority date for domestic students, 10/1 for international students. Applications are processed on a rolling basis. Application fee: $50 ($125 for international students). Electronic applications accepted. *Expenses:* Contact institution. *Financial support:* In 2009–10, 478 students received support. Scholarships/grants available. Financial award applicants required to submit FAFSA. *Unit head:* Dr. Janice Nelson, Dean, 949-854-8002 Ext. 1249, E-mail: janice.nelson@cui.edu. *Application contact:* Narleen Narciso, Assistant Director of School of Education Admissions, 949-854-8002 Ext. 1132, Fax: 949-854-6894, E-mail: narleen.narciso@cui.edu.

Concordia University Chicago, College of Education, Program in Curriculum and Instruction, River Forest, IL 60305-1499. Offers MA. MA offered jointly with the Chicago Consortium of

Colleges and Universities. *Accreditation:* NCATE. Part-time and evening/weekend programs available. *Degree requirements:* For master's, comprehensive exam, thesis. *Entrance requirements:* For master's, minimum GPA of 2.9. Additional exam requirements/recommendations for international students: Required—TOEFL (minimum score 550 paper-based; 195 computer-based). Electronic applications accepted. *Faculty research:* School discipline, school improvement, leadership.

Concordia University, St. Paul, College of Education, St. Paul, MN 55104-5494. Offers curriculum and instruction (MA Ed), including K-12 reading endorsement; differentiated instruction (MA Ed); early childhood education (MA Ed); educational leadership (MA Ed); family life education (MA); K-12 reading endorsement (Certificate); special education (Certificate); sports management (MA). *Accreditation:* NCATE. Evening/weekend programs available. Post-baccalaureate distance learning degree programs offered (minimal on-campus study). *Faculty:* 12 full-time (8 women), 59 part-time/adjunct (47 women). *Students:* 697 full-time (571 women), 13 part-time (12 women); includes 64 minority (31 African Americans, 1 American Indian/Alaska Native, 21 Asian Americans or Pacific Islanders, 11 Hispanic Americans), 1 international. Average age 34. In 2009, 402 master's, 29 other advanced degrees awarded. *Application deadline:* Applications are processed on a rolling basis. Application fee: $50. Electronic applications accepted. *Financial support:* Applicants required to submit FAFSA. *Unit head:* Dr. Donald Helmstetter, Dean, 651-641-8227, Fax: 651-641-8807, E-mail: helmstetter@csp.edu. *Application contact:* Kimberly Craig, Director of Graduate and Cohort Admission, 651-603-6223, Fax: 651-603-6320, E-mail: craig@csp.edu.

Concordia University Wisconsin, Graduate Programs, Department of Education, Program in Curriculum and Instruction, Mequon, WI 53097-2402. Offers MS Ed. Postbaccalaureate distance learning degree programs offered (minimal on-campus study). *Degree requirements:* For master's, comprehensive exam, thesis or alternative. *Entrance requirements:* For master's, minimum GPA of 3.0, teaching license. Additional exam requirements/recommendations for international students: Required—TOEFL.

Converse College, School of Education and Graduate Studies, Education Specialist Program, Spartanburg, SC 29302-0006. Offers administration and supervision (Ed S); curriculum and instruction (Ed S); marriage and family therapy (Ed S). *Accreditation:* AAMFT/COAMFTE. Part-time programs available. *Entrance requirements:* For degree, GRE or MAT (marriage and family therapy), minimum GPA of 3.0. Electronic applications accepted.

Coppin State University, Division of Graduate Studies, Division of Education, Baltimore, MD 21216-3698. Offers adult and general education (MS); curriculum and instruction (M Ed, MAT, MS), including curriculum and instruction (M Ed), reading education (MS), teaching (MAT); special education (M Ed). *Accreditation:* NCATE. Part-time and evening/weekend programs available. Postbaccalaureate distance learning degree programs offered. *Degree requirements:* For master's, comprehensive exam (for some programs), thesis (for some programs).

Coppin State University, Division of Graduate Studies, Division of Education, Department of Curriculum and Instruction, Program in Curriculum and Instruction, Baltimore, MD 21216-3698. Offers M Ed. Part-time and evening/weekend programs available. Postbaccalaureate distance learning degree programs offered. *Degree requirements:* For master's, thesis. *Entrance requirements:* For master's, GRE or MAT, minimum GPA of 3.0, teacher certification.

Cornell University, Graduate School, Graduate Fields of Agriculture and Life Sciences, Field of Education, Ithaca, NY 14853-0001. Offers agricultural education (MAT); biology (7-12) (MAT); chemistry (7-12) (MAT); curriculum and instruction (MPS, MS, PhD); earth science (7-12) (MAT); extension, and adult education (MPS, MS, PhD); mathematics (7-12) (MAT); physics (7-12) (MAT). *Faculty:* 26 full-time (9 women). *Students:* 65 full-time (50 women); includes 15 minority (4 African Americans, 7 Asian Americans or Pacific Islanders, 4 Hispanic Americans), 2 international. Average age 34. 96 applicants, 33% accepted, 21 enrolled. In 2009, 27 master's, 2 doctorates awarded. Terminal master's awarded for partial completion of doctoral program. *Degree requirements:* For master's, thesis (MS); for doctorate, comprehensive exam, thesis/dissertation. *Entrance requirements:* For master's and doctorate, GRE General Test, sample of written work (recommended), 2 letters of recommendation. Additional exam requirements/recommendations for international students: Required—TOEFL (minimum score 550 paper-based; 213 computer-based; 77 iBT). *Application deadline:* For fall admission, 2/15 for domestic students. Application fee: $70. Electronic applications accepted. *Expenses:* Tuition: Full-time $29,500. Required fees: $70. Full-time tuition and fees vary according to degree level, program and student level. *Financial support:* In 2009–10, 33 students received support, including 3 fellowships with full tuition reimbursements available, 5 teaching assistantships with full tuition reimbursements available; research assistantships with full tuition reimbursements available, institutionally sponsored loans, scholarships/grants, health care benefits, tuition waivers (full and partial), and unspecified assistantships also available. Financial award applicants required to submit FAFSA. *Faculty research:* Moral development and professional ethics; public issues education and community development; socio/political issues in public education; teacher education and curriculum in agricultural science, and mathematics; extension research. *Unit head:* Director of Graduate Studies, 607-255-4278, Fax: 607-255-7905. *Application contact:* Graduate Field Assistant, 607-255-4278, Fax: 607-255-7905, E-mail: rh22@cornell.edu.

Dakota Wesleyan University, Program in Education, Mitchell, SD 57301-4398. Offers curriculum and instruction (MA Ed); education (MA); educational policy and administration (MA Ed); pre K-12 principal with certification (MA Ed); secondary with certification (MA Ed). Part-time and evening/weekend programs available. *Faculty:* 12 part-time/adjunct (7 women). *Students:* 31 part-time (15 women); includes 4 African Americans. Average age 30. 9 applicants, 100% accepted, 9 enrolled. In 2009, 14 master's awarded. *Degree requirements:* For master's, comprehensive exam, thesis optional, electronic portfolio. *Entrance requirements:* For master's, minimum GPA of 2.7, elementary statistics course. Additional exam requirements/recommendations for international students: Required—TOEFL (minimum score 500 paper-based; 71 computer-based), IELTS (minimum score 6.5). *Application deadline:* For fall admission, 8/1 priority date for domestic and international students; for winter admission, 12/1 priority date for domestic students; for spring admission, 4/1 priority date for domestic students, 12/1 priority date for international students. Applications are processed on a rolling basis. Application fee: $50. Electronic applications accepted. *Expenses:* Tuition: Full-time $5400; part-time $300 per credit hour. *Faculty research:* Math, political policy, technology in the classroom. *Unit head:* Dr. Ruth Haidle, Director of Graduate Studies, 605-995-2630, Fax: 605-995-2609, E-mail: ruhaidle@dwv.edu. *Application contact:* Coordinator of Graduate Admissions, 800-333-8506, Fax: 605-995-2699, E-mail: admissions@dwv.edu.

Dallas Baptist University, Dorothy M. Bush College of Education, Program in Curriculum and Instruction, Dallas, TX 75211-9299. Offers M Ed. Part-time and evening/weekend programs available. *Entrance requirements:* For master's, GRE General Test, minimum GPA of 3.0. Additional exam requirements/recommendations for international students: Required—TOEFL, IELTS. *Expenses:* Tuition: Full-time $10,674; part-time $593 per credit hour.

Delaware State University, Graduate Programs, College of Education, Program in Curriculum and Instruction, Dover, DE 19901-2277. Offers MA. Part-time and evening/weekend programs available. *Degree requirements:* For master's, comprehensive exam, thesis optional. *Entrance requirements:* For master's, GRE General Test, minimum GPA of 3.0 in major, 2.75 overall. Additional exam requirements/recommendations for international students: Required—TOEFL (minimum score 550 paper-based). Electronic applications accepted.

Delaware Valley College, Program in Educational Leadership, Doylestown, PA 18901-2697. Offers instruction, curriculum and technology (MS); school administration and leadership (MS). Part-time and evening/weekend programs available. *Faculty:* 30 part-time/adjunct (11 women). *Students:* 119 full-time (84 women), 46 part-time (29 women); includes 12 minority (9 African Americans, 3 Hispanic Americans). Average age 36. 56 applicants, 100% accepted, 56 enrolled. In 2009, 33 master's awarded. *Entrance requirements:* For master's, minimum undergraduate GPA of 3.0. *Application deadline:* Applications are processed on a rolling basis. Application fee: $50. *Expenses:* Tuition: Full-time $6336; part-time $528 per credit hour. Required fees: $72 per semester. One-time fee: $90. Tuition and fees vary according to program. *Financial support:* Applicants required to submit FAFSA. *Unit head:* Dr. Patricia Carney-Dalton, Director/Intern Supervisor, 215-489-4833, Fax: 215-489-4832, E-mail: patricia.carney@delval.edu. *Application contact:* Dr. Patricia Carney-Dalton, Director/Intern Supervisor, 215-489-4833, Fax: 215-489-4832, E-mail: patricia.carney@delval.edu.

DePaul University, School of Education, Chicago, IL 60106. Offers bilingual and bicultural education (M Ed, MA); curriculum studies (M Ed, MA, Ed D); educational leadership (M Ed, MA, Ed D), including administration and supervision (M Ed, MA), Catholic school leadership (M Ed, MA), physical education (M Ed, MA); human development and learning (MA); human services and counseling (M Ed, MA), including agencies, family concerns, and higher education, elementary schools, human services management, secondary schools; reading and learning disabilities (M Ed, MA); social culture studies in education and development (M Ed, MA), including curriculum studies/development; teaching and learning (early childhood, elementary and secondary) (M Ed), including elementary education (M Ed, MA), secondary education (M Ed, MA); teaching and learning (early childhood, elementary, and secondary) (MA), including elementary education (M Ed, MA), secondary education (M Ed, MA). *Accreditation:* NCATE. Part-time and evening/weekend programs available. *Faculty:* 61 full-time (40 women), 66 part-time/adjunct (41 women). *Students:* 799 full-time (779 women), 470 part-time (365 women); includes 319 minority (153 African Americans, 3 American Indian/Alaska Native, 48 Asian Americans or Pacific Islanders, 115 Hispanic Americans), 15 international. Average age 30. 635 applicants, 74% accepted, 318 enrolled. In 2009, 604 master's, 5 doctorates awarded. *Degree requirements:* For doctorate, thesis/dissertation. *Entrance requirements:* For master's, interview, minimum GPA of 2.75, 2 letters of recommendation; for doctorate, interview, master's degree, writing sample, 3 letters of recommendation. Additional exam requirements/recommendations for international students: Required—TOEFL (minimum score 550 paper-based; 213 computer-based; 80 iBT). *Application deadline:* Applications are processed on a rolling basis. Application fee: $40. Electronic applications accepted. *Expenses:* Tuition: Full-time $37,525; part-time $620 per credit hour. *Financial support:* In 2009–10, 14 research assistantships with tuition reimbursements (averaging $5,800 per year) were awarded; career-related internships or fieldwork also available. *Faculty research:* Reflective teaching, children at risk, loss, ethnicity, urban education. Total annual research expenditures: $1.6 million. *Unit head:* Dr. Marie Donovan, Dean, 773-325-7581, Fax: 773-325-7713, E-mail: mdonovan@depaul.edu. *Application contact:* Brandon Washington, Data Project Manager, 773-325-1152, Fax: 773-325-2270, E-mail: bwashin3@depaul.edu.

Doane College, Program in Education, Crete, NE 68333-2430. Offers curriculum and instruction (M Ed); educational leadership (M Ed). *Accreditation:* NCATE. Part-time and evening/weekend programs available. *Students:* 156 full-time (123 women), 495 part-time (383 women); includes 20 minority (7 African Americans, 1 American Indian/Alaska Native, 4 Asian Americans or Pacific Islanders, 8 Hispanic Americans). Average age 33. In 2009, 274 master's awarded. *Degree requirements:* For master's, thesis. *Entrance requirements:* For master's, minimum GPA of 2.5. *Application deadline:* Applications are processed on a rolling basis. Application fee: $25. Electronic applications accepted. *Expenses:* Contact institution. *Financial support:* Applicants required to submit FAFSA. *Unit head:* Lyn C. Forester, Dean, 402-826-8604, Fax: 402-826-8278. *Application contact:* Wilma Daddario, Assistant Dean, 402-464-1223, Fax: 402-466-4228, E-mail: wdaddario@doane.edu.

Dominican University, School of Education, River Forest, IL 60305-1099. Offers curriculum and instruction (MA Ed); early childhood education (MS); education (MAT); educational administration (MA); elementary (online) (MS); English as a second language (online) (MS); reading (online) (MS); special education (MS). Part-time and evening/weekend programs available. Postbaccalaureate distance learning degree programs offered. *Faculty:* 16 full-time (12 women), 59 part-time/adjunct (46 women). *Students:* 236 full-time (182 women), 622 part-time (509 women); includes 180 minority (54 African Americans, 3 American Indian/Alaska Native, 36 Asian Americans or Pacific Islanders, 87 Hispanic Americans), 2 international. Average age 32. In 2009, 199 master's awarded. *Entrance requirements:* For master's, Illinois certification test of basic skills. Additional exam requirements/recommendations for international students: Required—TOEFL (minimum score 550 paper-based; 213 computer-based; 79 iBT). *Application deadline:* Applications are processed on a rolling basis. Application fee: $25. *Expenses:* Contact institution. *Financial support:* Career-related internships or fieldwork, scholarships/grants, and tuition waivers (partial) available. Support available to part-time students. Financial award application deadline: 8/15; financial award applicants required to submit FAFSA. *Faculty research:* Governance of private education institutions, reading and language arts, inclusion, organizational planning, leadership and vision. *Unit head:* Dr. Colleen Reardon, Dean, 718-524-6643, Fax: 708-524-6665, E-mail: creardon@dom.edu. *Application contact:* Keven Hansen, Coordinator of Recruitment and Admissions, 708-524-6921, Fax: 708-524-6665, E-mail: educate@dom.edu.

Drexel University, School of Education, Program in Science of Instruction, Philadelphia, PA 19104-2875. Offers MS. Part-time and evening/weekend programs available. *Entrance requirements:* For master's, GRE, bachelor's degree in related field. Additional exam requirements/recommendations for international students: Required—TOEFL. Electronic applications accepted.

Drexel University, School of Education, Program in Teaching, Learning and Curriculum, Philadelphia, PA 19104-2875. Offers MS.

Duquesne University, School of Education, Department of Foundations and Leadership, Program in School Administration and Supervision, Pittsburgh, PA 15282-0001. Offers school administration (MS Ed, Post-Master's Certificate), including curriculum and instruction (Post-Master's Certificate), K-12 administration (MS Ed), secondary administration (MS Ed); school supervision (MS Ed). Part-time and evening/weekend programs available. *Faculty:* 3 full-time (1 woman), 3 part-time/adjunct (1 woman). *Students:* 41 full-time (26 women), 23 part-time (18 women); includes 1 minority (African American), 1 international. Average age 39. 72 applicants, 71% accepted, 29 enrolled. In 2009, 26 master's awarded. *Degree requirements:* For master's, thesis. *Entrance requirements:* For master's, MAT, minimum GPA of 3.0. Additional exam requirements/recommendations for international students: Required—TOEFL (minimum score 550 paper-based; 80 computer-based). *Application deadline:* For fall admission, 8/1 for domestic students; for spring admission, 12/1 for domestic students. Applications are processed on a rolling basis. Application fee: $0. Electronic applications accepted. *Expenses:* Tuition: Part-time $851 per credit. Required fees: $81 per credit. *Financial support:* Research assistantships available. Support available to part-time students. *Unit head:* Dr. Robert Furman, Director, 412-396-5274, Fax: 412-396-1274, E-mail: furman@duq.edu. *Application contact:* Michael Dolinger, Director of Student and Academic Services, 412-396-6647, Fax: 412-396-5585, E-mail: dolingerm@duq.edu.

East Carolina University, Graduate School, College of Education, Department of Curriculum and Instruction, Greenville, NC 27858-4353. Offers behavior/emotional disabilities (MA Ed); elementary education (MA Ed); English education (MA Ed); learning disabilities (MA Ed); low incidence disabilities (MA Ed); mental retardation (MA Ed); middle grade education (MA Ed); reading education (MA Ed); social studies education (MA Ed). Part-time programs available. Postbaccalaureate distance learning degree programs offered. *Degree requirements:* For master's, comprehensive exam, thesis optional. *Entrance requirements:* For master's, GRE General Test or MAT, interview, bachelor's degree in related field, minimum GPA of 2.5, teaching license. Additional exam requirements/recommendations for international students: Required—TOEFL.

Eastern Kentucky University, The Graduate School, College of Education, Department of Curriculum and Instruction, Richmond, KY 40475-3102. Offers elementary education (MA Ed), including early elementary education, reading; library science (MA Ed); music education (MA Ed); secondary and higher education (MA Ed), including secondary education; teaching (MAT). *Accreditation:* NCATE. Part-time programs available. *Degree requirements:* For master's, portfolio is part of exam. *Entrance requirements:* For master's, GRE General Test, PRAXIS II (KY), minimum GPA of 2.5. *Faculty research:* Technology in education, reading instruction, e-portfolios, induction to teacher education, dispositions of teachers.

Curriculum and Instruction

Eastern Michigan University, Graduate School, College of Education, Department of Teacher Education, Program in K–12 Education, Ypsilanti, MI 48197. Offers curriculum and instruction (MA); elementary education (MA); K-12 education (MA); middle school education (MA); secondary school education (MA). *Accreditation:* NCATE. Part-time and evening/weekend programs available. Postbaccalaureate distance learning degree programs offered (minimal on-campus study). *Students:* 18 full-time (10 women), 103 part-time (83 women); includes 20 minority (11 African Americans, 2 American Indian/Alaska Native, 3 Asian Americans or Pacific Islanders, 4 Hispanic Americans), 1 international. Average age 36. In 2009, 10 master's awarded. *Entrance requirements:* For master's, GRE. Additional exam requirements/ recommendations for international students: Required—TOEFL. *Application deadline:* Applications are processed on a rolling basis. Application fee: $35. Tuition and fees vary according to course level. *Financial support:* Fellowships, research assistantships with full tuition reimbursements, teaching assistantships with full tuition reimbursements, career-related internships or fieldwork, Federal Work-Study, institutionally sponsored loans, scholarships/grants, tuition waivers (partial), and unspecified assistantships available. Support available to part-time students. Financial award applicants required to submit FAFSA. *Unit head:* Dr. Wendy Burke, Coordinator, 734-487-3260, Fax: 734-487-2101, E-mail: wendy.burke@emich.edu. *Application contact:* Dr. Wendy Burke, Coordinator, 734-487-3260, Fax: 734-487-2101, E-mail: wendy.burke@emich.edu.

Eastern Washington University, Graduate Studies, College of Education and Human Development, Department of Education, Program in Curriculum Development, Cheney, WA 99004-2431. Offers M Ed. *Accreditation:* NCATE. *Degree requirements:* For master's, comprehensive exam. *Entrance requirements:* For master's, minimum GPA of 3.0. *Expenses:* Tuition, state resident: full-time $7476; part-time $249 per quarter hour. Tuition, nonresident: full-time $18,030; part-time $601 per quarter hour. Required fees: $3.50 per quarter hour. $142 per quarter.

East Tennessee State University, School of Graduate Studies, College of Education, Department of Curriculum and Instruction, Johnson City, TN 37614. Offers 7-12 (MAT); classroom technology (M Ed); educational communication (M Ed); educational media/educational technology (M Ed); elementary education (M Ed, MAT); K-12 (MAT); reading and storytelling (M Ed, MA); reading education (M Ed, MA); school library media (M Ed); secondary education (M Ed, MAT). *Accreditation:* NCATE. Part-time and evening/weekend programs available. *Degree requirements:* For master's, thesis (for some programs). *Entrance requirements:* For master's, GRE, minimum GPA of 3.0. Additional exam requirements/recommendations for international students: Required—TOEFL (minimum score 550 paper-based; 213 computer-based). *Faculty research:* Critical thinking, curriculum development, cultural diversity, cognitive processes, effective teaching strategies.

Emporia State University, School of Graduate Studies, The Teachers College, Department of School Leadership/Middle and Secondary Teacher Education, Program in Curriculum and Instruction, Emporia, KS 66801-5087. Offers curriculum leadership (MS); effective practitioner (MS); national board certification (MS). *Accreditation:* NCATE. Part-time programs available. *Students:* 1 (woman) full-time, 134 part-time (116 women); includes 5 minority (1 African American, 4 Hispanic Americans). 33 applicants, 97% accepted, 30 enrolled. In 2009, 60 master's awarded. *Degree requirements:* For master's, comprehensive exam or thesis, practicum. *Entrance requirements:* For master's, GRE or MAT, appropriate bachelor's degree, teacher certification, 1 year of teaching experience, letters of recommendation. *Application deadline:* For fall admission, 8/15 priority date for domestic students. Applications are processed on a rolling basis. Application fee: $30 ($75 for international students). Electronic applications accepted. *Expenses:* Tuition, state resident: full-time $4154; part-time $173 per credit hour. Tuition, nonresident: full-time $12,864; part-time $536 per credit hour. Required fees: $948; $58 per credit hour. Tuition and fees vary according to campus/location. *Financial support:* Career-related internships or fieldwork, Federal Work-Study, institutionally sponsored loans, health care benefits, and unspecified assistantships available. Financial award application deadline: 3/15; financial award applicants required to submit FAFSA. *Unit head:* Dr. Jerry Will, Chair, 620-341-5777, E-mail: jwill@emporia.edu. *Application contact:* Mary Sewell, Admissions Coordinator, 800-950-GRAD, Fax: 620-341-5909, E-mail: msewell@emporia.edu.

Fairleigh Dickinson University, Metropolitan Campus, University College: Arts, Sciences, and Professional Studies, Peter Sammartino School of Education, Program in Teaching, Teaneck, NJ 07666-1914. Offers MAT. *Students:* 36 full-time (32 women), 110 part-time (89 women). Average age 33. 86 applicants, 87% accepted, 64 enrolled. In 2009, 76 master's awarded. *Application deadline:* Applications are processed on a rolling basis. Application fee: $40. *Application contact:* Susan Brooman, University Director of Graduate Admissions, 201-692-2554, Fax: 201-692-2560, E-mail: globaleducation@fdu.edu.

Ferris State University, College of Education and Human Services, School of Education, Big Rapids, MI 49307. Offers administration (MSCTE); curriculum and instruction (M Ed), including administration, elementary education, experiential education, philanthropic education, reading, secondary education, special education, subject matter option; education technology (MSCTE); instructor (MSCTE); post-secondary administration (MSCTE); training and development (MSCTE). Part-time and evening/weekend programs available. Postbaccalaureate distance learning degree programs offered. *Faculty:* 12 full-time (8 women), 11 part-time/adjunct (5 women). *Students:* 19 full-time (13 women), 185 part-time (122 women); includes 24 minority (20 African Americans, 1 Asian American or Pacific Islander, 3 Hispanic Americans), 1 international. Average age 36. 37 applicants, 32% accepted, 11 enrolled. In 2009, 73 master's awarded. *Degree requirements:* For master's, thesis, research paper. *Entrance requirements:* For master's, 2 years of work experience for vocational setting, minimum GPA of 2.75. Additional exam requirements/recommendations for international students: Recommended—TOEFL (minimum score 500 paper-based; 173 computer-based; 61 iBT). *Application deadline:* For fall admission, 7/1 priority date for domestic students; for spring admission, 11/1 priority date for domestic students. Applications are processed on a rolling basis. Application fee: $30. *Financial support:* Career-related internships or fieldwork and scholarships/grants available. Support available to part-time students. Financial award applicants required to submit FAFSA. *Faculty research:* Suicide prevention, reading, women in education, special needs, administration. *Unit head:* Dr. Liza Ing, Director, 231-591-5362, Fax: 231-591-2041. *Application contact:* Kimisue Worrall, Secretary, 231-591-5361, Fax: 231-591-2043.

Fitchburg State University, Division of Graduate and Continuing Education, Program in Curriculum and Teaching, Fitchburg, MA 01420-2697. Offers M Ed. Part-time and evening/weekend programs available. *Students:* 98 full-time (73 women), 156 part-time (122 women); includes 10 minority (3 African Americans, 3 Asian Americans or Pacific Islanders, 4 Hispanic Americans), 1 international. Average age 35. 111 applicants, 100% accepted, 103 enrolled. In 2009, 202 master's awarded. *Entrance requirements:* For master's, GRE General Test or MAT, letters of recommendation, resume. Additional exam requirements/recommendations for international students: Required—TOEFL (minimum score 550 paper-based; 213 computer-based; 79 iBT). *Application deadline:* Applications are processed on a rolling basis. Application fee: $25 ($50 for international students). *Expenses:* Tuition, area resident: Part-time $150 per credit. Tuition, state resident: part-time $150 per credit. Tuition, nonresident: part-time $150 per credit. Required fees: $120 per credit. *Financial support:* In 2009–10, research assistantships with partial tuition reimbursements (averaging $5,500 per year); Federal Work-Study, scholarships/grants, and unspecified assistantships also available. Support available to part-time students. Financial award application deadline: 3/1; financial award applicants required to submit FAFSA. *Unit head:* Dr. Patricia Smith, Chair, 978-665-3448, Fax: 978-665-3658, E-mail: gce@fsc.edu. *Application contact:* Director of Admissions, 978-665-3144, Fax: 978-665-4540, E-mail: admissions@fsc.edu.

Florida Atlantic University, College of Education, Department of Curriculum, Culture, and Educational Inquiry, Boca Raton, FL 33431-0991. Offers curriculum and instruction (Ed D, Ed S); early childhood education (M Ed); multicultural education (M Ed); teaching English to speakers of other languages (TESOL) (M Ed). *Faculty:* 11 full-time (8 women), 17 part-time/adjunct (13 women). *Students:* 38 full-time (26 women), 124 part-time (105 women); includes 40 minority (23 African Americans, 3 Asian Americans or Pacific Islanders, 14 Hispanic Americans), 4 international. Average age 36. 84 applicants, 56% accepted, 34 enrolled. In 2009, 39 master's, 5 doctorates awarded. *Application deadline:* For fall admission, 7/1 for domestic students, 2/15 for international students; for spring admission, 11/1 for domestic students, 7/15 for international students. *Expenses:* Tuition, state resident: full-time $7055; part-time $293.94 per credit hour. Tuition, nonresident: full-time $22,096; part-time $920.66 per credit hour. *Faculty research:* Multicultural education, early intervention strategies, family literacy, religious diversity in schools, early childhood curriculum. *Unit head:* Dr. James McLaughlin, Interim Chair, 561-297-3965, E-mail: jmclau17@fau.edu. *Application contact:* Dr. Eliah Watlington, Associate Dean, 561-296-8520, Fax: 261-297-2991, E-mail: ewatling@fau.edu.

Florida Atlantic University, College of Education, Department of Teaching and Learning, Boca Raton, FL 33431-0991. Offers curriculum and instruction (M Ed); elementary education (M Ed); environmental education (M Ed); reading education (M Ed); social foundations of education (M Ed). *Accreditation:* NCATE. Part-time and evening/weekend programs available. *Faculty:* 35 full-time (29 women), 92 part-time/adjunct (61 women). *Students:* 56 full-time (50 women), 134 part-time (128 women); includes 36 minority (15 African Americans, 4 Asian Americans or Pacific Islanders, 17 Hispanic Americans), 2 international. Average age 32. 162 applicants, 74% accepted, 66 enrolled. In 2009, 52 master's awarded. *Entrance requirements:* For master's, GRE General Test, minimum GPA of 3.0 in last 2 years of undergraduate course work. Additional exam requirements/recommendations for international students: Required—TOEFL. *Application deadline:* For fall admission, 7/1 for domestic students, 2/15 for international students; for spring admission, 11/1 for domestic students, 7/15 for international students. Applications are processed on a rolling basis. Application fee: $30. *Expenses:* Tuition, state resident: full-time $7055; part-time $293.94 per credit hour. Tuition, nonresident: full-time $22,096; part-time $920.66 per credit hour. *Financial support:* Fellowships with partial tuition reimbursements, research assistantships with partial tuition reimbursements, teaching assistantships with partial tuition reimbursements, career-related internships or fieldwork, scholarships/grants, and unspecified assistantships available. *Faculty research:* Technology, teaching English to speakers of other languages, math teaching, electronic portfolio assessment, global perspectives through social studies. *Unit head:* Dr. Barbara Ridener, Chairperson, 561-297-3588. *Application contact:* Dr. Barbara Ridener, Chairperson, 561-297-3588.

Florida Gulf Coast University, College of Education, Program in Curriculum and Instruction, Fort Myers, FL 33965-6565. Offers educational technology (M Ed, MA); English education (M Ed). Part-time and evening/weekend programs available. Postbaccalaureate distance learning degree programs offered (minimal on-campus study). *Faculty:* 31 full-time (23 women), 41 part-time/adjunct (29 women). *Students:* 54 full-time (42 women), 4 part-time (3 women); includes 7 minority (1 African American, 1 Asian American or Pacific Islander, 5 Hispanic Americans). Average age 35. 20 applicants, 70% accepted, 0 enrolled. In 2009, 8 master's awarded. *Degree requirements:* For master's, final project or portfolio. *Entrance requirements:* For master's, GRE General Test, MAT, minimum undergraduate GPA of 3.0 in last 2 years. Additional exam requirements/recommendations for international students: Required—TOEFL (minimum score 550 paper-based; 213 computer-based). *Application deadline:* For fall admission, 7/1 priority date for domestic students; for spring admission, 10/15 for domestic students. Applications are processed on a rolling basis. Application fee: $30. Electronic applications accepted. *Faculty research:* Internet in schools, technology in pre-service and in-service teacher training. *Unit head:* Dr. Pat Wachholz, Associate Dean, 239-590-7808, Fax: 239-590-7801, E-mail: wachhol@fgcu.edu. *Application contact:* Dr. Pat Wachholz, Associate Dean, 239-590-7808, Fax: 239-590-7801, E-mail: wachhol@fgcu.edu.

Florida Gulf Coast University, College of Education, Program in Elementary Education, Fort Myers, FL 33965-6565. Offers early childhood education (M Ed); elementary curriculum (M Ed); elementary education (MA). Part-time and evening/weekend programs available. Postbaccalaureate distance learning degree programs offered (minimal on-campus study). *Faculty:* 31 full-time (24 women), 39 part-time/adjunct (28 women). *Students:* 7 full-time (6 women), 1 (woman) part-time. Average age 40. 8 applicants, 25% accepted, 1 enrolled. In 2009, 4 master's awarded. *Degree requirements:* For master's, comprehensive exam, thesis or alternative, final project. *Entrance requirements:* For master's, GRE General Test, MAT, minimum GPA of 3.0. Additional exam requirements/recommendations for international students: Required—TOEFL (minimum score 550 paper-based; 213 computer-based). *Application deadline:* For fall admission, 7/1 priority date for domestic students; for spring admission, 10/15 for domestic students. Applications are processed on a rolling basis. Application fee: $30. Electronic applications accepted. *Faculty research:* Language acquisition, impact of literature on reading, action research in the classroom. *Unit head:* Dr. Patricia Wachholz, Head, 239-590-7808, Fax: 239-590-7801, E-mail: pwachhol@fgcu.edu. *Application contact:* Dr. Patricia Wachholz, Head, 239-590-7808, Fax: 239-590-7801, E-mail: pwachhol@fgcu.edu.

Florida International University, College of Education, Department of Curriculum and Instruction, Miami, FL 33199. Offers art education (MAT, MS, Ed D); curriculum and instruction (Ed S); curriculum development (MS); curriculum studies (PhD); early childhood education (MS, Ed D); elementary education (MS, Ed D); English education (MAT, MS, Ed D); foreign language education—teaching English to speakers of other languages (TESOL) (Certificate), including foreign language education; foreign language education- teaching English to speakers of other languages (TESOL) (MS), including teaching English; French education—initial teacher preparation (MAT); international and intercultural development education (Ed D); international and intercultural developmental education (MS); language, literacy and culture (PhD); learning technologies (MS, Ed D, PhD); mathematics education (MAT, MS, Ed D, PhD); modern language education/bilingual education (MS, Ed D); physical education (MS); reading education (MS, Ed D); science education (MAT, MS, Ed D, PhD); social studies education (MAT, MS, Ed D); Spanish education—initial teacher preparation (MAT); special education (MS). Part-time and evening/weekend programs available. *Degree requirements:* For doctorate, comprehensive exam, thesis/dissertation. *Entrance requirements:* For master's, GRE General Test, Florida General Knowledge Test or Florida College Level Academic Skills Test; for doctorate and other advanced degree, GRE General Test. Additional exam requirements/recommendations for international students: Required—TOEFL (minimum score 550 paper-based; 213 computer-based; 80 iBT), IELTS (minimum score 6.3). Electronic applications accepted. *Expenses:* Tuition, state resident: full-time $8008; part-time $4004 per year. Tuition, nonresident: full-time $20,104; part-time $10,052 per year. Required fees: $298; $149 per term.

Fordham University, Graduate School of Education, Division of Curriculum and Teaching, New York, NY 10023. Offers adult education (MS, MSE); bilingual teacher education (MSE); curriculum and teaching (MSE); early childhood education (MSE); elementary education (MST); language, literacy, and learning (PhD); reading education (MSE, Adv C); secondary education (MAT, MSE); special education (MSE, Adv C); teaching English as a second language (MSE). *Accreditation:* NCATE. *Degree requirements:* For doctorate, thesis/dissertation; for Adv C, thesis. *Entrance requirements:* For doctorate, MAT, GRE General Test.

Framingham State University, Division of Graduate and Continuing Education, Program in Curriculum and Instructional Technology, Framingham, MA 01701-9101. Offers M Ed. Postbaccalaureate distance learning degree programs offered.

Franciscan University of Steubenville, Graduate Programs, Department of Education, Steubenville, OH 43952-1763. Offers administration (MS Ed); teaching (MS Ed). Part-time and evening/weekend programs available. *Degree requirements:* For master's, project. *Entrance requirements:* For master's, minimum undergraduate GPA of 2.5 or written exam. *Expenses:* Contact institution.

Freed-Hardeman University, Program in Education, Henderson, TN 38340-2399. Offers curriculum and instruction (M Ed); school counseling (M Ed), including administration and supervision, special education; school leadership (Ed S). *Accreditation:* NCATE. Part-time and evening/weekend programs available. *Degree requirements:* For master's, comprehensive exam, thesis optional; for Ed S, thesis. *Entrance requirements:* For master's, GRE General Test or NTE; for Ed S, 3 years of teaching experience. Additional exam requirements/

recommendations for international students: Required—TOEFL (minimum score 500 paper-based; 173 computer-based).

Fresno Pacific University, Graduate Programs, School of Education, Fresno, CA 93702-4709. Offers administration (MA Ed), including administrative services; foundations, curriculum and teaching (MA Ed), including curriculum and teaching, school library and information technology; language, literacy, and culture (MA Ed), including bilingual/cross-cultural education, language development, multilingual contexts, reading; mathematics/science/computer education (MA Ed), including educational technology, integrated mathematics/science education, mathematics education; pupil personnel services (MA Ed), including school counseling, school psychology; special education (MA Ed), including mild/moderate, moderate/severe, physical and health impairments. Part-time and evening/weekend programs available. *Degree requirements:* For master's, thesis (for some programs). *Entrance requirements:* For master's, interview; GMAT, GRE, MAT, or 6 units of course work with a faculty recommendation. Additional exam requirements/recommendations for international students: Required—TOEFL (minimum score 550 paper-based; 213 computer-based). Electronic applications accepted.

Fresno Pacific University, Graduate Programs, School of Education, Division of Foundations, Curriculum and Teaching, Program in Curriculum and Teaching, Fresno, CA 93702-4709. Offers MA Ed. Part-time and evening/weekend programs available. Postbaccalaureate distance learning degree programs offered. *Degree requirements:* For master's, thesis or alternative. *Entrance requirements:* Additional exam requirements/recommendations for international students: Required—TOEFL (minimum score 550 paper-based; 213 computer-based). Electronic applications accepted.

Frostburg State University, Graduate School, College of Education, Department of Educational Professions, Program in Curriculum and Instruction, Frostburg, MD 21532-1099. Offers educational technology (M Ed); elementary education (M Ed); secondary education (M Ed). Part-time and evening/weekend programs available. *Faculty:* 2. *Students:* 5 full-time (all women), 42 part-time (36 women); includes 1 minority (Hispanic American). Average age 32. 20 applicants, 75% accepted, 13 enrolled. In 2009, 8 master's awarded. *Degree requirements:* For master's, thesis or alternative. *Entrance requirements:* For master's, teaching certificate. Additional exam requirements/recommendations for international students: Required—TOEFL. *Application deadline:* For fall admission, 7/15 priority date for domestic students. Applications are processed on a rolling basis. Application fee: $30. Electronic applications accepted. *Expenses:* Tuition, state resident: full-time $5706; part-time $317 per credit hour. Tuition, nonresident: full-time $6948; part-time $386 per credit hour. Required fees: $1476; $82 per credit hour. $11 per term. One-time fee: $30 full-time. *Financial support:* In 2009–10, 2 research assistantships with full tuition reimbursements (averaging $5,000 per year) were awarded. Financial award application deadline: 4/1; financial award applicants required to submit FAFSA. *Unit head:* Dr. Doris Santamaria-Makang, Coordinator, 301-687-7018, E-mail: dsantamaria@frostburg.edu. *Application contact:* Vickie Mazer, Director, Graduate Services, 301-687-7053, Fax: 301-687-4597, E-mail: vmmazer@frostburg.edu.

Furman University, Graduate Division, Department of Education, Greenville, SC 29613. Offers curriculum and instruction (MA); early childhood education (MA); English as a second language (MA); literacy (MA); school leadership (MA); special education (MA). *Accreditation:* NCATE. Part-time programs available. Postbaccalaureate distance learning degree programs offered (minimal on-campus study). *Faculty:* 14 full-time (8 women), 10 part-time/adjunct (6 women). *Students:* 114 part-time (93 women); includes 13 minority (10 African Americans, 3 Asian Americans or Pacific Islanders). Average age 29. 24 applicants, 100% accepted, 23 enrolled. In 2009, 71 master's awarded. *Degree requirements:* For master's, comprehensive exam (for some programs), thesis or alternative. *Entrance requirements:* For master's, PRAXIS II. *Application deadline:* For fall admission, 8/1 priority date for domestic students, 7/15 priority date for international students; for spring admission, 12/1 priority date for domestic and international students. Applications are processed on a rolling basis. Application fee: $50. *Financial support:* In 2009–10, 43 students received support; fellowships, scholarships/grants available. Financial award application deadline: 5/15; financial award applicants required to submit FAFSA. *Faculty research:* Literacy, pedagogy and practice, social justice, advanced leadership, achievement in high poverty schools. *Unit head:* Dr. Nelly Hecker, Head, 864-294-3385. *Application contact:* Helen Reynolds, Department Assistant, 864-294-2213, Fax: 864-294-3579, E-mail: helen.reynolds@furman.edu.

Gannon University, School of Graduate Studies, College of Humanities, Education, and Social Sciences, School of Education, Program in Curriculum and Instruction, Erie, PA 16541-0001. Offers M Ed. Part-time and evening/weekend programs available. Postbaccalaureate distance learning degree programs offered (no on-campus study). *Students:* 20 full-time (17 women), 340 part-time (256 women); includes 8 minority (7 African Americans, 1 Asian American or Pacific Islander). Average age 30. 83 applicants, 84% accepted, 35 enrolled. In 2009, 258 master's awarded. *Degree requirements:* For master's, thesis or alternative, portfolio project. *Entrance requirements:* For master's, bachelor's degree, minimum QPA of 3.0. Additional exam requirements/recommendations for international students: Required—TOEFL (minimum score 79 iBT). *Application deadline:* Applications are processed on a rolling basis. Application fee: $25. Electronic applications accepted. *Expenses:* Contact institution. *Financial support:* Scholarships/grants available. Financial award application deadline: 7/1; financial award applicants required to submit FAFSA. *Unit head:* Dr. Francis S. Grandinetti, Director, 814-871-7533, E-mail: grandine002@gannon.edu. *Application contact:* Kara Morgan, Assistant Director of Graduate Admissions, 814-871-5831, Fax: 814-871-5827, E-mail: graduate@gannon.edu.

Gardner-Webb University, Graduate School, School of Education, Program in Curriculum and Instruction, Boiling Springs, NC 28017. Offers Ed D. *Faculty:* 9 full-time (3 women). *Students:* 55 part-time (46 women); includes 14 minority (13 African Americans, 1 Hispanic American). Average age 38. *Expenses:* Tuition: Part-time $305 per credit hour. *Unit head:* Dr. Carroll Smith, Chair, 704-406-3913, Fax: 704-406-3921, E-mail: dsimmons@gardner-webb.edu. *Application contact:* Dr. Frank Burch, Dean, Graduate School, 704-406-4422, Fax: 704-406-4329, E-mail: gradschool@gardner-webb.edu.

George Fox University, School of Education, Educational Foundations and Leadership Program, Newberg, OR 97132-2697. Offers continuing administrator license (Certificate); curriculum and instruction (M Ed); educational leadership (M Ed, Ed D); higher education (M Ed); initial administrator license (Certificate); library media (M Ed, Certificate); literacy (M Ed); reading (M Ed); secondary education (M Ed). *Accreditation:* NCATE. Part-time and evening/weekend programs available. Postbaccalaureate distance learning degree programs offered (minimal on-campus study). *Faculty:* 10 full-time (3 women), 7 part-time/adjunct (3 women). *Students:* 1 (woman) full-time, 151 part-time (101 women); includes 15 minority (1 African American, 4 American Indian/Alaska Native, 4 Asian Americans or Pacific Islanders, 6 Hispanic Americans), 1 international. Average age 40. 44 applicants, 75% accepted, 26 enrolled. In 2009, 44 master's, 27 doctorates, 82 Certificates awarded. *Degree requirements:* For master's, thesis (for some programs); for doctorate, comprehensive exam, thesis/dissertation, project. *Entrance requirements:* For master's, minimum undergraduate GPA of 3.0 during previous 2 years of course work, resume, 3 professional recommendations on university forms, copy of teaching license (if applicable); for doctorate, GRE or MAT, master's degree with minimum GPA of 3.25, 3 years of relevant professional experience, interview, personal essay, scholarly work, 3 professional recommendations on university forms along with 3 written letters of recommendation, official transcripts. Additional exam requirements/recommendations for international students: Required—TOEFL (minimum score 577 paper-based; 233 computer-based; 90 iBT). *Application deadline:* For fall admission, 7/15 for domestic and international students; for winter admission, 11/1 for domestic and international students; for spring admission, 4/1 for domestic and international students. Applications are processed on a rolling basis. Application fee: $40. Electronic applications accepted. *Expenses:* Contact institution. *Financial support:* Career-related internships or fieldwork available. Financial award applicants required to submit FAFSA. *Unit head:* Dr. Scott Headley, Chair, 503-554-2836, E-mail: sheadley@georgefox.edu. *Application contact:* Kristie DeHaven, Admissions Counselor, 800-631-0921, Fax: 503-554-3110, E-mail: edfl@georgefox.edu.

George Mason University, College of Education and Human Development, Programs in Curriculum and Instruction, Fairfax, VA 22030. Offers curriculum and instruction (M Ed); special education (M Ed). Part-time and evening/weekend programs available. *Faculty:* 88 full-time (64 women), 120 part-time/adjunct (93 women). *Students:* 190 full-time (150 women), 836 part-time (694 women); includes 100 minority (25 African Americans, 1 American Indian/Alaska Native, 29 Asian Americans or Pacific Islanders, 45 Hispanic Americans), 50 international. Average age 31. 627 applicants, 76% accepted, 389 enrolled. In 2009, 383 master's awarded. *Degree requirements:* For master's, comprehensive exam, thesis (for some programs). *Entrance requirements:* For master's, PRAXIS I, PRAXIS II, Virginia Communication and Literacy Assessment Test (VCLA), minimum GPA of 3.0 in last 60 hours, licensed as teacher or educational administrator, 3 recommendation letters, interview. Additional exam requirements/recommendations for international students: Required—TOEFL. *Application deadline:* For fall admission, 5/1 for domestic students; for spring admission, 11/1 for domestic students. Applications are processed on a rolling basis. Application fee: $75. Electronic applications accepted. *Expenses:* Tuition, state resident: full-time $7568; part-time $315.33 per credit hour. Tuition, nonresident: full-time $21,704; part-time $904.33 per credit hour. Required fees: $2184; $91 per credit hour. *Financial support:* In 2009–10, 4 students received support, including 3 research assistantships with full and partial tuition reimbursements available (averaging $8,940 per year), 1 teaching assistantship with full and partial tuition reimbursement available (averaging $2,080 per year); Federal Work-Study, scholarships/grants, unspecified assistantships, and health care benefits (full-time research or teaching assistantship recipients) also available. Support available to part-time students. Financial award application deadline: 3/1; financial award applicants required to submit FAFSA. *Unit head:* Martin E. Ford, Acting Dean, College of Education and Human Development, 703-993-2004, E-mail: mford@gmu.edu. *Application contact:* Information Contact.

The George Washington University, Graduate School of Education and Human Development, Department of Teacher Preparation and Special Education, Program in Curriculum and Instruction, Washington, DC 20052. Offers MA Ed, Ed D, Ed S. *Accreditation:* NCATE. Evening/weekend programs available. *Students:* 15 full-time (13 women), 38 part-time (28 women); includes 8 minority (6 African Americans, 1 Asian American or Pacific Islander, 1 Hispanic American), 3 international. Average age 35. 41 applicants, 93% accepted, 16 enrolled. In 2009, 25 master's, 5 doctorates, 5 other advanced degrees awarded. *Degree requirements:* For master's and Ed S, comprehensive exam; for doctorate, comprehensive exam, thesis/dissertation. *Entrance requirements:* For master's, GRE General Test or MAT, minimum GPA of 2.75, resume; for doctorate and Ed S, GRE General Test or MAT, interview, minimum GPA of 3.3. *Application deadline:* For fall admission, 1/15 priority date for domestic students; for spring admission, 10/1 for domestic students. Applications are processed on a rolling basis. Application fee: $60. *Financial support:* In 2009–10, 25 students received support; fellowships, research assistantships, career-related internships or fieldwork, Federal Work-Study, and tuition waivers (partial) available. Financial award application deadline: 1/15; financial award applicants required to submit FAFSA. *Faculty research:* Cognitive skills-teaching, metacognitive strategies, adult basic literacy. *Unit head:* Dr. Sharon Lynch, Faculty Coordinator, 202-994-6174, E-mail: slynch@gwu.edu. *Application contact:* Sarah Lang, Director of Graduate Admissions, 202-994-1447, Fax: 202-994-7207, E-mail: slang@gwu.edu.

Georgia College & State University, Graduate School, The John H. Lounsbury College of Education, Department of Foundations and Secondary Education, Milledgeville, GA 31061. Offers curriculum and instruction (Ed S), including secondary education; instructional technology (M Ed); secondary education (M Ed, MAT). *Accreditation:* NCATE. Part-time and evening/weekend programs available. *Faculty:* 13 full-time (7 women). *Students:* 127 full-time (81 women), 99 part-time (83 women); includes 39 minority (34 African Americans, 5 Hispanic Americans). Average age 32. In 2009, 104 master's awarded. *Degree requirements:* For master's and Ed S, comprehensive exam. *Entrance requirements:* For master's, on-site writing assessment, 2 letters of recommendation, level 4 teaching certificate; for Ed S, on-site writing assessment, master's degree, 2 letters of recommendation, 2 years of teaching experience, level 5 teacher certification. Additional exam requirements/recommendations for international students: Recommended—TOEFL (minimum score 550 paper-based; 213 computer-based; 79 iBT). *Application deadline:* Applications are processed on a rolling basis. Application fee: $40. Electronic applications accepted. *Expenses:* Tuition, area resident: Part-time $241 per credit hour. Tuition, state resident: full-time $4338. Tuition, nonresident: full-time $17,352; part-time $964 per credit hour. Required fees: $609 per semester. Tuition and fees vary according to course load and campus/location. *Financial support:* In 2009–10, 12 research assistantships with full tuition reimbursements were awarded; career-related internships or fieldwork and Federal Work-Study also available. Support available to part-time students. Financial award applicants required to submit FAFSA. *Unit head:* Dr. Jane Hinson, Chair, 478-445-7368, Fax: 478-445-2513, E-mail: jane.hinson@gcsu.edu. *Application contact:* Shanda Brand, Graduate Advisor, 478-445-1383, E-mail: shanda.brand@gcsu.edu.

Georgia Southern University, Jack N. Averitt College of Graduate Studies, College of Education, Department of Curriculum, Foundations, and Reading, Program in Curriculum Studies, Statesboro, GA 30460. Offers Ed D. Part-time programs available. *Students:* 23 full-time (18 women), 209 part-time (173 women); includes 61 minority (50 African Americans, 2 American Indian/Alaska Native, 4 Asian Americans or Pacific Islanders, 5 Hispanic Americans). Average age 42. In 2009, 24 doctorates awarded. *Degree requirements:* For doctorate, thesis/dissertation, exams. *Entrance requirements:* For doctorate, GRE or MAT, letters of reference, minimum GPA of 3.5, writing sample. Additional exam requirements/recommendations for international students: Required—TOEFL (minimum score 550 paper-based; 213 computer-based; 80 iBT). Application fee: $50. Electronic applications accepted. *Expenses:* Tuition, state resident: full-time $5040; part-time $210 per credit hour. Tuition, nonresident: full-time $20,136; part-time $839 per credit hour. Required fees: $1644. *Financial support:* In 2009–10, 88 students received support, including research assistantships with partial tuition reimbursements available (averaging $9,500 per year), teaching assistantships with partial tuition reimbursements available (averaging $9,500 per year); career-related internships or fieldwork, Federal Work-Study, scholarships/grants, and unspecified assistantships also available. Support available to part-time students. Financial award application deadline: 4/15; financial award applicants required to submit FAFSA. *Unit head:* Dr. Grigory Dmitriyer, Coordinator, 912-478-5545, E-mail: gregodmi@georgiasouthern.edu. *Application contact:* Dr. Charles Ziglar, Coordinator for Graduate Student Recruitment, 912-478-5635, Fax: 912-478-0740, E-mail: gradadmissions@georgiasouthern.edu.

Grambling State University, School of Graduate Studies and Research, College of Education, Department of Educational Leadership, Grambling, LA 71245. Offers curriculum and instruction (Ed D); developmental education (MS, Ed D), including curriculum and instruction: reading (Ed D), English (MS), guidance and counseling (MS), higher education administration (Ed D), instructional systems and technology (Ed D), mathematics (MS), reading (MS), science (MS), student development and personnel services (Ed D); educational leadership (MS, Ed D). Part-time and evening/weekend programs available. *Faculty:* 19 full-time (12 women). *Students:* 23 full-time (18 women), 84 part-time (62 women); includes 81 minority (80 African Americans, 1 Asian American or Pacific Islander), 5 international. Average age 39. 72 applicants, 75% accepted, 39 enrolled. In 2009, 5 master's, 9 doctorates awarded. *Degree requirements:* For master's, comprehensive exam, thesis (for some programs); for doctorate, comprehensive exam, thesis/dissertation. *Entrance requirements:* For master's, GRE, minimum GPA of 2.5 on last degree; for doctorate, GRE (minimum 1000, 500 on Verbal), master's degree, minimum GPA of 3.0 on last degree. Additional exam requirements/recommendations for international students: Required—TOEFL (minimum score 500 paper-based; 173 computer-based; 61 iBT). *Application deadline:* For fall admission, 7/1 for domestic and international students; for spring admission, 12/1 for domestic and international students. Applications are processed on a rolling basis. Application fee: $20 ($30 for international students). Electronic applications accepted. *Expenses:* Tuition, state resident: full-time $2610. Tuition, nonresident: full-time $2610. *Financial support:* In 2009–10, 5 research assistantships (averaging $10,948 per year) were awarded; health care benefits, tuition waivers (full), and unspecified assistantships also available. Financial award application deadline: 5/31; financial award applicants required to

Curriculum and Instruction

Grambling State University (continued)
submit FAFSA. *Unit head:* Dr. Olatunde Ogunyemi, Director, 318-274-6105, Fax: 318-274-2799, E-mail: ogunyemio@gram.edu. *Application contact:* Laketha Richards, Administrative Assistant III, 318-274-6105, Fax: 318-274-6249, E-mail: richardsl@gram.edu.

Grand Canyon University, College of Education, Phoenix, AZ 85017-1097. Offers curriculum and instruction (M Ed); education administration (M Ed); elementary education (M Ed); organizational leadership (Ed D); secondary education (M Ed); special education (M Ed); teaching (MA). Part-time and evening/weekend programs available. Postbaccalaureate distance learning degree programs offered (no on-campus study). *Degree requirements:* For master's, publishable research paper (M Ed), e-portfolio. *Entrance requirements:* Additional exam requirements/recommendations for international students: Required—TOEFL (minimum score 550 paper-based; 213 computer-based; 79 iBT), IELTS (minimum score 6). Electronic applications accepted.

Grand Valley State University, College of Education, Program in Instruction and Curriculum, Allendale, MI 49401-9403. Offers M Ed. *Expenses:* Tuition, state resident: part-time $471 per credit hour. Tuition, nonresident: part-time $646 per credit hour. Tuition and fees vary according to course level.

Harvard University, Graduate School of Education, Master's Programs in Education, Cambridge, MA 02138. Offers arts in education (Ed M); education policy and management (Ed M); higher education (Ed M); human development and psychology (Ed M); international education policy (Ed M); language and literacy (Ed M); learning and teaching (Ed M); mid-career mathematics and science (teaching certificate) (Ed M); mind brain and education (Ed M); risk and prevention (Ed M); school leadership (Ed M); special studies (Ed M); teaching and curriculum (teaching certificate) (Ed M); technology innovation and education (Ed M). Part-time programs available. *Faculty:* 70 full-time (33 women), 36 part-time/adjunct (20 women). *Students:* 598 full-time (448 women), 76 part-time (60 women); includes 132 minority (40 African Americans, 2 American Indian/Alaska Native, 58 Asian Americans or Pacific Islanders, 32 Hispanic Americans), 103 international. Average age 28. 1,574 applicants, 58% accepted, 640 enrolled. In 2009, 556 master's awarded. *Entrance requirements:* For master's, GRE General Test, 3 letters of recommendation. Additional exam requirements/recommendations for international students: Required—TOEFL (minimum score 600 paper-based; 250 computer-based; 100 iBT), TWE (minimum score 5). *Application deadline:* For fall admission, 1/4 for domestic and international students. Application fee: $85. Electronic applications accepted. *Expenses:* Contact institution. *Financial support:* In 2009–10, 424 students received support, including 25 fellowships with full and partial tuition reimbursements available (averaging $15,890 per year); career-related internships or fieldwork, Federal Work-Study, institutionally sponsored loans, scholarships/grants, health care benefits, tuition waivers (full and partial), and unspecified assistantships also available. Support available to part-time students. Financial award application deadline: 2/1; financial award applicants required to submit FAFSA. *Faculty research:* Learning and development, educational leadership and organizations, educational policy analysis. Total annual research expenditures: $18.1 million. *Unit head:* Jennifer L. Petrallia, Assistant Dean, 617-495-8445. *Application contact:* Information Contact, 617-495-3414, Fax: 617-496-3577, E-mail: gseadmissions@harvard.edu.

Henderson State University, Graduate Studies, School of Education, Department of Advanced Instructional Studies, Arkadelphia, AR 71999-0001. Offers early childhood (P-4) (MSE); education (MAT); middle school (MSE); reading (MSE); special education (MSE). *Accreditation:* NCATE. Part-time programs available. *Faculty:* 7 full-time (4 women), 2 part-time/adjunct (both women). *Students:* 7 full-time (all women), 131 part-time (119 women); includes 16 minority (11 African Americans, 1 Asian American or Pacific Islander, 4 Hispanic Americans). Average age 33. 25 applicants, 100% accepted, 25 enrolled. In 2009, 53 master's awarded. *Entrance requirements:* For master's, GRE General Test or MAT, minimum GPA of 2.7, teacher certification. Additional exam requirements/recommendations for international students: Required—TOEFL (minimum score 550 paper-based; 213 computer-based); Recommended—IELTS (minimum score 6). *Application deadline:* For fall admission, 8/1 priority date for domestic students, 6/30 priority date for international students; for spring admission, 1/1 priority date for domestic students, 11/30 priority date for international students. Application fee: $25 ($75 for international students). Electronic applications accepted. *Expenses:* Tuition, state resident: full-time $3798; part-time $211 per credit hour. Tuition, nonresident: full-time $7596; part-time $422 per credit hour. Required fees: $903. *Financial support:* Research assistantships, teaching assistantships with tuition reimbursements available. *Unit head:* Dr. Gary Smithey, Chairperson, 870-230-5361, Fax: 870-230-5455, E-mail: smitheg@hsu.edu. *Application contact:* Dr. Marck L. Beggs, Graduate Dean, 870-230-5126, Fax: 870-230-5479, E-mail: beggsm@hsu.edu.

Hood College, Graduate School, Department of Education, Frederick, MD 21701-8575. Offers curriculum and instruction (MS), including early childhood education, elementary education, elementary school science and mathematics, secondary education, special education; educational leadership (MS, Certificate); reading specialization (MS). Part-time and evening/weekend programs available. *Faculty:* 4 full-time (all women), 39 part-time/adjunct (21 women). *Students:* 2 full-time (both women), 397 part-time (326 women); includes 41 minority (29 African Americans, 5 Asian Americans or Pacific Islanders, 7 Hispanic Americans). Average age 33. 100 applicants, 92% accepted, 84 enrolled. In 2009, 73 master's, 65 other advanced degrees awarded. *Degree requirements:* For master's, action research project, portfolio (reading). *Entrance requirements:* For master's, minimum GPA of 2.75, teaching certification. *Application deadline:* For fall admission, 7/15 for domestic and international students; for spring admission, 12/15 for domestic and international students. Applications are processed on a rolling basis. Application fee: $35. Electronic applications accepted. *Expenses:* Tuition: Full-time $6480; part-time $360 per credit. Required fees: $100; $50 per term. *Financial support:* Applicants required to submit FAFSA. *Faculty research:* Leadership, action research, brain research, learning styles. *Unit head:* Dr. John George, Chairperson, 301-696-3471, Fax: 301-696-3597, E-mail: george@hood.edu. *Application contact:* Dr. Allen P. Flora, Dean of Graduate School, 301-696-3811, Fax: 301-696-3597, E-mail: gofurther@hood.edu.

Houston Baptist University, College of Education and Behavioral Sciences, Programs in Education, Houston, TX 77074-3298. Offers bilingual education (M Ed); counselor education (M Ed); curriculum and instruction (M Ed); educational administration (M Ed); educational diagnostician (M Ed); reading education (M Ed). Part-time programs available. *Entrance requirements:* For master's, GRE General Test or MAT. Additional exam requirements/recommendations for international students: Required—TOEFL (minimum score 550 paper-based; 213 computer-based).

Idaho State University, Office of Graduate Studies, College of Education, Department of Educational Foundations, Pocatello, ID 83209-8059. Offers child and family studies (M Ed); curriculum leadership (M Ed); education (M Ed); educational administration (M Ed); educational foundations (5th Year Certificate); elementary education (M Ed), including K-12 education, literacy, secondary education. Part-time programs available. *Faculty:* 13 full-time (8 women). *Students:* 15 full-time (9 women), 100 part-time (64 women); includes 2 minority (1 African American, 1 Hispanic American), 3 international. Average age 39. In 2009, 25 master's awarded. *Degree requirements:* For master's, comprehensive exam, thesis optional, oral exam, written exam; for 5th Year Certificate, comprehensive exam, thesis (for some programs), oral exam, written exam. *Entrance requirements:* For master's, GRE General Test or MAT, minimum undergraduate GPA of 3.0; for 5th Year Certificate, GRE General Test, minimum undergraduate GPA of 3.0, master's degree. Additional exam requirements/recommendations for international students: Required—TOEFL (minimum score 550 paper-based; 213 computer-based; 80 iBT). *Application deadline:* For fall admission, 7/1 for domestic students, 6/1 for international students; for spring admission, 12/1 for domestic students, 11/1 for international students. Applications are processed on a rolling basis. Application fee: $55. Electronic applications accepted. *Expenses:* Tuition, state resident: full-time $3318; part-time $297 per credit hour. Tuition, nonresident: full-time $13,120; part-time $437 per credit hour. Required fees: $2530. Tuition and fees vary according to program. *Financial support:* Research assistantships with full and partial tuition reimbursements, teaching assistantships with full and partial tuition reimbursements, career-related internships or fieldwork, Federal Work-Study, institutionally sponsored loans, scholarships/grants, traineeships, health care benefits, tuition waivers (full and partial), and unspecified assistantships available. Support available to part-time students. Financial award application deadline: 1/1; financial award applicants required to submit FAFSA. *Faculty research:* Child and families studies; business education; special education; math, science, and technology education. *Unit head:* Dr. Beverly Ray, Chair, 208-282-4516, Fax: 208-282-3791, E-mail: raybeve@isu.edu. *Application contact:* Dr. Peter Denner, Assistant Dean, 208-282-3807, Fax: 208-282-4697, E-mail: dennpete@isu.edu.

Illinois State University, Graduate School, College of Education, Department of Curriculum and Instruction, Normal, IL 61790-2200. Offers curriculum and instruction (MS, MS Ed, Ed D); educational policies (Ed D); postsecondary education (Ed D); reading (MS Ed); supervision (Ed D). *Accreditation:* NCATE. *Degree requirements:* For master's, variable foreign language requirement, thesis or alternative; for doctorate, variable foreign language requirement, thesis/dissertation, 2 terms of residency, internship. *Entrance requirements:* For master's, GRE General Test, minimum GPA of 3.0 in last 60 hours of course work; for doctorate, GRE General Test. *Faculty research:* In-service and pre-service teacher education for teachers of English language learners; teachers for all children: developing a model for alternative, bilingual elementary certification for paraprofessionals in Illinois; Illinois Geographic Alliance, Connections Project.

Indiana State University, School of Graduate Studies, College of Education, Department of Curriculum, Instruction, and Media Technology, Terre Haute, IN 47809. Offers curriculum and instruction (M Ed, PhD); educational technology (MS). *Accreditation:* NCATE. *Degree requirements:* For doctorate, thesis/dissertation. *Entrance requirements:* For doctorate, GRE General Test. Electronic applications accepted. *Faculty research:* Discipline FERPA reading, teacher strengths and needs.

Indiana University Bloomington, School of Education, Department of Curriculum and Instruction, Bloomington, IN 47405-7000. Offers art education (MS, Ed D, PhD); curriculum studies (Ed D, PhD); elementary education (MS, Ed D, PhD, Ed S); mathematics education (MS, Ed D, PhD); science education (MS, Ed D, PhD); secondary education (MS, Ed D, PhD); social studies education (MS, PhD); special education (MS, Ed D, PhD, Ed S). *Accreditation:* NCATE. Part-time and evening/weekend programs available. *Students:* 208 full-time (155 women), 44 part-time (25 women); includes 28 minority (9 African Americans, 3 American Indian/Alaska Native, 9 Asian Americans or Pacific Islanders, 7 Hispanic Americans), 34 international. Average age 34. 100 applicants, 68% accepted, 39 enrolled. In 2009, 48 master's, 20 doctorates awarded. Terminal master's awarded for partial completion of doctoral program. *Degree requirements:* For doctorate, thesis/dissertation; for Ed S, comprehensive exam or project. *Entrance requirements:* For master's, doctorate, and Ed S, GRE General Test. *Application deadline:* For fall admission, 6/1 priority date for domestic students, 3/1 for international students; for winter admission, 11/1 priority date for domestic students; for spring admission, 9/1 for international students. Applications are processed on a rolling basis. Application fee: $55 ($65 for international students). Electronic applications accepted. *Financial support:* Fellowships with full and partial tuition reimbursements, research assistantships with full and partial tuition reimbursements, teaching assistantships with full and partial tuition reimbursements, career-related internships or fieldwork, Federal Work-Study, institutionally sponsored loans, and tuition waivers (partial) available. Support available to part-time students. *Unit head:* Cary Buzzelli, Chairperson, 812-856-8100. *Application contact:* Bobbie Partenheimer, Admissions Services Coordinator, 812-856-8127, Fax: 812-856-8333, E-mail: partenhe@indiana.edu.

Indiana University of Pennsylvania, School of Graduate Studies and Research, College of Education and Educational Technology, Department of Professional Studies in Education, Program in Curriculum and Instruction, Indiana, PA 15705-1087. Offers M Ed, D Ed. *Accreditation:* NCATE. *Faculty:* 1 (woman) full-time. *Students:* 8 full-time (6 women), 83 part-time (71 women); includes 5 minority (all African Americans), 5 international. Average age 39. 74 applicants, 61% accepted, 35 enrolled. In 2009, 3 doctorates awarded. *Degree requirements:* For doctorate, one foreign language, comprehensive exam, thesis/dissertation. *Entrance requirements:* For doctorate, 2 letters of recommendation. Additional exam requirements/recommendations for international students: Required—TOEFL. *Application deadline:* For fall admission, 7/1 priority date for domestic students; for spring admission, 11/1 for domestic students. Applications are processed on a rolling basis. Application fee: $40. *Expenses:* Tuition, state resident: full-time $6666; part-time $370 per credit hour. Tuition, nonresident: full-time $10,666; part-time $593 per credit hour. Required fees: $813 per semester. *Financial support:* In 2009–10, 4 fellowships (averaging $1,500 per year), 14 research assistantships with full and partial tuition reimbursements (averaging $5,234 per year), 3 teaching assistantships (averaging $12,563 per year) were awarded; career-related internships or fieldwork and Federal Work-Study also available. Support available to part-time students. Financial award application deadline: 3/15; financial award applicants required to submit FAFSA. *Unit head:* Dr. Mary R. Jalongo, Graduate Coordinator, 724-357-2417, E-mail: mjalongo@iup.edu. *Application contact:* Dr. Mary R. Jalongo, Graduate Coordinator, 724-357-2417, E-mail: mjalongo@iup.edu.

Indiana University–Purdue University Indianapolis, School of Education, Indianapolis, IN 46202-2896. Offers computer education (Certificate); curriculum and instruction (MS); early childhood (MS); educational leadership (MS, Certificate); English as a second language (Certificate); higher education and student affairs (MS); kindergarten (Certificate); language education (MS); reading (Certificate); school counseling (MS); special education (MS, Certificate). Part-time and evening/weekend programs available. *Faculty:* 41 full-time, 80 part-time/adjunct. *Students:* 72 full-time (60 women), 427 part-time (325 women); includes 57 minority (42 African Americans, 1 American Indian/Alaska Native, 4 Asian Americans or Pacific Islanders, 10 Hispanic Americans), 5 international. Average age 32. 181 applicants, 78% accepted, 112 enrolled. In 2009, 162 master's awarded. *Degree requirements:* For master's, thesis optional. *Entrance requirements:* For master's, GRE General Test, minimum GPA of 3.0. Additional exam requirements/recommendations for international students: Required—TOEFL. *Application deadline:* For fall admission, 5/1 priority date for domestic students; for spring admission, 11/1 for domestic students. Application fee: $55 ($65 for international students). *Financial support:* In 2009–10, 2 fellowships (averaging $780 per year), 18 teaching assistantships (averaging $9,756 per year) were awarded; research assistantships with partial tuition reimbursements, Federal Work-Study, institutionally sponsored loans, scholarships/grants, and tuition waivers (partial) also available. Support available to part-time students. *Faculty research:* Teachers in the process of change, learning cycles, children's concepts of science. Total annual research expenditures: $614,458. *Unit head:* Dr. Chris Leland, Interim Executive Associate Dean, 317-274-6801, Fax: 317-274-6864. *Application contact:* Sarah Brandenburg, Graduate Advisor, 317-274-6801, Fax: 317-274-6864, E-mail: edugrad@iupui.edu.

Indiana Wesleyan University, College of Adult and Professional Studies, Department of Master's Studies in Education, Marion, IN 46953. Offers curriculum and instruction (M Ed). *Accreditation:* NCATE. Part-time and evening/weekend programs available. Postbaccalaureate distance learning degree programs offered (no on-campus study). *Degree requirements:* For master's, portfolio. *Entrance requirements:* For master's, minimum GPA of 2.75, teaching experience, teaching license. Additional exam requirements/recommendations for international students: Required—TOEFL (minimum score 550 paper-based; 213 computer-based). Electronic applications accepted. *Expenses:* Tuition: Full-time $7380; part-time $410 per credit. One-time fee: $85. Tuition and fees vary according to campus/location. *Faculty research:* Mentoring, performance-based assessments, faith integration, integration of technology, program assessment.

Inter American University of Puerto Rico, Arecibo Campus, Programs in Education, Arecibo, PR 00614-4050. Offers administration and educational supervision (MA Ed); counseling and guidance (MA Ed); curriculum and teaching (MA Ed), including biology education, English as a second language, history education, math education, Spanish; elementary education (MA Ed). *Degree requirements:* For master's, comprehensive exam, thesis optional. *Entrance requirements:* For master's, GRE, EXADEP, bachelor's degree in education or teaching license (administration

and supervision) or courses in education and psychology (counseling and guidance), minimum GPA of 2.5 in last 60 credits.

Inter American University of Puerto Rico, Barranquitas Campus, Program in Education, Barranquitas, PR 00794. Offers curriculum and teaching (M Ed); educational administration and supervision (MA); elementary education (M Ed); information and library service technology (M Ed). *Degree requirements:* For master's, comprehensive exam, thesis optional. *Entrance requirements:* For master's, EXADEP, letter of recommendation. Electronic applications accepted.

Inter American University of Puerto Rico, Metropolitan Campus, Graduate Programs, Program in Education, San Juan, PR 00919-1293. Offers curriculum and instruction (Ed D); educational administration (Ed D); guidance and counseling (MA, Ed D); special education administration (Ed D). *Degree requirements:* For doctorate, comprehensive exam, thesis/dissertation. *Entrance requirements:* For doctorate, GRE, MAT, or EXADEP. Electronic applications accepted.

Inter American University of Puerto Rico, San Germán Campus, Graduate Studies Center, Program in Curriculum and Instruction, San Germán, PR 00683-5008. Offers Ed D.

Iowa State University of Science and Technology, Graduate College, College of Human Sciences, Department of Curriculum and Instruction, Ames, IA 50011. Offers curriculum and instructional technology (M Ed, MS, PhD); elementary education (M Ed, MS); historical, philosophical, and comparative studies in education (M Ed, MS); special education (M Ed, MS). *Faculty:* 26 full-time (16 women), 1 (woman) part-time/adjunct. *Students:* 51 full-time (34 women), 72 part-time (49 women); includes 11 minority (5 African Americans, 1 American Indian/Alaska Native, 4 Asian Americans or Pacific Islanders, 1 Hispanic American), 25 international. 54 applicants, 69% accepted, 25 enrolled. In 2009, 41 master's, 6 doctorates awarded. *Degree requirements:* For master's, thesis or alternative; for doctorate, thesis/dissertation. *Entrance requirements:* For doctorate, GRE General Test. Additional exam requirements/recommendations for international students: Required—TOEFL (minimum score 560 paper-based; 83 iBT) or IELTS (minimum score 6.5). *Application deadline:* For fall admission, 1/1 priority date for domestic and international students; for spring admission, 9/1 for domestic and international students. Application fee: $40 ($90 for international students). Electronic applications accepted. *Expenses:* Tuition, state resident: full-time $6716. Tuition, nonresident: full-time $8908. Tuition and fees vary according to course level, course load, program and student level. *Financial support:* In 2009–10, 21 research assistantships with full and partial tuition reimbursements (averaging $14,600 per year), 12 teaching assistantships with full and partial tuition reimbursements (averaging $14,600 per year) were awarded; fellowships, scholarships/grants, health care benefits, and unspecified assistantships also available. *Unit head:* Dr. Carl Smith, Director of Graduate Education, 515-294-0317, E-mail: cigrad@iastate.edu. *Application contact:* Dr. Patricia Leigh, Director of Graduate Education, 515-294-7021, E-mail: cigrad@iastate.edu.

The Johns Hopkins University, School of Education, Department of Teacher Preparation, Baltimore, MD 21218. Offers education (MS), including educational studies; elementary education (MAT); English for speakers of other languages (MAT); K-8 mathematics lead-teacher (Certificate); K-8 science lead-teacher (Certificate); secondary education (MAT), including biology, chemistry, earth/space/environmental science, English, French, mathematics, physics, social studies, Spanish. Part-time and evening/weekend programs available. *Faculty:* 13 full-time (11 women), 35 part-time/adjunct (21 women). *Students:* 162 full-time (119 women), 347 part-time (256 women); includes 138 minority (80 African Americans, 3 American Indian/Alaska Native, 38 Asian Americans or Pacific Islanders, 17 Hispanic Americans), 3 international. Average age 27. 89 applicants, 37% accepted, 24 enrolled. In 2009, 177 master's awarded. *Degree requirements:* For master's, portfolio, PRAXIS II, internship. *Entrance requirements:* For master's, PRAXIS I, SAT, ACT, or GRE (MAT), minimum undergraduate GPA of 3.0, interview, 1 letter of recommendation, curriculum vitae/resume; for Certificate, bachelor's degree, minimum undergraduate GPA of 3.0, essay/statement of goals, interview. Additional exam requirements/recommendations for international students: Required—TOEFL (minimum score 600 paper-based; 250 computer-based; 100 iBT). *Application deadline:* For fall admission, 5/1 for international students; for spring admission, 10/15 for international students. Applications are processed on a rolling basis. Application fee: $80. Electronic applications accepted. *Financial support:* Scholarships/grants available. Support available to part-time students. Financial award application deadline: 6/1; financial award applicants required to submit FAFSA. *Faculty research:* Teacher retention; STEM education reform; alternative certification programs; school-university partnerships; urban education; action research/data-informed instruction; family engagement. *Unit head:* Dr. Francis Masci, Chair, 410-516-9774, Fax: 410-516-9770, E-mail: matjhu@jhu.edu. *Application contact:* Jennifer Shaffer, Director of Admissions, 410-516-9797, Fax: 410-516-9799, E-mail: educationinfo@jhu.edu.

Johnson State College, Graduate Program in Education, Program in Curriculum and Instruction, Johnson, VT 05656. Offers MA Ed. Part-time programs available. *Degree requirements:* For master's, comprehensive exam, thesis or alternative. *Entrance requirements:* For master's, interview. Additional exam requirements/recommendations for international students: Required—TOEFL. *Expenses:* Tuition, area resident: Part-time $416 per credit. Tuition, state resident: part-time $416 per credit. Tuition, nonresident: part-time $899 per credit.

Jones International University, Graduate School of Education, Centennial, CO 80112. Offers adult education (M Ed); corporate training and knowledge management (M Ed); curriculum and instruction (M Ed), including elementary teacher licensure, secondary teacher licensure; e-learning technology and design (M Ed); educational leadership and administration (M Ed); educational leadership and administration: principal and administrator licensure (M Ed); elementary curriculum instruction and assessment (M Ed); higher education leadership and administration (M Ed); K-12 instructional technology (M Ed); K-12 instructional technology: teacher licensure (M Ed); secondary curriculum instruction and assessment (M Ed); technology and design (M Ed). Part-time and evening/weekend programs available. Postbaccalaureate distance learning degree programs offered (no on-campus study). *Entrance requirements:* For master's, minimum cumulative GPA of 2.5. Additional exam requirements/recommendations for international students: Recommended—TOEFL (minimum score 550 paper-based; 213 computer-based). Electronic applications accepted.

Kansas State University, Graduate School, College of Education, Program in Curriculum and Instruction, Manhattan, KS 66506. Offers MS, Ed D, PhD. *Accreditation:* NCATE. *Students:* 32 full-time (22 women), 153 part-time (124 women); includes 10 minority (3 African Americans, 1 Asian American or Pacific Islander, 6 Hispanic Americans), 6 international. Average age 37. 37 applicants, 89% accepted, 29 enrolled. In 2009, 49 master's, 15 doctorates awarded. *Degree requirements:* For doctorate, comprehensive exam, thesis/dissertation, preliminary exam. *Entrance requirements:* For doctorate, GRE or MAT. Additional exam requirements/recommendations for international students: Required—TOEFL. *Application deadline:* For fall admission, 2/1 priority date for domestic and international students; for spring admission, 8/1 priority date for domestic and international students. Applications are processed on a rolling basis. Application fee: $40 ($55 for international students). Electronic applications accepted. *Financial support:* Career-related internships or fieldwork, institutionally sponsored loans, and scholarships/grants available. Support available to part-time students. Financial award application deadline: 3/1; financial award applicants required to submit FAFSA. *Faculty research:* Narrative inquiry, literacy and technology, brain based research in reading, critical race theory and diversity, achievement gaps. *Unit head:* Gail Shroyer, Director, 785-532-6737, Fax: 785-532-7304, E-mail: gshroyer@ksu.edu. *Application contact:* Dona Deam, Application Contact, 785-532-5595, Fax: 785-532-7304, E-mail: ddeam@ksu.edu.

Kean University, College of Education, Program in Early Childhood Education, Union, NJ 07083. Offers administration in early childhood and family studies (MA); advanced curriculum and teaching (MA); classroom instruction (MA), including preschool-third grade; education for family living (MA). *Accreditation:* NCATE. Part-time and evening/weekend programs available. *Faculty:* 8 full-time (7 women). *Students:* 5 full-time (all women), 55 part-time (53 women); includes 17 minority (6 African Americans, 1 American Indian/Alaska Native, 3 Asian Americans

or Pacific Islanders, 7 Hispanic Americans), 1 international. Average age 32. 37 applicants, 95% accepted, 23 enrolled. In 2009, 25 master's awarded. *Degree requirements:* For master's, thesis, portfolio. *Entrance requirements:* For master's, GRE General Test, minimum GPA of 3.0, 2 letters of recommendation, interview, teacher certification (for some programs), writing sample. *Application deadline:* For fall admission, 5/1 for domestic students; for spring admission, 11/1 for domestic students. Application fee: $60 ($150 for international students). Electronic applications accepted. *Expenses:* Tuition, state resident: full-time $10,440; part-time $435 per credit. Tuition, nonresident: full-time $14,160; part-time $590 per credit. Required fees: $2642; $110 per credit. Part-time tuition and fees vary according to course load and degree level. *Financial support:* In 2009–10, 1 research assistantship with full tuition reimbursement (averaging $3,263 per year) was awarded; unspecified assistantships also available. *Unit head:* Dr. Polly Ashelman, Program Coordinator, 908-737-3780, E-mail: pashelma@kean.edu. *Application contact:* Ann-Marie Kay, Assistant Director of Graduate Admissions, 908-737-5922, Fax: 908-737-5965, E-mail: akay@kean.edu.

Kean University, College of Education, Program in Instruction and Curriculum, Union, NJ 07083. Offers bilingual/bicultural education (MA); classroom instruction (MA); earth science (MA); mathematics/science/computer education (MA); teaching (MA); teaching English as a second language (MA); world languages (Spanish) (MA). *Accreditation:* NCATE. Part-time and evening/weekend programs available. *Faculty:* 16 full-time (7 women). *Students:* 45 full-time (34 women), 131 part-time (104 women); includes 60 minority (11 African Americans, 6 Asian Americans or Pacific Islanders, 43 Hispanic Americans), 6 international. Average age 33. 64 applicants, 94% accepted, 46 enrolled. In 2009, 58 master's awarded. *Entrance requirements:* For master's, GRE General Test or MAT, PRAXIS, minimum GPA of 3.0, 2 letters of recommendation, interview, teacher certification (for some programs). *Application deadline:* For fall admission, 5/1 for domestic students; for spring admission, 11/1 for domestic students. Application fee: $60 ($150 for international students). Electronic applications accepted. *Expenses:* Tuition, state resident: full-time $10,440; part-time $435 per credit. Tuition, nonresident: full-time $14,160; part-time $590 per credit. Required fees: $2642; $110 per credit. Part-time tuition and fees vary according to course load and degree level. *Financial support:* In 2009–10, 1 research assistantship with full tuition reimbursement (averaging $3,263 per year) was awarded; unspecified assistantships also available. *Unit head:* Dr. Thomas Walsh, Program Coordinator, 908-737-4296, E-mail: twalsh@kean.edu. *Application contact:* Ann-Marie Kay, Assistant Director of Graduate Admissions, 908-737-5922, Fax: 908-737-5965, E-mail: akay@kean.edu.

Keene State College, School of Professional and Graduate Studies, Keene, NH 03435. Offers curriculum and instruction (M Ed); education leadership (PMC); educational leadership (M Ed); school counselor (M Ed, PMC); special education (M Ed); teacher certification (Postbaccalaureate Certificate). *Accreditation:* NCATE. Part-time and evening/weekend programs available. *Faculty:* 21 full-time (13 women), 14 part-time/adjunct (13 women). *Students:* 8 full-time (5 women), 80 part-time (56 women); includes 1 Asian American or Pacific Islander, 1 Hispanic American, 1 international. Average age 34. 94 applicants, 80% accepted, 62 enrolled. In 2009, 55 master's, 10 other advanced degrees awarded. *Entrance requirements:* For master's, PRAXIS I, resume; minimum GPA of 2.5. Additional exam requirements/recommendations for international students: Required—TOEFL (minimum score 550 paper-based; 173 computer-based; 61 iBT). *Application deadline:* For fall admission, 4/1 for domestic students; for spring admission, 12/1 for domestic students. Application fee: $40. *Expenses:* Tuition, state resident: part-time $320 per credit. Tuition, nonresident: part-time $350 per credit. Required fees: $92 per credit. $10 per term. Tuition and fees vary according to course load. *Financial support:* Research assistantships, career-related internships or fieldwork, Federal Work-Study, institutionally sponsored loans, and unspecified assistantships available. Support available to part-time students. Financial award application deadline: 3/1; financial award applicants required to submit FAFSA. *Unit head:* Dr. Melinda Treadwell, Dean, 603-358-2220. *Application contact:* Peggy Richmond, Director of Admissions, 603-358-2276, Fax: 603-358-2767, E-mail: admissions@keene.edu.

Kent State University, Graduate School of Education, Health, and Human Services, School of Teaching, Learning and Curriculum Studies, Program in Curriculum and Instruction, Kent, OH 44242-0001. Offers physical education teacher education (M Ed, MA, PhD, Ed S). *Accreditation:* NCATE. Part-time and evening/weekend programs available. *Faculty:* 32 full-time (21 women), 6 part-time/adjunct (5 women). *Students:* 91 full-time (72 women), 84 part-time (62 women); includes 17 minority (12 African Americans, 5 Asian Americans or Pacific Islanders), 8 international. 46 applicants, 50% accepted. In 2009, 40 master's, 10 doctorates, 2 other advanced degrees awarded. *Degree requirements:* For master's, thesis (for some programs); for doctorate, comprehensive exam, thesis/dissertation. *Entrance requirements:* For doctorate and Ed S, GRE General Test. Additional exam requirements/recommendations for international students: Required—TOEFL. *Application deadline:* Applications are processed on a rolling basis. Application fee: $30 ($60 for international students). Electronic applications accepted. *Financial support:* In 2009–10, 1 fellowship with full tuition reimbursement (averaging $13,500 per year), research assistantships with full tuition reimbursements (averaging $9,000 per year), 15 teaching assistantships with full tuition reimbursements (averaging $13,500 per year) were awarded; Federal Work-Study, scholarships/grants, and unspecified assistantships also available. Financial award application deadline: 4/1; financial award applicants required to submit FAFSA. *Faculty research:* Gender equity issues in teaching, learning math and science, teaching as inquiry artistry, curriculum studies for democratic humanism. *Unit head:* Dr. James Henderson, Coordinator, 330-672-0631, E-mail: jhenders@kent.edu. *Application contact:* Nancy Miller, Academic Program Coordinator, Office of Graduate Student Services, 330-672-2576, Fax: 330-672-9162, E-mail: ogs@kent.edu.

Kutztown University of Pennsylvania, College of Education, Program in Secondary Education, Kutztown, PA 19530-0730. Offers biology (M Ed); curriculum and instruction (M Ed); English (M Ed); mathematics (M Ed); secondary education (Certificate); social studies (M Ed). *Accreditation:* NCATE. Part-time and evening/weekend programs available. *Faculty:* 7 full-time (4 women). *Students:* 90 full-time (45 women), 84 part-time (56 women); includes 8 minority (4 African Americans, 1 Asian American or Pacific Islander, 3 Hispanic Americans), 2 international. Average age 29. 129 applicants, 76% accepted, 31 enrolled. In 2009, 36 master's awarded. *Degree requirements:* For master's, comprehensive exam, thesis optional. *Entrance requirements:* For master's, GRE General Test. Additional exam requirements/recommendations for international students: Required—TOEFL. *Application deadline:* For fall admission, 8/15 priority date for domestic and international students; for spring admission, 12/15 priority date for domestic and international students. Applications are processed on a rolling basis. Application fee: $35. Electronic applications accepted. *Expenses:* Tuition, state resident: full-time $6666; part-time $370 per credit. Tuition, nonresident: full-time $10,666; part-time $593 per credit. Required fees: $62 per credit. $60 per semester. *Financial support:* Career-related internships or fieldwork, Federal Work-Study, scholarships/grants, and unspecified assistantships available. Financial award application deadline: 3/1; financial award applicants required to submit FAFSA. *Unit head:* Dr. Theresa Stahler, Chairperson, 610-683-4259, Fax: 610-683-1338, E-mail: stahler@kutztown.edu. *Application contact:* Kelly D. Burr, Associate Director, Graduate Admissions, 610-683-4200, Fax: 610-683-1393, E-mail: graduate@kutztown.edu.

LaGrange College, Graduate Programs, Department of Education, LaGrange, GA 30240-2999. Offers curriculum and instruction (M Ed); middle grades (MAT); secondary education (MAT). Part-time and evening/weekend programs available. *Degree requirements:* For master's, comprehensive exam. *Entrance requirements:* For master's, GRE, MAT, minimum GPA of 2.5. Additional exam requirements/recommendations for international students: Required—TOEFL (minimum score 550 paper-based).

Lake Erie College, Division of Education, Painesville, OH 44077-3389. Offers curriculum and instruction (MS Ed); education (MS Ed); educational leadership (MS Ed); reading (MS Ed). Part-time and evening/weekend programs available. *Degree requirements:* For master's, comprehensive exam (for some programs), thesis optional, applied research project. *Entrance requirements:* For master's, GRE General Test or minimum GPA of 3.0. Additional exam requirements/recommendations for international students: Required—TOEFL (minimum score

Curriculum and Instruction

Lake Erie College *(continued)*

590 paper-based). Electronic applications accepted. *Expenses:* Contact institution. *Faculty research:* Cooperative learning, portfolio assessment, education systems abroad, Web-based instruction.

Lander University, School of Education, Greenwood, SC 29649-2099. Offers elementary education (M Ed); teaching (MAT). *Accreditation:* NCATE. Part-time programs available. *Degree requirements:* For master's, comprehensive exam, thesis or alternative. *Entrance requirements:* For master's, GRE General Test. Additional exam requirements/recommendations for international students: Required—TOEFL (minimum score 550 paper-based; 213 computer-based). Electronic applications accepted.

La Sierra University, School of Education, Department of Curriculum and Instruction, Riverside, CA 92515. Offers curriculum and instruction (MA, Ed D, Ed S); teaching (MAT). Part-time and evening/weekend programs available. *Degree requirements:* For doctorate, thesis/dissertation; for Ed S, thesis optional. *Entrance requirements:* For master's, minimum GPA of 3.0; for doctorate, GRE General Test, GRE Subject Test, minimum GPA of 3.3; for Ed S, minimum GPA of 3.3. *Faculty research:* New teacher success, politics of knowledge, computer-assisted instruction, diversity issues.

Lehigh University, College of Education, Program in Educational Leadership, Bethlehem, PA 18015. Offers educational leadership (M Ed, Ed D); principal certification K-12 (Certificate); pupil services (Certificate); special education (Certificate); superintendant certification (Certificate); supervisor of curriculum and instruction (Certificate); supervisor of pupil services (Certificate); MBA/M Ed. Part-time and evening/weekend programs available. Postbaccalaureate distance learning degree programs offered (minimal on-campus study). *Faculty:* 7 full-time (2 women), 16 part-time/adjunct (9 women). *Students:* 12 full-time (6 women), 174 part-time (102 women); includes 8 minority (4 African Americans, 1 Asian American or Pacific Islander, 3 Hispanic Americans), 20 international. Average age 37. 55 applicants, 73% accepted, 34 enrolled. In 2009, 39 master's, 4 doctorates awarded. *Degree requirements:* For doctorate, comprehensive exam, thesis/dissertation. *Entrance requirements:* For master's, minimum GPA of 3.0; for doctorate, GRE General Test or MAT, minimum graduate GPA of 3.6, 2 letters of recommendation, essay, transcript; for Certificate, minimum undergraduate GPA of 3.0. Additional exam requirements/recommendations for international students: Required—TOEFL (minimum score 600 paper-based; 250 computer-based; 93 iBT). *Application deadline:* For fall admission, 1/15 for domestic and international students; for spring admission, 11/1 for domestic and international students. Applications are processed on a rolling basis. Application fee: $65. Electronic applications accepted. *Financial support:* In 2009–10, 2 students received support, including 2 research assistantships with full and partial tuition reimbursements available (averaging $13,000 per year); fellowships with full and partial tuition reimbursements available, teaching assistantships with full and partial tuition reimbursements available, career-related internships or fieldwork, Federal Work-Study, institutionally sponsored loans, scholarships/grants, and tuition waivers (full and partial) also available. Financial award application deadline: 1/31. *Faculty research:* School finance and law, supervision of instruction, middle-level education, organizational change, leadership preparation and development, international school leadership, urban school leadership. *Unit head:* Dr. George P. White, Coordinator, 610-758-3250, Fax: 610-758-3227, E-mail: gpw1@lehigh.edu. *Application contact:* Donna M. Johnson, Coordinator, 610-758-3231, Fax: 610-758-6223, E-mail: dmj4@lehigh.edu.

Lesley University, School of Education, Cambridge, MA 02138-2790. Offers curriculum and instruction (M Ed, CAGS); early childhood education (M Ed); educational studies (PhD); elementary education (M Ed); individually designed (M Ed); middle school education (M Ed); moderate special needs (M Ed); reading (M Ed, CAGS); science in education (M Ed); severe special needs (M Ed); special needs (CAGS); technology in education (M Ed, CAGS). *Accreditation:* Teacher Education Accreditation Council. Part-time and evening/weekend programs available. Postbaccalaureate distance learning degree programs offered (no on-campus study). *Degree requirements:* For master's, practicum; for doctorate, thesis/dissertation. *Entrance requirements:* For doctorate, GRE General Test or MAT, interview, master's degree, resume; for CAGS, interview, master's degree. Additional exam requirements/recommendations for international students: Required—TOEFL (minimum score 550 paper-based; 213 computer-based; 80 iBT). Electronic applications accepted. *Faculty research:* Assessment in literacy, mathematics and science; autism spectrum disorders; instructional technology and online learning; multicultural education and ELL.

LeTourneau University, School of Graduate and Professional Studies, Longview, TX 75607-7001. Offers business administration (MBA); curriculum and instruction (M Ed); educational administration (M Ed); strategic leadership (MSL); teaching and learning (M Ed). Part-time and evening/weekend programs available. Postbaccalaureate distance learning degree programs offered (no on-campus study). *Faculty:* 8 full-time (1 woman), 19 part-time/adjunct (7 women). *Students:* 43 full-time (30 women), 245 part-time (164 women); includes 158 minority (130 African Americans, 2 American Indian/Alaska Native, 2 Asian Americans or Pacific Islanders, 24 Hispanic Americans). Average age 36. 1,717 applicants, 31% accepted, 288 enrolled. *Entrance requirements:* For master's, minimum GPA of 2.8. Additional exam requirements/recommendations for international students: Required—TOEFL. *Application deadline:* Applications are processed on a rolling basis. Electronic applications accepted. *Expenses:* Tuition: Full-time $10,710; part-time $595 per credit hour. *Financial support:* Applicants required to submit FAFSA. *Unit head:* Dr. Carol Green, Vice President, 903-233-3250, Fax: 903-233-3227, E-mail: carolgreen@letu.edu. *Application contact:* Chris Fontaine, Assistant Vice President for Enrollment Management and Market Research, 903-233-3250, Fax: 903-233-3227, E-mail: chrisfontaine@letu.edu.

Lewis University, College of Education, Program in Curriculum and Teacher Leadership, Romeoville, IL 60446. Offers M Ed. Part-time and evening/weekend programs available. *Degree requirements:* For master's, comprehensive exam. *Entrance requirements:* For master's, writing exam, interview. Additional exam requirements/recommendations for international students: Required—TOEFL (minimum score 550 paper-based; 213 computer-based). *Application deadline:* For fall admission, 5/1 priority date for international students; for spring admission, 11/15 priority date for international students. Applications are processed on a rolling basis. Application fee: $40. Electronic applications accepted. *Expenses:* Tuition: Full-time $6480; part-time $720 per credit. One-time fee: $40. Tuition and fees vary according to course load, degree level and program. *Financial support:* Federal Work-Study, scholarships/grants, tuition waivers (full and partial), and unspecified assistantships available. Financial award application deadline: 5/1; financial award applicants required to submit FAFSA. *Unit head:* Dr. Jane Petrek, Director, 815-838-0500 Ext. 5039, Fax: 815-836-5879, E-mail: petrekja@lewisu.edu. *Application contact:* Pat Levenda, Secretary, 815-836-5769, E-mail: levendpa@lewisu.edu.

Liberty University, School of Education, Lynchburg, VA 24502. Offers administration and supervision (M Ed); curriculum and instruction (M Ed); early childhood education (M Ed); education specialist (Ed S); educational leadership (Ed D); elementary education (M Ed); gifted education (M Ed); reading specialist (M Ed); school counseling (M Ed); secondary education (M Ed); special education (M Ed). *Accreditation:* NCATE. Part-time programs available. Postbaccalaureate distance learning degree programs offered (minimal on-campus study). *Degree requirements:* For doctorate, comprehensive exam, thesis/dissertation. *Entrance requirements:* For master's, GRE General Test or MAT (aken in or before 1999), 2 letters of recommendation, minimum undergraduate GPA of 3.0, curriculum vitae; for doctorate, GRE General Test or MAT (if taken before 1999), minimum master's GPA of 3.0, 3 years of teacher experience; for Ed S, GRE General Test or MAT (if taken before 1999), minimum master's GPA of 3.0, 3 years of teaching experience. Additional exam requirements/recommendations for international students: Required—TOEFL (minimum score 600 paper-based; 250 computer-based). Electronic applications accepted. *Expenses:* Contact institution. *Faculty research:* Self-determination, character education, bibliotherapy, learning styles, distance education.

Lincoln Memorial University, Carter and Moyers School of Education, Harrogate, TN 37752-1901. Offers administration and supervision (M Ed, Ed S); counseling and guidance (M Ed);

curriculum and instruction (M Ed, Ed S); English (M Ed). Part-time and evening/weekend programs available. Postbaccalaureate distance learning degree programs offered. *Faculty:* 31 full-time (13 women), 22 part-time/adjunct (11 women). *Students:* 190 full-time (151 women), 1,299 part-time (959 women); includes 144 minority (128 African Americans, 1 American Indian/Alaska Native, 5 Asian Americans or Pacific Islanders, 10 Hispanic Americans), 4 international. 1,562 applicants, 96% accepted, 1489 enrolled. In 2009, 173 master's, 901 Ed Ss awarded. *Degree requirements:* For master's, comprehensive exam, thesis optional; for Ed S, comprehensive exam. *Entrance requirements:* For master's, PRAXIS, NTE, GRE, MAT, letters of recommendation; for Ed S, graduate transcripts. *Application deadline:* For fall admission, 8/10 for domestic and international students; for spring admission, 1/10 for domestic and international students. Application fee: $25. *Expenses:* Tuition: Full-time $11,700; part-time $390 per hour. *Financial support:* In 2009–10, 973 students received support. Career-related internships or fieldwork, health care benefits, and unspecified assistantships available. Support available to part-time students. Financial award application deadline: 4/1; financial award applicants required to submit FAFSA. *Faculty research:* Brain compatible teaching and learning; poverty in Appalachia; leadership for change; ethics, moral responsibility and social justice; human and organizational learning. *Unit head:* Dr. David Hand, Dean, 423-869-6259, Fax: 423-869-6261, E-mail: david.hand@lmunet.edu. *Application contact:* Terri Knuckles, Office Manager, Graduate Education, 423-869-6223, Fax: 423-869-6261, E-mail: terri.knuckles@lmunet.edu.

Lipscomb University, Program in Education, Nashville, TN 37204-3951. Offers English language learners (MAT); instructional leadership (M Ed); instructional technology (M Ed); learning and teaching (MALT); math specialty (M Ed); school administration and supervision (M Ed); special education instruction, K-12 (MASE). *Accreditation:* NCATE. Part-time and evening/weekend programs available. *Faculty:* 4 full-time (1 woman), 12 part-time/adjunct (8 women). *Students:* 140 full-time (103 women), 200 part-time (144 women); includes 32 minority (29 African Americans, 3 Hispanic Americans). Average age 31. 206 applicants, 75% accepted. In 2009, 131 master's awarded. *Entrance requirements:* For master's, MAT or GRE General Test, 2 reference letters. Additional exam requirements/recommendations for international students: Required—TOEFL (minimum score 570 paper-based; 230 computer-based). *Application deadline:* For fall admission, 8/29 priority date for domestic students; for spring admission, 1/16 priority date for domestic students. Applications are processed on a rolling basis. Application fee: $50. *Expenses:* Tuition: Full-time $16,002; part-time $889 per credit hour. Tuition and fees vary according to program. *Financial support:* In 2009–10, 67 students received support. Federal Work-Study, tuition waivers (full), and unspecified assistantships available. Support available to part-time students. Financial award applicants required to submit FAFSA. *Faculty research:* Facilitative learning styles, leadership, student assessment, interactive multimedia inclusion. *Unit head:* Dr. Deborah Boyd, Director of M Ed Program, 615-966-6263. *Application contact:* Kristin Green, Administrative Assistant, 615-966-7628 Ext. 6081, Fax: 615-966-7628, E-mail: kristin.green@lipscomb.edu.

Louisiana State University in Shreveport, College of Education and Human Development, Program in Education, Shreveport, LA 71115-2399. Offers education (M Ed); education curriculum and instruction (M Ed); educational leadership (M Ed). Part-time programs available. *Students:* 3 full-time (all women), 43 part-time (32 women); includes 4 minority (all African Americans), 2 international. Average age 35. 22 applicants, 95% accepted, 10 enrolled. In 2009, 26 master's awarded. *Degree requirements:* For master's, orally presented project, 200-hour internship (educational leadership). *Entrance requirements:* For master's, GRE, minimum GPA of 2.5; teacher certification; recommendations and interview (for educational leadership). Additional exam requirements/recommendations for international students: Required—TOEFL (minimum score 500 paper-based; 173 computer-based; 61 iBT). *Application deadline:* For fall admission, 6/30 for domestic and international students; for spring admission, 11/30 for domestic and international students. Applications are processed on a rolling basis. Application fee: $10 ($20 for international students). *Financial support:* In 2009–10, 4 research assistantships with partial tuition reimbursements (averaging $10,000 per year) were awarded. *Unit head:* Dr. Julie Bergeron, Coordinator of Graduate Programs in Education, 318-797-5033, Fax: 318-798-4144, E-mail: julie.bergeron@lsus.edu. *Application contact:* Dr. Julie Bergeron, Coordinator of Graduate Programs in Education, 318-797-5033, Fax: 318-798-4144, E-mail: julie.bergeron@lsus.edu.

Louisiana Tech University, Graduate School, College of Education, Department of Curriculum, Instruction and Leadership, Ruston, LA 71272. Offers curriculum and instruction (MS, Ed D); educational leadership (Ed D); secondary education (M Ed), including business education, English education, foreign language education, health and physical education, mathematics education, science education, social studies education, speech education. *Accreditation:* NCATE. Part-time programs available. *Degree requirements:* For doctorate, thesis/dissertation. *Entrance requirements:* For master's and doctorate, GRE General Test.

Loyola University Chicago, School of Education, Program in Curriculum and Instruction, Chicago, IL 60660. Offers M Ed, Ed D. Part-time and evening/weekend programs available. *Faculty:* 4 full-time (3 women), 2 part-time/adjunct (1 woman). *Students:* 90. Average age 35. 28 applicants, 71% accepted, 14 enrolled. In 2009, 6 master's, 11 doctorates awarded. Terminal master's awarded for partial completion of doctoral program. *Degree requirements:* For master's, comprehensive exam; for doctorate, comprehensive exam, thesis/dissertation. *Entrance requirements:* For master's, 3 references, minimum GPA of 3.0, resume; for doctorate, GRE, 3 references, interview, minimum GPA of 3.0, resume. Additional exam requirements/recommendations for international students: Required—TOEFL (minimum score 550 paper-based; 213 computer-based; 79 iBT). *Application deadline:* For fall admission, 7/1 for domestic and international students; for spring admission, 11/1 for domestic and international students. Applications are processed on a rolling basis. Application fee: $50. Electronic applications accepted. *Expenses:* Tuition: Full-time $14,220; part-time $790 per credit hour. Required fees: $60 per semester hour. Tuition and fees vary according to program. *Financial support:* In 2009–10, 1 research assistantship with tuition reimbursement (averaging $11,000 per year) was awarded; Federal Work-Study and institutionally sponsored loans also available. Financial award application deadline: 2/15. *Faculty research:* School improvement, technology, change, reading. *Unit head:* Dr. David Ensminger, Director, 312-915-7257, E-mail: densmin@luc.edu. *Application contact:* Marie Rosin-Dittmar, Information Contact, 312-915-6800, E-mail: schleduc@luc.edu.

Loyola University Maryland, Graduate Programs, College of Arts and Sciences, Department of Education, Program in Curriculum and Instruction, Baltimore, MD 21210-2699. Offers M Ed, MA, CAS. Part-time and evening/weekend programs available. *Entrance requirements:* For master's and CAS, GRE General Test, GRE Subject Test (recommended). Additional exam requirements/recommendations for international students: Required—TOEFL (minimum score 550 paper-based; 213 computer-based).

Lynchburg College, Graduate Studies, School of Education and Human Development, Lynchburg, VA 24501-3199. Offers community counseling (M Ed); counselor education (M Ed), including community counseling; curriculum and instruction (M Ed); educational leadership (M Ed); English education (M Ed); reading (M Ed); school counseling (M Ed); science education (M Ed); special education (M Ed), including autism spectrum disorder, early childhood special education, mental retardation, teaching children with learning disabilities, teaching the emotionally disturbed. Part-time and evening/weekend programs available. *Degree requirements:* For master's, comprehensive exam. *Entrance requirements:* For master's, GRE, minimum undergraduate GPA of 3.0. Additional exam requirements/recommendations for international students: Required—TOEFL. *Expenses:* Tuition: Full-time $7020; part-time $390 per credit hour.

Lyndon State College, Graduate Programs in Education, Department of Education, Lyndonville, VT 05851-0919. Offers curriculum and instruction (M Ed); reading specialist (M Ed); special education (M Ed); teaching and counseling (M Ed). Part-time and evening/weekend programs available. *Degree requirements:* For master's, exam or major field project. *Entrance*

requirements: Additional exam requirements/recommendations for international students: Recommended—TOEFL (minimum score 500 paper-based; 173 computer-based).

Malone University, Graduate Program in Education, Canton, OH 44709. Offers curriculum and instruction (MA); curriculum, instruction, and professional development (MA); instructional technology (MA); intervention specialist (MA); reading (MA). Part-time and evening/weekend programs available. *Faculty:* 7 full-time (4 women), 7 part-time/adjunct (5 women). *Students:* 2 full-time (1 woman), 64 part-time (55 women); includes 1 minority (African American). Average age 34. In 2009, 27 master's awarded. *Degree requirements:* For master's, research project. *Entrance requirements:* For master's, minimum GPA of 3.0, teaching license. Additional exam requirements/recommendations for international students: Required—TOEFL (minimum score 550 paper-based; 213 computer-based; 79 iBT). *Application deadline:* Applications are processed on a rolling basis. Application fee: $25. *Expenses:* Tuition: Part-time $450 per semester hour. *Financial support:* Tuition waivers (partial) available. Support available to part-time students. Financial award application deadline: 6/30. *Faculty research:* The Bible as children's literature, special needs students and literacy development, middle level education, school/university partnerships and professional development, child/adolescent literature and popular culture. *Unit head:* Dr. Alice E. Christie, Director, 330-478-8541, Fax: 330-471-8563, E-mail: achristie@malone.edu. *Application contact:* David L. Kleffman, Assistant Director of Enrollment, 330-471-8447, Fax: 330-471-8343, E-mail: dkleffman@malone.edu.

Martin Luther College, Graduate Studies, New Ulm, MN 56073. Offers instruction (MS Ed); leadership (MS Ed); special education (MS Ed). Part-time programs available. Postbaccalaureate distance learning degree programs offered. *Degree requirements:* For master's, capstone project or comprehensive exam. *Entrance requirements:* For master's, undergraduate degree in education from an accredited college or university, minimum undergraduate GPA of 3.0. Electronic applications accepted.

Massachusetts College of Liberal Arts, Program in Education, North Adams, MA 01247-4100. Offers curriculum (M Ed); educational administration (M Ed); reading (M Ed); special education (M Ed). Part-time and evening/weekend programs available. *Degree requirements:* For master's, thesis. *Entrance requirements:* For master's, writing sample. *Faculty research:* Anxiety, methodology, mainstreaming.

McDaniel College, Graduate and Professional Studies, Program in Curriculum and Instruction, Westminster, MD 21157-4390. Offers MS. *Degree requirements:* For master's, comprehensive exam (for some programs), thesis optional. *Entrance requirements:* For master's, letter of reference. Additional exam requirements/recommendations for international students: Required—TOEFL (minimum score 213 computer-based). *Expenses:* Tuition: Part-time $325 per credit hour.

McGill University, Faculty of Graduate and Postdoctoral Studies, Faculty of Education, Department of Integrated Studies in Education, Montréal, QC H3A 2T5, Canada. Offers culture and values in education (MA, PhD); curriculum studies (MA); educational leadership (MA, Certificate); educational studies (PhD); integrated studies in education (M Ed); second language education (MA, PhD).

McNeese State University, Doré School of Graduate Studies, Burton College of Education, Department of Teacher Education, Program in Curriculum and Instruction, Lake Charles, LA 70609. Offers early childhood education (M Ed); elementary education (M Ed); secondary education (M Ed). Evening/weekend programs available. *Faculty:* 12 full-time (6 women). *Students:* 4 full-time (all women), 9 part-time (all women); includes 2 minority (both African Americans). In 2009, 3 master's awarded. *Entrance requirements:* For master's, GRE, teaching certificate. *Application deadline:* For fall admission, 5/15 priority date for domestic and international students; for spring admission, 10/15 priority date for domestic and international students. Applications are processed on a rolling basis. Application fee: $20 ($30 for international students). *Expenses:* Tuition, area resident: Full-time $2556. Tuition, state resident: full-time $2556. Required fees: $1031. Tuition and fees vary according to course load. *Financial support:* Application deadline: 5/1. *Unit head:* Dr. Royce Zant, Head, 337-475-5404, Fax: 337-475-5398, E-mail: rzant@mcneese.edu. *Application contact:* Dr. George F. Mead, Interim Dean of Dore' School of Graduate Studies, 337-475-5396, Fax: 337-475-5397, E-mail: admissions@mcneese.edu.

Medaille College, Program in Education, Buffalo, NY 14214-2695. Offers adolescent education (MS Ed); curriculum and instruction (MS Ed); education preparation (MS Ed); literacy (MS Ed); special education (MS). *Accreditation:* Teacher Education Accreditation Council. Part-time and evening/weekend programs available. *Faculty:* 22 full-time (16 women), 47 part-time/adjunct (36 women). *Students:* 721 full-time (596 women), 2 part-time (both women); includes 34 minority (16 African Americans, 1 American Indian/Alaska Native, 14 Asian Americans or Pacific Islanders, 3 Hispanic Americans). Average age 26. 621 applicants, 46% accepted, 288 enrolled. In 2009, 608 master's awarded. *Degree requirements:* For master's, thesis or alternative. *Entrance requirements:* For master's, minimum undergraduate GPA of 2.7. Additional exam requirements/recommendations for international students: Required—TOEFL (minimum score 550 paper-based; 213 computer-based). *Application deadline:* For fall admission, 8/15 priority date for domestic students; for spring admission, 1/15 priority date for domestic students. Applications are processed on a rolling basis. Application fee: $35. Electronic applications accepted. *Financial support:* In 2009–10, 501 students received support. Federal Work-Study available. Financial award applicants required to submit FAFSA. *Faculty research:* Curriculum planning, truancy, tracking minority students, curriculum design, mentoring students. *Unit head:* Dr. Robert DiSibio, Director of Graduate Programs, 716-932-2548, Fax: 716-631-1380, E-mail: rdisibio@medaille.edu. *Application contact:* Jacqueline Matheny, Executive Director of Marketing and Enrollment, 716-932-2541, Fax: 716-632-1811, E-mail: jmatheny@medaille.edu.

Memorial University of Newfoundland, School of Graduate Studies, Faculty of Education, St. John's, NL A1C 5S7, Canada. Offers counseling psychology (M Ed); curriculum, teaching, and learning studies (M Ed); education (PhD); educational leadership studies (M Ed); information technology (M Ed); post-secondary studies (M Ed, Diploma), including health professional education (Diploma). Part-time programs available. *Degree requirements:* For master's, thesis optional, internship, paper folio, project; for doctorate, comprehensive exam, thesis/dissertation, thesis seminar, oral defense of thesis. *Entrance requirements:* For master's, undergraduate degree with at least 2nd class standing, 1-2 years work experience; for doctorate, minimum A average in graduate course work, MA in education, 2 years professional experience; for Diploma, 2nd class degree, 2 years of work experience with adult learners, appropriate academic qualifications and work experience in a health-related field. Electronic applications accepted. *Faculty research:* Critical thinking, literacy, cognitive studies and counseling, educational change, technology in instruction.

Mercer University, Graduate Studies, Cecil B. Day Campus, Tift College of Education (Atlanta), Macon, GA 31207-0003. Offers curriculum and instruction (PhD); early childhood education (M Ed, MAT); educational leadership (PhD, Ed S); middle grades education (M Ed, MAT); reading education (M Ed); secondary education (M Ed, MAT); teacher leadership (Ed S). *Accreditation:* NCATE. Part-time and evening/weekend programs available. *Faculty:* 27 full-time (14 women), 6 part-time/adjunct (3 women). *Students:* 302 full-time (251 women), 543 part-time (430 women); includes 334 minority (311 African Americans, 1 American Indian/Alaska Native, 21 Asian Americans or Pacific Islanders, 1 Hispanic American), 7 international. Average age 34. In 2009, 195 master's, 20 doctorates awarded. *Degree requirements:* For master's and Ed S, research project; for doctorate, thesis/dissertation. *Entrance requirements:* For master's, GRE or MAT, minimum undergraduate GPA of 2.75; for doctorate, GRE; for Ed S, GRE or MAT, minimum GPA of 3.25, 3 years of teaching experience. Additional exam requirements/recommendations for international students: Required—TOEFL. *Application deadline:* For fall admission, 8/1 for domestic and international students; for spring admission, 12/1 for domestic and international students. Applications are processed on a rolling basis. Application fee: $25. *Expenses:* Contact institution. *Financial support:* Federal Work-Study available. Support available to part-time students. Financial award application deadline: 5/1. *Faculty research:* Educational computing, content area reading, concept learning, importance of play for young children, multicultural literature. *Unit head:* Dr. Carl R. Martray, Dean, 478-301-5397, Fax: 478-301-2280, E-mail: martray_cr@mercer.edu. *Application contact:* Dr. Allison Gilmore, Associate Dean for Graduate Teacher Education, 678-547-6330, Fax: 678-547-6055, E-mail: gilmore_a@mercer.edu.

Mercer University, Graduate Studies, Macon Campus, Tift College of Education (Macon), Macon, GA 31207-0003. Offers collaborative education (M Ed); curriculum and instruction (PhD); educational leadership (PhD, Ed S). *Accreditation:* NCATE. Part-time and evening/weekend programs available. *Faculty:* 14 full-time (8 women), 2 part-time/adjunct (1 woman). *Students:* 85 full-time (78 women), 86 part-time (66 women); includes 51 minority (49 African Americans, 1 Asian American or Pacific Islander, 1 Hispanic American). Average age 33. In 2009, 57 master's, 12 doctorates, 6 other advanced degrees awarded. *Degree requirements:* For master's, research project report; for doctorate, thesis/dissertation. *Entrance requirements:* For master's, GRE or MAT, minimum GPA of 2.75; for doctorate, GRE. Additional exam requirements/recommendations for international students: Required—TOEFL. *Application deadline:* For fall admission, 8/1 for domestic students; for spring admission, 12/1 for domestic students. Applications are processed on a rolling basis. Application fee: $25. *Expenses:* Contact institution. *Financial support:* Federal Work-Study and institutionally sponsored loans available. Support available to part-time students. Financial award application deadline: 5/1. *Faculty research:* Teacher effectiveness, specific learning disabilities, inclusion. *Unit head:* Dr. Carl R. Martray, Dean, 478-301-5397, Fax: 478-301-2280, E-mail: martray_cr@mercer.edu. *Application contact:* Dr. Penny Elkins, Associate Dean, 678-547-6556, Fax: 678-547-6389, E-mail: elkins_pl@mercer.edu.

Miami University, Graduate School, School of Education and Allied Professions, Department of Educational Leadership, Oxford, OH 45056. Offers curriculum and teacher leadership (M Ed); educational administration (Ed D, PhD); school leadership (MS); student affairs in higher education (MS, PhD). *Accreditation:* NCATE. Part-time programs available. *Students:* 78 full-time (51 women), 77 part-time (53 women); includes 38 minority (30 African Americans, 1 American Indian/Alaska Native, 4 Asian Americans or Pacific Islanders, 3 Hispanic Americans), 4 international. *Entrance requirements:* For master's, MAT or GRE, minimum undergraduate GPA of 3.0 during previous 2 years or 2.75 overall; for doctorate, GRE, minimum GPA of 2.75 (undergraduate), 3.0 (graduate). Additional exam requirements/recommendations for international students: Required—TOEFL. Application fee: $50. *Expenses:* Tuition, state resident: full-time $11,280. Tuition, nonresident: full-time $24,912. Required fees: $516. *Financial support:* Fellowships with full tuition reimbursements, research assistantships with full tuition reimbursements, teaching assistantships with full tuition reimbursements, career-related internships or fieldwork, Federal Work-Study, health care benefits, tuition waivers (full), and unspecified assistantships available. Financial award application deadline: 3/1. *Unit head:* Dr. Kate Rousmaniere, Chair, 513-529-6843, Fax: 513-529-1729, E-mail: roumak@muohio.edu. *Application contact:* Dr. Denise Taliaferri Baszile, Director of Graduate Studies, 513-529-1798, E-mail: taliafda@muohio.edu.

Michigan State University, The Graduate School, College of Education, Department of Teacher Education, East Lansing, MI 48824. Offers curriculum, instruction and teacher education (PhD, Ed S); teaching and curriculum (MA). *Faculty:* 47 full-time (35 women). *Students:* 148 full-time (104 women), 123 part-time (95 women); includes 23 minority (14 African Americans, 1 American Indian/Alaska Native, 6 Asian Americans or Pacific Islanders, 2 Hispanic Americans), 51 international. Average age 32. 119 applicants, 57% accepted. In 2009, 73 master's, 20 doctorates awarded. *Entrance requirements:* Additional exam requirements/recommendations for international students: Required—TOEFL. *Application deadline:* Applications are processed on a rolling basis. Electronic applications accepted. *Expenses:* Tuition, state resident: part-time $478.25 per credit hour. Tuition, nonresident: part-time $966.50 per credit hour. Part-time tuition and fees vary according to program. *Financial support:* In 2009–10, 37 research assistantships with tuition reimbursements (averaging $6,891 per year), 88 teaching assistantships with tuition reimbursements (averaging $6,811 per year) were awarded; scholarships/grants and unspecified assistantships also available. Total annual research expenditures: $3.3 million. *Unit head:* Dr. Suzanne M. Wilson, Chairperson, 517-353-9150, Fax: 517-432-5092, E-mail: swilson@msu.edu. *Application contact:* Department Information, 517-353-5091, Fax: 517-432-5092.

Middle Tennessee State University, College of Graduate Studies, College of Education and Behavioral Science, Department of Educational Leadership, Program in Curriculum and Instruction, Murfreesboro, TN 37132. Offers curriculum and instruction (M Ed, Ed S); English as a second language (M Ed, Ed S); secondary education (M Ed); technology and curriculum design (Ed S). *Accreditation:* NCATE. Part-time and evening/weekend programs available. Postbaccalaureate distance learning degree programs offered. *Students:* 14 full-time (7 women), 277 part-time (249 women); includes 39 minority (35 African Americans, 3 Asian Americans or Pacific Islanders, 1 Hispanic American). 80 applicants, 89% accepted, 71 enrolled. In 2009, 69 master's, 40 Ed Ss awarded. *Degree requirements:* For master's, comprehensive exam. *Entrance requirements:* For master's and Ed S, GRE, MAT or PRAXIS. Additional exam requirements/recommendations for international students: Required—TOEFL (minimum score 525 paper-based; 195 computer-based; 71 iBT) or IELTS (minimum score 6). *Application deadline:* For fall admission, 6/1 for domestic and international students. Applications are processed on a rolling basis. Application fee: $25 ($30 for international students). Electronic applications accepted. *Expenses:* Tuition, state resident: full-time $4404. Tuition, nonresident: full-time $10,956. *Financial support:* Application deadline: 5/1. *Unit head:* Dr. James Huffman, Chair, 615-898-2855, Fax: 615-898-2859. *Application contact:* Dr. Michael Allen, Dean and Vice Provost for Research, 615-898-2840, Fax: 615-904-8020, E-mail: mallen@mtsu.edu.

Midwestern State University, Graduate Studies, College of Education, Program in Curriculum and Instruction, Wichita Falls, TX 76308. Offers ME. Part-time and evening/weekend programs available. *Degree requirements:* For master's, comprehensive exam. *Entrance requirements:* For master's, GRE General Test, MAT, or GMAT. Additional exam requirements/recommendations for international students: Required—TOEFL (minimum score 550 paper-based; 213 computer-based). Electronic applications accepted. *Expenses:* Tuition, state resident: full-time $1620; part-time $90 per credit hour. Tuition, nonresident: full-time $2160; part-time $120 per credit hour. International tuition: $7506 full-time. Required fees: $3068.80; $145.60 per credit hour. $179 per semester.

Mills College, Graduate Studies, School of Education, Oakland, CA 94613-1000. Offers child life in hospitals (MA); early childhood education (MA); education (MA), including art education, curriculum and instruction, elementary education, English education, foreign language education, mathematics education, science education, secondary education, social studies education, teaching; educational leadership (MA, Ed D); infant mental health (MA). Part-time and evening/weekend programs available. *Faculty:* 11 full-time (9 women), 16 part-time/adjunct (14 women). *Students:* 138 full-time (119 women), 55 part-time (48 women); includes 71 minority (34 African Americans, 19 Asian Americans or Pacific Islanders, 18 Hispanic Americans), 3 international. Average age 34. 210 applicants, 82% accepted, 93 enrolled. In 2009, 54 master's, 15 doctorates awarded. Terminal master's awarded for partial completion of doctoral program. *Degree requirements:* For master's, comprehensive exam. *Entrance requirements:* For doctorate, GRE General Test. Additional exam requirements/recommendations for international students: Required—TOEFL. *Application deadline:* For fall admission, 2/1 for domestic and international students; for spring admission, 11/1 for domestic and international students. Applications are processed on a rolling basis. Application fee: $50. Electronic applications accepted. *Expenses:* Tuition: Full-time $26,326; part-time $6584 per course. Required fees: $896. One-time fee: $896 part-time. Tuition and fees vary according to program. *Financial support:* In 2009–10, 188 students received support, including 186 fellowships (averaging $6,499 per year), 28 teaching assistantships with partial tuition reimbursements available (averaging $3,187 per year); career-related internships or fieldwork and scholarships/grants also available. Support available to part-time students. Financial award application deadline: 2/1; financial award applicants required to submit FAFSA. *Faculty research:* Child development, gender and education, public policy, cross-cultural development, development of literacy. Total annual

Curriculum and Instruction

Mills College (continued)
research expenditures: $1.2 million. *Unit head:* Joseph Kahne, Chairperson, 510-430-3190, Fax: 510-430-3314, E-mail: grad-studies@mills.edu. *Application contact:* Jessica King, Graduate Admission Specialist, 510-430-3305, Fax: 510-430-2159, E-mail: grad-studies@mills.edu.

Minnesota State University Mankato, College of Graduate Studies, College of Education, Department of Educational Studies: K–12 and Secondary Programs, Mankato, MN 56001. Offers curriculum and instruction (SP); educational technology (MS); library media education (MS, Certificate); teacher licensure program (MAT); teaching and learning (MS, Certificate). *Accreditation:* NCATE. *Students:* 34 full-time (23 women), 100 part-time (75 women). *Degree requirements:* For master's, comprehensive exam, thesis or alternative; for other advanced degree, comprehensive exam, thesis. *Entrance requirements:* For master's, GRE General Test or MAT, minimum GPA of 3.0 during previous 2 years; for other advanced degree, GRE, minimum GPA of 3.0. Additional exam requirements/recommendations for international students: Required—TOEFL. *Application deadline:* For fall admission, 7/1 priority date for domestic students, 5/1 for international students; for spring admission, 11/1 for domestic students, 10/1 for international students. Applications are processed on a rolling basis. Application fee: $40. Electronic applications accepted. *Expenses:* Tuition, state resident: full-time $5364. Tuition, nonresident: full-time $8314. *Financial support:* Application deadline: 3/15. *Unit head:* Dr. Kitty Foord, Chairperson, 507-389-1965. *Application contact:* 507-389-2321, E-mail: grad@mnsu.edu.

Minnesota State University Moorhead, Graduate Studies, College of Education and Human Services, Program in Curriculum and Instruction, Moorhead, MN 56563-0002. Offers MS. *Accreditation:* NCATE. Part-time programs available. *Degree requirements:* For master's, comprehensive exam, final oral exam, project or thesis. *Entrance requirements:* For master's, MAT, bachelor's degree in education, minimum GPA of 2.75, one year teaching experience. Additional exam requirements/recommendations for international students: Required—TOEFL (minimum score 550 paper-based; 213 computer-based). Electronic applications accepted.

Misericordia University, College of Professional Studies and Social Sciences, Program in Education/Curriculum, Dallas, PA 18612-1098. Offers MS. Part-time and evening/weekend programs available. Postbaccalaureate distance learning degree programs offered. *Faculty:* 4 full-time (3 women), 9 part-time/adjunct (4 women). *Students:* 48 part-time (37 women); includes 2 minority (1 Asian American or Pacific Islander, 1 Hispanic American). Average age 32. In 2009, 9 master's awarded. *Degree requirements:* For master's, thesis or alternative. *Entrance requirements:* For master's, GRE General Test or MAT, minimum GPA of 3.0. *Application deadline:* For fall admission, 8/1 priority date for domestic students. Applications are processed on a rolling basis. Application fee: $25. Electronic applications accepted. *Financial support:* In 2009–10, 12 students received support. Scholarships/grants available. Support available to part-time students. Financial award application deadline: 6/30; financial award applicants required to submit FAFSA. *Unit head:* Dr. Catherine Kosenak, Director of Graduate Education Programs, 570-674-8058, E-mail: ckosenak@misericordia.edu. *Application contact:* Larree Brown, Coordinator of Part-Time Undergraduate and Graduate Programs, 570-674-6451, Fax: 570-674-6232, E-mail: lbrown@misericordia.edu.

Mississippi College, Graduate School, School of Education, Department of Teacher Education and Leadership, Clinton, MS 39058. Offers art (M Ed); biological science (M Ed); business education (M Ed); computer science (M Ed); dyslexia therapy (M Ed); educational leadership (M Ed, Ed D, Ed S); elementary education (M Ed, Ed S); English (M Ed); higher education administration (MS); mathematics (M Ed); secondary education (M Ed); social studies (history) (M Ed); teaching arts (M Ed). Part-time programs available. Postbaccalaureate distance learning degree programs offered (no on-campus study). *Faculty:* 11 full-time (7 women), 13 part-time/adjunct (7 women). *Students:* 33 full-time (22 women), 282 part-time (240 women); includes 148 minority (146 African Americans, 2 American Indian/Alaska Native), 1 international. Average age 34. In 2009, 147 master's awarded. *Degree requirements:* For master's, comprehensive exam, thesis optional. *Entrance requirements:* For master's, NTE. Additional exam requirements/recommendations for international students: Recommended—IELTS. *Application deadline:* For fall admission, 8/15 priority date for domestic students. Applications are processed on a rolling basis. Application fee: $30. Electronic applications accepted. *Expenses:* Tuition: Part-time $452 per credit hour. Required fees: $101 per semester. Tuition and fees vary according to degree level, campus/location, program and student level. *Financial support:* Teaching assistantships, career-related internships or fieldwork, Federal Work-Study, scholarships/grants, and unspecified assistantships available. Support available to part-time students. Financial award applicants required to submit FAFSA. *Unit head:* Dr. Tom Williams, Chair, 601-925-3844, E-mail: twilliams@mc.edu. *Application contact:* Elnora Lewis, Secretary, 601-925-3225, Fax: 601-925-3889, E-mail: lewis09@mc.edu.

Mississippi State University, College of Education, Department of Curriculum, Instruction and Special Education, Mississippi State, MS 39762. Offers curriculum and instruction (PhD); education (Ed D, Ed S), including elementary education, secondary education, special education (Ed S); elementary education (MS, PhD); secondary education (MS, PhD); secondary teacher alternate route (MAT); special education (MS). *Accreditation:* NCATE. Part-time and evening/weekend programs available. *Faculty:* 13 full-time (11 women). *Students:* 35 full-time (33 women), 126 part-time (103 women); includes 55 minority (all African Americans). Average age 35. 80 applicants, 60% accepted, 40 enrolled. In 2009, 60 master's, 6 doctorates, 7 other advanced degrees awarded. *Degree requirements:* For master's, comprehensive exam; for doctorate, thesis/dissertation; for Ed S, comprehensive exam, thesis or alternative. *Entrance requirements:* For master's, GRE, minimum GPA of 2.75 in junior and senior year, eligibility for initial teacher certification; for doctorate, GRE, minimum graduate GPA of 3.4; for Ed S, GRE, minimum graduate GPA of 3.2. Additional exam requirements/recommendations for international students: Required—TOEFL (minimum score 600 paper-based; 250 computer-based; 100 iBT); Recommended—IELTS (minimum score 7.5). *Application deadline:* For fall admission, 3/1 priority date for domestic students, 5/1 for international students; for spring admission, 9/1 priority date for domestic students, 9/1 for international students. Applications are processed on a rolling basis. Application fee: $40. Electronic applications accepted. *Expenses:* Tuition, state resident: full-time $2575.50; part-time $286.25 per credit hour. Tuition, nonresident: full-time $6510; part-time $723.50 per credit hour. Tuition and fees vary according to course load. *Financial support:* In 2009–10, 30 students received support, including 5 research assistantships with full and partial tuition reimbursements available (averaging $8,959 per year), 3 teaching assistantships (averaging $10,443 per year); Federal Work-Study, institutionally sponsored loans, scholarships/grants, and unspecified assistantships also available. Financial award applicants required to submit FAFSA. *Faculty research:* Early childhood education, reading, rural schools, multicultural education, use of technology in instruction. *Unit head:* Dr. Charlotte S. Burroughs, Associate Professor and Interim Head, 662-325-3747, Fax: 662-325-7857, E-mail: susie.burroughs@msstate.edu. *Application contact:* Dr. Kent Coffey, Professor and Graduate Coordinator, 662-325-2188, Fax: 662-325-7857, E-mail: kcoffey@colled.msstate.edu.

Mississippi University for Women, Graduate School, College of Education and Human Sciences, Columbus, MS 39701-9998. Offers differentiated instruction (M Ed); gifted studies (M Ed); teaching (MAT). *Accreditation:* ASHA; NCATE. Part-time programs available. *Degree requirements:* For master's, comprehensive exam, thesis optional. *Entrance requirements:* For master's, GRE General Test or NTE (M Ed in gifted education or MS in speech/language pathology), MAT (M Ed in instructional management), minimum QPA of 3.0.

Missouri State University, Graduate College, College of Education, Department of Reading, Foundations, and Technology, Program in Teaching, Springfield, MO 65897. Offers MAT. Part-time programs available. *Students:* 66 full-time (44 women), 94 part-time (54 women); includes 10 minority (1 African American, 1 American Indian/Alaska Native, 1 Asian American or Pacific Islander, 7 Hispanic Americans). Average age 35. 10 applicants, 100% accepted, 6 enrolled. In 2009, 30 master's awarded. *Degree requirements:* For master's, comprehensive exam, project. *Entrance requirements:* For master's, PRAXIS II. Additional exam requirements/recommendations for international students: Required—TOEFL (minimum score 550 paper-based; 213 computer-based; 79 iBT). *Application deadline:* For fall admission, 2/15 priority date for domestic and international students. Application fee: $35 ($50 for international students). Electronic applications accepted. *Expenses:* Tuition, state resident: full-time $3852; part-time $214 per credit hour. Tuition, nonresident: full-time $7524; part-time $418 per credit hour. Required fees: $696; $172 per semester. Tuition and fees vary according to course level, course load, degree level and program. *Financial support:* Federal Work-Study, institutionally sponsored loans, scholarships/grants, tuition waivers (full), and unspecified assistantships available. Financial award application deadline: 3/31; financial award applicants required to submit FAFSA. *Unit head:* Dr. Emmett Sawyer, Coordinator, 417-836-3170, E-mail: emmettsawyer@missouristate.edu. *Application contact:* Eric Eckert, Coordinator of Admissions and Recruitment, 417-836-5331, Fax: 417-836-6200, E-mail: ericeckert@missouristate.edu.

Montana State University, College of Graduate Studies, College of Education, Health, and Human Development, Department of Education, Bozeman, MT 59717. Offers adult and higher education (Ed D); curriculum and instruction (Ed D, Ed S); education (M Ed), including adult and higher education, curriculum and instruction, educational leadership, school counseling; educational leadership (Ed D, Ed S). Part-time programs available. Postbaccalaureate distance learning degree programs offered (minimal on-campus study). *Faculty:* 22 full-time (13 women), 18 part-time/adjunct (14 women). *Students:* 15 full-time (8 women), 210 part-time (126 women); includes 29 minority (27 American Indian/Alaska Native, 1 Asian American or Pacific Islander, 1 Hispanic American), 2 international. Average age 37. 52 applicants. In 2009, 62 master's, 9 doctorates awarded. *Degree requirements:* For master's, comprehensive exam; for doctorate, comprehensive exam, thesis/dissertation. *Entrance requirements:* For master's and doctorate, GRE General Test. Additional exam requirements/recommendations for international students: Required—TOEFL (minimum score 550 paper-based; 213 computer-based). *Application deadline:* For fall admission, 7/15 priority date for domestic students, 5/15 priority date for international students; for spring admission, 12/1 priority date for domestic students, 10/1 priority date for international students. Applications are processed on a rolling basis. Application fee: $30. Electronic applications accepted. *Expenses:* Tuition, state resident: full-time $5635; part-time $3492 per year. Tuition, nonresident: full-time $17,212; part-time $7865.10 per year. Required fees: $1441; $153.15 per credit. Tuition and fees vary according to course load and program. *Financial support:* In 2009–10, 45 students received support, including 5 teaching assistantships with tuition reimbursements available (averaging $9,000 per year); traineeships, tuition waivers (full and partial), and unspecified assistantships also available. Financial award application deadline: 3/1; financial award applicants required to submit FAFSA. *Faculty research:* Online teaching and learning, statistical strategies to course and student assessment, environmental education, copyright issues/web-based resources, multicultural education, curriculum design, preparation for North American teachers to be administrators, NCES data sets, relational trust in public school administration. Total annual research expenditures: $1.2 million. *Unit head:* Dr. Joanne Erickson, Interim Department Head, 406-994-6670, Fax: 406-994-3261, E-mail: jle@montana.edu. *Application contact:* Dr. Carl A. Fox, Vice Provost for Graduate Education, 406-994-4145, Fax: 406-994-7433, E-mail: gradstudy@montana.edu.

Montana State University Billings, College of Education, Department of Educational Theory and Practice, Option in General Curriculum, Billings, MT 59101-0298. Offers M Ed. *Accreditation:* NCATE. Part-time programs available. *Degree requirements:* For master's, thesis or professional paper and/or field experience. *Entrance requirements:* For master's, GRE General Test or MAT, minimum GPA of 3.0 (undergraduate), 3.25 (graduate). *Faculty research:* Social studies education, science education.

Montclair State University, The Graduate School, College of Education and Human Services, Center of Pedagogy, Montclair, NJ 07043-1624. Offers pedagogy and philosophy (Ed D). Part-time programs available. *Students:* 8 full-time (5 women), 16 part-time (7 women). Average age 37. 5 applicants, 40% accepted, 2 enrolled. In 2009, 2 doctorates awarded. *Degree requirements:* For doctorate, thesis/dissertation. *Entrance requirements:* For doctorate, GRE, 3 letters of recommendation. Additional exam requirements/recommendations for international students: Required—TOEFL, or IELTS. *Application deadline:* For fall admission, 2/1 for domestic students, 11/15 for international students. Application fee: $60. Electronic applications accepted. *Expenses:* Tuition, area resident: Part-time $486.74 per credit. Tuition, state resident: part-time $486.74 per credit. Tuition, nonresident: part-time $751.34 per credit. Tuition and fees vary according to degree level and program. *Financial support:* In 2009–10, 4 teaching assistantships (averaging $10,000 per year) were awarded; Federal Work-Study, institutionally sponsored loans, scholarships/grants, and unspecified assistantships also available. Support available to part-time students. Financial award application deadline: 3/1; financial award applicants required to submit FAFSA. *Unit head:* Jennifer Robinson, Director, 973-655-4262. *Application contact:* Amy Aiello, Director of Graduate Admissions and Operations, 973-655-5147, Fax: 973-655-7869, E-mail: graduate.school@montclair.edu.

Montclair State University, The Graduate School, College of Education and Human Services, Department of Curriculum and Teaching, Montclair, NJ 07043-1624. Offers education (M Ed); educational technology (M Ed); learning disabled teacher consultant (Certificate); school library media specialist (Certificate); teaching (MAT, Certificate), including art (MAT), biological science (MAT), early childhood education (P-3) (MAT), earth science (MAT), elementary education (K-8) (MAT), English (MAT), French (MAT), health and physical education (MAT), health education (MAT), home economics (MAT), mathematics (MAT), music (MAT), physical education (MAT), physical science (MAT), social studies (MAT), Spanish (MAT), teacher of ESL (MAT), teacher of students with disabilities (MAT). Part-time and evening/weekend programs available. *Faculty:* 17 full-time (12 women), 29 part-time/adjunct (21 women). *Students:* 124 full-time (63 women), 174 part-time (126 women). Average age 31. 112 applicants, 69% accepted, 59 enrolled. In 2009, 179 master's, 2 other advanced degrees awarded. *Degree requirements:* For master's, comprehensive exam, field experience. *Entrance requirements:* For master's, GRE, 2 letters of recommendation. Additional exam requirements/recommendations for international students: Required—TOEFL (minimum score 83 computer-based), or IELTS. *Application deadline:* For fall admission, 2/15 for domestic and international students; for spring admission, 9/15 for domestic and international students. Applications are processed on a rolling basis. Application fee: $60. Electronic applications accepted. *Expenses:* Tuition, area resident: Part-time $486.74 per credit. Tuition, state resident: part-time $486.74 per credit. Tuition, nonresident: part-time $751.34 per credit. Tuition and fees vary according to degree level and program. *Financial support:* In 2009–10, 12 research assistantships with full tuition reimbursements (averaging $7,000 per year) were awarded; Federal Work-Study, scholarships/grants, and unspecified assistantships also available. Support available to part-time students. Financial award application deadline: 3/1; financial award applicants required to submit FAFSA. *Unit head:* Dr. David Schwarzer, Chairperson, 973-655-5187. *Application contact:* Amy Aiello, Director of Graduate Admissions and Operations, 973-655-5147, Fax: 973-655-7869, E-mail: graduate.school@montclair.edu.

Moravian College, Moravian College Comenius Center, Education Programs, Bethlehem, PA 18018-6650. Offers curriculum and instruction (M Ed). Part-time and evening/weekend programs available. *Faculty:* 4 full-time (2 women), 11 part-time/adjunct (6 women). *Students:* 61 part-time (48 women). Average age 35. 23 applicants, 65% accepted, 13 enrolled. In 2009, 18 master's awarded. *Degree requirements:* For master's, thesis. *Entrance requirements:* For master's, state teacher certification. Application fee: $40. *Expenses:* Tuition: Part-time $1132 per course. Required fees: $40 per term. One-time fee: $30 part-time. *Unit head:* Dr. Joseph Shosh, Dean, Continuing and Graduate Studies, 610-861-1400, Fax: 610-861-1466, E-mail: comenius@moravian.edu. *Application contact:* Dr. Joseph Shosh, Dean, Continuing and Graduate Studies, 610-861-1400, Fax: 610-861-1466, E-mail: comenius@moravian.edu.

Morehead State University, Graduate Programs, College of Education, Department of Curriculum and Instruction, Morehead, KY 40351. Offers curriculum and instruction (Ed S); elementary education (MA Ed), including elementary education, international education, middle school education, reading; secondary education (MA Ed); special education (MA Ed); teaching (MAT). Part-time and evening/weekend programs available. *Faculty:* 25 full-time (17 women), 2 part-time/adjunct (1 woman). *Students:* 25 full-time (22 women), 165 part-time (139 women); includes 4 minority (1 African American, 2 American Indian/Alaska Native, 1 Hispanic American). Average age 33. 148 applicants, 68% accepted, 48 enrolled. In 2009, 178 master's awarded.

Degree requirements: For master's, comprehensive exam, thesis optional; for Ed S, thesis, oral exam. *Entrance requirements:* For master's, GRE General Test, minimum GPA of 2.75, teaching certificate; for Ed S, GRE General Test, interview, master's degree, minimum GPA of 3.5, work experience. Additional exam requirements/recommendations for international students: Required—TOEFL (minimum score 500 paper-based; 173 computer-based). *Application deadline:* For fall admission, 8/1 priority date for domestic and international students; for spring admission, 12/1 priority date for domestic and international students. Applications are processed on a rolling basis. Application fee: $30. Electronic applications accepted. *Expenses:* Tuition, state resident: full-time $6318; part-time $351 per credit hour. Tuition, nonresident: full-time $15,804; part-time $878 per credit hour. *Financial support:* In 2009–10, 2 teaching assistantships (averaging $6,000 per year) were awarded; career-related internships or fieldwork, Federal Work-Study, and unspecified assistantships also available. Financial award application deadline: 3/15; financial award applicants required to submit FAFSA. *Faculty research:* Communicative competence of learning-disabled students, teaching social studies in elementary schools, ungraded primary school organization, study skills. *Unit head:* Dr. James Knoll, Chair, 606-783-2598, Fax: 606-783-5044, E-mail: j.knoll@moreheadstate.edu. *Application contact:* Michelle Barber, Graduate Recruitment and Retention Assistant Director, 606-783-5127, Fax: 606-783-5061, E-mail: m.barber@moreheadstate.edu.

Morehead State University, Graduate Programs, College of Education, Department of Foundational and Graduate Studies in Education, Morehead, KY 40351. Offers adult and higher education (MA, Ed S); certified professional counselor (Ed S); counseling P-12 (MA); curriculum and instruction (Ed S); educational technology (MA Ed); instructional leadership (Ed S); school administration (MA); school counseling (Ed S); teacher leader business and marketing- content (MA Ed); teacher leader business and marketing- technology (MA Ed); teacher leader educational technology (MA Ed); teacher leader English (MA Ed); teacher leader gifted educ (MA Ed); teacher leader IECE—non-certification (MA Ed); teacher leader IECE certification (MA Ed); teacher leader interdisciplanary education P-5 (MA Ed); teacher leader middle grades 5-9 (MA Ed); teacher leader reading/writing—non-certification (MA Ed); teacher leader reading/writing certification (MA Ed); teacher leader school communication—non-certification (MA Ed); teacher leader school communication certification (MA Ed); teacher leader social studies (MA Ed); teacher leader special education (MA Ed). *Accreditation:* NCATE. Part-time and evening/weekend programs available. *Faculty:* 20 full-time (10 women), 7 part-time/adjunct (3 women). *Students:* 26 full-time (18 women), 371 part-time (295 women); includes 11 minority (9 African Americans, 1 American Indian/Alaska Native, 1 Hispanic American). Average age 35. 201 applicants, 73% accepted, 73 enrolled. In 2009, 105 master's, 5 other advanced degrees awarded. *Degree requirements:* For master's, thesis optional, oral and/or written comprehensive exams; for Ed S, thesis, oral exam. *Entrance requirements:* For master's, GRE General Test, minimum overall undergraduate GPA of 2.5; for Ed S, GRE General Test, interview, master's degree, minimum GPA of 3.5, work experience. Additional exam requirements/recommendations for international students: Required—TOEFL (minimum score 500 paper-based; 173 computer-based). *Application deadline:* For fall admission, 8/1 priority date for domestic and international students; for spring admission, 12/1 priority date for domestic and international students. Applications are processed on a rolling basis. Application fee: $30. Electronic applications accepted. *Expenses:* Tuition, state resident: full-time $6318; part-time $351 per credit hour. Tuition, nonresident: full-time $15,804; part-time $878 per credit hour. *Financial support:* In 2009–10, 2 research assistantships (averaging $10,000 per year) were awarded; career-related internships or fieldwork, Federal Work-Study, and unspecified assistantships also available. Financial award application deadline: 3/15; financial award applicants required to submit FAFSA. *Faculty research:* Character education, school accountability, computer applications for school administrators. *Unit head:* Dr. Cathy Gunn, Dean and Professor, 606-783-2040, Fax: 606-783-5029, E-mail: c.gunn@moreheadstate.edu. *Application contact:* Michelle Barber, Graduate Recruitment and Retention Assistant Director, 606-783-5127, Fax: 606-783-5061, E-mail: m.barber@moreheadstate.edu.

Mount Saint Vincent University, Graduate Programs, Faculty of Education, Program in Curriculum Studies, Halifax, NS B3M 2J6, Canada. Offers education of young adolescents (M Ed, MA Ed, MA-R); general studies (M Ed, MA Ed, MA-R); teaching English as a second language (M Ed, MA Ed, MA-R). Part-time and evening/weekend programs available. Postbaccalaureate distance learning degree programs offered (minimal on-campus study). *Degree requirements:* For master's, thesis (for some programs). *Entrance requirements:* For master's, bachelor's degree in related field, minimum B average, 1 year of teaching experience. Electronic applications accepted. *Faculty research:* Science education, cultural studies, international education, curriculum development.

National-Louis University, National College of Education, Doctoral Programs in Education, Program in Curriculum and Social Inquiry, Chicago, IL 60603. Offers Ed D. Part-time and evening/weekend programs available. *Degree requirements:* For doctorate, comprehensive exam, thesis/dissertation. *Entrance requirements:* For doctorate, GRE General Test, interview, minimum GPA of 3.25, resume, writing sample. *Expenses:* Tuition: Full-time $17,160; part-time $715 per semester hour. Tuition and fees vary according to course load, degree level, campus/location and program.

National-Louis University, National College of Education, Program in Curriculum and Instruction, Chicago, IL 60603. Offers M Ed, MS Ed, CAS. Part-time and evening/weekend programs available. *Entrance requirements:* For master's, GRE or MAT, minimum GPA of 3.0, teaching certificate; for CAS, master's degree, teaching certificate. *Expenses:* Tuition: Full-time $17,160; part-time $715 per semester hour. Tuition and fees vary according to course load, degree level, campus/location and program.

National-Louis University, National College of Education, Program in Interdisciplinary Studies in Curriculum and Instruction, Chicago, IL 60603. Offers M Ed. Part-time and evening/weekend programs available. *Entrance requirements:* For master's, GRE or MAT, minimum GPA of 3.0, teaching certificate. *Expenses:* Tuition: Full-time $17,160; part-time $715 per semester hour. Tuition and fees vary according to course load, degree level, campus/location and program.

Newman University, School of Education, Wichita, KS 67213-2097. Offers building leadership (MS Ed); curriculum and instruction (MS Ed), including accountability, English as a second language. *Accreditation:* NCATE. Part-time programs available. Postbaccalaureate distance learning degree programs offered (no on-campus study). *Faculty:* 3 full-time (0 women), 22 part-time/adjunct (all women). *Students:* 12 full-time (8 women), 329 part-time (263 women); includes 29 minority (5 African Americans, 2 American Indian/Alaska Native, 5 Asian Americans or Pacific Islanders, 17 Hispanic Americans), 4 international. Average age 37. 41 applicants, 76% accepted, 24 enrolled. In 2009, 57 master's awarded. *Degree requirements:* For master's, thesis optional. *Entrance requirements:* For master's, interview, minimum GPA of 3.0, writing sample, 3 letters of recommendation. Additional exam requirements/recommendations for international students: Required—TOEFL (minimum score 600 paper-based; 250 computer-based; 100 iBT). *Application deadline:* For fall admission, 8/15 priority date for domestic students, 7/15 priority date for international students; for spring admission, 1/10 priority date for domestic students, 11/15 priority date for international students. Applications are processed on a rolling basis. Application fee: $25 ($40 for international students). Electronic applications accepted. *Expenses:* Contact institution. *Financial support:* In 2009–10, 8 students received support. Federal Work-Study available. Financial award application deadline: 8/15; financial award applicants required to submit FAFSA. *Unit head:* Dr. Guy Glidden, Director, 316-942-4291 Ext. 2331, Fax: 316-942-4483, E-mail: gliddeng@newmanu.edu. *Application contact:* Linda Kay Sabala, Director of Graduate Admissions, 316-942-4291 Ext. 2230, Fax: 316-942-4483, E-mail: sabalal@newmanu.edu.

New Mexico Highlands University, Graduate Studies, School of Education, Las Vegas, NM 87701. Offers curriculum and instruction (MA); education (MA), including counseling, school counseling; educational leadership (MA); exercise and sport sciences (MA), including human performance and sport, sports administration, teacher education; guidance and counseling (MA), including professional counseling, rehabilitation counseling, school counseling; special education (MA), including). Part-time programs available. *Degree requirements:* For master's, comprehensive exam, thesis or alternative. *Entrance requirements:* For master's, minimum undergraduate GPA of 3.0. Additional exam requirements/recommendations for international students: Required—TOEFL (minimum score 540 paper-based; 207 computer-based). *Faculty research:* Teaching the United States Constitution, middle school curriculum, integrated computer applications for pre-service classroom teachers, adolescent literacy, narrative cognitive modes in NM multicultural setting.

New Mexico State University, Graduate School, College of Education, Department of Curriculum and Instruction, Las Cruces, NM 88003-8001. Offers curriculum and instruction (MAT, Ed D, PhD, Ed S); general education (MA). *Accreditation:* NCATE. Part-time programs available. Postbaccalaureate distance learning degree programs offered (minimal on-campus study). *Faculty:* 30 full-time (16 women), 18 part-time/adjunct (13 women). *Students:* 179 full-time (143 women), 346 part-time (257 women); includes 248 minority (22 African Americans, 9 American Indian/Alaska Native, 11 Asian Americans or Pacific Islanders, 206 Hispanic Americans), 29 international. Average age 37. 278 applicants, 95% accepted, 163 enrolled. In 2009, 148 master's, 10 doctorates, 1 other advanced degree awarded. *Degree requirements:* For master's, thesis optional; for doctorate, comprehensive exam, thesis/dissertation. *Entrance requirements:* For master's, minimum GPA of 2.5 in last 12 hours of course work; for doctorate, portfolio. *Application deadline:* For fall admission, 7/1 priority date for domestic students; for spring admission, 11/1 for domestic students. Applications are processed on a rolling basis. Application fee: $30 ($50 for international students). *Expenses:* Tuition, state resident: full-time $4080; part-time $223 per credit. Tuition, nonresident: full-time $14,256; part-time $647 per credit. Required fees: $1278; $639 per semester. *Financial support:* In 2009–10, 8 research assistantships (averaging $13,582 per year), 38 teaching assistantships (averaging $14,200 per year) were awarded; fellowships, career-related internships or fieldwork, Federal Work-Study, scholarships/grants, health care benefits, and unspecified assistantships also available. Support available to part-time students. Financial award application deadline: 3/1. *Faculty research:* Multicultural education, literacy/biliteracy education, bilingual and English as a second language education, critical pedagogy, education for democratic society. *Unit head:* Dr. Elizabeth Cahill, Head, 575-646-2990, Fax: 575-646-5436, E-mail: bcahill@nmsu.edu. *Application contact:* Dr. Elizabeth Cahill, Head, 575-646-2990, Fax: 575-646-5436, E-mail: bcahill@nmsu.edu.

New York University, Steinhardt School of Culture, Education, and Human Development, Department of Teaching and Learning, Program in English Education, New York, NY 10012-1019. Offers secondary and college (PhD), including applied linguistics, comparative education, curriculum, literature and reading, media education; teachers of English 7-12 (MA); teachers of English language and literature in college (Advanced Certificate). *Accreditation:* Teacher Education Accreditation Council. Part-time programs available. *Students:* 36 full-time (30 women), 30 part-time (25 women); includes 11 minority (4 African Americans, 3 Asian Americans or Pacific Islanders, 4 Hispanic Americans), 2 international. Average age 26. 91 applicants, 80% accepted, 21 enrolled. In 2009, 27 master's, 6 doctorates, 1 other advanced degree awarded. *Degree requirements:* For master's, thesis (for some programs); for doctorate, thesis/dissertation. *Entrance requirements:* For doctorate, GRE General Test, interview; for Advanced Certificate, master's degree. Additional exam requirements/recommendations for international students: Required—TOEFL. *Application deadline:* For fall admission, 12/15 priority date for domestic and international students; for spring admission, 11/1 for domestic and international students. Applications are processed on a rolling basis. Application fee: $75. Electronic applications accepted. *Expenses:* Tuition: Full-time $30,528; part-time $1272 per credit. Required fees: $2177. *Financial support:* Fellowships with full and partial tuition reimbursements, teaching assistantships with full and partial tuition reimbursements, career-related internships or fieldwork, Federal Work-Study, institutionally sponsored loans, scholarships/grants, tuition waivers (partial), and unspecified assistantships available. Support available to part-time students. Financial award application deadline: 2/1; financial award applicants required to submit FAFSA. *Faculty research:* Making meaning of literature, teaching of literature, urban adolescent literacy and equity, literacy development and globalization, digital media and literacy. *Unit head:* Director, 212-998-5460, Fax: 212-995-4049. *Application contact:* 212-998-5030, Fax: 212-995-4328, E-mail: steinhardt.gradadmissions@nyu.edu.

Nicholls State University, Graduate Studies, College of Education, Department of Teacher Education, Thibodaux, LA 70310. Offers administration and supervision (M Ed); counselor education (M Ed); curriculum and instruction (M Ed). *Accreditation:* NCATE. Part-time and evening/weekend programs available. *Degree requirements:* For master's, comprehensive exam, portfolio. *Entrance requirements:* For master's, GRE General Test, teaching license. Electronic applications accepted.

North Carolina Central University, Division of Academic Affairs, School of Education, Department of Curriculum, Instruction and Professional Studies, Durham, NC 27707-3129. Offers curriculum and instruction (MA), including elementary education, middle grades education. *Accreditation:* NCATE. Part-time and evening/weekend programs available. *Degree requirements:* For master's, comprehensive exam, thesis or alternative. *Entrance requirements:* For master's, minimum GPA of 3.0 in major, 2.5 overall. Additional exam requirements/recommendations for international students: Required—TOEFL. *Faculty research:* Simulation of decision-making behavior of school boards.

North Carolina State University, Graduate School, College of Education, Department of Curriculum and Instruction, Program in Curriculum and Instruction, Raleigh, NC 27695. Offers M Ed, MS, PhD. *Accreditation:* NCATE. *Degree requirements:* For master's, thesis (for some programs); for doctorate, thesis/dissertation. *Entrance requirements:* For master's, GRE General Test or MAT, minimum GPA of 3.0 in major; for doctorate, GRE General Test, minimum GPA of 3.0 in major. Electronic applications accepted. *Faculty research:* Curriculum development, teacher development, intervention for exceptional children, literacy development.

North Central College, Graduate Programs, Department of Education, Naperville, IL 60566-7063. Offers curriculum and instruction (MA Ed); leadership and administration (MA Ed). Part-time and evening/weekend programs available. *Degree requirements:* For master's, clinical practicum, project. *Entrance requirements:* For master's, interview. *Expenses:* Contact institution.

Northern Arizona University, Graduate College, College of Education, Department of Educational Specialties, Flagstaff, AZ 86011. Offers autism spectrum disorders (Certificate); bilingual/multicultural education (M Ed), including bilingual education, ESL education; career and technical education (M Ed, Certificate); curriculum and instruction (Ed D); early childhood special education (M Ed); early intervention (Certificate); educational technology (M Ed, Certificate); special education (M Ed). *Faculty:* 29 full-time (16 women). *Students:* 153 full-time (118 women), 360 part-time (291 women); includes 152 minority (12 African Americans, 43 American Indian/Alaska Native, 5 Asian Americans or Pacific Islanders, 92 Hispanic Americans), 9 international. Average age 30. 215 applicants, 87% accepted, 133 enrolled. In 2009, 200 master's, 8 doctorates awarded. *Degree requirements:* For master's, comprehensive exam (for some programs), thesis (for some programs). *Entrance requirements:* For master's, minimum GPA of 3.0. Additional exam requirements/recommendations for international students: Required—TOEFL (minimum score 550 paper-based; 213 computer-based; 80 iBT), IELTS (minimum score 7), or a bachelor's degree from an English-speaking university and demonstrated proficiency. *Application deadline:* For fall admission, 2/1 for domestic students, 8/1 for international students; for spring admission, 12/1 for domestic students. Applications are processed on a rolling basis. Application fee: $65. Electronic applications accepted. *Financial support:* In 2009–10, 2 research assistantships with partial tuition reimbursements (averaging $10,000 per year), 8 teaching assistantships with partial tuition reimbursements (averaging $10,000 per year) were awarded. Financial award application deadline: 3/30. *Unit head:* Dr. Lawrence Gallagher, Chair, 928-523-5083, E-mail: lawrence.gallagher@nau.edu. *Application contact:* Dr. Lawrence Gallagher, Chair, 928-523-5083, E-mail: lawrence.gallagher@nau.edu.

Northern Illinois University, Graduate School, College of Education, Department of Teaching and Learning, De Kalb, IL 60115-2854. Offers curriculum and instruction (MS Ed, Ed D), including curriculum leadership (Ed D), elementary education (Ed D), secondary education (Ed D); early childhood education (MS Ed); elementary education (MS Ed); special education

Curriculum and Instruction

Northern Illinois University *(continued)*

(MS Ed). Part-time and evening/weekend programs available. *Faculty:* 22 full-time (14 women), 2 part-time/adjunct (both women). *Students:* 50 full-time (38 women), 435 part-time (344 women); includes 107 minority (16 African Americans, 1 American Indian/Alaska Native, 12 Asian Americans or Pacific Islanders, 78 Hispanic Americans), 9 international. Average age 35. 154 applicants, 53% accepted, 57 enrolled. In 2009, 142 master's, 2 doctorates awarded. *Degree requirements:* For master's, comprehensive exam, thesis optional; for doctorate, thesis/dissertation, candidacy exam, dissertation defense. *Entrance requirements:* For master's, GRE General Test or MAT, minimum undergraduate GPA of 2.75; for doctorate, GRE General Test or MAT, minimum undergraduate GPA of 2.75, graduate 3.2. Additional exam requirements/recommendations for international students: Required—TOEFL (minimum score 550 paper-based; 213 computer-based). *Application deadline:* For fall admission, 6/1 for domestic students, 5/1 for international students; for spring admission, 11/1 for domestic students, 10/1 for international students. Applications are processed on a rolling basis. Application fee: $30. Electronic applications accepted. *Expenses:* Tuition, state resident: full-time $6576; part-time $274 per credit hour. Tuition, nonresident: full-time $13,152; part-time $548 per credit hour. Required fees: $1813; $75.53 per credit hour. Part-time tuition and fees vary according to course load. *Financial support:* In 2009–10, 20 research assistantships with full tuition reimbursements were awarded; fellowships with full tuition reimbursements, teaching assistantships with full tuition reimbursements, career-related internships or fieldwork, Federal Work-Study, scholarships/grants, tuition waivers (full), and unspecified assistantships also available. Support available to part-time students. Financial award applicants required to submit FAFSA. *Faculty research:* Teacher certification, stress reduction during student teaching, teaching history, portfolios in student teaching. *Unit head:* Dr. Helen Brantley, Chair, 815-753-0327, E-mail: tedur@niu.edu. *Application contact:* Gail Myers, E-mail: gmyers@niu.edu.

Northwestern State University of Louisiana, Graduate Studies and Research, College of Education, Program in Curriculum and Instruction, Natchitoches, LA 71497. Offers M Ed.

Northwest Nazarene University, Graduate Studies, Program in Teacher Education, Nampa, ID 83686-5897. Offers curriculum and instruction (M Ed); educational leadership (M Ed); exceptional child (M Ed); reading education (M Ed); school counseling (M Ed). *Accreditation:* ACA; NCATE. Part-time programs available. *Degree requirements:* For master's, comprehensive exam (for some programs), action research project. *Entrance requirements:* For master's, minimum undergraduate GPA of 2.8 overall or 3.0 during final 30 semester credits. *Faculty research:* Action research, cooperative learning, accountability, institutional accreditation.

Nova Southeastern University, Fischler School of Education and Human Services, Graduate Teacher Education Program, Fort Lauderdale, FL 33314-7796. Offers athletic administration (MS); brain research (MS, Ed S); charter school education/leadership (MS); cognitive and behavioral disabilities (MS); computer science education (Ed S); computer science education (K-12) (MS); curriculum and teaching (Ed S); curriculum, instruction and technology (MS); curriculum, instruction, management and administration (Ed S); early childhood education (MS); early literacy and reading (Ed S); early literacy education (MS); education technology (MS); educational leadership (administration K–12) (MS, Ed S); educational media (Ed S); educational media (K-12) (MS); elementary education (MS, Ed S), including ESOL endorsement (MS); English education (MS, Ed S); environmental education (MS); exceptional student education (MS), including ESOL endorsement; gifted education (MS, Ed S); interdisciplinary arts education (MS); management and administration of educational programs (MS); mathematics (MS); mathematics education (Ed S); multicultural early intervention (MS); pre-kindergarten/primary (MS); preschool education (MS); reading (MS); reading and TESOL (MS); reading education (Ed S); science (MS); science education (Ed S); secondary education (MS); social studies (MS, Ed S); Spanish language (MS); special education and reading (MS); teaching and learning (MA, MS), including curriculum and instruction (MA), elementary mathematics (MA), elementary reading (MA), K-12 technology integration (MA); teaching English to speakers of other languages (MS, Ed S); technology management and administration (Ed S); urban studies education (MS). Part-time and evening/weekend programs available. Postbaccalaureate distance learning degree programs offered (minimal on-campus study). *Faculty:* 72 full-time (43 women), 385 part-time/adjunct (252 women). *Students:* 196 full-time (175 women), 1,304 part-time (1,128 women); includes 594 minority (471 African Americans, 5 American Indian/Alaska Native, 18 Asian Americans or Pacific Islanders, 100 Hispanic Americans). Average age 37. 2,610 applicants, 72% accepted, 1352 enrolled. In 2009, 836 other advanced degrees awarded. *Degree requirements:* For master's and Ed S, thesis, practicum, internship. *Entrance requirements:* For master's, MAT, GRE, CLAST, CBEST, PRAXIS I, General Knowledge Test, minimum GPA of 2.5; for Ed S, MAT or GRE, master's degree, teaching certificate, minimum GPA of 3.0. Additional exam requirements/recommendations for international students: Required—TSE (recommended, minimum score 50); Recommended—TOEFL (minimum score 550 paper-based; 213 computer-based; 80 iBT), IELTS (minimum score 6). *Application deadline:* For fall admission, 9/25 priority date for domestic and international students; for winter admission, 2/23 priority date for domestic and international students; for spring admission, 4/25 priority date for domestic and international students. Applications are processed on a rolling basis. Application fee: $50. Electronic applications accepted. *Financial support:* Federal Work-Study available. Support available to part-time students. Financial award application deadline: 4/15; financial award applicants required to submit FAFSA. *Faculty research:* School effectiveness, critical thinking, leadership skills acquisition, child education, multicultural education. *Unit head:* Dr. Ronald Kern, Dean of Academic Affairs, 800-986-3223 Ext. 7809, Fax: 954-262-3606, E-mail: rk429@nsu.nova.edu. *Application contact:* Dr. Jennifer Quinones Nottingham, Dean of Student Affairs, 800-986-3223 Ext. 1559.

Ohio University, Graduate College, College of Education, Department of Teacher Education, Athens, OH 45701-2979. Offers adolescent to young adult education (M Ed); curriculum and instruction (M Ed, PhD); early childhood/special education (M Ed); intervention specialist/mild-moderate needs (M Ed); intervention specialist/moderate-intensive needs (M Ed); mathematics education (PhD); middle child education (M Ed); reading education (M Ed); social studies education (PhD). Part-time and evening/weekend programs available. *Faculty:* 21 full-time (13 women), 7 part-time/adjunct (all women). *Students:* 105 full-time (75 women), 183 part-time (161 women); includes 9 minority (5 African Americans, 3 American Indian/Alaska Native, 1 Asian American or Pacific Islander), 14 international. 190 applicants, 80% accepted, 72 enrolled. *Degree requirements:* For master's, thesis or alternative; for doctorate, comprehensive exam, thesis/dissertation. *Entrance requirements:* For master's, GRE General Test or MAT (if GPA is below 2.9); for doctorate, GRE General Test, minimum GPA of 3.4, work experience. Additional exam requirements/recommendations for international students: Required—TOEFL (minimum score 550 paper-based; 80 iBT) or IELTS Academic (minimum score 6.5). *Application deadline:* For fall admission, 5/1 priority date for domestic students, 4/1 priority date for international students; for winter admission, 11/1 priority date for domestic students, 10/1 priority date for international students; for spring admission, 2/15 priority date for domestic students, 1/1 priority date for international students. Applications are processed on a rolling basis. Application fee: $50 ($55 for international students). Electronic applications accepted. *Expenses:* Tuition, state resident: full-time $7839; part-time $323 per quarter hour. Tuition, nonresident: full-time $15,831; part-time $654 per quarter hour. Required fees: $2931. *Financial support:* Research assistantships with full tuition reimbursements, teaching assistantships with full tuition reimbursements, Federal Work-Study, institutionally sponsored loans, tuition waivers (partial), and unspecified assistantships available. Financial award application deadline: 3/1. *Faculty research:* Cognition literacy, character education, teacher's education reform, disabilities. Total annual research expenditures: $46,933. *Unit head:* Dr. John Henning, Chair, 740-597-1830, Fax: 740-593-0477, E-mail: henningj@ohio.edu. *Application contact:* Floyd J. Doney, Director of Student Affairs, 740-593-4400, Fax: 740-593-9310, E-mail: doney@ohio.edu.

Oklahoma State University, College of Education, School of Teaching and Curriculum Leadership, Stillwater, OK 74078. Offers MS, PhD. Part-time programs available. *Faculty:* 34 full-time (29 women), 25 part-time/adjunct (22 women). *Students:* 40 full-time (32 women), 218 part-time (175 women); includes 39 minority (11 African Americans, 20 American Indian/Alaska

Native, 3 Asian Americans or Pacific Islanders, 5 Hispanic Americans), 9 international. Average age 39. 109 applicants, 55% accepted, 40 enrolled. In 2009, 37 master's, 14 doctorates awarded. *Degree requirements:* For master's, thesis or alternative; for doctorate, comprehensive exam, thesis/dissertation. *Entrance requirements:* For master's and doctorate, GRE or GMAT. Additional exam requirements/recommendations for international students: Required—TOEFL (minimum score 550 paper-based; 79 iBT). *Application deadline:* For fall admission, 3/1 priority date for international students; for spring admission, 8/1 priority date for international students. Applications are processed on a rolling basis. Application fee: $40 ($75 for international students). Electronic applications accepted. *Expenses:* Tuition, state resident: full-time $3716; part-time $154.85 per credit hour. Tuition, nonresident: full-time $14,448; part-time $602 per credit hour. Required fees: $1772; $73.85 per credit hour. One-time fee: $50. Tuition and fees vary according to course load and campus/location. *Financial support:* In 2009–10, 18 research assistantships (averaging $7,889 per year), 15 teaching assistantships (averaging $11,004 per year) were awarded; career-related internships or fieldwork, Federal Work-Study, scholarships/grants, health care benefits, tuition waivers (partial), and unspecified assistantships also available. Support available to part-time students. Financial award application deadline: 3/1; financial award applicants required to submit FAFSA. *Unit head:* Dr. Christine Ormsbee, Head, 405-744-7125, Fax: 405-744-6290. *Application contact:* Dr. Gordon Emslie, Dean, 405-744-6368, Fax: 405-744-0355, E-mail: grad-i@okstate.edu.

Old Dominion University, Darden College of Education, Doctoral Program in Curriculum and Instruction, Norfolk, VA 23529. Offers PhD. Part-time and evening/weekend programs available. *Faculty:* 9 full-time (6 women). *Students:* 4 full-time (3 women), 18 part-time (13 women); includes 1 minority (African American), 1 international. Average age 39. 5 applicants, 100% accepted, 5 enrolled. In 2009, 1 doctorate awarded. *Degree requirements:* For doctorate, comprehensive exam, thesis/dissertation. *Entrance requirements:* For doctorate, GRE, letters of recommendation; minimum undergraduate GPA of 2.8, graduate 3.2. Additional exam requirements/recommendations for international students: Required—TOEFL (minimum score 600 paper-based; 250 computer-based). *Application deadline:* For fall admission, 3/15 priority date for domestic and international students; for spring admission, 11/15 for domestic and international students. Applications are processed on a rolling basis. Application fee: $50. Electronic applications accepted. *Expenses:* Tuition, state resident: full-time $8112; part-time $338 per credit. Tuition, nonresident: full-time $20,256; part-time $844 per credit. Required fees: $119 per semester. One-time fee: $50. *Financial support:* In 2009–10, fellowships with full tuition reimbursements (averaging $15,000 per year), 2 research assistantships with full tuition reimbursements (averaging $15,000 per year), 4 teaching assistantships with full tuition reimbursements (averaging $15,000 per year) were awarded; scholarships/grants and unspecified assistantships also available. Financial award application deadline: 4/15. *Faculty research:* Curriculum change, language arts, library science, multicultural education, foundations in education. *Unit head:* Dr. Charlene Fleener, Graduate Program Director, 757-683-4387, E-mail: cfleener@odu.edu. *Application contact:* Alice McAdory, Director of Admissions, 757-683-3685, Fax: 757-683-3255, E-mail: gradadmit@odu.edu.

Old Dominion University, Darden College of Education, Program in Physical Education, Curriculum and Instruction Emphasis, Norfolk, VA 23529. Offers MS Ed. Part-time and evening/weekend programs available. *Faculty:* 1 (woman) full-time, 1 (woman) part-time/adjunct. *Students:* 2 full-time (1 woman), 1 (woman) part-time. Average age 25. 6 applicants, 83% accepted, 1 enrolled. In 2009, 8 master's awarded. *Degree requirements:* For master's, comprehensive exam (for some programs), thesis or alternative, internship, research project. *Entrance requirements:* For master's, GRE, PRAXIS I (for licensure only), minimum GPA of 2.8 overall, 3.0 in major. Additional exam requirements/recommendations for international students: Required—TOEFL (minimum score 500 paper-based; 200 computer-based). *Application deadline:* For fall admission, 7/1 priority date for domestic students; for spring admission, 11/1 priority date for domestic students. Applications are processed on a rolling basis. Application fee: $40. Electronic applications accepted. *Expenses:* Tuition, state resident: full-time $8112; part-time $338 per credit. Tuition, nonresident: full-time $20,256; part-time $844 per credit. Required fees: $119 per semester. One-time fee: $50. *Financial support:* In 2009–10, 1 teaching assistantship with partial tuition reimbursement (averaging $9,000 per year) was awarded; career-related internships or fieldwork and scholarships/grants also available. Financial award application deadline: 4/15. *Faculty research:* Motor development, physical education, health education. *Unit head:* Xihu Zhu, Graduate Program Director, 757-683-4995, E-mail: lgagen@odu.edu. *Application contact:* Xihu Zhu, Graduate Program Director, 757-683-4995, E-mail: lgagen@odu.edu.

Olivet Nazarene University, Graduate School, Division of Education, Program in Curriculum and Instruction, Bourbonnais, IL 60914. Offers MAE. Evening/weekend programs available. *Degree requirements:* For master's, thesis or alternative.

Oral Roberts University, School of Education, Tulsa, OK 74171. Offers Christian school administration (K-12) (MA Ed, Ed D); Christian school curriculum development (MA Ed); college and higher education administration (Ed D); public school administration (K-12) (MA Ed, Ed D); public school teaching (MA Ed). *Accreditation:* NCATE. Part-time programs available. Postbaccalaureate distance learning degree programs offered (minimal on-campus study). *Faculty:* 7 full-time (2 women), 6 part-time/adjunct (2 women). *Students:* 344 full-time (223 women); includes 117 minority (93 African Americans, 7 American Indian/Alaska Native, 11 Asian Americans or Pacific Islanders, 6 Hispanic Americans). 80 applicants, 94% accepted, 65 enrolled. In 2009, 14 master's, 4 doctorates awarded. *Degree requirements:* For master's, comprehensive exam, thesis optional; for doctorate, comprehensive exam, thesis/dissertation. *Entrance requirements:* For master's, GRE General Test or MAT, minimum GPA of 3.0; for doctorate, minimum GPA of 3.0. Additional exam requirements/recommendations for international students: Required—TOEFL (minimum score 500 paper-based; 173 computer-based). *Application deadline:* For fall admission, 1/1 for domestic and international students; for spring admission, 1/1 priority date for domestic students, 1/1 for international students. Applications are processed on a rolling basis. *Expenses:* Contact institution. *Financial support:* In 2009–10, 4 research assistantships (averaging $5,000 per year) were awarded; scholarships/grants and unspecified assistantships also available. Financial award application deadline: 6/1; financial award applicants required to submit FAFSA. *Faculty research:* Teacher effectiveness, college success in high achieving African-Americans, professional development practices. *Unit head:* Dr. Kim Boyd, Dean, 918-495-7108, E-mail: kboyd@oru.edu. *Application contact:* Lance Miller, Graduate Admissions, 918-495-6553, Fax: 918-495-6222, E-mail: gradeducation@oru.edu.

Ottawa University, Graduate Studies-Arizona, Program in Education, Ottawa, KS 66067-3399. Offers community college counseling (MA); curriculum and instruction (MA); early childhood (MA); education intervention (MA); education leadership (MA); education technology (MA); Montessori early childhood education (MA); Montessori elementary education (MA); professional development (MA); school guidance counseling (MA); special education—cross categorical (MA). Programs offered in Mesa, Phoenix, Tempe and West Valley, AZ. *Accreditation:* NCATE. Part-time programs available. *Degree requirements:* For master's, thesis or alternative. *Entrance requirements:* For master's, minimum undergraduate GPA of 3.0, copy of current state certification or teaching license. Additional exam requirements/recommendations for international students: Required—TOEFL (minimum score 550 paper-based; 213 computer-based). Electronic applications accepted. *Expenses:* Contact institution.

Our Lady of Holy Cross College, Program in Education and Counseling, New Orleans, LA 70131-7399. Offers administration and supervision (M Ed); curriculum and instruction (M Ed); marriage and family counseling (MA); school counseling (M Ed, MA). *Accreditation:* ACA; NCATE. Part-time and evening/weekend programs available. *Degree requirements:* For master's, thesis. *Entrance requirements:* For master's, GRE General Test, minimum GPA of 2.7.

Our Lady of the Lake University of San Antonio, School of Professional Studies, Program in Curriculum and Instruction, San Antonio, TX 78207-4689. Offers bilingual (M Ed); early childhood education (M Ed); English as a second language (M Ed); integrated math teaching (M Ed); integrated science teaching (M Ed); master reading teacher (M Ed); master technology

teacher (M Ed); reading specialist (M Ed). *Students:* 2 full-time (1 woman), 112 part-time (94 women); includes 64 minority (5 African Americans, 1 American Indian/Alaska Native, 1 Asian American or Pacific Islander, 57 Hispanic Americans). Average age 38. In 2009, 49 master's awarded. *Expenses:* Tuition: Full-time $12,330; part-time $685 per contact hour. Required fees: $139; $12 per contact hour. $57 per semester. Tuition and fees vary according to campus/location. *Unit head:* Dr. Cullen Grinnan, 210-434-6711 Ext. 8928, E-mail: ctgrinnan@lake.ollusa.edu. *Application contact:* Dr. Cullen Grinnan, 210-434-6711 Ext. 8928, E-mail: ctgrinnan@lake.ollusa.edu.

Pace University, School of Education, New York, NY 10038. Offers administration and supervision (MS Ed); adolescent education (MST); childhood education (MST); curriculum and instruction (MS); education (MST); literacy (MSE); school business management (Certificate); teaching students with disabilities (MSE); teaching visual arts (MST). *Accreditation:* NCATE. Part-time and evening/weekend programs available. *Students:* 235 full-time (177 women), 766 part-time (515 women); includes 158 minority (58 African Americans, 1 American Indian/Alaska Native, 37 Asian Americans or Pacific Islanders, 62 Hispanic Americans), 7 international. Average age 30. 332 applicants, 83% accepted, 165 enrolled. In 2009, 669 master's, 34 other advanced degrees awarded. *Degree requirements:* For master's, internship. *Entrance requirements:* For master's, interview, teaching certificate. Additional exam requirements/recommendations for international students: Required—TOEFL. *Application deadline:* For fall admission, 7/31 priority date for domestic students; for spring admission, 11/30 for domestic students. Applications are processed on a rolling basis. Application fee: $70. Electronic applications accepted. *Expenses:* Contact institution. *Financial support:* Research assistantships, career-related internships or fieldwork and Federal Work-Study available. Support available to part-time students. Financial award applicants required to submit FAFSA. *Unit head:* Dr. Harriet Feldman, Interim Dean, 212-346-1512. *Application contact:* Susan Ford-Goldschein, Director of Admissions, 212-346-1652, Fax: 212-346-1585, E-mail: gradnyc@pace.edu.

Pacific Lutheran University, Division of Graduate Studies, School of Education, Program in Initial Teaching Certification, Tacoma, WA 98447. Offers MAE. *Accreditation:* NCATE. *Degree requirements:* For master's, comprehensive exam, thesis. *Entrance requirements:* For master's, GRE General Test or MAT, interview. Additional exam requirements/recommendations for international students: Required—TOEFL (minimum score 550 paper-based; 213 computer-based). *Expenses:* Contact institution.

Penn State University Park, Graduate School, College of Education, Department of Curriculum and Instruction, State College, University Park, PA 16802-1503. Offers M Ed, MS, D Ed, PhD. *Accreditation:* NCATE.

Peru State College, Graduate Programs, Program in Education, Peru, NE 68421. Offers curriculum and instruction (MS Ed). *Accreditation:* NCATE. Part-time programs available. *Degree requirements:* For master's, comprehensive exam (for some programs), thesis optional.

Philadelphia Biblical University, School of Education, Langhorne, PA 19047-2990. Offers educational leadership and administration (MS El); teacher education (MS Ed). Part-time and evening/weekend programs available. *Faculty:* 5 full-time (3 women), 2 part-time/adjunct (both women). *Students:* 14 full-time (9 women), 61 part-time (45 women); includes 11 minority (10 African Americans, 1 Asian American or Pacific Islander), 7 international. Average age 34. 45 applicants, 62% accepted, 23 enrolled. In 2009, 39 master's awarded. *Entrance requirements:* Additional exam requirements/recommendations for international students: Required—TOEFL (minimum score 550 paper-based; 213 computer-based). *Application deadline:* Applications are processed on a rolling basis. Application fee: $25. Electronic applications accepted. *Expenses:* Tuition: Full-time $10,350; part-time $575 per credit. Required fees: $10; $10 per year. Tuition and fees vary according to program. *Financial support:* In 2009–10, 14 students received support. Scholarships/grants available. Support available to part-time students. Financial award applicants required to submit FAFSA. *Unit head:* Dr. Martha MacCullough, Dean, 215-702-4387, E-mail: teacher.ed@pbu.edu. *Application contact:* Katerina Penkova, Enrollment Counselor, Graduate Education, 800-572-2472, Fax: 215-702-4248, E-mail: kpenkova@pbu.edu.

Piedmont College, School of Education, Demorest, GA 30535-0010. Offers early childhood education (MA, MAT); instruction (Ed S); secondary education (MA, MAT). Part-time and evening/weekend programs available. *Degree requirements:* For master's, thesis, field experience in the teaching classroom. *Entrance requirements:* For master's, GRE General Test, MAT, minimum undergraduate GPA of 2.5; for Ed S, minimum graduate GPA of 3.5, valid teaching certificate. Additional exam requirements/recommendations for international students: Required—TOEFL (minimum score 550 paper-based; 213 computer-based).

Point Park University, School of Arts and Sciences, Department of Education, Pittsburgh, PA 15222-1984. Offers curriculum and instruction (MA); educational administration (MA); teaching and leadership (M Ed). Part-time and evening/weekend programs available. *Faculty:* 2 full-time, 5 part-time/adjunct. *Students:* 9 full-time (7 women), 51 part-time (36 women); includes 11 minority (9 African Americans, 2 Asian Americans or Pacific Islanders), 1 international. Average age 36. 41 applicants, 68% accepted, 25 enrolled. In 2009, 12 master's awarded. *Degree requirements:* For master's, comprehensive exam (for some programs), thesis or alternative. *Entrance requirements:* For master's, minimum GPA of 3.0, resume, 2 letters of recommendation. Additional exam requirements/recommendations for international students: Required—TOEFL. *Application deadline:* Applications are processed on a rolling basis. Application fee: $30. Electronic applications accepted. *Expenses:* Tuition: Full-time $11,880; part-time $660 per credit. Required fees: $486; $27 per credit. *Financial support:* In 2009–10, 19 students received support, including 1 research assistantship with full tuition reimbursement available (averaging $6,400 per year); scholarships/grants also available. Financial award application deadline: 4/15; financial award applicants required to submit FAFSA. *Unit head:* Dr. Darlene Marnich, Chair, 412-392-3474, Fax: 412-392-3927, E-mail: dmarnich@pointpark.edu. *Application contact:* Lynn C. Ribar, Associate Director, Graduate and Adult Enrollment, 412-392-3908, Fax: 412-392-6164, E-mail: lribar@pointpark.edu.

Pontifical Catholic University of Puerto Rico, College of Education, Doctoral Program in Curriculum and Instruction, Ponce, PR 00717-0777. Offers PhD. *Degree requirements:* For doctorate, thesis/dissertation. *Entrance requirements:* For doctorate, EXADEP, GRE General Test or MAT, 3 letters of recommendation.

Pontifical Catholic University of Puerto Rico, College of Education, Master's Program in Curriculum and Instruction, Ponce, PR 00717-0777. Offers M Ed. *Degree requirements:* For master's, comprehensive exam, thesis (for some programs). *Entrance requirements:* For master's, GRE, 2 letters of recommendation, interview, minimum GPA of 2.75.

Portland State University, Graduate Studies, School of Education, Department of Curriculum and Instruction, Portland, OR 97207-0751. Offers early childhood education (MA, MS); education (M Ed, MA, MS); educational leadership: curriculum and instruction (Ed D); educational media/school librarianship (MA, MS); elementary education (M Ed, MAT, MST); reading (MA, MS); secondary education (M Ed, MAT, MST). *Accreditation:* NCATE. Part-time programs available. *Degree requirements:* For master's, comprehensive exam, thesis or alternative; for doctorate, thesis/dissertation. *Entrance requirements:* For master's, California Basic Educational Skills Test, minimum GPA of 3.0 in upper-division course work or 2.75 overall. Additional exam requirements/recommendations for international students: Required—TOEFL (minimum score 550 paper-based; 213 computer-based). *Faculty research:* Early literacy, characteristics of successful teachers of at-risk students, participation of women/minorities in technology courses, selection of cooperating teachers.

Prairie View A&M University, College of Education, Department of Curriculum and Instruction, Prairie View, TX 77446-0519. Offers curriculum and instruction (M Ed, MS Ed); special education (M Ed, MS Ed). *Accreditation:* NCATE. Part-time and evening/weekend programs available. *Faculty:* 7 full-time (4 women), 1 (woman) part-time/adjunct. *Students:* 20 full-time (18 women), 117 part-time (82 women); includes 113 African Americans, 3 international. Average age 36. 119 applicants, 87% accepted, 96 enrolled. In 2009, 51 master's awarded. *Degree requirements:* For master's, thesis optional. *Entrance requirements:* For master's, GRE, minimum GPA of 2.5, 3 references. *Application deadline:* For fall admission, 7/1 priority date for domestic students; for winter admission, 3/1 priority date for domestic students; for spring admission, 11/1 priority date for domestic students. Applications are processed on a rolling basis. Application fee: $50. Electronic applications accepted. *Expenses:* Tuition, state resident: full-time $2200. Tuition, nonresident: full-time $5600. Required fees: $1720. Tuition and fees vary according to course load. *Financial support:* In 2009–10, 1 research assistantship with tuition reimbursement (averaging $18,000 per year) was awarded; fellowships with tuition reimbursements, teaching assistantships, career-related internships or fieldwork, institutionally sponsored loans, scholarships/grants, health care benefits, tuition waivers (full and partial), and unspecified assistantships also available. Support available to part-time students. Financial award application deadline: 4/1. *Faculty research:* Metacognitive strategies, emotionally disturbed, language arts, teachers recruit, diversity, recruitment, retention, school collaboration. Total annual research expenditures: $25,000. *Unit head:* Dr. Edward Mason, Head, 936-261-3403, Fax: 936-261-3419, E-mail: elmason@pvamu.edu.

Purdue University, Graduate School, School of Education, Department of Curriculum and Instruction, West Lafayette, IN 47907. Offers agricultural and extension education (PhD, Ed S); agriculture and extension education (MS, MS Ed); art education (PhD); consumer and family sciences and extension education (MS Ed, PhD, Ed S); curriculum studies (MS Ed, PhD, Ed S); educational technology (MS Ed, PhD, Ed S); elementary education (MS Ed); foreign language education (MS Ed, PhD, Ed S); industrial technology (PhD, Ed S); language arts (MS Ed, PhD, Ed S); literacy (MS Ed, PhD, Ed S); mathematics/science education (MS, MS Ed, PhD, Ed S); social studies (MS Ed, PhD); social studies education (Ed S); vocational/industrial education (MS Ed, PhD, Ed S); vocational/technical education (MS Ed, PhD, Ed S). *Accreditation:* NCATE. Part-time and evening/weekend programs available. *Degree requirements:* For master's, thesis optional; for doctorate, thesis/dissertation, oral and written exams; for Ed S, oral presentation, project. *Entrance requirements:* For master's, GRE General Test, minimum B average; for doctorate, GRE General Test; for Ed S, GRE, minimum B average. Additional exam requirements/recommendations for international students: Required—TOEFL. Electronic applications accepted. *Faculty research:* Literacy acquisition and development, teacher beliefs and knowledge, recruitment and retention of underrepresented students, economic education, literacy discourse.

Quincy University, Program in Education, Quincy, IL 62301-2699. Offers curriculum and instruction (MS Ed); leadership (MRS); reading education (MS Ed); school administration (MS Ed); special education (MS Ed); teaching certification (MS Ed). Part-time programs available. Postbaccalaureate distance learning degree programs offered. *Faculty:* 3 full-time (2 women), 19 part-time/adjunct (16 women). *Students:* 328 full-time (222 women), 88 part-time (57 women); includes 60 African Americans, 9 Asian Americans or Pacific Islanders, 69 Hispanic Americans. In 2009, 10 master's awarded. *Degree requirements:* For master's, thesis. *Entrance requirements:* For master's, MAT or GRE. Additional exam requirements/recommendations for international students: Required—TOEFL. *Application deadline:* Applications are processed on a rolling basis. Application fee: $25. Electronic applications accepted. *Expenses:* Tuition: Full-time $8400; part-time $350 per credit hour. Required fees: $360; $15 per credit hour. Tuition and fees vary according to course load, campus/location and program. *Financial support:* Available to part-time students. Applicants required to submit FAFSA. *Unit head:* Dot Nelson, Director, 217-228-5432 Ext. 3111, E-mail: nelsodo@quincy.edu. *Application contact:* Jennifer O'Donnell, Coordinator of Adult Studies, 217-228-5404, Fax: 217-228-5479, E-mail: admissions@quincy.edu.

Randolph College, Programs in Education, Lynchburg, VA 24503. Offers curriculum and instruction (MAT); special education-learning disabilities (M Ed, MAT). *Accreditation:* Teacher Education Accreditation Council. *Entrance requirements:* For master's, minimum GPA of 3.0 in prerequisite education coursework, 2.7 in major or field of interest (MAT); teaching license (M Ed); 2 recommendations; interview.

Regis University, College for Professional Studies, Program in Teacher Education, Denver, CO 80221-1099. Offers adult learning, training, and development (M Ed); curriculum, instruction, and assessment (M Ed); early childhood (M Ed); educational technology (Certificate); elementary (M Ed); ESL (M Ed); fine arts (M Ed), including arts, music; instructional technology (M Ed); professional leadership (M Ed); reading (M Ed); secondary (M Ed); self-designed (M Ed); space studies (M Ed); special education (M Ed); teacher licensure (M Ed). Program also offered in Henderson and Las Vegas (Summerlin), NV. *Accreditation:* Teacher Education Accreditation Council. Part-time and evening/weekend programs available. Postbaccalaureate distance learning degree programs offered (no on-campus study). *Degree requirements:* For master's, thesis. *Entrance requirements:* For master's, resume, minimum GPA of 2.75, criminal background check. Additional exam requirements/recommendations for international students: Required—TOEFL (minimum score 213 computer-based), TWE (minimum score 5). Electronic applications accepted. *Faculty research:* Issues of equity in the middle school classroom, professional learning communities, school reform, socialinguistic and discursive obstacles to student integration, inclusive language arts curriculum.

Rider University, Department of Graduate Education, Leadership and Counseling, Program in Curriculum, Instruction and Supervision, Lawrenceville, NJ 08648-3001. Offers curriculum, instruction and supervision (MA); supervisor (Certificate). *Accreditation:* NCATE. Part-time and evening/weekend programs available. *Degree requirements:* For master's, comprehensive exam, practicum project. *Entrance requirements:* For master's, interview, 2 letters of recommendation from current supervisors, resume. Additional exam requirements/recommendations for international students: Required—TOEFL (minimum score 550 paper-based; 213 computer-based). Electronic applications accepted. *Faculty research:* Curriculum change, curriculum development, teacher evaluation.

Rivier College, School of Graduate Studies, Department of Education, Nashua, NH 03060. Offers curriculum and instruction (M Ed); early childhood education (M Ed); educational administration (M Ed); educational studies (M Ed); elementary education (M Ed); elementary education and general special education (M Ed); emotional and behavioral disorders (M Ed); general social education (M Ed); leadership and learning (Ed D, CAGS); learning disabilities (M Ed); learning disabilities and reading (M Ed); mental health counseling (MA); reading (M Ed); school counseling (M Ed). Part-time and evening/weekend programs available. *Faculty:* 13 full-time (9 women), 38 part-time/adjunct (25 women). *Students:* 87 full-time (78 women), 293 part-time (246 women); includes 10 minority (3 African Americans, 4 Asian Americans or Pacific Islanders, 3 Hispanic Americans). Average age 38. 182 applicants, 82% accepted, 72 enrolled. In 2009, 110 master's, 18 other advanced degrees awarded. *Degree requirements:* For master's, comprehensive exam (for some programs), internships. *Entrance requirements:* For master's, GRE General Test or MAT. *Application deadline:* Applications are processed on a rolling basis. Application fee: $25. *Expenses:* Tuition: Part-time $447 per credit. *Financial support:* Available to part-time students. Application deadline: 2/1. *Unit head:* Dr. Patricia Howson, Chairman, 603-897-8562, E-mail: phowson@rivier.edu. *Application contact:* Mathew Kittredge, Director of Graduate Admissions, 603-897-8129, Fax: 603-897-8810, E-mail: mkittredge@rivier.edu.

Rosemont College, Schools of Graduate and Professional Studies, Program in Curriculum and Instruction, Rosemont, PA 19010-1699. Offers elementary certification (MA). Part-time and evening/weekend programs available. *Entrance requirements:* For master's, minimum college GPA of 3.0, 3 letters of recommendation. Additional exam requirements/recommendations for international students: Required—TOEFL. Electronic applications accepted.

Rowan University, Graduate School, College of Education, Department of Educational Leadership, Program in Supervision and Curriculum Development, Glassboro, NJ 08028-1701. Offers MA. *Accreditation:* NCATE. Part-time and evening/weekend programs available. *Students:* 1 part-time (0 women); minority (Asian American or Pacific Islander). Average age 24. *Degree requirements:* For master's, comprehensive exam, thesis. *Entrance requirements:* For master's, GRE General Test, minimum GPA of 2.8, 2 years of teaching experience. Additional exam requirements/recommendations for international students: Required—TOEFL.

Curriculum and Instruction

Rowan University (continued)
Application deadline: Applications are processed on a rolling basis. Application fee: $50. Electronic applications accepted. *Expenses:* Tuition, state resident: full-time $10,624; part-time $590 per semester hour. Tuition, nonresident: full-time $10,624; part-time $590 per semester hour. Required fees: $2320; $125 per semester hour. *Financial support:* Career-related internships or fieldwork, scholarships/grants, health care benefits, and unspecified assistantships available. Support available to part-time students. *Unit head:* Dr. Mira Lalovic-Hand, Interim Associate Provost/Director of Graduate School, 856-256-5120, E-mail: lalovic-hand@rowan.edu. *Application contact:* Karen Haynes, Graduate Coordinator, 856-256-4052, Fax: 856-256-4436, E-mail: haynes@rowan.edu.

St. Cloud State University, School of Graduate Studies, College of Education, Department of Teacher Development, St. Cloud, MN 56301-4498. Offers curriculum and instruction (MS). *Faculty:* 17 full-time (9 women). *Students:* 7 full-time (5 women), 33 part-time (28 women), 2 international. 6 applicants, 100% accepted. In 2009, 14 master's awarded. *Degree requirements:* For master's, thesis or alternative. *Entrance requirements:* For master's, GRE General Test, minimum GPA of 2.75. Additional exam requirements/recommendations for international students: Required—Michigan English Language Assessment Battery; Recommended—TOEFL (minimum score 550 paper-based; 213 computer-based), IELTS (minimum score 6.5). *Application deadline:* For fall admission, 6/1 for domestic students, 4/1 for international students; for spring admission, 10/1 for domestic students, 8/1 for international students. Applications are processed on a rolling basis. Application fee: $35. Electronic applications accepted. *Financial support:* Federal Work-Study, scholarships/grants, and unspecified assistantships available. Financial award application deadline: 3/1. *Unit head:* Ramon Serrano, Chair, 320-308-4886, E-mail: raserrano@stcloudstate.edu. *Application contact:* Linda Lou Krueger, School of Graduate Studies, 320-308-2113, Fax: 320-308-5371, E-mail: lekrueger@stcloudstate.edu.

St. Francis Xavier University, Graduate Studies, Graduate Studies in Education, Antigonish, NS B2G 2W5, Canada. Offers curriculum and instruction (M Ed); educational administration and leadership (M Ed). Part-time programs available. Postbaccalaureate distance learning degree programs offered (minimal on-campus study). *Degree requirements:* For master's, thesis. *Entrance requirements:* For master's, minimum undergraduate B average, 2 years of teaching experience. *Faculty research:* Inclusive education, qualitative research.

Saint Leo University, Graduate Studies in Education, Saint Leo, FL 33574-6665. Offers educational leadership (M Ed, Ed S); exceptional student education (M Ed); higher education leadership (Ed S); instructional design (MS); instructional leadership (M Ed); reading (M Ed). Part-time and evening/weekend programs available. Postbaccalaureate distance learning degree programs offered (minimal on-campus study). *Faculty:* 13 full-time (10 women), 12 part-time/adjunct (9 women). *Students:* 432 full-time (355 women), 35 part-time (24 women); includes 56 minority (40 African Americans, 2 American Indian/Alaska Native, 2 Asian Americans or Pacific Islanders, 12 Hispanic Americans), 1 international. Average age 37. In 2009, 131 master's awarded. *Degree requirements:* For master's, comprehensive exam, appropriate State of Florida Certification Tests. *Entrance requirements:* For master's, GRE (minimum score of 1000) or MAT (minimum score of 410) if undergraduate GPA for last 60 hours of coursework was below 3.0 (for M Ed), bachelor's degree from regionally-accredited college or university with minimum GPA of 3.0 for last 60 hours of coursework, 2 recommendations, resume, statement of professional goals, copy of valid teaching certificate (for M Ed); for Ed S, GRE (minimum score 1000) or MAT (minimum score 410) if undergraduate GPA for last 60 hours of coursework less than 3.0, bachelor's degree from regionally-accredited college or university with minimum GPA of 3.0 for last 60 hours of coursework, 2 recommendations, resume, valid teaching certificate. Additional exam requirements/recommendations for international students: Required—TOEFL (minimum score 550 paper-based; 213 computer-based; 80 iBT). *Application deadline:* For fall admission, 7/1 priority date for domestic students; for spring admission, 11/12 priority date for domestic students. Applications are processed on a rolling basis. Application fee: $75. Electronic applications accepted. *Expenses:* Tuition: Part-time $1767 per course. Required fees: $115 per course. *Financial support:* Career-related internships or fieldwork, Federal Work-Study, and health care benefits available. Financial award application deadline: 3/1; financial award applicants required to submit FAFSA. *Faculty research:* The role of the school leader in data analysis of student achievement, teacher recruitment, and teacher effectiveness. *Unit head:* Dr. John Smith, Director, 352-588-8309, Fax: 352-588-8861, E-mail: med@saintleo.edu. *Application contact:* Jared Welling, Director, Graduate/Weekend and Evening Admission, 800-707-8846, Fax: 352-588-7873, E-mail: grad.admissions@saintleo.edu.

Saint Louis University, Graduate School, College of Education and Public Service and Graduate School, Department of Educational Studies, St. Louis, MO 63103-2097. Offers curriculum and instruction (MA, Ed D, PhD); educational foundations (MA, Ed D, PhD); special education (MA); teaching (MAT). *Accreditation:* NCATE. Part-time programs available. *Degree requirements:* For master's, comprehensive exam; for doctorate, comprehensive exam, thesis/dissertation, preliminary oral and written exams. *Entrance requirements:* For master's, GRE General Test or MAT, letters of recommendation, resume; for doctorate, GRE General Test, letters of recommendation, resumé, goal statement, transcripts. Additional exam requirements/recommendations for international students: Required—TOEFL (minimum score 525 paper-based; 194 computer-based). Electronic applications accepted. *Faculty research:* Teacher preparation, multicultural issues, children with special needs, qualitative research in education, inclusion.

Saint Mary's College of California, Kalmanovitz School of Education, Program in Instruction, Moraga, CA 94556. Offers M Ed. *Students:* 27 part-time (20 women); includes 5 minority (1 African American, 2 Asian Americans or Pacific Islanders, 2 Hispanic Americans). In 2009, 3 master's awarded. *Expenses:* Tuition: Full-time $35,087; part-time $956 per credit hour. One-time fee: $50 full-time. Part-time tuition and fees vary according to course level, course load, degree level, campus/location and program. *Unit head:* Dr. Mary Parish, Director, 925-631-4249, Fax: 925-376-8379, E-mail: mparish@stmarys-ca.edu. *Application contact:* Jane Joyce, Coordinator, Recruitment and Admissions, 925-631-4700, Fax: 925-376-8379, E-mail: soereq@stmarys-ca.edu.

Saint Michael's College, Graduate Programs, Program in Education, Colchester, VT 05439. Offers administration (M Ed, CAGS); arts in education (CAGS); curriculum and instruction (M Ed, CAGS); information technology (CAGS); reading (M Ed); special education (M Ed, CAGS); technology (M Ed). Part-time and evening/weekend programs available. *Degree requirements:* For master's, thesis. *Entrance requirements:* For master's, minimum GPA of 3.0. Electronic applications accepted. *Faculty research:* Integrative curriculum, moral and spiritual dimensions of education, learning styles, multiple intelligences, integrating technology into the curriculum.

Saint Peter's College, Graduate Programs in Education, Program in Teaching, Jersey City, NJ 07306-5997. Offers elementary teacher (Certificate); supervisor of instruction (Certificate); teaching (MA). Part-time and evening/weekend programs available. *Degree requirements:* For master's, comprehensive exam. *Entrance requirements:* For master's, GRE or MAT. Additional exam requirements/recommendations for international students: Required—TOEFL. *Application deadline:* Applications are processed on a rolling basis. Application fee: $0. Electronic applications accepted. *Expenses:* Tuition: Part-time $971 per credit. *Financial support:* Career-related internships or fieldwork, Federal Work-Study, and institutionally sponsored loans available. *Unit head:* Dr. Anthony Sciarrillo, Chairperson, 201-761-6473, Fax: 201-435-5270. *Application contact:* Dr. Anthony Sciarrillo, Chairperson, 201-761-6473, Fax: 201-435-5270.

Saint Vincent College, Program in Education, Latrobe, PA 15650-2690. Offers curriculum and instruction (MS); environmental education (MS); library media management (MS); school administration (MS); special education (MS). Part-time and evening/weekend programs available. *Degree requirements:* For master's, comprehensive exam. *Entrance requirements:* For master's, GRE (if undergraduate GPA less than 3.0). Additional exam requirements/recommendations for international students: Required—TOEFL (minimum score 550 paper-based; 213 computer-based). *Faculty research:* Assessment and instructional technology.

Saint Xavier University, Graduate Studies, School of Education, Chicago, IL 60655-3105. Offers counseling (MA); counselor education (MA); curriculum and instruction (MA); early childhood education (MA); education (CAS); educational administration (MA); elementary education (MA); field-based education (MA); general educational studies (MA); individualized program (MA); learning disabilities (MA); reading (MA); secondary education (MA). *Accreditation:* NCATE. Part-time and evening/weekend programs available. *Degree requirements:* For master's, thesis or project. *Entrance requirements:* For master's, minimum GPA of 3.0. *Expenses:* Contact institution.

Salem International University, School of Education, Salem, WV 26426-0500. Offers curriculum and instruction (M Ed); educational leadership (M Ed). Part-time and evening/weekend programs available. Postbaccalaureate distance learning degree programs offered. *Degree requirements:* For master's, comprehensive exam (for some programs), thesis (for some programs). *Entrance requirements:* For master's, GRE, MAT, NTE, 3 letters of recommendation. Additional exam requirements/recommendations for international students: Required—TOEFL (minimum score 550 paper-based; 213 computer-based). Electronic applications accepted. *Expenses:* Contact institution. *Faculty research:* Improved classroom effectiveness.

Sam Houston State University, College of Education and Applied Science, Department of Curriculum and Instruction, Huntsville, TX 77341. Offers curriculum and instruction (M Ed, MA); instructional technology (M Ed). *Accreditation:* NCATE. Part-time and evening/weekend programs available. *Faculty:* 10 full-time (5 women), 1 (woman) part-time/adjunct. *Students:* 34 full-time (26 women), 134 part-time (95 women); includes 37 minority (21 African Americans, 1 American Indian/Alaska Native, 4 Asian Americans or Pacific Islanders, 11 Hispanic Americans). Average age 32. 85 applicants, 94% accepted, 57 enrolled. In 2009, 85 master's awarded. *Entrance requirements:* For master's, GRE General Test. Additional exam requirements/recommendations for international students: Required—TOEFL (minimum score 550 paper-based; 213 computer-based; 79 iBT). *Application deadline:* For fall admission, 8/1 for domestic students; for spring admission, 12/1 for domestic students. Application fee: $20. *Expenses:* Tuition, state resident: full-time $3690; part-time $205 per credit hour. Tuition, nonresident: full-time $8676; part-time $482 per credit hour. Required fees: $1474. Tuition and fees vary according to course load and campus/location. *Financial support:* Teaching assistantships, institutionally sponsored loans available. Financial award application deadline: 5/31; financial award applicants required to submit FAFSA. *Unit head:* Dr. Daphne Johnson, Chair, 936-294-3875, Fax: 936-294-1056, E-mail: edu_dxe@shsu.edu. *Application contact:* Dr. Eren Johnson, Advisor, 936-294-1140, E-mail: edu_mej@shsu.edu.

San Diego State University, Graduate and Research Affairs, College of Education, School of Teacher Education, Program in Elementary Curriculum and Instruction, San Diego, CA 92182. Offers MA. *Accreditation:* NCATE. Evening/weekend programs available. *Entrance requirements:* For master's, GRE General Test, letters of reference. Additional exam requirements/recommendations for international students: Required—TOEFL. Electronic applications accepted.

San Diego State University, Graduate and Research Affairs, College of Education, School of Teacher Education, Program in Secondary Curriculum and Instruction, San Diego, CA 92182. Offers MA. *Accreditation:* NCATE. *Entrance requirements:* For master's, GRE General Test, letters of reference. Additional exam requirements/recommendations for international students: Required—TOEFL. Electronic applications accepted.

San Jose State University, Graduate Studies and Research, Connie L. Lurie College of Education, Department of Elementary Education, San Jose, CA 95192-0001. Offers curriculum and instruction (MA); reading (Certificate). *Accreditation:* NCATE. *Students:* 318 full-time (270 women), 163 part-time (140 women); includes 166 minority (5 African Americans, 97 Asian Americans or Pacific Islanders, 64 Hispanic Americans), 7 international. Average age 32. 257 applicants, 87% accepted, 189 enrolled. In 2009, 40 master's awarded. *Degree requirements:* For master's, thesis or alternative. *Application deadline:* For fall admission, 6/29 for domestic students; for spring admission, 11/30 for domestic students. Applications are processed on a rolling basis. Application fee: $59. Electronic applications accepted. *Financial support:* Career-related internships or fieldwork available. Financial award applicants required to submit FAFSA. *Unit head:* Dr. Andrea Whittaker, Chair, 408-924-3751, Fax: 408-924-3775. *Application contact:* Dr. Andrea Whittaker, Chair, 408-924-3751, Fax: 408-924-3775.

Santa Clara University, School of Education and Counseling Psychology, Department of Education, Program in Interdisciplinary Education, Santa Clara, CA 95053. Offers interdisciplinary education (MA), including Catholic education, curriculum and instruction, reading, STEEM, teaching and learning. Part-time and evening/weekend programs available. *Students:* 6 full-time (all women), 73 part-time (60 women); includes 18 minority (1 African American, 1 American Indian/Alaska Native, 9 Asian Americans or Pacific Islanders, 7 Hispanic Americans), 1 international. Average age 34. 35 applicants. In 2009, 36 master's awarded. *Degree requirements:* For master's, comprehensive exam. *Entrance requirements:* For master's, GRE or MAT, minimum GPA of 3.0. Additional exam requirements/recommendations for international students: Required—TOEFL. *Application deadline:* Applications are processed on a rolling basis. *Expenses:* Contact institution. *Financial support:* Fellowships, Federal Work-Study, institutionally sponsored loans, and scholarships/grants available. Support available to part-time students. Financial award application deadline: 5/15; financial award applicants required to submit FAFSA. *Unit head:* Dr. Sara Garcia, Director, 408-554-4507. *Application contact:* Dr. Sara Garcia, Director, 408-554-4507.

Seattle Pacific University, M Ed in Curriculum and Instruction Program, Seattle, WA 98119-1997. Offers reading/language arts education (M Ed). *Accreditation:* NCATE. Part-time and evening/weekend programs available. *Faculty:* 3 full-time (all women), 9 part-time/adjunct (6 women). *Students:* 7 full-time (6 women), 86 part-time (70 women); includes 4 minority (1 Asian American or Pacific Islander, 3 Hispanic Americans), 1 international. Average age 33. 35 applicants, 74% accepted, 26 enrolled. In 2009, 11 master's awarded. *Degree requirements:* For master's, comprehensive exam. *Entrance requirements:* For master's, GRE General Test or MAT, minimum GPA of 3.0. Additional exam requirements/recommendations for international students: Required—TOEFL (minimum score 550 paper-based). *Application deadline:* For fall admission, 7/1 priority date for domestic students, 7/1 for international students; for spring admission, 3/1 priority date for domestic students, 3/1 for international students. Applications are processed on a rolling basis. Application fee: $50. Electronic applications accepted. *Expenses:* Contact institution. *Financial support:* In 2009–10, 61 students received support. Applicants required to submit FAFSA. *Faculty research:* Educational technology, classroom environments, character education. *Unit head:* Dr. Andrew Lumpe, Chair, 206-281-2369. *Application contact:* The Grad Center, 206-281-2091.

Seattle University, College of Education, Program in Curriculum and Instruction, Seattle, WA 98122-1090. Offers M Ed, MA, Certificate. *Accreditation:* NCATE. Part-time and evening/weekend programs available. *Degree requirements:* For master's, comprehensive exam. *Entrance requirements:* For master's, GRE, MAT, or minimum GPA of 3.0; 1 year of related experience. Additional exam requirements/recommendations for international students: Required—TOEFL.

Shawnee State University, Program in Curriculum and Instruction, Portsmouth, OH 45662-4344. Offers M Ed. *Accreditation:* NCATE.

Shaw University, Department of Education, Raleigh, NC 27601-2399. Offers curriculum and instruction (MS). Part-time and evening/weekend programs available. *Degree requirements:* For master's, comprehensive exam, thesis, practicum/internship, PRAXIS II. *Entrance requirements:* For master's, GRE General Test, letters of recommendation. Additional exam requirements/recommendations for international students: Required—TOEFL (minimum score 500 paper-based). Electronic applications accepted. *Faculty research:* Multicultural education, instructional technology.

Shepherd University, Program in Curriculum and Instruction, Shepherdstown, WV 25443. Offers MA. *Accreditation:* NCATE.

Shippensburg University of Pennsylvania, School of Graduate Studies, College of Education and Human Services, Department of Teacher Education, Shippensburg, PA 17257-2299. Offers curriculum and instruction (M Ed), including biology, early childhood education, elementary education, English, foreign languages, geography/earth science, history, mathematics, middle school education; reading (M Ed). *Accreditation:* NCATE. Part-time and evening/weekend programs available. *Degree requirements:* For master's, comprehensive exam (for some programs), thesis optional, practicum or internship (for some programs). *Entrance requirements:* For master's, MAT (if GPA less than 2.75), interview, 3 letters of recommendation, writing sample of teaching background and future goals. Additional exam requirements/recommendations for international students: Required—TOEFL (minimum score 560 paper-based; 220 computer-based); Recommended—IELTS (minimum score 6). Electronic applications accepted.

Shorter University, Professional Studies, Rome, GA 30165. Offers business administration (MBA); curriculum and instruction (M Ed); leadership (MA). Evening/weekend programs available. *Degree requirements:* For master's, project. *Entrance requirements:* For master's, minimum undergraduate GPA of 2.75 in last 60 hours, 3 years of work experience. Additional exam requirements/recommendations for international students: Required—TOEFL (minimum score 550 paper-based; 213 computer-based; 79 iBT). *Faculty research:* Systems design, leadership, pedagogy using technology.

Simon Fraser University, Graduate Studies, Faculty of Education, Programs in Curriculum and Instruction, Burnaby, BC V5A 1S6, Canada. Offers curriculum theory and implementation (PhD); foundations (M Ed, MA); philosophy of education (PhD). *Degree requirements:* For master's, project or thesis; for doctorate, thesis/dissertation. *Entrance requirements:* For master's, minimum GPA of 3.0; for doctorate, GRE, master's degree or exceptional record in a bachelor's degree, minimum GPA of 3.5. Additional exam requirements/recommendations for international students: Required—TOEFL or IELTS.

Sonoma State University, School of Education, Department of Curriculum Studies and Secondary Education, Rohnert Park, CA 94928-3609. Offers education—curriculum, teaching and learning (MA). Part-time and evening/weekend programs available. *Degree requirements:* For master's, thesis or alternative. *Entrance requirements:* For master's, minimum GPA of 2.5. *Expenses:* Tuition, nonresident: full-time $11,160. Required fees: $6226. Full-time tuition and fees vary according to course load.

South Dakota State University, Graduate School, College of Education and Human Sciences, Department of Educational Leadership, Brookings, SD 57007. Offers curriculum and instruction (M Ed); educational administration (M Ed). Part-time and evening/weekend programs available. Postbaccalaureate distance learning degree programs offered (minimal on-campus study). *Degree requirements:* For master's, portfolio, oral exam. *Entrance requirements:* For master's, minimum GPA of 2.75. Additional exam requirements/recommendations for international students: Required—TOEFL (minimum score 550 paper-based; 213 computer-based; 80 iBT). *Faculty research:* Inclusion school climate, K-12 reform and restructuring, rural development, ESL, leadership.

Southeastern Louisiana University, College of Education and Human Development, Department of Teaching and Learning, Hammond, LA 70402. Offers curriculum and instruction (M Ed); elementary education (MAT); special education (M Ed, MAT), including mild/moderate grades K-12 (MAT). *Accreditation:* NCATE. Part-time programs available. *Faculty:* 16 full-time (14 women). *Students:* 20 full-time (all women), 107 part-time (99 women); includes 18 minority (11 African Americans, 1 American Indian/Alaska Native, 1 Asian American or Pacific Islander, 5 Hispanic Americans), 1 international. Average age 35. 16 applicants, 94% accepted, 13 enrolled. In 2009, 61 master's awarded. *Degree requirements:* For master's, comprehensive exam (for some programs), portfolio. *Entrance requirements:* For master's, GRE (verbal and quantitative), PRAXIS (MAT), bachelor's degree from an accredited U.S. institution or its foreign equivalent; minimum undergraduate GPA of 2.5 on all undergraduate work attempted or 2.75 on all undergraduate upper-level work attempted. Additional exam requirements/recommendations for international students: Required—TOEFL (minimum score 500 paper-based; 173 computer-based; 61 iBT). *Application deadline:* For fall admission, 7/15 priority date for domestic students, 6/1 priority date for international students; for spring admission, 12/1 priority date for domestic students, 10/1 priority date for international students. Applications are processed on a rolling basis. Application fee: $20 ($30 for international students). Electronic applications accepted. *Expenses:* Tuition, state resident: full-time $3086; part-time $225 per credit hour. Tuition, nonresident: part-time $529 per credit hour. Required fees: $1195. Tuition and fees vary according to course level and course load. *Financial support:* In 2009–10, 9 students received support. Federal Work-Study, institutionally sponsored loans, and administrative assistantship available. Support available to part-time students. Financial award application deadline: 5/1; financial award applicants required to submit FAFSA. *Faculty research:* Reading, instructional methodology, science education, math education, early childhood. Total annual research expenditures: $458,029. *Unit head:* Dr. Shirley Jacob, Department Head, 985-549-2221, Fax: 985-549-5009, E-mail: sjacob@selu.edu. *Application contact:* Sandra Meyers, Graduate Admissions Analyst, 985-549-5620, Fax: 985-549-5632, E-mail: admissions@selu.edu.

Southern Arkansas University–Magnolia, Graduate Programs, Magnolia, AR 71753. Offers agriculture (MS); business administration (MBA); computer and information sciences (MS); counseling (MS); education (M Ed), including counseling and development, curriculum and instruction emphasis, educational administration and supervision, elementary education, middle level emphasis, reading emphasis, secondary education, TESOL emphasis; kinesiology (MS); library media and information specialist (M Ed); mental health and clinical counseling (MS); public administration (EMPA); school counseling (M Ed); teaching (MAT). *Accreditation:* NCATE. Part-time and evening/weekend programs available. *Faculty:* 43 full-time (24 women), 12 part-time/adjunct (7 women). *Students:* 116 full-time (78 women), 333 part-time (255 women); includes 105 minority (98 African Americans, 3 American Indian/Alaska Native, 3 Asian Americans or Pacific Islanders, 1 Hispanic American), 11 international. Average age 33. In 2009, 88 master's awarded. *Degree requirements:* For master's, comprehensive exam, thesis optional. *Entrance requirements:* For master's, GRE, MAT or GMAT, minimum GPA of 2.75. *Application deadline:* For fall admission, 8/15 for domestic students; for winter admission, 1/8 for domestic students; for spring admission, 1/8 for domestic students. Applications are processed on a rolling basis. Application fee: $0. *Expenses:* Tuition, state resident: full-time $3798; part-time $211 per hour. Tuition, nonresident: full-time $5580; part-time $310 per hour. Required fees: $584. *Financial support:* Career-related internships or fieldwork, Federal Work-Study, scholarships/grants, tuition waivers (full), and unspecified assistantships available. Financial award applicants required to submit FAFSA. *Faculty research:* Alternative certification for teachers, supervision of instruction, instructional leadership, counseling. *Unit head:* Dr. Kim Bloss, Dean, Graduate Studies, 870-235-4150, Fax: 870-235-5227, E-mail: kkbloss@saumag.edu. *Application contact:* Dr. Kim Bloss, Dean, Graduate Studies, 870-235-4150, Fax: 870-235-5227, E-mail: kkbloss@saumag.edu.

Southern Illinois University Carbondale, Graduate School, College of Education, Department of Curriculum and Instruction, Carbondale, IL 62901-4701. Offers MS Ed, PhD. *Accreditation:* NCATE. Part-time programs available. *Degree requirements:* For doctorate, variable foreign language requirement, thesis/dissertation. *Entrance requirements:* For master's, minimum GPA of 2.7; for doctorate, GRE or MAT, minimum GPA of 3.25. Additional exam requirements/recommendations for international students: Required—TOEFL. *Faculty research:* Early childhood, science/environmental education, teacher education, instructional development/technology, reading.

Southern Illinois University Edwardsville, Graduate Studies and Research, School of Education, Department of Curriculum and Instruction, Program in Curriculum and Instruction, Edwardsville, IL 62026-0001. Offers MS Ed. *Accreditation:* NCATE. Part-time and evening/weekend programs available. *Faculty:* 20 full-time (12 women). *Students:* 7 full-time (5 women), 112 part-time (104 women); includes 10 minority (8 African Americans, 1 Asian American or Pacific Islander, 1 Hispanic American), 1 international. Average age 26. 35 applicants, 66% accepted. In 2009, 47 master's awarded. *Degree requirements:* For master's, thesis or alternative, final exam/paper. *Entrance requirements:* For master's, teaching certificate. Additional exam requirements/recommendations for international students: Required—TOEFL (minimum score 550 paper-based; 213 computer-based; 79 iBT), IELTS (minimum score 6.5). *Application deadline:* For fall admission, 7/23 for domestic students, 6/1 for international students; for spring admission, 12/11 for domestic students, 10/1 for international students. Applications are processed on a rolling basis. Application fee: $30. Electronic applications accepted. *Expenses:* Tuition, state resident: part-time $1252.50 per semester. Tuition, nonresident: part-time $3131.25 per semester. Required fees: $586.85 per semester. Tuition and fees vary according to course load. *Financial support:* In 2009–10, 1 research assistantship (averaging $8,064 per year) was awarded; fellowships, teaching assistantships, career-related internships or fieldwork, Federal Work-Study, institutionally sponsored loans, scholarships/grants, traineeships, and unspecified assistantships also available. Support available to part-time students. Financial award application deadline: 3/1; financial award applicants required to submit FAFSA. *Unit head:* Dr. Susan Breck, Director, 618-650-3444, E-mail: sbreck@siue.edu. *Application contact:* Dr. Susan Breck, Director, 618-650-3444, E-mail: sbreck@siue.edu.

Southern Nazarene University, Graduate College, School of Education, Bethany, OK 73008. Offers curriculum and instruction (MA); educational leadership (MA). *Accreditation:* NCATE. Part-time and evening/weekend programs available. *Degree requirements:* For master's, thesis optional. *Entrance requirements:* For master's, MAT, English proficiency exam, minimum GPA of 3.0 in last 60 hours/major, 2.7 overall.

Southern New Hampshire University, School of Education, Manchester, NH 03106-1045. Offers business education (MS); child development (M Ed); computer technology education (Certificate); curriculum and instruction (M Ed); education (M Ed, CAS); elementary education (M Ed); general special education (Certificate); school business administrator (Certificate); secondary education (M Ed); training and development (Certificate). Part-time and evening/weekend programs available. Postbaccalaureate distance learning degree programs offered (no on-campus study). *Degree requirements:* For master's, comprehensive exam (for some programs), thesis or alternative. *Entrance requirements:* For master's, PRAXIS I, minimum GPA of 2.75. Additional exam requirements/recommendations for international students: Required—TOEFL (minimum score 550 paper-based; 213 computer-based). Electronic applications accepted. *Expenses:* Contact institution.

Southwestern Adventist University, Education Department, Graduate Program, Keene, TX 76059. Offers curriculum and instruction with reading emphasis (M Ed); educational leadership (M Ed). Part-time and evening/weekend programs available. *Degree requirements:* For master's, thesis or alternative, professional paper. *Entrance requirements:* For master's, GRE General Test.

Southwestern Assemblies of God University, Thomas F. Harrison School of Graduate Studies, Program in Education, Waxahachie, TX 75165-5735. Offers Christian school administration (MS); curriculum development (MS); early education administration (M Ed); middle and secondary education (M Ed). *Degree requirements:* For master's, comprehensive written and oral exams. *Entrance requirements:* For master's, GRE General Test, minimum GPA of 2.5. Electronic applications accepted.

Southwestern College, Education Programs, Winfield, KS 67156-2499. Offers curriculum and instruction (M Ed); special education (M Ed); teaching (MA). *Accreditation:* NCATE. Part-time and evening/weekend programs available. Postbaccalaureate distance learning degree programs offered (minimal on-campus study). *Faculty:* 2 full-time (1 woman), 14 part-time/adjunct (12 women). *Students:* 1 (woman) full-time, 112 part-time (88 women); includes 9 minority (2 African Americans, 1 American Indian/Alaska Native, 3 Asian Americans or Pacific Islanders, 3 Hispanic Americans), 2 international. Average age 37. 50 applicants, 98% accepted, 46 enrolled. In 2009, 18 master's awarded. *Degree requirements:* For master's, practicum, portfolio. *Entrance requirements:* For master's, baccalaureate degree, minimum GPA of 2.5, valid teaching certificate (for special education). Additional exam requirements/recommendations for international students: Required—TOEFL (minimum score 550 paper-based; 213 computer-based). *Application deadline:* For fall admission, 8/1 for domestic students; for spring admission, 12/1 for domestic students. Applications are processed on a rolling basis. Application fee: $0. Electronic applications accepted. *Expenses:* Contact institution. *Financial support:* In 2009–10, 77 students received support. Federal Work-Study, tuition waivers (partial), and unspecified assistantships available. Financial award application deadline: 4/1; financial award applicants required to submit FAFSA. *Unit head:* Dr. David Hofmeister, Director of Teacher Education, 800-846-1543 Ext. 6115, Fax: 620-229-6341, E-mail: david.hofmeister@sckans.edu. *Application contact:* Lindy Kralicek, Education Program Representative, 888-684-5335 Ext. 130, Fax: 316-688-5218, E-mail: lindy.kralicek@sckans.edu.

Stanford University, School of Education, Program in Curriculum Studies and Teacher Education, Stanford, CA 94305-9991. Offers art education (MA, PhD); dance education (MA); English education (MA, PhD); general curriculum studies (MA, PhD); mathematics education (MA, PhD); science education (MA, PhD); social studies education (PhD); teacher education (MA, PhD). *Degree requirements:* For master's, thesis (for some programs); for doctorate, thesis/dissertation. *Entrance requirements:* For master's and doctorate, GRE General Test. Electronic applications accepted. *Expenses:* Tuition: Full-time $37,380; part-time $2760 per quarter. Required fees: $501.

State University of New York at Plattsburgh, Division of Education, Health, and Human Services, Program in Teacher Education: Curriculum and Instruction, Plattsburgh, NY 12901-2681. Offers MS Ed. Part-time and evening/weekend programs available. *Faculty:* 2 full-time (1 woman), 8 part-time/adjunct (2 women). *Students:* 15 full-time (11 women), 69 part-time (44 women). Average age 29. 35 applicants, 80% accepted, 24 enrolled. In 2009, 81 master's awarded. *Degree requirements:* For master's, portfolio. *Entrance requirements:* For master's, minimum GPA of 2.5. Additional exam requirements/recommendations for international students: Required—TOEFL (minimum score 550 paper-based; 213 computer-based; 79 iBT). *Application deadline:* For fall admission, 2/15 priority date for domestic students; for spring admission, 10/15 priority date for domestic students. Applications are processed on a rolling basis. Application fee: $75. *Expenses:* Tuition, state resident: full-time $8370; part-time $349 per credit hour. Tuition, nonresident: full-time $13,250; part-time $552 per credit hour. Required fees: $1130. *Financial support:* Application deadline: 4/15. *Unit head:* Dr. Heidi Schnackenberg, Coordinator, 518-564-5143, E-mail: schnachl@plattsburgh.edu. *Application contact:* Marguerite Adelman, Assistant Director, Graduate Admissions, 518-564-4723, Fax: 518-564-4722, E-mail: adelmaml@plattsburgh.edu.

State University of New York College at Potsdam, School of Education and Professional Studies, Program in Curriculum and Instruction, Potsdam, NY 13676. Offers childhood education (MST); childhood instruction (MST); curriculum and instruction (MS Ed). *Accreditation:* NCATE. Postbaccalaureate distance learning degree programs offered (minimal on-campus study). *Faculty:* 14 full-time (12 women), 8 part-time/adjunct (4 women). *Students:* 209 full-time (157 women), 55 part-time (49 women); includes 9 minority (4 African Americans, 2 American Indian/Alaska Native, 2 Asian Americans or Pacific Islanders, 1 Hispanic American), 138 international. 130 applicants, 85% accepted, 90 enrolled. In 2009, 188 master's awarded. *Degree requirements:* For master's, thesis. *Entrance requirements:* For master's, minimum GPA of 2.75 in last 60 credit hours of undergraduate study. Additional exam requirements/recommendations for international students: Required—TOEFL (minimum score 550 paper-based; 213 computer-based; 80 iBT), IELTS (minimum score 6). *Application deadline:* For fall admission, 4/1 priority date for domestic and international students; for spring admission, 10/15 priority date for domestic and international students. Applications are processed on a rolling basis. Application fee: $50. *Expenses:* Tuition, state resident: full-time $8370; part-time $349 per credit hour. Tuition, nonresident: full-time $13,250; part-time $552 per credit hour. Required fees: $942; $38.70 per credit hour. *Financial support:* Federal Work-Study, scholarships/

Curriculum and Instruction

State University of New York College at Potsdam *(continued)*
grants, and unspecified assistantships available. Support available to part-time students. Financial award application deadline: 3/1; financial award applicants required to submit FAFSA. *Unit head:* Dr. Kathleen Valentine, Chairperson, 315-267-3314, Fax: 315-267-4802, E-mail: valentkm@potsdam.edu. *Application contact:* Peter Cutler, Graduate Admissions Counselor, 315-267-3154, Fax: 315-267-4802, E-mail: cutlerpj@potsdam.edu.

Stephens College, Division of Graduate and Continuing Studies, Program in Curriculum and Instruction, Columbia, MO 65215-0002. Offers M Ed. Part-time programs available. Post-baccalaureate distance learning degree programs offered (minimal on-campus study). *Students:* 11 full-time (all women), 1 (woman) part-time. Average age 30. 1 applicant, 0% accepted, 0 enrolled. In 2009, 11 master's awarded. *Entrance requirements:* For master's, minimum GPA of 3.5 in last 60 hours. Additional exam requirements/recommendations for international students: Required—TOEFL (minimum score 213 computer-based). *Application deadline:* For fall admission, 7/25 priority date for domestic and international students; for winter admission, 12/1 priority date for domestic and international students; for spring admission, 4/25 priority date for domestic and international students. Applications are processed on a rolling basis. Application fee: $40. *Expenses:* Tuition: Part-time $350 per credit. Required fees: $25 per credit. *Financial support:* Scholarships/grants and unspecified assistantships available. Financial award application deadline: 12/5; financial award applicants required to submit FAFSA. *Unit head:* Dr. Leslie Willey, Department Chair, 800-388-7579, E-mail: online@stephens.edu. *Application contact:* Meredith Julian, Assistant Director of Marketing and Recruitment, 800-388-7579, E-mail: online@stephens.edu.

Syracuse University, School of Education, Program in Instructional Design, Development, and Evaluation, Syracuse, NY 13244. Offers MS, PhD, CAS. Part-time programs available. *Students:* 34 full-time (19 women), 38 part-time (22 women); includes 10 minority (3 African Americans, 1 American Indian/Alaska Native, 3 Asian Americans or Pacific Islanders, 3 Hispanic Americans), 16 international. Average age 39. 28 applicants, 61% accepted, 12 enrolled. In 2009, 9 master's, 3 doctorates awarded. *Degree requirements:* For master's, thesis or alternative; for doctorate, thesis/dissertation. *Entrance requirements:* For doctorate, GRE, interview, completion of master's degree; for CAS, GRE (recommended), interview. Additional exam requirements/recommendations for international students: Required—TOEFL (minimum score 100 iBT). *Application deadline:* For fall admission, 2/1 priority date for domestic and international students; for spring admission, 10/15 priority date for domestic and international students. Applications are processed on a rolling basis. Application fee: $75. Electronic applications accepted. *Expenses:* Tuition: Full-time $26,808; part-time $1117 per credit. Required fees: $1024. *Financial support:* Fellowships with full tuition reimbursements, research assistantships with full and partial tuition reimbursements, teaching assistantships with full tuition reimbursements available. Financial award application deadline: 1/1; financial award applicants required to submit FAFSA. *Faculty research:* Cultural pluralism and instructional design, corrections training, aging and learning, the University and social change, investigative evaluation. *Unit head:* Dr. Nick Smith, Chair, 315-443-2685, E-mail: nlsmith@syr.edu. *Application contact:* Liza Rochelson, Graduate Recruiter, School of Education, 315-443-2505, E-mail: e-gradrcrt@syr.edu.

Syracuse University, School of Education, Program in Teaching and Curriculum, Syracuse, NY 13244. Offers MS, PhD. Part-time and evening/weekend programs available. *Students:* 15 full-time (10 women), 19 part-time (15 women); includes 1 minority (Asian American or Pacific Islander), 5 international. Average age 41. 12 applicants, 67% accepted, 6 enrolled. In 2009, 6 master's, 3 doctorates awarded. *Degree requirements:* For master's, thesis or alternative; for doctorate, thesis/dissertation. *Entrance requirements:* For doctorate, GRE, MS. Additional exam requirements/recommendations for international students: Required—TOEFL (minimum score 100 iBT). *Application deadline:* For fall admission, 2/1 priority date for domestic and international students; for spring admission, 10/15 priority date for domestic and international students. Applications are processed on a rolling basis. Application fee: $75. Electronic applications accepted. *Expenses:* Tuition: Full-time $26,808; part-time $1117 per credit. Required fees: $1024. *Financial support:* Fellowships with tuition reimbursements, teaching assistantships with tuition reimbursements, tuition waivers (partial) available. Financial award application deadline: 1/1. *Unit head:* Dr. Gerald Mager, Program Coordinator, 315-443-2685, E-mail: gmmager@syr.edu. *Application contact:* Liza Rochelson, Graduate Recruiter, School of Education, 315-443-2505, E-mail: e-gradrcrt@syr.edu.

Tarleton State University, College of Graduate Studies, College of Education, Department of Curriculum and Instruction, Stephenville, TX 76402. Offers M Ed. Part-time and evening/weekend programs available. *Degree requirements:* For master's, comprehensive exam. *Entrance requirements:* For master's, GRE General Test, minimum GPA of 3.0. Additional exam requirements/recommendations for international students: Required—TOEFL (minimum score 550 paper-based; 213 computer-based; 80 iBT). Electronic applications accepted.

Teachers College, Columbia University, Graduate Faculty of Education, Department of Curriculum and Teaching, Program in Curriculum and Teaching, New York, NY 10027-6696. Offers Ed M, MA, Ed D. *Faculty:* 9 full-time (all women). *Students:* 75 full-time (59 women), 121 part-time (101 women); includes 59 minority (17 African Americans, 27 Asian Americans or Pacific Islanders, 15 Hispanic Americans), 21 international. Average age 33. 100 applicants, 71% accepted, 37 enrolled. In 2009, 26 master's, 23 doctorates awarded. *Degree requirements:* For doctorate, thesis/dissertation. *Entrance requirements:* For doctorate, GRE General Test or MAT. *Application deadline:* For fall admission, 5/15 for domestic students; for spring admission, 12/1 for domestic students. Application fee: $65. *Financial support:* Career-related internships or fieldwork, Federal Work-Study, institutionally sponsored loans, and tuition waivers (full and partial) available. Support available to part-time students. Financial award application deadline: 2/1. *Faculty research:* Teacher education, reading education, curriculum development. *Unit head:* Marjorie Siegel, Chair, 212-678-3765. *Application contact:* Peter Shon, Assistant Director of Admission, 212-678-3305, Fax: 212-678-4171, E-mail: shon@exchange.tc.columbia.edu.

Tennessee State University, The School of Graduate Studies and Research, College of Education, Department of Teaching and Learning, Program in Curriculum and Instruction, Nashville, TN 37209-1561. Offers M Ed, Ed D. *Accreditation:* NCATE. *Degree requirements:* For master's, thesis optional; for doctorate, thesis/dissertation. *Entrance requirements:* For master's, GRE General Test, GRE Subject Test, or MAT, minimum GPA of 2.5; for doctorate, GRE General Test, GRE Subject Test, or MAT. Additional exam requirements/recommendations for international students: Required—TOEFL.

Tennessee Technological University, Graduate School, College of Education, Department of Curriculum and Instruction, Program in Curriculum, Cookeville, TN 38505. Offers MA, Ed S. *Accreditation:* NCATE. Part-time and evening/weekend programs available. *Faculty:* 2 full-time (1 woman). *Students:* 18 full-time (11 women), 237 part-time (191 women); includes 7 minority (4 African Americans, 3 Hispanic Americans). Average age 27. 347 applicants, 97% accepted, 210 enrolled. In 2009, 16 master's, 6 other advanced degrees awarded. *Degree requirements:* For master's and Ed S, comprehensive exam, thesis or alternative. *Entrance requirements:* For master's and Ed S, MAT or GRE. Additional exam requirements/recommendations for international students: Required—TOEFL (minimum score 550 paper-based; 79 iBT), IELTS (minimum score 5.5). *Application deadline:* For fall admission, 8/1 for domestic students, 5/1 for international students; for spring admission, 12/1 for domestic students, 10/1 for international students. Application fee: $25 ($30 for international students). Electronic applications accepted. *Expenses:* Tuition, state resident: full-time $7034; part-time $368 per credit hour. *Financial support:* In 2009–10, 2 fellowships (averaging $8,000 per year), research assistantships (averaging $4,000 per year), 1 teaching assistantship (averaging $4,000 per year) were awarded. Financial award application deadline: 4/1. *Unit head:* Dr. Matthew R. SMith, Chairperson, 931-372-3181, Fax: 931-372-6270. *Application contact:* Shelia K. Kendrick, Coordinator of Graduate Studies, 931-372-3808, Fax: 931-372-3497, E-mail: skendrick@tntech.edu.

Tennessee Temple University, Graduate Studies in Education, Program in Instructional Effectiveness, Chattanooga, TN 37404-3587. Offers M Ed. *Degree requirements:* For master's, comprehensive exam, thesis or alternative. *Entrance requirements:* For master's, GRE, minimum cumulative undergraduate GPA of 3.0, 3 references.

Texas A&M International University, Office of Graduate Studies and Research, College of Education, Department of Curriculum and Instruction, Laredo, TX 78041-1900. Offers bilingual education (PhD); curriculum and instruction (MS, PhD); early childhood education (PhD); reading (MS). *Faculty:* 4 full-time (3 women). *Students:* 7 full-time (3 women), 120 part-time (105 women); includes 117 minority (all Hispanic Americans), 2 international. Average age 36. 50 applicants, 64% accepted, 29 enrolled. In 2009, 34 master's awarded. *Application deadline:* For fall admission, 4/30 priority date for domestic students; for spring admission, 11/30 for domestic students. *Unit head:* Dr. Cathy Guerra, Interim Chair, 956-326-2438, E-mail: cgsakta@tamiu.edu. *Application contact:* Rosie Dickinson, Director of Admissions, 956-326-2200.

Texas A&M University, College of Education and Human Development, Department of Teaching, Learning, and Culture, College Station, TX 77843. Offers curriculum and instruction (M Ed, MS, PhD); mathematics education (M Ed, MS, PhD); multicultural/urban/ESL/international education (M Ed, MS, PhD); reading/language arts (M Ed, MS, PhD); science education (M Ed, MS, PhD); social studies education (M Ed, MS, PhD). Part-time programs available. *Faculty:* 33. *Students:* 145 full-time (113 women), 270 part-time (214 women); includes 110 minority (60 African Americans, 4 American Indian/Alaska Native, 4 Asian Americans or Pacific Islanders, 42 Hispanic Americans), 47 international. Average age 36. In 2009, 114 master's, 17 doctorates awarded. *Degree requirements:* For master's, comprehensive exam, thesis (for some programs); for doctorate, comprehensive exam, thesis/dissertation. *Entrance requirements:* For master's, GRE General Test, minimum GPA of 3.0; for doctorate, GRE General Test, 3 years of teaching experience. Additional exam requirements/recommendations for international students: Required—TOEFL (minimum score 550 paper-based; 213 computer-based). *Application deadline:* For fall admission, 1/15 priority date for domestic and international students; for spring admission, 9/15 priority date for domestic and international students. Applications are processed on a rolling basis. Application fee: $50 ($75 for international students). Electronic applications accepted. *Expenses:* Tuition, state resident: full-time $3991; part-time $221.74 per credit hour. Tuition, nonresident: full-time $9049; part-time $502.74 per credit hour. *Financial support:* In 2009–10, fellowships with partial tuition reimbursements (averaging $3,000 per year), teaching assistantships with partial tuition reimbursements (averaging $7,200 per year) were awarded; research assistantships with partial tuition reimbursements, career-related internships or fieldwork, Federal Work-Study, institutionally sponsored loans, scholarships/grants, tuition waivers (partial), and unspecified assistantships also available. Support available to part-time students. Financial award application deadline: 4/1; financial award applicants required to submit FAFSA. *Unit head:* Dr. Dennie Smith, Head, 979-845-8384, Fax: 979-845-9663, E-mail: krsmith@tamu.edu. *Application contact:* Graduate Admissions Supervisor, 979-845-8382, Fax: 979-845-9663, E-mail: krsmith@tamu.edu.

Texas A&M University–Commerce, Graduate School, College of Education and Human Services, Department of Secondary and Higher Education, Commerce, TX 75429-3011. Offers higher education (MS), including administration, teaching; learning technology and information systems (M Ed, MS), including educational computing, library and information science, media and technology; secondary education (M Ed, MS); supervision, curriculum, and instruction (Ed D); training and development (MS). Part-time programs available. Terminal master's awarded for partial completion of doctoral program. *Degree requirements:* For master's, comprehensive exam, thesis (for some programs); for doctorate, thesis/dissertation, departmental qualifying exam. *Entrance requirements:* For master's and doctorate, GRE General Test. Electronic applications accepted. *Faculty research:* Deviance, migration.

Texas A&M University–Corpus Christi, Graduate Studies and Research, College of Education, Program in Curriculum and Instruction, Corpus Christi, TX 78412-5503. Offers MS, Ed D. Part-time and evening/weekend programs available. *Degree requirements:* For master's, comprehensive exam, thesis (for some programs). *Entrance requirements:* For master's, GRE General Test. Additional exam requirements/recommendations for international students: Required—TOEFL. Electronic applications accepted.

Texas A&M University–Texarkana, Graduate Studies and Research, College of Education and Liberal Arts, Texarkana, TX 75505-5518. Offers adult education (MS); curriculum and instruction (M Ed); education (MS); educational administration (M Ed); English (MA); instructional technology (MS); interdisciplinary studies (MA, MS); special education (MS). Part-time and evening/weekend programs available. *Degree requirements:* For master's, comprehensive exam (for some programs), thesis optional. *Entrance requirements:* For master's, minimum GPA of 2.5 on last 60 hours of bachelor's degree. Additional exam requirements/recommendations for international students: Required—TOEFL. Electronic applications accepted.

Texas Christian University, College of Education, Program in Curriculum Studies, Fort Worth, TX 76129-0002. Offers M Ed. Part-time and evening/weekend programs available. *Entrance requirements:* Additional exam requirements/recommendations for international students: Required—TOEFL (minimum score 550 paper-based; 213 computer-based; 80 iBT). *Application deadline:* For fall admission, 7/15 for domestic and international students; for spring admission, 11/15 for domestic and international students. Applications are processed on a rolling basis. Application fee: $50. *Expenses:* Tuition: Full-time $17,640; part-time $980 per credit hour. Tuition and fees vary according to program. *Financial support:* Teaching assistantships with full tuition reimbursements, unspecified assistantships available. Financial award application deadline: 3/15; financial award applicants required to submit FAFSA. *Unit head:* Dr. Kay B. Stevens, Associate Dean, 817-257-7661, E-mail: k.stevens2@tcu.edu. *Application contact:* Robyn P. Shepheard, Academic Program Specialist, 817-257-7661, E-mail: r.shepheard@tcu.edu.

Texas Southern University, College of Education, Area of Curriculum and Instruction, Houston, TX 77004-4584. Offers bilingual education (M Ed); curriculum and instruction (Ed D); secondary education (M Ed). Part-time and evening/weekend programs available. *Faculty:* 7 full-time (5 women), 1 part-time/adjunct (0 women). *Students:* 20 full-time (17 women), 50 part-time (43 women); includes 66 minority (64 African Americans, 1 Asian American or Pacific Islander, 1 Hispanic American), 1 international. Average age 37. 16 applicants, 100% accepted, 9 enrolled. In 2009, 12 master's, 5 doctorates awarded. *Degree requirements:* For master's, comprehensive exam; for doctorate, comprehensive exam, thesis/dissertation. *Entrance requirements:* For master's, GRE General Test, minimum GPA of 2.5; for doctorate, GRE General Test or MAT, master's degree, minimum B+ average. Additional exam requirements/recommendations for international students: Required—TOEFL. *Application deadline:* For fall admission, 7/1 for domestic and international students; for spring admission, 11/1 for domestic and international students. Applications are processed on a rolling basis. Application fee: $50 ($75 for international students). Electronic applications accepted. *Expenses:* Tuition, state resident: full-time $1805; part-time $100 per credit hour. Tuition, nonresident: full-time $6470; part-time $343 per credit hour. Tuition and fees vary according to course level, course load and degree level. *Financial support:* In 2009–10, 1 research assistantship (averaging $3,000 per year), 1 teaching assistantship (averaging $2,000 per year) were awarded; scholarships/grants and unspecified assistantships also available. Support available to part-time students. Financial award application deadline: 5/1. *Unit head:* Dr. Cherry Gooden, Chair, 713-313-7496, Fax: 713-313-7496, E-mail: gooden_cr@tsu.edu. *Application contact:* Dr. Gregory Maddox, Interim Dean of the Graduate School, 713-313-7011 Ext. 4410, Fax: 713-639-1876, E-mail: maddox_gh@tsu.edu.

Texas Tech University, Graduate School, College of Education, Division of Curriculum and Instruction, Lubbock, TX 79409. Offers bilingual education (M Ed); curriculum and instruction (M Ed, PhD); elementary education (M Ed); language and literacy education (M Ed); secondary education (M Ed). *Accreditation:* NCATE. Part-time programs available. *Students:* 72 full-time (54 women), 109 part-time (85 women); includes 50 minority (11 African Americans, 1 American Indian/Alaska Native, 4 Asian Americans or Pacific Islanders, 34 Hispanic Americans), 11 international. Average age 35. 228 applicants, 54% accepted, 56 enrolled. In 2009, 59 master's, 5 doctorates awarded. *Degree requirements:* For master's, thesis or alternative; for doctorate,

thesis/dissertation. *Entrance requirements:* For master's and doctorate, GRE General Test. Additional exam requirements/recommendations for international students: Required—TOEFL (minimum score 550 paper-based; 213 computer-based). *Application deadline:* For fall admission, 3/1 priority date for international students; for spring admission, 11/1 priority date for international students. Applications are processed on a rolling basis. Application fee: $50 ($75 for international students). Electronic applications accepted. *Expenses:* Tuition, state resident: full-time $5100; part-time $213 per credit hour. Tuition, nonresident: full-time $11,748; part-time $490 per credit hour. Required fees: $2298; $50 per credit hour. $555 per semester. *Financial support:* Research assistantships with partial tuition reimbursements, teaching assistantships with partial tuition reimbursements, career-related internships or fieldwork, Federal Work-Study, and institutionally sponsored loans available. Support available to part-time students. Financial award application deadline: 4/15; financial award applicants required to submit FAFSA. *Faculty research:* Multicultural foundations of education, teacher education, instruction and pedagogy in subject areas, curriculum theory, language and literary. *Unit head:* Dr. Walter Smith, Chair, 806-742-1988 Ext. 437, Fax: 806-742-2179, E-mail: walter.smith@ttu.edu. *Application contact:* Dr. Walter Smith, Chair, 806-742-1988 Ext. 437, Fax: 806-742-2179, E-mail: walter.smith@ttu.edu.

Texas Woman's University, Graduate School, College of Professional Education, Department of Teacher Education, Denton, TX 76201. Offers administration (M Ed, MA); elementary education (MA); special education (M Ed, MA, PhD), including educational diagnostician (M Ed, MA); teaching (MAT); teaching, learning, and curriculum (M Ed). Part-time programs available. *Faculty:* 19 full-time (13 women), 14 part-time/adjunct (11 women). *Students:* 36 full-time (29 women), 155 part-time (135 women); includes 65 minority (31 African Americans, 1 American Indian/Alaska Native, 3 Asian Americans or Pacific Islanders, 30 Hispanic Americans), 6 international. Average age 38. 48 applicants, 90% accepted, 21 enrolled. In 2009, 52 master's, 2 doctorates awarded. Terminal master's awarded for partial completion of doctoral program. *Degree requirements:* For master's, professional paper (MEd); for doctorate, comprehensive exam, thesis/dissertation. *Entrance requirements:* For master's, minimum GPA of 3.0, 3 letters of reference, curriculum vitae, copy of certifications, teacher service record; for doctorate, minimum GPA of 3.0, 3 letters of reference, curriculum vitae, copy of certifications, teacher service record, statement of intent. Additional exam requirements/recommendations for international students: Required—TOEFL (minimum score 550 paper-based; 213 computer-based; 79 iBT). *Application deadline:* For fall admission, 7/1 priority date for domestic students, 3/1 for international students; for spring admission, 11/1 priority date for domestic students, 7/1 for international students. Applications are processed on a rolling basis. Application fee: $50. Electronic applications accepted. *Expenses:* Tuition, state resident: full-time $3564; part-time $198 per credit hour. Tuition, nonresident: full-time $8550; part-time $475 per credit hour. Required fees: $69.26 per credit hour. Tuition and fees vary according to course load. *Financial support:* In 2009–10, 47 students received support, including 5 research assistantships (averaging $10,440 per year); career-related internships or fieldwork, Federal Work-Study, institutionally sponsored loans, scholarships/grants, traineeships, health care benefits, and unspecified assistantships also available. Support available to part-time students. Financial award application deadline: 3/1; financial award applicants required to submit FAFSA. *Faculty research:* Language and literacy, classroom management, learning disabilities, staff and professional development, leadership preparation practice. *Unit head:* Dr. Jane Pemberton, Interim Chair, 940-898-2271, Fax: 940-898-2270, E-mail: jpemberton@twu.edu. *Application contact:* Samuel Wheeler, Assistant Director of Admissions, 940-898-3188, Fax: 940-898-3081, E-mail: wheelersr@twu.edu.

Trevecca Nazarene University, Graduate Division, School of Education, Major in Instructional Effectiveness, Nashville, TN 37210-2877. Offers M Ed. Part-time and evening/weekend programs available. *Students:* 7 full-time (6 women), 3 part-time (all women); includes 3 minority (2 African Americans, 1 Asian American or Pacific Islander). In 2009, 15 master's awarded. *Degree requirements:* For master's, exit assessment. *Entrance requirements:* For master's, GRE General Test, MAT, minimum GPA of 2.7, 2 reference forms. Additional exam requirements/recommendations for international students: Required—TOEFL (minimum score 550 paper-based; 213 computer-based). *Application deadline:* Applications are processed on a rolling basis. Application fee: $25. *Expenses:* Contact institution. *Financial support:* Applicants required to submit FAFSA. *Unit head:* Dr. Esther Swink, Dean, School of Education/Director of Graduate Education Programs, 615-248-1201, Fax: 615-248-1597, E-mail: admissions_ged@trevecca.edu. *Application contact:* Admissions Office, 615-248-1201, Fax: 615-248-1597, E-mail: admissions_ged@trevecca.edu.

Trinity (Washington) University, School of Education, Washington, DC 20017-1094. Offers counseling (MA); early childhood education (MAT); educating for change (M Ed); educational administration (MSA); elementary education (MAT); school counseling (MA); secondary education (MAT), including English, social studies; special education (MAT); teaching English as a second language (MAT); teaching English to speakers of other languages (M Ed); the teaching of reading (M Ed). *Accreditation:* NCATE. Part-time and evening/weekend programs available. *Degree requirements:* For master's, thesis (for some programs), capstone project(s). *Entrance requirements:* For master's, PRAXIS I, minimum GPA of 2.8. Additional exam requirements/recommendations for international students: Required—TOEFL (minimum score 550 paper-based; 213 computer-based). *Faculty research:* Technology, literacy, special education, organizations, inclusion models.

Universidad Adventista de las Antillas, EGECED Department, Mayagüez, PR 00681-0118. Offers curriculum and instruction (MA), including secondary biology, secondary history, secondary Spanish; education (MA), including ESL (elementary school level), ESL (high school level), school administration and supervision. *Degree requirements:* For master's, comprehensive exam (for some programs), thesis (for some programs). *Entrance requirements:* For master's, EXADEP or GRE General Test, recommendations. Application fee: $175. Electronic applications accepted. *Expenses:* Tuition: Full-time $3990; part-time $190 per credit. Required fees: $570; $190 per credit. $1375 per summer. *Financial support:* Fellowships, Federal Work-Study available. *Unit head:* Dr. Zilma Sepulveda, Director, 787-834-9595 Ext. 2282, Fax: 787-834-9595, E-mail: zsantiago@uaa.edu. *Application contact:* Prof. Evelyn del Valle, Admissions Department Director, 787-834-9595 Ext. 2261, Fax: 787-834-9597, E-mail: admissions@uaa.edu.

Universidad del Turabo, Graduate Programs, Programs in Education, Program in Curriculum and Instruction and Appropriate Environment, Gurabo, PR 00778-3030. Offers D Ed. *Students:* 21 full-time (17 women), 76 part-time (59 women); includes 85 Hispanic Americans. Average age 41. 38 applicants, 95% accepted, 33 enrolled. In 2009, 4 doctorates awarded. *Unit head:* Angela Candelario, Dean, 787-743-7979 Ext. 4126. *Application contact:* Virginia Gonzalez, Admissions Officer, 787-746-3009.

Universidad del Turabo, Graduate Programs, Programs in Education, Program in Curriculum and Teaching, Gurabo, PR 00778-3030. Offers M Ed. *Students:* 41 full-time (39 women), 33 part-time (30 women); includes 68 Hispanic Americans. Average age 36. In 2009, 39 master's awarded. *Unit head:* Angela Candelario, Dean, 787-743-7979 Ext. 4126. *Application contact:* Virginia Gonzalez, Admissions Officer, 787-746-3009.

Universidad Metropolitana, Graduate Programs in Education, Program in Curriculum and Teaching, San Juan, PR 00928-1150. Offers M Ed. Part-time and evening/weekend programs available. *Degree requirements:* For master's, thesis or alternative. *Entrance requirements:* For master's, EXADEP, interview.

Université de Montréal, Faculty of Education, Department of Didactics, Montréal, QC H3C 3J7, Canada. Offers M Ed, MA, PhD, DESS. *Faculty:* 23 full-time (15 women), 5 part-time/adjunct (3 women). *Students:* 34 full-time (26 women), 212 part-time (151 women). 183 applicants, 55% accepted, 77 enrolled. In 2009, 13 master's, 5 doctorates, 17 other advanced degrees awarded. Terminal master's awarded for partial completion of doctoral program. *Degree requirements:* For master's, thesis (for some programs); for doctorate, thesis/dissertation, general exam. *Application deadline:* For fall admission, 2/1 priority date for domestic students; for winter admission, 11/1 priority date for domestic students; for spring

admission, 2/1 priority date for domestic students. Application fee: $100. Electronic applications accepted. *Financial support:* Fellowships, teaching assistantships available. *Faculty research:* Teaching of French as a first or second language, teaching of science and technology, teaching of mathematics, teaching of arts. *Unit head:* Marc-Andr?? ??thier, Director, 514-343-7247, Fax: 514-343-7286, E-mail: marc.andre.ethier@umontreal.ca. *Application contact:* Louise Poirier, Responsible for Graduate Studies, 514-343-6658, Fax: 514-343-7286, E-mail: louise.poirier.2@umontreal.ca.

Université Laval, Faculty of Education, Department of Teaching and Learning Studies, Programs in Didactics, Québec, QC G1K 7P4, Canada. Offers MA, PhD. Terminal master's awarded for partial completion of doctoral program. *Degree requirements:* For master's, thesis (for some programs); for doctorate, comprehensive exam, thesis/dissertation. *Entrance requirements:* For master's and doctorate, English exam (comprehension of written English), knowledge of French. Electronic applications accepted.

University at Albany, State University of New York, School of Education, Department of Educational Theory and Practice, Albany, NY 12222-0001. Offers curriculum and instruction (MS, Ed D, CAS); curriculum planning and development (MA); educational communications (MS, CAS). Evening/weekend programs available. *Degree requirements:* For doctorate, one foreign language, thesis/dissertation. *Entrance requirements:* For doctorate, GRE General Test. Additional exam requirements/recommendations for international students: Required—TOEFL (minimum score 550 paper-based; 213 computer-based). Electronic applications accepted.

University of Alaska Fairbanks, School of Education, Program in Education, Fairbanks, AK 99775. Offers curriculum and instruction (M Ed); education (M Ed); elementary education (M Ed); language and literacy (M Ed); reading (M Ed); secondary education (M Ed). *Faculty:* 23 full-time (15 women), 10 part-time/adjunct (9 women). *Students:* 35 full-time (26 women), 58 part-time (43 women); includes 25 minority (2 African Americans, 17 American Indian/Alaska Native, 4 Asian Americans or Pacific Islanders, 2 Hispanic Americans), 1 international. Average age 36. 94 applicants, 64% accepted, 42 enrolled. In 2009, 19 master's, 18 other advanced degrees awarded. *Degree requirements:* For master's, comprehensive exam, thesis, oral defense. *Entrance requirements:* Additional exam requirements/recommendations for international students: Required—TOEFL (minimum score 550 paper-based; 213 computer-based; 80 iBT). *Application deadline:* For fall admission, 5/1 for domestic students, 3/1 for international students; for spring admission, 10/15 for domestic students, 8/1 for international students. Applications are processed on a rolling basis. Application fee: $60. Electronic applications accepted. *Expenses:* Tuition, state resident: full-time $7584; part-time $316 per credit. Tuition, nonresident: full-time $15,504; part-time $646 per credit. Required fees: $23 per credit. $135 per semester. Tuition and fees vary according to course level, course load and reciprocity agreements. *Financial support:* In 2009–10, 1 teaching assistantship (averaging $11,955 per year) was awarded; fellowships, career-related internships or fieldwork, Federal Work-Study, scholarships/grants, health care benefits, and unspecified assistantships also available. Support available to part-time students. Financial award application deadline: 6/1; financial award applicants required to submit FAFSA. *Unit head:* Dr. Eric C. Madsen, Dean, 907-474-7341, Fax: 907-474-5451, E-mail: fysoed@uaf.edu. *Application contact:* Dr. Eric C. Madsen, Dean, 907-474-7341, Fax: 907-474-5451, E-mail: fysoed@uaf.edu.

University of Arkansas, Graduate School, College of Education and Health Professions, Department of Curriculum and Instruction, Program in Curriculum and Instruction, Fayetteville, AR 72701-1201. Offers PhD. Part-time programs available. *Students:* 17 full-time (12 women), 48 part-time (41 women); includes 11 minority (6 African Americans, 1 American Indian/Alaska Native, 1 Asian American or Pacific Islander, 3 Hispanic Americans), 7 international. In 2009, 4 doctorates awarded. *Degree requirements:* For doctorate, thesis/dissertation. *Entrance requirements:* For doctorate, GRE General Test. Application fee: $40 ($50 for international students). *Expenses:* Tuition, state resident: full-time $7355; part-time $356.58 per hour. Tuition, nonresident: full-time $17,401; part-time $775.17 per hour. Required fees: $1203. *Financial support:* In 2009–10, 3 fellowships with tuition reimbursements, 7 research assistantships, 6 teaching assistantships were awarded. Financial award application deadline: 4/1. *Unit head:* Dr. Michael Daugherty, Unit Head, 479-575-4209, E-mail: mkd03@uark.edu. *Application contact:* Dr. William McComas, Graduate Coordinator, 479-575-7525, E-mail: mccomas@uark.edu.

The University of British Columbia, Faculty of Education, Centre for Cross-Faculty Inquiry in Education, Vancouver, BC V6T 1Z1, Canada. Offers curriculum and instruction (M Ed, MA, PhD); early childhood education (M Ed, MA). Part-time and evening/weekend programs available. Terminal master's awarded for partial completion of doctoral program. *Degree requirements:* For master's, thesis (MA); for doctorate, thesis/dissertation. *Entrance requirements:* Additional exam requirements/recommendations for international students: Required—TOEFL (minimum score 567 paper-based; 227 computer-based). Electronic applications accepted.

The University of British Columbia, Faculty of Education, Department of Curriculum and Pedagogy, Vancouver, BC V6T 1Z4, Canada. Offers art education (M Ed, MA); business education (MA); curriculum studies (M Ed, MA, PhD); home economics education (M Ed, MA); math education (M Ed, MA); music education (M Ed, MA); physical education (M Ed, MA); science education (M Ed, MA); social studies education (M Ed, MA); technology studies education (M Ed, MA). Part-time programs available. *Degree requirements:* For master's, thesis (MA); for doctorate, comprehensive exam, thesis/dissertation. *Entrance requirements:* Additional exam requirements/recommendations for international students: Required—TOEFL (minimum score 580 paper-based; 237 computer-based; 92 iBT). Electronic applications accepted. *Expenses:* Contact institution. *Faculty research:* School subjects, teaching and learning.

University of Calgary, Faculty of Graduate Studies, Faculty of Education, Graduate Division of Educational Research, Calgary, AB T2N 1N4, Canada. Offers community rehabilitation and disability studies (M Ed, M Sc, Ed D, PhD, Graduate Certificate, Graduate Diploma); curriculum, teaching and learning (M Ed, M Sc, MA, Ed D, PhD, Graduate Certificate, Graduate Diploma); educational contexts (M Ed, MA, Ed D, PhD, Graduate Certificate, Graduate Diploma); educational leadership (M Ed, MA, Ed D, PhD, Graduate Certificate, Graduate Diploma); educational technology (M Ed, M Sc, MA, Ed D, PhD, Graduate Certificate, Graduate Diploma); gifted education (M Sc, MA, Ed D, PhD, Graduate Certificate, Graduate Diploma); higher education administration (Ed D); interpretive studies in education (M Ed, M Sc, MA, Ed D, PhD, Graduate Certificate, Graduate Diploma); second language teaching (M Ed, Ed D, PhD, Graduate Certificate, Graduate Diploma); teaching English as a second language (M Ed, M Sc, MA, Ed D, PhD, Graduate Certificate, Graduate Diploma); workplace and adult learning (M Ed, MA, Ed D, PhD, Graduate Certificate, Graduate Diploma). Ed D in both higher education administration and educational leadership offered via distance delivery. Part-time and evening/weekend programs available. Postbaccalaureate distance learning degree programs offered (minimal on-campus study). *Degree requirements:* For master's, thesis (for some programs); for doctorate, thesis/dissertation, candidacy exam. *Entrance requirements:* For master's, minimum GPA of 3.0, 3 letters of reference; for doctorate, minimum GPA of 3.5, 3 letters of reference; for other advanced degree, minimum GPA of 3.0. Additional exam requirements/recommendations for international students: Required—TOEFL, IELTS. Electronic applications accepted. *Faculty research:* Curriculum, leadership, technology, contexts, gifted, second language teaching, work place and adult learning.

University of California, Davis, Graduate Studies, Graduate Group in Education, Davis, CA 95616. Offers education (MA, Ed D); instructional studies (PhD); psychological studies (PhD); sociocultural studies (PhD). Terminal master's awarded for partial completion of doctoral program. *Degree requirements:* For master's, comprehensive exam (for some programs), thesis (for some programs); for doctorate, thesis/dissertation. *Entrance requirements:* For master's and doctorate, GRE. Additional exam requirements/recommendations for international students: Required—TOEFL (minimum score 550 paper-based; 213 computer-based). Electronic applications accepted. *Faculty research:* Language and literacy, mathematics education, science education, teacher development, school psychology.

Curriculum and Instruction

University of California, Riverside, Graduate Division, Graduate School of Education, Riverside, CA 92521-0102. Offers autism (M Ed); curriculum and instruction (MA, PhD); diversity and equity (M Ed); educational leadership and policy (MA, PhD); educational psychology (MA, PhD); general education (M Ed); higher education administration and policy (M Ed, PhD); leadership (M Ed); reading (M Ed); school psychology (PhD); special education (M Ed, MA, PhD). *Faculty:* 23 full-time (12 women), 12 part-time/adjunct (8 women). *Students:* 230 full-time (183 women), 6 part-time (3 women); includes 75 minority (12 African Americans, 1 American Indian/Alaska Native, 21 Asian Americans or Pacific Islanders, 41 Hispanic Americans), 6 international. Average age 32. 288 applicants, 60% accepted, 118 enrolled. In 2009, 68 master's, 13 doctorates awarded. Terminal master's awarded for partial completion of doctoral program. *Degree requirements:* For master's, comprehensive exam (for some programs), comprehensive exams or thesis (MA), case study or analytical report (M Ed); for doctorate, thesis/dissertation, written and oral qualifying exams, college teaching practicum. *Entrance requirements:* For master's, GRE General Test, GRE Subject Test, CBEST, CSET, minimum GPA of 3.2; for doctorate, GRE General Test, GRE Subject Test, master's degree (desirable), minimum GPA of 3.2. Additional exam requirements/recommendations for international students: Required—TOEFL (minimum score 550 paper-based; 213 computer-based; 80 iBT). *Application deadline:* For fall admission, 9/1 for domestic students, 4/1 for international students; for winter admission, 12/1 for domestic students, 9/1 for international students; for spring admission, 3/1 for domestic students, 10/1 for international students. Applications are processed on a rolling basis. Application fee: $70 ($85 for international students). Electronic applications accepted. *Financial support:* In 2009–10, 55 students received support, including 13 fellowships with full and partial tuition reimbursements available (averaging $26,809 per year), 21 research assistantships with full and partial tuition reimbursements available (averaging $14,238 per year), 1 teaching assistantship with full and partial tuition reimbursement available (averaging $16,638 per year); career-related internships or fieldwork, Federal Work-Study, institutionally sponsored loans, scholarships/grants, and unspecified assistantships also available. Financial award application deadline: 1/5; financial award applicants required to submit FAFSA. *Faculty research:* Responsiveness to intervention, faculty core, response to intervention of English language learners, advanced modeling techniques, study on social capital, trust, and motivation. Total annual research expenditures: $5.6 million. *Unit head:* Dr. Steven T. Bossert, Dean, 951-827-5802, Fax: 951-827-3942, E-mail: steven.bossert@ucr.edu. *Application contact:* Dr. John Wills, Graduate Advisor for Admission, 951-827-6362, Fax: 951-827-3942, E-mail: edgrad@ucr.edu.

University of Central Florida, College of Education, Department of Educational Studies, Orlando, FL 32816. Offers applied learning and instruction (MA); community college education (Certificate); curriculum and instruction (Ed S); education (Ed D, PhD, Ed S); gifted education (Certificate); global and comparative education (Certificate); initial teacher professional preparation (Certificate); teacher leadership (M Ed); urban education (Certificate). *Accreditation:* NCATE. Part-time and evening/weekend programs available. *Faculty:* 18 full-time (10 women), 16 part-time/adjunct (10 women). *Students:* 155 full-time (106 women), 156 part-time (131 women); includes 80 minority (37 African Americans, 5 Asian Americans or Pacific Islanders, 38 Hispanic Americans), 22 international. Average age 36. 200 applicants, 57% accepted, 77 enrolled. In 2009, 9 master's, 34 doctorates, 17 other advanced degrees awarded. *Degree requirements:* For other advanced degree, thesis or alternative, final exam. *Entrance requirements:* For degree, GRE General Test, minimum GPA of 3.0, resume. Additional exam requirements/recommendations for international students: Required—TOEFL. *Application deadline:* For fall admission, 2/20 for domestic students; for spring admission, 9/20 for domestic students. Application fee: $30. Electronic applications accepted. *Expenses:* Tuition, state resident: part-time $306.31 per credit hour. Tuition, nonresident: part-time $1099.01 per credit hour. Part-time tuition and fees vary according to degree level and program. *Financial support:* In 2009–10, 82 students received support, including 55 fellowships with partial tuition reimbursements available (averaging $8,300 per year), 29 research assistantships with partial tuition reimbursements available (averaging $7,000 per year), 43 teaching assistantships with partial tuition reimbursements available (averaging $8,000 per year); career-related internships or fieldwork, Federal Work-Study, institutionally sponsored loans, and unspecified assistantships also available. Financial award application deadline: 3/1; financial award applicants required to submit FAFSA. *Unit head:* Dr. Karen Biraimah, Chair, 407-823-2428, E-mail: biraimah@mail.ucf.edu. *Application contact:* Dr. Karen Biraimah, Chair, 407-823-2428, E-mail: biraimah@mail.ucf.edu.

University of Central Missouri, The Graduate School, College of Education, Warrensburg, MO 64093. Offers career and technical education administration (MS); career and technical education industry training (MS); career and technical education leadership/teaching (MS); college student personnel administration (MS); counseling (MS); curriculum and instruction (Ed S); educational leadership (Ed D); educational technology (MS); elementary education/educational foundations and literacy (MSE); elementary school administration (MSE); elementary school principalship (Ed S); human services/learning resources (Ed S); human services/professional counseling (Ed S); human services/special education (Ed S); human services/technology and occupational education (Ed S); K-12 education/educational foundations and literacy (MSE); K-12 special education (MSE); library science and information services (MS); literacy education (MSE); secondary education/educational foundations & literacy (MSE); secondary school administration (MSE); secondary school principalship (Ed S); superintendency (Ed S); teaching (MAT). Part-time programs available. Postbaccalaureate distance learning degree programs offered. *Faculty:* 42. *Students:* 123 full-time (82 women), 721 part-time (552 women); includes 58 minority (38 African Americans, 3 American Indian/Alaska Native, 6 Asian Americans or Pacific Islanders, 11 Hispanic Americans), 6 international. Average age 34. 229 applicants, 88% accepted, 190 enrolled. In 2009, 212 master's, 47 other advanced degrees awarded. *Entrance requirements:* Additional exam requirements/recommendations for international students: Required—TOEFL (minimum score 550 paper-based; 79 computer-based). *Application deadline:* For fall admission, 6/1 priority date for domestic students, 5/1 for international students; for spring admission, 10/1 priority date for domestic students, 10/1 for international students. Applications are processed on a rolling basis. Application fee: $30 ($75 for international students). Electronic applications accepted. *Expenses:* Tuition, area resident: Part-time $245.80 per credit hour. Tuition, nonresident: part-time $491.60 per credit hour. Required fees: $24.20 per credit hour. Full-time tuition and fees vary according to course load, degree level, campus/location and reciprocity agreements. *Financial support:* Research assistantships with full and partial tuition reimbursements, teaching assistantships with full and partial tuition reimbursements, career-related internships or fieldwork, Federal Work-Study, scholarships/grants, and administrative and laboratory assistantships available. Support available to part-time students. Financial award application deadline: 3/1; financial award applicants required to submit FAFSA. *Unit head:* Dr. Michael Wright, Dean, 660-543-4272, Fax: 660-543-8753, E-mail: mwright@ucmo.edu. *Application contact:* Laurie Delap, Admissions Coordinator, 660-543-4621, Fax: 660-543-4778, E-mail: gradinfo@ucmo.edu.

University of Cincinnati, Graduate School, College of Education, Criminal Justice, and Human Services, Division of Teacher Education, Program in Curriculum and Instruction, Cincinnati, OH 45221. Offers M Ed, Ed D. *Accreditation:* NCATE. Part-time programs available. *Degree requirements:* For master's, thesis; for doctorate, thesis/dissertation. *Entrance requirements:* For master's, GRE General Test; for doctorate, GRE General Test, GRE Subject Test. Additional exam requirements/recommendations for international students: Required—TOEFL (minimum score 550 paper-based; 213 computer-based), TWE (minimum score 4.5), OEPT. Electronic applications accepted.

University of Colorado at Boulder, Graduate School, School of Education, Division of Instruction and Curriculum, Boulder, CO 80309. Offers MA, PhD. *Accreditation:* NCATE. Part-time programs available. *Students:* 83 full-time (54 women), 65 part-time (58 women); includes 13 minority (1 American Indian/Alaska Native, 8 Asian Americans or Pacific Islanders, 4 Hispanic Americans). Average age 31. 170 applicants, 52% accepted, 48 enrolled. In 2009, 62 master's, 6 doctorates awarded. *Degree requirements:* For master's, comprehensive exam, thesis or alternative; for doctorate, one foreign language, comprehensive exam, thesis/dissertation. *Entrance requirements:* For master's, GRE General Test or MAT, minimum undergraduate GPA of 2.75; for doctorate, GRE General Test. *Application deadline:* For fall

admission, 2/1 priority date for domestic students, 12/1 for international students; for spring admission, 9/1 for domestic students, 12/1 for international students. Application fee: $50 ($60 for international students). *Financial support:* In 2009–10, 33 fellowships (averaging $2,561 per year), 18 research assistantships (averaging $13,655 per year) were awarded; career-related internships or fieldwork, Federal Work-Study, and scholarships/grants also available. Support available to part-time students. *Application contact:* E-mail: edadvise@colorado.edu.

University of Colorado at Colorado Springs, Graduate School, College of Education, Colorado Springs, CO 80933-7150. Offers counseling and human services (MA); curriculum and instruction (MA); educational administration (MA); educational leadership (MA, PhD); special education (MA). *Accreditation:* ACA; NCATE. Part-time and evening/weekend programs available. Postbaccalaureate distance learning degree programs offered (minimal on-campus study). *Faculty:* 23 full-time (15 women), 11 part-time/adjunct (8 women). *Students:* 317 full-time (243 women), 160 part-time (132 women); includes 81 minority (23 African Americans, 3 American Indian/Alaska Native, 13 Asian Americans or Pacific Islanders, 42 Hispanic Americans), 2 international. Average age 36. 375 applicants, 94% accepted, 254 enrolled. In 2009, 203 master's awarded. *Degree requirements:* For master's, comprehensive exam, thesis or alternative, microcomputer proficiency; for doctorate, comprehensive exam, research lab. *Entrance requirements:* For master's, GRE General Test, MAT. *Application deadline:* For fall admission, 6/15 for domestic students; for spring admission, 10/15 for domestic students. Applications are processed on a rolling basis. Application fee: $60 ($75 for international students). *Expenses:* Tuition, state resident: full-time $8922; part-time $639 per credit hour. Tuition, nonresident: full-time $19,372; part-time $1154 per credit hour. Tuition and fees vary according to course level, course load, degree level, program, reciprocity agreements and student level. *Financial support:* Fellowships, career-related internships or fieldwork, Federal Work-Study, and scholarships/grants available. Support available to part-time students. Financial award application deadline: 3/1; financial award applicants required to submit FAFSA. *Faculty research:* Job training for special populations, materials development for classroom. Total annual research expenditures: $1.4 million. *Unit head:* Dr. LaVonne Neal, Dean, 719-255-4111, Fax: 719-262-4110, E-mail: lneal@uccs.edu. *Application contact:* Melissa Schecter, Student Services Manager, 719-255-4526, Fax: 719-255-4110, E-mail: mschedte@uccs.edu.

University of Colorado Denver, School of Education and Human Development, Programs in Curriculum and Instruction, Denver, CO 80217-3364. Offers MA. *Accreditation:* NCATE. Part-time and evening/weekend programs available. *Students:* 217 full-time (167 women), 315 part-time (257 women); includes 52 minority (4 African Americans, 13 Asian Americans or Pacific Islanders, 35 Hispanic Americans), 8 international. 132 applicants, 92% accepted, 64 enrolled. In 2009, 175 master's awarded. *Degree requirements:* For master's, thesis or alternative. *Entrance requirements:* For master's, GRE, MAT, minimum GPA of 2.75, 3 letters of recommendation. Additional exam requirements/recommendations for international students: Required—TOEFL (minimum score 525 paper-based; 197 computer-based). *Application deadline:* For fall admission, 3/1 for domestic students; for spring admission, 9/15 for domestic students. Applications are processed on a rolling basis. Application fee: $50 ($75 for international students). Electronic applications accepted. *Financial support:* Research assistantships, teaching assistantships, Federal Work-Study available. Financial award application deadline: 4/1; financial award applicants required to submit FAFSA. *Unit head:* Carole Basile, Coordinator, 303-315-6031, E-mail: carole.basile@ucdenver.edu. *Application contact:* Lori Sisneros, Student Services Coordinator, 303-315-4979, Fax: 303-315-6311, E-mail: lori.sisneros@ucdenver.edu.

University of Delaware, College of Human Services, Education and Public Policy, School of Education, Newark, DE 19716. Offers education (PhD); educational leadership (Ed D); higher education (M Ed); instruction (MI); reading (M Ed); school leadership (M Ed); school psychology (MA, Ed S); teaching English as a second language (TESL) (MA). *Accreditation:* NCATE. Part-time and evening/weekend programs available. Terminal master's awarded for partial completion of doctoral program. *Degree requirements:* For master's, comprehensive exam (for some programs), thesis (for some programs); for doctorate, comprehensive exam (for some programs), thesis/dissertation. *Entrance requirements:* For master's and doctorate, GRE, 3 letters of recommendation. Additional exam requirements/recommendations for international students: Required—TOEFL (minimum score 600 paper-based; 250 computer-based). Electronic applications accepted. *Faculty research:* Teacher education; curriculum theory and development; community based education models, educational leadership.

University of Denver, College of Education, Denver, CO 80208. Offers counseling psychology (MA, PhD); curriculum and instruction (MA, PhD, Certificate), including curriculum leadership (MA, PhD); educational administration and policy studies (Certificate); educational psychology (MA, PhD, Ed S), including child and family studies (MA, PhD), quantitative research methods (MA, PhD), school psychology (PhD, Ed S); higher education and adult studies (MA, PhD); library and information science (MLIS); library and information sciences (Certificate); school administration (PhD). *Accreditation:* ALA; APA (one or more programs are accredited). Part-time and evening/weekend programs available. Postbaccalaureate distance learning degree programs offered (no on-campus study). *Faculty:* 33 full-time (24 women), 62 part-time/adjunct (41 women). *Students:* 384 full-time (305 women), 453 part-time (336 women); includes 164 minority (47 African Americans, 8 American Indian/Alaska Native, 14 Asian Americans or Pacific Islanders, 95 Hispanic Americans), 20 international. Average age 34. 1,065 applicants, 59% accepted, 433 enrolled. In 2009, 206 master's, 38 doctorates, 117 other advanced degrees awarded. Terminal master's awarded for partial completion of doctoral program. *Degree requirements:* For master's, comprehensive exam; for doctorate, 2 foreign languages, comprehensive exam, thesis/dissertation. *Entrance requirements:* For master's and doctorate, GRE General Test or MAT. *Application deadline:* Applications are processed on a rolling basis. Application fee: $50. Electronic applications accepted. *Expenses:* Tuition: Full-time $34,596; part-time $961 per quarter hour. Required fees: $4 per quarter hour. Tuition and fees vary according to course load, campus/location and program. *Financial support:* In 2009–10, 78 teaching assistantships with full and partial tuition reimbursements (averaging $11,700 per year) were awarded; career-related internships or fieldwork, Federal Work-Study, institutionally sponsored loans, and scholarships/grants also available. Support available to part-time students. Financial award application deadline: 3/1; financial award applicants required to submit FAFSA. *Faculty research:* Parkinson's disease, personnel training, development and assessments, gifted education, service-learning, transportation, public schools. Total annual research expenditures: $340,000. *Unit head:* Dr. Gregory M. Anderson, Dean, 303-871-3665. *Application contact:* Janet Erickson, Director of Graduate Admission, 303-871-2485, E-mail: edinfo@du.edu.

University of Detroit Mercy, College of Liberal Arts and Education, Department of Education, Program in Curriculum and Instruction, Detroit, MI 48221. Offers MA. Part-time and evening/weekend programs available. *Degree requirements:* For master's, thesis or alternative. *Entrance requirements:* For master's, minimum GPA of 2.75. *Faculty research:* Integrative curriculum planning, curriculum planning for ethical and character education.

University of Florida, Graduate School, College of Education, Department of Educational Administration and Policy, Gainesville, FL 32611. Offers curriculum and instruction (Ed D, PhD); educational leadership (M Ed, MAE, Ed D, PhD, Ed S); higher education administration (Ed D, PhD, Ed S); student personnel in higher education (M Ed, MAE); PhD/JD. *Accreditation:* NCATE. *Degree requirements:* For master's, thesis optional; for doctorate, variable foreign language requirement, thesis/dissertation. *Entrance requirements:* For master's, GRE General Test, minimum GPA of 3.0, teaching experience; for doctorate and Ed S, GRE General Test, minimum GPA of 3.0. Additional exam requirements/recommendations for international students: Required—TOEFL (minimum score 550 paper-based; 213 computer-based). Electronic applications accepted. *Faculty research:* Educational finance, community education, middle school curriculum, community college administration.

University of Florida, Graduate School, College of Education, School of Teaching and Learning, Gainesville, FL 32611. Offers bilingual/ESOL education (M Ed, MAE, Ed D, PhD, Ed S); curriculum and instruction (M Ed, MAE, Ed D, PhD, Ed S); early childhood education

(Ed D, PhD, Ed S); elementary education (M Ed, MAE); English education (M Ed, MAE); mathematics education (M Ed, MAE); reading education (M Ed, MAE); science education (M Ed, MAE); social foundations (M Ed, MAE, Ed D, PhD); social studies education (M Ed, MAE). *Accreditation:* NCATE. *Degree requirements:* For master's, thesis optional; for doctorate, variable foreign language requirement, thesis/dissertation. *Entrance requirements:* For master's and doctorate, GRE General Test, minimum GPA of 3.0; for Ed S, GRE General Test. Additional exam requirements/recommendations for international students: Required—TOEFL (minimum score 550 paper-based; 213 computer-based). Electronic applications accepted. *Faculty research:* Teacher education, inclusive education, classroom processes, curriculum and technology.

University of Hawaii at Manoa, Graduate Division, College of Education, Department of Curriculum Studies, Honolulu, HI 96822. Offers curriculum studies (M Ed); early childhood education (M Ed). Part-time programs available. *Faculty:* 34 full-time (20 women), 11 part-time/adjunct (8 women). *Students:* 31 full-time (26 women), 184 part-time (148 women); includes 156 minority (1 African American, 148 Asian Americans or Pacific Islanders, 7 Hispanic Americans), 15 international. Average age 35. 98 applicants, 79% accepted, 58 enrolled. In 2009, 89 master's awarded. *Degree requirements:* For master's, thesis optional. *Entrance requirements:* Additional exam requirements/recommendations for international students: Required—TOEFL (minimum score 500 paper-based; 173 computer-based; 61 iBT), IELTS (minimum score 5). *Application deadline:* For fall admission, 3/1 for domestic and international students; for spring admission, 9/1 for domestic and international students. Application fee: $60. *Expenses:* Tuition, state resident: full-time $8900; part-time $372 per credit. Tuition, nonresident: full-time $21,400; part-time $898 per credit. Required fees: $207 per semester. *Financial support:* In 2009–10, 1 student received support, including 8 fellowships (averaging $2,235 per year), 2 research assistantships (averaging $20,259 per year); career-related internships or fieldwork, Federal Work-Study, institutionally sponsored loans, and tuition waivers (full and partial) also available. Total annual research expenditures: $1.5 million. *Application contact:* Andrea Bartlett, Graduate Chairperson, 808-956-4401, Fax: 808-956-9905, E-mail: bartlett@hawaii.edu.

University of Hawaii at Manoa, Graduate Division, College of Education, Doctorate in Education Program, Honolulu, HI 96822. Offers curriculum and instruction (PhD); educational administration (PhD); educational foundations (PhD); educational policy studies (PhD); educational technology (PhD); exceptionalities (PhD); kinesiology (PhD). Part-time and evening/weekend programs available. *Faculty:* 65 full-time (40 women), 28 part-time/adjunct (17 women). *Students:* 74 full-time (44 women), 119 part-time (77 women); includes 101 minority (5 African Americans, 2 American Indian/Alaska Native, 86 Asian Americans or Pacific Islanders, 8 Hispanic Americans), 17 international. Average age 38. 98 applicants, 53% accepted, 35 enrolled. In 2009, 11 doctorates awarded. *Degree requirements:* For doctorate, thesis/dissertation. *Entrance requirements:* For doctorate, GRE General Test, sample of written work. Additional exam requirements/recommendations for international students: Required—TOEFL (minimum score 600 paper-based; 250 computer-based; 100 iBT), IELTS (minimum score 7). *Application deadline:* For fall admission, 2/1 for domestic students, 1/15 for international students. Application fee: $50. *Expenses:* Tuition, state resident: full-time $8900; part-time $372 per credit. Tuition, nonresident: full-time $21,400; part-time $898 per credit. Required fees: $207 per semester. *Financial support:* In 2009–10, 1 student received support, including 11 fellowships (averaging $4,147 per year), 17 research assistantships (averaging $17,392 per year), 4 teaching assistantships (averaging $14,670 per year); career-related internships or fieldwork, Federal Work-Study, and tuition waivers (full and partial) also available. *Application contact:* Dr. Helen Slaughter, Chairperson, 808-956-7913, Fax: 808-956-9905, E-mail: slaughte@hawaii.edu.

University of Houston, College of Education, Department of Curriculum and Instruction, Houston, TX 77204. Offers art education (M Ed); bilingual education (M Ed); curriculum and instruction (M Ed, Ed D); early childhood education (M Ed); elementary education (M Ed); gifted and talented education (M Ed); instructional technology (M Ed); mathematics education (M Ed); reading and language arts education (M Ed); science education (M Ed); second language education (M Ed); secondary education (M Ed); social studies education (M Ed); teaching (M Ed). *Accreditation:* NCATE. Part-time and evening/weekend programs available. *Faculty:* 20 full-time (9 women), 22 part-time/adjunct (17 women). *Students:* 113 full-time (81 women), 195 part-time (150 women); includes 107 minority (43 African Americans, 29 Asian Americans or Pacific Islanders, 35 Hispanic Americans), 29 international. Average age 35. 150 applicants, 77% accepted, 55 enrolled. In 2009, 75 master's, 31 doctorates awarded. *Degree requirements:* For master's, comprehensive exam, thesis optional; for doctorate, comprehensive exam, thesis/dissertation. *Entrance requirements:* For master's and doctorate, GRE, minimum cumulative undergraduate GPA of 2.6. Additional exam requirements/recommendations for international students: Required—TOEFL (minimum score 550 paper-based; 79 iBT). *Application deadline:* For fall admission, 3/1 for domestic and international students; for spring admission, 10/1 for domestic and international students. Application fee: $45 ($75 for international students). Electronic applications accepted. *Expenses:* Tuition, state resident: full-time $7676; part-time $320 per credit hour. Tuition, nonresident: full-time $14,324; part-time $597 per credit hour. Required fees: $3034. *Financial support:* In 2009–10, 4 fellowships with full tuition reimbursements (averaging $9,500 per year), 6 research assistantships with full tuition reimbursements (averaging $8,800 per year), 25 teaching assistantships with full tuition reimbursements (averaging $8,800 per year) were awarded; career-related internships or fieldwork, Federal Work-Study, institutionally sponsored loans, scholarships/grants, health care benefits, and unspecified assistantships also available. Support available to part-time students. Financial award application deadline: 2/1. *Faculty research:* Teaching-learning process, instructional technology in schools, teacher education, classroom management, at-risk students. *Unit head:* Dr. Laveria Hutchison, Chairperson, 713-743-4958, Fax: 713-743-4990, E-mail: lhutchison@uh.edu. *Application contact:* Renee C. Rattelade, Executive Secretary, 713-743-4997, Fax: 713-743-4990, E-mail: rrattelade@mail.coe.uh.edu.

University of Houston–Clear Lake, School of Education, Program in Curriculum and Instruction, Houston, TX 77058-1098. Offers curriculum and instruction (MS); early childhood education (MS); reading (MS); school library and information science (MS). Part-time and evening/weekend programs available. *Degree requirements:* For master's, thesis (for some programs). *Entrance requirements:* For master's, GRE or minimum GPA of 3.0 in last 60 hours. Additional exam requirements/recommendations for international students: Required—TOEFL (minimum score 550 paper-based; 213 computer-based). Electronic applications accepted.

University of Houston–Downtown, College of Public Service, Department of Urban Education, Houston, TX 77002. Offers bilingual education (MAT); curriculum and instruction (MAT); elementary education (MAT); secondary education (MAT). Part-time and evening/weekend programs available. *Faculty:* 8 full-time (5 women). *Students:* 1 (woman) full-time, 42 part-time (34 women); includes 27 minority (15 African Americans, 3 Asian Americans or Pacific Islanders, 9 Hispanic Americans). Average age 37. 16 applicants, 100% accepted, 12 enrolled. In 2009, 17 master's awarded. *Degree requirements:* For master's, capstone course with completed project, position paper, grant proposal, empirical study, curriculum development/revision, or advanced technology project presented at annual Graduate Project Exhibition. *Entrance requirements:* For master's, GRE, personal statement, 3 recommendation forms. Additional exam requirements/recommendations for international students: Required—TOEFL (minimum score 550 paper-based; 213 computer-based; 80 iBT). *Application deadline:* For fall admission, 6/1 for domestic and international students; for spring admission, 11/1 for domestic and international students. Applications are processed on a rolling basis. Application fee: $35 ($60 for international students). Electronic applications accepted. *Expenses:* Tuition, state resident: full-time $3150; part-time $175 per credit hour. Tuition, nonresident: full-time $7506; part-time $417 per credit hour. Required fees: $908; $322 per term. *Financial support:* Scholarships/grants available. Financial award applicants required to submit FAFSA. *Unit head:* Dr. Myrna Cohen, Chair, 713-221-2759, Fax: 713-226-5294, E-mail: cohenm@uhd.edu. *Application contact:* Traneshia Parker, Assistant Director, Admissions-Graduate, International and Residency, 713-221-8093, Fax: 713-221-8157, E-mail: parkert@uhd.edu.

University of Houston–Victoria, School of Education and Human Development, Victoria, TX 77901-4450. Offers administration and supervision (M Ed); counseling (M Ed); curriculum and instruction (M Ed); special education (M Ed). Part-time and evening/weekend programs available. Postbaccalaureate distance learning degree programs offered. *Degree requirements:* For master's, comprehensive exam, project or thesis. *Entrance requirements:* For master's, GRE General Test. Additional exam requirements/recommendations for international students: Required—TOEFL. Electronic applications accepted. *Faculty research:* Reading and language arts education, evaluation and diagnosis of special children's abilities.

University of Idaho, College of Graduate Studies, College of Education, Department of Curriculum and Instruction, Moscow, ID 83844-2282. Offers M Ed. *Faculty:* 23 full-time, 12 part-time/adjunct. *Students:* 17 full-time, 46 part-time. In 2009, 19 master's awarded. *Entrance requirements:* For master's, minimum GPA of 2.8. *Application deadline:* For fall admission, 8/1 for domestic students; for spring admission, 12/15 for domestic students. Application fee: $55 ($60 for international students). *Expenses:* Tuition, state resident: full-time $6120. Tuition, nonresident: full-time $17,712. *Financial support:* Research assistantships, teaching assistantships available. Financial award application deadline: 2/15. *Unit head:* Paul H. Gathercoal, Chair, 208-885-6587. *Application contact:* Paul H. Gathercoal, Chair, 208-885-6587.

University of Illinois at Chicago, Graduate College, College of Education, Department of Curriculum and Instruction, Chicago, IL 60607-7128. Offers curriculum studies (PhD); educational studies (M Ed); elementary education (M Ed); literacy, language and culture (M Ed, PhD); secondary education (M Ed). Part-time and evening/weekend programs available. *Degree requirements:* For doctorate, thesis/dissertation. *Entrance requirements:* For master's, minimum GPA of 2.75; for doctorate, GRE General Test, minimum GPA of 2.75. Additional exam requirements/recommendations for international students: Required—TOEFL. Electronic applications accepted. *Faculty research:* Curriculum theory, curriculum development, research on teaching, curriculum and context, reading/literacy.

University of Illinois at Urbana–Champaign, Graduate College, College of Education, Department of Curriculum and Instruction, Champaign, IL 61820. Offers curriculum and instruction (Ed M, MA, MS, Ed D, PhD, CAS); early childhood education (Ed M); elementary education (Ed M); secondary education (Ed M). Part-time programs available. Postbaccalaureate distance learning degree programs offered (minimal on-campus study). *Faculty:* 24 full-time (18 women). *Students:* 102 full-time (76 women), 116 part-time (95 women); includes 38 minority (16 African Americans, 14 Asian Americans or Pacific Islanders, 8 Hispanic Americans), 57 international. 185 applicants, 42% accepted, 36 enrolled. In 2009, 42 master's, 17 doctorates, 1 other advanced degree awarded. *Entrance requirements:* For master's, minimum GPA of 3.0; for doctorate, GRE General Test, writing sample. Additional exam requirements/recommendations for international students: Required—TOEFL (minimum score 550 paper-based; 213 computer-based; 79 iBT). *Application deadline:* Applications are processed on a rolling basis. Application fee: $60 ($75 for international students). Electronic applications accepted. *Financial support:* In 2009–10, 5 fellowships, 42 research assistantships, 43 teaching assistantships were awarded; tuition waivers (full and partial) also available. *Unit head:* Stafford Hood, Head, 217-244-8286, Fax: 217-244-4572, E-mail: slhood@illinois.edu. *Application contact:* Myranda Lyons, Office Support Associate, 217-244-8286, Fax: 217-244-4572, E-mail: mjlyons@illinois.edu.

University of Indianapolis, Graduate Programs, School of Education, Indianapolis, IN 46227-3697. Offers art education (MAT); biology (MAT); chemistry (MAT); curriculum and instruction (MA); earth sciences (MAT); education (MA, MAT); educational leadership (MA); elementary education (MA); English (MAT); French (MAT); math (MAT); physical education (MAT); physics (MAT); secondary education (MA), including art education, education, English education, social studies education; social studies (MAT); Spanish (MAT). *Accreditation:* NCATE. Part-time and evening/weekend programs available. *Faculty:* 4 full-time (3 women), 3 part-time/adjunct (2 women). *Students:* 52 full-time (28 women), 110 part-time (67 women); includes 3 minority (all African Americans), 2 international. Average age 33. *Entrance requirements:* For master's, GRE Subject Test, PRAXIS I, minimum GPA of 2.5, 3 letters of recommendation, interview, writing exercise. Additional exam requirements/recommendations for international students: Required—TOEFL (minimum score 550 paper-based; 213 computer-based). *Application deadline:* Applications are processed on a rolling basis. Application fee: $50. *Financial support:* Federal Work-Study available. Financial award application deadline: 5/1; financial award applicants required to submit FAFSA. *Faculty research:* Assessment of teacher education, perceptions of prospective teachers by parents. *Unit head:* Dr. Kathy Moran, Dean, 317-788-3285, Fax: 317-788-3300, E-mail: kmoran@uindy.edu. *Application contact:* Chemain Slater, 317-788-2051, E-mail: slaterc@uindy.edu.

The University of Iowa, Graduate College, College of Education, Department of Teaching and Learning, Program in Elementary Education, Iowa City, IA 52242-1316. Offers curriculum and supervision (MA, PhD); developmental reading (MA); early childhood education and care (MA); elementary education (MA, PhD); language, literature and culture (PhD). *Degree requirements:* For master's, thesis optional, exam; for doctorate, comprehensive exam, thesis/dissertation. *Entrance requirements:* For master's and doctorate, GRE General Test, minimum GPA of 3.0. Additional exam requirements/recommendations for international students: Required—TOEFL (minimum score 550 paper-based; 213 computer-based; 81 iBT). Electronic applications accepted.

The University of Iowa, Graduate College, College of Education, Department of Teaching and Learning, Program in Secondary Education, Iowa City, IA 52242-1316. Offers art education (PhD); curriculum and supervision (PhD); curriculum supervision (MA); developmental reading (MA); English education (MA, MAT); foreign language education (MA, MAT); foreign language/ESL education (PhD); language, literature and culture (PhD); math education (PhD); mathematics education (MA); social studies (MA, PhD). *Degree requirements:* For master's, thesis optional, exam; for doctorate, comprehensive exam, thesis/dissertation. *Entrance requirements:* For master's and doctorate, GRE General Test, minimum GPA of 3.0. Additional exam requirements/recommendations for international students: Required—TOEFL (minimum score 550 paper-based; 213 computer-based; 81 iBT). Electronic applications accepted.

The University of Kansas, Graduate Studies, School of Education, Department of Curriculum and Teaching, Lawrence, KS 66045-3101. Offers curriculum and instruction (MA, MS Ed, Ed D, PhD). Part-time and evening/weekend programs available. *Faculty:* 27 full-time (18 women), 6 part-time/adjunct (all women). *Students:* 262 full-time (181 women), 164 part-time (129 women); includes 42 minority (12 African Americans, 3 American Indian/Alaska Native, 17 Asian Americans or Pacific Islanders, 10 Hispanic Americans), 64 international. Average age 32. 228 applicants, 79% accepted, 135 enrolled. In 2009, 114 master's, 14 doctorates awarded. *Degree requirements:* For master's, comprehensive exam (for some programs), thesis optional; for doctorate, comprehensive exam, thesis/dissertation. *Entrance requirements:* For master's, minimum GPA of 3.0; for doctorate, GRE General Test, minimum graduate GPA of 3.5. Additional exam requirements/recommendations for international students: Required—TOEFL (minimum score 590 paper-based; 243 computer-based; 96 iBT), IELTS (minimum score 7.5). *Application deadline:* For fall admission, 2/1 priority date for domestic and international students; for spring admission, 10/15 priority date for domestic and international students. Applications are processed on a rolling basis. Application fee: $45 ($55 for international students). Electronic applications accepted. *Expenses:* Tuition, state resident: full-time $6492; part-time $270.50 per credit hour. Tuition, nonresident: full-time $15,510; part-time $646.25 per credit hour. Required fees: $847; $70.56 per credit hour. Tuition and fees vary according to course load and program. *Financial support:* Fellowships, research assistantships with full and partial tuition reimbursements, teaching assistantships with full and partial tuition reimbursements, Federal Work-Study, scholarships/grants, and unspecified assistantships available. Financial award application deadline: 3/15; financial award applicants required to submit FAFSA. *Faculty research:* Reading, teacher preparation, math education, science education, geographic literacy. *Unit head:* Steven Hugh White, Associate Professor and Chair, 785-864-9662, Fax: 785-864-5207, E-mail: s-white@ku.edu. *Application contact:* Jan Kazar, Graduate Admissions Coordinator, 785-864-4437, Fax: 785-864-5207, E-mail: jkazar@ku.edu.

Curriculum and Instruction

University of Kentucky, Graduate School, College of Education, Program in Curriculum and Instruction, Lexington, KY 40506-0032. Offers curriculum and instruction (MA Ed, Ed D); instruction and administration (Ed D); instruction system design (MS Ed); middle school education (MS Ed). *Accreditation:* NCATE. *Degree requirements:* For master's, comprehensive exam, thesis optional; for doctorate, comprehensive exam, thesis/dissertation. *Entrance requirements:* For master's, GRE General Test, minimum undergraduate GPA of 2.75; for doctorate, GRE General Test, minimum graduate GPA of 3.0. Additional exam requirements/recommendations for international students: Required—TOEFL (minimum score 550 paper-based; 213 computer-based). Electronic applications accepted. *Faculty research:* Educational reform, multicultural education, classroom instructional practices, performance based assessment, primary school programs.

University of Louisiana at Lafayette, College of Education, Graduate Studies and Research in Education, Program in Curriculum and Instruction, Lafayette, LA 70504. Offers M Ed. *Accreditation:* NCATE. *Degree requirements:* For master's, thesis or alternative. *Entrance requirements:* For master's, GRE General Test, teaching certificate. Additional exam requirements/recommendations for international students: Required—TOEFL (minimum score 550 paper-based; 213 computer-based). Electronic applications accepted.

University of Louisiana at Monroe, Graduate School, College of Education and Human Development, Department of Curriculum and Instruction, Program in Curriculum and Instruction, Monroe, LA 71209-0001. Offers curriculum and instruction (Ed D); elementary education (1-5) (M Ed); reading education (K-12) (M Ed); SPED-academically gifted education (K-12) (M Ed); SPED-early intervention education (birth-3) (M Ed); SPED-educational diagnostics education (PreK-12) (M Ed). *Accreditation:* NCATE. *Faculty:* 17 full-time (all women), 2 part-time/adjunct (both women). *Students:* 15 full-time (13 women), 125 part-time (118 women); includes 38 minority (36 African Americans, 1 Asian American or Pacific Islander, 1 Hispanic American). Average age 37. In 2009, 11 master's, 4 doctorates awarded. *Degree requirements:* For master's, comprehensive exam (for some programs), thesis; for doctorate, thesis/dissertation, internships. *Entrance requirements:* For master's, GRE General Test; for doctorate, GRE General Test, minimum undergraduate GPA of 2.75, graduate 3.25. Additional exam requirements/recommendations for international students: Required—TOEFL (minimum score 500 paper-based; 173 computer-based; 61 iBT). *Application deadline:* For fall admission, 8/24 priority date for domestic students, 7/1 for international students; for winter admission, 12/14 priority date for domestic students; for spring admission, 1/19 for domestic students, 11/1 for international students. Applications are processed on a rolling basis. Application fee: $20 ($30 for international students). Electronic applications accepted. *Expenses:* Tuition, state resident: part-time $159 per credit hour. Tuition, nonresident: part-time $159 per credit hour. Required fees: $1300 per year. Tuition and fees vary according to course load. *Financial support:* In 2009–10, 8 teaching assistantships with full tuition reimbursements (averaging $2,969 per year) were awarded; career-related internships or fieldwork, Federal Work-Study, and unspecified assistantships also available. Financial award application deadline: 4/1; financial award applicants required to submit FAFSA. *Unit head:* Dr. Dorothy Schween, Coordinator, 318-342-1269, Fax: 318-342-3131, E-mail: schween@ulm.edu. *Application contact:* Whitney Sutherland, Administrative Assistant to the Department Head, 318-342-1266, Fax: 318-342-3131, E-mail: sutherland@ulm.edu.

University of Louisville, Graduate School, College of Education and Human Development, Department of Teaching and Learning, Louisville, KY 40292-0001. Offers art education (MAT); curriculum and instruction (PhD); early elementary education (MAT); instructional technology (M Ed); interdisciplinary early childhood education (MAT); middle school education (MAT); music education (MAT); reading education (M Ed); secondary education (MAT); special education (M Ed, MAT); teacher leadership (M Ed). Part-time and evening/weekend programs available. *Faculty:* 43 full-time (33 women), 43 part-time/adjunct (36 women). *Students:* 207 full-time (144 women), 410 part-time (306 women); includes 68 minority (43 African Americans, 2 American Indian/Alaska Native, 14 Asian Americans or Pacific Islanders, 9 Hispanic Americans), 5 international. Average age 33. 216 applicants, 68% accepted, 112 enrolled. In 2009, 269 master's, 6 doctorates awarded. *Degree requirements:* For doctorate, comprehensive exam, thesis/dissertation. *Entrance requirements:* For master's, GRE General Test, PRAXIS II (for some programs); for doctorate, GRE General Test. Additional exam requirements/recommendations for international students: Required—TOEFL (minimum score 560 paper-based; 210 computer-based; 83 iBT). Application fee: $50. Electronic applications accepted. *Financial support:* In 2009–10, 172 students received support; fellowships, research assistantships, teaching assistantships, career-related internships or fieldwork, Federal Work-Study, scholarships/grants, and unspecified assistantships available. Financial award application deadline: 6/1; financial award applicants required to submit FAFSA. *Faculty research:* Assessment of cognitive and language abilities in infants and preschool children; mathematics teachers' conceptions and beliefs, effect, and understanding of mathematics; incorporating nanoscience and nanotechnology into middle and high school science classrooms; urban teacher preparation through inquiry, action and advocacy; impacts of cognitive coaching on teacher practice and student achievement. Total annual research expenditures: $3.7 million. *Unit head:* Dr. Ann E. Larson, Acting Chair, 502-852-6431, Fax: 502-852-1497, E-mail: ann@louisville.edu. *Application contact:* Libby Leggett, Director, Graduate Admissions, 502-852-3101, Fax: 502-852-6536, E-mail: gradadm@louisville.edu.

University of Maine, Graduate School, College of Education and Human Development, Program in Curriculum, Assessment, and Instruction, Orono, ME 04469. Offers elementary and secondary education (M Ed). *Students:* 3 full-time (0 women), 15 part-time (13 women). Average age 37. 6 applicants, 0% accepted, 0 enrolled. In 2009, 18 master's awarded. Application fee: $65. *Unit head:* Dr. Janet Spector, Dean, 207-581-2441, Fax: 207-581-2423. *Application contact:* Scott G. Delcourt, Associate Dean of the Graduate School, 207-581-3291, Fax: 207-581-3232, E-mail: graduate@maine.edu.

University of Manitoba, Faculty of Graduate Studies, Faculty of Education, Department of Curriculum, Teaching and Learning, Winnipeg, MB R3T 2N2, Canada. Offers language and literacy (M Ed); second language education (M Ed); studies in curriculum, teaching and learning (M Ed). *Degree requirements:* For master's, thesis or alternative.

University of Mary, Program in Education, Bismarck, ND 58504-9652. Offers college teaching (M Ed); curriculum, instruction and assessment (M Ed); early childhood education (M Ed); early childhood special education (M Ed); elementary education administration (M Ed); emotional disorders (M Ed); learning disabilities (M Ed); reading (M Ed); secondary education administration (M Ed); special education (M Ed); special education strategist (M Ed). Part-time programs available. *Degree requirements:* For master's, portfolio or thesis. *Entrance requirements:* For master's, interview, letters of reference. Additional exam requirements/recommendations for international students: Required—TOEFL (minimum score 550 paper-based). *Expenses:* Tuition: Full-time $10,062; part-time $430 per credit. Tuition and fees vary according to course load, degree level, program and student level. *Faculty research:* Innovative pedagogy in higher education, technology in education, content standards, children of poverty, children with diverse learning needs.

University of Maryland, Baltimore County, Graduate School, College of Arts, Humanities and Social Sciences, Department of Education, Baltimore, MD 21250. Offers computer/web-based instruction (Postbaccalaureate Certificate); distance education (Postbaccalaureate Certificate); education (MA), including mathematics education, science education, STEM education; elementary/middle science education (Postbaccalaureate Certificate); instructional systems development: training systems (MA, Graduate Certificate), including distance education (Graduate Certificate), e-learning in instructional design (Graduate Certificate), instructional systems development, instructional technology (Graduate Certificate); language, literacy, culture (PhD); math education (Postbaccalaureate Certificate); STEM education (Postbaccalaureate Certificate); teaching (MAT), including early childhood education, elementary education, secondary education; teaching English to speakers of other languages (MA, Postbaccalaureate Certificate). *Accreditation:* NCATE. Part-time and evening/weekend programs available. Postbaccalaureate distance learning degree programs offered (no on-campus study). *Faculty:* 24 full-time (18 women), 25 part-time/adjunct (19 women). *Students:* 90 full-time (79 women), 320 part-time (264 women); includes 64 minority (36 African Americans, 2 American Indian/Alaska Native, 16 Asian Americans or Pacific Islanders, 10 Hispanic Americans), 21 international. Average age 34. 209 applicants, 63% accepted, 98 enrolled. In 2009, 106 master's, 3 doctorates awarded. *Degree requirements:* For master's, comprehensive exam (for some programs), thesis (for some programs); for doctorate, comprehensive exam, thesis/dissertation. *Entrance requirements:* For master's, GRE General Test, GRE Subject Test (MA), PRAXIS I (MAT), minimum GPA of 3.0. Additional exam requirements/recommendations for international students: Required—TOEFL. *Application deadline:* For fall admission, 6/1 for domestic students; for spring admission, 11/1 for domestic students. Applications are processed on a rolling basis. Application fee: $50. Electronic applications accepted. *Financial support:* In 2009–10, 12 students received support, including research assistantships with full tuition reimbursements available (averaging $12,000 per year); fellowships, teaching assistantships, career-related internships or fieldwork, Federal Work-Study, scholarships/grants, tuition waivers (partial), and unspecified assistantships also available. Financial award application deadline: 3/1. *Faculty research:* Teacher leadership; STEM education; ESOL/bilingual education; early childhood education; language, literacy and culture. Total annual research expenditures: $1.3 million. *Unit head:* Dr. Eugene Schaffer, Department Chair, 410-455-2465, Fax: 410-455-3986, E-mail: schaffer@umbc.edu. *Application contact:* Dr. Susan M. Blunck, Director, 410-455-2869, Fax: 410-455-3986, E-mail: blunck@umbc.edu.

University of Maryland, College Park, Academic Affairs, College of Education, Department of Curriculum and Instruction, College Park, MD 20742. Offers reading (M Ed, MA, PhD, CAGS); secondary education (M Ed, MA, Ed D, PhD, CAGS); teaching English to speakers of other languages (M Ed). *Accreditation:* NCATE. Part-time and evening/weekend programs available. Postbaccalaureate distance learning degree programs offered (no on-campus study). *Faculty:* 57 full-time (36 women), 35 part-time/adjunct (30 women). *Students:* 280 full-time (216 women), 181 part-time (150 women); includes 117 minority (60 African Americans, 2 American Indian/Alaska Native, 33 Asian Americans or Pacific Islanders, 22 Hispanic Americans), 51 international. 300 applicants, 40% accepted, 85 enrolled. In 2009, 143 master's, 20 doctorates awarded. *Degree requirements:* For master's, comprehensive exam, seminar paper; for doctorate, comprehensive exam, thesis/dissertation, published paper, oral exam. *Entrance requirements:* For master's, GRE General Test or MAT, minimum GPA of 3.0, 3 letters of recommendation; for doctorate, GRE General Test or MAT, minimum undergraduate GPA of 3.0, graduate 3.5; 3 letters of recommendation. *Application deadline:* For fall admission, 1/20 priority date for domestic students, 1/20 for international students; for spring admission, 9/1 priority date for domestic students, 6/1 for international students. Applications are processed on a rolling basis. Application fee: $60. Electronic applications accepted. *Expenses:* Tuition, area resident: Part-time $471 per credit hour. Tuition, state resident: part-time $471 per credit hour. Tuition, nonresident: part-time $1016 per credit hour. Required fees: $337.04 per term. *Financial support:* In 2009–10, 19 research assistantships with tuition reimbursements (averaging $18,124 per year), 76 teaching assistantships with tuition reimbursements (averaging $17,105 per year) were awarded; fellowships, Federal Work-Study and scholarships/grants also available. Support available to part-time students. Financial award applicants required to submit FAFSA. *Faculty research:* Teacher preparation, curriculum study, inservice education. Total annual research expenditures: $3.9 million. *Unit head:* Dr. Linda M. Valli, Interim Chair, 301-405-3117, E-mail: lrv@umd.edu. *Application contact:* Dean of Graduate School, 301-405-0358.

University of Massachusetts Boston, Office of Graduate Studies, Graduate College of Education, Program in Instructional Design, Boston, MA 02125-3393. Offers M Ed. Part-time and evening/weekend programs available. *Degree requirements:* For master's, comprehensive exam, thesis optional, practicum. *Entrance requirements:* For master's, MAT, minimum GPA of 2.75. *Faculty research:* Distance education, adult education.

University of Massachusetts Lowell, Graduate School of Education, Lowell, MA 01854-2881. Offers administration, planning, and policy (CAGS); curriculum and instruction (M Ed, CAGS); educational administration (M Ed); language arts and literacy (Ed D); leadership in schooling (Ed D); math and science education (Ed D); reading and language (M Ed, CAGS). *Accreditation:* NCATE. Part-time and evening/weekend programs available. Postbaccalaureate distance learning degree programs offered (no on-campus study). Terminal master's awarded for partial completion of doctoral program. *Degree requirements:* For doctorate, thesis/dissertation. *Entrance requirements:* For master's, doctorate, and CAGS, GRE General Test. Additional exam requirements/recommendations for international students: Required—TOEFL. Electronic applications accepted.

University of Memphis, Graduate School, College of Education, Department of Instruction and Curriculum Leadership, Memphis, TN 38152. Offers early childhood education (MAT, MS, Ed D); elementary education (MAT); instruction and curriculum (MS, Ed D); instruction design and technology (MS, Ed D); middle grades education (MAT); reading (MS, Ed D); secondary education (MAT); special education (MAT, MS, Ed D). *Accreditation:* NCATE (one or more programs are accredited). Part-time programs available. *Faculty:* 40 full-time (28 women), 20 part-time/adjunct (15 women). *Students:* 119 full-time (90 women), 631 part-time (505 women); includes 348 minority (331 African Americans, 2 American Indian/Alaska Native, 4 Asian Americans or Pacific Islanders, 11 Hispanic Americans), 7 international. Average age 34. 202 applicants, 77% accepted, 29 enrolled. In 2009, 137 master's, 10 doctorates awarded. Terminal master's awarded for partial completion of doctoral program. *Degree requirements:* For master's, comprehensive exam, thesis or alternative; for doctorate, comprehensive exam, thesis/dissertation. *Entrance requirements:* For master's, GRE General Test, minimum GPA of 2.5; for doctorate, GRE General Test, GRE Subject Test, 2 years of teaching experience. *Application deadline:* For fall admission, 8/1 for domestic students; for spring admission, 12/1 for domestic students. Applications are processed on a rolling basis. Application fee: $35 ($60 for international students). Electronic applications accepted. *Expenses:* Tuition, state resident: full-time $6246; part-time $347 per credit hour. Tuition, nonresident: full-time $15,894; part-time $883 per credit hour. Required fees: $1160. Full-time tuition and fees vary according to course load, degree level and program. *Financial support:* In 2009–10, 635 students received support; research assistantships with full tuition reimbursements available, teaching assistantships with full tuition reimbursements available, career-related internships or fieldwork, Federal Work-Study, institutionally sponsored loans, scholarships/grants, traineeships, and unspecified assistantships available. Support available to part-time students. Financial award application deadline: 2/15; financial award applicants required to submit FAFSA. *Faculty research:* Effective urban teachers, preparation and retention of urban teachers, technology utilization in schools, field-based teacher preparation programs, effective use of online instruction. *Unit head:* Dr. Sandra Cooley-Nichols, Interim Chair, 901-678-2365. *Application contact:* Dr. Sally Blake, Director of Graduate Studies, 901-678-4861.

University of Michigan, Horace H. Rackham School of Graduate Studies, School of Education, Programs in Educational Studies, Ann Arbor, MI 48109. Offers cross specialization (PhD); curriculum development (MA); early childhood education (MA, PhD); educational administration and policy (MA, PhD); educational foundations and policy (MA, PhD); English education (MA); English language learning in school settings (MA); learning technologies (MA, PhD); literacy, language, and culture (MA, PhD); mathematics education (MA, PhD); postsecondary science education (MS); research methods (MA); science education (MA, PhD); social studies education (MA); teaching and teacher education (PhD); MA/Certification; MBA/MA; PhD/MA. Terminal master's awarded for partial completion of doctoral program. *Degree requirements:* For master's, thesis (for some programs); for doctorate, comprehensive exam, thesis/dissertation. *Entrance requirements:* For master's and doctorate, GRE General Test. Additional exam requirements/recommendations for international students: Required—TOEFL (minimum score 600 paper-based; 250 computer-based). *Application deadline:* For fall admission, 12/1 priority date for domestic students, 12/1 for international students. Application fee: $60 ($75 for international students). Electronic applications accepted. *Expenses:* Tuition, state resident: full-time $17,286; part-time $1099 per credit hour. Tuition, nonresident: full-time $34,944; part-time $2080 per credit hour. Required fees: $95 per semester. Tuition and fees vary according to course load, degree level and program. *Financial support:* Applicants required to submit FAFSA. *Unit head:*

Dr. Addison Stone, Chairperson, 734-763-7500, Fax: 734-615-1290, E-mail: addison@umich.edu. *Application contact:* Laura Mayers, Student Services Assistant, 734-764-7563, Fax: 734-763-1495, E-mail: ed.grad.admit@umich.edu.

University of Michigan–Dearborn, School of Education, Doctoral Program in Education, Dearborn, MI 48126. Offers curriculum and practice (Ed D); educational leadership (Ed D); educational psychology/special education (Ed D); metropolitan education (Ed D). Part-time and evening/weekend programs available. *Faculty:* 7 full-time (4 women). *Students:* 1 (woman) full-time, 17 part-time (9 women); includes 5 minority (3 African Americans, 1 Asian American or Pacific Islander, 1 Hispanic American). Average age 46. 62 applicants, 31% accepted, 18 enrolled. *Degree requirements:* For doctorate, comprehensive exam, thesis/dissertation. *Entrance requirements:* For doctorate, GRE (taken within the last 5 years), master's degree with minimum GPA of 3.3, 3 letters of recommendation (1 from faculty), 3 yearsprofessional and/or teaching experience. Additional exam requirements/recommendations for international students: Required—TOEFL (minimum score 550 paper-based), Test of Spoken English (TES). *Application deadline:* For fall admission, 3/1 for domestic and international students. Application fee: $60. *Expenses:* Tuition, state resident: part-time $504.10 per credit hour. Tuition, nonresident: part-time $957.90 per credit hour. *Faculty research:* Educational leadership, metropolitan education, curriculum and practice, educational psychology, special education, assessment. *Unit head:* Gail Luera, Associate Dean/Interim Coordinator, 313-593-5098, E-mail: grl@umich.edu. *Application contact:* Catherine Parkins, Customer Service Assistant, 313-583-6349, Fax: 313-593-4748, E-mail: cparkins@umd.umich.edu.

University of Minnesota, Twin Cities Campus, Graduate School, College of Education and Human Development, Department of Curriculum and Instruction, Minneapolis, MN 55455-0213. Offers art education (M Ed, MA, PhD); children's literature (M Ed, MA, PhD); curriculum and instruction (MA, PhD); early childhood education (M Ed, PhD); elementary education (M Ed, MA, PhD); English education (MA, PhD); environmental education (M Ed); family education (M Ed, MA, Ed D, PhD); instructional systems and technology (M Ed, MA, PhD); language arts (MA, PhD); language immersion education (Certificate); literacy education (MA); mathematics education (MA, PhD); reading education (MA, PhD); science education (MA, PhD); second languages and cultures education (MA, PhD); social studies education (MA, PhD); teaching (M Ed), including Chinese, earth science, elementary special education, English, English as a second language, French, German, Hebrew, Japanese, life sciences, mathematics, middle school science, science, second languages and cultures, social studies, Spanish; technology enhanced learning (Certificate); writing education (M Ed, MA, PhD). *Faculty:* 34 full-time (21 women). *Students:* 436 full-time (307 women), 375 part-time (280 women); includes 80 minority (30 African Americans, 6 American Indian/Alaska Native, 33 Asian Americans or Pacific Islanders, 11 Hispanic Americans), 40 international. Average age 32. 660 applicants, 64% accepted, 379 enrolled. In 2009, 552 master's, 14 doctorates, 7 other advanced degrees awarded. *Financial support:* In 2009–10, 5 fellowships (averaging $27,000 per year), 47 research assistantships with full tuition reimbursements (averaging $25,682 per year), 60 teaching assistantships with full tuition reimbursements (averaging $29,889 per year) were awarded. *Faculty research:* Teaching and learning; quality of education; influence of cultural, linguistic, social, political, technological and economic factors on teaching, learning and educational research; relationship between educational practice and a democratic and just society. Total annual research expenditures: $1.8 million. *Unit head:* Dr. Ruth Thomas, Chair, 612-624-4772, Fax: 612-624-8277, E-mail: thoma006@umn.edu. *Application contact:* Dr. Mary Trettin, Associate Dean, 612-625-6501, Fax: 612-626-1580, E-mail: mtrettin@umn.edu.

University of Mississippi, Graduate School, School of Education, Department of Curriculum and Instruction, Oxford, University, MS 38677. Offers curriculum and instruction (M Ed, Ed D, Ed S); education (PhD). *Accreditation:* NCATE. *Faculty:* 41 full-time (36 women), 23 part-time/adjunct (14 women). *Students:* 70 full-time (62 women), 334 part-time (283 women); includes 133 minority (129 African Americans, 1 American Indian/Alaska Native, 3 Hispanic Americans), 3 international. In 2009, 127 master's, 8 doctorates, 9 other advanced degrees awarded. *Degree requirements:* For master's, thesis (for some programs); for doctorate, one foreign language, thesis/dissertation. *Entrance requirements:* For master's, GRE General Test, minimum GPA of 3.0; for doctorate, GRE General Test. Additional exam requirements/recommendations for international students: Required—TOEFL. *Application deadline:* For fall admission, 7/1 for domestic students; for spring admission, 10/1 for domestic students. Applications are processed on a rolling basis. Application fee: $25. *Financial support:* Scholarships/grants available. Financial award application deadline: 3/1; financial award applicants required to submit FAFSA. *Unit head:* Dr. Kimberly Jeane Hartman, Chair, 662-915-5908, E-mail: khartman@olemiss.edu. *Application contact:* Dr. Christy M. Wyandt, Associate Dean, 662-915-7474, Fax: 662-915-7577, E-mail: cwyandt@olemiss.edu.

University of Missouri, Graduate School, College of Education, Department of Educational, School, and Counseling Psychology, Columbia, MO 65211. Offers counseling psychology (M Ed, MA, PhD, Ed S); educational psychology (M Ed, MA, PhD, Ed S); learning and instruction (M Ed); school psychology (M Ed, MA, PhD, Ed S). *Accreditation:* APA (one or more programs are accredited). Part-time programs available. *Degree requirements:* For doctorate, thesis/dissertation. *Entrance requirements:* For master's, doctorate, and Ed S, GRE General Test, minimum GPA of 3.0. Additional exam requirements/recommendations for international students: Required—TOEFL (minimum score 580 paper-based; 237 computer-based; 92 iBT).

University of Missouri, Graduate School, College of Education, Department of Learning, Teaching and Curriculum, Columbia, MO 65211. Offers agricultural education (M Ed, PhD, Ed S); art education (M Ed, PhD, Ed S); business and office education (M Ed, PhD, Ed S); early childhood education (M Ed, PhD, Ed S); elementary education (M Ed, PhD, Ed S); English education (M Ed, PhD, Ed S); foreign language education (M Ed, PhD, Ed S); health education and promotion (M Ed, PhD); learning and instruction (M Ed); marketing education (M Ed, PhD, Ed S); mathematics education (M Ed, PhD, Ed S); music education (M Ed, PhD, Ed S); reading education (M Ed, PhD, Ed S); science education (M Ed, PhD, Ed S); social studies education (M Ed, PhD, Ed S); vocational education (M Ed, PhD, Ed S). Part-time programs available. Terminal master's awarded for partial completion of doctoral program. *Degree requirements:* For doctorate, thesis/dissertation. *Entrance requirements:* For master's and Ed S, GRE General Test or MAT, minimum GPA of 3.0; for doctorate, GRE General Test, minimum GPA of 3.0. Additional exam requirements/recommendations for international students: Required—TOEFL (minimum score 600 paper-based; 250 computer-based; 100 iBT). Electronic applications accepted.

University of Missouri, Graduate School, College of Education, Department of Special Education, Columbia, MO 65211. Offers administration and supervision of special education (PhD); behavior disorders (M Ed, PhD); curriculum development of exceptional students (M Ed, PhD); early childhood special education (M Ed, PhD); general special education (M Ed, MA, PhD); learning and instruction (M Ed); learning disabilities (M Ed, PhD); mental retardation (M Ed, PhD). Part-time and evening/weekend programs available. Postbaccalaureate distance learning degree programs offered (no on-campus study). *Degree requirements:* For master's, comprehensive exam, thesis or alternative; for doctorate, comprehensive exam, thesis/dissertation. *Entrance requirements:* For master's and doctorate, GRE General Test, letters of recommendation. Additional exam requirements/recommendations for international students: Required—TOEFL (minimum score 500 paper-based; 173 computer-based; 61 iBT). Electronic applications accepted. *Faculty research:* Positive behavior support, applied behavior analysis, attention deficit disorder, pre-linguistic development, school discipline.

University of Missouri–Kansas City, School of Education, Kansas City, MO 64110-2499. Offers administration (Ed D); counseling and guidance (MA, Ed S); counseling psychology (PhD); curriculum and instruction (MA, Ed S); education (PhD); educational administration (Ed S); reading education (MA, Ed S); special education (MA). PhD with concentration in education (interdisciplinary) is offered through the School of Graduate Studies. *Accreditation:* NCATE. Part-time and evening/weekend programs available. *Faculty:* 62 full-time (52 women), 45 part-time/adjunct (34 women). *Students:* 207 full-time (154 women), 401 part-time (290 women); includes 142 minority (107 African Americans, 14 Asian Americans or Pacific Islanders,

21 Hispanic Americans), 18 international. Average age 34. 294 applicants, 61% accepted, 150 enrolled. In 2009, 184 master's, 9 doctorates, 49 other advanced degrees awarded. *Degree requirements:* For doctorate, thesis/dissertation, internship, practicum. *Entrance requirements:* For master's, GRE, minimum GPA of 2.75, 2 letters of reference, written statement of purpose; for doctorate, GRE, minimum GPA of 3.0; for Ed S, minimum GPA of 3.0. Additional exam requirements/recommendations for international students: Required—TOEFL (minimum score 550 paper-based; 213 computer-based; 80 iBT). *Application deadline:* For fall admission, 4/1 priority date for domestic and international students; for spring admission, 11/1 priority date for domestic and international students. Applications are processed on a rolling basis. Application fee: $45 ($50 for international students). *Expenses:* Tuition, state resident: full-time $5378; part-time $299 per credit hour. Tuition, nonresident: full-time $13,881; part-time $771 per credit hour. Required fees: $641; $71 per credit hour. Tuition and fees vary according to course load and program. *Financial support:* In 2009–10, 19 research assistantships with partial tuition reimbursements (averaging $9,821 per year) were awarded; career-related internships or fieldwork, Federal Work-Study, institutionally sponsored loans, and tuition waivers (full and partial) also available. Support available to part-time students. Financial award application deadline: 3/1; financial award applicants required to submit FAFSA. *Faculty research:* Urban education, inquiry-based field study, theories of counseling and psychotherapy, school literacy, educational technology. Total annual research expenditures: $2.9 million. *Unit head:* Dr. Wanda Blanchett, Dean, 816-235-2234, Fax: 816-235-5270, E-mail: education@umkc.edu. *Application contact:* Erica Hernandez-Scott, Student Recruiter, 816-235-1295, Fax: 816-235-5270, E-mail: hernandeze@umkc.edu.

University of Missouri–St. Louis, College of Education, Division of Teaching and Learning, St. Louis, MO 63121. Offers elementary education (M Ed), including early childhood, general, reading; secondary education (M Ed), including curriculum and instruction, general, middle level education, reading, teaching English to speakers of other languages (TESOL); secondary school teaching (Certificate); special education (M Ed), including behavioral disorders, early childhood special education, general, learning disabilities, mental retardation; teaching English to speakers of other languages (Certificate). Part-time and evening/weekend programs available. *Faculty:* 36 full-time (23 women), 51 part-time/adjunct (42 women). *Students:* 123 full-time (77 women), 569 part-time (435 women); includes 137 minority (110 African Americans, 4 American Indian/Alaska Native, 10 Asian Americans or Pacific Islanders, 13 Hispanic Americans), 11 international. Average age 32. In 2009, 1,852 master's awarded. *Degree requirements:* For master's, comprehensive exam. *Entrance requirements:* Additional exam requirements/recommendations for international students: Recommended—TOEFL (minimum score 550 paper-based; 213 computer-based). *Application deadline:* For fall admission, 7/1 priority date for domestic and international students; for spring admission, 12/1 priority date for domestic and international students. Application fee: $35 ($40 for international students). Electronic applications accepted. *Expenses:* Tuition, state resident: full-time $5377; part-time $297.70 per credit hour. Tuition, nonresident: full-time $13,882; part-time $771.20 per credit hour. Required fees: $220; $12.20 per credit hour. One-time fee: $12. Tuition and fees vary according to course level, campus/location and program. *Financial support:* In 2009–10, 5 research assistantships (averaging $10,339 per year), 2 teaching assistantships (averaging $6,800 per year) were awarded. Financial award application deadline: 4/1; financial award applicants required to submit FAFSA. *Unit head:* Dr. Joseph Polman, Chair, 314-516-5791. *Application contact:* 314-516-5458, Fax: 314-516-6996, E-mail: gadadm@umsl.edu.

The University of Montana, Graduate School, School of Education, Department of Curriculum and Instruction, Missoula, MT 59812-0002. Offers M Ed, Ed D. Part-time programs available. *Degree requirements:* For doctorate, thesis/dissertation. *Entrance requirements:* For master's, GRE General Test. Additional exam requirements/recommendations for international students: Required—TOEFL.

University of Nebraska at Kearney, College of Graduate Study, College of Education, Department of Teacher Education, Kearney, NE 68849-0001. Offers curriculum and instruction (MS Ed); instructional technology (MS Ed); reading education (MA Ed); special education (MA Ed). Part-time and evening/weekend programs available. *Degree requirements:* For master's, comprehensive exam, thesis optional. *Entrance requirements:* For master's, portfolio or GRE. Additional exam requirements/recommendations for international students: Required—TOEFL (minimum score 550 paper-based; 213 computer-based). Electronic applications accepted.

University of Nebraska–Lincoln, Graduate College, College of Education and Human Sciences, Department of Teaching, Learning and Teacher Education, Lincoln, NE 68588. Offers adult and continuing education (MA); educational studies (Ed D, PhD), including special education (Ed D); teaching, learning and teacher education (M Ed, MA, MST, Ed D, PhD); vocational and adult education (M Ed, MA). *Accreditation:* NCATE. *Degree requirements:* For master's, thesis optional. *Entrance requirements:* Additional exam requirements/recommendations for international students: Required—TOEFL (minimum score 550 paper-based; 213 computer-based). Electronic applications accepted. *Faculty research:* Teacher education, instructional leadership, literacy education, technology, improvement of school curriculum.

University of Nebraska–Lincoln, Graduate College, College of Education and Human Sciences, Interdepartmental Area of Administration, Curriculum and Instruction, Lincoln, NE 68588. Offers Ed D, PhD, JD/PhD. *Accreditation:* NCATE. Postbaccalaureate distance learning degree programs offered. *Degree requirements:* For doctorate, comprehensive exam, thesis/dissertation. *Entrance requirements:* For doctorate, GRE, curriculum vitae. Additional exam requirements/recommendations for international students: Required—TOEFL (minimum score 550 paper-based; 213 computer-based). Electronic applications accepted.

University of Nevada, Las Vegas, Graduate College, College of Education, Department of Curriculum and Instruction, Las Vegas, NV 89154-3005. Offers curriculum and instruction (M Ed, Ed D, PhD); teacher education (PhD). *Accreditation:* NCATE. Part-time and evening/weekend programs available. *Faculty:* 38 full-time (20 women), 16 part-time/adjunct (14 women). *Students:* 154 full-time (108 women), 385 part-time (297 women); includes 87 minority (19 African Americans, 28 Asian Americans or Pacific Islanders, 40 Hispanic Americans), 13 international. Average age 33. 201 applicants, 78% accepted, 120 enrolled. In 2009, 226 master's, 3 doctorates awarded. *Degree requirements:* For master's, comprehensive exam (for some programs), thesis (for some programs); for doctorate, comprehensive exam, thesis/dissertation, defense of dissertation, submit article for publication (curriculum and instruction). *Entrance requirements:* For doctorate, GRE General Test. Additional exam requirements/recommendations for international students: Required—TOEFL (minimum score 550 paper-based; 213 computer-based; 80 iBT), IELTS (minimum score 7). *Application deadline:* For fall admission, 3/1 priority date for domestic and international students; for spring admission, 11/1 priority date for domestic students, 10/1 for international students. Applications are processed on a rolling basis. Application fee: $60 ($95 for international students). Electronic applications accepted. *Financial support:* In 2009–10, 36 students received support, including 3 research assistantships with partial tuition reimbursements available (averaging $10,055 per year), 33 teaching assistantships with partial tuition reimbursements available (averaging $10,055 per year); institutionally sponsored loans, scholarships/grants, health care benefits, and unspecified assistantships also available. Financial award application deadline: 3/1. *Faculty research:* Teaching and learning in teacher education, mathematics education, literacy and teaching English as a second language, science education, technology education. *Unit head:* Dr. Sandra Odell, Chair/Professor, 702-895-3232, Fax: 702-895-4898, E-mail: odells@unlv.nevada.edu. *Application contact:* Graduate College Admissions Evaluator, 702-895-3320, Fax: 702-895-4180, E-mail: gradcollege@unlv.edu.

University of Nevada, Reno, Graduate School, College of Education, Department of Curriculum, Teaching and Learning, Program in Curriculum and Instruction, Reno, NV 89557. Offers PhD. *Degree requirements:* For doctorate, thesis/dissertation. *Entrance requirements:* For doctorate, GRE General Test, minimum GPA of 3.0. Additional exam requirements/recommendations for international students: Required—TOEFL (minimum score 500 paper-

Curriculum and Instruction

University of Nevada, Reno (continued)
based; 179 computer-based; 61 iBT), IELTS (minimum score 6). Electronic applications accepted. *Faculty research:* Education, development, pedagogy.

University of Nevada, Reno, Graduate School, College of Education, Department of Curriculum, Teaching and Learning, Program in Curriculum, Teaching and Learning, Reno, NV 89557. Offers Ed D, PhD. *Degree requirements:* For doctorate, comprehensive exam, thesis/dissertation. *Entrance requirements:* For doctorate, GRE General Test, minimum GPA of 3.0. Additional exam requirements/recommendations for international students: Required—TOEFL (minimum score 500 paper-based; 173 computer-based; 61 iBT), IELTS (minimum score 6). Electronic applications accepted. *Faculty research:* Education, trends, pedagogy.

University of New England, College of Arts and Sciences, Program in Education, Biddeford, ME 04005-9526. Offers curriculum and instruction strategy (MS Ed); educational leadership (MS Ed); general studies (MS Ed); literacy (MS Ed); teaching methodologies (MS Ed). Part-time programs available. Postbaccalaureate distance learning degree programs offered (minimal on-campus study). *Faculty:* 2 full-time (1 woman), 25 part-time/adjunct (15 women). *Students:* 473 full-time (362 women), 177 part-time (133 women); includes 29 African Americans, 12 Asian Americans or Pacific Islanders, 16 Hispanic Americans. In 2009, 319 master's awarded. *Degree requirements:* For master's, collaborative action research project, integrative seminar portfolio. *Entrance requirements:* For master's, teaching certificate, 2 years of teaching experience. Additional exam requirements/recommendations for international students: Required—TOEFL. *Application deadline:* For fall admission, 9/15 for domestic students; for spring admission, 1/15 for domestic students. Applications are processed on a rolling basis. Application fee: $40. Electronic applications accepted. *Expenses:* Contact institution. *Financial support:* Application deadline: 5/1. *Faculty research:* Distance learning, effective teaching, transition planning, adult learning. *Unit head:* Dr. Doug Lynch, Chair of Education Department, 207-283-0171 Ext. 2888, E-mail: dlynch@une.edu. *Application contact:* Stacy Gato, Assistant Director of Graduate Admissions, 207-221-4225, Fax: 207-221-4898, E-mail: gradadmissions@une.edu.

University of New Orleans, Graduate School, College of Education and Human Development, Department of Curriculum and Instruction, New Orleans, LA 70148. Offers M Ed, PhD, GCE. *Accreditation:* NCATE. Evening/weekend programs available. *Degree requirements:* For doctorate, variable foreign language requirement, thesis/dissertation. *Entrance requirements:* For master's, GRE General Test; for doctorate, GRE General Test, GRE Subject Test. Additional exam requirements/recommendations for international students: Required—TOEFL (minimum score 550 paper-based; 213 computer-based; 79 iBT). Electronic applications accepted.

The University of North Carolina at Chapel Hill, Graduate School, School of Education, Program in Education, Chapel Hill, NC 27599. Offers culture, curriculum and change (MA, PhD); early childhood, intervention and literacy (MA, PhD); educational psychology, measurement and evaluation (MA, PhD). *Accreditation:* NCATE. *Degree requirements:* For master's, thesis; for doctorate, comprehensive exam, thesis/dissertation. *Entrance requirements:* For master's, GRE General Test, minimum GPA of 3.0 during last 2 years of undergraduates course work; for doctorate, GRE General Test, minimum GPA of 3.0 during last 2 years of undergraduate course work. Additional exam requirements/recommendations for international students: Required—TOEFL (minimum score 550 paper-based; 213 computer-based). Electronic applications accepted.

The University of North Carolina at Charlotte, Graduate School, College of Education, Department of Educational Leadership, Charlotte, NC 28223-0001. Offers curriculum and supervision (M Ed); educational administration (CAS); educational leadership (Ed D); instructional systems technology (M Ed); school administration (MSA). Part-time and evening/weekend programs available. *Faculty:* 24 full-time (12 women). *Students:* 10 full-time (8 women), 73 part-time (40 women); includes 32 minority (31 African Americans, 1 American Indian/Alaska Native). Average age 43. 26 applicants, 81% accepted, 15 enrolled. In 2009, 2 doctorates awarded. *Entrance requirements:* For master's and doctorate, GRE or MAT. Additional exam requirements/recommendations for international students: Required—TOEFL (minimum score 550 paper-based; 220 computer-based; 83 iBT). *Application deadline:* For fall admission, 7/1 for domestic students, 5/1 for international students; for spring admission, 11/1 for domestic students, 10/1 for international students. Applications are processed on a rolling basis. Application fee: $55. Electronic applications accepted. *Financial support:* In 2009–10, 6 students received support, including 4 research assistantships (averaging $13,500 per year), 2 teaching assistantships (averaging $8,500 per year); career-related internships or fieldwork, institutionally sponsored loans, scholarships/grants, and unspecified assistantships also available. Support available to part-time students. Financial award application deadline: 4/1; financial award applicants required to submit FAFSA. *Faculty research:* Educational leadership theory and practice, instructional systems technology, educational research methodology, curriculum and supervision in the schools, school law and finance. Total annual research expenditures: $800,000. *Unit head:* Dr. Dawson R. Hancock, Chair, 704-687-8863, Fax: 704-687-3493, E-mail: dhancock@uncc.edu. *Application contact:* Kathy B. Giddings, Director of Graduate Admissions, 704-687-5503, Fax: 704-687-3279, E-mail: gradadm@uncc.edu.

The University of North Carolina at Charlotte, Graduate School, College of Education, Program in Curriculum and Instruction, Charlotte, NC 28223-0001. Offers urban education (PhD), including adult and continuing education leadership, educational administration; urban literacy (PhD); urban math (PhD). Part-time and evening/weekend programs available. *Faculty:* 7 full-time (5 women). *Students:* 10 full-time (all women), 55 part-time (36 women); includes 14 African Americans, 1 Asian American or Pacific Islander, 2 international. Average age 41. 24 applicants, 71% accepted, 15 enrolled. In 2009, 8 doctorates awarded. *Degree requirements:* For doctorate, thesis/dissertation. *Entrance requirements:* For doctorate, GRE or MAT. Additional exam requirements/recommendations for international students: Required—TOEFL (minimum score 557 paper-based; 220 computer-based; 83 iBT). *Application deadline:* For fall admission, 7/15 for domestic students, 5/1 for international students; for spring admission, 11/15 for domestic students, 10/1 for international students. Application fee: $55. *Financial support:* In 2009–10, 9 students received support, including 9 teaching assistantships (averaging $12,880 per year). Financial award application deadline: 4/1; financial award applicants required to submit FAFSA. Total annual research expenditures: $65,335. *Unit head:* Dr. Jeanneine Jones, Interim Chair, Department of Middle, Secondary, and K-12 Education, 704-687-8875, Fax: 704-687-6430, E-mail: jpjones@uncc.edu. *Application contact:* Dr. David K. Pugalee, Coordinator, 704-687-8887, Fax: 704-687-3216, E-mail: david.pugalee@uncc.edu.

The University of North Carolina at Greensboro, Graduate School, School of Education, Department of Curriculum and Instruction, Greensboro, NC 27412-5001. Offers college teaching and adult learning (Certificate); curriculum and instruction (M Ed), including chemistry education, elementary education, English as a second language, French education, instructional technology, mathematics education, middle grades education, reading education, science education, social studies education, Spanish education; curriculum and teaching (PhD), including higher education, teacher education and development; English as a second language (Certificate); higher education (M Ed); supervision (M Ed). *Accreditation:* NCATE. Part-time programs available. *Degree requirements:* For doctorate, thesis/dissertation. *Entrance requirements:* For master's and doctorate, GRE General Test. Additional exam requirements/recommendations for international students: Required—TOEFL. Electronic applications accepted. *Faculty research:* Community college literacy program, middle school mathematics/computer mathematics.

The University of North Carolina at Greensboro, Graduate School, School of Education, Department of Educational Leadership and Cultural Foundations, Greensboro, NC 27412-5001. Offers curriculum and teaching (PhD), including cultural studies; educational leadership (Ed D, Ed S); school administration (MSA). *Accreditation:* NCATE. *Degree requirements:* For doctorate, thesis/dissertation. *Entrance requirements:* For master's, doctorate, and Ed S, GRE General Test. Additional exam requirements/recommendations for international students: Required—TOEFL. Electronic applications accepted.

The University of North Carolina Wilmington, School of Education, Department of Educational Leadership, Program in Curriculum, Instruction and Supervision, Wilmington, NC 28403-3297. Offers M Ed. *Degree requirements:* For master's, comprehensive exam.

University of Northern Iowa, Graduate College, College of Education, Department of Curriculum and Instruction, Program in Curriculum and Instruction, Cedar Falls, IA 50614. Offers MAE, Ed D. Part-time and evening/weekend programs available. *Students:* 5 applicants, 60% accepted, 0 enrolled. In 2009, 3 doctorates awarded. *Degree requirements:* For doctorate, thesis/dissertation. *Entrance requirements:* For master's, minimum GPA of 3.0; for doctorate, GRE, minimum GPA of 3.0, master's degree. Additional exam requirements/recommendations for international students: Required—TOEFL (minimum score 500 paper-based; 180 computer-based; 61 iBT). *Application deadline:* For fall admission, 8/1 priority date for domestic students. Applications are processed on a rolling basis. Application fee: $30 ($50 for international students). *Financial support:* Career-related internships or fieldwork, Federal Work-Study, and tuition waivers (full and partial) available. Support available to part-time students. Financial award application deadline: 2/1. *Unit head:* Dr. Rebecca Edmiaston, Coordinator, 319-273-3250, Fax: 319-273-5886, E-mail: rebecca.edmiaston@uni.edu. *Application contact:* Laurie S. Russell, Record Analyst, 319-273-2623, Fax: 319-273-6792, E-mail: laurie.russell@uni.edu.

University of North Texas, Robert B. Toulouse School of Graduate Studies, College of Education, Department of Teacher Education and Administration, Program in Curriculum and Instruction, Denton, TX 76203. Offers M Ed, Ed D, PhD. *Accreditation:* NCATE. Part-time programs available. *Degree requirements:* For doctorate, thesis/dissertation. *Entrance requirements:* For doctorate, GRE General Test. Additional exam requirements/recommendations for international students: Required—proof of English language proficiency required for non-native English speakers; Recommended—TOEFL (minimum score 550 paper-based; 213 computer-based; 79 iBT). *Application deadline:* Applications are processed on a rolling basis. Application fee: $50 ($75 for international students). Electronic applications accepted. *Expenses:* Tuition, state resident: full-time $4298; part-time $239 per contact hour. Tuition, nonresident: full-time $9878; part-time $549 per contact hour. Required fees: $265 per contact hour. *Financial support:* Application deadline: 4/1. *Faculty research:* K-12 achievement gaps, early literacy, special action, GIs technologies and social studies, immigration.

University of Oklahoma, Graduate College, College of Education, Department of Instructional Leadership and Academic Curriculum, Norman, OK 73072. Offers education (Certificate); instructional leadership and academic curriculum (M Ed, PhD), including bilingual education, early childhood education, elementary education, English education, math education, reading education, science education, secondary education, social studies education. *Accreditation:* NCATE. Part-time and evening/weekend programs available. *Faculty:* 18 full-time (11 women). *Students:* 44 full-time (36 women), 117 part-time (92 women); includes 35 minority (11 African Americans, 14 American Indian/Alaska Native, 5 Asian Americans or Pacific Islanders, 5 Hispanic Americans), 2 international. 50 applicants, 84% accepted, 32 enrolled. In 2009, 31 master's, 6 doctorates awarded. Terminal master's awarded for partial completion of doctoral program. *Degree requirements:* For doctorate, thesis/dissertation. *Entrance requirements:* For master's, 12 hours of course work in education; for doctorate, GRE General Test, master's degree, minimum graduate GPA of 3.0. Additional exam requirements/recommendations for international students: Required—TOEFL (minimum score 550 paper-based; 213 computer-based). *Application deadline:* For fall admission, 6/1 priority date for domestic students, 4/1 for international students; for spring admission, 11/1 for domestic students, 9/1 for international students. Applications are processed on a rolling basis. Application fee: $40 ($90 for international students). Electronic applications accepted. *Expenses:* Tuition, state resident: full-time $3744; part-time $156 per credit hour. Tuition, nonresident: full-time $13,577; part-time $565.70 per credit hour. Required fees: $2415; $90.10 per credit hour. *Financial support:* In 2009–10, 107 students received support, including 1 research assistantship with partial tuition reimbursement available (averaging $9,630 per year), 6 teaching assistantships with partial tuition reimbursements available (averaging $10,801 per year); scholarships/grants, health care benefits, and unspecified assistantships also available. Financial award applicants required to submit FAFSA. *Faculty research:* English education, mathematics education, reading, science education, social studies education. Total annual research expenditures: $752,908. *Unit head:* Lawrence Baines, Chair, 405-325-1498, Fax: 405-325-4061, E-mail: lbaines@ou.edu. *Application contact:* Lynn Crussel, Administrative Assistant for Graduate Studies, 405-325-4843, Fax: 405-325-4061, E-mail: lcrussel@ou.edu.

University of Phoenix, College of Natural Sciences, College of Education, Phoenix, AZ 85034-7209. Offers administration and supervision (MAEd); adult education and training (MAEd); curriculum and instruction (MAEd); curriculum and instruction-adult education (MAEd); curriculum and instruction-computer education (MAEd); curriculum and instruction-English and language arts education (MAEd); curriculum and instruction-English as a second language (MAEd); curriculum and instruction-mathematics education (MAEd); curriculum education (MAEd); early childhood (MAEd); elementary teacher education (MAEd); secondary teacher education (MAEd); special education (MAEd); teacher leadership (MAEd). *Accreditation:* Teacher Education Accreditation Council. Evening/weekend programs available. Postbaccalaureate distance learning degree programs offered (no on-campus study). *Faculty:* 47 full-time (34 women), 844 part-time/adjunct (636 women). *Students:* 13,657 full-time (10,698 women); includes 4,000 minority (3,063 African Americans, 74 American Indian/Alaska Native, 241 Asian Americans or Pacific Islanders, 622 Hispanic Americans), 307 international. Average age 36. In 2009, 17,246 master's awarded. *Degree requirements:* For master's, thesis (for some programs). *Entrance requirements:* For master's, 3 years of work experience, minimum GPA of 2.5. Additional exam requirements/recommendations for international students: Required—TOEFL (minimum score 550 paper-based; 213 computer-based; 79 iBT). *Application deadline:* Applications are processed on a rolling basis. Application fee: $45. Electronic applications accepted. *Expenses:* Tuition: Full-time $13,272. Required fees: $660. Full-time tuition and fees vary according to course level, degree level and program. *Financial support:* Institutionally sponsored loans and scholarships/grants available. Financial award applicants required to submit FAFSA. *Unit head:* Dr. Meredith Curley, Dean/Executive Director, 480-557-1217, Fax: 480-557-1588, E-mail: meredith.curley@phoenix.edu. *Application contact:* Chair, 602-387-7000, Fax: 602-387-6020.

University of Phoenix, School of Advanced Studies, Phoenix, AZ 85034-7209. Offers business administration (DBA); education (Ed D); educational leadership (Ed D), including curriculum and instruction, educational leadership, educational technology; health administration (DHA); higher education administration (PhD); industrial/organizational psychology (PhD); nursing (PhD); organizational leadership (DM), including information systems and technology, organizational leadership. Evening/weekend programs available. *Faculty:* 83 full-time (47 women), 540 part-time/adjunct (264 women). *Students:* 7,749 full-time (5,032 women); includes 3,180 minority (2,473 African Americans, 61 American Indian/Alaska Native, 221 Asian Americans or Pacific Islanders, 425 Hispanic Americans), 490 international. Average age 44. In 2009, 467 doctorates awarded. *Degree requirements:* For doctorate, thesis/dissertation. *Entrance requirements:* For doctorate, 3 letters of recommendation, minimum master's GPA of 3.0, 3 years professional work experience. Additional exam requirements/recommendations for international students: Required—TOEFL (minimum score 550 paper-based; 213 computer-based; 79 iBT). *Application deadline:* Applications are processed on a rolling basis. Application fee: $45. Electronic applications accepted. *Expenses:* Tuition: Full-time $13,272. Required fees: $660. Full-time tuition and fees vary according to course level, degree level and program. *Financial support:* Institutionally sponsored loans and scholarships/grants available. Financial award applicants required to submit FAFSA. *Unit head:* Dr. Jeremy Moreland, Dean/Executive Director, 480-557-3231, E-mail: jeremy.moreland@phoenix.edu. *Application contact:* Information Contact, 800-697-8223.

University of Phoenix–Austin Campus, College of Education, Austin, TX 78759. Offers curriculum and instruction (MA Ed).

University of Phoenix–Bay Area Campus, The Artemis School, College of Education, Pleasanton, CA 94588-3677. Offers curriculum instruction (MA Ed); curriculum instruction—

adult education (MA Ed); elementary teacher education (MA Ed); secondary teacher education (MA Ed). Evening/weekend programs available. Postbaccalaureate distance learning degree programs offered (no on-campus study). *Degree requirements:* For master's, thesis (for some programs). *Entrance requirements:* For master's, minimum undergraduate GPA of 2.5, 3 years of work experience. Additional exam requirements/recommendations for international students: Required—TOEFL (minimum score 550 paper-based; 213 computer-based; 79 iBT). Electronic applications accepted.

University of Phoenix–Central Florida Campus, The Artemis School, College of Education, Maitland, FL 32751-7057. Offers administration and supervision (MA Ed); curriculum and instruction (MA Ed); curriculum and instruction-computer education (MA Ed); curriculum and instruction-mathematics education (MA Ed); early childhood education (MA Ed); elementary teacher education (MA Ed); secondary teacher education (MA Ed). Evening/weekend programs available. *Degree requirements:* For master's, thesis (for some programs). *Entrance requirements:* For master's, 3 years of work experience, minimum undergraduate GPA of 2.5. Additional exam requirements/recommendations for international students: Required—TOEFL (minimum score 550 paper-based; 213 computer-based; 79 iBT). Electronic applications accepted.

University of Phoenix–Central Valley Campus, College of Education, Fresno, CA 93720-1562. Offers curriculum and instruction (MA Ed); curriculum and instruction-computer education (MA Ed); elementary teacher education (MA Ed); secondary teacher education (MA Ed).

University of Phoenix–Chattanooga Campus, College of Education, Chattanooga, TN 37421-3707. Offers administration and supervision (MA Ed); curriculum and instruction (MA Ed); elementary teacher education (MA Ed); secondary teacher education (MA Ed).

University of Phoenix–Dallas Campus, The Artemis School, College of Education, Dallas, TX 75251-2009. Offers curriculum and instruction (MA Ed).

University of Phoenix–Denver Campus, The Artemis School, College of Education, Lone Tree, CO 80124-5453. Offers administration and supervision (MAEd); curriculum instruction (MAEd); elementary teacher education (MAEd); school counseling (MSC); secondary teacher education (MAEd). Evening/weekend programs available. *Degree requirements:* For master's, thesis (for some programs). *Entrance requirements:* For master's, minimum undergraduate GPA of 2.5, 3 years work experience. Additional exam requirements/recommendations for international students: Required—TOEFL (minimum score 550 paper-based; 213 computer-based; 79 iBT). Electronic applications accepted.

University of Phoenix–Hawaii Campus, The Artemis School, College of Education, Honolulu, HI 96813-4317. Offers administration and supervision (MA Ed); curriculum and instruction (MA Ed); elementary education (MA Ed); secondary education (MA Ed); special education (MA Ed); teacher education for elementary licensure (MA Ed). Evening/weekend programs available. *Degree requirements:* For master's, thesis (for some programs). *Entrance requirements:* For master's, minimum undergraduate GPA of 2.5, 3 years of work experience. Additional exam requirements/recommendations for international students: Required—TOEFL (minimum score 550 paper-based; 213 computer-based; 79 iBT). Electronic applications accepted.

University of Phoenix–Houston Campus, The Artemis School, College of Education, Houston, TX 77079-2004. Offers curriculum and instruction (MA Ed).

University of Phoenix–Idaho Campus, The Artemis School, College of Education, Meridian, ID 83642-3014. Offers administration and supervision (MA Ed); curriculum and instruction (MA Ed); elementary teacher education (MA Ed); secondary teacher education (MA Ed). Evening/weekend programs available. *Degree requirements:* For master's, thesis (for some programs). *Entrance requirements:* For master's, minimum undergraduate GPA of 2.5, 3 years of work experience. Additional exam requirements/recommendations for international students: Required—TOEFL (minimum score 550 paper-based; 213 computer-based). Electronic applications accepted.

University of Phoenix–Las Vegas Campus, The Artemis School, College of Education, Las Vegas, NV 89128. Offers administration and supervision (MA Ed); curriculum and instruction (MA Ed); school counseling (MSC); teacher education-elementary licensure (MA Ed). Evening/weekend programs available. *Degree requirements:* For master's, thesis (for some programs). *Entrance requirements:* For master's, minimum undergraduate GPA of 2.5, 3 years of work experience. Additional exam requirements/recommendations for international students: Required—TOEFL (minimum score 550 paper-based; 213 computer-based; 79 iBT). Electronic applications accepted.

University of Phoenix–Louisiana Campus, The Artemis School, College of Education, Metairie, LA 70001-2082. Offers curriculum and instruction (MA Ed); early childhood education (MA Ed). Postbaccalaureate distance learning degree programs offered. *Degree requirements:* For master's, thesis. *Entrance requirements:* For master's, minimum undergraduate GPA of 2.5, 3 years work experience. Additional exam requirements/recommendations for international students: Required—TOEFL (minimum score 550 paper-based; 213 computer-based; 79 iBT).

University of Phoenix–Memphis Campus, College of Education, Cordova, TN 38018. Offers administration and supervision (MA Ed); curriculum and instruction (MA Ed); elementary teacher education (MA Ed); secondary teacher education (MA Ed).

University of Phoenix–Nashville Campus, The Artemis School, College of Education, Nashville, TN 37214-5048. Offers administration and supervision (MA Ed); curriculum and instruction (MA Ed); elementary teacher education (MA Ed); secondary teacher education (MA Ed). Evening/weekend programs available. *Degree requirements:* For master's, thesis (for some programs). *Entrance requirements:* For master's, minimum undergraduate GPA of 2.5, 3 years work experience. Additional exam requirements/recommendations for international students: Required—TOEFL (minimum score 500 paper-based; 213 computer-based; 79 iBT). Electronic applications accepted.

University of Phoenix–New Mexico Campus, The Artemis School, College of Education, Albuquerque, NM 87113-1570. Offers administration and supervision (MAEd); curriculum and instruction (MAEd); elementary teacher education (MAEd); school counseling (MSC); secondary teacher education (MAEd). Evening/weekend programs available. *Degree requirements:* For master's, thesis (for some programs). *Entrance requirements:* For master's, minimum undergraduate GPA of 2.5, 3 years of work experience. Additional exam requirements/recommendations for international students: Required—TOEFL (minimum score 550 paper-based; 213 computer-based; 79 iBT). Electronic applications accepted.

University of Phoenix–Northern Nevada Campus, College of Education, Reno, NV 89521-5862. Offers administration and supervision (MA Ed); curriculum and instruction (MA Ed); elementary teacher education (MA Ed); secondary teacher education (MA Ed).

University of Phoenix–North Florida Campus, The Artemis School, College of Education, Jacksonville, FL 32216-0959. Offers administration and supervision (MA Ed); curriculum and instruction (MA Ed), including computer education, mathematics education; early childhood education (MA Ed); elementary teacher education (MA Ed); secondary teacher education (MA Ed). Evening/weekend programs available. *Degree requirements:* For master's, thesis (for some programs). *Entrance requirements:* For master's, 3 years of work experience, minimum undergraduate GPA of 2.5. Additional exam requirements/recommendations for international students: Required—TOEFL (minimum score 550 paper-based; 213 computer-based; 49 iBT). Electronic applications accepted.

University of Phoenix–Omaha Campus, College of Education, Omaha, NE 68154-5240. Offers administration and supervision (MA Ed); curriculum and instruction (MA Ed), including adult education, computer education, curriculum and instruction, English and language arts education, English as a second language, mathematics education; elementary teacher education (MA Ed); secondary teacher education (MA Ed); special education (MA Ed).

University of Phoenix–Oregon Campus, The Artemis School, College of Education, Tigard, OR 97223. Offers curriculum and instruction (MA Ed); early childhood education (MA Ed); elementary education (MA Ed), including early childhood specialization, middle level specialization; secondary education (MA Ed), including middle level specialization. Evening/weekend programs available. *Degree requirements:* For master's, thesis (for some programs). *Entrance requirements:* For master's, minimum undergraduate GPA of 2.5, 3 years work experience. Additional exam requirements/recommendations for international students: Required—TOEFL (minimum score 550 paper-based; 213 computer-based; 79 iBT). Electronic applications accepted.

University of Phoenix–Richmond Campus, The Artemis School, College of Education, Richmond, VA 23230. Offers administration and supervision (MA Ed); curriculum and instruction (MA Ed).

University of Phoenix–Sacramento Valley Campus, The Artemis School, College of Education, Sacramento, CA 95833-3632. Offers adult education (MA Ed); curriculum instruction (MA Ed); elementary teacher education (MA Ed); secondary teacher education (MA Ed); teacher education (Certificate). Evening/weekend programs available. *Degree requirements:* For master's, thesis (for some programs). *Entrance requirements:* For master's, 3 years of work experience, minimum undergraduate GPA of 2.5. Additional exam requirements/recommendations for international students: Required—TOEFL (minimum score 550 paper-based; 213 computer-based; 79 iBT). Electronic applications accepted.

University of Phoenix–San Antonio Campus, College of Education, San Antonio, TX 78230. Offers curriculum and instruction (MA Ed).

University of Phoenix–San Diego Campus, The Artemis School, College of Education, San Diego, CA 92123. Offers curriculum and instruction (MA Ed), including computer education, curriculum and instruction, English as a second language; elementary teacher education (MA Ed); secondary teacher education (MA Ed). Evening/weekend programs available. *Degree requirements:* For master's, thesis (for some programs). *Entrance requirements:* For master's, 3 years of work experience, minimum undergraduate GPA of 3.0. Additional exam requirements/recommendations for international students: Required—TOEFL (minimum score 550 paper-based; 213 computer-based; 79 iBT). Electronic applications accepted.

University of Phoenix–Southern Arizona Campus, The Artemis School, College of Education, Tucson, AZ 85711. Offers administration and supervision (MA Ed); adult education and training (MA Ed); curriculum instruction (MA Ed); educational counseling (MA Ed); elementary teacher education (MA Ed); school counseling (MSC); secondary teacher education (MA Ed); special education (MA Ed, Certificate). Evening/weekend programs available. *Degree requirements:* For master's, thesis (for some programs). *Entrance requirements:* For master's, minimum undergraduate GPA of 2.5, 3 years of work experience. Additional exam requirements/recommendations for international students: Required—TOEFL (minimum score 550 paper-based; 213 computer-based; 79 iBT). Electronic applications accepted.

University of Phoenix–Southern California Campus, College of Education, Costa Mesa, CA 92626. Offers administration and supervision (MA Ed); adult education and training (MA Ed); curriculum and instruction (MA Ed), including computer education, curriculum and instruction, English and language arts, English as a second language, mathematics education; early childhood education (MA Ed); special education (MA Ed); teacher leadership (MA Ed). Evening/weekend programs available. *Faculty:* 47 full-time (34 women), 844 part-time/adjunct (636 women). *Students:* 558 full-time (391 women); includes 222 minority (60 African Americans, 4 American Indian/Alaska Native, 26 Asian Americans or Pacific Islanders, 132 Hispanic Americans), 9 international. Average age 34. In 2009, 303 master's awarded. *Degree requirements:* For master's, thesis (for some programs). *Entrance requirements:* For master's, minimum undergraduate GPA of 2.5, 3 years work experience. Additional exam requirements/recommendations for international students: Required—TOEFL (minimum score 550 paper-based; 213 computer-based; 79 iBT). *Application deadline:* Applications are processed on a rolling basis. Application fee: $45. Electronic applications accepted. *Expenses:* Tuition: Full-time $15,120. Required fees: $660. *Financial support:* Institutionally sponsored loans and scholarships/grants available. Financial award applicants required to submit FAFSA. *Unit head:* Dr. Meredith Curley, Dean/Executive Director, 480-557-1217, Fax: 480-557-1588, E-mail: meredith.curley@phoenix.edu. *Application contact:* Campus College Chair, 714-378-1878, Fax: 714-378-5875.

University of Phoenix–Southern Colorado Campus, The Artemis School, College of Education, Colorado Springs, CO 80919-2335. Offers administration and supervision (MA Ed); curriculum and instruction (MA Ed); elementary teacher education (MA Ed); principal licensure certification (Certificate); school counseling (MSC); secondary teacher education (MA Ed). Evening/weekend programs available. *Degree requirements:* For master's, thesis (for some programs). *Entrance requirements:* For master's, minimum undergraduate GPA of 2.5, 3 years of work experience. Additional exam requirements/recommendations for international students: Required—TOEFL (minimum score 550 paper-based; 213 computer-based; 79 iBT). Electronic applications accepted.

University of Phoenix–South Florida Campus, The Artemis School, College of Education, Fort Lauderdale, FL 33309. Offers administration and supervision (MA Ed); curriculum and instruction (MA Ed), including computer education, curriculum and instruction, mathematics education; early childhood education (MA Ed); elementary teacher education (MA Ed); secondary teacher education (MA Ed). Evening/weekend programs available. *Degree requirements:* For master's, thesis (for some programs). *Entrance requirements:* For master's, 3 years of work experience, minimum undergraduate GPA of 2.5. Additional exam requirements/recommendations for international students: Required—TOEFL (minimum score 550 paper-based; 213 computer-based; 79 iBT). Electronic applications accepted.

University of Phoenix–Springfield Campus, College of Education, Springfield, MO 65804-7211. Offers administration and supervision (MA Ed); curriculum and instruction (MA Ed), including computer education, curriculum and instruction, English and language arts education, English as a second language, mathematics education; English and language arts education (MA Ed).

University of Phoenix–Utah Campus, The Artemis School, College of Education, Salt Lake City, UT 84123-4617. Offers administration and supervision (MA Ed); curriculum and instruction (MA Ed); elementary teacher education (MA Ed); school counseling (MSC); secondary teacher education (MA Ed); special education (MA Ed). Evening/weekend programs available. *Degree requirements:* For master's, thesis (for some programs). *Entrance requirements:* For master's, minimum undergraduate GPA of 2.5, 3 years work experience. Additional exam requirements/recommendations for international students: Required—TOEFL (minimum score 550 paper-based; 213 computer-based; 79 iBT). Electronic applications accepted.

University of Phoenix–Vancouver Campus, The Artemis School, College of Education, Burnaby, BC V5C 6G9, Canada. Offers administration and supervision (MA Ed); curriculum and instruction (MA Ed), including computer education, curriculum and instruction. Evening/weekend programs available. *Degree requirements:* For master's, thesis (for some programs). *Entrance requirements:* For master's, minimum undergraduate GPA of 2.5, 3 years work experience. Additional exam requirements/recommendations for international students: Required—TOEFL (minimum score 550 paper-based; 213 computer-based; 79 iBT). Electronic applications accepted.

University of Phoenix–West Florida Campus, The Artemis School, College of Education, Temple Terrace, FL 33637. Offers administration and supervision (MA Ed); curriculum and instruction (MA Ed), including computer education, curriculum and instruction, mathematics education; curriculum and technology (MA Ed); early childhood education (MA Ed); elementary teacher education (MA Ed); secondary teacher education (MA Ed). Evening/weekend programs available. *Degree requirements:* For master's, thesis (for some programs). *Entrance requirements:* For master's, 3 years of work experience, minimum undergraduate GPA of 2.5.

Curriculum and Instruction

University of Phoenix–West Florida Campus (continued)
Additional exam requirements/recommendations for international students: Required—TOEFL (minimum score 550 paper-based; 213 computer-based; 79 iBT).

University of Puerto Rico, Río Piedras, College of Education, Program in Curriculum and Teaching, San Juan, PR 00931-3300. Offers biology education (M Ed); chemistry education (M Ed); curriculum and teaching (Ed D); history education (M Ed); mathematics education (M Ed); physics education (M Ed); Spanish education (M Ed). Part-time programs available. *Degree requirements:* For master's, thesis; for doctorate, thesis/dissertation, internship. *Entrance requirements:* For master's, PAEG or GRE, minimum GPA of 3.0, letter of recommendation; for doctorate, GRE or PAEG, master's degree, minimum GPA of 3.0, letter of recommendation (2), interview. *Faculty research:* Curriculum, math teaching.

University of Regina, Faculty of Graduate Studies and Research, Faculty of Education, Department of Curriculum and Instruction, Regina, SK S4S 0A2, Canada. Offers M Ed. Part-time programs available. *Faculty:* 28 full-time (13 women), 2 part-time/adjunct (both women). *Students:* 19 full-time (15 women), 77 part-time (57 women). 31 applicants, 97% accepted. In 2009, 59 master's awarded. *Degree requirements:* For master's, thesis optional, practicum, project, or thesis. *Entrance requirements:* For master's, bachelor's degree in education, 2 years of teaching experience. Additional exam requirements/recommendations for international students: Required—TOEFL (minimum score 580 paper-based; 237 computer-based; 80 iBT). *Application deadline:* For fall admission, 2/15 for domestic students; for winter admission, 2/15 for domestic students; for spring admission, 2/15 for domestic students. Application fee: $90 ($100 for international students). Electronic applications accepted. *Financial support:* In 2009–10, 2 fellowships (averaging $19,000 per year), 1 teaching assistantship (averaging $6,650 per year) were awarded; research assistantships. Financial award application deadline: 6/15. *Unit head:* Dr. Warren Wessel, 306-585-4555, E-mail: warren.wessel@uregina.ca. *Application contact:* Tania Gates, Graduate Program Coordinator, 306-585-4506, Fax: 306-585-5387, E-mail: edgrad@uregina.ca.

University of St. Francis, College of Education, Joliet, IL 60435-6169. Offers educational leadership (MS), including reading; elementary education certification (M Ed); reading (MS); secondary education certification (M Ed), including English education, math education, science education, social studies education; special education (M Ed); teaching and learning (MS), including character education, curriculum and instruction, differentiated instruction, technology. *Accreditation:* NCATE. Part-time and evening/weekend programs available. *Faculty:* 10 full-time (8 women), 26 part-time/adjunct (18 women). *Students:* 60 full-time (45 women), 349 part-time (283 women); includes 36 minority (10 African Americans, 2 Asian Americans or Pacific Islanders, 24 Hispanic Americans). Average age 33, 211 applicants, 65% accepted, 102 enrolled. In 2009, 174 master's awarded. *Entrance requirements:* For master's, Illinois Basic Skills Test (M Ed), teaching certificate (MS), minimum undergraduate GPA of 2.75, 2 letters of recommendation, computer competency. Additional exam requirements/recommendations for international students: Required—TOEFL (minimum score 550 paper-based; 213 computer-based). *Application deadline:* Applications are processed on a rolling basis. Application fee: $30. Electronic applications accepted. *Expenses:* Contact institution. *Financial support:* In 2009–10, 254 students received support. Federal Work-Study, scholarships/grants; tuition waivers (partial), and unspecified assistantships available. Support available to part-time students. Financial award applicants required to submit FAFSA. *Unit head:* Dr. John Gambro, Dean, 815-740-3332, Fax: 815-740-2264, E-mail: jgambro@stfrancis.edu. *Application contact:* Sandra Sloka, Director of Admissions for Graduate and Degree Completion Programs, 800-735-7500, Fax: 815-740-5032, E-mail: ssloka@stfrancis.edu.

University of Saint Mary, Graduate Programs, Program in Education, Leavenworth, KS 66048-5082. Offers curriculum and instruction (MAT). *Accreditation:* NCATE. Part-time and evening/weekend programs available. Postbaccalaureate distance learning degree programs offered (no on-campus study). *Degree requirements:* For master's, thesis, oral presentation. *Entrance requirements:* For master's, minimum undergraduate GPA of 2.75. *Faculty research:* Curriculum and instruction.

University of St. Thomas, Graduate Studies, School of Education, Department of Leadership, Policy and Administration, St. Paul, MN 55105-1096. Offers athletics and activities administration (MA); community education administration (MA); critical pedagogy (Ed D); curriculum and instruction (Ed S); educational leadership (Ed S); educational leadership and administration (MA); international leadership (MA, Certificate); leadership (Ed D); leadership in student affairs (MA, Certificate); police leadership (MA); public policy and leadership (MA, Certificate). Part-time and evening/weekend programs available. *Faculty:* 8 full-time (3 women), 15 part-time/adjunct (7 women). *Students:* 36 full-time (29 women), 307 part-time (149 women); includes 44 minority (29 African Americans, 1 American Indian/Alaska Native, 11 Asian Americans or Pacific Islanders, 3 Hispanic Americans), 5 international. Average age 36. 398 applicants, 75% accepted, 267 enrolled. In 2009, 63 master's, 17 doctorates, 46 other advanced degrees awarded. Terminal master's awarded for partial completion of doctoral program. *Degree requirements:* For master's, thesis (for some programs); for doctorate, thesis/dissertation; for other advanced degree, thesis or alternative. *Entrance requirements:* For master's, minimum GPA of 3.0 or MAT; for doctorate, MAT, minimum graduate GPA of 3.5; for other advanced degree, minimum graduate GPA of 3.25 or MAT. Additional exam requirements/recommendations for international students: Required—TOEFL (minimum score 550 paper-based; 213 computer-based; 20 iBT). *Application deadline:* For fall admission, 6/1 priority date for domestic students; for spring admission, 11/1 priority date for domestic students. Applications are processed on a rolling basis. Application fee: $50. *Expenses:* Contact institution. *Financial support:* Fellowships, research assistantships, institutionally sponsored loans and scholarships/grants available. Support available to part-time students. Financial award applicants required to submit FAFSA. *Unit head:* Dr. Donald R. LaMagdeleine, Chair, 651-962-4893, Fax: 651-962-4169, E-mail: drlamagdelei@stthomas.edu. *Application contact:* Jackie Grossklaus, Department Assistant, 651-962-4885, Fax: 651-962-4169, E-mail: jmgrossklaus@stthomas.edu.

University of St. Thomas, Graduate Studies, School of Education, Department of Teacher Education, St. Paul, MN 55105-1096. Offers curriculum and instruction (MA), including elementary, individualized, K-12, secondary; elementary (MAT); multicultural education (Certificate); reading (MA, Certificate), including elementary (MA), K-12 (MA). *Accreditation:* NCATE. Part-time and evening/weekend programs available. *Faculty:* 10 full-time (7 women), 25 part-time/adjunct (16 women). *Students:* 31 full-time (25 women), 260 part-time (195 women); includes 19 minority (6 African Americans, 7 Asian Americans or Pacific Islanders, 6 Hispanic Americans), 3 international. Average age 34. 325 applicants, 72% accepted, 225 enrolled. In 2009, 135 master's, 17 other advanced degrees awarded. *Entrance requirements:* For master's, minimum GPA of 3.0 or MAT. Additional exam requirements/recommendations for international students: Required—TOEFL (minimum score 550 paper-based; 210 computer-based; 80 iBT). *Application deadline:* For fall admission, 6/1 for domestic students; for spring admission, 11/1 for domestic students. Applications are processed on a rolling basis. Application fee: $50. *Financial support:* Fellowships, research assistantships, institutionally sponsored loans and scholarships/grants available. Support available to part-time students. Financial award applicants required to submit FAFSA. *Unit head:* Dr. Douglas F. Warring, Department Chair, 651-962-4877, Fax: 651-962-4169, E-mail: dfwarring@stthomas.edu. *Application contact:* Kathy J. Neary, Department Assistant, 651-962-4420, Fax: 651-962-4169, E-mail: kjneary@stthomas.edu.

University of San Diego, School of Leadership and Education Sciences, Department of Learning and Teaching, San Diego, CA 92110-2492. Offers curriculum and instruction (M Ed); mathematics, science and technology education (M Ed); special education (M Ed); special education with deaf and hard of hearing (M Ed); teaching (MAT); TESOL, literacy and culture (M Ed). Part-time and evening/weekend programs available. *Faculty:* 13 full-time (9 women), 24 part-time/adjunct (21 women). *Students:* 77 full-time (63 women), 92 part-time (74 women); includes 46 minority (13 African Americans, 12 Asian Americans or Pacific Islanders, 21 Hispanic Americans), 6 international. Average age 31. 142 applicants, 75% accepted, 59 enrolled. In 2009, 64 master's awarded. *Degree requirements:* For master's, thesis (for some

programs). *Entrance requirements:* For master's, minimum GPA of 3.0. Additional exam requirements/recommendations for international students: Required—TOEFL (minimum score 580 paper-based; 237 computer-based; 83 iBT), TWE. *Application deadline:* For fall admission, 7/15 for domestic and international students; for spring admission, 12/1 for domestic and international students. Applications are processed on a rolling basis. Application fee: $45. Electronic applications accepted. *Expenses:* Tuition: Full-time $21,042; part-time $1169 per unit. Required fees: $224. Full-time tuition and fees vary according to course load and degree level. *Financial support:* In 2009–10, 113 students received support. Career-related internships or fieldwork, Federal Work-Study, institutionally sponsored loans, and stipends available. Support available to part-time students. Financial award application deadline: 4/1; financial award applicants required to submit FAFSA. *Faculty research:* Action research methodology, cultural studies, instructional theories and practices, second language acquisition, school reform. *Unit head:* Dr. Judy Mantle, Director, 619-260-7879, Fax: 619-260-6835, E-mail: jmantle@sandiego.edu. *Application contact:* Dr. John Mosby, Associate Director of Graduate Admissions, 619-260-4524, Fax: 619-260-4158, E-mail: grads@sandiego.edu.

University of San Francisco, School of Education, Department of Learning and Instruction, San Francisco, CA 94117-1080. Offers digital media and learning (MA); learning and instruction (MA, Ed D); teaching (MA); teaching reading (MA). *Faculty:* 10 full-time (6 women), 1 part-time/adjunct (0 women). *Students:* 89 full-time (64 women), 40 part-time (27 women); includes 36 minority (9 African Americans, 4 American Indian/Alaska Native, 13 Asian Americans or Pacific Islanders, 10 Hispanic Americans), 1 international. Average age 40. 88 applicants, 72% accepted, 42 enrolled. In 2009, 17 master's, 9 doctorates awarded. *Degree requirements:* For doctorate, thesis/dissertation. Application fee: $55 ($65 for international students). *Expenses:* Tuition: Full-time $19,710; part-time $1095 per unit. Part-time tuition and fees vary according to degree level, campus/location and program. *Financial support:* In 2009–10, 77 students received support; fellowships, research assistantships, teaching assistantships available. Financial award application deadline: 3/2; financial award applicants required to submit FAFSA. *Unit head:* Dr. Robert Burns, Chair, 415-422-6289. *Application contact:* Beth Teague, Associate Director of Graduate Outreach, 415-422-5467, E-mail: schoolofeducation@usfca.edu.

University of Saskatchewan, College of Graduate Studies and Research, College of Education, Department of Curriculum Studies, Saskatoon, SK S7N 5A2, Canada. Offers M Ed, PhD, Diploma. Part-time programs available. *Faculty:* 26. *Students:* 104. In 2009, 35 master's awarded. *Degree requirements:* For master's, thesis (for some programs); for doctorate, comprehensive exam (for some programs), thesis/dissertation. *Entrance requirements:* For master's, MAT. Additional exam requirements/recommendations for international students: Required—TOEFL (minimum score 80 iBT); Recommended—IELTS (minimum score 6.5). *Application deadline:* For fall admission, 7/1 priority date for domestic students. Applications are processed on a rolling basis. Application fee: $75. Electronic applications accepted. Tuition and fees charges are reported in Canadian dollars. *Expenses:* Tuition, area resident: Full-time $3000 Canadian dollars; part-time $500 Canadian dollars per term. Required fees: $700 Canadian dollars; $100 Canadian dollars per term. *Financial support:* Fellowships, research assistantships, teaching assistantships available. Financial award application deadline: 1/31. *Unit head:* Dr. Len Proctor, Head, 306-966-7550, Fax: 306-966-7658, E-mail: len.proctor@usask.ca. *Application contact:* Dr. Janet McVittie, Graduate Chair, 306-966-7583, Fax: 306-966-7658, E-mail: janet.mcvittie@usask.ca.

The University of Scranton, College of Graduate and Continuing Education, Department of Education, Program in Curriculum and Instruction, Scranton, PA 18510. Offers MA, MS. Part-time and evening/weekend programs available. Postbaccalaureate distance learning degree programs offered (no on-campus study). *Students:* 160 full-time (134 women), 189 part-time (160 women); includes 27 minority (15 African Americans, 2 American Indian/Alaska Native, 3 Asian Americans or Pacific Islanders, 7 Hispanic Americans), 6 international. Average age 33. 99 applicants, 98% accepted. In 2009, 172 master's awarded. *Degree requirements:* For master's, comprehensive exam, thesis (for some programs), capstone experience. *Entrance requirements:* For master's, minimum GPA of 2.75. Additional exam requirements/recommendations for international students: Required—TOEFL (minimum score 500 paper-based; 173 computer-based), IELTS (minimum score 5.3). *Application deadline:* Applications are processed on a rolling basis. Application fee: $0. *Financial support:* Federal Work-Study and unspecified assistantships available. Financial award application deadline: 3/1. *Unit head:* Dr. Art Chambers, Director, 570-941-4668, Fax: 570-941-5515, E-mail: chambersa2@scranton.edu. *Application contact:* Joseph M. Roback, Director of Admissions, 570-941-4385, Fax: 570-941-5928, E-mail: robackj2@scranton.edu.

University of South Africa, College of Human Sciences, Pretoria, South Africa. Offers adult education (M Ed); African languages (MA, PhD); African politics (MA, PhD); Afrikaans (MA, PhD); ancient history (MA, PhD); ancient Near Eastern studies (MA, PhD); anthropology (MA, PhD); applied linguistics (MA); Arabic (MA, PhD); archaeology (MA); art history (MA); Biblical archaeology (MA); Biblical studies (M Th, D Th, PhD); Christian spirituality (M Th, D Th); church history (M Th, D Th); classical studies (MA, PhD); clinical psychology (MA); communication (MA, PhD); comparative education (M Ed, Ed D); consulting psychology (D Admin, D Com, PhD); curriculum studies (M Ed, Ed D); development studies (M Admin, MA, D Admin, PhD); didactics (M Ed, Ed D); education (M Tech); education management (M Ed, Ed D); educational psychology (M Ed); English (MA); environmental education (M Ed); French (MA, PhD); German (MA, PhD); Greek (MA); guidance and counseling (M Ed); health studies (MA, PhD), including health sciences education (MA), health services management (MA), medical and surgical nursing science (critical care general) (MA), midwifery and neonatal nursing science (MA), trauma and emergency care (MA); history (MA, PhD); history of education (Ed D); inclusive education (M Ed, Ed D); information and communications technology policy and regulation (MA); information science (MA, MIS, PhD); international politics (MA, PhD); Islamic studies (MA, PhD); Italian (MA, PhD); Judaica (MA, PhD); linguistics (MA, PhD); mathematical education (M Ed); mathematics education (MA); missiology (M Th, D Th); modern Hebrew (MA, PhD); musicology (MA, MMus, D Mus, PhD); natural science education (M Ed); New Testament (M Th, D Th); Old Testament (D Th); pastoral therapy (M Th, D Th); philosophy (MA); philosophy of education (M Ed, Ed D); politics (MA, PhD); Portuguese (MA, PhD); practical theology (M Th, D Th); psychology (MA, MS, PhD); psychology of education (M Ed, Ed D); public health (MA); religious studies (MA, D Th, PhD); Romance languages (MA); Russian (MA, PhD); Semitic languages (MA, PhD); social behavior studies in HIV/AIDS (MA); social science (mental health) (MA); social science in development studies (MA); social science in psychology (MA); social science in social work (MA); social science in sociology (MA); social work (MSW, DSW, PhD); socio-education (M Ed, Ed D); sociolinguistics (MA); sociology (MA, PhD); Spanish (MA, PhD); systematic theology (M Th, D Th); TESOL (teaching English to speakers of other languages) (MA); theological ethics (M Th, D Th); theory of literature (MA, PhD); urban ministries (D Th); urban ministry (M Th).

University of South Carolina, The Graduate School, College of Education, Department of Instruction and Teacher Education, Program in Curriculum and Instruction, Columbia, SC 29208. Offers Ed D. This degree cuts across two departments and represents 6 different concentrations. *Accreditation:* NCATE. Part-time and evening/weekend programs available. *Degree requirements:* For doctorate, comprehensive exam, thesis/dissertation. *Entrance requirements:* For doctorate, GRE General Test or MAT, interview, resume, letter of intent, letters of reference. Electronic applications accepted. *Faculty research:* Teacher education, historian recording project, curriculum development in international areas, human sexuality.

The University of South Dakota, Graduate School, School of Education, Division of Curriculum and Instruction, Vermillion, SD 57069-2390. Offers curriculum and instruction (Ed D, Ed S); elementary education (MA); secondary education (MA); special education (MA); technology for education and training (MS, Ed S). *Accreditation:* NCATE. Part-time programs available. Postbaccalaureate distance learning degree programs offered. *Degree requirements:* For master's and Ed S, comprehensive exam, thesis or alternative; for doctorate, comprehensive exam, thesis/dissertation. *Entrance requirements:* For master's, doctorate, and Ed S, GRE General Test, MAT, minimum GPA of 2.7. Additional exam requirements/recommendations for

international students: Required—TOEFL (minimum score 550 paper-based; 213 computer-based; 79 iBT). Electronic applications accepted.

University of Southern Mississippi, Graduate School, College of Education and Psychology, Department of Curriculum, Instruction, and Special Education, Hattiesburg, MS 39406-0001. Offers alternative secondary teacher education (MAT); early childhood education (M Ed, Ed S); education of the gifted (M Ed, Ed D, PhD, Ed S); elementary education (M Ed, Ed D, PhD, Ed S); reading (M Ed, MS, Ed S); secondary education (M Ed, MS, Ed D, PhD, Ed S); special education (M Ed, Ed D, PhD, Ed S). *Faculty:* 23 full-time (17 women), 3 part-time/adjunct (2 women). *Students:* 31 full-time (26 women), 77 part-time (68 women); includes 18 minority (15 African Americans, 3 Hispanic Americans). Average age 37. 50 applicants, 52% accepted, 19 enrolled. In 2009, 43 master's, 3 doctorates, 2 other advanced degrees awarded. *Degree requirements:* For master's, comprehensive exam, thesis (for some programs); for doctorate, comprehensive exam, thesis/dissertation; for Ed S, comprehensive exam, thesis. *Entrance requirements:* For master's, GRE General Test, MAT, minimum GPA of 3.0; for doctorate, GRE General Test, minimum GPA of 3.5; for Ed S, GRE General Test, MAT, minimum GPA of 3.25. Additional exam requirements/recommendations for international students: Required—TOEFL. *Application deadline:* For fall admission, 3/1 priority date for domestic students, 3/1 for international students. Applications are processed on a rolling basis. Application fee: $35. *Expenses:* Tuition, state resident: full-time $5096; part-time $284 per hour. Tuition, nonresident: full-time $13,052; part-time $726 per hour. Required fees: $402. Tuition and fees vary according to course level and course load. *Financial support:* In 2009–10, 9 research assistantships with tuition reimbursements (averaging $18,316 per year), 2 teaching assistantships with full tuition reimbursements (averaging $8,500 per year) were awarded; Federal Work-Study, institutionally sponsored loans, and tuition waivers (partial) also available. Financial award application deadline: 3/15; financial award applicants required to submit FAFSA. *Faculty research:* Mathematical problem solving, integrative curriculum, writing process, teacher education models. Total annual research expenditures: $100,000. *Unit head:* Dr. David Daves, Chair, 601-266-4547, Fax: 601-266-4175. *Application contact:* Rachea Cawthorn, Administrative Assistant, 601-266-6987, Fax: 601-266-4548.

University of South Florida, Graduate School, College of Education–Main Campus, Department of Secondary Education, Tampa, FL 33620-9951. Offers English education (M Ed, MA, MAT, PhD); foreign language education/ESOL (M Ed, MA, MAT); instructional technology (M Ed, PhD, Ed S); mathematics education (M Ed, MA, MAT, PhD, Ed S); science education (M Ed, MA, MAT, PhD); second language acquisition/instructional technology (PhD); secondary education (M Ed, PhD); secondary education/TESOL (M Ed); social science education (M Ed, MA, MAT); teaching and learning in the content area (PhD). *Accreditation:* NCATE. Part-time and evening/weekend programs available. *Faculty:* 28 full-time (17 women), 3 part-time/adjunct (1 woman). *Students:* 144 full-time (97 women), 322 part-time (212 women); includes 100 minority (32 African Americans, 4 American Indian/Alaska Native, 17 Asian Americans or Pacific Islanders, 47 Hispanic Americans), 25 international. Average age 30. 230 applicants, 67% accepted, 122 enrolled. In 2009, 122 master's, 14 doctorates, 1 other advanced degree awarded. *Degree requirements:* For master's, variable foreign language requirement, comprehensive exam; for doctorate, variable foreign language requirement, comprehensive exam, thesis/dissertation. *Entrance requirements:* For master's, GRE General Test or General Knowledge Test, minimum GPA of 3.0; for doctorate, GRE General Test, minimum GPA of 3.5; for Ed S, GRE General Test. Additional exam requirements/recommendations for international students: Required—TOEFL (minimum score 550 paper-based; 213 computer-based; 79 iBT). *Application deadline:* For fall admission, 2/15 for domestic students, 1/2 for international students; for spring admission, 10/15 for domestic students, 6/1 for international students. Application fee: $30. Electronic applications accepted. *Financial support:* In 2009–10, 7 students received support, including 1 research assistantship with full tuition reimbursement available (averaging $10,000 per year), 55 teaching assistantships with full and partial tuition reimbursements available (averaging $7,900 per year); scholarships/grants and unspecified assistantships also available. Financial award application deadline: 4/15; financial award applicants required to submit FAFSA. *Faculty research:* English language learners/multicultural, social science education, mathematics education, science education, instructional technology. Total annual research expenditures: $336,023. *Unit head:* Dr. Stephen Thornton, Chairperson, 813-974-3533, Fax: 813-974-3837, E-mail: thornton@usf.edu. *Application contact:* Dr. James White, Program Director, 813-974-1629, Fax: 813-974-3837, E-mail: jwhite@usf.edu.

The University of Tampa, Program in Teaching, Tampa, FL 33606-1490. Offers curriculum and instruction (M Ed); math education (MAT); science education (MAT); social science education (MAT). Part-time and evening/weekend programs available. *Faculty:* 9 full-time (6 women), 5 part-time/adjunct (4 women). *Students:* 1 full-time (0 women), 68 part-time (51 women); includes 11 minority (3 African Americans, 1 Asian American or Pacific Islander, 7 Hispanic Americans), 1 international. Average age 30. 119 applicants, 71% accepted, 69 enrolled. In 2009, 36 master's awarded. *Degree requirements:* For master's, comprehensive exam, thesis. *Entrance requirements:* For master's, General Knowledge Test, GRE General Test, SAE Subject Area Exam, bachelor's degree in education or professional teaching certificate. Additional exam requirements/recommendations for international students: Required—TOEFL (minimum score 577 paper-based; 230 computer-based; 90 iBT), IELTS (minimum score 7). *Application deadline:* For fall admission, 5/1 for domestic students. Application fee: $40. *Expenses:* Tuition: Part-time $488 per credit hour. *Financial support:* In 2009–10, 67 students received support. Applicants required to submit FAFSA. *Unit head:* Dr. Martha Harrison, Associate Professor of Education, 813-253-3333 Ext. 3373, E-mail: mharrison@ut.edu. *Application contact:* Karen Full, Director of Admissions for Graduate and Continuing Studies, 813-257-3642, E-mail: kfull@ut.edu.

The University of Tennessee, Graduate School, College of Education, Health and Human Sciences, Program in Education, Knoxville, TN 37996. Offers art education (MS); counseling education (PhD); cultural studies in education (PhD); curriculum (MS, Ed S); curriculum, educational research and evaluation (Ed D, PhD); early childhood education (PhD); early childhood special education (MS); education of deaf and hard of hearing (MS); educational administration and policy studies (Ed D, PhD); educational administration and supervision (Ed S); educational psychology (Ed D, PhD); elementary education (MS, Ed S); elementary teaching (MS); English education (MS, Ed S); exercise science (PhD); foreign language/ESL education (MS, Ed S); instructional technology (MS, Ed D, PhD, Ed S); literacy, language and ESL education (PhD); literacy, language education, and ESL education (Ed D); mathematics education (MS, Ed S); modified and comprehensive special education (MS); reading education (MS, Ed S); school counseling (Ed S); school psychology (PhD, Ed S); science education (MS, Ed S); secondary teaching (MS); social foundations (MS); social science education (MS, Ed S); socio-cultural foundations of sports and education (PhD); special education (Ed S); teacher education (Ed D, PhD). *Accreditation:* NCATE. Part-time and evening/weekend programs available. *Degree requirements:* For master's and Ed S, thesis optional; for doctorate, variable foreign language requirement, thesis/dissertation. *Entrance requirements:* For master's, minimum GPA of 2.7; for doctorate and Ed S, GRE General Test, minimum GPA of 2.7. Additional exam requirements/recommendations for international students: Required—TOEFL. Electronic applications accepted. *Expenses:* Tuition, state resident: full-time $6826; part-time $380 per semester hour. Tuition, nonresident: full-time $21,844; part-time $1147 per semester hour. Tuition and fees vary according to program.

The University of Texas at Arlington, Graduate School, College of Education, Arlington, TX 76019. Offers curriculum and instruction (M Ed); educational leadership and policy studies (M Ed); K-16 educational, leadership and policy studies (PhD); physiology of exercise (MS); teaching (M Ed T). *Accreditation:* NCATE. Part-time and evening/weekend programs available. *Faculty:* 35 full-time (22 women), 4 part-time/adjunct (2 women). *Students:* 125 full-time (83 women), 586 part-time (479 women); includes 283 minority (125 African Americans, 4 American Indian/Alaska Native, 19 Asian Americans or Pacific Islanders, 135 Hispanic Americans), 15 international. Average age 35. 601 applicants, 99% accepted, 238 enrolled. In 2009, 161 degrees awarded. *Degree requirements:* For master's, comprehensive exam (for some programs), thesis (for some programs), comprehensive activity, research project; for doctorate, comprehensive exam, thesis/dissertation. *Entrance requirements:* For master's, GRE General Test, minimum undergraduate GPA of 3.0 in last 60 hours of course work, writing sample, 3 letters of recommendation; for doctorate, GRE General Test, interview, minimum GPA of 3.5, master's degree in education or other appropriate field, 3 years of documented experience in an education related work environment. Additional exam requirements/recommendations for international students: Required—TOEFL (minimum score 550 paper-based; 213 computer-based). *Application deadline:* For fall admission, 6/5 priority date for domestic students, 4/3 priority date for international students; for spring admission, 10/17 priority date for domestic students, 9/5 priority date for international students. Applications are processed on a rolling basis. Application fee: $35 ($50 for international students). Electronic applications accepted. *Financial support:* In 2009–10, 9 fellowships (averaging $1,000 per year), 6 research assistantships (averaging $6,250 per year), 10 teaching assistantships with full tuition reimbursements (averaging $5,200 per year) were awarded; career-related internships or fieldwork, Federal Work-Study, scholarships/grants, and unspecified assistantships also available. Financial award application deadline: 6/1; financial award applicants required to submit FAFSA. *Unit head:* Dr. Jeanne M. Gerlach, Dean, 817-272-2591, Fax: 817-272-2530, E-mail: coeadvising@uta.edu. *Application contact:* Kas McConnell, Graduate Advisor, 817-272-7489, Fax: 817-272-7624, E-mail: coedadvising@uta.edu.

The University of Texas at Austin, Graduate School, College of Education, Department of Curriculum and Instruction, Austin, TX 78712-1111. Offers M Ed, MA, Ed D, PhD. Terminal master's awarded for partial completion of doctoral program. *Degree requirements:* For doctorate, thesis/dissertation. *Entrance requirements:* For master's and doctorate, GRE General Test. Electronic applications accepted.

The University of Texas at Brownsville, Graduate Studies, School of Education, Brownsville, TX 78520-4991. Offers bilingual education (M Ed); counseling and guidance (M Ed); curriculum and instruction (M Ed); early childhood education (M Ed); educational administration (M Ed); educational technology (M Ed); English as a second language (M Ed); reading specialist (M Ed); special education/educational diagnostician (M Ed). Part-time and evening/weekend programs available. Postbaccalaureate distance learning degree programs offered (minimal on-campus study). *Degree requirements:* For master's, thesis optional. *Entrance requirements:* For master's, GRE General Test. Additional exam requirements/recommendations for international students: Required—TOEFL.

The University of Texas at El Paso, Graduate School, College of Education, Department of Teacher Education, El Paso, TX 79968-0001. Offers education (MA); instruction (M Ed); reading education (M Ed); teaching, learning, and culture (PhD). Part-time and evening/weekend programs available. *Degree requirements:* For master's, thesis optional. *Entrance requirements:* For master's, GRE General Test, minimum graduate GPA of 3.0. Additional exam requirements/recommendations for international students: Required—TOEFL. Electronic applications accepted.

The University of Texas at San Antonio, College of Education and Human Development, Department of Interdisciplinary Learning and Teaching, San Antonio, TX 78249-0617. Offers curriculum and instruction (MA); early childhood education (MA); instructional technology (MA); reading (MA); special education (MA). Part-time and evening/weekend programs available. *Faculty:* 28 full-time (24 women), 1 part-time/adjunct (0 women). *Students:* 103 full-time (83 women), 317 part-time (253 women); includes 227 minority (36 African Americans, 11 Asian Americans or Pacific Islanders, 180 Hispanic Americans), 17 international. Average age 33. 212 applicants, 90% accepted, 140 enrolled. In 2009, 74 master's awarded. *Degree requirements:* For master's, comprehensive exam (for some programs), thesis (for some programs). *Entrance requirements:* For master's, GRE General Test, minimum GPA of 3.0. Additional exam requirements/recommendations for international students: Required—TOEFL (minimum score 500 paper-based; 173 computer-based; 61 iBT), IELTS (minimum score 5). *Application deadline:* For fall admission, 7/1 for domestic students, 4/1 for international students; for spring admission, 11/1 for domestic students, 9/1 for international students. Applications are processed on a rolling basis. Application fee: $45 ($80 for international students). Electronic applications accepted. *Expenses:* Tuition, state resident: full-time $3975; part-time $221 per contact hour. Tuition, nonresident: full-time $13,947; part-time $775 per contact hour. Required fees: $1853. *Financial support:* In 2009–10, 76 students received support, including 25 research assistantships (averaging $11,599 per year), 4 teaching assistantships (averaging $8,800 per year); scholarships/grants, tuition waivers, and unspecified assistantships also available. Support available to part-time students. *Faculty research:* Adult education; early childhood education; literacy; special education; science, technology, engineering and math fields. Total annual research expenditures: $57,097. *Unit head:* Dr. Belinda B. Flores, Chair, 210-458-5969, Fax: 210-458-7281, E-mail: belinda.flores@utsa.edu. *Application contact:* Mari Cortez, Graduate Advisor, 210-458-4414, E-mail: mari.cortez@utsa.edu.

University of the Pacific, School of Education, Department of Curriculum and Instruction, Stockton, CA 95211-0197. Offers curriculum and instruction (M Ed, MA, Ed D); education (M Ed); special education (MA). *Accreditation:* NCATE. *Faculty:* 11 full-time (7 women), 2 part-time/adjunct (1 woman). *Students:* 24 full-time (18 women), 115 part-time (81 women); includes 52 minority (10 African Americans, 1 American Indian/Alaska Native, 32 Asian Americans or Pacific Islanders, 9 Hispanic Americans), 1 international. Average age 36. 93 applicants, 84% accepted, 52 enrolled. In 2009, 21 master's awarded. *Degree requirements:* For master's, thesis (for some programs). *Entrance requirements:* For master's, GRE General Test. Additional exam requirements/recommendations for international students: Required—TOEFL (minimum score 475 paper-based; 150 computer-based). *Application deadline:* For fall admission, 3/1 priority date for domestic students; for spring admission, 10/1 priority date for domestic students. Applications are processed on a rolling basis. Application fee: $75. *Financial support:* In 2009–10, 7 teaching assistantships were awarded. Financial award application deadline: 3/1; financial award applicants required to submit FAFSA. *Unit head:* Dr. Marilyn Draheim, Chairperson, 209-946-2685, E-mail: mdraheim@pacific.edu. *Application contact:* Office of Graduate Admissions, 209-946-2344.

University of the Southwest, Graduate Programs, Hobbs, NM 88240-9129. Offers business administration (MBA); curriculum and instruction (MSE); curriculum and instruction: bilingual (MSE); curriculum and instruction: reading (MSE); curriculum and instruction: TESOL (MSE); early childhood education (MSE); educational diagnostician (MSE); mental health counseling (MSE); school business administration (MSE); school counseling (MSE); special education (MSE). Part-time and evening/weekend programs available. Postbaccalaureate distance learning degree programs offered (no on-campus study). *Faculty:* 10 full-time (6 women), 10 part-time/adjunct (4 women). *Students:* 112 full-time (93 women), 99 part-time (72 women). Average age 35. 94 applicants, 47% accepted, 39 enrolled. In 2009, 32 master's awarded. *Degree requirements:* For master's, comprehensive exam. *Application deadline:* For fall admission, 3/1 priority date for domestic students; for spring admission, 10/1 for domestic students. Applications are processed on a rolling basis. Application fee: $25. Electronic applications accepted. *Expenses:* Tuition: Part-time $512 per hour. Tuition and fees vary according to course load. *Financial support:* In 2009–10, 196 students received support; research assistantships with partial tuition reimbursements available, Federal Work-Study, scholarships/grants, and tuition waivers (partial) available. Support available to part-time students. Financial award application deadline: 4/1; financial award applicants required to submit FAFSA. *Unit head:* Dr. Mary Harris, Dean of Education, 575-392-6561 Ext. 1056, Fax: 575-392-6006, E-mail: mharris@usw.edu. *Application contact:* Ryanne Evans, Assistant Registrar, 575-392-6561 Ext. 1031, Fax: 575-392-6006, E-mail: revans@usw.edu.

The University of Toledo, College of Graduate Studies, College of Education, Department of Curriculum and Instruction, Program in Curriculum and Instruction, Toledo, OH 43606-3390. Offers ME, DE, PhD, Ed S. *Entrance requirements:* For master's, minimum GPA of 2.7; for doctorate, GRE, minimum undergraduate GPA of 2.7.

University of Vermont, Graduate College, College of Education and Social Services, Department of Education, Program in Curriculum and Instruction, Burlington, VT 05405. Offers M Ed, MAT. *Accreditation:* NCATE. *Students:* 137 (107 women); includes 3 minority (1 African

Curriculum and Instruction

University of Vermont (continued)

American, 1 Asian American or Pacific Islander, 1 Hispanic American). 157 applicants, 71% accepted, 31 enrolled. In 2009, 47 master's awarded. *Entrance requirements:* Additional exam requirements/recommendations for international students: Required—TOEFL (minimum score 550 paper-based; 213 computer-based; 80 iBT). *Application deadline:* For fall admission, 4/1 priority date for domestic students. Applications are processed on a rolling basis. Application fee: $40. Electronic applications accepted. *Expenses:* Tuition, state resident: part-time $508 per credit hour. Tuition, nonresident: part-time $1281 per credit hour. *Financial support:* Fellowships, teaching assistantships, career-related internships or fieldwork available. Financial award application deadline: 3/1. *Unit head:* Dr. Cynthia Gerstl-Pepin, Chairperson, 802-656-3356. *Application contact:* Prof. Maureen Neumann, Coordinator, 802-656-3356.

University of Victoria, Faculty of Graduate Studies, Faculty of Education, Department of Curriculum and Instruction, Victoria, BC V8W 2Y2, Canada. Offers art education (M Ed, PhD); curriculum studies (M Ed, MA, PhD); early childhood education (M Ed, PhD); educational studies (PhD); language and literacy (M Ed, MA, PhD); mathematics (M Ed, MA, PhD); music education (M Ed, MA, PhD); science (M Ed, MA, PhD); social studies (M Ed, MA); social, cultural and foundational studies (MA, PhD); technology and environmental education (PhD). Part-time programs available. *Degree requirements:* For master's, thesis, project (M Ed); for doctorate, comprehensive exam, thesis/dissertation. *Entrance requirements:* For master's, minimum B average. Additional exam requirements/recommendations for international students: Required—TOEFL (minimum score 575 paper-based; 233 computer-based), IELTS (minimum score 7). Electronic applications accepted. *Faculty research:* Elementary and secondary English, language arts, curriculum theory and practice, educational media and technology, educational administration and leadership, history and philosophy of education.

University of Virginia, Curry School of Education, Department of Curriculum, Instruction, and Special Education, Program in Curriculum and Instruction, Charlottesville, VA 22903. Offers curriculum and instruction (M Ed, Ed S); elementary (M Ed, Ed D); English (M Ed, Ed D); foreign language (M Ed); mathematics (M Ed, Ed D); reading (M Ed, Ed D, Ed S); science (Ed D); social studies (M Ed). *Students:* 12 full-time (8 women), 30 part-time (24 women); includes 2 minority (1 Asian American or Pacific Islander, 1 Hispanic American), 1 international. Average age 36. 55 applicants, 69% accepted, 26 enrolled. In 2009, 247 master's, 14 doctorates, 10 other advanced degrees awarded. *Degree requirements:* For master's, comprehensive exam (for some programs); for doctorate, comprehensive exam, thesis/dissertation; for Ed S, comprehensive exam. *Entrance requirements:* For master's, doctorate, and Ed S, GRE General Test, 2 letters of recommendation. Additional exam requirements/recommendations for international students: Required—TOEFL (minimum score 600 paper-based; 250 computer-based; 90 iBT), IELTS (minimum score 7). *Application deadline:* Applications are processed on a rolling basis. Application fee: $60. Electronic applications accepted. *Financial support:* Fellowships with tuition reimbursements, research assistantships with tuition reimbursements, teaching assistantships with tuition reimbursements available. Financial award application deadline: 1/5; financial award applicants required to submit FAFSA.

University of Virginia, Curry School of Education, Program in Education, Charlottesville, VA 22903. Offers administration and supervision (PhD); applied developmental science (PhD); counselor education (PhD); curriculum and instruction (PhD); early childhood-developmental risk (MT); education evaluation (PhD); educational psychology (PhD); educational research (PhD); elementary (MT, PhD); English education (MT, PhD); foreign language education (MT); higher education (PhD); instructional technology (PhD); kinesiology (MT, PhD); math education (PhD); reading education (PhD); research statistics and evaluation (PhD); school psychology (PhD); science education (PhD); social studies education (MT, PhD); special education (PhD); world languages education (MT). *Students:* 336 full-time (239 women), 88 part-time (54 women); includes 43 minority (24 African Americans, 2 American Indian/Alaska Native, 11 Asian Americans or Pacific Islanders, 6 Hispanic Americans), 18 international. Average age 27. 199 applicants, 48% accepted, 55 enrolled. In 2009, 127 master's, 52 doctorates awarded. *Degree requirements:* For master's, comprehensive exam (for some programs), field project; for doctorate, comprehensive exam, thesis/dissertation. *Entrance requirements:* For doctorate, GRE General Test. Additional exam requirements/recommendations for international students: Required—TOEFL (minimum score 600 paper-based; 250 computer-based; 90 iBT), IELTS (minimum score 7). *Application deadline:* Applications are processed on a rolling basis. Application fee: $60. Electronic applications accepted. *Financial support:* Fellowships, research assistantships, teaching assistantships available. Financial award application deadline: 1/5; financial award applicants required to submit FAFSA.

University of Washington, Graduate School, College of Education, Seattle, WA 98195. Offers curriculum and instruction (M Ed, Ed D, PhD), including educational technology, general curriculum (Ed D, PhD), language, literacy, and culture, mathematics education, multicultural education, reading and language arts education (Ed D), science education, social studies education, teaching and curriculum (M Ed); educational leadership and policy studies (M Ed, Ed D, PhD), including administration (Ed D), educational policy, organization, and leadership (M Ed, PhD), higher education, leadership for learning (Ed D), social and cultural foundations of education (M Ed, PhD); educational psychology (M Ed, PhD), including educational psychology (PhD), human development and cognition (M Ed), learning sciences, measurement, statistics and research design (M Ed), school psychology (M Ed); instructional leadership (M Ed); intercollegiate athletic leadership (M Ed); special education (M Ed, Ed D, PhD), including early childhood special education (M Ed), emotional and behavioral disabilities (M Ed), learning disabilities (M Ed), low-incidence disabilities (M Ed), severe disabilities (M Ed), special education (Ed D, PhD); teacher education (MIT). *Accreditation:* APA. Part-time and evening/weekend programs available. *Degree requirements:* For master's, thesis optional; for doctorate, thesis/dissertation. *Entrance requirements:* For master's and doctorate, GRE General Test, minimum GPA of 3.0. Additional exam requirements/recommendations for international students: Required—TOEFL. Electronic applications accepted. *Faculty research:* School restructuring/effective schools, special education interventions, literacy and writing, technology, school partnerships, teacher preparation.

The University of Western Ontario, Faculty of Graduate Studies, Social Sciences Division, Faculty of Education, Program in Educational Studies, London, ON N6A 5B8, Canada. Offers curriculum studies (M Ed); educational policy studies (M Ed); educational psychology/special education (M Ed). Part-time programs available. *Faculty research:* Reflective practice, gender and schooling, feminist pedagogy, narrative inquiry, second language, multiculturalism in Canada, education and law.

University of West Florida, College of Professional Studies, Department of Engineering and Computer Technology, Specialization in Curriculum and Instruction: Specialist, Pensacola, FL 32514-5750. Offers Ed S. *Accreditation:* NCATE. Part-time and evening/weekend programs available. *Students:* 11 part-time (7 women); includes 4 minority (3 African Americans, 1 Hispanic American). Average age 41. 14 applicants, 79% accepted, 4 enrolled. In 2009, 14 Ed Ss awarded. *Entrance requirements:* Additional exam requirements/recommendations for international students: Required—TOEFL (minimum score 550 paper-based; 213 computer-based). *Application deadline:* For fall admission, 6/1 for domestic students, 5/15 for international students; for spring admission, 11/1 for domestic students, 10/1 for international students. Applications are processed on a rolling basis. Application fee: $30. *Expenses:* Tuition, state resident: full-time $4982; part-time $260 per credit hour. Tuition, nonresident: full-time $20,059; part-time $919 per credit hour. Required fees: $1247; $52 per credit hour. *Financial support:* Fellowships, career-related internships or fieldwork available. *Faculty research:* Dropout prevention, technology/educational enhancement. *Unit head:* Dr. Karen Rasmussen, Chairperson, 850-474-2301, Fax: 850-474-2804. *Application contact:* Terry McCray, Assistant Director of Graduate Admissions, 850-473-7718, Fax: 850-473-7714, E-mail: gradadmissions@uwf.edu.

University of West Florida, College of Professional Studies, Department of Professional and Community Leadership, Program in Curriculum and Instruction—Ed D, Pensacola, FL 32514-5750. Offers Ed D. *Accreditation:* NCATE. Evening/weekend programs available. *Students:* 7 full-time (5 women), 98 part-time (62 women); includes 36 minority (25 African Americans, 3 American Indian/Alaska Native, 5 Asian Americans or Pacific Islanders, 3 Hispanic Americans). Average age 43. 39 applicants, 64% accepted, 21 enrolled. In 2009, 26 doctorates awarded. *Degree requirements:* For doctorate, thesis/dissertation. *Entrance requirements:* Additional exam requirements/recommendations for international students: Required—TOEFL (minimum score 550 paper-based; 213 computer-based). *Application deadline:* For fall admission, 6/1 for domestic students, 5/15 for international students; for spring admission, 11/1 for domestic students, 10/1 for international students. Applications are processed on a rolling basis. Application fee: $30. *Expenses:* Tuition, state resident: full-time $4982; part-time $260 per credit hour. Tuition, nonresident: full-time $20,059; part-time $919 per credit hour. Required fees: $1247; $52 per credit hour. *Financial support:* Fellowships, Federal Work-Study, institutionally sponsored loans, scholarships/grants, and tuition waivers (partial) available. Support available to part-time students. Financial award application deadline: 4/15; financial award applicants required to submit FAFSA. *Unit head:* Dr. Thomas J. Kramer, Chairperson, 850-474-2949, Fax: 850-857-6288. *Application contact:* Terry McCray, Assistant Director of Graduate Admissions, 850-473-7718, Fax: 850-473-7714, E-mail: gradadmissions@uwf.edu.

University of Wisconsin–Madison, Graduate School, School of Education, Department of Curriculum and Instruction, Madison, WI 53706-1380. Offers art education (MA); curriculum and instruction (MS, PhD); education and mathematics (MA); French education (MA); German education (MA); music education (MS); science education (MS); Spanish education (MA). *Accreditation:* NASM (one or more programs are accredited). *Degree requirements:* For doctorate, thesis/dissertation. Application fee: $56. *Expenses:* Tuition, state resident: part-time $594 per credit. Tuition, nonresident: part-time $1504 per credit. Required fees: $65 per credit. Tuition and fees vary according to course load, program and reciprocity agreements. *Financial support:* Project assistantships available. *Unit head:* Dr. Gloria Ladson-Billings, Chair, 608-262-4000. *Application contact:* Dr. Gloria Ladson-Billings, Chair, 608-262-4000.

University of Wisconsin–Milwaukee, Graduate School, School of Education, Department of Curriculum and Instruction, Milwaukee, WI 53201-0413. Offers curriculum planning and instruction improvement (MS); early childhood education (MS); elementary education (MS); junior high/middle school education (MS); reading education (MS); secondary education (MS); teaching in an urban setting (MS). Part-time programs available. *Faculty:* 22 full-time (17 women). *Students:* 23 full-time (14 women), 64 part-time (58 women); includes 8 minority (4 African Americans, 1 American Indian/Alaska Native, 3 Hispanic Americans), 1 international. Average age 31. 46 applicants, 57% accepted, 12 enrolled. In 2009, 28 master's awarded. *Degree requirements:* For master's, thesis or alternative. *Entrance requirements:* Additional exam requirements/recommendations for international students: Required—TOEFL (minimum score 550 paper-based; 79 iBT), IELTS (minimum score 6.5). *Application deadline:* For fall admission, 1/1 priority date for domestic students; for spring admission, 9/1 for domestic students. Applications are processed on a rolling basis. Application fee: $45 ($75 for international students). *Expenses:* Tuition, state resident: full-time $8800. Tuition, nonresident: full-time $20,760. Tuition and fees vary according to program and reciprocity agreements. *Financial support:* Career-related internships or fieldwork and unspecified assistantships available. Support available to part-time students. Financial award application deadline: 4/15. Total annual research expenditures: $65,946. *Unit head:* Hope Longwell-Grice, Chair, 414-229-4884, Fax: 414-229-5571, E-mail: hope@uwm.edu. *Application contact:* General Information Contact, 414-229-4982, Fax: 414-229-6967, E-mail: gradschool@uwm.edu.

University of Wisconsin–Milwaukee, Graduate School, School of Education, Program in Urban Education, Milwaukee, WI 53201-0413. Offers adult and continuing education (PhD); curriculum and instruction (PhD); educational administration (PhD); educational and media technology (PhD); educational psychology (PhD); multicultural studies (PhD); social foundations of education (PhD). *Students:* 67 full-time (51 women), 44 part-time (30 women); includes 41 minority (23 African Americans, 2 American Indian/Alaska Native, 7 Asian Americans or Pacific Islanders, 9 Hispanic Americans), 4 international. Average age 41. 31 applicants, 45% accepted, 5 enrolled. In 2009, 11 doctorates awarded. *Degree requirements:* For doctorate, comprehensive exam, thesis/dissertation. *Entrance requirements:* For doctorate, GRE General Test, minimum undergraduate GPA of 2.85, graduate 3.5. Additional exam requirements/recommendations for international students: Required—TOEFL (minimum score 550 paper-based; 79 iBT), IELTS (minimum score 6.5). *Application deadline:* For fall admission, 1/1 priority date for domestic students; for spring admission, 9/1 for domestic students. Applications are processed on a rolling basis. Application fee: $45 ($75 for international students). *Expenses:* Tuition, state resident: full-time $8800. Tuition, nonresident: full-time $20,760. Tuition and fees vary according to program and reciprocity agreements. *Financial support:* Career-related internships or fieldwork and unspecified assistantships available. Support available to part-time students. Financial award application deadline: 4/15. *Unit head:* Larry Martin, Representative, 414-229-4729, Fax: 414-229-2920, E-mail: lmartin@uwm.edu. *Application contact:* General Information Contact, 414-229-4982, Fax: 414-229-6967, E-mail: gradschool@uwm.edu.

University of Wisconsin–Oshkosh, The Office of Graduate Studies, College of Education and Human Services, Department of Curriculum and Instruction, Oshkosh, WI 54901. Offers MSE. Part-time and evening/weekend programs available. *Degree requirements:* For master's, thesis or alternative, seminar paper. *Entrance requirements:* For master's, teaching license, letters of recommendation. Additional exam requirements/recommendations for international students: Required—TOEFL (minimum score 550 paper-based; 213 computer-based; 79 iBT). Electronic applications accepted. *Faculty research:* Early childhood, middle school teaching, literacy, elementary teaching, bilingual education.

University of Wisconsin–Superior, Graduate Division, Department of Teacher Education, Program in Instruction, Superior, WI 54880-4500. Offers MSE. Part-time and evening/weekend programs available. *Faculty:* 3 full-time (2 women). *Students:* 10 part-time (6 women); includes 1 minority (American Indian/Alaska Native). 3 applicants, 100% accepted. In 2009, 10 master's awarded. *Degree requirements:* For master's, comprehensive exam, thesis or alternative, research project. *Entrance requirements:* For master's, minimum GPA of 2.75, teaching certificate. *Application deadline:* For fall admission, 4/1 priority date for domestic students; for spring admission, 10/15 priority date for domestic students. Applications are processed on a rolling basis. Application fee: $45. *Financial support:* Career-related internships or fieldwork, Federal Work-Study, institutionally sponsored loans, scholarships/grants, and tuition waivers (partial) available. Support available to part-time students. Financial award application deadline: 4/15; financial award applicants required to submit FAFSA. *Unit head:* Terri Kronzer, Coordinator, 715-394-8506. *Application contact:* Sandy Wallgren, Program Assistant/Status Examiner, 715-394-8295, Fax: 715-394-8146, E-mail: gradstudy@uwsuper.edu.

University of Wisconsin–Whitewater, School of Graduate Studies, College of Education, Department of Curriculum and Instruction, Whitewater, WI 53190-1790. Offers MS. *Accreditation:* NCATE. Part-time and evening/weekend programs available. Postbaccalaureate distance learning degree programs offered. *Degree requirements:* For master's, thesis or integrated project. *Entrance requirements:* Additional exam requirements/recommendations for international students: Required—TOEFL (minimum score 550 paper-based; 213 computer-based). Electronic applications accepted. *Faculty research:* Hybrid of exercise physiology and psychology; gender equity; education, pedagogy, and technology; comprehensive school health education.

University of Wyoming, College of Education, Programs in Curriculum and Instruction, Laramie, WY 82070. Offers MA, Ed D, PhD. Part-time programs available. Postbaccalaureate distance learning degree programs offered. Terminal master's awarded for partial completion of doctoral program. *Degree requirements:* For master's, comprehensive exam, thesis; for doctorate, comprehensive exam, thesis/dissertation. *Entrance requirements:* For master's, minimum GPA of 3.0, 3 letters of reference, writing samples; for doctorate, accredited master's degree, 3 letters of reference, 3 years of teaching experience, writing sample. Additional exam requirements/recommendations for international students: Required—TOEFL (minimum score

525 paper-based). *Faculty research:* Teaching and learning teacher education, multi-cultural education, early childhood, discipline-specific pedagogy.

Utah State University, School of Graduate Studies, College of Education and Human Services, Doctoral Program in Education, Logan, UT 84322. Offers business information systems (Ed D, PhD); curriculum and instruction (Ed D, PhD); research and evaluation (PhD). *Degree requirements:* For doctorate, comprehensive exam, thesis/dissertation. *Entrance requirements:* For doctorate, GRE General Test, minimum GPA of 3.0, master's degree. Additional exam requirements/recommendations for international students: Required—TOEFL. Electronic applications accepted. *Faculty research:* Language and literacy development, math and science education, instructional technology, hearing problems/deafness, domestic violence and animal abuse.

Virginia Commonwealth University, Graduate School, School of Education, Program in Curriculum and Instruction, Richmond, VA 23284-9005. Offers M Ed. *Accreditation:* NCATE. Part-time programs available. *Degree requirements:* For master's, comprehensive exam. *Entrance requirements:* For master's, GRE General Test or MAT.

Virginia Commonwealth University, Graduate School, School of Education, Program in Teaching and Learning, Richmond, VA 23284-9005. Offers early education (MT); middle education (MT); secondary education (MT, Certificate); special education (MT). *Accreditation:* NCATE. Part-time programs available. *Entrance requirements:* For master's, GRE General Test or MAT.

Virginia Polytechnic Institute and State University, Graduate School, College of Liberal Arts and Human Sciences, School of Education, Department of Teaching and Learning, Blacksburg, VA 24061. Offers career and technical education (MS Ed, Ed D, PhD, Ed S); curriculum and instruction (MA Ed, Ed D, PhD, Ed S); health and physical education (MS Ed); mathematics education (MA Ed, PhD); secondary English education (MA Ed). *Accreditation:* NCATE. Postbaccalaureate distance learning degree programs offered (no on-campus study). *Students:* 295 full-time (186 women), 374 part-time (272 women); includes 104 minority (1 African American, 39 American Indian/Alaska Native, 54 Asian Americans or Pacific Islanders, 10 Hispanic Americans), 23 international. Average age 34. 324 applicants, 85% accepted, 205 enrolled. In 2009, 235 master's, 34 doctorates, 1 other advanced degree awarded. *Entrance requirements:* For master's and doctorate, GRE, GMAT. Additional exam requirements/recommendations for international students: Required—TOEFL (minimum score 550 paper-based; 213 computer-based). *Application deadline:* For fall admission, 5/15 for international students; for spring admission, 10/15 for international students. Applications are processed on a rolling basis. Application fee: $65. Electronic applications accepted. *Expenses:* Tuition, area resident: Full-time $10,228; part-time $459 per credit hour. Tuition, nonresident: full-time $17,892; part-time $865 per credit hour. Required fees: $1966; $451 per semester. *Financial support:* Career-related internships or fieldwork, Federal Work-Study, scholarships/grants, and unspecified assistantships available. Financial award application deadline: 1/15. *Faculty research:* Instructional technology, teacher evaluation, school change, literacy, teaching strategies. *Unit head:* Dr. Daisy L. Stewart, Dean, 540-231-8180, Fax: 540-231-3717, E-mail: daisys@vt.edu. *Application contact:* Dr. Daisy L. Stewart, Dean, 540-231-8180, Fax: 540-231-3717, E-mail: daisys@vt.edu.

Walden University, Graduate Programs, Richard W. Riley College of Education and Leadership, Minneapolis, MN 55401. Offers administrator leadership for teaching and learning (Ed D, Ed S); curriculum, instruction, and professional development (Ed S); early childhood education (birth-grade 3) (MAT); education (MS, PhD), including adolescent literacy and technology (grades 6-12) (MS), adult education leadership (PhD), community college leadership (PhD), curriculum, instruction, and assessment, early childhood education (PhD), educational leadership (MS), educational technology (PhD), elementary reading and literacy (MS), elementary reading and mathematics (MS), emotional/behavioral disorders (K-12) (MS), general program, higher education (PhD), integrating technology in the classroom (MS), K-12 educational leadership (PhD), learning disabilities (K-12) (MS), literacy and learning in the content areas (MS), mathematics (grades 6-8) (MS), mathematics (grades K-5) (MS), middle level education (grades 5-8) (MS), professional development (MS), science (grades K-8) (MS), self-designed (PhD), special education (PhD), special education (non-licensure) (MS), teacher leadership (grades K-12) (MS); educational leadership and administration (principal preparation) (Ed S); educational technology (Ed S); higher education and adult learning (Ed D); instructional design (Postbaccalaureate Certificate); instructional design and technology (MS), including general program (MS, PhD), online learning, training and performance improvement; special education: emotional/behavioral disorders (K-12) (MAT); special education: learning disabilities (K-12) (MAT); teacher leadership (Ed D, Ed S). Part-time and evening/weekend programs available. Postbaccalaureate distance learning degree programs offered (minimal on-campus study). *Faculty:* 54 full-time, 835 part-time/adjunct. *Students:* 13,940 full-time (11,339 women), 1,940 part-time (1,637 women); includes 4,626 minority (3,795 African Americans, 111 American Indian/Alaska Native, 199 Asian Americans or Pacific Islanders, 521 Hispanic Americans), 124 international. Average age 38. In 2009, 4,688 master's, 190 doctorates awarded. *Degree requirements:* For doctorate, thesis/dissertation (for some programs), residency; for other advanced degree, residency (for some programs). *Entrance requirements:* For master's, bachelor's degree or equivalent in related field; minimum GPA of 2.5; official transcripts; goal statement; access to computer and Internet; for doctorate, master's degree or equivalent in related field; minimum GPA of 3.0; official transcripts; three years' related professional/academic experience (preferred); access to computer and Internet; for other advanced degree, master's degree or equivalent in related field; minimum GPA of 3.0; 3 years related professional/academic experience (preferred); access to computer and Internet (Ed S). Additional exam requirements/recommendations for international students: Required—TOEFL (minimum score 550 paper-based; 213 computer-based), IELTS (minimum score 6.5), or Michigan English Language Assessment Battery (minimum score 82). *Application deadline:* Applications are processed on a rolling basis. Application fee: $50. Electronic applications accepted. *Expenses:* Tuition: Full-time $13,665; part-time $560 per credit. Required fees: $1375. Tuition and fees vary according to course load, degree level and program. *Financial support:* In 2009–10, 2,418 students received support; fellowships, Federal Work-Study, scholarships/grants, unspecified assistantships, and family tuition reduction, active duty/veteran tuition reduction, group tuition reduction, interest-free payment plans available. Support available to part-time students. Financial award applicants required to submit FAFSA. *Unit head:* Dr. Kate Steffens, Dean, 800-925-3368. *Application contact:* Jennifer Hall, Director of Enrollment, 866-4-WALDEN, E-mail: info@waldenu.edu.

Walla Walla University, Graduate School, School of Education and Psychology, College Place, WA 99324-1198. Offers counseling psychology (MA); curriculum and instruction (M Ed, MA, MAT); educational leadership (M Ed, MA, MAT); literacy instruction (M Ed, MA, MAT); students at risk (M Ed, MA, MAT); teaching (MAT). Part-time programs available. *Faculty:* 7 full-time (3 women), 1 part-time/adjunct (0 women). *Students:* 32 full-time (14 women), 9 part-time (7 women); includes 5 minority (1 African American, 1 American Indian/Alaska Native, 2 Asian Americans or Pacific Islanders, 1 Hispanic American). Average age 30. 41 applicants, 80% accepted, 21 enrolled. In 2009, 29 master's awarded. *Entrance requirements:* For master's, GRE General Test, minimum GPA of 2.75. Additional exam requirements/recommendations for international students: Required—TOEFL (minimum score 550 paper-based; 213 computer-based; 79 iBT). *Application deadline:* For fall admission, 4/1 priority date for domestic students. Applications are processed on a rolling basis. Application fee: $50. Electronic applications accepted. *Expenses:* Tuition: Full-time $19,929. *Financial support:* In 2009–10, 29 students received support; research assistantships, teaching assistantships, Federal Work-Study and tuition waivers (partial) available. Support available to part-time students. Financial award application deadline: 4/1; financial award applicants required to submit FAFSA. *Faculty research:* Admissions/retention, instructional psychology, moral development, teaching of reading. *Unit head:* Dr. Julian Melgosa, Dean, 509-527-2272, Fax: 509-527-2248, E-mail: julian.melgosa@wallawalla.edu. *Application contact:* Dr. Joe G. Galusha, Dean of Graduate Studies, 509-527-2421, Fax: 509-527-2237, E-mail: joe.galusha@wallawalla.edu.

Washburn University, College of Arts and Sciences, Department of Education, Program in Curriculum and Instruction, Topeka, KS 66621. Offers M Ed. *Accreditation:* NCATE.

Washington State University, Graduate School, College of Education, Department of Teaching and Learning, Pullman, WA 99164. Offers curriculum and instruction (Ed D, PhD); diverse languages (M Ed, MA); elementary education (M Ed, MA, MIT); exercise science (MS); literacy education (M Ed, MA, PhD); math education (PhD); secondary education (M Ed, MA). *Accreditation:* NCATE. *Degree requirements:* For master's, comprehensive exam (for some programs), thesis (for some programs), oral or written exam; for doctorate, comprehensive exam, thesis/dissertation, oral, written exam. *Entrance requirements:* For master's and doctorate, GRE General Test, minimum GPA of 3.0, 3 letters of recommendation. Additional exam requirements/recommendations for international students: Required—TOEFL. *Faculty research:* Evolution of middle school education issues in special education, computer-assisted language learning.

Wayne State College, School of Education and Counseling, Department of Educational Foundations and Leadership, Program in Curriculum and Instruction, Wayne, NE 68787. Offers alternative education (MSE); business and information technology education (MSE); communication arts education (MSE); early childhood education (MSE); elementary education (MSE); English as a second language (MSE); English education (MSE); family and consumer sciences education (MSE); industrial technology and vocational education (MSE); learning communities (MSE); mathematics education (MSE); music education (MSE); science education (MSE); social science education (MSE). *Accreditation:* NCATE. Part-time and evening/weekend programs available. *Degree requirements:* For master's, comprehensive exam, thesis optional. *Entrance requirements:* For master's, GRE General Test. Additional exam requirements/recommendations for international students: Required—TOEFL (minimum score 550 paper-based; 213 computer-based).

Wayne State University, College of Education, Division of Administrative and Organizational Studies, Detroit, MI 48202. Offers administration and supervision-secondary (Ed S); college and university teaching (Certificate); curriculum and instruction (PhD); educational leadership (M Ed, Ed S); educational leadership and policy studies (Ed D, PhD); elementary education curriculum and instruction (MA, Ed S); general administration and supervision (Ed D, PhD, Ed S); higher education (Ed D, PhD); instructional technology (M Ed, Ed D, PhD, Ed S); secondary curriculum and instruction (M Ed, Ed S). *Degree requirements:* For doctorate, thesis/dissertation. *Entrance requirements:* For doctorate, interview, minimum GPA of 3.0, an autobiography or curriculum vitae; references. Additional exam requirements/recommendations for international students: Required—TOEFL (minimum score 550 paper-based; 213 computer-based), TWE (minimum score 6). Electronic applications accepted. *Faculty research:* Total quality management, participatory management, administering educational technology, school improvement, principalship.

Wayne State University, College of Education, Division of Teacher Education, Detroit, MI 48202. Offers adult and continuing education (M Ed); art education (M Ed); bilingual/bicultural education (M Ed, MAT); business education (M Ed, MAT); career and technical education (M Ed, Ed D, PhD, Ed S); curriculum and instruction (Ed D, PhD, Ed S); distributive education (M Ed, MAT); early childhood education (M Ed); elementary education (M Ed, MAT, Ed D, PhD, Ed S); elementary education curriculum and instruction (M Ed); English education (M Ed); English education-secondary (M Ed, Ed S); foreign language education (M Ed); general education (Ed D, Ed S); health occupations education (M Ed); industrial education (M Ed); mathematics education (M Ed, Ed S); pre-school and parent education (M Ed); reading (M Ed, Ed D, Ed S); reading, languages and literature (Ed D); school music-vocal (M Ed); science education (M Ed, MAT, Ed S); secondary education (MAT); secondary school reading (M Ed); social studies education (M Ed, Ed S), including education-secondary (M Ed); special education (M Ed, Ed D, PhD, Ed S); teacher education (MAT, Ed D, PhD). *Degree requirements:* For doctorate, thesis/dissertation. *Entrance requirements:* For master's, Michigan Basic Skills Test (MA in teaching), minimum GPA of 2.6; for doctorate, minimum undergraduate GPA of 3.0, graduate 3.5; interview, curriculum vitae; references. Additional exam requirements/recommendations for international students: Required—TOEFL (minimum score 550 paper-based; 213 computer-based), TWE (minimum score 6). Electronic applications accepted. *Faculty research:* Reading and writing literacy and literature.

Weber State University, Jerry and Vickie Moyes College of Education, Program in Curriculum and Instruction, Ogden, UT 84408-1001. Offers M Ed. *Accreditation:* NCATE. Part-time and evening/weekend programs available. *Degree requirements:* For master's, thesis or alternative, project presentation and exam. *Entrance requirements:* For master's, MAT or GRE, minimum GPA of 3.0 in last 90 credits. Additional exam requirements/recommendations for international students: Required—TOEFL (minimum score 550 paper-based; 213 computer-based), American Council on the Teaching of Foreign Languages test. *Faculty research:* Special needs, best practices in education literacy, metacognition.

Western Connecticut State University, Division of Graduate Studies, School of Professional Studies, Department of Education and Educational Psychology, Curriculum Option, Danbury, CT 06810-6885. Offers MS. Part-time programs available. *Students:* 2 full-time (both women), 47 part-time (37 women); includes 1 minority (Hispanic American). Average age 29. 17 applicants, 82% accepted, 13 enrolled. In 2009, 16 master's awarded. *Degree requirements:* For master's, thesis or alternative, thesis research project or 3 extra classes and comprehensive exam, completion of program in 6 years. *Entrance requirements:* For master's, minimum GPA of 2.8 or MAT, teaching certificate in elementary or secondary education. Additional exam requirements/recommendations for international students: Recommended—TOEFL (minimum score 550 paper-based; 213 computer-based; 79 iBT), IELTS (minimum score 6). *Application deadline:* For fall admission, 8/5 priority date for domestic students; for spring admission, 1/5 priority date for domestic students. Applications are processed on a rolling basis. Application fee: $50. *Expenses:* Tuition, state resident: full-time $5012; part-time $278 per credit hour. Tuition, nonresident: full-time $13,962; part-time $284 per credit hour. Required fees: $3886; $139 per credit hour. Full-time tuition and fees vary according to course load and program. Part-time tuition and fees vary according to course level, degree level and program. *Financial support:* Application deadline: 5/1. *Unit head:* Dr. Theresa Canada, Chairperson, Department of Education and Educational Psychology, 203-837-8509, Fax: 203-837-8413, E-mail: canadat@wcsu.edu. *Application contact:* Chris Shankle, Associate Director of Graduate Studies, 203-837-9005, Fax: 203-837-8326, E-mail: shanklec@wcsu.edu.

West Texas A&M University, College of Education and Social Sciences, Division of Education, Program in Curriculum and Instruction, Canyon, TX 79016-0001. Offers M Ed. Part-time and evening/weekend programs available. Postbaccalaureate distance learning degree programs offered. *Degree requirements:* For master's, comprehensive exam, thesis optional. *Entrance requirements:* For master's, GRE General Test, 18 semester hours of education course work. Additional exam requirements/recommendations for international students: Required—TOEFL (minimum score 550 paper-based). Electronic applications accepted.

West Virginia University, College of Human Resources and Education, Department of Curriculum and Instruction-Literacy, Morgantown, WV 26506. Offers curriculum and instruction (Ed D); elementary education (MA); reading (MA); secondary education (MA), including higher education curriculum and teaching, secondary education; special education (Ed D), including special education. *Accreditation:* NCATE. Part-time and evening/weekend programs available. *Degree requirements:* For doctorate, comprehensive exam, thesis/dissertation. *Entrance requirements:* For master's, minimum GPA of 2.75; for doctorate, GRE General Test or MAT, 3 letters of recommendation, curriculum vitae. Additional exam requirements/recommendations for international students: Required—TOEFL. *Faculty research:* Teacher education, curriculum development, educational technology, curriculum assessment.

Wichita State University, Graduate School, College of Education, Department of Curriculum and Instruction, Wichita, KS 67260. Offers curriculum and instruction (M Ed); special education (M Ed), including adaptive, early childhood unified, functional, gifted; teaching (MAT). *Accreditation:* NCATE. Part-time and evening/weekend programs available. *Entrance requirements:*

Curriculum and Instruction

Wichita State University *(continued)*

For master's, MAT, minimum GPA of 2.75. *Expenses:* Tuition, state resident: full-time $4247; part-time $235.95 per credit hour. Tuition, nonresident: full-time $11,171; part-time $620.60 per credit hour. Required fees: $34; $3.60 per credit hour. $17 per term. Tuition and fees vary according to campus/location and program. *Unit head:* Dr. Janice Ewing, Chairperson, 316-978-3322, E-mail: janice.ewing@wichita.edu. *Application contact:* Dr. Janice Ewing, Chairperson, 316-978-3322, E-mail: janice.ewing@wichita.edu.

William Woods University, Graduate and Adult Studies, Fulton, MO 65251-1098. Offers administration (Ed S); agriculture (MBA); athletic/activities administration (M Ed); curriculum and instruction (M Ed); curriculum leadership (Ed S); elementary administration (M Ed); health management (MBA); human resources (MBA); principalship (Ed S); secondary administration (M Ed); special education director (M Ed). Evening/weekend programs available. *Degree requirements:* For master's, capstone course (MBA), action research (M Ed); for Ed S, field experience. *Entrance requirements:* For master's, 2 recommendations, resumé, BA/BS; teaching certification (M Ed); course work in economics and accounting (MBA); for Ed S, M Ed, 2 letters of recommendation, resume, teaching certification. Additional exam requirements/recommendations for international students: Required—TOEFL (minimum score 550 paper-based). Electronic applications accepted.

Wright State University, School of Graduate Studies, College of Education and Human Services, Department of Educational Leadership, Program in Advanced Educational Leadership, Dayton, OH 45435. Offers advanced curriculum and instruction (Ed S); higher education-adult education (Ed S); superintendent (Ed S). *Accreditation:* NCATE. *Degree requirements:* For Ed S, thesis. *Entrance requirements:* For degree, GRE General Test, MAT. Additional exam requirements/recommendations for international students: Required—TOEFL.

Wright State University, School of Graduate Studies, College of Education and Human Services, Department of Educational Leadership, Programs in Educational Leadership, Dayton, OH 45435. Offers curriculum and instruction: teacher leader (MA); educational administrative specialist: teacher leader (M Ed); educational administrative specialist: vocational education administration (M Ed, MA); student affairs in higher education-administration (M Ed, MA). *Accreditation:* NCATE. *Degree requirements:* For master's, thesis (for some programs). *Entrance requirements:* For master's, GRE General Test, MAT. Additional exam requirements/recommendations for international students: Required—TOEFL.

Xavier University of Louisiana, Graduate School, Programs in Education, New Orleans, LA 70125-1098. Offers curriculum and instruction (MA); education administration and supervision (MA); guidance and counseling (MA). *Accreditation:* NCATE. Part-time and evening/weekend programs available. *Degree requirements:* For master's, comprehensive exam, thesis or alternative. *Entrance requirements:* For master's, GRE General Test, MAT, minimum GPA of 2.5. Additional exam requirements/recommendations for international students: Required—TOEFL.

Youngstown State University, Graduate School, Beeghly College of Education, Department of Teacher Education, Youngstown, OH 44555-0001. Offers adolescent/young adult education (MS Ed); content area concentration (MS Ed); early childhood education (MS Ed); educational technology (MS Ed); literacy (MS Ed); middle childhood education (MS Ed); special education (MS Ed), including gifted and talented education, special education. *Accreditation:* NCATE. Part-time and evening/weekend programs available. *Degree requirements:* For master's, comprehensive exam. *Entrance requirements:* For master's, GRE, MAT, or teaching certificate; minimum GPA of 2.7. Additional exam requirements/recommendations for international students: Required—TOEFL. *Faculty research:* Multicultural literacy, hands-on mathematics teaching, integrated instruction, reading comprehension, emergent curriculum.

Distance Education Development

Athabasca University, Centre for Distance Education, Athabasca, AB T9S 3A3, Canada. Offers distance education (MDE); distance education technology (Advanced Diploma). Part-time programs available. Postbaccalaureate distance learning degree programs offered (no on-campus study). *Faculty:* 11 full-time (4 women), 1 (woman) part-time/adjunct. *Students:* 311 part-time. Average age 36. 135 applicants, 14 enrolled. In 2009, 46 master's, 10 other advanced degrees awarded. *Degree requirements:* For master's, thesis optional. *Entrance requirements:* For master's, 3 or 4 year baccalaureate degree. *Application deadline:* For fall admission, 3/1 for domestic and international students. Application fee: $80. Electronic applications accepted. *Expenses:* Contact institution. *Faculty research:* Role development, interaction, educational technology, and communities of practice in distance education; instructional design. *Unit head:* Dr. Mohamed Ally, Director, 866-916-8650, E-mail: mohameda@athabascau.ca. *Application contact:* Centre for Distance Education, 800-788-9041 Ext. 6179, Fax: 780-675-6170, E-mail: mde@athabascau.ca.

Barry University, School of Education, Graduate Certificate Programs, Miami Shores, FL 33161-6695. Offers advanced teaching and learning with technology (Certificate); distance education (Certificate); higher education technology integration (Certificate); human resources: not for profit and religious organizations (Certificate); K-12 technology integration (Certificate).

Endicott College, Van Loan School of Graduate and Professional Studies, Program in Integrative Learning, Beverly, MA 01915-2096. Offers M Ed. Part-time and evening/weekend programs available. Postbaccalaureate distance learning degree programs offered. *Faculty:* 2 full-time (1 woman), 5 part-time/adjunct (all women). *Students:* 14 full-time (10 women), 9 part-time (8 women). Average age 35. 11 applicants, 100% accepted, 11 enrolled. In 2009, 17 master's awarded. *Degree requirements:* For master's, thesis. *Entrance requirements:* Additional exam requirements/recommendations for international students: Required—TOEFL. *Application deadline:* Applications are processed on a rolling basis. Application fee: $50. *Expenses:* Contact institution. *Financial support:* Tuition waivers (partial) available. *Unit head:* Enid E. Larsen, Assistant Dean of Academic Programs, 978-232-2198, Fax: 978-232-3000, E-mail: elarsen@endicott.edu. *Application contact:* Dr. Phil Snow Gang, Dean, 406-387-5107, Fax: 413-778-9644, E-mail: ties@endicott.edu.

Fairmont State University, Graduate Studies, Programs in Education, Fairmont, WV 26554. Offers education (MAT); leadership studies (M Ed); online learning (M Ed); professional studies (M Ed); reading (M Ed); special education (M Ed). *Accreditation:* NCATE.

Florida State University, The Graduate School, College of Education, Department of Educational Psychology and Learning Systems, Program in Instructional Systems, Tallahassee, FL 32306. Offers instructional systems (MS, PhD, Ed S); open and distance learning (MS); performance improvement and human resources (MS). *Faculty:* 6 full-time (3 women), 4 part-time/adjunct (1 woman). *Students:* 51 full-time (34 women), 60 part-time (35 women); includes 19 minority (9 African Americans, 2 American Indian/Alaska Native, 5 Asian Americans or Pacific Islanders, 3 Hispanic Americans), 26 international. 68 applicants, 16% accepted, 11 enrolled. In 2009, 25 master's, 9 doctorates awarded. *Degree requirements:* For master's and Ed S, comprehensive exam, thesis optional; for doctorate, comprehensive exam, thesis/dissertation. *Entrance requirements:* For master's, doctorate, and Ed S, GRE General Test, minimum GPA of 3.0. Additional exam requirements/recommendations for international students: Required—TOEFL (minimum score 550 paper-based; 213 computer-based; 80 iBT). *Application deadline:* For fall admission, 6/1 priority date for domestic and international students; for spring admission, 10/1 priority date for domestic and international students. Applications are processed on a rolling basis. Application fee: $30. *Expenses:* Tuition, state resident: full-time $7413. Tuition, nonresident: full-time $22,567. *Financial support:* In 2009–10, 3 fellowships with full and partial tuition reimbursements, 8 research assistantships with full and partial tuition reimbursements, 6 teaching assistantships with full and partial tuition reimbursements were awarded; career-related internships or fieldwork and Federal Work-Study also available. Financial award applicants required to submit FAFSA. *Faculty research:* Human performance improvement, educational semiotics, development of software tools to measure online interaction among learners. *Unit head:* Dr. Vanessa Dennen, Program Coordinator, 850-644-8783, Fax: 850-644-8776, E-mail: vdennen@fsu.edu. *Application contact:* Mary Kate McKee, Program Coordinator, 850-644-8792, Fax: 850-644-8776, E-mail: mmckee@oddl.fsu.edu.

Jones International University, Graduate School of Education, Centennial, CO 80112. Offers adult education (M Ed); corporate training and knowledge management (M Ed); curriculum and instruction (M Ed), including elementary teacher licensure, secondary teacher licensure; e-learning technology and design (M Ed); educational leadership and administration (M Ed); educational leadership and administration: principal and administrator licensure (M Ed); elementary curriculum instruction and assessment (M Ed); higher education leadership and administration (M Ed); K-12 instructional technology (M Ed); K-12 instructional technology: teacher licensure (M Ed); secondary curriculum instruction and assessment (M Ed); technology and design (M Ed). Part-time and evening/weekend programs available. Postbaccalaureate distance learning degree programs offered (no on-campus study). *Entrance requirements:* For master's, minimum cumulative GPA of 2.5. Additional exam requirements/recommendations for international students: Recommended—TOEFL (minimum score 550 paper-based; 213 computer-based). Electronic applications accepted.

New York Institute of Technology, Graduate Division, School of Education, Program in Instructional Technology, Old Westbury, NY 11568-8000. Offers distance learning (Advanced Certificate); instructional technology (MS); multimedia (Advanced Certificate). Part-time and evening/weekend programs available. Postbaccalaureate distance learning degree programs offered. *Students:* 20 full-time (11 women), 211 part-time (115 women); includes 28 minority (10 African Americans, 7 Asian Americans or Pacific Islanders, 11 Hispanic Americans), 8 international. Average age 34. In 2009, 93 master's awarded. *Degree requirements:* For master's, thesis. *Entrance requirements:* For master's, minimum QPA of 3.0; for Advanced Certificate, master's degree, minimum GPA of 3.0, 3 years of teaching experience, New York teaching certificate, 2 letters of recommendation. Additional exam requirements/recommendations for international students: Required—TOEFL (minimum score 550 paper-based; 213 computer-based). *Application deadline:* For fall admission, 7/1 priority date for domestic students; for spring admission, 12/1 priority date for domestic students. Applications are processed on a rolling basis. Application fee: $50. Electronic applications accepted. *Expenses:* Tuition: Part-time $825 per credit. *Financial support:* Research assistantships with partial tuition reimbursements, career-related internships or fieldwork, institutionally sponsored loans, and tuition waivers (full and partial) available. Support available to part-time students. Financial award applicants required to submit FAFSA. *Faculty research:* Distance learning, teacher training resources and strategies. *Unit head:* Dr. Sarah McPherson, Coordinator, 516-686-1053, Fax: 516-686-7655, E-mail: smcphers@nyit.edu. *Application contact:* Dr. Jacquelyn Nealon, Vice President for Enrollment Services, 516-686-7925, Fax: 516-686-7597, E-mail: jnealon@nyit.edu.

Nova Southeastern University, Fischler School of Education and Human Services, Programs in Instructional Technology and Distance Education, Fort Lauderdale, FL 33314-7796. Offers MS, Ed D. Part-time and evening/weekend programs available. Postbaccalaureate distance learning degree programs offered (minimal on-campus study). *Faculty:* 9 full-time (2 women), 9 part-time/adjunct (5 women). *Students:* 150 full-time (109 women), 110 part-time (80 women); includes 227 minority (12 African Americans, 3 Asian Americans or Pacific Islanders, 212 Hispanic Americans), 2 international. Average age 42. 57 applicants, 70% accepted, 35 enrolled. In 2009, 20 master's, 26 doctorates awarded. *Degree requirements:* For master's, practicum; for doctorate, thesis/dissertation, practicum. *Entrance requirements:* For master's, interview, current employment in a position using technology; for doctorate, MAT, minimum GPA of 3.0, interview, current employment in a position using technology. Additional exam requirements/recommendations for international students: Recommended—TOEFL (minimum score 550 paper-based; 213 computer-based; 80 iBT), IELTS (minimum score 6). *Application deadline:* Applications are processed on a rolling basis. Application fee: $50. Electronic applications accepted. *Financial support:* Fellowships available. Financial award application deadline: 4/15; financial award applicants required to submit FAFSA. *Unit head:* Dr. Ronald Kern, Dean of Academic Affairs, 954-262-7809, Fax: 954-262-3606, E-mail: rk429@nsu.nova.edu. *Application contact:* Dr. Jennifer Quinones Nottingham, Dean of Student Affairs, 800-986-3223 Ext. 8500.

Saginaw Valley State University, College of Education, Program in E-Learning, University Center, MI 48710. Offers MA. *Students:* 3 full-time (2 women), 6 part-time (5 women); includes 1 minority (African American). Average age 40. 1 applicant, 100% accepted, 1 enrolled. *Entrance requirements:* Additional exam requirements/recommendations for international students: Required—TOEFL (minimum score 525 paper-based; 197 computer-based; 71 iBT). *Financial support:* Federal Work-Study and scholarships/grants available. Support available to part-time students. *Unit head:* Dr. Steve P. Barbus, Dean, 989-964-6067, Fax: 989-790-4385, E-mail: barbus@svsu.edu. *Application contact:* Kathy Lopez, Certification Officer, 989-964-4661, Fax: 989-964-4385, E-mail: klopez@svsu.edu.

Télé-université, Graduate Programs, Québec, QC G1K 9H5, Canada. Offers computer science (PhD); corporate finance (MS); distance learning (MS). Part-time programs available.

Thomas Edison State College, Heavin School of Arts and Sciences, Program in Online Learning and Teaching, Trenton, NJ 08608-1176. Offers Graduate Certificate. Part-time programs available. Postbaccalaureate distance learning degree programs offered (no on-campus study). *Students:* 28 part-time (21 women); includes 7 minority (6 African Americans, 1 Hispanic American), 1 international. Average age 47. In 2009, 7 Graduate Certificates awarded. *Entrance requirements:* Additional exam requirements/recommendations for international students: Required—TOEFL (minimum score 550 paper-based; 213 computer-based; 79 iBT). *Application deadline:* For fall admission, 8/15 priority date for domestic and international students; for winter admission, 11/15 priority date for domestic and international students; for spring admission, 2/15 priority date for domestic and international students. Applications are processed on a rolling basis. Application fee: $75. Electronic applications accepted. *Expenses:* Tuition, area resident: Part-time $479 per credit. Tuition, state resident: part-time $479 per credit. Tuition, nonresident: part-time $479 per credit. *Financial support:* Applicants required to submit FAFSA. *Unit head:* Dr. Susan Davenport, Dean, Heavin School of Arts and Sciences, 609-984-1130, Fax: 609-984-0740, E-mail: info@tesc.edu. *Application contact:* David Hoftiezer, Director of Admissions, 888-442-8372, Fax: 609-984-8447, E-mail: admissions@tesc.edu.

University of Maryland, Baltimore County, Graduate School, College of Arts, Humanities and Social Sciences, Department of Education, Program in Instructional Systems Development: Training Systems, Baltimore, MD 21250. Offers distance education (Graduate Certificate); e-learning in instructional design (Graduate Certificate); instructional systems development (MA, Graduate Certificate); instructional technology (Graduate Certificate). Part-time and evening/

weekend programs available. Postbaccalaureate distance learning degree programs offered (no on-campus study). *Faculty:* 2 full-time (0 women), 13 part-time/adjunct (5 women). *Students:* 107; includes 28 African Americans, 4 Asian Americans or Pacific Islanders, 7 Hispanic Americans. 48 applicants, 100% accepted, 42 enrolled. In 2009, 29 master's, 78 other advanced degrees awarded. *Degree requirements:* For master's, comprehensive exam. *Entrance requirements:* Additional exam requirements/recommendations for international students: Required—TOEFL. *Application deadline:* For fall admission, 7/1 priority date for domestic students, 1/1 for international students; for spring admission, 12/1 priority date for domestic students, 7/1 for international students. Application fee: $50. Electronic applications accepted. *Faculty research:* E-learning, distance education, instructional design. *Unit head:* Dr. Greg Williams, Department Chair, 410-455-6773, Fax: 410-455-1344, E-mail: gregw@umbc.edu. *Application contact:* Sharese Essien, Director, 410-455-8670, Fax: 410-455-1344, E-mail: sharese@umbc.edu.

University of Maryland University College, Graduate School of Management and Technology, Program in Distance Education, Adelphi, MD 20783. Offers MDE, Certificate. Part-time and evening/weekend programs available. Postbaccalaureate distance learning degree programs offered (no on-campus study). *Students:* 2 full-time (both women), 160 part-time (109 women); includes 58 minority (45 African Americans, 1 American Indian/Alaska Native, 6 Asian Americans or Pacific Islanders, 6 Hispanic Americans), 2 international. Average age 42. 87 applicants, 100% accepted, 32 enrolled. In 2009, 20 master's, 29 other advanced degrees awarded. *Degree requirements:* For master's, thesis or alternative. *Application deadline:* Applications are processed on a rolling basis. Application fee: $50. Electronic applications accepted. *Expenses:* Tuition, state resident: full-time $7704; part-time $428 per credit hour. Tuition, nonresident: full-time $11,862; part-time $659 per credit hour. *Financial support:* Federal Work-Study and scholarships/grants available. Support available to part-time students. Financial award application deadline: 6/1; financial award applicants required to submit FAFSA. *Unit head:* Dr. Stella Porto, Director, 240-684-2400, Fax: 240-684-2401, E-mail: sporto@umuc.edu. *Application contact:* Coordinator, Graduate Admissions, 800-888-UMUC, Fax: 240-684-2151, E-mail: newgrad@umuc.edu.

University of Nebraska–Lincoln, Graduate College, College of Agricultural Sciences and Natural Resources, Department of Agricultural Leadership, Education and Communication, Lincoln, NE 68588. Offers distance education specialization (MS); leadership development (MS); leadership education (MS); nutrition outreach education specialization (MS); teaching and extension education specialization (MS). *Degree requirements:* For master's, thesis optional. *Entrance requirements:* For master's, resume. Additional exam requirements/recommendations for international students: Required—TOEFL (minimum score 550 paper-based; 213 computer-based). Electronic applications accepted. *Faculty research:* Teaching and instruction, extension education, leadership and human resource development, international agricultural education.

University of Wyoming, College of Education, Department of Adult Learning and Technology, Laramie, WY 82070. Offers adult and postsecondary education (MA, Ed D, PhD, Ed S); distance education (Ed D, PhD); instructional technology (MS, Ed D, PhD). Part-time programs available. Postbaccalaureate distance learning degree programs offered (no on-campus study). *Degree requirements:* For master's, thesis or alternative; for doctorate, comprehensive exam, thesis/dissertation. *Entrance requirements:* For master's, GRE, minimum GPA of 3.0; for doctorate, MS or MA, minimum GPA of 3.0. Additional exam requirements/recommendations for international students: Required—TOEFL. Electronic applications accepted. *Faculty research:* Web based instruction, instructional decision, adult education history, literacy in adults, international distance education.

Virginia Polytechnic Institute and State University, VT Online, Blacksburg, VA 24061. Offers aerospace engineering (MS); business information systems (Graduate Certificate); career and technical education (MS); computer engineering (M Eng, MS); decision support systems (Graduate Certificate); eLearning leadership (MA); electrical engineering (M Eng, MS); engineering administration (MEA); environmental politics and policy (Graduate Certificate); foundations of political analysis (Graduate Certificate); health product risk management (Graduate Certificate); information policy and society (Graduate Certificate); information security (Graduate Certificate); instructional technology (MA); liberal arts (Graduate Certificate); life sciences: health product risk management (MS); natural resources (MNR, Graduate Certificate); networking (Graduate Certificate); nonprofit and nongovernmental organization management (Graduate Certificate); ocean engineering (MS); political science (MA); security studies (Graduate Certificate); software development (Graduate Certificate). *Expenses:* Tuition, area resident: Full-time $10,228; part-time $459 per credit hour. Tuition, nonresident: full-time $17,892; part-time $865 per credit hour. Required fees: $1966; $451 per semester.

Walden University, Graduate Programs, Richard W. Riley College of Education and Leadership, Minneapolis, MN 55401. Offers administrator leadership for teaching and learning (Ed D, Ed S); curriculum, instruction, and professional development (Ed S); early childhood education (birth-grade 3) (MAT); education (MS, PhD), including adolescent literacy and technology (grades 6-12) (MS), adult education leadership (PhD), community college leadership (PhD), curriculum, instruction, and assessment, early childhood education (PhD), educational leadership (MS), educational technology (PhD), elementary reading and literacy (MS), elementary reading and mathematics (MS), emotional/behavioral disorders (K-12) (MS), general program, higher education (PhD), integrating technology in the classroom (MS), K-12 educational leadership (PhD), learning disabilities (K-12) (MS), literacy and learning in the content areas (MS), mathematics (grades 6-8) (MS), mathematics (grades K-5) (MS), middle level education (grades 5-8) (MS), professional development (MS), science (grades K-8) (MS), self-designed (PhD), special education (PhD), special education (non-licensure) (MS), teacher leadership (grades K-12) (MS); educational leadership and administration (principal preparation) (Ed S); educational technology (Ed S); higher education and adult learning (Ed D); instructional design (Postbaccalaureate Certificate); instructional design and technology (MS), including general program (MS, PhD), online learning, training and performance improvement; special education: emotional/behavioral disorders (K-12) (MAT); special education: learning disabilities (K-12) (MAT); teacher leadership (Ed D, Ed S). Part-time and evening/weekend programs available. Postbaccalaureate distance learning degree programs offered (minimal on-campus study). *Faculty:* 54 full-time, 835 part-time/adjunct. *Students:* 13,940 full-time (11,339 women), 1,940 part-time (1,637 women); includes 4,626 minority (3,795 African Americans, 111 American Indian/Alaska Native, 199 Asian Americans or Pacific Islanders, 521 Hispanic Americans), 124 international. Average age 38. In 2009, 4,688 master's, 190 doctorates awarded. *Degree requirements:* For doctorate, thesis/dissertation (for some programs), residency; for other advanced degree, residency (for some programs). *Entrance requirements:* For master's, bachelor's degree or equivalent in related field; minimum GPA of 2.5; official transcripts; goal statement; access to computer and Internet; for doctorate, master's degree or equivalent in related field; minimum GPA of 3.0; official transcripts; three years' related professional/academic experience (preferred); access to computer and Internet; for other advanced degree, master's degree or equivalent in related field; minimum GPA of 3.0; 3 years related professional/academic experience (preferred); access to computer and Internet (Ed S). Additional exam requirements/recommendations for international students: Required—TOEFL (minimum score 550 paper-based; 213 computer-based), IELTS (minimum score 6.5), or Michigan English Language Assessment Battery (minimum score 82). *Application deadline:* Applications are processed on a rolling basis. Application fee: $50. Electronic applications accepted. *Expenses:* Tuition: Full-time $13,665; part-time $560 per credit. Required fees: $1375. Tuition and fees vary according to course load, degree level and program. *Financial support:* In 2009–10, 2,418 students received support; fellowships, Federal Work-Study, scholarships/grants, unspecified assistantships, and family tuition reduction, active duty/veteran tuition reduction, group tuition reduction, interest-free payment plans available. Support available to part-time students. Financial award applicants required to submit FAFSA. *Unit head:* Dr. Kate Steffens, Dean, 800-925-3368. *Application contact:* Jennifer Hall, Director of Enrollment, 866-4-WALDEN, E-mail: info@waldenu.edu.

Western Illinois University, School of Graduate Studies, College of Education and Human Services, Department of Instructional Design and Technology, Macomb, IL 61455-1390. Offers distance learning (Certificate); graphic applications (Certificate); instructional design and technology (MS); multimedia (Certificate); technology integration in education (Certificate); training development (Certificate). Part-time programs available. Postbaccalaureate distance learning degree programs offered (no on-campus study). *Students:* 23 full-time (13 women), 56 part-time (37 women); includes 18 minority (12 African Americans, 2 American Indian/Alaska Native, 3 Asian Americans or Pacific Islanders, 1 Hispanic American), 8 international. Average age 36. 18 applicants, 72% accepted. In 2009, 25 master's, 2 other advanced degrees awarded. *Degree requirements:* For master's, thesis or alternative. *Entrance requirements:* Additional exam requirements/recommendations for international students: Required—TOEFL (minimum score 550 paper-based; 213 computer-based; 80 iBT). *Application deadline:* Applications are processed on a rolling basis. Application fee: $30. Electronic applications accepted. *Expenses:* Tuition, state resident: full-time $4486; part-time $249.21 per credit hour. Tuition, nonresident: full-time $8972; part-time $498.42 per credit hour. Required fees: $72.62 per credit hour. *Financial support:* In 2009–10, 16 students received support, including 11 research assistantships with full tuition reimbursements available (averaging $7,280 per year), 5 teaching assistantships with full tuition reimbursements available (averaging $8,400 per year). Financial award applicants required to submit FAFSA. *Unit head:* Dr. Hoyet Hemphill, Chairperson, 309-298-1952. *Application contact:* Evelyn Hoing, Assistant Director of Graduate Studies, 309-298-1806, Fax: 309-298-2345, E-mail: grad-office@wiu.edu.

Wilkes University, College of Graduate and Professional Studies, School of Education, Wilkes-Barre, PA 18766-0002. Offers classroom technology (MS Ed); educational computing (MS Ed); educational development and strategies (MS Ed); educational leadership (MS Ed); educational technology (Ed D); elementary education (MS Ed); higher education administration (Ed D); instructional technology (MS Ed); K-12 administration (Ed D); online teaching (MS Ed); school business leadership (MS Ed); secondary education (MS Ed), including biology, chemistry, English, history; special education (MS Ed). Part-time and evening/weekend programs available. Postbaccalaureate distance learning degree programs offered (minimal on-campus study). *Students:* 89 full-time (60 women), 2,849 part-time (2,058 women); includes 52 minority (10 African Americans, 2 American Indian/Alaska Native, 13 Asian Americans or Pacific Islanders, 27 Hispanic Americans), 6 international. Average age 33. In 2009, 947 master's awarded. *Entrance requirements:* Additional exam requirements/recommendations for international students: Required—TOEFL (minimum score 500 paper-based; 173 computer-based; 79 iBT). *Application deadline:* Applications are processed on a rolling basis. Application fee: $45. *Expenses:* Contact institution. *Financial support:* Federal Work-Study and unspecified assistantships available. Financial award application deadline: 3/1; financial award applicants required to submit FAFSA. *Unit head:* Dr. Michael Speziale, Dean, 570-408-4679, Fax: 570-408-4905, E-mail: michael.speziale@wilkes.edu. *Application contact:* Kathleen Houlihan, Director of Graduate Studies, 570-408-3235, Fax: 570-408-7846, E-mail: kathleen.houlihan@wilkes.edu.

Educational Leadership and Administration

Abilene Christian University, Graduate School, College of Education and Human Services, Graduate Studies in Education, Leadership of Learning Program, Abilene, TX 79699-9100. Offers M Ed. Part-time programs available. Postbaccalaureate distance learning degree programs offered (no on-campus study). *Students:* 10 full-time (all women), 106 part-time (69 women); includes 14 minority (7 African Americans, 1 Asian American or Pacific Islander, 6 Hispanic Americans). 61 applicants, 61% accepted, 35 enrolled. In 2009, 38 master's awarded. *Degree requirements:* For master's, comprehensive exam. *Application deadline:* For fall admission, 4/1 priority date for domestic students; for spring admission, 11/1 for domestic students. Applications are processed on a rolling basis. Application fee: $40. Electronic applications accepted. *Expenses:* Tuition: Full-time $11,520; part-time $640 per hour. Required fees: $1090; $53.50 per hour. $10 per term. Tuition and fees vary according to program. *Financial support:* In 2009–10, 80 students received support. Application deadline: 4/1. *Unit head:* Dr. Donnie Snider, Graduate Advisor, 325-674-2977, Fax: 325-674-2123, E-mail: donnie.snider@acu.edu. *Application contact:* William Horn, Graduate Admissions Counselor, 325-674-2656, Fax: 325-674-6717, E-mail: gradinfo@acu.edu.

Acadia University, Faculty of Professional Studies, School of Education, Program in Leadership, Wolfville, NS B4P 2R6, Canada. Offers M Ed. Part-time and evening/weekend programs available. *Faculty:* 2 full-time (1 woman). *Students:* 2 full-time (0 women), 49 part-time (33 women). 83 applicants, 81% accepted. In 2009, 24 master's awarded. *Degree requirements:* For master's, thesis optional. *Entrance requirements:* For master's, B Ed or the equivalent, 2 years teaching or related experience. Additional exam requirements/recommendations for international students: Required—TOEFL (minimum score 580 paper-based; 237 computer-based; 93 iBT), IELTS (minimum score 6.5). *Application deadline:* For fall admission, 3/15 priority date for domestic and international students. Application fee: $50. Electronic applications accepted. *Financial support:* In 2009–10, teaching assistantships (averaging $4,000 per year). Financial award application deadline: 3/15. *Faculty research:* Organizational theory and structural change, professionalism, sexuality education. *Unit head:* Ann Vibert, Director, E-mail: ann.vibert@acadiau.ca. *Application contact:* Sheila Langille, Secretary, 902-585-1229, Fax: 902-585-1071, E-mail: sheila.langille@acadiau.ca.

Adelphi University, School of Education, Program in Educational Leadership and Technology, Garden City, NY 11530-0701. Offers MA, Certificate. *Students:* 11 full-time (7 women), 53 part-time (39 women); includes 36 minority (24 African Americans, 3 Asian Americans or Pacific Islanders, 9 Hispanic Americans). Average age 39. In 2009, 36 master's, 12 other advanced degrees awarded. *Entrance requirements:* For master's, 2 letters of recommendation, resume, letter attesting to teaching experience (3 years full-time K-12). Additional exam requirements/recommendations for international students: Required—TOEFL (minimum score 550 paper-based; 213 computer-based; 80 iBT). *Application deadline:* For fall admission, 8/15 priority date for domestic students, 4/1 for international students; for spring admission, 1/15 priority date for domestic students, 11/1 for international students. Applications are processed on a rolling basis. Application fee: $50. Electronic applications accepted. *Expenses:* Tuition: Full-time $28,340; part-time $830 per credit. Required fees: $600; $250 per credit. Full-time tuition and fees vary according to course load and program. *Financial support:* Research assistantships with partial tuition reimbursements, institutionally sponsored loans available. Financial award application deadline: 2/15; financial award applicants required to submit FAFSA. *Faculty research:* Technology methodology focusing on in-service and preservice curriculum. *Unit head:* Dr. Devin Thornburg, Director, 516-877-4026, E-mail: thornburg@adelphi.edu. *Application contact:* Christine Murphy, Director of Admissions, 516-877-3050, Fax: 516-877-3039, E-mail: graduateadmissions@adelphi.edu.

Alabama Agricultural and Mechanical University, School of Graduate Studies, School of Education, Area in Secondary Education, Huntsville, AL 35811. Offers education (M Ed, Ed S);

Educational Leadership and Administration

Alabama Agricultural and Mechanical University (continued)
higher administration (MS). *Accreditation:* NCATE. Evening/weekend programs available. *Degree requirements:* For master's, comprehensive exam; for Ed S, thesis. *Entrance requirements:* For master's, GRE General Test. Additional exam requirements/recommendations for international students: Required—TOEFL (minimum score 500 paper-based; 173 computer-based; 61 iBT). Electronic applications accepted. *Faculty research:* World peace through education, computer-assisted instruction.

Alabama State University, School of Graduate Studies, College of Education, Department of Instructional Support, Program in Educational Administration, Montgomery, AL 36101-0271. Offers educational administration (M Ed, Ed S); educational leadership, policy and law (Ed D). Part-time programs available. *Degree requirements:* For master's, comprehensive exam, thesis optional; for Ed S, thesis. *Entrance requirements:* For master's, GRE General Test, MAT, graduate writing competency test; for Ed S, graduate writing competency test, GRE, MAT. Additional exam requirements/recommendations for international students: Required—TOEFL (minimum score 500 paper-based; 173 computer-based). *Faculty research:* Nontraditional roles, computer applications for principals, women in educational administration.

Albany State University, College of Education, Program in Educational Leadership, Albany, GA 31705-2717. Offers M Ed, Ed S. *Accreditation:* NCATE. Evening/weekend programs available. *Students:* 10 full-time (6 women), 4 part-time (2 women); includes 9 minority (all African Americans). Average age 38. 3 applicants, 100% accepted, 3 enrolled. In 2009, 8 master's, 20 Ed Ss awarded. *Degree requirements:* For master's, comprehensive exam, internship. *Entrance requirements:* For master's, GRE General Test, MAT, GACE I, minimum overall GPA of 2.5, teacher certification, 3 letters of reference from individuals in the school or school system; for Ed S, GACE II in educational leadership, master's degree at accredited or approved institution, Georgia's Level 5 certification or higher, three letters of reference, letter of employment or intent to hire from the employing Superintendent for leadership position. Additional exam requirements/recommendations for international students: Required—TOEFL. *Application deadline:* For fall admission, 11/16 for domestic students, 9/16 for international students; for spring admission, 4/19 for domestic students, 2/19 for international students. Applications are processed on a rolling basis. Application fee: $20. Electronic applications accepted. *Expenses:* Tuition, state resident: full-time $2970; part-time $162 per credit hour. Tuition, nonresident: full-time $12,168; part-time $676 per credit hour. Required fees: $962; $75 per credit hour. *Financial support:* Application deadline: 6/30. *Unit head:* Dr. Deborah Bembry, Chair, 229-430-4715, Fax: 229-430-4993, E-mail: deborah.bembry@asurams.edu. *Application contact:* Nicole Lane, Interim Graduate Admissions Officer, 229-430-4862, Fax: 229-430-6398, E-mail: nicole.lane@asurams.edu.

Alliant International University–Fresno, Graduate School of Education, Program in Educational Leadership, Fresno, CA 93727. Offers educational leadership and management (Ed D). Part-time programs available. *Entrance requirements:* For doctorate, minimum GPA of 3.0, letters of recommendation. Additional exam requirements/recommendations for international students: Required—TOEFL (minimum score 550 paper-based; 213 computer-based), TWE (minimum score 5). Electronic applications accepted. *Faculty research:* School administration, cross cultural leadership.

Alliant International University–Irvine, Graduate School of Education, Educational Leadership Programs, Irvine, CA 92612. Offers educational administration (MA, Credential); educational leadership and management (K-12) (Ed D); higher education (Ed D); preliminary administrative services (Credential). Part-time programs available. *Entrance requirements:* For master's and doctorate, minimum GPA of 3.0, letters of recommendation. Additional exam requirements/recommendations for international students: Required—TOEFL (minimum score 550 paper-based; 213 computer-based), TWE (minimum score 5). Electronic applications accepted.

Alliant International University–Los Angeles, Graduate School of Education, Educational Leadership Programs, Alhambra, CA 91803-1360. Offers educational administration (MA); educational leadership and management (K-12) (Ed D); higher education (Ed D); preliminary administrative services (Credential). Part-time programs available. *Entrance requirements:* For master's and doctorate, minimum GPA of 3.0, letters of recommendation. Additional exam requirements/recommendations for international students: Required—TOEFL (minimum score 550 paper-based; 213 computer-based), TWE (minimum score 5).

Alliant International University–San Diego, Graduate School of Education, Educational Leadership Programs, San Diego, CA 92131-1799. Offers educational administration (MA); educational leadership and management (K-12) (Ed D); higher education (Ed D, Certificate); preliminary administrative services (Credential). Part-time programs available. *Entrance requirements:* For master's and doctorate, minimum GPA of 3.0, letters of recommendation. Additional exam requirements/recommendations for international students: Required—TOEFL (minimum score 550 paper-based; 213 computer-based), TWE (minimum score 5). Electronic applications accepted.

Alliant International University–San Francisco, Graduate School of Education, Educational Leadership Programs, San Francisco, CA 94133-1221. Offers community college administration (Ed D); educational administration (MA); educational leadership and management (K-12) (Ed D); higher education (Ed D); preliminary administrative services (Credential); university administration (Ed D). Part-time programs available. *Entrance requirements:* For master's and doctorate, minimum GPA of 3.0, letters of recommendation. Additional exam requirements/recommendations for international students: Required—TOEFL (minimum score 550 paper-based; 213 computer-based), TWE (minimum score 5). Electronic applications accepted. *Faculty research:* Leadership in higher education, community colleges.

Alverno College, School of Education, Milwaukee, WI 53234-3922. Offers adaptive education (MA); administrative leadership (MA); adult education and organizational development (MA); adult educational and instructional design (MA); adult educational and instructional technology (MA); global connections in the humanities (MA); instructional leadership (MA); instructional technology for K-12 settings (MA); professional development (MA); reading education (MA); reading education with adaptive education (MA); science education (MA); teaching in alternative schools (MA). *Accreditation:* NCATE. Part-time and evening/weekend programs available. *Faculty:* 10 full-time (all women), 17 part-time/adjunct (15 women). *Students:* 65 full-time (59 women), 82 part-time (75 women); includes 31 minority (24 African Americans, 1 American Indian/Alaska Native, 1 Asian American or Pacific Islander, 5 Hispanic Americans), 2 international. Average age 38. 113 applicants, 64% accepted, 61 enrolled. In 2009, 56 master's awarded. *Degree requirements:* For master's, presentation/defense of proposal, conference presentation of inquiry projects. *Entrance requirements:* For master's, bachelor's degree in related field, communication samples from work setting, 3 letters of recommendation. Additional exam requirements/recommendations for international students: Required—TOEFL. *Application deadline:* For fall admission, 7/15 priority date for domestic and international students; for spring admission, 12/15 priority date for domestic and international students. Applications are processed on a rolling basis. Application fee: $50. Electronic applications accepted. *Financial support:* In 2009–10, 92 students received support. Federal Work-Study available. Support available to part-time students. Financial award application deadline: 4/15; financial award applicants required to submit FAFSA. *Faculty research:* Student self-assessment, self-reflection, integration of curriculum, identifying needs of students in strategic situations and designing appropriate classroom strategies. *Unit head:* Dr. Mary Diez, Graduate Dean, 414-382-6214, Fax: 414-382-6332, E-mail: mary.diez@alverno.edu. *Application contact:* Angela Peterson-Adams, Graduate Recruiter, 414-382-6104, Fax: 414-382-6354, E-mail: angela.peterson-adams@alverno.edu.

American InterContinental University Online, Program in Education, Hoffman Estates, IL 60192. Offers curriculum and instruction (M Ed); educational assessment and evaluation (M Ed); instructional technology (M Ed); leadership of educational organizations (M Ed). Evening/weekend programs available. Postbaccalaureate distance learning degree programs offered (no on-campus study). *Entrance requirements:* Additional exam requirements/recommendations for international students: Required—TOEFL (minimum score 550 paper-based; 213 computer-based). Electronic applications accepted.

American International College, School of Arts, Education and Sciences, Department of Education, Springfield, MA 01109-3189. Offers early childhood education (M Ed, CAGS); educational leadership and supervision (Ed D); elementary education (M Ed, CAGS); middle/secondary education (M Ed, CAGS); moderate disabilities (M Ed, CAGS); reading (M Ed, CAGS); school adjustment counseling (MA, CAGS); school administration (M Ed, CAGS); school guidance counseling (MA, CAGS); teaching (MA, MS); teaching and learning (Ed D). Part-time and evening/weekend programs available. Terminal master's awarded for partial completion of doctoral program. *Degree requirements:* For master's, comprehensive exam (for some programs), thesis (for some programs), practicum; for doctorate, comprehensive exam (for some programs), thesis/dissertation; for CAGS, practicum. *Entrance requirements:* For master's, minimum B- average in undergraduate course work; for doctorate, GRE General Test, interview. Additional exam requirements/recommendations for international students: Required—TOEFL. Electronic applications accepted. *Expenses:* Tuition: Full-time $12,510; part-time $695 per credit hour. Required fees: $35 per term.

Andrews University, School of Graduate Studies, School of Education, Department of Leadership and Educational Administration, Program in Educational Administration and Leadership, Berrien Springs, MI 49104. Offers MA, Ed D, PhD, Ed S. *Faculty:* 4 full-time (0 women). *Students:* 6 full-time (2 women), 27 part-time (13 women); includes 13 minority (10 African Americans, 2 Asian Americans or Pacific Islanders, 1 Hispanic American), 13 international. Average age 42. 31 applicants, 58% accepted, 8 enrolled. In 2009, 1 master's awarded. *Degree requirements:* For master's, thesis or alternative; for doctorate, thesis/dissertation. *Entrance requirements:* For master's and doctorate, GRE Subject Test. Additional exam requirements/recommendations for international students: Required—TOEFL (minimum score 550 paper-based). *Application deadline:* Applications are processed on a rolling basis. Application fee: $40. *Financial support:* Research assistantships available. *Unit head:* Dr. Gary Gifford, Coordinator, 269-471-6682. *Application contact:* Carolyn Hurst, Supervisor of Graduate Admission, 800-253-2874, Fax: 269-471-6321, E-mail: graduate@andrews.edu.

Andrews University, School of Graduate Studies, School of Education, Department of Leadership and Educational Administration, Program in Leadership, Berrien Springs, MI 49104. Offers MA, Ed D, PhD. *Students:* 2 full-time (0 women), 114 part-time (57 women); includes 33 minority (17 African Americans, 3 American Indian/Alaska Native, 2 Asian Americans or Pacific Islanders, 11 Hispanic Americans), 13 international. Average age 49. 23 applicants, 43% accepted, 6 enrolled. In 2009, 1 master's, 7 doctorates awarded. *Entrance requirements:* For master's, GRE. Additional exam requirements/recommendations for international students: Required—TOEFL (minimum score 550 paper-based). Application fee: $40. *Unit head:* Dr. Erich Baumgartener, Chair, 269-471-2523. *Application contact:* Carolyn Hurst, Supervisor of Graduate Admission, 800-253-2874, Fax: 269-471-6321, E-mail: graduate@andrews.edu.

Angelo State University, College of Graduate Studies, College of Education, Department of Curriculum and Instruction, Program in School Administration, San Angelo, TX 76909. Offers principal (Certificate); school administration (M Ed); superintendent (Certificate). Part-time and evening/weekend programs available. *Faculty:* 17 full-time (12 women). *Students:* 5 full-time (2 women), 71 part-time (28 women); includes 14 minority (2 African Americans, 12 Hispanic Americans). Average age 40. 26 applicants, 100% accepted, 19 enrolled. In 2009, 13 master's awarded. *Degree requirements:* For master's, comprehensive exam. *Entrance requirements:* For master's, GRE General Test, minimum GPA of 2.5. Additional exam requirements/recommendations for international students: Required—TOEFL or IELTS. *Application deadline:* For fall admission, 7/15 priority date for domestic students, 6/10 for international students; for spring admission, 12/1 priority date for domestic students, 11/1 for international students. Applications are processed on a rolling basis. Application fee: $40 ($50 for international students). Electronic applications accepted. *Expenses:* Tuition, state resident: full-time $3396; part-time $142 per credit hour. Tuition, nonresident: full-time $10,152; part-time $423 per credit hour. Required fees: $1786; $36.25 per credit hour. $494 per semester. Full-time tuition and fees vary according to course load, degree level and program. *Financial support:* In 2009–10, 19 students received support. Career-related internships or fieldwork, Federal Work-Study, scholarships/grants, and unspecified assistantships available. Support available to part-time students. Financial award application deadline: 3/1; financial award applicants required to submit FAFSA. *Unit head:* Dr. James Summerlin, 325-942-2052 Ext. 266, Fax: 325-942-2039, E-mail: jsummerlin@angelo.edu. *Application contact:* Theresa Fortin, Graduate Admissions Assistant, 325-942-2169, Fax: 325-942-2194, E-mail: theresa.fortin@angelo.edu.

Antioch University New England, Graduate School, Department of Organization and Management, Program in Administration and Supervision, Keene, NH 03431-3552. Offers M Ed. *Degree requirements:* For master's, practicum. *Entrance requirements:* For master's, previous course work and work experience in organization and management. Additional exam requirements/recommendations for international students: Required—TOEFL (minimum score 600 paper-based; 250 computer-based). Electronic applications accepted. *Expenses:* Contact institution. *Faculty research:* Collaborative research programs in Waldorf schools and communities, shared decision making in schools, rational to creative problem solving, competency to shift paradigms of thinking.

Appalachian State University, Cratis D. Williams Graduate School, Department of Leadership and Educational Studies, Boone, NC 28608. Offers educational administration (Ed S); educational media (MA); higher education (MA, Ed S); library science (MLS); school administration (MSA). Part-time and evening/weekend programs available. Postbaccalaureate distance learning degree programs offered (no on-campus study). *Faculty:* 25 full-time (10 women), 28 part-time/adjunct (16 women). *Students:* 48 full-time (35 women), 474 part-time (373 women); includes 24 minority (21 African Americans, 2 Asian Americans or Pacific Islanders, 1 Hispanic American), 2 international. 229 applicants, 89% accepted, 156 enrolled. In 2009, 133 master's, 32 other advanced degrees awarded. *Degree requirements:* For master's and Ed S, comprehensive exam, thesis optional. *Entrance requirements:* For master's and Ed S, GRE or MAT, 3 letters of recommendation. Additional exam requirements/recommendations for international students: Required—TOEFL (minimum score 570 paper-based; 230 computer-based; 79 iBT), IELTS (minimum score 6.5). *Application deadline:* For fall admission, 7/1 for domestic students, 2/1 for international students; for spring admission, 11/1 for domestic students, 7/1 for international students. Applications are processed on a rolling basis. Application fee: $50. Electronic applications accepted. *Expenses:* Tuition, state resident: full-time $2960. Tuition, nonresident: full-time $14,051. Required fees: $2320. *Financial support:* In 2009–10, 10 research assistantships (averaging $8,000 per year) were awarded; career-related internships or fieldwork, scholarships/grants, and unspecified assistantships also available. Financial award application deadline: 4/1; financial award applicants required to submit FAFSA. *Faculty research:* Brain, learning and meditation; leadership of teaching and learning. Total annual research expenditures: $475,000. *Unit head:* Dr. Richard Riedl, Interim Director, 828-262-3112, E-mail: reidlr@appstate.edu. *Application contact:* Lori Dean, Graduate Student Coordinator, 828-262-6041, E-mail: deanlk@appstate.edu.

Appalachian State University, Cratis D. Williams Graduate School, Program in Educational Leadership, Boone, NC 28608. Offers Ed D. *Accreditation:* NCATE. Part-time programs available. Postbaccalaureate distance learning degree programs offered (no on-campus study). *Students:* 6 full-time (4 women), 87 part-time (48 women); includes 9 minority (7 African Americans, 1 Asian American or Pacific Islander, 1 Hispanic American), 1 international. 40 applicants, 75% accepted, 28 enrolled. In 2009, 5 doctorates awarded. *Degree requirements:* For doctorate, comprehensive exam, thesis/dissertation. *Entrance requirements:* For doctorate, GRE General Test, 4 letters of recommendation. Additional exam requirements/recommendations for international students: Required—TOEFL (minimum score 570 paper-based; 230 computer-based; 79 iBT), or IELTS (minimum score 6.5). *Application deadline:* For fall admission, 3/1 for domestic students, 2/1 for international students; for spring admission, 7/1 for international students. Application fee: $50. Electronic applications accepted. *Expenses:* Tuition, state resident: full-time $2960. Tuition, nonresident: full-time $14,051. Required fees: $2320. *Financial*

support: In 2009–10, 8 research assistantships (averaging $16,000 per year) were awarded; Federal Work-Study, scholarships/grants, and unspecified assistantships also available. Financial award application deadline: 4/1; financial award applicants required to submit FAFSA. *Faculty research:* Sustainability of organizations, cultural pedagogy. *Unit head:* Dr. C. James Killacky, Director, 828-262-3168, E-mail: killackycj@appstate.edu. *Application contact:* Susan Musilli, Graduate Student Coordinator, 828-262-3168, E-mail: musillism@appstate.edu.

Arcadia University, Graduate Studies, Department of Education, Glenside, PA 19038-3295. Offers art education (M Ed, MA Ed); biology education (MA Ed); chemistry education (MA Ed); child development (CAS); computer education (M Ed, CAS); computer education 7–12 (MA Ed); early childhood education (M Ed, CAS), including individualized (M Ed), master teacher (M Ed), research in child development (M Ed); educational leadership (M Ed, CAS); educational psychology (CAS); elementary education (M Ed, CAS); English education (MA Ed); environmental education (MA Ed, CAS); history education (MA Ed); language arts (M Ed, CAS); mathematics education (M Ed, MA Ed, CAS); music education (MA Ed); psychology (MA Ed); pupil personnel services (CAS); reading (M Ed, CAS); school library science (M Ed); science education (M Ed, CAS); secondary education (M Ed, CAS); special education (M Ed, Ed D, CAS); theater arts (MA Ed); written communication (MA Ed). *Accreditation:* NASAD. Part-time and evening/weekend programs available. Postbaccalaureate distance learning degree programs offered (minimal on-campus study). *Faculty:* 12 full-time (8 women), 38 part-time/adjunct (26 women). *Students:* 89 full-time (74 women), 622 part-time (487 women); includes 112 minority (94 African Americans, 9 Asian Americans or Pacific Islanders, 9 Hispanic Americans), 2 international. Average age 32. In 2009, 257 master's, 4 doctorates awarded. *Application deadline:* Applications are processed on a rolling basis. Application fee: $40. Electronic applications accepted. *Expenses:* Tuition: Full-time $30,450; part-time $620 per credit hour. Required fees: $165. Tuition and fees vary according to program. *Financial support:* Career-related internships or fieldwork, tuition waivers (partial), and unspecified assistantships available. *Unit head:* Dr. Steven P. Gulkus. *Application contact:* 215-572-2925, Fax: 215-572-2126, E-mail: grad@arcadia.edu.

Argosy University, Atlanta, College of Education, Atlanta, GA 30328. Offers educational leadership (MAEd, Ed D, Ed S), including higher education administration (Ed D), K-12 education (Ed D); teaching and learning (MAEd, Ed D, Ed S), including education technology (Ed D), higher education (Ed D), K-12 education (Ed D).

See Close-Up on page 887.

Argosy University, Chicago, College of Education, Chicago, IL 60601. Offers adult education and training (MA Ed); community college executive leadership (Ed D); educational leadership (MA Ed, Ed D, Ed S), including district leadership (Ed D), higher education administration (Ed D), K-12 education (Ed D); instructional leadership (Ed D, Ed S), including higher education (Ed D), K-12 education (Ed D). Postbaccalaureate distance learning degree programs offered (minimal on-campus study).

See Close-Up on page 675.

Argosy University, Dallas, College of Education, Farmers Branch, TX 75244. Offers educational administration (MA Ed); educational leadership (Ed D); higher and postsecondary education (MA Ed); instructional leadership (MA Ed); school psychology (MA).

See Close-Up on page 677.

Argosy University, Denver, College of Education, Denver, CO 80231. Offers community college executive leadership (Ed D); educational leadership (MA Ed, Ed D), including higher education (Ed D), K-12 education (Ed D); instructional leadership (MA Ed, Ed D), including higher education administration (Ed D), K-12 education (Ed D).

See Close-Up on page 679.

Argosy University, Hawai'i, College of Education, Honolulu, HI 96813. Offers adult education and training (MAEd); educational leadership (Ed D), including higher education administration, K-12 education; instructional leadership (Ed D), including higher education, K-12 education; school psychology (MA).

See Close-Up on page 681.

Argosy University, Inland Empire, College of Education, San Bernardino, CA 92408. Offers community college executive leadership (Ed D); educational leadership (MA Ed, Ed D), including higher education administration (Ed D), K-12 education (Ed D); instructional leadership (MA Ed, Ed D), including higher education (Ed D), K-12 education (Ed D), multiple subject teacher preparation (MA Ed), single subject teacher preparation (MA Ed).

See Close-Up on page 889.

Argosy University, Los Angeles, College of Education, Santa Monica, CA 90045. Offers community college executive leadership (Ed D); educational leadership (MA Ed, Ed D), including higher education administration (Ed D), K-12 education (Ed D); instructional leadership (MA Ed, Ed D), including higher education (Ed D), K-12 education (Ed D), multiple subject teacher preparation (MA Ed), single subject teacher preparation (MA Ed).

See Close-Up on page 683.

Argosy University, Nashville, College of Education, Program in Educational Leadership, Nashville, TN 37214. Offers educational leadership (MA Ed, Ed S); higher education administration (Ed D); K-12 education (Ed D).

See Close-Up on page 891.

Argosy University, Nashville, College of Education, Program in Instructional Leadership, Nashville, TN 37214. Offers education technology (Ed D); higher education administration (Ed D); instructional leadership (MA Ed, Ed S); K-12 education (Ed D).

See Close-Up on page 891.

Argosy University, Orange County, College of Education, Orange, CA 92868. Offers community college executive leadership (Ed D); educational leadership (MA Ed, Ed D), including higher education administration (Ed D), K-12 education (Ed D); instructional leadership (MA Ed, Ed D), including education technology (Ed D), higher education (Ed D), K-12 education (Ed D), multiple subject teacher preparation (MA Ed), single subject teacher preparation (MA Ed).

See Close-Up on page 685.

Argosy University, Phoenix, College of Education, Phoenix, AZ 85021. Offers adult education and training (MA Ed); advanced educational administration (Ed D, Ed S); community college executive leadership (Ed D); educational administration (MA Ed); educational leadership (MA Ed, Ed D, Ed S), including education technology (Ed D), higher education administration (Ed D), K-12 education (Ed D); higher and postsecondary education (MA Ed); initial educational administration (Ed D, Ed S); school psychology (MA); teaching and learning (MA Ed, Ed D, Ed S), including education technology (Ed D), higher education (Ed D), K-12 education (Ed D).

See Close-Up on page 687.

Argosy University, Salt Lake City, College of Education, Draper, UT 84020. Offers educational leadership (MA Ed, Ed D).

See Close-Up on page 689.

Argosy University, San Diego, College of Education, San Diego, CA 92108. Offers community college executive leadership (Ed D); educational leadership (MA Ed, Ed D), including higher education administration (Ed D), K-12 education (Ed D); instructional leadership (MA Ed, Ed D), including higher education (Ed D), K-12 education (Ed D).

See Close-Up on page 691.

Argosy University, San Francisco Bay Area, College of Education, Alameda, CA 94501. Offers community college executive leadership (Ed D); educational leadership (MA Ed, Ed D), including education technology (Ed D), higher education administration (Ed D), K-12 education (Ed D); instructional leadership (MA Ed, Ed D), including education technology (Ed D), higher education (Ed D), K-12 education (Ed D), multiple subject teacher preparation (MA Ed), single subject teacher preparation (MA Ed).

See Close-Up on page 693.

Argosy University, Sarasota, College of Education, Sarasota, FL 34235. Offers community college executive leadership (Ed D); educational leadership (MA Ed, Ed D, Ed S), including higher education administration (Ed D), K-12 education (Ed D); school counseling (MA, Ed S); school psychology (MA); teaching and learning (MA Ed, Ed D, Ed S), including education technology (Ed D), higher education (Ed D), K-12 education (Ed D).

See Close-Up on page 695.

Argosy University, Schaumburg, College of Education, Schaumburg, IL 60173-5403. Offers community college executive leadership (Ed D); educational leadership (MA Ed, Ed D, Ed S), including district leadership (Ed D), higher education administration (Ed D), K-12 education (Ed D); instructional leadership (Ed D, Ed S), including higher education (Ed D), K-12 education (Ed D).

See Close-Up on page 697.

Argosy University, Seattle, College of Education, Seattle, WA 98121. Offers adult education and training (MA Ed); community college executive leadership (Ed D); educational leadership (MA Ed, Ed D), including higher education administration (Ed D), K-12 education (Ed D); higher and postsecondary education (MA Ed); instructional leadership (MA Ed, Ed D), including education technology (Ed D), higher education (Ed D), K-12 education (Ed D).

See Close-Up on page 699.

Argosy University, Tampa, College of Education, Tampa, FL 33607. Offers community college executive leadership (Ed D); educational leadership (MA Ed, Ed D, Ed S), including higher education administration (Ed D), K-12 education (Ed D); school counseling (MA); teaching and learning (MA Ed, Ed D, Ed S), including higher education (Ed D), K-12 education (Ed D).

See Close-Up on page 701.

Argosy University, Twin Cities, College of Education, Eagan, MN 55121. Offers advanced educational administration (Ed D, Ed S); educational leadership (MA Ed, Ed D, Ed S), including higher education administration (Ed D), K-12 education (Ed D); higher and postsecondary education (MA Ed); initial educational administration (Ed D, Ed S); instructional leadership (MA Ed, Ed D, Ed S), including education technology (Ed D), higher education (Ed D), K-12 education (Ed D).

See Close-Up on page 703.

Argosy University, Washington DC, College of Education, Arlington, VA 22209. Offers community college executive leadership (Ed D); educational leadership (MA Ed, Ed D, Ed S), including higher education administration (Ed D), K-12 education (Ed D); instructional leadership (MA Ed, Ed D, Ed S), including higher education (Ed D), K-12 education (Ed D).

See Close-Up on page 705.

Arizona State University, Graduate College, College of Teacher Education and Leadership, Tempe, AZ 85287. Offers educational administration and supervision (M Ed); elementary education (M Ed, Certificate); leadership/innovation (administration) (Ed D); leadership/innovation (teaching) (Ed D); physical education (MPE); secondary education (M Ed, Certificate); special education (M Ed). Part-time and evening/weekend programs available. *Degree requirements:* For master's, applied project or comprehensive exams; for doctorate, comprehensive exam, thesis/dissertation. *Entrance requirements:* For master's, 3 letters of recommendation, minimum undergraduate GPA of 3.0, resume; for doctorate, master's degree in education or related field, 3 professional references, resumé, graduate GPA of 3.0, 3 letters of recommendation. Additional exam requirements/recommendations for international students: Required—TOEFL (minimum score 550 paper-based; 213 computer-based; 83 iBT), IELTS (minimum score 6.5). Electronic applications accepted. *Expenses:* Contact institution. *Faculty research:* Self-regulated learning in students, collaboration and consultation skills for educators, school reform and restructuring, hands-on science and mathematics programs, educational technology.

Arizona State University, Graduate College, Mary Lou Fulton College of Education, Division of Educational Leadership and Policy Studies, Program in Educational Administration and Supervision, Tempe, AZ 85287. Offers M Ed, Ed D. *Degree requirements:* For master's, thesis or alternative; for doctorate, thesis/dissertation. *Entrance requirements:* For master's and doctorate, GRE General Test or MAT.

Arizona State University, Graduate College, Mary Lou Fulton College of Education, Division of Educational Leadership and Policy Studies, Program in Educational Leadership and Policy Studies, Tempe, AZ 85287. Offers PhD. *Degree requirements:* For doctorate, thesis/dissertation. *Entrance requirements:* For doctorate, GRE General Test or MAT.

Arkansas State University—Jonesboro, Graduate School, College of Education, Department of Educational Leadership, Curriculum, and Special Education, Jonesboro, State University, AR 72467. Offers community college administration education (SCCT); curriculum and instruction (MSE); education theory and practice (MSE); educational leadership (MSE, Ed D, Ed S), including curriculum and instruction (MSE, Ed S); special education (MSE), including gifted and talented and creative, instructional specialist 4-12, instructional specialist P-4. *Accreditation:* NCATE. Part-time programs available. Postbaccalaureate distance learning degree programs offered (no on-campus study). *Faculty:* 15 full-time (6 women), 19 part-time/adjunct (11 women). *Students:* 16 full-time (11 women), 734 part-time (606 women); includes 111 minority (96 African Americans, 4 American Indian/Alaska Native, 4 Asian Americans or Pacific Islanders, 7 Hispanic Americans), 2 international. Average age 38. 882 applicants, 70% accepted, 240 enrolled. In 2009, 80 master's, 6 doctorates, 15 other advanced degrees awarded. *Degree requirements:* For master's, comprehensive exam, thesis or alternative; for doctorate, comprehensive exam, thesis/dissertation; for other advanced degree, comprehensive exam. *Entrance requirements:* For master's, GRE General Test or MAT, appropriate bachelor's degree, letters of reference, interview; for doctorate, GRE General Test or MAT, interview, master's degree, letters of reference, official transcript, personal statement, writing sample, immunization records; for other advanced degree, GRE General Test or MAT, interview, master's degree, letters of reference, official transcript, 3 years teaching experience, mentor, teaching license, immunization records. Additional exam requirements/recommendations for international students: Required—TOEFL (minimum score 550 paper-based; 213 computer-based; 79 iBT), IELTS (minimum score 6). *Application deadline:* Applications are processed on a rolling basis. Application fee: $50. Electronic applications accepted. *Expenses:* Tuition, state resident: full-time $3744; part-time $208 per credit hour. Tuition, nonresident: full-time $9540; part-time $530 per credit hour. Required fees: $896; $47 per credit hour. $25 per term. One-time fee: $50. Tuition and fees vary according to course load and program. *Financial support:* In 2009–10, 16 students received support; fellowships, teaching assistantships, career-related internships or fieldwork, scholarships/grants, and unspecified assistantships available. Financial award application deadline: 7/1; financial award applicants required to submit FAFSA. *Unit head:* Dr. Mitchell Holifield, Chair, 870-972-3062, Fax: 870-680-8130, E-mail: hfield@astate.edu. *Application contact:* Dr. Andrew Sustich, Dean of the Graduate School, 870-972-3029, Fax: 870-972-3857, E-mail: sustich@astate.edu.

Arkansas Tech University, Graduate College, College of Education, Russellville, AR 72801. Offers college student personnel (MS); educational leadership (M Ed, Ed S); English education (M Ed); instructional improvement (M Ed); secondary education (M Ed); teaching, learning and leadership (M Ed). *Accreditation:* NCATE. Part-time and evening/weekend programs available. Postbaccalaureate distance learning degree programs offered (no on-campus study). *Students:* 39 full-time (26 women), 246 part-time (179 women); includes 27 minority (18 African Americans, 4 American Indian/Alaska Native, 5 Hispanic Americans), 4 international. Average age 33. In 2009, 92 master's, 11 other advanced degrees awarded. *Degree requirements:* For master's, comprehensive exam, thesis optional, action research project. *Entrance requirements:* For master's, GRE General Test or MAT. Additional exam requirements/recommendations for

Educational Leadership and Administration

Arkansas Tech University (continued)

international students: Required—TOEFL (minimum score 550 paper-based; 213 computer-based; 79 iBT), IELTS (minimum score 6). *Application deadline:* For fall admission, 3/1 priority date for domestic students, 5/1 priority date for international students; for spring admission, 10/1 priority date for domestic and international students. Applications are processed on a rolling basis. Application fee: $0 ($50 for international students). Electronic applications accepted. *Expenses:* Tuition, state resident: full-time $3438; part-time $191 per hour. Tuition, nonresident: full-time $6876; part-time $382 per hour. Required fees: $482; $9 per credit hour. $140 per semester. Tuition and fees vary according to course load. *Financial support:* In 2009–10, teaching assistantships with full tuition reimbursements (averaging $4,000 per year); research assistantships, career-related internships or fieldwork, Federal Work-Study, scholarships/grants, health care benefits, and unspecified assistantships also available. Support available to part-time students. Financial award application deadline: 4/15; financial award applicants required to submit FAFSA. *Unit head:* Dr. Eldon G. Clary, Dean, 479-968-0350, Fax: 479-968-0350, E-mail: eclary@atu.edu. *Application contact:* Dr. Mary B. Gunter, Dean of Graduate College, 479-968-0398, Fax: 479-964-0542, E-mail: graduate.school@atu.edu.

Asbury University, School of Graduate and Professional Studies, Wilmore, KY 40390-1198. Offers biology: alternative certificate (MA Ed); chemistry: alternative certificate (MA Ed); English (MA Ed); English as a second language (MA Ed); ESL (MA Ed); French (MA Ed); Latin: alternative certificate (MA Ed); mathematics: alternative certificate (MA Ed); reading/writing endorsement (MA Ed); social studies (MA Ed); social work (MSW), including child and family services; Spanish (MA Ed); special education (MA Ed); special education: alternative certificate (MA Ed); teacher as leader endorsement (MA Ed). *Accreditation:* NCATE. Part-time programs available. *Faculty:* 8 full-time (7 women), 9 part-time/adjunct (4 women). *Students:* 108 part-time (87 women); includes 8 minority (4 African Americans, 2 Asian Americans or Pacific Islanders, 2 Hispanic Americans). Average age 36. 36 applicants, 86% accepted, 24 enrolled. In 2009, 20 master's awarded. *Degree requirements:* For master's, action research project, portfolio. *Entrance requirements:* For master's, PRAXIS/NTE, minimum GPA of 2.75, letters of recommendation. Additional exam requirements/recommendations for international students: Required—TOEFL (minimum score 550 paper-based). *Application deadline:* Applications are processed on a rolling basis. Application fee: $25. Electronic applications accepted. *Financial support:* Scholarships/grants and traineeships available. Financial award applicants required to submit FAFSA. *Unit head:* Dr. Bonnie J. Banker, Dean, School of Graduate and Professional Studies, 859-858-3511 Ext. 2221, Fax: 859-858-3921, E-mail: bonnie.banker@asbury.edu. *Application contact:* Lenore A. Sweigard, Graduate Program Assistant and Certification Specialist, 859-858-3511 Ext. 2502, Fax: 859-858-3921, E-mail: graded@asbury.edu.

Ashland University, Dwight Schar College of Education, Department of Educational Administration, Ashland, OH 44805-3702. Offers curriculum specialist (M Ed); principalship (M Ed); pupil services (M Ed). Part-time programs available. *Faculty:* 6 full-time (3 women), 31 part-time/adjunct (12 women). *Students:* 118 full-time (70 women), 239 part-time (135 women); includes 37 minority (29 African Americans, 1 American Indian/Alaska Native, 2 Asian Americans or Pacific Islanders, 5 Hispanic Americans), 2 international. Average age 33. 129 applicants, 98% accepted, 114 enrolled. In 2009, 166 master's awarded. *Degree requirements:* For master's, thesis or alternative, internship. *Entrance requirements:* For master's, teaching certificate or license, bachelor's degree, minimum cumulative GPA of 2.75. Additional exam requirements/recommendations for international students: Required—TOEFL. *Application deadline:* Applications are processed on a rolling basis. Application fee: $30. Electronic applications accepted. *Financial support:* Institutionally sponsored loans and scholarships/grants available. Financial award application deadline: 4/15. *Faculty research:* Gender and religious considerations in employment, ISLLC standards, adjunct faculty training, politics of school finance, ethnicity and employment. *Unit head:* Dr. Larry Cook, Chair, 419-289-5396, Fax: 419-208-5702, E-mail: lcook@ashland.edu. *Application contact:* Dr. Larry Cook, Chair, 419-289-5396, Fax: 419-208-5702, E-mail: lcook@ashland.edu.

Ashland University, Dwight Schar College of Education, Doctoral Program in Educational Leadership Studies, Ashland, OH 44805-3702. Offers Ed D. Evening/weekend programs available. *Faculty:* 9 full-time (7 women). *Students:* 6 full-time (3 women), 35 part-time (18 women); includes 8 minority (7 African Americans, 1 Hispanic American), 1 international. Average age 41. 2 applicants, 50% accepted, 1 enrolled. In 2009, 16 doctorates awarded. *Degree requirements:* For doctorate, comprehensive exam, thesis/dissertation. *Entrance requirements:* For doctorate, GRE, master's degree, minimum GPA of 3.3, writing sample, letters of recommendation. Additional exam requirements/recommendations for international students: Required—TOEFL. *Application deadline:* For spring admission, 3/1 for domestic students. Applications are processed on a rolling basis. Application fee: $30. Electronic applications accepted. *Expenses:* Contact institution. *Financial support:* In 2009–10, 21 students received support; teaching assistantships available. Financial award application deadline: 4/15. *Faculty research:* School funding, charter schools, administrative jobs, continuous improvement, marginalized groups, school finance, minority superintendent trends, teacher salaries, minority recruiting, women's issues. *Unit head:* Dr. Judy Alston, Director, 419-289-4983, Fax: 419-289-5097, E-mail: jalston@ashland.edu. *Application contact:* Administrative Assistant.

Auburn University, Graduate School, College of Education, Department of Educational Foundations, Leadership, and Technology, Auburn University, AL 36849. Offers adult education (M Ed, MS, Ed D); curriculum and instruction (M Ed, MS, Ed D, Ed S); curriculum supervision (M Ed, MS, Ed D, Ed S); educational psychology (PhD); higher education administration (M Ed, MS, Ed D, Ed S); media instructional design (MS); media specialist (M Ed); school administration (M Ed, MS, Ed D, Ed S). *Accreditation:* NCATE. Part-time programs available. *Faculty:* 21 full-time (11 women), 6 part-time/adjunct (4 women). *Students:* 68 full-time (40 women), 175 part-time (103 women); includes 87 minority (84 African Americans, 1 Asian American or Pacific Islander, 2 Hispanic Americans), 8 international. Average age 37. 112 applicants, 65% accepted, 53 enrolled. In 2009, 31 master's, 12 doctorates, 1 other advanced degree awarded. *Degree requirements:* For master's, thesis (for some programs); for doctorate, thesis/dissertation; for Ed S, field project. *Entrance requirements:* For master's, doctorate, and Ed S, GRE General Test. *Application deadline:* For fall admission, 7/7 for domestic students; for spring admission, 11/24 for domestic students. Applications are processed on a rolling basis. Application fee: $50 ($60 for international students). Electronic applications accepted. *Expenses:* Tuition, state resident: full-time $6240. Tuition, nonresident: full-time $18,720. International tuition: $18,938 full-time. Required fees: $492. Tuition and fees vary according to course load, program and reciprocity agreements. *Financial support:* Teaching assistantships, Federal Work-Study available. Support available to part-time students. Financial award application deadline: 3/15; financial award applicants required to submit FAFSA. *Unit head:* Dr. Jose Llanes, Head, 334-844-4460. *Application contact:* Dr. George Flowers, Dean of the Graduate School, 334-844-4700.

Auburn University Montgomery, School of Education, Department of Counselor, Leadership, and Special Education, Montgomery, AL 36124-4023. Offers counseling (M Ed, Ed S); education administration (M Ed, Ed S); special education (M Ed, Ed S). *Accreditation:* NCATE. Part-time and evening/weekend programs available. *Faculty:* 8 full-time (6 women), 3 part-time/adjunct (1 woman). *Students:* 30 full-time (27 women), 61 part-time (44 women); includes 61 minority (60 African Americans, 1 Hispanic American). Average age 34. In 2009, 19 master's awarded. *Degree requirements:* For master's and Ed S, comprehensive exam. *Entrance requirements:* For master's, GRE General Test or MAT, certification, BS in teaching; for Ed S, GRE General Test or MAT, certification. *Application deadline:* Applications are processed on a rolling basis. Electronic applications accepted. *Expenses:* Tuition, state resident: full-time $2841; part-time $225 per credit hour. Tuition, nonresident: full-time $8241; part-time $675 per credit hour. Required fees: $282; $8 per hour. $45 per term. *Financial support:* In 2009–10, 1 teaching assistantship was awarded; career-related internships or fieldwork and scholarships/grants also available. Support available to part-time students. Financial award application deadline: 3/1; financial award applicants required to submit FAFSA. *Unit head:* Dr. James V. Wright, Head, 334-244-3457, Fax: 334-344-3102, E-mail: jwright@mail.aum.edu. *Application contact:*

Dr. Sam Flynt, Associate Graduate Coordinator, 334-244-3270, Fax: 334-244-3835, E-mail: sflynt@mail.aum.edu.

Augusta State University, Graduate Studies, College of Education, Program in Educational Leadership, Augusta, GA 30904-2200. Offers M Ed, Ed S. *Accreditation:* NCATE. Part-time and evening/weekend programs available. *Degree requirements:* For master's, comprehensive exam; for Ed S, comprehensive exam, thesis. *Entrance requirements:* For master's, GRE, MAT, minimum GPA of 2.5; for Ed S, GRE, MAT. *Faculty research:* Restructuring schools, financing education, student transition.

Aurora University, College of Education, Aurora, IL 60506-4892. Offers curriculum and instruction (Ed D); education (MAT); education and administration (Ed D); educational leadership (MEL); reading instruction (MA). *Accreditation:* NCATE. Part-time and evening/weekend programs available. *Degree requirements:* For doctorate, thesis/dissertation. *Entrance requirements:* For master's, 2 years of teaching experience, valid teaching certificate. Additional exam requirements/recommendations for international students: Required—TOEFL (minimum score 550 paper-based; 213 computer-based). Electronic applications accepted. *Expenses:* Contact institution.

Austin Peay State University, College of Graduate Studies, College of Education, Department of Educational Specialties, Clarksville, TN 37044. Offers administration and supervision (Ed S); curriculum and instruction (MA Ed); education leadership (MA Ed); elementary education (Ed S); secondary education (Ed S); special education (MA Ed). Part-time and evening/weekend programs available. Postbaccalaureate distance learning degree programs offered. *Faculty:* 7 full-time (4 women), 4 part-time/adjunct (3 women). *Students:* 17 full-time (11 women), 96 part-time (76 women); includes 20 minority (12 African Americans, 1 American Indian/Alaska Native, 7 Hispanic Americans). Average age 36. 81 applicants, 99% accepted, 45 enrolled. In 2009, 47 master's awarded. *Degree requirements:* For master's, comprehensive exam, thesis optional. *Entrance requirements:* For master's, GRE General Test, 3 letters of recommendation, minimum undergraduate GPA of 2.75. Additional exam requirements/recommendations for international students: Required—TOEFL (minimum score 500 paper-based; 173 computer-based). *Application deadline:* For fall admission, 7/27 priority date for domestic students; for spring admission, 12/17 priority date for domestic students. Applications are processed on a rolling basis. Application fee: $25. Electronic applications accepted. *Expenses:* Tuition, state resident: full-time $6160; part-time $608 per credit hour. Tuition, nonresident: full-time $17,080; part-time $854 per credit hour. Required fees: $1224; $61.20 per credit hour. *Financial support:* Career-related internships or fieldwork, Federal Work-Study, institutionally sponsored loans, scholarships/grants, and unspecified assistantships available. Support available to part-time students. Financial award application deadline: 3/1; financial award applicants required to submit FAFSA. *Unit head:* Dr. Moniqueka Gold, Chair, 931-221-7696, Fax: 931-221-1292, E-mail: goldm@apsu.edu. *Application contact:* Dr. Dixie Dennis, Dean, College of Graduate Studies, 931-221-7662, Fax: 931-221-7641, E-mail: dennisdi@apsu.edu.

Azusa Pacific University, School of Behavioral and Applied Sciences, Department of Higher Education and Organizational Leadership, Program in Higher Education Leadership, Azusa, CA 91702-7000. Offers Ed D.

Azusa Pacific University, School of Education, Department of Education, Program in Educational Leadership, Azusa, CA 91702-7000. Offers Ed D. Part-time and evening/weekend programs available. *Degree requirements:* For doctorate, oral defense of dissertation, qualifying exam. *Entrance requirements:* For doctorate, GRE General Test or MAT, 5 years of experience, writing sample. Additional exam requirements/recommendations for international students: Required—TOEFL. *Expenses:* Contact institution. *Faculty research:* Ethics in educational administration.

Azusa Pacific University, School of Education, Program in School Administration, Azusa, CA 91702-7000. Offers MA. Part-time and evening/weekend programs available. *Degree requirements:* For master's, comprehensive exam or thesis, core exams, oral presentation. *Entrance requirements:* For master's, 12 units of course work in education, minimum GPA of 3.0. *Faculty research:* Instructional supervision, outcome-based education, technology and online searching, teacher preparation.

Baldwin-Wallace College, Graduate Programs, Division of Education, Leadership in Higher Education Program, Berea, OH 44017-2088. Offers MA Ed. Part-time and evening/weekend programs available. *Students:* 13 full-time (all women); includes 2 minority (both African Americans). Average age 25. 46 applicants, 50% accepted, 13 enrolled. *Entrance requirements:* For master's, bachelor's degree in field, MAT or minimum GPA of 2.75. Additional exam requirements/recommendations for international students: Required—TOEFL (minimum score 523 paper-based; 193 computer-based; 70 iBT). *Application deadline:* For fall admission, 8/15 for domestic students; for spring admission, 12/15 for domestic students. Applications are processed on a rolling basis. Application fee: $25. Electronic applications accepted. *Expenses:* Tuition: Full-time $14,174; part-time $682 per credit. Tuition and fees vary according to program. *Faculty research:* Program development in higher education; leadership styles; the psychology of leadership and learning in higher education. *Unit head:* Karen Kaye, Chair, 440-826-2168, Fax: 440-826-3779, E-mail: kkaye@bw.edu. *Application contact:* Winifred W. Gerhardt, Director of Admission for the Evening and Weekend College, 440-826-2222, Fax: 440-826-3830, E-mail: admission@bw.edu.

Baldwin-Wallace College, Graduate Programs, Division of Education, Specialization in School Leadership, Berea, OH 44017-2088. Offers MA Ed. Part-time and evening/weekend programs available. *Students:* 17 full-time (9 women), 19 part-time (11 women); includes 4 minority (3 African Americans, 1 Asian American or Pacific Islander). Average age 30. 12 applicants, 83% accepted, 6 enrolled. In 2009, 2 master's awarded. *Degree requirements:* For master's, comprehensive exam. *Entrance requirements:* For master's, bachelor's degree in field, MAT or minimum GPA of 2.75. Additional exam requirements/recommendations for international students: Required—TOEFL (minimum score 523 paper-based; 193 computer-based; 70 iBT). *Application deadline:* For fall admission, 8/15 priority date for domestic students; for spring admission, 12/15 priority date for domestic students. Applications are processed on a rolling basis. Application fee: $25. Electronic applications accepted. *Expenses:* Tuition: Full-time $14,174; part-time $682 per credit. Tuition and fees vary according to program. *Financial support:* Career-related internships or fieldwork available. Support available to part-time students. Financial award application deadline: 5/1; financial award applicants required to submit FAFSA. *Faculty research:* Leadership styles, instructional strategies, formative assessment. *Unit head:* Karen Kaye, Chair, 440-826-2168, Fax: 440-826-3779, E-mail: kkaye@bw.edu. *Application contact:* Winifred W. Gerhardt, Director of Admission for the Evening and Weekend College, 440-826-2222, Fax: 440-826-3830, E-mail: admission@bw.edu.

Ball State University, Graduate School, Teachers College, Department of Educational Leadership, Program in Educational Administration, Muncie, IN 47306-1099. Offers MAE, Ed D. *Accreditation:* NCATE. *Degree requirements:* For doctorate, thesis/dissertation. *Entrance requirements:* For doctorate, GRE General Test, interview, minimum graduate GPA of 3.2.

Ball State University, Graduate School, Teachers College, Department of Educational Leadership, Program in School Superintendency, Muncie, IN 47306-1099. Offers Ed S. *Accreditation:* NCATE. *Degree requirements:* For Ed S, thesis. *Entrance requirements:* For degree, GRE General Test, interview.

Ball State University, Graduate School, Teachers College, Department of Educational Studies, Program in Executive Development, Muncie, IN 47306-1099. Offers MA.

Ball State University, Graduate School, Teachers College, Department of Educational Studies, Program in Student Affairs Administration in Higher Education, Muncie, IN 47306-1099. Offers MA. *Accreditation:* NCATE. *Entrance requirements:* For master's, GRE General Test, interview.

Bank Street College of Education, Graduate School, Programs in Educational Leadership, New York, NY 10025. Offers early childhood leadership (MS Ed); educational leadership

(MS Ed); leadership for educational change (Ed M, MS Ed); leadership in mathematics education (MS Ed); leadership in museum education (MS Ed); leadership in the arts: creative writing (MS Ed); leadership in the arts: visual arts (MS Ed). *Students:* 76 full-time (60 women), 121 part-time (95 women); includes 67 minority (34 African Americans, 1 American Indian/Alaska Native, 6 Asian Americans or Pacific Islanders, 26 Hispanic Americans), 2 international. Average age 36. 124 applicants, 86% accepted, 98 enrolled. In 2009, 79 master's awarded. *Degree requirements:* For master's, thesis. *Entrance requirements:* For master's, interview, minimum of 2 years experience as a classroom teacher. Additional exam requirements/recommendations for international students: Required—TOEFL (minimum score 600 paper-based; 250 computer-based; 100 iBT), IELTS (minimum score 7). *Application deadline:* For fall admission, 3/1 priority date for domestic students; for spring admission, 11/1 priority date for domestic students. Applications are processed on a rolling basis. Application fee: $65. *Expenses:* Tuition: Part-time $1120 per credit. *Financial support:* Career-related internships or fieldwork, Federal Work-Study, scholarships/grants, and unspecified assistantships available. Support available to part-time students. Financial award application deadline: 4/15; financial award applicants required to submit FAFSA. *Faculty research:* Leadership in small schools, mathematics in elementary schools, professional development in early childhood, leadership in arts education, leadership in special education. *Unit head:* Dr. Rima Shore, Chairperson, 212-875-4478, Fax: 212-875-8753, E-mail: rshore@bankstreet.edu. *Application contact:* Ann Morgan, Director of Graduate Admissions, 212-875-4403, Fax: 212-875-4678, E-mail: amorgan@bankstreet.edu.

Barry University, School of Education, Program in Educational Leadership, Miami Shores, FL 33161-6695. Offers MS, Ed D, Certificate, Ed S. Part-time and evening/weekend programs available. *Degree requirements:* For master's and other advanced degree, comprehensive exam. *Entrance requirements:* For master's, GRE General Test or MAT, minimum GPA of 3.0; for other advanced degree, GRE General Test, minimum GPA of 3.0. Electronic applications accepted.

Barry University, School of Education, Program in Higher Education Administration, Miami Shores, FL 33161-6695. Offers MS. Part-time and evening/weekend programs available. *Degree requirements:* For master's, comprehensive exam. *Entrance requirements:* For master's, GRE General Test or MAT, minimum GPA of 3.0. Electronic applications accepted.

Barry University, School of Education, Program in Leadership and Education, Miami Shores, FL 33161-6695. Offers educational technology (PhD); exceptional student education (PhD); higher education administration (PhD); human resource development (PhD); leadership (PhD). Part-time and evening/weekend programs available. *Degree requirements:* For doctorate, thesis/dissertation. *Entrance requirements:* For doctorate, GRE General Test, minimum GPA of 3.25. Electronic applications accepted.

Bayamón Central University, Graduate Programs, Program in Education, Bayamón, PR 00960-1725. Offers administration and supervision (MA Ed); commercial education (MA Ed); education of the autistic (MA Ed); elementary education (K–3) (MA Ed); elementary education (K–6) (MA Ed); guidance and counseling (MA Ed); organizational psychology (MA); pre-elementary teacher (MA Ed); rehabilitation counseling (MA Ed); special education (MA Ed), including attention deficit disorder, learning disabilities. Part-time and evening/weekend programs available. *Degree requirements:* For master's, comprehensive exam. *Entrance requirements:* For master's, EXADEP, bachelor's degree in education or related field.

Baylor University, Graduate School, School of Education, Department of Educational Administration, Waco, TX 76798. Offers MS Ed, Ed S. *Accreditation:* NCATE. *Students:* 33 full-time (24 women), 10 part-time (8 women); includes 14 minority (5 African Americans, 9 Hispanic Americans). 90 applicants, 44% accepted. In 2009, 15 master's awarded. *Entrance requirements:* For master's, GRE General Test. *Application deadline:* Applications are processed on a rolling basis. Application fee: $25. *Financial support:* In 2009–10, 20 students received support, including 2 research assistantships; teaching assistantships, Federal Work-Study, institutionally sponsored loans, and scholarships/grants also available. *Unit head:* Dr. Frank Shushok, Graduate Program Director, 254-710-6957, Fax: 254-710-3265, E-mail: frank_shushok@baylor.edu. *Application contact:* Julie Baker, Administrative Assistant, 254-710-3050, Fax: 254-710-3870, E-mail: julie_l_baker@baylor.edu.

Bay Path College, Program in Higher Education Administration, Longmeadow, MA 01106-2292. Offers enrollment management (MS); general administration (MS); institutional advancement (MS). Postbaccalaureate distance learning degree programs offered (no on-campus study). Electronic applications accepted.

Bellarmine University, Annsley Frazier Thornton School of Education, Louisville, KY 40205-0671. Offers early elementary education (MA, MAT); instructional leadership and school administration/school principal (MA); learning and behavior disorders (MA); middle school education (MA, MAT); reading and writing endorsement (MA); secondary school education (MAT); Waldorf inspired curriculum (MA). *Accreditation:* NCATE. Part-time and evening/weekend programs available. *Faculty:* 16 full-time (11 women), 20 part-time/adjunct (13 women). *Students:* 67 full-time (47 women), 140 part-time (111 women); includes 14 minority (10 African Americans, 1 American Indian/Alaska Native, 3 Asian Americans or Pacific Islanders), 1 international. Average age 33. In 2009, 106 degrees awarded. *Degree requirements:* For master's, comprehensive exam, thesis (for some programs). *Entrance requirements:* For master's, GRE, baccalaureate degree from an accredited institution; minimum overall GPA of 2.75, 3.0 in major; letters of recommendation; valid Kentucky provisional or professional certificate. Additional exam requirements/recommendations for international students: Required—TOEFL (minimum score 550 paper-based; 213 computer-based; 80 iBT). *Application deadline:* Applications are processed on a rolling basis. Application fee: $25. *Expenses:* Contact institution. *Financial support:* Scholarships/grants available. Financial award applicants required to submit FAFSA. *Faculty research:* Literacy, service learning, dispositions, educational technology, special education. *Unit head:* Dr. Cindy Gnadinger, Dean, 502-452-8191, Fax: 502-452-8189, E-mail: cgnadinger@bellarmine.edu. *Application contact:* Theresa Klapheke, Administrative Director of Graduate Programs, 502-452-8271, Fax: 502-452-8002, E-mail: tklapheke@bellarmine.edu.

Benedictine College, Master of Arts Program in School Leadership, Atchison, KS 66002-1499. Offers MA. *Accreditation:* NCATE. Part-time and evening/weekend programs available. *Degree requirements:* For master's, comprehensive exam, practicum. *Entrance requirements:* For master's, minimum GPA of 3.0. *Expenses:* Contact institution. *Faculty research:* Teacher leadership, special education issues, diversity in schools, catholic school leadership, professional development.

Benedictine University, Graduate Programs, Program in Education, Lisle, IL 60532-0900. Offers curriculum and instruction and collaborative teaching (M Ed); elementary education (MA Ed); leadership and administration (M Ed); reading and literacy (M Ed); secondary education (MA Ed); special education (MA Ed). Part-time and evening/weekend programs available. *Faculty:* 4 full-time (2 women), 52 part-time/adjunct (30 women). *Students:* 286 full-time (252 women), 443 part-time (349 women); includes 61 minority (22 African Americans, 11 Asian Americans or Pacific Islanders, 28 Hispanic Americans), 5 international. Average age 33. 341 applicants, 90% accepted, 264 enrolled. In 2009, 299 master's awarded. *Degree requirements:* For master's, comprehensive exam, thesis (for some programs). *Entrance requirements:* For master's, GRE or MAT. Additional exam requirements/recommendations for international students: Required—TOEFL (minimum score 550 paper-based; 213 computer-based). *Application deadline:* For fall admission, 9/1 for domestic students; for winter admission, 12/1 for domestic students; for spring admission, 2/15 for domestic students. Applications are processed on a rolling basis. Application fee: $40. Electronic applications accepted. *Expenses:* Contact institution. *Financial support:* Career-related internships or fieldwork and health care benefits available. Support available to part-time students. *Unit head:* Dr. Richard Campbell, Director, 630-829-6242, Fax: 630-960-1126, E-mail: rcampbell@ben.edu. *Application contact:* Kari Gibbons, Director, Admissions, 630-829-6200, Fax: 630-829-6584, E-mail: kgibbons@ben.edu.

Benedictine University, Graduate Programs, Program in Higher Education and Organizational Change, Lisle, IL 60532-0900. Offers Ed D. *Students:* 41 full-time (29 women), 18 part-time (8 women); includes 19 minority (14 African Americans, 2 Asian Americans or Pacific Islanders, 3 Hispanic Americans). 64 applicants, 66% accepted, 36 enrolled. In 2009, 14 doctorates awarded. Application fee: $40. *Expenses:* Tuition: Part-time $750 per credit hour. Tuition and fees vary according to campus/location and program. *Unit head:* Dr. Donald Fouts, Director, 630-829-6343. *Application contact:* Kari Gibbons, Director, Admissions, 630-829-6200, Fax: 630-829-6584, E-mail: kgibbons@ben.edu.

Bernard M. Baruch College of the City University of New York, School of Public Affairs, Program in Educational Leadership, New York, NY 10010-5585. Offers educational leadership (MS Ed). Part-time and evening/weekend programs available. *Degree requirements:* For master's, internship. *Entrance requirements:* For master's, GRE or master's degree, minimum GPA of 3.0. Additional exam requirements/recommendations for international students: Recommended—TOEFL (minimum score 625 paper-based; 263 computer-based; 108 iBT). Electronic applications accepted. *Faculty research:* School administration, program development, school leadership, violence in schools, school leadership development, school reform, school discipline policy, program development.

Bernard M. Baruch College of the City University of New York, School of Public Affairs, Program in Higher Education Administration, New York, NY 10010-5585. Offers MS Ed. Part-time and evening/weekend programs available. *Degree requirements:* For master's, internship (for some students). *Entrance requirements:* For master's, GRE General Test. Additional exam requirements/recommendations for international students: Required—TOEFL (minimum score 625 paper-based; 263 computer-based; 106 iBT). Electronic applications accepted. *Expenses:* Contact institution.

Berry College, Graduate Programs, Graduate Programs in Education, Program in Leadership in Curriculum and Instruction, Mount Berry, GA 30149-0159. Offers curriculum and instruction (Ed S); educational leadership (Ed S). *Accreditation:* NCATE. *Faculty:* 4 part-time/adjunct (1 woman). *Students:* 11 part-time (10 women); includes 1 minority (African American). Average age 37. In 2009, 5 Ed Ss awarded. *Degree requirements:* For Ed S, thesis, portfolio, oral exams. *Entrance requirements:* For degree, M Ed from NCATE accredited school, minimum GPA of 3.25. Additional exam requirements/recommendations for international students: Required—TOEFL (minimum score 550 paper-based; 213 computer-based). *Application deadline:* For fall admission, 5/1 for domestic and international students; for spring admission, 10/1 for domestic and international students. Applications are processed on a rolling basis. Application fee: $25 ($30 for international students). *Expenses:* Contact institution. *Financial support:* In 2009–10, 5 students received support. Scholarships/grants available. Support available to part-time students. Financial award application deadline: 4/1; financial award applicants required to submit FAFSA. *Faculty research:* Curriculum development, teacher training, pedagogy. *Unit head:* Dr. Jacqueline McDowell, 706-236-1717, Fax: 706-238-5827, E-mail: jmcdowell@berry.edu. *Application contact:* Brett Kennedy, Director of Admissions, 706-236-2215, Fax: 706-290-2178, E-mail: admissions@berry.edu.

Bethany University, Program in Teacher Education, Scotts Valley, CA 95066-2820. Offers education (MA); educational leadership (MA). Part-time and evening/weekend programs available. *Degree requirements:* For master's, thesis. *Entrance requirements:* For master's, GRE General Test.

Bethel University, Graduate School, Department of Education, St. Paul, MN 55112-6999. Offers education K-12 (MA), including autism spectrum disorders, coordinator of work-based learning, differentiation, international baccalaureate, literacy, special education; educational administration (Ed D), including director of special education, K-12 principal license, superintendent license; literacy (Certificate); literacy education (MA); special education (MA), including autism spectrum disorders; teaching (MA). *Accreditation:* Teacher Education Accreditation Council. Evening/weekend programs available. Postbaccalaureate distance learning degree programs offered (minimal on-campus study). *Faculty:* 17 full-time (11 women), 37 part-time/adjunct (17 women). *Students:* 182 full-time (119 women), 172 part-time (120 women); includes 18 minority (2 African Americans, 1 American Indian/Alaska Native, 6 Asian Americans or Pacific Islanders, 9 Hispanic Americans), 1 international. Average age 35. 236 applicants, 79% accepted, 173 enrolled. In 2009, 51 master's, 5 doctorates awarded. *Degree requirements:* For master's, thesis, practicum; for doctorate, comprehensive exam, thesis/dissertation, internship. *Entrance requirements:* For master's, baccalaureate degree, statement of purpose essay, interview, current teaching license (if applicable), minimum GPA of 3.0, teaching experience (if applicable), letters of reference; for doctorate, MAT or GRE, minimum GPA of 3.0, letters of reference, statement of purpose essay, pre-assessment of prior experience and preparation, current license (if applicable), master's degree, interview, work experience in education. Additional exam requirements/recommendations for international students: Required—TOEFL (minimum score 550 paper-based; 213 computer-based; 80 iBT). *Application deadline:* For fall admission, 8/1 priority date for domestic students; for winter admission, 12/5 priority date for domestic students; for spring admission, 5/1 priority date for domestic students. Applications are processed on a rolling basis. Application fee: $25. Electronic applications accepted. *Expenses:* Contact institution. *Financial support:* Applicants required to submit FAFSA. *Unit head:* Dr. Judi Landrum, Assistant Dean, 651-635-8000, Fax: 651-638-8004, E-mail: j-landrum@bethel.edu. *Application contact:* Michael Price, Director of Admissions, 651-635-8000, Fax: 651-635-8004, E-mail: m-price@bethel.edu.

Bethel University, Program in Education, McKenzie, TN 38201. Offers administration and supervision (MA Ed); biology education K8-12 (MAT); elementary education (MAT); English education K8-12 (MAT); history education K8-12 (MAT); physical education K8-12 (MAT); special education K8-12 (MAT). Part-time and evening/weekend programs available. *Degree requirements:* For master's, thesis (for some programs). *Entrance requirements:* For master's, GRE General Test or MAT, minimum undergraduate GPA of 2.5.

Bob Jones University, Graduate Programs, Greenville, SC 29614. Offers accountancy (MS); Bible (MA); Bible translation (MA); Biblical studies (Certificate); broadcast management (MS); business administration (MBA); church history (MA, PhD); church ministries (MA); church music (MM); cinema and video production (MA); counseling (MS); curriculum and instruction (Ed D); divinity (M Div); dramatic production (MA); educational leadership (MS, Ed D, Ed S); elementary education (M Ed, MAT); English (M Ed, MA, MAT); fine arts (MA); graphic design (MA); history (M Ed, MA); illustration (MA); interpretative speech (MA); mathematics (M Ed, MAT); medical missions (Certificate); ministry (MM, D Min); multi-categorical special education (M Ed, MAT); music (M Ed); New Testament interpretation (PhD); Old Testament interpretation (PhD); orchestral instrument performance (MM); organ performance (MM); pastoral studies (MA); personnel services (MS, Ed S); piano pedagogy (MM); piano performance (MM); platform arts (MA); radio and television broadcasting (MS); rhetoric and public address (MA); secondary education (M Ed); studio art (MA); teaching Bible (MA); theology (MA, PhD); voice performance (MM); youth ministries (MA); M Div/MM.

Boise State University, Graduate College, College of Education, Department of Curriculum, Instruction and Foundational Studies, Boise, ID 83725-0399. Offers curriculum and instruction (Ed D); curriculum instruction (MA); educational leadership (M Ed). *Accreditation:* NCATE. Part-time programs available. *Degree requirements:* For master's, thesis optional. *Entrance requirements:* For master's, minimum GPA of 3.0. Electronic applications accepted. *Expenses:* Tuition, state resident: full-time $3106; part-time $209 per credit. Tuition, nonresident: part-time $284 per credit.

Boston College, Lynch Graduate School of Education, Department of Educational Administration and Higher Education, Educational Administration Specialization, Chestnut Hill, MA 02467-3800. Offers M Ed, CAES, JD/M Ed. Part-time and evening/weekend programs available. *Students:* 8 full-time (4 women), 49 part-time (19 women); includes 7 minority (5 African Americans, 1 Asian American or Pacific Islander, 1 Hispanic American), 7 international. 55 applicants, 58% accepted, 21 enrolled. In 2009, 14 master's, 6 CAESs awarded. Terminal master's awarded for partial completion of doctoral program. *Degree requirements:* For master's

Educational Leadership and Administration

Boston College (continued)
and CAES, comprehensive exam. *Entrance requirements:* For master's and CAES, GRE General Test or MAT. Additional exam requirements/recommendations for international students: Required—TOEFL (minimum score 550 paper-based; 213 computer-based; 81 iBT). Application fee: $60. Electronic applications accepted. *Financial support:* Fellowships with full and partial tuition reimbursements, research assistantships with full and partial tuition reimbursements, teaching assistantships with full and partial tuition reimbursements, career-related internships or fieldwork, Federal Work-Study, scholarships/grants, traineeships, health care benefits, tuition waivers (full and partial), and unspecified assistantships available. Support available to part-time students. Financial award applicants required to submit FAFSA. *Faculty research:* Politics of urban education; principalship; urban catholic schools; educational leadership; educational law and policy. *Unit head:* Dr. Ana M. Martinez-Aleman, Chairperson, 617-552-1760, Fax: 617-552-0812, E-mail: ana.aleman.1@bc.edu. *Application contact:* Adam Poluzzi, Director, Graduate Admission and Financial Aid, 617-552-4214, Fax: 617-552-0398, E-mail: poluzzi@bc.edu.

Boston College, Lynch Graduate School of Education, Department of Educational Administration and Higher Education, Higher Education Specialization, Chestnut Hill, MA 02467-3800. Offers MA, PhD, JD/MA, MBA/MA. *Accreditation:* Teacher Education Accreditation Council. Part-time and evening/weekend programs available. *Students:* 25 full-time (14 women), 109 part-time (75 women); includes 22 minority (5 African Americans, 13 Asian Americans or Pacific Islanders, 4 Hispanic Americans), 6 international. 250 applicants, 52% accepted, 55 enrolled. In 2009, 31 master's, 10 doctorates awarded. Terminal master's awarded for partial completion of doctoral program. *Degree requirements:* For master's, comprehensive exam; for doctorate, comprehensive exam, thesis/dissertation. *Entrance requirements:* For master's, GRE General Test or MAT; for doctorate, GRE General Test. Additional exam requirements/recommendations for international students: Required—TOEFL (minimum score 550 paper-based; 213 computer-based; 81 iBT). Application fee: $60. Electronic applications accepted. *Financial support:* Fellowships with full and partial tuition reimbursements, research assistantships with full and partial tuition reimbursements, teaching assistantships with full and partial tuition reimbursements, career-related internships or fieldwork, Federal Work-Study, scholarships/grants, traineeships, health care benefits, tuition waivers (full and partial), and unspecified assistantships available. Support available to part-time students. Financial award applicants required to submit FAFSA. *Faculty research:* Race, culture and gender in higher education; international education; college student development; Catholic higher education; organizational analysis. *Unit head:* Dr. Ana M. Martinez-Aleman, Chairperson, 617-552-1760, Fax: 617-552-0812, E-mail: ana.aleman.1@bc.edu. *Application contact:* Adam Poluzzi, Director, Graduate Admission and Financial Aid, 617-552-4214, Fax: 617-552-0398, E-mail: poluzzi@bc.edu.

Boston College, Lynch Graduate School of Education, Department of Educational Administration and Higher Education, Massachusetts Elementary School Principal Association/Professional School Administrator Program, Chestnut Hill, MA 02467-3800. Offers Ed D. Part-time and evening/weekend programs available. *Students:* 32 part-time (16 women); includes 7 minority (4 African Americans, 3 Hispanic Americans). 72 applicants, 44% accepted, 0 enrolled. In 2009, 16 doctorates awarded. *Degree requirements:* For doctorate, comprehensive exam, thesis/dissertation. *Entrance requirements:* For doctorate, GRE General Test. Additional exam requirements/recommendations for international students: Required—TOEFL. *Application deadline:* For fall admission, 2/1 for domestic students. Application fee: $60. Electronic applications accepted. *Financial support:* Fellowships with full and partial tuition reimbursements, research assistantships with full and partial tuition reimbursements, teaching assistantships with full and partial tuition reimbursements, career-related internships or fieldwork, Federal Work-Study, scholarships/grants, traineeships, health care benefits, tuition waivers (full and partial), and unspecified assistantships available. Support available to part-time students. Financial award applicants required to submit FAFSA. *Faculty research:* Educational leadership, diversity and social justice, data-based decision-making. *Unit head:* Dr. Ana M. Martinez-Aleman, Chairperson, 617-552-1760, Fax: 617-552-0812, E-mail: ana.aleman.1@bc.edu. *Application contact:* Adam Poluzzi, Director, Graduate Admission and Financial Aid, 617-552-4214, Fax: 617-552-0398, E-mail: poluzzi@bc.edu.

Boston University, School of Education, Department of Administration, Training, and Policy Studies, Program in Human Resource Education, Boston, MA 02215. Offers Ed M, CAGS. Part-time programs available. *Degree requirements:* For master's, thesis optional; for CAGS, comprehensive exam. *Entrance requirements:* For master's and CAGS, GRE General Test or MAT. Additional exam requirements/recommendations for international students: Required—TOEFL. Electronic applications accepted. *Expenses:* Tuition: Full-time $37,910; part-time $1184 per credit hour. Required fees: $386; $40 per semester. Part-time tuition and fees vary according to class time, course level, degree level and program.

Boston University, School of Education, Department of Administration, Training, and Policy Studies, Program in Policy, Planning, and Administration, Boston, MA 02215. Offers educational administration (Ed M); policy, planning, and administration (Ed M, CAGS); MSW/Ed M. Part-time programs available. *Degree requirements:* For master's, thesis optional; for CAGS, comprehensive exam. *Entrance requirements:* For master's and CAGS, GRE General Test or MAT. Additional exam requirements/recommendations for international students: Required—TOEFL. Electronic applications accepted. *Expenses:* Tuition: Full-time $37,910; part-time $1184 per credit hour. Required fees: $386; $40 per semester. Part-time tuition and fees vary according to class time, course level, degree level and program. *Faculty research:* School effectiveness, creative problem solving, parent involvement, community education, curriculum theory and evaluation.

Bowie State University, Graduate Programs, Program in Educational Leadership/Executive Fellows, Bowie, MD 20715-9465. Offers Ed D. Part-time and evening/weekend programs available. *Degree requirements:* For doctorate, comprehensive exam, thesis/dissertation. Electronic applications accepted.

Bowie State University, Graduate Programs, Program in Elementary and Secondary School Administration, Bowie, MD 20715-9465. Offers M Ed. Part-time and evening/weekend programs available. *Degree requirements:* For master's, comprehensive exam. *Entrance requirements:* For master's, copy of Advance Teaching Certificate, 3 years teaching experience, letter of recommendation from current supervisor. Electronic applications accepted.

Bowie State University, Graduate Programs, Program in School Administration and Supervision, Bowie, MD 20715-9465. Offers M Ed. Part-time and evening/weekend programs available. *Degree requirements:* For master's, comprehensive exam, thesis optional, research paper. *Entrance requirements:* For master's, minimum undergraduate GPA of 3.0, 3 years of teaching experience, teaching certificate.

Bowling Green State University, Graduate College, College of Education and Human Development, School of Leadership and Policy Studies, Program in Educational Administration and Supervision, Bowling Green, OH 43403. Offers educational administration and supervision (M Ed, Ed S); leadership studies (Ed D). *Accreditation:* NCATE. Part-time and evening/weekend programs available. *Degree requirements:* For master's, thesis or alternative; for doctorate, comprehensive exam, thesis/dissertation; for Ed S, thesis or alternative, field experience or internship. *Entrance requirements:* For master's, doctorate, and Ed S, GRE General Test. Additional exam requirements/recommendations for international students: Required—TOEFL. Electronic applications accepted. *Faculty research:* Professional development for school leaders, organizational development, school finance, legal challenges to school decision making, administering urban schools.

Bowling Green State University, Graduate College, College of Education and Human Development, School of Leadership and Policy Studies, Program in Higher Education Administration, Bowling Green, OH 43403. Offers PhD. *Accreditation:* NCATE. Part-time programs available. *Degree requirements:* For doctorate, comprehensive exam, thesis/dissertation. *Entrance requirements:* For doctorate, GRE General Test. Additional exam requirements/recommendations for international students: Required—TOEFL. Electronic applications accepted. *Faculty research:* Adult learners, legal issues, intellectual development.

Bradley University, Graduate School, College of Education and Health Sciences, Department of Educational Leadership and Human Development, Peoria, IL 61625-0002. Offers human development counseling (MA), including community and agency counseling, school counseling; leadership in educational administration (MA); leadership in human service administration (MA). *Accreditation:* ACA; NCATE. Part-time and evening/weekend programs available. *Degree requirements:* For master's, comprehensive exam, thesis optional. *Entrance requirements:* For master's, GRE General Test or MAT, interview, 3 letters of recommendation. Additional exam requirements/recommendations for international students: Required—TOEFL (minimum score 550 paper-based; 213 computer-based; 79 iBT).

Brandon University, Faculty of Education, Brandon, MB R7A 6A9, Canada. Offers curriculum and instruction (M Ed, Diploma); educational administration (M Ed, Diploma); guidance and counseling (M Ed, Diploma); special education (M Ed, Diploma). *Degree requirements:* For master's, thesis. *Entrance requirements:* For master's, minimum GPA of 3.0, teaching certificate or equivalent. Additional exam requirements/recommendations for international students: Required—TOEFL. *Faculty research:* Comparative education, environmental studies, parent/school council.

Bridgewater State University, School of Graduate Studies, School of Education and Allied Science, Department of Secondary Education and Professional Programs, Program in Educational Leadership, Bridgewater, MA 02325-0001. Offers M Ed, CAGS. *Accreditation:* NCATE. Part-time and evening/weekend programs available. *Degree requirements:* For master's and CAGS, comprehensive exam. *Entrance requirements:* For master's, GRE General Test or Massachusetts Test for Educator Licensure, work experience; for CAGS, master's degree.

Brigham Young University, Graduate Studies, David O. McKay School of Education, Department of Educational Leadership and Foundations, Provo, UT 84602. Offers M Ed. *Accreditation:* NCATE. Part-time and evening/weekend programs available. *Faculty:* 11 full-time (3 women), 1 part-time/adjunct (0 women). *Students:* 14 full-time (6 women), 106 part-time (59 women); includes 18 minority (11 American Indian/Alaska Native, 7 Hispanic Americans). Average age 35. 74 applicants, 54% accepted, 36 enrolled. In 2009, 26 master's awarded. *Degree requirements:* For master's, comprehensive exam, thesis or alternative. *Entrance requirements:* For master's, GRE, MAT, LSAT. Additional exam requirements/recommendations for international students: Required—TOEFL (minimum score 580 paper-based; 237 computer-based; 85 iBT). *Application deadline:* For fall admission, 2/15 for domestic and international students; for spring admission, 2/1 for domestic and international students. Application fee: $50. Electronic applications accepted. *Expenses:* Tuition: Full-time $5580; part-time $301 per credit hour. Tuition and fees vary according to student's religious affiliation. *Financial support:* In 2009–10, 42 students received support, including 4 research assistantships (averaging $27,480 per year); teaching assistantships, career-related internships or fieldwork, scholarships/grants, and unspecified assistantships also available. Financial award application deadline: 9/1. *Faculty research:* Mentoring, pre-service training of administrators, policy development, cross-cultural studies of educational leadership. *Unit head:* Dean Richard K. Young, Chair, 801-422-3695, Fax: 801-422-0200, E-mail: msesec@byu.edu. *Application contact:* Bonnie Bennett, Department Secretary, 801-422-3813, Fax: 801-422-0196, E-mail: bonnie_bennett@byu.edu.

Brooklyn College of the City University of New York, Division of Graduate Studies, School of Education, Program in Educational Leadership, Brooklyn, NY 11210-2889. Offers MS Ed. Part-time and evening/weekend programs available. *Students:* 90 full-time (72 women), 3 part-time (2 women); includes 43 minority (32 African Americans, 1 Asian American or Pacific Islander, 10 Hispanic Americans), 1 international. Average age 35. 45 applicants, 89% accepted, 35 enrolled. In 2009, 43 master's awarded. *Entrance requirements:* For master's, 2 supervisory letters of recommendation, essay, resume, teaching certificate, interview, supplemental application. Additional exam requirements/recommendations for international students: Required—TOEFL (minimum score 500 paper-based; 173 computer-based; 61 iBT). *Application deadline:* For fall admission, 7/1 for domestic students, 6/1 for international students; for spring admission, 12/31 for domestic students, 11/30 for international students. Applications are processed on a rolling basis. Application fee: $125. Electronic applications accepted. *Expenses:* Tuition, state resident: full-time $7360; part-time $310 per credit hour. Tuition, nonresident: full-time $13,800; part-time $575 per credit hour. Required fees: $140.10 per semester. *Financial support:* Career-related internships or fieldwork, Federal Work-Study, institutionally sponsored loans, and scholarships/grants available. Support available to part-time students. Financial award application deadline: 5/1; financial award applicants required to submit FAFSA. *Unit head:* Prof. David Bloomfield, Program Head, 718-951-5213, E-mail: davidb@brooklyn.cuny.edu. *Application contact:* Hernan Sierra, Graduate Admissions Coordinator, 718-951-4536, Fax: 718-951-4506, E-mail: grads@brooklyn.cuny.edu.

Bucknell University, Graduate Studies, College of Arts and Sciences, Department of Education, Specialization in Elementary and Secondary Principalship, Lewisburg, PA 17837. Offers MA, MS Ed. *Degree requirements:* For master's, thesis or alternative. *Entrance requirements:* For master's, GRE General Test, minimum GPA of 2.8. Additional exam requirements/recommendations for international students: Required—TOEFL.

Buffalo State College, State University of New York, The Graduate School, Faculty of Applied Science and Education, Department of Elementary Education and Reading, Program in Educational Leadership and Facilitation, Buffalo, NY 14222-1095. Offers CAS. *Accreditation:* NCATE. Part-time and evening/weekend programs available. *Degree requirements:* For CAS, internship. *Entrance requirements:* For degree, master's degree, New York teaching certificate, 3 years of teaching experience. Additional exam requirements/recommendations for international students: Required—TOEFL (minimum score 550 paper-based; 213 computer-based).

Butler University, College of Education, Indianapolis, IN 46208-3485. Offers administration (MS); elementary education (MS); reading (MS); school counseling (MS); secondary education (MS); special education (MS). *Accreditation:* ACA; NCATE. Part-time and evening/weekend programs available. *Faculty:* 9 full-time (7 women), 7 part-time/adjunct (6 women). *Students:* 18 full-time (11 women), 137 part-time (111 women); includes 17 minority (14 African Americans, 1 American Indian/Alaska Native, 2 Asian Americans or Pacific Islanders), 9 international. Average age 31. 57 applicants, 77% accepted, 24 enrolled. In 2009, 61 master's awarded. *Entrance requirements:* For master's, GRE General Test, MAT, interview. *Application deadline:* For fall admission, 8/15 priority date for domestic students. Applications are processed on a rolling basis. Application fee: $35. Electronic applications accepted. *Financial support:* Institutionally sponsored loans available. Support available to part-time students. Financial award application deadline: 7/15; financial award applicants required to submit FAFSA. *Faculty research:* Ethics in cybercounseling, history of sports for disabled, effect of fetal alcohol syndrome on perceptual learning, reading recovery's theoretical framework in teacher education. *Unit head:* Dr. Ena Shelley, Dean, 317-940-9752, Fax: 317-940-6481. *Application contact:* Karen Farrell, Department Secretary, 317-940-9220, E-mail: kfarrell@butler.edu.

Caldwell College, Graduate Studies, Program in Educational Administration, Caldwell, NJ 07006-6195. Offers MA. Part-time and evening/weekend programs available. *Degree requirements:* For master's, thesis, research paper. *Entrance requirements:* For master's, GRE General Test or MAT, interview, minimum GPA of 2.75, teaching certificate, 3 years of teaching experience, writing sample. Additional exam requirements/recommendations for international students: Required—TOEFL (minimum score 580 paper-based; 237 computer-based). Electronic applications accepted.

California Baptist University, Program in Education, Riverside, CA 92504-3206. Offers cross-cultural language and academic development (MA); educational leadership (MS); educational leadership and faith-based instruction (MS); educational technology (MS); instructional computer applications (MS); reading (MS); school counseling (MS); school psychology (MS); special education (MS); special education in mild/moderate disabilities (MS); special education in moderate/severe disabilities (MS); teaching (MS); teaching and learning (MS Ed). Part-time programs available. *Faculty:* 16 full-time (9 women), 10 part-time/adjunct

(all women). *Students:* 73 full-time (60 women), 368 part-time (298 women); includes 170 minority (34 African Americans, 4 American Indian/Alaska Native, 18 Asian Americans or Pacific Islanders, 114 Hispanic Americans). 266 applicants, 72% accepted, 169 enrolled. In 2009, 120 master's awarded. *Degree requirements:* For master's, comprehensive exam (for some programs), thesis optional. *Entrance requirements:* For master's, minimum undergraduate GPA of 2.75, 12 semester hours of pre-requisite course work in education. Additional exam requirements/recommendations for international students: Required—TOEFL (minimum score 575 paper-based; 230 computer-based; 89 iBT). *Application deadline:* For fall admission, 8/1 priority date for domestic students, 7/1 for international students; for spring admission, 12/1 priority date for domestic students, 10/15 priority date for international students. Applications are processed on a rolling basis. Application fee: $45. Electronic applications accepted. *Expenses:* Tuition: Full-time $8352; part-time $464 per semester hour. Required fees: $125 per semester. Tuition and fees vary according to course load, campus/location and program. *Financial support:* Career-related internships or fieldwork, Federal Work-Study, and scholarships/grants available. Support available to part-time students. Financial award applicants required to submit FAFSA. *Unit head:* Dr. Mary Crist, Dean, School of Education, 951-343-4313, Fax: 951-343-4516, E-mail: mcrist@calbaptist.edu. *Application contact:* Gail Ronveaux, Dean of Graduate Enrollment, 951-343-5045, Fax: 951-343-5095, E-mail: graduateadmissions@calbaptist.edu.

California Coast University, Programs in Education, Santa Ana, CA 92701. Offers administration (M Ed); curriculum and instruction (M Ed); educational psychology (D Ed); organizational leadership (D Ed). Part-time and evening/weekend programs available. Postbaccalaureate distance learning degree programs offered (no on-campus study). Application fee: $75. *Application contact:* Christi Okuma, 714-547-9625, Fax: 714-547-5777, E-mail: ccu@calcoast.edu.

California Lutheran University, Graduate Studies, School of Education, Emphasis in Educational Leadership, Thousand Oaks, CA 91360-2787. Offers educational leadership (MA); educational leadership (k-12) (Ed D); higher education leadership (Ed D). Part-time and evening/weekend programs available. *Degree requirements:* For master's, thesis or comprehensive exam. *Entrance requirements:* For master's, GRE General Test, interview, minimum GPA of 3.0.

California State University, Bakersfield, Division of Graduate Studies, School of Education, Program in Educational Administration, Bakersfield, CA 93311. Offers MA. *Degree requirements:* For master's, thesis or alternative, project or culminating exam.

California State University Channel Islands, Extended Education, Program in Educational Leadership, Camarillo, CA 93012. Offers MAEd.

California State University, Dominguez Hills, College of Professional Studies, School of Education, Division of Graduate Education, Program in Educational Administration, Carson, CA 90747-0001. Offers MA. Part-time and evening/weekend programs available. *Faculty:* 5 full-time (2 women), 8 part-time/adjunct (2 women). *Students:* 141 full-time (96 women), 50 part-time (29 women); includes 127 minority (35 African Americans, 2 American Indian/Alaska Native, 20 Asian Americans or Pacific Islanders, 70 Hispanic Americans). Average age 37. 159 applicants, 91% accepted, 98 enrolled. In 2009, 100 master's awarded. *Degree requirements:* For master's, comprehensive exam. *Entrance requirements:* For master's, minimum GPA of 2.75. *Application deadline:* For fall admission, 6/1 for domestic students. Applications are processed on a rolling basis. Application fee: $55. *Expenses:* Tuition, nonresident: full-time $6696; part-time $372 per unit. Required fees: $5946; $1752 per semester. *Faculty research:* Educational leadership, teacher retention, accountability, decision making. *Unit head:* Dr. Ann Chlebicki, Chairperson, 310-243-2517, E-mail: achlebicki@csudh.edu. *Application contact:* Admissions Office, 310-243-3530.

California State University, East Bay, Graduate Programs, College of Education and Allied Studies, Department of Educational Leadership, Hayward, CA 94542-3000. Offers educational leadership (MS, Ed D); specializing in urban teaching leadership (MS). *Accreditation:* NCATE. Part-time and evening/weekend programs available. Postbaccalaureate distance learning degree programs offered. *Faculty:* 10 full-time (5 women), 5 part-time/adjunct (3 women). *Students:* 101 full-time (68 women), 57 part-time (40 women); includes 55 minority (29 African Americans, 1 American Indian/Alaska Native, 13 Asian Americans or Pacific Islanders, 12 Hispanic Americans), 1 international. Average age 39. 110 applicants, 88% accepted, 85 enrolled. In 2009, 56 master's awarded. *Degree requirements:* For master's, comprehensive exam, project or thesis; for doctorate, thesis/dissertation. *Entrance requirements:* For master's, teaching or services credential and experience; for doctorate, GRE, MA with minimum GPA of 3.0; PK-12 leadership position; portfolio of work samples. Additional exam requirements/recommendations for international students: Required—TOEFL (minimum score 550 paper-based; 213 computer-based). *Application deadline:* For fall admission, 6/30 for domestic and international students. Application fee: $55. Electronic applications accepted. *Financial support:* Career-related internships or fieldwork, Federal Work-Study, and institutionally sponsored loans available. Support available to part-time students. Financial award application deadline: 3/1; financial award applicants required to submit FAFSA. *Unit head:* Prof. Gilberto Arriaza, Chair, 510-885-4151, Fax: 510-885-4642, E-mail: gilberto.arriaza@csueastbay.edu. *Application contact:* Donna Wiley, Interim Associate Director, 510-885-2928, Fax: 510-885-4777, E-mail: donna.wiley@csueastbay.edu.

California State University, Fresno, Division of Graduate Studies, School of Education and Human Development, Department of Educational Research and Administration, Fresno, CA 93740-8027. Offers education (MA), including administration and supervision. *Accreditation:* NCATE. Part-time and evening/weekend programs available. *Degree requirements:* For master's, thesis or alternative. *Entrance requirements:* For master's, GRE General Test, MAT, minimum GPA of 2.75. Additional exam requirements/recommendations for international students: Required—TOEFL. Electronic applications accepted. *Faculty research:* Substance abuse on youth education.

California State University, Fresno, Division of Graduate Studies, School of Education and Human Development, Doctoral Program in Educational Leadership, Fresno, CA 93740-8027. Offers Ed D. Part-time programs available. *Degree requirements:* For doctorate, thesis/dissertation. *Entrance requirements:* For doctorate, GRE or MAT, minimum GPA of 3.2, master's degree. Additional exam requirements/recommendations for international students: Required—TOEFL. Electronic applications accepted. *Faculty research:* Minority special education leadership, literacy, ethics of leadership, organizational planning, language development.

California State University, Fullerton, Graduate Studies, College of Education, Department of Educational Leadership, Fullerton, CA 92834-9480. Offers MS, Ed D. *Accreditation:* NCATE. Part-time programs available. *Students:* 6 full-time (3 women), 261 part-time (166 women); includes 107 minority (16 African Americans, 25 Asian Americans or Pacific Islanders, 66 Hispanic Americans), 7 international. Average age 36. 132 applicants, 75% accepted, 89 enrolled. In 2009, 48 master's awarded. *Degree requirements:* For master's, thesis or alternative, project. *Entrance requirements:* For master's, minimum GPA of 2.5. Application fee: $55. *Expenses:* Tuition, nonresident: full-time $11,160; part-time $373 per credit. Required fees: $1440 per term. Tuition and fees vary according to course load, degree level and program. *Financial support:* Career-related internships or fieldwork, Federal Work-Study, institutionally sponsored loans, and scholarships/grants available. Support available to part-time students. Financial award application deadline: 3/1; financial award applicants required to submit FAFSA. *Faculty research:* Creation of a substance abuse prevention training and demonstration program. *Unit head:* Dr. Louise Adler, Head, 657-278-3911. *Application contact:* Admissions/Applications, 657-278-2371.

California State University, Long Beach, Graduate Studies, College of Education, Department of Advanced Studies in Education and Counseling, Long Beach, CA 90840. Offers counseling (MS), including marriage and family therapy, school counseling, student development in higher education; education (MA, Ed D); educational administration (MA, Ed D); educational psychology (MA); special education (MS). Part-time and evening/weekend programs available. *Students:* 386 full-time (289 women), 430 part-time (319 women); includes 462 minority (90 African Americans, 4 American Indian/Alaska Native, 130 Asian Americans or Pacific Islanders, 238 Hispanic Americans), 17 international. Average age 33. 757 applicants, 28% accepted, 174 enrolled. *Entrance requirements:* For master's, GRE General Test, minimum GPA of 2.75. *Application deadline:* For fall admission, 3/1 for domestic students. Applications are processed on a rolling basis. Application fee: $55. Electronic applications accepted. *Expenses:* Required fees: $1802 per semester. Part-time tuition and fees vary according to course load. *Financial support:* Federal Work-Study, institutionally sponsored loans, and scholarships/grants available. Financial award application deadline: 3/2.

California State University, Northridge, Graduate Studies, College of Education, Department of Educational Leadership and Policy Studies, Northridge, CA 91330. Offers education (MA); educational administration (MA); educational leadership (Ed D). *Accreditation:* NCATE. Part-time and evening/weekend programs available. *Faculty:* 15 full-time (7 women), 26 part-time/adjunct (13 women). *Students:* 207 full-time (134 women), 267 part-time (181 women); includes 226 minority (43 African Americans, 3 American Indian/Alaska Native, 32 Asian Americans or Pacific Islanders, 148 Hispanic Americans), 6 international. Average age 37. 250 applicants, 91% accepted, 170 enrolled. In 2009, 364 master's awarded. *Entrance requirements:* For master's, 2 letters of recommendation. Additional exam requirements/recommendations for international students: Required—TOEFL. *Application deadline:* For fall admission, 11/30 for domestic students. Application fee: $55. *Financial support:* Fellowships available. Financial award application deadline: 3/1. *Faculty research:* Bilingual educational training. *Unit head:* Bronte Reynolds, Chair, 818-677-2591. *Application contact:* Bronte Reynolds, Chair, 818-677-2591.

California State University, Sacramento, Graduate Studies, College of Education, Department of Educational Leadership and Policy Studies, Sacramento, CA 95819. Offers educational leadership (MA). Part-time programs available. *Degree requirements:* For master's, thesis or alternative, writing proficiency exam. *Entrance requirements:* For master's, minimum GPA of 2.5. Additional exam requirements/recommendations for international students: Required—TOEFL. Electronic applications accepted.

California State University, San Bernardino, Graduate Studies, College of Education, Program in Educational Administration, San Bernardino, CA 92407-2397. Offers MA. Part-time and evening/weekend programs available. *Faculty:* 5 full-time (3 women), 7 part-time/adjunct (3 women). *Students:* 72 full-time (46 women), 76 part-time (50 women); includes 80 minority (10 African Americans, 5 Asian Americans or Pacific Islanders, 65 Hispanic Americans), 2 international. Average age 37. 59 applicants, 93% accepted, 35 enrolled. In 2009, 130 master's awarded. *Degree requirements:* For master's, thesis or alternative. *Entrance requirements:* For master's, minimum GPA of 3.0 in education. *Application deadline:* For fall admission, 8/31 priority date for domestic students. Application fee: $55. *Financial support:* Career-related internships or fieldwork available. Support available to part-time students. *Unit head:* Dr. Jay Fiene, Department Chair, 909-537-7621, Fax: 909-537-7510, E-mail: jfiene@csusb.edu. *Application contact:* Olivia Rosas, Director of Admissions, 909-537-7577, Fax: 909-537-7034, E-mail: orosas@csusb.edu.

California State University, San Bernardino, Graduate Studies, College of Education, Program in Educational Leadership and Curriculum, San Bernardino, CA 92407-2397. Offers Ed D. *Students:* 31 part-time (17 women); includes 13 minority (5 African Americans, 1 Asian American or Pacific Islander, 7 Hispanic Americans), 1 international. Average age 44. 28 applicants, 64% accepted, 14 enrolled. *Unit head:* Dr. David Stine, Interim Department Chair, 909-537-7621, E-mail: dstine@csusb.edu. *Application contact:* Olivia Rosas, Director of Admissions, 909-537-7577, Fax: 909-537-7034, E-mail: orosas@csusb.edu.

California State University, Stanislaus, College of Education, Department of Advanced Studies in Education, Turlock, CA 95382. Offers community college leadership (Ed D); education (MA); educational leadership (Ed D); educational technology (MA); P-12 leadership (Ed D); school administration (MA); school counseling (MA); special education (MA). Part-time and evening/weekend programs available. Postbaccalaureate distance learning degree programs offered. *Degree requirements:* For master's, thesis. *Entrance requirements:* For master's, MAT or GRE, BEST (depending on concentration), minimum GPA of 2.8, 3 letters of reference; for doctorate, GRE, 3.0 minimum GPA, 3 letters of reference and personal statement. Additional exam requirements/recommendations for international students: Required—TOEFL (minimum score 550 paper-based; 213 computer-based). *Faculty research:* Current school technology use, social aspects of technology, staff development.

California University of Pennsylvania, School of Graduate Studies and Research, School of Education, Program in School Administration, California, PA 15419-1394. Offers M Ed. *Accreditation:* NCATE. Part-time and evening/weekend programs available. *Degree requirements:* For master's, comprehensive exam, thesis optional. *Entrance requirements:* For master's, MAT, interview, minimum GPA of 3.0, teaching certificate, 2 years of teaching experience. Additional exam requirements/recommendations for international students: Required—TOEFL (minimum score 550 paper-based; 213 computer-based; 80 iBT). Electronic applications accepted. *Faculty research:* Educational leadership, peer coaching, online education-effective teaching strategies, instruction strategies, school law.

Calumet College of Saint Joseph, Program in Leadership in Teaching, Whiting, IN 46394-2195. Offers MS Ed.

Calvin College, Graduate Programs in Education, Grand Rapids, MI 49546-4388. Offers curriculum and instruction (M Ed); educational leadership (M Ed); learning disabilities (M Ed); literacy (M Ed). Part-time programs available. *Faculty:* 3 full-time (2 women), 4 part-time/adjunct (1 woman). *Students:* 7 full-time (6 women), 113 part-time (79 women); includes 9 minority (2 African Americans, 5 Asian Americans or Pacific Islanders, 2 Hispanic Americans). Average age 29. In 2009, 27 master's awarded. *Degree requirements:* For master's, thesis or seminar. *Entrance requirements:* For master's, teaching certificate. Additional exam requirements/recommendations for international students: Required—TOEFL (minimum score 550 paper-based; 213 computer-based). *Application deadline:* For fall admission, 8/1 priority date for domestic students, 6/1 priority date for international students; for spring admission, 1/1 priority date for domestic students, 2/1 priority date for international students. Applications are processed on a rolling basis. Application fee: $0. Electronic applications accepted. *Expenses:* Tuition: Full-time $10,080. *Financial support:* Federal Work-Study, scholarships/grants, and tuition waivers (full and partial) available. Support available to part-time students. Financial award application deadline: 4/3. *Faculty research:* Literacy, racialized gender and gendered identity, teacher learning, learning disabilities identification. *Unit head:* Dr. Debra Buursma, Graduate Program Director, 616-526-6231, Fax: 616-526-6505, E-mail: dbuursma@calvin.edu. *Application contact:* Cindi Hoekstra, Program Coordinator, 616-526-6158, Fax: 616-526-6505, E-mail: choekstr@calvin.edu.

Cambridge College, School of Education, Cambridge, MA 02138-5304. Offers autism specialist (M Ed); autism/behavior analyst (M Ed); behavior analyst (Post-Master's Certificate); behavioral management (M Ed); early childhood teacher (M Ed); education specialist in curriculum and instruction (CAGS); educational leadership (Ed D); elementary teacher (M Ed); English as a second language (M Ed, Certificate); general science (M Ed); health education, health promotion (Post-Master's Certificate); health/family and consumer sciences (M Ed); history (M Ed); individualized degree (M Ed); information technology literacy (M Ed); instructional technology (M Ed); interdisciplinary studies (M Ed); library teacher (M Ed); literacy education (M Ed); mathematics (M Ed); mathematics specialist (Certificate); middle school mathematics and science (M Ed); school administration (M Ed, CAGS); school guidance counselor (M Ed); school nurse education (M Ed); school social worker/school adjustment counselor (M Ed); special education administrator (CAGS); special education/moderate disabilities (M Ed); teaching skills and methodologies (M Ed). Part-time and evening/weekend programs available. Postbaccalaureate distance learning degree programs offered (minimal on-campus study). *Faculty:* 10 full-time (3 women), 283 part-time/adjunct (187 women). *Students:* 974 full-time (755 women), 1,071 part-time (835 women); includes 940 minority (762 African Americans, 4

Educational Leadership and Administration

Cambridge College (continued)
American Indian/Alaska Native, 22 Asian Americans or Pacific Islanders, 152 Hispanic Americans), 28 international. Average age 39. In 2009, 866 master's, 4 doctorates, 209 CAGSs awarded. *Degree requirements:* For master's, thesis, internship/practicum (licensure program only); for doctorate, thesis/dissertation; for other advanced degree, thesis. *Entrance requirements:* For master's, interview, resume, documentation of licensure, 2 professional references; for doctorate, official transcripts, interview, resume, documentation of licensure (if any), written personal statement/essay, portfolio of scholarly and professional work, qualifying assessment, 2 professional references, health insurance, immunizations form; for other advanced degree, official transcripts, interview, resume, documentation of licensure (if any), written personal statement/essay, 2 professional references, health insurance, immunizations form. Additional exam requirements/recommendations for international students: Required—TOEFL (minimum score 550 paper-based; 213 computer-based; 79 iBT); Recommended—IELTS (minimum score 6). *Application deadline:* Applications are processed on a rolling basis. Application fee: $30. Electronic applications accepted. *Expenses:* Contact institution. *Financial support:* In 2009–10, 1,373 students received support. Career-related internships or fieldwork, Federal Work-Study, and scholarships/grants available. Financial award applicants required to submit FAFSA. *Faculty research:* Adult education, accelerated learning, mathematics education, brain compatible learning, special education and law. *Unit head:* Dr. N. Alan Sheppard, Interim Associate Dean, 617-873-0619, E-mail: alan.sheppard@cambridgecollege.edu. *Application contact:* Stephen Lyons, Director of Enrollment, Graduate and N.I.T.E. Programs, 617-868-1000, Fax: 617-349-3561, E-mail: stephen.lyons@cambridgecollege.edu.

Cameron University, Office of Graduate Studies, Program in Educational Leadership, Lawton, OK 73505-6377. Offers MS. Part-time and evening/weekend programs available. *Degree requirements:* For master's, portfolio.

Campbell University, Graduate and Professional Programs, School of Education, Buies Creek, NC 27506. Offers administration (MSA); community counseling (MA); elementary education (M Ed); English education (M Ed); interdisciplinary studies (M Ed); mathematics education (M Ed); middle grades education (M Ed); physical education (M Ed); school counseling (M Ed); secondary education (M Ed); social science education (M Ed). *Accreditation:* NCATE. Part-time and evening/weekend programs available. *Degree requirements:* For master's, comprehensive exam. *Entrance requirements:* For master's, GRE General Test, minimum GPA of 2.7. *Faculty research:* Spiritual values and wellness issues in counseling, stress and professional burnout among counselors, thinking strategies, leadership, adaptive technology.

Canisius College, Graduate Division, School of Education and Human Services, Department of Graduate Education, Buffalo, NY 14208-1098. Offers adolescence education (grades 7-12) (MS); childhood education (grades 1-6) (MS); college student personnel administration (MS); deaf education (MS); differentiated instruction (MS Ed); educational administration and supervision (MS); general education (MS Ed); initial teacher certification (elementary education) (MS); initial teacher certification (secondary education) (MS); literacy (MS Ed); special education (MS). *Accreditation:* NCATE. Part-time and evening/weekend programs available. *Faculty:* 22 full-time (14 women), 84 part-time/adjunct (54 women). *Students:* 409 full-time (288 women), 261 part-time (187 women); includes 29 minority (24 African Americans, 5 Hispanic Americans), 156 international. Average age 30. 518 applicants, 74% accepted, 240 enrolled. In 2009, 346 master's awarded. Application fee: $25. *Financial support:* Research assistantships with full tuition reimbursements, career-related internships or fieldwork, institutionally sponsored loans, scholarships/grants, health care benefits, tuition waivers (full and partial), and unspecified assistantships available. *Faculty research:* Autism, Asperger's disease, private higher education, reading strategies. *Unit head:* Rev. Paul Nochelski, Chair of Graduate Education and Leadership, 716-888-3297, Fax: 716-888-3299. *Application contact:* James D. Bagwell, Director of Graduate Recruitment and Admissions, 716-888-2544, Fax: 716-888-3290, E-mail: bagwellj@canisius.edu.

Capella University, School of Education, Minneapolis, MN 55402. Offers college teaching (Certificate); curriculum and instruction (MS, PhD); education (MS); enrollment management (MS); instructional design for online learning (MS, PhD); k-12 studies in education (MS, PhD); leadership for higher education (MS, PhD); leadership in education administration (Certificate); leadership in educational administration (MS, PhD); postsecondary and adult education (MS, PhD); professional studies in education (MS, PhD); reading and literacy (MS); training and performance improvement (MS, PhD). Part-time and evening/weekend programs available. Postbaccalaureate distance learning degree programs offered (minimal on-campus study). Terminal master's awarded for partial completion of doctoral program. *Degree requirements:* For master's, thesis optional, integrative project; for doctorate, comprehensive exam, thesis/dissertation. *Entrance requirements:* Additional exam requirements/recommendations for international students: Required—TOEFL (minimum score 550 paper-based; 213 computer-based), TWE (minimum score 4). Electronic applications accepted. *Faculty research:* Higher education administration, distance learning, adult education, training and curriculum design.

Cardinal Stritch University, College of Education, Department of Education, Milwaukee, WI 53217-3985. Offers education (ME); educational leadership (MS); leadership for the advancement of learning and service (Ed D, PhD); teaching (MAT); urban education (MA). *Accreditation:* NCATE. Evening/weekend programs available. *Degree requirements:* For master's, comprehensive exam, thesis (for some programs), research project, faculty recommendation; for doctorate, thesis/dissertation, practica, field experience. *Entrance requirements:* For master's, letters of recommendation (3), minimum GPA of 3.0; for doctorate, minimum GPA of 3.5 in master's coursework, letters of recommendation (3).

Caribbean University, Graduate School, Bayamón, PR 00960-0493. Offers administration and supervision (MA Ed); criminal justice (MA); curriculum and instruction (MA Ed), including elementary education, English education, history education, mathematics education, primary education, science education, Spanish education; education (PhD); gerontology (MSN); human resources (MBA); museology, archiving and art history (MA Ed); neonatal pediatrics (MSN); physical education (MA Ed); special education (MA Ed). *Entrance requirements:* For master's, interview, minimum GPA of 2.5.

Carlow University, School of Education, Program in Educational Leadership, Pittsburgh, PA 15213-3165. Offers M Ed. Part-time and evening/weekend programs available. *Degree requirements:* For master's, thesis or alternative. *Entrance requirements:* Additional exam requirements/recommendations for international students: Required—TOEFL. Electronic applications accepted. *Expenses:* Tuition: Full-time $11,250; part-time $625 per credit. Tuition and fees vary according to course load, degree level and program.

Carson-Newman College, Graduate Program in Education, Jefferson City, TN 37760. Offers curriculum and instruction (M Ed); educational leadership (M Ed); elementary education (MAT); school counseling (MS); secondary education (MAT); teaching English as a second language (MATESL). *Accreditation:* NCATE. Part-time and evening/weekend programs available. *Faculty:* 5 full-time (2 women), 10 part-time/adjunct (3 women). *Students:* 112 full-time (84 women), 84 part-time (52 women); includes 5 African Americans, 17 international. Average age 32. 86 applicants, 98% accepted. In 2009, 55 master's awarded. *Degree requirements:* For master's, thesis or alternative. *Entrance requirements:* For master's, NTE, minimum GPA of 3.0 in major, 2.5 overall. *Application deadline:* For fall admission, 7/15 priority date for domestic students. Applications are processed on a rolling basis. Application fee: $25 ($50 for international students). *Expenses:* Tuition: Full-time $5490; part-time $305 per semester hour. Required fees: $200. *Financial support:* In 2009–10, 41 students received support. Federal Work-Study and unspecified assistantships available. Financial award application deadline: 4/1; financial award applicants required to submit FAFSA. *Unit head:* Dr. Sharon Teets, Chair, 865-471-3461. *Application contact:* Graduate Admissions and Services Adviser, 865-471-3460, Fax: 865-471-3875.

Carthage College, Division of Teacher Education, Kenosha, WI 53140. Offers classroom guidance and counseling (M Ed); creative arts (M Ed); gifted and talented children (M Ed); language arts (M Ed); modern language (M Ed); natural sciences (M Ed); reading (M Ed, Certificate); social sciences (M Ed); teacher leadership (M Ed). Part-time and evening/weekend programs available. *Degree requirements:* For master's, thesis optional. *Entrance requirements:* For master's, MAT, minimum B average, letters of reference.

Castleton State College, Division of Graduate Studies, Department of Education, Program in Educational Leadership, Castleton, VT 05735. Offers MA Ed, CAGS. Part-time and evening/weekend programs available. *Degree requirements:* For master's, thesis or alternative; for CAGS, publishable paper. *Entrance requirements:* For master's, GRE General Test, MAT, interview, minimum undergraduate GPA of 3.0; for CAGS, educational research, master's degree, minimum undergraduate GPA of 3.0. *Expenses:* Tuition, state resident: full-time $10,290; part-time $429 per credit. Tuition, nonresident: full-time $15,420; part-time $643 per credit. One-time fee: $200 full-time.

The Catholic University of America, School of Arts and Sciences, Department of Education, Washington, DC 20064. Offers Catholic educational leadership (PhD); education (Certificate); educational psychology (PhD); learning and instruction (MA); secondary education (MA); special education (MA). *Accreditation:* NCATE. Part-time programs available. *Faculty:* 11 full-time (8 women), 3 part-time/adjunct (0 women). *Students:* 6 full-time (5 women), 56 part-time (39 women); includes 9 minority (5 African Americans, 2 Asian Americans or Pacific Islanders, 2 Hispanic Americans), 2 international. Average age 38. 54 applicants, 59% accepted, 14 enrolled. In 2009, 14 master's, 6 doctorates, 1 other advanced degree awarded. *Degree requirements:* For master's, comprehensive exam, thesis or alternative; for doctorate, comprehensive exam, thesis/dissertation. *Entrance requirements:* For master's and doctorate, GRE General Test or MAT, statement of purpose, official copies of academic transcripts, three letters of recommendation. Additional exam requirements/recommendations for international students: Required—TOEFL (minimum score 580 paper-based; 237 computer-based). *Application deadline:* For fall admission, 8/1 priority date for domestic students, 7/15 for international students; for spring admission, 12/1 priority date for domestic students, 10/15 for international students. Applications are processed on a rolling basis. Application fee: $55. Electronic applications accepted. *Expenses:* Tuition: Full-time $31,740; part-time $1245 per credit hour. Required fees: $50; $25 per semester hour. One-time fee: $425. *Financial support:* Fellowships, research assistantships, teaching assistantships, Federal Work-Study, scholarships/grants, tuition waivers (full and partial), and unspecified assistantships available. Financial award application deadline: 2/1; financial award applicants required to submit FAFSA. *Faculty research:* Catholic school issues, reflective teaching, cognitive psychology, urban education. Total annual research expenditures: $68,905. *Unit head:* Dr. Merylann J. Schuttloffel, Chair, 202-319-5805, Fax: 202-319-5815, E-mail: schuttloffel@cua.edu. *Application contact:* Julie Schwing, Director of Graduate Admissions, 202-319-5057, Fax: 202-319-6533, E-mail: cua-admissions@cua.edu.

The Catholic University of America, School of Theology and Religious Studies, Washington, DC 20064. Offers Biblical studies (STB, MA, PhD, STL); Catholic educational leadership (MA); church history (PhD); Hispanic pastoral leadership (Certificate); Hispanic/Latino ministry (M Div); historical theology (STB, STD); history of religions (Hinduism/Islam) (MA, PhD); liturgical studies/sacramental theology (MA, PhD, STD, STL); moral theology/ethics (STB, MA, PhD, STD, STL); pastoral studies (M Div, Certificate); religion and culture (PhD); religious education/catechetics (MA, MRE, PhD); spirituality (STB, PhD, STD, STL); systematic and historical theology (MA, PhD, STD, STL). *Accreditation:* ATS (one or more programs are accredited). Part-time programs available. *Faculty:* 40 full-time (6 women), 10 part-time/adjunct (2 women). *Students:* 169 full-time (26 women), 225 part-time (57 women); includes 33 minority (10 African Americans, 1 American Indian/Alaska Native, 9 Asian Americans or Pacific Islanders, 13 Hispanic Americans), 73 international. Average age 36. 226 applicants, 72% accepted, 75 enrolled. In 2009, 9 first professional degrees, 14 master's, 26 doctorates awarded. *Degree requirements:* For master's, variable foreign language requirement, comprehensive exam, thesis (for some programs); for doctorate, variable foreign language requirement, comprehensive exam, thesis/dissertation; for first professional degree, comprehensive exam. *Entrance requirements:* For first professional degree and master's, GRE General Test, statement of purpose, official copies of academic transcripts, three letters of recommendation; for doctorate, GRE General Test, 3 letters of recommendation. Additional exam requirements/recommendations for international students: Required—TOEFL (minimum score 580 paper-based; 237 computer-based). *Application deadline:* For fall admission, 8/1 priority date for domestic students, 7/15 for international students; for spring admission, 12/1 priority date for domestic students, 10/15 for international students. Applications are processed on a rolling basis. Application fee: $55. Electronic applications accepted. *Expenses:* Tuition: Full-time $31,740; part-time $1245 per credit hour. Required fees: $50; $25 per semester hour. One-time fee: $425. *Financial support:* Fellowships, research assistantships, teaching assistantships, Federal Work-Study, scholarships/grants, tuition waivers (full and partial), and unspecified assistantships available. Financial award application deadline: 2/1; financial award applicants required to submit FAFSA. *Faculty research:* Historical and systematic theology, religious education and catechetics, moral theology and ethics, Biblical studies, liturgical studies and sacramental theology. Total annual research expenditures: $66,740. *Unit head:* Msgr. Kevin W. Irwin, Dean, 202-319-5683, Fax: 202-319-4967, E-mail: irwin@cua.edu. *Application contact:* Julie Schwing, Director of Graduate Admissions, 202-319-5057, Fax: 202-319-6533, E-mail: cua-admissions@cua.edu.

Centenary College, Program in Education, Hackettstown, NJ 07840-2100. Offers instructional leadership (MA); special education (MA). *Accreditation:* Teacher Education Accreditation Council. Part-time and evening/weekend programs available. Postbaccalaureate distance learning degree programs offered (minimal on-campus study). *Degree requirements:* For master's, thesis. *Entrance requirements:* For master's, interview, minimum undergraduate GPA of 2.8.

Centenary College of Louisiana, Graduate Programs, Department of Education, Shreveport, LA 71104. Offers administration (M Ed); elementary education (MAT); secondary education (MAT); supervision of instruction (M Ed). Part-time and evening/weekend programs available. *Degree requirements:* For master's, comprehensive exam. *Entrance requirements:* For master's, GRE General Test (M Ed), PRAXIS I and PRAXIS II (MAT), teacher certification (M Ed), minimum GPA of 2.5. *Expenses:* Contact institution. *Faculty research:* Teachers as advocates for teachers, portfolio assessment, disabled readers.

Central Connecticut State University, School of Graduate Studies, School of Education and Professional Studies, Department of Educational Leadership, Program in Educational Leadership, New Britain, CT 06050-4010. Offers MS, Ed D, Sixth Year Certificate. Part-time and evening/weekend programs available. *Students:* 10 full-time (7 women), 248 part-time (165 women); includes 30 minority (17 African Americans, 2 Asian Americans or Pacific Islanders, 11 Hispanic Americans), 3 international. Average age 42. 99 applicants, 72% accepted, 60 enrolled. In 2009, 44 master's, 10 doctorates, 71 other advanced degrees awarded. *Entrance requirements:* Additional exam requirements/recommendations for international students: Required—TOEFL. *Application deadline:* For fall admission, 7/1 for domestic students; for spring admission, 12/1 for domestic students. Applications are processed on a rolling basis. Application fee: $50. Electronic applications accepted. *Expenses:* Tuition, area resident: Full-time $4662; part-time $440 per credit. Tuition, state resident: full-time $6994; part-time $440 per credit. Tuition, nonresident: full-time $12,988; part-time $440 per credit. Required fees: $3606. One-time fee: $62 part-time. *Financial support:* Application deadline: 3/1.

Central Michigan University, Central Michigan University Off-Campus Programs, Program in Educational Leadership, Mount Pleasant, MI 48859. Offers educational administration (Ed S); educational administration and community leadership (Ed D); school principalship (MA). Part-time and evening/weekend programs available. *Entrance requirements:* For master's, minimum GPA of 2.7 in major. Additional exam requirements/recommendations for international students: Required—TOEFL. *Application deadline:* Applications are processed on a rolling basis. Application fee: $50. Electronic applications accepted. *Financial support:* Scholarships/grants available. Support available to part-time students. *Unit head:* Dr. Michael B. Gilbert, Chair, 989-774-7699, Fax: 989-774-4374, E-mail: gilbe1mb@cmich.edu. *Application contact:* 877-268-4636, E-mail: cmuoffcampus@cmich.edu.

Central Michigan University, College of Graduate Studies, College of Education and Human Services, Department of Educational Leadership, Mount Pleasant, MI 48859. Offers educational leadership (MA, Ed D), including charter school leadership (Ed D), educational technology (Ed D), general educational leadership, higher education administration (Ed D), higher education leadership (Ed D), K-12 curriculum (Ed D), K-12 leadership (Ed D), student affairs administration (Ed D); general educational administration (Ed S); school principalship (MA). Part-time and evening/weekend programs available. *Degree requirements:* For master's and Ed S, thesis or alternative; for doctorate, thesis/dissertation. *Entrance requirements:* For doctorate, GRE or MAT, master's degree, minimum GPA of 3.5, 3 years of professional education experience. Electronic applications accepted. *Faculty research:* Elementary administration, secondary administration, student achievement, in-service training, internships in administration.

Chadron State College, School of Professional and Graduate Studies, Department of Education, Chadron, NE 69337. Offers business (MA Ed); community counseling (MA Ed); educational administration (MS Ed, Sp Ed); elementary education (MS Ed); history (MA Ed); language and literature (MA Ed); secondary administration (MS Ed); secondary education (MS Ed). *Accreditation:* NCATE. Part-time and evening/weekend programs available. Postbaccalaureate distance learning degree programs offered. *Degree requirements:* For master's, thesis optional. *Entrance requirements:* For master's, GRE General Test, GRE Writing Test, minimum GPA of 2.75 or 12 graduate hours at CSC with minimum GPA of 3.25. Additional exam requirements/recommendations for international students: Required—TOEFL. Electronic applications accepted. *Faculty research:* Rural education, technology, mental health.

Chapman University, Graduate Studies, College of Educational Studies, Concentration in Educational Leadership and Administration, Orange, CA 92866. Offers administrative services (Tier I) (Credential). Part-time and evening/weekend programs available. *Faculty:* 19 full-time (13 women), 20 part-time/adjunct (12 women). *Students:* 2 full-time (both women), 17 part-time (9 women); includes 6 minority (2 Asian Americans or Pacific Islanders, 4 Hispanic Americans). Average age 33. 6 applicants, 67% accepted, 4 enrolled. In 2009, 12 master's awarded. *Degree requirements:* For master's, comprehensive exam, thesis optional. *Entrance requirements:* For master's, GRE General Test, MAT, or California Subject Examinations for Teachers, minimum undergraduate GPA of 2.5. Additional exam requirements/recommendations for international students: Required—TOEFL (minimum score 550 paper-based). *Application deadline:* Applications are processed on a rolling basis. Application fee: $55. Electronic applications accepted. *Expenses:* Contact institution. *Financial support:* Fellowships, Federal Work-Study and scholarships/grants available. Financial award application deadline: 6/30; financial award applicants required to submit FAFSA. *Unit head:* Dr. Penny Bryan, Coordinator, 714-997-6781. *Application contact:* Rika Judd, Information Contact, 714-997-6786, Fax: 714-997-6713, E-mail: rjudd@chapman.edu.

Chapman University, Graduate Studies, College of Educational Studies, Program in Education, Orange, CA 92866. Offers curriculum and foundations (MA); educational leadership and administration (MA); reading and literacy (MA). Part-time and evening/weekend programs available. *Faculty:* 24 full-time (15 women), 25 part-time/adjunct (16 women). *Students:* 7 full-time (all women), 35 part-time (25 women); includes 20 minority (1 African American, 8 Asian Americans or Pacific Islanders, 11 Hispanic Americans). Average age 32. 18 applicants, 89% accepted, 9 enrolled. In 2009, 32 master's awarded. *Degree requirements:* For master's, comprehensive exam, thesis optional. *Entrance requirements:* For master's, GRE General Test, MAT, or California Subject Examinations for Teachers, minimum undergraduate GPA of 2.5. Additional exam requirements/recommendations for international students: Required—TOEFL (minimum score 550 paper-based). *Application deadline:* Applications are processed on a rolling basis. Application fee: $55. Electronic applications accepted. *Expenses:* Contact institution. *Financial support:* Fellowships, Federal Work-Study and scholarships/grants available. Financial award application deadline: 6/30; financial award applicants required to submit FAFSA. *Unit head:* Dr. Barbara Tye, Coordinator, 714-997-6781. *Application contact:* Rika Judd, Information Contact, 714-997-6786, Fax: 714-997-6713, E-mail: rjudd@chapman.edu.

Charleston Southern University, School of Education, Charleston, SC 29423-8087. Offers administration and supervision (M Ed), including elementary, secondary; elementary education (M Ed); secondary education (M Ed). *Accreditation:* NCATE. Part-time and evening/weekend programs available. *Faculty:* 4 full-time (2 women). *Students:* 70 part-time (57 women); includes 17 minority (all African Americans). Average age 34. 48 applicants, 79% accepted, 22 enrolled. In 2009, 27 master's awarded. *Degree requirements:* For master's, thesis optional. *Entrance requirements:* For master's, GRE or MAT. Additional exam requirements/recommendations for international students: Required—TOEFL (minimum score 550 paper-based; 213 computer-based; 79 iBT). *Application deadline:* Applications are processed on a rolling basis. Application fee: $30. *Expenses:* Contact institution. *Financial support:* Research assistantships with full tuition reimbursements, career-related internships or fieldwork and Federal Work-Study available. Financial award application deadline: 4/15; financial award applicants required to submit FAFSA. *Unit head:* Dr. Norma Harper, Dean, 843-863-7765, Fax: 843-863-7085, E-mail: nharper@csuniv.edu. *Application contact:* Alison Harrison, Graduate Enrollment Counselor, 843-863-7534, Fax: 843-863-7070, E-mail: aharrison@cwuniv.edu.

Chestnut Hill College, School of Graduate Studies, Department of Education, Program in Educational Leadership, Philadelphia, PA 19118-2693. Offers M Ed. Part-time and evening/weekend programs available. *Degree requirements:* For master's, thesis optional. *Entrance requirements:* For master's, PRAXIS I or proof of teaching certification, letters of recommendation, writing sample, 6 graduate credits with minimum B grade if undergraduate GPA less than 3.0. Additional exam requirements/recommendations for international students: Required—TOEFL (minimum score 500 paper-based). *Faculty research:* Mentoring and induction programs.

Cheyney University of Pennsylvania, School of Education and Professional Studies, Program in Educational Administration and Supervision, Cheyney, PA 19319. Offers M Ed, Certificate. *Accreditation:* NCATE. Part-time and evening/weekend programs available. *Degree requirements:* For master's, thesis or alternative. *Entrance requirements:* For master's, GRE General Test, MAT, minimum GPA of 2.75. Electronic applications accepted. *Faculty research:* Teacher motivation, critical thinking.

Cheyney University of Pennsylvania, School of Education and Professional Studies, Program in Educational Administration of Adult and Continuing Education, Cheyney, PA 19319. Offers M Ed, MS. Part-time and evening/weekend programs available. *Degree requirements:* For master's, thesis or alternative. Electronic applications accepted.

Cheyney University of Pennsylvania, School of Education and Professional Studies, Program in Elementary and Secondary Principalship, Cheyney, PA 19319. Offers Certificate.

Chicago State University, School of Graduate and Professional Studies, College of Education, Department of Educational Leadership, Curriculum and Foundations, Program in Educational Leadership, Chicago, IL 60628. Offers educational leadership (Ed D); general administration (MA); higher education administration (MA). *Accreditation:* NCATE. *Degree requirements:* For master's, comprehensive exam, thesis optional. *Entrance requirements:* For master's, minimum GPA of 2.75.

Christian Brothers University, School of Arts, Memphis, TN 38104-5581. Offers Catholic studies (MACS); curriculum and instruction (M Ed); educational leadership (MSEL); teacher-leadership (M Ed); teaching (MAT). Part-time and evening/weekend programs available. *Faculty:* 7 full-time (4 women), 10 part-time/adjunct (7 women). *Students:* 62 full-time (49 women), 175 part-time (125 women); includes 70 minority (60 African Americans, 5 Asian Americans or Pacific Islanders, 5 Hispanic Americans). Average age 32. In 2009, 92 master's awarded. *Entrance requirements:* For master's, GRE, GMAT, PRAXIS II. *Application deadline:* Applications are processed on a rolling basis. Application fee: $35. *Expenses:* Contact institution. *Financial support:* Institutionally sponsored loans available. Support available to part-time students. *Unit head:* Dr. Marius Carriere, Dean, 901-321-3366, Fax: 901-321-4340, E-mail: mcarrier@cbu.edu. *Application contact:* Dr. Talana L. Vogel, Director, 901-321-4101, Fax: 901-321-3408, E-mail: tvogel@cbu.edu.

The Citadel, The Military College of South Carolina, Citadel Graduate College, School of Education, Program in Educational Administration, Charleston, SC 29409. Offers elementary/secondary school administration and supervision (M Ed); school superintendency (Ed S). *Accreditation:* NCATE. Part-time and evening/weekend programs available. *Faculty:* 12 full-time (7 women), 8 part-time/adjunct (5 women). *Students:* 63 part-time (40 women); includes 13 minority (10 African Americans, 3 Hispanic Americans). Average age 33. In 2009, 29 master's, 13 Ed Ss awarded. *Degree requirements:* For master's and Ed S, comprehensive exam, internship. *Entrance requirements:* For master's, GRE (minimum score 900) or MAT (minimum score 396), minimum undergraduate GPA of 2.5, valid South Carolina teaching certificate, one year of teaching experience; for Ed S, GRE (minimum 900) or MAT (minimum 396), minimum GPA of 3.5; South Carolina State Certificate in school administration or an administrative position equivalent to assistant principal or higher in education; valid South Carolina teaching certificate and three years teaching experience. Additional exam requirements/recommendations for international students: Required—TOEFL (minimum score 550 paper-based; 213 computer-based). *Application deadline:* Applications are processed on a rolling basis. Application fee: $30. Electronic applications accepted. *Expenses:* Tuition, state resident: part-time $400 per credit hour. Tuition, nonresident: part-time $657 per credit hour. Required fees: $40 per term. *Financial support:* Career-related internships or fieldwork, health care benefits, and unspecified assistantships available. Support available to part-time students. Financial award application deadline: 7/1; financial award applicants required to submit FAFSA. *Unit head:* Dr. Mary Lou Yeatts, Coordinator, 843-953-5097, Fax: 843-953-7258, E-mail: marylou.yeatts@citadel.edu. *Application contact:* Dr. Steve A. Nida, Associate Provost, The Citadel Graduate College, 843-953-5089, Fax: 843-953-7630, E-mail: cgc@citadel.edu.

City College of the City University of New York, Graduate School, School of Education, Department of Administration and Supervision, New York, NY 10031-9198. Offers MS, AC. *Degree requirements:* For master's, thesis, research paper. *Entrance requirements:* For master's, Liberal Arts and Sciences Test (LAST), Content Specialty Test (CST), interview; minimum GPA of 3.0 in major, 2.5 overall. Additional exam requirements/recommendations for international students: Required—TOEFL. *Expenses:* Tuition, state resident: part-time $310 per credit. Tuition, nonresident: part-time $575 per credit. Tuition and fees vary according to course load and program. *Faculty research:* Dynamics of organizational change, impact of laws on educational policy, leadership development in schools.

City University of Seattle, Graduate Division, Gordon Albright School of Education, Bellevue, WA 98005. Offers curriculum and instruction (M Ed); educational leadership (M Ed); educational leadership: administrator certification (Certificate); executive leadership: superintendent certification (Certificate); guidance and counseling (M Ed); leadership (M Ed); leadership and school counseling (M Ed); professional certification for teachers (Certificate); reading and literacy (M Ed); reading and literacy in education (M Ed); teacher certification (elementary K-8) (MIT); teacher certification (special education K-12) (MIT); technology, curriculum, and instruction (M Ed). Part-time and evening/weekend programs available. Postbaccalaureate distance learning degree programs offered (no on-campus study). *Entrance requirements:* Additional exam requirements/recommendations for international students: Required—TOEFL (minimum score 540 paper-based; 207 computer-based); Recommended—IELTS. Electronic applications accepted. *Expenses:* Contact institution.

Claremont Graduate University, Graduate Programs, School of Educational Studies, Claremont, CA 91711-6160. Offers Africana education (Certificate); education and policy (MA, PhD); higher education/student affairs (MA, PhD); human development (MA, PhD); public school administration (MA, PhD); quantitative evaluation (MA, PhD); special education (MA, PhD); teacher education (MA); teaching and learning (MA, PhD); urban leadership (PhD); MBA/PhD. Part-time programs available. *Faculty:* 18 full-time (12 women), 1 part-time/adjunct (0 women). *Students:* 279 full-time (190 women), 174 part-time (122 women); includes 196 minority (50 African Americans, 1 American Indian/Alaska Native, 37 Asian Americans or Pacific Islanders, 108 Hispanic Americans), 10 international. Average age 37. In 2009, 84 master's, 23 doctorates awarded. Terminal master's awarded for partial completion of doctoral program. *Entrance requirements:* For master's and doctorate, GRE General Test. Additional exam requirements/recommendations for international students: Required—TOEFL (minimum score 550 paper-based; 213 computer-based; 80 iBT). *Application deadline:* For fall admission, 2/1 priority date for domestic students. Applications are processed on a rolling basis. Application fee: $60. Electronic applications accepted. *Expenses:* Tuition: Full-time $35,046; part-time $1524 per credit. Required fees: $161 per semester. *Financial support:* Fellowships, research assistantships, Federal Work-Study, institutionally sponsored loans, and scholarships/grants available. Support available to part-time students. Financial award application deadline: 2/15; financial award applicants required to submit FAFSA. *Faculty research:* Education administration, K-12 and higher education, multicultural education, education policy, diversity in higher education, faculty issues. *Unit head:* Margaret Grogan, Dean, 909-621-8075, Fax: 909-621-8734, E-mail: margaret.grogan@cgu.edu.

Clark Atlanta University, School of Education, Department of Educational Leadership, Atlanta, GA 30314. Offers MA, Ed D, Ed S. Part-time and evening/weekend programs available. *Faculty:* 5 full-time (1 woman), 3 part-time/adjunct (0 women). *Students:* 17 full-time (12 women), 72 part-time (41 women); includes 83 minority (79 African Americans, 1 American Indian/Alaska Native, 1 Asian American or Pacific Islander, 2 Hispanic Americans). Average age 37. 31 applicants, 87% accepted, 16 enrolled. In 2009, 6 master's, 16 doctorates, 1 other advanced degree awarded. *Degree requirements:* For master's and Ed S, comprehensive exam; for doctorate, comprehensive exam, thesis/dissertation. *Entrance requirements:* For master's, GRE General Test, minimum undergraduate GPA of 2.6; for doctorate and Ed S, GRE General Test, minimum graduate GPA of 3.0. Additional exam requirements/recommendations for international students: Required—TOEFL (minimum score 500 paper-based; 173 computer-based). *Application deadline:* For fall admission, 4/1 for domestic and international students; for spring admission, 11/1 for domestic and international students. Applications are processed on a rolling basis. Application fee: $40 ($55 for international students). Electronic applications accepted. *Expenses:* Tuition: Full-time $12,240; part-time $680 per credit hour. Required fees: $710; $355 per semester. *Financial support:* Career-related internships or fieldwork, Federal Work-Study, scholarships/grants, and unspecified assistantships available. Support available to part-time students. Financial award application deadline: 4/30; financial award applicants required to submit FAFSA. *Unit head:* Dr. Moses Norman, Chairperson, 404-880-8495, E-mail: mnorman@cau.edu. *Application contact:* Michelle Clark-Davis, Graduate Program Admissions, 404-880-6605, E-mail: cauadmissions@cau.edu.

Clarke College, Program in Education, Dubuque, IA 52001-3198. Offers early childhood/special education (MAE); educational administration: elementary and secondary (MAE); educational media: elementary and secondary (MAE); multi-categorical resource k-12 (MAE); multidisciplinary studies (MAE); reading: elementary (MAE); technology in education (MAE). Part-time and evening/weekend programs available. Postbaccalaureate distance learning degree programs offered (minimal on-campus study). *Faculty:* 5 full-time (all women). *Students:* 1 (woman) full-time, 45 part-time (40 women). Average age 31. 19 applicants, 74% accepted, 13 enrolled. In 2009, 11 master's awarded. *Degree requirements:* For master's, comprehensive exam, thesis optional. *Entrance requirements:* For master's, GRE General Test or MAT, minimum GPA of 2.75. *Application deadline:* Applications are processed on a rolling basis. Application fee: $25. Electronic applications accepted. *Expenses:* Tuition: Full-time $10,836; part-time $602 per credit hour. Required fees: $30 per credit hour. *Financial support:* Career-related internships or fieldwork available. Financial award applicants required to submit FAFSA. *Unit head:* Dr. Larry Bice, Chair, 319-588-6397, Fax: 319-584-8604. *Application contact:* Joan Coates, Information Contact, 563-588-6354, Fax: 563-588-6789, E-mail: graduate@clarke.edu.

Clearwater Christian College, Program in Educational Leadership, Clearwater, FL 33759-4595. Offers M Ed. Postbaccalaureate distance learning degree programs offered (minimal on-campus study). *Degree requirements:* For master's, thesis or practicum.

Clemson University, Graduate School, College of Health, Education, and Human Development, School of Education, Program in Administration and Supervision, Clemson, SC 29634. Offers

Educational Leadership and Administration

Clemson University (continued)
M Ed, Ed S. *Students:* 2 full-time (0 women), 72 part-time (50 women); includes 6 minority (all African Americans), 1 international. Average age 34. 24 applicants, 71% accepted, 9 enrolled. In 2009, 35 master's, 1 Ed S awarded. *Entrance requirements:* For master's and Ed S, GRE General Test or MAT, 1 year of teaching experience. Additional exam requirements/recommendations for international students: Required—TOEFL. *Application deadline:* For fall admission, 3/1 for domestic and international students; for spring admission, 10/1 for domestic and international students. Applications are processed on a rolling basis. Application fee: $70 ($80 for international students). Electronic applications accepted. *Expenses:* Tuition, state resident: full-time $8684; part-time $528 per credit hour. Tuition, nonresident: full-time $15,330; part-time $1078 per credit hour. Required fees: $736; $37 per semester. Part-time tuition and fees vary according to course load and program. *Financial support:* Application deadline: 6/1. *Unit head:* Dr. Michael J. Padilla, Director/Associate Dean, 864-656-4444, Fax: 864-656-0311, E-mail: padilla@clemson.edu. *Application contact:* Dr. David Fleming, Graduate Coordinator, 864-656-1881, Fax: 864-656-0311, E-mail: dflemin@clemson.edu.

Clemson University, Graduate School, College of Health, Education, and Human Development, School of Education, Program in Educational Leadership, Clemson, SC 29634. Offers PhD. *Accreditation:* NCATE. *Students:* 18 full-time (11 women), 83 part-time (42 women); includes 19 minority (17 African Americans, 2 Asian Americans or Pacific Islanders), 1 international. Average age 38. 30 applicants, 70% accepted, 10 enrolled. In 2009, 19 doctorates awarded. *Degree requirements:* For doctorate, thesis/dissertation. *Entrance requirements:* For doctorate, GRE General Test, master's degree in related field. Additional exam requirements/recommendations for international students: Required—TOEFL. *Application deadline:* For fall admission, 3/1 for domestic and international students; for spring admission, 10/1 for domestic and international students. Applications are processed on a rolling basis. Application fee: $70 ($80 for international students). Electronic applications accepted. *Expenses:* Tuition, state resident: full-time $8684; part-time $528 per credit hour. Tuition, nonresident: full-time $15,330; part-time $1078 per credit hour. Required fees: $736; $37 per semester. Part-time tuition and fees vary according to course load and program. *Financial support:* In 2009–10, 10 students received support, including 1 fellowship with full and partial tuition reimbursement available (averaging $10,000 per year), 7 research assistantships with partial tuition reimbursements available (averaging $17,985 per year), 1 teaching assistantship with partial tuition reimbursement available (averaging $8,620 per year); career-related internships or fieldwork, institutionally sponsored loans, scholarships/grants, health care benefits, and unspecified assistantships also available. Support available to part-time students. Financial award application deadline: 6/1; financial award applicants required to submit FAFSA. *Unit head:* Dr. Michael J. Padilla, Director/Associate Dean, 864-656-4444, Fax: 864-656-0311, E-mail: padilla@clemson.edu. *Application contact:* Dr. David Fleming, Graduate Coordinator, 864-656-1881, Fax: 864-656-0311, E-mail: dflemin@clemson.edu.

Cleveland State University, College of Graduate Studies, College of Education and Human Services, Department of Counseling, Administration, Supervision and Adult Learning (CASAL), Cleveland, OH 44115. Offers accelerated degree in adult learning and development (M Ed); adult learning and development (M Ed); chemical dependency counseling (Certificate); community agency counseling (M Ed); counseling and pupil personnel administration (Ed S); early childhood mental health counseling (Certificate); educational administration and supervision (M Ed); school administration (Ed S); school counseling (M Ed). *Accreditation:* ACA (one or more programs are accredited). Part-time and evening/weekend programs available. *Degree requirements:* For master's, comprehensive exam (for some programs), thesis optional; for other advanced degree, comprehensive exam, thesis optional, internship. *Entrance requirements:* For master's, GRE General Test or MAT, letter of recommendation, minimum GPA of 2.75. Additional exam requirements/recommendations for international students: Required—TOEFL (minimum score 525 paper-based; 197 computer-based), IELTS (minimum score 6). Electronic applications accepted. *Faculty research:* Education law, career development, women in school administration, psychopharmacology, counseling and spirituality.

Cleveland State University, College of Graduate Studies, College of Education and Human Services, Program in Urban Education, Cleveland, OH 44115. Offers counseling (PhD); counseling psychology (PhD); leadership and lifelong learning (PhD); learning and development (PhD); policy studies (PhD); school administration (PhD). Part-time programs available. *Degree requirements:* For doctorate, one foreign language, comprehensive exam, thesis/dissertation. *Entrance requirements:* For doctorate, GRE General Test, minimum graduate GPA of 3.25. Additional exam requirements/recommendations for international students: Required—TOEFL (minimum score 525 paper-based; 197 computer-based), IELTS (minimum score 6). *Faculty research:* Equity issues (race, ethnicity, and gender), education development consequences for special needs of urban populations, urban education programming, counseling the violent or aggressive adolescent.

Coastal Carolina University, Spadoni College of Education, Conway, SC 29528-6054. Offers education (MAT); educational leadership (M Ed); learning and teaching (M Ed); secondary education (M Ed). *Accreditation:* NCATE. Part-time and evening/weekend programs available. *Faculty:* 12 full-time (4 women), 3 part-time/adjunct (1 woman). *Students:* 66 full-time (41 women), 138 part-time (105 women); includes 29 minority (24 African Americans, 1 American Indian/Alaska Native, 2 Asian Americans or Pacific Islanders, 2 Hispanic Americans), 3 international. Average age 33. 242 applicants, 88% accepted, 150 enrolled. In 2009, 76 master's awarded. *Degree requirements:* For master's, comprehensive exam. *Entrance requirements:* For master's, GRE General Test, MAT, 2 letters of recommendation, copy of teaching credential. Additional exam requirements/recommendations for international students: Required—TOEFL (minimum score 550 paper-based; 213 computer-based; 79 iBT). *Application deadline:* For fall admission, 7/1 priority date for domestic and international students; for spring admission, 11/15 priority date for domestic and international students. Applications are processed on a rolling basis. Application fee: $45. Electronic applications accepted. *Expenses:* Tuition, state resident: full-time $9600; part-time $400 per credit hour. Tuition, nonresident: full-time $11,880; part-time $495 per credit hour. Required fees: $80; $40 per term. *Financial support:* Fellowships, research assistantships, unspecified assistantships available. Support available to part-time students. Financial award application deadline: 3/1; financial award applicants required to submit FAFSA. *Unit head:* Dr. Diane L. Mark, Dean, 843-349-2629, Fax: 843-349-2106, E-mail: dmark@coastal.edu. *Application contact:* Dr. Richard L. Johnson, Director of Graduate Studies, 843-349-2192, Fax: 843-349-6444, E-mail: rjohnson@coastal.edu.

The College at Brockport, State University of New York, School of Education and Human Services, Department of Educational Administration, Brockport, NY 14420-2997. Offers educational administration (CAS); school business administration (CAS). Part-time programs available. *Students:* 10 full-time (7 women), 186 part-time (117 women); includes 14 minority (6 African Americans, 8 Hispanic Americans). 68 applicants, 93% accepted, 63 enrolled. In 2009, 93 CASs awarded. *Degree requirements:* For CAS, thesis or alternative, 6-hour internship. *Entrance requirements:* For degree, minimum GPA of 3.0. Additional exam requirements/recommendations for international students: Required—TOEFL (minimum score 550 paper-based; 213 computer-based; 79 iBT). *Application deadline:* For fall admission, 7/15 priority date for domestic and international students; for spring admission, 11/15 priority date for domestic and international students. Application fee: $80. Electronic applications accepted. *Expenses:* Tuition, state resident: full-time $8370; part-time $349 per credit. Tuition, nonresident: full-time $13,250; part-time $522 per credit. *Financial support:* Federal Work-Study, scholarships/grants, and unspecified assistantships available. Support available to part-time students. Financial award application deadline: 3/15; financial award applicants required to submit FAFSA. *Faculty research:* Superintendency, budgeting, school business administration, leadership, special education administration. *Unit head:* Donald R. Covell, Interim Chairperson, 585-395-2661, Fax: 585-395-2172, E-mail: dcovell@brockport.edu. *Application contact:* Donald R. Covell, Interim Chairperson, 585-395-2661, Fax: 585-395-2172, E-mail: dcovell@brockport.edu.

College of Mount St. Joseph, Graduate Education Program, Cincinnati, OH 45233-1670. Offers adolescent young adult education (MA); art (MA); inclusive early childhood education (MA); instructional leadership (MA); middle childhood education (MA); multi-age education (MA); multicultural special education (MA); music (MA); reading (MA). *Accreditation:* Teacher Education Accreditation Council. Part-time and evening/weekend programs available. *Faculty:* 15 full-time (11 women), 9 part-time/adjunct (6 women). *Students:* 93 full-time (75 women), 99 part-time (66 women); includes 19 minority (18 African Americans, 1 American Indian/Alaska Native). Average age 34. 116 applicants, 97% accepted, 94 enrolled. In 2009, 51 master's awarded. *Degree requirements:* For master's, research project, student teaching, clinical and field-based experiences. *Entrance requirements:* For master's, GRE, PRAXIS II in teaching content area (math or science), 2 letters of recommendation, interview, resume. Additional exam requirements/recommendations for international students: Required—TOEFL (minimum score 560 paper-based; 220 computer-based; 83 iBT). *Application deadline:* Applications are processed on a rolling basis. Application fee: $50. Electronic applications accepted. *Expenses:* Tuition: Part-time $500 per hour. Required fees: $200 per year. Tuition and fees vary according to degree level and program. *Financial support:* In 2009–10, 51 students received support. Scholarships/grants available. Financial award applicants required to submit FAFSA. *Faculty research:* Foreign and second language learning problems/reading disabilities/hyperlexia, multicultural/bilingual special education, alternative educator licensure, science education, pedagogical content knowledge. *Unit head:* Dr. Mary West, Chair of Graduate Education, 513-244-3263, Fax: 513-244-4867, E-mail: mary_west@mail.msj.edu. *Application contact:* Marilyn Hoskins, Assistant Director of Graduate Recruitment, 513-244-4723, Fax: 513-244-4629, E-mail: marilyn_hoskins@mail.msj.edu.

The College of New Jersey, Graduate Division, School of Education, Department of Educational Administration and Secondary Education, Program in Educational Leadership, Ewing, NJ 08628. Offers M Ed, Certificate. Part-time and evening/weekend programs available. *Students:* 32 full-time (23 women), 106 part-time (75 women); includes 24 minority (16 African Americans, 1 American Indian/Alaska Native, 3 Asian Americans or Pacific Islanders, 4 Hispanic Americans), 1 international. 253 applicants, 75% accepted. In 2009, 88 master's, 24 Certificates awarded. *Degree requirements:* For master's, comprehensive exam. *Entrance requirements:* For master's, GRE, minimum GPA of 3.0 in field or 2.75 overall; for Certificate, previous master's degree or higher. Additional exam requirements/recommendations for international students: Required—TOEFL. *Application deadline:* For fall admission, 2/1 priority date for domestic students; for spring admission, 10/1 priority date for domestic students. Application fee: $70. Electronic applications accepted. *Expenses:* Tuition, state resident: part-time $573.70 per credit. Tuition, nonresident: part-time $887.75 per credit. Required fees: $140.85 per credit. One-time fee: $10 part-time. *Financial support:* Tuition waivers (partial) and unspecified assistantships available. Financial award applicants required to submit FAFSA. *Unit head:* Dr. Jacqueline Norris, Coordinator, 609-771-2422, E-mail: norris@tcnj.edu. *Application contact:* Susan L. Hydro, Assistant Dean, Office of Graduate Studies, 609-771-2300, Fax: 609-637-5105, E-mail: graduate@tcnj.edu.

The College of New Rochelle, Graduate School, Division of Education, Program in School Administration and Supervision, New Rochelle, NY 10805-2308. Offers dual certification: school building leader/school district leader (MS); school building leader (MS, Advanced Certificate); school district leader (MS, Advanced Diploma). *Degree requirements:* For master's, internship. *Entrance requirements:* For master's, interview, minimum GPA of 3.0 in field, 2.7 overall, minimum 3 years teaching or education administration experience. *Faculty research:* Training administrators in Eastern Europe, leadership.

College of Notre Dame of Maryland, Graduate Studies, Leadership in Teaching Program, Baltimore, MD 21210-2476. Offers MA. *Entrance requirements:* For master's, interview, 1 year of teaching experience, minimum GPA of 3.0. Additional exam requirements/recommendations for international students: Required—TOEFL (minimum score 500 paper-based; 173 computer-based; 61 iBT). Electronic applications accepted.

College of Notre Dame of Maryland, Graduate Studies, Program in Instructional Leadership for Changing Populations, Baltimore, MD 21210-2476. Offers PhD. *Entrance requirements:* Additional exam requirements/recommendations for international students: Required—TOEFL (minimum score 500 paper-based; 173 computer-based; 61 iBT).

College of Saint Elizabeth, Department of Education, Morristown, NJ 07960-6989. Offers accelerated certification for teachers (Certificate); assistive technology (Certificate); education: human services leadership (MA); educational leadership (MA, Ed D); educational technology (MA). Part-time and evening/weekend programs available. *Faculty:* 10 full-time (3 women), 20 part-time/adjunct (11 women). *Students:* 119 full-time (88 women), 332 part-time (292 women); includes 63 minority (35 African Americans, 3 Asian Americans or Pacific Islanders, 25 Hispanic Americans), 1 international. Average age 37. 201 applicants, 82% accepted, 146 enrolled. In 2009, 140 master's, 81 other advanced degrees awarded. *Degree requirements:* For master's, thesis or alternative, portfolio. *Entrance requirements:* For master's, interview, minimum undergraduate GPA of 3.0. *Application deadline:* For fall admission, 6/30 priority date for domestic students; for spring admission, 11/30 for domestic students. Applications are processed on a rolling basis. Application fee: $35. Electronic applications accepted. *Expenses:* Tuition: Part-time $797 per credit hour. Required fees: $65 per credit hour. *Financial support:* Career-related internships or fieldwork, tuition waivers (partial), and unspecified assistantships available. Support available to part-time students. Financial award application deadline: 3/15; financial award applicants required to submit FAFSA. *Faculty research:* Developmental stages for teaching and human services professionals, effectiveness of humanities core curriculum. *Unit head:* Dr. Alan H. Markowitz, Director of Graduate Education Programs, 973-290-4374, Fax: 973-290-4389, E-mail: amarkowitz@cse.edu. *Application contact:* Donna Tatarka, Dean of Admission, 973-290-4705, Fax: 973-290-4710, E-mail: dtatarka@cse.edu.

College of Saint Mary, Program in Education, Omaha, NE 68106. Offers assessment leadership (MSE); English as a second language (MSE). Part-time programs available. *Entrance requirements:* For master's, technology competency test or equivalent, minimum cumulative GPA of 3.0, teaching certificate, 2 letters of reference, resume.

The College of Saint Rose, Graduate Studies, School of Education, Department of Counseling and Educational Administration, Program in Educational Administration and Supervision, Albany, NY 12203-1419. Offers college student services administration (MS Ed); educational administration and supervision (MS Ed, Certificate); school administrator and supervisor (Certificate). Part-time and evening/weekend programs available. *Degree requirements:* For master's, comprehensive exam or thesis. *Entrance requirements:* For master's, minimum undergraduate GPA of 3.0, timed writing sample, interview, permanent certification or 3 years teaching experience. Additional exam requirements/recommendations for international students: Required—TOEFL (minimum score 550 paper-based; 213 computer-based). Electronic applications accepted.

College of Santa Fe, Department of Education, Santa Fe, NM 87505-7634. Offers at-risk youth (MA), including bilingual/multicultural education, classroom teaching, community counseling, educational administration, leadership, school counseling, self-designed program, TESOL/Multicultural; curriculum and instruction (MA); multicultural special education (MA). Part-time and evening/weekend programs available. *Entrance requirements:* For master's, minimum GPA of 3.0. *Faculty research:* Integrated curriculum, child development, brain research, learning styles, systemic issues in education.

College of Staten Island of the City University of New York, Graduate Programs, Department of Education, Program in Leadership in Education, Staten Island, NY 10314-6600. Offers 6th Year Certificate. Part-time and evening/weekend programs available. *Faculty:* 3 full-time (all women). *Students:* 31 part-time (22 women); includes 2 minority (1 African American, 1 Hispanic American). Average age 36. 28 applicants, 75% accepted, 20 enrolled. In 2009, 15 6th Year Certificates awarded. *Entrance requirements:* For degree, master's degree, minimum GPA of 3.0, 4 years of teaching experience, 3 professional recommendations, interview. Additional exam requirements/recommendations for international students: Required—TOEFL (minimum score 550 paper-based; 213 computer-based; 79 iBT). *Application deadline:* For fall admission, 4/19 for domestic and international students; for spring admission, 11/16 for

domestic and international students. Applications are processed on a rolling basis. Application fee: $125. Electronic applications accepted. *Expenses:* Tuition, state resident: full-time $7360; part-time $310 per credit. Tuition, nonresident: part-time $575 per credit. Required fees: $378; $113 per semester. *Financial support:* Career-related internships or fieldwork, Federal Work-Study, and scholarships/grants available. Support available to part-time students. Financial award applicants required to submit FAFSA. Total annual research expenditures: $27,000. *Unit head:* Dr. Ruth Silverberg, Coordinator, 718-982-3726, Fax: 718-982-3743, E-mail: educationmasters@mail.csi.cuny.edu. *Application contact:* Sasha Spence, Assistant Director of Graduate Recruitment Admissions, 718-982-2699, Fax: 718-982-2500, E-mail: sasha.spence@csi.cuny.edu.

The College of William and Mary, School of Education, Program in Education Policy, Planning, and Leadership, Williamsburg, VA 23187-8795. Offers curriculum and educational technology (Ed D, PhD); curriculum leadership (Ed D, PhD); educational leadership (M Ed), including higher education administration (M Ed, Ed D, PhD), K-12 administration and supervision; educational policy, planning, and leadership (Ed D, PhD), including general education administration, gifted education administration, higher education administration (M Ed, Ed D, PhD), special education administration; gifted education administration (M Ed). *Accreditation:* NCATE. Part-time and evening/weekend programs available. *Faculty:* 12 full-time (6 women), 3 part-time/adjunct (1 woman). *Students:* 41 full-time (26 women), 134 part-time (93 women); includes 35 minority (32 African Americans, 3 Asian Americans or Pacific Islanders), 2 international. Average age 38. 108 applicants, 57% accepted, 44 enrolled. In 2009, 20 master's, 22 doctorates awarded. *Degree requirements:* For doctorate, comprehensive exam, thesis/dissertation. *Entrance requirements:* For master's, GRE or MAT, minimum GPA of 2.5; for doctorate, GRE or MAT, minimum GPA of 3.0. Additional exam requirements/recommendations for international students: Required—TOEFL. *Application deadline:* For fall admission, 1/15 for domestic and international students. Application fee: $45. Electronic applications accepted. *Expenses:* Tuition, state resident: full-time $6400; part-time $315 per credit hour. Tuition, nonresident: full-time $19,720; part-time $840 per credit hour. Required fees: $4114. *Financial support:* In 2009–10, 56 students received support, including 32 research assistantships with full and partial tuition reimbursements available (averaging $13,000 per year); career-related internships or fieldwork, Federal Work-Study, institutionally sponsored loans, scholarships/grants, and unspecified assistantships also available. Support available to part-time students. Financial award application deadline: 1/15; financial award applicants required to submit FAFSA. *Faculty research:* Higher education policy, faculty incentives, history of adversity, resilience, leadership. *Unit head:* Dr. Megan Tschannen-Moran, Area Coordinator, 757-221-2187, E-mail: mxtsch@wm.edu. *Application contact:* Dorothy Smith Osborne, Director of Admissions, 757-221-2317, Fax: 757-221-2293, E-mail: dsosbo@wm.edu.

Colorado State University, Graduate School, College of Applied Human Sciences, School of Education, Fort Collins, CO 80523-1588. Offers adult education and training (M Ed); community college leadership (PhD); counseling and career development (M Ed); education and human resource studies (M Ed, PhD); educational leadership (M Ed, PhD); interdisciplinary studies (PhD); organizational performance and change (M Ed, PhD); student affairs in higher education (MS). *Accreditation:* ACA; Teacher Education Accreditation Council. Part-time and evening/weekend programs available. *Faculty:* 21 full-time (10 women). *Students:* 195 full-time (132 women), 469 part-time (292 women); includes 114 minority (31 African Americans, 12 American Indian/Alaska Native, 22 Asian Americans or Pacific Islanders, 49 Hispanic Americans), 24 international. Average age 38. 451 applicants, 41% accepted, 141 enrolled. In 2009, 175 master's, 54 doctorates awarded. *Degree requirements:* For master's, comprehensive exam (for some programs), thesis optional; for doctorate, comprehensive exam, thesis/dissertation, minimum of 60 credits. *Entrance requirements:* For master's, GRE, minimum undergraduate GPA of 3.0, 3 letters of recommendation, curriculum vitae/resume; for doctorate, minimum GPA of 3.0, 3 letters of recommendation, curriculum vitae. Additional exam requirements/recommendations for international students: Required—TOEFL (minimum score 550 paper-based; 213 computer-based). *Application deadline:* For fall admission, 3/15 for domestic and international students; for spring admission, 11/1 for domestic students, 10/1 for international students. Applications are processed on a rolling basis. Application fee: $50. Electronic applications accepted. *Expenses:* Tuition, state resident: full-time $6434; part-time $359.10 per credit. Tuition, nonresident: full-time $18,116; part-time $1006.45 per credit. Required fees: $1496; $83 per credit. *Financial support:* In 2009–10, 8 students received support, including 3 research assistantships with full tuition reimbursements available (averaging $13,790 per year), 5 teaching assistantships with full tuition reimbursements available (averaging $10,253 per year); fellowships, Federal Work-Study, scholarships/grants, and unspecified assistantships also available. Financial award applicants required to submit FAFSA. *Faculty research:* Innovative instruction, diverse learners, transition, scientifically-based evaluation methods, leadership and organizational development. Total annual research expenditures: $655,700. *Unit head:* Dr. Carole Makela, Interim Director, 970-491-6317, Fax: 970-491-1317, E-mail: carole.makela@colostate.edu. *Application contact:* Dr. Sharon Anderson, Director of Graduate Programs, 970-491-6861, Fax: 970-491-1317, E-mail: sharon.anderson@colostate.edu.

Columbia International University, Columbia Graduate School, Columbia, SC 29230-3122. Offers Bible teaching (MABT); Christian higher education leadership (Ed D); Christian school educational leadership (Ed D); counseling (MACN); curriculum and instruction (M Ed), including Christian school guidance, English as a second language, learning disabilities, school technology; early childhood and elementary education (MAT); educational administration (M Ed); teaching English as a foreign language (Certificate); teaching English as a foreign language and intercultural studies (MATF). Part-time and evening/weekend programs available. *Degree requirements:* For master's, internships, professional project. *Entrance requirements:* For master's, Minnesota Multiphasic Personality Inventory, MAT, minimum GPA of 2.7. Additional exam requirements/recommendations for international students: Required—TOEFL. Electronic applications accepted.

Columbus State University, Graduate Studies, College of Education and Health Professions, Department of Counseling, Foundations, and Leadership, Columbus, GA 31907-5645. Offers community counseling (MS); curriculum and leadership (Ed D); educational leadership (M Ed, Ed S); school counseling (M Ed). *Accreditation:* ACA; NCATE. Part-time and evening/weekend programs available. Postbaccalaureate distance learning degree programs offered (minimal on-campus study). *Faculty:* 11 full-time (3 women), 7 part-time/adjunct (3 women). *Students:* 92 full-time (65 women), 110 part-time (88 women); includes 68 minority (62 African Americans, 1 American Indian/Alaska Native, 1 Asian American or Pacific Islander, 4 Hispanic Americans), 1 international. Average age 35. 134 applicants, 65% accepted, 61 enrolled. In 2009, 32 master's, 34 other advanced degrees awarded. *Degree requirements:* For master's, thesis, exit exam; for Ed S, thesis or alternative. *Entrance requirements:* For master's, GRE General Test, minimum GPA of 2.75; for doctorate, minimum graduate GPA of 3.5, four years of professional service; for Ed S, GRE General Test. Additional exam requirements/recommendations for international students: Required—TOEFL (minimum score 550 paper-based; 213 computer-based; 79 iBT). *Application deadline:* For fall admission, 5/1 priority date for domestic students, 5/1 for international students; for spring admission, 11/1 for domestic and international students. Applications are processed on a rolling basis. Application fee: $30. Electronic applications accepted. *Financial support:* In 2009–10, 110 students received support, including 7 research assistantships with partial tuition reimbursements available (averaging $3,000 per year); career-related internships or fieldwork, Federal Work-Study, institutionally sponsored loans, scholarships/grants, tuition waivers (partial), and unspecified assistantships also available. Support available to part-time students. Financial award application deadline: 5/1; financial award applicants required to submit FAFSA. *Unit head:* Dr. Paul Tom Hackett, Chair, 706-568-5061, Fax: 706-569-3134, E-mail: hackett_paul@colstate.edu. *Application contact:* Katie Thornton, Graduate Admissions Specialist, 706-568-2035, Fax: 706-568-2462, E-mail: thornton_katie@colstate.edu.

Concordia University, College of Education, Portland, OR 97211-6099. Offers curriculum and instruction (elementary) (M Ed); educational administration (M Ed); elementary education (MAT); secondary education (MAT). Part-time programs available. Postbaccalaureate distance learning degree programs offered (no on-campus study). *Degree requirements:* For master's, comprehensive exam, work samples/portfolio. *Entrance requirements:* For master's, California Basic Educational Skills Test or PRAXIS I, minimum undergraduate GPA of 2.8, graduate 3.0; 2 letters of recommendation. Additional exam requirements/recommendations for international students: Required—TOEFL (minimum score 525 paper-based; 195 computer-based). Electronic applications accepted. *Faculty research:* Learner centered classroom, brain-based learning future of on-line learning.

Concordia University, Graduate Programs, Ann Arbor, MI 48105-2797. Offers curriculum and instruction (MS); educational leadership (MS); organizational leadership and administration (MS). Part-time and evening/weekend programs available. *Faculty:* 3 full-time (2 women), 24 part-time/adjunct (10 women). *Students:* 179 full-time (117 women), 27 part-time (19 women). 84 applicants, 65% accepted, 43 enrolled. In 2009, 45 master's awarded. *Degree requirements:* For master's, thesis. *Entrance requirements:* Additional exam requirements/recommendations for international students: Required—TOEFL (minimum score 520 paper-based; 190 computer-based; 68 iBT); Recommended—IELTS, TWE. *Application deadline:* For fall admission, 9/1 priority date for domestic students, 8/1 priority date for international students; for winter admission, 1/5 priority date for domestic students, 12/1 priority date for international students; for spring admission, 5/12 priority date for domestic students, 4/1 priority date for international students. Applications are processed on a rolling basis. Application fee: $0 ($100 for international students). *Expenses:* Tuition: Full-time $7866; part-time $437 per credit hour. *Financial support:* Applicants required to submit FAFSA. *Unit head:* Dr. Dennis Genig, Vice President of Academics, 734-995-7383, Fax: 734-995-7448, E-mail: genigd@cuaa.edu. *Application contact:* Jean Christensen, Associate Director of Graduate Admission, 734-995-7521, Fax: 734-995-7530, E-mail: christj@cuaa.edu.

Concordia University, School of Education, Irvine, CA 92612-3299. Offers curriculum and instruction (MA); education and preliminary teaching credential (M Ed); educational administration and preliminary administrative services credential (MA). Part-time and evening/weekend programs available. Postbaccalaureate distance learning degree programs offered. *Faculty:* 18 full-time (9 women), 53 part-time/adjunct (25 women). *Students:* 569 full-time (439 women), 81 part-time (55 women); includes 160 minority (28 African Americans, 2 American Indian/Alaska Native, 38 Asian Americans or Pacific Islanders, 92 Hispanic Americans), 1 international. Average age 39. 263 applicants, 94% accepted, 203 enrolled. In 2009, 308 master's awarded. *Degree requirements:* For master's, action research project. *Entrance requirements:* For master's, California Basic Educational Skills Test, California Subject Examinations for Teachers, 2 references, copy of credential. Additional exam requirements/recommendations for international students: Required—TOEFL. *Application deadline:* For fall admission, 7/15 priority date for domestic students, 6/1 for international students; for spring admission, 11/30 priority date for domestic students, 10/1 for international students. Applications are processed on a rolling basis. Application fee: $50 ($125 for international students). Electronic applications accepted. *Expenses:* Contact institution. *Financial support:* In 2009–10, 478 students received support. Scholarships/grants available. Financial award applicants required to submit FAFSA. *Unit head:* Dr. Janice Nelson, Dean, 949-854-8002 Ext. 1249, E-mail: janice.nelson@cui.edu. *Application contact:* Narleen Narciso, Assistant Director of School of Education Admissions, 949-854-8002 Ext. 1132, Fax: 949-854-6894, E-mail: narleen.narciso@cui.edu.

Concordia University Chicago, College of Education, Program in School Leadership, River Forest, IL 60305-1499. Offers MA, Ed D, CAS. MA offered jointly with the Chicago Consortium of Colleges and Universities. *Accreditation:* NCATE. Part-time and evening/weekend programs available. *Degree requirements:* For master's, comprehensive exam, thesis optional; for CAS, thesis, final project. *Entrance requirements:* For master's, minimum GPA of 2.9; for CAS, master's degree. Additional exam requirements/recommendations for international students: Required—TOEFL (minimum score 550 paper-based; 195 computer-based). Electronic applications accepted. *Faculty research:* Effectiveness of urban Lutheran schools in impacting children's faith development, effectiveness of centers for urban ministries in supporting urban ministry and teaching science.

Concordia University, Nebraska, Graduate Programs in Education, Program in Educational Administration, Seward, NE 68434-1599. Offers elementary and secondary education (M Ed); elementary education (M Ed); secondary education (M Ed). *Accreditation:* NCATE. Part-time programs available. *Degree requirements:* For master's, thesis or alternative. *Entrance requirements:* For master's, GRE, MAT, or NTE, BS in education or equivalent, minimum GPA of 3.0.

Concordia University, St. Paul, College of Education, St. Paul, MN 55104-5494. Offers curriculum and instruction (MA Ed), including K-12 reading endorsement; differentiated instruction (MA Ed); early childhood education (MA Ed); educational leadership (MA Ed); family life education (MA); K-12 reading endorsement (Certificate); special education (Certificate); sports management (MA). *Accreditation:* NCATE. Evening/weekend programs available. Postbaccalaureate distance learning degree programs offered (minimal on-campus study). *Faculty:* 12 full-time (8 women), 59 part-time/adjunct (47 women). *Students:* 697 full-time (571 women), 13 part-time (12 women); includes 64 minority (31 African Americans, 1 American Indian/Alaska Native, 21 Asian Americans or Pacific Islanders, 11 Hispanic Americans), 1 international. Average age 34. In 2009, 402 master's, 29 other advanced degrees awarded. *Application deadline:* Applications are processed on a rolling basis. Application fee: $50. Electronic applications accepted. *Financial support:* Applicants required to submit FAFSA. *Unit head:* Dr. Donald Helmstetter, Dean, 651-641-8227, Fax: 651-641-8807, E-mail: helmstetter@csp.edu. *Application contact:* Kimberly Craig, Director of Graduate and Cohort Admission, 651-603-6223, Fax: 651-603-6320, E-mail: craig@csp.edu.

Concordia University Wisconsin, Graduate Programs, Department of Education, Program in Educational Administration, Mequon, WI 53097-2402. Offers MS Ed. Part-time and evening/weekend programs available. Postbaccalaureate distance learning degree programs offered (minimal on-campus study). *Degree requirements:* For master's, comprehensive exam, thesis or alternative. *Entrance requirements:* For master's, minimum GPA of 3.0. Additional exam requirements/recommendations for international students: Required—TOEFL.

Concord University, Graduate Studies, Athens, WV 24712-1000. Offers behavioral science (M Ed); educational leadership and supervision (M Ed); geography (M Ed); health promotion (M Ed); reading specialist (M Ed); social studies (M Ed). Postbaccalaureate distance learning degree programs offered. *Entrance requirements:* For master's, GRE or MAT, baccalaureate degree with minimum GPA of 2.5 GPA from regionally accredited institution; teaching license; 2 letters of recommendation.

Converse College, School of Education and Graduate Studies, Education Specialist Program, Spartanburg, SC 29302-0006. Offers administration and supervision (Ed S); curriculum and instruction (Ed S); marriage and family therapy (Ed S). *Accreditation:* AAMFT/COAMFTE. Part-time programs available. *Entrance requirements:* For degree, GRE or MAT (marriage and family therapy), minimum GPA of 3.0. Electronic applications accepted.

Converse College, School of Education and Graduate Studies, Program in Leadership, Spartanburg, SC 29302-0006. Offers M Ed. *Degree requirements:* For master's, capstone paper. *Entrance requirements:* For master's, NTE, minimum GPA of 2.75, nomination by school district, 3 recommendations. Electronic applications accepted.

Creighton University, Graduate School, College of Arts and Sciences, Department of Education, Program in Educational Leadership, Omaha, NE 68178-0001. Offers elementary school administration (MS); secondary school administration (MS); teacher leadership (MS). Part-time and evening/weekend programs available. *Students:* 47 part-time (27 women); includes 1 minority (Hispanic American), 1 international. Average age 35. 8 applicants, 75% accepted, 6 enrolled. In 2009, 8 master's awarded. *Degree requirements:* For master's, portfolio. *Entrance requirements:* For master's, 2 writing samples, 3 letters of recommendation. Additional exam requirements/recommendations for international students: Required—TOEFL (minimum score 550 paper-based; 213 computer-based; 80 iBT). *Application deadline:* For fall admission, 7/1

Educational Leadership and Administration

Creighton University (continued)
for domestic students, 3/1 for international students; for winter admission, 10/1 for domestic students, 5/1 for international students; for spring admission, 3/1 for domestic students, 10/1 for international students. Applications are processed on a rolling basis. Application fee: $50. Electronic applications accepted. *Expenses:* Tuition: Full-time $11,700; part-time $650 per credit hour. Required fees: $126 per semester. *Financial support:* Scholarships/grants and tuition waivers (partial) available. Support available to part-time students. Financial award application deadline: 5/1; financial award applicants required to submit FAFSA. *Unit head:* Dr. Barbara Brock, Professor of Education, 402-280-2551, E-mail: barbarabrock@creighton.edu. *Application contact:* Taunya Plater, Senior Program Coordinator, 402-280-2870, Fax: 402-280-2899, E-mail: taunyaplater@creighton.edu.

Curry College, Graduate Studies, Program in Education, Milton, MA 02186-9984. Offers educational administration (M Ed); educational diagnostic assessment (Certificate); educational therapy (Certificate); elementary education (M Ed); foundations (non-license) (M Ed); learning disabilities across the lifespan (Certificate); reading (M Ed, Certificate); special education (M Ed). Part-time and evening/weekend programs available. *Faculty:* 6 full-time (4 women), 12 part-time/adjunct (9 women). *Students:* 101 part-time (82 women). Average age 37. In 2009, 25 master's awarded. *Degree requirements:* For master's, project or thesis. *Entrance requirements:* For master's, MAT or GRE, interview, recommendations, resume, written statement. Additional exam requirements/recommendations for international students: Required—TOEFL (minimum score 550 paper-based; 213 computer-based; 80 iBT). *Application deadline:* For fall admission, 8/1 priority date for domestic students, 6/1 for international students; for winter admission, 10/1 for international students; for spring admission, 1/1 for domestic students, 1/28 for international students. Applications are processed on a rolling basis. Application fee: $50. *Expenses:* Contact institution. *Financial support:* Career-related internships or fieldwork and tuition waivers (partial) available. *Faculty research:* Classroom trauma, therapeutic writing, inclusionary practices. *Unit head:* Dr. Donald Gratz, Director and Associate Professor, 617-333-2243, E-mail: dgratz0703@curry.edu. *Application contact:* John Bresnahan, Director of Graduate Enrollment and Student Services, 617-333-2243, Fax: 617-979-3535, E-mail: jbresnah0104@curry.edu.

Dakota Wesleyan University, Program in Education, Mitchell, SD 57301-4398. Offers curriculum and instruction (MA Ed); education (MA); educational policy and administration (MA Ed); pre K-12 principal with certification (MA Ed); secondary with certification (MA Ed). Part-time and evening/weekend programs available. *Faculty:* 12 part-time/adjunct (7 women). *Students:* 31 part-time (15 women); includes 4 African Americans. Average age 30. 9 applicants, 100% accepted, 9 enrolled. In 2009, 14 master's awarded. *Degree requirements:* For master's, comprehensive exam, thesis optional, electronic portfolio. *Entrance requirements:* For master's, minimum GPA of 2.7, elementary statistics course. Additional exam requirements/recommendations for international students: Required—TOEFL (minimum score 500 paper-based; 71 computer-based), IELTS (minimum score 6.5). *Application deadline:* For fall admission, 8/1 priority date for domestic and international students; for winter admission, 12/1 priority date for domestic students; for spring admission, 4/1 priority date for domestic students, 12/1 priority date for international students. Applications are processed on a rolling basis. Application fee: $50. Electronic applications accepted. *Expenses:* Tuition: Full-time $5400; part-time $300 per credit hour. *Faculty research:* Math, political policy, technology in the classroom. *Unit head:* Dr. Ruth Haidle, Director of Graduate Studies, 605-995-2630, Fax: 605-995-2609, E-mail: ruhaidle@dwu.edu. *Application contact:* Coordinator of Graduate Admissions, 800-333-8506, Fax: 605-995-2699, E-mail: admissions@dwu.edu.

Dallas Baptist University, Dorothy M. Bush College of Education, Program in Educational Leadership, Dallas, TX 75211-9299. Offers M Ed. Part-time and evening/weekend programs available. *Entrance requirements:* For master's, GRE General Test, minimum GPA of 3.0. Additional exam requirements/recommendations for international students: Required—TOEFL, IELTS. Electronic applications accepted. *Expenses:* Tuition: Full-time $10,674; part-time $593 per credit hour. *Faculty research:* Emerging literacy, self-directed schools.

Delaware State University, Graduate Programs, College of Education, Program in Educational Leadership, Dover, DE 19901-2277. Offers MA, Ed D. *Entrance requirements:* Additional exam requirements/recommendations for international students: Required—TOEFL (minimum score 550 paper-based).

Delaware Valley College, Program in Educational Leadership, Doylestown, PA 18901-2697. Offers instruction, curriculum and technology (MS); school administration and leadership (MS). Part-time and evening/weekend programs available. *Faculty:* 30 part-time/adjunct (11 women). *Students:* 119 full-time (84 women), 46 part-time (29 women); includes 12 minority (9 African Americans, 3 Hispanic Americans). Average age 36. 56 applicants, 100% accepted, 56 enrolled. In 2009, 33 master's awarded. *Entrance requirements:* For master's, minimum undergraduate GPA of 3.0. *Application deadline:* Applications are processed on a rolling basis. Application fee: $50. *Expenses:* Tuition: Full-time $6336; part-time $528 per credit hour. Required fees: $72 per semester. One-time fee: $90. Tuition and fees vary according to program. *Financial support:* Applicants required to submit FAFSA. *Unit head:* Dr. Patricia Carney-Dalton, Director/Intern Supervisor, 215-489-4833, Fax: 215-489-4832, E-mail: patricia.carney@delval.edu. *Application contact:* Dr. Patricia Carney-Dalton, Director/Intern Supervisor, 215-489-4833, Fax: 215-489-4832, E-mail: patricia.carney@delval.edu.

Delta State University, Graduate Programs, College of Education, Thad Cochran Center for Rural School Leadership and Research, Program in Administration and Supervision, Cleveland, MS 38733-0001. Offers educational administration and supervision (Ed S); educational leadership (M Ed); elementary education (Ed S); secondary education (Ed S). *Accreditation:* NCATE. Part-time and evening/weekend programs available. *Degree requirements:* For master's, thesis optional. *Entrance requirements:* For master's, GRE General Test or MAT; for Ed S, master's degree, teaching certificate. *Expenses:* Tuition, state resident: full-time $4450; part-time $247 per credit hour. Tuition, nonresident: full-time $11,520; part-time $640 per credit hour.

Delta State University, Graduate Programs, College of Education, Thad Cochran Center for Rural School Leadership and Research, Program in Professional Studies, Cleveland, MS 38733-0001. Offers counselor education (Ed D); educational leadership (Ed D); elementary education (Ed D); higher education (Ed D). Part-time and evening/weekend programs available. *Degree requirements:* For doctorate, thesis/dissertation. *Entrance requirements:* For doctorate, GRE General Test. *Expenses:* Tuition, state resident: full-time $4450; part-time $247 per credit hour. Tuition, nonresident: full-time $11,520; part-time $640 per credit hour.

DePaul University, School of Education, Chicago, IL 60106. Offers bilingual and bicultural education (M Ed, MA); curriculum studies (M Ed, MA, Ed D); educational leadership (M Ed, MA, Ed D), including administration and supervision (M Ed, MA), Catholic school leadership (M Ed, MA), physical education (M Ed, MA); human development and learning (MA); human services and counseling (M Ed, MA), including agencies, family concerns, and higher education, elementary schools, human services management, secondary schools; reading and learning disabilities (M Ed, MA); social culture studies in education and development (M Ed, MA), including curriculum studies/development; teaching and learning (early childhood, elementary and secondary) (M Ed), including elementary education (M Ed, MA), secondary education (M Ed, MA); teaching and learning (early childhood, elementary, and secondary) (MA), including elementary education (M Ed, MA), secondary education (M Ed, MA). *Accreditation:* NCATE. Part-time and evening/weekend programs available. *Faculty:* 61 full-time (40 women), 66 part-time/adjunct (41 women). *Students:* 799 full-time (779 women), 470 part-time (365 women); includes 319 minority (153 African Americans, 3 American Indian/Alaska Native, 48 Asian Americans or Pacific Islanders, 115 Hispanic Americans), 15 international. Average age 30. 635 applicants, 74% accepted, 318 enrolled. In 2009, 604 master's, 5 doctorates awarded. *Degree requirements:* For doctorate, thesis/dissertation. *Entrance requirements:* For master's, interview, minimum GPA of 2.75, 2 letters of recommendation; for doctorate, interview, master's degree, writing sample, 3 letters of recommendation. Additional exam requirements/recommendations for international students: Required—TOEFL (minimum score 550 paper-

based; 213 computer-based; 80 iBT). *Application deadline:* Applications are processed on a rolling basis. Application fee: $40. Electronic applications accepted. *Expenses:* Tuition: Full-time $37,525; part-time $620 per credit hour. *Financial support:* In 2009–10, 14 research assistantships with tuition reimbursements (averaging $5,800 per year) were awarded; career-related internships or fieldwork also available. *Faculty research:* Reflective teaching, children at risk, loss, ethnicity, urban education. Total annual research expenditures: $1.6 million. *Unit head:* Dr. Marie Donovan, Dean, 773-325-7581, Fax: 773-325-7713, E-mail: mdonovan@depaul.edu. *Application contact:* Brandon Washington, Data Project Manager, 773-325-1152, Fax: 773-325-2270, E-mail: bwashin3@depaul.edu.

Doane College, Program in Education, Crete, NE 68333-2430. Offers curriculum and instruction (M Ed); educational leadership (M Ed). *Accreditation:* NCATE. Part-time and evening/weekend programs available. *Students:* 156 full-time (123 women), 495 part-time (383 women); includes 20 minority (7 African Americans, 1 American Indian/Alaska Native, 4 Asian Americans or Pacific Islanders, 8 Hispanic Americans). Average age 33. In 2009, 274 master's awarded. *Degree requirements:* For master's, thesis. *Entrance requirements:* For master's, minimum GPA of 2.5. *Application deadline:* Applications are processed on a rolling basis. Application fee: $25. Electronic applications accepted. *Expenses:* Contact institution. *Financial support:* Applicants required to submit FAFSA. *Unit head:* Lyn C. Forester, Dean, 402-826-8604, Fax: 402-826-8278. *Application contact:* Wilma Daddario, Assistant Dean, 402-464-1223, Fax: 402-466-4228, E-mail: wdaddario@doane.edu.

Dominican University, School of Education, River Forest, IL 60305-1099. Offers curriculum and instruction (MA Ed); early childhood education (MS); education (MAT); educational administration (MA); elementary (online) (MS); English as a second language (online) (MS); reading (online) (MS); special education (MS). Part-time and evening/weekend programs available. Postbaccalaureate distance learning degree programs offered. *Faculty:* 16 full-time (12 women), 59 part-time/adjunct (46 women). *Students:* 236 full-time (182 women), 622 part-time (509 women); includes 180 minority (54 African Americans, 3 American Indian/Alaska Native, 36 Asian Americans or Pacific Islanders, 87 Hispanic Americans), 2 international. Average age 32. In 2009, 199 master's awarded. *Entrance requirements:* For master's, Illinois certification test of basic skills. Additional exam requirements/recommendations for international students: Required—TOEFL (minimum score 550 paper-based; 213 computer-based; 79 iBT). *Application deadline:* Applications are processed on a rolling basis. Application fee: $25. *Expenses:* Contact institution. *Financial support:* Career-related internships or fieldwork, scholarships/grants, and tuition waivers (partial) available. Support available to part-time students. Financial award application deadline: 8/15; financial award applicants required to submit FAFSA. *Faculty research:* Governance of private education institutions, reading and language arts, inclusion, organizational planning, leadership and vision. *Unit head:* Dr. Colleen Reardon, Dean, 718-524-6643, Fax: 708-524-6665, E-mail: creardon@dom.edu. *Application contact:* Keven Hansen, Coordinator of Recruitment and Admissions, 708-524-6921, Fax: 708-524-6665, E-mail: educate@dom.edu.

Dowling College, Graduate Programs in Education, Oakdale, NY 11769-1999. Offers adolescence education (MS Ed), including educational administration; advanced certificate in gifted education (AC); childhood and early childhood education (MS Ed); childhood education (MS Ed); educational administration (AC, PD), including computers in education (PD), school administration and supervision (PD), school district administration (PD); educational technology specialist (AC); literacy (MS Ed); literacy/special education (MS Ed); secondary education (MS Ed); special education (MS Ed). *Accreditation:* NCATE. Part-time and evening/weekend programs available. Postbaccalaureate distance learning degree programs offered. *Faculty:* 32 full-time (18 women), 98 part-time/adjunct (59 women). *Students:* 563 full-time (393 women), 885 part-time (668 women); includes 133 minority (47 African Americans, 2 American Indian/Alaska Native, 10 Asian Americans or Pacific Islanders, 74 Hispanic Americans). Average age 32. 363 applicants, 89% accepted, 213 enrolled. In 2009, 459 master's, 85 ACs awarded. *Degree requirements:* For master's and other advanced degree, comprehensive exam. *Entrance requirements:* For master's, minimum GPA of 3.0; for other advanced degree, teaching certificate. Additional exam requirements/recommendations for international students: Required—TOEFL (minimum score 550 paper-based). *Application deadline:* For fall admission, 9/1 priority date for domestic students; for winter admission, 1/1 priority date for domestic students; for spring admission, 2/1 priority date for domestic students. Applications are processed on a rolling basis. Application fee: $50. Electronic applications accepted. *Expenses:* Tuition: Full-time $14,490; part-time $805 per credit. Required fees: $346 per term. *Financial support:* Career-related internships or fieldwork and Federal Work-Study available. Support available to part-time students. Financial award application deadline: 6/30; financial award applicants required to submit FAFSA. *Faculty research:* Natural readers, Korean styles and learning strategies, mothers of children with disabilities, computers in instruction, cultural background and organizational roadblocks to problem solving. *Unit head:* Dr. Clyde Payne, Dean of the School of Education, 631-244-3404, Fax: 631-589-6644, E-mail: paynec@dowling.edu. *Application contact:* Glenn M. Berman, Assistant Vice President for Enrollment Services/Dean of Admissions, 631-244-3357, Fax: 631-244-1059, E-mail: glenn.berman@dowling.edu.

Drexel University, School of Education, Program in Educational Administration, Philadelphia, PA 19104-2875. Offers MS.

Drexel University, School of Education, Program in Educational Leadership and Learning Technology, Philadelphia, PA 19104-2875. Offers PhD. *Degree requirements:* For doctorate, thesis/dissertation. Electronic applications accepted.

Duquesne University, School of Education, Department of Foundations and Leadership, Interdisciplinary Doctoral Program for Educational Leaders, Pittsburgh, PA 15282-0001. Offers Ed D. Part-time and evening/weekend programs available. *Faculty:* 2 full-time (1 woman), 4 part-time/adjunct (3 women). *Students:* 10 full-time (6 women), 25 part-time (13 women); includes 3 minority (all African Americans). Average age 46. 1 applicant, 0% accepted, 0 enrolled. In 2009, 27 doctorates awarded. *Degree requirements:* For doctorate, thesis/dissertation. *Entrance requirements:* For doctorate, GRE General Test, MAT, interview, minimum GPA of 3.25, writing sample. Additional exam requirements/recommendations for international students: Required—TOEFL (minimum score 550 paper-based; 80 computer-based). *Application deadline:* For fall admission, 2/1 priority date for domestic students. Application fee: $0. Electronic applications accepted. *Expenses:* Tuition: Part-time $851 per credit. Required fees: $81 per credit. *Financial support:* Research assistantships, career-related internships or fieldwork, institutionally sponsored loans, and tuition waivers (partial) available. Support available to part-time students. Financial award application deadline: 5/31. *Faculty research:* Leader effectiveness, shared decision making, organizational climate and health, leader authenticity. *Unit head:* Dr. James Henderson, Director, 412-396-4880, Fax: 412-396-6100, E-mail: henderson@duq.edu. *Application contact:* Michael Dolinger, Director of Student and Academic Services, 412-396-6647, Fax: 412-396-5585, E-mail: dolingerm@duq.edu.

Duquesne University, School of Education, Department of Foundations and Leadership, Program in School Administration and Supervision, Pittsburgh, PA 15282-0001. Offers school administration (MS Ed, Post-Master's Certificate), including curriculum and instruction (Post-Master's Certificate), K-12 administration (MS Ed), secondary administration (MS Ed); school supervision (MS Ed). Part-time and evening/weekend programs available. *Faculty:* 3 full-time (1 woman), 3 part-time/adjunct (1 woman). *Students:* 41 full-time (26 women), 23 part-time (18 women); includes 1 minority (African American), 1 international. Average age 39. 72 applicants, 71% accepted, 29 enrolled. In 2009, 26 master's awarded. *Degree requirements:* For master's, thesis. *Entrance requirements:* For master's, MAT, minimum GPA of 3.0. Additional exam requirements/recommendations for international students: Required—TOEFL (minimum score 550 paper-based; 80 computer-based). *Application deadline:* For fall admission, 8/1 for domestic students; for spring admission, 12/1 for domestic students. Applications are processed on a rolling basis. Application fee: $0. Electronic applications accepted. *Expenses:* Tuition: Part-time $851 per credit. Required fees: $81 per credit. *Financial support:* Research assistantships available. Support available to part-time students. *Unit head:* Dr. Robert Furman, Director, 412-396-5274, Fax: 412-396-1274, E-mail: furman@duq.edu. *Application contact:* Michael

Dolinger, Director of Student and Academic Services, 412-396-6647, Fax: 412-396-5585, E-mail: dolingerm@duq.edu.

D'Youville College, Doctoral Programs, Buffalo, NY 14201-1084. Offers educational leadership (Ed D); health education (Ed D); health policy (Ed D). Part-time and evening/weekend programs available. *Degree requirements:* For doctorate, comprehensive exam, thesis/dissertation, fieldwork. *Entrance requirements:* For doctorate, MS/MA; professional experience. *Faculty research:* Educational assessment, assessment reform, culture and education, market-based reform, men's health, electronic records.

East Carolina University, Graduate School, College of Education, Department of Educational Leadership, Greenville, NC 27858-4353. Offers educational administration and supervision (Ed S); educational leadership (Ed D); higher education administration (Ed D); school administration (MSA); supervision (MA Ed). *Accreditation:* NCATE. Part-time and evening/weekend programs available. Postbaccalaureate distance learning degree programs offered (minimal on-campus study). *Degree requirements:* For master's, comprehensive exam, thesis optional; for doctorate, thesis/dissertation. *Entrance requirements:* For master's, GRE General Test or MAT, interview, minimum GPA of 2.5, bachelor's degree in related field, teaching license (MA Ed); for doctorate, GRE or MAT, interview, minimum GPA of 3.5. Additional exam requirements/recommendations for international students: Required—TOEFL.

Eastern Illinois University, Graduate School, College of Education and Professional Studies, Department of Educational Leadership, Charleston, IL 61920-3099. Offers MS Ed, Ed S. *Accreditation:* NCATE. Part-time and evening/weekend programs available. *Faculty:* 5 full-time (1 woman). In 2009, 157 master's, 45 Ed Ss awarded. *Degree requirements:* For master's, fieldwork; for Ed S, thesis. *Application deadline:* For fall admission, 3/31 priority date for domestic students. Applications are processed on a rolling basis. Application fee: $30. *Expenses:* Tuition, state resident: full-time $9434; part-time $239 per credit hour. Tuition, nonresident: full-time $23,774; part-time $717 per credit hour. Required fees: $802.63. *Financial support:* In 2009–10, research assistantships with tuition reimbursements (averaging $8,100 per year), teaching assistantships with tuition reimbursements (averaging $8,100 per year) were awarded; career-related internships or fieldwork also available. *Unit head:* Dr. John Dively, Chairperson, 217-581-2919, Fax: 217-581-7147, E-mail: jdively@eiu.edu. *Application contact:* Bill Elliott, Assistant Dean of Graduate and International Admissions, 217-581-7489, Fax: 217-581-6020, E-mail: wjelliott@eiu.edu.

Eastern Kentucky University, The Graduate School, College of Education, Department of Counseling and Educational Leadership, Richmond, KY 40475-3102. Offers human services (MA); instructional leadership (MA Ed); mental health counseling (MA); school counseling (MA Ed). *Accreditation:* ACA (one or more programs are accredited); NCATE. Part-time programs available. Postbaccalaureate distance learning degree programs offered. *Entrance requirements:* For master's, GRE General Test, minimum GPA of 2.5.

Eastern Michigan University, Graduate School, College of Education, Department of Leadership and Counseling, Programs in Leadership, Ypsilanti, MI 48197. Offers college student personnel (MA); community college leadership (Graduate Certificate); educational leadership (MA, Ed D, SPA); higher education general administration (MA); higher education student affairs (MA); K-12 administration (MA). Part-time and evening/weekend programs available. Postbaccalaureate distance learning degree programs offered (no on-campus study). *Students:* 38 full-time (20 women), 422 part-time (282 women); includes 112 minority (92 African Americans, 7 American Indian/Alaska Native, 6 Asian Americans or Pacific Islanders, 7 Hispanic Americans), 7 international. Average age 37. In 2009, 79 master's, 8 doctorates, 19 other advanced degrees awarded. *Degree requirements:* For master's, portfolio. *Entrance requirements:* For doctorate, GRE. Additional exam requirements/recommendations for international students: Required—TOEFL. *Application deadline:* For winter admission, 2/1 for domestic and international students. Applications are processed on a rolling basis. Application fee: $35. Tuition and fees vary according to course level. *Financial support:* Fellowships, research assistantships with full tuition reimbursements, teaching assistantships with full tuition reimbursements, career-related internships or fieldwork, Federal Work-Study, institutionally sponsored loans, scholarships/grants, tuition waivers (partial), and unspecified assistantships available. Support available to part-time students. *Application contact:* Dr. Elizabeth Broughton, Advisor, 734-487-0255, Fax: 734-487-4608, E-mail: elizabeth.broughton@emich.edu.

Eastern Michigan University, Graduate School, College of Education, Department of Special Education, Programs in Special Education, Ypsilanti, MI 48197. Offers special education (MA); special education-administration and supervision (SPA); special education-curriculum development (SPA). *Accreditation:* NCATE. Part-time and evening/weekend programs available. Postbaccalaureate distance learning degree programs offered (minimal on-campus study). *Students:* 19 full-time (17 women), 44 part-time (37 women); includes 10 minority (4 African Americans, 1 American Indian/Alaska Native, 1 Asian American or Pacific Islander, 4 Hispanic Americans). Average age 36. In 2009, 5 master's, 4 other advanced degrees awarded. *Entrance requirements:* For master's, GRE General Test. Additional exam requirements/recommendations for international students: Required—TOEFL. *Application deadline:* Applications are processed on a rolling basis. Application fee: $35. Tuition and fees vary according to course level. *Financial support:* Fellowships, research assistantships with full tuition reimbursements, teaching assistantships with full tuition reimbursements, career-related internships or fieldwork, Federal Work-Study, institutionally sponsored loans, scholarships/grants, tuition waivers (partial), and unspecified assistantships available. Support available to part-time students. Financial award applicants required to submit FAFSA. *Application contact:* Graduate Admissions, 734-487-3400, Fax: 734-487-6559, E-mail: graduate.admissions@emich.edu.

Eastern Nazarene College, Adult and Graduate Studies, Division of Education, Quincy, MA 02170. Offers early childhood education (M Ed, Certificate); elementary education (M Ed, Certificate); English as a second language (M Ed, Certificate); instructional enrichment and development (M Ed, Certificate); middle school education (M Ed, Certificate); moderate special needs education (M Ed, Certificate); principal (Certificate); program development and supervision (M Ed, Certificate); secondary education (M Ed, Certificate); special education administrator (Certificate); supervisor (Certificate); teacher of reading (M Ed, Certificate). M Ed and Certificate also available through weekend program for administration, special needs, and reading only. Part-time and evening/weekend programs available. *Entrance requirements:* Additional exam requirements/recommendations for international students: Required—TOEFL (minimum score 550 paper-based).

Eastern Washington University, Graduate Studies, College of Education and Human Development, Department of Education, Program in Educational Leadership, Cheney, WA 99004-2431. Offers M Ed. *Accreditation:* NCATE. *Degree requirements:* For master's, comprehensive exam, thesis or alternative. *Entrance requirements:* For master's, minimum GPA of 3.0. *Expenses:* Tuition, state resident: full-time $7476; part-time $249 per quarter hour. Tuition, nonresident: full-time $18,030; part-time $601 per quarter hour. Required fees: $3.50 per quarter hour. $142 per quarter.

East Tennessee State University, School of Graduate Studies, College of Education, Department of Educational Leadership and Policy Analysis, Johnson City, TN 37614. Offers administrative endorsement (M Ed, Ed D, Ed S); classroom leadership (Ed D); educational leadership (M Ed, Ed D, Ed S); post secondary and private sector leadership (Ed D); school leadership (Ed D); school system leadership (Ed S); teacher leadership (Ed S). *Accreditation:* NCATE. Terminal master's awarded for partial completion of doctoral program. *Degree requirements:* For master's, oral exam or thesis; for doctorate, thesis/dissertation, oral and written exams; for Ed S, internship, practicum. *Entrance requirements:* For master's, GRE, interview, minimum GPA of 2.75, teaching certificate; for doctorate, GRE General Test, GRE Subject Test; for Ed S, GRE General Test, teaching certificate. Additional exam requirements/recommendations for international students: Required—TOEFL (minimum score 550 paper-based; 213 computer-based). *Faculty research:* Needs of principals in the new century, funding accountability and policy formulation for US community college systems, use of technology in principal preparation programs, multiple intelligence and the adult learner, leadership development in youth and young adults.

Edgewood College, Program in Education, Madison, WI 53711-1997. Offers director of instruction (Certificate); director of special education and pupil services (Certificate); education (MA Ed); educational administration (MA); educational leadership (Ed D); program coordinator (Certificate); school business administration (Certificate); school principalship K-12 (Certificate). *Accreditation:* NCATE (one or more programs are accredited). Part-time and evening/weekend programs available. *Students:* 36 full-time (21 women), 232 part-time (141 women); includes 39 minority (10 African Americans, 3 American Indian/Alaska Native, 9 Asian Americans or Pacific Islanders, 17 Hispanic Americans), 1 international. Average age 37. In 2009, 30 master's, 23 doctorates awarded. *Degree requirements:* For master's, practicum, research project. *Entrance requirements:* For master's, minimum GPA of 2.75, 2 letters of recommendation, personal statement; for doctorate, resume, 2 letters of recommendation, interview. Additional exam requirements/recommendations for international students: Required—TOEFL (minimum score 525 paper-based; 197 computer-based; 72 iBT). *Application deadline:* For fall admission, 8/24 for domestic students, 8/1 for international students; for spring admission, 1/10 for domestic students, 10/1 for international students. Applications are processed on a rolling basis. Application fee: $25. Electronic applications accepted. *Expenses:* Tuition: Part-time $688 per credit hour. *Unit head:* Dr. Jane Belmore, Interim Dean, 608-663-8336, Fax: 608-663-3291, E-mail: jbelmore@edgewood.edu. *Application contact:* Joann Eastman, Admissions Counselor, 608-663-3250, Fax: 608-663-2214, E-mail: gps@edgewood.edu.

Edinboro University of Pennsylvania, School of Graduate Studies and Research, School of Education, Department of Professional Studies, Edinboro, PA 16444. Offers counseling (MA), including community counseling, elementary guidance, rehabilitation counseling, secondary guidance, student personnel services; educational leadership (M Ed), including elementary school administration, secondary school administration; letter of eligibility (Certificate). Part-time and evening/weekend programs available. *Faculty:* 21 full-time (15 women), 12 part-time/adjunct (7 women). *Students:* 153 full-time (113 women), 785 part-time (598 women); includes 28 minority (19 African Americans, 3 American Indian/Alaska Native, 2 Asian Americans or Pacific Islanders, 4 Hispanic Americans). Average age 32. In 2009, 124 master's, 60 other advanced degrees awarded. *Degree requirements:* For master's, thesis or alternative, competency exam; for Certificate, thesis or alternative. *Entrance requirements:* For master's and Certificate, GRE or MAT, minimum QPA of 2.5. *Application deadline:* Applications are processed on a rolling basis. Application fee: $30. Electronic applications accepted. *Expenses:* Tuition, state resident: full-time $6666; part-time $370 per credit. Tuition, nonresident: full-time $10,666; part-time $593 per credit. Required fees: $2206.28. One-time fee: $204 part-time. *Financial support:* In 2009–10, 60 research assistantships with full and partial tuition reimbursements (averaging $4,050 per year) were awarded; career-related internships or fieldwork, Federal Work-Study, scholarships/grants, and unspecified assistantships also available. Support available to part-time students. Financial award application deadline: 2/15; financial award applicants required to submit FAFSA. *Unit head:* Dr. Susan Norton, Program Head, Counseling, 814-732-2260, E-mail: scnorton@edinboro.edu. *Application contact:* Dr. Andrew Pushchack, Program Head, Educational Leadership, 814-732-1548, E-mail: apushchack@edinboro.edu.

Elizabeth City State University, School of Education and Psychology, Program in School Administration, Elizabeth City, NC 27909-7806. Offers MSA. Part-time and evening/weekend programs available. *Degree requirements:* For master's, thesis. *Entrance requirements:* For master's, MAT, GRE, minimum GPA of 3.0. Additional exam requirements/recommendations for international students: Required—TOEFL. Electronic applications accepted.

Elmhurst College, Graduate Programs, Program in Teacher Leadership, Elmhurst, IL 60126-3296. Offers M Ed. Part-time and evening/weekend programs available. *Faculty:* 3 full-time (all women), 1 part-time/adjunct (0 women). *Students:* 12 part-time (all women). Average age 27. 8 applicants, 38% accepted, 2 enrolled. In 2009, 6 master's awarded. *Entrance requirements:* For master's, 3 recommendations. Additional exam requirements/recommendations for international students: Required—TOEFL (minimum score 550 paper-based; 213 computer-based). *Application deadline:* Applications are processed on a rolling basis. Application fee: $25. Electronic applications accepted. *Expenses:* Contact institution. *Financial support:* In 2009–10, 3 students received support. Federal Work-Study and scholarships/grants available. Support available to part-time students. Financial award application deadline: 6/1; financial award applicants required to submit FAFSA. *Unit head:* Dr. Ted Lerud, Associate Dean of the Faculty, 630-617-3661, Fax: 630-617-6415, E-mail: gradadm@elmhurst.edu. *Application contact:* Elizabeth D. Kuebler, Director of Adult and Graduate Admission, 630-617-3069, Fax: 630-617-5501, E-mail: betsyk@elmhurst.edu.

Emmanuel College, Graduate Programs, Programs in Education, Boston, MA 02115. Offers educational leadership (CAGS); elementary education (MAT); school administration (M Ed); secondary education (MAT). Part-time and evening/weekend programs available. *Faculty:* 6 part-time/adjunct (2 women). *Students:* 6 full-time (5 women), 46 part-time (33 women); includes 8 minority (4 African Americans, 4 Hispanic Americans). Average age 33. 16 applicants, 56% accepted, 9 enrolled. In 2009, 23 master's awarded. *Entrance requirements:* For master's, interview, resume, 2 letters of recommendation, essay, bachelor's degree; for CAGS, interview, leadership statement, resume, 2 letters of recommendation. Additional exam requirements/recommendations for international students: Required—TOEFL (minimum score 600 paper-based; 250 computer-based). *Application deadline:* For fall admission, 8/15 priority date for domestic students; for spring admission, 12/8 priority date for domestic students. Applications are processed on a rolling basis. Application fee: $50. Electronic applications accepted. *Expenses:* Tuition: Part-time $665 per credit. *Faculty research:* Literature/reading, history of education, multicultural education, special education. *Unit head:* Dr. Judith Marley, Dean, Graduate and Professional Programs, 617-735-9700, Fax: 617-507-0434, E-mail: gpp@emmanuel.edu. *Application contact:* Enrollment Counselor, 617-735-9700, Fax: 617-507-0434, E-mail: gpp@emmanuel.edu.

Emporia State University, School of Graduate Studies, The Teachers College, Department of School Leadership/Middle and Secondary Teacher Education, Program in Curriculum and Instruction, Emporia, KS 66801-5087. Offers curriculum leadership (MS); effective practitioner (MS); national board certification (MS). *Accreditation:* NCATE. Part-time programs available. *Students:* 1 (woman) full-time, 134 part-time (116 women); includes 5 minority (1 African American, 4 Hispanic Americans). 33 applicants, 97% accepted, 30 enrolled. In 2009, 60 master's awarded. *Degree requirements:* For master's, comprehensive exam or thesis, practicum. *Entrance requirements:* For master's, GRE or MAT, appropriate bachelor's degree, teacher certification, 1 year of teaching experience, letters of recommendation. *Application deadline:* For fall admission, 8/15 priority date for domestic students. Applications are processed on a rolling basis. Application fee: $30 ($75 for international students). Electronic applications accepted. *Expenses:* Tuition, state resident: full-time $4154; part-time $173 per credit hour. Tuition, nonresident: full-time $12,864; part-time $536 per credit hour. Required fees: $948; $58 per credit hour. Tuition and fees vary according to campus/location. *Financial support:* Career-related internships or fieldwork, Federal Work-Study, institutionally sponsored loans, health care benefits, and unspecified assistantships available. Financial award application deadline: 3/15; financial award applicants required to submit FAFSA. *Unit head:* Dr. Jerry Will, Chair, 620-341-5777, E-mail: jwill@emporia.edu. *Application contact:* Mary Sewell, Admissions Coordinator, 800-950-GRAD, Fax: 620-341-5909, E-mail: msewell@emporia.edu.

Emporia State University, School of Graduate Studies, The Teachers College, Department of School Leadership/Middle and Secondary Teacher Education, Program in Educational Administration, Emporia, KS 66801-5087. Offers elementary administration (MS); elementary/secondary administration (MS); secondary administration (MS). *Accreditation:* NCATE. Part-time programs available. *Students:* 2 full-time (both women), 146 part-time (62 women); includes 9 minority (1 African American, 2 American Indian/Alaska Native, 1 Asian American or Pacific Islander, 5 Hispanic Americans). 26 applicants, 92% accepted, 17 enrolled. In 2009, 72 master's awarded. *Degree requirements:* For master's, comprehensive exam or thesis, practicum. *Entrance requirements:* For master's, GRE or MAT, appropriate bachelor's degree,

Educational Leadership and Administration

Emporia State University *(continued)*
letters of recommendation, teacher certification, 1 year teaching experience. *Application deadline:* For fall admission, 8/15 priority date for domestic students. Applications are processed on a rolling basis. Application fee: $30 ($75 for international students). Electronic applications accepted. *Expenses:* Tuition, state resident: full-time $4154; part-time $173 per credit hour. Tuition, nonresident: full-time $12,864; part-time $536 per credit hour. Required fees: $948; $58 per credit hour. Tuition and fees vary according to campus/location. *Financial support:* Career-related internships or fieldwork, Federal Work-Study, institutionally sponsored loans, health care benefits, and unspecified assistantships available. Financial award application deadline: 3/15; financial award applicants required to submit FAFSA. *Unit head:* Dr. Jerry Will, Chair, 620-341-5777, E-mail: jwill@emporia.edu. *Application contact:* Mary Sewell, Admissions Coordinator, 800-950-GRAD, Fax: 620-341-5909, E-mail: msewell@emporia.edu.

Evangel University, Department of Education, Springfield, MO 65802. Offers educational leadership (M Ed); reading education (M Ed); secondary teaching (M Ed); teaching (MA). *Accreditation:* NCATE. Part-time and evening/weekend programs available. *Faculty:* 4 full-time (2 women), 5 part-time/adjunct (3 women). *Students:* 10 full-time (6 women), 40 part-time (31 women). Average age 33. 14 applicants, 86% accepted, 11 enrolled. In 2009, 23 master's awarded. *Degree requirements:* For master's, comprehensive exam, thesis optional. *Entrance requirements:* For master's, PRAXIS II (preferred) or GRE. Additional exam requirements/recommendations for international students: Required—TOEFL (minimum score 550 paper-based; 213 computer-based). *Application deadline:* For fall admission, 7/15 priority date for domestic students; for spring admission, 11/15 priority date for domestic students. Applications are processed on a rolling basis. Application fee: $25. *Financial support:* In 2009–10, 3 students received support. Career-related internships or fieldwork, institutionally sponsored loans, and scholarships/grants available. Support available to part-time students. Financial award application deadline: 3/1; financial award applicants required to submit FAFSA. *Unit head:* Dr. Colleen Hardy, Program Coordinator, 417-865-2815 Ext. 8553, E-mail: hardyc@evangel.edu. *Application contact:* Charity H. Fahlstrom, Admissions Representative, Graduate and Professional Studies, 417-865-2811 Ext. 7227, Fax: 417-865-9599.

Fairleigh Dickinson University, College at Florham, University College: Arts, Sciences, and Professional Studies, Peter Sammartino School of Education, Program in Educational Leadership, Madison, NJ 07940-1099. Offers MA. *Application contact:* Susan Brooman, University Director, Graduate Admissions, 973-443-8905, Fax: 973-443-8088, E-mail: grad@fdu.edu.

Fairleigh Dickinson University, Metropolitan Campus, University College: Arts, Sciences, and Professional Studies, Peter Sammartino School of Education, Program in Educational Leadership, Teaneck, NJ 07666-1914. Offers MA. *Students:* 2 full-time (both women), 64 part-time (41 women), 2 international. Average age 35. 27 applicants, 100% accepted, 27 enrolled. In 2009, 27 master's awarded. *Application deadline:* Applications are processed on a rolling basis. Application fee: $40. *Application contact:* Susan Brooman, University Director of Graduate Admissions, 201-692-2554, Fax: 201-692-2560, E-mail: globaleducation@fdu.edu.

Fairmont State University, Graduate Studies, Programs in Education, Fairmont, WV 26554. Offers education (MAT); leadership studies (M Ed); online learning (M Ed); professional studies (M Ed); reading (M Ed); special education (M Ed). *Accreditation:* NCATE.

Fayetteville State University, Graduate School, Programs in Educational Leadership and School Administration, Fayetteville, NC 28301-4298. Offers educational leadership (Ed D); school administration (MSA). *Accreditation:* NCATE (one or more programs are accredited). Part-time and evening/weekend programs available. *Faculty:* 7 full-time (1 woman), 3 part-time/adjunct (1 woman). *Students:* 47 full-time (33 women), 34 part-time (25 women); includes 61 minority (54 African Americans, 5 American Indian/Alaska Native, 2 Hispanic Americans), 1 international. Average age 42. 18 applicants, 100% accepted, 18 enrolled. In 2009, 31 master's, 9 doctorates awarded. *Degree requirements:* For master's, internship, written and oral exams. *Entrance requirements:* For master's, GRE or MAT, minimum GPA of 2.5. *Application deadline:* For fall admission, 4/1 for domestic students. Applications are processed on a rolling basis. Application fee: $35. Electronic applications accepted. *Faculty research:* First-generation college students and academic successes, educational law and higher education, educational policy and K-12/higher education. Total annual research expenditures: $20,000. *Unit head:* Dr. Terrance Hicks, Acting Director, 910-672-1731, E-mail: thicks@uncfsu.edu. *Application contact:* Katrina Hoffman, Associate Vice-Chancellor for Enrollment Management, 910-672-1374, Fax: 910-672-1470, E-mail: khoffma1@uncfsu.edu.

Felician College, Program in Education, Lodi, NJ 07644-2117. Offers education (MA); educational supervision (MA, PMC); elementary education (MA); principal (PMC); principal/supervision dual certification (MA); school nurse/health (MA); school nurse/health educator (Certificate); special education (MA). *Accreditation:* Teacher Education Accreditation Council. Part-time and evening/weekend programs available. *Students:* 12 full-time (9 women), 93 part-time (83 women); includes 5 African Americans, 1 Asian American or Pacific Islander, 9 Hispanic Americans, 3 international. Average age 37. 18 applicants, 50% accepted, 9 enrolled. *Degree requirements:* For master's, project. *Entrance requirements:* For master's, MAT, minimum GPA of 3.0, 3 letters of recommendation. Additional exam requirements/recommendations for international students: Recommended—TOEFL (minimum score 550 paper-based; 213 computer-based). *Application deadline:* Applications are processed on a rolling basis. Application fee: $40. *Financial support:* Federal Work-Study available. *Unit head:* Dr. Rosemarie Liebmann, Associate Dean, 201-559-3537, E-mail: liebmannr@felician.edu. *Application contact:* Dr. Wendy Lin-Cook, Director of Adult and Graduate Admission, 201-559-6077, Fax: 201-559-6138, E-mail: adultandgraduate@felician.edu.

See Close-Up on page 709.

Ferris State University, College of Education and Human Services, School of Education, Big Rapids, MI 49307. Offers administration (MSCTE); curriculum and instruction (M Ed), including administration, elementary education, experiential education, philanthropic education, reading, secondary education, special education, subject matter option; education technology (MSCTE); instructor (MSCTE); post-secondary administration (MSCTE); training and development (MSCTE). Part-time and evening/weekend programs available. Postbaccalaureate distance learning degree programs offered. *Faculty:* 12 full-time (8 women), 11 part-time/adjunct (5 women). *Students:* 19 full-time (13 women), 185 part-time (122 women); includes 24 minority (20 African Americans, 1 Asian American or Pacific Islander, 3 Hispanic Americans), 1 international. Average age 36. 37 applicants, 32% accepted, 11 enrolled. In 2009, 73 master's awarded. *Degree requirements:* For master's, thesis, research paper. *Entrance requirements:* For master's, 2 years of work experience for vocational setting, minimum GPA of 2.75. Additional exam requirements/recommendations for international students: Recommended—TOEFL (minimum score 500 paper-based; 173 computer-based; 61 iBT). *Application deadline:* For fall admission, 7/1 priority date for domestic students; for spring admission, 11/1 priority date for domestic students. Applications are processed on a rolling basis. Application fee: $30. *Financial support:* Career-related internships or fieldwork and scholarships/grants available. Support available to part-time students. Financial award applicants required to submit FAFSA. *Faculty research:* Suicide prevention, reading, women in education, special needs, administration. *Unit head:* Dr. Liza Ing, Director, 231-591-5362, Fax: 231-591-2041. *Application contact:* Kimisue Worrall, Secretary, 231-591-5361, Fax: 231-591-2043.

Fielding Graduate University, Graduate Programs, School of Educational Leadership and Change, Santa Barbara, CA 93105-3538. Offers collaborative educational leadership (MA); educational leadership and change (Ed D); teaching in the virtual classroom (Graduate Certificate). Postbaccalaureate distance learning degree programs offered (minimal on-campus study). *Faculty:* 17 full-time (9 women), 18 part-time/adjunct (9 women). *Students:* 409 full-time (289 women), 8 part-time (5 women); includes 156 minority (100 African Americans, 7 American Indian/Alaska Native, 13 Asian Americans or Pacific Islanders, 36 Hispanic Americans), 4 international. Average age 44. 75 applicants, 92% accepted, 45 enrolled. In 2009, 99 master's, 32 doctorates, 23 other advanced degrees awarded. *Degree requirements:* For master's,

capstone research project; for doctorate, comprehensive exam, thesis/dissertation. *Entrance requirements:* For master's, minimum GPA of 2.5; for doctorate, resume, 2 letters of recommendation, writing sample. *Application deadline:* For fall admission, 7/31 priority date for domestic students, 7/31 for international students; for spring admission, 11/19 priority date for domestic students, 11/19 for international students. Application fee: $75. Electronic applications accepted. *Expenses:* Contact institution. *Financial support:* In 2009–10, 293 students received support. Scholarships/grants, health care benefits, and tuition waivers (partial) available. Support available to part-time students. Financial award application deadline: 5/15; financial award applicants required to submit FAFSA. *Unit head:* Dr. Judy Witt, Dean, 805-898-2940, E-mail: jwitt@fielding.edu. *Application contact:* Kristin Kontilis, Admission Counselor, 800-340-1099, Fax: 805-687-9793, E-mail: kkontilis@fielding.edu.

Fitchburg State University, Division of Graduate and Continuing Education, Program in Educational Leadership and Management, Fitchburg, MA 01420-2697. Offers educational technology (Certificate); higher education administration (CAGS); non-licensure (M Ed, CAGS); school principal (M Ed, CAGS); supervisor director (M Ed, CAGS); technology leader (M Ed, CAGS). *Accreditation:* NCATE. Part-time and evening/weekend programs available. *Students:* 29 full-time (9 women), 66 part-time (30 women); includes 2 minority (1 Asian American or Pacific Islander, 1 Hispanic American). Average age 37. 23 applicants, 100% accepted, 22 enrolled. In 2009, 17 master's, 50 CAGSs awarded. *Degree requirements:* For master's, comprehensive exam, thesis or alternative. *Entrance requirements:* For master's, GRE General Test or MAT, 3 years of teaching experience, teaching certificate, letters of recommendation, resume; for other advanced degree, master's degree, letters of recommendation, resume. Additional exam requirements/recommendations for international students: Required—TOEFL (minimum score 550 paper-based; 213 computer-based; 79 iBT). *Application deadline:* Applications are processed on a rolling basis. Application fee: $25 ($50 for international students). *Expenses:* Tuition, area resident: Part-time $150 per credit. Tuition, state resident: part-time $150 per credit. Tuition, nonresident: part-time $150 per credit. Required fees: $120 per credit. *Financial support:* In 2009–10, research assistantships with partial tuition reimbursements (averaging $5,500 per year); Federal Work-Study, scholarships/grants, and unspecified assistantships also available. Support available to part-time students. Financial award application deadline: 3/1; financial award applicants required to submit FAFSA. *Unit head:* Dr. Randy Howe, Chair, 978-665-3544, Fax: 978-665-3658, E-mail: gce@fsc.edu. *Application contact:* Director of Admissions, 978-665-3144, Fax: 978-665-4540, E-mail: admissions@fsc.edu.

Florida Agricultural and Mechanical University, Division of Graduate Studies, Research, and Continuing Education, College of Education, Department of Educational Leadership and Human Services, Tallahassee, FL 32307-3200. Offers administration and supervision (M Ed, MS Ed, PhD); adult education (M Ed, MS Ed); educational leadership (PhD); guidance and counseling (M Ed, MS Ed). *Accreditation:* NCATE. *Faculty:* 15 full-time (8 women). *Students:* 58 full-time (31 women), 43 part-time (32 women); includes 94 minority (93 African Americans, 1 Asian American or Pacific Islander), 5 international. In 2009, 24 master's, 5 doctorates awarded. *Degree requirements:* For master's, thesis (for some programs); for doctorate, thesis/dissertation. *Entrance requirements:* For master's, GRE General Test, minimum GPA of 3.0. Additional exam requirements/recommendations for international students: Required—TOEFL. *Application deadline:* For fall admission, 5/18 for domestic students, 12/18 for international students; for spring admission, 11/12 for domestic students, 5/12 for international students. Application fee: $20. *Unit head:* Dr. Warren Hope, Interim Chairperson, 850-599-3191, Fax: 850-561-2211. *Application contact:* Dr. Chanta M. Haywood, Dean of Graduate Studies, Research, and Continuing Education, 850-599-3315, Fax: 850-599-3727.

Florida Atlantic University, College of Education, Department of Educational Leadership, Boca Raton, FL 33431-0991. Offers adult and community education (M Ed, PhD, Ed S); educational leadership (M Ed, PhD, Ed S); higher education (M Ed, PhD); K-12 school leadership (M Ed, PhD, Ed S). *Accreditation:* NCATE. Part-time and evening/weekend programs available. Postbaccalaureate distance learning degree programs offered (minimal on-campus study). *Faculty:* 16 full-time (8 women), 19 part-time/adjunct (10 women). *Students:* 103 full-time (63 women), 261 part-time (186 women); includes 119 minority (71 African Americans, 9 Asian Americans or Pacific Islanders, 39 Hispanic Americans), 1 international. Average age 36. 254 applicants, 57% accepted, 96 enrolled. In 2009, 123 master's, 22 doctorates awarded. *Degree requirements:* For doctorate, comprehensive exam, thesis/dissertation, departmental qualifying exam; for Ed S, departmental qualifying exam. *Entrance requirements:* For master's, GRE General Test, minimum GPA of 3.0 during previous 2 years; for doctorate, GRE General Test, minimum GPA of 3.5; for Ed S, GRE General Test. *Application deadline:* For fall admission, 7/1 for domestic students, 2/15 for international students; for spring admission, 9/15 for domestic students, 7/15 for international students. Applications are processed on a rolling basis. Application fee: $30. Electronic applications accepted. *Expenses:* Tuition, state resident: full-time $7055; part-time $293.94 per credit hour. Tuition, nonresident: full-time $22,096; part-time $920.66 per credit hour. *Financial support:* Fellowships, research assistantships, teaching assistantships, career-related internships or fieldwork and tuition waivers (partial) available. *Faculty research:* Self-directed learning, school reform issues, legal issues, mentoring, school leadership. *Unit head:* Dr. Robert Shockley, Chair, 561-297-3550, Fax: 561-297-3618, E-mail: shockley@fau.edu. *Application contact:* Catherine Politi, Senior Secretary, 561-297-3550, Fax: 561-297-3618, E-mail: edleadership@fau.edu.

Florida Gulf Coast University, College of Education, Program in Educational Leadership, Fort Myers, FL 33965-6565. Offers M Ed, MA. Part-time and evening/weekend programs available. *Faculty:* 31 full-time (23 women), 41 part-time/adjunct (29 women). *Students:* 35 full-time (28 women), 16 part-time (11 women); includes 8 minority (4 African Americans, 1 American Indian/Alaska Native, 1 Asian American or Pacific Islander, 2 Hispanic Americans). Average age 32. 38 applicants, 82% accepted, 21 enrolled. In 2009, 26 master's awarded. *Degree requirements:* For master's, thesis or alternative, learning and professional portfolios. *Entrance requirements:* For master's, GRE General Test, MAT, minimum GPA of 3.0. Additional exam requirements/recommendations for international students: Required—TOEFL (minimum score 550 paper-based; 213 computer-based). *Application deadline:* For fall admission, 7/1 priority date for domestic students; for spring admission, 10/15 for domestic students. Applications are processed on a rolling basis. Application fee: $30. Electronic applications accepted. *Faculty research:* Inclusion, technology in teaching, curriculum development in educational leadership, education policy and law. *Unit head:* Dr. Pat Wachholz, Associate Dean, 239-590-7808, Fax: 239-590-7801, E-mail: wachhol@fgcu.edu. *Application contact:* Dr. Pat Wachholz, Associate Dean, 239-590-7808, Fax: 239-590-7801, E-mail: wachhol@fgcu.edu.

Florida International University, College of Education, Department of Educational Leadership and Policy Studies, Program in Educational Administration and Supervision, Miami, FL 33199. Offers Ed D. *Accreditation:* NCATE. Part-time and evening/weekend programs available. *Degree requirements:* For doctorate, thesis/dissertation. *Entrance requirements:* For doctorate, GRE General Test, teaching certificate, 3 years full-time teaching. Additional exam requirements/recommendations for international students: Required—TOEFL (minimum score 550 paper-based; 213 computer-based; 80 iBT), IELTS (minimum score 6.3). Electronic applications accepted. *Expenses:* Tuition, state resident: full-time $8008; part-time $4004 per year. Tuition, nonresident: full-time $20,104; part-time $10,052 per year. Required fees: $298; $149 per term.

Florida International University, College of Education, Department of Educational Leadership and Policy Studies, Program in Educational Leadership, Miami, FL 33199. Offers MS, Certificate, Ed S. *Accreditation:* NCATE. Part-time and evening/weekend programs available. *Entrance requirements:* For master's, 3 years full-time teaching; for other advanced degree, GRE General Test, 3 years full-time teaching. Additional exam requirements/recommendations for international students: Required—TOEFL (minimum score 550 paper-based; 213 computer-based; 80 iBT), IELTS (minimum score 6.3). *Expenses:* Tuition, state resident: full-time $8008; part-time $4004 per year. Tuition, nonresident: full-time $20,104; part-time $10,052 per year. Required fees: $298; $149 per term.

Florida International University, College of Education, Department of Educational Leadership and Policy Studies, Program in Higher Education Administration, Miami, FL 33199. Offers MS.

Part-time and evening/weekend programs available. *Degree requirements:* For master's, comprehensive exam. *Entrance requirements:* For master's, minimum GPA of 3.0. Additional exam requirements/recommendations for international students: Required—TOEFL (minimum score 550 paper-based; 213 computer-based; 80 iBT), IELTS (minimum score 6.3). Electronic applications accepted. *Expenses:* Tuition, state resident: full-time $8008; part-time $4004 per year. Tuition, nonresident: full-time $20,104; part-time $10,052 per year. Required fees: $298; $149 per term. *Faculty research:* Access and equity in college admission, social justice, higher education law, faculty and tenure for individuals of color, affirmative action.

Florida State University, The Graduate School, College of Education, Department of Educational Leadership and Policy Studies, Program in Educational Leadership/Administration, Tallahassee, FL 32306. Offers educational administration/leadership (MS, Ed D, PhD, Ed S). Part-time and evening/weekend programs available. *Faculty:* 5 full-time (4 women), 8 part-time/adjunct (7 women). *Students:* 27 full-time (15 women), 102 part-time (70 women); includes 29 minority (23 African Americans, 1 Asian American or Pacific Islander, 5 Hispanic Americans), 5 international. 102 applicants, 38% accepted, 27 enrolled. In 2009, 28 master's, 1 doctorate, 2 other advanced degrees awarded. Terminal master's awarded for partial completion of doctoral program. *Degree requirements:* For master's and Ed S, comprehensive exam, thesis optional; for doctorate, comprehensive exam, thesis/dissertation. *Entrance requirements:* For master's, GRE General Test, minimum GPA of 3.0; for doctorate and Ed S, GRE General Test, minimum graduate GPA of 3.0. Additional exam requirements/recommendations for international students: Required—TOEFL (minimum score 550 paper-based; 213 computer-based; 80 iBT). *Application deadline:* For fall admission, 5/1 priority date for domestic and international students; for winter admission, 10/1 priority date for domestic and international students; for spring admission, 2/1 for domestic students, 1/1 priority date for international students. Application fee: $30. Electronic applications accepted. *Expenses:* Tuition, state resident: full-time $7413. Tuition, nonresident: full-time $22,567. *Financial support:* Fellowships with full and partial tuition reimbursements, research assistantships with full and partial tuition reimbursements, teaching assistantships with full and partial tuition reimbursements, career-related internships or fieldwork, scholarships/grants, and unspecified assistantships available. Financial award applicants required to submit FAFSA. *Faculty research:* Issues in higher education law; diversity, equity, and social justice; educational issues in Western and Non-Western countries. *Unit head:* Dr. Judith Irvin, Program Coordinator, 850-644-6777, Fax: 850-644-1258, E-mail: irvin@coe.fsu.edu. *Application contact:* Jimmy Pastrano, Program Assistant, 850-644-6777, Fax: 850-644-1258, E-mail: pastrano@coe.fsu.edu.

Fordham University, Graduate School of Education, Division of Educational Leadership, Administration and Policy, New York, NY 10023. Offers administration and supervision (MSE, Adv C); administration and supervision for church leaders (PhD); educational administration and supervision (Ed D, PhD); human resource program administration (MS). *Accreditation:* NCATE. *Degree requirements:* For doctorate, thesis/dissertation. *Entrance requirements:* For doctorate, MAT, GRE General Test.

Fort Hays State University, Graduate School, College of Education and Technology, Department of Educational Administration and Counseling, Program in Educational Administration, Hays, KS 67601-4099. Offers MS, Ed S. *Accreditation:* NCATE. *Degree requirements:* For master's and Ed S, comprehensive exam, thesis or alternative. *Entrance requirements:* For master's, GRE General Test or MAT. Additional exam requirements/recommendations for international students: Required—TOEFL (minimum score 550 paper-based; 213 computer-based). Electronic applications accepted. *Faculty research:* Guide to negotiations, nutrition program for disadvantaged, accountability, student insurance practices, student liability.

Framingham State University, Division of Graduate and Continuing Education, Program in Educational Leadership, Framingham, MA 01701-9101. Offers MA. Part-time and evening/weekend programs available. *Entrance requirements:* For master's, MAT.

Franciscan University of Steubenville, Graduate Programs, Department of Education, Steubenville, OH 43952-1763. Offers administration (MS Ed); teaching (MS Ed). Part-time and evening/weekend programs available. *Degree requirements:* For master's, project. *Entrance requirements:* For master's, minimum undergraduate GPA of 2.5 or written exam. *Expenses:* Contact institution.

Freed-Hardeman University, Program in Education, Henderson, TN 38340-2399. Offers curriculum and instruction (M Ed); school counseling (M Ed), including administration and supervision, special education; school leadership (Ed S). *Accreditation:* NCATE. Part-time and evening/weekend programs available. *Degree requirements:* For master's, comprehensive exam, thesis optional; for Ed S, thesis. *Entrance requirements:* For master's, GRE General Test or NTE; for Ed S, 3 years of teaching experience. Additional exam requirements/recommendations for international students: Required—TOEFL (minimum score 500 paper-based; 173 computer-based).

Fresno Pacific University, Graduate Programs, School of Education, Division of Administration, Fresno, CA 93702-4709. Offers administrative services (MA Ed). Part-time and evening/weekend programs available. *Degree requirements:* For master's, thesis or alternative, 4 practica. *Entrance requirements:* Additional exam requirements/recommendations for international students: Required—TOEFL (minimum score 550 paper-based; 213 computer-based). Electronic applications accepted.

Frostburg State University, Graduate School, College of Education, Department of Educational Professions, Program in Educational Administration and Supervision, Frostburg, MD 21532-1099. Offers elementary (M Ed); secondary (M Ed). Part-time and evening/weekend programs available. *Faculty:* 4. *Students:* 7 full-time (3 women), 98 part-time (57 women); includes 2 minority (1 African American, 1 American Indian/Alaska Native). Average age 30. 19 applicants, 84% accepted, 13 enrolled. In 2009, 20 master's awarded. *Degree requirements:* For master's, thesis or alternative. *Entrance requirements:* For master's, teaching certificate. Additional exam requirements/recommendations for international students: Required—TOEFL. *Application deadline:* For fall admission, 7/15 priority date for domestic students. Applications are processed on a rolling basis. Application fee: $30. Electronic applications accepted. *Expenses:* Tuition, state resident: full-time $5706; part-time $317 per credit hour. Tuition, nonresident: full-time $6948; part-time $386 per credit hour. Required fees: $1476; $82 per credit hour. $11 per term. One-time fee: $30 full-time. *Financial support:* In 2009–10, 1 research assistantship with full tuition reimbursement (averaging $5,000 per year) was awarded; career-related internships or fieldwork also available. Financial award application deadline: 4/1; financial award applicants required to submit FAFSA. *Faculty research:* Practicum experience in schools. *Unit head:* Dr. William Childs, Coordinator, 301-687-4216, E-mail: wchilds@frostburg.edu. *Application contact:* Vickie Mazer, Director, Graduate Services, 301-687-7053, Fax: 301-687-4597, E-mail: vmmazer@frostburg.edu.

Furman University, Graduate Division, Department of Education, Greenville, SC 29613. Offers curriculum and instruction (MA); early childhood education (MA); English as a second language (MA); literacy (MA); school leadership (MA); special education (MA). *Accreditation:* NCATE. Part-time programs available. Postbaccalaureate distance learning degree programs offered (minimal on-campus study). *Faculty:* 14 full-time (8 women), 10 part-time/adjunct (6 women). *Students:* 114 part-time (93 women); includes 13 minority (10 African Americans, 3 Asian Americans or Pacific Islanders). Average age 29. 24 applicants, 100% accepted, 23 enrolled. In 2009, 71 master's awarded. *Degree requirements:* For master's, comprehensive exam (for some programs), thesis or alternative. *Entrance requirements:* For master's, PRAXIS II. *Application deadline:* For fall admission, 8/1 priority date for domestic students, 7/15 priority date for international students; for spring admission, 12/1 priority date for domestic and international students. Applications are processed on a rolling basis. Application fee: $50. *Financial support:* In 2009–10, 43 students received support; fellowships, scholarships/grants available. Financial award application deadline: 5/15; financial award applicants required to submit FAFSA. *Faculty research:* Literacy, pedagogy and practice, social justice, advanced leadership, achievement in high poverty schools. *Unit head:* Dr. Nelly Hecker, Head, 864-294-3385. *Application contact:* Helen Reynolds, Department Assistant, 864-294-2213, Fax: 864-294-3579, E-mail: helen.reynolds@furman.edu.

Gallaudet University, The Graduate School, Department of Administration and Supervision, Washington, DC 20002-3625. Offers administration (MS); administration and supervision (PhD); change leadership on deaf education (Ed S); leadership (Certificate); management (Certificate); special education administration (PhD). *Degree requirements:* For master's, thesis optional; for doctorate, 2 foreign languages, thesis/dissertation; for other advanced degree, 2 foreign languages, thesis (for some programs). *Entrance requirements:* For master's, GRE General Test or MAT; for doctorate, GRE General Test or MAT, interview. Electronic applications accepted.

Gannon University, School of Graduate Studies, College of Humanities, Education, and Social Sciences, School of Education, Program in Educational Leadership, Erie, PA 16541-0001. Offers M Ed. Part-time and evening/weekend programs available. *Students:* 5 part-time (3 women); includes 1 minority (Hispanic American). Average age 37. In 2009, 7 master's awarded. *Entrance requirements:* For master's, bachelor's degree, minimum QPA of 3.0. Additional exam requirements/recommendations for international students: Required—TOEFL (minimum score 79 iBT). *Application deadline:* Applications are processed on a rolling basis. Application fee: $25. Electronic applications accepted. *Expenses:* Contact institution. *Financial support:* Application deadline: 7/1. *Faculty research:* English, natural sciences, environmental education. *Unit head:* Dr. Kathleen Kingston, Director, 814-871-5626, E-mail: kingston002@gannon.edu. *Application contact:* Kara Morgan, Director of Graduate Recruitment, 814-871-5831, Fax: 814-871-5827, E-mail: graduate@gannon.edu.

Gannon University, School of Graduate Studies, College of Humanities, Education, and Social Sciences, School of Education, Program in Principal Certification, Erie, PA 16541-0001. Offers Certificate. Part-time and evening/weekend programs available. Postbaccalaureate distance learning degree programs offered (no on-campus study). *Students:* 5 full-time (4 women), 49 part-time (26 women). Average age 36. 75 applicants, 97% accepted, 39 enrolled. *Entrance requirements:* For degree, master's degree, minimum QPA of 3.0, educational certification. Additional exam requirements/recommendations for international students: Required—TOEFL (minimum score 79 iBT). *Application deadline:* Applications are processed on a rolling basis. Application fee: $25. Electronic applications accepted. *Expenses:* Contact institution. *Financial support:* Scholarships/grants available. Financial award application deadline: 7/1; financial award applicants required to submit FAFSA. *Unit head:* Dr. Kathleen Kingston, Director, 814-871-5626, E-mail: kingston002@gannon.edu. *Application contact:* Kara Morgan, Assistant Director of Graduate Admissions, 814-871-5831, Fax: 814-871-5827, E-mail: graduate@gannon.edu.

Gannon University, School of Graduate Studies, College of Humanities, Education, and Social Sciences, School of Education, Program in Superintendent Letter of Eligibility Certification, Erie, PA 16541-0001. Offers Certificate. Part-time and evening/weekend programs available. Postbaccalaureate distance learning degree programs offered (no on-campus study). *Students:* 14 part-time (4 women). Average age 41. 24 applicants, 88% accepted, 12 enrolled. *Degree requirements:* For Certificate, superintendent internship. *Entrance requirements:* For degree, master's degree; minimum QPA of 3.0; 6 years of educational experience, 3 of which must be under administrative of supervisory certificate. Additional exam requirements/recommendations for international students: Required—TOEFL (minimum score 79 iBT). *Application deadline:* Applications are processed on a rolling basis. Application fee: $25. Electronic applications accepted. *Expenses:* Contact institution. *Financial support:* Scholarships/grants available. Financial award application deadline: 7/1; financial award applicants required to submit FAFSA. *Unit head:* Dr. Kathleen Kingston, Director, 814-871-5626, E-mail: kingston002@gannon.edu. *Application contact:* Kara Morgan, Assistant Director of Graduate Admission, 814-871-5831, Fax: 814-871-5827, E-mail: graduate@gannon.edu.

Gannon University, School of Graduate Studies, College of Humanities, Education, and Social Sciences, School of Humanities, Program in Organizational Learning and Leadership, Erie, PA 16541-0001. Offers PhD. Part-time and evening/weekend programs available. *Students:* 4 full-time (1 woman), 45 part-time (26 women); includes 4 minority (all African Americans), 1 international. Average age 41. 30 applicants, 80% accepted, 18 enrolled. *Degree requirements:* For doctorate, thesis/dissertation. *Entrance requirements:* For doctorate, GRE (verbal, quantitative and written sections taken within the last 3 years), minimum graduate GPA of 3.5, 2 years post-baccalaureate work experience. Additional exam requirements/recommendations for international students: Required—TOEFL (minimum score 79 iBT). *Application deadline:* For spring admission, 2/1 for domestic students. Application fee: $50. Electronic applications accepted. *Expenses:* Tuition: Full-time $13,590; part-time $755 per credit. Required fees: $524; $17 per credit. Tuition and fees vary according to course load, degree level, campus/location and program. *Financial support:* Scholarships/grants and unspecified assistantships available. Financial award applicants required to submit FAFSA. *Unit head:* Dr. David B. Barker, Director, 814-871-7700, E-mail: barker002@gannon.edu. *Application contact:* Kara Morgan, Director of Graduate Recruitment, 814-871-5831, Fax: 814-871-5827, E-mail: graduate@gannon.edu.

Gardner-Webb University, Graduate School, School of Education, Program in Educational Leadership, Boiling Springs, NC 28017. Offers Ed D. *Faculty:* 10 full-time (4 women). *Students:* 72 part-time (37 women); includes 28 minority (26 African Americans, 1 Asian American or Pacific Islander, 1 Hispanic American). Average age 42. In 2009, 15 doctorates awarded. *Expenses:* Tuition: Part-time $305 per credit hour. *Unit head:* Dr. Carrol Smith, Chair, 704-406-3913, Fax: 704-406-3921, E-mail: dsimmons@gardner-webb.edu. *Application contact:* Dr. Franki Burch, Dean, Graduate School, 704-406-4422, Fax: 704-406-4329, E-mail: gradschool@gardner-webb.edu.

Gardner-Webb University, Graduate School, School of Education, Program in School Administration, Boiling Springs, NC 28017. Offers MA. *Accreditation:* NCATE. Part-time and evening/weekend programs available. *Faculty:* 7 full-time (3 women), 2 part-time/adjunct (both women). *Students:* 9 full-time (5 women), 218 part-time (138 women); includes 69 minority (64 African Americans, 1 American Indian/Alaska Native, 1 Asian American or Pacific Islander, 3 Hispanic Americans). Average age 35. In 2009, 112 master's awarded. *Degree requirements:* For master's, comprehensive exam. *Entrance requirements:* For master's, GRE General Test or NTE, PRAXIS, minimum GPA of 2.5. *Application deadline:* For fall admission, 8/1 priority date for domestic students. Applications are processed on a rolling basis. Application fee: $25. Electronic applications accepted. *Expenses:* Tuition: Part-time $305 per credit hour. *Financial support:* Unspecified assistantships available. *Unit head:* Dr. Carrol Smith, 704-406-3913. *Application contact:* Dr. Franki Burch, Dean, Graduate School, 704-406-4422, Fax: 704-406-4329, E-mail: gradschool@gardner-webb.edu.

Geneva College, Program in Higher Education, Beaver Falls, PA 15010-3599. Offers campus ministry (MA); college teaching (MA); educational leadership (MA); student affairs administration (MA). Part-time and evening/weekend programs available. Postbaccalaureate distance learning degree programs offered (minimal on-campus study). *Faculty:* 2 full-time (0 women), 4 part-time/adjunct (0 women). *Students:* 28 full-time (13 women), 37 part-time (21 women); includes 2 minority (1 African American, 1 Asian American or Pacific Islander). Average age 25. 41 applicants, 98% accepted, 19 enrolled. In 2009, 29 master's awarded. *Degree requirements:* For master's, research seminar. *Entrance requirements:* For master's, minimum GPA of 3.0, writing sample, 3 letters of recommendation. Additional exam requirements/recommendations for international students: Required—TOEFL. *Application deadline:* For fall admission, 9/1 priority date for domestic students; for winter admission, 1/2 priority date for domestic students; for spring admission, 3/11 priority date for domestic students. Applications are processed on a rolling basis. Electronic applications accepted. *Expenses:* Tuition: Full-time $11,250; part-time $625 per credit. Tuition and fees vary according to program. *Financial support:* In 2009–10, 1 research assistantship with partial tuition reimbursement (averaging $4,500 per year), 1 teaching assistantship with partial tuition reimbursement (averaging $4,500 per year) were awarded; career-related internships or fieldwork and unspecified assistantships also available. Support available to part-time students. Financial award application deadline: 9/1; financial award

Educational Leadership and Administration

Geneva College (continued)

applicants required to submit FAFSA. *Faculty research:* Student development, learning theories, church-related higher education, assessment, organizational culture. *Unit head:* Dr. Donald Opitz, Director, 724-847-6883, Fax: 724-847-6107, E-mail: hed@geneva.edu. *Application contact:* Jerryn S. Carson, Coordinator, 724-847-6510, Fax: 724-847-6696, E-mail: hed@geneva.edu.

George Fox University, School of Education, Educational Foundations and Leadership Program, Newberg, OR 97132-2697. Offers continuing administrator license (Certificate); curriculum and instruction (M Ed); educational leadership (M Ed, Ed D); higher education (M Ed); initial administrator license (Certificate); library media (M Ed, Certificate); literacy (M Ed); reading (M Ed); secondary education (M Ed). *Accreditation:* NCATE. Part-time and evening/weekend programs available. Postbaccalaureate distance learning degree programs offered (minimal on-campus study). *Faculty:* 10 full-time (3 women), 7 part-time/adjunct (3 women). *Students:* 1 (woman) full-time, 151 part-time (101 women); includes 15 minority (1 African American, 4 American Indian/Alaska Native, 4 Asian Americans or Pacific Islanders, 6 Hispanic Americans), 1 international. Average age 40. 44 applicants, 75% accepted, 26 enrolled. In 2009, 44 master's, 27 doctorates, 82 Certificates awarded. *Degree requirements:* For master's, thesis (for some programs); for doctorate, comprehensive exam, thesis/dissertation, project. *Entrance requirements:* For master's, minimum undergraduate GPA of 3.0 during previous 2 years of course work, resume, 3 professional recommendations on university forms, copy of teaching license (if applicable); for doctorate, GRE or MAT, master's degree with minimum GPA of 3.25, 3 years of relevant professional experience, interview, personal essay, scholarly work, 3 professional recommendations on university forms along with 3 written letters of recommendation, official transcripts. Additional exam requirements/recommendations for international students: Required—TOEFL (minimum score 577 paper-based; 233 computer-based; 90 iBT). *Application deadline:* For fall admission, 7/15 for domestic and international students; for winter admission, 11/1 for domestic and international students; for spring admission, 4/1 for domestic and international students. Applications are processed on a rolling basis. Application fee: $40. Electronic applications accepted. *Expenses:* Contact institution. *Financial support:* Career-related internships or fieldwork available. Financial award applicants required to submit FAFSA. *Unit head:* Dr. Scott Headley, Chair, 503-554-2836, E-mail: sheadley@georgefox.edu. *Application contact:* Kristie DeHaven, Admissions Counselor, 800-631-0921, Fax: 503-554-3110, E-mail: edfl@georgefox.edu.

George Mason University, College of Education and Human Development, Program in Education Leadership, Fairfax, VA 22030. Offers M Ed. *Accreditation:* NCATE. Part-time and evening/weekend programs available. *Faculty:* 88 full-time (64 women), 120 part-time/adjunct (93 women). *Students:* 4 full-time (3 women), 323 part-time (221 women); includes 39 minority (27 African Americans, 2 Asian Americans or Pacific Islanders, 10 Hispanic Americans), 4 international. Average age 37. 133 applicants, 83% accepted, 89 enrolled. In 2009, 103 master's awarded. *Entrance requirements:* For master's, minimum GPA of 3.0 in last 60 hours, 3 letters of recommendation, 3 years of documented full-time experience in schools, interview. Additional exam requirements/recommendations for international students: Required—TOEFL. *Application deadline:* For fall admission, 3/1 priority date for domestic and international students; for spring admission, 11/1 for domestic and international students. Applications are processed on a rolling basis. Application fee: $75. Electronic applications accepted. *Expenses:* Tuition, state resident: full-time $7568; part-time $315.33 per credit hour. Tuition, nonresident: full-time $21,704; part-time $904.33 per credit hour. Required fees: $2184; $91 per credit hour. *Financial support:* In 2009–10, 1 student received support, including 1 teaching assistantship with full and partial tuition reimbursement available (averaging $1,010 per year); career-related internships or fieldwork, Federal Work-Study, unspecified assistantships, and health care benefits (full-time research or teaching assistantship recipients) also available. Financial award application deadline: 3/1; financial award applicants required to submit FAFSA. *Faculty research:* Understanding of the complexities of change in schools, communities, and organizations; education law; foundations of education leadership-history and leadership. *Unit head:* Scott Bauer, Coordinator, 703-993-3775, Fax: 703-993-3643. *Application contact:* David Brazer, Information Contact, 703-993-3634, E-mail: sbrazer@gmu.edu.

The George Washington University, Graduate School of Education and Human Development, Department of Educational Leadership, Program in Educational Administration and Policy Studies, Washington, DC 20052. Offers education policy (Ed D); educational administration (Ed D). Educational administration program offered at Newport News and Alexandria, VA. *Accreditation:* NCATE. *Students:* 6 full-time (3 women), 150 part-time (96 women); includes 62 minority (51 African Americans, 4 Asian Americans or Pacific Islanders, 7 Hispanic Americans), 7 international. Average age 40. 62 applicants, 50% accepted, 18 enrolled. In 2009, 21 doctorates awarded. *Degree requirements:* For doctorate, comprehensive exam, thesis/dissertation. *Entrance requirements:* For doctorate, GRE General Test or MAT, interview, minimum GPA of 3.3. *Application deadline:* For fall admission, 1/15 priority date for domestic students; for spring admission, 10/1 for domestic students. Applications are processed on a rolling basis. Application fee: $60. *Financial support:* In 2009–10, 9 students received support; fellowships, research assistantships, teaching assistantships, career-related internships or fieldwork, Federal Work-Study, and tuition waivers (partial) available. Financial award application deadline: 1/15; financial award applicants required to submit FAFSA. *Unit head:* Prof. Yas Nakib, Program Coordinator, 202-994-8816, E-mail: nakib@gwu.edu. *Application contact:* Sarah Lang, 202-994-1447, Fax: 202-994-7207, E-mail: slang@gwu.edu.

The George Washington University, Graduate School of Education and Human Development, Department of Educational Leadership, Program in Educational Leadership and Administration, Washington, DC 20052. Offers MA Ed, Certificate, Ed S. Programs offered at Newport News and Alexandria, VA. *Accreditation:* NCATE. Evening/weekend programs available. *Students:* 30 full-time (21 women), 168 part-time (121 women); includes 82 minority (65 African Americans, 1 American Indian/Alaska Native, 9 Asian Americans or Pacific Islanders, 7 Hispanic Americans), 2 international. Average age 37. 122 applicants, 99% accepted, 74 enrolled. In 2009, 80 master's, 53 Certificates awarded. *Degree requirements:* For master's, comprehensive exam. *Entrance requirements:* For master's, GRE General Test or MAT, interview, minimum GPA of 2.75. *Application deadline:* For fall admission, 1/15 priority date for domestic students; for spring admission, 10/1 for domestic students. Applications are processed on a rolling basis. Application fee: $60. *Financial support:* Fellowships, teaching assistantships, career-related internships or fieldwork and Federal Work-Study available. Financial award application deadline: 1/15; financial award applicants required to submit FAFSA. *Faculty research:* Organizational learning. *Unit head:* Dr. Linda K. Lemasters, Director, 757-269-2218, E-mail: lindal@gwu.edu. *Application contact:* Sarah Lang, Director of Graduate Admissions, 202-994-1447, Fax: 202-994-7207, E-mail: slang@gwu.edu.

The George Washington University, Graduate School of Education and Human Development, Department of Educational Leadership, Program in Higher Education Administration, Washington, DC 20052. Offers MA Ed, Ed D, Ed S. *Accreditation:* NCATE. *Students:* 26 full-time (20 women), 141 part-time (90 women); includes 44 minority (30 African Americans, 2 American Indian/Alaska Native, 7 Asian Americans or Pacific Islanders, 5 Hispanic Americans), 3 international. Average age 35. 136 applicants, 90% accepted, 45 enrolled. In 2009, 25 master's, 19 doctorates, 4 other advanced degrees awarded. *Degree requirements:* For master's and Ed S, comprehensive exam; for doctorate, comprehensive exam, thesis/dissertation. *Entrance requirements:* For master's, GRE General Test or MAT, minimum GPA of 2.75; for doctorate, GRE General Test or MAT, interview, minimum GPA of 3.3; for Ed S, GRE General Test or MAT, minimum GPA of 3.3. *Application deadline:* For fall admission, 1/15 priority date for domestic students; for spring admission, 10/1 for domestic students. Applications are processed on a rolling basis. Application fee: $60. *Financial support:* In 2009–10, 17 students received support; fellowships, research assistantships, career-related internships or fieldwork, Federal Work-Study, and tuition waivers (partial) available. Financial award application deadline: 1/15; financial award applicants required to submit FAFSA. *Faculty research:* Technology in higher education administration. *Application contact:* Sarah Lang, Director of Graduate Admissions, 202-994-1447, Fax: 202-994-7207, E-mail: slang@gwu.edu.

Georgia College & State University, Graduate School, The John H. Lounsbury College of Education, Department of Special Education and Educational Leadership, Program in Educational Leadership, Milledgeville, GA 31061. Offers M Ed, Ed S. *Accreditation:* NCATE. Part-time and evening/weekend programs available. *Students:* 119 full-time (80 women), 1 part-time (0 women); includes 39 minority (37 African Americans, 1 American Indian/Alaska Native, 1 Hispanic American). Average age 37. 146 applicants, 95% accepted, 101 enrolled. In 2009, 27 master's, 57 Ed Ss awarded. *Entrance requirements:* Additional exam requirements/recommendations for international students: Required—TOEFL (minimum score 550 paper-based; 213 computer-based; 79 iBT). Application fee: $40. Electronic applications accepted. *Expenses:* Tuition, area resident: Part-time $241 per credit hour. Tuition, state resident: full-time $4338. Tuition, nonresident: full-time $17,352; part-time $964 per credit hour. Required fees: $609 per semester. Tuition and fees vary according to course load and campus/location. *Unit head:* Dr. Craig Smith, Chair, Special Education and Educational Leadership, 478-445-4577, E-mail: craig.smith@gcsu.edu. *Application contact:* Shanda Brand, Graduate Admission Coordinator, 478-445-1383.

Georgian Court University, School of Arts and Humanities, Lakewood, NJ 08701-2697. Offers Catholic school leadership (Certificate); parish business management (Certificate); pastoral administration (Certificate); pastoral ministry (Certificate); religious education (Certificate); theology (MA, Certificate). Part-time and evening/weekend programs available. *Faculty:* 3 full-time (2 women), 1 (woman) part-time/adjunct. *Students:* 57 part-time (39 women); includes 8 minority (3 African Americans, 1 Asian American or Pacific Islander, 4 Hispanic Americans). Average age 52. 20 applicants, 100% accepted, 14 enrolled. In 2009, 6 master's awarded. *Degree requirements:* For master's, thesis (for some programs). *Entrance requirements:* For master's, 3 letters of recommendation. Additional exam requirements/recommendations for international students: Required—TOEFL (minimum score 550 paper-based; 213 computer-based). *Application deadline:* For fall admission, 8/1 priority date for domestic students, 4/1 for international students; for spring admission, 1/1 priority date for domestic students, 7/1 for international students. Applications are processed on a rolling basis. Application fee: $40. Electronic applications accepted. *Expenses:* Tuition: Full-time $12,510; part-time $695 per credit. Required fees: $416 per year. Tuition and fees vary according to campus/location. *Financial support:* Scholarships/grants, health care benefits, and unspecified assistantships available. Financial award application deadline: 4/15; financial award applicants required to submit FAFSA. *Unit head:* Dr. Linda James, Dean, 732-987-2617, Fax: 732-987-2007. *Application contact:* Eugene Soltys, Director of Graduate Admissions, 732-987-2770, Fax: 732-987-2084, E-mail: graduateadmissions@georgian.edu.

Georgian Court University, School of Education, Lakewood, NJ 08701-2697. Offers administration and leadership (MA); education (MA). *Accreditation:* Teacher Education Accreditation Council. Part-time and evening/weekend programs available. *Faculty:* 27 full-time (15 women), 45 part-time/adjunct (30 women). *Students:* 184 full-time (155 women), 525 part-time (444 women); includes 64 minority (15 African Americans, 2 American Indian/Alaska Native, 7 Asian Americans or Pacific Islanders, 40 Hispanic Americans), 1 international. Average age 32. 612 applicants, 77% accepted, 267 enrolled. In 2009, 91 master's awarded. *Degree requirements:* For master's, comprehensive exam (for some programs), thesis (for some programs). *Entrance requirements:* For master's, GRE, MAT or NTE/PRAXIS, 3 letters of recommendation. Additional exam requirements/recommendations for international students: Required—TOEFL (minimum score 550 paper-based; 213 computer-based). *Application deadline:* For fall admission, 8/1 priority date for domestic students, 4/1 for international students; for spring admission, 1/1 priority date for domestic students, 7/1 for international students. Applications are processed on a rolling basis. Application fee: $40. Electronic applications accepted. *Expenses:* Tuition: Full-time $12,510; part-time $695 per credit. Required fees: $416 per year. Tuition and fees vary according to campus/location. *Financial support:* In 2009–10, 183 students received support. Scholarships/grants, health care benefits, and unspecified assistantships available. Financial award application deadline: 4/15; financial award applicants required to submit FAFSA. *Unit head:* Dr. Jacqueline Kress, Dean, 732-987-2525. *Application contact:* Eugene Soltys, Director of Graduate Admissions, 732-987-2770, Fax: 732-987-2084, E-mail: graduateadmissions@georgian.edu.

Georgia Southern University, Jack N. Averitt College of Graduate Studies, College of Education, Department of Leadership, Technology, and Human Development, Program in Educational Administration, Statesboro, GA 30460. Offers Ed D. Part-time and evening/weekend programs available. *Students:* 7 full-time (4 women), 206 part-time (133 women); includes 97 minority (92 African Americans, 2 Asian Americans or Pacific Islanders, 3 Hispanic Americans), 1 international. Average age 43. 18 applicants, 100% accepted, 5 enrolled. In 2009, 31 doctorates awarded. *Degree requirements:* For doctorate, thesis/dissertation, exams. *Entrance requirements:* For doctorate, GRE General Test or MAT, minimum GPA of 3.5, letters of reference, resume. Additional exam requirements/recommendations for international students: Required—TOEFL (minimum score 550 paper-based; 213 computer-based; 80 iBT). *Application deadline:* For fall admission, 4/1 for domestic students, 3/1 priority date for international students; for spring admission, 11/1 for domestic students, 10/1 for international students. Applications are processed on a rolling basis. Application fee: $50. Electronic applications accepted. *Expenses:* Tuition, state resident: full-time $5040; part-time $210 per credit hour. Tuition, nonresident: full-time $20,136; part-time $839 per credit hour. Required fees: $1644. *Financial support:* In 2009–10, 93 students received support, including fellowships with partial tuition reimbursements available (averaging $9,500 per year), teaching assistantships with partial tuition reimbursements available (averaging $9,500 per year); research assistantships with partial tuition reimbursements available, Federal Work-Study, scholarships/grants, tuition waivers (partial), and unspecified assistantships also available. Support available to part-time students. Financial award application deadline: 4/15; financial award applicants required to submit FAFSA. *Unit head:* Dr. Linda Arthur, Coordinator, 912-478-0697, Fax: 912-478-7140, E-mail: larthur@georgiasouthern.edu. *Application contact:* Dr. Charles Ziglar, Coordinator for Graduate Student Recruitment, 912-478-5635, Fax: 912-478-0740, E-mail: gradadmissions@georgiasouthern.edu.

Georgia Southern University, Jack N. Averitt College of Graduate Studies, College of Education, Department of Leadership, Technology, and Human Development, Program in Educational Leadership, Statesboro, GA 30460. Offers M Ed, Ed S. *Accreditation:* NCATE. Part-time and evening/weekend programs available. *Students:* 27 full-time (16 women), 55 part-time (31 women); includes 28 minority (24 African Americans, 4 Hispanic Americans), 2 international. Average age 35. 40 applicants, 100% accepted, 20 enrolled. In 2009, 40 master's, 14 Ed Ss awarded. *Degree requirements:* For master's, comprehensive exam, transition point assessments; for Ed S, transition point assessments. *Entrance requirements:* For master's, GRE General Test or MAT, minimum GPA of 2.5, 3 years teaching experience; for Ed S, GRE General Test or MAT, minimum graduate GPA of 3.25. Additional exam requirements/recommendations for international students: Required—TOEFL (minimum score 550 paper-based; 213 computer-based; 80 iBT). *Application deadline:* For fall admission, 3/1 priority date for domestic and international students; for spring admission, 10/1 priority date for domestic students, 10/1 for international students. Applications are processed on a rolling basis. Application fee: $50. Electronic applications accepted. *Expenses:* Tuition, state resident: full-time $5040; part-time $210 per credit hour. Tuition, nonresident: full-time $20,136; part-time $839 per credit hour. Required fees: $1644. *Financial support:* In 2009–10, 46 students received support, including research assistantships with partial tuition reimbursements available (averaging $7,200 per year), teaching assistantships with partial tuition reimbursements available (averaging $7,200 per year); career-related internships or fieldwork, Federal Work-Study, scholarships/grants, tuition waivers (partial), and unspecified assistantships also available. Support available to part-time students. Financial award application deadline: 4/15; financial award applicants required to submit FAFSA. *Faculty research:* Principalship, school finance, supervision. *Unit head:* Dr. Barbara Mallory, Assistant Professor, 912-478-5307, Fax: 912-478-7104, E-mail: bmallory@georgiasouthern.edu. *Application contact:* Dr. Charles Ziglar, Coordinator for Graduate Student Recruitment, 912-478-5635, Fax: 912-478-0740, E-mail: gradadmissions@georgiasouthern.edu.

Georgia State University, College of Education, Department of Educational Policy Studies, Program in Educational Leadership, Atlanta, GA 30302-3083. Offers M Ed, PhD, Ed S. *Accreditation:* NCATE. Part-time and evening/weekend programs available. *Degree requirements:* For master's, comprehensive exam; for doctorate, comprehensive exam, thesis/dissertation. *Entrance requirements:* For master's, GRE General Test, minimum GPA of 2.5; for doctorate, GRE General Test or MAT, minimum GPA of 3.3; for Ed S, GRE General Test or MAT, minimum graduate GPA of 3.25. Electronic applications accepted. *Faculty research:* Principal effectiveness, teacher empowerment, restructuring of schools.

Golden Gate Baptist Theological Seminary, Graduate and Professional Programs, Mill Valley, CA 94941-3197. Offers divinity (M Div); early childhood education (Certificate); education leadership (MAEL, Diploma); ministry (D Min); theological studies (MTS); theology (Th M); youth ministry (Certificate). *Accreditation:* ACIPE; ATS (one or more programs are accredited). Part-time and evening/weekend programs available. *Degree requirements:* For master's, thesis (for some programs); for doctorate, 2 foreign languages, thesis/dissertation; for M Div, 2 foreign languages. *Entrance requirements:* For doctorate, MAT. Additional exam requirements/recommendations for international students: Required—TOEFL (minimum score 550 paper-based; 213 computer-based). Electronic applications accepted.

Gonzaga University, School of Education, Program in Administration and Curriculum, Spokane, WA 99258. Offers MAA. *Accreditation:* NCATE. *Faculty:* 3 full-time (1 woman), 21 part-time/adjunct (10 women). *Students:* 327 part-time (208 women); includes 9 minority (3 American Indian/Alaska Native, 2 Asian Americans or Pacific Islanders, 4 Hispanic Americans). Average age 39. In 2009, 203 master's awarded. *Degree requirements:* For master's, comprehensive exam. *Entrance requirements:* For master's, GRE General Test or MAT, minimum B average in undergraduate course work. Additional exam requirements/recommendations for international students: Required—TOEFL. *Application deadline:* For fall admission, 7/20 priority date for domestic students; for spring admission, 11/1 for domestic students. Applications are processed on a rolling basis. Application fee: $40. Tuition and fees vary according to course level, course load, degree level, campus/location and program. *Financial support:* Teaching assistantships available. Support available to part-time students. Financial award application deadline: 3/1. *Unit head:* Dr. Janet Brougher, Director, 509-328-4220 Ext. 3654. *Application contact:* Julie McCulloh, Dean of Admissions, 509-313-6592, Fax: 509-313-5780, E-mail: mcculloh@gu.gonzaga.edu.

Gonzaga University, School of Education, Program in Educational Administration, Spokane, WA 99258. Offers MA Ed Ad. *Faculty:* 1 full-time (0 women). *Students:* 6 part-time (3 women). Average age 34. In 2009, 5 master's awarded. Tuition and fees vary according to course level, course load, degree level, campus/location and program. *Unit head:* Dr. Dennis Conners, Chair, 509-323-3650. *Application contact:* Julie McCulloh, Dean of Admissions, 509-323-6592, Fax: 509-323-5780, E-mail: mcculloh@gu.gonzaga.edu.

Gonzaga University, School of Professional Studies, Program in Leadership Studies, Spokane, WA 99258. Offers PhD. *Faculty:* 5 full-time (2 women), 3 part-time/adjunct (1 woman). *Students:* 8 full-time (3 women), 107 part-time (52 women); includes 8 minority (1 African American, 3 American Indian/Alaska Native, 3 Asian Americans or Pacific Islanders, 1 Hispanic American), 4 international. Average age 43. In 2009, 17 doctorates awarded. *Entrance requirements:* For doctorate, MAT and/or GRE. Application fee: $50. Tuition and fees vary according to course level, course load, degree level, campus/location and program. *Unit head:* Dr. Sandra Wilson, Chairperson, 509-328-4220 Ext. 3517. *Application contact:* Dr. Sandra Wilson, Chairperson, 509-328-4220 Ext. 3517.

Governors State University, College of Education, Program in Educational Administration and Supervision, University Park, IL 60466-0975. Offers MA. Part-time and evening/weekend programs available. *Degree requirements:* For master's, comprehensive exam, practicum. *Entrance requirements:* For master's, minimum GPA of 2.75 in last 60 hours of undergraduate course work, minimum graduate GPA of 3.0.

Graceland University, Gleazer School of Education, Lamoni, IA 50140. Offers collaborative learning and teaching (M Ed); differentiated instruction (M Ed); instructional leadership (M Ed); mild/moderate special education (M Ed); quality schools (M Ed); technology integration (M Ed). *Accreditation:* NCATE. Part-time and evening/weekend programs available. Postbaccalaureate distance learning degree programs offered (no on-campus study). *Faculty:* 8 full-time (7 women), 25 part-time/adjunct (14 women). *Students:* 505 full-time (406 women); includes 18 minority (6 African Americans, 3 American Indian/Alaska Native, 4 Asian Americans or Pacific Islanders, 5 Hispanic Americans), 7 international. Average age 36. 167 applicants, 100% accepted, 160 enrolled. In 2009, 277 master's awarded. *Degree requirements:* For master's, action research project. *Entrance requirements:* For master's, minimum GPA of 3.0, teaching certificate, current teaching contract. *Application deadline:* For fall admission, 7/15 for domestic students; for winter admission, 10/15 for domestic students; for spring admission, 1/15 priority date for domestic students. Application fee: $50. Electronic applications accepted. *Expenses:* Tuition: Full-time $7110; part-time $395 per semester hour. Required fees: $1110; $185 per course. *Financial support:* In 2009–10, 437 students received support. Institutionally sponsored loans and scholarships/grants available. Financial award application deadline: 12/15; financial award applicants required to submit FAFSA. *Unit head:* Dr. Nancy Halferty, Dean, 641-784-5000 Ext. 5251, E-mail: halferty@graceland.edu. *Application contact:* Cathy Porter, Program Consultant, 816-833-0524 Ext. 4516, E-mail: cgporter@graceland.edu.

Grambling State University, School of Graduate Studies and Research, College of Education, Department of Educational Leadership, Grambling, LA 71245. Offers curriculum and instruction (Ed D); developmental education (MS, Ed D), including curriculum and instruction: reading (Ed D), English (MS), guidance and counseling (MS), higher education administration (Ed D), instructional systems and technology (Ed D), mathematics (MS), reading (MS), science (MS), student development and personnel services (Ed D); educational leadership (MS, Ed D). Part-time and evening/weekend programs available. *Faculty:* 19 full-time (12 women). *Students:* 23 full-time (18 women), 84 part-time (62 women); includes 81 minority (80 African Americans, 1 Asian American or Pacific Islander), 5 international. Average age 39. 72 applicants, 75% accepted, 39 enrolled. In 2009, 5 master's, 9 doctorates awarded. *Degree requirements:* For master's, comprehensive exam, thesis (for some programs); for doctorate, comprehensive exam, thesis/dissertation. *Entrance requirements:* For master's, GRE, minimum GPA of 2.5 on last degree; for doctorate, GRE (minimum 1000, 500 on Verbal), master's degree, minimum GPA of 3.0 on last degree. Additional exam requirements/recommendations for international students: Required—TOEFL (minimum score 500 paper-based; 173 computer-based; 61 iBT). *Application deadline:* For fall admission, 7/1 for domestic and international students; for spring admission, 12/1 for domestic and international students. Applications are processed on a rolling basis. Application fee: $20 ($30 for international students). Electronic applications accepted. *Expenses:* Tuition, state resident: full-time $2610. Tuition, nonresident: full-time $2610. *Financial support:* In 2009–10, 5 research assistantships (averaging $10,948 per year) were awarded; health care benefits, tuition waivers (full), and unspecified assistantships also available. Financial award application deadline: 5/31; financial award applicants required to submit FAFSA. *Unit head:* Dr. Olatunde Ogunyemi, Director, 318-274-6105, Fax: 318-274-2799, E-mail: ogunyemio@gram.edu. *Application contact:* Laketha Richards, Administrative Assistant III, 318-274-6105, Fax: 318-274-6249, E-mail: richardsl@gram.edu.

Grand Canyon University, College of Education, Phoenix, AZ 85017-1097. Offers curriculum and instruction (M Ed); education administration (M Ed); elementary education (M Ed); organizational leadership (Ed D); secondary education (M Ed); special education (M Ed); teaching (MA). Part-time and evening/weekend programs available. Postbaccalaureate distance learning degree programs offered (no on-campus study). *Degree requirements:* For master's, publishable research paper (M Ed), e-portfolio. *Entrance requirements:* Additional exam requirements/recommendations for international students: Required—TOEFL (minimum score 550 paper-based; 213 computer-based; 79 iBT), IELTS (minimum score 6). Electronic applications accepted.

Grand Valley State University, College of Education, Program in Educational Leadership, Allendale, MI 49401-9403. Offers M Ed. *Expenses:* Tuition, state resident: part-time $471 per credit hour. Tuition, nonresident: part-time $646 per credit hour. Tuition and fees vary according to course level.

Grand Valley State University, College of Education, Program in Leadership, Allendale, MI 49401-9403. Offers Ed S. *Entrance requirements:* For degree, GRE, master's degree with minimum GPA of 3.0, resume, 3 recommendations. Electronic applications accepted. *Expenses:* Tuition, state resident: part-time $471 per credit hour. Tuition, nonresident: part-time $646 per credit hour. Tuition and fees vary according to course level.

Grand Valley State University, College of Education, Programs in General Education, Allendale, MI 49401-9403. Offers adult and higher education (M Ed); early childhood education (M Ed); educational differentiation (M Ed); educational leadership (M Ed); educational technology integration (M Ed); elementary education (M Ed); middle level education (M Ed); school library media services (M Ed); secondary level education (M Ed); teaching English to speakers of other languages (M Ed). Part-time and evening/weekend programs available. Postbaccalaureate distance learning degree programs offered (minimal on-campus study). *Faculty:* 82 full-time (42 women), 43 part-time/adjunct (25 women). *Students:* 100 full-time (53 women), 723 part-time (478 women); includes 59 minority (25 African Americans, 4 American Indian/Alaska Native, 13 Asian Americans or Pacific Islanders, 17 Hispanic Americans), 10 international. Average age 33. 237 applicants, 96% accepted, 117 enrolled. In 2009, 291 master's awarded. *Degree requirements:* For master's, thesis. *Entrance requirements:* For master's, GRE General Test or minimum GPA of 3.0. Additional exam requirements/recommendations for international students: Required—TOEFL. *Application deadline:* Applications are processed on a rolling basis. Application fee: $30. Electronic applications accepted. *Expenses:* Tuition, state resident: part-time $471 per credit hour. Tuition, nonresident: part-time $646 per credit hour. Tuition and fees vary according to course level. *Financial support:* In 2009–10, 73 students received support, including 55 fellowships (averaging $2,273 per year), 19 research assistantships with full and partial tuition reimbursements available (averaging $8,000 per year); career-related internships or fieldwork, Federal Work-Study, scholarships/grants, and unspecified assistantships also available. *Faculty research:* Effectiveness of technology in education, parental involvement, effective teaching, effective schools research. *Unit head:* Dr. Linda McCrea, Director, 616-331-2080, E-mail: mccreal@gvsu.edu. *Application contact:* Thomas Owens, Student Information and Services Center, 616-331-6282, Fax: 616-331-2000, E-mail: owenst@gvsu.edu.

Gwynedd-Mercy College, School of Education, Gwynedd Valley, PA 19437-0901. Offers educational administration (MS); master teacher (MS); reading (MS); school counseling (MS); special education (MS). Part-time and evening/weekend programs available. *Degree requirements:* For master's, thesis, internship, practicum. *Entrance requirements:* For master's, GRE or MAT; PRAXIS I Test, minimum GPA of 3.0. *Faculty research:* Learning and the brain, reading literacy, ethics and moral judgment, leadership, teaching and multicultural education.

Harding University, College of Education, Searcy, AR 72149-0001. Offers advanced studies in teaching and learning (M Ed); art (MSE); behavioral science (MSE); counseling (MS, Ed S); early childhood special education (M Ed, MSE); education (MSE); educational leadership (M Ed, Ed S); elementary education (M Ed); English (MSE); family and consumer science (MSE); French (MSE); history/social science (MSE); kinesiology (MSE); math (MSE); physical science (MSE); reading (M Ed); secondary education (M Ed); Spanish (MSE); special education licensure (M Ed); teaching (MAT); teaching English as a second language (M Ed). *Accreditation:* NCATE. Part-time and evening/weekend programs available. *Faculty:* 11 full-time (4 women), 49 part-time/adjunct (26 women). *Students:* 104 full-time (85 women), 392 part-time (282 women); includes 77 minority (67 African Americans, 5 American Indian/Alaska Native, 1 Asian American or Pacific Islander, 4 Hispanic Americans), 5 international. Average age 36. 153 applicants, 92% accepted, 131 enrolled. In 2009, 153 master's, 6 other advanced degrees awarded. *Degree requirements:* For master's, comprehensive exam (for some programs), thesis optional, portfolio(s); for Ed S, comprehensive exam, portfolio, specialist project. *Entrance requirements:* For master's, GRE, MAT, PRAXIS; for Ed S, MAT or GRE. Additional exam requirements/recommendations for international students: Required—TOEFL (minimum score 550 paper-based; 79 iBT). *Application deadline:* For fall admission, 8/1 for domestic and international students; for spring admission, 1/1 for domestic and international students. Applications are processed on a rolling basis. Application fee: $35. *Expenses:* Tuition: Full-time $9720; part-time $540 per credit hour. Required fees: $22 per credit hour. Tuition and fees vary according to course load and program. *Financial support:* In 2009–10, 30 students received support. Unspecified assistantships available. *Faculty research:* Reading, comprehension, school violence, educational technology, behavior, college choice, differentiated instruction, brain-based teaching. *Unit head:* Dr. Clara Carroll, Chair, 501-279-4501, Fax: 501-279-4083, E-mail: ccarroll@harding.edu. *Application contact:* Information Contact, 501-279-4315, E-mail: gradstudiesedu@harding.edu.

Harvard University, Graduate School of Education, Doctoral Program in Education, Cambridge, MA 02138. Offers culture, communities and education (Ed D); education policy, leadership and instructional practice (Ed D); higher education (Ed D); human development and education (Ed D); quantitative policy analysis in education (Ed D); urban superintendency (Ed D). Part-time programs available. *Faculty:* 70 full-time (33 women), 36 part-time/adjunct (20 women). *Students:* 295 full-time (198 women), 23 part-time (11 women); includes 103 minority (40 African Americans, 4 American Indian/Alaska Native, 34 Asian Americans or Pacific Islanders, 25 Hispanic Americans), 33 international. Average age 32. 551 applicants, 9% accepted, 39 enrolled. In 2009, 41 doctorates awarded. Terminal master's awarded for partial completion of doctoral program. *Degree requirements:* For doctorate, thesis/dissertation. *Entrance requirements:* For doctorate, GRE General Test, 3 letters of recommendation. Additional exam requirements/recommendations for international students: Required—TOEFL (minimum score 600 paper-based; 250 computer-based; 100 iBT), TWE (minimum score 5). *Application deadline:* For fall admission, 12/14 for domestic and international students. Application fee: $85. Electronic applications accepted. *Expenses:* Contact institution. *Financial support:* In 2009–10, 265 students received support, including 129 fellowships with full and partial tuition reimbursements available (averaging $11,142 per year), 41 research assistantships (averaging $11,990 per year), 173 teaching assistantships (averaging $9,174 per year); career-related internships or fieldwork, Federal Work-Study, institutionally sponsored loans, scholarships/grants, health care benefits, tuition waivers (full and partial), and unspecified assistantships also available. Support available to part-time students. Financial award application deadline: 2/1; financial award applicants required to submit FAFSA. *Faculty research:* Learning and development, educational leadership and organizations, education policy analysis. Total annual research expenditures: $18.1 million. *Unit head:* Dr. Shu-Ling Chen, Assistant Dean, 617-496-4406. *Application contact:* Information Contact, 617-495-3414, Fax: 617-496-3577, E-mail: gseadmissions@harvard.edu.

Harvard University, Graduate School of Education, Master's Programs in Education, Cambridge, MA 02138. Offers arts in education (Ed M); education policy and management (Ed M); higher education (Ed M); human development and psychology (Ed M); international education policy (Ed M); language and literacy (Ed M); learning and teaching (Ed M); mid-career mathematics and science (teaching certificate) (Ed M); mind brain and education (Ed M); risk and prevention (Ed M); school leadership (Ed M); special studies (Ed M); teaching and curriculum (teaching certificate) (Ed M); technology innovation and education (Ed M). Part-time programs available. *Faculty:* 70 full-time (33 women), 36 part-time/adjunct (20 women). *Students:* 598 full-time (448 women), 76 part-time (60 women); includes 132 minority (40 African Americans, 2 American Indian/Alaska Native, 58 Asian Americans or Pacific Islanders, 32 Hispanic Americans), 103 international. Average age 28. 1,574 applicants, 58% accepted, 640 enrolled. In 2009, 556 master's awarded. *Entrance requirements:* For master's, GRE General Test, 3 letters of recommendation. Additional exam requirements/recommendations for international students: Required—TOEFL (minimum score 600 paper-based; 250 computer-based; 100 iBT), TWE (minimum score 5). *Application deadline:* For fall admission, 1/4 for domestic and international students. Application fee: $85. Electronic applications accepted. *Expenses:* Contact institution. *Financial support:* In 2009–10, 424 students received support, including 25 fellowships with full and partial tuition reimbursements available (averaging

Educational Leadership and Administration

Harvard University (continued)

$15,890 per year); career-related internships or fieldwork, Federal Work-Study, institutionally sponsored loans, scholarships/grants, health care benefits, tuition waivers (full and partial), and unspecified assistantships also available. Support available to part-time students. Financial award application deadline: 2/1; financial award applicants required to submit FAFSA. *Faculty research:* Learning and development, educational leadership and organizations, educational policy analysis. Total annual research expenditures: $18.1 million. *Unit head:* Jennifer L. Petrallia, Assistant Dean, 617-495-8445. *Application contact:* Information Contact, 617-495-3414, Fax: 617-496-3577, E-mail: gseadmissions@harvard.edu.

Henderson State University, Graduate Studies, School of Education, Department of Educational Leadership, Arkadelphia, AR 71999-0001. Offers educational leadership (Ed S); school administration (MSE). Part-time programs available. *Faculty:* 11 full-time (7 women), 3 part-time/adjunct (0 women). *Students:* 8 full-time (4 women), 38 part-time (23 women); includes 11 minority (all African Americans). Average age 38. 3 applicants, 100% accepted, 3 enrolled. In 2009, 7 master's, 5 other advanced degrees awarded. *Entrance requirements:* For master's, GRE or MAT. Additional exam requirements/recommendations for international students: Required—TOEFL (minimum score 550 paper-based; 213 computer-based); Recommended—IELTS (minimum score 6). *Application deadline:* For fall admission, 8/1 priority date for domestic students, 6/30 priority date for international students; for spring admission, 1/1 priority date for domestic students, 11/30 priority date for international students. Application fee: $25 ($75 for international students). Electronic applications accepted. *Expenses:* Tuition, state resident: full-time $3798; part-time $211 per credit hour. Tuition, nonresident: full-time $7596; part-time $422 per credit hour. Required fees: $903. *Unit head:* Dr. Sheldon Buxton, Chairperson, 870-230-5351, E-mail: buxtons@hsu.edu. *Application contact:* Dr. Marck L. Beggs, Graduate Dean, 870-230-5126, Fax: 870-230-5479, E-mail: beggsm@hsu.edu.

Heritage University, Graduate Programs in Education, Program in Educational Administration, Toppenish, WA 98948-9599. Offers M Ed. Part-time and evening/weekend programs available. *Degree requirements:* For master's, comprehensive exam, thesis optional, special project. *Entrance requirements:* For master's, valid teaching certificate, 3 years of teaching experience, interview, letters of recommendation.

High Point University, Norcross Graduate School, High Point, NC 27262-3598. Offers business administration (MBA); educational leadership (M Ed); elementary education (M Ed); history (MA); nonprofit management (MA); special education (M Ed); sport studies (MS). *Accreditation:* ACBSP; NCATE. Part-time and evening/weekend programs available. *Degree requirements:* For master's, comprehensive exam (for some programs), thesis (for some programs). *Entrance requirements:* For master's, GMAT (MBA), GRE General Test, MAT, minimum GPA of 3.0. Additional exam requirements/recommendations for international students: Required—TOEFL (minimum score 550 paper-based). Electronic applications accepted.

Hofstra University, School of Education, Health, and Human Services, Department of Foundations, Leadership, and Policy Studies, Program in Educational and Policy Leadership, Hempstead, NY 11549. Offers educational and policy leadership (Ed D); educational leadership (CAS); educational leadership and policy studies (MS Ed); school building leader (CAS); school district business leader (CAS). Part-time and evening/weekend programs available. *Students:* 12 full-time (5 women), 104 part-time (71 women); includes 33 minority (24 African Americans, 1 American Indian/Alaska Native, 3 Asian Americans or Pacific Islanders, 5 Hispanic Americans). Average age 37. 64 applicants, 95% accepted, 48 enrolled. In 2009, 7 master's, 7 doctorates, 11 CASs awarded. *Degree requirements:* For master's, thesis or alternative; for doctorate, comprehensive exam, thesis/dissertation. *Entrance requirements:* For doctorate, GMAT, GRE, LSAT, or MAT, 3 letters of recommendation, resume, interview. Additional exam requirements/recommendations for international students: Required—TOEFL (minimum score 550 paper-based; 213 computer-based; 80 iBT). *Application deadline:* Applications are processed on a rolling basis. Application fee: $60. Electronic applications accepted. *Expenses:* Tuition: Full-time $16,200; part-time $900 per credit hour. Required fees: $970; $145 per term. Tuition and fees vary according to program. *Financial support:* In 2009–10, 40 students received support, including 30 fellowships with full and partial tuition reimbursements available (averaging $4,809 per year), 3 research assistantships with full and partial tuition reimbursements available (averaging $6,367 per year); Federal Work-Study, institutionally sponsored loans, scholarships/grants, tuition waivers (full and partial), and unspecified assistantships also available. Support available to part-time students. Financial award applicants required to submit FAFSA. *Faculty research:* School improvement, student belonging, educational policy, professional development, race/gender in education. Total annual research expenditures: $36,000. *Unit head:* Dr. Monica C. Byrne-Jimenez, Program Director, 516-463-5763, Fax: 516-463-5949, E-mail: edamcb@hofstra.edu. *Application contact:* Carol Drummer, Dean of Graduate Admissions, 516-463-4876, Fax: 516-463-4664, E-mail: gradstudent@hofstra.edu.

Holy Family University, Graduate School, School of Education, Philadelphia, PA 19114. Offers education (M Ed); education leadership (M Ed); elementary education (M Ed); reading specialist (M Ed); secondary education (M Ed); special education (M Ed). Part-time and evening/weekend programs available. *Faculty:* 14 full-time (10 women), 42 part-time/adjunct (23 women). *Students:* 63 full-time (48 women), 608 part-time (487 women); includes 45 minority (23 African Americans, 7 Asian Americans or Pacific Islanders, 15 Hispanic Americans), 1 international. Average age 31. 202 applicants, 86% accepted, 146 enrolled. In 2009, 248 master's awarded. *Degree requirements:* For master's, thesis optional. *Entrance requirements:* For master's, GRE or MAT, interview. *Application deadline:* For fall admission, 7/1 priority date for domestic students; for winter admission, 11/1 priority date for domestic students. Applications are processed on a rolling basis. Application fee: $25. *Expenses:* Tuition: Part-time $600 per credit. Required fees: $58 per semester. *Financial support:* Research assistantships, Federal Work-Study available. Support available to part-time students. Financial award application deadline: 2/15; financial award applicants required to submit FAFSA. *Faculty research:* Cognition, developmental issues, sociological issues in education. *Unit head:* Dr. Leonard Soroka, Dean, 267-341-3565, Fax: 215-824-2438, E-mail: lsoroka@holyfanily.edu. *Application contact:* Gidget Marie Montelibano, Graduate Admissions Counselor, 267-341-3558, Fax: 215-637-1478, E-mail: gmontelibano@holyfamily.edu.

Hood College, Graduate School, Department of Education, Frederick, MD 21701-8575. Offers curriculum and instruction (MS), including early childhood education, elementary education, elementary school science and mathematics, secondary education, special education; educational leadership (MS, Certificate); reading specialization (MS). Part-time and evening/weekend programs available. *Faculty:* 4 full-time (all women), 39 part-time/adjunct (21 women). *Students:* 2 full-time (both women), 397 part-time (326 women); includes 41 minority (29 African Americans, 5 Asian Americans or Pacific Islanders, 7 Hispanic Americans). Average age 33. 100 applicants, 92% accepted, 84 enrolled. In 2009, 73 master's, 65 other advanced degrees awarded. *Degree requirements:* For master's, action research project, portfolio (reading). *Entrance requirements:* For master's, minimum GPA of 2.75, teaching certification. *Application deadline:* For fall admission, 7/15 for domestic and international students; for spring admission, 12/15 for domestic and international students. Applications are processed on a rolling basis. Application fee: $35. Electronic applications accepted. *Expenses:* Tuition: Full-time $6480; part-time $360 per credit. Required fees: $100; $50 per term. *Financial support:* Applicants required to submit FAFSA. *Faculty research:* Leadership, action research, brain research, learning styles. *Unit head:* Dr. John George, Chairperson, 301-696-3471, Fax: 301-696-3597, E-mail: george@hood.edu. *Application contact:* Dr. Allen P. Flora, Dean of Graduate School, 301-696-3811, Fax: 301-696-3597, E-mail: gofurther@hood.edu.

Hope International University, School of Graduate and Professional Studies, Program in Business Administration, Fullerton, CA 92831-3138. Offers business administration (MBA); educational administration (MSM); international development (MBA, MSM); management (MBA); nonprofit management (MBA). Part-time programs available. Postbaccalaureate distance learning degree programs offered (no on-campus study). *Degree requirements:* For master's, comprehensive exam (for some programs), thesis (for some programs), project. *Entrance requirements:* For master's, minimum GPA of 3.0; 2 references. Additional exam requirements/recommendations for international students: Required—TOEFL (minimum score 550 paper-based; 213 computer-based; 86 iBT); Recommended—IELTS (minimum score 6.5). Electronic applications accepted. *Expenses:* Contact institution.

Houston Baptist University, College of Education and Behavioral Sciences, Programs in Education, Houston, TX 77074-3298. Offers bilingual education (M Ed); counselor education (M Ed); curriculum and instruction (M Ed); educational administration (M Ed); educational diagnostician (M Ed); reading education (M Ed). Part-time programs available. *Entrance requirements:* For master's, GRE General Test or MAT. Additional exam requirements/recommendations for international students: Required—TOEFL (minimum score 550 paper-based; 213 computer-based).

Howard Payne University, Program in Instructional Leadership, Brownwood, TX 76801-2715. Offers M Ed. Postbaccalaureate distance learning degree programs offered (no on-campus study).

Howard University, School of Education, Department of Educational Administration and Policy, Program in Educational Administration and Policy, Washington, DC 20059-0002. Offers educational administration (M Ed, MA, CAGS); educational administration and policy (Ed D). MA offered through the Graduate School of Arts and Sciences. *Accreditation:* NCATE. Part-time programs available. *Faculty:* 6 full-time (4 women), 2 part-time/adjunct (1 woman). *Students:* 30 full-time (17 women), 28 part-time (17 women); includes 39 minority (38 African Americans, 1 Hispanic American), 3 international. Average age 38. 33 applicants, 64% accepted, 19 enrolled. In 2009, 3 master's, 2 doctorates, 1 other advanced degree awarded. *Degree requirements:* For master's, comprehensive exam, thesis (for some programs); for doctorate, comprehensive exam, thesis/dissertation, internship; for CAGS, thesis. *Entrance requirements:* For master's, GRE General Test (MA), minimum GPA of 3.0; for doctorate, minimum GPA of 3.0. *Application deadline:* For fall admission, 4/15 priority date for domestic students; for spring admission, 11/15 priority date for domestic students. Applications are processed on a rolling basis. Application fee: $45. Electronic applications accepted. *Financial support:* In 2009–10, 14 students received support, including fellowships with full and partial tuition reimbursements available (averaging $15,000 per year), 13 research assistantships with full and partial tuition reimbursements available (averaging $6,000 per year); career-related internships or fieldwork, Federal Work-Study, institutionally sponsored loans, scholarships/grants, and unspecified assistantships also available. Financial award application deadline: 4/1. *Faculty research:* Educational policy, reform, achievement gap, disability reform policy, school governance delivery of social services to students. *Unit head:* Dr. R. C. Saravanabhavan, Professor/Coordinator, Doctoral Program, 202-806-5782, E-mail: rsaravanabhavan@howard.edu. *Application contact:* Dr. Dawn G. Williams, Associate Professor, Master's Programs, 202-806-7060, E-mail: dgwilliams@howard.edu.

Hunter College of the City University of New York, Graduate School, School of Education, Department of Curriculum and Teaching, Program in Educational Supervision and Administration, New York, NY 10021-5085. Offers AC. *Faculty:* 12 full-time (6 women), 57 part-time/adjunct (42 women). *Students:* 103 part-time (74 women); includes 17 minority (5 African Americans, 2 Asian Americans or Pacific Islanders, 10 Hispanic Americans). Average age 35. 53 applicants, 68% accepted, 28 enrolled. In 2009, 76 ACs awarded. *Degree requirements:* For AC, portfolio review. *Entrance requirements:* For degree, minimum B average in graduate course work, teaching certificate, minimum 3 years of full-time teaching experience, interview, 2 letters of support. Additional exam requirements/recommendations for international students: Required—TOEFL. *Application deadline:* For fall admission, 4/1 for domestic students, 2/1 for international students; for spring admission, 11/1 for domestic students, 9/1 for international students. Applications are processed on a rolling basis. Application fee: $125. *Expenses:* Tuition, state resident: full-time $7360; part-time $310 per credit. Required fees: $250 per semester. *Financial support:* Federal Work-Study and tuition waivers (partial) available. Support available to part-time students. *Faculty research:* Supervision of instruction, theory in action, human relations and leadership. *Unit head:* Dr. Marcia Knoll, Coordinator, 212-772-4761, E-mail: mknoll@hunter.cuny.edu. *Application contact:* William Zlata, Director for Graduate Admissions, 212-772-4482, Fax: 212-650-3336, E-mail: admissions@hunter.cuny.edu.

Idaho State University, Office of Graduate Studies, College of Education, Department of Educational Foundations, Pocatello, ID 83209-8059. Offers child and family studies (M Ed); curriculum leadership (M Ed); education (M Ed); educational administration (M Ed); educational foundations (5th Year Certificate); elementary education (M Ed), including K-12 education, literacy, secondary education. Part-time programs available. *Faculty:* 13 full-time (8 women). *Students:* 15 full-time (9 women), 100 part-time (64 women); includes 2 minority (1 African American, 1 Hispanic American), 3 international. Average age 39. In 2009, 25 master's awarded. *Degree requirements:* For master's, comprehensive exam, thesis optional, oral exam, written exam; for 5th Year Certificate, comprehensive exam, thesis (for some programs), oral exam, written exam. *Entrance requirements:* For master's, GRE General Test or MAT, minimum undergraduate GPA of 3.0; for 5th Year Certificate, GRE General Test, minimum undergraduate GPA of 3.0, master's degree. Additional exam requirements/recommendations for international students: Required—TOEFL (minimum score 550 paper-based; 213 computer-based; 80 iBT). *Application deadline:* For fall admission, 7/1 for domestic students, 6/1 for international students; for spring admission, 12/1 for domestic students, 11/1 for international students. Applications are processed on a rolling basis. Application fee: $55. Electronic applications accepted. *Expenses:* Tuition, state resident: full-time $3318; part-time $297 per credit hour. Tuition, nonresident: full-time $13,120; part-time $437 per credit hour. Required fees: $2530. Tuition and fees vary according to program. *Financial support:* Research assistantships with full and partial tuition reimbursements, teaching assistantships with full and partial tuition reimbursements, career-related internships or fieldwork, Federal Work-Study, institutionally sponsored loans, scholarships/grants, traineeships, health care benefits, tuition waivers (full and partial), and unspecified assistantships available. Support available to part-time students. Financial award application deadline: 1/1; financial award applicants required to submit FAFSA. *Faculty research:* Child and families studies; business education; special education; math, science, and technology education. *Unit head:* Dr. Beverly Ray, Chair, 208-282-4516, Fax: 208-282-3791, E-mail: raybeve@isu.edu. *Application contact:* Dr. Peter Denner, Assistant Dean, 208-282-3807, Fax: 208-282-4697, E-mail: dennpete@isu.edu.

Idaho State University, Office of Graduate Studies, College of Education, Department of Educational Leadership and Instructional Design, Pocatello, ID 83209-8059. Offers educational administration (M Ed, 6th Year Certificate, Ed S); educational leadership (Ed D), including education training and development, educational administration, educational technology, higher education administration; instructional technology (M Ed). Part-time programs available. *Faculty:* 4 full-time (1 woman), 1 (woman) part-time/adjunct. *Students:* 17 full-time (8 women), 112 part-time (40 women); includes 10 minority (3 African Americans, 4 American Indian/Alaska Native, 1 Asian American or Pacific Islander, 2 Hispanic Americans), 9 international. Average age 42. In 2009, 4 master's, 8 doctorates, 15 other advanced degrees awarded. *Degree requirements:* For master's, comprehensive exam, thesis optional, internship, oral exam or deferred thesis; for doctorate, comprehensive exam, thesis/dissertation, written exam; for other advanced degree, comprehensive exam, thesis (for some programs), written and oral exam. *Entrance requirements:* For master's, MAT, bachelor's degree, minimum GPA of 3.0, 1 year of training experience; for doctorate, GRE General Test or MAT, minimum GPA of 3.0 (undergraduate), 3.5 (graduate); departmental interview; for other advanced degree, GRE General Test, minimum GPA of 3.0, master's degree. Additional exam requirements/recommendations for international students: Required—TOEFL (minimum score 550 paper-based; 213 computer-based; 80 iBT). *Application deadline:* For fall admission, 7/1 for domestic students, 6/1 for international students; for spring admission, 12/1 for domestic students, 11/1 for international students. Applications are processed on a rolling basis. Application fee: $55. Electronic applications accepted. *Expenses:* Tuition, state resident: full-time $3318; part-time $297 per credit hour. Tuition, nonresident: full-time $13,120; part-time $437 per credit hour. Required fees: $2530. Tuition and fees vary according to program. *Financial support:* Teaching assistantships with full and partial tuition reimbursements, career-related internships or fieldwork, Federal Work-Study, institutionally sponsored loans, scholarships/grants, health care benefits,

tuition waivers (full and partial), and unspecified assistantships available. Support available to part-time students. Financial award application deadline: 1/1; financial award applicants required to submit FAFSA. *Faculty research:* Educational leadership, gender issues in education and sport, staff development. *Unit head:* Dr. Jonathan Lawson, Chair, 208-282-1036, Fax: 208-282-4697, E-mail: lawsjona@isu.edu. *Application contact:* Dr. Peter Denner, Assistant Dean, 208-282-3807, Fax: 208-282-4697, E-mail: dennpete@isu.edu.

Illinois State University, Graduate School, College of Education, Department of Educational Administration and Foundations, Normal, IL 61790-2200. Offers college student personnel administration (MS); educational administration (MS, MS Ed, Ed D, PhD). *Accreditation:* NCATE. *Degree requirements:* For doctorate, variable foreign language requirement, thesis/dissertation, 2 terms of residency. *Entrance requirements:* For master's, GRE General Test, minimum GPA of 2.6 in last 60 hours of course work; for doctorate, GRE General Test, master's degree or equivalent, minimum GPA of 3.5. *Faculty research:* Illinois Association of School Administrators FY2007, Illinois Principals Association, special populations professional development and technical assistance project, Illinois state action for education leadership project.

Immaculata University, College of Graduate Studies, Program in Educational Leadership and Administration, Immaculata, PA 19345. Offers educational leadership and administration (MA, Ed D); elementary education (Certificate); school principal (Certificate); school superintendent (Certificate); secondary education (Certificate); special education (Certificate). Part-time and evening/weekend programs available. *Degree requirements:* For master's, comprehensive exam, thesis optional; for doctorate, comprehensive exam, thesis/dissertation. *Entrance requirements:* For master's, GRE or MAT, minimum GPA of 3.0; for doctorate, GRE General Test, minimum GPA of 3.5. Additional exam requirements/recommendations for international students: Required—TOEFL. *Faculty research:* Cooperative learning, school-based management, whole language, performance assessment.

Indiana State University, School of Graduate Studies, College of Education, Department of Educational Leadership, Administration, and Foundations, Terre Haute, IN 47809. Offers educational administration (PhD); leadership in higher education (PhD); school administration (Ed S); school administration and supervision (M Ed); student affairs in higher education (MS). *Accreditation:* NCATE. Part-time and evening/weekend programs available. Terminal master's awarded for partial completion of doctoral program. *Degree requirements:* For master's, thesis; for doctorate, thesis/dissertation. *Entrance requirements:* For master's, GRE General Test, minimum undergraduate GPA of 2.5; for doctorate, GRE General Test, minimum undergraduate GPA of 3.5; for Ed S, GRE General Test, minimum graduate GPA of 3.25. Electronic applications accepted.

Indiana University Bloomington, School of Education, Department of Educational Leadership and Policy Studies, Bloomington, IN 47405-7000. Offers education policy studies (PhD); educational leadership (MS, Ed D, PhD, Ed S); higher education (MS, Ed D, PhD); history and philosophy of education (MS); history of education (PhD); international and comparative education (MS, PhD); philosophy of education (PhD); student affairs administration (MS). *Accreditation:* NCATE. Part-time and evening/weekend programs available. *Faculty:* 31 full-time (16 women), 8 part-time/adjunct (4 women). *Students:* 195 full-time (120 women), 102 part-time (53 women); includes 78 minority (49 African Americans, 1 American Indian/Alaska Native, 6 Asian Americans or Pacific Islanders, 22 Hispanic Americans), 29 international. Average age 33. 331 applicants, 77% accepted, 75 enrolled. In 2009, 61 master's, 21 doctorates, 7 other advanced degrees awarded. *Degree requirements:* For master's, thesis optional; for doctorate, comprehensive exam, thesis/dissertation; for Ed S, comprehensive exam or project. *Entrance requirements:* For master's, doctorate, and Ed S, GRE General Test. Additional exam requirements/recommendations for international students: Required—TOEFL (minimum score 213 computer-based; 79 iBT). *Application deadline:* For fall admission, 1/15 priority date for domestic students, 12/1 priority date for international students; for spring admission, 9/1 priority date for domestic and international students. Applications are processed on a rolling basis. Application fee: $55 ($65 for international students). Electronic applications accepted. *Financial support:* In 2009–10, 73 students received support, including 34 fellowships with full and partial tuition reimbursements available (averaging $7,677 per year), 16 research assistantships with full and partial tuition reimbursements available (averaging $17,757 per year), 23 teaching assistantships with full and partial tuition reimbursements available (averaging $13,496 per year); career-related internships or fieldwork, Federal Work-Study, institutionally sponsored loans, and tuition waivers (full and partial) also available. Support available to part-time students. *Faculty research:* Student engagement at higher education institutions in the nation, Reading First professional development initiative, state finance policy on financial access to higher education, school reform, special needs studies. *Unit head:* Martha McCarthy, Chair, 812-856-8377. *Application contact:* Sandy Strain, Department Secretary, 812-856-8360, Fax: 812-856-8394, E-mail: strain@indiana.edu.

Indiana University of Pennsylvania, School of Graduate Studies and Research, College of Education and Educational Technology, Department of Professional Studies in Education, Certification Program for Principal, Indiana, PA 15705-1087. Offers Certificate. *Faculty:* 2 full-time (1 woman). *Students:* 33 part-time (16 women). Average age 36. 28 applicants, 93% accepted, 25 enrolled. *Entrance requirements:* For degree, GRE General Test, GRE Subject Test, 2 letters of recommendation. Additional exam requirements/recommendations for international students: Required—TOEFL. *Application deadline:* For fall admission, 7/1 priority date for domestic students; for spring admission, 11/1 for domestic students. Applications are processed on a rolling basis. Application fee: $40. *Expenses:* Tuition, state resident: full-time $6666; part-time $370 per credit hour. Tuition, nonresident: full-time $10,666; part-time $593 per credit hour. Required fees: $813 per semester. *Financial support:* Application deadline: 3/15. *Unit head:* Dr. Cathy Kauffman, Graduate Coordinator, 724-357-3928, E-mail: ckaufman@iup.edu. *Application contact:* Dr. Cathy Kauffman, Graduate Coordinator, 724-357-3928, E-mail: ckaufman@iup.edu.

Indiana University of Pennsylvania, School of Graduate Studies and Research, College of Education and Educational Technology, Department of Professional Studies in Education, Doctoral Program in Administration and Leadership Studies, Indiana, PA 15705-1087. Offers D Ed. Part-time and evening/weekend programs available. *Faculty:* 7 full-time (4 women). *Students:* 3 full-time (1 woman), 60 part-time (28 women); includes 5 minority (all African Americans). Average age 43. 15 applicants, 7% accepted, 1 enrolled. In 2009, 26 doctorates awarded. *Degree requirements:* For doctorate, one foreign language, comprehensive exam, thesis/dissertation, written exam. *Entrance requirements:* For doctorate, 2 letters of recommendation, interview. Additional exam requirements/recommendations for international students: Required—TOEFL. *Application deadline:* For fall admission, 7/1 priority date for domestic students; for spring admission, 11/1 for domestic students. Applications are processed on a rolling basis. Application fee: $40. *Expenses:* Tuition, state resident: full-time $6666; part-time $370 per credit hour. Tuition, nonresident: full-time $10,666; part-time $593 per credit hour. Required fees: $813 per semester. *Financial support:* In 2009–10, 5 fellowships (averaging $1,000 per year) were awarded; research assistantships with full and partial tuition reimbursements. Financial award application deadline: 3/15; financial award applicants required to submit FAFSA. *Unit head:* Dr. Cathy Kaufmann, Graduate Coordinator, 724-357-5593, E-mail: cathy.kaufmann@iup.edu. *Application contact:* Dr. Cathy Kaufmann, Graduate Coordinator, 724-357-5593, E-mail: cathy.kaufmann@iup.edu.

Indiana University of Pennsylvania, School of Graduate Studies and Research, College of Education and Educational Technology, Department of Student Affairs in Higher Education, Indiana, PA 15705-1087. Offers MA. *Accreditation:* NCATE. Part-time programs available. *Faculty:* 4 full-time (2 women). *Students:* 55 full-time (36 women), 5 part-time (2 women); includes 7 minority (4 African Americans, 1 American Indian/Alaska Native, 1 Asian American or Pacific Islander, 1 Hispanic American). Average age 24. 102 applicants, 38% accepted, 29 enrolled. In 2009, 25 master's awarded. *Degree requirements:* For master's, comprehensive exam, thesis optional. *Entrance requirements:* For master's, resume, interview, 2 letters of recommendation, writing sample. Additional exam requirements/recommendations for international students: Required—TOEFL. *Application deadline:* For fall admission, 7/1 priority date for domestic students; for spring admission, 11/1 for domestic students. Applications are processed on a rolling basis. Application fee: $40. *Expenses:* Tuition, state resident: full-time $6666; part-time $370 per credit hour. Tuition, nonresident: full-time $10,666; part-time $593 per credit hour. Required fees: $813 per semester. *Financial support:* In 2009–10, 1 fellowship (averaging $500 per year), 19 research assistantships with full and partial tuition reimbursements (averaging $5,440 per year) were awarded; career-related internships or fieldwork and Federal Work-Study also available. Support available to part-time students. Financial award application deadline: 3/15; financial award applicants required to submit FAFSA. *Unit head:* Dr. Linda W. Hall, Chairperson and Graduate Coordinator, 724-357-4535, E-mail: linda.hall@iup.edu. *Application contact:* Dr. Edward Nardi, Interim Associate Dean, 724-357-2480, Fax: 724-357-5595, E-mail: ewnardi@iup.edu.

Indiana University of Pennsylvania, School of Graduate Studies and Research, College of Humanities and Social Sciences, Department of Sociology, Program in Administration and Leadership Studies, Indiana, PA 15705-1087. Offers PhD. Part-time and evening/weekend programs available. *Faculty:* 13 full-time (6 women). *Students:* 3 full-time (2 women), 93 part-time (52 women); includes 9 minority (6 African Americans, 2 Asian Americans or Pacific Islanders, 1 Hispanic American), 2 international. Average age 43. 38 applicants, 45% accepted, 17 enrolled. In 2009, 7 doctorates awarded. *Degree requirements:* For doctorate, comprehensive exam, thesis/dissertation. *Entrance requirements:* For doctorate, GRE, resume, writing sample, 3 letters of recommendation. Additional exam requirements/recommendations for international students: Required—TOEFL. *Application deadline:* For fall admission, 7/1 priority date for domestic students; for spring admission, 11/1 for domestic students. Applications are processed on a rolling basis. Application fee: $40. *Expenses:* Tuition, state resident: full-time $6666; part-time $370 per credit hour. Tuition, nonresident: full-time $10,666; part-time $593 per credit hour. Required fees: $813 per semester. *Financial support:* In 2009–10, 3 fellowships (averaging $1,583 per year), 4 research assistantships with full and partial tuition reimbursements (averaging $5,981 per year) were awarded. Financial award applicants required to submit FAFSA. *Unit head:* Dr. John Anderson, Graduate Coordinator, 724-357-1291, E-mail: janderson@iup.edu. *Application contact:* Dr. John Anderson, Graduate Coordinator, 724-357-1291, E-mail: janderson@iup.edu.

Indiana University–Purdue University Fort Wayne, School of Education, Department of Professional Studies, Fort Wayne, IN 46805-1499. Offers counseling education (MS Ed); educational leadership (MS Ed); marriage and family therapy (MS Ed); school counseling (MS Ed); special education (MS Ed, Certificate). Part-time programs available. *Faculty:* 10 full-time (5 women). *Students:* 2 full-time (both women), 159 part-time (120 women); includes 19 minority (12 African Americans, 1 Asian American or Pacific Islander, 6 Hispanic Americans). Average age 35. 47 applicants, 98% accepted, 38 enrolled. In 2009, 64 master's awarded. *Degree requirements:* For master's, comprehensive exam, practicum, internship, portfolio. *Entrance requirements:* For master's, minimum GPA of 2.5. Additional exam requirements/recommendations for international students: Required—TOEFL (minimum score 550 paper-based; 213 computer-based; 77 iBT). *Application deadline:* For fall admission, 4/1 priority date for domestic and international students. Applications are processed on a rolling basis. Application fee: $55. *Expenses:* Tuition, state resident: full-time $4595; part-time $255 per credit. Tuition, nonresident: full-time $10,963; part-time $609 per credit. Required fees: $528; $29.35 per credit. Tuition and fees vary according to course load. *Financial support:* In 2009–10, 1 teaching assistantship with partial tuition reimbursement (averaging $12,740 per year) was awarded; research assistantships with partial tuition reimbursements, scholarships/grants also available. Support available to part-time students. Financial award application deadline: 3/1; financial award applicants required to submit FAFSA. *Unit head:* Dr. James Burg, Interim Chair, 260-481-5406, Fax: 260-481-5408, E-mail: burgj@ipfw.edu. *Application contact:* Vicky L. Schmidt, Graduate Recorder, 260-481-6450, Fax: 260-481-5408, E-mail: schmidt@ipfw.edu.

Indiana University–Purdue University Indianapolis, School of Education, Indianapolis, IN 46202-2896. Offers computer education (Certificate); curriculum and instruction (MS); early childhood (MS); educational leadership (MS, Certificate); English as a second language (Certificate); higher education and student affairs (MS); kindergarten (Certificate); language education (MS); reading (Certificate); school counseling (MS); special education (MS, Certificate). Part-time and evening/weekend programs available. *Faculty:* 41 full-time, 80 part-time/adjunct. *Students:* 72 full-time (60 women), 427 part-time (325 women); includes 57 minority (42 African Americans, 1 American Indian/Alaska Native, 4 Asian Americans or Pacific Islanders, 10 Hispanic Americans), 5 international. Average age 32. 181 applicants, 78% accepted, 112 enrolled. In 2009, 162 master's awarded. *Degree requirements:* For master's, thesis optional. *Entrance requirements:* For master's, GRE General Test, minimum GPA of 3.0. Additional exam requirements/recommendations for international students: Required—TOEFL. *Application deadline:* For fall admission, 5/1 priority date for domestic students; for spring admission, 11/1 for domestic students. Application fee: $55 ($65 for international students). *Financial support:* In 2009–10, 2 fellowships (averaging $780 per year), 18 teaching assistantships (averaging $9,756 per year) were awarded; research assistantships with partial tuition reimbursements, Federal Work-Study, institutionally sponsored loans, scholarships/grants, and tuition waivers (partial) also available. Support available to part-time students. *Faculty research:* Teachers in the process of change, learning cycles, children's concepts of science. Total annual research expenditures: $614,458. *Unit head:* Dr. Chris Leland, Interim Executive Associate Dean, 317-274-6801, Fax: 317-274-6864. *Application contact:* Sarah Brandenburg, Graduate Advisor, 317-274-6801, Fax: 317-274-6864, E-mail: edugrad@iupui.edu.

Instituto Tecnológico y de Estudios Superiores de Monterrey, Campus Central de Veracruz, Graduate Programs, Córdoba, Mexico. Offers administration (MA); administration of information technologies (MTI); computer sciences (MCC); education (MEE); educational institution administration (MAD); educational technology (MTE); electronic commerce (MCE); finance (MAF); humanistic studies (MEH); international business for Latin America (MNL); marketing (MMT); science (MCP); technology management (MTT). Part-time and evening/weekend programs available. Postbaccalaureate distance learning degree programs offered (minimal on-campus study). *Degree requirements:* For master's, thesis (for some programs). *Entrance requirements:* For master's, PAEP College Board. Electronic applications accepted.

Instituto Tecnológico y de Estudios Superiores de Monterrey, Campus Ciudad Juárez, Program in Educational Administration, Ciudad Juárez, Mexico. Offers MEA.

Instituto Tecnológico y de Estudios Superiores de Monterrey, Campus Estado de México, Professional and Graduate Division, Estado de Mexico, Mexico. Offers administration of information technologies (MITA); architecture (M Arch); business administration (GMBA, MBA); computer sciences (MCS, PhD); education (M Ed); educational institution administration (MAD); educational technology and innovation (PhD); electronic commerce (MEC); environmental systems (MS); finance (MAF); humanistic studies (MHS); information sciences and knowledge management (MISKM); information systems (MS); manufacturing systems (MS); marketing (MEM); quality systems and productivity (MS); science and materials engineering (PhD); telecommunications management (MTM). Part-time programs available. Postbaccalaureate distance learning degree programs offered (minimal on-campus study). *Degree requirements:* For master's, one foreign language, thesis (for some programs); for doctorate, one foreign language, thesis/dissertation. *Entrance requirements:* For master's, E-PAEP 500, interview; for doctorate, E-PAEP 500, research proposal. Additional exam requirements/recommendations for international students: Required—TOEFL (minimum score 550 paper-based). *Faculty research:* Surface treatments by plasmas, mechanical properties, robotics, graphical computing, mechatronics security protocols.

Instituto Tecnológico y de Estudios Superiores de Monterrey, Campus Irapuato, Graduate Programs, Irapuato, Mexico. Offers administration (MBA); administration of information technology (MAIT); administration of telecommunications (MAT); architecture (M Arch); computer science (MCS); education (M Ed); educational administration (MEA); educational innovation and technology (DEIT); educational technology (MET); electronic commerce (MBA); environmental administration and planning (MEAP); environmental systems (MES); finances (MBA);

Educational Leadership and Administration

Instituto Tecnológico y de Estudios Superiores de Monterrey, Campus Irapuato (continued)

humanistic studies (MHS); international management for Latin American executives (MIMLAE); library and information science (MLIS); manufacturing quality management (MMQM); marketing research (MBA).

Inter American University of Puerto Rico, Aguadilla Campus, Graduate School, Aguadilla, PR 00605. Offers accounting (MBA); business information systems (MBA); counseling psychology with an emphasis in family (MS); criminal justice (MA); educative management and leadership (MA); elementary education (MA); finance (MBA); human resources (MBA); industrial management (MBA); marketing (MBA). Part-time and evening/weekend programs available. *Degree requirements:* For master's, comprehensive exam. *Entrance requirements:* For master's, EXADEP, 2 letters of recommendation, minimum GPA of 2.5. Electronic applications accepted.

Inter American University of Puerto Rico, Arecibo Campus, Programs in Education, Arecibo, PR 00614-4050. Offers administration and educational supervision (MA Ed); counseling and guidance (MA Ed); curriculum and teaching (MA Ed), including biology education, English as a second language, history education, math education, Spanish; elementary education (MA Ed). *Degree requirements:* For master's, comprehensive exam, thesis optional. *Entrance requirements:* For master's, GRE, EXADEP, bachelor's degree in education or teaching license (administration and supervision) or courses in education and psychology (counseling and guidance), minimum GPA of 2.5 in last 60 credits.

Inter American University of Puerto Rico, Barranquitas Campus, Program in Education, Barranquitas, PR 00794. Offers curriculum and teaching (M Ed); educational administration and supervision (MA); elementary education (M Ed); information and library service technology (M Ed). *Degree requirements:* For master's, comprehensive exam, thesis optional. *Entrance requirements:* For master's, EXADEP, letter of recommendation. Electronic applications accepted.

Inter American University of Puerto Rico, Metropolitan Campus, Graduate Programs, Program in Education, San Juan, PR 00919-1293. Offers curriculum and instruction (Ed D); educational administration (Ed D); guidance and counseling (MA, Ed D); special education administration (Ed D). *Degree requirements:* For doctorate, comprehensive exam, thesis/dissertation. *Entrance requirements:* For doctorate, GRE, MAT, or EXADEP. Electronic applications accepted.

Inter American University of Puerto Rico, San Germán Campus, Graduate Studies Center, Program in Administration and Supervision, San Germán, PR 00683-5008. Offers MA, Ed D. Part-time and evening/weekend programs available. *Degree requirements:* For master's, comprehensive exam. *Entrance requirements:* For master's, GRE General Test or EXADEP, minimum GPA of 3.0.

Iona College, School of Arts and Science, Program in Education, New Rochelle, NY 10801-1890. Offers biology education (MS Ed, MST); educational leadership (MS Ed); English education (MS Ed, MST); literacy education (MS Ed); mathematics education (MS Ed, MST); social studies education (MS Ed, MST); Spanish education (MS Ed, MST); teaching in childhood education (MST). *Accreditation:* NCATE. Part-time and evening/weekend programs available. *Faculty:* 24 full-time (13 women), 16 part-time/adjunct (10 women). *Students:* 41 full-time (35 women), 118 part-time (87 women); includes 15 minority (5 African Americans, 1 Asian American or Pacific Islander, 9 Hispanic Americans). Average age 28. 91 applicants, 67% accepted, 41 enrolled. In 2009, 61 master's awarded. *Degree requirements:* For master's, thesis or alternative. *Entrance requirements:* For master's, minimum GPA of 2.5 (MST), New York teaching certificate (MS Ed). Additional exam requirements/recommendations for international students: Required—TOEFL (minimum score 550 paper-based; 213 computer-based). *Application deadline:* Applications are processed on a rolling basis. Application fee: $50. Electronic applications accepted. *Expenses:* Tuition: Part-time $830 per credit. *Financial support:* Unspecified assistantships available. Support available to part-time students. Financial award application deadline: 4/15; financial award applicants required to submit FAFSA. *Faculty research:* Reading/writing, educational technology, administration, early literacy assessment, literacy development. *Unit head:* Dr. Catherine O'Callaghan, Chair, 914-633-2210, Fax: 914-633-2608, E-mail: cocallaghan@iona.edu. *Application contact:* Veronica Jarek-Prinz, Director of Graduate Admissions, 914-633-2420, Fax: 914-633-2277, E-mail: vjarekprinz@iona.edu.

Iowa State University of Science and Technology, Graduate College, College of Human Sciences, Department of Educational Leadership and Policy Studies, Ames, IA 50011. Offers counselor education (M Ed, MS); educational administration (M Ed, MS); educational leadership (PhD); higher education (M Ed, MS); organizational learning and human resource development (M Ed, MS); research and evaluation (MS). *Faculty:* 21 full-time (10 women), 14 part-time/adjunct (8 women). *Students:* 116 full-time (68 women), 218 part-time (130 women); includes 58 minority (34 African Americans, 3 American Indian/Alaska Native, 4 Asian Americans or Pacific Islanders, 17 Hispanic Americans), 7 international. 138 applicants, 78% accepted, 74 enrolled. In 2009, 77 master's, 18 doctorates awarded. *Degree requirements:* For master's, thesis or alternative; for doctorate, thesis/dissertation. *Entrance requirements:* For doctorate, GRE General Test. Additional exam requirements/recommendations for international students: Required—TOEFL (minimum score 560 paper-based; 83 iBT) or IELTS (minimum score 6.5). *Application deadline:* For fall admission, 1/1 priority date for domestic and international students. Applications are processed on a rolling basis. Application fee: $40 ($90 for international students). Electronic applications accepted. *Expenses:* Tuition, state resident: full-time $6716. Tuition, nonresident: full-time $8908. Tuition and fees vary according to course level, course load, program and student level. *Financial support:* In 2009–10, 104 research assistantships with full and partial tuition reimbursements (averaging $13,500 per year), 2 teaching assistantships with full and partial tuition reimbursements (averaging $13,500 per year) were awarded; fellowships, scholarships/grants, health care benefits, and unspecified assistantships also available. *Unit head:* Dr. Laura Rendon, Chair, 515-294-7093, E-mail: lrendon@iastate.edu. *Application contact:* Dr. Daniel Robinson, Information Contact, 515-294-1241, E-mail: eldrshp@iastate.edu.

Jackson State University, Graduate School, School of Education, Department of Educational Foundations and Leadership, Jackson, MS 39217. Offers education administration (Ed S); educational administration (MS Ed, PhD); secondary education (MS Ed, Ed S), including educational technology (MS Ed). *Accreditation:* NCATE. Part-time and evening/weekend programs available. *Degree requirements:* For master's, comprehensive exam, thesis or alternative; for doctorate, comprehensive exam, thesis/dissertation; for Ed S, comprehensive exam, thesis. *Entrance requirements:* For master's, GRE General Test; for doctorate, MAT, GRE, teaching experience. Additional exam requirements/recommendations for international students: Required—TOEFL.

Jacksonville State University, College of Graduate Studies and Continuing Education, College of Education and Professional Studies, Program in Educational Administration, Jacksonville, AL 36265-1602. Offers MS Ed, Ed S. *Accreditation:* NCATE. Part-time and evening/weekend programs available. *Degree requirements:* For master's, comprehensive exam, thesis (for some programs). *Entrance requirements:* For master's, GRE General Test or MAT. Electronic applications accepted.

James Madison University, The Graduate School, College of Education, Adult Education Department, Program in Educational Leadership, Harrisonburg, VA 22807. Offers M Ed. *Accreditation:* NCATE. Part-time and evening/weekend programs available. *Students:* Average age 27. *Entrance requirements:* For master's, GRE General Test. Additional exam requirements/recommendations for international students: Required—TOEFL. *Application deadline:* For fall admission, 5/1 priority date for domestic students; for spring admission, 9/1 priority date for domestic students. Applications are processed on a rolling basis. Application fee: $55. Electronic applications accepted. *Expenses:* Tuition, area resident: Part-time $305 per credit hour. Tuition, state resident: part-time $305 per credit hour. Tuition, nonresident: part-time $890 per credit hour. *Financial support:* Federal Work-Study available. Financial award application deadline: 3/1; financial award applicants required to submit FAFSA. *Unit head:* Dr. Diane Foucar-Szocki,

Academic Unit Head, 540-568-6794. *Application contact:* Lynette M. Bible, Director of Graduate Admissions, 540-568-6395, Fax: 540-568-7860, E-mail: biblelm@jmu.edu.

John Carroll University, Graduate School, Department of Education and Allied Studies, Program in Administration, University Heights, OH 44118-4581. Offers M Ed, MA. *Accreditation:* NCATE. Part-time and evening/weekend programs available. *Degree requirements:* For master's, comprehensive exam, research essay or thesis (MA only). *Entrance requirements:* For master's, GRE General Test or MAT, minimum GPA of 2.75, interview, teachers license, 2 years experience. Electronic applications accepted.

The Johns Hopkins University, School of Education, Department of Interdisciplinary Studies in Education, Baltimore, MD 21218. Offers earth/space science (Certificate); education (MS), including educational studies; mind, brain, and teaching (Certificate); teaching the adult learner (Certificate); urban education (Certificate). Part-time and evening/weekend programs available. Postbaccalaureate distance learning degree programs offered (minimal on-campus study). *Faculty:* 2 full-time (1 woman), 6 part-time/adjunct (5 women). *Students:* 8 full-time (7 women), 171 part-time (150 women); includes 44 minority (29 African Americans, 1 American Indian/Alaska Native, 11 Asian Americans or Pacific Islanders, 3 Hispanic Americans), 7 international. Average age 34. 77 applicants, 68% accepted, 39 enrolled. In 2009, 69 master's, 17 other advanced degrees awarded. *Degree requirements:* For master's, capstone course. *Entrance requirements:* For master's and Certificate, minimum undergraduate GPA of 3.0. Additional exam requirements/recommendations for international students: Required—TOEFL (minimum score 600 paper-based; 250 computer-based; 100 iBT). *Application deadline:* For fall admission, 5/1 for international students; for spring admission, 10/15 for international students. Applications are processed on a rolling basis. Application fee: $80. Electronic applications accepted. *Financial support:* Scholarships/grants available. Support available to part-time students. Financial award application deadline: 6/1; financial award applicants required to submit FAFSA. *Faculty research:* Neuro-education; urban school reform; leadership development; teacher leadership; charter schools; techniques for teaching reading to adolescents with delayed reading skills; school culture. *Unit head:* Dr. Mariale Hardiman, Assistant Dean and Chair, 410-516-8225, Fax: 410-516-3939, E-mail: mclean@jhu.edu. *Application contact:* Jennifer Shaffer, Director of Admissions, 410-516-9797, Fax: 410-516-9799, E-mail: educationinfo@jhu.edu.

The Johns Hopkins University, School of Education, Department of Teacher Development and Leadership, Baltimore, MD 21218-2699. Offers adolescent literacy education (Certificate); data-based decision making and organizational improvement (Certificate); education (MS), including reading, school administration and supervision, technology for educators; educational leadership for independent schools (Certificate); effective teaching of reading (Certificate); emergent literacy education (Certificate); English as a second language instruction (Certificate); gifted education (Certificate); leadership for school, family, and community collaboration (Certificate); leadership in technology integration (Certificate); school administration and supervision (Certificate); teacher development and leadership (Ed D); teacher leadership (Certificate); technology for educators (MS). Part-time and evening/weekend programs available. Postbaccalaureate distance learning degree programs offered (minimal on-campus study). *Faculty:* 8 full-time (2 women), 53 part-time/adjunct (36 women). *Students:* 17 full-time (16 women), 462 part-time (358 women); includes 117 minority (77 African Americans, 25 Asian Americans or Pacific Islanders, 15 Hispanic Americans), 11 international. Average age 33. 217 applicants, 62% accepted, 107 enrolled. In 2009, 85 master's, 2 doctorates, 181 other advanced degrees awarded. *Degree requirements:* For master's and Certificate, portfolio; for doctorate, comprehensive exam (for some programs), thesis/dissertation, portfolio or comprehensive exam. *Entrance requirements:* For master's and Certificate, bachelor's degree; minimum undergraduate GPA of 3.0; essay/statement of goals; for doctorate, GRE, essay/statement of goals; three letters of recommendation; curriculum vitae/resume; K-12 professional experience; interview; writing assessment. Additional exam requirements/recommendations for international students: Required—TOEFL (minimum score 600 paper-based; 250 computer-based; 100 iBT). *Application deadline:* For fall admission, 5/1 for international students; for spring admission, 10/15 for international students. Applications are processed on a rolling basis. Application fee: $80. Electronic applications accepted. *Financial support:* In 2009–10, 5 research assistantships, 1 teaching assistantship were awarded; scholarships/grants also available. Support available to part-time students. Financial award application deadline: 6/1; financial award applicants required to submit FAFSA. *Faculty research:* Application of psychoanalytic concepts to teaching, schools, and education reform; adolescent literacies; use of emerging technologies for teaching, learning, and school leadership; quantitative analyses of the social contexts of education; school, family, and community collaboration; program evaluation methodologies. *Unit head:* Dr. Edward Pajak, Chair, 410-516-9755, Fax: 410-516-9770, E-mail: mbuckingham@jhu.edu. *Application contact:* Jennifer Shaffer, Director of Admissions, 410-516-9797, Fax: 410-516-9799, E-mail: educationinfo@jhu.edu.

Johnson & Wales University, The Alan Shawn Feinstein Graduate School, Ed D Program, Providence, RI 02903-3703. Offers higher education (Ed D); K-12 (Ed D). Part-time programs available. *Faculty:* 7 full-time (3 women), 3 part-time/adjunct (2 women). *Students:* 95 full-time (54 women); includes 3 minority (1 African American, 2 Asian Americans or Pacific Islanders). Average age 42. 27 applicants, 89% accepted, 22 enrolled. In 2009, 30 doctorates awarded. *Degree requirements:* For doctorate, thesis/dissertation. *Entrance requirements:* For doctorate, MAT, minimum GPA of 3.25. Additional exam requirements/recommendations for international students: Required—TOEFL (minimum score 550 paper-based; 210 computer-based) or IELTS recommended; Recommended—TWE. *Application deadline:* Applications are processed on a rolling basis. Application fee: $0. *Expenses:* Required fees: $340 per quarter hour. *Financial support:* Application deadline: 5/1. *Faculty research:* Site-based management, collaborative learning, technology and education, K–16 education. *Unit head:* Dr. Robert Gable, Director, 401-598-4738, Fax: 401-598-1162, E-mail: rgable@jwu.edu. *Application contact:* Dr. Allan G. Freedman, Director of Graduate Admissions, 401-598-1015, Fax: 401-598-1286, E-mail: gradadm@jwu.edu.

Jones International University, Graduate School of Education, Centennial, CO 80112. Offers adult education (M Ed); corporate training and knowledge management (M Ed); curriculum and instruction (M Ed), including elementary teacher licensure, secondary teacher licensure; e-learning technology and design (M Ed); educational leadership and administration (M Ed); educational leadership and administration: principal and administrator licensure (M Ed); elementary curriculum instruction and assessment (M Ed); higher education leadership and administration (M Ed); K-12 instructional technology (M Ed); K-12 instructional technology: teacher licensure (M Ed); secondary curriculum instruction and assessment (M Ed); technology and design (M Ed). Part-time and evening/weekend programs available. Postbaccalaureate distance learning degree programs offered (no on-campus study). *Entrance requirements:* For master's, minimum cumulative GPA of 2.5. Additional exam requirements/recommendations for international students: Recommended—TOEFL (minimum score 550 paper-based; 213 computer-based). Electronic applications accepted.

Kansas State University, Graduate School, College of Education, Department of Educational Leadership, Manhattan, KS 66506. Offers adult and continuing education (Ed D); adult, occupational and continuing education (MS); educational administration and leadership (MS, Ed D). *Accreditation:* NCATE. *Faculty:* 10 full-time (5 women), 3 part-time/adjunct (1 woman). *Students:* 41 full-time (27 women), 169 part-time (72 women); includes 19 minority (12 African Americans, 1 American Indian/Alaska Native, 3 Asian Americans or Pacific Islanders, 3 Hispanic Americans), 1 international. Average age 41. 46 applicants, 96% accepted, 39 enrolled. In 2009, 79 master's, 9 doctorates awarded. *Degree requirements:* For master's, thesis or alternative, final written exam; for doctorate, comprehensive exam, thesis/dissertation, preliminary exam, residency. *Entrance requirements:* For master's, GRE General Test, MAT, minimum undergraduate GPA of 3.0; for doctorate, GRE General Test, MAT, minimum GPA of 3.0. Additional exam requirements/recommendations for international students: Required—TOEFL. *Application deadline:* For fall admission, 2/1 priority date for domestic and international students; for spring admission, 8/1 priority date for domestic and international students. Applications are processed on a rolling basis. Application fee: $40 ($55 for international students). Electronic

applications accepted. *Financial support:* Career-related internships or fieldwork, institutionally sponsored loans, and scholarships/grants available. Support available to part-time students. Financial award application deadline: 3/1; financial award applicants required to submit FAFSA. *Faculty research:* Educational law, finance, technology ethics, application, and leadership in education; distance learning/education; program evaluation. Total annual research expenditures: $71,091. *Unit head:* David C. Thompson, Head, 785-532-5535, Fax: 785-532-7304, E-mail: thomsond@ksu.edu. *Application contact:* Gail Shroyer, Director, 785-532-6737, Fax: 785-532-7304, E-mail: gshroyer@ksu.edu.

Kaplan University, Davenport Campus, School of Higher Education Studies, Davenport, IA 52807-2095. Offers college administration and leadership (MS); college teaching and learning (MS); student services (MS). Part-time and evening/weekend programs available. Postbaccalaureate distance learning degree programs offered (no on-campus study). *Entrance requirements:* Additional exam requirements/recommendations for international students: Required—TOEFL (minimum score 550 paper-based; 218 computer-based; 80 iBT).

Kean University, Nathan Weiss Graduate College, Program in Educational Administration, Union, NJ 07083. Offers school business administration (MA); supervisors and principals (MA). *Accreditation:* NCATE. Part-time and evening/weekend programs available. *Faculty:* 7 full-time (2 women). *Students:* 16 full-time (10 women), 253 part-time (164 women); includes 74 minority (44 African Americans, 5 Asian Americans or Pacific Islanders, 25 Hispanic Americans). Average age 36. 118 applicants, 98% accepted, 79 enrolled. In 2009, 83 master's awarded. *Degree requirements:* For master's, comprehensive exam, portfolio, field experience, research component. *Entrance requirements:* For master's, GRE General Test or MAT, minimum GPA of 3.0, interview, 2 letters of recommendation, 1 year of teaching experience, teacher certification. *Application deadline:* For fall admission, 5/1 for domestic students; for spring admission, 11/1 for domestic students. Application fee: $60 ($150 for international students). Electronic applications accepted. *Expenses:* Tuition, state resident: full-time $10,440; part-time $435 per credit. Tuition, nonresident: full-time $14,160; part-time $590 per credit. Required fees: $2642; $110 per credit. Part-time tuition and fees vary according to course load and degree level. *Financial support:* In 2009–10, 1 research assistantship with full tuition reimbursement (averaging $3,263 per year) was awarded; unspecified assistantships also available. *Unit head:* Dr. Gerard Babo, Program Coordinator, 908-737-4270, E-mail: gbabo@kean.edu. *Application contact:* Ann-Marie Kay, Assistant Director of Graduate Admissions, 908-737-5922, Fax: 908-737-5965, E-mail: akay@kean.edu.

Kean University, Nathan Weiss Graduate College, Program in Urban Leadership, Union, NJ 07083. Offers Ed D. Evening/weekend programs available. *Faculty:* 7 full-time (2 women). *Students:* 33 part-time (20 women); includes 21 minority (17 African Americans, 4 Hispanic Americans). Average age 43. 28 applicants, 61% accepted, 16 enrolled. *Degree requirements:* For doctorate, comprehensive exam, thesis/dissertation. *Entrance requirements:* For doctorate, GRE General Test, GRE Subject Test in psychology (taken within the last 5 years), master's degree from an accredited college, minimum GPA of 3.0 in last degree attained (lower GPAs may be considered), substantial experience working in education or family support agencies, 2 letters of recommendation. *Application deadline:* For fall admission, 1/30 for domestic students. Application fee: $60 ($150 for international students). Electronic applications accepted. *Expenses:* Contact institution. *Financial support:* Research assistantships, unspecified assistantships available. *Unit head:* Dr. Columbus Salley, Program Director, 908-737-5978, E-mail: csalley@kean.edu. *Application contact:* Steven Koch, Pre-Admissions Coordinator, 908-737-5924, Fax: 908-737-5965, E-mail: skoch@kean.edu.

Keene State College, School of Professional and Graduate Studies, Keene, NH 03435. Offers curriculum and instruction (M Ed); education leadership (PMC); educational leadership (M Ed); school counselor (M Ed, PMC); special education (M Ed); teacher certification (Post-baccalaureate Certificate). *Accreditation:* NCATE. Part-time and evening/weekend programs available. *Faculty:* 21 full-time (13 women), 14 part-time/adjunct (13 women). *Students:* 8 full-time (5 women), 80 part-time (56 women); includes 1 Asian American or Pacific Islander, 1 Hispanic American, 1 international. Average age 34. 94 applicants, 80% accepted, 62 enrolled. In 2009, 55 master's, 10 other advanced degrees awarded. *Entrance requirements:* For master's, PRAXIS I, resume; minimum GPA of 2.5. Additional exam requirements/recommendations for international students: Required—TOEFL (minimum score 550 paper-based; 173 computer-based; 61 iBT). *Application deadline:* For fall admission, 4/1 for domestic students; for spring admission, 12/1 for domestic students. Application fee: $40. *Expenses:* Tuition, state resident: part-time $320 per credit. Tuition, nonresident: part-time $350 per credit. Required fees: $92 per credit. $10 per term. Tuition and fees vary according to course load. *Financial support:* Research assistantships, career-related internships or fieldwork, Federal Work-Study, institutionally sponsored loans, and unspecified assistantships available. Support available to part-time students. Financial award application deadline: 3/1; financial award applicants required to submit FAFSA. *Unit head:* Dr. Melinda Treadwell, Dean, 603-358-2220. *Application contact:* Peggy Richmond, Director of Admissions, 603-358-2276, Fax: 603-358-2767, E-mail: admissions@keene.edu.

Keiser University, Master of Science in Education Program, Fort Lauderdale, FL 33309. Offers college administration (MS); leadership (MS); teaching and learning (MS). Part-time programs available. Postbaccalaureate distance learning degree programs offered (no on-campus study). *Faculty:* 2 full-time (both women), 3 part-time/adjunct (2 women). *Students:* 9 full-time (7 women), 13 part-time (11 women); includes 17 minority (14 African Americans, 1 American Indian/Alaska Native, 2 Hispanic Americans). Average age 35. 16 applicants, 88% accepted, 11 enrolled. *Entrance requirements:* For master's, minimum GPA of 2.7 from an accredited institution. Additional exam requirements/recommendations for international students: Required—TOEFL. *Application deadline:* Applications are processed on a rolling basis. Application fee: $50. Electronic applications accepted. *Financial support:* In 2009–10, 10 students received support. Federal Work-Study available. Financial award applicants required to submit FAFSA. *Unit head:* Dr. Sara Malmstrom, Dean, Graduate School, 954-318-1620. *Application contact:* Manuel Christiansen, Associate Director of Admissions, 954-318-1620 Ext. 309, E-mail: mchristiansen@keiseruniversity.edu.

Keiser University, PhD in Educational Leadership Program, Fort Lauderdale, FL 33309. Offers PhD. *Application contact:* Manuel Christiansen, Associate Director of Admissions, 954-318-1620 Ext. 309, E-mail: mchristiansen@keiseruniversity.edu.

Kennesaw State University, Leland and Clarice C. Bagwell College of Education, Program in Graduate Education, Kennesaw, GA 30144-5591. Offers adolescent education (M Ed); educational leadership (M Ed); educational leadership technology (M Ed); elementary and early childhood education (M Ed); special education (M Ed); teaching English to speakers of other languages (M Ed). *Accreditation:* NCATE. Part-time programs available. *Faculty:* 60 full-time (38 women), 12 part-time/adjunct (4 women). *Students:* 140 full-time (116 women), 136 part-time (107 women); includes 51 minority (39 African Americans, 1 American Indian/Alaska Native, 3 Asian Americans or Pacific Islanders, 8 Hispanic Americans), 4 international. Average age 34. 113 applicants, 83% accepted, 69 enrolled. In 2009, 282 master's awarded. *Degree requirements:* For master's, thesis or alternative. *Entrance requirements:* For master's, GRE General Test, T-4 state certification, minimum GPA of 2.75. Additional exam requirements/recommendations for international students: Required—TOEFL (minimum score 550 paper-based; 213 computer-based; 80 iBT), IELTS (minimum score 6). *Application deadline:* For fall admission, 7/1 for domestic and international students; for spring admission, 10/1 for domestic and international students. Application fee: $60. Electronic applications accepted. *Expenses:* Tuition, state resident: full-time $2341; part-time $196 per credit hour. Tuition, nonresident: full-time $9396; part-time $783 per credit hour. Required fees: $573 per semester. *Financial support:* Federal Work-Study and unspecified assistantships available. Support available to part-time students. Financial award application deadline: 6/15; financial award applicants required to submit FAFSA. *Unit head:* Dr. Nita Paris, Associate Dean for Graduate Programs, 770-423-6636, E-mail: nparis@kennesaw.edu. *Application contact:* Alisha Bello, Administrative Coordinator, 770-423-6043, Fax: 770-420-4435, E-mail: abello1@kennesaw.edu.

Kennesaw State University, Leland and Clarice C. Bagwell College of Education, Program in Leadership for Learning, Kennesaw, GA 30144-5591. Offers Ed D, Ed S. Part-time and evening/weekend programs available. *Students:* 6 full-time (5 women), 55 part-time (41 women); includes 8 minority (4 African Americans, 4 Hispanic Americans), 1 international. Average age 42. In 2009, 14 other advanced degrees awarded. *Degree requirements:* For doctorate, thesis/dissertation. *Entrance requirements:* For doctorate, GRE General Test, minimum graduate GPA of 3.0, resume. Additional exam requirements/recommendations for international students: Required—TOEFL (minimum score 550 paper-based; 218 computer-based; 80 iBT), IELTS (minimum score 6). *Application deadline:* For spring admission, 9/1 for domestic and international students. Application fee: $60. Electronic applications accepted. *Expenses:* Tuition, state resident: full-time $2341; part-time $196 per credit hour. Tuition, nonresident: full-time $9396; part-time $783 per credit hour. Required fees: $573 per semester. *Financial support:* In 2009–10, 2 research assistantships with tuition reimbursements (averaging $4,000 per year) were awarded. Financial award application deadline: 6/15; financial award applicants required to submit FAFSA. *Unit head:* Dr. Nita Paris, Associate Dean for Graduate Programs, 770-423-6636, E-mail: nparis@kennesaw.edu. *Application contact:* Alisha Bello, Administrative Coordinator, 770-423-6043, Fax: 770-420-4435, E-mail: abello1@kennesaw.edu.

Kent State University, Graduate School of Education, Health, and Human Services, School of Foundations, Leadership and Administration, Program in K-12 Leadership, Kent, OH 44242-0001. Offers M Ed, MA, PhD, Ed S. *Faculty:* 4 full-time (3 women), 2 part-time/adjunct (1 woman). *Students:* 12 full-time (10 women), 58 part-time (41 women); includes 4 minority (3 African Americans, 1 Asian American or Pacific Islander). 16 applicants, 81% accepted. In 2009, 35 master's, 2 doctorates, 4 other advanced degrees awarded. *Entrance requirements:* For doctorate and Ed S, GRE. Additional exam requirements/recommendations for international students: Required—TOEFL. *Application deadline:* Applications are processed on a rolling basis. Application fee: $30. Electronic applications accepted. *Financial support:* In 2009–10, 1 fellowship (averaging $12,000 per year), 1 research assistantship (averaging $8,500 per year), teaching assistantships (averaging $12,000 per year) were awarded; career-related internships or fieldwork, Federal Work-Study, institutionally sponsored loans, scholarships/grants, health care benefits, and unspecified assistantships also available. Support available to part-time students. *Unit head:* Anita Varrati, Coordinator, 330-672-0630, E-mail: avarrati@kent.edu. *Application contact:* Nancy Miller, Academic Program Coordinator, Office of Graduate Student Services, 330-672-2576, Fax: 330-672-9162, E-mail: ogs@kent.edu.

Kutztown University of Pennsylvania, College of Education, Program in Student Affairs in Higher Education, Kutztown, PA 19530-0730. Offers M Ed. *Accreditation:* NCATE. Part-time and evening/weekend programs available. *Faculty:* 2 full-time (both women). *Students:* 16 full-time (14 women), 9 part-time (8 women); includes 4 minority (2 African Americans, 1 Asian American or Pacific Islander, 1 Hispanic American), 1 international. Average age 28. 16 applicants, 81% accepted, 3 enrolled. In 2009, 9 master's awarded. *Degree requirements:* For master's, comprehensive exam. *Entrance requirements:* For master's, GRE General Test, interview. Additional exam requirements/recommendations for international students: Required—TOEFL. *Application deadline:* For fall admission, 2/1 for domestic and international students; for spring admission, 8/1 for domestic and international students. Application fee: $35. Electronic applications accepted. *Expenses:* Tuition, state resident: full-time $6666; part-time $370 per credit. Tuition, nonresident: full-time $10,666; part-time $593 per credit. Required fees: $62 per credit. $60 per semester. *Financial support:* Career-related internships or fieldwork, Federal Work-Study, scholarships/grants, and unspecified assistantships available. Financial award application deadline: 3/1; financial award applicants required to submit FAFSA. *Unit head:* Dr. Deborah Barlieb, Chairperson, 610-683-4204, Fax: 610-683-1585, E-mail: barlieb@kutztown.edu. *Application contact:* Kelly D. Burr, Associate Director, Graduate Admissions, 610-683-4200, Fax: 610-683-1393, E-mail: graduate@kutztown.edu.

Lake Erie College, Division of Education, Painesville, OH 44077-3389. Offers curriculum and instruction (MS Ed); education (MS Ed); educational leadership (MS Ed); reading (MS Ed). Part-time and evening/weekend programs available. *Degree requirements:* For master's, comprehensive exam (for some programs), thesis optional, applied research project. *Entrance requirements:* For master's, GRE General Test or minimum GPA of 3.0. Additional exam requirements/recommendations for international students: Required—TOEFL (minimum score 590 paper-based). Electronic applications accepted. *Expenses:* Contact institution. *Faculty research:* Cooperative learning, portfolio assessment, education systems abroad, Web-based instruction.

Lamar University, College of Graduate Studies, College of Education and Human Development, Department of Educational Leadership, Beaumont, TX 77710. Offers counseling and development (M Ed, Certificate); education administration (M Ed); educational leadership (DE); principal (Certificate); school superintendent (Certificate); supervision (M Ed); technology application (Certificate). Part-time and evening/weekend programs available. *Faculty:* 14 full-time (7 women), 7 part-time/adjunct (2 women). *Students:* 14 full-time (8 women), 2,827 part-time (1,986 women); includes 798 minority (340 African Americans, 20 American Indian/Alaska Native, 31 Asian Americans or Pacific Islanders, 407 Hispanic Americans). Average age 40. 2,662 applicants, 75% accepted, 332 enrolled. In 2009, 199 master's, 21 doctorates awarded. Terminal master's awarded for partial completion of doctoral program. *Degree requirements:* For master's, comprehensive exam, thesis optional; for doctorate, thesis/dissertation. *Entrance requirements:* For master's, GRE General Test, minimum GPA of 2.5; for doctorate, GRE. Additional exam requirements/recommendations for international students: Required—TOEFL. *Application deadline:* For fall admission, 8/1 priority date for domestic students; for spring admission, 12/1 priority date for domestic students. Applications are processed on a rolling basis. Application fee: $25 ($50 for international students). *Financial support:* In 2009–10, 3 fellowships (averaging $20,000 per year), 1 research assistantship with tuition reimbursement (averaging $6,500 per year) were awarded; teaching assistantships with tuition reimbursements, career-related internships or fieldwork and scholarships/grants also available. Support available to part-time students. Financial award application deadline: 4/1. *Faculty research:* School dropouts, suicide prevention in public school students, school climate and gifted performance, teacher evaluation. *Unit head:* Dr. Carolyn Crawford, Chair, 409-880-8689, Fax: 409-880-8685. *Application contact:* Dr. Carolyn Crawford, Chair, 409-880-8689, Fax: 409-880-8685.

La Sierra University, School of Education, Department of Administration and Leadership, Riverside, CA 92515. Offers MA, Ed D, Ed S. Part-time and evening/weekend programs available. Terminal master's awarded for partial completion of doctoral program. *Degree requirements:* For master's, thesis optional; for doctorate, thesis/dissertation, fieldwork, qualifying exam; for Ed S, thesis optional, fieldwork. *Entrance requirements:* For master's, minimum GPA of 3.0; for doctorate, GRE General Test, GRE Subject Test, minimum GPA of 3.3, Ed S; for Ed S, master's degree, minimum GPA of 3.3.

Lee University, Program in Education, Cleveland, TN 37320-3450. Offers classroom teaching (M Ed, Ed S); educational leadership (M Ed, Ed S); elementary/secondary education (MAT); secondary education (MAT); special education (elementary) (M Ed); special education (secondary) (M Ed, MAT); special education (severe disabilities) (M Ed). Part-time programs available. *Faculty:* 11 full-time (4 women), 3 part-time/adjunct (2 women). *Students:* 65 full-time (45 women), 140 part-time (80 women); includes 8 minority (5 African Americans, 1 American Indian/Alaska Native, 2 Hispanic Americans), 6 international. Average age 31. 4 applicants, 100% accepted, 2 enrolled. In 2009, 75 master's, 7 other advanced degrees awarded. *Degree requirements:* For master's, variable foreign language requirement, comprehensive exam, thesis, internship. *Entrance requirements:* For master's, MAT or GRE General Test, minimum GPA of 2.75, 3 letters of recommendation, interview, writing sample. Additional exam requirements/recommendations for international students: Required—TOEFL (minimum score 450 paper-based; 45 computer-based). *Application deadline:* For fall admission, 4/1 priority date for domestic students; for spring admission, 10/1 priority date for domestic students. Applications are processed on a rolling basis. Application fee: $25. *Expenses:* Tuition: Full-time $11,100; part-time $463 per credit. Required fees: $305. *Financial support:* Career-related internships or fieldwork, Federal Work-Study, institutionally sponsored loans, scholarships/

Educational Leadership and Administration

Lee University (continued)

grants, and unspecified assistantships available. Financial award application deadline: 3/1; financial award applicants required to submit FAFSA. *Unit head:* Dr. Gary Riggins, Director, 423-614-8193. *Application contact:* Vicki Glasscock, Graduate Admissions Director, 423-614-8059, E-mail: vglasscock@leeuniversity.edu.

Lehigh University, College of Education, Program in Educational Leadership, Bethlehem, PA 18015. Offers educational leadership (M Ed, Ed D); principal certification K-12 (Certificate); pupil services (Certificate); special education (Certificate); superintendant certification (Certificate); supervisor of curriculum and instruction (Certificate); supervisor of pupil services (Certificate); MBA/M Ed. Part-time and evening/weekend programs available. Postbaccalaureate distance learning degree programs offered (minimal on-campus study). *Faculty:* 7 full-time (2 women), 16 part-time/adjunct (9 women). *Students:* 12 full-time (6 women), 174 part-time (102 women); includes 8 minority (4 African Americans, 1 Asian American or Pacific Islander, 3 Hispanic Americans), 20 international. Average age 37. 55 applicants, 73% accepted, 34 enrolled. In 2009, 39 master's, 4 doctorates awarded. *Degree requirements:* For doctorate, comprehensive exam, thesis/dissertation. *Entrance requirements:* For master's, minimum GPA of 3.0; for doctorate, GRE General Test or MAT, minimum graduate GPA of 3.6, 2 letters of recommendation, essay, transcript; for Certificate, minimum undergraduate GPA of 3.0. Additional exam requirements/recommendations for international students: Required—TOEFL (minimum score 600 paper-based; 250 computer-based; 93 iBT). *Application deadline:* For fall admission, 1/15 for domestic and international students; for spring admission, 11/1 for domestic and international students. Applications are processed on a rolling basis. Application fee: $65. Electronic applications accepted. *Financial support:* In 2009–10, 2 students received support, including 2 research assistantships with full and partial tuition reimbursements available (averaging $13,000 per year); fellowships with full and partial tuition reimbursements available, teaching assistantships with full and partial tuition reimbursements available, career-related internships or fieldwork, Federal Work-Study, institutionally sponsored loans, scholarships/grants, and tuition waivers (full and partial) also available. Financial award application deadline: 1/31. *Faculty research:* School finance and law, supervision of instruction, middle-level education, organizational change, leadership preparation and development, international school leadership, urban school leadership. *Unit head:* Dr. George P. White, Coordinator, 610-758-3250, Fax: 610-758-3227, E-mail: gpw1@lehigh.edu. *Application contact:* Donna M. Johnson, Coordinator, 610-758-3231, Fax: 610-758-6223, E-mail: dmj4@lehigh.edu.

Le Moyne College, Department of Education, Syracuse, NY 13214. Offers adolescent education (MS Ed, MST); adolescent education/special education (MS Ed, MST); adolescent English (grades 7-12) (MST); adolescent history (grades 7-12) (MST); childhood education (MS Ed); childhood education/special education (MS Ed); elementary education (MS Ed); general professional education (MS Ed); inclusive childhood education (MST); middle child specialist/special education (MS Ed); middle childhood specialist (MS Ed); school building leadership (MS Ed, CAS); school district business leader (MS Ed, CAS); school district leadership (MS Ed, CAS); secondary education (MS Ed); special education (MS Ed). *Accreditation:* Teacher Education Accreditation Council. Part-time and evening/weekend programs available. *Faculty:* 15 full-time (8 women), 61 part-time/adjunct (33 women). *Students:* 40 full-time (30 women), 260 part-time (180 women); includes 25 minority (11 African Americans, 3 American Indian/Alaska Native, 3 Asian Americans or Pacific Islanders, 8 Hispanic Americans). Average age 31. 168 applicants, 89% accepted, 140 enrolled. In 2009, 180 master's awarded. *Degree requirements:* For master's, thesis. *Entrance requirements:* For master's, GRE General Test, 2 letters of recommendation. Additional exam requirements/recommendations for international students: Required—TOEFL (minimum score 550 paper-based; 213 computer-based; 79 iBT). *Application deadline:* For fall admission, 4/1 priority date for domestic and international students; for spring admission, 10/1 priority date for domestic and international students. Applications are processed on a rolling basis. Application fee: $50. *Expenses:* Contact institution. *Financial support:* In 2009–10, 28 students received support. Career-related internships or fieldwork and health care benefits available. Support available to part-time students. Financial award applicants required to submit FAFSA. *Faculty research:* Recruitment/retention strategies, minority teachers, special education, multiculturalism, literacy, technology, video games learning, autism, school district organization. *Unit head:* Dr. Norbert J. Henry, Interim Chair/Director, 315-445-4376, Fax: 315-445-4744, E-mail: henry@lemoyne.edu. *Application contact:* Kristen P. Trapasso, Director of Graduate Admission, 315-445-4265, Fax: 315-445-6027, E-mail: trapaskp@lemoyne.edu.

LeTourneau University, School of Graduate and Professional Studies, Longview, TX 75607-7001. Offers business administration (MBA); curriculum and instruction (M Ed); educational administration (M Ed); strategic leadership (MSL); teaching and learning (M Ed). Part-time and evening/weekend programs available. Postbaccalaureate distance learning degree programs offered (no on-campus study). *Faculty:* 8 full-time (1 woman), 19 part-time/adjunct (7 women). *Students:* 43 full-time (30 women), 245 part-time (164 women); includes 158 minority (130 African Americans, 2 American Indian/Alaska Native, 2 Asian Americans or Pacific Islanders, 24 Hispanic Americans). Average age 36. 1,717 applicants, 31% accepted, 288 enrolled. *Entrance requirements:* For master's, minimum GPA of 2.8. Additional exam requirements/recommendations for international students: Required—TOEFL. *Application deadline:* Applications are processed on a rolling basis. Electronic applications accepted. *Expenses:* Tuition: Full-time $10,710; part-time $595 per credit hour. *Financial support:* Applicants required to submit FAFSA. *Unit head:* Dr. Carol Green, Vice President, 903-233-3250, Fax: 903-233-3227, E-mail: carolgreen@letu.edu. *Application contact:* Chris Fontaine, Assistant Vice President for Enrollment Management and Market Research, 903-233-3250, Fax: 903-233-3227, E-mail: chrisfontaine@letu.edu.

Lewis & Clark College, Graduate School of Education and Counseling, Department of Educational Leadership, Program in Educational Leadership, Portland, OR 97219-7899. Offers educational administration (M Ed); educational leadership (Ed D). Part-time and evening/weekend programs available. *Faculty:* 5 full-time (all women), 11 part-time/adjunct (7 women). *Students:* 55 part-time (32 women); includes 5 minority (3 African Americans, 1 Asian American or Pacific Islander, 1 Hispanic American). Average age 43. 74 applicants, 93% accepted, 44 enrolled. In 2009, 4 master's, 10 doctorates awarded. *Degree requirements:* For doctorate, thesis/dissertation. *Entrance requirements:* For master's, Minimum undergraduate GPA of 2.75. Applicants must hold an Oregon teaching or personnel service license and have three years of successful teaching and/or personnel service experience in the public schools or regionally accredited private schools.; for doctorate, Earned master's degree plus a minimum of 14 post master's, degree applicable, semester credits. Minimum undergraduate GPA of 2.75. Additional exam requirements/recommendations for international students: Required—TOEFL (minimum score 575 paper-based; 233 computer-based). *Application deadline:* For fall admission, 5/1 for domestic and international students. Applications are processed on a rolling basis. Application fee: $50. Electronic applications accepted. *Expenses:* Tuition: Part-time $713 per semester hour. Tuition and fees vary according to course level and campus/location. *Financial support:* In 2009–10, 30 students received support. Career-related internships or fieldwork, Federal Work-Study, institutionally sponsored loans, health care benefits, and tuition waivers (partial) available. Support available to part-time students. Financial award application deadline: 3/1; financial award applicants required to submit FAFSA. *Unit head:* Dr. Carolyn Carr, Department Chair, 503-768-6080, Fax: 503-768-6085, E-mail: eda@lclark.edu. *Application contact:* Becky Haas, Director of Admissions, 503-768-6200, Fax: 503-768-6205, E-mail: gseadmit@lclark.edu.

Lewis University, College of Arts and Sciences, Program in Organizational Leadership, Romeoville, IL 60446. Offers higher education/student services (MA); organizational management (MA); public administration (MA); training and development (MA). Part-time and evening/weekend programs available. *Faculty:* 2 full-time (0 women), 9 part-time/adjunct (2 women). *Students:* 24 full-time (11 women), 111 part-time (91 women); includes 42 minority (33 African Americans, 1 American Indian/Alaska Native, 1 Asian American or Pacific Islander, 7 Hispanic Americans), 1 international. Average age 38. In 2009, 41 master's awarded. *Entrance requirements:* For master's, bachelor's degree, at least 25 years of age, minimum of 3 years of work experience, minimum GPA of 3.0, letter of recommendation, interview. Additional exam requirements/recommendations for international students: Required—TOEFL (minimum score 550 paper-based; 213 computer-based). *Application deadline:* For fall admission, 5/1 priority date for international students; for spring admission, 11/15 priority date for international students. Applications are processed on a rolling basis. Application fee: $40. Electronic applications accepted. *Expenses:* Tuition: Full-time $6480; part-time $720 per credit. One-time fee: $40. Tuition and fees vary according to course load, degree level and program. *Financial support:* Federal Work-Study, scholarships/grants, tuition waivers, and unspecified assistantships available. Financial award application deadline: 5/1; financial award applicants required to submit FAFSA. *Unit head:* Dr. Rich Walsh, Director, 815-838-0500, E-mail: walshri@lewisu.edu. *Application contact:* Bernadette Valderrama, Information Contact, 815-838-0500 Ext. 5629.

Lewis University, College of Education, Program in Advanced Study in Education, Romeoville, IL 60446. Offers general administrative (CAS); superintendent endorsement (CAS). Part-time and evening/weekend programs available. *Students:* 3 full-time (1 woman), 37 part-time (17 women); includes 8 minority (7 African Americans, 1 Hispanic American). Average age 39. *Entrance requirements:* Additional exam requirements/recommendations for international students: Required—TOEFL (minimum score 550 paper-based; 213 computer-based). *Application deadline:* For fall admission, 5/1 priority date for international students; for spring admission, 11/15 priority date for international students. Applications are processed on a rolling basis. Application fee: $40. Electronic applications accepted. *Expenses:* Tuition: Full-time $6480; part-time $720 per credit. One-time fee: $40. Tuition and fees vary according to course load, degree level and program. *Financial support:* Institutionally sponsored loans and unspecified assistantships available. Support available to part-time students. Financial award application deadline: 5/1; financial award applicants required to submit FAFSA. *Unit head:* Dr. Barbara Mackey, Program Director, 815-838-0500 Ext. 5962, E-mail: mackeyba@lewisu.edu. *Application contact:* Julie Nickel, Assistant Director, Graduate and Adult Admission, 815-838-0500 Ext. 5574, E-mail: nickelju@lewisu.edu.

Lewis University, College of Education, Program in Educational Leadership, Romeoville, IL 60446. Offers M Ed, MA. Part-time and evening/weekend programs available. *Students:* 23 full-time (16 women), 78 part-time (49 women); includes 12 minority (8 African Americans, 1 Asian American or Pacific Islander, 3 Hispanic Americans), 1 international. Average age 40. 48 applicants, 75% accepted, 35 enrolled. In 2009, 34 master's awarded. *Entrance requirements:* For master's, departmental qualifying exams, writing exam, minimum GPA of 2.75, 2 letters of recommendation, interview. Additional exam requirements/recommendations for international students: Required—TOEFL (minimum score 550 paper-based; 213 computer-based). *Application deadline:* For fall admission, 5/1 priority date for international students; for spring admission, 11/15 priority date for international students. Application fee: $40. *Expenses:* Tuition: Full-time $6480; part-time $720 per credit. One-time fee: $40. Tuition and fees vary according to course load, degree level and program. *Financial support:* Federal Work-Study, scholarships/grants, and unspecified assistantships available. Financial award application deadline: 5/1; financial award applicants required to submit FAFSA. *Unit head:* Dr. Jane Petrek, Director, 815-838-0500 Ext. 5039, Fax: 815-836-5879, E-mail: petrekja@lewisu.edu. *Application contact:* Stormie Surles, Secretary, 815-838-0500 Ext. 5121, E-mail: surlesst@lewisu.edu.

Lewis University, College of Education, Program in Educational Leadership for Teaching and Learning, Romeoville, IL 60446. Offers Ed D. *Students:* 1 full-time (0 women), 47 part-time (32 women); includes 13 minority (9 African Americans, 4 Hispanic Americans), 1 international. Average age 40. *Degree requirements:* For doctorate, thesis/dissertation. *Entrance requirements:* For doctorate, GRE General Test. *Expenses:* Tuition: Full-time $6480; part-time $720 per credit. One-time fee: $40. Tuition and fees vary according to course load, degree level and program. *Financial support:* Application deadline: 5/1. *Unit head:* Dr. Lauren Hoffman, Program Director, 815-838-0500 Ext. 5501, E-mail: hoffmala@lewisu.edu. *Application contact:* Pat Levenda, Secretary, 815-838-0500 Ext. 5769, E-mail: levendpa@lewisu.edu.

Liberty University, School of Education, Lynchburg, VA 24502. Offers administration and supervision (M Ed); curriculum and instruction (M Ed); early childhood education (M Ed); education specialist (Ed S); educational leadership (Ed D); elementary education (M Ed); gifted education (M Ed); reading specialist (M Ed); school counseling (M Ed); secondary education (M Ed); special education (M Ed). *Accreditation:* NCATE. Part-time programs available. Postbaccalaureate distance learning degree programs offered (minimal on-campus study). *Degree requirements:* For doctorate, comprehensive exam, thesis/dissertation. *Entrance requirements:* For master's, GRE General Test or MAT (aken in or before 1999), 2 letters of recommendation, minimum undergraduate GPA of 3.0, curriculum vitae; for doctorate, GRE General Test or MAT (if taken before 1999), minimum master's GPA of 3.0, 3 years of teacher experience; for Ed S, GRE General Test or MAT (if taken before 1999), minimum master's GPA of 3.0, 3 years of teaching experience. Additional exam requirements/recommendations for international students: Required—TOEFL (minimum score 600 paper-based; 250 computer-based). Electronic applications accepted. *Expenses:* Contact institution. *Faculty research:* Self-determination, character education, bibliotherapy, learning styles, distance education.

Lincoln Memorial University, Carter and Moyers School of Education, Harrogate, TN 37752-1901. Offers administration and supervision (M Ed, Ed S); counseling and guidance (M Ed); curriculum and instruction (M Ed, Ed S); English (M Ed). Part-time and evening/weekend programs available. Postbaccalaureate distance learning degree programs offered. *Faculty:* 31 full-time (13 women), 22 part-time/adjunct (11 women). *Students:* 190 full-time (151 women), 1,299 part-time (959 women); includes 144 minority (128 African Americans, 1 American Indian/Alaska Native, 5 Asian Americans or Pacific Islanders, 10 Hispanic Americans), 4 international. 1,562 applicants, 96% accepted, 1489 enrolled. In 2009, 173 master's, 901 Ed Ss awarded. *Degree requirements:* For master's, comprehensive exam, thesis optional; for Ed S, comprehensive exam. *Entrance requirements:* For master's, PRAXIS, NTE, GRE, MAT, letters of recommendation; for Ed S, graduate transcripts. *Application deadline:* For fall admission, 8/10 for domestic and international students; for spring admission, 1/10 for domestic and international students. Application fee: $25. *Expenses:* Tuition: Full-time $11,700; part-time $390 per hour. *Financial support:* In 2009–10, 973 students received support. Career-related internships or fieldwork, health care benefits, and unspecified assistantships available. Support available to part-time students. Financial award application deadline: 4/1; financial award applicants required to submit FAFSA. *Faculty research:* Brain compatible teaching and learning; poverty in Appalachia; leadership for change; ethics, moral responsibility and social justice; human and organizational learning. *Unit head:* Dr. David Hand, Dean, 423-869-6259, Fax: 423-869-6261, E-mail: david.hand@lmunet.edu. *Application contact:* Terri Knuckles, Office Manager, Graduate Education, 423-869-6223, Fax: 423-869-6261, E-mail: terri.knuckles@lmunet.edu.

Lincoln University, School of Graduate Studies and Continuing Education, Jefferson City, MO 65102. Offers business administration (MBA), including accounting, entrepreneurship, management, public administration and policy; educational leadership (Ed S), including elementary leadership, secondary leadership, superintendency; guidance and counseling (M Ed), including community/agency counseling, elementary school, secondary school; history (MA); school administration and supervision (M Ed), including elementary school administration, secondary school administration, special education administration; school teaching (M Ed), including elementary school teaching, secondary school teaching; social science (MA), including history, political science, sociology; sociology (MA); sociology/criminal justice (MA). Part-time and evening/weekend programs available. *Students:* 52 full-time (27 women), 146 part-time (107 women); includes 40 minority (39 African Americans, 1 Asian American or Pacific Islander), 15 international. Average age 35. 76 applicants, 95% accepted, 46 enrolled. In 2009, 60 master's, 6 other advanced degrees awarded. *Degree requirements:* For master's and Ed S, comprehensive exam, thesis optional. *Entrance requirements:* For master's and Ed S, GRE, MAT or GMAT, minimum GPA of 2.75 in major, 2.5 overall; 3 letters of recommendation; minimum C average in English composition; personal statement of purpose. Additional exam requirements/recommendations for international students: Required—TOEFL (minimum score 500 paper-based; 173 computer-based; 61 iBT). *Application deadline:* For fall admission, 7/1

priority date for domestic and international students; for spring admission, 12/1 priority date for domestic and international students. Applications are processed on a rolling basis. Application fee: $20. *Expenses:* Tuition, state resident: full-time $4185; part-time $232.50 per credit hour. Tuition, nonresident: full-time $7767; part-time $431.50 per credit hour. Required fees: $270; $15 per credit hour. $20 per term. *Financial support:* Federal Work-Study and scholarships/grants available. Financial award application deadline: 4/1; financial award applicants required to submit FAFSA. *Faculty research:* Suicide prevention. *Unit head:* Dr. Linda S. Bickel, Dean, 573-681-5247, Fax: 573-681-5106, E-mail: gradschool@lincolnu.edu. *Application contact:* Irasema Steck, Administrative Assistant, 573-681-5247, Fax: 573-681-5106, E-mail: gradschool@lincolnu.edu.

Lindenwood University, Graduate Programs, School of Education, St. Charles, MO 63301-1695. Offers education (MA); educational administration (MA, Ed D, Ed S); instructional leadership (Ed D, Ed S); library media (MA); professional and school counseling (MA); professional counseling (MA); school administration (Ed S); school counseling (MA); teaching (MA). Part-time and evening/weekend programs available. *Faculty:* 33 full-time (13 women), 176 part-time/adjunct (83 women). *Students:* 558 full-time (415 women), 1,957 part-time (1,516 women); includes 580 minority (549 African Americans, 6 American Indian/Alaska Native, 16 Asian Americans or Pacific Islanders, 9 Hispanic Americans), 13 international. Average age 35. 248 applicants, 120 enrolled. In 2009, 730 master's, 62 doctorates, 67 other advanced degrees awarded. *Degree requirements:* For master's, thesis (for some programs); for doctorate, thesis/dissertation, minimum GPA of 3.0; for Ed S, comprehensive exam, specialist project, minimum GPA of 3.0. *Entrance requirements:* For master's, interview, minimum GPA of 3.0, writing sample, letter of recommendation; for doctorate, GRE, minimum graduate GPA of 3.4, resume, interview, writing sample, 4 letters of recommendation; for Ed S, master's degree in education, relevant work experience. Additional exam requirements/recommendations for international students: Required—TOEFL (minimum score 550 paper-based; 213 computer-based; 80 iBT). *Application deadline:* For fall admission, 8/27 priority date for domestic and international students; for spring admission, 1/28 priority date for domestic and international students. Applications are processed on a rolling basis. Application fee: $30 ($100 for international students). Electronic applications accepted. *Expenses:* Tuition: Full-time $12,960; part-time $370 per credit hour. Required fees: $340. One-time fee: $30 full-time. Tuition and fees vary according to course level and course load. *Financial support:* In 2009–10, 1,591 students received support. Career-related internships or fieldwork, institutionally sponsored loans, tuition waivers (partial), and unspecified assistantships available. Financial award application deadline: 6/30; financial award applicants required to submit FAFSA. *Unit head:* Dr. Cynthia Bice, Dean, 636-949-4618, Fax: 636-949-4197, E-mail: cbice@lindenwood.edu. *Application contact:* Brett Barger, Dean of Evening Admissions and Extension Campuses, 636-949-4934, Fax: 636-949-4109, E-mail: adultadmissions@lindenwood.edu.

Lipscomb University, Program in Education, Nashville, TN 37204-3951. Offers English language learners (MAT); instructional leadership (M Ed); instructional technology (M Ed); learning and teaching (MALT); math specialty (M Ed); school administration and supervision (M Ed); special education instruction, K-12 (MASE). *Accreditation:* NCATE. Part-time and evening/weekend programs available. *Faculty:* 4 full-time (1 woman), 12 part-time/adjunct (8 women). *Students:* 140 full-time (103 women), 200 part-time (144 women); includes 32 minority (29 African Americans, 3 Hispanic Americans). Average age 31. 206 applicants, 75% accepted. In 2009, 131 master's awarded. *Entrance requirements:* For master's, MAT or GRE General Test, 2 reference letters. Additional exam requirements/recommendations for international students: Required—TOEFL (minimum score 570 paper-based; 230 computer-based). *Application deadline:* For fall admission, 8/29 priority date for domestic students; for spring admission, 1/16 priority date for domestic students. Applications are processed on a rolling basis. Application fee: $50. *Expenses:* Tuition: Full-time $16,002; part-time $889 per credit hour. Tuition and fees vary according to program. *Financial support:* In 2009–10, 67 students received support. Federal Work-Study, tuition waivers (full), and unspecified assistantships available. Support available to part-time students. Financial award applicants required to submit FAFSA. *Faculty research:* Facilitative learning styles, leadership, student assessment, interactive multimedia inclusion. *Unit head:* Dr. Deborah Boyd, Director of M Ed Program, 615-966-6263. *Application contact:* Kristin Green, Administrative Assistant, 615-966-7628 Ext. 6081, Fax: 615-966-7628, E-mail: kristin.green@lipscomb.edu.

Long Island University, Brooklyn Campus, School of Education, Department of Human Development and Leadership, Program in Leadership and Policy, Brooklyn, NY 11201-8423. Offers MS. *Degree requirements:* For master's, thesis optional. *Entrance requirements:* For master's, 2 letters of recommendation. Additional exam requirements/recommendations for international students: Required—TOEFL (minimum score 500 paper-based; 173 computer-based).

Long Island University, C.W. Post Campus, School of Education, Department of Educational Leadership and Administration, Brookville, NY 11548-1300. Offers school administration and supervision (MS Ed); school building leader (AC); school district business leader (AC); school district leader (AC). Part-time and evening/weekend programs available. *Degree requirements:* For master's, comprehensive exam or research project, internship; for AC, internship. *Entrance requirements:* For master's, minimum GPA of 3.0, 3 years of teaching experience. Electronic applications accepted. *Faculty research:* Leadership administration, computers in decision making, curricular innovation and school business administration.

Long Island University, C.W. Post Campus, School of Education, Program in Interdisciplinary Educational Studies, Brookville, NY 11548-1300. Offers educational leadership (Ed D); teaching and learning (Ed D). Part-time programs available. *Degree requirements:* For doctorate, comprehensive exam, thesis/dissertation, portfolio. *Entrance requirements:* For doctorate, master's degree in education or a related field, 3 letters of recommendation, writing sample, curriculum vitae/resume. Additional exam requirements/recommendations for international students: Required—TOEFL (minimum score 600 paper-based).

Long Island University, Rockland Graduate Campus, Graduate School, Program in Educational Leadership, Orangeburg, NY 10962. Offers MS Ed, Advanced Certificate. Part-time programs available. *Faculty:* 2 full-time (0 women), 5 part-time/adjunct (1 woman). *Students:* 6 full-time (3 women), 30 part-time (19 women). In 2009, 11 master's awarded. *Application deadline:* Applications are processed on a rolling basis. Application fee: $30. *Expenses:* Tuition: Part-time $930 per credit. Required fees: $200 per semester. *Financial support:* Applicants required to submit FAFSA. *Unit head:* Dr. Charles Murphy, Program Director, 845-359-7200 Ext. 5428, Fax: 845-359-7248, E-mail: charles.murphy@liu.edu. *Application contact:* Peter S. Reiner, Director of Admissions and Marketing, 845-359-7200, Fax: 845-359-7248, E-mail: peter.reiner@liu.edu.

Longwood University, Office of Graduate Studies, College of Education and Human Services, Farmville, VA 23909. Offers communication sciences and disorders (MS); community and college counseling (MS); curriculum and instruction specialist-elementary (MS), including mild disabilities, modern languages; curriculum and instruction specialist-secondary (MS), including English, mild disabilities, modern languages; educational leadership (MS); guidance and counseling (MS); literacy and culture (MS); school library media (MS). *Accreditation:* NCATE. Part-time and evening/weekend programs available. *Degree requirements:* For master's, comprehensive exam, thesis optional. *Entrance requirements:* For master's, GRE (communication sciences and disorders), minimum GPA of 2.75. Additional exam requirements/recommendations for international students: Required—TOEFL (minimum score 550 paper-based; 213 computer-based).

Loras College, Graduate Division, Program in Educational Leadership, Dubuque, IA 52004-0178. Offers MA. Part-time and evening/weekend programs available. *Degree requirements:* For master's, comprehensive exam, thesis optional. *Entrance requirements:* For master's, minimum cumulative undergraduate GPA of 3.0.

Louisiana State University and Agricultural and Mechanical College, Graduate School, College of Education, Department of Educational Theory, Policy and Practice, Baton Rouge, LA 70803. Offers counseling (M Ed, MA, Ed S); educational administration (M Ed, MA, PhD, Ed S); educational technology (MA); elementary education (M Ed); higher education (PhD); research methodology (PhD); secondary education (M Ed). *Accreditation:* ACA (one or more programs are accredited); NCATE. Part-time and evening/weekend programs available. *Faculty:* 38 full-time (24 women). *Students:* 174 full-time (139 women), 154 part-time (129 women); includes 74 minority (66 African Americans, 3 Asian Americans or Pacific Islanders, 5 Hispanic Americans), 9 international. Average age 32. 122 applicants, 60% accepted, 48 enrolled. In 2009, 124 master's, 13 doctorates, 11 other advanced degrees awarded. Terminal master's awarded for partial completion of doctoral program. *Degree requirements:* For doctorate, thesis/dissertation; for Ed S, thesis optional. *Entrance requirements:* For master's and doctorate, GRE General Test, minimum GPA of 3.0. Additional exam requirements/recommendations for international students: Required—TOEFL (minimum score 550 paper-based; 213 computer-based; 79 iBT) or IELTS (minimum score 6.5). *Application deadline:* For fall admission, 1/25 priority date for domestic students, 5/15 for international students; for spring admission, 10/15 for international students. Applications are processed on a rolling basis. Application fee: $50 ($70 for international students). Electronic applications accepted. *Financial support:* In 2009–10, 226 students received support, including 1 fellowship (averaging $31,711 per year), 27 research assistantships with full and partial tuition reimbursements available (averaging $10,143 per year), 35 teaching assistantships with full and partial tuition reimbursements available (averaging $12,555 per year); career-related internships or fieldwork, Federal Work-Study, institutionally sponsored loans, health care benefits, and unspecified assistantships also available. Support available to part-time students. Financial award applicants required to submit FAFSA. *Faculty research:* Literary, curriculum studies, science education, K-12 leadership, higher education. Total annual research expenditures: $1.8 million. *Unit head:* Dr. Earl Cheek, Chair, 225-578-6867, Fax: 225-578-9135, E-mail: echeek@lsu.edu. *Application contact:* Dr., Graduate Coordinator, 225-578-2280, Fax: 225-578-9135.

Louisiana State University in Shreveport, College of Education and Human Development, Program in Education, Shreveport, LA 71115-2399. Offers education (M Ed); education curriculum and instruction (M Ed); educational leadership (M Ed). Part-time programs available. *Students:* 3 full-time (all women), 43 part-time (32 women); includes 4 minority (all African Americans), 2 international. Average age 35. 22 applicants, 95% accepted, 10 enrolled. In 2009, 26 master's awarded. *Degree requirements:* For master's, orally presented project, 200-hour internship (educational leadership). *Entrance requirements:* For master's, GRE, minimum GPA of 2.5; teacher certification; recommendations and interview (for educational leadership). Additional exam requirements/recommendations for international students: Required—TOEFL (minimum score 500 paper-based; 173 computer-based; 61 iBT). *Application deadline:* For fall admission, 6/30 for domestic and international students; for spring admission, 11/30 for domestic and international students. Applications are processed on a rolling basis. Application fee: $10 ($20 for international students). *Financial support:* In 2009–10, 4 research assistantships with partial tuition reimbursements (averaging $10,000 per year) were awarded. *Unit head:* Dr. Julie Bergeron, Coordinator of Graduate Programs in Education, 318-797-5033, Fax: 318-798-4144, E-mail: julie.bergeron@lsus.edu. *Application contact:* Dr. Julie Bergeron, Coordinator of Graduate Programs in Education, 318-797-5033, Fax: 318-798-4144, E-mail: julie.bergeron@lsus.edu.

Louisiana Tech University, Graduate School, College of Education, Department of Curriculum, Instruction and Leadership, Ruston, LA 71272. Offers curriculum and instruction (MS, Ed D); educational leadership (Ed D); secondary education (M Ed), including business education, English education, foreign language education, health and physical education, mathematics education, science education, social studies education, speech education. *Accreditation:* NCATE. Part-time programs available. *Degree requirements:* For doctorate, thesis/dissertation. *Entrance requirements:* For master's and doctorate, GRE General Test.

Loyola Marymount University, School of Education, Department of Educational Leadership, Doctorate in Educational Leadership in Social Justice Program, Los Angeles, CA 90045. Offers Ed D. Part-time programs available. *Faculty:* 7 full-time (5 women), 8 part-time/adjunct (5 women). *Students:* 15 full-time (10 women), 39 part-time (23 women); includes 26 minority (6 African Americans, 20 Hispanic Americans), 3 international. Average age 39. 36 applicants, 64% accepted, 15 enrolled. In 2009, 11 doctorates awarded. *Degree requirements:* For doctorate, thesis/dissertation. *Entrance requirements:* For doctorate, GRE, interview, resume, 3 letters of recommendation. Additional exam requirements/recommendations for international students: Required—TOEFL (minimum score 600 paper-based; 250 computer-based; 100 iBT). *Application deadline:* For fall admission, 1/25 for domestic students. Application fee: $50. Electronic applications accepted. *Financial support:* In 2009–10, 47 students received support, including 1 research assistantship (averaging $1,400 per year); institutionally sponsored loans, scholarships/grants, and unspecified assistantships also available. Support available to part-time students. Financial award application deadline: 1/25; financial award applicants required to submit FAFSA. *Unit head:* Fr. Michael Caruso, Chair, 310-338-7862, Fax: 310-338-1976, E-mail: mcaruso@lmu.edu. *Application contact:* Chake Kouyoumjian, Associate Dean of Graduate Studies, 310-338-2721, E-mail: ckouyoum@lmu.edu.

Loyola Marymount University, School of Education, Department of Educational Leadership, Program in Catholic School Administration, Los Angeles, CA 90045. Offers MA. Part-time programs available. *Faculty:* 7 full-time (5 women), 8 part-time/adjunct (5 women). *Students:* 25 full-time (21 women), 2 part-time (both women); includes 16 minority (1 Asian American or Pacific Islander, 15 Hispanic Americans), 1 international. Average age 38. 2 applicants, 100% accepted, 2 enrolled. In 2009, 28 master's awarded. *Degree requirements:* For master's, comprehensive exam. *Entrance requirements:* For master's, CBEST, CSET, 2 letters of recommendation, full-time employment in the Archdiocese of Los Angeles. Additional exam requirements/recommendations for international students: Required—TOEFL (minimum score 600 paper-based; 250 computer-based; 100 iBT). *Application deadline:* For fall admission, 6/15 for domestic students; for spring admission, 11/15 for domestic students. Application fee: $50. Electronic applications accepted. *Financial support:* In 2009–10, 27 students received support. Institutionally sponsored loans, scholarships/grants, and unspecified assistantships available. Financial award application deadline: 6/15; financial award applicants required to submit FAFSA. *Unit head:* Fr. Michael Caruso, Chair, 310-338-7862, E-mail: mcaruso@lmu.edu. *Application contact:* Chake H. Kouyoumjian, Associate Dean, Graduate Studies, 310-338-2721, Fax: 310-338-6086, E-mail: ckouyoum@lmu.edu.

Loyola Marymount University, School of Education, Department of Educational Leadership, Program in School Administration, Los Angeles, CA 90045. Offers MA. Part-time and evening/weekend programs available. *Faculty:* 7 full-time (5 women), 8 part-time/adjunct (5 women). *Students:* 16 full-time (10 women), 3 part-time (2 women); includes 12 minority (2 African Americans, 1 American Indian/Alaska Native, 2 Asian Americans or Pacific Islanders, 7 Hispanic Americans), 2 international. Average age 31. 20 applicants, 85% accepted, 12 enrolled. In 2009, 12 master's awarded. *Degree requirements:* For master's, comprehensive exam. *Entrance requirements:* For master's, CBEST, 2 letters of recommendation. Additional exam requirements/recommendations for international students: Required—TOEFL (minimum score 600 paper-based; 250 computer-based; 100 iBT). *Application deadline:* For fall admission, 5/1 for domestic students; for spring admission, 11/1 for domestic students. Application fee: $50. Electronic applications accepted. *Financial support:* In 2009–10, 18 students received support. Scholarships/grants and unspecified assistantships available. Support available to part-time students. Financial award application deadline: 5/1; financial award applicants required to submit FAFSA. *Unit head:* Fr. Michael Caruso, Chair, 310-338-7862, E-mail: mcaruso@lmu.edu. *Application contact:* Chake H. Kouyoumjian, Associate Dean of Graduate Studies, 310-338-2721, Fax: 310-338-6086, E-mail: ckouyoum@lmu.edu.

Loyola University Chicago, School of Education, Program in Administration and Supervision, Chicago, IL 60660. Offers M Ed, Ed D, Certificate. Part-time and evening/weekend programs available. *Faculty:* 3 full-time (all women), 4 part-time/adjunct (2 women). *Students:* 165. Average age 35. 34 applicants, 59% accepted, 14 enrolled. In 2009, 27 master's, 14 doctorates awarded. *Degree requirements:* For master's, comprehensive exam (MEd), thesis (MA); for doctorate, comprehensive exam, thesis/dissertation. *Entrance requirements:* For master's,

Educational Leadership and Administration

Loyola University Chicago (continued)
minimum GPA of 3.0, letters of recommendation, resume, transcripts; for doctorate, GRE General Test, MAT, interview, minimum GPA of 3.0, letters of recommendation, resume. Additional exam requirements/recommendations for international students: Required—TOEFL (minimum score 550 paper-based; 213 computer-based; 79 iBT). *Application deadline:* For fall admission, 7/1 for domestic and international students; for spring admission, 11/1 for domestic and international students. Applications are processed on a rolling basis. Application fee: $50. Electronic applications accepted. *Expenses:* Tuition: Full-time $14,220; part-time $790 per credit hour. Required fees: $60 per semester hour. Tuition and fees vary according to program. *Financial support:* Research assistantships with full tuition reimbursements, teaching assistantships, career-related internships or fieldwork and institutionally sponsored loans available. Financial award application deadline: 2/15; financial award applicants required to submit FAFSA. *Faculty research:* Leadership, school law, school administration, supervision, ethics. *Unit head:* Dr. Janis Fine, Director, 312-915-7022, Fax: 312-915-6980, E-mail: jfine@luc.edu. *Application contact:* Marie Rosin-Dittmar, Information Contact, 312-915-6800, E-mail: schleduc@luc.edu.

Loyola University Chicago, School of Education, Program in Instructional Leadership, Chicago, IL 60660. Offers M Ed. Part-time and evening/weekend programs available. *Faculty:* 7 full-time (6 women), 2 part-time/adjunct (1 woman). *Students:* 34. Average age 38. 15 applicants, 93% accepted, 11 enrolled. In 2009, 13 master's awarded. *Degree requirements:* For master's, comprehensive exam. *Entrance requirements:* For master's, minimum GPA of 3.0, letters of recommendation, resume. Additional exam requirements/recommendations for international students: Required—TOEFL (minimum score 550 paper-based; 213 computer-based; 79 iBT). *Application deadline:* For fall admission, 7/1 for domestic students; for spring admission, 11/1 for domestic students. Applications are processed on a rolling basis. Application fee: $50. Electronic applications accepted. *Expenses:* Tuition: Full-time $14,220; part-time $790 per credit hour. Required fees: $60 per semester hour. Tuition and fees vary according to program. *Financial support:* Application deadline: 5/1. *Faculty research:* Staff development, school leadership, school change. *Unit head:* Dr. Janis Fine, Director, 312-915-7022, Fax: 312-915-6980, E-mail: jfine@luc.edu. *Application contact:* Marie Rosin-Dittmar, Information Contact, 312-915-6800, E-mail: schleduc@luc.edu.

Loyola University Maryland, Graduate Programs, College of Arts and Sciences, Department of Education, Program in Administration and Supervision, Baltimore, MD 21210-2699. Offers M Ed, MA, CAS. Part-time and evening/weekend programs available. *Entrance requirements:* For master's and CAS, GRE General Test, GRE Subject Test (recommended). Additional exam requirements/recommendations for international students: Required—TOEFL (minimum score 550 paper-based; 213 computer-based).

Lynchburg College, Graduate Studies, School of Education and Human Development, Lynchburg, VA 24501-3199. Offers community counseling (M Ed); counselor education (M Ed), including community counseling; curriculum and instruction (M Ed); educational leadership (M Ed); English education (M Ed); reading (M Ed); school counseling (M Ed); science education (M Ed); special education (M Ed), including autism spectrum disorder, early childhood special education, mental retardation, teaching children with learning disabilities, teaching the emotionally disturbed. Part-time and evening/weekend programs available. *Degree requirements:* For master's, comprehensive exam. *Entrance requirements:* For master's, GRE, minimum undergraduate GPA of 3.0. Additional exam requirements/recommendations for international students: Required—TOEFL. *Expenses:* Tuition: Full-time $7020; part-time $390 per credit hour.

Lynn University, Donald and Helen Ross College of Education, Boca Raton, FL 33431-5598. Offers educational leadership (M Ed, PhD); exceptional student education (M Ed); teacher preparation (PhD). Part-time and evening/weekend programs available. *Degree requirements:* For master's, thesis (for some programs); for doctorate, thesis/dissertation, qualifying paper. *Entrance requirements:* For master's, GRE, minimum undergraduate GPA of 3.0, resume, 2 letters of recommendation; for doctorate, GRE or GMAT, minimum GPA of 3.25, resume, 2 letters of recommendation. Additional exam requirements/recommendations for international students: Required—TOEFL (minimum score 550 paper-based; 213 computer-based). *Application deadline:* Applications are processed on a rolling basis. Application fee: $50. Electronic applications accepted. *Expenses:* Tuition: Part-time $580 per credit. One-time fee: $200 part-time. Part-time tuition and fees vary according to degree level. *Financial support:* Career-related internships or fieldwork, Federal Work-Study, institutionally sponsored loans, scholarships/grants, tuition waivers (partial), and unspecified assistantships available. Support available to part-time students. Financial award application deadline: 8/1; financial award applicants required to submit FAFSA. *Faculty research:* Non-traditional education, innovative curricula, multicultural education, simulation games. *Application contact:* Dr. Larissa Baia, Assistant Director of Graduate Admissions, 561-237-7916, Fax: 561-237-7100, E-mail: lbaia@lynn.edu.

Madonna University, Programs in Education, Livonia, MI 48150-1173. Offers Catholic school leadership (MSA); educational leadership (MSA); learning disabilities (MAT); literacy education (MAT); teaching and learning (MAT). *Accreditation:* NCATE. Part-time and evening/weekend programs available. *Degree requirements:* For master's, thesis or alternative. Electronic applications accepted.

Manhattan College, Graduate Division, School of Education, Program in School Building Leadership, Riverdale, NY 10471. Offers MS Ed, Diploma. Part-time and evening/weekend programs available. *Degree requirements:* For master's, thesis, internship. *Entrance requirements:* For master's, minimum GPA of 3.0, 3 years teaching, professional recommendation; for Diploma, minimum GPA of 3.0. Additional exam requirements/recommendations for international students: Required—TOEFL. *Faculty research:* Distance learning and teacher efficacy, leadership and student achievement, professional development and student achievement, leadership development, professional development for teachers.

Manhattanville College, Graduate Programs, School of Education, Program in Educational Leadership, Purchase, NY 10577-2132. Offers MPS. Part-time and evening/weekend programs available. *Students:* 1 (woman) full-time, 6 part-time (5 women); includes 1 minority (African American). In 2009, 3 master's awarded. *Entrance requirements:* For master's, minimum undergraduate GPA of 3.0, 2 letters of recommendation. Additional exam requirements/recommendations for international students: Required—TOEFL. *Application deadline:* Applications are processed on a rolling basis. Application fee: $70. Electronic applications accepted. *Financial support:* Career-related internships or fieldwork, Federal Work-Study, institutionally sponsored loans, and unspecified assistantships available. Financial award application deadline: 3/1; financial award applicants required to submit FAFSA. *Unit head:* Dr. Shelley Wepner, Dean, 914-323-5192, Fax: 914-694-2386, E-mail: wepners@mville.edu. *Application contact:* Jeanine Pardey-Levine, Director of Admissions, 914-323-3208, Fax: 914-694-1732, E-mail: edschool@mville.edu.

Marian University, School of Education, Fond du Lac, WI 54935-4699. Offers educational leadership (MAE, PhD); teacher development (MAE). *Accreditation:* NCATE. Part-time programs available. *Faculty:* 16 full-time (8 women), 52 part-time/adjunct (37 women). *Students:* 31 full-time (19 women), 618 part-time (387 women); includes 35 minority (13 African Americans, 4 American Indian/Alaska Native, 8 Asian Americans or Pacific Islanders, 10 Hispanic Americans), 2 international. Average age 36. 105 applicants, 80% accepted, 84 enrolled. In 2009, 290 master's, 2 doctorates awarded. *Degree requirements:* For master's, exam, field-based experience project, portfolio; for doctorate, comprehensive exam, thesis/dissertation, field-based experience. *Entrance requirements:* For master's, minimum GPA of 3.0, BA in education or related field, teaching license; for doctorate, GRE, MAT, resume, 2 writing samples, interview. *Application deadline:* Applications are processed on a rolling basis. Application fee: $50. *Expenses:* Tuition: Part-time $380 per credit hour. Part-time tuition and fees vary according to course level and program. *Financial support:* In 2009–10, 200 students received support. Federal Work-Study and institutionally sponsored loans available. Support available to part-time students. Financial award application deadline: 3/1; financial award applicants required to submit FAFSA. *Faculty research:* At-risk youth, multicultural issues, values in education, teaching/learning strategies. *Unit head:* Sue Stoddart, Dean, 920-923-8099, Fax: 920-923-7663, E-mail: sstoddart@marianuniversity.edu. *Application contact:* Robert Bohnsack, Graduate Education Admissions, 920-923-8100, Fax: 920-923-7154, E-mail: bbohnsack@marianuniversity.edu.

Marshall University, Academic Affairs Division, Graduate School of Education and Professional Development, Program in Leadership Studies, Huntington, WV 25755. Offers MA, Ed D, Ed S. Part-time and evening/weekend programs available. *Faculty:* 10 full-time (4 women), 6 part-time/adjunct (5 women). *Students:* 34 full-time (22 women), 215 part-time (153 women); includes 13 minority (9 African Americans, 3 Asian Americans or Pacific Islanders, 1 Hispanic American), 1 international. Average age 39. In 2009, 35 master's, 12 doctorates, 1 other advanced degree awarded. *Degree requirements:* For master's, thesis optional, comprehensive or oral assessment. *Entrance requirements:* For master's, GRE General Test or MAT. Application fee: $40. *Financial support:* Career-related internships or fieldwork, Federal Work-Study, tuition waivers (full), and unspecified assistantships available. Support available to part-time students. Financial award applicants required to submit FAFSA. *Unit head:* Dr. Michael Cunningham, Program Director, 800-642-9842 Ext. 61912, E-mail: mcunningham@marshall.edu. *Application contact:* Information Contact, 304-746-1900, Fax: 304-746-1902, E-mail: services@marshall.edu.

Martin Luther College, Graduate Studies, New Ulm, MN 56073. Offers instruction (MS Ed); leadership (MS Ed); special education (MS Ed). Part-time programs available. Postbaccalaureate distance learning degree programs offered. *Degree requirements:* For master's, capstone project or comprehensive exam. *Entrance requirements:* For master's, undergraduate degree in education from an accredited college or university, minimum undergraduate GPA of 3.0. Electronic applications accepted.

Marygrove College, Graduate Division, Program in Educational Leadership, Detroit, MI 48221-2599. Offers MA. Part-time and evening/weekend programs available. *Degree requirements:* For master's, research project. *Entrance requirements:* For master's, MAT, interview, minimum undergraduate GPA of 3.0.

Marymount University, School of Education and Human Services, Program in Catholic School Leadership, Arlington, VA 22207-4299. Offers M Ed, Certificate. Part-time and evening/weekend programs available. Postbaccalaureate distance learning degree programs offered (minimal on-campus study). *Faculty:* 1 (woman) full-time, 2 part-time/adjunct (1 woman). *Students:* 35 part-time (32 women); includes 3 minority (all Hispanic Americans). Average age 45. 1 applicant, 100% accepted, 1 enrolled. In 2009, 22 master's, 1 Certificate awarded. *Degree requirements:* For master's, thesis or alternative. *Entrance requirements:* For master's, GRE General Test or MAT, 3 letters of recommendation, interview, resume; for Certificate, 3 letters of recommendation, interview, resume, essay. Additional exam requirements/recommendations for international students: Required—TOEFL (minimum score 600 paper-based; 250 computer-based; 96 iBT), IELTS (minimum score 6.5). Application fee: $40. Electronic applications accepted. *Expenses:* Tuition: Full-time $13,050; part-time $725 per credit hour. Required fees: $135; $7.50 per credit hour. *Financial support:* In 2009–10, 35 students received support; research assistantships with full tuition reimbursements available, career-related internships or fieldwork, Federal Work-Study, scholarships/grants, and unspecified assistantships available. Support available to part-time students. Financial award applicants required to submit FAFSA. *Unit head:* Sr. Patricia Earl, Coordinator, 703-284-1517, Fax: 703-284-1631, E-mail: patricia.earl@marymount.edu. *Application contact:* Francesca Reed, Director, Graduate Admissions, 703-284-5901, Fax: 703-527-3815, E-mail: grad.admissions@marymount.edu.

Maryville University of Saint Louis, School of Education, St. Louis, MO 63141-7299. Offers art education (MA Ed); early childhood education (MA Ed); educational leadership (Ed D); educational leadership: principal certification (MA Ed); elementary education (MA Ed); elementary education/English (MA Ed); elementary education/psychology (MA Ed); environmental education (MA Ed); gifted education (MA Ed); literacy specialist (MA Ed); middle grades education (MA Ed); secondary teaching and inquiry (MA Ed); teacher as leader (MA Ed). *Accreditation:* NASAD; NCATE. Part-time and evening/weekend programs available. *Students:* 25 full-time (18 women), 198 part-time (145 women); includes 33 minority (27 African Americans, 2 American Indian/Alaska Native, 1 Asian American or Pacific Islander, 3 Hispanic Americans). Average age 36. In 2009, 61 master's, 45 doctorates awarded. *Degree requirements:* For master's, thesis, project. *Entrance requirements:* For master's and doctorate, minimum GPA of 3.0, 3 professional recommendations. Additional exam requirements/recommendations for international students: Required—TOEFL (minimum score 550 paper-based). *Application deadline:* Applications are processed on a rolling basis. Application fee: $40 ($60 for international students). Electronic applications accepted. *Expenses:* Tuition: Full-time $20,384; part-time $627.50 per credit hour. Required fees: $100 per semester. *Financial support:* Career-related internships or fieldwork, Federal Work-Study, tuition waivers (partial), and professional educator discounts available. Financial award application deadline: 3/1; financial award applicants required to submit FAFSA. *Faculty research:* Collaboration with public schools, pre-service program development, mathematics, diversity, literacy. *Unit head:* Dr. Sam Hausfather, Dean, 314-529-9466, Fax: 314-529-9921, E-mail: shausfather@maryville.edu. *Application contact:* Holly Stanwich, Graduate Admissions Coordinator, 314-529-9542, Fax: 314-529-9921, E-mail: teachered@maryville.edu.

Marywood University, Academic Affairs, Reap College of Education and Human Development, Department of Education, Program in Higher Education Administration, Scranton, PA 18509-1598. Offers MS. Part-time and evening/weekend programs available. *Students:* 3 full-time (2 women), 15 part-time (12 women); includes 2 minority (both Hispanic Americans). Average age 39. 6 applicants, 100% accepted. In 2009, 3 master's awarded. *Entrance requirements:* Additional exam requirements/recommendations for international students: Required—TOEFL (minimum score 550 paper-based; 213 computer-based; 79 iBT). *Application deadline:* For fall admission, 4/1 priority date for domestic students, 3/31 priority date for international students; for spring admission, 11/1 priority date for domestic students, 8/31 priority date for international students. Applications are processed on a rolling basis. Application fee: $30. Electronic applications accepted. *Expenses:* Tuition: Part-time $715 per credit. Required fees: $270 per semester. Tuition and fees vary according to degree level, campus/location and program. *Financial support:* Research assistantships with tuition reimbursements, career-related internships or fieldwork, scholarships/grants, and unspecified assistantships available. Support available to part-time students. Financial award application deadline: 6/30; financial award applicants required to submit FAFSA. *Faculty research:* Integrated thematic instruction. *Unit head:* Sr. Ann Jablonski, Chair, 570-348-6211 Ext. 2638, E-mail: jablonski@marywood.edu. *Application contact:* Tammy Manka, Assistant Director of Graduate Admissions, 570-340-6002, E-mail: tmanka@marywood.edu.

Marywood University, Academic Affairs, Reap College of Education and Human Development, Department of Education, Program in Instructional Leadership, Scranton, PA 18509-1598. Offers M Ed. *Students:* 1 full-time (0 women), 6 part-time (all women). Average age 33. In 2009, 2 master's awarded. *Entrance requirements:* For master's, For most updated info go to: http://www.marywood.edu/academics/gradcatalog/. *Application deadline:* For fall admission, 4/1 for domestic students, 3/31 for international students; for spring admission, 11/1 for domestic students, 8/31 for international students. Applications are processed on a rolling basis. Electronic applications accepted. *Expenses:* Tuition: Part-time $715 per credit. Required fees: $270 per semester. Tuition and fees vary according to degree level, campus/location and program. *Financial support:* Career-related internships or fieldwork, scholarships/grants, and unspecified assistantships available. Support available to part-time students. Financial award application deadline: 6/30. *Unit head:* Sr. Ann Jablonski, Chair, 570-348-6211 Ext. 2638, E-mail: jablonski@marywood.edu. *Application contact:* Tammy Manka, Assistant Director of Graduate Admissions, 570-340-6002, E-mail: tmanka@marywood.edu.

Marywood University, Academic Affairs, Reap College of Education and Human Development, Department of Education, Program in School Leadership, Scranton, PA 18509-1598. Offers MS. *Accreditation:* NCATE. *Students:* 9 part-time (6 women). Average age 36. In 2009, 3 master's awarded. *Entrance requirements:* Additional exam requirements/recommendations for international students: Required—TOEFL (minimum score 550 paper-based; 213 computer-based; 79 iBT). *Application deadline:* For fall admission, 4/1 priority date for domestic students, 3/31 priority date for international students; for spring admission, 11/1 priority date for domestic students, 8/31 priority date for international students. Applications are processed on a rolling basis. Application fee: $35. Electronic applications accepted. *Expenses:* Tuition: Part-time $715 per credit. Required fees: $270 per semester. Tuition and fees vary according to degree level, campus/location and program. *Financial support:* Career-related internships or fieldwork, scholarships/grants, and unspecified assistantships available. Support available to part-time students. Financial award application deadline: 6/30; financial award applicants required to submit FAFSA. *Faculty research:* School board leadership and development, site-based decision making, educational administration. *Application contact:* Tammy Manka, Assistant Director of Graduate Admissions, 866-279-9663, E-mail: tmanka@marywood.edu.

Marywood University, Academic Affairs, Reap College of Education and Human Development, Department of Human Development, Emphasis in Educational Administration, Scranton, PA 18509-1598. Offers PhD. *Students:* 15 part-time (11 women). Average age 41. In 2009, 1 doctorate awarded. *Entrance requirements:* Additional exam requirements/recommendations for international students: Required—TOEFL (minimum score 550 paper-based; 213 computer-based; 79 iBT). *Application deadline:* For fall admission, 1/30 priority date for domestic and international students. Application fee: $35. Electronic applications accepted. *Expenses:* Contact institution. *Financial support:* Career-related internships or fieldwork, scholarships/grants, and unspecified assistantships available. Support available to part-time students. Financial award application deadline: 6/30; financial award applicants required to submit FAFSA. *Unit head:* Dr. Brook Cannon, Director, 570-348-6211 Ext. 2324, E-mail: cannon@marywood.edu. *Application contact:* Tammy Manka, Assistant Director of Graduate Admissions, 866-279-9663, E-mail: tmanka@marywood.edu.

Marywood University, Academic Affairs, Reap College of Education and Human Development, Department of Human Development, Emphasis in Higher Education Administration, Scranton, PA 18509-1598. Offers PhD. *Students:* 1 full-time (0 women), 24 part-time (16 women), 1 international. Average age 37. In 2009, 2 doctorates awarded. *Entrance requirements:* Additional exam requirements/recommendations for international students: Required—TOEFL (minimum score 550 paper-based; 213 computer-based; 79 iBT). *Application deadline:* For fall admission, 1/30 for domestic and international students. Application fee: $35. Electronic applications accepted. *Expenses:* Contact institution. *Financial support:* Career-related internships or fieldwork, scholarships/grants, and unspecified assistantships available. Support available to part-time students. Financial award application deadline: 6/30; financial award applicants required to submit FAFSA. *Unit head:* Dr. Brook Cannon, Director, 570-348-6211 Ext. 2324, E-mail: cannon@marywood.edu. *Application contact:* Tammy Manka, Assistant Director of Graduate Admissions, 866-279-9663, E-mail: tmanka@marywood.edu.

Marywood University, Academic Affairs, Reap College of Education and Human Development, Department of Human Development, Emphasis in Instructional Leadership, Scranton, PA 18509-1598. Offers PhD. *Students:* 1 (woman) full-time, 23 part-time (20 women); includes 4 minority (2 African Americans, 2 Hispanic Americans). Average age 40. In 2009, 4 doctorates awarded. *Entrance requirements:* Additional exam requirements/recommendations for international students: Required—TOEFL (minimum score 550 paper-based; 213 computer-based; 79 iBT). *Application deadline:* For fall admission, 1/30 priority date for domestic and international students. Application fee: $35. Electronic applications accepted. *Expenses:* Contact institution. *Financial support:* Career-related internships or fieldwork, scholarships/grants, and unspecified assistantships available. Support available to part-time students. Financial award application deadline: 6/30; financial award applicants required to submit FAFSA. *Unit head:* Dr. Brook Cannon, Director, 570-348-6211 Ext. 2324, E-mail: cannon@marywood.edu. *Application contact:* Tammy Manka, Assistant Director of Graduate Admissions, 866-279-9663, E-mail: tmanka@marywood.edu.

Massachusetts College of Liberal Arts, Program in Education, North Adams, MA 01247-4100. Offers curriculum (M Ed); educational administration (M Ed); reading (M Ed); special education (M Ed). Part-time and evening/weekend programs available. *Degree requirements:* For master's, thesis. *Entrance requirements:* For master's, writing sample. *Faculty research:* Anxiety, methodology, mainstreaming.

McDaniel College, Graduate and Professional Studies, Program in Educational Administration, Westminster, MD 21157-4390. Offers MS. Part-time and evening/weekend programs available. *Degree requirements:* For master's, comprehensive exam (for some programs), thesis optional, portfolio. *Entrance requirements:* For master's, GRE General Test, MAT, or NTE/PRAXIS I. Additional exam requirements/recommendations for international students: Required—TOEFL (minimum score 213 computer-based). *Expenses:* Tuition: Part-time $325 per credit hour.

McGill University, Faculty of Graduate and Postdoctoral Studies, Faculty of Education, Department of Integrated Studies in Education, Montréal, QC H3A 2T5, Canada. Offers culture and values in education (MA, PhD); curriculum studies (MA); educational leadership (MA, Certificate); educational studies (PhD); integrated studies in education (M Ed); second language education (MA, PhD).

McKendree University, Graduate Programs, Master of Arts in Education Program, Lebanon, IL 62254-1299. Offers certification (MA Ed); educational administration and leadership (MA Ed); educational studies (MA Ed); higher education administrative services (MA Ed); music education (MA Ed); special education (MA Ed); teacher leadership (MA Ed); transition to teaching (MA Ed). *Accreditation:* NCATE. Part-time and evening/weekend programs available. Postbaccalaureate distance learning degree programs offered (no on-campus study). *Faculty:* 18 full-time (7 women), 56 part-time/adjunct (34 women). *Students:* 107 full-time (83 women), 445 part-time (325 women); includes 41 minority (32 African Americans, 3 Asian Americans or Pacific Islanders, 6 Hispanic Americans). Average age 35. 225 applicants, 77% accepted, 129 enrolled. In 2009, 200 master's awarded. *Entrance requirements:* For master's, official transcripts from institutions attended, minimum GPA of 3.0, resume, references. Additional exam requirements/recommendations for international students: Required—TOEFL. *Application deadline:* Applications are processed on a rolling basis. Application fee: $0. Electronic applications accepted. *Expenses:* Tuition: Full-time $6300; part-time $350 per credit hour. One-time fee: $125. *Financial support:* In 2009–10, 1 student received support. Application deadline: 6/30. *Unit head:* Dr. Joseph J. Cipfl, Interim Chair of the School of Education, 618-537-6462, Fax: 618-537-6417, E-mail: jjcipfl@mckendree.edu. *Application contact:* Sabrina Storner, Director of Graduate Admission, 618-537-6477, Fax: 618-537-6410, E-mail: skstorner@mckendree.edu.

McNeese State University, Doré School of Graduate Studies, Burton College of Education, Department of Educational Leadership and Instructional Technology, Program in Educational Leadership, Lake Charles, LA 70609. Offers educational leadership (M Ed); educational technology (Ed S). Evening/weekend programs available. *Faculty:* 5 full-time (0 women). *Students:* 11 full-time (10 women), 65 part-time (44 women); includes 16 minority (15 African Americans, 1 Hispanic American). In 2009, 22 master's, 2 Ed Ss awarded. *Degree requirements:* For Ed S, comprehensive exam. *Entrance requirements:* For master's, GRE, teaching certificate, 3 years full-time teaching experience; for Ed S, teaching certificate, 3 years of teaching experience, 1 year of administration or supervision experience, master's degree with 12 semester hours in graduate education. *Application deadline:* For fall admission, 5/15 priority date for domestic and international students; for spring admission, 10/15 priority date for domestic and international students. Applications are processed on a rolling basis. Application fee: $20 ($30 for international students). *Expenses:* Tuition, area resident: Full-time $2556. Tuition, state resident: full-time $2556. Required fees: $1031. Tuition and fees vary according to course load. *Financial support:* Fellowships available. Financial award application deadline: 5/1. *Unit head:* Dr. Sharon Van Metre, Head, 337-475-5423, Fax: 337-475-5402, E-mail: svanmetre@mcneese.edu. *Application contact:* Dr. George F. Mead, Interim Dean of Dore' School of Graduate Studies, 337-475-5396, Fax: 337-475-5397, E-mail: admissions@mcneese.edu.

Memorial University of Newfoundland, School of Graduate Studies, Faculty of Education, St. John's, NL A1C 5S7, Canada. Offers counseling psychology (M Ed); curriculum, teaching, and learning studies (M Ed); education (PhD); educational leadership studies (M Ed); information technology (M Ed); post-secondary studies (M Ed, Diploma), including health professional education (Diploma). Part-time programs available. *Degree requirements:* For master's, thesis optional, internship, paper folio, project; for doctorate, comprehensive exam, thesis/dissertation, thesis seminar, oral defense of thesis. *Entrance requirements:* For master's, undergraduate degree with at least 2nd class standing, 1-2 years work experience; for doctorate, minimum A average in graduate course work, MA in education, 2 years professional experience; for Diploma, 2nd class degree, 2 years of work experience with adult learners, appropriate academic qualifications and work experience in a health-related field. Electronic applications accepted. *Faculty research:* Critical thinking, literacy, cognitive studies and counseling, educational change, technology in instruction.

Mercer University, Graduate Studies, Cecil B. Day Campus, Tift College of Education (Atlanta), Macon, GA 31207-0003. Offers curriculum and instruction (PhD); early childhood education (M Ed, MAT); educational leadership (PhD, Ed S); middle grades education (M Ed, MAT); reading education (M Ed); secondary education (M Ed, MAT); teacher leadership (Ed S). *Accreditation:* NCATE. Part-time and evening/weekend programs available. *Faculty:* 27 full-time (14 women), 6 part-time/adjunct (3 women). *Students:* 302 full-time (251 women), 543 part-time (430 women); includes 334 minority (311 African Americans, 1 American Indian/Alaska Native, 21 Asian Americans or Pacific Islanders, 1 Hispanic American), 7 international. Average age 34. In 2009, 195 master's, 20 doctorates awarded. *Degree requirements:* For master's and Ed S, research project; for doctorate, thesis/dissertation. *Entrance requirements:* For master's, GRE or MAT, minimum undergraduate GPA of 2.75; for doctorate, GRE; for Ed S, GRE or MAT, minimum GPA of 3.25, 3 years of teaching experience. Additional exam requirements/recommendations for international students: Required—TOEFL. *Application deadline:* For fall admission, 8/1 for domestic and international students; for spring admission, 12/1 for domestic and international students. Applications are processed on a rolling basis. Application fee: $25. *Expenses:* Contact institution. *Financial support:* Federal Work-Study available. Support available to part-time students. Financial award application deadline: 5/1. *Faculty research:* Educational computing, content area reading, concept learning, importance of play for young children, multicultural literature. *Unit head:* Dr. Carl R. Martray, Dean, 478-301-5397, Fax: 478-301-2280, E-mail: martray_cr@mercer.edu. *Application contact:* Dr. Allison Gilmore, Associate Dean for Graduate Teacher Education, 678-547-6330, Fax: 678-547-6055, E-mail: gilmore_a@mercer.edu.

Mercer University, Graduate Studies, Macon Campus, Tift College of Education (Macon), Macon, GA 31207-0003. Offers collaborative education (M Ed); curriculum and instruction (PhD); educational leadership (PhD, Ed S). *Accreditation:* NCATE. Part-time and evening/weekend programs available. *Faculty:* 14 full-time (8 women), 2 part-time/adjunct (1 woman). *Students:* 85 full-time (78 women), 86 part-time (66 women); includes 51 minority (49 African Americans, 1 Asian American or Pacific Islander, 1 Hispanic American). Average age 33. In 2009, 57 master's, 12 doctorates, 6 other advanced degrees awarded. *Degree requirements:* For master's, research project report; for doctorate, thesis/dissertation. *Entrance requirements:* For master's, GRE or MAT, minimum GPA of 2.75; for doctorate, GRE. Additional exam requirements/recommendations for international students: Required—TOEFL. *Application deadline:* For fall admission, 8/1 for domestic students; for spring admission, 12/1 for domestic students. Applications are processed on a rolling basis. Application fee: $25. *Expenses:* Contact institution. *Financial support:* Federal Work-Study and institutionally sponsored loans available. Support available to part-time students. Financial award application deadline: 5/1. *Faculty research:* Teacher effectiveness, specific learning disabilities, inclusion. *Unit head:* Dr. Carl R. Martray, Dean, 478-301-5397, Fax: 478-301-2280, E-mail: martray_cr@mercer.edu. *Application contact:* Dr. Penny Elkins, Associate Dean, 678-547-6556, Fax: 678-547-6389, E-mail: elkins_pl@mercer.edu.

Mercy College, School of Education, Certificate Program in School Building Leadership, Dobbs Ferry, NY 10522-1189. Offers Advanced Certificate. Part-time and evening/weekend programs available. *Students:* 2 full-time (both women), 18 part-time (14 women); includes 8 minority (5 African Americans, 1 Asian American or Pacific Islander, 2 Hispanic Americans). Average age 41. 12 applicants, 67% accepted, 7 enrolled. In 2009, 5 Advanced Certificates awarded. *Entrance requirements:* Additional exam requirements/recommendations for international students: Required—TOEFL (minimum score 600 paper-based; 250 computer-based; 100 iBT). *Application deadline:* For fall admission, 8/1 for international students. Applications are processed on a rolling basis. Application fee: $40. Electronic applications accepted. *Expenses:* Tuition: Full-time $13,158; part-time $731 per credit. Required fees: $500. Tuition and fees vary according to degree level and program. *Financial support:* In 2009–10, 10 students received support. Career-related internships or fieldwork, Federal Work-Study, scholarships/grants, and unspecified assistantships available. Support available to part-time students. Financial award applicants required to submit FAFSA. *Faculty research:* School law, leadership, supervision. *Unit head:* Dr. Andrew Peiser, Chairperson, 914-674-7489, Fax: 914-674-7352, E-mail: apeiser@mercy.edu. *Application contact:* Mary Ellen Hoffman, Director, Graduate Education Programs, 914-674-7334, E-mail: mhoffman@mercy.edu.

Mercy College, School of Education, Master's Program in School Building Leadership, Dobbs Ferry, NY 10522-1189. Offers MS. Part-time and evening/weekend programs available. *Students:* 43 full-time (31 women), 199 part-time (149 women); includes 75 African Americans, 4 Asian Americans or Pacific Islanders, 53 Hispanic Americans, 1 international. Average age 38. 90 applicants, 80% accepted, 62 enrolled. In 2009, 137 master's awarded. *Entrance requirements:* For master's, minimum undergraduate GPA of 3.0; resume; interview with program director; initial or professional teacher certification; two years of paid teaching or specialty area experience. Additional exam requirements/recommendations for international students: Required—TOEFL (minimum score 600 paper-based; 250 computer-based; 100 iBT). *Application deadline:* For fall admission, 8/1 for international students. Applications are processed on a rolling basis. Application fee: $40. Electronic applications accepted. *Expenses:* Tuition: Full-time $13,158; part-time $731 per credit. Required fees: $500. Tuition and fees vary according to degree level and program. *Financial support:* In 2009–10, 104 students received support. Career-related internships or fieldwork, Federal Work-Study, scholarships/grants, and unspecified assistantships available. Support available to part-time students. Financial award applicants required to submit FAFSA. *Faculty research:* Proper school management, decisive and visionary leadership, school law. *Unit head:* Dr. Andrew Peiser, Interim Dean, 914-674-7489, Fax: 914-674-7352, E-mail: apeiser@mercy.edu. *Application contact:* Mary Ellen Hoffman, Interim Associate Dean, 914-674-7334, E-mail: mhoffman@mercy.edu.

Mercyhurst College, Graduate Program, Program in Special Education, Erie, PA 16546. Offers bilingual/bicultural special education (MS); educational leadership (Certificate); special education (MS). Part-time and evening/weekend programs available. *Degree requirements:* For master's, thesis optional. *Entrance requirements:* For master's, GRE General Test, MAT, or minimum GPA of 3.0, interview. Additional exam requirements/recommendations for international students: Required—TOEFL. Electronic applications accepted. *Faculty research:* College age learning disabled program, teacher preparation/collaboration, applied behavior analysis, special education policy issues.

Mesa State College, Center for Teacher Education, Grand Junction, CO 81501-3122. Offers educational leadership (MAEd); ESOL (MAEd). *Accreditation:* NCATE. Part-time and evening/weekend programs available. Postbaccalaureate distance learning degree programs offered (minimal on-campus study). *Faculty:* 6 full-time (3 women), 8 part-time/adjunct (3 women). *Students:* 1 (woman) full-time, 71 part-time (50 women); includes 3 Hispanic Americans. Average age 37. 11 applicants, 27% accepted, 3 enrolled. In 2009, 29 master's awarded. *Degree requirements:* For master's, capstone course. *Entrance requirements:* For master's,

Educational Leadership and Administration

Mesa State College (continued)

GRE, 2 professional letters of recommendation. Additional exam requirements/recommendations for international students: Required—TOEFL (minimum score 550 paper-based; 207 computer-based). *Application deadline:* For fall admission, 4/1 for domestic students; for spring admission, 3/31 for domestic students. Applications are processed on a rolling basis. Application fee: $50. Electronic applications accepted. *Expenses:* Tuition, state resident: full-time $5400; part-time $300 per credit hour. Tuition, nonresident: full-time $16,200; part-time $900 per credit hour. Required fees: $460; $25 per credit hour. Tuition and fees vary according to program. *Financial support:* Applicants required to submit FAFSA. *Unit head:* Valerie Dobbs, Director of Teacher Education, 970-248-1953, Fax: 970-248-1112, E-mail: vdobbs@mesastate.edu. *Application contact:* Mary Kienietz, Administrative Assistant, 970-248-1785, Fax: 970-248-1112, E-mail: mkieniet@mesastate.edu.

Miami University, Graduate School, School of Education and Allied Professions, Department of Educational Leadership, Oxford, OH 45056. Offers curriculum and teacher leadership (M Ed); educational administration (Ed D, PhD); school leadership (MS); student affairs in higher education (MS, PhD). *Accreditation:* NCATE. Part-time programs available. *Students:* 78 full-time (51 women), 77 part-time (53 women); includes 38 minority (30 African Americans, 1 American Indian/Alaska Native, 4 Asian Americans or Pacific Islanders, 3 Hispanic Americans), 4 international. *Entrance requirements:* For master's, MAT or GRE, minimum undergraduate GPA of 3.0 during previous 2 years or 2.75 overall; for doctorate, GRE, minimum GPA of 2.75 (undergraduate), 3.0 (graduate). Additional exam requirements/recommendations for international students: Required—TOEFL. Application fee: $50. *Expenses:* Tuition, state resident: full-time $11,280. Tuition, nonresident: full-time $24,912. Required fees: $516. *Financial support:* Fellowships with full tuition reimbursements, research assistantships with full tuition reimbursements, teaching assistantships with full tuition reimbursements, career-related internships or fieldwork, Federal Work-Study, health care benefits, tuition waivers (full), and unspecified assistantships available. Financial award application deadline: 3/1. *Unit head:* Dr. Kate Rousmaniere, Chair, 513-529-6843, Fax: 513-529-1729, E-mail: roumak@muohio.edu. *Application contact:* Dr. Denise Taliaferri Baszile, Director of Graduate Studies, 513-529-1798, E-mail: taliafda@muohio.edu.

Michigan State University, The Graduate School, College of Education, Department of Educational Administration, East Lansing, MI 48824. Offers higher, adult and lifelong education (MA, PhD); K–12 educational administration (MA, PhD, Ed S); student affairs administration (MA). Part-time programs available. *Faculty:* 20 full-time (9 women). *Students:* 158 full-time (95 women), 158 part-time (92 women); includes 59 minority (33 African Americans, 5 American Indian/Alaska Native, 11 Asian Americans or Pacific Islanders, 10 Hispanic Americans), 33 international. Average age 33. 274 applicants, 52% accepted. In 2009, 73 master's, 27 doctorates awarded. *Entrance requirements:* Additional exam requirements/recommendations for international students: Required—TOEFL. Electronic applications accepted. *Expenses:* Tuition, state resident: part-time $478.25 per credit hour. Tuition, nonresident: part-time $966.50 per credit hour. Part-time tuition and fees vary according to program. *Financial support:* In 2009–10, 51 research assistantships with tuition reimbursements (averaging $6,633 per year), 3 teaching assistantships with tuition reimbursements (averaging $6,967 per year) were awarded. Total annual research expenditures: $365,790. *Unit head:* Dr. Marilyn J. Amey, Chairperson, 517-432-1056, Fax: 517-884-1392, E-mail: amey@msu.edu. *Application contact:* Cathy Ogar, Graduate Secretary, 517-355-4537, Fax: 517-884-1392, E-mail: cogar@msu.edu.

Middle Tennessee State University, College of Graduate Studies, College of Education and Behavioral Science, Department of Educational Leadership, Program in Administration and Supervision, Murfreesboro, TN 37132. Offers M Ed, Ed S. Part-time and evening/weekend programs available. Postbaccalaureate distance learning degree programs offered. *Students:* 19 full-time (14 women), 246 part-time (190 women); includes 55 minority (50 African Americans, 1 American Indian/Alaska Native, 2 Asian Americans or Pacific Islanders, 2 Hispanic Americans). 95 applicants, 84% accepted, 80 enrolled. In 2009, 97 master's, 47 Ed Ss awarded. *Degree requirements:* For master's, comprehensive exam. *Entrance requirements:* For master's and Ed S, GRE, MAT or current teaching license. Additional exam requirements/recommendations for international students: Required—TOEFL (minimum score 525 paper-based; 195 computer-based; 71 iBT) or IELTS (minimum score 6). *Application deadline:* For fall admission, 6/1 for domestic and international students. Applications are processed on a rolling basis. Application fee: $25 ($30 for international students). Electronic applications accepted. *Expenses:* Tuition, state resident: full-time $4404. Tuition, nonresident: full-time $10,956. *Financial support:* Application deadline: 5/1. *Unit head:* Dr. James Huffman, Chair, 615-898-2855, Fax: 615-898-2859. *Application contact:* Dr. Michael Allen, Dean and Vice Provost for Research, 615-898-2840, Fax: 615-904-8020, E-mail: mallen@mtsu.edu.

Midwestern State University, Graduate Studies, College of Education, Program in Educational Leadership and Technology, Wichita Falls, TX 76308. Offers ME. Part-time and evening/weekend programs available. *Degree requirements:* For master's, comprehensive exam. *Entrance requirements:* For master's, GRE General Test or MAT. Additional exam requirements/recommendations for international students: Required—TOEFL (minimum score 550 paper-based; 213 computer-based). Electronic applications accepted. *Expenses:* Tuition, state resident: full-time $1620; part-time $90 per credit hour. Tuition, nonresident: full-time $2160; part-time $120 per credit hour. International tuition: $7506 full-time. Required fees: $3068.80; $145.60 per credit hour. $179 per semester.

Mills College, Graduate Studies, School of Education, Oakland, CA 94613-1000. Offers child life in hospitals (MA); early childhood education (MA); education (MA), including art education, curriculum and instruction, elementary education, English education, foreign language education, mathematics education, science education, secondary education, social studies education, teaching; educational leadership (MA, Ed D); infant mental health (MA). Part-time and evening/weekend programs available. *Faculty:* 11 full-time (9 women), 16 part-time/adjunct (14 women). *Students:* 138 full-time (119 women), 55 part-time (48 women); includes 71 minority (34 African Americans, 19 Asian Americans or Pacific Islanders, 18 Hispanic Americans), 3 international. Average age 34. 210 applicants, 82% accepted, 93 enrolled. In 2009, 54 master's, 15 doctorates awarded. Terminal master's awarded for partial completion of doctoral program. *Degree requirements:* For master's, comprehensive exam. *Entrance requirements:* For doctorate, GRE General Test. Additional exam requirements/recommendations for international students: Required—TOEFL. *Application deadline:* For fall admission, 2/1 for domestic and international students; for spring admission, 11/1 for domestic and international students. Applications are processed on a rolling basis. Application fee: $50. Electronic applications accepted. *Expenses:* Tuition: Full-time $26,326; part-time $6584 per course. Required fees: $896. One-time fee: $896 part-time. Tuition and fees vary according to program. *Financial support:* In 2009–10, 188 students received support, including 186 fellowships (averaging $6,499 per year), 28 teaching assistantships with partial tuition reimbursements available (averaging $3,187 per year); career-related internships or fieldwork and scholarships/grants also available. Support available to part-time students. Financial award application deadline: 2/1; financial award applicants required to submit FAFSA. *Faculty research:* Child development, gender and education, public policy, cross-cultural development, development of literacy. Total annual research expenditures: $1.2 million. *Unit head:* Joseph Kahne, Chairperson, 510-430-3190, Fax: 510-430-3314, E-mail: grad-studies@mills.edu. *Application contact:* Jessica King, Graduate Admission Specialist, 510-430-3305, Fax: 510-430-2159, E-mail: grad-studies@mills.edu.

Minnesota State University Mankato, College of Graduate Studies, College of Education, Department of Educational Leadership, Program in Experiential Education, Mankato, MN 56001. Offers MS. *Accreditation:* NCATE. Part-time and evening/weekend programs available. *Students:* 16 full-time (7 women), 24 part-time (9 women). *Degree requirements:* For master's, thesis or alternative. *Entrance requirements:* For master's, minimum GPA of 3.0 during previous 2 years. Additional exam requirements/recommendations for international students: Required—TOEFL. *Application deadline:* For fall admission, 7/1 priority date for domestic students; for spring admission, 11/1 for domestic students. Applications are processed on a rolling basis. Application fee: $40. Electronic applications accepted. *Expenses:* Tuition, state resident: full-time $5364. Tuition, nonresident: full-time $8314. *Financial support:* Research assistantships with full tuition reimbursements, teaching assistantships with full tuition reimbursements, career-related internships or fieldwork, Federal Work-Study, and unspecified assistantships available. Support available to part-time students. Financial award application deadline: 3/15; financial award applicants required to submit FAFSA. *Unit head:* Dr. Jasper Hunt, Graduate Coordinator, 507-389-1116. *Application contact:* 507-389-2321, E-mail: grad@mnsu.edu.

Minnesota State University Moorhead, Graduate Studies, College of Education and Human Services, Program in Educational Leadership, Moorhead, MN 56563-0002. Offers MS, Ed S. *Accreditation:* NCATE. Part-time programs available. *Degree requirements:* For master's, comprehensive exam, final oral exam, project or thesis. *Entrance requirements:* For master's, 2 letters of recommendation, minimum GPA of 3.0. Additional exam requirements/recommendations for international students: Required—TOEFL (minimum score 550 paper-based; 213 computer-based). Electronic applications accepted.

Mississippi College, Graduate School, School of Education, Department of Teacher Education and Leadership, Clinton, MS 39058. Offers art (M Ed); biological science (M Ed); business education (M Ed); computer science (M Ed); dyslexia therapy (M Ed); educational leadership (M Ed, Ed D, Ed S); elementary education (M Ed, Ed S); English (M Ed); higher education administration (MS); mathematics (M Ed); secondary education (M Ed); social studies (history) (M Ed); teaching arts (M Ed). Part-time programs available. Postbaccalaureate distance learning degree programs offered (no on-campus study). *Faculty:* 11 full-time (7 women), 13 part-time/adjunct (7 women). *Students:* 33 full-time (22 women), 282 part-time (240 women); includes 148 minority (146 African Americans, 2 American Indian/Alaska Native), 1 international. Average age 34. In 2009, 147 master's awarded. *Degree requirements:* For master's, comprehensive exam, thesis optional. *Entrance requirements:* For master's, NTE. Additional exam requirements/recommendations for international students: Recommended—IELTS. *Application deadline:* For fall admission, 8/15 priority date for domestic students. Applications are processed on a rolling basis. Application fee: $30. Electronic applications accepted. *Expenses:* Tuition: Part-time $452 per credit hour. Required fees: $101 per semester. Tuition and fees vary according to degree level, campus/location, program and student level. *Financial support:* Teaching assistantships, career-related internships or fieldwork, Federal Work-Study, scholarships/grants, and unspecified assistantships available. Support available to part-time students. Financial award applicants required to submit FAFSA. *Unit head:* Dr. Tom Williams, Chair, 601-925-3844, E-mail: twilliams@mc.edu. *Application contact:* Elnora Lewis, Secretary, 601-925-3225, Fax: 601-925-3889, E-mail: lewis09@mc.edu.

Mississippi College, Graduate School, School of Education, Program in Higher Education Administration, Clinton, MS 39058. Offers MS. Part-time programs available. Postbaccalaureate distance learning degree programs offered (no on-campus study). *Faculty:* 4 part-time/adjunct (1 woman). *Students:* 4 full-time (2 women), 26 part-time (21 women); includes 13 minority (all African Americans). Average age 30. In 2009, 4 master's awarded. *Degree requirements:* For master's, comprehensive exam, thesis optional. *Entrance requirements:* For master's, GRE or GMAT, minimum GPA of 3.0. Additional exam requirements/recommendations for international students: Recommended—IELTS. *Application deadline:* For fall admission, 8/15 priority date for domestic students. Application fee: $30. *Expenses:* Tuition: Part-time $452 per credit hour. Required fees: $101 per semester. Tuition and fees vary according to degree level, campus/location, program and student level. *Financial support:* Teaching assistantships, career-related internships or fieldwork, Federal Work-Study, and unspecified assistantships available. Support available to part-time students. Financial award application deadline: 4/1; financial award applicants required to submit FAFSA. *Unit head:* Dr. Debbie C. Norris, Graduate Dean, 601-925-3260, Fax: 601-925-3889, E-mail: dnorris@mc.edu. *Application contact:* Elnora Lewis, Secretary, 601-925-3225, Fax: 601-925-3889, E-mail: lewis09@mc.edu.

Mississippi State University, College of Education, Department of Leadership and Foundations, Mississippi State, MS 39762. Offers community college education (MAT); community college leadership (PhD); education (Ed S), including school administration; elementary, middle school, and secondary education administration (PhD); school administration (MS); workforce educational leadership (MS). *Faculty:* 9 full-time (3 women). *Students:* 64 full-time (36 women), 196 part-time (139 women); includes 146 minority (143 African Americans, 1 American Indian/Alaska Native, 2 Hispanic Americans), 1 international. Average age 39. 96 applicants, 68% accepted, 53 enrolled. In 2009, 29 master's, 37 doctorates, 17 other advanced degrees awarded. *Degree requirements:* For master's and Ed S, comprehensive exam, thesis; for doctorate, comprehensive exam, thesis/dissertation. *Entrance requirements:* For master's, GRE, minimum GPA of 2.75 in junior and senior courses; for doctorate and Ed S, GRE. Additional exam requirements/recommendations for international students: Required—TOEFL (minimum score 550 paper-based; 213 computer-based; 79 iBT); Recommended—IELTS (minimum score 6.5). *Application deadline:* For fall admission, 7/1 for domestic students, 5/1 for international students; for spring admission, 11/1 for domestic students, 9/1 for international students. Application fee: $40. *Expenses:* Tuition, state resident: full-time $2575.50; part-time $286.25 per credit hour. Tuition, nonresident: full-time $6510; part-time $723.50 per credit hour. Tuition and fees vary according to course load. *Financial support:* In 2009–10, 1 research assistantship (averaging $8,029 per year) was awarded; Federal Work-Study and institutionally sponsored loans also available. Financial award application deadline: 4/1; financial award applicants required to submit FAFSA. *Unit head:* Dr. Frankie K. Williams, Associate Professor/Head, 662-325-0974, Fax: 662-325-0975, E-mail: fwilliams@colled.msstate.edu. *Application contact:* Bonnie Hays, Office Manager, 662-325-0969, Fax: 662-325-0975, E-mail: bhays@colled.msstate.edu.

Missouri Baptist University, Graduate Programs, St. Louis, MO 63141-8660. Offers business administration (MBA); Christian ministries (MACM); counseling (MAC); education (MSE); education administration (MEA); educational leadership (MSE, Ed S); teaching (MAT).

Missouri State University, Graduate College, College of Education, Department of Counseling, Leadership, and Special Education, Program in Educational Administration, Springfield, MO 65897. Offers educational administration (MS Ed, Ed S); elementary education (MS Ed); elementary principal (Ed S); secondary education (MS Ed); secondary principal (Ed S); superintendent (Ed S). Part-time and evening/weekend programs available. *Students:* 12 full-time (10 women), 161 part-time (98 women); includes 3 minority (1 Asian American or Pacific Islander, 2 Hispanic Americans), 3 international. Average age 36. 25 applicants, 96% accepted, 21 enrolled. In 2009, 42 master's, 23 Ed Ss awarded. *Degree requirements:* For master's and Ed S, comprehensive exam, thesis or alternative. *Entrance requirements:* For master's, minimum GPA of 2.75; for Ed S, GRE General Test, MAT, minimum GPA of 2.75. Additional exam requirements/recommendations for international students: Required—TOEFL (minimum score 550 paper-based; 213 computer-based; 79 iBT). *Application deadline:* For fall admission, 7/20 priority date for domestic students, 5/1 for international students; for spring admission, 12/20 priority date for domestic students, 9/1 for international students. Applications are processed on a rolling basis. Application fee: $35 ($50 for international students). Electronic applications accepted. *Expenses:* Tuition, state resident: full-time $3852; part-time $214 per credit hour. Tuition, nonresident: full-time $7524; part-time $418 per credit hour. Required fees: $696; $172 per semester. Tuition and fees vary according to course level, course load, degree level and program. *Financial support:* Career-related internships or fieldwork, Federal Work-Study, institutionally sponsored loans, scholarships/grants, and unspecified assistantships available. Financial award application deadline: 3/31; financial award applicants required to submit FAFSA. *Unit head:* Gerald Moseman, Graduate Program Coordinator, 417-836-5490, Fax: 417-836-4918, E-mail: geraldmoseman@missouristate.edu. *Application contact:* Eric Eckert, Coordinator of Admissions and Recruitment, 417-836-5331, Fax: 417-836-6200, E-mail: ericeckert@missouristate.edu.

Monmouth University, Graduate School, School of Education, West Long Branch, NJ 07764-1898. Offers education (M Ed); initial certification (MAT), including elementary level, K-12, secondary level; learning disabilities-teacher consultant (Certificate); principal (MS Ed); principal/school administrator (MS Ed); reading specialist (MS Ed, Certificate); school counseling (MS Ed); special education (MS Ed), including autism, learning disabilities teacher consultant, teacher

of students with disabilities, teaching in inclusive settings; supervisor (Certificate); teacher of the handicapped (Certificate); teaching english to speakers of other languages (TESOL) (Certificate). *Accreditation:* NCATE. Part-time and evening/weekend programs available. *Faculty:* 20 full-time (13 women), 32 part-time/adjunct (22 women). *Students:* 182 full-time (146 women), 353 part-time (286 women); includes 40 minority (15 African Americans, 3 American Indian/Alaska Native, 5 Asian Americans or Pacific Islanders, 17 Hispanic Americans), 1 international. Average age 29. 361 applicants, 96% accepted, 176 enrolled. In 2009, 178 master's awarded. *Entrance requirements:* For master's, minimum GPA of 3.0 in major, 2.75 overall; 2 letters of recommendation (for some programs). Additional exam requirements/recommendations for international students: Required—TOEFL (minimum score 550 paper-based; 213 computer-based; 79 iBT), IELTS (minimum score 5), Michigan English Language Assessment Battery (minimum score 77), Cambridge A, B, C. *Application deadline:* For fall admission, 7/15 priority date for domestic students, 7/1 for international students; for spring admission, 11/15 priority date for domestic students, 11/1 for international students. Applications are processed on a rolling basis. Application fee: $50. Electronic applications accepted. *Expenses:* Tuition: Part-time $773 per credit. Required fees: $157 per semester. *Financial support:* In 2009–10, 326 students received support, including 211 fellowships (averaging $1,824 per year), 23 research assistantships (averaging $7,943 per year); career-related internships or fieldwork, scholarships/grants, and unspecified assistantships also available. Support available to part-time students. Financial award applicants required to submit FAFSA. *Faculty research:* Multicultural literacy, science and mathematics teaching strategies, teacher as reflective practitioner, children with disabilities, varied contexts of learning. *Unit head:* Dr. Terri Rothman, Associate Dean, 732-571-7507, Fax: 732-263-5277, E-mail: trothman@monmouth.edu. *Application contact:* Kevin Roane, Director, Office of Graduate Admission, 732-571-3452, Fax: 732-263-5123, E-mail: gradadm@monmouth.edu.

Montana State University, College of Graduate Studies, College of Education, Health, and Human Development, Department of Education, Bozeman, MT 59717. Offers adult and higher education (Ed D); curriculum and instruction (Ed D, Ed S); education (M Ed), including adult and higher education, curriculum and instruction, educational leadership, school counseling; educational leadership (Ed D, Ed S). Part-time programs available. Postbaccalaureate distance learning degree programs offered (minimal on-campus study). *Faculty:* 22 full-time (13 women), 18 part-time/adjunct (14 women). *Students:* 15 full-time (8 women), 210 part-time (126 women); includes 29 minority (27 American Indian/Alaska Native, 1 Asian American or Pacific Islander, 1 Hispanic American), 2 international. Average age 37. 52 applicants. In 2009, 62 master's, 9 doctorates awarded. *Degree requirements:* For master's, comprehensive exam; for doctorate, comprehensive exam, thesis/dissertation. *Entrance requirements:* For master's and doctorate, GRE General Test. Additional exam requirements/recommendations for international students: Required—TOEFL (minimum score 550 paper-based; 213 computer-based). *Application deadline:* For fall admission, 7/15 priority date for domestic students, 5/15 priority date for international students; for spring admission, 12/1 priority date for domestic students, 10/1 priority date for international students. Applications are processed on a rolling basis. Application fee: $30. Electronic applications accepted. *Expenses:* Tuition, state resident: full-time $5635; part-time $3492 per year. Tuition, nonresident: full-time $17,212; part-time $7865.10 per year. Required fees: $1441; $153.15 per credit. Tuition and fees vary according to course load and program. *Financial support:* In 2009–10, 45 students received support, including 5 teaching assistantships with tuition reimbursements available (averaging $9,000 per year); traineeships, tuition waivers (full and partial), and unspecified assistantships also available. Financial award application deadline: 3/1; financial award applicants required to submit FAFSA. *Faculty research:* Online teaching and learning, statistical strategies to course and student assessment, environmental education, copyright issues/web-based resources, multicultural education, curriculum design, preparation for North American teachers to be administrators, NCES data sets, relational trust in public school administration. Total annual research expenditures: $1.2 million. *Unit head:* Dr. Joanne Erickson, Interim Department Head, 406-994-6670, Fax: 406-994-3261, E-mail: jle@montana.edu. *Application contact:* Dr. Carl A. Fox, Vice Provost for Graduate Education, 406-994-4145, Fax: 406-994-7433, E-mail: gradstudy@montana.edu.

Montclair State University, The Graduate School, College of Education and Human Services, Department of Counseling, Human Development, and Educational Leadership, Montclair, NJ 07043-1624. Offers administration and supervision (MA), including administration and supervision, educator/trainer; advanced counseling (Certificate); counseling and guidance (MA), including addictions counseling, community counseling, student affairs; counselor education (PhD); principal (Certificate); school administrator (Certificate); school business administrator (Certificate); school counselor (Certificate); substance awareness coordinator (Certificate). *Accreditation:* NCATE. Part-time and evening/weekend programs available. *Faculty:* 17 full-time (12 women), 13 part-time/adjunct (7 women). *Students:* 161 full-time (126 women), 425 part-time (325 women). Average age 33. 269 applicants, 55% accepted, 125 enrolled. In 2009, 91 master's awarded. *Degree requirements:* For master's, comprehensive exam, thesis or alternative; for doctorate, comprehensive exam, thesis/dissertation. *Entrance requirements:* For master's, GRE General Test, interview, 2 letters of recommendation; for doctorate, GRE General Test, interview, 3 letters of recommendation. Additional exam requirements/recommendations for international students: Required—TOEFL (minimum score 83 computer-based), or IELTS. *Application deadline:* For fall admission, 6/1 for international students; for spring admission, 10/1 for international students. Applications are processed on a rolling basis. Application fee: $60. Electronic applications accepted. *Expenses:* Tuition, area resident: Part-time $486.74 per credit. Tuition, state resident: part-time $486.74 per credit. Tuition, nonresident: part-time $751.34 per credit. Tuition and fees vary according to degree level and program. *Financial support:* In 2009–10, 28 research assistantships with full tuition reimbursements (averaging $7,000 per year), 2 teaching assistantships (averaging $15,000 per year) were awarded; Federal Work-Study, scholarships/grants, and unspecified assistantships also available. Support available to part-time students. Financial award application deadline: 3/1; financial award applicants required to submit FAFSA. *Faculty research:* K-12 education, data collection. *Unit head:* Dr. Larry Burlew, Chairperson, 973-655-7611. *Application contact:* Amy Aiello, Director of Graduate Admissions and Operations, 973-655-5147, Fax: 973-655-7869, E-mail: graduate.school@montclair.edu.

Morehead State University, Graduate Programs, College of Education, Department of Foundational and Graduate Studies in Education, Morehead, KY 40351. Offers adult and higher education (MA, Ed S); certified professional counselor (Ed S); counseling P-12 (MA); curriculum and instruction (Ed S); educational technology (MA Ed); instructional leadership (Ed S); school administration (MA); school counseling (Ed S); teacher leader business and marketing- content (MA Ed); teacher leader business and marketing- technology (MA Ed); teacher leader educational technology (MA Ed); teacher leader English (MA Ed); teacher leader gifted educ (MA Ed); teacher leader IECE—non-certification (MA Ed); teacher leader IECE certification (MA Ed); teacher leader interdisciplanary educaction P-5 (MA Ed); teacher leader middle grades 5-9 (MA Ed); teacher leader reading/writing—non-certification (MA Ed); teacher leader reading/writing certification (MA Ed); teacher leader school communication—non-certification (MA Ed); teacher leader school communication certification (MA Ed); teacher leader social studies (MA Ed); teacher leader special education (MA Ed). *Accreditation:* NCATE. Part-time and evening/weekend programs available. *Faculty:* 20 full-time (10 women), 7 part-time/adjunct (3 women). *Students:* 26 full-time (18 women), 371 part-time (295 women); includes 11 minority (9 African Americans, 1 American Indian/Alaska Native, 1 Hispanic American). Average age 35. 201 applicants, 73% accepted, 73 enrolled. In 2009, 105 master's, 5 other advanced degrees awarded. *Degree requirements:* For master's, thesis optional, oral and/or written comprehensive exams; for Ed S, thesis, oral exam. *Entrance requirements:* For master's, GRE General Test, minimum overall undergraduate GPA of 2.5; for Ed S, GRE General Test, interview, master's degree, minimum GPA of 3.5, work experience. Additional exam requirements/recommendations for international students: Required—TOEFL (minimum score 500 paper-based; 173 computer-based). *Application deadline:* For fall admission, 8/1 priority date for domestic and international students; for spring admission, 12/1 priority date for domestic and international students. Applications are processed on a rolling basis. Application fee: $30. Electronic applications accepted. *Expenses:* Tuition, state resident: full-time $6318; part-time $351 per credit hour. Tuition, nonresident: full-time $15,804; part-time $878 per credit hour. *Financial support:* In 2009–10, 2 research assistantships (averaging $10,000 per year) were awarded; career-related internships or fieldwork, Federal Work-Study, and unspecified assistantships also available. Financial award application deadline: 3/15; financial award applicants required to submit FAFSA. *Faculty research:* Character education, school accountability, computer applications for school administrators. *Unit head:* Dr. Cathy Gunn, Dean and Professor, 606-783-2040, Fax: 606-783-5029, E-mail: c.gunn@moreheadstate.edu. *Application contact:* Michelle Barber, Graduate Recruitment and Retention Assistant Director, 606-783-5127, Fax: 606-783-5061, E-mail: m.barber@moreheadstate.edu.

Morgan State University, School of Graduate Studies, School of Education and Urban Studies, Department of Advanced Studies, Leadership and Policy, Program in Educational Administration and Supervision, Baltimore, MD 21251. Offers MS. *Accreditation:* NCATE. Part-time and evening/weekend programs available. *Degree requirements:* For master's, comprehensive exam, thesis optional. *Entrance requirements:* For master's, GRE General Test or MAT. *Faculty research:* Multicultural education, cooperative learning, psychology of cognition.

Morgan State University, School of Graduate Studies, School of Education and Urban Studies, Department of Advanced Studies, Leadership and Policy, Program in Higher Education Administration, Baltimore, MD 21251. Offers PhD. *Degree requirements:* For doctorate, comprehensive exam, thesis/dissertation. *Entrance requirements:* For doctorate, GRE General Test or MAT, minimum GPA of 3.0.

Morgan State University, School of Graduate Studies, School of Education and Urban Studies, Department of Advanced Studies, Leadership and Policy, Program in Higher Education-Community College Leadership, Baltimore, MD 21251. Offers Ed D. *Accreditation:* NCATE. Part-time and evening/weekend programs available. *Degree requirements:* For doctorate, comprehensive exam, thesis/dissertation. *Entrance requirements:* For doctorate, GRE General Test or MAT. Additional exam requirements/recommendations for international students: Required—TOEFL (minimum score 550 paper-based; 213 computer-based). *Faculty research:* Multicultural education, cooperative learning, psychology of cognition.

Mount St. Mary's College, Graduate Division, Department of Education, Specialization in Administrative Services, Los Angeles, CA 90049-1599. Offers MS. Part-time and evening/weekend programs available. *Students:* 1 part-time (0 women); minority (Hispanic American). Average age 33. In 2009, 8 master's awarded. *Degree requirements:* For master's, thesis, research project. *Entrance requirements:* For master's, MAT, minimum GPA of 3.0. *Application deadline:* For fall admission, 7/15 priority date for domestic students; for spring admission, 11/15 priority date for domestic students. Application fee: $50 ($75 for international students). *Expenses:* Tuition: Part-time $730 per unit. Part-time tuition and fees vary according to degree level and program. *Financial support:* Institutionally sponsored loans and tuition waivers (full and partial) available. Support available to part-time students. Financial award application deadline: 3/15; financial award applicants required to submit FAFSA. *Application contact:* Director of Graduate Admission.

Murray State University, College of Education, Department of Educational Studies, Leadership and Counseling, Program in School Administration, Murray, KY 42071. Offers MA Ed, Ed S. *Accreditation:* NCATE. Part-time programs available. *Degree requirements:* For master's and Ed S, comprehensive exam. *Entrance requirements:* For degree, GRE General Test. Additional exam requirements/recommendations for international students: Required—TOEFL.

National-Louis University, College of Arts and Sciences, Division of Language and Academic Development, Chicago, IL 60603. Offers adult education (M Ed, Ed D, Certificate), including adult education administration (Certificate), adult education for professional development (M Ed), adult education leadership (M Ed), facilitating adult learning (Certificate), teaching and learning in community colleges (Certificate); adult literacy and developmental studies (M Ed, Certificate); adult, continuing, and literacy education (M Ed, Certificate). Part-time programs available. Postbaccalaureate distance learning degree programs offered (minimal on-campus study). *Degree requirements:* For doctorate, thesis/dissertation. *Entrance requirements:* For master's, GRE General Test, MAT, or Watson-Glaser Critical Thinking Appraisal, interview, minimum GPA of 3.0; for doctorate, GRE General Test, MAT, or Watson-Glaser Critical Thinking Appraisal, interview, master's degree, 3 years of experience in field, resume, writing sample; for Certificate, GRE, MAT, or Watson-Glaser Critical Thinking Appraisal, interview, minimum GPA of 3.0. *Expenses:* Tuition: Full-time $17,160; part-time $715 per semester hour. Tuition and fees vary according to course load, degree level, campus/location and program.

National-Louis University, National College of Education, Doctoral Programs in Education, Program in Educational Leadership, Chicago, IL 60603. Offers educational leadership/superintendent endorsement (Ed D). Part-time and evening/weekend programs available. *Degree requirements:* For doctorate, comprehensive exam, thesis/dissertation, internship. *Entrance requirements:* For doctorate, GRE General Test, minimum GPA of 3.25, interview, resume, writing sample. *Expenses:* Tuition: Full-time $17,160; part-time $715 per semester hour. Tuition and fees vary according to course load, degree level, campus/location and program.

National-Louis University, National College of Education, Program in Administration and Supervision, Chicago, IL 60603. Offers M Ed, CAS, Ed S. Part-time and evening/weekend programs available. *Degree requirements:* For other advanced degree, internship (Ed S). *Entrance requirements:* For master's, GRE or MAT, minimum GPA of 3.0, teaching certificate; for other advanced degree, GRE or MAT, master's degree, teaching certificate (CAS), writing sample, interview (Ed S). *Expenses:* Tuition: Full-time $17,160; part-time $715 per semester hour. Tuition and fees vary according to course load, degree level, campus/location and program.

National-Louis University, National College of Education, Program in Early Childhood Administration, Chicago, IL 60603. Offers M Ed, CAS. *Entrance requirements:* For master's, GRE or MAT, minimum GPA of 3.0, teaching certificate; for CAS, master's degree, teaching certificate. *Expenses:* Tuition: Full-time $17,160; part-time $715 per semester hour. Tuition and fees vary according to course load, degree level, campus/location and program.

National University, Academic Affairs, School of Education, Department of Educational Administration, La Jolla, CA 92037-1011. Offers applied school leadership (MS); educational administration (MS). Part-time and evening/weekend programs available. Postbaccalaureate distance learning degree programs offered (no on-campus study). *Faculty:* 15 full-time (4 women), 37 part-time/adjunct (15 women). *Students:* 176 full-time (165 women), 745 part-time (440 women); includes 389 minority (141 African Americans, 10 American Indian/Alaska Native, 38 Asian Americans or Pacific Islanders, 200 Hispanic Americans), 1 international. Average age 40. 510 applicants, 100% accepted, 433 enrolled. In 2009, 195 master's awarded. *Degree requirements:* For master's, thesis. *Entrance requirements:* For master's, interview, minimum GPA of 2.5. Additional exam requirements/recommendations for international students: Required—TOEFL (minimum score 550 paper-based; 213 computer-based; 79 iBT), IELTS (minimum score 6). *Application deadline:* Applications are processed on a rolling basis. Application fee: $60 ($65 for international students). Electronic applications accepted. *Expenses:* Tuition: Part-time $338 per quarter hour. *Financial support:* Career-related internships or fieldwork, institutionally sponsored loans, scholarships/grants, and tuition waivers (partial) available. Support available to part-time students. Financial award application deadline: 6/30; financial award applicants required to submit FAFSA. *Unit head:* Dr. Gary Hoban, Chair and Professor, 858-642-8320, Fax: 858-642-8724, E-mail: ghoban@nu.edu. *Application contact:* Dominick Giovanniello, Associate Regional Dean—San Diego, 800-NAT-UNIV, Fax: 858-541-7792, E-mail: dgiovann@nu.edu.

National University, Academic Affairs, School of Education, Department of Teacher Education, La Jolla, CA 92037-1011. Offers best practices (MA); cross-cultural teaching (M Ed); teacher leadership (MA); teaching (MA); teaching/learning in global society (MA). Part-time and evening/weekend programs available. Postbaccalaureate distance learning degree programs offered

Educational Leadership and Administration

National University (continued)

(no on-campus study). *Faculty:* 45 full-time (27 women), 293 part-time/adjunct (185 women). *Students:* 2,731 full-time (1,904 women), 4,477 part-time (3,008 women); includes 2,111 minority (481 African Americans, 35 American Indian/Alaska Native, 364 Asian Americans or Pacific Islanders, 1,231 Hispanic Americans), 10 international. Average age 35. 3,863 applicants, 100% accepted, 2916 enrolled. In 2009, 1,822 master's awarded. *Degree requirements:* For master's, thesis. *Entrance requirements:* For master's, interview, minimum GPA of 2.5. Additional exam requirements/recommendations for international students: Required—TOEFL (minimum score 550 paper-based; 213 computer-based; 79 iBT), IELTS (minimum score 6). *Application deadline:* Applications are processed on a rolling basis. Application fee: $60 ($65 for international students). Electronic applications accepted. *Expenses:* Tuition: Part-time $338 per quarter hour. *Financial support:* Career-related internships or fieldwork, institutionally sponsored loans, scholarships/grants, and tuition waivers (partial) available. Support available to part-time students. Financial award application deadline: 6/30; financial award applicants required to submit FAFSA. *Unit head:* Dr. Cynthia Schubert-Irastroza, Chair, 858-642-8320, Fax: 858-642-8724, E-mail: cshubert@nu.edu. *Application contact:* Dominick Giovanniello, Associate Regional Dean—San Diego, 800-NAT-UNIV, Fax: 858-541-7792, E-mail: dgiovann@nu.edu.

New England College, Program in Education, Henniker, NH 03242-3293. Offers higher education administration (MS); literacy and language arts (M Ed); meeting the needs of all learners/special education (M Ed); teacher leadership/school reform (M Ed). Part-time and evening/weekend programs available.

New Jersey City University, Graduate Studies and Continuing Education, Debra Cannon Partridge Wolfe College of Education, Department of Educational Leadership, Jersey City, NJ 07305-1597. Offers basics and urban studies (MA); bilingual/bicultural education and English as a second language (MA); educational administration and supervision (MA). Part-time and evening/weekend programs available. *Faculty:* 3. *Students:* 27 full-time (18 women), 187 part-time (115 women); includes 77 minority (18 African Americans, 6 Asian Americans or Pacific Islanders, 53 Hispanic Americans), 16 international. Average age 34. In 2009, 121 master's awarded. *Entrance requirements:* For master's, GRE General Test or MAT. Additional exam requirements/recommendations for international students: Required—TOEFL. *Application deadline:* For fall admission, 8/1 priority date for domestic students; for spring admission, 12/1 for domestic students. Applications are processed on a rolling basis. Application fee: $0. *Expenses:* Tuition, area resident: Part-time $456.75 per credit. Tuition, nonresident: part-time $842.55 per credit. Required fees: $65 per term. *Financial support:* Fellowships, teaching assistantships, career-related internships or fieldwork and unspecified assistantships available. *Unit head:* Dr. Susan Phifer, Chairperson, 201-200-3012, E-mail: sphifer@njcu.edu. *Application contact:* Dr. Susan Phifer, Chairperson, 201-200-3012, E-mail: sphifer@njcu.edu.

Newman Theological College, Religious Education Program, Edmonton, AB T6V 1H3, Canada. Offers Catholic school administration (CCSA); religious education (MRE, GDRE). Part-time programs available. Postbaccalaureate distance learning degree programs offered (no on-campus study). *Degree requirements:* For master's, thesis or alternative. *Entrance requirements:* For master's, 2 years of successful teaching experience, graduate diploma in religious education; for other advanced degree, bachelor's degree in education, teaching certificate. Additional exam requirements/recommendations for international students: Required—TOEFL (minimum score 560 paper-based; 220 computer-based). Tuition and fees charges are reported in Canadian dollars. *Expenses:* Tuition: Full-time $5150 Canadian dollars; part-time $515 Canadian dollars per course. Required fees: $40 Canadian dollars per semester. Tuition and fees vary according to course level, course load, campus/location and program.

Newman University, School of Education, Wichita, KS 67213-2097. Offers building leadership (MS Ed); curriculum and instruction (MS Ed), including accountability, English as a second language. *Accreditation:* NCATE. Part-time programs available. Postbaccalaureate distance learning degree programs offered (no on-campus study). *Faculty:* 3 full-time (0 women), 22 part-time/adjunct (all women). *Students:* 12 full-time (8 women), 329 part-time (263 women); includes 29 minority (5 African Americans, 2 American Indian/Alaska Native, 5 Asian Americans or Pacific Islanders, 17 Hispanic Americans), 4 international. Average age 37. 41 applicants, 76% accepted, 24 enrolled. In 2009, 57 master's awarded. *Degree requirements:* For master's, thesis optional. *Entrance requirements:* For master's, interview, minimum GPA of 3.0, writing sample, 3 letters of recommendation. Additional exam requirements/recommendations for international students: Required—TOEFL (minimum score 600 paper-based; 250 computer-based; 100 iBT). *Application deadline:* For fall admission, 8/15 priority date for domestic students, 7/15 priority date for international students; for spring admission, 1/10 priority date for domestic students, 11/15 priority date for international students. Applications are processed on a rolling basis. Application fee: $25 ($40 for international students). Electronic applications accepted. *Expenses:* Contact institution. *Financial support:* In 2009–10, 8 students received support. Federal Work-Study available. Financial award application deadline: 8/15; financial award applicants required to submit FAFSA. *Unit head:* Dr. Guy Glidden, Director, 316-942-4291 Ext. 2331, Fax: 316-942-4483, E-mail: gliddeng@newmanu.edu. *Application contact:* Linda Kay Sabala, Director of Graduate Admissions, 316-942-4291 Ext. 2230, Fax: 316-942-4483, E-mail: sabalal@newmanu.edu.

New Mexico Highlands University, Graduate Studies, School of Education, Las Vegas, NM 87701. Offers curriculum and instruction (MA); education (MA), including counseling, school counseling; educational leadership (MA); exercise and sport sciences (MA), including human performance and sport, sports administration, teacher education; guidance and counseling (MA), including professional counseling, rehabilitation counseling, school counseling; special education (MA), including). Part-time programs available. *Degree requirements:* For master's, comprehensive exam, thesis or alternative. *Entrance requirements:* For master's, minimum undergraduate GPA of 3.0. Additional exam requirements/recommendations for international students: Required—TOEFL (minimum score 540 paper-based; 207 computer-based). *Faculty research:* Teaching the United States Constitution, middle school curriculum, integrated computer applications for pre-service classroom teachers, adolescent literacy, narrative cognitive modes in NM multicultural setting.

New Mexico State University, Graduate School, College of Education, Department of Educational Management and Development, Las Cruces, NM 88003-8001. Offers educational administration (MA, PhD); educational management and development (Ed D). *Accreditation:* NCATE. Part-time and evening/weekend programs available. Postbaccalaureate distance learning degree programs offered (minimal on-campus study). *Faculty:* 11 full-time (5 women), 2 part-time/adjunct (1 woman). *Students:* 17 full-time (10 women), 130 part-time (95 women); includes 86 minority (2 African Americans, 13 American Indian/Alaska Native, 1 Asian American or Pacific Islander, 70 Hispanic Americans), 6 international. Average age 41. 127 applicants, 69% accepted, 48 enrolled. In 2009, 40 master's, 5 doctorates awarded. *Degree requirements:* For master's, comprehensive exam, internship; for doctorate, thesis/dissertation, internship. *Entrance requirements:* For master's and doctorate, minimum GPA of 3.0. Additional exam requirements/recommendations for international students: Required—TOEFL. *Application deadline:* Applications are processed on a rolling basis. Application fee: $30 ($50 for international students). Electronic applications accepted. *Expenses:* Tuition, state resident: full-time $4080; part-time $223 per credit. Tuition, nonresident: full-time $14,256; part-time $647 per credit. Required fees: $1278; $639 per semester. *Financial support:* In 2009–10, 1 research assistantship (averaging $8,100 per year), 5 teaching assistantships (averaging $6,350 per year) were awarded; fellowships with tuition reimbursements, career-related internships or fieldwork, Federal Work-Study, health care benefits, and unspecified assistantships also available. Financial award application deadline: 7/2. *Faculty research:* Leadership in K–12 and postsecondary education, management technology, community college administration, diversity in educational administration, program evaluation. *Unit head:* Dr. Gary Ivory, Head, 575-646-4050, Fax: 575-646-4767, E-mail: givory@nmsu.edu. *Application contact:* Herb Torres, College Instructor, 575-646-3495, Fax: 575-646-4767, E-mail: htorres@nmsu.edu.

New York Institute of Technology, Graduate Division, School of Education, Program in School Leadership and Technology, Old Westbury, NY 11568-8000. Offers Professional Diploma. Part-time and evening/weekend programs available. *Students:* 14 full-time (7 women), 14 part-time (9 women); includes 3 African Americans, 1 Asian American or Pacific Islander, 1 Hispanic American. Average age 36. 2 applicants, 50% accepted, 0 enrolled. In 2009, 2 Professional Diplomas awarded. *Degree requirements:* For Professional Diploma, internship. *Entrance requirements:* For degree, 3 years full-time teaching experience, permanent teacher certification in New York state. Additional exam requirements/recommendations for international students: Required—TOEFL (minimum score 550 paper-based; 213 computer-based). *Application deadline:* For fall admission, 7/1 for domestic students; for spring admission, 12/1 for domestic students. Application fee: $50. *Expenses:* Tuition: Part-time $825 per credit. *Financial support:* Career-related internships or fieldwork available. Financial award applicants required to submit FAFSA. *Unit head:* Dr. Jacqueline Kress, Dean, 516-686-7706, Fax: 516-686-7655. *Application contact:* Jacquelyn Nealon, Dean of Admissions and Financial Aid, 516-686-7925, Fax: 516-686-7613, E-mail: jnealon@nyit.edu.

New York University, Steinhardt School of Culture, Education, and Human Development, Department of Administration, Leadership, and Technology, Program in Educational Leadership, New York, NY 10012-1019. Offers educational leadership (Ed D, PhD); educational leadership, politics and advocacy (MA); school building leader (MA); school district leader (Advanced Certificate). Part-time and evening/weekend programs available. *Students:* 40 full-time (35 women), 76 part-time (54 women); includes 64 minority (30 African Americans, 10 Asian Americans or Pacific Islanders, 24 Hispanic Americans), 2 international. Average age 31. 165 applicants, 49% accepted, 39 enrolled. In 2009, 9 master's, 3 doctorates awarded. *Degree requirements:* For master's, thesis (for some programs); for doctorate, thesis/dissertation. *Entrance requirements:* For doctorate, GRE General Test, interview; for Advanced Certificate, master's degree. Additional exam requirements/recommendations for international students: Required—TOEFL. *Application deadline:* For fall admission, 12/15 priority date for domestic and international students; for spring admission, 11/1 for domestic and international students. Applications are processed on a rolling basis. Application fee: $75. Electronic applications accepted. *Expenses:* Tuition: Full-time $30,528; part-time $1272 per credit. Required fees: $2177. *Financial support:* Fellowships with full and partial tuition reimbursements, teaching assistantships with partial tuition reimbursements, career-related internships or fieldwork, Federal Work-Study, institutionally sponsored loans, scholarships/grants, tuition waivers (partial), and unspecified assistantships available. Support available to part-time students. Financial award application deadline: 2/1; financial award applicants required to submit FAFSA. *Faculty research:* Schools and communities; critical theories of race, class and gender; school restructuring; educational reform; social organization of schools, educational advocacy. *Unit head:* Dr. Colleen Larson, Director, 212-998-5520, Fax: 212-995-4041, E-mail: colleen.larson@nyu.edu. *Application contact:* 212-998-5030, Fax: 212-995-4328, E-mail: steinhardt.gradadmissions@nyu.edu.

New York University, Steinhardt School of Culture, Education, and Human Development, Department of Administration, Leadership, and Technology, Program in Higher Education, New York, NY 10012-1019. Offers higher and postsecondary education (PhD); higher education administration (Ed D); student personnel administration in higher education (MA). *Accreditation:* Teacher Education Accreditation Council. Part-time programs available. *Students:* 43 full-time (25 women), 93 part-time (73 women); includes 41 minority (18 African Americans, 10 Asian Americans or Pacific Islanders, 13 Hispanic Americans), 3 international. Average age 32. 199 applicants, 26% accepted, 41 enrolled. In 2009, 37 master's, 9 doctorates awarded. *Degree requirements:* For master's, thesis (for some programs); for doctorate, thesis/dissertation. *Entrance requirements:* For master's, interview, 2 letters of recommendation; for doctorate, GRE General Test, interview. Additional exam requirements/recommendations for international students: Required—TOEFL. *Application deadline:* For fall admission, 12/15 priority date for domestic and international students; for spring admission, 11/1 for domestic and international students. Applications are processed on a rolling basis. Application fee: $75. Electronic applications accepted. *Expenses:* Tuition: Full-time $30,528; part-time $1272 per credit. Required fees: $2177. *Financial support:* Fellowships with full and partial tuition reimbursements, career-related internships or fieldwork, Federal Work-Study, institutionally sponsored loans, scholarships/grants, tuition waivers (partial), and unspecified assistantships available. Support available to part-time students. Financial award application deadline: 2/1; financial award applicants required to submit FAFSA. *Faculty research:* Organizational theory and culture, systemic change, leadership development, access, equity and diversity. *Unit head:* Dr. Ann Marcus, Head, 212-998-4041, Fax: 212-995-4041. *Application contact:* 212-998-5030, Fax: 212-995-4328, E-mail: steinhardt.gradadmissions@nyu.edu.

New York University, Steinhardt School of Culture, Education, and Human Development, Department of Teaching and Learning, Program in Early Childhood and Childhood Education, New York, NY 10012-1019. Offers childhood education (MA); childhood education/special education: childhood (MA); early childhood education (MA); positions of leadership: early childhood and elementary education (PhD). *Accreditation:* Teacher Education Accreditation Council. Part-time programs available. *Students:* 40 full-time (all women), 19 part-time (all women); includes 20 minority (4 African Americans, 10 Asian Americans or Pacific Islanders, 6 Hispanic Americans), 2 international. Average age 25. 140 applicants, 72% accepted, 23 enrolled. In 2009, 47 master's awarded. *Degree requirements:* For master's, thesis (for some programs); for doctorate, thesis/dissertation. *Entrance requirements:* For doctorate, GRE General Test, interview. Additional exam requirements/recommendations for international students: Required—TOEFL. *Application deadline:* For fall admission, 12/15 priority date for domestic and international students; for spring admission, 11/1 for domestic and international students. Applications are processed on a rolling basis. Application fee: $75. Electronic applications accepted. *Expenses:* Tuition: Full-time $30,528; part-time $1272 per credit. Required fees: $2177. *Financial support:* Fellowships with full and partial tuition reimbursements, career-related internships or fieldwork, Federal Work-Study, institutionally sponsored loans, scholarships/grants, tuition waivers (partial), and unspecified assistantships available. Support available to part-time students. Financial award application deadline: 2/1; financial award applicants required to submit FAFSA. *Faculty research:* Teacher evaluation and beliefs about teaching, early literacy development, language arts, child development and education, cultural differences. *Application contact:* 212-998-5030, Fax: 212-995-4328, E-mail: steinhardt.gradadmissions@nyu.edu.

Niagara University, Graduate Division of Education, Concentration in Educational Leadership, Niagara Falls, Niagara University, NY 14109. Offers administration/supervision (Certificate); educational administration/supervision (MS Ed); educational leadership school district building (MS Ed); school business administration (Certificate); school business leadership (MS Ed); school district administration (Certificate). Part-time and evening/weekend programs available. *Entrance requirements:* For master's, GRE General Test or MAT; for Certificate, GRE General Test and GRE Subject Test or MAT. *Expenses:* Contact institution.

Nicholls State University, Graduate Studies, College of Education, Department of Teacher Education, Thibodaux, LA 70310. Offers administration and supervision (M Ed); counselor education (M Ed); curriculum and instruction (M Ed). *Accreditation:* NCATE. Part-time and evening/weekend programs available. *Degree requirements:* For master's, comprehensive exam, portfolio. *Entrance requirements:* For master's, GRE General Test, teaching license. Electronic applications accepted.

Norfolk State University, School of Graduate Studies, School of Education, Department of Secondary Education and School Leadership, Norfolk, VA 23504. Offers principal preparation (MA); secondary education (MAT); urban education/administration (MA), including teaching. *Accreditation:* NCATE. Part-time programs available. *Entrance requirements:* For master's, GRE General Test, PRAXIS I, minimum GPA of 3.0 in major, 2.5 overall. Additional exam requirements/recommendations for international students: Required—TOEFL (minimum score 500 paper-based).

North Carolina Agricultural and Technical State University, Graduate School, School of Education, Department of Human Development and Services, Greensboro, NC 27411. Offers adult education (MS); counselor education (MS); human resources-agency counseling (MS);

human resources-rehabilitation counseling (MS); leadership studies (PhD); school administration (MS). *Accreditation:* ACA. Part-time and evening/weekend programs available. *Degree requirements:* For master's, comprehensive exam, thesis, qualifying exam. *Entrance requirements:* For master's, GRE General Test, minimum GPA of 3.0.

North Carolina Central University, Division of Academic Affairs, School of Education, Program in School Administration, Durham, NC 27707-3129. Offers MSA.

North Carolina State University, Graduate School, College of Education, Department of Adult and Higher Education, Program in Higher Education Administration, Raleigh, NC 27695. Offers M Ed, MS, Ed D. *Degree requirements:* For master's, thesis (for some programs); for doctorate, thesis/dissertation. *Entrance requirements:* For master's and doctorate, GRE General Test or MAT, minimum GPA of 3.0 in major. Electronic applications accepted.

North Carolina State University, Graduate School, College of Education, Department of Educational Leadership and Policy Studies, Program in Educational Administration and Supervision, Raleigh, NC 27695. Offers Ed D. *Degree requirements:* For doctorate, thesis/ dissertation. *Entrance requirements:* For doctorate, GRE General Test or MAT, minimum GPA of 3.0, interview, sample of work. Electronic applications accepted.

North Carolina State University, Graduate School, College of Education, Department of Educational Leadership and Policy Studies, Program in School Administration, Raleigh, NC 27695. Offers MSA. *Degree requirements:* For master's, comprehensive exam, thesis optional. *Entrance requirements:* For master's, GRE General Test or MAT, minimum GPA of 3.0 in major, 3 years of teaching experience. Electronic applications accepted. *Faculty research:* State and national policy, educational evaluation, cohort preparation programs.

North Central College, Graduate Programs, Department of Education, Naperville, IL 60566-7063. Offers curriculum and instruction (MA Ed); leadership and administration (MA Ed). Part-time and evening/weekend programs available. *Degree requirements:* For master's, clinical practicum, project. *Entrance requirements:* For master's, interview. *Expenses:* Contact institution.

North Central College, Graduate Programs, Department of Leadership Studies, Naperville, IL 60566-7063. Offers MLD. Part-time and evening/weekend programs available. *Degree requirements:* For master's, project. *Entrance requirements:* For master's, interview. *Expenses:* Contact institution.

North Dakota State University, College of Graduate and Interdisciplinary Studies, College of Human Development and Education, School of Education, Program in Educational Leadership, Fargo, ND 58108. Offers M Ed, MS, Ed S. *Accreditation:* NCATE. Part-time and evening/ weekend programs available. Postbaccalaureate distance learning degree programs offered (minimal on-campus study). *Faculty:* 9. *Students:* 27 full-time (12 women), 40 part-time (20 women); includes 1 minority (American Indian/Alaska Native), 1 international. Average age 32. 17 applicants, 94% accepted. In 2009, 37 master's, 1 other advanced degree awarded. *Entrance requirements:* For degree, GRE General Test, master's degree, minimum GPA of 3.25. Additional exam requirements/recommendations for international students: Required—TOEFL. *Application deadline:* Applications are processed on a rolling basis. Application fee: $45 ($60 for international students). *Financial support:* In 2009–10, 1 teaching assistantship with full tuition reimbursement (averaging $800 per year) was awarded; career-related internships or fieldwork, Federal Work-Study, institutionally sponsored loans, and tuition waivers (full) also available. Financial award application deadline: 4/15. *Faculty research:* Organizational change and development, goal setting and systematic planning, beginning teacher assistance. *Unit head:* Dr. Thomas Hall, Chair, 701-231-5778, Fax: 701-231-7205, E-mail: thomas.e.hall@ndsu.edu. *Application contact:* Vicki Ihry, Administrative Assistant, 701-231-9732, Fax: 701-231-7205, E-mail: vicki.ihry@ndsu.edu.

Northeastern Illinois University, Graduate College, College of Education, Department of Educational Leadership and Development, Program in Educational Leadership, Chicago, IL 60625-4699. Offers educational administration and supervision (MA), including chief school business official, community college administration. Part-time and evening/weekend programs available. *Degree requirements:* For master's, comprehensive exam, practicum. *Entrance requirements:* For master's, 2 years of teaching experience, minimum GPA of 2.75. Additional exam requirements/recommendations for international students: Required—TOEFL (minimum score 550 paper-based; 213 computer-based; 80 iBT). Electronic applications accepted. *Faculty research:* Student motivation, leadership, teacher expectation, educational partnerships, community/school relations.

Northeastern State University, Graduate College, College of Education, Department of Educational Foundations and Leadership, Higher Education Administration and Services Program, Tahlequah, OK 74464-2399. Offers MS. *Degree requirements:* For master's, thesis. *Entrance requirements:* For master's, MAT or GRE. Additional exam requirements/ recommendations for international students: Required—TOEFL (minimum score 213 computer-based). Electronic applications accepted.

Northeastern State University, Graduate College, College of Education, Department of Educational Foundations and Leadership, Program in School Administration, Tahlequah, OK 74464-2399. Offers M Ed. Part-time and evening/weekend programs available. *Degree requirements:* For master's, thesis. *Entrance requirements:* For master's, MAT or GRE, minimum GPA of 3.0. Additional exam requirements/recommendations for international students: Required—TOEFL (minimum score 213 computer-based). Electronic applications accepted.

Northern Arizona University, Graduate College, College of Education, Department of Educational Leadership, Flagstaff, AZ 86011. Offers community college/higher education (M Ed); educational foundations (M Ed); educational leadership (M Ed, Ed D); principal (Certificate); principal K-12 (M Ed); school leadership K-12 (M Ed); superintendent (Certificate). *Faculty:* 21 full-time (11 women). *Students:* 196 full-time (128 women), 744 part-time (452 women); includes 249 minority (59 African Americans, 39 American Indian/Alaska Native, 21 Asian Americans or Pacific Islanders, 130 Hispanic Americans), 4 international. Average age 32. 267 applicants, 97% accepted, 185 enrolled. In 2009, 461 master's, 12 doctorates awarded. *Degree requirements:* For master's, comprehensive exam, thesis (for some programs); for doctorate, comprehensive exam, thesis/dissertation. *Entrance requirements:* For master's, minimum GPA of 3.0; for doctorate, GRE or MAT, minimum GPA of 3.5. Additional exam requirements/recommendations for international students: Required—TOEFL (minimum score 550 paper-based; 213 computer-based; 80 iBT), IELTS (minimum score 7), or a bachelor's degree from an English-speaking university and demonstrated proficiency. *Application deadline:* For fall admission, 2/1 priority date for domestic students, 9/15 priority date for international students; for spring admission, 12/1 for domestic students. Applications are processed on a rolling basis. Application fee: $65. Electronic applications accepted. *Financial support:* In 2009–10, 1 teaching assistantship with partial tuition reimbursement (averaging $10,000 per year) was awarded. Financial award application deadline: 3/30. *Unit head:* Dr. Michael Schwanenberger, Chair, 928-523-3202, Fax: 928-523-8950, E-mail: michael.schwanenberger@nau.edu. *Application contact:* Dr. Michael Schwanenberger, Chair, 928-523-3202, Fax: 928-523-8950, E-mail: michael.schwanenberger@nau.edu.

Northern Illinois University, Graduate School, College of Education, Department of Leadership, Educational Psychology and Foundations, De Kalb, IL 60115-2854. Offers educational administration (MS Ed, Ed D, Ed S); educational psychology (MS Ed, Ed D); foundations of education (MS Ed); school business management (MS Ed). Part-time and evening/weekend programs available. Postbaccalaureate distance learning degree programs offered (minimal on-campus study). *Faculty:* 23 full-time (12 women). *Students:* 17 full-time (14 women), 382 part-time (215 women); includes 63 minority (41 African Americans, 1 American Indian/Alaska Native, 6 Asian Americans or Pacific Islanders, 15 Hispanic Americans), 10 international. Average age 38. 117 applicants, 60% accepted, 53 enrolled. In 2009, 110 master's, 9 doctorates, 24 other advanced degrees awarded. *Degree requirements:* For master's, comprehensive exam, thesis optional; for doctorate, thesis/dissertation, candidacy exam, dissertation defense. *Entrance requirements:* For master's, minimum undergraduate GPA of 2.75; for doctorate, GRE General Test, minimum undergraduate GPA of 2.75, 3.2 graduate; for Ed S, GRE General Test, minimum GPA of 2.75 (undergraduate), 3.2 (graduate). Additional exam requirements/recommendations for international students: Required—TOEFL (minimum score 550 paper-based; 213 computer-based). *Application deadline:* For fall admission, 6/1 for domestic students, 5/1 for international students; for spring admission, 11/1 for domestic students, 10/1 for international students. Applications are processed on a rolling basis. Application fee: $30. Electronic applications accepted. *Expenses:* Tuition, state resident: full-time $6576; part-time $274 per credit hour. Tuition, nonresident: full-time $13,152; part-time $548 per credit hour. Required fees: $1813; $75.53 per credit hour. Part-time tuition and fees vary according to course load. *Financial support:* In 2009–10, 2 research assistantships with full tuition reimbursements, 12 teaching assistantships with full tuition reimbursements were awarded; fellowships with full tuition reimbursements, career-related internships or fieldwork, Federal Work-Study, scholarships/grants, tuition waivers (full), and staff assistantships also available. Support available to part-time students. Financial award applicants required to submit FAFSA. *Faculty research:* Interpersonal forgiveness, learner-centered education, psychedelic studies, senior theory, professional growth. *Unit head:* Dr. Charles L. Howell, Chair, 815-753-4404, E-mail: chowell@niu.edu. *Application contact:* Graduate School Office, 815-753-0395, E-mail: gradsch@niu.edu.

Northern Illinois University, Graduate School, College of Education, Department of Teaching and Learning, De Kalb, IL 60115-2854. Offers curriculum and instruction (MS Ed, Ed D), including curriculum leadership (Ed D), elementary education (Ed D), secondary education (Ed D); early childhood education (MS Ed); elementary education (MS Ed); special education (MS Ed). Part-time and evening/weekend programs available. *Faculty:* 22 full-time (14 women), 2 part-time/adjunct (both women). *Students:* 50 full-time (38 women), 435 part-time (344 women); includes 107 minority (16 African Americans, 1 American Indian/Alaska Native, 12 Asian Americans or Pacific Islanders, 78 Hispanic Americans), 9 international. Average age 35. 154 applicants, 53% accepted, 57 enrolled. In 2009, 142 master's, 2 doctorates awarded. *Degree requirements:* For master's, comprehensive exam, thesis optional; for doctorate, thesis/dissertation, candidacy exam, dissertation defense. *Entrance requirements:* For master's, GRE General Test or MAT, minimum undergraduate GPA of 2.75; for doctorate, GRE General Test or MAT, minimum undergraduate GPA of 2.75, graduate 3.2. Additional exam requirements/ recommendations for international students: Required—TOEFL (minimum score 550 paper-based; 213 computer-based). *Application deadline:* For fall admission, 6/1 for domestic students, 5/1 for international students; for spring admission, 11/1 for domestic students, 10/1 for international students. Applications are processed on a rolling basis. Application fee: $30. Electronic applications accepted. *Expenses:* Tuition, state resident: full-time $6576; part-time $274 per credit hour. Tuition, nonresident: full-time $13,152; part-time $548 per credit hour. Required fees: $1813; $75.53 per credit hour. Part-time tuition and fees vary according to course load. *Financial support:* In 2009–10, 20 research assistantships with full tuition reimbursements were awarded; fellowships with full tuition reimbursements, teaching assistantships with full tuition reimbursements, career-related internships or fieldwork, Federal Work-Study, scholarships/grants, tuition waivers (full), and unspecified assistantships also available. Support available to part-time students. Financial award applicants required to submit FAFSA. *Faculty research:* Teacher certification, stress reduction during student teaching, teaching history, portfolios in student teaching. *Unit head:* Dr. Helen Brantley, Chair, 815-753-0327, E-mail: tedur@niu.edu. *Application contact:* Gail Myers, E-mail: gmyers@niu.edu.

Northern Kentucky University, Office of Graduate Programs, College of Education and Human Services, Program in Education, Highland Heights, KY 41099. Offers teacher as a leader (MA). Part-time and evening/weekend programs available. Postbaccalaureate distance learning degree programs offered (no on-campus study). *Students:* 1 (woman) full-time, 111 part-time (99 women); includes 2 minority (1 American Indian/Alaska Native, 1 Hispanic American). Average age 32. 82 applicants, 59% accepted, 43 enrolled. In 2009, 165 master's awarded. *Degree requirements:* For master's, thesis optional, portfolio. *Entrance requirements:* For master's, GRE, teacher certification, bachelor's degree in appropriate subject area, minimum GPA of 2.5, 3 letters of recommendation, 1 year of teaching experience. Additional exam requirements/recommendations for international students: Required—TOEFL (minimum score 550 paper-based; 213 computer-based; 79 iBT); Recommended—IELTS (minimum score 6.5). *Application deadline:* For fall admission, 7/1 priority date for domestic students, 6/1 priority date for international students; for spring admission, 11/1 priority date for domestic students, 10/1 priority date for international students. Application fee: $40. Electronic applications accepted. *Expenses:* Tuition, state resident: full-time $6912; part-time $384 per credit hour. Tuition, nonresident: full-time $12,150; part-time $675 per credit hour. Tuition and fees vary according to course load, program and reciprocity agreements. *Financial support:* Fellowships with tuition reimbursements, Federal Work-Study, scholarships/grants, and unspecified assistantships available. *Faculty research:* Teaching with technology, middle school education, children with disabilities, teaching in the content areas, diversifying faculty. *Unit head:* Dr. Shawn Faulkner, Assistant Chair for Graduate Programs, 859-572-1910, Fax: 859-572-6096, E-mail: faulkners1@nku.edu. *Application contact:* Heidi Waters, Advising Coordinator, 859-572-5237, Fax: 859-572-1384, E-mail: watersh2@nku.edu.

Northern Kentucky University, Office of Graduate Programs, College of Education and Human Services, Program in Educational Leadership, Highland Heights, KY 41099. Offers Ed D. Part-time and evening/weekend programs available. *Students:* 7 full-time (4 women), 31 part-time (23 women); includes 4 minority (3 African Americans, 1 Asian American or Pacific Islander). Average age 41. 29 applicants, 55% accepted, 15 enrolled. *Entrance requirements:* Additional exam requirements/recommendations for international students: Required—TOEFL (minimum score 550 paper-based; 213 computer-based; 79 iBT); Recommended—IELTS (minimum score 6.5). *Application deadline:* For fall admission, 7/1 for domestic students, 6/1 for international students; for spring admission, 11/1 for domestic students, 10/1 for international students. Application fee: $40. Electronic applications accepted. *Expenses:* Tuition, state resident: full-time $6912; part-time $384 per credit hour. Tuition, nonresident: full-time $12,150; part-time $675 per credit hour. Tuition and fees vary according to course load, program and reciprocity agreements. *Financial support:* Application deadline: 5/1. *Unit head:* Dr. Elaine McNally Jarchow, Dean, 859-572-5229, Fax: 859-572-6623, E-mail: jarchowe1@nku.edu. *Application contact:* Dr. Peg Griffin, Director of Graduate Programs, 859-572-6934, Fax: 859-572-6670, E-mail: griffinp@nku.edu.

Northern Kentucky University, Office of Graduate Programs, College of Education and Human Services, Program in Instructional Leadership, Highland Heights, KY 41099. Offers MA. Part-time and evening/weekend programs available. Postbaccalaureate distance learning degree programs offered (no on-campus study). *Students:* 12 full-time (9 women), 142 part-time (101 women); includes 12 minority (5 African Americans, 3 Asian Americans or Pacific Islanders, 4 Hispanic Americans), 1 international. Average age 32. 19 applicants, 79% accepted, 15 enrolled. *Degree requirements:* For master's, comprehensive exam, portfolio. *Entrance requirements:* For master's, GRE, teaching certificate, 3 letters of recommendation, 3 years of teaching experience, letter of introduction and interest, 3 essays, interview. Additional exam requirements/recommendations for international students: Required—TOEFL (minimum score 550 paper-based; 213 computer-based; 79 iBT); Recommended—IELTS (minimum score 6.5). *Application deadline:* For fall admission, 7/1 priority date for domestic students, 6/1 for international students; for spring admission, 12/1 priority date for domestic students, 10/1 for international students. Applications are processed on a rolling basis. Application fee: $40. Electronic applications accepted. *Expenses:* Tuition, state resident: full-time $6912; part-time $384 per credit hour. Tuition, nonresident: full-time $12,150; part-time $675 per credit hour. Tuition and fees vary according to course load, program and reciprocity agreements. *Financial support:* Unspecified assistantships available. Financial award applicants required to submit FAFSA. *Faculty research:* Ethics, law, redesign of principal preparation, principal preparation for low-achieving poverty schools. *Unit head:* Dr. Rosa Weaver, Director, 859-572-5536, Fax: 859-572-6592, E-mail: weaverro@nku.edu. *Application contact:* Dr. Peg Griffin, Director of Graduate Programs, 859-572-6934, Fax: 859-572-6670, E-mail: griffinp@nku.edu.

Northern Kentucky University, Office of Graduate Programs, College of Education and Human Services, Program in Teaching, Highland Heights, KY 41099. Offers school

Educational Leadership and Administration

Northern Kentucky University (continued)
superintendent (Certificate); special education (Certificate); teaching (MA). Part-time programs available. *Students:* 4 full-time (2 women), 70 part-time (42 women); includes 3 minority (1 Asian American or Pacific Islander, 2 Hispanic Americans). Average age 32. 110 applicants, 36% accepted, 37 enrolled. In 2009, 45 master's awarded. *Degree requirements:* For master's, comprehensive exam, thesis optional, portfolio, student teaching or internship. *Entrance requirements:* For master's, GRE, PRAXIS II, minimum GPA of 2.5, 3 letters of recommendation, criminal background check (state and federal), resume, letter to the reviewer, interview. Additional exam requirements/recommendations for international students: Required—TOEFL (minimum score 550 paper-based; 213 computer-based; 79 iBT); Recommended—IELTS (minimum score 6.5). *Application deadline:* For fall admission, 6/1 priority date for domestic and international students; for spring admission, 10/1 priority date for international students. Application fee: $40. Electronic applications accepted. *Expenses:* Tuition, state resident: full-time $6912; part-time $384 per credit hour. Tuition, nonresident: full-time $12,150; part-time $675 per credit hour. Tuition and fees vary according to course load, program and reciprocity agreements. *Financial support:* Unspecified assistantships available. Financial award applicants required to submit FAFSA. *Faculty research:* Middle grades students, secondary students, rural classrooms, urban classrooms, teacher preparation. *Unit head:* Department Chair, 859-572-5942, Fax: 859-572-6623. *Application contact:* Melissa Decker, Alternative Certification Coordinator, 859-572-6330, Fax: 859-572-1384, E-mail: deckerm@nku.edu.

Northern Michigan University, College of Graduate Studies, College of Professional Studies, School of Education, Program in Administration and Supervision, Marquette, MI 49855-5301. Offers MA Ed, Ed S. Part-time programs available. *Degree requirements:* For master's, thesis or alternative. *Entrance requirements:* For master's, GRE General Test, minimum GPA of 3.0. *Faculty research:* Supervision and improvement of instruction, the principal as educational leader, women in K–12 educational administration.

Northern State University, Division of Graduate Studies in Education, Program in Elementary and Secondary School Administration, Aberdeen, SD 57401-7198. Offers elementary school administration (MS Ed); secondary school administration (MS Ed). *Accreditation:* NCATE. Part-time and evening/weekend programs available. *Faculty:* 3 full-time (1 woman). *Students:* 4 full-time (1 woman), 27 part-time (17 women). Average age 32. In 2009, 12 master's awarded. *Degree requirements:* For master's, thesis optional. *Entrance requirements:* For master's, minimum GPA of 2.75. Additional exam requirements/recommendations for international students: Required—TOEFL (minimum score 550 paper-based; 213 computer-based; 78 iBT). *Application deadline:* For fall admission, 8/15 priority date for domestic students; for spring admission, 12/15 for domestic students. Applications are processed on a rolling basis. Application fee: $35. Electronic applications accepted. *Financial support:* In 2009–10, 5 students received support, including 2 teaching assistantships with partial tuition reimbursements available (averaging $5,558 per year); career-related internships or fieldwork, Federal Work-Study, institutionally sponsored loans, scholarships/grants, and unspecified assistantships also available. Support available to part-time students. Financial award application deadline: 3/1; financial award applicants required to submit FAFSA. *Unit head:* Dr. Craig D. Kono, Head, 605-626-2448, E-mail: konoc@northern.edu. *Application contact:* Tammy K. Griffith, Program Assistant, 605-626-2558, Fax: 605-626-7190, E-mail: griffith@northern.edu.

North Georgia College & State University, Graduate Studies, Program in Teacher Education, Dahlonega, GA 30597. Offers early childhood education (M Ed); educational leadership (Ed S); middle grades education (M Ed); secondary education (M Ed), including art education, biology education, chemistry education, English education, history education, mathematics education, physical education, science education; special education (M Ed), including interrelated special education, learning disabilities. *Accreditation:* NCATE. Part-time and evening/weekend programs available. Postbaccalaureate distance learning degree programs offered (minimal on-campus study). *Degree requirements:* For master's, comprehensive exam, thesis optional. *Entrance requirements:* For master's, GRE General Test or MAT, minimum GPA of 2.75; for Ed S, GRE General Test or MAT, 3 years of teaching experience, master's degree, minimum graduate GPA of 3.25. Electronic applications accepted. *Faculty research:* Computers and teachers' attitudes, rural versus urban teacher attitudes, teacher leadership roles, minority recruitment in teaching force.

Northwestern State University of Louisiana, Graduate Studies and Research, College of Education, Programs in Education, Natchitoches, LA 71497. Offers business and distributive education (M Ed); counseling (M Ed); early childhood education (M Ed); education (M Ed); education leadership (M Ed); educational technology (M Ed); elementary teaching (M Ed); English education (M Ed); home economics education (M Ed); mathematics education (M Ed); reading (M Ed); science education (M Ed); secondary teaching (M Ed); social sciences education (M Ed). *Degree requirements:* For master's, comprehensive exam, thesis or alternative. *Entrance requirements:* For master's, GRE General Test, minimum undergraduate GPA of 2.5.

Northwestern State University of Louisiana, Graduate Studies and Research, College of Education, Programs in Educational Leadership and Instruction, Natchitoches, LA 71497. Offers counseling (Ed S); educational leadership (Ed S); educational technology (Ed S); elementary teaching (Ed S); reading (Ed S); secondary teaching (Ed S); special education (Ed S). *Entrance requirements:* For degree, GRE General Test.

Northwest Missouri State University, Graduate School, College of Education and Human Services, Department of Educational Leadership, Program in Educational Leadership, Maryville, MO 64468-6001. Offers educational leadership: elementary (MS Ed); educational leadership: secondary (MS Ed); elementary principalship (Ed S); secondary principalship (Ed S); superintendency (Ed S). *Accreditation:* NCATE. Part-time programs available. *Faculty:* 16 full-time (6 women). *Students:* 21 full-time (13 women), 60 part-time (39 women); includes 3 minority (1 African American, 1 Asian American or Pacific Islander, 1 Hispanic American). 30 applicants, 83% accepted, 17 enrolled. In 2009, 63 master's awarded. *Degree requirements:* For master's, comprehensive exam; for Ed S, comprehensive exam, thesis. *Entrance requirements:* For master's, GRE General Test, minimum undergraduate GPA of 2.75, teaching certificate, writing sample; for Ed S, minimum graduate GPA of 3.25. Additional exam requirements/recommendations for international students: Required—TOEFL (minimum score 550 paper-based; 213 computer-based). *Application deadline:* For fall admission, 7/1 for domestic and international students; for spring admission, 11/15 for domestic and international students. Application fee: $0 ($50 for international students). *Expenses:* Tuition, state resident: part-time $296.34 per credit hour. Tuition, nonresident: part-time $510.43 per credit hour. *Financial support:* In 2009–10, 5 research assistantships with full tuition reimbursements (averaging $6,000 per year), 1 teaching assistantship with full tuition reimbursement (averaging $6,000 per year) were awarded; unspecified assistantships also available. Financial award application deadline: 4/1; financial award applicants required to submit FAFSA. *Unit head:* Dr. Joyce Piveral, Chairperson, 660-562-1231. *Application contact:* Dr. Gregory Haddock, Dean of Graduate School, 660-562-1145, Fax: 660-562-1096, E-mail: gradsch@nwmissouri.edu.

Northwest Nazarene University, Graduate Studies, Program in Teacher Education, Nampa, ID 83686-5897. Offers curriculum and instruction (M Ed); educational leadership (M Ed); exceptional child (M Ed); reading education (M Ed); school counseling (M Ed). *Accreditation:* ACA; NCATE. Part-time programs available. *Degree requirements:* For master's, comprehensive exam (for some programs), action research project. *Entrance requirements:* For master's, minimum undergraduate GPA of 2.8 overall or 3.0 during final 30 semester credits. *Faculty research:* Action research, cooperative learning, accountability, institutional accreditation.

Notre Dame de Namur University, Division of Academic Affairs, School of Education and Leadership, Program in School Administration, Belmont, CA 94002-1908. Offers administrative services credential (Certificate); school administration (MA). Part-time programs available. In 2009, 8 master's awarded. *Degree requirements:* For master's, thesis. *Entrance requirements:* Additional exam requirements/recommendations for international students: Required—TOEFL (minimum score 550 paper-based; 213 computer-based; 79 iBT). *Application deadline:* For fall admission, 8/1 priority date for domestic students; for spring admission, 12/1 priority date for domestic students. Applications are processed on a rolling basis. Application fee: $50. Electronic applications accepted. *Expenses:* Tuition: Part-time $720 per credit. Required fees: $35 per semester hour. *Financial support:* Career-related internships or fieldwork available. Support available to part-time students. Financial award applicants required to submit FAFSA. *Unit head:* Dr. Judith Kell, Director, 650-508-3710, E-mail: jkell@ndnu.edu. *Application contact:* Candace Hallmark, Associate Director of Admissions, 650-508-3592, Fax: 650-508-3426, E-mail: grad.admit@ndnu.edu.

Nova Southeastern University, Fischler School of Education and Human Services, Graduate Teacher Education Program, Fort Lauderdale, FL 33314-7796. Offers athletic administration (MS); brain research (MS, Ed S); charter school education/leadership (MS); cognitive and behavioral disabilities (MS); computer science education (Ed S); computer science education (K-12) (MS); curriculum and teaching (Ed S); curriculum, instruction and technology (MS); curriculum, instruction, management and administration (Ed S); early childhood education (MS); early literacy and reading (Ed S); early literacy education (MS); education technology (MS); educational leadership (administration K–12) (MS, Ed S); educational media (Ed S); educational media (K-12) (MS); elementary education (MS, Ed S), including ESOL endorsement (MS); English education (MS, Ed S); environmental education (MS); exceptional student education (MS), including ESOL endorsement; gifted education (MS, Ed S); interdisciplinary arts education (MS); management and administration of educational programs (MS); mathematics (MS); mathematics education (Ed S); multicultural early intervention (MS); pre-kindergarten/primary (MS); preschool education (MS); reading (MS); reading and TESOL (MS); reading education (Ed S); science (MS); science education (Ed S); secondary education (MS); social studies (MS, Ed S); Spanish language (MS); special education and reading (MS); teaching and learning (MA, MS), including curriculum and instruction (MA), elementary mathematics (MA), elementary reading (MA), K-12 technology integration (MA); teaching English to speakers of other languages (MS, Ed S); technology management and administration (Ed S); urban studies education (MS). Part-time and evening/weekend programs available. Postbaccalaureate distance learning degree programs offered (minimal on-campus study). *Faculty:* 72 full-time (43 women), 385 part-time/adjunct (252 women). *Students:* 196 full-time (175 women), 1,304 part-time (1,128 women); includes 594 minority (471 African Americans, 5 American Indian/Alaska Native, 18 Asian Americans or Pacific Islanders, 100 Hispanic Americans). Average age 37. 2,610 applicants, 72% accepted, 1352 enrolled. In 2009, 836 other advanced degrees awarded. *Degree requirements:* For master's and Ed S, thesis, practicum, internship. *Entrance requirements:* For master's, MAT, GRE, CLAST, CBEST, PRAXIS I, General Knowledge Test, minimum GPA of 2.5; for Ed S, MAT or GRE, master's degree, teaching certificate, minimum GPA of 3.0. Additional exam requirements/recommendations for international students: Required—TSE (recommended, minimum score 50); Recommended—TOEFL (minimum score 550 paper-based; 213 computer-based; 80 iBT), IELTS (minimum score 6). *Application deadline:* For fall admission, 9/25 priority date for domestic and international students; for winter admission, 2/23 priority date for domestic and international students; for spring admission, 4/25 priority date for domestic and international students. Applications are processed on a rolling basis. Application fee: $50. Electronic applications accepted. *Financial support:* Federal Work-Study available. Support available to part-time students. Financial award application deadline: 4/15; financial award applicants required to submit FAFSA. *Faculty research:* School effectiveness, critical thinking, leadership skills acquisition, child education, multicultural education. *Unit head:* Dr. Ronald Kern, Dean of Academic Affairs, 800-986-3223 Ext. 7809, Fax: 954-262-3606, E-mail: rk429@nsu.nova.edu. *Application contact:* Dr. Jennifer Quinones Nottingham, Dean of Student Affairs, 800-986-3223 Ext. 1559.

Nova Southeastern University, Fischler School of Education and Human Services, National Program for Educational Leaders, Fort Lauderdale, FL 33314-7796. Offers Ed D. Part-time and evening/weekend programs available. Postbaccalaureate distance learning degree programs offered (minimal on-campus study). *Students:* 846 full-time (637 women), 35 part-time (25 women); includes 593 minority (552 African Americans, 2 American Indian/Alaska Native, 5 Asian Americans or Pacific Islanders, 34 Hispanic Americans), 1 international. Average age 38. 3 applicants, 67% accepted, 2 enrolled. In 2009, 310 doctorates awarded. *Degree requirements:* For doctorate, thesis/dissertation, research project. *Entrance requirements:* For doctorate, MAT or GRE, master's degree, professional certification, current position as a practicing school administrator, letter of recommendation, resume. Additional exam requirements/recommendations for international students: Required—TSE (recommended, minimum score 50); Recommended—TOEFL (minimum score 550 paper-based; 213 computer-based; 80 iBT), IELTS (minimum score 6). *Application deadline:* For fall admission, 8/11 priority date for domestic and international students; for winter admission, 12/28 priority date for domestic and international students; for spring admission, 4/22 priority date for domestic and international students. Applications are processed on a rolling basis. Application fee: $50. Electronic applications accepted. *Financial support:* Tuition waivers (full) available. Financial award application deadline: 1/7. *Unit head:* Dr. Karen D. Bowser, Associate Dean of Doctoral Programs, 954-262-8677, Fax: 954-262-3606, E-mail: bowserk@nova.edu. *Application contact:* Dr. Jennifer Quinones Nottingham, Dean of Student Affairs, 800-986-3223 Ext. 8624, Fax: 954-262-3883, E-mail: jlquinon@nova.edu.

Nova Southeastern University, Fischler School of Education and Human Services, Program in Education, Fort Lauderdale, FL 33314-7796. Offers educational leadership (Ed D); health care education (Ed D); higher education leadership (Ed D); human services administration (Ed D); instructional leadership (Ed D); instructional technology and distance education (Ed D); organizational leadership (Ed D); special education (Ed D); speech language pathology (Ed D). Part-time and evening/weekend programs available. Postbaccalaureate distance learning degree programs offered (minimal on-campus study). *Faculty:* 88 full-time (46 women), 132 part-time/adjunct (63 women). *Students:* 2,805 full-time (2,128 women), 1,411 part-time (1,081 women); includes 2,629 minority (2,034 African Americans, 19 American Indian/Alaska Native, 62 Asian Americans or Pacific Islanders, 514 Hispanic Americans), 30 international. Average age 41. 964 applicants, 69% accepted, 513 enrolled. In 2009, 445 doctorates awarded. *Degree requirements:* For doctorate, thesis/dissertation. *Entrance requirements:* For doctorate, MAT or GRE, master's degree, 2 letters of recommendation, work experience. Additional exam requirements/recommendations for international students: Required—TSE (recommended, minimum score 50); Recommended—TOEFL (minimum score 550 paper-based; 213 computer-based; 80 iBT), IELTS (minimum score 6). *Application deadline:* For fall admission, 8/20 priority date for domestic and international students; for winter admission, 12/19 priority date for domestic and international students; for spring admission, 4/26 priority date for domestic students, 4/25 priority date for international students. Applications are processed on a rolling basis. Application fee: $50. Electronic applications accepted. *Financial support:* In 2009–10, 2 fellowships with full tuition reimbursements (averaging $30,000 per year) were awarded; scholarships/grants and tuition waivers (full) also available. Support available to part-time students. Financial award application deadline: 4/15; financial award applicants required to submit FAFSA. *Unit head:* Dr. Ronald Kern, Dean of Academic Affairs, 800-986-3223 Ext. 7809, Fax: 954-262-3606, E-mail: rk429@nsu.nova.edu. *Application contact:* Dr. Jennifer Quinones Nottingham, Dean of Student Affairs, 800-986-3223 Ext. 1546.

Nova Southeastern University, Fischler School of Education and Human Services, Program in Leadership, Fort Lauderdale, FL 33314-7796. Offers MS. Part-time and evening/weekend programs available. Postbaccalaureate distance learning degree programs offered (minimal on-campus study). *Faculty:* 3 full-time (2 women), 6 part-time/adjunct (5 women). *Students:* 13 full-time (10 women), 79 part-time (55 women); includes 50 minority (35 African Americans, 1 Asian American or Pacific Islander, 14 Hispanic Americans). In 2009, 1 master's awarded. *Entrance requirements:* For master's, minimum GPA of 2.5. Additional exam requirements/recommendations for international students: Required—TSE (recommended, minimum score 50); Recommended—TOEFL (minimum score 550 paper-based; 213 computer-based; 80 iBT), IELTS (minimum score 6). *Application deadline:* For fall admission, 9/25 priority date for domestic and international students; for winter admission, 2/23 priority date for domestic students, 2/22 priority date for international students; for spring admission, 4/25 priority date for domestic and international students. Applications are processed on a rolling basis. Electronic

applications accepted. *Financial support:* Application deadline: 4/15. *Unit head:* Dr. Ronald Kern, Dean of Academic Affairs, 800-986-3223 Ext. 7809, Fax: 954-262-3606, E-mail: rk429@nsu.nova.edu. *Application contact:* Dr. Jennifer Quinones Nottingham, Dean of Student Affairs, 800-986-3223 Ext. 1559.

Oakland City University, School of Education and Technology, Oakland City, IN 47660-1099. Offers educational leadership (Ed D); teaching (MA). *Accreditation:* NCATE. Terminal master's awarded for partial completion of doctoral program. *Degree requirements:* For master's, thesis; for doctorate, comprehensive exam, thesis/dissertation. *Entrance requirements:* For master's, MAT, minimum GPA of 3.0, interview, resume, letters of recommendation; for doctorate, MAT, GRE, minimum GPA of 3.2, interview, resumé, letters of recommendation. *Expenses:* Contact institution. *Faculty research:* Assessment, cultural diversity, teacher education, education leadership.

Oakland University, Graduate Study and Lifelong Learning, School of Education and Human Services, Department of Educational Leadership, Rochester, MI 48309-4401. Offers educational leadership (M Ed, PhD); higher education (Certificate); higher education administration (Certificate); school administration (Ed S). *Entrance requirements:* Additional exam requirements/recommendations for international students: Required—TOEFL (minimum score 550 paper-based; 213 computer-based).

Oakland University, Graduate Study and Lifelong Learning, School of Education and Human Services, Department of Teacher Development and Educational Studies, Rochester, MI 48309-4401. Offers education studies (M Ed); secondary education (MAT). *Entrance requirements:* For master's, minimum GPA of 3.0 for unconditional admission. Electronic applications accepted. *Faculty research:* Earth science for middle and high school teachers through real world connections, learning communities, content enrichment.

Oglala Lakota College, Graduate Studies, Program in Educational Administration, Kyle, SD 57752-0490. Offers MA. Part-time and evening/weekend programs available. *Entrance requirements:* For master's, minimum GPA of 2.5.

The Ohio State University, Graduate School, College of Education and Human Ecology, School of Educational Policy and Leadership, Columbus, OH 43210. Offers M Ed, MA, PhD. *Accreditation:* NCATE. *Faculty:* 41. *Students:* 93 full-time (65 women), 203 part-time (136 women); includes 66 minority (47 African Americans, 1 American Indian/Alaska Native, 6 Asian Americans or Pacific Islanders, 12 Hispanic Americans), 20 international. Average age 35. In 2009, 72 master's, 21 doctorates awarded. *Degree requirements:* For master's, thesis optional; for doctorate, thesis/dissertation. *Entrance requirements:* For doctorate, GRE General Test. Additional exam requirements/recommendations for international students: Required—TOEFL (minimum score 600 paper-based; 250 computer-based). *Application deadline:* For fall admission, 8/15 priority date for domestic students, 7/1 priority date for international students; for winter admission, 12/1 priority date for domestic students, 11/1 priority date for international students; for spring admission, 3/1 priority date for domestic students, 2/1 priority date for international students. Applications are processed on a rolling basis. Application fee: $40 ($50 for international students). Electronic applications accepted. *Expenses:* Tuition, state resident: full-time $10,683. Tuition, nonresident: full-time $25,923. Tuition and fees vary according to course load and program. *Financial support:* Fellowships, research assistantships, teaching assistantships, Federal Work-Study, institutionally sponsored loans, and unspecified assistantships available. Support available to part-time students. *Unit head:* Eric Anderman, Interim Director, 614-688-4007, Fax: 614-292-5721, E-mail: anderman.1@osu.edu. *Application contact:* 614-292-9444, Fax: 614-292-3895, E-mail: domestic.grad@osu.edu.

Ohio University, Graduate College, College of Education, Department of Educational Studies, Athens, OH 45701-2979. Offers computer education and technology (M Ed); cultural studies (M Ed); educational administration (M Ed, Ed D); educational research and evaluation (M Ed, PhD); instructional technology (PhD). Part-time and evening/weekend programs available. Postbaccalaureate distance learning degree programs offered (minimal on-campus study). *Faculty:* 12 full-time (6 women), 2 part-time/adjunct (0 women). *Students:* 151 full-time (95 women), 142 part-time (105 women); includes 24 minority (19 African Americans, 1 American Indian/Alaska Native, 1 Asian American or Pacific Islander, 3 Hispanic Americans), 46 international. 107 applicants, 69% accepted, 50 enrolled. In 2009, 32 master's, 19 doctorates awarded. *Degree requirements:* For master's, thesis or alternative; for doctorate, comprehensive exam, thesis/dissertation. *Entrance requirements:* For master's, GRE General Test (if GPA less than 2.9); for doctorate, GRE General Test, GRE Subject Test, minimum GPA of 2.9, work experience, 3 letters of reference, autobiography. Additional exam requirements/recommendations for international students: Required—TOEFL (minimum score 550 paper-based; 80 iBT) or IELTS Academic (minimum score 6.5). *Application deadline:* For fall admission, 3/1 priority date for domestic and international students; for winter admission, 10/1 priority date for domestic and international students; for spring admission, 1/30 priority date for domestic students, 1/1 priority date for international students. Applications are processed on a rolling basis. Application fee: $50 ($55 for international students). Electronic applications accepted. *Expenses:* Tuition, state resident: full-time $7839; part-time $323 per quarter hour. Tuition, nonresident: full-time $15,831; part-time $654 per quarter hour. Required fees: $2931. *Financial support:* Research assistantships with full tuition reimbursements, teaching assistantships with full tuition reimbursements, Federal Work-Study, institutionally sponsored loans, tuition waivers (partial), and unspecified assistantships available. Financial award application deadline: 3/1. *Faculty research:* Race, class and gender; computer programs; development and organization theory; evaluation/development of instruments, leadership. Total annual research expenditures: $158,037. *Unit head:* Dr. Gordon Brooks, Chair, 740-593-4423, Fax: 740-593-0477, E-mail: brooksg@ohio.edu. *Application contact:* Floyd J. Doney, Director of Student Affairs, 740-593-4400, Fax: 740-593-9310, E-mail: doney@ohio.edu.

Oklahoma State University, College of Education, School of Teaching and Curriculum Leadership, Stillwater, OK 74078. Offers MS, PhD. Part-time programs available. *Faculty:* 34 full-time (29 women), 25 part-time/adjunct (22 women). *Students:* 40 full-time (32 women), 218 part-time (175 women); includes 39 minority (11 African Americans, 20 American Indian/Alaska Native, 3 Asian Americans or Pacific Islanders, 5 Hispanic Americans), 9 international. Average age 39. 109 applicants, 55% accepted, 40 enrolled. In 2009, 37 master's, 14 doctorates awarded. *Degree requirements:* For master's, thesis or alternative; for doctorate, comprehensive exam, thesis/dissertation. *Entrance requirements:* For master's and doctorate, GRE or GMAT. Additional exam requirements/recommendations for international students: Required—TOEFL (minimum score 550 paper-based; 79 iBT). *Application deadline:* For fall admission, 3/1 priority date for international students; for spring admission, 8/1 priority date for international students. Applications are processed on a rolling basis. Application fee: $40 ($75 for international students). Electronic applications accepted. *Expenses:* Tuition, state resident: full-time $3716; part-time $154.85 per credit hour. Tuition, nonresident: full-time $14,448; part-time $602 per credit hour. Required fees: $1772; $73.85 per credit hour. One-time fee: $50. Tuition and fees vary according to course load and campus/location. *Financial support:* In 2009–10, 18 research assistantships (averaging $7,889 per year), 15 teaching assistantships (averaging $11,004 per year) were awarded; career-related internships or fieldwork, Federal Work-Study, scholarships/grants, health care benefits, tuition waivers (partial), and unspecified assistantships also available. Support available to part-time students. Financial award application deadline: 3/1; financial award applicants required to submit FAFSA. *Unit head:* Dr. Christine Ormsbee, Head, 405-744-7125, Fax: 405-744-6290. *Application contact:* Dr. Gordon Emslie, Dean, 405-744-6368, Fax: 405-744-0355, E-mail: grad-i@okstate.edu.

Old Dominion University, Darden College of Education, Programs in Educational Leadership and Administration, Norfolk, VA 23529. Offers educational leadership (PhD, Ed S); educational training (MS Ed); principal preparation (MS Ed). *Accreditation:* NCATE. Part-time and evening/weekend programs available. Postbaccalaureate distance learning degree programs offered (minimal on-campus study). *Faculty:* 4 full-time (2 women), 5 part-time/adjunct (2 women). *Students:* 22 full-time (15 women), 89 part-time (67 women); includes 34 minority (30 African Americans, 1 American Indian/Alaska Native, 3 Hispanic Americans), 2 international. Average age 38. 29 applicants, 79% accepted, 20 enrolled. In 2009, 27 master's, 4 doctorates, 61 other advanced degrees awarded. *Degree requirements:* For master's, comprehensive exam, thesis optional, internship, portfolio, school leadership licensure assessment; for doctorate, comprehensive exam, thesis/dissertation; for Ed S, comprehensive exam, thesis optional, field research. *Entrance requirements:* For master's, GRE General Test or MAT, minimum GPA of 3.0 in major, letter of recommendation; for doctorate, GRE, minimum graduate GPA of 3.5, 3 letters of recommendation; for Ed S, GRE General Test or MAT, minimum GPA of 3.0 in major, 2 letters of recommendation. Additional exam requirements/recommendations for international students: Required—TOEFL (minimum score 550 paper-based). *Application deadline:* For fall admission, 6/1 priority date for domestic students, 2/15 priority date for international students; for winter admission, 10/1 priority date for international students; for spring admission, 11/1 priority date for domestic students, 2/1 priority date for international students. Applications are processed on a rolling basis. Application fee: $40. Electronic applications accepted. *Expenses:* Tuition, state resident: full-time $8112; part-time $338 per credit. Tuition, nonresident: full-time $20,256; part-time $844 per credit. Required fees: $119 per semester. One-time fee: $50. *Financial support:* In 2009–10, 48 students received support, including 1 fellowship with tuition reimbursement available (averaging $15,000 per year), 3 teaching assistantships with tuition reimbursements available (averaging $15,000 per year); career-related internships or fieldwork, scholarships/grants, and tuition waivers (partial) also available. Support available to part-time students. Financial award application deadline: 2/15; financial award applicants required to submit FAFSA. *Faculty research:* Principal and leadership preparation, supervision, policy studies, finance, teacher quality. Total annual research expenditures: $500,000. *Unit head:* Dr. William Owings, Graduate Program Director, 757-683-4954, Fax: 757-683-4413, E-mail: els@odu.edu. *Application contact:* Dr. William Owings, Graduate Program Director, 757-683-4954, Fax: 757-683-4413, E-mail: els@odu.edu.

Old Dominion University, Darden College of Education, Programs in Higher Education, Norfolk, VA 23529. Offers educational leadership (MS Ed, Ed S), including higher education. Part-time programs available. *Faculty:* 3 full-time (1 woman), 10 part-time/adjunct (5 women). *Students:* 38 full-time (26 women), 10 part-time (7 women); includes 15 minority (13 African Americans, 1 Asian American or Pacific Islander, 1 Hispanic American), 2 international. Average age 26. 43 applicants, 63% accepted, 20 enrolled. In 2009, 18 master's, 1 Ed S awarded. *Degree requirements:* For master's, comprehensive exam. *Entrance requirements:* For master's, GRE or MAT, minimum undergraduate GPA of 2.8; for Ed S, GRE or MAT, 2 letters of reference, minimum GPA of 3.5, master's degree. Additional exam requirements/recommendations for international students: Required—TOEFL. *Application deadline:* For fall admission, 3/1 priority date for domestic and international students; for winter admission, 10/1 for domestic and international students; for spring admission, 3/1 for domestic and international students. Applications are processed on a rolling basis. Application fee: $40. Electronic applications accepted. *Expenses:* Tuition, state resident: full-time $8112; part-time $338 per credit. Tuition, nonresident: full-time $20,256; part-time $844 per credit. Required fees: $119 per semester. One-time fee: $50. *Financial support:* Research assistantships with partial tuition reimbursements, career-related internships or fieldwork, scholarships/grants, and unspecified assistantships available. *Faculty research:* Law leadership, student development, research administration, international higher education administration. *Unit head:* Dr. Dana D. Burnett, Graduate Program Director, 757-683-3287, Fax: 757-683-5756, E-mail: hied@odu.edu. *Application contact:* Dr. Dana D. Burnett, Graduate Program Director, 757-683-3287, Fax: 757-683-5756, E-mail: hied@odu.edu.

Olivet Nazarene University, Graduate School, Division of Education, Program in School Leadership, Bourbonnais, IL 60914. Offers MAE.

Oral Roberts University, School of Education, Tulsa, OK 74171. Offers Christian school administration (K-12) (MA Ed, Ed D); Christian school curriculum development (MA Ed); college and higher education administration (Ed D); public school administration (K-12) (MA Ed, Ed D); public school teaching (MA Ed). *Accreditation:* NCATE. Part-time programs available. Postbaccalaureate distance learning degree programs offered (minimal on-campus study). *Faculty:* 7 full-time (2 women), 6 part-time/adjunct (2 women). *Students:* 344 full-time (223 women); includes 117 minority (93 African Americans, 7 American Indian/Alaska Native, 11 Asian Americans or Pacific Islanders, 6 Hispanic Americans). 80 applicants, 94% accepted, 65 enrolled. In 2009, 14 master's, 4 doctorates awarded. *Degree requirements:* For master's, comprehensive exam, thesis optional; for doctorate, comprehensive exam, thesis/dissertation. *Entrance requirements:* For master's, GRE General Test or MAT, minimum GPA of 3.0; for doctorate, minimum GPA of 3.0. Additional exam requirements/recommendations for international students: Required—TOEFL (minimum score 500 paper-based; 173 computer-based). *Application deadline:* For fall admission, 1/1 for domestic and international students; for spring admission, 1/1 priority date for domestic students, 1/1 for international students. Applications are processed on a rolling basis. *Expenses:* Contact institution. *Financial support:* In 2009–10, 4 research assistantships (averaging $5,000 per year) were awarded; scholarships/grants and unspecified assistantships also available. Financial award application deadline: 6/1; financial award applicants required to submit FAFSA. *Faculty research:* Teacher effectiveness, college success in high achieving African-Americans, professional development practices. *Unit head:* Dr. Kim Boyd, Dean, 918-495-7108, E-mail: kboyd@oru.edu. *Application contact:* Lance Miller, Graduate Admissions, 918-495-6553, Fax: 918-495-6222, E-mail: gradeducation@oru.edu.

Oregon State University, Graduate School, College of Education, Program in Adult Education and Higher Education Leadership, Corvallis, OR 97331. Offers Ed M, MAIS. *Accreditation:* NCATE. Part-time programs available. *Faculty:* 3 full-time (all women), 4 part-time/adjunct (1 woman). *Students:* 1 full-time (0 women), 45 part-time (34 women); includes 5 minority (1 African American, 2 American Indian/Alaska Native, 2 Hispanic Americans), 1 international. Average age 42. In 2009, 13 master's awarded. *Degree requirements:* For master's, thesis or alternative. *Entrance requirements:* For master's, minimum GPA of 3.0 in last 90 hours. Additional exam requirements/recommendations for international students: Required—TOEFL. *Application deadline:* For fall admission, 3/1 for domestic students. Applications are processed on a rolling basis. Application fee: $50. *Expenses:* Tuition, state resident: full-time $9774; part-time $362 per credit. Tuition, nonresident: full-time $15,849; part-time $587 per credit. Required fees: $1639. Full-time tuition and fees vary according to course load and program. *Financial support:* Research assistantships, teaching assistantships, career-related internships or fieldwork, Federal Work-Study, and institutionally sponsored loans available. Support available to part-time students. Financial award application deadline: 2/1. *Faculty research:* Adult training and developmental psychology, cross-cultural communication, leadership development and human relations, adult literacy. *Unit head:* Dr. Tom Scheuermann, Interim Chair, 541-737-9524, E-mail: tom.scheuermann@oregonstate.edu. *Application contact:* Rosemary Garagnani, Assistant Dean, 541-737-1465, Fax: 541-737-3313.

Ottawa University, Graduate Studies-Arizona, Program in Education, Ottawa, KS 66067-3399. Offers community college counseling (MA); curriculum and instruction (MA); early childhood (MA); education intervention (MA); education leadership (MA); education technology (MA); Montessori early childhood education (MA); Montessori elementary education (MA); professional development (MA); school guidance counseling (MA); special education—cross categorical (MA). Programs offered in Mesa, Phoenix, Tempe and West Valley, AZ. *Accreditation:* NCATE. Part-time programs available. *Degree requirements:* For master's, thesis or alternative. *Entrance requirements:* For master's, minimum undergraduate GPA of 3.0, copy of current state certification or teaching license. Additional exam requirements/recommendations for international students: Required—TOEFL (minimum score 550 paper-based; 213 computer-based). Electronic applications accepted. *Expenses:* Contact institution.

Our Lady of Holy Cross College, Program in Education and Counseling, New Orleans, LA 70131-7399. Offers administration and supervision (M Ed); curriculum and instruction (M Ed); marriage and family counseling (MA); school counseling (M Ed, MA). *Accreditation:* ACA; NCATE. Part-time and evening/weekend programs available. *Degree requirements:* For master's, thesis. *Entrance requirements:* For master's, GRE General Test, minimum GPA of 2.7.

Our Lady of the Lake University of San Antonio, School of Professional Studies, Program in Principal, San Antonio, TX 78207-4689. Offers M Ed. Part-time and evening/weekend

Educational Leadership and Administration

Our Lady of the Lake University of San Antonio (continued)
programs available. *Students:* 2 full-time (both women), 7 part-time (6 women); all minorities (1 Asian American or Pacific Islander, 8 Hispanic Americans). Average age 40. *Degree requirements:* For master's, exam, internship. *Entrance requirements:* For master's, GRE General Test or MAT. Additional exam requirements/recommendations for international students: Required—TOEFL. *Application deadline:* Applications are processed on a rolling basis. Application fee: $25 ($50 for international students). Electronic applications accepted. *Expenses:* Tuition: Full-time $12,330; part-time $685 per contact hour. Required fees: $139; $12 per contact hour. $57 per semester. Tuition and fees vary according to campus/location. *Financial support:* Career-related internships or fieldwork, institutionally sponsored loans, and scholarships/grants available. Financial award application deadline: 4/15. *Unit head:* Dr. Cullen Grinnan, Head, 210-434-6711 Ext. 8928, Fax: 210-431-3927, E-mail: ctgrinnan@lake.ollusa.edu. *Application contact:* 210-434-6711 Ext. 2314, Fax: 210-431-4036, E-mail: gradadm@lake.ollusa.edu.

Pace University, School of Education, New York, NY 10038. Offers administration and supervision (MS Ed); adolescent education (MST); childhood education (MST); curriculum and instruction (MS); education (MST); literacy (MSE); school business management (Certificate); teaching students with disabilities (MSE); teaching visual arts (MST). *Accreditation:* NCATE. Part-time and evening/weekend programs available. *Students:* 235 full-time (177 women), 766 part-time (515 women); includes 158 minority (58 African Americans, 1 American Indian/Alaska Native, 37 Asian Americans or Pacific Islanders, 62 Hispanic Americans), 7 international. Average age 30. 332 applicants, 83% accepted, 165 enrolled. In 2009, 669 master's, 34 other advanced degrees awarded. *Degree requirements:* For master's, internship. *Entrance requirements:* For master's, interview, teaching certificate. Additional exam requirements/recommendations for international students: Required—TOEFL. *Application deadline:* For fall admission, 7/31 priority date for domestic students; for spring admission, 11/30 for domestic students. Applications are processed on a rolling basis. Application fee: $70. Electronic applications accepted. *Expenses:* Contact institution. *Financial support:* Research assistantships, career-related internships or fieldwork and Federal Work-Study available. Support available to part-time students. Financial award applicants required to submit FAFSA. *Unit head:* Dr. Harriet Feldman, Interim Dean, 212-346-1512. *Application contact:* Susan Ford-Goldschein, Director of Admissions, 212-346-1652, Fax: 212-346-1585, E-mail: gradnyc@pace.edu.

Pacific Lutheran University, Division of Graduate Studies, School of Education, Program for Principal Certification, Tacoma, WA 98447. Offers MAE.

Pacific Lutheran University, Division of Graduate Studies, School of Education, Program in Educational Leadership, Tacoma, WA 98447. Offers MAE. *Accreditation:* NCATE. Part-time and evening/weekend programs available. *Degree requirements:* For master's, comprehensive exam, thesis or alternative. *Entrance requirements:* For master's, GRE General Test or MAT, interview. Additional exam requirements/recommendations for international students: Required—TOEFL (minimum score 550 paper-based; 213 computer-based).

Park University, College of Graduate and Professional Studies, Kansas City, MO 54105. Offers adult education (M Ed); at-risk students (M Ed); disaster and emergency management (MPA); educational administration (M Ed); entrepreneurship (MBA); general business (MBA); general education (M Ed); government/business relations (MPA); healthcare/services management (MBA, MPA); international business (MBA); K-12 certification (MAT); management information systems (MBA); management of information systems (MPA); middle school certification (MAT); multi-cultural education (M Ed); nonprofit management (MPA); public management (MPA); school law (M Ed); secondary school certification (MAT); special education (M Ed). Part-time and evening/weekend programs available. Postbaccalaureate distance learning degree programs offered (no on-campus study). *Degree requirements:* For master's, comprehensive exam, thesis (for some programs). *Entrance requirements:* For master's, GRE, GMAT, teacher certification (M Ed). Additional exam requirements/recommendations for international students: Required—TOEFL (minimum score 550 paper-based). Electronic applications accepted. *Faculty research:* Literacy, leadership, brain based research, multicultural education, diversity.

Pepperdine University, Graduate School of Education and Psychology, Division of Education, Ed D Program in Educational Leadership, Administration, and Policy, Malibu, CA 90263. Offers Ed D. *Degree requirements:* For doctorate, thesis/dissertation. *Entrance requirements:* For doctorate, GRE General Test, MAT, or GMAT. Additional exam requirements/recommendations for international students: Required—TOEFL. *Expenses:* Contact institution.

Pepperdine University, Graduate School of Education and Psychology, Division of Education, Ed D Program in Organizational Leadership, Malibu, CA 90263. Offers Ed D. Part-time and evening/weekend programs available. *Degree requirements:* For doctorate, thesis/dissertation. *Entrance requirements:* For doctorate, GMAT or GRE General Test, MAT. Additional exam requirements/recommendations for international students: Required—TOEFL. *Expenses:* Contact institution.

Pepperdine University, Graduate School of Education and Psychology, Division of Education, Ed D Program in Organization Change, Malibu, CA 90263. Offers Ed D. Part-time and evening/weekend programs available. *Degree requirements:* For doctorate, thesis/dissertation. *Entrance requirements:* For doctorate, GMAT, GRE General Test, MAT. Additional exam requirements/recommendations for international students: Required—TOEFL. *Expenses:* Contact institution.

Pepperdine University, Graduate School of Education and Psychology, Division of Education, MS Program in Administration and Preliminary Administrative Services Credential, Malibu, CA 90263. Offers MS. *Entrance requirements:* For master's, GRE General Test. Additional exam requirements/recommendations for international students: Required—TOEFL. *Expenses:* Tuition: Full-time $37,516; part-time $1310 per unit. Required fees: $80.

Philadelphia Biblical University, School of Education, Langhorne, PA 19047-2990. Offers educational leadership and administration (MS El); teacher education (MS Ed). Part-time and evening/weekend programs available. *Faculty:* 5 full-time (3 women), 2 part-time/adjunct (both women). *Students:* 14 full-time (9 women), 61 part-time (45 women); includes 11 minority (10 African Americans, 1 Asian American or Pacific Islander), 7 international. Average age 34. 45 applicants, 62% accepted, 23 enrolled. In 2009, 39 master's awarded. *Entrance requirements:* Additional exam requirements/recommendations for international students: Required—TOEFL (minimum score 550 paper-based; 213 computer-based). *Application deadline:* Applications are processed on a rolling basis. Application fee: $25. Electronic applications accepted. *Expenses:* Tuition: Full-time $10,350; part-time $575 per credit. Required fees: $10; $10 per year. Tuition and fees vary according to program. *Financial support:* In 2009–10, 14 students received support. Scholarships/grants available. Support available to part-time students. Financial award applicants required to submit FAFSA. *Unit head:* Dr. Martha MacCullough, Dean, 215-702-4387, E-mail: teacher.ed@pbu.edu. *Application contact:* Katerina Penkova, Enrollment Counselor, Graduate Education, 800-572-2472, Fax: 215-702-4248, E-mail: kpenkova@pbu.edu.

Pittsburg State University, Graduate School, College of Education, Department of Special Services and Leadership Studies, Program in Educational Leadership, Pittsburg, KS 66762. Offers MS. *Expenses:* Tuition, state resident: full-time $4212; part-time $176 per credit. Tuition, nonresident: full-time $11,530; part-time $480 per credit. Required fees: $940; $43 per credit. Tuition and fees vary according to course level, course load, degree level, campus/location, reciprocity agreements and student level.

Pittsburg State University, Graduate School, College of Education, Department of Special Services and Leadership Studies, Program in General School Administration, Pittsburg, KS 66762. Offers Ed S. *Expenses:* Tuition, state resident: full-time $4212; part-time $176 per credit. Tuition, nonresident: full-time $11,530; part-time $480 per credit. Required fees: $940; $43 per credit. Tuition and fees vary according to course level, course load, degree level, campus/location, reciprocity agreements and student level.

Plymouth State University, College of Graduate Studies, Graduate Studies in Education, Program in Educational Leadership, Plymouth, NH 03264-1595. Offers M Ed. *Accreditation:* NCATE. Part-time and evening/weekend programs available. *Degree requirements:* For master's, PRAXIS. *Entrance requirements:* For master's, MAT, minimum GPA of 3.0.

Point Park University, School of Arts and Sciences, Department of Education, Pittsburgh, PA 15222-1984. Offers curriculum and instruction (MA); educational administration (MA); teaching and leadership (M Ed). Part-time and evening/weekend programs available. *Faculty:* 2 full-time, 5 part-time/adjunct. *Students:* 9 full-time (7 women), 51 part-time (36 women); includes 11 minority (9 African Americans, 2 Asian Americans or Pacific Islanders), 1 international. Average age 36. 41 applicants, 68% accepted, 25 enrolled. In 2009, 12 master's awarded. *Degree requirements:* For master's, comprehensive exam (for some programs), thesis or alternative. *Entrance requirements:* For master's, minimum GPA of 3.0, resume, 2 letters of recommendation. Additional exam requirements/recommendations for international students: Required—TOEFL. *Application deadline:* Applications are processed on a rolling basis. Application fee: $30. Electronic applications accepted. *Expenses:* Tuition: Full-time $11,880; part-time $660 per credit. Required fees: $486; $27 per credit. *Financial support:* In 2009–10, 19 students received support, including 1 research assistantship with full tuition reimbursement available (averaging $6,400 per year); scholarships/grants also available. Financial award application deadline: 4/15; financial award applicants required to submit FAFSA. *Unit head:* Dr. Darlene Marnich, Chair, 412-392-3474, Fax: 412-392-3927, E-mail: dmarnich@pointpark.edu. *Application contact:* Lynn C. Ribar, Associate Director, Graduate and Adult Enrollment, 412-392-3908, Fax: 412-392-6164, E-mail: lribar@pointpark.edu.

Pontifical Catholic University of Puerto Rico, College of Education, Program in Educational Leadership and Administration, Ponce, PR 00717-0777. Offers PhD.

Portland State University, Graduate Studies, School of Education, Department of Educational Policy, Foundations, and Administrative Studies, Portland, OR 97207-0751. Offers educational leadership (MA, MS, Ed D); postsecondary, adult and continuing education (Ed D). *Accreditation:* NCATE. Part-time and evening/weekend programs available. *Degree requirements:* For master's, thesis or alternative, written exam or research project; for doctorate, comprehensive exam, thesis/dissertation. *Entrance requirements:* For master's, California Basic Educational Skills Test, minimum GPA of 3.0 in upper-division course work or 2.75 overall; for doctorate, GRE General Test or MAT. Additional exam requirements/recommendations for international students: Required—TOEFL (minimum score 550 paper-based; 213 computer-based). *Faculty research:* Leadership development and research, principals and urban schools, accelerated schools, cooperative learning, family involvement in schools.

Prairie View A&M University, College of Education, Department of Educational Leadership and Counseling, Prairie View, TX 77446-0519. Offers counseling (MA, MS Ed); educational administration (M Ed, MS Ed); educational leadership (PhD). *Accreditation:* NCATE. Part-time and evening/weekend programs available. *Faculty:* 21 full-time (8 women), 32 part-time/adjunct (13 women). *Students:* 84 full-time (65 women), 1,102 part-time (865 women); includes 1,033 minority (989 African Americans, 2 American Indian/Alaska Native, 3 Asian Americans or Pacific Islanders, 39 Hispanic Americans), 6 international. Average age 34. 1,341 applicants, 100% accepted. In 2009, 439 master's, 17 doctorates awarded. *Degree requirements:* For master's, thesis optional; for doctorate, comprehensive exam, thesis/dissertation. *Entrance requirements:* For master's, GRE General Test, 3 letters of reference, minimum undergraduate GPA of 2.5; for doctorate, GRE General Test, 3 letters of reference. Additional exam requirements/recommendations for international students: Required—TOEFL (minimum score 550 paper-based). *Application deadline:* For fall admission, 7/1 priority date for domestic students, 6/1 for international students; for spring admission, 11/1 priority date for domestic students, 10/1 for international students. Applications are processed on a rolling basis. Application fee: $50. Electronic applications accepted. *Expenses:* Tuition, state resident: full-time $2200. Tuition, nonresident: full-time $5600. Required fees: $1720. Tuition and fees vary according to course load. *Financial support:* In 2009–10, 600 students received support. Career-related internships or fieldwork available. Support available to part-time students. Financial award application deadline: 4/1; financial award applicants required to submit FAFSA. *Faculty research:* Mentoring, personality assessment, holistic/humanistic education. *Unit head:* Dr. Pamela Barber-Freeman, Interim Head, 936-261-3530, Fax: 936-261-3617. *Application contact:* Dr. Pamela Barber-Freeman, Interim Head, 936-261-3530, Fax: 936-261-3617.

Prescott College, Graduate Programs, Program in Education, Prescott, AZ 86301. Offers early childhood education (MA); early childhood special education (MA); education (MA); elementary education (MA); environmental education leadership and administration (MA); equine-assisted experiential learning (MA); school guidance counseling (MA); secondary education (MA); special education, learning disability (MA); special education, mental retardation (MA); special education, serious emotional disability (MA); student-directed independent study (MA); sustainability education (PhD). Part-time programs available. Postbaccalaureate distance learning degree programs offered (minimal on-campus study). *Faculty:* 3 full-time (1 woman), 79 part-time/adjunct (41 women). *Students:* 75 full-time (44 women), 46 part-time (36 women); includes 18 minority (8 African Americans, 3 American Indian/Alaska Native, 4 Asian Americans or Pacific Islanders, 8 Hispanic Americans), 2 international. Average age 39. 66 applicants, 67% accepted, 31 enrolled. In 2009, 22 master's, 4 doctorates awarded. *Degree requirements:* For master's, thesis, fieldwork or internship, practicum; for doctorate, thesis/dissertation. *Entrance requirements:* For master's, 2 letters of recommendation, resume; for doctorate, 3 letters of recommendation, resume, official transcripts, personal statement, program proposal. Additional exam requirements/recommendations for international students: Required—TOEFL (minimum score 500 paper-based; 173 computer-based). *Application deadline:* For fall admission, 4/15 priority date for domestic and international students; for spring admission, 9/15 priority date for domestic and international students. Applications are processed on a rolling basis. Application fee: $40. Electronic applications accepted. *Expenses:* Tuition: Full-time $14,712; part-time $613 per credit. Required fees: $50 per term. One-time fee: $150. Tuition and fees vary according to course load and degree level. *Financial support:* Career-related internships or fieldwork and Federal Work-Study available. Financial award applicants required to submit FAFSA. *Unit head:* Noel Caniglia, Chair, 928-358-3201, Fax: 928-776-5151, E-mail: ncaniglia@prescott.edu. *Application contact:* Kerstin Alicki, Admissions Counselor, 877-412-8705, Fax: 928-277-4695, E-mail: admissions@prescott.edu.

Providence College, Graduate Studies, Department of Education, Programs in Administration, Providence, RI 02918. Offers elementary administration (M Ed); secondary administration (M Ed). Part-time and evening/weekend programs available. *Faculty:* 4 full-time (3 women), 39 part-time/adjunct (22 women). *Students:* 7 full-time (3 women), 50 part-time (23 women); includes 1 minority (African American). Average age 36. 7 applicants, 100% accepted. In 2009, 23 master's awarded. *Degree requirements:* For master's, comprehensive exam. *Entrance requirements:* For master's, GRE General Test. Additional exam requirements/recommendations for international students: Required—TOEFL (minimum score 550 paper-based; 213 computer-based; 80 iBT). *Application deadline:* For fall admission, 8/1 priority date for domestic and international students; for spring admission, 12/1 priority date for domestic and international students. Applications are processed on a rolling basis. Application fee: $55. *Expenses:* Tuition: Full-time $9909; part-time $367 per credit. One-time fee: $200. Tuition and fees vary according to course load and program. *Financial support:* In 2009–10, research assistantships with full tuition reimbursements (averaging $8,400 per year); career-related internships or fieldwork, institutionally sponsored loans, and unspecified assistantships also available. Support available to part-time students. Financial award application deadline: 8/1; financial award applicants required to submit FAFSA. *Unit head:* Francis J. Leary, Director, 401-865-2247, Fax: 401-865-1147, E-mail: fleary@providence.edu. *Application contact:* Carol A. Daniels, Coordinator of Graduate Faculty and Administrative Services, 401-865-2247, Fax: 401-865-1147, E-mail: daniels@providence.edu.

Purdue University, Graduate School, School of Education, Department of Educational Studies, West Lafayette, IN 47907. Offers administration (MS Ed, PhD, Ed S); counseling and development (MS Ed, PhD); education of the gifted (MS Ed); educational psychology (MS Ed,

PhD); foundations of education (MS Ed, PhD); higher education administration (MS Ed, PhD); special education (MS Ed, PhD). *Accreditation:* ACA (one or more programs are accredited); NCATE (one or more programs are accredited). Part-time and evening/weekend programs available. *Degree requirements:* For master's, thesis optional; for doctorate, thesis/dissertation, oral and written exams; for Ed S, oral presentation, project. *Entrance requirements:* For master's, GRE General Test, minimum undergraduate GPA of 3.0; for doctorate, GRE General Test; for Ed S, GRE, minimum B average. Additional exam requirements/recommendations for international students: Required—TOEFL. Electronic applications accepted. *Faculty research:* Motivation, learning disabilities, school learning, group processes, cognitive development.

Purdue University Calumet, Graduate School, School of Education, Program in Educational Administration, Hammond, IN 46323-2094. Offers MS Ed. *Entrance requirements:* Additional exam requirements/recommendations for international students: Required—TOEFL.

Queens College of the City University of New York, Division of Graduate Studies, Division of Education, Department of Educational and Community Programs, Program in Educational Leadership, Flushing, NY 11367-1597. Offers AC. Part-time programs available. *Faculty:* 4 full-time (0 women). *Students:* 86 part-time (61 women). 61 applicants, 48% accepted, 22 enrolled. In 2009, 142 ACs awarded. *Degree requirements:* For AC, thesis optional, internship. *Entrance requirements:* For degree, master's degree or equivalent. Additional exam requirements/recommendations for international students: Required—TOEFL. *Application deadline:* For fall admission, 4/1 for domestic students; for spring admission, 11/1 for domestic students. Applications are processed on a rolling basis. Application fee: $125. *Expenses:* Tuition, state resident: full-time $7360; part-time $310 per credit. Tuition, nonresident: part-time $575 per credit. One-time fee: $195 full-time; $145.25 part-time. *Financial support:* Career-related internships or fieldwork, Federal Work-Study, institutionally sponsored loans, and tuition waivers (partial) available. Support available to part-time students. Financial award application deadline: 4/1; financial award applicants required to submit FAFSA. *Unit head:* Dr. Kenneth Dunn, Coordinator, 718-997-5240. *Application contact:* Mario Caruso, Director of Graduate Admissions, 718-997-5200, Fax: 718-997-5193, E-mail: graduate_admissions@qc.edu.

Queens University of Charlotte, Wayland H. Cato, Jr. School of Education, Charlotte, NC 28274-0002. Offers education in literacy (M Ed); elementary education (MAT); school administration (MSA). *Accreditation:* NCATE. Part-time and evening/weekend programs available. *Degree requirements:* For master's, comprehensive exam. *Entrance requirements:* For master's, GRE General Test. *Expenses:* Contact institution.

Quincy University, Program in Education, Quincy, IL 62301-2699. Offers curriculum and instruction (MS Ed); leadership (MRS); reading education (MS Ed); school administration (MS Ed); special education (MS Ed); teaching certification (MS Ed). Part-time programs available. Postbaccalaureate distance learning degree programs offered. *Faculty:* 3 full-time (2 women), 19 part-time/adjunct (16 women). *Students:* 328 full-time (222 women), 88 part-time (57 women); includes 60 African Americans, 9 Asian Americans or Pacific Islanders, 69 Hispanic Americans. In 2009, 10 master's awarded. *Degree requirements:* For master's, thesis. *Entrance requirements:* For master's, MAT or GRE. Additional exam requirements/recommendations for international students: Required—TOEFL. *Application deadline:* Applications are processed on a rolling basis. Application fee: $25. Electronic applications accepted. *Expenses:* Tuition: Full-time $8400; part-time $350 per credit hour. Required fees: $360; $15 per credit hour. Tuition and fees vary according to course load, campus/location and program. *Financial support:* Available to part-time students. Applicants required to submit FAFSA. *Unit head:* Dot Nelson, Director, 217-228-5432 Ext. 3111, E-mail: nelsodo@quincy.edu. *Application contact:* Jennifer O'Donnell, Coordinator of Adult Studies, 217-228-5404, Fax: 217-228-5479, E-mail: admissions@quincy.edu.

Radford University, College of Graduate and Professional Studies, College of Education and Human Development, School of Teacher Education and Leadership, Program in Educational Leadership, Radford, VA 24142. Offers licensure option (MS); non-licensure option (MS). *Accreditation:* NCATE. Part-time and evening/weekend programs available. *Faculty:* 2 full-time (0 women), 3 part-time/adjunct (0 women). *Students:* 5 full-time (3 women), 91 part-time (60 women); includes 9 minority (all African Americans). Average age 34. 48 applicants, 96% accepted, 41 enrolled. In 2009, 43 master's awarded. *Degree requirements:* For master's, comprehensive exam. *Entrance requirements:* For master's, GRE or MAT, minimum GPA of 2.75, 3 years of K-12 classroom experience, writing sample, 3 letters of reference. Additional exam requirements/recommendations for international students: Required—TOEFL (minimum score 550 paper-based; 213 computer-based; 79 iBT). *Application deadline:* For fall admission, 12/1 for international students; for spring admission, 7/1 for international students. Applications are processed on a rolling basis. Application fee: $50. Electronic applications accepted. *Expenses:* Tuition, state resident: full-time $5086; part-time $211 per credit hour. Tuition, nonresident: full-time $12,608; part-time $525 per credit hour. Required fees: $2508; $105 per credit hour. *Financial support:* In 2009–10, 2 students received support. Career-related internships or fieldwork, Federal Work-Study, institutionally sponsored loans, scholarships/grants, and unspecified assistantships available. Financial award application deadline: 3/1; financial award applicants required to submit FAFSA. *Unit head:* Dr. William F. Flora, Coordinator, 540-831-5140, Fax: 540-831-5059, E-mail: wfflora@radford.edu. *Application contact:* Graduate Admissions, 540-831-5431, Fax: 540-831-6061, E-mail: gradcollege@radford.edu.

Regent University, Graduate School, School of Education, Virginia Beach, VA 23464-9800. Offers career switcher (M Ed); Christian school program (M Ed); cross-categorical special education (M Ed); education (M Ed, Ed D); education licensure (M Ed); educational leadership (M Ed); elementary education (M Ed); individualized degree plan (M Ed); leadership in character education (M Ed); master teacher (M Ed); mathematics education (M Ed); special education leadership (Ed S); student affairs (M Ed); TESOL (M Ed). *Accreditation:* Teacher Education Accreditation Council. Part-time and evening/weekend programs available. Postbaccalaureate distance learning degree programs offered (minimal on-campus study). *Faculty:* 26 full-time (13 women), 104 part-time/adjunct (78 women). *Students:* 141 full-time (116 women), 622 part-time (488 women); includes 218 minority (186 African Americans, 1 American Indian/Alaska Native, 10 Asian Americans or Pacific Islanders, 21 Hispanic Americans), 8 international. Average age 39. 509 applicants, 60% accepted, 176 enrolled. In 2009, 212 master's, 15 doctorates awarded. *Degree requirements:* For master's, thesis or alternative; for doctorate, comprehensive exam, thesis/dissertation. *Entrance requirements:* For master's, MAT, minimum undergraduate GPA of 2.75, writing sample, resume, recommendations, interview; for doctorate, GRE, writing sample, 3 years of relevant professional experience, master's-level paper, copies of published work, resume, transcripts, interview, recommendations. Additional exam requirements/recommendations for international students: Required—TOEFL (minimum score 577 paper-based; 233 computer-based). *Application deadline:* For fall admission, 4/1 priority date for domestic students; for spring admission, 10/15 priority date for domestic students. Applications are processed on a rolling basis. Application fee: $50. Electronic applications accepted. *Expenses:* Contact institution. *Financial support:* In 2009–10, 480 students received support; fellowships, career-related internships or fieldwork, scholarships/grants, tuition waivers (full and partial), and unspecified assistantships available. Support available to part-time students. Financial award application deadline: 4/1; financial award applicants required to submit FAFSA. *Faculty research:* Character development and discipline for children, education leadership development, diversity in schools, classroom management, technology in education settings. *Unit head:* Dr. Alan A. Arroyo, Dean, 757-352-4261, Fax: 757-352-4318, E-mail: alanarr@regent.edu. *Application contact:* Matthew Chadwick, Director of Admissions, 800-373-5504, Fax: 757-352-4381, E-mail: admissions@regent.edu.

Regis University, College for Professional Studies, Program in Teacher Education, Denver, CO 80221-1099. Offers adult learning, training, and development (M Ed); curriculum, instruction, and assessment (M Ed); early childhood (M Ed); educational technology (Certificate); elementary (M Ed); ESL (M Ed); fine arts (M Ed), including arts, music; instructional technology (M Ed); professional leadership (M Ed); reading (M Ed); secondary (M Ed); self-designed (M Ed); space studies (M Ed); special education (M Ed); teacher licensure (M Ed). Program also offered in Henderson and Las Vegas (Summerlin), NV. *Accreditation:* Teacher Education Accreditation Council. Part-time and evening/weekend programs available. Postbaccalaureate distance learning degree programs offered (no on-campus study). *Degree requirements:* For master's, thesis. *Entrance requirements:* For master's, resume, minimum GPA of 2.75, criminal background check. Additional exam requirements/recommendations for international students: Required—TOEFL (minimum score 213 computer-based), TWE (minimum score 5). Electronic applications accepted. *Faculty research:* Issues of equity in the middle school classroom, professional learning communities, school reform, socialinguistic and discursive obstacles to student integration, inclusive language arts curriculum.

Rhode Island College, School of Graduate Studies, Feinstein School of Education and Human Development, Department of Counseling, Educational Leadership, and School Psychology, Providence, RI 02908-1991. Offers counseling (MA); educational leadership (M Ed); school administration (M Ed); school counseling (CAGS). *Accreditation:* NCATE. Part-time and evening/weekend programs available. *Faculty:* 10 full-time (5 women), 9 part-time/adjunct (5 women). *Students:* 39 full-time (30 women), 108 part-time (79 women); includes 7 minority (3 African Americans, 3 Asian Americans or Pacific Islanders, 1 Hispanic American). Average age 35. In 2009, 39 master's, 34 other advanced degrees awarded. *Degree requirements:* For master's and CAGS, comprehensive exam (for some programs), thesis (for some programs). *Entrance requirements:* For master's, GRE General Test or MAT, undergraduate transcripts; minimum undergraduate GPA of 3.0; for CAGS, GRE or MAT (for most programs), undergraduate transcripts; minimum undergraduate GPA of 3.0; copy of teaching certificate (when applicable); 3 letters of recommendation; current resume. Additional exam requirements/recommendations for international students: Recommended—TOEFL (minimum score 550 paper-based; 213 computer-based; 79 iBT). *Application deadline:* For fall admission, 3/15 for domestic students; for spring admission, 11/1 for domestic students. Applications are processed on a rolling basis. Application fee: $50. *Expenses:* Tuition, state resident: full-time $7440; part-time $310 per credit hour. Tuition, nonresident: full-time $14,784; part-time $616 per credit hour. Required fees: $552; $20 per credit. $70 per term. *Financial support:* Teaching assistantships with full tuition reimbursements, career-related internships or fieldwork, Federal Work-Study, scholarships/grants, health care benefits, and unspecified assistantships available. Support available to part-time students. Financial award application deadline: 5/15; financial award applicants required to submit FAFSA. *Unit head:* Dr. Monica Darcy, Chair, 401-456-8023. *Application contact:* Graduate Studies, 401-456-8700.

Rider University, Department of Graduate Education, Leadership and Counseling, Program in Curriculum, Instruction and Supervision, Lawrenceville, NJ 08648-3001. Offers curriculum, instruction and supervision (MA); supervisor (Certificate). *Accreditation:* NCATE. Part-time and evening/weekend programs available. *Degree requirements:* For master's, comprehensive exam, practicum project. *Entrance requirements:* For master's, interview, 2 letters of recommendation from current supervisors, resume. Additional exam requirements/recommendations for international students: Required—TOEFL (minimum score 550 paper-based; 213 computer-based). Electronic applications accepted. *Faculty research:* Curriculum change, curriculum development, teacher evaluation.

Rider University, Department of Graduate Education, Leadership and Counseling, Program in Educational Administration, Lawrenceville, NJ 08648-3001. Offers educational administration (MA); principal (Certificate); school administrator (Certificate). *Accreditation:* NCATE. Part-time and evening/weekend programs available. *Degree requirements:* For master's, comprehensive exam, research project. *Entrance requirements:* For master's, interview, resume, 2 letters of recommendation. Additional exam requirements/recommendations for international students: Required—TOEFL (minimum score 550 paper-based; 213 computer-based). Electronic applications accepted. *Faculty research:* National/state standards, urban education, administrative leadership, financing public education, community school linkages.

Rivier College, School of Graduate Studies, Department of Education, Nashua, NH 03060. Offers curriculum and instruction (M Ed); early childhood education (M Ed); educational administration (M Ed); educational studies (M Ed); elementary education (M Ed); elementary education and general special education (M Ed); emotional and behavioral disorders (M Ed); general social education (M Ed); leadership and learning (Ed D, CAGS); learning disabilities (M Ed); learning disabilities and reading (M Ed); mental health counseling (MA); reading (M Ed); school counseling (M Ed). Part-time and evening/weekend programs available. *Faculty:* 13 full-time (9 women), 38 part-time/adjunct (25 women). *Students:* 87 full-time (78 women), 293 part-time (246 women); includes 10 minority (3 African Americans, 4 Asian Americans or Pacific Islanders, 3 Hispanic Americans). Average age 38. 182 applicants, 82% accepted, 72 enrolled. In 2009, 110 master's, 18 other advanced degrees awarded. *Degree requirements:* For master's, comprehensive exam (for some programs), internships. *Entrance requirements:* For master's, GRE General Test or MAT. *Application deadline:* Applications are processed on a rolling basis. Application fee: $25. *Expenses:* Tuition: Part-time $447 per credit. *Financial support:* Available to part-time students. Application deadline: 2/1. *Unit head:* Dr. Patricia Howson, Chairman, 603-897-8562, E-mail: phowson@rivier.edu. *Application contact:* Mathew Kittredge, Director of Graduate Admissions, 603-897-8129, Fax: 603-897-8810, E-mail: mkittredge@rivier.edu.

Robert Morris University, Graduate Studies, School of Education and Social Sciences, Moon Township, PA 15108-1189. Offers business education (MS); education (Postbaccalaureate Certificate); instructional leadership (MS); instructional management and leadership (PhD). *Accreditation:* Teacher Education Accreditation Council. Part-time and evening/weekend programs available. *Faculty:* 14 full-time (3 women), 11 part-time/adjunct (6 women). *Students:* 353 part-time (229 women); includes 24 minority (21 African Americans, 1 Asian American or Pacific Islander, 2 Hispanic Americans), 1 international. Average age 31. 117 applicants, 96% accepted, 79 enrolled. In 2009, 79 master's, 14 doctorates, 97 other advanced degrees awarded. *Degree requirements:* For doctorate, thesis/dissertation. *Entrance requirements:* Additional exam requirements/recommendations for international students: Required—TOEFL (minimum score 550 paper-based; 213 computer-based; 79 iBT). *Application deadline:* For fall admission, 7/1 priority date for domestic and international students; for spring admission, 11/1 priority date for domestic and international students. Applications are processed on a rolling basis. Application fee: $35. Electronic applications accepted. *Expenses:* Contact institution. *Unit head:* Dr. John E. Graham, Dean, 412-397-3228, Fax: 412-397-2524, E-mail: graham@rmu.edu. *Application contact:* Debra Roach, Assistant Dean, Graduate Admissions, 412-397-5200, Fax: 412-397-2425, E-mail: graduateadmissions@rmu.edu.

Rocky Mountain College, Graduate Programs, Billings, MT 59102-1796. Offers accounting (M Acc); educational leadership (M Ed); physician assistant studies (MPAS). Part-time programs available. *Faculty:* 10 full-time (3 women), 12 part-time/adjunct (4 women). *Students:* 65 full-time (34 women), 1 part-time (0 women). Average age 28. In 2009, 55 master's awarded. *Entrance requirements:* Additional exam requirements/recommendations for international students: Required—TOEFL (minimum score 570 paper-based; 230 computer-based; 88 iBT), IELTS (minimum score 6.5). *Application deadline:* Applications are processed on a rolling basis. Application fee: $35 ($40 for international students). Electronic applications accepted. *Expenses:* Tuition: Full-time $25,070. Required fees: $450. Full-time tuition and fees vary according to program. *Financial support:* In 2009–10, 65 students received support. Federal Work-Study and scholarships/grants available. Financial award applicants required to submit FAFSA. *Unit head:* Anthony Piltz, Academic Vice President, 406-657-1020, Fax: 406-259-9751, E-mail: piltza@rocky.edu. *Application contact:* Kelly Edwards, Director of Admissions, 406-657-1026, Fax: 406-657-1189, E-mail: admissions@rocky.edu.

Roosevelt University, Graduate Division, College of Education, Program in Teacher Leadership (LEAD), Chicago, IL 60605. Offers MA.

Rowan University, Graduate School, College of Education, Department of Educational Leadership, Program in Educational Leadership, Glassboro, NJ 08028-1701. Offers Ed D. *Accreditation:* NCATE. Part-time and evening/weekend programs available. *Students:* 18 full-time (11 women), 182 part-time (126 women); includes 66 minority (57 African Americans, 1 American Indian/Alaska Native, 1 Asian American or Pacific Islander, 7 Hispanic Americans).

Educational Leadership and Administration

Rowan University (continued)

Average age 42. 69 applicants, 100% accepted, 62 enrolled. In 2009, 28 doctorates awarded. *Degree requirements:* For doctorate, thesis/dissertation. *Entrance requirements:* For doctorate, GRE General Test, master's degree. Additional exam requirements/recommendations for international students: Required—TOEFL. *Application deadline:* Applications are processed on a rolling basis. Application fee: $50. Electronic applications accepted. *Expenses:* Tuition, state resident: full-time $10,624; part-time $590 per semester hour. Tuition, nonresident: full-time $10,624; part-time $590 per semester hour. Required fees: $2320; $125 per semester hour. *Financial support:* Career-related internships or fieldwork, scholarships/grants, health care benefits, and unspecified assistantships available. Support available to part-time students. *Unit head:* Dr. Mira Lalovic-Hand, Interim Associate Provost/Director of Graduate School, 856-256-5120, E-mail: lalovic-hand@rowan.edu. *Application contact:* Karen Haynes, Graduate Coordinator, 856-256-4052, Fax: 856-256-4436, E-mail: haynes@rowan.edu.

Rowan University, Graduate School, College of Education, Department of Educational Leadership, Program in Higher Education Administration, Glassboro, NJ 08028-1701. Offers MA. *Accreditation:* NCATE. Part-time and evening/weekend programs available. *Students:* 17 full-time (11 women), 21 part-time (16 women); includes 12 minority (10 African Americans, 2 Hispanic Americans). Average age 25. 23 applicants, 91% accepted, 14 enrolled. In 2009, 19 master's awarded. *Degree requirements:* For master's, comprehensive exam, thesis. *Entrance requirements:* For master's, GRE General Test, minimum GPA of 2.8, 2 years of teaching experience. Additional exam requirements/recommendations for international students: Required—TOEFL. *Application deadline:* Applications are processed on a rolling basis. Application fee: $50. Electronic applications accepted. *Expenses:* Tuition, state resident: full-time $10,624; part-time $590 per semester hour. Tuition, nonresident: full-time $10,624; part-time $590 per semester hour. Required fees: $2320; $125 per semester hour. *Financial support:* Career-related internships or fieldwork, scholarships/grants, health care benefits, and unspecified assistantships available. Support available to part-time students. *Unit head:* Dr. Mira Lalovic-Hand, Interim Associate Provost/Director of Graduate School, 856-256-5120, E-mail: lalovic-hand@rowan.edu. *Application contact:* Karen Haynes, Graduate Coordinator, 856-256-4052, Fax: 856-256-4436, E-mail: haynes@rowan.edu.

Rowan University, Graduate School, College of Education, Department of Educational Leadership, Program in Principal Preparation, Glassboro, NJ 08028-1701. Offers CAGS. Part-time and evening/weekend programs available. *Students:* 10 part-time (8 women). Average age 41. 3 applicants, 100% accepted, 3 enrolled. *Degree requirements:* For CAGS, comprehensive exam, thesis, internship. *Entrance requirements:* For degree, GRE General Test, minimum GPA of 2.81, 1 year of teaching experience. Additional exam requirements/recommendations for international students: Required—TOEFL. *Application deadline:* Applications are processed on a rolling basis. Electronic applications accepted. *Expenses:* Tuition, state resident: full-time $10,624; part-time $590 per semester hour. Tuition, nonresident: full-time $10,624; part-time $590 per semester hour. Required fees: $2320; $125 per semester hour. *Financial support:* Career-related internships or fieldwork, Federal Work-Study, and unspecified assistantships available. Support available to part-time students. *Unit head:* Dr. Robert Campbell, Program Coordinator, 856-256-4500 Ext. 3817, E-mail: campbell@rowan.edu. *Application contact:* Karen Haynes, Graduate Coordinator, 856-256-4052, Fax: 856-256-4436, E-mail: haynes@rowan.edu.

Rowan University, Graduate School, College of Education, Department of Educational Leadership, Program in School Administration, Glassboro, NJ 08028-1701. Offers business administration (MA); principal preparation (MA). *Accreditation:* NCATE. Part-time and evening/weekend programs available. *Students:* 1 full-time (0 women), 44 part-time (23 women); includes 3 minority (2 African Americans, 1 Hispanic American). Average age 35. 5 applicants, 100% accepted, 5 enrolled. In 2009, 31 master's awarded. *Degree requirements:* For master's, comprehensive exam, thesis, internship. *Entrance requirements:* For master's, GRE General Test, NTE, minimum GPA of 2.8, 2 years of teaching experience. Additional exam requirements/recommendations for international students: Required—TOEFL. *Application deadline:* Applications are processed on a rolling basis. Application fee: $50. Electronic applications accepted. *Expenses:* Tuition, state resident: full-time $10,624; part-time $590 per semester hour. Tuition, nonresident: full-time $10,624; part-time $590 per semester hour. Required fees: $2320; $125 per semester hour. *Financial support:* Career-related internships or fieldwork, scholarships/grants, health care benefits, and unspecified assistantships available. Support available to part-time students. *Unit head:* Dr. Mira Lalovic-Hand, Interim Associate Provost/Director of Graduate School, 856-256-5120, E-mail: lalovic-hand@rowan.edu. *Application contact:* Karen Haynes, Graduate Coordinator, 856-256-4052, E-mail: haynes@rowan.edu.

Rowan University, Graduate School, College of Education, Department of Educational Leadership, Program in School Business Administration, Glassboro, NJ 08028-1701. Offers MA. Part-time and evening/weekend programs available. *Students:* 1 part-time (0 women). Average age 29. In 2009, 3 master's awarded. *Degree requirements:* For master's, comprehensive exam, thesis. *Entrance requirements:* For master's, GRE General Test. Additional exam requirements/recommendations for international students: Required—TOEFL. *Application deadline:* Applications are processed on a rolling basis. Application fee: $50. Electronic applications accepted. *Expenses:* Tuition, state resident: full-time $10,624; part-time $590 per semester hour. Tuition, nonresident: full-time $10,624; part-time $590 per semester hour. Required fees: $2320; $125 per semester hour. *Financial support:* Career-related internships or fieldwork, scholarships/grants, health care benefits, and unspecified assistantships available. *Unit head:* Dr. Mira Lalovic-Hand, Interim Associate Provost/Director of Graduate School, 856-256-5120, E-mail: lalovic-hand@rowan.edu. *Application contact:* Karen Haynes, Graduate Coordinator, 856-256-4052, Fax: 856-256-4436, E-mail: haynes@rowan.edu.

Rowan University, Graduate School, College of Education, Department of Teacher Education, Program in Standards-Based Practice, Glassboro, NJ 08028-1701. Offers M Ed. Part-time and evening/weekend programs available. *Students:* 1 (woman) part-time. Average age 47. 5 applicants, 60% accepted. In 2009, 9 master's awarded. *Degree requirements:* For master's, thesis. *Entrance requirements:* For master's, GRE General Test. Additional exam requirements/recommendations for international students: Required—TOEFL. *Application deadline:* Applications are processed on a rolling basis. Electronic applications accepted. *Expenses:* Tuition, state resident: full-time $10,624; part-time $590 per semester hour. Tuition, nonresident: full-time $10,624; part-time $590 per semester hour. Required fees: $2320; $125 per semester hour. *Financial support:* Career-related internships or fieldwork, scholarships/grants, health care benefits, and unspecified assistantships available. *Unit head:* Dr. Mira Lalovic-Hand, Interim Associate Provost/Director of Graduate School, 856-256-5120, E-mail: lalovic-hand@rowan.edu. *Application contact:* Karen Haynes, Graduate Coordinator, 856-256-4052, Fax: 856-256-4436, E-mail: haynes@rowan.edu.

Rowan University, Graduate School, College of Education, Department of Teacher Education, Program in Teacher Leadership, Glassboro, NJ 08028-1701. Offers M Ed. Part-time and evening/weekend programs available. *Students:* 7 full-time (all women), 35 part-time (33 women); includes 3 minority (2 African Americans, 1 Hispanic American). Average age 33. 20 applicants, 100% accepted, 17 enrolled. *Degree requirements:* For master's, thesis. *Entrance requirements:* For master's, GRE General Test, minimum GPA of 2.8, 1 year of teaching experience. Additional exam requirements/recommendations for international students: Required—TOEFL. *Application deadline:* Applications are processed on a rolling basis. Application fee: $50. Electronic applications accepted. *Expenses:* Tuition, state resident: full-time $10,624; part-time $590 per semester hour. Tuition, nonresident: full-time $10,624; part-time $590 per semester hour. Required fees: $2320; $125 per semester hour. *Financial support:* Career-related internships or fieldwork, scholarships/grants, health care benefits, and unspecified assistantships available. *Unit head:* Dr. Mira Lalovic-Hand, Interim Associate Provost/Director of Graduate School, 856-256-5120, E-mail: lalovic-hand@rowan.edu. *Application contact:* Karen Haynes, Graduate Coordinator, 856-256-4052, Fax: 856-256-4436, E-mail: haynes@rowan.edu.

Rutgers, The State University of New Jersey, Camden, Graduate School of Arts and Sciences, Department of Public Policy and Administration, Camden, NJ 08102-1401. Offers education policy and leadership (MPA); international public service and development (MPA); public management (MPA); JD/MPA; MPA/MA. *Accreditation:* NASPAA. Part-time and evening/weekend programs available. *Degree requirements:* For master's, directed study, research workshop. *Entrance requirements:* For master's, GRE General Test, GMAT or LSAT, 3 letters of recommendation; resume. Additional exam requirements/recommendations for international students: Required—TOEFL (minimum score 550 paper-based; 213 computer-based), IELTS. Electronic applications accepted. *Faculty research:* Nonprofit management, county and municipal administration, health and human services, government communication, administrative law, educational finance.

Rutgers, The State University of New Jersey, New Brunswick, Graduate School of Education, Department of Educational Theory, Policy and Administration, Programs in Educational Administration and Supervision, Piscataway, NJ 08854-8097. Offers Ed M, Ed D. Part-time and evening/weekend programs available. *Degree requirements:* For doctorate, thesis/dissertation, qualifying exam. *Entrance requirements:* For master's, GRE General Test, minimum GPA of 3.0; for doctorate, GRE General Test, minimum GPA of 3.0, master's degree in educational administration. Additional exam requirements/recommendations for international students: Required—TOEFL. Electronic applications accepted. *Faculty research:* 5.

Sacred Heart University, Graduate Programs, College of Education and Health Professions, Isabelle Farrington School of Education, Fairfield, CT 06825-1000. Offers administration (CAS); educational technology (MAT); elementary education (MAT); reading (CAS); secondary education (MAT); teaching (CAS). Part-time and evening/weekend programs available. Postbaccalaureate distance learning degree programs offered (minimal on-campus study). *Faculty:* 23 full-time (10 women). *Students:* 377 full-time (291 women), 691 part-time (495 women); includes 63 minority (31 African Americans, 2 American Indian/Alaska Native, 8 Asian Americans or Pacific Islanders, 22 Hispanic Americans), 2 international. Average age 34. 429 applicants, 90% accepted, 338 enrolled. In 2009, 409 master's, 66 other advanced degrees awarded. *Degree requirements:* For master's, thesis or alternative. *Entrance requirements:* For master's, PRAXIS (teacher certification/MAT); for CAS, PRAXIS I. Additional exam requirements/recommendations for international students: Required—TOEFL (minimum score 550 paper-based; 213 computer-based). *Application deadline:* Applications are processed on a rolling basis. Application fee: $50 ($100 for international students). Electronic applications accepted. *Expenses:* Contact institution. *Financial support:* Teaching assistantships with partial tuition reimbursements, career-related internships or fieldwork, institutionally sponsored loans, traineeships, tuition waivers (partial), and unspecified assistantships available. Support available to part-time students. Financial award applicants required to submit FAFSA. *Faculty research:* Reading education, learning theory, teacher preparation, education of underachievers. *Unit head:* Dr. Edward Malin, Director, 203-371-7800, Fax: 203-365-7513. *Application contact:* Kathy Dilks, Assistant Dean of Graduate Admissions, 203-365-7619, Fax: 203-365-4732, E-mail: gradstudies@sacredheart.edu.

Sage Graduate School, Graduate School, School of Education, Program in Educational Leadership, Troy, NY 12180-4115. Offers Ed D. Part-time programs available. *Faculty:* 15 full-time (9 women), 19 part-time/adjunct (16 women). *Students:* 30 part-time (15 women). Average age 45. 28 applicants, 54% accepted, 15 enrolled. *Degree requirements:* For doctorate, comprehensive exam. *Entrance requirements:* For doctorate, minimum GPA of 3.5, 60 graduate credits from an accredited institution, 3 references addressing leadership skill potential, writing sample, personal interview. Additional exam requirements/recommendations for international students: Required—TOEFL (minimum score 550 paper-based; 213 computer-based). *Application deadline:* Applications are processed on a rolling basis. Application fee: $40. *Expenses:* Tuition: Full-time $10,620; part-time $590 per credit hour. *Financial support:* Fellowships, research assistantships, Federal Work-Study, scholarships/grants, and unspecified assistantships available. Support available to part-time students. *Unit head:* Dr. Ann Myers, Director, 518-244-2347, E-mail: myersa1@sage.edu. *Application contact:* Wendy D. Diefendorf, Director of Graduate and Adult Admission, 518-244-2443, Fax: 518-244-6880, E-mail: diefew@sage.edu.

Saginaw Valley State University, College of Education, Program in Educational Leadership, University Center, MI 48710. Offers chief business officers (M Ed); education leadership (Ed S); educational administration and supervision (M Ed); principalship (M Ed); superintendency (M Ed). *Accreditation:* NCATE. Part-time and evening/weekend programs available. *Students:* 4 full-time (2 women), 119 part-time (68 women); includes 7 minority (4 African Americans, 1 American Indian/Alaska Native, 2 Hispanic Americans), 1 international. Average age 34. 24 applicants, 100% accepted, 16 enrolled. In 2009, 130 master's, 37 Ed Ss awarded. *Degree requirements:* For master's, practicum. *Entrance requirements:* For master's, minimum GPA of 3.0, teaching certificate. *Application deadline:* Applications are processed on a rolling basis. Application fee: $25. Electronic applications accepted. *Financial support:* Federal Work-Study and scholarships/grants available. Support available to part-time students. Financial award applicants required to submit FAFSA. *Unit head:* Dr. Steve P. Barbus, Dean, 989-964-6067, Fax: 989-790-4385, E-mail: barbus@svsu.edu. *Application contact:* Jeanne Chipman, Certification Officer, 989-964-4083, Fax: 989-964-4385, E-mail: jdc@svsu.edu.

St. Ambrose University, College of Education and Health Sciences, Program in Educational Administration, Davenport, IA 52803-2898. Offers MEA. Part-time and evening/weekend programs available. *Faculty:* 1 full-time (0 women), 2 part-time/adjunct (0 women). *Students:* 1 full-time (0 women), 18 part-time (9 women), 1 international. Average age 37. 12 applicants, 100% accepted, 12 enrolled. In 2009, 15 master's awarded. *Entrance requirements:* Additional exam requirements/recommendations for international students: Required—TOEFL. *Application deadline:* Applications are processed on a rolling basis. Application fee: $25. Electronic applications accepted. *Expenses:* Tuition: Part-time $702 per credit hour. Tuition and fees vary according to degree level, program and reciprocity agreements. *Financial support:* In 2009–10, 13 students received support. Scholarships/grants available. *Unit head:* Dr. Charles Manges, Director, 563-388-7652, Fax: 563-388-7662, E-mail: mangescharles@sau.edu. *Application contact:* Susan M. Jameson, Administrative Assistant, 563-388-7660, Fax: 563-388-7662, E-mail: lovelesselizabethb@sau.edu.

St. Bonaventure University, School of Graduate Studies, School of Education, Program in Educational Leadership, St. Bonaventure, NY 14778-2284. Offers educational leadership (MS Ed); school building leader (Adv C); school district leader (Adv C). Part-time and evening/weekend programs available. Postbaccalaureate distance learning degree programs offered (minimal on-campus study). *Faculty:* 1 full-time (0 women), 1 (woman) part-time/adjunct. *Students:* 5 full-time (all women), 32 part-time (20 women); includes 1 minority (American Indian/Alaska Native). Average age 37. 34 applicants, 85% accepted, 22 enrolled. In 2009, 4 master's awarded. *Degree requirements:* For master's, thesis optional. *Entrance requirements:* For master's, 3 years of teaching experience, teacher certification. Additional exam requirements/recommendations for international students: Required—TOEFL. *Application deadline:* For fall admission, 8/1 for domestic students. Applications are processed on a rolling basis. Application fee: $30. *Expenses:* Tuition: Full-time $11,700; part-time $650 per credit. *Financial support:* In 2009–10, 1 student received support; research assistantships, scholarships/grants available. Support available to part-time students. Financial award application deadline: 4/15; financial award applicants required to submit FAFSA. *Faculty research:* Collective bargaining, curriculum development, self-esteem, rural schools program, leadership issues, school safety. *Unit head:* Dr. Greg Gibbs, Director, 716-375-2315, Fax: 716-375-2363, E-mail: gibbs@sbu.edu. *Application contact:* Bruce Campbell, Director of Graduate Admissions, 716-375-2021.

St. Cloud State University, School of Graduate Studies, College of Education, Department of Counselor Education, Higher Education, and Educational Psychology, Program in Higher Education Administration, St. Cloud, MN 56301-4498. Offers MS, Ed D. *Students:* 16 full-time (9 women), 52 part-time (28 women); includes 9 minority (3 African Americans, 1 American Indian/Alaska Native, 5 Asian Americans or Pacific Islanders), 9 international. 19 applicants,

100% accepted. In 2009, 7 master's awarded. Application fee: $35. *Unit head:* Dr. Christine Imbra, Head, 320-308-4909, E-mail: cmimbra@stcloudstate.edu. *Application contact:* Linda Lou Krueger, School of Graduate Studies, 320-308-2113, Fax: 320-308-5371, E-mail: lekrueger@stcloudstate.edu.

St. Cloud State University, School of Graduate Studies, College of Education, Department of Educational Leadership and Community Psychology, Program in Educational Administration and Leadership, St. Cloud, MN 56301-4498. Offers MS. Part-time programs available. *Faculty:* 5 full-time (4 women), 3 part-time/adjunct (all women). *Students:* 17 full-time (9 women), 79 part-time (47 women); includes 7 minority (all African Americans), 4 international. 25 applicants, 100% accepted, 0 enrolled. In 2009, 8 master's awarded. *Degree requirements:* For master's, comprehensive exam (for some programs), thesis or alternative. *Entrance requirements:* For master's, GRE General Test, minimum GPA of 2.75. Additional exam requirements/recommendations for international students: Required—Michigan English Language Assessment Battery; Recommended—TOEFL (minimum score 550 paper-based; 213 computer-based), IELTS (minimum score 6.5). *Application deadline:* For fall admission, 6/1 priority date for domestic students, 4/1 for international students; for spring admission, 10/1 priority date for domestic students, 8/1 for international students. Applications are processed on a rolling basis. Application fee: $35. Electronic applications accepted. *Financial support:* Federal Work-Study, scholarships/grants, and unspecified assistantships available. *Unit head:* Dr. Janine Dahms-Walker, Coordinator, 320-308-2946, E-mail: jdwalker@stcloudstate.edu. *Application contact:* Linda Lou Krueger, School of Graduate Studies, 320-308-2113, Fax: 320-308-5371, E-mail: lekrueger@stcloudstate.edu.

St. Edward's University, School of Education, Program in Teaching, Austin, TX 78704. Offers curriculum leadership (Certificate); instructional technology (Certificate); mentoring and supervision (Certificate); sports management (Certificate); teaching (MA), including conflict resolution, initial teacher certification, liberal arts, organization development and training, sports management, teacher leadership. Part-time and evening/weekend programs available. *Students:* 5 full-time (4 women), 36 part-time (26 women); includes 10 minority (1 African American, 9 Hispanic Americans). Average age 30. 23 applicants, 70% accepted, 12 enrolled. In 2009, 9 master's awarded. *Degree requirements:* For master's, minimum of 24 resident hours. *Entrance requirements:* For master's, GRE General Test, minimum GPA of 3.0 in last 60 hours or 2.75 overall. Additional exam requirements/recommendations for international students: Required—TOEFL (minimum score 550 paper-based; 213 computer-based; 79 iBT) or IELTS (minimum score 6). *Application deadline:* For fall admission, 7/1 for domestic and international students; for spring admission, 11/1 for domestic and international students. Applications are processed on a rolling basis. Application fee: $45 ($50 for international students). Electronic applications accepted. *Expenses:* Tuition: Full-time $14,922; part-time $829 per credit hour. Required fees: $50 per trimester. Full-time tuition and fees vary according to course load and program. *Financial support:* In 2009–10, 3 students received support. Scholarships/grants available. *Unit head:* Dr. David Hollier, Director, 512-448-8666, Fax: 512-428-1372, E-mail: davidrh@stedwards.edu. *Application contact:* Kay L. Arnold, Assistant Director of Admissions, 512-233-1636, Fax: 512-428-1032, E-mail: kayla@stedwards.edu.

Saint Francis University, Graduate Education Program, Loretto, PA 15940-0600. Offers education (M Ed); leadership (M Ed); reading (M Ed). Part-time and evening/weekend programs available. *Faculty:* 29 part-time/adjunct (7 women). *Students:* 150 part-time (100 women); includes 3 minority (2 African Americans, 1 Hispanic American). Average age 30. 20 applicants, 100% accepted, 20 enrolled. In 2009, 50 master's awarded. *Degree requirements:* For master's, comprehensive exam, thesis optional. *Entrance requirements:* For master's, GRE or MAT (if undergraduate GPA less than 2.8), minimum undergraduate QPA of 2.5. *Application deadline:* Applications are processed on a rolling basis. Application fee: $30. *Expenses:* Contact institution. *Financial support:* Applicants required to submit FAFSA. *Unit head:* Dr. Janette D. Kelly, Director, Graduate Education, 814-472-3068, Fax: 814-472-3864, E-mail: jkelly@francis.edu. *Application contact:* Sherri L. Toth, Coordinator, 814-472-3058, Fax: 814-472-3864, E-mail: stoth@francis.edu.

St. Francis Xavier University, Graduate Studies, Graduate Studies in Education, Antigonish, NS B2G 2W5, Canada. Offers curriculum and instruction (M Ed); educational administration and leadership (M Ed). Part-time programs available. Postbaccalaureate distance learning degree programs offered (minimal on-campus study). *Degree requirements:* For master's, thesis. *Entrance requirements:* For master's, minimum undergraduate B average, 2 years of teaching experience. *Faculty research:* Inclusive education, qualitative research.

St. John Fisher College, Ralph C. Wilson Jr. School of Education, Educational Leadership Program, Rochester, NY 14618-3597. Offers MS Ed. Part-time and evening/weekend programs available. *Faculty:* 3 full-time (1 woman), 2 part-time/adjunct (both women). *Students:* 41 part-time (24 women); includes 12 minority (10 African Americans, 2 Hispanic Americans). Average age 36. 30 applicants, 93% accepted, 19 enrolled. In 2009, 37 master's awarded. *Degree requirements:* For master's, capstone project, internship. *Entrance requirements:* For master's, GRE (if GPA below 3.0), teacher certification, minimum 2 years of teaching experience, 2 letters of recommendation, current resume. Additional exam requirements/recommendations for international students: Required—TOEFL (minimum score 575 paper-based; 233 computer-based; 80 iBT). *Application deadline:* Applications are processed on a rolling basis. Application fee: $30. Electronic applications accepted. *Expenses:* Tuition: Part-time $680 per credit hour. Required fees: $25 per semester. Tuition and fees vary according to degree level and program. *Financial support:* In 2009–10, 36 students received support. Scholarships/grants available. Financial award applicants required to submit FAFSA. *Faculty research:* Urban school leadership, assessment, effective school leadership. *Unit head:* Dr. William Stroud, Co-Director, 585-385-7258, E-mail: wstroud@sjfc.edu. *Application contact:* Jose Perales, Director of Graduate Admissions, 585-385-8067, E-mail: jperales@sjfc.edu.

St. John Fisher College, Ralph C. Wilson Jr. School of Education, Executive Leadership Program, Rochester, NY 14618-3597. Offers Ed D. Part-time and evening/weekend programs available. *Faculty:* 7 full-time (3 women), 3 part-time/adjunct (0 women). *Students:* 75 full-time (57 women), 8 part-time (4 women); includes 38 minority (34 African Americans, 4 Hispanic Americans). Average age 45. 73 applicants, 89% accepted, 52 enrolled. In 2009, 25 doctorates awarded. *Degree requirements:* For doctorate, comprehensive exam, thesis/dissertation, field experiences. *Entrance requirements:* For doctorate, 3 professional writing samples, 2 letters of reference, interview, minimum 3 years management experience, completed master's degree. Additional exam requirements/recommendations for international students: Required—TOEFL (minimum score 575 paper-based; 233 computer-based; 80 iBT). *Application deadline:* For fall admission, 3/1 for domestic and international students. Applications are processed on a rolling basis. Electronic applications accepted. *Expenses:* Tuition: Part-time $680 per credit hour. Required fees: $25 per semester. Tuition and fees vary according to degree level and program. *Financial support:* In 2009–10, 70 students received support. Scholarships/grants available. Financial award applicants required to submit FAFSA. *Faculty research:* Leadership, organizational development. *Unit head:* Dr. Arthur Walton, Program Director, 585-385-8387, E-mail: awalton@sjfc.edu. *Application contact:* Jose Perales, Director of Graduate Admissions, 585-385-8067, E-mail: jperales@sjfc.edu.

St. John's University, The School of Education, Division of Administrative and Instructional Leadership, Instructional Leadership Program, Queens, NY 11439. Offers Ed D, PD. Part-time and evening/weekend programs available. *Students:* 4 full-time (2 women), 90 part-time (63 women); includes 21 minority (10 African Americans, 7 Asian Americans or Pacific Islanders, 4 Hispanic Americans), 3 international. Average age 42. 37 applicants, 62% accepted, 20 enrolled. In 2009, 16 doctorates, 10 other advanced degrees awarded. *Degree requirements:* For doctorate, comprehensive exam, thesis/dissertation. *Entrance requirements:* For doctorate, GRE General Test, interview, minimum GPA of 3.2, 2 letters of recommendation, resume, writing samples; for PD, official transcript, minimum GPA of 3.0, 2 letters of recommendation. Additional exam requirements/recommendations for international students: Required—TOEFL (minimum score 500 paper-based; 173 computer-based; 61 iBT), IELTS (minimum score 5.5). *Application deadline:* For fall admission, 4/15 priority date for domestic students, 6/1 priority date for international students; for spring admission, 11/1 priority date for domestic and international students. Applications are processed on a rolling basis. Application fee: $70. Electronic applications accepted. *Expenses:* Tuition: Full-time $16,290; part-time $905 per credit. Required fees: $300; $150 per semester. Tuition and fees vary according to program. *Financial support:* Fellowships, research assistantships, career-related internships or fieldwork and scholarships/grants available. Support available to part-time students. Financial award application deadline: 3/1; financial award applicants required to submit FAFSA. *Faculty research:* Learning styles, gifted and talented. *Unit head:* Dr. Gene Geisert, Chair, 718-990-6598, E-mail: geisertg@stjohns.edu. *Application contact:* Dr. Kelly K. Ronayne, Associate Dean of Graduate Admissions, 718-990-2303, Fax: 718-990-2343, E-mail: graded@stjohns.edu.

St. John's University, The School of Education, Division of Administrative and Instructional Leadership, Program in Educational Administration and Supervision, Queens, NY 11439. Offers administration and supervision (Ed D, PD). Part-time and evening/weekend programs available. *Students:* 3 full-time (1 woman), 100 part-time (65 women); includes 26 minority (20 African Americans, 6 Hispanic Americans), 3 international. Average age 43. 38 applicants, 58% accepted, 17 enrolled. In 2009, 18 doctorates, 21 other advanced degrees awarded. *Degree requirements:* For doctorate, thesis/dissertation, clinical residency. *Entrance requirements:* For doctorate, GRE General Test, interview, minimum GPA of 3.2, 2 letters of recommendation, resume, writing samples. Additional exam requirements/recommendations for international students: Required—TOEFL (minimum score 500 paper-based; 173 computer-based; 61 iBT), IELTS (minimum score 5.5). *Application deadline:* For fall admission, 4/15 priority date for domestic students, 6/1 priority date for international students; for spring admission, 11/1 priority date for domestic and international students. Applications are processed on a rolling basis. Application fee: $70. Electronic applications accepted. *Expenses:* Tuition: Full-time $16,290; part-time $905 per credit. Required fees: $300; $150 per semester. Tuition and fees vary according to program. *Financial support:* Research assistantships, career-related internships or fieldwork available. Support available to part-time students. Financial award application deadline: 3/1; financial award applicants required to submit FAFSA. *Faculty research:* Organizational theory, economics, bargaining and restructuring. *Unit head:* Dr. Gene Geisert, Chair, 718-990-6598, E-mail: geisertg@stjohns.edu. *Application contact:* Dr. Kelly K. Ronayne, Associate Dean of Graduate Admissions, 718-990-2303, Fax: 718-990-2343, E-mail: graded@stjohns.edu.

St. John's University, The School of Education, Division of Administrative and Instructional Leadership, Program in School Building Leadership, Queens, NY 11439. Offers MS Ed, PD. Part-time and evening/weekend programs available. Postbaccalaureate distance learning degree programs offered. *Students:* 15 full-time (9 women), 159 part-time (112 women); includes 48 minority (15 African Americans, 6 Asian Americans or Pacific Islanders, 27 Hispanic Americans), 5 international. Average age 36. 96 applicants, 88% accepted, 55 enrolled. In 2009, 124 master's, 2 other advanced degrees awarded. *Degree requirements:* For master's and PD, comprehensive exam, internship. *Entrance requirements:* For master's, official transcript with minimum GPA of 3.0, minimum 3 years successful teaching experience, New York State Permanent Teaching Certification; for PD, minimum GPA of 3.0, minimum 3 years successful teaching experience, New York State Permanent Teaching Certification. Additional exam requirements/recommendations for international students: Required—TOEFL (minimum score 500 paper-based; 173 computer-based; 61 iBT), IELTS (minimum score 5.5). *Application deadline:* For fall admission, 4/15 priority date for domestic students, 6/1 priority date for international students; for spring admission, 11/1 priority date for domestic and international students. Applications are processed on a rolling basis. Application fee: $70. Electronic applications accepted. *Expenses:* Contact institution. *Financial support:* Research assistantships, career-related internships or fieldwork and scholarships/grants available. Support available to part-time students. Financial award application deadline: 3/1; financial award applicants required to submit FAFSA. *Unit head:* Dr. Gene Geisert, Chair, 718-990-6598, E-mail: geisertg@stjohns.edu. *Application contact:* Dr. Kelly K. Ronayne, Associate Dean for Graduate Admissions, 718-990-2303, Fax: 718-990-2343, E-mail: graded@stjohns.edu.

St. John's University, The School of Education, Division of Administrative and Instructional Leadership, Program in School District Leadership, Queens, NY 11439. Offers PD. Part-time and evening/weekend programs available. *Students:* 1 (woman) full-time, 3 part-time (2 women); includes 1 minority (African American). Average age 30. 5 applicants, 40% accepted, 2 enrolled. *Degree requirements:* For PD, comprehensive exam. *Entrance requirements:* For degree, minimum GPA of 3.0, minimum 3 years successful teaching experience, New York State Permanent Teaching Certification. Additional exam requirements/recommendations for international students: Required—TOEFL (minimum score 500 paper-based; 173 computer-based; 61 iBT), IELTS (minimum score 5.5). *Application deadline:* For fall admission, 4/15 priority date for domestic students, 6/1 priority date for international students; for spring admission, 11/1 priority date for domestic and international students. Applications are processed on a rolling basis. Application fee: $70. Electronic applications accepted. *Expenses:* Tuition: Full-time $16,290; part-time $905 per credit. Required fees: $300; $150 per semester. Tuition and fees vary according to program. *Financial support:* Research assistantships, career-related internships or fieldwork available. Support available to part-time students. Financial award application deadline: 3/1; financial award applicants required to submit FAFSA. *Unit head:* Dr. Gene Geisert, Chair, 718-990-6598, E-mail: geisertg@stjohns.edu. *Application contact:* Dr. Kelly K. Ronayne, Associate Dean of Graduate Admissions, 718-990-2303, Fax: 718-990-2343, E-mail: graded@stjohns.edu.

Saint Joseph's University, College of Arts and Sciences, Department of Education, Philadelphia, PA 19131-1395. Offers educational leadership (Ed D); elementary education (MS); instructional technology (MS); organizational development and leadership (MS); professional education (MS); reading specialist (MS); secondary education (MS); special education (MS). Part-time and evening/weekend programs available. *Students:* 5 full-time (3 women), 750 part-time (561 women); includes 100 minority (76 African Americans, 1 American Indian/Alaska Native, 11 Asian Americans or Pacific Islanders, 12 Hispanic Americans), 3 international. Average age 33. In 2009, 210 master's, 14 doctorates awarded. *Entrance requirements:* For master's, 2 letters of recommendation, minimum GPA of 3.0, application, official transcripts, personal statement; for doctorate, GRE, master's degree from accredited institution, minimum graduate GPA of 3.5, computer competence, commitment to participate in cohort, interview with program director. Additional exam requirements/recommendations for international students: Required—TOEFL (minimum score 550 paper-based; 213 computer-based; 79 iBT). *Application deadline:* For fall admission, 7/15 priority date for domestic students, 4/15 for international students; for winter admission, 11/15 for domestic students, 1/15 for international students; for spring admission, 11/15 priority date for domestic students, 10/15 for international students. Applications are processed on a rolling basis. Application fee: $35. Electronic applications accepted. *Expenses:* Contact institution. *Financial support:* Unspecified assistantships available. Financial award applicants required to submit FAFSA. *Faculty research:* Early childhood course design, public education professional development. Total annual research expenditures: $91,900. *Unit head:* Dr. Teri Sosa, Director of Graduate Education, 610-660-3162, E-mail: tsosa@sju.edu. *Application contact:* Kate McConnell, Director, Graduate College of Arts and Sciences Admissions and Retention, 610-660-3184, Fax: 610-660-3230, E-mail: kate.mcconnell@sju.edu.

St. Lawrence University, Department of Education, Program in Educational Leadership, Canton, NY 13617-1455. Offers combined school building leadership/school district leadership (CAS); educational leadership (M Ed); school building leadership (M Ed); school district leadership (CAS). Part-time and evening/weekend programs available. *Entrance requirements:* For master's, GRE General Test. *Faculty research:* Leadership.

Saint Leo University, Graduate Studies in Education, Saint Leo, FL 33574-6665. Offers educational leadership (M Ed, Ed S); exceptional student education (M Ed); higher education leadership (Ed S); instructional design (MS); instructional leadership (M Ed); reading (M Ed). Part-time and evening/weekend programs available. Postbaccalaureate distance learning degree programs offered (minimal on-campus study). *Faculty:* 13 full-time (10 women), 12 part-time/adjunct (9 women). *Students:* 432 full-time (355 women), 35 part-time (24 women); includes

Educational Leadership and Administration

Saint Leo University (continued)

56 minority (40 African Americans, 2 American Indian/Alaska Native, 2 Asian Americans or Pacific Islanders, 12 Hispanic Americans), 1 international. Average age 37. In 2009, 131 master's awarded. *Degree requirements:* For master's, comprehensive exam, appropriate State of Florida Certification Tests. *Entrance requirements:* For master's, GRE (minimum score of 1000) or MAT (minimum score of 410) if undergraduate GPA for last 60 hours of coursework was below 3.0 (for M Ed), bachelor's degree from regionally-accredited college or university with minimum GPA of 3.0 for last 60 hours of coursework, 2 recommendations, resume, statement of professional goals, copy of valid teaching certificate (for M Ed); for Ed S, GRE (minimum score 1000) or MAT (minimum score 410) if undergraduate GPA for last 60 hours of coursework less than 3.0, bachelor's degree from regionally-accredited college or university with minimum GPA of 3.0 for last 60 hours of coursework, 2 recommendations, resume, valid teaching certificate. Additional exam requirements/recommendations for international students: Required—TOEFL (minimum score 550 paper-based; 213 computer-based; 80 iBT). *Application deadline:* For fall admission, 7/1 priority date for domestic students; for spring admission, 11/12 priority date for domestic students. Applications are processed on a rolling basis. Application fee: $75. Electronic applications accepted. *Expenses:* Tuition: Part-time $1767 per course. Required fees: $115 per course. *Financial support:* Career-related internships or fieldwork, Federal Work-Study, and health care benefits available. Financial award application deadline: 3/1; financial award applicants required to submit FAFSA. *Faculty research:* The role of the school leader in data analysis of student achievement, teacher recruitment, and teacher effectiveness. *Unit head:* Dr. John Smith, Director, 352-588-8309, Fax: 352-588-8861, E-mail: med@saintleo.edu. *Application contact:* Jared Welling, Director, Graduate/Weekend and Evening Admission, 800-707-8846, Fax: 352-588-7873, E-mail: grad.admissions@saintleo.edu.

Saint Louis University, Graduate School, College of Education and Public Service and Graduate School, Department of Educational Leadership and Higher Education, St. Louis, MO 63103-2097. Offers Catholic school leadership (MA); educational administration (MA, Ed D, PhD, Ed S); higher education (MA, Ed D, PhD); student personnel administration (MA). *Accreditation:* NCATE. Part-time programs available. *Degree requirements:* For master's, comprehensive written and oral exam; for doctorate, comprehensive exam, thesis/dissertation, preliminary oral and written exams. *Entrance requirements:* For master's, GRE General Test, MAT, LSAT, GMAT or MCAT, letters of recommendation, resume; for doctorate and Ed S, GRE General Test, LSAT, GMAT or MCAT, letters of recommendation, resumé, goal statement, transcripts. Additional exam requirements/recommendations for international students: Required—TOEFL (minimum score 525 paper-based; 194 computer-based). Electronic applications accepted. *Faculty research:* Superintendent of schools, school finance, school facilities, student personal administration, building leadership.

Saint Martin's University, Graduate Programs, College of Education, Lacey, WA 98503. Offers administration (M Ed); English as a second language (M Ed); guidance and counseling (M Ed); reading (M Ed); special education (M Ed); teaching (MIT); technology in education (M Ed). *Accreditation:* Teacher Education Accreditation Council. Part-time and evening/weekend programs available. *Faculty:* 13 full-time (9 women), 11 part-time/adjunct (7 women). *Students:* 61 full-time (42 women), 23 part-time (17 women); includes 7 minority (2 African Americans, 1 American Indian/Alaska Native, 3 Asian Americans or Pacific Islanders, 1 Hispanic American), 1 international. Average age 35. 26 applicants, 92% accepted, 22 enrolled. In 2009, 12 master's awarded. *Degree requirements:* For master's, comprehensive exam (for some programs), thesis or alternative, project or comprehensives. *Entrance requirements:* For master's, GRE General Test or MAT, resume. Additional exam requirements/recommendations for international students: Required—TOEFL (minimum score 560 paper-based; 220 computer-based; 83 iBT). *Application deadline:* For fall admission, 6/1 priority date for domestic and international students; for spring admission, 10/1 priority date for domestic and international students. Applications are processed on a rolling basis. Application fee: $35. *Expenses:* Tuition: Full-time $12,440; part-time $827 per credit hour. *Financial support:* In 2009–10, 62 students received support. Career-related internships or fieldwork, Federal Work-Study, institutionally sponsored loans, and unspecified assistantships available. Support available to part-time students. Financial award application deadline: 3/1; financial award applicants required to submit FAFSA. *Faculty research:* Reader's theatre and reader/writer workshops, curriculum and assessment integration, gender and equity, classroom evaluations, organizational leadership. *Unit head:* Dr. Joyce Westgard, Director, 360-438-4509, Fax: 360-438-4486, E-mail: westgard@stmartin.edu. *Application contact:* Ryan M. Smith, Administrative Assistant, 360-438-4333, Fax: 360-438-4486, E-mail: ryan.smith@stmartin.edu.

Saint Mary's College of California, Kalmanovitz School of Education, Program in Educational Leadership, Moraga, CA 94556. Offers M Ed, MA. Part-time and evening/weekend programs available. *Faculty:* 4 full-time (all women), 6 part-time/adjunct (4 women). *Students:* 29 full-time (16 women), 57 part-time (31 women); includes 18 minority (9 African Americans, 2 American Indian/Alaska Native, 4 Asian Americans or Pacific Islanders, 3 Hispanic Americans), 1 international. Average age 35. In 2009, 6 master's awarded. *Degree requirements:* For master's, thesis or alternative. *Entrance requirements:* For master's, interview, minimum GPA of 3.0, teaching credential. *Application deadline:* For fall admission, 12/15 priority date for domestic students; for spring admission, 4/15 priority date for domestic students. Applications are processed on a rolling basis. Application fee: $50. *Expenses:* Tuition: Full-time $35,087; part-time $956 per credit hour. One-time fee: $50 full-time. Part-time tuition and fees vary according to course level, course load, degree level, campus/location and program. *Financial support:* Career-related internships or fieldwork available. Support available to part-time students. Financial award application deadline: 2/15. *Faculty research:* Building communities, programs in educational leadership, alignment of curriculum to standards. *Unit head:* Dr. Rebecca A. Proehl, Director, 925-631-4994, Fax: 925-376-8379, E-mail: rproehl@stmarys-ca.edu. *Application contact:* Jane Joyce, Coordinator, Recruitment and Admissions, 925-631-4700, Fax: 925-376-8379, E-mail: soereq@stmarys-ca.edu.

Saint Mary's College of California, Kalmanovitz School of Education, Teaching Leadership Program, Moraga, CA 94556. Offers MA. *Faculty:* 1 (woman) full-time, 3 part-time/adjunct (2 women). *Students:* 42 part-time (31 women). In 2009, 42 master's awarded. *Expenses:* Tuition: Full-time $35,087; part-time $956 per credit hour. One-time fee: $50 full-time. Part-time tuition and fees vary according to course level, course load, degree level, campus/location and program. *Unit head:* Katherine D. Perez, Unit Head, 925-631-4350, Fax: 925-376-8379, E-mail: kperez@stmarys-ca.edu. *Application contact:* Jane Joyce, Coordinator, Recruitment and Admissions, 925-631-4700, Fax: 925-376-8379, E-mail: soereq@stmarys-ca.edu.

St. Mary's University, Graduate School, Department of Teacher Education, Program in Catholic School Leadership, San Antonio, TX 78228-8507. Offers Catholic school administrators (Certificate); Catholic school leadership (MA); Catholic school teachers (Certificate). Part-time and evening/weekend programs available. Postbaccalaureate distance learning degree programs offered (minimal on-campus study). *Degree requirements:* For master's, comprehensive exam. *Entrance requirements:* For master's, GRE General Test. Additional exam requirements/recommendations for international students: Required—TOEFL (minimum score 550 paper-based; 213 computer-based; 80 iBT). Electronic applications accepted. *Expenses:* Tuition: Full-time $8004. Required fees: $536. One-time fee: $5 full-time. Full-time tuition and fees vary according to program.

St. Mary's University, Graduate School, Department of Teacher Education, Program in Educational Leadership, San Antonio, TX 78228-8507. Offers educational leadership (MA); principalship (mid-management) (Certificate). Part-time programs available. *Degree requirements:* For master's, comprehensive exam. *Entrance requirements:* For master's, GRE. Additional exam requirements/recommendations for international students: Required—TOEFL (minimum score 550 paper-based; 213 computer-based; 80 iBT). Electronic applications accepted. *Expenses:* Tuition: Full-time $8004. Required fees: $536. One-time fee: $5 full-time. Full-time tuition and fees vary according to program.

Saint Mary's University of Minnesota, Schools of Graduate and Professional Programs, Graduate School of Education, Catholic School Leadership Program, Winona, MN 55987-1399. Offers MA. *Application contact:* Yasin Alsaidi, Director of Admissions for Graduate and Professional Programs, 612-728-5207, Fax: 612-728-5121, E-mail: yalsaidi@smumn.edu.

Saint Mary's University of Minnesota, Schools of Graduate and Professional Programs, Graduate School of Education, Educational Administration Program, Winona, MN 55987-1399. Offers educational administration (Certificate, Ed S), including director of special education, K-12 principal, superintendent. *Unit head:* Dr. William Bjorum, Director, 612-728-5126, Fax: 612-728-5121, E-mail: wbjorum@smumn.edu. *Application contact:* Yasin Alsaidi, Director of Admissions for Graduate and Professional Programs, 612-728-5207, Fax: 612-728-5121, E-mail: yalsaidi@smumn.edu.

Saint Mary's University of Minnesota, Schools of Graduate and Professional Programs, Graduate School of Education, Educational Leadership Program, Winona, MN 55987-1399. Offers MA, Ed D. *Unit head:* Dr. Nelson Updaw, Director, 612-728-5191, Fax: 612-728-5121, E-mail: nupdaw@smumn.edu. *Application contact:* Yasin Alsaidi, Director of Admissions for Graduate and Professional Programs, 612-728-5207, Fax: 612-728-5121, E-mail: yalsaidi@smumn.edu.

Saint Mary's University of Minnesota, Schools of Graduate and Professional Programs, Graduate School of Education, Institute for LaSallian Studies, Winona, MN 55987-1399. Offers LaSallian leadership (MA); LaSallian studies (MA). *Unit head:* Dr. Roxanne Eubank, Director, 612-728-5217, E-mail: reubank@smumn.edu. *Application contact:* Yasin Alsaidi, Director of Admissions for Graduate and Professional Programs, 612-728-5207, Fax: 612-728-5121, E-mail: yalsaidi@smumn.edu.

Saint Michael's College, Graduate Programs, Program in Education, Colchester, VT 05439. Offers administration (M Ed, CAGS); arts in education (CAGS); curriculum and instruction (M Ed, CAGS); information technology (CAGS); reading (M Ed); special education (M Ed, CAGS); technology (M Ed). Part-time and evening/weekend programs available. *Degree requirements:* For master's, thesis. *Entrance requirements:* For master's, minimum GPA of 3.0. Electronic applications accepted. *Faculty research:* Integrative curriculum, moral and spiritual dimensions of education, learning styles, multiple intelligences, integrating technology into the curriculum.

Saint Peter's College, Graduate Programs in Education, Program in Educational Leadership, Jersey City, NJ 07306-5997. Offers MA, Ed D. Part-time and evening/weekend programs available. *Degree requirements:* For master's, comprehensive exam. *Entrance requirements:* For master's, GRE or MAT. Additional exam requirements/recommendations for international students: Required—TOEFL. *Application deadline:* Applications are processed on a rolling basis. Electronic applications accepted. *Expenses:* Tuition: Part-time $971 per credit. *Financial support:* Career-related internships or fieldwork, Federal Work-Study, and institutionally sponsored loans available. *Unit head:* Dr. Anthony Sciarrillo, Chairperson, 201-761-6473, Fax: 201-435-5270. *Application contact:* Dr. Anthony Sciarrillo, Chairperson, 201-761-6473, Fax: 201-435-5270.

Saint Peter's College, Graduate Programs in Education, Program in Teaching, Jersey City, NJ 07306-5997. Offers elementary teacher (Certificate); supervisor of instruction (Certificate); teaching (MA). Part-time and evening/weekend programs available. *Degree requirements:* For master's, comprehensive exam. *Entrance requirements:* For master's, GRE or MAT. Additional exam requirements/recommendations for international students: Required—TOEFL. *Application deadline:* Applications are processed on a rolling basis. Application fee: $0. Electronic applications accepted. *Expenses:* Tuition: Part-time $971 per credit. *Financial support:* Career-related internships or fieldwork, Federal Work-Study, and institutionally sponsored loans available. *Unit head:* Dr. Anthony Sciarrillo, Chairperson, 201-761-6473, Fax: 201-435-5270. *Application contact:* Dr. Anthony Sciarrillo, Chairperson, 201-761-6473, Fax: 201-435-5270.

St. Thomas Aquinas College, Division of Teacher Education, Sparkill, NY 10976. Offers adolescence education (MST); childhood and special education (MST); childhood education (MST); educational leadership (MS Ed); reading (MS Ed, PMC); special education (MS Ed, PMC); teaching (MS Ed), including elementary education, middle school education, secondary education. *Accreditation:* NCATE. Part-time and evening/weekend programs available. *Degree requirements:* For master's, comprehensive exam, comprehensive professional portfolio; for PMC, action research project. *Entrance requirements:* For master's, New York State Qualifying Exam, GRE General Test or minimum GPA of 3.0, teaching certificate; for PMC, GRE General Test or minimum GPA of 3.0. Electronic applications accepted. *Faculty research:* Computer applications in education, adolescent special education students, literacy development, inclusive practices for special education students.

St. Thomas University, School of Leadership Studies, Institute for Education, Miami Gardens, FL 33054-6459. Offers earth/space science (Certificate); educational administration (MS, Certificate); educational leadership (Ed D); elementary education (MS); ESOL (Certificate); gifted education (Certificate); instructional technology (MS, Certificate); professional/studies (Certificate); reading (MS, Certificate); special education (MS). Part-time and evening/weekend programs available. *Degree requirements:* For master's, comprehensive exam; for doctorate, comprehensive exam, thesis/dissertation. *Entrance requirements:* For master's, interview, minimum GPA of 3.0 or GRE; for doctorate, GRE or MAT. Additional exam requirements/recommendations for international students: Required—TOEFL (minimum score 550 paper-based; 213 computer-based; 79 iBT). Electronic applications accepted.

Saint Vincent College, Program in Education, Latrobe, PA 15650-2690. Offers curriculum and instruction (MS); environmental education (MS); library media management (MS); school administration (MS); special education (MS). Part-time and evening/weekend programs available. *Degree requirements:* For master's, comprehensive exam. *Entrance requirements:* For master's, GRE (if undergraduate GPA less than 3.0). Additional exam requirements/recommendations for international students: Required—TOEFL (minimum score 550 paper-based; 213 computer-based). *Faculty research:* Assessment and instructional technology.

Saint Xavier University, Graduate Studies, School of Education, Chicago, IL 60655-3105. Offers counseling (MA); counselor education (MA); curriculum and instruction (MA); early childhood education (MA); education (CAS); educational administration (MA); elementary education (MA); field-based education (MA); general educational studies (MA); individualized program (MA); learning disabilities (MA); reading (MA); secondary education (MA). *Accreditation:* NCATE. Part-time and evening/weekend programs available. *Degree requirements:* For master's, thesis or project. *Entrance requirements:* For master's, minimum GPA of 3.0. *Expenses:* Contact institution.

Salem International University, School of Education, Salem, WV 26426-0500. Offers curriculum and instruction (M Ed); educational leadership (M Ed). Part-time and evening/weekend programs available. Postbaccalaureate distance learning degree programs offered. *Degree requirements:* For master's, comprehensive exam (for some programs), thesis (for some programs). *Entrance requirements:* For master's, GRE, MAT, NTE, 3 letters of recommendation. Additional exam requirements/recommendations for international students: Required—TOEFL (minimum score 550 paper-based; 213 computer-based). Electronic applications accepted. *Expenses:* Contact institution. *Faculty research:* Improved classroom effectiveness.

Salem State College, School of Graduate Studies, Program in Educational Leadership, Salem, MA 01970-5353. Offers M Ed. *Students:* 1 (woman) full-time, 10 part-time (5 women), 1 international. Average age 39. 1 applicant, 100% accepted, 1 enrolled. In 2009, 2 master's awarded. *Entrance requirements:* For master's, GRE or MAT. Additional exam requirements/recommendations for international students: Required—TOEFL (minimum score 550 paper-based; 80 iBT), or IELTS (minimum score 5.5). *Application deadline:* For fall admission, 5/1 for domestic students; for spring admission, 11/1 for domestic students. Applications are processed on a rolling basis. Application fee: $50. *Expenses:* Tuition, state resident: full-time $2520; part-time $275 per credit hour. Tuition, nonresident: full-time $4140; part-time $365 per credit hour. Required fees: $2430. *Financial support:* Career-related internships or fieldwork, Federal

Work-Study, scholarships/grants, and unspecified assistantships available. Support available to part-time students. Financial award application deadline: 5/1; financial award applicants required to submit FAFSA. *Unit head:* Linda Darisse, Coordinator, 978-542-2229, Fax: 978-542-7215, E-mail: ldarisse@salemstate.edu. *Application contact:* Dr. Lee A. Brossoit, Assistant Dean of Graduate Admissions, 978-542-6673, Fax: 978-542-7215, E-mail: lbrossoit@salemstate.edu.

Salem State College, School of Graduate Studies, Program in Higher Education in Student Affairs, Salem, MA 01970-5353. Offers M Ed. Part-time and evening/weekend programs available. *Students:* 13 full-time (12 women), 29 part-time (19 women); includes 6 minority (3 African Americans, 3 Hispanic Americans). Average age 32. 12 applicants, 100% accepted, 12 enrolled. In 2009, 8 master's awarded. *Entrance requirements:* For master's, GRE or MAT. Additional exam requirements/recommendations for international students: Required—TOEFL (minimum score 550 paper-based; 80 iBT), or IELTS (minimum score 5.5). *Application deadline:* For fall admission, 5/1 for domestic students. Application fee: $50. *Expenses:* Tuition, state resident: full-time $2520; part-time $275 per credit hour. Tuition, nonresident: full-time $4140; part-time $365 per credit hour. Required fees: $2430. *Financial support:* In 2009–10, 22 students received support. Career-related internships or fieldwork, Federal Work-Study, scholarships/grants, and unspecified assistantships available. Support available to part-time students. Financial award application deadline: 5/1; financial award applicants required to submit FAFSA. *Unit head:* Dr. Lee A. Brossoit, Program Coordinator, 978-542-6675, E-mail: lbrossoit@salemstate.edu. *Application contact:* Dr. Lee A. Brossoit, Assistant Dean of Graduate Admissions, 978-542-6675, Fax: 978-542-7215, E-mail: lbrossoit@salemstate.edu.

Salisbury University, Graduate Division, Department of Education, Salisbury, MD 21801-6837. Offers educational leadership (M Ed); general (M Ed); reading specialist (M Ed); teaching (MAT). *Accreditation:* NCATE. Part-time and evening/weekend programs available. *Faculty:* 23 full-time (14 women), 9 part-time/adjunct (8 women). *Students:* 33 full-time (18 women), 129 part-time (100 women); includes 14 minority (12 African Americans, 1 Asian American or Pacific Islander, 1 Hispanic American), 1 international. Average age 31. 71 applicants, 54% accepted, 12 enrolled. In 2009, 70 master's awarded. *Degree requirements:* For master's, comprehensive exam (for some programs). *Entrance requirements:* For master's, minimum GPA of 2.75. Additional exam requirements/recommendations for international students: Required—TOEFL (minimum score 550 paper-based; 213 computer-based). *Application deadline:* For fall admission, 3/3 for domestic students; for spring admission, 10/1 for domestic students. Applications are processed on a rolling basis. Application fee: $45. Electronic applications accepted. *Expenses:* Tuition, area resident: Part-time $278 per credit hour. Tuition, state resident: part-time $278 per credit hour. Tuition, nonresident: part-time $574 per credit hour. Required fees: $57 per credit hour. *Financial support:* In 2009–10, 30 students received support. Career-related internships or fieldwork and scholarships/grants available. Support available to part-time students. Financial award applicants required to submit FAFSA. *Unit head:* Dr. Laura Marasco, Program Coordinator, 410-546-6012, E-mail: llmarasco@salisbury.edu. *Application contact:* Tina Melczarek, Administrative Assistant I, 410-543-6281, Fax: 410-548-2593, E-mail: tmmelczarek@salisbury.edu.

Samford University, Orlean Bullard Beeson School of Education and Professional Studies, Birmingham, AL 35229. Offers early childhood education (Ed S); early childhood/elementary education (MS Ed); educational administration (Ed S); educational leadership (Ed D); elementary education (Ed S); gifted education (MS Ed); instructional leadership (MS Ed); secondary collaboration (MS Ed); M Div/MS Ed. *Accreditation:* NCATE. Part-time programs available. *Faculty:* 11 full-time (8 women), 9 part-time/adjunct (5 women). *Students:* 16 full-time (13 women), 173 part-time (131 women); includes 47 minority (46 African Americans, 1 American Indian/Alaska Native), 1 international. Average age 40. 15 applicants, 100% accepted, 15 enrolled. In 2009, 52 master's, 11 doctorates, 27 other advanced degrees awarded. *Degree requirements:* For master's, comprehensive exam; for doctorate, comprehensive exam, thesis/dissertation. *Entrance requirements:* For master's, GRE or MAT, minimum GPA of 3.0; for doctorate, minimum GPA of 3.7; for Ed S, GRE, master's degree, teaching certificate, minimum GPA of 3.25. Additional exam requirements/recommendations for international students: Required—TOEFL (minimum score 550 paper-based; 213 computer-based). *Application deadline:* Applications are processed on a rolling basis. Application fee: $25. *Expenses:* Tuition: Full-time $26,660; part-time $595 per credit hour. Required fees: $110 per semester. *Financial support:* In 2009–10, 127 students received support; research assistantships, career-related internships or fieldwork, Federal Work-Study, scholarships/grants, and tuition waivers (partial) available. Support available to part-time students. Financial award applicants required to submit FAFSA. *Faculty research:* School law, the characteristics of beginning teachers, the nature of school reform, school culture, quality improvement in education, K-12 student achievement. *Unit head:* Dr. Jean Ann Box, Dean, 205-726-2559, E-mail: jabox@samford.edu. *Application contact:* Dr. Maurice Persall, Director, Graduate Office, 205-726-2019, E-mail: jmpersal@samford.edu.

Sam Houston State University, College of Education and Applied Science, Department of Educational Leadership and Counseling, Huntsville, TX 77341. Offers administration (M Ed, MA); counseling (M Ed, MA); counselor education (MA, PhD); educational leadership (Ed D); instructional leadership (M Ed, MA). Part-time programs available. *Faculty:* 31 full-time (20 women), 8 part-time/adjunct (6 women). *Students:* 91 full-time (73 women), 581 part-time (464 women); includes 214 minority (107 African Americans, 2 American Indian/Alaska Native, 7 Asian Americans or Pacific Islanders, 98 Hispanic Americans), 10 international. Average age 36. 231 applicants, 91% accepted, 164 enrolled. In 2009, 280 master's, 16 doctorates awarded. *Entrance requirements:* For master's, GRE General Test. Additional exam requirements/recommendations for international students: Required—TOEFL (minimum score 550 paper-based; 213 computer-based; 79 iBT). *Application deadline:* For fall admission, 8/1 for domestic students; for spring admission, 12/1 for domestic students. Application fee: $20. *Expenses:* Tuition, state resident: full-time $3690; part-time $205 per credit hour. Tuition, nonresident: full-time $8676; part-time $482 per credit hour. Required fees: $1474. Tuition and fees vary according to course load and campus/location. *Financial support:* Career-related internships or fieldwork, Federal Work-Study, and institutionally sponsored loans available. Support available to part-time students. Financial award application deadline: 5/31; financial award applicants required to submit FAFSA. *Unit head:* Dr. Beverly Irby, Chair, 936-294-1134, Fax: 936-294-3886, E-mail: edu_bid@shsu.edu. *Application contact:* Dr. Stacey Edmondson, Advisor, 936-294-1752, E-mail: sedmonson@shsu.edu.

San Diego State University, Graduate and Research Affairs, College of Education, Department of Administration, Rehabilitation and Post-Secondary Education, San Diego, CA 92182. Offers educational leadership in post-secondary education (MA); rehabilitation counseling (MS), including deafness. Evening/weekend programs available. Postbaccalaureate distance learning degree programs offered. *Degree requirements:* For master's, comprehensive exam (for some programs), thesis (for some programs). *Entrance requirements:* For master's, GRE General Test, letters of reference. Additional exam requirements/recommendations for international students: Required—TOEFL. Electronic applications accepted. *Faculty research:* Rehabilitation in cultural diversity, distance learning technology.

San Diego State University, Graduate and Research Affairs, College of Education, Department of Educational Leadership, San Diego, CA 92182. Offers MA. *Accreditation:* NCATE. Evening/weekend programs available. *Entrance requirements:* For master's, GRE General Test, letters of reference. Additional exam requirements/recommendations for international students: Required—TOEFL. Electronic applications accepted.

San Francisco State University, Division of Graduate Studies, College of Education, Department of Administration and Interdisciplinary Studies, Program in Educational Administration, San Francisco, CA 94132-1722. Offers MA, AC. *Accreditation:* NCATE.

San Jose State University, Graduate Studies and Research, Connie L. Lurie College of Education, Department of Educational Leadership, San Jose, CA 95192-0001. Offers educational administration (K-12) (MA); higher education administration (MA). *Accreditation:* NCATE. *Students:* 185 full-time (128 women), 76 part-time (53 women); includes 99 minority (7 African Americans, 2 American Indian/Alaska Native, 34 Asian Americans or Pacific Islanders, 56 Hispanic Americans). Average age 38. 108 applicants, 83% accepted, 81 enrolled. In 2009, 157 master's awarded. *Degree requirements:* For master's, thesis or alternative. *Application deadline:* For fall admission, 6/29 for domestic students; for spring admission, 11/30 for domestic students. Applications are processed on a rolling basis. Application fee: $59. Electronic applications accepted. *Financial support:* Career-related internships or fieldwork available. Financial award applicants required to submit FAFSA. *Unit head:* Dr. Noni Mendoza Reis, Chair, 408-924-3616, Fax: 408-924-3713. *Application contact:* Dr. Noni Mendoza Reis, Chair, 408-924-3616, Fax: 408-924-3713.

Santa Clara University, School of Education and Counseling Psychology, Department of Education, Program in Educational Administration, Santa Clara, CA 95053. Offers educational administration (MA), including administrative services, higher education. Part-time and evening/weekend programs available. *Students:* 3 full-time (all women), 29 part-time (21 women); includes 4 minority (2 African Americans, 2 Hispanic Americans), 1 international. Average age 34. 21 applicants, 57% accepted, 11 enrolled. In 2009, 15 master's awarded. *Degree requirements:* For master's, comprehensive exam. *Entrance requirements:* For master's, GRE or MAT, minimum GPA of 3.0. Additional exam requirements/recommendations for international students: Required—TOEFL. *Application deadline:* Applications are processed on a rolling basis. *Expenses:* Contact institution. *Financial support:* Fellowships, Federal Work-Study, scholarships/grants, and traineeships available. Support available to part-time students. Financial award application deadline: 5/15; financial award applicants required to submit FAFSA. *Unit head:* Patricia DeMarlo, Director, 408-554-4696. *Application contact:* Patricia DeMarlo, Director, 408-554-4696.

Seattle Pacific University, Educational Leadership Program, Seattle, WA 98119-1997. Offers educational leadership (M Ed, Ed D); principal (Certificate); superintendent (Certificate). *Accreditation:* NCATE. Part-time and evening/weekend programs available. *Faculty:* 8 full-time (0 women), 3 part-time/adjunct (0 women). *Students:* 7 full-time (6 women), 55 part-time (38 women); includes 6 minority (1 African American, 1 American Indian/Alaska Native, 2 Asian Americans or Pacific Islanders, 2 Hispanic Americans), 4 international. Average age 40. 13 applicants, 46% accepted, 5 enrolled. In 2009, 9 master's awarded. *Degree requirements:* For master's, comprehensive exam; for doctorate, comprehensive exam, thesis/dissertation. *Entrance requirements:* For master's, GRE General Test or MAT, minimum GPA of 3.0; for doctorate, GRE General Test or MAT, minimum GPA of 3.0, formal interview. *Application deadline:* For fall admission, 7/1 priority date for domestic students; for spring admission, 3/1 priority date for domestic students. Applications are processed on a rolling basis. Application fee: $50. Electronic applications accepted. *Expenses:* Tuition: Part-time $485 per credit. Part-time tuition and fees vary according to course level, degree level and program. *Financial support:* In 2009–10, 35 students received support. Career-related internships or fieldwork available. Financial award applicants required to submit FAFSA. *Unit head:* Dr. Richard Smith, Chair, 206-281-2375, Fax: 206-281-2756, E-mail: rsmith@spu.edu. *Application contact:* The Grad Center, 206-281-2091.

Seattle University, College of Education, Program in Educational Administration, Seattle, WA 98122-1090. Offers M Ed, MA, Certificate, Ed S. *Accreditation:* NCATE. Part-time and evening/weekend programs available. *Degree requirements:* For master's and other advanced degree, comprehensive exam. *Entrance requirements:* For master's, GRE, MAT, or minimum GPA of 3.0; interview; 1 year of related experience. Additional exam requirements/recommendations for international students: Required—TOEFL.

Seattle University, College of Education, Program in Educational Leadership, Seattle, WA 98122-1090. Offers Ed D. *Accreditation:* NCATE. Part-time and evening/weekend programs available. *Degree requirements:* For doctorate, comprehensive exam, thesis/dissertation. *Entrance requirements:* For doctorate, GRE General Test, MAT, interview, MA, minimum GPA of 3.5, 3 years of related experience. Additional exam requirements/recommendations for international students: Required—TOEFL. *Expenses:* Contact institution.

Seattle University, College of Education, Program in Student Development Administration, Seattle, WA 98122-1090. Offers M Ed, MA. Part-time and evening/weekend programs available. *Degree requirements:* For master's, comprehensive exam. *Entrance requirements:* For master's, GRE, MAT, or minimum GPA of 3.0. Additional exam requirements/recommendations for international students: Required—TOEFL.

Seton Hall University, College of Education and Human Services, Department of Education Leadership, Management and Policy, Program in Higher Education Administration, South Orange, NJ 07079-2697. Offers Ed D, PhD. *Accreditation:* NCATE. Part-time and evening/weekend programs available. *Faculty:* 12 full-time (4 women), 1 part-time/adjunct (0 women). *Students:* 14 full-time (8 women), 62 part-time (39 women); includes 19 minority (13 African Americans, 6 Hispanic Americans), 9 international. Average age 41. 26 applicants, 81% accepted, 16 enrolled. In 2009, 6 doctorates awarded. *Degree requirements:* For doctorate, comprehensive exam, thesis/dissertation, internship. *Entrance requirements:* For doctorate, GRE or MAT, interview, minimum GPA of 3.5. Additional exam requirements/recommendations for international students: Required—TOEFL. *Application deadline:* For fall admission, 2/1 priority date for domestic students; for spring admission, 10/1 for domestic students. Applications are processed on a rolling basis. Application fee: $50. *Financial support:* In 2009–10, 7 research assistantships with tuition reimbursements (averaging $5,000 per year) were awarded. Financial award application deadline: 2/1.

Seton Hall University, College of Education and Human Services, Department of Education Leadership, Management and Policy, Program in K–12 Leadership, Management and Policy, South Orange, NJ 07079-2697. Offers Ed D, Exec Ed D, Ed S. Part-time and evening/weekend programs available. *Faculty:* 12 full-time (4 women), 1 part-time/adjunct (0 women). *Students:* 73 full-time (41 women), 273 part-time (164 women); includes 66 minority (47 African Americans, 4 Asian Americans or Pacific Islanders, 15 Hispanic Americans), 2 international. Average age 43. 48 applicants, 81% accepted, 22 enrolled. In 2009, 38 doctorates, 13 other advanced degrees awarded. *Degree requirements:* For doctorate, comprehensive exam, thesis/dissertation, internship. *Entrance requirements:* For doctorate, MAT, interview. *Application deadline:* For fall admission, 2/1 for domestic students; for spring admission, 12/1 for domestic students. Applications are processed on a rolling basis. Application fee: $50. *Financial support:* In 2009–10, 2 research assistantships with full tuition reimbursements (averaging $4,500 per year) were awarded; unspecified assistantships also available. Financial award application deadline: 2/1. *Application contact:* Information Contact, 973-761-9397.

Shasta Bible College, Program in School and Church Administration, Redding, CA 96002. Offers MS. Part-time and evening/weekend programs available. *Degree requirements:* For master's, comprehensive exam (for some programs), thesis or alternative. *Entrance requirements:* For master's, cumulative GPA of 3.0, 9 semester hours of education or psychology courses. Additional exam requirements/recommendations for international students: Required—TOEFL (minimum score 550 paper-based; 213 computer-based).

Shenandoah University, School of Education and Human Development, Winchester, VA 22601-5195. Offers administrative leadership (D Ed); advanced professional teaching English to speakers of other languages (Certificate); education (MSE); elementary education (Certificate); middle school education (Certificate); organizational leadership (MS); professional studies (Certificate); professional studies (for initial teacher licensure) (Certificate); professional studies (for special education teacher licensure) (Certificate); professional studies (for VA licensure reading specialists) (Certificate); professional studies (for VA licensure) (Certificate); professional teaching English to speakers of other languages (Certificate); public management (Certificate); school reform (Certificate); secondary education (Certificate). *Accreditation:* Teacher Education Accreditation Council. Part-time and evening/weekend programs available. Postbaccalaureate distance learning degree programs offered (minimal on-campus study). *Faculty:* 13 full-time (7 women), 27 part-time/adjunct (20 women). *Students:* 11 full-time (8 women), 382 part-time (276 women); includes 35 minority (17 African Americans, 1 American Indian/Alaska Native, 6 Asian Americans or Pacific Islanders, 11 Hispanic Americans), 4 international. Average age 39. 272 applicants, 95% accepted, 218 enrolled. In 2009, 103 master's, 2

Educational Leadership and Administration

Shenandoah University (continued)

doctorates awarded. *Degree requirements:* For master's, comprehensive exam (for some programs), thesis (for some programs), internship; for doctorate, comprehensive exam, thesis/dissertation; for Certificate, full time teaching in area for 1 year. *Entrance requirements:* For master's, minimum GPA of 3.0 or satisfactory GRE, 3 letters of recommendation, valid teaching license, essay; for doctorate, minimum graduate GPA of 3.5, 3 years of teaching experience, 3 letters of recommendation, writing samples; for Certificate, minimum undergraduate GPA of 3.0, essay, 3 letters of recommendation. Additional exam requirements/recommendations for international students: Required—TOEFL (minimum score 550 paper-based; 213 computer-based; 79 iBT), IELTS (minimum score 6.5). *Application deadline:* For fall admission, 7/1 for domestic and international students; for spring admission, 10/15 for domestic and international students. Application fee: $30. Electronic applications accepted. *Expenses:* Tuition: Full-time $11,925; part-time $695 per credit. Required fees: $400 per semester. *Financial support:* Application deadline: 3/15. *Unit head:* Dr. Steven E. Humphries, Dean, 540-535-3574, E-mail: shumphri@su.edu. *Application contact:* David Anthony, Dean of Admissions, 540-665-4581, Fax: 540-665-4627, E-mail: admit@su.edu.

Shippensburg University of Pennsylvania, School of Graduate Studies, College of Education and Human Services, Department of Educational Leadership and Special Education, Shippensburg, PA 17257-2299. Offers school administration principal K-12 (M Ed); special education (M Ed), including behavior disorders, comprehensive, learning disabilities, mental retardation. *Accreditation:* NCATE. Part-time and evening/weekend programs available. *Degree requirements:* For master's, candidacy, thesis, or practicum. *Entrance requirements:* For master's, instructional or educational specialist certificate; 2 letters of reference; 2 years of successful teaching experience; interview and GRE or MAT (if GPA is less than 2.75). Additional exam requirements/recommendations for international students: Required—TOEFL (minimum score 560 paper-based; 220 computer-based); Recommended—IELTS (minimum score 6). Electronic applications accepted.

Siena Heights University, Graduate College, Program in Educational Leadership, Adrian, MI 49221-1796. Offers MA.

Silver Lake College, Division of Graduate Studies, Program in Education, Manitowoc, WI 54220-9319. Offers administrative leadership (MA Ed); teacher leadership (MA Ed). Part-time and evening/weekend programs available. Postbaccalaureate distance learning degree programs offered (no on-campus study). *Faculty:* 1 (woman) full-time, 12 part-time/adjunct (10 women). *Students:* 43 part-time (28 women); includes 4 minority (2 African Americans, 2 Hispanic Americans). Average age 36. 22 applicants, 73% accepted, 15 enrolled. In 2009, 20 master's awarded. *Degree requirements:* For master's, comprehensive exam, thesis or alternative, public presentation of culminating project. *Entrance requirements:* For master's, interview, minimum undergraduate GPA of 3.0, writing sample, 3 letters of recommendation. Additional exam requirements/recommendations for international students: Required—TOEFL. *Application deadline:* For fall admission, 8/1 for domestic and international students; for spring admission, 12/1 for domestic and international students. Applications are processed on a rolling basis. Application fee: $50. Electronic applications accepted. *Expenses:* Tuition: Full-time $7380; part-time $410 per credit. Required fees: $10 per term. Part-time tuition and fees vary according to course load. *Financial support:* Scholarships/grants available. Support available to part-time students. Financial award applicants required to submit FAFSA. *Unit head:* Dr. Julie A. Mayrose, Director, 800-236-4752 Ext. 370, Fax: 920-684-7082, E-mail: mayrose@siler.sl.edu. *Application contact:* Jamie Grant, Associate Director of Admissions, 800-236-4752 Ext. 186, Fax: 920-686-6322, E-mail: jgrant@silver.sl.edu.

Simmons College, College of Arts and Sciences Graduate Studies, Department of Education, Program in Educational Leadership, Boston, MA 02115. Offers MS Ed, PhD, CAGS. Part-time programs available. *Students:* 28 part-time (21 women); includes 7 minority (all African Americans). 4 applicants, 100% accepted, 3 enrolled. In 2009, 4 master's, 9 other advanced degrees awarded. *Degree requirements:* For master's, practicum; for doctorate, thesis/dissertation. *Application deadline:* For fall admission, 8/1 for domestic and international students; for winter admission, 12/15 for domestic and international students; for spring admission, 5/1 for domestic and international students. Applications are processed on a rolling basis. Application fee: $35. Electronic applications accepted. *Expenses:* Tuition: Part-time $925 per credit hour. Part-time tuition and fees vary according to program. *Faculty research:* Work/life balance for female administrators, crisis management, leadership models during fiscal crises. *Unit head:* Roberta Kelly, Program Director, 617-521-2241, E-mail: roberta.kelly@simmons.edu. *Application contact:* Kristen Haack, Director, Graduate Studies Admission, 617-521-2917, Fax: 617-521-3058, E-mail: gsa@simmons.edu.

Simmons College, College of Arts and Sciences Graduate Studies, Department of Education, Program in Teacher Preparation, Boston, MA 02115. Offers educational leadership (MS Ed); elementary education (MAT); general education (CAGS); general purposes (MS); middle school education (MAT); professional license (CAGS); professional license: elementary (MS Ed); professional license: middle/high (MS Ed); secondary education (MAT); urban education (MS Ed, CAGS). Part-time programs available. *Students:* 68 full-time (58 women), 125 part-time (113 women); includes 25 minority (10 African Americans, 3 American Indian/Alaska Native, 8 Asian Americans or Pacific Islanders, 4 Hispanic Americans). Average age 27. 115 applicants, 88% accepted, 75 enrolled. In 2009, 137 master's, 14 other advanced degrees awarded. *Degree requirements:* For master's, practicum. *Entrance requirements:* For master's, GRE General Test, MAT or Massachusetts Tests for Educator Licensure (MTEL). Additional exam requirements/recommendations for international students: Required—TOEFL (minimum score 600 paper-based; 250 computer-based; 100 iBT). *Application deadline:* For fall admission, 8/1 priority date for domestic and international students; for winter admission, 12/15 priority date for domestic and international students; for spring admission, 12/15 priority date for domestic and international students. Applications are processed on a rolling basis. Application fee: $35. Electronic applications accepted. *Expenses:* Contact institution. *Financial support:* Application deadline: 3/1. *Faculty research:* Educational psychology, mentorship with first year teachers, urban classrooms, first generation college students. *Unit head:* Gary Oakes, Director, Master of Arts in Teaching (MAT) Program, 617-521-2203, Fax: 617-521-3133. *Application contact:* Kristen Haack, Director, Graduate Studies Admission, 617-521-2917, Fax: 617-521-3058, E-mail: gsa@simmons.edu.

Simon Fraser University, Graduate Studies, Faculty of Education, Program in Educational Leadership, Burnaby, BC V5A 1S6, Canada. Offers M Ed, MA, Ed D. *Degree requirements:* For master's, project or thesis. *Entrance requirements:* For master's, minimum GPA of 3.0. Additional exam requirements/recommendations for international students: Required—TOEFL or IELTS.

Simpson University, School of Education, Redding, CA 96003-8606. Offers education (MA); education and preliminary administrative services (MA); education and preliminary teaching (MA); teaching (MA). Part-time and evening/weekend programs available. *Faculty:* 6 full-time (3 women), 5 part-time/adjunct (1 woman). *Students:* 45 full-time (31 women), 90 part-time (62 women); includes 9 minority (1 African American, 4 Asian Americans or Pacific Islanders, 4 Hispanic Americans). In 2009, 42 master's awarded. *Degree requirements:* For master's, thesis optional. *Entrance requirements:* For master's, California Basic Educational Skills Test, CSET, 2 letters of reference. Additional exam requirements/recommendations for international students: Required—TOEFL (minimum score 550 paper-based; 180 computer-based). *Application deadline:* Applications are processed on a rolling basis. Application fee: $25. Electronic applications accepted. *Financial support:* Scholarships/grants available. Financial award applicants required to submit FAFSA. *Unit head:* Dr. Glee Brooks, Dean, 530-226-4606, Fax: 530-226-4861, E-mail: edadmissions@simpsonu.edu. *Application contact:* Marie Moe, Director of Continuing and Graduate Admissions, 530-226-4784, Fax: 530-226-4861, E-mail: edadmissions@simpsonu.edu.

Slippery Rock University of Pennsylvania, Graduate Studies (Recruitment), College of Education, Department of Special Education, Slippery Rock, PA 16057-1383. Offers master teacher (M Ed); supervision (M Ed). *Accreditation:* NCATE. Part-time and evening/weekend programs available. *Degree requirements:* For master's, comprehensive exam (for some programs), thesis (for some programs), portfolio presentation. *Entrance requirements:* For master's, GRE General Test, MAT, minimum GPA of 2.75 (3.0 for initial certification). Additional exam requirements/recommendations for international students: Required—TOEFL (minimum score 550 paper-based; 213 computer-based). *Application deadline:* For fall admission, 3/1 priority date for domestic students, 5/1 priority date for international students; for spring admission, 11/1 priority date for domestic students, 9/1 priority date for international students. Applications are processed on a rolling basis. Application fee: $25 ($30 for international students). Electronic applications accepted. *Expenses:* Tuition, state resident: full-time $6666; part-time $370 per credit. Tuition, nonresident: full-time $10,666; part-time $593 per credit. Required fees: $2184; $182 per credit. *Financial support:* Career-related internships or fieldwork, Federal Work-Study, scholarships/grants, and unspecified assistantships available. Support available to part-time students. Financial award application deadline: 5/1; financial award applicants required to submit FAFSA. *Faculty research:* In-service teacher education, contemporary issues in special education, education for developmentally disabled, educational assessment. *Unit head:* Dr. Dennis Fair, Graduate Coordinator, 724-738-2614, Fax: 724-738-4395, E-mail: dennis.fair@sru.edu. *Application contact:* Angela Piverotto, Interim Director of Graduate Studies, 724-738-2051, Fax: 724-738-2146, E-mail: graduate.admissions@sru.edu.

Sonoma State University, School of Education, Department of Educational Leadership and Special Education, Rohnert Park, CA 94928-3609. Offers educational leadership (MA); special education (MA). Part-time and evening/weekend programs available. *Degree requirements:* For master's, thesis or alternative. *Entrance requirements:* For master's, GRE General Test, minimum GPA of 2.5. *Expenses:* Tuition, nonresident: full-time $11,160. Required fees: $6226. Full-time tuition and fees vary according to course load.

South Carolina State University, School of Graduate Studies, Department of Educational Leadership, Orangeburg, SC 29117-0001. Offers educational leadership (Ed D, Ed S). *Accreditation:* ACA; NCATE. Part-time and evening/weekend programs available. *Degree requirements:* For doctorate, comprehensive exam, thesis/dissertation, preliminary exams, internship, practicum; for Ed S, thesis. *Entrance requirements:* For doctorate, GRE General Test or MAT, teaching certificate, teaching experience; for Ed S, GRE General Test or MAT, interview, teaching certificate, teaching experience. Electronic applications accepted. *Expenses:* Tuition, state resident: part-time $470 per credit hour. Tuition, nonresident: part-time $924 per credit hour. *Faculty research:* Decision making, relaxation theory, learning styles, student recruitment, academic achievement.

South Dakota State University, Graduate School, College of Education and Human Sciences, Department of Educational Leadership, Brookings, SD 57007. Offers curriculum and instruction (M Ed); educational administration (M Ed). Part-time and evening/weekend programs available. Postbaccalaureate distance learning degree programs offered (minimal on-campus study). *Degree requirements:* For master's, portfolio, oral exam. *Entrance requirements:* For master's, minimum GPA of 2.75. Additional exam requirements/recommendations for international students: Required—TOEFL (minimum score 550 paper-based; 213 computer-based; 80 iBT). *Faculty research:* Inclusion school climate, K-12 reform and restructuring, rural development, ESL, leadership.

Southeastern Louisiana University, College of Education and Human Development, Department of Educational Leadership and Technology, Hammond, LA 70402. Offers educational leadership (M Ed, Ed D); educational technology leadership (M Ed). Part-time and evening/weekend programs available. *Faculty:* 16 full-time (6 women). *Students:* 23 full-time (18 women), 224 part-time (177 women); includes 52 minority (47 African Americans, 1 Asian American or Pacific Islander, 4 Hispanic Americans), 1 international. Average age 38. 23 applicants, 100% accepted, 17 enrolled. In 2009, 52 master's awarded. *Degree requirements:* For master's, comprehensive exam (for some programs); for doctorate, thesis/dissertation. *Entrance requirements:* For master's, GRE (verbal and quantitative), 18 hours of course work in professional education or an undergraduate degree in education, standard teaching certificate; for doctorate, GRE, master's degree with minimum GPA of 3.25, 3.0 on the last 60 undergraduate hours. Additional exam requirements/recommendations for international students: Required—TOEFL (minimum score 500 paper-based; 173 computer-based; 61 iBT). *Application deadline:* For fall admission, 7/15 priority date for domestic students, 6/1 priority date for international students; for spring admission, 12/1 priority date for domestic students, 10/1 priority date for international students. Applications are processed on a rolling basis. Application fee: $20 ($30 for international students). Electronic applications accepted. *Expenses:* Tuition, state resident: full-time $3086; part-time $225 per credit hour. Tuition, nonresident: part-time $529 per credit hour. Required fees: $1195. Tuition and fees vary according to course level and course load. *Financial support:* In 2009–10, 9 students received support. Federal Work-Study, institutionally sponsored loans, scholarships/grants, and administrative assistantships available. Support available to part-time students. Financial award application deadline: 5/1; financial award applicants required to submit FAFSA. *Faculty research:* Using the Web and professional development in technology integration, legal and ethical issues in education, school culture and gender perceptions, training needs to prepare school board members and superintendents, data information for decision making. Total annual research expenditures: $90,477. *Unit head:* Dr. Michael D. Richardson, Department Head, 985-549-5713, Fax: 985-549-5712, E-mail: mrichardson@selu.edu. *Application contact:* Sandra Meyers, Graduate Admissions Analyst, 985-549-2066, Fax: 985-549-5632, E-mail: admissions@selu.edu.

Southeastern Oklahoma State University, School of Education, Durant, OK 74701-0609. Offers math specialist (M Ed); reading specialist (M Ed); school administration (M Ed); school counseling (M Ed). *Accreditation:* NCATE. Part-time and evening/weekend programs available. *Faculty:* 52 full-time (19 women), 1 (woman) part-time/adjunct. *Students:* 14 full-time (11 women), 73 part-time (58 women); includes 22 minority (4 African Americans, 17 American Indian/Alaska Native, 1 Hispanic American). Average age 32. 18 applicants, 100% accepted, 18 enrolled. *Degree requirements:* For master's, comprehensive exam, thesis optional, portfolio (M Ed). *Entrance requirements:* For master's, GRE General Test (MBS), minimum GPA of 3.0 in last 60 hours or 2.75 overall. Additional exam requirements/recommendations for international students: Required—TOEFL (minimum score 550 paper-based; 213 computer-based). *Application deadline:* For fall admission, 8/1 for domestic students, 6/1 for international students; for spring admission, 1/5 for domestic students, 11/1 for international students. Application fee: $20 ($55 for international students). Electronic applications accepted. *Financial support:* In 2009–10, 1 teaching assistantship with full tuition reimbursement (averaging $5,000 per year) was awarded; Federal Work-Study, institutionally sponsored loans, and tuition waivers (partial) also available. Support available to part-time students. Financial award application deadline: 6/15; financial award applicants required to submit FAFSA. *Unit head:* Dr. Melanie Price, Chair, 580-745-2602, Fax: 580-745-7474, E-mail: mprice@se.edu. *Application contact:* Carrie Williamson, Graduate Secretary, 580-745-2200, Fax: 580-745-7474, E-mail: cwilliamson@se.edu.

Southeastern University, College of Education, Lakeland, FL 33801-6099. Offers educational leadership (M Ed); elementary education (M Ed); teaching and learning (M Ed).

Southeast Missouri State University, School of Graduate Studies, Department of Educational Leadership and Counseling, Program in Educational Administration, Cape Girardeau, MO 63701-4799. Offers MA, Ed S. *Accreditation:* NCATE. Part-time and evening/weekend programs available. *Degree requirements:* For master's, comprehensive exam, thesis or alternative, graduate paper; for Ed S, comprehensive exam. *Entrance requirements:* For master's, GRE General Test, PRAXIS or MAT, minimum undergraduate GPA of 2.75, teacher certification; for Ed S, GRE General Test, PRAXIS or MAT, minimum graduate GPA of 3.5. Additional exam requirements/recommendations for international students: Required—TOEFL (minimum score 550 paper-based; 213 computer-based); Recommended—IELTS (minimum score 6). Electronic applications accepted. *Expenses:* Tuition, state resident: full-time $4266; part-time $237 per credit hour. Tuition, nonresident: full-time $7506; part-time $417 per credit hour. Required fees:

$427; $427. *Faculty research:* Web based instruction, school district leadership, teacher leadership, university/school district partnerships, aspiring school leaders.

Southern Adventist University, School of Education and Psychology, Collegedale, TN 37315-0370. Offers clinical mental health counseling (MS); inclusive education (MS Ed); instructional leadership (MS Ed); literacy education (MS Ed); outdoor teacher education (MS Ed); school counseling (MS). *Accreditation:* NCATE. Part-time and evening/weekend programs available. *Faculty:* 4 full-time (2 women), 8 part-time/adjunct (5 women). *Students:* 33 full-time (15 women), 17 part-time (13 women); includes 16 minority (7 African Americans, 9 Hispanic Americans). Average age 30. In 2009, 23 master's awarded. *Degree requirements:* For master's, comprehensive exam (for some programs), thesis optional, position paper (MS), portfolio (MS Ed in outdoor teacher education). *Entrance requirements:* For master's, interview (MS); 9 semester hours of upper division course work in psychology or related field, including 1 course in psychology research or statistics; 9 semester hours of education (MS Ed). Additional exam requirements/recommendations for international students: Required—TOEFL (minimum score 600 paper-based; 250 computer-based; 100 iBT). *Application deadline:* For fall admission, 7/1 priority date for domestic students, 6/1 priority date for international students; for winter admission, 11/1 priority date for domestic students, 10/1 priority date for international students; for spring admission, 4/1 priority date for domestic students, 3/1 priority date for international students. Applications are processed on a rolling basis. Application fee: $25. Electronic applications accepted. *Expenses:* Tuition: Full-time $13,149; part-time $487 per credit hour. *Financial support:* In 2009–10, 7 students received support, including 1 research assistantship with full tuition reimbursement available (averaging $15,000 per year), 5 teaching assistantships with full tuition reimbursements available (averaging $15,000 per year); career-related internships or fieldwork, scholarships/grants, tuition waivers (partial), and unspecified assistantships also available. Support available to part-time students. Financial award application deadline: 4/1; financial award applicants required to submit FAFSA. *Unit head:* Dr. Wesley Taylor, Dean, 423-236-2444, Fax: 423-236-1765, E-mail: jwtv@southern.edu. *Application contact:* Mikhaile Spence, Information Contact, 423-236-2496, Fax: 423-236-1765, E-mail: maspence@southern.edu.

Southern Arkansas University–Magnolia, Graduate Programs, Magnolia, AR 71753. Offers agriculture (MS); business administration (MBA); computer and information sciences (MS); counseling (MS); education (M Ed), including counseling and development, curriculum and instruction emphasis, educational administration and supervision, elementary education, middle level emphasis, reading emphasis, secondary education, TESOL emphasis; kinesiology (MS); library media and information specialist (M Ed); mental health and clinical counseling (MS); public administration (EMPA); school counseling (M Ed); teaching (MAT). *Accreditation:* NCATE. Part-time and evening/weekend programs available. *Faculty:* 43 full-time (24 women), 12 part-time/adjunct (7 women). *Students:* 116 full-time (78 women), 333 part-time (255 women); includes 105 minority (98 African Americans, 3 American Indian/Alaska Native, 3 Asian Americans or Pacific Islanders, 1 Hispanic American), 11 international. Average age 33. In 2009, 88 master's awarded. *Degree requirements:* For master's, comprehensive exam, thesis optional. *Entrance requirements:* For master's, GRE, MAT or GMAT, minimum GPA of 2.75. *Application deadline:* For fall admission, 8/15 for domestic students; for winter admission, 1/8 for domestic students; for spring admission, 1/8 for domestic students. Applications are processed on a rolling basis. Application fee: $0. *Expenses:* Tuition, state resident: full-time $3798; part-time $211 per hour. Tuition, nonresident: full-time $5580; part-time $310 per hour. Required fees: $584. *Financial support:* Career-related internships or fieldwork, Federal Work-Study, scholarships/grants, tuition waivers (full), and unspecified assistantships available. Financial award applicants required to submit FAFSA. *Faculty research:* Alternative certification for teachers, supervision of instruction, instructional leadership, counseling. *Unit head:* Dr. Kim Bloss, Dean, Graduate Studies, 870-235-4150, Fax: 870-235-5227, E-mail: kkbloss@saumag.edu. *Application contact:* Dr. Kim Bloss, Dean, Graduate Studies, 870-235-4150, Fax: 870-235-5227, E-mail: kkbloss@saumag.edu.

Southern Connecticut State University, School of Graduate Studies, School of Education, Department of Educational Leadership, New Haven, CT 06515-1355. Offers educational foundations (Diploma), including foundational studies; educational leadership (Ed D, Diploma); research, statistics, and measurement (MS). Part-time and evening/weekend programs available. *Faculty:* 6 full-time, 6 part-time/adjunct. *Students:* 7 full-time (5 women), 240 part-time (164 women); includes 33 minority (26 African Americans, 1 American Indian/Alaska Native, 6 Hispanic Americans), 1 international. 160 applicants, 54% accepted, 71 enrolled. In 2009, 98 other advanced degrees awarded. *Entrance requirements:* For degree, master's degree, minimum GPA of 3.0, writing sample. *Application deadline:* For fall admission, 7/15 priority date for domestic students. Applications are processed on a rolling basis. Application fee: $50. Electronic applications accepted. Tuition and fees vary according to program. *Financial support:* Application deadline: 4/15. *Unit head:* Dr. Peter Madonia, Chairperson, 203-392-5441, E-mail: madoniap1@southernct.edu. *Application contact:* Dr. Cathryn Magno, Graduate Coordinator, 203-392-5170, Fax: 203-392-5347, E-mail: magnoc1@southernct.edu.

Southern Illinois University Carbondale, Graduate School, College of Education, Department of Educational Administration and Higher Education, Program in Educational Administration, Carbondale, IL 62901-4701. Offers MS Ed, PhD. *Accreditation:* NCATE. Part-time programs available. *Degree requirements:* For master's, thesis or alternative; for doctorate, thesis/dissertation. *Entrance requirements:* For master's, GRE General Test, MAT, minimum GPA of 2.7; for doctorate, GRE General Test, MAT, minimum GPA of 3.5. Additional exam requirements/recommendations for international students: Required—TOEFL. *Faculty research:* School principalship, history and philosophy of education, supervision.

Southern Illinois University Edwardsville, Graduate Studies and Research, School of Education, Department of Educational Leadership, Program in Educational Administration, Edwardsville, IL 62026-0001. Offers MS Ed, Ed S. *Accreditation:* NCATE. Part-time and evening/weekend programs available. *Students:* 2 full-time (both women), 197 part-time (125 women); includes 25 minority (22 African Americans, 3 Hispanic Americans). Average age 26. 53 applicants, 42% accepted. In 2009, 44 master's, 12 Ed Ss awarded. *Degree requirements:* For master's, thesis or alternative, portfolio. *Entrance requirements:* Additional exam requirements/recommendations for international students: Required—TOEFL (minimum score 550 paper-based; 213 computer-based; 79 iBT), IELTS (minimum score 6.5). *Application deadline:* For fall admission, 7/23 for domestic students, 6/1 for international students; for spring admission, 12/11 for domestic students, 10/1 for international students. Applications are processed on a rolling basis. Application fee: $30. Electronic applications accepted. *Expenses:* Tuition, state resident: part-time $1252.50 per semester. Tuition, nonresident: part-time $3131.25 per semester. Required fees: $586.85 per semester. Tuition and fees vary according to course load. *Financial support:* Fellowships with tuition reimbursements, research assistantships with full tuition reimbursements, teaching assistantships with tuition reimbursements, career-related internships or fieldwork, Federal Work-Study, institutionally sponsored loans, scholarships/grants, traineeships, and unspecified assistantships available. Support available to part-time students. Financial award application deadline: 3/1; financial award applicants required to submit FAFSA. *Unit head:* Dr. Linda Morice, Director, 618-650-3277, E-mail: lmorice@siue.edu. *Application contact:* Dr. Linda Morice, Director, 618-650-3277, E-mail: lmorice@siue.edu.

Southern Nazarene University, Graduate College, School of Education, Bethany, OK 73008. Offers curriculum and instruction (MA); educational leadership (MA). *Accreditation:* NCATE. Part-time and evening/weekend programs available. *Degree requirements:* For master's, thesis optional. *Entrance requirements:* For master's, MAT, English proficiency exam, minimum GPA of 3.0 in last 60 hours/major, 2.7 overall.

Southern New Hampshire University, School of Education, Manchester, NH 03106-1045. Offers business education (MS); child development (M Ed); computer technology education (Certificate); curriculum and instruction (M Ed); education (M Ed, CAS); elementary education (M Ed); general special education (Certificate); school business administrator (Certificate); secondary education (M Ed); training and development (Certificate). Part-time and evening/weekend programs available. Postbaccalaureate distance learning degree programs offered (no on-campus study). *Degree requirements:* For master's, comprehensive exam (for some programs), thesis or alternative. *Entrance requirements:* For master's, PRAXIS I, minimum GPA of 2.75. Additional exam requirements/recommendations for international students: Required—TOEFL (minimum score 550 paper-based; 213 computer-based). Electronic applications accepted. *Expenses:* Contact institution.

Southern Oregon University, Graduate Studies, School of Education, Ashland, OR 97520. Offers elementary education (MA Ed, MS Ed), including classroom teacher, early childhood, handicapped learner, reading, supervision; secondary education (MA Ed, MS Ed), including classroom teacher, handicapped learner, reading, supervision; teaching (MAT). *Degree requirements:* For master's, thesis optional. *Entrance requirements:* For master's, GRE General Test, minimum GPA of 3.0. Electronic applications accepted.

Southern University and Agricultural and Mechanical College, Graduate School, College of Education, Department of Behavioral Studies and Educational Leadership, Program in Administration and Supervision, Baton Rouge, LA 70813. Offers M Ed.

Southern University and Agricultural and Mechanical College, Graduate School, College of Education, Department of Behavioral Studies and Educational Leadership, Program in Educational Leadership, Baton Rouge, LA 70813. Offers M Ed. *Entrance requirements:* For master's, GRE General Test.

Southwest Baptist University, Program in Education, Bolivar, MO 65613-2597. Offers education (MS); educational administration (MS, Ed S). Part-time programs available. *Degree requirements:* For master's, comprehensive exam, thesis optional, 6 hour residency; for Ed S, comprehensive exam, 5 hour residency. *Entrance requirements:* For master's, GRE or PRAXIS II, interviews, minimum GPA of 2.75; for Ed S, master's degree. Additional exam requirements/recommendations for international students: Required—TOEFL (minimum score 550 paper-based; 213 computer-based). *Faculty research:* At-risk programs, principal retention, mentoring beginning principals.

Southwestern Adventist University, Education Department, Graduate Program, Keene, TX 76059. Offers curriculum and instruction with reading emphasis (M Ed); educational leadership (M Ed). Part-time and evening/weekend programs available. *Degree requirements:* For master's, thesis or alternative, professional paper. *Entrance requirements:* For master's, GRE General Test.

Southwestern Assemblies of God University, Thomas F. Harrison School of Graduate Studies, Program in Education, Waxahachie, TX 75165-5735. Offers Christian school administration (MS); curriculum development (MS); early education administration (M Ed); middle and secondary education (M Ed). *Degree requirements:* For master's, comprehensive written and oral exams. *Entrance requirements:* For master's, GRE General Test, minimum GPA of 2.5. Electronic applications accepted.

Southwestern Oklahoma State University, College of Professional and Graduate Studies, School of Behavioral Sciences and Education, Specialization in Educational Administration, Weatherford, OK 73096-3098. Offers M Ed. M Ed distance learning degree program offered to Oklahoma residents only. *Accreditation:* NCATE. Part-time and evening/weekend programs available. Postbaccalaureate distance learning degree programs offered (minimal on-campus study). *Degree requirements:* For master's, exam. *Entrance requirements:* For master's, GRE General Test or minimum undergraduate GPA of 3.0, portfolio. Additional exam requirements/recommendations for international students: Required—TOEFL.

Spalding University, Graduate Studies, College of Education, Program in Leadership Education, Louisville, KY 40203-2188. Offers Ed D. *Accreditation:* NCATE. Part-time and evening/weekend programs available. *Faculty:* 4 full-time (2 women), 8 part-time/adjunct (3 women). *Students:* 25 full-time (19 women), 70 part-time (37 women); includes 20 minority (19 African Americans, 1 Asian American or Pacific Islander), 27 international. Average age 40. 22 applicants, 77% accepted, 16 enrolled. In 2009, 15 doctorates awarded. *Degree requirements:* For doctorate, comprehensive exam, thesis/dissertation. *Entrance requirements:* For doctorate, GRE General Test or MAT, interview, recommendations, resume. Additional exam requirements/recommendations for international students: Required—TOEFL (minimum score 535 paper-based; 203 computer-based). *Application deadline:* Applications are processed on a rolling basis. Electronic applications accepted. *Expenses:* Tuition: Full-time $11,340; part-time $630 per credit hour. Tuition and fees vary according to program. *Financial support:* In 2009–10, 15 students received support, including 1 research assistantship with partial tuition reimbursement available (averaging $3,780 per year); scholarships/grants and unspecified assistantships also available. Financial award application deadline: 3/15; financial award applicants required to submit FAFSA. *Faculty research:* Leadership of schools, achievement gap, women in leadership. *Unit head:* Dr. Beverly Keepers, Dean, 502-588-7121, Fax: 502-585-7123, E-mail: bkeepers@spalding.edu. *Application contact:* Admissions Office, 502-585-7111, E-mail: admissions@spalding.edu.

Spalding University, Graduate Studies, College of Education, Programs in Education, Louisville, KY 40203-2188. Offers elementary school education (MAT); general education (MA); high school education (MAT); middle school education (MAT); school administration (MA); special education (learning and behavioral disorders) (MAT); student guidance counselor (MA). MAT degree programs offered for first teaching certificate/license students. *Accreditation:* NCATE. Part-time and evening/weekend programs available. *Faculty:* 6 full-time (4 women), 32 part-time/adjunct (23 women). *Students:* 125 full-time (93 women), 64 part-time (49 women); includes 53 minority (50 African Americans, 2 American Indian/Alaska Native, 1 Hispanic American), 2 international. Average age 37. 57 applicants, 79% accepted, 41 enrolled. In 2009, 56 master's awarded. *Degree requirements:* For master's, portfolio, final project, clinical experience. *Entrance requirements:* For master's, GRE General Test or MAT, interview, recommendations, resume. Additional exam requirements/recommendations for international students: Required—TOEFL (minimum score 535 paper-based; 203 computer-based). *Application deadline:* Applications are processed on a rolling basis. Application fee: $30. Electronic applications accepted. *Expenses:* Tuition: Full-time $11,340; part-time $630 per credit hour. Tuition and fees vary according to program. *Financial support:* In 2009–10, 106 students received support, including 3 research assistantships with partial tuition reimbursements available (averaging $3,590 per year); scholarships/grants, traineeships, and unspecified assistantships also available. Financial award application deadline: 3/15; financial award applicants required to submit FAFSA. *Faculty research:* Instructional technology, achievement gap, classroom management, assessment. *Unit head:* Dr. Beverly Keepers, Dean, 502-588-7121, Fax: 502-585-7123, E-mail: bkeepers@spalding.edu. *Application contact:* Admissions Office, 502-585-7111, E-mail: admissions@spalding.edu.

Springfield College, Graduate Programs, Program in Education, Springfield, MA 01109-3797. Offers counseling and secondary education (M Ed, MS); early childhood education (M Ed, MS); education (M Ed, MS); educational administration (M Ed, MS); educational studies (M Ed, MS); elementary education (M Ed, MS); secondary education (M Ed, MS); special education (M Ed, MS). Part-time and evening/weekend programs available. *Entrance requirements:* Additional exam requirements/recommendations for international students: Required—TOEFL (minimum score 550 paper-based; 213 computer-based). Electronic applications accepted. *Expenses:* Tuition: Full-time $19,800; part-time $825 per credit hour. Required fees: $150.

Stanford University, School of Education, Program in Social Sciences, Policy, and Educational Practice, Stanford, CA 94305-9991. Offers administration and policy analysis (Ed D, PhD); anthropology of education (PhD); economics of education (PhD); educational linguistics (PhD); evaluation (MA), including interdisciplinary studies; higher education (PhD); history of education (PhD); interdisciplinary studies (PhD); international comparative education (MA, PhD); international education administration and policy analysis (MA); philosophy of education (PhD); policy analysis (MA); prospective principal's program (MA); sociology of education (PhD). *Degree requirements:* For master's, thesis (for some programs); for doctorate, thesis/dissertation. *Entrance requirements:* For master's and doctorate, GRE General Test. Electronic

Educational Leadership and Administration

Stanford University (continued)
applications accepted. *Expenses:* Tuition: Full-time $37,380; part-time $2760 per quarter. Required fees: $501.

State University of New York at Binghamton, Graduate School, College of Community and Public Affairs, Department of Student Affairs Administration, Binghamton, NY 13902-6000. Offers MS. *Students:* 21 full-time (11 women), 13 part-time (6 women); includes 6 minority (2 African Americans, 4 Hispanic Americans). Average age 29. 18 applicants, 67% accepted, 12 enrolled. In 2009, 11 master's awarded. *Financial support:* In 2009–10, 12 students received support, including 1 fellowship with full tuition reimbursement available (averaging $9,000 per year). *Unit head:* Dr. Sharon Holmes, Program Director, 607-777-9219, E-mail: slholmes@binghamton.edu. *Application contact:* Victoria Williams, Recruiting and Admissions Coordinator, 607-777-2151, Fax: 607-777-2501, E-mail: vwilliam@binghamton.edu.

State University of New York at Fredonia, Graduate Studies, College of Education, Program in Educational Administration, Fredonia, NY 14063-1136. Offers CAS. Part-time and evening/weekend programs available. *Degree requirements:* For CAS, thesis or alternative. *Expenses:* Tuition, state resident: full-time $8370; part-time $349 per credit. Tuition, nonresident: full-time $13,250; part-time $552 per credit. Required fees: $1289; $53.55 per credit.

State University of New York at New Paltz, Graduate School, School of Education, Department of Educational Administration, New Paltz, NY 12561. Offers alternative certificate: school district leader (transition D) (CAS); school business leadership (CAS); school leadership (MS Ed, CAS). Part-time and evening/weekend programs available. *Faculty:* 6 full-time (3 women), 1 part-time/adjunct (0 women). *Students:* 10 full-time (6 women), 128 part-time (80 women); includes 17 minority (3 African Americans, 2 American Indian/Alaska Native, 3 Asian Americans or Pacific Islanders, 9 Hispanic Americans). Average age 40. 32 applicants, 69% accepted, 20 enrolled. In 2009, 3 master's, 49 CASs awarded. *Degree requirements:* For CAS, internship. *Entrance requirements:* For master's, GRE General Test or MAT, minimum GPA of 3.0, NYS teaching certificate; for CAS, minimum GPA of 3.0, proof of 3 years teaching experience, NYS teaching certificate. Additional exam requirements/recommendations for international students: Required—TOEFL (minimum score 550 paper-based; 213 computer-based; 80 iBT), IELTS (minimum score 6.5). *Application deadline:* For fall admission, 5/15 priority date for domestic and international students; for spring admission, 11/15 priority date for domestic and international students. Applications are processed on a rolling basis. Application fee: $50. Electronic applications accepted. *Financial support:* Career-related internships or fieldwork, Federal Work-Study, and institutionally sponsored loans available. Financial award application deadline: 8/1; financial award applicants required to submit FAFSA. *Faculty research:* Time management of administrators, social justice, women in educational leadership, diversity in educational leadership, superintendency. *Unit head:* Dr. Edward Sullivan, Chair, 845-257-2810, E-mail: sullivae@newpaltz.edu. *Application contact:* Caroline Murphy, Graduate Admissions Advisor, 845-257-3285, Fax: 845-257-3284, E-mail: gradschool@newpaltz.edu.

State University of New York at Oswego, Graduate Studies, School of Education, Department of Educational Administration, Oswego, NY 13126. Offers educational administration and supervision (CAS); school building leadership (CAS); MS Ed/CAS. Part-time programs available. *Degree requirements:* For CAS, comprehensive exam, internship. *Entrance requirements:* For degree, interview, MA or MS, minimum GPA of 3.0, teaching certificate. Additional exam requirements/recommendations for international students: Required—TOEFL (minimum score 560 paper-based; 220 computer-based). *Faculty research:* Professional growth and development, leadership, governance, strategic planning, shared decision making.

State University of New York at Plattsburgh, Division of Education, Health, and Human Services, Program in Educational Leadership, Plattsburgh, NY 12901-2681. Offers CAS. Part-time and evening/weekend programs available. *Faculty:* 1 full-time (0 women), 13 part-time/adjunct (4 women). *Students:* 2 full-time (both women), 44 part-time (27 women); includes 3 minority (1 African American, 2 Hispanic Americans). Average age 40. 8 applicants, 100% accepted, 8 enrolled. In 2009, 20 CASs awarded. *Degree requirements:* For CAS, comprehensive exam, portfolio. *Entrance requirements:* Additional exam requirements/recommendations for international students: Required—TOEFL (minimum score 550 paper-based; 213 computer-based; 79 iBT). *Application deadline:* For fall admission, 2/15 priority date for domestic students; for spring admission, 10/15 priority date for domestic students. Applications are processed on a rolling basis. Application fee: $75. *Expenses:* Tuition, state resident: full-time $8370; part-time $349 per credit hour. Tuition, nonresident: full-time $13,250; part-time $552 per credit hour. Required fees: $1130. *Financial support:* Federal Work-Study available. Support available to part-time students. Financial award application deadline: 4/15; financial award applicants required to submit FAFSA. *Unit head:* Dr. Steven Black, Coordinator, 518-792-5425 Ext. 105, E-mail: blacksn@plattsburgh.edu. *Application contact:* Marguerite Adelman, Assistant Director, Graduate Admissions, 518-564-4723, Fax: 518-564-4722, E-mail: adelmaml@plattsburgh.edu.

State University of New York College at Cortland, Graduate Studies, School of Education, Program in Educational Leadership, Cortland, NY 13045. Offers CAS. Part-time and evening/weekend programs available. *Degree requirements:* For CAS, one foreign language. *Entrance requirements:* For degree, MS in education, permanent New York teaching certificate. Additional exam requirements/recommendations for international students: Required—TOEFL.

Stephen F. Austin State University, Graduate School, College of Education, Department of Secondary Education and Educational Leadership, Nacogdoches, TX 75962. Offers educational leadership (Ed D); secondary education (M Ed). *Accreditation:* NCATE. *Degree requirements:* For master's, comprehensive exam; for doctorate, thesis/dissertation. *Entrance requirements:* For master's, GRE General Test; for doctorate, GRE General Test, interview, writing sample. Additional exam requirements/recommendations for international students: Required—TOEFL. Electronic applications accepted.

Stetson University, College of Arts and Sciences, Division of Education, Department of Teacher Education, Program in Educational Leadership, DeLand, FL 32723. Offers M Ed. *Accreditation:* NCATE. Evening/weekend programs available. *Students:* 33 full-time (23 women), 2 part-time (1 woman); includes 7 minority (2 African Americans, 5 Hispanic Americans). Average age 34. In 2009, 53 master's awarded. *Degree requirements:* For master's, comprehensive exam. *Entrance requirements:* For master's, GRE General Test or MAT. *Application deadline:* For fall admission, 3/1 priority date for domestic students; for spring admission, 11/1 for domestic students. Applications are processed on a rolling basis. Application fee: $25. Tuition and fees vary according to course load, campus/location and program. *Financial support:* Career-related internships or fieldwork available. *Unit head:* Dr. Debra Touchton, Coordinator, 386-822-7075. *Application contact:* Diana Belian, Office of Graduate Studies, 386-822-7075, Fax: 386-822-7388, E-mail: dbelian@stetson.edu.

Stony Brook University, State University of New York, School of Professional Development, Stony Brook, NY 11794. Offers biology-grade 7-12 (MAT); chemistry-grade 7-12 (MAT); coaching (Graduate Certificate); computer integrated engineering (Graduate Certificate); earth science-grade 7-12 (MAT); educational computing (Graduate Certificate); educational leadership (Advanced Certificate); English-grade 7-12 (MAT); environmental management (Graduate Certificate); environmental/occupational health and safety (Graduate Certificate); French-grade 7-12 (MAT); German-grade 7-12 (MAT); human resource management (Graduate Certificate); information systems management (Graduate Certificate); Italian-grade 7-12 (MAT); liberal studies (MA); mathematics-grade 7-12 (MAT); operation research (Graduate Certificate); physics-grade 7-12 (MAT); school administration and supervision (Graduate Certificate); school building leadership (Graduate Certificate); school district administration (Graduate Certificate); school district business leadership (Advanced Certificate); school district leadership (Graduate Certificate); social science and the professions (MPS), including environmental waste management; human resource management; social studies-grade 7-12 (MAT); Spanish-grade 7-12 (MAT); waste management (Graduate Certificate). Part-time and evening/weekend programs available. Postbaccalaureate distance learning degree programs offered. *Faculty:* 5 full-time (3 women), 131 part-time/adjunct (53 women). *Students:* 317 full-time (187 women),

1,200 part-time (773 women); includes 187 minority (77 African Americans, 2 American Indian/Alaska Native, 22 Asian Americans or Pacific Islanders, 86 Hispanic Americans), 11 international. Average age 28. In 2009, 597 master's, 234 other advanced degrees awarded. *Degree requirements:* For master's, one foreign language, thesis or alternative. *Application deadline:* Applications are processed on a rolling basis. Application fee: $62. *Expenses:* Tuition, state resident: full-time $8370; part-time $349 per credit. Tuition, nonresident: full-time $13,250; part-time $552 per credit. Required fees: $933. *Financial support:* Fellowships, research assistantships, teaching assistantships, career-related internships or fieldwork available. Support available to part-time students. *Unit head:* Dr. Paul J. Edelson, Dean, 631-632-7052, Fax: 631-632-9046, E-mail: paul.edelson@stonybrook.edu. *Application contact:* Dr. Paul J. Edelson, Dean, 631-632-7052, Fax: 631-632-9046, E-mail: paul.edelson@stonybrook.edu.

Suffolk University, College of Arts and Sciences, Department of Education and Human Services, Program in Administration of Higher Education, Boston, MA 02108-2770. Offers administration of higher education (M Ed); leadership (CAGS). Part-time and evening/weekend programs available. *Entrance requirements:* For master's, GRE General Test or MAT, 2 letters of recommendation, resume. *Application deadline:* For fall admission, 6/15 priority date for domestic students, 6/15 for international students; for spring admission, 11/15 priority date for domestic students, 11/15 for international students. Applications are processed on a rolling basis. Application fee: $50. *Expenses:* Tuition: Full-time $33,000; part-time $1100 per credit. Required fees: $20. Tuition and fees vary according to program. *Financial support:* Fellowships, career-related internships or fieldwork, Federal Work-Study, and institutionally sponsored loans available. Support available to part-time students. Financial award application deadline: 4/1; financial award applicants required to submit FAFSA. *Faculty research:* History of universities, student financial aid, leadership. *Unit head:* Dr. Michael Siegel, Graduate Program Director, 617-994-6456, Fax: 617-305-1743, E-mail: msiegel@suffolk.edu. *Application contact:* Judith Reynolds, Director of Graduate Admissions, 617-573-8302, Fax: 617-305-1733, E-mail: grad.admission@suffolk.edu.

Sul Ross State University, Rio Grande College of Sul Ross State University, Alpine, TX 79832. Offers business administration (MBA); teacher education (M Ed), including bilingual education, counseling, educational diagnostics, elementary education, general education, reading, school administration, secondary education. Part-time and evening/weekend programs available. *Degree requirements:* For master's, thesis optional. *Entrance requirements:* For master's, GMAT or GRE General Test, minimum GPA of 2.5 in last 60 hours of undergraduate work. *Faculty research:* Drug and substance abuse counseling, U.S.-Mexico border economic development.

Sul Ross State University, School of Professional Studies, Department of Teacher Education, Program in School Administration, Alpine, TX 79832. Offers M Ed. Part-time and evening/weekend programs available. *Degree requirements:* For master's, thesis optional. *Entrance requirements:* For master's, GMAT or GRE General Test, minimum GPA of 2.5 in last 60 hours of undergraduate work.

Sul Ross State University, School of Professional Studies, Department of Teacher Education, Program in Supervision, Alpine, TX 79832. Offers M Ed. Part-time and evening/weekend programs available. *Degree requirements:* For master's, thesis optional. *Entrance requirements:* For master's, GMAT or GRE General Test, minimum GPA of 2.5 in last 60 hours of undergraduate work.

Syracuse University, School of Education, Program in Educational Leadership, Syracuse, NY 13244. Offers MS, Ed D, CAS. Part-time programs available. *Students:* 4 full-time (3 women), 59 part-time (37 women); includes 5 minority (4 African Americans, 1 Asian American or Pacific Islander), 1 international. Average age 40. 11 applicants, 91% accepted, 3 enrolled. In 2009, 10 other advanced degrees awarded. *Degree requirements:* For master's, thesis or alternative; for doctorate, thesis/dissertation; for CAS, thesis. *Entrance requirements:* For doctorate, GRE. Additional exam requirements/recommendations for international students: Required—TOEFL (minimum score 100 iBT). *Application deadline:* For fall admission, 2/1 priority date for domestic and international students; for spring admission, 10/15 priority date for domestic and international students. Applications are processed on a rolling basis. Application fee: $75. Electronic applications accepted. *Expenses:* Tuition: Full-time $26,808; part-time $1117 per credit. Required fees: $1024. *Financial support:* Fellowships with tuition reimbursements, teaching assistantships with tuition reimbursements available. Financial award application deadline: 1/1; financial award applicants required to submit FAFSA. *Unit head:* Dr. Joseph Shedd, Program Coordinator, 315-443-1468, E-mail: jbshedd@syr.edu. *Application contact:* Liza Rochelson, Graduate Recruiter, School of Education, 315-443-2505, E-mail: e-gradrcrt@syr.edu.

Tarleton State University, College of Graduate Studies, College of Education, Department of Educational Leadership and Policy Studies, Stephenville, TX 76402. Offers educational administration (M Ed); educational leadership (Ed D, Certificate). Part-time and evening/weekend programs available. Postbaccalaureate distance learning degree programs offered (minimal on-campus study). *Degree requirements:* For master's, comprehensive exam, thesis optional; for doctorate, thesis/dissertation. *Entrance requirements:* For master's, GRE General Test, minimum GPA of 3.0; for doctorate, GRE, 4 letters of reference, leadership portfolio. Additional exam requirements/recommendations for international students: Required—TOEFL (minimum score 550 paper-based; 213 computer-based; 80 iBT). Electronic applications accepted.

Tarleton State University, College of Graduate Studies, College of Education, Department of Psychology and Counseling, Stephenville, TX 76402. Offers counseling and psychology (M Ed), including counseling, counseling psychology, educational psychology; educational administration (M Ed); secondary education (Certificate); special education (Certificate). Part-time and evening/weekend programs available. Postbaccalaureate distance learning degree programs offered (minimal on-campus study). *Degree requirements:* For master's, comprehensive exam, thesis optional. *Entrance requirements:* For master's, GRE General Test, minimum GPA of 3.0. Additional exam requirements/recommendations for international students: Required—TOEFL (minimum score 550 paper-based; 213 computer-based; 80 iBT). Electronic applications accepted.

Teachers College, Columbia University, Graduate Faculty of Education, Department of Math, Science and Technology, Program in Supervision in Science Education, New York, NY 10027-6696. Offers MA.

Teachers College, Columbia University, Graduate Faculty of Education, Department of Organization and Leadership, Program in Education Leadership, New York, NY 10027-6696. Offers education leadership (PhD); education leadership studies (Ed M, MA, Ed D); leadership, policy and politics (Ed M, MA, Ed D, PhD); private school leadership (Ed M, MA, Ed D); public school and school district leadership (Ed M, MA, Ed D); MBA/Ed D. *Students:* 62 full-time (39 women), 180 part-time (105 women); includes 81 minority (54 African Americans, 17 Asian Americans or Pacific Islanders, 10 Hispanic Americans), 3 international. Average age 34. 173 applicants, 50% accepted, 45 enrolled. In 2009, 176 master's, 7 doctorates awarded. Application fee: $65. *Unit head:* Warner Burke, Chair, 212-678-3258. *Application contact:* Debbie Lesperance, Assistant Director of Admission, 212-678-3710, Fax: 212-678-4171.

Teachers College, Columbia University, Graduate Faculty of Education, Department of Organization and Leadership, Program in Leadership, Policy and Politics, New York, NY 10027-6696. Offers MA, ME, Ed D.

Teachers College, Columbia University, Graduate Faculty of Education, Department of Organization and Leadership, Program in Private School Leadership, New York, NY 10027-6696. Offers Ed M, MA.

Teachers College, Columbia University, Graduate Faculty of Education, Department of Organization and Leadership, Program in Public School Building Leadership, New York, NY 10027-6696. Offers Ed M, MA.

Teachers College, Columbia University, Graduate Faculty of Education, Department of Organization and Leadership, Urban Education Leaders Program, New York, NY 10027-6696. Offers Ed D.

Teachers College, Columbia University, Graduate Faculty of Education, Program in Administration and Supervision in Special Education, New York, NY 10027-6696. Offers Ed M, MA, Ed D, PhD. *Accreditation:* NCATE. *Students:* 1 (woman) full-time, 7 part-time (5 women); includes 1 minority (Asian American or Pacific Islander), 1 international. Average age 31. 3 applicants, 0% accepted, 0 enrolled. In 2009, 3 master's, 7 doctorates awarded. *Degree requirements:* For doctorate, thesis/dissertation. *Application deadline:* For fall admission, 5/15 for domestic students. Application fee: $65. *Financial support:* Career-related internships or fieldwork, Federal Work-Study, institutionally sponsored loans, and tuition waivers (full and partial) available. Support available to part-time students. Financial award application deadline: 2/1. *Faculty research:* Cognition and comprehension, disability studies, self-determination, literacy development. *Unit head:* Susan Furhman, President, 212-678-3050. *Application contact:* Ursula Felton, Office of Admissions, 212-678-3710, Fax: 212-678-4171.

Temple University, Graduate School, College of Education, Department of Educational Leadership and Policy Studies, Philadelphia, PA 19122-6096. Offers educational administration (Ed M, Ed D); urban education (Ed M, Ed D). Part-time and evening/weekend programs available. Terminal master's awarded for partial completion of doctoral program. *Degree requirements:* For master's, comprehensive exam, thesis or alternative; for doctorate, thesis/dissertation, preliminary exam. *Entrance requirements:* For master's and doctorate, GRE General Test or MAT, minimum GPA of 3.0. Additional exam requirements/recommendations for international students: Required—TOEFL (minimum score 550 paper-based; 213 computer-based; 79 iBT). Electronic applications accepted. *Faculty research:* Women in education, school effectiveness, financial policy, school improvement in city schools, nongraded schools.

Tennessee State University, The School of Graduate Studies and Research, College of Education, Department of Educational Administration, Nashville, TN 37209-1561. Offers administration and supervision (M Ed, Ed D, Ed S). *Accreditation:* NCATE. *Entrance requirements:* For master's, GRE General Test, GRE Subject Test, minimum GPA of 2.5; for doctorate, GRE General Test, MAT, interview, minimum GPA of 3.25, work experience.

Tennessee Technological University, Graduate School, College of Education, Department of Curriculum and Instruction, Program in Instructional Leadership, Cookeville, TN 38505. Offers MA, Ed S. *Accreditation:* NCATE. Part-time and evening/weekend programs available. *Faculty:* 9 full-time (3 women). *Students:* 237 full-time (169 women), 314 part-time (226 women); includes 39 minority (34 African Americans, 3 American Indian/Alaska Native, 1 Asian American or Pacific Islander, 1 Hispanic American). Average age 27. 362 applicants, 89% accepted, 272 enrolled. In 2009, 160 master's, 220 other advanced degrees awarded. *Degree requirements:* For master's and Ed S, comprehensive exam, thesis or alternative. *Entrance requirements:* For master's and Ed S, MAT or GRE. Additional exam requirements/recommendations for international students: Required—TOEFL (minimum score 550 paper-based; 79 iBT), IELTS (minimum score 5.5). *Application deadline:* For fall admission, 8/1 for domestic students, 5/1 for international students; for spring admission, 12/1 for domestic students, 10/1 for international students. Application fee: $25 ($30 for international students). Electronic applications accepted. *Expenses:* Tuition, state resident: full-time $7034; part-time $368 per credit hour. *Financial support:* In 2009–10, 33 fellowships (averaging $8,000 per year), 11 research assistantships (averaging $4,000 per year), 7 teaching assistantships (averaging $4,000 per year) were awarded; career-related internships or fieldwork also available. Financial award application deadline: 4/1. *Faculty research:* School board member training, community school education. *Unit head:* Dr. Matthew R. Smith, Chairperson, 931-372-3181, Fax: 931-372-6270. *Application contact:* Shelia K. Kendrick, Coordinator of Graduate Studies, 931-372-3808, Fax: 931-372-3497, E-mail: skendrick@tntech.edu.

Tennessee Temple University, Graduate Studies in Education, Program in Educational Leadership, Chattanooga, TN 37404-3587. Offers M Ed. *Degree requirements:* For master's, comprehensive exam, thesis or alternative. *Entrance requirements:* For master's, GRE, minimum cumulative undergraduate GPA of 3.0, 3 references.

Texas A&M International University, Office of Graduate Studies and Research, Department of Professional Programs, Laredo, TX 78041-1900. Offers educational administration (MS Ed); generic special education (MS Ed); school counseling (MS). *Faculty:* 9 full-time (3 women), 2 part-time/adjunct (1 woman). *Students:* 15 full-time (9 women), 152 part-time (120 women); includes 162 minority (1 African American, 161 Hispanic Americans). Average age 34. 59 applicants. In 2009, 74 master's awarded. *Application deadline:* For fall admission, 4/30 priority date for domestic students; for spring admission, 11/30 priority date for domestic students. *Financial support:* In 2009–10, 62 students received support, including 1 research assistantship. *Unit head:* Dr. Randel Brown, Interim Chair, 956-326-2679, E-mail: brown@tamiu.edu. *Application contact:* Rosie Dickinson, Director of Admissions, 956-326-2200.

Texas A&M University, College of Education and Human Development, Department of Educational Administration and Human Resource Development, College Station, TX 77843. Offers M Ed, MS, Ed D, PhD. Part-time programs available. *Faculty:* 30. *Students:* 132 full-time (90 women), 323 part-time (197 women); includes 165 minority (70 African Americans, 3 American Indian/Alaska Native, 9 Asian Americans or Pacific Islanders, 83 Hispanic Americans), 28 international. Average age 37. In 2009, 54 master's, 29 doctorates awarded. *Degree requirements:* For master's, thesis optional; for doctorate, thesis/dissertation. *Entrance requirements:* For master's, GRE General Test, writing exam, interview, professional experience; for doctorate, GRE General Test, writing exam, interview/presentation, professional experience. Additional exam requirements/recommendations for international students: Required—TOEFL. *Application deadline:* For fall admission, 12/1 for domestic and international students; for spring admission, 8/15 for domestic and international students. Application fee: $50 ($75 for international students). Electronic applications accepted. *Expenses:* Tuition, state resident: full-time $3991; part-time $221.74 per credit hour. Tuition, nonresident: full-time $9049; part-time $502.74 per credit hour. *Financial support:* In 2009–10, fellowships (averaging $20,000 per year), research assistantships (averaging $12,000 per year) were awarded; career-related internships or fieldwork and institutionally sponsored loans also available. Support available to part-time students. Financial award application deadline: 3/1; financial award applicants required to submit FAFSA. *Faculty research:* Higher education administration, public school administration, student affairs. *Application contact:* Joyce Nelson, Senior Academic Advisor, 979-847-9098, Fax: 979-862-4347, E-mail: jnelson@tamu.edu.

Texas A&M University–Commerce, Graduate School, College of Education and Human Services, Department of Educational Leadership, Commerce, TX 75429-3011. Offers educational administration (M Ed, Ed D); educational technology (M Ed, MS); higher education (MS, Ed D); training and development (MS). Part-time programs available. Terminal master's awarded for partial completion of doctoral program. *Degree requirements:* For master's, comprehensive exam, thesis (for some programs); for doctorate, thesis/dissertation, departmental qualifying exam. *Entrance requirements:* For master's, GRE General Test; for doctorate, GRE General Test, writing skills exam, interview. Electronic applications accepted. *Faculty research:* Property tax reform, politics of education, administrative stress.

Texas A&M University–Corpus Christi, Graduate Studies and Research, College of Education, Program in Educational Administration, Corpus Christi, TX 78412-5503. Offers MS. Part-time and evening/weekend programs available. *Degree requirements:* For master's, comprehensive exam, thesis (for some programs). *Entrance requirements:* For master's, GRE General Test. Additional exam requirements/recommendations for international students: Required—TOEFL. Electronic applications accepted.

Texas A&M University–Corpus Christi, Graduate Studies and Research, College of Education, Program in Educational Leadership, Corpus Christi, TX 78412-5503. Offers Ed D. Part-time and evening/weekend programs available. *Degree requirements:* For doctorate, comprehensive exam, thesis/dissertation. *Entrance requirements:* Additional exam requirements/recommendations for international students: Required—TOEFL. Electronic applications accepted.

Texas A&M University–Kingsville, College of Graduate Studies, College of Education, Department of Education, Program in Higher Education Administration Leadership, Kingsville, TX 78363. Offers PhD. *Degree requirements:* For doctorate, one foreign language, comprehensive exam, thesis/dissertation. *Entrance requirements:* For doctorate, GRE General Test, MAT, minimum GPA of 3.25.

Texas A&M University–Kingsville, College of Graduate Studies, College of Education, Department of Education, Program in School Administration, Kingsville, TX 78363. Offers MA, MS, Ed D. Part-time and evening/weekend programs available. *Degree requirements:* For master's, comprehensive exam, mini-thesis; for doctorate, one foreign language, comprehensive exam, thesis/dissertation. *Entrance requirements:* For master's, GRE General Test, MAT, minimum GPA of 3.0; for doctorate, GRE General Test, MAT, minimum GPA of 3.25. *Faculty research:* Funding sources in public education.

Texas A&M University–Kingsville, College of Graduate Studies, College of Education, Department of Education, Program in Supervision, Kingsville, TX 78363. Offers MA, MS. Part-time programs available. *Degree requirements:* For master's, comprehensive exam, mini-thesis. *Entrance requirements:* For master's, GRE General Test, MAT, minimum GPA of 3.0.

Texas A&M University–Texarkana, Graduate Studies and Research, College of Education and Liberal Arts, Texarkana, TX 75505-5518. Offers adult education (MS); curriculum and instruction (M Ed); education (MS); educational administration (M Ed); English (MA); instructional technology (MS); interdisciplinary studies (MA, MS); special education (MS). Part-time and evening/weekend programs available. *Degree requirements:* For master's, comprehensive exam (for some programs), thesis optional. *Entrance requirements:* For master's, minimum GPA of 2.5 on last 60 hours of bachelor's degree. Additional exam requirements/recommendations for international students: Required—TOEFL. Electronic applications accepted.

Texas Christian University, College of Education, Ed D in Educational Leadership Program, Fort Worth, TX 76129-0002. Offers Ed D. Part-time and evening/weekend programs available. *Degree requirements:* For doctorate, capstone project. *Entrance requirements:* For doctorate, GRE or MAT. Additional exam requirements/recommendations for international students: Required—TOEFL (minimum score 550 paper-based; 213 computer-based; 80 iBT). *Application deadline:* For fall admission, 2/1 for domestic and international students. *Expenses:* Tuition: Full-time $17,640; part-time $980 per credit hour. Tuition and fees vary according to program. *Financial support:* Teaching assistantships with full tuition reimbursements, career-related internships or fieldwork and unspecified assistantships available. Financial award application deadline: 3/15; financial award applicants required to submit FAFSA. *Unit head:* Dr. Kay B. Stevens, Dean, 817-257-7661, E-mail: k.stevens2@tcu.edu. *Application contact:* Robyn P. Shepheard, Academic Program Specialist, 817-257-7661, E-mail: r.shepheard@tcu.edu.

Texas Christian University, College of Education, Program in Educational Administration, Fort Worth, TX 76129-0002. Offers educational administration (M Ed); principal (Certificate). Part-time and evening/weekend programs available. *Entrance requirements:* Additional exam requirements/recommendations for international students: Required—TOEFL (minimum score 550 paper-based; 213 computer-based; 80 iBT). *Application deadline:* For fall admission, 7/15 for domestic and international students; for spring admission, 11/15 for domestic and international students. Applications are processed on a rolling basis. Application fee: $50. *Expenses:* Tuition: Full-time $17,640; part-time $980 per credit hour. Tuition and fees vary according to program. *Financial support:* Teaching assistantships with full tuition reimbursements, career-related internships or fieldwork and unspecified assistantships available. Financial award application deadline: 3/15; financial award applicants required to submit FAFSA. *Unit head:* Dr. Kay B. Stevens, Associate Dean, 817-257-7661, E-mail: m.patton@tcu.edu. *Application contact:* Robyn P. Shepheard, Academic Program Specialist, 817-257-7661, E-mail: r.shepheard@tcu.edu.

Texas Christian University, The Neeley School of Business at TCU, MBA/Ed D in Educational Leadership Joint Program, Fort Worth, TX 76129-0002. Offers MBA/Ed D. Part-time and evening/weekend programs available. *Entrance requirements:* Additional exam requirements/recommendations for international students: Required—TOEFL (minimum score 550 paper-based; 213 computer-based; 80 iBT). *Application deadline:* For fall admission, 2/1 for domestic and international students. Applications are processed on a rolling basis. Application fee: $50. *Expenses:* Tuition: Full-time $17,640; part-time $980 per credit hour. Tuition and fees vary according to program. *Financial support:* Teaching assistantships with full tuition reimbursements, career-related internships or fieldwork and unspecified assistantships available. Financial award application deadline: 3/15; financial award applicants required to submit FAFSA. *Unit head:* Dr. Kay B. Stevens, Associate Dean, 817-257-7661, E-mail: k.stevens2@tcu.edu. *Application contact:* Robyn P. Shepheard, Academic Program Specialist, 817-257-7661, E-mail: r.shepheard@tcu.edu.

Texas Southern University, College of Education, Department of Educational Administration and Foundation, Houston, TX 77004-4584. Offers educational administration (M Ed, Ed D). Part-time and evening/weekend programs available. *Faculty:* 11 full-time (5 women), 2 part-time/adjunct (0 women). *Students:* 37 full-time (27 women), 70 part-time (50 women); includes 97 minority (92 African Americans, 5 Hispanic Americans). Average age 38. 51 applicants, 100% accepted, 39 enrolled. In 2009, 27 master's, 5 doctorates awarded. *Degree requirements:* For master's, comprehensive exam; for doctorate, comprehensive exam, thesis/dissertation. *Entrance requirements:* For master's, GRE General Test, minimum GPA of 2.5; for doctorate, GRE General Test or MAT, master's degree, minimum B+ average. Additional exam requirements/recommendations for international students: Required—TOEFL. *Application deadline:* For fall admission, 7/1 for domestic and international students; for spring admission, 11/1 for domestic and international students. Applications are processed on a rolling basis. Application fee: $50 ($75 for international students). Electronic applications accepted. *Expenses:* Tuition, state resident: full-time $1805; part-time $100 per credit hour. Tuition, nonresident: full-time $6470; part-time $343 per credit hour. Tuition and fees vary according to course level, course load and degree level. *Financial support:* Scholarships/grants and unspecified assistantships available. Support available to part-time students. Financial award application deadline: 5/1. *Unit head:* Dr. Emmanuel Nwagwu, Chair, 713-313-1055, E-mail: nwagwu_ec@tsu.edu. *Application contact:* Dr. Gregory Maddox, Dean of the Graduate School, 713-313-7011 Ext. 4410, Fax: 713-639-1876, E-mail: maddox_gh@tsu.edu.

Texas State University–San Marcos, Graduate School, College of Education, Department of Counseling, Leadership, Adult Education, and School Psychology, Program in Educational Leadership, San Marcos, TX 78666. Offers educational leadership (M Ed, MA); school improvement (PhD). Part-time and evening/weekend programs available. *Faculty:* 17 full-time (8 women), 8 part-time/adjunct (5 women). *Students:* 11 full-time (3 women), 175 part-time (55 women); includes 63 minority (14 African Americans, 1 Asian American or Pacific Islander, 48 Hispanic Americans), 3 international. Average age 37. 81 applicants, 62% accepted, 44 enrolled. In 2009, 55 master's, 3 doctorates awarded. *Degree requirements:* For master's, comprehensive exam, thesis (for some programs); for doctorate, comprehensive exam, thesis/dissertation. *Entrance requirements:* For master's, GRE General Test, minimum GPA of 2.75 in last 60 hours of course work; for doctorate, master's degree with minimum GPA of 3.5, essay describing background and professional goals, program faculty interview, 3 recommendation forms, current resume. Additional exam requirements/recommendations for international students: Required—TOEFL (minimum score 550 paper-based; 213 computer-based). *Application deadline:* For fall admission, 6/15 for domestic students, 6/1 for international students. Applications are processed on a rolling basis. Application fee: $40 ($90 for international students). Electronic applications accepted. *Expenses:* Tuition, state resident: full-time $5784; part-time $241 per credit hour. Tuition, nonresident: full-time $13,224; part-time $551 per credit hour. Required fees: $1728; $48 per credit hour. $306. Tuition and fees vary according to course load. *Financial support:* In 2009–10, 96 students received support, including 1 research assistantship (averaging $9,264 per year), 3 teaching assistantships (averaging $9,264 per year); career-related internships or fieldwork, Federal Work-Study, and institutionally sponsored loans also available. Support available to part-time students. Financial award application deadline: 4/1; financial award applicants required to submit FAFSA. *Faculty research:*

Educational Leadership and Administration

Texas State University–San Marcos (continued)
Superintendency, middle management, supervision, junior college. *Unit head:* Dr. Miguel Guajardo, Graduate Advisor, 512-245-2575, E-mail: mg50@txstate.edu. *Application contact:* Dr. J. Michael Willoughby, Dean of Graduate School, 512-245-2581, Fax: 512-245-8365, E-mail: gradcollege@txstate.edu.

Texas State University–San Marcos, Graduate School, Interdisciplinary Studies Program in Educational Administration and Psychological Services, San Marcos, TX 78666. Offers MAIS. *Degree requirements:* For master's, comprehensive exam. *Application deadline:* For fall admission, 6/15 priority date for domestic students; for spring admission, 10/15 priority date for domestic students. Applications are processed on a rolling basis. Application fee: $40 ($90 for international students). *Expenses:* Tuition, state resident: full-time $5784; part-time $241 per credit hour. Tuition, nonresident: full-time $13,224; part-time $551 per credit hour. Required fees: $1728; $48 per credit hour. $306. Tuition and fees vary according to course load. *Financial support:* Application deadline: 4/1. *Unit head:* Dr. Stan Carpenter, Dean, 512-245-2575, Fax: 512-245-8345, E-mail: sc33@txstate.edu. *Application contact:* Dr. J. Michael Willoughby, Dean of Graduate School, 512-245-2581, Fax: 512-245-8365, E-mail: gradcollege@txstate.edu.

Texas Tech University, Graduate School, College of Education, Department of Educational Psychology and Leadership, Lubbock, TX 79409. Offers counselor education (M Ed, PhD); educational leadership (M Ed, Ed D); educational psychology (M Ed, PhD); higher education (M Ed, Ed D); higher education: higher education research (PhD); instructional technology (M Ed, Ed D); instructional technology: distance education (M Ed); special education (M Ed, Ed D). *Accreditation:* ACA; NCATE. Part-time programs available. *Students:* 137 full-time (94 women), 335 part-time (236 women); includes 90 minority (27 African Americans, 6 American Indian/Alaska Native, 3 Asian Americans or Pacific Islanders, 54 Hispanic Americans), 34 international. Average age 36. 390 applicants, 51% accepted, 90 enrolled. In 2009, 113 master's, 18 doctorates awarded. *Degree requirements:* For master's, thesis optional; for doctorate, thesis/dissertation. *Entrance requirements:* For master's and doctorate, GRE General Test. Additional exam requirements/recommendations for international students: Required—TOEFL (minimum score 550 paper-based; 213 computer-based). *Application deadline:* For fall admission, 3/1 priority date for international students; for spring admission, 11/1 priority date for international students. Applications are processed on a rolling basis. Application fee: $50 ($75 for international students). Electronic applications accepted. *Expenses:* Tuition, state resident: full-time $5100; part-time $213 per credit hour. Tuition, nonresident: full-time $11,748; part-time $490 per credit hour. Required fees: $2298; $50 per credit hour. $555 per semester. *Financial support:* Research assistantships with partial tuition reimbursements, teaching assistantships with partial tuition reimbursements, career-related internships or fieldwork, Federal Work-Study, and institutionally sponsored loans available. Support available to part-time students. Financial award application deadline: 4/15; financial award applicants required to submit FAFSA. *Faculty research:* Psychological processes of teaching and learning, teaching populations with special needs, instructional technology, educational administration in education, theories and practice in counseling and counselor education K-12 and higher. *Unit head:* Dr. William Lan, Chair, 806-742-1998 Ext. 436, Fax: 806-742-2179, E-mail: william.lan@ttu.edu. *Application contact:* Dr. Joseph G. Claudet, Graduate Adviser, 806-742-1998, Fax: 806-742-2179.

Texas Woman's University, Graduate School, College of Professional Education, Department of Teacher Education, Denton, TX 76201. Offers administration (M Ed, MA); elementary education (MA); special education (M Ed, MA, PhD), including educational diagnostician (M Ed, MA); teaching (MAT); teaching, learning, and curriculum (M Ed). Part-time programs available. *Faculty:* 19 full-time (13 women), 14 part-time/adjunct (11 women). *Students:* 36 full-time (29 women), 155 part-time (135 women); includes 65 minority (31 African Americans, 1 American Indian/Alaska Native, 3 Asian Americans or Pacific Islanders, 30 Hispanic Americans), 6 international. Average age 38. 48 applicants, 90% accepted, 21 enrolled. In 2009, 52 master's, 2 doctorates awarded. Terminal master's awarded for partial completion of doctoral program. *Degree requirements:* For master's, professional paper (MEd); for doctorate, comprehensive exam, thesis/dissertation. *Entrance requirements:* For master's, minimum GPA of 3.0, 3 letters of reference, curriculum vitae, copy of certifications, teacher service record; for doctorate, minimum GPA of 3.0, 3 letters of reference, curriculum vitae, copy of certifications, teacher service record, statement of intent. Additional exam requirements/recommendations for international students: Required—TOEFL (minimum score 550 paper-based; 213 computer-based; 79 iBT). *Application deadline:* For fall admission, 7/1 priority date for domestic students, 3/1 for international students; for spring admission, 11/1 priority date for domestic students, 7/1 for international students. Applications are processed on a rolling basis. Application fee: $50. Electronic applications accepted. *Expenses:* Tuition, state resident: full-time $3564; part-time $198 per credit hour. Tuition, nonresident: full-time $8550; part-time $475 per credit hour. Required fees: $69.26 per credit hour. Tuition and fees vary according to course load. *Financial support:* In 2009–10, 47 students received support, including 5 research assistantships (averaging $10,440 per year); career-related internships or fieldwork, Federal Work-Study, institutionally sponsored loans, scholarships/grants, traineeships, health care benefits, and unspecified assistantships also available. Support available to part-time students. Financial award application deadline: 3/1; financial award applicants required to submit FAFSA. *Faculty research:* Language and literacy, classroom management, learning disabilities, staff and professional development, leadership preparation practice. *Unit head:* Dr. Jane Pemberton, Interim Chair, 940-898-2271, Fax: 940-898-2270, E-mail: jpemberton@twu.edu. *Application contact:* Samuel Wheeler, Assistant Director of Admissions, 940-898-3188, Fax: 940-898-3081, E-mail: wheelersr@twu.edu.

Thomas Edison State College, Heavin School of Arts and Sciences, Program in Educational Leadership, Trenton, NJ 08608-1176. Offers MAEL. Part-time programs available. Postbaccalaureate distance learning degree programs offered (no on-campus study). *Students:* 69 part-time (41 women); includes 9 minority (5 African Americans, 1 Asian American or Pacific Islander, 3 Hispanic Americans). Average age 35. In 2009, 4 master's awarded. *Degree requirements:* For master's, field-based practicum, professional portfolio development. *Entrance requirements:* For master's, at least 3 years of teaching experience; valid teacher's certification; letter of recommendation from a building-level administrator; school setting and on-site mentor available to conduct site-based fieldwork and inquiry projects successfully for each course; statement of goals and objectives. Additional exam requirements/recommendations for international students: Required—TOEFL (minimum score 550 paper-based; 213 computer-based; 79 iBT). *Application deadline:* For fall admission, 8/15 priority date for domestic and international students; for winter admission, 11/15 priority date for domestic and international students; for spring admission, 2/15 priority date for domestic and international students. Applications are processed on a rolling basis. Application fee: $75. Electronic applications accepted. *Expenses:* Tuition, area resident: Part-time $479 per credit. Tuition, state resident: part-time $479 per credit. Tuition, nonresident: part-time $479 per credit. *Financial support:* Applicants required to submit FAFSA. *Unit head:* Dr. Susan Davenport, Dean, Heavin School of Arts and Sciences, 609-984-1130, Fax: 609-984-0740, E-mail: info@tesc.edu. *Application contact:* David Hoftiezer, Director of Admissions, 888-442-8372, Fax: 609-984-8447, E-mail: admissions@tese.edu.

Trevecca Nazarene University, Graduate Division, School of Education, Major in Educational Leadership, Nashville, TN 37210-2877. Offers M Ed. Part-time and evening/weekend programs available. *Students:* 150 full-time (97 women), 8 part-time (6 women); includes 44 minority (41 African Americans, 1 American Indian/Alaska Native, 1 Asian American or Pacific Islander, 1 Hispanic American). In 2009, 103 master's awarded. *Degree requirements:* For master's, exit assessment. *Entrance requirements:* For master's, GRE General Test, MAT, interview, minimum GPA of 2.7, 2 references. Additional exam requirements/recommendations for international students: Required—TOEFL (minimum score 550 paper-based; 213 computer-based). *Application deadline:* Applications are processed on a rolling basis. Application fee: $25. *Expenses:* Contact institution. *Financial support:* Applicants required to submit FAFSA. *Unit head:* Dr. Esther Swink, Dean, School of Education/Director of Graduate Education Programs, 615-248-1201, Fax: 615-248-1597, E-mail: admissions.ged@trevecca.edu. *Application contact:* Admissions Office, 615-248-1201, Fax: 615-248-1597, E-mail: admissions_ged@trevecca.edu.

Trevecca Nazarene University, Graduate Division, School of Education, Major in Leadership and Professional Practice, Nashville, TN 37210-2877. Offers Ed D. *Students:* 68 full-time (48 women), 49 part-time (32 women); includes 27 minority (23 African Americans, 1 Asian American or Pacific Islander, 3 Hispanic Americans). Average age 38. In 2009, 23 doctorates awarded. *Degree requirements:* For doctorate, thesis/dissertation, proposal study, symposium presentation. *Entrance requirements:* For doctorate, GMAT, GRE, MAT, or NTE, minimum GPA of 3.4, resume, writing sample, interview. Additional exam requirements/recommendations for international students: Required—TOEFL (minimum score 550 paper-based; 213 computer-based). *Application deadline:* Applications are processed on a rolling basis. Application fee: $50. *Expenses:* Contact institution. *Financial support:* Applicants required to submit FAFSA. *Unit head:* Dr. Esther Swink, Dean, School of Education/Director of Graduate Education Program, 615-248-1201, Fax: 615-248-1597, E-mail: admissions_ged@trevecca.edu. *Application contact:* Admissions Office, 615-248-1201, Fax: 615-248-1597, E-mail: admissions_ged@trevecca.edu.

Trinity Baptist College, Graduate Programs, Jacksonville, FL 32221. Offers Bible (M Ed); Christian school administration (M Ed); classroom practices (M Ed); ministry (M Min); special education (M Ed). Postbaccalaureate distance learning degree programs offered. *Entrance requirements:* For master's, GRE (M Ed), 2 letters of recommendation; minimum GPA of 2.5 (M Min) or 3.0 (M Ed); computer proficiency.

Trinity International University, Trinity Graduate School, Deerfield, IL 60015-1284. Offers bioethics (MA); communication and culture (MA); counseling psychology (MA); instructional leadership (M Ed); teaching (MA). Part-time and evening/weekend programs available. Postbaccalaureate distance learning degree programs offered (minimal on-campus study). *Degree requirements:* For master's, comprehensive exam. *Entrance requirements:* For master's, GRE General Test or MAT, minimum undergraduate GPA of 3.0. Additional exam requirements/recommendations for international students: Required—TOEFL (minimum score 580 paper-based; 237 computer-based), TWE (minimum score 4). Electronic applications accepted.

Trinity University, Department of Education, Program in School Administration, San Antonio, TX 78212-7200. Offers M Ed. *Accreditation:* NCATE. Part-time and evening/weekend programs available. *Entrance requirements:* For master's, GRE General Test, interview, minimum GPA of 3.0.

Trinity (Washington) University, School of Education, Washington, DC 20017-1094. Offers counseling (MA); early childhood education (MAT); educating for change (M Ed); educational administration (MSA); elementary education (MAT); school counseling (MA); secondary education (MAT), including English, social studies; special education (MAT); teaching English as a second language (MAT); teaching English to speakers of other languages (M Ed); the teaching of reading (M Ed). *Accreditation:* NCATE. Part-time and evening/weekend programs available. *Degree requirements:* For master's, thesis (for some programs), capstone project(s). *Entrance requirements:* For master's, PRAXIS I, minimum GPA of 2.8. Additional exam requirements/recommendations for international students: Required—TOEFL (minimum score 550 paper-based; 213 computer-based). *Faculty research:* Technology, literacy, special education, organizations, inclusion models.

Trinity Western University, School of Graduate Studies, Program in Leadership, Langley, BC V2Y 1Y1, Canada. Offers business (MA, Certificate); Christian ministry (MA); education (MA, Certificate); healthcare (MA, Certificate); non-profit (MA, Certificate). Postbaccalaureate distance learning degree programs offered (minimal on-campus study). *Degree requirements:* For master's, major project. *Entrance requirements:* For master's, minimum GPA of 2.7. Additional exam requirements/recommendations for international students: Required—TOEFL (minimum score 620 paper-based; 260 computer-based; 105 iBT). Electronic applications accepted. *Expenses:* Contact institution. *Faculty research:* Servant leadership.

Troy University, Graduate School, College of Education, Program in Educational Administration/Leadership, Troy, AL 36082. Offers educational administration (MS, Ed S). *Accreditation:* NCATE. Part-time and evening/weekend programs available. *Students:* 14 full-time (9 women), 40 part-time (20 women); includes 24 minority (all African Americans). Average age 38. 31 applicants, 90% accepted. In 2009, 83 master's, 15 other advanced degrees awarded. *Degree requirements:* For master's, comprehensive exam, thesis. *Entrance requirements:* For master's, minimum GPA of 2.5; for Ed S, MS. Additional exam requirements/recommendations for international students: Required—TOEFL (minimum score 523 paper-based; 193 computer-based; 70 iBT), IELTS. *Application deadline:* Applications are processed on a rolling basis. Application fee: $50. Electronic applications accepted. *Financial support:* Available to part-time students. Applicants required to submit FAFSA. *Unit head:* Larry Thacker, Chair, 334-448-5140, Fax: 334-448-5205, E-mail: lthacker@troy.edu. *Application contact:* Jessida McConnell, Graduate Admissions, 334-448-5106, Fax: 334-448-5299, E-mail: jcmcconnell@troy.edu.

Troy University, Graduate School, College of Education, Program in Postsecondary Education, Troy, AL 36082. Offers adult education (M Ed); biology (M Ed); criminal justice (M Ed); english (M Ed); foundations of education (M Ed); general science (M Ed); higher education administration (M Ed); history (M Ed); instructional technology (M Ed); mathematics (M Ed); music industry (M Ed); physical fitness (M Ed); political science (M Ed); public administration (M Ed); social science (M Ed); teaching english (M Ed). Also offered through the University College. *Accreditation:* NCATE. Part-time and evening/weekend programs available. *Students:* 267 full-time (192 women), 381 part-time (293 women); includes 326 minority (309 African Americans, 4 American Indian/Alaska Native, 5 Asian Americans or Pacific Islanders, 8 Hispanic Americans). Average age 34. 343 applicants, 90% accepted. In 2009, 480 master's awarded. *Degree requirements:* For master's, comprehensive exam, thesis. *Entrance requirements:* For master's, MAT (minimum score 385), minimum GPA of 2.5. Additional exam requirements/recommendations for international students: Required—TOEFL (minimum score 523 paper-based; 193 computer-based; 70 iBT), IELTS, or ACT Compass ESL (minimum score 270 on Listening, Reading, and Grammar with no individual score below 85 and a minimum score of 8 out of 12 on writing test). *Application deadline:* Applications are processed on a rolling basis. Application fee: $50. Electronic applications accepted. *Financial support:* Available to part-time students. Applicants required to submit FAFSA. *Unit head:* Dr. Andrew Creamer, Chair, 334-670-3350, E-mail: drcreamer@troy.edu. *Application contact:* Brenda K. Campbell, Director of Graduate Admissions, 334-670-3178, Fax: 334-670-3733, E-mail: bcamp@troy.edu.

TUI University, College of Education, Program in Educational Leadership, Cypress, CA 90630. Offers e-learning leadership (MA Ed, PhD); educational leadership (MA Ed); higher education leadership (PhD); K-12 leadership (PhD). Part-time and evening/weekend programs available. Postbaccalaureate distance learning degree programs offered (no on-campus study). *Degree requirements:* For doctorate, comprehensive exam, thesis/dissertation, defense of dissertation. *Entrance requirements:* For master's, minimum GPA of 2.5 (students with GPA 3.0 or greater may transfer up to 30% of graduate level credits); for doctorate, minimum GPA of 3.4, course work in research methods or statistics. Additional exam requirements/recommendations for international students: Required—TOEFL. Electronic applications accepted.

Union College, Graduate Programs, Department of Education, Barbourville, KY 40906-1499. Offers elementary education (MA); health and physical education (MA); middle grades (MA); music education (MA); principalship (MA); reading specialist (MA); secondary education (MA); special education (MA). *Degree requirements:* For master's, thesis optional. *Entrance requirements:* For master's, GRE General Test, NTE.

Union College, Graduate Programs, Educational Leadership Program, Barbourville, KY 40906-1499. Offers principalship (MA).

Union Graduate College, School of Education, Schenectady, NY 12308-3107. Offers biology (MAT, MS); chemistry (MAT); Chinese (MAT); earth science (MAT); English (MAT); French (MAT); general science (MAT); German (MAT); Greek (MAT); languages (MAT); Latin (MAT); mathematics (MAT); mathematics and technology (MS); mentoring and teacher leadership

(AC); middle childhood extension (AC); national board certificate and teacher leadership (AC); physical science (MS); physics (MAT); social studies (MAT); Spanish (MAT). *Accreditation:* Teacher Education Accreditation Council. *Faculty:* 3 full-time (1 woman), 39 part-time/adjunct (19 women). *Students:* 46 full-time (27 women), 45 part-time (39 women); includes 5 minority (1 Asian American or Pacific Islander, 4 Hispanic Americans), 2 international. Average age 33. 66 applicants, 73% accepted, 39 enrolled. In 2009, 44 master's awarded. *Degree requirements:* For master's, thesis or project. *Entrance requirements:* For master's, minimum GPA of 3.0, letters of recommendation. Additional exam requirements/recommendations for international students: Required—TOEFL (minimum score 550 paper-based; 213 computer-based). *Application deadline:* Applications are processed on a rolling basis. Application fee: $60. Electronic applications accepted. *Expenses:* Contact institution. *Financial support:* In 2009–10, 12 research assistantships with tuition reimbursements (averaging $3,000 per year) were awarded; Federal Work-Study, scholarships/grants, health care benefits, and tuition waivers (partial) also available. Support available to part-time students. Financial award applicants required to submit FAFSA. *Faculty research:* Transformative learning, science education, National Board Certification, teacher leadership, teacher quality. *Unit head:* Dr. Patrick Allen, Dean, 518-631-9870, Fax: 518-631-9901. *Application contact:* Christine Angley, Assistant, 518-631-9871, Fax: 518-631-9903, E-mail: angleyc@uniongraduatecollege.edu.

Union Institute & University, Doctor of Education Program, Cincinnati, OH 45206-1925. Offers educational leadership (Ed D); higher education (Ed D). Postbaccalaureate distance learning degree programs offered (minimal on-campus study). *Faculty:* 2 full-time (0 women), 7 part-time/adjunct (3 women). *Students:* 19 full-time (13 women); includes 5 minority (3 African Americans, 2 Hispanic Americans). Average age 49. *Application deadline:* Applications are processed on a rolling basis. Tuition and fees vary according to course load, degree level, campus/location and program. *Financial support:* Federal Work-Study and scholarships/grants available. *Unit head:* Dr. Arlene Sacks, Dean, 305-653-6713, E-mail: arlene.sacks@myunion.edu. *Application contact:* Michelle Flick, Admissions Counselor, 513-861-6400 Ext. 1225, E-mail: admissions@tui.edu.

Union Institute & University, Education Programs–Florida Center, North Miami Beach, FL 33162. Offers educational leadership (M Ed, Ed S); exceptional student education (M Ed, Ed S); guidance and counseling (M Ed, Ed S); reading (M Ed, Ed S). *Faculty:* 3 full-time (1 woman), 23 part-time/adjunct (19 women). *Students:* 32 full-time (21 women); includes 23 minority (21 African Americans, 2 Hispanic Americans). Average age 37. In 2009, 8 master's, 3 Ed Ss awarded. *Degree requirements:* For master's, thesis or alternative, portfolio. *Entrance requirements:* For master's, letters of recommendation. *Application deadline:* Applications are processed on a rolling basis. Application fee: $50. *Expenses:* Contact institution. *Financial support:* Federal Work-Study, scholarships/grants, and tuition waivers (partial) available. Financial award applicants required to submit FAFSA. *Unit head:* Dr. Arlene Sacks, Dean, 305-653-6713 Ext. 2152, E-mail: arlene.sacks@myunion.edu. *Application contact:* Josefina Rosario, Admissions Counselor, 305-653-6713 Ext. 2172, E-mail: admissions@tui.edu.

Union Institute & University, M Ed Program–Vermont Campus, Montpelier, VT 05602. Offers school administration (M Ed), including principalship; school counseling (M Ed); teaching (M Ed), including art, early childhood, elementary, English, math, middle schools, science, social studies, special education. *Faculty:* 3 full-time (1 woman), 23 part-time/adjunct (19 women). *Students:* 41 part-time (29 women). Average age 38. In 2009, 15 master's awarded. *Degree requirements:* For master's, thesis. *Entrance requirements:* For master's, 3 letters of reference. *Application deadline:* Applications are processed on a rolling basis. Application fee: $50. *Expenses:* Contact institution. *Financial support:* Federal Work-Study, scholarships/grants, and tuition waivers available. Financial award applicants required to submit FAFSA. *Unit head:* Dr. Arlene Sacks, Dean, Graduate Programs in Education, 305-653-6713 Ext. 2152, E-mail: arlene.sacks@myunion.edu. *Application contact:* Dr. Arlene Sacks, Dean, Graduate Programs in Education, 305-653-6713 Ext. 2152, E-mail: arlene.sacks@myunion.edu.

Union University, School of Education, Jackson, TN 38305-3697. Offers education (M Ed, MA Ed); education administration generalist (Ed S); educational leadership (Ed D); educational supervision (Ed S); higher education (Ed D). M Ed also available at Germantown campus. *Accreditation:* NCATE. Part-time and evening/weekend programs available. *Degree requirements:* For master's, thesis (for some programs), capstone research course; for doctorate, comprehensive exam, thesis/dissertation; for Ed S, thesis or alternative. *Entrance requirements:* For master's, MAT, PRAXIS II or GRE, minimum GPA of 3.0, teaching license, writing sample; for doctorate, GRE, minimum graduate GPA of 3.2, writing sample; for Ed S, PRAXIS II, minimum graduate GPA of 3.2, writing sample. *Faculty research:* Mathematics education, direct instruction, language disorders and special education, brain compatible learning, empathy and school leadership.

Universidad Adventista de las Antillas, EGECED Department, Mayagüez, PR 00681-0118. Offers curriculum and instruction (MA), including secondary biology, secondary history, secondary Spanish; education (MA), including ESL (elementary school level), ESL (high school level), school administration and supervision. *Degree requirements:* For master's, comprehensive exam (for some programs), thesis (for some programs). *Entrance requirements:* For master's, EXADEP or GRE General Test, recommendations. Application fee: $175. Electronic applications accepted. *Expenses:* Tuition: Full-time $3990; part-time $190 per credit. Required fees: $570; $190 per credit. $1375 per summer. *Financial support:* Fellowships, Federal Work-Study available. *Unit head:* Dr. Zilma Sepulveda, Director, 787-834-9595 Ext. 2282, Fax: 787-834-9595, E-mail: zsantiago@uaa.edu. *Application contact:* Prof. Evelyn del Valle, Admissions Department Director, 787-834-9595 Ext. 2261, Fax: 787-834-9597, E-mail: admissions@uaa.edu.

Universidad del Turabo, Graduate Programs, Programs in Education, Program in Administration of School Libraries, Gurabo, PR 00778-3030. Offers Certificate. *Students:* 1 (woman) full-time; minority (Hispanic American). Average age 39. *Unit head:* Angela Candelario, Dean, 787-743-7979 Ext. 4126. *Application contact:* Virginia Gonzalez, Admissions Officer, 787-746-3009.

Universidad del Turabo, Graduate Programs, Programs in Education, Program in Educational Administration, Gurabo, PR 00778-3030. Offers M Ed. *Students:* 22 full-time (14 women), 18 part-time (14 women); includes 37 Hispanic Americans. Average age 34. 32 applicants, 88% accepted, 14 enrolled. In 2009, 16 master's awarded. *Unit head:* Angela Candelario, Dean, 787-743-7979 Ext. 4126. *Application contact:* Virginia Gonzalez, Admissions Officer, 787-746-3009.

Universidad del Turabo, Graduate Programs, Programs in Education, Program in Educational Leadership, Gurabo, PR 00778-3030. Offers D Ed. *Students:* 9 full-time (7 women), 66 part-time (48 women); includes 64 Hispanic Americans. Average age 43. 34 applicants, 100% accepted, 34 enrolled. In 2009, 1 doctorate awarded. *Unit head:* Angela Candelario, Dean, 787-743-7979 Ext. 4126. *Application contact:* Virginia Gonzalez, Admissions Officer, 787-746-3009.

Universidad Iberoamericana, Graduate School, Santo Domingo D.N., Dominican Republic. Offers advertising management (MM); business (MBA); constitutional law (MA); dentistry (DMD); educational management (MA); integrated marketing communication (MA); psychopedagogical intervention (M Ed); strategic management of human talent (MM).

Universidad Metropolitana, Graduate Programs in Education, Program in Educational Administration and Supervision, San Juan, PR 00928-1150. Offers M Ed. Part-time programs available. *Degree requirements:* For master's, thesis or alternative. *Entrance requirements:* For master's, EXADEP, interview. Electronic applications accepted.

Universidad Metropolitana, Graduate Programs in Education, Program in Fitness Management, San Juan, PR 00928-1150. Offers M Ed. Part-time programs available. *Degree requirements:* For master's, thesis or alternative. *Entrance requirements:* For master's, EXADEP, interview. Electronic applications accepted.

Universidad Metropolitana, Graduate Programs in Education, Program in Pre-School Centers Administration, San Juan, PR 00928-1150. Offers M Ed. Part-time programs available. *Degree requirements:* For master's, thesis or alternative. *Entrance requirements:* For master's, EXADEP, interview. Electronic applications accepted.

Université de Moncton, Faculty of Education, Graduate Studies in Education, Moncton, NB E1A 3E9, Canada. Offers educational psychology (M Ed, MA Ed); guidance (M Ed, MA Ed); school administration (M Ed, MA Ed); teaching (M Ed, MA Ed). Part-time programs available. *Degree requirements:* For master's, proficiency in English and French. *Entrance requirements:* For master's, minimum GPA of 3.0. *Faculty research:* Guidance, ethnolinguistic vitality, children's rights, ecological education, entrepreneurship.

Université de Montréal, Faculty of Education, Department of Administration and Foundations of Education, Montréal, QC H3C 3J7, Canada. Offers M Ed, MA, PhD, DESS. Part-time programs available. *Faculty:* 20 full-time (6 women), 10 part-time/adjunct (4 women). *Students:* 19 full-time (12 women), 609 part-time (427 women). 307 applicants, 63% accepted, 103 enrolled. In 2009, 30 master's, 4 doctorates, 108 other advanced degrees awarded. *Degree requirements:* For master's, thesis; for doctorate, thesis/dissertation, general exam. *Entrance requirements:* For master's and DESS, bachelor's degree in related field with minimum B average; for doctorate, master's degree in related field with minimum B average. *Application deadline:* For fall admission, 2/1 priority date for domestic students; for winter admission, 11/1 priority date for domestic students; for spring admission, 2/1 priority date for domestic students. Application fee: $100. Electronic applications accepted. *Financial support:* Teaching assistantships available. *Faculty research:* Pluriethnicity, formative education, comparative education, diagnostic evaluation. *Unit head:* Gabriel Boileau, Director, 514-343-6659, Fax: 514-343-2497, E-mail: gabriel.boileau@umontreal.ca. *Application contact:* Marc-Andre Deniger, Responsible for Graduate Studies, 514-343-7079, Fax: 514-343-2497, E-mail: marc-andre.deniger@umontreal.ca.

Université de Sherbrooke, Faculty of Education, Program in School Administration, Sherbrooke, QC J1K 2R1, Canada. Offers M Ed. Part-time and evening/weekend programs available. *Degree requirements:* For master's, thesis.

Université du Québec à Trois-Rivières, Graduate Programs, Program in Educational Administration, Trois-Rivières, QC G9A 5H7, Canada. Offers DESS.

Université Laval, Faculty of Education, Department of Foundations and Interventions in Education, Programs in Educational Administration and Evaluation, Québec, QC G1K 7P4, Canada. Offers MA, PhD. Terminal master's awarded for partial completion of doctoral program. *Degree requirements:* For master's, thesis (for some programs); for doctorate, comprehensive exam, thesis/dissertation. *Entrance requirements:* For master's and doctorate, English exam (comprehension of written English), knowledge of French and English. Electronic applications accepted.

Université Laval, Faculty of Education, Department of Foundations and Interventions in Education, Programs in Educational Practice, Québec, QC G1K 7P4, Canada. Offers educational pedagogy (Diploma); pedagogy management and development (Diploma); school adaptation (Diploma). Part-time programs available. *Entrance requirements:* For degree, English exam (comprehension of written English), knowledge of French and English. Electronic applications accepted.

University at Albany, State University of New York, School of Education, Department of Educational Administration and Policy Studies, Albany, NY 12222-0001. Offers MS, PhD, CAS. Evening/weekend programs available. *Degree requirements:* For doctorate, one foreign language, thesis/dissertation. *Entrance requirements:* For doctorate, GRE General Test, GRE Subject Test. Additional exam requirements/recommendations for international students: Required—TOEFL (minimum score 550 paper-based; 213 computer-based). Electronic applications accepted.

University at Buffalo, the State University of New York, Graduate School, Graduate School of Education, Department of Educational Leadership and Policy, Buffalo, NY 14260. Offers educational administration (Ed M, Ed D, PhD); general education (Ed M); higher education administration (Ed M, Ed D, PhD), including student affairs (Ed D); school building leadership (LIFTS) (Certificate); school business and human resource administration (Certificate); school district business leadership (LIFTS) (Certificate); school district leadership (LIFTS) (Certificate); social foundations (PhD). Part-time and evening/weekend programs available. *Faculty:* 12 full-time (6 women), 13 part-time/adjunct (7 women). *Students:* 71 full-time (53 women), 159 part-time (99 women); includes 42 minority (27 African Americans, 1 American Indian/Alaska Native, 4 Asian Americans or Pacific Islanders, 10 Hispanic Americans), 20 international. Average age 36.7. 170 applicants, 59% accepted, 65 enrolled. In 2009, 29 master's, 24 doctorates, 29 other advanced degrees awarded. *Degree requirements:* For master's, comprehensive exam (for some programs), thesis optional; for doctorate, comprehensive exam, thesis/dissertation. *Entrance requirements:* For doctorate, GRE General Test or MAT, writing sample. Additional exam requirements/recommendations for international students: Required—TOEFL (minimum score 550 paper-based; 213 computer-based; 79 iBT). *Application deadline:* For fall admission, 3/1 priority date for domestic students, 3/1 for international students; for spring admission, 11/15 priority date for domestic students, 10/1 for international students. Applications are processed on a rolling basis. Application fee: $50. Electronic applications accepted. *Financial support:* In 2009–10, 6 fellowships with full tuition reimbursements (averaging $9,000 per year), 12 research assistantships with full tuition reimbursements (averaging $9,000 per year) were awarded; career-related internships or fieldwork, Federal Work-Study, institutionally sponsored loans, health care benefits, tuition waivers (full and partial), and unspecified assistantships also available. Financial award application deadline: 3/15; financial award applicants required to submit FAFSA. *Faculty research:* College access and choice, school leadership preparation and practice, public policy, curriculum and pedagogy, comparative and international education. Total annual research expenditures: $34,848. *Unit head:* Dr. William C. Barba, Chairman, 716-645-2471, Fax: 716-645-2481, E-mail: barba@buffalo.edu. *Application contact:* Bonnie Fisher, Admissions Assistant, 716-645-2110, Fax: 716-645-7937, E-mail: brfisher@buffalo.edu.

The University of Akron, Graduate School, College of Education, Department of Educational Foundations and Leadership, Program in Educational Leadership, Akron, OH 44325. Offers Ed D. *Accreditation:* NCATE. *Students:* 5 full-time (3 women), 25 part-time (14 women); includes 1 minority (African American), 2 international. Average age 42. 21 applicants, 48% accepted, 9 enrolled. In 2009, 4 doctorates awarded. Terminal master's awarded for partial completion of doctoral program. *Degree requirements:* For doctorate, one foreign language, comprehensive exam, thesis/dissertation, written and oral exams. *Entrance requirements:* For doctorate, GRE, interview, minimum GPA of 3.25 for master's degree, writing sample, letters of reference, resume. Additional exam requirements/recommendations for international students: Required—TOEFL (minimum score 550 paper-based; 213 computer-based; 79 iBT). *Application deadline:* For fall admission, 3/1 for domestic and international students; for spring admission, 10/15 for domestic and international students. Application fee: $30 ($40 for international students). Electronic applications accepted. *Expenses:* Tuition, state resident: full-time $6570; part-time $365 per credit hour. Tuition, nonresident: full-time $11,250; part-time $625 per credit hour. *Unit head:* Dr. Sharon Kruse, Coordinator, 330-972-7773, E-mail: skruse@uakron.edu. *Application contact:* Dr. Sharon Kruse, Coordinator, 330-972-7773, E-mail: skruse@uakron.edu.

The University of Akron, Graduate School, College of Education, Department of Educational Foundations and Leadership, Program in Higher Education Administration, Akron, OH 44325. Offers MA, MS. *Accreditation:* NCATE. *Students:* 64 full-time (46 women), 50 part-time (33 women); includes 23 minority (20 African Americans, 2 Asian Americans or Pacific Islanders, 1 Hispanic American), 3 international. Average age 35. 56 applicants, 88% accepted, 24 enrolled. In 2009, 20 master's awarded. *Degree requirements:* For master's, written comprehensive exam. *Entrance requirements:* For master's, minimum GPA of 2.75. Additional exam requirements/recommendations for international students: Required—TOEFL (minimum score 550 paper-based; 213 computer-based; 79 iBT). *Application deadline:* Applications are processed

Educational Leadership and Administration

The University of Akron (continued)

on a rolling basis. Application fee: $30 ($40 for international students). Electronic applications accepted. *Expenses:* Tuition, state resident: full-time $6570; part-time $365 per credit hour. Tuition, nonresident: full-time $11,250; part-time $625 per credit hour. *Financial support:* Fellowships, research assistantships, teaching assistantships available. *Unit head:* Dr. Sandra Coyner, Coordinator, 330-972-5822, E-mail: scoyner@uakron.edu. *Application contact:* Dr. Sandra Coyner, Coordinator, 330-972-5822, E-mail: scoyner@uakron.edu.

The University of Akron, Graduate School, College of Education, Department of Educational Foundations and Leadership, Program in Principalship, Akron, OH 44325. Offers MA, MS. *Students:* 1 full-time (0 women), 157 part-time (87 women); includes 13 minority (10 African Americans, 1 American Indian/Alaska Native, 2 Asian Americans or Pacific Islanders). Average age 36. 55 applicants, 89% accepted, 37 enrolled. In 2009, 63 master's awarded. *Degree requirements:* For master's, portfolio assessment. *Entrance requirements:* For master's, minimum GPA of 2.75, current teaching license, minimum three years working under valid Ohio teacher license. Additional exam requirements/recommendations for international students: Required—TOEFL (minimum score 550 paper-based; 213 computer-based; 79 iBT). *Application deadline:* Applications are processed on a rolling basis. Application fee: $30 ($40 for international students). Electronic applications accepted. *Expenses:* Tuition, state resident: full-time $6570; part-time $365 per credit hour. Tuition, nonresident: full-time $11,250; part-time $625 per credit hour. *Unit head:* Dr. Sharon Kruse, Coordinator, 330-972-7773, E-mail: skruse@uakron.edu. *Application contact:* Dr. Sharon Kruse, Coordinator, 330-972-7773, E-mail: skruse@uakron.edu.

The University of Alabama, Graduate School, College of Education, Department of Educational Leadership, Policy, and Technology Studies, Educational Administration Program, Tuscaloosa, AL 35487. Offers Ed D, PhD. Evening/weekend programs available. *Faculty:* 24 full-time (12 women), 1 (woman) part-time/adjunct. *Students:* 13 full-time (7 women), 75 part-time (36 women); includes 20 minority (18 African Americans, 2 American Indian/Alaska Native). Average age 41. 16 applicants, 19% accepted, 3 enrolled. In 2009, 12 degrees awarded. *Degree requirements:* For doctorate, comprehensive exam, thesis/dissertation. *Entrance requirements:* For doctorate, MAT, GRE, master's degree in field. *Application deadline:* For fall admission, 9/1 priority date for domestic and international students; for winter admission, 2/1 priority date for domestic and international students; for spring admission, 4/1 priority date for domestic and international students. Applications are processed on a rolling basis. Application fee: $50 ($60 for international students). Electronic applications accepted. *Expenses:* Tuition, state resident: full-time $7000. Tuition, nonresident: full-time $19,200. *Financial support:* In 2009–10, 3 research assistantships with tuition reimbursements (averaging $14,000 per year), teaching assistantships with tuition reimbursements (averaging $14,000 per year) were awarded; unspecified assistantships also available. Financial award application deadline: 4/1. *Unit head:* Dr. David R. Dagley, Professor of Educational Leadership, 205-348-5159, Fax: 205-348-2161, E-mail: ddagley@bamaed.ua.edu. *Application contact:* Dr. Kathy S. Wetzel, Assistant Dean for Student Services, 205-348-1154, Fax: 205-348-0080, E-mail: kwetzel@bamaed.ua.edu.

The University of Alabama, Graduate School, College of Education, Department of Educational Leadership, Policy, and Technology Studies, Educational Leadership Program, Tuscaloosa, AL 35487. Offers MA, Ed S. Part-time and evening/weekend programs available. Postbaccalaureate distance learning degree programs offered (minimal on-campus study). *Faculty:* 24 full-time (12 women), 1 (woman) part-time/adjunct. *Students:* 19 full-time (8 women), 37 part-time (26 women); includes 5 minority (4 African Americans, 1 American Indian/Alaska Native). Average age 38. 55 applicants, 45% accepted, 22 enrolled. In 2009, 3 master's, 20 other advanced degrees awarded. *Degree requirements:* For master's, comprehensive exam, internship. *Entrance requirements:* For master's, MAT, GRE, 3 years of teaching experience, teaching certification. *Application deadline:* For fall admission, 9/1 priority date for domestic and international students; for winter admission, 2/1 priority date for domestic and international students; for spring admission, 4/1 priority date for domestic and international students. Applications are processed on a rolling basis. Application fee: $50 ($60 for international students). Electronic applications accepted. *Expenses:* Tuition, state resident: full-time $7000. Tuition, nonresident: full-time $19,200. *Unit head:* Dr. David R. Dagley, Professor of Educational Leadership, 205-348-5159, Fax: 205-348-2161, E-mail: ddagley@bamaed.ua.edu. *Application contact:* Dr. Kathy S. Wetzel, Assistant Dean for Student Services, 205-348-1154, Fax: 205-348-0080, E-mail: kwetzel@bamaed.ua.edu.

The University of Alabama, Graduate School, College of Education, Department of Educational Leadership, Policy, and Technology Studies, Higher Education Administration Program, Tuscaloosa, AL 35487. Offers MA, Ed D, PhD. Evening/weekend programs available. *Faculty:* 24 full-time (12 women), 1 (woman) part-time/adjunct. *Students:* 42 full-time (24 women), 102 part-time (61 women); includes 28 minority (24 African Americans, 1 American Indian/Alaska Native, 1 Asian American or Pacific Islander, 2 Hispanic Americans), 1 international. Average age 37. 75 applicants, 48% accepted, 30 enrolled. In 2009, 12 master's, 21 doctorates awarded. Terminal master's awarded for partial completion of doctoral program. *Degree requirements:* For master's, comprehensive exam; for doctorate, comprehensive exam, thesis/dissertation. *Entrance requirements:* For master's, GRE, MAT or GMAT; for doctorate, GRE or MAT. Application fee: $50 ($60 for international students). Electronic applications accepted. *Expenses:* Tuition, state resident: full-time $7000. Tuition, nonresident: full-time $19,200. *Financial support:* In 2009–10, 5 students received support. Career-related internships or fieldwork, scholarships/grants, and unspecified assistantships available. *Unit head:* Dr. Claire H. Major, Coordinator and Associate Professor, 205-348-6871, Fax: 205-348-2161, E-mail: bea@bamaed.ua.edu. *Application contact:* Donna Smith, Administration Assistant, 205-348-6871, Fax: 205-348-2161, E-mail: dbsmith@bamaed.ua.edu.

The University of Alabama, Graduate School, College of Education, Department of Educational Leadership, Policy, and Technology Studies, Instructional Leadership Program, Tuscaloosa, AL 35487. Offers Ed D, PhD. Evening/weekend programs available. *Faculty:* 24 full-time (12 women), 1 (woman) part-time/adjunct. *Students:* 65 full-time (48 women), 89 part-time (64 women); includes 32 minority (30 African Americans, 1 American Indian/Alaska Native, 1 Asian American or Pacific Islander), 2 international. Average age 40. 70 applicants, 69% accepted, 43 enrolled. In 2009, 12 degrees awarded. *Degree requirements:* For doctorate, comprehensive exam, thesis/dissertation. *Entrance requirements:* For doctorate, GRE, MAT, master's degree. *Application deadline:* For fall admission, 9/1 priority date for domestic and international students; for winter admission, 2/1 priority date for domestic and international students; for spring admission, 4/1 priority date for domestic and international students. Applications are processed on a rolling basis. Application fee: $50 ($60 for international students). Electronic applications accepted. *Expenses:* Tuition, state resident: full-time $7000. Tuition, nonresident: full-time $19,200. *Financial support:* In 2009–10, 2 research assistantships (averaging $14,000 per year), 2 teaching assistantships (averaging $14,000 per year) were awarded; health care benefits and unspecified assistantships also available. *Unit head:* Dr. John Petroric, Professor in Foundations of Education, 205-348-0465, Fax: 205-348-2161, E-mail: petroric@bamaed.ua.edu. *Application contact:* Dr. Kathy S. Wetzel, Assistant Dean for Student Services, 205-348-1154, Fax: 205-348-0080, E-mail: kwetzel@bamaed.ua.edu.

The University of Alabama at Birmingham, College of Arts and Sciences, School of Education, Program in Educational Leadership, Birmingham, AL 35294. Offers MA Ed, Ed D, PhD, Ed S. *Accreditation:* NCATE. *Degree requirements:* For master's, thesis optional; for doctorate, thesis/dissertation; for Ed S, comprehensive exam, thesis optional. *Entrance requirements:* For master's, GRE General Test, MAT, or NTE, minimum GPA of 3.0; for doctorate, GRE General Test, MAT, minimum GPA of 3.25; for Ed S, GRE General Test, MAT, minimum GPA of 3.0, master's degree. Electronic applications accepted.

University of Alaska Anchorage, College of Education, Program in Educational Leadership, Anchorage, AK 99508. Offers educational leadership (M Ed); principal licensure (Certificate); superintendent (Certificate). Part-time programs available. *Entrance requirements:* For master's, GRE or MAT, interview, minimum GPA of 3.0. Additional exam requirements/recommendations for international students: Required—TOEFL (minimum score 550 paper-based; 213 computer-based).

University of Alberta, Faculty of Graduate Studies and Research, Department of Educational Policy Studies, Edmonton, AB T6G 2E1, Canada. Offers adult education (M Ed, Ed D, PhD); educational administration and leadership (M Ed, Ed D, PhD, Postgraduate Diploma); First Nations education (M Ed, Ed D, PhD); theoretical, cultural and international studies in education (M Ed, Ed D, PhD). *Faculty:* 19 full-time (10 women), 5 part-time/adjunct (1 woman). *Students:* 73 full-time (47 women), 144 part-time (86 women). 141 applicants, 44% accepted. In 2009, 52 master's, 20 doctorates awarded. *Degree requirements:* For master's, thesis (for some programs); for doctorate, thesis/dissertation. *Entrance requirements:* For master's, minimum GPA of 6.5 on a 9.0 scale; for doctorate, minimum GPA of 7.5 on a 9.0 scale. Additional exam requirements/recommendations for international students: Required—TOEFL (minimum score 580 paper-based; 237 computer-based). *Application deadline:* For spring admission, 2/1 for domestic and international students. Electronic applications accepted. Tuition and fees charges are reported in Canadian dollars. *Expenses:* Tuition, area resident: Full-time $4626 Canadian dollars; part-time $99.72 Canadian dollars per unit. International tuition: $8216 Canadian dollars full-time. Required fees: $3590 Canadian dollars; $99.72 Canadian dollars per unit. $215 Canadian dollars per term. *Financial support:* In 2009–10, 7 fellowships with partial tuition reimbursements, 10 research assistantships with partial tuition reimbursements (averaging $6,936 per year), 30 teaching assistantships with partial tuition reimbursements (averaging $11,130 per year) were awarded; scholarships/grants and unspecified assistantships also available. *Unit head:* Dr. Frank Peters, Graduate Coordinator, 780-492-3679, Fax: 780-492-2024, E-mail: epscoord@ualberta.ca. *Application contact:* Joan A. White, Secretary, 780-492-3679, Fax: 780-492-2024, E-mail: joan.white@ualberta.ca.

The University of Arizona, Graduate College, College of Education, Department of Educational Policy Studies and Practice, Program of Educational Leadership, Tucson, AZ 85721. Offers M Ed, Ed D, Ed S. Part-time programs available. *Faculty:* 3. *Students:* 8 full-time (6 women), 61 part-time (39 women); includes 2 minority (both Hispanic Americans), 3 international. Average age 40. 49 applicants, 53% accepted, 25 enrolled. In 2009, 15 master's, 9 doctorates awarded. *Degree requirements:* For master's and Ed S, capstone experience; for doctorate, comprehensive exam, thesis/dissertation. *Entrance requirements:* For master's, leadership experience; for doctorate, GRE General Test, minimum GPA of 3.5, 3 letters of recommendation, curriculum vitae, writing sample. Additional exam requirements/recommendations for international students: Required—TOEFL (minimum score 550 paper-based; 213 computer-based; 79 iBT). *Application deadline:* For fall admission, 3/1 for domestic students, 12/1 for international students. Applications are processed on a rolling basis. Application fee: $65. Electronic applications accepted. *Expenses:* Tuition, state resident: full-time $9028. Tuition, nonresident: full-time $24,890. *Financial support:* Career-related internships or fieldwork, scholarships/grants, health care benefits, and unspecified assistantships available. *Faculty research:* School governance, higher order thinking, restructuring schools, bilingual education policy, authority in education. Total annual research expenditures: $292,015. *Unit head:* Dr. Kris Bosworth, Department Head, 520-621-6658, Fax: 520-626-6005, E-mail: edlprog@email.arizona.edu. *Application contact:* Kathy Bayham, Administrative Assistant, 520-621-6658, Fax: 520-626-6005, E-mail: edlprog@email.arizona.edu.

University of Arkansas, Graduate School, College of Education and Health Professions, Department of Curriculum and Instruction, Program in Educational Leadership, Fayetteville, AR 72701-1201. Offers M Ed, Ed D, Ed S. *Accreditation:* NCATE. Part-time and evening/weekend programs available. *Students:* 5 full-time (4 women), 29 part-time (19 women); includes 5 minority (1 African American, 2 American Indian/Alaska Native, 2 Asian Americans or Pacific Islanders), 2 international. In 2009, 5 master's, 7 doctorates awarded. *Degree requirements:* For doctorate, thesis/dissertation. *Entrance requirements:* For master's, GRE General Test, MAT or minimum GPA of 3.0; for doctorate, GRE General Test or MAT. Application fee: $40 ($50 for international students). *Expenses:* Tuition, state resident: full-time $7355; part-time $356.58 per hour. Tuition, nonresident: full-time $17,401; part-time $775.17 per hour. Required fees: $1203. *Financial support:* In 2009–10, 1 research assistantship was awarded; fellowships with tuition reimbursements, teaching assistantships, career-related internships or fieldwork and Federal Work-Study also available. Support available to part-time students. Financial award application deadline: 4/1; financial award applicants required to submit FAFSA. *Unit head:* Dr. Michael Daugherty, Department Chairperson, 479-575-4209, Fax: 479-575-5119, E-mail: mkd03@uark.edu. *Application contact:* Dr. William McComas, Graduate Coordinator, 479-575-7525, E-mail: mccomas@uark.edu.

University of Arkansas at Little Rock, Graduate School, College of Education, Department of Educational Leadership, Program in Educational Administration, Little Rock, AR 72204-1099. Offers educational administration (M Ed, Ed S); educational administration and supervision (Ed D). Part-time and evening/weekend programs available. *Degree requirements:* For master's, comprehensive exam; for doctorate, comprehensive exam, oral defense of dissertation, residency; for Ed S, comprehensive exam, professional project. *Entrance requirements:* For master's, GRE General Test or MAT, 4 years of work experience (minimum 3 in teaching), interview, minimum GPA of 2.75, teaching certificate; for doctorate, GRE General Test or MAT, 4 years of work experience, minimum graduate GPA of 3.0, teaching certificate; for Ed S, GRE General Test or MAT, 4 years of work experience, minimum GPA of 2.75, teaching certificate.

University of Arkansas at Little Rock, Graduate School, College of Education, Department of Educational Leadership, Program in Higher Education Administration, Little Rock, AR 72204-1099. Offers Ed D. *Degree requirements:* For doctorate, comprehensive exam, oral defense of dissertation, residency. *Entrance requirements:* For doctorate, GRE General Test or MAT, interview, minimum graduate GPA of 3.0, teaching certificate, work experience.

University of Arkansas at Monticello, School of Education, Monticello, AR 71656. Offers education (M Ed, MAT); educational leadership (M Ed). *Accreditation:* NCATE. Part-time and evening/weekend programs available. Postbaccalaureate distance learning degree programs offered (minimal on-campus study). *Degree requirements:* For master's, comprehensive exam. *Entrance requirements:* For master's, minimum GPA of 3.0. Additional exam requirements/recommendations for international students: Required—TOEFL (minimum score 550 paper-based; 213 computer-based). Electronic applications accepted.

University of Atlanta, Graduate Programs, Atlanta, GA 30360. Offers business (MS); business administration (Exec MBA, MBA); computer science (MS); educational leadership (MS, Ed D); healthcare administration (MS, D Sc, Graduate Certificate); information technology for management (Graduate Certificate); international project management (Graduate Certificate); law (JD); managerial science (DBA); project management (Graduate Certificate); social science (MS). Postbaccalaureate distance learning degree programs offered. *Faculty:* 54 part-time/adjunct (10 women). *Students:* 251 full-time. *Entrance requirements:* For master's, minimum cumulative GPA of 2.5. *Expenses:* Tuition: Part-time $1000 per course. Part-time tuition and fees vary according to course load and degree level.

University of Bridgeport, School of Education and Human Resources, Division of Education, Program in Educational Management, Bridgeport, CT 06604. Offers intermediate administrator or supervisor (Diploma); leadership (Ed D). *Degree requirements:* For doctorate, comprehensive exam, thesis/dissertation; for Diploma, thesis or alternative, final project. *Entrance requirements:* For doctorate, GRE, MAT; for Diploma, GRE General Test or MAT, minimum graduate QPA of 3.0. Additional exam requirements/recommendations for international students: Recommended—TOEFL (minimum score 550 paper-based; 213 computer-based; 80 iBT), IELTS (minimum score 6.5). Electronic applications accepted. *Expenses:* Contact institution.

The University of British Columbia, Faculty of Education, Department of Educational Studies, Vancouver, BC V6T 1Z1, Canada. Offers adult education (M Ed, MA); adult learning and global change (M Ed); educational administration (M Ed, MA); educational leadership and policy (Ed D); educational studies (PhD); higher education (M Ed, MA); society, culture and politics in education (M Ed, MA). Part-time and evening/weekend programs available. Terminal master's awarded for partial completion of doctoral program. *Degree requirements:* For master's, thesis; for doctorate, comprehensive exam, thesis/dissertation, master's thesis. *Entrance requirements:* For master's, minimum B+ average, 4-year undergraduate degree, field-related experience; for doctorate, minimum B+ average, 4-year undergraduate degree, master's

degree, field-related experience. Additional exam requirements/recommendations for international students: Required—TOEFL (600 paper; 250 computer; 100 Internet-based) or IELTS (6.5). Electronic applications accepted. *Faculty research:* Educational leadership educational administration adult education politics in education, global change and adult learning.

University of Calgary, Faculty of Graduate Studies, Faculty of Education, Graduate Division of Educational Research, Calgary, AB T2N 1N4, Canada. Offers community rehabilitation and disability studies (M Ed, M Sc, Ed D, PhD, Graduate Certificate, Graduate Diploma); curriculum, teaching and learning (M Ed, M Sc, MA, Ed D, PhD, Graduate Certificate, Graduate Diploma); educational contexts (M Ed, MA, Ed D, PhD, Graduate Certificate, Graduate Diploma); educational leadership (M Ed, MA, Ed D, PhD, Graduate Certificate, Graduate Diploma); educational technology (M Ed, M Sc, MA, Ed D, PhD, Graduate Certificate, Graduate Diploma); gifted education (M Sc, MA, Ed D, PhD, Graduate Certificate, Graduate Diploma); higher education administration (Ed D); interpretive studies in education (M Ed, M Sc, MA, Ed D, PhD, Graduate Certificate, Graduate Diploma); second language teaching (M Ed, Ed D, PhD, Graduate Certificate, Graduate Diploma); teaching English as a second language (M Ed, M Sc, MA, Ed D, PhD, Graduate Certificate, Graduate Diploma); workplace and adult learning (M Ed, MA, Ed D, PhD, Graduate Certificate, Graduate Diploma). Ed D in both higher education administration and educational leadership offered via distance delivery. Part-time and evening/weekend programs available. Postbaccalaureate distance learning degree programs offered (minimal on-campus study). *Degree requirements:* For master's, thesis (for some programs); for doctorate, thesis/dissertation, candidacy exam. *Entrance requirements:* For master's, minimum GPA of 3.0, 3 letters of reference; for doctorate, minimum GPA of 3.5, 3 letters of reference; for other advanced degree, minimum GPA of 3.0. Additional exam requirements/recommendations for international students: Required—TOEFL, IELTS. Electronic applications accepted. *Faculty research:* Curriculum, leadership, technology, contexts, gifted, second language teaching, work place and adult learning.

University of California, Irvine, Office of Graduate Studies, Department of Education, Irvine, CA 92697. Offers educational administration (Ed D); educational administration and leadership (Ed D); elementary and secondary education (MAT). Part-time and evening/weekend programs available. *Students:* 292 full-time (210 women), 11 part-time (9 women); includes 114 minority (7 African Americans, 2 American Indian/Alaska Native, 64 Asian Americans or Pacific Islanders, 41 Hispanic Americans), 6 international. Average age 28. 523 applicants, 75% accepted, 233 enrolled. In 2009, 164 master's, 20 doctorates awarded. *Degree requirements:* For doctorate, thesis/dissertation. *Entrance requirements:* For master's, GRE, minimum GPA of 3.0; for doctorate, GRE General Test, minimum GPA of 3.0. Additional exam requirements/recommendations for international students: Required—TOEFL (minimum score 550 paper-based; 213 computer-based). *Application deadline:* For fall admission, 1/4 priority date for domestic students, 1/4 for international students. Application fee: $70 ($90 for international students). Electronic applications accepted. *Financial support:* Fellowships, research assistantships with full tuition reimbursements, institutionally sponsored loans, traineeships, health care benefits, and unspecified assistantships available. Financial award application deadline: 3/1; financial award applicants required to submit FAFSA. *Faculty research:* Education technology, learning theory, social theory, cultural diversity, postmodernism. *Unit head:* David Brant, Interim Chair, 949-824-7840, E-mail: dbrant@uci.edu. *Application contact:* Sarah K. Singh, Student Affairs Officer, 949-824-7832, Fax: 949-824-2965, E-mail: sksingh@uci.edu.

University of California, Los Angeles, Graduate Division, Graduate School of Education and Information Studies, Program in Educational Leadership, Los Angeles, CA 90095. Offers Ed D. Evening/weekend programs available. *Degree requirements:* For doctorate, thesis/dissertation, oral and written qualifying exams. *Entrance requirements:* For doctorate, GRE General Test, minimum undergraduate GPA of 3.0, resume. Electronic applications accepted.

University of California, Riverside, Graduate Division, Graduate School of Education, Riverside, CA 92521-0102. Offers autism (M Ed); curriculum and instruction (MA, PhD); diversity and equity (M Ed); educational leadership and policy (MA, PhD); educational psychology (MA, PhD); general education (M Ed); higher education administration and policy (M Ed, PhD); leadership (M Ed); reading (M Ed); school psychology (PhD); special education (M Ed, MA, PhD). *Faculty:* 23 full-time (12 women), 12 part-time/adjunct (8 women). *Students:* 230 full-time (183 women), 6 part-time (3 women); includes 75 minority (12 African Americans, 1 American Indian/Alaska Native, 21 Asian Americans or Pacific Islanders, 41 Hispanic Americans), 6 international. Average age 32. 288 applicants, 60% accepted, 118 enrolled. In 2009, 68 master's, 13 doctorates awarded. Terminal master's awarded for partial completion of doctoral program. *Degree requirements:* For master's, comprehensive exam (for some programs), comprehensive exams or thesis (MA), case study or analytical report (M Ed); for doctorate, thesis/dissertation, written and oral qualifying exams, college teaching practicum. *Entrance requirements:* For master's, GRE General Test, GRE Subject Test, CBEST, CSET, minimum GPA of 3.2; for doctorate, GRE General Test, GRE Subject Test, master's degree (desirable), minimum GPA of 3.2. Additional exam requirements/recommendations for international students: Required—TOEFL (minimum score 550 paper-based; 213 computer-based; 80 iBT). *Application deadline:* For fall admission, 9/1 for domestic students, 4/1 for international students; for winter admission, 12/1 for domestic students, 9/1 for international students; for spring admission, 3/1 for domestic students, 10/1 for international students. Applications are processed on a rolling basis. Application fee: $70 ($85 for international students). Electronic applications accepted. *Financial support:* In 2009–10, 55 students received support, including 13 fellowships with full and partial tuition reimbursements available (averaging $26,809 per year), 21 research assistantships with full and partial tuition reimbursements available (averaging $14,238 per year), 1 teaching assistantship with full and partial tuition reimbursement available (averaging $16,638 per year); career-related internships or fieldwork, Federal Work-Study, institutionally sponsored loans, scholarships/grants, and unspecified assistantships also available. Financial award application deadline: 1/5; financial award applicants required to submit FAFSA. *Faculty research:* Responsiveness to intervention, faculty core, response to intervention of English language learners, advanced modeling techniques, study on social capital, trust, and motivation. Total annual research expenditures: $5.6 million. *Unit head:* Dr. Steven T. Bossert, Dean, 951-827-5802, Fax: 951-827-3942, E-mail: steven.bossert@ucr.edu. *Application contact:* Dr. John Wills, Graduate Advisor for Admission, 951-827-6362, Fax: 951-827-3942, E-mail: edgrad@ucr.edu.

University of California, Santa Barbara, Graduate Division, Gevirtz Graduate School of Education, Santa Barbara, CA 93106-9490. Offers counseling, clinical and school psychology (PhD), including clinical psychology, counseling psychology, school psychology; education (M Ed, MA, PhD), including child and adolescent development (MA, PhD), cultural perspectives and comparative education (MA, PhD), educational leadership and organizations (MA, PhD), research methodology (MA, PhD), special education disabilities and risk studies (MA), special education, disabilities and risk studies (PhD), teaching (M Ed), teaching and learning (MA, PhD); educational leadership (Ed D); school psychology (M Ed); MA/PhD. *Accreditation:* APA (one or more programs are accredited). Postbaccalaureate distance learning degree programs offered (minimal on-campus study). *Faculty:* 42 full-time (20 women), 10 part-time/adjunct (4 women). *Students:* 390 full-time (303 women); includes 149 minority (14 African Americans, 3 American Indian/Alaska Native, 57 Asian Americans or Pacific Islanders, 75 Hispanic Americans), 16 international. Average age 31. 717 applicants, 40% accepted, 170 enrolled. In 2009, 140 master's, 46 doctorates awarded. Terminal master's awarded for partial completion of doctoral program. *Degree requirements:* For master's, comprehensive exam (for some programs), thesis (for some programs); for doctorate, comprehensive exam (for some programs), thesis/dissertation, qualifying exam. *Entrance requirements:* For master's, GRE, 3 letters of recommendation, resume/curriculum vitae; for doctorate, GRE, 3 letters of recommendation, statement of purpose, personal achievements/contributions statement, resume/curriculum vitae, transcripts for post-secondary institutions attended. Additional exam requirements/recommendations for international students: Required—TOEFL (minimum score 550 paper-based; 213 computer-based; 80 iBT) or IELTS (minimum score 7). Application fee: $70 ($90 for international students). Electronic applications accepted. *Financial support:* In 2009–10, 253 students received support, including 206 fellowships with full and partial tuition reimbursements available (averaging $5,000 per year), 62 research assistantships with full and partial tuition reimbursements available (averaging $6,200 per year), 87 teaching assistantships with partial tuition reimbursements available (averaging $6,500 per year); career-related internships or fieldwork, Federal Work-Study, institutionally sponsored loans, scholarships/grants, traineeships, health care benefits, and unspecified assistantships also available. Financial award applicants required to submit FAFSA. *Faculty research:* Professional development, early childhood development, school violence, literacy, science/math initiative. Total annual research expenditures: $4.4 million. *Unit head:* Dr. Jane Conoley, Chair, 805-893-2185, E-mail: jane-conoley@education.ucsb.edu. *Application contact:* Kathryn Marie Tucciarone, Student Affairs Officer, 805-893-2137, E-mail: katiet@education.ucsb.edu.

University of Central Arkansas, Graduate School, College of Education, Department of Leadership Studies, Conway, AR 72035-0001. Offers college student personnel (MS); educational leadership—district level (Ed S); school counseling (MS), including elementary school counseling, secondary school counseling; school leadership (MS). *Accreditation:* NCATE. Part-time programs available. *Students:* 31 full-time (19 women), 74 part-time (50 women); includes 27 minority (24 African Americans, 2 American Indian/Alaska Native, 1 Asian American or Pacific Islander), 1 international. Average age 33. 34 applicants, 97% accepted, 25 enrolled. In 2009, 54 master's awarded. *Degree requirements:* For Ed S, comprehensive exam. *Application deadline:* For fall admission, 3/1 priority date for domestic students; for spring admission, 10/1 priority date for domestic students. Applications are processed on a rolling basis. Application fee: $25 ($40 for international students). *Expenses:* Contact institution. *Financial support:* Federal Work-Study, scholarships/grants, and tuition waivers (partial) available. Financial award application deadline: 2/15; financial award applicants required to submit FAFSA. *Unit head:* Dr. Terry James, Interim Chair, 501-450-5209, Fax: 501-450-5302. *Application contact:* Brenda Herring, Admissions Assistant, 501-450-5065, Fax: 501-450-5678, E-mail: bherring@uca.edu.

University of Central Florida, College of Education, Department of Educational Research, Technology and Leadership, Program in Educational Leadership, Orlando, FL 32816. Offers educational leadership (M Ed, MA, Ed D, Ed S). Part-time and evening/weekend programs available. *Students:* 102 full-time (66 women), 184 part-time (132 women); includes 44 minority (22 African Americans, 4 Asian Americans or Pacific Islanders, 18 Hispanic Americans). Average age 35. 121 applicants, 68% accepted, 45 enrolled. In 2009, 5 master's, 8 doctorates, 11 other advanced degrees awarded. *Degree requirements:* For master's, thesis or alternative; for doctorate, thesis/dissertation, candidacy exam; for Ed S, thesis or alternative, final exam. *Entrance requirements:* For master's, GRE General Test; for doctorate, GRE General Test, GRE Subject Test, minimum GPA of 3.0, resume; for Ed S, GRE General Test, minimum GPA of 3.0, resume. Additional exam requirements/recommendations for international students: Required—TOEFL. *Application deadline:* For fall admission, 2/20 priority date for domestic students; for spring admission, 9/20 priority date for domestic students. Application fee: $30. Electronic applications accepted. *Expenses:* Tuition, state resident: part-time $306.31 per credit hour. Tuition, nonresident: part-time $1099.01 per credit hour. Part-time tuition and fees vary according to degree level and program. *Financial support:* In 2009–10, 2 students received support, including 2 research assistantships with partial tuition reimbursements available (averaging $7,550 per year); fellowships with partial tuition reimbursements available, teaching assistantships with partial tuition reimbursements available, career-related internships or fieldwork, Federal Work-Study, institutionally sponsored loans, tuition waivers (partial), and unspecified assistantships also available. Financial award application deadline: 3/1; financial award applicants required to submit FAFSA.

University of Central Florida, College of Education, Department of Educational Studies, Orlando, FL 32816. Offers applied learning and instruction (MA); community college education (Certificate); curriculum and instruction (Ed S); education (Ed D, PhD, Ed S); gifted education (Certificate); global and comparative education (Certificate); initial teacher professional preparation (Certificate); teacher leadership (M Ed); urban education (Certificate). *Accreditation:* NCATE. Part-time and evening/weekend programs available. *Faculty:* 18 full-time (10 women), 16 part-time/adjunct (10 women). *Students:* 155 full-time (106 women), 156 part-time (131 women); includes 80 minority (37 African Americans, 5 Asian Americans or Pacific Islanders, 38 Hispanic Americans), 22 international. Average age 36. 200 applicants, 57% accepted, 77 enrolled. In 2009, 9 master's, 34 doctorates, 17 other advanced degrees awarded. *Degree requirements:* For other advanced degree, thesis or alternative, final exam. *Entrance requirements:* For degree, GRE General Test, minimum GPA of 3.0, resume. Additional exam requirements/recommendations for international students: Required—TOEFL. *Application deadline:* For fall admission, 2/20 for domestic students; for spring admission, 9/20 for domestic students. Application fee: $30. Electronic applications accepted. *Expenses:* Tuition, state resident: part-time $306.31 per credit hour. Tuition, nonresident: part-time $1099.01 per credit hour. Part-time tuition and fees vary according to degree level and program. *Financial support:* In 2009–10, 82 students received support, including 55 fellowships with partial tuition reimbursements available (averaging $8,300 per year), 29 research assistantships with partial tuition reimbursements available (averaging $7,000 per year), 43 teaching assistantships with partial tuition reimbursements available (averaging $8,000 per year); career-related internships or fieldwork, Federal Work-Study, institutionally sponsored loans, and unspecified assistantships also available. Financial award application deadline: 3/1; financial award applicants required to submit FAFSA. *Unit head:* Dr. Karen Biraimah, Chair, 407-823-2428, E-mail: biraimah@mail.ucf.edu. *Application contact:* Dr. Karen Biraimah, Chair, 407-823-2428, E-mail: biraimah@mail.ucf.edu.

University of Central Missouri, The Graduate School, College of Education, Warrensburg, MO 64093. Offers career and technical education administration (MS); career and technical education industry training (MS); career and technical education leadership/teaching (MS); college student personnel administration (MS); counseling (MS); curriculum and instruction (Ed S); educational leadership (Ed D); educational technology (MS); elementary education/educational foundations and literacy (MSE); elementary school administration (MSE); elementary school principalship (Ed S); human services/learning resources (Ed S); human services/professional counseling (Ed S); human services/special education (Ed S); human services/technology and occupational education (Ed S); K-12 education/educational foundations and literacy (MSE); K-12 special education (MSE); library science and information services (MS); literacy education (MSE); secondary education/educational foundations & literacy (MSE); secondary school administration (MSE); secondary school principalship (Ed S); superintendency (Ed S); teaching (MAT). Part-time programs available. Postbaccalaureate distance learning degree programs offered. *Faculty:* 42. *Students:* 123 full-time (82 women), 721 part-time (552 women); includes 58 minority (38 African Americans, 3 American Indian/Alaska Native, 6 Asian Americans or Pacific Islanders, 11 Hispanic Americans), 6 international. Average age 34. 229 applicants, 88% accepted, 190 enrolled. In 2009, 212 master's, 47 other advanced degrees awarded. *Entrance requirements:* Additional exam requirements/recommendations for international students: Required—TOEFL (minimum score 550 paper-based; 79 computer-based). *Application deadline:* For fall admission, 6/1 priority date for domestic students, 5/1 for international students; for spring admission, 10/1 priority date for domestic students, 10/1 for international students. Applications are processed on a rolling basis. Application fee: $30 ($75 for international students). Electronic applications accepted. *Expenses:* Tuition, area resident: Part-time $245.80 per credit hour. Tuition, nonresident: part-time $491.60 per credit hour. Required fees: $24.20 per credit hour. Full-time tuition and fees vary according to course load, degree level, campus/location and reciprocity agreements. *Financial support:* Research assistantships with full and partial tuition reimbursements, teaching assistantships with full and partial tuition reimbursements, career-related internships or fieldwork, Federal Work-Study, scholarships/grants, and administrative and laboratory assistantships available. Support available to part-time students. Financial award application deadline: 3/1; financial award applicants required to submit FAFSA. *Unit head:* Dr. Michael Wright, Dean, 660-543-4272, Fax: 660-543-8753, E-mail: mwright@ucmo.edu. *Application contact:* Laurie Delap, Admissions Coordinator, 660-543-4621, Fax: 660-543-4778, E-mail: gradinfo@ucmo.edu.

University of Central Oklahoma, College of Graduate Studies and Research, College of Education, Department of Advanced Professional Services, Program in Educational Administration,

Educational Leadership and Administration

University of Central Oklahoma (continued)
Edmond, OK 73034-5209. Offers M Ed. *Accreditation:* NCATE. Part-time programs available. *Faculty:* 6 full-time (3 women), 3 part-time/adjunct (1 woman). *Students:* 4 full-time (3 women), 99 part-time (67 women); includes 9 minority (8 African Americans, 1 American Indian/Alaska Native). Average age 37. 21 applicants, 100% accepted. In 2009, 37 master's awarded. *Entrance requirements:* For master's, GRE General Test. Additional exam requirements/recommendations for international students: Required—TOEFL (minimum score 550 paper-based; 213 computer-based). *Application deadline:* For fall admission, 7/1 for international students; for spring admission, 11/1 for international students. Applications are processed on a rolling basis. Application fee: $25. Electronic applications accepted. *Expenses:* Tuition, state resident: full-time $4128; part-time $172 per credit hour. Tuition, nonresident: full-time $10,373; part-time $432.20 per credit hour. Required fees: $433.20; $18.05 per credit hour. *Financial support:* Unspecified assistantships available. Financial award application deadline: 3/31; financial award applicants required to submit FAFSA. *Unit head:* Dr. Pat Couts, Director, 405-974-5888, Fax: 405-974-3822. *Application contact:* Dr. Richard Bernard, Dean, Graduate College, 405-974-3493, Fax: 405-974-3852, E-mail: gradcoll@uco.edu.

University of Cincinnati, Graduate School, College of Education, Criminal Justice, and Human Services, Division of Educational Studies, Program in Educational Leadership, Cincinnati, OH 45221. Offers M Ed, Ed S. *Accreditation:* NCATE. Part-time programs available. Post-baccalaureate distance learning degree programs offered. *Degree requirements:* For master's, thesis or alternative. *Entrance requirements:* For master's, GRE General Test, 3 letters of reference, resume, minimum GPA of 2.8; for Ed S, references, interview. Additional exam requirements/recommendations for international students: Required—TOEFL (minimum score 550 paper-based). Electronic applications accepted.

University of Cincinnati, Graduate School, College of Education, Criminal Justice, and Human Services, Division of Educational Studies, Program in Urban Educational Leadership, Cincinnati, OH 45221. Offers Ed D. *Degree requirements:* For doctorate, thesis/dissertation. *Entrance requirements:* For doctorate, GRE General Test, GRE Subject Test. Additional exam requirements/recommendations for international students: Required—TOEFL (minimum score 550 paper-based), OEPT.

University of Colorado at Colorado Springs, Graduate School, College of Education, Colorado Springs, CO 80933-7150. Offers counseling and human services (MA); curriculum and instruction (MA); educational administration (MA); educational leadership (MA, PhD); special education (MA). *Accreditation:* ACA; NCATE. Part-time and evening/weekend programs available. Postbaccalaureate distance learning degree programs offered (minimal on-campus study). *Faculty:* 23 full-time (15 women), 11 part-time/adjunct (8 women). *Students:* 317 full-time (243 women), 160 part-time (132 women); includes 81 minority (23 African Americans, 3 American Indian/Alaska Native, 13 Asian Americans or Pacific Islanders, 42 Hispanic Americans), 2 international. Average age 36. 375 applicants, 94% accepted, 254 enrolled. In 2009, 203 master's awarded. *Degree requirements:* For master's, comprehensive exam, thesis or alternative, microcomputer proficiency; for doctorate, comprehensive exam, research lab. *Entrance requirements:* For master's, GRE General Test, MAT. *Application deadline:* For fall admission, 6/15 for domestic students; for spring admission, 10/15 for domestic students. Applications are processed on a rolling basis. Application fee: $60 ($75 for international students). *Expenses:* Tuition, state resident: full-time $8922; part-time $639 per credit hour. Tuition, nonresident: full-time $19,372; part-time $1154 per credit hour. Tuition and fees vary according to course level, course load, degree level, program, reciprocity agreements and student level. *Financial support:* Fellowships, career-related internships or fieldwork, Federal Work-Study, and scholarships/grants available. Support available to part-time students. Financial award application deadline: 3/1; financial award applicants required to submit FAFSA. *Faculty research:* Job training for special populations, materials development for classroom. Total annual research expenditures: $1.4 million. *Unit head:* Dr. LaVonne Neal, Dean, 719-255-4111, Fax: 719-262-4110, E-mail: lneal@uccs.edu. *Application contact:* Melissa Schecter, Student Services Manager, 719-255-4526, Fax: 719-255-4110, E-mail: mschedte@uccs.edu.

University of Colorado Denver, School of Education and Human Development, Administrative Leadership and Professional Studies Program, Denver, CO 80217-3364. Offers MA, Ed S. *Accreditation:* NCATE. Part-time and evening/weekend programs available. *Students:* 104 full-time (75 women), 14 part-time (7 women); includes 18 minority (6 African Americans, 1 Asian American or Pacific Islander, 11 Hispanic Americans). 37 applicants, 89% accepted, 30 enrolled. In 2009, 17 master's, 20 other advanced degrees awarded. *Degree requirements:* For master's, thesis or alternative, portfolio, final paper. *Entrance requirements:* For master's, GRE, MAT, minimum GPA of 2.75, interview, 3 letters of recommendation, resume. Additional exam requirements/recommendations for international students: Required—TOEFL (minimum score 525 paper-based; 197 computer-based). *Application deadline:* For fall admission, 5/15 for domestic students; for spring admission, 10/15 for domestic students. Applications are processed on a rolling basis. Application fee: $50 ($75 for international students). Electronic applications accepted. *Financial support:* Research assistantships, teaching assistantships, Federal Work-Study available. Financial award application deadline: 4/1; financial award applicants required to submit FAFSA. *Faculty research:* Learning cultures, teaching and learning in educational administration. *Unit head:* Connie Fulmer, Area Coordinator, 303-315-4962, E-mail: connie.fulmer@ucdenver.edu. *Application contact:* Lori Sisneros, Student Services Coordinator, 303-315-4979, Fax: 303-315-6311, E-mail: lori.sisneros@ucdenver.edu.

University of Colorado Denver, School of Education and Human Development, Program in Educational Leadership and Innovation, Denver, CO 80217-3364. Offers PhD. Part-time and evening/weekend programs available. *Students:* 12 full-time (6 women), 50 part-time (32 women); includes 17 minority (6 African Americans, 1 American Indian/Alaska Native, 6 Asian Americans or Pacific Islanders, 4 Hispanic Americans), 1 international. 3 applicants, 0% accepted, 0 enrolled. In 2009, 11 doctorates awarded. *Degree requirements:* For doctorate, one foreign language, comprehensive exam, thesis/dissertation. *Entrance requirements:* For doctorate, GRE or equivalent, resume. Additional exam requirements/recommendations for international students: Required—TOEFL (minimum score 525 paper-based; 197 computer-based). *Application deadline:* For fall admission, 1/15 for domestic students. Application fee: $50 ($75 for international students). *Financial support:* Application deadline: 4/1. *Faculty research:* Administrative leadership and policy studies, early childhood education, research in diversity, paraprofessionals in education, urban schools lab. *Unit head:* Dr. Wanda Blanchett, Associate Dean, 303-315-4956, E-mail: wanda.blanchett@ucdenver.edu. *Application contact:* Lori Sisneros, Student Services Coordinator, 303-315-4979, Fax: 303-315-6311, E-mail: lori.sisneros@ucdenver.edu.

University of Connecticut, Graduate School, Neag School of Education, Department of Educational Leadership, Field of Educational Administration, Storrs, CT 06269. Offers Ed D, PhD, Post-Master's Certificate. *Accreditation:* NCATE. *Faculty:* 6 full-time (3 women). *Students:* 93 part-time (58 women); includes 11 minority (5 African Americans, 3 Asian Americans or Pacific Islanders, 3 Hispanic Americans), 1 international. Average age 38. 65 applicants, 2% accepted, 0 enrolled. In 2009, 53 other advanced degrees awarded. *Degree requirements:* For doctorate, thesis/dissertation. *Entrance requirements:* For doctorate, GRE General Test. Additional exam requirements/recommendations for international students: Required—TOEFL (minimum score 550 paper-based; 213 computer-based). *Application deadline:* For fall admission, 2/1 priority date for domestic and international students; for spring admission, 11/1 for domestic students, 10/1 for international students. Applications are processed on a rolling basis. Electronic applications accepted. *Expenses:* Tuition, state resident: full-time $4725; part-time $525 per credit. Tuition, nonresident: full-time $12,267; part-time $1363 per credit. Required fees: $346 per semester. Tuition and fees vary according to course load. *Financial support:* Fellowships, research assistantships with full tuition reimbursements, teaching assistantships with full tuition reimbursements, Federal Work-Study, scholarships/grants, health care benefits, and unspecified assistantships available. Financial award application deadline: 2/1; financial award applicants required to submit FAFSA. *Unit head:* Barry G. Sheckley, Head, 860-486-2738, Fax:

860-486-4028, E-mail: barry.sheckley@uconn.edu. *Application contact:* Lisa Rasicot, Graduate Coordinator, 860-486-3065, Fax: 860-486-0210, E-mail: l.rasicot@uconn.edu.

University of Dayton, Graduate School, School of Education and Allied Professions, Department of Counselor Education and Human Services, Dayton, OH 45469-1300. Offers college student personnel (MS Ed); community counseling (MS Ed); higher education administration (MS Ed); human services (MS Ed); school counseling (MS Ed); school psychology (MS Ed, Ed S); teacher as child/youth development specialist (MS Ed). *Accreditation:* NCATE. Part-time and evening/weekend programs available. *Faculty:* 11 full-time (8 women), 33 part-time/adjunct (22 women). *Students:* 254 full-time (207 women), 207 part-time (180 women); includes 76 minority (69 African Americans, 3 Asian Americans or Pacific Islanders, 4 Hispanic Americans), 2 international. Average age 32. 359 applicants, 47% accepted, 114 enrolled. In 2009, 163 master's, 11 Ed Ss awarded. *Degree requirements:* For master's, comprehensive exam (for some programs), thesis (for some programs), exit exam. *Entrance requirements:* For master's, MAT or GRE (if GPA less than 2.75), interview, writing sample. Additional exam requirements/recommendations for international students: Required—TOEFL (minimum score 550 paper-based; 213 computer-based; 80 iBT). *Application deadline:* For fall admission, 4/10 for domestic students, 3/1 priority date for international students; for winter admission, 9/10 for domestic students, 7/1 priority date for international students; for spring admission, 1/10 for domestic students, 1/1 priority date for international students. Applications are processed on a rolling basis. Application fee: $0 ($50 for international students). Electronic applications accepted. *Expenses:* Tuition: Full-time $8412; part-time $701 per credit hour. Required fees: $325; $65 per course. $25 per semester. Tuition and fees vary according to course load, degree level and program. *Financial support:* In 2009–10, 7 research assistantships with full tuition reimbursements (averaging $8,000 per year), 1 teaching assistantship with full tuition reimbursement (averaging $8,000 per year) were awarded; career-related internships or fieldwork, institutionally sponsored loans, health care benefits, and unspecified assistantships also available. Financial award applicants required to submit FAFSA. *Faculty research:* Anger as part of the grief process, inclusion of children with severe disabilities, comparisons of school counselors in Bosnia and the U. S., graduate and professional student socialization, use of cohort groups in doctoral programs, bullying in schools, impact of space on learning, sophomore experience. *Unit head:* Dr. Alan Demmitt, Chairperson, 937-229-3644, Fax: 937-229-1055. *Application contact:* Graduate Admissions, 937-229-4411, Fax: 937-229-4729, E-mail: gradadmission@udayton.edu.

University of Dayton, Graduate School, School of Education and Allied Professions, Department of Educational Leadership, Doctoral Program in Educational Leadership, Dayton, OH 45469-1300. Offers PhD. Evening/weekend programs available. *Faculty:* 13 full-time (4 women). *Students:* 70 full-time (42 women); includes 7 minority (4 African Americans, 3 Asian Americans or Pacific Islanders), 1 international. Average age 43. 108 applicants, 64% accepted, 59 enrolled. In 2009, 5 doctorates awarded. *Degree requirements:* For doctorate, comprehensive exam, thesis/dissertation. *Entrance requirements:* For doctorate, GRE or MAT, administration experience, minimum GPA of 3.25. Additional exam requirements/recommendations for international students: Required—TOEFL (minimum score 550 paper-based; 213 computer-based; 80 iBT). *Application deadline:* For fall admission, 3/1 priority date for international students; for winter admission, 7/1 priority date for international students; for spring admission, 1/1 priority date for international students. Applications are processed on a rolling basis. Application fee: $0 ($50 for international students). Electronic applications accepted. *Expenses:* Tuition: Full-time $8412; part-time $701 per credit hour. Required fees: $325; $65 per course. $25 per semester. Tuition and fees vary according to course load, degree level and program. *Financial support:* In 2009–10, 5 research assistantships with full tuition reimbursements (averaging $11,725 per year) were awarded. Financial award applicants required to submit FAFSA. *Unit head:* Dr. Andrew William Place, Director, 937-229-4003, Fax: 937-229-4003, E-mail: andrew.place@notes.udayton.edu. *Application contact:* Nancy Crouchley, Administrative Assistant, 937-229-4003, E-mail: nancy.crouchley@notes.udayton.edu.

University of Dayton, Graduate School, School of Education and Allied Professions, Department of Educational Leadership, Program in Educational Leadership, Dayton, OH 45469-1300. Offers education administration (Ed S); educational leadership (MS Ed). Part-time and evening/weekend programs available. Postbaccalaureate distance learning degree programs offered (no on-campus study). *Faculty:* 10 full-time (2 women), 31 part-time/adjunct (12 women). *Students:* 146 full-time (88 women), 298 part-time (194 women); includes 41 minority (29 African Americans, 3 Asian Americans or Pacific Islanders, 9 Hispanic Americans), 9 international. Average age 33. 61 applicants, 87% accepted, 47 enrolled. In 2009, 139 master's awarded. *Degree requirements:* For master's, comprehensive exam (for some programs), thesis or alternative. *Entrance requirements:* For master's, MAT or GRE (if GPA less than 2.75), minimum GPA of 2.75. Additional exam requirements/recommendations for international students: Required—TOEFL (minimum score 550 paper-based; 213 computer-based; 80 iBT). *Application deadline:* For fall admission, 1/20 priority date for domestic students, 6/1 priority date for international students; for winter admission, 10/10 for domestic students, 10/1 priority date for international students; for spring admission, 1/14 for domestic students, 1/1 priority date for international students. Applications are processed on a rolling basis. Application fee: $0 ($50 for international students). Electronic applications accepted. *Expenses:* Tuition: Full-time $8412; part-time $701 per credit hour. Required fees: $325; $65 per course. $25 per semester. Tuition and fees vary according to course load, degree level and program. *Financial support:* In 2009–10, 2 research assistantships with full tuition reimbursements (averaging $8,500 per year) were awarded; career-related internships or fieldwork, institutionally sponsored loans, health care benefits, and unspecified assistantships also available. Financial award applicants required to submit FAFSA. *Faculty research:* Preparation for school superintendents, issues in diversity, legal issues in special education, online education, Catholic school leadership. *Unit head:* Rep. Joseph D. Massucci, Chair, 937-229-3737, E-mail: joseph.massucci@notes.udayton.edu. *Application contact:* Graduate Admissions, 937-229-4411, Fax: 937-229-4729, E-mail: gradadmission@udayton.edu.

University of Dayton, Graduate School, School of Education and Allied Professions, Department of Teacher Education, Dayton, OH 45469-1300. Offers adolescent/young adult (MS Ed); art education (MS Ed); early childhood education (MS Ed); inclusive early childhood (MS Ed); interdisciplinary education (MS Ed); intervention specialist education, mild/moderate (MS Ed); literacy (MS Ed); middle childhood (MS Ed); multi-age education (MS Ed); music education (MS Ed); teacher as leader (MS Ed); technology in education (MS Ed). Part-time and evening/weekend programs available. *Faculty:* 17 full-time (13 women), 27 part-time/adjunct (21 women). *Students:* 105 full-time (76 women), 152 part-time (131 women); includes 25 minority (21 African Americans, 1 Asian American or Pacific Islander, 3 Hispanic Americans), 8 international. Average age 33. 199 applicants, 58% accepted, 48 enrolled. In 2009, 139 master's awarded. *Degree requirements:* For master's, thesis, capstone research project. *Entrance requirements:* For master's, GRE General Test, minimum GPA of 2.75. Additional exam requirements/recommendations for international students: Required—TOEFL (minimum score 550 paper-based; 213 computer-based; 80 iBT). *Application deadline:* For fall admission, 3/15 priority date for domestic students, 3/1 priority date for international students; for winter admission, 7/1 priority date for international students; for spring admission, 1/1 priority date for international students. Applications are processed on a rolling basis. Application fee: $0 ($50 for international students). Electronic applications accepted. *Expenses:* Contact institution. *Financial support:* In 2009–10, 5 research assistantships with full and partial tuition reimbursements (averaging $8,000 per year) were awarded; career-related internships or fieldwork, institutionally sponsored loans, health care benefits, and unspecified assistantships also available. Financial award applicants required to submit FAFSA. *Faculty research:* Diversity, literacy, art representation by young children, preservice teacher preparation. *Unit head:* Dr. Katie A. Kinnucan-Welsch, Chair, 937-229-3346. *Application contact:* Graduate Admissions, 937-229-4411, Fax: 937-229-4729, E-mail: gradadmission@udayton.edu.

University of Delaware, College of Human Services, Education and Public Policy, School of Education, Newark, DE 19716. Offers education (PhD); educational leadership (Ed D); higher education (M Ed); instruction (MI); reading (M Ed); school leadership (M Ed); school psychology

(MA, Ed S); teaching English as a second language (TESL) (MA). *Accreditation:* NCATE. Part-time and evening/weekend programs available. Terminal master's awarded for partial completion of doctoral program. *Degree requirements:* For master's, comprehensive exam (for some programs), thesis (for some programs); for doctorate, comprehensive exam (for some programs), thesis/dissertation. *Entrance requirements:* For master's and doctorate, GRE, 3 letters of recommendation. Additional exam requirements/recommendations for international students: Required—TOEFL (minimum score 600 paper-based; 250 computer-based). Electronic applications accepted. *Faculty research:* Teacher education; curriculum theory and development; community based education models, educational leadership.

University of Denver, College of Education, Denver, CO 80208. Offers counseling psychology (MA, PhD); curriculum and instruction (MA, PhD, Certificate), including curriculum leadership (MA, PhD); educational administration and policy studies (Certificate); educational psychology (MA, PhD, Ed S), including child and family studies (MA, PhD), quantitative research methods (MA, PhD), school psychology (PhD, Ed S); higher education and adult studies (MA, PhD); library and information science (MLIS); library and information sciences (Certificate); school administration (PhD). *Accreditation:* ALA; APA (one or more programs are accredited). Part-time and evening/weekend programs available. Postbaccalaureate distance learning degree programs offered (no on-campus study). *Faculty:* 33 full-time (24 women), 62 part-time/adjunct (41 women). *Students:* 384 full-time (305 women), 453 part-time (336 women); includes 164 minority (47 African Americans, 8 American Indian/Alaska Native, 14 Asian Americans or Pacific Islanders, 95 Hispanic Americans), 20 international. Average age 34. 1,065 applicants, 59% accepted, 433 enrolled. In 2009, 206 master's, 38 doctorates, 117 other advanced degrees awarded. Terminal master's awarded for partial completion of doctoral program. *Degree requirements:* For master's, comprehensive exam; for doctorate, 2 foreign languages, comprehensive exam, thesis/dissertation. *Entrance requirements:* For master's and doctorate, GRE General Test or MAT. *Application deadline:* Applications are processed on a rolling basis. Application fee: $50. Electronic applications accepted. *Expenses:* Tuition: Full-time $34,596; part-time $961 per quarter hour. Required fees: $4 per quarter hour. Tuition and fees vary according to course load, campus/location and program. *Financial support:* In 2009–10, 78 teaching assistantships with full and partial tuition reimbursements (averaging $11,700 per year) were awarded; career-related internships or fieldwork, Federal Work-Study, institutionally sponsored loans, and scholarships/grants also available. Support available to part-time students. Financial award application deadline: 3/1; financial award applicants required to submit FAFSA. *Faculty research:* Parkinson's disease, personnel training, development and assessments, gifted education, service-learning, transportation, public schools. Total annual research expenditures: $340,000. *Unit head:* Dr. Gregory M. Anderson, Dean, 303-871-3665. *Application contact:* Janet Erickson, Director of Graduate Admission, 303-871-2485, E-mail: edinfo@du.edu.

University of Detroit Mercy, College of Liberal Arts and Education, Department of Education, Program in Educational Administration, Detroit, MI 48221. Offers MA. *Degree requirements:* For master's, thesis or alternative. *Entrance requirements:* For master's, minimum GPA of 2.75.

The University of Findlay, Graduate and Professional Studies, College of Education, Findlay, OH 45840-3653. Offers administration (MA Ed); early childhood (MA Ed); elementary education (MA Ed); human resource development (MA Ed); leadership (MA Ed); special education (MA Ed); technology (MA Ed); web instruction (MA Ed). *Accreditation:* NCATE. Part-time and evening/weekend programs available. *Degree requirements:* For master's, thesis, cumulative project. *Entrance requirements:* For master's, minimum undergraduate GPA of 2.75 in last 62 hours of course work. Additional exam requirements/recommendations for international students: Required—TOEFL (minimum score 550 paper-based; 213 computer-based; 80 iBT). Electronic applications accepted. *Expenses:* Contact institution. *Faculty research:* Children's literature, books and artwork, educational technology, professional development.

University of Florida, Graduate School, College of Education, Department of Educational Administration and Policy, Gainesville, FL 32611. Offers curriculum and instruction (Ed D, PhD); educational leadership (M Ed, MAE, Ed D, PhD, Ed S); higher education administration (Ed D, PhD, Ed S); student personnel in higher education (M Ed, MAE); PhD/JD. *Accreditation:* NCATE. *Degree requirements:* For master's, thesis optional; for doctorate, variable foreign language requirement, thesis/dissertation. *Entrance requirements:* For master's, GRE General Test, minimum GPA of 3.0, teaching experience; for doctorate and Ed S, GRE General Test, minimum GPA of 3.0. Additional exam requirements/recommendations for international students: Required—TOEFL (minimum score 550 paper-based; 213 computer-based). Electronic applications accepted. *Faculty research:* Educational finance, community education, middle school curriculum, community college administration.

University of Georgia, Graduate School, College of Education, Department of Lifelong Education, Administration and Policy, Athens, GA 30602. Offers adult education (M Ed, Ed D, PhD, Ed S); educational administration and policy (M Ed, PhD, Ed S); educational leadership (Ed D); human resource and organizational design (M Ed). *Accreditation:* NCATE. *Faculty:* 26 full-time (17 women). *Students:* 77 full-time (55 women), 181 part-time (124 women); includes 64 minority (54 African Americans, 1 American Indian/Alaska Native, 4 Asian Americans or Pacific Islanders, 5 Hispanic Americans), 28 international. 199 applicants, 60% accepted, 77 enrolled. In 2009, 43 master's, 21 doctorates, 5 other advanced degrees awarded. *Entrance requirements:* For master's and Ed S, GRE General Test or MAT; for doctorate, GRE General Test. *Application deadline:* For fall admission, 7/1 priority date for domestic students; for spring admission, 11/15 for domestic students. Application fee: $50. Electronic applications accepted. *Expenses:* Tuition, state resident: full-time $6000; part-time $250 per credit hour. Tuition, nonresident: full-time $20,904; part-time $871 per credit hour. Required fees: $730 per semester. *Unit head:* Dr. Ronald M. Cervero, Head, 706-542-2221, Fax: 706-542-5873, E-mail: rcervero@uga.edu. *Application contact:* Dr. Kathryn Roulston, Graduate Coordinator, 706-542-4060, Fax: 706-542-5873, E-mail: roulston@uga.edu.

University of Georgia, Graduate School, College of Education, Department of Workforce Education, Leadership and Social Foundations, Athens, GA 30602. Offers educational leadership (Ed D); human resources and organization design (M Ed); occupational studies (MAT, Ed D, PhD, Ed S); social foundations of education (PhD). *Accreditation:* NCATE. *Faculty:* 19 full-time (8 women). *Students:* 33 full-time (20 women), 127 part-time (81 women); includes 24 minority (19 African Americans, 2 American Indian/Alaska Native, 1 Asian American or Pacific Islander, 2 Hispanic Americans), 6 international. 140 applicants, 71% accepted, 46 enrolled. In 2009, 18 master's, 11 doctorates, 9 other advanced degrees awarded. *Entrance requirements:* For master's, GRE General Test, MAT; for doctorate, GRE General Test; for Ed S, GRE General Test or MAT. *Application deadline:* For fall admission, 7/1 priority date for domestic students; for spring admission, 11/15 for domestic students. Application fee: $50. Electronic applications accepted. *Expenses:* Tuition, state resident: full-time $6000; part-time $250 per credit hour. Tuition, nonresident: full-time $20,904; part-time $871 per credit hour. Required fees: $730 per semester. *Financial support:* Fellowships, research assistantships, teaching assistantships, unspecified assistantships available. *Unit head:* Dr. Roger B. Hill, Interim Head, 706-542-4100, Fax: 706-542-4054, E-mail: rbhill@uga.edu. *Application contact:* Dr. Myra N. Womble, Graduate Coordinator, 706-542-4091, Fax: 706-542-4054, E-mail: mwomble@uga.edu.

University of Guam, Office of Graduate Studies, School of Education, Program in Administration and Supervision, Mangilao, GU 96923. Offers M Ed. *Degree requirements:* For master's, comprehensive oral and written exams, special project or thesis. *Entrance requirements:* For master's, GRE General Test. Additional exam requirements/recommendations for international students: Required—TOEFL.

University of Hartford, College of Education, Nursing, and Health Professions, Program in Educational Leadership, West Hartford, CT 06117-1599. Offers administration and supervision (CAGS). *Accreditation:* NCATE. Part-time and evening/weekend programs available. *Degree requirements:* For CAGS, comprehensive exam or research project. *Entrance requirements:* For degree, GRE General Test or MAT, interview. Additional exam requirements/recommendations for international students: Required—TOEFL (minimum score 550 paper-based; 213 computer-based). Electronic applications accepted.

University of Hartford, College of Education, Nursing, and Health Professions, Program in Educational Leadership (Doctoral), West Hartford, CT 06117-1599. Offers Ed D. *Accreditation:* NCATE. Part-time and evening/weekend programs available. *Degree requirements:* For doctorate, thesis/dissertation. *Entrance requirements:* For doctorate, MAT, 3 letters of recommendation, writing samples, interview, resume, letter of support from employer. *Expenses:* Contact institution.

University of Hawaii at Manoa, Graduate Division, College of Education, Department of Educational Administration, Honolulu, HI 96822. Offers M Ed. Part-time programs available. *Faculty:* 7 full-time (5 women), 3 part-time/adjunct (all women). *Students:* 28 full-time (15 women), 48 part-time (25 women); includes 49 minority (1 African American, 47 Asian Americans or Pacific Islanders, 1 Hispanic American), 2 international. Average age 36. 45 applicants, 69% accepted, 22 enrolled. In 2009, 33 master's awarded. *Degree requirements:* For master's, thesis optional. *Entrance requirements:* Additional exam requirements/recommendations for international students: Required—TOEFL (minimum score 600 paper-based; 250 computer-based; 100 iBT), IELTS (minimum score 7). *Application deadline:* For fall admission, 3/1 for domestic students, 1/15 for international students; for spring admission, 9/1 for domestic students, 8/1 for international students. Application fee: $60. *Expenses:* Tuition, state resident: full-time $8900; part-time $372 per credit. Tuition, nonresident: full-time $21,400; part-time $898 per credit. Required fees: $207 per semester. *Financial support:* In 2009–10, 3 students received support, including 7 fellowships (averaging $2,091 per year), 2 research assistantships (averaging $15,558 per year); career-related internships or fieldwork, Federal Work-Study, institutionally sponsored loans, and tuition waivers (full and partial) also available. *Faculty research:* Leadership, educational policy, organizational processes, finance. *Application contact:* Stacey Roberts, Acting Graduate Chair, 808-956-7919, Fax: 808-956-4120, E-mail: sroberts@hawaii.edu.

University of Hawaii at Manoa, Graduate Division, College of Education, Doctorate in Education Program, Honolulu, HI 96822. Offers curriculum and instruction (PhD); educational administration (PhD); educational foundations (PhD); educational policy studies (PhD); educational technology (PhD); exceptionalities (PhD); kinesiology (PhD). Part-time and evening/weekend programs available. *Faculty:* 65 full-time (40 women), 28 part-time/adjunct (17 women). *Students:* 74 full-time (44 women), 119 part-time (77 women); includes 101 minority (5 African Americans, 2 American Indian/Alaska Native, 86 Asian Americans or Pacific Islanders, 8 Hispanic Americans), 17 international. Average age 38. 98 applicants, 53% accepted, 35 enrolled. In 2009, 11 doctorates awarded. *Degree requirements:* For doctorate, thesis/dissertation. *Entrance requirements:* For doctorate, GRE General Test, sample of written work. Additional exam requirements/recommendations for international students: Required—TOEFL (minimum score 600 paper-based; 250 computer-based; 100 iBT), IELTS (minimum score 7). *Application deadline:* For fall admission, 2/1 for domestic students, 1/15 for international students. Application fee: $50. *Expenses:* Tuition, state resident: full-time $8900; part-time $372 per credit. Tuition, nonresident: full-time $21,400; part-time $898 per credit. Required fees: $207 per semester. *Financial support:* In 2009–10, 1 student received support, including 11 fellowships (averaging $4,147 per year), 17 research assistantships (averaging $17,392 per year), 4 teaching assistantships (averaging $14,670 per year); career-related internships or fieldwork, Federal Work-Study, and tuition waivers (full and partial) also available. *Application contact:* Dr. Helen Slaughter, Chairperson, 808-956-7913, Fax: 808-956-9905, E-mail: slaughte@hawaii.edu.

University of Houston, College of Education, Department of Educational Leadership and Cultural Studies, Houston, TX 77204. Offers administration and supervison (M Ed, Ed D); higher education (M Ed); historical, social, and cultural foundations of education (M Ed). *Accreditation:* NCATE. Part-time and evening/weekend programs available. *Faculty:* 6 full-time (4 women), 3 part-time/adjunct (0 women). *Students:* 57 full-time (42 women), 113 part-time (70 women); includes 82 minority (44 African Americans, 1 American Indian/Alaska Native, 12 Asian Americans or Pacific Islanders, 25 Hispanic Americans), 4 international. Average age 35. 102 applicants, 85% accepted, 65 enrolled. In 2009, 38 master's, 8 doctorates awarded. *Degree requirements:* For master's, comprehensive exam or thesis; for doctorate, comprehensive exam, thesis/dissertation. *Entrance requirements:* For master's, GRE General Test or MAT, minimum GPA of 3.0 in last 60 hours of course work; for doctorate, GRE General Test, interview, minimum GPA of 3.0 in last 60 hours. *Application deadline:* Applications are processed on a rolling basis. Application fee: $75 for international students. Electronic applications accepted. *Expenses:* Tuition, state resident: full-time $7676; part-time $320 per credit hour. Tuition, nonresident: full-time $14,324; part-time $597 per credit hour. Required fees: $3034. *Financial support:* In 2009–10, 2 fellowships with full tuition reimbursements (averaging $9,500 per year), 2 teaching assistantships with full tuition reimbursements (averaging $9,500 per year) were awarded; career-related internships or fieldwork, Federal Work-Study, institutionally sponsored loans, scholarships/grants, health care benefits, and unspecified assistantships also available. Support available to part-time students. Financial award application deadline: 2/1; financial award applicants required to submit FAFSA. *Faculty research:* Change, supervision, multiculturalism, evaluation, policy.

University of Houston–Clear Lake, School of Education, Program in Educational Leadership, Houston, TX 77058-1098. Offers educational leadership (Ed D); educational management (MS). *Degree requirements:* For master's, thesis optional; for doctorate, comprehensive exam, thesis/dissertation.

University of Houston–Victoria, School of Education and Human Development, Victoria, TX 77901-4450. Offers administration and supervision (M Ed); counseling (M Ed); curriculum and instruction (M Ed); special education (M Ed). Part-time and evening/weekend programs available. Postbaccalaureate distance learning degree programs offered. *Degree requirements:* For master's, comprehensive exam, project or thesis. *Entrance requirements:* For master's, GRE General Test. Additional exam requirements/recommendations for international students: Required—TOEFL. Electronic applications accepted. *Faculty research:* Reading and language arts education, evaluation and diagnosis of special children's abilities.

University of Idaho, College of Graduate Studies, College of Education, Department of Counseling and School Psychology, Special Education, and Educational Leadership, Program in Educational Leadership, Moscow, ID 83844-2282. Offers M Ed, Ed S. *Accreditation:* NCATE. *Students:* 10 full-time, 193 part-time. In 2009, 42 master's, 32 Ed Ss awarded. *Entrance requirements:* For master's, minimum GPA of 2.8. *Application deadline:* For fall admission, 8/1 for domestic students; for spring admission, 12/15 for domestic students. Application fee: $55 ($60 for international students). *Expenses:* Tuition, state resident: full-time $6120. Tuition, nonresident: full-time $17,712. *Financial support:* Application deadline: 2/15. *Unit head:* Dr. Russell A. Joki, Chair, 208-364-4099, E-mail: rjoki@uidaho.edu. *Application contact:* Dr. Russell A. Joki, Chair, 208-364-4099, E-mail: rjoki@uidaho.edu.

University of Illinois at Chicago, Graduate College, College of Education, Department of Educational Policy Studies, Chicago, IL 60607-7128. Offers policy studies (M Ed); policy studies in urban education (PhD); urban education leadership (Ed D).

University of Illinois at Springfield, Graduate Programs, College of Education and Human Services, Program in Educational Leadership, Springfield, IL 62703-5407. Offers educational leadership (MA); teacher leadership (MA). Part-time and evening/weekend programs available. Postbaccalaureate distance learning degree programs offered (no on-campus study). *Faculty:* 10 full-time (2 women), 12 part-time/adjunct (6 women). *Students:* 7 full-time (all women), 294 part-time (206 women); includes 23 minority (17 African Americans, 2 American Indian/Alaska Native, 1 Asian American or Pacific Islander, 3 Hispanic Americans), 1 international. Average age 35. 69 applicants, 68% accepted, 38 enrolled. In 2009, 122 master's awarded. *Degree requirements:* For master's, project or thesis, capstone course (teacher leadership option). *Entrance requirements:* For master's, minimum undergraduate GPA of 3.0. Additional exam requirements/recommendations for international students: Required—TOEFL (minimum score

Educational Leadership and Administration

University of Illinois at Springfield (continued)

500 paper-based; 176 computer-based; 61 iBT). *Application deadline:* Applications are processed on a rolling basis. Application fee: $50 ($60 for international students). Electronic applications accepted. *Expenses:* Tuition, state resident: full-time $6390; part-time $266.25 per credit hour. Tuition, nonresident: full-time $14,226; part-time $592.75 per credit hour. Required fees: $2044; $14.36 per credit hour. $722.50 per term. *Financial support:* In 2009–10, research assistantships with full tuition reimbursements (averaging $8,109 per year), teaching assistantships with full tuition reimbursements (averaging $8,109 per year) were awarded; career-related internships or fieldwork, Federal Work-Study, scholarships/grants, health care benefits, and unspecified assistantships also available. Support available to part-time students. Financial award application deadline: 11/15; financial award applicants required to submit FAFSA. *Unit head:* Dr. Scott Day, Program Administrator, 217-206-7520, Fax: 217-206-6775, E-mail: day.scott@uis.edu. *Application contact:* Dr. Lynn Pardie, Office of Graduate Studies, 800-252-8533, Fax: 217-206-7623, E-mail: pardie.lynn@uis.edu.

University of Illinois at Urbana–Champaign, Graduate College, College of Education, Department of Educational Organization and Leadership, Champaign, IL 61820. Offers Ed M, MS, Ed D, PhD, CAS. Part-time programs available. Postbaccalaureate distance learning degree programs offered (minimal on-campus study). *Faculty:* 10 full-time (3 women), 2 part-time/adjunct (both women). *Students:* 50 full-time (33 women), 168 part-time (104 women); includes 41 minority (23 African Americans, 10 Asian Americans or Pacific Islanders, 8 Hispanic Americans), 3 international. 146 applicants, 56% accepted, 53 enrolled. In 2009, 48 master's, 12 doctorates, 3 other advanced degrees awarded. *Entrance requirements:* For master's, minimum GPA of 3.0; for doctorate, GRE General Test, minimum GPA of 3.0, writing samples, interview. Additional exam requirements/recommendations for international students: Required—TOEFL (minimum score 620 paper-based; 260 computer-based; 105 iBT). *Application deadline:* Applications are processed on a rolling basis. Application fee: $60 ($75 for international students). Electronic applications accepted. *Financial support:* In 2009–10, 5 fellowships, 18 research assistantships, 3 teaching assistantships were awarded; tuition waivers (full and partial) also available. *Unit head:* Donald Hackmann, Interim Head, 217-333-0230, Fax: 217-244-3378, E-mail: dghack@illinois.edu. *Application contact:* Laura A. Ketchum, 217-333-0807, Fax: 217-244-3378, E-mail: lirle@illinois.edu.

University of Indianapolis, Graduate Programs, School of Education, Indianapolis, IN 46227-3697. Offers art education (MAT); biology (MAT); chemistry (MAT); curriculum and instruction (MA); earth sciences (MAT); education (MA, MAT); educational leadership (MA); elementary education (MA); English (MAT); French (MAT); math (MAT); physical education (MAT); physics (MAT); secondary education (MA), including art education, education, English education, social studies education; social studies (MAT); Spanish (MAT). *Accreditation:* NCATE. Part-time and evening/weekend programs available. *Faculty:* 4 full-time (3 women), 3 part-time/adjunct (2 women). *Students:* 52 full-time (28 women), 110 part-time (67 women); includes 3 minority (all African Americans), 2 international. Average age 33. *Entrance requirements:* For master's, GRE Subject Test, PRAXIS I, minimum GPA of 2.5, 3 letters of recommendation, interview, writing exercise. Additional exam requirements/recommendations for international students: Required—TOEFL (minimum score 550 paper-based; 213 computer-based). *Application deadline:* Applications are processed on a rolling basis. Application fee: $50. *Financial support:* Federal Work-Study available. Financial award application deadline: 5/1; financial award applicants required to submit FAFSA. *Faculty research:* Assessment of teacher education, perceptions of prospective teachers by parents. *Unit head:* Dr. Kathy Moran, Dean, 317-788-3285, Fax: 317-788-3300, E-mail: kmoran@uindy.edu. *Application contact:* Chemain Slater, 317-788-2051, E-mail: slaterc@uindy.edu.

The University of Iowa, Graduate College, College of Education, Department of Counseling, Rehabilitation, and Student Development, Iowa City, IA 52242-1316. Offers administration and research (PhD); community/rehabilitation counseling (MA); counselor education and supervision (PhD); rehabilitation counselor education (PhD); school counseling (MA); student development (MA, PhD). *Accreditation:* ACA (one or more programs are accredited); CORE (one or more programs are accredited). *Degree requirements:* For master's, thesis optional, exam; for doctorate, comprehensive exam, thesis/dissertation. *Entrance requirements:* For master's and doctorate, GRE General Test, minimum GPA of 3.0. Additional exam requirements/recommendations for international students: Required—TOEFL (minimum score 550 paper-based; 213 computer-based; 81 iBT). Electronic applications accepted.

The University of Iowa, Graduate College, College of Education, Department of Educational Policy and Leadership Studies, Program in Educational Administration, Iowa City, IA 52242-1316. Offers MA, PhD, Ed S. *Degree requirements:* For master's and Ed S, exam; for doctorate, comprehensive exam, thesis/dissertation. *Entrance requirements:* For master's, doctorate, and Ed S, GRE General Test, minimum GPA of 3.0. Additional exam requirements/recommendations for international students: Required—TOEFL (minimum score 550 paper-based; 213 computer-based; 81 iBT). Electronic applications accepted.

The University of Kansas, Graduate Studies, School of Education, Department of Educational Leadership and Policy Studies, Program in Educational Administration, Lawrence, KS 66045-3101. Offers MS Ed. Program begins in summer semester only. Part-time and evening/weekend programs available. *Students:* 5 full-time (all women), 19 part-time (9 women); includes 1 minority (Hispanic American), 4 international. Average age 28. 15 applicants, 87% accepted, 10 enrolled. In 2009, 7 master's awarded. *Degree requirements:* For master's, comprehensive exam. *Entrance requirements:* For master's, minimum GPA of 3.0. Additional exam requirements/recommendations for international students: Required—TOEFL (minimum score 570 paper-based; 230 computer-based; 80 iBT). *Application deadline:* For fall admission, 3/1 for domestic and international students. Application fee: $45 ($55 for international students). Electronic applications accepted. *Expenses:* Tuition, state resident: full-time $6492; part-time $270.50 per credit hour. Tuition, nonresident: full-time $15,510; part-time $646.25 per credit hour. Required fees: $847; $70.56 per credit hour. Tuition and fees vary according to course load and program. *Faculty research:* Policy studies, law, personnel, leadership, organizational studies. *Unit head:* Dr. Susan Twombly, Chair, 785-864-9721, Fax: 785-864-4697, E-mail: stwombly@ku.edu. *Application contact:* Denise Brubaker, Admissions Coordinator, 785-864-4458, Fax: 785-864-4697, E-mail: elps@ku.edu.

The University of Kansas, Graduate Studies, School of Education, Department of Educational Leadership and Policy Studies, Program in Educational Policy and Leadership, Lawrence, KS 66045-3101. Offers educational administration (Ed D, PhD); foundations (PhD); higher education (Ed D, PhD); policy studies (PhD). Part-time and evening/weekend programs available. *Students:* 116 full-time (70 women), 58 part-time (32 women); includes 28 minority (12 African Americans, 4 American Indian/Alaska Native, 7 Asian Americans or Pacific Islanders, 5 Hispanic Americans), 9 international. Average age 38. 69 applicants, 68% accepted, 39 enrolled. In 2009, 11 doctorates awarded. *Degree requirements:* For doctorate, comprehensive exam, thesis/dissertation. *Entrance requirements:* For doctorate, GRE General Test, minimum graduate GPA of 3.5. Additional exam requirements/recommendations for international students: Required—TOEFL (minimum score 570 paper-based; 230 computer-based; 80 iBT). *Application deadline:* For fall admission, 7/1 for domestic and international students; for spring admission, 11/1 for domestic and international students. Applications are processed on a rolling basis. Application fee: $45 ($55 for international students). Electronic applications accepted. *Expenses:* Tuition, state resident: full-time $6492; part-time $270.50 per credit hour. Tuition, nonresident: full-time $15,510; part-time $646.25 per credit hour. Required fees: $847; $70.56 per credit hour. Tuition and fees vary according to course load and program. *Financial support:* Fellowships, research assistantships with full and partial tuition reimbursements, teaching assistantships with full and partial tuition reimbursements, scholarships/grants and unspecified assistantships available. Financial award application deadline: 3/15. *Faculty research:* Historical and philosophical issues in education, education policy and leadership, higher education faculty, research on college students, education technology. *Unit head:* Dr. Susan Twombly, Chair, 785-864-9721, Fax: 785-864-4697, E-mail: stwombly@ku.edu. *Application contact:* Denise Brubaker, Admissions Coordinator, 785-864-4458, Fax: 785-864-4697, E-mail: elps@ku.edu.

University of Kentucky, Graduate School, College of Education, Program in Educational Leadership Studies, Lexington, KY 40506-0032. Offers administration and supervision (Ed S); instruction and administration (Ed D); school administration (M Ed). *Degree requirements:* For master's and Ed S, comprehensive exam; for doctorate, comprehensive exam, thesis/dissertation. *Entrance requirements:* For master's, GRE General Test, minimum undergraduate GPA of 2.75; for doctorate, GRE General Test, minimum graduate GPA of 3.0. Additional exam requirements/recommendations for international students: Required—TOEFL (minimum score 550 paper-based; 213 computer-based). Electronic applications accepted. *Faculty research:* School governance, teacher empowerment, planned change, systemic reform, issues of equity and fairness.

University of La Verne, College of Education and Organizational Leadership, Doctoral Program in Organizational Leadership, La Verne, CA 91750-4443. Offers Ed D. Part-time programs available. *Faculty:* 19 full-time (14 women), 35 part-time/adjunct (27 women). *Students:* 138 full-time (89 women), 151 part-time (102 women); includes 97 minority (31 African Americans, 3 American Indian/Alaska Native, 13 Asian Americans or Pacific Islanders, 50 Hispanic Americans). Average age 45. In 2009, 58 doctorates awarded. *Degree requirements:* For doctorate, thesis/dissertation. *Entrance requirements:* For doctorate, GRE or MAT, minimum graduate GPA of 3.0, resume, 2 endorsement forms. Additional exam requirements/recommendations for international students: Required—TOEFL (minimum score 550 paper-based; 213 computer-based). *Application deadline:* Applications are processed on a rolling basis. Application fee: $75. *Expenses:* Contact institution. *Financial support:* Institutionally sponsored loans available. Financial award application deadline: 3/2; financial award applicants required to submit FAFSA. *Unit head:* Dr. William Bearley, Chairperson, 909-593-3511 Ext. 4163, Fax: 909-392-2700, E-mail: wbearley@laverne.edu. *Application contact:* Christy Ranells, Program and Admission Specialist, 909-593-3511 Ext. 4644, Fax: 909-392-2761, E-mail: cranells@laverne.edu.

University of La Verne, College of Education and Organizational Leadership, Program in Educational Management, La Verne, CA 91750-4443. Offers educational management (M Ed); preliminary administrative services (Credential); professional administrative services (Credential). *Faculty:* 19 full-time (14 women), 35 part-time/adjunct (27 women). *Students:* 2 full-time (1 woman), 21 part-time (15 women); includes 11 minority (2 African Americans, 9 Hispanic Americans). Average age 38. In 2009, 49 master's awarded. *Entrance requirements:* For master's, California Basic Educational Skills Test, 2 years experience in teaching, pupil personnel services, health, or librarian services; California teaching credential. Additional exam requirements/recommendations for international students: Required—TOEFL (minimum score 550 paper-based; 213 computer-based). *Application deadline:* Applications are processed on a rolling basis. Application fee: $50. *Expenses:* Contact institution. *Financial support:* Institutionally sponsored loans available. Financial award application deadline: 3/2; financial award applicants required to submit FAFSA. *Unit head:* Patricia Ensey, Chair, 909-593-3511 Ext. 4385, E-mail: pensey@laverne.edu. *Application contact:* Christy Ranells, Program and Admission Specialist, 909-593-3511 Ext. 4644, Fax: 909-392-2761, E-mail: cranells@laverne.edu.

University of La Verne, Regional Campus Administration, Master's Programs in Education, California Statewide Campus, La Verne, CA 91750-4443. Offers educational management (M Ed), including preliminary administrative services credential; multiple or single subject teaching credential (M Ed); school counseling (MS), including pupil personnel services credential. *Faculty:* 3 full-time (1 woman), 97 part-time/adjunct (58 women). *Students:* 145 full-time (117 women), 174 part-time (139 women); includes 165 minority (31 African Americans, 2 American Indian/Alaska Native, 12 Asian Americans or Pacific Islanders, 120 Hispanic Americans). Average age 34. In 2009, 208 master's awarded. *Entrance requirements:* For master's, California Basic Educational Skills Test, 3 letters of recommendation, teaching credential. *Application deadline:* Applications are processed on a rolling basis. Application fee: $50. *Expenses:* Contact institution. *Financial support:* Fellowships, institutionally sponsored loans available. Financial award application deadline: 3/2; financial award applicants required to submit FAFSA. *Unit head:* Juline Behrens, Director, 800-695-4858 Ext. 5400, Fax: 909-981-8695, E-mail: jbehrens@laverne.edu. *Application contact:* Juline Behrens, Director, 800-695-4858 Ext. 5400, Fax: 909-981-8695, E-mail: jbehrens@laverne.edu.

University of Lethbridge, School of Graduate Studies, Lethbridge, AB T1K 3M4, Canada. Offers accounting (MScM); addictions counseling (M Sc); agricultural biotechnology (M Sc); agricultural studies (M Sc, MA); anthropology (MA); archaeology (MA); art (MA, MFA); biochemistry (M Sc); biological sciences (M Sc); biomolecular science (PhD); biosystems and biodiversity (PhD); Canadian studies (MA); chemistry (M Sc); computer science (M Sc); computer science and geographical information science (M Sc); counseling psychology (M Ed); dramatic arts (MA); earth, space, and physical science (PhD); economics (MA); educational leadership (M Ed); English (MA); environmental science (M Sc); evolution and behavior (PhD); exercise science (M Sc); finance (MScM); French (MA); French/German (MA); French/Spanish (MA); general education (M Ed); general management (MScM); geography (M Sc, MA); German (MA); health science (M Sc); health sciences (MA); history (MA); human resource management and labour relations (MScM); individualized multidisciplinary (M Sc, MA); information systems (MScM); international management (MScM); kinesiology (M Sc, MA); management (M Sc, MA); marketing (MScM); mathematics (M Sc); music (M Mus, MA); Native American studies (MA); neuroscience (M Sc, PhD); new media (MA); nursing (M Sc); philosophy (MA); physics (M Sc); policy and strategy (MScM); political science (MA); psychology (M Sc, MA); religious studies (MA); social sciences (MA); sociology (MA); theatre and dramatic arts (MFA); theoretical and computational science (PhD); urban and regional studies (MA); women's studies (MA). Part-time and evening/weekend programs available. *Degree requirements:* For doctorate, comprehensive exam, thesis/dissertation. *Entrance requirements:* For master's, GMAT (M Sc in management), bachelor's degree in related field, minimum GPA of 3.0 during previous 20 graded semester courses, 2 years teaching or related experience (M Ed); for doctorate, master's degree, minimum graduate GPA of 3.5. Additional exam requirements/recommendations for international students: Required—TOEFL. *Faculty research:* Movement and brain plasticity, gibberellin physiology, photosynthesis, carbon cycling, molecular properties of main-group ring components.

University of Louisiana at Lafayette, College of Education, Graduate Studies and Research in Education, Program in Administration and Supervision, Lafayette, LA 70504. Offers M Ed. *Degree requirements:* For master's, thesis or alternative. *Entrance requirements:* For master's, GRE General Test, teaching certificate. Additional exam requirements/recommendations for international students: Required—TOEFL (minimum score 550 paper-based; 213 computer-based). Electronic applications accepted.

University of Louisiana at Lafayette, College of Education, Graduate Studies and Research in Education, Program in Educational Leadership, Lafayette, LA 70504. Offers M Ed, Ed D. *Entrance requirements:* Additional exam requirements/recommendations for international students: Required—TOEFL (minimum score 550 paper-based; 213 computer-based).

University of Louisiana at Monroe, Graduate School, College of Education and Human Development, Department of Educational Leadership and Counseling, Program in Administration and Supervision, Monroe, LA 71209-0001. Offers M Ed. *Accreditation:* NCATE. Part-time and evening/weekend programs available. *Faculty:* 3 full-time (2 women). *Students:* 2 part-time (1 woman). Average age 46. *Degree requirements:* For master's, comprehensive exam. *Entrance requirements:* For master's, GRE General Test, minimum undergraduate GPA of 2.5. Additional exam requirements/recommendations for international students: Required—TOEFL (minimum score 500 paper-based; 173 computer-based; 61 iBT). *Application deadline:* For fall admission, 8/24 priority date for domestic students, 7/1 for international students; for winter admission, 12/14 priority date for domestic students; for spring admission, 1/19 for domestic students, 11/1 for international students. Applications are processed on a rolling basis. Application fee: $20 ($30 for international students). *Expenses:* Tuition, state resident: part-time $159 per credit hour. Tuition, nonresident: part-time $159 per credit hour. Required fees: $1300 per year. Tuition and fees vary according to course load. *Financial support:* Career-related internships or fieldwork, Federal Work-Study, and unspecified assistantships available. Financial

award application deadline: 4/1; financial award applicants required to submit FAFSA. *Faculty research:* School facilities utilization.

University of Louisiana at Monroe, Graduate School, College of Education and Human Development, Department of Educational Leadership and Counseling, Program in Educational Leadership, Monroe, LA 71209-0001. Offers Ed D. *Accreditation:* NCATE. *Faculty:* 3 full-time (2 women), 2 part-time/adjunct (1 woman). *Students:* 27 full-time (18 women), 63 part-time (43 women); includes 32 minority (31 African Americans, 1 Hispanic American). Average age 38. In 2009, 2 doctorates awarded. *Degree requirements:* For doctorate, comprehensive exam, thesis/dissertation, internship. *Entrance requirements:* For doctorate, GRE General Test, minimum GPA of 2.75, 3 letters of recommendation. Additional exam requirements/recommendations for international students: Required—TOEFL (minimum score 500 paper-based; 173 computer-based; 61 iBT). *Application deadline:* For fall admission, 8/24 priority date for domestic students, 7/1 for international students; for winter admission, 12/14 for domestic students; for spring admission, 1/19 for domestic students, 11/1 for international students. Applications are processed on a rolling basis. Application fee: $20 ($30 for international students). Electronic applications accepted. *Expenses:* Tuition, state resident: part-time $159 per credit hour. Tuition, nonresident: part-time $159 per credit hour. Required fees: $1300 per year. Tuition and fees vary according to course load. *Financial support:* In 2009–10, 10 research assistantships with full tuition reimbursements (averaging $3,750 per year) were awarded; career-related internships or fieldwork, Federal Work-Study, and unspecified assistantships also available. Financial award application deadline: 4/1; financial award applicants required to submit FAFSA. *Unit head:* Dr. Bob Cage, Director, 318-342-1288, Fax: 318-342-3131, E-mail: cage@ulm.edu. *Application contact:* Dr. Bob Cage, Director, 318-342-1288, Fax: 318-342-3131, E-mail: cage@ulm.edu.

University of Louisville, Graduate School, College of Education and Human Development, Department of Leadership, Foundations and Human Resource Education, Louisville, KY 40292-0001. Offers educational leadership and organizational development (Ed D, PhD); higher education (MA); human resource education (MS); p-12 educational administration (M Ed, Ed S). *Accreditation:* NCATE. Part-time and evening/weekend programs available. Postbaccalaureate distance learning degree programs offered. *Faculty:* 23 full-time (11 women), 14 part-time/adjunct (7 women). *Students:* 57 full-time (37 women), 189 part-time (125 women); includes 32 minority (28 African Americans, 2 Asian Americans or Pacific Islanders, 2 Hispanic Americans), 7 international. Average age 39. 103 applicants, 63% accepted, 59 enrolled. In 2009, 35 master's, 27 doctorates, 12 other advanced degrees awarded. *Entrance requirements:* For master's, doctorate, and Ed S, GRE General Test. Additional exam requirements/recommendations for international students: Required—TOEFL (minimum score 560 paper-based; 210 computer-based; 83 iBT). *Application deadline:* Applications are processed on a rolling basis. Application fee: $50. Electronic applications accepted. *Financial support:* In 2009–10, 28 students received support; fellowships, research assistantships, teaching assistantships, career-related internships or fieldwork, Federal Work-Study, scholarships/grants, and unspecified assistantships available. Financial award application deadline: 6/1; financial award applicants required to submit FAFSA. *Faculty research:* Evaluation of programs to improve elementary and secondary education; research on organizational and human resource development; student access, retention and success in post-secondary education; educational policy analysis; multivariate quantitative research methods. Total annual research expenditures: $4.2 million. *Unit head:* Dr. Bridgette Pregliasco, Acting Chair, 502-852-6204, Fax: 502-852-4563, E-mail: bridgette.pregliasco@louisville.edu. *Application contact:* Libby Leggett, Director, Graduate Admissions, 502-852-3101, Fax: 502-852-6536, E-mail: gradadm@louisville.edu.

University of Louisville, Graduate School, College of Education and Human Development, Department of Teaching and Learning, Louisville, KY 40292-0001. Offers art education (MAT); curriculum and instruction (PhD); early elementary education (MAT); instructional technology (M Ed); interdisciplinary early childhood education (MAT); middle school education (MAT); music education (MAT); reading education (M Ed); secondary education (MAT); special education (M Ed, MAT); teacher leadership (M Ed). Part-time and evening/weekend programs available. *Faculty:* 43 full-time (33 women), 43 part-time/adjunct (36 women). *Students:* 207 full-time (144 women), 410 part-time (306 women); includes 68 minority (43 African Americans, 2 American Indian/Alaska Native, 14 Asian Americans or Pacific Islanders, 9 Hispanic Americans), 5 international. Average age 33. 216 applicants, 68% accepted, 112 enrolled. In 2009, 269 master's, 6 doctorates awarded. *Degree requirements:* For doctorate, comprehensive exam, thesis/dissertation. *Entrance requirements:* For master's, GRE General Test, PRAXIS II (for some programs); for doctorate, GRE General Test. Additional exam requirements/recommendations for international students: Required—TOEFL (minimum score 560 paper-based; 210 computer-based; 83 iBT). Application fee: $50. Electronic applications accepted. *Financial support:* In 2009–10, 172 students received support; fellowships, research assistantships, teaching assistantships, career-related internships or fieldwork, Federal Work-Study, scholarships/grants, and unspecified assistantships available. Financial award application deadline: 6/1; financial award applicants required to submit FAFSA. *Faculty research:* Assessment of cognitive and language abilities in infants and preschool children; mathematics teachers' conceptions and beliefs, effect, and understanding of mathematics; incorporating nanoscience and nanotechnology into middle and high school science classrooms; urban teacher preparation through inquiry, action and advocacy; impacts of cognitive coaching on teacher practice and student achievement. Total annual research expenditures: $3.7 million. *Unit head:* Dr. Ann E. Larson, Acting Chair, 502-852-6431, Fax: 502-852-1497, E-mail: ann@louisville.edu. *Application contact:* Libby Leggett, Director, Graduate Admissions, 502-852-3101, Fax: 502-852-6536, E-mail: gradadm@louisville.edu.

University of Maine, Graduate School, College of Education and Human Development, Program in Educational Leadership, Orono, ME 04469. Offers M Ed, Ed D, CAS. *Accreditation:* NCATE. Part-time and evening/weekend programs available. *Students:* 18 full-time (11 women), 71 part-time (41 women); includes 2 minority (1 African American, 1 Hispanic American). Average age 41. 33 applicants, 76% accepted, 25 enrolled. In 2009, 23 master's, 3 doctorates, 20 CASs awarded. *Degree requirements:* For master's, thesis or alternative; for doctorate, thesis/dissertation. *Entrance requirements:* For master's, MAT; for doctorate, GRE General Test, MA, M Ed, or MS; for CAS, MA, M Ed, or MS. Additional exam requirements/recommendations for international students: Required—TOEFL. *Application deadline:* For fall admission, 2/1 priority date for domestic students. Applications are processed on a rolling basis. Application fee: $65. Electronic applications accepted. *Financial support:* Career-related internships or fieldwork, Federal Work-Study, institutionally sponsored loans, tuition waivers (full and partial), and unspecified assistantships available. Support available to part-time students. Financial award application deadline: 3/1. *Unit head:* Dr. Janet Spector, Coordinator, 207-581-2444, Fax: 207-581-2423. *Application contact:* Scott G. Delcourt, Associate Dean of the Graduate School, 207-581-3291, Fax: 207-581-3232, E-mail: graduate@maine.edu.

University of Maine at Farmington, Program in Education, Farmington, ME 04938-1990. Offers administration (MS Ed); educational technology (MS Ed); studies in literature and literacy (MS Ed). *Accreditation:* NCATE. *Entrance requirements:* For master's, teaching certificate, 2 years' teaching experience.

University of Manitoba, Faculty of Graduate Studies, Faculty of Education, Department of Educational Administration, Foundations and Psychology, Winnipeg, MB R3T 2N2, Canada. Offers adult and post-secondary education (M Ed); educational administration (M Ed); guidance and counseling (M Ed); inclusive special education (M Ed); social foundations of education (M Ed). *Degree requirements:* For master's, thesis or alternative.

University of Mary, Program in Education, Bismarck, ND 58504-9652. Offers college teaching (M Ed); curriculum, instruction and assessment (M Ed); early childhood education (M Ed); early childhood special education (M Ed); elementary education administration (M Ed); emotional disorders (M Ed); learning disabilities (M Ed); reading (M Ed); secondary education administration (M Ed); special education (M Ed); special education strategist (M Ed). Part-time programs available. *Degree requirements:* For master's, portfolio or thesis. *Entrance requirements:* For master's, interview, letters of reference. Additional exam requirements/recommendations for international students: Required—TOEFL (minimum score 550 paper-based). *Expenses:* Tuition: Full-time $10,062; part-time $430 per credit. Tuition and fees vary according to course load, degree level, program and student level. *Faculty research:* Innovative pedagogy in higher education, technology in education, content standards, children of poverty, children with diverse learning needs.

University of Mary Hardin-Baylor, Graduate Studies in Education, Belton, TX 76513. Offers educational administration (M Ed, Ed D); educational psychology (M Ed); exercise and sport science (M Ed); general studies (M Ed); reading education (M Ed). Part-time and evening/weekend programs available. *Degree requirements:* For master's, comprehensive exam; for doctorate, thesis/dissertation. *Entrance requirements:* For master's, GRE General Test, minimum GPA of 2.75, Texas teaching certificate. Electronic applications accepted.

University of Maryland, College Park, Academic Affairs, College of Education, Department of Counseling and Personnel Services, College Park, MD 20742. Offers college student personnel (M Ed, MA); college student personnel administration (PhD); community counseling (CAGS); community/career counseling (M Ed, MA); counseling and personnel services (M Ed, MA, PhD), including art therapy (M Ed), college student personnel (M Ed), counseling and personnel services (PhD), counseling psychology (M Ed), mental health counseling (M Ed), school counseling (M Ed); counseling psychology (PhD); counselor education (PhD); rehabilitation counseling (M Ed, MA, AGSC); school counseling (M Ed, MA); school psychology (M Ed, MA, PhD). *Accreditation:* ACA (one or more programs are accredited); APA (one or more programs are accredited); CORE (one or more programs are accredited); NCATE. Part-time and evening/weekend programs available. Postbaccalaureate distance learning degree programs offered (no on-campus study). *Faculty:* 34 full-time (21 women), 8 part-time/adjunct (6 women). *Students:* 152 full-time (117 women), 25 part-time (18 women); includes 67 minority (32 African Americans, 2 American Indian/Alaska Native, 20 Asian Americans or Pacific Islanders, 13 Hispanic Americans), 16 international. 319 applicants, 15% accepted, 32 enrolled. In 2009, 24 master's, 15 doctorates, 4 other advanced degrees awarded. *Degree requirements:* For master's, thesis (for some programs); for doctorate, thesis/dissertation. *Entrance requirements:* For master's, GRE General Test or MAT, minimum GPA of 3.0, 3 letters of recommendation; for doctorate, GRE General Test or MAT, minimum GPA of 3.5, 3 letters of recommendation. Additional exam requirements/recommendations for international students: Required—TOEFL. *Application deadline:* For fall admission, 12/15 for domestic and international students; for spring admission, 10/1 for domestic students, 6/1 for international students. Applications are processed on a rolling basis. Application fee: $60. Electronic applications accepted. *Expenses:* Tuition, area resident: Part-time $471 per credit hour. Tuition, state resident: part-time $471 per credit hour. Tuition, nonresident: part-time $1016 per credit hour. Required fees: $337.04 per term. *Financial support:* In 2009–10, 4 fellowships with partial tuition reimbursements (averaging $10,402 per year), 8 research assistantships (averaging $16,454 per year), 93 teaching assistantships with tuition reimbursements (averaging $16,109 per year) were awarded; career-related internships or fieldwork, Federal Work-Study, and scholarships/grants also available. Support available to part-time students. Financial award applicants required to submit FAFSA. *Faculty research:* Educational psychology, counseling, health. Total annual research expenditures: $1.5 million. *Unit head:* Dr. Dennis Kivlighan, Chair, 301-405-2858, E-mail: dennisk@umd.edu. *Application contact:* Dean of Graduate School, 301-405-0358.

University of Maryland, College Park, Academic Affairs, College of Education, Department of Education Policy and Leadership, College Park, MD 20742. Offers curriculum and educational communications (M Ed, MA, Ed D, PhD); social foundations of education (M Ed, MA, Ed D, PhD, CAGS). *Accreditation:* NCATE. Part-time and evening/weekend programs available. Postbaccalaureate distance learning degree programs offered (minimal on-campus study). *Students:* 120 full-time (81 women), 52 part-time (37 women). 1 applicant, 100% accepted, 0 enrolled. In 2009, 25 master's, 15 doctorates, 1 other advanced degree awarded. *Degree requirements:* For master's, thesis or alternative, internship and/or field experience; for doctorate, comprehensive exam, thesis/dissertation, practicum or internship. *Entrance requirements:* For master's, GRE General Test or MAT, minimum GPA of 3.0, scholarly writing sample, 3 letters of recommendation; for doctorate, GRE General Test or MAT, scholarly writing sample; minimum undergraduate GPA of 3.0, graduate 3.5. *Application deadline:* For fall admission, 12/15 for domestic and international students; for spring admission, 6/1 for international students. Applications are processed on a rolling basis. Application fee: $60. Electronic applications accepted. *Expenses:* Tuition, area resident: Part-time $471 per credit hour. Tuition, state resident: part-time $471 per credit hour. Tuition, nonresident: part-time $1016 per credit hour. Required fees: $337.04 per term. *Financial support:* In 2009–10, 5 fellowships with full and partial tuition reimbursements (averaging $17,387 per year), 1 research assistantship with tuition reimbursement (averaging $24,000 per year), 26 teaching assistantships with tuition reimbursements (averaging $16,554 per year) were awarded; career-related internships or fieldwork, Federal Work-Study, and scholarships/grants also available. Support available to part-time students. Financial award applicants required to submit FAFSA. *Faculty research:* Educational technology, adult and higher education. Total annual research expenditures: $41,998. *Unit head:* Dr. Thomas Weible, Interim Chair, 301-405-3589, Fax: 301-405-3573, E-mail: tweible@umd.edu. *Application contact:* Dean of Graduate School, 301-405-0358.

University of Maryland Eastern Shore, Graduate Programs, Department of Education, Program in Education Leadership, Princess Anne, MD 21853-1299. Offers Ed D. Evening/weekend programs available. *Degree requirements:* For doctorate, comprehensive exam, thesis/dissertation, internship. *Entrance requirements:* For doctorate, interview, writing sample, state certification in a standard area, 3 years recent teaching or successful professional experience in a k-12 school setting. Additional exam requirements/recommendations for international students: Required—TOEFL (minimum score 213 computer-based; 80 iBT). Electronic applications accepted.

University of Maryland University College, Graduate School of Management and Technology, Doctor of Management in Community College Policy and Administration Program, Adelphi, MD 20783. Offers DM. *Students:* 27 part-time (15 women); includes 11 minority (all African Americans). Average age 47. 50 applicants, 100% accepted, 27 enrolled. *Degree requirements:* For doctorate, comprehensive exam, thesis/dissertation. *Application deadline:* Applications are processed on a rolling basis. Application fee: $100. Electronic applications accepted. *Expenses:* Tuition, state resident: full-time $7704; part-time $428 per credit hour. Tuition, nonresident: full-time $11,862; part-time $659 per credit hour. *Financial support:* Federal Work-Study and scholarships/grants available. Support available to part-time students. Financial award application deadline: 6/1; financial award applicants required to submit FAFSA. *Unit head:* Dr. Charlene Nunley, Director, 240-684-2400, Fax: 240-684-2401. *Application contact:* Coordinator, Graduate Admissions, 240-684-2400, Fax: 240-684-2151, E-mail: newgrad@umuc.edu.

University of Massachusetts Amherst, Graduate School, School of Education, Program in Education, Amherst, MA 01003. Offers bilingual, English as a second language, and multicultural education (M Ed, CAGS); child study and early education (M Ed); children, families and schools (Ed D, CAGS); early childhood and elementary teacher education (M Ed); education policy and leadership (CAGS); educational administration (M Ed, CAGS); educational policy and leadership (Ed D); higher education (M Ed, CAGS); international education (M Ed); language, literacy and culture (Ed D); learning, media and technology (M Ed, CAGS); mathematics, science, and learning technologies (Ed D); policy studies (M Ed); policy studies in education (CAGS); reading and writing (M Ed); research and evaluation methods (Ed D); school counselor education (M Ed, CAGS); school psychology (CAGS); science education (CAGS); secondary teacher education (M Ed); social justice education (M Ed, Ed D, CAGS); special education (M Ed, Ed D, CAGS). *Accreditation:* NCATE. Part-time programs available. Postbaccalaureate distance learning degree programs offered (minimal on-campus study). *Faculty:* 74 full-time (41 women). *Students:* 377 full-time (268 women), 347 part-time (232 women); includes 115 minority (59 African Americans, 2 American Indian/Alaska Native, 16 Asian Americans or Pacific Islanders, 38 Hispanic Americans), 108 international. Average age 35. 708 applicants, 68% accepted, 266 enrolled. In 2009, 183 master's, 17 doctorates awarded. Terminal master's awarded for partial completion of doctoral program. *Degree requirements:* For master's, thesis

Educational Leadership and Administration

University of Massachusetts Amherst (continued)

or alternative; for doctorate, comprehensive exam, thesis/dissertation. *Entrance requirements:* Additional exam requirements/recommendations for international students: Required—TOEFL (minimum score 550 paper-based; 213 computer-based; 80 iBT), IELTS (minimum score 6.5). *Application deadline:* For fall admission, 1/15 for domestic and international students. Applications are processed on a rolling basis. Application fee: $50 ($65 for international students). Electronic applications accepted. *Expenses:* Tuition, state resident: full-time $2640; part-time $110 per credit. Tuition, nonresident: full-time $9936; part-time $414 per credit. Tuition and fees vary according to course load. *Financial support:* In 2009–10, 1 fellowship with full tuition reimbursement (averaging $8,036 per year), 92 research assistantships with full tuition reimbursements (averaging $8,555 per year), 83 teaching assistantships with full tuition reimbursements (averaging $4,661 per year) were awarded; career-related internships or fieldwork, Federal Work-Study, scholarships/grants, traineeships, health care benefits, tuition waivers (full), and unspecified assistantships also available. Support available to part-time students. Financial award application deadline: 1/15. *Unit head:* Dr. Linda L. Griffin, Graduate Program Director, 413-545-6984, Fax: 413-545-2873. *Application contact:* Jean M. Ames, Supervisor of Admissions, 413-545-0722, Fax: 413-577-0010, E-mail: gradadm@grad.umass.edu.

University of Massachusetts Boston, Office of Graduate Studies, Graduate College of Education, School Organization, Curriculum and Instruction Department, Program in Educational Administration, Boston, MA 02125-3393. Offers M Ed, CAGS. Part-time and evening/weekend programs available. *Degree requirements:* For master's, comprehensive exam, practicum; for CAGS, comprehensive exam. *Entrance requirements:* For master's, GRE General Test or MAT, 2 years of teaching experience, minimum GPA of 2.75; for CAGS, minimum GPA of 2.75. *Faculty research:* Power in the classroom, teacher leadership, professional development schools.

University of Massachusetts Boston, Office of Graduate Studies, Graduate College of Education, School Organization, Curriculum and Instruction Department, Program in Education, Track in Higher Education Administration, Boston, MA 02125-3393. Offers Ed D. Part-time and evening/weekend programs available. *Degree requirements:* For doctorate, comprehensive exam, thesis/dissertation. *Entrance requirements:* For doctorate, GRE General Test or MAT, minimum GPA of 2.75. *Faculty research:* Women, higher education and professionalization, school reform, urban classroom, higher education policy.

University of Massachusetts Boston, Office of Graduate Studies, Graduate College of Education, School Organization, Curriculum and Instruction Department, Program in Education, Track in Urban School Leadership, Boston, MA 02125-3393. Offers Ed D. Part-time and evening/weekend programs available. *Degree requirements:* For doctorate, comprehensive exam, thesis/dissertation. *Entrance requirements:* For doctorate, GRE General Test or MAT, minimum GPA of 2.75. *Faculty research:* School reform, race and culture in schools, race and higher education, language, literacy and writing.

University of Massachusetts Lowell, Graduate School of Education, Lowell, MA 01854-2881. Offers administration, planning, and policy (CAGS); curriculum and instruction (M Ed, CAGS); educational administration (M Ed); language arts and literacy (Ed D); leadership in schooling (Ed D); math and science education (Ed D); reading and language (M Ed, CAGS). *Accreditation:* NCATE. Part-time and evening/weekend programs available. Postbaccalaureate distance learning degree programs offered (no on-campus study). Terminal master's awarded for partial completion of doctoral program. *Degree requirements:* For doctorate, thesis/dissertation. *Entrance requirements:* For master's, doctorate, and CAGS, GRE General Test. Additional exam requirements/recommendations for international students: Required—TOEFL. Electronic applications accepted.

University of Memphis, Graduate School, College of Education, Department of Leadership, Memphis, TN 38152. Offers adult education (Ed D); educational leadership (Ed D); higher education (Ed D); leadership (MS); policy studies (Ed D); school administration and supervision (MS). *Accreditation:* NCATE. Part-time and evening/weekend programs available. Postbaccalaureate distance learning degree programs offered (minimal on-campus study). *Faculty:* 10 full-time (5 women), 9 part-time/adjunct (2 women). *Students:* 34 full-time (21 women), 115 part-time (69 women); includes 87 minority (86 African Americans, 1 Hispanic American), 1 international. Average age 40. 27 applicants, 85% accepted, 5 enrolled. In 2009, 12 master's, 13 doctorates awarded. *Degree requirements:* For master's, comprehensive exam, thesis optional; for doctorate, comprehensive exam, thesis/dissertation. *Entrance requirements:* For master's and doctorate, GRE. *Application deadline:* For fall admission, 4/1 for domestic students; for spring admission, 10/1 for domestic students. Application fee: $35 ($60 for international students). Electronic applications accepted. *Expenses:* Tuition, state resident: full-time $6246; part-time $347 per credit hour. Tuition, nonresident: full-time $15,894; part-time $883 per credit hour. Required fees: $1160. Full-time tuition and fees vary according to course load, degree level and program. *Financial support:* In 2009–10, 70 students received support; research assistantships with full tuition reimbursements available, teaching assistantships, Federal Work-Study, scholarships/grants, and unspecified assistantships available. Financial award application deadline: 2/15; financial award applicants required to submit FAFSA. *Faculty research:* School improvement, social justice, online learning, adult learning, diversity. *Unit head:* Katrina Mayer, Interim Chair, E-mail: kmeyer@memphis.edu. *Application contact:* Larry McNeal, Professor, School Administration and Supervision Programs, E-mail: lmcneal1@memphis.edu.

University of Michigan, Horace H. Rackham School of Graduate Studies, School of Education, Center for the Study of Higher and Postsecondary Education, Ann Arbor, MI 48109. Offers academic affairs and student development (PhD); development (AM); higher education (AM); individually designed concentration (PhD); medical and professional education (AM); organizational behavior and management (PhD); public policy (PhD); research, evaluation, and assessment (PhD); MBA/MA; MPP/MA. Terminal master's awarded for partial completion of doctoral program. *Degree requirements:* For master's, thesis optional; for doctorate, comprehensive exam, thesis/dissertation. *Entrance requirements:* For master's and doctorate, GRE General Test. Additional exam requirements/recommendations for international students: Required—TOEFL (minimum score 600 paper-based; 250 computer-based). *Application deadline:* For fall admission, 12/1 priority date for domestic students, 12/1 for international students. Application fee: $60 ($75 for international students). Electronic applications accepted. *Expenses:* Tuition, state resident: full-time $17,286; part-time $1099 per credit hour. Tuition, nonresident: full-time $34,944; part-time $2080 per credit hour. Required fees: $95 per semester. Tuition and fees vary according to course load, degree level and program. *Financial support:* Applicants required to submit FAFSA. *Unit head:* Dr. Stephen DesJardins, Chairperson, 734-647-1981, Fax: 734-764-2510, E-mail: sdesj@umich.edu. *Application contact:* Laura Mayers, Student Services Assistant, 734-764-7563, Fax: 734-763-1495, E-mail: ed.grad.admit@umich.edu.

University of Michigan, Horace H. Rackham School of Graduate Studies, School of Education, Programs in Educational Studies, Ann Arbor, MI 48109. Offers cross specialization (PhD); curriculum development (MA); early childhood education (MA, PhD); educational administration and policy (MA, PhD); educational foundations and policy (MA, PhD); English education (MA); English language learning in school settings (MA); learning technologies (MA, PhD); literacy, language, and culture (MA, PhD); mathematics education (MA, PhD); postsecondary science education (MS); research methods (MA); science education (MA, PhD); social studies education (MA); teaching and teacher education (PhD); MA/Certification; MBA/MA; PhD/MA. Terminal master's awarded for partial completion of doctoral program. *Degree requirements:* For master's, thesis (for some programs); for doctorate, comprehensive exam, thesis/dissertation. *Entrance requirements:* For master's and doctorate, GRE General Test. Additional exam requirements/recommendations for international students: Required—TOEFL (minimum score 600 paper-based; 250 computer-based). *Application deadline:* For fall admission, 12/1 priority date for domestic students, 12/1 for international students. Application fee: $60 ($75 for international students). Electronic applications accepted. *Expenses:* Tuition, state resident: full-time $17,286;

part-time $1099 per credit hour. Tuition, nonresident: full-time $34,944; part-time $2080 per credit hour. Required fees: $95 per semester. Tuition and fees vary according to course load, degree level and program. *Financial support:* Applicants required to submit FAFSA. *Unit head:* Dr. Addison Stone, Chairperson, 734-763-7500, Fax: 734-615-1290, E-mail: addison@umich.edu. *Application contact:* Laura Mayers, Student Services Assistant, 734-764-7563, Fax: 734-763-1495, E-mail: ed.grad.admit@umich.edu.

University of Michigan–Dearborn, School of Education, Doctoral Program in Education, Dearborn, MI 48126. Offers curriculum and practice (Ed D); educational leadership (Ed D); educational psychology/special education (Ed D); metropolitan education (Ed D). Part-time and evening/weekend programs available. *Faculty:* 7 full-time (4 women). *Students:* 1 (woman) full-time, 17 part-time (9 women); includes 5 minority (3 African Americans, 1 Asian American or Pacific Islander, 1 Hispanic American). Average age 46. 62 applicants, 31% accepted, 18 enrolled. *Degree requirements:* For doctorate, comprehensive exam, thesis/dissertation. *Entrance requirements:* For doctorate, GRE (taken within the last 5 years), master's degree with minimum GPA of 3.3, 3 letters of recommendation (1 from faculty), 3 years professional and/or teaching experience. Additional exam requirements/recommendations for international students: Required—TOEFL (minimum score 550 paper-based), Test of Spoken English (TES). *Application deadline:* For fall admission, 3/1 for domestic and international students. Application fee: $60. *Expenses:* Tuition, state resident: part-time $504.10 per credit hour. Tuition, nonresident: part-time $957.90 per credit hour. *Faculty research:* Educational leadership, metropolitan education, curriculum and practice, educational psychology, special education, assessment. *Unit head:* Gail Luera, Associate Dean/Interim Coordinator, 313-593-5098, E-mail: grl@umich.edu. *Application contact:* Catherine Parkins, Customer Service Assistant, 313-583-6349, Fax: 313-593-4748, E-mail: cparkins@umd.umich.edu.

University of Michigan–Dearborn, School of Education, Program in Educational Leadership, Dearborn, MI 48126. Offers MA. Part-time and evening/weekend programs available. Postbaccalaureate distance learning degree programs offered (minimal on-campus study). *Faculty:* 1 (woman) full-time, 5 part-time/adjunct (4 women). *Students:* 1 (woman) full-time, 17 part-time (8 women); includes 1 African American, 1 Hispanic American. Average age 31. 4 applicants, 100% accepted, 4 enrolled. In 2009, 4 master's awarded. *Entrance requirements:* For master's, Michigan Test for Teacher Certification, minimum GPA of 3.0; 3 letters of recommendation; interview; teacher certification. Additional exam requirements/recommendations for international students: Required—TOEFL (minimum score 560 paper-based; 220 computer-based; 84 iBT). *Application deadline:* For fall admission, 9/15 for domestic students; for winter admission, 12/22 for domestic students; for spring admission, 5/5 for domestic students. Applications are processed on a rolling basis. Application fee: $60 ($75 for international students). Electronic applications accepted. *Expenses:* Tuition, state resident: part-time $504.10 per credit hour. Tuition, nonresident: part-time $957.90 per credit hour. *Financial support:* Applicants required to submit FAFSA. *Unit head:* Dr. Bonnie Beyer, Professor, 313-593-5583, Fax: 313-593-4748, E-mail: beyere@umd.umich.edu. *Application contact:* Graduate Secretary, 313-583-6333, Fax: 313-593-4748, E-mail: emorden@umd.umich.edu.

University of Minnesota, Twin Cities Campus, Graduate School, College of Education and Human Development, Department of Organizational Leadership, Policy and Development, Program in Educational Administration, Minneapolis, MN 55455-0213. Offers MA, Ed D, PhD. *Students:* 65 full-time (38 women), 153 part-time (95 women); includes 40 minority (18 African Americans, 6 American Indian/Alaska Native, 8 Asian Americans or Pacific Islanders, 8 Hispanic Americans), 9 international. Average age 34. 126 applicants, 82% accepted, 75 enrolled. In 2009, 14 master's, 21 doctorates awarded. *Application contact:* Dr. Mary Trettin, Associate Dean, 612-625-6501, Fax: 612-626-1580, E-mail: mtrettin@umn.edu.

University of Mississippi, Graduate School, School of Education, Department of Educational Leadership and Counselor Education, Oxford, University, MS 38677. Offers counselor education (M Ed, PhD, Specialist); educational leadership (PhD); educational leadership and counselor education (M Ed, MA, Ed D, Ed S); higher education/student personnel (MA). *Accreditation:* ACA; NCATE. *Faculty:* 14 full-time (5 women), 1 part-time/adjunct (0 women). *Students:* 107 full-time (83 women), 192 part-time (129 women); includes 94 minority (91 African Americans, 2 Asian Americans or Pacific Islanders, 1 Hispanic American), 7 international. In 2009, 48 master's, 13 doctorates, 18 other advanced degrees awarded. *Degree requirements:* For doctorate, thesis/dissertation. *Entrance requirements:* For master's, GRE General Test, minimum GPA of 3.0; for doctorate, GRE General Test. Additional exam requirements/recommendations for international students: Required—TOEFL. *Application deadline:* For fall admission, 4/1 for domestic students; for spring admission, 10/1 for domestic students. Applications are processed on a rolling basis. Application fee: $25. Electronic applications accepted. *Financial support:* Scholarships/grants available. Financial award application deadline: 3/1; financial award applicants required to submit FAFSA. *Unit head:* Dr. Timothy Letzring, Acting Chair, 662-915-7069, E-mail: fdl@olemiss.edu. *Application contact:* Dr. Christy M. Wyandt, Associate Dean, 662-915-7474, Fax: 662-915-7577, E-mail: cwyandt@olemiss.edu.

University of Missouri, Graduate School, College of Education, Department of Educational Leadership and Policy Analysis, Columbia, MO 65211. Offers education administration (M Ed, MA, Ed D, PhD, Ed S); higher and adult education (M Ed, MA, Ed D, PhD, Ed S). Part-time programs available. *Faculty:* 15 full-time (8 women), 5 part-time/adjunct (4 women). *Students:* 212 full-time (128 women), 160 part-time (97 women); includes 35 minority (22 African Americans, 2 American Indian/Alaska Native, 4 Asian Americans or Pacific Islanders, 7 Hispanic Americans), 12 international. Average age 39. 186 applicants, 74% accepted, 91 enrolled. In 2009, 7 master's, 19 doctorates, 7 other advanced degrees awarded. *Degree requirements:* For doctorate, variable foreign language requirement, comprehensive exam (for some programs), thesis/dissertation. *Entrance requirements:* For master's, doctorate, and Ed S, minimum GPA of 3.0. Additional exam requirements/recommendations for international students: Required—TOEFL (minimum score 500 paper-based; 173 computer-based; 61 iBT), IELTS (minimum score 5.5). *Application deadline:* For fall admission, 2/15 priority date for domestic students; for spring admission, 10/15 for domestic students. Applications are processed on a rolling basis. Application fee: $45 ($60 for international students). Electronic applications accepted. *Financial support:* In 2009–10, 2 fellowships with full tuition reimbursements, 32 research assistantships with full tuition reimbursements, 4 teaching assistantships with full tuition reimbursements were awarded; institutionally sponsored loans, scholarships/grants, health care benefits, and unspecified assistantships also available. *Faculty research:* Administrative communication and behavior, middle schools leadership, administration of special education. *Unit head:* Dr. Jay Scribner, Department Chair, E-mail: scribnerj@missouri.edu. *Application contact:* Betty Kissane, 573-882-8231, E-mail: kissaneb@missouri.edu.

University of Missouri–Kansas City, School of Education, Kansas City, MO 64110-2499. Offers administration (Ed D); counseling and guidance (MA, Ed S); counseling psychology (PhD); curriculum and instruction (MA, Ed S); education (PhD); educational administration (Ed S); reading education (MA, Ed S); special education (MA). PhD with concentration in education (interdisciplinary) is offered through the School of Graduate Studies. *Accreditation:* NCATE. Part-time and evening/weekend programs available. *Faculty:* 62 full-time (52 women), 45 part-time/adjunct (34 women). *Students:* 207 full-time (154 women), 401 part-time (290 women); includes 142 minority (107 African Americans, 14 Asian Americans or Pacific Islanders, 21 Hispanic Americans), 18 international. Average age 34. 294 applicants, 61% accepted, 150 enrolled. In 2009, 184 master's, 9 doctorates, 49 other advanced degrees awarded. *Degree requirements:* For doctorate, thesis/dissertation, internship, practicum. *Entrance requirements:* For master's, GRE, minimum GPA of 2.75, 2 letters of reference, written statement of purpose; for doctorate, GRE, minimum GPA of 3.0; for Ed S, minimum GPA of 3.0. Additional exam requirements/recommendations for international students: Required—TOEFL (minimum score 550 paper-based; 213 computer-based; 80 iBT). *Application deadline:* For fall admission, 4/1 priority date for domestic and international students; for spring admission, 11/1 priority date for domestic and international students. Applications are processed on a rolling basis. Application fee: $45 ($50 for international students). *Expenses:* Tuition, state resident: full-time $5378; part-time $299 per credit hour. Tuition, nonresident: full-time $13,881; part-time $771 per credit hour. Required fees: $641; $71 per credit hour. Tuition and fees vary according to course load

and program. *Financial support:* In 2009–10, 19 research assistantships with partial tuition reimbursements (averaging $9,821 per year) were awarded; career-related internships or fieldwork, Federal Work-Study, institutionally sponsored loans, and tuition waivers (full and partial) also available. Support available to part-time students. Financial award application deadline: 3/1; financial award applicants required to submit FAFSA. *Faculty research:* Urban education, inquiry-based field study, theories of counseling and psychotherapy, school literacy, educational technology. Total annual research expenditures: $2.9 million. *Unit head:* Dr. Wanda Blanchett, Dean, 816-235-2234, Fax: 816-235-5270, E-mail: education@umkc.edu. *Application contact:* Erica Hernandez-Scott, Student Recruiter, 816-235-1295, Fax: 816-235-5270, E-mail: hernandeze@umkc.edu.

University of Missouri–St. Louis, College of Education, Division of Educational Leadership and Policy Studies, St. Louis, MO 63121. Offers adult and higher education (M Ed), including adult education; educational administration (M Ed, Ed S), including community education (M Ed), elementary education (M Ed), secondary education (M Ed); institutional research (Certificate). *Accreditation:* NCATE. Part-time and evening/weekend programs available. *Faculty:* 19 full-time (8 women), 7 part-time/adjunct (4 women). *Students:* 25 full-time (21 women), 196 part-time (137 women); includes 88 minority (84 African Americans, 1 Asian American or Pacific Islander, 3 Hispanic Americans), 4 international. Average age 36. In 2009, 66 master's, 25 Certificates awarded. *Degree requirements:* For master's, comprehensive exam (for some programs). *Entrance requirements:* Additional exam requirements/recommendations for international students: Required—TOEFL (minimum score 550 paper-based; 213 computer-based). *Application deadline:* For fall admission, 7/1 priority date for domestic and international students; for spring admission, 12/1 priority date for domestic and international students. Applications are processed on a rolling basis. Application fee: $35 ($40 for international students). Electronic applications accepted. *Expenses:* Tuition, state resident: full-time $5377; part-time $297.70 per credit hour. Tuition, nonresident: full-time $13,882; part-time $771.20 per credit hour. Required fees: $220; $12.20 per credit hour. One-time fee: $12. Tuition and fees vary according to course level, campus/location and program. *Financial support:* In 2009–10, 3 research assistantships (averaging $5,133 per year) were awarded. Financial award application deadline: 4/1; financial award applicants required to submit FAFSA. *Faculty research:* Educational policy research; philosophy of education; higher, adult, and vocational education; school initiatives, change, and reform. *Unit head:* Dr. E. Paulette Savage, Chair, 514-516-5944. *Application contact:* 314-516-5458, Fax: 314-516-6996, E-mail: gradadm@umsl.edu.

University of Missouri–St. Louis, College of Education, Interdisciplinary Doctoral Programs, St. Louis, MO 63121. Offers adult and higher education (Ed D); counseling (PhD); counselor education (Ed D); educational administration (Ed D); educational leadership and policy studies (PhD); educational psychology (PhD). *Faculty:* 72 full-time (33 women). *Students:* 23 full-time (18 women), 240 part-time (159 women); includes 76 minority (61 African Americans, 2 American Indian/Alaska Native, 7 Asian Americans or Pacific Islanders, 6 Hispanic Americans), 5 international. Average age 40. In 2009, 19 doctorates awarded. *Degree requirements:* For doctorate, thesis/dissertation. *Entrance requirements:* For doctorate, GRE General Test, 3 letters of recommendation; personal interview. Additional exam requirements/recommendations for international students: Recommended—TOEFL (minimum score 550 paper-based; 230 computer-based). *Application deadline:* For fall admission, 2/15 for domestic and international students; for spring admission, 10/1 for domestic and international students. Application fee: $35 ($40 for international students). Electronic applications accepted. *Expenses:* Tuition, state resident: full-time $5377; part-time $297.70 per credit hour. Tuition, nonresident: full-time $13,882; part-time $771.20 per credit hour. Required fees: $220; $12.20 per credit hour. One-time fee: $12. Tuition and fees vary according to course level, campus/location and program. *Financial support:* In 2009–10, 15 research assistantships (averaging $12,240 per year), 8 teaching assistantships (averaging $12,240 per year) were awarded. Financial award application deadline: 4/1; financial award applicants required to submit FAFSA. *Faculty research:* Higher education law and policy, gender and higher education, student retention, lifelong learning orientation, school counselor's role in violence prevention. *Unit head:* Dr. Kathleen Haywood, Director of Graduate Studies, 314-516-5483, Fax: 314-516-5227, E-mail: kathleen_haywood@umsl.edu. *Application contact:* Dr. Kathleen Haywood, Director of Graduate Studies, 314-516-5483, Fax: 314-516-5227, E-mail: kathleen_haywood@umsl.edu.

The University of Montana, Graduate School, School of Education, Department of Educational Leadership and Counseling, Program in Educational Leadership, Missoula, MT 59812-0002. Offers M Ed, Ed D, Ed S. *Degree requirements:* For doctorate, thesis/dissertation; for Ed S, thesis. *Entrance requirements:* For master's and Ed S, GRE General Test. Additional exam requirements/recommendations for international students: Required—TOEFL.

University of Montevallo, College of Education, Program in Instructional Leadership, Montevallo, AL 35115. Offers M Ed, Ed S. *Accreditation:* NCATE. Part-time and evening/weekend programs available. *Students:* 1 (woman) full-time, 76 part-time (57 women); includes 27 minority (18 African Americans, 9 Asian Americans or Pacific Islanders). In 2009, 12 master's, 10 Ed Ss awarded. *Degree requirements:* For master's and Ed S, comprehensive exam. *Entrance requirements:* For master's, GRE General Test or MAT. Additional exam requirements/recommendations for international students: Required—TOEFL (minimum score 550 paper-based). *Application deadline:* For fall admission, 7/15 for domestic students; for spring admission, 11/15 for domestic students. Application fee: $25. *Expenses:* Tuition, state resident: full-time $5592; part-time $233 per credit. Tuition, nonresident: full-time $11,184; part-time $466 per credit hour. Required fees: $482; $241 per semester. One-time fee: $25 part-time. *Financial support:* Federal Work-Study, scholarships/grants, and unspecified assistantships available. *Unit head:* Dr. Leland Doebler, Chair, 205-665-6380. *Application contact:* Rebecca Hartley, Coordinator for Graduate Studies, 205-665-6350, Fax: 205-665-6353, E-mail: hartleyrs@montevallo.edu.

University of Nebraska at Kearney, College of Graduate Study, College of Education, Department of Educational Administration, Kearney, NE 68849-0001. Offers educational administration (MA Ed, Ed S); supervisor (MA Ed). *Accreditation:* NCATE. Part-time and evening/weekend programs available. *Degree requirements:* For master's, thesis optional; for Ed S, thesis. *Entrance requirements:* For master's, letters of recommendation. Additional exam requirements/recommendations for international students: Required—TOEFL (minimum score 550 paper-based; 213 computer-based). Electronic applications accepted. *Faculty research:* Leadership and organizational behavior.

University of Nebraska at Omaha, Graduate Studies, College of Education, Department of Counseling, Omaha, NE 68182. Offers community counseling (MA, MS); counseling gerontology (MA, MS); school counseling (MA, MS); student affairs practice in higher education (MA, MS). *Accreditation:* ACA (one or more programs are accredited); NCATE. Part-time and evening/weekend programs available. *Faculty:* 5 full-time (1 woman). *Students:* 34 full-time (28 women), 152 part-time (128 women); includes 14 minority (10 African Americans, 1 Asian American or Pacific Islander, 3 Hispanic Americans). Average age 29. 50 applicants, 38% accepted, 13 enrolled. In 2009, 46 master's awarded. *Degree requirements:* For master's, comprehensive exam, thesis (for some programs). *Entrance requirements:* For master's, GRE General Test, MAT, department test, interview, minimum GPA of 3.0. Additional exam requirements/recommendations for international students: Required—TOEFL (minimum score 550 paper-based; 213 computer-based; 80 iBT). *Application deadline:* For fall admission, 3/1 for domestic students; for spring admission, 10/1 for domestic students. Applications are processed on a rolling basis. Application fee: $45. Electronic applications accepted. *Financial support:* In 2009–10, 79 students received support, including 2 research assistantships with tuition reimbursements available; fellowships, Federal Work-Study, institutionally sponsored loans, scholarships/grants, tuition waivers (partial), and unspecified assistantships also available. Support available to part-time students. Financial award application deadline: 3/1; financial award applicants required to submit FAFSA. *Unit head:* Dr. Jeanette Seaberry, Chairperson, 402-554-2727. *Application contact:* Penny Harmoney, Director, Graduate Studies, 402-554-2341, Fax: 402-554-3143, E-mail: graduate@unomaha.edu.

University of Nebraska at Omaha, Graduate Studies, College of Education, Department of Educational Administration and Supervision, Omaha, NE 68182. Offers MS, Ed D, Ed S. *Accreditation:* NCATE. Part-time and evening/weekend programs available. *Faculty:* 6 full-time (3 women). *Students:* 1 full-time (0 women), 152 part-time (81 women); includes 18 minority (17 African Americans, 1 Asian American or Pacific Islander). Average age 41. 47 applicants, 45% accepted, 19 enrolled. In 2009, 43 master's, 12 doctorates awarded. *Degree requirements:* For master's, comprehensive exam, thesis (for some programs); for doctorate, comprehensive exam, thesis/dissertation; for Ed S, comprehensive exam, thesis. *Entrance requirements:* For master's, minimum GPA of 3.0; for doctorate, GRE General Test, resume, 3 samples of research/written work, letters of recommendation. Additional exam requirements/recommendations for international students: Required—TOEFL (minimum score 500 paper-based; 173 computer-based; 61 iBT). *Application deadline:* For fall admission, 2/1 priority date for domestic students; for spring admission, 10/15 priority date for domestic students. Applications are processed on a rolling basis. Application fee: $45. Electronic applications accepted. *Financial support:* In 2009–10, 45 students received support; research assistantships with tuition reimbursements available, Federal Work-Study, institutionally sponsored loans, scholarships/grants, tuition waivers (partial), and unspecified assistantships available. Support available to part-time students. Financial award application deadline: 3/1. *Unit head:* Dr. John Hill, Chairperson, 402-554-2721. *Application contact:* Penny Harmoney, Director, Graduate Studies, 402-554-2341, Fax: 402-554-3143, E-mail: graduate@unomaha.edu.

University of Nebraska–Lincoln, Graduate College, College of Education and Human Sciences, Department of Educational Administration, Lincoln, NE 68588. Offers M Ed, MA, Ed D, Certificate. *Accreditation:* NCATE. *Degree requirements:* For master's, thesis optional; for doctorate, comprehensive exam, thesis/dissertation. *Entrance requirements:* For master's, GRE or MAT; for doctorate, GRE General Test, administrative certification. Additional exam requirements/recommendations for international students: Required—TOEFL (minimum score 550 paper-based; 213 computer-based). Electronic applications accepted. *Faculty research:* Educational policy, school finance, school law, school restructuring, leadership behavior.

University of Nebraska–Lincoln, Graduate College, College of Education and Human Sciences, Interdepartmental Area of Administration, Curriculum and Instruction, Lincoln, NE 68588. Offers Ed D, PhD, JD/PhD. *Accreditation:* NCATE. Postbaccalaureate distance learning degree programs offered. *Degree requirements:* For doctorate, comprehensive exam, thesis/dissertation. *Entrance requirements:* For doctorate, GRE, curriculum vitae. Additional exam requirements/recommendations for international students: Required—TOEFL (minimum score 550 paper-based; 213 computer-based). Electronic applications accepted.

University of Nevada, Las Vegas, Graduate College, College of Education, Department of Educational Leadership, Las Vegas, NV 89154-3002. Offers M Ed, MS, Ed D, Exec Ed D, PhD. *Accreditation:* NCATE. Part-time and evening/weekend programs available. *Faculty:* 21 full-time (9 women), 4 part-time/adjunct (2 women). *Students:* 47 full-time (33 women), 229 part-time (134 women); includes 66 minority (22 African Americans, 4 American Indian/Alaska Native, 16 Asian Americans or Pacific Islanders, 24 Hispanic Americans), 4 international. Average age 39. 129 applicants, 83% accepted, 91 enrolled. In 2009, 101 master's, 10 doctorates awarded. *Degree requirements:* For master's, comprehensive exam (for some programs), thesis (for some programs); for doctorate, comprehensive exam (for some programs), thesis/dissertation. *Entrance requirements:* For master's, GMAT or GRE General Test; for doctorate, GRE General Test, writing exam. Additional exam requirements/recommendations for international students: Required—TOEFL (minimum score 550 paper-based; 213 computer-based; 80 iBT), IELTS (minimum score 7). *Application deadline:* For fall admission, 3/1 priority date for domestic and international students; for spring admission, 11/15 priority date for domestic students, 10/1 for international students. Applications are processed on a rolling basis. Application fee: $60 ($95 for international students). Electronic applications accepted. *Financial support:* In 2009–10, 15 students received support, including 15 research assistantships with partial tuition reimbursements available (averaging $11,650 per year); institutionally sponsored loans, scholarships/grants, health care benefits, and unspecified assistantships also available. Financial award application deadline: 3/1. *Faculty research:* Student retention and persistence, student development, student culture and student veterans; state higher education policy, finance, governance, and competency modeling; higher education foundations; higher education law and ethics; faculty and mid-level administrative work life issues and mobility. *Unit head:* Dr. Howard Gordon, Chair/ Professor, 702-895-2729, Fax: 702-895-3492, E-mail: howard.gordon@unlv.edu. *Application contact:* Graduate College Admissions Evaluator, 702-895-3320, Fax: 702-895-4180, E-mail: gradcollege@unlv.edu.

University of Nevada, Reno, Graduate School, College of Education, Department of Educational Leadership, Reno, NV 89557. Offers M Ed, MA, MS, Ed D, PhD, Ed S. *Accreditation:* NCATE. Terminal master's awarded for partial completion of doctoral program. *Degree requirements:* For master's, comprehensive exam, thesis optional; for doctorate, comprehensive exam, thesis/dissertation. *Entrance requirements:* For master's, minimum GPA of 2.75; for doctorate, GRE General Test, minimum GPA of 3.0. Additional exam requirements/recommendations for international students: Required—TOEFL (minimum score 500 paper-based; 173 computer-based; 61 iBT), IELTS (minimum score 6). Electronic applications accepted. *Faculty research:* Law, finance, supervision, organizational theory, principalship.

University of New England, College of Arts and Sciences, Program in Education, Biddeford, ME 04005-9526. Offers curriculm and instruction strategy (MS Ed); educational leadership (MS Ed); general studies (MS Ed); literacy (MS Ed); teaching methodologies (MS Ed). Part-time programs available. Postbaccalaureate distance learning degree programs offered (minimal on-campus study). *Faculty:* 2 full-time (1 woman), 25 part-time/adjunct (15 women). *Students:* 473 full-time (362 women), 177 part-time (133 women); includes 29 African Americans, 12 Asian Americans or Pacific Islanders, 16 Hispanic Americans. In 2009, 319 master's awarded. *Degree requirements:* For master's, collaborative action research project, integrative seminar portfolio. *Entrance requirements:* For master's, teaching certificate, 2 years of teaching experience. Additional exam requirements/recommendations for international students: Required—TOEFL. *Application deadline:* For fall admission, 9/15 for domestic students; for spring admission, 1/15 for domestic students. Applications are processed on a rolling basis. Application fee: $40. Electronic applications accepted. *Expenses:* Contact institution. *Financial support:* Application deadline: 5/1. *Faculty research:* Distance learning, effective teaching, transition planning, adult learning. *Unit head:* Dr. Doug Lynch, Chair of Education Department, 207-283-0171 Ext. 2888, E-mail: dlynch@une.edu. *Application contact:* Stacy Gato, Assistant Director of Graduate Admissions, 207-221-4225, Fax: 207-221-4898, E-mail: gradadmissions@une.edu.

University of New England, College of Arts and Sciences, Program in Educational Leadership, Biddeford, ME 04005-9526. Offers CAGS. Part-time programs available. Postbaccalaureate distance learning degree programs offered (minimal on-campus study). *Faculty:* 3 part-time/adjunct (0 women). *Students:* 69 full-time (47 women), 29 part-time (21 women); includes 3 minority (1 African American, 1 American Indian/Alaska Native, 1 Hispanic American). In 2009, 16 CAGSs awarded. *Entrance requirements:* For degree, 3 years of teaching experience in an accredited school, master's degree. *Application deadline:* For fall admission, 8/15 priority date for domestic students; for winter admission, 11/15 priority date for domestic students; for spring admission, 4/15 priority date for domestic students. Applications are processed on a rolling basis. Application fee: $40. Electronic applications accepted. *Expenses:* Contact institution. *Financial support:* Application deadline: 5/1. *Unit head:* Dr. Doug Lynch, Chair of Education Department, 207-283-0171 Ext. 2888, E-mail: dlynch@une.edu. *Application contact:* Stacy Gato, Assistant Director of Graduate Admissions, 207-221-4225, Fax: 207-221-4898, E-mail: gradadmissions@une.edu.

University of New Hampshire, Center for Graduate and Professional Studies, Manchester, NH 03101. Offers business administration (MBA); counseling (M Ed); education (M Ed, MAT); educational administration and supervision (M Ed, CAGS); industrial statistics (Certificate); public administration (MPA); public health (MPH, Certificate); social work (MSW). Part-time and evening/weekend programs available. *Students:* 86 full-time (57 women), 150 part-time (87 women); includes 13 minority (3 African Americans, 6 Asian Americans or Pacific Islanders, 4 Hispanic Americans), 7 international. 127 applicants, 73% accepted, 60 enrolled. In 2009, 81

Educational Leadership and Administration

University of New Hampshire (continued)

master's, 5 other advanced degrees awarded. *Degree requirements:* For master's, thesis or alternative. *Entrance requirements:* Additional exam requirements/recommendations for international students: Required—TOEFL (minimum score 550 paper-based; 213 computer-based; 80 iBT), TOEIC, TSE. *Application deadline:* For fall admission, 6/1 for domestic students, 4/1 for international students; for spring admission, 12/1 for domestic students. Applications are processed on a rolling basis. Application fee: $65. Electronic applications accepted. *Expenses:* Tuition, state resident: full-time $10,380; part-time $577 per credit hour. Tuition, nonresident: full-time $24,350; part-time $1002 per credit hour. Required fees: $1550; $387.50 per semester. Tuition and fees vary according to course load and program. *Financial support:* In 2009–10, 20 students received support, including 1 fellowship, 1 teaching assistantship; research assistantships, Federal Work-Study, scholarships/grants, health care benefits, and unspecified assistantships also available. Support available to part-time students. Financial award application deadline: 3/1; financial award applicants required to submit FAFSA. *Unit head:* Kate Ferreira, Director, 603-641-4313, E-mail: unhm.gradcenter@unh.edu. *Application contact:* Graduate Admissions Office, 603-862-3000, Fax: 603-862-0275, E-mail: grad.school@unh.edu.

University of New Hampshire, Graduate School, College of Liberal Arts, Department of Education, Program in Educational Administration, Durham, NH 03824. Offers M Ed, Ed S. Part-time programs available. *Faculty:* 32 full-time. *Students:* 1 (woman) full-time, 34 part-time (17 women); includes 1 minority (African American), 1 international. Average age 37. 9 applicants, 78% accepted, 2 enrolled. In 2009, 9 master's, 15 Ed Ss awarded. *Degree requirements:* For master's, thesis or alternative. *Entrance requirements:* For master's and Ed S, GRE General Test. Additional exam requirements/recommendations for international students: Required—TOEFL (minimum score 550 paper-based; 213 computer-based; 80 iBT). *Application deadline:* For fall admission, 2/1 priority date for domestic students, 2/1 for international students; for spring admission, 12/1 for domestic students. Applications are processed on a rolling basis. Application fee: $65. *Expenses:* Tuition, state resident: full-time $10,380; part-time $577 per credit hour. Tuition, nonresident: full-time $24,350; part-time $1002 per credit hour. Required fees: $1550; $387.50 per semester. Tuition and fees vary according to course load and program. *Financial support:* In 2009–10, 2 students received support; fellowships, research assistantships, teaching assistantships, career-related internships or fieldwork, Federal Work-Study, scholarships/grants, and tuition waivers (full and partial) available. Support available to part-time students. Financial award application deadline: 2/15. *Faculty research:* School principalship, supervision, superintendency. *Unit head:* Dr. Todd Demitchell, Chair, 603-862-5043, E-mail: education.department@unh.edu. *Application contact:* Dr. Todd Demitchell, Chair, 603-862-5043, E-mail: education.department@unh.edu.

University of New Hampshire, Graduate School, College of Liberal Arts, Department of Education, Program in Teacher Leadership, Durham, NH 03824. Offers M Ed, Postbaccalaureate Certificate. Part-time programs available. *Faculty:* 32 full-time. *Students:* 16 part-time (10 women). Average age 39. 2 applicants, 100% accepted, 0 enrolled. In 2009, 4 master's, 1 other advanced degree awarded. *Degree requirements:* For master's, oral exam or thesis. *Entrance requirements:* For master's, GRE. Additional exam requirements/recommendations for international students: Required—TOEFL (minimum score 550 paper-based; 213 computer-based; 80 iBT). *Application deadline:* For fall admission, 3/1 for domestic and international students; for spring admission, 4/1 for domestic students. Applications are processed on a rolling basis. Application fee: $65. Electronic applications accepted. *Expenses:* Tuition, state resident: full-time $10,380; part-time $577 per credit hour. Tuition, nonresident: full-time $24,350; part-time $1002 per credit hour. Required fees: $1550; $387.50 per semester. Tuition and fees vary according to course load and program. *Financial support:* In 2009–10, 2 students received support; fellowships, research assistantships, teaching assistantships, Federal Work-Study and scholarships/grants available. Support available to part-time students. Financial award application deadline: 2/15. *Unit head:* Dr. Michael D. Andrew, Coordinator, 603-862-2371, E-mail: education.department@unh.edu. *Application contact:* Dr. Michael D. Andrew, Coordinator, 603-862-2371, E-mail: education.department@unh.edu.

University of New Mexico, Graduate School, College of Education, Department of Educational Leadership and Organizational Learning, Program in Educational Leadership, Albuquerque, NM 87131-2039. Offers MA, Ed D, EDSPC. *Accreditation:* NCATE. Part-time and evening/weekend programs available. Postbaccalaureate distance learning degree programs offered. *Students:* 25 full-time (19 women), 82 part-time (53 women); includes 46 minority (1 African American, 6 American Indian/Alaska Native, 2 Asian Americans or Pacific Islanders, 37 Hispanic Americans). Average age 44. 38 applicants, 34% accepted, 11 enrolled. In 2009, 23 master's, 4 doctorates, 15 other advanced degrees awarded. *Degree requirements:* For master's, comprehensive exam; for doctorate, comprehensive exam, thesis/dissertation. *Entrance requirements:* For master's, bachelor's degree; for doctorate, GRE, master's degree. *Application deadline:* For fall admission, 6/1 for domestic students; for spring admission, 10/1 for domestic students. Applications are processed on a rolling basis. Application fee: $50. Electronic applications accepted. *Expenses:* Tuition, state resident: full-time $2099; part-time $233.20 per credit hour. Tuition, nonresident: full-time $6650. Required fees: $25 per semester. Tuition and fees vary according to course load, program and reciprocity agreements. *Financial support:* In 2009–10, 28 students received support, including 7 fellowships (averaging $14,000 per year), 4 teaching assistantships with tuition reimbursements available (averaging $7,371 per year); career-related internships or fieldwork and scholarships/grants also available. Financial award application deadline: 3/1; financial award applicants required to submit FAFSA. *Faculty research:* K-20 educational and organizational leadership, individual and organizational learning, policy, legal and political contexts. *Unit head:* Dr. Patricia Boverie, Head, 505-277-2408, Fax: 505-277-5553, E-mail: pboverie@unm.edu. *Application contact:* Linda Wood, Information Contact, 505-277-0441, Fax: 505-277-5553, E-mail: woodl@unm.edu.

University of New Orleans, Graduate School, College of Education and Human Development, Department of Educational Leadership, Counseling, and Foundations, Program in Educational Leadership, New Orleans, LA 70148. Offers M Ed, PhD, GCE. *Accreditation:* NCATE. Evening/weekend programs available. Terminal master's awarded for partial completion of doctoral program. *Degree requirements:* For doctorate, variable foreign language requirement, thesis/dissertation. *Entrance requirements:* For master's and doctorate, GRE General Test. Additional exam requirements/recommendations for international students: Required—TOEFL (minimum score 550 paper-based; 213 computer-based; 79 iBT). Electronic applications accepted.

University of North Alabama, College of Education, Department of Secondary Education, Program in Education Leadership, Florence, AL 35632-0001. Offers Ed S. *Accreditation:* NCATE. Part-time and evening/weekend programs available. *Faculty:* 1 (woman) full-time, 2 part-time/adjunct (0 women). *Students:* 1 full-time (0 women), 23 part-time (13 women); includes 2 minority (both African Americans). Average age 37. In 2009, 6 Ed Ss awarded. *Application deadline:* For fall admission, 7/1 priority date for domestic students; for spring admission, 12/1 for domestic students. Applications are processed on a rolling basis. Application fee: $25. Electronic applications accepted. *Expenses:* Tuition, state resident: full-time $5040; part-time $210 per credit hour. Tuition, nonresident: full-time $10,080; part-time $420 per credit hour. Required fees: $906. *Financial support:* Application deadline: 4/1. *Unit head:* Dr. Peggy Campbell, Coordinator, 256-765-4575, Fax: 256-765-4159, E-mail: pccampbell@una.edu. *Application contact:* Kim Mauldin, Director of Admissions, 256-765-4608, Fax: 256-765-4960, E-mail: komauldin@una.edu.

The University of North Carolina at Chapel Hill, Graduate School, School of Education, Programs in Educational Leadership and School Administration, Chapel Hill, NC 27599. Offers educational leadership (Ed D); school administration (MSA). *Accreditation:* NCATE. Part-time programs available. *Degree requirements:* For master's, comprehensive exam; for doctorate, comprehensive exam, thesis/dissertation. *Entrance requirements:* For master's, GRE General Test or MAT, minimum GPA of 3.2 during last 2 years of undergraduate course work, 3 years of school-based professional experience; for doctorate, GRE General Test, minimum GPA of 3.2 during last 2 years of undergraduate course work, 3 years of school-based professional experience. Additional exam requirements/recommendations for international students:

Required—TOEFL (minimum score 550 paper-based; 213 computer-based). *Faculty research:* Gender, race, and class issues; school leadership; school finance and reform.

The University of North Carolina at Charlotte, Graduate School, College of Education, Department of Educational Leadership, Charlotte, NC 28223-0001. Offers curriculum and supervision (M Ed); educational administration (CAS); educational leadership (Ed D); instructional systems technology (M Ed); school administration (MSA). Part-time and evening/weekend programs available. *Faculty:* 24 full-time (12 women). *Students:* 10 full-time (8 women), 73 part-time (40 women); includes 32 minority (31 African Americans, 1 American Indian/Alaska Native). Average age 43. 26 applicants, 81% accepted, 15 enrolled. In 2009, 2 doctorates awarded. *Entrance requirements:* For master's and doctorate, GRE or MAT. Additional exam requirements/recommendations for international students: Required—TOEFL (minimum score 550 paper-based; 220 computer-based; 83 iBT). *Application deadline:* For fall admission, 7/1 for domestic students, 5/1 for international students; for spring admission, 11/1 for domestic students, 10/1 for international students. Applications are processed on a rolling basis. Application fee: $55. Electronic applications accepted. *Financial support:* In 2009–10, 6 students received support, including 4 research assistantships (averaging $13,500 per year), 2 teaching assistantships (averaging $8,500 per year); career-related internships or fieldwork, institutionally sponsored loans, scholarships/grants, and unspecified assistantships also available. Support available to part-time students. Financial award application deadline: 4/1; financial award applicants required to submit FAFSA. *Faculty research:* Educational leadership theory and practice, instructional systems technology, educational research methodology, curriculum and supervision in the schools, school law and finance. Total annual research expenditures: $800,000. *Unit head:* Dr. Dawson R. Hancock, Chair, 704-687-8863, Fax: 704-687-3493, E-mail: dhancock@uncc.edu. *Application contact:* Kathy B. Giddings, Director of Graduate Admissions, 704-687-5503, Fax: 704-687-3279, E-mail: gradadm@uncc.edu.

The University of North Carolina at Charlotte, Graduate School, College of Education, Program in Curriculum and Instruction, Charlotte, NC 28223-0001. Offers urban education (PhD), including adult and continuing education leadership, educational administration; urban literacy (PhD); urban math (PhD). Part-time and evening/weekend programs available. *Faculty:* 7 full-time (5 women). *Students:* 10 full-time (all women), 55 part-time (36 women); includes 14 African Americans, 1 Asian American or Pacific Islander, 2 international. Average age 41. 24 applicants, 71% accepted, 15 enrolled. In 2009, 8 doctorates awarded. *Degree requirements:* For doctorate, thesis/dissertation. *Entrance requirements:* For doctorate, GRE or MAT. Additional exam requirements/recommendations for international students: Required—TOEFL (minimum score 557 paper-based; 220 computer-based; 83 iBT). *Application deadline:* For fall admission, 7/15 for domestic students, 5/1 for international students; for spring admission, 11/15 for domestic students, 10/1 for international students. Application fee: $55. *Financial support:* In 2009–10, 9 students received support, including 9 teaching assistantships (averaging $12,880 per year). Financial award application deadline: 4/1; financial award applicants required to submit FAFSA. Total annual research expenditures: $65,335. *Unit head:* Dr. Jeanneine Jones, Interim Chair, Department of Middle, Secondary, and K-12 Education, 704-687-8875, Fax: 704-687-6430, E-mail: jpjones@uncc.edu. *Application contact:* Dr. David K. Pugalee, Coordinator, 704-687-8887, Fax: 704-687-3216, E-mail: david.pugalee@uncc.edu.

The University of North Carolina at Greensboro, Graduate School, School of Education, Department of Curriculum and Instruction, Greensboro, NC 27412-5001. Offers college teaching and adult learning (Certificate); curriculum and instruction (M Ed), including chemistry education, elementary education, English as a second language, French education, instructional technology, mathematics education, middle grades education, reading education, science education, social studies education, Spanish education; curriculum and teaching (PhD), including higher education, teacher education and development; English as a second language (Certificate); higher education (M Ed); supervision (M Ed). *Accreditation:* NCATE. Part-time programs available. *Degree requirements:* For doctorate, thesis/dissertation. *Entrance requirements:* For master's and doctorate, GRE General Test. Additional exam requirements/recommendations for international students: Required—TOEFL. Electronic applications accepted. *Faculty research:* Community college literacy program, middle school mathematics/computer mathematics.

The University of North Carolina at Greensboro, Graduate School, School of Education, Department of Educational Leadership and Cultural Foundations, Greensboro, NC 27412-5001. Offers curriculum and teaching (PhD), including cultural studies; educational leadership (Ed D, Ed S); school administration (MSA). *Accreditation:* NCATE. *Degree requirements:* For doctorate, thesis/dissertation. *Entrance requirements:* For master's, doctorate, and Ed S, GRE General Test. Additional exam requirements/recommendations for international students: Required—TOEFL. Electronic applications accepted.

The University of North Carolina at Pembroke, Graduate Studies, School of Education, Program in School Administration, Pembroke, NC 28372-1510. Offers MSA. Part-time and evening/weekend programs available. *Degree requirements:* For master's, internship. *Entrance requirements:* For master's, GRE General Test or MAT, minimum GPA of 3.0 in major, 2.5 overall; 3 years teaching experience. Additional exam requirements/recommendations for international students: Required—TOEFL.

The University of North Carolina Wilmington, School of Education, Department of Educational Leadership, Program in Educational Leadership, Wilmington, NC 28403-3297. Offers MSA, Ed D. *Degree requirements:* For master's, comprehensive exam.

University of North Dakota, Graduate School, College of Education and Human Development, Program in Educational Leadership, Grand Forks, ND 58202. Offers M Ed, MS, Ed D, PhD, Specialist. *Accreditation:* NCATE. Part-time and evening/weekend programs available. Postbaccalaureate distance learning degree programs offered (minimal on-campus study). *Degree requirements:* For master's and Specialist, comprehensive exam, thesis or alternative; for doctorate, comprehensive exam, thesis/dissertation, final exam. *Entrance requirements:* For master's, minimum GPA of 3.0; for doctorate, minimum GPA of 3.5. Additional exam requirements/recommendations for international students: Required—TOEFL (minimum score 550 paper-based; 213 computer-based; 79 iBT), IELTS (minimum score 6.5). Electronic applications accepted.

University of Northern Colorado, Graduate School, College of Education and Behavioral Sciences, School of Educational Research, Leadership and Technology, Educational Leadership and Policy Studies Program, Greeley, CO 80639. Offers educational leadership (MA, Ed D, Ed S). *Accreditation:* NCATE. Part-time and evening/weekend programs available. Postbaccalaureate distance learning degree programs offered. *Faculty:* 3 full-time (2 women). *Students:* 21 full-time (15 women), 65 part-time (46 women); includes 18 minority (3 African Americans, 1 American Indian/Alaska Native, 14 Hispanic Americans). Average age 39. 46 applicants, 93% accepted, 12 enrolled. In 2009, 29 master's, 4 doctorates, 14 other advanced degrees awarded. *Degree requirements:* For master's, comprehensive exam, thesis or alternative; for doctorate, comprehensive exam, thesis/dissertation; for Ed S, comprehensive exam, thesis. *Entrance requirements:* For master's, resume, interview; for doctorate, GRE General Test, resume, interview; for Ed S, resume. *Application deadline:* For fall admission, 5/1 for domestic and international students. Applications are processed on a rolling basis. Application fee: $50 ($60 for international students). Electronic applications accepted. *Expenses:* Tuition, state resident: full-time $5770; part-time $320.55 per credit hour. Tuition, nonresident: full-time $13,847; part-time $769.27 per credit hour. Required fees: $948.78; $52.72 per credit hour. *Financial support:* In 2009–10, 38 students received support, including 2 research assistantships (averaging $13,465 per year), 1 teaching assistantship (averaging $1,899 per year); fellowships, unspecified assistantships also available. Financial award application deadline: 3/1; financial award applicants required to submit FAFSA. *Unit head:* Dr. Linda Vogel, Program Coordinator, 970-351-2861, E-mail: elps@unco.edu. *Application contact:* Linda Sisson, Graduate Student Admission Coordinator, 970-351-1807, Fax: 970-351-2371, E-mail: linda.sisson@unco.edu.

University of Northern Colorado, Graduate School, College of Education and Behavioral Sciences, School of Teacher Education, Program in Educational Studies, Greeley, CO 80639.

Offers MAT, Ed D. Part-time and evening/weekend programs available. *Faculty:* 11 full-time (7 women). *Students:* 7 full-time (all women), 21 part-time (all women); includes 2 minority (1 Asian American or Pacific Islander, 1 Hispanic American), 2 international. Average age 38. 6 applicants, 83% accepted, 4 enrolled. In 2009, 35 master's, 1 doctorate awarded. *Application deadline:* Applications are processed on a rolling basis. Application fee: $50 ($60 for international students). Electronic applications accepted. *Expenses:* Tuition, state resident: full-time $5770; part-time $320.55 per credit hour. Tuition, nonresident: full-time $13,847; part-time $769.27 per credit hour. Required fees: $948.78; $52.72 per credit. *Financial support:* Research assistantships, teaching assistantships available. Financial award application deadline: 3/1; financial award applicants required to submit FAFSA. *Unit head:* Dr. Alexander Sidorkin, Director, 970-351-2908, Fax: 970-351-1877. *Application contact:* Linda Sisson, Graduate Student Admission Coordinator, 970-351-1807, Fax: 970-351-2371, E-mail: linda.sisson@unco.edu.

University of Northern Iowa, Graduate College, College of Education, Department of Educational Leadership, Counseling, and Postsecondary Education, Program in Educational Leadership, Cedar Falls, IA 50614. Offers educational administration (Ed D); elementary principal (MAE); secondary principal (MAE). Part-time and evening/weekend programs available. *Students:* 1 (woman) full-time, 127 part-time (50 women); includes 11 minority (7 African Americans, 1 Asian American or Pacific Islander, 3 Hispanic Americans), 2 international. 51 applicants, 69% accepted, 34 enrolled. In 2009, 36 master's, 2 doctorates awarded. *Degree requirements:* For master's, comprehensive exam (for some programs), thesis or alternative, minimum of 1 year successful teaching appropriate to the major; for doctorate, thesis/dissertation. *Entrance requirements:* For master's, minimum GPA of 3.0; for doctorate, GRE, master's degree, minimum GPA of 3.5. Additional exam requirements/recommendations for international students: Required—TQEFL (minimum score 500 paper-based; 180 computer-based; 61 iBT). *Application deadline:* For fall admission, 8/1 priority date for domestic students. Applications are processed on a rolling basis. Application fee: $30 ($50 for international students). Electronic applications accepted. *Financial support:* Career-related internships or fieldwork, Federal Work-Study, and tuition waivers (full and partial) available. Support available to part-time students. Financial award application deadline: 2/1. *Unit head:* Dr. Robert Decker, Coordinator, 319-273-2443, Fax: 319-273-5175, E-mail: robert.decker@uni.edu. *Application contact:* Laurie S. Russell, Record Analyst, 319-273-2623, Fax: 319-273-6792, E-mail: laurie.russell@uni.edu.

University of North Florida, College of Education and Human Services, Department of Leadership, Counseling and Instructional Technology, Program in Educational Leadership, Jacksonville, FL 32224. Offers educational leadership (M Ed, Ed D); educational technology (M Ed); instructional leadership (M Ed). *Accreditation:* NCATE. Part-time and evening/weekend programs available. *Faculty:* 18 full-time (11 women). *Students:* 26 full-time (16 women), 185 part-time (129 women); includes 44 minority (31 African Americans, 3 American Indian/Alaska Native, 1 Asian American or Pacific Islander, 9 Hispanic Americans), 1 international. Average age 38. 64 applicants, 45% accepted, 18 enrolled. In 2009, 52 master's, 15 doctorates awarded. *Degree requirements:* For doctorate, thesis/dissertation. *Entrance requirements:* For master's, GRE General Test, minimum GPA of 3.0 in last 60 hours, interview, 3 letters of recommendation; for doctorate, GRE General Test, master's degree, interview, 3 letters of recommendation, writing sample. Additional exam requirements/recommendations for international students: Required—TOEFL (minimum score 500 paper-based; 173 computer-based). *Application deadline:* For fall admission, 7/1 priority date for domestic students, 5/1 for international students; for spring admission, 11/1 priority date for domestic students, 10/1 for international students. Applications are processed on a rolling basis. Application fee: $30. Electronic applications accepted. *Expenses:* Tuition, state resident: full-time $6649.20; part-time $277.05 per credit hour. Tuition, nonresident: full-time $22,970; part-time $957.08 per credit hour. Required fees: $985; $41.03 per credit hour. *Financial support:* In 2009–10, 100 students received support, including 1 research assistantship (averaging $680 per year), 1 teaching assistantship (averaging $5,700 per year); career-related internships or fieldwork, Federal Work-Study, and tuition waivers (partial) also available. Support available to part-time students. Financial award application deadline: 4/1; financial award applicants required to submit FAFSA. *Unit head:* Dr. Edgar Jackson, Chair, 904-620-2990, Fax: 904-620-2982, E-mail: newton.jackson@unf.edu. *Application contact:* Kiersten Jarvis, Graduate Admissions Coordinator, 904-620-1360, Fax: 904-620-1362, E-mail: kiersten.jarvis@unf.edu.

University of North Texas, Robert B. Toulouse School of Graduate Studies, College of Education, Department of Teacher Education and Administration, Program in Educational Administration, Denton, TX 76203. Offers M Ed, Ed D, PhD. *Accreditation:* NCATE. *Degree requirements:* For master's, internship/practicum; for doctorate, comprehensive exam, thesis/dissertation. *Entrance requirements:* For master's, GRE General Test, letter of recommendation, resume; for doctorate, GRE General Test, admission exam, 3 letters of recommendation, resume, teaching experience, essay, academic writing sample. Additional exam requirements/recommendations for international students: Required—proof of English language proficiency required for non-native English speakers; Recommended—TOEFL (minimum score 550 paper-based; 213 computer-based). *Application deadline:* Applications are processed on a rolling basis. Application fee: $50 ($75 for international students). Electronic applications accepted. *Expenses:* Tuition, state resident: full-time $4298; part-time $239 per contact hour. Tuition, nonresident: full-time $9878; part-time $549 per contact hour. Required fees: $265 per contact hour. *Financial support:* Fellowships, research assistantships, teaching assistantships, career-related internships or fieldwork, Federal Work-Study, and institutionally sponsored loans available. Financial award application deadline: 4/15; financial award applicants required to submit FAFSA. *Faculty research:* Professional learning communities, early college high schools, growth model analysis of student achievement.

University of Oklahoma, Graduate College, College of Education, Department of Educational Leadership and Policy Studies, Program in Educational Administration, Curriculum and Supervision, Norman, OK 73019. Offers M Ed, Ed D, PhD. *Accreditation:* NCATE. Part-time and evening/weekend programs available. *Students:* 32 full-time (28 women), 109 part-time (80 women); includes 40 minority (18 African Americans, 16 American Indian/Alaska Native, 2 Asian Americans or Pacific Islanders, 4 Hispanic Americans). 32 applicants, 81% accepted, 20 enrolled. In 2009, 40 master's, 10 doctorates awarded. Terminal master's awarded for partial completion of doctoral program. *Degree requirements:* For master's, thesis optional; for doctorate, variable foreign language requirement, thesis/dissertation, general exam. *Entrance requirements:* For master's, 12 hours of course work in education; for doctorate, GRE General Test, master's degree, 3 letters of reference, writing sample. Additional exam requirements/recommendations for international students: Required—TOEFL (minimum score 550 paper-based; 213 computer-based). *Application deadline:* For fall admission, 6/1 priority date for domestic students, 4/1 for international students; for spring admission, 10/1 for domestic students, 9/1 for international students. Application fee: $40 ($90 for international students). Electronic applications accepted. *Expenses:* Tuition, state resident: full-time $3744; part-time $156 per credit hour. Tuition, nonresident: full-time $13,577; part-time $565.70 per credit hour. Required fees: $2415; $90.10 per credit hour. *Financial support:* In 2009–10, 58 students received support. Career-related internships or fieldwork, health care benefits, and unspecified assistantships available. Financial award applicants required to submit FAFSA. *Faculty research:* Institutional control and trust, ethics, leadership, decision making, school law. *Unit head:* David Tan, Interim Chair, 405-325-5986, Fax: 405-325-2403, E-mail: dtan@ou.edu. *Application contact:* Dr. Patrick Forsyth, Program Area Coordinator, 918-660-3989, Fax: 918-660-3988, E-mail: patrick.forsyth@ou.edu.

University of Oklahoma—Tulsa, Executive Ed D Program, Tulsa, OK 74135-2512. Offers Ed D. *Degree requirements:* For doctorate, comprehensive exam, thesis/dissertation. *Entrance requirements:* For doctorate, GRE, letters of reference.

University of Pennsylvania, Graduate School of Education, Division of Foundations and Practices in Education, Program in Educational Leadership, Philadelphia, PA 19104. Offers MS Ed, Ed D, PhD. Part-time programs available. *Students:* 136 full-time (74 women), 18 part-time (8 women); includes 26 minority (18 African Americans, 1 American Indian/Alaska Native, 3 Asian Americans or Pacific Islanders, 4 Hispanic Americans), 4 international. 428 applicants, 34% accepted, 80 enrolled. In 2009, 19 master's, 28 doctorates awarded. *Degree requirements:* For master's, comprehensive exam, thesis; for doctorate, comprehensive exam, thesis/dissertation, oral exams. *Entrance requirements:* For master's, GRE or MAT; for doctorate, GRE. *Application deadline:* For fall admission, 12/15 priority date for domestic students; for spring admission, 12/1 for domestic students. Applications are processed on a rolling basis. Application fee: $70. Electronic applications accepted. *Expenses:* Contact institution. *Financial support:* Institutionally sponsored loans, scholarships/grants, traineeships, health care benefits, and unspecified assistantships available. *Faculty research:* Public policy, curriculum and instruction, organization theory/leadership, school reform.

University of Phoenix, College of Natural Sciences, College of Education, Phoenix, AZ 85034-7209. Offers administration and supervision (MAEd); adult education and training (MAEd); curriculum and instruction (MAEd); curriculum and instruction-adult education (MAEd); curriculum and instruction-computer education (MAEd); curriculum and instruction-English and language arts education (MAEd); curriculum and instruction-English as a second language (MAEd); curriculum and instruction-mathematics education (MAEd); curriculum education (MAEd); early childhood (MAEd); elementary teacher education (MAEd); secondary teacher education (MAEd); special education (MAEd); teacher leadership (MAEd). *Accreditation:* Teacher Education Accreditation Council. Evening/weekend programs available. Postbaccalaureate distance learning degree programs offered (no on-campus study). *Faculty:* 47 full-time (34 women), 844 part-time/adjunct (636 women). *Students:* 13,657 full-time (10,698 women); includes 4,000 minority (3,063 African Americans, 74 American Indian/Alaska Native, 241 Asian Americans or Pacific Islanders, 622 Hispanic Americans), 307 international. Average age 36. In 2009, 17,246 master's awarded. *Degree requirements:* For master's, thesis (for some programs). *Entrance requirements:* For master's, 3 years of work experience, minimum GPA of 2.5. Additional exam requirements/recommendations for international students: Required—TOEFL (minimum score 550 paper-based; 213 computer-based; 79 iBT). *Application deadline:* Applications are processed on a rolling basis. Application fee: $45. Electronic applications accepted. *Expenses:* Tuition: Full-time $13,272. Required fees: $660. Full-time tuition and fees vary according to course level, degree level and program. *Financial support:* Institutionally sponsored loans and scholarships/grants available. Financial award applicants required to submit FAFSA. *Unit head:* Dr. Meredith Curley, Dean/Executive Director, 480-557-1217, Fax: 480-557-1588, E-mail: meredith.curley@phoenix.edu. *Application contact:* Chair, 602-387-7000, Fax: 602-387-6020.

University of Phoenix, School of Advanced Studies, Phoenix, AZ 85034-7209. Offers business administration (DBA); education (Ed D); educational leadership (Ed D), including curriculum and instruction, educational leadership, educational technology; health administration (DHA); higher education administration (PhD); industrial/organizational psychology (PhD); nursing (PhD); organizational leadership (DM), including information systems and technology, organizational leadership. Evening/weekend programs available. *Faculty:* 83 full-time (47 women), 540 part-time/adjunct (264 women). *Students:* 7,749 full-time (5,032 women); includes 3,180 minority (2,473 African Americans, 61 American Indian/Alaska Native, 221 Asian Americans or Pacific Islanders, 425 Hispanic Americans), 490 international. Average age 44. In 2009, 467 doctorates awarded. *Degree requirements:* For doctorate, thesis/dissertation. *Entrance requirements:* For doctorate, 3 letters of recommendation, minimum master's GPA of 3.0, 3 years professional work experience. Additional exam requirements/recommendations for international students: Required—TOEFL (minimum score 550 paper-based; 213 computer-based; 79 iBT). *Application deadline:* Applications are processed on a rolling basis. Application fee: $45. Electronic applications accepted. *Expenses:* Tuition: Full-time $13,272. Required fees: $660. Full-time tuition and fees vary according to course level, degree level and program. *Financial support:* Institutionally sponsored loans and scholarships/grants available. Financial award applicants required to submit FAFSA. *Unit head:* Dr. Jeremy Moreland, Dean/Executive Director, 480-557-3231, E-mail: jeremy.moreland@phoenix.edu. *Application contact:* Information Contact, 800-697-8223.

University of Phoenix–Central Florida Campus, The Artemis School, College of Education, Maitland, FL 32751-7057. Offers administration and supervision (MA Ed); curriculum and instruction (MA Ed); curriculum and instruction-computer education (MA Ed); curriculum and instruction-mathematics education (MA Ed); early childhood education (MA Ed); elementary teacher education (MA Ed); secondary teacher education (MA Ed). Evening/weekend programs available. *Degree requirements:* For master's, thesis (for some programs). *Entrance requirements:* For master's, 3 years of work experience, minimum undergraduate GPA of 2.5. Additional exam requirements/recommendations for international students: Required—TOEFL (minimum score 550 paper-based; 213 computer-based; 79 iBT). Electronic applications accepted.

University of Phoenix–Chattanooga Campus, College of Education, Chattanooga, TN 37421-3707. Offers administration and supervision (MA Ed); curriculum and instruction (MA Ed); elementary teacher education (MA Ed); secondary teacher education (MA Ed).

University of Phoenix–Denver Campus, The Artemis School, College of Education, Lone Tree, CO 80124-5453. Offers administration and supervision (MAEd); curriculum instruction (MAEd); elementary teacher education (MAEd); school counseling (MSC); secondary teacher education (MAEd). Evening/weekend programs available. *Degree requirements:* For master's, thesis (for some programs). *Entrance requirements:* For master's, minimum undergraduate GPA of 2.5, 3 years work experience. Additional exam requirements/recommendations for international students: Required—TOEFL (minimum score 550 paper-based; 213 computer-based; 79 iBT). Electronic applications accepted.

University of Phoenix–Hawaii Campus, The Artemis School, College of Education, Honolulu, HI 96813-4317. Offers administration and supervision (MA Ed); curriculum and instruction (MA Ed); elementary education (MA Ed); secondary education (MA Ed); special education (MA Ed); teacher education for elementary licensure (MA Ed). Evening/weekend programs available. *Degree requirements:* For master's, thesis (for some programs). *Entrance requirements:* For master's, minimum undergraduate GPA of 2.5, 3 years of work experience. Additional exam requirements/recommendations for international students: Required—TOEFL (minimum score 550 paper-based; 213 computer-based; 79 iBT). Electronic applications accepted.

University of Phoenix–Idaho Campus, The Artemis School, College of Education, Meridian, ID 83642-3014. Offers administration and supervision (MA Ed); curriculum and instruction (MA Ed); elementary teacher education (MA Ed); secondary teacher education (MA Ed). Evening/weekend programs available. *Degree requirements:* For master's, thesis (for some programs). *Entrance requirements:* For master's, minimum undergraduate GPA of 2.5, 3 years of work experience. Additional exam requirements/recommendations for international students: Required—TOEFL (minimum score 550 paper-based; 213 computer-based). Electronic applications accepted.

University of Phoenix–Kansas City Campus, The Artemis School, College of Education, Kansas City, MO 64131-4517. Offers administration and supervision (MA Ed). Postbaccalaureate distance learning degree programs offered.

University of Phoenix–Las Vegas Campus, The Artemis School, College of Education, Las Vegas, NV 89128. Offers administration and supervision (MA Ed); curriculum and instruction (MA Ed); school counseling (MSC); teacher education-elementary licensure (MA Ed). Evening/weekend programs available. *Degree requirements:* For master's, thesis (for some programs). *Entrance requirements:* For master's, minimum undergraduate GPA of 2.5, 3 years of work experience. Additional exam requirements/recommendations for international students: Required—TOEFL (minimum score 550 paper-based; 213 computer-based; 79 iBT). Electronic applications accepted.

University of Phoenix–Memphis Campus, College of Education, Cordova, TN 38018. Offers administration and supervision (MA Ed); curriculum and instruction (MA Ed); elementary teacher education (MA Ed); secondary teacher education (MA Ed).

Educational Leadership and Administration

University of Phoenix–Metro Detroit Campus, College of Education, Troy, MI 48098-2623. Offers administration and supervision (MA Ed); elementary teacher education (MA Ed); secondary teacher education (MA Ed); special education (MA Ed). Evening/weekend programs available. *Faculty:* 3 full-time (1 woman), 2 part-time/adjunct (both women). *Students:* 34 full-time (30 women); includes 23 minority (all African Americans). Average age 44. In 2009, 44 master's awarded. *Degree requirements:* For master's, thesis (for some programs). *Entrance requirements:* For master's, 3 years of work experience, minimum undergraduate GPA of 2.5. Additional exam requirements/recommendations for international students: Required—TOEFL (minimum score 550 paper-based; 213 computer-based; 79 iBT). *Application deadline:* Applications are processed on a rolling basis. Application fee: $45. Electronic applications accepted. *Expenses:* Tuition: Full-time $14,136. Required fees: $660. *Financial support:* Institutionally sponsored loans and scholarships/grants available. Financial award applicants required to submit FAFSA. *Unit head:* Dr. Meredith Curley, Dean/Executive Director, 480-557-1217, E-mail: meredith.curley@phoenix.edu. *Application contact:* Chair, 800-834-2438, Fax: 248-267-0147.

University of Phoenix–Nashville Campus, The Artemis School, College of Education, Nashville, TN 37214-5048. Offers administration and supervision (MA Ed); curriculum and instruction (MA Ed); elementary teacher education (MA Ed); secondary teacher education (MA Ed). Evening/weekend programs available. *Degree requirements:* For master's, thesis (for some programs). *Entrance requirements:* For master's, minimum undergraduate GPA of 2.5, 3 years work experience. Additional exam requirements/recommendations for international students: Required—TOEFL (minimum score 500 paper-based; 213 computer-based; 79 iBT). Electronic applications accepted.

University of Phoenix–New Mexico Campus, The Artemis School, College of Education, Albuquerque, NM 87113-1570. Offers administration and supervision (MAEd); curriculum and instruction (MAEd); elementary teacher education (MAEd); school counseling (MSC); secondary teacher education (MAEd). Evening/weekend programs available. *Degree requirements:* For master's, thesis (for some programs). *Entrance requirements:* For master's, minimum undergraduate GPA of 2.5, 3 years of work experience. Additional exam requirements/recommendations for international students: Required—TOEFL (minimum score 550 paper-based; 213 computer-based; 79 iBT). Electronic applications accepted.

University of Phoenix–Northern Nevada Campus, College of Education, Reno, NV 89521-5862. Offers administration and supervision (MA Ed); curriculum and instruction (MA Ed); elementary teacher education (MA Ed); secondary teacher education (MA Ed).

University of Phoenix–Northern Virginia Campus, College of Education, Reston, VA 20190. Offers administration and supervision (MA Ed).

University of Phoenix–North Florida Campus, The Artemis School, College of Education, Jacksonville, FL 32216-0959. Offers administration and supervision (MA Ed); curriculum and instruction (MA Ed), including computer education, mathematics education; early childhood education (MA Ed); elementary teacher education (MA Ed); secondary teacher education (MA Ed). Evening/weekend programs available. *Degree requirements:* For master's, thesis (for some programs). *Entrance requirements:* For master's, 3 years of work experience, minimum undergraduate GPA of 2.5. Additional exam requirements/recommendations for international students: Required—TOEFL (minimum score 550 paper-based; 213 computer-based; 49 iBT). Electronic applications accepted.

University of Phoenix–Omaha Campus, College of Education, Omaha, NE 68154-5240. Offers administration and supervision (MA Ed); curriculum and instruction (MA Ed), including adult education, computer education, curriculum and instruction, English and language arts education, English as a second language, mathematics education; elementary teacher education (MA Ed); secondary teacher education (MA Ed); special education (MA Ed).

University of Phoenix–Phoenix Campus, College of Social Sciences, College of Education, Phoenix, AZ 85040-1958. Offers administration and supervision (MA Ed); elementary teacher education (MA Ed); secondary teacher education (MA Ed); special education (MA Ed). Evening/weekend programs available. *Faculty:* 39 full-time (23 women), 422 part-time/adjunct (255 women). *Students:* 443 full-time (297 women); includes 79 minority (32 African Americans, 8 American Indian/Alaska Native, 8 Asian Americans or Pacific Islanders, 31 Hispanic Americans), 6 international. Average age 35. In 2009, 199 master's awarded. *Degree requirements:* For master's, thesis (for some programs). *Entrance requirements:* For master's, 3 years of work experience, minimum undergraduate GPA of 2.5. Additional exam requirements/recommendations for international students: Required—TOEFL (minimum score 550 paper-based; 213 computer-based; 79 iBT). *Application deadline:* Applications are processed on a rolling basis. Application fee: $45. Electronic applications accepted. *Expenses:* Tuition: Full-time $10,272. Required fees: $760. *Financial support:* Institutionally sponsored loans and scholarships/grants available. Financial award applicants required to submit FAFSA. *Unit head:* Dr. Meredith Curley, Dean/Executive Director, 480-557-1217, Fax: 480-557-1588, E-mail: meredith.curley@phoenix.edu. *Application contact:* College Chair, 480-804-2000.

University of Phoenix–Puerto Rico Campus, The Artemis School, College of Education, Guaynabo, PR 00968. Offers administration and supervision (MA Ed); early childhood education (MA Ed); school counselor (MSC). Evening/weekend programs available. *Degree requirements:* For master's, thesis (for some programs). *Entrance requirements:* For master's, minimum undergraduate GPA of 2.5, 3 years work experience. Additional exam requirements/recommendations for international students: Required—TOEFL (minimum score 550 paper-based; 213 computer-based; 79 iBT). Electronic applications accepted.

University of Phoenix–Richmond Campus, The Artemis School, College of Education, Richmond, VA 23230. Offers administration and supervision (MA Ed); curriculum and instruction (MA Ed).

University of Phoenix–Southern Arizona Campus, The Artemis School, College of Education, Tucson, AZ 85711. Offers administration and supervision (MA Ed); adult education and training (MA Ed); curriculum instruction (MA Ed); educational counseling (MA Ed); elementary teacher education (MA Ed); school counseling (MSC); secondary teacher education (MA Ed); special education (MA Ed, Certificate). Evening/weekend programs available. *Degree requirements:* For master's, thesis (for some programs). *Entrance requirements:* For master's, minimum undergraduate GPA of 2.5, 3 years of work experience. Additional exam requirements/recommendations for international students: Required—TOEFL (minimum score 550 paper-based; 213 computer-based; 79 iBT). Electronic applications accepted.

University of Phoenix–Southern California Campus, College of Education, Costa Mesa, CA 92626. Offers administration and supervision (MA Ed); adult education and training (MA Ed); curriculum and instruction (MA Ed), including computer education, curriculum and instruction, English and language arts, English as a second language, mathematics education; early childhood education (MA Ed); special education (MA Ed); teacher leadership (MA Ed). Evening/weekend programs available. *Faculty:* 47 full-time (34 women), 844 part-time/adjunct (636 women). *Students:* 558 full-time (391 women); includes 222 minority (60 African Americans, 4 American Indian/Alaska Native, 26 Asian Americans or Pacific Islanders, 132 Hispanic Americans), 9 international. Average age 34. In 2009, 303 master's awarded. *Degree requirements:* For master's, thesis (for some programs). *Entrance requirements:* For master's, minimum undergraduate GPA of 2.5, 3 years work experience. Additional exam requirements/recommendations for international students: Required—TOEFL (minimum score 550 paper-based; 213 computer-based; 79 iBT). *Application deadline:* Applications are processed on a rolling basis. Application fee: $45. Electronic applications accepted. *Expenses:* Tuition: Full-time $15,120. Required fees: $660. *Financial support:* Institutionally sponsored loans and scholarships/grants available. Financial award applicants required to submit FAFSA. *Unit head:* Dr. Meredith Curley, Dean/Executive Director, 480-557-1217, Fax: 480-557-1588, E-mail: meredith.curley@phoenix.edu. *Application contact:* Campus College Chair, 714-378-1878, Fax: 714-378-5875.

University of Phoenix–Southern Colorado Campus, The Artemis School, College of Education, Colorado Springs, CO 80919-2335. Offers administration and supervision (MA Ed); curriculum and instruction (MA Ed); elementary teacher education (MA Ed); principal licensure certification (Certificate); school counseling (MSC); secondary teacher education (MA Ed). Evening/weekend programs available. *Degree requirements:* For master's, thesis (for some programs). *Entrance requirements:* For master's, minimum undergraduate GPA of 2.5, 3 years of work experience. Additional exam requirements/recommendations for international students: Required—TOEFL (minimum score 550 paper-based; 213 computer-based; 79 iBT). Electronic applications accepted.

University of Phoenix–South Florida Campus, The Artemis School, College of Education, Fort Lauderdale, FL 33309. Offers administration and supervision (MA Ed); curriculum and instruction (MA Ed), including computer education, curriculum and instruction, mathematics education; early childhood education (MA Ed); elementary teacher education (MA Ed); secondary teacher education (MA Ed). Evening/weekend programs available. *Degree requirements:* For master's, thesis (for some programs). *Entrance requirements:* For master's, 3 years of work experience, minimum undergraduate GPA of 2.5. Additional exam requirements/recommendations for international students: Required—TOEFL (minimum score 550 paper-based; 213 computer-based; 79 iBT). Electronic applications accepted.

University of Phoenix–Springfield Campus, College of Education, Springfield, MO 65804-7211. Offers administration and supervision (MA Ed); curriculum and instruction (MA Ed), including computer education, curriculum and instruction, English and language arts education, English as a second language, mathematics education; English and language arts education (MA Ed).

University of Phoenix–Utah Campus, The Artemis School, College of Education, Salt Lake City, UT 84123-4617. Offers administration and supervision (MA Ed); curriculum and instruction (MA Ed); elementary teacher education (MA Ed); school counseling (MSC); secondary teacher education (MA Ed); special education (MA Ed). Evening/weekend programs available. *Degree requirements:* For master's, thesis (for some programs). *Entrance requirements:* For master's, minimum undergraduate GPA of 2.5, 3 years work experience. Additional exam requirements/recommendations for international students: Required—TOEFL (minimum score 550 paper-based; 213 computer-based; 79 iBT). Electronic applications accepted.

University of Phoenix–Vancouver Campus, The Artemis School, College of Education, Burnaby, BC V5C 6G9, Canada. Offers administration and supervision (MA Ed); curriculum and instruction (MA Ed), including computer education, curriculum and instruction. Evening/weekend programs available. *Degree requirements:* For master's, thesis (for some programs). *Entrance requirements:* For master's, minimum undergraduate GPA of 2.5, 3 years work experience. Additional exam requirements/recommendations for international students: Required—TOEFL (minimum score 550 paper-based; 213 computer-based; 79 iBT). Electronic applications accepted.

University of Phoenix–West Florida Campus, The Artemis School, College of Education, Temple Terrace, FL 33637. Offers administration and supervision (MA Ed); curriculum and instruction (MA Ed), including computer education, curriculum and instruction, mathematics education; curriculum and technology (MA Ed); early childhood education (MA Ed); elementary teacher education (MA Ed); secondary teacher education (MA Ed). Evening/weekend programs available. *Degree requirements:* For master's, thesis (for some programs). *Entrance requirements:* For master's, 3 years of work experience, minimum undergraduate GPA of 2.5. Additional exam requirements/recommendations for international students: Required—TOEFL (minimum score 550 paper-based; 213 computer-based; 79 iBT).

University of Pittsburgh, School of Education, Department of Administrative and Policy Studies, Program in School Leadership, Pittsburgh, PA 15260. Offers M Ed, Ed D. Part-time and evening/weekend programs available. *Students:* 9 full-time (6 women), 142 part-time (79 women); includes 13 minority (12 African Americans, 1 Hispanic American), 2 international. Average age 37. 44 applicants, 77% accepted, 31 enrolled. In 2009, 17 master's, 7 doctorates awarded. *Degree requirements:* For master's, thesis; for doctorate, thesis/dissertation. *Entrance requirements:* For doctorate, GRE General Test. Additional exam requirements/recommendations for international students: Required—TOEFL (minimum score 213 computer-based; 80 iBT). *Application deadline:* For fall admission, 2/15 priority date for domestic and international students; for spring admission, 11/1 priority date for domestic and international students. Applications are processed on a rolling basis. Application fee: $50. Electronic applications accepted. *Expenses:* Tuition, state resident: full-time $16,402; part-time $665 per credit. Tuition, nonresident: full-time $28,694; part-time $1175 per credit. Required fees: $690; $175 per term. Tuition and fees vary according to program. *Financial support:* Fellowships, research assistantships, teaching assistantships, Federal Work-Study, institutionally sponsored loans, scholarships/grants, health care benefits, tuition waivers (partial), and unspecified assistantships available. Support available to part-time students. Financial award application deadline: 3/15; financial award applicants required to submit FAFSA. *Unit head:* Dr. John C. Weidman, Chair, 412-648-7114, Fax: 412-648-1784, E-mail: weidman@pitt.edu. *Application contact:* Lauren Pasquini, Enrollment Manager, 412-648-2230, Fax: 412-648-1899, E-mail: soeinfo@pitt.edu.

University of Prince Edward Island, Faculty of Education, Charlottetown, PE C1A 4P3, Canada. Offers leadership and learning (M Ed). Part-time programs available. *Degree requirements:* For master's, thesis. *Entrance requirements:* For master's, 2 years of professional experience, bachelor of education, professional certificate. Additional exam requirements/recommendations for international students: Required—TOEFL (minimum score 550 paper-based; 213 computer-based; 80 iBT), Canadian Academic English Language Assessment, Michigan English Language Assessment Battery, Canadian Test of English for Scholars and Trainees. *Faculty research:* Distance learning, aboriginal communities and education leadership development, international development, immersion language learning.

University of Puerto Rico, Río Piedras, College of Education, Program in School Administration and Supervision, San Juan, PR 00931-3300. Offers M Ed, Ed D. Part-time programs available. *Degree requirements:* For master's, thesis; for doctorate, thesis/dissertation, internship. *Entrance requirements:* For master's, PAEG or GRE, minimum GPA of 3.0, letter of recommendation; for doctorate, GRE or PAEG, interview, master's degree, minimum GPA of 3.0, letter of recommendation.

University of Regina, Faculty of Graduate Studies and Research, Faculty of Education, Department of Educational Administration, Regina, SK S4S 0A2, Canada. Offers M Ed. *Faculty:* 3 full-time (1 woman), 1 (woman) part-time/adjunct. *Students:* 3 full-time (1 woman), 30 part-time (14 women). 14 applicants, 86% accepted. In 2009, 20 master's awarded. *Degree requirements:* For master's, thesis optional, practicum, project, or thesis. *Entrance requirements:* For master's, bachelor's degree in education, 2 years of teaching experience. Additional exam requirements/recommendations for international students: Required—TOEFL (minimum score 580 paper-based; 237 computer-based; 80 iBT). *Application deadline:* For fall admission, 2/15 for domestic students; for winter admission, 2/15 for domestic students; for spring admission, 2/15 for domestic students. Application fee: $90 ($100 for international students). Electronic applications accepted. *Financial support:* In 2009–10, 1 research assistantship (averaging $16,910 per year), 1 teaching assistantship (averaging $6,650 per year) were awarded; fellowships also available. Financial award application deadline: 6/15. *Faculty research:* Administration, policy. *Unit head:* Dr. Warren Wessel, 306-585-4555, E-mail: warren.wessel@uregina.ca. *Application contact:* Tania Gates, Graduate Program Coordinator, 306-585-4506, Fax: 306-585-5387, E-mail: edgrad@uregina.ca.

University of St. Francis, College of Education, Joliet, IL 60435-6169. Offers educational leadership (MS), including reading; elementary education certification (M Ed); reading (MS); secondary education certification (M Ed), including English education, math education, science education, social studies education; special education (M Ed); teaching and learning (MS), including character education, curriculum and instruction, differentiated instruction, technology. *Accreditation:* NCATE. Part-time and evening/weekend programs available. *Faculty:* 10 full-time (8 women), 26 part-time/adjunct (18 women). *Students:* 60 full-time (45 women), 349 part-time (283 women); includes 36 minority (10 African Americans, 2 Asian Americans or Pacific

Islanders, 24 Hispanic Americans). Average age 33. 211 applicants, 65% accepted, 102 enrolled. In 2009, 174 master's awarded. *Entrance requirements:* For master's, Illinois Basic Skills Test (M Ed), teaching certificate (MS), minimum undergraduate GPA of 2.75, 2 letters of recommendation, computer competency. Additional exam requirements/recommendations for international students: Required—TOEFL (minimum score 550 paper-based; 213 computer-based). *Application deadline:* Applications are processed on a rolling basis. Application fee: $30. Electronic applications accepted. *Expenses:* Contact institution. *Financial support:* In 2009–10, 254 students received support. Federal Work-Study, scholarships/grants, tuition waivers (partial), and unspecified assistantships available. Support available to part-time students. Financial award applicants required to submit FAFSA. *Unit head:* Dr. John Gambro, Dean, 815-740-3332, Fax: 815-740-2264, E-mail: jgambro@stfrancis.edu. *Application contact:* Sandra Sloka, Director of Admissions for Graduate and Degree Completion Programs, 800-735-7500, Fax: 815-740-5032, E-mail: ssloka@stfrancis.edu.

University of St. Thomas, Graduate Studies, School of Education, Department of Leadership, Policy and Administration, St. Paul, MN 55105-1096. Offers athletics and activities administration (MA); community education administration (MA); critical pedagogy (Ed D); curriculum and instruction (Ed S); educational leadership (Ed S); educational leadership and administration (MA); international leadership (MA, Certificate); leadership (Ed D); leadership in student affairs (MA, Certificate); police leadership (MA); public policy and leadership (MA, Certificate). Part-time and evening/weekend programs available. *Faculty:* 8 full-time (3 women), 15 part-time/adjunct (7 women). *Students:* 36 full-time (29 women), 307 part-time (149 women); includes 44 minority (29 African Americans, 1 American Indian/Alaska Native, 11 Asian Americans or Pacific Islanders, 3 Hispanic Americans), 5 international. Average age 36. 398 applicants, 75% accepted, 267 enrolled. In 2009, 63 master's, 17 doctorates, 46 other advanced degrees awarded. Terminal master's awarded for partial completion of doctoral program. *Degree requirements:* For master's, thesis (for some programs); for doctorate, thesis/dissertation; for other advanced degree, thesis or alternative. *Entrance requirements:* For master's, minimum GPA of 3.0 or MAT; for doctorate, MAT, minimum graduate GPA of 3.5; for other advanced degree, minimum graduate GPA of 3.25 or MAT. Additional exam requirements/recommendations for international students: Required—TOEFL (minimum score 550 paper-based; 213 computer-based; 20 iBT). *Application deadline:* For fall admission, 6/1 priority date for domestic students; for spring admission, 11/1 priority date for domestic students. Applications are processed on a rolling basis. Application fee: $50. *Expenses:* Contact institution. *Financial support:* Fellowships, research assistantships, institutionally sponsored loans and scholarships/grants available. Support available to part-time students. Financial award applicants required to submit FAFSA. *Unit head:* Dr. Donald R. LaMagdeleine, Chair, 651-962-4893, Fax: 651-962-4169, E-mail: drlamagdelei@stthomas.edu. *Application contact:* Jackie Grossklaus, Department Assistant, 651-962-4885, Fax: 651-962-4169, E-mail: jmgrossklaus@stthomas.edu.

University of San Diego, School of Leadership and Education Sciences, Department of Leadership Studies, San Diego, CA 92110-2492. Offers higher education leadership (MA); leadership studies (MA, PhD); nonprofit leadership and management (MA, Certificate). Part-time and evening/weekend programs available. *Faculty:* 8 full-time (5 women), 13 part-time/adjunct (9 women). *Students:* 23 full-time (12 women), 189 part-time (137 women); includes 63 minority (14 African Americans, 1 American Indian/Alaska Native, 17 Asian Americans or Pacific Islanders, 31 Hispanic Americans), 4 international. Average age 35. 186 applicants, 53% accepted, 72 enrolled. In 2009, 37 master's, 9 doctorates awarded. *Degree requirements:* For master's, thesis (for some programs), portfolio; for doctorate, comprehensive exam, thesis/dissertation. *Entrance requirements:* For master's, minimum GPA of 3.0, interview; for doctorate, GRE, master's degree, minimum GPA of 3.5 (recommended), interview, writing sample, resume. Additional exam requirements/recommendations for international students: Required—TOEFL (minimum score 580 paper-based; 237 computer-based; 83 iBT), TWE. *Application deadline:* For fall admission, 3/1 for domestic and international students. Application fee: $45. Electronic applications accepted. *Expenses:* Tuition: Full-time $21,042; part-time $1169 per unit. Required fees: $224. Full-time tuition and fees vary according to course load and degree level. *Financial support:* In 2009–10, 182 students received support. Career-related internships or fieldwork, Federal Work-Study, institutionally sponsored loans, unspecified assistantships, and stipends available. Support available to part-time students. Financial award application deadline: 4/1; financial award applicants required to submit FAFSA. *Faculty research:* Educational leadership, higher education policy and relations, leadership development, nonprofits and philanthropy, peace studies. *Unit head:* Dr. Cheryl Getz, Graduate Program Director, 619-260-4289, Fax: 619-260-6835, E-mail: cgetz@sandiego.edu. *Application contact:* Dr. John Mosby, Associate Director of Graduate Admissions, 619-260-4524, Fax: 619-260-4158, E-mail: grads@sandiego.edu.

University of San Francisco, School of Education, Catholic Educational Leadership Program, San Francisco, CA 94117-1080. Offers Catholic school leadership (MA, Ed D); Catholic school teaching (MA). *Faculty:* 1 (woman) full-time, 3 part-time/adjunct (2 women). *Students:* 12 full-time (3 women), 21 part-time (8 women); includes 1 minority (Hispanic American), 2 international. Average age 42. 20 applicants, 65% accepted, 4 enrolled. In 2009, 13 master's, 2 doctorates awarded. *Degree requirements:* For doctorate, thesis/dissertation. Application fee: $55 ($65 for international students). *Expenses:* Tuition: Full-time $19,710; part-time $1095 per unit. Part-time tuition and fees vary according to degree level, campus/location and program. *Financial support:* In 2009–10, 6 students received support; fellowships, research assistantships, teaching assistantships available. Financial award application deadline: 3/2; financial award applicants required to submit FAFSA. *Unit head:* Br. Ray Vercruysse, Chair, 415-422-6226. *Application contact:* Beth Teague, Associate Director of Graduate Outreach, 415-422-5467, E-mail: schoolofeducation@usfca.edu.

University of San Francisco, School of Education, Organization and Leadership Program, San Francisco, CA 94117-1080. Offers MA, Ed D. *Faculty:* 2 full-time (both women), 12 part-time/adjunct (7 women). *Students:* 209 full-time (151 women), 69 part-time (46 women); includes 84 minority (26 African Americans, 2 American Indian/Alaska Native, 28 Asian Americans or Pacific Islanders, 28 Hispanic Americans), 7 international. Average age 33. 221 applicants, 66% accepted, 93 enrolled. In 2009, 70 master's, 26 doctorates awarded. *Degree requirements:* For doctorate, thesis/dissertation. Application fee: $55 ($65 for international students). *Expenses:* Tuition: Full-time $19,710; part-time $1095 per unit. Part-time tuition and fees vary according to degree level, campus/location and program. *Financial support:* In 2009–10, 166 students received support; fellowships, research assistantships, teaching assistantships available. Financial award application deadline: 3/2; financial award applicants required to submit FAFSA. *Unit head:* Br. Ray Vercruysse, Chair, 415-422-6551. *Application contact:* Beth Teague, Associate Director of Graduate Outreach, 415-422-5467, E-mail: schoolofeducation@usfca.edu.

University of Saskatchewan, College of Graduate Studies and Research, College of Education, Department of Educational Administration, Saskatoon, SK S7N 5A2, Canada. Offers M Ed, PhD, Diploma. Part-time programs available. *Faculty:* 15. *Students:* 221. In 2009, 35 master's, 6 doctorates awarded. *Degree requirements:* For master's, thesis (for some programs); for doctorate, comprehensive exam (for some programs), thesis/dissertation. *Entrance requirements:* Additional exam requirements/recommendations for international students: Required—TOEFL (minimum score 80 iBT); Recommended—IELTS (minimum score 6.5). *Application deadline:* For fall admission, 7/1 priority date for domestic students. Applications are processed on a rolling basis. Application fee: $75. Electronic applications accepted. Tuition and fees charges are reported in Canadian dollars. *Expenses:* Tuition, area resident: Full-time $3000 Canadian dollars; part-time $500 Canadian dollars per term. Required fees: $700 Canadian dollars; $100 Canadian dollars per term. *Financial support:* Fellowships, research assistantships, teaching assistantships available. Financial award application deadline: 1/31. *Unit head:* Dr. Sheila Carr-Stewart, Head, 306-966-7611, Fax: 306-966-7020, E-mail: sheila.carr-stewart@usask.ca. *Application contact:* Dr. Sheila Carr-Stewart, Graduate Chair, 306-966-7611, Fax: 306-966-7020, E-mail: sheila.carr-stewart@usask.ca.

The University of Scranton, College of Graduate and Continuing Education, Department of Education, Program in Educational Administration, Scranton, PA 18510. Offers MS. *Accreditation:* NCATE. Part-time and evening/weekend programs available. Postbaccalaureate distance learning degree programs offered (no on-campus study). *Students:* 142 full-time (83 women), 236 part-time (132 women); includes 57 minority (31 African Americans, 2 American Indian/Alaska Native, 4 Asian Americans or Pacific Islanders, 20 Hispanic Americans), 2 international. Average age 35. 103 applicants, 96% accepted. In 2009, 214 master's awarded. *Degree requirements:* For master's, comprehensive exam, capstone experience. *Entrance requirements:* For master's, minimum GPA of 2.75. Additional exam requirements/recommendations for international students: Required—TOEFL (minimum score 500 paper-based; 173 computer-based), IELTS (minimum score 5.5). *Application deadline:* Applications are processed on a rolling basis. Application fee: $50. *Financial support:* Teaching assistantships, career-related internships or fieldwork, Federal Work-Study, and unspecified assistantships available. Support available to part-time students. Financial award application deadline: 3/1. *Unit head:* Dr. Art Chambers, Director, 570-941-4668, Fax: 570-941-5515, E-mail: chambersa2@scranton.edu. *Application contact:* Joseph M. Roback, Director of Admissions, 570-941-4385, Fax: 570-941-5928, E-mail: robackj2@scranton.edu.

University of Sioux Falls, Fredrikson School of Education, Sioux Falls, SD 57105-1699. Offers leadership (M Ed); reading (M Ed); superintendent (Ed S); teaching (M Ed); technology (M Ed). Summer admission only. *Accreditation:* NCATE. Part-time and evening/weekend programs available. *Degree requirements:* For master's, comprehensive exam (for some programs), research application project; for Ed S, comprehensive exam, portfolio. *Entrance requirements:* For master's, minimum GPA of 3.0, 1 year of teaching experience; for Ed S, minimum 3 years of teaching experience, minimum cumulative GPA of 3.5, 1 year of administrative experience. Additional exam requirements/recommendations for international students: Required—TOEFL. *Faculty research:* Reading, literacy, leadership.

University of South Africa, College of Human Sciences, Pretoria, South Africa. Offers adult education (M Ed); African languages (MA, PhD); African politics (MA, PhD); Afrikaans (MA, PhD); ancient history (MA, PhD); ancient Near Eastern studies (MA, PhD); anthropology (MA, PhD); applied linguistics (MA); Arabic (MA, PhD); archaeology (MA); art history (MA); Biblical archaeology (MA); Biblical studies (M Th, D Th, PhD); Christian spirituality (M Th, D Th); church history (M Th, D Th); classical studies (MA, PhD); clinical psychology (MA); communication (MA, PhD); comparative education (M Ed, Ed D); consulting psychology (D Admin, D Com, PhD); curriculum studies (M Ed, Ed D); development studies (M Admin, MA, D Admin, PhD); didactics (M Ed, Ed D); education (M Tech); education management (M Ed, Ed D); educational psychology (M Ed); English (MA); environmental education (M Ed); French (MA, PhD); German (MA, PhD); Greek (MA); guidance and counseling (M Ed); health studies (MA, PhD), including health sciences education (MA), health services management (MA), medical and surgical nursing science (critical care general) (MA), midwifery and neonatal nursing science (MA), trauma and emergency care (MA); history (MA, PhD); history of education (Ed D); inclusive education (M Ed, Ed D); information and communications technology policy and regulation (MA); information science (MA, MIS, PhD); international politics (MA, PhD); Islamic studies (MA, PhD); Italian (MA, PhD); Judaica (MA, PhD); linguistics (MA, PhD); mathematical education (M Ed); mathematics education (MA); missiology (M Th, D Th); modern Hebrew (MA, PhD); musicology (MA, MMus, D Mus, PhD); natural science education (M Ed); New Testament (M Th, D Th); Old Testament (D Th); pastoral therapy (M Th, D Th); philosophy (MA); philosophy of education (M Ed, Ed D); politics (MA, PhD); Portuguese (MA, PhD); practical theology (M Th, D Th); psychology (MA, MS, PhD); psychology of education (M Ed, Ed D); public health (MA); religious studies (MA, D Th, PhD); Romance languages (MA); Russian (MA, PhD); Semitic languages (MA, PhD); social behavior studies in HIV/AIDS (MA); social science (mental health) (MA); social science in development studies (MA); social science in psychology (MA); social science in social work (MA); social science in sociology (MA); social work (MSW, DSW, PhD); socio-education (M Ed, Ed D); sociolinguistics (MA); sociology (MA, PhD); Spanish (MA, PhD); systematic theology (M Th, D Th); TESOL (teaching English to speakers of other languages) (MA); theological ethics (M Th, D Th); theory of literature (MA, PhD); urban ministries (D Th); urban ministry (M Th).

University of South Alabama, Graduate School, College of Education, Department of Leadership and Teacher Education, Mobile, AL 36688-0002. Offers early childhood education (M Ed); educational administration (Ed S); educational leadership (M Ed); elementary education (M Ed); reading education (M Ed); science education (M Ed); secondary education (M Ed); special education (M Ed, Ed S). *Accreditation:* NCATE. Part-time programs available. *Degree requirements:* For master's, comprehensive exam. *Entrance requirements:* For master's, GRE General Test or MAT, minimum GPA of 3.0. *Expenses:* Tuition, state resident: part-time $218 per contact hour. Required fees: $1102 per year.

University of South Carolina, The Graduate School, College of Education, Department of Educational Leadership and Policies, Program in Educational Administration, Columbia, SC 29208. Offers M Ed, PhD, Ed S. *Accreditation:* NCATE. Part-time and evening/weekend programs available. Postbaccalaureate distance learning degree programs offered (no on-campus study). *Degree requirements:* For master's, comprehensive exam, thesis (for some programs), foreign language (MA); for doctorate, comprehensive exam, thesis/dissertation. *Entrance requirements:* For master's, GRE General Test or MAT, letter of reference, resume; for doctorate and Ed S, GRE General Test or MAT, interview, letter of intent, letter of reference, transcripts, resum&e. Electronic applications accepted.

The University of South Dakota, Graduate School, School of Education, Division of Educational Administration, Vermillion, SD 57069-2390. Offers MA, Ed D, Ed S. *Accreditation:* NCATE. Part-time and evening/weekend programs available. Postbaccalaureate distance learning degree programs offered (no on-campus study). *Degree requirements:* For master's and Ed S, comprehensive exam, thesis or alternative; for doctorate, comprehensive exam, thesis/dissertation. *Entrance requirements:* For master's and doctorate, GRE General Test, MAT, minimum GPA of 2.7. Additional exam requirements/recommendations for international students: Required—TOEFL (minimum score 550 paper-based; 213 computer-based; 79 iBT). Electronic applications accepted.

University of Southern California, Graduate School, Rossier School of Education, Doctor of Education Programs, Los Angeles, CA 90089. Offers educational psychology (Ed D); higher education administration (Ed D); K-12 leadership in urban school settings (Ed D); teacher education in multicultural societies (Ed D). Part-time and evening/weekend programs available. *Faculty:* 59 full-time (32 women), 12 part-time/adjunct (3 women). *Students:* 567 full-time (361 women), 12 part-time (6 women); includes 339 minority (73 African Americans, 11 American Indian/Alaska Native, 129 Asian Americans or Pacific Islanders, 126 Hispanic Americans), 13 international. 300 applicants, 76% accepted, 182 enrolled. In 2009, 143 doctorates awarded. *Degree requirements:* For doctorate, thesis/dissertation. *Entrance requirements:* For doctorate, GRE. Additional exam requirements/recommendations for international students: Required—TOEFL (minimum score 250 computer-based; 100 iBT). *Application deadline:* For fall admission, 1/15 priority date for domestic and international students. Application fee: $85. Electronic applications accepted. *Expenses:* Tuition: Full-time $25,980; part-time $1315 per unit. Required fees: $554. One-time fee: $35 full-time. Full-time tuition and fees vary according to degree level and program. *Financial support:* In 2009–10, 385 students received support. Scholarships/grants available. Support available to part-time students. Financial award application deadline: 5/5. *Faculty research:* Data-driven decision-making in K-12 schools and districts; examination of college and university leadership and management in U. S. and Asia; studies in facilitating student learning; organizational change and the role of leaders; leadership, diversity, learning and accountability. *Unit head:* Dr. Kathy Stowe, Executive Director/Assistant Professor of Clinical Education, 213-740-9323. *Application contact:* Carolyn Stirling, Associate Director of Recruiting and Admissions, 213-740-0224, Fax: 213-740-9433, E-mail: soeinfo@usc.edu.

University of Southern California, Graduate School, Rossier School of Education, Doctor of Philosophy in Education Programs, Los Angeles, CA 90089. Offers educational psychology (PhD); higher education administration and policy (PhD); K-12 policy and practice (PhD). *Faculty:* 20 full-time (11 women). *Students:* 23 full-time (17 women); includes 12 minority (3 African Americans, 3 Asian Americans or Pacific Islanders, 6 Hispanic Americans), 1 international. 64 applicants, 17% accepted, 5 enrolled. In 2009, 14 doctorates awarded. *Degree requirements:*

Educational Leadership and Administration

University of Southern California (continued)

For doctorate, thesis/dissertation, qualifying exam, proposal and defense. *Entrance requirements:* For doctorate, GRE. Additional exam requirements/recommendations for international students: Required—TOEFL (minimum score 250 computer-based; 100 iBT). *Application deadline:* For fall admission, 12/1 for domestic and international students. Application fee: $85. Electronic applications accepted. *Expenses:* Tuition: Full-time $25,980; part-time $1315 per unit. Required fees: $554. One-time fee: $35 full-time. Full-time tuition and fees vary according to degree level and program. *Financial support:* In 2009–10, 5 fellowships with full tuition reimbursements (averaging $29,000 per year), 23 research assistantships with full tuition reimbursements (averaging $31,000 per year) were awarded; health care benefits and full tuition coverage for all required coursework, academic stipend, awards for professional development and academic conferences also available. *Faculty research:* Diversity in higher education, organizational change, educational psychology, policy and politics of educational reform, economics of education and education policy. *Unit head:* Dianne Morris, Director, 213-740-6303, Fax: 213-740-9433, E-mail: rsoephd@usc.edu. *Application contact:* Aba Cassell, 213-821-1517, Fax: 213-740-9433, E-mail: rossier.phd@usc.edu.

University of Southern Maine, College of Education and Human Development, Educational Leadership Program, Portland, ME 04104-9300. Offers assistant principal (Certificate); athletic administration (Certificate); educational leadership (MS Ed, CAS); middle-level education (Certificate). Part-time and evening/weekend programs available. Postbaccalaureate distance learning degree programs offered (minimal on-campus study). *Faculty:* 5 full-time (0 women), 2 part-time/adjunct (1 woman). *Students:* 15 full-time (6 women), 42 part-time (23 women); includes 1 minority (American Indian/Alaska Native). 20 applicants, 85% accepted, 10 enrolled. In 2009, 26 master's, 11 CASs awarded. *Degree requirements:* For master's, thesis or alternative, practicum, internship; for other advanced degree, thesis or alternative. *Entrance requirements:* For master's, three years of documented teaching; for other advanced degree, master's degree. Additional exam requirements/recommendations for international students: Required—TOEFL (minimum score 550 paper-based; 213 computer-based; 79 iBT). *Application deadline:* For fall admission, 5/1 priority date for domestic students; for spring admission, 10/15 priority date for domestic students. Applications are processed on a rolling basis. Application fee: $50. Electronic applications accepted. *Financial support:* Research assistantships with partial tuition reimbursements, career-related internships or fieldwork, Federal Work-Study, institutionally sponsored loans, scholarships/grants, and unspecified assistantships available. Financial award application deadline: 3/1; financial award applicants required to submit FAFSA. *Unit head:* Dr. James Curry, Chair, Professional Education Department, 270-780-5400, Fax: 270-780-5674, E-mail: jcurry@usm.maine.edu. *Application contact:* Mary Sloan, Director of Graduate Admissions, 207-780-4386, Fax: 207-780-4969, E-mail: msloan@usm.maine.edu.

University of Southern Mississippi, Graduate School, College of Education and Psychology, Department of Educational Leadership and Research, Hattiesburg, MS 39406-0001. Offers adult education (M Ed, Ed D, PhD, Ed S); educational administration (M Ed, Ed D, PhD, Ed S); higher education (PhD). *Faculty:* 7 full-time (1 woman), 5 part-time/adjunct (1 woman). *Students:* 45 full-time (34 women), 97 part-time (66 women); includes 42 minority (40 African Americans, 1 American Indian/Alaska Native, 1 Hispanic American), 2 international. Average age 36. 54 applicants, 67% accepted, 33 enrolled. In 2009, 26 master's, 11 doctorates, 3 other advanced degrees awarded. *Degree requirements:* For master's, comprehensive exam, thesis (for some programs), internship; for doctorate, comprehensive exam, thesis/dissertation; for Ed S, comprehensive exam, thesis (for some programs). *Entrance requirements:* For master's, GRE General Test, minimum GPA of 2.75; for doctorate, GRE General Test, minimum GPA of 3.5; for Ed S, GRE General Test, minimum GPA of 3.25. Additional exam requirements/recommendations for international students: Required—TOEFL. *Application deadline:* For fall admission, 3/1 priority date for domestic students, 3/1 for international students. Applications are processed on a rolling basis. Application fee: $35. *Expenses:* Tuition, state resident: full-time $5096; part-time $284 per hour. Tuition, nonresident: full-time $13,052; part-time $726 per hour. Required fees: $402. Tuition and fees vary according to course level and course load. *Financial support:* In 2009–10, 10 research assistantships with full tuition reimbursements (averaging $8,000 per year) were awarded; teaching assistantships, career-related internships or fieldwork, Federal Work-Study, and institutionally sponsored loans also available. Financial award application deadline: 3/15; financial award applicants required to submit FAFSA. *Faculty research:* Supervision, learning styles, education finance, higher education organization. Total annual research expenditures: $88,500. *Unit head:* Dr. Gaylynn Parker, Interim Chair, 601-266-4589, Fax: 601-266-5141. *Application contact:* Shonna Breland, Manager of Graduate Admissions, 601-266-6563, Fax: 601-266-5138.

University of Southern Mississippi, Graduate School, College of Education and Psychology, Department of Educational Leadership and School Counseling, Hattiesburg, MS 39401. Offers education (M Ed), including educational administration, educational administration and supervision, school business administration, secondary administration; education (Ed S), including elementary administration, higher education administration; educational administration (M Ed); educational administration and supervision (M Ed), including educational administration; educational leadership and school counseling (Ed D, PhD). *Faculty:* 9 full-time (5 women), 3 part-time/adjunct (1 woman). *Students:* 51 full-time (32 women), 217 part-time (158 women); includes 92 minority (84 African Americans, 2 Asian Americans or Pacific Islanders, 6 Hispanic Americans), 2 international. Average age 39. 84 applicants, 57% accepted, 45 enrolled. In 2009, 68 master's, 25 doctorates, 35 other advanced degrees awarded. *Degree requirements:* For master's, internship. *Entrance requirements:* For master's, doctorate, and Ed S, GRE General Test, minimum GPA of 2.75. *Application deadline:* For fall admission, 3/1 priority date for domestic and international students. Application fee: $35. *Expenses:* Tuition, state resident: full-time $5096; part-time $284 per hour. Tuition, nonresident: full-time $13,052; part-time $726 per hour. Required fees: $402. Tuition and fees vary according to course level and course load. *Financial support:* Career-related internships or fieldwork, Federal Work-Study, and institutionally sponsored loans available. Financial award application deadline: 3/15; financial award applicants required to submit FAFSA. *Unit head:* Dr. Mary Ann Adams, Interim Chair, 601-266-4579. *Application contact:* Shonna Breland, Manager of Graduate Admissions, 601-266-6563, Fax: 601-266-5138.

University of Southern Mississippi, Graduate School, College of Education and Psychology, Department of Educational Studies and Research, Hattiesburg, MS 39406-0001. Offers adult education (Graduate Certificate); community college leadership (Graduate Certificate); counseling and personnel services (college) (M Ed); education (PhD, Ed S), including adult education, research, evaluation and statistics (PhD); education (Ed D), including educational administration, educational research; education: educational leadership and research (Ed S), including higher education administration; educational administration and supervision (M Ed); higher education administration (Ed D, PhD); institutional research (Graduate Certificate). *Faculty:* 7 full-time (1 woman), 5 part-time/adjunct (1 woman). *Students:* 45 full-time (34 women), 97 part-time (66 women); includes 42 minority (40 African Americans, 1 American Indian/Alaska Native, 1 Hispanic American), 2 international. Average age 36. 54 applicants, 67% accepted, 33 enrolled. In 2009, 26 master's, 11 doctorates, 3 other advanced degrees awarded. *Degree requirements:* For master's and other advanced degree, comprehensive exam, thesis (for some programs); for doctorate, comprehensive exam, thesis/dissertation. *Entrance requirements:* For master's, doctorate, and other advanced degree, GRE General Test, minimum GPA of 2.75. Additional exam requirements/recommendations for international students: Required—TOEFL. *Application deadline:* For fall admission, 2/1 for domestic students, 3/1 for international students. Applications are processed on a rolling basis. Application fee: $35. *Expenses:* Tuition, state resident: full-time $5096; part-time $284 per hour. Tuition, nonresident: full-time $13,052; part-time $726 per hour. Required fees: $402. Tuition and fees vary according to course level and course load. *Financial support:* Career-related internships or fieldwork, Federal Work-Study, and institutionally sponsored loans available. Financial award application deadline: 3/15; financial award applicants required to submit FAFSA. Total annual research expenditures: $88,500. *Unit head:* Dr. Thomas V. O'Brien, Chair, 601-266-6093, E-mail: thomas.obrien@usm.edu. *Application contact:* Shonna Breland, Manager of Graduate Admissions, 601-266-6563, Fax: 601-266-5138.

University of South Florida, Graduate School, College of Education–Main Campus, Department of Educational Leadership and Policy Studies, Tampa, FL 33620-9951. Offers educational leadership (M Ed, Ed D, Ed S). Part-time programs available. *Faculty:* 10 full-time (5 women), 9 part-time/adjunct (4 women). *Students:* 42 full-time (27 women), 182 part-time (136 women); includes 48 minority (31 African Americans, 17 Hispanic Americans). Average age 30. 110 applicants, 65% accepted, 61 enrolled. In 2009, 82 master's, 5 doctorates, 2 other advanced degrees awarded. *Degree requirements:* For master's, comprehensive exam, portfolio; for doctorate, comprehensive exam, thesis/dissertation; for Ed S, comprehensive exam, thesis. *Entrance requirements:* For master's, minimum GPA of 3.0 in last 60 hours of coursework; Florida Professional Teaching Certificate; 2 years' postbachelor's teaching experience; for doctorate, GRE General Test, master's degree in educational leadership or educational leadership certification; for Ed S, GRE General Test, educational leadership certification. Additional exam requirements/recommendations for international students: Required—TOEFL (minimum score 550 paper-based; 213 computer-based; 79 iBT). *Application deadline:* For fall admission, 2/15 for domestic students, 1/2 for international students; for spring admission, 10/15 for domestic students, 6/1 for international students. Application fee: $30. Electronic applications accepted. *Financial support:* In 2009–10, 8 students received support, including 2 teaching assistantships with full tuition reimbursements available (averaging $10,500 per year); scholarships/grants, health care benefits, and unspecified assistantships also available. Financial award application deadline: 3/22; financial award applicants required to submit FAFSA. *Faculty research:* Multicultural education and social justice, educational accountability policy, school reform, community development and school success, school governance, teacher and principal preparation. Total annual research expenditures: $76,508. *Unit head:* Dr. Anthony Rolle, Chairperson, 813-974-6036, Fax: 813-974-5423. *Application contact:* Lisa Mullen, Academic Advisor, 813-974-1344, Fax: 813-974-5423, E-mail: lmullen@usf.edu.

The University of Tennessee, Graduate School, College of Education, Health and Human Sciences, Program in Education, Knoxville, TN 37996. Offers art education (MS); counseling education (PhD); cultural studies in education (PhD); curriculum (MS, Ed S); curriculum, educational research and evaluation (Ed D, PhD); early childhood education (PhD); early childhood special education (MS); education of deaf and hard of hearing (MS); educational administration and policy studies (Ed D, PhD); educational administration and supervision (Ed S); educational psychology (Ed D, PhD); elementary education (MS, Ed S); elementary teaching (MS); English education (MS, Ed S); exercise science (PhD); foreign language/ESL education (MS, Ed S); instructional technology (MS, Ed D, PhD, Ed S); literacy, language and ESL education (PhD); literacy, language education, and ESL education (Ed D); mathematics education (MS, Ed S); modified and comprehensive special education (MS); reading education (MS, Ed S); school counseling (Ed S); school psychology (PhD, Ed S); science education (MS, Ed S); secondary teaching (MS); social foundations (MS); social science education (MS, Ed S); socio-cultural foundations of sports and education (PhD); special education (Ed S); teacher education (Ed D, PhD). *Accreditation:* NCATE. Part-time and evening/weekend programs available. *Degree requirements:* For master's and Ed S, thesis optional; for doctorate, variable foreign language requirement, thesis/dissertation. *Entrance requirements:* For master's, minimum GPA of 2.7; for doctorate and Ed S, GRE General Test, minimum GPA of 2.7. Additional exam requirements/recommendations for international students: Required—TOEFL. Electronic applications accepted. *Expenses:* Tuition, state resident: full-time $6826; part-time $380 per semester hour. Tuition, nonresident: full-time $21,844; part-time $1147 per semester hour. Tuition and fees vary according to program.

The University of Tennessee, Graduate School, College of Education, Health and Human Sciences, Program in Educational Administration and Policy Studies, Knoxville, TN 37996. Offers educational administration and policy studies (Ed D); educational administration and supervision (MS). *Accreditation:* NCATE. Part-time and evening/weekend programs available. Postbaccalaureate distance learning degree programs offered (no on-campus study). *Degree requirements:* For master's, thesis optional. *Entrance requirements:* For master's, minimum GPA of 2.7. Additional exam requirements/recommendations for international students: Required—TOEFL. Electronic applications accepted. *Expenses:* Tuition, state resident: full-time $6826; part-time $380 per semester hour. Tuition, nonresident: full-time $21,844; part-time $1147 per semester hour. Tuition and fees vary according to program.

The University of Tennessee at Chattanooga, Graduate School, College of Health, Education and Professional Studies, Graduate Studies Division of Education, Program in Education, Chattanooga, TN 37403-2598. Offers elementary education (M Ed); school leadership (M Ed, Post-Master's Certificate); secondary education (M Ed); special education (M Ed). Part-time and evening/weekend programs available. Postbaccalaureate distance learning degree programs offered (no on-campus study). *Faculty:* 10 full-time (9 women), 6 part-time/adjunct (3 women). *Students:* 124 full-time (83 women), 208 part-time (150 women); includes 42 minority (32 African Americans, 2 American Indian/Alaska Native, 3 Asian Americans or Pacific Islanders, 5 Hispanic Americans), 1 international. Average age 33. 117 applicants, 97% accepted, 80 enrolled. In 2009, 97 master's, 4 other advanced degrees awarded. *Degree requirements:* For master's, comprehensive exam (for some programs), thesis (for some programs). *Entrance requirements:* For master's and Post-Master's Certificate, PRAXIS I, minimum GPA of 2.5 overall or 3.0 in senior year. Additional exam requirements/recommendations for international students: Required—TOEFL (minimum score 550 paper-based; 213 computer-based; 79 iBT), IELTS (minimum score 6). *Application deadline:* For fall admission, 8/1 for domestic students, 6/1 for international students; for spring admission, 12/1 for domestic students, 10/1 for international students. Applications are processed on a rolling basis. Application fee: $35. Electronic applications accepted. *Expenses:* Tuition, state resident: full-time $5404; part-time $300 per credit hour. Tuition, nonresident: full-time $16,702; part-time $928 per credit hour. Required fees: $1150; $130 per credit hour. *Financial support:* In 2009–10, 8 research assistantships with full and partial tuition reimbursements (averaging $5,500 per year) were awarded; career-related internships or fieldwork, scholarships/grants, and unspecified assistantships also available. Support available to part-time students. *Faculty research:* Elementary education, community counseling, school counseling, secondary education, special education. *Unit head:* Dr. John Freeman, Department Head, 423-425-4133, Fax: 423-425-5443, E-mail: john-freeman@utc.edu. *Application contact:* Dr. Stephanie Bellar, Dean of Graduate Studies, 423-425-4666, Fax: 423-425-5223, E-mail: stephanie-bellar@utc.edu.

The University of Tennessee at Chattanooga, Graduate School, College of Health, Education and Professional Studies, Graduate Studies Division of Education, Program in Learning and Leadership, Chattanooga, TN 37403. Offers educational leadership (Ed D). *Faculty:* 9 full-time (3 women), 1 part-time/adjunct (0 women). *Students:* 6 full-time (3 women), 74 part-time (44 women); includes 8 minority (5 African Americans, 1 American Indian/Alaska Native, 2 Hispanic Americans), 1 international. Average age 42. 26 applicants, 58% accepted, 12 enrolled. In 2009, 1 doctorate awarded. *Degree requirements:* For doctorate, comprehensive exam, thesis/dissertation, portfolio. *Entrance requirements:* For doctorate, GRE General Test, master's degree, two years of practical work experience in organizational environment. Additional exam requirements/recommendations for international students: Required—TOEFL (minimum score 550 paper-based; 213 computer-based; 79 iBT), IELTS (minimum score 6). *Application deadline:* For fall admission, 8/1 priority date for domestic students, 6/1 for international students; for spring admission, 12/1 priority date for domestic students, 10/1 for international students. Applications are processed on a rolling basis. Application fee: $35. Electronic applications accepted. *Expenses:* Tuition, state resident: full-time $5404; part-time $300 per credit hour. Tuition, nonresident: full-time $16,702; part-time $928 per credit hour. Required fees: $1150; $130 per credit hour. *Financial support:* In 2009–10, 5 research assistantships with full and partial tuition reimbursements (averaging $5,500 per year) were awarded; career-related internships or fieldwork, scholarships/grants, and unspecified assistantships also available. Support available to part-time students. *Faculty research:* Instructional design and development, curriculum inquiry/mapping, program evaluation, professional development and teacher training, fostering student diligence. *Unit head:* Becca McCashin, Director, 423-425-5445, Fax: 423-425-5443, E-mail: becca-mccashin@utc.edu. *Application contact:* Dr. Stephanie Bellar, Dean of Graduate Studies, 423-425-4666, Fax: 423-425-5223, E-mail: stephanie-bellar@utc.edu.

The University of Tennessee at Martin, Graduate Programs, College of Education and Behavioral Sciences, Program in Educational Leadership, Martin, TN 38238-1000. Offers MS Ed. Part-time programs available. Postbaccalaureate distance learning degree programs offered. *Students:* 46 (32 women). 27 applicants, 56% accepted, 13 enrolled. In 2009, 22 master's awarded. *Degree requirements:* For master's, comprehensive exam. *Entrance requirements:* For master's, GRE General Test, minimum GPA of 2.5, letters of reference, teaching license, resume, teaching experience. Additional exam requirements/recommendations for international students: Required—TOEFL (minimum score 525 paper-based; 197 computer-based; 71 iBT). *Application deadline:* For fall admission, 8/1 priority date for domestic students, 6/15 priority date for international students; for spring admission, 12/14 priority date for domestic students, 12/1 priority date for international students. Applications are processed on a rolling basis. Application fee: $30 ($130 for international students). Electronic applications accepted. *Expenses:* Tuition, state resident: full-time $6660; part-time $372 per hour. Tuition, nonresident: full-time $18,000; part-time $1005 per hour. *Financial support:* Research assistantships with full tuition reimbursements, teaching assistantships with full tuition reimbursements, scholarships/grants and unspecified assistantships available. Support available to part-time students. Financial award application deadline: 2/15; financial award applicants required to submit FAFSA. *Unit head:* Staci H. Fuqua, Staff Assistant, 731-881-7123, Fax: 731-881-7975, E-mail: sfuqua@utm.edu. *Application contact:* Linda S. Arant, Student Services Specialist, 731-881-7012, Fax: 731-881-7499, E-mail: larant@utm.edu.

The University of Texas at Arlington, Graduate School, College of Education, Arlington, TX 76019. Offers curriculum and instruction (M Ed); educational leadership and policy studies (M Ed); K-16 educational, leadership and policy studies (PhD); physiology of exercise (MS); teaching (M Ed T). *Accreditation:* NCATE. Part-time and evening/weekend programs available. *Faculty:* 35 full-time (22 women), 4 part-time/adjunct (2 women). *Students:* 125 full-time (83 women), 586 part-time (479 women); includes 283 minority (125 African Americans, 4 American Indian/Alaska Native, 19 Asian Americans or Pacific Islanders, 135 Hispanic Americans), 15 international. Average age 35. 601 applicants, 99% accepted, 238 enrolled. In 2009, 161 degrees awarded. *Degree requirements:* For master's, comprehensive exam (for some programs), thesis (for some programs), comprehensive activity, research project; for doctorate, comprehensive exam, thesis/dissertation. *Entrance requirements:* For master's, GRE General Test, minimum undergraduate GPA of 3.0 in last 60 hours of course work, writing sample, 3 letters of recommendation; for doctorate, GRE General Test, interview, minimum GPA of 3.5, master's degree in education or other appropriate field, 3 years of documented experience in an education related work environment. Additional exam requirements/recommendations for international students: Required—TOEFL (minimum score 550 paper-based; 213 computer-based). *Application deadline:* For fall admission, 6/5 priority date for domestic students, 4/3 priority date for international students; for spring admission, 10/17 priority date for domestic students, 9/5 priority date for international students. Applications are processed on a rolling basis. Application fee: $35 ($50 for international students). Electronic applications accepted. *Financial support:* In 2009–10, 9 fellowships (averaging $1,000 per year), 6 research assistantships (averaging $6,250 per year), 10 teaching assistantships with full tuition reimbursements (averaging $5,200 per year) were awarded; career-related internships or fieldwork, Federal Work-Study, scholarships/grants, and unspecified assistantships also available. Financial award application deadline: 6/1; financial award applicants required to submit FAFSA. *Unit head:* Dr. Jeanne M. Gerlach, Dean, 817-272-2591, Fax: 817-272-2530, E-mail: coeadvising@uta.edu. *Application contact:* Kas McConnell, Graduate Advisor, 817-272-7489, Fax: 817-272-7624, E-mail: coedadvising@uta.edu.

The University of Texas at Austin, Graduate School, College of Education, Department of Educational Administration, Austin, TX 78712-1111. Offers M Ed, Ed D, PhD. *Degree requirements:* For doctorate, thesis/dissertation. *Entrance requirements:* For master's and doctorate, GRE General Test. Electronic applications accepted.

The University of Texas at Brownsville, Graduate Studies, School of Education, Brownsville, TX 78520-4991. Offers bilingual education (M Ed); counseling and guidance (M Ed); curriculum and instruction (M Ed); early childhood education (M Ed); educational administration (M Ed); educational technology (M Ed); English as a second language (M Ed); reading specialist (M Ed); special education/educational diagnostician (M Ed). Part-time and evening/weekend programs available. Postbaccalaureate distance learning degree programs offered (minimal on-campus study). *Degree requirements:* For master's, thesis optional. *Entrance requirements:* For master's, GRE General Test. Additional exam requirements/recommendations for international students: Required—TOEFL.

The University of Texas at El Paso, Graduate School, College of Education, Department of Educational Leadership and Foundations, El Paso, TX 79968-0001. Offers educational administration (M Ed); educational leadership and administration (Ed D). Part-time and evening/weekend programs available. *Degree requirements:* For master's, thesis optional; for doctorate, thesis/dissertation. *Entrance requirements:* For doctorate, GRE General Test, minimum graduate GPA of 3.0. Additional exam requirements/recommendations for international students: Required—TOEFL. Electronic applications accepted.

The University of Texas at San Antonio, College of Education and Human Development, Department of Educational Leadership and Policy Studies, San Antonio, TX 78249-0617. Offers educational leadership (M Ed, Ed D). Part-time and evening/weekend programs available. *Faculty:* 17 full-time (7 women), 7 part-time/adjunct (2 women). *Students:* 41 full-time (25 women), 255 part-time (182 women); includes 197 minority (33 African Americans, 1 American Indian/Alaska Native, 4 Asian Americans or Pacific Islanders, 159 Hispanic Americans), 2 international. Average age 35. 93 applicants, 86% accepted, 59 enrolled. In 2009, 103 master's, 10 doctorates awarded. *Degree requirements:* For master's, comprehensive exam (for some programs), thesis (for some programs); for doctorate, comprehensive exam (for some programs), thesis/dissertation (for some programs). *Entrance requirements:* For master's and doctorate, GRE General Test. Additional exam requirements/recommendations for international students: Required—TOEFL (minimum score 500 paper-based; 173 computer-based; 61 iBT). *Application deadline:* For fall admission, 7/1 for domestic students, 4/1 for international students; for spring admission, 11/1 for domestic students, 9/1 for international students. Applications are processed on a rolling basis. Application fee: $45 ($80 for international students). Electronic applications accepted. *Expenses:* Tuition, state resident: full-time $3975; part-time $221 per contact hour. Tuition, nonresident: full-time $13,947; part-time $775 per contact hour. Required fees: $1853. *Financial support:* In 2009–10, 15 students received support, including 20 research assistantships (averaging $11,258 per year); career-related internships or fieldwork, scholarships/grants, tuition waivers, and unspecified assistantships also available. Support available to part-time students. *Faculty research:* Educational leadership and preparation, school-university collaboration, social justice in education, educational policy and politics, social and organizational contexts for education. Total annual research expenditures: $90,870. *Unit head:* Dr. David P. Thompson, Chair, 210-458-5436, Fax: 210-458-5848, E-mail: david.thompson@utsa.edu. *Application contact:* Elisha Reynolds, Graduate Advisor, 210-458-6620, E-mail: elisha.reynolds@utsa.edu.

The University of Texas at Tyler, College of Education and Psychology, Department of Educational Leadership, Tyler, TX 75799-0001. Offers M Ed. Part-time and evening/weekend programs available. Postbaccalaureate distance learning degree programs offered (no on-campus study). *Faculty:* 5 full-time (2 women). *Students:* 3 full-time (all women), 86 part-time (50 women); includes 11 minority (8 African Americans, 1 American Indian/Alaska Native, 2 Hispanic Americans). Average age 35. 57 applicants, 100% accepted, 46 enrolled. In 2009, 25 master's awarded. *Degree requirements:* For master's, comprehensive exam, 2 years of teaching experience. *Entrance requirements:* For master's, GRE General Test. Additional exam requirements/recommendations for international students: Required—TOEFL (minimum score 79 computer-based). *Application deadline:* For fall admission, 8/17 priority date for domestic students, 7/1 priority date for international students; for spring admission, 12/21 priority date for domestic students, 11/1 priority date for international students. Applications are processed on a rolling basis. Application fee: $25 ($50 for international students). *Expenses:* Tuition, state resident: part-time $665 per semester hour. Tuition, nonresident: part-time $942 per semester hour. Part-time tuition and fees vary according to degree level and program. *Financial support:* Fellowships, research assistantships, teaching assistantships, scholarships/grants available. Financial award application deadline: 7/1. *Faculty research:* Effective schools, restructuring of schools, leadership. Total annual research expenditures: $516,000. *Unit head:* Dr. Ross Sherman, Chair, 903-566-7218, Fax: 903-566-5527, E-mail: rsherman@mail.uttyl.edu. *Application contact:* Dr. Ross Sherman.

The University of Texas of the Permian Basin, Office of Graduate Studies, School of Education, Program in Educational Leadership, Odessa, TX 79762-0001. Offers MA. *Degree requirements:* For master's, comprehensive exam (for some programs), thesis (for some programs). *Entrance requirements:* For master's, GRE General Test. Additional exam requirements/recommendations for international students: Required—TOEFL (minimum score 550 paper-based; 213 computer-based).

The University of Texas–Pan American, College of Education, Department of Educational Leadership, Edinburg, TX 78539. Offers M Ed, Ed D. Part-time and evening/weekend programs available. *Degree requirements:* For master's, comprehensive exam, thesis optional; for doctorate, comprehensive exam, thesis/dissertation. *Entrance requirements:* For master's, GRE; for doctorate, master's degree. Additional exam requirements/recommendations for international students: Required—TOEFL. Electronic applications accepted. *Expenses:* Tuition, state resident: full-time $3630.60; part-time $201.70 per credit hour. Tuition, nonresident: full-time $8617; part-time $478.70 per credit hour. Required fees: $806.50. *Faculty research:* Community perceptions of education, leadership and gender studies, continuous improvement processes, leadership.

University of the Cumberlands, Graduate Programs in Education, Program in Elementary/Secondary Principalship, Williamsburg, KY 40769-1372. Offers MA Ed.

University of the Incarnate Word, School of Graduate Studies and Research, Dreeben School of Education, Programs in Education, San Antonio, TX 78209-6397. Offers adult education (M Ed, MA); cross-cultural education (M Ed, MA); early childhood literacy (M Ed, MA); general education (M Ed, MA); Higher Education (PhD); instructional technology (M Ed, MA); international education and entrepreneurship (PhD); kinesiology (M Ed, MA); literacy (M Ed, MA); organizational leadership (PhD); organizational learning and learning (M Ed, MA); reading (M Ed, MA); special education (M Ed, MA); teacher leadership (M Ed, MA). Part-time and evening/weekend programs available. *Students:* 20 full-time (11 women), 201 part-time (122 women); includes 113 minority (29 African Americans, 2 American Indian/Alaska Native, 2 Asian Americans or Pacific Islanders, 80 Hispanic Americans), 30 international. Average age 41. In 2009, 26 master's, 19 doctorates awarded. *Degree requirements:* For master's, capstone; for doctorate, thesis/dissertation, qualifying exam. *Entrance requirements:* For master's, baccalaureate degree; minimum foundation GPA of 2.5; interview; for doctorate, master's degree; interview; supervised writing sample. Additional exam requirements/recommendations for international students: Required—TOEFL (minimum score 560 paper-based; 220 computer-based; 83 iBT). *Application deadline:* Applications are processed on a rolling basis. Application fee: $20. Electronic applications accepted. *Expenses:* Tuition: Full-time $12,150; part-time $675 per credit hour. Required fees: $83 per credit hour. *Financial support:* Federal Work-Study and scholarships/grants available. Financial award applicants required to submit FAFSA. *Unit head:* Dr. Denise Staudt, Dean, Dreeben School of Education, 210-829-2762, E-mail: staudt@uiwtx.edu. *Application contact:* Andrea Cyterski-Acosta, Dean of Enrollment, 210-829-6005, Fax: 210-829-3921, E-mail: admis@uiwtx.edu.

University of the Pacific, School of Education, Department of Educational Administration and Leadership, Stockton, CA 95211-0197. Offers educational administration (MA, Ed D). *Accreditation:* NCATE. *Faculty:* 5 full-time (2 women). *Students:* 47 full-time (29 women), 71 part-time (46 women); includes 38 minority (17 African Americans, 8 Asian Americans or Pacific Islanders, 13 Hispanic Americans), 3 international. Average age 35. 39 applicants, 90% accepted, 26 enrolled. In 2009, 30 master's, 17 doctorates awarded. *Degree requirements:* For master's, thesis (for some programs); for doctorate, thesis/dissertation. *Entrance requirements:* For master's and doctorate, GRE General Test, GRE Subject Test. Additional exam requirements/recommendations for international students: Required—TOEFL (minimum score 475 paper-based; 150 computer-based). *Application deadline:* For fall admission, 3/1 priority date for domestic students; for spring admission, 10/1 priority date for domestic students. Applications are processed on a rolling basis. Application fee: $75. *Financial support:* Application deadline: 3/1. *Unit head:* Dr. Dennis Brennan, Chairperson, 209-946-2580, E-mail: dbrennan@pacific.edu. *Application contact:* Office of Graduate Admissions, 209-946-2344.

University of the Southwest, Graduate Programs, Hobbs, NM 88240-9129. Offers business administration (MBA); curriculum and instruction (MSE); curriculum and instruction: bilingual (MSE); curriculum and instruction: reading (MSE); curriculum and instruction: TESOL (MSE); early childhood education (MSE); educational diagnostician (MSE); mental health counseling (MSE); school business administration (MSE); school counseling (MSE); special education (MSE). Part-time and evening/weekend programs available. Postbaccalaureate distance learning degree programs offered (no on-campus study). *Faculty:* 10 full-time (6 women), 10 part-time/adjunct (4 women). *Students:* 112 full-time (93 women), 99 part-time (72 women). Average age 35. 94 applicants, 47% accepted, 39 enrolled. In 2009, 32 master's awarded. *Degree requirements:* For master's, comprehensive exam. *Application deadline:* For fall admission, 3/1 priority date for domestic students; for spring admission, 10/1 for domestic students. Applications are processed on a rolling basis. Application fee: $25. Electronic applications accepted. *Expenses:* Tuition: Part-time $512 per hour. Tuition and fees vary according to course load. *Financial support:* In 2009–10, 196 students received support; research assistantships with partial tuition reimbursements available, Federal Work-Study, scholarships/grants, and tuition waivers (partial) available. Support available to part-time students. Financial award application deadline: 4/1; financial award applicants required to submit FAFSA. *Unit head:* Dr. Mary Harris, Dean of Education, 575-392-6561 Ext. 1056, Fax: 575-392-6006, E-mail: mharris@usw.edu. *Application contact:* Ryanne Evans, Assistant Registrar, 575-392-6561 Ext. 1031, Fax: 575-392-6006, E-mail: revans@usw.edu.

The University of Toledo, College of Graduate Studies, College of Education, Department of Educational Foundations and Leadership, Program in Educational Administration and Supervision, Toledo, OH 43606-3390. Offers ME, DE, Ed S. *Accreditation:* NCATE. Evening/weekend programs available. *Degree requirements:* For master's, comprehensive exam, thesis or alternative; for doctorate, thesis/dissertation, comprehensive exams; for Ed S, thesis optional. *Entrance requirements:* For master's, minimum GPA of 2.7; for doctorate, GRE General Test, interview; minimum GPA of 2.7 (undergraduate), 3.0 (graduate); for Ed S, minimum GPA of 2.7 (undergraduate), 3.0 (graduate). Electronic applications accepted. *Faculty research:* School learning organizations, equity, access and equality in schools.

University of Utah, Graduate School, College of Education, Department of Educational Leadership and Policy, Salt Lake City, UT 84084. Offers M Ed, M Phil, Ed D, PhD, MPA/Ed D, MPA/PhD. Part-time programs available. *Faculty:* 12 full-time (7 women), 5 part-time/adjunct (all women). *Students:* 48 full-time (27 women), 87 part-time (47 women); includes 28 minority (4 African Americans, 1 American Indian/Alaska Native, 6 Asian Americans or Pacific Islanders, 17 Hispanic Americans), 1 international. Average age 37. 119 applicants, 66% accepted, 11 enrolled. In 2009, 34 master's, 10 doctorates awarded. *Degree requirements:* For master's, comprehensive exam, internship; for doctorate, thesis/dissertation, qualifying exam, capstone project (Ed D). *Entrance requirements:* For master's, minimum undergraduate GPA of 3.0, 2 years' teaching or leadership experience, Level 2 UT educator's license, valid bachelor's degree (for K-12 programs only); for doctorate, GRE General Test, minimum undergraduate GPA of 3.0, valid master's degree. Additional exam requirements/recommendations for international students: Required—TOEFL (minimum score 500 paper-based; 173 computer-based). *Application deadline:* For fall admission, 12/15 for domestic and international students. Application fee: $55 ($65 for international students). Electronic applications accepted. *Expenses:* Tuition, state resident: full-time $4004; part-time $1674 per semester. Tuition, nonresident: full-time $14,134; part-time $5915 per semester. Required fees: $324 per semester. Tuition and fees vary according to course load, degree level and program. *Financial support:* In

Educational Leadership and Administration

University of Utah (continued)

2009–10, 4 students received support, including 3 teaching assistantships with full tuition reimbursements available (averaging $11,500 per year); career-related internships or fieldwork, scholarships/grants, and unspecified assistantships also available. Financial award application deadline: 3/1; financial award applicants required to submit CSS PROFILE. *Faculty research:* Education accountability, college student diversity, social principalship, middle school teaming, comparative higher education. Total annual research expenditures: $6,587. *Unit head:* Dr. David Sperry, Interim Chair, 801-581-6714, Fax: 801-585-6756, E-mail: david.sperry@utah.edu. *Application contact:* Jinny Yeara McGavien, Academic Program Coordinator, 801-581-6714, Fax: 801-585-6756, E-mail: jinny.yeara@utah.edu.

University of Vermont, Graduate College, College of Education and Social Services, Department of Educational Leadership and Policy Studies, Burlington, VT 05405. Offers Ed D. *Accreditation:* NCATE. *Students:* 61 (38 women); includes 7 minority (6 African Americans, 1 Hispanic American), 1 international. 38 applicants, 66% accepted, 22 enrolled. In 2009, 18 doctorates awarded. *Degree requirements:* For doctorate, thesis/dissertation. *Entrance requirements:* Additional exam requirements/recommendations for international students: Required—TOEFL (minimum score 550 paper-based; 213 computer-based; 80 iBT). *Application deadline:* For fall admission, 2/1 priority date for domestic students. Application fee: $40. Electronic applications accepted. *Expenses:* Tuition, state resident: part-time $508 per credit hour. Tuition, nonresident: part-time $1281 per credit hour. *Financial support:* Research assistantships, teaching assistantships available. *Unit head:* Dr. Susan Hasazi, Chairperson, 802-656-1442. *Application contact:* Dr. Susan Hasazi, Chairperson, 802-656-1442.

University of Vermont, Graduate College, College of Education and Social Services, Department of Education, Program in Educational Leadership, Burlington, VT 05405. Offers M Ed. *Accreditation:* NCATE. *Students:* 25 (14 women); includes 1 minority (Asian American or Pacific Islander). 26 applicants, 85% accepted, 10 enrolled. In 2009, 8 master's awarded. *Degree requirements:* For master's, thesis or alternative. *Entrance requirements:* Additional exam requirements/recommendations for international students: Required—TOEFL (minimum score 550 paper-based; 213 computer-based; 80 iBT). *Application deadline:* For fall admission, 4/1 priority date for domestic students; for spring admission, 11/1 priority date for domestic students. Application fee: $40. Electronic applications accepted. *Expenses:* Tuition, state resident: part-time $508 per credit hour. Tuition, nonresident: part-time $1281 per credit hour. *Financial support:* Research assistantships, teaching assistantships, career-related internships or fieldwork available. Financial award application deadline: 3/1. *Unit head:* Kieran Killeen, Coordinator, 802-656-2936. *Application contact:* Kieran Killeen, Coordinator, 802-656-2936.

University of Vermont, Graduate College, College of Education and Social Services, Department of Integrated Professional Studies, Program in Higher Education and Student Affairs Administration, Burlington, VT 05405. Offers M Ed. *Accreditation:* NCATE. *Students:* 32 (21 women); includes 15 minority (4 African Americans, 6 Asian Americans or Pacific Islanders, 5 Hispanic Americans), 1 international. 148 applicants, 23% accepted, 17 enrolled. In 2009, 16 master's awarded. *Degree requirements:* For master's, thesis or alternative. *Entrance requirements:* For master's, resume. Additional exam requirements/recommendations for international students: Required—TOEFL (minimum score 550 paper-based; 213 computer-based; 80 iBT). *Application deadline:* For fall admission, 1/1 priority date for domestic students. Applications are processed on a rolling basis. Application fee: $40. Electronic applications accepted. *Expenses:* Tuition, state resident: part-time $508 per credit hour. Tuition, nonresident: part-time $1281 per credit hour. *Financial support:* Application deadline: 1/1. *Unit head:* Dr. D. Hunter, Coordinator, 802-656-2030. *Application contact:* Dr. D. Hunter, Coordinator, 802-656-2030.

University of Victoria, Faculty of Graduate Studies, Faculty of Education, Department of Educational Psychology and Leadership Studies, Victoria, BC V8W 2Y2, Canada. Offers aboriginal communities counseling (M Ed); counseling (M Ed, MA); educational psychology (M Ed, MA, PhD), including counseling psychology (M Ed, MA), leadership studies (PhD), learning and development (MA, PhD), measurement and evaluation, special education (M Ed, MA); leadership studies (M Ed, MA). Part-time programs available. *Degree requirements:* For master's, thesis (for some programs), comprehensive exam (M Ed); for doctorate, comprehensive exam, thesis/dissertation, candidacy exam. *Entrance requirements:* For master's, 2 years of work experience in a relevant field; for doctorate, GRE, 2 years of work experience in a relevant field, minimum B average. Additional exam requirements/recommendations for international students: Required—TOEFL (minimum score 575 paper-based; 233 computer-based), IELTS (minimum score 7). *Faculty research:* Learning and development (child, adolescent and adult), special education and exceptional children.

University of Virginia, Curry School of Education, Department of Leadership, Foundations and Policy, Program in Administration and Supervision, Charlottesville, VA 22903. Offers M Ed, Ed D, Ed S. *Students:* 7 full-time (3 women), 34 part-time (12 women); includes 2 minority (both African Americans). Average age 40. 19 applicants, 63% accepted, 11 enrolled. In 2009, 61 master's, 18 doctorates, 47 other advanced degrees awarded. *Entrance requirements:* For master's, doctorate, and Ed S, GRE General Test, letters of recommendation. *Application deadline:* Applications are processed on a rolling basis. Application fee: $60. Electronic applications accepted. *Financial support:* Fellowships, research assistantships, teaching assistantships available. Financial award applicants required to submit FAFSA. *Unit head:* Pam Tucker, Program Coordinator. *Application contact:* Pam Tucker, Program Coordinator.

University of Virginia, Curry School of Education, Program in Education, Charlottesville, VA 22903. Offers administration and supervision (PhD); applied developmental science (PhD); counselor education (PhD); curriculum and instruction (PhD); early childhood-developmental risk (MT); education evaluation (PhD); educational psychology (PhD); educational research (PhD); elementary (MT, PhD); English education (MT, PhD); foreign language education (MT); higher education (PhD); instructional technology (PhD); kinesiology (MT, PhD); math education (PhD); reading education (PhD); research statistics and evaluation (PhD); school psychology (PhD); science education (PhD); social studies education (MT, PhD); special education (PhD); world languages education (MT). *Students:* 336 full-time (239 women), 88 part-time (54 women); includes 43 minority (24 African Americans, 2 American Indian/Alaska Native, 11 Asian Americans or Pacific Islanders, 6 Hispanic Americans), 18 international. Average age 27. 199 applicants, 48% accepted, 55 enrolled. In 2009, 127 master's, 52 doctorates awarded. *Degree requirements:* For master's, comprehensive exam (for some programs), field project; for doctorate, comprehensive exam, thesis/dissertation. *Entrance requirements:* For doctorate, GRE General Test. Additional exam requirements/recommendations for international students: Required—TOEFL (minimum score 600 paper-based; 250 computer-based; 90 iBT), IELTS (minimum score 7). *Application deadline:* Applications are processed on a rolling basis. Application fee: $60. Electronic applications accepted. *Financial support:* Fellowships, research assistantships, teaching assistantships available. Financial award application deadline: 1/5; financial award applicants required to submit FAFSA.

University of Washington, Graduate School, College of Education, Seattle, WA 98195. Offers curriculum and instruction (M Ed, Ed D, PhD), including educational technology, general curriculum (Ed D, PhD), language, literacy, and culture, mathematics education, multicultural education, reading and language arts education (Ed D), science education, social studies education, teaching and curriculum (M Ed); educational leadership and policy studies (M Ed, Ed D, PhD), including administration (Ed D), educational policy, organization, and leadership (M Ed, PhD), higher education, leadership for learning (Ed D), social and cultural foundations of education (M Ed, PhD); educational psychology (M Ed, PhD), including educational psychology (PhD), human development and cognition (M Ed), learning sciences, measurement, statistics and research design (M Ed), school psychology (M Ed); instructional leadership (M Ed); intercollegiate athletic leadership (M Ed); special education (M Ed, Ed D, PhD), including early childhood special education (M Ed), emotional and behavioral disabilities (M Ed), learning disabilities (M Ed), low-incidence disabilities (M Ed), severe disabilities (M Ed), special education (Ed D, PhD); teacher education (MIT). *Accreditation:* APA. Part-time and evening/weekend programs available. *Degree requirements:* For master's, thesis optional; for doctorate, thesis/dissertation. *Entrance requirements:* For master's and doctorate, GRE General Test, minimum GPA of 3.0. Additional exam requirements/recommendations for international students: Required—TOEFL. Electronic applications accepted. *Faculty research:* School restructuring/effective schools, special education interventions, literacy and writing, technology, school partnerships, teacher preparation.

University of Washington, Bothell, Program in Education, Bothell, WA 98011-8246. Offers leadership development for educators (M Ed); secondary/middle level endorsement (M Ed). Part-time and evening/weekend programs available. *Faculty:* 9 full-time (7 women), 1 (woman) part-time/adjunct. *Students:* 25 full-time (15 women), 118 part-time (91 women); includes 17 minority (6 African Americans, 6 Asian Americans or Pacific Islanders, 5 Hispanic Americans). Average age 34. 78 applicants, 76% accepted, 55 enrolled. In 2009, 47 master's awarded. *Degree requirements:* For master's, thesis. *Entrance requirements:* Additional exam requirements/recommendations for international students: Required—TOEFL. *Application deadline:* For fall admission, 8/14 priority date for domestic and international students; for spring admission, 2/12 priority date for domestic and international students. Applications are processed on a rolling basis. Application fee: $65. Electronic applications accepted. *Expenses:* Tuition, state resident: full-time $10,160; part-time $484 per credit hour. Tuition, nonresident: full-time $23,500; part-time $1120 per credit hour. Required fees: $567; $21.50 per credit hour. Tuition and fees vary according to course load and program. *Financial support:* Federal Work-Study and unspecified assistantships available. *Faculty research:* Multicultural education in citizenship education, intercultural education, knowledge and practice in the principalship, educational public policy, national board certification for teachers, teacher learning in literacy, technology and its impact on teaching and learning of mathematics, reading assessments, professional development in literacy education and mobility, digital media, education and class. *Unit head:* Dr. Bradley S. Portin, Director and Professor, 425-352-3482, Fax: 425-352-5234, E-mail: bportin@uwb.edu. *Application contact:* Amelia Bowers, Education Program Advisor, 425-352-5274, Fax: 425-352-5434, E-mail: abowers@uwb.edu.

University of Washington, Tacoma, Graduate Programs, Program in Education, Tacoma, WA 98402-3100. Offers educational administrator (M Ed); K-8 teacher education (M Ed); professional certification (M Ed); secondary science (M Ed); special education (M Ed). Part-time and evening/weekend programs available. *Faculty:* 13 full-time (8 women), 9 part-time/adjunct (8 women). *Students:* 85 full-time (66 women), 118 part-time (99 women); includes 24 minority (4 African Americans, 9 Asian Americans or Pacific Islanders, 11 Hispanic Americans). Average age 33. 36 applicants, 75% accepted, 23 enrolled. In 2009, 68 master's awarded. *Entrance requirements:* For master's, official sealed transcript from every college/university attended, personal goal statement, letters of recommendation, copy of valid teaching certificate. *Application deadline:* For fall admission, 8/1 for domestic students; for winter admission, 11/1 priority date for domestic students; for spring admission, 2/1 priority date for domestic students. Applications are processed on a rolling basis. Application fee: $65. Electronic applications accepted. *Expenses:* Tuition, state resident: full-time $10,660; part-time $484 per credit. Tuition, nonresident: full-time $24,000; part-time $1119 per credit. Required fees: $150 per term. Tuition and fees vary according to course load and program. *Faculty research:* Global learning communities for English/Chinese languages, evaluation of mathematics and reading intervention programs, response to intervention, school wide behavioral and emotional support, mathematics education and culturally responsive mathematics education. *Unit head:* Dr. Karen Landenburger, Chancellor, 253-692-4430, Fax: 253-692-5612, E-mail: uwted@u.washington.edu. *Application contact:* Dr. Carla Van Rossum, Recruiter/Advisor, 253-692-4430, Fax: 253-692-5612, E-mail: uwted@u.washington.edu.

The University of West Alabama, School of Graduate Studies, College of Education, Department of Teacher Education, Program in School Administration, Livingston, AL 35470. Offers M Ed. *Accreditation:* NCATE. Part-time programs available. *Entrance requirements:* For master's, GRE General Test, MAT, minimum GPA of 2.75.

University of West Florida, College of Professional Studies, Department of Engineering and Computer Technology, Pensacola, FL 32514-5750. Offers career and technical education (M Ed); curriculum and instruction (Ed S); curriculum and instruction: instructional technology (Ed D); instructional technology (M Ed), including educational leadership, instructional technology. *Faculty:* 2 full-time (1 woman). *Students:* 6 full-time (5 women), 130 part-time (77 women); includes 24 minority (19 African Americans, 1 American Indian/Alaska Native, 2 Asian Americans or Pacific Islanders, 2 Hispanic Americans). Average age 43. 80 applicants, 73% accepted, 44 enrolled. In 2009, 18 master's, 14 other advanced degrees awarded. *Entrance requirements:* For master's, GRE, GMAT, or MAT, letter of intent, names of references. Additional exam requirements/recommendations for international students: Required—TOEFL (minimum score 550 paper-based; 213 computer-based). *Application deadline:* For fall admission, 6/1 for domestic students, 5/1 for international students; for spring admission, 11/1 for domestic students, 10/1 for international students. Applications are processed on a rolling basis. Electronic applications accepted. *Expenses:* Tuition, state resident: full-time $4982; part-time $260 per credit hour. Tuition, nonresident: full-time $20,059; part-time $919 per credit hour. Required fees: $1247; $52 per credit hour. *Financial support:* In 2009–10, 3 research assistantships (averaging $3,280 per year), 2 teaching assistantships (averaging $3,760 per year) were awarded; unspecified assistantships also available. *Unit head:* Dr. Karen Rasmussen, Chair, 850-474-2300. *Application contact:* Terry McCray, Assistant Director of Graduate Admissions, 850-473-7718, Fax: 850-473-7714, E-mail: gradadmissions@uwf.edu.

University of West Florida, College of Professional Studies, Department of Engineering and Computer Technology, Program in Instructional Technology, Specialization in Educational Leadership, Pensacola, FL 32514-5750. Offers M Ed. *Students:* 2 full-time (1 woman), 10 part-time (5 women); includes 1 African American. Average age 38. 8 applicants, 50% accepted, 4 enrolled. In 2009, 21 master's awarded. *Expenses:* Tuition, state resident: full-time $4982; part-time $260 per credit hour. Tuition, nonresident: full-time $20,059; part-time $919 per credit hour. Required fees: $1247; $52 per credit hour. *Unit head:* Dr. Karen Rasmussen. *Application contact:* Terry McCray, Assistant Director of Graduate Admissions, 850-473-7718, Fax: 850-473-7714, E-mail: gradadmissions@uwf.edu.

University of West Florida, College of Professional Studies, Department of Professional and Community Leadership, Program in Administration, Pensacola, FL 32514-5750. Offers acquisition and contract administration (MSA); biomedical/pharmaceutical (MSA); criminal justice administration (MSA); database administration (MSA); education leadership (MSA); healthcare administration (MSA); human performance technology (MSA); leadership (MSA); nursing administration (MSA); public administration (MSA); software engineering administration (MSA). Part-time and evening/weekend programs available. Postbaccalaureate distance learning degree programs offered (no on-campus study). *Students:* 33 full-time (21 women), 168 part-time (97 women); includes 53 minority (32 African Americans, 2 American Indian/Alaska Native, 5 Asian Americans or Pacific Islanders, 14 Hispanic Americans), 1 international. Average age 34. 103 applicants, 74% accepted, 64 enrolled. In 2009, 47 master's awarded. *Entrance requirements:* For master's, GRE General Test, letter of intent, names of references. Additional exam requirements/recommendations for international students: Required—TOEFL (minimum score 550 paper-based; 213 computer-based). *Application deadline:* For fall admission, 6/1 for domestic students, 5/15 for international students; for spring admission, 11/1 for domestic students, 10/1 for international students. Applications are processed on a rolling basis. Application fee: $30. *Expenses:* Tuition, state resident: full-time $4982; part-time $260 per credit hour. Tuition, nonresident: full-time $20,059; part-time $919 per credit hour. Required fees: $1247; $52 per credit hour. *Financial support:* Unspecified assistantships available. Financial award application deadline: 4/15; financial award applicants required to submit FAFSA. *Unit head:* Dr. Karen Rasmussen, Chairperson, 850-474-2301, Fax: 850-474-2804. *Application contact:* Terry McCray, Assistant Director of Graduate Admissions, 850-473-7718, Fax: 850-473-7714, E-mail: gradadmissions@uwf.edu.

University of West Florida, College of Professional Studies, Department of Professional and Community Leadership, Program in Educational Leadership, Pensacola, FL 32514-5750.

Offers M Ed. *Accreditation:* NCATE. Part-time and evening/weekend programs available. *Students:* 9 full-time (3 women), 77 part-time (23 women); includes 15 minority (11 African Americans, 4 Hispanic Americans). Average age 34. 25 applicants, 72% accepted, 12 enrolled. In 2009, 36 master's awarded. *Degree requirements:* For master's, thesis optional. *Entrance requirements:* For master's, GRE General Test or minimum GPA of 3.0. Additional exam requirements/recommendations for international students: Required—TOEFL (minimum score 550 paper-based; 213 computer-based). *Application deadline:* For fall admission, 6/1 for domestic students, 5/15 for international students; for spring admission, 11/1 for domestic students, 10/1 for international students. Applications are processed on a rolling basis. Application fee: $30. *Expenses:* Tuition, state resident: full-time $4982; part-time $260 per credit hour. Tuition, nonresident: full-time $20,059; part-time $919 per credit hour. Required fees: $1247; $52 per credit hour. *Financial support:* Career-related internships or fieldwork, Federal Work-Study, scholarships/grants, and tuition waivers (partial) available. Support available to part-time students. Financial award application deadline: 4/15; financial award applicants required to submit FAFSA. *Unit head:* Dr. Thomas J. Kramer, Chairperson, 850-474-2949, Fax: 850-857-6288. *Application contact:* Terry McCray, Assistant Director of Graduate Admissions, 850-473-7718, Fax: 850-473-7714, E-mail: gradadmissions@uwf.edu.

University of West Florida, College of Professional Studies, Department of Professional and Community Leadership, Program in Educational Leadership—Education Specialist, Pensacola, FL 32514-5750. Offers Ed S. *Students:* 7 full-time (6 women), 36 part-time (24 women); includes 13 minority (10 African Americans, 1 American Indian/Alaska Native, 2 Hispanic Americans). Average age 36. 25 applicants, 72% accepted, 12 enrolled. In 2009, 26 Ed Ss awarded. *Entrance requirements:* Additional exam requirements/recommendations for international students: Required—TOEFL (minimum score 550 paper-based; 213 computer-based). *Application deadline:* For fall admission, 6/1 for domestic students, 5/15 for international students; for spring admission, 11/1 for domestic students, 10/1 for international students. Applications are processed on a rolling basis. Application fee: $30. *Expenses:* Tuition, state resident: full-time $4982; part-time $260 per credit hour. Tuition, nonresident: full-time $20,059; part-time $919 per credit hour. Required fees: $1247; $52 per credit hour. *Financial support:* Unspecified assistantships available. *Unit head:* Dr. David Stout, Chairperson, 850-474-2284, Fax: 850-474-2844. *Application contact:* Terry McCray, Assistant Director of Graduate Admissions, 850-473-7718, Fax: 850-473-7714, E-mail: gradadmissions@uwf.edu.

University of West Georgia, Graduate School, College of Education, Department of Educational Leadership and Professional Studies, Carrollton, GA 30118. Offers administration and supervision (M Ed, Ed S). *Accreditation:* NCATE. Part-time and evening/weekend programs available. *Faculty:* 12 full-time (5 women), 4 part-time/adjunct (3 women). *Students:* 63 full-time (48 women), 18 part-time (12 women); includes 26 minority (all African Americans). Average age 35. 7 applicants, 43% accepted, 2 enrolled. In 2009, 24 master's, 37 Ed Ss awarded. *Degree requirements:* For master's, internship; for Ed S, research project. *Entrance requirements:* For master's, GRE General Test, minimum GPA of 2.7 in field, 3.0 overall; 3 letters of reference; for Ed S, GRE General Test, master's degree, minimum graduate GPA of 3.0, letters of recommendation. *Application deadline:* For fall admission, 7/17 for domestic students; for spring admission, 11/20 for domestic students. Applications are processed on a rolling basis. Application fee: $30. Electronic applications accepted. *Expenses:* Tuition, state resident: full-time $2952; part-time $164 per semester hour. Tuition, nonresident: full-time $11,808; part-time $656 per semester hour. Required fees: $42.90 per semester hour. $307 per semester. Tuition and fees vary according to course load. *Financial support:* In 2009–10, 1 research assistantship with full tuition reimbursement (averaging $7,444 per year) was awarded; career-related internships or fieldwork, scholarships/grants, and unspecified assistantships also available. Support available to part-time students. Financial award applicants required to submit FAFSA. *Faculty research:* Legal issues in schooling, school violence, transforming leadership, action research in professional practice. Total annual research expenditures: $5,000. *Unit head:* Dr. Myrna Gantner, Interim Chair, 678-839-6557, Fax: 678-839-6097, E-mail: mgantner@westga.edu. *Application contact:* Dr. Charles W. Clark, Dean, 678-839-6508, E-mail: cclark@westga.edu.

University of Wisconsin–Madison, Graduate School, School of Education, Department of Educational Leadership and Policy Analysis, Madison, WI 53706-1380. Offers administration (Certificate); educational policy (MS, PhD). *Degree requirements:* For doctorate, thesis/dissertation. *Entrance requirements:* For master's and doctorate, GRE General Test. *Application deadline:* For fall admission, 1/15 for domestic and international students. Application fee: $56. Electronic applications accepted. *Expenses:* Tuition, state resident: part-time $594 per credit. Tuition, nonresident: part-time $1504 per credit. Required fees: $65 per credit. Tuition and fees vary according to course load, program and reciprocity agreements. *Financial support:* Fellowships with full tuition reimbursements, research assistantships with full tuition reimbursements, teaching assistantships with full tuition reimbursements, project assistantships available. *Unit head:* Dr. Julie Mead, Chair, 608-262-3106. *Application contact:* Dr. Julie Mead, Chair, 608-262-3106.

University of Wisconsin–Milwaukee, Graduate School, School of Education, Department of Administrative Leadership, Milwaukee, WI 53201-0413. Offers administrative leadership and supervision in education (MS); specialist in administrative leadership (Certificate); teaching and learning in higher education (Certificate). Part-time programs available. *Faculty:* 7 full-time (5 women). *Students:* 22 full-time (10 women), 102 part-time (82 women); includes 30 minority (20 African Americans, 1 American Indian/Alaska Native, 5 Asian Americans or Pacific Islanders, 4 Hispanic Americans), 2 international. Average age 36. 63 applicants, 73% accepted, 14 enrolled. In 2009, 46 master's awarded. *Degree requirements:* For master's, comprehensive exam, thesis or alternative. *Entrance requirements:* For master's, GRE General Test. Additional exam requirements/recommendations for international students: Required—TOEFL (minimum score 550 paper-based; 79 iBT), IELTS (minimum score 6.5). *Application deadline:* For fall admission, 1/1 priority date for domestic students; for spring admission, 9/1 for domestic students. Applications are processed on a rolling basis. Application fee: $45 ($75 for international students). *Expenses:* Tuition, state resident: full-time $8800. Tuition, nonresident: full-time $20,760. Tuition and fees vary according to program and reciprocity agreements. *Financial support:* Career-related internships or fieldwork and unspecified assistantships available. Support available to part-time students. Financial award application deadline: 4/15. Total annual research expenditures: $135,576. *Unit head:* Barbara J. Daley, Chair, 414-229-4740, Fax: 414-229-5300, E-mail: bdaley@uwm.edu. *Application contact:* General Information Contact, 414-229-4982, Fax: 414-229-6967, E-mail: gradschool@uwm.edu.

University of Wisconsin–Milwaukee, Graduate School, School of Education, Program in Urban Education, Milwaukee, WI 53201-0413. Offers adult and continuing education (PhD); curriculum and instruction (PhD); educational administration (PhD); educational and media technology (PhD); educational psychology (PhD); multicultural studies (PhD); social foundations of education (PhD). *Students:* 67 full-time (51 women), 44 part-time (30 women); includes 41 minority (23 African Americans, 2 American Indian/Alaska Native, 7 Asian Americans or Pacific Islanders, 9 Hispanic Americans), 4 international. Average age 41. 31 applicants, 45% accepted, 5 enrolled. In 2009, 11 doctorates awarded. *Degree requirements:* For doctorate, comprehensive exam, thesis/dissertation. *Entrance requirements:* For doctorate, GRE General Test, minimum undergraduate GPA of 2.85, graduate 3.5. Additional exam requirements/recommendations for international students: Required—TOEFL (minimum score 550 paper-based; 79 iBT), IELTS (minimum score 6.5). *Application deadline:* For fall admission, 1/1 priority date for domestic students; for spring admission, 9/1 for domestic students. Applications are processed on a rolling basis. Application fee: $45 ($75 for international students). *Expenses:* Tuition, state resident: full-time $8800. Tuition, nonresident: full-time $20,760. Tuition and fees vary according to program and reciprocity agreements. *Financial support:* Career-related internships or fieldwork and unspecified assistantships available. Support available to part-time students. Financial award application deadline: 4/15. *Unit head:* Larry Martin, Representative, 414-229-4729, Fax: 414-229-2920, E-mail: lmartin@uwm.edu. *Application contact:* General Information Contact, 414-229-4982, Fax: 414-229-6967, E-mail: gradschool@uwm.edu.

University of Wisconsin–Oshkosh, The Office of Graduate Studies, College of Education and Human Services, Department of Educational Leadership and Human Services, Oshkosh, WI 54901. Offers educational leadership (MS). Part-time and evening/weekend programs available. *Degree requirements:* For master's, comprehensive exam, thesis optional. *Entrance requirements:* For master's, bachelor's degree in education or related field. Additional exam requirements/recommendations for international students: Required—TOEFL (minimum score 550 paper-based; 213 computer-based; 79 iBT). Electronic applications accepted. *Faculty research:* Supervision models, learning styles, total quality management, cooperative learning, school choice.

University of Wisconsin–Stevens Point, College of Professional Studies, School of Education, Program in Educational Administration, Stevens Point, WI 54481-3897. Offers MSE. *Degree requirements:* For master's, comprehensive exam, thesis or alternative. *Application deadline:* For fall admission, 5/1 priority date for domestic students. Applications are processed on a rolling basis. Application fee: $45. *Expenses:* Tuition, state resident: full-time $7740; part-time $430 per credit hour. Tuition, nonresident: full-time $17,804; part-time $989 per credit hour. Tuition and fees vary according to course load and reciprocity agreements. *Financial support:* Application deadline: 5/1. *Unit head:* Dr. JoAnne Katzmarek, Associate Dean, 715-346-4430, Fax: 715-346-4846, E-mail: jkatzmar@uwsp.edu. *Application contact:* Dr. Patricia Caro, Director, 715-346-4403, Fax: 715-346-4846, E-mail: pcaro@uwsp.edu.

University of Wisconsin–Superior, Graduate Division, Department of Educational Administration, Superior, WI 54880-4500. Offers MSE, Ed S. Part-time and evening/weekend programs available. Postbaccalaureate distance learning degree programs offered (minimal on-campus study). *Faculty:* 4 full-time (1 woman). *Students:* 22 full-time (11 women), 95 part-time (37 women); includes 3 minority (1 American Indian/Alaska Native, 2 Asian Americans or Pacific Islanders). Average age 37. 15 applicants, 100% accepted. In 2009, 19 master's awarded. *Degree requirements:* For master's, thesis or alternative, research project or position paper, written exam; for Ed S, thesis, internship, oral and written exams. *Entrance requirements:* For master's, GRE General Test or MAT, minimum GPA of 2.75, teaching license, 3 years teaching experience; for Ed S, MAT, GRE, master's degree, 3 years of teaching experience, teaching license. *Application deadline:* For fall admission, 4/1 priority date for domestic students; for spring admission, 10/15 priority date for domestic students. Applications are processed on a rolling basis. Application fee: $45. *Financial support:* In 2009–10, 1 fellowship with partial tuition reimbursement (averaging $6,500 per year), 1 research assistantship with partial tuition reimbursement (averaging $5,000 per year) were awarded; career-related internships or fieldwork, Federal Work-Study, institutionally sponsored loans, scholarships/grants, tuition waivers (partial), and unspecified assistantships also available. Support available to part-time students. Financial award application deadline: 4/15; financial award applicants required to submit FAFSA. *Faculty research:* Postsecondary disabilities, educational partnerships, K-12. *Unit head:* Dr. Terri Kronzer, Chairperson, 715-394-8506, E-mail: tkronzer@uwsuper.edu. *Application contact:* Sandy Wallgren, Program Assistant/Status Examiner, 715-394-8295, Fax: 715-394-8146, E-mail: gradstudy@uwsuper.edu.

University of Wisconsin–Whitewater, School of Graduate Studies, College of Business and Economics, Program in School Business Management, Whitewater, WI 53190-1790. Offers MS Ed. Part-time and evening/weekend programs available. Postbaccalaureate distance learning degree programs offered (no on-campus study). *Degree requirements:* For master's, thesis or alternative. *Entrance requirements:* For master's, minimum GPA of 2.75 or MAT. Additional exam requirements/recommendations for international students: Required—TOEFL (minimum score 550 paper-based; 213 computer-based). Electronic applications accepted.

University of Wyoming, College of Education, Department of Educational Leadership, Laramie, WY 82070. Offers MA, Ed D, Certificate. Part-time programs available. Postbaccalaureate distance learning degree programs offered (minimal on-campus study). *Degree requirements:* For master's, thesis; for doctorate, comprehensive exam, thesis/dissertation; for Certificate, comprehensive exam, thesis, residency. *Entrance requirements:* For master's and Certificate, GRE; for doctorate, MA, 3 years' teaching experience. Additional exam requirements/recommendations for international students: Required—TOEFL (minimum score 520 paper-based). *Faculty research:* School leadership, leadership preparation, leadership skills.

Upper Iowa University, Online Master's Programs, Fayette, IA 52142-1857. Offers accounting (MBA); corporate financial management (MBA); global business (MBA); health and human services (MPA); higher education administration (MHEA); homeland security (MPA); human resources management (MBA); justice administration (MPA); organizational development (MBA); public personnel management (MPA); quality management (MBA). MBA also available at Madison, WI campus. Part-time programs available. Postbaccalaureate distance learning degree programs offered (no on-campus study). *Faculty:* 3 full-time (0 women), 66 part-time/adjunct (27 women). *Students:* 723 full-time (442 women). *Degree requirements:* For master's, research project. *Entrance requirements:* For master's, GMAT, GRE, or minimum GPA of 2.7 during last 60 hours. Additional exam requirements/recommendations for international students: Required—TOEFL (minimum score 570 paper-based; 230 computer-based). *Application deadline:* Applications are processed on a rolling basis. Application fee: $50. Electronic applications accepted. *Expenses:* Tuition: Full-time $6948; part-time $386 per credit hour. *Financial support:* Available to part-time students. Applicants required to submit FAFSA. *Faculty research:* Total quality management, CQI, teams, organization culture and climate, management. *Application contact:* David Hannum, Admissions Advisor, 800-603-3756, E-mail: hannumd@uiu.edu.

Ursuline College, School of Graduate Studies, Program in Educational Administration, Pepper Pike, OH 44124-4398. Offers MA. Part-time programs available. *Faculty:* 1 full-time (0 women), 5 part-time/adjunct (2 women). *Students:* 2 full-time (both women), 66 part-time (43 women); includes 12 minority (all African Americans). Average age 37. 12 applicants, 100% accepted, 11 enrolled. In 2009, 17 master's awarded. *Degree requirements:* For master's, thesis or alternative. *Entrance requirements:* For master's, minimum undergraduate GPA of 3.0, teaching certificate, professional experience. Additional exam requirements/recommendations for international students: Required—TOEFL (minimum score 500 paper-based; 173 computer-based). *Application deadline:* For fall admission, 8/1 priority date for domestic students. Applications are processed on a rolling basis. Application fee: $25. *Expenses:* Contact institution. *Financial support:* Federal Work-Study available. Financial award application deadline: 3/1; financial award applicants required to submit FAFSA. *Unit head:* Martin Kane, Director, 440-646-8148, Fax: 440-646-8328, E-mail: mkane@ursuline.edu. *Application contact:* Melanie Steele, Secretary, 440-464-8199, Fax: 440-684-6138, E-mail: gradsch@ursuline.edu.

Valdosta State University, Graduate School, Program in Educational Leadership, Valdosta, GA 31698. Offers M Ed, Ed D, Ed S. *Accreditation:* NCATE. *Degree requirements:* For master's, thesis (for some programs), comprehensive written and/or oral exams; for doctorate, thesis/dissertation, comprehensive written and/or oral exams; for Ed S, thesis. *Entrance requirements:* For master's and Ed S, GRE General Test or MAT; for doctorate, GRE General Test, minimum GPA of 3.5, 3 years experience. Additional exam requirements/recommendations for international students: Required—TOEFL (minimum score 523 paper-based; 193 computer-based). Electronic applications accepted. *Faculty research:* Student transition, mentoring in higher education, contemporary issues in higher education.

Vanderbilt University, Graduate School, Program in Leadership and Policy Studies, Nashville, TN 37240-1001. Offers PhD. *Faculty:* 21 full-time (7 women). *Students:* 38 full-time (23 women), 2 part-time (1 woman); includes 7 minority (4 African Americans, 1 Asian American or Pacific Islander, 2 Hispanic Americans), 6 international. Average age 33. 109 applicants, 10% accepted, 5 enrolled. In 2009, 6 doctorates awarded. *Degree requirements:* For doctorate, comprehensive exam, thesis/dissertation. *Entrance requirements:* For doctorate, GRE General Test. Additional exam requirements/recommendations for international students: Required—TOEFL (minimum score 570 paper-based; 230 computer-based; 88 iBT). *Application deadline:* For fall admission, 12/31 for domestic and international students. Application fee: $0. Electronic applications accepted. *Financial support:* Fellowships with full and partial tuition reimbursements, research assistantships with full tuition reimbursements, teaching assistantships with

Educational Leadership and Administration

Vanderbilt University (continued)
full tuition reimbursements, Federal Work-Study, institutionally sponsored loans, scholarships/grants, traineeships, and health care benefits available. Financial award application deadline: 1/15; financial award applicants required to submit CSS PROFILE or FAFSA. *Unit head:* Ellen Goldring, Chair, 615-322-8000, Fax: 615-343-7094, E-mail: ellen.b.goldring@vanderbilt.edu. *Application contact:* Tom Smith, Director of Graduate Studies, 615-322-8000, Fax: 615-343-7094, E-mail: thomas.m.smith@vanderbilt.edu.

Vanderbilt University, Peabody College, Department of Leadership, Policy, and Organizations, Nashville, TN 37240-1001. Offers education policy (MPP); educational leadership and policy (Ed D); higher education (M Ed); higher education, leadership and policy (Ed D); human resource development (M Ed); international education policy and management (M Ed); organizational leadership (M Ed). Part-time and evening/weekend programs available. *Faculty:* 28 full-time (13 women), 8 part-time/adjunct (3 women). *Students:* 155 full-time (111 women), 95 part-time (52 women); includes 36 minority (27 African Americans, 6 Asian Americans or Pacific Islanders, 3 Hispanic Americans), 21 international. Average age 31. 298 applicants, 76% accepted, 94 enrolled. In 2009, 65 master's, 21 doctorates awarded. *Degree requirements:* For master's, comprehensive exam, thesis optional; for doctorate, thesis/dissertation, qualifying exams, residency. *Entrance requirements:* For master's and doctorate, GRE General Test. Additional exam requirements/recommendations for international students: Required—TOEFL (minimum score 550 paper-based; 213 computer-based). *Application deadline:* For fall admission, 12/31 priority date for domestic and international students; for spring admission, 11/1 priority date for domestic and international students. Applications are processed on a rolling basis. Application fee: $0. Electronic applications accepted. *Financial support:* In 2009–10, 155 students received support, including 3 fellowships with full and partial tuition reimbursements available, 61 research assistantships with full and partial tuition reimbursements available, 1 teaching assistantship with full and partial tuition reimbursement available; Federal Work-Study, institutionally sponsored loans, scholarships/grants, tuition waivers (partial), and unspecified assistantships also available. Support available to part-time students. Financial award application deadline: 2/1; financial award applicants required to submit FAFSA. *Faculty research:* Education and leadership policy, education finances/economics of education, higher education leadership and policy, educator pay for performance and school choice, international and comparative education and policy management. *Unit head:* Dr. Ellen B. Goldring, Chair, 615-322-8000, Fax: 615-343-7094, E-mail: ellen.b.goldring@vanderbilt.edu. *Application contact:* Rosie Moody, Educational Coordinator, 615-322-8019, Fax: 615-343-7094, E-mail: rosie.moody@vanderbilt.edu.

Villanova University, Graduate School of Liberal Arts and Sciences, Department of Education and Human Services, Program in Educational Leadership, Villanova, PA 19085-1699. Offers MA. Part-time and evening/weekend programs available. *Students:* 2 full-time (both women), 11 part-time (3 women); includes 1 minority (Asian American or Pacific Islander). Average age 29. In 2009, 6 master's awarded. *Degree requirements:* For master's, comprehensive exam. *Entrance requirements:* For master's, GRE or MAT, minimum GPA of 3.0. Additional exam requirements/recommendations for international students: Required—TOEFL. *Application deadline:* For fall admission, 3/1 priority date for domestic and international students; for spring admission, 11/15 priority date for domestic and international students. Applications are processed on a rolling basis. Application fee: $50. Electronic applications accepted. *Expenses:* Tuition: Part-time $630 per credit. Required fees: $60 per credit. Part-time tuition and fees vary according to degree level and program. *Financial support:* Career-related internships or fieldwork and Federal Work-Study available. Financial award applicants required to submit FAFSA. *Unit head:* Dr. Connie Titone, Chairperson, 610-519-4620. *Application contact:* Dr. Connie Titone, Chairperson, 610-519-4620.

Virginia Commonwealth University, Graduate School, School of Education, Doctoral Program in Education, Educational Leadership Track, Richmond, VA 23284-9005. Offers PhD.

Virginia Commonwealth University, Graduate School, School of Education, Doctoral Program in Education, Instructional Leadership Track, Richmond, VA 23284-9005. Offers PhD.

Virginia Polytechnic Institute and State University, Graduate School, College of Liberal Arts and Human Sciences, School of Education, Department of Educational Leadership and Policy Studies, Program in Administration and Supervision of Special Education, Blacksburg, VA 24061. Offers Ed D, PhD, Ed S. *Accreditation:* NCATE. Postbaccalaureate distance learning degree programs offered (minimal on-campus study). *Degree requirements:* For doctorate, thesis/dissertation, internship. *Entrance requirements:* For doctorate and Ed S, GRE General Test, teaching experience. Additional exam requirements/recommendations for international students: Required—TOEFL. Electronic applications accepted. *Expenses:* Tuition, area resident: Full-time $10,228; part-time $459 per credit hour. Tuition, nonresident: full-time $17,892; part-time $865 per credit hour. Required fees: $1966; $451 per semester.

Virginia State University, School of Graduate Studies, Research, and Outreach, School of Liberal Arts and Education, Department of Graduate Professional Education Programs, Program in Educational Administration and Supervision, Petersburg, VA 23806-0001. Offers M Ed, MS. *Accreditation:* NCATE. *Degree requirements:* For master's, thesis optional.

Wagner College, Division of Graduate Studies, Department of Education, Program in Educational Leadership, Staten Island, NY 10301-4495. Offers school building leader (Certificate); school district leader (Certificate). *Expenses:* Tuition: Full-time $15,570; part-time $865 per credit. Required fees: $2.

Walden University, Graduate Programs, Richard W. Riley College of Education and Leadership, Minneapolis, MN 55401. Offers administrator leadership for teaching and learning (Ed D, Ed S); curriculum, instruction, and professional development (Ed S); early childhood education (birth-grade 3) (MAT); education (MS, PhD), including adolescent literacy and technology (grades 6-12) (MS), adult education leadership (PhD), community college leadership (PhD), curriculum, instruction, and assessment, early childhood education (PhD), educational leadership (MS), educational technology (PhD), elementary reading and literacy (MS), elementary reading and mathematics (MS), emotional/behavioral disorders (K-12) (MS), general program, higher education (PhD), integrating technology in the classroom (MS), K-12 educational leadership (PhD), learning disabilities (K-12) (MS), literacy and learning in the content areas (MS), mathematics (grades 6-8) (MS), mathematics (grades K-5) (MS), middle level education (grades 5-8) (MS), professional development (MS), science (grades K-8) (MS), self-designed (PhD), special education (PhD), special education (non-licensure) (MS), teacher leadership (grades K-12) (MS); educational leadership and administration (principal preparation) (Ed S); educational technology (Ed S); higher education and adult learning (Ed D); instructional design (Postbaccalaureate Certificate); instructional design and technology (MS), including general program (MS, PhD), online learning, training and performance improvement; special education: emotional/behavioral disorders (K-12) (MAT); special education: learning disabilities (K-12) (MAT); teacher leadership (Ed D, Ed S). Part-time and evening/weekend programs available. Postbaccalaureate distance learning degree programs offered (minimal on-campus study). *Faculty:* 54 full-time, 835 part-time/adjunct. *Students:* 13,940 full-time (11,339 women), 1,940 part-time (1,637 women); includes 4,626 minority (3,795 African Americans, 111 American Indian/Alaska Native, 199 Asian Americans or Pacific Islanders, 521 Hispanic Americans), 124 international. Average age 38. In 2009, 4,688 master's, 190 doctorates awarded. *Degree requirements:* For doctorate, thesis/dissertation (for some programs), residency; for other advanced degree, residency (for some programs). *Entrance requirements:* For master's, bachelor's degree or equivalent in related field; minimum GPA of 2.5; official transcripts; goal statement; access to computer and Internet; for doctorate, master's degree or equivalent in related field; minimum GPA of 3.0; official transcripts; three years' related professional/academic experience (preferred); access to computer and Internet; for other advanced degree, master's degree or equivalent in related field; minimum GPA of 3.0; 3 years related professional/academic experience (preferred); access to computer and Internet (Ed S). Additional exam requirements/recommendations for international students: Required—TOEFL (minimum score 550 paper-based; 213 computer-based), IELTS (minimum score 6.5), or Michigan English Language Assessment Battery (minimum score 82). *Application deadline:* Applications are processed on a rolling basis. Application fee: $50. Electronic applications accepted. *Expenses:* Tuition: Full-time $13,665; part-time $560 per credit. Required fees: $1375. Tuition and fees vary according to course load, degree level and program. *Financial support:* In 2009–10, 2,418 students received support; fellowships, Federal Work-Study, scholarships/grants, unspecified assistantships, and family tuition reduction, active duty/veteran tuition reduction, group tuition reduction, interest-free payment plans available. Support available to part-time students. Financial award applicants required to submit FAFSA. *Unit head:* Dr. Kate Steffens, Dean, 800-925-3368. *Application contact:* Jennifer Hall, Director of Enrollment, 866-4-WALDEN, E-mail: info@waldenu.edu.

Walla Walla University, Graduate School, School of Education and Psychology, College Place, WA 99324-1198. Offers counseling psychology (MA); curriculum and instruction (M Ed, MA, MAT); educational leadership (M Ed, MA, MAT); literacy instruction (M Ed, MA, MAT); students at risk (M Ed, MA, MAT); teaching (MAT). Part-time programs available. *Faculty:* 7 full-time (3 women), 1 part-time/adjunct (0 women). *Students:* 32 full-time (14 women), 9 part-time (7 women); includes 5 minority (1 African American, 1 American Indian/Alaska Native, 2 Asian Americans or Pacific Islanders, 1 Hispanic American). Average age 30. 41 applicants, 80% accepted, 21 enrolled. In 2009, 29 master's awarded. *Entrance requirements:* For master's, GRE General Test, minimum GPA of 2.75. Additional exam requirements/recommendations for international students: Required—TOEFL (minimum score 550 paper-based; 213 computer-based; 79 iBT). *Application deadline:* For fall admission, 4/1 priority date for domestic students. Applications are processed on a rolling basis. Application fee: $50. Electronic applications accepted. *Expenses:* Tuition: Full-time $19,929. *Financial support:* In 2009–10, 29 students received support; research assistantships, teaching assistantships, Federal Work-Study and tuition waivers (partial) available. Support available to part-time students. Financial award application deadline: 4/1; financial award applicants required to submit FAFSA. *Faculty research:* Admissions/retention, instructional psychology, moral development, teaching of reading. *Unit head:* Dr. Julian Melgosa, Dean, 509-527-2272, Fax: 509-527-2248, E-mail: julian.melgosa@wallawalla.edu. *Application contact:* Dr. Joe G. Galusha, Dean of Graduate Studies, 509-527-2421, Fax: 509-527-2237, E-mail: joe.galusha@wallawalla.edu.

Washburn University, College of Arts and Sciences, Department of Education, Program in Educational Leadership, Topeka, KS 66621. Offers M Ed. *Accreditation:* NCATE. *Degree requirements:* For master's, portfolio.

Washington State University, Graduate School, College of Education, Department of Educational Leadership and Counseling Psychology, Program in Educational Leadership, Pullman, WA 99164. Offers M Ed, MA, Ed D, PhD. *Accreditation:* NCATE. *Degree requirements:* For master's, comprehensive exam (for some programs), thesis (for some programs), oral or written exam; for doctorate, comprehensive exam, thesis/dissertation, oral exam, written exam. *Entrance requirements:* For master's, minimum GPA of 3.0, 3 letters of recommendation; for doctorate, GRE General Test, minimum GPA of 3.0, 3 letters of recommendation. Additional exam requirements/recommendations for international students: Recommended—TOEFL (minimum score 550 paper-based; 213 computer-based). Electronic applications accepted. *Faculty research:* Cross cultural personality study, language, learning school as community.

Washington State University Spokane, Graduate Programs, Program in Education, Spokane, WA 99210. Offers educational leadership (Ed M, MA); principal (Certificate); professional certification for teachers (Certificate); program administrator (Certificate); school psychologist (Certificate); superintendent (Certificate); teaching (MIT). *Faculty:* 24. *Students:* 18 full-time (8 women), 38 part-time (25 women); includes 1 minority (Hispanic American). 22 applicants, 73% accepted, 8 enrolled. *Degree requirements:* For master's, comprehensive exam (for some programs), thesis (for some programs). *Entrance requirements:* For master's, GRE or GMAT, minimum GPA of 3.0, 3 letters of recommendation, resume. Additional exam requirements/recommendations for international students: Required—TOEFL (minimum score 550 paper-based; 213 computer-based). *Application deadline:* For fall admission, 1/10 priority date for domestic students, 1/10 for international students; for spring admission, 7/1 priority date for domestic students, 7/1 for international students. Application fee: $50. *Expenses:* Tuition, state resident: part-time $423 per credit. Tuition, nonresident: part-time $1032 per credit. *Financial support:* In 2009–10, 33 students received support, including research assistantships (averaging $14,634 per year), teaching assistantships (averaging $13,383 per year). Total annual research expenditures: $16,557. *Unit head:* Dr. Joan Kingrey, Director, 509-358-7939, Fax: 509-358-7900, E-mail: kingrey@wsu.edu. *Application contact:* Graduate School Admissions, 800-GRADWSU, Fax: 509-335-1949, E-mail: gradsch@wsu.edu.

Washington State University Tri-Cities, Graduate Programs, Program in Education, Richland, WA 99354. Offers counseling (Ed M); educational leadership (Ed M, Ed D); literacy (Ed M); secondary certification (Ed M); teaching (MIT). Part-time programs available. *Faculty:* 24. *Students:* 11 full-time (8 women), 97 part-time (80 women); includes 17 minority (1 African American, 3 Asian Americans or Pacific Islanders, 13 Hispanic Americans). Average age 36. In 2009, 39 master's awarded. *Degree requirements:* For master's, comprehensive exam, thesis or alternative; for doctorate, comprehensive exam, thesis/dissertation. *Entrance requirements:* For master's, GRE, minimum GPA of 3.0, Working with Youth form, Character and Fitness form, 3 letters of recommendation. Additional exam requirements/recommendations for international students: Required—TOEFL. *Application deadline:* For fall admission, 1/10 priority date for domestic students, 1/10 for international students; for spring admission, 7/1 priority date for domestic students, 7/1 for international students. Applications are processed on a rolling basis. Application fee: $50. Electronic applications accepted. *Expenses:* Tuition, state resident: part-time $423 per credit. Tuition, nonresident: part-time $1032 per credit. *Financial support:* In 2009–10, 59 students received support, including research assistantships (averaging $14,634 per year), teaching assistantships (averaging $13,383 per year); Federal Work-Study, scholarships/grants, and unspecified assistantships also available. Financial award application deadline: 2/15. *Faculty research:* Multicultural counseling, socio-cultural influences in schools, diverse learners, teacher education, K-12 educational leadership. *Unit head:* Dr. Elizabeth Nagel, Director, 509-372-7398, E-mail: elizabeth_nagel@tricity.wsu.edu. *Application contact:* Helen Berry, Academic Coordinator, 800-GRADWSU, Fax: 509-372-3796, E-mail: hberry@tricity.wsu.edu.

Wayland Baptist University, Graduate Programs, Program in Education, Plainview, TX 79072-6998. Offers education administration (M Ed); higher education administration (M Ed); instructional leadership (M Ed); instructional technology (M Ed); special education (M Ed). Part-time and evening/weekend programs available. Postbaccalaureate distance learning degree programs offered (no on-campus study). *Faculty:* 6 full-time (4 women). *Students:* 4 full-time (2 women), 45 part-time (26 women); includes 6 minority (3 African Americans, 3 Hispanic Americans). Average age 30. 26 applicants, 77% accepted, 9 enrolled. In 2009, 4 master's awarded. *Degree requirements:* For master's, comprehensive exam, capstone course. *Entrance requirements:* For master's, GRE, GMAT or MAT. Additional exam requirements/recommendations for international students: Required—TOEFL (minimum score 500 paper-based; 173 computer-based; 61 iBT). *Application deadline:* Applications are processed on a rolling basis. Application fee: $50. Electronic applications accepted. *Expenses:* Tuition: Full-time $5796; part-time $322 per credit hour. Required fees: $782; $9 per credit hour. $60 per semester. Tuition and fees vary according to course load and campus/location. *Financial support:* Federal Work-Study, institutionally sponsored loans, and scholarships/grants available. Support available to part-time students. Financial award application deadline: 5/1; financial award applicants required to submit FAFSA. *Unit head:* Dr. Jim Todd, Chairman, 806-291-1045, Fax: 806-291-1951. *Application contact:* Amanda Stanton, Graduate Studies, 806-291-3423, Fax: 806-291-1950, E-mail: stanton@wbu.edu.

Wayne State College, School of Education and Counseling, Department of Educational Foundations and Leadership, Program in Educational Administration, Wayne, NE 68787. Offers educational administration (Ed S); elementary administration (MSE); elementary and secondary administration (MSE); secondary administration (MSE). *Accreditation:* NCATE.

Part-time and evening/weekend programs available. *Degree requirements:* For master's, comprehensive exam, thesis optional, research paper. *Entrance requirements:* For master's, GRE General Test, minimum GPA of 2.5; for Ed S, GRE General Test, minimum GPA of 3.2. Additional exam requirements/recommendations for international students: Required—TOEFL (minimum score 550 paper-based; 213 computer-based). Electronic applications accepted.

Wayne State University, College of Education, Division of Administrative and Organizational Studies, Detroit, MI 48202. Offers administration and supervision-secondary (Ed S); college and university teaching (Certificate); curriculum and instruction (PhD); educational leadership (M Ed, Ed S); educational leadership and policy studies (Ed D, PhD); elementary education curriculum and instruction (MA, Ed S); general administration and supervision (Ed D, PhD, Ed S); higher education (Ed D, PhD); instructional technology (M Ed, Ed D, PhD, Ed S); secondary curriculum and instruction (M Ed, Ed S). *Degree requirements:* For doctorate, thesis/dissertation. *Entrance requirements:* For doctorate, interview, minimum GPA of 3.0, an autobiography or curriculum vitae; references. Additional exam requirements/recommendations for international students: Required—TOEFL (minimum score 550 paper-based; 213 computer-based), TWE (minimum score 6). Electronic applications accepted. *Faculty research:* Total quality management, participatory management, administering educational technology, school improvement, principalship.

Webster University, School of Education, Department of Multidisciplinary Studies, St. Louis, MO 63119-3194. Offers administrative leadership (Ed S); education leadership (Ed S); educational technology (MAT); mathematics (MAT); multidisciplinary studies (MAT); school systems, superintendency and leadership (Ed S); social science (MAT); special education (MAT). Part-time programs available. *Entrance requirements:* For master's, minimum GPA of 2.5. Additional exam requirements/recommendations for international students: Required—TOEFL. *Expenses:* Tuition: Part-time $565 per credit hour. Tuition and fees vary according to degree level, campus/location and program.

Western Carolina University, Graduate School, College of Education and Allied Professions, Department of Educational Leadership and Foundations, Program in Community College and Higher Education, Cullowhee, NC 28723. Offers community college administration (MA Ed); community college teaching (MA Ed). *Accreditation:* NCATE. Part-time and evening/weekend programs available. Postbaccalaureate distance learning degree programs offered. *Students:* 6 full-time (5 women), 25 part-time (17 women). Average age 40. 70 applicants, 13% accepted, 5 enrolled. In 2009, 8 master's awarded. *Degree requirements:* For master's, comprehensive exam. *Entrance requirements:* For master's, GRE General Test, appropriate undergraduate degree, 3 letters of recommendation. Additional exam requirements/recommendations for international students: Required—TOEFL (minimum score 550 paper-based; 270 computer-based; 79 iBT). *Application deadline:* For fall admission, 5/1 priority date for domestic students; for spring admission, 9/1 priority date for domestic students. Applications are processed on a rolling basis. Application fee: $45. *Financial support:* In 2009–10, 1 student received support, including 1 research assistantship with full and partial tuition reimbursement available (averaging $7,000 per year); fellowships, teaching assistantships with full and partial tuition reimbursements available, career-related internships or fieldwork, institutionally sponsored loans, scholarships/grants, and unspecified assistantships also available. Financial award application deadline: 3/31; financial award applicants required to submit FAFSA. *Faculty research:* Women leaders, program evaluation, organizational culture and change, rural education, democracy in education, faculty careers and development. *Unit head:* Dr. Jacqueline Jacobs, Head, 828-227-7415, Fax: 828-227-7607, E-mail: jjacobs@email.wcu.edu. *Application contact:* Admissions Specialist for Community College and Higher Education, 828-227-7398, Fax: 828-227-7480, E-mail: jbewsey@email.wcu.edu.

Western Carolina University, Graduate School, College of Education and Allied Professions, Department of Educational Leadership and Foundations, Program in Educational Leadership, Cullowhee, NC 28723. Offers educational leadership (MSA, Ed D, Ed S); educational supervision (MA Ed). *Accreditation:* NCATE. Part-time and evening/weekend programs available. Postbaccalaureate distance learning degree programs offered. *Students:* 13 full-time (9 women), 289 part-time (192 women). Average age 39. 112 applicants, 72% accepted, 72 enrolled. In 2009, 32 master's, 13 doctorates, 5 other advanced degrees awarded. *Degree requirements:* For doctorate, comprehensive exam, thesis/dissertation. *Entrance requirements:* For master's, GRE, appropriate undergraduate degree, 3 letters of recommendation; for doctorate, GRE General Test, minimum graduate GPA of 3.5, appropriate master's degree; for other advanced degree, GRE General Test, minimum graduate GPA of 3.5, work experience, appropriate master's degree. Additional exam requirements/recommendations for international students: Required—TOEFL (minimum score 550 paper-based; 270 computer-based; 79 iBT). *Application deadline:* For fall admission, 2/1 for domestic students; for spring admission, 9/1 priority date for domestic students. Applications are processed on a rolling basis. Application fee: $45. *Financial support:* In 2009–10, 1 student received support, including 1 fellowship (averaging $6,000 per year); research assistantships with full and partial tuition reimbursements available, teaching assistantships with full and partial tuition reimbursements available, career-related internships or fieldwork, institutionally sponsored loans, scholarships/grants, and unspecified assistantships also available. Financial award application deadline: 3/31; financial award applicants required to submit FAFSA. *Faculty research:* Moral development and leadership, role of the principal, special education, qualitative research, student retention and engagement, interinstitutional partnerships. *Unit head:* Dr. Jacqueline Jacobs, Head, 828-227-7415, Fax: 828-227-7607, E-mail: jjacobs@email.wcu.edu. *Application contact:* Admissions Specialist for Educational Leadership, 828-227-7398, Fax: 828-227-7480, E-mail: gradsch@email.wcu.edu.

Western Connecticut State University, Division of Graduate Studies, School of Professional Studies, Department of Education and Educational Psychology, Program in Instructional Leadership, Danbury, CT 06810-6885. Offers Ed D. Part-time programs available. *Faculty:* 4 full-time (3 women), 3 part-time/adjunct (2 women). *Students:* 4 full-time (all women), 62 part-time (43 women); includes 7 minority (2 African Americans, 2 American Indian/Alaska Native, 3 Hispanic Americans). Average age 45. In 2009, 2 doctorates awarded. *Degree requirements:* For doctorate, comprehensive exam, thesis/dissertation, completion of program in 6 years. *Entrance requirements:* For doctorate, GRE or MAT, resume, three recommendations (one in a supervisory capacity in an educational setting), satisfactory interview with WCSU representatives from the EdD Admissions Committee. Additional exam requirements/recommendations for international students: Recommended—TOEFL (minimum score 550 paper-based; 213 computer-based; 79 iBT), IELTS (minimum score 6). *Application deadline:* For fall admission, 3/30 priority date for domestic students. Application fee: $100. *Expenses:* Contact institution. *Unit head:* Dr. Marcia A. Delcourt, Coordinator, 203-837-9121, Fax: 203-837-8413, E-mail: delcourtm@wcsu.edu. *Application contact:* Chris Shankle, Associate Director of Graduate Studies, 203-837-9005, Fax: 203-837-8326, E-mail: shanklec@wcsu.edu.

Western Governors University, Teachers College, Salt Lake City, UT 84107. Offers English language learning (K-12) (MA); learning and technology (M Ed, MA); management and innovation (M Ed); mathematics education (5-12) (MA); mathematics education (5-9) (MA); mathematics education (K-6) (MA); measurement and evaluation (M Ed); science (5-12) (MA), including biology, geology; science education (5-9) (MA); teaching (MAT); technology for principals (Post-Graduate Certificate). *Accreditation:* NCATE. Part-time and evening/weekend programs available. Postbaccalaureate distance learning degree programs offered (no on-campus study). *Degree requirements:* For master's, comprehensive exam. *Entrance requirements:* Additional exam requirements/recommendations for international students: Required—TOEFL (minimum score 450 paper-based). Electronic applications accepted. *Expenses:* Contact institution.

Western Illinois University, School of Graduate Studies, College of Education and Human Services, Department of Educational Leadership, Macomb, IL 61455-1390. Offers MS Ed, Ed D, Ed S. *Accreditation:* NCATE. Part-time and evening/weekend programs available. *Students:* 12 full-time (10 women), 208 part-time (97 women); includes 10 minority (3 African Americans, 1 American Indian/Alaska Native, 3 Asian Americans or Pacific Islanders, 3 Hispanic Americans). Average age 39. 32 applicants, 47% accepted. In 2009, 59 master's, 6 doctorates, 14 other advanced degrees awarded. *Degree requirements:* For master's, thesis or alternative; for doctorate, comprehensive exam, thesis/dissertation, electronic portfolio. *Entrance requirements:* For master's and Ed S, interview; for doctorate, GRE General Test. Additional exam requirements/recommendations for international students: Required—TOEFL (minimum score 575 paper-based; 230 computer-based; 88 iBT). *Application deadline:* Applications are processed on a rolling basis. Application fee: $30. Electronic applications accepted. *Expenses:* Tuition, state resident: full-time $4486; part-time $249.21 per credit hour. Tuition, nonresident: full-time $8972; part-time $498.42 per credit hour. Required fees: $72.62 per credit hour. *Financial support:* Research assistantships with full tuition reimbursements available. Financial award applicants required to submit FAFSA. *Unit head:* Dr. Jess House, Interim Chairperson, 309-298-1070. *Application contact:* Evelyn Hoing, Assistant Director of Graduate Studies, 309-298-1806, Fax: 309-298-2345, E-mail: grad-office@wiu.edu.

Western Kentucky University, Graduate Studies, College of Education and Behavioral Sciences, Department of Educational Administration Leadership and Research, Bowling Green, KY 42101. Offers educational administration (MAE); school administration (Ed S). *Accreditation:* NCATE. Part-time and evening/weekend programs available. *Degree requirements:* For master's, comprehensive exam, thesis or applied project and oral defense; for Ed S, thesis. *Entrance requirements:* For master's, GRE General Test, minimum GPA of 2.75. Additional exam requirements/recommendations for international students: Required—TOEFL (minimum score 555 paper-based; 213 computer-based; 79 iBT). *Expenses:* Tuition, state resident: full-time $4160; part-time $416 per credit hour. Tuition, nonresident: full-time $9550; part-time $506 per credit hour. Tuition and fees vary according to campus/location and reciprocity agreements. *Faculty research:* Principal internship, superintendent assessment, administrative leadership, group training for residential workers.

Western Michigan University, Graduate College, College of Education, Department of Educational Leadership, Research and Technology, Kalamazoo, MI 49008. Offers educational leadership (MA, PhD, Ed S); educational technology (MA, Graduate Certificate); evaluation, measurement and research (MA, PhD). *Unit head:* Dr. David A. England, Dean, 269-387-2960. *Application contact:* Admissions and Orientation, 269-387-2000, Fax: 269-387-2355.

Western New Mexico University, Graduate Division, School of Education, Silver City, NM 88062-0680. Offers bilingual education (MAT); counseling (MA); educational leadership (MA); elementary education (MAT); reading (MAT); school psychology (MA); secondary education (MAT); special education (MAT); TESOL (teaching English to speakers of other languages) (MAT). *Accreditation:* NCATE. *Degree requirements:* For master's, comprehensive exam. *Entrance requirements:* For master's, GRE General Test, GRE Subject Test, minimum GPA of 3.2 in last 64 hours of undergraduate study. Additional exam requirements/recommendations for international students: Required—TOEFL (minimum score 550 paper-based; 213 computer-based). Electronic applications accepted.

Western Washington University, Graduate School, Woodring College of Education, Department of Educational Leadership, Educational Administration Program, Bellingham, WA 98225-5996. Offers M Ed. *Accreditation:* NCATE. Part-time programs available. *Degree requirements:* For master's, comprehensive exam, thesis optional. *Entrance requirements:* For master's, GRE General Test or MAT, minimum GPA of 3.0 in last 60 semester hours or last 90 quarter hours, certification. Additional exam requirements/recommendations for international students: Required—TOEFL (minimum score 567 paper-based; 227 computer-based). Electronic applications accepted. *Faculty research:* Principal efficacy, collaborative school leadership, school/university partnerships, case study methodology, ethical leadership.

Western Washington University, Graduate School, Woodring College of Education, Department of Educational Leadership, Program in Student Affairs Administration, Bellingham, WA 98225-5996. Offers M Ed. *Accreditation:* NCATE. Part-time programs available. *Degree requirements:* For master's, comprehensive exam, thesis optional, research project. *Entrance requirements:* For master's, GRE General Test or MAT, minimum GPA of 3.0 in last 60 semester hours or last 90 quarter hours. Additional exam requirements/recommendations for international students: Required—TOEFL (minimum score 567 paper-based; 227 computer-based). Electronic applications accepted. *Faculty research:* Outcomes assessment, adult learning, best practices/student affairs, college health promotion, cultural pluralism.

Westfield State College, Division of Graduate and Continuing Education, Department of Education, Program in School Administration, Westfield, MA 01086. Offers M Ed, CAGS. Part-time and evening/weekend programs available. *Degree requirements:* For master's, comprehensive exam, practicum; for CAGS, research-based field internship. *Entrance requirements:* For master's, GRE General Test or MAT, minimum undergraduate GPA of 2.7; for CAGS, master's degree. *Faculty research:* Collaborative teacher education, developmental early childhood education.

Westminster College, Programs in Education, Program in Administration, New Wilmington, PA 16172-0001. Offers M Ed, Certificate. Part-time and evening/weekend programs available. *Degree requirements:* For master's, comprehensive exam. *Entrance requirements:* For master's, GRE or MAT, minimum GPA of 3.0.

West Texas A&M University, College of Education and Social Sciences, Division of Education, Program in Administration, Canyon, TX 79016-0001. Offers M Ed. Part-time and evening/weekend programs available. Postbaccalaureate distance learning degree programs offered (minimal on-campus study). *Degree requirements:* For master's, comprehensive exam, thesis optional. *Entrance requirements:* For master's, GRE General Test. Additional exam requirements/recommendations for international students: Required—TOEFL (minimum score 550 paper-based). Electronic applications accepted. *Faculty research:* Teacher quality, leadership, recruitment, retention.

West Virginia University, College of Human Resources and Education, Department of Educational Leadership Studies, Morgantown, WV 26506. Offers educational leadership (Ed D); higher education administration (MA); public school administration (MA). *Accreditation:* NCATE. Part-time programs available. *Degree requirements:* For master's, content exams; for doctorate, comprehensive exam, thesis/dissertation. *Entrance requirements:* For master's, minimum GPA of 2.75 or MA Degree or MAT of 4107; for doctorate, GRE General Test or MAT, minimum GPA of 3.25. Additional exam requirements/recommendations for international students: Required—TOEFL. Electronic applications accepted. *Faculty research:* Evaluation, collective bargaining, educational law, international higher education, superintendency.

Wheelock College, Graduate Programs, Division of Education, Boston, MA 02215-4176. Offers early childhood education (MS); education leadership (MS); elementary education (MS); language, literacy, and reading (MS); teaching students with moderate disabilities (MS). *Accreditation:* NCATE. Postbaccalaureate distance learning degree programs offered (minimal on-campus study). *Degree requirements:* For master's, comprehensive exam. *Entrance requirements:* Additional exam requirements/recommendations for international students: Required—TOEFL. Electronic applications accepted. *Faculty research:* Symbolic learning, emergent literacy, diversity inclusion, beginning reading language and culture, math education.

Whittier College, Graduate Programs, Department of Education and Child Development, Program in Educational Administration, Whittier, CA 90608-0634. Offers MA Ed. Part-time and evening/weekend programs available. *Degree requirements:* For master's, thesis. *Entrance requirements:* For master's, GRE General Test, MAT. *Faculty research:* Candidate leadership development.

Whitworth University, School of Education, Graduate Studies in Education, Program in Administration, Spokane, WA 99251-0001. Offers M Ed. *Accreditation:* NCATE. Part-time and evening/weekend programs available. *Degree requirements:* For master's, comprehensive exam, internship, practicum, research project, or thesis. *Entrance requirements:* For master's, GRE General Test, MAT. Tuition and fees vary according to program. *Faculty research:* Rural staff development.

Wichita State University, Graduate School, College of Education, Department of Counseling, Educational and School Psychology, Wichita, KS 67260. Offers counseling (M Ed); educational

Educational Leadership and Administration

Wichita State University (continued)

psychology (M Ed); school psychology (Ed S). *Accreditation:* NCATE. Part-time and evening/weekend programs available. *Expenses:* Tuition, state resident: full-time $4247; part-time $235.95 per credit hour. Tuition, nonresident: full-time $11,171; part-time $620.60 per credit hour. Required fees: $34; $3.60 per credit hour. $17 per term. Tuition and fees vary according to campus/location and program. *Unit head:* Dr. Marlene Schommer-Aikins, Chairperson, 316-978-3326, Fax: 316-978-3102, E-mail: marlene.schommer-aikins@wichita.edu. *Application contact:* Dr. Marlene Schommer-Aikins, Chairperson, 316-978-3326, Fax: 316-978-3102, E-mail: marlene.schommer-aikins@wichita.edu.

Wichita State University, Graduate School, College of Education, Department of Educational Leadership, Wichita, KS 67260. Offers M Ed, Ed D. *Expenses:* Tuition, state resident: full-time $4247; part-time $235.95 per credit hour. Tuition, nonresident: full-time $11,171; part-time $620.60 per credit hour. Required fees: $34; $3.60 per credit hour. $17 per term. Tuition and fees vary according to campus/location and program.

Widener University, School of Human Service Professions, Center for Education, Chester, PA 19013-5792. Offers adult education (M Ed); counseling in higher education (M Ed); counselor education (M Ed); early childhood education (M Ed); educational foundations (M Ed); educational leadership (M Ed); educational psychology (M Ed); elementary education (M Ed); English and language arts (M Ed); health education (M Ed); higher education leadership (Ed D); home and school visitor (M Ed); human sexuality (M Ed); mathematics education (M Ed); middle school education (M Ed); principalship (M Ed); reading and language arts (Ed D); reading education (M Ed); school administration (Ed D); science education (M Ed); social studies education (M Ed); special education (M Ed); technology education (M Ed). *Accreditation:* NCATE. Part-time and evening/weekend programs available. *Faculty:* 34 full-time (22 women), 37 part-time/adjunct (14 women). *Students:* 203 full-time (154 women), 415 part-time (298 women); includes 50 minority (34 African Americans, 1 American Indian/Alaska Native, 5 Asian Americans or Pacific Islanders, 10 Hispanic Americans), 3 international. Average age 39. 139 applicants, 88% accepted. In 2009, 168 master's, 31 doctorates awarded. Terminal master's awarded for partial completion of doctoral program. *Degree requirements:* For doctorate, thesis/dissertation. *Entrance requirements:* For master's, minimum GPA of 2.5; for doctorate, GRE or MAT, minimum GPA of 2.0 (undergraduate), 3.5 (graduate). *Application deadline:* Applications are processed on a rolling basis. Application fee: $25 ($300 for international students). Electronic applications accepted. *Expenses:* Contact institution. *Financial support:* Career-related internships or fieldwork, tuition waivers (full and partial), and unspecified assistantships available. Support available to part-time students. Financial award application deadline: 5/1. *Faculty research:* Reading and cognition, adult education, technology education, educational leadership, special education. *Unit head:* Dr. Michael W. LeDoux, Associate Dean, 610-499-4294, Fax: 610-499-4623, E-mail: mwledoux@widener.edu. *Application contact:* Dr. Roberta D. Nolan, Director of Graduate Admissions, 610-499-4125, E-mail: rdnolan@widener.edu.

Wilkes University, College of Graduate and Professional Studies, School of Education, Wilkes-Barre, PA 18766-0002. Offers classroom technology (MS Ed); educational computing (MS Ed); educational development and strategies (MS Ed); educational leadership (MS Ed); educational technology (Ed D); elementary education (MS Ed); higher education administration (Ed D); instructional technology (MS Ed); K-12 administration (Ed D); online teaching (MS Ed); school business leadership (MS Ed); secondary education (MS Ed), including biology, chemistry, English, history; special education (MS Ed). Part-time and evening/weekend programs available. Postbaccalaureate distance learning degree programs offered (minimal on-campus study). *Students:* 89 full-time (60 women), 2,849 part-time (2,058 women); includes 52 minority (10 African Americans, 2 American Indian/Alaska Native, 13 Asian Americans or Pacific Islanders, 27 Hispanic Americans), 6 international. Average age 33. In 2009, 947 master's awarded. *Entrance requirements:* Additional exam requirements/recommendations for international students: Required—TOEFL (minimum score 500 paper-based; 173 computer-based; 79 iBT). *Application deadline:* Applications are processed on a rolling basis. Application fee: $45. *Expenses:* Contact institution. *Financial support:* Federal Work-Study and unspecified assistantships available. Financial award application deadline: 3/1; financial award applicants required to submit FAFSA. *Unit head:* Dr. Michael Speziale, Dean, 570-408-4679, Fax: 570-408-4905, E-mail: michael.speziale@wilkes.edu. *Application contact:* Kathleen Houlihan, Director of Graduate Studies, 570-408-3235, Fax: 570-408-7846, E-mail: kathleen.houlihan@wilkes.edu.

William Paterson University of New Jersey, College of Education, Wayne, NJ 07470-8420. Offers curriculum and learning (M Ed); educational leadership (M Ed); reading (M Ed); special education and counseling services (M Ed), including counseling services, special education; teaching (MAT). *Accreditation:* NCATE. Part-time and evening/weekend programs available. *Students:* 119 full-time (100 women), 662 part-time (550 women); includes 111 minority (25 African Americans, 1 American Indian/Alaska Native, 9 Asian Americans or Pacific Islanders, 76 Hispanic Americans), 2 international. *Degree requirements:* For master's, comprehensive exam. *Entrance requirements:* For master's, GRE General Test, MAT, minimum GPA of 2.75, teaching certificate. *Application deadline:* Applications are processed on a rolling basis. Application fee: $50. Electronic applications accepted. *Financial support:* Research assistantships with full tuition reimbursements, career-related internships or fieldwork, Federal Work-Study, and unspecified assistantships available. Support available to part-time students. Financial award application deadline: 4/1; financial award applicants required to submit FAFSA. *Faculty research:* Urban community service. *Unit head:* Dr. Candace Burns, Dean, 973-720-2137, Fax: 973-720-2955, E-mail: burnsc@wpunj.edu. *Application contact:* Liana Fornarotto, Assistant Director, Graduate Admissions, 973-720-3578, Fax: 973-720-2035, E-mail: fornarottol@wpunj.edu.

William Woods University, Graduate and Adult Studies, Fulton, MO 65251-1098. Offers administration (Ed S); agriculture (MBA); athletic/activities administration (M Ed); curriculum and instruction (M Ed); curriculum leadership (Ed S); elementary administration (M Ed); health management (MBA); human resources (MBA); principalship (Ed S); secondary administration (M Ed); special education director (M Ed). Evening/weekend programs available. *Degree requirements:* For master's, capstone course (MBA), action research (M Ed); for Ed S, field experience. *Entrance requirements:* For master's, 2 recommendations, resumé, BA/BS; teaching certification (M Ed); course work in economics and accounting (MBA); for Ed S, M Ed, 2 letters of recommendation, resume, teaching certification. Additional exam requirements/recommendations for international students: Required—TOEFL (minimum score 550 paper-based). Electronic applications accepted.

Wilmington University, College of Education, New Castle, DE 19720-6491. Offers applied education technology (M Ed); career and technical education (M Ed); elementary and secondary school counseling (M Ed); elementary special education (M Ed); elementary studies (M Ed); instruction: gifted and talented (M Ed); instruction: teaching and learning (M Ed); literacy (M Ed); reading (M Ed); school leadership (M Ed); secondary teaching (MAT). *Accreditation:* NCATE. Part-time and evening/weekend programs available. *Entrance requirements:* For master's, 2 letters of recommendation, interview. Additional exam requirements/recommendations for international students: Required—TOEFL (minimum score 500 paper-based; 173 computer-based). Electronic applications accepted.

Wilmington University, College of Health Professions, New Castle, DE 19720-6491. Offers adult nurse practitioner (MSN); family nurse practitioner (MSN); gerontology (MSN); leadership (MSN); nursing (MSN); women's nurse practitioner (MSN). *Accreditation:* AACN. Part-time programs available. *Degree requirements:* For master's, thesis. *Entrance requirements:* For master's, BSN, RN license, interview, 3 letters of recommendation. Additional exam requirements/recommendations for international students: Required—TOEFL (minimum score 500 paper-based; 173 computer-based). Electronic applications accepted. *Faculty research:* Outcomes assessment, student writing ability.

Wilmington University, Program in Innovation and Leadership, New Castle, DE 19720-6491. Offers education innovation (Ed D); organizational leadership (Ed D). Part-time programs available. *Degree requirements:* For doctorate, thesis/dissertation. *Entrance requirements:* For doctorate, 3 letters of recommendation. Additional exam requirements/recommendations for international students: Required—TOEFL (minimum score 500 paper-based; 173 computer-based). Electronic applications accepted.

Wingate University, Program in Education, Wingate, NC 28174-0159. Offers educational leadership (MA Ed); elementary education (MA Ed, MAT); physical education (MA Ed); sport administration (MA Ed). *Accreditation:* NCATE. Part-time and evening/weekend programs available. *Degree requirements:* For master's, portfolio. *Entrance requirements:* For master's, GRE General Test or MAT, teaching certificate (MA Ed).

Winona State University, College of Education, Department of Educational Leadership, Winona, MN 55987-5838. Offers educational leadership (Ed S), including general superintendency, K-12 prinicpalship; general school leadership (MS); K-12 principalship (MS); outdoor education/adventure based leadership (MS); sports management (MS); teacher leadership (MS). *Accreditation:* NCATE. Part-time and evening/weekend programs available. *Degree requirements:* For master's, comprehensive exam, thesis optional; for Ed S, thesis optional. *Faculty research:* Financial equity, democratic practices in the classroom.

Winthrop University, College of Education, Program in Educational Leadership, Rock Hill, SC 29733. Offers M Ed. *Entrance requirements:* For master's, GRE General Test or MAT, 3 years of experience, South Carolina Class III Teaching Certificate, recommendations from current principal and district-level administrator, pre-entrance assessment. Electronic applications accepted.

Worcester State College, Graduate Studies, Department of Education, Program in Leadership and Administration, Worcester, MA 01602-2597. Offers M Ed, CAGS. Part-time programs available. *Faculty:* 9 full-time (7 women), 19 part-time/adjunct (7 women). *Students:* 21 part-time (12 women); includes 1 minority (Hispanic American). Average age 37. 60 applicants, 80% accepted, 11 enrolled. In 2009, 14 master's, 32 CAGSs awarded. *Degree requirements:* For master's, comprehensive exam (for some programs), thesis optional. *Entrance requirements:* For master's, GRE General Test or MAT, teaching certificate. Additional exam requirements/recommendations for international students: Required—TOEFL (minimum score 550 paper-based; 213 computer-based; 79 iBT). *Application deadline:* Applications are processed on a rolling basis. Application fee: $30. *Expenses:* Tuition, area resident: Part-time $150 per credit. Tuition, state resident: part-time $150 per credit. Tuition, nonresident: part-time $150 per credit. Required fees: $85. *Financial support:* Career-related internships or fieldwork, scholarships/grants, and unspecified assistantships available. Financial award application deadline: 3/1; financial award applicants required to submit FAFSA. *Unit head:* Dr. Audrey Wright, Coordinator, 508-929-8594, Fax: 508-929-8164, E-mail: awright1@worcester.edu. *Application contact:* Nicole Brown, Assistant Dean of Graduate and Continuing Education, 508-929-8787, Fax: 508-929-8100, E-mail: nbrown@worcester.edu.

Wright State University, School of Graduate Studies, College of Education and Human Services, Department of Educational Leadership, Program in Advanced Educational Leadership, Dayton, OH 45435. Offers advanced curriculum and instruction (Ed S); higher education-adult education (Ed S); superintendent (Ed S). *Accreditation:* NCATE. *Degree requirements:* For Ed S, thesis. *Entrance requirements:* For degree, GRE General Test, MAT. Additional exam requirements/recommendations for international students: Required—TOEFL.

Wright State University, School of Graduate Studies, College of Education and Human Services, Department of Educational Leadership, Programs in Educational Leadership, Dayton, OH 45435. Offers curriculum and instruction: teacher leader (MA); educational administrative specialist: teacher leader (M Ed); educational administrative specialist: vocational education administration (M Ed, MA); student affairs in higher education-administration (M Ed, MA). *Accreditation:* NCATE. *Degree requirements:* For master's, thesis (for some programs). *Entrance requirements:* For master's, GRE General Test, MAT. Additional exam requirements/recommendations for international students: Required—TOEFL.

Xavier University, College of Social Sciences, Health and Education, School of Education, Department of Educational Leadership and Human Resource Development, Program in Educational Administration, Cincinnati, OH 45207. Offers M Ed. Part-time programs available. *Faculty:* 4 full-time (0 women), 23 part-time/adjunct (3 women). *Students:* 2 full-time (0 women), 87 part-time (55 women); includes 3 minority (all African Americans). Average age 33. In 2009, 48 master's awarded. *Degree requirements:* For master's, comprehensive exam, thesis. *Entrance requirements:* For master's, MAT or GRE. Additional exam requirements/recommendations for international students: Required—TOEFL (minimum score 550 paper-based; 213 computer-based; 79 iBT). *Application deadline:* Applications are processed on a rolling basis. Application fee: $35. Electronic applications accepted. *Expenses:* Tuition: Part-time $697 per credit hour. One-time fee: $35 part-time. *Financial support:* Tuition waivers (partial) and unspecified assistantships available. Financial award applicants required to submit FAFSA. *Faculty research:* Educational leadership, hidden curriculum, internship effectiveness, NeuroLeadership, school leadership, strategic thinking. *Unit head:* Dr. Leo Bradley, Chair, 513-745-3701, Fax: 513-745-3504, E-mail: bradley@xavier.edu. *Application contact:* Dr. Leo Bradley, Chair, 513-745-3701, Fax: 513-745-3504, E-mail: bradley@xavier.edu.

Xavier University of Louisiana, Graduate School, Programs in Education, New Orleans, LA 70125-1098. Offers curriculum and instruction (MA); education administration and supervision (MA); guidance and counseling (MA). *Accreditation:* NCATE. Part-time and evening/weekend programs available. *Degree requirements:* For master's, comprehensive exam, thesis or alternative. *Entrance requirements:* For master's, GRE General Test, MAT, minimum GPA of 2.5. Additional exam requirements/recommendations for international students: Required—TOEFL.

Yeshiva University, Azrieli Graduate School of Jewish Education and Administration, New York, NY 10033-4391. Offers MS, Ed D, Specialist. Part-time and evening/weekend programs available. *Faculty:* 3 full-time (0 women), 11 part-time/adjunct (5 women). *Students:* 67 full-time (30 women), 136 part-time (52 women); includes 1 African American. Average age 25. 47 applicants, 83% accepted. In 2009, 46 master's, 4 doctorates, 2 other advanced degrees awarded. Terminal master's awarded for partial completion of doctoral program. *Degree requirements:* For master's, one foreign language, student teaching experience, comprehensive exam or thesis; for doctorate, one foreign language, comprehensive exam, thesis/dissertation, certifying exams, internship; for Specialist, one foreign language, comprehensive exam, certifying exams, internship. *Entrance requirements:* For master's, GRE General Test, BA in Jewish studies or equivalent; for doctorate and Specialist, GRE General Test, master's degree in Jewish education, 2 years of teaching experience. *Application deadline:* Applications are processed on a rolling basis. Application fee: $35. *Expenses:* Contact institution. *Financial support:* In 2009–10, 149 students received support, including 39 fellowships with full and partial tuition reimbursements available (averaging $2,500 per year); institutionally sponsored loans, scholarships/grants, and tuition waivers (partial) also available. Support available to part-time students. Financial award application deadline: 4/1. *Faculty research:* Social patterns of American and Israeli Jewish population, special education, adult education, technology in education, return to religious values. *Unit head:* Dr. Yitzchak S. Handel, Associate Dean, 212-340-7705, Fax: 212-340-7787. *Application contact:* Michael Kranzler, Associate Director of Admissions, 212-960-5277, Fax: 212-960-0086.

Youngstown State University, Graduate School, Beeghly College of Education, Department of Educational Foundations, Research, Technology, and Leadership, Youngstown, OH 44555-0001. Offers educational administration (MS Ed); educational leadership (Ed D). *Accreditation:* NCATE. Part-time and evening/weekend programs available. *Degree requirements:* For master's, comprehensive exam; for doctorate, comprehensive exam, thesis/dissertation. *Entrance requirements:* For master's, GRE, MAT, or teaching certificate; minimum GPA of 2.7; for doctorate, GRE General Test, GRE Subject Test, interview, minimum GPA of 3.5. Additional exam requirements/recommendations for international students: Required—TOEFL. *Faculty research:* Administrative theory, computer applications, education law, school and community relations, finance principalship.

Educational Measurement and Evaluation

American InterContinental University Online, Program in Education, Hoffman Estates, IL 60192. Offers curriculum and instruction (M Ed); educational assessment and evaluation (M Ed); instructional technology (M Ed); leadership of educational organizations (M Ed). Evening/weekend programs available. Postbaccalaureate distance learning degree programs offered (no on-campus study). *Entrance requirements:* Additional exam requirements/recommendations for international students: Required—TOEFL (minimum score 550 paper-based; 213 computer-based). Electronic applications accepted.

Angelo State University, College of Graduate Studies, College of Education, Department of Teacher Education, Program in Educational Diagnostics, San Angelo, TX 76909. Offers M Ed. Part-time and evening/weekend programs available. *Faculty:* 17 full-time (12 women). *Students:* 5 full-time (all women), 7 part-time (all women); includes 2 minority (both Hispanic Americans). Average age 37. 4 applicants, 100% accepted, 4 enrolled. In 2009, 9 master's awarded. *Degree requirements:* For master's, comprehensive exam. *Entrance requirements:* For master's, GRE General Test. Additional exam requirements/recommendations for international students: Required—TOEFL or IELTS. *Application deadline:* For fall admission, 7/15 priority date for domestic students, 6/10 for international students; for spring admission, 12/1 priority date for domestic students, 11/1 for international students. Applications are processed on a rolling basis. Application fee: $40 ($50 for international students). Electronic applications accepted. *Expenses:* Tuition, state resident: full-time $3396; part-time $142 per credit hour. Tuition, nonresident: full-time $10,152; part-time $423 per credit hour. Required fees: $1786; $36.25 per credit hour. $494 per semester. Full-time tuition and fees vary according to course load, degree level and program. *Financial support:* In 2009–10, 3 students received support. Career-related internships or fieldwork, Federal Work-Study, scholarships/grants, and unspecified assistantships available. Support available to part-time students. Financial award application deadline: 3/1; financial award applicants required to submit FAFSA. *Unit head:* Dr. Mary E. Sanders, Graduate Advisor, 325-942-2052 Ext. 265, Fax: 325-942-2039, E-mail: mary.sanders@angelo.edu. *Application contact:* Theresa Fortin, Graduate Admissions Assistant, 325-942-2169, Fax: 325-942-2194, E-mail: theresa.fortin@angelo.edu.

Arkansas State University—Jonesboro, Graduate School, College of Education, Department of Psychology and Counseling, Jonesboro, State University, AR 72467. Offers college student personnel services (MS); counselor education (Ed S), including college student personnel services, psychoeducational diagnosis, school counseling; rehabilitation counseling (MRC); school counseling (MSE); student affairs (Certificate). *Accreditation:* ACA (one or more programs are accredited); CORE (one or more programs are accredited); NCATE. Part-time programs available. *Faculty:* 11 full-time (6 women), 6 part-time/adjunct (2 women). *Students:* 49 full-time (37 women), 100 part-time (81 women); includes 32 minority (31 African Americans, 1 American Indian/Alaska Native), 1 international. Average age 32. 70 applicants, 46% accepted, 30 enrolled. In 2009, 23 master's, 11 other advanced degrees awarded. *Degree requirements:* For master's and other advanced degree, comprehensive exam, thesis or alternative. *Entrance requirements:* For master's, GRE General Test or MAT (MSE), appropriate bachelor's degree, interview, letters of reference; for other advanced degree, GRE General Test, interview, master's degree, letters of reference, official transcript, personal statement, immunization records. Additional exam requirements/recommendations for international students: Required—TOEFL (minimum score 550 paper-based; 213 computer-based; 79 iBT), IELTS (minimum score 6). *Application deadline:* For fall admission, 7/15 for domestic students, 7/1 for international students; for spring admission, 12/1 for domestic students, 11/13 for international students. Applications are processed on a rolling basis. Application fee: $30 ($40 for international students). Electronic applications accepted. *Expenses:* Tuition, state resident: full-time $3744; part-time $208 per credit hour. Tuition, nonresident: full-time $9540; part-time $530 per credit hour. Required fees: $896; $47 per credit hour. $25 per term. One-time fee: $50. Tuition and fees vary according to course load and program. *Financial support:* In 2009–10, 24 students received support; teaching assistantships, career-related internships or fieldwork, scholarships/grants, and unspecified assistantships available. Financial award application deadline: 7/1; financial award applicants required to submit FAFSA. *Unit head:* Dr. Loretta McGregor, Chair, 870-972-3064, Fax: 870-972-3962, E-mail: lmcgregor@astate.edu. *Application contact:* Dr. Andrew Sustich, Dean of the Graduate School, 870-972-3029, Fax: 870-972-3857, E-mail: sustich@astate.edu.

Boston College, Lynch Graduate School of Education, Department of Educational Research, Measurement, and Evaluation, Chestnut Hill, MA 02467-3800. Offers M Ed, PhD. Part-time and evening/weekend programs available. *Students:* 19 full-time (12 women), 30 part-time (25 women); includes 10 minority (4 African Americans, 2 Asian Americans or Pacific Islanders, 4 Hispanic Americans), 11 international. 54 applicants, 14 enrolled. In 2009, 5 master's, 4 doctorates awarded. Terminal master's awarded for partial completion of doctoral program. *Degree requirements:* For master's, comprehensive exam; for doctorate, comprehensive exam, thesis/dissertation. *Entrance requirements:* For master's, GRE General Test or MAT; for doctorate, GRE General Test. Additional exam requirements/recommendations for international students: Required—TOEFL (minimum score 550 paper-based; 213 computer-based; 81 iBT). Application fee: $60. Electronic applications accepted. *Financial support:* Fellowships with full and partial tuition reimbursements, research assistantships with full and partial tuition reimbursements, teaching assistantships with full and partial tuition reimbursements, career-related internships or fieldwork, Federal Work-Study, institutionally sponsored loans, scholarships/grants, traineeships, health care benefits, tuition waivers (full and partial), and unspecified assistantships available. Support available to part-time students. Financial award applicants required to submit FAFSA. *Faculty research:* Testing and educational public policy; statistical modeling; classroom use of technology; international comparisons of student achievement; psychometrics. *Unit head:* Dr. Larry Ludlow, Chairperson, 617-552-4214, Fax: 617-552-0812. *Application contact:* Adam Poluzzi, Director, Graduate Admission and Financial Aid, 617-552-4214, Fax: 617-552-0398, E-mail: poluzzi@bc.edu.

Bucknell University, Graduate Studies, College of Arts and Sciences, Department of Education, Specialization in Educational Research, Lewisburg, PA 17837. Offers MS Ed. *Degree requirements:* For master's, thesis or alternative. *Entrance requirements:* For master's, GRE General Test, minimum GPA of 2.8. Additional exam requirements/recommendations for international students: Required—TOEFL.

Cambridge College, School of Education, Cambridge, MA 02138-5304. Offers autism specialist (M Ed); autism/behavior analyst (M Ed); behavior analyst (Post-Master's Certificate); behavioral management (M Ed); early childhood teacher (M Ed); education specialist in curriculum and instruction (CAGS); educational leadership (Ed D); elementary teacher (M Ed); English as a second language (M Ed, Certificate); general science (M Ed); health education, health promotion (Post-Master's Certificate); health/family and consumer sciences (M Ed); history (M Ed); individualized degree (M Ed); information technology literacy (M Ed); instructional technology (M Ed); interdisciplinary studies (M Ed); library teacher (M Ed); literacy education (M Ed); mathematics (M Ed); mathematics specialist (Certificate); middle school mathematics and science (M Ed); school administration (M Ed, CAGS); school guidance counselor (M Ed); school nurse education (M Ed); school social worker/school adjustment counselor (M Ed); special education administrator (CAGS); special education/moderate disabilities (M Ed); teaching skills and methodologies (M Ed). Part-time and evening/weekend programs available. Postbaccalaureate distance learning degree programs offered (minimal on-campus study). *Faculty:* 10 full-time (3 women), 283 part-time/adjunct (187 women). *Students:* 974 full-time (755 women), 1,071 part-time (835 women); includes 940 minority (762 African Americans, 4 American Indian/Alaska Native, 22 Asian Americans or Pacific Islanders, 152 Hispanic Americans), 28 international. Average age 39. In 2009, 866 master's, 4 doctorates, 209 CAGSs awarded. *Degree requirements:* For master's, thesis, internship/practicum (licensure program only); for doctorate, thesis/dissertation; for other advanced degree, thesis. *Entrance requirements:* For master's, interview, resume, documentation of licensure, 2 professional references; for doctorate, official transcripts, interview, resume, documentation of licensure (if any), written personal statement/essay, portfolio of scholarly and professional work, qualifying assessment, 2 professional references, health insurance, immunizations form; for other advanced degree, official transcripts, interview, resume, documentation of licensure (if any), written personal statement/essay, 2 professional references, health insurance, immunizations form. Additional exam requirements/recommendations for international students: Required—TOEFL (minimum score 550 paper-based; 213 computer-based; 79 iBT); Recommended—IELTS (minimum score 6). *Application deadline:* Applications are processed on a rolling basis. Application fee: $30. Electronic applications accepted. *Expenses:* Contact institution. *Financial support:* In 2009–10, 1,373 students received support. Career-related internships or fieldwork, Federal Work-Study, and scholarships/grants available. Financial award applicants required to submit FAFSA. *Faculty research:* Adult education, accelerated learning, mathematics education, brain compatible learning, special education and law. *Unit head:* Dr. N. Alan Sheppard, Interim Associate Dean, 617-873-0619, E-mail: alan.sheppard@cambridgecollege.edu. *Application contact:* Stephen Lyons, Director of Enrollment, Graduate and N.I.T.E. Programs, 617-868-1000, Fax: 617-349-3561, E-mail: stephen.lyons@cambridgecollege.edu.

Claremont Graduate University, Graduate Programs, School of Educational Studies, Claremont, CA 91711-6160. Offers Africana education (Certificate); education and policy (MA, PhD); higher education/student affairs (MA, PhD); human development (MA, PhD); public school administration (MA, PhD); quantitative evaluation (MA, PhD); special education (MA, PhD); teacher education (MA); teaching and learning (MA, PhD); urban leadership (PhD); MBA/PhD. Part-time programs available. *Faculty:* 18 full-time (12 women), 1 part-time/adjunct (0 women). *Students:* 279 full-time (190 women), 174 part-time (122 women); includes 196 minority (50 African Americans, 1 American Indian/Alaska Native, 37 Asian Americans or Pacific Islanders, 108 Hispanic Americans), 10 international. Average age 37. In 2009, 84 master's, 23 doctorates awarded. Terminal master's awarded for partial completion of doctoral program. *Entrance requirements:* For master's and doctorate, GRE General Test. Additional exam requirements/recommendations for international students: Required—TOEFL (minimum score 550 paper-based; 213 computer-based; 80 iBT). *Application deadline:* For fall admission, 2/1 priority date for domestic students. Applications are processed on a rolling basis. Application fee: $60. Electronic applications accepted. *Expenses:* Tuition: Full-time $35,046; part-time $1524 per credit. Required fees: $161 per semester. *Financial support:* Fellowships, research assistantships, Federal Work-Study, institutionally sponsored loans, and scholarships/grants available. Support available to part-time students. Financial award application deadline: 2/15; financial award applicants required to submit FAFSA. *Faculty research:* Education administration, K-12 and higher education, multicultural education, education policy, diversity in higher education, faculty issues. *Unit head:* Margaret Grogan, Dean, 909-621-8075, Fax: 909-621-8734, E-mail: margaret.grogan@cgu.edu.

College of Saint Mary, Program in Education, Omaha, NE 68106. Offers assessment leadership (MSE); English as a second language (MSE). Part-time programs available. *Entrance requirements:* For master's, technology competency test or equivalent, minimum cumulative GPA of 3.0, teaching certificate, 2 letters of reference, resume.

Curry College, Graduate Studies, Program in Education, Milton, MA 02186-9984. Offers educational administration (M Ed); educational diagnostic assessment (Certificate); educational therapy (Certificate); elementary education (M Ed); foundations (non-license) (M Ed); learning disabilities across the lifespan (Certificate); reading (M Ed, Certificate); special education (M Ed). Part-time and evening/weekend programs available. *Faculty:* 6 full-time (4 women), 12 part-time/adjunct (9 women). *Students:* 101 part-time (82 women). Average age 37. In 2009, 25 master's awarded. *Degree requirements:* For master's, project or thesis. *Entrance requirements:* For master's, MAT or GRE, interview, recommendations, resume, written statement. Additional exam requirements/recommendations for international students: Required—TOEFL (minimum score 550 paper-based; 213 computer-based; 80 iBT). *Application deadline:* For fall admission, 8/1 priority date for domestic students, 6/1 for international students; for winter admission, 10/1 for international students; for spring admission, 1/1 for domestic students, 1/28 for international students. Applications are processed on a rolling basis. Application fee: $50. *Expenses:* Contact institution. *Financial support:* Career-related internships or fieldwork and tuition waivers (partial) available. *Faculty research:* Classroom trauma, therapeutic writing, inclusionary practices. *Unit head:* Dr. Donald Gratz, Director and Associate Professor, 617-333-2243, E-mail: dgratz0703@curry.edu. *Application contact:* John Bresnahan, Director of Graduate Enrollment and Student Services, 617-333-2243, Fax: 617-979-3535, E-mail: jbresnah0104@curry.edu.

Eastern Michigan University, Graduate School, College of Education, Department of Teacher Education, Programs in Educational Psychology and Assessment, Ypsilanti, MI 48197. Offers educational assessment (Graduate Certificate); educational psychology (MA), including development/personality, research and assessment, research and evaluation, the developing learner. *Accreditation:* NCATE. Part-time and evening/weekend programs available. Postbaccalaureate distance learning degree programs offered (minimal on-campus study). *Students:* 17 part-time (14 women); includes 1 minority (African American). Average age 34. In 2009, 2 master's awarded. *Degree requirements:* For master's, thesis or alternative. *Entrance requirements:* For master's, GRE. Additional exam requirements/recommendations for international students: Required—TOEFL. *Application deadline:* Applications are processed on a rolling basis. Application fee: $35. Tuition and fees vary according to course level. *Financial support:* Fellowships, research assistantships with full tuition reimbursements, teaching assistantships with full tuition reimbursements, career-related internships or fieldwork, Federal Work-Study, institutionally sponsored loans, scholarships/grants, tuition waivers (partial), and unspecified assistantships available. Support available to part-time students. Financial award applicants required to submit FAFSA. *Unit head:* Dr. Rob Carpenter, Coordinator, 734-487-3260, Fax: 734-487-2101, E-mail: rcarpen1@emich.edu. *Application contact:* Dr. Rob Carpenter, Coordinator, 734-487-3260, Fax: 734-487-2101, E-mail: rcarpen1@emich.edu.

Florida State University, The Graduate School, College of Education, Department of Educational Leadership and Policy Studies, Program in Program Evaluation, Tallahassee, FL 32306. Offers MS, PhD, Ed S. *Faculty:* 1 (woman) full-time. *Students:* 2 full-time (1 woman), 5 part-time (4 women); includes 2 minority (both African Americans). In 2009, 1 master's awarded. *Entrance requirements:* Additional exam requirements/recommendations for international students: Required—TOEFL (minimum score 550 paper-based; 213 computer-based; 80 iBT). *Application deadline:* For fall admission, 5/1 priority date for domestic and international students; for spring admission, 10/1 priority date for domestic and international students. Application fee: $30. Electronic applications accepted. *Expenses:* Tuition, state resident: full-time $7413. Tuition, nonresident: full-time $22,567. *Financial support:* Fellowships with full and partial tuition reimbursements, research assistantships with full and partial tuition reimbursements, teaching assistantships with full and partial tuition reimbursements, career-related internships or fieldwork, scholarships/grants, and unspecified assistantships available. *Faculty research:* Evaluation services for state, federal and HR organizations; career counseling. *Unit head:* Dr. Linda Schrader, Head, 850-644-6777, Fax: 850-644-1258, E-mail: lschrade@coe.fsu.edu. *Application contact:* Jimmy Pastrano, Program Assistant, 850-644-6777, Fax: 850-644-1258, E-mail: pastrano@coe.fsu.edu.

Florida State University, The Graduate School, College of Education, Department of Educational Psychology and Learning Systems, Program in Measurement and Statistics,

Educational Measurement and Evaluation

Florida State University (continued)
Tallahassee, FL 32306. Offers MS, PhD, Ed S. *Faculty:* 4 full-time (2 women), 1 (woman) part-time/adjunct. *Students:* 23 full-time (18 women), 4 part-time (2 women); includes 3 minority (1 African American, 2 Asian Americans or Pacific Islanders), 19 international. 31 applicants, 29% accepted, 6 enrolled. In 2009, 1 master's, 3 doctorates awarded. *Degree requirements:* For master's, comprehensive exam; for doctorate, thesis/dissertation, preliminary exam, prospectus. *Entrance requirements:* Additional exam requirements/recommendations for international students: Required—TOEFL (minimum score 550 paper-based; 213 computer-based; 80 iBT). *Application deadline:* For fall admission, 6/1 priority date for domestic and international students; for spring admission, 10/1 priority date for domestic and international students. Application fee: $30. *Expenses:* Tuition, state resident: full-time $7413. Tuition, nonresident: full-time $22,567. *Financial support:* In 2009–10, 11 research assistantships with full and partial tuition reimbursements were awarded; fellowships with full and partial tuition reimbursements, teaching assistantships with full and partial tuition reimbursements also available. *Faculty research:* Methods for meta analysis; IRT/mixIRT; CBT; modeling, especially of large data sets. *Unit head:* Dr. Betsy Becker, Program Leader, 850-645-2371, Fax: 850-644-8776, E-mail: bjbecker@coe.fsu.edu. *Application contact:* Sally Gadson, Program Assistant, 850-644-8046, Fax: 850-644-5067, E-mail: gadson@coe.fsu.edu.

Gallaudet University, The Graduate School, Department of Educational Foundations and Research, Washington, DC 20002-3625. Offers international development (MA, Certificate). *Accreditation:* NCATE. *Degree requirements:* For Certificate, thesis optional. *Entrance requirements:* For degree, GRE General Test or MAT. Electronic applications accepted.

George Mason University, College of Education and Human Development, Program in New Professional Studies, Fairfax, VA 22030. Offers MA. *Faculty:* 88 full-time (64 women), 120 part-time/adjunct (93 women). *Students:* 5 full-time (4 women), 262 part-time (210 women); includes 22 minority (6 African Americans, 3 Asian Americans or Pacific Islanders, 13 Hispanic Americans). Average age 34. 128 applicants, 91% accepted, 104 enrolled. In 2009, 116 master's awarded. *Degree requirements:* For master's, comprehensive exam, final research presentation. *Entrance requirements:* For master's, GMAT, minimum GPA of 3.0 in last 60 hours, 3 letters of recommendation. Additional exam requirements/recommendations for international students: Required—TOEFL. *Application deadline:* For fall admission, 3/1 priority date for domestic and international students; for spring admission, 11/1 for domestic and international students. Application fee: $75. Electronic applications accepted. *Expenses:* Tuition, state resident: full-time $7568; part-time $315.33 per credit hour. Tuition, nonresident: full-time $21,704; part-time $904.33 per credit hour. Required fees: $2184; $91 per credit hour. *Financial support:* Federal Work-Study, scholarships/grants, unspecified assistantships, and health care benefits (full-time research or teaching assistantship recipients) available. Support available to part-time students. Financial award application deadline: 3/1; financial award applicants required to submit FAFSA. *Faculty research:* Peace building, educational relationships in Africa, research on peace with Africa, integrating technology ideas for teachers in classrooms. *Unit head:* Betsy De Mulder, Director, 703-993-8326, Fax: 703-993-8321, E-mail: iet@gmu.edu. *Application contact:* Ruth Potter, Office Manager, 703-993-8319, E-mail: rpotter@gmu.edu.

Georgia State University, College of Education, Department of Educational Policy Studies, Program in Educational Research, Atlanta, GA 30302-3083. Offers educational research (MS); research, measurements and statistics (PhD). *Accreditation:* NCATE. *Degree requirements:* For master's, thesis or project; for doctorate, comprehensive exam, thesis/dissertation. *Entrance requirements:* For master's, GRE General Test, minimum GPA of 2.5, 2 letters of recommendation, resume; for doctorate, GRE General Test or MAT, minimum GPA of 3.3, goals statement, 2 letters of recommendation, resumé/curriculum vitae. Electronic applications accepted. *Faculty research:* Educational statistics, item response theory, instructional computing, measurement.

Harvard University, Graduate School of Education, Doctoral Program in Education, Cambridge, MA 02138. Offers culture, communities and education (Ed D); education policy, leadership and instructional practice (Ed D); higher education (Ed D); human development and education (Ed D); quantitative policy analysis in education (Ed D); urban superintendency (Ed D). Part-time programs available. *Faculty:* 70 full-time (33 women), 36 part-time/adjunct (20 women). *Students:* 295 full-time (198 women), 23 part-time (11 women); includes 103 minority (40 African Americans, 4 American Indian/Alaska Native, 34 Asian Americans or Pacific Islanders, 25 Hispanic Americans), 33 international. Average age 32. 551 applicants, 9% accepted, 39 enrolled. In 2009, 41 doctorates awarded. Terminal master's awarded for partial completion of doctoral program. *Degree requirements:* For doctorate, thesis/dissertation. *Entrance requirements:* For doctorate, GRE General Test, 3 letters of recommendation. Additional exam requirements/recommendations for international students: Required—TOEFL (minimum score 600 paper-based; 250 computer-based; 100 iBT), TWE (minimum score 5). *Application deadline:* For fall admission, 12/14 for domestic and international students. Application fee: $85. Electronic applications accepted. *Expenses:* Contact institution. *Financial support:* In 2009–10, 265 students received support, including 129 fellowships with full and partial tuition reimbursements available (averaging $11,142 per year), 41 research assistantships (averaging $11,990 per year), 173 teaching assistantships (averaging $9,174 per year); career-related internships or fieldwork, Federal Work-Study, institutionally sponsored loans, scholarships/grants, health care benefits, tuition waivers (full and partial), and unspecified assistantships also available. Support available to part-time students. Financial award application deadline: 2/1; financial award applicants required to submit FAFSA. *Faculty research:* Learning and development, educational leadership and organizations, education policy analysis. Total annual research expenditures: $18.1 million. *Unit head:* Dr. Shu-Ling Chen, Assistant Dean, 617-496-4406. *Application contact:* Information Contact, 617-495-3414, Fax: 617-496-3577, E-mail: gseadmissions@harvard.edu.

Houston Baptist University, College of Education and Behavioral Sciences, Programs in Education, Houston, TX 77074-3298. Offers bilingual education (M Ed); counselor education (M Ed); curriculum and instruction (M Ed); educational administration (M Ed); educational diagnostician (M Ed); reading education (M Ed). Part-time programs available. *Entrance requirements:* For master's, GRE General Test or MAT. Additional exam requirements/recommendations for international students: Required—TOEFL (minimum score 550 paper-based; 213 computer-based).

Indiana University Bloomington, School of Education, Department of Counseling and Educational Psychology, Bloomington, IN 47405-1006. Offers counseling (MS, PhD, Ed S); counseling psychology (PhD); counselor education (MS, Ed S); educational psychology (MS, PhD); inquiry methodology (PhD); learning and developmental sciences (MS, PhD); school psychology (PhD, Ed S). *Accreditation:* ACA (one or more programs are accredited); APA (one or more programs are accredited); NCATE. *Faculty:* 32 full-time (13 women), 20 part-time/adjunct (10 women). *Students:* 218 full-time (165 women), 34 part-time (29 women); includes 45 minority (19 African Americans, 2 American Indian/Alaska Native, 12 Asian Americans or Pacific Islanders, 12 Hispanic Americans), 42 international. Average age 30. 348 applicants, 41% accepted, 53 enrolled. In 2009, 57 master's, 21 doctorates, 22 other advanced degrees awarded. Terminal master's awarded for partial completion of doctoral program. *Degree requirements:* For master's, thesis optional; for doctorate, thesis/dissertation; for Ed S, comprehensive exam or project. *Entrance requirements:* For master's, doctorate, and Ed S, GRE General Test. Additional exam requirements/recommendations for international students: Required—TOEFL. *Application deadline:* Applications are processed on a rolling basis. Application fee: $55 ($65 for international students). Electronic applications accepted. *Financial support:* In 2009–10, 58 students received support, including 7 fellowships with partial tuition reimbursements available (averaging $15,000 per year), 15 research assistantships with partial tuition reimbursements available (averaging $12,000 per year), 36 teaching assistantships with partial tuition reimbursements available (averaging $14,280 per year); career-related internships or fieldwork, Federal Work-Study, institutionally sponsored loans, scholarships/grants, and unspecified assistantships also available. Support available to part-time students. Financial award application deadline: 1/1; financial award applicants required to submit FAFSA. *Faculty research:* Counseling psychology, inquiry methodology, school psychology, learning sciences, human development, educational psychology. *Unit head:* Dr. Joyce Alexander, Chairperson, 812-856-8300, Fax: 812-856-8333, E-mail: cep@indiana.edu. *Application contact:* Jessica Durnal, Student Services Specialist, 812-856-8300, Fax: 812-856-8333, E-mail: cep@indiana.edu.

Indiana University Bloomington, School of Education, Program in Inquiry Methodology, Bloomington, IN 47405-7000. Offers PhD. *Students:* 5 full-time (2 women), all international. Average age 28. 1 applicant, 0% accepted, 0 enrolled.Application fee: $55 ($65 for international students). *Unit head:* Dr. Gerardo Gonzalez, Dean, 812-856-8001, Fax: 812-856-8088, E-mail: gonzalez@indiana.edu. *Application contact:* Elizabeth Tilghman, Admissions Coordinator, 812-856-8552, Fax: 812-856-8505, E-mail: etilghma@indiana.edu.

Iowa State University of Science and Technology, Graduate College, College of Human Sciences, Department of Educational Leadership and Policy Studies, Ames, IA 50011. Offers counselor education (M Ed, MS); educational administration (M Ed, MS); educational leadership (PhD); higher education (M Ed, MS); organizational learning and human resource development (M Ed, MS); research and evaluation (MS). *Faculty:* 21 full-time (10 women), 14 part-time/adjunct (8 women). *Students:* 116 full-time (68 women), 218 part-time (130 women); includes 58 minority (34 African Americans, 3 American Indian/Alaska Native, 4 Asian Americans or Pacific Islanders, 17 Hispanic Americans), 7 international. 138 applicants, 78% accepted, 74 enrolled. In 2009, 77 master's, 18 doctorates awarded. *Degree requirements:* For master's, thesis or alternative; for doctorate, thesis/dissertation. *Entrance requirements:* For doctorate, GRE General Test. Additional exam requirements/recommendations for international students: Required—TOEFL (minimum score 560 paper-based; 83 iBT) or IELTS (minimum score 6.5). *Application deadline:* For fall admission, 1/1 priority date for domestic and international students. Applications are processed on a rolling basis. Application fee: $40 ($90 for international students). Electronic applications accepted. *Expenses:* Tuition, state resident: full-time $6716. Tuition, nonresident: full-time $8908. Tuition and fees vary according to course level, course load, program and student level. *Financial support:* In 2009–10, 104 research assistantships with full and partial tuition reimbursements (averaging $13,500 per year), 2 teaching assistantships with full and partial tuition reimbursements (averaging $13,500 per year) were awarded; fellowships, scholarships/grants, health care benefits, and unspecified assistantships also available. *Unit head:* Dr. Laura Rendon, Chair, 515-294-7093, E-mail: lrendon@iastate.edu. *Application contact:* Dr. Daniel Robinson, Information Contact, 515-294-1241, E-mail: eldrshp@iastate.edu.

Kent State University, Graduate School of Education, Health, and Human Services, School of Foundations, Leadership and Administration, Program in Evaluation and Measurement, Kent, OH 44242-0001. Offers M Ed, MA, PhD. *Faculty:* 4 full-time (1 woman), 3 part-time/adjunct (2 women). *Students:* 27 full-time (20 women), 46 part-time (38 women); includes 3 minority (1 African American, 1 Asian American or Pacific Islander, 1 Hispanic American), 1 international. 29 applicants, 90% accepted. In 2009, 43 master's, 1 doctorate awarded. *Entrance requirements:* For doctorate, GRE. Application fee: $30. *Financial support:* In 2009–10, 1 fellowship (averaging $12,000 per year), 2 research assistantships (averaging $8,500 per year), teaching assistantships (averaging $12,000 per year) were awarded; career-related internships or fieldwork, Federal Work-Study, institutionally sponsored loans, scholarships/grants, health care benefits, and unspecified assistantships also available. Support available to part-time students. *Unit head:* Dr. Shawn Fitzgerald, Coordinator, 330-672-0583, E-mail: smfitzge@kent.edu. *Application contact:* Nancy Miller, Academic Program Coordinator, Office of Graduate Student Services, 330-672-2576, Fax: 330-672-9162, E-mail: ogs@kent.edu.

Kent State University, Graduate School of Education, Health, and Human Services, School of Lifespan Development and Educational Sciences, Kent, OH 44242-0001. Offers community counseling (MA); counseling (Ed S); counseling and human development services (PhD); cultural foundations (M Ed, MA, PhD); educational psychology (M Ed, MA, PhD); evaluation and measurement (M Ed, MA, PhD); family studies (MA), including gerontology, human development and family studies; instructional technology (M Ed, MA), including computer technology, general instructional technology, library media; intervention specialist (M Ed, MA), including deaf education, early childhood intervention specialist, educational interpreter K-12, general special education, gifted education, mild/moderate intervention, moderate/intensive intervention, transition to work; rehabilitation counseling (M Ed, MA, Ed S); school counseling (M Ed, MA); school psychology (M Ed, PhD, Ed S); special education (PhD, Ed S). Part-time and evening/weekend programs available. *Faculty:* 84 full-time (50 women), 116 part-time/adjunct (89 women). *Students:* 357 full-time (295 women), 325 part-time (256 women); includes 73 minority (55 African Americans, 1 American Indian/Alaska Native, 9 Asian Americans or Pacific Islanders, 8 Hispanic Americans), 10 international. 331 applicants, 66% accepted. In 2009, 134 master's, 9 doctorates, 22 other advanced degrees awarded. *Degree requirements:* For master's, thesis (for some programs); for doctorate, comprehensive exam, thesis/dissertation. *Entrance requirements:* For master's, doctorate, and Ed S, GRE General Test. Additional exam requirements/recommendations for international students: Required—TOEFL. *Application deadline:* Applications are processed on a rolling basis. Application fee: $30. Electronic applications accepted. *Financial support:* In 2009–10, 12 fellowships with full tuition reimbursements (averaging $11,000 per year), 28 research assistantships with full tuition reimbursements (averaging $8,313 per year), 3 teaching assistantships with full tuition reimbursements (averaging $11,000 per year) were awarded; Federal Work-Study, scholarships/grants, and unspecified assistantships also available. Financial award application deadline: 4/1. *Unit head:* Dr. Mary Dellmann-Jenkins, Director, 330-672-6958, E-mail: mdellman@kent.edu. *Application contact:* Nancy Miller, Academic Program Coordinator, Office of Graduate Student Services, 330-672-2576, Fax: 330-672-9162, E-mail: ogs@kent.edu.

Louisiana State University and Agricultural and Mechanical College, Graduate School, College of Education, Department of Educational Theory, Policy and Practice, Baton Rouge, LA 70803. Offers counseling (M Ed, MA, Ed S); educational administration (M Ed, MA, PhD, Ed S); educational technology (MA); elementary education (M Ed); higher education (PhD); research methodology (PhD); secondary education (M Ed). *Accreditation:* ACA (one or more programs are accredited); NCATE. Part-time and evening/weekend programs available. *Faculty:* 38 full-time (24 women). *Students:* 174 full-time (139 women), 154 part-time (129 women); includes 74 minority (66 African Americans, 3 Asian Americans or Pacific Islanders, 5 Hispanic Americans), 9 international. Average age 32. 122 applicants, 60% accepted, 48 enrolled. In 2009, 124 master's, 13 doctorates, 11 other advanced degrees awarded. Terminal master's awarded for partial completion of doctoral program. *Degree requirements:* For doctorate, thesis/dissertation; for Ed S, thesis optional. *Entrance requirements:* For master's and doctorate, GRE General Test, minimum GPA of 3.0. Additional exam requirements/recommendations for international students: Required—TOEFL (minimum score 550 paper-based; 213 computer-based; 79 iBT) or IELTS (minimum score 6.5). *Application deadline:* For fall admission, 1/25 priority date for domestic students, 5/15 for international students; for spring admission, 10/15 for international students. Applications are processed on a rolling basis. Application fee: $50 ($70 for international students). Electronic applications accepted. *Financial support:* In 2009–10, 226 students received support, including 1 fellowship (averaging $31,711 per year), 27 research assistantships with full and partial tuition reimbursements available (averaging $10,143 per year), 35 teaching assistantships with full and partial tuition reimbursements available (averaging $12,555 per year); career-related internships or fieldwork, Federal Work-Study, institutionally sponsored loans, health care benefits, and unspecified assistantships also available. Support available to part-time students. Financial award applicants required to submit FAFSA. *Faculty research:* Literary, curriculum studies, science education, K-12 leadership, higher education. Total annual research expenditures: $1.8 million. *Unit head:* Dr. Earl Cheek, Chair, 225-578-6867, Fax: 225-578-9135, E-mail: echeek@lsu.edu. *Application contact:* Dr., Graduate Coordinator, 225-578-2280, Fax: 225-578-9135.

Loyola University Chicago, School of Education, Program in Research Methods, Chicago, IL 60660. Offers M Ed, MA, PhD. MA and PhD offered through the Graduate School. Part-time and evening/weekend programs available. *Faculty:* 3 full-time (all women), 2 part-time/adjunct (both women). *Students:* 14. Average age 25. 2 applicants, 100% accepted, 2 enrolled. In

2009, 2 master's, 2 doctorates awarded. *Degree requirements:* For master's, comprehensive exam (M Ed), thesis (MA); for doctorate, comprehensive exam, thesis/dissertation. *Entrance requirements:* For master's, GRE General Test, letters of recommendation, resume, minimum GPA of 3.0; for doctorate, GRE General Test, interview. Additional exam requirements/recommendations for international students: Required—TOEFL (minimum score 550 paper-based; 213 computer-based; 79 iBT). *Application deadline:* For fall admission, 2/15 for domestic and international students. Applications are processed on a rolling basis. Application fee: $50. Electronic applications accepted. *Expenses:* Tuition: Full-time $14,220; part-time $790 per credit hour. Required fees: $60 per semester hour. Tuition and fees vary according to program. *Financial support:* In 2009–10, 1 fellowship (averaging $14,000 per year), 4 research assistantships with full tuition reimbursements (averaging $11,000 per year) were awarded. Financial award application deadline: 2/15; financial award applicants required to submit FAFSA. *Faculty research:* Circular statistics, program evaluation, psychological measurement, infant attachment, adolescent development. *Unit head:* Dr. Pamela Fenning, Director, 312-915-6803, E-mail: pfennin@luc.edu. *Application contact:* Marie Rosin-Dittmar, Information Contact, 312-915-6800, E-mail: schleduc@luc.edu.

Michigan State University, The Graduate School, College of Education, Department of Counseling, Educational Psychology and Special Education, East Lansing, MI 48824. Offers counseling (MA); educational psychology and educational technology (PhD); educational technology (MA); measurement and quantitative methods (PhD); rehabilitation counseling (MA); rehabilitation counselor education (PhD); school psychology (MA, PhD, Ed S); special education (MA, PhD). *Accreditation:* APA (one or more programs are accredited); CORE (one or more programs are accredited). Part-time programs available. *Faculty:* 35 full-time (13 women). *Students:* 217 full-time (154 women), 144 part-time (107 women); includes 48 minority (25 African Americans, 13 Asian Americans or Pacific Islanders, 10 Hispanic Americans), 71 international. Average age 32. 238 applicants, 46% accepted. In 2009, 117 master's, 36 doctorates awarded. *Entrance requirements:* Additional exam requirements/recommendations for international students: Required—TOEFL. Electronic applications accepted. *Expenses:* Tuition, state resident: part-time $478.25 per credit hour. Tuition, nonresident: part-time $966.50 per credit hour. Part-time tuition and fees vary according to program. *Financial support:* In 2009–10, 71 research assistantships with tuition reimbursements (averaging $6,836 per year), 74 teaching assistantships with tuition reimbursements (averaging $6,858 per year) were awarded. Total annual research expenditures: $2.3 million. *Unit head:* Dr. Richard S. Prawat, Chairperson, 517-353-6417, Fax: 517-353-6393, E-mail: rsprawat@msu.edu. *Application contact:* Kathy Dimoff, Graduate Admissions Coordinator, 517-355-6683, Fax: 517-353-6393, E-mail: dimoff@msu.edu.

North Carolina State University, Graduate School, College of Education, Department of Educational Leadership and Policy Studies, Program in Educational Research and Policy Analysis, Raleigh, NC 27695. Offers PhD. *Degree requirements:* For doctorate, thesis/dissertation. *Entrance requirements:* For doctorate, GRE General Test, minimum GPA of 3.0, interview, sample of work. Electronic applications accepted.

Ohio University, Graduate College, College of Education, Department of Educational Studies, Athens, OH 45701-2979. Offers computer education and technology (M Ed); cultural studies (M Ed); educational administration (M Ed, Ed D); educational research and evaluation (M Ed, PhD); instructional technology (PhD). Part-time and evening/weekend programs available. Postbaccalaureate distance learning degree programs offered (minimal on-campus study). *Faculty:* 12 full-time (6 women), 2 part-time/adjunct (0 women). *Students:* 151 full-time (95 women), 142 part-time (105 women); includes 24 minority (19 African Americans, 1 American Indian/Alaska Native, 1 Asian American or Pacific Islander, 3 Hispanic Americans), 46 international. 107 applicants, 69% accepted, 50 enrolled. In 2009, 32 master's, 19 doctorates awarded. *Degree requirements:* For master's, thesis or alternative; for doctorate, comprehensive exam, thesis/dissertation. *Entrance requirements:* For master's, GRE General Test (if GPA less than 2.9); for doctorate, GRE General Test, GRE Subject Test, minimum GPA of 2.9, work experience, 3 letters of reference, autobiography. Additional exam requirements/recommendations for international students: Required—TOEFL (minimum score 550 paper-based; 80 iBT) or IELTS Academic (minimum score 6.5). *Application deadline:* For fall admission, 3/1 priority date for domestic and international students; for winter admission, 10/1 priority date for domestic and international students; for spring admission, 1/30 priority date for domestic students, 1/1 priority date for international students. Applications are processed on a rolling basis. Application fee: $50 ($55 for international students). Electronic applications accepted. *Expenses:* Tuition, state resident: full-time $7839; part-time $323 per quarter hour. Tuition, nonresident: full-time $15,831; part-time $654 per quarter hour. Required fees: $2931. *Financial support:* Research assistantships with full tuition reimbursements, teaching assistantships with full tuition reimbursements, Federal Work-Study, institutionally sponsored loans, tuition waivers (partial), and unspecified assistantships available. Financial award application deadline: 3/1. *Faculty research:* Race, class and gender; computer programs; development and organization theory; evaluation/development of instruments, leadership. Total annual research expenditures: $158,037. *Unit head:* Dr. Gordon Brooks, Chair, 740-593-4423, Fax: 740-593-0477, E-mail: brooksg@ohio.edu. *Application contact:* Floyd J. Doney, Director of Student Affairs, 740-593-4400, Fax: 740-593-9310, E-mail: doney@ohio.edu.

Rutgers, The State University of New Jersey, New Brunswick, Graduate School of Education, Department of Educational Psychology, Program in Educational Statistics, Measurement and Evaluation, Piscataway, NJ 08854-8097. Offers Ed M. Part-time and evening/weekend programs available. *Entrance requirements:* For master's, GRE General Test, 3 letters of recommendation. Additional exam requirements/recommendations for international students: Required—TOEFL (minimum score 550 paper-based; 233 computer-based; 83 iBT). Electronic applications accepted. *Faculty research:* Program evaluation of student assessment, Type I error and power comparisons, test performance factors, theory building in participatory program evaluation, test validity in higher education admissions.

Seton Hall University, College of Education and Human Services, Department of Education Leadership, Management and Policy, South Orange, NJ 07079-2697. Offers college student personnel administration (MA); education research, assessment and program evaluation (PhD); higher education administration (Ed D, PhD); human resource training and development (MA); K–12 administration and supervision (Ed D, Exec Ed D, Ed S); K–12 leadership, management and policy (Ed D, Exec Ed D, Ed S). Part-time and evening/weekend programs available. Postbaccalaureate distance learning degree programs offered (no on-campus study). *Faculty:* 12 full-time (4 women), 1 part-time/adjunct (0 women). *Students:* 112 full-time (63 women), 444 part-time (232 women); includes 108 minority (71 African Americans, 7 Asian Americans or Pacific Islanders, 30 Hispanic Americans), 11 international. Average age 39. 135 applicants, 87% accepted, 90 enrolled. In 2009, 147 master's, 45 doctorates, 13 other advanced degrees awarded. *Degree requirements:* For master's, comprehensive exam, thesis or alternative; for doctorate, thesis/dissertation, oral exam, written exam; for Ed S, internship, research project. *Entrance requirements:* For master's, GRE or MAT, minimum GPA of 3.0; for doctorate, GRE or MAT, interview, minimum GPA of 3.5; for Ed S, GRE or MAT, minimum GPA of 3.5. *Application deadline:* Applications are processed on a rolling basis. Application fee: $50. *Financial support:* In 2009–10, 2 research assistantships with full tuition reimbursements (averaging $4,500 per year) were awarded; unspecified assistantships also available. Financial award application deadline: 2/1; financial award applicants required to submit FAFSA. *Unit head:* Dr. Michael Osnato, Chair, 973-275-2446, E-mail: osnatomi@shu.edu. *Application contact:* Dr. Michael Osnato, Chair, 973-275-2446, E-mail: osnatomi@shu.edu.

Southern Connecticut State University, School of Graduate Studies, School of Education, Department of Educational Leadership, Program in Research, Statistics, and Measurement, New Haven, CT 06515-1355. Offers MS. *Faculty:* 2 full-time (0 women). *Students:* 4 full-time (2 women), 18 part-time (16 women); includes 4 minority (2 African Americans, 2 Asian Americans or Pacific Islanders). 16 applicants, 69% accepted, 10 enrolled. In 2009, 12 master's awarded. *Degree requirements:* For master's, thesis. *Entrance requirements:* For master's, interview. *Application deadline:* For fall admission, 7/15 priority date for domestic students. Applications are processed on a rolling basis. Application fee: $50. Electronic applications accepted. Tuition and fees vary according to program. *Financial support:* Application deadline: 4/15. *Unit head:* Dr. Peter Madonia, Chairperson of Educational Leadership, E-mail: madoniap1@southernct.edu. *Application contact:* Dr. William Diffley, Coordinator, 203-392-5911, E-mail: diffleyw1@southernct.edu.

Southern Illinois University Carbondale, Graduate School, College of Education, Department of Educational Psychology and Special Education, Program in Educational Psychology, Carbondale, IL 62901-4701. Offers counselor education (MS Ed, PhD); educational psychology (PhD); human learning and development (MS Ed); measurement and statistics (PhD). *Accreditation:* NCATE. *Degree requirements:* For master's, thesis; for doctorate, thesis/dissertation. *Entrance requirements:* For master's, GRE General Test, minimum GPA of 2.7; for doctorate, minimum GPA of 3.25. Additional exam requirements/recommendations for international students: Required—TOEFL. *Faculty research:* Career development, problem solving, learning and instruction, cognitive development, family assessment.

Southwestern Oklahoma State University, College of Professional and Graduate Studies, School of Behavioral Sciences and Education, Specialization in School Psychometry, Weatherford, OK 73096-3098. Offers M Ed. M Ed distance learning degree program offered to Oklahoma residents only. *Accreditation:* NCATE. Part-time and evening/weekend programs available. *Degree requirements:* For master's, exam. *Entrance requirements:* For master's, GRE General Test or minimum undergraduate GPA of 3.0, portfolio. Additional exam requirements/recommendations for international students: Required—TOEFL.

Stanford University, School of Education, Program in Social Sciences, Policy, and Educational Practice, Stanford, CA 94305-9991. Offers administration and policy analysis (Ed D, PhD); anthropology of education (PhD); economics of education (PhD); educational linguistics (PhD); evaluation (MA), including interdisciplinary studies; higher education (PhD); history of education (PhD); interdisciplinary studies (PhD); international comparative education (MA, PhD); international education administration and policy analysis (MA); philosophy of education (PhD); policy analysis (MA); prospective principal's program (MA); sociology of education (PhD). *Degree requirements:* For master's, thesis (for some programs); for doctorate, thesis/dissertation. *Entrance requirements:* For master's and doctorate, GRE General Test. Electronic applications accepted. *Expenses:* Tuition: Full-time $37,380; part-time $2760 per quarter. Required fees: $501.

Sul Ross State University, Rio Grande College of Sul Ross State University, Alpine, TX 79832. Offers business administration (MBA); teacher education (M Ed), including bilingual education, counseling, educational diagnostics, elementary education, general education, reading, school administration, secondary education. Part-time and evening/weekend programs available. *Degree requirements:* For master's, thesis optional. *Entrance requirements:* For master's, GMAT or GRE General Test, minimum GPA of 2.5 in last 60 hours of undergraduate work. *Faculty research:* Drug and substance abuse counseling, U.S.-Mexico border economic development.

Sul Ross State University, School of Professional Studies, Department of Teacher Education, Program in Educational Diagnostics, Alpine, TX 79832. Offers M Ed. Part-time and evening/weekend programs available. *Degree requirements:* For master's, thesis optional. *Entrance requirements:* For master's, GMAT or GRE General Test, minimum GPA of 2.5 in last 60 hours of undergraduate work.

Syracuse University, School of Education, Program in Instructional Design, Development, and Evaluation, Syracuse, NY 13244. Offers MS, PhD, CAS. Part-time programs available. *Students:* 34 full-time (19 women), 38 part-time (22 women); includes 10 minority (3 African Americans, 1 American Indian/Alaska Native, 3 Asian Americans or Pacific Islanders, 3 Hispanic Americans), 16 international. Average age 39. 28 applicants, 61% accepted, 12 enrolled. In 2009, 9 master's, 3 doctorates awarded. *Degree requirements:* For master's, thesis or alternative; for doctorate, thesis/dissertation. *Entrance requirements:* For doctorate, GRE, interview, completion of master's degree; for CAS, GRE (recommended), interview. Additional exam requirements/recommendations for international students: Required—TOEFL (minimum score 100 iBT). *Application deadline:* For fall admission, 2/1 priority date for domestic and international students; for spring admission, 10/15 priority date for domestic and international students. Applications are processed on a rolling basis. Application fee: $75. Electronic applications accepted. *Expenses:* Tuition: Full-time $26,808; part-time $1117 per credit. Required fees: $1024. *Financial support:* Fellowships with full tuition reimbursements, research assistantships with full and partial tuition reimbursements, teaching assistantships with full tuition reimbursements available. Financial award application deadline: 1/1; financial award applicants required to submit FAFSA. *Faculty research:* Cultural pluralism and instructional design, corrections training, aging and learning, the University and social change, investigative evaluation. *Unit head:* Dr. Nick Smith, Chair, 315-443-2685, E-mail: nlsmith@syr.edu. *Application contact:* Liza Rochelson, Graduate Recruiter, School of Education, 315-443-2505, E-mail: e-gradrcrt@syr.edu.

Teachers College, Columbia University, Graduate Faculty of Education, Department of Human Development, Program in Measurement, Evaluation, and Statistics, New York, NY 10027-6696. Offers MA, MS, Ed D, PhD. *Faculty:* 4 full-time (2 women). *Students:* 11 full-time (8 women), 20 part-time (12 women); includes 16 minority (15 Asian Americans or Pacific Islanders, 1 Hispanic American), 4 international. Average age 32. 39 applicants, 62% accepted, 3 enrolled. In 2009, 10 master's, 2 doctorates awarded. *Entrance requirements:* For master's and doctorate, GRE. *Application deadline:* For fall admission, 5/15 for domestic students; for spring admission, 12/1 for domestic students. Application fee: $65. *Financial support:* Career-related internships or fieldwork, Federal Work-Study, institutionally sponsored loans, and tuition waivers (full and partial) available. Support available to part-time students. Financial award application deadline: 2/1. *Faculty research:* Probability and inference, potentially biased test items, research design, clustering and scaling methods for multivariate data. *Unit head:* James Corter, Chair, 212-678-4190. *Application contact:* Melba Remice, Assistant Director of Admission, 212-678-4035, Fax: 212-678-4171, E-mail: ms2545@columbia.edu.

Tennessee Technological University, Graduate School, College of Education, Department of Curriculum and Instruction, Program in Exceptional Learning, Cookeville, TN 38505. Offers applied behavior and learning (PhD); literacy (PhD); program planning and evaluation (PhD). *Students:* 11 full-time (10 women), 14 part-time (11 women); includes 3 minority (2 African Americans, 1 Asian American or Pacific Islander). 22 applicants, 18% accepted, 4 enrolled. In 2009, 4 doctorates awarded. *Degree requirements:* For doctorate, comprehensive exam, thesis/dissertation. *Entrance requirements:* For doctorate, GRE, minimum GPA of 3.0. Additional exam requirements/recommendations for international students: Required—TOEFL (minimum score 550 paper-based; 79 iBT), IELTS (minimum score 5.5). *Application deadline:* For fall admission, 8/1 for domestic students, 5/1 for international students; for spring admission, 12/1 for domestic students, 10/1 for international students. Application fee: $25 ($30 for international students). Electronic applications accepted. *Expenses:* Tuition, state resident: full-time $7034; part-time $368 per credit hour. *Financial support:* In 2009–10, 4 fellowships (averaging $8,000 per year), 10 research assistantships (averaging $12,000 per year), 1 teaching assistantship (averaging $12,000 per year) were awarded. Financial award application deadline: 4/1. *Unit head:* Dr. John J. Wheeler, Director, Doctoral Studies, 931-372-3078, Fax: 931-372-3517. *Application contact:* Shelia K. Kendrick, Coordinator of Graduate Studies, 931-372-3808, Fax: 931-372-3497, E-mail: skendrick@Tntech.edu.

Texas A&M University, College of Education and Human Development, Department of Educational Psychology, College Station, TX 77843. Offers counseling psychology (PhD); educational psychology (PhD); educational technology (M Ed); gifted and talented education (M Ed, MS); Hispanic bilingual education (M Ed, PhD); human learning and development (MS); intelligence, creativity, and giftedness (PhD); learning, development, and instruction (PhD); research, measurement and statistics (MS); research, measurement, and statistics (PhD); school counseling (M Ed); school psychology (PhD); special education (M Ed, PhD). *Accreditation:* APA (one or more programs are accredited). Part-time and evening/weekend programs available. Postbaccalaureate distance learning degree programs offered (no

Educational Measurement and Evaluation

Texas A&M University (continued)
on-campus study). *Faculty:* 45. *Students:* 160 full-time (126 women), 144 part-time (118 women); includes 99 minority (25 African Americans, 13 Asian Americans or Pacific Islanders, 61 Hispanic Americans), 41 international. In 2009, 53 master's, 30 doctorates awarded. *Degree requirements:* For master's, thesis optional; for doctorate, thesis/dissertation. *Entrance requirements:* For master's and doctorate, GRE General Test. Additional exam requirements/recommendations for international students: Required—TOEFL. Application fee: $50 ($75 for international students). Electronic applications accepted. *Expenses:* Tuition, state resident: full-time $3991; part-time $221.74 per credit hour. Tuition, nonresident: full-time $9049; part-time $502.74 per credit hour. *Financial support:* In 2009–10, fellowships (averaging $12,000 per year), research assistantships (averaging $9,000 per year), teaching assistantships (averaging $9,000 per year) were awarded; career-related internships or fieldwork, institutionally sponsored loans, scholarships/grants, and unspecified assistantships also available. Financial award applicants required to submit FAFSA. *Unit head:* Dr. Victor Willson, Head, 979-845-1800. *Application contact:* Carol A. Wagner, Director of Advising, 979-845-1833, Fax: 979-862-1256, E-mail: epsyadvisor@tamu.edu.

Université Laval, Faculty of Education, Department of Foundations and Interventions in Education, Québec, QC G1K 7P4, Canada. Offers educational administration and evaluation (MA, PhD); educational practice (Diploma), including educational pedagogy, pedagogy management and development, school adaptation; orientation sciences (MA, PhD). *Degree requirements:* For doctorate, comprehensive exam, thesis/dissertation. Electronic applications accepted.

University at Albany, State University of New York, School of Education, Department of Educational and Counseling Psychology, Albany, NY 12222-0001. Offers counseling psychology (MS, PhD, CAS); educational psychology (Ed D); educational psychology and statistics (MS); measurements and evaluation (Ed D); rehabilitation counseling (MS), including counseling psychology; school counselor (CAS); school psychology (Psy D, CAS); special education (MS); statistics and research design (Ed D). *Accreditation:* APA (one or more programs are accredited). Evening/weekend programs available. *Degree requirements:* For doctorate, thesis/dissertation. *Entrance requirements:* For doctorate, GRE General Test. Additional exam requirements/recommendations for international students: Required—TOEFL (minimum score 550 paper-based; 213 computer-based). Electronic applications accepted.

University of Arkansas, Graduate School, College of Education and Health Professions, Department of Curriculum and Instruction, Program in Educational Statistics and Research Methods, Fayetteville, AR 72701-1201. Offers MS, PhD. *Students:* 8 full-time (6 women), 4 part-time (3 women). Application fee: $40 ($50 for international students). *Expenses:* Tuition, state resident: full-time $7355; part-time $356.58 per hour. Tuition, nonresident: full-time $17,401; part-time $775.17 per hour. Required fees: $1203. *Financial support:* In 2009–10, 2 fellowships, 6 research assistantships, 2 teaching assistantships were awarded. *Unit head:* Michael Daugherty, Department Chairperson, 479-575-4209, Fax: 479-575-5119, E-mail: mkd03@uark.edu. *Application contact:* Dr. William McComas, Graduate Coordinator, 479-575-7525, E-mail: mccomas@uark.edu.

The University of British Columbia, Faculty of Education, Department of Educational and Counseling Psychology, and Special Education, Vancouver, BC V6T 1Z1, Canada. Offers counseling psychology (M Ed, MA, PhD); development, learning and culture (PhD); guidance studies (Diploma); human development, learning and culture (M Ed, MA); measurement and evaluation and research methodology (M Ed); measurement, evaluation and research methodology (MA); measurement, evaluation, and research methodology (PhD); school psychology (M Ed, MA, PhD); special education (M Ed, MA, PhD, Diploma). Part-time programs available. *Degree requirements:* For master's, thesis (for some programs); for doctorate, comprehensive exam, thesis/dissertation. *Entrance requirements:* For master's, GRE General Test (counseling psychology MA); for doctorate, GRE General Test. Additional exam requirements/recommendations for international students: Required—TOEFL. Electronic applications accepted. *Faculty research:* Women, family, social problems, career transition, stress and coping problems.

University of Calgary, Faculty of Graduate Studies, Faculty of Education, Graduate Division of Educational Research, Calgary, AB T2N 1N4, Canada. Offers community rehabilitation and disability studies (M Ed, M Sc, Ed D, PhD, Graduate Certificate, Graduate Diploma); curriculum, teaching and learning (M Ed, M Sc, MA, Ed D, PhD, Graduate Certificate, Graduate Diploma); educational contexts (M Ed, MA, Ed D, PhD, Graduate Certificate, Graduate Diploma); educational leadership (M Ed, MA, Ed D, PhD, Graduate Certificate, Graduate Diploma); educational technology (M Ed, M Sc, MA, Ed D, PhD, Graduate Certificate, Graduate Diploma); gifted education (M Sc, MA, Ed D, PhD, Graduate Certificate, Graduate Diploma); higher education administration (Ed D); interpretive studies in education (M Ed, M Sc, MA, Ed D, PhD, Graduate Certificate, Graduate Diploma); second language teaching (M Ed, Ed D, PhD, Graduate Certificate, Graduate Diploma); teaching English as a second language (M Ed, M Sc, MA, Ed D, PhD, Graduate Certificate, Graduate Diploma); workplace and adult learning (M Ed, MA, Ed D, PhD, Graduate Certificate, Graduate Diploma). Ed D in both higher education administration and educational leadership offered via distance delivery. Part-time and evening/weekend programs available. Postbaccalaureate distance learning degree programs offered (minimal on-campus study). *Degree requirements:* For master's, thesis (for some programs); for doctorate, thesis/dissertation, candidacy exam. *Entrance requirements:* For master's, minimum GPA of 3.0, 3 letters of reference; for doctorate, minimum GPA of 3.5, 3 letters of reference; for other advanced degree, minimum GPA of 3.0. Additional exam requirements/recommendations for international students: Required—TOEFL, IELTS. Electronic applications accepted. *Faculty research:* Curriculum, leadership, technology, contexts, gifted, second language teaching, work place and adult learning.

University of California, Santa Barbara, Graduate Division, Gevirtz Graduate School of Education, Santa Barbara, CA 93106-9490. Offers counseling, clinical and school psychology (PhD), including clinical psychology, counseling psychology, school psychology; education (M Ed, MA, PhD), including child and adolescent development (MA, PhD), cultural perspectives and comparative education (MA, PhD), educational leadership and organizations (MA, PhD), research methodology (MA, PhD), special education disabilities and risk studies (MA), special education, disabilities and risk studies (PhD), teaching (M Ed), teaching and learning (MA, PhD); educational leadership (Ed D); school psychology (M Ed); MA/PhD. *Accreditation:* APA (one or more programs are accredited). Postbaccalaureate distance learning degree programs offered (minimal on-campus study). *Faculty:* 42 full-time (20 women), 10 part-time/adjunct (4 women). *Students:* 390 full-time (303 women); includes 149 minority (14 African Americans, 3 American Indian/Alaska Native, 57 Asian Americans or Pacific Islanders, 75 Hispanic Americans), 16 international. Average age 31. 717 applicants, 40% accepted, 170 enrolled. In 2009, 140 master's, 46 doctorates awarded. Terminal master's awarded for partial completion of doctoral program. *Degree requirements:* For master's, comprehensive exam (for some programs), thesis (for some programs); for doctorate, comprehensive exam (for some programs), thesis/dissertation, qualifying exam. *Entrance requirements:* For master's, GRE, 3 letters of recommendation, resume/curriculum vitae; for doctorate, GRE, 3 letters of recommendation, statement of purpose, personal achievements/contributions statement, resume/curriculum vitae, transcripts for post-secondary institutions attended. Additional exam requirements/recommendations for international students: Required—TOEFL (minimum score 550 paper-based; 213 computer-based; 80 iBT) or IELTS (minimum score 7). Application fee: $70 ($90 for international students). Electronic applications accepted. *Financial support:* In 2009–10, 253 students received support, including 206 fellowships with full and partial tuition reimbursements available (averaging $5,000 per year), 62 research assistantships with full and partial tuition reimbursements available (averaging $6,200 per year), 87 teaching assistantships with partial tuition reimbursements available (averaging $6,500 per year); career-related internships or fieldwork, Federal Work-Study, institutionally sponsored loans, scholarships/grants, traineeships, health care benefits, and unspecified assistantships also available. Financial award applicants required to submit FAFSA. *Faculty research:* Professional development, early childhood development, school violence, literacy, science/math initiative. Total annual research expenditures: $4.4 million. *Unit head:* Dr. Jane Conoley, Chair, 805-893-2185, E-mail: jane-conoley@education.ucsb.edu. *Application contact:* Kathryn Marie Tucciarone, Student Affairs Officer, 805-893-2137, E-mail: katiet@education.ucsb.edu.

University of Colorado at Boulder, Graduate School, School of Education, Division of Research and Evaluation Methodologies, Boulder, CO 80309. Offers PhD. *Accreditation:* NCATE. *Students:* 9 full-time (4 women), 4 part-time (all women); includes 2 minority (both Hispanic Americans). Average age 33. 18 applicants, 6% accepted, 1 enrolled. *Degree requirements:* For doctorate, one foreign language, comprehensive exam, thesis/dissertation. *Entrance requirements:* For doctorate, GRE General Test, minimum undergraduate GPA of 2.75. *Application deadline:* For fall admission, 2/1 priority date for domestic students, 12/1 for international students; for spring admission, 9/1 for domestic students, 12/1 for international students. Application fee: $40 ($60 for international students). *Financial support:* In 2009–10, 2 fellowships (averaging $5,688 per year), 6 research assistantships (averaging $14,010 per year) were awarded; career-related internships or fieldwork, Federal Work-Study, and scholarships/grants also available. *Application contact:* E-mail: edadvise@colorado.edu.

University of Connecticut, Graduate School, Neag School of Education, Department of Educational Psychology, Program in Measurement, Evaluation, and Assessment, Storrs, CT 06269. Offers MA, PhD, Post-Master's Certificate. *Faculty:* 14 full-time (7 women). *Students:* 10 full-time (7 women), 4 part-time (3 women); includes 2 minority (1 Asian American or Pacific Islander, 1 Hispanic American), 6 international. Average age 35. 15 applicants, 13% accepted, 1 enrolled. In 2009, 1 doctorate awarded. Terminal master's awarded for partial completion of doctoral program. *Degree requirements:* For master's, comprehensive exam, thesis or alternative; for doctorate, thesis/dissertation. *Entrance requirements:* For doctorate, GRE General Test. Additional exam requirements/recommendations for international students: Required—TOEFL (minimum score 550 paper-based; 213 computer-based). *Application deadline:* For fall admission, 2/1 priority date for domestic and international students; for spring admission, 11/1 for domestic students, 10/1 for international students. Applications are processed on a rolling basis. Application fee: $55. Electronic applications accepted. *Expenses:* Tuition, state resident: full-time $4725; part-time $525 per credit. Tuition, nonresident: full-time $12,267; part-time $1363 per credit. Required fees: $346 per semester. Tuition and fees vary according to course load. *Financial support:* In 2009–10, 9 research assistantships with full tuition reimbursements were awarded; fellowships, teaching assistantships with full tuition reimbursements, Federal Work-Study, scholarships/grants, health care benefits, and unspecified assistantships also available. Financial award application deadline: 2/1; financial award applicants required to submit FAFSA. *Unit head:* Hariharan Swaminathan, Head, 860-486-4031, Fax: 860-486-0210, E-mail: hariharan.swaminathan@uconn.edu. *Application contact:* Cheryl Lowe, Program Assistant, 860-486-4031, Fax: 860-486-0180, E-mail: cheryl.lowe@uconn.edu.

University of Denver, College of Education, Denver, CO 80208. Offers counseling psychology (MA, PhD); curriculum and instruction (MA, PhD, Certificate), including curriculum leadership (MA, PhD); educational administration and policy studies (Certificate); educational psychology (MA, PhD, Ed S), including child and family studies (MA, PhD), quantitative research methods (MA, PhD), school psychology (PhD, Ed S); higher education and adult studies (MA, PhD); library and information science (MLIS); library and information sciences (Certificate); school administration (PhD). *Accreditation:* ALA; APA (one or more programs are accredited). Part-time and evening/weekend programs available. Postbaccalaureate distance learning degree programs offered (no on-campus study). *Faculty:* 33 full-time (24 women), 62 part-time/adjunct (41 women). *Students:* 384 full-time (305 women), 453 part-time (336 women); includes 164 minority (47 African Americans, 8 American Indian/Alaska Native, 14 Asian Americans or Pacific Islanders, 95 Hispanic Americans), 20 international. Average age 34. 1,065 applicants, 59% accepted, 433 enrolled. In 2009, 206 master's, 38 doctorates, 117 other advanced degrees awarded. Terminal master's awarded for partial completion of doctoral program. *Degree requirements:* For master's, comprehensive exam; for doctorate, 2 foreign languages, comprehensive exam, thesis/dissertation. *Entrance requirements:* For master's and doctorate, GRE General Test or MAT. *Application deadline:* Applications are processed on a rolling basis. Application fee: $50. Electronic applications accepted. *Expenses:* Tuition: Full-time $34,596; part-time $961 per quarter hour. Required fees: $4 per quarter hour. Tuition and fees vary according to course load, campus/location and program. *Financial support:* In 2009–10, 78 teaching assistantships with full and partial tuition reimbursements (averaging $11,700 per year) were awarded; career-related internships or fieldwork, Federal Work-Study, institutionally sponsored loans, and scholarships/grants also available. Support available to part-time students. Financial award application deadline: 3/1; financial award applicants required to submit FAFSA. *Faculty research:* Parkinson's disease, personnel training, development and assessments, gifted education, service-learning, transportation, public schools. Total annual research expenditures: $340,000. *Unit head:* Dr. Gregory M. Anderson, Dean, 303-871-3665. *Application contact:* Janet Erickson, Director of Graduate Admission, 303-871-2485, E-mail: edinfo@du.edu.

University of Florida, Graduate School, College of Education, Department of Educational Psychology, Gainesville, FL 32611. Offers educational psychology (M Ed, MAE, Ed D, PhD, Ed S); research and evaluation methodology (M Ed, MAE, Ed D, PhD, Ed S); school psychology (M Ed, MAE, Ed D, PhD, Ed S). *Accreditation:* NCATE. Terminal master's awarded for partial completion of doctoral program. *Degree requirements:* For master's, thesis (MAE); for doctorate, variable foreign language requirement, thesis/dissertation. *Entrance requirements:* For master's and doctorate, GRE General Test, minimum GPA of 3.0; for Ed S, GRE General Test. Additional exam requirements/recommendations for international students: Required—TOEFL (minimum score 550 paper-based; 213 computer-based). Electronic applications accepted. *Faculty research:* School improvement, teaching and learning, item response theory.

The University of Iowa, Graduate College, College of Education, Department of Psychological and Quantitative Foundations, Iowa City, IA 52242-1316. Offers counseling psychology (PhD); educational measurement and statistics (MA, PhD); educational psychology (MA, PhD); school psychology (PhD, Ed S); JD/PhD. *Accreditation:* APA. *Degree requirements:* For master's, thesis optional, exam; for doctorate, comprehensive exam, thesis/dissertation; for Ed S, exam. *Entrance requirements:* For master's, doctorate, and Ed S, GRE General Test, minimum GPA of 3.0. Additional exam requirements/recommendations for international students: Required—TOEFL (minimum score 550 paper-based; 213 computer-based; 81 iBT). Electronic applications accepted.

The University of Kansas, Graduate Studies, School of Education, Department of Psychology and Research in Education, Program in Educational Psychology and Research, Lawrence, KS 66045. Offers MS Ed, PhD. *Students:* 28 full-time (17 women), 10 part-time (6 women); includes 3 minority (2 African Americans, 1 Asian American or Pacific Islander), 17 international. Average age 32. 18 applicants, 72% accepted, 11 enrolled. *Degree requirements:* For master's, thesis; for doctorate, comprehensive exam, thesis/dissertation. *Entrance requirements:* For master's, GRE General Test, minimum GPA of 3.0; for doctorate, GRE General Test. Additional exam requirements/recommendations for international students: Required—TOEFL. *Application deadline:* For fall admission, 4/15 for domestic students; for spring admission, 11/15 for domestic students. Application fee: $45 ($55 for international students). Electronic applications accepted. *Expenses:* Tuition, state resident: full-time $6492; part-time $270.50 per credit hour. Tuition, nonresident: full-time $15,510; part-time $646.25 per credit hour. Required fees: $847; $70.56 per credit hour. Tuition and fees vary according to course load and program. *Financial support:* Fellowships, research assistantships with full and partial tuition reimbursements, teaching assistantships with full and partial tuition reimbursements, career-related internships or fieldwork, institutionally sponsored loans, scholarships/grants, traineeships, health care benefits, tuition waivers (full and partial), and unspecified assistantships available. Support available to part-time students. Financial award application deadline: 2/1. *Faculty research:* Educational measurement, applied statistics, research design, program evaluation, learning and development. *Unit head:* Bruce Frey, Faculty Coordinator, 785-864-3931, E-mail: bfrey@ku.edu. *Application contact:* Admissions Coordinator, 785-864-3931, Fax: 785-864-3820, E-mail: preadmit@ku.edu.

University of Kentucky, Graduate School, College of Education, Program in Educational Policy Studies and Evaluation, Lexington, KY 40506-0032. Offers educational policy studies and evaluation (Ed D); higher education (MS Ed, PhD). *Accreditation:* NCATE. Terminal master's awarded for partial completion of doctoral program. *Degree requirements:* For master's, comprehensive exam, thesis optional; for doctorate, comprehensive exam, thesis/dissertation. *Entrance requirements:* For master's, GRE General Test, minimum undergraduate GPA of 2.75; for doctorate, GRE General Test, minimum graduate GPA of 3.0. Additional exam requirements/recommendations for international students: Required—TOEFL (minimum score 550 paper-based; 213 computer-based). Electronic applications accepted. *Faculty research:* Studies in higher education; comparative and international education; evaluation of educational programs, policies, and reform; student, teacher, and faculty cultures; gender and education.

University of Louisiana at Monroe, Graduate School, College of Education and Human Development, Department of Curriculum and Instruction, Program in Curriculum and Instruction, Monroe, LA 71209-0001. Offers curriculum and instruction (Ed D); elementary education (1-5) (M Ed); reading education (K-12) (M Ed); SPED-academically gifted education (K-12) (M Ed); SPED-early intervention education (birth-3) (M Ed); SPED-educational diagnostics education (PreK-12) (M Ed). *Accreditation:* NCATE. *Faculty:* 17 full-time (all women), 2 part-time/adjunct (both women). *Students:* 15 full-time (13 women), 125 part-time (118 women); includes 38 minority (36 African Americans, 1 Asian American or Pacific Islander, 1 Hispanic American). Average age 37. In 2009, 11 master's, 4 doctorates awarded. *Degree requirements:* For master's, comprehensive exam (for some programs), thesis; for doctorate, thesis/dissertation, internships. *Entrance requirements:* For master's, GRE General Test; for doctorate, GRE General Test, minimum undergraduate GPA of 2.75, graduate 3.25. Additional exam requirements/recommendations for international students: Required—TOEFL (minimum score 500 paper-based; 173 computer-based; 61 iBT). *Application deadline:* For fall admission, 8/24 priority date for domestic students, 7/1 for international students; for winter admission, 12/14 priority date for domestic students; for spring admission, 1/19 for domestic students, 11/1 for international students. Applications are processed on a rolling basis. Application fee: $20 ($30 for international students). Electronic applications accepted. *Expenses:* Tuition, state resident: part-time $159 per credit hour. Tuition, nonresident: part-time $159 per credit hour. Required fees: $1300 per year. Tuition and fees vary according to course load. *Financial support:* In 2009–10, 8 teaching assistantships with full tuition reimbursements (averaging $2,969 per year) were awarded; career-related internships or fieldwork, Federal Work-Study, and unspecified assistantships also available. Financial award application deadline: 4/1; financial award applicants required to submit FAFSA. *Unit head:* Dr. Dorothy Schween, Coordinator, 318-342-1269, Fax: 318-342-3131, E-mail: schween@ulm.edu. *Application contact:* Whitney Sutherland, Administrative Assistant to the Department Head, 318-342-1266, Fax: 318-342-3131, E-mail: sutherland@ulm.edu.

University of Maryland, College Park, Academic Affairs, College of Education, Department of Measurement, Statistics, and Evaluation, College Park, MD 20742. Offers measurement (MA, PhD); program evaluation (MA, PhD); statistics (MA, PhD). *Accreditation:* NCATE. Part-time and evening/weekend programs available. Postbaccalaureate distance learning degree programs offered (minimal on-campus study). *Faculty:* 9 full-time (2 women), 2 part-time/adjunct (1 woman). *Students:* 37 full-time (28 women), 11 part-time (6 women). 36 applicants, 36% accepted, 9 enrolled. In 2009, 1 master's, 6 doctorates awarded. *Degree requirements:* For master's, comprehensive exam, thesis optional; for doctorate, thesis/dissertation, preliminary and comprehensive written exams. *Entrance requirements:* For master's and doctorate, GRE General Test or MAT, minimum GPA of 3.0, 3 letters of recommendation. Additional exam requirements/recommendations for international students: Required—TOEFL. *Application deadline:* For fall admission, 3/15 for domestic students, 2/1 for international students; for spring admission, 10/1 for domestic students, 6/1 for international students. Applications are processed on a rolling basis. Application fee: $60. Electronic applications accepted. *Expenses:* Tuition, area resident: Part-time $471 per credit hour. Tuition, state resident: part-time $471 per credit hour. Tuition, nonresident: part-time $1016 per credit hour. Required fees: $337.04 per term. *Financial support:* In 2009–10, 4 fellowships with full and partial tuition reimbursements (averaging $10,277 per year), 7 research assistantships with tuition reimbursements (averaging $16,157 per year), 14 teaching assistantships with tuition reimbursements (averaging $15,984 per year) were awarded; Federal Work-Study and scholarships/grants also available. Support available to part-time students. Financial award applicants required to submit FAFSA. Total annual research expenditures: $869,611. *Unit head:* Dr. Gregory Hancock, Chair, 301-405-3624, E-mail: ghancock@umd.edu. *Application contact:* Dean of Graduate School, 301-405-0358.

University of Massachusetts Amherst, Graduate School, School of Education, Program in Education, Amherst, MA 01003. Offers bilingual, English as a second language, and multicultural education (M Ed, CAGS); child study and early education (M Ed); children, families and schools (Ed D, CAGS); early childhood and elementary teacher education (M Ed); education policy and leadership (CAGS); educational administration (M Ed, CAGS); educational policy and leadership (Ed D); higher education (M Ed, CAGS); international education (M Ed); language, literacy and culture (Ed D); learning, media and technology (M Ed, CAGS); mathematics, science, and learning technologies (Ed D); policy studies (M Ed); policy studies in education (CAGS); reading and writing (M Ed); research and evaluation methods (Ed D); school counselor education (M Ed, CAGS); school psychology (CAGS); science education (CAGS); secondary teacher education (M Ed); social justice education (M Ed, Ed D, CAGS); special education (M Ed, Ed D, CAGS). *Accreditation:* NCATE. Part-time programs available. Postbaccalaureate distance learning degree programs offered (minimal on-campus study). *Faculty:* 74 full-time (41 women). *Students:* 377 full-time (268 women), 347 part-time (232 women); includes 115 minority (59 African Americans, 2 American Indian/Alaska Native, 16 Asian Americans or Pacific Islanders, 38 Hispanic Americans), 108 international. Average age 35. 708 applicants, 68% accepted, 266 enrolled. In 2009, 183 master's, 17 doctorates awarded. Terminal master's awarded for partial completion of doctoral program. *Degree requirements:* For master's, thesis or alternative; for doctorate, comprehensive exam, thesis/dissertation. *Entrance requirements:* Additional exam requirements/recommendations for international students: Required—TOEFL (minimum score 550 paper-based; 213 computer-based; 80 iBT), IELTS (minimum score 6.5). *Application deadline:* For fall admission, 1/15 for domestic and international students. Applications are processed on a rolling basis. Application fee: $50 ($65 for international students). Electronic applications accepted. *Expenses:* Tuition, state resident: full-time $2640; part-time $110 per credit. Tuition, nonresident: full-time $9936; part-time $414 per credit. Tuition and fees vary according to course load. *Financial support:* In 2009–10, 1 fellowship with full tuition reimbursement (averaging $8,036 per year), 92 research assistantships with full tuition reimbursements (averaging $8,555 per year), 83 teaching assistantships with full tuition reimbursements (averaging $4,661 per year) were awarded; career-related internships or fieldwork, Federal Work-Study, scholarships/grants, traineeships, health care benefits, tuition waivers (full), and unspecified assistantships also available. Support available to part-time students. Financial award application deadline: 1/15. *Unit head:* Dr. Linda L. Griffin, Graduate Program Director, 413-545-6984, Fax: 413-545-2873. *Application contact:* Jean M. Ames, Supervisor of Admissions, 413-545-0722, Fax: 413-577-0010, E-mail: gradadm@grad.umass.edu.

University of Memphis, Graduate School, College of Education, Department of Counseling, Educational Psychology and Research, Memphis, TN 38152. Offers counseling (MS, Ed D), including community counseling (MS), rehabilitation counseling (MS), school counseling (MS); counseling psychology (PhD); educational psychology and research (MS, PhD), including educational psychology, educational research. *Accreditation:* ACA (one or more programs are accredited); APA (one or more programs are accredited); CORE (one or more programs are accredited); NCATE. *Faculty:* 26 full-time (13 women), 9 part-time/adjunct (5 women). *Students:* 95 full-time (73 women), 104 part-time (81 women); includes 62 minority (56 African Americans, 3 American Indian/Alaska Native, 1 Asian American or Pacific Islander, 2 Hispanic Americans), 5 international. Average age 33. 118 applicants, 63% accepted, 36 enrolled. In 2009, 46 master's, 14 doctorates awarded. *Degree requirements:* For master's, comprehensive exam, thesis or alternative; for doctorate, comprehensive exam, thesis/dissertation. *Entrance requirements:* For master's, GRE General Test or MAT, minimum GPA of 2.5; for doctorate, GRE General Test. *Application deadline:* For fall admission, 10/1 for domestic students; for spring admission, 4/1 for domestic students. Application fee: $35 ($60 for international students). *Expenses:* Tuition, state resident: full-time $6246; part-time $347 per credit hour. Tuition, nonresident: full-time $15,894; part-time $883 per credit hour. Required fees: $1160. Full-time tuition and fees vary according to course load, degree level and program. *Financial support:* In 2009–10, 130 students received support; fellowships with full tuition reimbursements available, research assistantships with full tuition reimbursements available, teaching assistantships with full tuition reimbursements available, career-related internships or fieldwork, Federal Work-Study, scholarships/grants, and unspecified assistantships available. Financial award application deadline: 2/15; financial award applicants required to submit FAFSA. *Faculty research:* Anger management, aging and disability, supervision, multicultural counseling. *Unit head:* Dr. Douglas C. Strohmer, Chair, 901-678-2841, Fax: 901-678-5114. *Application contact:* Dr. Ernest A. Rakow, Associate Dean of Administration and Graduate Programs, 901-678-2399, Fax: 901-678-4778.

University of Miami, Graduate School, School of Education, Department of Educational and Psychological Studies, Program in Research, Measurement, and Evaluation, Coral Gables, FL 33124. Offers MS Ed, PhD. Part-time and evening/weekend programs available. *Students:* 5 full-time (all women); includes 1 minority (Hispanic American), 1 international. Average age 29. 11 applicants, 27% accepted, 1 enrolled. In 2009, 1 master's awarded. Terminal master's awarded for partial completion of doctoral program. *Degree requirements:* For master's, comprehensive exam, thesis optional; for doctorate, thesis/dissertation, qualifying exam. *Entrance requirements:* For master's and doctorate, GRE General Test. Additional exam requirements/recommendations for international students: Required—TOEFL (minimum score 550 paper-based; 80 iBT); Recommended—IELTS (minimum score 6.5). *Application deadline:* For fall admission, 2/1 for domestic students, 10/15 for international students. Applications are processed on a rolling basis. Application fee: $65. Electronic applications accepted. *Financial support:* In 2009–10, 5 students received support. Career-related internships or fieldwork, institutionally sponsored loans, health care benefits, and unspecified assistantships available. Support available to part-time students. Financial award application deadline: 3/1; financial award applicants required to submit FAFSA. *Faculty research:* Psychometric theory, computer-based testing, quantitative research methods. *Unit head:* Dr. Randall D. Penfield, Associate Professor and Program Director, 305-284-8340, Fax: 305-284-3003, E-mail: penfield@miami.edu. *Application contact:* Marissa Stevenson-Jacobs, Graduate Admissions Coordinator, 305-284-2167, Fax: 305-284-3003, E-mail: mstevenson@miami.edu.

University of Michigan, Horace H. Rackham School of Graduate Studies, School of Education, Center for the Study of Higher and Postsecondary Education, Ann Arbor, MI 48109. Offers academic affairs and student development (PhD); development (AM); higher education (AM); individually designed concentration (PhD); medical and professional education (AM); organizational behavior and management (PhD); public policy (PhD); research, evaluation, and assessment (PhD); MBA/MA; MPP/MA. Terminal master's awarded for partial completion of doctoral program. *Degree requirements:* For master's, thesis optional; for doctorate, comprehensive exam, thesis/dissertation. *Entrance requirements:* For master's and doctorate, GRE General Test. Additional exam requirements/recommendations for international students: Required—TOEFL (minimum score 600 paper-based; 250 computer-based). *Application deadline:* For fall admission, 12/1 priority date for domestic students, 12/1 for international students. Application fee: $60 ($75 for international students). Electronic applications accepted. *Expenses:* Tuition, state resident: full-time $17,286; part-time $1099 per credit hour. Tuition, nonresident: full-time $34,944; part-time $2080 per credit hour. Required fees: $95 per semester. Tuition and fees vary according to course load, degree level and program. *Financial support:* Applicants required to submit FAFSA. *Unit head:* Dr. Stephen DesJardins, Chairperson, 734-647-1981, Fax: 734-764-2510, E-mail: sdesj@umich.edu. *Application contact:* Laura Mayers, Student Services Assistant, 734-764-7563, Fax: 734-763-1495, E-mail: ed.grad.admit@umich.edu.

University of Michigan–Dearborn, College of Arts, Sciences, and Letters, Master of Public Administration Program, Dearborn, MI 48128. Offers assessment and evaluation (Certificate); nonprofit leadership (Certificate); public administration (MPA). Part-time and evening/weekend programs available. *Faculty:* 3 full-time (1 woman), 9 part-time/adjunct (2 women). *Students:* 13 full-time (10 women), 67 part-time (43 women); includes 20 minority (16 African Americans, 1 American Indian/Alaska Native, 2 Asian Americans or Pacific Islanders, 1 Hispanic American). Average age 35. 30 applicants, 90% accepted, 24 enrolled. In 2009, 36 master's awarded. *Degree requirements:* For master's, assessment seminar. *Entrance requirements:* For master's, GRE or minimum undergraduate GPA of 3.0, 3 letters of recommendation. Additional exam requirements/recommendations for international students: Required—TOEFL, TWE. *Application deadline:* For fall admission, 8/1 for domestic students, 4/1 for international students; for winter admission, 12/1 for domestic students, 11/1 for international students; for spring admission, 4/1 for domestic students, 3/1 for international students. Applications are processed on a rolling basis. Application fee: $60. *Expenses:* Tuition, state resident: part-time $504.10 per credit hour. Tuition, nonresident: part-time $957.90 per credit hour. *Financial support:* Career-related internships or fieldwork and Federal Work-Study available. Support available to part-time students. Financial award applicants required to submit FAFSA. *Faculty research:* Federal, state, and local agency management; independent sector management; educational administration. *Unit head:* Dr. Trevor Thrall, Director, 313-593-5282, Fax: 313-583-6700, E-mail: atthrall@umich.edu. *Application contact:* Carol Ligienza, Graduate Programs Coordinator, 313-593-1183, Fax: 313-583-6700, E-mail: caslgrad@umd.umich.edu.

University of Minnesota, Twin Cities Campus, Graduate School, College of Education and Human Development, Department of Organizational Leadership, Policy and Development, Program in Evaluation Studies, Minneapolis, MN 55455-0213. Offers MA, PhD. *Students:* 12 full-time (11 women), 18 part-time (15 women); includes 4 minority (1 African American, 3 Asian Americans or Pacific Islanders), 2 international. Average age 39. 8 applicants, 88% accepted, 3 enrolled. In 2009, 2 master's, 4 doctorates awarded. *Unit head:* Dr. Darwin Hendel, Chair, 612-625-0129, Fax: 612-624-3377, E-mail: hende001@umn.edu. *Application contact:* Dr. Mary Trettin, Associate Dean, 612-625-6501, Fax: 612-626-1580, E-mail: mtrettin@umn.edu.

University of Missouri–St. Louis, College of Education, Division of Educational Leadership and Policy Studies, St. Louis, MO 63121. Offers adult and higher education (M Ed), including adult education; educational administration (M Ed, Ed S), including community education (M Ed), elementary education (M Ed), secondary education (M Ed); institutional research (Certificate). *Accreditation:* NCATE. Part-time and evening/weekend programs available. *Faculty:* 19 full-time (8 women), 7 part-time/adjunct (4 women). *Students:* 25 full-time (21 women), 196 part-time (137 women); includes 88 minority (84 African Americans, 1 Asian American or Pacific Islander, 3 Hispanic Americans), 4 international. Average age 36. In 2009, 66 master's, 25 Certificates awarded. *Degree requirements:* For master's, comprehensive exam (for some programs). *Entrance requirements:* Additional exam requirements/recommendations for international students: Required—TOEFL (minimum score 550 paper-based; 213 computer-based). *Application deadline:* For fall admission, 7/1 priority date for domestic and international students; for spring admission, 12/1 priority date for domestic and international students. Applications are processed on a rolling basis. Application fee: $35 ($40 for international students). Electronic applications accepted. *Expenses:* Tuition, state resident: full-time $5377; part-time $297.70 per credit hour. Tuition, nonresident: full-time $13,882; part-time $771.20 per credit hour. Required fees: $220; $12.20 per credit hour. One-time fee: $12. Tuition and fees vary according to course level, campus/location and program. *Financial support:* In 2009–10, 3 research assistantships (averaging $5,133 per year) were awarded. Financial award application deadline: 4/1; financial award applicants required to submit FAFSA. *Faculty research:* Educational policy research; philosophy of education; higher, adult, and vocational education; school initiatives, change, and reform. *Unit head:* Dr. E. Paulette Savage, Chair, 514-516-5944. *Application contact:* 314-516-5458, Fax: 314-516-6996, E-mail: gradadm@umsl.edu.

University of Missouri–St. Louis, College of Education, Division of Educational Psychology, Research, and Evaluation, St. Louis, MO 63121. Offers education (Ed D); educational psychology

Educational Measurement and Evaluation

University of Missouri–St. Louis (continued)

(PhD); program evaluation and assessment (Certificate); school psychology (Ed S). *Faculty:* 13 full-time (4 women), 8 part-time/adjunct (4 women). *Students:* 27 full-time (24 women), 27 part-time (20 women); includes 12 minority (all African Americans), 2 international. Average age 36. In 2009, 39 doctorates awarded. *Degree requirements:* For other advanced degree, internship. *Entrance requirements:* For degree, GRE General Test, 2-4 letters of recommendation, personal interview. Additional exam requirements/recommendations for international students: Recommended—TOEFL (minimum score 550 paper-based; 213 computer-based). *Application deadline:* For fall admission, 3/1 for domestic and international students. Application fee: $35 ($40 for international students). Electronic applications accepted. *Expenses:* Tuition, state resident: full-time $5377; part-time $297.70 per credit hour. Tuition, nonresident: full-time $13,882; part-time $771.20 per credit hour. Required fees: $220; $12.20 per credit hour. One-time fee: $12. Tuition and fees vary according to course level, campus/location and program. *Financial support:* In 2009–10, 1 research assistantship (averaging $12,240 per year), 2 teaching assistantships (averaging $8,306 per year) were awarded. Financial award application deadline: 4/1; financial award applicants required to submit FAFSA. *Faculty research:* Child/adolescent psychology, quantitative and qualitative methodology, evaluation processes, measurement and assessment. *Unit head:* Dr. Matthew Keefer, Chairperson, 314-516-5783, Fax: 314-516-5784, E-mail: keefer@umsl.edu. *Application contact:* 314-516-5458, Fax: 314-516-6996, E-mail: gradadm@umsl.edu.

University of Nebraska–Lincoln, Graduate College, College of Education and Human Sciences, Department of Educational Psychology, Lincoln, NE 68588. Offers cognition, learning and development (MA); counseling psychology (MA); educational psychology (MA, Ed S); psychological studies in education (PhD), including cognition, learning and development, counseling psychology, quantitative, qualitative, and psychometric methods, school psychology; quantitative, qualitative, and psychometric methods (MA); school psychology (MA, Ed S). *Accreditation:* APA (one or more programs are accredited); NCATE. *Degree requirements:* For master's, thesis optional. *Entrance requirements:* For master's, GRE General Test. Additional exam requirements/recommendations for international students: Required—TOEFL (minimum score 500 paper-based; 173 computer-based). Electronic applications accepted. *Faculty research:* Measurement and assessment, metacognition, academic skills, child development, multicultural education and counseling.

University of New England, College of Arts and Sciences, Program in Education, Biddeford, ME 04005-9526. Offers curriculm and instruction strategy (MS Ed); educational leadership (MS Ed); general studies (MS Ed); literacy (MS Ed); teaching methodologies (MS Ed). Part-time programs available. Postbaccalaureate distance learning degree programs offered (minimal on-campus study). *Faculty:* 2 full-time (1 woman), 25 part-time/adjunct (15 women). *Students:* 473 full-time (362 women), 177 part-time (133 women); includes 29 African Americans, 12 Asian Americans or Pacific Islanders, 16 Hispanic Americans. In 2009, 319 master's awarded. *Degree requirements:* For master's, collaborative action research project, integrative seminar portfolio. *Entrance requirements:* For master's, teaching certificate, 2 years of teaching experience. Additional exam requirements/recommendations for international students: Required—TOEFL. *Application deadline:* For fall admission, 9/15 for domestic students; for spring admission, 1/15 for domestic students. Applications are processed on a rolling basis. Application fee: $40. Electronic applications accepted. *Expenses:* Contact institution. *Financial support:* Application deadline: 5/1. *Faculty research:* Distance learning, effective teaching, transition planning, adult learning. *Unit head:* Dr. Doug Lynch, Chair of Education Department, 207-283-0171 Ext. 2888, E-mail: dlynch@une.edu. *Application contact:* Stacy Gato, Assistant Director of Graduate Admissions, 207-221-4225, Fax: 207-221-4898, E-mail: gradadmissions@une.edu.

The University of North Carolina at Chapel Hill, Graduate School, School of Education, Program in Education, Chapel Hill, NC 27599. Offers culture, curriculum and change (MA, PhD); early childhood, intervention and literacy (MA, PhD); educational psychology, measurement and evaluation (MA, PhD). *Accreditation:* NCATE. *Degree requirements:* For master's, thesis; for doctorate, comprehensive exam, thesis/dissertation. *Entrance requirements:* For master's, GRE General Test, minimum GPA of 3.0 during last 2 years of undergraduates course work; for doctorate, GRE General Test, minimum GPA of 3.0 during last 2 years of undergraduate course work. Additional exam requirements/recommendations for international students: Required—TOEFL (minimum score 550 paper-based; 213 computer-based). Electronic applications accepted.

The University of North Carolina at Greensboro, Graduate School, School of Education, Department of Educational Research Methodology, Greensboro, NC 27412-5001. Offers educational research, measurement and evaluation (PhD); MS/PhD. *Accreditation:* NCATE. *Degree requirements:* For doctorate, thesis/dissertation. *Entrance requirements:* For doctorate, GRE General Test. Additional exam requirements/recommendations for international students: Required—TOEFL. Electronic applications accepted.

University of North Dakota, Graduate School, College of Education and Human Development, Teaching and Learning Program, Grand Forks, ND 58202. Offers elementary education (Ed D, PhD); measurement and statistics (Ed D, PhD); secondary education (Ed D, PhD); special education (Ed D, PhD). *Accreditation:* NCATE. Postbaccalaureate distance learning degree programs offered (minimal on-campus study). *Degree requirements:* For doctorate, comprehensive exam, thesis/dissertation, final exam. *Entrance requirements:* For doctorate, minimum GPA of 3.5. Additional exam requirements/recommendations for international students: Required—TOEFL (minimum score 550 paper-based; 213 computer-based; 79 iBT), IELTS (minimum score 6.5). Electronic applications accepted.

University of Northern Colorado, Graduate School, College of Education and Behavioral Sciences, School of Educational Research, Leadership and Technology, Program in Applied Statistics and Research Methods, Greeley, CO 80639. Offers MS, PhD. Part-time programs available. *Faculty:* 8 full-time (4 women). *Students:* 26 full-time (11 women), 21 part-time (10 women); includes 4 minority (1 African American, 1 Asian American or Pacific Islander, 2 Hispanic Americans), 9 international. Average age 37. 25 applicants, 80% accepted, 12 enrolled. In 2009, 4 master's, 9 doctorates awarded. *Degree requirements:* For master's, comprehensive exam; for doctorate, comprehensive exam, thesis/dissertation. *Entrance requirements:* For master's, 3 letters of reference; for doctorate, GRE General Test, 3 letters of reference. *Application deadline:* Applications are processed on a rolling basis. Application fee: $50 ($60 for international students). Electronic applications accepted. *Expenses:* Tuition, state resident: full-time $5770; part-time $320.55 per credit hour. Tuition, nonresident: full-time $13,847; part-time $769.27 per credit hour. Required fees: $948.78; $52.72 per credit. *Financial support:* In 2009–10, 7 research assistantships (averaging $2,908 per year), 5 teaching assistantships (averaging $3,419 per year) were awarded; fellowships also available. Financial award application deadline: 3/1. *Unit head:* Dr. Susan Hutchinson, Program Coordinator, 970-351-2807, Fax: 970-351-1669. *Application contact:* Linda Sisson, Graduate Student Admission Coordinator, 970-351-1807, Fax: 970-351-2371, E-mail: linda.sisson@unco.edu.

University of North Texas, Robert B. Toulouse School of Graduate Studies, College of Education, Department of Educational Psychology, Program in Educational Research, Denton, TX 76203. Offers PhD. *Accreditation:* NCATE. *Students:* Average age 39. *Degree requirements:* For doctorate, one foreign language, thesis/dissertation, internship. *Entrance requirements:* For doctorate, GRE General Test, admissions exam. Additional exam requirements/recommendations for international students: Recommended—TOEFL (minimum score 550 paper-based; 213 computer-based; 79 iBT). *Application deadline:* Applications are processed on a rolling basis. Application fee: $50 ($75 for international students). Electronic applications accepted. *Expenses:* Tuition, state resident: full-time $4298; part-time $239 per contact hour. Tuition, nonresident: full-time $9878; part-time $549 per contact hour. Required fees: $265 per contact hour. *Financial support:* Fellowships, research assistantships, teaching assistantships, career-related internships or fieldwork, Federal Work-Study, and institutionally sponsored loans available. Financial award applicants required to submit FAFSA. *Faculty research:* Applied general linear modeling, reliability, factor analysis, structural equation modeling, learning environments and social/historical factors. *Application contact:* Graduate Adviser, 940-369-8377, E-mail: kroberts@unt.edu.

University of Pennsylvania, Graduate School of Education, Division of Policy, Management and Evaluation, Philadelphia, PA 19104. Offers education policy (MS Ed, PhD); policy research, evaluation, and measurement (M Phil, PhD). Part-time programs available. *Students:* 192 full-time (122 women), 58 part-time (35 women); includes 37 minority (20 African Americans, 1 American Indian/Alaska Native, 11 Asian Americans or Pacific Islanders, 5 Hispanic Americans), 9 international. 438 applicants, 46% accepted, 107 enrolled. In 2009, 49 master's, 31 doctorates awarded. Terminal master's awarded for partial completion of doctoral program. *Degree requirements:* For master's, comprehensive exam; for doctorate, comprehensive exam, thesis/dissertation. *Entrance requirements:* For master's and doctorate, GRE. *Application deadline:* For fall admission, 12/15 for domestic students. Applications are processed on a rolling basis. Application fee: $70. Electronic applications accepted. *Expenses:* Contact institution. *Financial support:* Fellowships, institutionally sponsored loans, scholarships/grants, traineeships, health care benefits, and unspecified assistantships available. *Faculty research:* Institutional research, strategic planning, governance and administration, public policy, budgeting and finance.

University of Pittsburgh, School of Education, Department of Psychology in Education, Program in Research Methodology, Pittsburgh, PA 15260. Offers M Ed, MA, PhD. Part-time and evening/weekend programs available. *Students:* 16 full-time (11 women), 12 part-time (8 women); includes 2 minority (both Asian Americans or Pacific Islanders), 13 international. Average age 32. 18 applicants, 83% accepted, 10 enrolled. In 2009, 6 master's, 2 doctorates awarded. Terminal master's awarded for partial completion of doctoral program. *Degree requirements:* For master's, thesis; for doctorate, thesis/dissertation. *Entrance requirements:* For doctorate, GRE General Test. Additional exam requirements/recommendations for international students: Required—TOEFL. *Application deadline:* For fall admission, 2/1 for domestic students. Application fee: $50. Electronic applications accepted. *Expenses:* Tuition, state resident: full-time $16,402; part-time $665 per credit. Tuition, nonresident: full-time $28,694; part-time $1175 per credit. Required fees: $690; $175 per term. Tuition and fees vary according to program. *Financial support:* Fellowships, research assistantships with partial tuition reimbursements, Federal Work-Study, tuition waivers (partial), and unspecified assistantships available. Support available to part-time students. Financial award application deadline: 3/15; financial award applicants required to submit FAFSA. *Unit head:* Dr. Carl N. Johnson, Chairman, 412-624-6942, Fax: 412-624-7231, E-mail: johnson@pitt.edu. *Application contact:* Lauren Pasquini, Graduate Enrollment Manager, 412-648-2230, Fax: 412-648-1899, E-mail: soeinfo@pitt.edu.

University of Puerto Rico, Río Piedras, College of Education, Program in Educational Research and Evaluation, San Juan, PR 00931-3300. Offers M Ed. Part-time programs available. *Degree requirements:* For master's, thesis. *Entrance requirements:* For master's, PAEG or GRE, interview, minimum GPA of 3.0, letter of recommendation.

University of South Carolina, The Graduate School, College of Education, Department of Educational Studies, Program in Educational Psychology, Research, Columbia, SC 29208. Offers M Ed, PhD. *Accreditation:* NCATE. Part-time programs available. *Degree requirements:* For master's, comprehensive exam, thesis (for some programs); for doctorate, comprehensive exam, thesis/dissertation. *Entrance requirements:* For master's, GRE General Test; for doctorate, GRE General Test, interview. Electronic applications accepted. *Faculty research:* Problem solving, higher order thinking skills, psychometric research, methodology.

University of Southern Mississippi, Graduate School, College of Education and Psychology, Department of Educational Studies and Research, Hattiesburg, MS 39406-0001. Offers adult education (Graduate Certificate); community college leadership (Graduate Certificate); counseling and personnel services (college) (M Ed); education (PhD, Ed S), including adult education, research, evaluation and statistics (PhD); education (Ed D), including educational administration, educational research; education: educational leadership and research (Ed S), including higher education administration; educational administration and supervision (M Ed); higher education administration (Ed D, PhD); institutional research (Graduate Certificate). *Faculty:* 7 full-time (1 woman), 5 part-time/adjunct (1 woman). *Students:* 45 full-time (34 women), 97 part-time (66 women); includes 42 minority (40 African Americans, 1 American Indian/Alaska Native, 1 Hispanic American), 2 international. Average age 36. 54 applicants, 67% accepted, 33 enrolled. In 2009, 26 master's, 11 doctorates, 3 other advanced degrees awarded. *Degree requirements:* For master's and other advanced degree, comprehensive exam, thesis (for some programs); for doctorate, comprehensive exam, thesis/dissertation. *Entrance requirements:* For master's, doctorate, and other advanced degree, GRE General Test, minimum GPA of 2.75. Additional exam requirements/recommendations for international students: Required—TOEFL. *Application deadline:* For fall admission, 2/1 for domestic students, 3/1 for international students. Applications are processed on a rolling basis. Application fee: $35. *Expenses:* Tuition, state resident: full-time $5096; part-time $284 per hour. Tuition, nonresident: full-time $13,052; part-time $726 per hour. Required fees: $402. Tuition and fees vary according to course level and course load. *Financial support:* Career-related internships or fieldwork, Federal Work-Study, and institutionally sponsored loans available. Financial award application deadline: 3/15; financial award applicants required to submit FAFSA. Total annual research expenditures: $88,500. *Unit head:* Dr. Thomas V. O'Brien, Chair, 601-266-6093, E-mail: thomas.obrien@usm.edu. *Application contact:* Shonna Breland, Manager of Graduate Admissions, 601-266-6563, Fax: 601-266-5138.

University of South Florida, Graduate School, College of Education–Main Campus, Department of Educational Measurement and Research, Tampa, FL 33620-9951. Offers measurement and evaluation (M Ed, PhD, Ed S). *Accreditation:* NCATE. Part-time programs available. *Faculty:* 7 full-time (2 women), 3 part-time/adjunct (2 women). *Students:* 24 full-time (15 women), 23 part-time (13 women); includes 7 minority (3 African Americans, 1 Asian American or Pacific Islander, 3 Hispanic Americans), 9 international. Average age 30. 12 applicants, 92% accepted, 10 enrolled. In 2009, 3 master's, 2 doctorates awarded. *Degree requirements:* For master's, comprehensive exam; for doctorate, comprehensive exam, thesis/dissertation. *Entrance requirements:* For master's, GRE General Test, minimum GPA of 3.0 in last 60 hours of course work; for doctorate, GRE General Test, minimum undergraduate GPA of 3.0 on upper-division coursework, master's degree or Ed S from regionally-accredited institution; for Ed S, GRE General Test, minimum undergraduate GPA of 3.0 on upper-division coursework, master's degree from regionally-accredited institution. Additional exam requirements/recommendations for international students: Required—TOEFL (minimum score 550 paper-based; 213 computer-based; 79 iBT). *Application deadline:* For fall admission, 2/15 for domestic students, 1/2 for international students; for spring admission, 10/15 for domestic students, 6/1 for international students. Applications are processed on a rolling basis. Application fee: $30. Electronic applications accepted. *Financial support:* In 2009–10, 1 student received support, including 1 fellowship with full tuition reimbursement available (averaging $10,000 per year), 8 research assistantships with full tuition reimbursements available (averaging $10,553 per year), 4 teaching assistantships with full tuition reimbursements available (averaging $10,553 per year); career-related internships or fieldwork, scholarships/grants, health care benefits, and unspecified assistantships also available. Financial award application deadline: 6/15; financial award applicants required to submit FAFSA. *Faculty research:* Multilevel modeling, methods for analyzing single case data, collaborative evaluation, validity of statistical inferences, secondary data analysis, effect sizes, meta-analyses. Total annual research expenditures: $252,886. *Unit head:* Dr. Constance Hines, Chairperson, 813-974-0370, Fax: 813-974-4495, E-mail: hines@tempest.coedu.usf.edu. *Application contact:* Dr. John Ferron, Program Director, 813-974-3220, Fax: 813-974-4495, E-mail: ferron@tempest.cordu.usf.edu.

The University of Tennessee, Graduate School, College of Education, Health and Human Sciences, Program in Education, Knoxville, TN 37996. Offers art education (MS); counseling education (PhD); cultural studies in education (PhD); curriculum (MS, Ed S); curriculum, educational research and evaluation (Ed D, PhD); early childhood education (PhD); early childhood special education (MS); education of deaf and hard of hearing (MS); educational administration and policy studies (Ed D, PhD); educational administration and supervision

(Ed S); educational psychology (Ed D, PhD); elementary education (MS, Ed S); elementary teaching (MS); English education (MS, Ed S); exercise science (PhD); foreign language/ESL education (MS, Ed S); instructional technology (MS, Ed D, PhD, Ed S); literacy, language and ESL education (PhD); literacy, language education, and ESL education (Ed D); mathematics education (MS, Ed S); modified and comprehensive special education (MS); reading education (MS, Ed S); school counseling (Ed S); school psychology (PhD, Ed S); science education (MS, Ed S); secondary teaching (MS); social foundations (MS); social science education (MS, Ed S); socio-cultural foundations of sports and education (PhD); special education (Ed S); teacher education (Ed D, PhD). *Accreditation:* NCATE. Part-time and evening/weekend programs available. *Degree requirements:* For master's and Ed S, thesis optional; for doctorate, variable foreign language requirement, thesis/dissertation. *Entrance requirements:* For master's, minimum GPA of 2.7; for doctorate and Ed S, GRE General Test, minimum GPA of 2.7. Additional exam requirements/recommendations for international students: Required—TOEFL. Electronic applications accepted. *Expenses:* Tuition, state resident: full-time $6826; part-time $380 per semester hour. Tuition, nonresident: full-time $21,844; part-time $1147 per semester hour. Tuition and fees vary according to program.

The University of Texas at El Paso, Graduate School, College of Education, Department of Educational Psychology and Special Services, El Paso, TX 79968-0001. Offers educational diagnostics (M Ed); guidance and counseling (M Ed); special education (M Ed). Part-time and evening/weekend programs available. *Degree requirements:* For master's, thesis optional. *Entrance requirements:* For master's, minimum graduate GPA of 3.0. Additional exam requirements/recommendations for international students: Required—TOEFL. Electronic applications accepted.

The University of Texas–Pan American, College of Education, Department of Educational Psychology, Edinburg, TX 78539. Offers counseling (M Ed); educational diagnostician (M Ed); gifted education (M Ed); school psychology (MA); special education (M Ed). Part-time and evening/weekend programs available. *Degree requirements:* For master's, comprehensive exam (for some programs), thesis (for some programs). *Entrance requirements:* For master's, GRE General Test, interview. *Expenses:* Tuition, state resident: full-time $3630.60; part-time $201.70 per credit hour. Tuition, nonresident: full-time $8617; part-time $478.70 per credit hour. Required fees: $806.50. *Faculty research:* Reading instruction, assessment practice, behavior interventions consultation, mental retardation.

University of the Southwest, Graduate Programs, Hobbs, NM 88240-9129. Offers business administration (MBA); curriculum and instruction (MSE); curriculum and instruction: bilingual (MSE); curriculum and instruction: reading (MSE); curriculum and instruction: TESOL (MSE); early childhood education (MSE); educational diagnostician (MSE); mental health counseling (MSE); school business administration (MSE); school counseling (MSE); special education (MSE). Part-time and evening/weekend programs available. Postbaccalaureate distance learning degree programs offered (no on-campus study). *Faculty:* 10 full-time (6 women), 10 part-time/adjunct (4 women). *Students:* 112 full-time (93 women), 99 part-time (72 women). Average age 35. 94 applicants, 47% accepted, 39 enrolled. In 2009, 32 master's awarded. *Degree requirements:* For master's, comprehensive exam. *Application deadline:* For fall admission, 3/1 priority date for domestic students; for spring admission, 10/1 for domestic students. Applications are processed on a rolling basis. Application fee: $25. Electronic applications accepted. *Expenses:* Tuition: Part-time $512 per hour. Tuition and fees vary according to course load. *Financial support:* In 2009–10, 196 students received support; research assistantships with partial tuition reimbursements available, Federal Work-Study, scholarships/grants, and tuition waivers (partial) available. Support available to part-time students. Financial award application deadline: 4/1; financial award applicants required to submit FAFSA. *Unit head:* Dr. Mary Harris, Dean of Education, 575-392-6561 Ext. 1056, Fax: 575-392-6006, E-mail: mharris@usw.edu. *Application contact:* Ryanne Evans, Assistant Registrar, 575-392-6561 Ext. 1031, Fax: 575-392-6006, E-mail: revans@usw.edu.

The University of Toledo, College of Graduate Studies, College of Education, Department of Educational Foundations and Leadership, Program in Educational Research and Measurement, Toledo, OH 43606-3390. Offers ME, PhD.

University of Victoria, Faculty of Graduate Studies, Faculty of Education, Department of Educational Psychology and Leadership Studies, Victoria, BC V8W 2Y2, Canada. Offers aboriginal communities counseling (M Ed); counseling (M Ed, MA); educational psychology (M Ed, MA, PhD), including counseling psychology (M Ed, MA), leadership studies (PhD), learning and development (MA, PhD), measurement and evaluation, special education (M Ed, MA); leadership studies (M Ed, MA). Part-time programs available. *Degree requirements:* For master's, thesis (for some programs), comprehensive exam (M Ed); for doctorate, comprehensive exam, thesis/dissertation, candidacy exam. *Entrance requirements:* For master's, 2 years of work experience in a relevant field; for doctorate, GRE, 2 years of work experience in a relevant field, minimum B average. Additional exam requirements/recommendations for international students: Required—TOEFL (minimum score 575 paper-based; 233 computer-based), IELTS (minimum score 7). *Faculty research:* Learning and development (child, adolescent and adult), special education and exceptional children.

University of Virginia, Curry School of Education, Department of Leadership, Foundations and Policy, Educational Policy Studies Program, Charlottesville, VA 22903. Offers M Ed, Ed D. *Students:* 1 full-time (0 women), 1 part-time (0 women). Average age 45. 1 applicant, 0% accepted, 0 enrolled. In 2009, 1 doctorate awarded. *Entrance requirements:* For master's and doctorate, GRE General Test, 2 letters of recommendation. Additional exam requirements/recommendations for international students: Required—TOEFL (minimum score 600 paper-based; 250 computer-based; 90 iBT), IELTS (minimum score 7). *Application deadline:* Applications are processed on a rolling basis. Application fee: $60. Electronic applications accepted. *Financial support:* Fellowships, research assistantships, teaching assistantships available. Financial award application deadline: 1/5; financial award applicants required to submit FAFSA.

University of Virginia, Curry School of Education, Department of Leadership, Foundations and Policy, Program in Educational Psychology, Charlottesville, VA 22903. Offers applied developmental science (M Ed); educational evaluation (M Ed); educational psychology (M Ed, Ed D, Ed S); educational research (Ed D); gifted education (M Ed); instructional technology (M Ed, Ed S); research statistics and evaluation (Ed D); school psychology (Ed D). *Students:* 28 full-time (22 women), 18 part-time (13 women); includes 3 minority (1 African American, 1 Asian American or Pacific Islander, 1 Hispanic American), 7 international. Average age 31. 130 applicants, 36% accepted, 31 enrolled. In 2009, 50 master's, 25 doctorates, 1 other advanced degree awarded. *Degree requirements:* For master's, comprehensive exam. *Entrance requirements:* For master's and doctorate, GRE General Test, 2 letters of recommendation. Additional exam requirements/recommendations for international students: Required—TOEFL (minimum score 600 paper-based; 250 computer-based; 90 iBT), IELTS (minimum score 7). *Application deadline:* Applications are processed on a rolling basis. Application fee: $60. Electronic applications accepted. *Financial support:* Fellowships, research assistantships, teaching assistantships available. Financial award application deadline: 1/5; financial award applicants required to submit FAFSA. *Unit head:* Jen Mashburn, Program Coordinator, E-mail: jmashburn@virginia.edu. *Application contact:* Jen Mashburn, Program Coordinator, E-mail: jmashburn@virginia.edu.

University of Virginia, Curry School of Education, Program in Education, Charlottesville, VA 22903. Offers administration and supervision (PhD); applied developmental science (PhD); counselor education (PhD); curriculum and instruction (PhD); early childhood-developmental risk (MT); education evaluation (PhD); educational psychology (PhD); educational research (PhD); elementary (MT, PhD); English education (MT, PhD); foreign language education (MT); higher education (PhD); instructional technology (PhD); kinesiology (MT, PhD); math education (PhD); reading education (PhD); research statistics and evaluation (PhD); school psychology (PhD); science education (PhD); social studies education (MT, PhD); special education (PhD); world languages education (MT). *Students:* 336 full-time (239 women), 88 part-time (54 women); includes 43 minority (24 African Americans, 2 American Indian/Alaska Native, 11 Asian Americans or Pacific Islanders, 6 Hispanic Americans), 18 international. Average age 27. 199 applicants, 48% accepted, 55 enrolled. In 2009, 127 master's, 52 doctorates awarded. *Degree requirements:* For master's, comprehensive exam (for some programs), field project; for doctorate, comprehensive exam, thesis/dissertation. *Entrance requirements:* For doctorate, GRE General Test. Additional exam requirements/recommendations for international students: Required—TOEFL (minimum score 600 paper-based; 250 computer-based; 90 iBT), IELTS (minimum score 7). *Application deadline:* Applications are processed on a rolling basis. Application fee: $60. Electronic applications accepted. *Financial support:* Fellowships, research assistantships, teaching assistantships available. Financial award application deadline: 1/5; financial award applicants required to submit FAFSA.

University of Washington, Graduate School, College of Education, Program in Educational Psychology, Seattle, WA 98195. Offers educational psychology (PhD); human development and cognition (M Ed); learning sciences (M Ed, PhD); measurement, statistics and research design (M Ed); school psychology (M Ed). *Accreditation:* APA. *Degree requirements:* For master's, thesis optional; for doctorate, thesis/dissertation. *Entrance requirements:* For master's and doctorate, GRE General Test, minimum GPA of 3.0. Additional exam requirements/recommendations for international students: Required—TOEFL.

University of West Georgia, Graduate School, College of Education, Program in School Improvement, Carrollton, GA 30118. Offers Ed D. Part-time and evening/weekend programs available. *Students:* 74 part-time (53 women); includes 26 minority (24 African Americans, 2 Hispanic Americans). Average age 41. 2 applicants, 50% accepted, 0 enrolled. In 2009, 8 doctorates awarded. *Degree requirements:* For doctorate, thesis/dissertation, research project, professional portfolio. *Entrance requirements:* For doctorate, GRE, curriculum vitae, minimum GPA of 3.0 in graduate education, interview, references, 2 writing samples. *Application deadline:* For fall admission, 7/17 for domestic students; for spring admission, 11/20 for domestic students. Applications are processed on a rolling basis. Application fee: $30. Electronic applications accepted. *Expenses:* Tuition, state resident: full-time $2952; part-time $164 per semester hour. Tuition, nonresident: full-time $11,808; part-time $656 per semester hour. Required fees: $42.90 per semester hour. $307 per semester. Tuition and fees vary according to course load. *Financial support:* In 2009–10, 1 student received support, including 1 research assistantship with full tuition reimbursement available (averaging $6,000 per year). Financial award application deadline: 4/30; financial award applicants required to submit FAFSA. *Faculty research:* School-based partnerships, school change, action research, teacher leadership, teacher certification. *Unit head:* Dr. Cher Hendricks, Director, 678-839-6134, Fax: 678-839-6063, E-mail: cher@westga.edu. *Application contact:* Dr. Charles W. Clark, Dean, 678-839-6508, E-mail: cclark@westga.edu.

University of Wisconsin–Milwaukee, Graduate School, School of Education, Department of Educational Psychology, Milwaukee, WI 53201-0413. Offers counseling (school, community) (MS); counseling psychology (PhD); learning and development (MS); research methodology (MS, PhD); school psychology (PhD). *Accreditation:* APA. Part-time programs available. *Faculty:* 22 full-time (14 women). *Students:* 124 full-time (107 women), 47 part-time (35 women); includes 20 minority (10 African Americans, 4 Asian Americans or Pacific Islanders, 6 Hispanic Americans), 2 international. Average age 30. 263 applicants, 52% accepted, 51 enrolled. In 2009, 55 master's, 13 doctorates awarded. *Degree requirements:* For master's, comprehensive exam, thesis; for doctorate, thesis/dissertation. *Entrance requirements:* For master's, minimum GPA of 3.0; for doctorate, GRE General Test, minimum GPA of 3.0. Additional exam requirements/recommendations for international students: Required—TOEFL (minimum score 550 paper-based; 79 iBT), IELTS (minimum score 6.5). *Application deadline:* For fall admission, 1/1 priority date for domestic students; for spring admission, 9/1 for domestic students. Applications are processed on a rolling basis. Application fee: $45 ($75 for international students). *Expenses:* Tuition, state resident: full-time $8800. Tuition, nonresident: full-time $20,760. Tuition and fees vary according to program and reciprocity agreements. *Financial support:* In 2009–10, 9 teaching assistantships were awarded; career-related internships or fieldwork and unspecified assistantships also available. Support available to part-time students. Financial award application deadline: 4/15. Total annual research expenditures: $1.3 million. *Unit head:* Bo Zhang, Graduate Program Representative, 414-229-5742, Fax: 414-229-4939, E-mail: boz@uwm.edu. *Application contact:* General Information Contact, 414-229-4982, Fax: 414-229-6967, E-mail: gradschool@uwm.edu.

Utah State University, School of Graduate Studies, College of Education and Human Services, Department of Psychology, Logan, UT 84322. Offers clinical/counseling/school psychology (PhD); research and evaluation methodology (PhD); school counseling (MS); school psychology (MS). *Accreditation:* APA (one or more programs are accredited). Part-time and evening/weekend programs available. Postbaccalaureate distance learning degree programs offered (no on-campus study). Terminal master's awarded for partial completion of doctoral program. *Degree requirements:* For master's, thesis (for some programs); for doctorate, thesis/dissertation. *Entrance requirements:* For master's, GRE General Test (school psychology), MAT (school counseling), minimum GPA of 3.5; for doctorate, GRE General Test, minimum GPA of 3.5. Additional exam requirements/recommendations for international students: Required—TOEFL. *Faculty research:* Hearing loss detection in infancy, ADHD, eating disorders, domestic violence, neuropsychology, bilingual/Spanish speaking students/parents.

Utah State University, School of Graduate Studies, College of Education and Human Services, Doctoral Program in Education, Logan, UT 84322. Offers business information systems (Ed D, PhD); curriculum and instruction (Ed D, PhD); research and evaluation (PhD). *Degree requirements:* For doctorate, comprehensive exam, thesis/dissertation. *Entrance requirements:* For doctorate, GRE General Test, minimum GPA of 3.0, master's degree. Additional exam requirements/recommendations for international students: Required—TOEFL. Electronic applications accepted. *Faculty research:* Language and literacy development, math and science education, instructional technology, hearing problems/deafness, domestic violence and animal abuse.

Vanderbilt University, Graduate School, Department of Physics and Astronomy, Nashville, TN 37240-1001. Offers astronomy (MS); physics (MA, MAT, MS, PhD). *Faculty:* 52 full-time (5 women). *Students:* 66 full-time (16 women), 2 part-time (1 woman); includes 11 minority (5 African Americans, 2 Asian Americans or Pacific Islanders, 4 Hispanic Americans), 16 international. Average age 29. 167 applicants, 21% accepted, 13 enrolled. In 2009, 10 master's, 6 doctorates awarded. *Degree requirements:* For master's, thesis; for doctorate, comprehensive exam, thesis/dissertation, final and qualifying exams. *Entrance requirements:* For master's, GRE General Test; for doctorate, GRE General Test, GRE Subject Test. Additional exam requirements/recommendations for international students: Required—TOEFL (minimum score 570 paper-based; 230 computer-based; 88 iBT). *Application deadline:* For fall admission, 1/15 for domestic and international students. Application fee: $0. Electronic applications accepted. *Financial support:* Fellowships with full and partial tuition reimbursements, research assistantships with full tuition reimbursements, teaching assistantships with full tuition reimbursements, career-related internships or fieldwork, Federal Work-Study, and institutionally sponsored loans available. Financial award application deadline: 1/15; financial award applicants required to submit CSS PROFILE or FAFSA. *Faculty research:* Experimental and theoretical physics, free electron laser, living-state physics, heavy-ion physics, nuclear structure. *Unit head:* Robert J. Scherrer, Chair, 615-322-2828, Fax: 615-343-7263, E-mail: robert.scherrer@vanderbilt.edu. *Application contact:* Richard Haglund, Director of Graduate Studies, 615-322-2828, Fax: 615-343-7263, E-mail: physastro-grad@vanderbilt.edu.

Virginia Commonwealth University, Graduate School, School of Education, Doctoral Program in Education, Research and Evaluation Track, Richmond, VA 23284-9005. Offers PhD.

Virginia Polytechnic Institute and State University, Graduate School, College of Liberal Arts and Human Sciences, School of Education, Department of Educational Leadership and Policy Studies, Program in Educational Research and Evaluation, Blacksburg, VA 24061. Offers PhD. *Accreditation:* NCATE. *Entrance requirements:* Additional exam requirements/recommendations for international students: Required—TOEFL. *Application deadline:* Applications are processed on a rolling basis. Application fee: $65. Electronic applications accepted.

Educational Measurement and Evaluation

Virginia Polytechnic Institute and State University (continued)
Expenses: Tuition, area resident: Full-time $10,228; part-time $459 per credit hour. Tuition, nonresident: full-time $17,892; part-time $865 per credit hour. Required fees: $1966; $451 per semester. *Financial support:* Research assistantships with full tuition reimbursements available. *Unit head:* Kusum Singh, Program Area Leader and Professor, 540-231-9729, Fax: 540-231-7845, E-mail: ksingh@vt.edu. *Application contact:* Kusum Singh, Program Area Leader and Professor, 540-231-9729, Fax: 540-231-7845, E-mail: ksingh@vt.edu.

Walden University, Graduate Programs, Richard W. Riley College of Education and Leadership, Minneapolis, MN 55401. Offers administrator leadership for teaching and learning (Ed D, Ed S); curriculum, instruction, and professional development (Ed S); early childhood education (birth-grade 3) (MAT); education (MS, PhD), including adolescent literacy and technology (grades 6-12) (MS), adult education leadership (PhD), community college leadership (PhD), curriculum, instruction, and assessment, early childhood education (PhD), educational leadership (MS), educational technology (PhD), elementary reading and literacy (MS), elementary reading and mathematics (MS), emotional/behavioral disorders (K-12) (MS), general program, higher education (PhD), integrating technology in the classroom (MS), K-12 educational leadership (PhD), learning disabilities (K-12) (MS), literacy and learning in the content areas (MS), mathematics (grades 6-8) (MS), mathematics (grades K-5) (MS), middle level education (grades 5-8) (MS), professional development (MS), science (grades K-8) (MS), self-designed (PhD), special education (PhD), special education (non-licensure) (MS), teacher leadership (grades K-12) (MS); educational leadership and administration (principal preparation) (Ed S); educational technology (Ed S); higher education and adult learning (Ed D); instructional design (Postbaccalaureate Certificate); instructional design and technology (MS), including general program (MS, PhD), online learning, training and performance improvement; special education: emotional/behavioral disorders (K-12) (MAT); special education: learning disabilities (K-12) (MAT); teacher leadership (Ed D, Ed S). Part-time and evening/weekend programs available. Postbaccalaureate distance learning degree programs offered (minimal on-campus study). *Faculty:* 54 full-time, 835 part-time/adjunct. *Students:* 13,940 full-time (11,339 women), 1,940 part-time (1,637 women); includes 4,626 minority (3,795 African Americans, 111 American Indian/Alaska Native, 199 Asian Americans or Pacific Islanders, 521 Hispanic Americans), 124 international. Average age 38. In 2009, 4,688 master's, 190 doctorates awarded. *Degree requirements:* For doctorate, thesis/dissertation (for some programs), residency; for other advanced degree, residency (for some programs). *Entrance requirements:* For master's, bachelor's degree or equivalent in related field; minimum GPA of 2.5; official transcripts; goal statement; access to computer and Internet; for doctorate, master's degree or equivalent in related field; minimum GPA of 3.0; official transcripts; three years' related professional/academic experience (preferred); access to computer and Internet; for other advanced degree, master's degree or equivalent in related field; minimum GPA of 3.0; 3 years related professional/academic experience (preferred); access to computer and Internet (Ed S). Additional exam requirements/recommendations for international students: Required—TOEFL (minimum score 550 paper-based; 213 computer-based), IELTS (minimum score 6.5), or Michigan English Language Assessment Battery (minimum score 82). *Application deadline:* Applications are processed on a rolling basis. Application fee: $50. Electronic applications accepted. *Expenses:* Tuition: Full-time $13,665; part-time $560 per credit. Required fees: $1375. Tuition and fees vary according to course load, degree level and program. *Financial support:* In 2009-10, 2,418 students received support; fellowships, Federal Work-Study, scholarships/grants, unspecified assistantships, and family tuition reduction, active duty/veteran tuition reduction, group tuition reduction, interest-free payment plans available. Support available to part-time students. Financial award applicants required to submit FAFSA. *Unit head:* Dr. Kate Steffens, Dean, 800-925-3368. *Application contact:* Jennifer Hall, Director of Enrollment, 866-4-WALDEN, E-mail: info@waldenu.edu.

Washington University in St. Louis, Graduate School of Arts and Sciences, Department of Education, Program in Educational Research, St. Louis, MO 63130-4899. Offers PhD. *Entrance requirements:* For doctorate, GRE General Test. Electronic applications accepted.

Wayne State University, College of Education, Division of Theoretical and Behavioral Foundations, Detroit, MI 48202. Offers counseling (M Ed, MA, Ed D, PhD, Ed S); education evaluation and research (M Ed, Ed D, PhD); educational psychology (M Ed, Ed D, PhD, Ed S); educational sociology (M Ed, Ed D, PhD, Ed S); history and philosophy of education (M Ed, Ed D, PhD); rehabilitation counseling and community inclusion (MA, Ed S); school and community psychology (MA, Ed S); school clinical psychology (Ed S). *Accreditation:* ACA (one or more programs are accredited); CORE (one or more programs are accredited). Evening/weekend programs available. *Degree requirements:* For doctorate, thesis/dissertation. *Entrance requirements:* For master's, GRE; for doctorate, GRE, interview, minimum GPA of 3.0, curriculum vitae, references. Additional exam requirements/recommendations for international students: Required—TOEFL (minimum score 550 paper-based; 213 computer-based), TWE (minimum score 6). Electronic applications accepted. *Faculty research:* Adolescents at risk, supervision of counseling.

Western Governors University, Teachers College, Salt Lake City, UT 84107. Offers English language learning (K-12) (MA); learning and technology (M Ed, MA); management and innovation (M Ed); mathematics education (5-12) (MA); mathematics education (5-9) (MA); mathematics education (K-6) (MA); measurement and evaluation (M Ed); science (5-12) (MA), including biology, geology; science education (5-9) (MA); teaching (MAT); technology for principals (Post-Graduate Certificate). *Accreditation:* NCATE. Part-time and evening/weekend programs available. Postbaccalaureate distance learning degree programs offered (no on-campus study). *Degree requirements:* For master's, comprehensive exam. *Entrance requirements:* Additional exam requirements/recommendations for international students: Required—TOEFL (minimum score 450 paper-based). Electronic applications accepted. *Expenses:* Contact institution.

Western Michigan University, Graduate College, College of Education, Department of Educational Leadership, Research and Technology, Kalamazoo, MI 49008. Offers educational leadership (MA, PhD, Ed S); educational technology (MA, Graduate Certificate); evaluation, measurement and research (MA, PhD). *Unit head:* Dr. David A. England, Dean, 269-387-2960. *Application contact:* Admissions and Orientation, 269-387-2000, Fax: 269-387-2355.

Western Michigan University, Graduate College, The Evaluation Center, Kalamazoo, MI 49008. Offers PhD. *Unit head:* Dr. Stephen Magura, Director, 269-387-5895, E-mail: stephen.magura@wmich.edu. *Application contact:* Admissions and Orientation, 269-387-2000, Fax: 269-387-2355.

West Texas A&M University, College of Education and Social Sciences, Division of Education, Program in Educational Diagnostician, Canyon, TX 79016-0001. Offers M Ed. Part-time programs available. Postbaccalaureate distance learning degree programs offered (minimal on-campus study). *Degree requirements:* For master's, comprehensive exam, thesis optional. *Entrance requirements:* For master's, GRE General Test, 3 years teaching experience, competency in diagnosis and prescription. Additional exam requirements/recommendations for international students: Required—TOEFL (minimum score 550 paper-based). Electronic applications accepted. *Faculty research:* Teacher preparation through web-based instruction, developmental disabilities.

Wilkes University, College of Graduate and Professional Studies, School of Education, Wilkes-Barre, PA 18766-0002. Offers classroom technology (MS Ed); educational computing (MS Ed); educational development and strategies (MS Ed); educational leadership (MS Ed); educational technology (Ed D); elementary education (MS Ed); higher education administration (Ed D); instructional technology (MS Ed); K-12 administration (Ed D); online teaching (MS Ed); school business leadership (MS Ed); secondary education (MS Ed), including biology, chemistry, English, history; special education (MS Ed). Part-time and evening/weekend programs available. Postbaccalaureate distance learning degree programs offered (minimal on-campus study). *Students:* 89 full-time (60 women), 2,849 part-time (2,058 women); includes 52 minority (10 African Americans, 2 American Indian/Alaska Native, 13 Asian Americans or Pacific Islanders, 27 Hispanic Americans), 6 international. Average age 33. In 2009, 947 master's awarded. *Entrance requirements:* Additional exam requirements/recommendations for international students: Required—TOEFL (minimum score 500 paper-based; 173 computer-based; 79 iBT). *Application deadline:* Applications are processed on a rolling basis. Application fee: $45. *Expenses:* Contact institution. *Financial support:* Federal Work-Study and unspecified assistantships available. Financial award application deadline: 3/1; financial award applicants required to submit FAFSA. *Unit head:* Dr. Michael Speziale, Dean, 570-408-4679, Fax: 570-408-4905, E-mail: michael.speziale@wilkes.edu. *Application contact:* Kathleen Houlihan, Director of Graduate Studies, 570-408-3235, Fax: 570-408-7846, E-mail: kathleen.houlihan@wilkes.edu.

Educational Media/Instructional Technology

Acadia University, Faculty of Professional Studies, School of Education, Program in Curriculum Studies, Wolfville, NS B4P 2R6, Canada. Offers cultural and media studies (M Ed); learning and technology (M Ed); science, math and technology (M Ed). Evening/weekend programs available. *Faculty:* 12 full-time (5 women). *Students:* 7 full-time (all women), 49 part-time (33 women). 61 applicants, 80% accepted. In 2009, 32 master's awarded. *Degree requirements:* For master's, thesis optional. *Entrance requirements:* For master's, B Ed or the equivalent, minimum B average in undergraduate course work, 2 years of teaching experience. Additional exam requirements/recommendations for international students: Required—TOEFL (minimum score 580 paper-based; 237 computer-based; 93 iBT), IELTS (minimum score 6.5). *Application deadline:* For fall admission, 3/15 priority date for domestic and international students. Applications are processed on a rolling basis. Application fee: $50. *Financial support:* Teaching assistantships available. Financial award application deadline: 3/15. *Faculty research:* Literacy development, postmodern philosophy and curriculum theory, historiography, philosophy of education, learning and technology. *Unit head:* Ann Vibert, Director, E-mail: ann.vibert@acadiau.ca. *Application contact:* Sheila Langille, Secretary, 902-585-1229, Fax: 902-585-1071, E-mail: sheila.langille@acadiau.ca.

Adelphi University, School of Education, Program in Educational Leadership and Technology, Garden City, NY 11530-0701. Offers MA, Certificate. *Students:* 11 full-time (7 women), 53 part-time (39 women); includes 36 minority (24 African Americans, 3 Asian Americans or Pacific Islanders, 9 Hispanic Americans). Average age 39. In 2009, 36 master's, 12 other advanced degrees awarded. *Entrance requirements:* For master's, 2 letters of recommendation, resume, letter attesting to teaching experience (3 years full-time K-12). Additional exam requirements/recommendations for international students: Required—TOEFL (minimum score 550 paper-based; 213 computer-based; 80 iBT). *Application deadline:* For fall admission, 8/15 priority date for domestic students, 4/1 for international students; for spring admission, 1/15 priority date for domestic students, 11/1 for international students. Applications are processed on a rolling basis. Application fee: $50. Electronic applications accepted. *Expenses:* Tuition: Full-time $28,340; part-time $830 per credit. Required fees: $600; $250 per credit. Full-time tuition and fees vary according to course load and program. *Financial support:* Research assistantships with partial tuition reimbursements, institutionally sponsored loans available. Financial award application deadline: 2/15; financial award applicants required to submit FAFSA. *Faculty research:* Technology methodology focusing on in-service and pre-service curriculum. *Unit head:* Dr. Devin Thornburg, Director, 516-877-4026, E-mail: thornburg@adelphi.edu. *Application contact:* Christine Murphy, Director of Admissions, 516-877-3050, Fax: 516-877-3039, E-mail: graduateadmissions@adelphi.edu.

Alabama State University, School of Graduate Studies, College of Education, Department of Instructional Support, Library Education Media Program, Montgomery, AL 36101-0271. Offers M Ed, Ed S. Part-time programs available. *Degree requirements:* For master's, comprehensive exam; for Ed S, comprehensive exam, thesis. *Entrance requirements:* For master's, GRE General Test or MAT, graduate writing competency test, 2 letters of recommendation; for Ed S, graduate writing competency test, GRE or MAT, 2 letters of recommendation. Additional exam requirements/recommendations for international students: Required—TOEFL (minimum score 500 paper-based; 173 computer-based). *Faculty research:* Developing research capabilities through media, computer and media usage for teaching young children, use of media for in-service.

Alliant International University–Irvine, Graduate School of Education, Teacher Education Programs, Irvine, CA 92612. Offers auditory oral education (Certificate); CLAD (Certificate); preliminary multiple subject (Credential); preliminary multiple subject with BCLAD (Credential); preliminary single subject (Credential); professional clear multiple subject (Credential); professional clear single subject (Credential); teaching (MA, Credential); technology and learning (MA). Part-time and evening/weekend programs available. *Entrance requirements:* For degree, California Basic Educational Skills Test, minimum GPA of 2.5. Additional exam requirements/recommendations for international students: Required—TOEFL (minimum score 550 paper-based; 213 computer-based), TWE. Electronic applications accepted.

Alverno College, School of Education, Milwaukee, WI 53234-3922. Offers adaptive education (MA); administrative leadership (MA); adult education and organizational development (MA); adult educational and instructional design (MA); adult educational and instructional technology (MA); global connections in the humanities (MA); instructional leadership (MA); instructional technology for K-12 settings (MA); professional development (MA); reading education (MA); reading education with adaptive education (MA); science education (MA); teaching in alternative schools (MA). *Accreditation:* NCATE. Part-time and evening/weekend programs available. *Faculty:* 10 full-time (all women), 17 part-time/adjunct (15 women). *Students:* 65 full-time (59 women), 82 part-time (75 women); includes 31 minority (24 African Americans, 1 American Indian/Alaska Native, 1 Asian American or Pacific Islander, 5 Hispanic Americans), 2 international. Average age 38. 113 applicants, 64% accepted, 61 enrolled. In 2009, 56 master's awarded. *Degree requirements:* For master's, presentation/defense of proposal, conference presentation of inquiry projects. *Entrance requirements:* For master's, bachelor's degree in related field, communication samples from work setting, 3 letters of recommendation. Additional exam requirements/recommendations for international students: Required—TOEFL. *Application deadline:* For fall admission, 7/15 priority date for domestic and international students; for spring admission, 12/15 priority date for domestic and international students. Applications are processed on a rolling basis. Application fee: $50. Electronic applications accepted. *Financial support:* In 2009-10, 92 students received support. Federal Work-Study available. Support available to part-time students. Financial award application deadline: 4/15; financial award applicants required to submit FAFSA. *Faculty research:* Student self-assessment, self-reflection, integration of curriculum, identifying needs of students in strategic situations and designing appropriate classroom strategies. *Unit head:* Dr. Mary Diez, Graduate Dean, 414-382-6214, Fax: 414-382-6332, E-mail: mary.diez@alverno.edu. *Application contact:* Angela Peterson-Adams, Graduate Recruiter, 414-382-6104, Fax: 414-382-6354, E-mail: angela.peterson-adams@alverno.edu.

American InterContinental University Online, Program in Education, Hoffman Estates, IL 60192. Offers curriculum and instruction (M Ed); educational assessment and evaluation (M Ed); instructional technology (M Ed); leadership of educational organizations (M Ed). Evening/weekend programs available. Postbaccalaureate distance learning degree programs offered (no on-campus study). *Entrance requirements:* Additional exam requirements/recommendations for international students: Required—TOEFL (minimum score 550 paper-based; 213 computer-based). Electronic applications accepted.

American InterContinental University South Florida, Program in Instructional Technology, Weston, FL 33326. Offers M Ed. Part-time and evening/weekend programs available. *Entrance requirements:* Additional exam requirements/recommendations for international students: Required—TOEFL (minimum score 670 paper-based). Electronic applications accepted.

Appalachian State University, Cratis D. Williams Graduate School, Department of Curriculum and Instruction, Boone, NC 28608. Offers curriculum specialist (MA); educational media (MA); elementary education (MA); middle grades education (MA), including language arts, mathematics, science, social studies. *Accreditation:* NCATE. Part-time and evening/weekend programs available. Postbaccalaureate distance learning degree programs offered (no on-campus study). *Faculty:* 32 full-time (22 women), 9 part-time/adjunct (3 women). *Students:* 16 full-time (12 women), 168 part-time (140 women); includes 2 minority (both African Americans), 1 international. 97 applicants, 99% accepted, 77 enrolled. In 2009, 78 master's awarded. *Degree requirements:* For master's, comprehensive exam, thesis or alternative. *Entrance requirements:* For master's, GRE General Test or MAT, 3 letters of recommendation. Additional exam requirements/recommendations for international students: Required—TOEFL (minimum score 570 paper-based; 230 computer-based; 79 iBT), IELTS (minimum score 6.5). *Application deadline:* For fall admission, 7/1 for domestic students, 2/1 for international students; for spring admission, 11/1 for domestic students, 7/1 for international students. Applications are processed on a rolling basis. Application fee: $50. Electronic applications accepted. *Expenses:* Tuition, state resident: full-time $2960. Tuition, nonresident: full-time $14,051. Required fees: $2320. *Financial support:* In 2009–10, 8 teaching assistantships (averaging $8,000 per year) were awarded; fellowships, research assistantships, career-related internships or fieldwork, Federal Work-Study, scholarships/grants, and unspecified assistantships also available. Financial award application deadline: 4/1; financial award applicants required to submit FAFSA. *Faculty research:* Media literacy, elementary teaching, curriculum development, online learning environments. Total annual research expenditures: $690,000. *Unit head:* Dr. Michael Jacobson, Chairperson, 828-262-2224. *Application contact:* Sandy Krause, Director of Admissions and Recruiting, 828-262-2130, Fax: 828-262-2709, E-mail: krausesl@appstate.edu.

Appalachian State University, Cratis D. Williams Graduate School, Department of Leadership and Educational Studies, Boone, NC 28608. Offers educational administration (Ed S); educational media (MA); higher education (MA, Ed S); library science (MLS); school administration (MSA). Part-time and evening/weekend programs available. Postbaccalaureate distance learning degree programs offered (no on-campus study). *Faculty:* 25 full-time (10 women), 28 part-time/adjunct (16 women). *Students:* 48 full-time (35 women), 474 part-time (373 women); includes 24 minority (21 African Americans, 2 Asian Americans or Pacific Islanders, 1 Hispanic American), 2 international. 229 applicants, 89% accepted, 156 enrolled. In 2009, 133 master's, 32 other advanced degrees awarded. *Degree requirements:* For master's and Ed S, comprehensive exam, thesis optional. *Entrance requirements:* For master's and Ed S, GRE or MAT, 3 letters of recommendation. Additional exam requirements/recommendations for international students: Required—TOEFL (minimum score 570 paper-based; 230 computer-based; 79 iBT), IELTS (minimum score 6.5). *Application deadline:* For fall admission, 7/1 for domestic students, 2/1 for international students; for spring admission, 11/1 for domestic students, 7/1 for international students. Applications are processed on a rolling basis. Application fee: $50. Electronic applications accepted. *Expenses:* Tuition, state resident: full-time $2960. Tuition, nonresident: full-time $14,051. Required fees: $2320. *Financial support:* In 2009–10, 10 research assistantships (averaging $8,000 per year) were awarded; career-related internships or fieldwork, scholarships/grants, and unspecified assistantships also available. Financial award application deadline: 4/1; financial award applicants required to submit FAFSA. *Faculty research:* Brain, learning and meditation; leadership of teaching and learning. Total annual research expenditures: $475,000. *Unit head:* Dr. Richard Riedl, Interim Director, 828-262-3112, E-mail: reidlr@appstate.edu. *Application contact:* Lori Dean, Graduate Student Coordinator, 828-262-6041, E-mail: deanlk@appstate.edu.

Arcadia University, Graduate Studies, Department of Education, Glenside, PA 19038-3295. Offers art education (M Ed, MA Ed); biology education (MA Ed); chemistry education (MA Ed); child development (CAS); computer education (M Ed, CAS); computer education 7–12 (MA Ed); early childhood education (M Ed, CAS), including individualized (M Ed), master teacher (M Ed), research in child development (M Ed); educational leadership (M Ed, CAS); educational psychology (CAS); elementary education (M Ed, CAS); English education (MA Ed); environmental education (MA Ed, CAS); history education (MA Ed); language arts (M Ed, CAS); mathematics education (M Ed, MA Ed, CAS); music education (MA Ed); psychology (MA Ed); pupil personnel services (CAS); reading (M Ed, CAS); school library science (M Ed); science education (M Ed, CAS); secondary education (M Ed, CAS); special education (M Ed, Ed D, CAS); theater arts (MA Ed); written communication (MA Ed). *Accreditation:* NASAD. Part-time and evening/weekend programs available. Postbaccalaureate distance learning degree programs offered (minimal on-campus study). *Faculty:* 12 full-time (8 women), 38 part-time/adjunct (26 women). *Students:* 89 full-time (74 women), 622 part-time (487 women); includes 112 minority (94 African Americans, 9 Asian Americans or Pacific Islanders, 9 Hispanic Americans), 2 international. Average age 32. In 2009, 257 master's, 4 doctorates awarded. *Application deadline:* Applications are processed on a rolling basis. Application fee: $40. Electronic applications accepted. *Expenses:* Tuition: Full-time $30,450; part-time $620 per credit hour. Required fees: $165. Tuition and fees vary according to program. *Financial support:* Career-related internships or fieldwork, tuition waivers (partial), and unspecified assistantships available. *Unit head:* Dr. Steven P. Gulkus. *Application contact:* 215-572-2925, Fax: 215-572-2126, E-mail: grad@arcadia.edu.

Argosy University, Atlanta, College of Education, Atlanta, GA 30328. Offers educational leadership (MAEd, Ed D, Ed S), including higher education administration (Ed D), K-12 education (Ed D); teaching and learning (MAEd, Ed D, Ed S), including education technology (Ed D), higher education (Ed D), K-12 education (Ed D).

See Close-Up on page 887.

Argosy University, Denver, College of Education, Denver, CO 80231. Offers community college executive leadership (Ed D); educational leadership (MA Ed, Ed D), including higher education (Ed D), K-12 education (Ed D); instructional leadership (MA Ed, Ed D), including higher education administration (Ed D), K-12 education (Ed D).

See Close-Up on page 679.

Argosy University, Nashville, College of Education, Program in Instructional Leadership, Nashville, TN 37214. Offers education technology (Ed D); higher education administration (Ed D); instructional leadership (MA Ed, Ed S); K-12 education (Ed D).

See Close-Up on page 891.

Argosy University, Orange County, College of Education, Orange, CA 92868. Offers community college executive leadership (Ed D); educational leadership (MA Ed, Ed D), including higher education administration (Ed D), K-12 education (Ed D); instructional leadership (MA Ed, Ed D), including education technology (Ed D), higher education (Ed D), K-12 education (Ed D), multiple subject teacher preparation (MA Ed), single subject teacher preparation (MA Ed).

See Close-Up on page 685.

Argosy University, Phoenix, College of Education, Phoenix, AZ 85021. Offers adult education and training (MA Ed); advanced educational administration (Ed D, Ed S); community college executive leadership (Ed D); educational administration (MA Ed); educational leadership (MA Ed, Ed D, Ed S), including education technology (Ed D), higher education administration (Ed D), K-12 education (Ed D); higher and postsecondary education (MA Ed); initial educational administration (Ed D, Ed S); school psychology (MA); teaching and learning (MA Ed, Ed D, Ed S), including education technology (Ed D), higher education (Ed D), K-12 education (Ed D).

See Close-Up on page 687.

Argosy University, San Francisco Bay Area, College of Education, Alameda, CA 94501. Offers community college executive leadership (Ed D); educational leadership (MA Ed, Ed D), including education technology (Ed D), higher education administration (Ed D), K-12 education (Ed D); instructional leadership (MA Ed, Ed D), including education technology (Ed D), higher education (Ed D), K-12 education (Ed D), multiple subject teacher preparation (MA Ed), single subject teacher preparation (MA Ed).

See Close-Up on page 693.

Argosy University, Sarasota, College of Education, Sarasota, FL 34235. Offers community college executive leadership (Ed D); educational leadership (MA Ed, Ed D, Ed S), including higher education administration (Ed D), K-12 education (Ed D); school counseling (MA, Ed S); school psychology (MA); teaching and learning (MA Ed, Ed D, Ed S), including education technology (Ed D), higher education (Ed D), K-12 education (Ed D).

See Close-Up on page 695.

Argosy University, Seattle, College of Education, Seattle, WA 98121. Offers adult education and training (MA Ed); community college executive leadership (Ed D); educational leadership (MA Ed, Ed D), including higher education administration (Ed D), K-12 education (Ed D); higher and postsecondary education (MA Ed); instructional leadership (MA Ed, Ed D), including education technology (Ed D), higher education (Ed D), K-12 education (Ed D).

See Close-Up on page 699.

Argosy University, Twin Cities, College of Education, Eagan, MN 55121. Offers advanced educational administration (Ed D, Ed S); educational leadership (MA Ed, Ed D, Ed S), including higher education administration (Ed D), K-12 education (Ed D); higher and postsecondary education (MA Ed); initial educational administration (Ed D, Ed S); instructional leadership (MA Ed, Ed D, Ed S), including education technology (Ed D), higher education (Ed D), K-12 education (Ed D).

See Close-Up on page 703.

Arizona State University, Graduate College, Mary Lou Fulton College of Education, Division of Psychology in Education, Program in Educational Technology, Tempe, AZ 85287. Offers M Ed, PhD. *Degree requirements:* For master's, thesis or alternative; for doctorate, thesis/dissertation. *Entrance requirements:* For master's and doctorate, GRE General Test or MAT.

Ashland University, Dwight Schar College of Education, Department of Curriculum and Instruction, Ashland, OH 44805-3702. Offers intervention specialist–mild/moderate (M Ed); intervention specialist–moderate/intensive (M Ed); literacy (M Ed); technology facilitator (M Ed). *Accreditation:* NCATE. Part-time and evening/weekend programs available. *Faculty:* 20 full-time (14 women), 83 part-time/adjunct (53 women). *Students:* 137 full-time (116 women), 309 part-time (278 women); includes 22 minority (16 African Americans, 2 American Indian/Alaska Native, 4 Hispanic Americans), 1 international. Average age 33. 160 applicants, 98% accepted, 152 enrolled. In 2009, 245 master's awarded. *Degree requirements:* For master's, thesis or alternative, internship, practicum, inquiry seminar. *Entrance requirements:* For master's, teaching certificate or license, bachelor's degree, minimum cumulative GPA of 2.75. Additional exam requirements/recommendations for international students: Required—TOEFL. *Application deadline:* For fall admission, 8/27 for domestic students; for spring admission, 1/14 for domestic students. Applications are processed on a rolling basis. Application fee: $30. Electronic applications accepted. *Financial support:* In 2009–10, 192 students received support. Institutionally sponsored loans and scholarships/grants available. Financial award application deadline: 4/15. *Faculty research:* Gender equity, postmodern children's and young adult literature, outdoor/experimental education, re-examining literature study in middle grades, morality and giftedness. *Unit head:* Dr. David J. Kommer, Chair, 419-289-5203, E-mail: dkommer@ashland.edu. *Application contact:* Dr. David J. Kommer, Chair, 419-289-5203, E-mail: dkommer@ashland.edu.

Auburn University, Graduate School, College of Education, Department of Educational Foundations, Leadership, and Technology, Auburn University, AL 36849. Offers adult education (M Ed, MS, Ed D); curriculum and instruction (M Ed, MS, Ed D, Ed S); curriculum supervision (M Ed, MS, Ed D, Ed S); educational psychology (PhD); higher education administration (M Ed, MS, Ed D, Ed S); media instructional design (MS); media specialist (M Ed); school administration (M Ed, MS, Ed D, Ed S). *Accreditation:* NCATE. Part-time programs available. *Faculty:* 21 full-time (11 women), 6 part-time/adjunct (4 women). *Students:* 68 full-time (40 women), 175 part-time (103 women); includes 87 minority (84 African Americans, 1 Asian American or Pacific Islander, 2 Hispanic Americans), 8 international. Average age 37. 112 applicants, 65% accepted, 53 enrolled. In 2009, 31 master's, 12 doctorates, 1 other advanced degree awarded. *Degree requirements:* For master's, thesis (for some programs); for doctorate, thesis/dissertation; for Ed S, field project. *Entrance requirements:* For master's, doctorate, and Ed S, GRE General Test. *Application deadline:* For fall admission, 7/7 for domestic students; for spring admission, 11/24 for domestic students. Applications are processed on a rolling basis. Application fee: $50 ($60 for international students). Electronic applications accepted. *Expenses:* Tuition, state resident: full-time $6240. Tuition, nonresident: full-time $18,720. International tuition: $18,938 full-time. Required fees: $492. Tuition and fees vary according to course load, program and reciprocity agreements. *Financial support:* Teaching assistantships, Federal Work-Study available. Support available to part-time students. Financial award application deadline: 3/15; financial award applicants required to submit FAFSA. *Unit head:* Dr. Jose Llanes, Head, 334-844-4460. *Application contact:* Dr. George Flowers, Dean of the Graduate School, 334-844-4700.

Azusa Pacific University, School of Education, Department of Advanced Studies, Program in Educational Technology, Azusa, CA 91702-7000. Offers M Ed. Part-time and evening/weekend programs available. *Degree requirements:* For master's, comprehensive exam, core exam, oral presentation. *Entrance requirements:* For master's, 12 units of course work in education, minimum GPA of 3.0.

Baldwin-Wallace College, Graduate Programs, Division of Education, Specialization in Educational Technology, Berea, OH 44017-2088. Offers MA Ed. Part-time and evening/weekend programs available. *Students:* 22 full-time (14 women), 36 part-time (28 women); includes 1 minority (African American). Average age 32. 17 applicants, 71% accepted, 11 enrolled. In 2009, 37 master's awarded. *Entrance requirements:* For master's, bachelor's degree in field, MAT or minimum GPA of 2.75. Additional exam requirements/recommendations for international students: Required—TOEFL (minimum score 523 paper-based; 193 computer-based; 70 iBT). *Application deadline:* For fall admission, 8/15 priority date for domestic students; for spring admission, 12/15 priority date for domestic students. Applications are processed on a rolling basis. Application fee: $25. Electronic applications accepted. *Expenses:* Tuition: Full-time $14,174; part-time $682 per credit. Tuition and fees vary according to program. *Financial support:* Career-related internships or fieldwork available. Support available to part-time students. Financial award application deadline: 5/1. *Faculty research:* No cost software, online resources for building a classroom learning management system. *Unit head:* Karen Kaye, Chair, 440-826-2168, Fax: 440-826-3779, E-mail: kkaye@bw.edu. *Application contact:* Winifred W. Gerhardt, Director of Admission for the Evening and Weekend College, 440-826-2222, Fax: 440-826-3830, E-mail: admission@bw.edu.

Barry University, School of Education, Graduate Certificate Programs, Miami Shores, FL 33161-6695. Offers advanced teaching and learning with technology (Certificate); distance education (Certificate); higher education technology integration (Certificate); human resources: not for profit and religious organizations (Certificate); K-12 technology integration (Certificate).

Barry University, School of Education, Program in Educational Technology Applications, Miami Shores, FL 33161-6695. Offers educational computing and technology (MS, Ed S). Part-time and evening/weekend programs available. Postbaccalaureate distance learning degree

Educational Media/Instructional Technology

Barry University (continued)

programs offered (minimal on-campus study). *Degree requirements:* For master's and Ed S, comprehensive exam. *Entrance requirements:* For master's, GRE General Test or MAT, minimum GPA of 3.0; for Ed S, GRE General Test, minimum GPA of 3.0.

Barry University, School of Education, Program in Leadership and Education, Miami Shores, FL 33161-6695. Offers educational technology (PhD); exceptional student education (PhD); higher education administration (PhD); human resource development (PhD); leadership (PhD). Part-time and evening/weekend programs available. *Degree requirements:* For doctorate, thesis/dissertation. *Entrance requirements:* For doctorate, GRE General Test, minimum GPA of 3.25. Electronic applications accepted.

Barry University, School of Education, Program in Technology and TESOL, Miami Shores, FL 33161-6695. Offers MS, Ed S.

Bellevue University, Graduate School, Bellevue, NE 68005-3098. Offers acquisition and contract management (MS); business administration (MBA); clinical counseling (MS); computer information systems (MS); healthcare administration (MA, MHA, MS), including healthcare administration (MHA), human services (MA, MS); human capital management (MS, PhD); instructional design and development (MS); leadership (MA); management (MA); management information systems (MS); organizational performance (MS); public administration (MPA); public health (MPH); security management (MS). Part-time and evening/weekend programs available. Postbaccalaureate distance learning degree programs offered (no on-campus study). *Degree requirements:* For master's, thesis or project. *Entrance requirements:* For master's, minimum GPA of 2.5 in last 60 hours. Additional exam requirements/recommendations for international students: Required—TOEFL (minimum score 538 paper-based; 200 computer-based).

Bloomsburg University of Pennsylvania, School of Graduate Studies, College of Science and Technology, Department of Instructional Technology, Bloomsburg, PA 17815-1301. Offers instructional technology (MS), including corporate track, education track, eLearning certificate. Postbaccalaureate distance learning degree programs offered (no on-campus study). *Degree requirements:* For master's, thesis or alternative. *Entrance requirements:* For master's, minimum QPA of 3.0, 3 letters of recommendation. Additional exam requirements/recommendations for international students: Required—TOEFL (minimum score 550 paper-based; 213 computer-based; 79 iBT). Electronic applications accepted. *Faculty research:* Instructional design and computing, interactive graphics, authoring tools.

Boise State University, Graduate College, College of Education, Programs in Teacher Education, Department of Educational Technology, Boise, ID 83725-0399. Offers MET, MS, MS Ed. *Accreditation:* NCATE. Part-time programs available. Postbaccalaureate distance learning degree programs offered (no on-campus study). *Degree requirements:* For master's, thesis optional. *Entrance requirements:* For master's, minimum GPA of 3.0. Electronic applications accepted. *Expenses:* Tuition, state resident: full-time $3106; part-time $209 per credit. Tuition, nonresident: part-time $284 per credit.

Boise State University, Graduate College, College of Engineering, Department of Instructional and Performance Technology, Boise, ID 83725-0399. Offers MS. Part-time programs available. Postbaccalaureate distance learning degree programs offered (no on-campus study). *Degree requirements:* For master's, thesis optional. *Entrance requirements:* For master's, minimum GPA of 3.0. Electronic applications accepted. *Expenses:* Tuition, state resident: full-time $3106; part-time $209 per credit. Tuition, nonresident: part-time $284 per credit.

Boston University, School of Education, Department of Curriculum and Teaching, Program in Educational Media and Technology, Boston, MA 02215. Offers Ed M, Ed D, CAGS. *Degree requirements:* For master's, thesis optional; for doctorate, comprehensive exam, thesis/dissertation; for CAGS, comprehensive exam. *Entrance requirements:* For master's, doctorate, and CAGS, GRE General Test or MAT. Additional exam requirements/recommendations for international students: Required—TOEFL. Electronic applications accepted. *Expenses:* Tuition: Full-time $37,910; part-time $1184 per credit hour. Required fees: $386; $40 per semester. Part-time tuition and fees vary according to class time, course level, degree level and program. *Faculty research:* Facilities design, program evaluation, human factors, computer-based technologies.

Bowling Green State University, Graduate College, College of Education and Human Development, School of Education and Intervention Services, Intervention Services Division, Program in Special Education, Bowling Green, OH 43403. Offers assistive technology (M Ed); early childhood intervention (M Ed); gifted education (M Ed); hearing impaired intervention (M Ed); mild/moderate intervention (M Ed); moderate/intensive intervention (M Ed). *Accreditation:* NCATE. Part-time programs available. *Degree requirements:* For master's, thesis or alternative. *Entrance requirements:* For master's, GRE General Test. Additional exam requirements/recommendations for international students: Required—TOEFL. Electronic applications accepted. *Faculty research:* Reading and special populations, deafness, early childhood, gifted and talented, behavior disorders.

Bowling Green State University, Graduate College, College of Education and Human Development, School of Education and Intervention Services, Teaching and Learning Division, Program in Classroom Technology, Bowling Green, OH 43403. Offers M Ed. *Accreditation:* NCATE. Part-time and evening/weekend programs available. *Degree requirements:* For master's, thesis or alternative. *Entrance requirements:* For master's, GRE General Test. Additional exam requirements/recommendations for international students: Required—TOEFL. Electronic applications accepted.

Bridgewater State University, School of Graduate Studies, School of Education and Allied Science, Department of Secondary Education and Professional Programs, Program in Instructional Technology, Bridgewater, MA 02325-0001. Offers M Ed. Part-time and evening/weekend programs available. *Entrance requirements:* For master's, GRE General Test or Massachusetts Test for Educator Licensure.

Brigham Young University, Graduate Studies, David O. McKay School of Education, Department of Instructional Psychology and Technology, Provo, UT 84602. Offers MS, PhD. *Faculty:* 9 full-time (0 women), 10 part-time/adjunct (2 women). *Students:* 50 full-time (22 women), 36 part-time (16 women); includes 3 minority (1 Asian American or Pacific Islander, 2 Hispanic Americans), 12 international. Average age 35. 23 applicants, 74% accepted, 15 enrolled. In 2009, 7 master's, 6 doctorates awarded. *Degree requirements:* For master's, thesis; for doctorate, comprehensive exam, thesis/dissertation. *Entrance requirements:* For master's and doctorate, GRE General Test. Additional exam requirements/recommendations for international students: Required—TOEFL. *Application deadline:* For fall and winter admission, 2/1 for domestic and international students. Application fee: $50. Electronic applications accepted. *Expenses:* Tuition: Full-time $5580; part-time $301 per credit hour. Tuition and fees vary according to student's religious affiliation. *Financial support:* In 2009–10, 32 students received support, including 9 research assistantships with full and partial tuition reimbursements available (averaging $10,000 per year), 15 teaching assistantships with full and partial tuition reimbursements available (averaging $6,000 per year); career-related internships or fieldwork, scholarships/grants, tuition waivers (full and partial), and unspecified assistantships also available. Support available to part-time students. *Faculty research:* Interactive learning, learning theory, instructional designed development, research and evaluation, measurement. *Unit head:* Dr. Andrew S. Gibbons, Chair, 801-422-5097, Fax: 801-422-0314, E-mail: andy_gibbons@byu.edu. *Application contact:* Michele Bray, Department Secretary, 801-422-2746, Fax: 801-422-0314, E-mail: michele_bray@byu.edu.

Brigham Young University, Graduate Studies, Ira A. Fulton College of Engineering and Technology, School of Technology, Provo, UT 84602-1001. Offers construction management (MS); information technology (MS); manufacturing systems (MS); technology and engineering education (MS). *Faculty:* 25 full-time (0 women). *Students:* 23 full-time (3 women); includes 3 minority (2 Asian Americans or Pacific Islanders, 1 Hispanic American). Average age 25. 14 applicants, 71% accepted, 6 enrolled. In 2009, 13 master's awarded. *Degree requirements:* For master's, thesis. *Entrance requirements:* For master's, GRE General Test, GMAT (construction management), minimum GPA of 3.0 in last 60 hours of course work. Additional exam requirements/recommendations for international students: Required—TOEFL (minimum score 580 paper-based; 237 computer-based; 85 iBT). *Application deadline:* For fall admission, 2/15 for domestic and international students; for winter admission, 9/15 for domestic and international students; for spring admission, 2/15 for domestic and international students. Application fee: $50. Electronic applications accepted. *Expenses:* Tuition: Full-time $5580; part-time $301 per credit hour. Tuition and fees vary according to student's religious affiliation. *Financial support:* In 2009–10, 9 research assistantships (averaging $4,774 per year), 7 teaching assistantships (averaging $4,481 per year) were awarded; fellowships, career-related internships or fieldwork also available. Financial award application deadline: 2/1. *Faculty research:* Real time process control in IT, electronic physical design, processing and non-linear systems, networking, computerized systems in CM. Total annual research expenditures: $52,000. *Unit head:* Val D. Hawks, Director, 801-422-6300, Fax: 801-422-0490, E-mail: hawksv@byu.edu. *Application contact:* Ronald E. Terry, Graduate Coordinator, 801-422-4297, Fax: 801-422-0490, E-mail: ralowe@byu.edu.

Buffalo State College, State University of New York, The Graduate School, Faculty of Applied Science and Education, Department of Computer Information Systems, Program in Educational Computing, Buffalo, NY 14222-1095. Offers MS Ed. *Accreditation:* NCATE. Part-time and evening/weekend programs available. *Degree requirements:* For master's, thesis, project. *Entrance requirements:* Additional exam requirements/recommendations for international students: Required—TOEFL (minimum score 550 paper-based; 213 computer-based).

California Baptist University, Program in Education, Riverside, CA 92504-3206. Offers cross-cultural language and academic development (MA); educational leadership (MS); educational leadership and faith-based instruction (MS); educational technology (MS); instructional computer applications (MS); reading (MS); school counseling (MS); school psychology (MS); special education (MS); special education in mild/moderate disabilities (MS); special education in moderate/severe disabilities (MS); teaching (MS); teaching and learning (MS Ed). Part-time programs available. *Faculty:* 16 full-time (9 women), 10 part-time/adjunct (all women). *Students:* 73 full-time (60 women), 368 part-time (298 women); includes 170 minority (34 African Americans, 4 American Indian/Alaska Native, 18 Asian Americans or Pacific Islanders, 114 Hispanic Americans). 266 applicants, 72% accepted, 169 enrolled. In 2009, 120 master's awarded. *Degree requirements:* For master's, comprehensive exam (for some programs), thesis optional. *Entrance requirements:* For master's, minimum undergraduate GPA of 2.75, 12 semester hours of pre-requisite course work in education. Additional exam requirements/recommendations for international students: Required—TOEFL (minimum score 575 paper-based; 230 computer-based; 89 iBT). *Application deadline:* For fall admission, 8/1 priority date for domestic students, 7/1 for international students; for spring admission, 12/1 priority date for domestic students, 10/15 priority date for international students. Applications are processed on a rolling basis. Application fee: $45. Electronic applications accepted. *Expenses:* Tuition: Full-time $8352; part-time $464 per semester hour. Required fees: $125 per semester. Tuition and fees vary according to course load, campus/location and program. *Financial support:* Career-related internships or fieldwork, Federal Work-Study, and scholarships/grants available. Support available to part-time students. Financial award applicants required to submit FAFSA. *Unit head:* Dr. Mary Crist, Dean, School of Education, 951-343-4313, Fax: 951-343-4516, E-mail: mcrist@calbaptist.edu. *Application contact:* Gail Ronveaux, Dean of Graduate Enrollment, 951-343-5045, Fax: 951-343-5095, E-mail: graduateadmissions@calbaptist.edu.

California State University, Bakersfield, Division of Graduate Studies, School of Education, Program in Curriculum and Instruction, Bakersfield, CA 93311. Offers curriculum and instruction (MA Ed); educational technology (MA Ed). *Accreditation:* NCATE. Postbaccalaureate distance learning degree programs offered. *Degree requirements:* For master's, thesis or alternative, culminating projects. *Entrance requirements:* For master's, CBEST, copy of current teaching credential, minimum GPA of 3.0 for last 90 units, 3 letters of recommendation.

California State University, East Bay, Graduate Programs, College of Education and Allied Studies, Department of Teacher Education, Hayward, CA 94542-3000. Offers education (MS), including curriculum, early childhood education, educational technology leadership, reading instruction. *Faculty:* 18 full-time (10 women), 4 part-time/adjunct (3 women). *Students:* Average age 37. In 2009, 135 master's awarded. *Degree requirements:* For master's, project or thesis. *Entrance requirements:* For master's, minimum GPA of 3.0 in field, 2.5 overall; teaching experience. Additional exam requirements/recommendations for international students: Required—TOEFL (minimum score 550 paper-based; 213 computer-based). *Application deadline:* For fall admission, 6/30 for domestic and international students. Application fee: $55. Electronic applications accepted. *Financial support:* Career-related internships or fieldwork, Federal Work-Study, and institutionally sponsored loans available. Support available to part-time students. Financial award application deadline: 3/1; financial award applicants required to submit FAFSA. *Unit head:* Dr. Jeanette Bicais, Chair, 510-885-3027, E-mail: jeanette.bicais@csueastbay.edu. *Application contact:* Donna Wiley, Interim Associate Director, 510-885-2928, Fax: 510-885-4777, E-mail: donna.wiley@csueastbay.edu.

California State University, Fullerton, Graduate Studies, College of Education, Program of Instructional Design and Technology, Fullerton, CA 92834-9480. Offers MS. Part-time programs available. Postbaccalaureate distance learning degree programs offered. *Students:* 47 part-time (31 women); includes 13 minority (1 African American, 7 Asian Americans or Pacific Islanders, 5 Hispanic Americans). Average age 38. 38 applicants, 68% accepted, 25 enrolled. In 2009, 21 master's awarded. Application fee: $55. *Expenses:* Tuition, nonresident: full-time $11,160; part-time $373 per credit. Required fees: $1440 per term. Tuition and fees vary according to course load, degree level and program. *Financial support:* Career-related internships or fieldwork, Federal Work-Study, institutionally sponsored loans, and scholarships/grants available. Support available to part-time students. Financial award application deadline: 3/1; financial award applicants required to submit FAFSA. *Unit head:* Dr. Jo Ann Carter-Wells, Chair, 657-278-3357. *Application contact:* Admissions/Applications, 657-278-2371.

California State University, Monterey Bay, College of Science, Media Arts and Technology, School of Information Technology and Communication Design, Seaside, CA 93955-8001. Offers interdisciplinary studies (MA), including instructional science and technology; management and information technology (MA). *Degree requirements:* For master's, capstone or thesis. *Entrance requirements:* For master's, GRE, 2 letters of recommendation, minimum GPA of 3.0, technology screening assessment. Additional exam requirements/recommendations for international students: Required—TOEFL (minimum score 550 paper-based; 213 computer-based; 71 iBT). Electronic applications accepted. *Faculty research:* Electronic commerce, e-learning, knowledge management, international business, business and public policy.

California State University, Northridge, Graduate Studies, College of Education, Department of Secondary Education, Northridge, CA 91330. Offers educational technology (MA); English education (MA); mathematics education (MA); secondary science education (MA); teaching and learning (MA). *Accreditation:* NCATE. Part-time programs available. *Faculty:* 13 full-time (7 women), 41 part-time/adjunct (20 women). *Students:* 10 full-time (6 women), 99 part-time (65 women); includes 40 minority (6 African Americans, 2 American Indian/Alaska Native, 13 Asian Americans or Pacific Islanders, 19 Hispanic Americans). Average age 34. 86 applicants, 60% accepted, 40 enrolled. *Degree requirements:* For master's, thesis optional. *Entrance requirements:* For master's, GRE General Test or minimum GPA of 3.0. Additional exam requirements/recommendations for international students: Required—TOEFL. *Application deadline:* For fall admission, 11/30 for domestic students. Application fee: $55. *Financial support:* Application deadline: 3/1. *Unit head:* Dr. Bonnie Ericson, Chair, 818-677-2580. *Application contact:* Dr. Michael Rivas, Graduate Advisor, 818-677-6792, E-mail: michael.rivas@csun.edu.

California State University, San Bernardino, Graduate Studies, College of Education, Program in Instructional Technology, San Bernardino, CA 92407-2397. Offers MA. *Faculty:* 1 full-time (0

women). *Students:* 17 full-time (9 women), 25 part-time (14 women); includes 18 minority (2 African Americans, 1 American Indian/Alaska Native, 6 Asian Americans or Pacific Islanders, 9 Hispanic Americans), 3 international. Average age 37. 23 applicants, 74% accepted, 11 enrolled. In 2009, 21 master's awarded. *Degree requirements:* For master's, comprehensive exam (for some programs), thesis optional, advancement to candidacy. *Entrance requirements:* For master's, minimum GPA of 2.5. *Application deadline:* For fall admission, 8/31 priority date for domestic students. Application fee: $55. *Unit head:* Dr. Herbert Brunkhorst, Chair, 909-537-5613, Fax: 909-537-7522, E-mail: hkbrunkh@csusb.edu. *Application contact:* Olivia Rosas, Director of Admissions, 909-537-7577, Fax: 909-537-7034, E-mail: orosas@csusb.edu.

California State University, Stanislaus, College of Education, Department of Advanced Studies in Education, Turlock, CA 95382. Offers community college leadership (Ed D); education (MA); educational leadership (Ed D); educational technology (MA); P-12 leadership (Ed D); school administration (MA); school counseling (MA); special education (MA). Part-time and evening/weekend programs available. Postbaccalaureate distance learning degree programs offered. *Degree requirements:* For master's, thesis. *Entrance requirements:* For master's, MAT or GRE, BEST (depending on concentration), minimum GPA of 2.8, 3 letters of reference; for doctorate, GRE, 3.0 minimum GPA, 3 letters of reference and personal statement. Additional exam requirements/recommendations for international students: Required—TOEFL (minimum score 550 paper-based; 213 computer-based). *Faculty research:* Current school technology use, social aspects of technology, staff development.

Cambridge College, School of Education, Cambridge, MA 02138-5304. Offers autism specialist (M Ed); autism/behavior analyst (M Ed); behavior analyst (Post-Master's Certificate); behavioral management (M Ed); early childhood teacher (M Ed); education specialist in curriculum and instruction (CAGS); educational leadership (Ed D); elementary teacher (M Ed); English as a second language (M Ed, Certificate); general science (M Ed); health education, health promotion (Post-Master's Certificate); health/family and consumer sciences (M Ed); history (M Ed); individualized degree (M Ed); information technology literacy (M Ed); instructional technology (M Ed); interdisciplinary studies (M Ed); library teacher (M Ed); literacy education (M Ed); mathematics (M Ed); mathematics specialist (Certificate); middle school mathematics and science (M Ed); school administration (M Ed, CAGS); school guidance counselor (M Ed); school nurse education (M Ed); school social worker/school adjustment counselor (M Ed); special education administrator (CAGS); special education/moderate disabilities (M Ed); teaching skills and methodologies (M Ed). Part-time and evening/weekend programs available. Postbaccalaureate distance learning degree programs offered (minimal on-campus study). *Faculty:* 10 full-time (3 women), 283 part-time/adjunct (187 women). *Students:* 974 full-time (755 women), 1,071 part-time (835 women); includes 940 minority (762 African Americans, 4 American Indian/Alaska Native, 22 Asian Americans or Pacific Islanders, 152 Hispanic Americans), 28 international. Average age 39. In 2009, 866 master's, 4 doctorates, 209 CAGSs awarded. *Degree requirements:* For master's, thesis, internship/practicum (licensure program only); for doctorate, thesis/dissertation; for other advanced degree, thesis. *Entrance requirements:* For master's, interview, resume, documentation of licensure, 2 professional references; for doctorate, official transcripts, interview, resume, documentation of licensure (if any), written personal statement/essay, portfolio of scholarly and professional work, qualifying assessment, 2 professional references, health insurance, immunizations form; for other advanced degree, official transcripts, interview, resume, documentation of licensure (if any), written personal statement/essay, 2 professional references, health insurance, immunizations form. Additional exam requirements/recommendations for international students: Required—TOEFL (minimum score 550 paper-based; 213 computer-based; 79 iBT); Recommended—IELTS (minimum score 6). *Application deadline:* Applications are processed on a rolling basis. Application fee: $30. Electronic applications accepted. *Expenses:* Contact institution. *Financial support:* In 2009–10, 1,373 students received support. Career-related internships or fieldwork, Federal Work-Study, and scholarships/grants available. Financial award applicants required to submit FAFSA. *Faculty research:* Adult education, accelerated learning, mathematics education, brain compatible learning, special education and law. *Unit head:* Dr. N. Alan Sheppard, Interim Associate Dean, 617-873-0619, E-mail: alan.sheppard@cambridgecollege.edu. *Application contact:* Stephen Lyons, Director of Enrollment, Graduate and N.I.T.E. Programs, 617-868-1000, Fax: 617-349-3561, E-mail: stephen.lyons@cambridgecollege.edu.

Cape Breton University, School of Education, Health, and Wellness, Sydney, NS B1P 6L2, Canada. Offers educational counseling (Diploma); educational curriculum (Diploma); educational studies in arts education (Certificate); educational technology (Diploma). Part-time and evening/weekend programs available. Postbaccalaureate distance learning degree programs offered (no on-campus study). *Faculty:* 15 part-time/adjunct (5 women). *Students:* 171 part-time (103 women). Average age 30. *Application deadline:* For fall admission, 8/1 priority date for domestic students. Applications are processed on a rolling basis. Application fee: $50. Electronic applications accepted. *Unit head:* Susan Basso, Coordinator of the Education Program, 902-563-1651, Fax: 902-563-1861. *Application contact:* Terry MacDonald, Coordinator, Teacher Education Program, 902-563-1647, Fax: 902-563-1449, E-mail: terry_macdonald@cbu.ca.

Capella University, School of Education, Minneapolis, MN 55402. Offers college teaching (Certificate); curriculum and instruction (MS, PhD); education (MS, PhD); enrollment management (MS); instructional design for online learning (MS, PhD); k-12 studies in education (MS, PhD); leadership for higher education (MS, PhD); leadership in education administration (Certificate); leadership in educational administration (MS, PhD); postsecondary and adult education (MS, PhD); professional studies in education (MS, PhD); reading and literacy (MS); training and performance improvement (MS, PhD). Part-time and evening/weekend programs available. Postbaccalaureate distance learning degree programs offered (minimal on-campus study). Terminal master's awarded for partial completion of doctoral program. *Degree requirements:* For master's, thesis optional, integrative project; for doctorate, comprehensive exam, thesis/dissertation. *Entrance requirements:* Additional exam requirements/recommendations for international students: Required—TOEFL (minimum score 550 paper-based; 213 computer-based), TWE (minimum score 4). Electronic applications accepted. *Faculty research:* Higher education administration, distance learning, adult education, training and curriculum design.

Cardinal Stritch University, College of Education, Department of Educational Computing, Milwaukee, WI 53217-3985. Offers instructional technology (ME, MS). Part-time and evening/weekend programs available. *Degree requirements:* For master's, comprehensive exam, thesis, faculty recommendation. *Entrance requirements:* For master's, letters of recommendation (2), minimum GPA of 2.75.

Carlow University, School of Education, Program in Education, Pittsburgh, PA 15213-3165. Offers elementary education (M Ed); instructional technology specialist (M Ed); secondary education (M Ed); special education (M Ed). Part-time and evening/weekend programs available. *Entrance requirements:* For master's, resume, 3 letters of recommendation, minimum GPA of 3.0, interview. Electronic applications accepted. *Expenses:* Tuition: Full-time $11,250; part-time $625 per credit. Tuition and fees vary according to course load, degree level and program.

Central Connecticut State University, School of Graduate Studies, School of Education and Professional Studies, Department of Educational Leadership, Program in Educational Technology and Media, New Britain, CT 06050-4010. Offers MS. Part-time and evening/weekend programs available. *Students:* 3 full-time (2 women), 37 part-time (19 women); includes 3 minority (all Hispanic Americans). Average age 33. 13 applicants, 77% accepted, 10 enrolled. In 2009, 22 master's awarded. *Entrance requirements:* Additional exam requirements/recommendations for international students: Required—TOEFL. *Application deadline:* For fall admission, 7/1 for domestic students; for spring admission, 12/1 for domestic students. Applications are processed on a rolling basis. Application fee: $50. Electronic applications accepted. *Expenses:* Tuition, area resident: Full-time $4662; part-time $440 per credit. Tuition, state resident: full-time $6994; part-time $440 per credit. Tuition, nonresident: full-time $12,988; part-time $440 per credit. Required fees: $3606. One-time fee: $62 part-time. *Financial support:* Application deadline: 3/1. *Faculty research:* Design and development of multimedia packages, semiotics, perceptual theories, integrated media presentations, distance teaching.

Central Michigan University, College of Graduate Studies, College of Education and Human Services, Department of Educational Leadership, Mount Pleasant, MI 48859. Offers educational leadership (MA, Ed D), including charter school leadership (Ed D), educational technology (Ed D), general educational leadership, higher education administration (Ed D), higher education leadership (Ed D), K-12 curriculum (Ed D), K-12 leadership (Ed D), student affairs administration (Ed D), general educational administration (Ed S); school principalship (MA). Part-time and evening/weekend programs available. *Degree requirements:* For master's and Ed S, thesis or alternative; for doctorate, thesis/dissertation. *Entrance requirements:* For doctorate, GRE or MAT, master's degree, minimum GPA of 3.5, 3 years of professional education experience. Electronic applications accepted. *Faculty research:* Elementary administration, secondary administration, student achievement, in-service training, internships in administration.

Central Michigan University, College of Graduate Studies, College of Education and Human Services, Department of Teacher Education and Professional Development, Mount Pleasant, MI 48859. Offers educational technology (MA); elementary education (MA), including classroom teaching, early childhood; middle level education (MA); reading and literacy K-12 (MA); secondary education (MA). Part-time and evening/weekend programs available. *Degree requirements:* For master's, thesis or alternative. Electronic applications accepted. *Faculty research:* Integrating literacy across the curriculum; science teaching and aesthetic learning in science; diversity education; educational technology; educational psychology and child development.

Chestnut Hill College, School of Graduate Studies, Program in Instructional Technology, Philadelphia, PA 19118-2693. Offers MS, CAS. Part-time and evening/weekend programs available. *Degree requirements:* For master's, special project/internship. *Entrance requirements:* For master's, GRE General Test or MAT, letters of recommendation, writing sample, 300 volunteer hours or 1 year work-related experience in human services, computer course; for CAS, GRE or MAT, transcripts, letters of recommendation, statement of professional goals, writing sample, 300 volunteer hours or 1 year work-related experience in human services, prerequisite computer course. Additional exam requirements/recommendations for international students: Required—TOEFL (minimum score 500 paper-based; 213 computer-based). *Faculty research:* Second Life: a social virtual environment, immersive learning simulations, video as a learning tool;, web 2.0 technologies as a learning tool, utilization of laptops in the classroom.

Chicago State University, School of Graduate and Professional Studies, College of Education, Department of Reading, Elementary Education, Library Information and Media Studies, Program in Library Information and Media Studies, Chicago, IL 60628. Offers MS Ed. *Entrance requirements:* For master's, minimum GPA of 2.75.

Chicago State University, School of Graduate and Professional Studies, College of Education, Department of Technology and Education, Chicago, IL 60628. Offers secondary education (MAT); technology and education (MS Ed). Postbaccalaureate distance learning degree programs offered. *Degree requirements:* For master's, thesis optional. *Entrance requirements:* For master's, minimum GPA of 2.75.

City University of Seattle, Graduate Division, Gordon Albright School of Education, Bellevue, WA 98005. Offers curriculum and instruction (M Ed); educational leadership (M Ed); educational leadership: administrator certification (Certificate); executive leadership: superintendent certification (Certificate); guidance and counseling (M Ed); leadership (M Ed); leadership and school counseling (M Ed); professional certification for teachers (Certificate); reading and literacy (M Ed); reading and literacy in education (M Ed); teacher certification (elementary K-8) (MIT); teacher certification (special education K-12) (MIT); technology, curriculum, and instruction (M Ed). Part-time and evening/weekend programs available. Postbaccalaureate distance learning degree programs offered (no on-campus study). *Entrance requirements:* Additional exam requirements/recommendations for international students: Required—TOEFL (minimum score 540 paper-based; 207 computer-based); Recommended—IELTS. Electronic applications accepted. *Expenses:* Contact institution.

Clarke College, Program in Education, Dubuque, IA 52001-3198. Offers early childhood/special education (MAE); educational administration: elementary and secondary (MAE); educational media: elementary and secondary (MAE); multi-categorical resource k-12 (MAE); multidisciplinary studies (MAE); reading: elementary (MAE); technology in education (MAE). Part-time and evening/weekend programs available. Postbaccalaureate distance learning degree programs offered (minimal on-campus study). *Faculty:* 5 full-time (all women). *Students:* 1 (woman) full-time, 45 part-time (40 women). Average age 31. 19 applicants, 74% accepted, 13 enrolled. In 2009, 11 master's awarded. *Degree requirements:* For master's, comprehensive exam, thesis optional. *Entrance requirements:* For master's, GRE General Test or MAT, minimum GPA of 2.75. *Application deadline:* Applications are processed on a rolling basis. Application fee: $25. Electronic applications accepted. *Expenses:* Tuition: Full-time $10,836; part-time $602 per credit hour. Required fees: $30 per credit hour. *Financial support:* Career-related internships or fieldwork available. Financial award applicants required to submit FAFSA. *Unit head:* Dr. Larry Bice, Chair, 319-588-6397, Fax: 319-584-8604. *Application contact:* Joan Coates, Information Contact, 563-588-6354, Fax: 563-588-6789, E-mail: graduate@clarke.edu.

College of Mount Saint Vincent, School of Professional and Continuing Studies, Department of Teacher Education, Riverdale, NY 10471-1093. Offers instructional technology and global perspectives (Certificate); middle level education (Certificate); multicultural studies (Certificate); urban and multicultural education (MS Ed). *Accreditation:* Teacher Education Accreditation Council. Part-time programs available. *Degree requirements:* For master's, comprehensive exam. *Entrance requirements:* For master's, interview, New York teaching certificate. Additional exam requirements/recommendations for international students: Required—TOEFL.

College of Saint Elizabeth, Department of Education, Morristown, NJ 07960-6989. Offers accelerated certification for teachers (Certificate); assistive technology (Certificate); education: human services leadership (MA); educational leadership (MA, Ed D); educational technology (MA). Part-time and evening/weekend programs available. *Faculty:* 10 full-time (3 women), 20 part-time/adjunct (11 women). *Students:* 119 full-time (88 women), 332 part-time (292 women); includes 63 minority (35 African Americans, 3 Asian Americans or Pacific Islanders, 25 Hispanic Americans), 1 international. Average age 37. 201 applicants, 82% accepted, 146 enrolled. In 2009, 140 master's, 81 other advanced degrees awarded. *Degree requirements:* For master's, thesis or alternative, portfolio. *Entrance requirements:* For master's, interview, minimum undergraduate GPA of 3.0. *Application deadline:* For fall admission, 6/30 priority date for domestic students; for spring admission, 11/30 for domestic students. Applications are processed on a rolling basis. Application fee: $35. Electronic applications accepted. *Expenses:* Tuition: Part-time $797 per credit hour. Required fees: $65 per credit hour. *Financial support:* Career-related internships or fieldwork, tuition waivers (partial), and unspecified assistantships available. Support available to part-time students. Financial award application deadline: 3/15; financial award applicants required to submit FAFSA. *Faculty research:* Developmental stages for teaching and human services professionals, effectiveness of humanities core curriculum. *Unit head:* Dr. Alan H. Markowitz, Director of Graduate Education Programs, 973-290-4374, Fax: 973-290-4389, E-mail: amarkowitz@cse.edu. *Application contact:* Donna Tatarka, Dean of Admission, 973-290-4705, Fax: 973-290-4710, E-mail: dtatarka@cse.edu.

The College of Saint Rose, Graduate Studies, School of Education, Educational and School Psychology Department, Albany, NY 12203-1419. Offers applied technology education (MS Ed); educational psychology (MS Ed); school psychology (MS, Certificate). Part-time and evening/weekend programs available. *Entrance requirements:* For master's, minimum undergraduate GPA of 3.0. Additional exam requirements/recommendations for international students: Required—TOEFL (minimum score 550 paper-based; 213 computer-based). Electronic applications accepted.

The College of St. Scholastica, Graduate Studies, Program in Educational Media and Technology, Duluth, MN 55811-4199. Offers M Ed. Part-time and evening/weekend programs available. Postbaccalaureate distance learning degree programs offered (no on-campus study). *Degree requirements:* For master's, thesis. *Entrance requirements:* For master's, interview,

Educational Media/Instructional Technology

The College of St. Scholastica (continued)

minimum GPA of 2.7. Additional exam requirements/recommendations for international students: Required—TOEFL (minimum score 550 paper-based; 213 computer-based; 79 iBT). Electronic applications accepted. *Expenses:* Contact institution. *Faculty research:* The current standards environment.

The College of William and Mary, School of Education, Program in Education Policy, Planning, and Leadership, Williamsburg, VA 23187-8795. Offers curriculum and educational technology (Ed D, PhD); curriculum leadership (Ed D, PhD); educational leadership (M Ed), including higher education administration (M Ed, Ed D, PhD), K-12 administration and supervision; educational policy, planning, and leadership (Ed D, PhD), including general education administration, gifted education administration, higher education administration (M Ed, Ed D, PhD), special education administration; gifted education administration (M Ed). *Accreditation:* NCATE. Part-time and evening/weekend programs available. *Faculty:* 12 full-time (6 women), 3 part-time/adjunct (1 woman). *Students:* 41 full-time (26 women), 134 part-time (93 women); includes 35 minority (32 African Americans, 3 Asian Americans or Pacific Islanders), 2 international. Average age 38. 108 applicants, 57% accepted, 44 enrolled. In 2009, 20 master's, 22 doctorates awarded. *Degree requirements:* For doctorate, comprehensive exam, thesis/dissertation. *Entrance requirements:* For master's, GRE or MAT, minimum GPA of 2.5; for doctorate, GRE or MAT, minimum GPA of 3.0. Additional exam requirements/recommendations for international students: Required—TOEFL. *Application deadline:* For fall admission, 1/15 for domestic and international students. Application fee: $45. Electronic applications accepted. *Expenses:* Tuition, state resident: full-time $6400; part-time $315 per credit hour. Tuition, nonresident: full-time $19,720; part-time $840 per credit hour. Required fees: $4114. *Financial support:* In 2009–10, 56 students received support, including 32 research assistantships with full and partial tuition reimbursements available (averaging $13,000 per year); career-related internships or fieldwork, Federal Work-Study, institutionally sponsored loans, scholarships/grants, and unspecified assistantships also available. Support available to part-time students. Financial award application deadline: 1/15; financial award applicants required to submit FAFSA. *Faculty research:* Higher education policy, faculty incentives, history of adversity, resilience, leadership. *Unit head:* Dr. Megan Tschannen-Moran, Area Coordinator, 757-221-2187, E-mail: mxtsch@wm.edu. *Application contact:* Dorothy Smith Osborne, Director of Admissions, 757-221-2317, Fax: 757-221-2293, E-mail: dsosbo@wm.edu.

Colorado State University–Pueblo, College of Education, Engineering and Professional Studies, Education Program, Pueblo, CO 81001-4901. Offers art education (M Ed); foreign language education (M Ed); health and physical education (M Ed); instructional technology (M Ed); linguistically diverse education (M Ed); music education (M Ed); special education (M Ed). *Accreditation:* Teacher Education Accreditation Council. Part-time programs available. *Degree requirements:* For master's, portfolio. *Entrance requirements:* For master's, 3 recommendations, teaching license. Additional exam requirements/recommendations for international students: Required—TOEFL (minimum score 500 paper-based; 173 computer-based). Electronic applications accepted. *Faculty research:* Portfolio assessment, math education, science education.

Columbia International University, Columbia Graduate School, Columbia, SC 29230-3122. Offers Bible teaching (MABT); Christian higher education leadership (Ed D); Christian school educational leadership (Ed D); counseling (MACN); curriculum and instruction (M Ed), including Christian school guidance, English as a second language, learning disabilities, school technology; early childhood and elementary education (MAT); educational administration (M Ed); teaching English as a foreign language (Certificate); teaching English as a foreign language and intercultural studies (MATF). Part-time and evening/weekend programs available. *Degree requirements:* For master's, internships, professional project. *Entrance requirements:* For master's, Minnesota Multiphasic Personality Inventory, MAT, minimum GPA of 2.7. Additional exam requirements/recommendations for international students: Required—TOEFL. Electronic applications accepted.

Concordia University, School of Graduate Studies, Faculty of Arts and Science, Department of Education, Program in Educational Technology, Montréal, QC H3G 1M8, Canada. Offers MA, PhD. *Degree requirements:* For master's, one foreign language, thesis optional, internship; for doctorate, comprehensive exam, thesis/dissertation. *Entrance requirements:* For doctorate, MA in educational technology or equivalent. *Faculty research:* Instructional design and tele-education, educational cybernetics and systems analysis, media research and theory development, distance education.

Concordia University, School of Graduate Studies, Faculty of Arts and Science, Department of Education, Program in Instructional Technology, Montréal, QC H3G 1M8, Canada. Offers Diploma. *Entrance requirements:* For degree, BA in related field.

Concordia University Chicago, College of Graduate and Innovative Programs, Program in Educational Technology, River Forest, IL 60305-1499. Offers MA.

Dakota State University, College of Education, Madison, SD 57042-1799. Offers instructional technology (MSET). *Accreditation:* NCATE. Part-time programs available. Postbaccalaureate distance learning degree programs offered (minimal on-campus study). *Faculty:* 7 full-time (3 women), 3 part-time/adjunct (0 women). *Students:* 1 full-time (0 women), 31 part-time (18 women), 1 international. Average age 34. 12 applicants, 92% accepted, 10 enrolled. In 2009, 22 master's awarded. *Degree requirements:* For master's, thesis, electronic portfolio. *Entrance requirements:* For master's, GRE General Test, demonstration of technology skills, minimum GPA of 2.7. Additional exam requirements/recommendations for international students: Required—TOEFL. *Application deadline:* For fall admission, 8/1 for domestic students, 6/1 for international students. Applications are processed on a rolling basis. Application fee: $35 ($85 for international students). Electronic applications accepted. *Financial support:* In 2009–10, 15 students received support; research assistantships, teaching assistantships, Federal Work-Study, scholarships/grants, tuition waivers (partial), and administrative assistantships available. Support available to part-time students. Financial award applicants required to submit FAFSA. *Faculty research:* Educational technology evaluation, computer supported collaborative learning, cognitive theory and visual representation of the effects of ambiquitous wireless computing on student learning and productivity. *Unit head:* Dr. Judy Dittman, Dean, 605-256-5177, Fax: 605-256-7300, E-mail: judy.dittman@dsu.edu. *Application contact:* Annette Miller, Secretary, Office of Graduate Studies and Research, 605-256-5799, Fax: 605-256-5093, E-mail: annette.miller@dsu.edu.

Delaware Valley College, Program in Educational Leadership, Doylestown, PA 18901-2697. Offers instruction, curriculum and technology (MS); school administration and leadership (MS). Part-time and evening/weekend programs available. *Faculty:* 30 part-time/adjunct (11 women). *Students:* 119 full-time (84 women), 46 part-time (29 women); includes 12 minority (9 African Americans, 3 Hispanic Americans). Average age 36. 56 applicants, 100% accepted, 56 enrolled. In 2009, 33 master's awarded. *Entrance requirements:* For master's, minimum undergraduate GPA of 3.0. *Application deadline:* Applications are processed on a rolling basis. Application fee: $50. *Expenses:* Tuition: Full-time $6336; part-time $528 per credit hour. Required fees: $72 per semester. One-time fee: $90. Tuition and fees vary according to program. *Financial support:* Applicants required to submit FAFSA. *Unit head:* Dr. Patricia Carney-Dalton, Director/Intern Supervisor, 215-489-4833, Fax: 215-489-4832, E-mail: patricia.carney@delval.edu. *Application contact:* Dr. Patricia Carney-Dalton, Director/Intern Supervisor, 215-489-4833, Fax: 215-489-4832, E-mail: patricia.carney@delval.edu.

DeSales University, Graduate Division, Program in Education, Center Valley, PA 18034-9568. Offers elementary education (M Ed); instructional technology for K-12 (M Ed); interdisciplinary (M Ed); mathematics (M Ed); special education (M Ed); TESOL/ESL (M Ed). Part-time and evening/weekend programs available. Postbaccalaureate distance learning degree programs offered (no on-campus study). *Students:* 218 part-time. *Degree requirements:* For master's, thesis project. *Entrance requirements:* For master's, teaching certificate. Additional exam requirements/recommendations for international students: Required—TOEFL. *Application deadline:* Applications are processed on a rolling basis. Application fee: $35. Electronic applications accepted. *Expenses:* Tuition: Full-time $17,500; part-time $665 per credit. Full-time tuition and fees vary according to program. Part-time tuition and fees vary according to course load. *Financial support:* Application deadline: 5/1. *Faculty research:* Effective teaching, computer interfacing in chemistry labs, computer applications to teaching, history of philosophy, aesthetics multidrug-resistant cancer. *Unit head:* Dr. Lujean Baab, Director, 610-282-1100 Ext. 1739, Fax: 610-282-3734, E-mail: lujean.baab@desales.edu. *Application contact:* Caryn Stopper, Director of Graduate Admissions, 610-282-1100 Ext. 1768, Fax: 610-282-0525, E-mail: caryn.stopper@desales.edu.

Dowling College, Graduate Programs in Education, Oakdale, NY 11769-1999. Offers adolescence education (MS Ed), including educational administration; advanced certificate in gifted education (AC); childhood and early childhood education (MS Ed); childhood education (MS Ed); educational administration (AC, PD), including computers in education (PD), school administration and supervision (PD), school district administration (PD); educational technology specialist (AC); literacy (MS Ed); literacy/special education (MS Ed); secondary education (MS Ed); special education (MS Ed). *Accreditation:* NCATE. Part-time and evening/weekend programs available. Postbaccalaureate distance learning degree programs offered. *Faculty:* 32 full-time (18 women), 98 part-time/adjunct (59 women). *Students:* 563 full-time (393 women), 885 part-time (668 women); includes 133 minority (47 African Americans, 2 American Indian/Alaska Native, 10 Asian Americans or Pacific Islanders, 74 Hispanic Americans). Average age 32. 363 applicants, 89% accepted, 213 enrolled. In 2009, 459 master's, 85 ACs awarded. *Degree requirements:* For master's and other advanced degree, comprehensive exam. *Entrance requirements:* For master's, minimum GPA of 3.0; for other advanced degree, teaching certificate. Additional exam requirements/recommendations for international students: Required—TOEFL (minimum score 550 paper-based). *Application deadline:* For fall admission, 9/1 priority date for domestic students; for winter admission, 1/1 priority date for domestic students; for spring admission, 2/1 priority date for domestic students. Applications are processed on a rolling basis. Application fee: $50. Electronic applications accepted. *Expenses:* Tuition: Full-time $14,490; part-time $805 per credit. Required fees: $346 per term. *Financial support:* Career-related internships or fieldwork and Federal Work-Study available. Support available to part-time students. Financial award application deadline: 6/30; financial award applicants required to submit FAFSA. *Faculty research:* Natural readers, Korean styles and learning strategies, mothers of children with disabilities, computers in instruction, cultural background and organizational roadblocks to problem solving. *Unit head:* Dr. Clyde Payne, Dean of the School of Education, 631-244-3404, Fax: 631-589-6644, E-mail: paynec@dowling.edu. *Application contact:* Glenn M. Berman, Assistant Vice President for Enrollment Services/Dean of Admissions, 631-244-3357, Fax: 631-244-1059, E-mail: glenn.berman@dowling.edu.

Drexel University, The iSchool at Drexel, College of Information Science and Technology, Master of Science (Library and Information Science) Program, Philadelphia, PA 19104-2875. Offers archival studies (MS); competitive intelligence and knowledge management (MS); digital libraries (MS); library and information services (MS); school library media (MS); youth services (MS). Part-time and evening/weekend programs available. Postbaccalaureate distance learning degree programs offered (no on-campus study). *Faculty:* 34 full-time (19 women), 24 part-time/adjunct (9 women). *Students:* 248 full-time (187 women), 363 part-time (289 women); includes 47 minority (16 African Americans, 1 American Indian/Alaska Native, 17 Asian Americans or Pacific Islanders, 13 Hispanic Americans), 9 international. Average age 34. 465 applicants, 50% accepted, 224 enrolled. In 2009, 272 master's awarded. *Entrance requirements:* For master's, GRE General Test. Additional exam requirements/recommendations for international students: Required—TOEFL (minimum score 600 paper-based; 250 computer-based; 100 iBT). *Application deadline:* For fall admission, 8/1 for domestic and international students; for spring admission, 2/1 for domestic and international students. Applications are processed on a rolling basis. Electronic applications accepted. *Expenses:* Contact institution. *Financial support:* In 2009–10, 217 students received support, including 213 fellowships with partial tuition reimbursements available (averaging $225 per year); institutionally sponsored loans, scholarships/grants, and fellowships also available. Support available to part-time students. Financial award applicants required to submit FAFSA. *Faculty research:* Library and information resources and services, knowledge organization and representation, information retrieval/information visualization/bibliometrics, information needs and behaviors, digital libraries. Total annual research expenditures: $2 million. *Unit head:* Dr. David E. Fenske, Dean and Isaac L. Auerbach Professor of Information Science, 215-895-2475, Fax: 215-895-6378, E-mail: fenske@drexel.edu. *Application contact:* Matthew Lechtenberg, Graduate Admissions Manager, 215-895-1951, Fax: 215-895-2303, E-mail: ml333@drexel.edu.

Drexel University, School of Education, Program in Educational Leadership and Learning Technology, Philadelphia, PA 19104-2875. Offers PhD. *Degree requirements:* For doctorate, thesis/dissertation. Electronic applications accepted.

Drexel University, School of Technology and Professional Studies, Philadelphia, PA 19104-2875. Offers construction management (MS); engineering technology (MS); food science (MS); hospitality management (MS); professional studies: creativity studies (MS); professional studies: e-learning leadership (MS); professional studies: homeland security management (MS); project management (MS); property management (MS); sport management (MS). Postbaccalaureate distance learning degree programs offered.

Drury University, Graduate Programs in Education, Springfield, MO 65802. Offers elementary education (M Ed); gifted education (M Ed); human services (M Ed); instructional mathematics K-8 (M Ed); instructional technology (M Ed); middle school teaching (M Ed); secondary education (M Ed); special education (M Ed); special reading (M Ed). *Accreditation:* NCATE. Part-time and evening/weekend programs available. *Degree requirements:* For master's, thesis. *Entrance requirements:* For master's, GRE or MAT, minimum GPA of 2.75. Additional exam requirements/recommendations for international students: Required—TOEFL. Electronic applications accepted. *Faculty research:* Cultural enrichment, research skills, parental involvement relating to reading skills, reading strategies for mainstreaming children.

Duquesne University, School of Education, Department of Instruction and Leadership, Program in Instructional Technology, Pittsburgh, PA 15282-0001. Offers MS Ed, Ed D. Part-time programs available. Postbaccalaureate distance learning degree programs offered (minimal on-campus study). *Faculty:* 3 full-time (1 woman), 4 part-time/adjunct (2 women). *Students:* 50 full-time (32 women), 42 part-time (23 women); includes 7 minority (3 African Americans, 3 Asian Americans or Pacific Islanders, 1 Hispanic American), 8 international. Average age 36. 21 applicants, 81% accepted, 12 enrolled. In 2009, 23 master's, 9 doctorates awarded. *Entrance requirements:* For master's, MAT, minimum GPA of 3.0; for doctorate, GRE. Additional exam requirements/recommendations for international students: Required—TOEFL (minimum score 550 paper-based; 80 computer-based). *Application deadline:* For fall admission, 8/1 priority date for domestic students; for spring admission, 12/1 priority date for domestic students. Applications are processed on a rolling basis. Application fee: $0. Electronic applications accepted. *Expenses:* Tuition: Part-time $851 per credit. Required fees: $81 per credit. *Financial support:* Available to part-time students. *Unit head:* Dr. David Carbonara, Director, 412-396-4039, Fax: 412-396-1997, E-mail: carbonara@duq.edu. *Application contact:* Michael Dolinger, Director of Student and Academic Services, 412-396-6647, Fax: 412-396-5585, E-mail: dolingerm@duq.edu.

East Carolina University, Graduate School, College of Education, Department of Library Science and Instructional Technology, Greenville, NC 27858-4353. Offers instruction technology specialist (MA Ed); library science (MLS, CAS). *Accreditation:* NCATE. Part-time and evening/weekend programs available. Postbaccalaureate distance learning degree programs offered (no on-campus study). *Degree requirements:* For master's, comprehensive exam, thesis optional. *Entrance requirements:* For master's, GRE General Test or MAT, interview, minimum GPA of 2.5, bachelor's degree in related field, teaching license (MA Ed). Additional exam requirements/recommendations for international students: Required—TOEFL.

Eastern Connecticut State University, School of Education and Professional Studies/Graduate Division, Program in Educational Technology, Willimantic, CT 06226-2295. Offers

MS. Part-time and evening/weekend programs available. *Degree requirements:* For master's, comprehensive exam or thesis. *Entrance requirements:* For master's, minimum GPA of 2.7. Additional exam requirements/recommendations for international students: Required—TOEFL (minimum score 550 paper-based; 213 computer-based). Electronic applications accepted.

Eastern Michigan University, Graduate School, College of Education, Department of Teacher Education, Program in Educational Media and Technology, Ypsilanti, MI 48197. Offers MA, Graduate Certificate. Part-time and evening/weekend programs available. Postbaccalaureate distance learning degree programs offered (minimal on-campus study). *Students:* 1 (woman) full-time, 48 part-time (32 women); includes 5 minority (2 African Americans, 1 American Indian/Alaska Native, 1 Asian American or Pacific Islander, 1 Hispanic American). Average age 33. In 2009, 7 master's, 1 other advanced degree awarded. *Entrance requirements:* Additional exam requirements/recommendations for international students: Required—TOEFL. *Application deadline:* Applications are processed on a rolling basis. Application fee: $35. Tuition and fees vary according to course level. *Financial support:* Fellowships, research assistantships with full tuition reimbursements, teaching assistantships with full tuition reimbursements, career-related internships or fieldwork, Federal Work-Study, institutionally sponsored loans, scholarships/grants, tuition waivers (partial), and unspecified assistantships available. Support available to part-time students. Financial award applicants required to submit FAFSA. *Unit head:* Dr. Jon Margerum-Leys, Coordinator, 734-487-3260, Fax: 734-487-2101, E-mail: jon.margerum-leys@emich.edu. *Application contact:* Dr. Jon Margerum-Leys, Coordinator, 734-487-3260, Fax: 734-487-2101, E-mail: jon.margerum-leys@emich.edu.

Eastern Washington University, Graduate Studies, College of Education and Human Development, Department of Education, Program in Instructional Media and Technology, Cheney, WA 99004-2431. Offers M Ed. *Expenses:* Tuition, state resident: full-time $7476; part-time $249 per quarter hour. Tuition, nonresident: full-time $18,030; part-time $601 per quarter hour. Required fees: $3.50 per quarter hour. $142 per quarter.

East Stroudsburg University of Pennsylvania, Graduate School, College of Education, Department of Media Communications and Technology, East Stroudsburg, PA 18301-2999. Offers instructional technology (M Ed). Part-time and evening/weekend programs available. *Faculty:* 4 full-time (3 women), 1 (woman) part-time/adjunct. *Students:* 6 full-time (2 women), 19 part-time (12 women); includes 4 minority (2 Asian Americans or Pacific Islanders, 2 Hispanic Americans), 2 international. Average age 34. In 2009, 5 master's awarded. *Degree requirements:* For master's, comprehensive exam, comprehensive portfolio, internship. *Entrance requirements:* For master's, two letters of recommendation, portfolio or interview, minimum overall undergraduate QPA of 2.5, internship. Additional exam requirements/recommendations for international students: Required—TOEFL (minimum score 560 paper-based; 220 computer-based; 83 iBT). *Application deadline:* For fall admission, 7/31 priority date for domestic students, 5/1 priority date for international students; for spring admission, 11/30 for domestic students, 10/1 for international students. Application fee: $50. *Expenses:* Tuition, state resident: full-time $9942; part-time $387 per credit. Tuition, nonresident: full-time $14,240; part-time $619 per credit. *Financial support:* In 2009–10, 8 research assistantships with full and partial tuition reimbursements (averaging $2,189 per year) were awarded; career-related internships or fieldwork, Federal Work-Study, and institutionally sponsored loans also available. Financial award application deadline: 3/1; financial award applicants required to submit FAFSA. *Unit head:* Dr. Beth Sockman, Graduate Coordinator, 570-422-3621, Fax: 570-422-3506, E-mail: bsockman@po-box.esu.edu. *Application contact:* Kevin Quintero, Graduate Admissions Coordinator, 570-422-3890, Fax: 570-422-2711, E-mail: kquintero@po-box.esu.edu.

East Tennessee State University, School of Graduate Studies, College of Education, Department of Curriculum and Instruction, Johnson City, TN 37614. Offers 7-12 (MAT); classroom technology (M Ed); educational communication (M Ed); educational media/educational technology (M Ed); elementary education (M Ed, MAT); K-12 (MAT); reading and storytelling (M Ed, MA); reading education (M Ed, MA); school library media (M Ed); secondary education (M Ed, MAT). *Accreditation:* NCATE. Part-time and evening/weekend programs available. *Degree requirements:* For master's, thesis (for some programs). *Entrance requirements:* For master's, GRE, minimum GPA of 3.0. Additional exam requirements/recommendations for international students: Required—TOEFL (minimum score 550 paper-based; 213 computer-based). *Faculty research:* Critical thinking, curriculum development, cultural diversity, cognitive processes, effective teaching strategies.

Emporia State University, School of Graduate Studies, The Teachers College, Department of Instructional Design and Technology, Emporia, KS 66801-5087. Offers MS. *Accreditation:* NCATE. Part-time programs available. Postbaccalaureate distance learning degree programs offered (minimal on-campus study). *Faculty:* 6 full-time (3 women), 1 part-time/adjunct (0 women). *Students:* 21 full-time (13 women), 96 part-time (67 women); includes 5 minority (4 African Americans, 1 Hispanic American), 13 international. 18 applicants, 89% accepted, 16 enrolled. In 2009, 41 master's awarded. *Degree requirements:* For master's, comprehensive exam (for some programs), thesis (for some programs), project. *Entrance requirements:* For master's, appropriate bachelor's degree, letters of recommendation. Additional exam requirements/recommendations for international students: Required—TOEFL (minimum score 520 paper-based; 133 computer-based; 68 iBT). *Application deadline:* For fall admission, 8/15 priority date for domestic students. Applications are processed on a rolling basis. Application fee: $30 ($75 for international students). Electronic applications accepted. *Expenses:* Tuition, state resident: full-time $4154; part-time $173 per credit hour. Tuition, nonresident: full-time $12,864; part-time $536 per credit hour. Required fees: $948; $58 per credit hour. Tuition and fees vary according to campus/location. *Financial support:* In 2009–10, 4 teaching assistantships with full tuition reimbursements (averaging $3,751 per year) were awarded; Federal Work-Study, institutionally sponsored loans, health care benefits, and unspecified assistantships also available. Financial award application deadline: 3/15; financial award applicants required to submit FAFSA. *Unit head:* Dr. Marcus Childress, Chair, 620-341-5627, E-mail: mchildre@emporia.edu. *Application contact:* Mary Sewell, Admissions Coordinator, 800-950-GRAD, Fax: 620-341-5909, E-mail: msewell@emporia.edu.

Fairfield University, Graduate School of Education and Allied Professions, Department of Curriculum and Instruction, Fairfield, CT 06824-5195. Offers bilingual education (CAS); elementary education (MA); media/educational technology (MA); secondary education (MA); teaching and foundations (MA, CAS); TESOL, foreign language and bilingual/multicultural education (MA, CAS). Part-time and evening/weekend programs available. *Degree requirements:* For master's, comprehensive exam, thesis or alternative. *Entrance requirements:* For master's, PRAXIS I (PPST), minimum QPA of 3.0, 2 recommendations, resume. Additional exam requirements/recommendations for international students: Required—TOEFL (minimum score 550 paper-based; 213 computer-based; 80 iBT). Electronic applications accepted. *Faculty research:* Urban and multicultural education; participatory action for social justice; culture and family; second language acquisition; science, technology and social education.

Fairfield University, Graduate School of Education and Allied Professions, Department of Psychological and Educational Consultation, Fairfield, CT 06824-5195. Offers applied psychology (MA), including foundations of advanced psychology, human services, industrial/organizational/personnel; media/educational technology (MA); school media specialist (MA); school psychology (MA, CAS); special education (MA, CAS). Part-time and evening/weekend programs available. *Degree requirements:* For master's, comprehensive exam, thesis optional. *Entrance requirements:* For master's, PRAXIS I (PPST), minimum QPA of 3.0, 2 recommendations, resume. Additional exam requirements/recommendations for international students: Required—TOEFL (minimum score 550 paper-based; 213 computer-based; 80 iBT). Electronic applications accepted. *Faculty research:* Child neuropsychology, disabilities, effect of pre-treatment orientation on treatment, autism, technology in business and classroom, collaboration with schools, communities and industry.

Fairleigh Dickinson University, College at Florham, University College: Arts, Sciences, and Professional Studies, Peter Sammartino School of Education, Madison, NJ 07940-1099. Offers education for certified teachers (MA, Certificate); educational leadership (MA); instructional technology (Certificate); literacy/reading (Certificate); teaching (MAT). *Students:* 66 full-time (53 women), 49 part-time (25 women). Average age 27. 91 applicants, 87% accepted, 68 enrolled. In 2009, 74 master's awarded. *Application deadline:* Applications are processed on a rolling basis. Application fee: $40. *Application contact:* Susan Brooman, University Director, Graduate Admissions, 973-443-8905, Fax: 973-443-8088, E-mail: grad@fdu.edu.

Fairleigh Dickinson University, Metropolitan Campus, University College: Arts, Sciences, and Professional Studies, Peter Sammartino School of Education, Teaneck, NJ 07666-1914. Offers dyslexia specialist (Certificate); education for certified teachers (MA); educational leadership (MA); instructional technology (Certificate); learning disabilities (MA); literacy/reading (Certificate); multilingual education (MA); teacher of the handicapped (Certificate); teaching (MAT). *Accreditation:* Teacher Education Accreditation Council. Part-time programs available. *Students:* 61 full-time (56 women), 530 part-time (464 women), 10 international. Average age 36. 283 applicants, 93% accepted, 231 enrolled. In 2009, 152 master's awarded. *Degree requirements:* For master's, research project (MAT). *Application deadline:* Applications are processed on a rolling basis. Application fee: $40. *Unit head:* Dr. Vicki Cohen, Director, 201-692-2525, Fax: 201-692-2603, E-mail: vicki_cohen@fdu.edu. *Application contact:* Susan Brooman, University Director of Graduate Admissions, 201-692-2554, Fax: 201-692-2560, E-mail: globaleducation@fdu.edu.

Ferris State University, College of Education and Human Services, School of Education, Big Rapids, MI 49307. Offers administration (MSCTE); curriculum and instruction (M Ed), including administration, elementary education, experiential education, philanthropic education, reading, secondary education, special education, subject matter option; education technology (MSCTE); instructor (MSCTE); post-secondary administration (MSCTE); training and development (MSCTE). Part-time and evening/weekend programs available. Postbaccalaureate distance learning degree programs offered. *Faculty:* 12 full-time (8 women), 11 part-time/adjunct (5 women). *Students:* 19 full-time (13 women), 185 part-time (122 women); includes 24 minority (20 African Americans, 1 Asian American or Pacific Islander, 3 Hispanic Americans), 1 international. Average age 36. 37 applicants, 32% accepted, 11 enrolled. In 2009, 73 master's awarded. *Degree requirements:* For master's, thesis, research paper. *Entrance requirements:* For master's, 2 years of work experience for vocational setting, minimum GPA of 2.75. Additional exam requirements/recommendations for international students: Recommended—TOEFL (minimum score 500 paper-based; 173 computer-based; 61 iBT). *Application deadline:* For fall admission, 7/1 priority date for domestic students; for spring admission, 11/1 priority date for domestic students. Applications are processed on a rolling basis. Application fee: $30. *Financial support:* Career-related internships or fieldwork and scholarships/grants available. Support available to part-time students. Financial award applicants required to submit FAFSA. *Faculty research:* Suicide prevention, reading, women in education, special needs, administration. *Unit head:* Dr. Liza Ing, Director, 231-591-5362, Fax: 231-591-2041. *Application contact:* Kimisue Worrall, Secretary, 231-591-5361, Fax: 231-591-2043.

Fielding Graduate University, Graduate Programs, School of Educational Leadership and Change, Santa Barbara, CA 93105-3538. Offers collaborative educational leadership (MA); educational leadership and change (Ed D); teaching in the virtual classroom (Graduate Certificate). Postbaccalaureate distance learning degree programs offered (minimal on-campus study). *Faculty:* 17 full-time (9 women), 18 part-time/adjunct (9 women). *Students:* 409 full-time (289 women), 8 part-time (5 women); includes 156 minority (100 African Americans, 7 American Indian/Alaska Native, 13 Asian Americans or Pacific Islanders, 36 Hispanic Americans), 4 international. Average age 44. 75 applicants, 92% accepted, 45 enrolled. In 2009, 99 master's, 32 doctorates, 23 other advanced degrees awarded. *Degree requirements:* For master's, capstone research project; for doctorate, comprehensive exam, thesis/dissertation. *Entrance requirements:* For master's, minimum GPA of 2.5; for doctorate, resume, 2 letters of recommendation, writing sample. *Application deadline:* For fall admission, 7/31 priority date for domestic students, 7/31 for international students; for spring admission, 11/19 priority date for domestic students, 11/19 for international students. Application fee: $75. Electronic applications accepted. *Expenses:* Contact institution. *Financial support:* In 2009–10, 293 students received support. Scholarships/grants, health care benefits, and tuition waivers (partial) available. Support available to part-time students. Financial award application deadline: 5/15; financial award applicants required to submit FAFSA. *Unit head:* Dr. Judy Witt, Dean, 805-898-2940, E-mail: jwitt@fielding.edu. *Application contact:* Kristin Kontilis, Admission Counselor, 800-340-1099, Fax: 805-687-9793, E-mail: kkontilis@fielding.edu.

Fitchburg State University, Division of Graduate and Continuing Education, Program in Applied Communications, Fitchburg, MA 01420-2697. Offers applied communications (MS, Certificate); library media (MS); technical and professional writing (MS). Part-time and evening/weekend programs available. *Students:* 3 full-time (2 women), 18 part-time (10 women), 2 international. Average age 33. 8 applicants, 88% accepted, 6 enrolled. In 2009, 10 master's awarded. *Entrance requirements:* For master's, GRE General Test or MAT, minimum 2 years of related experience, letters of recommendation, resume. Additional exam requirements/recommendations for international students: Required—TOEFL (minimum score 550 paper-based; 213 computer-based; 79 iBT). *Application deadline:* Applications are processed on a rolling basis. Application fee: $25 ($50 for international students). *Expenses:* Tuition, area resident: Part-time $150 per credit. Tuition, state resident: part-time $150 per credit. Tuition, nonresident: part-time $150 per credit. Required fees: $120 per credit. *Financial support:* In 2009–10, research assistantships with partial tuition reimbursements (averaging $5,500 per year); Federal Work-Study, scholarships/grants, and unspecified assistantships also available. Support available to part-time students. Financial award application deadline: 3/1; financial award applicants required to submit FAFSA. *Unit head:* Dr. John Chetro-Szivos, Chair, 978-665-3261, Fax: 978-665-3658, E-mail: gce@fsc.edu. *Application contact:* Director of Admissions, 978-665-3144, Fax: 978-665-4540, E-mail: admissions@fsc.edu.

Florida Gulf Coast University, College of Education, Program in Curriculum and Instruction, Fort Myers, FL 33965-6565. Offers educational technology (M Ed, MA); English education (M Ed). Part-time and evening/weekend programs available. Postbaccalaureate distance learning degree programs offered (minimal on-campus study). *Faculty:* 31 full-time (23 women), 41 part-time/adjunct (29 women). *Students:* 54 full-time (42 women), 4 part-time (3 women); includes 7 minority (1 African American, 1 Asian American or Pacific Islander, 5 Hispanic Americans). Average age 35. 20 applicants, 70% accepted, 0 enrolled. In 2009, 8 master's awarded. *Degree requirements:* For master's, final project or portfolio. *Entrance requirements:* For master's, GRE General Test, MAT, minimum undergraduate GPA of 3.0 in last 2 years. Additional exam requirements/recommendations for international students: Required—TOEFL (minimum score 550 paper-based; 213 computer-based). *Application deadline:* For fall admission, 7/1 priority date for domestic students; for spring admission, 10/15 for domestic students. Applications are processed on a rolling basis. Application fee: $30. Electronic applications accepted. *Faculty research:* Internet in schools, technology in pre-service and in-service teacher training. *Unit head:* Dr. Pat Wachholz, Associate Dean, 239-590-7808, Fax: 239-590-7801, E-mail: wachhol@fgcu.edu. *Application contact:* Dr. Pat Wachholz, Associate Dean, 239-590-7808, Fax: 239-590-7801, E-mail: wachhol@fgcu.edu.

Florida International University, College of Education, Department of Curriculum and Instruction, Miami, FL 33199. Offers art education (MAT, MS, Ed D); curriculum and instruction (Ed S); curriculum development (MS); curriculum studies (PhD); early childhood education (MS, Ed D); elementary education (MS, Ed D); English education (MAT, MS, Ed D); foreign language education—teaching English to speakers of other languages (TESOL) (Certificate), including foreign language education; foreign language education- teaching English to speakers of other languages (TESOL) (MS), including teaching English; French education—initial teacher preparation (MAT); international and intercultural development education (Ed D); international and intercultural developmental education (MS); language, literacy and culture (PhD); learning technologies (MS, Ed D, PhD); mathematics education (MAT, MS, Ed D, PhD); modern language education/bilingual education (MS, Ed D); physical education (MS); reading education (MS, Ed D); science education (MAT, MS, Ed D, PhD); social studies education (MAT, MS, Ed D); Spanish education—initial teacher preparation (MAT); special education (MS). Part-time and evening/weekend programs available. *Degree requirements:* For doctorate, comprehensive exam, thesis/dissertation. *Entrance requirements:* For master's, GRE General Test, Florida

Educational Media/Instructional Technology

Florida International University (continued)
General Knowledge Test or Florida College Level Academic Skills Test; for doctorate and other advanced degree, GRE General Test. Additional exam requirements/recommendations for international students: Required—TOEFL (minimum score 550 paper-based; 213 computer-based; 80 iBT), IELTS (minimum score 6.3). Electronic applications accepted. *Expenses:* Tuition, state resident: full-time $8008; part-time $4004 per year. Tuition, nonresident: full-time $20,104; part-time $10,052 per year. Required fees: $298; $149 per term.

Florida State University, The Graduate School, College of Education, Department of Educational Psychology and Learning Systems, Program in Instructional Systems, Tallahassee, FL 32306. Offers instructional systems (MS, PhD, Ed S); open and distance learning (MS); performance improvement and human resources (MS). *Faculty:* 6 full-time (3 women), 4 part-time/adjunct (1 woman). *Students:* 51 full-time (34 women), 60 part-time (35 women); includes 19 minority (9 African Americans, 2 American Indian/Alaska Native, 5 Asian Americans or Pacific Islanders, 3 Hispanic Americans), 26 international. 68 applicants, 16% accepted, 11 enrolled. In 2009, 25 master's, 9 doctorates awarded. *Degree requirements:* For master's and Ed S, comprehensive exam, thesis optional; for doctorate, comprehensive exam, thesis/dissertation. *Entrance requirements:* For master's, doctorate, and Ed S, GRE General Test, minimum GPA of 3.0. Additional exam requirements/recommendations for international students: Required—TOEFL (minimum score 550 paper-based; 213 computer-based; 80 iBT). *Application deadline:* For fall admission, 6/1 priority date for domestic and international students; for spring admission, 10/1 priority date for domestic and international students. Applications are processed on a rolling basis. Application fee: $30. *Expenses:* Tuition, state resident: full-time $7413. Tuition, nonresident: full-time $22,567. *Financial support:* In 2009–10, 3 fellowships with full and partial tuition reimbursements, 8 research assistantships with full and partial tuition reimbursements, 6 teaching assistantships with full and partial tuition reimbursements were awarded; career-related internships or fieldwork and Federal Work-Study also available. Financial award applicants required to submit FAFSA. *Faculty research:* Human performance improvement, educational semiotics, development of software tools to measure online interaction among learners. *Unit head:* Dr. Vanessa Dennen, Program Coordinator, 850-644-8783, Fax: 850-644-8776, E-mail: vdennen@fsu.edu. *Application contact:* Mary Kate McKee, Program Coordinator, 850-644-8792, Fax: 850-644-8776, E-mail: mmckee@oddl.fsu.edu.

Fort Hays State University, Graduate School, College of Education and Technology, Department of Technology Studies, Hays, KS 67601-4099. Offers instructional technology (MS). *Degree requirements:* For master's, comprehensive exam, thesis or alternative. *Entrance requirements:* Additional exam requirements/recommendations for international students: Required—TOEFL (minimum score 550 paper-based; 213 computer-based). Electronic applications accepted.

Framingham State University, Division of Graduate and Continuing Education, Program in Curriculum and Instructional Technology, Framingham, MA 01701-9101. Offers M Ed. Postbaccalaureate distance learning degree programs offered.

Fresno Pacific University, Graduate Programs, School of Education, Fresno, CA 93702-4709. Offers administration (MA Ed), including administrative services; foundations, curriculum and teaching (MA Ed), including curriculum and teaching, school library and information technology; language, literacy, and culture (MA Ed), including bilingual/cross-cultural education, language development, multilingual contexts, reading; mathematics/science/computer education (MA Ed), including educational technology, integrated mathematics/science education, mathematics education; pupil personnel services (MA Ed), including school counseling, school psychology; special education (MA Ed), including mild/moderate, moderate/severe, physical and health impairments. Part-time and evening/weekend programs available. *Degree requirements:* For master's, thesis (for some programs). *Entrance requirements:* For master's, interview; GMAT, GRE, MAT, or 6 units of course work with a faculty recommendation. Additional exam requirements/recommendations for international students: Required—TOEFL (minimum score 550 paper-based; 213 computer-based). Electronic applications accepted.

Fresno Pacific University, Graduate Programs, School of Education, Division of Foundations, Curriculum and Teaching, Program in School Library and Information Technology, Fresno, CA 93702-4709. Offers MA Ed. Part-time and evening/weekend programs available. *Degree requirements:* For master's, thesis or alternative. *Entrance requirements:* Additional exam requirements/recommendations for international students: Required—TOEFL (minimum score 550 paper-based; 213 computer-based). Electronic applications accepted.

Fresno Pacific University, Graduate Programs, School of Education, Division of Mathematics/Science/Computer Education, Program in Educational Technology, Fresno, CA 93702-4709. Offers MA Ed. Part-time and evening/weekend programs available. *Degree requirements:* For master's, thesis or alternative. *Entrance requirements:* Additional exam requirements/recommendations for international students: Required—TOEFL (minimum score 550 paper-based; 213 computer-based).

Frostburg State University, Graduate School, College of Education, Department of Educational Professions, Program in Curriculum and Instruction, Frostburg, MD 21532-1099. Offers educational technology (M Ed); elementary education (M Ed); secondary education (M Ed). Part-time and evening/weekend programs available. *Faculty:* 2. *Students:* 5 full-time (all women), 42 part-time (36 women); includes 1 minority (Hispanic American). Average age 32. 20 applicants, 75% accepted, 13 enrolled. In 2009, 8 master's awarded. *Degree requirements:* For master's, thesis or alternative. *Entrance requirements:* For master's, teaching certificate. Additional exam requirements/recommendations for international students: Required—TOEFL. *Application deadline:* For fall admission, 7/15 priority date for domestic students. Applications are processed on a rolling basis. Application fee: $30. Electronic applications accepted. *Expenses:* Tuition, state resident: full-time $5706; part-time $317 per credit hour. Tuition, nonresident: full-time $6948; part-time $386 per credit hour. Required fees: $1476; $82 per credit hour. $11 per term. One-time fee: $30 full-time. *Financial support:* In 2009–10, 2 research assistantships with full tuition reimbursements (averaging $5,000 per year) were awarded. Financial award application deadline: 4/1; financial award applicants required to submit FAFSA. *Unit head:* Dr. Doris Santamaria-Makang, Coordinator, 301-687-7018, E-mail: dsantamaria@frostburg.edu. *Application contact:* Vickie Mazer, Director, Graduate Services, 301-687-7053, Fax: 301-687-4597, E-mail: vmmazer@frostburg.edu.

Full Sail University, Education Media Design and Technology Master of Science Program—Online, Winter Park, FL 32792-7437. Offers MS. Postbaccalaureate distance learning degree programs offered (no on-campus study). *Entrance requirements:* Additional exam requirements/recommendations for international students: Required—TOEFL (minimum score 550 paper-based; 213 computer-based; 79 iBT).

Gannon University, School of Graduate Studies, College of Humanities, Education, and Social Sciences, School of Education, Program in Educational Computing Technology, Erie, PA 16541-0001. Offers M Ed. Part-time and evening/weekend programs available. *Degree requirements:* For master's, comprehensive exam, thesis. *Entrance requirements:* For master's, GRE or MAT, interview, teaching certificate. Additional exam requirements/recommendations for international students: Required—TOEFL (minimum score 79 iBT). *Application deadline:* Applications are processed on a rolling basis. Application fee: $25. Electronic applications accepted. *Expenses:* Contact institution. *Financial support:* Application deadline: 7/1. *Application contact:* Kara Morgan, Assistant Director of Graduate Admissions, 814-871-5831, Fax: 814-871-5827, E-mail: graduate@gannon.edu.

Gannon University, School of Graduate Studies, College of Humanities, Education, and Social Sciences, School of Education, Program in Instructional Technology Specialist, Erie, PA 16541-0001. Offers Certificate. Part-time and evening/weekend programs available. *Entrance requirements:* Additional exam requirements/recommendations for international students: Required—TOEFL (minimum score 500 paper-based; 173 computer-based). *Application deadline:* Applications are processed on a rolling basis. Application fee: $25. Electronic applications accepted. *Expenses:* Contact institution. *Financial support:* Application deadline: 7/1. *Unit head:* Dr. Francis S. Grandinetti, Director, 814-871-7533, E-mail: grandine002@gannon.edu. *Application contact:* Kara Morgan, Assistant Director of Graduate Admissions, 814-871-5831, Fax: 814-871-5827, E-mail: graduate@gannon.edu.

George Fox University, School of Education, Educational Foundations and Leadership Program, Newberg, OR 97132-2697. Offers continuing administrator license (Certificate); curriculum and instruction (M Ed); educational leadership (M Ed, Ed D); higher education (M Ed); initial administrator license (Certificate); library media (M Ed, Certificate); literacy (M Ed); reading (M Ed); secondary education (M Ed). *Accreditation:* NCATE. Part-time and evening/weekend programs available. Postbaccalaureate distance learning degree programs offered (minimal on-campus study). *Faculty:* 10 full-time (3 women), 7 part-time/adjunct (3 women). *Students:* 1 (woman) full-time, 151 part-time (101 women); includes 15 minority (1 African American, 4 American Indian/Alaska Native, 4 Asian Americans or Pacific Islanders, 6 Hispanic Americans), 1 international. Average age 40. 44 applicants, 75% accepted, 26 enrolled. In 2009, 44 master's, 27 doctorates, 82 Certificates awarded. *Degree requirements:* For master's, thesis (for some programs); for doctorate, comprehensive exam, thesis/dissertation, project. *Entrance requirements:* For master's, minimum undergraduate GPA of 3.0 during previous 2 years of course work, resume, 3 professional recommendations on university forms, copy of teaching license (if applicable); for doctorate, GRE or MAT, master's degree with minimum GPA of 3.25, 3 years of relevant professional experience, interview, personal essay, scholarly work, 3 professional recommendations on university forms along with 3 written letters of recommendation, official transcripts. Additional exam requirements/recommendations for international students: Required—TOEFL (minimum score 577 paper-based; 233 computer-based; 90 iBT). *Application deadline:* For fall admission, 7/15 for domestic and international students; for winter admission, 11/1 for domestic and international students; for spring admission, 4/1 for domestic and international students. Applications are processed on a rolling basis. Application fee: $40. Electronic applications accepted. *Expenses:* Contact institution. *Financial support:* Career-related internships or fieldwork available. Financial award applicants required to submit FAFSA. *Unit head:* Dr. Scott Headley, Chair, 503-554-2836, E-mail: sheadley@georgefox.edu. *Application contact:* Kristie DeHaven, Admissions Counselor, 800-631-0921, Fax: 503-554-3110, E-mail: edfl@georgefox.edu.

The George Washington University, Graduate School of Education and Human Development, Department of Educational Leadership, Program in Educational Technology Leadership, Washington, DC 20052. Offers MA Ed. *Accreditation:* NCATE. Part-time and evening/weekend programs available. *Students:* 3 full-time (all women), 54 part-time (32 women); includes 13 minority (5 African Americans, 2 Asian Americans or Pacific Islanders, 6 Hispanic Americans), 2 international. Average age 37. 26 applicants, 100% accepted, 16 enrolled. In 2009, 29 master's awarded. *Degree requirements:* For master's, comprehensive exam, thesis or alternative. *Entrance requirements:* For master's, GRE General Test or MAT, minimum GPA of 2.75. *Application deadline:* For fall admission, 1/15 priority date for domestic students; for spring admission, 10/1 for domestic students. Applications are processed on a rolling basis. Application fee: $60. *Expenses:* Contact institution. *Financial support:* Fellowships, research assistantships, teaching assistantships, career-related internships or fieldwork available. Financial award application deadline: 1/15. *Faculty research:* Interactive multimedia, distance education, federal technology policy. *Unit head:* Dr. Michael Corry, Director, 202-994-9295, E-mail: mcorry@gwu.edu. *Application contact:* Sarah Lang, Director of Graduate Admissions, 202-994-1447, Fax: 202-994-7207, E-mail: slang@gwu.edu.

Georgia College & State University, Graduate School, The John H. Lounsbury College of Education, Department of Foundations and Secondary Education, Milledgeville, GA 31061. Offers curriculum and instruction (Ed S), including secondary education; instructional technology (M Ed); secondary education (M Ed, MAT). *Accreditation:* NCATE. Part-time and evening/weekend programs available. *Faculty:* 13 full-time (7 women). *Students:* 127 full-time (81 women), 99 part-time (83 women); includes 39 minority (34 African Americans, 5 Hispanic Americans). Average age 32. In 2009, 104 master's awarded. *Degree requirements:* For master's and Ed S, comprehensive exam. *Entrance requirements:* For master's, on-site writing assessment, 2 letters of recommendation, level 4 teaching certificate; for Ed S, on-site writing assessment, master's degree, 2 letters of recommendation, 2 years of teaching experience, level 5 teacher certification. Additional exam requirements/recommendations for international students: Recommended—TOEFL (minimum score 550 paper-based; 213 computer-based; 79 iBT). *Application deadline:* Applications are processed on a rolling basis. Application fee: $40. Electronic applications accepted. *Expenses:* Tuition, area resident: Part-time $241 per credit hour. Tuition, state resident: full-time $4338. Tuition, nonresident: full-time $17,352; part-time $964 per credit hour. Required fees: $609 per semester. Tuition and fees vary according to course load and campus/location. *Financial support:* In 2009–10, 12 research assistantships with full tuition reimbursements were awarded; career-related internships or fieldwork and Federal Work-Study also available. Support available to part-time students. Financial award applicants required to submit FAFSA. *Unit head:* Dr. Jane Hinson, Chair, 478-445-7368, Fax: 478-445-2513, E-mail: jane.hinson@gcsu.edu. *Application contact:* Shanda Brand, Graduate Advisor, 478-445-1383, E-mail: shanda.brand@gcsu.edu.

Georgia Southern University, Jack N. Averitt College of Graduate Studies, College of Education, Department of Leadership, Technology, and Human Development, Program in Instructional Technology, Statesboro, GA 30460. Offers M Ed. Part-time and evening/weekend programs available. Postbaccalaureate distance learning degree programs offered (no on-campus study). *Students:* 38 full-time (32 women), 180 part-time (164 women); includes 36 minority (33 African Americans, 1 Asian American or Pacific Islander, 2 Hispanic Americans), 1 international. Average age 35. 78 applicants, 100% accepted, 56 enrolled. In 2009, 25 master's awarded. *Degree requirements:* For master's, portfolio, transition point assessments. *Entrance requirements:* For master's, GRE General Test or MAT, minimum GPA of 2.5. Additional exam requirements/recommendations for international students: Required—TOEFL (minimum score 550 paper-based; 213 computer-based; 80 iBT). *Application deadline:* For fall admission, 3/1 priority date for domestic and international students; for spring admission, 10/1 priority date for domestic students, 10/1 for international students. Applications are processed on a rolling basis. Application fee: $50. Electronic applications accepted. *Expenses:* Tuition, state resident: full-time $5040; part-time $210 per credit hour. Tuition, nonresident: full-time $20,136; part-time $839 per credit hour. Required fees: $1644. *Financial support:* In 2009–10, 136 students received support; research assistantships, teaching assistantships, career-related internships or fieldwork and scholarships/grants available. Support available to part-time students. Financial award application deadline: 4/15; financial award applicants required to submit FAFSA. *Unit head:* Dr. Judith Repman, Coordinator, 912-478-5394, Fax: 912-478-7104, E-mail: edowns@georgiasouthern.edu. *Application contact:* Dr. Charles Ziglar, Coordinator for Graduate Student Recruitment, 912-478-5635, Fax: 912-478-0740, E-mail: gradadmissions@georgiasouthern.edu.

Georgia State University, College of Education, Department of Middle-Secondary Education and Instructional Technology, Library Science/Media Unit, Atlanta, GA 30302-3083. Offers instructional technology (MS, PhD, Ed S); library media technology (MLM, PhD, Ed S). Part-time and evening/weekend programs available. *Degree requirements:* For master's, comprehensive exam; for doctorate, comprehensive exam, thesis/dissertation; for Ed S, project/exam. *Entrance requirements:* For master's, GRE General Test, minimum GPA of 2.5; for doctorate, GRE General Test or MAT, minimum GPA of 3.3; for Ed S, GRE General Test or MAT, minimum graduate GPA of 3.25. *Faculty research:* Automation, children's literature, cataloging, electronic resources.

Governors State University, College of Arts and Sciences, Program in Communication and Training, University Park, IL 60466-0975. Offers communication studies (MA); instructional and training technology (MA); media communication (MA). Part-time and evening/weekend programs available. *Degree requirements:* For master's, thesis or alternative.

Graceland University, Gleazer School of Education, Lamoni, IA 50140. Offers collaborative learning and teaching (M Ed); differentiated instruction (M Ed); instructional leadership (M Ed); mild/moderate special education (M Ed); quality schools (M Ed); technology integration (M Ed). *Accreditation:* NCATE. Part-time and evening/weekend programs available. Postbaccalaureate

distance learning degree programs offered (no on-campus study). *Faculty:* 8 full-time (7 women), 25 part-time/adjunct (14 women). *Students:* 505 full-time (406 women); includes 18 minority (6 African Americans, 3 American Indian/Alaska Native, 4 Asian Americans or Pacific Islanders, 5 Hispanic Americans), 7 international. Average age 36. 167 applicants, 100% accepted, 160 enrolled. In 2009, 277 master's awarded. *Degree requirements:* For master's, action research project. *Entrance requirements:* For master's, minimum GPA of 3.0, teaching certificate, current teaching contract. *Application deadline:* For fall admission, 7/15 for domestic students; for winter admission, 10/15 for domestic students; for spring admission, 1/15 priority date for domestic students. Application fee: $50. Electronic applications accepted. *Expenses:* Tuition: Full-time $7110; part-time $395 per semester hour. Required fees: $1110; $185 per course. *Financial support:* In 2009–10, 437 students received support. Institutionally sponsored loans and scholarships/grants available. Financial award application deadline: 12/15; financial award applicants required to submit FAFSA. *Unit head:* Dr. Nancy Halferty, Dean, 641-784-5000 Ext. 5251, E-mail: halferty@graceland.edu. *Application contact:* Cathy Porter, Program Consultant, 816-833-0524 Ext. 4516, E-mail: cgporter@graceland.edu.

Grambling State University, School of Graduate Studies and Research, College of Education, Department of Educational Leadership, Grambling, LA 71245. Offers curriculum and instruction (Ed D); developmental education (MS, Ed D), including curriculum and instruction: reading (Ed D), English (MS), guidance and counseling (MS), higher education administration (Ed D), instructional systems and technology (Ed D), mathematics (MS), reading (MS), science (MS), student development and personnel services (Ed D); educational leadership (MS, Ed D). Part-time and evening/weekend programs available. *Faculty:* 19 full-time (12 women). *Students:* 23 full-time (18 women), 84 part-time (62 women); includes 81 minority (80 African Americans, 1 Asian American or Pacific Islander), 5 international. Average age 39. 72 applicants, 75% accepted, 39 enrolled. In 2009, 5 master's, 9 doctorates awarded. *Degree requirements:* For master's, comprehensive exam, thesis (for some programs); for doctorate, comprehensive exam, thesis/dissertation. *Entrance requirements:* For master's, GRE, minimum GPA of 2.5 on last degree; for doctorate, GRE (minimum 1000, 500 on Verbal), master's degree, minimum GPA of 3.0 on last degree. Additional exam requirements/recommendations for international students: Required—TOEFL (minimum score 500 paper-based; 173 computer-based; 61 iBT). *Application deadline:* For fall admission, 7/1 for domestic and international students; for spring admission, 12/1 for domestic and international students. Applications are processed on a rolling basis. Application fee: $20 ($30 for international students). Electronic applications accepted. *Expenses:* Tuition, state resident: full-time $2610. Tuition, nonresident: full-time $2610. *Financial support:* In 2009–10, 5 research assistantships (averaging $10,948 per year) were awarded; health care benefits, tuition waivers (full), and unspecified assistantships also available. Financial award application deadline: 5/31; financial award applicants required to submit FAFSA. *Unit head:* Dr. Olatunde Ogunyemi, Director, 318-274-6105, Fax: 318-274-2799, E-mail: ogunyemio@gram.edu. *Application contact:* Laketha Richards, Administrative Assistant III, 318-274-6105, Fax: 318-274-6249, E-mail: richardsl@gram.edu.

Grand Valley State University, College of Education, Programs in General Education, Allendale, MI 49401-9403. Offers adult and higher education (M Ed); early childhood education (M Ed); educational differentiation (M Ed); educational leadership (M Ed); educational technology integration (M Ed); elementary education (M Ed); middle level education (M Ed); school library media services (M Ed); secondary level education (M Ed); teaching English to speakers of other languages (M Ed). Part-time and evening/weekend programs available. Postbaccalaureate distance learning degree programs offered (minimal on-campus study). *Faculty:* 82 full-time (42 women), 43 part-time/adjunct (25 women). *Students:* 100 full-time (53 women), 723 part-time (478 women); includes 59 minority (25 African Americans, 4 American Indian/Alaska Native, 13 Asian Americans or Pacific Islanders, 17 Hispanic Americans), 10 international. Average age 33. 237 applicants, 96% accepted, 117 enrolled. In 2009, 291 master's awarded. *Degree requirements:* For master's, thesis. *Entrance requirements:* For master's, GRE General Test or minimum GPA of 3.0. Additional exam requirements/recommendations for international students: Required—TOEFL. *Application deadline:* Applications are processed on a rolling basis. Application fee: $30. Electronic applications accepted. *Expenses:* Tuition, state resident: part-time $471 per credit hour. Tuition, nonresident: part-time $646 per credit hour. Tuition and fees vary according to course level. *Financial support:* In 2009–10, 73 students received support, including 55 fellowships (averaging $2,273 per year), 19 research assistantships with full and partial tuition reimbursements available (averaging $8,000 per year); career-related internships or fieldwork, Federal Work-Study, scholarships/grants, and unspecified assistantships also available. *Faculty research:* Effectiveness of technology in education, parental involvement, effective teaching, effective schools research. *Unit head:* Dr. Linda McCrea, Director, 616-331-2080, E-mail: mccreal@gvsu.edu. *Application contact:* Thomas Owens, Student Information and Services Center, 616-331-6282, Fax: 616-331-2000, E-mail: owenst@gvsu.edu.

Harrisburg University of Science and Technology, Program in Learning Technologies, Harrisburg, PA 17101. Offers learning technologies (MS). Part-time and evening/weekend programs available. *Faculty:* 1 full-time (0 women), 4 part-time/adjunct (2 women). *Students:* 33 part-time (20 women). Average age 30. 37 applicants, 89% accepted, 33 enrolled. *Entrance requirements:* Additional exam requirements/recommendations for international students: Required—TOEFL (minimum score 520 paper-based; 200 computer-based; 80 iBT). *Application deadline:* For fall admission, 8/1 priority date for domestic students, 7/1 priority date for international students. Applications are processed on a rolling basis. Application fee: $0. Electronic applications accepted. *Expenses:* Tuition: Full-time $18,000; part-time $650 per semester hour. *Financial support:* In 2009–10, 2 students received support. Scholarships/grants available. Financial award applicants required to submit FAFSA. *Unit head:* Andy Petroski, Director of Learning Technologies and Assistant Professor, 717-901-5167, Fax: 717-901-3167, E-mail: apetroski@harrisburgu.edu. *Application contact:* Julie Cullings, Information Contact, 717-901-5163, Fax: 717-901-3163, E-mail: admissions@harrisburgu.edu.

Harvard University, Extension School, Cambridge, MA 02138-3722. Offers applied sciences (CAS); biotechnology (ALM); educational technologies (ALM); educational technology (CET); English for graduate and professional studies (DGP); environmental management (ALM, CEM); information technology (ALM); journalism (ALM); liberal arts (ALM); management (ALM, CM); mathematics for teaching (ALM); museum studies (ALM); premedical studies (Diploma); publication and communication (CPC). Part-time and evening/weekend programs available. *Degree requirements:* For master's, thesis. *Entrance requirements:* For master's, 3 completed graduate courses with grade of B or higher. Additional exam requirements/recommendations for international students: Required—TOEFL (minimum score 600 paper-based; 250 computer-based), TWE (minimum score 5). *Expenses:* Contact institution.

Harvard University, Graduate School of Education, Master's Programs in Education, Cambridge, MA 02138. Offers arts in education (Ed M); education policy and management (Ed M); higher education (Ed M); human development and psychology (Ed M); international education policy (Ed M); language and literacy (Ed M); learning and teaching (Ed M); mid-career mathematics and science (teaching certificate) (Ed M); mind brain and education (Ed M); risk and prevention (Ed M); school leadership (Ed M); special studies (Ed M); teaching and curriculum (teaching certificate) (Ed M); technology innovation and education (Ed M). Part-time programs available. *Faculty:* 70 full-time (33 women), 36 part-time/adjunct (20 women). *Students:* 598 full-time (448 women), 76 part-time (60 women); includes 132 minority (40 African Americans, 2 American Indian/Alaska Native, 58 Asian Americans or Pacific Islanders, 32 Hispanic Americans), 103 international. Average age 28. 1,574 applicants, 58% accepted, 640 enrolled. In 2009, 556 master's awarded. *Entrance requirements:* For master's, GRE General Test, 3 letters of recommendation. Additional exam requirements/recommendations for international students: Required—TOEFL (minimum score 600 paper-based; 250 computer-based; 100 iBT), TWE (minimum score 5). *Application deadline:* For fall admission, 1/4 for domestic and international students. Application fee: $85. Electronic applications accepted. *Expenses:* Contact institution. *Financial support:* In 2009–10, 424 students received support, including 25 fellowships with full and partial tuition reimbursements available (averaging $15,890 per year); career-related internships or fieldwork, Federal Work-Study, institutionally sponsored loans, scholarships/grants, health care benefits, tuition waivers (full and partial), and unspecified assistantships also available. Support available to part-time students. Financial award application deadline: 2/1; financial award applicants required to submit FAFSA. *Faculty research:* Learning and development, educational leadership and organizations, educational policy analysis. Total annual research expenditures: $18.1 million. *Unit head:* Jennifer L. Petrallia, Assistant Dean, 617-495-8445. *Application contact:* Information Contact, 617-495-3414, Fax: 617-496-3577, E-mail: gseadmissions@harvard.edu.

Hofstra University, School of Education, Health, and Human Services, Department of Curriculum and Teaching, Program in Educational Technology, Hempstead, NY 11549. Offers CAS. Part-time and evening/weekend programs available. Postbaccalaureate distance learning degree programs offered. *Students:* 1 applicant, 100% accepted, 0 enrolled. *Entrance requirements:* Additional exam requirements/recommendations for international students: Required—TOEFL (minimum score 550 paper-based; 213 computer-based; 80 iBT). *Application deadline:* Applications are processed on a rolling basis. Application fee: $60. Electronic applications accepted. *Expenses:* Tuition: Full-time $16,200; part-time $900 per credit hour. Required fees: $970; $145 per term. Tuition and fees vary according to program. *Financial support:* Fellowships with full and partial tuition reimbursements, research assistantships with full and partial tuition reimbursements, Federal Work-Study, institutionally sponsored loans, scholarships/grants, and tuition waivers (full and partial) available. Support available to part-time students. Financial award applicants required to submit FAFSA. *Faculty research:* Culture and educational technology, systemic change in education, digital divide. *Unit head:* Dr. Roberto Joseph, Program Director, 516-463-5086, Fax: 516-463-6196, E-mail: catrzj@hofstra.edu. *Application contact:* Carol Drummer, Dean of Graduate Admissions, 516-463-4876, Fax: 516-463-4664, E-mail: gradstudent@hofstra.edu.

Hofstra University, School of Education, Health, and Human Services, Department of Curriculum and Teaching, Program in Elementary Education—Math, Science, and Technology, Hempstead, NY 11549. Offers MA. Part-time and evening/weekend programs available. *Students:* 3 full-time (all women), 12 part-time (all women); includes 1 minority (Hispanic American). Average age 25. 7 applicants, 100% accepted, 5 enrolled. In 2009, 10 master's awarded. *Degree requirements:* For master's, thesis. *Entrance requirements:* For master's, 2 letters of recommendation, interview, teaching certificate (MA), essay. Additional exam requirements/recommendations for international students: Required—TOEFL (minimum score 550 paper-based; 213 computer-based; 80 iBT). *Application deadline:* Applications are processed on a rolling basis. Application fee: $60. Electronic applications accepted. *Expenses:* Tuition: Full-time $16,200; part-time $900 per credit hour. Required fees: $970; $145 per term. Tuition and fees vary according to program. *Financial support:* In 2009–10, 8 students received support, including 3 fellowships with full and partial tuition reimbursements available (averaging $3,167 per year); research assistantships with full and partial tuition reimbursements available, Federal Work-Study, institutionally sponsored loans, scholarships/grants, tuition waivers (full and partial), and unspecified assistantships also available. Support available to part-time students. Financial award applicants required to submit FAFSA. *Faculty research:* Constructivism, interdisciplinary curriculum, design and technology education, science inquiry, problem-based learning. *Unit head:* Dr. Irene Plonczak, Program Director, 516-463-5768, Fax: 516-463-6196, E-mail: catizp@hofstra.edu. *Application contact:* Carol Drummer, Dean of Graduate Admissions, 516-463-4876, Fax: 516-463-4664, E-mail: gradstudent@hofstra.edu.

Idaho State University, Office of Graduate Studies, College of Education, Department of Educational Leadership and Instructional Design, Pocatello, ID 83209-8059. Offers educational administration (M Ed, 6th Year Certificate, Ed S); educational leadership (Ed D), including education training and development, educational administration, educational technology, higher education administration; instructional technology (M Ed). Part-time programs available. *Faculty:* 4 full-time (1 woman), 1 (woman) part-time/adjunct. *Students:* 17 full-time (8 women), 112 part-time (40 women); includes 10 minority (3 African Americans, 4 American Indian/Alaska Native, 1 Asian American or Pacific Islander, 2 Hispanic Americans), 9 international. Average age 42. In 2009, 4 master's, 8 doctorates, 15 other advanced degrees awarded. *Degree requirements:* For master's, comprehensive exam, thesis optional, internship, oral exam or deferred thesis; for doctorate, comprehensive exam, thesis/dissertation, written exam; for other advanced degree, comprehensive exam, thesis (for some programs), written and oral exam. *Entrance requirements:* For master's, MAT, bachelor's degree, minimum GPA of 3.0, 1 year of training experience; for doctorate, GRE General Test or MAT, minimum GPA of 3.0 (undergraduate), 3.5 (graduate); departmental interview; for other advanced degree, GRE General Test, minimum GPA of 3.0, master's degree. Additional exam requirements/recommendations for international students: Required—TOEFL (minimum score 550 paper-based; 213 computer-based; 80 iBT). *Application deadline:* For fall admission, 7/1 for domestic students, 6/1 for international students; for spring admission, 12/1 for domestic students, 11/1 for international students. Applications are processed on a rolling basis. Application fee: $55. Electronic applications accepted. *Expenses:* Tuition, state resident: full-time $3318; part-time $297 per credit hour. Tuition, nonresident: full-time $13,120; part-time $437 per credit hour. Required fees: $2530. Tuition and fees vary according to program. *Financial support:* Teaching assistantships with full and partial tuition reimbursements, career-related internships or fieldwork, Federal Work-Study, institutionally sponsored loans, scholarships/grants, health care benefits, tuition waivers (full and partial), and unspecified assistantships available. Support available to part-time students. Financial award application deadline: 1/1; financial award applicants required to submit FAFSA. *Faculty research:* Educational leadership, gender issues in education and sport, staff development. *Unit head:* Dr. Jonathan Lawson, Chair, 208-282-1036, Fax: 208-282-4697, E-mail: lawsjona@isu.edu. *Application contact:* Dr. Peter Denner, Assistant Dean, 208-282-3807, Fax: 208-282-4697, E-mail: dennpete@isu.edu.

Idaho State University, Office of Graduate Studies, College of Education, Program in Instructional Methods and Technology, Pocatello, ID 83209. Offers instructional design (PhD); instructional technology (M Ed). Part-time programs available. *Faculty:* 4 full-time (2 women). *Students:* 6 full-time (2 women), 35 part-time (10 women); includes 4 minority (1 African American, 1 American Indian/Alaska Native, 1 Asian American or Pacific Islander, 1 Hispanic American), 1 international. Average age 38. In 2009, 7 master's awarded. *Degree requirements:* For master's, comprehensive exam, thesis optional, minimum 36 credits; for doctorate, comprehensive exam, thesis/dissertation (for some programs). *Entrance requirements:* For master's, GRE or MAT, bachelor's degree; for doctorate, GRE or MAT, master's degree. Additional exam requirements/recommendations for international students: Required—TOEFL (minimum score 550 paper-based; 213 computer-based; 80 iBT). *Application deadline:* For fall admission, 7/1 for domestic students, 6/1 for international students; for spring admission, 12/1 for domestic students, 11/1 for international students. Applications are processed on a rolling basis. Application fee: $55. Electronic applications accepted. *Expenses:* Tuition, state resident: full-time $3318; part-time $297 per credit hour. Tuition, nonresident: full-time $13,120; part-time $437 per credit hour. Required fees: $2530. Tuition and fees vary according to program. *Financial support:* In 2009–10, teaching assistantships with full and partial tuition reimbursements (averaging $9,128 per year); career-related internships or fieldwork, Federal Work-Study, institutionally sponsored loans, scholarships/grants, health care benefits, and unspecified assistantships also available. Support available to part-time students. Financial award application deadline: 1/1; financial award applicants required to submit FAFSA. *Unit head:* Dr. Jonathan Lawson, Chairman, 208-282-1036, Fax: 208-282-4697, E-mail: lawsjona@isu.edu. *Application contact:* Dr. Peter Denner, Assistant Dean, 208-282-3807, Fax: 208-282-4697, E-mail: dennpete@isu.edu.

Indiana State University, School of Graduate Studies, College of Education, Department of Curriculum, Instruction, and Media Technology, Terre Haute, IN 47809. Offers curriculum and instruction (M Ed, PhD); educational technology (MS). *Accreditation:* NCATE. *Degree requirements:* For doctorate, thesis/dissertation. *Entrance requirements:* For doctorate, GRE General Test. Electronic applications accepted. *Faculty research:* Discipline FERPA reading, teacher strengths and needs.

Indiana University Bloomington, School of Education, Department of Instructional Systems Technology, Bloomington, IN 47405-1006. Offers MS, PhD, Ed S. Postbaccalaureate distance

Educational Media/Instructional Technology

Indiana University Bloomington *(continued)*
learning degree programs offered (no on-campus study). *Faculty:* 11 full-time (4 women), 6 part-time/adjunct (2 women). *Students:* 75 full-time (34 women), 28 part-time (23 women); includes 10 minority (4 African Americans, 3 Asian Americans or Pacific Islanders, 3 Hispanic Americans), 38 international. Average age 45. 47 applicants, 64% accepted, 13 enrolled. In 2009, 16 master's, 7 doctorates, 2 other advanced degrees awarded. Terminal master's awarded for partial completion of doctoral program. *Degree requirements:* For master's, thesis optional, portfolio; for doctorate, comprehensive exam, thesis/dissertation, dossier review. *Entrance requirements:* For master's and doctorate, GRE General Test, minimum GPA of 2.75. Additional exam requirements/recommendations for international students: Required—TOEFL. *Application deadline:* For fall admission, 6/1 for domestic students, 3/1 for international students; for winter admission, 11/1 for domestic students; for spring admission, 9/1 for international students. Application fee: $55 ($65 for international students). Electronic applications accepted. *Financial support:* In 2009–10, 25 students received support, including 2 fellowships with full and partial tuition reimbursements available (averaging $32,000 per year), 3 research assistantships with partial tuition reimbursements available (averaging $31,000 per year), 12 teaching assistantships with full and partial tuition reimbursements available (averaging $33,000 per year); career-related internships or fieldwork, Federal Work-Study, institutionally sponsored loans, health care benefits, and unspecified assistantships also available. Financial award application deadline: 1/15. *Faculty research:* Instructional design and theory development, e-learning and distance education, systemic change, serious simulations and games, human performance improvement, technology integration in education. Total annual research expenditures: $392,000. *Unit head:* Prof. Elizabeth Boling, Chairperson, 812-856-8450, E-mail: istdept@indiana.edu. *Application contact:* Ruth Teh, Office Manager, 812-856-8455, E-mail: istdept@indiana.edu.

Indiana University of Pennsylvania, School of Graduate Studies and Research, College of Education and Educational Technology, Department of Adult and Community Education, Program in Adult Education and Communication Technology, Indiana, PA 15705-1087. Offers communications technology (MA). Part-time and evening/weekend programs available. *Faculty:* 2 full-time (0 women). *Students:* 21 full-time (9 women), 15 part-time (9 women); includes 6 minority (4 African Americans, 2 Asian Americans or Pacific Islanders). Average age 31. 54 applicants, 59% accepted, 23 enrolled. In 2009, 22 master's awarded. *Degree requirements:* For master's, thesis optional. *Entrance requirements:* For master's, 2 letters of recommendation, writing sample. Additional exam requirements/recommendations for international students: Required—TOEFL. *Application deadline:* For fall admission, 7/1 priority date for domestic students; for spring admission, 11/1 for domestic students. Applications are processed on a rolling basis. Application fee: $40. *Expenses:* Tuition, state resident: full-time $6666; part-time $370 per credit hour. Tuition, nonresident: full-time $10,666; part-time $593 per credit hour. Required fees: $813 per semester. *Financial support:* In 2009–10, 7 research assistantships with full and partial tuition reimbursements (averaging $5,440 per year) were awarded; career-related internships or fieldwork and Federal Work-Study also available. Support available to part-time students. Financial award application deadline: 3/15; financial award applicants required to submit FAFSA. *Unit head:* Dr. Gary Dean, Chairperson, 724-357-2470, E-mail: gjdean@iup.edu. *Application contact:* Dr. Gary Dean, Chairperson, 724-357-2470, E-mail: gjdean@iup.edu.

Indiana University of Pennsylvania, School of Graduate Studies and Research, College of Education and Educational Technology, Department of Communications Media, Indiana, PA 15705-1087. Offers adult education and communications technology (MA); communications media and instructional technology (PhD). *Faculty:* 8 full-time (1 woman). *Students:* 16 full-time (7 women), 24 part-time (13 women); includes 3 minority (2 African Americans, 1 Asian American or Pacific Islander), 2 international. Average age 35. 40 applicants, 53% accepted, 20 enrolled. Application fee: $40. *Expenses:* Tuition, state resident: full-time $6666; part-time $370 per credit hour. Tuition, nonresident: full-time $10,666; part-time $593 per credit hour. Required fees: $813 per semester. *Financial support:* In 2009–10, 4 fellowships (averaging $1,000 per year), 8 research assistantships (averaging $5,936 per year), 3 teaching assistantships (averaging $21,536 per year) were awarded. *Unit head:* Dr. Mark Piwinsky, Chairperson, 724-357-3954, Fax: 724-357-5503, E-mail: mark.piwinsky@iup.edu. *Application contact:* Dr. Edward Nardi, Associate Dean, 724-357-2480, Fax: 724-357-5595, E-mail: ewnardi@iup.edu.

Instituto Tecnológico y de Estudios Superiores de Monterrey, Campus Central de Veracruz, Graduate Programs, Córdoba, Mexico. Offers administration (MA); administration of information technologies (MTI); computer sciences (MCC); education (MEE); educational institution administration (MAD); educational technology (MTE); electronic commerce (MCE); finance (MAF); humanistic studies (MEH); international business for Latin America (MNL); marketing (MMT); science (MCP); technology management (MTT). Part-time and evening/weekend programs available. Postbaccalaureate distance learning degree programs offered (minimal on-campus study). *Degree requirements:* For master's, thesis (for some programs). *Entrance requirements:* For master's, PAEP College Board. Electronic applications accepted.

Instituto Tecnológico y de Estudios Superiores de Monterrey, Campus Ciudad de México, Virtual University Division, Ciudad de Mexico, Mexico. Offers administration of information technologies (MA); computer sciences (MA); education (MA, PhD); educational technology (MA); environmental engineering (MA); environmental systems (MA); humanistic studies (MA); industrial engineering (MA); international business for Latin America (MA); quality systems (MA); quality systems and productivity (MA). Part-time and evening/weekend programs available. Postbaccalaureate distance learning degree programs offered (minimal on-campus study). *Entrance requirements:* For master's and doctorate, Instituto entrance exam. Additional exam requirements/recommendations for international students: Required—TOEFL.

Instituto Tecnológico y de Estudios Superiores de Monterrey, Campus Ciudad Juárez, Program in Educational Innovation, Ciudad Juárez, Mexico. Offers DE.

Instituto Tecnológico y de Estudios Superiores de Monterrey, Campus Ciudad Juárez, Program in Educational Technology, Ciudad Juárez, Mexico. Offers MTE.

Instituto Tecnológico y de Estudios Superiores de Monterrey, Campus Estado de México, Professional and Graduate Division, Estado de Mexico, Mexico. Offers administration of information technologies (MITA); architecture (M Arch); business administration (GMBA, MBA); computer sciences (MCS, PhD); education (M Ed); educational institution administration (MAD); educational technology and innovation (PhD); electronic commerce (MEC); environmental systems (MS); finance (MAF); humanistic studies (MHS); information sciences and knowledge management (MISKM); information systems (MS); manufacturing systems (MS); marketing (MEM); quality systems and productivity (MS); science and materials engineering (PhD); telecommunications management (MTM). Part-time programs available. Postbaccalaureate distance learning degree programs offered (minimal on-campus study). *Degree requirements:* For master's, one foreign language, thesis (for some programs); for doctorate, one foreign language, thesis/dissertation. *Entrance requirements:* For master's, E-PAEP 500, interview; for doctorate, E-PAEP 500, research proposal. Additional exam requirements/recommendations for international students: Required—TOEFL (minimum score 550 paper-based). *Faculty research:* Surface treatments by plasmas, mechanical properties, robotics, graphical computing, mechatronics security protocols.

Instituto Tecnológico y de Estudios Superiores de Monterrey, Campus Irapuato, Graduate Programs, Irapuato, Mexico. Offers administration (MBA); administration of information technology (MAIT); administration of telecommunications (MAT); architecture (M Arch); computer science (MCS); education (M Ed); educational administration (MEA); educational innovation and technology (DEIT); educational technology (MET); electronic commerce (MBA); environmental administration and planning (MEAP); environmental systems (MES); finances (MBA); humanistic studies (MHS); international management for Latin American executives (MIMLAE); library and information science (MLIS); manufacturing quality management (MMQM); marketing research (MBA).

Inter American University of Puerto Rico, Metropolitan Campus, Graduate Programs, Program in Educational Computing, San Juan, PR 00919-1293. Offers MA. *Degree requirements:* For master's, comprehensive exam, portfolio. *Entrance requirements:* For master's, GRE or EXADEP, minimum GPA of 2.5. Electronic applications accepted. *Faculty research:* Effectiveness of multimedia, World Wide Web for distance learning.

Iowa State University of Science and Technology, Graduate College, College of Human Sciences, Department of Curriculum and Instruction, Ames, IA 50011. Offers curriculum and instructional technology (M Ed, MS, PhD); elementary education (M Ed, MS); historical, philosophical, and comparative studies in education (M Ed, MS); special education (M Ed, MS). *Faculty:* 26 full-time (16 women), 1 (woman) part-time/adjunct. *Students:* 51 full-time (34 women), 72 part-time (49 women); includes 11 minority (5 African Americans, 1 American Indian/Alaska Native, 4 Asian Americans or Pacific Islanders, 1 Hispanic American), 25 international. 54 applicants, 69% accepted, 25 enrolled. In 2009, 41 master's, 6 doctorates awarded. *Degree requirements:* For master's, thesis or alternative; for doctorate, thesis/dissertation. *Entrance requirements:* For doctorate, GRE General Test. Additional exam requirements/recommendations for international students: Required—TOEFL (minimum score 560 paper-based; 83 iBT) or IELTS (minimum score 6.5). *Application deadline:* For fall admission, 1/1 priority date for domestic and international students; for spring admission, 9/1 for domestic and international students. Application fee: $40 ($90 for international students). Electronic applications accepted. *Expenses:* Tuition, state resident: full-time $6716. Tuition, nonresident: full-time $8908. Tuition and fees vary according to course level, course load, program and student level. *Financial support:* In 2009–10, 21 research assistantships with full and partial tuition reimbursements (averaging $14,600 per year), 12 teaching assistantships with full and partial tuition reimbursements (averaging $14,600 per year) were awarded; fellowships, scholarships/grants, health care benefits, and unspecified assistantships also available. *Unit head:* Dr. Carl Smith, Director of Graduate Education, 515-294-0317, E-mail: cigrad@iastate.edu. *Application contact:* Dr. Patricia Leigh, Director of Graduate Education, 515-294-7021, E-mail: cigrad@iastate.edu.

Jackson State University, Graduate School, School of Education, Department of Educational Foundations and Leadership, Jackson, MS 39217. Offers education administration (Ed S); educational administration (MS Ed, PhD); secondary education (MS Ed, Ed S), including educational technology (MS Ed). *Accreditation:* NCATE. Part-time and evening/weekend programs available. *Degree requirements:* For master's, comprehensive exam, thesis or alternative; for doctorate, comprehensive exam, thesis/dissertation; for Ed S, comprehensive exam, thesis. *Entrance requirements:* For master's, GRE General Test; for doctorate, MAT, GRE, teaching experience. Additional exam requirements/recommendations for international students: Required—TOEFL.

Jacksonville State University, College of Graduate Studies and Continuing Education, College of Education and Professional Studies, Program in Instructional Media, Jacksonville, AL 36265-1602. Offers MS Ed. Part-time and evening/weekend programs available. *Degree requirements:* For master's, comprehensive exam, thesis (for some programs). *Entrance requirements:* For master's, GRE General Test or MAT. Electronic applications accepted.

Jacksonville University, College of Arts and Sciences, School of Education, Program in Integrated Learning with Educational Technology, Jacksonville, FL 32211. Offers MAT. *Degree requirements:* For master's, comprehensive exam. *Entrance requirements:* For master's, GRE General Test, minimum GPA of 3.0. Additional exam requirements/recommendations for international students: Required—TOEFL.

The Johns Hopkins University, School of Education, Department of Special Education, Baltimore, MD 21218. Offers advanced methods for differentiated instruction and inclusive education (Certificate); assistive technology (Certificate); early intervention/preschool special education specialist (Certificate); education of students with autism and other pervasive developmental disorders (Certificate); education of students with severe disabilities (Certificate); special education (MS, Ed D, CAGS), including early childhood special education (MS), general special education studies (MS), mild to moderate disabilities (MS), severe disabilities (MS), technology in special education (MS). *Accreditation:* NCATE. Part-time and evening/weekend programs available. Postbaccalaureate distance learning degree programs offered (minimal on-campus study). *Faculty:* 6 full-time (5 women), 21 part-time/adjunct (18 women). *Students:* 19 full-time (18 women), 270 part-time (243 women); includes 45 minority (35 African Americans, 6 Asian Americans or Pacific Islanders, 4 Hispanic Americans), 10 international. Average age 31. 114 applicants, 56% accepted, 46 enrolled. In 2009, 88 master's, 34 other advanced degrees awarded. *Degree requirements:* For master's, internships, professional portfolio, and PRAXIS II (for licensure); for doctorate, comprehensive exam, thesis/dissertation. *Entrance requirements:* For master's, PRAXIS I, SAT, ACT, or GRE, minimum undergraduate GPA of 3.0, 2 letters of recommendation (for cohort programs); for doctorate, GRE, degree in special education (or related field); minimum GPA of 3.0 in all prior academic work; 3 letters of recommendation; curriculum vitae/resume; professional experience; for other advanced degree, minimum undergraduate GPA of 3.0, master's degree (for CAGS). Additional exam requirements/recommendations for international students: Required—TOEFL (minimum score 600 paper-based; 250 computer-based; 100 iBT). *Application deadline:* For fall admission, 5/1 for international students; for spring admission, 10/15 for international students. Applications are processed on a rolling basis. Application fee: $80. Electronic applications accepted. *Financial support:* In 2009–10, 9 fellowships were awarded; scholarships/grants also available. Support available to part-time students. Financial award application deadline: 6/1; financial award applicants required to submit FAFSA. *Faculty research:* Alternative licensure programs for special educators; collaborative programming; data-based decision making and knowledge management as keys to school reform; parent training; natural environment teaching (NET). *Unit head:* Dr. Laurie U. deBettencourt, Chair, 301-294-7054, Fax: 410-516-8474, E-mail: specialed@jhu.edu. *Application contact:* Jennifer Shaffer, Director of Admissions, 410-516-9797, Fax: 410-516-9799, E-mail: educationinfo@jhu.edu.

The Johns Hopkins University, School of Education, Department of Teacher Development and Leadership, Baltimore, MD 21218-2699. Offers adolescent literacy education (Certificate); data-based decision making and organizational improvement (Certificate); education (MS), including reading, school administration and supervision, technology for educators; educational leadership for independent schools (Certificate); effective teaching of reading (Certificate); emergent literacy education (Certificate); English as a second language instruction (Certificate); gifted education (Certificate); leadership for school, family, and community collaboration (Certificate); leadership in technology integration (Certificate); school administration and supervision (Certificate); teacher development and leadership (Ed D); teacher leadership (Certificate); technology for educators (MS). Part-time and evening/weekend programs available. Postbaccalaureate distance learning degree programs offered (minimal on-campus study). *Faculty:* 8 full-time (2 women), 53 part-time/adjunct (36 women). *Students:* 17 full-time (16 women), 462 part-time (358 women); includes 117 minority (77 African Americans, 25 Asian Americans or Pacific Islanders, 15 Hispanic Americans), 11 international. Average age 33. 217 applicants, 62% accepted, 107 enrolled. In 2009, 85 master's, 2 doctorates, 181 other advanced degrees awarded. *Degree requirements:* For master's and Certificate, portfolio; for doctorate, comprehensive exam (for some programs), thesis/dissertation, portfolio or comprehensive exam. *Entrance requirements:* For master's and Certificate, bachelor's degree; minimum undergraduate GPA of 3.0; essay/statement of goals; for doctorate, GRE, essay/statement of goals; three letters of recommendation; curriculum vitae/resume; K-12 professional experience; interview; writing assessment. Additional exam requirements/recommendations for international students: Required—TOEFL (minimum score 600 paper-based; 250 computer-based; 100 iBT). *Application deadline:* For fall admission, 5/1 for international students; for spring admission, 10/15 for international students. Applications are processed on a rolling basis. Application fee: $80. Electronic applications accepted. *Financial support:* In 2009–10, 5 research assistantships, 1 teaching assistantship were awarded; scholarships/grants also available. Support available to part-time students. Financial award application deadline: 6/1; financial award applicants required to submit FAFSA. *Faculty research:* Application of psychoanalytic concepts to teaching, schools, and education reform; adolescent literacies; use of emerging

technologies for teaching, learning, and school leadership; quantitative analyses of the social contexts of education; school, family, and community collaboration; program evaluation methodologies. *Unit head:* Dr. Edward Pajak, Chair, 410-516-9755, Fax: 410-516-9770, E-mail: mbuckingham@jhu.edu. *Application contact:* Jennifer Shaffer, Director of Admissions, 410-516-9797, Fax: 410-516-9799, E-mail: educationinfo@jhu.edu.

Johnson Bible College, Teacher Education Program, Knoxville, TN 37998-1001. Offers Bible and educational technology (MA); holistic education (MA). Part-time programs available. *Degree requirements:* For master's, multimedia action research presentation. *Entrance requirements:* For master's, interview, minimum GPA of 3.0, portfolio, teaching license. Additional exam requirements/recommendations for international students: Required—TOEFL. *Faculty research:* Instructional technology.

Jones International University, Graduate School of Education, Centennial, CO 80112. Offers adult education (M Ed); corporate training and knowledge management (M Ed); curriculum and instruction (M Ed), including elementary teacher licensure, secondary teacher licensure; e-learning technology and design (M Ed); educational leadership and administration (M Ed); educational leadership and administration: principal and administrator licensure (M Ed); elementary curriculum instruction and assessment (M Ed); higher education leadership and administration (M Ed); K-12 instructional technology (M Ed); K-12 instructional technology: teacher licensure (M Ed); secondary curriculum instruction and assessment (M Ed); technology and design (M Ed). Part-time and evening/weekend programs available. Postbaccalaureate distance learning degree programs offered (no on-campus study). *Entrance requirements:* For master's, minimum cumulative GPA of 2.5. Additional exam requirements/recommendations for international students: Recommended—TOEFL (minimum score 550 paper-based; 213 computer-based). Electronic applications accepted.

Kaplan University, Davenport Campus, School of Teacher Education, Davenport, IA 52807-2095. Offers education (M Ed); secondary education (M Ed); teaching and learning (MA); teaching literacy and language: grades 6-12 (MA); teaching literacy and language: grades K-6 (MA); teaching mathematics: grades 6-8 (MA); teaching mathematics: grades 9-12 (MA); teaching mathematics: grades K-5 (MA); teaching science: grades 6-12 (MA); teaching science: grades K-6 (MA); teaching students with special needs (MA); teaching with technology (MA). Part-time and evening/weekend programs available. Postbaccalaureate distance learning degree programs offered (no on-campus study). *Entrance requirements:* Additional exam requirements/recommendations for international students: Required—TOEFL (minimum score 550 paper-based; 218 computer-based; 80 iBT).

Kennesaw State University, Leland and Clarice C. Bagwell College of Education, Program in Graduate Education, Kennesaw, GA 30144-5591. Offers adolescent education (M Ed); educational leadership (M Ed); educational leadership technology (M Ed); elementary and early childhood education (M Ed); special education (M Ed); teaching English to speakers of other languages (M Ed). *Accreditation:* NCATE. Part-time programs available. *Faculty:* 60 full-time (38 women), 12 part-time/adjunct (4 women). *Students:* 140 full-time (116 women), 136 part-time (107 women); includes 51 minority (39 African Americans, 1 American Indian/Alaska Native, 3 Asian Americans or Pacific Islanders, 8 Hispanic Americans), 4 international. Average age 34. 113 applicants, 83% accepted, 69 enrolled. In 2009, 282 master's awarded. *Degree requirements:* For master's, thesis or alternative. *Entrance requirements:* For master's, GRE General Test, T-4 state certification, minimum GPA of 2.75. Additional exam requirements/recommendations for international students: Required—TOEFL (minimum score 550 paper-based; 213 computer-based; 80 iBT), IELTS (minimum score 6). *Application deadline:* For fall admission, 7/1 for domestic and international students; for spring admission, 10/1 for domestic and international students. Application fee: $60. Electronic applications accepted. *Expenses:* Tuition, state resident: full-time $2341; part-time $196 per credit hour. Tuition, nonresident: full-time $9396; part-time $783 per credit hour. Required fees: $573 per semester. *Financial support:* Federal Work-Study and unspecified assistantships available. Support available to part-time students. Financial award application deadline: 6/15; financial award applicants required to submit FAFSA. *Unit head:* Dr. Nita Paris, Associate Dean for Graduate Programs, 770-423-6636, E-mail: nparis@kennesaw.edu. *Application contact:* Alisha Bello, Administrative Coordinator, 770-423-6043, Fax: 770-420-4435, E-mail: abello1@kennesaw.edu.

Kent State University, Graduate School of Education, Health, and Human Services, School of Lifespan Development and Educational Sciences, Program in Instructional Technology, Kent, OH 44242-0001. Offers computer technology (M Ed, MA); general instructional technology (M Ed, MA); library media (M Ed, MA). *Accreditation:* NCATE. *Faculty:* 7 full-time (3 women), 1 (woman) part-time/adjunct. *Students:* 16 full-time (13 women), 53 part-time (39 women); includes 3 minority (all African Americans). 22 applicants, 77% accepted. In 2009, 20 master's awarded. *Degree requirements:* For master's, thesis (for some programs). *Entrance requirements:* For master's, GRE General Test. Additional exam requirements/recommendations for international students: Required—TOEFL. *Application deadline:* Applications are processed on a rolling basis. Application fee: $30. *Financial support:* In 2009–10, 2 research assistantships with full tuition reimbursements (averaging $8,313 per year) were awarded; fellowships with full tuition reimbursements, teaching assistantships with full tuition reimbursements, Federal Work-Study, scholarships/grants, and unspecified assistantships also available. Financial award application deadline: 4/1; financial award applicants required to submit FAFSA. *Faculty research:* Cooperative learning, aesthetics, computers in schools. *Unit head:* Dr. Drew Tiene, Coordinator, 330-672-0607, E-mail: dtiene@kent.edu. *Application contact:* Nancy Miller, Academic Program Coordinator, Office of Graduate Student Services, 330-672-2576, Fax: 330-672-9162, E-mail: ogs@kent.edu.

Kutztown University of Pennsylvania, College of Education, Program in Instructional Technology, Kutztown, PA 19530-0730. Offers M Ed, Certificate. Part-time and evening/weekend programs available. *Students:* 1 full-time (0 women), 21 part-time (8 women). Average age 31. 18 applicants, 67% accepted, 2 enrolled. In 2009, 14 master's awarded. *Degree requirements:* For master's, comprehensive exam. *Entrance requirements:* Additional exam requirements/recommendations for international students: Required—TOEFL. *Application deadline:* For fall admission, 8/15 priority date for domestic and international students; for spring admission, 12/15 priority date for domestic and international students. Applications are processed on a rolling basis. Application fee: $35. Electronic applications accepted. *Expenses:* Tuition, state resident: full-time $6666; part-time $370 per credit. Tuition, nonresident: full-time $10,666; part-time $593 per credit. Required fees: $62 per credit. $60 per semester. *Financial support:* Career-related internships or fieldwork, Federal Work-Study, scholarships/grants, and unspecified assistantships available. Financial award application deadline: 3/1; financial award applicants required to submit FAFSA. *Unit head:* Dr. Eloise Long, Chairperson, 610-683-4302, Fax: 610-683-1326, E-mail: long@kutztown.edu. *Application contact:* Kelly D. Burr, Associate Director, Graduate Admissions, 610-683-4200, Fax: 610-683-1393, E-mail: graduate@kutztown.edu.

Lamar University, College of Graduate Studies, College of Education and Human Development, Department of Educational Leadership, Beaumont, TX 77710. Offers counseling and development (M Ed, Certificate); education administration (M Ed); educational leadership (DE); principal (Certificate); school superintendent (Certificate); supervision (M Ed); technology application (Certificate). Part-time and evening/weekend programs available. *Faculty:* 14 full-time (7 women), 7 part-time/adjunct (2 women). *Students:* 14 full-time (8 women), 2,827 part-time (1,986 women); includes 798 minority (340 African Americans, 20 American Indian/Alaska Native, 31 Asian Americans or Pacific Islanders, 407 Hispanic Americans). Average age 40. 2,662 applicants, 75% accepted, 332 enrolled. In 2009, 199 master's, 21 doctorates awarded. Terminal master's awarded for partial completion of doctoral program. *Degree requirements:* For master's, comprehensive exam, thesis optional; for doctorate, thesis/dissertation. *Entrance requirements:* For master's, GRE General Test, minimum GPA of 2.5; for doctorate, GRE. Additional exam requirements/recommendations for international students: Required—TOEFL. *Application deadline:* For fall admission, 8/1 priority date for domestic students; for spring admission, 12/1 priority date for domestic students. Applications are processed on a rolling basis. Application fee: $25 ($50 for international students). *Financial support:* In 2009–10, 3 fellowships (averaging $20,000 per year), 1 research assistantship with tuition reimbursement (averaging $6,500 per year) were awarded; teaching assistantships with tuition reimbursements, career-related internships or fieldwork and scholarships/grants also available. Support available to part-time students. Financial award application deadline: 4/1. *Faculty research:* School dropouts, suicide prevention in public school students, school climate and gifted performance, teacher evaluation. *Unit head:* Dr. Carolyn Crawford, Chair, 409-880-8689, Fax: 409-880-8685. *Application contact:* Dr. Carolyn Crawford, Chair, 409-880-8689, Fax: 409-880-8685.

La Salle University, Program in Instructional Technology Management, Philadelphia, PA 19141-1199. Offers MS. *Degree requirements:* For master's, capstone project. *Entrance requirements:* For master's, GRE, MAT, or GMAT, 3 to 5 years professional experience in corporate training, human resources, information technology or business; resume; 2 letters of recommendation. Additional exam requirements/recommendations for international students: Required—TOEFL. Electronic applications accepted.

Lawrence Technological University, College of Arts and Sciences, Southfield, MI 48075-1058. Offers computer science (MS); educational technology (MET); science education (MSE); technical communication (MS). Part-time and evening/weekend programs available. *Faculty:* 14 full-time (6 women), 14 part-time/adjunct (4 women). *Students:* 6 full-time (3 women), 80 part-time (49 women); includes 19 minority (14 African Americans, 5 Asian Americans or Pacific Islanders), 12 international. Average age 35. 87 applicants, 57% accepted, 20 enrolled. In 2009, 34 master's awarded. *Degree requirements:* For master's, thesis (for some programs). *Entrance requirements:* For master's, GRE. Additional exam requirements/recommendations for international students: Required—TOEFL (minimum score 550 paper-based; 213 computer-based; 79 iBT). *Application deadline:* For fall admission, 8/1 priority date for domestic students, 6/1 for international students; for winter admission, 12/1 priority date for domestic students, 10/1 for international students; for spring admission, 5/1 priority date for domestic students, 3/1 for international students. Applications are processed on a rolling basis. Application fee: $50. Electronic applications accepted. *Expenses:* Tuition: Full-time $11,320; part-time $798 per credit hour. *Financial support:* Federal Work-Study available. Financial award application deadline: 4/1; financial award applicants required to submit FAFSA. *Unit head:* Dr. Hsiao-Ping Moore, Dean, 248-204-3500, Fax: 248-204-3518, E-mail: scidean@ltu.edu. *Application contact:* Jane Rohrback, Director of Admissions, 248-204-3160, Fax: 248-204-3188, E-mail: admissions@ltu.edu.

Lehigh University, College of Education, Program in Teaching, Learning and Technology, Bethlehem, PA 18015. Offers elementary education with certification (M Ed); instructional technology (MS); learning sciences and technology (PhD); secondary education with certification (M Ed); teaching and learning (M Ed, MA); technology use in the schools (Graduate Certificate). Part-time programs available. *Faculty:* 7 full-time (4 women), 7 part-time/adjunct (3 women). *Students:* 48 full-time (39 women), 61 part-time (41 women); includes 11 minority (3 African Americans, 4 Asian Americans or Pacific Islanders, 4 Hispanic Americans), 5 international. Average age 31. 81 applicants, 67% accepted, 23 enrolled. In 2009, 48 master's awarded. Terminal master's awarded for partial completion of doctoral program. *Degree requirements:* For master's, comprehensive exam and dissertation (M Ed); for doctorate, comprehensive exam, thesis/dissertation. *Entrance requirements:* For master's, minimum GPA of 3.0, 2 letters of recommendation, essay, transcript; for doctorate, GRE General Test, minimum graduate GPA of 3.0, writing sample, 2 letters of recommendation, essay, transcript. Additional exam requirements/recommendations for international students: Required—TOEFL (minimum score 600 paper-based; 250 computer-based; 93 iBT). *Application deadline:* For fall admission, 2/1 for domestic and international students; for spring admission, 11/1 for domestic and international students. Applications are processed on a rolling basis. Application fee: $65. Electronic applications accepted. *Financial support:* In 2009–10, 18 students received support, including 1 fellowship with full and partial tuition reimbursement available (averaging $16,000 per year), 2 research assistantships with full and partial tuition reimbursements available (averaging $18,000 per year); career-related internships or fieldwork, institutionally sponsored loans, scholarships/grants, and tuition waivers (full and partial) also available. Financial award application deadline: 1/31. *Faculty research:* Instructional media and delivery systems, technologies to enhance education, technical and informal education, Web-based learning. *Unit head:* Dr. MJ Bishop, Coordinator, 610-758-3235, Fax: 610-758-3243, E-mail: mjba@lehigh.edu. *Application contact:* Donna M. Johnson, Coordinator, 610-758-3231, Fax: 610-758-6223, E-mail: dmj4@lehigh.edu.

Lewis University, College of Education, Program in Curriculum and Instruction: Instructional Technology, Romeoville, IL 60446. Offers M Ed. Part-time and evening/weekend programs available. *Students:* 40 part-time (31 women). Average age 31. In 2009, 3 master's awarded. *Entrance requirements:* For master's, departmental qualifying exam, writing exam, minimum GPA of 2.75, 2 letters of recommendation, interview. Additional exam requirements/recommendations for international students: Required—TOEFL (minimum score 550 paper-based; 213 computer-based). *Application deadline:* For fall admission, 5/1 priority date for international students; for spring admission, 11/15 priority date for international students. Applications are processed on a rolling basis. Application fee: $40. Electronic applications accepted. *Expenses:* Tuition: Full-time $6480; part-time $720 per credit. One-time fee: $40. Tuition and fees vary according to course load, degree level and program. *Financial support:* Institutionally sponsored loans and unspecified assistantships available. Support available to part-time students. Financial award application deadline: 5/1; financial award applicants required to submit FAFSA. *Unit head:* Dr. Seung Kim, Program Director, 815-838-0500, E-mail: kimse@lewisu.edu. *Application contact:* Sandy Zigrossi, Information Contact, 815-838-0500 Ext. 5398, E-mail: zigrossa@lewisu.edu.

Lindenwood University, Graduate Programs, School of Education, St. Charles, MO 63301-1695. Offers education (MA); educational administration (MA, Ed D, Ed S); instructional leadership (Ed D, Ed S); library media (MA); professional and school counseling (MA); professional counseling (MA); school administration (Ed S); school counseling (MA); teaching (MA). Part-time and evening/weekend programs available. *Faculty:* 33 full-time (13 women), 176 part-time/adjunct (83 women). *Students:* 558 full-time (415 women), 1,957 part-time (1,516 women); includes 580 minority (549 African Americans, 6 American Indian/Alaska Native, 16 Asian Americans or Pacific Islanders, 9 Hispanic Americans), 13 international. Average age 35. 248 applicants, 120 enrolled. In 2009, 730 master's, 62 doctorates, 67 other advanced degrees awarded. *Degree requirements:* For master's, thesis (for some programs); for doctorate, thesis/dissertation, minimum GPA of 3.0; for Ed S, comprehensive exam, specialist project, minimum GPA of 3.0. *Entrance requirements:* For master's, interview, minimum GPA of 3.0, writing sample, letter of recommendation; for doctorate, GRE, minimum graduate GPA of 3.4, resume, interview, writing sample, 4 letters of recommendation; for Ed S, master's degree in education, relevant work experience. Additional exam requirements/recommendations for international students: Required—TOEFL (minimum score 550 paper-based; 213 computer-based; 80 iBT). *Application deadline:* For fall admission, 8/27 priority date for domestic and international students; for spring admission, 1/28 priority date for domestic and international students. Applications are processed on a rolling basis. Application fee: $30 ($100 for international students). Electronic applications accepted. *Expenses:* Tuition: Full-time $12,960; part-time $370 per credit hour. Required fees: $340. One-time fee: $30 full-time. Tuition and fees vary according to course level and course load. *Financial support:* In 2009–10, 1,591 students received support. Career-related internships or fieldwork, institutionally sponsored loans, tuition waivers (partial), and unspecified assistantships available. Financial award application deadline: 6/30; financial award applicants required to submit FAFSA. *Unit head:* Dr. Cynthia Bice, Dean, 636-949-4618, Fax: 636-949-4197, E-mail: cbice@lindenwood.edu. *Application contact:* Brett Barger, Dean of Evening Admissions and Extension Campuses, 636-949-4934, Fax: 636-949-4109, E-mail: adultadmissions@lindenwood.edu.

Lipscomb University, Program in Education, Nashville, TN 37204-3951. Offers English language learners (MAT); instructional leadership (M Ed); instructional technology (M Ed); learning and teaching (MALT); math specialty (M Ed); school administration and supervision (M Ed); special education instruction, K-12 (MASE). *Accreditation:* NCATE. Part-time and

Educational Media/Instructional Technology

Lipscomb University *(continued)*
evening/weekend programs available. *Faculty:* 4 full-time (1 woman), 12 part-time/adjunct (8 women). *Students:* 140 full-time (103 women), 200 part-time (144 women); includes 32 minority (29 African Americans, 3 Hispanic Americans). Average age 31. 206 applicants, 75% accepted. In 2009, 131 master's awarded. *Entrance requirements:* For master's, MAT or GRE General Test, 2 reference letters. Additional exam requirements/recommendations for international students: Required—TOEFL (minimum score 570 paper-based; 230 computer-based). *Application deadline:* For fall admission, 8/29 priority date for domestic students; for spring admission, 1/16 priority date for domestic students. Applications are processed on a rolling basis. Application fee: $50. *Expenses:* Tuition: Full-time $16,002; part-time $889 per credit hour. Tuition and fees vary according to program. *Financial support:* In 2009–10, 67 students received support. Federal Work-Study, tuition waivers (full), and unspecified assistantships available. Support available to part-time students. Financial award applicants required to submit FAFSA. *Faculty research:* Facilitative learning styles, leadership, student assessment, interactive multimedia inclusion. *Unit head:* Dr. Deborah Boyd, Director of M Ed Program, 615-966-6263. *Application contact:* Kristin Green, Administrative Assistant, 615-966-7628 Ext. 6081, Fax: 615-966-7628, E-mail: kristin.green@lipscomb.edu.

Long Island University, Brooklyn Campus, School of Education, Department of Teaching and Learning, Program in Computers in Education, Brooklyn, NY 11201-8423. Offers MS. *Degree requirements:* For master's, thesis optional. *Entrance requirements:* For master's, 2 letters of recommendation. Additional exam requirements/recommendations for international students: Required—TOEFL (minimum score 500 paper-based; 173 computer-based).

Long Island University, C.W. Post Campus, School of Education, Department of Educational Technology, Brookville, NY 11548-1300. Offers computers in education (MS). Part-time and evening/weekend programs available. *Degree requirements:* For master's, research project. *Entrance requirements:* For master's, interview; minimum GPA of 2.75 in major, 2.5 overall. Electronic applications accepted. *Faculty research:* Desktop publishing, higher-order thinking skills, interactive learning environments.

Longwood University, Office of Graduate Studies, College of Education and Human Services, Farmville, VA 23909. Offers communication sciences and disorders (MS); community and college counseling (MS); curriculum and instruction specialist-elementary (MS), including mild disabilities, modern languages; curriculum and instruction specialist-secondary (MS), including English, mild disabilities, modern languages; educational leadership (MS); guidance and counseling (MS); literacy and culture (MS); school library media (MS). *Accreditation:* NCATE. Part-time and evening/weekend programs available. *Degree requirements:* For master's, comprehensive exam, thesis optional. *Entrance requirements:* For master's, GRE (communication sciences and disorders), minimum GPA of 2.75. Additional exam requirements/recommendations for international students: Required—TOEFL (minimum score 550 paper-based; 213 computer-based).

Louisiana State University and Agricultural and Mechanical College, Graduate School, College of Education, Department of Educational Theory, Policy and Practice, Baton Rouge, LA 70803. Offers counseling (M Ed, MA, Ed S); educational administration (M Ed, MA, PhD, Ed S); educational technology (MA); elementary education (M Ed); higher education (PhD); research methodology (PhD); secondary education (M Ed). *Accreditation:* ACA (one or more programs are accredited); NCATE. Part-time and evening/weekend programs available. *Faculty:* 38 full-time (24 women). *Students:* 174 full-time (139 women), 154 part-time (129 women); includes 74 minority (66 African Americans, 3 Asian Americans or Pacific Islanders, 5 Hispanic Americans), 9 international. Average age 32. 122 applicants, 60% accepted, 48 enrolled. In 2009, 124 master's, 13 doctorates, 11 other advanced degrees awarded. Terminal master's awarded for partial completion of doctoral program. *Degree requirements:* For doctorate, thesis/dissertation; for Ed S, thesis optional. *Entrance requirements:* For master's and doctorate, GRE General Test, minimum GPA of 3.0. Additional exam requirements/recommendations for international students: Required—TOEFL (minimum score 550 paper-based; 213 computer-based; 79 iBT) or IELTS (minimum score 6.5). *Application deadline:* For fall admission, 1/25 priority date for domestic students, 5/15 for international students; for spring admission, 10/15 for international students. Applications are processed on a rolling basis. Application fee: $50 ($70 for international students). Electronic applications accepted. *Financial support:* In 2009–10, 226 students received support, including 1 fellowship (averaging $31,711 per year), 27 research assistantships with full and partial tuition reimbursements available (averaging $10,143 per year), 35 teaching assistantships with full and partial tuition reimbursements available (averaging $12,555 per year); career-related internships or fieldwork, Federal Work-Study, institutionally sponsored loans, health care benefits, and unspecified assistantships also available. Support available to part-time students. Financial award applicants required to submit FAFSA. *Faculty research:* Literary, curriculum studies, science education, K-12 leadership, higher education. Total annual research expenditures: $1.8 million. *Unit head:* Dr. Earl Cheek, Chair, 225-578-6867, Fax: 225-578-9135, E-mail: echeek@lsu.edu. *Application contact:* Dr., Graduate Coordinator, 225-578-2280, Fax: 225-578-9135.

Lourdes College, School of Graduate and Professional Studies, Program in Education, Sylvania, OH 43560-2898. Offers endorsement in computer technology (M Ed). *Accreditation:* Teacher Education Accreditation Council. Evening/weekend programs available. *Entrance requirements:* Additional exam requirements/recommendations for international students: Required—TOEFL.

Loyola University Chicago, School of Education, Program in Initial Teacher Preparation, Chicago, IL 60660. Offers elementary education (M Ed); math education (M Ed); reading specialist (M Ed); school technology (M Ed); science education (M Ed); secondary education (M Ed); special education (M Ed). *Accreditation:* NCATE. *Faculty:* 12 full-time (9 women), 12 part-time/adjunct (6 women). *Students:* 154. Average age 28. 125 applicants, 69% accepted, 38 enrolled. In 2009, 89 master's awarded. *Degree requirements:* For master's, comprehensive exam. *Entrance requirements:* For master's, Illinois Basic Skills Test, 3 letters of recommendation, minimum GPA of 3.0, resume. Additional exam requirements/recommendations for international students: Required—TOEFL (minimum score 550 paper-based; 213 computer-based; 79 iBT). *Application deadline:* For fall admission, 7/1 priority date for domestic and international students; for spring admission, 11/1 priority date for domestic and international students. Applications are processed on a rolling basis. Application fee: $50. Electronic applications accepted. *Expenses:* Tuition: Full-time $14,220; part-time $790 per credit hour. Required fees: $60 per semester hour. Tuition and fees vary according to program. *Financial support:* In 2009–10, 1 research assistantship with full tuition reimbursement (averaging $8,500 per year), 1 teaching assistantship were awarded. Financial award application deadline: 2/15. *Faculty research:* Positive behavior support, school reform, school improvement. *Unit head:* Dr. Dorothy Giroux, Director, 312-915-7027, E-mail: dgiroux@luc.edu. *Application contact:* Marie Rosin-Dittmar, Information Contact, 312-915-6800, E-mail: schleduc@luc.edu.

Loyola University Maryland, Graduate Programs, College of Arts and Sciences, Department of Education, Program in Educational Technology, Baltimore, MD 21210-2699. Offers M Ed. *Entrance requirements:* For master's, GRE General Test, GRE Subject Test (recommended). Additional exam requirements/recommendations for international students: Required—TOEFL (minimum score 550 paper-based; 213 computer-based).

Malone University, Graduate Program in Education, Canton, OH 44709. Offers curriculum and instruction (MA); curriculum, instruction, and professional development (MA); instructional technology (MA); intervention specialist (MA); reading (MA). Part-time and evening/weekend programs available. *Faculty:* 7 full-time (4 women), 7 part-time/adjunct (5 women). *Students:* 2 full-time (1 woman), 64 part-time (55 women); includes 1 minority (African American). Average age 34. In 2009, 27 master's awarded. *Degree requirements:* For master's, research project. *Entrance requirements:* For master's, minimum GPA of 3.0, teaching license. Additional exam requirements/recommendations for international students: Required—TOEFL (minimum score 550 paper-based; 213 computer-based; 79 iBT). *Application deadline:* Applications are processed on a rolling basis. Application fee: $25. *Expenses:* Tuition: Part-time $450 per semester hour.

Financial support: Tuition waivers (partial) available. Support available to part-time students. Financial award application deadline: 6/30. *Faculty research:* The Bible as children's literature, special needs students and literacy development, middle level education, school/university partnerships and professional development, child/adolescent literature and popular culture. *Unit head:* Dr. Alice E. Christie, Director, 330-478-8541, Fax: 330-471-8563, E-mail: achristie@malone.edu. *Application contact:* David L. Kleffman, Assistant Director of Enrollment, 330-471-8447, Fax: 330-471-8343, E-mail: dkleffman@malone.edu.

Marywood University, Academic Affairs, Insalaco College of Creative and Performing Arts, Department of Communication Arts, Program in Information Sciences, Scranton, PA 18509-1598. Offers corporate communication (Certificate); e-business (Certificate); health communication (Certificate); information sciences (MS), including library science/information specialist; instructional technology (Certificate). *Students:* 1 full-time (0 women), 4 part-time (3 women). Average age 32. In 2009, 3 master's awarded. *Entrance requirements:* Additional exam requirements/recommendations for international students: Required—TOEFL (minimum score 550 paper-based; 213 computer-based; 79 iBT). *Application deadline:* For fall admission, 4/1 priority date for domestic students, 3/31 priority date for international students; for spring admission, 11/1 priority date for domestic students, 8/31 priority date for international students. Applications are processed on a rolling basis. Application fee: $35. Electronic applications accepted. *Expenses:* Tuition: Part-time $715 per credit. Required fees: $270 per semester. Tuition and fees vary according to degree level, campus/location and program. *Financial support:* Career-related internships or fieldwork, scholarships/grants, and unspecified assistantships available. Support available to part-time students. Financial award application deadline: 6/30; financial award applicants required to submit FAFSA. *Application contact:* Tammy Manka, Assistant Director of Graduate Admissions, 866-279-9663, E-mail: tmanka@marywood.edu.

McDaniel College, Graduate and Professional Studies, Program in Media/Library Science, Westminster, MD 21157-4390. Offers MS. Part-time and evening/weekend programs available. *Degree requirements:* For master's, comprehensive exam, thesis optional. *Entrance requirements:* For master's, GRE General Test, MAT, or NTE/PRAXIS I, letters of reference (3). Additional exam requirements/recommendations for international students: Required—TOEFL (minimum score 213 computer-based). *Expenses:* Tuition: Part-time $325 per credit hour.

McNeese State University, Doré School of Graduate Studies, Burton College of Education, Department of Educational Leadership and Instructional Technology, Program in Educational Leadership, Lake Charles, LA 70609. Offers educational leadership (M Ed); educational technology (Ed S). Evening/weekend programs available. *Faculty:* 5 full-time (0 women). *Students:* 11 full-time (10 women), 65 part-time (44 women); includes 16 minority (15 African Americans, 1 Hispanic American). In 2009, 22 master's, 2 Ed Ss awarded. *Degree requirements:* For Ed S, comprehensive exam. *Entrance requirements:* For master's, GRE, teaching certificate, 3 years full-time teaching experience; for Ed S, teaching certificate, 3 years of teaching experience, 1 year of administration or supervision experience, master's degree with 12 semester hours in graduate education. *Application deadline:* For fall admission, 5/15 priority date for domestic and international students; for spring admission, 10/15 priority date for domestic and international students. Applications are processed on a rolling basis. Application fee: $20 ($30 for international students). *Expenses:* Tuition, area resident: Full-time $2556. Tuition, state resident: full-time $2556. Required fees: $1031. Tuition and fees vary according to course load. *Financial support:* Fellowships available. Financial award application deadline: 5/1. *Unit head:* Dr. Sharon Van Metre, Head, 337-475-5423, Fax: 337-475-5402, E-mail: svanmetre@mcneese.edu. *Application contact:* Dr. George F. Mead, Interim Dean of Dore' School of Graduate Studies, 337-475-5396, Fax: 337-475-5397, E-mail: admissions@mcneese.edu.

McNeese State University, Doré School of Graduate Studies, Burton College of Education, Department of Educational Leadership and Instructional Technology, Program in Educational Technology Leadership, Lake Charles, LA 70609. Offers M Ed. Evening/weekend programs available. *Faculty:* 4 full-time (2 women). *Students:* 5 full-time (all women), 18 part-time (17 women); includes 3 minority (all African Americans), 1 international. In 2009, 5 master's awarded. *Entrance requirements:* For master's, GRE, teaching certificate. *Application deadline:* For fall admission, 5/15 priority date for domestic and international students; for spring admission, 10/15 priority date for domestic and international students. Applications are processed on a rolling basis. Application fee: $20 ($30 for international students). *Expenses:* Tuition, area resident: Full-time $2556. Tuition, state resident: full-time $2556. Required fees: $1031. Tuition and fees vary according to course load. *Financial support:* Fellowships available. Financial award application deadline: 5/1. *Unit head:* Dr. Sharon Van Metre, Head, 337-475-5423, Fax: 337-475-5402, E-mail: svanmetre@mcneese.edu. *Application contact:* Dr. George F. Mead, Interim Dean of Dore' School of Graduate Studies, 337-475-5396, Fax: 337-475-5397, E-mail: admissions@mcneese.edu.

McNeese State University, Doré School of Graduate Studies, Burton College of Education, Department of Educational Leadership and Instructional Technology, Program in Instructional Technology, Lake Charles, LA 70609. Offers MS. Evening/weekend programs available. *Faculty:* 4 full-time (2 women). *Students:* 16 full-time (12 women), 9 part-time (all women); includes 5 minority (all African Americans), 6 international. In 2009, 12 master's awarded. *Entrance requirements:* For master's, GRE. *Application deadline:* For fall admission, 5/15 priority date for domestic and international students; for spring admission, 10/15 priority date for domestic and international students. Applications are processed on a rolling basis. Application fee: $20 ($30 for international students). *Expenses:* Tuition, area resident: Full-time $2556. Tuition, state resident: full-time $2556. Required fees: $1031. Tuition and fees vary according to course load. *Financial support:* Application deadline: 5/1. *Unit head:* Dr. Sharon Van Metre, Head, 337-475-5423, Fax: 337-475-5402, E-mail: svanmetre@mcneese.edu. *Application contact:* Dr. George F. Mead, Interim Dean of Dore' School of Graduate Studies, 337-475-5396, Fax: 337-475-5397, E-mail: admissions@mcneese.edu.

Memorial University of Newfoundland, School of Graduate Studies, Faculty of Education, St. John's, NL A1C 5S7, Canada. Offers counseling psychology (M Ed); curriculum, teaching, and learning studies (M Ed); education (PhD); educational leadership studies (M Ed); information technology (M Ed); post-secondary studies (M Ed, Diploma), including health professional education (Diploma). Part-time programs available. *Degree requirements:* For master's, thesis optional, internship, paper folio, project; for doctorate, comprehensive exam, thesis/dissertation, thesis seminar, oral defense of thesis. *Entrance requirements:* For master's, undergraduate degree with at least 2nd class standing, 1-2 years work experience; for doctorate, minimum A average in graduate course work, MA in education, 2 years professional experience; for Diploma, 2nd class degree, 2 years of work experience with adult learners, appropriate academic qualifications and work experience in a health-related field. Electronic applications accepted. *Faculty research:* Critical thinking, literacy, cognitive studies and counseling, educational change, technology in instruction.

Miami University, Graduate School, School of Education and Allied Professions, Department of Educational Psychology, Oxford, OH 45056. Offers educational psychology (M Ed); instructional design and technology (M Ed, MA); school psychology (MS, Ed S); special education (M Ed). *Accreditation:* NCATE. *Students:* 39 full-time (34 women), 42 part-time (39 women); includes 5 minority (2 African Americans, 2 Asian Americans or Pacific Islanders, 1 Hispanic American), 9 international. *Entrance requirements:* For master's, GRE General Test or MAT, minimum undergraduate GPA of 3.0 during previous 2 years or 2.75 overall; for Ed S, GRE General Test or MAT. Additional exam requirements/recommendations for international students: Required—TOEFL. Application fee: $50. *Expenses:* Tuition, state resident: full-time $11,280. Tuition, nonresident: full-time $24,912. Required fees: $516. *Financial support:* Fellowships with full tuition reimbursements, research assistantships with full tuition reimbursements, teaching assistantships with full tuition reimbursements, career-related internships or fieldwork, Federal Work-Study, health care benefits, tuition waivers (full), and unspecified assistantships available. Financial award application deadline: 3/1. *Unit head:* Dr. Nelda Cambron-McCabe, Chair, 513-529-6836, Fax: 513-529-6621, E-mail: edp@muohio.edu. *Application contact:* Dr. Nelda Cambron-McCabe, Chair, 513-529-6836, Fax: 513-529-6621, E-mail: edp@muohio.edu.

Michigan State University, The Graduate School, College of Education, Department of Counseling, Educational Psychology and Special Education, East Lansing, MI 48824. Offers counseling (MA); educational psychology and educational technology (PhD); educational technology (MA); measurement and quantitative methods (PhD); rehabilitation counseling (MA); rehabilitation counselor education (PhD); school psychology (MA, PhD, Ed S); special education (MA, PhD). *Accreditation:* APA (one or more programs are accredited); CORE (one or more programs are accredited). Part-time programs available. *Faculty:* 35 full-time (13 women). *Students:* 217 full-time (154 women), 144 part-time (107 women); includes 48 minority (25 African Americans, 13 Asian Americans or Pacific Islanders, 10 Hispanic Americans), 71 international. Average age 32. 238 applicants, 46% accepted. In 2009, 117 master's, 36 doctorates awarded. *Entrance requirements:* Additional exam requirements/recommendations for international students: Required—TOEFL. Electronic applications accepted. *Expenses:* Tuition, state resident: part-time $478.25 per credit hour. Tuition, nonresident: part-time $966.50 per credit hour. Part-time tuition and fees vary according to program. *Financial support:* In 2009–10, 71 research assistantships with tuition reimbursements (averaging $6,836 per year), 74 teaching assistantships with tuition reimbursements (averaging $6,858 per year) were awarded. Total annual research expenditures: $2.3 million. *Unit head:* Dr. Richard S. Prawat, Chairperson, 517-353-6417, Fax: 517-353-6393, E-mail: rsprawat@msu.edu. *Application contact:* Kathy Dimoff, Graduate Admissions Coordinator, 517-355-6683, Fax: 517-353-6393, E-mail: dimoff@msu.edu.

MidAmerica Nazarene University, Graduate Studies in Education, Olathe, KS 66062-1899. Offers ESOL (M Ed); professional teaching (M Ed); special education (MA); technology enhanced teaching (M Ed). *Accreditation:* NCATE. Part-time and evening/weekend programs available. Postbaccalaureate distance learning degree programs offered (no on-campus study). *Faculty:* 6 full-time (2 women), 14 part-time/adjunct (8 women). *Students:* 2 full-time (1 woman), 148 part-time (120 women); includes 15 minority (7 African Americans, 3 American Indian/Alaska Native, 1 Asian American or Pacific Islander, 4 Hispanic Americans). Average age 36. In 2009, 72 master's awarded. *Degree requirements:* For master's, thesis or alternative, creative project, technology leadership practicum. *Entrance requirements:* For master's, minimum undergraduate GPA of 2.8, 2 years of teaching experience. *Application deadline:* Applications are processed on a rolling basis. Application fee: $25. *Expenses:* Contact institution. *Financial support:* Applicants required to submit FAFSA. *Unit head:* Dr. Martin Dunlap, Director, 913-971-3292, Fax: 913-971-3407, E-mail: mhdunlap@mnu.edu. *Application contact:* Glenna Murray, Administrative Assistant, 913-971-3292, Fax: 913-971-3407, E-mail: gkmurray@mnu.edu.

Middle Tennessee State University, College of Graduate Studies, College of Education and Behavioral Science, Department of Educational Leadership, Program in Curriculum and Instruction, Murfreesboro, TN 37132. Offers curriculum and instruction (M Ed, Ed S); English as a second language (M Ed, Ed S); secondary education (M Ed); technology and curriculum design (Ed S). *Accreditation:* NCATE. Part-time and evening/weekend programs available. Postbaccalaureate distance learning degree programs offered. *Students:* 14 full-time (7 women), 277 part-time (249 women); includes 39 minority (35 African Americans, 3 Asian Americans or Pacific Islanders, 1 Hispanic American). 80 applicants, 89% accepted, 71 enrolled. In 2009, 69 master's, 40 Ed Ss awarded. *Degree requirements:* For master's, comprehensive exam. *Entrance requirements:* For master's and Ed S, GRE, MAT or PRAXIS. Additional exam requirements/recommendations for international students: Required—TOEFL (minimum score 525 paper-based; 195 computer-based; 71 iBT) or IELTS (minimum score 6). *Application deadline:* For fall admission, 6/1 for domestic and international students. Applications are processed on a rolling basis. Application fee: $25 ($30 for international students). Electronic applications accepted. *Expenses:* Tuition, state resident: full-time $4404. Tuition, nonresident: full-time $10,956. *Financial support:* Application deadline: 5/1. *Unit head:* Dr. James Huffman, Chair, 615-898-2855, Fax: 615-898-2859. *Application contact:* Dr. Michael Allen, Dean and Vice Provost for Research, 615-898-2840, Fax: 615-904-8020, E-mail: mallen@mtsu.edu.

Midwestern State University, Graduate Studies, College of Education, Program in Educational Leadership and Technology, Wichita Falls, TX 76308. Offers ME. Part-time and evening/weekend programs available. *Degree requirements:* For master's, comprehensive exam. *Entrance requirements:* For master's, GRE General Test or MAT. Additional exam requirements/recommendations for international students: Required—TOEFL (minimum score 550 paper-based; 213 computer-based). Electronic applications accepted. *Expenses:* Tuition, state resident: full-time $1620; part-time $90 per credit hour. Tuition, nonresident: full-time $2160; part-time $120 per credit hour. International tuition: $7506 full-time. Required fees: $3068.80; $145.60 per credit hour. $179 per semester.

Minnesota State University Mankato, College of Graduate Studies, College of Education, Department of Educational Studies: K–12 and Secondary Programs, Program in Library Media Education, Mankato, MN 56001. Offers MS, Certificate. *Accreditation:* NCATE. Part-time programs available. *Students:* 27 part-time (26 women). *Degree requirements:* For master's, comprehensive exam, thesis or alternative; for Certificate, comprehensive exam, thesis. *Entrance requirements:* For master's, GRE General Test (if GPA less than 3.0), minimum GPA of 3.0 during previous 2 years; for Certificate, minimum GPA of 3.0. Additional exam requirements/recommendations for international students: Required—TOEFL. *Application deadline:* For fall admission, 7/1 priority date for domestic students; for spring admission, 11/1 for domestic students. Applications are processed on a rolling basis. Application fee: $40. Electronic applications accepted. *Expenses:* Tuition, state resident: full-time $5364. Tuition, nonresident: full-time $8314. *Financial support:* Research assistantships with full tuition reimbursements, teaching assistantships with full tuition reimbursements, career-related internships or fieldwork, Federal Work-Study, and institutionally sponsored loans available. Support available to part-time students. Financial award application deadline: 3/15; financial award applicants required to submit FAFSA. *Unit head:* Dr. Deborah Jesseman, Graduate Coordinator, 507-389-1965. *Application contact:* 507-389-2321, E-mail: grad@mnsu.edu.

Mississippi State University, College of Education, Department of Instructional Systems and Workforce Development, Mississippi State, MS 39762. Offers education (Ed D, Ed S), including technology; instructional systems and workforce development (PhD); instructional technology (MSIT); technology (MS). *Faculty:* 10 full-time (7 women). *Students:* 29 full-time (14 women), 115 part-time (97 women); includes 69 minority (all African Americans), 5 international. Average age 36. 35 applicants, 74% accepted, 19 enrolled. In 2009, 30 master's, 11 doctorates, 1 other advanced degree awarded. *Degree requirements:* For master's, comprehensive exam, thesis optional, comprehensive oral or written exam; for doctorate, comprehensive exam, thesis/dissertation, comprehensive oral and written exam; for Ed S, comprehensive exam, thesis, comprehensive written exam. *Entrance requirements:* For master's, GRE, minimum GPA of 2.75 in junior and senior courses; for doctorate and Ed S, GRE. Additional exam requirements/recommendations for international students: Required—TOEFL (minimum score 550 paper-based; 213 computer-based; 79 iBT); Recommended—IELTS (minimum score 6.5). *Application deadline:* For fall admission, 7/1 for domestic students, 5/1 for international students; for spring admission, 11/1 for domestic students, 9/1 for international students. Applications are processed on a rolling basis. Application fee: $40. Electronic applications accepted. *Expenses:* Tuition, state resident: full-time $2575.50; part-time $286.25 per credit hour. Tuition, nonresident: full-time $6510; part-time $723.50 per credit hour. Tuition and fees vary according to course load. *Financial support:* In 2009–10, 5 teaching assistantships with full tuition reimbursements (averaging $10,078 per year) were awarded; Federal Work-Study, institutionally sponsored loans, and unspecified assistantships also available. Financial award application deadline: 4/1; financial award applicants required to submit FAFSA. *Faculty research:* Computer technology, nontraditional students, interactive video, instructional technology, educational leadership. *Unit head:* Dr. Linda Cornelius, Professor and Interim Head, 662-325-2281, Fax: 662-325-7599, E-mail: lcornelius@colled.msstate.edu. *Application contact:* Interim Associate Vice President for Academic Affairs/Interim Dean of Graduate Studies.

Missouri Southern State University, Program in Instructional Technology, Joplin, MO 64801-1595. Offers MS Ed. *Degree requirements:* For master's, comprehensive exam. *Entrance requirements:* For master's, GRE, minimum GPA of 3.0.

Missouri State University, Graduate College, College of Education, Department of Reading, Foundations, and Technology, Program in Instructional Media Technology, Springfield, MO 65897. Offers MS Ed. Part-time programs available. *Students:* 1 full-time (0 women), 13 part-time (9 women), 1 international. Average age 39. 3 applicants, 100% accepted, 3 enrolled. In 2009, 6 master's awarded. *Degree requirements:* For master's, comprehensive exam, thesis or alternative. *Entrance requirements:* Additional exam requirements/recommendations for international students: Required—TOEFL (minimum score 550 paper-based; 213 computer-based; 79 iBT). *Application deadline:* For fall admission, 7/20 for domestic students, 5/1 for international students; for spring admission, 12/20 for domestic students, 9/1 for international students. Applications are processed on a rolling basis. Application fee: $35 ($50 for international students). Electronic applications accepted. *Expenses:* Tuition, state resident: full-time $3852; part-time $214 per credit hour. Tuition, nonresident: full-time $7524; part-time $418 per credit hour. Required fees: $696; $172 per semester. Tuition and fees vary according to course level, course load, degree level and program. *Financial support:* Federal Work-Study, institutionally sponsored loans, scholarships/grants, and unspecified assistantships available. Financial award application deadline: 3/31; financial award applicants required to submit FAFSA. *Unit head:* Dr. Fred Groves, Graduate Program Coordinator, 417-836-6769, E-mail: fredgroves@missouristate.edu. *Application contact:* Eric Eckert, Coordinator of Graduate Admissions and Recruitment, 417-836-5331, Fax: 417-836-6200, E-mail: ericeckert@missouristate.edu.

Montana State University Billings, College of Education, Department of Educational Theory and Practice, Option in Educational Technology, Billings, MT 59101-0298. Offers M Ed. *Accreditation:* NCATE. Part-time programs available. *Degree requirements:* For master's, professional paper or thesis. *Entrance requirements:* For master's, GRE General Test or MAT, minimum GPA of 3.0 (undergraduate), 3.25 (graduate).

Montclair State University, The Graduate School, College of Education and Human Services, Department of Curriculum and Teaching, Montclair, NJ 07043-1624. Offers education (M Ed); educational technology (M Ed); learning disabled teacher consultant (Certificate); school library media specialist (Certificate); teaching (MAT, Certificate), including art (MAT), biological science (MAT), early childhood education (P-3) (MAT), earth science (MAT), elementary education (K-8) (MAT), English (MAT), French (MAT), health and physical education (MAT), health education (MAT), home economics (MAT), mathematics (MAT), music (MAT), physical education (MAT), physical science (MAT), social studies (MAT), Spanish (MAT), teacher of ESL (MAT), teacher of students with disabilities (MAT). Part-time and evening/weekend programs available. *Faculty:* 17 full-time (12 women), 29 part-time/adjunct (21 women). *Students:* 124 full-time (63 women), 174 part-time (126 women). Average age 31. 112 applicants, 69% accepted, 59 enrolled. In 2009, 179 master's, 2 other advanced degrees awarded. *Degree requirements:* For master's, comprehensive exam, field experience. *Entrance requirements:* For master's, GRE, 2 letters of recommendation. Additional exam requirements/recommendations for international students: Required—TOEFL (minimum score 83 computer-based), or IELTS. *Application deadline:* For fall admission, 2/15 for domestic and international students; for spring admission, 9/15 for domestic and international students. Applications are processed on a rolling basis. Application fee: $60. Electronic applications accepted. *Expenses:* Tuition, area resident: Part-time $486.74 per credit. Tuition, state resident: part-time $486.74 per credit. Tuition, nonresident: part-time $751.34 per credit. Tuition and fees vary according to degree level and program. *Financial support:* In 2009–10, 12 research assistantships with full tuition reimbursements (averaging $7,000 per year) were awarded; Federal Work-Study, scholarships/grants, and unspecified assistantships also available. Support available to part-time students. Financial award application deadline: 3/1; financial award applicants required to submit FAFSA. *Unit head:* Dr. David Schwarzer, Chairperson, 973-655-5187. *Application contact:* Amy Aiello, Director of Graduate Admissions and Operations, 973-655-5147, Fax: 973-655-7869, E-mail: graduate.school@montclair.edu.

Morehead State University, Graduate Programs, College of Education, Department of Foundational and Graduate Studies in Education, Morehead, KY 40351. Offers adult and higher education (MA, Ed S); certified professional counselor (Ed S); counseling P-12 (MA); curriculum and instruction (Ed S); educational technology (MA Ed); instructional leadership (Ed S); school administration (MA); school counseling (Ed S); teacher leader business and marketing- content (MA Ed); teacher leader business and marketing- technology (MA Ed); teacher leader educational technology (MA Ed); teacher leader English (MA Ed); teacher leader gifted educ (MA Ed); teacher leader IECE—non-certification (MA Ed); teacher leader IECE certification (MA Ed); teacher leader interdisciplanary educaction P-5 (MA Ed); teacher leader middle grades 5-9 (MA Ed); teacher leader reading/writing—non-certification (MA Ed); teacher leader reading/writing certification (MA Ed); teacher leader school communication—non-certification (MA Ed); teacher leader school communication certification (MA Ed); teacher leader social studies (MA Ed); teacher leader special education (MA Ed). *Accreditation:* NCATE. Part-time and evening/weekend programs available. *Faculty:* 20 full-time (10 women), 7 part-time/adjunct (3 women). *Students:* 26 full-time (18 women), 371 part-time (295 women); includes 11 minority (9 African Americans, 1 American Indian/Alaska Native, 1 Hispanic American). Average age 35. 201 applicants, 73% accepted, 73 enrolled. In 2009, 105 master's, 5 other advanced degrees awarded. *Degree requirements:* For master's, thesis optional, oral and/or written comprehensive exams; for Ed S, thesis, oral exam. *Entrance requirements:* For master's, GRE General Test, minimum overall undergraduate GPA of 2.5; for Ed S, GRE General Test, interview, master's degree, minimum GPA of 3.5, work experience. Additional exam requirements/recommendations for international students: Required—TOEFL (minimum score 500 paper-based; 173 computer-based). *Application deadline:* For fall admission, 8/1 priority date for domestic and international students; for spring admission, 12/1 priority date for domestic and international students. Applications are processed on a rolling basis. Application fee: $30. Electronic applications accepted. *Expenses:* Tuition, state resident: full-time $6318; part-time $351 per credit hour. Tuition, nonresident: full-time $15,804; part-time $878 per credit hour. *Financial support:* In 2009–10, 2 research assistantships (averaging $10,000 per year) were awarded; career-related internships or fieldwork, Federal Work-Study, and unspecified assistantships also available. Financial award application deadline: 3/15; financial award applicants required to submit FAFSA. *Faculty research:* Character education, school accountability, computer applications for school administrators. *Unit head:* Dr. Cathy Gunn, Dean and Professor, 606-783-2040, Fax: 606-783-5029, E-mail: c.gunn@moreheadstate.edu. *Application contact:* Michelle Barber, Graduate Recruitment and Retention Assistant Director, 606-783-5127, Fax: 606-783-5061, E-mail: m.barber@moreheadstate.edu.

National-Louis University, National College of Education, Program in Technology in Education, Chicago, IL 60603. Offers M Ed, MS Ed, CAS. Part-time and evening/weekend programs available. *Degree requirements:* For master's, thesis (for some programs). *Entrance requirements:* For master's, GRE or MAT, minimum GPA of 3.0, teaching certificate; for CAS, master's degree, teaching certificate. *Expenses:* Tuition: Full-time $17,160; part-time $715 per semester hour. Tuition and fees vary according to course load, degree level, campus/location and program.

National University, Academic Affairs, School of Media and Communication, Department of Media, La Jolla, CA 92037-1011. Offers digital cinema (MFA); educational and instructional technology (MS); video game production and design (MFA). Part-time and evening/weekend programs available. Postbaccalaureate distance learning degree programs offered (no on-campus study). *Faculty:* 9 full-time (4 women), 13 part-time/adjunct (4 women). *Students:* 68 full-time (26 women), 118 part-time (45 women); includes 64 minority (29 African Americans, 10 Asian Americans or Pacific Islanders, 25 Hispanic Americans), 1 international. Average age 39. 118 applicants, 100% accepted, 70 enrolled. In 2009, 58 master's awarded. *Degree requirements:* For master's, thesis. *Entrance requirements:* For master's, interview, minimum GPA of 2.5. Additional exam requirements/recommendations for international students: Required—TOEFL (minimum score 550 paper-based; 213 computer-based; 79 iBT), IELTS (minimum score 6). *Application deadline:* Applications are processed on a rolling basis. Application fee: $60 ($65 for international students). Electronic applications accepted. *Expenses:* Tuition: Part-time $338 per quarter hour. *Financial support:* Career-related internships or

Educational Media/Instructional Technology

National University *(continued)*
fieldwork, institutionally sponsored loans, scholarships/grants, and tuition waivers (partial) available. Support available to part-time students. Financial award application deadline: 6/30; financial award applicants required to submit FAFSA. *Unit head:* Dr. Timothy Langdell, Department Chair, 310-662-2149, Fax: 858-309-3450, E-mail: tlangdell@nu.edu. *Application contact:* Dominick Giovanniello, Associate Regional Dean—San Diego, 800-NAT-UNIV, Fax: 858-541-7792, E-mail: dgiovann@nu.edu.

Nazareth College of Rochester, Graduate Studies, Department of Education, Program in Educational Technology/Computer Education, Rochester, NY 14618-3790. Offers MS Ed. Part-time and evening/weekend programs available. *Entrance requirements:* For master's, minimum GPA of 3.0.

New Jersey City University, Graduate Studies and Continuing Education, Debra Cannon Partridge Wolfe College of Education, Concentration in Educational Technology, Jersey City, NJ 07305-1597. Offers MA. *Accreditation:* NCATE. Part-time and evening/weekend programs available. Postbaccalaureate distance learning degree programs offered (minimal on-campus study). *Faculty:* 3. *Students:* 5 full-time (4 women), 99 part-time (75 women); includes 14 minority (1 African American, 2 Asian Americans or Pacific Islanders, 11 Hispanic Americans), 3 international. Average age 37. In 2009, 54 master's awarded. *Degree requirements:* For master's, internship. *Entrance requirements:* For master's, GRE General Test or MAT. Additional exam requirements/recommendations for international students: Required—TOEFL. *Application deadline:* For fall admission, 8/1 priority date for domestic students; for spring admission, 12/1 for domestic students. Applications are processed on a rolling basis. Application fee: $0. *Expenses:* Tuition, area resident: Part-time $456.75 per credit. Tuition, nonresident: part-time $842.55 per credit. Required fees: $65 per term. *Financial support:* Unspecified assistantships available. *Unit head:* Dr. Cordelia Twomey, Chairperson, 201-200-3421, E-mail: ctwomey@njcu.edu. *Application contact:* Dr. Cordelia Twomey, Chairperson, 201-200-3421, E-mail: ctwomey@njcu.edu.

New York Institute of Technology, Graduate Division, School of Education, Program in Instructional Technology, Old Westbury, NY 11568-8000. Offers distance learning (Advanced Certificate); instructional technology (MS); multimedia (Advanced Certificate). Part-time and evening/weekend programs available. Postbaccalaureate distance learning degree programs offered. *Students:* 20 full-time (11 women), 211 part-time (115 women); includes 28 minority (10 African Americans, 7 Asian Americans or Pacific Islanders, 11 Hispanic Americans), 8 international. Average age 34. In 2009, 93 master's awarded. *Degree requirements:* For master's, thesis. *Entrance requirements:* For master's, minimum QPA of 3.0; for Advanced Certificate, master's degree, minimum GPA of 3.0, 3 years of teaching experience, New York teaching certificate, 2 letters of recommendation. Additional exam requirements/recommendations for international students: Required—TOEFL (minimum score 550 paper-based; 213 computer-based). *Application deadline:* For fall admission, 7/1 priority date for domestic students; for spring admission, 12/1 priority date for domestic students. Applications are processed on a rolling basis. Application fee: $50. Electronic applications accepted. *Expenses:* Tuition: Part-time $825 per credit. *Financial support:* Research assistantships with partial tuition reimbursements, career-related internships or fieldwork, institutionally sponsored loans, and tuition waivers (full and partial) available. Support available to part-time students. Financial award applicants required to submit FAFSA. *Faculty research:* Distance learning, teacher training resources and strategies. *Unit head:* Dr. Sarah McPherson, Coordinator, 516-686-1053, Fax: 516-686-7655, E-mail: smcphers@nyit.edu. *Application contact:* Dr. Jacquelyn Nealon, Vice President for Enrollment Services, 516-686-7925, Fax: 516-686-7597, E-mail: jnealon@nyit.edu.

New York Institute of Technology, Graduate Division, School of Education, Program in School Leadership and Technology, Old Westbury, NY 11568-8000. Offers Professional Diploma. Part-time and evening/weekend programs available. *Students:* 14 full-time (7 women), 14 part-time (9 women); includes 3 African Americans, 1 Asian American or Pacific Islander, 1 Hispanic American. Average age 36. 2 applicants, 50% accepted, 0 enrolled. In 2009, 2 Professional Diplomas awarded. *Degree requirements:* For Professional Diploma, internship. *Entrance requirements:* For degree, 3 years full-time teaching experience, permanent teacher certification in New York state. Additional exam requirements/recommendations for international students: Required—TOEFL (minimum score 550 paper-based; 213 computer-based). *Application deadline:* For fall admission, 7/1 for domestic students; for spring admission, 12/1 for domestic students. Application fee: $50. *Expenses:* Tuition: Part-time $825 per credit. *Financial support:* Career-related internships or fieldwork available. Financial award applicants required to submit FAFSA. *Unit head:* Dr. Jacqueline Kress, Dean, 516-686-7706, Fax: 516-686-7655. *Application contact:* Jacquelyn Nealon, Dean of Admissions and Financial Aid, 516-686-7925, Fax: 516-686-7613, E-mail: jnealon@nyit.edu.

New York University, Steinhardt School of Culture, Education, and Human Development, Department of Administration, Leadership, and Technology, Program in Educational Communication and Technology, New York, NY 10012-1019. Offers MA, PhD, Advanced Certificate. Part-time programs available. *Students:* 22 full-time (12 women), 38 part-time (18 women); includes 15 minority (3 African Americans, 1 American Indian/Alaska Native, 6 Asian Americans or Pacific Islanders, 5 Hispanic Americans), 14 international. Average age 34. 55 applicants, 69% accepted, 11 enrolled. In 2009, 12 master's, 1 doctorate awarded. *Degree requirements:* For master's, thesis (for some programs); for doctorate, thesis/dissertation. *Entrance requirements:* For doctorate, GRE General Test, interview; for Advanced Certificate, master's degree. Additional exam requirements/recommendations for international students: Required—TOEFL. *Application deadline:* For fall admission, 12/15 priority date for domestic and international students; for spring admission, 11/1 for domestic and international students. Applications are processed on a rolling basis. Application fee: $75. Electronic applications accepted. *Expenses:* Tuition: Full-time $30,528; part-time $1272 per credit. Required fees: $2177. *Financial support:* Fellowships with full and partial tuition reimbursements, research assistantships with full and partial tuition reimbursements, teaching assistantships with partial tuition reimbursements, career-related internships or fieldwork, Federal Work-Study, institutionally sponsored loans, scholarships/grants, tuition waivers (partial), and unspecified assistantships available. Support available to part-time students. Financial award application deadline: 2/1; financial award applicants required to submit FAFSA. *Faculty research:* Digital design for learning, critical evaluation of games, multimedia, cognitive science, individual differences in multimedia learning, serious games. *Unit head:* Dr. Francine Shuchat Shaw, Director, 212-998-5520, Fax: 212-995-4047. *Application contact:* 212-998-5030, Fax: 212-995-4328, E-mail: steinhardt.gradadmissions@nyu.edu.

North Carolina Agricultural and Technical State University, Graduate School, School of Education, Department of Curriculum and Instruction, Greensboro, NC 27411. Offers elementary education (MA Ed); instructional technology (MS); reading (MA Ed); teaching (MAT). *Accreditation:* NCATE. Part-time and evening/weekend programs available. *Degree requirements:* For master's, comprehensive exam, qualifying exam. *Entrance requirements:* For master's, GRE General Test, minimum GPA of 3.0.

North Carolina Central University, Division of Academic Affairs, School of Education, Program in Educational Technology, Durham, NC 27707-3129. Offers MA. *Accreditation:* NCATE. Part-time and evening/weekend programs available. *Degree requirements:* For master's, comprehensive exam, thesis or alternative. *Entrance requirements:* For master's, GRE, minimum GPA of 3.0 in major, 2.5 overall. Additional exam requirements/recommendations for international students: Required—TOEFL. *Faculty research:* Role of media in school libraries, media and implications for educational gerontology.

North Carolina Central University, Division of Academic Affairs, School of Education, Program in Instructional Technology, Durham, NC 27707-3129. Offers M Ed.

North Carolina State University, Graduate School, College of Education, Department of Curriculum and Instruction, Program in Instructional Technology, Raleigh, NC 27695. Offers M Ed, MS. *Entrance requirements:* For master's, MAT or GRE, minimum GPA of 3.0, 3 letters of reference.

North Carolina State University, Graduate School, College of Education, Department of Mathematics, Science, and Technology Education, Program in Technology Education, Raleigh, NC 27695. Offers M Ed, MS, Ed D. *Degree requirements:* For master's, thesis (for some programs); for doctorate, thesis/dissertation. *Entrance requirements:* For master's, GRE or MAT; for doctorate, GRE General Test or MAT, minimum GPA of 3.0, interview. Electronic applications accepted.

Northeastern State University, Graduate College, College of Education, Program in Library Media and Information Technology, Tahlequah, OK 74464-2399. Offers MS Ed. *Entrance requirements:* Additional exam requirements/recommendations for international students: Required—TOEFL (minimum score 213 computer-based).

Northern Arizona University, Graduate College, College of Education, Department of Educational Specialties, Flagstaff, AZ 86011. Offers autism spectrum disorders (Certificate); bilingual/multicultural education (M Ed), including bilingual education, ESL education; career and technical education (M Ed, Certificate); curriculum and instruction (Ed D); early childhood special education (M Ed); early intervention (Certificate); educational technology (M Ed, Certificate); special education (M Ed). *Faculty:* 29 full-time (16 women). *Students:* 153 full-time (118 women), 360 part-time (291 women); includes 152 minority (12 African Americans, 43 American Indian/Alaska Native, 5 Asian Americans or Pacific Islanders, 92 Hispanic Americans), 9 international. Average age 30. 215 applicants, 87% accepted, 133 enrolled. In 2009, 200 master's, 8 doctorates awarded. *Degree requirements:* For master's, comprehensive exam (for some programs), thesis (for some programs). *Entrance requirements:* For master's, minimum GPA of 3.0. Additional exam requirements/recommendations for international students: Required—TOEFL (minimum score 550 paper-based; 213 computer-based; 80 iBT), IELTS (minimum score 7), or a bachelor's degree from an English-speaking university and demonstrated proficiency. *Application deadline:* For fall admission, 2/1 for domestic students, 8/1 for international students; for spring admission, 12/1 for domestic students. Applications are processed on a rolling basis. Application fee: $65. Electronic applications accepted. *Financial support:* In 2009–10, 2 research assistantships with partial tuition reimbursements (averaging $10,000 per year), 8 teaching assistantships with partial tuition reimbursements (averaging $10,000 per year) were awarded. Financial award application deadline: 3/30. *Unit head:* Dr. Lawrence Gallagher, Chair, 928-523-5083, E-mail: lawrence.gallagher@nau.edu. *Application contact:* Dr. Lawrence Gallagher, Chair, 928-523-5083, E-mail: lawrence.gallagher@nau.edu.

Northern Illinois University, Graduate School, College of Education, Department of Educational Technology, Research and Assessment, De Kalb, IL 60115-2854. Offers educational research and evaluation (MS); instructional technology (MS Ed, Ed D). Part-time and evening/weekend programs available. *Faculty:* 13 full-time (7 women). *Students:* 38 full-time (21 women), 137 part-time (95 women); includes 34 minority (18 African Americans, 9 Asian Americans or Pacific Islanders, 7 Hispanic Americans), 11 international. Average age 40. 41 applicants, 59% accepted, 19 enrolled. In 2009, 25 master's, 16 doctorates awarded. Terminal master's awarded for partial completion of doctoral program. *Degree requirements:* For master's, comprehensive exam, thesis optional; for doctorate, thesis/dissertation, candidacy exam, dissertation defense. *Entrance requirements:* For master's, GRE General Test or MAT, minimum GPA of 2.75; for doctorate, GRE General Test or MAT, minimum undergraduate GPA of 2.75, 3.2 graduate. Additional exam requirements/recommendations for international students: Required—TOEFL (minimum score 550 paper-based; 213 computer-based). *Application deadline:* For fall admission, 6/1 for domestic students, 5/1 for international students; for spring admission, 11/1 for domestic students, 10/1 for international students. Applications are processed on a rolling basis. Application fee: $30. Electronic applications accepted. *Expenses:* Tuition, state resident: full-time $6576; part-time $274 per credit hour. Tuition, nonresident: full-time $13,152; part-time $548 per credit hour. Required fees: $1813; $75.53 per credit hour. Part-time tuition and fees vary according to course load. *Financial support:* In 2009–10, 5 research assistantships with full tuition reimbursements, 1 teaching assistantship with full tuition reimbursement were awarded; fellowships with full tuition reimbursements, career-related internships or fieldwork, Federal Work-Study, scholarships/grants, tuition waivers (full), and unspecified assistantships also available. Support available to part-time students. Financial award applicants required to submit FAFSA. *Faculty research:* Distance education, Web-based training, copyright assessment during student teaching, instructional software. *Unit head:* Dr. Laura Leutkehans, Chair, 815-753-9939, E-mail: etra@niu.edu. *Application contact:* Graduate School Office, 815-753-0395, E-mail: gradsch@niu.edu.

Northern State University, Division of Graduate Studies in Education, Center for Statewide E-Learning, Aberdeen, SD 57401-7198. Offers e-learning design and instruction (MS Ed); e-learning technology and administration (MS). Part-time and evening/weekend programs available. *Faculty:* 1 full-time (0 women), 2 part-time/adjunct (1 woman). *Students:* 5 full-time (2 women), 4 part-time (2 women); includes 5 minority (2 African Americans, 2 Asian Americans or Pacific Islanders, 1 Hispanic American). Average age 32. In 2009, 3 master's awarded. *Degree requirements:* For master's, thesis optional. *Entrance requirements:* For master's, minimum GPA of 2.75. Additional exam requirements/recommendations for international students: Required—TOEFL (minimum score 550 paper-based; 213 computer-based; 78 iBT). *Application deadline:* For fall admission, 8/15 priority date for domestic students; for spring admission, 12/15 for domestic students. Applications are processed on a rolling basis. Application fee: $35. Electronic applications accepted. *Financial support:* In 2009–10, 7 teaching assistantships with partial tuition reimbursements (averaging $5,558 per year) were awarded; career-related internships or fieldwork, Federal Work-Study, institutionally sponsored loans, scholarships/grants, and unspecified assistantships also available. Support available to part-time students. Financial award application deadline: 3/1; financial award applicants required to submit FAFSA. *Unit head:* Mark Zaidel, Head, 605-626-3397. *Application contact:* Tammy K. Griffith, Program Assistant, 605-626-2558, Fax: 605-626-7190, E-mail: griffith@northern.edu.

Northwestern State University of Louisiana, Graduate Studies and Research, College of Education, Program in Educational Technology Leadership, Natchitoches, LA 71497. Offers M Ed.

Northwestern State University of Louisiana, Graduate Studies and Research, College of Education, Programs in Education, Natchitoches, LA 71497. Offers business and distributive education (M Ed); counseling (M Ed); early childhood education (M Ed); education (M Ed); education leadership (M Ed); educational technology (M Ed); elementary teaching (M Ed); English education (M Ed); home economics education (M Ed); mathematics education (M Ed); reading (M Ed); science education (M Ed); secondary teaching (M Ed); social sciences education (M Ed). *Degree requirements:* For master's, comprehensive exam, thesis or alternative. *Entrance requirements:* For master's, GRE General Test, minimum undergraduate GPA of 2.5.

Northwestern State University of Louisiana, Graduate Studies and Research, College of Education, Programs in Educational Leadership and Instruction, Natchitoches, LA 71497. Offers counseling (Ed S); educational leadership (Ed S); educational technology (Ed S); elementary teaching (Ed S); reading (Ed S); secondary teaching (Ed S); special education (Ed S). *Entrance requirements:* For degree, GRE General Test.

Northwestern University, The Graduate School, School of Education and Social Policy, Program in Learning Sciences, Evanston, IL 60208. Offers MA, PhD. Admissions and degrees offered through The Graduate School. *Faculty:* 17 full-time (6 women), 10 part-time/adjunct (4 women). *Students:* 43 full-time (32 women); includes 12 minority (5 African Americans, 1 American Indian/Alaska Native, 5 Asian Americans or Pacific Islanders, 1 Hispanic American), 4 international. Average age 31. 61 applicants, 15% accepted, 7 enrolled. In 2009, 10 master's, 11 doctorates awarded. Terminal master's awarded for partial completion of doctoral program. *Degree requirements:* For master's, thesis or alternative, portfolio; for doctorate, thesis/dissertation, qualifying exam. *Entrance requirements:* For doctorate, GRE General Test. Additional exam requirements/recommendations for international students: Required—TOEFL (minimum score 600 paper-based; 250 computer-based; 100 iBT). *Application deadline:* For fall admission, 12/31 for domestic and international students. Application fee: $75. Electronic applications accepted. *Expenses:* Contact institution. *Financial support:* In 2009–10, 26 students received support, including 10 fellowships with full tuition reimbursements available, 8 research

assistantships with full tuition reimbursements available, 8 teaching assistantships with full tuition reimbursements available; institutionally sponsored loans, scholarships/grants, health care benefits, and unspecified assistantships also available. Financial award application deadline: 12/31; financial award applicants required to submit FAFSA. *Faculty research:* Technologically supported learning environments; inquiry-based learning in mathematics, science, and literacy; learning social contexts; cognitive models of learning and problem solving; changing roles for teachers involved in innovative design and practice. *Unit head:* Prof. David N. Rapp, Coordinator of Doctoral Program, 847-491-7494, Fax: 847-491-8999. *Application contact:* Pauline Shih, Department Assistant, 847-491-7494, Fax: 847-491-8999, E-mail: ls-programs@mail.sesp.northwestern.edu.

Northwest Missouri State University, Graduate School, Melvin and Valorie Booth College of Business and Professional Studies, Department of Computer Science and Information Systems, Program in Teaching Instructional Technology, Maryville, MO 64468-6001. Offers MS Ed. Part-time programs available. *Faculty:* 11 full-time (5 women). *Students:* 1 full-time (0 women), 24 part-time (20 women). 5 applicants, 60% accepted, 2 enrolled. In 2009, 9 master's awarded. *Degree requirements:* For master's, comprehensive exam. *Entrance requirements:* For master's, GRE General Test, GRE Subject Test, minimum GPA of 2.5, teaching certificate, writing sample. Additional exam requirements/recommendations for international students: Required—TOEFL (minimum score 550 paper-based; 213 computer-based). *Application deadline:* For fall admission, 7/1 for domestic and international students; for spring admission, 12/1 for domestic students, 11/15 for international students. Applications are processed on a rolling basis. Application fee: $0 ($50 for international students). *Expenses:* Tuition, state resident: part-time $296.34 per credit hour. Tuition, nonresident: part-time $510.43 per credit hour. *Financial support:* Application deadline: 4/1. *Unit head:* Dr. Matt Symonds, Director, 660-562-1069. *Application contact:* Dr. Gregory Haddock, Dean of Graduate School, 660-562-1145, Fax: 660-562-1096, E-mail: gradsch@nwmissouri.edu.

Nova Southeastern University, Fischler School of Education and Human Services, Graduate Teacher Education Program, Fort Lauderdale, FL 33314-7796. Offers athletic administration (MS); brain research (MS, Ed S); charter school education/leadership (MS); cognitive and behavioral disabilities (MS); computer science education (Ed S); computer science education (K-12) (MS); curriculum and teaching (Ed S); curriculum, instruction and technology (MS); curriculum, instruction, management and administration (Ed S); early childhood education (MS); early literacy and reading (Ed S); early literacy education (MS); education technology (MS); educational leadership (administration K–12) (MS, Ed S); educational media (Ed S); educational media (K-12) (MS); elementary education (MS, Ed S), including ESOL endorsement (MS); English education (MS, Ed S); environmental education (MS); exceptional student education (MS), including ESOL endorsement; gifted education (MS, Ed S); interdisciplinary arts education (MS); management and administration of educational programs (MS); mathematics (MS); mathematics education (Ed S); multicultural early intervention (MS); pre-kindergarten/primary (MS); preschool education (MS); reading (MS); reading and TESOL (MS); reading education (Ed S); science (MS); science education (Ed S); secondary education (MS); social studies (MS, Ed S); Spanish language (MS); special education and reading (MS); teaching and learning (MA, MS), including curriculum and instruction (MA), elementary mathematics (MA), elementary reading (MA), K-12 technology integration (MA); teaching English to speakers of other languages (MS, Ed S); technology management and administration (Ed S); urban studies education (MS). Part-time and evening/weekend programs available. Postbaccalaureate distance learning degree programs offered (minimal on-campus study). *Faculty:* 72 full-time (43 women), 385 part-time/adjunct (252 women). *Students:* 196 full-time (175 women), 1,304 part-time (1,128 women); includes 594 minority (471 African Americans, 5 American Indian/Alaska Native, 18 Asian Americans or Pacific Islanders, 100 Hispanic Americans). Average age 37. 2,610 applicants, 72% accepted, 1352 enrolled. In 2009, 836 other advanced degrees awarded. *Degree requirements:* For master's and Ed S, thesis, practicum, internship. *Entrance requirements:* For master's, MAT, GRE, CLAST, CBEST, PRAXIS I, General Knowledge Test, minimum GPA of 2.5; for Ed S, MAT or GRE, master's degree, teaching certificate, minimum GPA of 3.0. Additional exam requirements/recommendations for international students: Required—TSE (recommended, minimum score 50); Recommended—TOEFL (minimum score 550 paper-based; 213 computer-based; 80 iBT), IELTS (minimum score 6). *Application deadline:* For fall admission, 9/25 priority date for domestic and international students; for winter admission, 2/23 priority date for domestic and international students; for spring admission, 4/25 priority date for domestic and international students. Applications are processed on a rolling basis. Application fee: $50. Electronic applications accepted. *Financial support:* Federal Work-Study available. Support available to part-time students. Financial award application deadline: 4/15; financial award applicants required to submit FAFSA. *Faculty research:* School effectiveness, critical thinking, leadership skills acquisition, child education, multicultural education. *Unit head:* Dr. Ronald Kern, Dean of Academic Affairs, 800-986-3223 Ext. 7809, Fax: 954-262-3606, E-mail: rk429@nsu.nova.edu. *Application contact:* Dr. Jennifer Quinones Nottingham, Dean of Student Affairs, 800-986-3223 Ext. 1559.

Nova Southeastern University, Fischler School of Education and Human Services, Program in Education, Fort Lauderdale, FL 33314-7796. Offers educational leadership (Ed D); health care education (Ed D); higher education leadership (Ed D); human services administration (Ed D); instructional leadership (Ed D); instructional technology and distance education (Ed D); organizational leadership (Ed D); special education (Ed D); speech language pathology (Ed D). Part-time and evening/weekend programs available. Postbaccalaureate distance learning degree programs offered (minimal on-campus study). *Faculty:* 88 full-time (46 women), 132 part-time/adjunct (63 women). *Students:* 2,805 full-time (2,128 women), 1,411 part-time (1,081 women); includes 2,629 minority (2,034 African Americans, 19 American Indian/Alaska Native, 62 Asian Americans or Pacific Islanders, 514 Hispanic Americans), 30 international. Average age 41. 964 applicants, 69% accepted, 513 enrolled. In 2009, 445 doctorates awarded. *Degree requirements:* For doctorate, thesis/dissertation. *Entrance requirements:* For doctorate, MAT or GRE, master's degree, 2 letters of recommendation, work experience. Additional exam requirements/recommendations for international students: Required—TSE (recommended, minimum score 50); Recommended—TOEFL (minimum score 550 paper-based; 213 computer-based; 80 iBT), IELTS (minimum score 6). *Application deadline:* For fall admission, 8/20 priority date for domestic and international students; for winter admission, 12/19 priority date for domestic and international students; for spring admission, 4/26 priority date for domestic students, 4/25 priority date for international students. Applications are processed on a rolling basis. Application fee: $50. Electronic applications accepted. *Financial support:* In 2009–10, 2 fellowships with full tuition reimbursements (averaging $30,000 per year) were awarded; scholarships/grants and tuition waivers (full) also available. Support available to part-time students. Financial award application deadline: 4/15; financial award applicants required to submit FAFSA. *Unit head:* Dr. Ronald Kern, Dean of Academic Affairs, 800-986-3223 Ext. 7809, Fax: 954-262-3606, E-mail: rk429@nsu.nova.edu. *Application contact:* Dr. Jennifer Quinones Nottingham, Dean of Student Affairs, 800-986-3223 Ext. 1546.

Nova Southeastern University, Fischler School of Education and Human Services, Programs in Instructional Technology and Distance Education, Fort Lauderdale, FL 33314-7796. Offers MS, Ed D. Part-time and evening/weekend programs available. Postbaccalaureate distance learning degree programs offered (minimal on-campus study). *Faculty:* 9 full-time (2 women), 9 part-time/adjunct (5 women). *Students:* 150 full-time (109 women), 110 part-time (80 women); includes 227 minority (12 African Americans, 3 Asian Americans or Pacific Islanders, 212 Hispanic Americans), 2 international. Average age 42. 57 applicants, 70% accepted, 35 enrolled. In 2009, 20 master's, 26 doctorates awarded. *Degree requirements:* For master's, practicum; for doctorate, thesis/dissertation, practicum. *Entrance requirements:* For master's, interview, current employment in a position using technology; for doctorate, MAT, minimum GPA of 3.0, interview, current employment in a position using technology. Additional exam requirements/recommendations for international students: Recommended—TOEFL (minimum score 550 paper-based; 213 computer-based; 80 iBT), IELTS (minimum score 6). *Application deadline:* Applications are processed on a rolling basis. Application fee: $50. Electronic applications accepted. *Financial support:* Fellowships available. Financial award application deadline: 4/15; financial award applicants required to submit FAFSA. *Unit head:* Dr. Ronald Kern, Dean of Academic Affairs, 954-262-7809, Fax: 954-262-3606, E-mail: rk429@nsu.nova.edu. *Application contact:* Dr. Jennifer Quinones Nottingham, Dean of Student Affairs, 800-986-3223 Ext. 8500.

Nova Southeastern University, Graduate School of Computer and Information Sciences, Program in Computing Technology in Education, Fort Lauderdale, FL 33314-7796. Offers PhD. Part-time and evening/weekend programs available. Postbaccalaureate distance learning degree programs offered (no on-campus study). *Students:* 17 full-time (9 women), 143 part-time (78 women); includes 44 minority (24 African Americans, 1 American Indian/Alaska Native, 4 Asian Americans or Pacific Islanders, 15 Hispanic Americans), 6 international. In 2009, 9 doctorates awarded. *Degree requirements:* For doctorate, thesis/dissertation. *Application deadline:* Applications are processed on a rolling basis. Electronic applications accepted. *Financial support:* Application deadline: 5/1. *Unit head:* Dr. Amon Seagull, Interim Dean, 954-262-7300. *Application contact:* 954-262-2000, Fax: 954-262-2752, E-mail: scisinfo@nova.edu.

Oakland University, Graduate Study and Lifelong Learning, School of Education and Human Services, Program in Microcomputer Applications in Education, Rochester, MI 48309-4401. Offers advanced microcomputer applications (Certificate); microcomputer applications (Certificate). *Entrance requirements:* Additional exam requirements/recommendations for international students: Required—TOEFL (minimum score 550 paper-based; 213 computer-based). Electronic applications accepted.

Ohio University, Graduate College, College of Education, Department of Educational Studies, Athens, OH 45701-2979. Offers computer education and technology (M Ed); cultural studies (M Ed); educational administration (M Ed, Ed D); educational research and evaluation (M Ed, PhD); instructional technology (PhD). Part-time and evening/weekend programs available. Postbaccalaureate distance learning degree programs offered (minimal on-campus study). *Faculty:* 12 full-time (6 women), 2 part-time/adjunct (0 women). *Students:* 151 full-time (95 women), 142 part-time (105 women); includes 24 minority (19 African Americans, 1 American Indian/Alaska Native, 1 Asian American or Pacific Islander, 3 Hispanic Americans), 46 international. 107 applicants, 69% accepted, 50 enrolled. In 2009, 32 master's, 19 doctorates awarded. *Degree requirements:* For master's, thesis or alternative; for doctorate, comprehensive exam, thesis/dissertation. *Entrance requirements:* For master's, GRE General Test (if GPA less than 2.9); for doctorate, GRE General Test, GRE Subject Test, minimum GPA of 2.9, work experience, 3 letters of reference, autobiography. Additional exam requirements/recommendations for international students: Required—TOEFL (minimum score 550 paper-based; 80 iBT) or IELTS Academic (minimum score 6.5). *Application deadline:* For fall admission, 3/1 priority date for domestic and international students; for winter admission, 10/1 priority date for domestic and international students; for spring admission, 1/30 priority date for domestic students, 1/1 priority date for international students. Applications are processed on a rolling basis. Application fee: $50 ($55 for international students). Electronic applications accepted. *Expenses:* Tuition, state resident: full-time $7839; part-time $323 per quarter hour. Tuition, nonresident: full-time $15,831; part-time $654 per quarter hour. Required fees: $2931. *Financial support:* Research assistantships with full tuition reimbursements, teaching assistantships with full tuition reimbursements, Federal Work-Study, institutionally sponsored loans, tuition waivers (partial), and unspecified assistantships available. Financial award application deadline: 3/1. *Faculty research:* Race, class and gender; computer programs; development and organization theory; evaluation/development of instruments, leadership. Total annual research expenditures: $158,037. *Unit head:* Dr. Gordon Brooks, Chair, 740-593-4423, Fax: 740-593-0477, E-mail: brooksg@ohio.edu. *Application contact:* Floyd J. Doney, Director of Student Affairs, 740-593-4400, Fax: 740-593-9310, E-mail: doney@ohio.edu.

Old Dominion University, Darden College of Education, Program in Elementary/Middle Education, Norfolk, VA 23529. Offers elementary education (MS Ed); instructional technology (MS Ed); library science (MS Ed); middle school education (MS Ed). *Accreditation:* NCATE. Part-time and evening/weekend programs available. Postbaccalaureate distance learning degree programs offered (no on-campus study). *Faculty:* 20 full-time (16 women), 22 part-time/adjunct (2 women). *Students:* 109 full-time (103 women), 171 part-time (148 women); includes 41 minority (22 African Americans, 1 American Indian/Alaska Native, 10 Asian Americans or Pacific Islanders, 8 Hispanic Americans). Average age 33. 191 applicants, 76% accepted, 123 enrolled. In 2009, 155 master's awarded. *Degree requirements:* For master's, comprehensive exam. *Entrance requirements:* For master's, GRE General Test or MAT; PRAXIS I, SAT or ACT, minimum GPA of 2.8. Additional exam requirements/recommendations for international students: Required—TOEFL (minimum score 600 paper-based; 250 computer-based). *Application deadline:* For fall admission, 6/1 priority date for domestic students; for winter admission, 11/1 priority date for domestic students; for spring admission, 3/1 priority date for domestic students. Applications are processed on a rolling basis. Application fee: $50. Electronic applications accepted. *Expenses:* Tuition, state resident: full-time $8112; part-time $338 per credit. Tuition, nonresident: full-time $20,256; part-time $844 per credit. Required fees: $119 per semester. One-time fee: $50. *Financial support:* In 2009–10, 180 students received support, including teaching assistantships (averaging $9,000 per year); career-related internships or fieldwork, Federal Work-Study, institutionally sponsored loans, and scholarships/grants also available. Support available to part-time students. Financial award application deadline: 2/15; financial award applicants required to submit FAFSA. *Faculty research:* Education pre-K to 6, school librarianship. *Unit head:* Dr. Charlene Fleener, Graduate Program Director, 757-683-4374, E-mail: cfleener@odu.edu. *Application contact:* Alice McAdory, Director of Admissions, 757-683-3685, Fax: 757-683-3255, E-mail: gradadmit@odu.edu.

Old Dominion University, Darden College of Education, Program in Instructional Design and Technology, Norfolk, VA 23529. Offers PhD. Part-time and evening/weekend programs available. Postbaccalaureate distance learning degree programs offered (no on-campus study). *Faculty:* 6 full-time (3 women). *Students:* 10 full-time (7 women), 30 part-time (15 women); includes 7 minority (6 African Americans, 1 American Indian/Alaska Native), 3 international. Average age 43. 10 applicants, 60% accepted, 6 enrolled. In 2009, 1 doctorate awarded. *Degree requirements:* For doctorate, comprehensive exam, thesis/dissertation. *Entrance requirements:* For doctorate, GRE, references, interview. Additional exam requirements/recommendations for international students: Required—TOEFL (minimum score 550 paper-based; 213 computer-based). *Application deadline:* For fall admission, 6/1 priority date for domestic students, 2/1 priority date for international students; for winter admission, 11/1 priority date for domestic and international students. Applications are processed on a rolling basis. Application fee: $40. Electronic applications accepted. *Expenses:* Tuition, state resident: full-time $8112; part-time $338 per credit. Tuition, nonresident: full-time $20,256; part-time $844 per credit. Required fees: $119 per semester. One-time fee: $50. *Financial support:* In 2009–10, 4 students received support, including 3 research assistantships with full tuition reimbursements available (averaging $12,500 per year); career-related internships or fieldwork and unspecified assistantships also available. Financial award application deadline: 2/15; financial award applicants required to submit FAFSA. *Faculty research:* Instructional design, cognitive load, distance education, pedagogical agents, human performance technology, gaming, simulation design, distance education. Total annual research expenditures: $2 million. *Unit head:* Dr. Gary R. Morrison, Graduate Program Director, 757-683-4305, Fax: 757-683-5227, E-mail: gmorriso@odu.edu. *Application contact:* Alice McAdory, Director of Admissions, 757-683-3685, Fax: 757-683-3255, E-mail: gradadmit@odu.edu.

Old Dominion University, Darden College of Education, Programs in Secondary Education, Norfolk, VA 23529. Offers biology (MS Ed); chemistry (MS Ed); English (MS Ed); instructional technology (MS Ed); library science (MS Ed); secondary education (MS Ed). *Accreditation:* NCATE. Part-time and evening/weekend programs available. Postbaccalaureate distance learning degree programs offered (minimal on-campus study). *Faculty:* 20 full-time (16 women). *Students:* 74 full-time (54 women), 137 part-time (92 women); includes 41 minority (22 African Americans, 1 American Indian/Alaska Native, 11 Asian Americans or Pacific Islanders, 7 Hispanic Americans). Average age 33. 67 applicants, 79% accepted, 53 enrolled. In 2009, 131 master's awarded. *Degree requirements:* For master's, comprehensive exam, thesis. *Entrance requirements:* For master's, GRE General Test or MAT, PRAXIS I (for licensure), minimum

Educational Media/Instructional Technology

Old Dominion University (continued)

GPA of 2.8, teaching certificate. Additional exam requirements/recommendations for international students: Required—TOEFL. *Application deadline:* For fall admission, 6/1 for domestic and international students; for winter admission, 11/1 for domestic and international students; for spring admission, 3/1 for domestic and international students. Applications are processed on a rolling basis. Application fee: $50. Electronic applications accepted. *Expenses:* Tuition, state resident: full-time $8112; part-time $338 per credit. Tuition, nonresident: full-time $20,256; part-time $844 per credit. Required fees: $119 per semester. One-time fee: $50. *Financial support:* In 2009–10, 56 students received support, including fellowships (averaging $15,000 per year), 2 research assistantships with tuition reimbursements available (averaging $9,000 per year), 3 teaching assistantships with tuition reimbursements available (averaging $12,500 per year); career-related internships or fieldwork, Federal Work-Study, institutionally sponsored loans, scholarships/grants, and tuition waivers (partial) also available. Support available to part-time students. Financial award application deadline: 2/15; financial award applicants required to submit FAFSA. *Faculty research:* Use of technology, writing project for teachers, geography teaching, reading. *Unit head:* Dr. Robert Lucking, Graduate Program Director, 757-683-5545, Fax: 757-683-5862, E-mail: rlucking@odu.edu. *Application contact:* Dr. Robert Lucking, Graduate Program Director, 757-683-5545, Fax: 757-683-5862, E-mail: rlucking@odu.edu.

Ottawa University, Graduate Studies-Arizona, Program in Education, Ottawa, KS 66067-3399. Offers community college counseling (MA); curriculum and instruction (MA); early childhood (MA); education intervention (MA); education leadership (MA); education technology (MA); Montessori early childhood education (MA); Montessori elementary education (MA); professional development (MA); school guidance counseling (MA); special education—cross categorical (MA). Programs offered in Mesa, Phoenix, Tempe and West Valley, AZ. *Accreditation:* NCATE. Part-time programs available. *Degree requirements:* For master's, thesis or alternative. *Entrance requirements:* For master's, minimum undergraduate GPA of 3.0, copy of current state certification or teaching license. Additional exam requirements/recommendations for international students: Required—TOEFL (minimum score 550 paper-based; 213 computer-based). Electronic applications accepted. *Expenses:* Contact institution.

Our Lady of the Lake University of San Antonio, School of Professional Studies, Program in Learning Resources Specialist, San Antonio, TX 78207-4689. Offers M Ed. Part-time and evening/weekend programs available. *Students:* 6 full-time (5 women), 25 part-time (21 women); includes 18 minority (1 African American, 17 Hispanic Americans). Average age 38. In 2009, 9 master's awarded. *Degree requirements:* For master's, comprehensive exam. *Entrance requirements:* For master's, GRE General Test or MAT. Additional exam requirements/recommendations for international students: Required—TOEFL. *Application deadline:* Applications are processed on a rolling basis. Application fee: $25 ($50 for international students). Electronic applications accepted. *Expenses:* Tuition: Full-time $12,330; part-time $685 per contact hour. Required fees: $139; $12 per contact hour. $57 per semester. Tuition and fees vary according to campus/location. *Financial support:* Application deadline: 4/15. *Faculty research:* Automation and libraries, electronic books. *Unit head:* Dr. Cullen Grinnan, Head, 210-434-6711 Ext. 8928, Fax: 210-436-0824, E-mail: ctgrinnan@lake.ollusa.edu. *Application contact:* 210-434-6711 Ext. 2314, Fax: 210-431-4036, E-mail: gradadm@lake.ollusa.edu.

Penn State University Park, Graduate School, College of Education, Department of Learning and Performance Systems, State College, University Park, PA 16802-1503. Offers M Ed, MS, D Ed, PhD.

Pepperdine University, Graduate School of Education and Psychology, Division of Education, Programs in Learning Technologies, Malibu, CA 90263. Offers MA, Ed D. Part-time and evening/weekend programs available. Postbaccalaureate distance learning degree programs offered (minimal on-campus study). *Degree requirements:* For doctorate, thesis/dissertation. *Entrance requirements:* For doctorate, GMAT, GRE General Test, MAT. Additional exam requirements/recommendations for international students: Required—TOEFL. *Expenses:* Contact institution.

Pittsburg State University, Graduate School, College of Education, Department of Special Services and Leadership Studies, Program in Educational Technology, Pittsburg, KS 66762. Offers MS. *Accreditation:* NCATE. *Degree requirements:* For master's, thesis or alternative. *Entrance requirements:* For master's, GRE General Test or MAT. *Expenses:* Tuition, state resident: full-time $4212; part-time $176 per credit. Tuition, nonresident: full-time $11,530; part-time $480 per credit. Required fees: $940; $43 per credit. Tuition and fees vary according to course level, course load, degree level, campus/location, reciprocity agreements and student level.

Portland State University, Graduate Studies, School of Education, Department of Curriculum and Instruction, Portland, OR 97207-0751. Offers early childhood education (MA, MS); education (M Ed, MA, MS); educational leadership: curriculum and instruction (Ed D); educational media/school librarianship (MA, MS); elementary education (M Ed, MAT, MST); reading (MA, MS); secondary education (M Ed, MAT, MST). *Accreditation:* NCATE. Part-time programs available. *Degree requirements:* For master's, comprehensive exam, thesis or alternative; for doctorate, thesis/dissertation. *Entrance requirements:* For master's, California Basic Educational Skills Test, minimum GPA of 3.0 in upper-division course work or 2.75 overall. Additional exam requirements/recommendations for international students: Required—TOEFL (minimum score 550 paper-based; 213 computer-based). *Faculty research:* Early literacy, characteristics of successful teachers of at-risk students, participation of women/minorities in technology courses, selection of cooperating teachers.

Post University, Program in Education, Waterbury, CT 06723-2540. Offers education (M Ed); instructional design and technology (M Ed); teaching and learning (M Ed). Postbaccalaureate distance learning degree programs offered.

Purdue University, Graduate School, School of Education, Department of Curriculum and Instruction, West Lafayette, IN 47907. Offers agricultural and extension education (PhD, Ed S); agriculture and extension education (MS, MS Ed); art education (PhD); consumer and family sciences and extension education (MS Ed, PhD, Ed S); curriculum studies (MS Ed, PhD, Ed S); educational technology (MS Ed, PhD, Ed S); elementary education (MS Ed); foreign language education (MS Ed, PhD, Ed S); industrial technology (PhD, Ed S); language arts (MS Ed, PhD, Ed S); literacy (MS Ed, PhD, Ed S); mathematics/science education (MS, MS Ed, PhD, Ed S); social studies (MS Ed, PhD); social studies education (Ed S); vocational/industrial education (MS Ed, PhD, Ed S); vocational/technical education (MS Ed, PhD, Ed S). *Accreditation:* NCATE. Part-time and evening/weekend programs available. *Degree requirements:* For master's, thesis optional; for doctorate, thesis/dissertation, oral and written exams; for Ed S, oral presentation, project. *Entrance requirements:* For master's, GRE General Test, minimum B average; for doctorate, GRE General Test; for Ed S, GRE, minimum B average. Additional exam requirements/recommendations for international students: Required—TOEFL. Electronic applications accepted. *Faculty research:* Literacy acquisition and development, teacher beliefs and knowledge, recruitment and retention of underrepresented students, economic education, literacy discourse.

Purdue University Calumet, Graduate School, School of Education, Program in Instructional Technology, Hammond, IN 46323-2094. Offers MS Ed. *Entrance requirements:* Additional exam requirements/recommendations for international students: Required—TOEFL.

Ramapo College of New Jersey, Master of Science in Educational Technology Program, Mahwah, NJ 07430. Offers MS. Part-time programs available. *Faculty:* 12 part-time/adjunct (8 women). *Students:* 138 full-time (103 women), 1 part-time (0 women); includes 12 minority (5 African Americans, 2 Asian Americans or Pacific Islanders, 5 Hispanic Americans), 2 international. Average age 35. 173 applicants, 100% accepted, 70 enrolled. In 2009, 81 master's awarded. *Entrance requirements:* For master's, interview. Additional exam requirements/recommendations for international students: Required—TOEFL (minimum score 550 paper-based; 213 computer-based; 90 iBT). *Application deadline:* Applications are processed on a rolling basis. Application fee: $60. *Expenses:* Tuition, state resident: part-time $525.30 per credit. Tuition, nonresident: part-time $675.20 per credit. Required fees: $53.55 per credit. *Financial support:* Scholarships/grants available. Financial award application deadline: 3/1; financial award applicants required to submit FAFSA. *Faculty research:* Integrity technology in the curriculum of K-12 learning environment. *Unit head:* Dr. Angela Cristini, Dean/Executive Director of Special Programs, Office of the Provost, 201-684-7721, Fax: 201-684-6699, E-mail: acristin@ramapo.edu. *Application contact:* Joyce Wilson, Administrative Assistant, 201-684-7721, Fax: 201-684-6699, E-mail: mlafayet@ramapo.edu.

Regis University, College for Professional Studies, Program in Teacher Education, Denver, CO 80221-1099. Offers adult learning, training, and development (M Ed); curriculum, instruction, and assessment (M Ed); early childhood (M Ed); educational technology (Certificate); elementary (M Ed); ESL (M Ed); fine arts (M Ed), including arts, music; instructional technology (M Ed); professional leadership (M Ed); reading (M Ed); secondary (M Ed); self-designed (M Ed); space studies (M Ed); special education (M Ed); teacher licensure (M Ed). Program also offered in Henderson and Las Vegas (Summerlin), NV. *Accreditation:* Teacher Education Accreditation Council. Part-time and evening/weekend programs available. Postbaccalaureate distance learning degree programs offered (no on-campus study). *Degree requirements:* For master's, thesis. *Entrance requirements:* For master's, resume, minimum GPA of 2.75, criminal background check. Additional exam requirements/recommendations for international students: Required—TOEFL (minimum score 213 computer-based), TWE (minimum score 5). Electronic applications accepted. *Faculty research:* Issues of equity in the middle school classroom, professional learning communities, school reform, socialinguistic and discursive obstacles to student integration, inclusive language arts curriculum.

The Richard Stockton College of New Jersey, School of Graduate and Continuing Education, Program in Instructional Technology, Pomona, NJ 08240-0195. Offers MA. Part-time programs available. *Degree requirements:* For master's, final project. *Entrance requirements:* For master's, GRE, minimum GPA of 3.0. Additional exam requirements/recommendations for international students: Required—TOEFL. Electronic applications accepted. *Expenses:* Tuition, state resident: part-time $497.36 per credit hour. Tuition, nonresident: part-time $765.61 per credit hour. Required fees: $129.12 per credit hour. Tuition and fees vary according to degree level. *Faculty research:* Ethics, digital imaging, virtual reality in the classroom, 3-D art in multimedia, technology projects for job-skills training, community computing networks.

Sacred Heart University, Graduate Programs, College of Education and Health Professions, Isabelle Farrington School of Education, Fairfield, CT 06825-1000. Offers administration (CAS); educational technology (MAT); elementary education (MAT); reading (CAS); secondary education (MAT); teaching (CAS). Part-time and evening/weekend programs available. Postbaccalaureate distance learning degree programs offered (minimal on-campus study). *Faculty:* 23 full-time (10 women). *Students:* 377 full-time (291 women), 691 part-time (495 women); includes 63 minority (31 African Americans, 2 American Indian/Alaska Native, 8 Asian Americans or Pacific Islanders, 22 Hispanic Americans), 2 international. Average age 34. 429 applicants, 90% accepted, 338 enrolled. In 2009, 409 master's, 66 other advanced degrees awarded. *Degree requirements:* For master's, thesis or alternative. *Entrance requirements:* For master's, PRAXIS (teacher certification/MAT); for CAS, PRAXIS I. Additional exam requirements/recommendations for international students: Required—TOEFL (minimum score 550 paper-based; 213 computer-based). *Application deadline:* Applications are processed on a rolling basis. Application fee: $50 ($100 for international students). Electronic applications accepted. *Expenses:* Contact institution. *Financial support:* Teaching assistantships with partial tuition reimbursements, career-related internships or fieldwork, institutionally sponsored loans, traineeships, tuition waivers (partial), and unspecified assistantships available. Support available to part-time students. Financial award applicants required to submit FAFSA. *Faculty research:* Reading education, learning theory, teacher preparation, education of underachievers. *Unit head:* Dr. Edward Malin, Director, 203-371-7800, Fax: 203-365-7513. *Application contact:* Kathy Dilks, Assistant Dean of Graduate Admissions, 203-365-7619, Fax: 203-365-4732, E-mail: gradstudies@sacredheart.edu.

Saginaw Valley State University, College of Education, Program in Instructional Technology, University Center, MI 48710. Offers MAT. Part-time and evening/weekend programs available. *Students:* 5 full-time (4 women), 48 part-time (31 women); includes 3 minority (1 African American, 1 American Indian/Alaska Native, 1 Hispanic American), 2 international. Average age 34. 14 applicants, 100% accepted, 10 enrolled. In 2009, 4 master's awarded. *Entrance requirements:* Additional exam requirements/recommendations for international students: Required—TOEFL (minimum score 525 paper-based; 197 computer-based; 71 iBT). Application fee: $25. *Financial support:* Federal Work-Study and scholarships/grants available. Support available to part-time students. Financial award applicants required to submit FAFSA. *Unit head:* Dr. Steve P. Barbus, Dean, 989-964-6067, Fax: 989-790-4385, E-mail: barbus@svsu.edu. *Application contact:* Kathy Lopez, Certification Officer, 989-964-4661, Fax: 989-964-4385, E-mail: klopez@svsu.edu.

St. Cloud State University, School of Graduate Studies, College of Education, Center for Information Media, St. Cloud, MN 56301-4498. Offers MS. *Faculty:* 11 full-time (5 women), 6 part-time/adjunct (3 women). *Students:* 6 full-time (5 women), 26 part-time (16 women), 10 international. 8 applicants, 100% accepted. In 2009, 8 master's awarded. *Degree requirements:* For master's, comprehensive exam, thesis or alternative. *Entrance requirements:* For master's, GRE General Test, minimum GPA of 2.75. Additional exam requirements/recommendations for international students: Required—Michigan English Language Assessment Battery; Recommended—TOEFL (minimum score 550 paper-based; 213 computer-based), IELTS (minimum score 6.5). *Application deadline:* For fall admission, 6/1 priority date for domestic students, 4/1 for international students; for spring admission, 10/1 priority date for domestic students, 8/1 for international students. Applications are processed on a rolling basis. Application fee: $35. Electronic applications accepted. *Financial support:* Federal Work-Study, scholarships/grants, and unspecified assistantships available. Financial award application deadline: 3/1. *Unit head:* Dr. Kristi Tornquist, Dean, 320-308-2022, E-mail: kmtornquist@stcloudstate.edu. *Application contact:* Linda Lou Krueger, School of Graduate Studies, 320-308-2113, Fax: 320-308-5371, E-mail: lekrueger@stcloudstate.edu.

St. Edward's University, School of Education, Program in Teaching, Austin, TX 78704. Offers curriculum leadership (Certificate); instructional technology (Certificate); mentoring and supervision (Certificate); sports management (Certificate); teaching (MA), including conflict resolution, initial teacher certification, liberal arts, organization development and training, sports management, teacher leadership. Part-time and evening/weekend programs available. *Students:* 5 full-time (4 women), 36 part-time (26 women); includes 10 minority (1 African American, 9 Hispanic Americans). Average age 30. 23 applicants, 70% accepted, 12 enrolled. In 2009, 9 master's awarded. *Degree requirements:* For master's, minimum of 24 resident hours. *Entrance requirements:* For master's, GRE General Test, minimum GPA of 3.0 in last 60 hours or 2.75 overall. Additional exam requirements/recommendations for international students: Required—TOEFL (minimum score 550 paper-based; 213 computer-based; 79 iBT) or IELTS (minimum score 6). *Application deadline:* For fall admission, 7/1 for domestic and international students; for spring admission, 11/1 for domestic and international students. Applications are processed on a rolling basis. Application fee: $45 ($50 for international students). Electronic applications accepted. *Expenses:* Tuition: Full-time $14,922; part-time $829 per credit hour. Required fees: $50 per trimester. Full-time tuition and fees vary according to course load and program. *Financial support:* In 2009–10, 3 students received support. Scholarships/grants available. *Unit head:* Dr. David Hollier, Director, 512-448-8666, Fax: 512-428-1372, E-mail: davidrh@stedwards.edu. *Application contact:* Kay L. Arnold, Assistant Director of Admissions, 512-233-1636, Fax: 512-428-1032, E-mail: kayla@stedwards.edu.

Saint Joseph's University, College of Arts and Sciences, Department of Education, Philadelphia, PA 19131-1395. Offers educational leadership (Ed D); elementary education (MS); instructional technology (MS); organizational development and leadership (MS); professional education (MS); reading specialist (MS); secondary education (MS); special education (MS). Part-time and evening/weekend programs available. *Students:* 5 full-time (3 women),

750 part-time (561 women); includes 100 minority (76 African Americans, 1 American Indian/Alaska Native, 11 Asian Americans or Pacific Islanders, 12 Hispanic Americans), 3 international. Average age 33. In 2009, 210 master's, 14 doctorates awarded. *Entrance requirements:* For master's, 2 letters of recommendation, minimum GPA of 3.0, application, official transcripts, personal statement; for doctorate, GRE, master's degree from accredited institution, minimum graduate GPA of 3.5, computer competence, commitment to participate in cohort, interview with program director. Additional exam requirements/recommendations for international students: Required—TOEFL (minimum score 550 paper-based; 213 computer-based; 79 iBT). *Application deadline:* For fall admission, 7/15 priority date for domestic students, 4/15 for international students; for winter admission, 11/15 for domestic students, 1/15 for international students; for spring admission, 11/15 priority date for domestic students, 10/15 for international students. Applications are processed on a rolling basis. Application fee: $35. Electronic applications accepted. *Expenses:* Contact institution. *Financial support:* Unspecified assistantships available. Financial award applicants required to submit FAFSA. *Faculty research:* Early childhood course design, public education professional development. Total annual research expenditures: $91,900. *Unit head:* Dr. Teri Sosa, Director of Graduate Education, 610-660-3162, E-mail: tsosa@sju.edu. *Application contact:* Kate McConnell, Director, Graduate College of Arts and Sciences Admissions and Retention, 610-660-3184, Fax: 610-660-3230, E-mail: kate.mcconnell@sju.edu.

Saint Leo University, Graduate Studies in Education, Saint Leo, FL 33574-6665. Offers educational leadership (M Ed, Ed S); exceptional student education (M Ed); higher education leadership (Ed S); instructional design (MS); instructional leadership (M Ed); reading (M Ed). Part-time and evening/weekend programs available. Postbaccalaureate distance learning degree programs offered (minimal on-campus study). *Faculty:* 13 full-time (10 women), 12 part-time/adjunct (9 women). *Students:* 432 full-time (355 women), 35 part-time (24 women); includes 56 minority (40 African Americans, 2 American Indian/Alaska Native, 2 Asian Americans or Pacific Islanders, 12 Hispanic Americans), 1 international. Average age 37. In 2009, 131 master's awarded. *Degree requirements:* For master's, comprehensive exam, appropriate State of Florida Certification Tests. *Entrance requirements:* For master's, GRE (minimum score of 1000) or MAT (minimum score of 410) if undergraduate GPA for last 60 hours of coursework was below 3.0 (for M Ed), bachelor's degree from regionally-accredited college or university with minimum GPA of 3.0 for last 60 hours of coursework, 2 recommendations, resume, statement of professional goals, copy of valid teaching certificate (for M Ed); for Ed S, GRE (minimum score 1000) or MAT (minimum score 410) if undergraduate GPA for last 60 hours of coursework less than 3.0, bachelor's degree from regionally-accredited college or university with minimum GPA of 3.0 for last 60 hours of coursework, 2 recommendations, resume, valid teaching certificate. Additional exam requirements/recommendations for international students: Required—TOEFL (minimum score 550 paper-based; 213 computer-based; 80 iBT). *Application deadline:* For fall admission, 7/1 priority date for domestic students; for spring admission, 11/12 priority date for domestic students. Applications are processed on a rolling basis. Application fee: $75. Electronic applications accepted. *Expenses:* Tuition: Part-time $1767 per course. Required fees: $115 per course. *Financial support:* Career-related internships or fieldwork, Federal Work-Study, and health care benefits available. Financial award application deadline: 3/1; financial award applicants required to submit FAFSA. *Faculty research:* The role of the school leader in data analysis of student achievement, teacher recruitment, and teacher effectiveness. *Unit head:* Dr. John Smith, Director, 352-588-8309, Fax: 352-588-8861, E-mail: med@saintleo.edu. *Application contact:* Jared Welling, Director, Graduate/Weekend and Evening Admission, 800-707-8846, Fax: 352-588-7873, E-mail: grad.admissions@saintleo.edu.

Saint Michael's College, Graduate Programs, Program in Education, Colchester, VT 05439. Offers administration (M Ed, CAGS); arts in education (CAGS); curriculum and instruction (M Ed, CAGS); information technology (CAGS); reading (M Ed); special education (M Ed, CAGS); technology (M Ed). Part-time and evening/weekend programs available. *Degree requirements:* For master's, thesis. *Entrance requirements:* For master's, minimum GPA of 3.0. Electronic applications accepted. *Faculty research:* Integrative curriculum, moral and spiritual dimensions of education, learning styles, multiple intelligences, integrating technology into the curriculum.

St. Thomas University, School of Leadership Studies, Institute for Education, Miami Gardens, FL 33054-6459. Offers earth/space science (Certificate); educational administration (MS, Certificate); educational leadership (Ed D); elementary education (MS); ESOL (Certificate); gifted education (Certificate); instructional technology (MS, Certificate); professional/studies (Certificate); reading (MS, Certificate); special education (MS). Part-time and evening/weekend programs available. *Degree requirements:* For master's, comprehensive exam; for doctorate, comprehensive exam, thesis/dissertation. *Entrance requirements:* For master's, interview, minimum GPA of 3.0 or GRE; for doctorate, GRE or MAT. Additional exam requirements/recommendations for international students: Required—TOEFL (minimum score 550 paper-based; 213 computer-based; 79 iBT). Electronic applications accepted.

Saint Vincent College, Program in Education, Latrobe, PA 15650-2690. Offers curriculum and instruction (MS); environmental education (MS); library media management (MS); school administration (MS); special education (MS). Part-time and evening/weekend programs available. *Degree requirements:* For master's, comprehensive exam. *Entrance requirements:* For master's, GRE (if undergraduate GPA less than 3.0). Additional exam requirements/recommendations for international students: Required—TOEFL (minimum score 550 paper-based; 213 computer-based). *Faculty research:* Assessment and instructional technology.

Salem State College, School of Graduate Studies, Program in Library Media Studies, Salem, MA 01970-5353. Offers M Ed. *Accreditation:* NCATE. Part-time and evening/weekend programs available. *Students:* 3 full-time (all women), 33 part-time (32 women). Average age 43. 9 applicants, 100% accepted, 9 enrolled. In 2009, 9 master's awarded. *Entrance requirements:* For master's, GRE or MAT. Additional exam requirements/recommendations for international students: Required—TOEFL (minimum score 550 paper-based; 80 iBT), or IELTS (minimum score 5.5). *Application deadline:* For fall admission, 5/1 for domestic students; for spring admission, 10/1 for domestic students. Applications are processed on a rolling basis. Application fee: $50. *Expenses:* Tuition, state resident: full-time $2520; part-time $275 per credit hour. Tuition, nonresident: full-time $4140; part-time $365 per credit hour. Required fees: $2430. *Financial support:* In 2009–10, 8 students received support. Career-related internships or fieldwork, Federal Work-Study, scholarships/grants, and unspecified assistantships available. Support available to part-time students. Financial award application deadline: 5/1; financial award applicants required to submit FAFSA. *Unit head:* Elizabeth Dole, Program Coordinator, 978-542-6310, Fax: 978-744-6596, E-mail: edole@salemstate.edu. *Application contact:* Dr. Lee A. Brossoit, Assistant Dean of Graduate Admissions, 978-542-6675, Fax: 978-542-7215, E-mail: lbrossoit@salemstate.edu.

Salem State College, School of Graduate Studies, Program in Technology in Education, Salem, MA 01970-5353. Offers M Ed. Part-time and evening/weekend programs available. *Students:* 1 (woman) full-time, 13 part-time (8 women). Average age 37. 1 applicant, 100% accepted, 1 enrolled. In 2009, 3 master's awarded. *Entrance requirements:* For master's, GRE or MAT. Additional exam requirements/recommendations for international students: Required—TOEFL (minimum score 550 paper-based; 80 iBT), or IELTS (minimum score 5.5). *Application deadline:* For fall admission, 5/1 for domestic students; for spring admission, 10/1 for domestic students. Applications are processed on a rolling basis. Application fee: $50. *Expenses:* Tuition, state resident: full-time $2520; part-time $275 per credit hour. Tuition, nonresident: full-time $4140; part-time $365 per credit hour. Required fees: $2430. *Financial support:* In 2009–10, 4 students received support. Career-related internships or fieldwork, Federal Work-Study, scholarships/grants, and unspecified assistantships available. Support available to part-time students. Financial award application deadline: 5/1; financial award applicants required to submit FAFSA. *Unit head:* Peter Smith, Professor, 978-542-6310, E-mail: psmith@salemstate.edu. *Application contact:* Dr. Lee A. Brossoit, Assistant Dean of Graduate Admissions, 978-542-6675, Fax: 978-542-7215, E-mail: lbrossoit@salemstate.edu.

Sam Houston State University, College of Education and Applied Science, Department of Curriculum and Instruction, Huntsville, TX 77341. Offers curriculum and instruction (M Ed, MA); instructional technology (M Ed). *Accreditation:* NCATE. Part-time and evening/weekend programs available. *Faculty:* 10 full-time (5 women), 1 (woman) part-time/adjunct. *Students:* 34 full-time (26 women), 134 part-time (95 women); includes 37 minority (21 African Americans, 1 American Indian/Alaska Native, 4 Asian Americans or Pacific Islanders, 11 Hispanic Americans). Average age 32. 85 applicants, 94% accepted, 57 enrolled. In 2009, 85 master's awarded. *Entrance requirements:* For master's, GRE General Test. Additional exam requirements/recommendations for international students: Required—TOEFL (minimum score 550 paper-based; 213 computer-based; 79 iBT). *Application deadline:* For fall admission, 8/1 for domestic students; for spring admission, 12/1 for domestic students. Application fee: $20. *Expenses:* Tuition, state resident: full-time $3690; part-time $205 per credit hour. Tuition, nonresident: full-time $8676; part-time $482 per credit hour. Required fees: $1474. Tuition and fees vary according to course load and campus/location. *Financial support:* Teaching assistantships, institutionally sponsored loans available. Financial award application deadline: 5/31; financial award applicants required to submit FAFSA. *Unit head:* Dr. Daphne Johnson, Chair, 936-294-3875, Fax: 936-294-1056, E-mail: edu_dxe@shsu.edu. *Application contact:* Dr. Eren Johnson, Advisor, 936-294-1140, E-mail: edu_mej@shsu.edu.

San Diego State University, Graduate and Research Affairs, College of Education, Department of Educational Technology, San Diego, CA 92182. Offers educational technology (MA); educational technology and teaching and learning (Ed D). *Accreditation:* NCATE. Evening/weekend programs available. *Entrance requirements:* For master's, GRE General Test, letters of reference. Additional exam requirements/recommendations for international students: Required—TOEFL. Electronic applications accepted.

San Francisco State University, Division of Graduate Studies, College of Education, Department of Instructional Technologies, San Francisco, CA 94132-1722. Offers educational technology (MA); training systems development (AC).

Seton Hall University, College of Education and Human Services, Department of Educational Studies, Program in Instructional Design, South Orange, NJ 07079-2697. Offers MA. Part-time and evening/weekend programs available. *Faculty:* 10 full-time (7 women). *Students:* 7 full-time (6 women), 22 part-time (17 women); includes 7 minority (3 African Americans, 4 Hispanic Americans). Average age 38. 6 applicants, 100% accepted, 6 enrolled. In 2009, 5 master's awarded. *Degree requirements:* For master's, comprehensive exam. *Entrance requirements:* For master's, GRE General Test or MAT, minimum GPA of 2.75. *Application deadline:* For fall admission, 5/1 for domestic students; for spring admission, 10/1 for domestic students. Applications are processed on a rolling basis. Application fee: $50. *Financial support:* Application deadline: 2/1. *Unit head:* Dr. Rosemary Skeele, Head, 973-761-9393, E-mail: skeelero@shu.edu. *Application contact:* Dr. Rosemary Skeele, Head, 973-761-9393, E-mail: skeelero@shu.edu.

Simmons College, College of Arts and Sciences Graduate Studies, Department of Education, Program in Special Education, Boston, MA 02115. Offers applied behavior analysis (PhD); assistive technology (MS Ed, Ed S); behavioral education (MS Ed, Ed S); health professions education (PhD); language and literacy (MS Ed, Ed S); moderate disabilities (Ed S); moderate special needs (MS Ed); severe disabilities (Ed S); severe special needs (MS Ed); special education administration (MS Ed, PhD, Ed S). Part-time and evening/weekend programs available. *Students:* 45 full-time (40 women), 316 part-time (271 women); includes 19 minority (7 African Americans, 1 American Indian/Alaska Native, 7 Asian Americans or Pacific Islanders, 4 Hispanic Americans), 2 international. 95 applicants, 89% accepted, 65 enrolled. In 2009, 145 master's awarded. *Degree requirements:* For master's, student teaching. *Entrance requirements:* For doctorate, GRE, research proposal, interview, BCBA credential. Additional exam requirements/recommendations for international students: Required—TOEFL (minimum score 600 paper-based; 250 computer-based; 100 iBT). *Application deadline:* For fall admission, 8/1 priority date for domestic and international students; for winter admission, 12/15 priority date for domestic students; for spring admission, 12/15 priority date for domestic and international students. Applications are processed on a rolling basis. Application fee: $35. Electronic applications accepted. *Expenses:* Contact institution. *Financial support:* Application deadline: 3/1. *Faculty research:* Development and application of the IEP for teachers, assistive technology, language-based disabilities, applied behavior analysis, communication challenges between general and special education teachers. *Unit head:* Paul Abraham, Chair, Department of Education, 617-521-2575, E-mail: paul.abraham@simmons.edu. *Application contact:* Kristen Haack, Director, Graduate Studies Admission, 617-521-2917, Fax: 617-521-3058, E-mail: gsa@simmons.edu.

Simmons College, Graduate School of Library and Information Science, Program in School Library Teacher, Boston, MA 02115. Offers MS, Certificate. Part-time programs available. *Faculty:* 25 full-time (17 women), 34 part-time/adjunct (22 women). *Students:* 2 full-time (both women), 63 part-time (60 women); includes 4 minority (1 African American, 2 Asian Americans or Pacific Islanders, 1 Hispanic American). Average age 32. 36 applicants, 69% accepted, 17 enrolled. *Entrance requirements:* For master's, GRE General Test or minimum cumulative GPA of 3.0; interview; for Certificate, GRE General Test or minimum GPA of 3.0, interview. Additional exam requirements/recommendations for international students: Required—TOEFL (minimum score 550 paper-based; 213 computer-based; 79 iBT). *Application deadline:* For fall admission, 3/1 priority date for domestic students, 3/1 for international students; for spring admission, 9/1 priority date for domestic students, 9/1 for international students. Applications are processed on a rolling basis. Application fee: $50. Electronic applications accepted. *Expenses:* Tuition: Part-time $925 per credit hour. Part-time tuition and fees vary according to program. *Financial support:* Application deadline: 3/1. *Faculty research:* Library leadership, organization, information use and users, children's literature, youth services. Total annual research expenditures: $253,656. *Unit head:* Michele V. Cloonan, Dean, 617-521-2806. *Application contact:* Sarah Petrakos, Assistant Dean, Admission and Recruitment, 617-521-2868, Fax: 617-521-3192, E-mail: gslisadm@simmons.edu.

Simon Fraser University, Graduate Studies, Faculty of Education, Program in Educational Technology and Learning Design, Burnaby, BC V5A 1S6, Canada. Offers M Ed, MA, PhD. *Degree requirements:* For master's, thesis or comprehensive exam.

Southeastern Louisiana University, College of Education and Human Development, Department of Educational Leadership and Technology, Hammond, LA 70402. Offers educational leadership (M Ed, Ed D); educational technology leadership (M Ed). Part-time and evening/weekend programs available. *Faculty:* 16 full-time (6 women). *Students:* 23 full-time (18 women), 224 part-time (177 women); includes 52 minority (47 African Americans, 1 Asian American or Pacific Islander, 4 Hispanic Americans), 1 international. Average age 38. 23 applicants, 100% accepted, 17 enrolled. In 2009, 52 master's awarded. *Degree requirements:* For master's, comprehensive exam (for some programs); for doctorate, thesis/dissertation. *Entrance requirements:* For master's, GRE (verbal and quantitative), 18 hours of course work in professional education or an undergraduate degree in education, standard teaching certificate; for doctorate, GRE, master's degree with minimum GPA of 3.25, 3.0 on the last 60 undergraduate hours. Additional exam requirements/recommendations for international students: Required—TOEFL (minimum score 500 paper-based; 173 computer-based; 61 iBT). *Application deadline:* For fall admission, 7/15 priority date for domestic students, 6/1 priority date for international students; for spring admission, 12/1 priority date for domestic students, 10/1 priority date for international students. Applications are processed on a rolling basis. Application fee: $20 ($30 for international students). Electronic applications accepted. *Expenses:* Tuition, state resident: full-time $3086; part-time $225 per credit hour. Tuition, nonresident: part-time $529 per credit hour. Required fees: $1195. Tuition and fees vary according to course level and course load. *Financial support:* In 2009–10, 9 students received support. Federal Work-Study, institutionally sponsored loans, scholarships/grants, and administrative assistantships available. Support available to part-time students. Financial award application deadline: 5/1; financial award applicants required to submit FAFSA. *Faculty research:* Using the Web and professional development in technology integration, legal and ethical issues in education, school culture

Educational Media/Instructional Technology

Southeastern Louisiana University (continued)
and gender perceptions, training needs to prepare school board members and superintendents, data information for decision making. Total annual research expenditures: $90,477. Unit head: Dr. Michael D. Richardson, Department Head, 985-549-5713, Fax: 985-549-5712, E-mail: mrichardson@selu.edu. Application contact: Sandra Meyers, Graduate Admissions Analyst, 985-549-2066, Fax: 985-549-5632, E-mail: admissions@selu.edu.

Southern Illinois University Edwardsville, Graduate Studies and Research, School of Education, Department of Educational Leadership, Program in Instructional Technology, Edwardsville, IL 62026-0001. Offers MS Ed. Accreditation: NCATE. Part-time and evening/weekend programs available. Students: 5 full-time (2 women), 31 part-time (19 women); includes 2 minority (both African Americans). Average age 26. 12 applicants, 58% accepted. In 2009, 6 master's awarded. Degree requirements: For master's, thesis or alternative, portfolio. Entrance requirements: Additional exam requirements/recommendations for international students: Required—TOEFL (minimum score 550 paper-based; 213 computer-based; 79 iBT), IELTS (minimum score 6.5). Application deadline: For fall admission, 7/23 for domestic students, 6/1 for international students; for spring admission, 12/11 for domestic students, 10/1 for international students. Applications are processed on a rolling basis. Application fee: $30. Electronic applications accepted. Expenses: Tuition, state resident: part-time $1252.50 per semester. Tuition, nonresident: part-time $3131.25 per semester. Required fees: $586.85 per semester. Tuition and fees vary according to course load. Financial support: In 2009–10, 4 teaching assistantships (averaging $8,064 per year) were awarded; fellowships, research assistantships, career-related internships or fieldwork, Federal Work-Study, institutionally sponsored loans, scholarships/grants, traineeships, and unspecified assistantships also available. Support available to part-time students. Financial award application deadline: 3/1; financial award applicants required to submit FAFSA. Unit head: Dr. Yuliang Liu, Program Director, 618-650-3293, E-mail: yliu@siue.edu. Application contact: Dr. Yuliang Liu, Program Director, 618-650-3293, E-mail: yliu@siue.edu.

Southern Illinois University Edwardsville, Graduate Studies and Research, School of Education, Department of Educational Leadership, Program in Web-Based Learning, Edwardsville, IL 62026-0001. Offers Postbaccalaureate Certificate. Part-time programs available. Students: 1 (woman) part-time. Average age 26. 7 applicants, 43% accepted. Entrance requirements: Additional exam requirements/recommendations for international students: Required—TOEFL (minimum score 550 paper-based; 213 computer-based; 79 iBT), IELTS (minimum score 6.5). Application deadline: For fall admission, 7/23 for domestic students, 6/1 for international students; for spring admission, 12/11 for domestic students, 10/1 for international students. Applications are processed on a rolling basis. Application fee: $30. Electronic applications accepted. Expenses: Tuition, state resident: part-time $1252.50 per semester. Tuition, nonresident: part-time $3131.25 per semester. Required fees: $586.85 per semester. Tuition and fees vary according to course load. Financial support: Career-related internships or fieldwork, Federal Work-Study, institutionally sponsored loans, scholarships/grants, traineeships, and unspecified assistantships available. Support available to part-time students. Financial award application deadline: 3/1; financial award applicants required to submit FAFSA. Unit head: Dr. Yuliang Liu, Director, 618-650-3293, E-mail: yliu@siue.edu. Application contact: Dr. Yuliang Liu, Director, 618-650-3293, E-mail: yliu@siue.edu.

Southern Polytechnic State University, School of Arts and Sciences, Department of English, Technical Communication, and Media Arts, Marietta, GA 30060-2896. Offers communications management (Graduate Certificate); content development (Graduate Certificate); information and instructional design (MSIID); information design and communication (MS); instructional design (Graduate Certificate); technical and professional communication (Graduate Certificate); visual communication and graphics (Graduate Certificate). Part-time and evening/weekend programs available. Postbaccalaureate distance learning degree programs offered (no on-campus study). Faculty: 4 full-time (3 women), 1 part-time/adjunct (0 women). Students: 5 full-time (all women), 50 part-time (32 women); includes 18 African Americans, 2 international. Average age 38. 32 applicants, 94% accepted, 26 enrolled. In 2009, 8 master's awarded. Degree requirements: For master's, thesis or internship; for Graduate Certificate, thesis optional, 18 hours completed through thesis option (6 hours), internship option (6 hours) or advanced coursework option (6 hours). Entrance requirements: For master's, GRE, statement of purpose, writing sample, professional recommendations, timed essay; for Graduate Certificate, writing sample, professional recommendations. Additional exam requirements/recommendations for international students: Required—TOEFL (minimum score 550 paper-based; 213 computer-based; 79 iBT), IELTS (minimum score 6.5). Application deadline: For fall admission, 5/1 priority date for domestic students, 7/1 priority date for international students; for spring admission, 9/1 priority date for domestic students, 11/1 priority date for international students. Applications are processed on a rolling basis. Application fee: $20. Electronic applications accepted. Expenses: Tuition, state resident: full-time $2896; part-time $181 per credit hour. Tuition, nonresident: full-time $11,552; part-time $722 per credit hour. Required fees: $1096. Financial support: In 2009–10, 1 research assistantship with full tuition reimbursement (averaging $4,000 per year), 1 teaching assistantship with partial tuition reimbursement (averaging $4,000 per year) were awarded; career-related internships or fieldwork, Federal Work-Study, scholarships/grants, and unspecified assistantships also available. Support available to part-time students. Financial award application deadline: 5/1; financial award applicants required to submit FAFSA. Faculty research: Usability, user-centered design, instructional design, information architecture, information design. Unit head: Dr. Mark Nunes, Chair, 678-915-7202, Fax: 678-915-7425, E-mail: mnunes@spsu.edu. Application contact: Nikki Palamiotis, Director of Graduate Studies, 678-915-4276, Fax: 678-915-7292, E-mail: npalamio@spsu.edu.

Southern University and Agricultural and Mechanical College, Graduate School, College of Education, Department of Curriculum and Instruction, Baton Rouge, LA 70813. Offers elementary education (M Ed); media (M Ed); secondary education (M Ed). Degree requirements: For master's, comprehensive exam, thesis optional. Entrance requirements: For master's, GMAT or GRE General Test. Additional exam requirements/recommendations for international students: Required—TOEFL (minimum score 525 paper-based; 193 computer-based).

State University of New York College at Oneonta, Graduate Education, Division of Education, Oneonta, NY 13820-4015. Offers educational psychology and counseling (MS Ed, CAS), including school counselor K-12; educational technology specialist (MS Ed); elementary education and reading (MS Ed), including childhood education, literacy education; secondary education (MS Ed); including adolescence education, family and consumer science education; special education (MS Ed), including adolescence, childhood. Accreditation: NCATE. Part-time and evening/weekend programs available. Students: 16 full-time (10 women), 66 part-time (39 women). Average age 25. 80 applicants, 94% accepted, 75 enrolled. In 2009, 18 master's awarded. Entrance requirements: For master's, GRE General Test. Application deadline: For fall admission, 3/25 priority date for domestic students; for spring admission, 10/1 priority date for domestic students. Applications are processed on a rolling basis. Application fee: $50. Expenses: Tuition, state resident: part-time $349 per credit hour. Tuition, nonresident: full-time $12,870; part-time $552 per credit hour. Required fees: $1280; $15.85 per credit hour. Unit head: Dr. Joanne Curran, Associate Dean, 607-436-2541, Fax: 607-436-2554, E-mail: curranjm@oneonta.edu. Application contact: Dean, 607-436-2523, Fax: 607-436-3084, E-mail: gradoffice@oneonta.edu.

State University of New York College at Potsdam, School of Education and Professional Studies, Program in Information and Communication Technology, Potsdam, NY 13676. Offers educational technology specialist (MS Ed); human performance technology (MS Ed); information technology (MS Ed); organizational leadership (MS Ed); technology educator (MS Ed). Part-time and evening/weekend programs available. Postbaccalaureate distance learning degree programs offered. Faculty: 4 full-time (1 woman), 2 part-time/adjunct (1 woman). Students: 22 full-time (12 women), 28 part-time (17 women); includes 4 minority (3 African Americans, 1 Asian American or Pacific Islander), 7 international. 28 applicants, 100% accepted, 20 enrolled. In 2009, 21 master's awarded. Degree requirements: For master's, thesis optional, culminating experience. Entrance requirements: For master's, minimum GPA of 2.75 in last 60 hours of

course work. Additional exam requirements/recommendations for international students: Required—TOEFL (minimum score 550 paper-based; 213 computer-based; 80 iBT), IELTS (minimum score 6). Application deadline: For fall admission, 4/1 priority date for domestic and international students; for spring admission, 10/15 priority date for domestic and international students. Applications are processed on a rolling basis. Application fee: $50. Expenses: Tuition, state resident: full-time $8370; part-time $349 per credit hour. Tuition, nonresident: full-time $13,250; part-time $552 per credit hour. Required fees: $942; $38.70 per credit hour. Financial support: In 2009–10, 1 student received support; fellowships, teaching assistantships, career-related internships or fieldwork, Federal Work-Study, scholarships/grants, and unspecified assistantships available. Support available to part-time students. Financial award application deadline: 3/1; financial award applicants required to submit FAFSA. Unit head: Dr. Anthony Betrus, Chairperson, 315-267-2535, Fax: 315-267-4802, E-mail: betrusak@potsdam.edu. Application contact: Peter Cutler, Graduate Admissions Counselor, 315-267-3154, Fax: 315-267-4802, E-mail: cutlerpj@potsdam.edu.

Stony Brook University, State University of New York, Graduate School, College of Engineering and Applied Sciences, Department of Technology and Society, Program in Educational Technology, Stony Brook, NY 11794. Offers MS. Accreditation: NCATE. Application deadline: For fall admission, 5/1 for domestic students; for spring admission, 11/1 for domestic students. Electronic applications accepted. Expenses: Tuition, state resident: full-time $8370; part-time $349 per credit. Tuition, nonresident: full-time $13,250; part-time $552 per credit. Required fees: $933. Financial support: Research assistantships, teaching assistantships available. Unit head: David Ferguson, Chair, 631-632-8770, E-mail: david.ferguson@stonybrook.edu. Application contact: Sheldon Reaven, 631-632-8770, E-mail: sheldon.raven@sunysb.edu.

Stony Brook University, State University of New York, School of Professional Development, Stony Brook, NY 11794. Offers biology-grade 7-12 (MAT); chemistry-grade 7-12 (MAT); coaching (Graduate Certificate); computer integrated engineering (Graduate Certificate); earth science-grade 7-12 (MAT); educational computing (Graduate Certificate); educational leadership (Advanced Certificate); English-grade 7-12 (MAT); environmental management (Graduate Certificate); environmental/occupational health and safety (Graduate Certificate); French-grade 7-12 (MAT); German-grade 7-12 (MAT); human resource management (Graduate Certificate); information systems management (Graduate Certificate); Italian-grade 7-12 (MAT); liberal studies (MA); mathematics-grade 7-12 (MAT); operation research (Graduate Certificate); physics-grade 7-12 (MAT); school administration and supervision (Graduate Certificate); school building leadership (Graduate Certificate); school district administration (Graduate Certificate); school district business leadership (Advanced Certificate); school district leadership (Graduate Certificate); social science and the professions (MPS), including environmental waste management, human resource management; social studies-grade 7-12 (MAT); Spanish-grade 7-12 (MAT); waste management (Graduate Certificate). Part-time and evening/weekend programs available. Postbaccalaureate distance learning degree programs offered. Faculty: 5 full-time (3 women), 131 part-time/adjunct (53 women). Students: 317 full-time (187 women), 1,200 part-time (773 women); includes 187 minority (77 African Americans, 2 American Indian/Alaska Native, 22 Asian Americans or Pacific Islanders, 86 Hispanic Americans), 11 international. Average age 28. In 2009, 597 master's, 234 other advanced degrees awarded. Degree requirements: For master's, one foreign language, thesis or alternative. Application deadline: Applications are processed on a rolling basis. Application fee: $62. Expenses: Tuition, state resident: full-time $8370; part-time $349 per credit. Tuition, nonresident: full-time $13,250; part-time $552 per credit. Required fees: $933. Financial support: Fellowships, research assistantships, teaching assistantships, career-related internships or fieldwork available. Support available to part-time students. Unit head: Dr. Paul J. Edelson, Dean, 631-632-7052, Fax: 631-632-9046, E-mail: paul.edelson@stonybrook.edu. Application contact: Dr. Paul J. Edelson, Dean, 631-632-7052, Fax: 631-632-9046, E-mail: paul.edelson@stonybrook.edu.

Strayer University, Graduate Studies, Washington, DC 20005-2603. Offers accounting (MS); acquisition (MBA); business administration (MBA); communications technology (MS); educational management (M Ed); finance (MBA); health services administration (MHSA); hospitality and tourism management (MBA); human resource management (MBA); information systems (MS), including computer security management, decision support system management, enterprise resource management, network management, software engineering management, systems development management; management (MBA); management information systems (MS); marketing (MBA); professional accounting (MS), including accounting information systems, controllership, taxation; public administration (MPA); supply chain management (MBA); technology in education (M Ed). Programs also offered at campus locations in Birmingham, AL; Chamblee, GA; Cobb County, GA; Morrow, GA; White Marsh, MD; Charleston, SC; Columbia, SC; Greensboro, NC; Greenville, SC; Lexington, KY; Louisville, KY; Nashville, TN; North Raleigh, NC; Washington, DC. Part-time and evening/weekend programs available. Postbaccalaureate distance learning degree programs offered (minimal on-campus study). Degree requirements: For master's, thesis. Entrance requirements: For master's, GMAT, GRE General Test, bachelor's degree from an accredited college or university, minimum undergraduate GPA of 2.75. Electronic applications accepted.

Syracuse University, School of Education, Program in Educational Technology, Syracuse, NY 13244. Offers CAS. Accreditation: ACA. Part-time programs available. Students: 1 (woman) part-time; minority (African American). Average age 47. In 2009, 1 CAS awarded. Degree requirements: For CAS, thesis or alternative. Entrance requirements: Additional exam requirements/recommendations for international students: Required—TOEFL (minimum score 100 iBT). Application deadline: For fall admission, 2/1 priority date for domestic and international students; for spring admission, 10/15 priority date for domestic and international students. Applications are processed on a rolling basis. Application fee: $75. Electronic applications accepted. Expenses: Tuition: Full-time $26,808; part-time $1117 per credit. Required fees: $1024. Financial support: Fellowships, research assistantships, teaching assistantships available. Financial award application deadline: 1/1. Faculty research: Academics and athletics, drug free schools, group counseling, prejudice prevention, culture-centered counseling. Unit head: Dr. Janine Bernard, Chair, 315-443-5266, Fax: 315-443-5732, E-mail: bernard@syr.edu. Application contact: Liza Rochelson, Graduate Recruiter, School of Education, 315-443-2505, E-mail: e-gradrcrt@syr.edu.

Syracuse University, School of Education, Program in Instructional Technology, Syracuse, NY 13244. Offers MS. Students: 1 applicant, 0% accepted, 0 enrolled. Entrance requirements: Additional exam requirements/recommendations for international students: Required—TOEFL (minimum score 100 iBT). Application deadline: For fall admission, 2/1 for domestic students, 2/1 priority date for international students. Application fee: $75. Electronic applications accepted. Expenses: Tuition: Full-time $26,808; part-time $1117 per credit. Required fees: $1024. Financial support: Fellowships with tuition reimbursements, research assistantships with tuition reimbursements available. Financial award application deadline: 1/1. Unit head: Dr. Nick Smith, Department Chair, 315-443-5293, E-mail: nlsmith@syr.edu. Application contact: Liza Rochelson, Graduate Recruiter, School of Education, 315-443-2505, E-mail: e-gradrcrt@syr.edu.

Syracuse University, School of Information Studies, Program in Library and Information Science: School Media, Syracuse, NY 13244. Offers MS. Part-time and evening/weekend programs available. Postbaccalaureate distance learning degree programs offered (minimal on-campus study). Students: 13 full-time (all women), 50 part-time (48 women); includes 5 minority (3 African Americans, 1 Asian American or Pacific Islander, 1 Hispanic American). Average age 36. 49 applicants, 84% accepted, 25 enrolled. In 2009, 36 master's awarded. Entrance requirements: For master's, GRE. Additional exam requirements/recommendations for international students: Required—TOEFL (minimum score 100 iBT). Application deadline: For fall admission, 2/1 priority date for domestic and international students; for spring admission, 10/15 priority date for domestic and international students. Applications are processed on a rolling basis. Application fee: $75. Electronic applications accepted. Expenses: Tuition: Full-time $26,808; part-time $1117 per credit. Required fees: $1024. Financial support: Tuition waivers (partial) available. Financial award application deadline: 1/1. Unit head: R. David Lankes,

Director, 315-443-1707, E-mail: rdlankes@iis.syr.edu. *Application contact:* Susan Corieri, Director of Enrollment Management, 315-443-2575, E-mail: ist@syr.edu.

Syracuse University, School of Information Studies, Program in School Media, Syracuse, NY 13244. Offers CAS. Part-time and evening/weekend programs available. Postbaccalaureate distance learning degree programs offered. *Students:* 1 (woman) full-time, 5 part-time (all women); includes 1 minority (African American). Average age 33. 1 applicant, 0% accepted, 0 enrolled. In 2009, 1 CAS awarded. *Entrance requirements:* For degree, MS in library and information science. Additional exam requirements/recommendations for international students: Required—TOEFL (minimum score 100 iBT). *Application deadline:* For fall admission, 2/1 priority date for domestic and international students; for spring admission, 10/15 priority date for domestic and international students. Applications are processed on a rolling basis. Application fee: $75. Electronic applications accepted. *Expenses:* Tuition: Full-time $26,808; part-time $1117 per credit. Required fees: $1024. *Financial support:* Application deadline: 1/1. *Unit head:* R. David Lankes, Director, 315-443-1707, E-mail: rdlankes@iis.syr.edu. *Application contact:* Susan Corieri, Director of Enrollment Management, 315-443-2575, E-mail: ist@syr.edu.

Teachers College, Columbia University, Graduate Faculty of Education, Department of Math, Science and Technology, Program in Educational Media/Instructional Technology, New York, NY 10027-6696. Offers Ed M, MA, Ed D. *Faculty:* 4 full-time (2 women). *Students:* 23 full-time (19 women), 97 part-time (56 women); includes 38 minority (10 African Americans, 24 Asian Americans or Pacific Islanders, 4 Hispanic Americans), 20 international. Average age 34. 56 applicants, 64% accepted, 18 enrolled. In 2009, 25 master's, 7 doctorates awarded. *Degree requirements:* For doctorate, thesis/dissertation. *Entrance requirements:* For doctorate, GRE General Test or MAT. *Application deadline:* For fall admission, 5/15 for domestic students; for spring admission, 12/1 for domestic students. Application fee: $65. *Financial support:* Career-related internships or fieldwork, Federal Work-Study, institutionally sponsored loans, and tuition waivers (full and partial) available. Support available to part-time students. Financial award application deadline: 2/1. *Faculty research:* Video and interactive learning. *Unit head:* Dr. O. Roger Anderson, Chair, 212-678-3405. *Application contact:* Deanna Ghozati, Assistant Director of Admission, 212-678-4018, Fax: 212-678-4171, E-mail: ghozati@tc.edu.

Texas A&M University, College of Education and Human Development, Department of Educational Psychology, College Station, TX 77843. Offers counseling psychology (PhD); educational psychology (PhD); educational technology (M Ed); gifted and talented education (M Ed, MS); Hispanic bilingual education (M Ed, PhD); human learning and development (MS); intelligence, creativity, and giftedness (PhD); learning, development, and instruction (PhD); research, measurement and statistics (MS); research, measurement, and statistics (PhD); school counseling (M Ed); school psychology (PhD); special education (M Ed, PhD). *Accreditation:* APA (one or more programs are accredited). Part-time and evening/weekend programs available. Postbaccalaureate distance learning degree programs offered (no on-campus study). *Faculty:* 45. *Students:* 160 full-time (126 women), 144 part-time (118 women); includes 99 minority (25 African Americans, 13 Asian Americans or Pacific Islanders, 61 Hispanic Americans), 41 international. In 2009, 53 master's, 30 doctorates awarded. *Degree requirements:* For master's, thesis optional; for doctorate, thesis/dissertation. *Entrance requirements:* For master's and doctorate, GRE General Test. Additional exam requirements/recommendations for international students: Required—TOEFL. Application fee: $50 ($75 for international students). Electronic applications accepted. *Expenses:* Tuition, state resident: full-time $3991; part-time $221.74 per credit hour. Tuition, nonresident: full-time $9049; part-time $502.74 per credit hour. *Financial support:* In 2009–10, fellowships (averaging $12,000 per year), research assistantships (averaging $9,000 per year), teaching assistantships (averaging $9,000 per year) were awarded; career-related internships or fieldwork, institutionally sponsored loans, scholarships/grants, and unspecified assistantships also available. Financial award applicants required to submit FAFSA. *Unit head:* Dr. Victor Willson, Head, 979-845-1800. *Application contact:* Carol A. Wagner, Director of Advising, 979-845-1833, Fax: 979-862-1256, E-mail: epsyadvisor@tamu.edu.

Texas A&M University–Commerce, Graduate School, College of Education and Human Services, Department of Educational Leadership, Commerce, TX 75429-3011. Offers educational administration (M Ed, Ed D); educational technology (M Ed, MS); higher education (MS, Ed D); training and development (MS). Part-time programs available. Terminal master's awarded for partial completion of doctoral program. *Degree requirements:* For master's, comprehensive exam, thesis (for some programs); for doctorate, thesis/dissertation, departmental qualifying exam. *Entrance requirements:* For master's, GRE General Test; for doctorate, GRE General Test, writing skills exam, interview. Electronic applications accepted. *Faculty research:* Property tax reform, politics of education, administrative stress.

Texas A&M University–Commerce, Graduate School, College of Education and Human Services, Department of Secondary and Higher Education, Commerce, TX 75429-3011. Offers higher education (MS), including administration, teaching; learning technology and information systems (M Ed, MS), including educational computing, library and information science, media and technology; secondary education (M Ed, MS); supervision, curriculum, and instruction (Ed D); training and development (MS). Part-time programs available. Terminal master's awarded for partial completion of doctoral program. *Degree requirements:* For master's, comprehensive exam, thesis (for some programs); for doctorate, thesis/dissertation, departmental qualifying exam. *Entrance requirements:* For master's and doctorate, GRE General Test. Electronic applications accepted. *Faculty research:* Deviance, migration.

Texas A&M University–Corpus Christi, Graduate Studies and Research, College of Education, Corpus Christi, TX 78412-5503. Offers counseling (MS, PhD), including counseling (MS), counselor education (PhD); curriculum and instruction (MS, Ed D); early childhood education (MS); educational administration (MS); educational leadership (Ed D); educational technology (MS); elementary education (MS); kinesiology (MS); reading (MS); secondary education (MS); special education (MS). Part-time and evening/weekend programs available. *Degree requirements:* For master's, comprehensive exam, thesis (for some programs); for doctorate, comprehensive exam, thesis/dissertation. *Entrance requirements:* For master's, GRE General Test. Additional exam requirements/recommendations for international students: Required—TOEFL. Electronic applications accepted.

Texas A&M University–Texarkana, Graduate Studies and Research, College of Education and Liberal Arts, Texarkana, TX 75505-5518. Offers adult education (MS); curriculum and instruction (M Ed); education (MS); educational administration (M Ed); English (MA); instructional technology (MS); interdisciplinary studies (MA, MS); special education (MS). Part-time and evening/weekend programs available. *Degree requirements:* For master's, comprehensive exam (for some programs), thesis optional. *Entrance requirements:* For master's, minimum GPA of 2.5 on last 60 hours of bachelor's degree. Additional exam requirements/recommendations for international students: Required—TOEFL. Electronic applications accepted.

Texas Tech University, Graduate School, College of Education, Department of Educational Psychology and Leadership, Lubbock, TX 79409. Offers counselor education (M Ed, PhD); educational leadership (M Ed, Ed D); educational psychology (M Ed, PhD); higher education (M Ed, Ed D); higher education: higher education research (PhD); instructional technology (M Ed, Ed D); instructional technology: distance education (M Ed); special education (M Ed, Ed D). *Accreditation:* ACA; NCATE. Part-time programs available. *Students:* 137 full-time (94 women), 335 part-time (236 women); includes 90 minority (27 African Americans, 6 American Indian/Alaska Native, 3 Asian Americans or Pacific Islanders, 54 Hispanic Americans), 34 international. Average age 36. 390 applicants, 51% accepted, 90 enrolled. In 2009, 113 master's, 18 doctorates awarded. *Degree requirements:* For master's, thesis optional; for doctorate, thesis/dissertation. *Entrance requirements:* For master's and doctorate, GRE General Test. Additional exam requirements/recommendations for international students: Required—TOEFL (minimum score 550 paper-based; 213 computer-based). *Application deadline:* For fall admission, 3/1 priority date for international students; for spring admission, 11/1 priority date for international students. Applications are processed on a rolling basis. Application fee: $50 ($75 for international students). Electronic applications accepted. *Expenses:* Tuition, state resident: full-time $5100; part-time $213 per credit hour. Tuition, nonresident: full-time $11,748; part-time $490 per credit hour. Required fees: $2298; $50 per credit hour. $555 per semester. *Financial support:* Research assistantships with partial tuition reimbursements, teaching assistantships with partial tuition reimbursements, career-related internships or fieldwork, Federal Work-Study, and institutionally sponsored loans available. Support available to part-time students. Financial award application deadline: 4/15; financial award applicants required to submit FAFSA. *Faculty research:* Psychological processes of teaching and learning, teaching populations with special needs, instructional technology, educational administration in education, theories and practice in counseling and counselor education K-12 and higher. *Unit head:* Dr. William Lan, Chair, 806-742-1998 Ext. 436, Fax: 806-742-2179, E-mail: william.lan@ttu.edu. *Application contact:* Dr. Joseph G. Claudet, Graduate Adviser, 806-742-1998, Fax: 806-742-2179.

Thomas Edison State College, Heavin School of Arts and Sciences, Program in Online Learning and Teaching, Trenton, NJ 08608-1176. Offers Graduate Certificate. Part-time programs available. Postbaccalaureate distance learning degree programs offered (no on-campus study). *Students:* 28 part-time (21 women); includes 7 minority (6 African Americans, 1 Hispanic American), 1 international. Average age 47. In 2009, 7 Graduate Certificates awarded. *Entrance requirements:* Additional exam requirements/recommendations for international students: Required—TOEFL (minimum score 550 paper-based; 213 computer-based; 79 iBT). *Application deadline:* For fall admission, 8/15 priority date for domestic and international students; for winter admission, 11/15 priority date for domestic and international students; for spring admission, 2/15 priority date for domestic and international students. Applications are processed on a rolling basis. Application fee: $75. Electronic applications accepted. *Expenses:* Tuition, area resident: Part-time $479 per credit. Tuition, state resident: part-time $479 per credit. Tuition, nonresident: part-time $479 per credit. *Financial support:* Applicants required to submit FAFSA. *Unit head:* Dr. Susan Davenport, Dean, Heavin School of Arts and Sciences, 609-984-1130, Fax: 609-984-0740, E-mail: info@tesc.edu. *Application contact:* David Hoftiezer, Director of Admissions, 888-442-8372, Fax: 609-984-8447, E-mail: admissions@tesc.edu.

Towson University, College of Graduate Studies and Research, Program in Instructional Technology, Towson, MD 21252-0001. Offers instructional design and training (MS); instructional technology (Ed D). Part-time and evening/weekend programs available. *Degree requirements:* For master's, thesis optional; for doctorate, comprehensive exam, thesis/dissertation. *Entrance requirements:* For master's, minimum GPA of 3.0, technological literacy; for doctorate, GRE, writing sample, letters of recommendation. Additional exam requirements/recommendations for international students: Required—TOEFL (minimum score 600 paper-based). Electronic applications accepted. *Faculty research:* Training and commercial vehicle inspections.

Trevecca Nazarene University, Graduate Division, School of Education, Major in Instructional Technology, Nashville, TN 37210-2877. Offers M Ed. *Accreditation:* NCATE. Part-time and evening/weekend programs available. *Students:* 10 full-time (5 women); includes 4 minority (2 African Americans, 2 Hispanic Americans). *Degree requirements:* For master's, exit assessment. *Entrance requirements:* For master's, GRE General Test, MAT, minimum GPA of 2.7, 2 reference forms. Additional exam requirements/recommendations for international students: Required—TOEFL (minimum score 550 paper-based; 213 computer-based). *Application deadline:* Applications are processed on a rolling basis. Application fee: $25. *Expenses:* Contact institution. *Financial support:* Applicants required to submit FAFSA. *Unit head:* Dr. Esther Swink, Dean, School of Education/Director of Graduate Education Program, 615-248-1201, Fax: 615-248-1597, E-mail: admissions_ged@trevecca.edu. *Application contact:* Admissions Office, 615-248-1201, Fax: 615-248-1597, E-mail: admissions_ged@trevecca.edu.

Troy University, Graduate School, College of Education, Program in Postsecondary Education, Troy, AL 36082. Offers adult education (M Ed); biology (M Ed); criminal justice (M Ed); english (M Ed); foundations of education (M Ed); general science (M Ed); higher education administration (M Ed); history (M Ed); instructional technology (M Ed); mathematics (M Ed); music industry (M Ed); physical fitness (M Ed); political science (M Ed); public administration (M Ed); social science (M Ed); teaching english (M Ed). Also offered through the University College. *Accreditation:* NCATE. Part-time and evening/weekend programs available. *Students:* 267 full-time (192 women), 381 part-time (293 women); includes 326 minority (309 African Americans, 4 American Indian/Alaska Native, 5 Asian Americans or Pacific Islanders, 8 Hispanic Americans). Average age 34. 343 applicants, 90% accepted. In 2009, 480 master's awarded. *Degree requirements:* For master's, comprehensive exam, thesis. *Entrance requirements:* For master's, MAT (minimum score 385), minimum GPA of 2.5. Additional exam requirements/recommendations for international students: Required—TOEFL (minimum score 523 paper-based; 193 computer-based; 70 iBT), IELTS, or ACT Compass ESL (minimum score 270 on Listening, Reading, and Grammar with no individual score below 85 and a minimum score of 8 out of 12 on writing test). *Application deadline:* Applications are processed on a rolling basis. Application fee: $50. Electronic applications accepted. *Financial support:* Available to part-time students. Applicants required to submit FAFSA. *Unit head:* Dr. Andrew Creamer, Chair, 334-670-3350, E-mail: drcreamer@troy.edu. *Application contact:* Brenda K. Campbell, Director of Graduate Admissions, 334-670-3178, Fax: 334-670-3733, E-mail: bcamp@troy.edu.

TUI University, College of Education, Program in Educational Leadership, Cypress, CA 90630. Offers e-learning leadership (MA Ed, PhD); educational leadership (MA Ed); higher education leadership (PhD); K-12 leadership (PhD). Part-time and evening/weekend programs available. Postbaccalaureate distance learning degree programs offered (no on-campus study). *Degree requirements:* For doctorate, comprehensive exam, thesis/dissertation, defense of dissertation. *Entrance requirements:* For master's, minimum GPA of 2.5 (students with GPA 3.0 or greater may transfer up to 30% of graduate level credits); for doctorate, minimum GPA of 3.4, course work in research methods or statistics. Additional exam requirements/recommendations for international students: Required—TOEFL. Electronic applications accepted.

Université Laval, Faculty of Education, Department of Teaching and Learning Studies, Programs in Teaching Technology, Québec, QC G1K 7P4, Canada. Offers MA, PhD. Terminal master's awarded for partial completion of doctoral program. *Degree requirements:* For master's, thesis (for some programs); for doctorate, comprehensive exam, thesis/dissertation. *Entrance requirements:* For master's and doctorate, English exam (comprehension of written English), knowledge of French. Electronic applications accepted.

University at Albany, State University of New York, School of Education, Department of Educational Theory and Practice, Albany, NY 12222-0001. Offers curriculum and instruction (MS, Ed D, CAS); curriculum planning and development (MA); educational communications (MS, CAS). Evening/weekend programs available. *Degree requirements:* For doctorate, one foreign language, thesis/dissertation. *Entrance requirements:* For doctorate, GRE General Test. Additional exam requirements/recommendations for international students: Required—TOEFL (minimum score 550 paper-based; 213 computer-based). Electronic applications accepted.

University of Alaska Southeast, Graduate Programs, Program in Education, Juneau, AK 99801. Offers early childhood education (M Ed, MAT); educational technology (M Ed); elementary education (MAT); reading (M Ed); secondary education (MAT). *Accreditation:* NCATE. Part-time and evening/weekend programs available. Postbaccalaureate distance learning degree programs offered (minimal on-campus study). *Degree requirements:* For master's, comprehensive exam or project, portfolio. *Entrance requirements:* For master's, PRAXIS, minimum GPA of 3.0, writing sample, letters of recommendation. Electronic applications accepted. *Faculty research:* Applied classroom research, culturally responsive practices, action research, teaching effectiveness.

University of Alberta, Faculty of Graduate Studies and Research, Department of Educational Psychology, Edmonton, AB T6G 2E1, Canada. Offers counseling psychology (M Ed, PhD); educational psychology (M Ed, PhD); instructional technology (M Ed); school counseling (M Ed); school psychology (M Ed, PhD); special education (M Ed, PhD); special education-deafness studies (M Ed); teaching English as a second language (M Ed). Part-time programs available. *Faculty:* 34 full-time (14 women), 12 part-time/adjunct (6 women). *Students:* 117 full-time (93

Educational Media/Instructional Technology

University of Alberta (continued)

women), 173 part-time (121 women). Average age 36. 252 applicants, 34% accepted. In 2009, 30 master's, 10 doctorates awarded. *Degree requirements:* For master's, thesis optional; for doctorate, comprehensive exam, thesis/dissertation. *Entrance requirements:* For master's and doctorate, minimum GPA of 3.0. Additional exam requirements/recommendations for international students: Required—TOEFL. *Application deadline:* For fall admission, 2/1 priority date for domestic and international students. Applications are processed on a rolling basis. Tuition and fees charges are reported in Canadian dollars. *Expenses:* Tuition, area resident: Full-time $4626 Canadian dollars; part-time $99.72 Canadian dollars per unit. International tuition: $8216 Canadian dollars full-time. Required fees: $3590 Canadian dollars; $99.72 Canadian dollars per unit. $215 Canadian dollars per term. *Financial support:* In 2009–10, 10 fellowships with full tuition reimbursements (averaging $16,120 per year), 36 research assistantships with full tuition reimbursements (averaging $12,614 per year), 46 teaching assistantships with full tuition reimbursements (averaging $5,462 per year) were awarded; career-related internships or fieldwork and scholarships/grants also available. *Faculty research:* Human learning, development and assessment. *Unit head:* Dr. Linda M. McDonald, Chair, 780-492-1149, Fax: 780-492-1318, E-mail: linda.mcdonald@ualberta.ca. *Application contact:* Judy Maynes, Information Contact, 780-492-1149, Fax: 780-492-1318, E-mail: edpygrad@ualberta.ca.

University of Arkansas, Graduate School, College of Education and Health Professions, Department of Curriculum and Instruction, Program in Educational Technology, Fayetteville, AR 72701-1201. Offers M Ed. *Accreditation:* NCATE. Part-time and evening/weekend programs available. *Students:* 6 full-time (3 women), 23 part-time (18 women); includes 2 minority (both African Americans), 1 international. In 2009, 2 master's awarded. *Entrance requirements:* For master's, GRE General Test, MAT or minimum GPA of 3.0. Application fee: $40 ($50 for international students). *Expenses:* Tuition, state resident: full-time $7355; part-time $356.58 per hour. Tuition, nonresident: full-time $17,401; part-time $775.17 per hour. Required fees: $1203. *Financial support:* In 2009–10, 1 research assistantship was awarded; fellowships with tuition reimbursements, teaching assistantships, career-related internships or fieldwork and Federal Work-Study also available. Support available to part-time students. Financial award application deadline: 4/1; financial award applicants required to submit FAFSA. *Unit head:* Dr. Michael Daugherty, Department Chairperson, 479-575-4209, E-mail: mkd03@uark.edu. *Application contact:* Dr. William McComas, Graduate Coordinator, 479-575-7525, E-mail: mccomas@uark.edu.

University of Arkansas at Little Rock, Graduate School, College of Education, Department of Educational Leadership, Program in Learning Systems Technology, Little Rock, AR 72204-1099. Offers M Ed. *Degree requirements:* For master's, comprehensive exam or defense of portfolio. *Entrance requirements:* For master's, GRE General Test, interview, minimum GPA of 2.75. *Faculty research:* Instructional program development, educational technology product development, educational technology management.

University of Calgary, Faculty of Graduate Studies, Faculty of Education, Graduate Division of Educational Research, Calgary, AB T2N 1N4, Canada. Offers community rehabilitation and disability studies (M Ed, M Sc, Ed D, PhD, Graduate Certificate, Graduate Diploma); curriculum, teaching and learning (M Ed, M Sc, MA, Ed D, PhD, Graduate Certificate, Graduate Diploma); educational contexts (M Ed, MA, Ed D, PhD, Graduate Certificate, Graduate Diploma); educational leadership (M Ed, MA, Ed D, PhD, Graduate Certificate, Graduate Diploma); educational technology (M Ed, M Sc, MA, Ed D, PhD, Graduate Certificate, Graduate Diploma); gifted education (M Sc, MA, Ed D, PhD, Graduate Certificate, Graduate Diploma); higher education administration (Ed D); interpretive studies in education (M Ed, M Sc, MA, Ed D, PhD, Graduate Certificate, Graduate Diploma); second language teaching (M Ed, Ed D, PhD, Graduate Certificate, Graduate Diploma); teaching English as a second language (M Ed, M Sc, MA, Ed D, PhD, Graduate Certificate, Graduate Diploma); workplace and adult learning (M Ed, MA, Ed D, PhD, Graduate Certificate, Graduate Diploma). Ed D in both higher education administration and educational leadership offered via distance delivery. Part-time and evening/weekend programs available. Postbaccalaureate distance learning degree programs offered (minimal on-campus study). *Degree requirements:* For master's, thesis (for some programs); for doctorate, thesis/dissertation, candidacy exam. *Entrance requirements:* For master's, minimum GPA of 3.0, 3 letters of reference; for doctorate, minimum GPA of 3.5, 3 letters of reference; for other advanced degree, minimum GPA of 3.0. Additional exam requirements/recommendations for international students: Required—TOEFL, IELTS. Electronic applications accepted. *Faculty research:* Curriculum, leadership, technology, contexts, gifted, second language teaching, work place and adult learning.

University of Central Arkansas, Graduate School, College of Education, Department of Teaching, Learning, and Technology, Program in Education Media and Library Science, Conway, AR 72035-0001. Offers MS. Part-time programs available. *Students:* 4 full-time (0 women), 5 part-time (4 women). Average age 37. 29 applicants, 100% accepted. In 2009, 41 master's awarded. *Degree requirements:* For master's, comprehensive exam. *Entrance requirements:* For master's, GRE General Test, minimum GPA of 2.7. Additional exam requirements/recommendations for international students: Required—TOEFL (minimum score 550 paper-based; 213 computer-based). *Application deadline:* For fall admission, 3/1 priority date for domestic and international students; for spring admission, 10/1 priority date for domestic and international students. Applications are processed on a rolling basis. Application fee: $25 ($50 for international students). *Expenses:* Tuition, state resident: full-time $5136; part-time $214 per credit hour. Required fees: $379.50; $127 per term. Tuition and fees vary according to course level, course load and campus/location. *Financial support:* Federal Work-Study, scholarships/grants, and tuition waivers (partial) available. Financial award application deadline: 2/15; financial award applicants required to submit FAFSA. *Unit head:* Stephanie Huffman, Head, 501-450-5430, Fax: 501-450-5680, E-mail: stephanieh@uca.edu. *Application contact:* Brenda Herring, Admissions Assistant, 501-450-5065, Fax: 501-450-5678, E-mail: bherring@uca.edu.

University of Central Arkansas, Graduate School, College of Education, Department of Teaching, Learning, and Technology, Program in Training Systems, Conway, AR 72035-0001. Offers MS. Part-time programs available. *Students:* 5 part-time (4 women); includes 3 minority (all African Americans). Average age 40. 2 applicants, 100% accepted, 0 enrolled. In 2009, 7 master's awarded. *Degree requirements:* For master's, comprehensive exam, thesis optional. *Entrance requirements:* For master's, GRE General Test, minimum GPA of 2.7. Additional exam requirements/recommendations for international students: Required—TOEFL (minimum score 550 paper-based; 213 computer-based). *Application deadline:* For fall admission, 3/1 priority date for domestic and international students; for spring admission, 10/1 priority date for domestic and international students. Applications are processed on a rolling basis. Application fee: $25 ($50 for international students). *Expenses:* Tuition, state resident: full-time $5136; part-time $214 per credit hour. Required fees: $379.50; $127 per term. Tuition and fees vary according to course level, course load and campus/location. *Financial support:* Federal Work-Study, scholarships/grants, tuition waivers (partial), and unspecified assistantships available. Support available to part-time students. Financial award application deadline: 2/15; financial award applicants required to submit FAFSA. *Application contact:* Brenda Herring, Admissions Assistant, 501-450-5065, Fax: 501-450-5678, E-mail: bherring@uca.edu.

University of Central Florida, College of Education, Department of Educational Research, Technology and Leadership, Program in Educational Technology, Orlando, FL 32816. Offers MA. *Students:* 11 applicants, 91% accepted, 7 enrolled. *Degree requirements:* For master's, thesis or alternative. *Application deadline:* For fall admission, 7/15 for domestic students; for spring admission, 12/1 for domestic students. Application fee: $30. Electronic applications accepted. *Expenses:* Tuition, state resident: part-time $306.31 per credit hour. Tuition, nonresident: part-time $1099.01 per credit hour. Part-time tuition and fees vary according to degree level and program. *Financial support:* Fellowships with partial tuition reimbursements, research assistantships with partial tuition reimbursements, career-related internships or fieldwork, Federal Work-Study, institutionally sponsored loans, tuition waivers (partial), and unspecified assistantships available. *Unit head:* Dr. Glenda Gunter, Coordinator, 407-823-3502, E-mail: ggunter@pegasus.cc.ucf.edu. *Application contact:* Dr. Glenda Gunter, Coordinator, 407-823-3502, E-mail: ggunter@pegasus.cc.ucf.edu.

University of Central Florida, College of Education, Department of Educational Research, Technology and Leadership, Program in e-Learning, Orlando, FL 32816. Offers e-learning professional development (Certificate); instructional technology/media and e-learning (MA). *Expenses:* Tuition, state resident: part-time $306.31 per credit hour. Tuition, nonresident: part-time $1099.01 per credit hour. Part-time tuition and fees vary according to degree level and program. *Financial support:* In 2009–10, 1 research assistantship (averaging $6,200 per year) was awarded. *Unit head:* Dr. Atusi Hirumi, Coordinator, 407-823-1760, E-mail: hirumi@mail.ucf.edu. *Application contact:* Dr. Atusi Hirumi, Coordinator, 407-823-1760, E-mail: hirumi@mail.ucf.edu.

University of Central Florida, College of Education, Department of Educational Research, Technology and Leadership, Program in Instructional Systems, Orlando, FL 32816. Offers MA. *Students:* Average age 34.Application fee: $30. Electronic applications accepted. *Expenses:* Tuition, state resident: part-time $306.31 per credit hour. Tuition, nonresident: part-time $1099.01 per credit hour. Part-time tuition and fees vary according to degree level and program. *Financial support:* Fellowships with partial tuition reimbursements, research assistantships with partial tuition reimbursements, teaching assistantships with partial tuition reimbursements available. *Unit head:* Dr. Atusi Hirumi, Coordinator, 407-823-1760, E-mail: hirumi@mail.ucf.edu. *Application contact:* Dr. Atusi Hirumi, Coordinator, 407-823-1760, E-mail: hirumi@mail.ucf.edu.

University of Central Florida, College of Education, Department of Educational Research, Technology and Leadership, Program in Instructional Technology/Media, Orlando, FL 32816. Offers e-learning (Certificate); educational technology (MA); instructional design for simulations (Certificate); instructional/educational technology (Certificate). *Students:* 18 full-time (16 women), 83 part-time (56 women); includes 18 minority (6 African Americans, 1 American Indian/Alaska Native, 2 Asian Americans or Pacific Islanders, 9 Hispanic Americans), 4 international. Average age 35. 59 applicants, 92% accepted, 38 enrolled. In 2009, 20 master's, 15 other advanced degrees awarded. Application fee: $30. Electronic applications accepted. *Expenses:* Tuition, state resident: part-time $306.31 per credit hour. Tuition, nonresident: part-time $1099.01 per credit hour. Part-time tuition and fees vary according to degree level and program.

University of Central Florida, College of Education, Education PhD Program, Orlando, FL 32816. Offers communication sciences and disorders (PhD); counselor education (PhD); elementary education (PhD); exceptional education (PhD); higher education (PhD); hospitality education (PhD); instructional technology (PhD); mathematics education (PhD); science education (PhD); social science education (PhD). *Students:* 99 full-time (70 women), 14 part-time (9 women); includes 28 minority (17 African Americans, 2 Asian Americans or Pacific Islanders, 9 Hispanic Americans), 20 international. In 2009, 15 doctorates awarded. Application fee: $30. Electronic applications accepted. *Expenses:* Tuition, state resident: part-time $306.31 per credit hour. Tuition, nonresident: part-time $1099.01 per credit hour. Part-time tuition and fees vary according to degree level and program. *Financial support:* In 2009–10, 40 fellowships with partial tuition reimbursements (averaging $9,200 per year), 61 research assistantships with partial tuition reimbursements (averaging $7,800 per year), 18 teaching assistantships with partial tuition reimbursements (averaging $6,500 per year) were awarded. *Unit head:* Dr. B. Grant Hayes, Associate Dean, 407-823-5391, E-mail: ghayes@mail.ucf.edu. *Application contact:* Dr. B. Grant Hayes, Associate Dean, 407-823-5391, E-mail: ghayes@mail.ucf.edu.

University of Central Missouri, The Graduate School, College of Education, Warrensburg, MO 64093. Offers career and technical education administration (MS); career and technical education industry training (MS); career and technical education leadership/teaching (MS); college student personnel administration (MS); counseling (MS); curriculum and instruction (Ed S); educational leadership (Ed D); educational technology (MS); elementary education/educational foundations and literacy (MSE); elementary school administration (MSE); elementary school principalship (Ed S); human services/learning resources (Ed S); human services/professional counseling (Ed S); human services/special education (Ed S); human services/technology and occupational education (Ed S); K-12 education/educational foundations and literacy (MSE); K-12 special education (MSE); library science and information services (MS); literacy education (MSE); secondary education/educational foundations & literacy (MSE); secondary school administration (MSE); secondary school principalship (Ed S); superintendency (Ed S); teaching (MAT). Part-time programs available. Postbaccalaureate distance learning degree programs offered. *Faculty:* 42. *Students:* 123 full-time (82 women), 721 part-time (552 women); includes 58 minority (38 African Americans, 3 American Indian/Alaska Native, 6 Asian Americans or Pacific Islanders, 11 Hispanic Americans), 6 international. Average age 34. 229 applicants, 88% accepted, 190 enrolled. In 2009, 212 master's, 47 other advanced degrees awarded. *Entrance requirements:* Additional exam requirements/recommendations for international students: Required—TOEFL (minimum score 550 paper-based; 79 computer-based). *Application deadline:* For fall admission, 6/1 priority date for domestic students, 5/1 for international students; for spring admission, 10/1 priority date for domestic students, 10/1 for international students. Applications are processed on a rolling basis. Application fee: $30 ($75 for international students). Electronic applications accepted. *Expenses:* Tuition, area resident: Part-time $245.80 per credit hour. Tuition, nonresident: part-time $491.60 per credit hour. Required fees: $24.20 per credit hour. Full-time tuition and fees vary according to course load, degree level, campus/location and reciprocity agreements. *Financial support:* Research assistantships with full and partial tuition reimbursements, teaching assistantships with full and partial tuition reimbursements, career-related internships or fieldwork, Federal Work-Study, scholarships/grants, and administrative and laboratory assistantships available. Support available to part-time students. Financial award application deadline: 3/1; financial award applicants required to submit FAFSA. *Unit head:* Dr. Michael Wright, Dean, 660-543-4272, Fax: 660-543-8753, E-mail: mwright@ucmo.edu. *Application contact:* Laurie Delap, Admissions Coordinator, 660-543-4621, Fax: 660-543-4778, E-mail: gradinfo@ucmo.edu.

University of Central Oklahoma, College of Graduate Studies and Research, College of Education, Department of Advanced Professional Services, Program in Instructional Media, Edmond, OK 73034-5209. Offers M Ed. *Accreditation:* NCATE. Part-time programs available. *Faculty:* 3 full-time (all women). *Students:* 5 full-time (all women), 54 part-time (52 women); includes 5 minority (2 African Americans, 2 American Indian/Alaska Native, 1 Hispanic American). Average age 38. 9 applicants, 100% accepted. In 2009, 12 master's awarded. *Entrance requirements:* For master's, GRE General Test. Additional exam requirements/recommendations for international students: Required—TOEFL (minimum score 550 paper-based; 213 computer-based). *Application deadline:* For fall admission, 7/1 for international students; for spring admission, 11/1 for international students. Applications are processed on a rolling basis. Application fee: $25. Electronic applications accepted. *Expenses:* Tuition, state resident: full-time $4128; part-time $172 per credit hour. Tuition, nonresident: full-time $10,373; part-time $432.20 per credit hour. Required fees: $433.20; $18.05 per credit hour. *Financial support:* Unspecified assistantships available. Financial award application deadline: 3/31; financial award applicants required to submit FAFSA. *Unit head:* Dr. Pat Couts, Adviser, 405-974-5888, Fax: 405-974-3822. *Application contact:* Dr. Richard Bernard, Dean, Graduate College, 405-974-3493, Fax: 405-974-3852, E-mail: gradcoll@uco.edu.

University of Colorado Denver, School of Education and Human Development, Information and Learning Technologies Program, Denver, CO 80217-3364. Offers MA. *Students:* 20 full-time (14 women), 123 part-time (98 women); includes 13 minority (3 African Americans, 2 Asian Americans or Pacific Islanders, 8 Hispanic Americans), 2 international. 45 applicants, 100% accepted, 22 enrolled. In 2009, 53 master's awarded. *Degree requirements:* For master's, thesis or alternative. *Entrance requirements:* For master's, GRE, MAT, minimum GPA of 2.75. Additional exam requirements/recommendations for international students: Required—TOEFL (minimum score 525 paper-based; 197 computer-based). *Application deadline:* For fall admission, 4/15 for domestic students; for spring admission, 9/15 for domestic students. Applications are processed on a rolling basis. Application fee: $50 ($75 for international students). Electronic

applications accepted. *Financial support:* Research assistantships, teaching assistantships, Federal Work-Study available. Financial award application deadline: 4/1; financial award applicants required to submit FAFSA. *Unit head:* Nancy Shanklin, Program Coordinator, 303-315-4999, E-mail: nancy.shanklin@ucdenver.edu. *Application contact:* Lori Sisneros, Student Services Coordinator, 303-315-4979, Fax: 303-315-6311, E-mail: lori.sisneros@ucdenver.edu.

University of Connecticut, Graduate School, Neag School of Education, Department of Educational Psychology, Program in Learning Technology, Storrs, CT 06269. Offers MA, PhD, Post-Master's Certificate. *Accreditation:* NCATE. *Faculty:* 13 full-time (5 women). *Students:* 20 full-time (11 women), 18 part-time (11 women); includes 6 minority (4 Asian Americans or Pacific Islanders, 2 Hispanic Americans), 2 international. Average age 39. 34 applicants, 0% accepted, 0 enrolled. In 2009, 26 master's, 8 other advanced degrees awarded. Terminal master's awarded for partial completion of doctoral program. *Degree requirements:* For master's, comprehensive exam, thesis or alternative; for doctorate, thesis/dissertation. *Entrance requirements:* For master's and doctorate, GRE General Test. Additional exam requirements/recommendations for international students: Required—TOEFL (minimum score 550 paper-based; 213 computer-based). *Application deadline:* For fall admission, 2/1 priority date for domestic and international students; for spring admission, 11/1 for domestic students, 10/1 for international students. Applications are processed on a rolling basis. Application fee: $55. Electronic applications accepted. *Expenses:* Tuition, state resident: full-time $4725; part-time $525 per credit. Tuition, nonresident: full-time $12,267; part-time $1363 per credit. Required fees: $346 per semester. Tuition and fees vary according to course load. *Financial support:* In 2009–10, 5 research assistantships with full tuition reimbursements were awarded; fellowships, teaching assistantships with full tuition reimbursements, Federal Work-Study, scholarships/grants, health care benefits, and unspecified assistantships also available. Financial award application deadline: 2/1; financial award applicants required to submit FAFSA. *Unit head:* Hariharan Swaminathan, Head, 860-486-4031, Fax: 860-486-0210, E-mail: hariharan.swaminathan@uconn.edu. *Application contact:* Cheryl Lowe, Program Assistant, 860-486-4031, Fax: 860-486-0180, E-mail: cheryl.lowe@uconn.edu.

University of Dayton, Graduate School, School of Education and Allied Professions, Department of Teacher Education, Dayton, OH 45469-1300. Offers adolescent/young adult (MS Ed); art education (MS Ed); early childhood education (MS Ed); inclusive early childhood (MS Ed); interdisciplinary education (MS Ed); intervention specialist education, mild/moderate (MS Ed); literacy (MS Ed); middle childhood (MS Ed); multi-age education (MS Ed); music education (MS Ed); teacher as leader (MS Ed); technology in education (MS Ed). Part-time and evening/weekend programs available. *Faculty:* 17 full-time (13 women), 27 part-time/adjunct (21 women). *Students:* 105 full-time (76 women), 152 part-time (131 women); includes 25 minority (21 African Americans, 1 Asian American or Pacific Islander, 3 Hispanic Americans), 8 international. Average age 33. 199 applicants, 58% accepted, 48 enrolled. In 2009, 139 master's awarded. *Degree requirements:* For master's, thesis, capstone research project. *Entrance requirements:* For master's, GRE General Test, minimum GPA of 2.75. Additional exam requirements/recommendations for international students: Required—TOEFL (minimum score 550 paper-based; 213 computer-based; 80 iBT). *Application deadline:* For fall admission, 3/15 priority date for domestic students, 3/1 priority date for international students; for winter admission, 7/1 priority date for international students; for spring admission, 1/1 priority date for international students. Applications are processed on a rolling basis. Application fee: $0 ($50 for international students). Electronic applications accepted. *Expenses:* Contact institution. *Financial support:* In 2009–10, 5 research assistantships with full and partial tuition reimbursements (averaging $8,000 per year) were awarded; career-related internships or fieldwork, institutionally sponsored loans, health care benefits, and unspecified assistantships also available. Financial award applicants required to submit FAFSA. *Faculty research:* Diversity, literacy, art representation by young children, preservice teacher preparation. *Unit head:* Dr. Katie A. Kinnucan-Welsch, Chair, 937-229-3346. *Application contact:* Graduate Admissions, 937-229-4411, Fax: 937-229-4729, E-mail: gradadmission@udayton.edu.

The University of Findlay, Graduate and Professional Studies, College of Education, Findlay, OH 45840-3653. Offers administration (MA Ed); early childhood (MA Ed); elementary education (MA Ed); human resource development (MA Ed); leadership (MA Ed); special education (MA Ed); technology (MA Ed); web instruction (MA Ed). *Accreditation:* NCATE. Part-time and evening/weekend programs available. *Degree requirements:* For master's, thesis, cumulative project. *Entrance requirements:* For master's, minimum undergraduate GPA of 2.75 in last 62 hours of course work. Additional exam requirements/recommendations for international students: Required—TOEFL (minimum score 550 paper-based; 213 computer-based; 80 iBT). Electronic applications accepted. *Expenses:* Contact institution. *Faculty research:* Children's literature, books and artwork, educational technology, professional development.

University of Georgia, Graduate School, College of Education, Department of Educational Psychology and Instructional Technology, Athens, GA 30602. Offers education of the gifted (Ed D); educational psychology (M Ed, MA, Ed D, PhD, Ed S); instructional technology (M Ed, PhD, Ed S). *Accreditation:* NCATE. *Faculty:* 27 full-time (11 women). *Students:* 112 full-time (84 women), 107 part-time (80 women); includes 38 minority (25 African Americans, 2 American Indian/Alaska Native, 4 Asian Americans or Pacific Islanders, 7 Hispanic Americans), 40 international. 281 applicants, 44% accepted, 78 enrolled. In 2009, 42 master's, 13 doctorates, 24 other advanced degrees awarded. *Entrance requirements:* For master's and Ed S, GRE General Test or MAT; for doctorate, GRE General Test. *Application deadline:* For fall admission, 7/1 priority date for domestic students; for spring admission, 11/15 for domestic students. Application fee: $50. Electronic applications accepted. *Expenses:* Tuition, state resident: full-time $6000; part-time $250 per credit hour. Tuition, nonresident: full-time $20,904; part-time $871 per credit hour. Required fees: $730 per semester. *Financial support:* Fellowships, research assistantships, teaching assistantships, unspecified assistantships available. *Unit head:* Dr. Robert M. Branch, Head, 706-542-4110, Fax: 706-542-4240, E-mail: rbranch@uga.edu. *Application contact:* Dr. Stacey Neuharth-Pritchett, Graduate Coordinator, 706-542-4247, E-mail: sneuhart@uga.edu.

University of Hartford, College of Education, Nursing, and Health Professions, Program in Educational Technology, West Hartford, CT 06117-1599. Offers M Ed. *Accreditation:* NCATE. Part-time and evening/weekend programs available. *Degree requirements:* For master's, comprehensive exam. *Entrance requirements:* For master's, interview, 2 letters of recommendation. Additional exam requirements/recommendations for international students: Required—TOEFL (minimum score 550 paper-based; 213 computer-based). Electronic applications accepted.

University of Hawaii at Manoa, Graduate Division, College of Education, Department of Educational Technology, Honolulu, HI 96822. Offers M Ed. Part-time programs available. *Faculty:* 4 full-time (2 women), 5 part-time/adjunct (2 women). *Students:* 31 full-time (17 women), 49 part-time (30 women); includes 47 minority (44 Asian Americans or Pacific Islanders, 3 Hispanic Americans), 6 international. Average age 35. 52 applicants, 79% accepted, 35 enrolled. In 2009, 21 master's awarded. *Degree requirements:* For master's, thesis optional. *Entrance requirements:* Additional exam requirements/recommendations for international students: Required—TOEFL (minimum score 650 paper-based; 280 computer-based; 114 iBT), IELTS (minimum score 7). *Application deadline:* For fall admission, 3/1 for domestic and international students. Application fee: $60. *Expenses:* Tuition, state resident: full-time $8900; part-time $372 per credit. Tuition, nonresident: full-time $21,400; part-time $898 per credit. Required fees: $207 per semester. *Financial support:* In 2009–10, 2 students received support, including 3 fellowships (averaging $2,075 per year), 4 research assistantships (averaging $14,825 per year), 1 teaching assistantship (averaging $14,382 per year); tuition waivers (full and partial) also available. *Faculty research:* Distance education-interaction via electronic means. Total annual research expenditures: $1.1 million. *Application contact:* Catherine Fulford, Graduate Chair, 808-956-7671, Fax: 808-956-3905, E-mail: fulford@hawaii.edu.

University of Hawaii at Manoa, Graduate Division, College of Education, Doctorate in Education Program, Honolulu, HI 96822. Offers curriculum and instruction (PhD); educational administration (PhD); educational foundations (PhD); educational policy studies (PhD); educational technology (PhD); exceptionalities (PhD); kinesiology (PhD). Part-time and evening/weekend programs available. *Faculty:* 65 full-time (40 women), 28 part-time/adjunct (17 women). *Students:* 74 full-time (44 women), 119 part-time (77 women); includes 101 minority (5 African Americans, 2 American Indian/Alaska Native, 86 Asian Americans or Pacific Islanders, 8 Hispanic Americans), 17 international. Average age 38. 98 applicants, 53% accepted, 35 enrolled. In 2009, 11 doctorates awarded. *Degree requirements:* For doctorate, thesis/dissertation. *Entrance requirements:* For doctorate, GRE General Test, sample of written work. Additional exam requirements/recommendations for international students: Required—TOEFL (minimum score 600 paper-based; 250 computer-based; 100 iBT), IELTS (minimum score 7). *Application deadline:* For fall admission, 2/1 for domestic students, 1/15 for international students. Application fee: $50. *Expenses:* Tuition, state resident: full-time $8900; part-time $372 per credit. Tuition, nonresident: full-time $21,400; part-time $898 per credit. Required fees: $207 per semester. *Financial support:* In 2009–10, 1 student received support, including 11 fellowships (averaging $4,147 per year), 17 research assistantships (averaging $17,392 per year), 4 teaching assistantships (averaging $14,670 per year); career-related internships or fieldwork, Federal Work-Study, and tuition waivers (full and partial) also available. *Application contact:* Dr. Helen Slaughter, Chairperson, 808-956-7913, Fax: 808-956-9905, E-mail: slaughte@hawaii.edu.

University of Houston, College of Education, Department of Curriculum and Instruction, Houston, TX 77204. Offers art education (M Ed); bilingual education (M Ed); curriculum and instruction (M Ed, Ed D); early childhood education (M Ed); elementary education (M Ed); gifted and talented education (M Ed); instructional technology (M Ed); mathematics education (M Ed); reading and language arts education (M Ed); science education (M Ed); second language education (M Ed); secondary education (M Ed); social studies education (M Ed); teaching (M Ed). *Accreditation:* NCATE. Part-time and evening/weekend programs available. *Faculty:* 20 full-time (9 women), 22 part-time/adjunct (17 women). *Students:* 113 full-time (81 women), 195 part-time (150 women); includes 107 minority (43 African Americans, 29 Asian Americans or Pacific Islanders, 35 Hispanic Americans), 29 international. Average age 35. 150 applicants, 77% accepted, 55 enrolled. In 2009, 75 master's, 31 doctorates awarded. *Degree requirements:* For master's, comprehensive exam, thesis optional; for doctorate, comprehensive exam, thesis/dissertation. *Entrance requirements:* For master's and doctorate, GRE, minimum cumulative undergraduate GPA of 2.6. Additional exam requirements/recommendations for international students: Required—TOEFL (minimum score 550 paper-based; 79 iBT). *Application deadline:* For fall admission, 3/1 for domestic and international students; for spring admission, 10/1 for domestic and international students. Application fee: $45 ($75 for international students). Electronic applications accepted. *Expenses:* Tuition, state resident: full-time $7676; part-time $320 per credit hour. Tuition, nonresident: full-time $14,324; part-time $597 per credit hour. Required fees: $3034. *Financial support:* In 2009–10, 4 fellowships with full tuition reimbursements (averaging $9,500 per year), 6 research assistantships with full tuition reimbursements (averaging $8,800 per year), 25 teaching assistantships with full tuition reimbursements (averaging $8,800 per year) were awarded; career-related internships or fieldwork, Federal Work-Study, institutionally sponsored loans, scholarships/grants, health care benefits, and unspecified assistantships also available. Support available to part-time students. Financial award application deadline: 2/1. *Faculty research:* Teaching-learning process, instructional technology in schools, teacher education, classroom management, at-risk students. *Unit head:* Dr. Laveria Hutchison, Chairperson, 713-743-4958, Fax: 713-743-4990, E-mail: lhutchison@uh.edu. *Application contact:* Renee C. Rattelade, Executive Secretary, 713-743-4997, Fax: 713-743-4990, E-mail: rrattelade@mail.coe.uh.edu.

University of Houston–Clear Lake, School of Education, Program in Curriculum and Instruction, Houston, TX 77058-1098. Offers curriculum and instruction (MS); early childhood education (MS); reading (MS); school library and information science (MS). Part-time and evening/weekend programs available. *Degree requirements:* For master's, thesis (for some programs). *Entrance requirements:* For master's, GRE or minimum GPA of 3.0 in last 60 hours. Additional exam requirements/recommendations for international students: Required—TOEFL (minimum score 550 paper-based; 213 computer-based). Electronic applications accepted.

University of Houston–Clear Lake, School of Education, Program in Foundations and Professional Studies, Houston, TX 77058-1098. Offers counseling (MS); instructional technology (MS); multicultural studies (MS). Part-time and evening/weekend programs available. *Degree requirements:* For master's, thesis optional. *Entrance requirements:* For master's, GRE or minimum GPA of 3.0 in last 60 hours. Additional exam requirements/recommendations for international students: Required—TOEFL (minimum score 550 paper-based; 213 computer-based). Electronic applications accepted.

University of Kentucky, Graduate School, College of Education, Program in Curriculum and Instruction, Lexington, KY 40506-0032. Offers curriculum and instruction (MA Ed, Ed D); instruction and administration (Ed D); instruction system design (MS Ed); middle school education (MS Ed). *Accreditation:* NCATE. *Degree requirements:* For master's, comprehensive exam, thesis optional; for doctorate, comprehensive exam, thesis/dissertation. *Entrance requirements:* For master's, GRE General Test, minimum undergraduate GPA of 2.75; for doctorate, GRE General Test, minimum graduate GPA of 3.0. Additional exam requirements/recommendations for international students: Required—TOEFL (minimum score 550 paper-based; 213 computer-based). Electronic applications accepted. *Faculty research:* Educational reform, multicultural education, classroom instructional practices, performance based assessment, primary school programs.

University of Maine, Graduate School, College of Education and Human Development, Program in Instructional Technology, Orono, ME 04469. Offers M Ed. Part-time and evening/weekend programs available. *Students:* 4 full-time (1 woman), 15 part-time (11 women). Average age 37. 8 applicants, 50% accepted, 4 enrolled. In 2009, 4 master's awarded. *Degree requirements:* For master's, thesis or alternative. *Entrance requirements:* For master's, MAT. Additional exam requirements/recommendations for international students: Required—TOEFL. *Application deadline:* Applications are processed on a rolling basis. Application fee: $65. Electronic applications accepted. *Financial support:* Application deadline: 3/1. *Unit head:* Dr. Janet Spector, Coordinator, 207-581-2444, Fax: 207-581-2423. *Application contact:* Scott G. Delcourt, Associate Dean of the Graduate School, 207-581-3291, Fax: 207-581-3232, E-mail: graduate@maine.edu.

University of Maine at Farmington, Program in Education, Farmington, ME 04938-1990. Offers administration (MS Ed); educational technology (MS Ed); studies in literature and literacy (MS Ed). *Accreditation:* NCATE. *Entrance requirements:* For master's, teaching certificate, 2 years' teaching experience.

University of Maryland, Baltimore County, Graduate School, College of Arts, Humanities and Social Sciences, Department of Education, Program in Instructional Systems Development: Training Systems, Baltimore, MD 21250. Offers distance education (Graduate Certificate); e-learning in instructional design (Graduate Certificate); instructional systems development (MA, Graduate Certificate); instructional technology (Graduate Certificate). Part-time and evening/weekend programs available. Postbaccalaureate distance learning degree programs offered (no on-campus study). *Faculty:* 2 full-time (0 women), 13 part-time/adjunct (5 women). *Students:* 107; includes 28 African Americans, 4 Asian Americans or Pacific Islanders, 7 Hispanic Americans. 48 applicants, 100% accepted, 42 enrolled. In 2009, 29 master's, 78 other advanced degrees awarded. *Degree requirements:* For master's, comprehensive exam. *Entrance requirements:* Additional exam requirements/recommendations for international students: Required—TOEFL. *Application deadline:* For fall admission, 7/1 priority date for domestic students, 1/1 for international students; for spring admission, 12/1 priority date for domestic students, 7/1 for international students. Application fee: $50. Electronic applications accepted. *Faculty research:* E-learning, distance education, instructional design. *Unit head:* Dr. Greg Williams, Department Chair, 410-455-6773, Fax: 410-455-1344, E-mail: gregw@umbc.edu. *Application contact:* Sharese Essien, Director, 410-455-8670, Fax: 410-455-1344, E-mail: sharese@umbc.edu.

University of Maryland, College Park, Academic Affairs, College of Education, Department of Education Policy and Leadership, College Park, MD 20742. Offers curriculum and educational

Educational Media/Instructional Technology

University of Maryland, College Park (continued)
communications (M Ed, MA, Ed D, PhD); social foundations of education (M Ed, MA, Ed D, PhD, CAGS). *Accreditation:* NCATE. Part-time and evening/weekend programs available. Postbaccalaureate distance learning degree programs offered (minimal on-campus study). *Students:* 120 full-time (81 women), 52 part-time (37 women). 1 applicant, 100% accepted, 0 enrolled. In 2009, 25 master's, 15 doctorates, 1 other advanced degree awarded. *Degree requirements:* For master's, thesis or alternative, internship and/or field experience; for doctorate, comprehensive exam, thesis/dissertation, practicum or internship. *Entrance requirements:* For master's, GRE General Test or MAT, minimum GPA of 3.0, scholarly writing sample, 3 letters of recommendation; for doctorate, GRE General Test or MAT, scholarly writing sample; minimum undergraduate GPA of 3.0, graduate 3.5. *Application deadline:* For fall admission, 12/15 for domestic and international students; for spring admission, 6/1 for international students. Applications are processed on a rolling basis. Application fee: $60. Electronic applications accepted. *Expenses:* Tuition, area resident: Part-time $471 per credit hour. Tuition, state resident: part-time $471 per credit hour. Tuition, nonresident: part-time $1016 per credit hour. Required fees: $337.04 per term. *Financial support:* In 2009–10, 5 fellowships with full and partial tuition reimbursements (averaging $17,387 per year), 1 research assistantship with tuition reimbursement (averaging $24,000 per year), 26 teaching assistantships with tuition reimbursements (averaging $16,554 per year) were awarded; career-related internships or fieldwork, Federal Work-Study, and scholarships/grants also available. Support available to part-time students. Financial award applicants required to submit FAFSA. *Faculty research:* Educational technology, adult and higher education. Total annual research expenditures: $41,998. *Unit head:* Dr. Thomas Weible, Interim Chair, 301-405-3589, Fax: 301-405-3573, E-mail: tweible@umd.edu. *Application contact:* Dean of Graduate School, 301-405-0358.

University of Massachusetts Amherst, Graduate School, School of Education, Program in Education, Amherst, MA 01003. Offers bilingual, English as a second language, and multicultural education (M Ed, CAGS); child study and early education (M Ed); children, families and schools (Ed D, CAGS); early childhood and elementary teacher education (M Ed); education policy and leadership (CAGS); educational administration (M Ed, CAGS); educational policy and leadership (Ed D); higher education (M Ed, CAGS); international education (M Ed); language, literacy and culture (Ed D); learning, media and technology (M Ed, CAGS); mathematics, science, and learning technologies (Ed D); policy studies (M Ed); policy studies in education (CAGS); reading and writing (M Ed); research and evaluation methods (Ed D); school counselor education (M Ed, CAGS); school psychology (CAGS); science education (CAGS); secondary teacher education (M Ed); social justice education (M Ed, Ed D, CAGS); special education (M Ed, Ed D, CAGS). *Accreditation:* NCATE. Part-time programs available. Postbaccalaureate distance learning degree programs offered (minimal on-campus study). *Faculty:* 74 full-time (41 women). *Students:* 377 full-time (268 women), 347 part-time (232 women); includes 115 minority (59 African Americans, 2 American Indian/Alaska Native, 16 Asian Americans or Pacific Islanders, 38 Hispanic Americans), 108 international. Average age 35. 708 applicants, 68% accepted, 266 enrolled. In 2009, 183 master's, 17 doctorates awarded. Terminal master's awarded for partial completion of doctoral program. *Degree requirements:* For master's, thesis or alternative; for doctorate, comprehensive exam, thesis/dissertation. *Entrance requirements:* Additional exam requirements/recommendations for international students: Required—TOEFL (minimum score 550 paper-based; 213 computer-based; 80 iBT), IELTS (minimum score 6.5). *Application deadline:* For fall admission, 1/15 for domestic and international students. Applications are processed on a rolling basis. Application fee: $50 ($65 for international students). Electronic applications accepted. *Expenses:* Tuition, state resident: full-time $2640; part-time $110 per credit. Tuition, nonresident: full-time $9936; part-time $414 per credit. Tuition and fees vary according to course load. *Financial support:* In 2009–10, 1 fellowship with full tuition reimbursement (averaging $8,036 per year), 92 research assistantships with full tuition reimbursements (averaging $8,555 per year), 83 teaching assistantships with full tuition reimbursements (averaging $4,661 per year) were awarded; career-related internships or fieldwork, Federal Work-Study, scholarships/grants, traineeships, health care benefits, tuition waivers (full), and unspecified assistantships also available. Support available to part-time students. Financial award application deadline: 1/15. *Unit head:* Dr. Linda L. Griffin, Graduate Program Director, 413-545-6984, Fax: 413-545-2873. *Application contact:* Jean M. Ames, Supervisor of Admissions, 413-545-0722, Fax: 413-577-0010, E-mail: gradadm@grad.umass.edu.

University of Memphis, Graduate School, College of Education, Department of Instruction and Curriculum Leadership, Memphis, TN 38152. Offers early childhood education (MAT, MS, Ed D); elementary education (MAT); instruction and curriculum (MS, Ed D); instruction design and technology (MS, Ed D); middle grades education (MAT); reading (MS, Ed D); secondary education (MAT); special education (MAT, MS, Ed D). *Accreditation:* NCATE (one or more programs are accredited). Part-time programs available. *Faculty:* 40 full-time (28 women), 20 part-time/adjunct (15 women). *Students:* 119 full-time (90 women), 631 part-time (505 women); includes 348 minority (331 African Americans, 2 American Indian/Alaska Native, 4 Asian Americans or Pacific Islanders, 11 Hispanic Americans), 7 international. Average age 34. 202 applicants, 77% accepted, 29 enrolled. In 2009, 137 master's, 10 doctorates awarded. Terminal master's awarded for partial completion of doctoral program. *Degree requirements:* For master's, comprehensive exam, thesis or alternative; for doctorate, comprehensive exam, thesis/dissertation. *Entrance requirements:* For master's, GRE General Test, minimum GPA of 2.5; for doctorate, GRE General Test, GRE Subject Test, 2 years of teaching experience. *Application deadline:* For fall admission, 8/1 for domestic students; for spring admission, 12/1 for domestic students. Applications are processed on a rolling basis. Application fee: $35 ($60 for international students). Electronic applications accepted. *Expenses:* Tuition, state resident: full-time $6246; part-time $347 per credit hour. Tuition, nonresident: full-time $15,894; part-time $883 per credit hour. Required fees: $1160. Full-time tuition and fees vary according to course load, degree level and program. *Financial support:* In 2009–10, 635 students received support; research assistantships with full tuition reimbursements available, teaching assistantships with full tuition reimbursements available, career-related internships or fieldwork, Federal Work-Study, institutionally sponsored loans, scholarships/grants, traineeships, and unspecified assistantships available. Support available to part-time students. Financial award application deadline: 2/15; financial award applicants required to submit FAFSA. *Faculty research:* Effective urban teachers, preparation and retention of urban teachers, technology utilization in schools, field-based teacher preparation programs, effective use of online instruction. *Unit head:* Dr. Sandra Cooley-Nichols, Interim Chair, 901-678-2365. *Application contact:* Dr. Sally Blake, Director of Graduate Studies, 901-678-4861.

University of Michigan, Horace H. Rackham School of Graduate Studies, School of Education, Programs in Educational Studies, Ann Arbor, MI 48109. Offers cross specialization (PhD); curriculum development (MA); early childhood education (MA, PhD); educational administration and policy (MA, PhD); educational foundations and policy (MA, PhD); English education (MA); English language learning in school settings (MA); learning technologies (MA, PhD); literacy, language, and culture (MA, PhD); mathematics education (MA, PhD); postsecondary science education (MS); research methods (MA); science education (MA, PhD); social studies education (MA); teaching and teacher education (PhD); MA/Certification; MBA/MA; PhD/MA. Terminal master's awarded for partial completion of doctoral program. *Degree requirements:* For master's, thesis (for some programs); for doctorate, comprehensive exam, thesis/dissertation. *Entrance requirements:* For master's and doctorate, GRE General Test. Additional exam requirements/recommendations for international students: Required—TOEFL (minimum score 600 paper-based; 250 computer-based). *Application deadline:* For fall admission, 12/1 priority date for domestic students, 12/1 for international students. Application fee: $60 ($75 for international students). Electronic applications accepted. *Expenses:* Tuition, state resident: full-time $17,286; part-time $1099 per credit hour. Tuition, nonresident: full-time $34,944; part-time $2080 per credit hour. Required fees: $95 per semester. Tuition and fees vary according to course load, degree level and program. *Financial support:* Applicants required to submit FAFSA. *Unit head:* Dr. Addison Stone, Chairperson, 734-763-7500, Fax: 734-615-1290, E-mail: addison@umich.edu. *Application contact:* Laura Mayers, Student Services Assistant, 734-764-7563, Fax: 734-763-1495, E-mail: ed.grad.admit@umich.edu.

University of Michigan–Flint, School of Education and Human Services, Department of Education, Flint, MI 48502-1950. Offers education (MA); elementary education with teaching certification (MA); literacy (K-12) (MA); special education (MA); technology in education (MA). Part-time programs available. *Faculty:* 14 full-time (12 women), 8 part-time/adjunct (4 women). *Students:* 27 full-time (24 women), 215 part-time (186 women); includes 22 minority (20 African Americans, 2 American Indian/Alaska Native). Average age 35. 63 applicants, 86% accepted, 43 enrolled. In 2009, 91 master's awarded. *Entrance requirements:* For master's, BS with minimum GPA of 3.0. Additional exam requirements/recommendations for international students: Required—TOEFL (minimum score 560 paper-based; 220 computer-based; 84 iBT), IELTS (minimum score 6.5). *Application deadline:* For fall admission, 8/1 priority date for domestic students, 5/1 priority date for international students; for winter admission, 11/15 priority date for domestic students, 9/15 priority date for international students; for spring admission, 3/15 priority date for domestic students, 1/15 priority date for international students. Application fee: $55. *Expenses:* Contact institution. *Financial support:* Federal Work-Study, scholarships/grants, and unspecified assistantships available. Support available to part-time students. Financial award application deadline: 6/1; financial award applicants required to submit FAFSA. *Unit head:* Dr. Beverly Schumer, Director, 810-424-5215, E-mail: bschumer@umflint.edu. *Application contact:* Beulah Alexander, Executive Secretary, 810-766-6879, Fax: 810-766-6891, E-mail: beulaha@umflint.edu.

University of Minnesota, Twin Cities Campus, Graduate School, College of Education and Human Development, Department of Curriculum and Instruction, Minneapolis, MN 55455-0213. Offers art education (M Ed, MA, PhD); children's literature (M Ed, MA, PhD); curriculum and instruction (MA, PhD); early childhood education (M Ed, PhD); elementary education (M Ed, MA, PhD); English education (MA, PhD); environmental education (M Ed); family education (M Ed, MA, Ed D, PhD); instructional systems and technology (M Ed, MA, PhD); language arts (MA, PhD); language immersion education (Certificate); literacy education (MA); mathematics education (MA, PhD); reading education (MA, PhD); science education (MA, PhD); second languages and cultures education (MA, PhD); social studies education (MA, PhD); teaching (M Ed), including Chinese, earth science, elementary special education, English, English as a second language, French, German, Hebrew, Japanese, life sciences, mathematics, middle school science, science, second languages and cultures, social studies, Spanish; technology enhanced learning (Certificate); writing education (M Ed, MA, PhD). *Faculty:* 34 full-time (21 women). *Students:* 436 full-time (307 women), 375 part-time (280 women); includes 80 minority (30 African Americans, 6 American Indian/Alaska Native, 33 Asian Americans or Pacific Islanders, 11 Hispanic Americans), 40 international. Average age 32. 660 applicants, 64% accepted, 379 enrolled. In 2009, 552 master's, 14 doctorates, 7 other advanced degrees awarded. *Financial support:* In 2009–10, 5 fellowships (averaging $27,000 per year), 47 research assistantships with full tuition reimbursements (averaging $25,682 per year), 60 teaching assistantships with full tuition reimbursements (averaging $29,889 per year) were awarded. *Faculty research:* Teaching and learning; quality of education; influence of cultural, linguistic, social, political, technological and economic factors on teaching, learning and educational research; relationship between educational practice and a democratic and just society. Total annual research expenditures: $1.8 million. *Unit head:* Dr. Ruth Thomas, Chair, 612-624-4772, Fax: 612-624-8277, E-mail: thoma006@umn.edu. *Application contact:* Dr. Mary Trettin, Associate Dean, 612-625-6501, Fax: 612-626-1580, E-mail: mtrettin@umn.edu.

University of Missouri, Graduate School, College of Education, School of Information Science and Learning Technologies, Columbia, MO 65211. Offers educational technology (M Ed, Ed S); information science and learning technology (PhD); library science (MA). *Accreditation:* ALA (one or more programs are accredited). Part-time and evening/weekend programs available. *Entrance requirements:* For master's, GRE General Test or MAT, minimum GPA of 3.0. Additional exam requirements/recommendations for international students: Required—TOEFL (minimum score 540 paper-based; 207 computer-based; 76 iBT).

University of Nebraska at Kearney, College of Graduate Study, College of Education, Department of Teacher Education, Kearney, NE 68849-0001. Offers curriculum and instruction (MS Ed); instructional technology (MS Ed); reading education (MA Ed); special education (MA Ed). Part-time and evening/weekend programs available. *Degree requirements:* For master's, comprehensive exam, thesis optional. *Entrance requirements:* For master's, portfolio or GRE. Additional exam requirements/recommendations for international students: Required—TOEFL (minimum score 550 paper-based; 213 computer-based). Electronic applications accepted.

University of Nebraska at Omaha, Graduate Studies, College of Education, Department of Teacher Education, Omaha, NE 68182. Offers elementary education (MA, MS); instruction in urban schools (Certificate); instructional technology (Certificate); reading education (MS); secondary education (MA, MS). Part-time and evening/weekend programs available. *Faculty:* 25 full-time (15 women). *Students:* 24 full-time (18 women), 330 part-time (284 women); includes 17 minority (6 African Americans, 11 Hispanic Americans), 4 international. Average age 33. 81 applicants, 83% accepted, 51 enrolled. In 2009, 110 master's, 7 other advanced degrees awarded. *Degree requirements:* For master's, comprehensive exam, thesis (for some programs). *Entrance requirements:* For master's, minimum GPA of 3.0. Additional exam requirements/recommendations for international students: Required—TOEFL (minimum score 550 paper-based; 213 computer-based; 80 iBT). *Application deadline:* For fall admission, 7/1 priority date for domestic students; for spring admission, 12/1 priority date for domestic students. Applications are processed on a rolling basis. Application fee: $45. Electronic applications accepted. *Financial support:* In 2009–10, 114 students received support; fellowships, teaching assistantships with tuition reimbursements available, Federal Work-Study, institutionally sponsored loans, scholarships/grants, tuition waivers (partial), and unspecified assistantships available. Support available to part-time students. Financial award application deadline: 3/1; financial award applicants required to submit FAFSA. *Unit head:* Dr. Lana Danielson, Advisor, 402-554-2212. *Application contact:* Dr. Wilma Kuhlman, Student Contact, 402-554-2212.

University of Nevada, Las Vegas, Graduate College, College of Education, Department of Educational Psychology, Las Vegas, NV 89154-3003. Offers educational psychology (MS, PhD); learning and technology (PhD); school psychology (Ed S). *Accreditation:* ACA (one or more programs are accredited); NCATE. Part-time and evening/weekend programs available. *Faculty:* 19 full-time (12 women), 1 part-time/adjunct (0 women). *Students:* 51 full-time (37 women), 68 part-time (48 women); includes 24 minority (10 African Americans, 6 Asian Americans or Pacific Islanders, 8 Hispanic Americans), 3 international. Average age 39. 69 applicants, 65% accepted, 36 enrolled. In 2009, 11 master's, 6 doctorates, 13 other advanced degrees awarded. *Degree requirements:* For master's, comprehensive exam (for some programs), thesis (for some programs); for doctorate, comprehensive exam, thesis/dissertation, research study submitted to refereed journal or proposal for presentation at conference of a national organization. *Entrance requirements:* For master's, doctorate, and Ed S, GRE General Test. Additional exam requirements/recommendations for international students: Required—TOEFL (minimum score 550 paper-based; 213 computer-based; 80 iBT), IELTS (minimum score 7). *Application deadline:* For fall admission, 2/1 priority date for domestic and international students. Applications are processed on a rolling basis. Application fee: $60 ($95 for international students). Electronic applications accepted. *Financial support:* In 2009–10, 23 students received support, including 1 fellowship with full tuition reimbursement available (averaging $14,000 per year), 8 research assistantships with partial tuition reimbursements available (averaging $11,650 per year), 14 teaching assistantships with partial tuition reimbursements available (averaging $12,000 per year); institutionally sponsored loans, scholarships/grants, health care benefits, and unspecified assistantships also available. Financial award application deadline: 3/1. *Faculty research:* Conceptual change, prose attention and comprehension, psychoeducational assessment, personal epistemology, statistical modeling. *Unit head:* Dr. W. Paul Jones, Chair/ Professor, 702-895-3937, Fax: 702-895-1658, E-mail: paul.jones@unlv.edu. *Application contact:* Graduate College Admissions Evaluator, 702-895-3320, Fax: 702-895-4180, E-mail: gradcollege@unlv.edu.

University of New Mexico, Graduate School, College of Education, Department of Educational Leadership and Organizational Learning, Program in Organizational Learning and Instructional

Technologies, Albuquerque, NM 87131-2039. Offers MA, PhD, EDSPC. *Accreditation:* NCATE. Part-time and evening/weekend programs available. Postbaccalaureate distance learning degree programs offered (no on-campus study). *Faculty:* 14 full-time (8 women), 3 part-time/adjunct (2 women). *Students:* 30 full-time (19 women), 91 part-time (65 women); includes 39 minority (3 African Americans, 4 American Indian/Alaska Native, 3 Asian Americans or Pacific Islanders, 29 Hispanic Americans), 6 international. Average age 44. 46 applicants, 67% accepted, 26 enrolled. In 2009, 9 master's, 3 doctorates awarded. *Degree requirements:* For master's, comprehensive exam, thesis or alternative; for doctorate, comprehensive exam, thesis/dissertation. *Entrance requirements:* For master's, minimum GPA of 3.0 in last 60 hours of course work, bachelor's degree; for doctorate, GRE General Test, MAT, master's degree, minimum GPA of 3.5. Additional exam requirements/recommendations for international students: Required—TOEFL. *Application deadline:* For fall admission, 3/15 for domestic and international students; for spring admission, 10/15 for domestic and international students. Application fee: $50. Electronic applications accepted. *Expenses:* Tuition, state resident: full-time $2099; part-time $233.20 per credit hour. Tuition, nonresident: full-time $6650. Required fees: $25 per semester. Tuition and fees vary according to course load, program and reciprocity agreements. *Financial support:* In 2009–10, 17 students received support, including 16 fellowships (averaging $24,356 per year), 7 teaching assistantships with tuition reimbursements available (averaging $7,371 per year); career-related internships or fieldwork also available. Financial award application deadline: 3/1; financial award applicants required to submit FAFSA. *Faculty research:* Adult learning, distance education, instructional multimedia, organizational learning and development, transformational learning, workplace and learning environment factors that enhance learning and productivity, program and organization evaluation and reform, effects of technology on learning and problem solving. Total annual research expenditures: $40,000. *Unit head:* Dr. Patricia Boverie, Head, 505-277-2408, Fax: 505-277-5553, E-mail: pboverie@unm.edu. *Application contact:* Loretta Brown, Administrative Assistant, 505-277-4131, Fax: 505-277-5553, E-mail: loribrwn@unm.edu.

The University of North Carolina at Charlotte, Graduate School, College of Education, Department of Educational Leadership, Charlotte, NC 28223-0001. Offers curriculum and supervision (M Ed); educational administration (CAS); educational leadership (Ed D); instructional systems technology (M Ed); school administration (MSA). Part-time and evening/weekend programs available. *Faculty:* 24 full-time (12 women). *Students:* 10 full-time (8 women), 73 part-time (40 women); includes 32 minority (31 African Americans, 1 American Indian/Alaska Native). Average age 43. 26 applicants, 81% accepted, 15 enrolled. In 2009, 2 doctorates awarded. *Entrance requirements:* For master's and doctorate, GRE or MAT. Additional exam requirements/recommendations for international students: Required—TOEFL (minimum score 550 paper-based; 220 computer-based; 83 iBT). *Application deadline:* For fall admission, 7/1 for domestic students, 5/1 for international students; for spring admission, 11/1 for domestic students, 10/1 for international students. Applications are processed on a rolling basis. Application fee: $55. Electronic applications accepted. *Financial support:* In 2009–10, 6 students received support, including 4 research assistantships (averaging $13,500 per year), 2 teaching assistantships (averaging $8,500 per year); career-related internships or fieldwork, institutionally sponsored loans, scholarships/grants, and unspecified assistantships also available. Support available to part-time students. Financial award application deadline: 4/1; financial award applicants required to submit FAFSA. *Faculty research:* Educational leadership theory and practice, instructional systems technology, educational research methodology, curriculum and supervision in the schools, school law and finance. Total annual research expenditures: $800,000. *Unit head:* Dr. Dawson R. Hancock, Chair, 704-687-8863, Fax: 704-687-3493, E-mail: dhancock@uncc.edu. *Application contact:* Kathy B. Giddings, Director of Graduate Admissions, 704-687-5503, Fax: 704-687-3279, E-mail: gradadm@uncc.edu.

The University of North Carolina at Greensboro, Graduate School, School of Education, Department of Curriculum and Instruction, Greensboro, NC 27412-5001. Offers college teaching and adult learning (Certificate); curriculum and instruction (M Ed), including chemistry education, elementary education, English as a second language, French education, instructional technology, mathematics education, middle grades education, reading education, science education, social studies education, Spanish education; curriculum and teaching (PhD), including higher education, teacher education and development; English as a second language (Certificate); higher education (M Ed); supervision (M Ed). *Accreditation:* NCATE. Part-time programs available. *Degree requirements:* For doctorate, thesis/dissertation. *Entrance requirements:* For master's and doctorate, GRE General Test. Additional exam requirements/recommendations for international students: Required—TOEFL. Electronic applications accepted. *Faculty research:* Community college literacy program, middle school mathematics/computer mathematics.

The University of North Carolina Wilmington, School of Education, Department of Instructional Technology, Foundations and Secondary Education, Wilmington, NC 28403-3297. Offers instructional technology (MS). *Degree requirements:* For master's, comprehensive exam, thesis or alternative. *Entrance requirements:* Additional exam requirements/recommendations for international students: Required—TOEFL (minimum score 550 paper-based; 217 computer-based; 79 iBT), IELTS (minimum score 6.5).

University of North Dakota, Graduate School, College of Education and Human Development, Department of Instructional Design and Technology, Grand Forks, ND 58202. Offers M Ed, MS. *Degree requirements:* For master's, comprehensive exam, thesis or alternative. *Entrance requirements:* For master's, minimum GPA of 3.0. Additional exam requirements/recommendations for international students: Required—TOEFL (minimum score 550 paper-based; 213 computer-based; 79 iBT), IELTS (minimum score 6.5). Electronic applications accepted.

University of Northern Colorado, Graduate School, College of Education and Behavioral Sciences, School of Educational Research, Leadership and Technology, Program in Educational Technology, Greeley, CO 80639. Offers educational media (MA); educational technology (MA, PhD). *Accreditation:* NCATE. Part-time programs available. Postbaccalaureate distance learning degree programs offered (minimal on-campus study). *Faculty:* 5 full-time (1 woman). *Students:* 23 full-time (17 women), 27 part-time (7 women); includes 5 minority (2 African Americans, 1 Asian American or Pacific Islander, 2 Hispanic Americans), 16 international. Average age 37. 12 applicants, 75% accepted, 6 enrolled. In 2009, 7 master's awarded. *Degree requirements:* For master's, comprehensive exam, thesis or alternative; for doctorate, comprehensive exam, thesis/dissertation. *Entrance requirements:* For master's and doctorate, GRE General Test, 3 letters of reference. *Application deadline:* For fall admission, 2/10 for domestic and international students; for spring admission, 10/10 for domestic and international students. Applications are processed on a rolling basis. Application fee: $50 ($60 for international students). Electronic applications accepted. *Expenses:* Tuition, state resident: full-time $5770; part-time $320.55 per credit hour. Tuition, nonresident: full-time $13,847; part-time $769.27 per credit hour. Required fees: $948.78; $52.72 per credit. *Financial support:* In 2009–10, 5 research assistantships (averaging $1,496 per year), 4 teaching assistantships (averaging $4,488 per year) were awarded; fellowships, unspecified assistantships also available. Financial award application deadline: 3/1; financial award applicants required to submit FAFSA. *Unit head:* Dr. Heng-Yu Ku, Program Coordinator, 970-351-2816. *Application contact:* Linda Sisson, Graduate Student Admission Coordinator, 970-351-1807, Fax: 970-351-2371, E-mail: linda.sisson@unco.edu.

University of Northern Colorado, Graduate School, College of Education and Behavioral Sciences, School of Educational Research, Leadership and Technology, Program in School Library Education, Greeley, CO 80639. Offers MA. Part-time programs available. *Faculty:* 5 full-time (1 woman). *Students:* 2 full-time (both women), 20 part-time (11 women); includes 1 minority (Asian American or Pacific Islander). Average age 34. 6 applicants, 100% accepted, 5 enrolled. In 2009, 8 master's awarded. *Application deadline:* Applications are processed on a rolling basis. Application fee: $50 ($60 for international students). Electronic applications accepted. *Expenses:* Tuition, state resident: full-time $5770; part-time $320.55 per credit hour. Tuition, nonresident: full-time $13,847; part-time $769.27 per credit hour. Required fees: $948.78; $52.72 per credit. *Financial support:* Application deadline: 3/1. *Unit head:* Berlinda

Saenz, Program Coordinator, 970-351-2816. *Application contact:* Linda Sisson, Graduate Student Admission Coordinator, 970-351-1807, Fax: 970-351-2371, E-mail: linda.sisson@unco.edu.

University of Northern Iowa, Graduate College, College of Education, Department of Curriculum and Instruction, Program in Educational Technology, Cedar Falls, IA 50614. Offers communication and training technology (MA); educational media (MA). *Students:* 3 full-time (all women), 19 part-time (12 women); includes 2 minority (both African Americans), 1 international. 9 applicants, 44% accepted, 2 enrolled. In 2009, 13 master's awarded. *Degree requirements:* For master's, comprehensive exam, thesis or alternative. *Entrance requirements:* For master's, minimum GPA of 3.0. Additional exam requirements/recommendations for international students: Required—TOEFL (minimum score 500 paper-based; 180 computer-based; 61 iBT). *Application deadline:* For fall admission, 8/1 priority date for domestic students. Applications are processed on a rolling basis. Application fee: $30 ($50 for international students). Electronic applications accepted. *Financial support:* Application deadline: 2/1. *Unit head:* Dr. Judith A. Donaldson, Coordinator, 319-273-2873, Fax: 319-273-5886, E-mail: ana.donaldson@uni.edu. *Application contact:* Laurie S. Russell, Record Analyst, 319-273-2623, Fax: 319-273-6792, E-mail: laurie.russell@uni.edu.

University of Northern Iowa, Graduate College, College of Education, Department of Curriculum and Instruction, Program in School Library Media Studies, Cedar Falls, IA 50614. Offers MA. Part-time and evening/weekend programs available. *Students:* 4 full-time (all women), 52 part-time (51 women); includes 3 minority (2 Asian Americans or Pacific Islanders, 1 Hispanic American). 13 applicants, 77% accepted, 2 enrolled. In 2009, 14 master's awarded. *Degree requirements:* For master's, comprehensive exam (for some programs), thesis or alternative, comprehensive portfolio. *Entrance requirements:* For master's, minimum GPA of 3.0. Additional exam requirements/recommendations for international students: Required—TOEFL (minimum score 500 paper-based; 180 computer-based; 61 iBT). *Application deadline:* For fall admission, 8/1 priority date for domestic students. Applications are processed on a rolling basis. Application fee: $30 ($50 for international students). Electronic applications accepted. *Financial support:* Career-related internships or fieldwork, Federal Work-Study, scholarships/grants, and tuition waivers (full and partial) available. Support available to part-time students. Financial award application deadline: 2/1. *Unit head:* Dr. Karla Krueger, Coordinator, 319-273-2551, Fax: 319-273-5886, E-mail: karla.krueger@uni.edu. *Application contact:* Laurie S. Russell, Record Analyst, 319-273-2623, Fax: 319-273-6792, E-mail: laurie.russell@uni.edu.

University of North Florida, College of Education and Human Services, Department of Foundations and Secondary Education, Jacksonville, FL 32224. Offers adult learning (M Ed); instructional technology (M Ed); professional education (M Ed). *Accreditation:* NCATE. Part-time and evening/weekend programs available. *Faculty:* 11 full-time (5 women). *Students:* 12 full-time (8 women), 27 part-time (17 women); includes 9 minority (7 African Americans, 1 Asian American or Pacific Islander, 1 Hispanic American). Average age 37. 13 applicants, 23% accepted, 2 enrolled. In 2009, 13 master's awarded. *Entrance requirements:* For master's, GRE General Test, minimum GPA of 3.0 in last 60 hours, interview, 3 letters of recommendation. Additional exam requirements/recommendations for international students: Required—TOEFL (minimum score 500 paper-based; 173 computer-based). *Application deadline:* For fall admission, 7/1 priority date for domestic students, 5/1 for international students; for spring admission, 11/1 priority date for domestic students, 10/1 for international students. Applications are processed on a rolling basis. Application fee: $30. Electronic applications accepted. *Expenses:* Tuition, state resident: full-time $6649.20; part-time $277.05 per credit hour. Tuition, nonresident: full-time $22,970; part-time $957.08 per credit hour. Required fees: $985; $41.03 per credit hour. *Financial support:* In 2009–10, 19 students received support; teaching assistantships, career-related internships or fieldwork, Federal Work-Study, and tuition waivers (partial) available. Support available to part-time students. Financial award application deadline: 4/1; financial award applicants required to submit FAFSA. *Faculty research:* Using children's literature to enhance metalinguistic awareness, education, oral language diagnosis of middle-schoolers, science inquiry teaching and learning. Total annual research expenditures: $8,501. *Unit head:* Dr. Jeffery Cornett, Chair, 904-620-2610, Fax: 904-620-1821, E-mail: jcornett@unf.edu. *Application contact:* Dr. John Kemppainen, Director of Academic Advising, 904-620-2530, Fax: 904-620-1135, E-mail: jkemppai@unf.edu.

University of North Florida, College of Education and Human Services, Department of Leadership, Counseling and Instructional Technology, Program in Educational Leadership, Jacksonville, FL 32224. Offers educational leadership (M Ed, Ed D); educational technology (M Ed); instructional leadership (M Ed). *Accreditation:* NCATE. Part-time and evening/weekend programs available. *Faculty:* 18 full-time (11 women). *Students:* 26 full-time (16 women), 185 part-time (129 women); includes 44 minority (31 African Americans, 3 American Indian/Alaska Native, 1 Asian American or Pacific Islander, 9 Hispanic Americans), 1 international. Average age 38. 64 applicants, 45% accepted, 18 enrolled. In 2009, 52 master's, 15 doctorates awarded. *Degree requirements:* For doctorate, thesis/dissertation. *Entrance requirements:* For master's, GRE General Test, minimum GPA of 3.0 in last 60 hours, interview, 3 letters of recommendation; for doctorate, GRE General Test, master's degree, interview, 3 letters of recommendation, writing sample. Additional exam requirements/recommendations for international students: Required—TOEFL (minimum score 500 paper-based; 173 computer-based). *Application deadline:* For fall admission, 7/1 priority date for domestic students, 5/1 for international students; for spring admission, 11/1 priority date for domestic students, 10/1 for international students. Applications are processed on a rolling basis. Application fee: $30. Electronic applications accepted. *Expenses:* Tuition, state resident: full-time $6649.20; part-time $277.05 per credit hour. Tuition, nonresident: full-time $22,970; part-time $957.08 per credit hour. Required fees: $985; $41.03 per credit hour. *Financial support:* In 2009–10, 100 students received support, including 1 research assistantship (averaging $680 per year), 1 teaching assistantship (averaging $5,700 per year); career-related internships or fieldwork, Federal Work-Study, and tuition waivers (partial) also available. Support available to part-time students. Financial award application deadline: 4/1; financial award applicants required to submit FAFSA. *Unit head:* Dr. Edgar Jackson, Chair, 904-620-2990, Fax: 904-620-2982, E-mail: newton.jackson@unf.edu. *Application contact:* Kiersten Jarvis, Graduate Admissions Coordinator, 904-620-1360, Fax: 904-620-1362, E-mail: kiersten.jarvis@unf.edu.

University of North Texas, College of Information, Department of Learning Technologies, Program in Educational Computing, Denton, TX 76203. Offers PhD. *Entrance requirements:* Additional exam requirements/recommendations for international students: Recommended—TOEFL (minimum score 550 paper-based; 213 computer-based; 79 iBT). *Application deadline:* Applications are processed on a rolling basis. Application fee: $50 ($75 for international students). Electronic applications accepted. *Expenses:* Tuition, state resident: full-time $4298; part-time $239 per contact hour. Tuition, nonresident: full-time $9878; part-time $549 per contact hour. Required fees: $265 per contact hour. *Financial support:* Application deadline: 4/1.

University of North Texas, College of Information, Department of Library and Information Sciences, Denton, TX 76203-5017. Offers information science (MS, PhD); learning technologies (M Ed, Ed D), including applied technology, training and development (M Ed), computer education and cognitive systems, educational computing; library science (MS). *Accreditation:* ALA (one or more programs are accredited). Part-time and evening/weekend programs available. *Degree requirements:* For master's, comprehensive exam; for doctorate, comprehensive exam, thesis/dissertation. *Entrance requirements:* For master's, GRE General Test, MAT; for doctorate, GRE General Test. Additional exam requirements/recommendations for international students: Required—proof of English language proficiency required for non-native English speakers; Recommended—TOEFL (minimum score 550 paper-based; 213 computer-based; 79 iBT). *Application deadline:* Applications are processed on a rolling basis. Application fee: $50 ($75 for international students). Electronic applications accepted. *Expenses:* Tuition, state resident: full-time $4298; part-time $239 per contact hour. Tuition, nonresident: full-time $9878; part-time $549 per contact hour. Required fees: $265 per contact hour. *Financial support:* Fellowships, research assistantships, teaching assistantships, career-related internships or fieldwork, Federal Work-Study, institutionally sponsored loans, scholarships/grants, health care benefits, and

Educational Media/Instructional Technology

University of North Texas (continued)
library assistantships available. Financial award application deadline: 4/1; financial award applicants required to submit FAFSA. *Faculty research:* Information resources and services, information management and retrieval, computer-based information systems, human information behavior. *Application contact:* Graduate Academic Counselor, 940-369-2873, Fax: 940-565-3101.

University of Pennsylvania, Graduate School of Education, Division of Foundations and Practices in Education, Programs in Learning Science and Technologies, Philadelphia, PA 19104. Offers MS Ed. *Students:* 2 full-time (both women), 1 (woman) part-time, 1 international. 16 applicants, 25% accepted, 1 enrolled. *Degree requirements:* For master's, comprehensive exam or portfolio. *Entrance requirements:* For master's, GRE, MAT. *Application deadline:* For fall admission, 12/15 priority date for domestic students. Applications are processed on a rolling basis. Application fee: $70. Electronic applications accepted. *Expenses:* Contact institution. *Financial support:* Applicants required to submit FAFSA.

University of Phoenix, College of Natural Sciences, College of Education, Phoenix, AZ 85034-7209. Offers administration and supervision (MAEd); adult education and training (MAEd); curriculum and instruction (MAEd); curriculum and instruction-adult education (MAEd); curriculum and instruction-computer education (MAEd); curriculum and instruction-English and language arts education (MAEd); curriculum and instruction-English as a second language (MAEd); curriculum and instruction-mathematics education (MAEd); curriculum education (MAEd); early childhood (MAEd); elementary teacher education (MAEd); secondary teacher education (MAEd); special education (MAEd); teacher leadership (MAEd). *Accreditation:* Teacher Education Accreditation Council. Evening/weekend programs available. Postbaccalaureate distance learning degree programs offered (no on-campus study). *Faculty:* 47 full-time (34 women), 844 part-time/adjunct (636 women). *Students:* 13,657 full-time (10,698 women); includes 4,000 minority (3,063 African Americans, 74 American Indian/Alaska Native, 241 Asian Americans or Pacific Islanders, 622 Hispanic Americans), 307 international. Average age 36. In 2009, 17,246 master's awarded. *Degree requirements:* For master's, thesis (for some programs). *Entrance requirements:* For master's, 3 years of work experience, minimum GPA of 2.5. Additional exam requirements/recommendations for international students: Required—TOEFL (minimum score 550 paper-based; 213 computer-based; 79 iBT). *Application deadline:* Applications are processed on a rolling basis. Application fee: $45. Electronic applications accepted. *Expenses:* Tuition: Full-time $13,272. Required fees: $660. Full-time tuition and fees vary according to course level, degree level and program. *Financial support:* Institutionally sponsored loans and scholarships/grants available. Financial award applicants required to submit FAFSA. *Unit head:* Dr. Meredith Curley, Dean/Executive Director, 480-557-1217, Fax: 480-557-1588, E-mail: meredith.curley@phoenix.edu. *Application contact:* Chair, 602-387-7000, Fax: 602-387-6020.

University of Phoenix, School of Advanced Studies, Phoenix, AZ 85034-7209. Offers business administration (DBA); education (Ed D); educational leadership (Ed D), including curriculum and instruction, educational leadership, educational technology; health administration (DHA); higher education administration (PhD); industrial/organizational psychology (PhD); nursing (PhD); organizational leadership (DM), including information systems and technology, organizational leadership. Evening/weekend programs available. *Faculty:* 83 full-time (47 women), 540 part-time/adjunct (264 women). *Students:* 7,749 full-time (5,032 women); includes 3,180 minority (2,473 African Americans, 61 American Indian/Alaska Native, 221 Asian Americans or Pacific Islanders, 425 Hispanic Americans), 490 international. Average age 44. In 2009, 467 doctorates awarded. *Degree requirements:* For doctorate, thesis/dissertation. *Entrance requirements:* For doctorate, 3 letters of recommendation, minimum master's GPA of 3.0, 3 years professional work experience. Additional exam requirements/recommendations for international students: Required—TOEFL (minimum score 550 paper-based; 213 computer-based; 79 iBT). *Application deadline:* Applications are processed on a rolling basis. Application fee: $45. Electronic applications accepted. *Expenses:* Tuition: Full-time $13,272. Required fees: $660. Full-time tuition and fees vary according to course level, degree level and program. *Financial support:* Institutionally sponsored loans and scholarships/grants available. Financial award applicants required to submit FAFSA. *Unit head:* Dr. Jeremy Moreland, Dean/Executive Director, 480-557-3231, E-mail: jeremy.moreland@phoenix.edu. *Application contact:* Information Contact, 800-697-8223.

University of Phoenix–West Florida Campus, The Artemis School, College of Education, Temple Terrace, FL 33637. Offers administration and supervision (MA Ed); curriculum and instruction (MA Ed), including computer education, curriculum and instruction, mathematics education; curriculum and technology (MA Ed); early childhood education (MA Ed); elementary teacher education (MA Ed); secondary teacher education (MA Ed). Evening/weekend programs available. *Degree requirements:* For master's, thesis (for some programs). *Entrance requirements:* For master's, 3 years of work experience, minimum undergraduate GPA of 2.5. Additional exam requirements/recommendations for international students: Required—TOEFL (minimum score 550 paper-based; 213 computer-based; 79 iBT).

University of St. Thomas, Graduate Studies, School of Education, Program in Organization Learning and Development, St. Paul, MN 55105-1096. Offers career development (Certificate); e-learning (Certificate); human resource management (Certificate); human resources and change leadership (MA); learning technology (Certificate); learning technology for learning development and change (MA); organization development (Ed D, Certificate). Part-time and evening/weekend programs available. Postbaccalaureate distance learning degree programs offered (minimal on-campus study). *Faculty:* 5 full-time (4 women), 6 part-time/adjunct (2 women). *Students:* 6 full-time (5 women), 161 part-time (130 women); includes 24 minority (13 African Americans, 7 Asian Americans or Pacific Islanders, 4 Hispanic Americans), 1 international. Average age 37. 115 applicants, 75% accepted, 85 enrolled. In 2009, 29 master's, 7 doctorates, 18 other advanced degrees awarded. *Degree requirements:* For doctorate, comprehensive exam, thesis/dissertation. *Entrance requirements:* For master's, minimum GPA of 3.0, 2 letters of reference, personal statement; for doctorate, minimum GPA of 3.5, interview; for Certificate, minimum graduate GPA of 3.25. Additional exam requirements/recommendations for international students: Required—TOEFL (minimum score 550 paper-based; 213 computer-based). *Application deadline:* For fall admission, 8/1 priority date for domestic and international students; for winter admission, 12/1 priority date for domestic students, 12/1 for international students; for spring admission, 12/1 priority date for domestic and international students. Applications are processed on a rolling basis. Application fee: $50. *Expenses:* Contact institution. *Financial support:* Fellowships, research assistantships, institutionally sponsored loans and scholarships/grants available. Support available to part-time students. Financial award applicants required to submit FAFSA. *Faculty research:* Workplace conflict, physician leaders, entrepreneurship education, mentoring. *Unit head:* Dr. Christopher S. Vye, Acting Department Chair, 651-962-4666, Fax: 651-962-4169, E-mail: csvye@stthomas.edu. *Application contact:* Liz G. Knight, Department Coordinator, 651-962-4459, Fax: 651-962-4169, E-mail: egknight@stthomas.edu.

University of San Francisco, School of Education, Department of Learning and Instruction, San Francisco, CA 94117-1080. Offers digital media and learning (MA); learning and instruction (MA, Ed D); teaching (MA); teaching reading (MA). *Faculty:* 10 full-time (6 women), 1 part-time/adjunct (0 women). *Students:* 89 full-time (64 women), 40 part-time (27 women); includes 36 minority (9 African Americans, 4 American Indian/Alaska Native, 13 Asian Americans or Pacific Islanders, 10 Hispanic Americans), 1 international. Average age 40. 88 applicants, 72% accepted, 42 enrolled. In 2009, 17 master's, 9 doctorates awarded. *Degree requirements:* For doctorate, thesis/dissertation. Application fee: $55 ($65 for international students). *Expenses:* Tuition: Full-time $19,710; part-time $1095 per unit. Part-time tuition and fees vary according to degree level, campus/location and program. *Financial support:* In 2009–10, 77 students received support; fellowships, research assistantships, teaching assistantships available. Financial award application deadline: 3/2; financial award applicants required to submit FAFSA. *Unit head:* Dr. Robert Burns, Chair, 415-422-6289. *Application contact:* Beth Teague, Associate Director of Graduate Outreach, 415-422-5467, E-mail: schoolofeducation@usfca.edu.

University of Sioux Falls, Fredrikson School of Education, Sioux Falls, SD 57105-1699. Offers leadership (M Ed); reading (M Ed); superintendent (Ed S); teaching (M Ed); technology (M Ed). Summer admission only. *Accreditation:* NCATE. Part-time and evening/weekend programs available. *Degree requirements:* For master's, comprehensive exam (for some programs), research application project; for Ed S, comprehensive exam, portfolio. *Entrance requirements:* For master's, minimum GPA of 3.0, 1 year of teaching experience; for Ed S, minimum 3 years of teaching experience, minimum cumulative GPA of 3.5, 1 year of administrative experience. Additional exam requirements/recommendations for international students: Required—TOEFL. *Faculty research:* Reading, literacy, leadership.

University of South Africa, College of Human Sciences, Pretoria, South Africa. Offers adult education (M Ed); African languages (MA, PhD); African politics (MA, PhD); Afrikaans (MA, PhD); ancient history (MA, PhD); ancient Near Eastern studies (MA, PhD); anthropology (MA, PhD); applied linguistics (MA); Arabic (MA, PhD); archaeology (MA); art history (MA); Biblical archaeology (MA); Biblical studies (M Th, D Th, PhD); Christian spirituality (M Th, D Th); church history (M Th, D Th); classical studies (MA, PhD); clinical psychology (MA); communication (MA, PhD); comparative education (M Ed, Ed D); consulting psychology (D Admin, D Com, PhD); curriculum studies (M Ed, Ed D); development studies (M Admin, MA, D Admin, PhD); didactics (M Ed, Ed D); education (M Tech); education management (M Ed, Ed D); educational psychology (M Ed); English (MA); environmental education (M Ed); French (MA, PhD); German (MA, PhD); Greek (MA); guidance and counseling (M Ed); health studies (MA, PhD), including health sciences education (MA), health services management (MA), medical and surgical nursing science (critical care general) (MA), midwifery and neonatal nursing science (MA), trauma and emergency care (MA); history (MA, PhD); history of education (Ed D); inclusive education (M Ed, Ed D); information and communications technology policy and regulation (MA); information science (MA, MIS, PhD); international politics (MA, PhD); Islamic studies (MA, PhD); Italian (MA, PhD); Judaica (MA, PhD); linguistics (MA, PhD); mathematical education (M Ed); mathematics education (MA); missiology (M Th, D Th); modern Hebrew (MA, PhD); musicology (MA, MMus, D Mus, PhD); natural science education (M Ed); New Testament (M Th, D Th); Old Testament (D Th); pastoral therapy (M Th, D Th); philosophy (MA); philosophy of education (M Ed, Ed D); politics (MA, PhD); Portuguese (MA, PhD); practical theology (M Th, D Th); psychology (MA, MS, PhD); psychology of education (M Ed, Ed D); public health (MA); religious studies (MA, D Th, PhD); Romance languages (MA); Russian (MA, PhD); Semitic languages (MA, PhD); social behavior studies in HIV/AIDS (MA); social science (mental health) (MA); social science in development studies (MA); social science in psychology (MA); social science in social work (MA); social science in sociology (MA); social work (MSW, DSW, PhD); socio-education (M Ed, Ed D); sociolinguistics (MA); sociology (MA, PhD); Spanish (MA, PhD); systematic theology (M Th, D Th); TESOL (teaching English to speakers of other languages) (MA); theological ethics (M Th, D Th); theory of literature (MA, PhD); urban ministries (D Th); urban ministry (M Th).

University of South Alabama, Graduate School, College of Education, Department of Professional Studies, Mobile, AL 36688-0002. Offers community counseling (MS); educational media (M Ed, MS); instructional design and development (MS, PhD); rehabilitation counseling (MS); school counseling (M Ed); school psychometry (M Ed). *Accreditation:* NCATE. Part-time programs available. *Degree requirements:* For master's, comprehensive exam. *Entrance requirements:* For master's, GRE General Test or MAT, minimum GPA of 3.0. *Expenses:* Tuition, state resident: part-time $218 per contact hour. Required fees: $1102 per year. *Faculty research:* Agency counseling, rehabilitation counseling, school psychometry.

University of South Carolina, The Graduate School, College of Education, Department of Educational Studies, Program in Educational Technology, Columbia, SC 29208. Offers M Ed. *Accreditation:* NCATE. Part-time programs available. Postbaccalaureate distance learning degree programs offered. *Degree requirements:* For master's, comprehensive exam. *Entrance requirements:* For master's, GRE or MAT, interview, letters of intent and reference.

University of South Carolina Aiken, School of Education, Program in Educational Technology, Aiken, SC 29801-6309. Offers M Ed. Part-time and evening/weekend programs available. *Entrance requirements:* For master's, GRE or MAT. Electronic applications accepted.

The University of South Dakota, Graduate School, School of Education, Division of Curriculum and Instruction, Program in Technology for Education and Training, Vermillion, SD 57069-2390. Offers MS, Ed S. Part-time and evening/weekend programs available. Postbaccalaureate distance learning degree programs offered (no on-campus study). *Degree requirements:* For master's and Ed S, comprehensive exam, thesis or alternative. *Entrance requirements:* For master's and Ed S, GRE, minimum GPA of 2.7. Additional exam requirements/recommendations for international students: Required—TOEFL (minimum score 550 paper-based; 213 computer-based; 79 iBT). Electronic applications accepted.

University of South Florida, Graduate School, College of Education–Main Campus, Department of Secondary Education, Tampa, FL 33620-9951. Offers English education (M Ed, MA, MAT, PhD); foreign language education/ESOL (M Ed, MA, MAT); instructional technology (M Ed, PhD, Ed S); mathematics education (M Ed, MA, MAT, PhD, Ed S); science education (M Ed, MA, MAT, PhD); second language acquisition/instructional technology (PhD); secondary education (M Ed, PhD); secondary education/TESOL (M Ed); social science education (M Ed, MA, MAT); teaching and learning in the content area (PhD). *Accreditation:* NCATE. Part-time and evening/weekend programs available. *Faculty:* 28 full-time (17 women), 3 part-time/adjunct (1 woman). *Students:* 144 full-time (97 women), 322 part-time (212 women); includes 100 minority (32 African Americans, 4 American Indian/Alaska Native, 17 Asian Americans or Pacific Islanders, 47 Hispanic Americans), 25 international. Average age 30. 230 applicants, 67% accepted, 122 enrolled. In 2009, 122 master's, 14 doctorates, 1 other advanced degree awarded. *Degree requirements:* For master's, variable foreign language requirement, comprehensive exam; for doctorate, variable foreign language requirement, comprehensive exam, thesis/dissertation. *Entrance requirements:* For master's, GRE General Test or General Knowledge Test, minimum GPA of 3.0; for doctorate, GRE General Test, minimum GPA of 3.5; for Ed S, GRE General Test. Additional exam requirements/recommendations for international students: Required—TOEFL (minimum score 550 paper-based; 213 computer-based; 79 iBT). *Application deadline:* For fall admission, 2/15 for domestic students, 1/2 for international students; for spring admission, 10/15 for domestic students, 6/1 for international students. Application fee: $30. Electronic applications accepted. *Financial support:* In 2009–10, 7 students received support, including 1 research assistantship with full tuition reimbursement available (averaging $10,000 per year), 55 teaching assistantships with full and partial tuition reimbursements available (averaging $7,900 per year); scholarships/grants and unspecified assistantships also available. Financial award application deadline: 4/15; financial award applicants required to submit FAFSA. *Faculty research:* English language learners/multicultural, social science education, mathematics education, science education, instructional technology. Total annual research expenditures: $336,023. *Unit head:* Dr. Stephen Thornton, Chairperson, 813-974-3533, Fax: 813-974-3837, E-mail: thornton@usf.edu. *Application contact:* Dr. James White, Program Director, 813-974-1629, Fax: 813-974-3837, E-mail: jwhite@usf.edu.

The University of Tennessee, Graduate School, College of Education, Health and Human Sciences, Program in Education, Knoxville, TN 37996. Offers art education (MS); counseling education (PhD); cultural studies in education (PhD); curriculum (MS, Ed S); curriculum, educational research and evaluation (Ed D, PhD); early childhood education (PhD); early childhood special education (MS); education of deaf and hard of hearing (MS); educational administration and policy studies (Ed D, PhD); educational administration and supervision (Ed S); educational psychology (Ed D, PhD); elementary education (MS, Ed S); elementary teaching (MS); English education (MS, Ed S); exercise science (PhD); foreign language/ESL education (MS, Ed S); instructional technology (MS, Ed D, PhD, Ed S); literacy, language and ESL education (PhD); literacy, language education, and ESL education (Ed D); mathematics education (MS, Ed S); modified and comprehensive special education (MS); reading education (MS, Ed S); school counseling (Ed S); school psychology (PhD, Ed S); science education (MS, Ed S); secondary teaching (MS); social foundations (MS); social science education (MS, Ed S); socio-cultural foundations of sports and education (PhD); special education (Ed S);

teacher education (Ed D, PhD). *Accreditation:* NCATE. Part-time and evening/weekend programs available. *Degree requirements:* For master's and Ed S, thesis optional; for doctorate, variable foreign language requirement, thesis/dissertation. *Entrance requirements:* For master's, minimum GPA of 2.7; for doctorate and Ed S, GRE General Test, minimum GPA of 2.7. Additional exam requirements/recommendations for international students: Required—TOEFL. Electronic applications accepted. *Expenses:* Tuition, state resident: full-time $6826; part-time $380 per semester hour. Tuition, nonresident: full-time $21,844; part-time $1147 per semester hour. Tuition and fees vary according to program.

The University of Tennessee at Chattanooga, Graduate School, College of Health, Education and Professional Studies, Graduate Studies Division of Education, Program for Educational Specialist, Chattanooga, TN 37403-2598. Offers educational technology (Ed S); school psychology (Ed S). Part-time and evening/weekend programs available. *Faculty:* 4 full-time (0 women), 1 part-time/adjunct (0 women). *Students:* 27 full-time (23 women), 14 part-time (10 women); includes 6 minority (5 African Americans, 1 Hispanic American). Average age 39. 14 applicants, 86% accepted, 6 enrolled. In 2009, 27 Ed Ss awarded. *Degree requirements:* For Ed S, internship. *Entrance requirements:* For degree, GRE (minimum score 1350), letters of reference. Additional exam requirements/recommendations for international students: Required—TOEFL (minimum score 550 paper-based; 213 computer-based; 79 iBT), IELTS (minimum score 6). *Application deadline:* For fall admission, 8/1 priority date for domestic students, 6/1 for international students; for spring admission, 12/1 priority date for domestic students, 10/1 for international students. Applications are processed on a rolling basis. Application fee: $35. Electronic applications accepted. *Expenses:* Tuition, state resident: full-time $5404; part-time $300 per credit hour. Tuition, nonresident: full-time $16,702; part-time $928 per credit hour. Required fees: $1150; $130 per credit hour. *Financial support:* In 2009–10, 5 research assistantships with full and partial tuition reimbursements (averaging $5,500 per year) were awarded; career-related internships or fieldwork, scholarships/grants, and unspecified assistantships also available. Support available to part-time students. *Faculty research:* Educational technology, using technology in the classroom, interactive media, distance learning, instructional design technological implementation. *Unit head:* Dr. Lloyd D. Davis, Coordinator, 423-425-4161, Fax: 423-425-5380, E-mail: lloyd-davis@utc.edu. *Application contact:* Dr. Stephanie Bellar, Dean of Graduate Studies, 423-425-4666, Fax: 423-425-5223, E-mail: stephanie-bellar@utc.edu.

The University of Texas at Brownsville, Graduate Studies, School of Education, Brownsville, TX 78520-4991. Offers bilingual education (M Ed); counseling and guidance (M Ed); curriculum and instruction (M Ed); early childhood education (M Ed); educational administration (M Ed); educational technology (M Ed); English as a second language (M Ed); reading specialist (M Ed); special education/educational diagnostician (M Ed). Part-time and evening/weekend programs available. Postbaccalaureate distance learning degree programs offered (minimal on-campus study). *Degree requirements:* For master's, thesis optional. *Entrance requirements:* For master's, GRE General Test. Additional exam requirements/recommendations for international students: Required—TOEFL.

The University of Texas at San Antonio, College of Education and Human Development, Department of Interdisciplinary Learning and Teaching, San Antonio, TX 78249-0617. Offers curriculum and instruction (MA); early childhood education (MA); instructional technology (MA); reading (MA); special education (MA). Part-time and evening/weekend programs available. *Faculty:* 28 full-time (24 women), 1 part-time/adjunct (0 women). *Students:* 103 full-time (83 women), 317 part-time (253 women); includes 227 minority (36 African Americans, 11 Asian Americans or Pacific Islanders, 180 Hispanic Americans), 17 international. Average age 33. 212 applicants, 90% accepted, 140 enrolled. In 2009, 74 master's awarded. *Degree requirements:* For master's, comprehensive exam (for some programs), thesis (for some programs). *Entrance requirements:* For master's, GRE General Test, minimum GPA of 3.0. Additional exam requirements/recommendations for international students: Required—TOEFL (minimum score 500 paper-based; 173 computer-based; 61 iBT), IELTS (minimum score 5). *Application deadline:* For fall admission, 7/1 for domestic students, 4/1 for international students; for spring admission, 11/1 for domestic students, 9/1 for international students. Applications are processed on a rolling basis. Application fee: $45 ($80 for international students). Electronic applications accepted. *Expenses:* Tuition, state resident: full-time $3975; part-time $221 per contact hour. Tuition, nonresident: full-time $13,947; part-time $775 per contact hour. Required fees: $1853. *Financial support:* In 2009–10, 76 students received support, including 25 research assistantships (averaging $11,599 per year), 4 teaching assistantships (averaging $8,800 per year); scholarships/grants, tuition waivers, and unspecified assistantships also available. Support available to part-time students. *Faculty research:* Adult education; early childhood education; literacy; special education; science, technology, engineering and math fields. Total annual research expenditures: $57,097. *Unit head:* Dr. Belinda B. Flores, Chair, 210-458-5969, Fax: 210-458-7281, E-mail: belinda.flores@utsa.edu. *Application contact:* Mari Cortez, Graduate Advisor, 210-458-4414, E-mail: mari.cortez@utsa.edu.

University of the Incarnate Word, School of Graduate Studies and Research, Dreeben School of Education, Programs in Education, San Antonio, TX 78209-6397. Offers adult education (M Ed, MA); cross-cultural education (M Ed, MA); early childhood literacy (M Ed, MA); general education (M Ed, MA); Higher Education (PhD); instructional technology (M Ed, MA); international education and entrepreneurship (PhD); kinesiology (M Ed, MA); literacy (M Ed, MA); organizational leadership (PhD); organizational learning and learning (M Ed, MA); reading (M Ed, MA); special education (M Ed, MA); teacher leadership (M Ed, MA). Part-time and evening/weekend programs available. *Students:* 20 full-time (11 women), 201 part-time (122 women); includes 113 minority (29 African Americans, 2 American Indian/Alaska Native, 2 Asian Americans or Pacific Islanders, 80 Hispanic Americans), 30 international. Average age 41. In 2009, 26 master's, 19 doctorates awarded. *Degree requirements:* For master's, capstone; for doctorate, thesis/dissertation, qualifying exam. *Entrance requirements:* For master's, baccalaureate degree; minimum foundation GPA of 2.5; interview; for doctorate, master's degree; interview; supervised writing sample. Additional exam requirements/recommendations for international students: Required—TOEFL (minimum score 560 paper-based; 220 computer-based; 83 iBT). *Application deadline:* Applications are processed on a rolling basis. Application fee: $20. Electronic applications accepted. *Expenses:* Tuition: Full-time $12,150; part-time $675 per credit hour. Required fees: $83 per credit hour. *Financial support:* Federal Work-Study and scholarships/grants available. Financial award applicants required to submit FAFSA. *Unit head:* Dr. Denise Staudt, Dean, Dreeben School of Education, 210-829-2762, E-mail: staudt@uiwtx.edu. *Application contact:* Andrea Cyterski-Acosta, Dean of Enrollment, 210-829-6005, Fax: 210-829-3921, E-mail: admis@uiwtx.edu.

University of the Incarnate Word, School of Graduate Studies and Research, H-E-B School of Business and Administration, Programs in Administration, San Antonio, TX 78209-6397. Offers adult education (MAA); applied administration (MAA); communication arts (MAA); healthcare administration (MAA); instructional technology (MAA); international business (Certificate); nutrition (MAA); organizational development (MAA, Certificate); project management (Certificate); sports management (MAA). Part-time and evening/weekend programs available. Postbaccalaureate distance learning degree programs offered (no on-campus study). *Students:* 30 full-time (17 women), 163 part-time (114 women); includes 128 minority (18 African Americans, 3 Asian Americans or Pacific Islanders, 107 Hispanic Americans), 8 international. Average age 35. In 2009, 68 master's awarded. *Degree requirements:* For master's, capstone. *Entrance requirements:* For master's, GRE, GMAT, undergraduate degree, minimum GPA of 2.5. Additional exam requirements/recommendations for international students: Required—TOEFL (minimum score 560 paper-based; 220 computer-based; 83 iBT). *Application deadline:* Applications are processed on a rolling basis. Application fee: $20. Electronic applications accepted. *Expenses:* Tuition: Full-time $12,150; part-time $675 per credit hour. Required fees: $83 per credit hour. *Financial support:* Federal Work-Study and scholarships/grants available. Financial award applicants required to submit FAFSA. *Unit head:* Dr. Daniel Dominguez, MAA Director, 210-829-3180, Fax: 210-805-3564, E-mail: domingue@uiwtx.edu. *Application contact:* Andrea Cyterski-Acosta, Dean of Enrollment, 210-829-6005, Fax: 210-829-3921, E-mail: admis@uiwtx.edu.

University of the Sacred Heart, Graduate Programs, Department of Education, Program in Instruction Systems and Education Technology, San Juan, PR 00914-0383. Offers M Ed. Part-time and evening/weekend programs available. *Degree requirements:* For master's, thesis. *Entrance requirements:* For master's, EXADEP, interview, minimum undergraduate GPA of 2.75.

The University of Toledo, College of Graduate Studies, College of Education, Department of Curriculum and Instruction, Program in Educational Media, Toledo, OH 43606-3390. Offers DE, PhD, Ed S.

The University of Toledo, College of Graduate Studies, College of Education, Department of Curriculum and Instruction, Program in Educational Technology, Toledo, OH 43606-3390. Offers ME.

University of Utah, Graduate School, College of Education, Department of Educational Psychology, Salt Lake City, UT 84112. Offers counseling psychology (PhD); educational psychology (MA); instructional design and educational technology (M Ed); learning and cognition (MS, PhD); professional counseling (MS); professional psychology (M Ed); reading and literacy (M Ed, PhD); school counseling (M Ed, MS); school psychology (MS, PhD); statistics (M Stat). *Accreditation:* APA (one or more programs are accredited). Evening/weekend programs available. Postbaccalaureate distance learning degree programs offered (minimal on-campus study). *Faculty:* 21 full-time (11 women), 8 part-time/adjunct (5 women). *Students:* 92 full-time (67 women), 74 part-time (43 women); includes 16 minority (4 Asian Americans or Pacific Islanders, 12 Hispanic Americans), 2 international. Average age 33. 177 applicants, 34% accepted, 50 enrolled. In 2009, 44 master's, 9 doctorates awarded. *Degree requirements:* For master's, variable foreign language requirement, comprehensive exam, thesis (for some programs); for doctorate, variable foreign language requirement, thesis/dissertation, oral exam. *Entrance requirements:* For master's and doctorate, GRE General Test, minimum GPA of 3.0. Additional exam requirements/recommendations for international students: Required—TOEFL (minimum score 500 paper-based; 173 computer-based). *Application deadline:* For fall admission, 4/1 for domestic and international students; for spring admission, 11/1 for domestic and international students. Application fee: $55 ($65 for international students). *Expenses:* Tuition, state resident: full-time $4004; part-time $1674 per semester. Tuition, nonresident: full-time $14,134; part-time $5915 per semester. Required fees: $324 per semester. Tuition and fees vary according to course load, degree level and program. *Financial support:* In 2009–10, 55 students received support, including 20 fellowships with full tuition reimbursements available (averaging $11,000 per year), 5 research assistantships with full tuition reimbursements available (averaging $11,000 per year), 32 teaching assistantships with full and partial tuition reimbursements available (averaging $11,000 per year); career-related internships or fieldwork, Federal Work-Study, institutionally sponsored loans, scholarships/grants, and unspecified assistantships also available. Financial award application deadline: 2/1; financial award applicants required to submit FAFSA. *Faculty research:* Autism, computer technology and instruction, cognitive behavior, aging, group counseling. Total annual research expenditures: $151,911. *Unit head:* Dr. Elaine Clark, Chair, 801-581-7148, Fax: 801-581-5566, E-mail: clark@ed.utah.edu. *Application contact:* Jenna Atkinson, Academic Program Specialist, 801-581-7148, Fax: 801-581-5566, E-mail: jenna.atkinson@utah.edu.

University of Virginia, Curry School of Education, Department of Leadership, Foundations and Policy, Program in Educational Psychology, Charlottesville, VA 22903. Offers applied developmental science (M Ed); educational evaluation (M Ed); educational psychology (M Ed, Ed D, Ed S); educational research (Ed D); gifted education (M Ed); instructional technology (M Ed, Ed S); research statistics and evaluation (Ed D); school psychology (Ed D). *Students:* 28 full-time (22 women), 18 part-time (13 women); includes 3 minority (1 African American, 1 Asian American or Pacific Islander, 1 Hispanic American), 7 international. Average age 31. 130 applicants, 36% accepted, 31 enrolled. In 2009, 50 master's, 25 doctorates, 1 other advanced degree awarded. *Degree requirements:* For master's, comprehensive exam. *Entrance requirements:* For master's and doctorate, GRE General Test, 2 letters of recommendation. Additional exam requirements/recommendations for international students: Required—TOEFL (minimum score 600 paper-based; 250 computer-based; 90 iBT), IELTS (minimum score 7). *Application deadline:* Applications are processed on a rolling basis. Application fee: $60. Electronic applications accepted. *Financial support:* Fellowships, research assistantships, teaching assistantships available. Financial award application deadline: 1/5; financial award applicants required to submit FAFSA. *Unit head:* Jen Mashburn, Program Coordinator, E-mail: jmashburn@virginia.edu. *Application contact:* Jen Mashburn, Program Coordinator, E-mail: jmashburn@virginia.edu.

University of Virginia, Curry School of Education, Program in Education, Charlottesville, VA 22903. Offers administration and supervision (PhD); applied developmental science (PhD); counselor education (PhD); curriculum and instruction (PhD); early childhood-developmental risk (MT); education evaluation (PhD); educational psychology (PhD); educational research (PhD); elementary (MT, PhD); English education (MT, PhD); foreign language education (MT); higher education (PhD); instructional technology (PhD); kinesiology (MT, PhD); math education (PhD); reading education (PhD); research statistics and evaluation (PhD); school psychology (PhD); science education (PhD); social studies education (MT, PhD); special education (PhD); world languages education (MT). *Students:* 336 full-time (239 women), 88 part-time (54 women); includes 43 minority (24 African Americans, 2 American Indian/Alaska Native, 11 Asian Americans or Pacific Islanders, 6 Hispanic Americans), 18 international. Average age 27. 199 applicants, 48% accepted, 55 enrolled. In 2009, 127 master's, 52 doctorates awarded. *Degree requirements:* For master's, comprehensive exam (for some programs), field project; for doctorate, comprehensive exam, thesis/dissertation. *Entrance requirements:* For doctorate, GRE General Test. Additional exam requirements/recommendations for international students: Required—TOEFL (minimum score 600 paper-based; 250 computer-based; 90 iBT), IELTS (minimum score 7). *Application deadline:* Applications are processed on a rolling basis. Application fee: $60. Electronic applications accepted. *Financial support:* Fellowships, research assistantships, teaching assistantships available. Financial award application deadline: 1/5; financial award applicants required to submit FAFSA.

University of Washington, Graduate School, College of Education, Seattle, WA 98195. Offers curriculum and instruction (M Ed, Ed D, PhD), including educational technology, general curriculum (Ed D, PhD), language, literacy, and culture, mathematics education, multicultural education, reading and language arts education (Ed D), science education, social studies education, teaching and curriculum (M Ed); educational leadership and policy studies (M Ed, Ed D, PhD), including administration (Ed D), educational policy, organization, and leadership (M Ed, PhD), higher education, leadership for learning (Ed D), social and cultural foundations of education (M Ed, PhD); educational psychology (M Ed, PhD), including educational psychology (PhD), human development and cognition (M Ed), learning sciences, measurement, statistics and research design (M Ed), school psychology (M Ed); instructional leadership (M Ed); intercollegiate athletic leadership (M Ed); special education (M Ed, Ed D, PhD), including early childhood special education (M Ed), emotional and behavioral disabilities (M Ed), learning disabilities (M Ed), low-incidence disabilities (M Ed), severe disabilities (M Ed), special education (Ed D, PhD); teacher education (MIT). *Accreditation:* APA. Part-time and evening/weekend programs available. *Degree requirements:* For master's, thesis optional; for doctorate, thesis/dissertation. *Entrance requirements:* For master's and doctorate, GRE General Test, minimum GPA of 3.0. Additional exam requirements/recommendations for international students: Required—TOEFL. Electronic applications accepted. *Faculty research:* School restructuring/effective schools, special education interventions, literacy and writing, technology, school partnerships, teacher preparation.

The University of West Alabama, School of Graduate Studies, College of Education, Department of Teacher Education, Program in Library Media, Livingston, AL 35470. Offers M Ed. Part-time programs available. *Entrance requirements:* For master's, GRE General Test, MAT, minimum GPA of 2.75.

University of West Florida, College of Professional Studies, Department of Engineering and Computer Technology, Program in Instructional Technology, Pensacola, FL 32514-5750. Offers educational leadership (M Ed); instructional technology (M Ed). *Students:* 5 full-time (4 women), 40 part-time (20 women); includes 9 minority (7 African Americans, 1 Asian American or Pacific

Educational Media/Instructional Technology

University of West Florida (continued)

Islander, 1 Hispanic American). Average age 38. 11 applicants, 91% accepted, 6 enrolled. In 2009, 14 master's awarded. *Entrance requirements:* For master's, MAT, GRE or GMAT, letter of intent, names of references. Additional exam requirements/recommendations for international students: Required—TOEFL (minimum score 550 paper-based; 213 computer-based). *Application deadline:* For fall admission, 6/1 for domestic students, 5/15 for international students; for spring admission, 11/1 for domestic students, 10/1 for international students. Applications are processed on a rolling basis. Application fee: $30. Electronic applications accepted. *Expenses:* Tuition, state resident: full-time $4982; part-time $260 per credit hour. Tuition, nonresident: full-time $20,059; part-time $919 per credit hour. Required fees: $1247; $52 per credit hour. *Financial support:* Application deadline: 4/15. *Unit head:* Dr. Karen Rasmussen, Chairperson, 850-474-2301, Fax: 850-474-2804. *Application contact:* Terry McCray, Assistant Director of Graduate Admissions, 850-473-7718, Fax: 850-473-7714, E-mail: gradadmissions@uwf.edu.

University of West Florida, College of Professional Studies, Department of Engineering and Computer Technology, Specialization in Curriculum and Instruction: Instructional Technology, Pensacola, FL 32514-5750. Offers Ed D. *Students:* 80 part-time (51 women); includes 9 African Americans, 1 American Indian/Alaska Native, 1 Asian American or Pacific Islander. Average age 46. 47 applicants, 70% accepted, 30 enrolled. *Expenses:* Tuition, state resident: full-time $4982; part-time $260 per credit hour. Tuition, nonresident: full-time $20,059; part-time $919 per credit hour. Required fees: $1247; $52 per credit hour. *Unit head:* Dr. Karen Rasmussen. *Application contact:* Terry McCray, Assistant Director of Graduate Admissions, 850-473-7718, Fax: 850-473-7714, E-mail: gradadmissions@uwf.edu.

University of West Georgia, Graduate School, College of Education, Department of Media and Instructional Technology, Carrollton, GA 30118. Offers media (M Ed, Ed S). Part-time and evening/weekend programs available. Postbaccalaureate distance learning degree programs offered (minimal on-campus study). *Faculty:* 9 full-time (6 women), 5 part-time/adjunct (3 women). *Students:* 20 full-time (15 women), 271 part-time (235 women); includes 37 minority (36 African Americans, 1 Hispanic American). Average age 37. 43 applicants. In 2009, 40 master's, 45 Ed Ss awarded. *Degree requirements:* For master's, comprehensive exam, electronic portfolio; for Ed S, comprehensive exam, research project. *Entrance requirements:* For master's, GRE General Test, MAT, minimum GPA of 2.7, teaching certificate; for Ed S, GRE General Test, MAT, master's degree, minimum graduate GPA of 3.0. *Application deadline:* For fall admission, 7/17 priority date for domestic students; for spring admission, 11/20 priority date for domestic students. Applications are processed on a rolling basis. Application fee: $30. Electronic applications accepted. *Expenses:* Tuition, state resident: full-time $2952; part-time $164 per semester hour. Tuition, nonresident: full-time $11,808; part-time $656 per semester hour. Required fees: $42.90 per semester hour. $307 per semester. Tuition and fees vary according to course load. *Financial support:* In 2009–10, 2 students received support, including 2 research assistantships with full tuition reimbursements available (averaging $6,000 per year); career-related internships or fieldwork, scholarships/grants, and unspecified assistantships also available. Support available to part-time students. Financial award application deadline: 2/1; financial award applicants required to submit FAFSA. *Faculty research:* Distance education, technology integration, collaboration, e-books for children, instructional design. *Unit head:* Dr. Elizabeth Kirby Bennett, Interim Chair, 678-839-6558, Fax: 678-839-6153, E-mail: ebennett@westga.edu. *Application contact:* Dr. Charles W. Clark, Dean, 678-839-6508, E-mail: cclark@westga.edu.

University of Wisconsin–Milwaukee, Graduate School, School of Education, Program in Urban Education, Milwaukee, WI 53201-0413. Offers adult and continuing education (PhD); curriculum and instruction (PhD); educational administration (PhD); educational and media technology (PhD); educational psychology (PhD); multicultural studies (PhD); social foundations of education (PhD). *Students:* 67 full-time (51 women), 44 part-time (30 women); includes 41 minority (23 African Americans, 2 American Indian/Alaska Native, 7 Asian Americans or Pacific Islanders, 9 Hispanic Americans), 4 international. Average age 41. 31 applicants, 45% accepted, 5 enrolled. In 2009, 11 doctorates awarded. *Degree requirements:* For doctorate, comprehensive exam, thesis/dissertation. *Entrance requirements:* For doctorate, GRE General Test, minimum undergraduate GPA of 2.85, graduate 3.5. Additional exam requirements/recommendations for international students: Required—TOEFL (minimum score 550 paper-based; 79 iBT), IELTS (minimum score 6.5). *Application deadline:* For fall admission, 1/1 priority date for domestic students; for spring admission, 9/1 for domestic students. Applications are processed on a rolling basis. Application fee: $45 ($75 for international students). *Expenses:* Tuition, state resident: full-time $8800. Tuition, nonresident: full-time $20,760. Tuition and fees vary according to program and reciprocity agreements. *Financial support:* Career-related internships or fieldwork and unspecified assistantships available. Support available to part-time students. Financial award application deadline: 4/15. *Unit head:* Larry Martin, Representative, 414-229-4729, Fax: 414-229-2920, E-mail: lmartin@uwm.edu. *Application contact:* General Information Contact, 414-229-4982, Fax: 414-229-6967, E-mail: gradschool@uwm.edu.

University of Wyoming, College of Education, Department of Adult Learning and Technology, Laramie, WY 82070. Offers adult and postsecondary education (MA, Ed D, PhD, Ed S); distance education (Ed D, PhD); instructional technology (MS, Ed D, PhD). Part-time programs available. Postbaccalaureate distance learning degree programs offered (no on-campus study). *Degree requirements:* For master's, thesis or alternative; for doctorate, comprehensive exam, thesis/dissertation. *Entrance requirements:* For master's, GRE, minimum GPA of 3.0; for doctorate, MS or MA, minimum GPA of 3.0. Additional exam requirements/recommendations for international students: Required—TOEFL. Electronic applications accepted. *Faculty research:* Web based instruction, instructional decision, adult education history, literacy in adults, international distance education.

Utah State University, School of Graduate Studies, College of Education and Human Services, Department of Instructional Technology, Logan, UT 84322. Offers M Ed, MS, PhD, Ed S. Part-time and evening/weekend programs available. Postbaccalaureate distance learning degree programs offered (minimal on-campus study). Terminal master's awarded for partial completion of doctoral program. *Degree requirements:* For master's, thesis (for some programs); for doctorate, comprehensive exam, thesis/dissertation. *Entrance requirements:* For master's, GRE General Test or MAT, minimum GPA of 3.0, 3 recommendation letters; for doctorate, GRE General Test, minimum GPA of 3.0, 3 recommendation letters, transcripts, letter of intent; for Ed S, GRE General Test, GRE Subject Test, minimum GPA of 3.0. Additional exam requirements/recommendations for international students: Required—TOEFL (minimum score 550 paper-based; 213 computer-based). Electronic applications accepted. *Faculty research:* Interactive learning environments, computer-assisted instruction, learning, distance education, corporate training.

Valley City State University, School of Education and Graduate Studies, Valley City, ND 58072. Offers English language learners (ELL) (M Ed); library and information technologies (M Ed); teaching and technology (M Ed); technology education (M Ed). *Accreditation:* NCATE. Part-time and evening/weekend programs available. Postbaccalaureate distance learning degree programs offered (no on-campus study). *Faculty:* 19 full-time (13 women), 4 part-time/adjunct (3 women). *Students:* 7 full-time (4 women), 115 part-time (73 women); includes 4 minority (1 African American, 1 American Indian/Alaska Native, 1 Asian American or Pacific Islander, 1 Hispanic American). Average age 36. 33 applicants, 97% accepted, 22 enrolled. In 2009, 22 master's awarded. *Degree requirements:* For master's, action research report, comprehensive portfolio. *Entrance requirements:* For master's, GRE, MAT, PRAXIS II or National Teaching Board for Professional Standards (if GPAless than 3.0). Additional exam requirements/recommendations for international students: Required—TOEFL (minimum score 525 paper-based; 193 computer-based). *Application deadline:* For fall admission, 5/24 priority date for domestic and international students; for winter admission, 12/11 priority date for domestic and international students; for spring admission, 4/24 priority date for domestic and international students. Applications are processed on a rolling basis. Application fee: $35. Electronic applications accepted. *Expenses:* Tuition, state resident: full-time $4266; part-time $237.40 per credit hour. Tuition, nonresident: full-time $4266; part-time $237.40 per credit hour. Required fees: $237.40 per credit hour. One-time fee: $35. *Financial support:* In 2009–10, 30 students received support. Applicants required to submit FAFSA. *Faculty research:* Academically at-risk students in higher education, communication pedagogy and technology, gender communication, computer mediated communication, creativity in music. Total annual research expenditures: $26,000. *Unit head:* Dr. Gary Thompson, Dean, 701-845-7197, E-mail: gary.thompson@vcsu.edu. *Application contact:* Misty Lindgren, 701-845-7303, Fax: 701-845-7305, E-mail: misty.lindgren@vcsu.edu.

Virginia Polytechnic Institute and State University, Graduate School, College of Liberal Arts and Human Sciences, School of Education, Department of Learning Sciences and Technologies, Blacksburg, VA 24061. Offers educational psychology (PhD); instructional design and technology (MA, Ed D, PhD, Ed S). Postbaccalaureate distance learning degree programs offered. *Entrance requirements:* For master's, minimum GPA of 3.0; for doctorate, GRE, 3 letters of reference, interview, curriculum vitae, writing sample. *Expenses:* Tuition, area resident: Full-time $10,228; part-time $459 per credit hour. Tuition, nonresident: full-time $17,892; part-time $865 per credit hour. Required fees: $1966; $451 per semester.

Virginia Polytechnic Institute and State University, VT Online, Blacksburg, VA 24061. Offers aerospace engineering (MS); business information systems (Graduate Certificate); career and technical education (MS); computer engineering (M Eng, MS); decision support systems (Graduate Certificate); eLearning leadership (MA); electrical engineering (M Eng, MS); engineering administration (MEA); environmental politics and policy (Graduate Certificate); foundations of political analysis (Graduate Certificate); health product risk management (Graduate Certificate); information policy and society (Graduate Certificate); information security (Graduate Certificate); instructional technology (MA); liberal arts (Graduate Certificate); life sciences: health product risk management (MS); natural resources (MNR, Graduate Certificate); networking (Graduate Certificate); nonprofit and nongovernmental organization management (Graduate Certificate); ocean engineering (MS); political science (MA); security studies (Graduate Certificate); software development (Graduate Certificate). *Expenses:* Tuition, area resident: Full-time $10,228; part-time $459 per credit hour. Tuition, nonresident: full-time $17,892; part-time $865 per credit hour. Required fees: $1966; $451 per semester.

Walden University, Graduate Programs, Richard W. Riley College of Education and Leadership, Minneapolis, MN 55401. Offers administrator leadership for teaching and learning (Ed D, Ed S); curriculum, instruction, and professional development (Ed S); early childhood education (birth-grade 3) (MAT); education (MS, PhD), including adolescent literacy and technology (grades 6-12) (MS), adult education leadership (PhD), community college leadership (PhD), curriculum, instruction, and assessment, early childhood education (PhD), educational leadership (MS), educational technology (PhD), elementary reading and literacy (MS), elementary reading and mathematics (MS), emotional/behavioral disorders (K-12) (MS), general program, higher education (PhD), integrating technology in the classroom (MS), K-12 educational leadership (PhD), learning disabilities (K-12) (MS), literacy and learning in the content areas (MS), mathematics (grades 6-8) (MS), mathematics (grades K-5) (MS), middle level education (grades 5-8) (MS), professional development (MS), science (grades K-8) (MS), self-designed (PhD), special education (PhD), special education (non-licensure) (MS), teacher leadership (grades K-12) (MS); educational leadership and administration (principal preparation) (Ed S); educational technology (Ed S); higher education and adult learning (Ed D); instructional design (Postbaccalaureate Certificate); instructional design and technology (MS), including general program (MS, PhD), online learning, training and performance improvement; special education: emotional/behavioral disorders (K-12) (MAT); special education: learning disabilities (K-12) (MAT); teacher leadership (Ed D, Ed S). Part-time and evening/weekend programs available. Postbaccalaureate distance learning degree programs offered (minimal on-campus study). *Faculty:* 54 full-time, 835 part-time/adjunct. *Students:* 13,940 full-time (11,339 women), 1,940 part-time (1,637 women); includes 4,626 minority (3,795 African Americans, 111 American Indian/Alaska Native, 199 Asian Americans or Pacific Islanders, 521 Hispanic Americans), 124 international. Average age 38. In 2009, 4,688 master's, 190 doctorates awarded. *Degree requirements:* For doctorate, thesis/dissertation (for some programs), residency; for other advanced degree, residency (for some programs). *Entrance requirements:* For master's, bachelor's degree or equivalent in related field; minimum GPA of 2.5; official transcripts; goal statement; access to computer and Internet; for doctorate, master's degree or equivalent in related field; minimum GPA of 3.0; official transcripts; three years' related professional/academic experience (preferred); access to computer and Internet; for other advanced degree, master's degree or equivalent in related field; minimum GPA of 3.0; 3 years related professional/academic experience (preferred); access to computer and Internet (Ed S). Additional exam requirements/recommendations for international students: Required—TOEFL (minimum score 550 paper-based; 213 computer-based), IELTS (minimum score 6.5), or Michigan English Language Assessment Battery (minimum score 82). *Application deadline:* Applications are processed on a rolling basis. Application fee: $50. Electronic applications accepted. *Expenses:* Tuition: Full-time $13,665; part-time $560 per credit. Required fees: $1375. Tuition and fees vary according to course load, degree level and program. *Financial support:* In 2009–10, 2,418 students received support; fellowships, Federal Work-Study, scholarships/grants, unspecified assistantships, and family tuition reduction, active duty/veteran tuition reduction, group tuition reduction, interest-free payment plans available. Support available to part-time students. Financial award applicants required to submit FAFSA. *Unit head:* Dr. Kate Steffens, Dean, 800-925-3368. *Application contact:* Jennifer Hall, Director of Enrollment, 866-4-WALDEN, E-mail: info@waldenu.edu.

Walden University, Graduate Programs, School of Psychology, Minneapolis, MN 55401. Offers clinical child psychology (Post-Doctoral Certificate); clinical psychology (Post-Doctoral Certificate); counseling psychology (Post-Doctoral Certificate); forensic psychology (MS), including forensic psychology in the community, general program, mental health applications, program planning and evaluation in forensic settings, psychology and legal systems; general psychology (Post-Doctoral Certificate); health psychology (Post-Doctoral Certificate); organizational psychology (Post-Doctoral Certificate); organizational psychology and development (Postbaccalaureate Certificate); psychology (MS, PhD), including clinical psychology (PhD), counseling psychology (PhD), crisis management and response (MS), general program (MS), general psychology (PhD), health psychology, leadership development and coaching (MS), media psychology (MS), organizational psychology (PhD), organizational psychology and development (MS), organizational psychology and nonprofit management (MS), program evaluation and research (MS), psychology of culture (MS), psychology, public administration, and social change (MS), social psychology (MS), terrorism and security (MS); teaching online (Post-Master's Certificate). Part-time and evening/weekend programs available. Postbaccalaureate distance learning degree programs offered (minimal on-campus study). *Faculty:* 33 full-time, 222 part-time/adjunct. *Students:* 3,546 full-time (2,761 women), 1,133 part-time (908 women); includes 1,723 minority (1,319 African Americans, 56 American Indian/Alaska Native, 101 Asian Americans or Pacific Islanders, 247 Hispanic Americans), 80 international. Average age 41. In 2009, 495 master's, 70 doctorates, 2 other advanced degrees awarded. Terminal master's awarded for partial completion of doctoral program. *Degree requirements:* For master's, thesis optional; for doctorate, thesis/dissertation, residency. *Entrance requirements:* For master's, bachelor's degree or equivalent in related field; minimum GPA of 2.5; official transcripts; goal statement; access to computer and Internet; for doctorate, master's degree or equivalent in related field; minimum GPA of 3.0;3 years of related professional/academic experience (preferred). Additional exam requirements/recommendations for international students: Required—TOEFL (minimum score 550 paper-based; 213 computer-based), IELTS (minimum score 6.5), or Michigan English Language Assessment Battery (minimum score 82). *Application deadline:* Applications are processed on a rolling basis. Application fee: $50. Electronic applications accepted. *Expenses:* Tuition: Full-time $13,665; part-time $560 per credit. Required fees: $1375. Tuition and fees vary according to course load, degree level and program. *Financial support:* In 2009–10, 290 students received support; fellowships, Federal Work-Study, scholarships/grants, unspecified assistantships, and family tuition reduction, active duty/veteran tuition reduction, group tuition reduction, interest-free payment plans available.

Support available to part-time students. Financial award applicants required to submit FAFSA. *Unit head:* Dr. Melanie Storms, Associate Dean, 800-925-3368. *Application contact:* Jennifer Hall, Director of Enrollment, 866-4-WALDEN, E-mail: info@waldenu.edu.

Wayland Baptist University, Graduate Programs, Program in Education, Plainview, TX 79072-6998. Offers education administration (M Ed); higher education administration (M Ed); instructional leadership (M Ed); instructional technology (M Ed); special education (M Ed). Part-time and evening/weekend programs available. Postbaccalaureate distance learning degree programs offered (no on-campus study). *Faculty:* 6 full-time (4 women). *Students:* 4 full-time (2 women), 45 part-time (26 women); includes 6 minority (3 African Americans, 3 Hispanic Americans). Average age 30. 26 applicants, 77% accepted, 9 enrolled. In 2009, 4 master's awarded. *Degree requirements:* For master's, comprehensive exam, capstone course. *Entrance requirements:* For master's, GRE, GMAT or MAT. Additional exam requirements/recommendations for international students: Required—TOEFL (minimum score 500 paper-based; 173 computer-based; 61 iBT). *Application deadline:* Applications are processed on a rolling basis. Application fee: $50. Electronic applications accepted. *Expenses:* Tuition: Full-time $5796; part-time $322 per credit hour. Required fees: $782; $9 per credit hour. $60 per semester. Tuition and fees vary according to course load and campus/location. *Financial support:* Federal Work-Study, institutionally sponsored loans, and scholarships/grants available. Support available to part-time students. Financial award application deadline: 5/1; financial award applicants required to submit FAFSA. *Unit head:* Dr. Jim Todd, Chairman, 806-291-1045, Fax: 806-291-1951. *Application contact:* Amanda Stanton, Graduate Studies, 806-291-3423, Fax: 806-291-1950, E-mail: stanton@wbu.edu.

Waynesburg University, Graduate and Professional Studies, Waynesburg, PA 15370-1222. Offers business (MBA), including finance, health systems, human resources, leadership, market development; counseling (MA), including addictions counseling, clinical mental health; education (MAT); nursing (MSN), including administration, education, informatics, palliative care; nursing practice (DNP); special education (M Ed); technology (M Ed); MSN/MBA. *Accreditation:* AACN. Part-time and evening/weekend programs available. *Faculty:* 11 full-time (5 women), 136 part-time/adjunct (80 women). *Students:* 116 full-time (85 women), 984 part-time (682 women). 711 applicants, 80% accepted, 485 enrolled. In 2009, 320 master's, 41 doctorates awarded. *Degree requirements:* For doctorate, thesis/dissertation. *Entrance requirements:* Additional exam requirements/recommendations for international students: Required—TOEFL. *Application deadline:* For fall admission, 8/1 priority date for domestic students. Applications are processed on a rolling basis. Electronic applications accepted. *Expenses:* Tuition: Part-time $520 per credit. *Financial support:* Available to part-time students. Application deadline: 5/1. *Unit head:* David Mariner, Dean, 724-743-4420, Fax: 724-743-4425, E-mail: dmariner@waynesburg.edu. *Application contact:* Michael Bednarski, Director of Admissions, 724-743-4420, Fax: 724-743-4425, E-mail: mbednars@waynesburg.edu.

Wayne State University, College of Education, Division of Administrative and Organizational Studies, Detroit, MI 48202. Offers administration and supervision-secondary (Ed S); college and university teaching (Certificate); curriculum and instruction (PhD); educational leadership (M Ed, Ed S); educational leadership and policy studies (Ed D, PhD); elementary education curriculum and instruction (MA, Ed S); general administration and supervision (Ed D, PhD, Ed S); higher education (Ed D, PhD); instructional technology (M Ed, Ed D, PhD, Ed S); secondary curriculum and instruction (M Ed, Ed S). *Degree requirements:* For doctorate, thesis/dissertation. *Entrance requirements:* For doctorate, interview, minimum GPA of 3.0, an autobiography or curriculum vitae; references. Additional exam requirements/recommendations for international students: Required—TOEFL (minimum score 550 paper-based; 213 computer-based), TWE (minimum score 6). Electronic applications accepted. *Faculty research:* Total quality management, participatory management, administering educational technology, school improvement, principalship.

Wayne State University, College of Education, Division of Teacher Education, Detroit, MI 48202. Offers adult and continuing education (M Ed); art education (M Ed); bilingual/bicultural education (M Ed, MAT); business education (M Ed, MAT); career and technical education (M Ed, Ed D, PhD, Ed S); curriculum and instruction (Ed D, PhD, Ed S); distributive education (M Ed, MAT); early childhood education (M Ed); elementary education (M Ed, MAT, Ed D, PhD, Ed S); elementary education curriculum and instruction (M Ed); English education (M Ed); English education-secondary (M Ed, Ed S); foreign language education (M Ed); general education (Ed D, Ed S); health occupations education (M Ed); industrial education (M Ed); mathematics education (M Ed, Ed S); pre-school and parent education (M Ed); reading (M Ed, Ed D, Ed S); reading, languages and literature (Ed D); school music-vocal (M Ed); science education (M Ed, MAT, Ed S); secondary education (MAT); secondary school reading (M Ed); social studies education (M Ed, Ed S), including education-secondary (M Ed); special education (M Ed, Ed D, PhD, Ed S); teacher education (MAT, Ed D, PhD). *Degree requirements:* For doctorate, thesis/dissertation. *Entrance requirements:* For master's, Michigan Basic Skills Test (MA in teaching), minimum GPA of 2.6; for doctorate, minimum undergraduate GPA of 3.0, graduate 3.5; interview, curriculum vitae; references. Additional exam requirements/recommendations for international students: Required—TOEFL (minimum score 550 paper-based; 213 computer-based), TWE (minimum score 6). Electronic applications accepted. *Faculty research:* Reading and writing literacy and literature.

Webster University, School of Education, Department of Multidisciplinary Studies, St. Louis, MO 63119-3194. Offers administrative leadership (Ed S); education leadership (Ed S); educational technology (MAT); mathematics (MAT); multidisciplinary studies (MAT); school systems, superintendency and leadership (Ed S); social science (MAT); special education (MAT). Part-time programs available. *Entrance requirements:* For master's, minimum GPA of 2.5. Additional exam requirements/recommendations for international students: Required—TOEFL. *Expenses:* Tuition: Part-time $565 per credit hour. Tuition and fees vary according to degree level, campus/location and program.

West Chester University of Pennsylvania, Office of Graduate Studies, College of Education, Department of Professional and Secondary Education, West Chester, PA 19383. Offers education for sustainability (Certificate); entrepreneurial education (Certificate); secondary education (M Ed, Teaching Certificate); teaching and learning with technology (Certificate). Part-time and evening/weekend programs available. *Students:* 4 full-time (3 women), 39 part-time (27 women); includes 2 minority (both Asian Americans or Pacific Islanders). Average age 30. 33 applicants, 97% accepted, 16 enrolled. In 2009, 13 master's, 3 Certificates awarded. *Degree requirements:* For master's, comprehensive exam, thesis (for some programs). *Entrance requirements:* For master's, GRE or MAT, teaching certificate. Additional exam requirements/recommendations for international students: Required—TOEFL (minimum score 550 paper-based; 213 computer-based; 80 iBT). *Application deadline:* For fall admission, 4/15 priority date for domestic students, 3/15 for international students; for spring admission, 10/15 priority date for domestic students, 9/1 for international students. Applications are processed on a rolling basis. Application fee: $35. Electronic applications accepted. *Expenses:* Tuition, state resident: full-time $6666; part-time $370 per credit. Tuition, nonresident: full-time $10,666; part-time $593 per credit. Required fees: $122.56 per credit. *Financial support:* In 2009–10, research assistantships with full and partial tuition reimbursements (averaging $5,000 per year); unspecified assistantships also available. Support available to part-time students. Financial award application deadline: 2/15; financial award applicants required to submit FAFSA. *Faculty research:* Technology integration: preparing our teachers for the twenty-first century. *Unit head:* Dr. John Kinslow, Chair, 610-436-3108, E-mail: jkinslow@wcupa.edu. *Application contact:* Dr. Cynthia Haggard, Graduate Coordinator, 610-436-6934, E-mail: chaggard@wcupa.edu.

Western Connecticut State University, Division of Graduate Studies, School of Professional Studies, Department of Education and Educational Psychology, Instructional Technology Option, Danbury, CT 06810-6885. Offers MS. Part-time programs available. *Students:* 1 (woman) full-time, 30 part-time (21 women). Average age 29. 14 applicants, 79% accepted, 11 enrolled. In 2009, 20 master's awarded. *Degree requirements:* For master's, thesis or research project, completion of program in 6 years. *Entrance requirements:* For master's, minimum GPA of 2.8, teaching certificate. Additional exam requirements/recommendations for international students: Recommended—TOEFL (minimum score 550 paper-based; 213 computer-based; 79 iBT), IELTS (minimum score 6). *Application deadline:* For fall admission, 8/5 priority date for domestic students; for spring admission, 1/5 priority date for domestic students. Applications are processed on a rolling basis. Application fee: $50. *Expenses:* Tuition, state resident: full-time $5012; part-time $278 per credit hour. Tuition, nonresident: full-time $13,962; part-time $284 per credit hour. Required fees: $3886; $139 per credit hour. Full-time tuition and fees vary according to course load and program. Part-time tuition and fees vary according to course level, degree level and program. *Financial support:* Application deadline: 5/1. *Unit head:* Dr. Theresa Canada, Chairperson, Department of Education and Educational Psychology, 203-837-8509, Fax: 203-837-8413. *Application contact:* Chris Shankle, Associate Director of Graduate Studies, 203-837-9005, Fax: 203-837-8326, E-mail: shanklec@wcsu.edu.

Western Governors University, Teachers College, Salt Lake City, UT 84107. Offers English language learning (K-12) (MA); learning and technology (M Ed, MA); management and innovation (M Ed); mathematics education (5-12) (MA); mathematics education (5-9) (MA); mathematics education (K-6) (MA); measurement and evaluation (M Ed); science (5-12) (MA), including biology, geology; science education (5-9) (MA); teaching (MAT); technology for principals (Post-Graduate Certificate). *Accreditation:* NCATE. Part-time and evening/weekend programs available. Postbaccalaureate distance learning degree programs offered (no on-campus study). *Degree requirements:* For master's, comprehensive exam. *Entrance requirements:* Additional exam requirements/recommendations for international students: Required—TOEFL (minimum score 450 paper-based). Electronic applications accepted. *Expenses:* Contact institution.

Western Illinois University, School of Graduate Studies, College of Education and Human Services, Department of Instructional Design and Technology, Macomb, IL 61455-1390. Offers distance learning (Certificate); graphic applications (Certificate); instructional design and technology (MS); multimedia (Certificate); technology integration in education (Certificate); training development (Certificate). Part-time programs available. Postbaccalaureate distance learning degree programs offered (no on-campus study). *Students:* 23 full-time (13 women), 56 part-time (37 women); includes 18 minority (12 African Americans, 2 American Indian/Alaska Native, 3 Asian Americans or Pacific Islanders, 1 Hispanic American), 8 international. Average age 36. 18 applicants, 72% accepted. In 2009, 25 master's, 2 other advanced degrees awarded. *Degree requirements:* For master's, thesis or alternative. *Entrance requirements:* Additional exam requirements/recommendations for international students: Required—TOEFL (minimum score 550 paper-based; 213 computer-based; 80 iBT). *Application deadline:* Applications are processed on a rolling basis. Application fee: $30. Electronic applications accepted. *Expenses:* Tuition, state resident: full-time $4486; part-time $249.21 per credit hour. Tuition, nonresident: full-time $8972; part-time $498.42 per credit hour. Required fees: $72.62 per credit hour. *Financial support:* In 2009–10, 16 students received support, including 11 research assistantships with full tuition reimbursements available (averaging $7,280 per year), 5 teaching assistantships with full tuition reimbursements available (averaging $8,400 per year). Financial award applicants required to submit FAFSA. *Unit head:* Dr. Hoyet Hemphill, Chairperson, 309-298-1952. *Application contact:* Evelyn Hoing, Assistant Director of Graduate Studies, 309-298-1806, Fax: 309-298-2345, E-mail: grad-office@wiu.edu.

Western Kentucky University, Graduate Studies, College of Education and Behavioral Sciences, Department of Special Instructional Programs, Bowling Green, KY 42101. Offers exceptional child education (MAE); interdisciplinary early child education (MAE); library media education (MS); literacy (MAE). Part-time and evening/weekend programs available. Postbaccalaureate distance learning degree programs offered (minimal on-campus study). *Degree requirements:* For master's, comprehensive exam. *Entrance requirements:* For master's, GRE General Test. Additional exam requirements/recommendations for international students: Required—TOEFL (minimum score 555 paper-based; 213 computer-based; 79 iBT). *Expenses:* Tuition, state resident: full-time $4160; part-time $416 per credit hour. Tuition, nonresident: full-time $9550; part-time $506 per credit hour. Tuition and fees vary according to campus/location and reciprocity agreements. *Faculty research:* Teacher preparation in moderate/severe disabilities.

Western Michigan University, Graduate College, College of Education, Department of Educational Leadership, Research and Technology, Kalamazoo, MI 49008. Offers educational leadership (MA, PhD, Ed S); educational technology (MA, Graduate Certificate); evaluation, measurement and research (MA, PhD). *Unit head:* Dr. David A. England, Dean, 269-387-2960. *Application contact:* Admissions and Orientation, 269-387-2000, Fax: 269-387-2355.

Western Oregon University, Graduate Programs, College of Education, Division of Teacher Education, Program in Information Technology, Monmouth, OR 97361-1394. Offers MS Ed. *Accreditation:* NCATE. Part-time and evening/weekend programs available. Postbaccalaureate distance learning degree programs offered (minimal on-campus study). *Degree requirements:* For master's, written exams. *Entrance requirements:* For master's, interview, minimum GPA of 3.0, teaching license. Additional exam requirements/recommendations for international students: Required—TOEFL (minimum score 550 paper-based; 213 computer-based; 79 iBT), IELTS (minimum score 6.5). *Faculty research:* Impact of technology on teaching and learning.

Westfield State College, Division of Graduate and Continuing Education, Department of Education, Program in Technology for Educators, Westfield, MA 01086. Offers M Ed. Part-time and evening/weekend programs available. *Degree requirements:* For master's, comprehensive exam or project. *Entrance requirements:* For master's, GRE General Test or MAT, minimum undergraduate GPA of 2.7.

West Texas A&M University, College of Education and Social Sciences, Division of Education, Program in Educational Technology, Canyon, TX 79016-0001. Offers M Ed. Part-time and evening/weekend programs available. Postbaccalaureate distance learning degree programs offered (minimal on-campus study). *Degree requirements:* For master's, comprehensive exam, thesis optional. *Entrance requirements:* For master's, GRE General Test, approval from the instructional technology admissions committee. Additional exam requirements/recommendations for international students: Required—TOEFL (minimum score 550 paper-based). Electronic applications accepted. *Faculty research:* Mathematics and science instruction, technology, developing online courses for freshmen, integrity of online courses.

West Virginia University, College of Human Resources and Education, Department of Technology, Learning and Culture, Program in Instructional Design and Technology, Morgantown, WV 26506. Offers MA, Ed D. *Accreditation:* NCATE. *Degree requirements:* For master's, thesis; for doctorate, thesis/dissertation. *Entrance requirements:* For master's, GRE General Test, minimum GPA of 2.75; for doctorate, GRE, minimum GPA of 2.75. Additional exam requirements/recommendations for international students: Required—TOEFL. *Faculty research:* Appropriate technology, alternative energy, computer applications for education and training, telecommunication, professional development.

Widener University, School of Human Service Professions, Center for Education, Chester, PA 19013-5792. Offers adult education (M Ed); counseling in higher education (M Ed); counselor education (M Ed); early childhood education (M Ed); educational foundations (M Ed); educational leadership (M Ed); educational psychology (M Ed); elementary education (M Ed); English and language arts (M Ed); health education (M Ed); higher education leadership (Ed D); home and school visitor (M Ed); human sexuality (M Ed); mathematics education (M Ed); middle school education (M Ed); principalship (M Ed); reading and language arts (Ed D); reading education (M Ed); school administration (Ed D); science education (M Ed); social studies education (M Ed); special education (M Ed); technology education (M Ed). *Accreditation:* NCATE. Part-time and evening/weekend programs available. *Faculty:* 34 full-time (22 women), 37 part-time/adjunct (14 women). *Students:* 203 full-time (154 women), 415 part-time (298 women); includes 50 minority (34 African Americans, 1 American Indian/Alaska Native, 5 Asian Americans or Pacific Islanders, 10 Hispanic Americans), 3 international. Average age 39. 139 applicants, 88% accepted. In 2009, 168 master's, 31 doctorates awarded. Terminal master's awarded for partial completion of doctoral program. *Degree requirements:* For doctorate, thesis/dissertation. *Entrance requirements:* For master's, minimum GPA of 2.5; for doctorate, GRE or MAT, minimum GPA of 2.0 (undergraduate), 3.5 (graduate). *Application deadline:* Applications are

Educational Media/Instructional Technology

Widener University (continued)

processed on a rolling basis. Application fee: $25 ($300 for international students). Electronic applications accepted. *Expenses:* Contact institution. *Financial support:* Career-related internships or fieldwork, tuition waivers (full and partial), and unspecified assistantships available. Support available to part-time students. Financial award application deadline: 5/1. *Faculty research:* Reading and cognition, adult education, technology education, educational leadership, special education. *Unit head:* Dr. Michael W. LeDoux, Associate Dean, 610-499-4294, Fax: 610-499-4623, E-mail: mwledoux@widener.edu. *Application contact:* Dr. Roberta D. Nolan, Director of Graduate Admissions, 610-499-4125, E-mail: rdnolan@widener.edu.

Wilkes University, College of Graduate and Professional Studies, School of Education, Wilkes-Barre, PA 18766-0002. Offers classroom technology (MS Ed); educational computing (MS Ed); educational development and strategies (MS Ed); educational leadership (MS Ed); educational technology (Ed D); elementary education (MS Ed); higher education administration (Ed D); instructional technology (MS Ed); K-12 administration (Ed D); online teaching (MS Ed); school business leadership (MS Ed); secondary education (MS Ed), including biology, chemistry, English, history; special education (MS Ed). Part-time and evening/weekend programs available. Postbaccalaureate distance learning degree programs offered (minimal on-campus study). *Students:* 89 full-time (60 women), 2,849 part-time (2,058 women); includes 52 minority (10 African Americans, 2 American Indian/Alaska Native, 13 Asian Americans or Pacific Islanders, 27 Hispanic Americans), 6 international. Average age 33. In 2009, 947 master's awarded. *Entrance requirements:* Additional exam requirements/recommendations for international students: Required—TOEFL (minimum score 500 paper-based; 173 computer-based; 79 iBT). *Application deadline:* Applications are processed on a rolling basis. Application fee: $45. *Expenses:* Contact institution. *Financial support:* Federal Work-Study and unspecified assistantships available. Financial award application deadline: 3/1; financial award applicants required to submit FAFSA. *Unit head:* Dr. Michael Speziale, Dean, 570-408-4679, Fax: 570-408-4905, E-mail: michael.speziale@wilkes.edu. *Application contact:* Kathleen Houlihan, Director of Graduate Studies, 570-408-3235, Fax: 570-408-7846, E-mail: kathleen.houlihan@wilkes.edu.

Wilmington University, College of Education, New Castle, DE 19720-6491. Offers applied education technology (M Ed); career and technical education (M Ed); elementary and secondary school counseling (M Ed); elementary special education (M Ed); elementary studies (M Ed); instruction: gifted and talented (M Ed); instruction: teaching and learning (M Ed); literacy (M Ed); reading (M Ed); school leadership (M Ed); secondary teaching (MAT). *Accreditation:* NCATE. Part-time and evening/weekend programs available. *Entrance requirements:* For master's, 2 letters of recommendation, interview. Additional exam requirements/recommendations for international students: Required—TOEFL (minimum score 500 paper-based; 173 computer-based). Electronic applications accepted.

Youngstown State University, Graduate School, Beeghly College of Education, Department of Teacher Education, Youngstown, OH 44555-0001. Offers adolescent/young adult education (MS Ed); content area concentration (MS Ed); early childhood education (MS Ed); educational technology (MS Ed); literacy (MS Ed); middle childhood education (MS Ed); special education (MS Ed), including gifted and talented education, special education. *Accreditation:* NCATE. Part-time and evening/weekend programs available. *Degree requirements:* For master's, comprehensive exam. *Entrance requirements:* For master's, GRE, MAT, or teaching certificate; minimum GPA of 2.7. Additional exam requirements/recommendations for international students: Required—TOEFL. *Faculty research:* Multicultural literacy, hands-on mathematics teaching, integrated instruction, reading comprehension, emergent curriculum.

Educational Policy

Alabama State University, School of Graduate Studies, College of Education, Department of Instructional Support, Program in Educational Administration, Montgomery, AL 36101-0271. Offers educational administration (M Ed, Ed S); educational leadership, policy and law (Ed D). Part-time programs available. *Degree requirements:* For master's, comprehensive exam, thesis optional; for Ed S, thesis. *Entrance requirements:* For master's, GRE General Test, MAT, graduate writing competency test; for Ed S, graduate writing competency test, GRE, MAT. Additional exam requirements/recommendations for international students: Required—TOEFL (minimum score 500 paper-based; 173 computer-based). *Faculty research:* Nontraditional roles, computer applications for principals, women in educational administration.

The College of William and Mary, School of Education, Program in Education Policy, Planning, and Leadership, Williamsburg, VA 23187-8795. Offers curriculum and educational technology (Ed D, PhD); curriculum leadership (Ed D, PhD); educational leadership (M Ed), including higher education administration (M Ed, Ed D, PhD), K-12 administration and supervision; educational policy, planning, and leadership (Ed D, PhD), including general education administration, gifted education administration, higher education administration (M Ed, Ed D, PhD), special education administration; gifted education administration (M Ed). *Accreditation:* NCATE. Part-time and evening/weekend programs available. *Faculty:* 12 full-time (6 women), 3 part-time/adjunct (1 woman). *Students:* 41 full-time (26 women), 134 part-time (93 women); includes 35 minority (32 African Americans, 3 Asian Americans or Pacific Islanders), 2 international. Average age 38. 108 applicants, 57% accepted, 44 enrolled. In 2009, 20 master's, 22 doctorates awarded. *Degree requirements:* For doctorate, comprehensive exam, thesis/dissertation. *Entrance requirements:* For master's, GRE or MAT, minimum GPA of 2.5; for doctorate, GRE or MAT, minimum GPA of 3.0. Additional exam requirements/recommendations for international students: Required—TOEFL. *Application deadline:* For fall admission, 1/15 for domestic and international students. Application fee: $45. Electronic applications accepted. *Expenses:* Tuition, state resident: full-time $6400; part-time $315 per credit hour. Tuition, nonresident: full-time $19,720; part-time $840 per credit hour. Required fees: $4114. *Financial support:* In 2009–10, 56 students received support, including 32 research assistantships with full and partial tuition reimbursements available (averaging $13,000 per year); career-related internships or fieldwork, Federal Work-Study, institutionally sponsored loans, scholarships/grants, and unspecified assistantships also available. Support available to part-time students. Financial award application deadline: 1/15; financial award applicants required to submit FAFSA. *Faculty research:* Higher education policy, faculty incentives, history of adversity, resilience, leadership. *Unit head:* Dr. Megan Tschannen-Moran, Area Coordinator, 757-221-2187, E-mail: mxtsch@wm.edu. *Application contact:* Dorothy Smith Osborne, Director of Admissions, 757-221-2317, Fax: 757-221-2293, E-mail: dsosbo@wm.edu.

Florida State University, The Graduate School, College of Education, Department of Educational Leadership and Policy Studies, Tallahassee, FL 32306-4452. Offers educational leadership/administration (MS, Ed D, PhD, Ed S), including educational administration/leadership; educational policy and planning analysis (PhD, Ed S); higher education (MS, Ed D, PhD, Ed S), including higher education; program evaluation (MS, PhD, Ed S); social, history and philosophy of education (MS, PhD, Ed S), including history and philosophy of education, international and intercultural education (PhD); sociocultural and international developmental education (MS, PhD, Ed S). Part-time and evening/weekend programs available. *Faculty:* 15 full-time (8 women), 15 part-time/adjunct (10 women). *Students:* 130 full-time (75 women), 148 part-time (95 women); includes 71 minority (47 African Americans, 1 American Indian/Alaska Native, 6 Asian Americans or Pacific Islanders, 17 Hispanic Americans), 22 international. Average age 24. 154 applicants, 60% accepted, 52 enrolled. In 2009, 60 master's, 7 doctorates, 2 other advanced degrees awarded. Terminal master's awarded for partial completion of doctoral program. *Degree requirements:* For master's and Ed S, comprehensive exam, thesis optional; for doctorate, comprehensive exam, thesis/dissertation. *Entrance requirements:* For master's, doctorate, and Ed S, GRE General Test, minimum GPA of 3.0. Additional exam requirements/recommendations for international students: Required—TOEFL (minimum score 550 paper-based; 213 computer-based; 80 iBT). *Application deadline:* For fall admission, 5/1 priority date for domestic and international students; for winter admission, 10/1 priority date for domestic and international students; for spring admission, 2/1 priority date for domestic and international students. Application fee: $30. Electronic applications accepted. *Expenses:* Tuition, state resident: full-time $7413. Tuition, nonresident: full-time $22,567. *Financial support:* In 2009–10, 3 fellowships with full and partial tuition reimbursements, 18 research assistantships with full and partial tuition reimbursements, 52 teaching assistantships with full and partial tuition reimbursements were awarded; career-related internships or fieldwork and scholarships/grants also available. Financial award applicants required to submit FAFSA. *Faculty research:* Study and implementation of educational policy on all applicable levels, from neighborhood schools to international agencies. *Unit head:* Dr. Patrice Iatrola, Chair, 850-644-6777, Fax: 850-644-1258, E-mail: iatrola@coe.fsu.edu. *Application contact:* Jimmy Pastrano, Program Assistant, 850-644-6777, Fax: 850-644-1258, E-mail: pastrano@coe.fsu.edu.

The George Washington University, Graduate School of Education and Human Development, Department of Educational Leadership, Program in Educational Administration and Policy Studies, Washington, DC 20052. Offers education policy (Ed D); educational administration (Ed D). Educational administration program offered at Newport News and Alexandria, VA. *Accreditation:* NCATE. *Students:* 6 full-time (3 women), 150 part-time (96 women); includes 62 minority (51 African Americans, 4 Asian Americans or Pacific Islanders, 7 Hispanic Americans), 7 international. Average age 40. 62 applicants, 50% accepted, 18 enrolled. In 2009, 21 doctorates awarded. *Degree requirements:* For doctorate, comprehensive exam, thesis/dissertation. *Entrance requirements:* For doctorate, GRE General Test or MAT, interview, minimum GPA of 3.3. *Application deadline:* For fall admission, 1/15 priority date for domestic students; for spring admission, 10/1 for domestic students. Applications are processed on a rolling basis. Application fee: $60. *Financial support:* In 2009–10, 9 students received support; fellowships, research assistantships, teaching assistantships, career-related internships or fieldwork, Federal Work-Study, and tuition waivers (partial) available. Financial award application deadline: 1/15; financial award applicants required to submit FAFSA. *Unit head:* Prof. Yas Nakib, Program Coordinator, 202-994-8816, E-mail: nakib@gwu.edu. *Application contact:* Sarah Lang, 202-994-1447, Fax: 202-994-7207, E-mail: slang@gwu.edu.

The George Washington University, Graduate School of Education and Human Development, Department of Educational Leadership, Program in Education Policy Studies, Washington, DC 20052. Offers MA Ed. *Accreditation:* NCATE. *Students:* 11 full-time (8 women), 14 part-time (13 women); includes 1 minority (African American). Average age 26. 63 applicants, 79% accepted, 12 enrolled. In 2009, 8 master's awarded. *Degree requirements:* For master's, comprehensive exam. *Entrance requirements:* For master's, GRE General Test or MAT, interview, minimum GPA of 2.75. *Application deadline:* For fall admission, 1/15 priority date for domestic students; for spring admission, 10/1 for domestic students. Applications are processed on a rolling basis. Application fee: $60. *Financial support:* In 2009–10, 10 students received support; fellowships, career-related internships or fieldwork, Federal Work-Study, and tuition waivers (partial) available. Financial award application deadline: 1/15. *Unit head:* Prof. Yas Nakib, Coordinator, 202-994-8816, E-mail: nakib@gwu.edu. *Application contact:* Sarah Lang, Director of Graduate Admissions, 202-994-1447, Fax: 202-994-7207, E-mail: slang@gwu.edu.

Georgia State University, College of Education, Department of Educational Policy Studies, Atlanta, GA 30302-3083. Offers educational leadership (M Ed, PhD, Ed S); educational research (MS, PhD), including educational research (MS), research, measurements and statistics (PhD); social foundations of education (MS, PhD). Part-time and evening/weekend programs available. *Degree requirements:* For master's, thesis or project; for doctorate, thesis/dissertation. *Entrance requirements:* For master's, GRE General Test, minimum GPA of 2.5, 2 letters of recommendation, resume; for doctorate, GRE General Test or MAT, minimum GPA of 3.3, goal statement, 2 letters of recommendation, resumé; for Ed S, GRE General Test or MAT, minimum GPA of 3.25, goal statement, 1 letter of recommendation. Electronic applications accepted. *Faculty research:* Policy studies, organizational studies, education and culture.

Harvard University, Graduate School of Education, Master's Programs in Education, Cambridge, MA 02138. Offers arts in education (Ed M); education policy and management (Ed M); higher education (Ed M); human development and psychology (Ed M); international education policy (Ed M); language and literacy (Ed M); learning and teaching (Ed M); mid-career mathematics and science (teaching certificate) (Ed M); mind brain and education (Ed M); risk and prevention (Ed M); school leadership (Ed M); special studies (Ed M); teaching and curriculum (teaching certificate) (Ed M); technology innovation and education (Ed M). Part-time programs available. *Faculty:* 70 full-time (33 women), 36 part-time/adjunct (20 women). *Students:* 598 full-time (448 women), 76 part-time (60 women); includes 132 minority (40 African Americans, 2 American Indian/Alaska Native, 58 Asian Americans or Pacific Islanders, 32 Hispanic Americans), 103 international. Average age 28. 1,574 applicants, 58% accepted, 640 enrolled. In 2009, 556 master's awarded. *Entrance requirements:* For master's, GRE General Test, 3 letters of recommendation. Additional exam requirements/recommendations for international students: Required—TOEFL (minimum score 600 paper-based; 250 computer-based; 100 iBT), TWE (minimum score 5). *Application deadline:* For fall admission, 1/4 for domestic and international students. Application fee: $85. Electronic applications accepted. *Expenses:* Contact institution. *Financial support:* In 2009–10, 424 students received support, including 25 fellowships with full and partial tuition reimbursements available (averaging $15,890 per year); career-related internships or fieldwork, Federal Work-Study, institutionally sponsored loans, scholarships/grants, health care benefits, tuition waivers (full and partial), and unspecified assistantships also available. Support available to part-time students. Financial award application deadline: 2/1; financial award applicants required to submit FAFSA. *Faculty research:* Learning and development, educational leadership and organizations, educational policy analysis. Total annual research expenditures: $18.1 million. *Unit head:* Jennifer L. Petrallia, Assistant Dean, 617-495-8445. *Application contact:* Information Contact, 617-495-3414, Fax: 617-496-3577, E-mail: gseadmissions@harvard.edu.

Illinois State University, Graduate School, College of Education, Department of Curriculum and Instruction, Normal, IL 61790-2200. Offers curriculum and instruction (MS, MS Ed, Ed D); educational policies (Ed D); postsecondary education (Ed D); reading (MS Ed); supervision (Ed D). *Accreditation:* NCATE. *Degree requirements:* For master's, variable foreign language requirement, thesis or alternative; for doctorate, variable foreign language requirement, thesis/dissertation, 2 terms of residency, internship. *Entrance requirements:* For master's, GRE General Test, minimum GPA of 3.0 in last 60 hours of course work; for doctorate, GRE General Test. *Faculty research:* In-service and pre-service teacher education for teachers of English language learners; teachers for all children: developing a model for alternative, bilingual elementary certification for paraprofessionals in Illinois; Illinois Geographic Alliance, Connections Project.

Indiana University Bloomington, School of Education, Department of Educational Leadership and Policy Studies, Bloomington, IN 47405-7000. Offers education policy studies (PhD); educational leadership (MS, Ed D, PhD, Ed S); higher education (MS, Ed D, PhD); history and

philosophy of education (MS); history of education (PhD); international and comparative education (MS, PhD); philosophy of education (PhD); student affairs administration (MS). *Accreditation:* NCATE. Part-time and evening/weekend programs available. *Faculty:* 31 full-time (16 women), 8 part-time/adjunct (4 women). *Students:* 195 full-time (120 women), 102 part-time (53 women); includes 78 minority (49 African Americans, 1 American Indian/Alaska Native, 6 Asian Americans or Pacific Islanders, 22 Hispanic Americans), 29 international. Average age 33. 331 applicants, 77% accepted, 75 enrolled. In 2009, 61 master's, 21 doctorates, 7 other advanced degrees awarded. *Degree requirements:* For master's, thesis optional; for doctorate, comprehensive exam, thesis/dissertation; for Ed S, comprehensive exam or project. *Entrance requirements:* For master's, doctorate, and Ed S, GRE General Test. Additional exam requirements/recommendations for international students: Required—TOEFL (minimum score 213 computer-based; 79 iBT). *Application deadline:* For fall admission, 1/15 priority date for domestic students, 12/1 priority date for international students; for spring admission, 9/1 priority date for domestic and international students. Applications are processed on a rolling basis. Application fee: $55 ($65 for international students). Electronic applications accepted. *Financial support:* In 2009–10, 73 students received support, including 34 fellowships with full and partial tuition reimbursements available (averaging $7,677 per year), 16 research assistantships with full and partial tuition reimbursements available (averaging $17,757 per year), 23 teaching assistantships with full and partial tuition reimbursements available (averaging $13,496 per year); career-related internships or fieldwork, Federal Work-Study, institutionally sponsored loans, and tuition waivers (full and partial) also available. Support available to part-time students. *Faculty research:* Student engagement at higher education institutions in the nation, Reading First professional development initiative, state finance policy on financial access to higher education, school reform, special needs studies. *Unit head:* Martha McCarthy, Chair, 812-856-8377. *Application contact:* Sandy Strain, Department Secretary, 812-856-8360, Fax: 812-856-8394, E-mail: strain@indiana.edu.

Loyola University Chicago, School of Education, Program in Cultural and Educational Policy Studies, Chicago, IL 60660. Offers M Ed, MA, Ed D, PhD. Part-time programs available. *Faculty:* 4 full-time (1 woman), 4 part-time/adjunct (2 women). *Students:* 75. Average age 30. 71 applicants, 48% accepted, 20 enrolled. In 2009, 8 master's, 6 doctorates awarded. *Degree requirements:* For master's, comprehensive exam (M Ed), thesis (MA); for doctorate, comprehensive exam, thesis/dissertation, oral candidacy exam. *Entrance requirements:* For master's, letters of recommendation, minimum GPA of 3.0; for doctorate, GRE General Test or MAT, interview, letter of recommendation, resume, minimum GPA of 3.0. Additional exam requirements/recommendations for international students: Required—TOEFL (minimum score 550 paper-based; 218 computer-based; 79 iBT). *Application deadline:* For fall admission, 7/1 for domestic and international students; for winter admission, 4/1 for domestic and international students; for spring admission, 11/1 for domestic and international students. Applications are processed on a rolling basis. Application fee: $50. *Expenses:* Tuition: Full-time $14,220; part-time $790 per credit hour. Required fees: $60 per semester hour. Tuition and fees vary according to program. *Financial support:* In 2009–10, 3 fellowships (averaging $13,000 per year), 6 research assistantships with full tuition reimbursements (averaging $11,000 per year) were awarded; career-related internships or fieldwork, Federal Work-Study, institutionally sponsored loans, and tuition waivers (partial) also available. Support available to part-time students. Financial award application deadline: 2/1; financial award applicants required to submit FAFSA. *Faculty research:* Politics of education, cultural foundations, policy studies, qualitative research methods, multicultural diversity. *Unit head:* Dr. Robert Roemer, Director, 312-915-6883, E-mail: rroemer@luc.edu. *Application contact:* Marie Rosin-Dittmar, Information Contact, 312-915-6800, E-mail: schleduc@luc.edu.

Michigan State University, The Graduate School, College of Education, Program in Educational Policy, East Lansing, MI 48824. Offers PhD. *Students:* 34 full-time (22 women); includes 7 minority (5 African Americans, 1 Asian American or Pacific Islander, 1 Hispanic American), 8 international. Average age 30. 25 applicants, 44% accepted. In 2009, 3 doctorates awarded. *Entrance requirements:* Additional exam requirements/recommendations for international students: Required—TOEFL. Electronic applications accepted. *Expenses:* Tuition, state resident: part-time $478.25 per credit hour. Tuition, nonresident: part-time $966.50 per credit hour. Part-time tuition and fees vary according to program. *Financial support:* In 2009–10, 28 research assistantships with tuition reimbursements (averaging $6,736 per year), 1 teaching assistantship with tuition reimbursement (averaging $6,922 per year) were awarded. *Unit head:* Dr. Michael W. Sedlak, Associate Dean, 517-432-1260, E-mail: msedlak@msu.edu. *Application contact:* Dr. Michael W. Sedlak, Associate Dean, 517-432-1260, E-mail: msedlak@msu.edu.

New York University, Steinhardt School of Culture, Education, and Human Development, Department of Humanities and Social Sciences in the Professions, Program in Sociology of Education, New York, NY 10012-1019. Offers education and social policy (MA); sociology of education (MA, PhD), including education policy (MA), social and cultural studies of education (MA). Part-time programs available. *Students:* 16 full-time (14 women), 7 part-time (4 women); includes 3 minority (1 African American, 1 American Indian/Alaska Native, 1 Hispanic American), 3 international. Average age 27. 35 applicants, 57% accepted, 6 enrolled. In 2009, 6 master's awarded. *Degree requirements:* For master's, thesis (for some programs); for doctorate, thesis/dissertation. *Entrance requirements:* For master's, letters of recommendation; for doctorate, GRE General Test, interview. Additional exam requirements/recommendations for international students: Required—TOEFL. *Application deadline:* For fall admission, 12/15 priority date for domestic and international students; for spring admission, 11/1 for domestic and international students. Applications are processed on a rolling basis. Application fee: $75. Electronic applications accepted. *Expenses:* Tuition: Full-time $30,528; part-time $1272 per credit. Required fees: $2177. *Financial support:* Fellowships with full and partial tuition reimbursements, Federal Work-Study, institutionally sponsored loans, scholarships/grants, and tuition waivers (partial) available. Support available to part-time students. Financial award application deadline: 2/1; financial award applicants required to submit FAFSA. *Faculty research:* Legal and institutional environments of schools; social inequality; high school reform and achievement; urban schooling, economics and education, educational policy . *Unit head:* Dr. Floyd M. Hammack, Program Director, 212-998-5542, Fax: 212-995-4832, E-mail: fmhl@nyu.edu. *Application contact:* 212-998-5030, Fax: 212-995-4328, E-mail: steinhardt.gradadmissions@nyu.edu.

The Ohio State University, Graduate School, College of Education and Human Ecology, School of Educational Policy and Leadership, Columbus, OH 43210. Offers M Ed, MA, PhD. *Accreditation:* NCATE. *Faculty:* 41. *Students:* 93 full-time (65 women), 203 part-time (136 women); includes 66 minority (47 African Americans, 1 American Indian/Alaska Native, 6 Asian Americans or Pacific Islanders, 12 Hispanic Americans), 20 international. Average age 35. In 2009, 72 master's, 21 doctorates awarded. *Degree requirements:* For master's, thesis optional; for doctorate, thesis/dissertation. *Entrance requirements:* For doctorate, GRE General Test. Additional exam requirements/recommendations for international students: Required—TOEFL (minimum score 600 paper-based; 250 computer-based). *Application deadline:* For fall admission, 8/15 priority date for domestic students, 7/1 priority date for international students; for winter admission, 12/1 priority date for domestic students, 11/1 priority date for international students; for spring admission, 3/1 priority date for domestic students, 2/1 priority date for international students. Applications are processed on a rolling basis. Application fee: $40 ($50 for international students). Electronic applications accepted. *Expenses:* Tuition, state resident: full-time $10,683. Tuition, nonresident: full-time $25,923. Tuition and fees vary according to course load and program. *Financial support:* Fellowships, research assistantships, teaching assistantships, Federal Work-Study, institutionally sponsored loans, and unspecified assistantships available. Support available to part-time students. *Unit head:* Eric Anderman, Interim Director, 614-688-4007, Fax: 614-292-5721, E-mail: anderman.1@osu.edu. *Application contact:* 614-292-9444, Fax: 614-292-3895, E-mail: domestic.grad@osu.edu.

Penn State University Park, Graduate School, College of Education, Department of Education Policy Studies, State College, University Park, PA 16802-1503. Offers M Ed, MA, MS, D Ed, PhD. *Accreditation:* NCATE.

Portland State University, Graduate Studies, School of Education, Department of Educational Policy, Foundations, and Administrative Studies, Portland, OR 97207-0751. Offers educational leadership (MA, MS, Ed D); postsecondary, adult and continuing education (Ed D). *Accreditation:* NCATE. Part-time and evening/weekend programs available. *Degree requirements:* For master's, thesis or alternative, written exam or research project; for doctorate, comprehensive exam, thesis/dissertation. *Entrance requirements:* For master's, California Basic Educational Skills Test, minimum GPA of 3.0 in upper-division course work or 2.75 overall; for doctorate, GRE General Test or MAT. Additional exam requirements/recommendations for international students: Required—TOEFL (minimum score 550 paper-based; 213 computer-based). *Faculty research:* Leadership development and research, principals and urban schools, accelerated schools, cooperative learning, family involvement in schools.

Rutgers, The State University of New Jersey, Camden, Graduate School of Arts and Sciences, Department of Public Policy and Administration, Camden, NJ 08102-1401. Offers education policy and leadership (MPA); international public service and development (MPA); public management (MPA); JD/MPA; MPA/MA. *Accreditation:* NASPAA. Part-time and evening/weekend programs available. *Degree requirements:* For master's, directed study, research workshop. *Entrance requirements:* For master's, GRE General Test, GMAT or LSAT, 3 letters of recommendation; resume. Additional exam requirements/recommendations for international students: Required—TOEFL (minimum score 550 paper-based; 213 computer-based), IELTS. Electronic applications accepted. *Faculty research:* Nonprofit management, county and municipal administration, health and human services, government communication, administrative law, educational finance.

Rutgers, The State University of New Jersey, New Brunswick, Graduate School of Education, Doctoral Program in Education, Piscataway, NJ 08854-8097. Offers educational policy (PhD); educational psychology (PhD); literacy education (PhD); mathematics education (PhD). Part-time programs available. *Degree requirements:* For doctorate, thesis/dissertation, qualifying exam. *Entrance requirements:* For doctorate, GRE General Test, GRE Subject Test (mathematics education). Additional exam requirements/recommendations for international students: Required—TOEFL (minimum score 575 paper-based; 233 computer-based; 83 iBT). Electronic applications accepted. *Faculty research:* Literacy education, math education, educational psychology, educational policy.

Teachers College, Columbia University, Graduate Faculty of Education, Department of Organization and Leadership, Program in Leadership, Policy and Politics, New York, NY 10027-6696. Offers MA, ME, Ed D.

Universidad Central del Este, Graduate School, San Pedro de Macoris, Dominican Republic. Offers administration (M Ad); dentistry (DMD); development of educational and social policies (PhD); environmental engineering (ME); financial management (M Ad); higher education (M Ed); human resources (M Ad); public health (MPH). *Entrance requirements:* For master's, letters of recommendation.

University of Alberta, Faculty of Graduate Studies and Research, Department of Educational Policy Studies, Edmonton, AB T6G 2E1, Canada. Offers adult education (M Ed, Ed D, PhD); educational administration and leadership (M Ed, Ed D, PhD, Postgraduate Diploma); First Nations education (M Ed, Ed D, PhD); theoretical, cultural and international studies in education (M Ed, Ed D, PhD). *Faculty:* 19 full-time (10 women), 5 part-time/adjunct (1 woman). *Students:* 73 full-time (47 women), 144 part-time (86 women). 141 applicants, 44% accepted. In 2009, 52 master's, 20 doctorates awarded. *Degree requirements:* For master's, thesis (for some programs); for doctorate, thesis/dissertation. *Entrance requirements:* For master's, minimum GPA of 6.5 on a 9.0 scale; for doctorate, minimum GPA of 7.5 on a 9.0 scale. Additional exam requirements/recommendations for international students: Required—TOEFL (minimum score 580 paper-based; 237 computer-based). *Application deadline:* For spring admission, 2/1 for domestic and international students. Electronic applications accepted. Tuition and fees charges are reported in Canadian dollars. *Expenses:* Tuition, area resident: Full-time $4626 Canadian dollars; part-time $99.72 Canadian dollars per unit. International tuition: $8216 Canadian dollars full-time. Required fees: $3590 Canadian dollars; $99.72 Canadian dollars per unit. $215 Canadian dollars per term. *Financial support:* In 2009–10, 7 fellowships with partial tuition reimbursements, 10 research assistantships with partial tuition reimbursements (averaging $6,936 per year), 30 teaching assistantships with partial tuition reimbursements (averaging $11,130 per year) were awarded; scholarships/grants and unspecified assistantships also available. *Unit head:* Dr. Frank Peters, Graduate Coordinator, 780-492-3679, Fax: 780-492-2024, E-mail: epscoord@ualberta.ca. *Application contact:* Joan A. White, Secretary, 780-492-3679, Fax: 780-492-2024, E-mail: joan.white@ualberta.ca.

University of Arkansas, Graduate School, College of Education and Health Professions, Program in Education Policy, Fayetteville, AR 72701-1201. Offers PhD. *Students:* 6 full-time (0 women). *Expenses:* Tuition, state resident: full-time $7355; part-time $356.58 per hour. Tuition, nonresident: full-time $17,401; part-time $775.17 per hour. Required fees: $1203. *Unit head:* Dr. Michael Daugherty, Department Head, 479-575-4209, E-mail: mkd03@uark.edu. *Application contact:* Dr. William McComas, Graduate Admissions, 479-575-7525, E-mail: mccomas@uark.edu.

The University of British Columbia, Faculty of Education, Department of Educational Studies, Vancouver, BC V6T 1Z1, Canada. Offers adult education (M Ed, MA); adult learning and global change (M Ed); educational administration (M Ed, MA); educational leadership and policy (Ed D); educational studies (PhD); higher education (M Ed, MA); society, culture and politics in education (M Ed, MA). Part-time and evening/weekend programs available. Terminal master's awarded for partial completion of doctoral program. *Degree requirements:* For master's, thesis; for doctorate, comprehensive exam, thesis/dissertation, master's thesis. *Entrance requirements:* For master's, minimum B+ average, 4-year undergraduate degree, field-related experience; for doctorate, minimum B+ average, 4-year undergraduate degree, master's degree, field-related experience. Additional exam requirements/recommendations for international students: Required—TOEFL (600 paper; 250 computer; 100 Internet-based) or IELTS (6.5). Electronic applications accepted. *Faculty research:* Educational leadership educational administration adult education politics in education, global change and adult learning.

University of California, Riverside, Graduate Division, Graduate School of Education, Riverside, CA 92521-0102. Offers autism (M Ed); curriculum and instruction (MA, PhD); diversity and equity (M Ed); educational leadership and policy (MA, PhD); educational psychology (MA, PhD); general education (M Ed); higher education administration and policy (M Ed, PhD); leadership (M Ed); reading (M Ed); school psychology (PhD); special education (M Ed, MA, PhD). *Faculty:* 23 full-time (12 women), 12 part-time/adjunct (8 women). *Students:* 230 full-time (183 women), 6 part-time (3 women); includes 75 minority (12 African Americans, 1 American Indian/Alaska Native, 21 Asian Americans or Pacific Islanders, 41 Hispanic Americans), 6 international. Average age 32. 288 applicants, 60% accepted, 118 enrolled. In 2009, 68 master's, 13 doctorates awarded. Terminal master's awarded for partial completion of doctoral program. *Degree requirements:* For master's, comprehensive exam (for some programs), comprehensive exams or thesis (MA), case study or analytical report (M Ed); for doctorate, thesis/dissertation, written and oral qualifying exams, college teaching practicum. *Entrance requirements:* For master's, GRE General Test, GRE Subject Test, CBEST, CSET, minimum GPA of 3.2; for doctorate, GRE General Test, GRE Subject Test, master's degree (desirable), minimum GPA of 3.2. Additional exam requirements/recommendations for international students: Required—TOEFL (minimum score 550 paper-based; 213 computer-based; 80 iBT). *Application deadline:* For fall admission, 9/1 for domestic students, 4/1 for international students; for winter admission, 12/1 for domestic students, 9/1 for international students; for spring admission, 3/1 for domestic students, 10/1 for international students. Applications are processed on a rolling basis. Application fee: $70 ($85 for international students). Electronic applications accepted. *Financial support:* In 2009–10, 55 students received support, including 13 fellowships with full and partial tuition reimbursements available (averaging $26,809 per year), 21 research assistantships with full and partial tuition reimbursements available (averaging $14,238 per year), 1 teaching assistantship with full and partial tuition reimbursement available (averaging $16,638 per year); career-related internships or fieldwork, Federal Work-Study, institutionally sponsored

Educational Policy

University of California, Riverside (continued)
loans, scholarships/grants, and unspecified assistantships also available. Financial award application deadline: 1/5; financial award applicants required to submit FAFSA. *Faculty research:* Responsiveness to intervention, faculty core, response to intervention of English language learners, advanced modeling techniques, study on social capital, trust, and motivation. Total annual research expenditures: $5.6 million. *Unit head:* Dr. Steven T. Bossert, Dean, 951-827-5802, Fax: 951-827-3942, E-mail: steven.bossert@ucr.edu. *Application contact:* Dr. John Wills, Graduate Advisor for Admission, 951-827-6362, Fax: 951-827-3942, E-mail: edgrad@ucr.edu.

University of California, Santa Cruz, Division of Graduate Studies, Division of Social Sciences, Department of Education, Santa Cruz, CA 95064. Offers education (MA); language and literacy studies (PhD); mathematics and science education (PhD); social context and policy studies of education (PhD). Terminal master's awarded for partial completion of doctoral program. *Degree requirements:* For master's, thesis; for doctorate, thesis/dissertation. *Faculty research:* Bilingual/multicultural education, special education, curriculum and instruction, child development.

University of Georgia, Graduate School, College of Education, Department of Lifelong Education, Administration and Policy, Athens, GA 30602. Offers adult education (M Ed, Ed D, PhD, Ed S); educational administration and policy (M Ed, PhD, Ed S); educational leadership (Ed D); human resource and organizational design (M Ed). *Accreditation:* NCATE. *Faculty:* 26 full-time (17 women). *Students:* 77 full-time (55 women), 181 part-time (124 women); includes 64 minority (54 African Americans, 1 American Indian/Alaska Native, 4 Asian Americans or Pacific Islanders, 5 Hispanic Americans), 28 international. 199 applicants, 60% accepted, 77 enrolled. In 2009, 43 master's, 21 doctorates, 5 other advanced degrees awarded. *Entrance requirements:* For master's and Ed S, GRE General Test or MAT; for doctorate, GRE General Test. *Application deadline:* For fall admission, 7/1 priority date for domestic students; for spring admission, 11/15 for domestic students. Application fee: $50. Electronic applications accepted. *Expenses:* Tuition, state resident: full-time $6000; part-time $250 per credit hour. Tuition, nonresident: full-time $20,904; part-time $871 per credit hour. Required fees: $730 per semester. *Unit head:* Dr. Ronald M. Cervero, Head, 706-542-2221, Fax: 706-542-5873, E-mail: rcervero@uga.edu. *Application contact:* Dr. Kathryn Roulston, Graduate Coordinator, 706-542-4060, Fax: 706-542-5873, E-mail: roulston@uga.edu.

University of Hawaii at Manoa, Graduate Division, College of Education, Doctorate in Education Program, Honolulu, HI 96822. Offers curriculum and instruction (PhD); educational administration (PhD); educational foundations (PhD); educational policy studies (PhD); educational technology (PhD); exceptionalities (PhD); kinesiology (PhD). Part-time and evening/weekend programs available. *Faculty:* 65 full-time (40 women), 28 part-time/adjunct (17 women). *Students:* 74 full-time (44 women), 119 part-time (77 women); includes 101 minority (5 African Americans, 2 American Indian/Alaska Native, 86 Asian Americans or Pacific Islanders, 8 Hispanic Americans), 17 international. Average age 38. 98 applicants, 53% accepted, 35 enrolled. In 2009, 11 doctorates awarded. *Degree requirements:* For doctorate, thesis/dissertation. *Entrance requirements:* For doctorate, GRE General Test, sample of written work. Additional exam requirements/recommendations for international students: Required—TOEFL (minimum score 600 paper-based; 250 computer-based; 100 iBT), IELTS (minimum score 7). *Application deadline:* For fall admission, 2/1 for domestic students, 1/15 for international students. Application fee: $50. *Expenses:* Tuition, state resident: full-time $8900; part-time $372 per credit. Tuition, nonresident: full-time $21,400; part-time $898 per credit. Required fees: $207 per semester. *Financial support:* In 2009–10, 1 student received support, including 11 fellowships (averaging $4,147 per year), 17 research assistantships (averaging $17,392 per year), 4 teaching assistantships (averaging $14,670 per year); career-related internships or fieldwork, Federal Work-Study, and tuition waivers (full and partial) also available. *Application contact:* Dr. Helen Slaughter, Chairperson, 808-956-7913, Fax: 808-956-9905, E-mail: slaughte@hawaii.edu.

University of Illinois at Chicago, Graduate College, College of Education, Department of Educational Policy Studies, Chicago, IL 60607-7128. Offers policy studies (M Ed); policy studies in urban education (PhD); urban education leadership (Ed D).

University of Illinois at Urbana–Champaign, Graduate College, College of Education, Department of Educational Policy Studies, Champaign, IL 61820. Offers Ed M, MA, PhD. Part-time programs available. Postbaccalaureate distance learning degree programs offered. *Faculty:* 15 full-time (5 women). *Students:* 116 full-time (74 women), 135 part-time (87 women); includes 113 minority (59 African Americans, 6 American Indian/Alaska Native, 12 Asian Americans or Pacific Islanders, 36 Hispanic Americans), 24 international. 166 applicants, 50% accepted, 47 enrolled. In 2009, 28 master's, 10 doctorates awarded. *Entrance requirements:* Additional exam requirements/recommendations for international students: Required—TOEFL (minimum score 590 paper-based; 243 computer-based). *Application deadline:* Applications are processed on a rolling basis. Application fee: $60 ($75 for international students). Electronic applications accepted. *Financial support:* In 2009–10, 32 fellowships, 34 research assistantships, 56 teaching assistantships were awarded; tuition waivers (full and partial) also available. *Unit head:* James D. Anderson, Head, 217-333-7404, Fax: 217-244-7064, E-mail: janders@illinois.edu. *Application contact:* Linda Michelle Meccoli, Clerical Assistant, 217-333-9449, Fax: 217-244-7064, E-mail: lmeccoli@illinois.edu.

The University of Iowa, Graduate College, College of Education, Department of Educational Policy and Leadership Studies, Iowa City, IA 52242-1316. Offers educational administration (MA, PhD, Ed S); higher education (MA, PhD, Ed S); social foundations (MA, PhD); JD/PhD. *Degree requirements:* For master's and Ed S, exam; for doctorate, comprehensive exam, thesis/dissertation. *Entrance requirements:* For master's, doctorate, and Ed S, GRE General Test, minimum GPA of 3.0. Additional exam requirements/recommendations for international students: Required—TOEFL (minimum score 550 paper-based; 213 computer-based; 81 iBT). Electronic applications accepted.

The University of Kansas, Graduate Studies, School of Education, Department of Educational Leadership and Policy Studies, Program in Educational Policy and Leadership, Lawrence, KS 66045-3101. Offers educational administration (Ed D, PhD); foundations (PhD); higher education (Ed D, PhD); policy studies (PhD). Part-time and evening/weekend programs available. *Students:* 116 full-time (70 women), 58 part-time (32 women); includes 28 minority (12 African Americans, 4 American Indian/Alaska Native, 7 Asian Americans or Pacific Islanders, 5 Hispanic Americans), 9 international. Average age 38. 69 applicants, 68% accepted, 39 enrolled. In 2009, 11 doctorates awarded. *Degree requirements:* For doctorate, comprehensive exam, thesis/dissertation. *Entrance requirements:* For doctorate, GRE General Test, minimum graduate GPA of 3.5. Additional exam requirements/recommendations for international students: Required—TOEFL (minimum score 570 paper-based; 230 computer-based; 80 iBT). *Application deadline:* For fall admission, 7/1 for domestic and international students; for spring admission, 11/1 for domestic and international students. Applications are processed on a rolling basis. Application fee: $45 ($55 for international students). Electronic applications accepted. *Expenses:* Tuition, state resident: full-time $6492; part-time $270.50 per credit hour. Tuition, nonresident: full-time $15,510; part-time $646.25 per credit hour. Required fees: $847; $70.56 per credit hour. Tuition and fees vary according to course load and program. *Financial support:* Fellowships, research assistantships with full and partial tuition reimbursements, teaching assistantships with full and partial tuition reimbursements, scholarships/grants and unspecified assistantships available. Financial award application deadline: 3/15. *Faculty research:* Historical and philosophical issues in education, education policy and leadership, higher education faculty, research on college students, education technology. *Unit head:* Dr. Susan Twombly, Chair, 785-864-9721, Fax: 785-864-4697, E-mail: stwombly@ku.edu. *Application contact:* Denise Brubaker, Admissions Coordinator, 785-864-4458, Fax: 785-864-4697, E-mail: elps@ku.edu.

University of Kentucky, Graduate School, College of Education, Program in Educational Policy Studies and Evaluation, Lexington, KY 40506-0032. Offers educational policy studies and evaluation (Ed D); higher education (MS Ed, PhD). *Accreditation:* NCATE. Terminal master's awarded for partial completion of doctoral program. *Degree requirements:* For master's, comprehensive exam, thesis optional; for doctorate, comprehensive exam, thesis/dissertation. *Entrance requirements:* For master's, GRE General Test, minimum undergraduate GPA of 2.75; for doctorate, GRE General Test, minimum graduate GPA of 3.0. Additional exam requirements/recommendations for international students: Required—TOEFL (minimum score 550 paper-based; 213 computer-based). Electronic applications accepted. *Faculty research:* Studies in higher education; comparative and international education; evaluation of educational programs, policies, and reform; student, teacher, and faculty cultures; gender and education.

University of Maryland, Baltimore County, Graduate School, College of Arts, Humanities and Social Sciences, Department of Public Policy, Program in Public Policy, Baltimore, MD 21250. Offers economics (PhD); education (MPP, PhD); evaluation (MPP); health (MPP, PhD); legal (MPP, PhD); management (MPP, PhD); urban (MPP, PhD). Part-time and evening/weekend programs available. *Faculty:* 40 full-time (12 women), 2 part-time/adjunct (1 woman). *Students:* 57 full-time (34 women), 114 part-time (61 women); includes 47 minority (26 African Americans, 21 Hispanic Americans). Average age 33. 89 applicants, 47% accepted, 24 enrolled. In 2009, 12 master's, 5 doctorates awarded. Terminal master's awarded for partial completion of doctoral program. *Degree requirements:* For master's, thesis optional, public analysis paper; for doctorate, comprehensive exam, thesis/dissertation, comprehensive and field qualifying exams. *Entrance requirements:* For master's, GRE General Test, 3 academic letters of reference, transcripts, resume; for doctorate, GRE General Test, 3 academic letters of reference, transcripts, resume, research paper. Additional exam requirements/recommendations for international students: Required—TOEFL (minimum score 550 paper-based; 213 computer-based; 80 iBT). *Application deadline:* For fall admission, 1/15 priority date for domestic students, 1/1 priority date for international students; for spring admission, 11/1 priority date for domestic students, 5/1 priority date for international students. Applications are processed on a rolling basis. Application fee: $50. Electronic applications accepted. *Financial support:* In 2009–10, 32 students received support, including 1 fellowship (averaging $3,000 per year), 17 research assistantships with full tuition reimbursements available (averaging $17,400 per year); career-related internships or fieldwork, Federal Work-Study, scholarships/grants, health care benefits, and unspecified assistantships also available. Support available to part-time students. Financial award application deadline: 2/1; financial award applicants required to submit FAFSA. *Faculty research:* Health policy, education policy, urban policy, public management, evaluation and analytical method. *Unit head:* Dr. Donald Norris, Chair, 410-455-1455, E-mail: norris@umbc.edu. *Application contact:* Sally F. Helms, Administrator of Academic Affairs, 410-455-3202, Fax: 410-455-1172, E-mail: gradposi@umbc.edu.

University of Maryland, College Park, Academic Affairs, College of Education, Department of Education Policy Studies, College Park, MD 20742. Offers M Ed, MA, PhD. *Faculty:* 6 full-time (3 women), 5 part-time/adjunct (2 women). *Students:* 9 full-time (7 women), 7 part-time (all women); includes 4 minority (1 African American, 2 Asian Americans or Pacific Islanders, 1 Hispanic American), 2 international. 65 applicants, 34% accepted, 11 enrolled. *Application deadline:* For fall admission, 12/15 for domestic and international students; for spring admission, 6/1 for domestic and international students. *Expenses:* Tuition, area resident: Part-time $471 per credit hour. Tuition, state resident: part-time $471 per credit hour. Tuition, nonresident: part-time $1016 per credit hour. Required fees: $337.04 per term. *Financial support:* In 2009–10, 1 fellowship (averaging $7,504 per year), 1 research assistantship (averaging $15,863 per year), 3 teaching assistantships (averaging $15,707 per year) were awarded. Total annual research expenditures: $8,170. *Unit head:* Dr. Francine Hultgren, Interim Department Chair, 301-405-4562, E-mail: fh@umd.edu. *Application contact:* Dean of Graduate School, 301-405-0358, Fax: 301-314-9305.

University of Massachusetts Amherst, Graduate School, School of Education, Program in Education, Amherst, MA 01003. Offers bilingual, English as a second language, and multicultural education (M Ed, CAGS); child study and early education (M Ed); children, families and schools (Ed D, CAGS); early childhood and elementary teacher education (M Ed); education policy and leadership (CAGS); educational administration (M Ed, CAGS); educational policy and leadership (Ed D); higher education (M Ed, CAGS); international education (M Ed); language, literacy and culture (Ed D); learning, media and technology (M Ed, CAGS); mathematics, science, and learning technologies (Ed D); policy studies (M Ed); policy studies in education (CAGS); reading and writing (M Ed); research and evaluation methods (Ed D); school counselor education (M Ed, CAGS); school psychology (CAGS); science education (CAGS); secondary teacher education (M Ed); social justice education (M Ed, Ed D, CAGS); special education (M Ed, Ed D, CAGS). *Accreditation:* NCATE. Part-time programs available. Postbaccalaureate distance learning degree programs offered (minimal on-campus study). *Faculty:* 74 full-time (41 women). *Students:* 377 full-time (268 women), 347 part-time (232 women); includes 115 minority (59 African Americans, 2 American Indian/Alaska Native, 16 Asian Americans or Pacific Islanders, 38 Hispanic Americans), 108 international. Average age 35. 708 applicants, 68% accepted, 266 enrolled. In 2009, 183 master's, 17 doctorates awarded. Terminal master's awarded for partial completion of doctoral program. *Degree requirements:* For master's, thesis or alternative; for doctorate, comprehensive exam, thesis/dissertation. *Entrance requirements:* Additional exam requirements/recommendations for international students: Required—TOEFL (minimum score 550 paper-based; 213 computer-based; 80 iBT), IELTS (minimum score 6.5). *Application deadline:* For fall admission, 1/15 for domestic and international students. Applications are processed on a rolling basis. Application fee: $50 ($65 for international students). Electronic applications accepted. *Expenses:* Tuition, state resident: full-time $2640; part-time $110 per credit. Tuition, nonresident: full-time $9936; part-time $414 per credit. Tuition and fees vary according to course load. *Financial support:* In 2009–10, 1 fellowship with full tuition reimbursement (averaging $8,036 per year), 92 research assistantships with full tuition reimbursements (averaging $8,555 per year), 83 teaching assistantships with full tuition reimbursements (averaging $4,661 per year) were awarded; career-related internships or fieldwork, Federal Work-Study, scholarships/grants, traineeships, health care benefits, tuition waivers (full), and unspecified assistantships also available. Support available to part-time students. Financial award application deadline: 1/15. *Unit head:* Dr. Linda L. Griffin, Graduate Program Director, 413-545-6984, Fax: 413-545-2873. *Application contact:* Jean M. Ames, Supervisor of Admissions, 413-545-0722, Fax: 413-577-0010, E-mail: gradadm@grad.umass.edu.

University of Minnesota, Twin Cities Campus, Graduate School, College of Education and Human Development, Department of Organizational Leadership, Policy and Development, Minneapolis, MN 55455-0213. Offers adult education (M Ed, MA, Ed D, PhD, Certificate); agricultural, food and environmental education (M Ed, MA, Ed D, PhD); business and industry education (M Ed, MA, Ed D, PhD); business education (M Ed); comparative and international development education (MA, PhD); disability policy and services (Certificate); educational administration (MA, Ed D, PhD); evaluation studies (MA, PhD); higher education (MA, PhD); human resource development (M Ed, MA, Ed D, PhD, Certificate); marketing education (M Ed); postsecondary administration (Ed D); program evaluation (Certificate); school-to-work (Certificate); staff development (Certificate); teacher leadership (M Ed); technical education (Certificate); technology education (M Ed, MA); work and human resource education (M Ed, MA, Ed D, PhD); youth development leadership (M Ed). *Faculty:* 24 full-time (11 women). *Students:* 334 full-time (220 women), 479 part-time (307 women); includes 120 minority (60 African Americans, 9 American Indian/Alaska Native, 30 Asian Americans or Pacific Islanders, 21 Hispanic Americans), 92 international. Average age 38. 452 applicants, 79% accepted, 261 enrolled. In 2009, 109 master's, 55 doctorates, 134 other advanced degrees awarded. *Financial support:* In 2009–10, 4 fellowships (averaging $32,881 per year), 34 research assistantships with full tuition reimbursements (averaging $24,977 per year), 16 teaching assistantships with full tuition reimbursements (averaging $26,078 per year) were awarded. *Faculty research:* Organization effects of schools, postsecondary institutions and business entities on leadership; program evaluation in shaping organizational reforms; international human resource development and change; effects of gender and race/ethnicity on learning and leadership; effects of initiatives to develop intercultural sensitivity and global awareness; the development of theory and pedagogy in pre-K through graduate school and in work contexts (including adult education and literacy). Total annual research expenditures: $757,278. *Unit head:* Dr. Darwin Hendel,

Chair, 612-625-0129, Fax: 612-624-3377, E-mail: hende001@umn.edu. *Application contact:* Dr. Mary Trettin, Associate Dean, 612-625-6501, Fax: 612-626-1580, E-mail: mtrettin@umn.edu.

University of Pennsylvania, Graduate School of Education, Division of Policy, Management and Evaluation, Program in Education Policy, Philadelphia, PA 19104. Offers MS Ed, PhD. *Expenses:* Tuition: Full-time $25,660; part-time $4758 per course. Required fees: $2152; $270 per course. Tuition and fees vary according to course load, degree level and program.

University of Pittsburgh, School of Education, Learning Sciences and Policy Program, Pittsburgh, PA 15260. Offers PhD. Part-time and evening/weekend programs available. *Students:* 11 full-time (5 women), 2 international. Average age 30. 17 applicants, 29% accepted, 4 enrolled. *Degree requirements:* For doctorate, comprehensive exam, thesis/dissertation. *Entrance requirements:* Additional exam requirements/recommendations for international students: Required—TOEFL (minimum score 550 paper-based; 213 computer-based; 80 iBT). *Application deadline:* For fall admission, 2/1 priority date for domestic and international students; for spring admission, 11/15 for domestic students, 7/1 priority date for international students. Application fee: $50. *Expenses:* Tuition, state resident: full-time $16,402; part-time $665 per credit. Tuition, nonresident: full-time $28,694; part-time $1175 per credit. Required fees: $690; $175 per term. Tuition and fees vary according to program. *Financial support:* Fellowships with full and partial tuition reimbursements, research assistantships with full and partial tuition reimbursements, teaching assistantships with full and partial tuition reimbursements available. Financial award applicants required to submit FAFSA. *Unit head:* Dr. Mary Kay Stein, Head, 412-648-7116, E-mail: mkstein@pitt.edu. *Application contact:* Marianne L. Budziszewski, Director of Admissions and Enrollment Services, 412-648-7056, Fax: 412-648-1899, E-mail: soeinfo@pitt.edu.

University of St. Thomas, Graduate Studies, School of Education, Department of Leadership, Policy and Administration, St. Paul, MN 55105-1096. Offers athletics and activities administration (MA); community education administration (MA); critical pedagogy (Ed D); curriculum and instruction (Ed S); educational leadership (Ed S); educational leadership and administration (MA); international leadership (MA, Certificate); leadership (Ed D); leadership in student affairs (MA, Certificate); police leadership (MA); public policy and leadership (MA, Certificate). Part-time and evening/weekend programs available. *Faculty:* 8 full-time (3 women), 15 part-time/adjunct (7 women). *Students:* 36 full-time (29 women), 307 part-time (149 women); includes 44 minority (29 African Americans, 1 American Indian/Alaska Native, 11 Asian Americans or Pacific Islanders, 3 Hispanic Americans), 5 international. Average age 36. 398 applicants, 75% accepted, 267 enrolled. In 2009, 63 master's, 17 doctorates, 46 other advanced degrees awarded. Terminal master's awarded for partial completion of doctoral program. *Degree requirements:* For master's, thesis (for some programs); for doctorate, thesis/dissertation; for other advanced degree, thesis or alternative. *Entrance requirements:* For master's, minimum GPA of 3.0 or MAT; for doctorate, MAT, minimum graduate GPA of 3.5; for other advanced degree, minimum graduate GPA of 3.25 or MAT. Additional exam requirements/recommendations for international students: Required—TOEFL (minimum score 550 paper-based; 213 computer-based; 20 iBT). *Application deadline:* For fall admission, 6/1 priority date for domestic students; for spring admission, 11/1 priority date for domestic students. Applications are processed on a rolling basis. Application fee: $50. *Expenses:* Contact institution. *Financial support:* Fellowships, research assistantships, institutionally sponsored loans and scholarships/grants available. Support available to part-time students. Financial award applicants required to submit FAFSA. *Unit head:* Dr. Donald R. LaMagdeleine, Chair, 651-962-4893, Fax: 651-962-4169, E-mail: drlamagdelei@stthomas.edu. *Application contact:* Jackie Grossklaus, Department Assistant, 651-962-4885, Fax: 651-962-4169, E-mail: jmgrossklaus@stthomas.edu.

University of Southern California, Graduate School, Rossier School of Education, Doctor of Philosophy in Education Programs, Los Angeles, CA 90089. Offers educational psychology (PhD); higher education administration and policy (PhD); K-12 policy and practice (PhD). *Faculty:* 20 full-time (11 women). *Students:* 23 full-time (17 women); includes 12 minority (3 African Americans, 3 Asian Americans or Pacific Islanders, 6 Hispanic Americans), 1 international. 64 applicants, 17% accepted, 5 enrolled. In 2009, 14 doctorates awarded. *Degree requirements:* For doctorate, thesis/dissertation, qualifying exam, proposal and defense. *Entrance requirements:* For doctorate, GRE. Additional exam requirements/recommendations for international students: Required—TOEFL (minimum score 250 computer-based; 100 iBT). *Application deadline:* For fall admission, 12/1 for domestic and international students. Application fee: $85. Electronic applications accepted. *Expenses:* Tuition: Full-time $25,980; part-time $1315 per unit. Required fees: $554. One-time fee: $35 full-time. Full-time tuition and fees vary according to degree level and program. *Financial support:* In 2009–10, 5 fellowships with full tuition reimbursements (averaging $29,000 per year), 23 research assistantships with full tuition reimbursements (averaging $31,000 per year) were awarded; health care benefits and full tuition coverage for all required coursework, academic stipend, awards for professional development and academic conferences also available. *Faculty research:* Diversity in higher education, organizational change, educational psychology, policy and politics of educational reform, economics of education and education policy. *Unit head:* Dianne Morris, Director, 213-740-6303, Fax: 213-740-9433, E-mail: rsoephd@usc.edu. *Application contact:* Aba Cassell, 213-821-1517, Fax: 213-740-9433, E-mail: rossier.phd@usc.edu.

University of Washington, Graduate School, College of Education, Seattle, WA 98195. Offers curriculum and instruction (M Ed, Ed D, PhD), including educational technology, general curriculum (Ed D, PhD), language, literacy, and culture, mathematics education, multicultural education, reading and language arts education (Ed D), science education, social studies education, teaching and curriculum (M Ed); educational leadership and policy studies (M Ed, Ed D, PhD), including administration (Ed D), educational policy, organization, and leadership (M Ed, PhD), higher education, leadership for learning (Ed D), social and cultural foundations of education (M Ed, PhD); educational psychology (M Ed, PhD), including educational psychology (PhD), human development and cognition (M Ed), learning sciences, measurement, statistics and research design (M Ed), school psychology (M Ed); instructional leadership (M Ed); intercollegiate athletic leadership (M Ed); special education (M Ed, Ed D, PhD), including early childhood special education (M Ed), emotional and behavioral disabilities (M Ed), learning disabilities (M Ed), low-incidence disabilities (M Ed), severe disabilities (M Ed), special education (Ed D, PhD); teacher education (MIT). *Accreditation:* APA. Part-time and evening/weekend programs available. *Degree requirements:* For master's, thesis optional; for doctorate, thesis/dissertation. *Entrance requirements:* For master's and doctorate, GRE General Test, minimum GPA of 3.0. Additional exam requirements/recommendations for international students: Required—TOEFL. Electronic applications accepted. *Faculty research:* School restructuring/effective schools, special education interventions, literacy and writing, technology, school partnerships, teacher preparation.

The University of Western Ontario, Faculty of Graduate Studies, Social Sciences Division, Faculty of Education, Program in Educational Studies, London, ON N6A 5B8, Canada. Offers curriculum studies (M Ed); educational policy studies (M Ed); educational psychology/special education (M Ed). Part-time programs available. *Faculty research:* Reflective practice, gender and schooling, feminist pedagogy, narrative inquiry, second language, multiculturalism in Canada, education and law.

University of Wisconsin–Madison, Graduate School, School of Education, Department of Educational Leadership and Policy Analysis, Madison, WI 53706-1380. Offers administration (Certificate); educational policy (MS, PhD). *Degree requirements:* For doctorate, thesis/dissertation. *Entrance requirements:* For master's and doctorate, GRE General Test. *Application deadline:* For fall admission, 1/15 for domestic and international students. Application fee: $56. Electronic applications accepted. *Expenses:* Tuition, state resident: part-time $594 per credit. Tuition, nonresident: part-time $1504 per credit. Required fees: $65 per credit. Tuition and fees vary according to course load, program and reciprocity agreements. *Financial support:* Fellowships with full tuition reimbursements, research assistantships with full tuition reimbursements, teaching assistantships with full tuition reimbursements, project assistantships available. *Unit head:* Dr. Julie Mead, Chair, 608-262-3106. *Application contact:* Dr. Julie Mead, Chair, 608-262-3106.

University of Wisconsin–Madison, Graduate School, School of Education, Department of Educational Policy Studies, Madison, WI 53706-1380. Offers MA, PhD. *Degree requirements:* For doctorate, thesis/dissertation. *Entrance requirements:* For master's and doctorate, GRE General Test. *Application deadline:* For fall admission, 1/1 for domestic and international students; for spring admission, 10/15 for domestic and international students. Application fee: $56. Electronic applications accepted. *Expenses:* Tuition, state resident: part-time $594 per credit. Tuition, nonresident: part-time $1504 per credit. Required fees: $65 per credit. Tuition and fees vary according to course load, program and reciprocity agreements. *Financial support:* Project assistantships available. *Unit head:* Dr. Stacey Lee, Chair, 608-262-1760. *Application contact:* Dr. Stacey Lee, Chair, 608-262-1760.

Vanderbilt University, Peabody College, Department of Leadership, Policy, and Organizations, Nashville, TN 37240-1001. Offers education policy (MPP); educational leadership and policy (Ed D); higher education (M Ed); higher education, leadership and policy (Ed D); human resource development (M Ed); international education policy and management (M Ed); organizational leadership (M Ed). Part-time and evening/weekend programs available. *Faculty:* 28 full-time (13 women), 8 part-time/adjunct (3 women). *Students:* 155 full-time (111 women), 95 part-time (52 women); includes 36 minority (27 African Americans, 6 Asian Americans or Pacific Islanders, 3 Hispanic Americans), 21 international. Average age 31. 298 applicants, 76% accepted, 94 enrolled. In 2009, 65 master's, 21 doctorates awarded. *Degree requirements:* For master's, comprehensive exam, thesis optional; for doctorate, thesis/dissertation, qualifying exams, residency. *Entrance requirements:* For master's and doctorate, GRE General Test. Additional exam requirements/recommendations for international students: Required—TOEFL (minimum score 550 paper-based; 213 computer-based). *Application deadline:* For fall admission, 12/31 priority date for domestic and international students; for spring admission, 11/1 priority date for domestic and international students. Applications are processed on a rolling basis. Application fee: $0. Electronic applications accepted. *Financial support:* In 2009–10, 155 students received support, including 3 fellowships with full and partial tuition reimbursements available, 61 research assistantships with full and partial tuition reimbursements available, 1 teaching assistantship with full and partial tuition reimbursement available; Federal Work-Study, institutionally sponsored loans, scholarships/grants, tuition waivers (partial), and unspecified assistantships also available. Support available to part-time students. Financial award application deadline: 2/1; financial award applicants required to submit FAFSA. *Faculty research:* Education and leadership policy, education finances/economics of education, higher education leadership and policy, educator pay for performance and school choice, international and comparative education and policy management. *Unit head:* Dr. Ellen B. Goldring, Chair, 615-322-8000, Fax: 615-343-7094, E-mail: ellen.b.goldring@vanderbilt.edu. *Application contact:* Rosie Moody, Educational Coordinator, 615-322-8019, Fax: 615-343-7094, E-mail: rosie.moody@vanderbilt.edu.

Virginia Commonwealth University, Graduate School, School of Education, Doctoral Program in Education, Richmond, VA 23284-9005. Offers educational leadership (PhD); educational psychology (PhD); instructional leadership (PhD); research and evaluation (PhD); special education and disability leadership (PhD); urban services leadership (PhD). *Accreditation:* NCATE. Part-time programs available. *Degree requirements:* For doctorate, thesis/dissertation. *Entrance requirements:* For doctorate, GRE, interview, master's degree, writing sample.

Wayne State University, College of Education, Division of Administrative and Organizational Studies, Detroit, MI 48202. Offers administration and supervision-secondary (Ed S); college and university teaching (Certificate); curriculum and instruction (PhD); educational leadership (M Ed, Ed S); educational leadership and policy studies (Ed D, PhD); elementary education curriculum and instruction (MA, Ed S); general administration and supervision (Ed D, PhD, Ed S); higher education (Ed D, PhD); instructional technology (M Ed, Ed D, PhD, Ed S); secondary curriculum and instruction (M Ed, Ed S). *Degree requirements:* For doctorate, thesis/dissertation. *Entrance requirements:* For doctorate, interview, minimum GPA of 3.0, an autobiography or curriculum vitae; references. Additional exam requirements/recommendations for international students: Required—TOEFL (minimum score 550 paper-based; 213 computer-based), TWE (minimum score 6). Electronic applications accepted. *Faculty research:* Total quality management, participatory management, administering educational technology, school improvement, principalship.

Educational Psychology

Alliant International University–Irvine, Graduate School of Education, Educational Psychology Programs, Irvine, CA 92612. Offers educational psychology (Psy D); pupil personnel services (Credential); school psychology (MA). Part-time programs available. *Degree requirements:* For doctorate, thesis/dissertation. *Entrance requirements:* For master's, minimum GPA of 3.0, letters of recommendation; for doctorate, interview, minimum GPA of 3.0, letters of recommendation. Additional exam requirements/recommendations for international students: Required—TOEFL (minimum score 550 paper-based; 213 computer-based), TWE (minimum score 5). *Faculty research:* School based mental health.

Alliant International University–Los Angeles, Graduate School of Education, Educational Psychology Programs, Alhambra, CA 91803-1360. Offers educational psychology (Psy D); pupil personnel services (Credential); school psychology (MA). Part-time programs available. *Degree requirements:* For doctorate, thesis/dissertation. *Entrance requirements:* For master's, minimum GPA of 3.0, letters of recommendation; for doctorate, interview, minimum GPA of 3.0, letters of recommendation. Additional exam requirements/recommendations for international students: Required—TOEFL (minimum score 550 paper-based; 213 computer-based), TWE (minimum score 5). Electronic applications accepted. *Faculty research:* Early identification and intervention with high-risk preschoolers, pediatric neuropsychology, interpersonal violence, ADHD, learning theories.

Alliant International University–San Diego, Graduate School of Education, Educational Psychology Programs, San Diego, CA 92131-1799. Offers educational psychology (Psy D); pupil personnel services (Credential); school psychology (MA); student personnel services (Certificate). Part-time programs available. *Degree requirements:* For doctorate, thesis/dissertation. *Entrance requirements:* For master's, minimum GPA of 3.0, letters of recommendation; for doctorate, interview, letters of recommendation. Additional exam requirements/recommendations for international students: Required—TOEFL (minimum score 550 paper-based; 213 computer-based), TWE (minimum score 5). Electronic applications accepted.

Alliant International University–San Francisco, Graduate School of Education, Educational Psychology Programs, San Francisco, CA 94133-1221. Offers educational psychology (Psy D); pupil personnel services (Credential); school psychology (MA). Part-time programs available.

Educational Psychology

Alliant International University–San Francisco (continued)
Degree requirements: For doctorate, thesis/dissertation. *Entrance requirements:* For master's, minimum GPA of 3.0, letters of recommendation; for doctorate, interview, minimum GPA of 3.0, letters of recommendation. Additional exam requirements/recommendations for international students: Required—TOEFL (minimum score 550 paper-based; 213 computer-based), TWE (minimum score 5). Electronic applications accepted. *Faculty research:* Social skills, ADHD, effects of sightedness on areas of knowledge.

American International College, School of Arts, Education and Sciences, Department of Psychology, Springfield, MA 01109-3189. Offers clinical psychology (MA); educational psychology (MA, Ed D); forensic psychology (MS). Part-time and evening/weekend programs available. *Degree requirements:* For master's, comprehensive exam (for some programs), thesis (for some programs), practicum. *Entrance requirements:* For master's, minimum GPA of 3.0; for doctorate, GRE General Test, interview. Additional exam requirements/recommendations for international students: Required—TOEFL. Electronic applications accepted. *Expenses:* Tuition: Full-time $12,510; part-time $695 per credit hour. Required fees: $35 per term.

Andrews University, School of Graduate Studies, School of Education, Department of Educational and Counseling Psychology, Program in Educational and Developmental Psychology, Berrien Springs, MI 49104. Offers educational and developmental psychology (MA); educational psychology (Ed D, PhD). *Students:* 9 full-time (7 women), 10 part-time (7 women); includes 9 minority (5 African Americans, 1 Asian American or Pacific Islander, 3 Hispanic Americans), 4 international. Average age 34. 16 applicants, 75% accepted, 8 enrolled. In 2009, 2 master's awarded. *Degree requirements:* For master's, thesis optional. *Entrance requirements:* For master's, GRE. Additional exam requirements/recommendations for international students: Required—TOEFL (minimum score 550 paper-based). *Application deadline:* Applications are processed on a rolling basis. Application fee: $40. *Unit head:* Dr. Jimmy Kijai, Coordinator, 269-471-6240. *Application contact:* Carolyn Hurst, Supervisor of Graduate Admission, 800-253-2874, Fax: 269-471-6321, E-mail: graduate@andrews.edu.

Arcadia University, Graduate Studies, Department of Education, Glenside, PA 19038-3295. Offers art education (M Ed, MA Ed); biology education (MA Ed); chemistry education (MA Ed); child development (CAS); computer education (M Ed, CAS); computer education 7–12 (MA Ed); early childhood education (M Ed, CAS), including individualized (M Ed), master teacher (M Ed), research in child development (M Ed); educational leadership (M Ed, CAS); educational psychology (CAS); elementary education (M Ed, CAS); English education (MA Ed); environmental education (MA Ed, CAS); history education (MA Ed); language arts (M Ed, CAS); mathematics education (M Ed, MA Ed, CAS); music education (MA Ed); psychology (MA Ed); pupil personnel services (CAS); reading (M Ed, CAS); school library science (M Ed); science education (M Ed, CAS); secondary education (M Ed, CAS); special education (M Ed, Ed D, CAS); theater arts (MA Ed); written communication (MA Ed). *Accreditation:* NASAD. Part-time and evening/weekend programs available. Postbaccalaureate distance learning degree programs offered (minimal on-campus study). *Faculty:* 12 full-time (8 women), 38 part-time/adjunct (26 women). *Students:* 89 full-time (74 women), 622 part-time (487 women); includes 112 minority (94 African Americans, 9 Asian Americans or Pacific Islanders, 9 Hispanic Americans), 2 international. Average age 32. In 2009, 257 master's, 4 doctorates awarded. *Application deadline:* Applications are processed on a rolling basis. Application fee: $40. Electronic applications accepted. *Expenses:* Tuition: Full-time $30,450; part-time $620 per credit hour. Required fees: $165. Tuition and fees vary according to program. *Financial support:* Career-related internships or fieldwork, tuition waivers (partial), and unspecified assistantships available. *Unit head:* Dr. Steven P. Gulkus. *Application contact:* 215-572-2925, Fax: 215-572-2126, E-mail: grad@arcadia.edu.

Arizona State University, Graduate College, Mary Lou Fulton College of Education, Division of Psychology in Education, Program in Educational Psychology, Tempe, AZ 85287. Offers M Ed, MA, PhD. *Accreditation:* APA. *Degree requirements:* For master's, thesis; for doctorate, thesis/dissertation. *Entrance requirements:* For master's and doctorate, GRE General Test or MAT.

Auburn University, Graduate School, College of Education, Department of Educational Foundations, Leadership, and Technology, Auburn University, AL 36849. Offers adult education (M Ed, MS, Ed D); curriculum and instruction (M Ed, MS, Ed D, Ed S); curriculum supervision (M Ed, MS, Ed D, Ed S); educational psychology (PhD); higher education administration (M Ed, MS, Ed D, Ed S); media instructional design (MS); media specialist (M Ed); school administration (M Ed, MS, Ed D, Ed S). *Accreditation:* NCATE. Part-time programs available. *Faculty:* 21 full-time (11 women), 6 part-time/adjunct (4 women). *Students:* 68 full-time (40 women), 175 part-time (103 women); includes 87 minority (84 African Americans, 1 Asian American or Pacific Islander, 2 Hispanic Americans), 8 international. Average age 37. 112 applicants, 65% accepted, 53 enrolled. In 2009, 31 master's, 12 doctorates, 1 other advanced degree awarded. *Degree requirements:* For master's, thesis (for some programs); for doctorate, thesis/dissertation; for Ed S, field project. *Entrance requirements:* For master's, doctorate, and Ed S, GRE General Test. *Application deadline:* For fall admission, 7/7 for domestic students; for spring admission, 11/24 for domestic students. Applications are processed on a rolling basis. Application fee: $50 ($60 for international students). Electronic applications accepted. *Expenses:* Tuition, state resident: full-time $6240. Tuition, nonresident: full-time $18,720. International tuition: $18,938 full-time. Required fees: $492. Tuition and fees vary according to course load, program and reciprocity agreements. *Financial support:* Teaching assistantships, Federal Work-Study available. Support available to part-time students. Financial award application deadline: 3/15; financial award applicants required to submit FAFSA. *Unit head:* Dr. Jose Llanes, Head, 334-844-4460. *Application contact:* Dr. George Flowers, Dean of the Graduate School, 334-844-4700.

Ball State University, Graduate School, Teachers College, Department of Educational Psychology, Program in Educational Psychology, Muncie, IN 47306-1099. Offers MA, PhD, Ed S. *Accreditation:* NCATE. *Degree requirements:* For doctorate, thesis/dissertation; for Ed S, thesis. *Entrance requirements:* For master's and Ed S, GRE General Test; for doctorate, GRE General Test, minimum graduate GPA of 3.2.

Baylor University, Graduate School, School of Education, Department of Educational Psychology, Waco, TX 76798. Offers MA, MS Ed, PhD, Ed S. *Accreditation:* NCATE. Part-time programs available. *Faculty:* 6 full-time (3 women), 2 part-time/adjunct (1 woman). *Students:* 36 full-time (30 women), 11 part-time (8 women); includes 10 minority (5 African Americans, 1 Asian American or Pacific Islander, 4 Hispanic Americans), 3 international. In 2009, 5 master's, 4 other advanced degrees awarded. *Degree requirements:* For doctorate, thesis/dissertation. *Entrance requirements:* For master's, GRE General Test; for doctorate, GRE General Test, master's degree. *Application deadline:* For fall admission, 8/1 for domestic students. Applications are processed on a rolling basis. Application fee: $25. *Financial support:* Federal Work-Study and institutionally sponsored loans available. *Faculty research:* Medical education, cross-cultural learning disabilities, characteristics of an ideal special education teacher, verbal following behavior in adult counseling groups. *Unit head:* Dr. Terrill Saxon, Chair, 254-710-3112, Fax: 254-710-3987, E-mail: terrill_saxon@baylor.edu. *Application contact:* Angela Love, Administrative Assistant, 254-710-3112, Fax: 254-710-3870, E-mail: angela_love@baylor.edu.

Boston College, Lynch Graduate School of Education, Department of Counseling Psychology, Developmental, and Educational Psychology, Program in Developmental and Educational Psychology, Chestnut Hill, MA 02467-3800. Offers MA, PhD. Part-time and evening/weekend programs available. *Students:* 15 full-time (13 women), 30 part-time (all women); includes 7 minority (1 African American, 3 Asian Americans or Pacific Islanders, 3 Hispanic Americans), 9 international. 122 applicants, 48% accepted, 26 enrolled. In 2009, 19 master's, 3 doctorates awarded. Terminal master's awarded for partial completion of doctoral program. *Degree requirements:* For master's, comprehensive exam; for doctorate, comprehensive exam, thesis/dissertation. *Entrance requirements:* For master's and doctorate, GRE General Test. Additional exam requirements/recommendations for international students: Required—TOEFL (minimum score 550 paper-based; 213 computer-based; 81 iBT). Application fee: $60. Electronic applications accepted. *Financial support:* Fellowships with full and partial tuition reimbursements, research assistantships with full and partial tuition reimbursements, teaching assistantships with full and partial tuition reimbursements, career-related internships or fieldwork, Federal Work-Study, scholarships/grants, traineeships, health care benefits, tuition waivers (full and partial), and unspecified assistantships available. Support available to part-time students. Financial award applicants required to submit FAFSA. *Faculty research:* Cognitive learning and culture, effects of social policy reform on children and families, psychosocial trauma, human rights and international justice; positive youth development; children and adolescents living in poverty. *Unit head:* Dr. M. Brinton Lykes, Chairperson, 617-552-4214, Fax: 617-552-0812. *Application contact:* Adam Poluzzi, Director, Graduate Admission and Financial Aid, 617-552-4214, Fax: 617-552-0398, E-mail: poluzzi@bc.edu.

Brigham Young University, Graduate Studies, David O. McKay School of Education, Department of Instructional Psychology and Technology, Provo, UT 84602. Offers MS, PhD. *Faculty:* 9 full-time (0 women), 10 part-time/adjunct (2 women). *Students:* 50 full-time (22 women), 36 part-time (16 women); includes 3 minority (1 Asian American or Pacific Islander, 2 Hispanic Americans), 12 international. Average age 35. 23 applicants, 74% accepted, 15 enrolled. In 2009, 7 master's, 6 doctorates awarded. *Degree requirements:* For master's, thesis; for doctorate, comprehensive exam, thesis/dissertation. *Entrance requirements:* For master's and doctorate, GRE General Test. Additional exam requirements/recommendations for international students: Required—TOEFL. *Application deadline:* For fall and winter admission, 2/1 for domestic and international students. Application fee: $50. Electronic applications accepted. *Expenses:* Tuition: Full-time $5580; part-time $301 per credit hour. Tuition and fees vary according to student's religious affiliation. *Financial support:* In 2009–10, 32 students received support, including 9 research assistantships with full and partial tuition reimbursements available (averaging $10,000 per year), 15 teaching assistantships with full and partial tuition reimbursements available (averaging $6,000 per year); career-related internships or fieldwork, scholarships/grants, tuition waivers (full and partial), and unspecified assistantships also available. Support available to part-time students. *Faculty research:* Interactive learning, learning theory, instructional designed development, research and evaluation, measurement. *Unit head:* Dr. Andrew S. Gibbons, Chair, 801-422-5097, Fax: 801-422-0314, E-mail: andy_gibbons@byu.edu. *Application contact:* Michele Bray, Department Secretary, 801-422-2746, Fax: 801-422-0314, E-mail: michele_bray@byu.edu.

California Coast University, Programs in Education, Santa Ana, CA 92701. Offers administration (M Ed); curriculum and instruction (M Ed); educational psychology (D Ed); organizational leadership (D Ed). Part-time and evening/weekend programs available. Postbaccalaureate distance learning degree programs offered (no on-campus study). Application fee: $75. *Application contact:* Christi Okuma, 714-547-9625, Fax: 714-547-5777, E-mail: ccu@calcoast.edu.

California State University, Long Beach, Graduate Studies, College of Education, Department of Advanced Studies in Education and Counseling, Long Beach, CA 90840. Offers counseling (MS), including marriage and family therapy, school counseling, student development in higher education; education (MA, Ed D); educational administration (MA, Ed D); educational psychology (MA); special education (MS). Part-time and evening/weekend programs available. *Students:* 386 full-time (289 women), 430 part-time (319 women); includes 462 minority (90 African Americans, 4 American Indian/Alaska Native, 130 Asian Americans or Pacific Islanders, 238 Hispanic Americans), 17 international. Average age 33. 757 applicants, 28% accepted, 174 enrolled. *Entrance requirements:* For master's, GRE General Test, minimum GPA of 2.75. *Application deadline:* For fall admission, 3/1 for domestic students. Applications are processed on a rolling basis. Application fee: $55. Electronic applications accepted. *Expenses:* Required fees: $1802 per semester. Part-time tuition and fees vary according to course load. *Financial support:* Federal Work-Study, institutionally sponsored loans, and scholarships/grants available. Financial award application deadline: 3/2.

California State University, Northridge, Graduate Studies, College of Education, Department of Educational Psychology and Counseling, Northridge, CA 91330. Offers counseling (MS), including career counseling, college counseling and student services, marriage and family therapy, school counseling, school psychology; educational psychology (MA Ed), including development, learning, and instruction, early childhood education. *Accreditation:* ACA (one or more programs are accredited); NCATE. Part-time and evening/weekend programs available. *Faculty:* 19 full-time (11 women), 42 part-time/adjunct (26 women). *Students:* 341 full-time (301 women), 135 part-time (121 women); includes 21 African Americans, 31 Asian Americans or Pacific Islanders, 149 Hispanic Americans, 11 international. Average age 31. 498 applicants, 39% accepted, 167 enrolled. In 2009, 119 master's awarded. *Entrance requirements:* For master's, GRE General Test or minimum GPA of 3.0. Additional exam requirements/recommendations for international students: Required—TOEFL. *Application deadline:* For fall admission, 11/30 for domestic students. Application fee: $55. *Financial support:* Scholarships/grants available. Support available to part-time students. Financial award application deadline: 3/1. *Unit head:* Dr. Shari Tarver-Behring, Chair, 818-677-2599. *Application contact:* Dr. Shari Tarver-Behring, Chair, 818-677-2599.

Capella University, Harold Abel School of Psychology, Minneapolis, MN 55402. Offers child and adolescent development (MS); clinical psychology (MS, Psy D); counseling psychology (MS); educational psychology (MS, PhD); evaluation, research, and measurement (MS); general psychology (MS, PhD); industrial/organizational psychology (MS, PhD); leadership coaching psychology (MS); organizational leader development (MS); school psychology (MS); sport psychology (MS). Part-time and evening/weekend programs available. Postbaccalaureate distance learning degree programs offered (minimal on-campus study). Terminal master's awarded for partial completion of doctoral program. *Degree requirements:* For master's, thesis optional, project; for doctorate, thesis/dissertation. *Entrance requirements:* For degree, master's degree in school psychology. Additional exam requirements/recommendations for international students: Required—TOEFL (minimum score 550 paper-based; 213 computer-based), TWE (minimum score 4); Recommended—IELTS. Electronic applications accepted.

The Catholic University of America, School of Arts and Sciences, Department of Education, Washington, DC 20064. Offers Catholic educational leadership (PhD); education (Certificate); educational psychology (PhD); learning and instruction (MA); secondary education (MA); special education (MA). *Accreditation:* NCATE. Part-time programs available. *Faculty:* 11 full-time (8 women), 3 part-time/adjunct (0 women). *Students:* 6 full-time (5 women), 56 part-time (39 women); includes 9 minority (5 African Americans, 2 Asian Americans or Pacific Islanders, 2 Hispanic Americans), 2 international. Average age 38. 54 applicants, 59% accepted, 14 enrolled. In 2009, 14 master's, 6 doctorates, 1 other advanced degree awarded. *Degree requirements:* For master's, comprehensive exam, thesis or alternative; for doctorate, comprehensive exam, thesis/dissertation. *Entrance requirements:* For master's and doctorate, GRE General Test or MAT, statement of purpose, official copies of academic transcripts, three letters of recommendation. Additional exam requirements/recommendations for international students: Required—TOEFL (minimum score 580 paper-based; 237 computer-based). *Application deadline:* For fall admission, 8/1 priority date for domestic students, 7/15 for international students; for spring admission, 12/1 priority date for domestic students, 10/15 for international students. Applications are processed on a rolling basis. Application fee: $55. Electronic applications accepted. *Expenses:* Tuition: Full-time $31,740; part-time $1245 per credit hour. Required fees: $50; $25 per semester hour. One-time fee: $425. *Financial support:* Fellowships, research assistantships, teaching assistantships, Federal Work-Study, scholarships/grants, tuition waivers (full and partial), and unspecified assistantships available. Financial award application deadline: 2/1; financial award applicants required to submit FAFSA. *Faculty research:* Catholic school issues, reflective teaching, cognitive psychology, urban education. Total annual research expenditures: $68,905. *Unit head:* Dr. Merylann J. Schuttloffel, Chair, 202-319-5805, Fax: 202-319-5815, E-mail: schuttloffel@cua.edu. *Application contact:* Julie Schwing, Director of Graduate Admissions, 202-319-5057, Fax: 202-319-6533, E-mail: cua-admissions@cua.edu.

Chapman University, Graduate Studies, College of Educational Studies, Program in School Psychology, Orange, CA 92866. Offers educational psychology (MA); school psychology

(Ed S). Part-time and evening/weekend programs available. *Faculty:* 24 full-time (15 women), 25 part-time/adjunct (16 women). *Students:* 41 full-time (38 women), 16 part-time (15 women); includes 26 minority (9 Asian Americans or Pacific Islanders, 17 Hispanic Americans). Average age 27. 52 applicants, 38% accepted, 11 enrolled. In 2009, 40 master's awarded. *Degree requirements:* For master's, comprehensive exam. *Entrance requirements:* For master's, GRE General Test, MAT, or California Subject Examinations for Teachers, minimum undergraduate GPA of 2.75. Additional exam requirements/recommendations for international students: Required—TOEFL (minimum score 550 paper-based). *Application deadline:* Applications are processed on a rolling basis. Application fee: $55. Electronic applications accepted. *Expenses:* Contact institution. *Financial support:* Fellowships, Federal Work-Study and scholarships/grants available. Financial award application deadline: 6/30; financial award applicants required to submit FAFSA. *Unit head:* Dr. Michael Hass, Coordinator, 714-997-6781, E-mail: hass@chapman.edu. *Application contact:* Rika Judd, Information Contact, 714-997-6786, Fax: 714-997-6713, E-mail: rjudd@chapman.edu.

Clark Atlanta University, School of Education, Department of Counseling and Psychological Studies, Atlanta, GA 30314. Offers MA. Part-time programs available. *Faculty:* 5 full-time (4 women). *Students:* 18 full-time (13 women), 28 part-time (22 women); includes 43 minority (42 African Americans, 1 Hispanic American), 1 international. Average age 28. 31 applicants, 81% accepted, 11 enrolled. In 2009, 10 master's awarded. *Degree requirements:* For master's, comprehensive exam. *Entrance requirements:* For master's, GRE General Test, minimum undergraduate GPA of 2.6. Additional exam requirements/recommendations for international students: Required—TOEFL (minimum score 500 paper-based, 173 computer-based). *Application deadline:* For fall admission, 4/1 for domestic and international students; for spring admission, 11/1 for domestic and international students. Applications are processed on a rolling basis. Application fee: $40 ($55 for international students). Electronic applications accepted. *Expenses:* Tuition: Full-time $12,240; part-time $680 per credit hour. Required fees: $710; $355 per semester. *Financial support:* Career-related internships or fieldwork, Federal Work-Study, scholarships/grants, and unspecified assistantships available. Support available to part-time students. Financial award application deadline: 4/30; financial award applicants required to submit FAFSA. *Unit head:* Dr. Jill Thompson, Chairperson, 404-880-7519, E-mail: jthompson@cau.edu. *Application contact:* Michelle Clark-Davis, Graduate Program Admissions, 404-880-6605, E-mail: cauadmissions@cau.edu.

The College of Saint Rose, Graduate Studies, School of Education, Educational and School Psychology Department, Albany, NY 12203-1419. Offers applied technology education (MS Ed); educational psychology (MS Ed); school psychology (MS, Certificate). Part-time and evening/weekend programs available. *Entrance requirements:* For master's, minimum undergraduate GPA of 3.0. Additional exam requirements/recommendations for international students: Required—TOEFL (minimum score 550 paper-based; 213 computer-based). Electronic applications accepted.

Dowling College, Graduate Programs in Education, Oakdale, NY 11769-1999. Offers adolescence education (MS Ed), including educational administration; advanced certificate in gifted education (AC); childhood and early childhood education (MS Ed); childhood education (MS Ed); educational administration (AC, PD), including computers in education (PD); school administration and supervision (PD), school district administration (PD); educational technology specialist (AC); literacy (MS Ed); literacy/special education (MS Ed); secondary education (MS Ed); special education (MS Ed). *Accreditation:* NCATE. Part-time and evening/weekend programs available. Postbaccalaureate distance learning degree programs offered. *Faculty:* 32 full-time (18 women), 98 part-time/adjunct (59 women). *Students:* 563 full-time (393 women), 885 part-time (668 women); includes 133 minority (47 African Americans, 2 American Indian/Alaska Native, 10 Asian Americans or Pacific Islanders, 74 Hispanic Americans). Average age 32. 363 applicants, 89% accepted, 213 enrolled. In 2009, 459 master's, 85 ACs awarded. *Degree requirements:* For master's and other advanced degree, comprehensive exam. *Entrance requirements:* For master's, minimum GPA of 3.0; for other advanced degree, teaching certificate. Additional exam requirements/recommendations for international students: Required—TOEFL (minimum score 550 paper-based). *Application deadline:* For fall admission, 9/1 priority date for domestic students; for winter admission, 1/1 priority date for domestic students; for spring admission, 2/1 priority date for domestic students. Applications are processed on a rolling basis. Application fee: $50. Electronic applications accepted. *Expenses:* Tuition: Full-time $14,490; part-time $805 per credit. Required fees: $346 per term. *Financial support:* Career-related internships or fieldwork and Federal Work-Study available. Support available to part-time students. Financial award application deadline: 6/30; financial award applicants required to submit FAFSA. *Faculty research:* Natural readers, Korean styles and learning strategies, mothers of children with disabilities, computers in instruction, cultural background and organizational roadblocks to problem solving. *Unit head:* Dr. Clyde Payne, Dean of the School of Education, 631-244-3404, Fax: 631-589-6644, E-mail: paynec@dowling.edu. *Application contact:* Glenn M. Berman, Assistant Vice President for Enrollment Services/Dean of Admissions, 631-244-3357, Fax: 631-244-1059, E-mail: glenn.berman@dowling.edu.

Eastern Michigan University, Graduate School, College of Education, Department of Teacher Education, Programs in Educational Psychology and Assessment, Ypsilanti, MI 48197. Offers educational assessment (Graduate Certificate); educational psychology (MA), including development/personality, research and assessment, research and evaluation, the developing learner. *Accreditation:* NCATE. Part-time and evening/weekend programs available. Postbaccalaureate distance learning degree programs offered (minimal on-campus study). *Students:* 17 part-time (14 women); includes 1 minority (African American). Average age 34. In 2009, 2 master's awarded. *Degree requirements:* For master's, thesis or alternative. *Entrance requirements:* For master's, GRE. Additional exam requirements/recommendations for international students: Required—TOEFL. *Application deadline:* Applications are processed on a rolling basis. Application fee: $35. Tuition and fees vary according to course level. *Financial support:* Fellowships, research assistantships with full tuition reimbursements, teaching assistantships with full tuition reimbursements, career-related internships or fieldwork, Federal Work-Study, institutionally sponsored loans, scholarships/grants, tuition waivers (partial), and unspecified assistantships available. Support available to part-time students. Financial award applicants required to submit FAFSA. *Unit head:* Dr. Rob Carpenter, Coordinator, 734-487-3260, Fax: 734-487-2101, E-mail: rcarpen1@emich.edu. *Application contact:* Dr. Rob Carpenter, Coordinator, 734-487-3260, Fax: 734-487-2101, E-mail: rcarpen1@emich.edu.

Edinboro University of Pennsylvania, School of Graduate Studies and Research, School of Education, Department of Early Childhood and Special Education, Edinboro, PA 16444. Offers behavior management (Certificate); educational psychology (M Ed); special education (M Ed). Part-time and evening/weekend programs available. *Faculty:* 8 full-time (7 women), 5 part-time/adjunct (3 women). *Students:* 20 full-time (15 women), 122 part-time (105 women); includes 7 minority (5 African Americans, 1 Asian American or Pacific Islander, 1 Hispanic American). Average age 31. In 2009, 16 master's, 7 Certificates awarded. *Degree requirements:* For master's, thesis or alternative, competency exam; for Certificate, thesis or alternative. *Entrance requirements:* For master's and Certificate, GRE or MAT, minimum QPA of 2.5. *Application deadline:* Applications are processed on a rolling basis. Application fee: $30. Electronic applications accepted. *Expenses:* Tuition, state resident: full-time $6666; part-time $370 per credit. Tuition, nonresident: full-time $10,666; part-time $593 per credit. Required fees: $2206.28. One-time fee: $204 part-time. *Financial support:* In 2009–10, 4 research assistantships with full and partial tuition reimbursements (averaging $4,050 per year) were awarded; career-related internships or fieldwork, Federal Work-Study, scholarships/grants, and unspecified assistantships also available. Support available to part-time students. Financial award application deadline: 2/15; financial award applicants required to submit FAFSA. *Unit head:* Dr. Edward Snyder, Program Head, Educational Psychology, 814-732-1098, E-mail: jkasper@edinboro.edu. *Application contact:* Dr. Susan Criswell, Program Head, Special Education, 814-732-2287, E-mail: scriswell@edinboro.edu.

Florida State University, The Graduate School, College of Education, Department of Educational Psychology and Learning Systems, Program in Educational Psychology, Tallahassee, FL 32306. Offers learning and cognition (MS, PhD, Ed S); sports psychology (MS,

PhD). *Faculty:* 5 full-time (3 women), 6 part-time/adjunct (2 women). *Students:* 58 full-time (32 women), 13 part-time (8 women); includes 16 minority (10 African Americans, 2 Asian Americans or Pacific Islanders, 4 Hispanic Americans), 12 international. 100 applicants, 39% accepted, 24 enrolled. In 2009, 10 master's, 8 doctorates awarded. *Degree requirements:* For master's, comprehensive exam, thesis optional; for doctorate, comprehensive exam, thesis/dissertation. *Entrance requirements:* For master's and doctorate, GRE General Test, minimum GPA of 3.0. Additional exam requirements/recommendations for international students: Required—TOEFL (minimum score 550 paper-based; 213 computer-based; 80 iBT). *Application deadline:* For fall admission, 7/1 priority date for domestic students; for spring admission, 11/1 for domestic students. Applications are processed on a rolling basis. Application fee: $30. *Expenses:* Tuition, state resident: full-time $7413. Tuition, nonresident: full-time $22,567. *Financial support:* In 2009–10, 1 fellowship with full and partial tuition reimbursement, 3 research assistantships with full and partial tuition reimbursements, 10 teaching assistantships with full and partial tuition reimbursements were awarded; career-related internships or fieldwork also available. Financial award applicants required to submit FAFSA. *Faculty research:* Learning and cognition, skill acquisition, self-perception, processes of motivation. *Unit head:* Dr. Susan Losh, Program Leader, 850-644-8776, Fax: 850-644-8776, E-mail: slosh@coe.fsu.edu. *Application contact:* Sally Gadson, Program Assistant, 850-644-8046, Fax: 850-644-5067, E-mail: gadson@coe.fsu.edu.

Fordham University, Graduate School of Education, Division of Psychological and Educational Services, New York, NY 10023. Offers counseling and personnel services (MSE, Adv C); counseling psychology (PhD); educational psychology (MSE, PhD); school psychology (PhD); urban and urban bilingual school psychology (Adv C). *Accreditation:* APA (one or more programs are accredited); NCATE. *Degree requirements:* For doctorate, thesis/dissertation. *Entrance requirements:* For doctorate, GRE General Test.

George Mason University, College of Education and Human Development, Program in Educational Psychology, Fairfax, VA 22030. Offers MS. *Faculty:* 88 full-time (64 women), 120 part-time/adjunct (93 women). *Students:* 5 full-time (all women), 18 part-time (14 women); includes 4 minority (1 African American, 2 Asian Americans or Pacific Islanders, 1 Hispanic American), 2 international. Average age 31. 13 applicants, 77% accepted, 6 enrolled. In 2009, 6 master's awarded. *Entrance requirements:* For master's, GRE, bachelor's degree, transcripts, 3 letters of recommendation, expanded goals statement. Additional exam requirements/recommendations for international students: Required—TOEFL. *Application deadline:* For fall admission, 4/1 for domestic students; for spring admission, 11/1 for domestic students. Application fee: $75. *Expenses:* Tuition, state resident: full-time $7568; part-time $315.33 per credit hour. Tuition, nonresident: full-time $21,704; part-time $904.33 per credit hour. Required fees: $2184; $91 per credit hour. *Financial support:* In 2009–10, 4 students received support, including 4 research assistantships with full and partial tuition reimbursements available (averaging $9,276 per year); career-related internships or fieldwork, Federal Work-Study, scholarships/grants, unspecified assistantships, and health care benefits (full-time research or teaching assistantship recipients) also available. Support available to part-time students. Financial award application deadline: 3/1. *Unit head:* Martin Ford, Acting Dean, College of Education and Human Development, 703-993-2004, E-mail: mford@gmu.edu.

Georgian Court University, School of Sciences and Mathematics, Lakewood, NJ 08701-2697. Offers biology (MS); counseling psychology (MA); holistic health (Certificate); holistic health studies (MA); mathematics (MA); professional counselor (Certificate); school psychology (Certificate). Part-time and evening/weekend programs available. *Faculty:* 18 full-time (11 women), 9 part-time/adjunct (6 women). *Students:* 74 full-time (67 women), 79 part-time (67 women); includes 19 minority (8 African Americans, 1 American Indian/Alaska Native, 2 Asian Americans or Pacific Islanders, 8 Hispanic Americans), 2 international. Average age 32. 137 applicants, 50% accepted, 54 enrolled. In 2009, 27 master's, 2 other advanced degrees awarded. *Degree requirements:* For master's, comprehensive exam (for some programs), thesis (for some programs). *Entrance requirements:* For master's, GRE General Test, GRE Subject Test in biology (MS), 3 letters of recommendation. Additional exam requirements/recommendations for international students: Required—TOEFL (minimum score 550 paper-based; 213 computer-based). *Application deadline:* For fall admission, 8/1 priority date for domestic students, 4/1 for international students; for spring admission, 1/1 priority date for domestic students, 7/1 for international students. Applications are processed on a rolling basis. Application fee: $40. Electronic applications accepted. *Expenses:* Tuition: Full-time $12,510; part-time $695 per credit. Required fees: $416 per year. Tuition and fees vary according to campus/location. *Financial support:* Scholarships/grants, health care benefits, and unspecified assistantships available. Financial award application deadline: 4/15; financial award applicants required to submit FAFSA. *Unit head:* Dr. Linda James, Dean, 732-987-2617, Fax: 732-987-2007. *Application contact:* Eugene Soltys, Director of Graduate Admissions, 732-987-2770, Fax: 732-987-2084, E-mail: graduateadmissions@georgian.edu.

Georgia State University, College of Education, Department of Educational Psychology and Special Education, Program in Educational Psychology, Atlanta, GA 30302-3083. Offers MS, PhD. *Accreditation:* NCATE. Part-time and evening/weekend programs available. *Degree requirements:* For master's, thesis or project; for doctorate, comprehensive exam, thesis/dissertation. *Entrance requirements:* For master's, GRE General Test, minimum GPA of 2.5; for doctorate, GRE General Test, minimum GPA of 3.3. *Faculty research:* Cognitive and language development, language development of deaf children, reading in adult populations.

Graduate School and University Center of the City University of New York, Graduate Studies, Program in Educational Psychology, New York, NY 10016-4039. Offers PhD. *Accreditation:* APA. *Faculty:* 19 full-time (9 women). *Students:* 118 full-time (98 women), 13 part-time (9 women); includes 16 minority (5 African Americans, 7 Asian Americans or Pacific Islanders, 4 Hispanic Americans), 5 international. Average age 36. 85 applicants, 34% accepted, 15 enrolled. In 2009, 12 doctorates awarded. *Degree requirements:* For doctorate, 2 foreign languages, thesis/dissertation. *Entrance requirements:* For doctorate, GRE General Test, interview, minimum GPA of 3.0. Additional exam requirements/recommendations for international students: Required—TOEFL. *Application deadline:* For fall admission, 1/15 for domestic students. Application fee: $125. Electronic applications accepted. *Financial support:* In 2009–10, 50 students received support, including 37 fellowships, 4 research assistantships, 2 teaching assistantships; career-related internships or fieldwork, Federal Work-Study, institutionally sponsored loans, and tuition waivers (full and partial) also available. Financial award application deadline: 2/1; financial award applicants required to submit FAFSA. *Unit head:* Dr. Alan Gross, Executive Officer, 212-817-8286, Fax: 212-817-1516. *Application contact:* Les Gribben, Director of Admissions, 212-817-7470, Fax: 212-817-1624, E-mail: lgribben@gc.cuny.edu.

Harvard University, Graduate School of Education, Master's Programs in Education, Cambridge, MA 02138. Offers arts in education (Ed M); education policy and management (Ed M); higher education (Ed M); human development and psychology (Ed M); international education policy (Ed M); language and literacy (Ed M); learning and teaching (Ed M); mid-career mathematics and science (teaching certificate) (Ed M); mind brain and education (Ed M); risk and prevention (Ed M); school leadership (Ed M); special studies (Ed M); teaching and curriculum (teaching certificate) (Ed M); technology innovation and education (Ed M). Part-time programs available. *Faculty:* 70 full-time (33 women), 36 part-time/adjunct (20 women). *Students:* 598 full-time (448 women), 76 part-time (60 women); includes 132 minority (40 African Americans, 2 American Indian/Alaska Native, 58 Asian Americans or Pacific Islanders, 32 Hispanic Americans), 103 international. Average age 28. 1,574 applicants, 58% accepted, 640 enrolled. In 2009, 556 master's awarded. *Entrance requirements:* For master's, GRE General Test, 3 letters of recommendation. Additional exam requirements/recommendations for international students: Required—TOEFL (minimum score 600 paper-based; 250 computer-based; 100 iBT), TWE (minimum score 5). *Application deadline:* For fall admission, 1/4 for domestic and international students. Application fee: $85. Electronic applications accepted. *Expenses:* Contact institution. *Financial support:* In 2009–10, 424 students received support, including 25 fellowships with full and partial tuition reimbursements available (averaging $15,890 per year); career-related internships or fieldwork, Federal Work-Study, institutionally sponsored loans, scholarships/grants, health care benefits, tuition waivers (full and partial),

Educational Psychology

Harvard University (continued)

and unspecified assistantships also available. Support available to part-time students. Financial award application deadline: 2/1; financial award applicants required to submit FAFSA. *Faculty research:* Learning and development, educational leadership and organizations, educational policy analysis. Total annual research expenditures: $18.1 million. *Unit head:* Jennifer L. Petrallia, Assistant Dean, 617-495-8445. *Application contact:* Information Contact, 617-495-3414, Fax: 617-496-3577, E-mail: gseadmissions@harvard.edu.

Holy Names University, Graduate Division, Department of Education, Oakland, CA 94619-1699. Offers educational therapy (Certificate); level 1 education specialist mild/moderate disabilities (Credential); level 2 education specialist mild/moderate disabilities (Credential); multiple subject teaching credential (Credential); single subject teaching credential (Credential); teaching English as a second language (TESL) (M Ed); urban education: educational therapy (M Ed); urban education: K-12 education (M Ed); urban education: special education (M Ed). Part-time programs available. *Degree requirements:* For master's, comprehensive exam, research paper, thesis or project. *Entrance requirements:* For master's, minimum undergraduate GPA of 2.6 overall, 3.0 in major. Additional exam requirements/recommendations for international students: Required—TOEFL (minimum score 550 paper-based; 213 computer-based; 80 iBT). *Faculty research:* Cognitive development, language development, learning handicaps.

Howard University, School of Education, Department of Human Development and Psychoeducational Studies, Program in Educational Psychology, Washington, DC 20059-0002. Offers M Ed, MA, Ed D, PhD, CAGS. MA and PhD offered through the Graduate School of Arts and Sciences. Part-time programs available. *Faculty:* 3 full-time (2 women), 2 part-time/adjunct (both women). *Students:* 13 full-time (11 women), 9 part-time (7 women); includes 18 minority (all African Americans), 2 international. Average age 33. 13 applicants, 54% accepted, 5 enrolled. In 2009, 3 doctorates awarded. Terminal master's awarded for partial completion of doctoral program. *Degree requirements:* For master's, comprehensive exam, thesis (for some programs), expository writing exam; for doctorate, one foreign language, comprehensive exam, thesis/dissertation, expository writing exam, internship. *Entrance requirements:* For master's, GRE General Test, minimum GPA of 2.7; for doctorate, GRE General Test, minimum GPA of 3.4; for CAGS, GRE General Test, minimum graduate GPA of 3.0. *Application deadline:* For fall admission, 2/15 priority date for domestic students; for spring admission, 11/1 for domestic students. Applications are processed on a rolling basis. Application fee: $45. Electronic applications accepted. *Financial support:* In 2009–10, 2 students received support, including 2 fellowships with full and partial tuition reimbursements available (averaging $15,000 per year), research assistantships with full and partial tuition reimbursements available (averaging $13,000 per year); teaching assistantships, career-related internships or fieldwork, Federal Work-Study, institutionally sponsored loans, and scholarships/grants also available. Financial award application deadline: 2/15. *Unit head:* Dr. Kimberly E. Freeman, Assistant Professor/Coordinator, 202-806-6514, Fax: 202-806-5205, E-mail: kefreeman@howard.edu. *Application contact:* Frazier Tate-Jackson, Administration Assistant, Department of Human Development and Psychoeducational Studies, 202-806-7350, Fax: 202-806-5205, E-mail: fjackson@howard.edu.

Illinois State University, Graduate School, College of Arts and Sciences, Department of Psychology, Normal, IL 61790-2200. Offers psychology (MA, MS), including clinical psychology, counseling psychology, developmental psychology, educational psychology, experimental psychology, measurement-evaluation, organizational-industrial psychology; school psychology (PhD, SSP). *Accreditation:* APA. *Degree requirements:* For master's, thesis or alternative; for doctorate, variable foreign language requirement, thesis/dissertation, 2 terms of residency, internship, practicum. *Entrance requirements:* For master's, GRE General Test, GRE Subject Test, minimum GPA of 3.0 in last 60 hours of course work; for doctorate, GRE General Test. *Faculty research:* Comprehensive evaluation system for the central region professional development grant, Illinois school psychology internship consortium, for children's sake.

Indiana University Bloomington, School of Education, Department of Counseling and Educational Psychology, Bloomington, IN 47405-1006. Offers counseling (MS, PhD, Ed S); counseling psychology (PhD); counselor education (MS, Ed S); educational psychology (MS, PhD); inquiry methodology (PhD); learning and developmental sciences (MS, PhD); school psychology (PhD, Ed S). *Accreditation:* ACA (one or more programs are accredited); APA (one or more programs are accredited); NCATE. *Faculty:* 32 full-time (13 women), 20 part-time/adjunct (10 women). *Students:* 218 full-time (165 women), 34 part-time (29 women); includes 45 minority (19 African Americans, 2 American Indian/Alaska Native, 12 Asian Americans or Pacific Islanders, 12 Hispanic Americans), 42 international. Average age 30. 348 applicants, 41% accepted, 53 enrolled. In 2009, 57 master's, 21 doctorates, 22 other advanced degrees awarded. Terminal master's awarded for partial completion of doctoral program. *Degree requirements:* For master's, thesis optional; for doctorate, thesis/dissertation; for Ed S, comprehensive exam or project. *Entrance requirements:* For master's, doctorate, and Ed S, GRE General Test. Additional exam requirements/recommendations for international students: Required—TOEFL. *Application deadline:* Applications are processed on a rolling basis. Application fee: $55 ($65 for international students). Electronic applications accepted. *Financial support:* In 2009–10, 58 students received support, including 7 fellowships with partial tuition reimbursements available (averaging $15,000 per year), 15 research assistantships with partial tuition reimbursements available (averaging $12,000 per year), 36 teaching assistantships with partial tuition reimbursements available (averaging $14,280 per year); career-related internships or fieldwork, Federal Work-Study, institutionally sponsored loans, scholarships/grants, and unspecified assistantships also available. Support available to part-time students. Financial award application deadline: 1/1; financial award applicants required to submit FAFSA. *Faculty research:* Counseling psychology, inquiry methodology, school psychology, learning sciences, human development, educational psychology. *Unit head:* Dr. Joyce Alexander, Chairperson, 812-856-8300, Fax: 812-856-8333, E-mail: cep@indiana.edu. *Application contact:* Jessica Durnal, Student Services Specialist, 812-856-8300, Fax: 812-856-8333, E-mail: cep@indiana.edu.

Indiana University of Pennsylvania, School of Graduate Studies and Research, College of Education and Educational Technology, Department of Educational and School Psychology, Program in Educational Psychology, Indiana, PA 15705-1087. Offers M Ed, Certificate. *Accreditation:* NCATE. Part-time and evening/weekend programs available. *Faculty:* 14 full-time (8 women). *Students:* 16 full-time (15 women), 2 part-time (both women), 3 international. Average age 26. 45 applicants, 31% accepted, 14 enrolled. In 2009, 22 master's awarded. *Degree requirements:* For master's, thesis optional. *Entrance requirements:* For master's, GRE General Test, GRE Subject Test, 2 letters of recommendation. Additional exam requirements/recommendations for international students: Required—TOEFL. *Application deadline:* For fall admission, 7/1 priority date for domestic students; for spring admission, 11/1 for domestic students. Applications are processed on a rolling basis. Application fee: $40. *Expenses:* Tuition, state resident: full-time $6666; part-time $370 per credit hour. Tuition, nonresident: full-time $10,666; part-time $593 per credit hour. Required fees: $813 per semester. *Financial support:* In 2009–10, 15 research assistantships with full and partial tuition reimbursements (averaging $4,533 per year) were awarded; fellowships, career-related internships or fieldwork and Federal Work-Study also available. Support available to part-time students. Financial award application deadline: 3/15; financial award applicants required to submit FAFSA. *Unit head:* Dr. Victoria Damiani, Graduate Coordinator, 724-357-3783, E-mail: vdamiani@iup.edu. *Application contact:* Dr. Edward Nardi, Interim Associate Dean, 724-357-2480, Fax: 724-357-5595, E-mail: ewnardi@iup.edu.

John Carroll University, Graduate School, Department of Education and Allied Studies, Program in Educational and School Psychology, University Heights, OH 44118-4581. Offers M Ed, MA. *Accreditation:* NCATE. Part-time and evening/weekend programs available. *Degree requirements:* For master's, comprehensive exam, research essay or thesis (MA only). *Entrance requirements:* For master's, GRE General Test or MAT, minimum GPA of 2.75, Educ. or Psych. degree, questionnaire, interview. Electronic applications accepted.

The Johns Hopkins University, School of Education, Department of Interdisciplinary Studies in Education, Baltimore, MD 21218. Offers earth/space science (Certificate); education (MS),

including educational studies; mind, brain, and teaching (Certificate); teaching the adult learner (Certificate); urban education (Certificate). Part-time and evening/weekend programs available. Postbaccalaureate distance learning degree programs offered (minimal on-campus study). *Faculty:* 2 full-time (1 woman), 6 part-time/adjunct (5 women). *Students:* 8 full-time (7 women), 171 part-time (150 women); includes 44 minority (29 African Americans, 1 American Indian/Alaska Native, 11 Asian Americans or Pacific Islanders, 3 Hispanic Americans), 7 international. Average age 34. 77 applicants, 68% accepted, 39 enrolled. In 2009, 69 master's, 17 other advanced degrees awarded. *Degree requirements:* For master's, capstone course. *Entrance requirements:* For master's and Certificate, minimum undergraduate GPA of 3.0. Additional exam requirements/recommendations for international students: Required—TOEFL (minimum score 600 paper-based; 250 computer-based; 100 iBT). *Application deadline:* For fall admission, 5/1 for international students; for spring admission, 10/15 for international students. Applications are processed on a rolling basis. Application fee: $80. Electronic applications accepted. *Financial support:* Scholarships/grants available. Support available to part-time students. Financial award application deadline: 6/1; financial award applicants required to submit FAFSA. *Faculty research:* Neuro-education; urban school reform; leadership development; teacher leadership; charter schools; techniques for teaching reading to adolescents with delayed reading skills; school culture. *Unit head:* Dr. Mariale Hardiman, Assistant Dean and Chair, 410-516-8225, Fax: 410-516-3939, E-mail: mclean@jhu.edu. *Application contact:* Jennifer Shaffer, Director of Admissions, 410-516-9797, Fax: 410-516-9799, E-mail: educationinfo@jhu.edu.

Johnson State College, Graduate Program in Education, Program in Applied Behavior Analysis, Johnson, VT 05656. Offers children's mental health (MA Ed). *Entrance requirements:* Additional exam requirements/recommendations for international students: Required—TOEFL. *Expenses:* Tuition, area resident: Part-time $416 per credit. Tuition, state resident: part-time $416 per credit. Tuition, nonresident: part-time $899 per credit.

Kean University, College of Humanities and Social Sciences, Program in Educational Psychology, Union, NJ 07083. Offers MA. Part-time and evening/weekend programs available. *Faculty:* 15 full-time (13 women). *Students:* 6 full-time (all women), 8 part-time (all women); includes 4 minority (1 Asian American or Pacific Islander, 3 Hispanic Americans). Average age 29. 8 applicants, 50% accepted, 4 enrolled. In 2009, 8 master's awarded. *Degree requirements:* For master's, comprehensive exam, thesis, research. *Entrance requirements:* For master's, GRE General Test, minimum GPA of 3.0, interview, 3 letters of recommendation, prerequisites in psychology. *Application deadline:* For fall admission, 3/15 for domestic students. Application fee: $60 ($150 for international students). Electronic applications accepted. *Expenses:* Tuition, state resident: full-time $10,440; part-time $435 per credit. Tuition, nonresident: full-time $14,160; part-time $590 per credit. Required fees: $2642; $110 per credit. Part-time tuition and fees vary according to course load and degree level. *Financial support:* In 2009–10, 2 research assistantships with full tuition reimbursements (averaging $3,263 per year) were awarded; unspecified assistantships also available. *Unit head:* Dr. Dennis Finger, Program Coordinator, 908-737-5879, E-mail: dfinger@kean.edu. *Application contact:* Ann-Marie Kay, Assistant Director of Graduate Admissions, 908-737-5922, Fax: 908-737-5965, E-mail: akay@kean.edu.

Kent State University, Graduate School of Education, Health, and Human Services, School of Lifespan Development and Educational Sciences, Program in Educational Psychology, Kent, OH 44242-0001. Offers M Ed, MA, PhD. *Faculty:* 7 full-time (3 women), 1 (woman) part-time/adjunct. *Students:* 25 full-time (14 women), 27 part-time (19 women); includes 2 minority (1 African American, 1 American Indian/Alaska Native), 1 international. 18 applicants, 56% accepted. In 2009, 2 master's awarded. *Entrance requirements:* For doctorate, GRE. *Application deadline:* Applications are processed on a rolling basis. Application fee: $30. Electronic applications accepted. *Financial support:* In 2009–10, 6 fellowships (averaging $11,000 per year), research assistantships (averaging $8,313 per year) were awarded; career-related internships or fieldwork, Federal Work-Study, institutionally sponsored loans, scholarships/grants, health care benefits, and unspecified assistantships also available. Support available to part-time students. *Unit head:* Dr. Christopher Was, Coordinator, 330-672-2929, E-mail: cwas@kent.edu. *Application contact:* Nancy Miller, Academic Program Coordinator, Office of Graduate Student Services, 330-672-2576, Fax: 330-672-9162, E-mail: ogs@kent.edu.

La Sierra University, School of Education, Department of School Psychology and Counseling, Riverside, CA 92515. Offers counseling (MA); educational psychology (Ed S); school psychology (Ed S). Part-time and evening/weekend programs available. *Degree requirements:* For master's, thesis optional; for Ed S, practicum (educational psychology). *Entrance requirements:* For master's, California Basic Educational Skills Test, NTE, minimum GPA of 3.0; for Ed S, minimum GPA of 3.3. *Faculty research:* Equivalent score scales, self perception.

Long Island University, Westchester Graduate Campus, Programs in Education-School Counselor and School Psychology, Purchase, NY 10577. Offers school counselor (MS Ed); school psychologist (MS Ed). Part-time and evening/weekend programs available.

Loyola University Chicago, School of Education, Program in Educational Psychology, Chicago, IL 60660. Offers M Ed. Part-time and evening/weekend programs available. *Faculty:* 7 full-time (5 women), 4 part-time/adjunct (2 women). *Students:* 32. Average age 28. 137 applicants, 34% accepted, 16 enrolled. In 2009, 28 master's awarded. Terminal master's awarded for partial completion of doctoral program. *Degree requirements:* For master's, comprehensive exam, thesis (for some programs). *Entrance requirements:* For master's, GRE General Test, letters of recommendation, minimum GPA of 3.0. Additional exam requirements/recommendations for international students: Required—TOEFL (minimum score 550 paper-based; 213 computer-based; 79 iBT). *Application deadline:* For fall admission, 12/15 for domestic and international students. Application fee: $50. Electronic applications accepted. *Expenses:* Tuition: Full-time $14,220; part-time $790 per credit hour. Required fees: $60 per semester hour. Tuition and fees vary according to program. *Financial support:* In 2009–10, 1 fellowship (averaging $14,000 per year) was awarded; institutionally sponsored loans, scholarships/grants, and tuition waivers (full and partial) also available. Financial award application deadline: 2/15. *Faculty research:* Learning theory and teaching; cognitive, social, and cultural constructivism; school reform; workplace training and adult education. *Unit head:* Dr. Pamela Fenning, Director, 312-915-6803, E-mail: pfennin@luc.edu. *Application contact:* Marie Rosin-Dittmar, Information Contact, 312-915-6800, E-mail: schleduc@luc.edu.

Marist College, Graduate Programs, School of Social and Behavioral Sciences, Poughkeepsie, NY 12601-1387. Offers counseling psychology (MA); education (M Ed); education psychology (MA); school psychology (MA, Adv C). Part-time and evening/weekend programs available. *Degree requirements:* For master's, thesis optional. *Entrance requirements:* For master's, GRE General Test, letters of recommendation, minimum undergraduate GPA of 3.0, interview. Additional exam requirements/recommendations for international students: Required—TOEFL (minimum score 550 paper-based; 213 computer-based; 80 iBT); Recommended—IELTS (minimum score 6.5). Electronic applications accepted. *Expenses:* Tuition: Full-time $12,510; part-time $695 per credit hour. *Faculty research:* AIDS prevention, educational intervention, humanistic counseling research, aging and development, neuroimaging.

Maryville University of Saint Louis, School of Education, St. Louis, MO 63141-7299. Offers art education (MA Ed); early childhood education (MA Ed); educational leadership (Ed D); educational leadership: principal certification (MA Ed); elementary education (MA Ed); elementary education/English (MA Ed); elementary education/psychology (MA Ed); environmental education (MA Ed); gifted education (MA Ed); literacy specialist (MA Ed); middle grades education (MA Ed); secondary teaching and inquiry (MA Ed); teacher as leader (MA Ed). *Accreditation:* NASAD; NCATE. Part-time and evening/weekend programs available. *Students:* 25 full-time (18 women), 198 part-time (145 women); includes 33 minority (27 African Americans, 2 American Indian/Alaska Native, 1 Asian American or Pacific Islander, 3 Hispanic Americans). Average age 36. In 2009, 61 master's, 45 doctorates awarded. *Degree requirements:* For master's, thesis, project. *Entrance requirements:* For master's and doctorate, minimum GPA of 3.0, 3 professional recommendations. Additional exam requirements/recommendations for international students: Required—TOEFL (minimum score 550 paper-based). *Application deadline:* Applications are processed on a rolling basis. Application fee: $40 ($60 for international students).

Electronic applications accepted. *Expenses:* Tuition: Full-time $20,384; part-time $627.50 per credit hour. Required fees: $100 per semester. *Financial support:* Career-related internships or fieldwork, Federal Work-Study, tuition waivers (partial), and professional educator discounts available. Financial award application deadline: 3/1; financial award applicants required to submit FAFSA. *Faculty research:* Collaboration with public schools, pre-service program development, mathematics, diversity, literacy. *Unit head:* Dr. Sam Hausfather, Dean, 314-529-9466, Fax: 314-529-9921, E-mail: shausfather@maryville.edu. *Application contact:* Holly Stanwich, Graduate Admissions Coordinator, 314-529-9542, Fax: 314-529-9921, E-mail: teachered@maryville.edu.

McGill University, Faculty of Graduate and Postdoctoral Studies, Faculty of Education, Department of Educational and Counseling Psychology, Montréal, QC H3A 2T5, Canada. Offers counseling psychology (MA, PhD); educational psychology (M Ed, MA, PhD); school/applied child psychology and applied developmental psychology (M Ed, MA, PhD, Diploma), including school psychology. *Accreditation:* APA.

Memorial University of Newfoundland, School of Graduate Studies, Faculty of Education, St. John's, NL A1C 5S7, Canada. Offers counseling psychology (M Ed); curriculum, teaching, and learning studies (M Ed); education (PhD); educational leadership studies (M Ed); information technology (M Ed); post-secondary studies (M Ed, Diploma), including health professional education (Diploma). Part-time programs available. *Degree requirements:* For master's, thesis optional, internship, paper folio, project; for doctorate, comprehensive exam, thesis/dissertation, thesis seminar, oral defense of thesis. *Entrance requirements:* For master's, undergraduate degree with at least 2nd class standing, 1-2 years work experience; for doctorate, minimum A average in graduate course work, MA in education, 2 years professional experience; for Diploma, 2nd class degree, 2 years of work experience with adult learners, appropriate academic qualifications and work experience in a health-related field. Electronic applications accepted. *Faculty research:* Critical thinking, literacy, cognitive studies and counseling, educational change, technology in instruction.

Miami University, Graduate School, School of Education and Allied Professions, Department of Educational Psychology, Oxford, OH 45056. Offers educational psychology (M Ed); instructional design and technology (M Ed, MA); school psychology (MS, Ed S); special education (M Ed). *Accreditation:* NCATE. *Students:* 39 full-time (34 women), 42 part-time (39 women); includes 5 minority (2 African Americans, 2 Asian Americans or Pacific Islanders, 1 Hispanic American), 9 international. *Entrance requirements:* For master's, GRE General Test or MAT, minimum undergraduate GPA of 3.0 during previous 2 years or 2.75 overall; for Ed S, GRE General Test or MAT. Additional exam requirements/recommendations for international students: Required—TOEFL. Application fee: $50. *Expenses:* Tuition, state resident: full-time $11,280. Tuition, nonresident: full-time $24,912. Required fees: $516. *Financial support:* Fellowships with full tuition reimbursements, research assistantships with full tuition reimbursements, teaching assistantships with full tuition reimbursements, career-related internships or fieldwork, Federal Work-Study, health care benefits, tuition waivers (full), and unspecified assistantships available. Financial award application deadline: 3/1. *Unit head:* Dr. Nelda Cambron-McCabe, Chair, 513-529-6836, Fax: 513-529-6621, E-mail: edp@muohio.edu. *Application contact:* Dr. Nelda Cambron-McCabe, Chair, 513-529-6836, Fax: 513-529-6621, E-mail: edp@muohio.edu.

Michigan School of Professional Psychology, Program in Clinical Psychology, Farmington Hills, MI 48334. Offers MA, Psy D. *Students:* 111 full-time (92 women), 15 part-time (all women); includes 20 minority (13 African Americans, 7 Asian Americans or Pacific Islanders). Average age 38. *Degree requirements:* For master's, thesis, practicum; for doctorate, thesis/dissertation, internship, practicum. *Entrance requirements:* For master's, 1 year of work experience, interview, minimum GPA of 3.0, curriculum vitae, personal essay, bachelor's degree, 3 letters of recommendation; for doctorate, 3 years of work experience, 2 interviews, minimum graduate GPA of 3.0, scholarly writing sample, curriculum vitae, personal essay, MA, 3 letters of recommendation. Additional exam requirements/recommendations for international students: Required—TOEFL. *Application deadline:* For fall admission, 1/15 priority date for domestic students. Applications are processed on a rolling basis. Application fee: $75. Electronic applications accepted. *Financial support:* Application deadline: 6/30. *Faculty research:* Qualitative research, existential-phenomenological psychology, applications to clinical practice. *Unit head:* Dr. Kerry Moustakas, President, 248-476-1122, Fax: 248-476-1125, E-mail: kmoustakas@mispp.edu. *Application contact:* Linda Potter-Gallant, Admissions Advisor, 248-476-1122 Ext. 117, Fax: 248-476-1125, E-mail: lpgallant@mispp.edu.

Michigan State University, The Graduate School, College of Education, Department of Counseling, Educational Psychology and Special Education, East Lansing, MI 48824. Offers counseling (MA); educational psychology and educational technology (PhD); educational technology (MA); measurement and quantitative methods (PhD); rehabilitation counseling (MA); rehabilitation counselor education (PhD); school psychology (MA, PhD, Ed S); special education (MA, PhD). *Accreditation:* APA (one or more programs are accredited); CORE (one or more programs are accredited). Part-time programs available. *Faculty:* 35 full-time (13 women). *Students:* 217 full-time (154 women), 144 part-time (107 women); includes 48 minority (25 African Americans, 13 Asian Americans or Pacific Islanders, 10 Hispanic Americans), 71 international. Average age 32. 238 applicants, 46% accepted. In 2009, 117 master's, 36 doctorates awarded. *Entrance requirements:* Additional exam requirements/recommendations for international students: Required—TOEFL. Electronic applications accepted. *Expenses:* Tuition, state resident: part-time $478.25 per credit hour. Tuition, nonresident: part-time $966.50 per credit hour. Part-time tuition and fees vary according to program. *Financial support:* In 2009–10, 71 research assistantships with tuition reimbursements (averaging $6,836 per year), 74 teaching assistantships with tuition reimbursements (averaging $6,858 per year) were awarded. Total annual research expenditures: $2.3 million. *Unit head:* Dr. Richard S. Prawat, Chairperson, 517-353-6417, Fax: 517-353-6393, E-mail: rsprawat@msu.edu. *Application contact:* Kathy Dimoff, Graduate Admissions Coordinator, 517-355-6683, Fax: 517-353-6393, E-mail: dimoff@msu.edu.

Mississippi State University, College of Education, Department of Counseling and Educational Psychology, Mississippi State, MS 39762. Offers college/postsecondary student counseling and personnel services (PhD); counselor education (MS); counselor education/student counseling and guidance services (PhD); education (Ed S), including counselor education, school psychology; educational psychology (MS, PhD). *Accreditation:* ACA (one or more programs are accredited); APA; CORE (one or more programs are accredited); NCATE. Part-time programs available. Postbaccalaureate distance learning degree programs offered (minimal on-campus study). *Faculty:* 14 full-time (10 women), 1 (woman) part-time/adjunct. *Students:* 116 full-time (95 women), 99 part-time (84 women); includes 63 minority (57 African Americans, 2 American Indian/Alaska Native, 2 Asian Americans or Pacific Islanders, 2 Hispanic Americans), 3 international. Average age 32. 154 applicants, 62% accepted, 69 enrolled. In 2009, 56 master's, 9 doctorates, 17 other advanced degrees awarded. Terminal master's awarded for partial completion of doctoral program. *Degree requirements:* For master's, comprehensive exam, thesis optional; for doctorate, thesis/dissertation, comprehensive oral and written exam. *Entrance requirements:* For master's, GRE, minimum QPA of 3.0; for doctorate, GRE, interview, minimum GPA of 3.4; for Ed S, GRE, MS in counseling or related field. Additional exam requirements/recommendations for international students: Required—TOEFL (minimum score 475 paper-based; 153 computer-based; 53 iBT); Recommended—IELTS (minimum score 4.5). *Application deadline:* For fall admission, 2/1 priority date for domestic and international students. Applications are processed on a rolling basis. Application fee: $40. Electronic applications accepted. *Expenses:* Tuition, state resident: full-time $2575.50; part-time $286.25 per credit hour. Tuition, nonresident: full-time $6510; part-time $723.50 per credit hour. Tuition and fees vary according to course load. *Financial support:* In 2009–10, 4 teaching assistantships with full tuition reimbursements (averaging $8,603 per year) were awarded; career-related internships or fieldwork, Federal Work-Study, institutionally sponsored loans, and unspecified assistantships also available. Financial award application deadline: 2/1; financial award applicants required to submit FAFSA. *Faculty research:* HIV-AIDS in college population, substance abuse in youth and college students, ADHD and conduct disorders in youth, assessment and identification of early childhood disabilities, assessment and vocational transition of the disabled. *Unit head:* Dr. Daniel Wong, Professor/Head, 662-325-7928, Fax: 662-325-3263, E-mail: dwong@colled.msstate.edu. *Application contact:* Dr. Tony Doggett, Associate Professor and Graduate Coordinator, 662-325-3312, Fax: 662-325-3263, E-mail: tdoggett@colled.msstate.edu.

Montclair State University, The Graduate School, College of Humanities and Social Sciences, Department of Psychology, Montclair, NJ 07043-1624. Offers educational psychology (MA), including child/adolescent clinical psychology, clinical psychology for Spanish/English bilinguals; psychology (MA, Certificate), including industrial and organizational psychology (MA); school psychologist (Certificate). Part-time and evening/weekend programs available. *Faculty:* 29 full-time (14 women), 26 part-time/adjunct (14 women). *Students:* 37 full-time (27 women), 33 part-time (23 women). Average age 27. 72 applicants, 47% accepted, 20 enrolled. In 2009, 7 master's awarded. *Degree requirements:* For master's, comprehensive exam, thesis or alternative. *Entrance requirements:* For master's, GRE General Test, 2 letters of recommendation. Additional exam requirements/recommendations for international students: Required—TOEFL (minimum score 83 computer-based), or IELTS. *Application deadline:* For fall admission, 2/1 for domestic and international students; for spring admission, 10/1 for domestic and international students. Applications are processed on a rolling basis. Application fee: $60. Electronic applications accepted. *Expenses:* Tuition, area resident: Part-time $486.74 per credit. Tuition, state resident: part-time $486.74 per credit. Tuition, nonresident: part-time $751.34 per credit. Tuition and fees vary according to degree level and program. *Financial support:* In 2009–10, 17 research assistantships with full tuition reimbursements (averaging $7,000 per year) were awarded; Federal Work-Study, scholarships/grants, and unspecified assistantships also available. Support available to part-time students. Financial award application deadline: 3/1; financial award applicants required to submit FAFSA. *Faculty research:* Engaged learning, academic and civic development. Total annual research expenditures: $10,000. *Unit head:* Dr. Peter Vietze, Chairperson, 973-655-5201. *Application contact:* Amy Aiello, Director of Admissions and Operations, 973-655-5147, Fax: 973-655-7869, E-mail: graduate.school@montclair.edu.

Mount Saint Vincent University, Graduate Programs, Faculty of Education, Program in Educational Psychology, Halifax, NS B3M 2J6, Canada. Offers education of the blind or visually impaired (M Ed, MA Ed); education of the deaf or hard of hearing (M Ed, MA Ed); educational psychology (MA-R); human relations (M Ed, MA Ed). Part-time and evening/weekend programs available. Postbaccalaureate distance learning degree programs offered (minimal on-campus study). *Degree requirements:* For master's, thesis (for some programs). *Entrance requirements:* For master's, bachelor's degree in related field, 1 year of teaching experience. Electronic applications accepted. *Faculty research:* Personality measurement, values reasoning, aggression and sexuality, power and control, quantitative and qualitative research methodologies.

National-Louis University, National College of Education, Doctoral Programs in Education, Program in Educational Psychology/School Psychology, Chicago, IL 60603. Offers Ed D. Part-time and evening/weekend programs available. *Degree requirements:* For doctorate, comprehensive exam, thesis/dissertation, internship. *Entrance requirements:* For doctorate, GRE General Test, minimum GPA of 3.25, interview, resume, writing sample. *Expenses:* Tuition: Full-time $17,160; part-time $715 per semester hour. Tuition and fees vary according to course load, degree level, campus/location and program.

National-Louis University, National College of Education, Program in Educational Psychology/Human Learning and Development, Chicago, IL 60603. Offers educational psychology (CAS, Ed S); educational psychology/human learning and development (M Ed, MS Ed). Part-time and evening/weekend programs available. *Degree requirements:* For master's, thesis (for some programs). *Entrance requirements:* For master's, MAT or GRE, minimum GPA of 3.0, teaching certificate; for other advanced degree, master's degree, teaching certificate. Electronic applications accepted. *Expenses:* Tuition: Full-time $17,160; part-time $715 per semester hour. Tuition and fees vary according to course load, degree level, campus/location and program.

National-Louis University, National College of Education, Programs in School Psychology, Chicago, IL 60603. Offers M Ed, Ed S. *Degree requirements:* For master's and Ed S, internship. *Entrance requirements:* For master's, GRE or MAT, minimum GPA of 3.0; for Ed S, GRE, interview, master's degree, writing sample. *Expenses:* Tuition: Full-time $17,160; part-time $715 per semester hour. Tuition and fees vary according to course load, degree level, campus/location and program.

New Jersey City University, Graduate Studies and Continuing Education, William J. Maxwell College of Arts and Sciences, Program in Educational Psychology, Jersey City, NJ 07305-1597. Offers educational psychology (MA); school psychology (PD). Part-time and evening/weekend programs available. *Faculty:* 9. *Students:* 12 full-time (11 women), 13 part-time (11 women); includes 14 minority (2 African Americans, 3 Asian Americans or Pacific Islanders, 9 Hispanic Americans), 1 international. Average age 30. In 2009, 12 master's, 5 other advanced degrees awarded. *Degree requirements:* For PD, summer internship or externship. *Entrance requirements:* For master's, GRE General Test or MAT; for PD, GRE General Test. Additional exam requirements/recommendations for international students: Required—TOEFL. *Application deadline:* For fall admission, 8/1 priority date for domestic students; for spring admission, 12/1 for domestic students. Applications are processed on a rolling basis. Application fee: $0. *Expenses:* Tuition, area resident: Part-time $456.75 per credit. Tuition, nonresident: part-time $842.55 per credit. Required fees: $65 per term. *Financial support:* Unspecified assistantships available. *Unit head:* Dr. James Lennon, Director, 201-200-3309, E-mail: jlennon@njcu.edu. *Application contact:* Dr. James Lennon, Director, 201-200-3309, E-mail: jlennon@njcu.edu.

New York University, Steinhardt School of Culture, Education, and Human Development, Department of Applied Psychology, Programs in Educational and Developmental Psychology, New York, NY 10012-1019. Offers educational psychology (MA); human development and social intervention (MA); psychological development (PhD); psychology and social intervention (PhD). *Accreditation:* APA (one or more programs are accredited). Part-time programs available. *Students:* 48 full-time (42 women), 36 part-time (30 women); includes 24 minority (9 African Americans, 4 Asian Americans or Pacific Islanders, 11 Hispanic Americans), 11 international. Average age 29. 233 applicants, 30% accepted, 26 enrolled. In 2009, 29 master's, 9 doctorates awarded. *Degree requirements:* For master's, thesis (for some programs); for doctorate, thesis/dissertation. *Entrance requirements:* For doctorate, GRE General Test, interview. Additional exam requirements/recommendations for international students: Required—TOEFL. *Application deadline:* For fall admission, 12/15 priority date for domestic and international students. Applications are processed on a rolling basis. Application fee: $75. Electronic applications accepted. *Expenses:* Tuition: Full-time $30,528; part-time $1272 per credit. Required fees: $2177. *Financial support:* Teaching assistantships with partial tuition reimbursements, career-related internships or fieldwork, Federal Work-Study, institutionally sponsored loans, and tuition waivers (partial) available. Support available to part-time students. Financial award application deadline: 2/1; financial award applicants required to submit FAFSA. *Faculty research:* High risk children and youth; child and adolescent developments; families and schooling; infant cognition; exploration, language, and symbolic play in toddlerhood. *Unit head:* Dr. LaRue Allen, Director, 212-998-5555, Fax: 212-995-4358. *Application contact:* 212-998-5030, Fax: 212-995-4328, E-mail: steinhardt.gradadmissions@nyu.edu.

Northern Arizona University, Graduate College, College of Education, Department of Educational Psychology, Flagstaff, AZ 86011. Offers counseling (MA); educational psychology (PhD), including counseling psychology, learning and instruction, school psychology; human relations (M Ed); school counseling (M Ed); school psychology (MA, Certificate); student affairs (M Ed). Part-time programs available. Postbaccalaureate distance learning degree programs offered. *Faculty:* 20 full-time (10 women). *Students:* 200 full-time (151 women), 241 part-time (189 women); includes 165 minority (28 African Americans, 21 American Indian/Alaska Native, 7 Asian Americans or Pacific Islanders, 109 Hispanic Americans), 1 international. In 2009, 167 master's, 7 doctorates awarded. Terminal master's awarded for partial completion of doctoral program. *Median time to degree:* Of those who began their doctoral program in fall 2001, 75%

Educational Psychology

Northern Arizona University (continued)
received their degree in 8 years or less. *Degree requirements:* For master's, internship (for some programs); for doctorate, comprehensive exam, thesis/dissertation, internship. *Entrance requirements:* Additional exam requirements/recommendations for international students: Required—TOEFL (minimum score 550 paper-based; 213 computer-based; 80 iBT), IELTS (minimum score 7), or a bachelor's degree from an English-speaking university and demonstrated proficiency. *Application deadline:* For fall admission, 9/15 for domestic students; for spring admission, 1/15 for domestic students. Application fee: $65. Electronic applications accepted. *Financial support:* In 2009–10, 20 students received support, including 2 research assistantships with partial tuition reimbursements available, 12 teaching assistantships with partial tuition reimbursements available; career-related internships or fieldwork, Federal Work-Study, scholarships/grants, health care benefits, tuition waivers (full and partial), and unspecified assistantships also available. Support available to part-time students. Financial award applicants required to submit FAFSA. *Unit head:* Dr. Kathy Bohan, Chair, 928-523-0362, E-mail: kathy.bohan@nau.edu. *Application contact:* Shirley Robinson, Director of Graduate Admissions, 928-523-4348, Fax: 928-523-8950, E-mail: graduate.college@nau.edu.

Northern Illinois University, Graduate School, College of Education, Department of Leadership, Educational Psychology and Foundations, De Kalb, IL 60115-2854. Offers educational administration (MS Ed, Ed D, Ed S); educational psychology (MS Ed, Ed D); foundations of education (MS Ed); school business management (MS Ed). Part-time and evening/weekend programs available. Postbaccalaureate distance learning degree programs offered (minimal on-campus study). *Faculty:* 23 full-time (12 women). *Students:* 17 full-time (14 women), 382 part-time (215 women); includes 63 minority (41 African Americans, 1 American Indian/Alaska Native, 6 Asian Americans or Pacific Islanders, 15 Hispanic Americans), 10 international. Average age 38. 117 applicants, 60% accepted, 53 enrolled. In 2009, 110 master's, 9 doctorates, 24 other advanced degrees awarded. *Degree requirements:* For master's, comprehensive exam, thesis optional; for doctorate, thesis/dissertation, candidacy exam, dissertation defense. *Entrance requirements:* For master's, minimum undergraduate GPA of 2.75; for doctorate, GRE General Test, minimum undergraduate GPA of 2.75, 3.2 graduate; for Ed S, GRE General Test, minimum GPA of 2.75 (undergraduate), 3.2 (graduate). Additional exam requirements/recommendations for international students: Required—TOEFL (minimum score 550 paper-based; 213 computer-based). *Application deadline:* For fall admission, 6/1 for domestic students, 5/1 for international students; for spring admission, 11/1 for domestic students, 10/1 for international students. Applications are processed on a rolling basis. Application fee: $30. Electronic applications accepted. *Expenses:* Tuition, state resident: full-time $6576; part-time $274 per credit hour. Tuition, nonresident: full-time $13,152; part-time $548 per credit hour. Required fees: $1813; $75.53 per credit hour. Part-time tuition and fees vary according to course load. *Financial support:* In 2009–10, 2 research assistantships with full tuition reimbursements, 12 teaching assistantships with full tuition reimbursements were awarded; fellowships with full tuition reimbursements, career-related internships or fieldwork, Federal Work-Study, scholarships/grants, tuition waivers (full), and staff assistantships also available. Support available to part-time students. Financial award applicants required to submit FAFSA. *Faculty research:* Interpersonal forgiveness, learner-centered education, psychedelic studies, senior theory, professional growth. *Unit head:* Dr. Charles L. Howell, Chair, 815-753-4404, E-mail: chowell@niu.edu. *Application contact:* Graduate School Office, 815-753-0395, E-mail: gradsch@niu.edu.

Oklahoma City University, Petree College of Arts and Sciences, Division of Education and Kinesiology Exercise Studies, Programs in Education, Oklahoma City, OK 73106-1402. Offers applied behavioral studies (M Ed); early childhood education (M Ed); elementary education (M Ed). Part-time and evening/weekend programs available. *Faculty:* 2 full-time (1 woman), 3 part-time/adjunct (all women). *Students:* 25 full-time (20 women), 13 part-time (9 women); includes 10 minority (8 African Americans, 2 American Indian/Alaska Native), 5 international. Average age 32. 45 applicants, 78% accepted, 18 enrolled. In 2009, 12 master's awarded. *Degree requirements:* For master's, thesis optional. *Entrance requirements:* For master's, minimum GPA of 3.0. Additional exam requirements/recommendations for international students: Required—TOEFL (minimum score 550 paper-based). *Application deadline:* For fall admission, 8/20 for domestic students; for spring admission, 1/6 for domestic students. Applications are processed on a rolling basis. Application fee: $50 ($70 for international students). *Expenses:* Tuition: Full-time $15,930; part-time $885 per hour. *Financial support:* Fellowships with partial tuition reimbursements, career-related internships or fieldwork, Federal Work-Study, and tuition waivers (partial) available. Support available to part-time students. Financial award application deadline: 8/1; financial award applicants required to submit FAFSA. *Faculty research:* Adult literacy, cognition, reading strategies. *Unit head:* Dr. Lois Lawler-Brown, Chair, 405-208-5374, Fax: 405-208-6012, E-mail: llbrown@okcu.edu. *Application contact:* Michelle Lockhart, Director, Admissions, 800-633-7242, Fax: 405-208-5916, E-mail: gadmissions@okcu.edu.

Oklahoma State University, College of Education, School of Applied Health and Educational Psychology, Stillwater, OK 74078. Offers applied behavioral studies (Ed D). *Accreditation:* APA (one or more programs are accredited). Part-time programs available. *Faculty:* 38 full-time (17 women), 15 part-time/adjunct (10 women). *Students:* 188 full-time (141 women), 179 part-time (122 women); includes 73 minority (27 African Americans, 26 American Indian/Alaska Native, 9 Asian Americans or Pacific Islanders, 11 Hispanic Americans), 13 international. Average age 33. 267 applicants, 30% accepted, 58 enrolled. In 2009, 65 master's, 50 doctorates awarded. *Degree requirements:* For master's, thesis (for some programs); for doctorate, comprehensive exam, thesis/dissertation. *Entrance requirements:* For master's and doctorate, GRE or GMAT. Additional exam requirements/recommendations for international students: Required—TOEFL (minimum score 550 paper-based; 79 iBT). *Application deadline:* For fall admission, 3/1 priority date for international students; for spring admission, 8/1 priority date for international students. Applications are processed on a rolling basis. Application fee: $40 ($75 for international students). Electronic applications accepted. *Expenses:* Tuition, state resident: full-time $3716; part-time $154.85 per credit hour. Tuition, nonresident: full-time $14,448; part-time $602 per credit hour. Required fees: $1772; $73.85 per credit hour. One-time fee: $50. Tuition and fees vary according to course load and campus/location. *Financial support:* In 2009–10, 31 research assistantships (averaging $6,378 per year), 67 teaching assistantships (averaging $8,252 per year) were awarded; career-related internships or fieldwork, Federal Work-Study, scholarships/grants, health care benefits, tuition waivers (partial), and unspecified assistantships also available. Support available to part-time students. Financial award application deadline: 3/1; financial award applicants required to submit FAFSA. *Unit head:* Dr. John Romans, Head, 405-744-6040, Fax: 405-744-6779. *Application contact:* Dr. Gordon Emslie, Dean, 405-744-6368, Fax: 405-744-0355, E-mail: grad-i@okstate.edu.

Penn State University Park, Graduate School, College of Education, Department of Educational and School Psychology and Special Education, State College, University Park, PA 16802-1503. Offers M Ed, MS, PhD.

Pontifical Catholic University of Puerto Rico, College of Education, Program in Educational Psychology, Ponce, PR 00717-0777. Offers M Ed. *Degree requirements:* For master's, comprehensive exam, thesis (for some programs). *Entrance requirements:* For master's, GRE, 2 letters of recommendation, interview, minimum GPA of 2.75.

Purdue University, Graduate School, School of Education, Department of Educational Studies, West Lafayette, IN 47907. Offers administration (MS Ed, PhD, Ed S); counseling and development (MS Ed, PhD); education of the gifted (MS Ed); educational psychology (MS Ed, PhD); foundations of education (MS Ed, PhD); higher education administration (MS Ed, PhD); special education (MS Ed, PhD). *Accreditation:* ACA (one or more programs are accredited); NCATE (one or more programs are accredited). Part-time and evening/weekend programs available. *Degree requirements:* For master's, thesis optional; for doctorate, thesis/dissertation, oral and written exams; for Ed S, oral presentation, project. *Entrance requirements:* For master's, GRE General Test, minimum undergraduate GPA of 3.0; for doctorate, GRE General Test; for Ed S, GRE, minimum B average. Additional exam requirements/recommendations for international students: Required—TOEFL. Electronic applications accepted. *Faculty research:* Motivation, learning disabilities, school learning, group processes, cognitive development.

Rutgers, The State University of New Jersey, New Brunswick, Graduate School of Education, Department of Educational Psychology, Program in Learning, Cognition and Development, Piscataway, NJ 08854-8097. Offers Ed M. Part-time and evening/weekend programs available. *Entrance requirements:* For master's, GRE General Test, 3 letters of recommendation. Additional exam requirements/recommendations for international students: Required—TOEFL (minimum score 550 paper-based; 233 computer-based; 83 iBT). Electronic applications accepted. *Faculty research:* Cognitive development, gender roles, cognition and instruction, peer learning, infancy and early childhood.

Rutgers, The State University of New Jersey, New Brunswick, Graduate School of Education, Doctoral Program in Education, Piscataway, NJ 08854-8097. Offers educational policy (PhD); educational psychology (PhD); literacy education (PhD); mathematics education (PhD). Part-time programs available. *Degree requirements:* For doctorate, thesis/dissertation, qualifying exam. *Entrance requirements:* For doctorate, GRE General Test, GRE Subject Test (mathematics education). Additional exam requirements/recommendations for international students: Required—TOEFL (minimum score 575 paper-based; 233 computer-based; 83 iBT). Electronic applications accepted. *Faculty research:* Literacy education, math education, educational psychology, educational policy.

Simon Fraser University, Graduate Studies, Faculty of Education, Program in Educational Psychology, Burnaby, BC V5A 1S6, Canada. Offers M Ed, MA, PhD. *Degree requirements:* For master's, project or thesis; for doctorate, thesis/dissertation. *Entrance requirements:* For master's, minimum GPA of 3.0; for doctorate, GRE, master's degree or exceptional record in a bachelor's degree, minimum GPA of 3.5. Additional exam requirements/recommendations for international students: Required—TOEFL or IELTS.

Southern Illinois University Carbondale, Graduate School, College of Education, Department of Educational Psychology and Special Education, Program in Educational Psychology, Carbondale, IL 62901-4701. Offers counselor education (MS Ed, PhD); educational psychology (PhD); human learning and development (MS Ed); measurement and statistics (PhD). *Accreditation:* NCATE. *Degree requirements:* For master's, thesis; for doctorate, thesis/dissertation. *Entrance requirements:* For master's, GRE General Test, minimum GPA of 2.7; for doctorate, minimum GPA of 3.25. Additional exam requirements/recommendations for international students: Required—TOEFL. *Faculty research:* Career development, problem solving, learning and instruction, cognitive development, family assessment.

Stanford University, School of Education, Program in Psychological Studies in Education, Stanford, CA 94305-9991. Offers child and adolescent development (PhD); counseling psychology (PhD); educational psychology (PhD). *Degree requirements:* For doctorate, thesis/dissertation. *Entrance requirements:* For doctorate, GRE General Test. Electronic applications accepted. *Expenses:* Tuition: Full-time $37,380; part-time $2760 per quarter. Required fees: $501.

State University of New York College at Oneonta, Graduate Education, Division of Education, Department of Educational Psychology and Counseling, Oneonta, NY 13820-4015. Offers school counselor K-12 (MS Ed, CAS). *Accreditation:* NCATE. Part-time and evening/weekend programs available. *Students:* 23 full-time (18 women), 17 part-time (11 women). Average age 28. 30 applicants, 50% accepted, 15 enrolled. In 2009, 10 master's, 2 CASs awarded. *Degree requirements:* For master's, comprehensive exam. *Entrance requirements:* For master's, GRE General Test. *Application deadline:* For fall admission, 3/1 for domestic students. Application fee: $50. *Expenses:* Tuition, state resident: part-time $349 per credit hour. Tuition, nonresident: full-time $12,870; part-time $552 per credit hour. Required fees: $1280; $15.85 per credit hour. *Unit head:* Dr. Anuradhaa Shastri, Chair, 607-436-3554, Fax: 607-436-3799, E-mail: shastra@oneonta.edu. *Application contact:* Dean, 607-436-2523, Fax: 607-436-3084, E-mail: gradoffice@oneonta.edu.

Teachers College, Columbia University, Graduate Faculty of Education, Department of Health and Behavioral Studies, Program in Applied Educational Psychology–School Psychology, New York, NY 10027-6696. Offers Ed M, MA, Ed D, PhD. *Accreditation:* APA (one or more programs are accredited). *Students:* 37 full-time (31 women), 56 part-time (52 women); includes 20 minority (5 African Americans, 12 Asian Americans or Pacific Islanders, 3 Hispanic Americans), 2 international. Average age 26. 166 applicants, 35% accepted, 23 enrolled. In 2009, 22 master's, 5 doctorates awarded. *Degree requirements:* For master's, integrative paper; for doctorate, thesis/dissertation, integrative project. *Entrance requirements:* For doctorate, GRE General Test. *Application deadline:* For fall admission, 5/15 for domestic students. Application fee: $65. *Financial support:* Fellowships, research assistantships, career-related internships or fieldwork, Federal Work-Study, institutionally sponsored loans, and tuition waivers (full and partial) available. Support available to part-time students. Financial award application deadline: 2/1. *Faculty research:* Psychoeducational assessment, observation and concept acquisition in young children, reading, mathematical thinking, memory. *Unit head:* Dr. Chuck Basch, Chair, 212-678-3964, E-mail: ceb35@columbia.edu. *Application contact:* Peter Shon, Assistant Director of Admission, 212-678-3305, Fax: 212-678-4171, E-mail: shon@exchange.tc.columbia.edu.

Teachers College, Columbia University, Graduate Faculty of Education, Department of Human Development, Program in Educational Psychology-Human Cognition and Learning, New York, NY 10027-6696. Offers Ed M, MA, Ed D, PhD. *Accreditation:* APA (one or more programs are accredited). Part-time programs available. *Faculty:* 4 full-time (2 women). *Students:* 22 full-time (12 women), 66 part-time (49 women); includes 24 minority (3 African Americans, 18 Asian Americans or Pacific Islanders, 3 Hispanic Americans), 11 international. Average age 33. 44 applicants, 84% accepted, 13 enrolled. In 2009, 14 master's, 5 doctorates awarded. Terminal master's awarded for partial completion of doctoral program. *Degree requirements:* For master's, integrative paper; for doctorate, thesis/dissertation, integrative project. *Entrance requirements:* For doctorate, GRE General Test. *Application deadline:* For fall admission, 5/15 for domestic students; for spring admission, 12/1 for domestic students. Application fee: $65. *Financial support:* Fellowships, research assistantships, career-related internships or fieldwork, Federal Work-Study, institutionally sponsored loans, and tuition waivers (full and partial) available. Support available to part-time students. Financial award application deadline: 2/1. *Faculty research:* Early reading, text comprehension, learning disabilities, mathematical thinking, reasoning. *Unit head:* James Corter, Chair, 212-678-4190. *Application contact:* Melba Remice, Assistant Director of Admission, 212-678-4035, Fax: 212-678-4171, E-mail: ms2545@columbia.edu.

Temple University, Graduate School, College of Education, Department of Psychological Studies in Education, Program in Educational Psychology, Philadelphia, PA 19122-6096. Offers Ed M, PhD. Part-time and evening/weekend programs available. Terminal master's awarded for partial completion of doctoral program. *Degree requirements:* For master's, thesis or alternative; for doctorate, thesis/dissertation. *Entrance requirements:* For master's and doctorate, GRE General Test or MAT, minimum GPA of 3.0. Additional exam requirements/recommendations for international students: Required—TOEFL (minimum score 550 paper-based; 213 computer-based; 79 iBT). Electronic applications accepted. *Faculty research:* Computers in education, student motivation, school improvement in city schools, individual differences in learning, teaching strategies.

Tennessee Technological University, Graduate School, College of Education, Department of Counseling and Psychology, Cookeville, TN 38505. Offers educational psychology (MA, Ed S); educational psychology and student personnel (MA, Ed S). *Accreditation:* NCATE (one or more programs are accredited). Part-time and evening/weekend programs available. *Faculty:* 24 full-time (6 women). *Students:* 64 full-time (52 women), 42 part-time (33 women); includes 9 minority (5 African Americans, 1 Asian American or Pacific Islander, 3 Hispanic Americans). Average age 27. 71 applicants, 79% accepted, 37 enrolled. In 2009, 18 master's, 9 other advanced degrees awarded. *Degree requirements:* For master's and Ed S, comprehensive exam, thesis or alternative. *Entrance requirements:* For master's and Ed S, MAT or GRE.

Additional exam requirements/recommendations for international students: Required—TOEFL (minimum score 550 paper-based; 79 iBT), IELTS (minimum score 5.5). *Application deadline:* For fall admission, 8/1 for domestic students, 5/1 for international students; for spring admission, 12/1 for domestic students, 10/1 for international students. Application fee: $25 ($30 for international students). Electronic applications accepted. *Expenses:* Tuition, state resident: full-time $7034; part-time $368 per credit hour. *Financial support:* In 2009–10, 1 fellowship (averaging $8,000 per year), 8 research assistantships (averaging $4,000 per year), 3 teaching assistantships (averaging $4,000 per year) were awarded; career-related internships or fieldwork also available. Financial award application deadline: 4/1. *Unit head:* Dr. Barry Stein, Interim Chairperson, 931-372-3457, Fax: 931-372-6319. *Application contact:* Shelia K. Kendrick, Coordinator of Graduate Studies, 931-372-3808, Fax: 931-372-3497, E-mail: skendrick@tntech.edu.

Tennessee Technological University, Graduate School, College of Education, Department of Curriculum and Instruction, Program in Exceptional Learning, Cookeville, TN 38505. Offers applied behavior and learning (PhD); literacy (PhD); program planning and evaluation (PhD). *Students:* 11 full-time (10 women), 14 part-time (11 women); includes 3 minority (2 African Americans, 1 Asian American or Pacific Islander). 22 applicants, 18% accepted, 4 enrolled. In 2009, 4 doctorates awarded. *Degree requirements:* For doctorate, comprehensive exam, thesis/dissertation. *Entrance requirements:* For doctorate, GRE, minimum GPA of 3.0. Additional exam requirements/recommendations for international students: Required—TOEFL (minimum score 550 paper-based; 79 iBT), IELTS (minimum score 5.5). *Application deadline:* For fall admission, 8/1 for domestic students, 5/1 for international students; for spring admission, 12/1 for domestic students, 10/1 for international students. Application fee: $25 ($30 for international students). Electronic applications accepted. *Expenses:* Tuition, state resident: full-time $7034; part-time $368 per credit hour. *Financial support:* In 2009–10, 4 fellowships (averaging $8,000 per year), 10 research assistantships (averaging $12,000 per year), 1 teaching assistantship (averaging $12,000 per year) were awarded. Financial award application deadline: 4/1. *Unit head:* Dr. John J. Wheeler, Director, Doctoral Studies, 931-372-3078, Fax: 931-372-3517. *Application contact:* Shelia K. Kendrick, Coordinator of Graduate Studies, 931-372-3808, Fax: 931-372-3497, E-mail: skendrick@Tntech.edu.

Texas A&M University, College of Education and Human Development, Department of Educational Psychology, College Station, TX 77843. Offers counseling psychology (PhD); educational psychology (PhD); educational technology (M Ed); gifted and talented education (M Ed, MS); Hispanic bilingual education (M Ed, PhD); human learning and development (MS); intelligence, creativity, and giftedness (PhD); learning, development, and instruction (PhD); research, measurement and statistics (MS); research, measurement, and statistics (PhD); school counseling (M Ed); school psychology (PhD); special education (M Ed, PhD). *Accreditation:* APA (one or more programs are accredited). Part-time and evening/weekend programs available. Postbaccalaureate distance learning degree programs offered (no on-campus study). *Faculty:* 45. *Students:* 160 full-time (126 women), 144 part-time (118 women); includes 99 minority (25 African Americans, 13 Asian Americans or Pacific Islanders, 61 Hispanic Americans), 41 international. In 2009, 53 master's, 30 doctorates awarded. *Degree requirements:* For master's, thesis optional; for doctorate, thesis/dissertation. *Entrance requirements:* For master's and doctorate, GRE General Test. Additional exam requirements/recommendations for international students: Required—TOEFL. Application fee: $50 ($75 for international students). Electronic applications accepted. *Expenses:* Tuition, state resident: full-time $3991; part-time $221.74 per credit hour. Tuition, nonresident: full-time $9049; part-time $502.74 per credit hour. *Financial support:* In 2009–10, fellowships (averaging $12,000 per year), research assistantships (averaging $9,000 per year), teaching assistantships (averaging $9,000 per year) were awarded; career-related internships or fieldwork, institutionally sponsored loans, scholarships/grants, and unspecified assistantships also available. Financial award applicants required to submit FAFSA. *Unit head:* Dr. Victor Willson, Head, 979-845-1800. *Application contact:* Carol A. Wagner, Director of Advising, 979-845-1833, Fax: 979-862-1256, E-mail: epsyadvisor@tamu.edu.

Texas Christian University, College of Education, Program in Counseling, Fort Worth, TX 76129-0002. Offers counseling (M Ed); LPC (Certificate); school counseling (Certificate). Part-time and evening/weekend programs available. *Degree requirements:* For master's, oral exams. *Entrance requirements:* Additional exam requirements/recommendations for international students: Required—TOEFL (minimum score 550 paper-based; 213 computer-based; 80 iBT). *Application deadline:* For fall admission, 7/15 for domestic and international students; for spring admission, 11/15 for domestic and international students. Applications are processed on a rolling basis. Application fee: $50. *Expenses:* Tuition: Full-time $17,640; part-time $980 per credit hour. Tuition and fees vary according to program. *Financial support:* Teaching assistantships with full tuition reimbursements, career-related internships or fieldwork and unspecified assistantships available. Financial award application deadline: 3/15; financial award applicants required to submit FAFSA. *Unit head:* Dr. Kay B. Stevens, Associate Dean, 817-257-7661, E-mail: k.stevens2@tcu.edu. *Application contact:* Robyn P. Shepheard, Academic Program Specialist, 817-257-7661, E-mail: r.shepheard@tcu.edu.

Texas Christian University, College of Science and Engineering, Department of Psychology, Fort Worth, TX 76129-0002. Offers experimental psychology (PhD), including cognitive psychology, learning, neuropsychology, social psychology; psychology (MA, MS). *Degree requirements:* For master's, thesis; for doctorate, thesis/dissertation. *Entrance requirements:* For master's and doctorate, GRE General Test. Additional exam requirements/recommendations for international students: Required—TOEFL. *Application deadline:* For fall admission, 3/1 for domestic and international students; for spring admission, 12/1 for domestic students. Applications are processed on a rolling basis. Application fee: $50. *Expenses:* Tuition: Full-time $17,640; part-time $980 per credit hour. Tuition and fees vary according to program. *Financial support:* In 2009–10, 20 students received support; teaching assistantships with full tuition reimbursements available, unspecified assistantships available. Financial award application deadline: 3/1. *Unit head:* Dr. Charles Lord, Graduate Director, 817-257-7410, E-mail: c.lord@tcu.edu. *Application contact:* Marilyn Eudaly, Department Manager, 817-257-6437.

Texas Tech University, Graduate School, College of Education, Department of Educational Psychology and Leadership, Lubbock, TX 79409. Offers counselor education (M Ed, PhD); educational leadership (M Ed, Ed D); educational psychology (M Ed, PhD); higher education (M Ed, Ed D); higher education: higher education research (PhD); instructional technology (M Ed, Ed D); instructional technology: distance education (M Ed); special education (M Ed, Ed D). *Accreditation:* ACA; NCATE. Part-time programs available. *Students:* 137 full-time (94 women), 335 part-time (236 women); includes 90 minority (27 African Americans, 6 American Indian/Alaska Native, 3 Asian Americans or Pacific Islanders, 54 Hispanic Americans), 34 international. Average age 36. 390 applicants, 51% accepted, 90 enrolled. In 2009, 113 master's, 18 doctorates awarded. *Degree requirements:* For master's, thesis optional; for doctorate, thesis/dissertation. *Entrance requirements:* For master's and doctorate, GRE General Test. Additional exam requirements/recommendations for international students: Required—TOEFL (minimum score 550 paper-based; 213 computer-based). *Application deadline:* For fall admission, 3/1 priority date for international students; for spring admission, 11/1 priority date for international students. Applications are processed on a rolling basis. Application fee: $50 ($75 for international students). Electronic applications accepted. *Expenses:* Tuition, state resident: full-time $5100; part-time $213 per credit hour. Tuition, nonresident: full-time $11,748; part-time $490 per credit hour. Required fees: $2298; $50 per credit hour. $555 per semester. *Financial support:* Research assistantships with partial tuition reimbursements, teaching assistantships with partial tuition reimbursements, career-related internships or fieldwork, Federal Work-Study, and institutionally sponsored loans available. Support available to part-time students. Financial award application deadline: 4/15; financial award applicants required to submit FAFSA. *Faculty research:* Psychological processes of teaching and learning, teaching populations with special needs, instructional technology, educational administration in education, theories and practice in counseling and counselor education K-12 and higher. *Unit head:* Dr. William Lan, Chair, 806-742-1998 Ext. 436, Fax: 806-742-2179, E-mail: william.lan@ttu.edu. *Application contact:* Dr. Joseph G. Claudet, Graduate Adviser, 806-742-1998, Fax: 806-742-2179.

Union Institute & University, MA Program in Psychology and Counseling, Brattleboro, VT 05301. Offers clinical mental health counseling (MA); clinical psychology (MA); counseling psychology (MA); developmental psychology (MA); educational psychology (MA); organizational psychology (MA). Postbaccalaureate distance learning degree programs offered (minimal on-campus study). *Faculty:* 2 full-time (1 woman), 8 part-time/adjunct (2 women). *Students:* 57 full-time (50 women), 20 part-time (16 women); includes 4 minority (1 African American, 3 Hispanic Americans). Average age 41. In 2009, 23 master's awarded. *Degree requirements:* For master's, thesis, internship (depending on concentration). *Application deadline:* Applications are processed on a rolling basis. Electronic applications accepted. Tuition and fees vary according to course load, degree level, campus/location and program. *Unit head:* Dr. Nicholas Young, Director, 802-257-8911, E-mail: nick.young@myunion.edu. *Application contact:* Diane Robinson, Director of Admissions, Brattleboro, 800-336-6794, E-mail: diane.robinson@myunion.edu.

Universidad de Iberoamerica, Graduate School, San Jose, Costa Rica. Offers clinical neuropsychology (PhD); clinical psychology (M Psych); educational psychology (M Psych); forensic psychology (M Psych); hospital management (MHA); intensive care nursing (MN); medicine (MD). *Entrance requirements:* For master's, 2 letters of recommendation, interview.

Université de Moncton, Faculty of Education, Graduate Studies in Education, Moncton, NB E1A 3E9, Canada. Offers educational psychology (M Ed, MA Ed); guidance (M Ed, MA Ed); school administration (M Ed, MA Ed); teaching (M Ed, MA Ed). Part-time programs available. *Degree requirements:* For master's, proficiency in English and French. *Entrance requirements:* For master's, minimum GPA of 3.0. *Faculty research:* Guidance, ethnolinguistic vitality, children's rights, ecological education, entrepreneurship.

Université de Montréal, Faculty of Education, Department of Psychopedagogy and Andragogy, Montréal, QC H3C 3J7, Canada. Offers M Ed, MA, PhD, DESS. Part-time and evening/weekend programs available. *Faculty:* 28 full-time (18 women), 4 part-time/adjunct (2 women). *Students:* 104 full-time (56 women), 332 part-time (235 women). 362 applicants, 57% accepted, 148 enrolled. In 2009, 23 master's, 4 doctorates, 19 other advanced degrees awarded. Terminal master's awarded for partial completion of doctoral program. *Degree requirements:* For master's, thesis (for some programs); for doctorate, thesis/dissertation, general exam. *Entrance requirements:* For doctorate, MA or M Ed. *Application deadline:* For fall admission, 2/1 priority date for domestic students; for winter admission, 11/1 priority date for domestic students; for spring admission, 2/1 priority date for domestic students. Application fee: $100. Electronic applications accepted. *Financial support:* Teaching assistantships available. *Unit head:* Colette Gervais, Director, 514-343-7035, Fax: 514-343-7660, E-mail: colette.gervais@umontreal.ca. *Application contact:* Mohamed Hrimech, Responsible for Graduate Studies, 514-343-6167, Fax: 514-343-7660, E-mail: mohamed.hrimech@umontreal.ca.

Université du Québec à Trois-Rivières, Graduate Programs, Program in Psychoeducation, Trois-Rivières, QC G9A 5H7, Canada. Offers M Ed, PhD. *Entrance requirements:* For master's, appropriate bachelor's degree, proficiency in French. *Faculty research:* Troubled youth intervention.

Université du Québec en Outaouais, Graduate Programs, Program in Psychoéducation, Gatineau, QC J8X 3X7, Canada. Offers M Ed, MA. Part-time programs available. *Entrance requirements:* For master's, appropriate bachelor's degree, proficiency in French.

Université Laval, Faculty of Education, Department of Teaching and Learning Studies, Programs in Educational Psychology, Québec, QC G1K 7P4, Canada. Offers MA, PhD. Terminal master's awarded for partial completion of doctoral program. *Degree requirements:* For master's, thesis (for some programs); for doctorate, comprehensive exam, thesis/dissertation. *Entrance requirements:* For master's and doctorate, English exam (comprehension of written English), knowledge of French. Electronic applications accepted. *Faculty research:* Emotional, social, and cognitive development; learning and motivation in school; language development; reading acquisition; computer and learning strategies.

University at Albany, State University of New York, School of Education, Department of Educational and Counseling Psychology, Albany, NY 12222-0001. Offers counseling psychology (MS, PhD, CAS); educational psychology (Ed D); educational psychology and statistics (MS); measurements and evaluation (Ed D); rehabilitation counseling (MS), including counseling psychology; school counselor (CAS); school psychology (Psy D, CAS); special education (MS); statistics and research design (Ed D). *Accreditation:* APA (one or more programs are accredited). Evening/weekend programs available. *Degree requirements:* For doctorate, thesis/dissertation. *Entrance requirements:* For doctorate, GRE General Test. Additional exam requirements/recommendations for international students: Required—TOEFL (minimum score 550 paper-based; 213 computer-based). Electronic applications accepted.

University at Buffalo, the State University of New York, Graduate School, Graduate School of Education, Department of Counseling, School, and Educational Psychology, Buffalo, NY 14260. Offers counseling/school psychology (PhD); counselor education (PhD); educational psychology (MA, PhD); general education (Ed M); mental health counseling (MS); rehabilitation counseling (MS); school counseling (Ed M, Certificate); Singapore school counseling (Ed M). *Accreditation:* CORE (one or more programs are accredited). Postbaccalaureate distance learning degree programs offered (no on-campus study). *Faculty:* 17 full-time (8 women), 36 part-time/adjunct (28 women). *Students:* 152 full-time (125 women), 127 part-time (97 women); includes 33 minority (22 African Americans, 2 American Indian/Alaska Native, 3 Asian Americans or Pacific Islanders, 6 Hispanic Americans), 27 international. Average age 30. 396 applicants, 41% accepted, 119 enrolled. In 2009, 60 master's, 12 doctorates, 24 other advanced degrees awarded. *Degree requirements:* For master's, comprehensive exam (for some programs), thesis (for some programs); for doctorate, comprehensive exam, thesis/dissertation. *Entrance requirements:* For master's and doctorate, GRE General Test, interview, letters of reference. Additional exam requirements/recommendations for international students: Required—TOEFL (minimum score 79 iBT). *Application deadline:* For fall admission, 2/1 priority date for domestic and international students. Application fee: $50. Electronic applications accepted. *Financial support:* In 2009–10, 14 fellowships with full tuition reimbursements (averaging $9,000 per year), 28 research assistantships with full tuition reimbursements (averaging $9,000 per year) were awarded; teaching assistantships with tuition reimbursements, career-related internships or fieldwork, Federal Work-Study, institutionally sponsored loans, and unspecified assistantships also available. Financial award application deadline: 2/1; financial award applicants required to submit FAFSA. *Faculty research:* Multicultural counseling, class size effects, good work in counseling, eating disorders, outcome assessment, change agents and therapeutic factors in group counseling. Total annual research expenditures: $3.7 million. *Unit head:* Dr. Timothy Janikowski, Chair, 716-645-2484, Fax: 716-645-6616, E-mail: tjanikow@buffalo.edu. *Application contact:* Rochelle Cohen, Admissions Assistant, 716-645-2110, Fax: 716-645-7937, E-mail: recohen@buffalo.edu.

University of Alberta, Faculty of Graduate Studies and Research, Department of Educational Psychology, Edmonton, AB T6G 2E1, Canada. Offers counseling psychology (M Ed, PhD); educational psychology (M Ed, PhD); instructional technology (M Ed); school counseling (M Ed); school psychology (M Ed, PhD); special education (M Ed, PhD); special education-deafness studies (M Ed); teaching English as a second language (M Ed). Part-time programs available. *Faculty:* 34 full-time (14 women), 12 part-time/adjunct (6 women). *Students:* 117 full-time (93 women), 173 part-time (121 women). Average age 36. 252 applicants, 34% accepted. In 2009, 30 master's, 10 doctorates awarded. *Degree requirements:* For master's, thesis optional; for doctorate, comprehensive exam, thesis/dissertation. *Entrance requirements:* For master's and doctorate, minimum GPA of 3.0. Additional exam requirements/recommendations for international students: Required—TOEFL. *Application deadline:* For fall admission, 2/1 priority date for domestic and international students. Applications are processed on a rolling basis. Tuition and fees charges are reported in Canadian dollars. *Expenses:* Tuition, area resident: Full-time $4626 Canadian dollars; part-time $99.72 Canadian dollars per unit. International tuition: $8216 Canadian dollars full-time. Required fees: $3590 Canadian dollars; $99.72 Canadian dollars per unit. $215 Canadian dollars per term. *Financial support:* In 2009–10, 10 fellowships

Educational Psychology

University of Alberta (continued)
with full tuition reimbursements (averaging $16,120 per year), 36 research assistantships with full tuition reimbursements (averaging $12,614 per year), 46 teaching assistantships with full tuition reimbursements (averaging $5,462 per year) were awarded; career-related internships or fieldwork and scholarships/grants also available. *Faculty research:* Human learning, development and assessment. *Unit head:* Dr. Linda M. McDonald, Chair, 780-492-1149, Fax: 780-492-1318, E-mail: linda.mcdonald@ualberta.ca. *Application contact:* Judy Maynes, Information Contact, 780-492-1149, Fax: 780-492-1318, E-mail: edpygrad@ualberta.ca.

The University of Arizona, Graduate College, College of Education, Department of Educational Psychology, Tucson, AZ 85721. Offers educational psychology (MA, PhD, Ed S); school counseling and guidance (M Ed). *Accreditation:* APA (one or more programs are accredited). Part-time programs available. *Faculty:* 5 full-time (3 women). *Students:* 14 full-time (13 women), 25 part-time (19 women); includes 8 minority (2 African Americans, 2 Asian Americans or Pacific Islanders, 4 Hispanic Americans), 5 international. Average age 32. 36 applicants, 36% accepted, 9 enrolled. In 2009, 5 master's, 3 doctorates awarded. Terminal master's awarded for partial completion of doctoral program. *Degree requirements:* For master's, comprehensive exam (for some programs), thesis optional; for doctorate, comprehensive exam, thesis/dissertation. *Entrance requirements:* For master's, minimum GPA of 3.0, 3 letters of recommendation, 500-word professional writing sample; for doctorate, GRE General Test, minimum GPA of 3.0, 3 letters of recommendation, statement of purpose, 500-word professional writing sample. Additional exam requirements/recommendations for international students: Required—TOEFL (minimum score 600 paper-based; 250 computer-based). *Application deadline:* For fall admission, 3/1 for domestic students; for spring admission, 10/1 for domestic students. Applications are processed on a rolling basis. Application fee: $65. Electronic applications accepted. *Expenses:* Tuition, state resident: full-time $9028. Tuition, nonresident: full-time $24,890. *Financial support:* In 2009–10, 7 research assistantships with full tuition reimbursements (averaging $12,551 per year), 10 teaching assistantships with full tuition reimbursements (averaging $11,928 per year) were awarded; career-related internships or fieldwork, scholarships/grants, health care benefits, tuition waivers (partial), and unspecified assistantships also available. *Faculty research:* School reform, motivational learning in classroom settings, measurement and evaluation of learning outcomes, student resilience, preadolescent and adolescent development. Total annual research expenditures: $32,464. *Unit head:* Dr. Thomas Good, Department Head, 520-621-7828, Fax: 520-621-2909, E-mail: goodt@u.arizona.edu. *Application contact:* Toni Sollars, Administrative Associate, 520-621-7828, Fax: 520-621-2909, E-mail: tsollars@u.arizona.edu.

University of Calgary, Faculty of Graduate Studies, Faculty of Education, Division of Applied Psychology, Calgary, AB T2N 1N4, Canada. Offers counseling psychology (M Ed, M Sc, PhD); human development and learning (M Ed, M Sc, PhD); school psychology (M Ed, M Sc, PhD); special education (M Ed, M Sc, PhD). Part-time programs available. *Degree requirements:* For master's, thesis (for some programs), final oral exam; for doctorate, thesis/dissertation, candidacy exam, final oral exam. *Entrance requirements:* For master's, minimum GPA of 3.0, 3 letters of reference; for doctorate, minimum GPA of 3.5, 3 letters of reference. *Faculty research:* Counselor education, family life studies, learning and cognition.

University of California, Davis, Graduate Studies, Graduate Group in Education, Davis, CA 95616. Offers education (MA, Ed D); instructional studies (PhD); psychological studies (PhD); sociocultural studies (PhD). Terminal master's awarded for partial completion of doctoral program. *Degree requirements:* For master's, comprehensive exam (for some programs), thesis (for some programs); for doctorate, thesis/dissertation. *Entrance requirements:* For master's and doctorate, GRE. Additional exam requirements/recommendations for international students: Required—TOEFL (minimum score 550 paper-based; 213 computer-based). Electronic applications accepted. *Faculty research:* Language and literacy, mathematics education, science education, teacher development, school psychology.

University of California, Riverside, Graduate Division, Graduate School of Education, Riverside, CA 92521-0102. Offers autism (M Ed); curriculum and instruction (MA, PhD); diversity and equity (M Ed); educational leadership and policy (MA, PhD); educational psychology (MA, PhD); general education (M Ed); higher education administration and policy (M Ed, PhD); leadership (M Ed); reading (M Ed); school psychology (PhD); special education (M Ed, MA, PhD). *Faculty:* 23 full-time (12 women), 12 part-time/adjunct (8 women). *Students:* 230 full-time (183 women), 6 part-time (3 women); includes 75 minority (12 African Americans, 1 American Indian/Alaska Native, 21 Asian Americans or Pacific Islanders, 41 Hispanic Americans), 6 international. Average age 32. 288 applicants, 60% accepted, 118 enrolled. In 2009, 68 master's, 13 doctorates awarded. Terminal master's awarded for partial completion of doctoral program. *Degree requirements:* For master's, comprehensive exam (for some programs), comprehensive exams or thesis (MA), case study or analytical report (M Ed); for doctorate, thesis/dissertation, written and oral qualifying exams, college teaching practicum. *Entrance requirements:* For master's, GRE General Test, GRE Subject Test, CBEST, CSET, minimum GPA of 3.2; for doctorate, GRE General Test, GRE Subject Test, master's degree (desirable), minimum GPA of 3.2. Additional exam requirements/recommendations for international students: Required—TOEFL (minimum score 550 paper-based; 213 computer-based; 80 iBT). *Application deadline:* For fall admission, 9/1 for domestic students, 4/1 for international students; for winter admission, 12/1 for domestic students, 9/1 for international students; for spring admission, 3/1 for domestic students, 10/1 for international students. Applications are processed on a rolling basis. Application fee: $70 ($85 for international students). Electronic applications accepted. *Financial support:* In 2009–10, 55 students received support, including 13 fellowships with full and partial tuition reimbursements available (averaging $26,809 per year), 21 research assistantships with full and partial tuition reimbursements available (averaging $14,238 per year), 1 teaching assistantship with full and partial tuition reimbursement available (averaging $16,638 per year); career-related internships or fieldwork, Federal Work-Study, institutionally sponsored loans, scholarships/grants, and unspecified assistantships also available. Financial award application deadline: 1/5; financial award applicants required to submit FAFSA. *Faculty research:* Responsiveness to intervention, faculty core, response to intervention of English language learners, advanced modeling techniques, study on social capital, trust, and motivation. Total annual research expenditures: $5.6 million. *Unit head:* Dr. Steven T. Bossert, Dean, 951-827-5802, Fax: 951-827-3942, E-mail: steven.bossert@ucr.edu. *Application contact:* Dr. John Wills, Graduate Advisor for Admission, 951-827-6362, Fax: 951-827-3942, E-mail: edgrad@ucr.edu.

University of Colorado at Boulder, Graduate School, School of Education, Division of Educational and Psychological Studies, Boulder, CO 80309. Offers MA, PhD. *Accreditation:* NCATE. Part-time programs available. *Students:* 14 full-time (10 women), 5 part-time (all women); includes 3 minority (1 American Indian/Alaska Native, 2 Hispanic Americans). Average age 33. 24 applicants, 38% accepted, 6 enrolled. In 2009, 1 master's awarded. *Degree requirements:* For master's, comprehensive exam, thesis or alternative; for doctorate, one foreign language, comprehensive exam, thesis/dissertation. *Entrance requirements:* For master's, GRE General Test or MAT, minimum undergraduate GPA of 2.75; for doctorate, GRE General Test. *Application deadline:* For fall admission, 2/1 priority date for domestic students, 12/1 for international students; for spring admission, 9/1 for domestic students, 12/1 for international students. Application fee: $50 ($60 for international students). *Financial support:* In 2009–10, 6 fellowships (averaging $8,551 per year), 3 research assistantships (averaging $11,048 per year) were awarded. *Application contact:* E-mail: edadvise@colorado.edu.

University of Connecticut, Graduate School, Neag School of Education, Department of Educational Psychology, Storrs, CT 06269. Offers cognition and instruction (MA, PhD, Post-Master's Certificate); counseling psychology (MA, PhD, Post-Master's Certificate), including counseling psychology (PhD), school counseling (MA, Post-Master's Certificate); gifted and talented education (MA, PhD, Post-Master's Certificate); learning technology (MA, PhD, Post-Master's Certificate); measurement, evaluation, and assessment (MA, PhD, Post-Master's Certificate); school psychology (MA, PhD, Post-Master's Certificate); special education (MA, PhD, Post-Master's Certificate). *Faculty:* 37 full-time (18 women). *Students:* 172 full-time (134 women), 124 part-time (87 women); includes 31 minority (10 African Americans, 1 American Indian/Alaska Native, 8 Asian Americans or Pacific Islanders, 12 Hispanic Americans), 24 international. Average age 34. 299 applicants, 28% accepted, 46 enrolled. In 2009, 103 master's, 12 doctorates, 18 other advanced degrees awarded. *Degree requirements:* For master's, comprehensive exam; for doctorate, thesis/dissertation. *Entrance requirements:* For doctorate, GRE General Test. Additional exam requirements/recommendations for international students: Required—TOEFL (minimum score 550 paper-based; 213 computer-based). *Application deadline:* For fall admission, 2/1 priority date for domestic and international students; for spring admission, 11/1 for domestic students, 10/1 for international students. Applications are processed on a rolling basis. Application fee: $55. Electronic applications accepted. *Expenses:* Tuition, state resident: full-time $4725; part-time $525 per credit. Tuition, nonresident: full-time $12,267; part-time $1363 per credit. Required fees: $346 per semester. Tuition and fees vary according to course load. *Financial support:* In 2009–10, 86 research assistantships with full tuition reimbursements, 4 teaching assistantships with full tuition reimbursements were awarded; fellowships, Federal Work-Study, scholarships/grants, health care benefits, and unspecified assistantships also available. Financial award application deadline: 2/1; financial award applicants required to submit FAFSA. *Unit head:* Hariharan Swaminathan, Head, 860-486-4031, Fax: 860-486-0210, E-mail: hariharan.swaminathan@uconn.edu. *Application contact:* Cheryl Lowe, Program Assistant, 860-486-4031, Fax: 860-486-0180, E-mail: cheryl.lowe@uconn.edu.

University of Denver, College of Education, Denver, CO 80208. Offers counseling psychology (MA, PhD); curriculum and instruction (MA, PhD, Certificate), including curriculum leadership (MA, PhD); educational administration and policy studies (Certificate); educational psychology (MA, PhD, Ed S), including child and family studies (MA, PhD), quantitative research methods (MA, PhD), school psychology (PhD, Ed S); higher education and adult studies (MA, PhD); library and information science (MLIS); library and information sciences (Certificate); school administration (PhD). *Accreditation:* ALA; APA (one or more programs are accredited). Part-time and evening/weekend programs available. Postbaccalaureate distance learning degree programs offered (no on-campus study). *Faculty:* 33 full-time (24 women), 62 part-time/adjunct (41 women). *Students:* 384 full-time (305 women), 453 part-time (336 women); includes 164 minority (47 African Americans, 8 American Indian/Alaska Native, 14 Asian Americans or Pacific Islanders, 95 Hispanic Americans), 20 international. Average age 34. 1,065 applicants, 59% accepted, 433 enrolled. In 2009, 206 master's, 38 doctorates, 117 other advanced degrees awarded. Terminal master's awarded for partial completion of doctoral program. *Degree requirements:* For master's, comprehensive exam; for doctorate, 2 foreign languages, comprehensive exam, thesis/dissertation. *Entrance requirements:* For master's and doctorate, GRE General Test or MAT. *Application deadline:* Applications are processed on a rolling basis. Application fee: $50. Electronic applications accepted. *Expenses:* Tuition: Full-time $34,596; part-time $961 per quarter hour. Required fees: $4 per quarter hour. Tuition and fees vary according to course load, campus/location and program. *Financial support:* In 2009–10, 78 teaching assistantships with full and partial tuition reimbursements (averaging $11,700 per year) were awarded; career-related internships or fieldwork, Federal Work-Study, institutionally sponsored loans, and scholarships/grants also available. Support available to part-time students. Financial award application deadline: 3/1; financial award applicants required to submit FAFSA. *Faculty research:* Parkinson's disease, personnel training, development and assessments, gifted education, service-learning, transportation, public schools. Total annual research expenditures: $340,000. *Unit head:* Dr. Gregory M. Anderson, Dean, 303-871-3665. *Application contact:* Janet Erickson, Director of Graduate Admission, 303-871-2485, E-mail: edinfo@du.edu.

University of Florida, Graduate School, College of Education, Department of Educational Psychology, Gainesville, FL 32611. Offers educational psychology (M Ed, MAE, Ed D, PhD, Ed S); research and evaluation methodology (M Ed, MAE, Ed D, PhD, Ed S); school psychology (M Ed, MAE, Ed D, PhD, Ed S). *Accreditation:* NCATE. Terminal master's awarded for partial completion of doctoral program. *Degree requirements:* For master's, thesis (MAE); for doctorate, variable foreign language requirement, thesis/dissertation. *Entrance requirements:* For master's and doctorate, GRE General Test, minimum GPA of 3.0; for Ed S, GRE General Test. Additional exam requirements/recommendations for international students: Required—TOEFL (minimum score 550 paper-based; 213 computer-based). Electronic applications accepted. *Faculty research:* School improvement, teaching and learning, item response theory.

University of Georgia, Graduate School, College of Education, Department of Educational Psychology and Instructional Technology, Athens, GA 30602. Offers education of the gifted (Ed D); educational psychology (M Ed, MA, Ed D, PhD, Ed S); instructional technology (M Ed, PhD, Ed S). *Accreditation:* NCATE. *Faculty:* 27 full-time (11 women). *Students:* 112 full-time (84 women), 107 part-time (80 women); includes 38 minority (25 African Americans, 2 American Indian/Alaska Native, 4 Asian Americans or Pacific Islanders, 7 Hispanic Americans), 40 international. 281 applicants, 44% accepted, 78 enrolled. In 2009, 42 master's, 13 doctorates, 24 other advanced degrees awarded. *Entrance requirements:* For master's and Ed S, GRE General Test or MAT; for doctorate, GRE General Test. *Application deadline:* For fall admission, 7/1 priority date for domestic students; for spring admission, 11/15 for domestic students. Application fee: $50. Electronic applications accepted. *Expenses:* Tuition, state resident: full-time $6000; part-time $250 per credit hour. Tuition, nonresident: full-time $20,904; part-time $871 per credit hour. Required fees: $730 per semester. *Financial support:* Fellowships, research assistantships, teaching assistantships, unspecified assistantships available. *Unit head:* Dr. Robert M. Branch, Head, 706-542-4110, Fax: 706-542-4240, E-mail: rbranch@uga.edu. *Application contact:* Dr. Stacey Neuharth-Pritchett, Graduate Coordinator, 706-542-4247, E-mail: sneuhart@uga.edu.

University of Hawaii at Manoa, Graduate Division, College of Education, Department of Educational Psychology, Honolulu, HI 96822. Offers M Ed, PhD. Part-time programs available. *Faculty:* 13 full-time (6 women), 2 part-time/adjunct (both women). *Students:* 24 full-time (19 women), 27 part-time (19 women); includes 22 minority (1 African American, 21 Asian Americans or Pacific Islanders), 4 international. Average age 31. 53 applicants, 45% accepted, 19 enrolled. In 2009, 8 master's, 5 doctorates awarded. *Degree requirements:* For master's, thesis optional; for doctorate, comprehensive exam, thesis/dissertation. *Entrance requirements:* Additional exam requirements/recommendations for international students: Required—TOEFL (minimum score 600 paper-based; 250 computer-based; 100 iBT), IELTS (minimum score 7). *Application deadline:* For fall admission, 2/1 for domestic students, 1/15 for international students. Application fee: $60. *Expenses:* Tuition, state resident: full-time $8900; part-time $372 per credit. Tuition, nonresident: full-time $21,400; part-time $898 per credit. Required fees: $207 per semester. *Financial support:* In 2009–10, 1 student received support, including 5 fellowships (averaging $1,580 per year), 10 research assistantships (averaging $17,740 per year); career-related internships or fieldwork, institutionally sponsored loans, and tuition waivers (full) also available. Financial award application deadline: 3/1; financial award applicants required to submit FAFSA. *Faculty research:* Human learning and development, measurement, research methods, statistics. Total annual research expenditures: $339,000. *Application contact:* Katherine Ratliffe, Graduate Chair, 808-956-7775, Fax: 808-956-6615, E-mail: ratliffe@hawaii.edu.

University of Houston, College of Education, Department of Educational Psychology, Houston, TX 77204. Offers counseling (M Ed); counseling psychology (PhD); educational psychology (M Ed); school psychology (PhD); school psychology and individual differences (PhD); special education (M Ed, Ed D). *Accreditation:* NCATE. Part-time and evening/weekend programs available. *Faculty:* 21 full-time (11 women), 12 part-time/adjunct (8 women). *Students:* 121 full-time (103 women), 123 part-time (106 women); includes 86 minority (23 African Americans, 3 American Indian/Alaska Native, 24 Asian Americans or Pacific Islanders, 36 Hispanic Americans), 11 international. Average age 30. 139 applicants, 52% accepted, 38 enrolled. In 2009, 32 master's, 16 doctorates awarded. *Degree requirements:* For master's, comprehensive exam or thesis; for doctorate, comprehensive exam, thesis/dissertation. *Entrance requirements:* For master's, GRE, recommendations, curriculum vitae/resume; for doctorate, GRE, recommendations, curriculum vitae/resume, goal statement, writing sample. Additional exam requirements/recommendations for international students: Required—TOEFL. *Application*

deadline: For fall admission, 12/1 for domestic and international students; for spring admission, 9/15 for domestic and international students. Application fee: $45 ($75 for international students). *Expenses:* Tuition, state resident: full-time $7676; part-time $320 per credit hour. Tuition, nonresident: full-time $14,324; part-time $597 per credit hour. Required fees: $3034. *Financial support:* In 2009–10, 2 fellowships with full tuition reimbursements (averaging $9,500 per year), 2 research assistantships with full tuition reimbursements (averaging $10,225 per year), 46 teaching assistantships with full tuition reimbursements (averaging $10,225 per year) were awarded; career-related internships or fieldwork, Federal Work-Study, institutionally sponsored loans, scholarships/grants, health care benefits, and unspecified assistantships also available. Support available to part-time students. Financial award application deadline: 2/1. *Faculty research:* Evidence-based assessment and intervention, multicultural issues in psychology, social and cultural context of learning, systemic barriers to college, motivational aspects of self-regulated learning. *Unit head:* Dr. Tom Kubiszyn, Chairperson, 713-743-9865, Fax: 713-743-4996, E-mail: tkubiszyn@uh.edu. *Application contact:* Kimberly A. Zainfeld, Academic Advisor, 713-743-9830, Fax: 713-743-4996, E-mail: kzainfeld@uh.edu.

University of Illinois at Chicago, Graduate College, College of Education, Department of Educational Psychology, Chicago, IL 60607-7128. Offers PhD.

University of Illinois at Urbana–Champaign, Graduate College, College of Education, Department of Educational Psychology, Champaign, IL 61820. Offers Ed M, MA, MS, PhD, CAS. *Accreditation:* APA (one or more programs are accredited). Part-time programs available. Postbaccalaureate distance learning degree programs offered. *Faculty:* 19 full-time (11 women). *Students:* 72 full-time (51 women), 73 part-time (53 women); includes 32 minority (15 African Americans, 6 Asian Americans or Pacific Islanders, 11 Hispanic Americans), 37 international. 159 applicants, 25% accepted, 28 enrolled. In 2009, 36 master's, 23 doctorates awarded. *Entrance requirements:* For master's, minimum GPA of 3.5; for doctorate, GRE General Test, minimum GPA of 3.5. Additional exam requirements/recommendations for international students: Required—TOEFL (minimum score 610 paper-based; 253 computer-based; 102 iBT). *Application deadline:* Applications are processed on a rolling basis. Application fee: $60 ($75 for international students). Electronic applications accepted. *Financial support:* In 2009–10, 7 fellowships, 39 research assistantships, 40 teaching assistantships were awarded; tuition waivers (full and partial) also available. *Unit head:* Thomas A. Schwandt, Chair, 217-333-5350, Fax: 217-244-7620, E-mail: tschwand@illinois.edu. *Application contact:* Helen N. Katz, Office Support Specialist, 217-333-5242, Fax: 217-244-7620, E-mail: hnkatz@illinois.edu.

The University of Iowa, Graduate College, College of Education, Department of Psychological and Quantitative Foundations, Iowa City, IA 52242-1316. Offers counseling psychology (PhD); educational measurement and statistics (MA, PhD); educational psychology (MA, PhD); school psychology (PhD, Ed S); JD/PhD. *Accreditation:* APA. *Degree requirements:* For master's, thesis optional, exam; for doctorate, comprehensive exam, thesis/dissertation; for Ed S, exam. *Entrance requirements:* For master's, doctorate, and Ed S, GRE General Test, minimum GPA of 3.0. Additional exam requirements/recommendations for international students: Required—TOEFL (minimum score 550 paper-based; 213 computer-based; 81 iBT). Electronic applications accepted.

The University of Kansas, Graduate Studies, School of Education, Department of Psychology and Research in Education, Program in Educational Psychology and Research, Lawrence, KS 66045. Offers MS Ed, PhD. *Students:* 28 full-time (17 women), 10 part-time (6 women); includes 3 minority (2 African Americans, 1 Asian American or Pacific Islander), 17 international. Average age 32. 18 applicants, 72% accepted, 11 enrolled. *Degree requirements:* For master's, thesis; for doctorate, comprehensive exam, thesis/dissertation. *Entrance requirements:* For master's, GRE General Test, minimum GPA of 3.0; for doctorate, GRE General Test. Additional exam requirements/recommendations for international students: Required—TOEFL. *Application deadline:* For fall admission, 4/15 for domestic students; for spring admission, 11/15 for domestic students. Application fee: $45 ($55 for international students). Electronic applications accepted. *Expenses:* Tuition, state resident: full-time $6492; part-time $270.50 per credit hour. Tuition, nonresident: full-time $15,510; part-time $646.25 per credit hour. Required fees: $847; $70.56 per credit hour. Tuition and fees vary according to course load and program. *Financial support:* Fellowships, research assistantships with full and partial tuition reimbursements, teaching assistantships with full and partial tuition reimbursements, career-related internships or fieldwork, institutionally sponsored loans, scholarships/grants, traineeships, health care benefits, tuition waivers (full and partial), and unspecified assistantships available. Support available to part-time students. Financial award application deadline: 2/1. *Faculty research:* Educational measurement, applied statistics, research design, program evaluation, learning and development. *Unit head:* Bruce Frey, Faculty Coordinator, 785-864-3931, E-mail: bfrey@ku.edu. *Application contact:* Admissions Coordinator, 785-864-3931, Fax: 785-864-3820, E-mail: preadmit@ku.edu.

University of Kentucky, Graduate School, College of Education, Program in Educational and Counseling Psychology, Lexington, KY 40506-0032. Offers counseling psychology (MS Ed, PhD, Ed S); educational and counseling psychology (MS Ed); educational psychology (Ed D, PhD, Ed S); school psychometrist and school psychology (MA Ed). *Accreditation:* APA (one or more programs are accredited); NCATE. *Degree requirements:* For master's, comprehensive exam, thesis optional; for doctorate, comprehensive exam, thesis/dissertation; for Ed S, comprehensive exam. *Entrance requirements:* For master's, GRE General Test, minimum undergraduate GPA of 2.75; for doctorate, GRE General Test, minimum graduate GPA of 3.0; for Ed S, GRE General Test. Additional exam requirements/recommendations for international students: Required—TOEFL (minimum score 550 paper-based; 213 computer-based). Electronic applications accepted.

University of Louisville, Graduate School, College of Education and Human Development, Department of Educational and Counseling Psychology, Louisville, KY 40292-0001. Offers counseling and personnel services (M Ed, PhD). *Accreditation:* APA; NCATE. Part-time and evening/weekend programs available. *Faculty:* 16 full-time (8 women), 8 part-time/adjunct (5 women). *Students:* 184 full-time (146 women), 105 part-time (83 women); includes 54 minority (49 African Americans, 3 Asian Americans or Pacific Islanders, 2 Hispanic Americans), 1 international. Average age 31. 241 applicants, 41% accepted, 73 enrolled. In 2009, 58 master's, 9 doctorates awarded. *Degree requirements:* For doctorate, comprehensive exam, thesis/dissertation. *Entrance requirements:* For master's and doctorate, GRE General Test. Additional exam requirements/recommendations for international students: Required—TOEFL (minimum score 560 paper-based; 210 computer-based; 83 iBT). Application fee: $50. Electronic applications accepted. *Financial support:* In 2009–10, 51 students received support; fellowships, research assistantships, teaching assistantships, career-related internships or fieldwork, Federal Work-Study, scholarships/grants, and unspecified assistantships available. Financial award application deadline: 6/1; financial award applicants required to submit FAFSA. *Faculty research:* Temperament, psychological development, classroom processes, school outcomes, adolescent and adult development issues/prevention and treatment, multicultural counseling, spirituality, therapeutic outcomes, college student success, college student affairs administration, career development. Total annual research expenditures: $17,276. *Unit head:* Dr. Linda T. Shapiro, Acting Chair, 502-852-5716, Fax: 502-852-0629, E-mail: linda.shapiro@louisville.edu. *Application contact:* Libby Leggett, Director, Graduate Admissions, 502-852-3101, Fax: 502-852-6536, E-mail: gradadm@louisville.edu.

University of Manitoba, Faculty of Graduate Studies, Faculty of Education, Department of Educational Administration, Foundations and Psychology, Winnipeg, MB R3T 2N2, Canada. Offers adult and post-secondary education (M Ed); educational administration (M Ed); guidance and counseling (M Ed); inclusive special education (M Ed); social foundations of education (M Ed). *Degree requirements:* For master's, thesis or alternative.

University of Mary Hardin-Baylor, Graduate Studies in Education, Belton, TX 76513. Offers educational administration (M Ed, Ed D); educational psychology (M Ed); exercise and sport science (M Ed); general studies (M Ed); reading education (M Ed). Part-time and evening/weekend programs available. *Degree requirements:* For master's, comprehensive exam; for doctorate, thesis/dissertation. *Entrance requirements:* For master's, GRE General Test, minimum GPA of 2.75, Texas teaching certificate. Electronic applications accepted.

University of Maryland, College Park, Academic Affairs, College of Education, Department of Human Development, College Park, MD 20742. Offers early childhood/elementary education (M Ed, MA, Ed D, PhD); human development (M Ed, MA, Ed D, PhD). *Accreditation:* NCATE. Part-time and evening/weekend programs available. Postbaccalaureate distance learning degree programs offered. *Faculty:* 52 full-time (45 women), 18 part-time/adjunct (14 women). *Students:* 54 full-time (48 women), 35 part-time (24 women); includes 18 minority (8 African Americans, 7 Asian Americans or Pacific Islanders, 3 Hispanic Americans), 8 international. 86 applicants, 35% accepted, 21 enrolled. In 2009, 24 master's, 7 doctorates awarded. *Degree requirements:* For master's, comprehensive exam, thesis optional; for doctorate, comprehensive exam, thesis/dissertation, essay, exam, research paper. *Entrance requirements:* For master's, GRE General Test, minimum GPA of 3.0, 3 letters of recommendation; for doctorate, GRE General Test or MAT, minimum undergraduate GPA of 3.0, graduate 3.5; 3 letters of recommendation. Additional exam requirements/recommendations for international students: Required—TOEFL. *Application deadline:* For fall admission, 3/15 for domestic students, 12/15 for international students; for spring admission, 10/1 priority date for domestic students, 6/1 for international students. Applications are processed on a rolling basis. Application fee: $60. Electronic applications accepted. *Expenses:* Tuition, area resident: Part-time $471 per credit hour. Tuition, state resident: part-time $471 per credit hour. Tuition, nonresident: part-time $1016 per credit hour. Required fees: $337.04 per term. *Financial support:* In 2009–10, 12 fellowships with full and partial tuition reimbursements (averaging $14,577 per year), 3 research assistantships with tuition reimbursements (averaging $17,558 per year), 29 teaching assistantships with tuition reimbursements (averaging $17,113 per year) were awarded; Federal Work-Study and scholarships/grants also available. Support available to part-time students. Financial award applicants required to submit FAFSA. *Faculty research:* Developmental science, educational psychology, cognitive development, language development. Total annual research expenditures: $2.4 million. *Unit head:* Dr. Allan L. Wigfield, Chair, 301-405-1659, Fax: 301-405-2891, E-mail: awigfield@umd.edu. *Application contact:* Dean of Graduate School, 301-405-0358, Fax: 301-314-9305.

University of Memphis, Graduate School, College of Education, Department of Counseling, Educational Psychology and Research, Memphis, TN 38152. Offers counseling (MS, Ed D), including community counseling (MS), rehabilitation counseling (MS), school counseling (MS); counseling psychology (PhD); educational psychology and research (MS, PhD), including educational psychology, educational research. *Accreditation:* ACA (one or more programs are accredited); APA (one or more programs are accredited); CORE (one or more programs are accredited); NCATE. *Faculty:* 26 full-time (13 women), 9 part-time/adjunct (5 women). *Students:* 95 full-time (73 women), 104 part-time (81 women); includes 62 minority (56 African Americans, 3 American Indian/Alaska Native, 1 Asian American or Pacific Islander, 2 Hispanic Americans), 5 international. Average age 33. 118 applicants, 63% accepted, 36 enrolled. In 2009, 46 master's, 14 doctorates awarded. *Degree requirements:* For master's, comprehensive exam, thesis or alternative; for doctorate, comprehensive exam, thesis/dissertation. *Entrance requirements:* For master's, GRE General Test or MAT, minimum GPA of 2.5; for doctorate, GRE General Test. *Application deadline:* For fall admission, 10/1 for domestic students; for spring admission, 4/1 for domestic students. Application fee: $35 ($60 for international students). *Expenses:* Tuition, state resident: full-time $6246; part-time $347 per credit hour. Tuition, nonresident: full-time $15,894; part-time $883 per credit hour. Required fees: $1160. Full-time tuition and fees vary according to course load, degree level and program. *Financial support:* In 2009–10, 130 students received support; fellowships with full tuition reimbursements available, research assistantships with full tuition reimbursements available, teaching assistantships with full tuition reimbursements available, career-related internships or fieldwork, Federal Work-Study, scholarships/grants, and unspecified assistantships available. Financial award application deadline: 2/15; financial award applicants required to submit FAFSA. *Faculty research:* Anger management, aging and disability, supervision, multicultural counseling. *Unit head:* Dr. Douglas C. Strohmer, Chair, 901-678-2841, Fax: 901-678-5114. *Application contact:* Dr. Ernest A. Rakow, Associate Dean of Administration and Graduate Programs, 901-678-2399, Fax: 901-678-4778.

University of Michigan–Dearborn, School of Education, Doctoral Program in Education, Dearborn, MI 48126. Offers curriculum and practice (Ed D); educational leadership (Ed D); educational psychology/special education (Ed D); metropolitan education (Ed D). Part-time and evening/weekend programs available. *Faculty:* 7 full-time (4 women). *Students:* 1 (woman) full-time, 17 part-time (9 women); includes 5 minority (3 African Americans, 1 Asian American or Pacific Islander, 1 Hispanic American). Average age 46. 62 applicants, 31% accepted, 18 enrolled. *Degree requirements:* For doctorate, comprehensive exam, thesis/dissertation. *Entrance requirements:* For doctorate, GRE (taken within the last 5 years), master's degree with minimum GPA of 3.3, 3 letters of recommendation (1 from faculty), 3 yearsprofessional and/or teaching experience. Additional exam requirements/recommendations for international students: Required—TOEFL (minimum score 550 paper-based), Test of Spoken English (TES). *Application deadline:* For fall admission, 3/1 for domestic and international students. Application fee: $60. *Expenses:* Tuition, state resident: part-time $504.10 per credit hour. Tuition, nonresident: part-time $957.90 per credit hour. *Faculty research:* Educational leadership, metropolitan education, curriculum and practice, educational psychology, special education, assessment. *Unit head:* Gail Luera, Associate Dean/Interim Coordinator, 313-593-5098, E-mail: grl@umich.edu. *Application contact:* Catherine Parkins, Customer Service Assistant, 313-583-6349, Fax: 313-593-4748, E-mail: cparkins@umd.umich.edu.

University of Minnesota, Twin Cities Campus, Graduate School, College of Education and Human Development, Department of Educational Psychology, Minneapolis, MN 55455-0213. Offers counseling and student personnel psychology (MA, PhD, Ed S); early childhood education (M Ed, MA, PhD); educational psychology (PhD); psychological foundations of education (MA, PhD, Ed S); school psychology (MA, PhD, Ed S); special education (M Ed, MA, PhD, Ed S); talent development and gifted education (Certificate). *Accreditation:* APA (one or more programs are accredited). *Faculty:* 34 full-time (12 women). *Students:* 286 full-time (214 women), 93 part-time (73 women); includes 43 minority (14 African Americans, 2 American Indian/Alaska Native, 19 Asian Americans or Pacific Islanders, 8 Hispanic Americans), 50 international. Average age 31. 395 applicants, 42% accepted, 107 enrolled. In 2009, 72 master's, 30 doctorates, 17 other advanced degrees awarded. *Financial support:* In 2009–10, 20 fellowships (averaging $26,215 per year), 61 research assistantships (averaging $26,184 per year), 38 teaching assistantships (averaging $28,004 per year) were awarded. *Faculty research:* Learning, cognitive and social processes; multicultural education and counseling; measurement and statistical processes; performance assessment; instructional design/strategies for students with special needs. Total annual research expenditures: $3 million. *Unit head:* Dr. Susan Hupp, Chair, 612-624-1003, Fax: 612-624-8241, E-mail: shupp@umn.edu. *Application contact:* Dr. Mary Trettin, Associate Dean, 612-625-6501, Fax: 612-626-1580, E-mail: mtrettin@umn.edu.

University of Missouri, Graduate School, College of Education, Department of Educational, School, and Counseling Psychology, Columbia, MO 65211. Offers counseling psychology (M Ed, MA, PhD, Ed S); educational psychology (M Ed, MA, PhD, Ed S); learning and instruction (M Ed); school psychology (M Ed, MA, PhD, Ed S). *Accreditation:* APA (one or more programs are accredited). Part-time programs available. *Degree requirements:* For doctorate, thesis/dissertation. *Entrance requirements:* For master's, doctorate, and Ed S, GRE General Test, minimum GPA of 3.0. Additional exam requirements/recommendations for international students: Required—TOEFL (minimum score 580 paper-based; 237 computer-based; 92 iBT).

University of Missouri–St. Louis, College of Education, Division of Educational Psychology, Research, and Evaluation, St. Louis, MO 63121. Offers education (Ed D); educational psychology (PhD); program evaluation and assessment (Certificate); school psychology (Ed S). *Faculty:* 13 full-time (4 women), 8 part-time/adjunct (4 women). *Students:* 27 full-time (24 women), 27 part-time (20 women); includes 12 minority (all African Americans), 2 international. Average age 36. In 2009, 39 doctorates awarded. *Degree requirements:* For other advanced degree, internship. *Entrance requirements:* For degree, GRE General Test, 2-4 letters of recom-

Educational Psychology

University of Missouri–St. Louis (continued)

mendation, personal interview. Additional exam requirements/recommendations for international students: Recommended—TOEFL (minimum score 550 paper-based; 213 computer-based). *Application deadline:* For fall admission, 3/1 for domestic and international students. Application fee: $35 ($40 for international students). Electronic applications accepted. *Expenses:* Tuition, state resident: full-time $5377; part-time $297.70 per credit hour. Tuition, nonresident: full-time $13,882; part-time $771.20 per credit hour. Required fees: $220; $12.20 per credit hour. One-time fee: $12. Tuition and fees vary according to course level, campus/location and program. *Financial support:* In 2009–10, 1 research assistantship (averaging $12,240 per year), 2 teaching assistantships (averaging $8,306 per year) were awarded. Financial award application deadline: 4/1; financial award applicants required to submit FAFSA. *Faculty research:* Child/adolescent psychology, quantitative and qualitative methodology, evaluation processes, measurement and assessment. *Unit head:* Dr. Matthew Keefer, Chairperson, 314-516-5783, Fax: 314-516-5784, E-mail: keefer@umsl.edu. *Application contact:* 314-516-5458, Fax: 314-516-6996, E-mail: gradadm@umsl.edu.

University of Missouri–St. Louis, College of Education, Interdisciplinary Doctoral Programs, St. Louis, MO 63121. Offers adult and higher education (Ed D); counseling (PhD); counselor education (Ed D); educational administration (Ed D); educational leadership and policy studies (PhD); educational psychology (PhD). *Faculty:* 72 full-time (33 women). *Students:* 23 full-time (18 women), 240 part-time (159 women); includes 76 minority (61 African Americans, 2 American Indian/Alaska Native, 7 Asian Americans or Pacific Islanders, 6 Hispanic Americans), 5 international. Average age 40. In 2009, 19 doctorates awarded. *Degree requirements:* For doctorate, thesis/dissertation. *Entrance requirements:* For doctorate, GRE General Test, 3 letters of recommendation; personal interview. Additional exam requirements/recommendations for international students: Recommended—TOEFL (minimum score 550 paper-based; 230 computer-based). *Application deadline:* For fall admission, 2/15 for domestic and international students; for spring admission, 10/1 for domestic and international students. Application fee: $35 ($40 for international students). Electronic applications accepted. *Expenses:* Tuition, state resident: full-time $5377; part-time $297.70 per credit hour. Tuition, nonresident: full-time $13,882; part-time $771.20 per credit hour. Required fees: $220; $12.20 per credit hour. One-time fee: $12. Tuition and fees vary according to course level, campus/location and program. *Financial support:* In 2009–10, 15 research assistantships (averaging $12,240 per year), 8 teaching assistantships (averaging $12,240 per year) were awarded. Financial award application deadline: 4/1; financial award applicants required to submit FAFSA. *Faculty research:* Higher education law and policy, gender and higher education, student retention, lifelong learning orientation, school counselor's role in violence prevention. *Unit head:* Dr. Kathleen Haywood, Director of Graduate Studies, 314-516-5483, Fax: 314-516-5227, E-mail: kathleen_haywood@umsl.edu. *Application contact:* Dr. Kathleen Haywood, Director of Graduate Studies, 314-516-5483, Fax: 314-516-5227, E-mail: kathleen_haywood@umsl.edu.

University of Nebraska at Omaha, Graduate Studies, College of Arts and Sciences, Department of Psychology, Omaha, NE 68182. Offers developmental psychology (PhD); industrial/organizational psychology (MS, PhD); psychobiology (PhD); psychology (MA); school psychology (MS, Ed S). Part-time programs available. *Faculty:* 18 full-time (8 women). *Students:* 44 full-time (36 women), 23 part-time (18 women); includes 3 minority (1 African American, 1 Asian American or Pacific Islander, 1 Hispanic American), 2 international. Average age 26. 116 applicants, 34% accepted, 28 enrolled. In 2009, 30 master's, 5 other advanced degrees awarded. *Degree requirements:* For master's, comprehensive exam, thesis (for some programs). *Entrance requirements:* For master's, GRE General Test, GRE Subject Test, previous course work in psychology, including statistics and a laboratory course; minimum GPA of 3.0, 3 letters of recommendation; for doctorate, GRE General Test. Additional exam requirements/recommendations for international students: Required—TOEFL (minimum score 500 paper-based; 173 computer-based; 61 iBT). *Application deadline:* For fall admission, 1/5 for domestic students. Application fee: $45. Electronic applications accepted. *Financial support:* In 2009–10, 44 students received support; fellowships, research assistantships with tuition reimbursements available, teaching assistantships with tuition reimbursements available, career-related internships or fieldwork, Federal Work-Study, institutionally sponsored loans, scholarships/grants, tuition waivers (partial), and unspecified assistantships available. Support available to part-time students. Financial award application deadline: 3/1; financial award applicants required to submit FAFSA. *Unit head:* Dr. Kenneth Deffenbacher, Chairperson, 402-554-2592. *Application contact:* Dr. Joseph Brown, Student Contact, 402-554-2592.

University of Nebraska–Lincoln, Graduate College, College of Education and Human Sciences, Department of Educational Psychology, Lincoln, NE 68588. Offers cognition, learning and development (MA); counseling psychology (MA); educational psychology (MA, Ed S); psychological studies in education (PhD), including cognition, learning and development, counseling psychology, quantitative, qualitative, and psychometric methods, school psychology; quantitative, qualitative, and psychometric methods (MA); school psychology (MA, Ed S). *Accreditation:* APA (one or more programs are accredited); NCATE. *Degree requirements:* For master's, thesis optional. *Entrance requirements:* For master's, GRE General Test. Additional exam requirements/recommendations for international students: Required—TOEFL (minimum score 500 paper-based; 173 computer-based). Electronic applications accepted. *Faculty research:* Measurement and assessment, metacognition, academic skills, child development, multicultural education and counseling.

University of Nevada, Las Vegas, Graduate College, College of Education, Department of Educational Psychology, Las Vegas, NV 89154-3003. Offers educational psychology (MS, PhD); learning and technology (PhD); school psychology (Ed S). *Accreditation:* ACA (one or more programs are accredited); NCATE. Part-time and evening/weekend programs available. *Faculty:* 19 full-time (12 women), 1 part-time/adjunct (0 women). *Students:* 51 full-time (37 women), 68 part-time (48 women); includes 24 minority (10 African Americans, 6 Asian Americans or Pacific Islanders, 8 Hispanic Americans), 3 international. Average age 39. 69 applicants, 65% accepted, 36 enrolled. In 2009, 11 master's, 6 doctorates, 13 other advanced degrees awarded. *Degree requirements:* For master's, comprehensive exam (for some programs), thesis (for some programs); for doctorate, comprehensive exam, thesis/dissertation, research study submitted to refereed journal or proposal for presentation at conference of a national organization. *Entrance requirements:* For master's, doctorate, and Ed S, GRE General Test. Additional exam requirements/recommendations for international students: Required—TOEFL (minimum score 550 paper-based; 213 computer-based; 80 iBT), IELTS (minimum score 7). *Application deadline:* For fall admission, 2/1 priority date for domestic and international students. Applications are processed on a rolling basis. Application fee: $60 ($95 for international students). Electronic applications accepted. *Financial support:* In 2009–10, 23 students received support, including 1 fellowship with full tuition reimbursement available (averaging $14,000 per year), 8 research assistantships with partial tuition reimbursements available (averaging $11,650 per year), 14 teaching assistantships with partial tuition reimbursements available (averaging $12,000 per year); institutionally sponsored loans, scholarships/grants, health care benefits, and unspecified assistantships also available. Financial award application deadline: 3/1. *Faculty research:* Conceptual change, prose attention and comprehension, psychoeducational assessment, personal epistemology, statistical modeling. *Unit head:* Dr. W. Paul Jones, Chair/ Professor, 702-895-3937, Fax: 702-895-1658, E-mail: paul.jones@unlv.edu. *Application contact:* Graduate College Admissions Evaluator, 702-895-3320, Fax: 702-895-4180, E-mail: gradcollege@unlv.edu.

University of Nevada, Reno, Graduate School, College of Education, Department of Counseling and Educational Psychology, Reno, NV 89557. Offers M Ed, MA, MS, Ed D, PhD, Ed S. *Accreditation:* ACA (one or more programs are accredited); NCATE. Terminal master's awarded for partial completion of doctoral program. *Degree requirements:* For master's, comprehensive exam, thesis optional; for doctorate, comprehensive exam, thesis/dissertation, qualifying exam. *Entrance requirements:* For master's, GRE, minimum GPA of 2.75; for doctorate, GRE, minimum GPA of 3.0. Additional exam requirements/recommendations for international students: Required—TOEFL (minimum score 500 paper-based; 173 computer-based; 61 iBT), IELTS (minimum score 6). Electronic applications accepted. *Faculty research:* Marriage and family counseling, substance abuse attitudes of teachers, current supply of counseling educators, HIV-positive services for patients, family counseling for youth at risk.

University of New Mexico, Graduate School, College of Education, Department of Individual, Family and Community Education, Program in Educational Psychology, Albuquerque, NM 87131-2039. Offers MA, PhD. *Accreditation:* NCATE. Part-time and evening/weekend programs available. *Students:* 16 full-time (13 women), 17 part-time (14 women); includes 10 minority (2 African Americans, 1 American Indian/Alaska Native, 7 Hispanic Americans). Average age 41. 10 applicants, 40% accepted, 4 enrolled. In 2009, 2 master's awarded. Terminal master's awarded for partial completion of doctoral program. *Degree requirements:* For master's, comprehensive exam (for some programs), thesis (for some programs); for doctorate, comprehensive exam, thesis/dissertation. *Entrance requirements:* For master's, GRE General Test or MAT, minimum GPA of 3.0 in last 2 years of undergraduate study, 3 letters of reference, interview with 3 faculty; for doctorate, GRE General Test or MAT, minimum GPA of 3.0 in last 2 years of undergraduate study, 3 letters of reference, interview with 3 faculty, writing sample. *Application deadline:* For fall admission, 2/15 priority date for domestic students; for spring admission, 10/15 priority date for domestic students. Applications are processed on a rolling basis. Application fee: $50. Electronic applications accepted. *Expenses:* Tuition, state resident: full-time $2099; part-time $233.20 per credit hour. Tuition, nonresident: full-time $6650. Required fees: $25 per semester. Tuition and fees vary according to course load, program and reciprocity agreements. *Financial support:* In 2009–10, 13 students received support, including 6 research assistantships with partial tuition reimbursements available (averaging $6,057 per year), 12 teaching assistantships with full and partial tuition reimbursements available (averaging $13,445 per year). Financial award application deadline: 3/1; financial award applicants required to submit FAFSA. *Faculty research:* Measurement and assessment, cognitive strategies, accountability, motivation, instructional technology, educational research, human lifespan development. *Unit head:* Dr. Deborah Rifenbary, Program Coordinator, 505-277-4535, Fax: 505-277-8361, E-mail: edpsy@unm.edu. *Application contact:* Cynthia Salas, Department Administrator, 505-277-4535, Fax: 505-277-8361, E-mail: divbse@unm.edu.

The University of North Carolina at Chapel Hill, Graduate School, School of Education, Program in Education, Chapel Hill, NC 27599. Offers culture, curriculum and change (MA, PhD); early childhood, intervention and literacy (MA, PhD); educational psychology, measurement and evaluation (MA, PhD). *Accreditation:* NCATE. *Degree requirements:* For master's, thesis; for doctorate, comprehensive exam, thesis/dissertation. *Entrance requirements:* For master's, GRE General Test, minimum GPA of 3.0 during last 2 years of undergraduate course work; for doctorate, GRE General Test, minimum GPA of 3.0 during last 2 years of undergraduate course work. Additional exam requirements/recommendations for international students: Required—TOEFL (minimum score 550 paper-based; 213 computer-based). Electronic applications accepted.

University of Northern Colorado, Graduate School, College of Education and Behavioral Sciences, School of Psychological Sciences, Program in Educational Psychology, Greeley, CO 80639. Offers early childhood education (MA); educational psychology (MA, PhD). *Accreditation:* NCATE. Part-time programs available. *Faculty:* 15 full-time (6 women). *Students:* 23 full-time (11 women), 16 part-time (14 women); includes 3 minority (1 Asian American or Pacific Islander, 2 Hispanic Americans), 8 international. Average age 33. 11 applicants, 91% accepted, 8 enrolled. In 2009, 6 master's, 4 doctorates awarded. *Degree requirements:* For master's, comprehensive exam, thesis or alternative; for doctorate, comprehensive exam, thesis/dissertation. *Entrance requirements:* For master's, GRE General Test, letters of recommendation; for doctorate, GRE General Test, letters of recommendation, resume. *Application deadline:* Applications are processed on a rolling basis. Application fee: $50 ($60 for international students). Electronic applications accepted. *Expenses:* Tuition, state resident: full-time $5770; part-time $320.55 per credit hour. Tuition, nonresident: full-time $13,847; part-time $769.27 per credit hour. Required fees: $948.78; $52.72 per credit. *Financial support:* In 2009–10, 1 teaching assistantship (averaging $6,732 per year) was awarded; fellowships, research assistantships, unspecified assistantships also available. Financial award application deadline: 3/1; financial award applicants required to submit FAFSA. *Unit head:* Dr. Marilyn Welsh, Program Coordinator, 970-351-2957, Fax: 970-351-1103. *Application contact:* Linda Sisson, Graduate Student Admission Coordinator, 970-351-1807, Fax: 970-351-2371, E-mail: linda.sisson@unco.edu.

University of Northern Iowa, Graduate College, College of Education, Department of Educational Psychology and Foundations, Cedar Falls, IA 50614. Offers educational psychology (MAE); professional development for teachers (MAE); school psychology (Ed S). Part-time and evening/weekend programs available. *Students:* 19 full-time (14 women), 16 part-time (11 women); includes 1 minority (Hispanic American), 2 international. 40 applicants, 48% accepted, 17 enrolled. In 2009, 20 master's, 6 other advanced degrees awarded. *Degree requirements:* For master's, comprehensive exam (for some programs), thesis or alternative; for Ed S, thesis or alternative. *Entrance requirements:* For master's, GRE General Test, minimum GPA of 3.0; for Ed S, GRE General Test. Additional exam requirements/recommendations for international students: Required—TOEFL (minimum score 500 paper-based; 180 computer-based; 61 iBT). *Application deadline:* For fall admission, 8/1 priority date for domestic students. Applications are processed on a rolling basis. Application fee: $30 ($50 for international students). Electronic applications accepted. *Financial support:* Career-related internships or fieldwork, Federal Work-Study, scholarships/grants, and tuition waivers (full and partial) available. Support available to part-time students. Financial award application deadline: 2/1. *Unit head:* Dr. Radhi Al-Mabuk, Interim Head, 319-273-2609, Fax: 319-273-5175, E-mail: radhi.al-mabuk@uni.edu. *Application contact:* Laurie S. Russell, Record Analyst, 319-273-2623, Fax: 319-273-6792, E-mail: laurie.russell@uni.edu.

University of North Texas, Robert B. Toulouse School of Graduate Studies, College of Education, Department of Educational Psychology, Program in Educational Psychology, Denton, TX 76203. Offers MS. *Degree requirements:* For master's, thesis optional. *Entrance requirements:* For master's, GRE General Test. Additional exam requirements/recommendations for international students: Required—proof of English language proficiency required for non-native English speakers; Recommended—TOEFL (minimum score 550 paper-based; 213 computer-based; 79 iBT). Application fee: $50 ($75 for international students). *Expenses:* Tuition, state resident: full-time $4298; part-time $239 per contact hour. Tuition, nonresident: full-time $9878; part-time $549 per contact hour. Required fees: $265 per contact hour. *Financial support:* Applicants required to submit FAFSA. *Faculty research:* Structural equation modeling, applied general linear modeling, reliability, factor analysis, learning environments, social historical factors. *Application contact:* Graduate Advisor, 940-565-8377, Fax: 940-565-2185, E-mail: young@coe.unt.edu.

University of Oklahoma, Graduate College, College of Education, Department of Educational Psychology, Program in Instructional Psychology, Norman, OK 73019. Offers M Ed, PhD. Part-time and evening/weekend programs available. *Students:* 24 full-time (15 women), 29 part-time (24 women); includes 9 minority (5 African Americans, 1 Asian American or Pacific Islander, 3 Hispanic Americans), 12 international. 21 applicants, 57% accepted, 9 enrolled. In 2009, 8 master's, 1 doctorate awarded. Terminal master's awarded for partial completion of doctoral program. *Degree requirements:* For master's, comprehensive exam (for some programs), thesis optional; for doctorate, thesis/dissertation, general exam. *Entrance requirements:* For master's, minimum GPA of 3.0; for doctorate, GRE General Test, master's degree, minimum graduate GPA of 3.25. Additional exam requirements/recommendations for international students: Required—TOEFL (minimum score 550 paper-based; 213 computer-based). *Application deadline:* For fall admission, 3/15 for domestic students, 7/1 for international students; for spring admission, 10/15 for domestic and international students. Applications are processed on a rolling basis. Application fee: $40 ($90 for international students). Electronic applications accepted. *Expenses:* Tuition, state resident: full-time $3744; part-time $156 per credit hour. Tuition, nonresident: full-time $13,577; part-time $565.70 per credit hour. Required fees: $2415; $90.10 per credit hour. *Financial support:* In 2009–10, 19 students received support. Career-related internships or fieldwork, Federal Work-Study, institutionally sponsored loans, scholarships/grants, health care benefits, and unspecified

assistantships available. Support available to part-time students. Financial award applicants required to submit FAFSA. *Faculty research:* Cognition and instruction, achievement motivation, digital learning environments, integration of instructional technology. *Unit head:* Dr. Terri K. Debacker, Chair, 405-325-1068, Fax: 405-325-6655, E-mail: debacker@ou.edu. *Application contact:* Rashida Y. Douglas, Graduate Programs Officer, 405-325-4525, Fax: 405-325-6655, E-mail: ryd618@ou.edu.

University of Phoenix–Southern Arizona Campus, The Artemis School, College of Education, Tucson, AZ 85711. Offers administration and supervision (MA Ed); adult education and training (MA Ed); curriculum instruction (MA Ed); educational counseling (MA Ed); elementary teacher education (MA Ed); school counseling (MSC); secondary teacher education (MA Ed); special education (MA Ed, Certificate). Evening/weekend programs available. *Degree requirements:* For master's, thesis (for some programs). *Entrance requirements:* For master's, minimum undergraduate GPA of 2.5, 3 years of work experience. Additional exam requirements/recommendations for international students: Required—TOEFL (minimum score 550 paper-based; 213 computer-based; 79 iBT). Electronic applications accepted.

University of Regina, Faculty of Graduate Studies and Research, Faculty of Education, Department of Educational Psychology, Regina, SK S4S 0A2, Canada. Offers M Ed. Part-time programs available. *Faculty:* 5 full-time (2 women), 1 part-time/adjunct (0 women). *Students:* 21 full-time (18 women), 34 part-time (25 women). 40 applicants, 50% accepted. In 2009, 11 master's awarded. *Degree requirements:* For master's, practicum, project, or thesis. *Entrance requirements:* For master's, bachelor's degree in education. Additional exam requirements/recommendations for international students: Required—TOEFL (minimum score 580 paper-based; 237 computer-based; 80 iBT). *Application deadline:* For fall admission, 2/15 for domestic students; for winter admission, 2/15 for domestic students; for spring admission, 2/15 for domestic students. Application fee: $90 ($100 for international students). Electronic applications accepted. *Financial support:* In 2009–10, 5 fellowships (averaging $19,000 per year), 1 research assistantship (averaging $16,910 per year), 2 teaching assistantships (averaging $6,650 per year) were awarded; career-related internships or fieldwork also available. Financial award application deadline: 6/15. *Unit head:* Dr. Warren Wessel, 306-585-4555, E-mail: warren.wessel@uregina.ca. *Application contact:* Tania Gates, Graduate Program Coordinator, 306-585-4506, Fax: 306-585-5387, E-mail: edgrad@uregina.ca.

University of Saskatchewan, College of Graduate Studies and Research, College of Education, Department of Educational Psychology and Special Education, Saskatoon, SK S7N 5A2, Canada. Offers M Ed, PhD, Diploma. *Faculty:* 20. *Students:* 69. In 2009, 13 master's awarded. *Degree requirements:* For master's, thesis (for some programs); for doctorate, comprehensive exam (for some programs), thesis/dissertation. *Entrance requirements:* Additional exam requirements/recommendations for international students: Required—TOEFL (minimum score 80 iBT); Recommended—IELTS (minimum score 6.5). *Application deadline:* For fall admission, 7/1 priority date for domestic students. Applications are processed on a rolling basis. Application fee: $75. Electronic applications accepted. Tuition and fees charges are reported in Canadian dollars. *Expenses:* Tuition, area resident: Full-time $3000 Canadian dollars; part-time $500 Canadian dollars per term. Required fees: $700 Canadian dollars; $100 Canadian dollars per term. *Financial support:* Fellowships, research assistantships, teaching assistantships available. Financial award application deadline: 1/31. *Unit head:* Dr. David Mykota, Head, 306-966-5246, Fax: 306-966-7719, E-mail: david.mykota@usask.ca. *Application contact:* Dr. Laure-Ann Hellsten, Graduate Chair, 306-966-7728, Fax: 306-966-7719, E-mail: laurie.hellsten@usask.ca.

University of South Africa, College of Human Sciences, Pretoria, South Africa. Offers adult education (M Ed); African languages (MA, PhD); African politics (MA, PhD); Afrikaans (MA, PhD); ancient history (MA, PhD); ancient Near Eastern studies (MA, PhD); anthropology (MA, PhD); applied linguistics (MA); Arabic (MA, PhD); archaeology (MA); art history (MA); Biblical archaeology (MA); Biblical studies (M Th, D Th, PhD); Christian spirituality (M Th, D Th); church history (M Th, D Th); classical studies (MA, PhD); clinical psychology (MA); communication (MA, PhD); comparative education (M Ed, Ed D); consulting psychology (D Admin, D Com, PhD); curriculum studies (M Ed, Ed D); development studies (M Admin, MA, D Admin, PhD); didactics (M Ed, Ed D); education (M Tech); education management (M Ed, Ed D); educational psychology (M Ed); English (MA); environmental education (M Ed); French (MA, PhD); German (MA, PhD); Greek (MA); guidance and counseling (M Ed); health studies (MA, PhD), including health sciences education (MA), health services management (MA), medical and surgical nursing science (critical care general) (MA), midwifery and neonatal nursing science (MA), trauma and emergency care (MA); history (MA, PhD); history of education (Ed D); inclusive education (M Ed, Ed D); information and communications technology policy and regulation (MA); information science (MA, MIS, PhD); international politics (MA, PhD); Islamic studies (MA, PhD); Italian (MA, PhD); Judaica (MA, PhD); linguistics (MA, PhD); mathematical education (M Ed); mathematics education (MA); missiology (M Th, D Th); modern Hebrew (MA, PhD); musicology (MA, MMus, D Mus, PhD); natural science education (M Ed); New Testament (M Th, D Th); Old Testament (D Th); pastoral therapy (M Th, D Th); philosophy (MA); philosophy of education (M Ed, Ed D); politics (MA, PhD); Portuguese (MA, PhD); practical theology (M Th, D Th); psychology (MA, MS, PhD); psychology of education (M Ed, Ed D); public health (MA); religious studies (MA, D Th, PhD); Romance languages (MA); Russian (MA, PhD); Semitic languages (MA, PhD); social behavior studies in HIV/AIDS (MA); social science (mental health) (MA); social science in development studies (MA); social science in psychology (MA); social science in social work (MA); social science in sociology (MA); social work (MSW, DSW, PhD); socio-education (M Ed, Ed D); sociolinguistics (MA); sociology (MA, PhD); Spanish (MA, PhD); systematic theology (M Th, D Th); TESOL (teaching English to speakers of other languages) (MA); theological ethics (M Th, D Th); theory of literature (MA, PhD); urban ministries (D Th); urban ministry (M Th).

University of South Carolina, The Graduate School, College of Education, Department of Educational Studies, Program in Educational Psychology, Research, Columbia, SC 29208. Offers M Ed, PhD. *Accreditation:* NCATE. Part-time programs available. *Degree requirements:* For master's, comprehensive exam, thesis (for some programs); for doctorate, comprehensive exam, thesis/dissertation. *Entrance requirements:* For master's, GRE General Test; for doctorate, GRE General Test, interview. Electronic applications accepted. *Faculty research:* Problem solving, higher order thinking skills, psychometric research, methodology.

The University of South Dakota, Graduate School, School of Education, Division of Counseling and Psychology in Education, Vermillion, SD 57069-2390. Offers MA, PhD, Ed S. *Accreditation:* ACA (one or more programs are accredited); NCATE. Part-time programs available. *Degree requirements:* For master's and Ed S, comprehensive exam, thesis or alternative; for doctorate, comprehensive exam, thesis/dissertation. *Entrance requirements:* For master's and doctorate, GRE General Test, minimum GPA of 3.0. Additional exam requirements/recommendations for international students: Required—TOEFL (minimum score 550 paper-based; 213 computer-based; 79 iBT). Electronic applications accepted.

University of Southern California, Graduate School, Rossier School of Education, Doctor of Education Programs, Los Angeles, CA 90089. Offers educational psychology (Ed D); higher education administration (Ed D); K-12 leadership in urban school settings (Ed D); teacher education in multicultural societies (Ed D). Part-time and evening/weekend programs available. *Faculty:* 59 full-time (32 women), 12 part-time/adjunct (3 women). *Students:* 567 full-time (361 women), 12 part-time (6 women); includes 339 minority (73 African Americans, 11 American Indian/Alaska Native, 129 Asian Americans or Pacific Islanders, 126 Hispanic Americans), 13 international. 300 applicants, 76% accepted, 182 enrolled. In 2009, 143 doctorates awarded. *Degree requirements:* For doctorate, thesis/dissertation. *Entrance requirements:* For doctorate, GRE. Additional exam requirements/recommendations for international students: Required—TOEFL (minimum score 250 computer-based; 100 iBT). *Application deadline:* For fall admission, 1/15 priority date for domestic and international students. Application fee: $85. Electronic applications accepted. *Expenses:* Tuition: Full-time $25,980; part-time $1315 per unit. Required fees: $554. One-time fee: $35 full-time. Full-time tuition and fees vary according to degree level and program. *Financial support:* In 2009–10, 385 students received support. Scholarships/grants available. Support available to part-time students. Financial award application deadline: 5/5. *Faculty research:* Data-driven decision-making in K-12 schools and districts; examination of college and university leadership and management in U. S. and Asia; studies in facilitating student learning; organizational change and the role of leaders; leadership, diversity, learning and accountability. *Unit head:* Dr. Kathy Stowe, Executive Director/Assistant Professor of Clinical Education, 213-740-9323. *Application contact:* Carolyn Stirling, Associate Director of Recruiting and Admissions, 213-740-0224, Fax: 213-740-9433, E-mail: soeinfo@usc.edu.

University of Southern California, Graduate School, Rossier School of Education, Doctor of Philosophy in Education Programs, Los Angeles, CA 90089. Offers educational psychology (PhD); higher education administration and policy (PhD); K-12 policy and practice (PhD). *Faculty:* 20 full-time (11 women). *Students:* 23 full-time (17 women); includes 12 minority (3 African Americans, 3 Asian Americans or Pacific Islanders, 6 Hispanic Americans), 1 international. 64 applicants, 17% accepted, 5 enrolled. In 2009, 14 doctorates awarded. *Degree requirements:* For doctorate, thesis/dissertation, qualifying exam, proposal and defense. *Entrance requirements:* For doctorate, GRE. Additional exam requirements/recommendations for international students: Required—TOEFL (minimum score 250 computer-based; 100 iBT). *Application deadline:* For fall admission, 12/1 for domestic and international students. Application fee: $85. Electronic applications accepted. *Expenses:* Tuition: Full-time $25,980; part-time $1315 per unit. Required fees: $554. One-time fee: $35 full-time. Full-time tuition and fees vary according to degree level and program. *Financial support:* In 2009–10, 5 fellowships with full tuition reimbursements (averaging $29,000 per year), 23 research assistantships with full tuition reimbursements (averaging $31,000 per year) were awarded; health care benefits and full tuition coverage for all required coursework, academic stipend, awards for professional development and academic conferences also available. *Faculty research:* Diversity in higher education, organizational change, educational psychology, policy and politics of educational reform, economics of education and education policy. *Unit head:* Dianne Morris, Director, 213-740-6303, Fax: 213-740-9433, E-mail: rsoephd@usc.edu. *Application contact:* Aba Cassell, 213-821-1517, Fax: 213-740-9433, E-mail: rossier.phd@usc.edu.

University of Southern Maine, College of Education and Human Development, Program in Educational Psychology, Portland, ME 04104-9300. Offers applied behavior analysis (MS, Certificate). Part-time and evening/weekend programs available. *Students:* 3 full-time (all women), 1 (woman) part-time. 7 applicants, 100% accepted, 4 enrolled. In 2009, 3 master's awarded. *Entrance requirements:* For master's, GRE or MAT. Additional exam requirements/recommendations for international students: Required—TOEFL (minimum score 550 paper-based; 213 computer-based; 79 iBT). *Application deadline:* For fall admission, 5/1 priority date for domestic students; for spring admission, 10/15 priority date for domestic students. Applications are processed on a rolling basis. Application fee: $50. Electronic applications accepted. *Financial support:* Federal Work-Study, institutionally sponsored loans, scholarships/grants, and unspecified assistantships available. Support available to part-time students. Financial award application deadline: 3/1. *Unit head:* Dr. E. Michael Brady, Chair, Human Resource Development Department, 207-780-5316, Fax: 207-780-5043, E-mail: mbrady@usm.maine.edu. *Application contact:* Mary Sloan, Director of Graduate Admissions, 207-780-4386, Fax: 207-780-4969, E-mail: msloan@usm.maine.edu.

The University of Tennessee, Graduate School, College of Education, Health and Human Sciences, Department of Educational Psychology and Counseling, Knoxville, TN 37996. Offers adult education (MS); applied educational psychology (MS); collaborative learning (Ed D); college student personnel (MS); mental health counseling (MS); rehabilitation counseling (MS); school counseling (MS). *Accreditation:* ACA (one or more programs are accredited); CORE (one or more programs are accredited); NCATE. Part-time and evening/weekend programs available. *Degree requirements:* For master's, thesis optional. *Entrance requirements:* For master's, GRE General Test, minimum GPA of 2.7. Additional exam requirements/recommendations for international students: Required—TOEFL. Electronic applications accepted. *Expenses:* Tuition, state resident: full-time $6826; part-time $380 per semester hour. Tuition, nonresident: full-time $21,844; part-time $1147 per semester hour. Tuition and fees vary according to program.

The University of Tennessee, Graduate School, College of Education, Health and Human Sciences, Program in Education, Knoxville, TN 37996. Offers art education (MS); counseling education (PhD); cultural studies in education (PhD); curriculum (MS, Ed S); curriculum, educational research and evaluation (Ed D, PhD); early childhood education (PhD); early childhood special education (MS); education of deaf and hard of hearing (MS); educational administration and policy studies (Ed D, PhD); educational administration and supervision (Ed S); educational psychology (Ed D, PhD); elementary education (MS, Ed S); elementary teaching (MS); English education (MS, Ed S); exercise science (PhD); foreign language/ESL education (MS, Ed S); instructional technology (MS, Ed D, PhD, Ed S); literacy, language and ESL education (PhD); literacy, language education, and ESL education (Ed D); mathematics education (MS, Ed S); modified and comprehensive special education (MS); reading education (MS, Ed S); school counseling (Ed S); school psychology (PhD, Ed S); science education (MS, Ed S); secondary teaching (MS); social foundations (MS); social science education (MS, Ed S); socio-cultural foundations of sports and education (PhD); special education (Ed S); teacher education (Ed D, PhD). *Accreditation:* NCATE. Part-time and evening/weekend programs available. *Degree requirements:* For master's and Ed S, thesis optional; for doctorate, variable foreign language requirement, thesis/dissertation. *Entrance requirements:* For master's, minimum GPA of 2.7; for doctorate and Ed S, GRE General Test, minimum GPA of 2.7. Additional exam requirements/recommendations for international students: Required—TOEFL. Electronic applications accepted. *Expenses:* Tuition, state resident: full-time $6826; part-time $380 per semester hour. Tuition, nonresident: full-time $21,844; part-time $1147 per semester hour. Tuition and fees vary according to program.

The University of Texas at Austin, Graduate School, College of Education, Department of Educational Psychology, Austin, TX 78712-1111. Offers academic educational psychology (M Ed, MA); counseling psychology (PhD); counselor education (M Ed); human development and culture (PhD); learning, cognition and instruction (PhD); quantitative methods (PhD); school psychology (PhD). *Accreditation:* APA (one or more programs are accredited). *Degree requirements:* For master's, thesis optional; for doctorate, thesis/dissertation. *Entrance requirements:* For master's and doctorate, GRE General Test, 3 letters of recommendation. Additional exam requirements/recommendations for international students: Required—TOEFL.

The University of Texas at El Paso, Graduate School, College of Education, Department of Educational Psychology and Special Services, El Paso, TX 79968-0001. Offers educational diagnostics (M Ed); guidance and counseling (M Ed); special education (M Ed). Part-time and evening/weekend programs available. *Degree requirements:* For master's, thesis optional. *Entrance requirements:* For master's, minimum graduate GPA of 3.0. Additional exam requirements/recommendations for international students: Required—TOEFL. Electronic applications accepted.

The University of Texas–Pan American, College of Education, Department of Educational Psychology, Edinburg, TX 78539. Offers counseling (M Ed); educational diagnostician (M Ed); gifted education (M Ed); school psychology (MA); special education (M Ed). Part-time and evening/weekend programs available. *Degree requirements:* For master's, comprehensive exam (for some programs), thesis (for some programs). *Entrance requirements:* For master's, GRE General Test, interview. *Expenses:* Tuition, state resident: full-time $3630.60; part-time $201.70 per credit hour. Tuition, nonresident: full-time $8617; part-time $478.70 per credit hour. Required fees: $806.50. *Faculty research:* Reading instruction, assessment practice, behavior interventions consultation, mental retardation.

University of the Pacific, School of Education, Department of Educational and School Psychology, Stockton, CA 95211-0197. Offers educational psychology (MA, Ed D); school psychology (Ed S). *Accreditation:* NCATE. *Faculty:* 4 full-time (3 women), 1 (woman) part-time/adjunct. *Students:* 18 full-time (12 women), 13 part-time (11 women); includes 14 minority (1 African American, 6 Asian Americans or Pacific Islanders, 7 Hispanic Americans). Average age 29. 14 applicants, 86% accepted, 9 enrolled. In 2009, 6 master's, 3 doctorates awarded. *Degree requirements:* For master's, thesis (for some programs); for doctorate, thesis/

Educational Psychology

University of the Pacific (continued)

dissertation. *Entrance requirements:* For master's and doctorate, GRE General Test, GRE Subject Test. Additional exam requirements/recommendations for international students: Required—TOEFL (minimum score 475 paper-based; 150 computer-based). *Application deadline:* For fall admission, 3/1 priority date for domestic students; for spring admission, 10/1 priority date for domestic students. Applications are processed on a rolling basis. Application fee: $75. *Financial support:* In 2009–10, 6 teaching assistantships were awarded. Financial award application deadline: 3/1; financial award applicants required to submit FAFSA. *Unit head:* Dr. Linda Webster, Chairperson, 209-946-2559, E-mail: lwebster@pacific.edu. *Application contact:* Office of Graduate Admissions, 209-946-2344.

The University of Toledo, College of Graduate Studies, College of Education, Department of Educational Foundations and Leadership, Program in Educational Psychology, Toledo, OH 43606-3390. Offers ME, DE, PhD.

University of Utah, Graduate School, College of Education, Department of Educational Psychology, Salt Lake City, UT 84112. Offers counseling psychology (PhD); educational psychology (MA); instructional design and educational technology (M Ed); learning and cognition (MS, PhD); professional counseling (MS); professional psychology (M Ed); reading and literacy (M Ed, PhD); school counseling (M Ed, MS); school psychology (MS, PhD); statistics (M Stat). *Accreditation:* APA (one or more programs are accredited). Evening/weekend programs available. Postbaccalaureate distance learning degree programs offered (minimal on-campus study). *Faculty:* 21 full-time (11 women), 8 part-time/adjunct (5 women). *Students:* 92 full-time (67 women), 74 part-time (43 women); includes 16 minority (4 Asian Americans or Pacific Islanders, 12 Hispanic Americans), 2 international. Average age 33. 177 applicants, 34% accepted, 50 enrolled. In 2009, 44 master's, 9 doctorates awarded. *Degree requirements:* For master's, variable foreign language requirement, comprehensive exam, thesis (for some programs); for doctorate, variable foreign language requirement, thesis/dissertation, oral exam. *Entrance requirements:* For master's and doctorate, GRE General Test, minimum GPA of 3.0. Additional exam requirements/recommendations for international students: Required—TOEFL (minimum score 500 paper-based; 173 computer-based). *Application deadline:* For fall admission, 4/1 for domestic and international students; for spring admission, 11/1 for domestic and international students. Application fee: $55 ($65 for international students). *Expenses:* Tuition, state resident: full-time $4004; part-time $1674 per semester. Tuition, nonresident: full-time $14,134; part-time $5915 per semester. Required fees: $324 per semester. Tuition and fees vary according to course load, degree level and program. *Financial support:* In 2009–10, 55 students received support, including 20 fellowships with full tuition reimbursements available (averaging $11,000 per year), 5 research assistantships with full tuition reimbursements available (averaging $11,000 per year), 32 teaching assistantships with full and partial tuition reimbursements available (averaging $11,000 per year); career-related internships or fieldwork, Federal Work-Study, institutionally sponsored loans, scholarships/grants, and unspecified assistantships also available. Financial award application deadline: 2/1; financial award applicants required to submit FAFSA. *Faculty research:* Autism, computer technology and instruction, cognitive behavior, aging, group counseling. Total annual research expenditures: $151,911. *Unit head:* Dr. Elaine Clark, Chair, 801-581-7148, Fax: 801-581-5566, E-mail: clark@ed.utah.edu. *Application contact:* Jenna Atkinson, Academic Program Specialist, 801-581-7148, Fax: 801-581-5566, E-mail: jenna.atkinson@utah.edu.

University of Utah, Graduate School, Interdepartmental Program in Statistics, Salt Lake City, UT 84112-1107. Offers biostatistics (M Stat); econometrics (M Stat); educational psychology (M Stat); mathematics (M Stat); sociology (M Stat); statistics (M Stat). Part-time programs available. *Students:* 25 full-time (11 women), 15 part-time (6 women); includes 4 minority (3 Asian Americans or Pacific Islanders, 1 Hispanic American), 12 international. Average age 30. 59 applicants, 44% accepted, 12 enrolled. In 2009, 15 master's awarded. *Degree requirements:* For master's, comprehensive exam, projects. *Entrance requirements:* For master's, GRE General Test (sociology and educational psychology), minimum GPA of 3.0; course work in calculus, matrix theory, statistics. Additional exam requirements/recommendations for international students: Required—TOEFL (minimum score 500 paper-based; 173 computer-based). *Application deadline:* For fall admission, 7/1 for domestic students, 4/1 for international students. Applications are processed on a rolling basis. Application fee: $55 ($65 for international students). *Expenses:* Tuition, state resident: full-time $4004; part-time $1674 per semester. Tuition, nonresident: full-time $14,134; part-time $5915 per semester. Required fees: $324 per semester. Tuition and fees vary according to course load, degree level and program. *Financial support:* Career-related internships or fieldwork available. *Faculty research:* Biostatistics, management, economics, educational psychology, mathematics. *Unit head:* Tariq Mughal, Chair, University Statistics Committee, 801-585-9547, E-mail: tariq.mughal@business.utah.edu. *Application contact:* Laura Egbert, Coordinator, 801-585-6853, E-mail: laura.demattia@utah.edu.

University of Victoria, Faculty of Graduate Studies, Faculty of Education, Department of Educational Psychology and Leadership Studies, Victoria, BC V8W 2Y2, Canada. Offers aboriginal communities counseling (M Ed); counseling (M Ed, MA); educational psychology (M Ed, MA, PhD), including counseling psychology (M Ed, MA), leadership studies (PhD), learning and development (MA, PhD), measurement and evaluation, special education (M Ed, MA); leadership studies (M Ed, MA). Part-time programs available. *Degree requirements:* For master's, thesis (for some programs), comprehensive exam (M Ed); for doctorate, comprehensive exam, thesis/dissertation, candidacy exam. *Entrance requirements:* For master's, 2 years of work experience in a relevant field; for doctorate, GRE, 2 years of work experience in a relevant field, minimum B average. Additional exam requirements/recommendations for international students: Required—TOEFL (minimum score 575 paper-based; 233 computer-based), IELTS (minimum score 7). *Faculty research:* Learning and development (child, adolescent and adult), special education and exceptional children.

University of Virginia, Curry School of Education, Department of Leadership, Foundations and Policy, Program in Educational Psychology, Charlottesville, VA 22903. Offers applied developmental science (M Ed); educational evaluation (M Ed); educational psychology (M Ed, Ed D, Ed S); educational research (Ed D); gifted education (M Ed); instructional technology (M Ed, Ed S); research statistics and evaluation (Ed D); school psychology (Ed D). *Students:* 28 full-time (22 women), 18 part-time (13 women); includes 3 minority (1 African American, 1 Asian American or Pacific Islander, 1 Hispanic American), 7 international. Average age 31. 130 applicants, 36% accepted, 31 enrolled. In 2009, 50 master's, 25 doctorates, 1 other advanced degree awarded. *Degree requirements:* For master's, comprehensive exam. *Entrance requirements:* For master's and doctorate, GRE General Test, 2 letters of recommendation. Additional exam requirements/recommendations for international students: Required—TOEFL (minimum score 600 paper-based; 250 computer-based; 90 iBT), IELTS (minimum score 7). *Application deadline:* Applications are processed on a rolling basis. Application fee: $60. Electronic applications accepted. *Financial support:* Fellowships, research assistantships, teaching assistantships available. Financial award application deadline: 1/5; financial award applicants required to submit FAFSA. *Unit head:* Jen Mashburn, Program Coordinator, E-mail: jmashburn@virginia.edu. *Application contact:* Jen Mashburn, Program Coordinator, E-mail: jmashburn@virginia.edu.

University of Virginia, Curry School of Education, Program in Education, Charlottesville, VA 22903. Offers administration and supervision (PhD); applied developmental science (PhD); counselor education (PhD); curriculum and instruction (PhD); early childhood-developmental risk (MT); education evaluation (PhD); educational psychology (PhD); educational research (PhD); elementary (MT, PhD); English education (MT, PhD); foreign language education (MT); higher education (PhD); instructional technology (PhD); kinesiology (MT, PhD); math education (PhD); reading education (PhD); research statistics and evaluation (PhD); school psychology (PhD); science education (PhD); social studies education (MT, PhD); special education (PhD); world languages education (MT). *Students:* 336 full-time (239 women), 88 part-time (54 women); includes 43 minority (24 African Americans, 2 American Indian/Alaska Native, 11 Asian Americans or Pacific Islanders, 6 Hispanic Americans), 18 international. Average age 27. 199 applicants, 48% accepted, 55 enrolled. In 2009, 127 master's, 52 doctorates awarded. *Degree requirements:* For master's, comprehensive exam (for some programs), field project; for doctorate, comprehensive exam, thesis/dissertation. *Entrance requirements:* For doctorate, GRE General Test. Additional exam requirements/recommendations for international students: Required—TOEFL (minimum score 600 paper-based; 250 computer-based; 90 iBT), IELTS (minimum score 7). *Application deadline:* Applications are processed on a rolling basis. Application fee: $60. Electronic applications accepted. *Financial support:* Fellowships, research assistantships, teaching assistantships available. Financial award application deadline: 1/5; financial award applicants required to submit FAFSA.

University of Washington, Graduate School, College of Education, Program in Educational Psychology, Seattle, WA 98195. Offers educational psychology (PhD); human development and cognition (M Ed); learning sciences (M Ed, PhD); measurement, statistics and research design (M Ed); school psychology (M Ed). *Accreditation:* APA. *Degree requirements:* For master's, thesis optional; for doctorate, thesis/dissertation. *Entrance requirements:* For master's and doctorate, GRE General Test, minimum GPA of 3.0. Additional exam requirements/recommendations for international students: Required—TOEFL.

The University of Western Ontario, Faculty of Graduate Studies, Social Sciences Division, Faculty of Education, Program in Educational Studies, London, ON N6A 5B8, Canada. Offers curriculum studies (M Ed); educational policy studies (M Ed); educational psychology/special education (M Ed). Part-time programs available. *Faculty research:* Reflective practice, gender and schooling, feminist pedagogy, narrative inquiry, second language, multiculturalism in Canada, education and law.

University of Wisconsin–Madison, Graduate School, School of Education, Department of Educational Psychology, Madison, WI 53706-1380. Offers MS, PhD. *Accreditation:* APA (one or more programs are accredited). *Degree requirements:* For doctorate, thesis/dissertation. *Entrance requirements:* For master's and doctorate, GRE General Test. *Application deadline:* For fall admission, 12/1 for domestic and international students; for spring admission, 10/1 for domestic and international students. Application fee: $56. Electronic applications accepted. *Expenses:* Tuition, state resident: part-time $594 per credit. Tuition, nonresident: part-time $1504 per credit. Required fees: $65 per credit. Tuition and fees vary according to course load, program and reciprocity agreements. *Financial support:* Fellowships with full tuition reimbursements, research assistantships with full tuition reimbursements, teaching assistantships with full tuition reimbursements, project assistantships available. *Unit head:* Dr. Charles Kalish, Chair, 608-262-9920. *Application contact:* Dr. Charles Kalish, Chair, 608-262-9920.

University of Wisconsin–Milwaukee, Graduate School, School of Education, Department of Educational Psychology, Milwaukee, WI 53201-0413. Offers counseling (school, community) (MS); counseling psychology (PhD); learning and development (MS); research methodology (MS, PhD); school psychology (PhD). *Accreditation:* APA. Part-time programs available. *Faculty:* 22 full-time (14 women). *Students:* 124 full-time (107 women), 47 part-time (35 women); includes 20 minority (10 African Americans, 4 Asian Americans or Pacific Islanders, 6 Hispanic Americans), 2 international. Average age 30. 263 applicants, 52% accepted, 51 enrolled. In 2009, 55 master's, 13 doctorates awarded. *Degree requirements:* For master's, comprehensive exam, thesis; for doctorate, thesis/dissertation. *Entrance requirements:* For master's, minimum GPA of 3.0; for doctorate, GRE General Test, minimum GPA of 3.0. Additional exam requirements/recommendations for international students: Required—TOEFL (minimum score 550 paper-based; 79 iBT), IELTS (minimum score 6.5). *Application deadline:* For fall admission, 1/1 priority date for domestic students; for spring admission, 9/1 for domestic students. Applications are processed on a rolling basis. Application fee: $45 ($75 for international students). *Expenses:* Tuition, state resident: full-time $8800. Tuition, nonresident: full-time $20,760. Tuition and fees vary according to program and reciprocity agreements. *Financial support:* In 2009–10, 9 teaching assistantships were awarded; career-related internships or fieldwork and unspecified assistantships also available. Support available to part-time students. Financial award application deadline: 4/15. Total annual research expenditures: $1.3 million. *Unit head:* Bo Zhang, Graduate Program Representative, 414-229-5742, Fax: 414-229-4939, E-mail: boz@uwm.edu. *Application contact:* General Information Contact, 414-229-4982, Fax: 414-229-6967, E-mail: gradschool@uwm.edu.

University of Wisconsin–Milwaukee, Graduate School, School of Education, Program in Urban Education, Milwaukee, WI 53201-0413. Offers adult and continuing education (PhD); curriculum and instruction (PhD); educational administration (PhD); educational and media technology (PhD); educational psychology (PhD); multicultural studies (PhD); social foundations of education (PhD). *Students:* 67 full-time (51 women), 44 part-time (30 women); includes 41 minority (23 African Americans, 2 American Indian/Alaska Native, 7 Asian Americans or Pacific Islanders, 9 Hispanic Americans), 4 international. Average age 41. 31 applicants, 45% accepted, 5 enrolled. In 2009, 11 doctorates awarded. *Degree requirements:* For doctorate, comprehensive exam, thesis/dissertation. *Entrance requirements:* For doctorate, GRE General Test, minimum undergraduate GPA of 2.85, graduate 3.5. Additional exam requirements/recommendations for international students: Required—TOEFL (minimum score 550 paper-based; 79 iBT), IELTS (minimum score 6.5). *Application deadline:* For fall admission, 1/1 priority date for domestic students; for spring admission, 9/1 for domestic students. Applications are processed on a rolling basis. Application fee: $45 ($75 for international students). *Expenses:* Tuition, state resident: full-time $8800. Tuition, nonresident: full-time $20,760. Tuition and fees vary according to program and reciprocity agreements. *Financial support:* Career-related internships or fieldwork and unspecified assistantships available. Support available to part-time students. Financial award application deadline: 4/15. *Unit head:* Larry Martin, Representative, 414-229-4729, Fax: 414-229-2920, E-mail: lmartin@uwm.edu. *Application contact:* General Information Contact, 414-229-4982, Fax: 414-229-6967, E-mail: gradschool@uwm.edu.

Virginia Commonwealth University, Graduate School, School of Education, Doctoral Program in Education, Educational Psychology Track, Richmond, VA 23284-9005. Offers PhD.

Virginia Polytechnic Institute and State University, Graduate School, College of Liberal Arts and Human Sciences, School of Education, Department of Learning Sciences and Technologies, Blacksburg, VA 24061. Offers educational psychology (PhD); instructional design and technology (MA, Ed D, PhD, Ed S). Postbaccalaureate distance learning degree programs offered. *Entrance requirements:* For master's, minimum GPA of 3.0; for doctorate, GRE, 3 letters of reference, interview, curriculum vitae, writing sample. *Expenses:* Tuition, area resident: Full-time $10,228; part-time $459 per credit hour. Tuition, nonresident: full-time $17,892; part-time $865 per credit hour. Required fees: $1966; $451 per semester.

Washington State University, Graduate School, College of Education, Department of Educational Leadership and Counseling Psychology, Pullman, WA 99164. Offers counseling psychology (Ed M, MA, PhD, Certificate), including counseling psychology (Ed M, MA, PhD), school psychologist (Certificate); educational leadership (M Ed, MA, Ed D, PhD); educational psychology (Ed M, MA, PhD); higher education (Ed M, MA, Ed D, PhD), including higher education administration (PhD), sport management (PhD), student affairs (PhD); higher education with sport management (Ed M). *Accreditation:* NCATE. Terminal master's awarded for partial completion of doctoral program. *Degree requirements:* For master's, comprehensive exam (for some programs), thesis (for some programs), oral exam or written exam; for doctorate, comprehensive exam, thesis/dissertation, oral and written exams. *Entrance requirements:* For master's and doctorate, GRE General Test, minimum GPA of 3.0, 3 letters of recommendation. Additional exam requirements/recommendations for international students: Required—TOEFL (minimum score 550 paper-based; 213 computer-based). *Faculty research:* Attentional processes, cross cultural psychology, faculty development in higher education.

Wayne State University, College of Education, Division of Theoretical and Behavioral Foundations, Detroit, MI 48202. Offers counseling (M Ed, MA, Ed D, PhD, Ed S); education evaluation and research (M Ed, Ed D, PhD); educational psychology (M Ed, Ed D, PhD, Ed S); educational sociology (M Ed, Ed D, PhD, Ed S); history and philosophy of education (M Ed, Ed D, PhD); rehabilitation counseling and community inclusion (MA, Ed S); school and community psychology

(MA, Ed S); school clinical psychology (Ed S). *Accreditation:* ACA (one or more programs are accredited); CORE (one or more programs are accredited). Evening/weekend programs available. *Degree requirements:* For doctorate, thesis/dissertation. *Entrance requirements:* For master's, GRE; for doctorate, GRE, interview, minimum GPA of 3.0, curriculum vitae, references. Additional exam requirements/recommendations for international students: Required—TOEFL (minimum score 550 paper-based; 213 computer-based), TWE (minimum score 6). Electronic applications accepted. *Faculty research:* Adolescents at risk, supervision of counseling.

Western Kentucky University, Graduate Studies, College of Education and Behavioral Sciences, Department of Counseling and Student Affairs, Bowling Green, KY 42101. Offers business and marketing education (MA Ed); counseling (MA Ed); counselor education (Ed S); education and behavioral science (MA Ed); elementary education (MA Ed, Ed S); middle years education (MA Ed); secondary education (MA Ed, Ed S); student affairs (MA Ed). *Accreditation:* ACA; NCATE. Part-time and evening/weekend programs available. *Degree requirements:* For master's, comprehensive exam, thesis optional. *Entrance requirements:* For master's, GRE General Test. Additional exam requirements/recommendations for international students: Required—TOEFL (minimum score 555 paper-based; 213 computer-based; 79 iBT). *Expenses:* Tuition, state resident: full-time $4160; part-time $416 per credit hour. Tuition, nonresident: full-time $9550; part-time $506 per credit hour. Tuition and fees vary according to campus/location and reciprocity agreements. *Faculty research:* Counselor education, research for residential workers.

West Virginia University, College of Human Resources and Education, Department of Technology, Learning and Culture, Program in Educational Psychology, Morgantown, WV 26506. Offers MA. *Accreditation:* NCATE. Evening/weekend programs available. *Degree requirements:* For master's, thesis, content exams. *Entrance requirements:* For master's, GRE General Test (minimum score 1100 verbal and quantitative) or MAT (minimum score 55), minimum GPA of 3.0, interview. Additional exam requirements/recommendations for international students: Required—TOEFL (minimum score 550 paper-based). *Faculty research:* Learning, development, instructional design, stimulus control, rehabilitation.

Wichita State University, Graduate School, College of Education, Department of Counseling, Educational and School Psychology, Wichita, KS 67260. Offers counseling (M Ed); educational psychology (M Ed); school psychology (Ed S). *Accreditation:* NCATE. Part-time and evening/weekend programs available. *Expenses:* Tuition, state resident: full-time $4247; part-time $235.95 per credit hour. Tuition, nonresident: full-time $11,171; part-time $620.60 per credit hour. Required fees: $34; $3.60 per credit hour. $17 per term. Tuition and fees vary according to campus/location and program. *Unit head:* Dr. Marlene Schommer-Aikins, Chairperson, 316-978-3326, Fax: 316-978-3102, E-mail: marlene.schommer-aikins@wichita.edu. *Application contact:* Dr. Marlene Schommer-Aikins, Chairperson, 316-978-3326, Fax: 316-978-3102, E-mail: marlene.schommer-aikins@wichita.edu.

Widener University, School of Human Service Professions, Center for Education, Chester, PA 19013-5792. Offers adult education (M Ed); counseling in higher education (M Ed); counselor education (M Ed); early childhood education (M Ed); educational foundations (M Ed); educational leadership (M Ed); educational psychology (M Ed); elementary education (M Ed); English and language arts (M Ed); health education (M Ed); higher education leadership (Ed D); home and school visitor (M Ed); human sexuality (M Ed); mathematics education (M Ed); middle school education (M Ed); principalship (M Ed); reading and language arts (Ed D); reading education (M Ed); school administration (Ed D); science education (M Ed); social studies education (M Ed); special education (M Ed); technology education (M Ed). *Accreditation:* NCATE. Part-time and evening/weekend programs available. *Faculty:* 34 full-time (22 women), 37 part-time/adjunct (14 women). *Students:* 203 full-time (154 women), 415 part-time (298 women); includes 50 minority (34 African Americans, 1 American Indian/Alaska Native, 5 Asian Americans or Pacific Islanders, 10 Hispanic Americans), 3 international. Average age 39. 139 applicants, 88% accepted. In 2009, 168 master's, 31 doctorates awarded. Terminal master's awarded for partial completion of doctoral program. *Degree requirements:* For doctorate, thesis/dissertation. *Entrance requirements:* For master's, minimum GPA of 2.5; for doctorate, GRE or MAT, minimum GPA of 2.0 (undergraduate), 3.5 (graduate). *Application deadline:* Applications are processed on a rolling basis. Application fee: $25 ($300 for international students). Electronic applications accepted. *Expenses:* Contact institution. *Financial support:* Career-related internships or fieldwork, tuition waivers (full and partial), and unspecified assistantships available. Support available to part-time students. Financial award application deadline: 5/1. *Faculty research:* Reading and cognition, adult education, technology education, educational leadership, special education. *Unit head:* Dr. Michael W. LeDoux, Associate Dean, 610-499-4294, Fax: 610-499-4623, E-mail: mwledoux@widener.edu. *Application contact:* Dr. Roberta D. Nolan, Director of Graduate Admissions, 610-499-4125, E-mail: rdnolan@widener.edu.

Foundations and Philosophy of Education

Antioch University New England, Graduate School, Department of Education, Experienced Educators Program, Keene, NH 03431-3552. Offers M Ed. *Degree requirements:* For master's, thesis, practicum. *Entrance requirements:* For master's, previous course work and work experience in education. Additional exam requirements/recommendations for international students: Required—TOEFL (minimum score 600 paper-based; 250 computer-based). Electronic applications accepted. *Expenses:* Contact institution. *Faculty research:* Classroom action research, school restructuring, problem-based learning, brain-based learning.

Arizona State University, Graduate College, Mary Lou Fulton College of Education, Division of Educational Leadership and Policy Studies, Program in Social and Philosophical Foundations of Education, Tempe, AZ 85287. Offers MA. *Degree requirements:* For master's, thesis or alternative. *Entrance requirements:* For master's, GRE General Test or MAT.

Arkansas State University—Jonesboro, Graduate School, College of Education, Department of Educational Leadership, Curriculum, and Special Education, Jonesboro, State University, AR 72467. Offers community college administration education (SCCT); curriculum and instruction (MSE); education theory and practice (MSE); educational leadership (MSE, Ed D, Ed S), including curriculum and instruction (MSE, Ed S); special education (MSE), including gifted and talented and creative, instructional specialist 4-12, instructional specialist P-4. *Accreditation:* NCATE. Part-time programs available. Postbaccalaureate distance learning degree programs offered (no on-campus study). *Faculty:* 15 full-time (6 women), 19 part-time/adjunct (11 women). *Students:* 16 full-time (11 women), 734 part-time (606 women); includes 111 minority (96 African Americans, 4 American Indian/Alaska Native, 4 Asian Americans or Pacific Islanders, 7 Hispanic Americans), 2 international. Average age 38. 882 applicants, 70% accepted, 240 enrolled. In 2009, 80 master's, 6 doctorates, 15 other advanced degrees awarded. *Degree requirements:* For master's, comprehensive exam, thesis or alternative; for doctorate, comprehensive exam, thesis/dissertation; for other advanced degree, comprehensive exam. *Entrance requirements:* For master's, GRE General Test or MAT, appropriate bachelor's degree, letters of reference, interview; for doctorate, GRE General Test or MAT, interview, master's degree, letters of reference, official transcript, personal statement, writing sample, immunization records; for other advanced degree, GRE General Test or MAT, interview, master's degree, letters of reference, official transcript, 3 years teaching experience, mentor, teaching license, immunization records. Additional exam requirements/recommendations for international students: Required—TOEFL (minimum score 550 paper-based; 213 computer-based; 79 iBT), IELTS (minimum score 6). *Application deadline:* Applications are processed on a rolling basis. Application fee: $50. Electronic applications accepted. *Expenses:* Tuition, state resident: full-time $3744; part-time $208 per credit hour. Tuition, nonresident: full-time $9540; part-time $530 per credit hour. Required fees: $896; $47 per credit hour. $25 per term. One-time fee: $50. Tuition and fees vary according to course load and program. *Financial support:* In 2009–10, 16 students received support; fellowships, teaching assistantships, career-related internships or fieldwork, scholarships/grants, and unspecified assistantships available. Financial award application deadline: 7/1; financial award applicants required to submit FAFSA. *Unit head:* Dr. Mitchell Holifield, Chair, 870-972-3062, Fax: 870-680-8130, E-mail: hfield@astate.edu. *Application contact:* Dr. Andrew Sustich, Dean of the Graduate School, 870-972-3029, Fax: 870-972-3857, E-mail: sustich@astate.edu.

Ashland University, Dwight Schar College of Education, Department of Educational Foundations, Ashland, OH 44805-3702. Offers curriculum and instruction (M Ed), including classroom instruction. Part-time and evening/weekend programs available. *Faculty:* 13 full-time (9 women), 60 part-time/adjunct (31 women). *Students:* 92 full-time (83 women), 242 part-time (194 women); includes 20 minority (13 African Americans, 2 Asian Americans or Pacific Islanders, 5 Hispanic Americans), 7 international. Average age 34. 161 applicants, 99% accepted, 146 enrolled. In 2009, 166 master's awarded. *Degree requirements:* For master's, inquiry seminar, internship, or thesis. *Entrance requirements:* For master's, teaching certificate or license, bachelor's degree, minimum cumulative GPA of 2.75. Additional exam requirements/recommendations for international students: Required—TOEFL. *Application deadline:* Applications are processed on a rolling basis. Application fee: $30. Electronic applications accepted. *Financial support:* In 2009–10, 229 students received support. Application deadline: 4/15. *Faculty research:* Character education, teacher reflection, religion and education, professional education, environmental education. *Unit head:* Dr. Louise Fleming, Chair, 419-289-5347, E-mail: lfleming@ashland.edu. *Application contact:* Dr. Louise Fleming, Chair, 419-289-5347, E-mail: lfleming@ashland.edu.

Ball State University, Graduate School, Teachers College, Department of Educational Studies, Program in Educational Studies, Muncie, IN 47306-1099. Offers PhD.

Bank Street College of Education, Graduate School, Studies in Education, New York, NY 10025. Offers Ed M, MS Ed. *Students:* 4 full-time (all women), 7 part-time (all women); includes 5 minority (3 African Americans, 2 Hispanic Americans). Average age 34. 5 applicants, 60% accepted, 3 enrolled. In 2009, 2 master's awarded. *Degree requirements:* For master's, thesis. *Entrance requirements:* For master's, interview. Additional exam requirements/recommendations for international students: Required—TOEFL (minimum score 600 paper-based; 250 computer-based; 100 iBT), IELTS (minimum score 7). *Application deadline:* For fall admission, 3/1 priority date for domestic students; for spring admission, 11/1 priority date for domestic students. Applications are processed on a rolling basis. Application fee: $65. *Expenses:* Tuition: Part-time $1120 per credit. *Financial support:* Career-related internships or fieldwork, Federal Work-Study, scholarships/grants, and unspecified assistantships available. Support available to part-time students. Financial award application deadline: 4/15; financial award applicants required to submit FAFSA. *Unit head:* Lia Gelb, Head, 212-875-4489, Fax: 212-875-4753, E-mail: liag@bankstreet.edu. *Application contact:* Ann Morgan, Director of Graduate Admissions, 212-875-4403, Fax: 212-875-4678, E-mail: amorgan@bankstreet.edu.

Brigham Young University, Graduate Studies, David O. McKay School of Education, Department of Educational Leadership and Foundations, Provo, UT 84602. Offers M Ed. *Accreditation:* NCATE. Part-time and evening/weekend programs available. *Faculty:* 11 full-time (3 women), 1 part-time/adjunct (0 women). *Students:* 14 full-time (6 women), 106 part-time (59 women); includes 18 minority (11 American Indian/Alaska Native, 7 Hispanic Americans). Average age 35. 74 applicants, 54% accepted, 36 enrolled. In 2009, 26 master's awarded. *Degree requirements:* For master's, comprehensive exam, thesis or alternative. *Entrance requirements:* For master's, GRE, MAT, LSAT. Additional exam requirements/recommendations for international students: Required—TOEFL (minimum score 580 paper-based; 237 computer-based; 85 iBT). *Application deadline:* For fall admission, 2/15 for domestic and international students; for spring admission, 2/1 for domestic and international students. Application fee: $50. Electronic applications accepted. *Expenses:* Tuition: Full-time $5580; part-time $301 per credit hour. Tuition and fees vary according to student's religious affiliation. *Financial support:* In 2009–10, 42 students received support, including 4 research assistantships (averaging $27,480 per year); teaching assistantships, career-related internships or fieldwork, scholarships/grants, and unspecified assistantships also available. Financial award application deadline: 9/1. *Faculty research:* Mentoring, pre-service training of administrators, policy development, cross-cultural studies of educational leadership. *Unit head:* Dean Richard K. Young, Chair, 801-422-3695, Fax: 801-422-0200, E-mail: msesec@byu.edu. *Application contact:* Bonnie Bennett, Department Secretary, 801-422-3813, Fax: 801-422-0196, E-mail: bonnie_bennett@byu.edu.

Central Connecticut State University, School of Graduate Studies, School of Education and Professional Studies, Department of Teacher Education, Program in Educational Foundations Policy/Secondary Education, New Britain, CT 06050-4010. Offers MS. Part-time and evening/weekend programs available. *Students:* 23 part-time (13 women); includes 1 minority (African American). Average age 35. 7 applicants, 43% accepted, 3 enrolled. In 2009, 7 master's awarded. *Degree requirements:* For master's, comprehensive exam, thesis or alternative. *Entrance requirements:* For master's, minimum undergraduate GPA of 2.7. Additional exam requirements/recommendations for international students: Required—TOEFL. *Application deadline:* For fall admission, 7/1 for domestic students; for spring admission, 12/1 for domestic students. Applications are processed on a rolling basis. Application fee: $50. Electronic applications accepted. *Expenses:* Tuition, area resident: Full-time $4662; part-time $440 per credit. Tuition, state resident: full-time $6994; part-time $440 per credit. Tuition, nonresident: full-time $12,988; part-time $440 per credit. Required fees: $3606. One-time fee: $62 part-time. *Financial support:* Application deadline: 3/1.

Chicago State University, School of Graduate and Professional Studies, College of Education, Department of Educational Leadership, Curriculum and Foundations, Program in Curriculum and Instruction, Chicago, IL 60628. Offers instructional foundations (MS Ed). *Degree requirements:* For master's, comprehensive exam, thesis optional. *Entrance requirements:* For master's, minimum GPA of 2.75.

Curry College, Graduate Studies, Program in Education, Milton, MA 02186-9984. Offers educational administration (M Ed); educational diagnostic assessment (Certificate); educational therapy (Certificate); elementary education (M Ed); foundations (non-license) (M Ed); learning disabilities across the lifespan (Certificate); reading (M Ed, Certificate); special education (M Ed). Part-time and evening/weekend programs available. *Faculty:* 6 full-time (4 women), 12 part-time/adjunct (9 women). *Students:* 101 part-time (82 women). Average age 37. In 2009, 25 master's awarded. *Degree requirements:* For master's, project or thesis. *Entrance requirements:* For master's, MAT or GRE, interview, recommendations, resume, written statement. Additional exam requirements/recommendations for international students: Required—TOEFL (minimum score 550 paper-based; 213 computer-based; 80 iBT). *Application deadline:* For fall admission, 8/1 priority date for domestic students, 6/1 for international students; for winter admission, 10/1 for international students; for spring admission, 1/1 for domestic students, 1/28 for international students. Applications are processed on a rolling basis. Application fee: $50. *Expenses:* Contact institution. *Financial support:* Career-related internships or fieldwork

Foundations and Philosophy of Education

Curry College (continued)
and tuition waivers (partial) available. *Faculty research:* Classroom trauma, therapeutic writing, inclusionary practices. *Unit head:* Dr. Donald Gratz, Director and Associate Professor, 617-333-2243, E-mail: dgratz0703@curry.edu. *Application contact:* John Bresnahan, Director of Graduate Enrollment and Student Services, 617-333-2243, Fax: 617-979-3535, E-mail: jbresnah0104@curry.edu.

Duquesne University, School of Education, Department of Foundations and Leadership, Program in Educational Studies, Pittsburgh, PA 15282-0001. Offers MS Ed. Part-time and evening/weekend programs available. Postbaccalaureate distance learning degree programs offered (minimal on-campus study). *Faculty:* 1 (woman) full-time. *Students:* 17 full-time (15 women), 11 part-time (9 women); includes 1 minority (African American). Average age 41. 13 applicants, 92% accepted, 8 enrolled. In 2009, 5 master's awarded. *Degree requirements:* For master's, thesis optional. *Entrance requirements:* For master's, MAT, minimum GPA of 3.0. Additional exam requirements/recommendations for international students: Required—TOEFL (minimum score 550 paper-based; 80 computer-based). *Application deadline:* For fall admission, 8/1 for domestic students; for spring admission, 12/1 for domestic students. Applications are processed on a rolling basis. Application fee: $0. Electronic applications accepted. *Expenses:* Tuition: Part-time $851 per credit. Required fees: $81 per credit. *Financial support:* Research assistantships available. Support available to part-time students. *Unit head:* Dr. Connie Marie Moss, Director, 412-396-4778, Fax: 412-396-5454, E-mail: moss@duq.edu. *Application contact:* Michael Dolinger, Director of Student and Academic Services, 412-396-6647, Fax: 412-396-5585, E-mail: dolingerm@duq.edu.

Eastern Michigan University, Graduate School, College of Education, Department of Teacher Education, Program in Social Foundations, Ypsilanti, MI 48197. Offers MA. *Accreditation:* NCATE. Part-time and evening/weekend programs available. Postbaccalaureate distance learning degree programs offered (minimal on-campus study). *Students:* 14 part-time (8 women); includes 4 minority (1 American Indian/Alaska Native, 2 Asian Americans or Pacific Islanders, 1 Hispanic American), 1 international. Average age 29. In 2009, 5 master's awarded. *Entrance requirements:* For master's, GRE. Additional exam requirements/recommendations for international students: Required—TOEFL. *Application deadline:* Applications are processed on a rolling basis. Application fee: $35. Tuition and fees vary according to course level. *Financial support:* Fellowships, research assistantships with full tuition reimbursements, teaching assistantships with full tuition reimbursements, career-related internships or fieldwork, Federal Work-Study, institutionally sponsored loans, scholarships/grants, tuition waivers (partial), and unspecified assistantships available. Support available to part-time students. Financial award applicants required to submit FAFSA. *Unit head:* Dr. Joe Bishop, Coordinator, 734-487-3260, Fax: 734-487-2101, E-mail: joe.bishop@emich.edu. *Application contact:* Dr. Joe Bishop, Coordinator, 734-487-3260, Fax: 734-487-2101, E-mail: joe.bishop@emich.edu.

Eastern Washington University, Graduate Studies, College of Education and Human Development, Department of Education, Program in Foundations of Education, Cheney, WA 99004-2431. Offers M Ed. *Accreditation:* NCATE. *Degree requirements:* For master's, comprehensive exam. *Entrance requirements:* For master's, minimum GPA of 3.0. *Expenses:* Tuition, state resident: full-time $7476; part-time $249 per quarter hour. Tuition, nonresident: full-time $18,030; part-time $601 per quarter hour. Required fees: $3.50 per quarter hour. $142 per quarter.

Fairfield University, Graduate School of Education and Allied Professions, Department of Curriculum and Instruction, Fairfield, CT 06824-5195. Offers bilingual education (CAS); elementary education (MA); media/educational technology (MA); secondary education (MA); teaching and foundations (MA, CAS); TESOL, foreign language and bilingual/multicultural education (MA, CAS). Part-time and evening/weekend programs available. *Degree requirements:* For master's, comprehensive exam, thesis or alternative. *Entrance requirements:* For master's, PRAXIS I (PPST), minimum QPA of 3.0, 2 recommendations, resume. Additional exam requirements/recommendations for international students: Required—TOEFL (minimum score 550 paper-based; 213 computer-based; 80 iBT). Electronic applications accepted. *Faculty research:* Urban and multicultural education; participatory action for social justice; culture and family; second language acquisition; science, technology and social education.

Fairleigh Dickinson University, Metropolitan Campus, University College: Arts, Sciences, and Professional Studies, School of Computer Sciences and Engineering, Program in Mathematical Foundation, Teaneck, NJ 07666-1914. Offers MS. *Students:* 31 part-time (27 women). Average age 37. In 2009, 12 master's awarded. *Application deadline:* Applications are processed on a rolling basis. Application fee: $40. *Application contact:* Susan Brooman, University Director of Graduate Admissions, 201-692-2554, Fax: 201-692-2560, E-mail: globaleducation@fdu.edu.

Florida Atlantic University, College of Education, Department of Teaching and Learning, Boca Raton, FL 33431-0991. Offers curriculum and instruction (M Ed); elementary education (M Ed); environmental education (M Ed); reading education (M Ed); social foundations of education (M Ed). *Accreditation:* NCATE. Part-time and evening/weekend programs available. *Faculty:* 35 full-time (29 women), 92 part-time/adjunct (61 women). *Students:* 56 full-time (50 women), 134 part-time (128 women); includes 36 minority (15 African Americans, 4 Asian Americans or Pacific Islanders, 17 Hispanic Americans), 2 international. Average age 32. 162 applicants, 74% accepted, 66 enrolled. In 2009, 52 master's awarded. *Entrance requirements:* For master's, GRE General Test, minimum GPA of 3.0 in last 2 years of undergraduate course work. Additional exam requirements/recommendations for international students: Required—TOEFL. *Application deadline:* For fall admission, 7/1 for domestic students, 2/15 for international students; for spring admission, 11/1 for domestic students, 7/15 for international students. Applications are processed on a rolling basis. Application fee: $30. *Expenses:* Tuition, state resident: full-time $7055; part-time $293.94 per credit hour. Tuition, nonresident: full-time $22,096; part-time $920.66 per credit hour. *Financial support:* Fellowships with partial tuition reimbursements, research assistantships with partial tuition reimbursements, teaching assistantships with partial tuition reimbursements, career-related internships or fieldwork, scholarships/grants, and unspecified assistantships available. *Faculty research:* Technology, teaching English to speakers of other languages, math teaching, electronic portfolio assessment, global perspectives through social studies. *Unit head:* Dr. Barbara Ridener, Chairperson, 561-297-3588. *Application contact:* Dr. Barbara Ridener, Chairperson, 561-297-3588.

Florida State University, The Graduate School, College of Education, Department of Educational Leadership and Policy Studies, Program in Social, History and Philosophy of Education, Tallahassee, FL 32306. Offers history and philosophy of education (MS, PhD, Ed S); international and intercultural education (PhD). *Faculty:* 2 full-time (both women), 1 part-time/adjunct (0 women). *Students:* 29 full-time (14 women), 12 part-time (7 women); includes 8 minority (4 African Americans, 1 Asian American or Pacific Islander, 3 Hispanic Americans), 14 international. 103 applicants, 29% accepted, 11 enrolled. In 2009, 4 master's, 4 doctorates awarded. *Degree requirements:* For master's and Ed S, comprehensive exam, thesis optional; for doctorate, comprehensive exam, thesis/dissertation. *Entrance requirements:* For master's, doctorate, and Ed S, GRE General Test, minimum GPA of 3.0. Additional exam requirements/recommendations for international students: Required—TOEFL (minimum score 550 paper-based; 213 computer-based; 80 iBT). *Application deadline:* For fall admission, 5/1 priority date for domestic and international students; for spring admission, 10/1 priority date for domestic and international students. Application fee: $30. Electronic applications accepted. *Expenses:* Tuition, state resident: full-time $7413. Tuition, nonresident: full-time $22,567. *Financial support:* Fellowships with full and partial tuition reimbursements, research assistantships with full and partial tuition reimbursements, teaching assistantships with full and partial tuition reimbursements, career-related internships or fieldwork, scholarships/grants, and unspecified assistantships available. Financial award applicants required to submit FAFSA. *Faculty research:* Social, historical, philosophical content of educational policies; religion, gender, diversity, and social justice in educational policy; interdisciplinary. *Unit head:* Dr. Jeffrey Milligan, Assistant Professor and Program Coordinator, 850-644-8171, Fax: 850-644-1258, E-mail: milligan@coe.fsu.edu. *Application contact:* Jimmy Pastrano, Program Assistant, 850-644-6777, Fax: 850-644-1258, E-mail: pastrano@coe.fsu.edu.

Georgia State University, College of Education, Department of Educational Policy Studies, Program in Social Foundations of Education, Atlanta, GA 30302-3083. Offers MS, PhD. *Accreditation:* NCATE. Part-time and evening/weekend programs available. *Degree requirements:* For master's, thesis or project; for doctorate, comprehensive exam, thesis/dissertation. *Entrance requirements:* For master's, GRE General Test, minimum GPA of 2.5, 2 letters of recommendation, resume; for doctorate, GRE General Test or MAT, minimum GPA of 3.3, 3 letters of recommendation, resumé/curriculum vitae, statement of goals. *Faculty research:* Teacher unionism, African and African-American history and culture, multicultural and workplace education, teacher autonomy and epistemology.

Harvard University, Extension School, Cambridge, MA 02138-3722. Offers applied sciences (CAS); biotechnology (ALM); educational technologies (ALM); educational technology (CET); English for graduate and professional studies (DGP); environmental management (ALM, CEM); information technology (ALM); journalism (ALM); liberal arts (ALM); management (ALM, CM); mathematics for teaching (ALM); museum studies (ALM); premedical studies (Diploma); publication and communication (CPC). Part-time and evening/weekend programs available. *Degree requirements:* For master's, thesis. *Entrance requirements:* For master's, 3 completed graduate courses with grade of B or higher. Additional exam requirements/recommendations for international students: Required—TOEFL (minimum score 600 paper-based; 250 computer-based), TWE (minimum score 5). *Expenses:* Contact institution.

Hofstra University, School of Education, Health, and Human Services, Department of Foundations, Leadership, and Policy Studies, Program in Foundations of Education, Hempstead, NY 11549. Offers MA, CAS. Part-time and evening/weekend programs available. *Students:* 1 (woman) full-time, 3 part-time (2 women). Average age 33. 3 applicants, 100% accepted, 1 enrolled. In 2009, 6 master's awarded. *Degree requirements:* For master's, comprehensive exam, thesis or alternative. *Entrance requirements:* For master's, interview, writing sample, essay; for CAS, interview, writing sample. Additional exam requirements/recommendations for international students: Required—TOEFL (minimum score 550 paper-based; 213 computer-based; 80 iBT). *Application deadline:* Applications are processed on a rolling basis. Application fee: $60. Electronic applications accepted. *Expenses:* Tuition: Full-time $16,200; part-time $900 per credit hour. Required fees: $970; $145 per term. Tuition and fees vary according to program. *Financial support:* In 2009–10, 1 student received support, including 1 fellowship with full and partial tuition reimbursement available (averaging $8,100 per year); research assistantships with full and partial tuition reimbursements available, Federal Work-Study, institutionally sponsored loans, scholarships/grants, and tuition waivers (full and partial) also available. Support available to part-time students. Financial award applicants required to submit FAFSA. *Faculty research:* Philosophy of education, post-modernism, critical race theory, existentialism, ecological thinking. *Unit head:* Dr. Donna R. Barnes, Director, 516-463-5781, Fax: 516-463-5949, E-mail: edadrb@hofstra.edu. *Application contact:* Carol Drummer, Dean of Graduate Admissions, 516-463-4876, Fax: 516-463-4664, E-mail: gradstudent@hofstra.edu.

Indiana University Bloomington, School of Education, Department of Educational Leadership and Policy Studies, Bloomington, IN 47405-7000. Offers education policy studies (PhD); educational leadership (MS, Ed D, PhD, Ed S); higher education (MS, Ed D, PhD); history and philosophy of education (MS); history of education (PhD); international and comparative education (MS, PhD); philosophy of education (PhD); student affairs administration (MS). *Accreditation:* NCATE. Part-time and evening/weekend programs available. *Faculty:* 61 full-time (16 women), 8 part-time/adjunct (4 women). *Students:* 195 full-time (120 women), 102 part-time (53 women); includes 78 minority (49 African Americans, 1 American Indian/Alaska Native, 6 Asian Americans or Pacific Islanders, 22 Hispanic Americans), 29 international. Average age 33. 331 applicants, 77% accepted, 75 enrolled. In 2009, 61 master's, 21 doctorates, 7 other advanced degrees awarded. *Degree requirements:* For master's, thesis optional; for doctorate, comprehensive exam, thesis/dissertation; for Ed S, comprehensive exam or project. *Entrance requirements:* For master's, doctorate, and Ed S, GRE General Test. Additional exam requirements/recommendations for international students: Required—TOEFL (minimum score 213 computer-based; 79 iBT). *Application deadline:* For fall admission, 1/15 priority date for domestic students, 12/1 priority date for international students; for spring admission, 9/1 priority date for domestic and international students. Applications are processed on a rolling basis. Application fee: $55 ($65 for international students). Electronic applications accepted. *Financial support:* In 2009–10, 73 students received support, including 34 fellowships with full and partial tuition reimbursements available (averaging $7,677 per year), 16 research assistantships with full and partial tuition reimbursements available (averaging $17,757 per year), 23 teaching assistantships with full and partial tuition reimbursements available (averaging $13,496 per year); career-related internships or fieldwork, Federal Work-Study, institutionally sponsored loans, and tuition waivers (full and partial) also available. Support available to part-time students. *Faculty research:* Student engagement at higher education institutions in the nation, Reading First professional development initiative, state finance policy on financial access to higher education, school reform, special needs studies. *Unit head:* Martha McCarthy, Chair, 812-856-8377. *Application contact:* Sandy Strain, Department Secretary, 812-856-8360, Fax: 812-856-8394, E-mail: strain@indiana.edu.

Iowa State University of Science and Technology, Graduate College, College of Human Sciences, Department of Curriculum and Instruction, Ames, IA 50011. Offers curriculum and instructional technology (M Ed, MS, PhD); elementary education (M Ed, MS); historical, philosophical, and comparative studies in education (M Ed, MS); special education (M Ed, MS). *Faculty:* 26 full-time (16 women), 1 (woman) part-time/adjunct. *Students:* 51 full-time (34 women), 72 part-time (49 women); includes 11 minority (5 African Americans, 1 American Indian/Alaska Native, 4 Asian Americans or Pacific Islanders, 1 Hispanic American), 25 international. 54 applicants, 69% accepted, 25 enrolled. In 2009, 41 master's, 6 doctorates awarded. *Degree requirements:* For master's, thesis or alternative; for doctorate, thesis/dissertation. *Entrance requirements:* For doctorate, GRE General Test. Additional exam requirements/recommendations for international students: Required—TOEFL (minimum score 560 paper-based; 83 iBT) or IELTS (minimum score 6.5). *Application deadline:* For fall admission, 1/1 priority date for domestic and international students; for spring admission, 9/1 for domestic and international students. Application fee: $40 ($90 for international students). Electronic applications accepted. *Expenses:* Tuition, state resident: full-time $6716. Tuition, nonresident: full-time $8908. Tuition and fees vary according to course level, course load, program and student level. *Financial support:* In 2009–10, 21 research assistantships with full and partial tuition reimbursements (averaging $14,600 per year), 12 teaching assistantships with full and partial tuition reimbursements (averaging $14,600 per year) were awarded; fellowships, scholarships/grants, health care benefits, and unspecified assistantships also available. *Unit head:* Dr. Carl Smith, Director of Graduate Education, 515-294-0317, E-mail: cigrad@iastate.edu. *Application contact:* Dr. Patricia Leigh, Director of Graduate Education, 515-294-7021, E-mail: cigrad@iastate.edu.

Kent State University, Graduate School of Education, Health, and Human Services, School of Foundations, Leadership and Administration, Program in Cultural Foundations, Kent, OH 44242-0001. Offers M Ed, MA, PhD. *Accreditation:* NCATE. *Faculty:* 4 full-time (all women), 1 part-time/adjunct (0 women). *Students:* 25 full-time (21 women), 27 part-time (21 women); includes 16 minority (8 African Americans, 4 Asian Americans or Pacific Islanders, 4 Hispanic Americans), 1 international. 23 applicants, 78% accepted. In 2009, 3 master's awarded. *Degree requirements:* For master's, thesis (for some programs); for doctorate, comprehensive exam, thesis/dissertation. *Entrance requirements:* For master's and doctorate, GRE General Test. Additional exam requirements/recommendations for international students: Required—TOEFL. *Application deadline:* Applications are processed on a rolling basis. Application fee: $30. Electronic applications accepted. *Financial support:* In 2009–10, 1 fellowship with full tuition reimbursement (averaging $12,000 per year), research assistantships with full tuition reimbursements (averaging $8,500 per year), 8 teaching assistantships with full tuition reimbursements (averaging $12,000 per year) were awarded; career-related internships or fieldwork, Federal Work-Study, institutionally sponsored loans, scholarships/grants, health care benefits,

and unspecified assistantships also available. Support available to part-time students. Financial award application deadline: 4/1; financial award applicants required to submit FAFSA. *Faculty research:* Public politics, intercultural communication and training, research paradigms, comparative and international education. *Unit head:* Dr. Averil McClelland, Coordinator, 330-672-0594, E-mail: amcclell@kent.edu. *Application contact:* Nancy Miller, Academic Program Coordinator, Office of Graduate Student Services, 330-672-2576, Fax: 330-672-9162, E-mail: ogs@kent.edu.

Kent State University, Graduate School of Education, Health, and Human Services, School of Lifespan Development and Educational Sciences, Kent, OH 44242-0001. Offers community counseling (MA); counseling (Ed S); counseling and human development services (PhD); cultural foundations (M Ed, MA, PhD); educational psychology (M Ed, MA, PhD); evaluation and measurement (M Ed, MA, PhD); family studies (MA), including gerontology, human development and family studies; instructional technology (M Ed, MA), including computer technology, general instructional technology, library media; intervention specialist (M Ed, MA), including deaf education, early childhood intervention specialist, educational interpreter K-12, general special education, gifted education, mild/moderate intervention, moderate/intensive intervention, transition to work; rehabilitation counseling (M Ed, MA, Ed S); school counseling (M Ed, MA); school psychology (M Ed, PhD, Ed S); special education (PhD, Ed S). Part-time and evening/weekend programs available. *Faculty:* 84 full-time (50 women), 116 part-time/adjunct (89 women). *Students:* 357 full-time (295 women), 325 part-time (256 women); includes 73 minority (55 African Americans, 1 American Indian/Alaska Native, 9 Asian Americans or Pacific Islanders, 8 Hispanic Americans), 10 international. 331 applicants, 66% accepted. In 2009, 134 master's, 9 doctorates, 22 other advanced degrees awarded. *Degree requirements:* For master's, thesis (for some programs); for doctorate, comprehensive exam, thesis/dissertation. *Entrance requirements:* For master's, doctorate, and Ed S, GRE General Test. Additional exam requirements/recommendations for international students: Required—TOEFL. *Application deadline:* Applications are processed on a rolling basis. Application fee: $30. Electronic applications accepted. *Financial support:* In 2009–10, 12 fellowships with full tuition reimbursements (averaging $11,000 per year), 28 research assistantships with full tuition reimbursements (averaging $8,313 per year), 3 teaching assistantships with full tuition reimbursements (averaging $11,000 per year) were awarded; Federal Work-Study, scholarships/grants, and unspecified assistantships also available. Financial award application deadline: 4/1. *Unit head:* Dr. Mary Dellmann-Jenkins, Director, 330-672-6958, E-mail: mdellman@kent.edu. *Application contact:* Nancy Miller, Academic Program Coordinator, Office of Graduate Student Services, 330-672-2576, Fax: 330-672-9162, E-mail: ogs@kent.edu.

McGill University, Faculty of Graduate and Postdoctoral Studies, Faculty of Education, Department of Integrated Studies in Education, Montréal, QC H3A 2T5, Canada. Offers culture and values in education (MA, PhD); curriculum studies (MA); educational leadership (MA, Certificate); educational studies (PhD); integrated studies in education (M Ed); second language education (MA, PhD).

Millersville University of Pennsylvania, College of Graduate and Professional Studies, School of Education, Department of Educational Foundations, Millersville, PA 17551-0302. Offers leadership for teaching and learning (M Ed). Part-time and evening/weekend programs available. *Faculty:* 13 full-time (7 women), 11 part-time/adjunct (7 women). *Students:* 1 (woman) full-time, 29 part-time (16 women); includes 2 minority (1 African American, 1 Hispanic American). Average age 33. 3 applicants, 100% accepted, 3 enrolled. In 2009, 14 master's awarded. *Degree requirements:* For master's, graded portfolio. *Entrance requirements:* For master's, GRE or MAT, 3 letters of recommendation; interview (in-person). Additional exam requirements/recommendations for international students: Required—TOEFL (minimum score 500 paper-based; 183 computer-based; 65 iBT) or IELTS (minimum score 6). *Application deadline:* For fall admission, 1/15 priority date for domestic and international students; for winter admission, 10/1 priority date for domestic and international students; for spring admission, 10/1 priority date for domestic and international students. Applications are processed on a rolling basis. Application fee: $40 ($50 for international students). Electronic applications accepted. *Expenses:* Tuition, state resident: full-time $6666; part-time $370 per credit. Tuition, nonresident: full-time $10,666; part-time $593 per credit. Required fees: $1578.50; $76.25 per credit. One-time fee: $60 part-time. Tuition and fees vary according to course load. *Financial support:* Research assistantships, institutionally sponsored loans and unspecified assistantships available. Support available to part-time students. Financial award application deadline: 3/15; financial award applicants required to submit FAFSA. *Faculty research:* Reflection teacher education, urban education—color of teaching, social learning technology, math learning disabilities, metacognitive aspects of leadership. Total annual research expenditures: $15,000. *Unit head:* Dr. John K. Ward, Chair, 717-871-3835, Fax: 717-872-3856, E-mail: john.ward@millersville.edu. *Application contact:* Dr. Victor S. DeSantis, Dean of Graduate and Professional Studies, 717-872-3099, Fax: 717-872-3453, E-mail: victor.desantis@millersville.edu.

Montclair State University, The Graduate School, College of Education and Human Services, Department of Educational Foundations, Montclair, NJ 07043-1624. Offers critical thinking (M Ed); philosophy for children (M Ed). Part-time and evening/weekend programs available. *Faculty:* 11 full-time (5 women), 21 part-time/adjunct (10 women). *Students:* 5 part-time (all women). Average age 38. 2 applicants, 100% accepted, 2 enrolled. *Degree requirements:* For master's, comprehensive exam, field experience. *Entrance requirements:* For master's, GRE or MAT, 2 letters of recommendation, teaching certificate. Additional exam requirements/recommendations for international students: Required—TOEFL (minimum score 83 computer-based), or IELTS. *Application deadline:* For fall admission, 2/1 for domestic students, 2/15 for international students; for spring admission, 10/15 for domestic and international students. Applications are processed on a rolling basis. Application fee: $60. Electronic applications accepted. *Expenses:* Tuition, area resident: Part-time $486.74 per credit. Tuition, state resident: part-time $486.74 per credit. Tuition, nonresident: part-time $751.34 per credit. Tuition and fees vary according to degree level and program. *Financial support:* In 2009–10, 5 research assistantships with full tuition reimbursements (averaging $7,000 per year) were awarded; Federal Work-Study and scholarships/grants also available. Support available to part-time students. Financial award application deadline: 3/1; financial award applicants required to submit FAFSA. *Unit head:* Dr. Jeremy Price, Chairperson, 973-655-7039. *Application contact:* Amy Aiello, Director of Graduate Admissions and Operations, 973-655-5147, Fax: 973-655-7869, E-mail: graduate.school@montclair.edu.

Mount Saint Vincent University, Graduate Programs, Faculty of Education, Program in Educational Foundations, Halifax, NS B3M 2J6, Canada. Offers M Ed, MA Ed, MA-R. Part-time and evening/weekend programs available. *Degree requirements:* For master's, thesis (for some programs). *Entrance requirements:* For master's, bachelor's degree in related field, minimum B average. Electronic applications accepted. *Faculty research:* Research paradigms, moral aspects of education and teaching, private/independent schools, theory of critical thinking, teachers as workers and as agents of social change.

New York University, Steinhardt School of Culture, Education, and Human Development, Department of Humanities and Social Sciences in the Professions, Program in History of Education, New York, NY 10012-1019. Offers MA, PhD. Part-time programs available. *Students:* 2 full-time (1 woman), 5 part-time (4 women); includes 1 minority (African American). Average age 37. 13 applicants, 23% accepted, 0 enrolled. In 2009, 1 doctorate awarded. *Degree requirements:* For master's, thesis (for some programs); for doctorate, thesis/dissertation. *Entrance requirements:* For doctorate, GRE General Test, interview. Additional exam requirements/recommendations for international students: Required—TOEFL. *Application deadline:* For fall admission, 12/15 priority date for domestic and international students; for spring admission, 11/1 for domestic and international students. Applications are processed on a rolling basis. Application fee: $75. Electronic applications accepted. *Expenses:* Tuition: Full-time $30,528; part-time $1272 per credit. Required fees: $2177. *Financial support:* Fellowships with full and partial tuition reimbursements, Federal Work-Study, institutionally sponsored loans, scholarships/grants, and tuition waivers (partial) available. Support available to part-time students. Financial award application deadline: 2/1; financial award applicants required to submit FAFSA. *Faculty research:* American educational thought, democratic community and education, twentieth century history of education, Jewish history. *Unit head:* Dr. Jonathan L. Zimmerman, Director, 212-992-9475, Fax: 212-995-4832, E-mail: jlzimm@aol.com. *Application contact:* 212-998-5030, Fax: 212-995-4328, E-mail: steinhardt.gradadmissions@nyu.edu.

Niagara University, Graduate Division of Education, Concentration in Foundations of Teaching, Niagara Falls, Niagara University, NY 14109. Offers MA, MS Ed. *Accreditation:* NCATE. Part-time and evening/weekend programs available. *Degree requirements:* For master's, thesis. *Entrance requirements:* For master's, GRE General Test or MAT. *Expenses:* Contact institution.

Northeastern State University, Graduate College, College of Education, Department of Educational Foundations and Leadership, Tahlequah, OK 74464-2399. Offers collegiate scholarship and services (MS); higher education administration and services (MS); school administration (M Ed); teaching (M Ed). Part-time and evening/weekend programs available. *Degree requirements:* For master's, thesis. *Entrance requirements:* For master's, MAT or GRE. Additional exam requirements/recommendations for international students: Required—TOEFL (minimum score 213 computer-based). Electronic applications accepted.

Northern Arizona University, Graduate College, College of Education, Department of Educational Leadership, Flagstaff, AZ 86011. Offers community college/higher education (M Ed); educational foundations (M Ed); educational leadership (M Ed, Ed D); principal (Certificate); principal K-12 (M Ed); school leadership K-12 (M Ed); superintendent (Certificate). *Faculty:* 21 full-time (11 women). *Students:* 196 full-time (128 women), 744 part-time (452 women); includes 249 minority (59 African Americans, 39 American Indian/Alaska Native, 21 Asian Americans or Pacific Islanders, 130 Hispanic Americans), 4 international. Average age 32. 267 applicants, 97% accepted, 185 enrolled. In 2009, 461 master's, 12 doctorates awarded. *Degree requirements:* For master's, comprehensive exam, thesis (for some programs); for doctorate, comprehensive exam, thesis/dissertation. *Entrance requirements:* For master's, minimum GPA of 3.0; for doctorate, GRE or MAT, minimum GPA of 3.5. Additional exam requirements/recommendations for international students: Required—TOEFL (minimum score 550 paper-based; 213 computer-based; 80 iBT), IELTS (minimum score 7), or a bachelor's degree from an English-speaking university and demonstrated proficiency. *Application deadline:* For fall admission, 2/1 priority date for domestic students, 9/15 priority date for international students; for spring admission, 12/1 for domestic students. Applications are processed on a rolling basis. Application fee: $65. Electronic applications accepted. *Financial support:* In 2009–10, 1 teaching assistantship with partial tuition reimbursement (averaging $10,000 per year) was awarded. Financial award application deadline: 3/30. *Unit head:* Dr. Michael Schwanenberger, Chair, 928-523-3202, Fax: 928-523-8950, E-mail: michael.schwanenberger@nau.edu. *Application contact:* Dr. Michael Schwanenberger, Chair, 928-523-3202, Fax: 928-523-8950, E-mail: michael.schwanenberger@nau.edu.

Northern Illinois University, Graduate School, College of Education, Department of Leadership, Educational Psychology and Foundations, De Kalb, IL 60115-2854. Offers educational administration (MS Ed, Ed D, Ed S); educational psychology (MS Ed, Ed D); foundations of education (MS Ed); school business management (MS Ed). Part-time and evening/weekend programs available. Postbaccalaureate distance learning degree programs offered (minimal on-campus study). *Faculty:* 23 full-time (12 women). *Students:* 17 full-time (14 women), 382 part-time (215 women); includes 63 minority (41 African Americans, 1 American Indian/Alaska Native, 6 Asian Americans or Pacific Islanders, 15 Hispanic Americans), 10 international. Average age 38. 117 applicants, 60% accepted, 53 enrolled. In 2009, 110 master's, 9 doctorates, 24 other advanced degrees awarded. *Degree requirements:* For master's, comprehensive exam, thesis optional; for doctorate, thesis/dissertation, candidacy exam, dissertation defense. *Entrance requirements:* For master's, minimum undergraduate GPA of 2.75; for doctorate, GRE General Test, minimum undergraduate GPA of 2.75, 3.2 graduate; for Ed S, GRE General Test, minimum GPA of 2.75 (undergraduate), 3.2 (graduate). Additional exam requirements/recommendations for international students: Required—TOEFL (minimum score 550 paper-based; 213 computer-based). *Application deadline:* For fall admission, 6/1 for domestic students, 5/1 for international students; for spring admission, 11/1 for domestic students, 10/1 for international students. Applications are processed on a rolling basis. Application fee: $30. Electronic applications accepted. *Expenses:* Tuition, state resident: full-time $6576; part-time $274 per credit hour. Tuition, nonresident: full-time $13,152; part-time $548 per credit hour. Required fees: $1813; $75.53 per credit hour. Part-time tuition and fees vary according to course load. *Financial support:* In 2009–10, 2 research assistantships with full tuition reimbursements, 12 teaching assistantships with full tuition reimbursements were awarded; fellowships with full tuition reimbursements, career-related internships or fieldwork, Federal Work-Study, scholarships/grants, tuition waivers (full), and staff assistantships also available. Support available to part-time students. Financial award applicants required to submit FAFSA. *Faculty research:* Interpersonal forgiveness, learner-centered education, psychedelic studies, senior theory, professional growth. *Unit head:* Dr. Charles L. Howell, Chair, 815-753-4404, E-mail: chowell@niu.edu. *Application contact:* Graduate School Office, 815-753-0395, E-mail: gradsch@niu.edu.

Oakland University, Graduate Study and Lifelong Learning, School of Education and Human Services, Department of Teacher Development and Educational Studies, Rochester, MI 48309-4401. Offers education studies (M Ed); secondary education (MAT). *Entrance requirements:* For master's, minimum GPA of 3.0 for unconditional admission. Electronic applications accepted. *Faculty research:* Earth science for middle and high school teachers through real world connections, learning communities, content enrichment.

Purdue University, Graduate School, School of Education, Department of Educational Studies, West Lafayette, IN 47907. Offers administration (MS Ed, PhD, Ed S); counseling and development (MS Ed, PhD); education of the gifted (MS Ed); educational psychology (MS Ed, PhD); foundations of education (MS Ed, PhD); higher education administration (MS Ed, PhD); special education (MS Ed, PhD). *Accreditation:* ACA (one or more programs are accredited); NCATE (one or more programs are accredited). Part-time and evening/weekend programs available. *Degree requirements:* For master's, thesis optional; for doctorate, thesis/dissertation, oral and written exams; for Ed S, oral presentation, project. *Entrance requirements:* For master's, GRE General Test, minimum undergraduate GPA of 3.0; for doctorate, GRE General Test; for Ed S, GRE, minimum B average. Additional exam requirements/recommendations for international students: Required—TOEFL. Electronic applications accepted. *Faculty research:* Motivation, learning disabilities, school learning, group processes, cognitive development.

Regis University, College for Professional Studies, Program in Teacher Education, Denver, CO 80221-1099. Offers adult learning, training, and development (M Ed); curriculum, instruction, and assessment (M Ed); early childhood (M Ed); educational technology (Certificate); elementary (M Ed); ESL (M Ed); fine arts (M Ed), including arts, music; instructional technology (M Ed); professional leadership (M Ed); reading (M Ed); secondary (M Ed); self-designed (M Ed); space studies (M Ed); special education (M Ed); teacher licensure (M Ed). Program also offered in Henderson and Las Vegas (Summerlin), NV. *Accreditation:* Teacher Education Accreditation Council. Part-time and evening/weekend programs available. Postbaccalaureate distance learning degree programs offered (no on-campus study). *Degree requirements:* For master's, thesis. *Entrance requirements:* For master's, resume, minimum GPA of 2.75, criminal background check. Additional exam requirements/recommendations for international students: Required—TOEFL (minimum score 213 computer-based), TWE (minimum score 5). Electronic applications accepted. *Faculty research:* Issues of equity in the middle school classroom, professional learning communities, school reform, socialinguistic and discursive obstacles to student integration, inclusive language arts curriculum.

Rutgers, The State University of New Jersey, New Brunswick, Graduate School of Education, Department of Educational Theory, Policy and Administration, Program in Social and Philosophical Foundations of Education, Piscataway, NJ 08854-8097. Offers Ed M, Ed D. Part-time and evening/weekend programs available. *Degree requirements:* For doctorate, thesis/dissertation, qualifying exam. *Entrance requirements:* For master's, GRE General Test; for doctorate, GRE General Test, writing sample. Additional exam requirements/recommendations for international students: Required—TOEFL. Electronic applications accepted.

Foundations and Philosophy of Education

Saint Louis University, Graduate School, College of Education and Public Service and Graduate School, Department of Educational Studies, St. Louis, MO 63103-2097. Offers curriculum and instruction (MA, Ed D, PhD); educational foundations (MA, Ed D, PhD); special education (MA); teaching (MAT). *Accreditation:* NCATE. Part-time programs available. *Degree requirements:* For master's, comprehensive exam; for doctorate, comprehensive exam, thesis/dissertation, preliminary oral and written exams. *Entrance requirements:* For master's, GRE General Test or MAT, letters of recommendation, resume; for doctorate, GRE General Test, letters of recommendation, resumé, goal statement, transcripts. Additional exam requirements/recommendations for international students: Required—TOEFL (minimum score 525 paper-based; 194 computer-based). Electronic applications accepted. *Faculty research:* Teacher preparation, multicultural issues, children with special needs, qualitative research in education, inclusion.

Simon Fraser University, Graduate Studies, Faculty of Education, Programs in Curriculum and Instruction, Burnaby, BC V5A 1S6, Canada. Offers curriculum theory and implementation (PhD); foundations (M Ed, MA); philosophy of education (PhD). *Degree requirements:* For master's, project or thesis; for doctorate, thesis/dissertation. *Entrance requirements:* For master's, minimum GPA of 3.0; for doctorate, GRE, master's degree or exceptional record in a bachelor's degree, minimum GPA of 3.5. Additional exam requirements/recommendations for international students: Required—TOEFL or IELTS.

Southeast Missouri State University, School of Graduate Studies, Department of Middle and Secondary Education, Cape Girardeau, MO 63701-4799. Offers educational studies (MA); middle level education (MA). *Accreditation:* NCATE. Part-time and evening/weekend programs available. *Degree requirements:* For master's, thesis or alternative. *Entrance requirements:* For master's, GRE General Test, MAT, PRAXIS II, minimum undergraduate GPA of 2.75. Additional exam requirements/recommendations for international students: Required—TOEFL (minimum score 550 paper-based; 213 computer-based); Recommended—IELTS (minimum score 6). Electronic applications accepted. *Expenses:* Tuition, state resident: full-time $4266; part-time $237 per credit hour. Tuition, nonresident: full-time $7506; part-time $417 per credit hour. Required fees: $427; $427. *Faculty research:* Educational administration issues in K-12, leadership in educational setting, counselor education and supervision issues, rural education issues.

Southern Connecticut State University, School of Graduate Studies, School of Education, Department of Educational Leadership, New Haven, CT 06515-1355. Offers educational foundations (Diploma), including foundational studies; educational leadership (Ed D, Diploma); research, statistics, and measurement (MS). Part-time and evening/weekend programs available. *Faculty:* 6 full-time, 6 part-time/adjunct. *Students:* 7 full-time (5 women), 240 part-time (164 women); includes 33 minority (26 African Americans, 1 American Indian/Alaska Native, 6 Hispanic Americans), 1 international. 160 applicants, 54% accepted, 71 enrolled. In 2009, 98 other advanced degrees awarded. *Entrance requirements:* For degree, master's degree, minimum GPA of 3.0, writing sample. *Application deadline:* For fall admission, 7/15 priority date for domestic students. Applications are processed on a rolling basis. Application fee: $50. Electronic applications accepted. Tuition and fees vary according to program. *Financial support:* Application deadline: 4/15. *Unit head:* Dr. Peter Madonia, Chairperson, 203-392-5441, E-mail: madoniap1@southernct.edu. *Application contact:* Dr. Cathryn Magno, Graduate Coordinator, 203-392-5170, Fax: 203-392-5347, E-mail: magnoc1@southernct.edu.

Southern Illinois University Edwardsville, Graduate Studies and Research, School of Education, Department of Educational Leadership, Program in Learning, Culture, and Society, Edwardsville, IL 62026-0001. Offers MS Ed. Part-time programs available. *Students:* 13 part-time (11 women); includes 5 minority (all African Americans). Average age 26. 6 applicants, 33% accepted. In 2009, 3 master's awarded. *Degree requirements:* For master's, thesis or alternative, project, oral defense. *Entrance requirements:* Additional exam requirements/recommendations for international students: Required—TOEFL (minimum score 550 paper-based; 213 computer-based; 79 iBT), IELTS (minimum score 6.5). *Application deadline:* For fall admission, 7/23 for domestic students, 6/1 for international students; for spring admission, 12/11 for domestic students, 10/1 for international students. Applications are processed on a rolling basis. Application fee: $30. Electronic applications accepted. *Expenses:* Tuition, state resident: part-time $1252.50 per semester. Tuition, nonresident: part-time $3131.25 per semester. Required fees: $586.85 per semester. Tuition and fees vary according to course load. *Financial support:* In 2009–10, 3 teaching assistantships with full tuition reimbursements (averaging $8,064 per year) were awarded; fellowships, research assistantships, career-related internships or fieldwork, Federal Work-Study, institutionally sponsored loans, scholarships/grants, and traineeships also available. Support available to part-time students. Financial award application deadline: 3/1; financial award applicants required to submit FAFSA. *Unit head:* Dr. Laurel Puchner, Director, 618-650-3286, E-mail: lpuchne@siue.edu. *Application contact:* Dr. Laurel Puchner, Director, 618-650-3286, E-mail: lpuchne@siue.edu.

Spring Hill College, Graduate Programs, Program in Education, Mobile, AL 36608-1791. Offers early childhood education (MAT, MS Ed); educational theory (MS Ed); elementary education (MAT, MS Ed); secondary education (MAT, MS Ed). Part-time programs available. *Faculty:* 3 full-time (all women), 3 part-time/adjunct (2 women). *Students:* 9 full-time (7 women), 26 part-time (21 women); includes 6 minority (5 African Americans, 1 Asian American or Pacific Islander). Average age 31. 33 applicants, 48% accepted, 9 enrolled. In 2009, 14 master's awarded. *Degree requirements:* For master's, comprehensive exam, completion of program within 6 calendar years of entrance into graduate studies at Spring Hill. *Entrance requirements:* For master's, GRE, MAT, NTE, or PRAXIS, bachelor's degree. Additional exam requirements/recommendations for international students: Required—TOEFL (minimum score 550 paper-based; 213 computer-based; 80 iBT), IELTS (minimum score 6.5). *Application deadline:* For fall admission, 8/1 priority date for domestic and international students; for spring admission, 12/1 priority date for domestic and international students. Applications are processed on a rolling basis. Application fee: $25 ($35 for international students). Electronic applications accepted. *Expenses:* Contact institution. *Financial support:* In 2009–10, 24 students received support. Career-related internships or fieldwork, institutionally sponsored loans, and scholarships/grants available. Support available to part-time students. Financial award applicants required to submit FAFSA. *Unit head:* Dr. Ann A. Adams, Chair of Teacher Education, 251-380-3479, Fax: 251-460-2184, E-mail: aadams@shc.edu. *Application contact:* Donna B. Tarasavage, Director of Marketing and Recruiting, Graduate and Continuing Studies, 251-380-3067, Fax: 251-460-2190, E-mail: dtarasavage@shc.edu.

Stanford University, School of Education, Program in Social Sciences, Policy, and Educational Practice, Stanford, CA 94305-9991. Offers administration and policy analysis (Ed D, PhD); anthropology of education (PhD); economics of education (PhD); educational linguistics (PhD); evaluation (MA), including interdisciplinary studies; higher education (PhD); history of education (PhD); interdisciplinary studies (PhD); international comparative education (MA, PhD); international education administration and policy analysis (MA); philosophy of education (PhD); policy analysis (MA); prospective principal's program (MA); sociology of education (PhD). *Degree requirements:* For master's, thesis (for some programs); for doctorate, thesis/dissertation. *Entrance requirements:* For master's and doctorate, GRE General Test. Electronic applications accepted. *Expenses:* Tuition: Full-time $37,380; part-time $2760 per quarter. Required fees: $501.

State University of New York at Binghamton, Graduate School, School of Education, Program in Educational Theory and Practice, Binghamton, NY 13902-6000. Offers Ed D. *Students:* 10 full-time (9 women), 65 part-time (47 women); includes 5 minority (3 African Americans, 1 American Indian/Alaska Native, 1 Asian American or Pacific Islander), 6 international. Average age 41. 22 applicants, 55% accepted, 12 enrolled. In 2009, 1 doctorate awarded. *Degree requirements:* For doctorate, thesis/dissertation. *Entrance requirements:* For doctorate, GRE General Test, writing sample. Additional exam requirements/recommendations for international students: Required—TOEFL (minimum score 550 paper-based; 213 computer-based; 80 iBT). *Application deadline:* For fall admission, 2/1 priority date for domestic and international students. Applications are processed on a rolling basis. Application fee: $60. Electronic applications accepted. *Financial support:* Fellowships, research assistantships, teaching assistantships with full tuition reimbursements, career-related internships or fieldwork, Federal Work-Study, institutionally sponsored loans, scholarships/grants, health care benefits, and unspecified assistantships available. Financial award application deadline: 2/15. *Unit head:* Dr. James Carpenter, Coordinator, 607-777-4678, E-mail: jcarpent@binghamton.edu. *Application contact:* Victoria Williams, Recruiting and Admissions Coordinator, 607-777-2151, Fax: 607-777-2501, E-mail: vwilliam@binghamton.edu.

Suffolk University, College of Arts and Sciences, Department of Education and Human Services, Programs in School Teaching, Boston, MA 02108-2770. Offers foundations of education (M Ed); middle school teaching (M Ed); school teaching (CAGS); secondary school teaching (M Ed). Part-time and evening/weekend programs available. *Entrance requirements:* For master's, GRE General Test, MAT, or Massachusetts Test for Educator Licensure, 2 letters of recommendation, resume. *Application deadline:* For fall admission, 6/15 priority date for domestic students, 6/15 for international students; for spring admission, 11/15 priority date for domestic students, 11/15 for international students. Applications are processed on a rolling basis. Application fee: $50. *Expenses:* Tuition: Full-time $33,000; part-time $1100 per credit. Required fees: $20. Tuition and fees vary according to program. *Financial support:* Fellowships, career-related internships or fieldwork, Federal Work-Study, and institutionally sponsored loans available. Support available to part-time students. Financial award application deadline: 4/1; financial award applicants required to submit FAFSA. *Faculty research:* Assessment systems, reflection, teamwork, learning environment. *Unit head:* Dr. Sarah M. Carroll, Graduate Program Director, 617-573-8015, Fax: 617-305-1743, E-mail: scarroll@suffolk.edu. *Application contact:* Judith Reynolds, Director of Graduate Admissions, 617-573-8302, Fax: 617-305-1733, E-mail: grad.admission@suffolk.edu.

Syracuse University, School of Education, Program in Cultural Foundations of Education, Syracuse, NY 13244. Offers MS, PhD. Part-time programs available. *Students:* 38 full-time (28 women), 22 part-time (13 women); includes 12 minority (7 African Americans, 2 American Indian/Alaska Native, 2 Asian Americans or Pacific Islanders, 1 Hispanic American), 16 international. Average age 35. 36 applicants, 72% accepted, 10 enrolled. In 2009, 14 master's, 4 doctorates awarded. *Degree requirements:* For master's, thesis or alternative; for doctorate, thesis/dissertation. *Entrance requirements:* For doctorate, GRE, completion of master's degree. Additional exam requirements/recommendations for international students: Required—TOEFL (minimum score 100 iBT). *Application deadline:* For fall admission, 2/1 priority date for domestic and international students; for spring admission, 10/15 priority date for domestic and international students. Applications are processed on a rolling basis. Application fee: $75. Electronic applications accepted. *Expenses:* Tuition: Full-time $26,808; part-time $1117 per credit. Required fees: $1024. *Financial support:* Fellowships with full tuition reimbursements, research assistantships with full tuition reimbursements, teaching assistantships with full and partial tuition reimbursements available. Financial award application deadline: 1/1; financial award applicants required to submit FAFSA. *Faculty research:* Gender and education, history of women's education, the role of science in liberal education, student attrition. *Unit head:* Dr. Sari Knopp Biklen, Chair, 315-443-9075. *Application contact:* Liza Rochelson, Graduate Recruiter, School of Education, 315-443-2505, E-mail: e-gradrcrt@syr.edu.

Teachers College, Columbia University, Graduate Faculty of Education, Department of Arts and Humanities, Program in Philosophy and Education, New York, NY 10027-6696. Offers Ed M, MA, Ed D, PhD. *Faculty:* 2 full-time (1 woman). *Students:* 15 full-time (8 women), 40 part-time (14 women); includes 11 minority (4 African Americans, 4 Asian Americans or Pacific Islanders, 3 Hispanic Americans), 5 international. Average age 33. 26 applicants, 65% accepted, 12 enrolled. In 2009, 10 master's, 2 doctorates awarded. *Degree requirements:* For doctorate, thesis/dissertation. *Entrance requirements:* For master's, previous course work in philosophy; for doctorate, previous course work in philosophy (Ed D), undergraduate degree in philosophy (PhD). *Application deadline:* For fall admission, 5/15 for domestic students; for spring admission, 12/1 for domestic students. Application fee: $65. *Financial support:* Career-related internships or fieldwork, Federal Work-Study, institutionally sponsored loans, and tuition waivers (full and partial) available. Support available to part-time students. Financial award application deadline: 2/1. *Faculty research:* Philosophy and its relationship to educational thought, ethics and education, social theory and ideology. *Unit head:* Graeme Sullivan, Chair, 212-678-3799. *Application contact:* Mark E. Stearns, Associate Director of Admission, 212-678-3710, Fax: 212-678-4171.

Texas A&M University, College of Education and Human Development, Department of Teaching, Learning, and Culture, College Station, TX 77843. Offers curriculum and instruction (M Ed, MS, PhD); mathematics education (M Ed, MS, PhD); multicultural/urban/ESL/international education (M Ed, MS, PhD); reading/language arts (M Ed, MS, PhD); science education (M Ed, MS, PhD); social studies education (M Ed, MS, PhD). Part-time programs available. *Faculty:* 33. *Students:* 145 full-time (113 women), 270 part-time (214 women); includes 110 minority (60 African Americans, 4 American Indian/Alaska Native, 4 Asian Americans or Pacific Islanders, 42 Hispanic Americans), 47 international. Average age 36. In 2009, 114 master's, 17 doctorates awarded. *Degree requirements:* For master's, comprehensive exam, thesis (for some programs); for doctorate, comprehensive exam, thesis/dissertation. *Entrance requirements:* For master's, GRE General Test, minimum GPA of 3.0; for doctorate, GRE General Test, 3 years of teaching experience. Additional exam requirements/recommendations for international students: Required—TOEFL (minimum score 550 paper-based; 213 computer-based). *Application deadline:* For fall admission, 1/15 priority date for domestic and international students; for spring admission, 9/15 priority date for domestic and international students. Applications are processed on a rolling basis. Application fee: $50 ($75 for international students). Electronic applications accepted. *Expenses:* Tuition, state resident: full-time $3991; part-time $221.74 per credit hour. Tuition, nonresident: full-time $9049; part-time $502.74 per credit hour. *Financial support:* In 2009–10, fellowships with partial tuition reimbursements (averaging $3,000 per year), teaching assistantships with partial tuition reimbursements (averaging $7,200 per year) were awarded; research assistantships with partial tuition reimbursements, career-related internships or fieldwork, Federal Work-Study, institutionally sponsored loans, scholarships/grants, tuition waivers (partial), and unspecified assistantships also available. Support available to part-time students. Financial award application deadline: 4/1; financial award applicants required to submit FAFSA. *Unit head:* Dr. Dennie Smith, Head, 979-845-8384, Fax: 979-845-9663, E-mail: krsmith@tamu.edu. *Application contact:* Graduate Admissions Supervisor, 979-845-8382, Fax: 979-845-9663, E-mail: krsmith@tamu.edu.

Troy University, Graduate School, College of Education, Program in Postsecondary Education, Troy, AL 36082. Offers adult education (M Ed); biology (M Ed); criminal justice (M Ed); english (M Ed); foundations of education (M Ed); general science (M Ed); higher education administration (M Ed); history (M Ed); instructional technology (M Ed); mathematics (M Ed); music industry (M Ed); physical fitness (M Ed); political science (M Ed); public administration (M Ed); social science (M Ed); teaching english (M Ed). Also offered through the University College. *Accreditation:* NCATE. Part-time and evening/weekend programs available. *Students:* 267 full-time (192 women), 381 part-time (293 women); includes 326 minority (309 African Americans, 4 American Indian/Alaska Native, 5 Asian Americans or Pacific Islanders, 8 Hispanic Americans). Average age 34. 343 applicants, 90% accepted. In 2009, 480 master's awarded. *Degree requirements:* For master's, comprehensive exam, thesis. *Entrance requirements:* For master's, MAT (minimum score 385), minimum GPA of 2.5. Additional exam requirements/recommendations for international students: Required—TOEFL (minimum score 523 paper-based; 193 computer-based; 70 iBT), IELTS, or ACT Compass ESL (minimum score 270 on Listening, Reading, and Grammar with no individual score below 85 and a minimum score of 8 out of 12 on writing test). *Application deadline:* Applications are processed on a rolling basis. Application fee: $50. Electronic applications accepted. *Financial support:* Available to part-time students. Applicants required to submit FAFSA. *Unit head:* Dr. Andrew Creamer, Chair, 334-670-3350, E-mail: drcreamer@troy.edu. *Application contact:* Brenda K. Campbell, Director of Graduate Admissions, 334-670-3178, Fax: 334-670-3733, E-mail: bcamp@troy.edu.

The University of British Columbia, Faculty of Education, Department of Educational Studies, Vancouver, BC V6T 1Z1, Canada. Offers adult education (M Ed, MA); adult learning and global

change (M Ed); educational administration (M Ed, MA); educational leadership and policy (Ed D); educational studies (PhD); higher education (M Ed, MA); society, culture and politics in education (M Ed, MA). Part-time and evening/weekend programs available. Terminal master's awarded for partial completion of doctoral program. *Degree requirements:* For master's, thesis; for doctorate, comprehensive exam, thesis/dissertation, master's thesis. *Entrance requirements:* For master's, minimum B+ average, 4-year undergraduate degree, field-related experience; for doctorate, minimum B+ average, 4-year undergraduate degree, master's degree, field-related experience. Additional exam requirements/recommendations for international students: Required—TOEFL (600 paper; 250 computer; 100 Internet-based) or IELTS (6.5). Electronic applications accepted. *Faculty research:* Educational leadership educational administration adult education politics in education, global change and adult learning.

University of Calgary, Faculty of Graduate Studies, Faculty of Education, Graduate Division of Educational Research, Calgary, AB T2N 1N4, Canada. Offers community rehabilitation and disability studies (M Ed, M Sc, Ed D, PhD, Graduate Certificate, Graduate Diploma); curriculum, teaching and learning (M Ed, M Sc, MA, Ed D, PhD, Graduate Certificate, Graduate Diploma); educational contexts (M Ed, MA, Ed D, PhD, Graduate Certificate, Graduate Diploma); educational leadership (M Ed, MA, Ed D, PhD, Graduate Certificate, Graduate Diploma); educational technology (M Ed, M Sc, MA, Ed D, PhD, Graduate Certificate, Graduate Diploma); gifted education (M Sc, MA, Ed D, PhD, Graduate Certificate, Graduate Diploma); higher education administration (Ed D); interpretive studies in education (M Ed, M Sc, MA, Ed D, PhD, Graduate Certificate, Graduate Diploma); second language teaching (M Ed, Ed D, PhD, Graduate Certificate, Graduate Diploma); teaching English as a second language (M Ed, M Sc, MA, Ed D, PhD, Graduate Certificate, Graduate Diploma); workplace and adult learning (M Ed, MA, Ed D, PhD, Graduate Certificate, Graduate Diploma). Ed D in both higher education administration and educational leadership offered via distance delivery. Part-time and evening/weekend programs available. Postbaccalaureate distance learning degree programs offered (minimal on-campus study). *Degree requirements:* For master's, thesis (for some programs); for doctorate, thesis/dissertation, candidacy exam. *Entrance requirements:* For master's, minimum GPA of 3.0, 3 letters of reference; for doctorate, minimum GPA of 3.5, 3 letters of reference; for other advanced degree, minimum GPA of 3.0. Additional exam requirements/recommendations for international students: Required—TOEFL, IELTS. Electronic applications accepted. *Faculty research:* Curriculum, leadership, technology, contexts, gifted, second language teaching, work place and adult learning.

University of Central Missouri, The Graduate School, College of Education, Warrensburg, MO 64093. Offers career and technical education administration (MS); career and technical education industry training (MS); career and technical education leadership/teaching (MS); college student personnel administration (MS); counseling (MS); curriculum and instruction (Ed S); educational leadership (Ed D); educational technology (MS); elementary education/educational foundations and literacy (MSE); elementary school administration (MSE); elementary school principalship (Ed S); human services/learning resources (Ed S); human services/professional counseling (Ed S); human services/special education (Ed S); human services/technology and occupational education (Ed S); K-12 education/educational foundations and literacy (MSE); K-12 special education (MSE); library science and information services (MS); literacy education (MSE); secondary education/educational foundations & literacy (MSE); secondary school administration (MSE); secondary school principalship (Ed S); superintendency (Ed S); teaching (MAT). Part-time programs available. Postbaccalaureate distance learning degree programs offered. *Faculty:* 42. *Students:* 123 full-time (82 women), 721 part-time (552 women); includes 58 minority (38 African Americans, 3 American Indian/Alaska Native, 6 Asian Americans or Pacific Islanders, 11 Hispanic Americans), 6 international. Average age 34. 229 applicants, 88% accepted, 190 enrolled. In 2009, 212 master's, 47 other advanced degrees awarded. *Entrance requirements:* Additional exam requirements/recommendations for international students: Required—TOEFL (minimum score 550 paper-based; 79 computer-based). *Application deadline:* For fall admission, 6/1 priority date for domestic students, 5/1 for international students; for spring admission, 10/1 priority date for domestic students, 10/1 for international students. Applications are processed on a rolling basis. Application fee: $30 ($75 for international students). Electronic applications accepted. *Expenses:* Tuition, area resident: Part-time $245.80 per credit hour. Tuition, nonresident: part-time $491.60 per credit hour. Required fees: $24.20 per credit hour. Full-time tuition and fees vary according to course load, degree level, campus/location and reciprocity agreements. *Financial support:* Research assistantships with full and partial tuition reimbursements, teaching assistantships with full and partial tuition reimbursements, career-related internships or fieldwork, Federal Work-Study, scholarships/grants, and administrative and laboratory assistantships available. Support available to part-time students. Financial award application deadline: 3/1; financial award applicants required to submit FAFSA. *Unit head:* Dr. Michael Wright, Dean, 660-543-4272, Fax: 660-543-8753, E-mail: mwright@ucmo.edu. *Application contact:* Laurie Delap, Admissions Coordinator, 660-543-4621, Fax: 660-543-4778, E-mail: gradinfo@ucmo.edu.

University of Cincinnati, Graduate School, College of Education, Criminal Justice, and Human Services, Division of Educational Studies, Program in Educational Studies, Cincinnati, OH 45221. Offers M Ed, PhD. *Accreditation:* NCATE. Part-time programs available. *Degree requirements:* For master's, thesis optional; for doctorate, comprehensive exam, thesis/dissertation. *Entrance requirements:* For master's, GRE General Test; for doctorate, GRE General Test, GRE Subject Test. Additional exam requirements/recommendations for international students: Required—TOEFL (minimum score 520 paper-based; 190 computer-based), OEPT 3. Electronic applications accepted.

University of Connecticut, Graduate School, Neag School of Education, Department of Educational Leadership, Center for Education Policy Analysis, Storrs, CT 06269. Offers PhD. *Accreditation:* NCATE. *Faculty:* 6 full-time (3 women). *Degree requirements:* For doctorate, thesis/dissertation. *Entrance requirements:* For doctorate, GRE General Test. Additional exam requirements/recommendations for international students: Required—TOEFL (minimum score 550 paper-based; 213 computer-based). *Application deadline:* For fall admission, 2/1 priority date for domestic and international students; for spring admission, 11/1 for domestic students, 10/1 for international students. Applications are processed on a rolling basis. Application fee: $55. Electronic applications accepted. *Expenses:* Tuition, state resident: full-time $4725; part-time $525 per credit. Tuition, nonresident: full-time $12,267; part-time $1363 per credit. Required fees: $346 per semester. Tuition and fees vary according to course load. *Financial support:* Fellowships, research assistantships with full tuition reimbursements, teaching assistantships with full tuition reimbursements, Federal Work-Study, scholarships/grants, health care benefits, and unspecified assistantships available. Financial award application deadline: 2/1; financial award applicants required to submit FAFSA. *Unit head:* Barry G. Sheckley, Head, 860-486-2738, Fax: 860-486-4028, E-mail: barry.sheckley@uconn.edu. *Application contact:* Lisa Rasicot, Graduate Coordinator, 860-486-3065, Fax: 860-486-0210, E-mail: l.rasicot@uconn.edu.

University of Florida, Graduate School, College of Education, School of Teaching and Learning, Gainesville, FL 32611. Offers bilingual/ESOL education (M Ed, MAE, Ed D, PhD, Ed S); curriculum and instruction (M Ed, MAE, Ed D, PhD, Ed S); early childhood education (Ed D, PhD, Ed S); elementary education (M Ed, MAE); English education (M Ed, MAE); mathematics education (M Ed, MAE); reading education (M Ed, MAE); science education (M Ed, MAE); social foundations (M Ed, MAE, Ed D, PhD); social studies education (M Ed, MAE). *Accreditation:* NCATE. *Degree requirements:* For master's, thesis optional; for doctorate, variable foreign language requirement, thesis/dissertation. *Entrance requirements:* For master's and doctorate, GRE General Test, minimum GPA of 3.0; for Ed S, GRE General Test. Additional exam requirements/recommendations for international students: Required—TOEFL (minimum score 550 paper-based; 213 computer-based). Electronic applications accepted. *Faculty research:* Teacher education, inclusive education, classroom processes, curriculum and technology.

University of Georgia, Graduate School, College of Education, Department of Workforce Education, Leadership and Social Foundations, Athens, GA 30602. Offers educational leadership (Ed D); human resources and organization design (M Ed); occupational studies (MAT, Ed D, PhD, Ed S); social foundations of education (PhD). *Accreditation:* NCATE. *Faculty:* 19 full-time (8 women). *Students:* 33 full-time (20 women), 127 part-time (81 women); includes 24 minority (19 African Americans, 2 American Indian/Alaska Native, 1 Asian American or Pacific Islander, 2 Hispanic Americans), 6 international. 140 applicants, 71% accepted, 46 enrolled. In 2009, 18 master's, 11 doctorates, 9 other advanced degrees awarded. *Entrance requirements:* For master's, GRE General Test, MAT; for doctorate, GRE General Test; for Ed S, GRE General Test or MAT. *Application deadline:* For fall admission, 7/1 priority date for domestic students; for spring admission, 11/15 for domestic students. Application fee: $50. Electronic applications accepted. *Expenses:* Tuition, state resident: full-time $6000; part-time $250 per credit hour. Tuition, nonresident: full-time $20,904; part-time $871 per credit hour. Required fees: $730 per semester. *Financial support:* Fellowships, research assistantships, teaching assistantships, unspecified assistantships available. *Unit head:* Dr. Roger B. Hill, Interim Head, 706-542-4100, Fax: 706-542-4054, E-mail: rbhill@uga.edu. *Application contact:* Dr. Myra N. Womble, Graduate Coordinator, 706-542-4091, Fax: 706-542-4054, E-mail: mwomble@uga.edu.

University of Hawaii at Manoa, Graduate Division, College of Education, Department of Educational Foundations, Honolulu, HI 96822. Offers M Ed. Part-time and evening/weekend programs available. *Faculty:* 9 full-time (6 women), 4 part-time/adjunct (2 women). *Students:* 6 full-time (5 women), 54 part-time (40 women); includes 32 minority (all Asian Americans or Pacific Islanders), 4 international. Average age 36. 27 applicants, 63% accepted, 10 enrolled. In 2009, 48 master's awarded. *Degree requirements:* For master's, thesis optional. *Entrance requirements:* Additional exam requirements/recommendations for international students: Required—TOEFL (minimum score 580 paper-based; 237 computer-based; 92 iBT), IELTS (minimum score 5). *Application deadline:* For fall admission, 3/1 for domestic students, 1/15 for international students; for spring admission, 9/1 for domestic students, 8/1 for international students. Applications are processed on a rolling basis. Application fee: $60. *Expenses:* Tuition, state resident: full-time $8900; part-time $372 per credit. Tuition, nonresident: full-time $21,400; part-time $898 per credit. Required fees: $207 per semester. *Financial support:* In 2009–10, 2 fellowships (averaging $1,650 per year) were awarded; institutionally sponsored loans and tuition waivers (full and partial) also available. Support available to part-time students. Financial award application deadline: 9/26. *Faculty research:* Multicultural-ethnic education, comparative education, educational policy, interdisciplinary inquiry, moral/political education. *Application contact:* Hannah Tavares, Graduate Chair, 808-956-7817, Fax: 808-956-9100, E-mail: hannaht@hawaii.edu.

University of Hawaii at Manoa, Graduate Division, College of Education, Doctorate in Education Program, Honolulu, HI 96822. Offers curriculum and instruction (PhD); educational administration (PhD); educational foundations (PhD); educational policy studies (PhD); educational technology (PhD); exceptionalities (PhD); kinesiology (PhD). Part-time and evening/weekend programs available. *Faculty:* 65 full-time (40 women), 28 part-time/adjunct (17 women). *Students:* 74 full-time (44 women), 119 part-time (77 women); includes 101 minority (5 African Americans, 2 American Indian/Alaska Native, 86 Asian Americans or Pacific Islanders, 8 Hispanic Americans), 17 international. Average age 38. 98 applicants, 53% accepted, 35 enrolled. In 2009, 11 doctorates awarded. *Degree requirements:* For doctorate, thesis/dissertation. *Entrance requirements:* For doctorate, GRE General Test, sample of written work. Additional exam requirements/recommendations for international students: Required—TOEFL (minimum score 600 paper-based; 250 computer-based; 100 iBT), IELTS (minimum score 7). *Application deadline:* For fall admission, 2/1 for domestic students, 1/15 for international students. Application fee: $50. *Expenses:* Tuition, state resident: full-time $8900; part-time $372 per credit. Tuition, nonresident: full-time $21,400; part-time $898 per credit. Required fees: $207 per semester. *Financial support:* In 2009–10, 1 student received support, including 11 fellowships (averaging $4,147 per year), 17 research assistantships (averaging $17,392 per year), 4 teaching assistantships (averaging $14,670 per year); career-related internships or fieldwork, Federal Work-Study, and tuition waivers (full and partial) also available. *Application contact:* Dr. Helen Slaughter, Chairperson, 808-956-7913, Fax: 808-956-9905, E-mail: slaughte@hawaii.edu.

University of Houston, College of Education, Department of Educational Leadership and Cultural Studies, Houston, TX 77204. Offers administration and supervison (M Ed, Ed D); higher education (M Ed); historical, social, and cultural foundations of education (M Ed). *Accreditation:* NCATE. Part-time and evening/weekend programs available. *Faculty:* 6 full-time (4 women), 3 part-time/adjunct (0 women). *Students:* 57 full-time (42 women), 113 part-time (70 women); includes 82 minority (44 African Americans, 1 American Indian/Alaska Native, 12 Asian Americans or Pacific Islanders, 25 Hispanic Americans), 4 international. Average age 35. 102 applicants, 85% accepted, 65 enrolled. In 2009, 38 master's, 8 doctorates awarded. *Degree requirements:* For master's, comprehensive exam or thesis; for doctorate, comprehensive exam, thesis/dissertation. *Entrance requirements:* For master's, GRE General Test or MAT, minimum GPA of 3.0 in last 60 hours of course work; for doctorate, GRE General Test, interview, minimum GPA of 3.0 in last 60 hours. *Application deadline:* Applications are processed on a rolling basis. Application fee: $75 for international students. Electronic applications accepted. *Expenses:* Tuition, state resident: full-time $7676; part-time $320 per credit hour. Tuition, nonresident: full-time $14,324; part-time $597 per credit hour. Required fees: $3034. *Financial support:* In 2009–10, 2 fellowships with full tuition reimbursements (averaging $9,500 per year), 2 teaching assistantships with full tuition reimbursements (averaging $9,500 per year) were awarded; career-related internships or fieldwork, Federal Work-Study, institutionally sponsored loans, scholarships/grants, health care benefits, and unspecified assistantships also available. Support available to part-time students. Financial award application deadline: 2/1; financial award applicants required to submit FAFSA. *Faculty research:* Change, supervision, multiculturalism, evaluation, policy.

University of Houston–Clear Lake, School of Education, Program in Foundations and Professional Studies, Houston, TX 77058-1098. Offers counseling (MS); instructional technology (MS); multicultural studies (MS). Part-time and evening/weekend programs available. *Degree requirements:* For master's, thesis optional. *Entrance requirements:* For master's, GRE or minimum GPA of 3.0 in last 60 hours. Additional exam requirements/recommendations for international students: Required—TOEFL (minimum score 550 paper-based; 213 computer-based). Electronic applications accepted.

The University of Iowa, Graduate College, College of Education, Department of Educational Policy and Leadership Studies, Program in Social Foundations, Iowa City, IA 52242-1316. Offers MA, PhD. *Degree requirements:* For master's, thesis optional, exam; for doctorate, comprehensive exam, thesis/dissertation. *Entrance requirements:* For master's and doctorate, GRE General Test, minimum GPA of 3.0. Additional exam requirements/recommendations for international students: Required—TOEFL (minimum score 550 paper-based; 213 computer-based; 81 iBT). Electronic applications accepted.

The University of Iowa, Graduate College, College of Education, Department of Psychological and Quantitative Foundations, Iowa City, IA 52242-1316. Offers counseling psychology (PhD); educational measurement and statistics (MA, PhD); educational psychology (MA, PhD); school psychology (PhD, Ed S); JD/PhD. *Accreditation:* APA. *Degree requirements:* For master's, thesis optional, exam; for doctorate, comprehensive exam, thesis/dissertation; for Ed S, exam. *Entrance requirements:* For master's, doctorate, and Ed S, GRE General Test, minimum GPA of 3.0. Additional exam requirements/recommendations for international students: Required—TOEFL (minimum score 550 paper-based; 213 computer-based; 81 iBT). Electronic applications accepted.

The University of Kansas, Graduate Studies, School of Education, Department of Educational Leadership and Policy Studies, Program in Educational Policy and Leadership, Lawrence, KS 66045-3101. Offers educational administration (Ed D, PhD); foundations (PhD); higher education (Ed D, PhD); policy studies (PhD). Part-time and evening/weekend programs available. *Students:* 116 full-time (70 women), 58 part-time (32 women); includes 28 minority (12 African Americans, 4 American Indian/Alaska Native, 7 Asian Americans or Pacific Islanders, 5 Hispanic Americans), 9 international. Average age 38. 69 applicants, 68% accepted, 39 enrolled. In 2009, 11 doctorates awarded. *Degree requirements:* For doctorate, comprehensive exam, thesis/

Foundations and Philosophy of Education

The University of Kansas (continued)
dissertation. *Entrance requirements:* For doctorate, GRE General Test, minimum graduate GPA of 3.5. Additional exam requirements/recommendations for international students: Required—TOEFL (minimum score 570 paper-based; 230 computer-based; 80 iBT). *Application deadline:* For fall admission, 7/1 for domestic and international students; for spring admission, 11/1 for domestic and international students. Applications are processed on a rolling basis. Application fee: $45 ($55 for international students). Electronic applications accepted. *Expenses:* Tuition, state resident: full-time $6492; part-time $270.50 per credit hour. Tuition, nonresident: full-time $15,510; part-time $646.25 per credit hour. Required fees: $847; $70.56 per credit hour. Tuition and fees vary according to course load and program. *Financial support:* Fellowships, research assistantships with full and partial tuition reimbursements, teaching assistantships with full and partial tuition reimbursements, scholarships/grants and unspecified assistantships available. Financial award application deadline: 3/15. *Faculty research:* Historical and philosophical issues in education, education policy and leadership, higher education faculty, research on college students, education technology. *Unit head:* Dr. Susan Twombly, Chair, 785-864-9721, Fax: 785-864-4697, E-mail: stwombly@ku.edu. *Application contact:* Denise Brubaker, Admissions Coordinator, 785-864-4458, Fax: 785-864-4697, E-mail: elps@ku.edu.

University of Manitoba, Faculty of Graduate Studies, Faculty of Education, Department of Educational Administration, Foundations and Psychology, Winnipeg, MB R3T 2N2, Canada. Offers adult and post-secondary education (M Ed); educational administration (M Ed); guidance and counseling (M Ed); inclusive special education (M Ed); social foundations of education (M Ed). *Degree requirements:* For master's, thesis or alternative.

University of Maryland, College Park, Academic Affairs, College of Education, Department of Education Policy and Leadership, College Park, MD 20742. Offers curriculum and educational communications (M Ed, MA, Ed D, PhD); social foundations of education (M Ed, MA, Ed D, PhD, CAGS). *Accreditation:* NCATE. Part-time and evening/weekend programs available. Postbaccalaureate distance learning degree programs offered (minimal on-campus study). *Students:* 120 full-time (81 women), 52 part-time (37 women). 1 applicant, 100% accepted, 0 enrolled. In 2009, 25 master's, 15 doctorates, 1 other advanced degree awarded. *Degree requirements:* For master's, thesis or alternative, internship and/or field experience; for doctorate, comprehensive exam, thesis/dissertation, practicum or internship. *Entrance requirements:* For master's, GRE General Test or MAT, minimum GPA of 3.0, scholarly writing sample, 3 letters of recommendation; for doctorate, GRE General Test or MAT, scholarly writing sample; minimum undergraduate GPA of 3.0, graduate 3.5. *Application deadline:* For fall admission, 12/15 for domestic and international students; for spring admission, 6/1 for international students. Applications are processed on a rolling basis. Application fee: $60. Electronic applications accepted. *Expenses:* Tuition, area resident: Part-time $471 per credit hour. Tuition, state resident: part-time $471 per credit hour. Tuition, nonresident: part-time $1016 per credit hour. Required fees: $337.04 per term. *Financial support:* In 2009–10, 5 fellowships with full and partial tuition reimbursements (averaging $17,387 per year), 1 research assistantship with tuition reimbursement (averaging $24,000 per year), 26 teaching assistantships with tuition reimbursements (averaging $16,554 per year) were awarded; career-related internships or fieldwork, Federal Work-Study, and scholarships/grants also available. Support available to part-time students. Financial award applicants required to submit FAFSA. *Faculty research:* Educational technology, adult and higher education. Total annual research expenditures: $41,998. *Unit head:* Dr. Thomas Weible, Interim Chair, 301-405-3589, Fax: 301-405-3573, E-mail: tweible@umd.edu. *Application contact:* Dean of Graduate School, 301-405-0358.

University of Michigan, Horace H. Rackham School of Graduate Studies, School of Education, Programs in Educational Studies, Ann Arbor, MI 48109. Offers cross specialization (PhD); curriculum development (MA); early childhood education (MA, PhD); educational administration and policy (MA, PhD); educational foundations and policy (MA, PhD); English education (MA); English language learning in school settings (MA); learning technologies (MA, PhD); literacy, language, and culture (MA, PhD); mathematics education (MA, PhD); postsecondary science education (MS); research methods (MA); science education (MA, PhD); social studies education (MA); teaching and teacher education (PhD); MA/Certification; MBA/MA; PhD/MA. Terminal master's awarded for partial completion of doctoral program. *Degree requirements:* For master's, thesis (for some programs); for doctorate, comprehensive exam, thesis/dissertation. *Entrance requirements:* For master's and doctorate, GRE General Test. Additional exam requirements/recommendations for international students: Required—TOEFL (minimum score 600 paper-based; 250 computer-based). *Application deadline:* For fall admission, 12/1 priority date for domestic students, 12/1 for international students. Application fee: $60 ($75 for international students). Electronic applications accepted. *Expenses:* Tuition, state resident: full-time $17,286; part-time $1099 per credit hour. Tuition, nonresident: full-time $34,944; part-time $2080 per credit hour. Required fees: $95 per semester. Tuition and fees vary according to course load, degree level and program. *Financial support:* Applicants required to submit FAFSA. *Unit head:* Dr. Addison Stone, Chairperson, 734-763-7500, Fax: 734-615-1290, E-mail: addison@umich.edu. *Application contact:* Laura Mayers, Student Services Assistant, 734-764-7563, Fax: 734-763-1495, E-mail: ed.grad.admit@umich.edu.

University of Minnesota, Twin Cities Campus, Graduate School, College of Education and Human Development, Department of Educational Psychology, Program in Psychological Foundations of Education, Minneapolis, MN 55455-0213. Offers MA, PhD, Ed S. *Students:* 55 full-time (32 women), 26 part-time (16 women); includes 7 minority (3 African Americans, 2 Asian Americans or Pacific Islanders, 2 Hispanic Americans), 22 international. Average age 35. 53 applicants, 40% accepted, 7 enrolled. In 2009, 4 master's, 8 doctorates awarded. *Unit head:* Dr. Susan Hupp, Chair, 612-624-1003, Fax: 612-624-8241, E-mail: shupp@umn.edu. *Application contact:* Dr. Mary Trettin, Associate Dean, 612-625-6501, Fax: 612-626-1580, E-mail: mtrettin@umn.edu.

University of New Mexico, Graduate School, College of Education, Department of Language, Literacy and Sociocultural Studies, Program in Language, Literacy and Sociocultural Studies, Albuquerque, NM 87131-2039. Offers MA, PhD. Part-time programs available. *Faculty:* 23 full-time (17 women), 4 part-time/adjunct (3 women). *Students:* 72 full-time (59 women), 99 part-time (81 women); includes 73 minority (3 African Americans, 23 American Indian/Alaska Native, 4 Asian Americans or Pacific Islanders, 43 Hispanic Americans), 25 international. Average age 40. 48 applicants, 63% accepted, 22 enrolled. In 2009, 44 master's, 9 doctorates awarded. *Degree requirements:* For master's, comprehensive exam, thesis optional; for doctorate, comprehensive exam, thesis/dissertation, research skills. *Entrance requirements:* For master's, letter of intent, 3 letters of recommendation, resume, BA/BS, department demographic form; for doctorate, writing sample, letter of intent, 3 letters of recommendation, resume, BA/BS, department demographic form. Additional exam requirements/recommendations for international students: Required—TOEFL. *Application deadline:* For fall admission, 12/1 for domestic students; for spring admission, 9/15 for domestic students. Application fee: $50. Electronic applications accepted. *Expenses:* Tuition, state resident: full-time $2099; part-time $233.20 per credit hour. Tuition, nonresident: full-time $6650. Required fees: $25 per semester. Tuition and fees vary according to course load, program and reciprocity agreements. *Financial support:* In 2009–10, 137 students received support, including 35 fellowships (averaging $16,435 per year), 3 research assistantships (averaging $10,862 per year), 17 teaching assistantships with tuition reimbursements available (averaging $4,562 per year); career-related internships or fieldwork, institutionally sponsored loans, scholarships/grants, and unspecified assistantships also available. Support available to part-time students. Financial award application deadline: 3/1; financial award applicants required to submit FAFSA. *Faculty research:* School reform, professional development, history of education, Native American education, politics of education, feminism and issues of sexual identity, critical race theory, bilingualism, literacy reading, adolescent literature, second language acquisition, critical theory and schooling, indigenous languages. *Unit head:* Dr. Don Zancanella, Chair, 505-277-0437, Fax: 505-277-7782, E-mail: zanc@unm.edu. *Application contact:* Debra Schaffer, Administrative Assistant, 505-277-0437, Fax: 505-277-8362, E-mail: schaffer@unm.edu.

University of Oklahoma, Graduate College, College of Education, Department of Educational Leadership and Policy Studies, Norman, OK 73019-0390. Offers adult and higher education (M Ed, PhD); educational administration, curriculum and supervision (M Ed, Ed D, PhD); educational studies (M Ed, PhD); historical, philosophical, and social foundations of education (M Ed, PhD). *Accreditation:* NCATE. Part-time programs available. *Faculty:* 34 full-time (18 women), 3 part-time/adjunct (0 women). *Students:* 157 full-time (81 women), 226 part-time (148 women); includes 101 minority (46 African Americans, 35 American Indian/Alaska Native, 8 Asian Americans or Pacific Islanders, 12 Hispanic Americans), 8 international. 162 applicants, 83% accepted, 80 enrolled. In 2009, 113 master's, 19 doctorates awarded. Terminal master's awarded for partial completion of doctoral program. *Degree requirements:* For master's, comprehensive exam; for doctorate, thesis/dissertation, general exam. *Entrance requirements:* For master's, 12 hours of course work in education; for doctorate, GRE General Test, master's degree, minimum graduate GPA of 3.25. Additional exam requirements/recommendations for international students: Required—TOEFL (minimum score 550 paper-based; 213 computer-based). *Application deadline:* For fall admission, 6/1 for domestic students, 4/1 for international students; for spring admission, 11/1 for domestic students, 9/1 for international students. Application fee: $40 ($90 for international students). Electronic applications accepted. *Expenses:* Tuition, state resident: full-time $3744; part-time $156 per credit hour. Tuition, nonresident: full-time $13,577; part-time $565.70 per credit hour. Required fees: $2415; $90.10 per credit hour. *Financial support:* In 2009–10, 221 students received support, including 55 research assistantships with partial tuition reimbursements available (averaging $9,663 per year); Federal Work-Study, institutionally sponsored loans, and tuition waivers (full) also available. Financial award applicants required to submit FAFSA. Total annual research expenditures: $1.1 million. *Unit head:* David Tan, Interim Chair, 405-325-5986, Fax: 405-325-2403, E-mail: dtan@ou.edu. *Application contact:* Geri Evans, Programs Officer, 405-325-5978, Fax: 405-325-2403, E-mail: gevans@ou.edu.

University of Pittsburgh, School of Education, Department of Administrative and Policy Studies, Program in Social and Comparative Analysis in Education, Pittsburgh, PA 15260. Offers M Ed, MA, Ed D, PhD. Evening/weekend programs available. *Students:* 55 full-time (35 women), 41 part-time (28 women); includes 16 minority (9 African Americans, 5 Asian Americans or Pacific Islanders, 2 Hispanic Americans), 19 international. Average age 37. 48 applicants, 83% accepted, 21 enrolled. In 2009, 6 master's, 6 doctorates awarded. *Degree requirements:* For master's, thesis; for doctorate, thesis/dissertation. *Entrance requirements:* For doctorate, GRE General Test. Additional exam requirements/recommendations for international students: Required—TOEFL (minimum score 213 computer-based; 80 iBT). *Application deadline:* For fall admission, 2/1 priority date for domestic and international students; for spring admission, 11/15 priority date for domestic students, 7/1 priority date for international students. Applications are processed on a rolling basis. Application fee: $50. Electronic applications accepted. *Expenses:* Tuition, state resident: full-time $16,402; part-time $665 per credit. Tuition, nonresident: full-time $28,694; part-time $1175 per credit. Required fees: $690; $175 per term. Tuition and fees vary according to program. *Financial support:* Research assistantships, teaching assistantships, Federal Work-Study, institutionally sponsored loans, scholarships/grants, health care benefits, tuition waivers (partial), and unspecified assistantships available. Support available to part-time students. Financial award application deadline: 3/15; financial award applicants required to submit FAFSA. *Unit head:* Dr. John C. Weidman, Chair, 412-648-7114, Fax: 412-648-1784, E-mail: weidman@pitt.edu. *Application contact:* Lauren Pasquini, Enrollment Manager, 412-648-2230, Fax: 412-648-1899, E-mail: soeinfo@pitt.edu.

University of Saskatchewan, College of Graduate Studies and Research, College of Education, Department of Educational Foundations, Saskatoon, SK S7N 5A2, Canada. Offers M Ed, MC Ed, PhD, Diploma. Part-time programs available. *Faculty:* 14. *Students:* 60. In 2009, 18 master's awarded. *Degree requirements:* For master's, thesis (for some programs); for doctorate, comprehensive exam (for some programs), thesis/dissertation. *Entrance requirements:* Additional exam requirements/recommendations for international students: Required—TOEFL (minimum score 80 iBT); Recommended—IELTS (minimum score 6.5). *Application deadline:* For fall admission, 7/1 priority date for domestic students. Applications are processed on a rolling basis. Application fee: $75. Electronic applications accepted. Tuition and fees charges are reported in Canadian dollars. *Expenses:* Tuition, area resident: Full-time $3000 Canadian dollars; part-time $500 Canadian dollars per term. Required fees: $700 Canadian dollars; $100 Canadian dollars per term. *Financial support:* Fellowships, research assistantships, teaching assistantships available. Financial award application deadline: 1/31. *Faculty research:* Indian and northern education, adult and continuing education, international education. *Unit head:* Dr. Dianne Mller, Acting Head, 306- 966-7724, Fax: 306-966-7549, E-mail: dianne.miller@usask.ca. *Application contact:* Dr. Dianne Miller, Graduate Chair, 306-966-7552, Fax: 306-966-7549, E-mail: dianne.miller@usask.ca.

University of South Africa, College of Human Sciences, Pretoria, South Africa. Offers adult education (M Ed); African languages (MA, PhD); African politics (MA, PhD); Afrikaans (MA, PhD); ancient history (MA, PhD); ancient Near Eastern studies (MA, PhD); anthropology (MA, PhD); applied linguistics (MA); Arabic (MA, PhD); archaeology (MA); art history (MA); Biblical archaeology (MA); Biblical studies (M Th, D Th, PhD); Christian spirituality (M Th, D Th); church history (M Th, D Th); classical studies (MA, PhD); clinical psychology (MA); communication (MA, PhD); comparative education (M Ed, Ed D); consulting psychology (D Admin, D Com, PhD); curriculum studies (M Ed, Ed D); development studies (M Admin, MA, D Admin, PhD); didactics (M Ed, Ed D); education (M Tech); education management (M Ed, Ed D); educational psychology (M Ed); English (MA); environmental education (M Ed); French (MA, PhD); German (MA, PhD); Greek (MA); guidance and counseling (M Ed); health studies (MA, PhD), including health sciences education (MA), health services management (MA), medical and surgical nursing science (critical care general) (MA), midwifery and neonatal nursing science (MA), trauma and emergency care (MA); history (MA, PhD); history of education (Ed D); inclusive education (M Ed, Ed D); information and communications technology policy and regulation (MA); information science (MA, MIS, PhD); international politics (MA, PhD); Islamic studies (MA, PhD); Italian (MA, PhD); Judaica (MA, PhD); linguistics (MA, PhD); mathematical education (M Ed); mathematics education (MA); missiology (M Th, D Th); modern Hebrew (MA, PhD); musicology (MA, MMus, D Mus, PhD); natural science education (M Ed); New Testament (M Th, D Th); Old Testament (D Th); pastoral therapy (M Th, D Th); philosophy (MA); philosophy of education (M Ed, Ed D); politics (MA, PhD); Portuguese (MA, PhD); practical theology (M Th, D Th); psychology (MA, MS, PhD); psychology of education (M Ed, Ed D); public health (MA); religious studies (MA, D Th, PhD); Romance languages (MA); Russian (MA, PhD); Semitic languages (MA, PhD); social behavior studies in HIV/AIDS (MA); social science (mental health) (MA); social science in development studies (MA); social science in psychology (MA); social science in social work (MA); social science in sociology (MA); social work (MSW, DSW, PhD); socio-education (M Ed, Ed D); sociolinguistics (MA); sociology (MA, PhD); Spanish (MA, PhD); systematic theology (M Th, D Th); TESOL (teaching English to speakers of other languages) (MA); theological ethics (M Th, D Th); theory of literature (MA, PhD); urban ministries (D Th); urban ministry (M Th).

University of South Carolina, The Graduate School, College of Education, Department of Educational Studies, Program in Foundations in Education, Columbia, SC 29208. Offers PhD. *Accreditation:* NCATE. Part-time programs available. *Degree requirements:* For doctorate, comprehensive exam, thesis/dissertation. *Entrance requirements:* For doctorate, GRE General Test or MAT, interview. Electronic applications accepted. *Faculty research:* Oral history, educational biography, home schooling, international education.

The University of Tennessee, Graduate School, College of Education, Health and Human Sciences, Program in Education, Knoxville, TN 37996. Offers art education (MS); counseling education (PhD); cultural studies in education (PhD); curriculum (MS, Ed S); curriculum, educational research and evaluation (Ed D, PhD); early childhood education (PhD); early childhood special education (MS); education of deaf and hard of hearing (MS); educational administration and policy studies (Ed D, PhD); educational administration and supervision (Ed S); educational psychology (Ed D, PhD); elementary education (MS, Ed S); elementary teaching (MS); English education (MS, Ed S); exercise science (PhD); foreign language/ESL education (MS, Ed S); instructional technology (MS, Ed D, PhD, Ed S); literacy, language and ESL education (PhD); literacy, language education, and ESL education (Ed D); mathematics

education (MS, Ed S); modified and comprehensive special education (MS); reading education (MS, Ed S); school counseling (Ed S); school psychology (PhD, Ed S); science education (MS, Ed S); secondary teaching (MS); social foundations (MS); social science education (MS, Ed S); socio-cultural foundations of sports and education (PhD); special education (Ed S); teacher education (Ed D, PhD). *Accreditation:* NCATE. Part-time and evening/weekend programs available. *Degree requirements:* For master's and Ed S, thesis optional; for doctorate, variable foreign language requirement, thesis/dissertation. *Entrance requirements:* For master's, minimum GPA of 2.7; for doctorate and Ed S, GRE General Test, minimum GPA of 2.7. Additional exam requirements/recommendations for international students: Required—TOEFL. Electronic applications accepted. *Expenses:* Tuition, state resident: full-time $6826; part-time $380 per semester hour. Tuition, nonresident: full-time $21,844; part-time $1147 per semester hour. Tuition and fees vary according to program.

The University of Texas of the Permian Basin, Office of Graduate Studies, School of Education, Program in Professional Education, Odessa, TX 79762-0001. Offers MA. *Degree requirements:* For master's, comprehensive exam (for some programs), thesis (for some programs). *Entrance requirements:* For master's, GRE General Test. Additional exam requirements/recommendations for international students: Required—TOEFL (minimum score 550 paper-based; 213 computer-based).

The University of Toledo, College of Graduate Studies, College of Education, Department of Educational Foundations and Leadership, Program in Educational Sociology, Toledo, OH 43606-3390. Offers DE, PhD.

The University of Toledo, College of Graduate Studies, College of Education, Department of Educational Foundations and Leadership, Program in Educational Theory and Social Foundations, Toledo, OH 43606-3390. Offers ME.

The University of Toledo, College of Graduate Studies, College of Education, Department of Educational Foundations and Leadership, Program in Foundations of Education, Toledo, OH 43606-3390. Offers DE, PhD.

The University of Toledo, College of Graduate Studies, College of Education, Department of Educational Foundations and Leadership, Program in History of Education, Toledo, OH 43606-3390. Offers DE, PhD.

The University of Toledo, College of Graduate Studies, College of Education, Department of Educational Foundations and Leadership, Program in Philosophy of Education, Toledo, OH 43606-3390. Offers DE, PhD.

University of Utah, Graduate School, College of Education, Department of Education, Culture, and Society, Salt Lake City, UT 84112-1107. Offers M Ed, MA, MS, PhD. Evening/weekend programs available. *Faculty:* 12 full-time (7 women). *Students:* 32 full-time (20 women), 41 part-time (28 women); includes 30 minority (8 African Americans, 2 American Indian/Alaska Native, 6 Asian Americans or Pacific Islanders, 14 Hispanic Americans), 5 international. Average age 37. 59 applicants, 54% accepted, 24 enrolled. In 2009, 13 master's, 3 doctorates awarded. *Degree requirements:* For master's, comprehensive exam, thesis (for some programs); for doctorate, thesis/dissertation. *Entrance requirements:* For master's and doctorate, minimum GPA of 3.0. Additional exam requirements/recommendations for international students: Required—TOEFL (minimum score 650 paper-based; 278 computer-based). *Application deadline:* For fall admission, 2/15 priority date for domestic and international students. Application fee: $55 ($65 for international students). *Expenses:* Tuition, state resident: full-time $4004; part-time $1674 per semester. Tuition, nonresident: full-time $14,134; part-time $5915 per semester. Required fees: $324 per semester. Tuition and fees vary according to course load, degree level and program. *Financial support:* In 2009–10, 13 students received support, including 9 teaching assistantships with full tuition reimbursements available (averaging $13,000 per year); tuition waivers (full) and unspecified assistantships also available. Financial award application deadline: 3/1; financial award applicants required to submit FAFSA. *Faculty research:* History, philosophy and sociology of education, language, culture and curriculum. *Unit head:* Dr. Harvey Kantor, Chair, 801-581-7805, Fax: 801-587-7801, E-mail: harvey.kantor@.utah.edu. *Application contact:* Dr. Audrey Thompson, Advisor, 801-581-7803, Fax: 801-587-7801, E-mail: audrey.thompson@.utah.edu.

University of Victoria, Faculty of Graduate Studies, Faculty of Education, Department of Curriculum and Instruction, Victoria, BC V8W 2Y2, Canada. Offers art education (M Ed, PhD); curriculum studies (M Ed, MA, PhD); early childhood education (M Ed, PhD); educational studies (PhD); language and literacy (M Ed, MA, PhD); mathematics (M Ed, MA, PhD); music education (M Ed, MA, PhD); science (M Ed, MA, PhD); social studies (M Ed, MA); social, cultural and foundational studies (MA, PhD); technology and environmental education (PhD). Part-time programs available. *Degree requirements:* For master's, thesis, project (M Ed); for doctorate, comprehensive exam, thesis/dissertation. *Entrance requirements:* For master's, minimum B average. Additional exam requirements/recommendations for international students: Required—TOEFL (minimum score 575 paper-based; 233 computer-based), IELTS (minimum score 7). Electronic applications accepted. *Faculty research:* Elementary and secondary English, language arts, curriculum theory and practice, educational media and technology, educational administration and leadership, history and philosophy of education.

University of Washington, Graduate School, College of Education, Seattle, WA 98195. Offers curriculum and instruction (M Ed, Ed D, PhD), including educational technology, general curriculum (Ed D, PhD), language, literacy, and culture, mathematics education, multicultural education, reading and language arts education (Ed D), science education, social studies education, teaching and curriculum (M Ed); educational leadership and policy studies (M Ed, Ed D, PhD), including administration (Ed D), educational policy, organization, and leadership (M Ed, PhD), higher education, leadership for learning (Ed D), social and cultural foundations of education (M Ed, PhD); educational psychology (M Ed, PhD), including educational psychology (PhD), human development and cognition (M Ed), learning sciences, measurement, statistics and research design (M Ed), school psychology (M Ed); instructional leadership (M Ed); intercollegiate athletic leadership (M Ed); special education (M Ed, Ed D, PhD), including early childhood special education (M Ed), emotional and behavioral disabilities (M Ed), learning disabilities (M Ed), low-incidence disabilities (M Ed), severe disabilities (M Ed), special education (Ed D, PhD); teacher education (MIT). *Accreditation:* APA. Part-time and evening/weekend programs available. *Degree requirements:* For master's, thesis optional; for doctorate, thesis/dissertation. *Entrance requirements:* For master's and doctorate, GRE General Test, minimum GPA of 3.0. Additional exam requirements/recommendations for international students: Required—TOEFL. Electronic applications accepted. *Faculty research:* School restructuring/effective schools, special education interventions, literacy and writing, technology, school partnerships, teacher preparation.

The University of West Alabama, School of Graduate Studies, College of Education, Department of Teacher Education, Livingston, AL 35470. Offers continuing education (MSCE); early childhood education (M Ed); elementary education (M Ed); guidance and counseling (M Ed, MSCE), including continuing education (MSCE), guidance and counseling (M Ed); library media (M Ed); school administration (M Ed); secondary education (MAT); special education (M Ed). *Accreditation:* NCATE. Part-time programs available. *Degree requirements:* For master's, comprehensive exam. *Entrance requirements:* For master's, GRE General Test, MAT, minimum GPA of 2.75.

University of Wisconsin–Milwaukee, Graduate School, School of Education, MS Program in Cultural Foundations of Education, Milwaukee, WI 53201-0413. Offers MS. Part-time programs available. *Faculty:* 9 full-time (4 women). *Students:* 11 full-time (6 women), 13 part-time (12 women); includes 12 minority (8 African Americans, 4 Hispanic Americans). Average age 38. 17 applicants, 59% accepted, 5 enrolled. In 2009, 5 master's awarded. *Degree requirements:* For master's, thesis or alternative. *Entrance requirements:* Additional exam requirements/recommendations for international students: Required—TOEFL (minimum score 550 paper-based; 79 iBT), IELTS (minimum score 6.5). *Application deadline:* For fall admission, 1/1 priority date for domestic students; for spring admission, 9/1 for domestic students. Applications are processed on a rolling basis. Application fee: $45 ($75 for international students). *Expenses:* Tuition, state resident: full-time $8800. Tuition, nonresident: full-time $20,760. Tuition and fees vary according to program and reciprocity agreements. *Financial support:* Career-related internships or fieldwork available. Support available to part-time students. Financial award application deadline: 4/15. *Faculty research:* Human relations in education, international and multicultural education. Total annual research expenditures: $3,005. *Unit head:* Michael Bonds, Representative, 414-229-2256, Fax: 414-229-3700, E-mail: mbonds@uwm.edu. *Application contact:* General Information Contact, 414-229-4982, Fax: 414-229-6967, E-mail: gradschool@uwm.edu.

University of Wisconsin–Milwaukee, Graduate School, School of Education, Program in Urban Education, Milwaukee, WI 53201-0413. Offers adult and continuing education (PhD); curriculum and instruction (PhD); educational administration (PhD); educational and media technology (PhD); educational psychology (PhD); multicultural studies (PhD); social foundations of education (PhD). *Students:* 67 full-time (51 women), 44 part-time (30 women); includes 41 minority (23 African Americans, 2 American Indian/Alaska Native, 7 Asian Americans or Pacific Islanders, 9 Hispanic Americans), 4 international. Average age 41. 31 applicants, 45% accepted, 5 enrolled. In 2009, 11 doctorates awarded. *Degree requirements:* For doctorate, comprehensive exam, thesis/dissertation. *Entrance requirements:* For doctorate, GRE General Test, minimum undergraduate GPA of 2.85, graduate 3.5. Additional exam requirements/recommendations for international students: Required—TOEFL (minimum score 550 paper-based; 79 iBT), IELTS (minimum score 6.5). *Application deadline:* For fall admission, 1/1 priority date for domestic students; for spring admission, 9/1 for domestic students. Applications are processed on a rolling basis. Application fee: $45 ($75 for international students). *Expenses:* Tuition, state resident: full-time $8800. Tuition, nonresident: full-time $20,760. Tuition and fees vary according to program and reciprocity agreements. *Financial support:* Career-related internships or fieldwork and unspecified assistantships available. Support available to part-time students. Financial award application deadline: 4/15. *Unit head:* Larry Martin, Representative, 414-229-4729, Fax: 414-229-2920, E-mail: lmartin@uwm.edu. *Application contact:* General Information Contact, 414-229-4982, Fax: 414-229-6967, E-mail: gradschool@uwm.edu.

Wayne State University, College of Education, Division of Theoretical and Behavioral Foundations, Detroit, MI 48202. Offers counseling (M Ed, MA, Ed D, PhD, Ed S); education evaluation and research (M Ed, Ed D, PhD); educational psychology (M Ed, Ed D, PhD, Ed S); educational sociology (M Ed, Ed D, PhD, Ed S); history and philosophy of education (M Ed, Ed D, PhD); rehabilitation counseling and community inclusion (MA, Ed S); school and community psychology (MA, Ed S); school clinical psychology (Ed S). *Accreditation:* ACA (one or more programs are accredited); CORE (one or more programs are accredited). Evening/weekend programs available. *Degree requirements:* For doctorate, thesis/dissertation. *Entrance requirements:* For master's, GRE; for doctorate, GRE, interview, minimum GPA of 3.0, curriculum vitae, references. Additional exam requirements/recommendations for international students: Required—TOEFL (minimum score 550 paper-based; 213 computer-based), TWE (minimum score 6). Electronic applications accepted. *Faculty research:* Adolescents at risk, supervision of counseling.

Western Illinois University, School of Graduate Studies, College of Education and Human Services, Department of Educational and Interdisciplinary Studies, Program in Educational and Interdisciplinary Studies, Macomb, IL 61455-1390. Offers MS Ed. *Accreditation:* NCATE. Part-time programs available. *Students:* 20 full-time (15 women), 39 part-time (29 women); includes 8 minority (1 African American, 1 Asian American or Pacific Islander, 6 Hispanic Americans), 1 international. Average age 37. 9 applicants, 56% accepted. In 2009, 16 master's awarded. *Degree requirements:* For master's, thesis or alternative. *Entrance requirements:* For master's, minimum GPA of 2.75, interview. Additional exam requirements/recommendations for international students: Required—TOEFL (minimum score 550 paper-based; 213 computer-based; 80 iBT). *Application deadline:* Applications are processed on a rolling basis. Application fee: $30. Electronic applications accepted. *Expenses:* Tuition, state resident: full-time $4486; part-time $249.21 per credit hour. Tuition, nonresident: full-time $8972; part-time $498.42 per credit hour. Required fees: $72.62 per credit hour. *Financial support:* In 2009–10, 9 students received support, including 9 research assistantships with full tuition reimbursements available (averaging $7,280 per year). Financial award applicants required to submit FAFSA. *Unit head:* Dr. Tom Cody, Graduate Committee Chairperson, 309-298-1183. *Application contact:* Evelyn Hoing, Assistant Director of Graduate Studies, 309-298-1806, Fax: 309-298-2345, E-mail: grad-office@wiu.edu.

Widener University, School of Human Service Professions, Center for Education, Chester, PA 19013-5792. Offers adult education (M Ed); counseling in higher education (M Ed); counselor education (M Ed); early childhood education (M Ed); educational foundations (M Ed); educational leadership (M Ed); educational psychology (M Ed); elementary education (M Ed); English and language arts (M Ed); health education (M Ed); higher education leadership (Ed D); home and school visitor (M Ed); human sexuality (M Ed); mathematics education (M Ed); middle school education (M Ed); principalship (M Ed); reading and language arts (Ed D); reading education (M Ed); school administration (Ed D); science education (M Ed); social studies education (M Ed); special education (M Ed); technology education (M Ed). *Accreditation:* NCATE. Part-time and evening/weekend programs available. *Faculty:* 34 full-time (22 women), 37 part-time/adjunct (14 women). *Students:* 203 full-time (154 women), 415 part-time (298 women); includes 50 minority (34 African Americans, 1 American Indian/Alaska Native, 5 Asian Americans or Pacific Islanders, 10 Hispanic Americans), 3 international. Average age 39. 139 applicants, 88% accepted. In 2009, 168 master's, 31 doctorates awarded. Terminal master's awarded for partial completion of doctoral program. *Degree requirements:* For doctorate, thesis/dissertation. *Entrance requirements:* For master's, minimum GPA of 2.5; for doctorate, GRE or MAT, minimum GPA of 2.0 (undergraduate), 3.5 (graduate). *Application deadline:* Applications are processed on a rolling basis. Application fee: $25 ($300 for international students). Electronic applications accepted. *Expenses:* Contact institution. *Financial support:* Career-related internships or fieldwork, tuition waivers (full and partial), and unspecified assistantships available. Support available to part-time students. Financial award application deadline: 5/1. *Faculty research:* Reading and cognition, adult education, technology education, educational leadership, special education. *Unit head:* Dr. Michael W. LeDoux, Associate Dean, 610-499-4294, Fax: 610-499-4623, E-mail: mwledoux@widener.edu. *Application contact:* Dr. Roberta D. Nolan, Director of Graduate Admissions, 610-499-4125, E-mail: rdnolan@widener.edu.

Wilfrid Laurier University, Faculty of Graduate Studies, Faculty of Arts, Cultural Analysis and Social Theory Program, Waterloo, ON N2L 3C5, Canada. Offers MA. *Entrance requirements:* For master's, honours BA in humanities, social science or interdisciplinary program with social theory, minimum B+ in final year of full-time study. Additional exam requirements/recommendations for international students: Required—TOEFL (minimum score 230 computer-based; 89 iBT). Electronic applications accepted. *Faculty research:* Globalization, identify and social movements, body politics: gender, sexuality and embodiment, cultural representation and social theory.

Youngstown State University, Graduate School, Beeghly College of Education, Department of Educational Foundations, Research, Technology, and Leadership, Youngstown, OH 44555-0001. Offers educational administration (MS Ed); educational leadership (Ed D). *Accreditation:* NCATE. Part-time and evening/weekend programs available. *Degree requirements:* For master's, comprehensive exam; for doctorate, comprehensive exam, thesis/dissertation. *Entrance requirements:* For master's, GRE, MAT, or teaching certificate; minimum GPA of 2.7; for doctorate, GRE General Test, GRE Subject Test, interview, minimum GPA of 3.5. Additional exam requirements/recommendations for international students: Required—TOEFL. *Faculty research:* Administrative theory, computer applications, education law, school and community relations, finance principalship.

International and Comparative Education

American University, College of Arts and Sciences, School of Education, Teaching, and Health, Program in International Training and Education, Washington, DC 20016-8030. Offers MA. *Students:* 25 full-time (21 women), 18 part-time (16 women); includes 4 minority (2 African Americans, 1 Asian American or Pacific Islander, 1 Hispanic American), 1 international. Average age 27. 68 applicants, 87% accepted, 21 enrolled. In 2009, 17 master's awarded. *Degree requirements:* For master's, one foreign language, comprehensive exam, volunteer experience. *Entrance requirements:* For master's, GRE General Test, minimum GPA of 3.0, six months international/cultural experience (preferred). *Application deadline:* For fall admission, 2/1 priority date for domestic students; for spring admission, 10/1 priority date for domestic students. Applications are processed on a rolling basis. Application fee: $80. *Expenses:* Tuition: Full-time $22,266; part-time $1237 per credit hour. Required fees: $430. Tuition and fees vary according to program. *Financial support:* Application deadline: 2/1. *Unit head:* Karen DiGiovanni, Director, Teacher Education, 202-885-3727, Fax: 202-885-1187, E-mail: digiovanni@american.edu. *Application contact:* Kathleen Clowery, Director, Graduate Admissions, 202-885-3621, Fax: 202-885-1505.

Boston University, School of Education, Department of Administration, Training, and Policy Studies, International Educational Development Program, Boston, MA 02215. Offers Ed M. Part-time programs available. *Degree requirements:* For master's, thesis. *Entrance requirements:* For master's, GRE General Test or MAT. Additional exam requirements/recommendations for international students: Required—TOEFL. Electronic applications accepted. *Expenses:* Tuition: Full-time $37,910; part-time $1184 per credit hour. Required fees: $386; $40 per semester. Part-time tuition and fees vary according to class time, course level, degree level and program. *Faculty research:* Formal and nonformal education for social and economic development, industrialized and agrarian societies.

Bowling Green State University, Graduate College, College of Education and Human Development, School of Leadership and Policy Studies, Program in Cross-Cultural and International Education, Bowling Green, OH 43403. Offers MA. Part-time programs available. *Degree requirements:* For master's, thesis or alternative. *Entrance requirements:* For master's, GRE General Test. Additional exam requirements/recommendations for international students: Required—TOEFL.

California State University, Dominguez Hills, College of Extended and International Education, Carson, CA 90747-0001. Offers MA, MS. Part-time and evening/weekend programs available. Postbaccalaureate distance learning degree programs offered. *Faculty:* 10 full-time (0 women), 27 part-time/adjunct (12 women). *Students:* 13 full-time (7 women), 612 part-time (319 women); includes 127 minority (26 African Americans, 6 American Indian/Alaska Native, 52 Asian Americans or Pacific Islanders, 43 Hispanic Americans). Average age 42. 292 applicants, 85% accepted, 87 enrolled. In 2009, 82 master's awarded. *Degree requirements:* For master's, thesis. *Entrance requirements:* Additional exam requirements/recommendations for international students: Required—TOEFL. Application fee: $55. Electronic applications accepted. *Expenses:* Contact institution. *Unit head:* Dr. Margaret Gordon, Dean, 310-243-3737, Fax: 310-516-4423, E-mail: mgordon@csudh.edu. *Application contact:* Dr. Gayle Ball-Parker, Director of Admissions, 310-243-3645, E-mail: gball@csudh.edu.

The College of New Jersey, Graduate Division, Office of Global Programs, Program in Overseas Education, Ewing, NJ 08628. Offers M Ed, Certificate. Part-time programs available. *Students:* 2 full-time (both women), 54 part-time (30 women); includes 11 minority (7 Asian Americans or Pacific Islanders, 4 Hispanic Americans), 1 international. 179 applicants, 77% accepted. In 2009, 31 master's, 68 Certificates awarded. *Degree requirements:* For master's, comprehensive exam. *Entrance requirements:* For master's, GRE, minimum GPA of 3.0 in field or 2.75 overall; for Certificate, previous master's degree or higher. Additional exam requirements/recommendations for international students: Required—TOEFL. *Application deadline:* For fall admission, 2/1 priority date for domestic students; for spring admission, 10/1 priority date for domestic students. Application fee: $70. Electronic applications accepted. *Expenses:* Tuition, state resident: part-time $573.70 per credit. Tuition, nonresident: part-time $887.75 per credit. Required fees: $140.85 per credit. One-time fee: $10 part-time. *Financial support:* Application deadline: 5/1. *Unit head:* Dr. Stuart Carroll, Coordinator, 609-771-2221. *Application contact:* Susan L. Hydro, Assistant Dean, Office of Graduate Studies, 609-771-2300, Fax: 609-637-5105, E-mail: graduate@tcnj.edu.

Drexel University, School of Education, Program in Global and International Education, Philadelphia, PA 19104-2875. Offers MS.

Florida International University, College of Education, Department of Curriculum and Instruction, Program in International and Intercultural Development Education, Miami, FL 33199. Offers MS, Ed D. *Accreditation:* NCATE. Part-time and evening/weekend programs available. *Entrance requirements:* Additional exam requirements/recommendations for international students: Required—TOEFL. *Expenses:* Tuition, state resident: full-time $8008; part-time $4004 per year. Tuition, nonresident: full-time $20,104; part-time $10,052 per year. Required fees: $298; $149 per term.

Florida State University, The Graduate School, College of Education, Department of Educational Leadership and Policy Studies, Program in Social, History and Philosophy of Education, Tallahassee, FL 32306. Offers history and philosophy of education (MS, PhD, Ed S); international and intercultural education (PhD). *Faculty:* 2 full-time (both women), 1 part-time/adjunct (0 women). *Students:* 29 full-time (14 women), 12 part-time (7 women); includes 8 minority (4 African Americans, 1 Asian American or Pacific Islander, 3 Hispanic Americans), 14 international. 103 applicants, 29% accepted, 11 enrolled. In 2009, 4 master's, 4 doctorates awarded. *Degree requirements:* For master's and Ed S, comprehensive exam, thesis optional; for doctorate, comprehensive exam, thesis/dissertation. *Entrance requirements:* For master's, doctorate, and Ed S, GRE General Test, minimum GPA of 3.0. Additional exam requirements/recommendations for international students: Required—TOEFL (minimum score 550 paper-based; 213 computer-based; 80 iBT). *Application deadline:* For fall admission, 5/1 priority date for domestic and international students; for spring admission, 10/1 priority date for domestic and international students. Application fee: $30. Electronic applications accepted. *Expenses:* Tuition, state resident: full-time $7413. Tuition, nonresident: full-time $22,567. *Financial support:* Fellowships with full and partial tuition reimbursements, research assistantships with full and partial tuition reimbursements, teaching assistantships with full and partial tuition reimbursements, career-related internships or fieldwork, scholarships/grants, and unspecified assistantships available. Financial award applicants required to submit FAFSA. *Faculty research:* Social, historical, philosophical content of educational policies; religion, gender, diversity, and social justice in educational policy; interdisciplinary. *Unit head:* Dr. Jeffrey Milligan, Assistant Professor and Program Coordinator, 850-644-8171, Fax: 850-644-1258, E-mail: milligan@coe.fsu.edu. *Application contact:* Jimmy Pastrano, Program Assistant, 850-644-6777, Fax: 850-644-1258, E-mail: pastrano@coe.fsu.edu.

Gallaudet University, The Graduate School, Department of Educational Foundations and Research, Washington, DC 20002-3625. Offers international development (MA, Certificate). *Accreditation:* NCATE. *Degree requirements:* For Certificate, thesis optional. *Entrance requirements:* For degree, GRE General Test or MAT. Electronic applications accepted.

The George Washington University, Graduate School of Education and Human Development, Department of Educational Leadership, Program in International Education, Washington, DC 20052. Offers MA Ed. *Accreditation:* NCATE. *Students:* 24 full-time (23 women), 38 part-time (31 women); includes 8 minority (3 African Americans, 1 American Indian/Alaska Native, 4 Asian Americans or Pacific Islanders), 6 international. Average age 29. 89 applicants, 93% accepted, 21 enrolled. In 2009, 38 master's awarded. *Degree requirements:* For master's, comprehensive exam. *Entrance requirements:* For master's, GRE General Test or MAT, minimum GPA of 2.75. *Application deadline:* For fall admission, 1/15 priority date for domestic students; for spring admission, 10/1 for domestic students. Applications are processed on a rolling basis. Application fee: $60. *Financial support:* In 2009–10, 13 students received support; fellowships, research assistantships, career-related internships or fieldwork, Federal Work-Study, and tuition waivers available. Financial award application deadline: 1/15; financial award applicants required to submit FAFSA. *Faculty research:* Education and development. *Unit head:* Dr. William K. Cummings, Coordinator, 202-994-4698, E-mail: wkcum@gwu.edu. *Application contact:* Sarah Lang, Director of Graduate Admissions, 202-994-1447, Fax: 202-994-7207, E-mail: slang@gwu.edu.

Harvard University, Graduate School of Education, Master's Programs in Education, Cambridge, MA 02138. Offers arts in education (Ed M); education policy and management (Ed M); higher education (Ed M); human development and psychology (Ed M); international education policy (Ed M); language and literacy (Ed M); learning and teaching (Ed M); mid-career mathematics and science (teaching certificate) (Ed M); mind brain and education (Ed M); risk and prevention (Ed M); school leadership (Ed M); special studies (Ed M); teaching and curriculum (teaching certificate) (Ed M); technology innovation and education (Ed M). Part-time programs available. *Faculty:* 70 full-time (33 women), 36 part-time/adjunct (20 women). *Students:* 598 full-time (448 women), 76 part-time (60 women); includes 132 minority (40 African Americans, 2 American Indian/Alaska Native, 58 Asian Americans or Pacific Islanders, 32 Hispanic Americans), 103 international. Average age 28. 1,574 applicants, 58% accepted, 640 enrolled. In 2009, 556 master's awarded. *Entrance requirements:* For master's, GRE General Test, 3 letters of recommendation. Additional exam requirements/recommendations for international students: Required—TOEFL (minimum score 600 paper-based; 250 computer-based; 100 iBT), TWE (minimum score 5). *Application deadline:* For fall admission, 1/4 for domestic and international students. Application fee: $85. Electronic applications accepted. *Expenses:* Contact institution. *Financial support:* In 2009–10, 424 students received support, including 25 fellowships with full and partial tuition reimbursements available (averaging $15,890 per year); career-related internships or fieldwork, Federal Work-Study, institutionally sponsored loans, scholarships/grants, health care benefits, tuition waivers (full and partial), and unspecified assistantships also available. Support available to part-time students. Financial award application deadline: 2/1; financial award applicants required to submit FAFSA. *Faculty research:* Learning and development, educational leadership and organizations, educational policy analysis. Total annual research expenditures: $18.1 million. *Unit head:* Jennifer L. Petrallia, Assistant Dean, 617-495-8445. *Application contact:* Information Contact, 617-495-3414, Fax: 617-496-3577, E-mail: gseadmissions@harvard.edu.

Indiana University Bloomington, School of Education, Department of Educational Leadership and Policy Studies, Bloomington, IN 47405-7000. Offers education policy studies (PhD); educational leadership (MS, Ed D, PhD, Ed S); higher education (MS, Ed D, PhD); history and philosophy of education (MS); history of education (PhD); international and comparative education (MS, PhD); philosophy of education (PhD); student affairs administration (MS). *Accreditation:* NCATE. Part-time and evening/weekend programs available. *Faculty:* 31 full-time (16 women), 8 part-time/adjunct (4 women). *Students:* 195 full-time (120 women), 102 part-time (53 women); includes 78 minority (49 African Americans, 1 American Indian/Alaska Native, 6 Asian Americans or Pacific Islanders, 22 Hispanic Americans), 29 international. Average age 33. 331 applicants, 77% accepted, 75 enrolled. In 2009, 61 master's, 21 doctorates, 7 other advanced degrees awarded. *Degree requirements:* For master's, thesis optional; for doctorate, comprehensive exam, thesis/dissertation; for Ed S, comprehensive exam or project. *Entrance requirements:* For master's, doctorate, and Ed S, GRE General Test. Additional exam requirements/recommendations for international students: Required—TOEFL (minimum score 213 computer-based; 79 iBT). *Application deadline:* For fall admission, 1/15 priority date for domestic students, 12/1 priority date for international students; for spring admission, 9/1 priority date for domestic and international students. Applications are processed on a rolling basis. Application fee: $55 ($65 for international students). Electronic applications accepted. *Financial support:* In 2009–10, 73 students received support, including 34 fellowships with full and partial tuition reimbursements available (averaging $7,677 per year), 16 research assistantships with full and partial tuition reimbursements available (averaging $17,757 per year), 23 teaching assistantships with full and partial tuition reimbursements available (averaging $13,496 per year); career-related internships or fieldwork, Federal Work-Study, institutionally sponsored loans, and tuition waivers (full and partial) also available. Support available to part-time students. *Faculty research:* Student engagement at higher education institutions in the nation, Reading First professional development initiative, state finance policy on financial access to higher education, school reform, special needs studies. *Unit head:* Martha McCarthy, Chair, 812-856-8377. *Application contact:* Sandy Strain, Department Secretary, 812-856-8360, Fax: 812-856-8394, E-mail: strain@indiana.edu.

Lehigh University, College of Education, Program in Comparative and International Education, Bethlehem, PA 18015. Offers comparative and international education (MA); globalization and educational change (M Ed); international counseling (Certificate); international development in education (Certificate); special education (Certificate); TESOL (Certificate). Part-time and evening/weekend programs available. Postbaccalaureate distance learning degree programs offered (no on-campus study). *Faculty:* 2 full-time (1 woman). *Students:* 9 full-time (6 women), 40 part-time (39 women); includes 3 minority (2 African Americans, 1 Hispanic American), 10 international. Average age 36. 46 applicants, 67% accepted, 18 enrolled. In 2009, 11 master's awarded. *Degree requirements:* For master's, thesis (MA). *Entrance requirements:* For master's, 2 letters of recommendation. Additional exam requirements/recommendations for international students: Required—TOEFL (minimum score 600 paper-based; 250 computer-based; 93 iBT). *Application deadline:* For fall admission, 5/15 for domestic and international students; for spring admission, 11/1 for domestic and international students. Applications are processed on a rolling basis. Application fee: $65. Electronic applications accepted. *Financial support:* In 2009–10, 4 students received support, including 4 research assistantships with full and partial tuition reimbursements available (averaging $13,000 per year). Financial award application deadline: 3/15. *Faculty research:* Gender equity in education, post-socialist education transformation, educational borrowing, comparing education systems, education policy and globalization. *Unit head:* Dr. Alexander W. Wiseman, Coordinator, 610-758-5740, Fax: 610-758-6223, E-mail: aww207@lehigh.edu. *Application contact:* Donna M. Johnson, Coordinator, 610-758-3231, Fax: 610-758-6223, E-mail: dmj4@lehigh.edu.

Louisiana State University and Agricultural and Mechanical College, Graduate School, College of Agriculture, School of Human Resource Education and Workforce Development, Baton Rouge, LA 70803. Offers agriculture and extension education and youth development (MS, PhD); career and technical education (MS, PhD); comprehensive vocational education (MS, PhD); extension and international education (MS, PhD); human resource and leadership development (MS, PhD); industrial education (MS); vocational agriculture education (MS, PhD); vocational business education (MS); vocational home economics education (MS). *Accreditation:* NCATE. Part-time programs available. *Faculty:* 11 full-time (5 women), 2 part-time/adjunct (both women). *Students:* 39 full-time (22 women), 75 part-time (51 women); includes 14 African Americans, 1 Asian American or Pacific Islander, 2 Hispanic Americans, 7 international. Average age 37. 40 applicants, 93% accepted, 18 enrolled. In 2009, 16 master's, 13 doctorates awarded. Terminal master's awarded for partial completion of doctoral program. *Degree requirements:* For master's, thesis (for some programs); for doctorate, thesis/dissertation. *Entrance requirements:* For master's and doctorate, GRE General Test, minimum GPA of 3.0. Additional exam requirements/recommendations for international students: Required—TOEFL (minimum score 550 paper-based; 213 computer-based; 79 iBT) or IELTS (minimum score 6.5). *Application deadline:* For fall admission, 1/25 priority date for domestic students, 5/15 for international students; for spring admission, 10/15 for international students. Applications are processed on a rolling basis. Application fee: $50 ($70 for international

students). Electronic applications accepted. *Financial support:* In 2009–10, 63 students received support, including 3 fellowships with full and partial tuition reimbursements available (averaging $24,885 per year), 5 research assistantships with full and partial tuition reimbursements available (averaging $14,440 per year), 4 teaching assistantships with partial tuition reimbursements available (averaging $13,750 per year); career-related internships or fieldwork, Federal Work-Study, institutionally sponsored loans, health care benefits, tuition waivers (full and partial), and unspecified assistantships also available. Financial award application deadline: 3/1; financial award applicants required to submit FAFSA. *Faculty research:* Adult education, history and philosophy of vocational education, curriculum and instruction, career decision making. Total annual research expenditures: $21,538. *Unit head:* Dr. Michael F. Burnett, Director, 225-578-5748, Fax: 225-578-2526, E-mail: vocbur@lsu.edu. *Application contact:* Paula Beecher, Recruiting Coordinator, 225-578-2468, E-mail: pbeeche@lsu.edu.

Morehead State University, Graduate Programs, College of Education, Department of Curriculum and Instruction, Morehead, KY 40351. Offers curriculum and instruction (Ed S); elementary education (MA Ed), including elementary education, international education, middle school education, reading; secondary education (MA Ed); special education (MA Ed); teaching (MAT). Part-time and evening/weekend programs available. *Faculty:* 25 full-time (17 women), 2 part-time/adjunct (1 woman). *Students:* 25 full-time (22 women), 165 part-time (139 women); includes 4 minority (1 African American, 2 American Indian/Alaska Native, 1 Hispanic American). Average age 33. 148 applicants, 68% accepted, 48 enrolled. In 2009, 178 master's awarded. *Degree requirements:* For master's, comprehensive exam, thesis optional; for Ed S, thesis, oral exam. *Entrance requirements:* For master's, GRE General Test, minimum GPA of 2.75, teaching certificate; for Ed S, GRE General Test, interview, master's degree, minimum GPA of 3.5, work experience. Additional exam requirements/recommendations for international students: Required—TOEFL (minimum score 500 paper-based; 173 computer-based). *Application deadline:* For fall admission, 8/1 priority date for domestic and international students; for spring admission, 12/1 priority date for domestic and international students. Applications are processed on a rolling basis. Application fee: $30. Electronic applications accepted. *Expenses:* Tuition, state resident: full-time $6318; part-time $351 per credit hour. Tuition, nonresident: full-time $15,804; part-time $878 per credit hour. *Financial support:* In 2009–10, 2 teaching assistantships (averaging $6,000 per year) were awarded; career-related internships or fieldwork, Federal Work-Study, and unspecified assistantships also available. Financial award application deadline: 3/15; financial award applicants required to submit FAFSA. *Faculty research:* Communicative competence of learning-disabled students, teaching social studies in elementary schools, ungraded primary school organization, study skills. *Unit head:* Dr. James Knoll, Chair, 606-783-2598, Fax: 606-783-5044, E-mail: j.knoll@moreheadstate.edu. *Application contact:* Michelle Barber, Graduate Recruitment and Retention Assistant Director, 606-783-5127, Fax: 606-783-5061, E-mail: m.barber@moreheadstate.edu.

New York University, Steinhardt School of Culture, Education, and Human Development, Department of Humanities and Social Sciences in the Professions, Program in International Education, New York, NY 10012-1019. Offers human development and social intervention (MA); international education (MA, PhD, Advanced Certificate), including cross cultural exchange and training (PhD), global education (PhD), international development education (PhD). Part-time programs available. *Students:* 68 full-time (61 women), 63 part-time (55 women); includes 32 minority (5 African Americans, 13 Asian Americans or Pacific Islanders, 14 Hispanic Americans), 21 international. Average age 27. 217 applicants, 70% accepted, 40 enrolled. In 2009, 46 master's, 3 doctorates awarded. *Degree requirements:* For master's, thesis (for some programs); for doctorate, thesis/dissertation. *Entrance requirements:* For doctorate, GRE General Test, interview; for Advanced Certificate, master's degree. Additional exam requirements/recommendations for international students: Required—TOEFL. *Application deadline:* For fall admission, 12/15 priority date for domestic and international students; for spring admission, 11/1 for domestic and international students. Applications are processed on a rolling basis. Application fee: $75. Electronic applications accepted. *Expenses:* Tuition: Full-time $30,528; part-time $1272 per credit. Required fees: $2177. *Financial support:* Fellowships with full and partial tuition reimbursements, career-related internships or fieldwork, Federal Work-Study, institutionally sponsored loans, and scholarships/grants available. Support available to part-time students. Financial award application deadline: 2/1; financial award applicants required to submit FAFSA. *Faculty research:* Civic education; ethnic identity among students and teachers; comparative education; education during emergencies; cross-cultural exchange. *Unit head:* Dr. Philip Hosay, Director, 212-998-5496, Fax: 212-995-4832, E-mail: pmh2@nyu.edu. *Application contact:* 212-998-5030, Fax: 212-995-4328, E-mail: steinhardt.gradadmissions@nyu.edu.

New York University, Steinhardt School of Culture, Education, and Human Development, Department of Teaching and Learning, Program in English Education, New York, NY 10012-1019. Offers secondary and college (PhD), including applied linguistics, comparative education, curriculum, literature and reading, media education; teachers of English 7-12 (MA); teachers of English language and literature in college (Advanced Certificate). *Accreditation:* Teacher Education Accreditation Council. Part-time programs available. *Students:* 36 full-time (30 women), 30 part-time (25 women); includes 11 minority (4 African Americans, 3 Asian Americans or Pacific Islanders, 4 Hispanic Americans), 2 international. Average age 26. 91 applicants, 80% accepted, 21 enrolled. In 2009, 27 master's, 6 doctorates, 1 other advanced degree awarded. *Degree requirements:* For master's, thesis (for some programs); for doctorate, thesis/dissertation. *Entrance requirements:* For doctorate, GRE General Test, interview; for Advanced Certificate, master's degree. Additional exam requirements/recommendations for international students: Required—TOEFL. *Application deadline:* For fall admission, 12/15 priority date for domestic and international students; for spring admission, 11/1 for domestic and international students. Applications are processed on a rolling basis. Application fee: $75. Electronic applications accepted. *Expenses:* Tuition: Full-time $30,528; part-time $1272 per credit. Required fees: $2177. *Financial support:* Fellowships with full and partial tuition reimbursements, teaching assistantships with full and partial tuition reimbursements, career-related internships or fieldwork, Federal Work-Study, institutionally sponsored loans, scholarships/grants, tuition waivers (partial), and unspecified assistantships available. Support available to part-time students. Financial award application deadline: 2/1; financial award applicants required to submit FAFSA. *Faculty research:* Making meaning of literature, teaching of literature, urban adolescent literacy and equity, literacy development and globalization, digital media and literacy. *Unit head:* Director, 212-998-5460, Fax: 212-995-4049. *Application contact:* 212-998-5030, Fax: 212-995-4328, E-mail: steinhardt.gradadmissions@nyu.edu.

SIT Graduate Institute, Graduate Programs, Master's Programs in Intercultural Service, Leadership, and Management, Brattleboro, VT 05302-0676. Offers conflict transformation (MA); intercultural service, leadership, and management (MA); international education (MA); management (MS); social justice in intercultural relations (MA); sustainable development (MA). Postbaccalaureate distance learning degree programs offered (minimal on-campus study). *Degree requirements:* For master's, one foreign language, thesis. *Entrance requirements:* For master's, 3 letters of reference. Additional exam requirements/recommendations for international students: Required—TOEFL. *Faculty research:* Intercultural communication, conflict resolution, advising and training, world issues, international business.

Stanford University, School of Education, Program in Social Sciences, Policy, and Educational Practice, Stanford, CA 94305-9991. Offers administration and policy analysis (Ed D, PhD); anthropology of education (PhD); economics of education (PhD); educational linguistics (PhD); evaluation (MA), including interdisciplinary studies; higher education (PhD); history of education (PhD); interdisciplinary studies (PhD); international comparative education (MA, PhD); international education administration and policy analysis (MA); philosophy of education (PhD); policy analysis (MA); prospective principal's program (MA); sociology of education (PhD). *Degree requirements:* For master's, thesis (for some programs); for doctorate, thesis/dissertation. *Entrance requirements:* For master's and doctorate, GRE General Test. Electronic

applications accepted. *Expenses:* Tuition: Full-time $37,380; part-time $2760 per quarter. Required fees: $501.

Teachers College, Columbia University, Graduate Faculty of Education, Department of International and Transcultural Studies, Program in Comparative and International Education, New York, NY 10027-6696. Offers Ed M, MA, Ed D, PhD. *Faculty:* 1 (woman) full-time, 1 part-time/adjunct. *Students:* 21 full-time (16 women), 26 part-time (22 women); includes 15 minority (4 African Americans, 8 Asian Americans or Pacific Islanders, 3 Hispanic Americans), 10 international. Average age 33. 71 applicants, 46% accepted, 10 enrolled. In 2009, 6 master's, 2 doctorates awarded. *Degree requirements:* For doctorate, thesis/dissertation. *Application deadline:* For fall admission, 5/15 for domestic students; for spring admission, 12/1 for domestic students. Application fee: $65. *Financial support:* Career-related internships or fieldwork, Federal Work-Study, institutionally sponsored loans, and tuition waivers (full and partial) available. Support available to part-time students. Financial award application deadline: 2/1. *Faculty research:* Comparative analysis of national educational systems, identity and community in local and transcultural settings. *Unit head:* Dr. George Bond, Chair, 212-678-3947. *Application contact:* Deanna Ghozati, Assistant Director of Admission, 212-678-4018, Fax: 212-678-4171, E-mail: ghozati@tc.edu.

Teachers College, Columbia University, Graduate Faculty of Education, Department of International and Transcultural Studies, Program in International Educational Development, New York, NY 10027-6696. Offers Ed M, MA, Ed D, PhD. *Faculty:* 5 full-time (4 women). *Students:* 77 full-time (66 women), 135 part-time (111 women); includes 58 minority (5 African Americans, 31 Asian Americans or Pacific Islanders, 22 Hispanic Americans), 39 international. Average age 30. 275 applicants, 67% accepted, 79 enrolled. In 2009, 65 master's, 13 doctorates awarded. *Degree requirements:* For doctorate, thesis/dissertation. *Application deadline:* For fall admission, 5/15 for domestic students; for spring admission, 12/1 for domestic students. Application fee: $65. *Financial support:* Career-related internships or fieldwork, Federal Work-Study, institutionally sponsored loans, and tuition waivers (full and partial) available. Support available to part-time students. Financial award application deadline: 2/1. *Faculty research:* Application of formal and nonformal education to programs of social and economic development in Third World countries. *Unit head:* Dr. George Bond, Chair, 212-678-3947. *Application contact:* Deanna Ghozati, Assistant Director of Admission, 212-678-4018, Fax: 212-678-4171, E-mail: ghozati@tc.edu.

Tufts University, Fletcher School of Law and Diplomacy, Medford, MA 02155. Offers LL M, MA, MAHA, MALD, MIB, PhD, DVM/MA, JD/MALD, MALD/MA, MALD/MBA, MALD/MS, MD/MA. Postbaccalaureate distance learning degree programs offered (minimal on-campus study). *Faculty:* 34 full-time (7 women), 31 part-time/adjunct (8 women). *Students:* 443 full-time (224 women), 7 part-time (4 women); includes 51 minority (6 African Americans, 1 American Indian/Alaska Native, 26 Asian Americans or Pacific Islanders, 18 Hispanic Americans), 165 international. Average age 31. 1,866 applicants, 40% accepted, 292 enrolled. In 2009, 364 master's, 12 doctorates awarded. *Degree requirements:* For master's, one foreign language, thesis; for doctorate, one foreign language, comprehensive exam, thesis/dissertation, dissertation defense. *Entrance requirements:* For master's and doctorate, GMAT or GRE General Test. Additional exam requirements/recommendations for international students: Required—TOEFL (minimum score 600 paper-based; 250 computer-based; 100 iBT), IELTS (minimum score 7). *Application deadline:* For fall admission, 1/15 for domestic and international students; for spring admission, 10/15 for domestic and international students. Application fee: $70. Electronic applications accepted. *Expenses:* Contact institution. *Financial support:* Federal Work-Study, institutionally sponsored loans, scholarships/grants, and tuition waivers (partial) available. Financial award application deadline: 1/15; financial award applicants required to submit FAFSA. *Faculty research:* Negotiation and conflict resolution, international organizations, international business and economic law, security studies, development economics. *Unit head:* Stephen W. Bosworth, Dean, 617-627-3050, Fax: 617-627-3712. *Application contact:* Laurie A. Hurley, E-mail: fletcheradmissions@tufts.edu.

University of Bridgeport, School of Education and Human Resources, Division of Education, Program in Secondary Education, Bridgeport, CT 06604. Offers computer specialist (Diploma); international education (Diploma); reading specialist (MS, Diploma); secondary education (MS, Diploma). Part-time and evening/weekend programs available. *Degree requirements:* For master's, final exam, final project, or thesis; for Diploma, thesis or alternative, final project. *Entrance requirements:* For master's, minimum undergraduate QPA of 2.67; for Diploma, minimum graduate QPA of 3.0. Additional exam requirements/recommendations for international students: Recommended—TOEFL (minimum score 550 paper-based; 213 computer-based; 80 iBT), IELTS (minimum score 6.5). Electronic applications accepted. *Faculty research:* Self-concept, internship assessment, stress and situational development, follow-up of graduation, trend analysis.

University of California, Santa Barbara, Graduate Division, Gevirtz Graduate School of Education, Santa Barbara, CA 93106-9490. Offers counseling, clinical and school psychology (PhD), including clinical psychology, counseling psychology, school psychology; education (M Ed, MA, PhD), including child and adolescent development (MA, PhD), cultural perspectives and comparative education (MA, PhD), educational leadership and organizations (MA, PhD), research methodology (MA, PhD), special education disabilities and risk studies (MA), special education, disabilities and risk studies (PhD), teaching (M Ed), teaching and learning (MA, PhD); educational leadership (Ed D); school psychology (M Ed); MA/PhD. *Accreditation:* APA (one or more programs are accredited). Postbaccalaureate distance learning degree programs offered (minimal on-campus study). *Faculty:* 42 full-time (20 women), 10 part-time/adjunct (4 women). *Students:* 390 full-time (303 women); includes 149 minority (14 African Americans, 3 American Indian/Alaska Native, 57 Asian Americans or Pacific Islanders, 75 Hispanic Americans), 16 international. Average age 31. 717 applicants, 40% accepted, 170 enrolled. In 2009, 140 master's, 46 doctorates awarded. Terminal master's awarded for partial completion of doctoral program. *Degree requirements:* For master's, comprehensive exam (for some programs), thesis (for some programs); for doctorate, comprehensive exam (for some programs), thesis/dissertation, qualifying exam. *Entrance requirements:* For master's, GRE, 3 letters of recommendation, resume/curriculum vitae; for doctorate, GRE, 3 letters of recommendation, statement of purpose, personal achievements/contributions statement, resume/curriculum vitae, transcripts for post-secondary institutions attended. Additional exam requirements/recommendations for international students: Required—TOEFL (minimum score 550 paper-based; 213 computer-based; 80 iBT) or IELTS (minimum score 7). Application fee: $70 ($90 for international students). Electronic applications accepted. *Financial support:* In 2009–10, 253 students received support, including 206 fellowships with full and partial tuition reimbursements available (averaging $5,000 per year), 62 research assistantships with full and partial tuition reimbursements available (averaging $6,200 per year), 87 teaching assistantships with partial tuition reimbursements available (averaging $6,500 per year); career-related internships or fieldwork, Federal Work-Study, institutionally sponsored loans, scholarships/grants, traineeships, health care benefits, and unspecified assistantships also available. Financial award applicants required to submit FAFSA. *Faculty research:* Professional development, early childhood development, school violence, literacy, science/math initiative. Total annual research expenditures: $4.4 million. *Unit head:* Dr. Jane Conoley, Chair, 805-893-2185, E-mail: jane-conoley@education.ucsb.edu. *Application contact:* Kathryn Marie Tucciarone, Student Affairs Officer, 805-893-2137, E-mail: katiet@education.ucsb.edu.

University of Central Florida, College of Education, Department of Educational Studies, Orlando, FL 32816. Offers applied learning and instruction (MA); community college education (Certificate); curriculum and instruction (Ed S); education (Ed D, PhD, Ed S); gifted education (Certificate); global and comparative education (Certificate); initial teacher professional preparation (Certificate); teacher leadership (M Ed); urban education (Certificate). *Accreditation:* NCATE. Part-time and evening/weekend programs available. *Faculty:* 18 full-time (10 women), 16 part-time/adjunct (10 women). *Students:* 155 full-time (106 women), 156 part-time (131 women); includes 80 minority (37 African Americans, 5 Asian Americans or Pacific Islanders, 38 Hispanic Americans), 22 international. Average age 36. 200 applicants, 57% accepted, 77

International and Comparative Education

University of Central Florida (continued)

enrolled. In 2009, 9 master's, 34 doctorates, 17 other advanced degrees awarded. *Degree requirements:* For other advanced degree, thesis or alternative, final exam. *Entrance requirements:* For degree, GRE General Test, minimum GPA of 3.0, resume. Additional exam requirements/recommendations for international students: Required—TOEFL. *Application deadline:* For fall admission, 2/20 for domestic students; for spring admission, 9/20 for domestic students. Application fee: $30. Electronic applications accepted. *Expenses:* Tuition, state resident: part-time $306.31 per credit hour. Tuition, nonresident: part-time $1099.01 per credit hour. Part-time tuition and fees vary according to degree level and program. *Financial support:* In 2009–10, 82 students received support, including 55 fellowships with partial tuition reimbursements available (averaging $8,300 per year), 29 research assistantships with partial tuition reimbursements available (averaging $7,000 per year), 43 teaching assistantships with partial tuition reimbursements available (averaging $8,000 per year); career-related internships or fieldwork, Federal Work-Study, institutionally sponsored loans, and unspecified assistantships also available. Financial award application deadline: 3/1; financial award applicants required to submit FAFSA. *Unit head:* Dr. Karen Biraimah, Chair, 407-823-2428, E-mail: biraimah@mail.ucf.edu. *Application contact:* Dr. Karen Biraimah, Chair, 407-823-2428, E-mail: biraimah@mail.ucf.edu.

University of Maryland, College Park, Academic Affairs, College of Education, Department of Education Leadership, Higher Education and International Education, College Park, MD 20742. Offers MA, Ed D, PhD. *Faculty:* 11 full-time (6 women), 3 part-time/adjunct (1 woman). *Students:* 53 full-time (40 women), 26 part-time (18 women); includes 22 minority (15 African Americans, 1 Asian American or Pacific Islander, 6 Hispanic Americans), 8 international. 245 applicants, 36% accepted, 44 enrolled. *Application deadline:* For fall admission, 12/15 for domestic students, 2/1 for international students; for spring admission, 6/1 for international students. *Expenses:* Tuition, area resident: Part-time $471 per credit hour. Tuition, state resident: part-time $471 per credit hour. Tuition, nonresident: part-time $1016 per credit hour. Required fees: $337.04 per term. *Financial support:* In 2009–10, 2 fellowships (averaging $11,756 per year), 1 research assistantship (averaging $15,349 per year), 37 teaching assistantships (averaging $15,814 per year) were awarded. Total annual research expenditures: $157,387. *Unit head:* Dr. Thomas Weible, Acting Chair, 301-405-3589, Fax: 301-405-3573, E-mail: tweible@umd.edu. *Application contact:* Dean of Graduate School, 301-405-0358.

University of Massachusetts Amherst, Graduate School, School of Education, Program in Education, Amherst, MA 01003. Offers bilingual, English as a second language, and multicultural education (M Ed, CAGS); child study and early education (M Ed); children, families and schools (Ed D, CAGS); early childhood and elementary teacher education (M Ed); education policy and leadership (CAGS); educational administration (M Ed, CAGS); educational policy and leadership (Ed D); higher education (M Ed, CAGS); international education (M Ed); language, literacy and culture (Ed D); learning, media and technology (M Ed, CAGS); mathematics, science, and learning technologies (Ed D); policy studies (M Ed); policy studies in education (CAGS); reading and writing (M Ed); research and evaluation methods (Ed D); school counselor education (M Ed, CAGS); school psychology (CAGS); science education (CAGS); secondary teacher education (M Ed); social justice education (M Ed, Ed D, CAGS); special education (M Ed, Ed D, CAGS). *Accreditation:* NCATE. Part-time programs available. Postbaccalaureate distance learning degree programs offered (minimal on-campus study). *Faculty:* 74 full-time (41 women). *Students:* 377 full-time (268 women), 347 part-time (232 women); includes 115 minority (59 African Americans, 2 American Indian/Alaska Native, 16 Asian Americans or Pacific Islanders, 38 Hispanic Americans), 108 international. Average age 35. 708 applicants, 68% accepted, 266 enrolled. In 2009, 183 master's, 17 doctorates awarded. Terminal master's awarded for partial completion of doctoral program. *Degree requirements:* For master's, thesis or alternative; for doctorate, comprehensive exam, thesis/dissertation. *Entrance requirements:* Additional exam requirements/recommendations for international students: Required—TOEFL (minimum score 550 paper-based; 213 computer-based; 80 iBT), IELTS (minimum score 6.5). *Application deadline:* For fall admission, 1/15 for domestic and international students. Applications are processed on a rolling basis. Application fee: $50 ($65 for international students). Electronic applications accepted. *Expenses:* Tuition, state resident: full-time $2640; part-time $110 per credit. Tuition, nonresident: full-time $9936; part-time $414 per credit. Tuition and fees vary according to course load. *Financial support:* In 2009–10, 1 fellowship with full tuition reimbursement (averaging $8,036 per year), 92 research assistantships with full tuition reimbursements (averaging $8,555 per year), 83 teaching assistantships with full tuition reimbursements (averaging $4,661 per year) were awarded; career-related internships or fieldwork, Federal Work-Study, scholarships/grants, traineeships, health care benefits, tuition waivers (full), and unspecified assistantships also available. Support available to part-time students. Financial award application deadline: 1/15. *Unit head:* Dr. Linda L. Griffin, Graduate Program Director, 413-545-6984, Fax: 413-545-2873. *Application contact:* Jean M. Ames, Supervisor of Admissions, 413-545-0722, Fax: 413-577-0010, E-mail: gradadm@grad.umass.edu.

University of Minnesota, Twin Cities Campus, Graduate School, College of Education and Human Development, Department of Organizational Leadership, Policy and Development, Program in Comparative and International Development Education, Minneapolis, MN 55455-0213. Offers MA, PhD. *Students:* 83 full-time (64 women), 37 part-time (26 women); includes 13 minority (4 African Americans, 7 Asian Americans or Pacific Islanders, 2 Hispanic Americans), 29 international. Average age 33. 70 applicants, 83% accepted, 28 enrolled. In 2009, 2 master's, 8 doctorates awarded. *Unit head:* Dr. Darwin Hendel, Chair, 612-625-0129, Fax: 612-624-3377, E-mail: hende001@umn.edu. *Application contact:* Dr. Mary Trettin, Associate Dean, 612-625-6501, Fax: 612-626-1580, E-mail: mtrettin@umn.edu.

University of North Texas, Robert B. Toulouse School of Graduate Studies, College of Public Affairs and Community Service, Department of Sociology, Denton, TX 76203-5017. Offers global and comparative (PhD); health and illness (PhD); social stratification and inequality (PhD); sociology (MA, MS). Terminal master's awarded for partial completion of doctoral program. *Degree requirements:* For master's, variable foreign language requirement, comprehensive exam, thesis (for some programs); for doctorate, variable foreign language requirement, comprehensive exam, thesis/dissertation. *Entrance requirements:* For master's, GRE General Test, 4 letters of recommendation; for doctorate, GRE General Test, master's degree, 4 letters of recommendation. Additional exam requirements/recommendations for international students: Required—TOEFL (minimum score 550 paper-based; 213 computer-based; 79 iBT), proof of English language proficiency required for non-native English speakers. *Application deadline:* Applications are processed on a rolling basis. Application fee: $50 ($75 for international students). Electronic applications accepted. *Expenses:* Tuition, state resident: full-time $4298; part-time $239 per contact hour. Tuition, nonresident: full-time $9878; part-time $549 per contact hour. Required fees: $265 per contact hour. *Financial support:* Fellowships, research assistantships, teaching assistantships, career-related internships or fieldwork, Federal Work-Study, institutionally sponsored loans, scholarships/grants, health care benefits, tuition waivers (partial), and unspecified assistantships available. Support available to part-time students. Financial award applicants required to submit FAFSA. *Faculty research:* Health and illness, social inequality, globalization and development, family. *Application contact:* Graduate Adviser, 940-565-2296, Fax: 940-369-7035, E-mail: seward@unt.edu.

University of Pennsylvania, Graduate School of Education, Division of Foundations and Practices in Education, Programs in Education, Culture and Society, Philadelphia, PA 19104. Offers MS Ed, PhD. *Students:* 31 full-time (25 women), 10 part-time (8 women); includes 2 minority (1 African American, 1 Hispanic American), 10 international. 119 applicants, 32% accepted, 19 enrolled. In 2009, 9 master's, 1 doctorate awarded. Application fee: $70. *Expenses:* Tuition: Full-time $25,660; part-time $4758 per course. Required fees: $2152; $270 per course. Tuition and fees vary according to course load, degree level and program. *Financial support:* Institutionally sponsored loans, scholarships/grants, traineeships, health care benefits, and unspecified assistantships available.

University of Pittsburgh, School of Education, Department of Administrative and Policy Studies, Program in Social and Comparative Analysis in Education, Pittsburgh, PA 15260. Offers M Ed, MA, Ed D, PhD. Evening/weekend programs available. *Students:* 55 full-time (35 women), 41 part-time (28 women); includes 16 minority (9 African Americans, 5 Asian Americans or Pacific Islanders, 2 Hispanic Americans), 19 international. Average age 37. 48 applicants, 83% accepted, 21 enrolled. In 2009, 6 master's, 6 doctorates awarded. *Degree requirements:* For master's, thesis; for doctorate, thesis/dissertation. *Entrance requirements:* For doctorate, GRE General Test. Additional exam requirements/recommendations for international students: Required—TOEFL (minimum score 213 computer-based; 80 iBT). *Application deadline:* For fall admission, 2/1 priority date for domestic and international students; for spring admission, 11/15 priority date for domestic students, 7/1 priority date for international students. Applications are processed on a rolling basis. Application fee: $50. Electronic applications accepted. *Expenses:* Tuition, state resident: full-time $16,402; part-time $665 per credit. Tuition, nonresident: full-time $28,694; part-time $1175 per credit. Required fees: $690; $175 per term. Tuition and fees vary according to program. *Financial support:* Research assistantships, teaching assistantships, Federal Work-Study, institutionally sponsored loans, scholarships/grants, health care benefits, tuition waivers (partial), and unspecified assistantships available. Support available to part-time students. Financial award application deadline: 3/15; financial award applicants required to submit FAFSA. *Unit head:* Dr. John C. Weidman, Chair, 412-648-7114, Fax: 412-648-1784, E-mail: weidman@pitt.edu. *Application contact:* Lauren Pasquini, Enrollment Manager, 412-648-2230, Fax: 412-648-1899, E-mail: soeinfo@pitt.edu.

University of San Francisco, School of Education, Department of International and Multicultural Education, San Francisco, CA 94117-1080. Offers international and multicultural education (MA, Ed D); multicultural literature for children and young adults (MA); teaching English as a second language (MA). *Faculty:* 2 full-time (both women), 6 part-time/adjunct (3 women). *Students:* 31 full-time (12 women), 54 part-time (42 women). Average age 36. 191 applicants, 69% accepted, 48 enrolled. In 2009, 32 master's, 10 doctorates awarded. *Degree requirements:* For doctorate, thesis/dissertation. Application fee: $55 ($65 for international students). *Expenses:* Tuition: Full-time $19,710; part-time $1095 per unit. Part-time tuition and fees vary according to degree level, campus/location and program. *Financial support:* In 2009–10, 56 students received support; fellowships, research assistantships, teaching assistantships available. Financial award application deadline: 3/2; financial award applicants required to submit FAFSA. *Unit head:* Dr. Katz Susan, Chair, 415-422-6878. *Application contact:* Beth Teague, Associate Director of Graduate Outreach, 415-422-5467, E-mail: schoolofeducation@usfca.edu.

University of South Africa, College of Human Sciences, Pretoria, South Africa. Offers adult education (M Ed); African languages (MA, PhD); African politics (MA, PhD); Afrikaans (MA, PhD); ancient history (MA, PhD); ancient Near Eastern studies (MA, PhD); anthropology (MA, PhD); applied linguistics (MA); Arabic (MA, PhD); archaeology (MA); art history (MA); Biblical archaeology (MA); Biblical studies (M Th, D Th, PhD); Christian spirituality (M Th, D Th); church history (M Th, D Th); classical studies (MA, PhD); clinical psychology (MA); communication (MA, PhD); comparative education (M Ed, Ed D); consulting psychology (D Admin, D Com, PhD); curriculum studies (M Ed, Ed D); development studies (M Admin, MA, D Admin, PhD); didactics (M Ed, Ed D); education (M Tech); education management (M Ed, Ed D); educational psychology (M Ed); English (MA); environmental education (M Ed); French (MA, PhD); German (MA, PhD); Greek (MA); guidance and counseling (M Ed); health studies (MA, PhD), including health sciences education (MA), health services management (MA), medical and surgical nursing science (critical care general) (MA), midwifery and neonatal nursing science (MA), trauma and emergency care (MA); history (MA, PhD); history of education (Ed D); inclusive education (M Ed, Ed D); information and communications technology policy and regulation (MA); information science (MA, MIS, PhD); international politics (MA, PhD); Islamic studies (MA, PhD); Italian (MA, PhD); Judaica (MA, PhD); linguistics (MA, PhD); mathematical education (M Ed); mathematics education (MA); missiology (M Th, D Th); modern Hebrew (MA, PhD); musicology (MA, MMus, D Mus, PhD); natural science education (M Ed); New Testament (M Th, D Th); Old Testament (D Th); pastoral therapy (M Th, D Th); philosophy (MA); philosophy of education (M Ed, Ed D); politics (MA, PhD); Portuguese (MA, PhD); practical theology (M Th, D Th); psychology (MA, MS, PhD); psychology of education (M Ed, Ed D); public health (MA); religious studies (MA, D Th, PhD); Romance languages (MA); Russian (MA, PhD); Semitic languages (MA, PhD); social behavior studies in HIV/AIDS (MA); social science (mental health) (MA); social science in development studies (MA); social science in psychology (MA); social science in social work (MA); social science in sociology (MA); social work (MSW, DSW, PhD); socio-education (M Ed, Ed D); sociolinguistics (MA); sociology (MA, PhD); Spanish (MA, PhD); systematic theology (M Th, D Th); TESOL (teaching English to speakers of other languages) (MA); theological ethics (M Th, D Th); theory of literature (MA, PhD); urban ministries (D Th); urban ministry (M Th).

Vanderbilt University, Peabody College, Department of Leadership, Policy, and Organizations, Nashville, TN 37240-1001. Offers education policy (MPP); educational leadership and policy (Ed D); higher education (M Ed); higher education, leadership and policy (Ed D); human resource development (M Ed); international education policy and management (M Ed); organizational leadership (M Ed). Part-time and evening/weekend programs available. *Faculty:* 28 full-time (13 women), 8 part-time/adjunct (3 women). *Students:* 155 full-time (111 women), 95 part-time (52 women); includes 36 minority (27 African Americans, 6 Asian Americans or Pacific Islanders, 3 Hispanic Americans), 21 international. Average age 31. 298 applicants, 76% accepted, 94 enrolled. In 2009, 65 master's, 21 doctorates awarded. *Degree requirements:* For master's, comprehensive exam, thesis optional; for doctorate, thesis/dissertation, qualifying exams, residency. *Entrance requirements:* For master's and doctorate, GRE General Test. Additional exam requirements/recommendations for international students: Required—TOEFL (minimum score 550 paper-based; 213 computer-based). *Application deadline:* For fall admission, 12/31 priority date for domestic and international students; for spring admission, 11/1 priority date for domestic and international students. Applications are processed on a rolling basis. Application fee: $0. Electronic applications accepted. *Financial support:* In 2009–10, 155 students received support, including 3 fellowships with full and partial tuition reimbursements available, 61 research assistantships with full and partial tuition reimbursements available, 1 teaching assistantship with full and partial tuition reimbursement available; Federal Work-Study, institutionally sponsored loans, scholarships/grants, tuition waivers (partial), and unspecified assistantships also available. Support available to part-time students. Financial award application deadline: 2/1; financial award applicants required to submit FAFSA. *Faculty research:* Education and leadership policy, education finances/economics of education, higher education leadership and policy, educator pay for performance and school choice, international and comparative education and policy management. *Unit head:* Dr. Ellen B. Goldring, Chair, 615-322-8000, Fax: 615-343-7094, E-mail: ellen.b.goldring@vanderbilt.edu. *Application contact:* Rosie Moody, Educational Coordinator, 615-322-8019, Fax: 615-343-7094, E-mail: rosie.moody@vanderbilt.edu.

Wright State University, School of Graduate Studies, College of Liberal Arts, Program in Applied Behavioral Science, Dayton, OH 45435. Offers criminal justice and social problems (MA); international and comparative politics (MA). *Degree requirements:* For master's, thesis optional. *Entrance requirements:* Additional exam requirements/recommendations for international students: Required—TOEFL. *Faculty research:* Training and development, criminal justice and social problems, community systems, human factors, industrial/organizational psychology.

Student Affairs

Alliant International University–Los Angeles, Graduate School of Education, Educational Psychology Programs, Alhambra, CA 91803-1360. Offers educational psychology (Psy D); pupil personnel services (Credential); school psychology (MA). Part-time programs available. *Degree requirements:* For doctorate, thesis/dissertation. *Entrance requirements:* For master's, minimum GPA of 3.0, letters of recommendation; for doctorate, interview, minimum GPA of 3.0, letters of recommendation. Additional exam requirements/recommendations for international students: Required—TOEFL (minimum score 550 paper-based; 213 computer-based), TWE (minimum score 5). Electronic applications accepted. *Faculty research:* Early identification and intervention with high-risk preschoolers, pediatric neuropsychology, interpersonal violence, ADHD, learning theories.

Alliant International University–San Diego, Graduate School of Education, Educational Psychology Programs, San Diego, CA 92131-1799. Offers educational psychology (Psy D); pupil personnel services (Credential); school psychology (MA); student personnel services (Certificate). Part-time programs available. *Degree requirements:* For doctorate, thesis/dissertation. *Entrance requirements:* For master's, minimum GPA of 3.0, letters of recommendation; for doctorate, interview, letters of recommendation. Additional exam requirements/recommendations for international students: Required—TOEFL (minimum score 550 paper-based; 213 computer-based), TWE (minimum score 5). Electronic applications accepted.

Appalachian State University, Cratis D. Williams Graduate School, Department of Human Development and Psychological Counseling, Boone, NC 28608. Offers college student development (MA); community counseling (MA); marriage and family therapy (MA); school counseling (MA). *Accreditation:* AAMFT/COAMFTE; ACA; NCATE. Part-time programs available. *Faculty:* 15 full-time (5 women), 21 part-time/adjunct (14 women). *Students:* 98 full-time (95 women), 32 part-time (25 women); includes 8 minority (5 African Americans, 2 Asian Americans or Pacific Islanders, 1 Hispanic American), 1 international. 149 applicants, 54% accepted, 59 enrolled. In 2009, 78 master's awarded. *Degree requirements:* For master's, comprehensive exam (for some programs), thesis optional, internships. *Entrance requirements:* For master's, GRE General Test, 3 letters of recommendation. Additional exam requirements/recommendations for international students: Required—TOEFL (minimum score 570 paper-based; 230 computer-based; 79 iBT), IELTS (minimum score 6.5). *Application deadline:* For fall admission, 2/1 priority date for domestic students, 2/1 for international students; for spring admission, 2/1 for international students. Applications are processed on a rolling basis. Application fee: $50. Electronic applications accepted. *Expenses:* Tuition, state resident: full-time $2960. Tuition, nonresident: full-time $14,051. Required fees: $2320. *Financial support:* In 2009–10, 20 research assistantships (averaging $8,000 per year), 7 teaching assistantships (averaging $8,000 per year) were awarded; fellowships, career-related internships or fieldwork, Federal Work-Study, scholarships/grants, and unspecified assistantships also available. Financial award application deadline: 4/1; financial award applicants required to submit FAFSA. *Faculty research:* Multicultural counseling, addictions counseling, play therapy, expressive arts, child and adolescent therapy, sexual abuse counseling. *Unit head:* Dr. Lee Baruth, Chairman, 828-262-2055, E-mail: baruthlg@appstate.edu. *Application contact:* Sandy Krause, Director of Admissions and Recruiting, 828-262-2130, Fax: 828-262-2709, E-mail: krausesl@appstate.edu.

Arkansas State University—Jonesboro, Graduate School, College of Education, Department of Psychology and Counseling, Jonesboro, State University, AR 72467. Offers college student personnel services (MS); counselor education (Ed S), including college student personnel services, psychoeducational diagnosis, school counseling; rehabilitation counseling (MRC); school counseling (MSE); student affairs (Certificate). *Accreditation:* ACA (one or more programs are accredited); CORE (one or more programs are accredited); NCATE. Part-time programs available. *Faculty:* 11 full-time (6 women), 6 part-time/adjunct (2 women). *Students:* 49 full-time (37 women), 100 part-time (81 women); includes 32 minority (31 African Americans, 1 American Indian/Alaska Native), 1 international. Average age 32. 70 applicants, 46% accepted, 30 enrolled. In 2009, 23 master's, 11 other advanced degrees awarded. *Degree requirements:* For master's and other advanced degree, comprehensive exam, thesis or alternative. *Entrance requirements:* For master's, GRE General Test or MAT (MSE), appropriate bachelor's degree, interview, letters of reference; for other advanced degree, GRE General Test, interview, master's degree, letters of reference, official transcript, personal statement, immunization records. Additional exam requirements/recommendations for international students: Required—TOEFL (minimum score 550 paper-based; 213 computer-based; 79 iBT), IELTS (minimum score 6). *Application deadline:* For fall admission, 7/15 for domestic students, 7/1 for international students; for spring admission, 12/1 for domestic students, 11/13 for international students. Applications are processed on a rolling basis. Application fee: $30 ($40 for international students). Electronic applications accepted. *Expenses:* Tuition, state resident: full-time $3744; part-time $208 per credit hour. Tuition, nonresident: full-time $9540; part-time $530 per credit hour. Required fees: $896; $47 per credit hour. $25 per term. One-time fee: $50. Tuition and fees vary according to course load and program. *Financial support:* In 2009–10, 24 students received support; teaching assistantships, career-related internships or fieldwork, scholarships/grants, and unspecified assistantships available. Financial award application deadline: 7/1; financial award applicants required to submit FAFSA. *Unit head:* Dr. Loretta McGregor, Chair, 870-972-3064, Fax: 870-972-3962, E-mail: lmcgregor@astate.edu. *Application contact:* Dr. Andrew Sustich, Dean of the Graduate School, 870-972-3029, Fax: 870-972-3857, E-mail: sustich@astate.edu.

Arkansas Tech University, Graduate College, College of Education, Russellville, AR 72801. Offers college student personnel (MS); educational leadership (M Ed, Ed S); English education (M Ed); instructional improvement (M Ed); secondary education (M Ed); teaching, learning and leadership (M Ed). *Accreditation:* NCATE. Part-time and evening/weekend programs available. Postbaccalaureate distance learning degree programs offered (no on-campus study). *Students:* 39 full-time (26 women), 246 part-time (179 women); includes 27 minority (18 African Americans, 4 American Indian/Alaska Native, 5 Hispanic Americans), 4 international. Average age 33. In 2009, 92 master's, 11 other advanced degrees awarded. *Degree requirements:* For master's, comprehensive exam, thesis optional, action research project. *Entrance requirements:* For master's, GRE General Test or MAT. Additional exam requirements/recommendations for international students: Required—TOEFL (minimum score 550 paper-based; 213 computer-based; 79 iBT), IELTS (minimum score 6). *Application deadline:* For fall admission, 3/1 priority date for domestic students, 5/1 priority date for international students; for spring admission, 10/1 priority date for domestic and international students. Applications are processed on a rolling basis. Application fee: $0 ($50 for international students). Electronic applications accepted. *Expenses:* Tuition, state resident: full-time $3438; part-time $191 per hour. Tuition, nonresident: full-time $6876; part-time $382 per hour. Required fees: $482; $9 per credit hour. $140 per semester. Tuition and fees vary according to course load. *Financial support:* In 2009–10, teaching assistantships with full tuition reimbursements (averaging $4,000 per year); research assistantships, career-related internships or fieldwork, Federal Work-Study, scholarships/grants, health care benefits, and unspecified assistantships also available. Support available to part-time students. Financial award application deadline: 4/15; financial award applicants required to submit FAFSA. *Unit head:* Dr. Eldon G. Clary, Dean, 479-968-0350, Fax: 479-968-0350, E-mail: eclary@atu.edu. *Application contact:* Dr. Mary B. Gunter, Dean of Graduate College, 479-968-0398, Fax: 479-964-0542, E-mail: graduate.school@atu.edu.

Ashland University, Dwight Schar College of Education, Department of Educational Administration, Ashland, OH 44805-3702. Offers curriculum specialist (M Ed); principalship (M Ed); pupil services (M Ed). Part-time programs available. *Faculty:* 6 full-time (3 women), 31 part-time/adjunct (12 women). *Students:* 118 full-time (70 women), 239 part-time (135 women); includes 37 minority (29 African Americans, 1 American Indian/Alaska Native, 2 Asian Americans or Pacific Islanders, 5 Hispanic Americans), 2 international. Average age 33. 129 applicants, 98% accepted, 114 enrolled. In 2009, 166 master's awarded. *Degree requirements:* For master's, thesis or alternative, internship. *Entrance requirements:* For master's, teaching certificate or license, bachelor's degree, minimum cumulative GPA of 2.75. Additional exam requirements/recommendations for international students: Required—TOEFL. *Application deadline:* Applications are processed on a rolling basis. Application fee: $30. Electronic applications accepted. *Financial support:* Institutionally sponsored loans and scholarships/grants available. Financial award application deadline: 4/15. *Faculty research:* Gender and religious considerations in employment, ISLLC standards, adjunct faculty training, politics of school finance, ethnicity and employment. *Unit head:* Dr. Larry Cook, Chair, 419-289-5396, Fax: 419-208-5702, E-mail: lcook@ashland.edu. *Application contact:* Dr. Larry Cook, Chair, 419-289-5396, Fax: 419-208-5702, E-mail: lcook@ashland.edu.

Azusa Pacific University, School of Behavioral and Applied Sciences, Department of Higher Education and Organizational Leadership, Program in College Student Affairs, Azusa, CA 91702-7000. Offers M Ed. Part-time and evening/weekend programs available. *Degree requirements:* For master's, exam. *Entrance requirements:* For master's, 12 units of course work in social science, minimum GPA of 3.0.

Azusa Pacific University, School of Education, Department of Education, Program in Pupil Personnel Services, Azusa, CA 91702-7000. Offers MA. Part-time and evening/weekend programs available. *Degree requirements:* For master's, core exams, oral presentation. *Entrance requirements:* For master's, 12 units of course work in education, minimum GPA of 3.0.

Bloomsburg University of Pennsylvania, School of Graduate Studies, College of Professional Studies, School of Education, Department of Educational Studies and Secondary Education, Program in Guidance Counseling and Student Affairs, Bloomsburg, PA 17815-1301. Offers M Ed. *Entrance requirements:* For master's, GRE, 3 letters of recommendation, resume.

Bob Jones University, Graduate Programs, Greenville, SC 29614. Offers accountancy (MS); Bible (MA); Bible translation (MA); Biblical studies (Certificate); broadcast management (MS); business administration (MBA); church history (MA, PhD); church ministries (MA); church music (MM); cinema and video production (MA); counseling (MS); curriculum and instruction (Ed D); divinity (M Div); dramatic production (MA); educational leadership (MS, Ed D, Ed S); elementary education (M Ed, MAT); English (M Ed, MA, MAT); fine arts (MA); graphic design (MA); history (M Ed, MA); illustration (MA); interpretative speech (MA); mathematics (M Ed, MAT); medical missions (Certificate); ministry (MM, D Min); multi-categorical special education (M Ed, MAT); music (M Ed); New Testament interpretation (PhD); Old Testament interpretation (PhD); orchestral instrument performance (MM); organ performance (MM); pastoral studies (MA); personnel services (MS, Ed S); piano pedagogy (MM); piano performance (MM); platform arts (MA); radio and television broadcasting (MS); rhetoric and public address (MA); secondary education (M Ed); studio art (MA); teaching Bible (MA); theology (MA, PhD); voice performance (MM); youth ministries (MA); M Div/MM.

Bowling Green State University, Graduate College, College of Education and Human Development, School of Leadership and Policy Studies, Program in College Student Personnel, Bowling Green, OH 43403. Offers MA. Part-time programs available. *Degree requirements:* For master's, thesis or alternative. *Entrance requirements:* For master's, GRE General Test, interview. Additional exam requirements/recommendations for international students: Required—TOEFL. Electronic applications accepted. *Faculty research:* Adult learning, legal issues, moral and ethical development.

Buffalo State College, State University of New York, The Graduate School, Faculty of Applied Science and Education, Department of Educational Foundations, Program in Student Personnel Administration, Buffalo, NY 14222-1095. Offers MS. *Degree requirements:* For master's, comprehensive exam. *Entrance requirements:* For master's, minimum GPA of 2.75 in last 60 hours of undergraduate course work. Additional exam requirements/recommendations for international students: Required—TOEFL (minimum score 550 paper-based; 213 computer-based).

California State University, Bakersfield, Division of Graduate Studies, School of Education, Program in Counseling, Bakersfield, CA 93311. Offers school counseling (MS); student affairs (MS). *Accreditation:* NCATE. *Degree requirements:* For master's, thesis or alternative, culminating projects. *Entrance requirements:* For master's, CBEST (school counseling).

California State University, Long Beach, Graduate Studies, College of Education, Department of Advanced Studies in Education and Counseling, Master of Science in Counseling Program, Long Beach, CA 90840. Offers marriage and family therapy (MS); school counseling (MS); student development in higher education (MS). *Accreditation:* NCATE. *Students:* 139 full-time (103 women), 73 part-time (54 women); includes 137 minority (27 African Americans, 35 Asian Americans or Pacific Islanders, 75 Hispanic Americans), 5 international. Average age 30. *Degree requirements:* For master's, comprehensive exam or thesis. *Application deadline:* For fall admission, 3/1 for domestic students. Applications are processed on a rolling basis. Application fee: $55. Electronic applications accepted. *Expenses:* Required fees: $1802 per semester. Part-time tuition and fees vary according to course load. *Financial support:* Federal Work-Study, institutionally sponsored loans, and scholarships/grants available. Financial award application deadline: 3/2. *Unit head:* Dr. Jennifer Coots, Chair, 562-985-4517, Fax: 562-985-4534, E-mail: jcoots@csulb.edu. *Application contact:* Dr. Bita Ghafoori, Assistant Chair, 562-985-7864, Fax: 562-985-4534, E-mail: bghafoor@csulb.edu.

Canisius College, Graduate Division, School of Education and Human Services, Department of Graduate Education, Buffalo, NY 14208-1098. Offers adolescence education (grades 7-12) (MS); childhood education (grades 1-6) (MS); college student personnel administration (MS); deaf education (MS); differentiated instruction (MS Ed); educational administration and supervision (MS); general education (MS Ed); initial teacher certification (elementary education) (MS); initial teacher certification (secondary education) (MS); literacy (MS Ed); special education (MS). *Accreditation:* NCATE. Part-time and evening/weekend programs available. *Faculty:* 22 full-time (14 women), 84 part-time/adjunct (54 women). *Students:* 409 full-time (288 women), 261 part-time (187 women); includes 29 minority (24 African Americans, 5 Hispanic Americans), 156 international. Average age 30. 518 applicants, 74% accepted, 240 enrolled. In 2009, 346 master's awarded. Application fee: $25. *Financial support:* Research assistantships with full tuition reimbursements, career-related internships or fieldwork, institutionally sponsored loans, scholarships/grants, health care benefits, tuition waivers (full and partial), and unspecified assistantships available. *Faculty research:* Autism, Asperger's disease, private higher education, reading strategies. *Unit head:* Rev. Paul Nochelski, Chair of Graduate Education and Leadership, 716-888-3297, Fax: 716-888-3299. *Application contact:* James D. Bagwell, Director of Graduate Recruitment and Admissions, 716-888-2544, Fax: 716-888-3290, E-mail: bagwellj@canisius.edu.

Central Michigan University, College of Graduate Studies, College of Education and Human Services, Department of Educational Leadership, Mount Pleasant, MI 48859. Offers educational leadership (MA, Ed D), including charter school leadership (Ed D), educational technology (Ed D), general educational leadership, higher education administration (Ed D), higher education leadership (Ed D), K-12 curriculum (Ed D), K-12 leadership (Ed D), student affairs administration (Ed D); general educational administration (Ed S); school principalship (MA). Part-time and evening/weekend programs available. *Degree requirements:* For master's and Ed S, thesis or alternative; for doctorate, thesis/dissertation. *Entrance requirements:* For doctorate, GRE or MAT, master's degree, minimum GPA of 3.5, 3 years of professional education experience.

Student Affairs

Central Michigan University *(continued)*
Electronic applications accepted. *Faculty research:* Elementary administration, secondary administration, student achievement, in-service training, internships in administration.

The Citadel, The Military College of South Carolina, Citadel Graduate College, School of Education, Program in Guidance and Counseling, Charleston, SC 29409. Offers elementary/secondary school counseling (M Ed); student affairs and college counseling (M Ed). *Accreditation:* ACA; NCATE. Part-time and evening/weekend programs available. *Faculty:* 12 full-time (7 women), 8 part-time/adjunct (5 women). *Students:* 16 full-time (15 women), 34 part-time (32 women); includes 10 minority (9 African Americans, 1 Hispanic American). Average age 29. In 2009, 16 master's awarded. *Degree requirements:* For master's, comprehensive exam, practicum or internship. *Entrance requirements:* For master's, GRE (minimum score 900) or MAT (minimum score 396), minimum undergraduate GPA of 3.0, 3 letters of reference, group admissions interview. Additional exam requirements/recommendations for international students: Required—TOEFL (minimum score 550 paper-based; 213 computer-based; 79 iBT). *Application deadline:* For fall admission, 6/1 for domestic students; for spring admission, 10/1 for domestic students. Application fee: $30. Electronic applications accepted. *Expenses:* Tuition, state resident: part-time $400 per credit hour. Tuition, nonresident: part-time $657 per credit hour. Required fees: $40 per term. *Financial support:* Career-related internships or fieldwork, health care benefits, and unspecified assistantships available. Support available to part-time students. Financial award application deadline: 7/1; financial award applicants required to submit FAFSA. *Unit head:* Dr. George T. Williams, Director, 843-953-2205, Fax: 843-953-7258, E-mail: williamsg@citadel.edu. *Application contact:* Dr. Steve A. Nida, Associate Provost, The Citadel Graduate College, 843-953-5089, Fax: 843-953-7630, E-mail: cgc@citadel.edu.

Claremont Graduate University, Graduate Programs, School of Educational Studies, Claremont, CA 91711-6160. Offers Africana education (Certificate); education and policy (MA, PhD); higher education/student affairs (MA, PhD); human development (MA, PhD); public school administration (MA, PhD); quantitative evaluation (MA, PhD); special education (MA, PhD); teacher education (MA); teaching and learning (MA, PhD); urban leadership (PhD); MBA/PhD. Part-time programs available. *Faculty:* 18 full-time (12 women), 1 part-time/adjunct (0 women). *Students:* 279 full-time (190 women), 174 part-time (122 women); includes 196 minority (50 African Americans, 1 American Indian/Alaska Native, 37 Asian Americans or Pacific Islanders, 108 Hispanic Americans), 10 international. Average age 37. In 2009, 84 master's, 23 doctorates awarded. Terminal master's awarded for partial completion of doctoral program. *Entrance requirements:* For master's and doctorate, GRE General Test. Additional exam requirements/recommendations for international students: Required—TOEFL (minimum score 550 paper-based; 213 computer-based; 80 iBT). *Application deadline:* For fall admission, 2/1 priority date for domestic students. Applications are processed on a rolling basis. Application fee: $60. Electronic applications accepted. *Expenses:* Tuition: Full-time $35,046; part-time $1524 per credit. Required fees: $161 per semester. *Financial support:* Fellowships, research assistantships, Federal Work-Study, institutionally sponsored loans, and scholarships/grants available. Support available to part-time students. Financial award application deadline: 2/15; financial award applicants required to submit FAFSA. *Faculty research:* Education administration, K-12 and higher education, multicultural education, education policy, diversity in higher education, faculty issues. *Unit head:* Margaret Grogan, Dean, 909-621-8075, Fax: 909-621-8734, E-mail: margaret.grogan@cgu.edu.

Cleveland State University, College of Graduate Studies, College of Education and Human Services, Department of Counseling, Administration, Supervision and Adult Learning (CASAL), Cleveland, OH 44115. Offers accelerated degree in adult learning and development (M Ed); adult learning and development (M Ed); chemical dependency counseling (Certificate); community agency counseling (M Ed); counseling and pupil personnel administration (Ed S); early childhood mental health counseling (Certificate); educational administration and supervision (M Ed); school administration (Ed S); school counseling (M Ed). *Accreditation:* ACA (one or more programs are accredited). Part-time and evening/weekend programs available. *Degree requirements:* For master's, comprehensive exam (for some programs), thesis optional; for other advanced degree, comprehensive exam, thesis optional, internship. *Entrance requirements:* For master's, GRE General Test or MAT, letter of recommendation, minimum GPA of 2.75. Additional exam requirements/recommendations for international students: Required—TOEFL (minimum score 525 paper-based; 197 computer-based), IELTS (minimum score 6). Electronic applications accepted. *Faculty research:* Education law, career development, women in school administration, psychopharmacology, counseling and spirituality.

College of Saint Elizabeth, Department of Psychology, Morristown, NJ 07960-6989. Offers counseling psychology (MA); forensic psychology (MA); student affairs in higher education (Certificate). Part-time and evening/weekend programs available. *Faculty:* 5 full-time (2 women), 10 part-time/adjunct (9 women). *Students:* 23 full-time (19 women), 73 part-time (67 women); includes 25 minority (12 African Americans, 2 Asian Americans or Pacific Islanders, 11 Hispanic Americans), 2 international. Average age 32. 104 applicants, 58% accepted, 47 enrolled. In 2009, 10 master's awarded. *Degree requirements:* For master's, thesis or alternative, portfolio. *Entrance requirements:* For master's, minimum GPA of 3.0, BA in psychology (preferred), 12 credits of course work in psychology. *Application deadline:* For fall admission, 4/14 priority date for domestic students; for spring admission, 11/15 for domestic students. Applications are processed on a rolling basis. Application fee: $35. Electronic applications accepted. *Expenses:* Tuition: Part-time $797 per credit hour. Required fees: $65 per credit hour. *Financial support:* Career-related internships or fieldwork, tuition waivers (partial), and unspecified assistantships available. Support available to part-time students. Financial award application deadline: 3/15; financial award applicants required to submit FAFSA. *Faculty research:* Family systems, dissociative identity disorder, multicultural counseling, outcomes assessment. *Unit head:* Dr. Valerie Scott, Director of the Graduate Program in Counseling Psychology, 973-290-4102, Fax: 973-290-4676, E-mail: vscott@cse.edu. *Application contact:* Donna Tatarka, Dean of Admission, 973-290-4705, Fax: 973-290-4710, E-mail: dtatarka@cse.edu.

The College of Saint Rose, Graduate Studies, School of Education, Department of Counseling and Educational Administration, Program in Counseling, Albany, NY 12203-1419. Offers college student personnel (MS Ed); community counseling (MS Ed); school counseling (MS Ed). *Accreditation:* NCATE. Part-time and evening/weekend programs available. *Degree requirements:* For master's, comprehensive exam or thesis. *Entrance requirements:* For master's, interview, minimum undergraduate GPA of 3.0, 9 hours of psychology coursework. Additional exam requirements/recommendations for international students: Required—TOEFL (minimum score 550 paper-based; 213 computer-based). Electronic applications accepted.

The College of Saint Rose, Graduate Studies, School of Education, Department of Counseling and Educational Administration, Program in Educational Administration and Supervision, Albany, NY 12203-1419. Offers college student services administration (MS Ed); educational administration and supervision (MS Ed, Certificate); school administrator and supervisor (Certificate). Part-time and evening/weekend programs available. *Degree requirements:* For master's, comprehensive exam or thesis. *Entrance requirements:* For master's, minimum undergraduate GPA of 3.0, timed writing sample, interview, permanent certification or 3 years teaching experience. Additional exam requirements/recommendations for international students: Required—TOEFL (minimum score 550 paper-based; 213 computer-based). Electronic applications accepted.

Colorado State University, Graduate School, College of Applied Human Sciences, School of Education, Fort Collins, CO 80523-1588. Offers adult education and training (M Ed); community college leadership (PhD); counseling and career development (M Ed); education and human resource studies (M Ed, PhD); educational leadership (M Ed, PhD); interdisciplinary studies (PhD); organizational performance and change (M Ed, PhD); student affairs in higher education (MS). *Accreditation:* ACA; Teacher Education Accreditation Council. Part-time and evening/weekend programs available. *Faculty:* 21 full-time (10 women). *Students:* 195 full-time (132 women), 469 part-time (292 women); includes 114 minority (31 African Americans, 12 American Indian/Alaska Native, 22 Asian Americans or Pacific Islanders, 49 Hispanic Americans),

24 international. Average age 38. 451 applicants, 41% accepted, 141 enrolled. In 2009, 175 master's, 54 doctorates awarded. *Degree requirements:* For master's, comprehensive exam (for some programs), thesis optional; for doctorate, comprehensive exam, thesis/dissertation, minimum of 60 credits. *Entrance requirements:* For master's, GRE, minimum undergraduate GPA of 3.0, 3 letters of recommendation, curriculum vitae/resume; for doctorate, minimum GPA of 3.0, 3 letters of recommendation, curriculum vitae. Additional exam requirements/recommendations for international students: Required—TOEFL (minimum score 550 paper-based; 213 computer-based). *Application deadline:* For fall admission, 3/15 for domestic and international students; for spring admission, 11/1 for domestic students, 10/1 for international students. Applications are processed on a rolling basis. Application fee: $50. Electronic applications accepted. *Expenses:* Tuition, state resident: full-time $6434; part-time $359.10 per credit. Tuition, nonresident: full-time $18,116; part-time $1006.45 per credit. Required fees: $1496; $83 per credit. *Financial support:* In 2009–10, 8 students received support, including 3 research assistantships with full tuition reimbursements available (averaging $13,790 per year), 5 teaching assistantships with full tuition reimbursements available (averaging $10,253 per year); fellowships, Federal Work-Study, scholarships/grants, and unspecified assistantships also available. Financial award applicants required to submit FAFSA. *Faculty research:* Innovative instruction, diverse learners, transition, scientifically-based evaluation methods, leadership and organizational development. Total annual research expenditures: $655,700. *Unit head:* Dr. Carole Makela, Interim Director, 970-491-6317, Fax: 970-491-1317, E-mail: carole.makela@colostate.edu. *Application contact:* Dr. Sharon Anderson, Director of Graduate Programs, 970-491-6861, Fax: 970-491-1317, E-mail: sharon.anderson@colostate.edu.

Concordia University Wisconsin, Graduate Programs, School of Business and Legal Studies, Program in Student Personnel Administration, Mequon, WI 53097-2402. Offers MSSPA. *Degree requirements:* For master's, comprehensive exam, thesis or alternative. *Entrance requirements:* Additional exam requirements/recommendations for international students: Required—TOEFL.

Creighton University, Graduate School, College of Arts and Sciences, Department of Education, Program in Counselor Education, Omaha, NE 68178-0001. Offers college student affairs (MS); community counseling (MS); elementary school guidance (MS); secondary school guidance (MS). Part-time and evening/weekend programs available. *Faculty:* 13 full-time (8 women). *Students:* 1 full-time (0 women), 42 part-time (33 women); includes 8 minority (3 African Americans, 1 American Indian/Alaska Native, 2 Asian Americans or Pacific Islanders, 2 Hispanic Americans), 4 international. Average age 32. 10 applicants, 60% accepted, 6 enrolled. In 2009, 18 master's awarded. *Entrance requirements:* For master's, GRE General Test, resume, 3 letters of recommendation. Additional exam requirements/recommendations for international students: Required—TOEFL (minimum score 550 paper-based; 213 computer-based; 80 iBT). *Application deadline:* For fall admission, 7/1 for domestic students, 3/1 for international students; for winter admission, 10/1 for domestic students, 7/1 for international students; for spring admission, 3/1 for domestic students, 9/1 for international students. Applications are processed on a rolling basis. Application fee: $50. Electronic applications accepted. *Expenses:* Tuition: Full-time $11,700; part-time $650 per credit hour. Required fees: $126 per semester. *Financial support:* Scholarships/grants available. Support available to part-time students. Financial award applicants required to submit FAFSA. *Unit head:* Dr. Debra L. Ponec, Associate Professor of Education, 402-280-2557, E-mail: dlponec@creighton.edu. *Application contact:* Taunya Plater, Senior Program Coordinator, 402-280-2870, Fax: 402-280-2899, E-mail: taunyaplater@creighton.edu.

Eastern Illinois University, Graduate School, College of Education and Professional Studies, Department of Counseling and Student Development, Charleston, IL 61920-3099. Offers clinical counseling (MS); college student affairs (MS); school counseling (MS). *Accreditation:* ACA; NCATE. Part-time and evening/weekend programs available. *Faculty:* 8 full-time (2 women). In 2009, 61 master's awarded. *Degree requirements:* For master's, comprehensive exam. *Entrance requirements:* For master's, GRE General Test or MAT. *Application deadline:* For fall admission, 3/31 priority date for domestic students. Applications are processed on a rolling basis. Application fee: $30. *Expenses:* Tuition, state resident: full-time $9434; part-time $239 per credit hour. Tuition, nonresident: full-time $23,774; part-time $717 per credit hour. Required fees: $802.63. *Financial support:* In 2009–10, research assistantships with tuition reimbursements (averaging $8,100 per year), 4 teaching assistantships with tuition reimbursements (averaging $8,100 per year) were awarded. *Unit head:* Dr. Rick Roberts, Chairperson, 217-581-2400, Fax: 217-581-7417, E-mail: rlroberts@eiu.edu. *Application contact:* Bill Elliott, Director of Graduate Admissions, 217-581-7489, Fax: 217-581-6020, E-mail: wjelliott@eiu.edu.

Fresno Pacific University, Graduate Programs, School of Education, Division of Pupil Personnel Services, Fresno, CA 93702-4709. Offers school counseling (MA Ed); school psychology (MA Ed). Part-time programs available. *Degree requirements:* For master's, thesis or alternative. *Entrance requirements:* Additional exam requirements/recommendations for international students: Required—TOEFL (minimum score 550 paper-based; 213 computer-based).

Grambling State University, School of Graduate Studies and Research, College of Education, Department of Educational Leadership, Grambling, LA 71245. Offers curriculum and instruction (Ed D); developmental education (MS, Ed D), including curriculum and instruction: reading (Ed D), English (MS); guidance and counseling (MS); higher education administration (Ed D); instructional systems and technology (Ed D); mathematics (MS); reading (MS); science (MS); student development and personnel services (Ed D); educational leadership (MS, Ed D). Part-time and evening/weekend programs available. *Faculty:* 19 full-time (12 women). *Students:* 23 full-time (18 women), 84 part-time (62 women); includes 81 minority (80 African Americans, 1 Asian American or Pacific Islander), 5 international. Average age 39. 72 applicants, 75% accepted, 39 enrolled. In 2009, 5 master's, 9 doctorates awarded. *Degree requirements:* For master's, comprehensive exam, thesis (for some programs); for doctorate, comprehensive exam, thesis/dissertation. *Entrance requirements:* For master's, GRE, minimum GPA of 2.5 on last degree; for doctorate, GRE (minimum 1000, 500 on Verbal), master's degree, minimum GPA of 3.0 on last degree. Additional exam requirements/recommendations for international students: Required—TOEFL (minimum score 500 paper-based; 173 computer-based; 61 iBT). *Application deadline:* For fall admission, 7/1 for domestic and international students; for spring admission, 12/1 for domestic and international students. Applications are processed on a rolling basis. Application fee: $20 ($30 for international students). Electronic applications accepted. *Expenses:* Tuition, state resident: full-time $2610. Tuition, nonresident: full-time $2610. *Financial support:* In 2009–10, 5 research assistantships (averaging $10,948 per year) were awarded; health care benefits, tuition waivers (full), and unspecified assistantships also available. Financial award application deadline: 5/31; financial award applicants required to submit FAFSA. *Unit head:* Dr. Olatunde Ogunyemi, Director, 318-274-6105, Fax: 318-274-2799, E-mail: ogunyemio@gram.edu. *Application contact:* Laketha Richards, Administrative Assistant III, 318-274-6105, Fax: 318-274-6249, E-mail: richardsl@gram.edu.

Hampton University, Graduate College, Department of Education, Program in Counseling, Hampton, VA 23668. Offers college student development (MA); community agency counseling (MA); pastoral counseling (MA); school counseling (MA). *Accreditation:* NCATE. Part-time and evening/weekend programs available. *Entrance requirements:* For master's, GRE General Test.

Illinois State University, Graduate School, College of Education, Department of Educational Administration and Foundations, Program in College Student Personnel Administration, Normal, IL 61790-2200. Offers MS.

Indiana State University, School of Graduate Studies, College of Education, Department of Educational Leadership, Administration, and Foundations, Terre Haute, IN 47809. Offers educational administration (PhD); leadership in higher education (PhD); school administration (Ed S); school administration and supervision (M Ed); student affairs in higher education (MS). *Accreditation:* NCATE. Part-time and evening/weekend programs available. Terminal master's awarded for partial completion of doctoral program. *Degree requirements:* For master's, thesis; for doctorate, thesis/dissertation. *Entrance requirements:* For master's, GRE General Test, minimum undergraduate GPA of 2.5; for doctorate, GRE General Test, minimum

undergraduate GPA of 3.5; for Ed S, GRE General Test, minimum graduate GPA of 3.25. Electronic applications accepted.

Indiana University–Purdue University Indianapolis, School of Education, Indianapolis, IN 46202-2896. Offers computer education (Certificate); curriculum and instruction (MS); early childhood (MS); educational leadership (MS, Certificate); English as a second language (Certificate); higher education and student affairs (MS); kindergarten (Certificate); language education (MS); reading (Certificate); school counseling (MS); special education (MS, Certificate). Part-time and evening/weekend programs available. *Faculty:* 41 full-time, 80 part-time/adjunct. *Students:* 72 full-time (60 women), 427 part-time (325 women); includes 57 minority (42 African Americans, 1 American Indian/Alaska Native, 4 Asian Americans or Pacific Islanders, 10 Hispanic Americans), 5 international. Average age 32. 181 applicants, 78% accepted, 112 enrolled. In 2009, 162 master's awarded. *Degree requirements:* For master's, thesis optional. *Entrance requirements:* For master's, GRE General Test, minimum GPA of 3.0. Additional exam requirements/recommendations for international students: Required—TOEFL. *Application deadline:* For fall admission, 5/1 priority date for domestic students; for spring admission, 11/1 for domestic students. Application fee: $55 ($65 for international students). *Financial support:* In 2009–10, 2 fellowships (averaging $780 per year), 18 teaching assistantships (averaging $9,756 per year) were awarded; research assistantships with partial tuition reimbursements, Federal Work-Study, institutionally sponsored loans, scholarships/grants, and tuition waivers (partial) also available. Support available to part-time students. *Faculty research:* Teachers in the process of change, learning cycles, children's concepts of science. Total annual research expenditures: $614,458. *Unit head:* Dr. Chris Leland, Interim Executive Associate Dean, 317-274-6801, Fax: 317-274-6864. *Application contact:* Sarah Brandenburg, Graduate Advisor, 317-274-6801, Fax: 317-274-6864, E-mail: edugrad@iupui.edu.

Kansas State University, Graduate School, College of Education, Department of Special Education, Counseling and Student Affairs, Manhattan, KS 66506. Offers academic advising (MS); college student development (MS); counseling and student development (Ed D); counselor education and supervision (PhD); school counseling (MS); special education (MS, Ed D); student affairs in higher education (PhD). *Accreditation:* NCATE. Part-time programs available. *Faculty:* 10 full-time (4 women), 3 part-time/adjunct (1 woman). *Students:* 64 full-time (38 women), 256 part-time (197 women); includes 33 minority (16 African Americans, 3 American Indian/Alaska Native, 6 Asian Americans or Pacific Islanders, 8 Hispanic Americans), 2 international. Average age 36. 100 applicants, 97% accepted, 73 enrolled. In 2009, 31 master's, 5 doctorates awarded. *Degree requirements:* For master's, thesis or alternative, final written exam. *Entrance requirements:* For master's, GRE General Test or MAT, teaching experience, BS in education with minimum B average. Additional exam requirements/recommendations for international students: Required—TOEFL. *Application deadline:* For fall admission, 2/1 priority date for domestic and international students; for spring admission, 8/1 priority date for domestic and international students. Applications are processed on a rolling basis. Application fee: $40 ($55 for international students). Electronic applications accepted. *Financial support:* In 2009–10, 1 research assistantship (averaging $12,134 per year) was awarded; career-related internships or fieldwork, Federal Work-Study, institutionally sponsored loans, and scholarships/grants also available. Support available to part-time students. Financial award application deadline: 3/1; financial award applicants required to submit FAFSA. *Faculty research:* Application of principles of universal design for learning, on-line applications for supervision of practicum students, interpretation of facial expressions by students with EBD and ASD, school-wide screening techniques for behavioral concerns, field-based observation technique refinements. Total annual research expenditures: $2,948. *Unit head:* Kenneth Hughey, Head, 785-532-6445, Fax: 785-532-7304, E-mail: khughey@ksu.edu. *Application contact:* Gail Shroyer, Director, 785-532-6737, Fax: 785-532-7304, E-mail: gshroyer@ksu.edu.

Kaplan University, Davenport Campus, School of Higher Education Studies, Davenport, IA 52807-2095. Offers college administration and leadership (MS); college teaching and learning (MS); student services (MS). Part-time and evening/weekend programs available. Postbaccalaureate distance learning degree programs offered (no on-campus study). *Entrance requirements:* Additional exam requirements/recommendations for international students: Required—TOEFL (minimum score 550 paper-based; 218 computer-based; 80 iBT).

Kent State University, Graduate School of Education, Health, and Human Services, School of Foundations, Leadership and Administration, Program in Higher Education and Student Personnel, Kent, OH 44242-0001. Offers M Ed, MA. *Accreditation:* NCATE. Part-time and evening/weekend programs available. *Faculty:* 7 full-time (4 women), 2 part-time/adjunct (0 women). *Students:* 66 full-time (47 women), 24 part-time (20 women); includes 7 minority (5 African Americans, 2 Hispanic Americans), 2 international. 107 applicants, 64% accepted. In 2009, 43 master's awarded. *Degree requirements:* For master's, thesis (for some programs). *Entrance requirements:* Additional exam requirements/recommendations for international students: Required—TOEFL. *Application deadline:* Applications are processed on a rolling basis. Application fee: $30. Electronic applications accepted. *Financial support:* In 2009–10, 10 research assistantships with full tuition reimbursements (averaging $8,500 per year) were awarded; teaching assistantships with full tuition reimbursements, Federal Work-Study, scholarships/grants, and unspecified assistantships also available. Financial award application deadline: 4/1; financial award applicants required to submit FAFSA. *Faculty research:* History/sociology of higher education, organization and administration in higher education. *Unit head:* Dr. Mark Kretovics, Coordinator, 330-672-0642, E-mail: mkretov1@kent.edu. *Application contact:* Nancy Miller, Academic Program Coordinator, Office of Graduate Student Services, 330-672-2576, Fax: 330-672-9162, E-mail: ogs@kent.edu.

Lehigh University, College of Education, Program in Educational Leadership, Bethlehem, PA 18015. Offers educational leadership (M Ed, Ed D); principal certification K-12 (Certificate); pupil services (Certificate); special education (Certificate); superintendant certification (Certificate); supervisor of curriculum and instruction (Certificate); supervisor of pupil services (Certificate); MBA/M Ed. Part-time and evening/weekend programs available. Postbaccalaureate distance learning degree programs offered (minimal on-campus study). *Faculty:* 7 full-time (2 women), 16 part-time/adjunct (9 women). *Students:* 12 full-time (6 women), 174 part-time (102 women); includes 8 minority (4 African Americans, 1 Asian American or Pacific Islander, 3 Hispanic Americans), 20 international. Average age 37. 55 applicants, 73% accepted, 34 enrolled. In 2009, 39 master's, 4 doctorates awarded. *Degree requirements:* For doctorate, comprehensive exam, thesis/dissertation. *Entrance requirements:* For master's, minimum GPA of 3.0; for doctorate, GRE General Test or MAT, minimum graduate GPA of 3.6, 2 letters of recommendation, essay, transcript; for Certificate, minimum undergraduate GPA of 3.0. Additional exam requirements/recommendations for international students: Required—TOEFL (minimum score 600 paper-based; 250 computer-based; 93 iBT). *Application deadline:* For fall admission, 1/15 for domestic and international students; for spring admission, 11/1 for domestic and international students. Applications are processed on a rolling basis. Application fee: $65. Electronic applications accepted. *Financial support:* In 2009–10, 2 students received support, including 2 research assistantships with full and partial tuition reimbursements available (averaging $13,000 per year); fellowships with full and partial tuition reimbursements available, teaching assistantships with full and partial tuition reimbursements available, career-related internships or fieldwork, Federal Work-Study, institutionally sponsored loans, scholarships/grants, and tuition waivers (full and partial) also available. Financial award application deadline: 1/31. *Faculty research:* School finance and law, supervision of instruction, middle-level education, organizational change, leadership preparation and development, international school leadership, urban school leadership. *Unit head:* Dr. George P. White, Coordinator, 610-758-3250, Fax: 610-758-3227, E-mail: gpw1@lehigh.edu. *Application contact:* Donna M. Johnson, Coordinator, 610-758-3231, Fax: 610-758-6223, E-mail: dmj4@lehigh.edu.

Lewis University, College of Arts and Sciences, Program in Organizational Leadership, Romeoville, IL 60446. Offers higher education/student services (MA); organizational management (MA); public administration (MA); training and development (MA). Part-time and evening/weekend programs available. *Faculty:* 2 full-time (0 women), 9 part-time/adjunct (2 women). *Students:* 24 full-time (11 women), 111 part-time (91 women); includes 42 minority (33 African Americans, 1 American Indian/Alaska Native, 1 Asian American or Pacific Islander, 7 Hispanic Americans), 1 international. Average age 38. In 2009, 41 master's awarded. *Entrance requirements:* For master's, bachelor's degree, at least 25 years of age, minimum of 3 years of work experience, minimum GPA of 3.0, letter of recommendation, interview. Additional exam requirements/recommendations for international students: Required—TOEFL (minimum score 550 paper-based; 213 computer-based). *Application deadline:* For fall admission, 5/1 priority date for international students; for spring admission, 11/15 priority date for international students. Applications are processed on a rolling basis. Application fee: $40. Electronic applications accepted. *Expenses:* Tuition: Full-time $6480; part-time $720 per credit. One-time fee: $40. Tuition and fees vary according to course load, degree level and program. *Financial support:* Federal Work-Study, scholarships/grants, tuition waivers, and unspecified assistantships available. Financial award application deadline: 5/1; financial award applicants required to submit FAFSA. *Unit head:* Dr. Rich Walsh, Director, 815-838-0500, E-mail: walshri@lewisu.edu. *Application contact:* Bernadette Valderrama, Information Contact, 815-838-0500 Ext. 5629.

Miami University, Graduate School, School of Education and Allied Professions, Department of Educational Leadership, Oxford, OH 45056. Offers curriculum and teacher leadership (M Ed); educational administration (Ed D, PhD); school leadership (MS); student affairs in higher education (MS, PhD). *Accreditation:* NCATE. Part-time programs available. *Students:* 78 full-time (51 women), 77 part-time (53 women); includes 38 minority (30 African Americans, 1 American Indian/Alaska Native, 4 Asian Americans or Pacific Islanders, 3 Hispanic Americans), 4 international. *Entrance requirements:* For master's, MAT or GRE, minimum undergraduate GPA of 3.0 during previous 2 years or 2.75 overall; for doctorate, GRE, minimum GPA of 2.75 (undergraduate), 3.0 (graduate). Additional exam requirements/recommendations for international students: Required—TOEFL. Application fee: $50. *Expenses:* Tuition, state resident: full-time $11,280. Tuition, nonresident: full-time $24,912. Required fees: $516. *Financial support:* Fellowships with full tuition reimbursements, research assistantships with full tuition reimbursements, teaching assistantships with full tuition reimbursements, career-related internships or fieldwork, Federal Work-Study, health care benefits, tuition waivers (full), and unspecified assistantships available. Financial award application deadline: 3/1. *Unit head:* Dr. Kate Rousmaniere, Chair, 513-529-6843, Fax: 513-529-1729, E-mail: roumak@muohio.edu. *Application contact:* Dr. Denise Taliaferri Baszile, Director of Graduate Studies, 513-529-1798, E-mail: taliafda@muohio.edu.

Minnesota State University Mankato, College of Graduate Studies, College of Education, Department of Counseling and Student Personnel, Mankato, MN 56001. Offers college student affairs (MS); counselor education and supervision (Ed D); marriage and family counseling (Certificate); professional community counseling (MS); professional school counseling (MS). *Accreditation:* ACA (one or more programs are accredited); NCATE. *Students:* 67 full-time (57 women), 41 part-time (32 women). *Degree requirements:* For master's, comprehensive exam, thesis or alternative. *Entrance requirements:* For master's, GRE General Test or MAT (if GPA less than 3.0 for last 2 years), minimum GPA of 3.0 during previous 2 years, 3 letters of reference. Additional exam requirements/recommendations for international students: Required—TOEFL. *Application deadline:* For fall admission, 1/15 priority date for domestic students. Applications are processed on a rolling basis. Application fee: $40. Electronic applications accepted. *Expenses:* Tuition, state resident: full-time $5364. Tuition, nonresident: full-time $8314. *Financial support:* Research assistantships with full tuition reimbursements, teaching assistantships with full tuition reimbursements, career-related internships or fieldwork, Federal Work-Study, institutionally sponsored loans, and unspecified assistantships available. Support available to part-time students. Financial award application deadline: 3/15; financial award applicants required to submit FAFSA. *Unit head:* Dr. Jacqueline Lewis, Chairperson, 507-389-5658. *Application contact:* 507-389-2321, E-mail: grad@mnsu.edu.

Mississippi State University, College of Education, Department of Counseling and Educational Psychology, Mississippi State, MS 39762. Offers college/postsecondary student counseling and personnel services (PhD); counselor education (MS); counselor education/student counseling and guidance services (PhD); education (Ed S), including counselor education, school psychology; educational psychology (MS, PhD). *Accreditation:* ACA (one or more programs are accredited); APA; CORE (one or more programs are accredited); NCATE. Part-time programs available. Postbaccalaureate distance learning degree programs offered (minimal on-campus study). *Faculty:* 14 full-time (10 women), 1 (woman) part-time/adjunct. *Students:* 116 full-time (95 women), 99 part-time (84 women); includes 63 minority (57 African Americans, 2 American Indian/Alaska Native, 2 Asian Americans or Pacific Islanders, 2 Hispanic Americans), 3 international. Average age 32. 154 applicants, 62% accepted, 69 enrolled. In 2009, 56 master's, 9 doctorates, 17 other advanced degrees awarded. Terminal master's awarded for partial completion of doctoral program. *Degree requirements:* For master's, comprehensive exam, thesis optional; for doctorate, thesis/dissertation, comprehensive oral and written exam. *Entrance requirements:* For master's, GRE, minimum QPA of 3.0; for doctorate, GRE, interview, minimum GPA of 3.4; for Ed S, GRE, MS in counseling or related field. Additional exam requirements/recommendations for international students: Required—TOEFL (minimum score 475 paper-based; 153 computer-based; 53 iBT); Recommended—IELTS (minimum score 4.5). *Application deadline:* For fall admission, 2/1 priority date for domestic and international students. Applications are processed on a rolling basis. Application fee: $40. Electronic applications accepted. *Expenses:* Tuition, state resident: full-time $2575.50; part-time $286.25 per credit hour. Tuition, nonresident: full-time $6510; part-time $723.50 per credit hour. Tuition and fees vary according to course load. *Financial support:* In 2009–10, 4 teaching assistantships with full tuition reimbursements (averaging $8,603 per year) were awarded; career-related internships or fieldwork, Federal Work-Study, institutionally sponsored loans, and unspecified assistantships also available. Financial award application deadline: 2/1; financial award applicants required to submit FAFSA. *Faculty research:* HIV-AIDS in college population, substance abuse in youth and college students, ADHD and conduct disorders in youth, assessment and identification of early childhood disabilities, assessment and vocational transition of the disabled. *Unit head:* Dr. Daniel Wong, Professor/Head, 662-325-7928, Fax: 662-325-3263, E-mail: dwong@colled.msstate.edu. *Application contact:* Dr. Tony Doggett, Associate Professor and Graduate Coordinator, 662-325-3312, Fax: 662-325-3263, E-mail: tdoggett@colled.msstate.edu.

Missouri State University, Graduate College, College of Education, Department of Counseling, Leadership, and Special Education, Program in Student Affairs, Springfield, MO 65897. Offers MS. Part-time programs available. *Students:* 31 full-time (18 women), 9 part-time (5 women); includes 5 minority (2 African Americans, 2 Asian Americans or Pacific Islanders, 1 Hispanic American), 3 international. Average age 28. 18 applicants, 100% accepted, 12 enrolled. In 2009, 14 master's awarded. *Degree requirements:* For master's, comprehensive exam, thesis or alternative. *Entrance requirements:* For master's, statement of purpose; three references. Additional exam requirements/recommendations for international students: Required—TOEFL (minimum score 550 paper-based; 213 computer-based; 79 iBT). *Application deadline:* For fall admission, 7/20 priority date for domestic students, 5/1 for international students; for spring admission, 12/20 priority date for domestic students, 9/1 for international students. Applications are processed on a rolling basis. Application fee: $35 ($50 for international students). Electronic applications accepted. *Expenses:* Tuition, state resident: full-time $3852; part-time $214 per credit hour. Tuition, nonresident: full-time $7524; part-time $418 per credit hour. Required fees: $696; $172 per semester. Tuition and fees vary according to course level, course load, degree level and program. *Financial support:* Federal Work-Study, institutionally sponsored loans, scholarships/grants, and unspecified assistantships available. Financial award application deadline: 3/31; financial award applicants required to submit FAFSA. *Unit head:* Dr. Gilbert Brown, Program Director, 417-836-4428, E-mail: gilbertbrown@missouristate.edu. *Application contact:* Eric Eckert, Coordinator of Admissions and Recruitment, 417-836-5331, Fax: 417-836-6200, E-mail: ericeckert@missouristate.edu.

New York University, Steinhardt School of Culture, Education, and Human Development, Department of Administration, Leadership, and Technology, Program in Higher Education, New York, NY 10012-1019. Offers higher and postsecondary education (PhD); higher education administration (Ed D); student personnel administration in higher education (MA). *Accreditation:* Teacher Education Accreditation Council. Part-time programs available. *Students:* 43 full-time

Student Affairs

New York University (continued)

(25 women), 93 part-time (73 women); includes 41 minority (18 African Americans, 10 Asian Americans or Pacific Islanders, 13 Hispanic Americans), 3 international. Average age 32. 199 applicants, 26% accepted, 41 enrolled. In 2009, 37 master's, 9 doctorates awarded. *Degree requirements:* For master's, thesis (for some programs); for doctorate, thesis/dissertation. *Entrance requirements:* For master's, interview, 2 letters of recommendation; for doctorate, GRE General Test, interview. Additional exam requirements/recommendations for international students: Required—TOEFL. *Application deadline:* For fall admission, 12/15 priority date for domestic and international students; for spring admission, 11/1 for domestic and international students. Applications are processed on a rolling basis. Application fee: $75. Electronic applications accepted. *Expenses:* Tuition: Full-time $30,528; part-time $1272 per credit. Required fees: $2177. *Financial support:* Fellowships with full and partial tuition reimbursements, career-related internships or fieldwork, Federal Work-Study, institutionally sponsored loans, scholarships/grants, tuition waivers (partial), and unspecified assistantships available. Support available to part-time students. Financial award application deadline: 2/1; financial award applicants required to submit FAFSA. *Faculty research:* Organizational theory and culture, systemic change, leadership development, access, equity and diversity. *Unit head:* Dr. Ann Marcus, Head, 212-998-4041, Fax: 212-995-4041. *Application contact:* 212-998-5030, Fax: 212-995-4328, E-mail: steinhardt.gradadmissions@nyu.edu.

Northeastern University, Bouvé College of Health Sciences Graduate School, Department of Counseling and Applied Educational Psychology, Program in College Student Development and Counseling, Boston, MA 02115-5096. Offers MS, CAGS. Part-time and evening/weekend programs available. *Faculty:* 1 (woman) full-time, 4 part-time/adjunct (all women). *Students:* 35 full-time (29 women), 4 part-time (all women); includes 6 minority (3 African Americans, 2 Asian Americans or Pacific Islanders, 1 Hispanic American). 71 applicants, 72% accepted, 25 enrolled. In 2009, 17 master's awarded. *Entrance requirements:* For master's, GRE General Test or MAT. Additional exam requirements/recommendations for international students: Required—TOEFL (minimum score 100 iBT). *Application deadline:* For fall admission, 8/1 for domestic students; for spring admission, 12/1 for domestic students. Applications are processed on a rolling basis. Application fee: $50. Electronic applications accepted. *Financial support:* Career-related internships or fieldwork, Federal Work-Study, scholarships/grants, tuition waivers (partial), and unspecified assistantships available. Support available to part-time students. Financial award application deadline: 3/1; financial award applicants required to submit FAFSA. *Unit head:* Prof. Vanessa Johnson, Director, 617-373-4634, E-mail: v.johnson@neu.edu. *Application contact:* Margaret Schnabel, Director of Graduate Admissions, 617-373-2708, E-mail: bouvegrad@neu.edu.

Northern Arizona University, Graduate College, College of Education, Department of Educational Psychology, Flagstaff, AZ 86011. Offers counseling (MA); educational psychology (PhD), including counseling psychology, learning and instruction, school psychology; human relations (M Ed); school counseling (M Ed); school psychology (MA, Certificate); student affairs (M Ed). Part-time programs available. Postbaccalaureate distance learning degree programs offered. *Faculty:* 20 full-time (10 women). *Students:* 200 full-time (151 women), 241 part-time (189 women); includes 165 minority (28 African Americans, 21 American Indian/Alaska Native, 7 Asian Americans or Pacific Islanders, 109 Hispanic Americans), 1 international. In 2009, 167 master's, 7 doctorates awarded. Terminal master's awarded for partial completion of doctoral program. *Median time to degree:* Of those who began their doctoral program in fall 2001, 75% received their degree in 8 years or less. *Degree requirements:* For master's, internship (for some programs); for doctorate, comprehensive exam, thesis/dissertation, internship. *Entrance requirements:* Additional exam requirements/recommendations for international students: Required—TOEFL (minimum score 550 paper-based; 213 computer-based; 80 iBT), IELTS (minimum score 7), or a bachelor's degree from an English-speaking university and demonstrated proficiency. *Application deadline:* For fall admission, 9/15 for domestic students; for spring admission, 1/15 for domestic students. Application fee: $65. Electronic applications accepted. *Financial support:* In 2009–10, 20 students received support, including 2 research assistantships with partial tuition reimbursements available, 12 teaching assistantships with partial tuition reimbursements available; career-related internships or fieldwork, Federal Work-Study, scholarships/grants, health care benefits, tuition waivers (full and partial), and unspecified assistantships also available. Support available to part-time students. Financial award applicants required to submit FAFSA. *Unit head:* Dr. Kathy Bohan, Chair, 928-523-0362, E-mail: kathy.bohan@nau.edu. *Application contact:* Shirley Robinson, Director of Graduate Admissions, 928-523-4348, Fax: 928-523-8950, E-mail: graduate.college@nau.edu.

Northern Kentucky University, Office of Graduate Programs, College of Education and Human Services, Program in Community Counseling, Highland Heights, KY 41099. Offers college student development administration (Certificate); community counseling (MS). Part-time and evening/weekend programs available. *Students:* 13 full-time (12 women), 32 part-time (22 women); includes 3 minority (2 African Americans, 1 Asian American or Pacific Islander). Average age 29. 36 applicants, 47% accepted, 15 enrolled. In 2009, 9 master's, 2 other advanced degrees awarded. *Degree requirements:* For master's, comprehensive exam, internship. *Entrance requirements:* For master's, GRE, minimum GPA of 2.75, 3 letters of reference, criminal background check (state and federal), resume. Additional exam requirements/recommendations for international students: Required—TOEFL (minimum score 550 paper-based; 213 computer-based; 79 iBT); Recommended—IELTS (minimum score 6.5). *Application deadline:* For fall admission, 8/1 for domestic students, 6/1 priority date for international students; for spring admission, 10/1 priority date for international students. Applications are processed on a rolling basis. Application fee: $40. Electronic applications accepted. *Expenses:* Tuition, state resident: full-time $6912; part-time $384 per credit hour. Tuition, nonresident: full-time $12,150; part-time $675 per credit hour. Tuition and fees vary according to course load, program and reciprocity agreements. *Financial support:* Applicants required to submit FAFSA. *Faculty research:* Ethical decision making in counseling, clinical supervision in counseling, expectations about counseling inventory development. *Unit head:* Dr. Jacqueline Smith, Director, 859-572-6149, E-mail: smithjac@nku.edu. *Application contact:* Dr. Peg Griffin, Director, Graduate Programs, 859-572-6934, Fax: 859-572-6670, E-mail: griffinp@nku.edu.

Northwestern State University of Louisiana, Graduate Studies and Research, College of Education, Program in Student Personnel Services, Natchitoches, LA 71497. Offers counseling and guidance (M Ed, Ed S); special education (M Ed, Ed S); student personnel services (MA). *Accreditation:* NCATE (one or more programs are accredited). *Degree requirements:* For master's, comprehensive exam, thesis or alternative. *Entrance requirements:* For master's, GRE General Test, GRE Subject Test, minimum undergraduate GPA of 2.5.

Nova Southeastern University, Graduate School of Humanities and Social Sciences, Department of Multi-Disciplinary Studies, Program in College Student Affairs, Fort Lauderdale, FL 33314-7796. Offers MS. Part-time programs available. Postbaccalaureate distance learning degree programs offered. *Degree requirements:* For master's, comprehensive exam. *Financial support:* Unspecified assistantships available. *Unit head:* Dr. Judith McKay, Chair, 954-262-3060. *Application contact:* Marcia Arango, Student Recruitment Coordinator, 954-262-3006, Fax: 954-262-3968, E-mail: marango@nsu.nova.edu.

Ohio University, Graduate College, College of Education, Department of Counseling and Higher Education, Athens, OH 45701-2979. Offers college student personnel (M Ed); community/agency counseling (M Ed); counselor education (PhD); higher education (PhD); rehabilitation counseling (M Ed); school counseling (M Ed). *Accreditation:* ACA; CORE. Part-time and evening/weekend programs available. *Faculty:* 12 full-time (6 women), 7 part-time/adjunct (1 woman). *Students:* 164 full-time (120 women), 51 part-time (30 women); includes 36 minority (27 African Americans, 3 American Indian/Alaska Native, 3 Asian Americans or Pacific Islanders, 3 Hispanic Americans), 9 international. 129 applicants, 58% accepted, 57 enrolled. In 2009, 60 master's, 16 doctorates awarded. *Degree requirements:* For master's, comprehensive exam (for some programs), thesis or alternative; for doctorate, comprehensive exam, thesis/dissertation. *Entrance requirements:* For master's, GRE General Test or MAT (if GPA less than 2.9), 3 letters of reference; for doctorate, GRE General Test, work experience, minimum GPA of 3.4. Additional exam requirements/recommendations for international students: Required—TOEFL (minimum score 550 paper-based; 80 iBT) or IELTS Academic (minimum score 6.5). *Application deadline:* For fall admission, 1/15 for domestic and international students. Application fee: $50 ($55 for international students). Electronic applications accepted. *Expenses:* Tuition, state resident: full-time $7839; part-time $323 per quarter hour. Tuition, nonresident: full-time $15,831; part-time $654 per quarter hour. Required fees: $2931. *Financial support:* Research assistantships with full tuition reimbursements, teaching assistantships with full tuition reimbursements, Federal Work-Study, institutionally sponsored loans, tuition waivers (partial), and unspecified assistantships available. Financial award application deadline: 1/15. *Faculty research:* Youth violence, gender studies, student affairs, chemical dependency, disabilities issues. Total annual research expenditures: $527,983. *Unit head:* Dr. Tracy Leinbaugh, Chair, 740-593-0846, Fax: 740-593-0477, E-mail: leinbaug@ohio.edu. *Application contact:* Floyd J. Doney, Director of Student Affairs, 740-593-4400, Fax: 740-593-9310, E-mail: doney@ohio.edu.

Oregon State University, Graduate School, College of Education, Program in College Student Service Administration, Corvallis, OR 97331. Offers Ed M, MS. *Students:* 36 full-time (30 women), 10 part-time (6 women); includes 9 minority (2 African Americans, 1 American Indian/Alaska Native, 2 Asian Americans or Pacific Islanders, 4 Hispanic Americans), 3 international. Average age 29. In 2009, 16 master's awarded. *Degree requirements:* For master's, thesis or alternative. *Entrance requirements:* For master's, minimum GPA of 3.0 in last 90 hours of course work. Additional exam requirements/recommendations for international students: Required—TOEFL. *Application deadline:* For fall admission, 3/1 for domestic students. Applications are processed on a rolling basis. Application fee: $50. *Expenses:* Tuition, state resident: full-time $9774; part-time $362 per credit. Tuition, nonresident: full-time $15,849; part-time $587 per credit. Required fees: $1639. Full-time tuition and fees vary according to course load and program. *Financial support:* Teaching assistantships, career-related internships or fieldwork, Federal Work-Study, and institutionally sponsored loans available. Support available to part-time students. Financial award application deadline: 2/1. *Faculty research:* Improvement of student activities, administering recreational sports programs. *Unit head:* Dr. Tom Scheuermann, Interim Chair, 541-737-9524, E-mail: tom.scheuermann@oregonstate.edu. *Application contact:* Dr. Tom Scheuermann, Interim Chair, 541-737-9524, E-mail: tom.scheuermann@oregonstate.edu.

Providence College and Theological Seminary, Theological Seminary, Otterburne, MB R0A 1G0, Canada. Offers children's ministry (Certificate); Christian studies (MA, Certificate); counseling (MA); cross-cultural discipleship (Certificate); divinity (M Div); educational studies (MA), including counseling psychology, educational ministries, student development, teaching English to speakers of other languages, training teachers of English to speakers of other languages; global studies (MA); lay counseling (Diploma); ministry (D Min); teaching English to speakers of other languages (Certificate); theological studies (MA); training teacher of English to speakers of other languages (Certificate); youth ministry (Certificate). *Accreditation:* ATS. Part-time programs available. *Degree requirements:* For master's, variable foreign language requirement, thesis (for some programs); for doctorate, thesis/dissertation; for M Div, 2 foreign languages, comprehensive exam, thesis/dissertation (for some programs). *Entrance requirements:* Additional exam requirements/recommendations for international students: Recommended—TOEFL (minimum score 550 paper-based; 213 computer-based). *Faculty research:* Studies in Isaiah, theology of sin.

Radford University, College of Graduate and Professional Studies, College of Education and Human Development, Department of Counselor Education, Radford, VA 24142. Offers community counseling (MS); school counseling (MS); student affairs—administration (MS); student affairs—counseling (MS). *Accreditation:* ACA; NCATE. Part-time and evening/weekend programs available. *Faculty:* 7 full-time (4 women), 20 part-time/adjunct (13 women). *Students:* 62 full-time (50 women), 60 part-time (50 women); includes 11 minority (8 African Americans, 1 American Indian/Alaska Native, 1 Asian American or Pacific Islander, 1 Hispanic American). Average age 29. 85 applicants, 88% accepted, 38 enrolled. In 2009, 53 master's awarded. *Degree requirements:* For master's, comprehensive exam, thesis optional. *Entrance requirements:* For master's, GRE or MAT, minimum GPA of 2.75, 3 letters of reference. Additional exam requirements/recommendations for international students: Required—TOEFL (minimum score 550 paper-based; 213 computer-based; 79 iBT). *Application deadline:* For fall admission, 4/15 priority date for domestic students, 12/1 for international students. Applications are processed on a rolling basis. Application fee: $50. Electronic applications accepted. *Expenses:* Tuition, state resident: full-time $5086; part-time $211 per credit hour. Tuition, nonresident: full-time $12,608; part-time $525 per credit hour. Required fees: $2508; $105 per credit hour. *Financial support:* In 2009–10, 27 students received support, including 11 research assistantships with partial tuition reimbursements available (averaging $8,000 per year), 9 teaching assistantships with partial tuition reimbursements available (averaging $8,700 per year); career-related internships or fieldwork, Federal Work-Study, institutionally sponsored loans, scholarships/grants, and unspecified assistantships also available. Financial award application deadline: 3/1; financial award applicants required to submit FAFSA. *Unit head:* Dr. Alan Forrest, Chair, 540-831-5487, Fax: 540-831-6755, E-mail: aforrest@radford.edu. *Application contact:* Graduate Admissions, 540-831-5431, Fax: 540-831-6061, E-mail: gradcollege@radford.edu.

Regent University, Graduate School, School of Education, Virginia Beach, VA 23464-9800. Offers career switcher (M Ed); Christian school program (M Ed); cross-categorical special education (M Ed); education (M Ed, Ed D); education licensure (M Ed); educational leadership (M Ed); elementary education (M Ed); individualized degree plan (M Ed); leadership in character education (M Ed); master teacher (M Ed); mathematics education (M Ed); special education leadership (Ed S); student affairs (M Ed); TESOL (M Ed). *Accreditation:* Teacher Education Accreditation Council. Part-time and evening/weekend programs available. Postbaccalaureate distance learning degree programs offered (minimal on-campus study). *Faculty:* 26 full-time (13 women), 104 part-time/adjunct (78 women). *Students:* 141 full-time (116 women), 622 part-time (488 women); includes 218 minority (186 African Americans, 1 American Indian/Alaska Native, 10 Asian Americans or Pacific Islanders, 21 Hispanic Americans), 8 international. Average age 39. 509 applicants, 60% accepted, 176 enrolled. In 2009, 212 master's, 15 doctorates awarded. *Degree requirements:* For master's, thesis or alternative; for doctorate, comprehensive exam, thesis/dissertation. *Entrance requirements:* For master's, MAT, minimum undergraduate GPA of 2.75, writing sample, resume, recommendations, interview; for doctorate, GRE, writing sample, 3 years of relevant professional experience, master's-level paper, copies of published work, resume, transcripts, interview, recommendations. Additional exam requirements/recommendations for international students: Required—TOEFL (minimum score 577 paper-based; 233 computer-based). *Application deadline:* For fall admission, 4/1 priority date for domestic students; for spring admission, 10/15 priority date for domestic students. Applications are processed on a rolling basis. Application fee: $50. Electronic applications accepted. *Expenses:* Contact institution. *Financial support:* In 2009–10, 480 students received support; fellowships, career-related internships or fieldwork, scholarships/grants, tuition waivers (full and partial), and unspecified assistantships available. Support available to part-time students. Financial award application deadline: 4/1; financial award applicants required to submit FAFSA. *Faculty research:* Character development and discipline for children, education leadership development, diversity in schools, classroom management, technology in education settings. *Unit head:* Dr. Alan A. Arroyo, Dean, 757-352-4261, Fax: 757-352-4318, E-mail: alanarr@regent.edu. *Application contact:* Matthew Chadwick, Director of Admissions, 800-373-5504, Fax: 757-352-4381, E-mail: admissions@regent.edu.

St. Cloud State University, School of Graduate Studies, College of Education, Department of Counselor Education, Higher Education, and Educational Psychology, Program in College Counseling and Student Development, St. Cloud, MN 56301-4498. Offers MS. *Faculty:* 12 full-time (5 women). *Students:* 25 full-time (18 women), 11 part-time (8 women); includes 2 minority (both Asian Americans or Pacific Islanders), 3 international. 15 applicants, 93% accepted. In 2009, 10 master's awarded. *Degree requirements:* For master's, comprehensive exam, thesis or alternative. *Entrance requirements:* For master's, GRE General Test, minimum GPA of 2.75. Additional exam requirements/recommendations for international students: Required—Michigan English Language Assessment Battery; Recommended—TOEFL (minimum

score 550 paper-based; 213 computer-based), IELTS (minimum score 6.5). *Application deadline:* For fall admission, 3/1 for domestic and international students. Application fee: $35. Electronic applications accepted. *Financial support:* Federal Work-Study, scholarships/grants, and unspecified assistantships available. Financial award application deadline: 3/1. *Unit head:* Dr. Dan Macari, Coordinator, 320-308-1044, E-mail: dpmacari@stcloudstate.edu. *Application contact:* Linda Lou Krueger, School of Graduate Studies, 320-308-2113, Fax: 320-308-5371, E-mail: lekrueger@stcloudstate.edu.

St. Edward's University, New College, Program in College Student Development, Austin, TX 78704. Offers MA. Part-time and evening/weekend programs available. *Students:* 16 part-time (11 women); includes 10 minority (2 African Americans, 8 Hispanic Americans). Average age 31. 7 applicants, 57% accepted, 2 enrolled. In 2009, 1 master's awarded. *Entrance requirements:* For master's, GRE, minimum GPA of 3.0 in last 60 hours or 2.75 overall. Additional exam requirements/recommendations for international students: Required—TOEFL (minimum score 550 paper-based; 213 computer-based; 79 iBT) or IELTS (minimum score 6). *Application deadline:* For fall admission, 7/1 for domestic and international students; for spring admission, 11/1 for domestic and international students. Applications are processed on a rolling basis. Application fee: $45 ($50 for international students). Electronic applications accepted. *Expenses:* Tuition: Full-time $14,922; part-time $829 per credit hour. Required fees: $50 per trimester. Full-time tuition and fees vary according to course load and program. *Financial support:* Scholarships/grants available. *Unit head:* Dr. Richard A. Parsells, Dean, 512-637-1978, Fax: 512-448-8492, E-mail: richp@stedwards.edu. *Application contact:* Anna Alkin, Graduate Admissions Coordinator, 512-448-8745, Fax: 512-428-1032, E-mail: annaa@stedwards.edu.

Saint Louis University, Graduate School, College of Education and Public Service and Graduate School, Department of Educational Leadership and Higher Education, St. Louis, MO 63103-2097. Offers Catholic school leadership (MA); educational administration (MA, Ed D, PhD, Ed S); higher education (MA, Ed D, PhD); student personnel administration (MA). *Accreditation:* NCATE. Part-time programs available. *Degree requirements:* For master's, comprehensive written and oral exam; for doctorate, comprehensive exam, thesis/dissertation, preliminary oral and written exams. *Entrance requirements:* For master's, GRE General Test, MAT, LSAT, GMAT or MCAT, letters of recommendation, resume; for doctorate and Ed S, GRE General Test, LSAT, GMAT or MCAT, letters of recommendation, resumé, goal statement, transcripts. Additional exam requirements/recommendations for international students: Required—TOEFL (minimum score 525 paper-based; 194 computer-based). Electronic applications accepted. *Faculty research:* Superintendent of schools, school finance, school facilities, student personal administration, building leadership.

San Jose State University, Graduate Studies and Research, Connie L. Lurie College of Education, Department of Counselor Education, San Jose, CA 95192-0001. Offers MA. *Accreditation:* NCATE. Evening/weekend programs available. *Students:* 176 full-time (136 women), 73 part-time (57 women); includes 153 minority (19 African Americans, 35 Asian Americans or Pacific Islanders, 99 Hispanic Americans), 5 international. Average age 30. 135 applicants, 53% accepted, 51 enrolled. In 2009, 122 master's awarded. *Degree requirements:* For master's, thesis or alternative. *Application deadline:* For fall admission, 6/29 for domestic students; for spring admission, 11/30 for domestic students. Applications are processed on a rolling basis. Application fee: $59. Electronic applications accepted. *Financial support:* Career-related internships or fieldwork available. Financial award applicants required to submit FAFSA. *Unit head:* Dr. Xiaolu Hu, Chair, 408-924-3668, Fax: 408-924-3713. *Application contact:* Dr. Xiaolu Hu, Chair, 408-924-3668, Fax: 408-924-3713.

Seton Hall University, College of Education and Human Services, Department of Education Leadership, Management and Policy, Program in College Student Personnel Administration, South Orange, NJ 07079-2697. Offers MA. Part-time and evening/weekend programs available. *Faculty:* 12 full-time (4 women), 1 part-time/adjunct (0 women). *Students:* 5 full-time (3 women), 5 part-time (2 women); includes 2 minority (both African Americans). Average age 33. 12 applicants, 100% accepted, 4 enrolled. In 2009, 3 master's awarded. *Entrance requirements:* For master's, GRE or MAT (within past 5 years), minimum GPA of 3.0. *Application deadline:* Applications are processed on a rolling basis. Application fee: $50. *Application contact:* Information Contact, 973-761-9668.

Shippensburg University of Pennsylvania, School of Graduate Studies, College of Education and Human Services, Department of Counseling, Shippensburg, PA 17257-2299. Offers Adlerian studies (Certificate); advanced study in counseling (Certificate); alcohol and drug counseling (Certificate); counseling (M Ed, MS), including college counseling (MS), community counseling (MS), elementary school counseling, mental health counseling (MS), secondary school counseling (MS), student personnel services (MS); couple and family counseling (Certificate). *Accreditation:* ACA (one or more programs are accredited); NCATE. Part-time and evening/weekend programs available. *Degree requirements:* For master's, fieldwork, research project, internship, candidacy. *Entrance requirements:* For master's, GRE or MAT (community, mental health, student personnel, and college counseling applicants if GPA is less than 2.75), minimum GPA of 2.75 (3.0 for M Ed), interview, resume, 3 letters of recommendation, supplemental data forms, one year of relevant work experience, on-campus interview. Additional exam requirements/recommendations for international students: Required—TOEFL (minimum score 560 paper-based; 220 computer-based); Recommended—IELTS (minimum score 6). Electronic applications accepted.

Slippery Rock University of Pennsylvania, Graduate Studies (Recruitment), College of Education, Department of Counseling and Development, Slippery Rock, PA 16057-1383. Offers community counseling (MA), including addiction, adult, child and adolescent; elementary guidance and counseling (M Ed); secondary guidance and counseling (M Ed); student personnel (MA). *Accreditation:* ACA (one or more programs are accredited); NCATE. Part-time and evening/weekend programs available. *Degree requirements:* For master's, thesis (for some programs), oral comprehensive exam. *Entrance requirements:* For master's, GRE General Test, MAT, minimum GPA of 2.75. Additional exam requirements/recommendations for international students: Required—TOEFL (minimum score 550 paper-based; 213 computer-based). *Application deadline:* For fall admission, 3/1 priority date for domestic students, 5/1 priority date for international students; for spring admission, 11/1 priority date for domestic students, 9/1 priority date for international students. Applications are processed on a rolling basis. Application fee: $25 ($30 for international students). Electronic applications accepted. *Expenses:* Tuition, state resident: full-time $6666; part-time $370 per credit. Tuition, nonresident: full-time $10,666; part-time $593 per credit. Required fees: $2184; $182 per credit. *Financial support:* Career-related internships or fieldwork, Federal Work-Study, scholarships/grants, and unspecified assistantships available. Support available to part-time students. Financial award application deadline: 5/1; financial award applicants required to submit FAFSA. *Unit head:* Dr. Jared Colbert, Graduate Coordinator, 724-738-2272, Fax: 724-738-2880, E-mail: jared.kolbert@sru.edu. *Application contact:* Angela Piverotto, Interim Director of Graduate Studies, 724-738-2051, Fax: 724-738-2146, E-mail: graduate.admissions@sru.edu.

Springfield College, Graduate Programs, Programs in Psychology and Counseling, Springfield, MA 01109-3797. Offers athletic counseling (M Ed, MS, CAGS); industrial/organizational psychology (M Ed, MS, CAGS); marriage and family therapy (M Ed, MS, CAGS); mental health counseling (M Ed, MS, CAGS); school guidance and counseling (M Ed, MS, CAGS); student personnel in higher education (M Ed, MS, CAGS). Part-time programs available. *Degree requirements:* For master's, research project, portfolio. *Entrance requirements:* Additional exam requirements/recommendations for international students: Required—TOEFL (minimum score 550 paper-based; 213 computer-based). Electronic applications accepted. *Expenses:* Tuition: Full-time $19,800; part-time $825 per credit hour. Required fees: $150.

State University of New York at Binghamton, Graduate School, College of Community and Public Affairs, Department of Student Affairs Administration, Binghamton, NY 13902-6000. Offers MS. *Students:* 21 full-time (11 women), 13 part-time (6 women); includes 6 minority (2 African Americans, 4 Hispanic Americans). Average age 29. 18 applicants, 67% accepted, 12 enrolled. In 2009, 11 master's awarded. *Financial support:* In 2009–10, 12 students received support, including 1 fellowship with full tuition reimbursement available (averaging $9,000 per year). *Unit head:* Dr. Sharon Holmes, Program Director, 607-777-9219, E-mail: slholmes@binghamton.edu. *Application contact:* Victoria Williams, Recruiting and Admissions Coordinator, 607-777-2151, Fax: 607-777-2501, E-mail: vwilliam@binghamton.edu.

Syracuse University, School of Education, Program in Student Affairs Counseling, Syracuse, NY 13244. Offers MS. *Students:* 2 full-time (1 woman), 2 part-time (both women). Average age 26. 7 applicants, 57% accepted, 1 enrolled. In 2009, 3 master's awarded. *Entrance requirements:* For master's, GRE General Test or MAT, interview. Additional exam requirements/recommendations for international students: Required—TOEFL (minimum score 100 iBT). *Application deadline:* For fall admission, 2/1 for domestic students, 2/1 priority date for international students; for spring admission, 10/15 for domestic students, 10/15 priority date for international students. Applications are processed on a rolling basis. Application fee: $75. Electronic applications accepted. *Expenses:* Tuition: Full-time $26,808; part-time $1117 per credit. Required fees: $1024. *Financial support:* Fellowships with tuition reimbursements, teaching assistantships with tuition reimbursements, tuition waivers (partial) available. Financial award application deadline: 1/1; financial award applicants required to submit FAFSA. *Unit head:* Dr. Dennis Gilbride, Chair, 315-443-2266, E-mail: ddgilbr@syr.edu. *Application contact:* Liza Rochelson, Graduate Recruiter, School of Education, 315-443-2505, E-mail: e-gradrcrt@syr.edu.

Teachers College, Columbia University, Graduate Faculty of Education, Department of Organization and Leadership, New York, NY 10027-6696. Offers adult education (MA, Ed D); education leadership (Ed M, MA, Ed D, PhD), including education leadership (PhD), education leadership studies (Ed M, MA, Ed D), leadership, policy and politics, private school leadership (Ed M, MA, Ed D), public school and school district leadership (Ed M, MA, Ed D); educational administration (Ed M, MA, Ed D, PhD); higher education (Ed M, MA, Ed D, PhD); inquiry in education leadership (Ed D); nurse executive (Ed M, MA, Ed D); politics and education (Ed M, MA, Ed D, PhD); social and organizational psychology (MA, Ed D, PhD), including organizational psychology, social psychology (Ed D, PhD); student personnel administration (Ed M, MA, Ed D); MBA/Ed D. Part-time and evening/weekend programs available. *Faculty:* 23 full-time (12 women). *Students:* 347 full-time (235 women), 549 part-time (362 women); includes 297 minority (144 African Americans, 85 Asian Americans or Pacific Islanders, 68 Hispanic Americans), 49 international. Average age 34. 657 applicants, 60% accepted, 188 enrolled. In 2009, 371 master's, 34 doctorates awarded. *Degree requirements:* For doctorate, thesis/dissertation. *Application deadline:* For fall admission, 5/15 for domestic students. Application fee: $65. *Financial support:* Fellowships, research assistantships, career-related internships or fieldwork, Federal Work-Study, institutionally sponsored loans, and tuition waivers (full and partial) available. Support available to part-time students. Financial award application deadline: 2/1. *Unit head:* Warner Burke, Chair, 212-678-3258. *Application contact:* Debbie Lesperance, Assistant Director of Admission, 212-678-3710, Fax: 212-678-4171.

Tennessee Technological University, Graduate School, College of Education, Department of Counseling and Psychology, Cookeville, TN 38505. Offers educational psychology (MA, Ed S); educational psychology and student personnel (MA, Ed S). *Accreditation:* NCATE (one or more programs are accredited). Part-time and evening/weekend programs available. *Faculty:* 24 full-time (6 women). *Students:* 64 full-time (52 women), 42 part-time (33 women); includes 9 minority (5 African Americans, 1 Asian American or Pacific Islander, 3 Hispanic Americans). Average age 27. 71 applicants, 79% accepted, 37 enrolled. In 2009, 18 master's, 9 other advanced degrees awarded. *Degree requirements:* For master's and Ed S, comprehensive exam, thesis or alternative. *Entrance requirements:* For master's and Ed S, MAT or GRE. Additional exam requirements/recommendations for international students: Required—TOEFL (minimum score 550 paper-based; 79 iBT), IELTS (minimum score 5.5). *Application deadline:* For fall admission, 8/1 for domestic students, 5/1 for international students; for spring admission, 12/1 for domestic students, 10/1 for international students. Application fee: $25 ($30 for international students). Electronic applications accepted. *Expenses:* Tuition, state resident: full-time $7034; part-time $368 per credit hour. *Financial support:* In 2009–10, 1 fellowship (averaging $8,000 per year), 8 research assistantships (averaging $4,000 per year), 3 teaching assistantships (averaging $4,000 per year) were awarded; career-related internships or fieldwork also available. Financial award application deadline: 4/1. *Unit head:* Dr. Barry Stein, Interim Chairperson, 931-372-3457, Fax: 931-372-6319. *Application contact:* Shelia K. Kendrick, Coordinator of Graduate Studies, 931-372-3808, Fax: 931-372-3497, E-mail: skendrick@tntech.edu.

University at Buffalo, the State University of New York, Graduate School, Graduate School of Education, Department of Educational Leadership and Policy, Buffalo, NY 14260. Offers educational administration (Ed M, Ed D, PhD); general education (Ed M); higher education administration (Ed M, Ed D, PhD), including student affairs (Ed D); school building leadership (LIFTS) (Certificate); school business and human resource administration (Certificate); school district business leadership (LIFTS) (Certificate); school district leadership (LIFTS) (Certificate); social foundations (PhD). Part-time and evening/weekend programs available. *Faculty:* 12 full-time (6 women), 13 part-time/adjunct (7 women). *Students:* 71 full-time (53 women), 159 part-time (99 women); includes 42 minority (27 African Americans, 1 American Indian/Alaska Native, 4 Asian Americans or Pacific Islanders, 10 Hispanic Americans), 20 international. Average age 36.7. 170 applicants, 59% accepted, 65 enrolled. In 2009, 29 master's, 24 doctorates, 29 other advanced degrees awarded. *Degree requirements:* For master's, comprehensive exam (for some programs), thesis optional; for doctorate, comprehensive exam, thesis/dissertation. *Entrance requirements:* For doctorate, GRE General Test or MAT, writing sample. Additional exam requirements/recommendations for international students: Required—TOEFL (minimum score 550 paper-based; 213 computer-based; 79 iBT). *Application deadline:* For fall admission, 3/1 priority date for domestic students, 3/1 for international students; for spring admission, 11/15 priority date for domestic students, 10/1 for international students. Applications are processed on a rolling basis. Application fee: $50. Electronic applications accepted. *Financial support:* In 2009–10, 6 fellowships with full tuition reimbursements (averaging $9,000 per year), 12 research assistantships with full tuition reimbursements (averaging $9,000 per year) were awarded; career-related internships or fieldwork, Federal Work-Study, institutionally sponsored loans, health care benefits, tuition waivers (full and partial), and unspecified assistantships also available. Financial award application deadline: 3/15; financial award applicants required to submit FAFSA. *Faculty research:* College access and choice, school leadership preparation and practice, public policy, curriculum and pedagogy, comparative and international education. Total annual research expenditures: $34,848. *Unit head:* Dr. William C. Barba, Chairman, 716-645-2471, Fax: 716-645-2481, E-mail: barba@buffalo.edu. *Application contact:* Bonnie Fisher, Admissions Assistant, 716-645-2110, Fax: 716-645-7937, E-mail: brfisher@buffalo.edu.

University of Bridgeport, School of Education and Human Resources, Division of Human Resources, Bridgeport, CT 06604. Offers college student personnel (MS); community counseling (MS); human resource development (MS); human service (MS). Part-time and evening/weekend programs available. *Degree requirements:* For master's, thesis, project. *Entrance requirements:* Additional exam requirements/recommendations for international students: Recommended—TOEFL (minimum score 550 paper-based; 213 computer-based; 80 iBT), IELTS (minimum score 6.5). Electronic applications accepted. *Faculty research:* Corporate elder care programs.

University of Central Arkansas, Graduate School, College of Education, Department of Leadership Studies, Program in College Student Personnel, Conway, AR 72035-0001. Offers MS. *Students:* 28 full-time (16 women), 8 part-time (5 women); includes 9 minority (8 African Americans, 1 Asian American or Pacific Islander), 1 international. Average age 25. 23 applicants, 96% accepted, 17 enrolled. In 2009, 20 master's awarded. *Degree requirements:* For master's, comprehensive exam, thesis. *Entrance requirements:* For master's, GRE General Test, minimum GPA of 2.7. Additional exam requirements/recommendations for international students: Required—TOEFL (minimum score 550 paper-based; 213 computer-based). *Application deadline:* For fall admission, 3/1 priority date for domestic students; for spring admission, 10/1 priority date for domestic students. Applications are processed on a rolling basis. Application fee: $25 ($40 for international students). *Expenses:* Contact institution. *Financial support:*

Student Affairs

University of Central Arkansas (continued)

Applicants required to submit FAFSA. *Unit head:* Dr. Charlotte Cone, Coordinator, 501-450-5303, Fax: 501-450-5469, E-mail: johns@uca.edu. *Application contact:* Brenda Herring, Admissions Assistant, 501-450-5065, Fax: 501-450-5678, E-mail: bherring@uca.edu.

University of Central Missouri, The Graduate School, College of Education, Warrensburg, MO 64093. Offers career and technical education administration (MS); career and technical education industry training (MS); career and technical education leadership/teaching (MS); college student personnel administration (MS); counseling (MS); curriculum and instruction (Ed S); educational leadership (Ed D); educational technology (MS); elementary education/educational foundations and literacy (MSE); elementary school administration (MSE); elementary school principalship (Ed S); human services/learning resources (Ed S); human services/professional counseling (Ed S); human services/special education (Ed S); human services/technology and occupational education (Ed S); K-12 education/educational foundations and literacy (MSE); K-12 special education (MSE); library science and information services (MS); literacy education (MSE); secondary education/educational foundations & literacy (MSE); secondary school administration (MSE); secondary school principalship (Ed S); superintendency (Ed S); teaching (MAT). Part-time programs available. Postbaccalaureate distance learning degree programs offered. *Faculty:* 42. *Students:* 123 full-time (82 women), 721 part-time (552 women); includes 58 minority (38 African Americans, 3 American Indian/Alaska Native, 6 Asian Americans or Pacific Islanders, 11 Hispanic Americans), 6 international. Average age 34. 229 applicants, 88% accepted, 190 enrolled. In 2009, 212 master's, 47 other advanced degrees awarded. *Entrance requirements:* Additional exam requirements/recommendations for international students: Required—TOEFL (minimum score 550 paper-based; 79 computer-based). *Application deadline:* For fall admission, 6/1 priority date for domestic students, 5/1 for international students; for spring admission, 10/1 priority date for domestic students, 10/1 for international students. Applications are processed on a rolling basis. Application fee: $30 ($75 for international students). Electronic applications accepted. *Expenses:* Tuition, area resident: Part-time $245.80 per credit hour. Tuition, nonresident: part-time $491.60 per credit hour. Required fees: $24.20 per credit hour. Full-time tuition and fees vary according to course load, degree level, campus/location and reciprocity agreements. *Financial support:* Research assistantships with full and partial tuition reimbursements, teaching assistantships with full and partial tuition reimbursements, career-related internships or fieldwork, Federal Work-Study, scholarships/grants, and administrative and laboratory assistantships available. Support available to part-time students. Financial award application deadline: 3/1; financial award applicants required to submit FAFSA. *Unit head:* Dr. Michael Wright, Dean, 660-543-4272, Fax: 660-543-8753, E-mail: mwright@ucmo.edu. *Application contact:* Laurie Delap, Admissions Coordinator, 660-543-4621, Fax: 660-543-4778, E-mail: gradinfo@ucmo.edu.

University of Dayton, Graduate School, School of Education and Allied Professions, Department of Counselor Education and Human Services, Dayton, OH 45469-1300. Offers college student personnel (MS Ed); community counseling (MS Ed); higher education administration (MS Ed); human services (MS Ed); school counseling (MS Ed); school psychology (MS Ed, Ed S); teacher as child/youth development specialist (MS Ed). *Accreditation:* NCATE. Part-time and evening/weekend programs available. *Faculty:* 11 full-time (8 women), 33 part-time/adjunct (22 women). *Students:* 254 full-time (207 women), 207 part-time (180 women); includes 76 minority (69 African Americans, 3 Asian Americans or Pacific Islanders, 4 Hispanic Americans), 2 international. Average age 32. 359 applicants, 47% accepted, 114 enrolled. In 2009, 163 master's, 11 Ed Ss awarded. *Degree requirements:* For master's, comprehensive exam (for some programs), thesis (for some programs), exit exam. *Entrance requirements:* For master's, MAT or GRE (if GPA less than 2.75), interview, writing sample. Additional exam requirements/recommendations for international students: Required—TOEFL (minimum score 550 paper-based; 213 computer-based; 80 iBT). *Application deadline:* For fall admission, 4/10 for domestic students, 3/1 priority date for international students; for winter admission, 9/10 for domestic students, 7/1 priority date for international students; for spring admission, 1/10 for domestic students; 1/1 priority date for international students. Applications are processed on a rolling basis. Application fee: $0 ($50 for international students). Electronic applications accepted. *Expenses:* Tuition: Full-time $8412; part-time $701 per credit hour. Required fees: $325; $65 per course. $25 per semester. Tuition and fees vary according to course load, degree level and program. *Financial support:* In 2009–10, 7 research assistantships with full tuition reimbursements (averaging $8,000 per year), 1 teaching assistantship with full tuition reimbursement (averaging $8,000 per year) were awarded; career-related internships or fieldwork, institutionally sponsored loans, health care benefits, and unspecified assistantships also available. Financial award applicants required to submit FAFSA. *Faculty research:* Anger as part of the grief process, inclusion of children with severe disabilities, comparisons of school counselors in Bosnia and the U. S., graduate and professional student socialization, use of cohort groups in doctoral programs, bullying in schools, impact of space on learning, sophomore experience. *Unit head:* Dr. Alan Demmitt, Chairperson, 937-229-3644, Fax: 937-229-1055. *Application contact:* Graduate Admissions, 937-229-4411, Fax: 937-229-4729, E-mail: gradadmission@udayton.edu.

University of Florida, Graduate School, College of Education, Department of Educational Administration and Policy, Gainesville, FL 32611. Offers curriculum and instruction (Ed D, PhD); educational leadership (M Ed, MAE, Ed D, PhD, Ed S); higher education administration (Ed D, PhD, Ed S); student personnel in higher education (M Ed, MAE); PhD/JD. *Accreditation:* NCATE. *Degree requirements:* For master's, thesis optional; for doctorate, variable foreign language requirement, thesis/dissertation. *Entrance requirements:* For master's, GRE General Test, minimum GPA of 3.0, teaching experience; for doctorate and Ed S, GRE General Test, minimum GPA of 3.0. Additional exam requirements/recommendations for international students: Required—TOEFL (minimum score 550 paper-based; 213 computer-based). Electronic applications accepted. *Faculty research:* Educational finance, community education, middle school curriculum, community college administration.

University of Georgia, Graduate School, College of Education, Department of Counseling and Human Development Services, Athens, GA 30602. Offers college student affairs administration (M Ed, PhD); counseling and student personnel (PhD); counseling psychology (PhD); professional counseling (M Ed); professional school counseling (Ed S); recreation and leisure studies (M Ed, MA, PhD). *Accreditation:* ACA (one or more programs are accredited); APA (one or more programs are accredited); NCATE. *Faculty:* 22 full-time (13 women). *Students:* 147 full-time (102 women), 56 part-time (30 women); includes 45 minority (36 African Americans, 5 Asian Americans or Pacific Islanders, 4 Hispanic Americans), 1 international. 278 applicants, 27% accepted, 69 enrolled. In 2009, 49 master's, 13 doctorates, 4 other advanced degrees awarded. *Degree requirements:* For master's, thesis (MA); for doctorate, variable foreign language requirement, thesis/dissertation. *Entrance requirements:* For master's, GRE General Test or MAT; for doctorate, GRE General Test. *Application deadline:* For fall admission, 7/1 priority date for domestic students; for spring admission, 11/15 for domestic students. Application fee: $50. Electronic applications accepted. *Expenses:* Tuition, state resident: full-time $6000; part-time $250 per credit hour. Tuition, nonresident: full-time $20,904; part-time $871 per credit hour. Required fees: $730 per semester. *Financial support:* Fellowships, research assistantships, teaching assistantships, unspecified assistantships available. *Unit head:* Dr. Rosemary E. Phelps, Head, 706-542-4221, Fax: 706-542-4130, E-mail: rephelps@uga.edu. *Application contact:* Dr. Georgia B. Calhoun, Graduate Coordinator, 706-542-4103, Fax: 706-542-4130, E-mail: gcalhoun@uga.edu.

The University of Iowa, Graduate College, College of Education, Department of Counseling, Rehabilitation, and Student Development, Iowa City, IA 52242-1316. Offers administration and research (PhD); community/rehabilitation counseling (MA); counselor education and supervision (PhD); rehabilitation counselor education (PhD); school counseling (MA); student development (MA, PhD). *Accreditation:* ACA (one or more programs are accredited); CORE (one or more programs are accredited). *Degree requirements:* For master's, thesis optional, exam; for doctorate, comprehensive exam, thesis/dissertation. *Entrance requirements:* For master's and doctorate, GRE General Test, minimum GPA of 3.0. Additional exam requirements/recommendations for international students: Required—TOEFL (minimum score 550 paper-based; 213 computer-based; 81 iBT). Electronic applications accepted.

University of La Verne, College of Arts and Sciences, Department of Psychology, Programs in Counseling, La Verne, CA 91750-4443. Offers counseling (MS), including student services; marriage and family therapy (MS). Part-time programs available. *Faculty:* 12 full-time (5 women), 22 part-time/adjunct (14 women). *Students:* 29 full-time (25 women), 73 part-time (68 women); includes 69 minority (17 African Americans, 5 Asian Americans or Pacific Islanders, 47 Hispanic Americans). Average age 29. In 2009, 36 master's awarded. *Degree requirements:* For master's, thesis, competency exam, personal psychotherapy. *Entrance requirements:* For master's, minimum undergraduate GPA of 3.0; 3 letters of recommendations; interview. Additional exam requirements/recommendations for international students: Required—TOEFL (minimum score 600 paper-based; 250 computer-based). *Application deadline:* Applications are processed on a rolling basis. Application fee: $50. *Expenses:* Contact institution. *Financial support:* Career-related internships or fieldwork, institutionally sponsored loans, and scholarships/grants available. Financial award application deadline: 3/2; financial award applicants required to submit FAFSA. *Unit head:* Patricia Long, 909-593-3511 Ext. 4091, E-mail: plong@laverne.edu. *Application contact:* Connie Hamlow, Admissions Information Specialist, 909-593-3511 Ext. 4519, Fax: 909-392-2761, E-mail: gradadmission@laverne.edu.

University of Louisville, Graduate School, College of Education and Human Development, Department of Educational and Counseling Psychology, Louisville, KY 40292-0001. Offers counseling and personnel services (M Ed, PhD). *Accreditation:* APA; NCATE. Part-time and evening/weekend programs available. *Faculty:* 16 full-time (8 women), 8 part-time/adjunct (5 women). *Students:* 184 full-time (146 women), 105 part-time (83 women); includes 54 minority (49 African Americans, 3 Asian Americans or Pacific Islanders, 2 Hispanic Americans), 1 international. Average age 31. 241 applicants, 41% accepted, 73 enrolled. In 2009, 58 master's, 9 doctorates awarded. *Degree requirements:* For doctorate, comprehensive exam, thesis/dissertation. *Entrance requirements:* For master's and doctorate, GRE General Test. Additional exam requirements/recommendations for international students: Required—TOEFL (minimum score 560 paper-based; 210 computer-based; 83 iBT). Application fee: $50. Electronic applications accepted. *Financial support:* In 2009–10, 51 students received support; fellowships, research assistantships, teaching assistantships, career-related internships or fieldwork, Federal Work-Study, scholarships/grants, and unspecified assistantships available. Financial award application deadline: 6/1; financial award applicants required to submit FAFSA. *Faculty research:* Temperament, psychological development, classroom processes, school outcomes, adolescent and adult development issues/prevention and treatment, multicultural counseling, spirituality, therapeutic outcomes, college student success, college student affairs administration, career development. Total annual research expenditures: $17,276. *Unit head:* Dr. Linda T. Shapiro, Acting Chair, 502-852-5716, Fax: 502-852-0629, E-mail: linda.shapiro@louisville.edu. *Application contact:* Libby Leggett, Director, Graduate Admissions, 502-852-3101, Fax: 502-852-6536, E-mail: gradadm@louisville.edu.

University of Maryland, College Park, Academic Affairs, College of Education, Department of Counseling and Personnel Services, College Park, MD 20742. Offers college student personnel (M Ed, MA); college student personnel administration (PhD); community counseling (CAGS); community/career counseling (M Ed, MA); counseling and personnel services (M Ed, MA, PhD), including art therapy (M Ed), college student personnel (M Ed), counseling and personnel services (PhD), counseling psychology (M Ed), mental health counseling (M Ed), school counseling (M Ed); counseling psychology (PhD); counselor education (PhD); rehabilitation counseling (M Ed, MA, AGSC); school counseling (M Ed, MA); school psychology (M Ed, MA, PhD). *Accreditation:* ACA (one or more programs are accredited); APA (one or more programs are accredited); CORE (one or more programs are accredited); NCATE. Part-time and evening/weekend programs available. Postbaccalaureate distance learning degree programs offered (no on-campus study). *Faculty:* 34 full-time (21 women), 8 part-time/adjunct (6 women). *Students:* 152 full-time (117 women), 25 part-time (18 women); includes 67 minority (32 African Americans, 2 American Indian/Alaska Native, 20 Asian Americans or Pacific Islanders, 13 Hispanic Americans), 16 international. 319 applicants, 15% accepted, 32 enrolled. In 2009, 24 master's, 15 doctorates, 4 other advanced degrees awarded. *Degree requirements:* For master's, thesis (for some programs); for doctorate, thesis/dissertation. *Entrance requirements:* For master's, GRE General Test or MAT, minimum GPA of 3.0, 3 letters of recommendation; for doctorate, GRE General Test or MAT, minimum GPA of 3.5, 3 letters of recommendation. Additional exam requirements/recommendations for international students: Required—TOEFL. *Application deadline:* For fall admission, 12/15 for domestic and international students; for spring admission, 10/1 for domestic students, 6/1 for international students. Applications are processed on a rolling basis. Application fee: $60. Electronic applications accepted. *Expenses:* Tuition, area resident: Part-time $471 per credit hour. Tuition, state resident: part-time $471 per credit hour. Tuition, nonresident: part-time $1016 per credit hour. Required fees: $337.04 per term. *Financial support:* In 2009–10, 4 fellowships with partial tuition reimbursements (averaging $10,402 per year), 8 research assistantships (averaging $16,454 per year), 93 teaching assistantships with tuition reimbursements (averaging $16,109 per year) were awarded; career-related internships or fieldwork, Federal Work-Study, and scholarships/grants also available. Support available to part-time students. Financial award applicants required to submit FAFSA. *Faculty research:* Educational psychology, counseling, health. Total annual research expenditures: $1.5 million. *Unit head:* Dr. Dennis Kivlighan, Chair, 301-405-2858, E-mail: dennisk@umd.edu. *Application contact:* Dean of Graduate School, 301-405-0358.

University of Minnesota, Twin Cities Campus, Graduate School, College of Education and Human Development, Department of Educational Psychology, Program in Counseling and Student Personnel Psychology, Minneapolis, MN 55455-0213. Offers MA, PhD, Ed S. *Students:* 99 full-time (74 women), 15 part-time (12 women); includes 18 minority (6 African Americans, 1 American Indian/Alaska Native, 9 Asian Americans or Pacific Islanders, 2 Hispanic Americans), 20 international. Average age 28. 171 applicants, 37% accepted, 38 enrolled. In 2009, 32 master's, 9 doctorates awarded. *Unit head:* Dr. Susan Hupp, Chair, 612-624-1003, Fax: 612-624-8241, E-mail: shupp@umn.edu. *Application contact:* Dr. Mary Trettin, Associate Dean, 612-625-6501, Fax: 612-626-1580, E-mail: mtrettin@umn.edu.

University of Mississippi, Graduate School, School of Education, Department of Educational Leadership and Counselor Education, Oxford, University, MS 38677. Offers counselor education (M Ed, PhD, Specialist); educational leadership (PhD); educational leadership and counselor education (M Ed, MA, Ed D, Ed S); higher education/student personnel (MA). *Accreditation:* ACA; NCATE. *Faculty:* 14 full-time (5 women), 1 part-time/adjunct (0 women). *Students:* 107 full-time (83 women), 192 part-time (129 women); includes 94 minority (91 African Americans, 2 Asian Americans or Pacific Islanders, 1 Hispanic American), 7 international. In 2009, 48 master's, 13 doctorates, 18 other advanced degrees awarded. *Degree requirements:* For doctorate, thesis/dissertation. *Entrance requirements:* For master's, GRE General Test, minimum GPA of 3.0; for doctorate, GRE General Test. Additional exam requirements/recommendations for international students: Required—TOEFL. *Application deadline:* For fall admission, 4/1 for domestic students; for spring admission, 10/1 for domestic students. Applications are processed on a rolling basis. Application fee: $25. Electronic applications accepted. *Financial support:* Scholarships/grants available. Financial award application deadline: 3/1; financial award applicants required to submit FAFSA. *Unit head:* Dr. Timothy Letzring, Acting Chair, 662-915-7069, E-mail: fdl@olemiss.edu. *Application contact:* Dr. Christy M. Wyandt, Associate Dean, 662-915-7474, Fax: 662-915-7577, E-mail: cwyandt@olemiss.edu.

University of Northern Colorado, Graduate School, College of Education and Behavioral Sciences, School of Educational Research, Leadership and Technology, Program in Higher Education and Student Affairs Leadership, Greeley, CO 80639. Offers PhD. Part-time programs available. *Faculty:* 1 full-time (0 women). *Students:* 13 full-time (10 women), 20 part-time (11 women); includes 6 minority (2 African Americans, 1 American Indian/Alaska Native, 3 Hispanic Americans), 1 international. Average age 33. 14 applicants, 79% accepted, 11 enrolled. In 2009, 4 doctorates awarded. *Entrance requirements:* For doctorate, GRE General Test, transcripts, 3 letters of recommendation. *Application deadline:* Applications are processed on

a rolling basis. Application fee: $50 ($60 for international students). Electronic applications accepted. *Expenses:* Tuition, state resident: full-time $5770; part-time $320.55 per credit hour. Tuition, nonresident: full-time $13,847; part-time $769.27 per credit hour. Required fees: $948.78; $52.72 per credit. *Financial support:* Research assistantships, teaching assistantships available. Financial award application deadline: 3/1; financial award applicants required to submit FAFSA. *Unit head:* Katrina Rodriguez, Program Coordinator, 970-351-2861, E-mail: hesal@unco.edu. *Application contact:* Linda Sisson, Graduate Student Admission Coordinator, 970-351-1807, Fax: 970-351-2371, E-mail: linda.sisson@unco.edu.

University of Northern Iowa, Graduate College, College of Education, Department of Educational Leadership, Counseling, and Postsecondary Education, Program in Postsecondary Education, Cedar Falls, IA 50614. Offers student affairs (MAE). *Students:* 17 full-time (14 women), 14 part-time (10 women); includes 3 minority (2 African Americans, 1 Hispanic American), 1 international. 35 applicants, 60% accepted, 11 enrolled. In 2009, 12 master's awarded. *Degree requirements:* For master's, comprehensive exam, thesis or alternative. *Entrance requirements:* For master's, minimum GPA of 3.0. Additional exam requirements/recommendations for international students: Required—TOEFL (minimum score 500 paper-based; 180 computer-based; 61 iBT). *Application deadline:* For fall admission, 8/1 priority date for domestic students. Applications are processed on a rolling basis. Application fee: $30 ($50 for international students). Electronic applications accepted. *Financial support:* Career-related internships or fieldwork, Federal Work-Study, scholarships/grants, and tuition waivers (full) available. Financial award application deadline: 2/1. *Unit head:* Dr. Michael Waggoner, Professor, 319-273-2605, Fax: 319-273-5175, E-mail: mike.waggoner@uni.edu. *Application contact:* Laurie S. Russell, Record Analyst, 319-273-2623, Fax: 319-273-6792, E-mail: laurie.russell@uni.edu.

University of Rhode Island, Graduate School, College of Human Science and Services, Department of Human Development and Family Studies, Kingston, RI 02881. Offers college student personnel (MS); human development and family studies (MS); marriage and family therapy (MS). *Accreditation:* AAMFT/COAMFTE. Part-time programs available. *Faculty:* 14 full-time (11 women), 4 part-time/adjunct (2 women). *Students:* 36 full-time (31 women), 18 part-time (16 women); includes 11 minority (6 African Americans, 2 Asian Americans or Pacific Islanders, 3 Hispanic Americans). In 2009, 27 master's awarded. *Degree requirements:* For master's, comprehensive exam (for some programs), thesis optional. *Entrance requirements:* For master's, GRE or MAT, 2 letters of recommendation. Additional exam requirements/recommendations for international students: Required—TOEFL (minimum score 550 paper-based; 213 computer-based). Application fee: $65. Electronic applications accepted. *Expenses:* Tuition, state resident: full-time $8828; part-time $490 per credit hour. Tuition, nonresident: full-time $22,100; part-time $1228 per credit hour. Required fees: $1118; $57 per semester. Tuition and fees vary according to program. *Financial support:* In 2009–10, 3 research assistantships with full and partial tuition reimbursements (averaging $10,421 per year), 4 teaching assistantships with full and partial tuition reimbursements (averaging $7,443 per year) were awarded. Financial award applicants required to submit FAFSA. Total annual research expenditures: $833,866. *Unit head:* Dr. Jerome Adams, Chair, 401-874-5962, Fax: 401-874-4020, E-mail: jadams@uri.edu. *Application contact:* Dr. Jerome Adams, Chair, 401-874-5962, Fax: 401-874-4020, E-mail: jadams@uri.edu.

University of St. Thomas, Graduate Studies, School of Education, Department of Leadership, Policy and Administration, St. Paul, MN 55105-1096. Offers athletics and activities administration (MA); community education administration (MA); critical pedagogy (Ed D); curriculum and instruction (Ed S); educational leadership (Ed S); educational leadership and administration (MA); international leadership (MA, Certificate); leadership (Ed D); leadership in student affairs (MA, Certificate); police leadership (MA); public policy and leadership (MA, Certificate). Part-time and evening/weekend programs available. *Faculty:* 8 full-time (3 women), 15 part-time/adjunct (7 women). *Students:* 36 full-time (29 women), 307 part-time (149 women); includes 44 minority (29 African Americans, 1 American Indian/Alaska Native, 11 Asian Americans or Pacific Islanders, 3 Hispanic Americans), 5 international. Average age 36. 398 applicants, 75% accepted, 267 enrolled. In 2009, 63 master's, 17 doctorates, 46 other advanced degrees awarded. Terminal master's awarded for partial completion of doctoral program. *Degree requirements:* For master's, thesis (for some programs); for doctorate, thesis/dissertation; for other advanced degree, thesis or alternative. *Entrance requirements:* For master's, minimum GPA of 3.0 or MAT; for doctorate, MAT, minimum graduate GPA of 3.5; for other advanced degree, minimum graduate GPA of 3.25 or MAT. Additional exam requirements/recommendations for international students: Required—TOEFL (minimum score 550 paper-based; 213 computer-based; 20 iBT). *Application deadline:* For fall admission, 6/1 priority date for domestic students; for spring admission, 11/1 priority date for domestic students. Applications are processed on a rolling basis. Application fee: $50. *Expenses:* Contact institution. *Financial support:* Fellowships, research assistantships, institutionally sponsored loans and scholarships/grants available. Support available to part-time students. Financial award applicants required to submit FAFSA. *Unit head:* Dr. Donald R. LaMagdeleine, Chair, 651-962-4893, Fax: 651-962-4169, E-mail: drlamagdelei@stthomas.edu. *Application contact:* Jackie Grossklaus, Department Assistant, 651-962-4885, Fax: 651-962-4169, E-mail: jmgrossklaus@stthomas.edu.

University of South Carolina, The Graduate School, College of Education, Department of Educational Leadership and Policies, Program in Higher Education and Student Affairs, Columbia, SC 29208. Offers M Ed. *Accreditation:* NCATE. Part-time programs available. *Degree requirements:* For master's, comprehensive exam, thesis (for some programs). *Entrance requirements:* For master's, GRE General Test or MAT, letters of reference. Electronic applications accepted. *Faculty research:* Minorities in higher education, community college transfer problem, federal role in educational research.

University of Southern California, Graduate School, Rossier School of Education, Master's Programs in Education, Los Angeles, CA 90089-4038. Offers marriage, family and child counseling (MMFT); postsecondary administration and student affairs [PASA] (ME); school counseling (ME); teaching (MA); teaching and teaching credential (MAT); teaching English to speakers of other languages (MAT, MS). Part-time and evening/weekend programs available. Postbaccalaureate distance learning degree programs offered (no on-campus study). *Faculty:* 26 full-time (17 women), 24 part-time/adjunct (14 women). *Students:* 579 full-time (455 women), 85 part-time (56 women); includes 302 minority (50 African Americans, 4 American Indian/Alaska Native, 110 Asian Americans or Pacific Islanders, 138 Hispanic Americans), 62 international. 1,282 applicants, 67% accepted, 484 enrolled. In 2009, 228 master's awarded. *Degree requirements:* For master's, thesis optional. *Entrance requirements:* For master's, GRE (for all programs except MAT). Additional exam requirements/recommendations for international students: Required—TOEFL (minimum score 250 computer-based; 100 iBT). Application fee: $85. Electronic applications accepted. *Expenses:* Tuition: Full-time $25,980; part-time $1315 per unit. Required fees: $554. One-time fee: $35 full-time. Full-time tuition and fees vary according to degree level and program. *Financial support:* Career-related internships or fieldwork, Federal Work-Study, scholarships/grants, traineeships, and unspecified assistantships available. Support available to part-time students. Financial award application deadline: 4/10; financial award applicants required to submit FAFSA. *Faculty research:* College access and equity; preparing teachers for culturally diverse populations; sociocultural basis of learning as mediated by instruction with focus on reading and literacy in English learners; social and political aspects of teaching and learning English; school counselor development and training. *Unit head:* Dr. Kristan Venegas, Director/Assistant Professor of Clinical Education, 213-740-3255, E-mail: rsoemast@usc.edu. *Application contact:* Michael Jackson, 213-740-0224, E-mail: soeinfo@usc.edu.

University of Southern Mississippi, Graduate School, College of Education and Psychology, Department of Educational Studies and Research, Hattiesburg, MS 39406-0001. Offers adult education (Graduate Certificate); community college leadership (Graduate Certificate); counseling and personnel services (college) (M Ed); education (PhD, Ed S), including adult education, research, evaluation and statistics (PhD); education (Ed D), including educational administration, educational research; education: educational leadership and research (Ed S), including higher education administration; educational administration and supervision (M Ed); higher education administration (Ed D, PhD); institutional research (Graduate Certificate). *Faculty:* 7 full-time (1 woman), 5 part-time/adjunct (1 woman). *Students:* 45 full-time (34 women), 97 part-time (66 women); includes 42 minority (40 African Americans, 1 American Indian/Alaska Native, 1 Hispanic American), 2 international. Average age 36. 54 applicants, 67% accepted, 33 enrolled. In 2009, 26 master's, 11 doctorates, 3 other advanced degrees awarded. *Degree requirements:* For master's and other advanced degree, comprehensive exam, thesis (for some programs); for doctorate, comprehensive exam, thesis/dissertation. *Entrance requirements:* For master's, doctorate, and other advanced degree, GRE General Test, minimum GPA of 2.75. Additional exam requirements/recommendations for international students: Required—TOEFL. *Application deadline:* For fall admission, 2/1 for domestic students, 3/1 for international students. Applications are processed on a rolling basis. Application fee: $35. *Expenses:* Tuition, state resident: full-time $5096; part-time $284 per hour. Tuition, nonresident: full-time $13,052; part-time $726 per hour. Required fees: $402. Tuition and fees vary according to course level and course load. *Financial support:* Career-related internships or fieldwork, Federal Work-Study, and institutionally sponsored loans available. Financial award application deadline: 3/15; financial award applicants required to submit FAFSA. Total annual research expenditures: $88,500. *Unit head:* Dr. Thomas V. O'Brien, Chair, 601-266-6093, E-mail: thomas.obrien@usm.edu. *Application contact:* Shonna Breland, Manager of Graduate Admissions, 601-266-6563, Fax: 601-266-5138.

University of South Florida, Graduate School, College of Education–Main Campus, Department of Psychological and Social Foundations of Education, Tampa, FL 33620-9951. Offers college student affairs (M Ed); counselor education (MA, PhD, Ed S); interdisciplinary (PhD, Ed S); school psychology (PhD, Ed S). Part-time and evening/weekend programs available. *Faculty:* 22 full-time (13 women), 6 part-time/adjunct (4 women). *Students:* 154 full-time (123 women), 88 part-time (69 women); includes 62 minority (28 African Americans, 8 Asian Americans or Pacific Islanders, 26 Hispanic Americans), 7 international. Average age 30. 260 applicants, 43% accepted, 97 enrolled. In 2009, 41 master's, 7 doctorates, 5 other advanced degrees awarded. *Degree requirements:* For master's, comprehensive exam, thesis (for some programs); for doctorate, comprehensive exam, thesis/dissertation. *Entrance requirements:* For master's, GRE General Test, minimum GPA of 3.5 in last 60 hours of course work; for doctorate, GRE General Test, MAT, minimum GPA of 3.5 in last 60 hours of course work; for Ed S, GRE General Test. Additional exam requirements/recommendations for international students: Required—TOEFL (minimum score 550 paper-based; 213 computer-based; 79 iBT). *Application deadline:* For fall admission, 1/1 for domestic and international students. Application fee: $30. Electronic applications accepted. *Financial support:* In 2009–10, 47 students received support, including 6 fellowships with full tuition reimbursements available (averaging $10,000 per year), 21 teaching assistantships with full tuition reimbursements available (averaging $10,200 per year); career-related internships or fieldwork, scholarships/grants, and unspecified assistantships also available. Financial award application deadline: 1/1; financial award applicants required to submit CSS PROFILE. *Faculty research:* College student affairs, counselor education, educational psychology, school psychology, social foundations. Total annual research expenditures: $4.2 million. *Unit head:* Dr. Herbert Exum, Chairperson, 813-974-8395, Fax: 813-974-5814, E-mail: exum@tempest.coedu.usf.edu. *Application contact:* Dr. Kathy Bradley, Program Director, School Psychology, 813-974-9486, Fax: 813-974-5814, E-mail: kbradley@usf.edu.

The University of Tennessee, Graduate School, College of Education, Health and Human Sciences, Department of Educational Psychology and Counseling, Program in College Student Personnel, Knoxville, TN 37996. Offers MS. *Accreditation:* NCATE. Part-time programs available. *Degree requirements:* For master's, thesis optional. *Entrance requirements:* For master's, GRE General Test, minimum GPA of 2.7. Additional exam requirements/recommendations for international students: Required—TOEFL. Electronic applications accepted. *Expenses:* Tuition, state resident: full-time $6826; part-time $380 per semester hour. Tuition, nonresident: full-time $21,844; part-time $1147 per semester hour. Tuition and fees vary according to program.

University of Virginia, Curry School of Education, Department of Leadership, Foundations and Policy, Program in Higher Education, Charlottesville, VA 22903. Offers higher education (Ed S); student affairs practice (M Ed). *Students:* 7 full-time (6 women), 8 part-time (5 women). Average age 35. 2 applicants, 50% accepted, 1 enrolled. In 2009, 15 master's, 5 doctorates awarded. *Entrance requirements:* For master's, doctorate, and Ed S, GRE General Test, 2 letters of recommendation. Additional exam requirements/recommendations for international students: Required—TOEFL (minimum score 600 paper-based; 250 computer-based; 90 iBT), IELTS (minimum score 7). *Application deadline:* Applications are processed on a rolling basis. Application fee: $60. Electronic applications accepted. *Financial support:* Fellowships, research assistantships, teaching assistantships available. Financial award applicants required to submit FAFSA. *Unit head:* Brian Pusser, Associate Professor and Director, 434-924-7782, E-mail: highered@virginia.edu. *Application contact:* Brian Pusser, Associate Professor and Director, 434-924-7782, E-mail: highered@virginia.edu.

University of West Florida, College of Professional Studies, Department of Professional and Community Leadership, Program in College Student Personnel Administration, Pensacola, FL 32514-5750. Offers college personnel administration (M Ed); guidance and counseling (M Ed). Part-time and evening/weekend programs available. *Students:* 16 full-time (10 women), 29 part-time (25 women); includes 11 minority (8 African Americans, 3 Hispanic Americans). Average age 29. 13 applicants, 92% accepted, 11 enrolled. In 2009, 8 master's awarded. *Degree requirements:* For master's, internship. *Entrance requirements:* For master's, GRE General Test, minimum GPA of 3.0. Additional exam requirements/recommendations for international students: Required—TOEFL (minimum score 550 paper-based; 213 computer-based). *Application deadline:* For fall admission, 6/1 for domestic students, 5/15 for international students; for spring admission, 11/1 for domestic students, 10/1 for international students. Application fee: $30. *Expenses:* Tuition, state resident: full-time $4982; part-time $260 per credit hour. Tuition, nonresident: full-time $20,059; part-time $919 per credit hour. Required fees: $1247; $52 per credit hour. *Financial support:* Application deadline: 4/15. *Unit head:* Dr. Thomas J. Kramer, Chairperson, 850-474-2949, Fax: 850-857-6288. *Application contact:* Terry McCray, Assistant Director of Graduate Admissions, 850-473-7718, Fax: 850-473-7714, E-mail: gradadmissions@uwf.edu.

University of Wisconsin–La Crosse, Office of University Graduate Studies, College of Liberal Studies, Department of Educational Studies, La Crosse, WI 54601-3742. Offers college student development and administration (MS Ed); professional development (MEPD), including elementary education, K–12, professional development, secondary education; special education (MS Ed), including emotional disturbance, learning disabilities. Part-time programs available. *Faculty:* 27 full-time (19 women), 18 part-time/adjunct (13 women). *Students:* 17 full-time (11 women), 350 part-time (280 women); includes 8 minority (3 Asian Americans or Pacific Islanders, 5 Hispanic Americans), 6 international. Average age 33. 136 applicants, 89% accepted, 78 enrolled. In 2009, 247 master's awarded. *Degree requirements:* For master's, thesis optional. *Entrance requirements:* For master's, minimum GPA of 2.85. Additional exam requirements/recommendations for international students: Required—TOEFL (minimum score 550 paper-based; 213 computer-based; 79 iBT). *Application deadline:* Applications are processed on a rolling basis. Application fee: $56. Electronic applications accepted. *Financial support:* In 2009–10, 4 research assistantships with partial tuition reimbursements (averaging $6,648 per year) were awarded; career-related internships or fieldwork, Federal Work-Study, institutionally sponsored loans, health care benefits, unspecified assistantships, and grant-funded positions also available. Support available to part-time students. Financial award application deadline: 3/15; financial award applicants required to submit FAFSA. *Unit head:* Dr. Dan Duquette, Acting Chair, 608-785-8132, E-mail: duquette.rode@uwlax.edu. *Application contact:* Kathryn Kiefer, Director of Admissions, 608-785-8939, E-mail: admissions@uwlax.edu.

University of Wisconsin–La Crosse, Office of University Graduate Studies, College of Liberal Studies, Department of Psychology, Program in Student Affairs Administration, La Crosse, WI 54601-3742. Offers MS Ed. Part-time programs available. Postbaccalaureate distance learning degree programs offered (no on-campus study). *Students:* 32 full-time (25 women), 38 part-time (30 women); includes 8 minority (1 African American, 1 American Indian/Alaska Native, 3 Asian Americans or Pacific Islanders, 3 Hispanic Americans), 1

Student Affairs

University of Wisconsin–La Crosse *(continued)*
international. Average age 28. 100 applicants, 42% accepted, 36 enrolled. In 2009, 26 master's awarded. *Degree requirements:* For master's, comprehensive exam (for some programs), thesis optional. *Entrance requirements:* For master's, interview, writing sample, references, experience in the field. Additional exam requirements/recommendations for international students: Required—TOEFL (minimum score 550 paper-based; 213 computer-based; 79 iBT). *Application deadline:* For fall admission, 2/1 priority date for domestic students. Application fee: $56. Electronic applications accepted. *Financial support:* Research assistantships with tuition reimbursements, career-related internships or fieldwork, Federal Work-Study, health care benefits, and unspecified assistantships available. Support available to part-time students. Financial award application deadline: 3/15; financial award applicants required to submit FAFSA. *Unit head:* Dr. Jodie Rindt, Director, 608-785-6450, E-mail: rindt.jodi@uwlax.edu. *Application contact:* Kathryn Kiefer, Director of Admissions, 608-785-8939, E-mail: admissions@uwlax.edu.

University of Wyoming, College of Education, Department of Counselor Education, Laramie, WY 82070. Offers community mental health (MS); counselor education and supervision (PhD); school counseling (MS); student affairs (MS). *Accreditation:* ACA (one or more programs are accredited). *Degree requirements:* For master's, comprehensive exam (for some programs), thesis optional; for doctorate, thesis/dissertation, video demonstration. *Entrance requirements:* For master's, interview, background check; for doctorate, video tape session, interview, writing sample, master's degree, background check. Additional exam requirements/recommendations for international students: Required—TOEFL. *Faculty research:* Wyoming SAGE photovoice project; accountable school counseling programs; GLBT issues; addictions; play therapy-early childhood mental health.

Washington State University, Graduate School, College of Education, Department of Educational Leadership and Counseling Psychology, Pullman, WA 99164. Offers counseling psychology (Ed M, MA, PhD, Certificate), including counseling psychology (Ed M, MA, PhD), school psychologist (Certificate); educational leadership (M Ed, MA, Ed D, PhD); educational psychology (Ed M, MA, PhD); higher education (Ed M, MA, Ed D, PhD), including higher education administration (PhD), sport management (PhD), student affairs (PhD); higher education with sport management (Ed M). *Accreditation:* NCATE. Terminal master's awarded for partial completion of doctoral program. *Degree requirements:* For master's, comprehensive exam (for some programs), thesis (for some programs), oral exam or written exam; for doctorate, comprehensive exam, thesis/dissertation, oral and written exams. *Entrance requirements:* For

master's and doctorate, GRE General Test, minimum GPA of 3.0, 3 letters of recommendation. Additional exam requirements/recommendations for international students: Required—TOEFL (minimum score 550 paper-based; 213 computer-based). *Faculty research:* Attentional processes, cross cultural psychology, faculty development in higher education.

Western Illinois University, School of Graduate Studies, College of Education and Human Services, Department of Educational and Interdisciplinary Studies, Program in College Student Personnel, Macomb, IL 61455-1390. Offers MS. *Accreditation:* NCATE. Part-time programs available. *Students:* 42 full-time (28 women); includes 3 minority (all African Americans). Average age 24. 68 applicants, 32% accepted. In 2009, 23 master's awarded. *Degree requirements:* For master's, thesis or alternative. *Entrance requirements:* For master's, interview. Additional exam requirements/recommendations for international students: Required—TOEFL (minimum score 550 paper-based; 213 computer-based; 80 iBT). *Application deadline:* For fall admission, 2/1 priority date for domestic students. Applications are processed on a rolling basis. Application fee: $30. Electronic applications accepted. *Expenses:* Tuition, state resident: full-time $4486; part-time $249.21 per credit hour. Tuition, nonresident: full-time $8972; part-time $498.42 per credit hour. Required fees: $72.62 per credit hour. *Financial support:* In 2009–10, 42 students received support, including 42 research assistantships with full tuition reimbursements available (averaging $7,280 per year). Financial award applicants required to submit FAFSA. *Unit head:* Dr. Tracy Davis, Coordinator, 309-298-1183. *Application contact:* Evelyn Hoing, Assistant Director of Graduate Studies, 309-298-1806, Fax: 309-298-2345, E-mail: grad-office@wiu.edu.

Western Kentucky University, Graduate Studies, College of Education and Behavioral Sciences, Department of Counseling and Student Affairs, Bowling Green, KY 42101. Offers business and marketing education (MA Ed); counseling (MA Ed); counselor education (Ed S); education and behavioral science (MA Ed); elementary education (MA Ed, Ed S); middle years education (MA Ed); secondary education (MA Ed, Ed S); student affairs (MA Ed). *Accreditation:* ACA; NCATE. Part-time and evening/weekend programs available. *Degree requirements:* For master's, comprehensive exam, thesis optional. *Entrance requirements:* For master's, GRE General Test. Additional exam requirements/recommendations for international students: Required—TOEFL (minimum score 555 paper-based; 213 computer-based; 79 iBT). *Expenses:* Tuition, state resident: full-time $4160; part-time $416 per credit hour. Tuition, nonresident: full-time $9550; part-time $506 per credit hour. Tuition and fees vary according to campus/location and reciprocity agreements. *Faculty research:* Counselor education, research for residential workers.

ARGOSY UNIVERSITY

ARGOSY UNIVERSITY, ATLANTA

College of Education

Programs of Study	Argosy University, Atlanta, offers the Master of Arts in Education (M.A.Ed.) degree in educational leadership and instructional leadership; the Education Specialist (Ed.S.) degree in educational leadership and instructional leadership; and the Doctor of Education (Ed.D.) degrees in educational leadership or instructional leadership.
	The M.A.Ed. in educational leadership program is designed to instill key philosophies, theories, and values that impact education. It prepares students to improve policies and practices within organizations through the motivation and supervision of others. Students develop skills needed to design, implement, and evaluate educational programs and curricula. Courses include educational law, educational finance, organizational communication, human resource management, instruction supervision, and organizational management.
	The M.A.Ed. in instructional leadership program examines the challenges and problems encountered in today's educational environment. Course work encompasses the historical, philosophical, psychological, social, technical, and theoretical aspects of education. Students develop skills in analysis, oral and written communication, problem solving, critical thinking, team building, and computer technology. The program is designed for those who wish to develop or enhance classroom skills, become curriculum supervisors, or become educational leaders with a focus on instruction.
	The Ed.S. in educational leadership program concentrates on applied organizational theory within the context of educational organizations. This specialized program develops the competencies required to secure educational administrator positions at the elementary or secondary school level.
	The Ed.S. in instructional leadership program enables experienced teachers to become more effective practitioners and educational leaders with a focus on instruction. Course work is designed to satisfy the requirements of students seeking career advancement and those who are working toward a doctoral degree.
	The Ed.D. in educational leadership program is designed to enhance educational leadership strengths. Students learn innovative and collaborative techniques used to manage and govern educational institutions. The program prepares students for leadership positions at the district, regional, state, or national level. Students must choose a concentration in higher education administration or K–12 education.
	The Ed.D. in instructional leadership program draws upon educational theories and practices to help students discover new learning techniques for diverse audiences. Students enrolled in this program master teaching methodologies, hone classroom skills, and gain the knowledge required to become curriculum administrators or educational leaders with a focus on instruction. Students must choose a concentration in higher education or K–12 education.
	Note: These programs do not lead to teacher or administrator certification, licensure, or endorsement in any state in the United States.
Research Facilities	Argosy University libraries provide curriculum support and educational resources, including current text materials, diagnostic training documents, reference materials and databases, journals and dissertations, and major and current titles in program areas. There is an online public-access catalog of library resources available throughout the Argosy University system. Students have remote access to the campus library database, enabling them to study and conduct research at home. Academic databases offer dissertation abstracts, academic journals, and professional periodicals. All library computers are Internet accessible. Software applications include Word, Excel, PowerPoint, SPSS, and various test-scoring programs.
Financial Aid	Financial aid is available to those who qualify. Argosy University, Atlanta, offers access to federal and state aid programs, merit-based awards, grants, loans, and a work-study program. As a first step, students should complete the Free Application for Federal Student Aid (FAFSA). Prospective students can apply electronically at http://www.fafsa.ed.gov or at the campus.
Cost of Study	Tuition varies by program. Students should contact Argosy University, Atlanta, for tuition information.
Living and Housing Costs	Students typically live in apartments in the metropolitan Atlanta area. Living expenses vary according to each student's preferred standard of living, housing, and transportation. The University does not offer or operate student housing. Most of the students are full-time working professionals who live within driving distance of the campus. Several nearby hotels offer special rates for those who commute from long distances. The Admissions Department also maintains a list of housing options, including contact information for University students who wish to share housing. For more information, students should contact the Admissions Department.
Student Group	Admission to Argosy University, Atlanta, is selective to ensure a dynamic and engaged student body. It encourages diversity in academic and employment backgrounds and promotes integration of the student body into professional life through established connections with local and national professional associations. Argosy University offers a professionally oriented education with rich opportunities to gain practical experience in class, field placements, and internships. Full-time students and working professionals gain the extensive knowledge and range of skills necessary for effective performance in their chosen fields.
Student Outcomes	Students can register with the University's online career-services system and use select services from a distance, such as degree-specific career e-mail lists, national job posts, and virtual job fairs. Students should contact the University for more information.
Location	Argosy University, Atlanta, is housed in a modern building in Sandy Springs, a northern suburb of Atlanta. The campus features a cafe and outdoor lakeside terrace. Beyond the University, students find a wide selection of affordable housing options. This major metropolitan area offers many social and recreational opportunities, from clubs and concerts to galleries and museums, from a growing restaurant scene to Braves baseball games and rollerblading in Piedmont Park.
	Many educational institutions and agencies in the area provide varied opportunities for student training. Atlanta's business environment includes technology companies such as EarthLink and Macquarium, as well as corporate giants such as the Coca-Cola Company, CNN, Delta Air Lines, AT&T, and Georgia Pacific.
The University	Argosy University is a private institution with nineteen locations across the nation. Argosy University, Atlanta, provides students with a career resources office, an academic resources center, and extensive information access for research. It offers the resources of a large university, plus the friendliness and personal attention of a small campus. Argosy University, Atlanta, is closely associated with the Franklin, Tennessee, campus, an approved degree site near Nashville.
	The innovative programs feature dynamic, relevant, and practical curricula delivered in flexible class formats. Students enjoy scheduling options that make it easier to fit school into their busy lives, choosing from day and evening courses, on campus or online. Many students find a combination of class formats to be an ideal way of continuing their education while meeting family and professional demands.
	Argosy University is accredited by the Higher Learning Commission and a member of the North Central Association (30 North LaSalle Street, Suite 2400, Chicago, Illinois 60602; 800-621-7440 (toll-free); http://www.ncahlc.org).
Applying	Argosy University, Atlanta, accepts students year-round on a rolling admissions basis, depending on availability of required courses. Applications for admission are available online or by contacting the campus.
Correspondence and Information	Argosy University, Atlanta 990 Hammond Drive, Suite 100 Atlanta, Georgia 30328 Phone: 770-671-1200 888-671-4777 (toll-free) Fax: 770-671-0476 E-mail: auadmissions@argosy.edu Web site: http://www.argosy.edu/atlanta

Argosy University, Atlanta

THE FACULTY

The Argosy University faculty comprises working professionals who are eager to help students succeed. Members bring real-world experience and the latest practice innovations to the academic setting. The diverse faculty members of the College of Education are widely recognized for contributions to the field. Many are published scholars, and most hold doctoral degrees. They provide a substantive education that combines comprehensive knowledge with critical skills and practical workplace relevance. Above all, faculty members are committed to their students' personal and professional development.

ARGOSY UNIVERSITY

ARGOSY UNIVERSITY, INLAND EMPIRE

College of Education

Programs of Study
Argosy University, Inland Empire, offers the Master of Arts in Education (M.A.Ed.) degree in educational leadership, instructional leadership, instructional specialist in English language learners/English second language (ELL/ESL), instructional specialist in reading (elementary), and instructional specialist in reading (middle/secondary); and the Doctor of Education (Ed.D.) degree in community college executive leadership, educational leadership, and instructional leadership.

The M.A.Ed. in educational leadership program is designed to instill key philosophies, theories, and values that impact education. It prepares students to improve policies and practices within organizations through the motivation and supervision of others. Students develop skills needed to design, implement, and evaluate educational programs and curricula. Courses include educational law, educational finance, organizational communication, human resource management, instruction supervision, and organizational management.

The M.A.Ed. in instructional leadership program examines the challenges and problems encountered in today's educational environment. Course work encompasses the historical, philosophical, psychological, social, technical, and theoretical aspects of education. Students develop skills in analysis, oral and written communication, problem solving, critical thinking, team building, and computer technology. The program is designed for those who wish to develop or enhance classroom skills, become curriculum supervisors, or become educational leaders with a focus on instruction. Students may choose optional concentrations in single- or multiple-subject teacher credential preparation.

The M.A.Ed. instructional specialist in ELL/ESL program prepares teachers to work with ELL/ESL students. Upon completion of the program, teachers are equipped to effectively support the learning of such students.

The M.A.Ed. instructional specialist in reading (elementary) program prepares teachers to work with beginning and developing readers. As a result of this program, teachers are prepared to integrate reading across the curriculum and increase students' vocabulary and reading fluency.

The M.A.Ed. instructional specialist in reading (middle/secondary) program prepares teachers to work with beginning and developing readers. As a result of this program, teachers are prepared to integrate reading across the curriculum and increase students' vocabulary and reading fluency.

The Ed.D. in community college executive leadership program offers an accelerated course of study intended to meet the needs of community college administrators who are looking to move into senior administrative positions (such as president, vice president, dean, and director) in community colleges.

The Ed.D. in educational leadership program is designed to enhance educational leadership strengths. Students learn innovative and collaborative techniques used to manage and govern educational institutions. The program prepares students for administrative leadership positions at the district, regional, state, or national level. Students must choose a concentration in higher education administration or K–12 education.

The Ed.D. in instructional leadership program draws upon educational theories and practices to help students discover new learning techniques for diverse audiences. Students enrolled in this program master teaching methodologies, hone classroom skills, and gain the knowledge required to become curriculum administrators or educational leaders with a focus on instruction. Students must choose a concentration in higher education or K–12 education.

Note: The M.A.Ed. in instructional leadership (multiple subject teacher credential prep) and the M.A.Ed. in instructional leadership (single subject teacher credential prep) programs can lead to multiple subject teaching credential or single subject teaching credential depending on the program concentration selected. All other programs offered through the College of Education do not lead to teacher or administrator certification, licensure, or endorsement in any state in the United States. The programs offered through Argosy University online programs do not lead to teacher or administrator certification, licensure, or endorsement in any state in the United States regardless of the state in which the student resides.

Research Facilities
Argosy University libraries provide curriculum support and educational resources, including current text materials, diagnostic training documents, reference materials and databases, journals and dissertations, and major and current titles in program areas. There is an online public-access catalog of library resources available throughout the Argosy University system. Students have remote access to the campus library database, enabling them to study and conduct research at home. Academic databases offer dissertation abstracts, academic journals, and professional periodicals. All library computers are Internet accessible. Software applications include Word, Excel, PowerPoint, SPSS, and various test-scoring programs.

Financial Aid
Financial aid is available to those who qualify. Argosy University, Inland Empire, offers access to federal and state aid programs, merit-based awards, grants, loans, and a work-study program. As a first step, students should complete the Free Application for Federal Student Aid (FAFSA). Prospective students can apply electronically at http://www.fafsa.ed.gov or at the campus.

Cost of Study
Tuition varies by program. Students should contact Argosy University, Inland Empire, for tuition information.

Living and Housing Costs
Students typically live in apartments in the metropolitan area. Living expenses vary according to each student's preferred standard of living, housing, and transportation. The University does not offer or operate student housing. Most of the students are full-time working professionals who live within driving distance of the campus. Several nearby hotels offer special rates for those who commute from long distances. The Admissions Department also maintains a list of housing options, including contact information for University students who wish to share housing. For more information, students should contact the Admissions Department.

Student Group
Admission to Argosy University, Inland Empire, is selective to ensure a dynamic and engaged student body. It encourages diversity in academic and employment backgrounds and promotes integration of the student body into professional life through established connections with local and national professional associations. Argosy University offers a professionally oriented education with rich opportunities to gain practical experience in class, field placements, and internships. Full-time students and working professionals gain the extensive knowledge and range of skills necessary for effective performance in their chosen fields.

Student Outcomes
Students can register with the University's online career-services system and use select services from a distance, such as degree-specific career e-mail lists, national job posts, and virtual job fairs. Students should contact the University for more information.

Location
Argosy University, Inland Empire, is located in the Hospitality Lane section of San Bernardino, California. The facility features classrooms, computer labs, a resource center with Internet access, a student lounge, staff and faculty offices, and proximity to the region's many cultural and recreational attractions. Argosy University provides a supportive educational environment with convenient class options that enable students to earn a degree while fulfilling other life responsibilities. All of the programs are thoroughly oriented to the real working world. The University focuses on developing technical proficiency in each student's field, as well as an overall professional career approach. Many educational institutions and agencies in the area provide varied opportunities for student training.

The University
Argosy University is a private institution with nineteen locations across the nation. Argosy University, Inland Empire, provides students with a career resources office, an academic resources center, and extensive information access for research. It offers the resources of a large university, plus the friendliness and personal attention of a small campus.

The innovative programs feature dynamic, relevant, and practical curricula delivered in flexible class formats. Students enjoy scheduling options that make it easier to fit school into their busy lives, choosing from day and evening courses, on campus or online. Many students find a combination of class formats to be an ideal way of continuing their education while meeting family and professional demands.

Argosy University is accredited by the Higher Learning Commission and a member of the North Central Association (30 North LaSalle Street, Suite 2400, Chicago, Illinois 60602; 800-621-7440 (toll-free); http://www.ncahlc.org).

Applying
Argosy University, Inland Empire, accepts students year-round on a rolling admissions basis, depending on availability of required courses. Applications for admission are available online or by contacting the campus.

Correspondence and Information
Argosy University, Inland Empire
636 East Brier Drive, Suite 120
San Bernardino, California 92408

Phone: 909-915-3800
      866-217-9075 (toll-free)
Fax: 909-915-3810
E-mail: auadmissions@argosy.edu
Web site: http://www.argosy.edu/inlandempire

Argosy University, Inland Empire

THE FACULTY

The Argosy University faculty comprises working professionals who are eager to help students succeed. Members bring real-world experience and the latest practice innovations to the academic setting. The diverse faculty members of the College of Education are widely recognized for contributions to the field. Most hold doctoral degrees. They provide a substantive education that combines comprehensive knowledge with critical skills and practical workplace relevance. Above all, faculty members are committed to their students' personal and professional development.

ARGOSY UNIVERSITY

ARGOSY UNIVERSITY, NASHVILLE

College of Education

Programs of Study	Argosy University, Nashville, offers the Master of Arts in Education (M.A.Ed.) degree in educational leadership and instructional leadership; the Education Specialist (Ed.S.) degree in educational leadership and instructional leadership; and the Doctor of Education (Ed.D.) degree in educational leadership and instructional leadership.
	The M.A.Ed. in educational leadership program is designed to instill key philosophies, theories, and values that impact education. It prepares students to improve policies and practices within organizations through the motivation and supervision of others. Students develop skills needed to design, implement, and evaluate educational programs and curricula. Courses include educational law, educational finance, organizational communication, human resource management, instruction supervision, and organizational management.
	The M.A.Ed. in instructional leadership program examines the challenges and problems encountered in today's educational environment. Course work encompasses the historical, philosophical, psychological, social, technical, and theoretical aspects of education. Students develop skills in analysis, oral and written communication, problem solving, critical thinking, team building, and computer technology. The program is designed for those who wish to develop or enhance classroom skills, become curriculum supervisors, or become educational leaders with a focus on instruction.
	The Ed.S. in educational leadership program concentrates on applied organizational theory within the context of educational organizations. This specialized program develops the competencies required to secure educational administrator positions at the elementary or secondary school level.
	The Ed.S. in instructional leadership program enables experienced teachers to become more effective practitioners and educational leaders with a focus on instruction. Course work is designed to satisfy the requirements of students seeking career advancement and those who are working toward a doctoral degree.
	The Ed.D. in educational leadership program is designed to enhance educational leadership strengths. Students learn innovative and collaborative techniques used to manage and govern educational institutions. The program prepares students for administrative leadership positions at the district, regional, state, or national level. Students must choose a concentration in higher education administration or K–12 education.
	The Ed.D. in instructional leadership program draws upon educational theories and practices to help students discover new learning techniques for diverse audiences. Students enrolled in this program master teaching methodologies, hone classroom skills, and gain the knowledge required to become curriculum administrators or educational leaders with a focus on instruction. Students must choose a concentration in higher education administration or K–12 education.
	Note: These programs do not lead to teacher or administrator certification, licensure, or endorsement in any state in the United States.
Research Facilities	Argosy University libraries provide curriculum support and educational resources, including current text materials, diagnostic training documents, reference materials and databases, journals and dissertations, and major and current titles in program areas. There is an online public-access catalog of library resources available throughout the Argosy University system. Students have remote access to the campus library database, enabling them to study and conduct research at home. Academic databases offer dissertation abstracts, academic journals, and professional periodicals. All library computers are Internet accessible. Software applications include Word, Excel, PowerPoint, SPSS, and various test-scoring programs.
Financial Aid	Financial aid is available to those who qualify. Argosy University, Nashville, offers access to federal and state aid programs, merit-based awards, grants, loans, and a work-study program. As a first step, students should complete the Free Application for Federal Student Aid (FAFSA). Prospective students can apply electronically at http://www.fafsa.ed.gov or at the campus.
Cost of Study	Tuition varies by program. Students should contact Argosy University, Nashville, for tuition information.
Living and Housing Costs	Students typically live in apartments in the metropolitan Nashville area. Living expenses vary according to each student's preferred standard of living, housing, and transportation. The University does not offer or operate student housing. Most of the students are full-time working professionals who live within driving distance of the campus. Several nearby hotels offer special rates for those who commute from long distances. The Admissions Department also maintains a list of housing options, including contact information, for University students who wish to share housing. For more information, students should contact the Admissions Department.
Student Group	Admission to Argosy University, Nashville, is selective to ensure a dynamic and engaged student body. It encourages diversity in academic and employment backgrounds and promotes integration of the student body into professional life through established connections with local and national professional associations. Argosy University offers a professionally oriented education with rich opportunities to gain practical experience in class, field placements, and internships. Full-time students and working professionals gain the extensive knowledge and range of skills necessary for effective performance in their chosen fields.
Student Outcomes	Students can register with the University's online career-services system and use select services from a distance, such as degree-specific career e-mail lists, national job posts, and virtual job fairs. Students should contact the University for more information.
Location	Argosy University, Nashville, is located at 100 Centerview Drive in Nashville, Tennessee. This growing city offers a variety of recreational activities, including the ballet and symphony, the newly established Frist Museum of Art, and professional sports. Nashville is known as Music City, USA, and is home to the Country Music Hall of Fame. Many educational institutions and agencies in the area provide varied opportunities for student training. The business environment includes companies such as Moses Cone Health Systems, Inc., and Novant Health, Inc.
The University	Argosy University is a private institution with nineteen locations across the nation. Argosy University, Nashville, provides students with a career resources office, an academic resources center, and extensive information access for research. It offers the resources of a large university, plus the friendliness and personal attention of a small campus. The innovative programs feature dynamic, relevant, and practical curricula delivered in flexible class formats. Students enjoy scheduling options that make it easier to fit school into their busy lives, choosing from day and evening courses, on campus or online. Many students find a combination of class formats to be an ideal way of continuing their education while meeting family and professional demands.
	Argosy University is accredited by the Higher Learning Commission and a member of the North Central Association (30 North LaSalle Street, Suite 2400, Chicago, Illinois 60602; 800-621-7440 (toll-free); http://www.ncahlc.org).
Applying	Argosy University, Nashville, accepts students year-round on a rolling admissions basis, depending on availability of required courses. Applications for admission are available online or by contacting the campus.
Correspondence and Information	Argosy University, Nashville 100 Centerview Drive, Suite 225 Nashville, Tennessee 37214 Phone: 615-525-2800 866-833-6598 (toll-free) Fax: 615-525-2900 E-mail: auadmissions@argosy.edu Web site: http://www.argosy.edu/nashville

Argosy University, Nashville

THE FACULTY

The Argosy University faculty comprises working professionals who are eager to help students succeed. Members bring real-world experience and the latest practice innovations to the academic setting. The diverse faculty members of the College of Education are widely recognized for contributions to the field. Most hold doctoral degrees. They provide a substantive education that combines comprehensive knowledge with critical skills and practical workplace relevance. Above all, faculty members are committed to their students' personal and professional development.

Section 24
Instructional Levels

This section contains a directory of institutions offering graduate work in instructional levels. Additional information about programs listed in the directory may be obtained by writing directly to the dean of a graduate school or chair of a department at the address given in the directory.

For programs offering related work, see also in this book *Administration, Instruction, and Theory; Education; Health-Related Professions; Leisure Studies and Recreation; Physical Education and Kinesiology; Special Focus;* and *Subject Areas.* In another guide in this series:

Graduate Programs in the Humanities, Arts & Social Sciences
See *Psychology and Counseling (School Psychology)*

CONTENTS

Program Directories

Adult Education

Alverno College, School of Education, Milwaukee, WI 53234-3922. Offers adaptive education (MA); administrative leadership (MA); adult education and organizational development (MA); adult educational and instructional design (MA); adult educational and instructional technology (MA); global connections in the humanities (MA); instructional leadership (MA); instructional technology for K-12 settings (MA); professional development (MA); reading education (MA); reading education with adaptive education (MA); science education (MA); teaching in alternative schools (MA). *Accreditation:* NCATE. Part-time and evening/weekend programs available. *Faculty:* 10 full-time (all women), 17 part-time/adjunct (15 women). *Students:* 65 full-time (59 women), 82 part-time (75 women); includes 31 minority (24 African Americans, 1 American Indian/Alaska Native, 1 Asian American or Pacific Islander, 5 Hispanic Americans), 2 international. Average age 38. 113 applicants, 64% accepted, 61 enrolled. In 2009, 56 master's awarded. *Degree requirements:* For master's, presentation/defense of proposal, conference presentation of inquiry projects. *Entrance requirements:* For master's, bachelor's degree in related field, communication samples from work setting, 3 letters of recommendation. Additional exam requirements/recommendations for international students: Required—TOEFL. *Application deadline:* For fall admission, 7/15 priority date for domestic and international students; for spring admission, 12/15 priority date for domestic and international students. Applications are processed on a rolling basis. Application fee: $50. Electronic applications accepted. *Financial support:* In 2009–10, 92 students received support. Federal Work-Study available. Support available to part-time students. Financial award application deadline: 4/15; financial award applicants required to submit FAFSA. *Faculty research:* Student self-assessment, self-reflection, integration of curriculum, identifying needs of students in strategic situations and designing appropriate classroom strategies. *Unit head:* Dr. Mary Diez, Graduate Dean, 414-382-6214, Fax: 414-382-6332, E-mail: mary.diez@alverno.edu. *Application contact:* Angela Peterson-Adams, Graduate Recruiter, 414-382-6104, Fax: 414-382-6354, E-mail: angela.peterson-adams@alverno.edu.

Argosy University, Chicago, College of Education, Chicago, IL 60601. Offers adult education and training (MA Ed); community college executive leadership (Ed D); educational leadership (MA Ed, Ed D, Ed S), including district leadership (Ed D), higher education administration (Ed D), K-12 education (Ed D); instructional leadership (Ed D, Ed S), including higher education (Ed D), K-12 education (Ed D). Postbaccalaureate distance learning degree programs offered (minimal on-campus study).

See Close-Up on page 675.

Argosy University, Hawai'i, College of Education, Honolulu, HI 96813. Offers adult education and training (MAEd); educational leadership (Ed D), including higher education administration, K-12 education; instructional leadership (Ed D), including higher education, K-12 education; school psychology (MA).

See Close-Up on page 681.

Argosy University, Phoenix, College of Education, Phoenix, AZ 85021. Offers adult education and training (MA Ed); advanced educational administration (Ed D, Ed S); community college executive leadership (Ed D); educational administration (MA Ed); educational leadership (MA Ed, Ed D, Ed S), including education technology (Ed D), higher education administration (Ed D), K-12 education (Ed D); higher and postsecondary education (MA Ed); initial educational administration (Ed D, Ed S); school psychology (MA); teaching and learning (MA Ed, Ed D, Ed S), including education technology (Ed D), higher education (Ed D), K-12 education (Ed D).

See Close-Up on page 687.

Argosy University, Seattle, College of Education, Seattle, WA 98121. Offers adult education and training (MA Ed); community college executive leadership (Ed D); educational leadership (MA Ed, Ed D), including higher education administration (Ed D), K-12 education (Ed D); higher and postsecondary education (MA Ed); instructional leadership (MA Ed, Ed D), including education technology (Ed D), higher education (Ed D), K-12 education (Ed D).

See Close-Up on page 699.

Armstrong Atlantic State University, School of Graduate Studies, Program in Education, Savannah, GA 31419-1997. Offers adult education (M Ed); curriculum and instruction (M Ed); early childhood education (M Ed); education (M Ed); elementary education (M Ed); middle grades education (M Ed); secondary education (M Ed), including business education, English education, mathematics education, science education, social science education; special education (M Ed), including behavioral disorders, learning disabilities, speech-language pathology. *Accreditation:* NCATE. Part-time and evening/weekend programs available. Postbaccalaureate distance learning degree programs offered (minimal on-campus study). *Degree requirements:* For master's, comprehensive exam, portfolio. *Entrance requirements:* For master's, GRE General Test or MAT, minimum GPA of 2.5, letters of recommendation. Additional exam requirements/recommendations for international students: Required—TOEFL (minimum score 523 paper-based; 193 computer-based). Electronic applications accepted.

Athabasca University, Centre for Integrated Studies, Athabasca, AB T9S 3A3, Canada. Offers adult education (MA); community studies (MA); cultural studies (MA); educational studies (MA); global change (MA); work, organization, and leadership (MA). Part-time and evening/weekend programs available. Postbaccalaureate distance learning degree programs offered (no on-campus study). *Faculty:* 10 full-time (4 women), 12 part-time/adjunct (9 women). *Students:* 705 part-time. Average age 35. 195 applicants, 38 enrolled. In 2009, 52 master's awarded. *Degree requirements:* For master's, project. *Entrance requirements:* Additional exam requirements/recommendations for international students: Required—TOEFL (minimum score 560 paper-based; 220 computer-based). *Application deadline:* For fall admission, 3/1 for domestic and international students; for winter admission, 9/1 for domestic and international students. Application fee: $80. Electronic applications accepted. *Expenses:* Tuition: Part-time $16,500 per degree program. Required fees: $200 per year. One-time fee: $80 part-time. *Faculty research:* Women's history, literature and culture studies, sustainable development, labor and education. *Unit head:* Dr. Michael Gismondi, Program Director, 780-675-6218, Fax: 780-675-6921, E-mail: mikeg@athabascau.ca. *Application contact:* Derek Stovin, Program Administrator, 780-675-6236, Fax: 780-675-6921, E-mail: dereks@athabascau.ca.

Auburn University, Graduate School, College of Education, Department of Educational Foundations, Leadership, and Technology, Auburn University, AL 36849. Offers adult education (M Ed, MS, Ed D); curriculum and instruction (M Ed, MS, Ed D, Ed S); curriculum supervision (M Ed, MS, Ed D, Ed S); educational psychology (PhD); higher education administration (M Ed, MS, Ed D, Ed S); media instructional design (MS); media specialist (M Ed); school administration (M Ed, MS, Ed D, Ed S). *Accreditation:* NCATE. Part-time programs available. *Faculty:* 21 full-time (11 women), 6 part-time/adjunct (4 women). *Students:* 68 full-time (40 women), 175 part-time (103 women); includes 87 minority (84 African Americans, 1 Asian American or Pacific Islander, 2 Hispanic Americans), 8 international. Average age 37. 112 applicants, 65% accepted, 53 enrolled. In 2009, 31 master's, 12 doctorates, 1 other advanced degree awarded. *Degree requirements:* For master's, thesis (for some programs); for doctorate, thesis/dissertation; for Ed S, field project. *Entrance requirements:* For master's, doctorate, and Ed S, GRE General Test. *Application deadline:* For fall admission, 7/7 for domestic students; for spring admission, 11/24 for domestic students. Applications are processed on a rolling basis. Application fee: $50 ($60 for international students). Electronic applications accepted. *Expenses:* Tuition, state resident: full-time $6240. Tuition, nonresident: full-time $18,720. International tuition: $18,938 full-time. Required fees: $492. Tuition and fees vary according to course load, program and reciprocity agreements. *Financial support:* Teaching assistantships, Federal Work-Study available. Support available to part-time students. Financial award application deadline: 3/15; financial award applicants required to submit FAFSA. *Unit head:* Dr. Jose Llanes, Head, 334-844-4460. *Application contact:* Dr. George Flowers, Dean of the Graduate School, 334-844-4700.

Ball State University, Graduate School, Teachers College, Department of Educational Studies, Program in Adult Education, Muncie, IN 47306-1099. Offers adult and community education (MA); adult, community, and higher education (Ed D). *Accreditation:* NCATE. *Degree requirements:* For doctorate, thesis/dissertation. *Entrance requirements:* For doctorate, GRE General Test, minimum graduate GPA of 3.2. *Faculty research:* Community education, executive development for public services, applied gerontology.

Buffalo State College, State University of New York, The Graduate School, Faculty of Applied Science and Education, Department of Educational Foundations, Program in Adult Education, Buffalo, NY 14222-1095. Offers adult education (MS, Certificate); human resources development (Certificate). Part-time and evening/weekend programs available. Postbaccalaureate distance learning degree programs offered (no on-campus study). *Degree requirements:* For master's, comprehensive exam. *Entrance requirements:* Additional exam requirements/recommendations for international students: Required—TOEFL (minimum score 550 paper-based; 213 computer-based).

Capella University, School of Education, Minneapolis, MN 55402. Offers college teaching (Certificate); curriculum and instruction (MS, PhD); education (MS); enrollment management (MS); instructional design for online learning (MS, PhD); k-12 studies in education (MS, PhD); leadership for higher education (MS, PhD); leadership in education administration (Certificate); leadership in educational administration (MS, PhD); postsecondary and adult education (MS, PhD); professional studies in education (MS, PhD); reading and literacy (MS); training and performance improvement (MS, PhD). Part-time and evening/weekend programs available. Postbaccalaureate distance learning degree programs offered (minimal on-campus study). Terminal master's awarded for partial completion of doctoral program. *Degree requirements:* For master's, thesis optional, integrative project; for doctorate, comprehensive exam, thesis/dissertation. *Entrance requirements:* Additional exam requirements/recommendations for international students: Required—TOEFL (minimum score 550 paper-based; 213 computer-based), TWE (minimum score 4). Electronic applications accepted. *Faculty research:* Higher education administration, distance learning, adult education, training and curriculum design.

Central Michigan University, Central Michigan University Off-Campus Programs, Program in Education, Mount Pleasant, MI 48859. Offers adult education (MA); community college (MA); education (MA); guidance and development (MA); instructional (MA); reading and literacy K-12 (MA). Part-time and evening/weekend programs available. *Entrance requirements:* For master's, minimum GPA of 2.7 in major. Additional exam requirements/recommendations for international students: Required—TOEFL. *Application deadline:* Applications are processed on a rolling basis. Application fee: $50. Electronic applications accepted. *Financial support:* Scholarships/grants available. Support available to part-time students. *Unit head:* Jennifer Cochran, Director, 989-774-2584, E-mail: jennifer.cochran@cmich.edu. *Application contact:* 877-268-4636, E-mail: cmuoffcampus@cmich.edu.

Cheyney University of Pennsylvania, School of Education and Professional Studies, Program in Adult and Continuing Education, Cheyney, PA 19319. Offers MS. Part-time and evening/weekend programs available. *Degree requirements:* For master's, thesis or alternative. *Entrance requirements:* For master's, GRE General Test, MAT, minimum GPA of 2.75. Electronic applications accepted.

Cheyney University of Pennsylvania, School of Education and Professional Studies, Program in Educational Administration of Adult and Continuing Education, Cheyney, PA 19319. Offers M Ed, MS. Part-time and evening/weekend programs available. *Degree requirements:* For master's, thesis or alternative. Electronic applications accepted.

Cleveland State University, College of Graduate Studies, College of Education and Human Services, Department of Counseling, Administration, Supervision and Adult Learning (CASAL), Cleveland, OH 44115. Offers accelerated degree in adult learning and development (M Ed); adult learning and development (M Ed); chemical dependency counseling (Certificate); community agency counseling (M Ed); counseling and pupil personnel administration (Ed S); early childhood mental health counseling (Certificate); educational administration and supervision (M Ed); school administration (Ed S); school counseling (M Ed). *Accreditation:* ACA (one or more programs are accredited). Part-time and evening/weekend programs available. *Degree requirements:* For master's, comprehensive exam (for some programs), thesis optional; for other advanced degree, comprehensive exam, thesis optional, internship. *Entrance requirements:* For master's, GRE General Test or MAT, letter of recommendation, minimum GPA of 2.75. Additional exam requirements/recommendations for international students: Required—TOEFL (minimum score 525 paper-based; 197 computer-based), IELTS (minimum score 6). Electronic applications accepted. *Faculty research:* Education law, career development, women in school administration, psychopharmacology, counseling and spirituality.

Colorado State University, Graduate School, College of Applied Human Sciences, School of Education, Fort Collins, CO 80523-1588. Offers adult education and training (M Ed); community college leadership (PhD); counseling and career development (M Ed); education and human resource studies (M Ed, PhD); educational leadership (M Ed, PhD); interdisciplinary studies (PhD); organizational performance and change (M Ed, PhD); student affairs in higher education (MS). *Accreditation:* ACA; Teacher Education Accreditation Council. Part-time and evening/weekend programs available. *Faculty:* 21 full-time (10 women). *Students:* 195 full-time (132 women), 469 part-time (292 women); includes 114 minority (31 African Americans, 12 American Indian/Alaska Native, 22 Asian Americans or Pacific Islanders, 49 Hispanic Americans), 24 international. Average age 38. 451 applicants, 41% accepted, 141 enrolled. In 2009, 175 master's, 54 doctorates awarded. *Degree requirements:* For master's, comprehensive exam (for some programs), thesis optional; for doctorate, comprehensive exam, thesis/dissertation, minimum of 60 credits. *Entrance requirements:* For master's, GRE, minimum undergraduate GPA of 3.0, 3 letters of recommendation, curriculum vitae/resume; for doctorate, minimum GPA of 3.0, 3 letters of recommendation, curriculum vitae. Additional exam requirements/recommendations for international students: Required—TOEFL (minimum score 550 paper-based; 213 computer-based). *Application deadline:* For fall admission, 3/15 for domestic and international students; for spring admission, 11/1 for domestic students, 10/1 for international students. Applications are processed on a rolling basis. Application fee: $50. Electronic applications accepted. *Expenses:* Tuition, state resident: full-time $6434; part-time $359.10 per credit. Tuition, nonresident: full-time $18,116; part-time $1006.45 per credit. Required fees: $1496; $83 per credit. *Financial support:* In 2009–10, 8 students received support, including 3 research assistantships with full tuition reimbursements available (averaging $13,790 per year), 5 teaching assistantships with full tuition reimbursements available (averaging $10,253 per year); fellowships, Federal Work-Study, scholarships/grants, and unspecified assistantships also available. Financial award applicants required to submit FAFSA. *Faculty research:* Innovative instruction, diverse learners, transition, scientifically-based evaluation methods, leadership and organizational development. Total annual research expenditures: $655,700. *Unit head:* Dr. Carole Makela, Interim Director, 970-491-6317, Fax: 970-491-1317, E-mail: carole.makela@colostate.edu. *Application contact:* Dr. Sharon Anderson, Director of Graduate Programs, 970-491-6861, Fax: 970-491-1317, E-mail: sharon.anderson@colostate.edu.

Concordia University, School of Graduate Studies, Faculty of Arts and Science, Department of Education, Program in Adult Education, Montréal, QC H3G 1M8, Canada. Offers Diploma. *Degree requirements:* For Diploma, internship. *Entrance requirements:* For degree, interview. *Faculty research:* Staff development, human relations training, adult learning, professional development, learning in the workplace.

Concordia University, School of Graduate Studies, Faculty of Arts and Science, Department of Education, Program in Educational Studies, Montréal, QC H3G 1M8, Canada. Offers MA. *Degree requirements:* For master's, one foreign language, thesis optional. *Faculty research:* Social aspects of microtechnology, gender and education, minorities and immigrants in Canadian education, professional development, political education.

Coppin State University, Division of Graduate Studies, Division of Education, Department of Adult and General Education, Baltimore, MD 21216-3698. Offers MS. Part-time and evening/weekend programs available. *Degree requirements:* For master's, thesis optional, research paper, internship. *Entrance requirements:* For master's, GRE or PRAXIS, minimum GPA of 2.5, interview, resume, references.

Cornell University, Graduate School, Graduate Fields of Agriculture and Life Sciences, Field of Education, Ithaca, NY 14853-0001. Offers agricultural education (MAT); biology (7-12) (MAT); chemistry (7-12) (MAT); curriculum and instruction (MPS, MS, PhD); earth science (7-12) (MAT); extension, and adult education (MPS, MS, PhD); mathematics (7-12) (MAT); physics (7-12) (MAT). *Faculty:* 26 full-time (9 women). *Students:* 65 full-time (50 women); includes 15 minority (4 African Americans, 7 Asian Americans or Pacific Islanders, 4 Hispanic Americans), 2 international. Average age 34. 96 applicants, 33% accepted, 21 enrolled. In 2009, 27 master's, 2 doctorates awarded. Terminal master's awarded for partial completion of doctoral program. *Degree requirements:* For master's, thesis (MS); for doctorate, comprehensive exam, thesis/dissertation. *Entrance requirements:* For master's and doctorate, GRE General Test, sample of written work (recommended), 2 letters of recommendation. Additional exam requirements/recommendations for international students: Required—TOEFL (minimum score 550 paper-based; 213 computer-based; 77 iBT). *Application deadline:* For fall admission, 2/15 for domestic students. Application fee: $70. Electronic applications accepted. *Expenses:* Tuition: Full-time $29,500. Required fees: $70. Full-time tuition and fees vary according to degree level, program and student level. *Financial support:* In 2009–10, 33 students received support, including 3 fellowships with full tuition reimbursements available, 5 teaching assistantships with full tuition reimbursements available; research assistantships with full tuition reimbursements available, institutionally sponsored loans, scholarships/grants, health care benefits, tuition waivers (full and partial), and unspecified assistantships also available. Financial award applicants required to submit FAFSA. *Faculty research:* Moral development and professional ethics; public issues education and community development; socio/political issues in public education; teacher education and curriculum in agricultural science, and mathematics; extension research. *Unit head:* Director of Graduate Studies, 607-255-4278, Fax: 607-255-7905. *Application contact:* Graduate Field Assistant, 607-255-4278, Fax: 607-255-7905, E-mail: rh22@cornell.edu.

Defiance College, Program in Education, Defiance, OH 43512-1610. Offers adolescent and young adult (MA); mild and moderate intervention specialist (MA); sport science (MA). Part-time programs available. *Degree requirements:* For master's, thesis (for some programs). *Entrance requirements:* For master's, teaching certificate.

Delaware State University, Graduate Programs, College of Education, Program in Adult Literacy and Basic Education, Dover, DE 19901-2277. Offers MA. *Entrance requirements:* Additional exam requirements/recommendations for international students: Required—TOEFL (minimum score 550 paper-based). Electronic applications accepted.

DePaul University, School for New Learning, Chicago, IL 60604. Offers applied technology (MS); educating adults (MA); integrated professional studies (MA). Part-time and evening/weekend programs available. *Faculty:* 8 full-time (2 women), 9 part-time/adjunct (5 women). *Students:* 12 full-time (7 women), 107 part-time (78 women); includes 62 minority (50 African Americans, 1 Asian American or Pacific Islander, 11 Hispanic Americans). Average age 42. 30 applicants, 80% accepted. In 2009, 20 master's awarded. *Degree requirements:* For master's, thesis or alternative. *Entrance requirements:* For master's, 3 years of work experience, current related employment. *Application deadline:* For fall admission, 9/1 priority date for domestic students; for spring admission, 3/1 priority date for domestic students. Applications are processed on a rolling basis. Application fee: $25. Electronic applications accepted. *Expenses:* Tuition: Full-time $37,525; part-time $620 per credit hour. *Financial support:* In 2009–10, 7 students received support. Scholarships/grants and tuition waivers (partial) available. Financial award applicants required to submit FAFSA. *Faculty research:* Interactive problem-based learning, liberal learning and professional competence, effective instructional practice. *Unit head:* Dr. Russ Rogers, Program Director, 312-362-8512, Fax: 312-362-8809, E-mail: rrogers@depaul.edu. *Application contact:* Sarah Hellstrom, Assistant Director, 312-362-5744, Fax: 312-362-8809, E-mail: shellstr@depaul.edu.

East Carolina University, Graduate School, College of Education, Department of Counselor and Adult Education, Greenville, NC 27858-4353. Offers adult education (MA Ed); counselor education (MS, Ed S). *Accreditation:* NCATE. Part-time and evening/weekend programs available. *Degree requirements:* For master's, comprehensive exam, thesis optional. *Entrance requirements:* For master's, GRE General Test or MAT, interview, minimum GPA of 2.5, bachelor's degree in related field, teaching license (MA Ed). Additional exam requirements/recommendations for international students: Required—TOEFL.

Eastern Washington University, Graduate Studies, College of Education and Human Development, Department of Education, Program in Adult Education, Cheney, WA 99004-2431. Offers M Ed. *Accreditation:* NCATE. *Degree requirements:* For master's, comprehensive exam, thesis or alternative. *Entrance requirements:* For master's, minimum GPA of 3.0. *Expenses:* Tuition, state resident: full-time $7476; part-time $249 per quarter hour. Tuition, nonresident: full-time $18,030; part-time $601 per quarter hour. Required fees: $3.50 per quarter hour. $142 per quarter.

Florida Agricultural and Mechanical University, Division of Graduate Studies, Research, and Continuing Education, College of Education, Department of Educational Leadership and Human Services, Tallahassee, FL 32307-3200. Offers administration and supervision (M Ed, MS Ed, PhD); adult education (M Ed, MS Ed); educational leadership (PhD); guidance and counseling (M Ed, MS Ed). *Accreditation:* NCATE. *Faculty:* 15 full-time (8 women). *Students:* 58 full-time (31 women), 43 part-time (32 women); includes 94 minority (93 African Americans, 1 Asian American or Pacific Islander), 5 international. In 2009, 24 master's, 5 doctorates awarded. *Degree requirements:* For master's, thesis (for some programs); for doctorate, thesis/dissertation. *Entrance requirements:* For master's, GRE General Test, minimum GPA of 3.0. Additional exam requirements/recommendations for international students: Required—TOEFL. *Application deadline:* For fall admission, 5/18 for domestic students, 12/18 for international students; for spring admission, 11/12 for domestic students, 5/12 for international students. Application fee: $20. *Unit head:* Dr. Warren Hope, Interim Chairperson, 850-599-3191, Fax: 850-561-2211. *Application contact:* Dr. Chanta M. Haywood, Dean of Graduate Studies, Research, and Continuing Education, 850-599-3315, Fax: 850-599-3727.

Florida Atlantic University, College of Education, Department of Educational Leadership, Boca Raton, FL 33431-0991. Offers adult and community education (M Ed, PhD, Ed S); educational leadership (M Ed, PhD, Ed S); higher education (M Ed, PhD); K-12 school leadership (M Ed, PhD, Ed S). *Accreditation:* NCATE. Part-time and evening/weekend programs available. Postbaccalaureate distance learning degree programs offered (minimal on-campus study). *Faculty:* 16 full-time (8 women), 19 part-time/adjunct (10 women). *Students:* 103 full-time (63 women), 261 part-time (186 women); includes 119 minority (71 African Americans, 9 Asian Americans or Pacific Islanders, 39 Hispanic Americans), 1 international. Average age 36. 254 applicants, 57% accepted, 96 enrolled. In 2009, 123 master's, 22 doctorates awarded. *Degree requirements:* For doctorate, comprehensive exam, thesis/dissertation, departmental qualifying exam; for Ed S, departmental qualifying exam. *Entrance requirements:* For master's, GRE General Test, minimum GPA of 3.0 during previous 2 years; for doctorate, GRE General Test, minimum GPA of 3.5; for Ed S, GRE General Test. *Application deadline:* For fall admission, 7/1 for domestic students, 2/15 for international students; for spring admission, 9/15 for domestic students, 7/15 for international students. Applications are processed on a rolling basis. Application fee: $30. Electronic applications accepted. *Expenses:* Tuition, state resident: full-time $7055; part-time $293.94 per credit hour. Tuition, nonresident: full-time $22,096; part-time $920.66 per credit hour. *Financial support:* Fellowships, research assistantships, teaching assistantships, career-related internships or fieldwork and tuition waivers (partial) available. *Faculty research:* Self-directed learning, school reform issues, legal issues, mentoring, school leadership. *Unit head:* Dr. Robert Shockley, Chair, 561-297-3550, Fax: 561-297-3618, E-mail: shockley@fau.edu. *Application contact:* Catherine Politi, Senior Secretary, 561-297-3550, Fax: 561-297-3618, E-mail: edleadership@fau.edu.

Florida International University, College of Education, Department of Educational Leadership and Policy Studies, Program in Adult Education, Miami, FL 33199. Offers MS. *Accreditation:* NCATE. Part-time and evening/weekend programs available. *Entrance requirements:* Additional exam requirements/recommendations for international students: Required—TOEFL (minimum score 550 paper-based; 213 computer-based; 80 iBT), IELTS (minimum score 6.3). *Expenses:* Tuition, state resident: full-time $8008; part-time $4004 per year. Tuition, nonresident: full-time $20,104; part-time $10,052 per year. Required fees: $298; $149 per term. *Faculty research:* Adult education, family literacy, learning technology.

Florida International University, College of Education, Department of Educational Leadership and Policy Studies, Program in Adult Education in Human Resource Development, Miami, FL 33199. Offers Ed D. Part-time and evening/weekend programs available. *Degree requirements:* For doctorate, thesis/dissertation. *Entrance requirements:* For doctorate, GRE General Test. Additional exam requirements/recommendations for international students: Required—TOEFL (minimum score 550 paper-based; 213 computer-based; 80 iBT), IELTS (minimum score 6.3). Electronic applications accepted. *Expenses:* Tuition, state resident: full-time $8008; part-time $4004 per year. Tuition, nonresident: full-time $20,104; part-time $10,052 per year. Required fees: $298; $149 per term. *Faculty research:* Adult education, family literacy, learning technologies.

Fordham University, Graduate School of Education, Division of Curriculum and Teaching, New York, NY 10023. Offers adult education (MS, MSE); bilingual teacher education (MSE); curriculum and teaching (MSE); early childhood education (MSE); elementary education (MST); language, literacy, and learning (PhD); reading education (MSE, Adv C); secondary education (MAT, MSE); special education (MSE, Adv C); teaching English as a second language (MSE). *Accreditation:* NCATE. *Degree requirements:* For doctorate, thesis/dissertation; for Adv C, thesis. *Entrance requirements:* For doctorate, MAT, GRE General Test.

Grand Valley State University, College of Education, Programs in General Education, Allendale, MI 49401-9403. Offers adult and higher education (M Ed); early childhood education (M Ed); educational differentiation (M Ed); educational leadership (M Ed); educational technology integration (M Ed); elementary education (M Ed); middle level education (M Ed); school library media services (M Ed); secondary level education (M Ed); teaching English to speakers of other languages (M Ed). Part-time and evening/weekend programs available. Postbaccalaureate distance learning degree programs offered (minimal on-campus study). *Faculty:* 82 full-time (42 women), 43 part-time/adjunct (25 women). *Students:* 100 full-time (53 women), 723 part-time (478 women); includes 59 minority (25 African Americans, 4 American Indian/Alaska Native, 13 Asian Americans or Pacific Islanders, 17 Hispanic Americans), 10 international. Average age 33. 237 applicants, 96% accepted, 117 enrolled. In 2009, 291 master's awarded. *Degree requirements:* For master's, thesis. *Entrance requirements:* For master's, GRE General Test or minimum GPA of 3.0. Additional exam requirements/recommendations for international students: Required—TOEFL. *Application deadline:* Applications are processed on a rolling basis. Application fee: $30. Electronic applications accepted. *Expenses:* Tuition, state resident: part-time $471 per credit hour. Tuition, nonresident: part-time $646 per credit hour. Tuition and fees vary according to course level. *Financial support:* In 2009–10, 73 students received support, including 55 fellowships (averaging $2,273 per year), 19 research assistantships with full and partial tuition reimbursements available (averaging $8,000 per year); career-related internships or fieldwork, Federal Work-Study, scholarships/grants, and unspecified assistantships also available. *Faculty research:* Effectiveness of technology in education, parental involvement, effective teaching, effective schools research. *Unit head:* Dr. Linda McCrea, Director, 616-331-2080, E-mail: mccreal@gvsu.edu. *Application contact:* Thomas Owens, Student Information and Services Center, 616-331-6282, Fax: 616-331-2000, E-mail: owenst@gvsu.edu.

Indiana University of Pennsylvania, School of Graduate Studies and Research, College of Education and Educational Technology, Department of Adult and Community Education, Program in Adult Education and Communication Technology, Indiana, PA 15705-1087. Offers communications technology (MA). Part-time and evening/weekend programs available. *Faculty:* 2 full-time (0 women). *Students:* 21 full-time (9 women), 15 part-time (9 women); includes 6 minority (4 African Americans, 2 Asian Americans or Pacific Islanders). Average age 31. 54 applicants, 59% accepted, 23 enrolled. In 2009, 22 master's awarded. *Degree requirements:* For master's, thesis optional. *Entrance requirements:* For master's, 2 letters of recommendation, writing sample. Additional exam requirements/recommendations for international students: Required—TOEFL. *Application deadline:* For fall admission, 7/1 priority date for domestic students; for spring admission, 11/1 for domestic students. Applications are processed on a rolling basis. Application fee: $40. *Expenses:* Tuition, state resident: full-time $6666; part-time $370 per credit hour. Tuition, nonresident: full-time $10,666; part-time $593 per credit hour. Required fees: $813 per semester. *Financial support:* In 2009–10, 7 research assistantships with full and partial tuition reimbursements (averaging $5,440 per year) were awarded; career-related internships or fieldwork and Federal Work-Study also available. Support available to part-time students. Financial award application deadline: 3/15; financial award applicants required to submit FAFSA. *Unit head:* Dr. Gary Dean, Chairperson, 724-357-2470, E-mail: gjdean@iup.edu. *Application contact:* Dr. Gary Dean, Chairperson, 724-357-2470, E-mail: gjdean@iup.edu.

Indiana University of Pennsylvania, School of Graduate Studies and Research, College of Education and Educational Technology, Department of Communications Media, Indiana, PA 15705-1087. Offers adult education and communications technology (MA); communications media and instructional technology (PhD). *Faculty:* 8 full-time (1 woman). *Students:* 16 full-time (7 women), 24 part-time (13 women); includes 3 minority (2 African Americans, 1 Asian American or Pacific Islander), 2 international. Average age 35. 40 applicants, 53% accepted, 20 enrolled.Application fee: $40. *Expenses:* Tuition, state resident: full-time $6666; part-time $370 per credit hour. Tuition, nonresident: full-time $10,666; part-time $593 per credit hour. Required fees: $813 per semester. *Financial support:* In 2009–10, 4 fellowships (averaging $1,000 per year), 8 research assistantships (averaging $5,936 per year), 3 teaching assistantships (averaging $21,536 per year) were awarded. *Unit head:* Dr. Mark Piwinsky, Chairperson, 724-357-3954, Fax: 724-357-5503, E-mail: mark.piwinsky@iup.edu. *Application contact:* Dr. Edward Nardi, Associate Dean, 724-357-2480, Fax: 724-357-5595, E-mail: ewnardi@iup.edu.

Indiana University–Purdue University Indianapolis, School of Continuing Studies, Program in Adult Education, Indianapolis, IN 46202-2896. Offers MS. *Students:* 3 full-time (all women), 69 part-time (55 women); includes 4 minority (3 African Americans, 1 Hispanic American). Average age 41. 31 applicants, 87% accepted, 24 enrolled. *Degree requirements:* For master's, thesis optional. *Entrance requirements:* For master's, GRE General Test, minimum GPA of 3.2. *Application deadline:* For fall admission, 7/1 for domestic students; for spring admission, 11/1 for domestic students. Application fee: $55 ($65 for international students). *Financial support:* In 2009–10, 2 fellowships (averaging $780 per year) were awarded; research assistantships with partial tuition reimbursements, scholarships/grants also available. *Unit head:* Dr. Henry Merrill, Chair, 317-274-5555. *Application contact:* Jeani Young, Coordinator, 317-274-3456, E-mail: adulted@iupui.edu.

The Johns Hopkins University, School of Education, Department of Interdisciplinary Studies in Education, Baltimore, MD 21218. Offers earth/space science (Certificate); education (MS), including educational studies; mind, brain, and teaching (Certificate); teaching the adult learner (Certificate); urban education (Certificate). Part-time and evening/weekend programs available. Postbaccalaureate distance learning degree programs offered (minimal on-campus study). *Faculty:* 2 full-time (1 woman), 6 part-time/adjunct (5 women). *Students:* 8 full-time (7 women), 171 part-time (150 women); includes 44 minority (29 African Americans, 1 American Indian/Alaska Native, 11 Asian Americans or Pacific Islanders, 3 Hispanic Americans), 7 international. Average age 34. 77 applicants, 68% accepted, 39 enrolled. In 2009, 69 master's, 17 other advanced degrees awarded. *Degree requirements:* For master's, capstone course. *Entrance requirements:* For master's and Certificate, minimum undergraduate GPA of 3.0. Additional exam requirements/recommendations for international students: Required—TOEFL (minimum score 600 paper-based; 250 computer-based; 100 iBT). *Application deadline:* For fall admission,

Adult Education

The Johns Hopkins University (continued)
5/1 for international students; for spring admission, 10/15 for international students. Applications are processed on a rolling basis. Application fee: $80. Electronic applications accepted. *Financial support:* Scholarships/grants available. Support available to part-time students. Financial award application deadline: 6/1; financial award applicants required to submit FAFSA. *Faculty research:* Neuro-education; urban school reform; leadership development; teacher leadership; charter schools; techniques for teaching reading to adolescents with delayed reading skills; school culture. *Unit head:* Dr. Mariale Hardiman, Assistant Dean and Chair, 410-516-8225, Fax: 410-516-3939, E-mail: mclean@jhu.edu. *Application contact:* Jennifer Shaffer, Director of Admissions, 410-516-9797, Fax: 410-516-9799, E-mail: educationinfo@jhu.edu.

Jones International University, Graduate School of Education, Centennial, CO 80112. Offers adult education (M Ed); corporate training and knowledge management (M Ed); curriculum and instruction (M Ed), including elementary teacher licensure, secondary teacher licensure; e-learning technology and design (M Ed); educational leadership and administration (M Ed); educational leadership and administration: principal and administrator licensure (M Ed); elementary curriculum instruction and assessment (M Ed); higher education leadership and administration (M Ed); K-12 instructional technology (M Ed); K-12 instructional technology: teacher licensure (M Ed); secondary curriculum instruction and assessment (M Ed); technology and design (M Ed). Part-time and evening/weekend programs available. Postbaccalaureate distance learning degree programs offered (no on-campus study). *Entrance requirements:* For master's, minimum cumulative GPA of 2.5. Additional exam requirements/recommendations for international students: Recommended—TOEFL (minimum score 550 paper-based; 213 computer-based). Electronic applications accepted.

Kansas State University, Graduate School, College of Education, Department of Educational Leadership, Manhattan, KS 66506. Offers adult and continuing education (Ed D); adult, occupational and continuing education (MS); educational administration and leadership (MS, Ed D). *Accreditation:* NCATE. *Faculty:* 10 full-time (5 women), 3 part-time/adjunct (1 woman). *Students:* 41 full-time (27 women), 169 part-time (72 women); includes 19 minority (12 African Americans, 1 American Indian/Alaska Native, 3 Asian Americans or Pacific Islanders, 3 Hispanic Americans), 1 international. Average age 41. 46 applicants, 96% accepted, 39 enrolled. In 2009, 79 master's, 9 doctorates awarded. *Degree requirements:* For master's, thesis or alternative, final written exam; for doctorate, comprehensive exam, thesis/dissertation, preliminary exam, residency. *Entrance requirements:* For master's, GRE General Test, MAT, minimum undergraduate GPA of 3.0; for doctorate, GRE General Test, MAT, minimum GPA of 3.0. Additional exam requirements/recommendations for international students: Required—TOEFL. *Application deadline:* For fall admission, 2/1 priority date for domestic and international students; for spring admission, 8/1 priority date for domestic and international students. Applications are processed on a rolling basis. Application fee: $40 ($55 for international students). Electronic applications accepted. *Financial support:* Career-related internships or fieldwork, institutionally sponsored loans, and scholarships/grants available. Support available to part-time students. Financial award application deadline: 3/1; financial award applicants required to submit FAFSA. *Faculty research:* Educational law, finance, technology ethics, application, and leadership in education; distance learning/education; program evaluation. Total annual research expenditures: $71,091. *Unit head:* David C. Thompson, Head, 785-532-5535, Fax: 785-532-7304, E-mail: thomsond@ksu.edu. *Application contact:* Gail Shroyer, Director, 785-532-6737, Fax: 785-532-7304, E-mail: gshroyer@ksu.edu.

Kean University, College of Education, Program in Reading Specialization, Union, NJ 07083. Offers adult literacy (MA); basic skills (MA); reading specialization (MA). *Faculty:* 15 full-time (13 women). *Students:* 3 full-time (all women), 69 part-time (63 women); includes 8 minority (3 African Americans, 4 Asian Americans or Pacific Islanders, 1 Hispanic American). Average age 32. 22 applicants, 100% accepted, 19 enrolled. In 2009, 28 master's awarded. *Degree requirements:* For master's, thesis, practicum, clinical, research seminar. *Entrance requirements:* For master's, GRE General Test or MAT, minimum GPA of 3.0, 2 letters of recommendation, interview, teaching certification. *Application deadline:* For fall admission, 5/1 for domestic students; for spring admission, 11/1 for domestic students. Application fee: $60 ($150 for international students). Electronic applications accepted. *Expenses:* Tuition, state resident: full-time $10,440; part-time $435 per credit. Tuition, nonresident: full-time $14,160; part-time $590 per credit. Required fees: $2642; $110 per credit. Part-time tuition and fees vary according to course load and degree level. *Financial support:* In 2009–10, research assistantships with full tuition reimbursements (averaging $3,263 per year); unspecified assistantships also available. *Unit head:* Dr. Joan M. Kastner, Program Coordinator, 908-737-3942, E-mail: jkastner@kean.edu. *Application contact:* Reenat Hasan, Pre-Admission Coordinator, 908-737-5923, Fax: 908-737-5965, E-mail: rhasan@exchange.kean.edu.

Marshall University, Academic Affairs Division, College of Education and Human Services, Division of Human Development and Allied Technology, Program in Adult and Technical Education, Huntington, WV 25755. Offers MS. *Accreditation:* NCATE. Evening/weekend programs available. *Faculty:* 7 full-time (4 women), 15 part-time/adjunct (8 women). *Students:* 88 full-time (57 women), 93 part-time (65 women); includes 22 minority (18 African Americans, 2 Asian Americans or Pacific Islanders, 2 Hispanic Americans), 40 international. Average age 35. In 2009, 71 master's awarded. *Degree requirements:* For master's, thesis optional, comprehensive assessment. Application fee: $40. *Unit head:* Dr. Lee Olson, Program Coordinator, 304-696-6757, E-mail: olsonl@marshall.edu. *Application contact:* Graduate Admission.

Memorial University of Newfoundland, School of Graduate Studies, Faculty of Education, St. John's, NL A1C 5S7, Canada. Offers counseling psychology (M Ed); curriculum, teaching, and learning studies (M Ed); education (PhD); educational leadership studies (M Ed); information technology (M Ed); post-secondary studies (M Ed, Diploma), including health professional education (Diploma). Part-time programs available. *Degree requirements:* For master's, thesis optional, internship, paper folio, project; for doctorate, comprehensive exam, thesis/dissertation, thesis seminar, oral defense of thesis. *Entrance requirements:* For master's, undergraduate degree with at least 2nd class standing, 1-2 years work experience; for doctorate, minimum A average in graduate course work, MA in education, 2 years professional experience; for Diploma, 2nd class degree, 2 years of work experience with adult learners, appropriate academic qualifications and work experience in a health-related field. Electronic applications accepted. *Faculty research:* Critical thinking, literacy, cognitive studies and counseling, educational change, technology in instruction.

Michigan State University, The Graduate School, College of Education, Department of Educational Administration, East Lansing, MI 48824. Offers higher, adult and lifelong education (MA, PhD); K–12 educational administration (MA, PhD, Ed S); student affairs administration (MA). Part-time programs available. *Faculty:* 20 full-time (9 women). *Students:* 158 full-time (95 women), 158 part-time (92 women); includes 59 minority (33 African Americans, 5 American Indian/Alaska Native, 11 Asian Americans or Pacific Islanders, 10 Hispanic Americans), 33 international. Average age 33. 274 applicants, 52% accepted. In 2009, 73 master's, 27 doctorates awarded. *Entrance requirements:* Additional exam requirements/recommendations for international students: Required—TOEFL. Electronic applications accepted. *Expenses:* Tuition, state resident: part-time $478.25 per credit hour. Tuition, nonresident: part-time $966.50 per credit hour. Part-time tuition and fees vary according to program. *Financial support:* In 2009–10, 51 research assistantships with tuition reimbursements (averaging $6,633 per year), 3 teaching assistantships with tuition reimbursements (averaging $6,967 per year) were awarded. Total annual research expenditures: $365,790. *Unit head:* Dr. Marilyn J. Amey, Chairperson, 517-432-1056, Fax: 517-884-1392, E-mail: amey@msu.edu. *Application contact:* Cathy Ogar, Graduate Secretary, 517-355-4537, Fax: 517-884-1392, E-mail: cogar@msu.edu.

Montana State University, College of Graduate Studies, College of Education, Health, and Human Development, Department of Education, Bozeman, MT 59717. Offers adult and higher education (Ed D); curriculum and instruction (Ed D, Ed S); education (M Ed), including adult and higher education, curriculum and instruction, educational leadership, school counseling;

educational leadership (Ed D, Ed S). Part-time programs available. Postbaccalaureate distance learning degree programs offered (minimal on-campus study). *Faculty:* 22 full-time (13 women), 18 part-time/adjunct (14 women). *Students:* 15 full-time (8 women), 210 part-time (126 women); includes 29 minority (27 American Indian/Alaska Native, 1 Asian American or Pacific Islander, 1 Hispanic American), 2 international. Average age 37. 52 applicants. In 2009, 62 master's, 9 doctorates awarded. *Degree requirements:* For master's, comprehensive exam; for doctorate, comprehensive exam, thesis/dissertation. *Entrance requirements:* For master's and doctorate, GRE General Test. Additional exam requirements/recommendations for international students: Required—TOEFL (minimum score 550 paper-based; 213 computer-based). *Application deadline:* For fall admission, 7/15 priority date for domestic students, 5/15 priority date for international students; for spring admission, 12/1 priority date for domestic students, 10/1 priority date for international students. Applications are processed on a rolling basis. Application fee: $30. Electronic applications accepted. *Expenses:* Tuition, state resident: full-time $5635; part-time $3492 per year. Tuition, nonresident: full-time $17,212; part-time $7865.10 per year. Required fees: $1441; $153.15 per credit. Tuition and fees vary according to course load and program. *Financial support:* In 2009–10, 45 students received support, including 5 teaching assistantships with tuition reimbursements available (averaging $9,000 per year); traineeships, tuition waivers (full and partial), and unspecified assistantships also available. Financial award application deadline: 3/1; financial award applicants required to submit FAFSA. *Faculty research:* Online teaching and learning, statistical strategies to course and student assessment, environmental education, copyright issues/web-based resources, multicultural education, curriculum design, preparation for North American teachers to be administrators, NCES data sets, relational trust in public school administration. Total annual research expenditures: $1.2 million. *Unit head:* Dr. Joanne Erickson, Interim Department Head, 406-994-6670, Fax: 406-994-3261, E-mail: jle@montana.edu. *Application contact:* Dr. Carl A. Fox, Vice Provost for Graduate Education, 406-994-4145, Fax: 406-994-7433, E-mail: gradstudy@montana.edu.

Morehead State University, Graduate Programs, College of Education, Department of Foundational and Graduate Studies in Education, Morehead, KY 40351. Offers adult and higher education (MA, Ed S); certified professional counselor (Ed S); counseling P-12 (MA); curriculum and instruction (Ed S); educational technology (MA Ed); instructional leadership (Ed S); school administration (MA); school counseling (Ed S); teacher leader business and marketing- content (MA Ed); teacher leader business and marketing- technology (MA Ed); teacher leader educational technology (MA Ed); teacher leader English (MA Ed); teacher leader gifted educ (MA Ed); teacher leader IECE—non-certification (MA Ed); teacher leader IECE certification (MA Ed); teacher leader interdisciplanary educaction P-5 (MA Ed); teacher leader middle grades 5-9 (MA Ed); teacher leader reading/writing—non-certification (MA Ed); teacher leader reading/writing certification (MA Ed); teacher leader school communication—non-certification (MA Ed); teacher leader school communication certification (MA Ed); teacher leader social studies (MA Ed); teacher leader special education (MA Ed). *Accreditation:* NCATE. Part-time and evening/weekend programs available. *Faculty:* 20 full-time (10 women), 7 part-time/adjunct (3 women). *Students:* 26 full-time (18 women), 371 part-time (295 women); includes 11 minority (9 African Americans, 1 American Indian/Alaska Native, 1 Hispanic American). Average age 35. 201 applicants, 73% accepted, 73 enrolled. In 2009, 105 master's, 5 other advanced degrees awarded. *Degree requirements:* For master's, thesis optional, oral and/or written comprehensive exams; for Ed S, thesis, oral exam. *Entrance requirements:* For master's, GRE General Test, minimum overall undergraduate GPA of 2.5; for Ed S, GRE General Test, interview, master's degree, minimum GPA of 3.5, work experience. Additional exam requirements/recommendations for international students: Required—TOEFL (minimum score 500 paper-based; 173 computer-based). *Application deadline:* For fall admission, 8/1 priority date for domestic and international students; for spring admission, 12/1 priority date for domestic and international students. Applications are processed on a rolling basis. Application fee: $30. Electronic applications accepted. *Expenses:* Tuition, state resident: full-time $6318; part-time $351 per credit hour. Tuition, nonresident: full-time $15,804; part-time $878 per credit hour. *Financial support:* In 2009–10, 2 research assistantships (averaging $10,000 per year) were awarded; career-related internships or fieldwork, Federal Work-Study, and unspecified assistantships also available. Financial award application deadline: 3/15; financial award applicants required to submit FAFSA. *Faculty research:* Character education, school accountability, computer applications for school administrators. *Unit head:* Dr. Cathy Gunn, Dean and Professor, 606-783-2040, Fax: 606-783-5029, E-mail: c.gunn@moreheadstate.edu. *Application contact:* Michelle Barber, Graduate Recruitment and Retention Assistant Director, 606-783-5127, Fax: 606-783-5061, E-mail: m.barber@moreheadstate.edu.

Mount Saint Vincent University, Graduate Programs, Faculty of Education, Program in Adult Education, Halifax, NS B3M 2J6, Canada. Offers M Ed, MA Ed, MA-R. Part-time and evening/weekend programs available. Postbaccalaureate distance learning degree programs offered (minimal on-campus study). *Degree requirements:* For master's, thesis (for some programs), practicum. *Entrance requirements:* For master's, bachelor's degree in related field, minimum B average. Electronic applications accepted.

National-Louis University, College of Arts and Sciences, Division of Language and Academic Development, Program in Adult, Continuing, and Literacy Education, Chicago, IL 60603. Offers M Ed, Certificate. Part-time and evening/weekend programs available. Postbaccalaureate distance learning degree programs offered (minimal on-campus study). *Degree requirements:* For master's, thesis or alternative. *Entrance requirements:* For master's, GRE General Test, MAT, or Watson-Glaser Critical Thinking Appraisal, interview, minimum GPA of 3.0; for Certificate, GRE, MAT, or Watson-Glaser Critical Thinking Appraisal, interview, minimum GPA of 3.0. *Expenses:* Tuition: Full-time $17,160; part-time $715 per semester hour. Tuition and fees vary according to course load, degree level, campus/location and program.

National-Louis University, College of Arts and Sciences, Division of Language and Academic Development, Program in Adult Literacy and Developmental Studies, Chicago, IL 60603. Offers M Ed, Certificate. Part-time and evening/weekend programs available. *Entrance requirements:* For master's, GRE General Test, MAT, or Watson-Glaser Critical Thinking Appraisal, interview, minimum GPA of 3.0; for Certificate, GRE, MAT, or Watson-Glaser Critical Thinking Appraisal, interview, minimum GPA of 3.0. *Expenses:* Tuition: Full-time $17,160; part-time $715 per semester hour. Tuition and fees vary according to course load, degree level, campus/location and program. *Faculty research:* Adult learning and development, learner-centered development, political and social foundations, reading development, curricular processes.

National-Louis University, National College of Education, Doctoral Programs in Education, Program in Adult Education, Chicago, IL 60603. Offers Ed D. Part-time and evening/weekend programs available. *Degree requirements:* For doctorate, thesis/dissertation. *Entrance requirements:* For doctorate, GRE General Test, MAT, or Watson-Glaser Critical Thinking Appraisal, 3 years of experience in field, interview, master's degree, resume, writing sample. *Expenses:* Tuition: Full-time $17,160; part-time $715 per semester hour. Tuition and fees vary according to course load, degree level, campus/location and program.

North Carolina Agricultural and Technical State University, Graduate School, School of Education, Department of Human Development and Services, Greensboro, NC 27411. Offers adult education (MS); counselor education (MS); human resources-agency counseling (MS); human resources-rehabilitation counseling (MS); leadership studies (PhD); school administration (MS). *Accreditation:* ACA. Part-time and evening/weekend programs available. *Degree requirements:* For master's, comprehensive exam, thesis, qualifying exam. *Entrance requirements:* For master's, GRE General Test, minimum GPA of 3.0.

North Carolina State University, Graduate School, College of Education, Department of Adult and Higher Education, Program in Adult and Community College Education, Raleigh, NC 27695. Offers M Ed, MS, Ed D. *Degree requirements:* For master's, thesis (for some programs); for doctorate, thesis/dissertation. *Entrance requirements:* For master's and doctorate, GRE or MAT. Electronic applications accepted.

North Dakota State University, College of Graduate and Interdisciplinary Studies, College of Human Development and Education, School of Education, Fargo, ND 58108. Offers agricultural

education (M Ed, MS), including agricultural education, agricultural extension education (MS); counseling (M Ed, MS, PhD); curriculum and instruction (M Ed, MS), including pedagogy, physical education and athletic administration; education (PhD); educational leadership (M Ed, MS, Ed S); family and consumer sciences education (M Ed, MS); history education (M Ed, MS); institutional analysis (Ed D); mathematics education (M Ed, MS); music education (M Ed, MS); occupational and adult education (Ed D); science education (M Ed, MS). *Accreditation:* NCATE. Part-time and evening/weekend programs available. Postbaccalaureate distance learning degree programs offered (minimal on-campus study). *Faculty:* 25 full-time (9 women), 3 part-time/adjunct (1 woman). *Students:* 29 full-time (25 women), 207 part-time (132 women); includes 15 minority (4 African Americans, 6 American Indian/Alaska Native, 3 Asian Americans or Pacific Islanders, 2 Hispanic Americans), 4 international. 88 applicants, 67% accepted, 56 enrolled. In 2009, 44 master's, 5 doctorates awarded. *Degree requirements:* For master's, comprehensive exam; for doctorate, thesis/dissertation; for Ed S, thesis. *Entrance requirements:* For degree, GRE General Test, master's degree, minimum GPA of 3.25. Additional exam requirements/recommendations for international students: Required—TOEFL. *Application deadline:* Applications are processed on a rolling basis. Application fee: $45 ($60 for international students). *Financial support:* Research assistantships, teaching assistantships, career-related internships or fieldwork, Federal Work-Study, institutionally sponsored loans, and tuition waivers (full) available. Financial award application deadline: 4/15. *Unit head:* Dr. William Martin, Chair, 701-231-7202, Fax: 701-231-7416, E-mail: william.martin@ndsu.edu. *Application contact:* Dr. William Martin, Chair, 701-231-7202, Fax: 701-231-7416, E-mail: william.martin@ndsu.edu.

Northern Illinois University, Graduate School, College of Education, Department of Counseling, Adult and Higher Education, De Kalb, IL 60115-2854. Offers adult and higher education (MS Ed, Ed D); counseling (MS Ed, Ed D). *Accreditation:* ACA. Part-time and evening/weekend programs available. *Faculty:* 19 full-time (11 women), 2 part-time/adjunct (1 woman). *Students:* 119 full-time (80 women), 280 part-time (198 women); includes 126 minority (93 African Americans, 4 American Indian/Alaska Native, 8 Asian Americans or Pacific Islanders, 21 Hispanic Americans), 18 international. Average age 38. 118 applicants, 53% accepted, 45 enrolled. In 2009, 76 master's, 12 doctorates awarded. Terminal master's awarded for partial completion of doctoral program. *Degree requirements:* For master's, comprehensive exam, thesis optional; for doctorate, thesis/dissertation, candidacy exam, dissertation defense. *Entrance requirements:* For master's, GRE General Test or MAT, minimum undergraduate GPA of 2.75, interview (counseling); for doctorate, GRE General Test, minimum undergraduate GPA of 2.75, 3.2 graduate, interview (counseling). Additional exam requirements/recommendations for international students: Required—TOEFL (minimum score 550 paper-based; 213 computer-based). *Application deadline:* For fall admission, 6/1 for domestic students, 5/1 for international students; for spring admission, 11/1 for domestic students, 10/1 for international students. Applications are processed on a rolling basis. Application fee: $30. Electronic applications accepted. *Expenses:* Tuition, state resident: full-time $6576; part-time $274 per credit hour. Tuition, nonresident: full-time $13,152; part-time $548 per credit hour. Required fees: $1813; $75.53 per credit hour. Part-time tuition and fees vary according to course load. *Financial support:* In 2009–10, 1 teaching assistantship with full tuition reimbursement was awarded; fellowships with full tuition reimbursements, research assistantships with full tuition reimbursements, career-related internships or fieldwork, Federal Work-Study, scholarships/grants, tuition waivers (full), and staff assistantships also available. Support available to part-time students. Financial award applicants required to submit FAFSA. *Unit head:* Dr. Barbara Johnson, Interim Chair, 815-753-1448, E-mail: cahe@niu.edu. *Application contact:* Graduate School Office, 815-753-0395, E-mail: gradsch@niu.edu.

Northwestern State University of Louisiana, Graduate Studies and Research, College of Education, Program in Adult and Continuing Education, Natchitoches, LA 71497. Offers M Ed. *Degree requirements:* For master's, comprehensive exam, thesis or alternative. *Entrance requirements:* For master's, GRE General Test, minimum undergraduate GPA of 2.5.

Nova Southeastern University, Fischler School of Education and Human Services, Programs for Higher Education, Fort Lauderdale, FL 33314-7796. Offers adult education (Ed D); computing and information technology (Ed D); health care education (Ed D); higher education (Ed D); vocational, occupational and technical education (Ed D). Part-time and evening/weekend programs available. Postbaccalaureate distance learning degree programs offered (minimal on-campus study). *Faculty:* 6 full-time (3 women), 8 part-time/adjunct (2 women). *Students:* 113 full-time (81 women), 2 part-time (both women); includes 57 minority (51 African Americans, 6 Hispanic Americans). 4 applicants, 75% accepted, 3 enrolled. In 2009, 13 doctorates awarded. *Degree requirements:* For doctorate, thesis/dissertation, practicum. *Entrance requirements:* For doctorate, MAT or GRE, master's degree, work experience in field, minimum GPA of 3.0. Additional exam requirements/recommendations for international students: Required—TSE (recommended, minimum score 50); Recommended—TOEFL (minimum score 550 paper-based; 213 computer-based; 80 iBT), IELTS (minimum score 6). *Application deadline:* For fall admission, 8/11 priority date for domestic and international students; for winter admission, 12/28 priority date for domestic and international students; for spring admission, 4/22 priority date for domestic and international students. Applications are processed on a rolling basis. Application fee: $50. Electronic applications accepted. *Expenses:* Contact institution. *Financial support:* Career-related internships or fieldwork and tuition waivers (full) available. Financial award application deadline: 1/7. *Unit head:* Dr. Karen D. Bowser, Associate Dean of Doctoral Programs, 954-262-8677, Fax: 954-262-3606, E-mail: bowserk@nova.edu. *Application contact:* Dr. Jennifer Quinones Nottingham, Dean of Student Affairs, 800-986-3223 Ext. 8624, Fax: 954-262-3883, E-mail: jlquinon@nova.edu.

Oregon State University, Graduate School, College of Education, Program in Adult Education and Higher Education Leadership, Corvallis, OR 97331. Offers Ed M, MAIS. *Accreditation:* NCATE. Part-time programs available. *Faculty:* 3 full-time (all women), 4 part-time/adjunct (1 woman). *Students:* 1 full-time (0 women), 45 part-time (34 women); includes 5 minority (1 African American, 2 American Indian/Alaska Native, 2 Hispanic Americans), 1 international. Average age 42. In 2009, 13 master's awarded. *Degree requirements:* For master's, thesis or alternative. *Entrance requirements:* For master's, minimum GPA of 3.0 in last 90 hours. Additional exam requirements/recommendations for international students: Required—TOEFL. *Application deadline:* For fall admission, 3/1 for domestic students. Applications are processed on a rolling basis. Application fee: $50. *Expenses:* Tuition, state resident: full-time $9774; part-time $362 per credit. Tuition, nonresident: full-time $15,849; part-time $587 per credit. Required fees: $1639. Full-time tuition and fees vary according to course load and program. *Financial support:* Research assistantships, teaching assistantships, career-related internships or fieldwork, Federal Work-Study, and institutionally sponsored loans available. Support available to part-time students. Financial award application deadline: 2/1. *Faculty research:* Adult training and developmental psychology, cross-cultural communication, leadership development and human relations, adult literacy. *Unit head:* Dr. Tom Scheuermann, Interim Chair, 541-737-9524, E-mail: tom.scheuermann@oregonstate.edu. *Application contact:* Rosemary Garagnani, Assistant Dean, 541-737-1465, Fax: 541-737-3313.

Plymouth State University, College of Graduate Studies, Graduate Studies in Education, Program in Learning, Leadership and Community, Plymouth, NH 03264-1595. Offers Ed D.

Portland State University, Graduate Studies, School of Education, Department of Educational Policy, Foundations, and Administrative Studies, Portland, OR 97207-0751. Offers educational leadership (MA, MS, Ed D); postsecondary, adult and continuing education (Ed D). *Accreditation:* NCATE. Part-time and evening/weekend programs available. *Degree requirements:* For master's, thesis or alternative, written exam or research project; for doctorate, comprehensive exam, thesis/dissertation. *Entrance requirements:* For master's, California Basic Educational Skills Test, minimum GPA of 3.0 in upper-division course work or 2.75 overall; for doctorate, GRE General Test or MAT. Additional exam requirements/recommendations for international students: Required—TOEFL (minimum score 550 paper-based; 213 computer-based). *Faculty research:* Leadership development and research, principals and urban schools, accelerated schools, cooperative learning, family involvement in schools.

Regis University, College for Professional Studies, Program in Teacher Education, Denver, CO 80221-1099. Offers adult learning, training, and development (M Ed); curriculum, instruction, and assessment (M Ed); early childhood (M Ed); educational technology (Certificate); elementary (M Ed); ESL (M Ed); fine arts (M Ed), including arts, music; instructional technology (M Ed); professional leadership (M Ed); reading (M Ed); secondary (M Ed); self-designed (M Ed); space studies (M Ed); special education (M Ed); teacher licensure (M Ed). Program also offered in Henderson and Las Vegas (Summerlin), NV. *Accreditation:* Teacher Education Accreditation Council. Part-time and evening/weekend programs available. Postbaccalaureate distance learning degree programs offered (no on-campus study). *Degree requirements:* For master's, thesis. *Entrance requirements:* For master's, resume, minimum GPA of 2.75, criminal background check. Additional exam requirements/recommendations for international students: Required—TOEFL (minimum score 213 computer-based), TWE (minimum score 5). Electronic applications accepted. *Faculty research:* Issues of equity in the middle school classroom, professional learning communities, school reform, socialinguistic and discursive obstacles to student integration, inclusive language arts curriculum.

St. Francis Xavier University, Graduate Studies, Department of Adult Education, Antigonish, NS B2G 2W5, Canada. Offers M Ad Ed. Part-time programs available. Postbaccalaureate distance learning degree programs offered (minimal on-campus study). *Degree requirements:* For master's, thesis. *Entrance requirements:* For master's, minimum undergraduate B average, 2 years of work experience in field. Additional exam requirements/recommendations for international students: Required—TOEFL (minimum score .580 paper-based; 236 computer-based). *Faculty research:* Adult learning and development, religious education, women's issues, literacy, action research.

Saint Joseph's University, College of Arts and Sciences, Organization Development and Leadership Programs, Philadelphia, PA 19131-1395. Offers adult learning and training (MS, Certificate); organization dynamics and leadership (MS, Certificate); organizational psychology and development (MS, Certificate). Part-time and evening/weekend programs available. Postbaccalaureate distance learning degree programs offered (no on-campus study). *Students:* 9 full-time (6 women), 75 part-time (50 women); includes 23 minority (20 African Americans, 1 Asian American or Pacific Islander, 2 Hispanic Americans), 10 international. Average age 37. In 2009, 29 master's awarded. *Entrance requirements:* For master's, GRE (if GPA less than 2.7), minimum GPA of 2.7, 2 letters of recommendation, resume. Additional exam requirements/recommendations for international students: Required—TOEFL (minimum score 550 paper-based; 213 computer-based; 79 iBT). *Application deadline:* For fall admission, 7/15 priority date for domestic students, 4/15 for international students; for winter admission, 1/15 for international students; for spring admission, 11/15 priority date for domestic students, 10/15 for international students. Applications are processed on a rolling basis. Application fee: $35. Electronic applications accepted. *Expenses:* Tuition: Part-time $729 per credit hour. Tuition and fees vary according to degree level and program. *Financial support:* Applicants required to submit FAFSA. *Unit head:* Dr. Felice Tilin, Director, 610-660-1575, E-mail: ftilin@sju.edu. *Application contact:* Kate McConnell, Director, Graduate College of Arts and Sciences Admissions and Retention, 610-660-3184, Fax: 610-660-3230, E-mail: kate.mcconnell@sju.edu.

San Francisco State University, Division of Graduate Studies, College of Education, Department of Administration and Interdisciplinary Studies, Program in Adult Education, San Francisco, CA 94132-1722. Offers MA Ed, AC. *Accreditation:* NCATE.

Seattle University, College of Education, Program in Adult Education and Training, Seattle, WA 98122-1090. Offers M Ed, MA, Certificate. *Accreditation:* NCATE. Part-time and evening/weekend programs available. *Degree requirements:* For master's, comprehensive exam. *Entrance requirements:* For master's, GRE, MAT, or minimum GPA of 3.0; 1 year of related experience. Additional exam requirements/recommendations for international students: Required—TOEFL.

Suffolk University, College of Arts and Sciences, Department of Education and Human Services, Programs in Human Resource, Learning and Performance, Boston, MA 02108-2770. Offers global human resources (Graduate Certificate); human resources (MS, Graduate Certificate); organizational development (CAGS, Graduate Certificate); organizational learning and development (MS, Graduate Certificate); MS/Certificate. Part-time and evening/weekend programs available. *Entrance requirements:* For master's, GRE General Test or MAT, 2 letters of recommendation, resume. *Application deadline:* For fall admission, 6/15 priority date for domestic students, 6/15 for international students; for spring admission, 11/15 priority date for domestic students, 11/15 for international students. Applications are processed on a rolling basis. Application fee: $50. *Expenses:* Tuition: Full-time $33,000; part-time $1100 per credit. Required fees: $20. Tuition and fees vary according to program. *Financial support:* Fellowships available. Financial award application deadline: 4/1. *Faculty research:* Adult training methods, adult learning theory, instructional design, learning and teaching styles, systems thinking. *Unit head:* Christine M. Westphal, Graduate Program Director, 617-994-6455, Fax: 617-305-1743, E-mail: cwestpha@suffolk.edu. *Application contact:* Judith Reynolds, Director of Graduate Admissions, 617-573-8302, Fax: 617-305-1733, E-mail: grad.admission@suffolk.edu.

Teachers College, Columbia University, Graduate Faculty of Education, Department of Organization and Leadership, Program in Adult Education, New York, NY 10027-6696. Offers MA, Ed D. *Accreditation:* NCATE. *Faculty:* 3 full-time (2 women). *Students:* 48 full-time (37 women), 100 part-time (61 women); includes 51 minority (26 African Americans, 11 Asian Americans or Pacific Islanders, 14 Hispanic Americans), 13 international. Average age 42. 33 applicants, 70% accepted, 17 enrolled. In 2009, 32 master's, 13 doctorates awarded. *Degree requirements:* For doctorate, variable foreign language requirement, thesis/dissertation. *Entrance requirements:* For doctorate, 3-5 years of professional experience. *Application deadline:* For fall admission, 5/15 for domestic students. Application fee: $65. *Financial support:* Career-related internships or fieldwork, Federal Work-Study, institutionally sponsored loans, and tuition waivers (full and partial) available. Support available to part-time students. Financial award application deadline: 2/1. *Faculty research:* Adult learning, perspective transformation, training and evaluation, workplace learning, theory to practice. *Unit head:* Warner Burke, Chair, 212-678-3258. *Application contact:* Debbie Lesperance, Assistant Director of Admission, 212-678-3710, Fax: 212-678-4171.

Teachers College, Columbia University, Graduate Faculty of Education, Department of Organization and Leadership, Program in Adult Learning and Leadership, New York, NY 10027-6696. Offers Ed M, MA, Ed D.

Texas A&M University–Kingsville, College of Graduate Studies, College of Education, Department of Education, Program in Adult Education, Kingsville, TX 78363. Offers M Ed. Part-time and evening/weekend programs available. *Degree requirements:* For master's, comprehensive exam, mini-thesis. *Entrance requirements:* For master's, GRE General Test, MAT, minimum GPA of 3.0. *Faculty research:* Continuing education efforts in south Texas, adult education methodologies.

Texas A&M University–Texarkana, Graduate Studies and Research, College of Education and Liberal Arts, Texarkana, TX 75505-5518. Offers adult education (MS); curriculum and instruction (M Ed); education (MS); educational administration (M Ed); English (MA); instructional technology (MS); interdisciplinary studies (MA, MS); special education (MS). Part-time and evening/weekend programs available. *Degree requirements:* For master's, comprehensive exam (for some programs), thesis optional. *Entrance requirements:* For master's, minimum GPA of 2.5 on last 60 hours of bachelor's degree. Additional exam requirements/recommendations for international students: Required—TOEFL. Electronic applications accepted.

Texas State University–San Marcos, Graduate School, College of Education, Department of Counseling, Leadership, Adult Education, and School Psychology, Program in Developmental and Adult Education, San Marcos, TX 78666. Offers adult, professional, and community education (PhD); developmental and adult education (MA). Part-time programs available. *Faculty:* 16 full-time (6 women). *Students:* 13 full-time (7 women), 71 part-time (23 women); includes 40 minority (14 African Americans, 4 Asian Americans or Pacific Islanders, 22 Hispanic

Adult Education

Texas State University–San Marcos (continued)

Americans). Average age 44. 51 applicants, 29% accepted, 11 enrolled. In 2009, 3 master's, 5 doctorates awarded. *Degree requirements:* For master's, comprehensive exam, thesis, internship. *Entrance requirements:* For master's, minimum GPA of 2.75 in last 60 hours of course work. Additional exam requirements/recommendations for international students: Required—TOEFL (minimum score 550 paper-based; 213 computer-based). *Application deadline:* For fall admission, 6/15 for domestic students, 6/1 for international students; for spring admission, 10/1 for domestic and international students. Applications are processed on a rolling basis. Application fee: $40 ($90 for international students). Electronic applications accepted. *Expenses:* Tuition, state resident: full-time $5784; part-time $241 per credit hour. Tuition, nonresident: full-time $13,224; part-time $551 per credit hour. Required fees: $1728; $48 per credit hour. $306. Tuition and fees vary according to course load. *Financial support:* In 2009–10, 8 students received support, including 3 research assistantships (averaging $8,129 per year), 5 teaching assistantships (averaging $7,811 per year); career-related internships or fieldwork, Federal Work-Study, and institutionally sponsored loans also available. Support available to part-time students. Financial award application deadline: 4/1; financial award applicants required to submit FAFSA. *Unit head:* Dr. Jovita Ross-Gordan, Graduate Advisor, 512-245-3083, Fax: 512-245-8872. *Application contact:* Dr. J. Michael Willoughby, Dean of Graduate School, 512-245-2581, Fax: 512-245-8365, E-mail: gradcollege@txstate.edu.

Troy University, Graduate School, College of Education, Program in Adult Education, Troy, AL 36082. Offers MS. Part-time and evening/weekend programs available. *Students:* 11 full-time (6 women), 52 part-time (36 women); includes 36 minority (35 African Americans, 1 Asian American or Pacific Islander). Average age 41. 29 applicants, 97% accepted. In 2009, 7 master's awarded. *Degree requirements:* For master's, comprehensive exam, thesis or alternative. *Entrance requirements:* For master's, MAT (minimum score 385). Additional exam requirements/recommendations for international students: Required—TOEFL (minimum score 523 paper-based; 193 computer-based; 70 iBT), IELTS, or ACT Compass ESL (minimum score 270 on Listening, Reading, and Grammar with no individual score below 85 and a minimum score of 8 out of 12 on writing test). *Application deadline:* Applications are processed on a rolling basis. Application fee: $50. Electronic applications accepted. *Unit head:* Dr. Joe H. Reynolds, Coordinator, 334-241-8577, Fax: 334-240-7320, E-mail: jreynolds45@troy.edu. *Application contact:* Beth Potts, Graduate Actions Coordinator, 334-241-9707, Fax: 334-241-9586, E-mail: lizrichmond@troy.edu.

Troy University, Graduate School, College of Education, Program in Postsecondary Education, Troy, AL 36082. Offers adult education (M Ed); biology (M Ed); criminal justice (M Ed); english (M Ed); foundations of education (M Ed); general science (M Ed); higher education administration (M Ed); history (M Ed); instructional technology (M Ed); mathematics (M Ed); music industry (M Ed); physical fitness (M Ed); political science (M Ed); public administration (M Ed); social science (M Ed); teaching english (M Ed). Also offered through the University College. *Accreditation:* NCATE. Part-time and evening/weekend programs available. *Students:* 267 full-time (192 women), 381 part-time (293 women); includes 326 minority (309 African Americans, 4 American Indian/Alaska Native, 5 Asian Americans or Pacific Islanders, 8 Hispanic Americans). Average age 34. 343 applicants, 90% accepted. In 2009, 480 master's awarded. *Degree requirements:* For master's, comprehensive exam, thesis. *Entrance requirements:* For master's, MAT (minimum score 385), minimum GPA of 2.5. Additional exam requirements/recommendations for international students: Required—TOEFL (minimum score 523 paper-based; 193 computer-based; 70 iBT), IELTS, or ACT Compass ESL (minimum score 270 on Listening, Reading, and Grammar with no individual score below 85 and a minimum score of 8 out of 12 on writing test). *Application deadline:* Applications are processed on a rolling basis. Application fee: $50. Electronic applications accepted. *Financial support:* Available to part-time students. Applicants required to submit FAFSA. *Unit head:* Dr. Andrew Creamer, Chair, 334-670-3350, E-mail: drcreamer@troy.edu. *Application contact:* Brenda K. Campbell, Director of Graduate Admissions, 334-670-3178, Fax: 334-670-3733, E-mail: bcamp@troy.edu.

TUI University, College of Education, Program in Education, Cypress, CA 90630. Offers adult education (MA Ed); aviation education (MA Ed); children's literacy development (MA Ed); e-learning (MA Ed); early childhood education (MA Ed); enrollment management (MA Ed); higher education (MA Ed); teaching and instruction (MA Ed); training and development (MA Ed). Part-time and evening/weekend programs available. Postbaccalaureate distance learning degree programs offered (no on-campus study). *Degree requirements:* For master's, capstone project with integrative paper. *Entrance requirements:* For master's, minimum GPA of 2.5 (students with GPA 3.0 or greater may transfer up to 30% of graduate level credits). Additional exam requirements/recommendations for international students: Required—TOEFL (minimum score 525 paper-based). Electronic applications accepted.

Tusculum College, Graduate School, Program in Education, Greeneville, TN 37743-9997. Offers adult education (MA Ed); K–12 (MA Ed). Evening/weekend programs available. *Degree requirements:* For master's, thesis or alternative. *Entrance requirements:* For master's, 3 years of work experience, minimum GPA of 2.75.

Universidad del Este, Graduate School, Carolina, PR 00984. Offers accounting (MBA); adult education (M Ed); agribusiness (MBA); bilingual education (M Ed); criminal justice and criminology (MA); early education (M Ed); elementary education (M Ed); human resources (MBA); information security management (MBA); information technology and Web business development (MBA); management (MBA); public policy (MPA); social work (MA), including clinical social work; special education (M Ed); strategic leadership (MBA); teaching English (M Ed); teaching Spanish (M Ed).

Université du Québec en Outaouais, Graduate Programs, Program in Adult Education, Gatineau, QC J8X 3X7, Canada. Offers andragogy (DESS). Part-time programs available. *Entrance requirements:* For degree, appropriate bachelor's degree, proficiency in French.

University of Alaska Anchorage, College of Education, Program in Adult Education, Anchorage, AK 99508. Offers M Ed. Part-time programs available. *Degree requirements:* For master's, thesis or alternative. *Entrance requirements:* For master's, interview, minimum GPA of 3.0, writing exercise. Additional exam requirements/recommendations for international students: Required—TOEFL (minimum score 550 paper-based; 213 computer-based).

University of Alberta, Faculty of Graduate Studies and Research, Department of Educational Policy Studies, Edmonton, AB T6G 2E1, Canada. Offers adult education (M Ed, Ed D, PhD); educational administration and leadership (M Ed, Ed D, PhD, Postgraduate Diploma); First Nations education (M Ed, Ed D, PhD); theoretical, cultural and international studies in education (M Ed, Ed D, PhD). *Faculty:* 19 full-time (10 women), 5 part-time/adjunct (1 woman). *Students:* 73 full-time (47 women), 144 part-time (86 women). 141 applicants, 44% accepted. In 2009, 52 master's, 20 doctorates awarded. *Degree requirements:* For master's, thesis (for some programs); for doctorate, thesis/dissertation. *Entrance requirements:* For master's, minimum GPA of 6.5 on a 9.0 scale; for doctorate, minimum GPA of 7.5 on a 9.0 scale. Additional exam requirements/recommendations for international students: Required—TOEFL (minimum score 580 paper-based; 237 computer-based). *Application deadline:* For spring admission, 2/1 for domestic and international students. Electronic applications accepted. Tuition and fees charges are reported in Canadian dollars. *Expenses:* Tuition, area resident: Full-time $4626 Canadian dollars; part-time $99.72 Canadian dollars per unit. International tuition: $8216 Canadian dollars full-time. Required fees: $3590 Canadian dollars; $99.72 Canadian dollars per unit. $215 Canadian dollars per term. *Financial support:* In 2009–10, 7 fellowships with partial tuition reimbursements, 10 research assistantships with partial tuition reimbursements (averaging $6,936 per year), 30 teaching assistantships with partial tuition reimbursements (averaging $11,130 per year) were awarded; scholarships/grants and unspecified assistantships also available. *Unit head:* Dr. Frank Peters, Graduate Coordinator, 780-492-3679, Fax: 780-492-2024, E-mail: epscoord@ualberta.ca. *Application contact:* Joan A. White, Secretary, 780-492-3679, Fax: 780-492-2024, E-mail: joan.white@ualberta.ca.

University of Arkansas at Little Rock, Graduate School, College of Education, Department of Counseling and Rehabilitation Education, Program in Adult Education, Little Rock, AR 72204-1099. Offers M Ed. *Accreditation:* NCATE. Part-time programs available. *Degree requirements:* For master's, comprehensive exam. *Entrance requirements:* For master's, interview, minimum GPA of 2.75, GRE General Test or teaching certificate. *Faculty research:* Adult literacy, volunteer training, in-services education.

The University of British Columbia, Faculty of Education, Department of Educational Studies, Vancouver, BC V6T 1Z1, Canada. Offers adult education (M Ed, MA); adult learning and global change (M Ed); educational administration (M Ed, MA); educational leadership and policy (Ed D); educational studies (PhD); higher education (M Ed, MA); society, culture and politics in education (M Ed, MA). Part-time and evening/weekend programs available. Terminal master's awarded for partial completion of doctoral program. *Degree requirements:* For master's, thesis; for doctorate, comprehensive exam, thesis/dissertation, master's thesis. *Entrance requirements:* For master's, minimum B+ average, 4-year undergraduate degree, field-related experience; for doctorate, minimum B+ average, 4-year undergraduate degree, master's degree, field-related experience. Additional exam requirements/recommendations for international students: Required—TOEFL (600 paper; 250 computer; 100 Internet-based) or IELTS (6.5). Electronic applications accepted. *Faculty research:* Educational leadership educational administration adult education politics in education, global change and adult learning.

University of Central Oklahoma, College of Graduate Studies and Research, College of Education, Department of Occupational and Technical Education, Program in Adult Education, Edmond, OK 73034-5209. Offers community services (M Ed); gerontology (M Ed). *Accreditation:* NCATE. Part-time programs available. *Faculty:* 4 full-time (1 woman), 3 part-time/adjunct (1 woman). *Students:* 19 full-time (16 women), 73 part-time (51 women); includes 25 minority (17 African Americans, 3 American Indian/Alaska Native, 3 Asian Americans or Pacific Islanders, 2 Hispanic Americans), 1 international. Average age 37. 34 applicants, 100% accepted. In 2009, 30 master's awarded. *Entrance requirements:* For master's, GRE General Test. Additional exam requirements/recommendations for international students: Required—TOEFL (minimum score 550 paper-based; 213 computer-based). *Application deadline:* For fall admission, 7/1 for international students; for spring admission, 11/1 for international students. Applications are processed on a rolling basis. Application fee: $25. Electronic applications accepted. *Expenses:* Tuition, state resident: full-time $4128; part-time $172 per credit hour. Tuition, nonresident: full-time $10,373; part-time $432.20 per credit hour. Required fees: $433.20; $18.05 per credit hour. *Financial support:* Unspecified assistantships available. Financial award application deadline: 3/31; financial award applicants required to submit FAFSA. *Unit head:* Candy Sebert, Head, 405-974-5780. *Application contact:* Dr. Richard Bernard, Dean, Graduate College, 405-974-3493, Fax: 405-974-3852, E-mail: gradcoll@uco.edu.

University of Cincinnati, Graduate School, College of Education, Criminal Justice, and Human Services, Division of Teacher Education, Cincinnati, OH 45221. Offers curriculum and instruction (M Ed, Ed D); deaf studies (Certificate); early childhood education (M Ed); middle childhood education (M Ed); postsecondary literacy instruction (Certificate); reading/literacy (M Ed, Ed D); secondary education (M Ed); special education (M Ed, Ed D); teaching English as a second language (M Ed, Ed D, Certificate); teaching science (MS). Part-time programs available. *Degree requirements:* For doctorate, thesis/dissertation. *Entrance requirements:* For master's, GRE General Test. Electronic applications accepted.

University of Connecticut, Graduate School, Neag School of Education, Department of Educational Leadership, Field of Adult Learning, Storrs, CT 06269. Offers MA, PhD. *Accreditation:* NCATE. *Faculty:* 16 full-time (11 women). *Students:* 9 full-time (5 women), 22 part-time (15 women); includes 1 minority (African American), 4 international. Average age 40. 11 applicants, 45% accepted, 1 enrolled. In 2009, 1 master's, 4 doctorates awarded. Terminal master's awarded for partial completion of doctoral program. *Degree requirements:* For master's, comprehensive exam, thesis or alternative; for doctorate, thesis/dissertation. *Entrance requirements:* For master's and doctorate, GRE General Test. Additional exam requirements/recommendations for international students: Required—TOEFL (minimum score 550 paper-based; 213 computer-based). *Application deadline:* For fall admission, 2/1 priority date for domestic and international students; for spring admission, 11/1 for domestic students, 10/1 for international students. Applications are processed on a rolling basis. Application fee: $55. Electronic applications accepted. *Expenses:* Tuition, state resident: full-time $4725; part-time $525 per credit. Tuition, nonresident: full-time $12,267; part-time $1363 per credit. Required fees: $346 per semester. Tuition and fees vary according to course load. *Financial support:* In 2009–10, 4 research assistantships with full tuition reimbursements, 2 teaching assistantships with full tuition reimbursements were awarded; fellowships, Federal Work-Study, scholarships/grants, health care benefits, and unspecified assistantships also available. Financial award application deadline: 2/1; financial award applicants required to submit FAFSA. *Unit head:* Barry G. Sheckley, Head, 860-486-2738, Fax: 860-486-4028, E-mail: barry.sheckley@uconn.edu. *Application contact:* Lisa Rasicot, Graduate Coordinator, 860-486-3065, Fax: 860-486-0210, E-mail: l.rasicot@uconn.edu.

University of Denver, College of Education, Denver, CO 80208. Offers counseling psychology (MA, PhD); curriculum and instruction (MA, PhD, Certificate), including curriculum leadership (MA, PhD); educational administration and policy studies (Certificate); educational psychology (MA, PhD, Ed S), including child and family studies (MA, PhD), quantitative research methods (MA, PhD), school psychology (PhD, Ed S); higher education and adult studies (MA, PhD); library and information science (MLIS); library and information sciences (Certificate); school administration (PhD). *Accreditation:* ALA; APA (one or more programs are accredited). Part-time and evening/weekend programs available. Postbaccalaureate distance learning degree programs offered (no on-campus study). *Faculty:* 33 full-time (24 women), 62 part-time/adjunct (41 women). *Students:* 384 full-time (305 women), 453 part-time (336 women); includes 164 minority (47 African Americans, 8 American Indian/Alaska Native, 14 Asian Americans or Pacific Islanders, 95 Hispanic Americans), 20 international. Average age 34. 1,065 applicants, 59% accepted, 433 enrolled. In 2009, 206 master's, 38 doctorates, 117 other advanced degrees awarded. Terminal master's awarded for partial completion of doctoral program. *Degree requirements:* For master's, comprehensive exam; for doctorate, 2 foreign languages, comprehensive exam, thesis/dissertation. *Entrance requirements:* For master's and doctorate, GRE General Test or MAT. *Application deadline:* Applications are processed on a rolling basis. Application fee: $50. Electronic applications accepted. *Expenses:* Tuition: Full-time $34,596; part-time $961 per quarter hour. Required fees: $4 per quarter hour. Tuition and fees vary according to course load, campus/location and program. *Financial support:* In 2009–10, 78 teaching assistantships with full and partial tuition reimbursements (averaging $11,700 per year) were awarded; career-related internships or fieldwork, Federal Work-Study, institutionally sponsored loans, and scholarships/grants also available. Support available to part-time students. Financial award application deadline: 3/1; financial award applicants required to submit FAFSA. *Faculty research:* Parkinson's disease, personnel training, development and assessments, gifted education, service-learning, transportation, public schools. Total annual research expenditures: $340,000. *Unit head:* Dr. Gregory M. Anderson, Dean, 303-871-3665. *Application contact:* Janet Erickson, Director of Graduate Admission, 303-871-2485, E-mail: edinfo@du.edu.

University of Georgia, Graduate School, College of Education, Department of Lifelong Education, Administration and Policy, Athens, GA 30602. Offers adult education (M Ed, Ed D, PhD, Ed S); educational administration and policy (M Ed, PhD, Ed S); educational leadership (Ed D); human resource and organizational design (M Ed). *Accreditation:* NCATE. *Faculty:* 26 full-time (17 women). *Students:* 77 full-time (55 women), 181 part-time (124 women); includes 64 minority (54 African Americans, 1 American Indian/Alaska Native, 4 Asian Americans or Pacific Islanders, 5 Hispanic Americans), 28 international. 199 applicants, 60% accepted, 77 enrolled. In 2009, 43 master's, 21 doctorates, 5 other advanced degrees awarded. *Entrance requirements:* For master's and Ed S, GRE General Test or MAT; for doctorate, GRE General Test. *Application deadline:* For fall admission, 7/1 priority date for domestic students; for spring admission, 11/15 for domestic students. Application fee: $50. Electronic applications accepted. *Expenses:* Tuition, state resident: full-time $6000; part-time $250 per credit hour. Tuition, nonresident: full-time $20,904; part-time $871 per credit hour. Required fees: $730 per semester. *Unit head:* Dr. Ronald M. Cervero, Head, 706-542-2221, Fax: 706-542-5873, E-mail: rcervero@.

uga.edu. *Application contact:* Dr. Kathryn Roulston, Graduate Coordinator, 706-542-4060, Fax: 706-542-5873, E-mail: roulston@uga.edu.

University of Idaho, College of Graduate Studies, College of Education, Department of Adult, Career, and Technology Education, Program in Adult and Organizational Learning, Moscow, ID 83844-2282. Offers MS, Ed S. *Accreditation:* NCATE. *Students:* 4 part-time. In 2009, 12 master's, 1 other advanced degree awarded. *Entrance requirements:* For master's, minimum GPA of 2.8. *Application deadline:* For fall admission, 8/1 for domestic students; for spring admission, 12/15 for domestic students. Application fee: $55 ($60 for international students). *Expenses:* Tuition, state resident: full-time $6120. Tuition, nonresident: full-time $17,712. *Financial support:* Application deadline: 2/15. *Unit head:* Dr. Charles W. Gagel, Head, 208-885-6492. *Application contact:* Dr. Charles W. Gagel, Head, 208-885-6492.

University of Manitoba, Faculty of Graduate Studies, Faculty of Education, Department of Educational Administration, Foundations and Psychology, Winnipeg, MB R3T 2N2, Canada. Offers adult and post-secondary education (M Ed); educational administration (M Ed); guidance and counseling (M Ed); inclusive special education (M Ed); social foundations of education (M Ed). *Degree requirements:* For master's, thesis or alternative.

University of Memphis, Graduate School, College of Education, Department of Leadership, Memphis, TN 38152. Offers adult education (Ed D); educational leadership (Ed D); higher education (Ed D); leadership (MS); policy studies (Ed D); school administration and supervision (MS). *Accreditation:* NCATE. Part-time and evening/weekend programs available. Post-baccalaureate distance learning degree programs offered (minimal on-campus study). *Faculty:* 10 full-time (5 women), 9 part-time/adjunct (2 women). *Students:* 34 full-time (21 women), 115 part-time (69 women); includes 87 minority (86 African Americans, 1 Hispanic American), 1 international. Average age 40. 27 applicants, 85% accepted, 5 enrolled. In 2009, 12 master's, 13 doctorates awarded. *Degree requirements:* For master's, comprehensive exam, thesis optional; for doctorate, comprehensive exam, thesis/dissertation. *Entrance requirements:* For master's and doctorate, GRE. *Application deadline:* For fall admission, 4/1 for domestic students; for spring admission, 10/1 for domestic students. Application fee: $35 ($60 for international students). Electronic applications accepted. *Expenses:* Tuition, state resident: full-time $6246; part-time $347 per credit hour. Tuition, nonresident: full-time $15,894; part-time $883 per credit hour. Required fees: $1160. Full-time tuition and fees vary according to course load, degree level and program. *Financial support:* In 2009–10, 70 students received support; research assistantships with full tuition reimbursements available, teaching assistantships, Federal Work-Study, scholarships/grants, and unspecified assistantships available. Financial award application deadline: 2/15; financial award applicants required to submit FAFSA. *Faculty research:* School improvement, social justice, online learning, adult learning, diversity. *Unit head:* Katrina Mayer, Interim Chair, E-mail: kmeyer@memphis.edu. *Application contact:* Larry McNeal, Professor, School Administration and Supervision Programs, E-mail: lmcneal1@memphis.edu.

University of Minnesota, Twin Cities Campus, Graduate School, College of Education and Human Development, Department of Organizational Leadership, Policy and Development, Program in Adult Education, Minneapolis, MN 55455-0213. Offers M Ed, MA, Ed D, PhD, Certificate. *Students:* 7 full-time (6 women), 14 part-time (10 women); includes 3 minority (1 African American, 2 Hispanic Americans). Average age 43. 24 applicants, 67% accepted, 14 enrolled. In 2009, 10 master's, 9 other advanced degrees awarded. *Unit head:* Ken Bartlett, Chair, 612-624-4935, Fax: 612-624-2231. *Application contact:* Dr. Mary Trettin, Associate Dean, 612-625-6501, Fax: 612-626-1580, E-mail: mtrettin@umn.edu.

University of Missouri, Graduate School, College of Education, Department of Educational Leadership and Policy Analysis, Columbia, MO 65211. Offers education administration (M Ed, MA, Ed D, PhD, Ed S); higher and adult education (M Ed, MA, Ed D, PhD, Ed S). Part-time programs available. *Faculty:* 15 full-time (8 women), 5 part-time/adjunct (4 women). *Students:* 212 full-time (128 women), 160 part-time (97 women); includes 35 minority (22 African Americans, 2 American Indian/Alaska Native, 4 Asian Americans or Pacific Islanders, 7 Hispanic Americans), 12 international. Average age 39. 186 applicants, 74% accepted, 91 enrolled. In 2009, 7 master's, 19 doctorates, 7 other advanced degrees awarded. *Degree requirements:* For doctorate, variable foreign language requirement, comprehensive exam (for some programs), thesis/dissertation. *Entrance requirements:* For master's, doctorate, and Ed S, minimum GPA of 3.0. Additional exam requirements/recommendations for international students: Required—TOEFL (minimum score 500 paper-based; 173 computer-based; 61 iBT), IELTS (minimum score 5.5). *Application deadline:* For fall admission, 2/15 priority date for domestic students; for spring admission, 10/15 for domestic students. Applications are processed on a rolling basis. Application fee: $45 ($60 for international students). Electronic applications accepted. *Financial support:* In 2009–10, 2 fellowships with full tuition reimbursements, 32 research assistantships with full tuition reimbursements, 4 teaching assistantships with full tuition reimbursements were awarded; institutionally sponsored loans, scholarships/grants, health care benefits, and unspecified assistantships also available. *Faculty research:* Administrative communication and behavior, middle schools leadership, administration of special education. *Unit head:* Dr. Jay Scribner, Department Chair, E-mail: scribnerj@missouri.edu. *Application contact:* Betty Kissane, 573-882-8231, E-mail: kissaneb@missouri.edu.

University of Missouri–St. Louis, College of Education, Division of Educational Leadership and Policy Studies, St. Louis, MO 63121. Offers adult and higher education (M Ed), including adult education; educational administration (M Ed, Ed S), including community education (M Ed), elementary education (M Ed), secondary education (M Ed); institutional research (Certificate). *Accreditation:* NCATE. Part-time and evening/weekend programs available. *Faculty:* 19 full-time (8 women), 7 part-time/adjunct (4 women). *Students:* 25 full-time (21 women), 196 part-time (137 women); includes 88 minority (84 African Americans, 1 Asian American or Pacific Islander, 3 Hispanic Americans), 4 international. Average age 36. In 2009, 66 master's, 25 Certificates awarded. *Degree requirements:* For master's, comprehensive exam (for some programs). *Entrance requirements:* Additional exam requirements/recommendations for international students: Required—TOEFL (minimum score 550 paper-based; 213 computer-based). *Application deadline:* For fall admission, 7/1 priority date for domestic and international students; for spring admission, 12/1 priority date for domestic and international students. Applications are processed on a rolling basis. Application fee: $35 ($40 for international students). Electronic applications accepted. *Expenses:* Tuition, state resident: full-time $5377; part-time $297.70 per credit hour. Tuition, nonresident: full-time $13,882; part-time $771.20 per credit hour. Required fees: $220; $12.20 per credit hour. One-time fee: $12. Tuition and fees vary according to course level, campus/location and program. *Financial support:* In 2009–10, 3 research assistantships (averaging $5,133 per year) were awarded. Financial award application deadline: 4/1; financial award applicants required to submit FAFSA. *Faculty research:* Educational policy research; philosophy of education; higher, adult, and vocational education; school initiatives, change, and reform. *Unit head:* Dr. E. Paulette Savage, Chair, 514-516-5944. *Application contact:* 314-516-5458, Fax: 314-516-6996, E-mail: gradadm@umsl.edu.

University of Missouri–St. Louis, College of Education, Interdisciplinary Doctoral Programs, St. Louis, MO 63121. Offers adult and higher education (Ed D); counseling (PhD); counselor education (Ed D); educational administration (Ed D); educational leadership and policy studies (PhD); educational psychology (PhD). *Faculty:* 72 full-time (33 women). *Students:* 23 full-time (18 women), 240 part-time (159 women); includes 76 minority (61 African Americans, 2 American Indian/Alaska Native, 7 Asian Americans or Pacific Islanders, 6 Hispanic Americans), 5 international. Average age 40. In 2009, 19 doctorates awarded. *Degree requirements:* For doctorate, thesis/dissertation. *Entrance requirements:* For doctorate, GRE General Test, 3 letters of recommendation; personal interview. Additional exam requirements/recommendations for international students: Recommended—TOEFL (minimum score 550 paper-based; 230 computer-based). *Application deadline:* For fall admission, 2/15 for domestic and international students; for spring admission, 10/1 for domestic and international students. Application fee: $35 ($40 for international students). Electronic applications accepted. *Expenses:* Tuition, state resident: full-time $5377; part-time $297.70 per credit hour. Tuition, nonresident: full-time $13,882; part-time $771.20 per credit hour. Required fees: $220; $12.20 per credit hour. One-time fee: $12. Tuition and fees vary according to course level, campus/location and program. *Financial support:* In 2009–10, 15 research assistantships (averaging $12,240 per year), 8 teaching assistantships (averaging $12,240 per year) were awarded. Financial award application deadline: 4/1; financial award applicants required to submit FAFSA. *Faculty research:* Higher education law and policy, gender and higher education, student retention, lifelong learning orientation, school counselor's role in violence prevention. *Unit head:* Dr. Kathleen Haywood, Director of Graduate Studies, 314-516-5483, Fax: 314-516-5227, E-mail: kathleen_haywood@umsl.edu. *Application contact:* Dr. Kathleen Haywood, Director of Graduate Studies, 314-516-5483, Fax: 314-516-5227, E-mail: kathleen_haywood@umsl.edu.

University of Nebraska–Lincoln, Graduate College, College of Education and Human Sciences, Department of Teaching, Learning and Teacher Education, Lincoln, NE 68588. Offers adult and continuing education (MA); educational studies (Ed D, PhD), including special education (Ed D); teaching, learning and teacher education (M Ed, MA, MST, Ed D, PhD); vocational and adult education (M Ed, MA). *Accreditation:* NCATE. *Degree requirements:* For master's, thesis optional. *Entrance requirements:* Additional exam requirements/recommendations for international students: Required—TOEFL (minimum score 550 paper-based; 213 computer-based). Electronic applications accepted. *Faculty research:* Teacher education, instructional leadership, literacy education, technology, improvement of school curriculum.

The University of North Carolina at Charlotte, Graduate School, College of Education, Program in Curriculum and Instruction, Charlotte, NC 28223-0001. Offers urban education (PhD), including adult and continuing education leadership, educational administration; urban literacy (PhD); urban math (PhD). Part-time and evening/weekend programs available. *Faculty:* 7 full-time (5 women). *Students:* 10 full-time (all women), 55 part-time (36 women); includes 14 African Americans, 1 Asian American or Pacific Islander, 2 international. Average age 41. 24 applicants, 71% accepted, 15 enrolled. In 2009, 8 doctorates awarded. *Degree requirements:* For doctorate, thesis/dissertation. *Entrance requirements:* For doctorate, GRE or MAT. Additional exam requirements/recommendations for international students: Required—TOEFL (minimum score 557 paper-based; 220 computer-based; 83 iBT). *Application deadline:* For fall admission, 7/15 for domestic students, 5/1 for international students; for spring admission, 11/15 for domestic students, 10/1 for international students. Application fee: $55. *Financial support:* In 2009–10, 9 students received support, including 9 teaching assistantships (averaging $12,880 per year). Financial award application deadline: 4/1; financial award applicants required to submit FAFSA. Total annual research expenditures: $65,335. *Unit head:* Dr. Jeanneine Jones, Interim Chair, Department of Middle, Secondary, and K-12 Education, 704-687-8875, Fax: 704-687-6430, E-mail: jpjones@uncc.edu. *Application contact:* Dr. David K. Pugalee, Coordinator, 704-687-8887, Fax: 704-687-3216, E-mail: david.pugalee@uncc.edu.

The University of North Carolina at Greensboro, Graduate School, School of Education, Department of Curriculum and Instruction, Greensboro, NC 27412-5001. Offers college teaching and adult learning (Certificate); curriculum and instruction (M Ed), including chemistry education, elementary education, English as a second language, French education, instructional technology, mathematics education, middle grades education, reading education, science education, social studies education, Spanish education; curriculum and teaching (PhD), including higher education, teacher education and development; English as a second language (Certificate); higher education (M Ed); supervision (M Ed). *Accreditation:* NCATE. Part-time programs available. *Degree requirements:* For doctorate, thesis/dissertation. *Entrance requirements:* For master's and doctorate, GRE General Test. Additional exam requirements/recommendations for international students: Required—TOEFL. Electronic applications accepted. *Faculty research:* Community college literacy program, middle school mathematics/computer mathematics.

University of North Florida, College of Education and Human Services, Department of Foundations and Secondary Education, Jacksonville, FL 32224. Offers adult learning (M Ed); instructional technology (M Ed); professional education (M Ed). *Accreditation:* NCATE. Part-time and evening/weekend programs available. *Faculty:* 11 full-time (5 women). *Students:* 12 full-time (8 women), 27 part-time (17 women); includes 9 minority (7 African Americans, 1 Asian American or Pacific Islander, 1 Hispanic American). Average age 37. 13 applicants, 23% accepted, 2 enrolled. In 2009, 13 master's awarded. *Entrance requirements:* For master's, GRE General Test, minimum GPA of 3.0 in last 60 hours, interview, 3 letters of recommendation. Additional exam requirements/recommendations for international students: Required—TOEFL (minimum score 500 paper-based; 173 computer-based). *Application deadline:* For fall admission, 7/1 priority date for domestic students, 5/1 for international students; for spring admission, 11/1 priority date for domestic students, 10/1 for international students. Applications are processed on a rolling basis. Application fee: $30. Electronic applications accepted. *Expenses:* Tuition, state resident: full-time $6649.20; part-time $277.05 per credit hour. Tuition, nonresident: full-time $22,970; part-time $957.08 per credit hour. Required fees: $985; $41.03 per credit hour. *Financial support:* In 2009–10, 19 students received support; teaching assistantships, career-related internships or fieldwork, Federal Work-Study, and tuition waivers (partial) available. Support available to part-time students. Financial award application deadline: 4/1; financial award applicants required to submit FAFSA. *Faculty research:* Using children's literature to enhance metalinguistic awareness, education, oral language diagnosis of middle-schoolers, science inquiry teaching and learning. Total annual research expenditures: $8,501. *Unit head:* Dr. Jeffery Cornett, Chair, 904-620-2610, Fax: 904-620-1821, E-mail: jcornett@unf.edu. *Application contact:* Dr. John Kemppainen, Director of Academic Advising, 904-620-2530, Fax: 904-620-1135, E-mail: jkemppai@unf.edu.

University of Oklahoma, Graduate College, College of Education, Department of Educational Leadership and Policy Studies, Program in Adult and Higher Education, Norman, OK 73019. Offers M Ed, PhD. *Accreditation:* NCATE. Part-time and evening/weekend programs available. *Students:* 112 full-time (45 women), 91 part-time (48 women); includes 51 minority (23 African Americans, 14 American Indian/Alaska Native, 6 Asian Americans or Pacific Islanders, 8 Hispanic Americans), 7 international. 124 applicants, 85% accepted, 58 enrolled. In 2009, 51 master's, 5 doctorates awarded. Terminal master's awarded for partial completion of doctoral program. *Degree requirements:* For master's, comprehensive exam; for doctorate, variable foreign language requirement, thesis/dissertation, general exam. *Entrance requirements:* For master's, minimum GPA of 3.0 in last 60 hours of undergraduate course work; for doctorate, GRE General Test, resume, 3 letters of reference, scholarly writing sample. Additional exam requirements/recommendations for international students: Required—TOEFL (minimum score 550 paper-based; 213 computer-based). *Application deadline:* For fall admission, 6/1 for domestic students, 4/1 for international students; for spring admission, 10/1 for domestic students, 9/1 for international students. Application fee: $40 ($90 for international students). Electronic applications accepted. *Expenses:* Tuition, state resident: full-time $3744; part-time $156 per credit hour. Tuition, nonresident: full-time $13,577; part-time $565.70 per credit hour. Required fees: $2415; $90.10 per credit hour. *Financial support:* In 2009–10, 148 students received support. Career-related internships or fieldwork, traineeships, health care benefits, and unspecified assistantships available. Financial award applicants required to submit FAFSA. *Faculty research:* Diversity, leadership, intercollegiate athletics, technology in learning, democratic education. *Unit head:* David Tan, Interim Chair, 405-325-5986, Fax: 405-325-2403, E-mail: dtan@ou.edu. *Application contact:* Dr. Kathleen Rager, Program Area Coordinator, 405-325-0548, Fax: 405-325-2403, E-mail: kbrager@ou.edu.

University of Phoenix, College of Natural Sciences, College of Education, Phoenix, AZ 85034-7209. Offers administration and supervision (MAEd); adult education and training (MAEd); curriculum and instruction (MAEd); curriculum and instruction-adult education (MAEd); curriculum and instruction-computer education (MAEd); curriculum and instruction-English and language arts education (MAEd); curriculum and instruction-English as a second language (MAEd); curriculum and instruction-mathematics education (MAEd); curriculum education (MAEd); early childhood (MAEd); elementary teacher education (MAEd); secondary teacher education (MAEd); special education (MAEd); teacher leadership (MAEd). *Accreditation:* Teacher Education Accreditation Council. Evening/weekend programs available. Postbaccalaureate distance learning degree programs offered (no on-campus study). *Faculty:* 47 full-time (34 women), 844 part-time/adjunct (636 women). *Students:* 13,657 full-time (10,698 women);

Adult Education

University of Phoenix (continued)

includes 4,000 minority (3,063 African Americans, 74 American Indian/Alaska Native, 241 Asian Americans or Pacific Islanders, 622 Hispanic Americans), 307 international. Average age 36. In 2009, 17,246 master's awarded. *Degree requirements:* For master's, thesis (for some programs). *Entrance requirements:* For master's, 3 years of work experience, minimum GPA of 2.5. Additional exam requirements/recommendations for international students: Required—TOEFL (minimum score 550 paper-based; 213 computer-based; 79 iBT). *Application deadline:* Applications are processed on a rolling basis. Application fee: $45. Electronic applications accepted. *Expenses:* Tuition: Full-time $13,272. Required fees: $660. Full-time tuition and fees vary according to course level, degree level and program. *Financial support:* Institutionally sponsored loans and scholarships/grants available. Financial award applicants required to submit FAFSA. *Unit head:* Dr. Meredith Curley, Dean/Executive Director, 480-557-1217, Fax: 480-557-1588, E-mail: meredith.curley@phoenix.edu. *Application contact:* Chair, 602-387-7000, Fax: 602-387-6020.

University of Phoenix–Bay Area Campus, The Artemis School, College of Education, Pleasanton, CA 94588-3677. Offers curriculum instruction (MA Ed); curriculum instruction—adult education (MA Ed); elementary teacher education (MA Ed); secondary teacher education (MA Ed). Evening/weekend programs available. Postbaccalaureate distance learning degree programs offered (no on-campus study). *Degree requirements:* For master's, thesis (for some programs). *Entrance requirements:* For master's, minimum undergraduate GPA of 2.5, 3 years of work experience. Additional exam requirements/recommendations for international students: Required—TOEFL (minimum score 550 paper-based; 213 computer-based; 79 iBT). Electronic applications accepted.

University of Phoenix–Omaha Campus, College of Education, Omaha, NE 68154-5240. Offers administration and supervision (MA Ed); curriculum and instruction (MA Ed), including adult education, computer education, curriculum and instruction, English and language arts education, English as a second language, mathematics education; elementary teacher education (MA Ed); secondary teacher education (MA Ed); special education (MA Ed).

University of Phoenix–Sacramento Valley Campus, The Artemis School, College of Education, Sacramento, CA 95833-3632. Offers adult education (MA Ed); curriculum instruction (MA Ed); elementary teacher education (MA Ed); secondary teacher education (MA Ed); teacher education (Certificate). Evening/weekend programs available. *Degree requirements:* For master's, thesis (for some programs). *Entrance requirements:* For master's, 3 years of work experience, minimum undergraduate GPA of 2.5. Additional exam requirements/recommendations for international students: Required—TOEFL (minimum score 550 paper-based; 213 computer-based; 79 iBT). Electronic applications accepted.

University of Phoenix–Southern Arizona Campus, The Artemis School, College of Education, Tucson, AZ 85711. Offers administration and supervision (MA Ed); adult education and training (MA Ed); curriculum instruction (MA Ed); educational counseling (MA Ed); elementary teacher education (MA Ed); school counseling (MSC); secondary teacher education (MA Ed); special education (MA Ed, Certificate). Evening/weekend programs available. *Degree requirements:* For master's, thesis (for some programs). *Entrance requirements:* For master's, minimum undergraduate GPA of 2.5, 3 years of work experience. Additional exam requirements/recommendations for international students: Required—TOEFL (minimum score 550 paper-based; 213 computer-based; 79 iBT). Electronic applications accepted.

University of Phoenix–Southern California Campus, College of Education, Costa Mesa, CA 92626. Offers administration and supervision (MA Ed); adult education and training (MA Ed); curriculum and instruction (MA Ed), including computer education, curriculum and instruction, English and language arts, English as a second language, mathematics education; early childhood education (MA Ed); special education (MA Ed); teacher leadership (MA Ed). Evening/weekend programs available. *Faculty:* 47 full-time (34 women), 844 part-time/adjunct (636 women). *Students:* 558 full-time (391 women); includes 222 minority (60 African Americans, 4 American Indian/Alaska Native, 26 Asian Americans or Pacific Islanders, 132 Hispanic Americans), 9 international. Average age 34. In 2009, 303 master's awarded. *Degree requirements:* For master's, thesis (for some programs). *Entrance requirements:* For master's, minimum undergraduate GPA of 2.5, 3 years work experience. Additional exam requirements/recommendations for international students: Required—TOEFL (minimum score 550 paper-based; 213 computer-based; 79 iBT). *Application deadline:* Applications are processed on a rolling basis. Application fee: $45. Electronic applications accepted. *Expenses:* Tuition: Full-time $15,120. Required fees: $660. *Financial support:* Institutionally sponsored loans and scholarships/grants available. Financial award applicants required to submit FAFSA. *Unit head:* Dr. Meredith Curley, Dean/Executive Director, 480-557-1217, Fax: 480-557-1588, E-mail: meredith.curley@phoenix.edu. *Application contact:* Campus College Chair, 714-378-1878, Fax: 714-378-5875.

University of Regina, Faculty of Graduate Studies and Research, Faculty of Education, Department of Adult Education, Regina, SK S4S 0A2, Canada. Offers M Ad Ed. Part-time programs available. *Faculty:* 3 full-time (2 women). *Students:* 4 full-time (2 women), 19 part-time (17 women). 14 applicants, 86% accepted. In 2009, 8 master's awarded. *Degree requirements:* For master's, practicum, project, or thesis. *Entrance requirements:* For master's, bachelor's degree in education, 2 years of teaching experience. Additional exam requirements/recommendations for international students: Required—TOEFL (minimum score 580 paper-based; 237 computer-based; 80 iBT). *Application deadline:* For fall admission, 2/15 for domestic students; for winter admission, 2/15 for domestic students; for spring admission, 2/15 for domestic students. Application fee: $90 ($100 for international students). Electronic applications accepted. *Financial support:* In 2009–10, 1 fellowship (averaging $19,000 per year), 1 research assistantship (averaging $16,910 per year), 1 teaching assistantship (averaging $6,650 per year) were awarded. Financial award application deadline: 6/15. *Faculty research:* Program and instruction. *Unit head:* Dr. Warren Wessel, 306-585-4555, E-mail: warren.wessel@uregina.ca. *Application contact:* Tania Gates, Graduate Program Coordinator, 306-585-4506, Fax: 306-585-5387, E-mail: edgrad@uregina.ca.

University of Rhode Island, Graduate School, College of Human Science and Services, School of Education, Kingston, RI 02881. Offers adult education (MA); education (PhD); elementary education (MA); music education (MM); reading education (MA); secondary education (MA); special education (MA); MS/PhD. *Accreditation:* NCATE. Part-time and evening/weekend programs available. *Faculty:* 19 full-time (12 women), 5 part-time/adjunct (1 woman). *Students:* 44 full-time (33 women), 128 part-time (101 women); includes 14 minority (8 African Americans, 2 American Indian/Alaska Native, 2 Asian Americans or Pacific Islanders, 2 Hispanic Americans), 3 international. In 2009, 44 master's, 7 doctorates awarded. *Degree requirements:* For master's, comprehensive exam (for some programs), thesis optional; for doctorate, comprehensive exam, thesis/dissertation. *Entrance requirements:* For master's, 2 letters of recommendation; interview (for special education applicants); for doctorate, GRE, 3 letters of recommendation, resume. Additional exam requirements/recommendations for international students: Required—TOEFL (minimum score 600 paper-based; 250 computer-based; 100 iBT). *Application deadline:* For fall admission, 1/31 for international students. Application fee: $65. Electronic applications accepted. *Expenses:* Tuition, state resident: full-time $8828; part-time $490 per credit hour. Tuition, nonresident: full-time $22,100; part-time $1228 per credit hour. Required fees: $1118; $57 per semester. Tuition and fees vary according to program. *Financial support:* In 2009–10, 5 research assistantships with full and partial tuition reimbursements (averaging $11,518 per year), 3 teaching assistantships with full and partial tuition reimbursements (averaging $10,421 per year) were awarded; career-related internships or fieldwork also available. Financial award applicants required to submit FAFSA. Total annual research expenditures: $3.4 million. *Unit head:* Dr. David Byrd, Director, 401-874-5484, Fax: 401-874-5471, E-mail: dbyrd@uri.edu. *Application contact:* Dr. John Boulmetis, Coordinator of Graduate Studies, 401-874-4159, Fax: 401-874-7610, E-mail: johnb@uri.edu.

University of South Africa, College of Human Sciences, Pretoria, South Africa. Offers adult education (M Ed); African languages (MA, PhD); African politics (MA, PhD); Afrikaans (MA, PhD); ancient history (MA, PhD); ancient Near Eastern studies (MA, PhD); anthropology (MA, PhD); applied linguistics (MA); Arabic (MA, PhD); archaeology (MA); art history (MA); Biblical archaeology (MA); Biblical studies (M Th, D Th, PhD); Christian spirituality (M Th, D Th); church history (M Th, D Th); classical studies (MA, PhD); clinical psychology (MA); communication (MA, PhD); comparative education (M Ed, Ed D); consulting psychology (D Admin, D Com, PhD); curriculum studies (M Ed, Ed D); development studies (M Admin, MA, D Admin, PhD); didactics (M Ed, Ed D); education (M Tech); education management (M Ed, Ed D); educational psychology (M Ed); English (MA); environmental education (M Ed); French (MA, PhD); German (MA, PhD); Greek (MA); guidance and counseling (M Ed); health studies (MA, PhD), including health sciences education (MA), health services management (MA), medical and surgical nursing science (critical care general) (MA), midwifery and neonatal nursing science (MA), trauma and emergency care (MA); history (MA, PhD); history of education (Ed D); inclusive education (M Ed, Ed D); information and communications technology policy and regulation (MA); information science (MA, MIS, PhD); international politics (MA, PhD); Islamic studies (MA, PhD); Italian (MA, PhD); Judaica (MA, PhD); linguistics (MA, PhD); mathematical education (M Ed); mathematics education (MA); missiology (M Th, D Th); modern Hebrew (MA, PhD); musicology (MA, MMus, D Mus, PhD); natural science education (M Ed); New Testament (M Th, D Th); Old Testament (D Th); pastoral therapy (M Th, D Th); philosophy (MA); philosophy of education (M Ed, Ed D); politics (MA, PhD); Portuguese (MA, PhD); practical theology (M Th, D Th); psychology (MA, MS, PhD); psychology of education (M Ed, Ed D); public health (MA); religious studies (MA, D Th, PhD); Romance languages (MA); Russian (MA, PhD); Semitic languages (MA, PhD); social behavior studies in HIV/AIDS (MA); social science (mental health) (MA); social science in development studies (MA); social science in psychology (MA); social science in social work (MA); social science in sociology (MA); social work (MSW, DSW, PhD); socio-education (M Ed, Ed D); sociolinguistics (MA); sociology (MA, PhD); Spanish (MA, PhD); systematic theology (M Th, D Th); TESOL (teaching English to speakers of other languages) (MA); theological ethics (M Th, D Th); theory of literature (MA, PhD); urban ministries (D Th); urban ministry (M Th).

University of Southern Maine, College of Education and Human Development, Program in Adult Education, Portland, ME 04104-9300. Offers adult education (MS); adult learning (CAS). *Accreditation:* Teacher Education Accreditation Council. Part-time and evening/weekend programs available. Postbaccalaureate distance learning degree programs offered (minimal on-campus study). *Faculty:* 2 full-time (1 woman), 1 part-time/adjunct (0 women). *Students:* 17 full-time (14 women), 23 part-time (17 women); includes 2 minority (1 African American, 1 Hispanic American). 19 applicants, 100% accepted, 18 enrolled. In 2009, 8 master's, 1 other advanced degree awarded. *Degree requirements:* For master's and CAS, thesis or alternative. *Entrance requirements:* For master's, interview; for CAS, master's degree. Additional exam requirements/recommendations for international students: Required—TOEFL (minimum score 550 paper-based; 213 computer-based; 79 iBT). *Application deadline:* For fall admission, 5/1 priority date for domestic students; for spring admission, 10/15 priority date for domestic students. Applications are processed on a rolling basis. Application fee: $50. Electronic applications accepted. *Financial support:* In 2009–10, 3 students received support, including 1 research assistantship with partial tuition reimbursement available (averaging $4,500 per year); career-related internships or fieldwork, Federal Work-Study, institutionally sponsored loans, scholarships/grants, and unspecified assistantships also available. Support available to part-time students. Financial award application deadline: 3/1; financial award applicants required to submit FAFSA. *Faculty research:* Workplace education. *Unit head:* Dr. E. Michael Brady, Chair, Human Resource Development Department, 207-780-5316, Fax: 207-780-5043, E-mail: mbrady@usm.maine.edu. *Application contact:* Mary Sloan, Director of Graduate Admissions, 207-780-4386, Fax: 207-780-4969, E-mail: msloan@usm.maine.edu.

University of Southern Mississippi, Graduate School, College of Education and Psychology, Department of Educational Leadership and Research, Hattiesburg, MS 39406-0001. Offers adult education (M Ed, Ed D, PhD, Ed S); educational administration (M Ed, Ed D, PhD, Ed S); higher education (PhD). *Faculty:* 7 full-time (1 woman), 5 part-time/adjunct (1 woman). *Students:* 45 full-time (34 women), 97 part-time (66 women); includes 42 minority (40 African Americans, 1 American Indian/Alaska Native, 1 Hispanic American), 2 international. Average age 36. 54 applicants, 67% accepted, 33 enrolled. In 2009, 26 master's, 11 doctorates, 3 other advanced degrees awarded. *Degree requirements:* For master's, comprehensive exam, thesis (for some programs), internship; for doctorate, comprehensive exam, thesis/dissertation; for Ed S, comprehensive exam, thesis (for some programs). *Entrance requirements:* For master's, GRE General Test, minimum GPA of 2.75; for doctorate, GRE General Test, minimum GPA of 3.5; for Ed S, GRE General Test, minimum GPA of 3.25. Additional exam requirements/recommendations for international students: Required—TOEFL. *Application deadline:* For fall admission, 3/1 priority date for domestic students, 3/1 for international students. Applications are processed on a rolling basis. Application fee: $35. *Expenses:* Tuition, state resident: full-time $5096; part-time $284 per hour. Tuition, nonresident: full-time $13,052; part-time $726 per hour. Required fees: $402. Tuition and fees vary according to course level and course load. *Financial support:* In 2009–10, 10 research assistantships with full tuition reimbursements (averaging $8,000 per year) were awarded; teaching assistantships, career-related internships or fieldwork, Federal Work-Study, and institutionally sponsored loans also available. Financial award application deadline: 3/15; financial award applicants required to submit FAFSA. *Faculty research:* Supervision, learning styles, education finance, higher education organization. Total annual research expenditures: $88,500. *Unit head:* Dr. Gaylynn Parker, Interim Chair, 601-266-4589, Fax: 601-266-5141. *Application contact:* Shonna Breland, Manager of Graduate Admissions, 601-266-6563, Fax: 601-266-5138.

University of Southern Mississippi, Graduate School, College of Education and Psychology, Department of Educational Studies and Research, Hattiesburg, MS 39406-0001. Offers adult education (Graduate Certificate); community college leadership (Graduate Certificate); counseling and personnel services (college) (M Ed); education (PhD, Ed S), including adult education, research, evaluation and statistics (PhD); education (Ed D), including educational administration, educational research; education: educational leadership and research (Ed S), including higher education administration; educational administration and supervision (M Ed); higher education administration (Ed D, PhD); institutional research (Graduate Certificate). *Faculty:* 7 full-time (1 woman), 5 part-time/adjunct (1 woman). *Students:* 45 full-time (34 women), 97 part-time (66 women); includes 42 minority (40 African Americans, 1 American Indian/Alaska Native, 1 Hispanic American), 2 international. Average age 36. 54 applicants, 67% accepted, 33 enrolled. In 2009, 26 master's, 11 doctorates, 3 other advanced degrees awarded. *Degree requirements:* For master's and other advanced degree, comprehensive exam, thesis (for some programs); for doctorate, comprehensive exam, thesis/dissertation. *Entrance requirements:* For master's, doctorate, and other advanced degree, GRE General Test, minimum GPA of 2.75. Additional exam requirements/recommendations for international students: Required—TOEFL. *Application deadline:* For fall admission, 2/1 for domestic students, 3/1 for international students. Applications are processed on a rolling basis. Application fee: $35. *Expenses:* Tuition, state resident: full-time $5096; part-time $284 per hour. Tuition, nonresident: full-time $13,052; part-time $726 per hour. Required fees: $402. Tuition and fees vary according to course level and course load. *Financial support:* Career-related internships or fieldwork, Federal Work-Study, and institutionally sponsored loans available. Financial award application deadline: 3/15; financial award applicants required to submit FAFSA. Total annual research expenditures: $88,500. *Unit head:* Dr. Thomas V. O'Brien, Chair, 601-266-6093, E-mail: thomas.obrien@usm.edu. *Application contact:* Shonna Breland, Manager of Graduate Admissions, 601-266-6563, Fax: 601-266-5138.

University of South Florida, Graduate School, College of Education–Main Campus, Department of Adult, Career and Higher Education, Tampa, FL 33620-9951. Offers adult education (MA, Ed D, PhD, Ed S); career and technical education (MA); career and workforce education (PhD); higher education/community college teaching (MA, Ed D, PhD); vocational education (Ed S). Part-time programs available. *Faculty:* 9 full-time (3 women), 4 part-time/adjunct (3 women). *Students:* 52 full-time (34 women), 211 part-time (149 women); includes 71 minority (41 African Americans, 1 American Indian/Alaska Native, 5 Asian Americans or Pacific Islanders, 24 Hispanic Americans), 6 international. Average age 30. 94 applicants, 69%

accepted, 58 enrolled. In 2009, 31 master's, 11 doctorates awarded. *Degree requirements:* For master's, comprehensive exam; for doctorate, comprehensive exam, thesis/dissertation; for Ed S, comprehensive exam, thesis. *Entrance requirements:* For master's, minimum GPA of 3.0 in last 60 hours of course work; for doctorate and Ed S, GRE General Test, GRE Writing Test. Additional exam requirements/recommendations for international students: Required—TOEFL (minimum score 500 paper-based; 213 computer-based; 91 iBT). *Application deadline:* For fall admission, 2/15 for domestic students, 1/2 for international students; for spring admission, 10/15 for domestic students, 6/1 for international students. Applications are processed on a rolling basis. Application fee: $30. Electronic applications accepted. *Financial support:* Career-related internships or fieldwork, scholarships/grants, and unspecified assistantships available. Financial award applicants required to submit FAFSA. *Faculty research:* Community college leadership; integration of academic, career and technical education; competency-based education; continuing education administration; adult learning and development. Total annual research expenditures: $9,807. *Unit head:* Dr. Ann Cranston-Gingras, Chairperson, 813-974-6036, Fax: 813-974-3366, E-mail: cranston@usf.edu. *Application contact:* Dr. William Young, Program Director, 813-974-1861, Fax: 813-974-3366, E-mail: williamyoung@usf.edu.

The University of Tennessee, Graduate School, College of Education, Health and Human Sciences, Department of Educational Psychology and Counseling, Knoxville, TN 37996. Offers adult education (MS); applied educational psychology (MS); collaborative learning (Ed D); college student personnel (MS); mental health counseling (MS); rehabilitation counseling (MS); school counseling (MS). *Accreditation:* ACA (one or more programs are accredited); CORE (one or more programs are accredited); NCATE. Part-time and evening/weekend programs available. *Degree requirements:* For master's, thesis optional. *Entrance requirements:* For master's, GRE General Test, minimum GPA of 2.7. Additional exam requirements/recommendations for international students: Required—TOEFL. Electronic applications accepted. *Expenses:* Tuition, state resident: full-time $6826; part-time $380 per semester hour. Tuition, nonresident: full-time $21,844; part-time $1147 per semester hour. Tuition and fees vary according to program.

University of the Incarnate Word, School of Graduate Studies and Research, Dreeben School of Education, Programs in Education, San Antonio, TX 78209-6397. Offers adult education (M Ed, MA); cross-cultural education (M Ed, MA); early childhood literacy (M Ed, MA); general education (M Ed, MA); Higher Education (PhD); instructional technology (M Ed, MA); international education and entrepreneurship (PhD); kinesiology (M Ed, MA); literacy (M Ed, MA); organizational leadership (PhD); organizational learning and learning (M Ed, MA); reading (M Ed, MA); special education (M Ed, MA); teacher leadership (M Ed, MA). Part-time and evening/weekend programs available. *Students:* 20 full-time (11 women), 201 part-time (122 women); includes 113 minority (29 African Americans, 2 American Indian/Alaska Native, 2 Asian Americans or Pacific Islanders, 80 Hispanic Americans), 30 international. Average age 41. In 2009, 26 master's, 19 doctorates awarded. *Degree requirements:* For master's, capstone; for doctorate, thesis/dissertation, qualifying exam. *Entrance requirements:* For master's, baccalaureate degree; minimum foundation GPA of 2.5; interview; for doctorate, master's degree; interview; supervised writing sample. Additional exam requirements/recommendations for international students: Required—TOEFL (minimum score 560 paper-based; 220 computer-based; 83 iBT). *Application deadline:* Applications are processed on a rolling basis. Application fee: $20. Electronic applications accepted. *Expenses:* Tuition: Full-time $12,150; part-time $675 per credit hour. Required fees: $83 per credit hour. *Financial support:* Federal Work-Study and scholarships/grants available. Financial award applicants required to submit FAFSA. *Unit head:* Dr. Denise Staudt, Dean, Dreeben School of Education, 210-829-2762, E-mail: staudt@uiwtx.edu. *Application contact:* Andrea Cyterski-Acosta, Dean of Enrollment, 210-829-6005, Fax: 210-829-3921, E-mail: admis@uiwtx.edu.

University of the Incarnate Word, School of Graduate Studies and Research, H-E-B School of Business and Administration, Programs in Administration, San Antonio, TX 78209-6397. Offers adult education (MAA); applied administration (MAA); communication arts (MAA); healthcare administration (MAA); instructional technology (MAA); international business (Certificate); nutrition (MAA); organizational development (MAA, Certificate); project management (Certificate); sports management (MAA). Part-time and evening/weekend programs available. Postbaccalaureate distance learning degree programs offered (no on-campus study). *Students:* 30 full-time (17 women), 163 part-time (114 women); includes 128 minority (18 African Americans, 3 Asian Americans or Pacific Islanders, 107 Hispanic Americans), 8 international. Average age 35. In 2009, 68 master's awarded. *Degree requirements:* For master's, capstone. *Entrance requirements:* For master's, GRE, GMAT, undergraduate degree, minimum GPA of 2.5. Additional exam requirements/recommendations for international students: Required—TOEFL (minimum score 560 paper-based; 220 computer-based; 83 iBT). *Application deadline:* Applications are processed on a rolling basis. Application fee: $20. Electronic applications accepted. *Expenses:* Tuition: Full-time $12,150; part-time $675 per credit hour. Required fees: $83 per credit hour. *Financial support:* Federal Work-Study and scholarships/grants available. Financial award applicants required to submit FAFSA. *Unit head:* Dr. Daniel Dominguez, MAA Director, 210-829-3180, Fax: 210-805-3564, E-mail: domingue@uiwtx.edu. *Application contact:* Andrea Cyterski-Acosta, Dean of Enrollment, 210-829-6005, Fax: 210-829-3921, E-mail: admis@uiwtx.edu.

The University of West Alabama, School of Graduate Studies, College of Education, Department of Teacher Education, Program in Continuing Education, Livingston, AL 35470. Offers MSCE. *Accreditation:* NCATE. Part-time programs available. *Degree requirements:* For master's, comprehensive exam. *Entrance requirements:* For master's, GRE General Test, MAT, minimum GPA of 2.75.

The University of West Alabama, School of Graduate Studies, College of Education, Department of Teacher Education, Program in Guidance and Counseling, Livingston, AL 35470. Offers continuing education (MSCE); guidance and counseling (M Ed). *Accreditation:* NCATE. Part-time and evening/weekend programs available. *Entrance requirements:* For master's, GRE General Test, MAT, minimum GPA of 2.75.

University of Wisconsin–Milwaukee, Graduate School, School of Education, Program in Urban Education, Milwaukee, WI 53201-0413. Offers adult and continuing education (PhD); curriculum and instruction (PhD); educational administration (PhD); educational and media technology (PhD); educational psychology (PhD); multicultural studies (PhD); social foundations of education (PhD). *Students:* 67 full-time (51 women), 44 part-time (30 women); includes 41 minority (23 African Americans, 2 American Indian/Alaska Native, 7 Asian Americans or Pacific Islanders, 9 Hispanic Americans), 4 international. Average age 41. 31 applicants, 45% accepted, 5 enrolled. In 2009, 11 doctorates awarded. *Degree requirements:* For doctorate, comprehensive exam, thesis/dissertation. *Entrance requirements:* For doctorate, GRE General Test, minimum undergraduate GPA of 2.85, graduate 3.5. Additional exam requirements/recommendations for international students: Required—TOEFL (minimum score 550 paper-based; 79 iBT), IELTS (minimum score 6.5). *Application deadline:* For fall admission, 1/1 priority date for domestic students; for spring admission, 9/1 for domestic students. Applications are processed on a rolling basis. Application fee: $45 ($75 for international students). *Expenses:* Tuition, state resident: full-time $8800. Tuition, nonresident: full-time $20,760. Tuition and fees vary according to program and reciprocity agreements. *Financial support:* Career-related internships or fieldwork and unspecified assistantships available. Support available to part-time students. Financial award application deadline: 4/15. *Unit head:* Larry Martin, Representative, 414-229-4729, Fax: 414-229-2920, E-mail: lmartin@uwm.edu. *Application contact:* General Information Contact, 414-229-4982, Fax: 414-229-6967, E-mail: gradschool@uwm.edu.

University of Wisconsin–Platteville, School of Graduate Studies, College of Liberal Arts and Education, School of Education, Platteville, WI 53818-3099. Offers adult education (MSE); elementary education (MSE); English education (MSE); middle school education (MSE); secondary education (MSE); vocational and technical education (MSE). *Accreditation:* NCATE. Part-time programs available. *Faculty:* 8 part-time/adjunct (3 women). *Students:* 16 full-time (12 women), 183 part-time (137 women); includes 35 minority (27 African Americans, 1 American Indian/Alaska Native, 1 Asian American or Pacific Islander, 6 Hispanic Americans), 63 international. 23 applicants, 100% accepted, 23 enrolled. In 2009, 85 master's awarded. *Degree requirements:* For master's, comprehensive exam, thesis or alternative. *Entrance requirements:* Additional exam requirements/recommendations for international students: Required—TOEFL (minimum score 500 paper-based; 173 computer-based; 61 iBT). *Application deadline:* For fall admission, 7/1 priority date for domestic students; for spring admission, 11/1 for domestic students. Applications are processed on a rolling basis. Application fee: $56. Electronic applications accepted. *Expenses:* Tuition, state resident: full-time $6706. Tuition, nonresident: full-time $16,772. *Financial support:* Research assistantships with partial tuition reimbursements, career-related internships or fieldwork, Federal Work-Study, institutionally sponsored loans, scholarships/grants, and unspecified assistantships available. Support available to part-time students. *Unit head:* Dr. Karen Stinson, Director, 608-342-1131, Fax: 608-342-1133. *Application contact:* Lisa Popp, School of Graduate Studies, 608-342-1322, Fax: 608-342-1389, E-mail: poppl@uwplatt.edu.

University of Wyoming, College of Education, Department of Adult Learning and Technology, Laramie, WY 82070. Offers adult and postsecondary education (MA, Ed D, PhD, Ed S); distance education (Ed D, PhD); instructional technology (MS, Ed D, PhD). Part-time programs available. Postbaccalaureate distance learning degree programs offered (no on-campus study). *Degree requirements:* For master's, thesis or alternative; for doctorate, comprehensive exam, thesis/dissertation. *Entrance requirements:* For master's, GRE, minimum GPA of 3.0; for doctorate, MS or MA, minimum GPA of 3.0. Additional exam requirements/recommendations for international students: Required—TOEFL. Electronic applications accepted. *Faculty research:* Web based instruction, instructional decision, adult education history, literacy in adults, international distance education.

Virginia Commonwealth University, Graduate School, School of Education, Program in Adult and Organizational Learning, Richmond, VA 23284-9005. Offers adult literacy (M Ed); adults with disabilities (M Ed); human resource development (M Ed). *Accreditation:* NCATE. Part-time programs available. *Entrance requirements:* For master's, GRE General Test or MAT. *Faculty research:* Adult development and learning, program planning and evaluation.

Virginia Polytechnic Institute and State University, Graduate School, College of Liberal Arts and Human Sciences, Department of Human Development, Blacksburg, VA 24061. Offers adult development and aging (MS, PhD); adult learning and human resource development (MS, PhD); child development (MS, PhD); family studies (MS, PhD); marriage and family therapy (MS, PhD). *Accreditation:* AAMFT/COAMFTE (one or more programs are accredited). *Faculty:* 22 full-time (18 women). *Students:* 49 full-time (38 women), 64 part-time (44 women); includes 30 minority (1 African American, 7 American Indian/Alaska Native, 16 Asian Americans or Pacific Islanders, 6 Hispanic Americans), 2 international. Average age 34. 64 applicants, 34% accepted, 16 enrolled. In 2009, 10 master's, 14 doctorates awarded. *Entrance requirements:* For master's and doctorate, GRE, GMAT. Additional exam requirements/recommendations for international students: Required—TOEFL (minimum score 550 paper-based; 213 computer-based). *Application deadline:* For fall admission, 5/15 for international students; for spring admission, 10/15 for international students. Applications are processed on a rolling basis. Application fee: $65. Electronic applications accepted. *Expenses:* Tuition, area resident: Full-time $10,228; part-time $459 per credit hour. Tuition, nonresident: full-time $17,892; part-time $865 per credit hour. Required fees: $1966; $451 per semester. *Financial support:* In 2009–10, 7 research assistantships with full tuition reimbursements (averaging $10,933 per year), 25 teaching assistantships with full tuition reimbursements (averaging $9,387 per year) were awarded; career-related internships or fieldwork, Federal Work-Study, scholarships/grants, and unspecified assistantships also available. Financial award application deadline: 1/15. *Faculty research:* Stress management, children's play, dual-career families, social cognition, relationships of elderly. Total annual research expenditures: $823,581. *Unit head:* Dr. Shannon E. Jarrott, Head, 540-231-4794, Fax: 540-231-7012, E-mail: sjarrott@vt.edu. *Application contact:* Mark Benson, Information Contact, 540-231-5720, Fax: 540-231-7012, E-mail: mbenson@vt.edu.

Walden University, Graduate Programs, Richard W. Riley College of Education and Leadership, Minneapolis, MN 55401. Offers administrator leadership for teaching and learning (Ed D, Ed S); curriculum, instruction, and professional development (Ed S); early childhood education (birth-grade 3) (MAT); education (MS, PhD), including adolescent literacy and technology (grades 6-12) (MS), adult education leadership (PhD), community college leadership (PhD), curriculum, instruction, and assessment, early childhood education (PhD), educational leadership (MS), educational technology (PhD), elementary reading and literacy (MS), elementary reading and mathematics (MS), emotional/behavioral disorders (K-12) (MS), general program, higher education (PhD), integrating technology in the classroom (MS), K-12 educational leadership (PhD), learning disabilities (K-12) (MS), literacy and learning in the content areas (MS), mathematics (grades 6-8) (MS), mathematics (grades K-5) (MS), middle level education (grades 5-8) (MS), professional development (MS), science (grades K-8) (MS), self-designed (PhD), special education (PhD), special education (non-licensure) (MS), teacher leadership (grades K-12) (MS); educational leadership and administration (principal preparation) (Ed S); educational technology (Ed S); higher education and adult learning (Ed D); instructional design (Postbaccalaureate Certificate); instructional design and technology (MS), including general program (MS, PhD), online learning, training and performance improvement; special education: emotional/behavioral disorders (K-12) (MAT); special education: learning disabilities (K-12) (MAT); teacher leadership (Ed D, Ed S). Part-time and evening/weekend programs available. Postbaccalaureate distance learning degree programs offered (minimal on-campus study). *Faculty:* 54 full-time, 835 part-time/adjunct. *Students:* 13,940 full-time (11,339 women), 1,940 part-time (1,637 women); includes 4,626 minority (3,795 African Americans, 111 American Indian/Alaska Native, 199 Asian Americans or Pacific Islanders, 521 Hispanic Americans), 124 international. Average age 38. In 2009, 4,688 master's, 190 doctorates awarded. *Degree requirements:* For doctorate, thesis/dissertation (for some programs), residency; for other advanced degree, residency (for some programs). *Entrance requirements:* For master's, bachelor's degree or equivalent in related field; minimum GPA of 2.5; official transcripts; goal statement; access to computer and Internet; for doctorate, master's degree or equivalent in related field; minimum GPA of 3.0; official transcripts; three years' related professional/academic experience (preferred); access to computer and Internet; for other advanced degree, master's degree or equivalent in related field; minimum GPA of 3.0; 3 years related professional/academic experience (preferred); access to computer and Internet (Ed S). Additional exam requirements/recommendations for international students: Required—TOEFL (minimum score 550 paper-based; 213 computer-based), IELTS (minimum score 6.5), or Michigan English Language Assessment Battery (minimum score 82). *Application deadline:* Applications are processed on a rolling basis. Application fee: $50. Electronic applications accepted. *Expenses:* Tuition: Full-time $13,665; part-time $560 per credit. Required fees: $1375. Tuition and fees vary according to course load, degree level and program. *Financial support:* In 2009–10, 2,418 students received support; fellowships, Federal Work-Study, scholarships/grants, unspecified assistantships, and family tuition reduction, active duty/veteran tuition reduction, group tuition reduction, interest-free payment plans available. Support available to part-time students. Financial award applicants required to submit FAFSA. *Unit head:* Dr. Kate Steffens, Dean, 800-925-3368. *Application contact:* Jennifer Hall, Director of Enrollment, 866-4-WALDEN, E-mail: info@waldenu.edu.

Wayne State University, College of Education, Division of Teacher Education, Detroit, MI 48202. Offers adult and continuing education (M Ed); art education (M Ed); bilingual/bicultural education (M Ed, MAT); business education (M Ed, MAT); career and technical education (M Ed, Ed D, PhD, Ed S); curriculum and instruction (Ed D, PhD, Ed S); distributive education (M Ed, MAT); early childhood education (M Ed); elementary education (M Ed, MAT, Ed D, PhD, Ed S); elementary education curriculum and instruction (M Ed); English education (M Ed); English education-secondary (M Ed, Ed S); foreign language education (M Ed); general education (Ed D, Ed S); health occupations education (M Ed); industrial education (M Ed); mathematics education (M Ed, Ed S); pre-school and parent education (M Ed); reading (M Ed, Ed D, Ed S); reading, languages and literature (Ed D); school music-vocal (M Ed); science

Adult Education

Wayne State University (continued)
education (M Ed, MAT, Ed S); secondary education (MAT); secondary school reading (M Ed); social studies education (M Ed, Ed S), including education-secondary (M Ed); special education (M Ed, Ed D, PhD, Ed S); teacher education (MAT, Ed D, PhD). *Degree requirements:* For doctorate, thesis/dissertation. *Entrance requirements:* For master's, Michigan Basic Skills Test (MA in teaching), minimum GPA of 2.6; for doctorate, minimum undergraduate GPA of 3.0, graduate 3.5; interview, curriculum vitae; references. Additional exam requirements/recommendations for international students: Required—TOEFL (minimum score 550 paper-based; 213 computer-based), TWE (minimum score 6). Electronic applications accepted. *Faculty research:* Reading and writing literacy and literature.

Western Washington University, Graduate School, Woodring College of Education, Department of Educational Leadership, Program in Continuing and College Education, Bellingham, WA 98225-5996. Offers M Ed. Part-time and evening/weekend programs available. Postbaccalaureate distance learning degree programs offered (minimal on-campus study). *Degree requirements:* For master's, comprehensive exam, thesis optional. *Entrance requirements:* For master's, GRE General Test or MAT, minimum GPA of 3.0 in last 60 semester hours or last 90 quarter hours. Additional exam requirements/recommendations for international students: Required—TOEFL (minimum score 567 paper-based; 227 computer-based). Electronic applications accepted. *Faculty research:* Transfer of learning, postsecondary faculty development, action research as professional development, literacy education in community colleges, adult education in the Middle East, distance learning tools for graduate students.

Widener University, School of Human Service Professions, Center for Education, Chester, PA 19013-5792. Offers adult education (M Ed); counseling in higher education (M Ed); counselor education (M Ed); early childhood education (M Ed); educational foundations (M Ed); educational leadership (M Ed); educational psychology (M Ed); elementary education (M Ed); English and language arts (M Ed); health education (M Ed); higher education leadership (Ed D); home and school visitor (M Ed); human sexuality (M Ed); mathematics education (M Ed); middle school education (M Ed); principalship (M Ed); reading and language arts (Ed D); reading education (M Ed); school administration (Ed D); science education (M Ed); social studies education (M Ed); special education (M Ed); technology education (M Ed). *Accreditation:* NCATE. Part-time and evening/weekend programs available. *Faculty:* 34 full-time (22 women), 37 part-time/adjunct (14 women). *Students:* 203 full-time (154 women), 415 part-time (298 women); includes 50 minority (34 African Americans, 1 American Indian/Alaska Native, 5 Asian Americans or Pacific Islanders, 10 Hispanic Americans), 3 international. Average age 39. 139 applicants, 88% accepted. In 2009, 168 master's, 31 doctorates awarded. Terminal master's awarded for partial completion of doctoral program. *Degree requirements:* For doctorate, thesis/dissertation. *Entrance requirements:* For master's, minimum GPA of 2.5; for doctorate, GRE or MAT, minimum GPA of 2.0 (undergraduate), 3.5 (graduate). *Application deadline:* Applications are processed on a rolling basis. Application fee: $25 ($300 for international students). Electronic applications accepted. *Expenses:* Contact institution. *Financial support:* Career-related internships or fieldwork, tuition waivers (full and partial), and unspecified assistantships available. Support available to part-time students. Financial award application deadline: 5/1. *Faculty research:* Reading and cognition, adult education, technology education, educational leadership, special education. *Unit head:* Dr. Michael W. LeDoux, Associate Dean, 610-499-4294, Fax: 610-499-4623, E-mail: mwledoux@widener.edu. *Application contact:* Dr. Roberta D. Nolan, Director of Graduate Admissions, 610-499-4125, E-mail: rdnolan@widener.edu.

Wright State University, School of Graduate Studies, College of Education and Human Services, Department of Educational Leadership, Program in Advanced Educational Leadership, Dayton, OH 45435. Offers advanced curriculum and instruction (Ed S); higher education-adult education (Ed S); superintendent (Ed S). *Accreditation:* NCATE. *Degree requirements:* For Ed S, thesis. *Entrance requirements:* For degree, GRE General Test, MAT. Additional exam requirements/recommendations for international students: Required—TOEFL.

Community College Education

Argosy University, Chicago, College of Education, Chicago, IL 60601. Offers adult education and training (MA Ed); community college executive leadership (Ed D); educational leadership (MA Ed, Ed D, Ed S), including district leadership (Ed D), higher education administration (Ed D), K-12 education (Ed D); instructional leadership (Ed D, Ed S), including higher education (Ed D), K-12 education (Ed D). Postbaccalaureate distance learning degree programs offered (minimal on-campus study).

See Close-Up on page 675.

Argosy University, Denver, College of Education, Denver, CO 80231. Offers community college executive leadership (Ed D); educational leadership (MA Ed, Ed D), including higher education (Ed D), K-12 education (Ed D); instructional leadership (MA Ed, Ed D), including higher education administration (Ed D), K-12 education (Ed D).

See Close-Up on page 679.

Argosy University, Inland Empire, College of Education, San Bernardino, CA 92408. Offers community college executive leadership (Ed D); educational leadership (MA Ed, Ed D), including higher education administration (Ed D), K-12 education (Ed D); instructional leadership (MA Ed, Ed D), including higher education (Ed D), K-12 education (Ed D), multiple subject teacher preparation (MA Ed), single subject teacher preparation (MA Ed).

See Close-Up on page 889.

Argosy University, Los Angeles, College of Education, Santa Monica, CA 90045. Offers community college executive leadership (Ed D); educational leadership (MA Ed, Ed D), including higher education administration (Ed D), K-12 education (Ed D); instructional leadership (MA Ed, Ed D), including higher education (Ed D), K-12 education (Ed D), multiple subject teacher preparation (MA Ed), single subject teacher preparation (MA Ed).

See Close-Up on page 683.

Argosy University, Orange County, College of Education, Orange, CA 92868. Offers community college executive leadership (Ed D); educational leadership (MA Ed, Ed D), including higher education administration (Ed D), K-12 education (Ed D); instructional leadership (MA Ed, Ed D), including education technology (Ed D), higher education (Ed D), K-12 education (Ed D), multiple subject teacher preparation (MA Ed), single subject teacher preparation (MA Ed).

See Close-Up on page 685.

Argosy University, Phoenix, College of Education, Phoenix, AZ 85021. Offers adult education and training (MA Ed); advanced educational administration (Ed D, Ed S); community college executive leadership (Ed D); educational administration (MA Ed); educational leadership (MA Ed, Ed D, Ed S), including education technology (Ed D), higher education administration (Ed D), K-12 education (Ed D); higher and postsecondary education (MA Ed); initial educational administration (Ed D, Ed S); school psychology (MA); teaching and learning (MA Ed, Ed D, Ed S), including education technology (Ed D), higher education (Ed D), K-12 education (Ed D).

See Close-Up on page 687.

Argosy University, San Diego, College of Education, San Diego, CA 92108. Offers community college executive leadership (Ed D); educational leadership (MA Ed, Ed D), including higher education administration (Ed D), K-12 education (Ed D); instructional leadership (MA Ed, Ed D), including higher education (Ed D), K-12 education (Ed D).

See Close-Up on page 691.

Argosy University, San Francisco Bay Area, College of Education, Alameda, CA 94501. Offers community college executive leadership (Ed D); educational leadership (MA Ed, Ed D), including education technology (Ed D), higher education administration (Ed D), K-12 education (Ed D); instructional leadership (MA Ed, Ed D), including education technology (Ed D), higher education (Ed D), K-12 education (Ed D), multiple subject teacher preparation (MA Ed), single subject teacher preparation (MA Ed).

See Close-Up on page 693.

Argosy University, Schaumburg, College of Education, Schaumburg, IL 60173-5403. Offers community college executive leadership (Ed D); educational leadership (MA Ed, Ed D, Ed S), including district leadership (Ed D), higher education administration (Ed D), K-12 education (Ed D); instructional leadership (Ed D, Ed S), including higher education (Ed D), K-12 education (Ed D).

See Close-Up on page 697.

Argosy University, Seattle, College of Education, Seattle, WA 98121. Offers adult education and training (MA Ed); community college executive leadership (Ed D); educational leadership (MA Ed, Ed D), including higher education administration (Ed D), K-12 education (Ed D); higher and postsecondary education (MA Ed); instructional leadership (MA Ed, Ed D), including education technology (Ed D), higher education (Ed D), K-12 education (Ed D).

See Close-Up on page 699.

Argosy University, Tampa, College of Education, Tampa, FL 33607. Offers community college executive leadership (Ed D); educational leadership (MA Ed, Ed D, Ed S), including higher education administration (Ed D), K-12 education (Ed D); school counseling (MA); teaching and learning (MA Ed, Ed D, Ed S), including higher education (Ed D), K-12 education (Ed D).

See Close-Up on page 701.

Argosy University, Washington DC, College of Education, Arlington, VA 22209. Offers community college executive leadership (Ed D); educational leadership (MA Ed, Ed D, Ed S), including higher education administration (Ed D), K-12 education (Ed D); instructional leadership (MA Ed, Ed D, Ed S), including higher education (Ed D), K-12 education (Ed D).

See Close-Up on page 705.

Arkansas State University—Jonesboro, Graduate School, College of Education, Department of Educational Leadership, Curriculum, and Special Education, Jonesboro, State University, AR 72467. Offers community college administration education (SCCT); curriculum and instruction (MSE); education theory and practice (MSE); educational leadership (MSE, Ed D, Ed S), including curriculum and instruction (MSE, Ed S); special education (MSE), including gifted and talented and creative, instructional specialist 4-12, instructional specialist P-4. *Accreditation:* NCATE. Part-time programs available. Postbaccalaureate distance learning degree programs offered (no on-campus study). *Faculty:* 15 full-time (6 women), 19 part-time/adjunct (11 women). *Students:* 16 full-time (11 women), 734 part-time (606 women); includes 111 minority (96 African Americans, 4 American Indian/Alaska Native, 4 Asian Americans or Pacific Islanders, 7 Hispanic Americans), 2 international. Average age 38. 882 applicants, 70% accepted, 240 enrolled. In 2009, 80 master's, 6 doctorates, 15 other advanced degrees awarded. *Degree requirements:* For master's, comprehensive exam, thesis or alternative; for doctorate, comprehensive exam, thesis/dissertation; for other advanced degree, comprehensive exam. *Entrance requirements:* For master's, GRE General Test or MAT, appropriate bachelor's degree, letters of reference, interview; for doctorate, GRE General Test or MAT, interview, master's degree, letters of reference, official transcript, personal statement, writing sample, immunization records; for other advanced degree, GRE General Test or MAT, interview, master's degree, letters of reference, official transcript, 3 years teaching experience, mentor, teaching license, immunization records. Additional exam requirements/recommendations for international students: Required—TOEFL (minimum score 550 paper-based; 213 computer-based; 79 iBT), IELTS (minimum score 6). *Application deadline:* Applications are processed on a rolling basis. Application fee: $50. Electronic applications accepted. *Expenses:* Tuition, state resident: full-time $3744; part-time $208 per credit hour. Tuition, nonresident: full-time $9540; part-time $530 per credit hour. Required fees: $896; $47 per credit hour. $25 per term. One-time fee: $50. Tuition and fees vary according to course load and program. *Financial support:* In 2009–10, 16 students received support; fellowships, teaching assistantships, career-related internships or fieldwork, scholarships/grants, and unspecified assistantships available. Financial award application deadline: 7/1; financial award applicants required to submit FAFSA. *Unit head:* Dr. Mitchell Holifield, Chair, 870-972-3062, Fax: 870-680-8130, E-mail: hfield@astate.edu. *Application contact:* Dr. Andrew Sustich, Dean of the Graduate School, 870-972-3029, Fax: 870-972-3857, E-mail: sustich@astate.edu.

California State University, Stanislaus, College of Education, Department of Advanced Studies in Education, Turlock, CA 95382. Offers community college leadership (Ed D); education (MA); educational leadership (Ed D); educational technology (MA); P-12 leadership (Ed D); school administration (MA); school counseling (MA); special education (MA). Part-time and evening/weekend programs available. Postbaccalaureate distance learning degree programs offered. *Degree requirements:* For master's, thesis. *Entrance requirements:* For master's, MAT or GRE, BEST (depending on concentration), minimum GPA of 2.8, 3 letters of reference; for doctorate, GRE, 3.0 minimum GPA, 3 letters of reference and personal statement. Additional exam requirements/recommendations for international students: Required—TOEFL (minimum score 550 paper-based; 213 computer-based). *Faculty research:* Current school technology use, social aspects of technology, staff development.

Central Michigan University, Central Michigan University Off-Campus Programs, Program in Education, Mount Pleasant, MI 48859. Offers adult education (MA); community college (MA); education (MA); guidance and development (MA); instructional (MA); reading and literacy K-12 (MA). Part-time and evening/weekend programs available. *Entrance requirements:* For master's, minimum GPA of 2.7 in major. Additional exam requirements/recommendations for international students: Required—TOEFL. *Application deadline:* Applications are processed on a rolling basis. Application fee: $50. Electronic applications accepted. *Financial support:* Scholarships/grants available. Support available to part-time students. *Unit head:* Jennifer Cochran, Director, 989-774-2584, E-mail: jennifer.cochran@cmich.edu. *Application contact:* 877-268-4636, E-mail: cmuoffcampus@cmich.edu.

Colorado State University, Graduate School, College of Applied Human Sciences, School of Education, Fort Collins, CO 80523-1588. Offers adult education and training (M Ed); community college leadership (PhD); counseling and career development (M Ed); education and human resource studies (M Ed, PhD); educational leadership (M Ed, PhD); interdisciplinary studies (PhD); organizational performance and change (M Ed, PhD); student affairs in higher education (MS). *Accreditation:* ACA; Teacher Education Accreditation Council. Part-time and evening/weekend programs available. *Faculty:* 21 full-time (10 women). *Students:* 195 full-time (132 women), 469 part-time (292 women); includes 114 minority (31 African Americans, 12 American Indian/Alaska Native, 22 Asian Americans or Pacific Islanders, 49 Hispanic Americans),

24 international. Average age 38. 451 applicants, 41% accepted, 141 enrolled. In 2009, 175 master's, 54 doctorates awarded. *Degree requirements:* For master's, comprehensive exam (for some programs), thesis optional; for doctorate, comprehensive exam, thesis/dissertation, minimum of 60 credits. *Entrance requirements:* For master's, GRE, minimum undergraduate GPA of 3.0, 3 letters of recommendation, curriculum vitae/resume; for doctorate, minimum GPA of 3.0, 3 letters of recommendation, curriculum vitae. Additional exam requirements/recommendations for international students: Required—TOEFL (minimum score 550 paper-based; 213 computer-based). *Application deadline:* For fall admission, 3/15 for domestic and international students; for spring admission, 11/1 for domestic students, 10/1 for international students. Applications are processed on a rolling basis. Application fee: $50. Electronic applications accepted. *Expenses:* Tuition, state resident: full-time $6434; part-time $359.10 per credit. Tuition, nonresident: full-time $18,116; part-time $1006.45 per credit. Required fees: $1496; $83 per credit. *Financial support:* In 2009–10, 8 students received support, including 3 research assistantships with full tuition reimbursements available (averaging $13,790 per year), 5 teaching assistantships with full tuition reimbursements available (averaging $10,253 per year); fellowships, Federal Work-Study, scholarships/grants, and unspecified assistantships also available. Financial award applicants required to submit FAFSA. *Faculty research:* Innovative instruction, diverse learners, transition, scientifically-based evaluation methods, leadership and organizational development. Total annual research expenditures: $655,700. *Unit head:* Dr. Carole Makela, Interim Director, 970-491-6317, Fax: 970-491-1317, E-mail: carole.makela@colostate.edu. *Application contact:* Dr. Sharon Anderson, Director of Graduate Programs, 970-491-6861, Fax: 970-491-1317, E-mail: sharon.anderson@colostate.edu.

George Mason University, College of Humanities and Social Sciences, Higher Education Program, Fairfax, VA 22030. Offers college teaching (Certificate); community college education (DA Ed); higher education administration (Certificate). *Faculty:* 5 full-time (4 women). *Students:* 4 full-time (3 women), 54 part-time (33 women); includes 15 minority (11 African Americans, 3 Asian Americans or Pacific Islanders, 1 Hispanic American). Average age 48. 19 applicants, 58% accepted, 7 enrolled. In 2009, 8 doctorates, 3 Certificates awarded. *Degree requirements:* For doctorate, thesis/dissertation, internship. *Entrance requirements:* For doctorate, GRE (taken within the last 5 years), writing sample, 3 letters of recommendation, resume. Additional exam requirements/recommendations for international students: Required—TOEFL. *Application deadline:* For fall admission, 3/1 for domestic students; for spring admission, 10/15 for domestic students. Applications are processed on a rolling basis. Application fee: $75. Electronic applications accepted. *Expenses:* Tuition, state resident: full-time $7568; part-time $315.33 per credit hour. Tuition, nonresident: full-time $21,704; part-time $904.33 per credit hour. Required fees: $2184; $91 per credit hour. *Financial support:* In 2009–10, 2 students received support, including 1 research assistantship with full and partial tuition reimbursement available (averaging $6,000 per year), 1 teaching assistantship with full and partial tuition reimbursement available (averaging $985 per year); Federal Work-Study, scholarships/grants, unspecified assistantships, and health care benefits (full-time research or teaching assistantship recipients) also available. Support available to part-time students. Financial award application deadline: 3/1; financial award applicants required to submit FAFSA. *Faculty research:* Leadership, the scholarship of teaching, learning, and assessment; ethical leadership; assessment; information technology; diversity. *Unit head:* John O'Connor, Director, 703-993-2310, E-mail: joconnor@gmu.edu. *Application contact:* Nina Joshi, Administrative Coordinator, 703-993-2310, E-mail: njoshi@gmu.edu.

Mississippi State University, College of Education, Department of Leadership and Foundations, Mississippi State, MS 39762. Offers community college education (MAT); community college leadership (PhD); education (Ed S), including school administration; elementary, middle school, and secondary education administration (PhD); school administration (MS); workforce educational leadership (MS). *Faculty:* 9 full-time (3 women). *Students:* 64 full-time (36 women), 196 part-time (139 women); includes 146 minority (143 African Americans, 1 American Indian/Alaska Native, 2 Hispanic Americans), 1 international. Average age 39. 96 applicants, 68% accepted, 53 enrolled. In 2009, 29 master's, 37 doctorates, 17 other advanced degrees awarded. *Degree requirements:* For master's and Ed S, comprehensive exam, thesis; for doctorate, comprehensive exam, thesis/dissertation. *Entrance requirements:* For master's, GRE, minimum GPA of 2.75 in junior and senior courses; for doctorate and Ed S, GRE. Additional exam requirements/recommendations for international students: Required—TOEFL (minimum score 550 paper-based; 213 computer-based; 79 iBT); Recommended—IELTS (minimum score 6.5). *Application deadline:* For fall admission, 7/1 for domestic students, 5/1 for international students; for spring admission, 11/1 for domestic students, 9/1 for international students. Application fee: $40. *Expenses:* Tuition, state resident: full-time $2575.50; part-time $286.25 per credit hour. Tuition, nonresident: full-time $6510; part-time $723.50 per credit hour. Tuition and fees vary according to course load. *Financial support:* In 2009–10, 1 research assistantship (averaging $8,029 per year) was awarded; Federal Work-Study and institutionally sponsored loans also available. Financial award application deadline: 4/1; financial award applicants required to submit FAFSA. *Unit head:* Dr. Frankie K. Williams, Associate Professor/Head, 662-325-0974, Fax: 662-325-0975, E-mail: fwilliams@colled.msstate.edu. *Application contact:* Bonnie Hays, Office Manager, 662-325-0969, Fax: 662-325-0975, E-mail: bhays@colled.msstate.edu.

Morgan State University, School of Graduate Studies, School of Education and Urban Studies, Department of Advanced Studies, Leadership and Policy, Program in Higher Education-Community College Leadership, Baltimore, MD 21251. Offers Ed D. *Accreditation:* NCATE. Part-time and evening/weekend programs available. *Degree requirements:* For doctorate, comprehensive exam, thesis/dissertation. *Entrance requirements:* For doctorate, GRE General Test or MAT. Additional exam requirements/recommendations for international students: Required—TOEFL (minimum score 550 paper-based; 213 computer-based). *Faculty research:* Multicultural education, cooperative learning, psychology of cognition.

National-Louis University, College of Arts and Sciences, Division of Language and Academic Development, Chicago, IL 60603. Offers adult education (M Ed, Ed D, Certificate), including adult education administration (Certificate), adult education for professional development (M Ed), adult education leadership (M Ed), facilitating adult learning (Certificate), teaching and learning in community colleges (Certificate); adult literacy and developmental studies (M Ed, Certificate); adult, continuing, and literacy education (M Ed, Certificate). Part-time programs available. Postbaccalaureate distance learning degree programs offered (minimal on-campus study). *Degree requirements:* For doctorate, thesis/dissertation. *Entrance requirements:* For master's, GRE General Test, MAT, or Watson-Glaser Critical Thinking Appraisal, interview, minimum GPA of 3.0; for doctorate, GRE General Test, MAT, or Watson-Glaser Critical Thinking Appraisal, interview, master's degree, 3 years of experience in field, resume, writing sample; for Certificate, GRE, MAT, or Watson-Glaser Critical Thinking Appraisal, interview, minimum GPA of 3.0. *Expenses:* Tuition: Full-time $17,160; part-time $715 per semester hour. Tuition and fees vary according to course load, degree level, campus/location and program.

North Carolina State University, Graduate School, College of Education, Department of Adult and Higher Education, Program in Adult and Community College Education, Raleigh, NC 27695. Offers M Ed, MS, Ed D. *Degree requirements:* For master's, thesis (for some programs); for doctorate, thesis/dissertation. *Entrance requirements:* For master's and doctorate, GRE or MAT. Electronic applications accepted.

Northern Arizona University, Graduate College, College of Education, Department of Educational Leadership, Flagstaff, AZ 86011. Offers community college/higher education (M Ed); educational foundations (M Ed); educational leadership (M Ed, Ed D); principal (Certificate); principal K-12 (M Ed); school leadership K-12 (M Ed); superintendent (Certificate). *Faculty:* 21 full-time (11 women). *Students:* 196 full-time (128 women), 744 part-time (452 women); includes 249 minority (59 African Americans, 39 American Indian/Alaska Native, 21 Asian Americans or Pacific Islanders, 130 Hispanic Americans), 4 international. Average age 32. 267 applicants, 97% accepted, 185 enrolled. In 2009, 461 master's, 12 doctorates awarded. *Degree requirements:* For master's, comprehensive exam, thesis (for some programs); for doctorate, comprehensive exam, thesis/dissertation. *Entrance requirements:* For master's, minimum GPA of 3.0; for doctorate, GRE or MAT, minimum GPA of 3.5. Additional exam requirements/recommendations for international students: Required—TOEFL (minimum score 550 paper-based; 213 computer-based; 80 iBT), IELTS (minimum score 7), or a bachelor's degree from an English-speaking university and demonstrated proficiency. *Application deadline:* For fall admission, 2/1 priority date for domestic students, 9/15 priority date for international students; for spring admission, 12/1 for domestic students. Applications are processed on a rolling basis. Application fee: $65. Electronic applications accepted. *Financial support:* In 2009–10, 1 teaching assistantship with partial tuition reimbursement (averaging $10,000 per year) was awarded. Financial award application deadline: 3/30. *Unit head:* Dr. Michael Schwanenberger, Chair, 928-523-3202, Fax: 928-523-8950, E-mail: michael.schwanenberger@nau.edu. *Application contact:* Dr. Michael Schwanenberger, Chair, 928-523-3202, Fax: 928-523-8950, E-mail: michael.schwanenberger@nau.edu.

Old Dominion University, Darden College of Education, Program in Community College Leadership, Norfolk, VA 23529. Offers PhD. Part-time programs available. Postbaccalaureate distance learning degree programs offered (minimal on-campus study). *Faculty:* 3 full-time (2 women), 11 part-time/adjunct (2 women). *Students:* 2 full-time (both women), 49 part-time (33 women); includes 6 minority (4 African Americans, 1 American Indian/Alaska Native, 1 Hispanic American). Average age 45. 30 applicants, 43% accepted, 13 enrolled. In 2009, 4 doctorates awarded. *Degree requirements:* For doctorate, comprehensive exam, thesis/dissertation, internship. *Entrance requirements:* For doctorate, GRE, master's degree, minimum GPA of 3.5, 3 letters of reference. Additional exam requirements/recommendations for international students: Required—TOEFL (minimum score 600 paper-based). *Application deadline:* For spring admission, 2/1 for domestic students, 2/1 priority date for international students. Application fee: $40. Electronic applications accepted. *Expenses:* Tuition, state resident: full-time $8112; part-time $338 per credit. Tuition, nonresident: full-time $20,256; part-time $844 per credit. Required fees: $119 per semester. One-time fee: $50. *Financial support:* In 2009–10, 12 fellowships with full tuition reimbursements (averaging $2,500 per year), 2 research assistantships with full tuition reimbursements (averaging $15,000 per year) were awarded; career-related internships or fieldwork and unspecified assistantships also available. Financial award application deadline: 4/15. *Faculty research:* Legal issues, leadership, distance education. *Unit head:* Dr. Ted Raspiller, Graduate Program Director, 757-683-4375, Fax: 757-683-5756, E-mail: eraspill@odu.edu. *Application contact:* Alice McAdory, Director of Admissions, 757-683-3685, Fax: 757-683-3255, E-mail: gradadmit@odu.edu.

Old Dominion University, Darden College of Education, Programs in Occupational and Technical Studies, Norfolk, VA 23529. Offers business and industry training (MS); career and technical education (MS, PhD); community college teaching (MS); human resources training (PhD); technology education (PhD). *Accreditation:* NCATE (one or more programs are accredited). Part-time and evening/weekend programs available. Postbaccalaureate distance learning degree programs offered (minimal on-campus study). *Faculty:* 6 full-time (1 woman), 8 part-time/adjunct (3 women). *Students:* 17 full-time (12 women), 67 part-time (39 women); includes 21 minority (17 African Americans, 1 Asian American or Pacific Islander, 3 Hispanic Americans), 2 international. Average age 41. 44 applicants, 95% accepted, 37 enrolled. In 2009, 18 master's, 7 doctorates awarded. *Degree requirements:* For master's, comprehensive exam, thesis optional, writing exam, candidacy exam; for doctorate, comprehensive exam, thesis/dissertation, writing exam, candidacy exam. *Entrance requirements:* For master's, GRE General Test or MAT, minimum GPA of 2.8, 2 letters of reference; for doctorate, GRE, minimum GPA of 3.0, 3 letters of reference. Additional exam requirements/recommendations for international students: Required—TOEFL. *Application deadline:* For fall admission, 6/1 priority date for domestic students, 6/1 for international students; for winter admission, 11/1 priority date for domestic students, 11/1 for international students; for spring admission, 3/1 priority date for domestic students, 3/1 for international students. Applications are processed on a rolling basis. Application fee: $40. Electronic applications accepted. *Expenses:* Tuition, state resident: full-time $8112; part-time $338 per credit. Tuition, nonresident: full-time $20,256; part-time $844 per credit. Required fees: $119 per semester. One-time fee: $50. *Financial support:* In 2009–10, 19 students received support, including 1 fellowship with full tuition reimbursement available (averaging $15,000 per year), 2 research assistantships with partial tuition reimbursements available (averaging $9,000 per year), 4 teaching assistantships with partial tuition reimbursements available (averaging $15,000 per year); career-related internships or fieldwork, scholarships/grants, tuition waivers (partial), and unspecified assistantships also available. Support available to part-time students. Financial award application deadline: 2/15; financial award applicants required to submit FAFSA. *Faculty research:* Training and development, marketing, technology, special populations, support of academic subjects. Total annual research expenditures: $799,773. *Unit head:* Dr. John M. Ritz, Graduate Program Director, 757-683-4305, Fax: 757-683-5227, E-mail: jritz@odu.edu. *Application contact:* Dr. John M. Ritz, Graduate Program Director, 757-683-4305, Fax: 757-683-5227, E-mail: jritz@odu.edu.

Pittsburg State University, Graduate School, College of Education, Department of Special Services and Leadership Studies, Program in Community College and Higher Education, Pittsburg, KS 66762. Offers Ed S. *Accreditation:* NCATE. *Expenses:* Tuition, state resident: full-time $4212; part-time $176 per credit. Tuition, nonresident: full-time $11,530; part-time $480 per credit. Required fees: $940; $43 per credit. Tuition and fees vary according to course level, course load, degree level, campus/location, reciprocity agreements and student level.

University of Central Florida, College of Education, Department of Educational Studies, Orlando, FL 32816. Offers applied learning and instruction (MA); community college education (Certificate); curriculum and instruction (Ed S); education (Ed D, PhD, Ed S); gifted education (Certificate); global and comparative education (Certificate); initial teacher professional preparation (Certificate); teacher leadership (M Ed); urban education (Certificate). *Accreditation:* NCATE. Part-time and evening/weekend programs available. *Faculty:* 18 full-time (10 women), 16 part-time/adjunct (10 women). *Students:* 155 full-time (106 women), 156 part-time (131 women); includes 80 minority (37 African Americans, 5 Asian Americans or Pacific Islanders, 38 Hispanic Americans), 22 international. Average age 36. 200 applicants, 57% accepted, 77 enrolled. In 2009, 9 master's, 34 doctorates, 17 other advanced degrees awarded. *Degree requirements:* For other advanced degree, thesis or alternative, final exam. *Entrance requirements:* For degree, GRE General Test, minimum GPA of 3.0, resume. Additional exam requirements/recommendations for international students: Required—TOEFL. *Application deadline:* For fall admission, 2/20 for domestic students; for spring admission, 9/20 for domestic students. Application fee: $30. Electronic applications accepted. *Expenses:* Tuition, state resident: part-time $306.31 per credit hour. Tuition, nonresident: part-time $1099.01 per credit hour. Part-time tuition and fees vary according to degree level and program. *Financial support:* In 2009–10, 82 students received support, including 55 fellowships with partial tuition reimbursements available (averaging $8,300 per year), 29 research assistantships with partial tuition reimbursements available (averaging $7,000 per year), 43 teaching assistantships with partial tuition reimbursements available (averaging $8,000 per year); career-related internships or fieldwork, Federal Work-Study, institutionally sponsored loans, and unspecified assistantships also available. Financial award application deadline: 3/1; financial award applicants required to submit FAFSA. *Unit head:* Dr. Karen Biraimah, Chair, 407-823-2428, E-mail: biraimah@mail.ucf.edu. *Application contact:* Dr. Karen Biraimah, Chair, 407-823-2428, E-mail: biraimah@mail.ucf.edu.

University of Maryland University College, Graduate School of Management and Technology, Doctor of Management in Community College Policy and Administration Program, Adelphi, MD 20783. Offers DM. *Students:* 27 part-time (15 women); includes 11 minority (all African Americans). Average age 47. 50 applicants, 100% accepted, 27 enrolled. *Degree requirements:* For doctorate, comprehensive exam, thesis/dissertation. *Application deadline:* Applications are processed on a rolling basis. Application fee: $100. Electronic applications accepted. *Expenses:* Tuition, state resident: full-time $7704; part-time $428 per credit hour. Tuition, nonresident: full-time $11,862; part-time $659 per credit hour. *Financial support:* Federal Work-Study and scholarships/grants available. Support available to part-time students. Financial award application deadline: 6/1; financial award applicants required to submit FAFSA. *Unit head:* Dr. Charlene Nunley, Director, 240-684-2400, Fax: 240-684-2401. *Application contact:* Coordinator, Graduate Admissions, 240-684-2400, Fax: 240-684-2151, E-mail: newgrad@umuc.edu.

Community College Education

University of Southern Mississippi, Graduate School, College of Education and Psychology, Department of Educational Studies and Research, Hattiesburg, MS 39406-0001. Offers adult education (Graduate Certificate); community college leadership (Graduate Certificate); counseling and personnel services (college) (M Ed); education (PhD, Ed S), including adult education, research, evaluation and statistics (PhD); education (Ed D), including educational administration, educational research; education: educational leadership and research (Ed S), including higher education administration; educational administration and supervision (M Ed); higher education administration (Ed D, PhD); institutional research (Graduate Certificate). *Faculty:* 7 full-time (1 woman), 5 part-time/adjunct (1 woman). *Students:* 45 full-time (34 women), 97 part-time (66 women); includes 42 minority (40 African Americans, 1 American Indian/Alaska Native, 1 Hispanic American), 2 international. Average age 36. 54 applicants, 67% accepted, 33 enrolled. In 2009, 26 master's, 11 doctorates, 3 other advanced degrees awarded. *Degree requirements:* For master's and other advanced degree, comprehensive exam, thesis (for some programs); for doctorate, comprehensive exam, thesis/dissertation. *Entrance requirements:* For master's, doctorate, and other advanced degree, GRE General Test, minimum GPA of 2.75. Additional exam requirements/recommendations for international students: Required—TOEFL. *Application deadline:* For fall admission, 2/1 for domestic students, 3/1 for international students. Applications are processed on a rolling basis. Application fee: $35. *Expenses:* Tuition, state resident: full-time $5096; part-time $284 per hour. Tuition, nonresident: full-time $13,052; part-time $726 per hour. Required fees: $402. Tuition and fees vary according to course level and course load. *Financial support:* Career-related internships or fieldwork, Federal Work-Study, and institutionally sponsored loans available. Financial award application deadline: 3/15; financial award applicants required to submit FAFSA. Total annual research expenditures: $88,500. *Unit head:* Dr. Thomas V. O'Brien, Chair, 601-266-6093, E-mail: thomas.obrien@usm.edu. *Application contact:* Shonna Breland, Manager of Graduate Admissions, 601-266-6563, Fax: 601-266-5138.

University of South Florida, Graduate School, College of Education–Main Campus, Department of Adult, Career and Higher Education, Tampa, FL 33620-9951. Offers adult education (MA, Ed D, PhD, Ed S); career and technical education (MA); career and workforce education (PhD); higher education/community college teaching (MA, Ed D, PhD); vocational education (Ed S). Part-time programs available. *Faculty:* 9 full-time (3 women), 4 part-time/adjunct (3 women). *Students:* 52 full-time (34 women), 211 part-time (149 women); includes 71 minority (41 African Americans, 1 American Indian/Alaska Native, 5 Asian Americans or Pacific Islanders, 24 Hispanic Americans), 6 international. Average age 30. 94 applicants, 69% accepted, 58 enrolled. In 2009, 31 master's, 11 doctorates awarded. *Degree requirements:* For master's, comprehensive exam; for doctorate, comprehensive exam, thesis/dissertation; for Ed S, comprehensive exam, thesis. *Entrance requirements:* For master's, minimum GPA of 3.0 in last 60 hours of course work; for doctorate and Ed S, GRE General Test, GRE Writing Test. Additional exam requirements/recommendations for international students: Required—TOEFL (minimum score 500 paper-based; 213 computer-based; 91 iBT). *Application deadline:* For fall admission, 2/15 for domestic students, 1/2 for international students; for spring admission, 10/15 for domestic students, 6/1 for international students. Applications are processed on a rolling basis. Application fee: $30. Electronic applications accepted. *Financial support:* Career-related internships or fieldwork, scholarships/grants, and unspecified assistantships available. Financial award applicants required to submit FAFSA. *Faculty research:* Community college leadership; integration of academic, career and technical education; competency-based education; continuing education administration; adult learning and development. Total annual research expenditures: $9,807. *Unit head:* Dr. Ann Cranston-Gingras, Chairperson, 813-974-6036, Fax: 813-974-3366, E-mail: cranston@usf.edu. *Application contact:* Dr. William Young, Program Director, 813-974-1861, Fax: 813-974-3366, E-mail: williamyoung@usf.edu.

Walden University, Graduate Programs, Richard W. Riley College of Education and Leadership, Minneapolis, MN 55401. Offers administrator leadership for teaching and learning (Ed D, Ed S); curriculum, instruction, and professional development (Ed S); early childhood education (birth-grade 3) (MAT); education (MS, PhD), including adolescent literacy and technology (grades 6-12) (MS), adult education leadership (PhD), community college leadership (PhD), curriculum, instruction, and assessment, early childhood education (PhD), educational leadership (MS), educational technology (PhD), elementary reading and literacy (MS), elementary reading and mathematics (MS), emotional/behavioral disorders (K-12) (MS), general program, higher education (PhD), integrating technology in the classroom (MS), K-12 educational leadership (PhD), learning disabilities (K-12) (MS), literacy and learning in the content areas (MS), mathematics (grades 6-8) (MS), mathematics (grades K-5) (MS), middle level education (grades 5-8) (MS), professional development (MS), science (grades K-8) (MS), self-designed (PhD), special education (PhD), special education (non-licensure) (MS), teacher leadership (grades K-12) (MS); educational leadership and administration (principal preparation) (Ed S); educational technology (Ed S); higher education and adult learning (Ed D); instructional design (Postbaccalaureate Certificate); instructional design and technology (MS), including general program (MS, PhD), online learning, training and performance improvement; special education: emotional/behavioral disorders (K-12) (MAT); special education: learning disabilities (K-12) (MAT); teacher leadership (Ed D, Ed S). Part-time and evening/weekend programs available. Postbaccalaureate distance learning degree programs offered (minimal on-campus study). *Faculty:* 54 full-time, 835 part-time/adjunct. *Students:* 13,940 full-time (11,339 women), 1,940 part-time (1,637 women); includes 4,626 minority (3,795 African Americans, 111 American Indian/Alaska Native, 199 Asian Americans or Pacific Islanders, 521 Hispanic Americans), 124 international. Average age 38. In 2009, 4,688 master's, 190 doctorates awarded. *Degree requirements:* For doctorate, thesis/dissertation (for some programs), residency; for other advanced degree, residency (for some programs). *Entrance requirements:* For master's, bachelor's degree or equivalent in related field; minimum GPA of 2.5; official transcripts; goal statement; access to computer and Internet; for doctorate, master's degree or equivalent in related field; minimum GPA of 3.0; official transcripts; three years' related professional/academic experience (preferred); access to computer and Internet; for other advanced degree, master's degree or equivalent in related field; minimum GPA of 3.0; 3 years related professional/academic experience (preferred); access to computer and Internet (Ed S). Additional exam requirements/recommendations for international students: Required—TOEFL (minimum score 550 paper-based; 213 computer-based), IELTS (minimum score 6.5), or Michigan English Language Assessment Battery (minimum score 82). *Application deadline:* Applications are processed on a rolling basis. Application fee: $50. Electronic applications accepted. *Expenses:* Tuition: Full-time $13,665; part-time $560 per credit. Required fees: $1375. Tuition and fees vary according to course load, degree level and program. *Financial support:* In 2009–10, 2,418 students received support; fellowships, Federal Work-Study, scholarships/grants, unspecified assistantships, and family tuition reduction, active duty/veteran tuition reduction, group tuition reduction, interest-free payment plans available. Support available to part-time students. Financial award applicants required to submit FAFSA. *Unit head:* Dr. Kate Steffens, Dean, 800-925-3368. *Application contact:* Jennifer Hall, Director of Enrollment, 866-4-WALDEN, E-mail: info@waldenu.edu.

Western Carolina University, Graduate School, College of Education and Allied Professions, Department of Educational Leadership and Foundations, Program in Community College and Higher Education, Cullowhee, NC 28723. Offers community college administration (MA Ed); community college teaching (MA Ed). *Accreditation:* NCATE. Part-time and evening/weekend programs available. Postbaccalaureate distance learning degree programs offered. *Students:* 6 full-time (5 women), 25 part-time (17 women). Average age 40. 70 applicants, 13% accepted, 5 enrolled. In 2009, 8 master's awarded. *Degree requirements:* For master's, comprehensive exam. *Entrance requirements:* For master's, GRE General Test, appropriate undergraduate degree, 3 letters of recommendation. Additional exam requirements/recommendations for international students: Required—TOEFL (minimum score 550 paper-based; 270 computer-based; 79 iBT). *Application deadline:* For fall admission, 5/1 priority date for domestic students; for spring admission, 9/1 priority date for domestic students. Applications are processed on a rolling basis. Application fee: $45. *Financial support:* In 2009–10, 1 student received support, including 1 research assistantship with full and partial tuition reimbursement available (averaging $7,000 per year); fellowships, teaching assistantships with full and partial tuition reimbursements available, career-related internships or fieldwork, institutionally sponsored loans, scholarships/grants, and unspecified assistantships also available. Financial award application deadline: 3/31; financial award applicants required to submit FAFSA. *Faculty research:* Women leaders, program evaluation, organizational culture and change, rural education, democracy in education, faculty careers and development. *Unit head:* Dr. Jacqueline Jacobs, Head, 828-227-7415, Fax: 828-227-7607, E-mail: jjacobs@email.wcu.edu. *Application contact:* Admissions Specialist for Community College and Higher Education, 828-227-7398, Fax: 828-227-7480, E-mail: jbewsey@email.wcu.edu.

Western Carolina University, Graduate School, College of Education and Allied Professions, Department of Educational Leadership and Foundations, Teaching Degree Programs, Cullowhee, NC 28723. Offers comprehensive education (MA Ed); physical education (MA Ed); teaching (MAT). *Accreditation:* NCATE. Part-time and evening/weekend programs available. Postbaccalaureate distance learning degree programs offered. *Students:* 62 full-time (46 women), 172 part-time (148 women). Average age 33. 125 applicants, 77% accepted, 64 enrolled. In 2009, 46 master's awarded. *Degree requirements:* For master's, comprehensive exam. *Entrance requirements:* For master's, GRE General Test or MAT, appropriate undergraduate degree, letters of recommendation. Additional exam requirements/recommendations for international students: Required—TOEFL (minimum score 550 paper-based; 270 computer-based; 79 iBT). *Application deadline:* For fall admission, 5/1 priority date for domestic students; for spring admission, 9/1 priority date for domestic students. Applications are processed on a rolling basis. Application fee: $45. *Financial support:* In 2009–10, 35 students received support, including 1 fellowship (averaging $6,000 per year), 20 research assistantships with full and partial tuition reimbursements available (averaging $7,716 per year), 14 teaching assistantships with full and partial tuition reimbursements available (averaging $7,143 per year); career-related internships or fieldwork, institutionally sponsored loans, scholarships/grants, and unspecified assistantships also available. Financial award application deadline: 3/31; financial award applicants required to submit FAFSA. *Faculty research:* Educational leadership; organizational theory and practice; women's access to leadership positions; preparation, evaluation and professional development of teachers. *Unit head:* Dr. Jacqueline Jacobs, Head, 828-227-7415, Fax: 828-227-7607, E-mail: jjacobs@email.wcu.edu. *Application contact:* Admissions Specialist for Teaching Degrees, 828-227-7398, Fax: 828-227-7480, E-mail: gradsch@email.wcu.edu.

Early Childhood Education

Adelphi University, School of Education, Program in Early Childhood Education, Garden City, NY 11530-0701. Offers early childhood education (Certificate); in-service (MA); pre-certification (MA). *Students:* 7 full-time (all women), 37 part-time (all women); includes 14 minority (9 African Americans, 1 Asian American or Pacific Islander, 4 Hispanic Americans). Average age 33. In 2009, 18 master's awarded. *Entrance requirements:* For master's, 2 letters of recommendation, resume; for Certificate, 2 letters of recommendation, resume, 6 credits in literacy. Additional exam requirements/recommendations for international students: Required—TOEFL (minimum score 550 paper-based; 213 computer-based; 80 iBT). *Application deadline:* For fall admission, 4/1 for domestic and international students; for spring admission, 11/1 for domestic and international students. Application fee: $50. Electronic applications accepted. *Expenses:* Tuition: Full-time $28,340; part-time $830 per credit. Required fees: $600; $250 per credit. Full-time tuition and fees vary according to course load and program. *Faculty research:* Gifted education; impact of family, culture and school in child development; teacher training; assessment of young children; classrooms as respectful communities. *Unit head:* Dr. Esther Kogan, Director, 516-877-4474, E-mail: kogan@adelphi.edu. *Application contact:* Christine Murphy, Director of Admissions, 516-877-3050, Fax: 516-877-3039, E-mail: graduateadmissions@adelphi.edu.

Alabama Agricultural and Mechanical University, School of Graduate Studies, School of Education, Area in Elementary and Early Childhood Education, Huntsville, AL 35811. Offers early childhood education (MS Ed, Ed S); elementary education (MS Ed, Ed S). *Accreditation:* NCATE. Evening/weekend programs available. *Degree requirements:* For master's, comprehensive exam; for Ed S, thesis. *Entrance requirements:* For master's, GRE General Test. Additional exam requirements/recommendations for international students: Required—TOEFL (minimum score 500 paper-based; 173 computer-based; 61 iBT). Electronic applications accepted. *Faculty research:* Multicultural education, learning styles, diagnostic-prescriptive instruction.

Alabama State University, School of Graduate Studies, College of Education, Department of Curriculum and Instruction, Program in Early Childhood Education, Montgomery, AL 36101-0271. Offers M Ed, Ed S. Part-time programs available. *Degree requirements:* For master's, comprehensive exam; for Ed S, comprehensive exam, thesis. *Entrance requirements:* For master's, GRE General Test, MAT or NTE, graduate writing competency test; for Ed S, graduate writing competency test, GRE, MAT. Additional exam requirements/recommendations for international students: Required—TOEFL (minimum score 500 paper-based; 173 computer-based).

Albany State University, College of Education, Program in Early Childhood Education, Albany, GA 31705-2717. Offers M Ed. *Accreditation:* NCATE. Part-time programs available. *Students:* 39 full-time (37 women), 34 part-time (32 women); includes 60 minority (all African Americans). Average age 32. 14 applicants, 100% accepted, 10 enrolled. In 2009, 11 master's awarded. *Degree requirements:* For master's, comprehensive exam, GACE II. *Entrance requirements:* For master's, GRE General Test or MAT, GACE I, clear renewable teaching certificate, 3 work-related letters of recommendation, writing sample (certified teachers); 3 letters of reference, writing sample, minimum GPA of 2.5, education standards (non-certified teachers). Additional exam requirements/recommendations for international students: Required—TOEFL. *Application deadline:* For fall admission, 11/16 for domestic students, 9/16 for international students; for spring admission, 4/19 for domestic students, 2/19 for international students. Applications are processed on a rolling basis. Application fee: $20. Electronic applications accepted. *Expenses:* Tuition, state resident: full-time $2970; part-time $162 per credit hour. Tuition, nonresident: full-time $12,168; part-time $676 per credit hour. Required fees: $962; $75 per credit hour. *Financial support:* Application deadline: 6/30. *Unit head:* Dr. Audrey Beard, Chair, 229-430-4715, Fax: 229-430-4993, E-mail: audrey.beard@asurams.edu. *Application contact:* Nicole Lane, Interim Graduate Admissions Officer, 229-430-4862, Fax: 229-430-6398, E-mail: nicole.lane@asurams.edu.

Albright College, Department of Education—Graduate Division, Reading, PA 19612-5234. Offers early childhood education (MS); elementary education (MS); English as a second language (MA); general education (MA); special education (MS). Part-time and evening/weekend programs available. *Degree requirements:* For master's, thesis. *Entrance requirements:* For master's, GRE General Test or MAT, minimum undergraduate GPA of 3.0, 2 letters of

recommendation, interview. Additional exam requirements/recommendations for international students: Recommended—TOEFL (minimum score 525 paper-based; 197 computer-based). Electronic applications accepted.

American International College, School of Arts, Education and Sciences, Department of Education, Springfield, MA 01109-3189. Offers early childhood education (M Ed, CAGS); educational leadership and supervision (Ed D); elementary education (M Ed, CAGS); middle/secondary education (M Ed, CAGS); moderate disabilities (M Ed, CAGS); reading (M Ed, CAGS); school adjustment counseling (MA, CAGS); school administration (M Ed, CAGS); school guidance counseling (MA, CAGS); teaching (MA, MS); teaching and learning (Ed D). Part-time and evening/weekend programs available. Terminal master's awarded for partial completion of doctoral program. *Degree requirements:* For master's, comprehensive exam (for some programs), thesis (for some programs), practicum; for doctorate, comprehensive exam (for some programs), thesis/dissertation; for CAGS, practicum. *Entrance requirements:* For master's, minimum B- average in undergraduate course work; for doctorate, GRE General Test, interview. Additional exam requirements/recommendations for international students: Required—TOEFL. Electronic applications accepted. *Expenses:* Tuition: Full-time $12,510; part-time $695 per credit hour. Required fees: $35 per term.

American University, College of Arts and Sciences, School of Education, Teaching, and Health, Washington, DC 20016-8030. Offers curriculum and instruction (M Ed, Certificate); early childhood education (MAT, Certificate); elementary education (MAT); English for speakers of other languages (MAT, Certificate); health promotion management (MS); international training and development (MAT); international training and education (MA); nutrition education (Certificate); secondary teaching (MAT, Certificate); special education (MA), including special education: learning disabilities; MAT/MA. *Accreditation:* NCATE. Part-time and evening/weekend programs available. *Faculty:* 15 full-time (9 women), 68 part-time/adjunct (45 women). *Students:* 74 full-time (56 women), 392 part-time (293 women); includes 110 minority (71 African Americans, 9 American Indian/Alaska Native, 11 Asian Americans or Pacific Islanders, 19 Hispanic Americans), 3 international. Average age 27. 354 applicants, 87% accepted, 218 enrolled. In 2009, 196 master's awarded. *Degree requirements:* For master's, comprehensive exam, thesis or alternative, PRAXIS II. *Entrance requirements:* For master's, GRE General Test, minimum GPA of 3.0; for Certificate, bachelor's degree. Additional exam requirements/recommendations for international students: Required—TOEFL. *Application deadline:* For fall admission, 2/1 priority date for domestic students; for spring admission, 10/1 priority date for domestic students. Applications are processed on a rolling basis. Application fee: $80. *Expenses:* Tuition: Full-time $22,266; part-time $1237 per credit hour. Required fees: $430. Tuition and fees vary according to program. *Financial support:* Fellowships, research assistantships with full and partial tuition reimbursements, teaching assistantships with full and partial tuition reimbursements, career-related internships or fieldwork, Federal Work-Study, and institutionally sponsored loans available. Support available to part-time students. Financial award application deadline: 2/1; financial award applicants required to submit FAFSA. *Faculty research:* Gender equity, socioeconomic technology, learning disabilities, gifted and talented education. *Unit head:* Dr. Sarah Irvine-Belson, Dean, 202-885-3714, Fax: 202-885-1187, E-mail: educate@american.edu. *Application contact:* Kathleen Clowery, Director, Graduate Admissions, 202-885-3621, Fax: 202-885-1505.

Anna Maria College, Graduate Division, Program in Education, Paxton, MA 01612. Offers early childhood education (M Ed); education (CAGS); elementary education (M Ed); English language arts (M Ed); visual arts (M Ed). Part-time and evening/weekend programs available. *Entrance requirements:* For master's, bachelor's degree in liberal arts or sciences, minimum GPA of 3.0. Additional exam requirements/recommendations for international students: Required—TOEFL (minimum score 500 paper-based). Electronic applications accepted.

Antioch University New England, Graduate School, Department of Education, Keene, NH 03431-3552. Offers experienced educators (M Ed); integrated learning (M Ed), including early childhood education, elementary education; Waldorf teacher training (M Ed). *Degree requirements:* For master's, thesis (for some programs), internship. *Entrance requirements:* Additional exam requirements/recommendations for international students: Required—TOEFL (minimum score 600 paper-based; 250 computer-based). *Expenses:* Contact institution. *Faculty research:* Classroom and school restructuring, problem-based learning, Waldorf collaborative leadership, ecological literacy.

Antioch University New England, Graduate School, Department of Education, Integrated Learning Program, Concentration in Early Childhood Education, Keene, NH 03431-3552. Offers M Ed.

Arcadia University, Graduate Studies, Department of Education, Glenside, PA 19038-3295. Offers art education (M Ed, MA Ed); biology education (MA Ed); chemistry education (MA Ed); child development (CAS); computer education (M Ed, CAS); computer education 7–12 (MA Ed); early childhood education (M Ed, CAS), including individualized (M Ed), master teacher (M Ed), research in child development (M Ed); educational leadership (M Ed, CAS); educational psychology (CAS); elementary education (M Ed, CAS); English education (MA Ed); environmental education (MA Ed, CAS); history education (MA Ed); language arts (M Ed, CAS); mathematics education (M Ed, MA Ed, CAS); music education (MA Ed); psychology (MA Ed); pupil personnel services (CAS); reading (M Ed, CAS); school library science (M Ed); science education (M Ed, CAS); secondary education (M Ed, CAS); special education (M Ed, Ed D, CAS); theater arts (MA Ed); written communication (MA Ed). *Accreditation:* NASAD. Part-time and evening/weekend programs available. Postbaccalaureate distance learning degree programs offered (minimal on-campus study). *Faculty:* 12 full-time (8 women), 38 part-time/adjunct (26 women). *Students:* 89 full-time (74 women), 622 part-time (487 women); includes 112 minority (94 African Americans, 9 Asian Americans or Pacific Islanders, 9 Hispanic Americans), 2 international. Average age 32. In 2009, 257 master's, 4 doctorates awarded. *Application deadline:* Applications are processed on a rolling basis. Application fee: $40. Electronic applications accepted. *Expenses:* Tuition: Full-time $30,450; part-time $620 per credit hour. Required fees: $165. Tuition and fees vary according to program. *Financial support:* Career-related internships or fieldwork, tuition waivers (partial), and unspecified assistantships available. *Unit head:* Dr. Steven P. Gulkus. *Application contact:* 215-572-2925, Fax: 215-572-2126, E-mail: grad@arcadia.edu.

Arkansas State University—Jonesboro, Graduate School, College of Education, Department of Teacher Education, Jonesboro, State University, AR 72467. Offers early childhood education (MSE); early childhood services (MS); middle level education (MSE); reading (MSE, SCCT). *Accreditation:* NCATE. Part-time programs available. *Faculty:* 5 full-time (4 women), 4 part-time/adjunct (3 women). *Students:* 10 full-time (all women), 87 part-time (84 women); includes 40 minority (39 African Americans, 1 American Indian/Alaska Native). Average age 35. 63 applicants, 79% accepted, 39 enrolled. In 2009, 31 master's awarded. *Degree requirements:* For master's, comprehensive exam, thesis or alternative; for SCCT, comprehensive exam. *Entrance requirements:* For master's, GRE General Test or MAT, appropriate bachelor's degree; for SCCT, GRE General Test or MAT, interview, master's degree, official transcript, immunization records. Additional exam requirements/recommendations for international students: Required—TOEFL (minimum score 550 paper-based; 213 computer-based; 79 iBT), IELTS (minimum score 6). *Application deadline:* For fall admission, 7/15 for domestic students, 7/1 for international students; for spring admission, 12/1 for domestic students, 11/13 for international students. Applications are processed on a rolling basis. Application fee: $30 ($40 for international students). Electronic applications accepted. *Expenses:* Tuition, state resident: full-time $3744; part-time $208 per credit hour. Tuition, nonresident: full-time $9540; part-time $530 per credit hour. Required fees: $896; $47 per credit hour. $25 per term. One-time fee: $50. Tuition and fees vary according to course load and program. *Financial support:* In 2009–10, 16 students received support; teaching assistantships, career-related internships or fieldwork, scholarships/grants, and unspecified assistantships available. Financial award application deadline: 7/1; financial award applicants required to submit FAFSA. *Unit head:* Dr. Dianne Lawler-Prince, Chair, 870-972-3059, Fax: 870-972-3344, E-mail: dprince@astate.edu. *Application contact:* Dr. Andrew Sustich, Dean of the Graduate School, 870-972-3029, Fax: 870-972-3857, E-mail: sustich@astate.edu.

Armstrong Atlantic State University, School of Graduate Studies, Program in Education, Savannah, GA 31419-1997. Offers adult education (M Ed); curriculum and instruction (M Ed); early childhood education (M Ed); education (M Ed); elementary education (M Ed); middle grades education (M Ed); secondary education (M Ed), including business education, English education, mathematics education, science education, social science education; special education (M Ed), including behavioral disorders, learning disabilities, speech-language pathology. *Accreditation:* NCATE. Part-time and evening/weekend programs available. Postbaccalaureate distance learning degree programs offered (minimal on-campus study). *Degree requirements:* For master's, comprehensive exam, portfolio. *Entrance requirements:* For master's, GRE General Test or MAT, minimum GPA of 2.5, letters of recommendation. Additional exam requirements/recommendations for international students: Required—TOEFL (minimum score 523 paper-based; 193 computer-based). Electronic applications accepted.

Auburn University, Graduate School, College of Education, Department of Curriculum and Teaching, Auburn University, AL 36849. Offers business education (M Ed, MS, PhD); early childhood education (M Ed, MS, PhD, Ed S); elementary education (M Ed, MS, PhD, Ed S); foreign languages (M Ed, MS); music education (M Ed, MS, PhD, Ed S); postsecondary education (PhD); reading education (PhD, Ed S); secondary education (M Ed, MS, PhD, Ed S), including English language arts, mathematics, science, social studies. *Accreditation:* NASM (one or more programs are accredited); NCATE. Part-time programs available. *Faculty:* 28 full-time (21 women), 8 part-time/adjunct (5 women). *Students:* 76 full-time (55 women), 186 part-time (139 women); includes 43 minority (29 African Americans, 1 American Indian/Alaska Native, 4 Asian Americans or Pacific Islanders, 9 Hispanic Americans), 4 international. Average age 33. 248 applicants, 65% accepted, 110 enrolled. In 2009, 102 master's, 12 doctorates, 6 other advanced degrees awarded. *Degree requirements:* For master's, thesis (for some programs); for doctorate, thesis/dissertation; for Ed S, field project. *Entrance requirements:* For master's, doctorate, and Ed S, GRE General Test. *Application deadline:* For fall admission, 7/7 for domestic students; for spring admission, 11/24 for domestic students. Applications are processed on a rolling basis. Application fee: $50 ($60 for international students). Electronic applications accepted. *Expenses:* Tuition, state resident: full-time $6240. Tuition, nonresident: full-time $18,720. International tuition: $18,938 full-time. Required fees: $492. Tuition and fees vary according to course load, program and reciprocity agreements. *Financial support:* Fellowships, teaching assistantships, career-related internships or fieldwork and Federal Work-Study available. Support available to part-time students. Financial award application deadline: 3/15; financial award applicants required to submit FAFSA. *Faculty research:* Emerging literacy, reading attitudes, music for at-risk youth, portfolio assessment. *Unit head:* Dr. Nancy H. Barry, Head, 334-844-4434. *Application contact:* Dr. George Flowers, Dean of the Graduate School, 334-844-2125.

Auburn University, Graduate School, College of Education, Department of Special Education, Rehabilitation, Counseling and School Psychology, Auburn University, AL 36849. Offers collaborative teacher special education (M Ed, MS); early childhood special education (M Ed, MS); rehabilitation counseling (M Ed, MS, PhD). *Accreditation:* CORE; NCATE. Part-time programs available. *Faculty:* 20 full-time (13 women), 8 part-time/adjunct (6 women). *Students:* 149 full-time (117 women), 94 part-time (78 women); includes 63 minority (56 African Americans, 1 American Indian/Alaska Native, 2 Asian Americans or Pacific Islanders, 4 Hispanic Americans), 4 international. Average age 31. 226 applicants, 51% accepted, 87 enrolled. In 2009, 48 master's, 20 doctorates awarded. *Degree requirements:* For master's, thesis (for some programs); for doctorate, thesis/dissertation. *Entrance requirements:* For master's, GRE General Test; for doctorate, GRE General Test, interview. *Application deadline:* For fall admission, 7/17 for domestic students; for spring admission, 11/24 for domestic students. Applications are processed on a rolling basis. Application fee: $50 ($60 for international students). Electronic applications accepted. *Expenses:* Tuition, state resident: full-time $6240. Tuition, nonresident: full-time $18,720. International tuition: $18,938 full-time. Required fees: $492. Tuition and fees vary according to course load, program and reciprocity agreements. *Financial support:* Research assistantships, teaching assistantships, Federal Work-Study available. Support available to part-time students. Financial award application deadline: 3/15; financial award applicants required to submit FAFSA. *Faculty research:* Emotional conflict/behavior disorders, gifted and talented, learning disabilities, mental retardation, multi-handicapped. *Unit head:* Dr. Philip L. Browning, Head, 334-844-5943. *Application contact:* Dr. George Flowers, Dean of the Graduate School, 334-844-2125.

Auburn University Montgomery, School of Education, Department of Early Childhood, Elementary, and Reading Education, Montgomery, AL 36124-4023. Offers early childhood education (M Ed, Ed S); elementary education (M Ed, Ed S); reading education (M Ed, Ed S). *Accreditation:* NCATE. Part-time and evening/weekend programs available. *Faculty:* 5 full-time (all women). *Students:* 56 full-time (54 women), 71 part-time (65 women); includes 45 minority (all African Americans). Average age 31. In 2009, 42 master's awarded. *Degree requirements:* For master's and Ed S, comprehensive exam. *Entrance requirements:* For master's, GRE General Test or MAT, certification, BS in teaching; for Ed S, GRE General Test or MAT, certification. *Application deadline:* Applications are processed on a rolling basis. Electronic applications accepted. *Expenses:* Tuition, state resident: full-time $2841; part-time $225 per credit hour. Tuition, nonresident: full-time $8241; part-time $675 per credit hour. Required fees: $282; $8 per hour. $45 per term. *Financial support:* In 2009–10, 1 teaching assistantship was awarded; career-related internships or fieldwork and scholarships/grants also available. Support available to part-time students. Financial award application deadline: 3/1; financial award applicants required to submit FAFSA. *Unit head:* Dr. Lynne Mills, Head, 334-244-3283, Fax: 334-244-3835, E-mail: lmills@mail.aum.edu. *Application contact:* Dr. Sam Flynt, Associate Graduate Coordinator, 334-244-3270, Fax: 334-244-3835, E-mail: sflynt@mail.aum.edu.

Bank Street College of Education, Graduate School, Program in Early Childhood Education, New York, NY 10025. Offers MS Ed. *Students:* 30 full-time (28 women), 57 part-time (54 women); includes 17 minority (3 African Americans, 8 Asian Americans or Pacific Islanders, 6 Hispanic Americans). Average age 30. 49 applicants, 82% accepted, 32 enrolled. In 2009, 19 master's awarded. *Degree requirements:* For master's, thesis. *Entrance requirements:* For master's, interview. Additional exam requirements/recommendations for international students: Required—TOEFL (minimum score 600 paper-based; 250 computer-based; 100 iBT), IELTS (minimum score 7). *Application deadline:* For fall admission, 3/1 priority date for domestic students; for spring admission, 11/1 priority date for domestic students. Applications are processed on a rolling basis. Application fee: $65. *Expenses:* Tuition: Part-time $1120 per credit. *Financial support:* Career-related internships or fieldwork, Federal Work-Study, scholarships/grants, and unspecified assistantships available. Support available to part-time students. Financial award application deadline: 4/15; financial award applicants required to submit FAFSA. *Faculty research:* Play in early childhood settings, early childhood learning environments, family-teacher interaction, child-centered education, developmental interaction. *Unit head:* Adrianne Kamsler, Chairperson, 212-875-4571, Fax: 212-875-4753, E-mail: akamsler@bankstreet.edu. *Application contact:* Ann Morgan, Director of Graduate Admissions, 212-875-4403, Fax: 212-875-4678, E-mail: amorgan@bankstreet.edu.

Bank Street College of Education, Graduate School, Program in Reading and Literacy, New York, NY 10025. Offers advanced literacy specialization (Ed M); reading and literacy (MS Ed); teaching literacy (MS Ed); teaching literacy and childhood general education (MS Ed). *Students:* 29 full-time (all women), 50 part-time (45 women); includes 13 minority (6 African Americans, 4 Asian Americans or Pacific Islanders, 3 Hispanic Americans). Average age 31. 48 applicants, 81% accepted, 28 enrolled. In 2009, 50 master's awarded. *Degree requirements:* For master's, thesis. *Entrance requirements:* For master's, interview. Additional exam requirements/recommendations for international students: Required—TOEFL (minimum score 600 paper-based; 250 computer-based; 100 iBT), IELTS (minimum score 7). *Application deadline:* For fall admission, 3/1 priority date for domestic students; for spring admission, 11/1 priority date for domestic students. Applications are processed on a rolling basis. Application fee: $65. *Expenses:* Tuition: Part-time $1120 per credit. *Financial support:* Career-related internships or fieldwork,

Early Childhood Education

Bank Street College of Education (continued)

Federal Work-Study, scholarships/grants, and unspecified assistantships available. Support available to part-time students. Financial award application deadline: 4/15; financial award applicants required to submit FAFSA. *Faculty research:* Language development, children's literature, whole language, the reading and writing processes, reading difficulties in multicultural classrooms. *Unit head:* Dr. Susan Goetz-Haver, Director, 212-875-4692, Fax: 212-875-4753, E-mail: sgoetz-haver@bankstreet.edu. *Application contact:* Ann Morgan, Director of Graduate Admissions, 212-875-4403, Fax: 212-875-4678, E-mail: amorgan@bankstreet.edu.

Bank Street College of Education, Graduate School, Programs in Educational Leadership, New York, NY 10025. Offers early childhood leadership (MS Ed); educational leadership (MS Ed); leadership for educational change (Ed M, MS Ed); leadership in mathematics education (MS Ed); leadership in museum education (MS Ed); leadership in the arts: creative writing (MS Ed); leadership in the arts: visual arts (MS Ed). *Students:* 76 full-time (60 women), 121 part-time (95 women); includes 67 minority (34 African Americans, 1 American Indian/Alaska Native, 6 Asian Americans or Pacific Islanders, 26 Hispanic Americans), 2 international. Average age 36. 124 applicants, 86% accepted, 98 enrolled. In 2009, 79 master's awarded. *Degree requirements:* For master's, thesis. *Entrance requirements:* For master's, interview, minimum of 2 years experience as a classroom teacher. Additional exam requirements/recommendations for international students: Required—TOEFL (minimum score 600 paper-based; 250 computer-based; 100 iBT), IELTS (minimum score 7). *Application deadline:* For fall admission, 3/1 priority date for domestic students; for spring admission, 11/1 priority date for domestic students. Applications are processed on a rolling basis. Application fee: $65. *Expenses:* Tuition: Part-time $1120 per credit. *Financial support:* Career-related internships or fieldwork, Federal Work-Study, scholarships/grants, and unspecified assistantships available. Support available to part-time students. Financial award application deadline: 4/15; financial award applicants required to submit FAFSA. *Faculty research:* Leadership in small schools, mathematics in elementary schools, professional development in early childhood, leadership in arts education, leadership in special education. *Unit head:* Dr. Rima Shore, Chairperson, 212-875-4478, Fax: 212-875-8753, E-mail: rshore@bankstreet.edu. *Application contact:* Ann Morgan, Director of Graduate Admissions, 212-875-4403, Fax: 212-875-4678, E-mail: amorgan@bankstreet.edu.

Barry University, School of Education, Program in Curriculum and Instruction, Miami Shores, FL 33161-6695. Offers accomplished teacher (Ed S); culture, language and literacy (TESOL) (PhD); curriculum evaluation and research (PhD); early childhood (Ed S); early childhood education (PhD); elementary (Ed S); elementary education (PhD); ESOL (Ed S); gifted (Ed S); Montessori (Ed S); PKP/elementary (Ed S); reading (Ed S); reading, language and cognition (PhD). *Entrance requirements:* For doctorate, GRE, minimum GPA of 3.25.

Barry University, School of Education, Program in Montessori Education, Miami Shores, FL 33161-6695. Offers MS, Ed S. Part-time and evening/weekend programs available. *Degree requirements:* For master's, comprehensive exam, practicum; for Ed S, practicum. *Entrance requirements:* For master's, GRE General Test or MAT, minimum GPA of 3.0; for Ed S, GRE General Test, minimum GPA of 3.0. Electronic applications accepted.

Barry University, School of Education, Program in Pre-Kindergarten and Primary Education, Miami Shores, FL 33161-6695. Offers pre-k/primary (MS); pre-k/primary/ESOL (MS). Part-time and evening/weekend programs available. *Degree requirements:* For master's, comprehensive exam, practicum. *Entrance requirements:* For master's, GRE General Test or MAT, minimum GPA of 3.0. Electronic applications accepted.

Bayamón Central University, Graduate Programs, Program in Education, Bayamón, PR 00960-1725. Offers administration and supervision (MA Ed); commercial education (MA Ed); education of the autistic (MA Ed); elementary education (K–3) (MA Ed); elementary education (K–6) (MA Ed); guidance and counseling (MA Ed); organizational psychology (MA); pre-elementary teacher (MA Ed); rehabilitation counseling (MA Ed); special education (MA Ed), including attention deficit disorder, learning disabilities. Part-time and evening/weekend programs available. *Degree requirements:* For master's, comprehensive exam. *Entrance requirements:* For master's, EXADEP, bachelor's degree in education or related field.

Bellarmine University, Annsley Frazier Thornton School of Education, Louisville, KY 40205-0671. Offers early elementary education (MA, MAT); instructional leadership and school administration/school principal (MA); learning and behavior disorders (MA); middle school education (MA, MAT); reading and writing endorsement (MA); secondary school education (MAT); Waldorf inspired curriculum (MA). *Accreditation:* NCATE. Part-time and evening/weekend programs available. *Faculty:* 16 full-time (11 women), 20 part-time/adjunct (13 women). *Students:* 67 full-time (47 women), 140 part-time (111 women); includes 14 minority (10 African Americans, 1 American Indian/Alaska Native, 3 Asian Americans or Pacific Islanders), 1 international. Average age 33. In 2009, 106 degrees awarded. *Degree requirements:* For master's, comprehensive exam, thesis (for some programs). *Entrance requirements:* For master's, GRE, baccalaureate degree from an accredited institution; minimum overall GPA of 2.75, 3.0 in major; letters of recommendation; valid Kentucky provisional or professional certificate. Additional exam requirements/recommendations for international students: Required—TOEFL (minimum score 550 paper-based; 213 computer-based; 80 iBT). *Application deadline:* Applications are processed on a rolling basis. Application fee: $25. *Expenses:* Contact institution. *Financial support:* Scholarships/grants available. Financial award applicants required to submit FAFSA. *Faculty research:* Literacy, service learning, dispositions, educational technology, special education. *Unit head:* Dr. Cindy Gnadinger, Dean, 502-452-8191, Fax: 502-452-8189, E-mail: cgnadinger@bellarmine.edu. *Application contact:* Theresa Klapheke, Administrative Director of Graduate Programs, 502-452-8271, Fax: 502-452-8002, E-mail: tklapheke@bellarmine.edu.

Belmont University, College of Arts and Sciences, School of Education, Nashville, TN 37212-3757. Offers education (M Ed); elementary education (MAT), including early childhood education, elementary education, language arts education; English (MAT); history (MAT); mathematics (MAT); middle grade education (MAT); science (MAT); secondary education (MAT); special education (MAT); sports administration (MSA). *Accreditation:* NCATE. Part-time and evening/weekend programs available. *Degree requirements:* For master's, comprehensive exam, thesis, culminating portfolio. *Entrance requirements:* For master's, MAT or GRE and/or LSAT or GMAT, minimum GPA of 2.75. Additional exam requirements/recommendations for international students: Required—TOEFL. *Expenses:* Contact institution. *Faculty research:* Improving secondary literacy, Montessori, classroom management strategies, teacher residency programs, online professional development, mentoring, leadership, sociological issues in sport, faculty development, coaching.

Bennington College, Graduate Programs, MA in Teaching Program, Bennington, VT 05201. Offers art education (MAT); early childhood (MAT); elementary education (MAT); English education (MAT); foreign language education (MAT); k-12 education (MAT); mathematics education (MAT); music education (MAT); science education (MAT); secondary education (MAT); social studies education (MAT); theater arts (MAT). *Faculty:* 5 part-time/adjunct (3 women). *Students:* 8 full-time (5 women), 1 part-time (0 women). Average age 28. 11 applicants, 27% accepted, 1 enrolled. In 2009, 4 master's awarded. *Degree requirements:* For master's, comprehensive exam, 1 year teaching practicum, professional portfolio. *Entrance requirements:* For master's, interview. *Application deadline:* For fall admission, 3/1 for domestic students. Application fee: $60. *Expenses:* Contact institution. *Financial support:* In 2009–10, 6 students received support, including 4 fellowships (averaging $10,475 per year); scholarships/grants and unspecified assistantships also available. Financial award application deadline: 4/1; financial award applicants required to submit FAFSA. *Unit head:* Carol Meyer, Director of Programs in Teacher Education, 802-440-4375, E-mail: cmeyer@bennington.edu. *Application contact:* Nancy Pearlman, Assistant Director of Programs in Teacher Education, 802-440-4710, Fax: 802-440-4383, E-mail: npearlman@bennington.edu.

Berry College, Graduate Programs, Graduate Programs in Education, Program in Early Childhood Education, Mount Berry, GA 30149-0159. Offers M Ed. *Accreditation:* NCATE. Part-time programs available. *Faculty:* 13 part-time/adjunct (8 women). *Students:* 2 full-time (1 woman), 34 part-time (32 women); includes 4 minority (2 African Americans, 2 Hispanic Americans). Average age 31. In 2009, 10 master's awarded. *Degree requirements:* For master's, thesis optional, oral exams. *Entrance requirements:* For master's, GRE General Test, MAT, or NTE, minimum GPA of 2.5. Additional exam requirements/recommendations for international students: Required—TOEFL (minimum score 550 paper-based; 213 computer-based). *Application deadline:* For fall admission, 5/1 for domestic and international students; for spring admission, 10/1 for domestic and international students. Applications are processed on a rolling basis. Application fee: $25 ($30 for international students). *Expenses:* Contact institution. *Financial support:* In 2009–10, 11 students received support, including 3 research assistantships with full tuition reimbursements available (averaging $3,708 per year); scholarships/grants and unspecified assistantships also available. Support available to part-time students. Financial award application deadline: 4/1; financial award applicants required to submit FAFSA. *Faculty research:* Curriculum development, teacher training, pedagogy. *Unit head:* Dr. Jacqueline McDowell, 706-236-1717, Fax: 706-238-5827, E-mail: jmcdowell@berry.edu. *Application contact:* Brett Kennedy, Director of Admissions, 706-236-2215, Fax: 706-290-2178, E-mail: admissions@berry.edu.

Bloomsburg University of Pennsylvania, School of Graduate Studies, College of Professional Studies, School of Education, Department of Elementary and Early Childhood Education, Program in Early Childhood Education, Bloomsburg, PA 17815-1301. Offers MS. *Accreditation:* NCATE. *Degree requirements:* For master's, thesis optional. *Entrance requirements:* For master's, MAT, minimum QPA of 3.0. Additional exam requirements/recommendations for international students: Required—TOEFL. Electronic applications accepted. *Faculty research:* Child development, children's literature, theory, administration.

Boise State University, Graduate College, College of Education, Programs in Teacher Education, Program in Early Childhood Education, Boise, ID 83725-0399. Offers M Ed, MA. *Accreditation:* NCATE. Part-time programs available. *Degree requirements:* For master's, thesis optional. *Entrance requirements:* For master's, minimum GPA of 3.0. Electronic applications accepted. *Expenses:* Tuition, state resident: full-time $3106; part-time $209 per credit. Tuition, nonresident: part-time $284 per credit.

Boston College, Lynch Graduate School of Education, Department of Counseling Psychology, Developmental, and Educational Psychology, Program in Early Childhood/Specialist Option, Chestnut Hill, MA 02467-3800. Offers MA. *Accreditation:* Teacher Education Accreditation Council. Part-time and evening/weekend programs available. *Students:* 1 (woman) full-time, 1 (woman) part-time. 9 applicants, 44% accepted, 2 enrolled. In 2009, 4 master's awarded. *Degree requirements:* For master's, comprehensive exam. *Entrance requirements:* For master's, GRE General Test or MAT. Additional exam requirements/recommendations for international students: Required—TOEFL (minimum score 550 paper-based; 213 computer-based; 81 iBT). *Application deadline:* For fall admission, 1/1 priority date for domestic students. Application fee: $60. Electronic applications accepted. *Financial support:* Fellowships with full and partial tuition reimbursements, research assistantships with full and partial tuition reimbursements, teaching assistantships with full and partial tuition reimbursements, career-related internships or fieldwork, Federal Work-Study, scholarships/grants, traineeships, health care benefits, tuition waivers (full and partial), and unspecified assistantships available. Support available to part-time students. Financial award applicants required to submit FAFSA. *Faculty research:* School preparedness, educational leadership in early childhood, dual language literacy in young children. *Unit head:* Dr. M. Brinton Lykes, Chairperson, 617-552-4214, Fax: 617-552-0812. *Application contact:* Adam Poluzzi, Director, Graduate Admission and Financial Aid, 617-552-4214, Fax: 617-552-0398, E-mail: poluzzi@bc.edu.

Boston College, Lynch Graduate School of Education, Department of Teacher Education/Special Education and Curriculum and Instruction, Early Childhood Education/Teacher Option Program, Chestnut Hill, MA 02467-3800. Offers M Ed. *Accreditation:* Teacher Education Accreditation Council. Part-time and evening/weekend programs available. *Students:* 1 (woman) full-time, 11 part-time (all women); includes 2 minority (1 Asian American or Pacific Islander, 1 Hispanic American). 39 applicants, 51% accepted, 10 enrolled. In 2009, 4 master's awarded. *Degree requirements:* For master's, comprehensive exam. *Entrance requirements:* For master's, GRE General Test or MAT. Additional exam requirements/recommendations for international students: Required—TOEFL (minimum score 550 paper-based; 213 computer-based; 81 iBT). *Application deadline:* For fall admission, 1/1 priority date for domestic students. Application fee: $60. Electronic applications accepted. *Financial support:* Fellowships with full and partial tuition reimbursements, research assistantships with full and partial tuition reimbursements, teaching assistantships with full and partial tuition reimbursements, career-related internships or fieldwork, Federal Work-Study, scholarships/grants, traineeships, health care benefits, tuition waivers (full and partial), and unspecified assistantships available. Support available to part-time students. Financial award applicants required to submit FAFSA. *Faculty research:* Early childhood testing and assessment, selective attention abilities in children, problem-solving, dual language learning and literacy. *Unit head:* Dr. Maria E. Brisk, Chairperson, 617-552-4216, Fax: 617-552-0812, E-mail: brisk@bc.edu. *Application contact:* Adam Poluzzi, Director, Graduate Admission and Financial Aid, 617-552-4214, Fax: 617-552-0398, E-mail: poluzzi@bc.edu.

Boston University, School of Education, Department of Curriculum and Teaching, Program in Early Childhood Education, Boston, MA 02215. Offers Ed M, Ed D, CAGS. *Degree requirements:* For master's, thesis optional; for doctorate, comprehensive exam, thesis/dissertation; for CAGS, comprehensive exam. *Entrance requirements:* For master's, doctorate, and CAGS, GRE General Test or MAT. Additional exam requirements/recommendations for international students: Required—TOEFL. Electronic applications accepted. *Expenses:* Tuition: Full-time $37,910; part-time $1184 per credit hour. Required fees: $386; $40 per semester. Part-time tuition and fees vary according to class time, course level, degree level and program. *Faculty research:* Language acquisition, child development, needs of handicapped children.

Bowling Green State University, Graduate College, College of Education and Human Development, School of Education and Intervention Services, Intervention Services Division, Program in Special Education, Bowling Green, OH 43403. Offers assistive technology (M Ed); early childhood intervention (M Ed); gifted education (M Ed); hearing impaired intervention (M Ed); mild/moderate intervention (M Ed); moderate/intensive intervention (M Ed). *Accreditation:* NCATE. Part-time programs available. *Degree requirements:* For master's, thesis or alternative. *Entrance requirements:* For master's, GRE General Test. Additional exam requirements/recommendations for international students: Required—TOEFL. Electronic applications accepted. *Faculty research:* Reading and special populations, deafness, early childhood, gifted and talented, behavior disorders.

Brenau University, Graduate Programs, School of Education, Gainesville, GA 30501. Offers early childhood (Ed S); early childhood education (M Ed, MAT); middle grades (Ed S); middle grades education (M Ed, MAT); secondary education (MAT); special education (M Ed, MAT). *Accreditation:* NCATE. Part-time and evening/weekend programs available. Postbaccalaureate distance learning degree programs offered (no on-campus study). *Faculty:* 12 full-time (7 women), 25 part-time/adjunct (21 women). *Students:* 161 full-time (146 women), 143 part-time (122 women); includes 43 minority (30 African Americans, 5 Asian Americans or Pacific Islanders, 8 Hispanic Americans), 1 international. Average age 35. 163 applicants, 34% accepted, 47 enrolled. In 2009, 154 master's, 20 other advanced degrees awarded. *Degree requirements:* For master's, thesis optional, comprehensive exam or applied research project, effective portfolio; for Ed S, applied research project. *Entrance requirements:* For master's, GRE, MAT, interview, minimum GPA of 3.0, 3 references, writing samples; for Ed S, GRE, MAT, master's degree, minimum GPA of 3.0, writing sample, letters of reference. Additional exam requirements/recommendations for international students: Required—TOEFL (minimum score 500 paper-based). *Application deadline:* Applications are processed on a rolling basis. Application fee: $35. Electronic applications accepted. *Expenses:* Contact institution. *Financial support:* In 2009–10, 2 students received support. Scholarships/grants available. Support available to part-time students. Financial award application deadline: 7/15; financial award applicants required to submit FAFSA. *Unit head:* Dr. Lora Bailey, Dean, 770-534-6220, Fax:

770-534-6221, E-mail: lbailey@brenau.edu. *Application contact:* Christina White, Dean of Admissions, 770-718-5320, Fax: 770-718-5337, E-mail: cwhite@brenau.edu.

Bridgewater State University, School of Graduate Studies, School of Education and Allied Science, Department of Elementary and Early Childhood Education, Program in Early Childhood Education, Bridgewater, MA 02325-0001. Offers M Ed. *Accreditation:* NCATE. Part-time and evening/weekend programs available. *Entrance requirements:* For master's, GRE General Test or Massachusetts Test for Educator Licensure.

Brooklyn College of the City University of New York, Division of Graduate Studies, School of Education, Program in Early Childhood Education, Brooklyn, NY 11210-2889. Offers birth-grade 2 (MS Ed). Part-time and evening/weekend programs available. *Students:* 2 full-time (both women), 140 part-time (137 women); includes 81 minority (54 African Americans, 7 Asian Americans or Pacific Islanders, 20 Hispanic Americans), 1 international. Average age 33. 61 applicants, 79% accepted, 29 enrolled. In 2009, 29 master's awarded. *Entrance requirements:* For master's, LAST, bachelor's degree in early childhood education, resume, 2 letters of recommendation, essay. Additional exam requirements/recommendations for international students: Required—TOEFL (minimum score 500 paper-based; 173 computer-based; 61 iBT). *Application deadline:* For fall admission, 3/1 priority date for domestic students, 2/1 priority date for international students; for spring admission, 11/1 priority date for domestic students, 10/1 priority date for international students. Applications are processed on a rolling basis. Application fee: $125. Electronic applications accepted. *Expenses:* Tuition, state resident: full-time $7360; part-time $310 per credit hour. Tuition, nonresident: full-time $13,800; part-time $575 per credit hour. Required fees: $140.10 per semester. *Financial support:* Career-related internships or fieldwork, Federal Work-Study, institutionally sponsored loans, and scholarships/grants available. Support available to part-time students. Financial award application deadline: 5/1; financial award applicants required to submit FAFSA. *Faculty research:* Children's narrations, language acquisition, culture and education. *Unit head:* Dr. Jacquelin Shannon, Program Head, 718-951-5214, Fax: 718-951-4816, E-mail: shannon@brooklyn.cuny.edu. *Application contact:* Hernan Sierra, Graduate Admissions Coordinator, 718-951-4536, Fax: 718-951-4506, E-mail: grads@brooklyn.cuny.edu.

Buffalo State College, State University of New York, The Graduate School, Faculty of Applied Science and Education, Department of Elementary Education and Reading, Program in Elementary Education, Buffalo, NY 14222-1095. Offers childhood education (grades 1-6) (MS Ed); early childhood and childhood curriculum and instruction (MS Ed); early childhood education (birth-grade 2) (MS Ed). *Accreditation:* NCATE. Part-time programs available. *Degree requirements:* For master's, thesis or project. *Entrance requirements:* For master's, minimum GPA of 2.5 in last 60 hours, New York teaching certificate. Additional exam requirements/recommendations for international students: Required—TOEFL (minimum score 550 paper-based; 213 computer-based).

California State University, Bakersfield, Division of Graduate Studies, School of Education, Program in Child, Adolescent, and Family Studies, Bakersfield, CA 93311. Offers early childhood education (MA). *Degree requirements:* For master's, thesis, project, or examination. *Entrance requirements:* For master's, valid basic California teaching credential.

California State University, East Bay, Graduate Programs, College of Education and Allied Studies, Department of Teacher Education, Hayward, CA 94542-3000. Offers education (MS), including curriculum, early childhood education, educational technology leadership, reading instruction. *Faculty:* 18 full-time (10 women), 4 part-time/adjunct (3 women). *Students:* Average age 37. In 2009, 135 master's awarded. *Degree requirements:* For master's, project or thesis. *Entrance requirements:* For master's, minimum GPA of 3.0 in field, 2.5 overall; teaching experience. Additional exam requirements/recommendations for international students: Required—TOEFL (minimum score 550 paper-based; 213 computer-based). *Application deadline:* For fall admission, 6/30 for domestic and international students. Application fee: $55. Electronic applications accepted. *Financial support:* Career-related internships or fieldwork, Federal Work-Study, and institutionally sponsored loans available. Support available to part-time students. Financial award application deadline: 3/1; financial award applicants required to submit FAFSA. *Unit head:* Dr. Jeanette Bicais, Chair, 510-885-3027, E-mail: jeanette.bicais@csueastbay.edu. *Application contact:* Donna Wiley, Interim Associate Director, 510-885-2928, Fax: 510-885-4777, E-mail: donna.wiley@csueastbay.edu.

California State University, Fresno, Division of Graduate Studies, School of Education and Human Development, Department of Literacy and Early Education, Fresno, CA 93740-8027. Offers education (MA), including early childhood education, reading/language arts. *Accreditation:* NCATE. Part-time and evening/weekend programs available. *Degree requirements:* For master's, thesis or alternative. *Entrance requirements:* For master's, GRE General Test, MAT, minimum GPA of 2.75. Additional exam requirements/recommendations for international students: Required—TOEFL. Electronic applications accepted. *Faculty research:* Reading recovery, monitoring/tutoring programs, character and academics, professional ethics, low-performing partnership schools.

California State University, Northridge, Graduate Studies, College of Education, Department of Educational Psychology and Counseling, Northridge, CA 91330. Offers counseling (MS), including career counseling, college counseling and student services, marriage and family therapy, school counseling, school psychology; educational psychology (MA Ed), including development, learning, and instruction, early childhood education. *Accreditation:* ACA (one or more programs are accredited); NCATE. Part-time and evening/weekend programs available. *Faculty:* 19 full-time (11 women), 42 part-time/adjunct (26 women). *Students:* 341 full-time (301 women), 135 part-time (121 women); includes 21 African Americans, 31 Asian Americans or Pacific Islanders, 149 Hispanic Americans, 11 international. Average age 31. 498 applicants, 39% accepted, 167 enrolled. In 2009, 119 master's awarded. *Entrance requirements:* For master's, GRE General Test or minimum GPA of 3.0. Additional exam requirements/recommendations for international students: Required—TOEFL. *Application deadline:* For fall admission, 11/30 for domestic students. Application fee: $55. *Financial support:* Scholarships/grants available. Support available to part-time students. Financial award application deadline: 3/1. *Unit head:* Dr. Shari Tarver-Behring, Chair, 818-677-2599. *Application contact:* Dr. Shari Tarver-Behring, Chair, 818-677-2599.

California State University, Sacramento, Graduate Studies, College of Education, Department of Teacher Education, Sacramento, CA 95819. Offers curriculum and instruction (MA); early childhood education (MA); reading education (MA). Part-time programs available. *Degree requirements:* For master's, thesis or alternative, writing proficiency exam. *Entrance requirements:* Additional exam requirements/recommendations for international students: Required—TOEFL. Electronic applications accepted.

Cambridge College, School of Education, Cambridge, MA 02138-5304. Offers autism specialist (M Ed); autism/behavior analyst (M Ed); behavior analyst (Post-Master's Certificate); behavioral management (M Ed); early childhood teacher (M Ed); education specialist in curriculum and instruction (CAGS); educational leadership (Ed D); elementary teacher (M Ed); English as a second language (M Ed, Certificate); general science (M Ed); health education, health promotion (Post-Master's Certificate); health/family and consumer sciences (M Ed); history (M Ed); individualized degree (M Ed); information technology literacy (M Ed); instructional technology (M Ed); interdisciplinary studies (M Ed); library teacher (M Ed); literacy education (M Ed); mathematics (M Ed); mathematics specialist (Certificate); middle school mathematics and science (M Ed); school administration (M Ed, CAGS); school guidance counselor (M Ed); school nurse education (M Ed); school social worker/school adjustment counselor (M Ed); special education administrator (CAGS); special education/moderate disabilities (M Ed); teaching skills and methodologies (M Ed). Part-time and evening/weekend programs available. Post-baccalaureate distance learning degree programs offered (minimal on-campus study). *Faculty:* 10 full-time (3 women), 283 part-time/adjunct (187 women). *Students:* 974 full-time (755 women), 1,071 part-time (835 women); includes 940 minority (762 African Americans, 4 American Indian/Alaska Native, 22 Asian Americans or Pacific Islanders, 152 Hispanic Americans), 28 international. Average age 39. In 2009, 866 master's, 4 doctorates, 209 CAGSs awarded. *Degree requirements:* For master's, thesis, internship/practicum (licensure program only); for doctorate, thesis/dissertation; for other advanced degree, thesis. *Entrance requirements:* For master's, interview, resume, documentation of licensure, 2 professional references; for doctorate, official transcripts, interview, resume, documentation of licensure (if any), written personal statement/essay, portfolio of scholarly and professional work, qualifying assessment, 2 professional references, health insurance, immunizations form; for other advanced degree, official transcripts, interview, resume, documentation of licensure (if any), written personal statement/essay, 2 professional references, health insurance, immunizations form. Additional exam requirements/recommendations for international students: Required—TOEFL (minimum score 550 paper-based; 213 computer-based; 79 iBT); Recommended—IELTS (minimum score 6). *Application deadline:* Applications are processed on a rolling basis. Application fee: $30. Electronic applications accepted. *Expenses:* Contact institution. *Financial support:* In 2009–10, 1,373 students received support. Career-related internships or fieldwork, Federal Work-Study, and scholarships/grants available. Financial award applicants required to submit FAFSA. *Faculty research:* Adult education, accelerated learning, mathematics education, brain compatible learning, special education and law. *Unit head:* Dr. N. Alan Sheppard, Interim Associate Dean, 617-873-0619, E-mail: alan.sheppard@cambridgecollege.edu. *Application contact:* Stephen Lyons, Director of Enrollment, Graduate and N.I.T.E. Programs, 617-868-1000, Fax: 617-349-3561, E-mail: stephen.lyons@cambridgecollege.edu.

Canisius College, Graduate Division, School of Education and Human Services, Department of Graduate Education, Buffalo, NY 14208-1098. Offers adolescence education (grades 7-12) (MS); childhood education (grades 1-6) (MS); college student personnel administration (MS); deaf education (MS); differentiated instruction (MS Ed); educational administration and supervision (MS); general education (MS Ed); initial teacher certification (elementary education) (MS); initial teacher certification (secondary education) (MS); literacy (MS Ed); special education (MS). *Accreditation:* NCATE. Part-time and evening/weekend programs available. *Faculty:* 22 full-time (14 women), 84 part-time/adjunct (54 women). *Students:* 409 full-time (288 women), 261 part-time (187 women); includes 29 minority (24 African Americans, 5 Hispanic Americans), 156 international. Average age 30. 518 applicants, 74% accepted, 240 enrolled. In 2009, 346 master's awarded. Application fee: $25. *Financial support:* Research assistantships with full tuition reimbursements, career-related internships or fieldwork, institutionally sponsored loans, scholarships/grants, health care benefits, tuition waivers (full and partial), and unspecified assistantships available. *Faculty research:* Autism, Asperger's disease, private higher education, reading strategies. *Unit head:* Rev. Paul Nochelski, Chair of Graduate Education and Leadership, 716-888-3297, Fax: 716-888-3299. *Application contact:* James D. Bagwell, Director of Graduate Recruitment and Admissions, 716-888-2544, Fax: 716-888-3290, E-mail: bagwellj@canisius.edu.

Caribbean University, Graduate School, Bayamón, PR 00960-0493. Offers administration and supervision (MA Ed); criminal justice (MA); curriculum and instruction (MA Ed), including elementary education, English education, history education, mathematics education, primary education, science education, Spanish education; education (PhD); gerontology (MSN); human resources (MBA); museology, archiving and art history (MA Ed); neonatal pediatrics (MSN); physical education (MA Ed); special education (MA Ed). *Entrance requirements:* For master's, interview, minimum GPA of 2.5.

Carlow University, School of Education, Program in Early Childhood Education, Pittsburgh, PA 15213-3165. Offers M Ed. Part-time and evening/weekend programs available. *Degree requirements:* For master's, thesis or alternative. *Entrance requirements:* Additional exam requirements/recommendations for international students: Required—TOEFL. Electronic applications accepted. *Expenses:* Tuition: Full-time $11,250; part-time $625 per credit. Tuition and fees vary according to course load, degree level and program. *Faculty research:* Understanding children's play, infant and toddler development, effects of violence on children, supervision and staff development.

Carlow University, School of Education, Program in Early Childhood Supervision, Pittsburgh, PA 15213-3165. Offers M Ed. Part-time and evening/weekend programs available. *Degree requirements:* For master's, thesis or alternative. *Entrance requirements:* Additional exam requirements/recommendations for international students: Required—TOEFL. Electronic applications accepted. *Expenses:* Tuition: Full-time $11,250; part-time $625 per credit. Tuition and fees vary according to course load, degree level and program. *Faculty research:* Leadership styles, learning styles, feminist pedagogy.

Central Connecticut State University, School of Graduate Studies, School of Education and Professional Studies, Department of Teacher Education, Program in Early Childhood Education, New Britain, CT 06050-4010. Offers MS. Part-time and evening/weekend programs available. *Students:* 1 (woman) full-time, 23 part-time (all women); includes 5 minority (2 African Americans, 1 Asian American or Pacific Islander, 2 Hispanic Americans). Average age 32. 15 applicants, 33% accepted, 4 enrolled. In 2009, 7 master's awarded. *Degree requirements:* For master's, comprehensive exam, thesis or alternative. *Entrance requirements:* For master's, minimum undergraduate GPA of 2.7. Additional exam requirements/recommendations for international students: Required—TOEFL. *Application deadline:* For fall admission, 7/1 for domestic students; for spring admission, 12/1 for domestic students. Applications are processed on a rolling basis. Application fee: $50. Electronic applications accepted. *Expenses:* Tuition, area resident: Full-time $4662; part-time $440 per credit. Tuition, state resident: full-time $6994; part-time $440 per credit. Tuition, nonresident: full-time $12,988; part-time $440 per credit. Required fees: $3606. One-time fee: $62 part-time. *Faculty research:* Pre-kindergarten and early learning research, early learning environments.

Central Michigan University, College of Graduate Studies, College of Education and Human Services, Department of Teacher Education and Professional Development, Mount Pleasant, MI 48859. Offers educational technology (MA); elementary education (MA), including classroom teaching, early childhood; middle level education (MA); reading and literacy K-12 (MA); secondary education (MA). Part-time and evening/weekend programs available. *Degree requirements:* For master's, thesis or alternative. Electronic applications accepted. *Faculty research:* Integrating literacy across the curriculum; science teaching and aesthetic learning in science; diversity education; educational technology; educational psychology and child development.

Chatham University, Program in Education, Pittsburgh, PA 15232-2826. Offers early childhood education (MAT); elementary education (MAT); English—secondary (MAT); environmental education (K-12) (MAT); secondary art (MAT); secondary biology education (MAT); secondary chemistry education (MAT); secondary English education (MAT); secondary math education (MAT); secondary physics education (MAT); secondary social studies education (MAT); special education (MAT). *Students:* 52 full-time (41 women), 20 part-time (16 women). Average age 30. 39 applicants, 79% accepted, 26 enrolled. In 2009, 37 master's awarded. *Degree requirements:* For master's, thesis, teaching experience. *Entrance requirements:* For master's, PRAXIS I, minimum GPA of 3.0, sample of written work, recommendation letters. Additional exam requirements/recommendations for international students: Required—TOEFL (minimum score 600 paper-based; 250 computer-based; 100 iBT), IELTS (minimum score 6.5), TWE. *Application deadline:* For fall admission, 5/1 priority date for domestic and international students; for spring admission, 10/15 priority date for domestic and international students. Applications are processed on a rolling basis. Application fee: $45. Electronic applications accepted. *Financial support:* Career-related internships or fieldwork available. Financial award applicants required to submit FAFSA. *Faculty research:* Gifted education, environmental education, technology in education, writing as learning, class size and achievement. *Unit head:* Dr. Barbara Biglan, Interim Director, 412-365-1170, E-mail: biglan@chatham.edu. *Application contact:* Dory Perry, Associate Director of Graduate Admissions, 412-365-2758, Fax: 412-365-1609, E-mail: gradadmissions@chatham.edu.

Chestnut Hill College, School of Graduate Studies, Department of Education, Program in Early Childhood Education, Philadelphia, PA 19118-2693. Offers M Ed. Part-time and evening/weekend programs available. *Degree requirements:* For master's, thesis optional. *Entrance requirements:* For master's, PRAXIS I or proof of teaching certification, writing sample, letters of recommendation, 6 graduate credits with minimum B grade if undergraduate GPA is below

Early Childhood Education

Chestnut Hill College (continued)

3.0. Additional exam requirements/recommendations for international students: Required—TOEFL (minimum score 500 paper-based). *Faculty research:* Gender issues, ECE standardized testing.

Cheyney University of Pennsylvania, School of Education and Professional Studies, Program in Early Childhood Education, Cheyney, PA 19319. Offers Certificate. Part-time and evening/weekend programs available. *Degree requirements:* For Certificate, thesis or alternative. *Entrance requirements:* For degree, GRE General Test, MAT, minimum GPA of 2.75. Electronic applications accepted.

Chicago State University, School of Graduate and Professional Studies, College of Education, Department of Special Education, Early Childhood Education and Bilingual Education, Program in Early Childhood Education, Chicago, IL 60628. Offers MAT, MS Ed. *Accreditation:* NCATE. *Degree requirements:* For master's, thesis optional. *Entrance requirements:* For master's, minimum GPA of 2.75.

City College of the City University of New York, Graduate School, School of Education, Department of Childhood Education, New York, NY 10031-9198. Offers MS. *Accreditation:* NCATE. *Degree requirements:* For master's, thesis. *Entrance requirements:* For master's, Liberal Arts and Sciences Test (LAST), Content Specialty Test (CST). Additional exam requirements/recommendations for international students: Required—TOEFL. *Expenses:* Tuition, state resident: part-time $310 per credit. Tuition, nonresident: part-time $575 per credit. Tuition and fees vary according to course load and program.

Clarion University of Pennsylvania, Office of Research and Graduate Studies, College of Education and Human Services, Department of Education, Program in Education, Clarion, PA 16214. Offers curriculum and instruction (M Ed); early childhood (M Ed); English (M Ed); history (M Ed); literacy (M Ed); science (M Ed); technology (M Ed). *Accreditation:* NCATE. Part-time programs available. *Degree requirements:* For master's, comprehensive exam, thesis or alternative. *Entrance requirements:* For master's, minimum QPA of 3.0, teacher certification. Additional exam requirements/recommendations for international students: Required—TOEFL (minimum score 550 paper-based; 213 computer-based; 80 iBT). Electronic applications accepted.

Clarke College, Program in Education, Dubuque, IA 52001-3198. Offers early childhood/special education (MAE); educational administration: elementary and secondary (MAE); educational media: elementary and secondary (MAE); multi-categorical resource k-12 (MAE); multidisciplinary studies (MAE); reading: elementary (MAE); technology in education (MAE). Part-time and evening/weekend programs available. Postbaccalaureate distance learning degree programs offered (minimal on-campus study). *Faculty:* 5 full-time (all women). *Students:* 1 (woman) full-time, 45 part-time (40 women). Average age 31. 19 applicants, 74% accepted, 13 enrolled. In 2009, 11 master's awarded. *Degree requirements:* For master's, comprehensive exam, thesis optional. *Entrance requirements:* For master's, GRE General Test or MAT, minimum GPA of 2.75. *Application deadline:* Applications are processed on a rolling basis. Application fee: $25. Electronic applications accepted. *Expenses:* Tuition: Full-time $10,836; part-time $602 per credit hour. Required fees: $30 per credit hour. *Financial support:* Career-related internships or fieldwork available. Financial award applicants required to submit FAFSA. *Unit head:* Dr. Larry Bice, Chair, 319-588-6397, Fax: 319-584-8604. *Application contact:* Joan Coates, Information Contact, 563-588-6354, Fax: 563-588-6789, E-mail: graduate@clarke.edu.

Clemson University, Graduate School, College of Health, Education, and Human Development, School of Education, Program in Early Childhood Education, Clemson, SC 29634. Offers M Ed. Part-time programs available. *Students:* 2 full-time (both women), 2 part-time (both women). Average age 26. 5 applicants, 40% accepted, 1 enrolled. In 2009, 2 master's awarded. *Degree requirements:* For master's, thesis optional. *Entrance requirements:* For master's, GRE, valid teaching certificate. Additional exam requirements/recommendations for international students: Required—TOEFL. *Application deadline:* Applications are processed on a rolling basis. Application fee: $70 ($80 for international students). Electronic applications accepted. *Expenses:* Contact institution. *Financial support:* Career-related internships or fieldwork, institutionally sponsored loans, scholarships/grants, health care benefits, and unspecified assistantships available. Support available to part-time students. *Unit head:* Dr. Michael J. Padilla, Director/Associate Dean, 864-656-4444, Fax: 864-656-0311, E-mail: padilla@clemson.edu. *Application contact:* Dr. David Fleming, Graduate Programs Coordinator, 864-656-1881, Fax: 864-656-0311, E-mail: dflemin@clemson.edu.

Cleveland State University, College of Graduate Studies, College of Education and Human Services, Department of Teacher Education, Cleveland, OH 44115. Offers art education (M Ed); early childhood education (M Ed); foreign language education (M Ed); mathematics and science education (M Ed); middle childhood education (M Ed); special education (M Ed), including mild/moderate disabilities, moderate/intensive disabilities; teaching English to speakers of other languages (M Ed). Part-time and evening/weekend programs available. *Degree requirements:* For master's, comprehensive exam (for some programs), thesis or alternative. *Entrance requirements:* For master's, GRE General Test or MAT, minimum GPA of 2.75. Additional exam requirements/recommendations for international students: Required—TOEFL (minimum score 525 paper-based; 197 computer-based), IELTS (minimum score 6). *Faculty research:* Early literacy, professional development in reading, reading recovery, dual language, induction programs.

College of Charleston, Graduate School, School of Education, Health, and Human Performance, Department of Elementary and Early Childhood Education, Program in Early Childhood Education, Charleston, SC 29424-0001. Offers MAT. *Accreditation:* NCATE. Part-time and evening/weekend programs available. *Faculty:* 31 full-time (26 women), 11 part-time/adjunct (10 women). *Students:* 37 full-time (32 women), 6 part-time (all women); includes 3 minority (all African Americans), 1 international. Average age 29. 23 applicants, 70% accepted, 16 enrolled. In 2009, 5 master's awarded. *Degree requirements:* For master's, thesis or alternative, written qualifying exam, student teaching experience (MAT). *Entrance requirements:* For master's, GRE, minimum GPA of 2.5, 2 letters of recommendation. Additional exam requirements/recommendations for international students: Required—TOEFL. *Application deadline:* For fall admission, 4/1 for domestic students; for spring admission, 11/1 for domestic students. Applications are processed on a rolling basis. Application fee: $45. Electronic applications accepted. *Financial support:* In 2009–10, teaching assistantships (averaging $13,300 per year); research assistantships, Federal Work-Study and unspecified assistantships also available. Support available to part-time students. Financial award application deadline: 4/1; financial award applicants required to submit FAFSA. *Faculty research:* Teacher education and creative arts, integrated curriculum, multicultural awareness, teaching models, cooperative learning. *Unit head:* Dr. Angela Cozart, Director, 843-953-6353, E-mail: cozarta@cofc.edu. *Application contact:* Susan Hallatt, Director of Graduate Admissions, 843-953-5614, Fax: 843-953-1434, E-mail: hallats@cofc.edu.

College of Mount St. Joseph, Graduate Education Program, Cincinnati, OH 45233-1670. Offers adolescent young adult education (MA); art (MA); inclusive early childhood education (MA); instructional leadership (MA); middle childhood education (MA); multi-age education (MA); multicultural special education (MA); music (MA); reading (MA). *Accreditation:* Teacher Education Accreditation Council. Part-time and evening/weekend programs available. *Faculty:* 15 full-time (11 women), 9 part-time/adjunct (6 women). *Students:* 93 full-time (75 women), 99 part-time (66 women); includes 19 minority (18 African Americans, 1 American Indian/Alaska Native). Average age 34. 116 applicants, 97% accepted, 94 enrolled. In 2009, 51 master's awarded. *Degree requirements:* For master's, research project, student teaching, clinical and field-based experiences. *Entrance requirements:* For master's, GRE, PRAXIS II in teaching content area (math or science), 2 letters of recommendation, interview, resume. Additional exam requirements/recommendations for international students: Required—TOEFL (minimum score 560 paper-based; 220 computer-based; 83 iBT). *Application deadline:* Applications are processed on a rolling basis. Application fee: $50. Electronic applications accepted. *Expenses:* Tuition: Part-time $500 per hour. Required fees: $200 per year. Tuition and fees vary according

to degree level and program. *Financial support:* In 2009–10, 51 students received support. Scholarships/grants available. Financial award applicants required to submit FAFSA. *Faculty research:* Foreign and second language learning problems/reading disabilities/hyperlexia, multicultural/bilingual special education, alternative educator licensure, science education, pedagogical content knowledge. *Unit head:* Dr. Mary West, Chair of Graduate Education, 513-244-3263, Fax: 513-244-4867, E-mail: mary_west@mail.msj.edu. *Application contact:* Marilyn Hoskins, Assistant Director of Graduate Recruitment, 513-244-4723, Fax: 513-244-4629, E-mail: marilyn_hoskins@mail.msj.edu.

The College of New Jersey, Graduate Division, School of Education, Department of Elementary and Early Childhood Education, Program in School Personnel Licensure: Preschool-Grade 3, Ewing, NJ 08628. Offers M Ed, MAT. Part-time programs available. *Students:* 2 full-time (1 woman), 19 part-time (all women); includes 4 minority (3 African Americans, 1 Hispanic American). 21 applicants, 71% accepted. *Entrance requirements:* For master's, GRE, minimum GPA of 3.0 in field or 2.75 overall. Additional exam requirements/recommendations for international students: Required—TOEFL. *Application deadline:* For fall admission, 2/1 priority date for domestic students; for spring admission, 10/1 priority date for domestic students. Application fee: $70. Electronic applications accepted. *Expenses:* Tuition, state resident: part-time $573.70 per credit. Tuition, nonresident: part-time $887.75 per credit. Required fees: $140.85 per credit. One-time fee: $10 part-time. *Financial support:* Tuition waivers (partial) and unspecified assistantships available. Financial award application deadline: 5/1; financial award applicants required to submit FAFSA. *Unit head:* Dr. Jody Eberly, Coordinator, 609-771-3093. *Application contact:* Susan L. Hydro, Assistant Dean, Office of Graduate Studies, 609-771-2300, Fax: 609-637-5105, E-mail: graduate@tcnj.edu.

The College of New Rochelle, Graduate School, Division of Education, Program in Elementary Education/Early Childhood Education, New Rochelle, NY 10805-2308. Offers MS Ed. Part-time programs available. *Degree requirements:* For master's, comprehensive exam (for some programs), thesis (for some programs), practicum. *Entrance requirements:* For master's, interview, minimum GPA of 3.0 in field, 2.7 overall.

The College of Saint Rose, Graduate Studies, School of Education, Teacher Education Department, Albany, NY 12203-1419. Offers business and marketing (MS Ed); childhood education (MS Ed); curriculum and instruction (MS Ed); early childhood education (MS Ed); elementary education (K-6) (MS Ed); secondary education (MS Ed, Certificate); teacher education (MS Ed, Certificate), including bilingual pupil personnel services (Certificate), teacher education (MS Ed). Part-time and evening/weekend programs available. *Entrance requirements:* For master's, minimum undergraduate GPA of 3.0. Additional exam requirements/recommendations for international students: Required—TOEFL (minimum score 550 paper-based; 213 computer-based). Electronic applications accepted.

Columbia International University, Columbia Graduate School, Columbia, SC 29230-3122. Offers Bible teaching (MABT); Christian higher education leadership (Ed D); Christian school educational leadership (Ed D); counseling (MACN); curriculum and instruction (M Ed), including Christian school guidance, English as a second language, learning disabilities, school technology; early childhood and elementary education (MAT); educational administration (M Ed); teaching English as a foreign language (Certificate); teaching English as a foreign language and intercultural studies (MATF). Part-time and evening/weekend programs available. *Degree requirements:* For master's, internships, professional project. *Entrance requirements:* For master's, Minnesota Multiphasic Personality Inventory, MAT, minimum GPA of 2.7. Additional exam requirements/recommendations for international students: Required—TOEFL. Electronic applications accepted.

Columbus State University, Graduate Studies, College of Education and Health Professions, Department of Teacher Education, Columbus, GA 31907-5645. Offers accomplished teaching (M Ed); early childhood education (M Ed, Ed S); health administration (MPA); instructional technology (MS); middle grades education (M Ed, Ed S); physical education (M Ed); secondary education (M Ed, MAT, Ed S), including English/language arts (M Ed, Ed S), general science (M Ed), mathematics (M Ed), social science (M Ed); special education (M Ed), including behavior disorders, mental retardation. *Accreditation:* NCATE. Part-time and evening/weekend programs available. Postbaccalaureate distance learning degree programs offered (minimal on-campus study). *Faculty:* 18 full-time (15 women), 14 part-time/adjunct (10 women). *Students:* 146 full-time (113 women), 312 part-time (261 women); includes 142 minority (120 African Americans, 1 American Indian/Alaska Native, 8 Asian Americans or Pacific Islanders, 13 Hispanic Americans), 2 international. Average age 31. 248 applicants, 64% accepted, 114 enrolled. In 2009, 103 master's, 22 other advanced degrees awarded. *Degree requirements:* For master's, thesis, exit exam; for Ed S, thesis or alternative. *Entrance requirements:* For master's, GRE General Test, minimum GPA of 2.75; for Ed S, GRE General Test. Additional exam requirements/recommendations for international students: Required—TOEFL (minimum score 550 paper-based; 213 computer-based; 79 iBT). *Application deadline:* For fall admission, 5/1 priority date for domestic students, 5/1 for international students; for spring admission, 11/1 for domestic and international students. Applications are processed on a rolling basis. Application fee: $30. Electronic applications accepted. *Financial support:* In 2009–10, 305 students received support, including 36 research assistantships with partial tuition reimbursements available (averaging $3,000 per year); career-related internships or fieldwork, Federal Work-Study, institutionally sponsored loans, scholarships/grants, tuition waivers (partial), and unspecified assistantships also available. Support available to part-time students. Financial award application deadline: 5/1; financial award applicants required to submit FAFSA. *Unit head:* Dr. Deborah Gober, Acting Chair, 706-568-2255, Fax: 706-568-3134, E-mail: gober_deborah@colstate.edu. *Application contact:* Katie Thornton, Graduate Admissions Specialist, 706-568-2035, Fax: 706-568-2462, E-mail: thornton_katie@colstate.edu.

Concordia University Chicago, College of Education, Program in Early Childhood Education, River Forest, IL 60305-1499. Offers MA, Ed D. Part-time and evening/weekend programs available. *Degree requirements:* For master's, comprehensive exam, thesis. *Entrance requirements:* For master's, minimum GPA of 2.9; for doctorate, MAT or GRE, minimum graduate GPA of 3.5. Additional exam requirements/recommendations for international students: Required—TOEFL (minimum score 550 paper-based; 195 computer-based). Electronic applications accepted. *Faculty research:* Child care training project, 'Children in Worship" project, ethical development of children.

Concordia University Chicago, College of Education, Program in Teaching, River Forest, IL 60305-1499. Offers early childhood education (MAT); elementary education (MAT); secondary education (MAT). *Degree requirements:* For master's, thesis or alternative. *Entrance requirements:* For master's, minimum GPA of 2.9. Additional exam requirements/recommendations for international students: Required—TOEFL (minimum score 550 paper-based; 195 computer-based). Electronic applications accepted.

Concordia University, Nebraska, Graduate Programs in Education, Program in Early Childhood Education, Seward, NE 68434-1599. Offers M Ed. *Accreditation:* NCATE. Part-time programs available. *Degree requirements:* For master's, comprehensive exam, thesis or alternative. *Entrance requirements:* For master's, GRE, MAT, or NTE, minimum GPA of 3.0, BS in education or equivalent. Additional exam requirements/recommendations for international students: Required—TOEFL.

Concordia University, St. Paul, College of Education, St. Paul, MN 55104-5494. Offers curriculum and instruction (MA Ed), including K-12 reading endorsement; differentiated instruction (MA Ed); early childhood education (MA Ed); educational leadership (MA Ed); family life education (MA); K-12 reading endorsement (Certificate); special education (Certificate); sports management (MA). *Accreditation:* NCATE. Evening/weekend programs available. Postbaccalaureate distance learning degree programs offered (minimal on-campus study). *Faculty:* 12 full-time (8 women), 59 part-time/adjunct (47 women). *Students:* 697 full-time (571 women), 13 part-time (12 women); includes 64 minority (31 African Americans, 1 American Indian/Alaska Native, 21 Asian Americans or Pacific Islanders, 11 Hispanic Americans), 1 international. Average age 34. In 2009, 402 master's, 29 other advanced degrees awarded. *Application*

deadline: Applications are processed on a rolling basis. Application fee: $50. Electronic applications accepted. *Financial support:* Applicants required to submit FAFSA. *Unit head:* Dr. Donald Helmstetter, Dean, 651-641-8227, Fax: 651-641-8807, E-mail: helmstetter@csp.edu. *Application contact:* Kimberly Craig, Director of Graduate and Cohort Admission, 651-603-6223, Fax: 651-603-6320, E-mail: craig@csp.edu.

Concordia University Wisconsin, Graduate Programs, Department of Education, Program in Early Childhood, Mequon, WI 53097-2402. Offers MS Ed. *Degree requirements:* For master's, comprehensive exam, thesis or alternative. *Entrance requirements:* For master's, minimum GPA of 3.0, teaching license. Additional exam requirements/recommendations for international students: Required—TOEFL.

Converse College, School of Education and Graduate Studies, Spartanburg, SC 29302-0006. Offers art education (M Ed); early childhood education (MAT); education (Ed S), including administration and supervision, curriculum and instruction, marriage and family therapy; elementary education (M Ed, MAT); gifted education (M Ed); leadership (M Ed); liberal arts (MLA), including English (M Ed, MAT, MLA), history, political science; secondary education (M Ed, MAT), including biology (MAT), chemistry (MAT), English (M Ed, MAT, MLA), mathematics, natural sciences (M Ed), social sciences; special education (M Ed, MAT), including learning disabilities (MAT), mental disabilities (MAT), special education (M Ed). *Accreditation:* NCATE. Part-time and evening/weekend programs available. *Entrance requirements:* For master's, PRAXIS II (M Ed), minimum GPA of 2.75; for Ed S, GRE or MAT, minimum GPA of 3.0. Electronic applications accepted. *Faculty research:* Motivation, classroom management, predictors of success in classroom teaching, sex equity in public education, gifted research.

Daemen College, Education Department, Amherst, NY 14226-3592. Offers adolescence education (MS); childhood education (MS); childhood special education (MS); childhood special-alternative certification (MS); early childhood special-alternative certification (MS). Part-time programs available. *Faculty:* 14 full-time (11 women), 42 part-time/adjunct (36 women). *Students:* 320 full-time (292 women), 225 part-time (202 women); includes 5 minority (3 African Americans, 1 American Indian/Alaska Native, 1 Hispanic American), 135 international. Average age 25. 331 applicants, 82% accepted, 220 enrolled. In 2009, 302 master's awarded. *Degree requirements:* For master's, comprehensive exam, thesis optional, completion of degree within 5 years. *Entrance requirements:* For master's, 2 letters of recommendation, proof of initial certificate of licensure for professional programs, resume, minimum undergraduate GPA of 3.0. Additional exam requirements/recommendations for international students: Required—TOEFL (minimum score 500 paper-based; 173 computer-based; 61 iBT). *Application deadline:* For fall admission, 3/1 priority date for domestic and international students; for spring admission, 10/1 priority date for domestic and international students. Applications are processed on a rolling basis. Application fee: $25. Electronic applications accepted. *Expenses:* Tuition: Part-time $770 per credit hour. Tuition and fees vary according to course load, program and reciprocity agreements. *Financial support:* In 2009–10, 16 students received support. Institutionally sponsored loans, scholarships/grants, and some discounted programs available. Financial award application deadline: 2/15; financial award applicants required to submit FAFSA. *Faculty research:* Transition for students with disabilities, early childhood special education, traumatic brain injury (TBI), reading assessment. *Unit head:* Dr. Mary H. Fox, Chair, 716-839-8530, Fax: 716-839-8516, E-mail: mfox@daemen.edu. *Application contact:* Scott Rowe, Associate Director of Graduate Admissions, 716-839-8225, Fax: 716-839-8229, E-mail: srowe@daemen.edu.

Dominican University, School of Education, River Forest, IL 60305-1099. Offers curriculum and instruction (MA Ed); early childhood education (MS); education (MAT); educational administration (MA); elementary (online) (MS); English as a second language (online) (MS); reading (online) (MS); special education (MS). Part-time and evening/weekend programs available. Postbaccalaureate distance learning degree programs offered. *Faculty:* 16 full-time (12 women), 59 part-time/adjunct (46 women). *Students:* 236 full-time (182 women), 622 part-time (509 women); includes 180 minority (54 African Americans, 3 American Indian/Alaska Native, 36 Asian Americans or Pacific Islanders, 87 Hispanic Americans), 2 international. Average age 32. In 2009, 199 master's awarded. *Entrance requirements:* For master's, Illinois certification test of basic skills. Additional exam requirements/recommendations for international students: Required—TOEFL (minimum score 550 paper-based; 213 computer-based; 79 iBT). *Application deadline:* Applications are processed on a rolling basis. Application fee: $25. *Expenses:* Contact institution. *Financial support:* Career-related internships or fieldwork, scholarships/grants, and tuition waivers (partial) available. Support available to part-time students. Financial award application deadline: 8/15; financial award applicants required to submit FAFSA. *Faculty research:* Governance of private education institutions, reading and language arts, inclusion, organizational planning, leadership and vision. *Unit head:* Dr. Colleen Reardon, Dean, 718-524-6643, Fax: 708-524-6665, E-mail: creardon@dom.edu. *Application contact:* Keven Hansen, Coordinator of Recruitment and Admissions, 708-524-6921, Fax: 708-524-6665, E-mail: educate@dom.edu.

Dowling College, Graduate Programs in Education, Oakdale, NY 11769-1999. Offers adolescence education (MS Ed), including educational administration; advanced certificate in gifted education (AC); childhood and early childhood education (MS Ed); childhood education (MS Ed); educational administration (AC, PD), including computers in education (PD), school administration and supervision (PD), school district administration (PD); educational technology specialist (AC); literacy (MS Ed); literacy/special education (MS Ed); secondary education (MS Ed); special education (MS Ed). *Accreditation:* NCATE. Part-time and evening/weekend programs available. Postbaccalaureate distance learning degree programs offered. *Faculty:* 32 full-time (18 women), 98 part-time/adjunct (59 women). *Students:* 563 full-time (393 women), 885 part-time (668 women); includes 133 minority (47 African Americans, 2 American Indian/Alaska Native, 10 Asian Americans or Pacific Islanders, 74 Hispanic Americans). Average age 32. 363 applicants, 89% accepted, 213 enrolled. In 2009, 459 master's, 85 ACs awarded. *Degree requirements:* For master's and other advanced degree, comprehensive exam. *Entrance requirements:* For master's, minimum GPA of 3.0; for other advanced degree, teaching certificate. Additional exam requirements/recommendations for international students: Required—TOEFL (minimum score 550 paper-based). *Application deadline:* For fall admission, 9/1 priority date for domestic students; for winter admission, 1/1 priority date for domestic students; for spring admission, 2/1 priority date for domestic students. Applications are processed on a rolling basis. Application fee: $50. Electronic applications accepted. *Expenses:* Tuition: Full-time $14,490; part-time $805 per credit. Required fees: $346 per term. *Financial support:* Career-related internships or fieldwork and Federal Work-Study available. Support available to part-time students. Financial award application deadline: 6/30; financial award applicants required to submit FAFSA. *Faculty research:* Natural readers, Korean styles and learning strategies, mothers of children with disabilities, computers in instruction, cultural background and organizational roadblocks to problem solving. *Unit head:* Dr. Clyde Payne, Dean of the School of Education, 631-244-3404, Fax: 631-589-6644, E-mail: paynec@dowling.edu. *Application contact:* Glenn M. Berman, Assistant Vice President for Enrollment Services/Dean of Admissions, 631-244-3357, Fax: 631-244-1059, E-mail: glenn.berman@dowling.edu.

Duquesne University, School of Education, Department of Instruction and Leadership, Program in Early Childhood Education, Pittsburgh, PA 15282-0001. Offers MS Ed. Part-time and evening/weekend programs available. *Faculty:* 3 full-time (all women), 3 part-time/adjunct (all women). *Students:* 2 full-time (both women); both minorities (both African Americans). Average age 33. 9 applicants, 67% accepted, 1 enrolled. In 2009, 1 master's awarded. *Degree requirements:* For master's, thesis optional. *Entrance requirements:* For master's, MAT, minimum GPA of 3.0. Additional exam requirements/recommendations for international students: Required—TOEFL (minimum score 550 paper-based; 80 computer-based). *Application deadline:* For fall admission, 8/1 priority date for domestic students; for spring admission, 12/1 priority date for domestic students. Applications are processed on a rolling basis. Application fee: $0. Electronic applications accepted. *Expenses:* Tuition: Part-time $851 per credit. Required fees: $81 per credit. *Financial support:* Available to part-time students. *Unit head:* Dr. Julia Williams, Assistant Professor, 412-396-6098, Fax: 412-396-5388, E-mail: williamsj@duq.edu. *Application contact:* Michael Dolinger, Director of Student and Academic Services, 412-396-6647, Fax: 412-396-5585, E-mail: dolingerm@duq.edu.

Duquesne University, School of Education, Department of Instruction and Leadership, Program in Elementary Education, Pittsburgh, PA 15282-0001. Offers elementary education (MS Ed); elementary education/early childhood (MS Ed). Part-time and evening/weekend programs available. *Faculty:* 5 full-time (3 women), 4 part-time/adjunct (2 women). *Students:* 54 full-time (50 women), 3 part-time (all women); includes 4 minority (2 African Americans, 2 Hispanic Americans). Average age 29. 49 applicants, 67% accepted, 19 enrolled. In 2009, 19 master's awarded. *Degree requirements:* For master's, thesis optional. *Entrance requirements:* For master's, MAT, minimum GPA of 3.0. Additional exam requirements/recommendations for international students: Required—TOEFL (minimum score 550 paper-based; 80 computer-based). *Application deadline:* For fall admission, 8/1 for domestic students; for spring admission, 12/1 for domestic students. Applications are processed on a rolling basis. Application fee: $0. Electronic applications accepted. *Expenses:* Tuition: Part-time $851 per credit. Required fees: $81 per credit. *Financial support:* Research assistantships, Federal Work-Study available. Support available to part-time students. *Unit head:* Dr. Kimberly Hyatt, Director, 412-396-4794, Fax: 412-396-5388, E-mail: hyatt@duq.edu. *Application contact:* Michael Dolinger, Director of Student and Academic Services, 412-396-6647, Fax: 412-396-5585, E-mail: dolingerm@duq.edu.

Eastern Connecticut State University, School of Education and Professional Studies/Graduate Division, Program in Early Childhood Education, Willimantic, CT 06226-2295. Offers MS. *Accreditation:* NCATE. Part-time and evening/weekend programs available. *Degree requirements:* For master's, comprehensive exam or thesis. *Entrance requirements:* For master's, PRAXIS I, minimum GPA of 2.7. Additional exam requirements/recommendations for international students: Required—TOEFL (minimum score 550 paper-based; 213 computer-based).

Eastern Illinois University, Graduate School, College of Education and Professional Studies, Department of Early Childhood, Elementary and Middle Level Education, Charleston, IL 61920-3099. Offers elementary education (MS Ed). *Accreditation:* NCATE. Part-time programs available. *Faculty:* 14 full-time (6 women). In 2009, 55 master's awarded. *Degree requirements:* For master's, comprehensive exam. *Application deadline:* For fall admission, 3/31 priority date for domestic students. Applications are processed on a rolling basis. Application fee: $30. *Expenses:* Tuition, state resident: full-time $9434; part-time $239 per credit hour. Tuition, nonresident: full-time $23,774; part-time $717 per credit hour. Required fees: $802.63. *Financial support:* In 2009–10, research assistantships with tuition reimbursements (averaging $8,100 per year), 5 teaching assistantships with tuition reimbursements (averaging $8,100 per year) were awarded. *Unit head:* Dr. Joy Russell, Chairperson, 217-581-5728, E-mail: jlrussell@eiu.edu. *Application contact:* Dr. Linda Reven, Coordinator of Graduate Studies, 217-581-7883, E-mail: lmreven@eiu.edu.

Eastern Michigan University, Graduate School, College of Education, Department of Teacher Education, Program in Early Childhood Education, Ypsilanti, MI 48197. Offers MA. *Accreditation:* NCATE. Part-time and evening/weekend programs available. *Students:* 1 (woman) full-time, 83 part-time (80 women); includes 6 minority (3 African Americans, 1 American Indian/Alaska Native, 2 Hispanic Americans). Average age 33. In 2009, 23 master's awarded. *Degree requirements:* For master's, thesis optional. *Entrance requirements:* For master's, GRE. Additional exam requirements/recommendations for international students: Required—TOEFL. *Application deadline:* Applications are processed on a rolling basis. Application fee: $35. Tuition and fees vary according to course level. *Financial support:* Fellowships, teaching assistantships available. Support available to part-time students. Financial award applicants required to submit FAFSA. *Unit head:* Dr. Brigid Beaubien, Coordinator, 734-487-3260, Fax: 734-487-2101, E-mail: bbeaubi1@emich.edu. *Application contact:* Dr. Brigid Beaubien, Coordinator, 734-487-3260, Fax: 734-487-2101, E-mail: bbeaubi1@emich.edu.

Eastern Nazarene College, Adult and Graduate Studies, Division of Education, Quincy, MA 02170. Offers early childhood education (M Ed, Certificate); elementary education (M Ed, Certificate); English as a second language (M Ed, Certificate); instructional enrichment and development (M Ed, Certificate); middle school education (M Ed, Certificate); moderate special needs education (M Ed, Certificate); principal (Certificate); program development and supervision (M Ed, Certificate); secondary education (M Ed, Certificate); special education administrator (Certificate); supervisor (Certificate); teacher of reading (M Ed, Certificate). M Ed and Certificate also available through weekend program for administration, special needs, and reading only. Part-time and evening/weekend programs available. *Entrance requirements:* Additional exam requirements/recommendations for international students: Required—TOEFL (minimum score 550 paper-based).

Eastern Washington University, Graduate Studies, College of Education and Human Development, Department of Education, Program in Early Childhood Education, Cheney, WA 99004-2431. Offers M Ed. *Expenses:* Tuition, state resident: full-time $7476; part-time $249 per quarter hour. Tuition, nonresident: full-time $18,030; part-time $601 per quarter hour. Required fees: $3.50 per quarter hour. $142 per quarter.

East Tennessee State University, School of Graduate Studies, College of Education, Department of Human Development and Learning, Johnson City, TN 37614. Offers advanced practitioner (M Ed); community agency counseling (M Ed, MA); comprehensive concentration (M Ed); counseling (M Ed, MA); early childhood education (M Ed, MA); early childhood general (M Ed); early childhood special education (M Ed); early childhood teaching (M Ed); elementary and secondary (school counseling) (M Ed, MA); marriage and family therapy (M Ed, MA); modified concentration (M Ed). *Accreditation:* ACA; NCATE. Part-time programs available. *Degree requirements:* For master's, comprehensive exam, thesis (for some programs). *Entrance requirements:* For master's, GRE General Test, minimum GPA of 3.0. Additional exam requirements/recommendations for international students: Required—TOEFL (minimum score 550 paper-based; 213 computer-based). *Faculty research:* Drug and alcohol abuse, marriage and family counseling, severe mental retardation, parenting of children with disabilities.

Edinboro University of Pennsylvania, School of Graduate Studies and Research, School of Education, Department of Early Childhood and Special Education, Edinboro, PA 16444. Offers behavior management (Certificate); educational psychology (M Ed); special education (M Ed). Part-time and evening/weekend programs available. *Faculty:* 8 full-time (7 women), 5 part-time/adjunct (3 women). *Students:* 20 full-time (15 women), 122 part-time (105 women); includes 7 minority (5 African Americans, 1 Asian American or Pacific Islander, 1 Hispanic American). Average age 31. In 2009, 16 master's, 7 Certificates awarded. *Degree requirements:* For master's, thesis or alternative, competency exam; for Certificate, thesis or alternative. *Entrance requirements:* For master's and Certificate, GRE or MAT, minimum QPA of 2.5. *Application deadline:* Applications are processed on a rolling basis. Application fee: $30. Electronic applications accepted. *Expenses:* Tuition, state resident: full-time $6666; part-time $370 per credit. Tuition, nonresident: full-time $10,666; part-time $593 per credit. Required fees: $2206.28. One-time fee: $204 part-time. *Financial support:* In 2009–10, 4 research assistantships with full and partial tuition reimbursements (averaging $4,050 per year) were awarded; career-related internships or fieldwork, Federal Work-Study, scholarships/grants, and unspecified assistantships also available. Support available to part-time students. Financial award application deadline: 2/15; financial award applicants required to submit FAFSA. *Unit head:* Dr. Edward Snyder, Program Head, Educational Psychology, 814-732-1098, E-mail: jkasper@edinboro.edu. *Application contact:* Dr. Susan Criswell, Program Head, Special Education, 814-732-2287, E-mail: scriswell@edinboro.edu.

Edinboro University of Pennsylvania, School of Graduate Studies and Research, School of Education, Department of Elementary, Middle and Secondary Education, Edinboro, PA 16444. Offers character education (Certificate); elementary education (M Ed), including character education, early childhood education, elementary education; reading (M Ed, Certificate), including reading (M Ed), reading specialist (Certificate). Part-time and evening/weekend programs available. *Faculty:* 10 full-time (6 women), 3 part-time/adjunct (2 women). *Students:* 106 full-time (63 women), 172 part-time (126 women); includes 7 minority (4 African Americans, 3 Hispanic Americans). Average age 31. In 2009, 153 master's, 7 Certificates awarded. *Degree requirements:* For master's, comprehensive exam, thesis or alternative, project; for Certificate,

Early Childhood Education

Edinboro University of Pennsylvania (continued)

thesis or alternative, exam. *Entrance requirements:* For master's and Certificate, GRE or MAT, minimum QPA of 2.5. *Application deadline:* Applications are processed on a rolling basis. Application fee: $30. Electronic applications accepted. *Expenses:* Tuition, state resident: full-time $6666; part-time $370 per credit. Tuition, nonresident: full-time $10,666; part-time $593 per credit. Required fees: $2206.28. One-time fee: $204 part-time. *Financial support:* In 2009–10, 14 research assistantships with full and partial tuition reimbursements (averaging $4,050 per year) were awarded; career-related internships or fieldwork, Federal Work-Study, scholarships/grants, and unspecified assistantships also available. Support available to part-time students. Financial award application deadline: 2/15; financial award applicants required to submit FAFSA. *Unit head:* Dr. Maureen Walcavich, Program Head, Elementary Education, 814-732-2303, E-mail: mwalcavich@edinboro.edu.

Elms College, Division of Education, Chicopee, MA 01013-2839. Offers early childhood education (MAT); education (M Ed, CAGS); elementary education (MAT); English as a second language (MAT); reading (MAT); secondary education (MAT), including biology education, English education, Spanish education; special education (MAT). Part-time and evening/weekend programs available. *Faculty:* 12 full-time (8 women), 4 part-time/adjunct (2 women). *Students:* 17 full-time (14 women), 153 part-time (136 women); includes 5 minority (1 American Indian/Alaska Native, 4 Hispanic Americans). Average age 36. 43 applicants, 88% accepted, 37 enrolled. In 2009, 23 master's, 8 other advanced degrees awarded. *Degree requirements:* For master's, thesis (for some programs). *Entrance requirements:* For master's, Massachusetts Educators Certification Test, minimum GPA of 3.0; for CAGS, master's degree in education. Additional exam requirements/recommendations for international students: Required—TOEFL. *Application deadline:* For fall admission, 7/1 priority date for domestic students; for spring admission, 11/1 priority date for domestic students. Applications are processed on a rolling basis. Application fee: $30. *Financial support:* In 2009–10, 2 teaching assistantships with partial tuition reimbursements were awarded; tuition waivers (partial) also available. Support available to part-time students. Financial award applicants required to submit FAFSA. *Unit head:* Dr. Mary Janeczek, Director, 413-594-2761, Fax: 413-592-4871, E-mail: janeczeke@elms.edu. *Application contact:* Dana Malone, Associate Director for Graduate Studies and Continuing Education, 413-265-2445, Fax: 413-265-2459, E-mail: maloned@elms.edu.

Emporia State University, School of Graduate Studies, The Teachers College, Department of Early Childhood/Elementary Teacher Education, Program in Early Childhood Education, Emporia, KS 66801-5087. Offers early childhood curriculum (MS); early childhood special education (MS). *Accreditation:* NCATE. Part-time programs available. Postbaccalaureate distance learning degree programs offered. *Students:* 1 (woman) full-time, 52 part-time (all women); includes 1 minority (Hispanic American). 6 applicants, 100% accepted, 6 enrolled. In 2009, 10 master's awarded. *Degree requirements:* For master's, comprehensive exam or thesis, practicum. *Entrance requirements:* For master's, GRE General Test or MAT, graduate essay exam, appropriate bachelor's degree, letters of recommendation. Additional exam requirements/recommendations for international students: Required—TOEFL (minimum score 520 paper-based; 133 computer-based; 68 iBT). *Application deadline:* For fall admission, 8/15 priority date for domestic students. Applications are processed on a rolling basis. Application fee: $30 ($75 for international students). Electronic applications accepted. *Expenses:* Tuition, state resident: full-time $4154; part-time $173 per credit hour. Tuition, nonresident: full-time $12,864; part-time $536 per credit hour. Required fees: $948; $58 per credit hour. Tuition and fees vary according to campus/location. *Financial support:* Federal Work-Study, institutionally sponsored loans, health care benefits, and unspecified assistantships available. Financial award application deadline: 3/15; financial award applicants required to submit FAFSA. *Unit head:* Dr. Jean Morrow, Chair, 620-341-5766, E-mail: jmorrow@emporia.edu. *Application contact:* Mary Sewell, Admissions Coordinator, 800-950-GRAD, Fax: 620-341-5909, E-mail: msewell@emporia.edu.

Endicott College, Van Loan School of Graduate and Professional Studies, Program in Montessori Early Childhood Education, Beverly, MA 01915-2096. Offers M Ed. *Faculty:* 4 part-time/adjunct (all women). *Students:* 18 part-time (all women). Average age 36. 9 applicants, 100% accepted, 9 enrolled. In 2009, 3 master's awarded. *Degree requirements:* For master's, thesis, practicum. *Entrance requirements:* For master's, GRE, GMAT. Additional exam requirements/recommendations for international students: Required—TOEFL. Application fee: $50. *Expenses:* Contact institution. *Unit head:* Enid E. Larsen, Assistant Dean of Academic Programs, 978-232-2198, Fax: 978-232-3000, E-mail: elarsen@endicott.edu. *Application contact:* Dr. Mary Huegel, Dean of Graduate and Professional Studies, 978-232-2084, Fax: 978-232-3000, E-mail: mhuegel@endicott.edu.

Erikson Institute, Erikson Institute, Chicago, IL 60654. Offers child development (MS); early childhood education (M Ed, MS, PhD). PhD offered through the Graduate School. *Accreditation:* NCA. *Degree requirements:* For master's, comprehensive exam, internship; for doctorate, one foreign language, comprehensive exam, thesis/dissertation. *Entrance requirements:* For master's, experience working with young children, interview; for doctorate, GRE General Test, interview. *Faculty research:* Early childhood development, cognitive development, sociocultural contexts, early childhood education, family and culture, early literacy.

Erikson Institute, Academic Programs, Program in Early Childhood Education, Chicago, IL 60654. Offers MS. *Degree requirements:* For master's, comprehensive exam. *Entrance requirements:* For master's, 3 letters of recommendation, minimum GPA of 2.75. Additional exam requirements/recommendations for international students: Required—TOEFL.

Fitchburg State University, Division of Graduate and Continuing Education, Program in Early Childhood Education, Fitchburg, MA 01420-2697. Offers M Ed. *Accreditation:* NCATE. Part-time and evening/weekend programs available. *Students:* 25 part-time (24 women). Average age 32. 5 applicants, 100% accepted, 3 enrolled. In 2009, 4 master's awarded. *Entrance requirements:* For master's, GRE General Test or MAT, teaching certificate, letters of recommendation, resume. Additional exam requirements/recommendations for international students: Recommended—TOEFL (minimum score 550 paper-based; 213 computer-based; 79 iBT). *Application deadline:* Applications are processed on a rolling basis. Application fee: $25 ($50 for international students). *Expenses:* Tuition, area resident: Part-time $150 per credit. Tuition, state resident: part-time $150 per credit. Tuition, nonresident: part-time $150 per credit. Required fees: $120 per credit. *Financial support:* In 2009–10, research assistantships with partial tuition reimbursements (averaging $5,500 per year); Federal Work-Study, scholarships/grants, and unspecified assistantships also available. Support available to part-time students. Financial award application deadline: 3/1; financial award applicants required to submit FAFSA. *Unit head:* Dr. Pam Hill, Chair, 978-665-3515, Fax: 978-665-3658, E-mail: gce@fsc.edu. *Application contact:* Director of Admissions, 978-665-3144, Fax: 978-665-4540, E-mail: admissions@fsc.edu.

Florida Agricultural and Mechanical University, Division of Graduate Studies, Research, and Continuing Education, College of Education, Department of Elementary Education, Tallahassee, FL 32307-3200. Offers early childhood and elementary education (M Ed, MS Ed). *Accreditation:* NCATE. *Faculty:* 8 full-time (7 women). *Students:* 4 full-time (all women), 3 part-time (all women); all minorities (all African Americans). In 2009, 1 master's awarded. *Degree requirements:* For master's, thesis (for some programs). *Entrance requirements:* For master's, GRE General Test, minimum GPA of 3.0. Additional exam requirements/recommendations for international students: Required—TOEFL. *Application deadline:* For fall admission, 5/18 for domestic students, 12/18 for international students; for spring admission, 11/12 for domestic students, 5/12 for international students. Application fee: $20. *Unit head:* Dr. Marian Smith, Chairperson, 850-599-3397, Fax: 850-561-2211. *Application contact:* Dr. Chanta M. Haywood, Dean of Graduate Studies, Research, and Continuing Education, 850-599-3315, Fax: 850-599-3727.

Florida Atlantic University, College of Education, Department of Curriculum, Culture, and Educational Inquiry, Boca Raton, FL 33431-0991. Offers curriculum and instruction (Ed D, Ed S); early childhood education (M Ed); multicultural education (M Ed); teaching English to speakers of other languages (TESOL) (M Ed). *Faculty:* 11 full-time (8 women), 17 part-time/adjunct (13 women). *Students:* 38 full-time (26 women), 124 part-time (105 women); includes 40 minority (23 African Americans, 3 Asian Americans or Pacific Islanders, 14 Hispanic Americans), 4 international. Average age 36. 84 applicants, 56% accepted, 34 enrolled. In 2009, 39 master's, 5 doctorates awarded. *Application deadline:* For fall admission, 7/1 for domestic students, 2/15 for international students; for spring admission, 11/1 for domestic students, 7/15 for international students. *Expenses:* Tuition, state resident: full-time $7055; part-time $293.94 per credit hour. Tuition, nonresident: full-time $22,096; part-time $920.66 per credit hour. *Faculty research:* Multicultural education, early intervention strategies, family literacy, religious diversity in schools, early childhood curriculum. *Unit head:* Dr. James McLaughlin, Interim Chair, 561-297-3965, E-mail: jmclau17@fau.edu. *Application contact:* Dr. Eliah Watlington, Associate Dean, 561-296-8520, Fax: 261-297-2991, E-mail: ewatling@fau.edu.

Florida Gulf Coast University, College of Education, Program in Elementary Education, Fort Myers, FL 33965-6565. Offers early childhood education (M Ed); elementary curriculum (M Ed); elementary education (MA). Part-time and evening/weekend programs available. Postbaccalaureate distance learning degree programs offered (minimal on-campus study). *Faculty:* 31 full-time (24 women), 39 part-time/adjunct (28 women). *Students:* 7 full-time (6 women), 1 (woman) part-time. Average age 40. 8 applicants, 25% accepted, 1 enrolled. In 2009, 4 master's awarded. *Degree requirements:* For master's, comprehensive exam, thesis or alternative, final project. *Entrance requirements:* For master's, GRE General Test, MAT, minimum GPA of 3.0. Additional exam requirements/recommendations for international students: Required—TOEFL (minimum score 550 paper-based; 213 computer-based). *Application deadline:* For fall admission, 7/1 priority date for domestic students; for spring admission, 10/15 for domestic students. Applications are processed on a rolling basis. Application fee: $30. Electronic applications accepted. *Faculty research:* Language acquisition, impact of literature on reading, action research in the classroom. *Unit head:* Dr. Patricia Wachholz, Head, 239-590-7808, Fax: 239-590-7801, E-mail: pwachhol@fgcu.edu. *Application contact:* Dr. Patricia Wachholz, Head, 239-590-7808, Fax: 239-590-7801, E-mail: pwachhol@fgcu.edu.

Florida International University, College of Education, Department of Curriculum and Instruction, Program in Early Childhood Education, Miami, FL 33199. Offers MS, Ed D. *Accreditation:* NCATE. Part-time and evening/weekend programs available. *Entrance requirements:* For master's, GRE General Test or minimum GPA of 3.0, teaching certificate. Additional exam requirements/recommendations for international students: Required—TOEFL (minimum score 550 paper-based; 213 computer-based; 80 iBT), IELTS (minimum score 6.3). Electronic applications accepted. *Expenses:* Tuition, state resident: full-time $8008; part-time $4004 per year. Tuition, nonresident: full-time $20,104; part-time $10,052 per year. Required fees: $298; $149 per term. *Faculty research:* Children's literature, parental involvement.

Florida State University, The Graduate School, College of Education, School of Teacher Education, Tallahassee, FL 32306. Offers early childhood education (MS, Ed D, PhD, Ed S); elementary education (MS, Ed D, PhD, Ed S); English education (MS, PhD, Ed S); mathematics education (MS, PhD, Ed S); reading education/language arts (MS, Ed D, PhD, Ed S); science education (MS, PhD, Ed S); social science education (MS, PhD, Ed S); special education (MS, PhD, Ed S), including emotional disturbance/learning disabilities (MS), mental retardation (MS), rehabilitation counseling, special education (PhD, Ed S), visual disabilities (MS). Part-time programs available. *Faculty:* 24 full-time (19 women), 3 part-time/adjunct (all women). *Students:* 85 full-time (73 women), 205 part-time (189 women); includes 60 minority (36 African Americans, 2 American Indian/Alaska Native, 13 Asian Americans or Pacific Islanders, 9 Hispanic Americans). 189 applicants, 61% accepted, 71 enrolled. In 2009, 76 master's, 7 doctorates, 5 other advanced degrees awarded. *Degree requirements:* For master's and Ed S, comprehensive exam, thesis optional; for doctorate, comprehensive exam, thesis/dissertation, preliminary exam, prospectus defense. *Entrance requirements:* For master's, doctorate, and Ed S, GRE General Test, minimum GPA of 3.0. Additional exam requirements/recommendations for international students: Required—TOEFL (minimum score 550 paper-based; 213 computer-based; 80 iBT). *Application deadline:* For fall admission, 7/1 priority date for domestic students; for spring admission, 11/1 for domestic students. Applications are processed on a rolling basis. Application fee: $30. *Expenses:* Tuition, state resident: full-time $7413. Tuition, nonresident: full-time $22,567. *Financial support:* In 2009–10, 2 fellowships with full and partial tuition reimbursements, 4 research assistantships with full and partial tuition reimbursements, 12 teaching assistantships with full and partial tuition reimbursements were awarded; career-related internships or fieldwork, Federal Work-Study, scholarships/grants, and unspecified assistantships also available. Financial award applicants required to submit FAFSA. *Faculty research:* Teaching and learning practices and policies, twenty-first century literacies, impact of teacher education programs of student gains. *Unit head:* Dr. Walt Wager, Chair, 850-644-6553, Fax: 850-644-1880, E-mail: wwager@fsu.edu. *Application contact:* Timolin Lynette Bodison-Baker, Program Assistant, 850-644-5458, Fax: 850-644-7736, E-mail: bodison@coe.fsu.edu.

Fordham University, Graduate School of Education, Division of Curriculum and Teaching, New York, NY 10023. Offers adult education (MS, MSE); bilingual teacher education (MSE); curriculum and teaching (MSE); early childhood education (MSE); elementary education (MST); language, literacy, and learning (PhD); reading education (MSE, Adv C); secondary education (MAT, MSE); special education (MSE, Adv C); teaching English as a second language (MSE). *Accreditation:* NCATE. *Degree requirements:* For doctorate, thesis/dissertation; for Adv C, thesis. *Entrance requirements:* For doctorate, MAT, GRE General Test.

Framingham State University, Division of Graduate and Continuing Education, Program in Early Childhood Education, Framingham, MA 01701-9101. Offers M Ed.

Francis Marion University, Graduate Programs, School of Education, Florence, SC 29502-0547. Offers early childhood education (M Ed); elementary education (M Ed); learning disabilities (M Ed, MAT); remedial education (M Ed); secondary education (M Ed). *Accreditation:* NCATE. Part-time programs available. *Faculty:* 20 full-time (15 women). *Students:* 8 full-time (7 women), 107 part-time (90 women); includes 33 minority (all African Americans), 1 international. Average age 34. 221 applicants, 94% accepted, 94 enrolled. In 2009, 57 degrees awarded. *Degree requirements:* For master's, comprehensive exam. *Entrance requirements:* For master's, GRE General Test, MAT, NTE, or PRAXIS II. *Application deadline:* For fall admission, 3/15 priority date for domestic students; for spring admission, 10/15 priority date for domestic students. Applications are processed on a rolling basis. Application fee: $30. *Expenses:* Tuition, state resident: full-time $8345; part-time $417.25 per semester hour. Tuition, nonresident: full-time $16,690; part-time $814.50 per semester hour. Required fees: $335; $12.25 per semester hour. $30 per semester. *Financial support:* In 2009–10, 4 research assistantships (averaging $6,000 per year) were awarded; unspecified assistantships also available. Support available to part-time students. Financial award application deadline: 3/1; financial award applicants required to submit FAFSA. *Faculty research:* Identification and alternate assessment of at-risk students. *Unit head:* Dr. James R. Faulkenberry, Dean, 843-661-1460, Fax: 843-661-4647. *Application contact:* Dr. James R. Faulkenberry, Dean, 843-661-1460, Fax: 843-661-4647.

Furman University, Graduate Division, Department of Education, Greenville, SC 29613. Offers curriculum and instruction (MA); early childhood education (MA); English as a second language (MA); literacy (MA); school leadership (MA); special education (MA). *Accreditation:* NCATE. Part-time programs available. Postbaccalaureate distance learning degree programs offered (minimal on-campus study). *Faculty:* 14 full-time (8 women), 10 part-time/adjunct (6 women). *Students:* 114 part-time (93 women); includes 13 minority (10 African Americans, 3 Asian Americans or Pacific Islanders). Average age 29. 24 applicants, 100% accepted, 23 enrolled. In 2009, 71 master's awarded. *Degree requirements:* For master's, comprehensive exam (for some programs), thesis or alternative. *Entrance requirements:* For master's, PRAXIS II. *Application deadline:* For fall admission, 8/1 priority date for domestic students, 7/15 priority date for international students; for spring admission, 12/1 priority date for domestic and international students. Applications are processed on a rolling basis. Application fee: $50. *Financial support:* In 2009–10, 43 students received support; fellowships, scholarships/grants

available. Financial award application deadline: 5/15; financial award applicants required to submit FAFSA. *Faculty research:* Literacy, pedagogy and practice, social justice, advanced leadership, achievement in high poverty schools. *Unit head:* Dr. Nelly Hecker, Head, 864-294-3385. *Application contact:* Helen Reynolds, Department Assistant, 864-294-2213, Fax: 864-294-3579, E-mail: helen.reynolds@furman.edu.

Gallaudet University, The Graduate School, Department of Education, Washington, DC 20002-3625. Offers early childhood education (MA, Ed S); education of deaf and hard of hearing students and multihandicapped deaf and hard of hearing students (MA, Ed S); elementary education (MA, Ed S); individualized program of study (PhD); parent/infant specialty (MA, Ed S); secondary education (MA, Ed S). *Accreditation:* NCATE. *Degree requirements:* For master's, thesis optional; for doctorate, thesis/dissertation. *Entrance requirements:* For doctorate, GRE General Test or MAT, interview. Electronic applications accepted.

Gannon University, School of Graduate Studies, College of Humanities, Education, and Social Sciences, School of Education, Program in Early Intervention, Erie, PA 16541-0001. Offers MS. Part-time and evening/weekend programs available. *Degree requirements:* For master's, comprehensive exam, research project. *Entrance requirements:* For master's, interview, teaching certificate. Additional exam requirements/recommendations for international students: Required—TOEFL (minimum score 79 iBT). *Application deadline:* Applications are processed on a rolling basis. Application fee: $25. Electronic applications accepted. *Expenses:* Contact institution. *Financial support:* Career-related internships or fieldwork available. Financial award application deadline: 7/1; financial award applicants required to submit FAFSA. *Unit head:* Dr. Francis S. Grandinetti, Director, 814-871-7533, E-mail: grandine002@gannon.edu. *Application contact:* Kara Morgan, Assistant Director of Graduate Admissions, 814-871-5831, Fax: 814-871-5827, E-mail: graduate@gannon.edu.

The George Washington University, Graduate School of Education and Human Development, Department of Teacher Preparation and Special Education, Program in Early Childhood Special Education, Washington, DC 20052. Offers MA Ed. *Accreditation:* NCATE. *Students:* 12 full-time (all women), 38 part-time (31 women); includes 17 minority (10 African Americans, 4 Asian Americans or Pacific Islanders, 3 Hispanic Americans), 2 international. Average age 29. 28 applicants, 93% accepted, 16 enrolled. In 2009, 25 master's awarded. *Degree requirements:* For master's, comprehensive exam. *Entrance requirements:* For master's, GRE General Test or MAT, minimum GPA of 2.75. *Application deadline:* For fall admission, 1/15 priority date for domestic students; for spring admission, 10/1 for domestic students. Applications are processed on a rolling basis. Application fee: $60. *Financial support:* In 2009–10, 19 students received support; fellowships, career-related internships or fieldwork, Federal Work-Study, and tuition waivers (full) available. Financial award application deadline: 1/15; financial award applicants required to submit FAFSA. *Faculty research:* Computer-assisted instruction and learning, disabled learner assessment of preschool, handicapped children. *Unit head:* Dr. Marian H. Jarrett, Faculty Coordinator, 202-994-1509, E-mail: mjarrett@gwu.edu. *Application contact:* Sarah Lang, Director of Graduate Admissions, 202-994-1447, Fax: 202-994-7207, E-mail: slang@gwu.edu.

Georgia College & State University, Graduate School, The John H. Lounsbury College of Education, Department of Early Childhood and Middle Grades Education, Milledgeville, GA 31061. Offers early childhood education (M Ed, Ed S); middle grades education (M Ed, Ed S). *Accreditation:* NCATE. Part-time and evening/weekend programs available. *Faculty:* 20 full-time (17 women). *Students:* 7 full-time (5 women), 47 part-time (44 women); includes 10 minority (8 African Americans, 2 Hispanic Americans), 1 international. Average age 29. 57 applicants, 100% accepted, 36 enrolled. In 2009, 10 master's, 44 other advanced degrees awarded. *Degree requirements:* For master's and Ed S, comprehensive exam. *Entrance requirements:* For master's, on-site writing assessment, level 4 teaching certificate, 2 recommendations; for Ed S, on-site writing assessment, master's degree, 2 years of teaching experience, 2 professional recommendations, level 5 teacher certification. Additional exam requirements/recommendations for international students: Recommended—TOEFL (minimum score 550 paper-based; 213 computer-based; 79 iBT). *Application deadline:* For fall admission, 7/1 for domestic students; for spring admission, 11/15 for domestic students. Applications are processed on a rolling basis. Application fee: $40. Electronic applications accepted. *Expenses:* Tuition, area resident: Part-time $241 per credit hour. Tuition, state resident: full-time $4338. Tuition, nonresident: full-time $17,352; part-time $964 per credit hour. Required fees: $609 per semester. Tuition and fees vary according to course load and campus/location. *Financial support:* In 2009–10, 2 research assistantships were awarded; career-related internships or fieldwork, Federal Work-Study, and unspecified assistantships also available. Support available to part-time students. Financial award applicants required to submit FAFSA. *Unit head:* Dr. Nancy Mizelle, Chair, 478-445-5479, Fax: 478-445-6695, E-mail: nancy.mizelle@gcsu.edu. *Application contact:* Shanda Brand, Graduate Coordinator, 478-445-1383, E-mail: shanda.brand@gcsu.edu.

Georgia Southern University, Jack N. Averitt College of Graduate Studies, College of Education, Department of Teaching and Learning, Program in Early Childhood Education, Statesboro, GA 30460. Offers M Ed, MAT. *Accreditation:* NCATE. Part-time and evening/weekend programs available. In 2009, 5 master's awarded. *Degree requirements:* For master's, portfolio, transition point assessments, exit assessment. *Entrance requirements:* For master's, GRE General Test or MAT, minimum cumulative GPA of 2.5. Additional exam requirements/recommendations for international students: Required—TOEFL (minimum score 550 paper-based; 213 computer-based; 80 iBT). *Application deadline:* For fall admission, 3/1 priority date for domestic and international students; for spring admission, 10/1 priority date for domestic students, 10/1 for international students. Applications are processed on a rolling basis. Application fee: $50. Electronic applications accepted. *Expenses:* Tuition, state resident: full-time $5040; part-time $210 per credit hour. Tuition, nonresident: full-time $20,136; part-time $839 per credit hour. Required fees: $1644. *Financial support:* In 2009–10, research assistantships with partial tuition reimbursements (averaging $7,200 per year), teaching assistantships with partial tuition reimbursements (averaging $7,200 per year) were awarded; career-related internships or fieldwork, Federal Work-Study, scholarships/grants, tuition waivers (partial), and unspecified assistantships also available. Support available to part-time students. Financial award application deadline: 4/15; financial award applicants required to submit FAFSA. *Faculty research:* Technology, effective instructional strategies, multiculturalism, children's literature, school violence. *Unit head:* Dr. Ronnie Sheppard, Department Chair, 912-478-5203, Fax: 912-478-0026, E-mail: sheppard@georgiasouthern.edu. *Application contact:* Dr. Charles Ziglar, Coordinator for Graduate Student Recruitment, 912-478-5635, Fax: 912-478-0740, E-mail: gradadmissions@georgiasouthern.edu.

Georgia Southwestern State University, Graduate Studies, School of Education, Americus, GA 31709-4693. Offers early childhood education (M Ed, Ed S); health and physical education (M Ed); middle grades education (M Ed, Ed S); reading (M Ed); secondary education (M Ed); special education (M Ed). *Accreditation:* NCATE. *Degree requirements:* For master's, comprehensive exam. *Entrance requirements:* For master's, GRE General Test or MAT, minimum GPA of 2.5; for Ed S, GRE General Test or MAT, minimum graduate GPA of 3.25, M Ed from accredited college or university, 3 years teaching experience. Electronic applications accepted.

Georgia State University, College of Education, Department of Early Childhood Education, Atlanta, GA 30302-3083. Offers M Ed, MAT, PhD, Ed S. *Accreditation:* NCATE. Part-time and evening/weekend programs available. *Degree requirements:* For master's, comprehensive exam; for doctorate, comprehensive exam, thesis/dissertation. *Entrance requirements:* For master's, GRE General Test, minimum GPA of 2.75; for doctorate, GRE General Test, minimum GPA of 3.3; for Ed S, GRE General Test or MAT, minimum graduate GPA of 3.25. Electronic applications accepted. *Faculty research:* Teacher training program evaluation, pre-kindergarten program evaluation, literacy development, children's literature, alternative assessment strategies, children in poverty.

Golden Gate Baptist Theological Seminary, Graduate and Professional Programs, Mill Valley, CA 94941-3197. Offers divinity (M Div); early childhood education (Certificate); education leadership (MAEL, Diploma); ministry (D Min); theological studies (MTS); theology (Th M); youth ministry (Certificate). *Accreditation:* ACIPE; ATS (one or more programs are accredited). Part-time and evening/weekend programs available. *Degree requirements:* For master's, thesis (for some programs); for doctorate, 2 foreign languages, thesis/dissertation; for M Div, 2 foreign languages. *Entrance requirements:* For doctorate, MAT. Additional exam requirements/recommendations for international students: Required—TOEFL (minimum score 550 paper-based; 213 computer-based). Electronic applications accepted.

Governors State University, College of Education, Program in Early Childhood Education, University Park, IL 60466-0975. Offers MA. *Accreditation:* NCATE. *Degree requirements:* For master's, comprehensive exam, practicum. *Entrance requirements:* For master's, minimum GPA of 2.75 in last 60 hours of undergraduate course work, minimum graduate GPA of 3.0.

Grand Valley State University, College of Education, Program in Special Education, Allendale, MI 49401-9403. Offers cognitive impairment (M Ed); early childhood developmental delay (M Ed); emotional impairment (M Ed); learning disabilities (M Ed); special education endorsements (M Ed). *Accreditation:* NCATE. Part-time and evening/weekend programs available. *Faculty:* 10 full-time (6 women), 6 part-time/adjunct (3 women). *Students:* 19 full-time (all women), 234 part-time (206 women); includes 17 minority (10 African Americans, 1 American Indian/Alaska Native, 4 Asian Americans or Pacific Islanders, 2 Hispanic Americans). Average age 35. 42 applicants, 100% accepted, 32 enrolled. In 2009, 63 master's awarded. *Degree requirements:* For master's, thesis. *Entrance requirements:* For master's, GRE General Test or minimum GPA of 3.0. Additional exam requirements/recommendations for international students: Required—TOEFL. *Application deadline:* Applications are processed on a rolling basis. Application fee: $30. Electronic applications accepted. *Expenses:* Tuition, state resident: part-time $471 per credit hour. Tuition, nonresident: part-time $646 per credit hour. Tuition and fees vary according to course level. *Financial support:* In 2009–10, 30 students received support, including 30 fellowships (averaging $2,168 per year); career-related internships or fieldwork, Federal Work-Study, scholarships/grants, and unspecified assistantships also available. *Faculty research:* Evaluation of special education program effects, adaptive behavior assessment, language development, writing disorders, comparative effects of presentation methods. *Unit head:* Dr. Sandy Miller, Director, 616-331-3344. *Application contact:* Thomas Owens, Student Information and Services Center, 616-331-6282, Fax: 616-331-2000, E-mail: owenst@gvsu.edu.

Grand Valley State University, College of Education, Programs in General Education, Allendale, MI 49401-9403. Offers adult and higher education (M Ed); early childhood education (M Ed); educational differentiation (M Ed); educational leadership (M Ed); educational technology integration (M Ed); elementary education (M Ed); middle level education (M Ed); school library media services (M Ed); secondary level education (M Ed); teaching English to speakers of other languages (M Ed). Part-time and evening/weekend programs available. Postbaccalaureate distance learning degree programs offered (minimal on-campus study). *Faculty:* 82 full-time (42 women), 43 part-time/adjunct (25 women). *Students:* 100 full-time (53 women), 723 part-time (478 women); includes 59 minority (25 African Americans, 4 American Indian/Alaska Native, 13 Asian Americans or Pacific Islanders, 17 Hispanic Americans), 10 international. Average age 33. 237 applicants, 96% accepted, 117 enrolled. In 2009, 291 master's awarded. *Degree requirements:* For master's, thesis. *Entrance requirements:* For master's, GRE General Test or minimum GPA of 3.0. Additional exam requirements/recommendations for international students: Required—TOEFL. *Application deadline:* Applications are processed on a rolling basis. Application fee: $30. Electronic applications accepted. *Expenses:* Tuition, state resident: part-time $471 per credit hour. Tuition, nonresident: part-time $646 per credit hour. Tuition and fees vary according to course level. *Financial support:* In 2009–10, 73 students received support, including 55 fellowships (averaging $2,273 per year), 19 research assistantships with full and partial tuition reimbursements available (averaging $8,000 per year); career-related internships or fieldwork, Federal Work-Study, scholarships/grants, and unspecified assistantships also available. *Faculty research:* Effectiveness of technology in education, parental involvement, effective teaching, effective schools research. *Unit head:* Dr. Linda McCrea, Director, 616-331-2080, E-mail: mccreal@gvsu.edu. *Application contact:* Thomas Owens, Student Information and Services Center, 616-331-6282, Fax: 616-331-2000, E-mail: owenst@gvsu.edu.

Hampton University, Graduate College, Department of Education, Program in Teaching, Hampton, VA 23668. Offers early childhood education (MT); middle school education (MT); music education (MT); secondary education (MT); special education (MT). *Entrance requirements:* For master's, GRE General Test.

Harding University, College of Education, Searcy, AR 72149-0001. Offers advanced studies in teaching and learning (M Ed); art (MSE); behavioral science (MSE); counseling (MS, Ed S); early childhood special education (M Ed, MSE); education (MSE); educational leadership (M Ed, Ed S); elementary education (M Ed); English (MSE); family and consumer science (MSE); French (MSE); history/social science (MSE); kinesiology (MSE); math (MSE); physical science (MSE); reading (M Ed); secondary education (M Ed); Spanish (MSE); special education licensure (M Ed); teaching (MAT); teaching English as a second language (M Ed). *Accreditation:* NCATE. Part-time and evening/weekend programs available. *Faculty:* 11 full-time (4 women), 49 part-time/adjunct (26 women). *Students:* 104 full-time (85 women), 392 part-time (282 women); includes 77 minority (67 African Americans, 5 American Indian/Alaska Native, 1 Asian American or Pacific Islander, 4 Hispanic Americans), 5 international. Average age 36. 153 applicants, 92% accepted, 131 enrolled. In 2009, 153 master's, 6 other advanced degrees awarded. *Degree requirements:* For master's, comprehensive exam (for some programs), thesis optional, portfolio(s); for Ed S, comprehensive exam, portfolio, specialist project. *Entrance requirements:* For master's, GRE, MAT, PRAXIS; for Ed S, MAT or GRE. Additional exam requirements/recommendations for international students: Required—TOEFL (minimum score 550 paper-based; 79 iBT). *Application deadline:* For fall admission, 8/1 for domestic and international students; for spring admission, 1/1 for domestic and international students. Applications are processed on a rolling basis. Application fee: $35. *Expenses:* Tuition: Full-time $9720; part-time $540 per credit hour. Required fees: $22 per credit hour. Tuition and fees vary according to course load and program. *Financial support:* In 2009–10, 30 students received support. Unspecified assistantships available. *Faculty research:* Reading, comprehension, school violence, educational technology, behavior, college choice, differentiated instruction, brain-based teaching. *Unit head:* Dr. Clara Carroll, Chair, 501-279-4501, Fax: 501-279-4083, E-mail: ccarroll@harding.edu. *Application contact:* Information Contact, 501-279-4315, E-mail: gradstudiesedu@harding.edu.

Hebrew College, Shoolman Graduate School of Education, Newton Centre, MA 02459. Offers early childhood Jewish education (Certificate); Jewish day school education (Certificate); Jewish education (MJ Ed); Jewish family education (Certificate); Jewish special education (Certificate); Jewish youth education, informal education and camping (Certificate). Part-time and evening/weekend programs available. Postbaccalaureate distance learning degree programs offered. *Degree requirements:* For master's, one foreign language. *Entrance requirements:* For master's, GRE, interview. Additional exam requirements/recommendations for international students: Required—TOEFL.

Henderson State University, Graduate Studies, School of Education, Department of Advanced Instructional Studies, Arkadelphia, AR 71999-0001. Offers early childhood (P-4) (MSE); education (MAT); middle school (MSE); reading (MSE); special education (MSE). *Accreditation:* NCATE. Part-time programs available. *Faculty:* 7 full-time (4 women), 2 part-time/adjunct (both women). *Students:* 7 full-time (all women), 131 part-time (119 women); includes 16 minority (11 African Americans, 1 Asian American or Pacific Islander, 4 Hispanic Americans). Average age 33. 25 applicants, 100% accepted, 25 enrolled. In 2009, 53 master's awarded. *Entrance requirements:* For master's, GRE General Test or MAT, minimum GPA of 2.7, teacher certification. Additional exam requirements/recommendations for international students: Required—TOEFL (minimum score 550 paper-based; 213 computer-based); Recommended—IELTS (minimum score 6). *Application deadline:* For fall admission, 8/1 priority date for domestic students, 6/30 priority date for international students; for spring admission, 1/1 priority date for domestic students, 11/30 priority date for international students. Application fee: $25 ($75 for international students). Electronic applications accepted. *Expenses:* Tuition, state resident: full-time $3798; part-time

Early Childhood Education

Henderson State University (continued)
$211 per credit hour. Tuition, nonresident: full-time $7596; part-time $422 per credit hour. Required fees: $903. *Financial support:* Research assistantships, teaching assistantships with tuition reimbursements available. *Unit head:* Dr. Gary Smithey, Chairperson, 870-230-5361, Fax: 870-230-5455, E-mail: smitheg@hsu.edu. *Application contact:* Dr. Marck L. Beggs, Graduate Dean, 870-230-5126, Fax: 870-230-5479, E-mail: beggsm@hsu.edu.

Hofstra University, School of Education, Health, and Human Services, Department of Counseling, Research, Special Education and Rehabilitation, Program in Special Education, Hempstead, NY 11549. Offers early childhood special education (MS Ed, Advanced Certificate); gifted education (Advanced Certificate); inclusive early childhood special education (MS Ed); inclusive elementary special education (MS Ed); inclusive secondary special education (MS Ed); literacy studies and special education (MS Ed); special education (MA, MS Ed, PD); special education assessment and diagnosis (Advanced Certificate); teaching students with severe or multiple disabilities (Advanced Certificate). Part-time and evening/weekend programs available. *Students:* 113 full-time (96 women), 105 part-time (95 women); includes 39 minority (18 African Americans, 1 American Indian/Alaska Native, 3 Asian Americans or Pacific Islanders, 17 Hispanic Americans). Average age 29. 134 applicants, 71% accepted, 74 enrolled. In 2009, 88 master's, 7 other advanced degrees awarded. *Degree requirements:* For master's, comprehensive exam (for some programs), thesis (for some programs), seminars, student teaching. *Entrance requirements:* For master's, interview, 3 letters of reference, initial/professional certification; for other advanced degree, interview, 3 letters of recommendation, resume, master's degree, certification. Additional exam requirements/recommendations for international students: Required—TOEFL (minimum score 550 paper-based; 213 computer-based; 80 iBT). *Application deadline:* Applications are processed on a rolling basis. Application fee: $60. Electronic applications accepted. *Expenses:* Tuition: Full-time $16,200; part-time $900 per credit hour. Required fees: $970; $145 per term. Tuition and fees vary according to program. *Financial support:* In 2009–10, 78 students received support, including 10 fellowships with full and partial tuition reimbursements available (averaging $2,541 per year), 4 research assistantships with full and partial tuition reimbursements available (averaging $7,210 per year); Federal Work-Study, institutionally sponsored loans, scholarships/grants, tuition waivers (full and partial), and unspecified assistantships also available. Support available to part-time students. Financial award applicants required to submit FAFSA. *Faculty research:* Inclusive schooling, autism spectrum disorders related services, cultural competency and culturally responsive instruction, co-teaching student teaching, universal design for learning. *Unit head:* Dr. George Guiliani, Director, 516-463-5143, Fax: 516-463-6184, E-mail: cprgag@hofstra.edu. *Application contact:* Carol Drummer, Dean of Graduate Admissions, 516-463-4876, Fax: 516-463-4664, E-mail: gradstudent@hofstra.edu.

Hofstra University, School of Education, Health, and Human Services, Department of Curriculum and Teaching, Program in Early Childhood Education, Hempstead, NY 11549. Offers early childhood and childhood education (MS Ed); early childhood education (MA, MS Ed). Part-time and evening/weekend programs available. Postbaccalaureate distance learning degree programs offered. *Students:* 26 full-time (24 women), 15 part-time (all women); includes 7 minority (4 African Americans, 2 Asian Americans or Pacific Islanders, 1 Hispanic American). Average age 28. 33 applicants, 82% accepted, 16 enrolled. In 2009, 13 master's awarded. *Degree requirements:* For master's, comprehensive exam, thesis (for some programs). *Entrance requirements:* For master's, 2 letters of recommendation, teacher certification (MA), interview. Additional exam requirements/recommendations for international students: Required—TOEFL (minimum score 550 paper-based; 213 computer-based; 80 iBT). *Application deadline:* Applications are processed on a rolling basis. Application fee: $60. Electronic applications accepted. *Expenses:* Tuition: Full-time $16,200; part-time $900 per credit hour. Required fees: $970; $145 per term. Tuition and fees vary according to program. *Financial support:* In 2009–10, 19 students received support, including 1 fellowship with full and partial tuition reimbursement available (averaging $2,600 per year), 1 research assistantship with full and partial tuition reimbursement available (averaging $15,300 per year); Federal Work-Study, institutionally sponsored loans, scholarships/grants, tuition waivers (full and partial), and unspecified assistantships also available. Support available to part-time students. Financial award applicants required to submit FAFSA. *Faculty research:* Play and meaning, dynamic curriculum, early childhood teacher education policy. *Unit head:* Dr. Doris P. Fromberg, Program Director, 516-463-5768, Fax: 516-463-6196, E-mail: dorisp@Hofstra.edu. *Application contact:* Carol Drummer, Dean of Graduate Admissions, 516-463-4876, Fax: 516-463-4664, E-mail: gradstudent@hofstra.edu.

Hofstra University, School of Education, Health, and Human Services, Department of Curriculum and Teaching, Program in Learning and Teaching, Hempstead, NY 11549. Offers learning and teaching (Ed D), including applied linguistics, art education, arts and humanities, early childhood education, English education, human development, math education, math, science, and technology, multicultural education, physical education, science education, social studies education, special education. Part-time and evening/weekend programs available. *Students:* 5 full-time (all women), 21 part-time (17 women); includes 2 minority (1 African American, 1 Hispanic American), 1 international. Average age 38. 22 applicants, 68% accepted, 11 enrolled. *Degree requirements:* For doctorate, comprehensive exam, thesis/dissertation. *Entrance requirements:* For doctorate, GRE, 3 letters of recommendation, interview, 2 years full-time teaching experience. Additional exam requirements/recommendations for international students: Required—TOEFL (minimum score 550 paper-based; 213 computer-based; 80 iBT). *Application deadline:* Applications are processed on a rolling basis. Application fee: $60. Electronic applications accepted. *Expenses:* Tuition: Full-time $16,200; part-time $900 per credit hour. Required fees: $970; $145 per term. Tuition and fees vary according to program. *Financial support:* In 2009–10, 24 students received support, including 20 fellowships with full and partial tuition reimbursements available (averaging $4,906 per year); research assistantships with full and partial tuition reimbursements available, Federal Work-Study, institutionally sponsored loans, scholarships/grants, and tuition waivers (full and partial) also available. Support available to part-time students. Financial award applicants required to submit FAFSA. *Faculty research:* Critical thinking, professional development, teacher quality, quantitative research. *Unit head:* Dr. Bruce A. Torff, Director, 516-463-5803, Fax: 516-463-6196, E-mail: catajs@hofstra.edu. *Application contact:* Carol Drummer, Dean of Graduate Admissions, 516-463-4876, Fax: 516-463-4664, E-mail: gradstudent@hofstra.edu.

Hood College, Graduate School, Department of Education, Frederick, MD 21701-8575. Offers curriculum and instruction (MS), including early childhood education, elementary education, elementary school science and mathematics, secondary education, special education; educational leadership (MS, Certificate); reading specialization (MS). Part-time and evening/weekend programs available. *Faculty:* 4 full-time (all women), 39 part-time/adjunct (21 women). *Students:* 2 full-time (both women), 397 part-time (326 women); includes 41 minority (29 African Americans, 5 Asian Americans or Pacific Islanders, 7 Hispanic Americans). Average age 33. 100 applicants, 92% accepted, 84 enrolled. In 2009, 73 master's, 65 other advanced degrees awarded. *Degree requirements:* For master's, action research project, portfolio (reading). *Entrance requirements:* For master's, minimum GPA of 2.75, teaching certification. *Application deadline:* For fall admission, 7/15 for domestic and international students; for spring admission, 12/15 for domestic and international students. Applications are processed on a rolling basis. Application fee: $35. Electronic applications accepted. *Expenses:* Tuition: Full-time $6480; part-time $360 per credit. Required fees: $100; $50 per term. *Financial support:* Applicants required to submit FAFSA. *Faculty research:* Leadership, action research, brain research, learning styles. *Unit head:* Dr. John George, Chairperson, 301-696-3471, Fax: 301-696-3597, E-mail: george@hood.edu. *Application contact:* Dr. Allen P. Flora, Dean of Graduate School, 301-696-3811, Fax: 301-696-3597, E-mail: gofurther@hood.edu.

Howard University, School of Education, Department of Curriculum and Instruction, Program in Early Childhood Education, Washington, DC 20059-0002. Offers M Ed, MA, MAT, CAGS. MA offered through the Graduate School of Arts and Sciences. *Accreditation:* NCATE. Part-time programs available. *Faculty:* 2 full-time (both women). *Students:* 9 full-time (all women), 1 (woman) part-time; all minorities (all African Americans). Average age 22. 8 applicants, 50% accepted, 3 enrolled. In 2009, 1 master's awarded. *Degree requirements:* For master's, comprehensive exam, thesis (for some programs), expository writing exam, internships, practicum; for CAGS, thesis optional. *Entrance requirements:* For master's, GRE General Test (MA), minimum GPA of 2.7. *Application deadline:* For fall admission, 2/15 priority date for domestic students; for spring admission, 11/1 for domestic students. Applications are processed on a rolling basis. Application fee: $45. Electronic applications accepted. *Financial support:* In 2009–10, 2 students received support, including 2 fellowships with full and partial tuition reimbursements available (averaging $15,000 per year), research assistantships with full and partial tuition reimbursements available (averaging $13,000 per year); career-related internships or fieldwork, Federal Work-Study, institutionally sponsored loans, scholarships/grants, tuition waivers (full and partial), and unspecified assistantships also available. Financial award application deadline: 2/15. *Faculty research:* Parental factors on child development, early attachment, cross–culture. *Unit head:* Dr. Rosa Trapp-Dail, Associate Professor/Coordinator, 202-806-6764, Fax: 202-806-5297, E-mail: rtrapp-dail@howard.edu. *Application contact:* June L. Harris, Administrative Assistant, Department of Curriculum and Instruction, 202-806-7343, Fax: 202-806-5297, E-mail: jlharris@howard.edu.

Hunter College of the City University of New York, Graduate School, School of Education, Department of Curriculum and Teaching, New York, NY 10021-5085. Offers bilingual education (MS); corrective reading (K-12) (MS Ed); early childhood education (MS); educational supervision and administration (AC); elementary education (MS); literacy education (MS); teaching English as a second language (MA). *Faculty:* 30 full-time (22 women), 122 part-time/adjunct (95 women). *Students:* 170 full-time (157 women), 1,035 part-time (889 women); includes 268 minority (74 African Americans, 5 American Indian/Alaska Native, 71 Asian Americans or Pacific Islanders, 118 Hispanic Americans). Average age 31. 1,339 applicants, 43% accepted, 410 enrolled. In 2009, 365 master's, 90 other advanced degrees awarded. *Degree requirements:* For master's, thesis; for AC, portfolio review. *Entrance requirements:* For degree, minimum B average in graduate course work, teaching certificate, minimum 3 years of full-time teaching experience, interview, 2 letters of support. Additional exam requirements/recommendations for international students: Required—TOEFL, TWE. *Application deadline:* For fall admission, 4/1 for domestic students; for spring admission, 11/1 for domestic students. Applications are processed on a rolling basis. Application fee: $125. *Expenses:* Tuition, state resident: full-time $7360; part-time $310 per credit. Required fees: $250 per semester. *Financial support:* Federal Work-Study, scholarships/grants, and tuition waivers (partial) available. Support available to part-time students. *Faculty research:* Teacher opportunity corps-mentor program for first-year teachers, adult literacy, student literacy corporation. *Unit head:* Dr. Anne M. Ediger, Head, 212-777-4686, E-mail: anne.ediger@hunter.cuny.edu. *Application contact:* Milena Solo, Director for Graduate Admissions, 212-772-4482, Fax: 212-650-3336, E-mail: milena.solo@hunter.cuny.edu.

Indiana State University, School of Graduate Studies, College of Education, Department of Elementary, Early and Special Education, Terre Haute, IN 47809. Offers early childhood education (M Ed); elementary education (M Ed); MA/MS. *Accreditation:* NCATE. Electronic applications accepted.

Indiana University–Purdue University Indianapolis, School of Education, Indianapolis, IN 46202-2896. Offers computer education (Certificate); curriculum and instruction (MS); early childhood (MS); educational leadership (MS, Certificate); English as a second language (Certificate); higher education and student affairs (MS); kindergarten (Certificate); language education (MS); reading (Certificate); school counseling (MS); special education (MS, Certificate). Part-time and evening/weekend programs available. *Faculty:* 41 full-time, 80 part-time/adjunct. *Students:* 72 full-time (60 women), 427 part-time (325 women); includes 57 minority (42 African Americans, 1 American Indian/Alaska Native, 4 Asian Americans or Pacific Islanders, 10 Hispanic Americans), 5 international. Average age 32. 181 applicants, 78% accepted, 112 enrolled. In 2009, 162 master's awarded. *Degree requirements:* For master's, thesis optional. *Entrance requirements:* For master's, GRE General Test, minimum GPA of 3.0. Additional exam requirements/recommendations for international students: Required—TOEFL. *Application deadline:* For fall admission, 5/1 priority date for domestic students; for spring admission, 11/1 for domestic students. Application fee: $55 ($65 for international students). *Financial support:* In 2009–10, 2 fellowships (averaging $780 per year), 18 teaching assistantships (averaging $9,756 per year) were awarded; research assistantships with partial tuition reimbursements, Federal Work-Study, institutionally sponsored loans, scholarships/grants, and tuition waivers (partial) also available. Support available to part-time students. *Faculty research:* Teachers in the process of change, learning cycles, children's concepts of science. Total annual research expenditures: $614,458. *Unit head:* Dr. Chris Leland, Interim Executive Associate Dean, 317-274-6801, Fax: 317-274-6864. *Application contact:* Sarah Brandenburg, Graduate Advisor, 317-274-6801, Fax: 317-274-6864, E-mail: edugrad@iupui.edu.

Inter American University of Puerto Rico, Guayama Campus, Department of Education and Social Sciences, Guayama, PR 00785. Offers early childhood education (MA); elementary education (MA). Part-time programs available. *Entrance requirements:* For master's, GRE, MAT, EXADEP, letters of recommendation, minimum GPA of 2.5. Electronic applications accepted.

Jackson State University, Graduate School, School of Education, Department of Curriculum and Instruction, Jackson, MS 39217. Offers early childhood education (MS Ed, Ed D); elementary education (MS Ed, Ed S). *Accreditation:* NCATE. Evening/weekend programs available. Terminal master's awarded for partial completion of doctoral program. *Degree requirements:* For master's, comprehensive exam, thesis or alternative; for doctorate, comprehensive exam, thesis/dissertation. *Entrance requirements:* For master's, GRE General Test; for doctorate, MAT, teaching experience. Additional exam requirements/recommendations for international students: Required—TOEFL.

Jacksonville State University, College of Graduate Studies and Continuing Education, College of Education and Professional Studies, Program in Early Childhood Education, Jacksonville, AL 36265-1602. Offers MS Ed. *Accreditation:* NCATE. Part-time and evening/weekend programs available. *Degree requirements:* For master's, comprehensive exam, thesis (for some programs). *Entrance requirements:* For master's, GRE General Test or MAT. Electronic applications accepted.

Jacksonville University, College of Arts and Sciences, School of Education, Jacksonville, FL 32211. Offers computer sciences (MAT); early childhood education (Certificate); elementary education (MAT); integrated learning with educational technology (MAT); mathematics education (MAT); music education (MAT); reading education (MAT); second careers as a teacher (Certificate). Part-time and evening/weekend programs available. *Degree requirements:* For master's, comprehensive exam. *Entrance requirements:* For master's, GRE General Test, minimum GPA of 3.0. Additional exam requirements/recommendations for international students: Required—TOEFL (minimum score 550 paper-based), TWE. *Expenses:* Contact institution.

James Madison University, The Graduate School, College of Education, Early, Elementary, and Reading Education Department, Program in Early Childhood Education, Harrisonburg, VA 22807. Offers M Ed. *Accreditation:* NCATE. Part-time programs available. *Students:* Average age 27. *Entrance requirements:* For master's, GRE General Test or MAT, PRAXIS I and II, 2-3 page written statement, faculty interview, admission into teacher education, minimum undergraduate GPA of 2.75. Additional exam requirements/recommendations for international students: Required—TOEFL. *Application deadline:* For fall admission, 5/1 priority date for domestic students; for spring admission, 9/1 priority date for domestic students. Applications are processed on a rolling basis. Application fee: $55. Electronic applications accepted. *Expenses:* Tuition, area resident: Part-time $305 per credit hour. Tuition, state resident: part-time $305 per credit hour. Tuition, nonresident: part-time $890 per credit hour. *Financial support:* Career-related internships or fieldwork and unspecified assistantships available. Financial award application deadline: 3/1; financial award applicants required to submit FAFSA. *Unit head:* Dr. Martha Ross, Academic Unit Head, 540-568-6255. *Application contact:* Lynette M. Bible, Director of Graduate Admissions, 540-568-6395, Fax: 540-568-7860, E-mail: biblelm@jmu.edu.

John Carroll University, Graduate School, Department of Education and Allied Studies, Program in School Based Early Childhood Education, University Heights, OH 44118-4581. Offers M Ed. *Accreditation:* NCATE. *Degree requirements:* For master's, comprehensive exam. *Entrance requirements:* For master's, GRE General Test or MAT, minimum GPA of 2.75, interview. Additional exam requirements/recommendations for international students: Required—TOEFL. Electronic applications accepted.

The Johns Hopkins University, School of Education, Department of Special Education, Baltimore, MD 21218. Offers advanced methods for differentiated instruction and inclusive education (Certificate); assistive technology (Certificate); early intervention/preschool special education specialist (Certificate); education of students with autism and other pervasive developmental disorders (Certificate); education of students with severe disabilities (Certificate); special education (MS, Ed D, CAGS), including early childhood special education (MS), general special education studies (MS), mild to moderate disabilities (MS), severe disabilities (MS), technology in special education (MS). *Accreditation:* NCATE. Part-time and evening/weekend programs available. Postbaccalaureate distance learning degree programs offered (minimal on-campus study). *Faculty:* 6 full-time (5 women), 21 part-time/adjunct (18 women). *Students:* 19 full-time (18 women), 270 part-time (243 women); includes 45 minority (35 African Americans, 6 Asian Americans or Pacific Islanders, 4 Hispanic Americans), 10 international. Average age 31. 114 applicants, 56% accepted, 46 enrolled. In 2009, 88 master's, 34 other advanced degrees awarded. *Degree requirements:* For master's, internships, professional portfolio, and PRAXIS II (for licensure); for doctorate, comprehensive exam, thesis/dissertation. *Entrance requirements:* For master's, PRAXIS I, SAT, ACT, or GRE, minimum undergraduate GPA of 3.0, 2 letters of recommendation (for cohort programs); for doctorate, GRE, degree in special education (or related field); minimum GPA of 3.0 in all prior academic work; 3 letters of recommendation; curriculum vitae/resume; professional experience; for other advanced degree, minimum undergraduate GPA of 3.0, master's degree (for CAGS). Additional exam requirements/recommendations for international students: Required—TOEFL (minimum score 600 paper-based; 250 computer-based; 100 iBT). *Application deadline:* For fall admission, 5/1 for international students; for spring admission, 10/15 for international students. Applications are processed on a rolling basis. Application fee: $80. Electronic applications accepted. *Financial support:* In 2009–10, 9 fellowships were awarded; scholarships/grants also available. Support available to part-time students. Financial award application deadline: 6/1; financial award applicants required to submit FAFSA. *Faculty research:* Alternative licensure programs for special educators; collaborative programming; data-based decision making and knowledge management as keys to school reform; parent training; natural environment teaching (NET). *Unit head:* Dr. Laurie U. deBettencourt, Chair, 301-294-7054, Fax: 410-516-8474, E-mail: specialed@jhu.edu. *Application contact:* Jennifer Shaffer, Director of Admissions, 410-516-9797, Fax: 410-516-9799, E-mail: educationinfo@jhu.edu.

Kansas State University, Graduate School, College of Human Ecology, School of Family Studies and Human Services, Manhattan, KS 66506. Offers communication sciences and disorders (MS); early childhood education (MS); family studies (MS); life span human development (MS); marriage and family therapy (MS). *Accreditation:* AAMFT/COAMFTE; ASHA. Part-time programs available. *Faculty:* 25 full-time (15 women), 3 part-time/adjunct (2 women). *Students:* 76 full-time (67 women), 101 part-time (61 women); includes 17 minority (7 African Americans, 1 American Indian/Alaska Native, 2 Asian Americans or Pacific Islanders, 7 Hispanic Americans), 1 international. Average age 32. 117 applicants, 68% accepted, 47 enrolled. In 2009, 63 master's awarded. *Degree requirements:* For master's, thesis or alternative, oral exam, residency. *Entrance requirements:* For master's, GRE, minimum GPA of 3.0 in last 2 years of undergraduate study. Additional exam requirements/recommendations for international students: Required—TOEFL (minimum score 600 paper-based; 250 computer-based). *Application deadline:* For fall admission, 2/1 priority date for domestic and international students; for spring admission, 8/1 priority date for domestic and international students. Applications are processed on a rolling basis. Application fee: $40 ($55 for international students). Electronic applications accepted. *Financial support:* In 2009–10, 26 research assistantships (averaging $10,867 per year), 17 teaching assistantships with full and partial tuition reimbursements (averaging $11,635 per year) were awarded; Federal Work-Study, institutionally sponsored loans, scholarships/grants, and unspecified assistantships also available. Support available to part-time students. Financial award application deadline: 3/1; financial award applicants required to submit FAFSA. *Faculty research:* Health and security of military families, personal and family risk assessment and evaluation, disorders of communication and swallowing, families and health. Total annual research expenditures: $10.1 million. *Unit head:* Dr. Maurice McDonald, Head, 785-532-1472, E-mail: morey@ksu.edu. *Application contact:* Connie Fechter, Administrative Specialist, 785-532-1473, Fax: 785-532-5505, E-mail: fechter@ksu.edu.

Kean University, College of Education, Program in Early Childhood Education, Union, NJ 07083. Offers administration in early childhood and family studies (MA); advanced curriculum and teaching (MA); classroom instruction (MA), including preschool-third grade; education for family living (MA). *Accreditation:* NCATE. Part-time and evening/weekend programs available. *Faculty:* 8 full-time (7 women). *Students:* 5 full-time (all women), 55 part-time (53 women); includes 17 minority (6 African Americans, 1 American Indian/Alaska Native, 3 Asian Americans or Pacific Islanders, 7 Hispanic Americans), 1 international. Average age 32. 37 applicants, 95% accepted, 23 enrolled. In 2009, 25 master's awarded. *Degree requirements:* For master's, thesis, portfolio. *Entrance requirements:* For master's, GRE General Test, minimum GPA of 3.0, 2 letters of recommendation, interview, teacher certification (for some programs), writing sample. *Application deadline:* For fall admission, 5/1 for domestic students; for spring admission, 11/1 for domestic students. Application fee: $60 ($150 for international students). Electronic applications accepted. *Expenses:* Tuition, state resident: full-time $10,440; part-time $435 per credit. Tuition, nonresident: full-time $14,160; part-time $590 per credit. Required fees: $2642; $110 per credit. Part-time tuition and fees vary according to course load and degree level. *Financial support:* In 2009–10, 1 research assistantship with full tuition reimbursement (averaging $3,263 per year) was awarded; unspecified assistantships also available. *Unit head:* Dr. Polly Ashelman, Program Coordinator, 908-737-3780, E-mail: pashelma@kean.edu. *Application contact:* Ann-Marie Kay, Assistant Director of Graduate Admissions, 908-737-5922, Fax: 908-737-5965, E-mail: akay@kean.edu.

Kennesaw State University, Leland and Clarice C. Bagwell College of Education, Program in Graduate Education, Kennesaw, GA 30144-5591. Offers adolescent education (M Ed); educational leadership (M Ed); educational leadership technology (M Ed); elementary and early childhood education (M Ed); special education (M Ed); teaching English to speakers of other languages (M Ed). *Accreditation:* NCATE. Part-time programs available. *Faculty:* 60 full-time (38 women), 12 part-time/adjunct (4 women). *Students:* 140 full-time (116 women), 136 part-time (107 women); includes 51 minority (39 African Americans, 1 American Indian/Alaska Native, 3 Asian Americans or Pacific Islanders, 8 Hispanic Americans), 4 international. Average age 34. 113 applicants, 83% accepted, 69 enrolled. In 2009, 282 master's awarded. *Degree requirements:* For master's, thesis or alternative. *Entrance requirements:* For master's, GRE General Test, T-4 state certification, minimum GPA of 2.75. Additional exam requirements/recommendations for international students: Required—TOEFL (minimum score 550 paper-based; 213 computer-based; 80 iBT), IELTS (minimum score 6). *Application deadline:* For fall admission, 7/1 for domestic and international students; for spring admission, 10/1 for domestic and international students. Application fee: $60. Electronic applications accepted. *Expenses:* Tuition, state resident: full-time $2341; part-time $196 per credit hour. Tuition, nonresident: full-time $9396; part-time $783 per credit hour. Required fees: $573 per semester. *Financial support:* Federal Work-Study and unspecified assistantships available. Support available to part-time students. Financial award application deadline: 6/15; financial award applicants required to submit FAFSA. *Unit head:* Dr. Nita Paris, Associate Dean for Graduate Programs, 770-423-6636, E-mail: nparis@kennesaw.edu. *Application contact:* Alisha Bello, Administrative Coordinator, 770-423-6043, Fax: 770-420-4435, E-mail: abello1@kennesaw.edu.

Kent State University, Graduate School of Education, Health, and Human Services, School of Teaching, Learning and Curriculum Studies, MAT Program in Early Childhood Education,

Kent, OH 44242-0001. Offers MAT. *Faculty:* 6 full-time (4 women), 3 part-time/adjunct (all women). *Students:* 19 full-time (18 women); includes 1 minority (Hispanic American). 19 applicants, 84% accepted. In 2009, 7 master's awarded. *Entrance requirements:* Additional exam requirements/recommendations for international students: Required—TOEFL. Application fee: $30 ($60 for international students). *Financial support:* In 2009–10, research assistantships (averaging $9,000 per year); Federal Work-Study, scholarships/grants, and unspecified assistantships also available. *Unit head:* Janice Kroeger, Coordinator, 330-672-0617, E-mail: jkroege1@kent.edu. *Application contact:* Nancy Miller, Academic Program Coordinator, Office of Graduate Student Services, 330-672-2576, Fax: 330-672-9162, E-mail: ogs@kent.edu.

Kent State University, Graduate School of Education, Health, and Human Services, School of Teaching, Learning and Curriculum Studies, Program in Early Childhood Education, Kent, OH 44242-0001. Offers M Ed, MA. *Accreditation:* NCATE. *Faculty:* 6 full-time (4 women), 3 part-time/adjunct (all women). *Students:* 4 full-time (all women), 7 part-time (all women); includes 2 minority (both Hispanic Americans). 8 applicants, 25% accepted. In 2009, 25 master's awarded. *Degree requirements:* For master's, thesis (for some programs). *Entrance requirements:* For master's, GRE General Test. Additional exam requirements/recommendations for international students: Required—TOEFL. *Application deadline:* For spring admission, 3/1 for domestic students. Applications are processed on a rolling basis. Application fee: $30 ($60 for international students). Electronic applications accepted. *Financial support:* In 2009–10, 2 research assistantships with full tuition reimbursements (averaging $9,000 per year) were awarded; Federal Work-Study, scholarships/grants, and unspecified assistantships also available. Financial award application deadline: 4/1; financial award applicants required to submit FAFSA. *Faculty research:* Parent-child relationships, professional preparation, curriculum and assessment. *Unit head:* Martha Lash, Coordinator, 330-672-0628, E-mail: mlash@kent.edu. *Application contact:* Nancy Miller, Academic Program Coordinator, Office of Graduate Student Services, 330-672-2576, Fax: 330-672-9162, E-mail: ogs@kent.edu.

Keuka College, Program in Childhood Education/Literacy, Keuka Park, NY 14478-0098. Offers MS. Part-time and evening/weekend programs available. *Faculty:* 5 part-time/adjunct (3 women). *Students:* 18 part-time (15 women). 9 applicants, 100% accepted, 9 enrolled. *Degree requirements:* For master's, thesis, research project, portfolio. *Entrance requirements:* For master's, minimum undergraduate GPA of 3.0, 2 letters of recommendation, provisional New York state certification. Additional exam requirements/recommendations for international students: Required—TOEFL (minimum score 550 paper-based; 213 computer-based). *Application deadline:* For fall admission, 8/15 priority date for domestic students; for winter admission, 12/15 priority date for domestic students; for spring admission, 4/15 priority date for domestic students. Applications are processed on a rolling basis. Application fee: $30. *Expenses:* Contact institution. *Faculty research:* Reading and writing across the curriculum, science education, elementary mathematics education, special education, critical thinking. *Unit head:* Dr. Diane Burke, Director of Graduate Program in Education, 315-279-5688. *Application contact:* Dr. Diane Burke, Director of Graduate Program in Education, 315-279-5688.

Kutztown University of Pennsylvania, College of Education, Program in Elementary Education, Kutztown, PA 19530-0730. Offers early childhood education (Certificate); elementary education (M Ed, Certificate); special education (Certificate). *Accreditation:* NCATE. Part-time and evening/weekend programs available. *Faculty:* 7 full-time (all women), 2 part-time/adjunct (both women). *Students:* 25 full-time (18 women), 27 part-time (25 women); includes 2 minority (both Hispanic Americans). Average age 29. 46 applicants, 83% accepted, 15 enrolled. In 2009, 23 master's awarded. *Degree requirements:* For master's, comprehensive exam, thesis optional, comprehensive project. *Entrance requirements:* For master's, GRE General Test. Additional exam requirements/recommendations for international students: Required—TOEFL. *Application deadline:* For fall admission, 8/15 priority date for domestic and international students; for spring admission, 12/15 priority date for domestic and international students. Applications are processed on a rolling basis. Application fee: $35. Electronic applications accepted. *Expenses:* Tuition, state resident: full-time $6666; part-time $370 per credit. Tuition, nonresident: full-time $10,666; part-time $593 per credit. Required fees: $62 per credit. $60 per semester. *Financial support:* Career-related internships or fieldwork, Federal Work-Study, scholarships/grants, and unspecified assistantships available. Financial award application deadline: 3/1; financial award applicants required to submit FAFSA. *Faculty research:* Whole language, middle schools, cooperative learning discussion techniques, oral reading techniques, hemisphericity. *Unit head:* Dr. Elsa Geskus, Chairperson, 610-683-4262, Fax: 610-683-1327, E-mail: geskus@kutztown.edu. *Application contact:* Kelly D. Burr, Associate Director, Graduate Admissions, 610-683-4200, Fax: 610-683-1393, E-mail: graduate@kutztown.edu.

Lehman College of the City University of New York, Division of Education, Department of Early Childhood and Elementary Education, Program in Early Childhood Education, Bronx, NY 10468-1589. Offers MS Ed. *Accreditation:* NCATE. Part-time and evening/weekend programs available. *Entrance requirements:* For master's, minimum GPA of 2.7. *Faculty research:* TV programming, literacy, children's trauma conceptualization.

Le Moyne College, Department of Education, Syracuse, NY 13214. Offers adolescent education (MS Ed, MST); adolescent education/special education (MS Ed, MST); adolescent English (grades 7-12) (MST); adolescent history (grades 7-12) (MST); childhood education (MS Ed); childhood education/special education (MS Ed); elementary education (MS Ed); general professional education (MS Ed); inclusive childhood education (MST); middle child specialist/special education (MS Ed); middle childhood specialist (MS Ed); school building leadership (MS Ed, CAS); school district business leader (MS Ed, CAS); school district leadership (MS Ed, CAS); secondary education (MS Ed); special education (MS Ed). *Accreditation:* Teacher Education Accreditation Council. Part-time and evening/weekend programs available. *Faculty:* 15 full-time (8 women), 61 part-time/adjunct (33 women). *Students:* 40 full-time (30 women), 260 part-time (180 women); includes 25 minority (11 African Americans, 3 American Indian/Alaska Native, 3 Asian Americans or Pacific Islanders, 8 Hispanic Americans). Average age 31. 168 applicants, 89% accepted, 140 enrolled. In 2009, 180 master's awarded. *Degree requirements:* For master's, thesis. *Entrance requirements:* For master's, GRE General Test, 2 letters of recommendation. Additional exam requirements/recommendations for international students: Required—TOEFL (minimum score 550 paper-based; 213 computer-based; 79 iBT). *Application deadline:* For fall admission, 4/1 priority date for domestic and international students; for spring admission, 10/1 priority date for domestic and international students. Applications are processed on a rolling basis. Application fee: $50. *Expenses:* Contact institution. *Financial support:* In 2009–10, 28 students received support. Career-related internships or fieldwork and health care benefits available. Support available to part-time students. Financial award applicants required to submit FAFSA. *Faculty research:* Recruitment/retention strategies, minority teachers, special education, multiculturalism, literacy, technology, video games learning, autism, school district organization. *Unit head:* Dr. Norbert J. Henry, Interim Chair/Director, 315-445-4376, Fax: 315-445-4744, E-mail: henry@lemoyne.edu. *Application contact:* Kristen P. Trapasso, Director of Graduate Admission, 315-445-4265, Fax: 315-445-6027, E-mail: trapaskp@lemoyne.edu.

Lenoir-Rhyne University, Graduate Programs, School of Education, Program in Birth through Kindergarten Education, Hickory, NC 28601. Offers MA. Part-time and evening/weekend programs available. *Degree requirements:* For master's, comprehensive exam, thesis optional. *Entrance requirements:* For master's, GRE General Test or MAT, minimum undergraduate GPA of 2.7, graduate 3.0. Additional exam requirements/recommendations for international students: Required—TOEFL (minimum score 600 paper-based). Electronic applications accepted.

Lesley University, School of Education, Cambridge, MA 02138-2790. Offers curriculum and instruction (M Ed, CAGS); early childhood education (M Ed); educational studies (PhD); elementary education (M Ed); individually designed (M Ed); middle school education (M Ed); moderate special needs (M Ed); reading (M Ed, CAGS); science in education (M Ed); severe special needs (M Ed); special needs (CAGS); technology in education (M Ed, CAGS). *Accreditation:* Teacher Education Accreditation Council. Part-time and evening/weekend programs available. Postbaccalaureate distance learning degree programs offered (no

Early Childhood Education

Lesley University (continued)
on-campus study). Degree requirements: For master's, practicum; for doctorate, thesis/dissertation. Entrance requirements: For doctorate, GRE General Test or MAT, interview, master's degree, resume; for CAGS, interview, master's degree. Additional exam requirements/recommendations for international students: Required—TOEFL (minimum score 550 paper-based; 213 computer-based; 80 iBT). Electronic applications accepted. Faculty research: Assessment in literacy, mathematics and science; autism spectrum disorders; instructional technology and online learning; multicultural education and ELL.

Lewis & Clark College, Graduate School of Education and Counseling, Department of Teacher Education, Program in Early Childhood/Elementary Education, Portland, OR 97219-7899. Offers MAT. Accreditation: NCATE. Faculty: 3 full-time (1 woman), 2 part-time/adjunct (both women). Students: 66 full-time (55 women), 1 part-time (0 women); includes 8 minority (1 American Indian/Alaska Native, 3 Asian Americans or Pacific Islanders, 4 Hispanic Americans), 2 international. Average age 28. 115 applicants, 89% accepted, 66 enrolled. In 2009, 61 master's awarded. Entrance requirements: For master's, minimum undergraduate GPA of 2.75. Candidates for admission must have a history of work, either volunteer or paid, with children in grades K-6. Additional exam requirements/recommendations for international students: Required—TOEFL (minimum score 575 paper-based; 233 computer-based). Application deadline: For fall admission, 12/1 priority date for domestic and international students. Application fee: $50. Electronic applications accepted. Expenses: Tuition: Part-time $713 per semester hour. Tuition and fees vary according to course level and campus/location. Financial support: In 2009–10, 64 students received support. Career-related internships or fieldwork, Federal Work-Study, institutionally sponsored loans, scholarships/grants, health care benefits, and tuition waivers (partial) available. Support available to part-time students. Financial award application deadline: 3/1; financial award applicants required to submit FAFSA. Faculty research: Classroom ethnography, assessing student learning, reading, moral development, language arts. Unit head: Dr. Vern Jones, Chair of Teacher Education Department, 503-768-6100, Fax: 503-768-6115, E-mail: lcteach@lclark.edu. Application contact: Becky Haas, Director of Admissions, 503-768-6200, Fax: 503-768-6205, E-mail: gseadmit@lclark.edu.

Liberty University, School of Education, Lynchburg, VA 24502. Offers administration and supervision (M Ed); curriculum and instruction (M Ed); early childhood education (M Ed); education specialist (Ed S); educational leadership (Ed D); elementary education (M Ed); gifted education (M Ed); reading specialist (M Ed); school counseling (M Ed); secondary education (M Ed); special education (M Ed). Accreditation: NCATE. Part-time programs available. Postbaccalaureate distance learning degree programs offered (minimal on-campus study). Degree requirements: For doctorate, comprehensive exam, thesis/dissertation. Entrance requirements: For master's, GRE General Test or MAT (aken in or before 1999), 2 letters of recommendation, minimum undergraduate GPA of 3.0, curriculum vitae; for doctorate, GRE General Test or MAT (if taken before 1999), minimum master's GPA of 3.0, 3 years of teacher experience; for Ed S, GRE General Test or MAT (if taken before 1999), minimum master's GPA of 3.0, 3 years of teaching experience. Additional exam requirements/recommendations for international students: Required—TOEFL (minimum score 600 paper-based; 250 computer-based). Electronic applications accepted. Expenses: Contact institution. Faculty research: Self-determination, character education, bibliotherapy, learning styles, distance education.

Lincoln University, Graduate Center, Lincoln University, PA 19352. Offers administration (MSA), including finance, human resources management; early childhood education (M Ed); elementary education (M Ed); human services (M Hum Svcs); reading (MSR). Evening/weekend programs available. Degree requirements: For master's, thesis. Entrance requirements: For master's, 5 years of work experience in human services. Faculty research: Gerontology/minority aging, computers in composition instruction.

Long Island University at Riverhead, Education Division, Program in Childhood Education, Riverhead, NY 11901. Offers childhood education (MS Ed); elementary education (MS Ed). Accreditation: Teacher Education Accreditation Council. Faculty: 1 full-time (0 women), 11 part-time/adjunct (7 women). Students: 23 full-time (19 women), 25 part-time (23 women); includes 1 African American, 1 Hispanic American. Average age 30. In 2009, 22 master's awarded. Degree requirements: For master's, thesis. Entrance requirements: For master's, minimum undergraduate GPA of 2.75, on-campus writing sample. Additional exam requirements/recommendations for international students: Required—TOEFL (minimum score 550 paper-based; 250 computer-based). Application deadline: Applications are processed on a rolling basis. Application fee: $30. Electronic applications accepted. Financial support: In 2009–10, 1 research assistantship with full tuition reimbursement was awarded; scholarships/grants and unspecified assistantships also available. Support available to part-time students. Financial award applicants required to submit FAFSA. Unit head: Prof. David S. Schultz, Head, 631-287-8010, Fax: 631-287-8253. Application contact: Andrea Borra, Admissions Counselor, 631-287-8010, Fax: 631-287-8253, E-mail: andrea.borra@liu.edu.

Long Island University, Brentwood Campus, School of Education, Brentwood, NY 11717. Offers childhood education (MS); early childhood education (MS); literacy (MS); mental health counseling (MS); school counseling (MS); special education (MS). Part-time and evening/weekend programs available.

Long Island University, C.W. Post Campus, School of Education, Department of Curriculum and Instruction, Brookville, NY 11548-1300. Offers adolescence education (MS); adolescence education: biology (MS); adolescence education: earth science (MS); adolescence education: English (MS); adolescence education: mathematics (MS); adolescence education: social studies (MS); adolescence education: Spanish (MS); art education (MS); bilingual education (MS); childhood education (MS); early childhood education (MS); middle childhood education (MS); music education (MS); teaching English to speakers of other languages (MS). Part-time and evening/weekend programs available. Degree requirements: For master's, comprehensive exam or thesis, student teaching. Entrance requirements: For master's, minimum GPA of 2.75 in major, 2.5 overall. Electronic applications accepted. Faculty research: Ethics and education, teaching strategies.

Long Island University, Rockland Graduate Campus, Graduate School, Program in Curriculum and Instruction, Orangeburg, NY 10962. Offers adolescence education (MS Ed); childhood education (MS). Faculty: 1 (woman) full-time, 8 part-time/adjunct (3 women). Students: 18 full-time (15 women), 46 part-time (40 women). In 2009, 35 master's awarded. Entrance requirements: For master's, GRE General Test. Application deadline: Applications are processed on a rolling basis. Application fee: $30. Expenses: Tuition: Part-time $930 per credit. Required fees: $200 per semester. Financial support: Scholarships/grants available. Support available to part-time students. Financial award applicants required to submit FAFSA. Unit head: Dr. Nancy T. Goldman, Program Director, 845-359-7200 Ext. 5409, Fax: 845-359-7248, E-mail: nancy.goldman@liu.edu. Application contact: Peter S. Reiner, Director of Admissions and Marketing, 845-359-7200, Fax: 845-359-7248, E-mail: peter.reiner@liu.edu.

Long Island University, Westchester Graduate Campus, Programs in Education-Teaching, Program in Early Childhood Education, Purchase, NY 10577. Offers MS Ed, Advanced Certificate.

Loyola Marymount University, School of Education, Department of Elementary and Secondary Education, Program in Early Childhood Education, Los Angeles, CA 90045. Offers MA. Part-time and evening/weekend programs available. Faculty: 6 full-time (5 women), 11 part-time/adjunct (6 women). Students: 32 full-time (31 women); includes 20 minority (8 African Americans, 7 Asian Americans or Pacific Islanders, 5 Hispanic Americans). Average age 26. 22 applicants, 82% accepted, 15 enrolled. Degree requirements: For master's, comprehensive exam. Entrance requirements: For master's, 3 letters of recommendation. Additional exam requirements/recommendations for international students: Required—TOEFL (minimum score 600 paper-based; 250 computer-based; 100 iBT). Application deadline: For fall admission, 6/15 for domestic students. Application fee: $50. Electronic applications accepted. Financial support: In 2009–10, 25 students received support, including 3 research assistantships (averaging $1,432 per year); scholarships/grants and unspecified assistantships also available. Support available

to part-time students. Financial award application deadline: 6/15; financial award applicants required to submit FAFSA. Unit head: Dr. Irene Oliver, Chair, 310-338-7302, Fax: 310-338-7302, E-mail: ioliver@lmu.edu. Application contact: Chake H. Kouyoumjian, Director, Graduate Admissions, 310-338-2721, Fax: 310-338-6086, E-mail: ckouyoum@lmu.edu.

Loyola University Maryland, Graduate Programs, College of Arts and Sciences, Department of Education, Program in Montessori Education, Baltimore, MD 21210-2699. Offers M Ed, CAS. Accreditation: NCATE. Part-time and evening/weekend programs available. Entrance requirements: For master's and CAS, GRE General Test, GRE Subject Test (recommended). Additional exam requirements/recommendations for international students: Required—TOEFL (minimum score 550 paper-based; 213 computer-based).

Manhattan College, Graduate Division, School of Education, Program in Special Education, Riverdale, NY 10471. Offers 5 year dual childhood/special education (MS Ed); dual childhood/special education (MS Ed); special education (MS Ed). Part-time and evening/weekend programs available. Degree requirements: For master's, thesis, internship. Entrance requirements: For master's, minimum GPA of 3.0, NYSTE Last Test. Additional exam requirements/recommendations for international students: Required—TOEFL (minimum score 550 paper-based). Expenses: Contact institution. Faculty research: Adapted physical education.

Manhattanville College, Graduate Programs, School of Education, Program in Childhood Education, Purchase, NY 10577-2132. Offers childhood and special education (MPS); childhood education (MAT); special education childhood (MPS). Part-time and evening/weekend programs available. Students: 67 full-time (62 women), 150 part-time (120 women); includes 6 African Americans, 3 Asian Americans or Pacific Islanders, 10 Hispanic Americans, 2 international. In 2009, 65 master's awarded. Degree requirements: For master's, comprehensive exam or research project, field experience. Entrance requirements: For master's, minimum undergraduate GPA of 3.0, 2 letters of recommendation. Additional exam requirements/recommendations for international students: Required—TOEFL. Application deadline: Applications are processed on a rolling basis. Application fee: $70. Financial support: Career-related internships or fieldwork and institutionally sponsored loans available. Support available to part-time students. Financial award applicants required to submit FAFSA. Unit head: Dr. Shelley Wepner, Dean, 914-323-5192, Fax: 914-694-2386, E-mail: wepners@mville.edu. Application contact: Jeanine Pardey-Levine, Director of Admissions, 914-323-3208, Fax: 914-694-1732, E-mail: edschool@mville.edu.

Manhattanville College, Graduate Programs, School of Education, Program in Early Childhood Education, Purchase, NY 10577-2132. Offers childhood and early childhood education (MAT); early childhood education (birth-grade 2) (MAT); literacy (birth-grade 6) (MPS), including reading, writing; literacy (birth-grade 6) and special education (grades 1-6) (MPS); special education (birth-grade 2) (MPS); special education (birth-grade 6) (MPS). Part-time and evening/weekend programs available. Students: 43 full-time (42 women), 62 part-time (59 women); includes 1 African American, 1 Asian American or Pacific Islander, 7 Hispanic Americans. In 2009, 5 master's awarded. Degree requirements: For master's, comprehensive exam or research project, field experience. Entrance requirements: For master's, minimum undergraduate GPA of 3.0, 2 letters of recommendation. Additional exam requirements/recommendations for international students: Required—TOEFL. Application deadline: Applications are processed on a rolling basis. Application fee: $70. Electronic applications accepted. Financial support: Career-related internships or fieldwork and institutionally sponsored loans available. Support available to part-time students. Unit head: Dr. Shelley Wepner, Dean, 914-323-5192, Fax: 914-694-2386, E-mail: wepners@mville.edu. Application contact: Jeanine Pardey-Levine, Director of Admissions, 914-323-3208, Fax: 914-694-1732, E-mail: edschool@mville.edu.

Marshall University, Academic Affairs Division, Graduate School of Education and Professional Development, Program in Early Childhood Education, Huntington, WV 25755. Offers MA. Accreditation: NCATE. Evening/weekend programs available. Faculty: 8 full-time (5 women). Students: 9 full-time (all women), 11 part-time (all women); includes 1 minority (African American), 1 international. Average age 30. In 2009, 4 master's awarded. Degree requirements: For master's, thesis optional, comprehensive or oral assessment. Entrance requirements: For master's, GRE General Test or MAT. Application fee: $40. Unit head: Dr. Calvin Meyer, Director, 304-746-1936, E-mail: meyer@marshall.edu. Application contact: Graduate Admissions, 304-746-1900, Fax: 304-746-1902, E-mail: services@marshall.edu.

Maryville University of Saint Louis, School of Education, St. Louis, MO 63141-7299. Offers art education (MA Ed); early childhood education (MA Ed); educational leadership (Ed D); educational leadership: principal certification (MA Ed); elementary education (MA Ed); elementary education/English (MA Ed); elementary education/psychology (MA Ed); environmental education (MA Ed); gifted education (MA Ed); literacy specialist (MA Ed); middle grades education (MA Ed); secondary teaching and inquiry (MA Ed); teacher as leader (MA Ed). Accreditation: NASAD; NCATE. Part-time and evening/weekend programs available. Students: 25 full-time (18 women), 198 part-time (145 women); includes 33 minority (27 African Americans, 2 American Indian/Alaska Native, 1 Asian American or Pacific Islander, 3 Hispanic Americans). Average age 36. In 2009, 61 master's, 45 doctorates awarded. Degree requirements: For master's, thesis, project. Entrance requirements: For master's and doctorate, minimum GPA of 3.0, 3 professional recommendations. Additional exam requirements/recommendations for international students: Required—TOEFL (minimum score 550 paper-based). Application deadline: Applications are processed on a rolling basis. Application fee: $40 ($60 for international students). Electronic applications accepted. Expenses: Tuition: Full-time $20,384; part-time $627.50 per credit hour. Required fees: $100 per semester. Financial support: Career-related internships or fieldwork, Federal Work-Study, tuition waivers (partial), and professional educator discounts available. Financial award application deadline: 3/1; financial award applicants required to submit FAFSA. Faculty research: Collaboration with public schools, pre-service program development, mathematics, diversity, literacy. Unit head: Dr. Sam Hausfather, Dean, 314-529-9466, Fax: 314-529-9921, E-mail: shausfather@maryville.edu. Application contact: Holly Stanwich, Graduate Admissions Coordinator, 314-529-9542, Fax: 314-529-9921, E-mail: teachered@maryville.edu.

Marywood University, Academic Affairs, Reap College of Education and Human Development, Department of Education, Program in Early Childhood Intervention, Scranton, PA 18509-1598. Offers MS. Accreditation: NCATE. Students: 2 full-time (both women), 9 part-time (all women); includes 1 minority (African American). Average age 30. 1 applicant, 0% accepted. In 2009, 3 master's awarded. Entrance requirements: Additional exam requirements/recommendations for international students: Required—TOEFL (minimum score 550 paper-based; 213 computer-based; 79 iBT). Application deadline: For fall admission, 4/1 priority date for domestic students, 3/31 priority date for international students; for spring admission, 11/1 priority date for domestic students, 8/31 priority date for international students. Applications are processed on a rolling basis. Application fee: $35. Electronic applications accepted. Expenses: Tuition: Part-time $715 per credit. Required fees: $270 per semester. Tuition and fees vary according to degree level, campus/location and program. Financial support: Career-related internships or fieldwork, scholarships/grants, and unspecified assistantships available. Support available to part-time students. Financial award application deadline: 6/30; financial award applicants required to submit FAFSA. Faculty research: Montessori education, developmentally appropriate practice, child care environment. Application contact: Tammy Manka, Assistant Director of Graduate Admissions, 866-279-9663, E-mail: tmanka@marywood.edu.

McNeese State University, Doré School of Graduate Studies, Burton College of Education, Department of Teacher Education, Program in Curriculum and Instruction, Lake Charles, LA 70609. Offers early childhood education (M Ed); elementary education (M Ed); secondary education (M Ed). Evening/weekend programs available. Faculty: 12 full-time (6 women). Students: 4 full-time (all women), 9 part-time (all women); includes 2 minority (both African Americans). In 2009, 3 master's awarded. Entrance requirements: For master's, GRE, teaching certificate. Application deadline: For fall admission, 5/15 priority date for domestic and international students; for spring admission, 10/15 priority date for domestic and international students. Applications are processed on a rolling basis. Application fee: $20 ($30 for international students). Expenses: Tuition, area resident: Full-time $2556. Tuition, state resident:

full-time $2556. Required fees: $1031. Tuition and fees vary according to course load. *Financial support:* Application deadline: 5/1. *Unit head:* Dr. Royce Zant, Head, 337-475-5404, Fax: 337-475-5398, E-mail: rzant@mcneese.edu. *Application contact:* Dr. George F. Mead, Interim Dean of Dore' School of Graduate Studies, 337-475-5396, Fax: 337-475-5397, E-mail: admissions@mcneese.edu.

Mercer University, Graduate Studies, Cecil B. Day Campus, Tift College of Education (Atlanta), Macon, GA 31207-0003. Offers curriculum and instruction (PhD); early childhood education (M Ed, MAT); educational leadership (PhD, Ed S); middle grades education (M Ed, MAT); reading education (M Ed); secondary education (M Ed, MAT); teacher leadership (Ed S). *Accreditation:* NCATE. Part-time and evening/weekend programs available. *Faculty:* 27 full-time (14 women), 6 part-time/adjunct (3 women). *Students:* 302 full-time (251 women), 543 part-time (430 women); includes 334 minority (311 African Americans, 1 American Indian/Alaska Native, 21 Asian Americans or Pacific Islanders, 1 Hispanic American), 7 international. Average age 34. In 2009, 195 master's, 20 doctorates awarded. *Degree requirements:* For master's and Ed S, research project; for doctorate, thesis/dissertation. *Entrance requirements:* For master's, GRE or MAT, minimum undergraduate GPA of 2.75; for doctorate, GRE; for Ed S, GRE or MAT, minimum GPA of 3.25, 3 years of teaching experience. Additional exam requirements/recommendations for international students: Required—TOEFL. *Application deadline:* For fall admission, 8/1 for domestic and international students; for spring admission, 12/1 for domestic and international students. Applications are processed on a rolling basis. Application fee: $25. *Expenses:* Contact institution. *Financial support:* Federal Work-Study available. Support available to part-time students. Financial award application deadline: 5/1. *Faculty research:* Educational computing, content area reading, concept learning, importance of play for young children, multicultural literature. *Unit head:* Dr. Carl R. Martray, Dean, 478-301-5397, Fax: 478-301-2280, E-mail: martray_cr@mercer.edu. *Application contact:* Dr. Allison Gilmore, Associate Dean for Graduate Teacher Education, 678-547-6330, Fax: 678-547-6055, E-mail: gilmore_a@mercer.edu.

Mercy College, School of Education, Program in Early Childhood Education, Birth-Grade 2, Dobbs Ferry, NY 10522-1189. Offers MS. Part-time and evening/weekend programs available. *Students:* 192 full-time (190 women), 229 part-time (222 women); includes 60 African Americans, 8 Asian Americans or Pacific Islanders, 57 Hispanic Americans, 1 international. Average age 31. 185 applicants, 82% accepted, 134 enrolled. In 2009, 100 master's awarded. *Degree requirements:* For master's, comprehensive exam. *Entrance requirements:* Additional exam requirements/recommendations for international students: Required—TOEFL (minimum score 600 paper-based; 250 computer-based; 100 iBT). *Application deadline:* For fall admission, 8/1 for international students. Applications are processed on a rolling basis. Application fee: $40. Electronic applications accepted. *Expenses:* Tuition: Full-time $13,158; part-time $731 per credit. Required fees: $500. Tuition and fees vary according to degree level and program. *Financial support:* In 2009–10, 9 students received support. Career-related internships or fieldwork, Federal Work-Study, scholarships/grants, and unspecified assistantships available. Support available to part-time students. Financial award applicants required to submit FAFSA. *Faculty research:* Correcting literacy problems, teaching-learning process, behavior management application for children. *Unit head:* Dr. Andrew Peiser, Interim Dean, School of Education, 914-674-7489, Fax: 914-674-7352, E-mail: apeiser@mercy.edu. *Application contact:* Mary Ellen Hoffman, Interim Associate Dean, 914-674-7334, E-mail: mhoffman@mercy.edu.

Miami University, Graduate School, School of Education and Allied Professions, Department of Teacher Education, Oxford, OH 45056. Offers elementary education (M Ed, MAT); reading education (M Ed); secondary education (M Ed, MAT), including adolescent education (MAT), elementary mathematics education (M Ed), secondary education. Part-time programs available. *Students:* 48 full-time (31 women), 70 part-time (60 women); includes 6 minority (3 African Americans, 3 Hispanic Americans), 5 international. *Entrance requirements:* For master's, GRE (MAT), minimum undergraduate GPA of 3.0 during previous 2 years or 2.75 overall. Application fee: $50. *Expenses:* Tuition, state resident: full-time $11,280. Tuition, nonresident: full-time $24,912. Required fees: $516. *Financial support:* Fellowships with full tuition reimbursements, research assistantships, teaching assistantships, career-related internships or fieldwork, Federal Work-Study, scholarships/grants, health care benefits, tuition waivers (full), and unspecified assistantships available. Financial award application deadline: 3/1. *Unit head:* Dr. James Shiveley, Chair, 513-529-6443, Fax: 513-529-4931, E-mail: shiveljm@muohio.edu. *Application contact:* Dr. Iris Johnson, Assistant Chair and Graduate Coordinator, 513-529-6443, Fax: 513-529-4931, E-mail: johnsoid@muohio.edu.

Middle Tennessee State University, College of Graduate Studies, College of Education and Behavioral Science, Department of Elementary and Special Education, Major in Curriculum and Instruction, Murfreesboro, TN 37132. Offers early childhood education (M Ed); elementary education (M Ed, Ed S); middle school education (M Ed). *Accreditation:* NCATE. Part-time and evening/weekend programs available. Postbaccalaureate distance learning degree programs offered. *Students:* 14 full-time (12 women), 126 part-time (118 women); includes 11 minority (8 African Americans, 2 Asian Americans or Pacific Islanders, 1 Hispanic American). 39 applicants, 72% accepted. In 2009, 55 master's awarded. *Degree requirements:* For master's, comprehensive exam; for Ed S, thesis. *Entrance requirements:* For master's and Ed S, GRE, MAT or PRAXIS. Additional exam requirements/recommendations for international students: Required—TOEFL (minimum score 525 paper-based; 195 computer-based; 71 iBT) or IELTS (minimum score 6). *Application deadline:* For fall admission, 8/1 priority date for domestic students. Applications are processed on a rolling basis. Application fee: $25. Electronic applications accepted. *Expenses:* Tuition, state resident: full-time $4404. Tuition, nonresident: full-time $10,956. *Financial support:* Institutionally sponsored loans available. Support available to part-time students. Financial award application deadline: 5/1. *Unit head:* Dr. Kathy Burriss, Director, 615-898-2323, Fax: 615-898-5309, E-mail: kburriss@mtsu.edu. *Application contact:* Dr. Michael Allen, Dean and Vice Provost for Research, 615-898-2840, Fax: 615-904-8020, E-mail: mallen@mtsu.edu.

Millersville University of Pennsylvania, College of Graduate and Professional Studies, School of Education, Department of Elementary and Early Childhood Education, Program in Early Childhood Education, Millersville, PA 17551-0302. Offers M Ed. Part-time and evening/weekend programs available. *Faculty:* 18 full-time (14 women), 15 part-time/adjunct (7 women). *Students:* 14 part-time (all women). Average age 31. 2 applicants, 100% accepted, 2 enrolled. In 2009, 4 master's awarded. *Degree requirements:* For master's, thesis optional. *Entrance requirements:* For master's, 3 letters of recommendation; copy of teaching certificate. Additional exam requirements/recommendations for international students: Required—TOEFL (minimum score 500 paper-based; 183 computer-based; 65 iBT) or IELTS (minimum score 6). *Application deadline:* For fall admission, 1/15 priority date for domestic and international students; for winter admission, 10/1 priority date for domestic and international students; for spring admission, 10/1 priority date for domestic and international students. Applications are processed on a rolling basis. Application fee: $40 ($50 for international students). Electronic applications accepted. *Expenses:* Tuition, state resident: full-time $6666; part-time $370 per credit. Tuition, nonresident: full-time $10,666; part-time $593 per credit. Required fees: $1578.50; $76.25 per credit. One-time fee: $60 part-time. Tuition and fees vary according to course load. *Financial support:* Research assistantships, institutionally sponsored loans and unspecified assistantships available. Support available to part-time students. Financial award application deadline: 3/15; financial award applicants required to submit FAFSA. *Faculty research:* Play, creative expression, alternative method of education, parent involvement in education. *Unit head:* Dr. Christine M. Anthony, Coordinator, 717-872-3922, Fax: 717-871-5462, E-mail: christine.anthony@millersville.edu. *Application contact:* Dr. Victor S. DeSantis, Dean of Graduate and Professional Studies, 717-872-3099, Fax: 717-872-3453, E-mail: victor.desantis@millersville.edu.

Mills College, Graduate Studies, School of Education, Oakland, CA 94613-1000. Offers child life in hospitals (MA); early childhood education (MA); education (MA), including art education, curriculum and instruction, elementary education, English education, foreign language education, mathematics education, science education, secondary education, social studies education, teaching; educational leadership (MA, Ed D); infant mental health (MA). Part-time and evening/weekend programs available. *Faculty:* 11 full-time (9 women), 16 part-time/adjunct (14 women). *Students:* 138 full-time (119 women), 55 part-time (48 women); includes 71 minority (34 African Americans, 19 Asian Americans or Pacific Islanders, 18 Hispanic Americans), 3 international. Average age 34. 210 applicants, 82% accepted, 93 enrolled. In 2009, 54 master's, 15 doctorates awarded. Terminal master's awarded for partial completion of doctoral program. *Degree requirements:* For master's, comprehensive exam. *Entrance requirements:* For doctorate, GRE General Test. Additional exam requirements/recommendations for international students: Required—TOEFL. *Application deadline:* For fall admission, 2/1 for domestic and international students; for spring admission, 11/1 for domestic and international students. Applications are processed on a rolling basis. Application fee: $50. Electronic applications accepted. *Expenses:* Tuition: Full-time $26,326; part-time $6584 per course. Required fees: $896. One-time fee: $896 part-time. Tuition and fees vary according to program. *Financial support:* In 2009–10, 188 students received support, including 186 fellowships (averaging $6,499 per year), 28 teaching assistantships with partial tuition reimbursements available (averaging $3,187 per year); career-related internships or fieldwork and scholarships/grants also available. Support available to part-time students. Financial award application deadline: 2/1; financial award applicants required to submit FAFSA. *Faculty research:* Child development, gender and education, public policy, cross-cultural development, development of literacy. Total annual research expenditures: $1.2 million. *Unit head:* Joseph Kahne, Chairperson, 510-430-3190, Fax: 510-430-3314, E-mail: grad-studies@mills.edu. *Application contact:* Jessica King, Graduate Admission Specialist, 510-430-3305, Fax: 510-430-2159, E-mail: grad-studies@mills.edu.

Minnesota State University Mankato, College of Graduate Studies, College of Education, Department of Elementary and Early Childhood Education, Mankato, MN 56001. Offers MS, Certificate. *Accreditation:* NCATE. Part-time programs available. *Students:* 2 full-time (1 woman), 62 part-time (59 women). *Degree requirements:* For master's, comprehensive exam, thesis or alternative. *Entrance requirements:* For master's, GRE General Test or MAT, minimum GPA of 3.0 during previous 2 years. Additional exam requirements/recommendations for international students: Required—TOEFL. *Application deadline:* For fall admission, 7/1 priority date for domestic students; for spring admission, 11/1 for domestic students. Applications are processed on a rolling basis. Application fee: $40. Electronic applications accepted. *Expenses:* Tuition, state resident: full-time $5364. Tuition, nonresident: full-time $8314. *Financial support:* Application deadline: 3/15. *Unit head:* Dr. Peggy Ballard, Graduate Coordinator, 507-389-1516. *Application contact:* 507-389-2321, E-mail: grad@mnsu.edu.

Minot State University, Graduate School, Program in Special Education, Minot, ND 58707-0002. Offers education of the deaf (MS); learning disabilities (MS); special education strategist (MS), including early childhood special education, severe multiple handicaps. *Accreditation:* NCATE. *Degree requirements:* For master's, comprehensive exam (for some programs), thesis (for some programs). *Entrance requirements:* For master's, GRE General Test or minimum GPA of 3.0. Additional exam requirements/recommendations for international students: Required—TOEFL. *Expenses:* Tuition, state resident: full-time $5720; part-time $283 per credit hour. Tuition, nonresident: full-time $5720; part-time $283 per credit hour. Required fees: $1034; $1034 per year. Tuition and fees vary according to course load, degree level and program. *Faculty research:* Special education team diagnostic unit; individual diagnostic assessments of mentally retarded, learning-disabled, hearing-impaired, and speech-impaired youth; educational programming for the hearing impaired.

Missouri Southern State University, Program in Early Childhood Education, Joplin, MO 64801-1595. Offers MS Ed. *Accreditation:* NCATE. *Entrance requirements:* For master's, GRE.

Missouri State University, Graduate College, College of Education, Department of Childhood Education and Family Studies, Springfield, MO 65897. Offers early childhood and family development (MS); elementary education (MS Ed). Part-time programs available. *Faculty:* 12 full-time (8 women), 1 (woman) part-time/adjunct. *Students:* 29 full-time (27 women), 68 part-time (63 women); includes 2 minority (1 African American, 1 Hispanic American). Average age 31. 17 applicants, 100% accepted, 7 enrolled. In 2009, 34 master's awarded. *Degree requirements:* For master's, comprehensive exam. *Entrance requirements:* For master's, GRE, minimum GPA of 3.0. Additional exam requirements/recommendations for international students: Required—TOEFL (minimum score 550 paper-based; 213 computer-based; 79 iBT). *Application deadline:* For fall admission, 7/20 priority date for domestic students, 5/1 for international students; for spring admission, 12/20 priority date for domestic students, 9/1 for international students. Applications are processed on a rolling basis. Application fee: $35 ($50 for international students). Electronic applications accepted. *Expenses:* Tuition, state resident: full-time $3852; part-time $214 per credit hour. Tuition, nonresident: full-time $7524; part-time $418 per credit hour. Required fees: $696; $172 per semester. Tuition and fees vary according to course level, course load, degree level and program. *Financial support:* Teaching assistantships, Federal Work-Study, institutionally sponsored loans, scholarships/grants, and unspecified assistantships available. Financial award applicants required to submit FAFSA. *Unit head:* Dr. Rebecca Swearingen, Acting Head, 417-836-3262, Fax: 417-836-8900. *Application contact:* Eric Eckert, Coordinator of Admissions and Recruitment, 417-836-5331, Fax: 417-836-6200, E-mail: ericeckert@missouristate.edu.

Montana State University Billings, College of Education, Department of Special Education, Counseling, Reading and Early Childhood, Option in Early Childhood Education, Billings, MT 59101-0298. Offers M Ed. *Accreditation:* NCATE. Part-time programs available. *Degree requirements:* For master's, thesis or professional paper and/or field experience. *Entrance requirements:* For master's, GRE General Test or MAT, minimum GPA of 3.0 (undergraduate), 3.25 (graduate). *Faculty research:* Bilingual education.

Montclair State University, The Graduate School, College of Education and Human Services, Department of Curriculum and Teaching, Montclair, NJ 07043-1624. Offers education (M Ed); educational technology (M Ed); learning disabled teacher consultant (Certificate); school library media specialist (Certificate); teaching (MAT, Certificate), including art (MAT), biological science (MAT), early childhood education (P-3) (MAT), earth science (MAT), elementary education (K-8) (MAT), English (MAT), French (MAT), health and physical education (MAT), health education (MAT), home economics (MAT), mathematics (MAT), music (MAT), physical education (MAT), physical science (MAT), social studies (MAT), Spanish (MAT), teacher of ESL (MAT), teacher of students with disabilities (MAT). Part-time and evening/weekend programs available. *Faculty:* 17 full-time (12 women), 29 part-time/adjunct (21 women). *Students:* 124 full-time (63 women), 174 part-time (126 women). Average age 31. 112 applicants, 69% accepted, 59 enrolled. In 2009, 179 master's, 2 other advanced degrees awarded. *Degree requirements:* For master's, comprehensive exam, field experience. *Entrance requirements:* For master's, GRE, 2 letters of recommendation. Additional exam requirements/recommendations for international students: Required—TOEFL (minimum score 83 computer-based), or IELTS. *Application deadline:* For fall admission, 2/15 for domestic and international students; for spring admission, 9/15 for domestic and international students. Applications are processed on a rolling basis. Application fee: $60. Electronic applications accepted. *Expenses:* Tuition, area resident: Part-time $486.74 per credit. Tuition, state resident: part-time $486.74 per credit. Tuition, nonresident: part-time $751.34 per credit. Tuition and fees vary according to degree level and program. *Financial support:* In 2009–10, 12 research assistantships with full tuition reimbursements (averaging $7,000 per year) were awarded; Federal Work-Study, scholarships/grants, and unspecified assistantships also available. Support available to part-time students. Financial award application deadline: 3/1; financial award applicants required to submit FAFSA. *Unit head:* Dr. David Schwarzer, Chairperson, 973-655-5187. *Application contact:* Amy Aiello, Director of Graduate Admissions and Operations, 973-655-5147, Fax: 973-655-7869, E-mail: graduate.school@montclair.edu.

Montclair State University, The Graduate School, College of Education and Human Services, Department of Early Childhood, Elementary and Literacy Education, Montclair, NJ 07043-1624. Offers early childhood education and teaching students with disabilities (MAT); early childhood special education (M Ed, Certificate); early childhood/elementary education (M Ed); elementary education with disabilities (MAT); elementary school teacher (Certificate); learning disabilities (Certificate); reading (MA, Certificate); reading specialist (Certificate). Part-time and evening/weekend programs available. *Faculty:* 17 full-time (15 women), 68 part-time/adjunct

Early Childhood Education

Montclair State University *(continued)*
(52 women). *Students:* 124 full-time (105 women), 274 part-time (257 women). Average age 31. 139 applicants, 65% accepted, 75 enrolled. In 2009, 85 master's awarded. *Degree requirements:* For master's, comprehensive exam, clinical experience, portfolio. *Entrance requirements:* For master's, GRE, 2 letters of recommendation. Additional exam requirements/recommendations for international students: Required—TOEFL (minimum score 83 computer-based), or IELTS. *Application deadline:* For fall admission, 6/1 for international students; for spring admission, 10/1 for international students. Applications are processed on a rolling basis. Application fee: $60. Electronic applications accepted. *Expenses:* Tuition, area resident: Part-time $486.74 per credit. Tuition, state resident: part-time $486.74 per credit. Tuition, nonresident: part-time $751.34 per credit. Tuition and fees vary according to degree level and program. *Financial support:* In 2009–10, 12 research assistantships with full tuition reimbursements (averaging $7,000 per year) were awarded; Federal Work-Study, scholarships/grants, and unspecified assistantships also available. Support available to part-time students. Financial award application deadline: 3/1; financial award applicants required to submit FAFSA. *Unit head:* Dr. Tina Jacobowitz, Chairperson, 973-655-7191. *Application contact:* Amy Aiello, Director of Graduate Admissions and Operations, 973-655-5147, Fax: 973-655-7869, E-mail: graduate.school@montclair.edu.

Mount Saint Mary College, Division of Education, Newburgh, NY 12550-3494. Offers adolescence and special education (MS Ed); adolescence education (MS Ed); childhood and special education (MS Ed); childhood education (MS Ed); literacy (5-12) (Advanced Certificate); literacy (birth-6) (Advanced Certificate); literacy and special education (MS Ed); literacy/childhood (MS Ed); middle school (5-6) (MS Ed); middle school (7-9) (MS Ed); special education (1-6) (MS Ed); special education (7-12) (MS Ed). *Accreditation:* NCATE. Part-time and evening/weekend programs available. *Faculty:* 15 full-time (13 women), 16 part-time/adjunct (10 women). *Students:* 76 full-time (63 women), 226 part-time (188 women); includes 27 minority (7 African Americans, 3 Asian Americans or Pacific Islanders, 17 Hispanic Americans). Average age 30. 141 applicants, 56% accepted, 44 enrolled. In 2009, 142 master's awarded. *Application deadline:* Applications are processed on a rolling basis. Application fee: $45. *Expenses:* Tuition: Full-time $13,356; part-time $742 per credit. Required fees: $50 per semester. *Financial support:* In 2009–10, 106 students received support. Unspecified assistantships available. Financial award application deadline: 4/15; financial award applicants required to submit FAFSA. *Faculty research:* Learning and teaching styles, computers in special education, language development. *Unit head:* Dr. Theresa Lewis, Coordinator, 845-569-3149, Fax: 845-569-3535, E-mail: tlewis@msmc.edu. *Application contact:* Dr. Theresa Lewis, Coordinator, 845-569-3149, Fax: 845-569-3535, E-mail: tlewis@msmc.edu.

Murray State University, College of Education, Department of Early Childhood and Elementary Education, Program in Interdisciplinary Early Childhood Education, Murray, KY 42071. Offers MA Ed. Part-time programs available. *Degree requirements:* For master's, portfolio. *Entrance requirements:* For master's, minimum GPA of 2.5 for conditional admittance, 3.0 for unconditional.

National-Louis University, National College of Education, Program in Early Childhood Administration, Chicago, IL 60603. Offers M Ed, CAS. *Entrance requirements:* For master's, GRE or MAT, minimum GPA of 3.0, teaching certificate; for CAS, master's degree, teaching certificate. *Expenses:* Tuition: Full-time $17,160; part-time $715 per semester hour. Tuition and fees vary according to course load, degree level, campus/location and program.

National-Louis University, National College of Education, Program in Early Childhood Education, Chicago, IL 60603. Offers early childhood curriculum and instruction specialist (M Ed, MS Ed, CAS); early childhood education (M Ed, MAT, CAS). Part-time and evening/weekend programs available. *Degree requirements:* For master's, thesis (for some programs), student teaching experience (MAT). *Entrance requirements:* For master's, GRE or MAT, minimum GPA of 3.0, teaching certificate (M Ed, MS Ed); for CAS, GRE or MAT, master's degree, teaching certificate. *Expenses:* Tuition: Full-time $17,160; part-time $715 per semester hour. Tuition and fees vary according to course load, degree level, campus/location and program. *Faculty research:* Head Start training.

Nazareth College of Rochester, Graduate Studies, Department of Education, Program in Inclusive Education-Early Childhood Level, Rochester, NY 14618-3790. Offers MS Ed. *Accreditation:* Teacher Education Accreditation Council. Part-time and evening/weekend programs available. *Entrance requirements:* For master's, minimum GPA of 3.0.

New Jersey City University, Graduate Studies and Continuing Education, Debra Cannon Partridge Wolfe College of Education, Department of Early Childhood Education, Jersey City, NJ 07305-1597. Offers MA. Part-time and evening/weekend programs available. *Faculty:* 6. *Students:* 13 full-time (all women), 67 part-time (64 women); includes 41 minority (19 African Americans, 2 Asian Americans or Pacific Islanders, 20 Hispanic Americans). Average age 34. In 2009, 52 master's awarded. *Entrance requirements:* For master's, GRE General Test or MAT. Additional exam requirements/recommendations for international students: Required—TOEFL. *Application deadline:* For fall admission, 8/1 priority date for domestic students; for spring admission, 12/1 for domestic students. Applications are processed on a rolling basis. Application fee: $0. *Expenses:* Tuition, area resident: Part-time $456.75 per credit. Tuition, nonresident: part-time $842.55 per credit. Required fees: $65 per term. *Financial support:* Career-related internships or fieldwork and unspecified assistantships available. *Unit head:* Dr. Regina Adesanya, Coordinator, 201-200-2114, E-mail: radesanya@njcu.edu. *Application contact:* Dr. Regina Adesanya, Coordinator, 201-200-2114, E-mail: radesanya@njcu.edu.

New York University, Steinhardt School of Culture, Education, and Human Development, Department of Teaching and Learning, Program in Early Childhood and Childhood Education, New York, NY 10012-1019. Offers childhood education (MA); childhood education/special education: childhood (MA); early childhood education (MA); positions of leadership: early childhood and elementary education (PhD). *Accreditation:* Teacher Education Accreditation Council. Part-time programs available. *Students:* 40 full-time (all women), 19 part-time (all women); includes 20 minority (4 African Americans, 10 Asian Americans or Pacific Islanders, 6 Hispanic Americans), 2 international. Average age 25. 140 applicants, 72% accepted, 23 enrolled. In 2009, 47 master's awarded. *Degree requirements:* For master's, thesis (for some programs); for doctorate, thesis/dissertation. *Entrance requirements:* For doctorate, GRE General Test, interview. Additional exam requirements/recommendations for international students: Required—TOEFL. *Application deadline:* For fall admission, 12/15 priority date for domestic and international students; for spring admission, 11/1 for domestic and international students. Applications are processed on a rolling basis. Application fee: $75. Electronic applications accepted. *Expenses:* Tuition: Full-time $30,528; part-time $1272 per credit. Required fees: $2177. *Financial support:* Fellowships with full and partial tuition reimbursements, career-related internships or fieldwork, Federal Work-Study, institutionally sponsored loans, scholarships/grants, tuition waivers (partial), and unspecified assistantships available. Support available to part-time students. Financial award application deadline: 2/1; financial award applicants required to submit FAFSA. *Faculty research:* Teacher evaluation and beliefs about teaching, early literacy development, language arts, child development and education, cultural differences. *Application contact:* 212-998-5030, Fax: 212-995-4328, E-mail: steinhardt.gradadmissions@nyu.edu.

New York University, Steinhardt School of Culture, Education, and Human Development, Department of Teaching and Learning, Program in Special Education, New York, NY 10012-1019. Offers childhood special education (MA); early childhood special education (MA). *Accreditation:* Teacher Education Accreditation Council. Part-time programs available. *Students:* 81 full-time (77 women), 18 part-time (15 women); includes 18 minority (3 African Americans, 11 Asian Americans or Pacific Islanders, 4 Hispanic Americans), 5 international. Average age 25. 112 applicants, 74% accepted, 34 enrolled. In 2009, 73 master's awarded. *Degree requirements:* For master's, thesis (for some programs). *Entrance requirements:* Additional exam requirements/recommendations for international students: Required—TOEFL. *Application deadline:* For fall admission, 12/15 priority date for domestic and international students. Applications are processed on a rolling basis. Application fee: $75. Electronic applications

accepted. *Expenses:* Tuition: Full-time $30,528; part-time $1272 per credit. Required fees: $2177. *Financial support:* Career-related internships or fieldwork, Federal Work-Study, institutionally sponsored loans, scholarships/grants, and tuition waivers (partial) available. Support available to part-time students. Financial award application deadline: 2/1; financial award applicants required to submit FAFSA. *Faculty research:* Special education referrals, attention deficit disorders in children, mainstreaming, curriculum-based assessment and program implementation, special education policy. *Application contact:* 212-998-5030, Fax: 212-995-4328, E-mail: steinhardt.gradadmissions@nyu.edu.

Niagara University, Graduate Division of Education, Concentration in Teacher Education, Niagara Falls, Niagara University, NY 14109. Offers early childhood and childhood education (MS Ed); middle and adolescence education (MS Ed); special education (grades 1-12) (MS Ed). *Accreditation:* NCATE. *Entrance requirements:* For master's, GRE General Test or MAT. *Expenses:* Contact institution.

Norfolk State University, School of Graduate Studies, School of Education, Department of Early Childhood and Elementary Education, Norfolk, VA 23504. Offers early childhood education (MAT); pre-elementary education (MA). *Accreditation:* NCATE. Part-time programs available. *Degree requirements:* For master's, comprehensive exam, thesis or alternative. *Entrance requirements:* For master's, PRAXIS I and II, minimum GPA of 2.5, letters of recommendation, interview. *Faculty research:* Parent involvement in education.

Northeastern State University, Graduate College, College of Education, Department of Curriculum and Instruction, Program in Early Childhood Education, Tahlequah, OK 74464-2399. Offers M Ed. Part-time and evening/weekend programs available. *Degree requirements:* For master's, thesis. *Entrance requirements:* For master's, GRE or MAT, minimum GPA of 2.5. Additional exam requirements/recommendations for international students: Required—TOEFL (minimum score 213 computer-based). Electronic applications accepted.

Northern Arizona University, Graduate College, College of Education, Department of Teaching and Learning, Flagstaff, AZ 86011. Offers early childhood education (M Ed); elementary education—certification (M Ed); elementary education—continuing professional (M Ed); secondary education—certification (M Ed); secondary education—continuing professional (M Ed). *Faculty:* 40 full-time (32 women). *Students:* 488 full-time (397 women), 599 part-time (535 women); includes 250 minority (25 African Americans, 77 American Indian/Alaska Native, 23 Asian Americans or Pacific Islanders, 125 Hispanic Americans), 2 international. Average age 29. 271 applicants, 93% accepted, 188 enrolled. In 2009, 555 master's awarded. *Degree requirements:* For master's, comprehensive exam (for some programs), thesis (for some programs). *Entrance requirements:* For master's, minimum GPA of 3.0. Additional exam requirements/recommendations for international students: Required—TOEFL (minimum score 550 paper-based; 213 computer-based; 80 iBT), IELTS (minimum score 7), or a bachelor's degree from an English-speaking university and demonstrated proficiency. *Application deadline:* For fall admission, 2/1 for domestic students, 9/1 for international students; for spring admission, 12/1 for domestic students. Applications are processed on a rolling basis. Application fee: $65. Electronic applications accepted. *Financial support:* In 2009–10, 7 teaching assistantships with partial tuition reimbursements (averaging $10,000 per year) were awarded. Financial award application deadline: 3/30. *Unit head:* Dr. Sandra J. Stone, Chair, 928-523-6166, E-mail: sandra.stone@nau.edu. *Application contact:* Dr. Sandra J. Stone, Chair, 928-523-6166, E-mail: sandra.stone@nau.edu.

Northern Illinois University, Graduate School, College of Education, Department of Teaching and Learning, De Kalb, IL 60115-2854. Offers curriculum and instruction (MS Ed, Ed D), including curriculum leadership (Ed D); elementary education (Ed D); secondary education (Ed D); early childhood education (MS Ed); elementary education (MS Ed); special education (MS Ed). Part-time and evening/weekend programs available. *Faculty:* 22 full-time (14 women), 2 part-time/adjunct (both women). *Students:* 50 full-time (38 women), 435 part-time (344 women); includes 107 minority (16 African Americans, 1 American Indian/Alaska Native, 12 Asian Americans or Pacific Islanders, 78 Hispanic Americans), 9 international. Average age 35. 154 applicants, 53% accepted, 57 enrolled. In 2009, 142 master's, 2 doctorates awarded. *Degree requirements:* For master's, comprehensive exam, thesis optional; for doctorate, thesis/dissertation, candidacy exam, dissertation defense. *Entrance requirements:* For master's, GRE General Test or MAT, minimum undergraduate GPA of 2.75; for doctorate, GRE General Test or MAT, minimum undergraduate GPA of 2.75, graduate 3.2. Additional exam requirements/recommendations for international students: Required—TOEFL (minimum score 550 paper-based; 213 computer-based). *Application deadline:* For fall admission, 6/1 for domestic students, 5/1 for international students; for spring admission, 11/1 for domestic students, 10/1 for international students. Applications are processed on a rolling basis. Application fee: $30. Electronic applications accepted. *Expenses:* Tuition, state resident: full-time $6576; part-time $274 per credit hour. Tuition, nonresident: full-time $13,152; part-time $548 per credit hour. Required fees: $1813; $75.53 per credit hour. Part-time tuition and fees vary according to course load. *Financial support:* In 2009–10, 20 research assistantships with full tuition reimbursements were awarded; fellowships with full tuition reimbursements, teaching assistantships with full tuition reimbursements, career-related internships or fieldwork, Federal Work-Study, scholarships/grants, tuition waivers (full), and unspecified assistantships also available. Support available to part-time students. Financial award applicants required to submit FAFSA. *Faculty research:* Teacher certification, stress reduction during student teaching, teaching history, portfolios in student teaching. *Unit head:* Dr. Helen Brantley, Chair, 815-753-0327, E-mail: tedur@niu.edu. *Application contact:* Gail Myers, E-mail: gmyers@niu.edu.

North Georgia College & State University, Graduate Studies, Program in Teacher Education, Dahlonega, GA 30597. Offers early childhood education (M Ed); educational leadership (Ed S); middle grades education (M Ed); secondary education (M Ed), including art education, biology education, chemistry education, English education, history education, mathematics education, physical education, science education; special education (M Ed), including interrelated special education, learning disabilities. *Accreditation:* NCATE. Part-time and evening/weekend programs available. Postbaccalaureate distance learning degree programs offered (minimal on-campus study). *Degree requirements:* For master's, comprehensive exam, thesis optional. *Entrance requirements:* For master's, GRE General Test or MAT, minimum GPA of 2.75; for Ed S, GRE General Test or MAT, 3 years of teaching experience, master's degree, minimum graduate GPA of 3.25. Electronic applications accepted. *Faculty research:* Computers and teachers' attitudes, rural versus urban teacher attitudes, teacher leadership roles, minority recruitment in teaching force.

Northwestern State University of Louisiana, Graduate Studies and Research, College of Education, Program in Early Childhood Education, Natchitoches, LA 71497. Offers early childhood education and teaching (M Ed); teacher education and professional development, specific levels and methods (M Ed).

Northwestern State University of Louisiana, Graduate Studies and Research, College of Education, Programs in Education, Natchitoches, LA 71497. Offers business and distributive education (M Ed); counseling (M Ed); early childhood education (M Ed); education (M Ed); education leadership (M Ed); educational technology (M Ed); elementary teaching (M Ed); English education (M Ed); home economics education (M Ed); mathematics education (M Ed); reading (M Ed); science education (M Ed); secondary teaching (M Ed); social sciences education (M Ed). *Degree requirements:* For master's, comprehensive exam, thesis or alternative. *Entrance requirements:* For master's, GRE General Test, minimum undergraduate GPA of 2.5.

Northwest Missouri State University, Graduate School, College of Education and Human Services, Department of Curriculum and Instruction, Program in Teaching: Early Childhood, Maryville, MO 64468-6001. Offers MS Ed. *Accreditation:* NCATE. Part-time programs available. *Faculty:* 12 full-time (all women). *Students:* 1 (woman) full-time, 6 part-time (all women). 5 applicants, 60% accepted, 2 enrolled. In 2009, 2 master's awarded. *Degree requirements:* For master's, comprehensive exam. *Entrance requirements:* For master's, GRE General Test, teaching certificate, minimum undergraduate GPA of 2.75, writing sample. Additional exam requirements/recommendations for international students: Required—TOEFL (minimum score

550 paper-based; 213 computer-based). *Application deadline:* For fall admission, 7/1 for domestic and international students; for spring admission, 11/15 for domestic and international students. Applications are processed on a rolling basis. Application fee: $0 ($50 for international students). *Expenses:* Tuition, state resident: part-time $296.34 per credit hour. Tuition, nonresident: part-time $510.43 per credit hour. *Financial support:* Teaching assistantships available. Financial award application deadline: 4/1; financial award applicants required to submit FAFSA. *Unit head:* Dr. Carolyn McCall, Director, 660-562-1236. *Application contact:* Dr. Gregory Haddock, Dean of Graduate School, 660-562-1145, Fax: 660-562-1096, E-mail: gradsch@nwmissouri.edu.

Nova Southeastern University, Fischler School of Education and Human Services, Graduate Teacher Education Program, Fort Lauderdale, FL 33314-7796. Offers athletic administration (MS); brain research (MS, Ed S); charter school education/leadership (MS); cognitive and behavioral disabilities (MS); computer science education (Ed S); computer science education (K-12) (MS); curriculum and teaching (Ed S); curriculum, instruction and technology (MS); curriculum, instruction, management and administration (Ed S); early childhood education (MS); early literacy and reading (Ed S); early literacy education (MS); education technology (MS); educational leadership (administration K–12) (MS, Ed S); educational media (Ed S); educational media (K-12) (MS); elementary education (MS, Ed S), including ESOL endorsement (MS); English education (MS, Ed S); environmental education (MS); exceptional student education (MS), including ESOL endorsement; gifted education (MS, Ed S); interdisciplinary arts education (MS); management and administration of educational programs (MS); mathematics (MS); mathematics education (Ed S); multicultural early intervention (MS); pre-kindergarten/primary (MS); preschool education (MS); reading (MS); reading and TESOL (MS); reading education (Ed S); science (MS); science education (Ed S); secondary education (MS); social studies (MS, Ed S); Spanish language (MS); special education and reading (MS); teaching and learning (MA, MS), including curriculum and instruction (MA), elementary mathematics (MA), elementary reading (MA), K-12 technology integration (MA); teaching English to speakers of other languages (MS, Ed S); technology management and administration (Ed S); urban studies education (MS). Part-time and evening/weekend programs available. Postbaccalaureate distance learning degree programs offered (minimal on-campus study). *Faculty:* 72 full-time (43 women), 385 part-time/adjunct (252 women). *Students:* 196 full-time (175 women), 1,304 part-time (1,128 women); includes 594 minority (471 African Americans, 5 American Indian/Alaska Native, 18 Asian Americans or Pacific Islanders, 100 Hispanic Americans). Average age 37. 2,610 applicants, 72% accepted, 1352 enrolled. In 2009, 836 other advanced degrees awarded. *Degree requirements:* For master's and Ed S, thesis, practicum, internship. *Entrance requirements:* For master's, MAT, GRE, CLAST, CBEST, PRAXIS I, General Knowledge Test, minimum GPA of 2.5; for Ed S, MAT or GRE, master's degree, teaching certificate, minimum GPA of 3.0. Additional exam requirements/recommendations for international students: Required—TSE (recommended, minimum score 50); Recommended—TOEFL (minimum score 550 paper-based; 213 computer-based; 80 iBT), IELTS (minimum score 6). *Application deadline:* For fall admission, 9/25 priority date for domestic and international students; for winter admission, 2/23 priority date for domestic and international students; for spring admission, 4/25 priority date for domestic and international students. Applications are processed on a rolling basis. Application fee: $50. Electronic applications accepted. *Financial support:* Federal Work-Study available. Support available to part-time students. Financial award application deadline: 4/15; financial award applicants required to submit FAFSA. *Faculty research:* School effectiveness, critical thinking, leadership skills acquisition, child education, multicultural education. *Unit head:* Dr. Ronald Kern, Dean of Academic Affairs, 800-986-3223 Ext. 7809, Fax: 954-262-3606, E-mail: rk429@nsu.nova.edu. *Application contact:* Dr. Jennifer Quinones Nottingham, Dean of Student Affairs, 800-986-3223 Ext. 1559.

Oakland University, Graduate Study and Lifelong Learning, School of Education and Human Services, Department of Human Development and Child Studies, Program in Early Childhood Education, Rochester, MI 48309-4401. Offers early childhood education (M Ed, PhD, Certificate); early mathematics education (Certificate). *Accreditation:* Teacher Education Accreditation Council. *Degree requirements:* For doctorate, thesis/dissertation. *Entrance requirements:* For master's, minimum GPA of 3.0 for unconditional admission; for doctorate, GRE General Test, minimum GPA of 3.0 for unconditional admission. Additional exam requirements/recommendations for international students: Required—TOEFL (minimum score 550 paper-based; 213 computer-based).

Oberlin College, Graduate Teacher Education Program, Oberlin, OH 44074. Offers early childhood education (M Ed); middle childhood education (M Ed). *Degree requirements:* For master's, comprehensive exam, portfolio. *Entrance requirements:* For master's, GRE General Test, PRAXIS II. *Faculty research:* Literacy learning, teacher education reform, program development.

Oglethorpe University, Division of Education, Atlanta, GA 30319-2797. Offers early childhood education (MAT). Part-time programs available. *Degree requirements:* For master's, comprehensive exam. *Entrance requirements:* For master's, GRE General Test, PRAXIS, minimum GPA of 2.8, 3 recommendations.

The Ohio State University at Lima, Graduate Programs, Lima, OH 45804. Offers early childhood education (M Ed); education (MA); middle childhood education (M Ed); social work (MSW). *Students:* 23 full-time (18 women), 83 part-time (72 women); includes 1 minority (African American). Average age 34. *Degree requirements:* For master's, comprehensive exam (for some programs), thesis (for some programs). *Entrance requirements:* For master's, GRE, minimum GPA of 3.0. Additional exam requirements/recommendations for international students: Required—TOEFL, IELTS or Michigan English Language Assessment Battery. *Application deadline:* For fall admission, 8/15 priority date for domestic students, 7/1 priority date for international students; for winter admission, 12/1 priority date for domestic students, 11/1 priority date for international students; for spring admission, 3/1 priority date for domestic students, 2/1 priority date for international students. Applications are processed on a rolling basis. Application fee: $40 ($50 for international students). Electronic applications accepted. *Expenses:* Tuition, state resident: full-time $10,155. Tuition, nonresident: full-time $25,395. Tuition and fees vary according to course load. *Unit head:* Dr. John Snyder, Dean/Director, 419-995-8481, E-mail: snyder.4@osu.edu. *Application contact:* Graduate Admissions, 614-292-9444, Fax: 614-292-3895, E-mail: domestic.grad@osu.edu.

The Ohio State University at Marion, Graduate Programs, Marion, OH 43302-5695. Offers early childhood education (pre-K to grade 3) (M Ed); integrated teaching and learning (MA); middle childhood education (grades 4-9) (M Ed); nursing (MS, PhD); social work (MSW); MS/PhD. Part-time programs available. *Students:* 49 full-time (38 women), 34 part-time (25 women); includes 2 minority (both African Americans). Average age 31. *Degree requirements:* For master's, comprehensive exam (for some programs), thesis (for some programs). *Entrance requirements:* For master's and doctorate, GRE, minimum undergraduate GPA of 3.0. Additional exam requirements/recommendations for international students: Required—TOEFL, IELTS or Michigan English Language Assessment Battery. *Application deadline:* For fall admission, 8/15 priority date for domestic students, 7/1 priority date for international students; for winter admission, 12/1 priority date for domestic students, 11/1 priority date for international students; for spring admission, 3/1 priority date for domestic students, 2/1 priority date for international students. Applications are processed on a rolling basis. Application fee: $40 ($50 for international students). Electronic applications accepted. *Expenses:* Tuition, state resident: full-time $10,155. Tuition, nonresident: full-time $25,395. Tuition and fees vary according to course load. *Unit head:* Gregory S. Rose, Dean/Director, 740-389-6786 Ext. 6218, E-mail: rose.9@osu.edu. *Application contact:* Graduate Admissions, 614-292-9444, Fax: 614-292-3895, E-mail: domestic.grad@osu.edu.

The Ohio State University–Mansfield Campus, Graduate Programs, Mansfield, OH 44906-1599. Offers early and middle childhood education (MA); early childhood education (M Ed); middle childhood education (M Ed); social work (MSW). *Faculty:* 8 full-time (4 women). *Students:* 31 full-time (29 women), 32 part-time (29 women); includes 1 minority (Asian American or Pacific Islander), 1 international. Average age 31. *Degree requirements:* For master's, comprehensive exam (for some programs), thesis (for some programs). *Entrance requirements:* For master's, GRE, minimum GPA of 3.0. Additional exam requirements/recommendations for international students: Required—TOEFL (minimum score 550 paper-based; 213 computer-based). *Application deadline:* For fall admission, 8/15 priority date for domestic students, 7/1 priority date for international students; for winter admission, 12/1 priority date for domestic students, 11/1 priority date for international students; for spring admission, 3/1 priority date for domestic students, 2/1 priority date for international students. Applications are processed on a rolling basis. Application fee: $40 ($50 for international students). Electronic applications accepted. *Expenses:* Tuition, state resident: full-time $10,155. Tuition, nonresident: full-time $25,395. Tuition and fees vary according to course load. *Financial support:* In 2009–10, 14 students received support, including 3 teaching assistantships with full tuition reimbursements available (averaging $9,000 per year); Federal Work-Study and scholarships/grants also available. Support available to part-time students. Financial award application deadline: 7/1. *Application contact:* Graduate Admissions, 614-292-9444, Fax: 614-292-3895, E-mail: domestic.grad@osu.edu.

The Ohio State University–Newark Campus, Graduate Programs, Newark, OH 43055-1797. Offers early/middle childhood education (M Ed); integrated teaching and learning (MA); social work (MSW). *Students:* 40 full-time (36 women), 64 part-time (59 women); includes 5 minority (4 African Americans, 1 Asian American or Pacific Islander), 1 international. Average age 31. *Degree requirements:* For master's, comprehensive exam (for some programs), thesis (for some programs). *Entrance requirements:* For master's, GRE, minimum GPA of 3.0. Additional exam requirements/recommendations for international students: Required—TOEFL, IELTS or Michigan English Language Assessment Battery. *Application deadline:* For fall admission, 8/15 priority date for domestic students, 7/1 priority date for international students; for winter admission, 12/1 priority date for domestic students, 11/1 priority date for international students; for spring admission, 3/1 priority date for domestic students, 2/1 priority date for international students. Applications are processed on a rolling basis. Application fee: $40 ($50 for international students). Electronic applications accepted. *Expenses:* Tuition, state resident: full-time $10,155. Tuition, nonresident: full-time $25,395. Tuition and fees vary according to course load. *Unit head:* Dr. William L. MacDonald, Dean/Director, 740-366-9333 Ext. 330, E-mail: macdonald.24@osu.edu. *Application contact:* Graduate Admissions, 614-292-9444, Fax: 614-292-3985, E-mail: domestic.grad@osu.edu.

Ohio University, Graduate College, College of Health and Human Services, School of Human and Consumer Sciences, Athens, OH 45701-2979. Offers apparel, textiles, and merchandising (MS); child development and family life (MS); early childhood education (MS); family studies (MS); food and nutrition (MS). Part-time programs available. *Faculty:* 13 full-time (9 women), 5 part-time/adjunct (all women). *Students:* 18 full-time (14 women), 7 part-time (all women); includes 2 minority (1 African American, 1 Asian American or Pacific Islander), 3 international. 21 applicants, 81% accepted, 8 enrolled. In 2009, 6 master's awarded. *Degree requirements:* For master's, comprehensive exam (for some programs), thesis. *Entrance requirements:* For master's, GRE. Additional exam requirements/recommendations for international students: Required—TOEFL (minimum score 550 paper-based; 80 iBT) or IELTS Academic (minimum score 6.5). *Application deadline:* For fall admission, 3/1 priority date for domestic and international students. Applications are processed on a rolling basis. Application fee: $50 ($55 for international students). Electronic applications accepted. *Expenses:* Tuition, state resident: full-time $7839; part-time $323 per quarter hour. Tuition, nonresident: full-time $15,831; part-time $654 per quarter hour. Required fees: $2931. *Financial support:* Research assistantships, teaching assistantships, career-related internships or fieldwork, Federal Work-Study, institutionally sponsored loans, and unspecified assistantships available. Financial award application deadline: 3/15. *Faculty research:* Diversity, developmentally appropriate activities, death and dying, gerontology, sexuality education. *Unit head:* Dr. V. Ann Paulins, Director, 740-593-2880, Fax: 740-593-0289, E-mail: paulins@ohio.edu. *Application contact:* Dr. Annette Graham, Graduate Coordinator, 740-593-0700, E-mail: grahama@ohio.edu.

Oklahoma City University, Petree College of Arts and Sciences, Division of Education and Kinesiology Exercise Studies, Programs in Education, Oklahoma City, OK 73106-1402. Offers applied behavioral studies (M Ed); early childhood education (M Ed); elementary education (M Ed). Part-time and evening/weekend programs available. *Faculty:* 2 full-time (1 woman), 3 part-time/adjunct (all women). *Students:* 25 full-time (20 women), 13 part-time (9 women); includes 10 minority (8 African Americans, 2 American Indian/Alaska Native), 5 international. Average age 32. 45 applicants, 78% accepted, 18 enrolled. In 2009, 12 master's awarded. *Degree requirements:* For master's, thesis optional. *Entrance requirements:* For master's, minimum GPA of 3.0. Additional exam requirements/recommendations for international students: Required—TOEFL (minimum score 550 paper-based). *Application deadline:* For fall admission, 8/20 for domestic students; for spring admission, 1/6 for domestic students. Applications are processed on a rolling basis. Application fee: $50 ($70 for international students). *Expenses:* Tuition: Full-time $15,930; part-time $885 per hour. *Financial support:* Fellowships with partial tuition reimbursements, career-related internships or fieldwork, Federal Work-Study, and tuition waivers (partial) available. Support available to part-time students. Financial award application deadline: 8/1; financial award applicants required to submit FAFSA. *Faculty research:* Adult literacy, cognition, reading strategies. *Unit head:* Dr. Lois Lawler-Brown, Chair, 405-208-5374, Fax: 405-208-6012, E-mail: llbrown@okcu.edu. *Application contact:* Michelle Lockhart, Director, Admissions, 800-633-7242, Fax: 405-208-5916, E-mail: gadmissions@okcu.edu.

Old Dominion University, Darden College of Education, Program in Early Childhood Education, Norfolk, VA 23529. Offers MS Ed, PhD. *Accreditation:* NCATE. Part-time and evening/weekend programs available. *Faculty:* 4 full-time (3 women), 6 part-time/adjunct (5 women). *Students:* 15 full-time (13 women), 45 part-time (44 women); includes 9 minority (6 African Americans, 1 American Indian/Alaska Native, 1 Asian American or Pacific Islander, 1 Hispanic American), 4 international. Average age 29. 35 applicants, 91% accepted. In 2009, 34 master's, 1 doctorate awarded. *Degree requirements:* For master's, comprehensive exam, thesis or alternative, written exams. *Entrance requirements:* For master's, GRE General Test, PRAXIS I, minimum undergraduate GPA of 2.5; for doctorate, GRE General Test. Additional exam requirements/recommendations for international students: Required—TOEFL. *Application deadline:* For fall admission, 7/1 for domestic students; for winter admission, 7/1 for domestic students; for spring admission, 11/1 for domestic students. Applications are processed on a rolling basis. Application fee: $40. *Expenses:* Tuition, state resident: full-time $8112; part-time $338 per credit. Tuition, nonresident: full-time $20,256; part-time $844 per credit. Required fees: $119 per semester. One-time fee: $50. *Financial support:* In 2009–10, 40 students received support, including 4 fellowships with full tuition reimbursements available (averaging $15,000 per year), 2 research assistantships with tuition reimbursements available (averaging $9,000 per year), 3 teaching assistantships with tuition reimbursements available (averaging $9,000 per year); career-related internships or fieldwork, scholarships/grants, and tuition waivers (partial) also available. Support available to part-time students. Financial award application deadline: 2/15; financial award applicants required to submit FAFSA. *Faculty research:* Child abuse, day care, parenting, discipline (positive), bullying. *Unit head:* Dr. Andrea Debruin-Parecki, Graduate Program Director, 757-683-6759, Fax: 757-683-5593, E-mail: adebruin@odu.edu. *Application contact:* Dr. Andrea Debruin-Parecki, Graduate Program Director, 757-683-6759, Fax: 757-683-5593, E-mail: adebruin@odu.edu.

Ottawa University, Graduate Studies-Arizona, Program in Education, Ottawa, KS 66067-3399. Offers community college counseling (MA); curriculum and instruction (MA); early childhood (MA); education intervention (MA); education leadership (MA); education technology (MA); Montessori early childhood education (MA); Montessori elementary education (MA); professional development (MA); school guidance counseling (MA); special education—cross categorical (MA). Programs offered in Mesa, Phoenix, Tempe and West Valley, AZ. *Accreditation:* NCATE. Part-time programs available. *Degree requirements:* For master's, thesis or alternative. *Entrance requirements:* For master's, minimum undergraduate GPA of 3.0, copy of current state certification or teaching license. Additional exam requirements/recommendations for international students: Required—TOEFL (minimum score 550 paper-based; 213 computer-based). Electronic applications accepted. *Expenses:* Contact institution.

Early Childhood Education

Our Lady of the Lake University of San Antonio, School of Professional Studies, Program in Curriculum and Instruction, San Antonio, TX 78207-4689. Offers bilingual (M Ed); early childhood education (M Ed); English as a second language (M Ed); integrated math teaching (M Ed); integrated science teaching (M Ed); master reading teacher (M Ed); master technology teacher (M Ed); reading specialist (M Ed). *Students:* 2 full-time (1 woman), 112 part-time (94 women); includes 64 minority (5 African Americans, 1 American Indian/Alaska Native, 1 Asian American or Pacific Islander, 57 Hispanic Americans). Average age 38. In 2009, 49 master's awarded. *Expenses:* Tuition: Full-time $12,330; part-time $685 per contact hour. Required fees: $139; $12 per contact hour. $57 per semester. Tuition and fees vary according to campus/location. *Unit head:* Dr. Cullen Grinnan, 210-434-6711 Ext. 8928, E-mail: ctgrinnan@lake.ollusa.edu. *Application contact:* Dr. Cullen Grinnan, 210-434-6711 Ext. 8928, E-mail: ctgrinnan@lake.ollusa.edu.

Pace University, School of Education, New York, NY 10038. Offers administration and supervision (MS Ed); adolescent education (MST); childhood education (MST); curriculum and instruction (MS); education (MST); literacy (MSE); school business management (Certificate); teaching students with disabilities (MSE); teaching visual arts (MST). *Accreditation:* NCATE. Part-time and evening/weekend programs available. *Students:* 235 full-time (177 women), 766 part-time (515 women); includes 158 minority (58 African Americans, 1 American Indian/Alaska Native, 37 Asian Americans or Pacific Islanders, 62 Hispanic Americans), 7 international. Average age 30. 332 applicants, 83% accepted, 165 enrolled. In 2009, 669 master's, 34 other advanced degrees awarded. *Degree requirements:* For master's, internship. *Entrance requirements:* For master's, interview, teaching certificate. Additional exam requirements/recommendations for international students: Required—TOEFL. *Application deadline:* For fall admission, 7/31 priority date for domestic students; for spring admission, 11/30 for domestic students. Applications are processed on a rolling basis. Application fee: $70. Electronic applications accepted. *Expenses:* Contact institution. *Financial support:* Research assistantships, career-related internships or fieldwork and Federal Work-Study available. Support available to part-time students. Financial award applicants required to submit FAFSA. *Unit head:* Dr. Harriet Feldman, Interim Dean, 212-346-1512. *Application contact:* Susan Ford-Goldschein, Director of Admissions, 212-346-1652, Fax: 212-346-1585, E-mail: gradnyc@pace.edu.

Pacific University, College of Education, Forest Grove, OR 97116-1797. Offers early childhood education (MAT); education (MAE); elementary education (MAT); high school education (MAT); middle school education (MAT); special education (MAT); visual function in learning (M Ed). *Accreditation:* NCATE. Part-time and evening/weekend programs available. *Degree requirements:* For master's, research project. *Entrance requirements:* For master's, California Basic Educational Skills Test, PRAXIS II, minimum undergraduate GPA of 2.75, 3.0 graduate. Additional exam requirements/recommendations for international students: Required—TOEFL. Electronic applications accepted. *Expenses:* Contact institution. *Faculty research:* Defining a culturally competent classroom, technology in the k-12 classroom, Socratic seminars, social studies education.

Piedmont College, School of Education, Demorest, GA 30535-0010. Offers early childhood education (MA, MAT); instruction (Ed S); secondary education (MA, MAT). Part-time and evening/weekend programs available. *Degree requirements:* For master's, thesis, field experience in the teaching classroom. *Entrance requirements:* For master's, GRE General Test, MAT, minimum undergraduate GPA of 2.5; for Ed S, minimum graduate GPA of 3.5, valid teaching certificate. Additional exam requirements/recommendations for international students: Required—TOEFL (minimum score 550 paper-based; 213 computer-based).

Pittsburg State University, Graduate School, College of Education, Department of Curriculum and Instruction, Pittsburg, KS 66762. Offers classroom reading teacher (MS); early childhood education (MS); elementary education (MS); reading (MS); reading specialist (MS); secondary education (MS); teaching (MAT). *Accreditation:* NCATE. *Degree requirements:* For master's, thesis or alternative. *Entrance requirements:* For master's, GRE or MAT. *Expenses:* Tuition, state resident: full-time $4212; part-time $176 per credit. Tuition, nonresident: full-time $11,530; part-time $480 per credit. Required fees: $940; $43 per credit. Tuition and fees vary according to course level, course load, degree level, campus/location, reciprocity agreements and student level.

Portland State University, Graduate Studies, School of Education, Department of Curriculum and Instruction, Portland, OR 97207-0751. Offers early childhood education (MA, MS); education (M Ed, MA, MS); educational leadership: curriculum and instruction (Ed D); educational media/school librarianship (MA, MS); elementary education (M Ed, MAT, MST); reading (MA, MS); secondary education (M Ed, MAT, MST). *Accreditation:* NCATE. Part-time programs available. *Degree requirements:* For master's, comprehensive exam, thesis or alternative; for doctorate, thesis/dissertation. *Entrance requirements:* For master's, California Basic Educational Skills Test, minimum GPA of 3.0 in upper-division course work or 2.75 overall. Additional exam requirements/recommendations for international students: Required—TOEFL (minimum score 550 paper-based; 213 computer-based). *Faculty research:* Early literacy, characteristics of successful teachers of at-risk students, participation of women/minorities in technology courses, selection of cooperating teachers.

Prescott College, Graduate Programs, Program in Education, Prescott, AZ 86301. Offers early childhood education (MA); early childhood special education (MA); education (MA); elementary education (MA); environmental education leadership and administration (MA); equine-assisted experiential learning (MA); school guidance counseling (MA); secondary education (MA); special education, learning disability (MA); special education, mental retardation (MA); special education, serious emotional disability (MA); student-directed independent study (MA); sustainability education (PhD). Part-time programs available. Postbaccalaureate distance learning degree programs offered (minimal on-campus study). *Faculty:* 3 full-time (1 woman), 79 part-time/adjunct (41 women). *Students:* 75 full-time (44 women), 46 part-time (36 women); includes 18 minority (3 African Americans, 3 American Indian/Alaska Native, 4 Asian Americans or Pacific Islanders, 8 Hispanic Americans), 2 international. Average age 39. 66 applicants, 67% accepted, 31 enrolled. In 2009, 22 master's, 4 doctorates awarded. *Degree requirements:* For master's, thesis, fieldwork or internship, practicum; for doctorate, thesis/dissertation. *Entrance requirements:* For master's, 2 letters of recommendation, resume; for doctorate, 3 letters of recommendation, resume, official transcripts, personal statement, program proposal. Additional exam requirements/recommendations for international students: Required—TOEFL (minimum score 500 paper-based; 173 computer-based). *Application deadline:* For fall admission, 4/15 priority date for domestic and international students; for spring admission, 9/15 priority date for domestic and international students. Applications are processed on a rolling basis. Application fee: $40. Electronic applications accepted. *Expenses:* Tuition: Full-time $14,712; part-time $613 per credit. Required fees: $50 per term. One-time fee: $150. Tuition and fees vary according to course load and degree level. *Financial support:* Career-related internships or fieldwork and Federal Work-Study available. Financial award applicants required to submit FAFSA. *Unit head:* Noel Caniglia, Chair, 928-358-3201, Fax: 928-776-5151, E-mail: ncaniglia@prescott.edu. *Application contact:* Kerstin Alicki, Admissions Counselor, 877-412-8705, Fax: 928-277-4695, E-mail: admissions@prescott.edu.

Queens College of the City University of New York, Division of Graduate Studies, Division of Education, Department of Elementary and Early Childhood Education, Flushing, NY 11367-1597. Offers bilingual education (MS Ed); childhood education (MA); early childhood education (MA); elementary education (MS Ed, AC); literacy (MS Ed). Part-time and evening/weekend programs available. *Faculty:* 31 full-time (25 women). *Students:* 98 full-time (88 women), 430 part-time (392 women). 436 applicants, 64% accepted, 212 enrolled. In 2009, 220 master's awarded. *Degree requirements:* For master's, research project; for AC, thesis optional. *Entrance requirements:* For master's, minimum GPA of 3.0. Additional exam requirements/recommendations for international students: Required—TOEFL. *Application deadline:* For fall admission, 4/1 for domestic students; for spring admission, 11/1 for domestic students. Applications are processed on a rolling basis. Application fee: $125. *Expenses:* Tuition, state resident: full-time $7360; part-time $310 per credit. Tuition, nonresident: part-time $575 per credit. One-time fee: $195 full-time; $145.25 part-time. *Financial support:* Career-related internships or fieldwork, Federal Work-Study, institutionally sponsored loans, and tuition waivers (partial) available. Support available to part-time students. Financial award application deadline: 4/1; financial award applicants required to submit FAFSA. *Unit head:* Dr. Myra Zarnowski, Chairperson, 718-997-5328. *Application contact:* Mario Caruso, Director of Graduate Admissions, 718-997-5200, Fax: 718-997-5193, E-mail: graduate_admissions@qc.edu.

Regis University, College for Professional Studies, Program in Teacher Education, Denver, CO 80221-1099. Offers adult learning, training, and development (M Ed); curriculum, instruction, and assessment (M Ed); early childhood (M Ed); educational technology (Certificate); elementary (M Ed); ESL (M Ed); fine arts (M Ed), including arts, music; instructional technology (M Ed); professional leadership (M Ed); reading (M Ed); secondary (M Ed); self-designed (M Ed); space studies (M Ed); special education (M Ed); teacher licensure (M Ed). Program also offered in Henderson and Las Vegas (Summerlin), NV. *Accreditation:* Teacher Education Accreditation Council. Part-time and evening/weekend programs available. Postbaccalaureate distance learning degree programs offered (no on-campus study). *Degree requirements:* For master's, thesis. *Entrance requirements:* For master's, resume, minimum GPA of 2.75, criminal background check. Additional exam requirements/recommendations for international students: Required—TOEFL (minimum score 213 computer-based), TWE (minimum score 5). Electronic applications accepted. *Faculty research:* Issues of equity in the middle school classroom, professional learning communities, school reform, socialinguistic and discursive obstacles to student integration, inclusive language arts curriculum.

Reinhardt University, Program in Early Childhood Education, Waleska, GA 30183-2981. Offers MAT. Part-time and evening/weekend programs available. Postbaccalaureate distance learning degree programs offered. *Faculty:* 3 full-time (all women), 1 (woman) part-time/adjunct. *Students:* 43 full-time (39 women), 1 (woman) part-time; includes 5 minority (4 African Americans, 1 Hispanic American). Average age 31. 54 applicants, 87% accepted. *Degree requirements:* For master's, comprehensive exam. *Entrance requirements:* For master's, GACE, background check. Additional exam requirements/recommendations for international students: Required—TOEFL. *Application deadline:* For fall admission, 5/7 for domestic and international students. Applications are processed on a rolling basis. Application fee: $25. Electronic applications accepted. *Expenses:* Tuition: Full-time $16,500; part-time $325 per credit hour. One-time fee: $100. Tuition and fees vary according to course load and program. *Financial support:* Application deadline: 5/1. *Unit head:* Nancy Carter, Coordinator, 770-720-5948, Fax: 770-720-9173, E-mail: ntc@reinhardt.edu. *Application contact:* Ray Schumacher, Admissions Counselor, 770-993-6971, Fax: 770-475-0263, E-mail: res@reinhardt.edu.

Rhode Island College, School of Graduate Studies, Feinstein School of Education and Human Development, Department of Elementary Education, Providence, RI 02908-1991. Offers early childhood education (M Ed); elementary education (M Ed, MAT); reading (M Ed). *Accreditation:* NCATE. Part-time and evening/weekend programs available. *Faculty:* 10 full-time (6 women), 7 part-time/adjunct (5 women). *Students:* 15 full-time (12 women), 40 part-time (all women); includes 1 minority (Asian American or Pacific Islander), 1 international. Average age 32. In 2009, 47 master's awarded. *Degree requirements:* For master's, comprehensive exam (for some programs), comprehensive assessment. *Entrance requirements:* For master's, GRE General Test or MAT, PRAXIS II (elementary content knowledge), undergraduate transcripts; minimum undergraduate GPA of 3.0; copy of teaching certificate (when applicable); 3 letters of recommendation. Additional exam requirements/recommendations for international students: Recommended—TOEFL (minimum score 550 paper-based; 213 computer-based; 79 iBT). *Application deadline:* For fall admission, 3/15 for domestic students; for spring admission, 11/1 for domestic students. Applications are processed on a rolling basis. Application fee: $50. *Expenses:* Tuition, state resident: full-time $7440; part-time $310 per credit hour. Tuition, nonresident: full-time $14,784; part-time $616 per credit hour. Required fees: $552; $20 per credit. $70 per term. *Financial support:* Teaching assistantships with full tuition reimbursements, Federal Work-Study, scholarships/grants, and health care benefits available. Support available to part-time students. Financial award application deadline: 5/15; financial award applicants required to submit FAFSA. *Unit head:* Dr. Patricia Cordeiro, Chair, 401-456-8016. *Application contact:* Graduate Studies, 401-456-8700.

Rivier College, School of Graduate Studies, Department of Education, Nashua, NH 03060. Offers curriculum and instruction (M Ed); early childhood education (M Ed); educational administration (M Ed); educational studies (M Ed); elementary education (M Ed); elementary education and general special education (M Ed); emotional and behavioral disorders (M Ed); general social education (M Ed); leadership and learning (Ed D, CAGS); learning disabilities (M Ed); learning disabilities and reading (M Ed); mental health counseling (MA); reading (M Ed); school counseling (M Ed). Part-time and evening/weekend programs available. *Faculty:* 13 full-time (9 women), 38 part-time/adjunct (25 women). *Students:* 87 full-time (78 women), 293 part-time (246 women); includes 10 minority (3 African Americans, 4 Asian Americans or Pacific Islanders, 3 Hispanic Americans). Average age 38. 182 applicants, 82% accepted, 72 enrolled. In 2009, 110 master's, 18 other advanced degrees awarded. *Degree requirements:* For master's, comprehensive exam (for some programs), internships. *Entrance requirements:* For master's, GRE General Test or MAT. *Application deadline:* Applications are processed on a rolling basis. Application fee: $25. *Expenses:* Tuition: Part-time $447 per credit. *Financial support:* Available to part-time students. Application deadline: 2/1. *Unit head:* Dr. Patricia Howson, Chairman, 603-897-8562, E-mail: phowson@rivier.edu. *Application contact:* Mathew Kittredge, Director of Graduate Admissions, 603-897-8129, Fax: 603-897-8810, E-mail: mkittredge@rivier.edu.

Roberts Wesleyan College, Division of Teacher Education, Rochester, NY 14624-1997. Offers adolescence education (M Ed); childhood and special education (M Ed); literacy education (M Ed); urban education (M Ed). Part-time and evening/weekend programs available. *Degree requirements:* For master's, thesis.

Roosevelt University, Graduate Division, College of Education, Department of Teaching and Learning, Chicago, IL 60605. Offers early childhood education (MA); elementary education (MA); special education (MA).

Rutgers, The State University of New Jersey, New Brunswick, Graduate School of Education, Department of Learning and Teaching, Program in Early Childhood/Elementary Education, Piscataway, NJ 08854-8097. Offers Ed M, Ed D. Part-time programs available. Terminal master's awarded for partial completion of doctoral program. *Degree requirements:* For master's, comprehensive exam (for some programs); for doctorate, thesis/dissertation, qualifying exam. *Entrance requirements:* For master's, GRE General Test, minimum GPA of 3.0; for doctorate, GRE General Test, minimum GPA of 3.5. Additional exam requirements/recommendations for international students: Required—TOEFL. Electronic applications accepted.

Saginaw Valley State University, College of Education, Program in Early Childhood Education, University Center, MI 48710. Offers MAT. *Accreditation:* NCATE. Part-time and evening/weekend programs available. *Students:* 7 full-time (all women), 146 part-time (141 women); includes 2 minority (1 African American, 1 Hispanic American). Average age 31. 26 applicants, 100% accepted, 20 enrolled. In 2009, 35 master's awarded. *Degree requirements:* For master's, practicum. *Entrance requirements:* For master's, minimum GPA of 3.0, teaching certificate. Additional exam requirements/recommendations for international students: Required—TOEFL (minimum score 525 paper-based; 197 computer-based; 71 iBT). *Application deadline:* Applications are processed on a rolling basis. Application fee: $25. Electronic applications accepted. *Financial support:* Federal Work-Study and scholarships/grants available. Support available to part-time students. Financial award applicants required to submit FAFSA. *Unit head:* Dr. Steve P. Barbus, Dean, 989-964-6067, Fax: 989-790-4385, E-mail: barbus@svsu.edu. *Application contact:* Dr. Steve P. Barbus, Dean, 989-964-6067, Fax: 989-790-4385, E-mail: barbus@svsu.edu.

St. Bonaventure University, School of Graduate Studies, School of Education, Literacy Programs, St. Bonaventure, NY 14778-2284. Offers adolescent literacy 5-12 (MS Ed); childhood literacy B-6 (MS Ed). *Accreditation:* NCATE. Part-time and evening/weekend programs available. *Faculty:* 2 full-time (1 woman), 1 (woman) part-time/adjunct. *Students:* 37 full-time (33 women), 33 part-time (31 women); includes 1 minority (Hispanic American). Average age 27. 37

applicants, 86% accepted, 26 enrolled. In 2009, 45 master's awarded. *Degree requirements:* For master's, comprehensive exam, thesis optional. *Entrance requirements:* For master's, interview, writing sample, minimum undergraduate GPA of 3.0. Additional exam requirements/recommendations for international students: Required—TOEFL. *Application deadline:* For fall admission, 8/1 for domestic students; for spring admission, 11/1 priority date for domestic students. Applications are processed on a rolling basis. Application fee: $30. Electronic applications accepted. *Expenses:* Tuition: Full-time $11,700; part-time $650 per credit. *Financial support:* In 2009–10, 9 research assistantships with full and partial tuition reimbursements were awarded; scholarships/grants also available. Support available to part-time students. Financial award application deadline: 4/15; financial award applicants required to submit FAFSA. *Faculty research:* Children's literary tastes, reading diagnosis. *Unit head:* Dr. Joseph Zimmer, Director, 716-375-2388. *Application contact:* Bruce Campbell, 716-375-2429, E-mail: gradsch@sbu.edu.

St. John's University, The School of Education, Department of Curriculum and Instruction, Program in Early Childhood Education, Queens, NY 11439. Offers MS Ed. *Students:* 12 full-time (all women), 29 part-time (28 women); includes 19 minority (11 African Americans, 2 Asian Americans or Pacific Islanders, 6 Hispanic Americans). Average age 29. 37 applicants, 78% accepted, 15 enrolled. In 2009, 15 master's awarded. *Degree requirements:* For master's, comprehensive exam. *Entrance requirements:* For master's, minimum GPA of 3.0, 2 letters of recommendation, qualification for the New York State provisional (initial) teaching certificate. Additional exam requirements/recommendations for international students: Required—TOEFL (minimum score 500 paper-based; 173 computer-based; 61 iBT), IELTS (minimum score 5.5). *Application deadline:* For fall admission, 4/1 priority date for domestic students, 6/1 priority date for international students; for spring admission, 11/1 priority date for domestic and international students. Applications are processed on a rolling basis. Application fee: $70. Electronic applications accepted. *Expenses:* Tuition: Full-time $16,290; part-time $905 per credit. Required fees: $300; $150 per semester. Tuition and fees vary according to program. *Financial support:* Research assistantships available. *Faculty research:* Improving children's learning in math, science and technology; health and nutrition education to prevent obesity; oral language and literacy development in diverse populations; home-school collaborations in literacy among young ELLS; multicultural and international education; bilingual education; at-risk children; arts education; parent, home and community partnership; special needs and inclusive education. *Unit head:* Dr. Peter Quinn, Chair, 718-990-6775, Fax: 718-990-3803, E-mail: quinnp@stjohns.edu. *Application contact:* Dr. Kelly K. Ronayne, Associate Dean for Graduate Admissions, 718-990-2303, Fax: 718-990-2343, E-mail: graded@stjohns.edu.

St. Joseph's College, Long Island Campus, Program in Infant/Toddler Early Childhood Special Education, Patchogue, NY 11772-2399. Offers MA. Part-time and evening/weekend programs available. *Degree requirements:* For master's, thesis, full-time practicum experience. *Entrance requirements:* For master's, 1 course in child development, 2 courses in special education, minimum undergraduate GPA of 3.0, New York state teaching certificate, interview. Additional exam requirements/recommendations for international students: Required—TOEFL (minimum score 550 paper-based; 213 computer-based).

St. Joseph's College, New York, Graduate Programs, Program in Education, Field of Infant/Toddler Early Childhood Special Education, Brooklyn, NY 11205-3688. Offers MA.

Saint Mary's College of California, Kalmanovitz School of Education, Program in Early Childhood Education and Montessori Teacher Training, Moraga, CA 94556. Offers M Ed, MA. Part-time and evening/weekend programs available. *Faculty:* 2 full-time (both women), 2 part-time/adjunct (both women). *Students:* 15 full-time (all women), 30 part-time (all women); includes 12 minority (2 African Americans, 10 Asian Americans or Pacific Islanders), 4 international. Average age 25. In 2009, 3 master's awarded. *Degree requirements:* For master's, thesis or alternative. *Entrance requirements:* For master's, interview, minimum GPA of 3.0. *Application deadline:* Applications are processed on a rolling basis. Application fee: $50. *Expenses:* Tuition: Full-time $35,087; part-time $956 per credit hour. One-time fee: $50 full-time. Part-time tuition and fees vary according to course level, course load, degree level, campus/location and program. *Financial support:* Career-related internships or fieldwork available. Support available to part-time students. Financial award application deadline: 2/15. *Unit head:* Patricia Chambers, Coordinator, 925-631-4036, Fax: 925-376-8379, E-mail: pchambers@stmarys-ca.edu. *Application contact:* Jane Joyce, Coordinator, Recruitment and Admissions, 925-631-4700, Fax: 925-376-8379, E-mail: soereq@stmarys-ca.edu.

Saint Xavier University, Graduate Studies, School of Education, Chicago, IL 60655-3105. Offers counseling (MA); counselor education (MA); curriculum and instruction (MA); early childhood education (MA); education (CAS); educational administration (MA); elementary education (MA); field-based education (MA); general educational studies (MA); individualized program (MA); learning disabilities (MA); reading (MA); secondary education (MA). *Accreditation:* NCATE. Part-time and evening/weekend programs available. *Degree requirements:* For master's, thesis or project. *Entrance requirements:* For master's, minimum GPA of 3.0. *Expenses:* Contact institution.

Salem College, Department of Education, Winston-Salem, NC 27101. Offers early education and leadership (MAT); elementary education (MAT); English as a second language (MAT); language and literacy (M Ed); middle school education (MAT); secondary education (MAT); special education (MAT). *Accreditation:* NCATE. Part-time and evening/weekend programs available. *Degree requirements:* For master's, comprehensive exam, practicum (MAT), project (M Ed), oral and written comprehensive exams. *Entrance requirements:* For master's, GRE, minimum GPA of 2.5. *Faculty research:* Content area reading strategies, literacy development, brain compatible instruction.

Salem State College, School of Graduate Studies, Program in Early Childhood Education, Salem, MA 01970-5353. Offers M Ed. *Accreditation:* NCATE. Part-time and evening/weekend programs available. *Students:* 6 full-time (all women), 47 part-time (all women); includes 2 minority (1 African American, 1 Asian American or Pacific Islander), 2 international. Average age 33. 9 applicants, 100% accepted, 9 enrolled. In 2009, 13 master's awarded. *Entrance requirements:* For master's, GRE or MAT. Additional exam requirements/recommendations for international students: Required—TOEFL (minimum score 550 paper-based; 80 iBT), or IELTS (minimum score 5.5). *Application deadline:* For fall admission, 4/1 for domestic students; for spring admission, 10/1 for domestic students. Applications are processed on a rolling basis. Application fee: $50. *Expenses:* Tuition, state resident: full-time $2520; part-time $275 per credit hour. Tuition, nonresident: full-time $4140; part-time $365 per credit hour. Required fees: $2430. *Financial support:* In 2009–10, 14 students received support. Career-related internships or fieldwork, Federal Work-Study, scholarships/grants, and unspecified assistantships available. Support available to part-time students. Financial award application deadline: 4/1; financial award applicants required to submit FAFSA. *Unit head:* Dr. Clarke Fowler, Coordinator, 978-542-6310, Fax: 978-542-7215, E-mail: rfowler@salemstate.edu. *Application contact:* Dr. Lee A. Brossoit, Assistant Dean of Graduate Admissions, 978-542-6673, Fax: 978-542-7215, E-mail: lbrossoit@salemstate.edu.

Samford University, Orlean Bullard Beeson School of Education and Professional Studies, Birmingham, AL 35229. Offers early childhood education (Ed S); early childhood/elementary education (MS Ed); educational administration (Ed S); educational leadership (Ed D); elementary education (Ed S); gifted education (MS Ed); instructional leadership (MS Ed); secondary collaboration (MS Ed); M Div/MS Ed. *Accreditation:* NCATE. Part-time programs available. *Faculty:* 11 full-time (8 women), 9 part-time/adjunct (5 women). *Students:* 16 full-time (13 women), 173 part-time (131 women); includes 47 minority (46 African Americans, 1 American Indian/Alaska Native), 1 international. Average age 40. 15 applicants, 100% accepted, 15 enrolled. In 2009, 52 master's, 11 doctorates, 27 other advanced degrees awarded. *Degree requirements:* For master's, comprehensive exam; for doctorate, comprehensive exam, thesis/dissertation. *Entrance requirements:* For master's, GRE or MAT, minimum GPA of 3.0; for doctorate, minimum GPA of 3.7; for Ed S, GRE, master's degree, teaching certificate, minimum GPA of 3.25. Additional exam requirements/recommendations for international students: Required—TOEFL (minimum score 550 paper-based; 213 computer-based). *Application deadline:* Applications are processed on a rolling basis. Application fee: $25. *Expenses:* Tuition: Full-time $26,660; part-time $595 per credit hour. Required fees: $110 per semester. *Financial support:* In 2009–10, 127 students received support; research assistantships, career-related internships or fieldwork, Federal Work-Study, scholarships/grants, and tuition waivers (partial) available. Support available to part-time students. Financial award applicants required to submit FAFSA. *Faculty research:* School law, the characteristics of beginning teachers, the nature of school reform, school culture, quality improvement in education, K-12 student achievement. *Unit head:* Dr. Jean Ann Box, Dean, 205-726-2559, E-mail: jabox@samford.edu. *Application contact:* Dr. Maurice Persall, Director, Graduate Office, 205-726-2019, E-mail: jmpersal@samford.edu.

San Francisco State University, Division of Graduate Studies, College of Education, Department of Elementary Education, Program in Early Childhood Education, San Francisco, CA 94132-1722. Offers MA. *Accreditation:* NCATE.

Santa Clara University, School of Education and Counseling Psychology, Department of Education, Program in Special Education, Santa Clara, CA 95053. Offers early childhood special education (Certificate); special education (MA), including early childhood education, mild moderate disabilities. Part-time and evening/weekend programs available. *Students:* 8 full-time (7 women), 71 part-time (63 women); includes 24 minority (1 African American, 15 Asian Americans or Pacific Islanders, 8 Hispanic Americans), 3 international. Average age 39. 48 applicants, 85% accepted, 39 enrolled. In 2009, 11 master's, 28 other advanced degrees awarded. *Degree requirements:* For master's, comprehensive exam. *Entrance requirements:* For master's, GRE or MAT, minimum GPA of 3.0. Additional exam requirements/recommendations for international students: Required—TOEFL. *Application deadline:* Applications are processed on a rolling basis. *Expenses:* Contact institution. *Financial support:* Fellowships, Federal Work-Study, institutionally sponsored loans, and scholarships/grants available. Support available to part-time students. Financial award application deadline: 5/15; financial award applicants required to submit FAFSA. *Unit head:* Dr. Ruth E. Cook, Interim Chair, 408-554-4119. *Application contact:* Dr. Ruth E. Cook, Interim Chair, 408-554-4119.

Shippensburg University of Pennsylvania, School of Graduate Studies, College of Education and Human Services, Department of Teacher Education, Shippensburg, PA 17257-2299. Offers curriculum and instruction (M Ed), including biology, early childhood education, elementary education, English, foreign languages, geography/earth science, history, mathematics, middle school education; reading (M Ed). *Accreditation:* NCATE. Part-time and evening/weekend programs available. *Degree requirements:* For master's, comprehensive exam (for some programs), thesis optional, practicum or internship (for some programs). *Entrance requirements:* For master's, MAT (if GPA less than 2.75), interview, 3 letters of recommendation, writing sample of teaching background and future goals. Additional exam requirements/recommendations for international students: Required—TOEFL (minimum score 560 paper-based; 220 computer-based); Recommended—IELTS (minimum score 6). Electronic applications accepted.

Siena Heights University, Graduate College, Program in Teacher Education, Concentration in Early Childhood Education, Adrian, MI 49221-1796. Offers Montessori education (MA). Part-time programs available. *Degree requirements:* For master's, thesis, presentation. *Entrance requirements:* For master's, interview, minimum GPA of 3.0.

South Carolina State University, School of Graduate Studies, Department of Education, Orangeburg, SC 29117-0001. Offers early childhood and special education (M Ed); early childhood education (MAT); elementary education (M Ed, MAT); engineering (MAT); general science (MAT); mathematics (MAT); secondary education (M Ed), including biology education, business education, counselor education, English education, home economics education, industrial education, mathematics education, science education, social studies education; special education (M Ed), including emotionally handicapped, learning disabilities, mentally handicapped. *Accreditation:* NCATE. Part-time and evening/weekend programs available. *Degree requirements:* For master's, thesis optional, departmental qualifying exam. *Entrance requirements:* For master's, GRE General Test, NTE, interview, teaching certificate. Electronic applications accepted. *Expenses:* Tuition, state resident: part-time $470 per credit hour. Tuition, nonresident: part-time $924 per credit hour. *Faculty research:* Critical thinking, child abuse, stress, test-taking skills, conflict resolution, mainstreaming.

Southern Oregon University, Graduate Studies, School of Education, Ashland, OR 97520. Offers elementary education (MA Ed, MS Ed), including classroom teacher, early childhood, handicapped learner, reading, supervision; secondary education (MA Ed, MS Ed), including classroom teacher, handicapped learner, reading, supervision; teaching (MAT). *Degree requirements:* For master's, thesis optional. *Entrance requirements:* For master's, GRE General Test, minimum GPA of 3.0. Electronic applications accepted.

Southwestern Oklahoma State University, College of Professional and Graduate Studies, School of Behavioral Sciences and Education, Specialization in Early Childhood Education, Weatherford, OK 73096-3098. Offers M Ed. M Ed distance learning degree program offered to Oklahoma residents only. *Accreditation:* NCATE. Part-time and evening/weekend programs available. *Degree requirements:* For master's, exam. *Entrance requirements:* For master's, GRE General Test or minimum undergraduate GPA of 3.0. Additional exam requirements/recommendations for international students: Required—TOEFL.

Springfield College, Graduate Programs, Program in Education, Springfield, MA 01109-3797. Offers counseling and secondary education (M Ed, MS); early childhood education (M Ed, MS); education (M Ed, MS); educational administration (M Ed, MS); educational studies (M Ed, MS); elementary education (M Ed, MS); secondary education (M Ed, MS); special education (M Ed, MS). Part-time and evening/weekend programs available. *Entrance requirements:* Additional exam requirements/recommendations for international students: Required—TOEFL (minimum score 550 paper-based; 213 computer-based). Electronic applications accepted. *Expenses:* Tuition: Full-time $19,800; part-time $825 per credit hour. Required fees: $150.

Spring Hill College, Graduate Programs, Program in Education, Mobile, AL 36608-1791. Offers early childhood education (MAT, MS Ed); educational theory (MS Ed); elementary education (MAT, MS Ed); secondary education (MAT, MS Ed). Part-time programs available. *Faculty:* 3 full-time (all women), 3 part-time/adjunct (2 women). *Students:* 9 full-time (7 women), 26 part-time (21 women); includes 6 minority (5 African Americans, 1 Asian American or Pacific Islander). Average age 31. 33 applicants, 48% accepted, 9 enrolled. In 2009, 14 master's awarded. *Degree requirements:* For master's, comprehensive exam, completion of program within 6 calendar years of entrance into graduate studies at Spring Hill. *Entrance requirements:* For master's, GRE, MAT, NTE, or PRAXIS, bachelor's degree. Additional exam requirements/recommendations for international students: Required—TOEFL (minimum score 550 paper-based; 213 computer-based; 80 iBT), IELTS (minimum score 6.5). *Application deadline:* For fall admission, 8/1 priority date for domestic and international students; for spring admission, 12/1 priority date for domestic and international students. Applications are processed on a rolling basis. Application fee: $25 ($35 for international students). Electronic applications accepted. *Expenses:* Contact institution. *Financial support:* In 2009–10, 24 students received support. Career-related internships or fieldwork, institutionally sponsored loans, and scholarships/grants available. Support available to part-time students. Financial award applicants required to submit FAFSA. *Unit head:* Dr. Ann A. Adams, Chair of Teacher Education, 251-380-3479, Fax: 251-460-2184, E-mail: aadams@shc.edu. *Application contact:* Donna B. Tarasavage, Director of Marketing and Recruiting, Graduate and Continuing Studies, 251-380-3067, Fax: 251-460-2190, E-mail: dtarasavage@shc.edu.

State University of New York at Binghamton, Graduate School, School of Education, Program in Childhood Education, Binghamton, NY 13902-6000. Offers MS Ed. *Accreditation:* Teacher Education Accreditation Council. Part-time and evening/weekend programs available. *Students:* 37 full-time (31 women), 6 part-time (all women); includes 3 minority (1 Asian American or Pacific Islander, 2 Hispanic Americans). Average age 27. 36 applicants, 67% accepted, 20 enrolled. In 2009, 5 master's awarded. *Entrance requirements:* For master's, GRE General Test. Additional exam requirements/recommendations for international students: Required—TOEFL (minimum score 550 paper-based; 213 computer-based; 80 iBT). *Application*

Early Childhood Education

State University of New York at Binghamton (continued)
deadline: For fall admission, 2/1 priority date for domestic and international students; for spring admission, 10/15 priority date for domestic and international students. Applications are processed on a rolling basis. Application fee: $60. Electronic applications accepted. *Financial support:* Fellowships, research assistantships, teaching assistantships, career-related internships or fieldwork, Federal Work-Study, institutionally sponsored loans, scholarships/grants, health care benefits, tuition waivers (full), and unspecified assistantships available. Financial award application deadline: 2/15; financial award applicants required to submit FAFSA. *Unit head:* Dr. Jenny Gordon, Coordinator, 607-777-4184, E-mail: gordon@binghamton.edu. *Application contact:* Victoria Williams, Recruiting and Admissions Coordinator, 607-777-2151, Fax: 607-777-2501, E-mail: vwilliam@binghamton.edu.

State University of New York at New Paltz, Graduate School, School of Education, Department of Educational Studies, Program in Special Education, New Paltz, NY 12561. Offers adolescence (7-12) (MS Ed); adolescence special education and literacy education (MS Ed); childhood (1-6) (MS Ed); childhood special education and literacy education (MS Ed); early childhood (B-2) (MS Ed). *Accreditation:* NCATE. Part-time and evening/weekend programs available. *Faculty:* 5 full-time (3 women), 7 part-time/adjunct (all women). *Students:* 33 full-time (30 women), 73 part-time (58 women); includes 4 minority (1 African American, 1 American Indian/Alaska Native, 1 Asian American or Pacific Islander, 1 Hispanic American). Average age 31. 53 applicants, 45% accepted, 19 enrolled. In 2009, 48 master's awarded. *Degree requirements:* For master's, portfolio. *Entrance requirements:* For master's, minimum GPA of 3.0 (3.2 for special education and literacy programs), NYS teaching certificate. Additional exam requirements/recommendations for international students: Required—TOEFL (minimum score 550 paper-based; 213 computer-based; 80 iBT), IELTS (minimum score 6.5). *Application deadline:* For fall admission, 3/15 priority date for domestic students, 3/15 for international students; for spring admission, 11/1 for domestic and international students. Application fee: $50. Electronic applications accepted. *Financial support:* In 2009–10, 1 student received support, including 1 fellowship (averaging $9,000 per year); career-related internships or fieldwork, Federal Work-Study, and institutionally sponsored loans also available. Financial award application deadline: 8/1; financial award applicants required to submit FAFSA. *Faculty research:* Grouping formats. *Unit head:* Dr. Spencer Salend, Coordinator, 845-257-2831, E-mail: salends@newpaltz.edu. *Application contact:* Dr. Catherine Whittaker, Coordinator, 845-257-2831, E-mail: whittakc@newpaltz.edu.

State University of New York College at Cortland, Graduate Studies, School of Education, Program in Childhood/Early Child Education, Cortland, NY 13045. Offers MS Ed, MST. *Accreditation:* NCATE.

State University of New York College at Geneseo, Graduate Studies, School of Education, Program in Early Childhood Education, Geneseo, NY 14454-1401. Offers MS Ed. Part-time and evening/weekend programs available. *Faculty:* 3 full-time (all women). *Students:* 1 (woman) full-time, 4 part-time (all women). Average age 24. 6 applicants, 100% accepted, 5 enrolled. In 2009, 2 master's awarded. *Degree requirements:* For master's, thesis optional. *Application deadline:* For fall admission, 3/1 priority date for domestic students; for spring admission, 10/1 for domestic students. Application fee: $50. *Expenses:* Tuition, state resident: full-time $8370; part-time $349 per credit hour. Tuition, nonresident: full-time $13,250; part-time $552 per credit hour. Required fees: $700.52; $29 per credit hour. *Financial support:* Scholarships/grants, health care benefits, and unspecified assistantships available. Support available to part-time students. Financial award application deadline: 4/1; financial award applicants required to submit FAFSA. *Unit head:* Dr. Osman Alawiye, Dean/Chairperson, 585-245-5560, Fax: 585-245-5220, E-mail: alawiyeo@geneseo.edu. *Application contact:* Dr. Susan Salmon, Assistant to the Dean/Graduate Liaison, 585-245-5560, Fax: 585-245-5220, E-mail: salmon@geneseo.edu.

State University of New York College at Potsdam, School of Education and Professional Studies, Program in Curriculum and Instruction, Potsdam, NY 13676. Offers childhood education (MST); childhood instruction (MST); curriculum and instruction (MS Ed). *Accreditation:* NCATE. Postbaccalaureate distance learning degree programs offered (minimal on-campus study). *Faculty:* 14 full-time (12 women), 8 part-time/adjunct (4 women). *Students:* 209 full-time (157 women), 55 part-time (49 women); includes 9 minority (4 African Americans, 2 American Indian/Alaska Native, 2 Asian Americans or Pacific Islanders, 1 Hispanic American), 138 international. 130 applicants, 85% accepted, 90 enrolled. In 2009, 188 master's awarded. *Degree requirements:* For master's, thesis. *Entrance requirements:* For master's, minimum GPA of 2.75 in last 60 credit hours of undergraduate study. Additional exam requirements/recommendations for international students: Required—TOEFL (minimum score 550 paper-based; 213 computer-based; 80 iBT), IELTS (minimum score 6). *Application deadline:* For fall admission, 4/1 priority date for domestic and international students; for spring admission, 10/15 priority date for domestic and international students. Applications are processed on a rolling basis. Application fee: $50. *Expenses:* Tuition, state resident: full-time $8370; part-time $349 per credit hour. Tuition, nonresident: full-time $13,250; part-time $552 per credit hour. Required fees: $942; $38.70 per credit hour. *Financial support:* Federal Work-Study, scholarships/grants, and unspecified assistantships available. Support available to part-time students. Financial award application deadline: 3/1; financial award applicants required to submit FAFSA. *Unit head:* Dr. Kathleen Valentine, Chairperson, 315-267-3314, Fax: 315-267-4802, E-mail: valentkm@potsdam.edu. *Application contact:* Peter Cutler, Graduate Admissions Counselor, 315-267-3154, Fax: 315-267-4802, E-mail: cutlerpj@potsdam.edu.

State University of New York College at Potsdam, School of Education and Professional Studies, Program in Special Education, Potsdam, NY 13676. Offers birth-grade 2 (MS Ed); grades 1-6 (MS Ed); grades 5-9 (MS Ed); grades 7-12 (MS Ed). *Accreditation:* NCATE. *Faculty:* 3 full-time (1 woman), 5 part-time/adjunct (4 women). *Students:* 19 full-time (17 women), 6 part-time (4 women); includes 2 minority (1 African American, 1 American Indian/Alaska Native). 18 applicants, 100% accepted, 16 enrolled. In 2009, 11 master's awarded. *Degree requirements:* For master's, thesis optional, culminating experience. *Entrance requirements:* For master's, minimum GPA of 3.0 in last 60 hours of undergraduate course work. Additional exam requirements/recommendations for international students: Required—TOEFL (minimum score 550 paper-based; 213 computer-based; 80 iBT), IELTS (minimum score 6). *Application deadline:* For fall admission, 4/1 priority date for domestic and international students. Applications are processed on a rolling basis. Application fee: $50. *Expenses:* Tuition, state resident: full-time $8370; part-time $349 per credit hour. Tuition, nonresident: full-time $13,250; part-time $552 per credit hour. Required fees: $942; $38.70 per credit hour. *Financial support:* Unspecified assistantships available. Financial award application deadline: 3/1; financial award applicants required to submit FAFSA. *Unit head:* Dr. Anjali Misra, Chairperson, 315-267-2764, Fax: 315-267-4802, E-mail: misraa@potsdam.edu. *Application contact:* Peter Cutler, Graduate Admissions Counselor, 315-267-3154, Fax: 315-267-4802, E-mail: cutlerpj@potsdam.edu.

Stephen F. Austin State University, Graduate School, College of Education, Department of Elementary Education, Program in Early Childhood Education, Nacogdoches, TX 75962. Offers M Ed. *Accreditation:* NCATE. *Degree requirements:* For master's, comprehensive exam. *Entrance requirements:* For master's, GRE General Test. Additional exam requirements/recommendations for international students: Required—TOEFL (minimum score 550 paper-based; 213 computer-based).

Syracuse University, School of Education, Program in Childhood Education: (1-6) Preparation, Syracuse, NY 13244. Offers MS. *Students:* 12 full-time (all women); includes 3 minority (all African Americans). Average age 24. 20 applicants, 85% accepted, 10 enrolled. In 2009, 7 master's awarded. *Entrance requirements:* For master's, interview. Additional exam requirements/recommendations for international students: Required—TOEFL (minimum score 100 iBT). *Application deadline:* For fall admission, 2/1 priority date for domestic and international students. Application fee: $75. Electronic applications accepted. *Expenses:* Tuition: Full-time $26,808; part-time $1117 per credit. Required fees: $1024. *Financial support:* Fellowships with tuition reimbursements, teaching assistantships with tuition reimbursements available. Financial award application deadline: 1/1; financial award applicants required to submit FAFSA. *Unit head:* Dr. Patricia Tinto, Program Director, 315-443-2684, E-mail: pptinto@syr.edu. *Application contact:* Traci Washburn, Graduate Recruiter, School of Education, 315-443-2505, E-mail: e-gradrcrt@syr.edu.

Syracuse University, School of Education, Program in Early Childhood Special Education, Syracuse, NY 13244. Offers MS. Part-time programs available. *Students:* 18 full-time (17 women), 16 part-time (15 women); includes 10 minority (6 African Americans, 1 American Indian/Alaska Native, 2 Asian Americans or Pacific Islanders, 1 Hispanic American). Average age 33. 21 applicants, 81% accepted, 8 enrolled. In 2009, 16 master's awarded. *Entrance requirements:* For master's, interview. Additional exam requirements/recommendations for international students: Required—TOEFL (minimum score 100 iBT). *Application deadline:* For fall admission, 2/1 for domestic students, 2/1 priority date for international students; for spring admission, 10/15 priority date for domestic and international students. Applications are processed on a rolling basis. Application fee: $75. Electronic applications accepted. *Expenses:* Tuition: Full-time $26,808; part-time $1117 per credit. Required fees: $1024. *Financial support:* Fellowships with tuition reimbursements, teaching assistantships with tuition reimbursements available. Financial award application deadline: 1/1; financial award applicants required to submit FAFSA. *Unit head:* Dr. Gail Ensher, Director, 315-443-9650. *Application contact:* Liza Rochelson, Graduate Recruiter, School of Education, 315-443-2505, E-mail: e-gradrcrt@syr.edu.

Teachers College, Columbia University, Graduate Faculty of Education, Department of Curriculum and Teaching, Program in Early Childhood Education, New York, NY 10027-6696. Offers Ed M, MA, Ed D. *Accreditation:* NCATE. *Faculty:* 3 full-time (all women). *Students:* 10 full-time (all women), 43 part-time (42 women); includes 22 minority (3 African Americans, 14 Asian Americans or Pacific Islanders, 5 Hispanic Americans), 5 international. Average age 29. 70 applicants, 47% accepted, 19 enrolled. In 2009, 11 master's, 6 doctorates awarded. *Degree requirements:* For doctorate, variable foreign language requirement, thesis/dissertation. *Entrance requirements:* For doctorate, GRE General Test or MAT. *Application deadline:* For fall admission, 5/15 for domestic students; for spring admission, 12/1 for domestic students. Application fee: $65. *Financial support:* Career-related internships or fieldwork, Federal Work-Study, institutionally sponsored loans, and tuition waivers (full and partial) available. Support available to part-time students. Financial award application deadline: 2/1. *Faculty research:* Infancy, child development, children and family, policy and program, childhood bilingualism. *Unit head:* Marjorie Siegel, Chair, 212-678-3765. *Application contact:* Peter Shon, Assistant Director of Admission, 212-678-3305, Fax: 212-678-4171, E-mail: shon@exchange.tc.columbia.edu.

Teachers College, Columbia University, Graduate Faculty of Education, Department of Curriculum and Teaching, Program in Early Childhood Special Education, New York, NY 10027-6696. Offers Ed M, MA. *Accreditation:* NCATE. Evening/weekend programs available. *Faculty:* 1 (woman) full-time. *Students:* 36 full-time (34 women), 130 part-time (118 women); includes 42 minority (11 African Americans, 20 Asian Americans or Pacific Islanders, 11 Hispanic Americans), 16 international. Average age 26. 254 applicants, 56% accepted, 55 enrolled. In 2009, 78 master's awarded. *Application deadline:* For fall admission, 5/15 for domestic students; for spring admission, 12/1 for domestic students. Application fee: $65. *Financial support:* Research assistantships, teaching assistantships, career-related internships or fieldwork, Federal Work-Study, institutionally sponsored loans, and tuition waivers (full and partial) available. Support available to part-time students. Financial award application deadline: 2/1. *Faculty research:* Curriculum development, infants, urban education, visually impaired infants. *Unit head:* Marjorie Siegel, Chair, 212-678-3765. *Application contact:* Peter Shon, Assistant Director of Admission, 212-678-3305, Fax: 212-678-4171, E-mail: shon@exchange.tc.columbia.edu.

Teachers College, Columbia University, Graduate Faculty of Education, Department of Curriculum and Teaching, Program in Elementary/Childhood Education, Preservice, New York, NY 10027-6696. Offers MA. *Accreditation:* NCATE. *Faculty:* 3 full-time (all women). *Students:* 3 full-time (all women), 2 part-time (1 woman); includes 2 minority (1 Asian American or Pacific Islander, 1 Hispanic American). Average age 26. *Application deadline:* For fall admission, 5/15 for domestic students; for spring admission, 12/1 for domestic students. Application fee: $65. *Financial support:* Career-related internships or fieldwork, Federal Work-Study, and tuition waivers (full and partial) available. Financial award application deadline: 2/1. *Faculty research:* Teaching of reading and writing, reforming schools, urban education, curriculum development. *Unit head:* Marjorie Siegel, Chair, 212-678-3765. *Application contact:* Peter Shon, Assistant Director of Admission, 212-678-3305, Fax: 212-678-4171, E-mail: shon@exchange.tc.columbia.edu.

Temple University, Graduate School, College of Education, Department of Curriculum, Instruction, and Technology in Education, Philadelphia, PA 19122-6096. Offers applied behavioral analysis (MS Ed); career and technical education (MS Ed); early childhood education and elementary education (MS Ed); English education (MS Ed); language arts education (Ed D); math/science education (Ed D); mathematics education (MS Ed); science education (MS Ed); second and foreign language education (MS Ed); special education (MS Ed); teaching English as a second language (MS Ed). Part-time and evening/weekend programs available. Terminal master's awarded for partial completion of doctoral program. *Degree requirements:* For master's, thesis or alternative; for doctorate, thesis/dissertation. *Entrance requirements:* For master's and doctorate, GRE General Test or MAT, minimum GPA of 3.0. Additional exam requirements/recommendations for international students: Required—TOEFL (minimum score 550 paper-based; 213 computer-based; 79 iBT). Electronic applications accepted. *Faculty research:* School improvement, problem solving, literacy, language development.

Tennessee Technological University, Graduate School, College of Education, Department of Curriculum and Instruction, Program in Early Childhood Education, Cookeville, TN 38505. Offers MA, Ed S. *Accreditation:* NCATE. Part-time and evening/weekend programs available. *Faculty:* 2 full-time (both women). *Students:* 2 full-time (both women), 11 part-time (all women); includes 1 minority (Hispanic American). Average age 27. 7 applicants, 86% accepted, 2 enrolled. In 2009, 5 master's, 1 other advanced degree awarded. *Degree requirements:* For master's and Ed S, comprehensive exam, thesis or alternative. *Entrance requirements:* For master's and Ed S, MAT or GRE. Additional exam requirements/recommendations for international students: Required—TOEFL (minimum score 550 paper-based; 79 iBT), IELTS (minimum score 5.5). *Application deadline:* For fall admission, 8/1 priority date for domestic students, 5/1 for international students; for spring admission, 12/1 for domestic students. Application fee: $25 ($30 for international students). Electronic applications accepted. *Expenses:* Tuition, state resident: full-time $7034; part-time $368 per credit hour. *Financial support:* In 2009–10, research assistantships (averaging $4,000 per year), teaching assistantships (averaging $4,000 per year) were awarded; fellowships, career-related internships or fieldwork also available. Financial award application deadline: 4/1. *Unit head:* Dr. Matthew R. Smith, Chairperson, 931-372-3181, Fax: 931-372-6270. *Application contact:* Shelia K. Kendrick, Coordinator of Graduate Studies, 931-372-3808, Fax: 931-372-3497, E-mail: skendrick@tntech.edu.

Texas A&M International University, Office of Graduate Studies and Research, College of Education, Department of Curriculum and Instruction, Laredo, TX 78041-1900. Offers bilingual education (PhD); curriculum and instruction (MS, PhD); early childhood education (PhD); reading (MS). *Faculty:* 4 full-time (3 women). *Students:* 7 full-time (3 women), 120 part-time (105 women); includes 117 minority (all Hispanic Americans), 2 international. Average age 36. 50 applicants, 64% accepted, 29 enrolled. In 2009, 34 master's awarded. *Application deadline:* For fall admission, 4/30 priority date for domestic students; for spring admission, 11/30 for domestic students. *Unit head:* Dr. Cathy Guerra, Interim Chair, 956-326-2438, E-mail: cgsakta@tamiu.edu. *Application contact:* Rosie Dickinson, Director of Admissions, 956-326-2200.

Texas A&M University–Commerce, Graduate School, College of Education and Human Services, Department of Curriculum and Instruction, Commerce, TX 75429-3011. Offers bilingual/ESL education (M Ed, MS); early childhood education (M Ed, MS); elementary education (M Ed, MS); reading (M Ed, MS); secondary education (M Ed, MS); supervision, curriculum and instruction: elementary education (Ed D). Part-time programs available. Terminal master's

awarded for partial completion of doctoral program. *Degree requirements:* For master's, comprehensive exam, thesis (for some programs); for doctorate, 2 foreign languages, thesis/dissertation, departmental qualifying exam. *Entrance requirements:* For master's and doctorate, GRE General Test. Electronic applications accepted. *Faculty research:* Literacy and learning, early childhood, preservice teacher education, technology.

Texas A&M University–Corpus Christi, Graduate Studies and Research, College of Education, Corpus Christi, TX 78412-5503. Offers counseling (MS, PhD), including counseling (MS), counselor education (PhD); curriculum and instruction (MS, Ed D); early childhood education (MS); educational administration (MS); educational leadership (Ed D); educational technology (MS); elementary education (MS); kinesiology (MS); reading (MS); secondary education (MS); special education (MS). Part-time and evening/weekend programs available. *Degree requirements:* For master's, comprehensive exam, thesis (for some programs); for doctorate, comprehensive exam, thesis/dissertation. *Entrance requirements:* For master's, GRE General Test. Additional exam requirements/recommendations for international students: Required—TOEFL. Electronic applications accepted.

Texas A&M University–Kingsville, College of Graduate Studies, College of Education, Department of Education, Program in Early Childhood Education, Kingsville, TX 78363. Offers M Ed. Part-time and evening/weekend programs available. *Degree requirements:* For master's, comprehensive exam, mini-thesis. *Entrance requirements:* For master's, GRE General Test, MAT, minimum GPA of 3.0.

Texas State University–San Marcos, Graduate School, College of Education, Department of Curriculum and Instruction, Program in Early Childhood Education, San Marcos, TX 78666. Offers M Ed, MA. *Faculty:* 1 (woman) part-time/adjunct. *Students:* 5 part-time (all women); includes 4 minority (all Hispanic Americans). Average age 28. 2 applicants, 100% accepted, 0 enrolled. In 2009, 2 master's awarded. *Degree requirements:* For master's, comprehensive exam, thesis optional. *Entrance requirements:* For master's, minimum GPA of 2.75 in undergraduate work. Additional exam requirements/recommendations for international students: Required—TOEFL (minimum score 550 paper-based; 213 computer-based). *Application deadline:* For fall admission, 6/15 priority date for domestic students; for spring admission, 10/15 priority date for domestic students. Applications are processed on a rolling basis. Application fee: $40 ($90 for international students). Electronic applications accepted. *Expenses:* Tuition, state resident: full-time $5784; part-time $241 per credit hour. Tuition, nonresident: full-time $13,224; part-time $551 per credit hour. Required fees: $1728; $48 per credit hour. $306. Tuition and fees vary according to course load. *Financial support:* In 2009–10, 3 students received support. Application deadline: 4/1. *Unit head:* Carolyn McCall, Graduate Advisor, 512-245-3701, Fax: 512-245-7911, E-mail: cm06@txstate.edu. *Application contact:* Dr. J. Michael Willoughby, Dean of Graduate School, 512-245-2581, Fax: 512-245-8365, E-mail: gradcollege@txstate.edu.

Texas Woman's University, Graduate School, College of Professional Education, Department of Family Sciences, Denton, TX 76201. Offers child development (MS, PhD); counseling and development (MS); early childhood education (M Ed, MA, MS, Ed D); family studies (MS, PhD); family therapy (MS, PhD). *Accreditation:* ACA (one or more programs are accredited). Part-time and evening/weekend programs available. *Faculty:* 25 full-time (21 women), 4 part-time/adjunct (all women). *Students:* 111 full-time (105 women), 294 part-time (269 women); includes 149 minority (99 African Americans, 3 American Indian/Alaska Native, 7 Asian Americans or Pacific Islanders, 40 Hispanic Americans), 22 international. Average age 36. 179 applicants, 86% accepted, 72 enrolled. In 2009, 86 master's, 22 doctorates awarded. Terminal master's awarded for partial completion of doctoral program. *Degree requirements:* For master's, portfolio; for doctorate, comprehensive exam, thesis/dissertation. *Entrance requirements:* For master's, interview, letter of intent, curriculum vitae; for doctorate, interview, minimum GPA of 3.5 in last 60 hours of course work. Additional exam requirements/recommendations for international students: Required—TOEFL (minimum score 550 paper-based; 213 computer-based; 79 iBT). *Application deadline:* For fall admission, 2/15 priority date for domestic students, 3/1 for international students; for spring admission, 9/15 priority date for domestic students, 8/1 for international students. Applications are processed on a rolling basis. Application fee: $50. Electronic applications accepted. *Expenses:* Tuition, state resident: full-time $3564; part-time $198 per credit hour. Tuition, nonresident: full-time $8550; part-time $475 per credit hour. Required fees: $69.26 per credit hour. Tuition and fees vary according to course load. *Financial support:* In 2009–10, 96 students received support, including 13 research assistantships (averaging $10,746 per year), 7 teaching assistantships (averaging $10,746 per year); career-related internships or fieldwork, Federal Work-Study, institutionally sponsored loans, scholarships/grants, traineeships, health care benefits, and unspecified assistantships also available. Support available to part-time students. Financial award application deadline: 3/1; financial award applicants required to submit FAFSA. *Faculty research:* Parenting/parent education, distance education, play therapy, family sexuality, diversity, ANTHEM healthy marriages initiative. *Unit head:* Dr. Larry LeFlore, Chair, 940-898-2685, Fax: 940-898-2676, E-mail: famsci@twu.edu. *Application contact:* Samuel Wheeler, Assistant Director of Admissions, 940-898-3188, Fax: 940-898-3081, E-mail: wheelersr@twu.edu.

Towson University, College of Graduate Studies and Research, Program in Early Childhood Education, Towson, MD 21252-0001. Offers M Ed, CAS. *Accreditation:* NCATE. Part-time and evening/weekend programs available. *Degree requirements:* For master's, thesis optional. *Entrance requirements:* For master's, minimum GPA of 3.0, teacher certification, work experience or course work in early childhood education. Electronic applications accepted. *Faculty research:* Developmental programs, training caregivers for HIV/AIDS children.

Trinity (Washington) University, School of Education, Washington, DC 20017-1094. Offers counseling (MA); early childhood education (MAT); educating for change (M Ed); educational administration (MSA); elementary education (MAT); school counseling (MA); secondary education (MAT), including English, social studies; special education (MAT); teaching English as a second language (MAT); teaching English to speakers of other languages (M Ed); the teaching of reading (M Ed). *Accreditation:* NCATE. Part-time and evening/weekend programs available. *Degree requirements:* For master's, thesis (for some programs), capstone project(s). *Entrance requirements:* For master's, PRAXIS I, minimum GPA of 2.8. Additional exam requirements/recommendations for international students: Required—TOEFL (minimum score 550 paper-based; 213 computer-based). *Faculty research:* Technology, literacy, special education, organizations, inclusion models.

Troy University, Graduate School, College of Education, Program in Early Childhood Education, Troy, AL 36082. Offers 5th year early childhood (MS); early childhood education (Ed S); traditional early childhood (MS). Part-time and evening/weekend programs available. Post-baccalaureate distance learning degree programs offered. *Students:* 4 full-time (all women), 12 part-time (all women); includes 4 minority (all African Americans). Average age 37. 11 applicants, 73% accepted. In 2009, 3 master's awarded. *Entrance requirements:* For master's, GRE, MAT, or GMAT. Additional exam requirements/recommendations for international students: Required—TOEFL (minimum score 523 paper-based; 193 computer-based; 70 iBT), IELTS (minimum score 6), or ACT Compass ESL (minimum score 270 on Listening, Reading, and Grammar with no individual score below 85 and a minimum score of 8 out of 12 on writing test). Application fee: $50. *Unit head:* Dr. Darrell Pearson, Interim Chair, 334-670-3444, Fax: 334-670-3474, E-mail: dpearson@troy.edu. *Application contact:* Brenda K. Campbell, Director of Graduate Admissions, 334-670-3178, Fax: 334-670-3733, E-mail: bcamp@troy.edu.

Tufts University, Graduate School of Arts and Sciences, Department of Child Development, Medford, MA 02155. Offers child development (MA, PhD, CAGS); early childhood education (MAT). Part-time programs available. *Faculty:* 16 full-time, 12 part-time/adjunct. *Students:* 66 (61 women). Average age 27. 113 applicants, 68% accepted, 35 enrolled. In 2009, 34 master's, 6 doctorates awarded. *Degree requirements:* For master's, thesis (for some programs); for doctorate, thesis/dissertation. *Entrance requirements:* For master's and doctorate, GRE General Test. Additional exam requirements/recommendations for international students: Required—TOEFL (minimum score 550 paper-based; 213 computer-based; 80 iBT). *Application deadline:* For fall admission, 1/15 for domestic students, 12/15 for international students. Applications are processed on a rolling basis. Application fee: $75. Electronic applications accepted. *Expenses:* Tuition: Full-time $38,096; part-time $3962 per credit. Required fees: $686; $40 per year. Tuition and fees vary according to course level, course load, degree level, program and student level. *Financial support:* Fellowships, research assistantships with full and partial tuition reimbursements, teaching assistantships with full and partial tuition reimbursements, Federal Work-Study, scholarships/grants, tuition waivers (partial), and unspecified assistantships available. Support available to part-time students. Financial award application deadline: 1/15; financial award applicants required to submit FAFSA. *Unit head:* Jayanthi Mistry, Chair, 617-627-3355. *Application contact:* Fred Rothbaum, Graduate Advisor, 617-627-3355.

TUI University, College of Education, Program in Education, Cypress, CA 90630. Offers adult education (MA Ed); aviation education (MA Ed); children's literacy development (MA Ed); e-learning (MA Ed); early childhood education (MA Ed); enrollment management (MA Ed); higher education (MA Ed); teaching and instruction (MA Ed); training and development (MA Ed). Part-time and evening/weekend programs available. Postbaccalaureate distance learning degree programs offered (no on-campus study). *Degree requirements:* For master's, capstone project with integrative paper. *Entrance requirements:* For master's, minimum GPA of 2.5 (students with GPA 3.0 or greater may transfer up to 30% of graduate level credits). Additional exam requirements/recommendations for international students: Required—TOEFL (minimum score 525 paper-based). Electronic applications accepted.

Union Institute & University, M Ed Program–Vermont Campus, Montpelier, VT 05602. Offers school administration (M Ed), including principalship; school counseling (M Ed); teaching (M Ed), including art, early childhood, elementary, English, math, middle schools, science, social studies, special education. *Faculty:* 3 full-time (1 woman), 23 part-time/adjunct (19 women). *Students:* 41 part-time (29 women). Average age 38. In 2009, 15 master's awarded. *Degree requirements:* For master's, thesis. *Entrance requirements:* For master's, 3 letters of reference. *Application deadline:* Applications are processed on a rolling basis. Application fee: $50. *Expenses:* Contact institution. *Financial support:* Federal Work-Study, scholarships/grants, and tuition waivers available. Financial award applicants required to submit FAFSA. *Unit head:* Dr. Arlene Sacks, Dean, Graduate Programs in Education, 305-653-6713 Ext. 2152, E-mail: arlene.sacks@myunion.edu. *Application contact:* Dr. Arlene Sacks, Dean, Graduate Programs in Education, 305-653-6713 Ext. 2152, E-mail: arlene.sacks@myunion.edu.

Universidad del Turabo, Graduate Programs, Programs in Education, Program in Teaching at Primary Level, Gurabo, PR 00778-3030. Offers M Ed. *Students:* 30 full-time (all women), 25 part-time (24 women); includes 52 Hispanic Americans. Average age 38. 19 applicants, 74% accepted, 10 enrolled. In 2009, 97 master's awarded. *Unit head:* Angela Candelario, Dean, 787-743-7979 Ext. 4126. *Application contact:* Virginia Gonzalez, Admissions Officer, 787-746-3009.

Universidad Metropolitana, Graduate Programs in Education, Program in Pre-School Education, San Juan, PR 00928-1150. Offers M Ed. *Degree requirements:* For master's, thesis or alternative. *Entrance requirements:* For master's, EXADEP, interview.

University at Buffalo, the State University of New York, Graduate School, Graduate School of Education, Department of Learning and Instruction, Buffalo, NY 14260. Offers biology education (Ed M, Certificate); chemistry education (Ed M, Certificate); childhood education (Ed M); childhood education with bilingual extension (Ed M); early childhood education (Ed M); earth science education (Ed M, Certificate); elementary education (Ed D, PhD); English education (Ed M, PhD, Certificate); English for speakers of other languages (Ed M); foreign and second language education (PhD); French education (Ed M, Certificate); general education (Ed M); German education (Ed M, Certificate); gifted education (online) (Certificate); Latin education (Ed M, Certificate); literary specialist (Ed M); mathematics education (Ed M, PhD, Certificate); music education (Ed M, Certificate); physics education (Ed M, Certificate); reading education (PhD); science and the public (online) (Ed M); science education (PhD); social studies education (Ed M, Certificate); Spanish education (Ed M, Certificate); special education (PhD); teaching and leading for diversity (Certificate); teaching English to speakers of other languages (Ed M). Part-time and evening/weekend programs available. Postbaccalaureate distance learning degree programs offered (no on-campus study). *Faculty:* 34 full-time (24 women), 50 part-time/adjunct (39 women). *Students:* 332 full-time (245 women), 365 part-time (272 women); includes 50 minority (18 African Americans, 4 American Indian/Alaska Native, 10 Asian Americans or Pacific Islanders, 18 Hispanic Americans), 55 international. Average age 30. 627 applicants, 78% accepted, 286 enrolled. In 2009, 255 master's, 16 doctorates, 51 other advanced degrees awarded. *Degree requirements:* For master's, comprehensive exam; for doctorate, thesis/dissertation, research analysis exam, research experience component. *Entrance requirements:* For doctorate, GRE General Test or MAT, interview, writing sample, letters of recommendation. Additional exam requirements/recommendations for international students: Required—TOEFL (minimum score 600 paper-based; 250 computer-based; 96 iBT). *Application deadline:* For fall admission, 2/1 priority date for domestic and international students; for spring admission, 11/15 priority date for domestic students, 10/1 for international students. Applications are processed on a rolling basis. Application fee: $50. Electronic applications accepted. *Financial support:* In 2009–10, 23 fellowships with full tuition reimbursements (averaging $9,000 per year), 42 research assistantships with full tuition reimbursements (averaging $10,000 per year) were awarded; teaching assistantships with full tuition reimbursements, career-related internships or fieldwork, Federal Work-Study, institutionally sponsored loans, scholarships/grants, tuition waivers (partial), and unspecified assistantships also available. Financial award application deadline: 2/28; financial award applicants required to submit FAFSA. *Faculty research:* Science assessment, foreign language teaching and learning, early learning, new literacies, gender and education. Total annual research expenditures: $1.8 million. *Unit head:* Dr. Suzanne Miller, Chair, 716-645-2455, Fax: 716-645-3161, E-mail: smiller@buffalo.edu. *Application contact:* Cathy Dimino, Admissions Assistant, 716-645-2110, Fax: 716-645-7937, E-mail: cadimino@buffalo.edu.

The University of Alabama at Birmingham, College of Arts and Sciences, School of Education, Program in Early Childhood Education, Birmingham, AL 35294. Offers MA Ed, PhD. *Accreditation:* NCATE. *Degree requirements:* For master's, comprehensive exam, thesis optional; for doctorate, thesis/dissertation. *Entrance requirements:* For master's, GRE General Test, MAT, or NTE, minimum GPA of 3.0; for doctorate, GRE General Test, MAT, minimum GPA of 3.25. Electronic applications accepted.

University of Alaska Anchorage, College of Education, Program in Special Education, Anchorage, AK 99508. Offers early childhood special education (M Ed); special education (M Ed, Certificate). Part-time programs available. *Degree requirements:* For master's, comprehensive exam (for some programs), thesis or alternative. *Entrance requirements:* For master's, GRE or MAT, interview, minimum GPA of 2.75. Additional exam requirements/recommendations for international students: Required—TOEFL (minimum score 550 paper-based; 213 computer-based). *Faculty research:* Mild disabilities, substance abuse issues for educators, partnerships to improve at-risk youth, analysis of planning models for teachers in special education.

University of Alaska Southeast, Graduate Programs, Program in Education, Juneau, AK 99801. Offers early childhood education (M Ed, MAT); educational technology (M Ed); elementary education (MAT); reading (M Ed); secondary education (MAT). *Accreditation:* NCATE. Part-time and evening/weekend programs available. Postbaccalaureate distance learning degree programs offered (minimal on-campus study). *Degree requirements:* For master's, comprehensive exam or project, portfolio. *Entrance requirements:* For master's, PRAXIS, minimum GPA of 3.0, writing sample, letters of recommendation. Electronic applications accepted. *Faculty research:* Applied classroom research, culturally responsive practices, action research, teaching effectiveness.

University of Arkansas, Graduate School, College of Education and Health Professions, Department of Curriculum and Instruction, Program in Childhood Education, Fayetteville, AR 72701-1201. Offers MAT. *Accreditation:* NCATE. *Students:* 66 full-time (63 women); includes 2 minority (both Asian Americans or Pacific Islanders), 2 international. In 2009, 59 master's

Early Childhood Education

University of Arkansas (continued)

awarded. Application fee: $40 ($50 for international students). *Expenses:* Tuition, state resident: full-time $7355; part-time $356.58 per hour. Tuition, nonresident: full-time $17,401; part-time $775.17 per hour. Required fees: $1203. *Financial support:* Fellowships, research assistantships, teaching assistantships available. *Unit head:* Dr. Michael Daugherty, Unit Head, 479-575-4201, E-mail: mkd03@uark.edu. *Application contact:* Dr. William McComas, Graduate Coordinator, 479-575-7525, E-mail: mccomas@uark.edu.

University of Arkansas at Little Rock, Graduate School, College of Education, Department of Teacher Education, Program in Early Childhood Education, Little Rock, AR 72204-1099. Offers M Ed.

University of Bridgeport, School of Education and Human Resources, Division of Education, Program in Elementary Education, Bridgeport, CT 06604. Offers early childhood education (MS, Diploma); elementary education (MS, Diploma). Evening/weekend programs available. *Degree requirements:* For master's, final exam, final project, or thesis; for Diploma, thesis or alternative, final project. *Entrance requirements:* For master's, minimum undergraduate QPA of 2.67; for Diploma, GRE General Test or MAT, minimum graduate QPA of 3.0. Additional exam requirements/recommendations for international students: Recommended—TOEFL (minimum score 550 paper-based; 213 computer-based; 80 iBT), IELTS (minimum score 6.5). Electronic applications accepted. *Faculty research:* Self-concept, internship assessment, stress and situational development, follow-up of graduation.

The University of British Columbia, Faculty of Education, Centre for Cross-Faculty Inquiry in Education, Vancouver, BC V6T 1Z1, Canada. Offers curriculum and instruction (M Ed, MA, PhD); early childhood education (M Ed, MA). Part-time and evening/weekend programs available. Terminal master's awarded for partial completion of doctoral program. *Degree requirements:* For master's, thesis (MA); for doctorate, thesis/dissertation. *Entrance requirements:* Additional exam requirements/recommendations for international students: Required—TOEFL (minimum score 567 paper-based; 227 computer-based). Electronic applications accepted.

University of Central Arkansas, Graduate School, College of Education, Department of Early Childhood and Special Education, Program in Early Childhood Education, Conway, AR 72035-0001. Offers MSE. *Accreditation:* NCATE. Part-time programs available. *Students:* 6 part-time (all women); includes 1 minority (African American). Average age 29. 6 applicants, 50% accepted, 3 enrolled. In 2009, 2 master's awarded. *Degree requirements:* For master's, comprehensive exam, thesis optional. *Entrance requirements:* For master's, GRE General Test, minimum GPA of 2.7. Additional exam requirements/recommendations for international students: Required—TOEFL (minimum score 550 paper-based; 213 computer-based). *Application deadline:* For fall admission, 3/1 priority date for domestic and international students; for spring admission, 10/1 priority date for domestic and international students. Applications are processed on a rolling basis. Application fee: $25 ($40 for international students). *Expenses:* Tuition, state resident: full-time $5136; part-time $214 per credit hour. Required fees: $379.50; $127 per term. Tuition and fees vary according to course level, course load and campus/location. *Financial support:* Federal Work-Study, scholarships/grants, tuition waivers (partial), and unspecified assistantships available. Financial award application deadline: 2/15. *Unit head:* Dr. Janet Filer, Coordinator, 501-450-3171, Fax: 501-450-5457. *Application contact:* Brenda Herring, Admissions Assistant, 501-450-5065, Fax: 501-450-5678, E-mail: bherring@uca.edu.

University of Central Florida, College of Education, Department of Child, Family and Community Sciences, Program in Early Childhood Education, Orlando, FL 32816. Offers early childhood development and education (MS). *Accreditation:* NCATE. *Students:* 8 full-time (7 women), 14 part-time (13 women); includes 3 minority (1 Asian American or Pacific Islander, 2 Hispanic Americans), 1 international. Average age 28. 14 applicants, 57% accepted, 6 enrolled. In 2009, 10 master's awarded. Application fee: $30. Electronic applications accepted. *Expenses:* Tuition, state resident: part-time $306.31 per credit hour. Tuition, nonresident: part-time $1099.01 per credit hour. Part-time tuition and fees vary according to degree level and program.

University of Central Oklahoma, College of Graduate Studies and Research, College of Education, Department of Curriculum and Instruction, Program in Early Childhood Education, Edmond, OK 73034-5209. Offers M Ed. *Accreditation:* NCATE. Part-time programs available. *Faculty:* 6 full-time (3 women), 4 part-time/adjunct (2 women). *Students:* 8 full-time (all women), 16 part-time (15 women); includes 3 minority (1 African American, 1 American Indian/Alaska Native, 1 Asian American or Pacific Islander), 1 international. Average age 25. 8 applicants, 100% accepted. In 2009, 5 master's awarded. *Entrance requirements:* For master's, GRE General Test. Additional exam requirements/recommendations for international students: Required—TOEFL (minimum score 550 paper-based; 213 computer-based). *Application deadline:* For fall admission, 7/1 for international students; for spring admission, 11/1 for international students. Applications are processed on a rolling basis. Application fee: $25. Electronic applications accepted. *Expenses:* Tuition, state resident: full-time $4128; part-time $172 per credit hour. Tuition, nonresident: full-time $10,373; part-time $432.20 per credit hour. Required fees: $433.20; $18.05 per credit hour. *Financial support:* Unspecified assistantships available. Financial award application deadline: 3/31; financial award applicants required to submit FAFSA. *Unit head:* Dr. Paulette Shreck, Adviser, 405-974-5721, Fax: 405-974-3822. *Application contact:* Dr. Richard Bernard, Dean, Graduate College, 405-974-3493, Fax: 405-974-3852, E-mail: gradcoll@uco.edu.

University of Cincinnati, Graduate School, College of Education, Criminal Justice, and Human Services, Division of Teacher Education, Program in Early Childhood Education, Cincinnati, OH 45221. Offers M Ed. *Accreditation:* NCATE. Part-time programs available. *Degree requirements:* For master's, thesis or alternative. *Entrance requirements:* For master's, GRE General Test. Additional exam requirements/recommendations for international students: Required—TOEFL (minimum score 610 paper-based), TWE (minimum score 5), OEPT. Electronic applications accepted.

University of Colorado Denver, School of Education and Human Development, Early Childhood Education Program, Denver, CO 80217-3364. Offers early childhood education/special education (MA). *Accreditation:* NCATE. Part-time and evening/weekend programs available. *Students:* 53 full-time (45 women), 109 part-time (98 women); includes 19 minority (4 African Americans, 5 Asian Americans or Pacific Islanders, 10 Hispanic Americans), 7 international. 93 applicants, 63% accepted, 48 enrolled. In 2009, 46 master's awarded. *Degree requirements:* For master's, comprehensive exam, thesis optional. *Entrance requirements:* For master's, GRE, minimum GPA of 2.75 or MAT. Additional exam requirements/recommendations for international students: Required—TOEFL (minimum score 525 paper-based; 197 computer-based). *Application deadline:* For fall admission, 4/15 for domestic students; for spring admission, 9/15 for domestic students. Applications are processed on a rolling basis. Application fee: $50 ($75 for international students). Electronic applications accepted. *Financial support:* Research assistantships, teaching assistantships, Federal Work-Study available. Financial award application deadline: 4/1; financial award applicants required to submit FAFSA. *Faculty research:* Early childhood growth and development, faculty development, adult learning, gender and equity issues, research methodology. *Unit head:* William Goodwin, Area Coordinator, 303-315-6323, E-mail: bill.goodwin@ucdenver.edu. *Application contact:* Meredith Lopez, Academic Advisor, 303-315-4980, Fax: 303-315-6311, E-mail: meredith.lopez@ucdenver.edu.

University of Dayton, Graduate School, School of Education and Allied Professions, Department of Teacher Education, Dayton, OH 45469-1300. Offers adolescent/young adult (MS Ed); art education (MS Ed); early childhood education (MS Ed); inclusive early childhood (MS Ed); interdisciplinary education (MS Ed); intervention specialist education, mild/moderate (MS Ed); literacy (MS Ed); middle childhood (MS Ed); multi-age education (MS Ed); music education (MS Ed); teacher as leader (MS Ed); technology in education (MS Ed). Part-time and evening/weekend programs available. *Faculty:* 17 full-time (13 women), 27 part-time/adjunct (21 women). *Students:* 105 full-time (76 women), 152 part-time (131 women); includes 25 minority (21 African Americans, 1 Asian American or Pacific Islander, 3 Hispanic Americans), 8 international. Average age 33. 199 applicants, 58% accepted, 48 enrolled. In 2009, 139 master's awarded. *Degree requirements:* For master's, thesis, capstone research project. *Entrance requirements:* For master's, GRE General Test, minimum GPA of 2.75. Additional exam requirements/recommendations for international students: Required—TOEFL (minimum score 550 paper-based; 213 computer-based; 80 iBT). *Application deadline:* For fall admission, 3/15 priority date for domestic students, 3/1 priority date for international students; for winter admission, 7/1 priority date for international students; for spring admission, 1/1 priority date for international students. Applications are processed on a rolling basis. Application fee: $0 ($50 for international students). Electronic applications accepted. *Expenses:* Contact institution. *Financial support:* In 2009–10, 5 research assistantships with full and partial tuition reimbursements (averaging $8,000 per year) were awarded; career-related internships or fieldwork, institutionally sponsored loans, health care benefits, and unspecified assistantships also available. Financial award applicants required to submit FAFSA. *Faculty research:* Diversity, literacy, art representation by young children, preservice teacher preparation. *Unit head:* Dr. Katie A. Kinnucan-Welsch, Chair, 937-229-3346. *Application contact:* Graduate Admissions, 937-229-4411, Fax: 937-229-4729, E-mail: gradadmission@udayton.edu.

The University of Findlay, Graduate and Professional Studies, College of Education, Findlay, OH 45840-3653. Offers administration (MA Ed); early childhood (MA Ed); elementary education (MA Ed); human resource development (MA Ed); leadership (MA Ed); special education (MA Ed); technology (MA Ed); web instruction (MA Ed). *Accreditation:* NCATE. Part-time and evening/weekend programs available. *Degree requirements:* For master's, thesis, cumulative project. *Entrance requirements:* For master's, minimum undergraduate GPA of 2.75 in last 62 hours of course work. Additional exam requirements/recommendations for international students: Required—TOEFL (minimum score 550 paper-based; 213 computer-based; 80 iBT). Electronic applications accepted. *Expenses:* Contact institution. *Faculty research:* Children's literature, books and artwork, educational technology, professional development.

University of Florida, Graduate School, College of Education, School of Teaching and Learning, Gainesville, FL 32611. Offers bilingual/ESOL education (M Ed, MAE, Ed D, PhD, Ed S); curriculum and instruction (M Ed, MAE, Ed D, PhD, Ed S); early childhood education (Ed D, PhD, Ed S); elementary education (M Ed, MAE); English education (M Ed, MAE); mathematics education (M Ed, MAE); reading education (M Ed, MAE); science education (M Ed, MAE); social foundations (M Ed, MAE, Ed D, PhD); social studies education (M Ed, MAE). *Accreditation:* NCATE. *Degree requirements:* For master's, thesis optional; for doctorate, variable foreign language requirement, thesis/dissertation. *Entrance requirements:* For master's and doctorate, GRE General Test, minimum GPA of 3.0; for Ed S, GRE General Test. Additional exam requirements/recommendations for international students: Required—TOEFL (minimum score 550 paper-based; 213 computer-based). Electronic applications accepted. *Faculty research:* Teacher education, inclusive education, classroom processes, curriculum and technology.

University of Georgia, Graduate School, College of Education, Department of Elementary and Social Studies Education, Athens, GA 30602. Offers early childhood education (M Ed, MAT, PhD, Ed S), including child and family development (MAT); elementary education (PhD); middle school education (M Ed, PhD, Ed S); social studies education (M Ed, Ed D, PhD, Ed S). *Faculty:* 14 full-time (9 women). *Students:* 114 full-time (94 women), 130 part-time (112 women); includes 37 minority (20 African Americans, 1 American Indian/Alaska Native, 11 Asian Americans or Pacific Islanders, 5 Hispanic Americans), 9 international. 168 applicants, 57% accepted, 48 enrolled. In 2009, 75 master's, 9 doctorates, 12 other advanced degrees awarded. *Entrance requirements:* For master's and Ed S, GRE General Test or MAT; for doctorate, GRE General Test. *Application deadline:* For fall admission, 7/1 priority date for domestic students; for spring admission, 11/15 for domestic students. Application fee: $50. Electronic applications accepted. *Expenses:* Tuition, state resident: full-time $6000; part-time $250 per credit hour. Tuition, nonresident: full-time $20,904; part-time $871 per credit hour. Required fees: $730 per semester. *Financial support:* Fellowships, research assistantships, teaching assistantships, unspecified assistantships available. *Unit head:* Dr. Ronald L. VanSickle, Interim Head, 706-542-7265, Fax: 706-542-6506, E-mail: rvansick@uga.edu. *Application contact:* Dr. Ronald E. Butchart, Graduate Coordinator, 706-542-6490, Fax: 706-542-8996, E-mail: essegrad@uga.edu.

University of Hartford, College of Education, Nursing, and Health Professions, Program in Early Childhood Education, West Hartford, CT 06117-1599. Offers M Ed. *Accreditation:* NCATE. Part-time and evening/weekend programs available. *Degree requirements:* For master's, comprehensive exam. *Entrance requirements:* For master's, PRAXIS I or waiver, interview, 2 letters of recommendation. Additional exam requirements/recommendations for international students: Required—TOEFL (minimum score 550 paper-based; 213 computer-based). Electronic applications accepted.

University of Hawaii at Manoa, Graduate Division, College of Education, Department of Curriculum Studies, Program in Early Childhood Education, Honolulu, HI 96822. Offers M Ed. *Accreditation:* NCATE. Part-time programs available. *Students:* 3 full-time (all women), 20 part-time (18 women); includes 16 minority (15 Asian Americans or Pacific Islanders, 1 Hispanic American). Average age 38. 1 applicant, 100% accepted, 0 enrolled. *Degree requirements:* For master's, thesis optional. *Entrance requirements:* Additional exam requirements/recommendations for international students: Required—TOEFL (minimum score 580 paper-based; 237 computer-based; 92 iBT), IELTS (minimum score 5). *Application deadline:* For fall admission, 1/31 for domestic and international students. Application fee: $50. *Expenses:* Tuition, state resident: full-time $8900; part-time $372 per credit. Tuition, nonresident: full-time $21,400; part-time $898 per credit. Required fees: $207 per semester. *Application contact:* Neil Pateman, Graduate Chairperson, 808-956-4401, Fax: 808-956-9905, E-mail: pateman@hawaii.edu.

University of Houston, College of Education, Department of Curriculum and Instruction, Houston, TX 77204. Offers art education (M Ed); bilingual education (M Ed); curriculum and instruction (M Ed, Ed D); early childhood education (M Ed); elementary education (M Ed); gifted and talented education (M Ed); instructional technology (M Ed); mathematics education (M Ed); reading and language arts education (M Ed); science education (M Ed); second language education (M Ed); secondary education (M Ed); social studies education (M Ed); teaching (M Ed). *Accreditation:* NCATE. Part-time and evening/weekend programs available. *Faculty:* 20 full-time (9 women), 22 part-time/adjunct (17 women). *Students:* 113 full-time (81 women), 195 part-time (150 women); includes 107 minority (43 African Americans, 29 Asian Americans or Pacific Islanders, 35 Hispanic Americans), 29 international. Average age 35. 150 applicants, 77% accepted, 55 enrolled. In 2009, 75 master's, 31 doctorates awarded. *Degree requirements:* For master's, comprehensive exam, thesis optional; for doctorate, comprehensive exam, thesis/dissertation. *Entrance requirements:* For master's and doctorate, GRE, minimum cumulative undergraduate GPA of 2.6. Additional exam requirements/recommendations for international students: Required—TOEFL (minimum score 550 paper-based; 79 iBT). *Application deadline:* For fall admission, 3/1 for domestic and international students; for spring admission, 10/1 for domestic and international students. Application fee: $45 ($75 for international students). Electronic applications accepted. *Expenses:* Tuition, state resident: full-time $7676; part-time $320 per credit hour. Tuition, nonresident: full-time $14,324; part-time $597 per credit hour. Required fees: $3034. *Financial support:* In 2009–10, 4 fellowships with full tuition reimbursements (averaging $9,500 per year), 6 research assistantships with full tuition reimbursements (averaging $8,800 per year), 25 teaching assistantships with full tuition reimbursements (averaging $8,800 per year) were awarded; career-related internships or fieldwork, Federal Work-Study, institutionally sponsored loans, scholarships/grants, health care benefits, and unspecified assistantships also available. Support available to part-time students. Financial award application deadline: 2/1. *Faculty research:* Teaching-learning process, instructional technology in schools, teacher education, classroom management, at-risk students. *Unit head:* Dr. Laveria Hutchison, Chairperson, 713-743-4958, Fax: 713-743-4990, E-mail: lhutchison@uh.edu. *Application contact:* Renee C. Rattelade, Executive Secretary, 713-743-4997, Fax: 713-743-4990, E-mail: rrattelade@mail.coe.uh.edu.

University of Houston–Clear Lake, School of Education, Program in Curriculum and Instruction, Houston, TX 77058-1098. Offers curriculum and instruction (MS); early childhood education

(MS); reading (MS); school library and information science (MS). Part-time and evening/weekend programs available. *Degree requirements:* For master's, thesis (for some programs). *Entrance requirements:* For master's, GRE or minimum GPA of 3.0 in last 60 hours. Additional exam requirements/recommendations for international students: Required—TOEFL (minimum score 550 paper-based; 213 computer-based). Electronic applications accepted.

The University of Iowa, Graduate College, College of Education, Department of Teaching and Learning, Program in Elementary Education, Iowa City, IA 52242-1316. Offers curriculum and supervision (MA, PhD); developmental reading (MA); early childhood education and care (MA); elementary education (MA, PhD); language, literature and culture (PhD). *Degree requirements:* For master's, thesis optional, exam; for doctorate, comprehensive exam, thesis/dissertation. *Entrance requirements:* For master's and doctorate, GRE General Test, minimum GPA of 3.0. Additional exam requirements/recommendations for international students: Required—TOEFL (minimum score 550 paper-based; 213 computer-based; 81 iBT). Electronic applications accepted.

University of Kentucky, Graduate School, College of Education, Program in Special Education, Lexington, KY 40506-0032. Offers early childhood special education (MS Ed); rehabilitation counseling (MRC); special education (MS Ed); special education leadership personnel preparation (Ed D). *Accreditation:* CORE; NCATE. Terminal master's awarded for partial completion of doctoral program. *Degree requirements:* For master's, comprehensive exam, thesis optional; for doctorate, comprehensive exam, thesis/dissertation. *Entrance requirements:* For master's, GRE General Test, minimum undergraduate GPA of 2.75; for doctorate, GRE General Test, minimum graduate GPA of 3.0. Additional exam requirements/recommendations for international students: Required—TOEFL (minimum score 550 paper-based; 213 computer-based). Electronic applications accepted. *Faculty research:* Applied behavior analysis applications in special education, single subject research design in classroom settings, transition research across life span, rural special education personnel.

University of Louisville, Graduate School, College of Education and Human Development, Department of Teaching and Learning, Louisville, KY 40292-0001. Offers art education (MAT); curriculum and instruction (PhD); early elementary education (MAT); instructional technology (M Ed); interdisciplinary early childhood education (MAT); middle school education (MAT); music education (MAT); reading education (M Ed); secondary education (MAT); special education (M Ed, MAT); teacher leadership (M Ed). Part-time and evening/weekend programs available. *Faculty:* 43 full-time (33 women), 43 part-time/adjunct (36 women). *Students:* 207 full-time (144 women), 410 part-time (306 women); includes 68 minority (43 African Americans, 2 American Indian/Alaska Native, 14 Asian Americans or Pacific Islanders, 9 Hispanic Americans), 5 international. Average age 33. 216 applicants, 68% accepted, 112 enrolled. In 2009, 269 master's, 6 doctorates awarded. *Degree requirements:* For doctorate, comprehensive exam, thesis/dissertation. *Entrance requirements:* For master's, GRE General Test, PRAXIS II (for some programs); for doctorate, GRE General Test. Additional exam requirements/recommendations for international students: Required—TOEFL (minimum score 560 paper-based; 210 computer-based; 83 iBT). Application fee: $50. Electronic applications accepted. *Financial support:* In 2009–10, 172 students received support; fellowships, research assistantships, teaching assistantships, career-related internships or fieldwork, Federal Work-Study, scholarships/grants, and unspecified assistantships available. Financial award application deadline: 6/1; financial award applicants required to submit FAFSA. *Faculty research:* Assessment of cognitive and language abilities in infants and preschool children; mathematics teachers' conceptions and beliefs, effect, and understanding of mathematics; incorporating nanoscience and nanotechnology into middle and high school science classrooms; urban teacher preparation through inquiry, action and advocacy; impacts of cognitive coaching on teacher practice and student achievement. Total annual research expenditures: $3.7 million. *Unit head:* Dr. Ann E. Larson, Acting Chair, 502-852-6431, Fax: 502-852-1497, E-mail: ann@louisville.edu. *Application contact:* Libby Leggett, Director, Graduate Admissions, 502-852-3101, Fax: 502-852-6536, E-mail: gradadm@louisville.edu.

University of Mary, Program in Education, Bismarck, ND 58504-9652. Offers college teaching (M Ed); curriculum, instruction and assessment (M Ed); early childhood education (M Ed); early childhood special education (M Ed); elementary education administration (M Ed); emotional disorders (M Ed); learning disabilities (M Ed); reading (M Ed); secondary education administration (M Ed); special education (M Ed); special education strategist (M Ed). Part-time programs available. *Degree requirements:* For master's, portfolio or thesis. *Entrance requirements:* For master's, interview, letters of reference. Additional exam requirements/recommendations for international students: Required—TOEFL (minimum score 550 paper-based). *Expenses:* Tuition: Full-time $10,062; part-time $430 per credit. Tuition and fees vary according to course load, degree level, program and student level. *Faculty research:* Innovative pedagogy in higher education, technology in education, content standards, children of poverty, children with diverse learning needs.

University of Maryland, Baltimore County, Graduate School, College of Arts, Humanities and Social Sciences, Department of Education, Program in Teaching, Baltimore, MD 21250. Offers early childhood education (MAT); elementary education (MAT); secondary education (MAT), including art, biology, chemistry, dance, earth/space science, English, foreign language, mathematics, music, physics, theatre; secondary science (MAT), including social studies. Part-time and evening/weekend programs available. *Faculty:* 24 full-time (18 women), 25 part-time/adjunct (19 women). *Students:* 52 full-time (41 women), 64 part-time (55 women); includes 20 minority (5 African Americans, 1 American Indian/Alaska Native, 10 Asian Americans or Pacific Islanders, 4 Hispanic Americans), 3 international. Average age 31. 88 applicants, 57% accepted, 39 enrolled. In 2009, 106 master's awarded. *Degree requirements:* For master's, comprehensive exam (for some programs), thesis (for some programs). *Entrance requirements:* For master's, PRAXIS I and II, minimum GPA of 3.0. Additional exam requirements/recommendations for international students: Required—TOEFL. *Application deadline:* For fall admission, 6/1 for domestic students; for spring admission, 11/1 for domestic students. Applications are processed on a rolling basis. Application fee: $50. Electronic applications accepted. *Financial support:* In 2009–10, 6 students received support, including research assistantships with full tuition reimbursements available (averaging $12,000 per year); career-related internships or fieldwork, Federal Work-Study, scholarships/grants, tuition waivers, and unspecified assistantships also available. Financial award application deadline: 3/1. *Faculty research:* STEM teacher education, culturally sensitive pedagogy, ESOL/bilingual education, early childhood education, language, literacy and culture. *Unit head:* Dr. Susan M. Blunck, Director, 410-455-2869, Fax: 410-455-3986, E-mail: blunck@umbc.edu. *Application contact:* Dr. Susan M. Blunck, Director, 410-455-2869, Fax: 410-455-3986, E-mail: blunck@umbc.edu.

University of Maryland, College Park, Academic Affairs, College of Education, Department of Human Development, College Park, MD 20742. Offers early childhood/elementary education (M Ed, MA, Ed D, PhD); human development (M Ed, MA, Ed D, PhD). *Accreditation:* NCATE. Part-time and evening/weekend programs available. Postbaccalaureate distance learning degree programs offered. *Faculty:* 52 full-time (45 women), 18 part-time/adjunct (14 women). *Students:* 54 full-time (48 women), 35 part-time (24 women); includes 18 minority (8 African Americans, 7 Asian Americans or Pacific Islanders, 3 Hispanic Americans), 8 international. 86 applicants, 35% accepted, 21 enrolled. In 2009, 24 master's, 7 doctorates awarded. *Degree requirements:* For master's, comprehensive exam, thesis optional; for doctorate, comprehensive exam, thesis/dissertation, essay, exam, research paper. *Entrance requirements:* For master's, GRE General Test, minimum GPA of 3.0, 3 letters of recommendation; for doctorate, GRE General Test or MAT, minimum undergraduate GPA of 3.0, graduate 3.5; 3 letters of recommendation. Additional exam requirements/recommendations for international students: Required—TOEFL. *Application deadline:* For fall admission, 3/15 for domestic students, 12/15 for international students; for spring admission, 10/1 priority date for domestic students, 6/1 for international students. Applications are processed on a rolling basis. Application fee: $60. Electronic applications accepted. *Expenses:* Tuition, area resident: Part-time $471 per credit hour. Tuition, state resident: part-time $471 per credit hour. Tuition, nonresident: part-time $1016 per credit hour. Required fees: $337.04 per term. *Financial support:* In 2009–10, 12 fellowships with full and partial tuition reimbursements (averaging $14,577 per year), 3 research assistantships with

tuition reimbursements (averaging $17,558 per year), 29 teaching assistantships with tuition reimbursements (averaging $17,113 per year) were awarded; Federal Work-Study and scholarships/grants also available. Support available to part-time students. Financial award applicants required to submit FAFSA. *Faculty research:* Developmental science, educational psychology, cognitive development, language development. Total annual research expenditures: $2.4 million. *Unit head:* Dr. Allan L. Wigfield, Chair, 301-405-1659, Fax: 301-405-2891, E-mail: awigfield@umd.edu. *Application contact:* Dean of Graduate School, 301-405-0358, Fax: 301-314-9305.

University of Massachusetts Amherst, Graduate School, School of Education, Program in Education, Amherst, MA 01003. Offers bilingual, English as a second language, and multi-cultural education (M Ed, CAGS); child study and early education (M Ed); children, families and schools (Ed D, CAGS); early childhood and elementary teacher education (M Ed); education policy and leadership (CAGS); educational administration (M Ed, CAGS); educational policy and leadership (Ed D); higher education (M Ed, CAGS); international education (M Ed); language, literacy and culture (Ed D); learning, media and technology (M Ed, CAGS); mathematics, science, and learning technologies (Ed D); policy studies (M Ed); policy studies in education (CAGS); reading and writing (M Ed); research and evaluation methods (Ed D); school counselor education (M Ed, CAGS); school psychology (CAGS); science education (CAGS); secondary teacher education (M Ed); social justice education (M Ed, Ed D, CAGS); special education (M Ed, Ed D, CAGS). *Accreditation:* NCATE. Part-time programs available. Postbaccalaureate distance learning degree programs offered (minimal on-campus study). *Faculty:* 74 full-time (41 women). *Students:* 377 full-time (268 women), 347 part-time (232 women); includes 115 minority (59 African Americans, 2 American Indian/Alaska Native, 16 Asian Americans or Pacific Islanders, 38 Hispanic Americans), 108 international. Average age 35. 708 applicants, 68% accepted, 266 enrolled. In 2009, 183 master's, 17 doctorates awarded. Terminal master's awarded for partial completion of doctoral program. *Degree requirements:* For master's, thesis or alternative; for doctorate, comprehensive exam, thesis/dissertation. *Entrance requirements:* Additional exam requirements/recommendations for international students: Required—TOEFL (minimum score 550 paper-based; 213 computer-based; 80 iBT), IELTS (minimum score 6.5). *Application deadline:* For fall admission, 1/15 for domestic and international students. Applications are processed on a rolling basis. Application fee: $50 ($65 for international students). Electronic applications accepted. *Expenses:* Tuition, state resident: full-time $2640; part-time $110 per credit. Tuition, nonresident: full-time $9936; part-time $414 per credit. Tuition and fees vary according to course load. *Financial support:* In 2009–10, 1 fellowship with full tuition reimbursement (averaging $8,036 per year), 92 research assistantships with full tuition reimbursements (averaging $8,555 per year), 83 teaching assistantships with full tuition reimbursements (averaging $4,661 per year) were awarded; career-related internships or fieldwork, Federal Work-Study, scholarships/grants, traineeships, health care benefits, tuition waivers (full), and unspecified assistantships also available. Support available to part-time students. Financial award application deadline: 1/15. *Unit head:* Dr. Linda L. Griffin, Graduate Program Director, 413-545-6984, Fax: 413-545-2873. *Application contact:* Jean M. Ames, Supervisor of Admissions, 413-545-0722, Fax: 413-577-0010, E-mail: gradadm@grad.umass.edu.

University of Memphis, Graduate School, College of Education, Department of Instruction and Curriculum Leadership, Memphis, TN 38152. Offers early childhood education (MAT, MS, Ed D); elementary education (MAT); instruction and curriculum (MS, Ed D); instruction design and technology (MS, Ed D); middle grades education (MAT); reading (MS, Ed D); secondary education (MAT); special education (MAT, MS, Ed D). *Accreditation:* NCATE (one or more programs are accredited). Part-time programs available. *Faculty:* 40 full-time (28 women), 20 part-time/adjunct (15 women). *Students:* 119 full-time (90 women), 631 part-time (505 women); includes 348 minority (331 African Americans, 2 American Indian/Alaska Native, 4 Asian Americans or Pacific Islanders, 11 Hispanic Americans), 7 international. Average age 34. 202 applicants, 77% accepted, 29 enrolled. In 2009, 137 master's, 10 doctorates awarded. Terminal master's awarded for partial completion of doctoral program. *Degree requirements:* For master's, comprehensive exam, thesis or alternative; for doctorate, comprehensive exam, thesis/dissertation. *Entrance requirements:* For master's, GRE General Test, minimum GPA of 2.5; for doctorate, GRE General Test, GRE Subject Test, 2 years of teaching experience. *Application deadline:* For fall admission, 8/1 for domestic students; for spring admission, 12/1 for domestic students. Applications are processed on a rolling basis. Application fee: $35 ($60 for international students). Electronic applications accepted. *Expenses:* Tuition, state resident: full-time $6246; part-time $347 per credit hour. Tuition, nonresident: full-time $15,894; part-time $883 per credit hour. Required fees: $1160. Full-time tuition and fees vary according to course load, degree level and program. *Financial support:* In 2009–10, 635 students received support; research assistantships with full tuition reimbursements available, teaching assistantships with full tuition reimbursements available, career-related internships or fieldwork, Federal Work-Study, institutionally sponsored loans, scholarships/grants, traineeships, and unspecified assistantships available. Support available to part-time students. Financial award application deadline: 2/15; financial award applicants required to submit FAFSA. *Faculty research:* Effective urban teachers, preparation and retention of urban teachers, technology utilization in schools, field-based teacher preparation programs, effective use of online instruction. *Unit head:* Dr. Sandra Cooley-Nichols, Interim Chair, 901-678-2365. *Application contact:* Dr. Sally Blake, Director of Graduate Studies, 901-678-4861.

University of Miami, Graduate School, School of Education, Department of Teaching and Learning, Coral Gables, FL 33124. Offers exceptional student education, pre-k disabilities and ESOL (MS Ed, Ed S); advanced professional studies (MS Ed); early childhood special education (MS Ed, Ed S); teaching and learning (PhD), including language and literacy learning in multilingual settings, mathematics and science education, special education. Part-time and evening/weekend programs available. *Faculty:* 14 full-time (9 women). *Students:* 40 full-time (30 women), 7 part-time (5 women); includes 22 minority (5 African Americans, 17 Hispanic Americans), 7 international. Average age 36. 37 applicants, 46% accepted, 10 enrolled. In 2009, 38 master's, 5 doctorates, 5 other advanced degrees awarded. Terminal master's awarded for partial completion of doctoral program. *Degree requirements:* For master's, electronic portfolio; for doctorate, thesis/dissertation, qualifying exam. *Entrance requirements:* For master's and doctorate, GRE General Test. Additional exam requirements/recommendations for international students: Required—TOEFL (minimum score 550 paper-based; 80 iBT); Recommended—IELTS (minimum score 6.5). *Application deadline:* For fall admission, 2/15 for domestic students, 10/15 for international students. Applications are processed on a rolling basis. Application fee: $65. Electronic applications accepted. *Financial support:* In 2009–10, 28 students received support, including 1 fellowship with full tuition reimbursement available (averaging $18,900 per year), 14 research assistantships with full and partial tuition reimbursements available (averaging $18,900 per year), 5 teaching assistantships with full and partial tuition reimbursements available (averaging $18,900 per year); career-related internships or fieldwork, institutionally sponsored loans, scholarships/grants, traineeships, health care benefits, and unspecified assistantships also available. Support available to part-time students. Financial award application deadline: 3/1; financial award applicants required to submit FAFSA. *Faculty research:* Exceptional students, math education, science education, literacy. Total annual research expenditures: $3.6 million. *Unit head:* Dr. Walter Secada, Department Chairperson, 305-284-4961, Fax: 305-284-6998, E-mail: wsecada@miami.edu. *Application contact:* Dr. Walter Secada, Department Chairperson, 305-284-4961, Fax: 305-284-6998, E-mail: wsecada@miami.edu.

University of Michigan, Horace H. Rackham School of Graduate Studies, School of Education, Programs in Educational Studies, Ann Arbor, MI 48109. Offers cross specialization (PhD); curriculum development (MA); early childhood education (MA, PhD); educational administration and policy (MA, PhD); educational foundations and policy (MA, PhD); English education (MA); English language learning in school settings (MA); learning technologies (MA, PhD); literacy, language, and culture (MA, PhD); mathematics education (MA, PhD); postsecondary science education (MS); research methods (MA); science education (MA, PhD); social studies education (MA); teaching and teacher education (PhD); MA/Certification; MBA/MA; PhD/MA. Terminal master's awarded for partial completion of doctoral program. *Degree requirements:* For master's,

Early Childhood Education

University of Michigan (continued)

thesis (for some programs); for doctorate, comprehensive exam, thesis/dissertation. *Entrance requirements:* For master's and doctorate, GRE General Test. Additional exam requirements/recommendations for international students: Required—TOEFL (minimum score 600 paper-based; 250 computer-based). *Application deadline:* For fall admission, 12/1 priority date for domestic students, 12/1 for international students. Application fee: $60 ($75 for international students). Electronic applications accepted. *Expenses:* Tuition, state resident: full-time $17,286; part-time $1099 per credit hour. Tuition, nonresident: full-time $34,944; part-time $2080 per credit hour. Required fees: $95 per semester. Tuition and fees vary according to course load, degree level and program. *Financial support:* Applicants required to submit FAFSA. *Unit head:* Dr. Addison Stone, Chairperson, 734-763-7500, Fax: 734-615-1290, E-mail: addison@umich.edu. *Application contact:* Laura Mayers, Student Services Assistant, 734-764-7563, Fax: 734-763-1495, E-mail: ed.grad.admit@umich.edu.

University of Minnesota, Twin Cities Campus, Graduate School, College of Education and Human Development, Department of Curriculum and Instruction, Minneapolis, MN 55455-0213. Offers art education (M Ed, MA, PhD); children's literature (M Ed, MA, PhD); curriculum and instruction (MA, PhD); early childhood education (M Ed, PhD); elementary education (M Ed, MA, PhD); English education (MA, PhD); environmental education (M Ed); family education (M Ed, MA, Ed D, PhD); instructional systems and technology (M Ed, MA, PhD); language arts (MA, PhD); language immersion education (Certificate); literacy education (MA); mathematics education (MA, PhD); reading education (MA, PhD); science education (MA, PhD); second languages and cultures education (MA, PhD); social studies education (MA, PhD); teaching (M Ed), including Chinese, earth science, elementary special education, English, English as a second language, French, German, Hebrew, Japanese, life sciences, mathematics, middle school science, science, second languages and cultures, social studies, Spanish; technology enhanced learning (Certificate); writing education (M Ed, MA, PhD). *Faculty:* 34 full-time (21 women). *Students:* 436 full-time (307 women), 375 part-time (280 women); includes 80 minority (30 African Americans, 6 American Indian/Alaska Native, 33 Asian Americans or Pacific Islanders, 11 Hispanic Americans), 40 international. Average age 32. 660 applicants, 64% accepted, 379 enrolled. In 2009, 552 master's, 14 doctorates, 7 other advanced degrees awarded. *Financial support:* In 2009–10, 5 fellowships (averaging $27,000 per year), 47 research assistantships with full tuition reimbursements (averaging $25,682 per year), 60 teaching assistantships with full tuition reimbursements (averaging $29,889 per year) were awarded. *Faculty research:* Teaching and learning; quality of education; influence of cultural, linguistic, social, political, technological and economic factors on teaching, learning and educational research; relationship between educational practice and a democratic and just society. Total annual research expenditures: $1.8 million. *Unit head:* Dr. Ruth Thomas, Chair, 612-624-4772, Fax: 612-624-8277, E-mail: thoma006@umn.edu. *Application contact:* Dr. Mary Trettin, Associate Dean, 612-625-6501, Fax: 612-626-1580, E-mail: mtrettin@umn.edu.

University of Minnesota, Twin Cities Campus, Graduate School, College of Education and Human Development, Department of Educational Psychology, Minneapolis, MN 55455-0213. Offers counseling and student personnel psychology (MA, PhD, Ed S); early childhood education (M Ed, MA, PhD); educational psychology (PhD); psychological foundations of education (MA, PhD, Ed S); school psychology (MA, PhD, Ed S); special education (M Ed, MA, PhD, Ed S); talent development and gifted education (Certificate). *Accreditation:* APA (one or more programs are accredited). *Faculty:* 34 full-time (12 women). *Students:* 286 full-time (214 women), 93 part-time (73 women); includes 43 minority (14 African Americans, 2 American Indian/Alaska Native, 19 Asian Americans or Pacific Islanders, 8 Hispanic Americans), 50 international. Average age 31. 395 applicants, 42% accepted, 107 enrolled. In 2009, 72 master's, 30 doctorates, 17 other advanced degrees awarded. *Financial support:* In 2009–10, 20 fellowships (averaging $26,215 per year), 61 research assistantships (averaging $26,184 per year), 38 teaching assistantships (averaging $28,004 per year) were awarded. *Faculty research:* Learning, cognitive and social processes; multicultural education and counseling; measurement and statistical processes; performance assessment; instructional design/strategies for students with special needs. Total annual research expenditures: $3 million. *Unit head:* Dr. Susan Hupp, Chair, 612-624-1003, Fax: 612-624-8241, E-mail: shupp@umn.edu. *Application contact:* Dr. Mary Trettin, Associate Dean, 612-625-6501, Fax: 612-626-1580, E-mail: mtrettin@umn.edu.

University of Minnesota, Twin Cities Campus, Graduate School, College of Education and Human Development, Institute of Child Development, Minneapolis, MN 55455-0213. Offers child psychology (MA, PhD); early childhood education (M Ed, MA, PhD); school psychology (MA, PhD). *Faculty:* 17 full-time (7 women). *Students:* 108 full-time (99 women), 34 part-time (32 women); includes 13 minority (2 African Americans, 3 American Indian/Alaska Native, 5 Asian Americans or Pacific Islanders, 3 Hispanic Americans), 11 international. Average age 31. 149 applicants, 29% accepted, 37 enrolled. In 2009, 45 master's, 7 doctorates awarded. *Financial support:* In 2009–10, 26 fellowships (averaging $24,044 per year), 23 research assistantships with full tuition reimbursements (averaging $26,058 per year), 39 teaching assistantships with full tuition reimbursements (averaging $27,413 per year) were awarded. *Faculty research:* Developmental affective and cognitive neuroscience; developmental psychopathology; intervention and prevention science; social and emotional development; cognitive, language, and perceptual development. Total annual research expenditures: $3.8 million. *Unit head:* Dr. Nicki Crick, Director, 612-625-8879, Fax: 612-624-6373, E-mail: crick001@umn.edu. *Application contact:* Claudia Johnston, Information Contact, 612-624-2576, Fax: 612-624-6373, E-mail: johnstc@staff.tc.umn.edu.

University of Missouri, Graduate School, College of Education, Department of Learning, Teaching and Curriculum, Columbia, MO 65211. Offers agricultural education (M Ed, PhD, Ed S); art education (M Ed, PhD, Ed S); business and office education (M Ed, PhD, Ed S); early childhood education (M Ed, PhD, Ed S); elementary education (M Ed, PhD, Ed S); English education (M Ed, PhD, Ed S); foreign language education (M Ed, PhD, Ed S); health education and promotion (M Ed, PhD); learning and instruction (M Ed); marketing education (M Ed, PhD, Ed S); mathematics education (M Ed, PhD, Ed S); music education (M Ed, PhD, Ed S); reading education (M Ed, PhD, Ed S); science education (M Ed, PhD, Ed S); social studies education (M Ed, PhD, Ed S); vocational education (M Ed, PhD, Ed S). Part-time programs available. Terminal master's awarded for partial completion of doctoral program. *Degree requirements:* For doctorate, thesis/dissertation. *Entrance requirements:* For master's and Ed S, GRE General Test or MAT, minimum GPA of 3.0; for doctorate, GRE General Test, minimum GPA of 3.0. Additional exam requirements/recommendations for international students: Required—TOEFL (minimum score 600 paper-based; 250 computer-based; 100 iBT). Electronic applications accepted.

University of Missouri–St. Louis, College of Education, Division of Teaching and Learning, St. Louis, MO 63121. Offers elementary education (M Ed), including early childhood, general, reading; secondary education (M Ed), including curriculum and instruction, general, middle level education, reading, teaching English to speakers of other languages (TESOL); secondary school teaching (Certificate); special education (M Ed), including behavioral disorders, early childhood special education, general, learning disabilities, mental retardation; teaching English to speakers of other languages (Certificate). Part-time and evening/weekend programs available. *Faculty:* 36 full-time (23 women), 51 part-time/adjunct (42 women). *Students:* 123 full-time (77 women), 569 part-time (435 women); includes 137 minority (110 African Americans, 4 American Indian/Alaska Native, 10 Asian Americans or Pacific Islanders, 13 Hispanic Americans), 11 international. Average age 32. In 2009, 1,852 master's awarded. *Degree requirements:* For master's, comprehensive exam. *Entrance requirements:* Additional exam requirements/recommendations for international students: Recommended—TOEFL (minimum score 550 paper-based; 213 computer-based). *Application deadline:* For fall admission, 7/1 priority date for domestic and international students; for spring admission, 12/1 priority date for domestic and international students. Application fee: $35 ($40 for international students). Electronic applications accepted. *Expenses:* Tuition, state resident: full-time $5377; part-time $297.70 per credit hour. Tuition, nonresident: full-time $13,882; part-time $771.20 per credit hour. Required fees: $220; $12.20 per credit hour. One-time fee: $12. Tuition and fees vary according to course level, campus/location and program. *Financial support:* In 2009–10, 5 research assistantships (averaging $10,339 per year), 2 teaching assistantships (averaging $6,800 per year) were awarded. Financial award application deadline: 4/1; financial award applicants required to submit FAFSA. *Unit head:* Dr. Joseph Polman, Chair, 314-516-5791. *Application contact:* 314-516-5458, Fax: 314-516-6996, E-mail: gadadm@umsl.edu.

University of Nebraska–Lincoln, Graduate College, College of Education and Human Sciences, Department of Child, Youth and Family Studies, Lincoln, NE 68588. Offers child development/early childhood education (MS, PhD); child, youth and family studies (MS); family and consumer sciences education (MS, PhD); family financial planning (MS); family science (MS, PhD); gerontology (PhD); human sciences (PhD), including child, youth and family studies, gerontology, medical family therapy; marriage and family therapy (MS); medical family therapy (PhD); youth development (MS). *Accreditation:* AAMFT/COAMFTE (one or more programs are accredited). Postbaccalaureate distance learning degree programs offered. *Degree requirements:* For master's, thesis optional. *Entrance requirements:* For master's, GRE. Additional exam requirements/recommendations for international students: Required—TOEFL (minimum score 550 paper-based; 213 computer-based). Electronic applications accepted. *Faculty research:* Marriage and family therapy, child development/early childhood education, family financial management.

University of Nevada, Las Vegas, Graduate College, College of Education, Department of Special Education, Las Vegas, NV 89154-3014. Offers early childhood education (M Ed); special education (MS, Ed D, PhD, Ed S). *Accreditation:* NCATE. Part-time and evening/weekend programs available. *Faculty:* 15 full-time (10 women), 12 part-time/adjunct (all women). *Students:* 203 full-time (168 women), 116 part-time (98 women); includes 79 minority (31 African Americans, 2 American Indian/Alaska Native, 19 Asian Americans or Pacific Islanders, 27 Hispanic Americans), 7 international. Average age 38. 144 applicants, 88% accepted, 105 enrolled. In 2009, 168 master's, 8 doctorates, 2 other advanced degrees awarded. *Degree requirements:* For master's, comprehensive exam (for some programs), thesis (for some programs), comprehensive portfolio (M Ed); for doctorate, comprehensive exam, thesis/dissertation. *Entrance requirements:* For doctorate and Ed S, GRE General Test. Additional exam requirements/recommendations for international students: Required—TOEFL (minimum score 550 paper-based; 213 computer-based; 80 iBT), IELTS (minimum score 7). *Application deadline:* For fall admission, 3/1 priority date for domestic and international students; for spring admission, 9/1 priority date for domestic and international students. Applications are processed on a rolling basis. Application fee: $60 ($95 for international students). Electronic applications accepted. *Financial support:* In 2009–10, 22 students received support, including 14 research assistantships with partial tuition reimbursements available (averaging $10,000 per year), 8 teaching assistantships with partial tuition reimbursements available (averaging $12,318 per year); institutionally sponsored loans, scholarships/grants, health care benefits, and unspecified assistantships also available. Financial award application deadline: 3/1. *Faculty research:* Autism, early childhood education, special education reneralist, early childhood special education, mental retardation. *Unit head:* Dr. Tom Pierce, Chair/ Professor, 702-895-3205, Fax: 702-895-0984, E-mail: tom.pierce@unlv.edu. *Application contact:* Graduate College Admissions Evaluator, 702-895-3320, Fax: 702-895-4180, E-mail: gradcollege@unlv.edu.

University of New Hampshire, Graduate School, College of Liberal Arts, Department of Education, Program in Early Childhood Education, Durham, NH 03824. Offers early childhood education (M Ed); special needs (M Ed). Part-time programs available. *Faculty:* 32 full-time. *Students:* 9 full-time (8 women), 8 part-time (7 women). Average age 31. 11 applicants, 91% accepted, 6 enrolled. In 2009, 13 master's awarded. *Degree requirements:* For master's, thesis or alternative. *Entrance requirements:* For master's, GRE General Test. Additional exam requirements/recommendations for international students: Required—TOEFL (minimum score 550 paper-based; 213 computer-based; 80 iBT). *Application deadline:* For fall admission, 2/1 priority date for domestic students, 2/1 for international students; for spring admission, 12/1 for domestic students. Applications are processed on a rolling basis. Application fee: $65. Electronic applications accepted. *Expenses:* Tuition, state resident: full-time $10,380; part-time $577 per credit hour. Tuition, nonresident: full-time $24,350; part-time $1002 per credit hour. Required fees: $1550; $387.50 per semester. Tuition and fees vary according to course load and program. *Financial support:* In 2009–10, 12 students received support; fellowships, research assistantships, teaching assistantships, career-related internships or fieldwork, Federal Work-Study, scholarships/grants, and tuition waivers (full and partial) available. Support available to part-time students. Financial award application deadline: 2/15. *Faculty research:* Young children with special needs. *Unit head:* Dr. Todd Demitchell, Coordinator, 603-862-5043, E-mail: education.department@unh.edu. *Application contact:* Dr. Todd Demitchell, Coordinator, 603-862-5043, E-mail: education.department@unh.edu.

University of New Mexico, Graduate School, College of Education, Department of Individual, Family and Community Education, Program in Multicultural Teacher and Childhood Education, Albuquerque, NM 87131-2039. Offers Ed D, PhD. *Accreditation:* NCATE. Part-time programs available. *Students:* 9 full-time (5 women), 16 part-time (11 women); includes 7 minority (1 African American, 1 American Indian/Alaska Native, 1 Asian American or Pacific Islander, 4 Hispanic Americans). Average age 48. 6 applicants, 50% accepted, 3 enrolled. *Degree requirements:* For doctorate, comprehensive exam, thesis/dissertation (for some programs). *Entrance requirements:* For doctorate, GRE, master's degree, minimum GPA of 3.0, 3 years teaching experience, 3-5 letters of reference, 1 letter of intent, professional writing sample. Additional exam requirements/recommendations for international students: Required—TOEFL (minimum score 550 paper-based; 213 computer-based). *Application deadline:* For fall admission, 3/1 priority date for domestic students, 3/1 for international students; for spring admission, 10/30 for domestic and international students. Application fee: $50. Electronic applications accepted. *Expenses:* Tuition, state resident: full-time $2099; part-time $233.20 per credit hour. Tuition, nonresident: full-time $6650. Required fees: $25 per semester. Tuition and fees vary according to course load, program and reciprocity agreements. *Financial support:* In 2009–10, 2 teaching assistantships with partial tuition reimbursements (averaging $12,805 per year) were awarded; fellowships, career-related internships or fieldwork, scholarships/grants, and unspecified assistantships also available. Financial award application deadline: 4/15; financial award applicants required to submit FAFSA. *Faculty research:* Mathematics/science/technology education, diversity, curriculum development, reflective practice, social justice, student learning, teacher education. *Unit head:* Dr. Rosalita Mitchell, Department Chair, 505-277-9611, Fax: 505-277-0455, E-mail: ted@unm.edu. *Application contact:* Robert Romero, Program Coordinator, 505-277-0513, Fax: 505-277-0455, E-mail: ted@unm.edu.

The University of North Carolina at Chapel Hill, Graduate School, School of Education, Master of Education Program for Experienced Teachers: Early Childhood Intervention and Family Support, Chapel Hill, NC 27599. Offers M Ed. *Accreditation:* NCATE. Part-time programs available. *Students:* 3 full-time (all women), 34 part-time (all women); includes 10 minority (all African Americans). Average age 33. 23 applicants, 78% accepted, 11 enrolled. In 2009, 17 master's awarded. *Degree requirements:* For master's, comprehensive exam. *Entrance requirements:* For master's, minimum GPA of 3.0 during last 2 years of undergraduate course work. *Application deadline:* For fall admission, 5/1 for domestic and international students. Applications are processed on a rolling basis. Application fee: $77. Electronic applications accepted. *Financial support:* Application deadline: 3/1. *Unit head:* Dr. Harriet Able, Coordinator, 919-962-9371, Fax: 919-962-1533. *Application contact:* Amy Butler, Student Services Assistant, 919-966-1346, Fax: 919-962-1533, E-mail: abutler@email.unc.edu.

The University of North Carolina at Chapel Hill, Graduate School, School of Education, Program in Education, Chapel Hill, NC 27599. Offers culture, curriculum and change (MA, PhD); early childhood, intervention and literacy (MA, PhD); educational psychology, measurement and evaluation (MA, PhD). *Accreditation:* NCATE. *Degree requirements:* For master's, thesis; for doctorate, comprehensive exam, thesis/dissertation. *Entrance requirements:* For master's, GRE General Test, minimum GPA of 3.0 during last 2 years of undergraduate course work; for doctorate, GRE General Test, minimum GPA of 3.0 during last 2 years of undergraduate course work. Additional exam requirements/recommendations for international students: Required—TOEFL (minimum score 550 paper-based; 213 computer-based). Electronic applications accepted.

The University of North Carolina at Greensboro, Graduate School, School of Education, Department of Specialized Education Services, Greensboro, NC 27412-5001. Offers cross-categorical special education (M Ed); interdisciplinary studies in special education (M Ed); leadership early care and education (Certificate); special education (M Ed, PhD). *Degree requirements:* For master's, thesis or alternative. *Entrance requirements:* For master's, GRE General Test. Additional exam requirements/recommendations for international students: Required—TOEFL. Electronic applications accepted.

University of North Dakota, Graduate School, College of Education and Human Development, Program in Early Childhood Education, Grand Forks, ND 58202. Offers MS. *Accreditation:* NCATE. Part-time programs available. *Degree requirements:* For master's, comprehensive exam, thesis or alternative. *Entrance requirements:* For master's, minimum GPA of 3.0. Additional exam requirements/recommendations for international students: Required—TOEFL (minimum score 550 paper-based; 213 computer-based; 79 iBT), IELTS (minimum score 6.5). Electronic applications accepted.

University of Northern Colorado, Graduate School, College of Education and Behavioral Sciences, School of Psychological Sciences, Program in Educational Psychology, Greeley, CO 80639. Offers early childhood education (MA); educational psychology (MA, PhD). *Accreditation:* NCATE. Part-time programs available. *Faculty:* 15 full-time (6 women). *Students:* 23 full-time (11 women), 16 part-time (14 women); includes 3 minority (1 Asian American or Pacific Islander, 2 Hispanic Americans), 8 international. Average age 33. 11 applicants, 91% accepted, 8 enrolled. In 2009, 6 master's, 4 doctorates awarded. *Degree requirements:* For master's, comprehensive exam, thesis or alternative; for doctorate, comprehensive exam, thesis/dissertation. *Entrance requirements:* For master's, GRE General Test, letters of recommendation; for doctorate, GRE General Test, letters of recommendation, resume. *Application deadline:* Applications are processed on a rolling basis. Application fee: $50 ($60 for international students). Electronic applications accepted. *Expenses:* Tuition, state resident: full-time $5770; part-time $320.55 per credit hour. Tuition, nonresident: full-time $13,847; part-time $769.27 per credit hour. Required fees: $948.78; $52.72 per credit. *Financial support:* In 2009–10, 1 teaching assistantship (averaging $6,732 per year) was awarded; fellowships, research assistantships, unspecified assistantships also available. Financial award application deadline: 3/1; financial award applicants required to submit FAFSA. *Unit head:* Dr. Marilyn Welsh, Program Coordinator, 970-351-2957, Fax: 970-351-1103. *Application contact:* Linda Sisson, Graduate Student Admission Coordinator, 970-351-1807, Fax: 970-351-2371, E-mail: linda.sisson@unco.edu.

University of Northern Iowa, Graduate College, College of Education, Department of Curriculum and Instruction, Program in Early Childhood Education, Cedar Falls, IA 50614. Offers MAE. *Students:* 28 part-time (27 women); includes 1 minority (Hispanic American), 1 international. 12 applicants, 92% accepted, 10 enrolled. In 2009, 1 master's awarded. *Degree requirements:* For master's, comprehensive exam, thesis or alternative. *Entrance requirements:* For master's, minimum GPA of 3.0. Additional exam requirements/recommendations for international students: Required—TOEFL (minimum score 500 paper-based; 180 computer-based; 61 iBT). *Application deadline:* For fall admission, 8/1 priority date for domestic students. Applications are processed on a rolling basis. Application fee: $30 ($50 for international students). Electronic applications accepted. *Financial support:* Application deadline: 2/1. *Unit head:* Dr. Fitzgerald Linda, Coordinator, 319-273-2214, Fax: 319-273-5886, E-mail: linda.fitzgerald@uni.edu. *Application contact:* Laurie S. Russell, Record Analyst, 319-273-2623, Fax: 319-273-6792, E-mail: laurie.russell@uni.edu.

University of North Texas, Robert B. Toulouse School of Graduate Studies, College of Education, Department of Educational Psychology, Program in Development and Family Studies, Denton, TX 76203. Offers MS, Certificate. Evening/weekend programs available. *Degree requirements:* For master's, comprehensive exam, thesis optional. *Entrance requirements:* For master's, GRE General Test, resume, references. Additional exam requirements/recommendations for international students: Recommended—TOEFL (minimum score 550 paper-based; 213 computer-based). *Application deadline:* Applications are processed on a rolling basis. Application fee: $50 ($75 for international students). Electronic applications accepted. *Expenses:* Tuition, state resident: full-time $4298; part-time $239 per contact hour. Tuition, nonresident: full-time $9878; part-time $549 per contact hour. Required fees: $265 per contact hour. *Financial support:* Teaching assistantships, career-related internships or fieldwork, Federal Work-Study, and institutionally sponsored loans available. Financial award applicants required to submit FAFSA. *Faculty research:* Parent-child issues, cognitive development, social development. *Application contact:* Becky Glover, Graduate Advisor, 940-565-4876, E-mail: becky.glover@unt.edu.

University of North Texas, Robert B. Toulouse School of Graduate Studies, College of Education, Department of Teacher Education and Administration, Program in Early Childhood Education, Denton, TX 76203. Offers MS, Ed D. Part-time programs available. *Students:* 22. In 2009, 6 master's awarded. Terminal master's awarded for partial completion of doctoral program. *Degree requirements:* For master's, comprehensive exam, thesis optional; for doctorate, comprehensive exam, thesis/dissertation. *Entrance requirements:* For master's, GRE General Test, 3 letters of reference, goal statement; for doctorate, GRE General Test, minimum graduate GPA of 3.5, 3 letters of reference, goal statement. Additional exam requirements/recommendations for international students: Required—proof of English language proficiency required for non-native English speakers; Recommended—TOEFL (minimum score 550 paper-based; 213 computer-based; 79 iBT). *Application deadline:* Applications are processed on a rolling basis. Application fee: $50 ($75 for international students). Electronic applications accepted. *Expenses:* Tuition, state resident: full-time $4298; part-time $239 per contact hour. Tuition, nonresident: full-time $9878; part-time $549 per contact hour. Required fees: $265 per contact hour. *Financial support:* Research assistantships, scholarships/grants available. Financial award application deadline: 4/15; financial award applicants required to submit FAFSA. *Faculty research:* Early literacy programs, African-American student achievement in the early grades, cross-cultural approaches to early childhood education.

University of Oklahoma, Graduate College, College of Education, Department of Instructional Leadership and Academic Curriculum, Norman, OK 73072. Offers education (Certificate); instructional leadership and academic curriculum (M Ed, PhD), including bilingual education, early childhood education, elementary education, English education, math education, reading education, science education, secondary education, social studies education. *Accreditation:* NCATE. Part-time and evening/weekend programs available. *Faculty:* 18 full-time (11 women). *Students:* 44 full-time (36 women), 117 part-time (92 women); includes 35 minority (11 African Americans, 14 American Indian/Alaska Native, 5 Asian Americans or Pacific Islanders, 5 Hispanic Americans), 2 international. 50 applicants, 84% accepted, 32 enrolled. In 2009, 31 master's, 6 doctorates awarded. Terminal master's awarded for partial completion of doctoral program. *Degree requirements:* For doctorate, thesis/dissertation. *Entrance requirements:* For master's, 12 hours of course work in education; for doctorate, GRE General Test, master's degree, minimum graduate GPA of 3.0. Additional exam requirements/recommendations for international students: Required—TOEFL (minimum score 550 paper-based; 213 computer-based). *Application deadline:* For fall admission, 6/1 priority date for domestic students, 4/1 for international students; for spring admission, 11/1 for domestic students, 9/1 for international students. Applications are processed on a rolling basis. Application fee: $40 ($90 for international students). Electronic applications accepted. *Expenses:* Tuition, state resident: full-time $3744; part-time $156 per credit hour. Tuition, nonresident: full-time $13,577; part-time $565.70 per credit hour. Required fees: $2415; $90.10 per credit hour. *Financial support:* In 2009–10, 107 students received support, including 1 research assistantship with partial tuition reimbursement available (averaging $9,630 per year), 6 teaching assistantships with partial tuition reimbursements available (averaging $10,801 per year); scholarships/grants, health care benefits, and unspecified assistantships also available. Financial award applicants required to submit FAFSA. *Faculty research:* English education, mathematics education, reading, science education, social studies education. Total annual research expenditures: $752,908. *Unit head:* Lawrence Baines, Chair, 405-325-1498, Fax: 405-325-4061, E-mail: lbaines@ou.edu. *Application*

contact: Lynn Crussel, Administrative Assistant for Graduate Studies, 405-325-4843, Fax: 405-325-4061, E-mail: lcrussel@ou.edu.

University of Phoenix, College of Natural Sciences, College of Education, Phoenix, AZ 85034-7209. Offers administration and supervision (MAEd); adult education and training (MAEd); curriculum and instruction (MAEd); curriculum and instruction-adult education (MAEd); curriculum and instruction-computer education (MAEd); curriculum and instruction-English and language arts education (MAEd); curriculum and instruction-English as a second language (MAEd); curriculum and instruction-mathematics education (MAEd); curriculum education (MAEd); early childhood (MAEd); elementary teacher education (MAEd); secondary teacher education (MAEd); special education (MAEd); teacher leadership (MAEd). *Accreditation:* Teacher Education Accreditation Council. Evening/weekend programs available. Postbaccalaureate distance learning degree programs offered (no on-campus study). *Faculty:* 47 full-time (34 women), 844 part-time/adjunct (636 women). *Students:* 13,657 full-time (10,698 women); includes 4,000 minority (3,063 African Americans, 74 American Indian/Alaska Native, 241 Asian Americans or Pacific Islanders, 622 Hispanic Americans), 307 international. Average age 36. In 2009, 17,246 master's awarded. *Degree requirements:* For master's, thesis (for some programs). *Entrance requirements:* For master's, 3 years of work experience, minimum GPA of 2.5. Additional exam requirements/recommendations for international students: Required—TOEFL (minimum score 550 paper-based; 213 computer-based; 79 iBT). *Application deadline:* Applications are processed on a rolling basis. Application fee: $45. Electronic applications accepted. *Expenses:* Tuition: Full-time $13,272. Required fees: $660. Full-time tuition and fees vary according to course level, degree level and program. *Financial support:* Institutionally sponsored loans and scholarships/grants available. Financial award applicants required to submit FAFSA. *Unit head:* Dr. Meredith Curley, Dean/Executive Director, 480-557-1217, Fax: 480-557-1588, E-mail: meredith.curley@phoenix.edu. *Application contact:* Chair, 602-387-7000, Fax: 602-387-6020.

University of Phoenix–Central Florida Campus, The Artemis School, College of Education, Maitland, FL 32751-7057. Offers administration and supervision (MA Ed); curriculum and instruction (MA Ed); curriculum and instruction-computer education (MA Ed); curriculum and instruction-mathematics education (MA Ed); early childhood education (MA Ed); elementary teacher education (MA Ed); secondary teacher education (MA Ed). Evening/weekend programs available. *Degree requirements:* For master's, thesis (for some programs). *Entrance requirements:* For master's, 3 years of work experience, minimum undergraduate GPA of 2.5. Additional exam requirements/recommendations for international students: Required—TOEFL (minimum score 550 paper-based; 213 computer-based; 79 iBT). Electronic applications accepted.

University of Phoenix–Louisiana Campus, The Artemis School, College of Education, Metairie, LA 70001-2082. Offers curriculum and instruction (MA Ed); early childhood education (MA Ed). Postbaccalaureate distance learning degree programs offered. *Degree requirements:* For master's, thesis. *Entrance requirements:* For master's, minimum undergraduate GPA of 2.5, 3 years work experience. Additional exam requirements/recommendations for international students: Required—TOEFL (minimum score 550 paper-based; 213 computer-based; 79 iBT).

University of Phoenix–North Florida Campus, The Artemis School, College of Education, Jacksonville, FL 32216-0959. Offers administration and supervision (MA Ed); curriculum and instruction (MA Ed), including computer education, mathematics education; early childhood education (MA Ed); elementary teacher education (MA Ed); secondary teacher education (MA Ed). Evening/weekend programs available. *Degree requirements:* For master's, thesis (for some programs). *Entrance requirements:* For master's, 3 years of work experience, minimum undergraduate GPA of 2.5. Additional exam requirements/recommendations for international students: Required—TOEFL (minimum score 550 paper-based; 213 computer-based; 49 iBT). Electronic applications accepted.

University of Phoenix–Oregon Campus, The Artemis School, College of Education, Tigard, OR 97223. Offers curriculum and instruction (MA Ed); early childhood education (MA Ed); elementary education (MA Ed), including early childhood specialization, middle level specialization; secondary education (MA Ed), including middle level specialization. Evening/weekend programs available. *Degree requirements:* For master's, thesis (for some programs). *Entrance requirements:* For master's, minimum undergraduate GPA of 2.5, 3 years work experience. Additional exam requirements/recommendations for international students: Required—TOEFL (minimum score 550 paper-based; 213 computer-based; 79 iBT). Electronic applications accepted.

University of Phoenix–Puerto Rico Campus, The Artemis School, College of Education, Guaynabo, PR 00968. Offers administration and supervision (MA Ed); early childhood education (MA Ed); school counselor (MSC). Evening/weekend programs available. *Degree requirements:* For master's, thesis (for some programs). *Entrance requirements:* For master's, minimum undergraduate GPA of 2.5, 3 years work experience. Additional exam requirements/recommendations for international students: Required—TOEFL (minimum score 550 paper-based; 213 computer-based; 79 iBT). Electronic applications accepted.

University of Phoenix–Southern California Campus, College of Education, Costa Mesa, CA 92626. Offers administration and supervision (MA Ed); adult education and training (MA Ed); curriculum and instruction (MA Ed), including computer education, curriculum and instruction, English and language arts, English as a second language, mathematics education; early childhood education (MA Ed); special education (MA Ed); teacher leadership (MA Ed). Evening/weekend programs available. *Faculty:* 47 full-time (34 women), 844 part-time/adjunct (636 women). *Students:* 558 full-time (391 women); includes 222 minority (60 African Americans, 4 American Indian/Alaska Native, 26 Asian Americans or Pacific Islanders, 132 Hispanic Americans), 9 international. Average age 34. In 2009, 303 master's awarded. *Degree requirements:* For master's, thesis (for some programs). *Entrance requirements:* For master's, minimum undergraduate GPA of 2.5, 3 years work experience. Additional exam requirements/recommendations for international students: Required—TOEFL (minimum score 550 paper-based; 213 computer-based; 79 iBT). *Application deadline:* Applications are processed on a rolling basis. Application fee: $45. Electronic applications accepted. *Expenses:* Tuition: Full-time $15,120. Required fees: $660. *Financial support:* Institutionally sponsored loans and scholarships/grants available. Financial award applicants required to submit FAFSA. *Unit head:* Dr. Meredith Curley, Dean/Executive Director, 480-557-1217, Fax: 480-557-1588, E-mail: meredith.curley@phoenix.edu. *Application contact:* Campus College Chair, 714-378-1878, Fax: 714-378-5875.

University of Phoenix–South Florida Campus, The Artemis School, College of Education, Fort Lauderdale, FL 33309. Offers administration and supervision (MA Ed); curriculum and instruction (MA Ed), including computer education, curriculum and instruction, mathematics education; early childhood education (MA Ed); elementary teacher education (MA Ed); secondary teacher education (MA Ed). Evening/weekend programs available. *Degree requirements:* For master's, thesis (for some programs). *Entrance requirements:* For master's, 3 years of work experience, minimum undergraduate GPA of 2.5. Additional exam requirements/recommendations for international students: Required—TOEFL (minimum score 550 paper-based; 213 computer-based; 79 iBT). Electronic applications accepted.

University of Phoenix–West Florida Campus, The Artemis School, College of Education, Temple Terrace, FL 33637. Offers administration and supervision (MA Ed); curriculum and instruction (MA Ed), including computer education, curriculum and instruction, mathematics education; curriculum and technology (MA Ed); early childhood education (MA Ed); elementary teacher education (MA Ed); secondary teacher education (MA Ed). Evening/weekend programs available. *Degree requirements:* For master's, thesis (for some programs). *Entrance requirements:* For master's, 3 years of work experience, minimum undergraduate GPA of 2.5. Additional exam requirements/recommendations for international students: Required—TOEFL (minimum score 550 paper-based; 213 computer-based; 79 iBT).

Early Childhood Education

University of Pittsburgh, School of Education, Department of Instruction and Learning, Program in Early Childhood Education, Pittsburgh, PA 15260. Offers M Ed. Part-time and evening/weekend programs available. *Students:* 12 full-time (all women), 5 part-time (all women); includes 2 minority (both African Americans), 1 international. Average age 24. 7 applicants, 71% accepted, 4 enrolled. In 2009, 3 master's awarded. *Degree requirements:* For master's, thesis. *Entrance requirements:* For master's, PRAXIS I. Additional exam requirements/recommendations for international students: Required—TOEFL. *Application deadline:* For fall admission, 2/1 for domestic students. Application fee: $50. Electronic applications accepted. *Expenses:* Tuition, state resident: full-time $16,402; part-time $665 per credit. Tuition, nonresident: full-time $28,694; part-time $1175 per credit. Required fees: $690; $175 per term. Tuition and fees vary according to program. *Financial support:* Career-related internships or fieldwork, Federal Work-Study, institutionally sponsored loans, and tuition waivers (partial) available. Support available to part-time students. Financial award application deadline: 3/15; financial award applicants required to submit FAFSA. *Unit head:* Dr. Richard Donato, Chairman, 412-624-7248, Fax: 412-648-7081, E-mail: donato@pitt.edu. *Application contact:* Dr. Marjie Schermer, Graduate Enrollment Manager, 412-648-2230, Fax: 412-648-1899, E-mail: soeinfo@pitt.edu.

University of Puerto Rico, Río Piedras, College of Education, Program in Child Education, San Juan, PR 00931-3300. Offers M Ed. Part-time programs available. *Degree requirements:* For master's, thesis. *Entrance requirements:* For master's, EXADEP, GRE General Test or PAEG, interview, minimum GPA of 3.0, letter of recommendation.

University of St. Thomas, Graduate Studies, School of Education, Department of Special and Gifted Education, St. Paul, MN 55105-1096. Offers autism spectrum disorders (Certificate); autism spectrum disorders (MA); developmental disabilities (MA); director of special education (Ed S); early childhood special education (MA); gifted, creative, and talented education (MA); learning disabilities (MA); Orton-Gillingham reading (Certificate); special education (MA). *Accreditation:* NCATE. Part-time and evening/weekend programs available. *Faculty:* 7 full-time (6 women), 16 part-time/adjunct (14 women). *Students:* 25 full-time (23 women), 226 part-time (180 women); includes 16 minority (6 African Americans, 6 Asian Americans or Pacific Islanders, 4 Hispanic Americans), 3 international. Average age 34. 447 applicants, 60% accepted. In 2009, 65 master's, 65 other advanced degrees awarded. *Degree requirements:* For master's, thesis; for other advanced degree, professional portfolio. *Entrance requirements:* For master's, minimum GPA of 3.0 or MAT; for other advanced degree, MAT or minimum GPA of 2.75. Additional exam requirements/recommendations for international students: Required—TOEFL (minimum score 550 paper-based; 213 computer-based; 80 iBT). *Application deadline:* For fall admission, 6/1 priority date for domestic students; for spring admission, 11/1 priority date for domestic students. Applications are processed on a rolling basis. Application fee: $50. *Financial support:* Fellowships, research assistantships, institutionally sponsored loans and scholarships/grants available. Support available to part-time students. Financial award applicants required to submit FAFSA. *Faculty research:* Reading and math fluency, inclusion curriculum for developmental disorders, parent involvement in positive behavior supports, children's friendships, preschool inclusion. *Unit head:* Dr. Terri L. Vandercook, Chair, 651-962-4389, Fax: 651-962-4169, E-mail: tlvandercook@stthomas.edu. *Application contact:* Patricia L. Thomas, Department Assistant, 651-962-4980, Fax: 651-962-4169, E-mail: plhelland@stthomas.edu.

The University of Scranton, College of Graduate and Continuing Education, Department of Education, Program in Early Childhood Education, Scranton, PA 18510. Offers MA, MS. Part-time and evening/weekend programs available. *Students:* 1 (woman) part-time. Average age 27. 1 applicant, 100% accepted. *Degree requirements:* For master's, comprehensive exam, thesis (for some programs), capstone experience. *Entrance requirements:* For master's, minimum GPA of 2.75. Additional exam requirements/recommendations for international students: Required—TOEFL (minimum score 500 paper-based; 173 computer-based), IELTS (minimum score 5.5). *Application deadline:* Applications are processed on a rolling basis. Application fee: $0. *Financial support:* Unspecified assistantships available. Financial award application deadline: 3/1. *Unit head:* Dr. Art Chambers, Director, 570-941-4668, Fax: 570-941-5515, E-mail: chambersa2@scranton.edu. *Application contact:* Joseph M. Roback, Director of Admissions, 570-941-4385, Fax: 570-941-5928, E-mail: robackj2@scranton.edu.

University of South Alabama, Graduate School, College of Education, Department of Leadership and Teacher Education, Mobile, AL 36688-0002. Offers early childhood education (M Ed); educational administration (Ed S); educational leadership (M Ed); elementary education (M Ed); reading education (M Ed); science education (M Ed); secondary education (M Ed); special education (M Ed, Ed S). *Accreditation:* NCATE. Part-time programs available. *Degree requirements:* For master's, comprehensive exam. *Entrance requirements:* For master's, GRE General Test or MAT, minimum GPA of 3.0. *Expenses:* Tuition, state resident: part-time $218 per contact hour. Required fees: $1102 per year.

University of South Carolina, The Graduate School, College of Education, Department of Instruction and Teacher Education, Program in Early Childhood Education, Columbia, SC 29208. Offers M Ed, Ed D, PhD. *Accreditation:* NCATE. *Degree requirements:* For master's, comprehensive exam; for doctorate, one foreign language, comprehensive exam, thesis/dissertation. *Entrance requirements:* For master's, GRE General Test, MAT, interview; for doctorate, GRE General Test, MAT, interview, teaching experience. *Faculty research:* Parent involvement, play, multicultural education, global education.

University of South Carolina Upstate, Graduate Programs, Spartanburg, SC 29303-4999. Offers early childhood education (M Ed); elementary education (M Ed); special education: visual impairment (M Ed). *Accreditation:* NCATE. Part-time and evening/weekend programs available. *Faculty:* 8 full-time (7 women), 4 part-time/adjunct (2 women). *Students:* 5 full-time (all women), 107 part-time (102 women). Average age 34. *Degree requirements:* For master's, professional portfolio. *Entrance requirements:* For master's, GRE General Test or MAT, interview, minimum undergraduate GPA of 2.5, teaching certificate, 2 letters of recommendation. *Application deadline:* Applications are processed on a rolling basis. Application fee: $40. *Expenses:* Tuition, state resident: full-time $9436; part-time $467 per credit hour. Tuition, nonresident: full-time $20,336; part-time $992 per credit hour. Required fees: $500. Tuition and fees vary according to course load. *Financial support:* Institutionally sponsored loans and institutional work-study available. Financial award application deadline: 7/15; financial award applicants required to submit FAFSA. *Faculty research:* Rough and tumble play, social justice education, American Indian literatures and cultures, diversity and multicultural education, science teaching strategy. *Unit head:* Dr. Rebecca L. Stevens, Director of Graduate Programs, 864-503-5521, Fax: 864-503-5574, E-mail: rstevens@uscupstate.edu. *Application contact:* Donette Stewart, Associate Vice Chancellor for Enrollment Services, 864-503-5280, E-mail: dstewart@uscupstate.edu.

University of Southern Mississippi, Graduate School, College of Education and Psychology, Department of Curriculum, Instruction, and Special Education, Hattiesburg, MS 39406-0001. Offers alternative secondary teacher education (MAT); early childhood education (M Ed, Ed S); education of the gifted (M Ed, Ed D, PhD, Ed S); elementary education (M Ed, Ed D, PhD, Ed S); reading (M Ed, MS, Ed S); secondary education (M Ed, MS, Ed D, PhD, Ed S); special education (M Ed, Ed D, PhD, Ed S). *Faculty:* 23 full-time (17 women), 3 part-time/adjunct (2 women). *Students:* 31 full-time (26 women), 77 part-time (68 women); includes 18 minority (15 African Americans, 3 Hispanic Americans). Average age 37. 50 applicants, 52% accepted, 19 enrolled. In 2009, 43 master's, 3 doctorates, 2 other advanced degrees awarded. *Degree requirements:* For master's, comprehensive exam, thesis (for some programs); for doctorate, comprehensive exam, thesis/dissertation; for Ed S, comprehensive exam, thesis. *Entrance requirements:* For master's, GRE General Test, MAT, minimum GPA of 3.0; for doctorate, GRE General Test, minimum GPA of 3.5; for Ed S, GRE General Test, MAT, minimum GPA of 3.25. Additional exam requirements/recommendations for international students: Required—TOEFL. *Application deadline:* For fall admission, 3/1 priority date for domestic students, 3/1 for international students. Applications are processed on a rolling basis. Application fee: $35. *Expenses:* Tuition, state resident: full-time $5096; part-time $284 per hour. Tuition, nonresident: full-time $13,052; part-time $726 per hour. Required fees: $402. Tuition and fees vary according to course level and course load. *Financial support:* In 2009–10, 9 research assistantships with tuition reimbursements (averaging $18,316 per year), 2 teaching assistantships with full tuition reimbursements (averaging $8,500 per year) were awarded; Federal Work-Study, institutionally sponsored loans, and tuition waivers (partial) also available. Financial award application deadline: 3/15; financial award applicants required to submit FAFSA. *Faculty research:* Mathematical problem solving, integrative curriculum, writing process, teacher education models. Total annual research expenditures: $100,000. *Unit head:* Dr. David Daves, Chair, 601-266-4547, Fax: 601-266-4175. *Application contact:* Rachea Cawthorn, Administrative Assistant, 601-266-6987, Fax: 601-266-4548.

University of South Florida, Graduate School, College of Education–Main Campus, Department of Childhood Education, Tampa, FL 33620-9951. Offers early childhood education (M Ed, MA, PhD); elementary education (MA, MAT); reading/language arts (MA, PhD, Ed S). *Accreditation:* NCATE. Part-time and evening/weekend programs available. *Faculty:* 24 full-time (21 women), 2 part-time/adjunct (both women). *Students:* 92 full-time (84 women), 165 part-time (157 women); includes 62 minority (36 African Americans, 1 American Indian/Alaska Native, 6 Asian Americans or Pacific Islanders, 19 Hispanic Americans), 9 international. Average age 30. 192 applicants, 76% accepted, 113 enrolled. In 2009, 94 master's, 11 doctorates awarded. *Degree requirements:* For master's, comprehensive exam; for doctorate, comprehensive exam, thesis/dissertation. *Entrance requirements:* For master's, GRE (if GPA less than 3.0), minimum GPA of 3.0 in last 60 hours of course work; for doctorate, GRE General Test, minimum GPA of 3.0 undergraduate, 3.5 graduate; interview; for Ed S, GRE General Test, interview. Additional exam requirements/recommendations for international students: Required—TOEFL (minimum score 550 paper-based; 213 computer-based). *Application deadline:* For fall admission, 2/15 for domestic students, 1/2 for international students; for winter admission, 2/15 for domestic students, 1/2 for international students; for spring admission, 10/15 for domestic students, 6/1 for international students. Application fee: $30. Electronic applications accepted. *Financial support:* In 2009–10, 7 teaching assistantships with full tuition reimbursements (averaging $10,300 per year) were awarded; institutionally sponsored loans, scholarships/grants, and unspecified assistantships also available. Financial award applicants required to submit FAFSA. *Faculty research:* Evaluating interventions for struggling users, prevention and intervention services for young children at risk for behavioral and mental health challenges, preservice teacher education and young adolescent middle school experience, art and inquiry-based approaches to teaching and learning, study of children's writing development. Total annual research expenditures: $381,048. *Unit head:* Dr. Diane Yendol-Hoppey, Chairperson, 813-974-3460, Fax: 813-974-0938. *Application contact:* Dr. Diane Yendol-Hoppey, Chairperson, 813-974-3460, Fax: 813-974-0938.

The University of Tennessee, Graduate School, College of Education, Health and Human Sciences, Department of Child and Family Studies, Knoxville, TN 37996. Offers child and family studies (MS); early childhood education (MS). Part-time programs available. *Degree requirements:* For master's, thesis or alternative. *Entrance requirements:* For master's, GRE General Test, minimum GPA of 2.7. Additional exam requirements/recommendations for international students: Required—TOEFL. Electronic applications accepted. *Expenses:* Tuition, state resident: full-time $6826; part-time $380 per semester hour. Tuition, nonresident: full-time $21,844; part-time $1147 per semester hour. Tuition and fees vary according to program.

The University of Tennessee, Graduate School, College of Education, Health and Human Sciences, Program in Education, Knoxville, TN 37996. Offers art education (MS); counseling education (PhD); cultural studies in education (PhD); curriculum (MS, Ed S); curriculum, educational research and evaluation (Ed D, PhD); early childhood education (PhD); early childhood special education (MS); education of deaf and hard of hearing (MS); educational administration and policy studies (Ed D, PhD); educational administration and supervision (Ed S); educational psychology (Ed D, PhD); elementary education (MS, Ed S); elementary teaching (MS); English education (MS, Ed S); exercise science (PhD); foreign language/ESL education (MS, Ed S); instructional technology (MS, Ed D, PhD, Ed S); literacy, language and ESL education (PhD); literacy, language education, and ESL education (Ed D); mathematics education (MS, Ed S); modified and comprehensive special education (MS); reading education (MS, Ed S); school counseling (Ed S); school psychology (PhD, Ed S); science education (MS, Ed S); secondary teaching (MS); social foundations (MS); social science education (MS, Ed S); socio-cultural foundations of sports and education (PhD); special education (Ed S); teacher education (Ed D, PhD). *Accreditation:* NCATE. Part-time and evening/weekend programs available. *Degree requirements:* For master's and Ed S, thesis optional; for doctorate, variable foreign language requirement, thesis/dissertation. *Entrance requirements:* For master's, minimum GPA of 2.7; for doctorate and Ed S, GRE General Test, minimum GPA of 2.7. Additional exam requirements/recommendations for international students: Required—TOEFL. Electronic applications accepted. *Expenses:* Tuition, state resident: full-time $6826; part-time $380 per semester hour. Tuition, nonresident: full-time $21,844; part-time $1147 per semester hour. Tuition and fees vary according to program.

The University of Texas at Brownsville, Graduate Studies, School of Education, Brownsville, TX 78520-4991. Offers bilingual education (M Ed); counseling and guidance (M Ed); curriculum and instruction (M Ed); early childhood education (M Ed); educational administration (M Ed); educational technology (M Ed); English as a second language (M Ed); reading specialist (M Ed); special education/educational diagnostician (M Ed). Part-time and evening/weekend programs available. Postbaccalaureate distance learning degree programs offered (minimal on-campus study). *Degree requirements:* For master's, thesis optional. *Entrance requirements:* For master's, GRE General Test. Additional exam requirements/recommendations for international students: Required—TOEFL.

The University of Texas at San Antonio, College of Education and Human Development, Department of Interdisciplinary Learning and Teaching, San Antonio, TX 78249-0617. Offers curriculum and instruction (MA); early childhood education (MA); instructional technology (MA); reading (MA); special education (MA). Part-time and evening/weekend programs available. *Faculty:* 28 full-time (24 women), 1 part-time/adjunct (0 women). *Students:* 103 full-time (83 women), 317 part-time (253 women); includes 227 minority (36 African Americans, 11 Asian Americans or Pacific Islanders, 180 Hispanic Americans), 17 international. Average age 33. 212 applicants, 90% accepted, 140 enrolled. In 2009, 74 master's awarded. *Degree requirements:* For master's, comprehensive exam (for some programs), thesis (for some programs). *Entrance requirements:* For master's, GRE General Test, minimum GPA of 3.0. Additional exam requirements/recommendations for international students: Required—TOEFL (minimum score 500 paper-based; 173 computer-based; 61 iBT), IELTS (minimum score 5). *Application deadline:* For fall admission, 7/1 for domestic students, 4/1 for international students; for spring admission, 11/1 for domestic students, 9/1 for international students. Applications are processed on a rolling basis. Application fee: $45 ($80 for international students). Electronic applications accepted. *Expenses:* Tuition, state resident: full-time $3975; part-time $221 per contact hour. Tuition, nonresident: full-time $13,947; part-time $775 per contact hour. Required fees: $1853. *Financial support:* In 2009–10, 76 students received support, including 25 research assistantships (averaging $11,599 per year), 4 teaching assistantships (averaging $8,800 per year); scholarships/grants, tuition waivers, and unspecified assistantships also available. Support available to part-time students. *Faculty research:* Adult education; early childhood education; literacy; special education; science, technology, engineering and math fields. Total annual research expenditures: $57,097. *Unit head:* Dr. Belinda B. Flores, Chair, 210-458-5969, Fax: 210-458-7281, E-mail: belinda.flores@utsa.edu. *Application contact:* Mari Cortez, Graduate Advisor, 210-458-4414, E-mail: mari.cortez@utsa.edu.

The University of Texas at Tyler, College of Education and Psychology, School of Education, Tyler, TX 75799-0001. Offers early childhood education (M Ed, MA); reading (M Ed, MA); special education (M Ed, MA). Part-time and evening/weekend programs available. *Faculty:* 18 full-time (8 women). *Students:* 4 full-time (3 women), 30 part-time (all women); includes 4 minority (3 African Americans, 1 Hispanic American), 2 international. Average age 37. 13 applicants, 100% accepted, 6 enrolled. In 2009, 14 master's awarded. *Degree requirements:* For master's, comprehensive exam, thesis (for some programs), research project. *Entrance requirements:* For master's, GRE General Test. Additional exam requirements/recommendations

for international students: Required—TOEFL (minimum score 79 computer-based). *Application deadline:* For fall admission, 8/17 priority date for domestic students, 7/1 priority date for international students; for spring admission, 12/21 priority date for domestic students, 11/1 priority date for international students. Applications are processed on a rolling basis. Application fee: $25 ($50 for international students). Electronic applications accepted. *Expenses:* Tuition, state resident: part-time $665 per semester hour. Tuition, nonresident: part-time $942 per semester hour. Part-time tuition and fees vary according to degree level and program. *Financial support:* In 2009–10, 2 research assistantships (averaging $12,000 per year) were awarded; scholarships/grants also available. Financial award application deadline: 7/1. *Faculty research:* Improving quality in childcare settings, play and creativity, teacher interactions, effects of modeling on early childhood teachers, biofeedback, literacy instruction. *Unit head:* Dr. Kathy L. Morrison, Interim Director, 903-566-7016, Fax: 903-565-5560, E-mail: kmorrison@uttyler.edu. *Application contact:* Dr. Kathy Morrison, Program Director for Curriculum and Instruction and Early Childhood, 903-566-7016, Fax: 903-565-5560, E-mail: kmorrison@uttyler.edu.

The University of Texas of the Permian Basin, Office of Graduate Studies, School of Education, Program in Early Childhood Education, Odessa, TX 79762-0001. Offers MA. *Degree requirements:* For master's, comprehensive exam (for some programs), thesis (for some programs). *Entrance requirements:* For master's, GRE General Test. Additional exam requirements/recommendations for international students: Required—TOEFL (minimum score 550 paper-based; 213 computer-based).

The University of Texas–Pan American, College of Education, Department of Curriculum and Instruction: Elementary and Secondary, Edinburg, TX 78539. Offers bilingual education (M Ed); early childhood education (M Ed); elementary education (M Ed); reading (M Ed); secondary education (M Ed). Part-time programs available. *Degree requirements:* For master's, comprehensive exam, thesis optional. *Entrance requirements:* For master's, GRE. Additional exam requirements/recommendations for international students: Required—TOEFL, IELTS. *Expenses:* Tuition, state resident: full-time $3630.60; part-time $201.70 per credit hour. Tuition, nonresident: full-time $8617; part-time $478.70 per credit hour. Required fees: $806.50. *Faculty research:* Dual language instruction, literacy and technology, teacher education in diverse populations, mathematics and science education.

University of the Cumberlands, Graduate Programs in Education, Program in Early Childhood Education, Williamsburg, KY 40769-1372. Offers MA Ed. Part-time and evening/weekend programs available. *Degree requirements:* For master's, comprehensive exam. *Entrance requirements:* For master's, GRE or NTE, Kentucky teaching certificate.

University of the District of Columbia, College of Arts and Sciences, Department of Education, Program in Early Childhood Education, Washington, DC 20008-1175. Offers MA. *Accreditation:* NCATE. Part-time programs available. *Students:* 1 (woman) part-time; includes Asian American or Pacific Islander. Average age 34. 16 applicants, 94% accepted. In 2009, 4 master's awarded. *Degree requirements:* For master's, comprehensive exam, research paper. *Entrance requirements:* For master's, GRE General Test, writing proficiency exam, minimum GPA of 3.0. *Application deadline:* For fall admission, 6/15 priority date for domestic students; for spring admission, 11/1 for domestic students. Applications are processed on a rolling basis. Application fee: $20. *Expenses:* Tuition, state resident: full-time $7580. Tuition, nonresident: full-time $14,580. Required fees: $620. *Financial support:* Fellowships, research assistantships available. *Unit head:* Dr. Rosemary Bolig, Professor, 202-274-5216. *Application contact:* Ann Marie Waterman, Associate Vice President for Admission, Recruitment and Financial Aid, 202-274-6069.

University of the Incarnate Word, School of Graduate Studies and Research, Dreeben School of Education, Programs in Education, San Antonio, TX 78209-6397. Offers adult education (M Ed, MA); cross-cultural education (M Ed, MA); early childhood literacy (M Ed, MA); general education (M Ed, MA); Higher Education (PhD); instructional technology (M Ed, MA); international education and entrepreneurship (PhD); kinesiology (M Ed, MA); literacy (M Ed, MA); organizational leadership (PhD); organizational learning and learning (M Ed, MA); reading (M Ed, MA); special education (M Ed, MA); teacher leadership (M Ed, MA). Part-time and evening/weekend programs available. *Students:* 20 full-time (11 women), 201 part-time (122 women); includes 113 minority (29 African Americans, 2 American Indian/Alaska Native, 2 Asian Americans or Pacific Islanders, 80 Hispanic Americans), 30 international. Average age 41. In 2009, 26 master's, 19 doctorates awarded. *Degree requirements:* For master's, capstone; for doctorate, thesis/dissertation, qualifying exam. *Entrance requirements:* For master's, baccalaureate degree; minimum foundation GPA of 2.5; interview; for doctorate, master's degree; interview; supervised writing sample. Additional exam requirements/recommendations for international students: Required—TOEFL (minimum score 560 paper-based; 220 computer-based; 83 iBT). *Application deadline:* Applications are processed on a rolling basis. Application fee: $20. Electronic applications accepted. *Expenses:* Tuition: Full-time $12,150; part-time $675 per credit hour. Required fees: $83 per credit hour. *Financial support:* Federal Work-Study and scholarships/grants available. Financial award applicants required to submit FAFSA. *Unit head:* Dr. Denise Staudt, Dean, Dreeben School of Education, 210-829-2762, E-mail: staudt@uiwtx.edu. *Application contact:* Andrea Cyterski-Acosta, Dean of Enrollment, 210-829-6005, Fax: 210-829-3921, E-mail: admis@uiwtx.edu.

University of the Sacred Heart, Graduate Programs, Department of Education, San Juan, PR 00914-0383. Offers early childhood education (M Ed); information technology and multimedia (Certificate); instruction systems and education technology (M Ed), including English, information technology and multimedia, instructional design, mathematics, Spanish. Part-time and evening/weekend programs available. *Degree requirements:* For master's, thesis. *Entrance requirements:* For master's, EXADEP, minimum undergraduate GPA of 2.75, interview.

University of the Southwest, Graduate Programs, Hobbs, NM 88240-9129. Offers business administration (MBA); curriculum and instruction (MSE); curriculum and instruction: bilingual (MSE); curriculum and instruction: reading (MSE); curriculum and instruction: TESOL (MSE); early childhood education (MSE); educational diagnostician (MSE); mental health counseling (MSE); school business administration (MSE); school counseling (MSE); special education (MSE). Part-time and evening/weekend programs available. Postbaccalaureate distance learning degree programs offered (no on-campus study). *Faculty:* 10 full-time (6 women), 10 part-time/adjunct (4 women). *Students:* 112 full-time (93 women), 99 part-time (72 women). Average age 35. 94 applicants, 47% accepted, 39 enrolled. In 2009, 32 master's awarded. *Degree requirements:* For master's, comprehensive exam. *Application deadline:* For fall admission, 3/1 priority date for domestic students; for spring admission, 10/1 for domestic students. Applications are processed on a rolling basis. Application fee: $25. Electronic applications accepted. *Expenses:* Tuition: Part-time $512 per hour. Tuition and fees vary according to course load. *Financial support:* In 2009–10, 196 students received support; research assistantships with partial tuition reimbursements available, Federal Work-Study, scholarships/grants, and tuition waivers (partial) available. Support available to part-time students. Financial award application deadline: 4/1; financial award applicants required to submit FAFSA. *Unit head:* Dr. Mary Harris, Dean of Education, 575-392-6561 Ext. 1056, Fax: 575-392-6006, E-mail: mharris@usw.edu. *Application contact:* Ryanne Evans, Assistant Registrar, 575-392-6561 Ext. 1031, Fax: 575-392-6006, E-mail: revans@usw.edu.

The University of Toledo, College of Graduate Studies, College of Education, Department of Curriculum and Instruction, Program in Early Childhood Education, Toledo, OH 43606-3390. Offers ME.

The University of Toledo, College of Graduate Studies, College of Education, Department of Early Childhood, Physical and Special Education, Program in Early Childhood Education, Toledo, OH 43606-3390. Offers ME, Ed S.

University of Utah, Graduate School, College of Education, Department of Special Education, Salt Lake City, UT 84112. Offers early childhood hearing impairments (M Ed, MS); early childhood special education (M Ed, PhD); early childhood vision impairments (M Ed, MS); hearing impairments (M Ed, MS); mild/moderate disabilities (M Ed, MS, PhD); professional practice (M Ed); research in special education (MS); severe disabilities (M Ed, MS, PhD); vision impairments (M Ed). Part-time and evening/weekend programs available. Postbaccalaureate distance learning degree programs offered (no on-campus study). *Faculty:* 17 full-time (12 women), 7 part-time/adjunct (5 women). *Students:* 41 full-time (40 women), 20 part-time (16 women); includes 5 minority (1 African American, 2 American Indian/Alaska Native, 2 Hispanic Americans), 3 international. Average age 35. 34 applicants, 65% accepted, 11 enrolled. In 2009, 27 master's, 2 doctorates awarded. Terminal master's awarded for partial completion of doctoral program. *Degree requirements:* For master's, comprehensive exam, thesis (for some programs), qualifying exam; for doctorate, thesis/dissertation, qualifying exam. *Entrance requirements:* For master's, GRE or Analytical/Writing portion of GRE plus PRAXIS I; Basic Skills Test, minimum GPA of 3.0; for doctorate, GRE General Test (minimum score: Verbal-600; Quantitative-600; Analytical/Writing-4), minimum GPA of 3.0, 3.5 (recommended). Additional exam requirements/recommendations for international students: Required—TOEFL (minimum score 600 paper-based; 250 computer-based; 100 iBT). *Application deadline:* For fall admission, 3/1 for domestic and international students; for spring admission, 11/1 for domestic and international students. Application fee: $55 ($65 for international students). *Expenses:* Contact institution. *Financial support:* In 2009–10, 44 students received support, including 44 fellowships with full and partial tuition reimbursements available (averaging $8,800 per year), 1 research assistantship (averaging $4,500 per year), 3 teaching assistantships (averaging $3,000 per year); career-related internships or fieldwork and scholarships/grants also available. Support available to part-time students. Financial award application deadline: 3/1; financial award applicants required to submit FAFSA. *Faculty research:* Inclusive education, positive behavior support, reading, instruction and intervention strategies. *Unit head:* Dr. Andrea P. McDonnell, Chair, 801-581-8121, Fax: 801-585-6476, E-mail: andrea.mcdonnell@utah.edu. *Application contact:* Patty Davis, Academic Advisor, 801-581-4764, Fax: 801-585-6476, E-mail: patty.davis@utah.edu.

University of Victoria, Faculty of Graduate Studies, Faculty of Education, Department of Curriculum and Instruction, Victoria, BC V8W 2Y2, Canada. Offers art education (M Ed, PhD); curriculum studies (M Ed, MA, PhD); early childhood education (M Ed, PhD); educational studies (PhD); language and literacy (M Ed, MA, PhD); mathematics (M Ed, MA, PhD); music education (M Ed, MA, PhD); science (M Ed, MA, PhD); social studies (M Ed, MA); social, cultural and foundational studies (MA, PhD); technology and environmental education (PhD). Part-time programs available. *Degree requirements:* For master's, thesis, project (M Ed); for doctorate, comprehensive exam, thesis/dissertation. *Entrance requirements:* For master's, minimum B average. Additional exam requirements/recommendations for international students: Required—TOEFL (minimum score 575 paper-based; 233 computer-based), IELTS (minimum score 7). Electronic applications accepted. *Faculty research:* Elementary and secondary English, language arts, curriculum theory and practice, educational media and technology, educational administration and leadership, history and philosophy of education.

University of Virginia, Curry School of Education, Program in Education, Charlottesville, VA 22903. Offers administration and supervision (PhD); applied developmental science (PhD); counselor education (PhD); curriculum and instruction (PhD); early childhood-developmental risk (MT); education evaluation (PhD); educational psychology (PhD); educational research (PhD); elementary (MT, PhD); English education (MT, PhD); foreign language education (MT); higher education (PhD); instructional technology (PhD); kinesiology (MT, PhD); math education (PhD); reading education (PhD); research statistics and evaluation (PhD); school psychology (PhD); science education (PhD); social studies education (MT, PhD); special education (PhD); world languages education (MT). *Students:* 336 full-time (239 women), 88 part-time (54 women); includes 43 minority (24 African Americans, 2 American Indian/Alaska Native, 11 Asian Americans or Pacific Islanders, 6 Hispanic Americans), 18 international. Average age 27. 199 applicants, 48% accepted, 55 enrolled. In 2009, 127 master's, 52 doctorates awarded. *Degree requirements:* For master's, comprehensive exam (for some programs), field project; for doctorate, comprehensive exam, thesis/dissertation. *Entrance requirements:* For doctorate, GRE General Test. Additional exam requirements/recommendations for international students: Required—TOEFL (minimum score 600 paper-based; 250 computer-based; 90 iBT), IELTS (minimum score 7). *Application deadline:* Applications are processed on a rolling basis. Application fee: $60. Electronic applications accepted. *Financial support:* Fellowships, research assistantships, teaching assistantships available. Financial award application deadline: 1/5; financial award applicants required to submit FAFSA.

The University of West Alabama, School of Graduate Studies, College of Education, Department of Teacher Education, Program in Early Childhood Education, Livingston, AL 35470. Offers M Ed. *Accreditation:* NCATE. Part-time programs available. *Entrance requirements:* For master's, GRE General Test, MAT, minimum GPA of 2.75.

University of West Florida, College of Professional Studies, School of Education, Master's Program in Curriculum and Instruction, Pensacola, FL 32514-5750. Offers curriculum and instruction: special education (M Ed); elementary education (M Ed); primary education (M Ed). Part-time and evening/weekend programs available. *Students:* 12 full-time (all women), 108 part-time (96 women); includes 16 minority (11 African Americans, 2 Asian Americans or Pacific Islanders, 3 Hispanic Americans), 2 international. Average age 36. 36 applicants, 25% accepted, 9 enrolled. In 2009, 35 master's awarded. *Entrance requirements:* For master's, GRE (minimum score 450 verbal) or MAT (minimum score 396) if bachelor's GPA less than 3.0, state teaching certification; letter of intent; two professional references. Additional exam requirements/recommendations for international students: Required—TOEFL (minimum score 550 paper-based; 213 computer-based). *Application deadline:* For fall admission, 6/1 for domestic students, 5/15 for international students; for spring admission, 11/1 for domestic students, 10/1 for international students. Applications are processed on a rolling basis. Application fee: $30. *Expenses:* Tuition, state resident: full-time $4982; part-time $260 per credit hour. Tuition, nonresident: full-time $20,059; part-time $919 per credit hour. Required fees: $1247; $52 per credit hour. *Financial support:* Career-related internships or fieldwork, Federal Work-Study, scholarships/grants, and tuition waivers (partial) available. Support available to part-time students. Financial award application deadline: 4/15; financial award applicants required to submit FAFSA. *Unit head:* Dr. David Stout, Interim Chairperson, 850-474-2284, Fax: 850-474-2844. *Application contact:* Terry McCray, Assistant Director of Graduate Admissions, 850-473-7718, Fax: 850-473-7714, E-mail: gradadmissions@uwf.edu.

University of West Georgia, Graduate School, College of Education, Department of Curriculum and Instruction, Carrollton, GA 30118. Offers art education (M Ed); art teacher education (Ed S); biology/secondary education (Ed S); business education (M Ed, Ed S); early childhood education (M Ed, Ed S); economics/secondary teacher education (Ed S); English teacher education (Ed S); French language teacher education (Ed S); history teacher education (Ed S); mathematics teacher education (Ed S); middle grades education (M Ed, Ed S); reading education (M Ed, Ed S); science teacher education (Ed S); secondary education (M Ed, Ed S); social science teacher education (Ed S); Spanish language teacher education (Ed S). Part-time and evening/weekend programs available. *Faculty:* 18 full-time (15 women), 7 part-time/adjunct (6 women). *Students:* 119 full-time (101 women), 358 part-time (280 women); includes 109 minority (97 African Americans, 3 American Indian/Alaska Native, 2 Asian Americans or Pacific Islanders, 7 Hispanic Americans). Average age 33. 193 applicants, 82% accepted, 34 enrolled. In 2009, 109 master's, 27 Ed Ss awarded. *Degree requirements:* For master's, comprehensive exam; for Ed S, research project. *Entrance requirements:* For master's, GRE General Test or MAT, minimum GPA of 2.7; for Ed S, GRE General Test, master's degree, minimum graduate GPA of 2.7. *Application deadline:* For fall admission, 7/17 for domestic students; for spring admission, 11/20 for domestic students. Applications are processed on a rolling basis. Application fee: $30. Electronic applications accepted. *Expenses:* Tuition, state resident: full-time $2952; part-time $164 per semester hour. Tuition, nonresident: full-time $11,808; part-time $656 per semester hour. Required fees: $42.90 per semester hour. $307 per semester. Tuition and fees vary according to course load. *Financial support:* In 2009–10, 5 research assistantships with full tuition reimbursements (averaging $3,000 per year) were awarded; career-related internships or fieldwork and scholarships/grants also available. Support available to part-time students. Financial award applicants required to submit FAFSA. *Unit head:* Dr. Donna Harkins, Chair, 678-839-6066, Fax: 678-839-6559, E-mail: dharkins@westga.edu. *Application contact:* Dr. Charles W. Clark, Dean, 678-839-6508, E-mail: cclark@westga.edu.

Early Childhood Education

University of Wisconsin–Milwaukee, Graduate School, School of Education, Department of Curriculum and Instruction, Milwaukee, WI 53201-0413. Offers curriculum planning and instruction improvement (MS); early childhood education (MS); elementary education (MS); junior high/middle school education (MS); reading education (MS); secondary education (MS); teaching in an urban setting (MS). Part-time programs available. *Faculty:* 22 full-time (17 women). *Students:* 23 full-time (14 women), 64 part-time (58 women); includes 8 minority (4 African Americans, 1 American Indian/Alaska Native, 3 Hispanic Americans), 1 international. Average age 31. 46 applicants, 57% accepted, 12 enrolled. In 2009, 28 master's awarded. *Degree requirements:* For master's, thesis or alternative. *Entrance requirements:* Additional exam requirements/recommendations for international students: Required—TOEFL (minimum score 550 paper-based; 79 iBT), IELTS (minimum score 6.5). *Application deadline:* For fall admission, 1/1 priority date for domestic students; for spring admission, 9/1 for domestic students. Applications are processed on a rolling basis. Application fee: $45 ($75 for international students). *Expenses:* Tuition, state resident: full-time $8800. Tuition, nonresident: full-time $20,760. Tuition and fees vary according to program and reciprocity agreements. *Financial support:* Career-related internships or fieldwork and unspecified assistantships available. Support available to part-time students. Financial award application deadline: 4/15. Total annual research expenditures: $65,946. *Unit head:* Hope Longwell-Grice, Chair, 414-229-4884, Fax: 414-229-5571, E-mail: hope@uwm.edu. *Application contact:* General Information Contact, 414-229-4982, Fax: 414-229-6967, E-mail: gradschool@uwm.edu.

University of Wisconsin–Oshkosh, The Office of Graduate Studies, College of Education and Human Services, Department of Special Education, Oshkosh, WI 54901. Offers cross-categorical (MSE); early childhood: exceptional education needs (MSE); non-licensure (MSE). Part-time and evening/weekend programs available. *Degree requirements:* For master's, comprehensive exam (for some programs), thesis or alternative, field report. *Entrance requirements:* For master's, interview, minimum GPA of 3.0, teaching license, letters of recommendation. Additional exam requirements/recommendations for international students: Required—TOEFL (minimum score 550 paper-based; 213 computer-based; 79 iBT). Electronic applications accepted. *Faculty research:* Private agency contributions to the disabled, graduation requirements for exceptional education needs students, direct instruction in spelling for learning disabled, effects of behavioral parent training, secondary education programming issues.

Ursuline College, School of Graduate Studies, Program in Education, Pepper Pike, OH 44124-4398. Offers art education (MA); early childhood education (MA); language arts education (MA); life science education (MA); math education (MA); middle school education (MA); social studies education (MA); special education (MA). *Accreditation:* NCATE. *Faculty:* 1 (woman) full-time, 10 part-time/adjunct (8 women). *Students:* 53 full-time (40 women), 3 part-time (all women); includes 8 minority (7 African Americans, 1 Hispanic American). Average age 34. In 2009, 11 master's awarded. *Degree requirements:* For master's, comprehensive exam. *Entrance requirements:* For master's, minimum undergraduate GPA of 3.0. Additional exam requirements/recommendations for international students: Required—TOEFL (minimum score 500 paper-based; 173 computer-based). *Application deadline:* For fall admission, 8/1 priority date for domestic students. Applications are processed on a rolling basis. Application fee: $25. *Expenses:* Contact institution. *Financial support:* Federal Work-Study available. Financial award application deadline: 3/1. *Unit head:* Karen Godenschwager Nelson, Director, 440-684-8338, Fax: 440-684-6088, E-mail: kgodenschwager@ursuline.edu. *Application contact:* Melanie Steele, Secretary, 440-646-8199, Fax: 440-684-6138, E-mail: gradsch@ursuline.edu.

Valdosta State University, Graduate School, Department of Early Childhood and Reading Education, Valdosta, GA 31698. Offers early childhood education (M Ed, Ed S); reading education (M Ed). *Accreditation:* NCATE. Part-time and evening/weekend programs available. *Degree requirements:* For master's, comprehensive written and/or oral exams; for Ed S, thesis. *Entrance requirements:* For master's and Ed S, GRE General Test or MAT. Additional exam requirements/recommendations for international students: Required—TOEFL (minimum score 523 paper-based; 193 computer-based). Electronic applications accepted.

Virginia Commonwealth University, Graduate School, School of Education, Program in Special Education, Richmond, VA 23284-9005. Offers early childhood (M Ed); emotionally disturbed (M Ed, MT); learning disabilities (M Ed); mentally retarded (M Ed, MT); severely/profoundly handicapped (M Ed). *Accreditation:* NCATE. *Degree requirements:* For master's, comprehensive exam. *Entrance requirements:* For master's, GRE General Test or MAT.

Virginia Commonwealth University, Graduate School, School of Education, Program in Teaching and Learning, Richmond, VA 23284-9005. Offers early education (MT); middle education (MT); secondary education (MT, Certificate); special education (MT). *Accreditation:* NCATE. Part-time programs available. *Entrance requirements:* For master's, GRE General Test or MAT.

Wagner College, Division of Graduate Studies, Department of Education, Program in Early Childhood Education (Birth-Grade 2), Staten Island, NY 10301-4495. Offers MS Ed. Part-time and evening/weekend programs available. *Degree requirements:* For master's, thesis. *Entrance requirements:* For master's, minimum GPA of 2.75. Additional exam requirements/recommendations for international students: Required—TOEFL (minimum score 550 paper-based; 217 computer-based). *Expenses:* Tuition: Full-time $15,570; part-time $865 per credit. Required fees: $2.

Walden University, Graduate Programs, Richard W. Riley College of Education and Leadership, Minneapolis, MN 55401. Offers administrator leadership for teaching and learning (Ed D, Ed S); curriculum, instruction, and professional development (Ed S); early childhood education (birth-grade 3) (MAT); education (MS, PhD), including adolescent literacy and technology (grades 6-12) (MS), adult education leadership (PhD), community college leadership (PhD), curriculum, instruction, and assessment, early childhood education (PhD), educational leadership (MS), educational technology (PhD), elementary reading and literacy (MS), elementary reading and mathematics (MS), emotional/behavioral disorders (K-12) (MS), general program, higher education (PhD), integrating technology in the classroom (MS), K-12 educational leadership (PhD), learning disabilities (K-12) (MS), literacy and learning in the content areas (MS), mathematics (grades 6-8) (MS), mathematics (grades K-5) (MS), middle level education (grades 5-8) (MS), professional development (MS), science (grades K-8) (MS), self-designed (PhD), special education (PhD), special education (non-licensure) (MS), teacher leadership (grades K-12) (MS); educational leadership and administration (principal preparation) (Ed S); educational technology (Ed S); higher education and adult learning (Ed D); instructional design (Postbaccalaureate Certificate); instructional design and technology (MS), including general program (MS, PhD), online learning, training and performance improvement; special education: emotional/behavioral disorders (K-12) (MAT); special education: learning disabilities (K-12) (MAT); teacher leadership (Ed D, Ed S). Part-time and evening/weekend programs available. Postbaccalaureate distance learning degree programs offered (minimal on-campus study). *Faculty:* 54 full-time, 835 part-time/adjunct. *Students:* 13,940 full-time (11,339 women), 1,940 part-time (1,637 women); includes 4,626 minority (3,795 African Americans, 111 American Indian/Alaska Native, 199 Asian Americans or Pacific Islanders, 521 Hispanic Americans), 124 international. Average age 38. In 2009, 4,688 master's, 190 doctorates awarded. *Degree requirements:* For doctorate, thesis/dissertation (for some programs), residency; for other advanced degree, residency (for some programs). *Entrance requirements:* For master's, bachelor's degree or equivalent in related field; minimum GPA of 2.5; official transcripts; goal statement; access to computer and Internet; for doctorate, master's degree or equivalent in related field; minimum GPA of 3.0; official transcripts; three years' related professional/academic experience (preferred); access to computer and Internet; for other advanced degree, master's degree or equivalent in related field; minimum GPA of 3.0; 3 years related professional/academic experience (preferred); access to computer and Internet (Ed S). Additional exam requirements/recommendations for international students: Required—TOEFL (minimum score 550 paper-based; 213 computer-based), IELTS (minimum score 6.5), or Michigan English Language Assessment Battery (minimum score 82). *Application deadline:* Applications are processed on a rolling basis. Application fee: $50. Electronic applications accepted. *Expenses:* Tuition: Full-time $13,665; part-time $560 per credit. Required fees: $1375. Tuition and fees vary according to course load, degree level and program. *Financial support:* In 2009–10, 2,418 students received support; fellowships, Federal Work-Study, scholarships/grants, unspecified assistantships, and family tuition reduction, active duty/veteran tuition reduction, group tuition reduction, interest-free payment plans available. Support available to part-time students. Financial award applicants required to submit FAFSA. *Unit head:* Dr. Kate Steffens, Dean, 800-925-3368. *Application contact:* Jennifer Hall, Director of Enrollment, 866-4-WALDEN, E-mail: info@waldenu.edu.

Wayne State College, School of Education and Counseling, Department of Educational Foundations and Leadership, Program in Curriculum and Instruction, Wayne, NE 68787. Offers alternative education (MSE); business and information technology education (MSE); communication arts education (MSE); early childhood education (MSE); elementary education (MSE); English as a second language (MSE); English education (MSE); family and consumer sciences education (MSE); industrial technology and vocational education (MSE); learning communities (MSE); mathematics education (MSE); music education (MSE); science education (MSE); social science education (MSE). *Accreditation:* NCATE. Part-time and evening/weekend programs available. *Degree requirements:* For master's, comprehensive exam, thesis optional. *Entrance requirements:* For master's, GRE General Test. Additional exam requirements/recommendations for international students: Required—TOEFL (minimum score 550 paper-based; 213 computer-based).

Wayne State University, College of Education, Division of Teacher Education, Detroit, MI 48202. Offers adult and continuing education (M Ed); art education (M Ed); bilingual/bicultural education (M Ed, MAT); business education (M Ed, MAT); career and technical education (M Ed, Ed D, PhD, Ed S); curriculum and instruction (Ed D, PhD, Ed S); distributive education (M Ed, MAT); early childhood education (M Ed); elementary education (M Ed, MAT, Ed D, PhD, Ed S); elementary education curriculum and instruction (M Ed); English education (M Ed); English education-secondary (M Ed, Ed S); foreign language education (M Ed); general education (Ed D, Ed S); health occupations education (M Ed); industrial education (M Ed); mathematics education (M Ed, Ed S); pre-school and parent education (M Ed); reading (M Ed, Ed D, Ed S); reading, languages and literature (Ed D); school music-vocal (M Ed); science education (M Ed, MAT, Ed S); secondary education (MAT); secondary school reading (M Ed); social studies education (M Ed, Ed S), including education-secondary (M Ed); special education (M Ed, Ed D, PhD, Ed S); teacher education (MAT, Ed D, PhD). *Degree requirements:* For doctorate, thesis/dissertation. *Entrance requirements:* For master's, Michigan Basic Skills Test (MA in teaching), minimum GPA of 2.6; for doctorate, minimum undergraduate GPA of 3.0, graduate 3.5; interview, curriculum vitae; references. Additional exam requirements/recommendations for international students: Required—TOEFL (minimum score 550 paper-based; 213 computer-based), TWE (minimum score 6). Electronic applications accepted. *Faculty research:* Reading and writing literacy and literature.

Webster University, School of Education, Department of Communication Arts, Reading and Early Childhood, St. Louis, MO 63119-3194. Offers communications (MAT); early childhood education (MAT). *Entrance requirements:* For master's, minimum GPA of 2.5. Additional exam requirements/recommendations for international students: Required—TOEFL. *Expenses:* Tuition: Part-time $565 per credit hour. Tuition and fees vary according to degree level, campus/location and program.

Wesleyan College, Department of Education, Program in Early Childhood Education, Macon, GA 31210-4462. Offers MA. Part-time programs available. *Degree requirements:* For master's, thesis or alternative, practicum, professional portfolio. *Entrance requirements:* For master's, GRE or MAT, interview, teaching certificate, 3 letters of recommendation. Additional exam requirements/recommendations for international students: Required—TOEFL.

West Chester University of Pennsylvania, Office of Graduate Studies, College of Education, Department of Early and Middle Grades, West Chester, PA 19383. Offers early childhood education (M Ed, Teaching Certificate); elementary education (M Ed). *Accreditation:* NCATE. Part-time and evening/weekend programs available. *Students:* 32 full-time (28 women), 148 part-time (132 women); includes 13 minority (6 African Americans, 4 Asian Americans or Pacific Islanders, 3 Hispanic Americans). Average age 30. 96 applicants, 96% accepted, 55 enrolled. In 2009, 67 master's awarded. *Degree requirements:* For master's, comprehensive exam, thesis optional. *Entrance requirements:* For master's, GMAT, GRE General Test, or MAT, interview, minimum GPA of 3.0. Additional exam requirements/recommendations for international students: Required—TOEFL (minimum score 550 paper-based; 213 computer-based; 80 iBT). *Application deadline:* For fall admission, 4/15 priority date for domestic students, 3/15 for international students; for spring admission, 10/15 for domestic students. Applications are processed on a rolling basis. Application fee: $35. Electronic applications accepted. *Expenses:* Tuition, state resident: full-time $6666; part-time $370 per credit. Tuition, nonresident: full-time $10,666; part-time $593 per credit. Required fees: $122.56 per credit. *Financial support:* In 2009–10, research assistantships with full and partial tuition reimbursements (averaging $5,000 per year); unspecified assistantships also available. Support available to part-time students. Financial award application deadline: 2/15; financial award applicants required to submit FAFSA. *Faculty research:* Cooperative learning, peer mediation in schools, creative thinking and questioning. *Unit head:* Dr. Heather Leaman, Chair, 610-738-0515, E-mail: hleaman@wcupa.edu. *Application contact:* Dr. Connie DiLucchio, Graduate Coordinator, 610-436-3323, E-mail: cdilucchio@wcupa.edu.

Western Kentucky University, Graduate Studies, College of Education and Behavioral Sciences, Department of Special Instructional Programs, Bowling Green, KY 42101. Offers exceptional child education (MAE); interdisciplinary early child education (MAE); library media education (MS); literacy (MAE). Part-time and evening/weekend programs available. Post-baccalaureate distance learning degree programs offered (minimal on-campus study). *Degree requirements:* For master's, comprehensive exam. *Entrance requirements:* For master's, GRE General Test. Additional exam requirements/recommendations for international students: Required—TOEFL (minimum score 555 paper-based; 213 computer-based; 79 iBT). *Expenses:* Tuition, state resident: full-time $4160; part-time $416 per credit hour. Tuition, nonresident: full-time $9550; part-time $506 per credit hour. Tuition and fees vary according to campus/location and reciprocity agreements. *Faculty research:* Teacher preparation in moderate/severe disabilities.

Western Oregon University, Graduate Programs, College of Education, Division of Special Education, Program in Early Childhood Special Education, Monmouth, OR 97361-1394. Offers MS Ed. *Accreditation:* NCATE. Part-time and evening/weekend programs available. *Degree requirements:* For master's, thesis optional, written exam, portfolio. *Entrance requirements:* For master's, CBEST, PRAXIS or GRE General Test, minimum GPA of 3.0, teaching license. Additional exam requirements/recommendations for international students: Required—TOEFL (minimum score 550 paper-based; 213 computer-based; 79 iBT), IELTS (minimum score 6.5). *Faculty research:* High school through university articulation, career development for early childhood educators professional collaboration/cooperation.

Westfield State College, Division of Graduate and Continuing Education, Department of Education, Program in Early Childhood Education, Westfield, MA 01086. Offers M Ed. *Accreditation:* NCATE. Part-time and evening/weekend programs available. *Degree requirements:* For master's, comprehensive exam, practicum. *Entrance requirements:* For master's, GRE General Test or MAT, minimum undergraduate GPA of 2.7.

West Virginia University, College of Human Resources and Education, Department of Special Education, Morgantown, WV 26506. Offers autism spectrum disorder (5-adult) (MA); autism spectrum disorder (K-6) (MA); early intervention/early childhood special education (MA); gifted education (1-12) (MA); low vision (PreK-adult) (MA); multicategorical special education (5-adult) (MA); multicategorical special education (K-6) (MA); severe/multiple disabilities (K-adult) (MA); special education (MA, Ed D); vision impairments (PreK-adult) (MA). *Accreditation:* NCATE. Part-time and evening/weekend programs available. Postbaccalaureate distance learning degree programs offered (no on-campus study). *Degree requirements:* For master's, thesis optional;

for doctorate, comprehensive exam, thesis/dissertation. *Entrance requirements:* For master's, minimum GPA of 2.75 passing scores on PRAXIS PPST; for doctorate, GRE General Test or MAT. Additional exam requirements/recommendations for international students: Required—TOEFL.

Wheelock College, Graduate Programs, Division of Education, Boston, MA 02215-4176. Offers early childhood education (MS); education leadership (MS); elementary education (MS); language, literacy, and reading (MS); teaching students with moderate disabilities (MS). *Accreditation:* NCATE. Postbaccalaureate distance learning degree programs offered (minimal on-campus study). *Degree requirements:* For master's, comprehensive exam. *Entrance requirements:* Additional exam requirements/recommendations for international students: Required—TOEFL. Electronic applications accepted. *Faculty research:* Symbolic learning, emergent literacy, diversity inclusion, beginning reading language and culture, math education.

Widener University, School of Human Service Professions, Center for Education, Chester, PA 19013-5792. Offers adult education (M Ed); counseling in higher education (M Ed); counselor education (M Ed); early childhood education (M Ed); educational foundations (M Ed); educational leadership (M Ed); educational psychology (M Ed); elementary education (M Ed); English and language arts (M Ed); health education (M Ed); higher education leadership (Ed D); home and school visitor (M Ed); human sexuality (M Ed); mathematics education (M Ed); middle school education (M Ed); principalship (M Ed); reading and language arts (Ed D); reading education (M Ed); school administration (Ed D); science education (M Ed); social studies education (M Ed); special education (M Ed); technology education (M Ed). *Accreditation:* NCATE. Part-time and evening/weekend programs available. *Faculty:* 34 full-time (22 women), 37 part-time/adjunct (14 women). *Students:* 203 full-time (154 women), 415 part-time (298 women); includes 50 minority (34 African Americans, 1 American Indian/Alaska Native, 5 Asian Americans or Pacific Islanders, 10 Hispanic Americans), 3 international. Average age 39. 139 applicants, 88% accepted. In 2009, 168 master's, 31 doctorates awarded. Terminal master's awarded for partial completion of doctoral program. *Degree requirements:* For doctorate, thesis/dissertation. *Entrance requirements:* For master's, minimum GPA of 2.5; for doctorate, GRE or MAT, minimum GPA of 2.0 (undergraduate), 3.5 (graduate). *Application deadline:* Applications are processed on a rolling basis. Application fee: $25 ($300 for international students). Electronic applications accepted. *Expenses:* Contact institution. *Financial support:* Career-related internships or fieldwork, tuition waivers (full and partial), and unspecified assistantships available. Support available to part-time students. Financial award application deadline: 5/1. *Faculty research:* Reading and cognition, adult education, technology education, educational leadership, special education. *Unit head:* Dr. Michael W. LeDoux, Associate Dean, 610-499-4294, Fax: 610-499-4623, E-mail: mwledoux@widener.edu. *Application contact:* Dr. Roberta D. Nolan, Director of Graduate Admissions, 610-499-4125, E-mail: rdnolan@widener.edu.

Worcester State College, Graduate Studies, Department of Education, Program in Early Childhood Education, Worcester, MA 01602-2597. Offers M Ed. Part-time and evening/weekend programs available. *Faculty:* 9 full-time (7 women), 19 part-time/adjunct (7 women). *Students:* 1 (woman) full-time, 11 part-time (all women). Average age 34. 10 applicants, 60% accepted, 2 enrolled. In 2009, 12 master's awarded. *Degree requirements:* For master's, comprehensive exam (for some programs), thesis optional. *Entrance requirements:* For master's, GRE General Test or MAT, teaching certificate. Additional exam requirements/recommendations for international students: Required—TOEFL (minimum score 550 paper-based; 213 computer-based; 79 iBT). *Application deadline:* Applications are processed on a rolling basis. Application fee: $30. *Expenses:* Tuition, area resident: Part-time $150 per credit. Tuition, state resident: part-time $150 per credit. Tuition, nonresident: part-time $150 per credit. Required fees: $85. *Financial support:* Career-related internships or fieldwork, scholarships/grants, and unspecified assistantships available. Financial award application deadline: 3/1; financial award applicants required to submit FAFSA. *Unit head:* Dr. Carol Donnelly, Coordinator, 508-929-8667, Fax: 508-929-8164, E-mail: cdonnelly@worcester.edu. *Application contact:* Nicole Brown, Assistant Dean of Graduate and Continuing Education, 508-929-8787, Fax: 508-929-8100, E-mail: nbrown@worcester.edu.

Wright State University, School of Graduate Studies, College of Education and Human Services, Department of Teacher Education, Program in Early Childhood Education, Dayton, OH 45435. Offers M Ed, MA. *Accreditation:* NCATE. *Degree requirements:* For master's, thesis (for some programs). *Entrance requirements:* For master's, GRE General Test, MAT. Additional exam requirements/recommendations for international students: Required—TOEFL.

Xavier University, College of Social Sciences, Health and Education, School of Education, Department of Childhood Education and Literacy, Montessori Program, Cincinnati, OH 45207. Offers M Ed. Part-time programs available. *Faculty:* 4 full-time (3 women), 9 part-time/adjunct (all women). *Students:* 30 full-time (25 women), 21 part-time (17 women); includes 7 minority (3 African Americans, 3 Asian Americans or Pacific Islanders, 1 Hispanic American), 1 international. Average age 34. 20 applicants, 70% accepted, 11 enrolled. In 2009, 23 master's awarded. *Degree requirements:* For master's, comprehensive exam, research paper. *Entrance requirements:* For master's, MAT or GRE. Additional exam requirements/recommendations for international students: Required—TOEFL (minimum score 79 iBT). *Application deadline:* Applications are processed on a rolling basis. Application fee: $35. Electronic applications accepted. *Expenses:* Tuition: Part-time $697 per credit hour. One-time fee: $35 part-time. *Financial support:* In 2009–10, 25 students received support. Applicants required to submit FAFSA. *Faculty research:* Public Montessori, reading, language curriculum. *Unit head:* Gina Taliaferro Lofquist, Director, 513-745-1072, Fax: 513-745-4378, E-mail: lofquistgm@xavier.edu. *Application contact:* Gina Taliaferro Lofquist, Director, 513-745-1072, Fax: 513-745-4378, E-mail: lofquistgm@xavier.edu.

Youngstown State University, Graduate School, Beeghly College of Education, Department of Teacher Education, Program in Early Childhood Education, Youngstown, OH 44555-0001. Offers MS Ed. *Accreditation:* NCATE. Part-time and evening/weekend programs available. *Degree requirements:* For master's, comprehensive exam. *Entrance requirements:* For master's, GRE, MAT, or teaching certificate; minimum GPA of 2.7. Additional exam requirements/recommendations for international students: Required—TOEFL.

Elementary Education

Adelphi University, School of Education, Program in Childhood Education, Garden City, NY 11530-0701. Offers elementary teachers pre K-6 (MA); grades 1-6 (MA). Part-time and evening/weekend programs available. *Students:* 84 full-time (72 women), 82 part-time (67 women); includes 27 minority (18 African Americans, 1 Asian American or Pacific Islander, 8 Hispanic Americans), 1 international. Average age 27. In 2009, 101 master's awarded. *Entrance requirements:* For master's, 2 letters of recommendation, resume. Additional exam requirements/recommendations for international students: Required—TOEFL (minimum score 550 paper-based; 213 computer-based; 80 iBT). *Application deadline:* For fall admission, 4/1 for international students; for spring admission, 11/1 for international students. Application fee: $50. Electronic applications accepted. *Expenses:* Tuition: Full-time $28,340; part-time $830 per credit. Required fees: $600; $250 per credit. Full-time tuition and fees vary according to course load and program. *Financial support:* Fellowships, research assistantships with partial tuition reimbursements, teaching assistantships, career-related internships or fieldwork, Federal Work-Study, institutionally sponsored loans, and tuition waivers (full) available. Support available to part-time students. Financial award application deadline: 2/15; financial award applicants required to submit FAFSA. *Faculty research:* Diversity; parental involvement; teacher education; psychoanalytic understanding of racial formation; relationships between ideology, language, culture and individual subject formation. *Unit head:* Dr. Renee White-Clark, Director, 516-877-4397, E-mail: whiteclark@adelphi.edu. *Application contact:* Christine Murphy, Director of Admissions, 516-877-3050, Fax: 516-877-3039, E-mail: graduateadmissions@adelphi.edu.

Alabama Agricultural and Mechanical University, School of Graduate Studies, School of Education, Area in Elementary and Early Childhood Education, Huntsville, AL 35811. Offers early childhood education (MS Ed, Ed S); elementary education (MS Ed, Ed S). *Accreditation:* NCATE. Evening/weekend programs available. *Degree requirements:* For master's, comprehensive exam; for Ed S, thesis. *Entrance requirements:* For master's, GRE General Test. Additional exam requirements/recommendations for international students: Required—TOEFL (minimum score 500 paper-based; 173 computer-based; 61 iBT). Electronic applications accepted. *Faculty research:* Multicultural education, learning styles, diagnostic-prescriptive instruction.

Alabama State University, School of Graduate Studies, College of Education, Department of Curriculum and Instruction, Program in Elementary Education, Montgomery, AL 36101-0271. Offers M Ed, Ed S. Part-time programs available. *Degree requirements:* For master's, comprehensive exam, thesis optional; for Ed S, comprehensive exam, thesis. *Entrance requirements:* For master's, GRE General Test, MAT, graduate writing competency test; for Ed S, graduate writing competency test, GRE, MAT. Additional exam requirements/recommendations for international students: Required—TOEFL (minimum score 500 paper-based; 173 computer-based).

Alaska Pacific University, Graduate Programs, Education Department, Program in Teaching, Anchorage, AK 99508-4672. Offers teaching (K-8) (MAT). *Degree requirements:* For master's, research project. *Entrance requirements:* For master's, GRE or MAT, PRAXIS, minimum GPA of 3.0.

Albright College, Department of Education—Graduate Division, Reading, PA 19612-5234. Offers early childhood education (MS); elementary education (MS); English as a second language (MA); general education (MA); special education (MS). Part-time and evening/weekend programs available. *Degree requirements:* For master's, thesis. *Entrance requirements:* For master's, GRE General Test or MAT, minimum undergraduate GPA of 3.0, 2 letters of recommendation, interview. Additional exam requirements/recommendations for international students: Recommended—TOEFL (minimum score 525 paper-based; 197 computer-based). Electronic applications accepted.

Alcorn State University, School of Graduate Studies, School of Psychology and Education, Alcorn State, MS 39096-7500. Offers agricultural education (MS Ed); elementary education (MS Ed, Ed S); guidance and counseling (MS Ed); industrial education (MS Ed); secondary education (MS Ed), including health and physical education; special education (MS Ed). *Accreditation:* NCATE. *Degree requirements:* For master's, thesis optional.

American International College, School of Arts, Education and Sciences, Department of Education, Springfield, MA 01109-3189. Offers early childhood education (M Ed, CAGS); educational leadership and supervision (Ed D); elementary education (M Ed, CAGS); middle/secondary education (M Ed, CAGS); moderate disabilities (M Ed, CAGS); reading (M Ed, CAGS); school adjustment counseling (MA, CAGS); school administration (M Ed, CAGS); school guidance counseling (MA, CAGS); teaching (MA, MS); teaching and learning (Ed D). Part-time and evening/weekend programs available. Terminal master's awarded for partial completion of doctoral program. *Degree requirements:* For master's, comprehensive exam (for some programs), thesis (for some programs), practicum; for doctorate, comprehensive exam (for some programs), thesis/dissertation; for CAGS, practicum. *Entrance requirements:* For master's, minimum B- average in undergraduate course work; for doctorate, GRE General Test, interview. Additional exam requirements/recommendations for international students: Required—TOEFL. Electronic applications accepted. *Expenses:* Tuition: Full-time $12,510; part-time $695 per credit hour. Required fees: $35 per term.

American University, College of Arts and Sciences, School of Education, Teaching, and Health, Program in Elementary Education, Washington, DC 20016-8030. Offers MAT, Certificate. *Students:* 9 full-time (6 women), 95 part-time (81 women); includes 32 minority (29 African Americans, 1 Asian American or Pacific Islander, 2 Hispanic Americans). Average age 30. 43 applicants, 88% accepted, 25 enrolled. In 2009, 51 master's, 1 other advanced degree awarded. *Degree requirements:* For master's, comprehensive exam, PRAXIS II. *Entrance requirements:* For master's, GRE, PRAXIS I, minimum GPA of 3.0, 2 recommendations; for Certificate, bachelor's degree. Additional exam requirements/recommendations for international students: Required—TOEFL. *Application deadline:* For fall admission, 2/1 priority date for domestic students; for spring admission, 10/1 priority date for domestic students. Applications are processed on a rolling basis. Application fee: $80. *Expenses:* Tuition: Full-time $22,266; part-time $1237 per credit hour. Required fees: $430. Tuition and fees vary according to program. *Financial support:* Research assistantships with partial tuition reimbursements available. Financial award application deadline: 2/1. *Unit head:* Karen DiGiovanni, Director, Teacher Education, 202-885-3727, Fax: 202-885-1187, E-mail: digiovanni@american.edu. *Application contact:* Karen DiGiovanni, Director, Teacher Education, 202-885-3727, Fax: 202-885-1187, E-mail: digiovanni@american.edu.

American University of Puerto Rico, Program in Education, Bayamón, PR 00960-2037. Offers art history (M Ed); elementary education (4-6) (M Ed); elementary education (k-3) (M Ed); general science education (M Ed); physical education (k-12) (M Ed); special education at secondary level (transition) (M Ed). *Faculty:* 1 full-time (0 women), 22 part-time/adjunct (6 women). *Students:* 121 full-time (98 women), 64 part-time (50 women); includes all Hispanic Americans. Average age 30. 250 applicants, 80% accepted, 185 enrolled. *Entrance requirements:* For master's, EXADEP or GRE or MAT, 2 letters of recommendation, minimum GPA of 2.5. *Application deadline:* For fall admission, 8/4 for domestic students; for winter admission, 10/18 for domestic students; for spring admission, 3/22 for domestic students. Applications are processed on a rolling basis. Application fee: $50. *Application contact:* Information Contact, E-mail: oficnaadmisiones@aupr.edu.

Andrews University, School of Graduate Studies, School of Education, Department of Teaching, Learning, and Curriculum, Berrien Springs, MI 49104. Offers curriculum and instruction (MA, Ed D, PhD, Ed S); elementary education (MAT); reading (MA); secondary education (MAT), including biology, education, English, English as a second language, French, history, physics; special education/learning disabilities (MS); teacher education (MAT). *Students:* 12 full-time (8 women), 30 part-time (19 women); includes 17 minority (14 African Americans, 1 Asian American or Pacific Islander, 2 Hispanic Americans), 10 international. Average age 43. 28 applicants, 54% accepted, 6 enrolled. In 2009, 11 master's, 4 doctorates, 1 other advanced degree awarded. *Entrance requirements:* For master's, GRE Subject Test. Additional exam requirements/recommendations for international students: Required—TOEFL (minimum score 550 paper-based). *Application deadline:* For fall admission, 8/15 for domestic students. Applications are processed on a rolling basis. Application fee: $40. *Unit head:* Dr. Lee C. Davidson, Chair, 269-471-6364. *Application contact:* Carolyn Hurst, Supervisor of Graduate Admission, 800-253-2874, Fax: 269-471-6321, E-mail: graduate@andrews.edu.

Anna Maria College, Graduate Division, Program in Education, Paxton, MA 01612. Offers early childhood education (M Ed); education (CAGS); elementary education (M Ed); English

Elementary Education

Anna Maria College (continued)
language arts (M Ed); visual arts (M Ed). Part-time and evening/weekend programs available. *Entrance requirements:* For master's, bachelor's degree in liberal arts or sciences, minimum GPA of 3.0. Additional exam requirements/recommendations for international students: Required—TOEFL (minimum score 500 paper-based). Electronic applications accepted.

Antioch University New England, Graduate School, Department of Education, Keene, NH 03431-3552. Offers experienced educators (M Ed); integrated learning (M Ed), including early childhood education, elementary education; Waldorf teacher training (M Ed). *Degree requirements:* For master's, thesis (for some programs), internship. *Entrance requirements:* Additional exam requirements/recommendations for international students: Required—TOEFL (minimum score 600 paper-based; 250 computer-based). *Expenses:* Contact institution. *Faculty research:* Classroom and school restructuring, problem-based learning, Waldorf collaborative leadership, ecological literacy.

Antioch University New England, Graduate School, Department of Education, Integrated Learning Program, Concentration in Elementary Education, Keene, NH 03431-3552. Offers M Ed.

Appalachian State University, Cratis D. Williams Graduate School, Department of Curriculum and Instruction, Boone, NC 28608. Offers curriculum specialist (MA); educational media (MA); elementary education (MA); middle grades education (MA), including language arts, mathematics, science, social studies. *Accreditation:* NCATE. Part-time and evening/weekend programs available. Postbaccalaureate distance learning degree programs offered (no on-campus study). *Faculty:* 32 full-time (22 women), 9 part-time/adjunct (3 women). *Students:* 16 full-time (12 women), 168 part-time (140 women); includes 2 minority (both African Americans), 1 international. 97 applicants, 99% accepted, 77 enrolled. In 2009, 78 master's awarded. *Degree requirements:* For master's, comprehensive exam, thesis or alternative. *Entrance requirements:* For master's, GRE General Test or MAT, 3 letters of recommendation. Additional exam requirements/recommendations for international students: Required—TOEFL (minimum score 570 paper-based; 230 computer-based; 79 iBT), IELTS (minimum score 6.5). *Application deadline:* For fall admission, 7/1 for domestic students, 2/1 for international students; for spring admission, 11/1 for domestic students, 7/1 for international students. Applications are processed on a rolling basis. Application fee: $50. Electronic applications accepted. *Expenses:* Tuition, state resident: full-time $2960. Tuition, nonresident: full-time $14,051. Required fees: $2320. *Financial support:* In 2009–10, 8 teaching assistantships (averaging $8,000 per year) were awarded; fellowships, research assistantships, career-related internships or fieldwork, Federal Work-Study, scholarships/grants, and unspecified assistantships also available. Financial award application deadline: 4/1; financial award applicants required to submit FAFSA. *Faculty research:* Media literacy, elementary teaching, curriculum development, online learning environments. Total annual research expenditures: $690,000. *Unit head:* Dr. Michael Jacobson, Chairperson, 828-262-2224. *Application contact:* Sandy Krause, Director of Admissions and Recruiting, 828-262-2130, Fax: 828-262-2709, E-mail: krausesl@appstate.edu.

Arcadia University, Graduate Studies, Department of Education, Glenside, PA 19038-3295. Offers art education (M Ed, MA Ed); biology education (MA Ed); chemistry education (MA Ed); child development (CAS); computer education (M Ed, CAS); computer education 7–12 (MA Ed); early childhood education (M Ed, CAS), including individualized (M Ed), master teacher (M Ed), research in child development (M Ed); educational leadership (M Ed, CAS); educational psychology (CAS); elementary education (M Ed, CAS); English education (MA Ed); environmental education (MA Ed, CAS); history education (MA Ed); language arts (M Ed, CAS); mathematics education (M Ed, MA Ed, CAS); music education (MA Ed); psychology (MA Ed); pupil personnel services (CAS); reading (M Ed, CAS); school library science (M Ed); science education (M Ed, CAS); secondary education (M Ed, CAS); special education (M Ed, Ed D, CAS); theater arts (MA Ed); written communication (MA Ed). *Accreditation:* NASAD. Part-time and evening/weekend programs available. Postbaccalaureate distance learning degree programs offered (minimal on-campus study). *Faculty:* 12 full-time (8 women), 38 part-time/adjunct (26 women). *Students:* 89 full-time (74 women), 622 part-time (487 women); includes 112 minority (94 African Americans, 9 Asian Americans or Pacific Islanders, 9 Hispanic Americans), 2 international. Average age 32. In 2009, 257 master's, 4 doctorates awarded. *Application deadline:* Applications are processed on a rolling basis. Application fee: $40. Electronic applications accepted. *Expenses:* Tuition: Full-time $30,450; part-time $620 per credit hour. Required fees: $165. Tuition and fees vary according to program. *Financial support:* Career-related internships or fieldwork, tuition waivers (partial), and unspecified assistantships available. *Unit head:* Dr. Steven P. Gulkus. *Application contact:* 215-572-2925, Fax: 215-572-2126, E-mail: grad@arcadia.edu.

Argosy University, Atlanta, College of Education, Atlanta, GA 30328. Offers educational leadership (MAEd, Ed D, Ed S), including higher education administration (Ed D), K-12 education (Ed D); teaching and learning (MAEd, Ed D, Ed S), including education technology (Ed D), higher education (Ed D), K-12 education (Ed D).

See Close-Up on page 887.

Argosy University, Chicago, College of Education, Chicago, IL 60601. Offers adult education and training (MA Ed); community college executive leadership (Ed D); educational leadership (MA Ed, Ed D, Ed S), including district leadership (Ed D), higher education administration (Ed D), K-12 education (Ed D); instructional leadership (Ed D, Ed S), including higher education (Ed D), K-12 education (Ed D). Postbaccalaureate distance learning degree programs offered (minimal on-campus study).

See Close-Up on page 675.

Argosy University, Denver, College of Education, Denver, CO 80231. Offers community college executive leadership (Ed D); educational leadership (MA Ed, Ed D), including higher education (Ed D), K-12 education (Ed D); instructional leadership (MA Ed, Ed D), including higher education administration (Ed D), K-12 education (Ed D).

See Close-Up on page 679.

Argosy University, Hawai'i, College of Education, Honolulu, HI 96813. Offers adult education and training (MAEd); educational leadership (Ed D), including higher education administration, K-12 education; instructional leadership (Ed D), including higher education, K-12 education; school psychology (MA).

See Close-Up on page 681.

Argosy University, Inland Empire, College of Education, San Bernardino, CA 92408. Offers community college executive leadership (Ed D); educational leadership (MA Ed, Ed D), including higher education administration (Ed D), K-12 education (Ed D); instructional leadership (MA Ed, Ed D), including higher education (Ed D), K-12 education (Ed D), multiple subject teacher preparation (MA Ed), single subject teacher preparation (MA Ed).

See Close-Up on page 889.

Argosy University, Los Angeles, College of Education, Santa Monica, CA 90045. Offers community college executive leadership (Ed D); educational leadership (MA Ed, Ed D), including higher education administration (Ed D), K-12 education (Ed D); instructional leadership (MA Ed, Ed D), including higher education (Ed D), K-12 education (Ed D), multiple subject teacher preparation (MA Ed), single subject teacher preparation (MA Ed).

See Close-Up on page 683.

Argosy University, Nashville, College of Education, Program in Educational Leadership, Nashville, TN 37214. Offers educational leadership (MA Ed, Ed S); higher education administration (Ed D); K-12 education (Ed D).

See Close-Up on page 891.

Argosy University, Nashville, College of Education, Program in Instructional Leadership, Nashville, TN 37214. Offers education technology (Ed D); higher education administration (Ed D); instructional leadership (MA Ed, Ed S); K-12 education (Ed D).

See Close-Up on page 891.

Argosy University, Orange County, College of Education, Orange, CA 92868. Offers community college executive leadership (Ed D); educational leadership (MA Ed, Ed D), including higher education administration (Ed D), K-12 education (Ed D); instructional leadership (MA Ed, Ed D), including education technology (Ed D), higher education (Ed D), K-12 education (Ed D), multiple subject teacher preparation (MA Ed), single subject teacher preparation (MA Ed).

See Close-Up on page 685.

Argosy University, Phoenix, College of Education, Phoenix, AZ 85021. Offers adult education and training (MA Ed); advanced educational administration (Ed D, Ed S); community college executive leadership (Ed D); educational administration (MA Ed); educational leadership (MA Ed, Ed D, Ed S), including education technology (Ed D), higher education administration (Ed D), K-12 education (Ed D); higher and postsecondary education (MA Ed); initial educational administration (Ed D, Ed S); school psychology (MA); teaching and learning (MA Ed, Ed D, Ed S), including education technology (Ed D), higher education (Ed D), K-12 education (Ed D).

See Close-Up on page 687.

Argosy University, San Diego, College of Education, San Diego, CA 92108. Offers community college executive leadership (Ed D); educational leadership (MA Ed, Ed D), including higher education administration (Ed D), K-12 education (Ed D); instructional leadership (MA Ed, Ed D), including higher education (Ed D), K-12 education (Ed D).

See Close-Up on page 691.

Argosy University, San Francisco Bay Area, College of Education, Alameda, CA 94501. Offers community college executive leadership (Ed D); educational leadership (MA Ed, Ed D), including education technology (Ed D), higher education administration (Ed D), K-12 education (Ed D); instructional leadership (MA Ed, Ed D), including education technology (Ed D), higher education (Ed D), K-12 education (Ed D), multiple subject teacher preparation (MA Ed), single subject teacher preparation (MA Ed).

See Close-Up on page 693.

Argosy University, Sarasota, College of Education, Sarasota, FL 34235. Offers community college executive leadership (Ed D); educational leadership (MA Ed, Ed D, Ed S), including higher education administration (Ed D), K-12 education (Ed D); school counseling (MA, Ed S); school psychology (MA); teaching and learning (MA Ed, Ed D, Ed S), including education technology (Ed D), higher education (Ed D), K-12 education (Ed D).

See Close-Up on page 695.

Argosy University, Schaumburg, College of Education, Schaumburg, IL 60173-5403. Offers community college executive leadership (Ed D); educational leadership (MA Ed, Ed D, Ed S), including district leadership (Ed D), higher education administration (Ed D), K-12 education (Ed D); instructional leadership (Ed D, Ed S), including higher education (Ed D), K-12 education (Ed D).

See Close-Up on page 697.

Argosy University, Seattle, College of Education, Seattle, WA 98121. Offers adult education and training (MA Ed); community college executive leadership (Ed D); educational leadership (MA Ed, Ed D), including higher education administration (Ed D), K-12 education (Ed D); higher and postsecondary education (MA Ed); instructional leadership (MA Ed, Ed D), including education technology (Ed D), higher education (Ed D), K-12 education (Ed D).

See Close-Up on page 699.

Argosy University, Tampa, College of Education, Tampa, FL 33607. Offers community college executive leadership (Ed D); educational leadership (MA Ed, Ed D, Ed S), including higher education administration (Ed D), K-12 education (Ed D); school counseling (MA); teaching and learning (MA Ed, Ed D, Ed S), including higher education (Ed D), K-12 education (Ed D).

See Close-Up on page 701.

Argosy University, Twin Cities, College of Education, Eagan, MN 55121. Offers advanced educational administration (Ed D, Ed S); educational leadership (MA Ed, Ed D, Ed S), including higher education administration (Ed D), K-12 education (Ed D); higher and postsecondary education (MA Ed); initial educational administration (Ed D, Ed S); instructional leadership (MA Ed, Ed D, Ed S), including education technology (Ed D), higher education (Ed D), K-12 education (Ed D).

See Close-Up on page 703.

Argosy University, Washington DC, College of Education, Arlington, VA 22209. Offers community college executive leadership (Ed D); educational leadership (MA Ed, Ed D, Ed S), including higher education administration (Ed D), K-12 education (Ed D); instructional leadership (MA Ed, Ed D, Ed S), including higher education (Ed D), K-12 education (Ed D).

See Close-Up on page 705.

Arizona State University, Graduate College, College of Teacher Education and Leadership, Tempe, AZ 85287. Offers educational administration and supervision (M Ed); elementary education (M Ed, Certificate); leadership/innovation (administration) (Ed D); leadership/innovation (teaching) (Ed D); physical education (MPE); secondary education (M Ed, Certificate); special education (M Ed). Part-time and evening/weekend programs available. *Degree requirements:* For master's, applied project or comprehensive exams; for doctorate, comprehensive exam, thesis/dissertation. *Entrance requirements:* For master's, 3 letters of recommendation, minimum undergraduate GPA of 3.0, resume; for doctorate, master's degree in education or related field, 3 professional references, resumé, graduate GPA of 3.0, 3 letters of recommendation. Additional exam requirements/recommendations for international students: Required—TOEFL (minimum score 550 paper-based; 213 computer-based; 83 iBT), IELTS (minimum score 6.5). Electronic applications accepted. *Expenses:* Contact institution. *Faculty research:* Self-regulated learning in students, collaboration and consultation skills for educators, school reform and restructuring, hands-on science and mathematics programs, educational technology.

Arkansas State University—Jonesboro, Graduate School, College of Education, Department of Teacher Education, Jonesboro, State University, AR 72467. Offers early childhood education (MSE); early childhood services (MS); middle level education (MSE); reading (MSE, SCCT). *Accreditation:* NCATE. Part-time programs available. *Faculty:* 5 full-time (4 women), 4 part-time/adjunct (3 women). *Students:* 10 full-time (all women), 87 part-time (84 women); includes 40 minority (39 African Americans, 1 American Indian/Alaska Native). Average age 35. 63 applicants, 79% accepted, 39 enrolled. In 2009, 31 master's awarded. *Degree requirements:* For master's, comprehensive exam, thesis or alternative; for SCCT, comprehensive exam. *Entrance requirements:* For master's, GRE General Test or MAT, appropriate bachelor's degree; for SCCT, GRE General Test or MAT, interview, master's degree, official transcript, immunization records. Additional exam requirements/recommendations for international students: Required—TOEFL (minimum score 550 paper-based; 213 computer-based; 79 iBT), IELTS (minimum score 6). *Application deadline:* For fall admission, 7/15 for domestic students, 7/1 for international students; for spring admission, 12/1 for domestic students, 11/13 for international students. Applications are processed on a rolling basis. Application fee: $30 ($40 for international students). Electronic applications accepted. *Expenses:* Tuition, state resident: full-time $3744; part-time $208 per credit hour. Tuition, nonresident: full-time $9540; part-time $530 per credit hour. Required fees: $896; $47 per credit hour. $25 per term. One-time fee: $50. Tuition and fees vary according to course load and program. *Financial support:* In 2009–10, 16 students received support; teaching assistantships, career-related internships or fieldwork, scholarships/grants, and unspecified assistantships available. Financial award application deadline: 7/1; financial award applicants required to submit FAFSA. *Unit head:* Dr. Dianne Lawler-Prince, Chair, 870-972-3059, Fax: 870-972-3344, E-mail: dprince@astate.edu. *Application*

contact: Dr. Andrew Sustich, Dean of the Graduate School, 870-972-3029, Fax: 870-972-3857, E-mail: sustich@astate.edu.

Armstrong Atlantic State University, School of Graduate Studies, Program in Education, Savannah, GA 31419-1997. Offers adult education (M Ed); curriculum and instruction (M Ed); early childhood education (M Ed); education (M Ed); elementary education (M Ed); middle grades education (M Ed); secondary education (M Ed), including business education, English education, mathematics education, science education, social science education; special education (M Ed), including behavioral disorders, learning disabilities, speech-language pathology. *Accreditation:* NCATE. Part-time and evening/weekend programs available. Post-baccalaureate distance learning degree programs offered (minimal on-campus study). *Degree requirements:* For master's, comprehensive exam, portfolio. *Entrance requirements:* For master's, GRE General Test or MAT, minimum GPA of 2.5, letters of recommendation. Additional exam requirements/recommendations for international students: Required—TOEFL (minimum score 523 paper-based; 193 computer-based). Electronic applications accepted.

Auburn University, Graduate School, College of Education, Department of Curriculum and Teaching, Auburn University, AL 36849. Offers business education (M Ed, MS, PhD); early childhood education (M Ed, MS, PhD, Ed S); elementary education (M Ed, MS, PhD, Ed S); foreign languages (M Ed, MS); music education (M Ed, MS, PhD, Ed S); postsecondary education (PhD); reading education (PhD, Ed S); secondary education (M Ed, MS, PhD, Ed S), including English language arts, mathematics, science, social studies. *Accreditation:* NASM (one or more programs are accredited); NCATE. Part-time programs available. *Faculty:* 28 full-time (21 women), 8 part-time/adjunct (5 women). *Students:* 76 full-time (55 women), 186 part-time (139 women); includes 43 minority (29 African Americans, 1 American Indian/Alaska Native, 4 Asian Americans or Pacific Islanders, 9 Hispanic Americans), 4 international. Average age 33. 248 applicants, 65% accepted, 110 enrolled. In 2009, 102 master's, 12 doctorates, 6 other advanced degrees awarded. *Degree requirements:* For master's, thesis (for some programs); for doctorate, thesis/dissertation; for Ed S, field project. *Entrance requirements:* For master's, doctorate, and Ed S, GRE General Test. *Application deadline:* For fall admission, 7/7 for domestic students; for spring admission, 11/24 for domestic students. Applications are processed on a rolling basis. Application fee: $50 ($60 for international students). Electronic applications accepted. *Expenses:* Tuition, state resident: full-time $6240. Tuition, nonresident: full-time $18,720. International tuition: $18,938 full-time. Required fees: $492. Tuition and fees vary according to course load, program and reciprocity agreements. *Financial support:* Fellowships, teaching assistantships, career-related internships or fieldwork and Federal Work-Study available. Support available to part-time students. Financial award application deadline: 3/15; financial award applicants required to submit FAFSA. *Faculty research:* Emerging literacy, reading attitudes, music for at-risk youth, portfolio assessment. *Unit head:* Dr. Nancy H. Barry, Head, 334-844-4434. *Application contact:* Dr. George Flowers, Dean of the Graduate School, 334-844-2125.

Auburn University Montgomery, School of Education, Department of Early Childhood, Elementary, and Reading Education, Montgomery, AL 36124-4023. Offers early childhood education (M Ed, Ed S); elementary education (M Ed, Ed S); reading education (M Ed, Ed S). *Accreditation:* NCATE. Part-time and evening/weekend programs available. *Faculty:* 5 full-time (all women). *Students:* 56 full-time (54 women), 71 part-time (65 women); includes 45 minority (all African Americans). Average age 31. In 2009, 42 master's awarded. *Degree requirements:* For master's and Ed S, comprehensive exam. *Entrance requirements:* For master's, GRE General Test or MAT, certification, BS in teaching; for Ed S, GRE General Test or MAT, certification. *Application deadline:* Applications are processed on a rolling basis. Electronic applications accepted. *Expenses:* Tuition, state resident: full-time $2841; part-time $225 per credit hour. Tuition, nonresident: full-time $8241; part-time $675 per credit hour. Required fees: $282; $8 per hour. $45 per term. *Financial support:* In 2009–10, 1 teaching assistantship was awarded; career-related internships or fieldwork and scholarships/grants also available. Support available to part-time students. Financial award application deadline: 3/1; financial award applicants required to submit FAFSA. *Unit head:* Dr. Lynne Mills, Head, 334-244-3283, Fax: 334-244-3835, E-mail: lmills@mail.aum.edu. *Application contact:* Dr. Sam Flynt, Associate Graduate Coordinator, 334-244-3270, Fax: 334-244-3835, E-mail: sflynt@mail.aum.edu.

Austin College, Program in Education, Sherman, TX 75090-4400. Offers art education (MA); elementary education (MA); middle school education (MA); music education (MA); physical education and coaching (MA); secondary education (MA); theatre education (MA). Part-time programs available. *Faculty:* 5 full-time (3 women), 1 (woman) part-time/adjunct. *Students:* 29 full-time (21 women); includes 3 minority (1 Asian American or Pacific Islander, 2 Hispanic Americans). Average age 23. In 2009, 23 master's awarded. *Degree requirements:* For master's, one foreign language, thesis or alternative. *Entrance requirements:* For master's, Texas Academic Skills Program Test. *Application deadline:* For fall admission, 5/1 priority date for domestic students; for spring admission, 1/15 priority date for domestic students. Applications are processed on a rolling basis. Application fee: $35. Electronic applications accepted. *Expenses:* Tuition: Full-time $31,575. Required fees: $160. *Financial support:* Career-related internships or fieldwork, Federal Work-Study, scholarships/grants, and unspecified assistantships available. Support available to part-time students. Financial award application deadline: 4/1; financial award applicants required to submit FAFSA. *Unit head:* Dr. Barbara Sylvester, Director of Teaching Program, 903-813-2327, Fax: 903-813-2326, E-mail: bsylvester@austincollege.edu. *Application contact:* Dr. Barbara Sylvester, Director of Teaching Program, 903-813-2327, Fax: 903-813-2326, E-mail: bsylvester@austincollege.edu.

Austin Peay State University, College of Graduate Studies, College of Education, Department of Educational Specialties, Clarksville, TN 37044. Offers administration and supervision (Ed S); curriculum and instruction (MA Ed); education leadership (MA Ed); elementary education (Ed S); secondary education (Ed S); special education (MA Ed). Part-time and evening/weekend programs available. Postbaccalaureate distance learning degree programs offered. *Faculty:* 7 full-time (4 women), 4 part-time/adjunct (3 women). *Students:* 17 full-time (11 women), 96 part-time (76 women); includes 20 minority (12 African Americans, 1 American Indian/Alaska Native, 7 Hispanic Americans). Average age 36. 81 applicants, 99% accepted, 45 enrolled. In 2009, 47 master's awarded. *Degree requirements:* For master's, comprehensive exam, thesis optional. *Entrance requirements:* For master's, GRE General Test, 3 letters of recommendation, minimum undergraduate GPA of 2.75. Additional exam requirements/recommendations for international students: Required—TOEFL (minimum score 500 paper-based; 173 computer-based). *Application deadline:* For fall admission, 7/27 priority date for domestic students; for spring admission, 12/17 priority date for domestic students. Applications are processed on a rolling basis. Application fee: $25. Electronic applications accepted. *Expenses:* Tuition, state resident: full-time $6160; part-time $608 per credit hour. Tuition, nonresident: full-time $17,080; part-time $854 per credit hour. Required fees: $1224; $61.20 per credit hour. *Financial support:* Career-related internships or fieldwork, Federal Work-Study, institutionally sponsored loans, scholarships/grants, and unspecified assistantships available. Support available to part-time students. Financial award application deadline: 3/1; financial award applicants required to submit FAFSA. *Unit head:* Dr. Moniqueka Gold, Chair, 931-221-7696, Fax: 931-221-1292, E-mail: goldm@apsu.edu. *Application contact:* Dr. Dixie Dennis, Dean, College of Graduate Studies, 931-221-7662, Fax: 931-221-7641, E-mail: dennisdi@apsu.edu.

Austin Peay State University, College of Graduate Studies, College of Education, Department of Teaching and Learning, Clarksville, TN 37044. Offers elementary education K-6 (MAT); reading (MA Ed); secondary education 7-12 (MAT); special education K-12 (MAT). Part-time and evening/weekend programs available. Postbaccalaureate distance learning degree programs offered. *Faculty:* 8 full-time (6 women), 3 part-time/adjunct (all women). *Students:* 91 full-time (74 women), 84 part-time (67 women); includes 14 minority (12 African Americans, 2 Asian Americans or Pacific Islanders), 1 international. Average age 32. 122 applicants, 94% accepted, 75 enrolled. In 2009, 61 master's awarded. *Degree requirements:* For master's, comprehensive exam, thesis optional. *Entrance requirements:* For master's, GRE General Test, 3 letters of recommendation, minimum undergraduate GPA of 2.75. Additional exam requirements/recommendations for international students: Required—TOEFL (minimum score 500 paper-

based; 173 computer-based). *Application deadline:* For fall admission, 7/27 priority date for domestic students; for spring admission, 12/17 priority date for domestic students. Applications are processed on a rolling basis. Application fee: $25. Electronic applications accepted. *Expenses:* Tuition, state resident: full-time $6160; part-time $608 per credit hour. Tuition, nonresident: full-time $17,080; part-time $854 per credit hour. Required fees: $1224; $61.20 per credit hour. *Financial support:* Career-related internships or fieldwork, Federal Work-Study, institutionally sponsored loans, scholarships/grants, and unspecified assistantships available. Support available to part-time students. Financial award application deadline: 3/1; financial award applicants required to submit FAFSA. *Unit head:* Dr. Rebecca McMahan, Interim Chair, 931-221-7513, Fax: 931-221-1292, E-mail: mcmahanb@apsu.edu. *Application contact:* Dr. Dixie Dennis, Dean, College of Graduate Studies, 931-221-7662, Fax: 931-221-7641, E-mail: dennisdi@apsu.edu.

Averett University, Master in Education Program, Danville, VA 24541-3692. Offers art education (M Ed); biology (M Ed); biology education (M Ed); chemistry (M Ed); chemistry education (M Ed); curriculum and instruction (M Ed); elementary education (M Ed); English (M Ed); English education (M Ed); health and physical education (M Ed); history and social studies education (M Ed); math (M Ed); mathematics education (M Ed); physical science (M Ed); reading specialization (M Ed); special education (learning disabilities specialization PK-12) (M Ed). Program also offered at Richmond, VA regional campus location. Part-time and evening/weekend programs available. *Faculty:* 4 full-time (3 women), 36 part-time/adjunct (22 women). *Students:* 182 full-time (160 women), 110 part-time (94 women); includes 113 minority (94 African Americans, 1 American Indian/Alaska Native, 7 Asian Americans or Pacific Islanders, 11 Hispanic Americans). Average age 37. 119 applicants, 99% accepted, 98 enrolled. In 2009, 92 master's awarded. *Degree requirements:* For master's, comprehensive exam, thesis optional. *Entrance requirements:* For master's, PRAXIS, GRE General Test, MAT or NTE, writing proficiency exam, 3 letters of recommendation, current teacher's licensure or eligibility for licensure, minimum undergraduate GPA of 3.0 in previous 2 years. Additional exam requirements/recommendations for international students: Required—TOEFL (minimum score 600 paper-based; 200 computer-based). *Application deadline:* Applications are processed on a rolling basis. *Expenses:* Contact institution. *Financial support:* Career-related internships or fieldwork, Federal Work-Study, and scholarships/grants available. Financial award application deadline: 4/1; financial award applicants required to submit FAFSA. *Faculty research:* Literary assessment-PreK-6, handwriting instruction and assessment-PreK-6, written language instruction and assessment-PreK-6 and special needs students learning styles, curriculum and instruction processes. *Unit head:* Dr. Lynn H. Wolf, Chair/Associate Professor/Director, 434-793-3995, Fax: 434-791-4392, E-mail: lynn.wolf@averett.edu. *Application contact:* Dr. Lynn H. Wolf, Chair/Associate Professor/Director, 434-793-3995, Fax: 434-791-4392, E-mail: lynn.wolf@averett.edu.

Ball State University, Graduate School, Teachers College, Department of Elementary Education, Muncie, IN 47306-1099. Offers MAE, Ed D, PhD. *Accreditation:* NCATE. *Degree requirements:* For doctorate, thesis/dissertation. *Entrance requirements:* For doctorate, GRE General Test, interview, minimum graduate GPA of 3.2.

Bank Street College of Education, Graduate School, Program in Elementary/Childhood Education, New York, NY 10025. Offers early childhood and elementary/childhood education (MS Ed); elementary/childhood education (MS Ed). *Students:* 41 full-time (34 women), 69 part-time (58 women); includes 9 minority (3 African Americans, 6 Asian Americans or Pacific Islanders). Average age 30. 95 applicants, 82% accepted, 52 enrolled. In 2009, 33 master's awarded. *Degree requirements:* For master's, thesis. *Entrance requirements:* For master's, interview. Additional exam requirements/recommendations for international students: Required—TOEFL (minimum score 600 paper-based; 250 computer-based; 100 iBT), IELTS (minimum score 7). *Application deadline:* For fall admission, 3/1 priority date for domestic students; for spring admission, 11/1 priority date for domestic students. Applications are processed on a rolling basis. Application fee: $65. *Expenses:* Tuition: Part-time $1120 per credit. *Financial support:* Career-related internships or fieldwork, Federal Work-Study, scholarships/grants, and unspecified assistantships available. Support available to part-time students. Financial award application deadline: 4/15; financial award applicants required to submit FAFSA. *Faculty research:* Social studies in the elementary grades, urban education, experiential learning, child-centered classrooms. *Unit head:* Adrianne Kamsler, Chairperson, 212-875-4571, Fax: 212-875-4753, E-mail: akamsler@bankstreet.edu. *Application contact:* Ann Morgan, Director of Graduate Admissions, 212-875-4403, Fax: 212-875-4678, E-mail: amorgan@bankstreet.edu.

Barry University, School of Education, Program in Curriculum and Instruction, Miami Shores, FL 33161-6695. Offers accomplished teacher (Ed S); culture, language and literacy (TESOL) (PhD); curriculum evaluation and research (PhD); early childhood (Ed S); early childhood education (PhD); elementary (Ed S); elementary education (PhD); ESOL (Ed S); gifted (Ed S); Montessori (Ed S); PKP/elementary (Ed S); reading (Ed S); reading, language and cognition (PhD). *Entrance requirements:* For doctorate, GRE, minimum GPA of 3.25.

Barry University, School of Education, Program in Elementary Education, Miami Shores, FL 33161-6695. Offers elementary education (MS); elementary education/ESOL (MS). Part-time and evening/weekend programs available. *Degree requirements:* For master's, comprehensive exam, practicum. *Entrance requirements:* For master's, GRE General Test or MAT, minimum GPA of 3.0. Electronic applications accepted.

Bayamón Central University, Graduate Programs, Program in Education, Bayamón, PR 00960-1725. Offers administration and supervision (MA Ed); commercial education (MA Ed); education of the autistic (MA Ed); elementary education (K–3) (MA Ed); elementary education (K–6) (MA Ed); guidance and counseling (MA Ed); organizational psychology (MA); pre-elementary teacher (MA Ed); rehabilitation counseling (MA Ed); special education (MA Ed), including attention deficit disorder, learning disabilities. Part-time and evening/weekend programs available. *Degree requirements:* For master's, comprehensive exam. *Entrance requirements:* For master's, EXADEP, bachelor's degree in education or related field.

Belhaven University, School of Education, Jackson, MS 39202-1789. Offers elementary education (M Ed, MAT); secondary education (M Ed, MAT). Part-time and evening/weekend programs available. *Faculty:* 4 full-time (all women), 19 part-time/adjunct (10 women). *Students:* 159 full-time (132 women), 51 part-time (42 women); includes 108 African Americans, 1 American Indian/Alaska Native, 7 Hispanic Americans. Average age 34. 392 applicants, 70% accepted, 140 enrolled. In 2009, 44 master's awarded. *Degree requirements:* For master's, comprehensive exam, portfolio. *Entrance requirements:* For master's, PRAXIS I, PRAXIS II, minimum GPA of 2.8. *Application deadline:* Applications are processed on a rolling basis. Application fee: $25. Electronic applications accepted. *Expenses:* Tuition: Full-time $8730; part-time $485 per credit hour. Required fees: $1260; $70 per credit hour. Tuition and fees vary according to campus/location. *Financial support:* Federal Work-Study, scholarships/grants, tuition waivers (full), and unspecified assistantships available. Support available to part-time students. Financial award applicants required to submit FAFSA. *Unit head:* Dr. Sandra L. Rasberry, Dean, 601-968-8703, Fax: 601-974-6461, E-mail: srasberry@belhaven.edu. *Application contact:* Jenny Mixon, Director of Graduate and Online Admission, 601-968-8947, Fax: 601-968-5953, E-mail: gradadmission@belhaven.edu.

Belmont University, College of Arts and Sciences, School of Education, Nashville, TN 37212-3757. Offers education (M Ed); elementary education (MAT), including early childhood education, elementary education, language arts education; English (MAT); history (MAT); mathematics (MAT); middle grade education (MAT); science (MAT); secondary education (MAT); special education (MAT); sports administration (MSA). *Accreditation:* NCATE. Part-time and evening/weekend programs available. *Degree requirements:* For master's, comprehensive exam, thesis, culminating portfolio. *Entrance requirements:* For master's, MAT or GRE and/or LSAT or GMAT, minimum GPA of 2.75. Additional exam requirements/recommendations for international students: Required—TOEFL. *Expenses:* Contact institution. *Faculty research:* Improving secondary literacy, Montessori, classroom management strategies, teacher residency programs, online professional development, mentoring, leadership, sociological issues in sport, faculty development, coaching.

Elementary Education

Benedictine University, Graduate Programs, Program in Education, Lisle, IL 60532-0900. Offers curriculum and instruction and collaborative teaching (M Ed); elementary education (MA Ed); leadership and administration (M Ed); reading and literacy (M Ed); secondary education (MA Ed); special education (MA Ed). Part-time and evening/weekend programs available. *Faculty:* 4 full-time (2 women), 52 part-time/adjunct (30 women). *Students:* 286 full-time (252 women), 443 part-time (349 women); includes 61 minority (22 African Americans, 11 Asian Americans or Pacific Islanders, 28 Hispanic Americans), 5 international. Average age 33. 341 applicants, 90% accepted, 264 enrolled. In 2009, 299 master's awarded. *Degree requirements:* For master's, comprehensive exam, thesis (for some programs). *Entrance requirements:* For master's, GRE or MAT. Additional exam requirements/recommendations for international students: Required—TOEFL (minimum score 550 paper-based; 213 computer-based). *Application deadline:* For fall admission, 9/1 for domestic students; for winter admission, 12/1 for domestic students; for spring admission, 2/15 for domestic students. Applications are processed on a rolling basis. Application fee: $40. Electronic applications accepted. *Expenses:* Contact institution. *Financial support:* Career-related internships or fieldwork and health care benefits available. Support available to part-time students. *Unit head:* Dr. Richard Campbell, Director, 630-829-6242, Fax: 630-960-1126, E-mail: rcampbell@ben.edu. *Application contact:* Kari Gibbons, Director, Admissions, 630-829-6200, Fax: 630-829-6584, E-mail: kgibbons@ben.edu.

Bennington College, Graduate Programs, MA in Teaching Program, Bennington, VT 05201. Offers art education (MAT); early childhood (MAT); elementary education (MAT); English education (MAT); foreign language education (MAT); k-12 education (MAT); mathematics education (MAT); music education (MAT); science education (MAT); secondary education (MAT); social studies education (MAT); theater arts (MAT). *Faculty:* 5 part-time/adjunct (3 women). *Students:* 8 full-time (5 women), 1 part-time (0 women). Average age 28. 11 applicants, 27% accepted, 1 enrolled. In 2009, 4 master's awarded. *Degree requirements:* For master's, comprehensive exam, 1 year teaching practicum, professional portfolio. *Entrance requirements:* For master's, interview. *Application deadline:* For fall admission, 3/1 for domestic students. Application fee: $60. *Expenses:* Contact institution. *Financial support:* In 2009–10, 6 students received support, including 4 fellowships (averaging $10,475 per year); scholarships/grants and unspecified assistantships also available. Financial award application deadline: 4/1; financial award applicants required to submit FAFSA. *Unit head:* Carol Meyer, Director of Programs in Teacher Education, 802-440-4375, E-mail: cmeyer@bennington.edu. *Application contact:* Nancy Pearlman, Assistant Director of Programs in Teacher Education, 802-440-4710, Fax: 802-440-4383, E-mail: npearlman@bennington.edu.

Bethel University, Program in Education, McKenzie, TN 38201. Offers administration and supervision (MA Ed); biology education K8-12 (MAT); elementary education (MAT); English education K8-12 (MAT); history education K8-12 (MAT); physical education K8-12 (MAT); special education K8-12 (MAT). Part-time and evening/weekend programs available. *Degree requirements:* For master's, thesis (for some programs). *Entrance requirements:* For master's, GRE General Test or MAT, minimum undergraduate GPA of 2.5.

Bloomsburg University of Pennsylvania, School of Graduate Studies, College of Professional Studies, School of Education, Department of Elementary and Early Childhood Education, Program in Elementary Education, Bloomsburg, PA 17815-1301. Offers M Ed. *Accreditation:* NCATE. *Degree requirements:* For master's, thesis or alternative. *Entrance requirements:* For master's, MAT or PRAXIS, minimum QPA of 3.0, teaching certificate. Additional exam requirements/recommendations for international students: Required—TOEFL (minimum score 550 paper-based; 213 computer-based; 79 iBT). Electronic applications accepted. *Faculty research:* Supervision, computing, measurement, mathematics, school law.

Bob Jones University, Graduate Programs, Greenville, SC 29614. Offers accountancy (MS); Bible (MA); Bible translation (MA); Biblical studies (Certificate); broadcast management (MS); business administration (MBA); church history (MA, PhD); church ministries (MA); church music (MM); cinema and video production (MA); counseling (MS); curriculum and instruction (Ed D); divinity (M Div); dramatic production (MA); educational leadership (MS, Ed D, Ed S); elementary education (M Ed, MAT); English (M Ed, MA, MAT); fine arts (MA); graphic design (MA); history (M Ed, MA); illustration (MA); interpretative speech (MA); mathematics (M Ed, MAT); medical missions (Certificate); ministry (MM, D Min); multi-categorical special education (M Ed, MAT); music (M Ed); New Testament interpretation (PhD); Old Testament interpretation (PhD); orchestral instrument performance (MM); organ performance (MM); pastoral studies (MA); personnel services (MS, Ed S); piano pedagogy (MM); piano performance (MM); platform arts (MA); radio and television broadcasting (MS); rhetoric and public address (MA); secondary education (M Ed); studio art (MA); teaching Bible (MA); theology (MA, PhD); voice performance (MM); youth ministries (MA); M Div/MM.

Boston College, Lynch Graduate School of Education, Department of Teacher Education/Special Education and Curriculum and Instruction, Program in Elementary Education, Chestnut Hill, MA 02467-3800. Offers M Ed. *Accreditation:* Teacher Education Accreditation Council. Part-time and evening/weekend programs available. *Students:* 7 full-time (6 women), 28 part-time (22 women); includes 4 minority (2 African Americans, 1 Asian American or Pacific Islander, 1 Hispanic American), 1 international. 108 applicants, 70% accepted, 25 enrolled. In 2009, 27 master's awarded. *Degree requirements:* For master's, comprehensive exam. *Entrance requirements:* For master's, GRE General Test or MAT. Additional exam requirements/recommendations for international students: Required—TOEFL (minimum score 550 paper-based; 213 computer-based; 81 iBT). *Application deadline:* For fall admission, 1/1 priority date for domestic students. Application fee: $60. Electronic applications accepted. *Financial support:* Fellowships with full and partial tuition reimbursements, research assistantships with full and partial tuition reimbursements, teaching assistantships with full and partial tuition reimbursements, career-related internships or fieldwork, Federal Work-Study, scholarships/grants, traineeships, health care benefits, tuition waivers (full and partial), and unspecified assistantships available. Support available to part-time students. Financial award applicants required to submit FAFSA. *Faculty research:* Cross-cultural studies in teaching, learning or supervision, curriculum design, teacher research. *Unit head:* Dr. Maria E. Brisk, Chairperson, 617-552-4216, Fax: 617-552-0812, E-mail: brisk@bc.edu. *Application contact:* Adam Poluzzi, Director, Graduate Admission and Financial Aid, 617-552-4214, Fax: 617-552-0398, E-mail: poluzzi@bc.edu.

Boston University, School of Education, Department of Curriculum and Teaching, Program in Elementary Education, Boston, MA 02215. Offers Ed M. *Entrance requirements:* For master's, GRE General Test or MAT. Additional exam requirements/recommendations for international students: Required—TOEFL. Electronic applications accepted. *Expenses:* Tuition: Full-time $37,910; part-time $1184 per credit hour. Required fees: $386; $40 per semester. Part-time tuition and fees vary according to class time, course level, degree level and program. *Faculty research:* Learning theory, program evaluation, preservice field experiences.

Bowie State University, Graduate Programs, Program in Elementary Education, Bowie, MD 20715-9465. Offers M Ed. *Accreditation:* NCATE. Part-time and evening/weekend programs available. *Degree requirements:* For master's, comprehensive exam, thesis optional, research paper. *Entrance requirements:* For master's, minimum GPA of 2.5, teaching certificate, teaching experience. Electronic applications accepted.

Brandeis University, Graduate School of Arts and Sciences, Teaching Program, Waltham, MA 02454-9110. Offers elementary education (public) (MAT); Jewish day school (MAT); secondary education (English, history, biology, Bible) (MAT). *Faculty:* 4 full-time (3 women), 12 part-time/adjunct (9 women). *Students:* 24 full-time (20 women), 1 part-time (0 women), 2 international. Average age 27. 61 applicants, 70% accepted, 24 enrolled. In 2009, 31 master's awarded. *Entrance requirements:* For master's, GRE General Test, 3 letters of recommendation, resume. Additional exam requirements/recommendations for international students: Required—TOEFL (minimum score 600 paper-based; 250 computer-based; 100 iBT); Recommended—IELTS (minimum score 7). *Application deadline:* For fall admission, 1/15 priority date for domestic and international students. Applications are processed on a rolling basis. Application fee: $75. Electronic applications accepted. *Expenses:* Contact institution. *Financial support:* Scholarships/grants and tuition waivers (partial) available. Financial award applicants required to submit FAFSA. *Faculty research:* Teacher education, induction, philosophy, education, democracy education, social justice. *Unit head:* Prof. Dirck Roosevelt, Director, MAT Program, 781-736-2020, Fax: 781-736-5020, E-mail: drooseve@brandeis.edu. *Application contact:* Manuel Tuan, Department Administrator, 781-736-2633, Fax: 781-736-5020, E-mail: tuan@brandeis.edu.

Bridgewater State University, School of Graduate Studies, School of Education and Allied Science, Department of Elementary and Early Childhood Education, Program in Elementary Education, Bridgewater, MA 02325-0001. Offers M Ed. *Accreditation:* NCATE. Part-time and evening/weekend programs available. *Entrance requirements:* For master's, GRE General Test or Massachusetts Test for Educator Licensure.

Brooklyn College of the City University of New York, Division of Graduate Studies, School of Education, Program in Childhood Education, Brooklyn, NY 11210-2889. Offers bilingual education (MS Ed); liberal arts (MS Ed); mathematics (MS Ed); science/environmental education (MS Ed). Part-time and evening/weekend programs available. *Students:* 14 full-time (13 women), 245 part-time (209 women); includes 129 minority (60 African Americans, 2 American Indian/Alaska Native, 20 Asian Americans or Pacific Islanders, 47 Hispanic Americans), 6 international. Average age 30. 114 applicants, 85% accepted, 65 enrolled. In 2009, 118 master's awarded. *Entrance requirements:* For master's, LAST, interview, previous course work in education, writing sample, resume, 2 letters of recommendation. Additional exam requirements/recommendations for international students: Required—TOEFL (minimum score 500 paper-based; 173 computer-based; 61 iBT). *Application deadline:* For fall admission, 3/1 priority date for domestic students, 2/1 priority date for international students; for spring admission, 11/1 priority date for domestic students, 10/1 priority date for international students. Applications are processed on a rolling basis. Application fee: $125. Electronic applications accepted. *Expenses:* Tuition, state resident: full-time $7360; part-time $310 per credit hour. Tuition, nonresident: full-time $13,800; part-time $575 per credit hour. Required fees: $140.10 per semester. *Financial support:* Career-related internships or fieldwork, Federal Work-Study, institutionally sponsored loans, and scholarships/grants available. Support available to part-time students. Financial award application deadline: 5/1; financial award applicants required to submit FAFSA. *Faculty research:* Emotional intelligence, multiculturalism, arts immersion, the Holocaust. *Unit head:* Dr. Wayne Reed, Program Head, 718-951-5214, E-mail: wreed@brooklyn.cuny.edu. *Application contact:* Hernan Sierra, Graduate Admissions Coordinator, 718-951-4536, Fax: 718-951-4506, E-mail: grads@brooklyn.cuny.edu.

Brown University, Graduate School, Department of Education, Program in Teaching, Providence, RI 02912. Offers biology (MAT); elementary education (MAT); English (MAT); history/social studies (MAT). *Faculty:* 4 full-time (3 women), 6 part-time/adjunct (all women). *Students:* 27 full-time (21 women); includes 3 minority (2 African Americans, 1 Asian American or Pacific Islander). Average age 26. 94 applicants, 62% accepted, 27 enrolled. In 2009, 21 master's awarded. *Degree requirements:* For master's, student teaching, portfolio. *Entrance requirements:* For master's, GRE General Test, transcript, personal statement, letters of recommendation, interview, writing sample (English applicants only). Additional exam requirements/recommendations for international students: Required—TOEFL (minimum score 577 paper-based; 90 computer-based). *Application deadline:* For winter admission, 1/15 for domestic students. Application fee: $75. Electronic applications accepted. *Financial support:* In 2009–10, 23 students received support, including 4 fellowships; Federal Work-Study, institutionally sponsored loans, scholarships/grants, tuition waivers (partial), and proctorships also available. Financial award application deadline: 2/1; financial award applicants required to submit FAFSA. *Faculty research:* Literacy, biodiversity, English language learners, diversity, special education. *Unit head:* Laura Snyder, Director of Graduate Study for the MAT. *Application contact:* Carin Algava, Assistant Director, 401-863-3364, Fax: 401-863-1276, E-mail: carin_algava@brown.edu.

Buffalo State College, State University of New York, The Graduate School, Faculty of Applied Science and Education, Department of Elementary Education and Reading, Program in Elementary Education, Buffalo, NY 14222-1095. Offers childhood education (grades 1-6) (MS Ed); early childhood and childhood curriculum and instruction (MS Ed); early childhood education (birth-grade 2) (MS Ed). *Accreditation:* NCATE. Part-time programs available. *Degree requirements:* For master's, thesis or project. *Entrance requirements:* For master's, minimum GPA of 2.5 in last 60 hours, New York teaching certificate. Additional exam requirements/recommendations for international students: Required—TOEFL (minimum score 550 paper-based; 213 computer-based).

Butler University, College of Education, Indianapolis, IN 46208-3485. Offers administration (MS); elementary education (MS); reading (MS); school counseling (MS); secondary education (MS); special education (MS). *Accreditation:* ACA; NCATE. Part-time and evening/weekend programs available. *Faculty:* 9 full-time (7 women), 7 part-time/adjunct (6 women). *Students:* 18 full-time (11 women), 137 part-time (111 women); includes 17 minority (14 African Americans, 1 American Indian/Alaska Native, 2 Asian Americans or Pacific Islanders), 9 international. Average age 31. 57 applicants, 77% accepted, 24 enrolled. In 2009, 61 master's awarded. *Entrance requirements:* For master's, GRE General Test, MAT, interview. *Application deadline:* For fall admission, 8/15 priority date for domestic students. Applications are processed on a rolling basis. Application fee: $35. Electronic applications accepted. *Financial support:* Institutionally sponsored loans available. Support available to part-time students. Financial award application deadline: 7/15; financial award applicants required to submit FAFSA. *Faculty research:* Ethics in cybercounseling, history of sports for disabled, effect of fetal alcohol syndrome on perceptual learning, reading recovery's theoretical framework in teacher education. *Unit head:* Dr. Ena Shelley, Dean, 317-940-9752, Fax: 317-940-6481. *Application contact:* Karen Farrell, Department Secretary, 317-940-9220, E-mail: kfarrell@butler.edu.

California Lutheran University, Graduate Studies, School of Education, Emphasis in Educational Leadership, Thousand Oaks, CA 91360-2787. Offers educational leadership (MA); educational leadership (k-12) (Ed D); higher education leadership (Ed D). Part-time and evening/weekend programs available. *Degree requirements:* For master's, thesis or comprehensive exam. *Entrance requirements:* For master's, GRE General Test, interview, minimum GPA of 3.0.

California State University, Fullerton, Graduate Studies, College of Education, Department of Elementary and Bilingual Education, Fullerton, CA 92834-9480. Offers bilingual/bicultural education (MS); elementary curriculum and instruction (MS). *Accreditation:* NCATE. Part-time programs available. *Students:* 39 full-time (36 women), 132 part-time (121 women); includes 80 minority (3 African Americans, 28 Asian Americans or Pacific Islanders, 49 Hispanic Americans), 2 international. Average age 31. 78 applicants, 76% accepted, 43 enrolled. In 2009, 78 master's awarded. *Degree requirements:* For master's, comprehensive exam, project or thesis. *Entrance requirements:* For master's, minimum GPA of 2.5, teaching certificate. Application fee: $55. *Expenses:* Tuition, nonresident: full-time $11,160; part-time $373 per credit. Required fees: $1440 per term. Tuition and fees vary according to course load, degree level and program. *Financial support:* Career-related internships or fieldwork, Federal Work-Study, institutionally sponsored loans, and scholarships/grants available. Support available to part-time students. Financial award application deadline: 3/1; financial award applicants required to submit FAFSA. *Faculty research:* Teacher training and tracking, model for improvement of teaching. *Unit head:* Dr. Karen Ivers, Chair, 657-278-2470. *Application contact:* Admissions/Applications, 657-278-2371.

California State University, Los Angeles, Graduate Studies, Charter College of Education, Division of Curriculum and Instruction, Los Angeles, CA 90032-8530. Offers elementary teaching (MA); reading (MA); secondary teaching (MA). Part-time and evening/weekend programs available. *Faculty:* 8 full-time (6 women), 7 part-time/adjunct (4 women). *Students:* 308 full-time (217 women), 297 part-time (211 women); includes 399 minority (22 African Americans, 98 Asian Americans or Pacific Islanders, 279 Hispanic Americans), 19 international. Average age 32. 53 applicants, 100% accepted, 30 enrolled. In 2009, 101 master's awarded. *Entrance requirements:* For master's, minimum GPA of 2.75 in last 90 units of course work, teaching

certificate. Additional exam requirements/recommendations for international students: Required—TOEFL (minimum score 500 paper-based; 173 computer-based). *Application deadline:* For fall admission, 5/1 for domestic and international students. Applications are processed on a rolling basis. Application fee: $55. Electronic applications accepted. *Financial support:* Federal Work-Study available. Support available to part-time students. Financial award application deadline: 3/1. *Faculty research:* Media, language arts, mathematics, computers, drug-free schools. *Unit head:* Dr. Ramakrishan Menon, Chair, 323-343-4350, Fax: 323-343-5458, E-mail: rmenon@calstatela.edu. *Application contact:* Dr. Cheryl L. Ney, Associate Vice President for Academic Affairs and Dean of Graduate Studies, 323-343-3820 Ext. 3827, Fax: 323-343-5653, E-mail: cney@cslanet.calstatela.edu.

California State University, Northridge, Graduate Studies, College of Education, Department of Elementary Education, Northridge, CA 91330. Offers curriculum and instruction (MA); language and literacy (MA); multilingual/multicultural education (MA); teaching and learning (MA). *Accreditation:* NCATE. Part-time and evening/weekend programs available. *Faculty:* 18 full-time (14 women), 32 part-time/adjunct (24 women). *Students:* 29 full-time (all women), 61 part-time (57 women); includes 38 minority (1 African American, 10 Asian Americans or Pacific Islanders, 27 Hispanic Americans), 1 international. Average age 31. 64 applicants, 64% accepted, 28 enrolled. *Degree requirements:* For master's, comprehensive exam. *Entrance requirements:* For master's, GRE General Test or minimum GPA of 3.0. Additional exam requirements/recommendations for international students: Required—TOEFL. *Application deadline:* For fall admission, 11/30 for domestic students. Application fee: $55. *Financial support:* Federal Work-Study available. Financial award application deadline: 3/1. *Unit head:* Dr. David Kretschmer, Chair, 818-677-2621. *Application contact:* Joyce Burstein, Graduate Coordinator, 818-677-2621 Ext. 6850, E-mail: joyce.burstein@csun.edu.

California State University, San Bernardino, Graduate Studies, College of Education, Program in Elementary Education, San Bernardino, CA 92407-2397. Offers MA. *Accreditation:* NCATE. *Faculty:* 1 full-time (0 women), 1 (woman) part-time/adjunct. *Application deadline:* For fall admission, 8/31 priority date for domestic students. Application fee: $55. *Unit head:* Dr. Patricia Arlin, Interim Chair, 909-537-5600, Fax: 909-537-7510, E-mail: parlin@csusb.edu. *Application contact:* Olivia Rosas, Director of Admissions, 909-537-7577, Fax: 909-537-7034, E-mail: orosas@csusb.edu.

California State University, Stanislaus, College of Education, Department of Teacher Education, Turlock, CA 95382. Offers curriculum and instruction (MA), including elementary education, multilingual education, reading, secondary education; education (MA); middle/junior high studies (Graduate Certificate). Part-time and evening/weekend programs available. *Degree requirements:* For master's, thesis. *Entrance requirements:* For master's, MAT or GRE, 3 letters of recommendation. Additional exam requirements/recommendations for international students: Required—TOEFL (minimum score 550 paper-based; 213 computer-based). Electronic applications accepted. *Faculty research:* Children's perspectives on historical events, method elementary schools dual language education, K-12 reading and CYRM programs.

California University of Pennsylvania, School of Graduate Studies and Research, School of Education, Department of Elementary Education, California, PA 15419-1394. Offers reading specialist (M Ed). *Accreditation:* NCATE. Part-time and evening/weekend programs available. *Degree requirements:* For master's, comprehensive exam, thesis optional. *Entrance requirements:* For master's, MAT, PRAXIS, minimum GPA of 3.0, state police clearances. Additional exam requirements/recommendations for international students: Required—TOEFL (minimum score 550 paper-based; 213 computer-based; 80 iBT). Electronic applications accepted. *Faculty research:* English as a second language, adult literacy, emerging literacy, diagnosis and remediation, phonemic awareness.

Cambridge College, School of Education, Cambridge, MA 02138-5304. Offers autism specialist (M Ed); autism/behavior analyst (M Ed); behavior analyst (Post-Master's Certificate); behavioral management (M Ed); early childhood teacher (M Ed); education specialist in curriculum and instruction (CAGS); educational leadership (Ed D); elementary teacher (M Ed); English as a second language (M Ed, Certificate); general science (M Ed); health education, health promotion (Post-Master's Certificate); health/family and consumer sciences (M Ed); history (M Ed); individualized degree (M Ed); information technology literacy (M Ed); instructional technology (M Ed); interdisciplinary studies (M Ed); library teacher (M Ed); literacy education (M Ed); mathematics (M Ed); mathematics specialist (Certificate); middle school mathematics and science (M Ed); school administration (M Ed, CAGS); school guidance counselor (M Ed); school nurse education (M Ed); school social worker/school adjustment counselor (M Ed); special education administrator (CAGS); special education/moderate disabilities (M Ed); teaching skills and methodologies (M Ed). Part-time and evening/weekend programs available. Post-baccalaureate distance learning degree programs offered (minimal on-campus study). *Faculty:* 10 full-time (3 women), 283 part-time/adjunct (187 women). *Students:* 974 full-time (755 women), 1,071 part-time (835 women); includes 940 minority (762 African Americans, 4 American Indian/Alaska Native, 22 Asian Americans or Pacific Islanders, 152 Hispanic Americans), 28 international. Average age 39. In 2009, 866 master's, 4 doctorates, 209 CAGSs awarded. *Degree requirements:* For master's, thesis, internship/practicum (licensure program only); for doctorate, thesis/dissertation; for other advanced degree, thesis. *Entrance requirements:* For master's, interview, resume, documentation of licensure, 2 professional references; for doctorate, official transcripts, interview, resume, documentation of licensure (if any), written personal statement/essay, portfolio of scholarly and professional work, qualifying assessment, 2 professional references, health insurance, immunizations form; for other advanced degree, official transcripts, interview, resume, documentation of licensure (if any), written personal statement/essay, 2 professional references, health insurance, immunizations form. Additional exam requirements/recommendations for international students: Required—TOEFL (minimum score 550 paper-based; 213 computer-based; 79 iBT); Recommended—IELTS (minimum score 6). *Application deadline:* Applications are processed on a rolling basis. Application fee: $30. Electronic applications accepted. *Expenses:* Contact institution. *Financial support:* In 2009–10, 1,373 students received support. Career-related internships or fieldwork, Federal Work-Study, and scholarships/grants available. Financial award applicants required to submit FAFSA. *Faculty research:* Adult education, accelerated learning, mathematics education, brain compatible learning, special education and law. *Unit head:* Dr. N. Alan Sheppard, Interim Associate Dean, 617-873-0619, E-mail: alan.sheppard@cambridgecollege.edu. *Application contact:* Stephen Lyons, Director of Enrollment, Graduate and N.I.T.E. Programs, 617-868-1000, Fax: 617-349-3561, E-mail: stephen.lyons@cambridgecollege.edu.

Campbell University, Graduate and Professional Programs, School of Education, Buies Creek, NC 27506. Offers administration (MSA); community counseling (MA); elementary education (M Ed); English education (M Ed); interdisciplinary studies (M Ed); mathematics education (M Ed); middle grades education (M Ed); physical education (M Ed); school counseling (M Ed); secondary education (M Ed); social science education (M Ed). *Accreditation:* NCATE. Part-time and evening/weekend programs available. *Degree requirements:* For master's, comprehensive exam. *Entrance requirements:* For master's, GRE General Test, minimum GPA of 2.7. *Faculty research:* Spiritual values and wellness issues in counseling, stress and professional burnout among counselors, thinking strategies, leadership, adaptive technology.

Canisius College, Graduate Division, School of Education and Human Services, Department of Graduate Education, Buffalo, NY 14208-1098. Offers adolescence education (grades 7-12) (MS); childhood education (grades 1-6) (MS); college student personnel administration (MS); deaf education (MS); differentiated instruction (MS Ed); educational administration and supervision (MS); general education (MS Ed); initial teacher certification (elementary education) (MS); initial teacher certification (secondary education) (MS); literacy (MS Ed); special education (MS). *Accreditation:* NCATE. Part-time and evening/weekend programs available. *Faculty:* 22 full-time (14 women), 84 part-time/adjunct (54 women). *Students:* 409 full-time (288 women), 261 part-time (187 women); includes 29 minority (24 African Americans, 5 Hispanic Americans), 156 international. Average age 30. 518 applicants, 74% accepted, 240 enrolled. In 2009, 346 master's awarded. Application fee: $25. *Financial support:* Research assistantships with full tuition reimbursements, career-related internships or fieldwork, institutionally sponsored loans,

scholarships/grants, health care benefits, tuition waivers (full and partial), and unspecified assistantships available. *Faculty research:* Autism, Asperger's disease, private higher education, reading strategies. *Unit head:* Rev. Paul Nochelski, Chair of Graduate Education and Leadership, 716-888-3297, Fax: 716-888-3299. *Application contact:* James D. Bagwell, Director of Graduate Recruitment and Admissions, 716-888-2544, Fax: 716-888-3290, E-mail: bagwellj@canisius.edu.

Capella University, School of Education, Minneapolis, MN 55402. Offers college teaching (Certificate); curriculum and instruction (MS, PhD); education (MS); enrollment management (MS); instructional design for online learning (MS, PhD); k-12 studies in education (MS, PhD); leadership for higher education (MS, PhD); leadership in education administration (Certificate); leadership in educational administration (MS, PhD); postsecondary and adult education (MS, PhD); professional studies in education (MS, PhD); reading and literacy (MS); training and performance improvement (MS, PhD). Part-time and evening/weekend programs available. Postbaccalaureate distance learning degree programs offered (minimal on-campus study). Terminal master's awarded for partial completion of doctoral program. *Degree requirements:* For master's, thesis optional, integrative project; for doctorate, comprehensive exam, thesis/dissertation. *Entrance requirements:* Additional exam requirements/recommendations for international students: Required—TOEFL (minimum score 550 paper-based; 213 computer-based), TWE (minimum score 4). Electronic applications accepted. *Faculty research:* Higher education administration, distance learning, adult education, training and curriculum design.

Caribbean University, Graduate School, Bayamón, PR 00960-0493. Offers administration and supervision (MA Ed); criminal justice (MA); curriculum and instruction (MA Ed), including elementary education, English education, history education, mathematics education, primary education, science education, Spanish education; education (PhD); gerontology (MSN); human resources (MBA); museology, archiving and art history (MA Ed); neonatal pediatrics (MSN); physical education (MA Ed); special education (MA Ed). *Entrance requirements:* For master's, interview, minimum GPA of 2.5.

Carlow University, School of Education, Program in Education, Pittsburgh, PA 15213-3165. Offers elementary education (M Ed); instructional technology specialist (M Ed); secondary education (M Ed); special education (M Ed). Part-time and evening/weekend programs available. *Entrance requirements:* For master's, resume, 3 letters of recommendation, minimum GPA of 3.0, interview. Electronic applications accepted. *Expenses:* Tuition: Full-time $11,250; part-time $625 per credit. Tuition and fees vary according to course load, degree level and program.

Carson-Newman College, Graduate Program in Education, Jefferson City, TN 37760. Offers curriculum and instruction (M Ed); educational leadership (M Ed); elementary education (MAT); school counseling (MS); secondary education (MAT); teaching English as a second language (MATESL). *Accreditation:* NCATE. Part-time and evening/weekend programs available. *Faculty:* 5 full-time (2 women), 10 part-time/adjunct (3 women). *Students:* 112 full-time (84 women), 84 part-time (52 women); includes 5 African Americans, 17 international. Average age 32. 86 applicants, 98% accepted. In 2009, 55 master's awarded. *Degree requirements:* For master's, thesis or alternative. *Entrance requirements:* For master's, NTE, minimum GPA of 3.0 in major, 2.5 overall. *Application deadline:* For fall admission, 7/15 priority date for domestic students. Applications are processed on a rolling basis. Application fee: $25 ($50 for international students). *Expenses:* Tuition: Full-time $5490; part-time $305 per semester hour. Required fees: $200. *Financial support:* In 2009–10, 41 students received support. Federal Work-Study and unspecified assistantships available. Financial award application deadline: 4/1; financial award applicants required to submit FAFSA. *Unit head:* Dr. Sharon Teets, Chair, 865-471-3461. *Application contact:* Graduate Admissions and Services Adviser, 865-471-3460, Fax: 865-471-3875.

Catawba College, Program in Education, Salisbury, NC 28144-2488. Offers elementary education (M Ed). *Accreditation:* NCATE. Part-time and evening/weekend programs available. *Faculty:* 4 full-time (3 women). *Students:* 39 part-time (all women). *Degree requirements:* For master's, portfolio. *Entrance requirements:* For master's, NTE, PRAXIS II, minimum undergraduate GPA of 3.0, valid teaching license, official transcripts, 3 references, essay, interview. *Application deadline:* Applications are processed on a rolling basis. Application fee: $25. *Expenses:* Tuition: Part-time $160 per credit hour. *Financial support:* Scholarships/grants available. Financial award applicants required to submit FAFSA. *Faculty research:* Integrated arts in elementary schools, professional development schools. *Unit head:* Dr. Rhonda Truitt, Chair, Department of Teacher Education, 704-637-4468, Fax: 704-637-4732, E-mail: rltruitt@catawba.edu. *Application contact:* Dr. Lou W. Kasias, Director, Graduate Program, 704-637-4462, Fax: 704-637-4732, E-mail: lakasias@catawba.edu.

Centenary College of Louisiana, Graduate Programs, Department of Education, Shreveport, LA 71104. Offers administration (M Ed); elementary education (MAT); secondary education (MAT); supervision of instruction (M Ed). Part-time and evening/weekend programs available. *Degree requirements:* For master's, comprehensive exam. *Entrance requirements:* For master's, GRE General Test (M Ed), PRAXIS I and PRAXIS II (MAT), teacher certification (M Ed), minimum GPA of 2.5. *Expenses:* Contact institution. *Faculty research:* Teachers as advocates for teachers, portfolio assessment, disabled readers.

Central Connecticut State University, School of Graduate Studies, School of Education and Professional Studies, Department of Teacher Education, Program in Elementary Education, New Britain, CT 06050-4010. Offers MS, Certificate. Part-time and evening/weekend programs available. *Students:* 23 full-time (22 women), 54 part-time (49 women); includes 3 minority (1 Asian American or Pacific Islander, 2 Hispanic Americans). Average age 31. 59 applicants, 47% accepted, 15 enrolled. In 2009, 29 master's, 2 other advanced degrees awarded. *Degree requirements:* For master's, comprehensive exam, thesis or alternative; for Certificate, qualifying exam. *Entrance requirements:* For master's, minimum undergraduate GPA of 2.7. Additional exam requirements/recommendations for international students: Required—TOEFL. *Application deadline:* For fall admission, 7/1 for domestic students; for spring admission, 12/1 for domestic students. Applications are processed on a rolling basis. Application fee: $50. Electronic applications accepted. *Expenses:* Tuition, area resident: Full-time $4662; part-time $440 per credit. Tuition, state resident: full-time $6994; part-time $440 per credit. Tuition, nonresident: full-time $12,988; part-time $440 per credit. Required fees: $3606. One-time fee: $62 part-time. *Financial support:* Application deadline: 3/1. *Faculty research:* Elementary school curriculum, changing school populations, multicultural education, professional development.

Central Michigan University, College of Graduate Studies, College of Education and Human Services, Department of Teacher Education and Professional Development, Mount Pleasant, MI 48859. Offers educational technology (MA); elementary education (MA), including classroom teaching, early childhood; middle level education (MA); reading and literacy K-12 (MA); secondary education (MA). Part-time and evening/weekend programs available. *Degree requirements:* For master's, thesis or alternative. Electronic applications accepted. *Faculty research:* Integrating literacy across the curriculum; science teaching and aesthetic learning in science; diversity education; educational technology; educational psychology and child development.

Chadron State College, School of Professional and Graduate Studies, Department of Education, Chadron, NE 69337. Offers business (MA Ed); community counseling (MA Ed); educational administration (MS Ed, Sp Ed); elementary education (MS Ed); history (MA Ed); language and literature (MA Ed); secondary administration (MS Ed); secondary education (MS Ed). *Accreditation:* NCATE. Part-time and evening/weekend programs available. Postbaccalaureate distance learning degree programs offered. *Degree requirements:* For master's, thesis optional. *Entrance requirements:* For master's, GRE General Test, GRE Writing Test, minimum GPA of 2.75 or 12 graduate hours at CSC with minimum GPA of 3.25. Additional exam requirements/recommendations for international students: Required—TOEFL. Electronic applications accepted. *Faculty research:* Rural education, technology, mental health.

Chapman University, Graduate Studies, College of Educational Studies, Program in Teaching, Orange, CA 92866. Offers elementary education (MA); multiple subjects with bilingual emphasis (Credential); professional clear (ryan fifth year) (Credential); single subject (Credential). Part-time and evening/weekend programs available. *Faculty:* 24 full-time (15 women), 25 part-time/

Elementary Education

Chapman University (continued)

adjunct (16 women). *Students:* 58 full-time (44 women), 48 part-time (37 women); includes 35 minority (18 Asian Americans or Pacific Islanders, 17 Hispanic Americans). Average age 28. 34 applicants, 76% accepted, 21 enrolled. In 2009, 30 master's awarded. *Degree requirements:* For master's, thesis. *Entrance requirements:* For master's, GRE General Test, MAT, or California Subject Examinations for Teachers, minimum GPA of 2.75. Additional exam requirements/recommendations for international students: Required—TOEFL (minimum score 550 paper-based). *Application deadline:* Applications are processed on a rolling basis. Application fee: $55. Electronic applications accepted. *Expenses:* Contact institution. *Financial support:* Fellowships, Federal Work-Study and scholarships/grants available. Financial award application deadline: 6/30; financial award applicants required to submit FAFSA. *Unit head:* Dr. Anaida Colon-Muniz, Coordinator, 714-997-6781, E-mail: acolon@chapman.edu. *Application contact:* Rika Judd, Graduate Admission Counselor, 714-997-6786, Fax: 714-997-6713, E-mail: rjudd@chapman.edu.

Charleston Southern University, School of Education, Charleston, SC 29423-8087. Offers administration and supervision (M Ed), including elementary, secondary; elementary education (M Ed); secondary education (M Ed). *Accreditation:* NCATE. Part-time and evening/weekend programs available. *Faculty:* 4 full-time (2 women). *Students:* 70 part-time (57 women); includes 17 minority (all African Americans). Average age 34. 48 applicants, 79% accepted, 22 enrolled. In 2009, 27 master's awarded. *Degree requirements:* For master's, thesis optional. *Entrance requirements:* For master's, GRE or MAT. Additional exam requirements/recommendations for international students: Required—TOEFL (minimum score 550 paper-based; 213 computer-based; 79 iBT). *Application deadline:* Applications are processed on a rolling basis. Application fee: $30. *Expenses:* Contact institution. *Financial support:* Research assistantships with full tuition reimbursements, career-related internships or fieldwork and Federal Work-Study available. Financial award application deadline: 4/15; financial award applicants required to submit FAFSA. *Unit head:* Dr. Norma Harper, Dean, 843-863-7765, Fax: 843-863-7085, E-mail: nharper@csuniv.edu. *Application contact:* Alison Harrison, Graduate Enrollment Counselor, 843-863-7534, Fax: 843-863-7070, E-mail: aharrison@cwuniv.edu.

Chatham University, Program in Education, Pittsburgh, PA 15232-2826. Offers early childhood education (MAT); elementary education (MAT); English—secondary (MAT); environmental education (K-12) (MAT); secondary art (MAT); secondary biology education (MAT); secondary chemistry education (MAT); secondary English education (MAT); secondary math education (MAT); secondary physics education (MAT); secondary social studies education (MAT); special education (MAT). *Students:* 52 full-time (41 women), 20 part-time (16 women). Average age 30. 39 applicants, 79% accepted, 26 enrolled. In 2009, 37 master's awarded. *Degree requirements:* For master's, thesis, teaching experience. *Entrance requirements:* For master's, PRAXIS I, minimum GPA of 3.0, sample of written work, recommendation letters. Additional exam requirements/recommendations for international students: Required—TOEFL (minimum score 600 paper-based; 250 computer-based; 100 iBT), IELTS (minimum score 6.5), TWE. *Application deadline:* For fall admission, 5/1 priority date for domestic and international students; for spring admission, 10/15 priority date for domestic and international students. Applications are processed on a rolling basis. Application fee: $45. Electronic applications accepted. *Financial support:* Career-related internships or fieldwork available. Financial award applicants required to submit FAFSA. *Faculty research:* Gifted education, environmental education, technology in education, writing as learning, class size and achievement. *Unit head:* Dr. Barbara Biglan, Interim Director, 412-365-1170, E-mail: biglan@chatham.edu. *Application contact:* Dory Perry, Associate Director of Graduate Admissions, 412-365-2758, Fax: 412-365-1609, E-mail: gradadmissions@chatham.edu.

Chestnut Hill College, School of Graduate Studies, Department of Education, Program in Elementary Education, Philadelphia, PA 19118-2693. Offers M Ed. Part-time and evening/weekend programs available. *Degree requirements:* For master's, thesis optional. *Entrance requirements:* For master's, PRAXIS I or proof of teaching certification, letters of recommendation, writing sample, 6 graduate credits with minimum B grade if undergraduate GPA less than 3.0. Additional exam requirements/recommendations for international students: Required—TOEFL (minimum score 500 paper-based; 213 computer-based). *Expenses:* Contact institution. *Faculty research:* Inclusive education, cultural issues in education.

Cheyney University of Pennsylvania, School of Education and Professional Studies, Program in Elementary Education, Cheyney, PA 19319. Offers M Ed, MAT. *Accreditation:* NCATE. Part-time and evening/weekend programs available. *Degree requirements:* For master's, thesis or alternative. *Entrance requirements:* For master's, GRE General Test, MAT, minimum GPA of 2.75. Electronic applications accepted.

Chicago State University, School of Graduate and Professional Studies, College of Education, Department of Reading, Elementary Education, Library Information and Media Studies, Program in Elementary Education, Chicago, IL 60628. Offers MAT. *Accreditation:* NCATE. *Degree requirements:* For master's, comprehensive exam, thesis optional. *Entrance requirements:* For master's, minimum GPA of 3.0 in last 60 hours.

Christopher Newport University, Graduate Studies, Department of Teacher Preparation, Newport News, VA 23606-2998. Offers art (PK-12) (MAT); biology (6-12) (MAT); computer science (6-12) (MAT); elementary (PK-6) (MAT); English (6-12) (MAT); French (PK-12) (MAT); history and social science (6-12) (MAT); mathematics (6-12) (MAT); music (PK-12) (MAT), including choral, instrumental; physics (6-12) (MAT); Spanish (PK-12) (MAT). Part-time and evening/weekend programs available. *Faculty:* 24 full-time (13 women), 4 part-time/adjunct (2 women). *Students:* 76 full-time (66 women), 12 part-time (10 women); includes 3 minority (2 African Americans, 1 Hispanic American). Average age 24. 3 applicants, 100% accepted, 2 enrolled. In 2009, 58 master's awarded. *Degree requirements:* For master's, comprehensive exam, thesis or alternative. *Entrance requirements:* For master's, PRAXIS I, minimum GPA of 3.0. Additional exam requirements/recommendations for international students: Required—TOEFL (minimum score 580 paper-based; 237 computer-based; 92 iBT). *Application deadline:* For fall admission, 8/15 for domestic students, 4/1 for international students; for spring admission, 10/15 for domestic students, 10/1 for international students. Applications are processed on a rolling basis. Application fee: $45. Electronic applications accepted. *Expenses:* Tuition, area resident: Part-time $384 per credit hour. Tuition, state resident: part-time $384 per credit hour. Tuition, nonresident: part-time $701 per credit hour. *Financial support:* In 2009–10, 3 research assistantships with full and partial tuition reimbursements (averaging $2,000 per year) were awarded; career-related internships or fieldwork, Federal Work-Study, and unspecified assistantships also available. Support available to part-time students. Financial award application deadline: 3/1; financial award applicants required to submit FAFSA. *Faculty research:* Early literacy development, instructional innovations, professional teaching standards, multicultural issues, aesthetic education. *Unit head:* Dr. Marsha Sprague, Director, 757-594-7388, Fax: 757-594-7803, E-mail: msprague@cnu.edu. *Application contact:* Lyn Sawyer, Associate Director, Graduate Admissions, 757-594-7544, Fax: 757-594-7649, E-mail: gradstdy@cnu.edu.

The Citadel, The Military College of South Carolina, Citadel Graduate College, School of Education, Program in Guidance and Counseling, Charleston, SC 29409. Offers elementary/secondary school counseling (M Ed); student affairs and college counseling (M Ed). *Accreditation:* ACA; NCATE. Part-time and evening/weekend programs available. *Faculty:* 12 full-time (7 women), 8 part-time/adjunct (5 women). *Students:* 16 full-time (15 women), 34 part-time (32 women); includes 10 minority (9 African Americans, 1 Hispanic American). Average age 29. In 2009, 16 master's awarded. *Degree requirements:* For master's, comprehensive exam, practicum or internship. *Entrance requirements:* For master's, GRE (minimum score 900) or MAT (minimum score 396), minimum undergraduate GPA of 3.0, 3 letters of reference, group admissions interview. Additional exam requirements/recommendations for international students: Required—TOEFL (minimum score 550 paper-based; 213 computer-based; 79 iBT). *Application deadline:* For fall admission, 6/1 for domestic students; for spring admission, 10/1 for domestic students. Application fee: $30. Electronic applications accepted. *Expenses:* Tuition, state resident: part-time $400 per credit hour. Tuition, nonresident: part-time $657 per credit hour. Required fees: $40 per term. *Financial support:* Career-related internships or fieldwork, health care benefits, and unspecified assistantships available. Support available to part-time students. Financial award application deadline: 7/1; financial award applicants required to submit FAFSA. *Unit head:* Dr. George T. Williams, Director, 843-953-2205, Fax: 843-953-7258, E-mail: williamsg@citadel.edu. *Application contact:* Dr. Steve A. Nida, Associate Provost, The Citadel Graduate College, 843-953-5089, Fax: 843-953-7630, E-mail: cgc@citadel.edu.

City University of Seattle, Graduate Division, Gordon Albright School of Education, Bellevue, WA 98005. Offers curriculum and instruction (M Ed); educational leadership (M Ed); educational leadership: administrator certification (Certificate); executive leadership: superintendent certification (Certificate); guidance and counseling (M Ed); leadership (M Ed); leadership and school counseling (M Ed); professional certification for teachers (Certificate); reading and literacy (M Ed); reading and literacy in education (M Ed); teacher certification (elementary K-8) (MIT); teacher certification (special education K-12) (MIT); technology, curriculum, and instruction (M Ed). Part-time and evening/weekend programs available. Postbaccalaureate distance learning degree programs offered (no on-campus study). *Entrance requirements:* Additional exam requirements/recommendations for international students: Required—TOEFL (minimum score 540 paper-based; 207 computer-based); Recommended—IELTS. Electronic applications accepted. *Expenses:* Contact institution.

Clarion University of Pennsylvania, Office of Research and Graduate Studies, College of Education and Human Services, Department of Education, Program in Education, Clarion, PA 16214. Offers curriculum and instruction (M Ed); early childhood (M Ed); English (M Ed); history (M Ed); literacy (M Ed); science (M Ed); technology (M Ed). *Accreditation:* NCATE. Part-time programs available. *Degree requirements:* For master's, comprehensive exam, thesis or alternative. *Entrance requirements:* For master's, minimum QPA of 3.0, teacher certification. Additional exam requirements/recommendations for international students: Required—TOEFL (minimum score 550 paper-based; 213 computer-based; 80 iBT). Electronic applications accepted.

Clemson University, Graduate School, College of Health, Education, and Human Development, School of Education, Program in Elementary Education, Clemson, SC 29634. Offers M Ed. *Accreditation:* NCATE. *Students:* 2 full-time (1 woman), 2 part-time (both women). Average age 24. 8 applicants, 63% accepted, 2 enrolled. In 2009, 11 master's awarded. *Degree requirements:* For master's, comprehensive exam. *Entrance requirements:* For master's, GRE General Test, teaching certificate. Additional exam requirements/recommendations for international students: Required—TOEFL. *Application deadline:* Applications are processed on a rolling basis. Application fee: $70 ($80 for international students). Electronic applications accepted. *Expenses:* Contact institution. *Financial support:* In 2009–10, 1 student received support, including 1 teaching assistantship with partial tuition reimbursement available (averaging $9,083 per year); career-related internships or fieldwork, institutionally sponsored loans, scholarships/grants, health care benefits, and unspecified assistantships also available. Support available to part-time students. Financial award application deadline: 6/1; financial award applicants required to submit FAFSA. *Unit head:* Dr. Michael J. Padilla, Director/Associate Dean, 864-656-4444, Fax: 864-656-0311, E-mail: padilla@clemson.edu. *Application contact:* Dr. David Fleming, Graduate Coordinator, 864-656-1881, Fax: 864-656-0311, E-mail: dflemin@clemson.edu.

College of Charleston, Graduate School, School of Education, Health, and Human Performance, Department of Elementary and Early Childhood Education, Program in Elementary Education, Charleston, SC 29424-0001. Offers MAT. *Accreditation:* NCATE. Part-time and evening/weekend programs available. *Faculty:* 31 full-time (26 women), 11 part-time/adjunct (10 women). *Students:* 47 full-time (40 women), 3 part-time (all women); includes 3 minority (1 African American, 2 American Indian/Alaska Native), 1 international. Average age 28. 15 applicants, 53% accepted, 6 enrolled. In 2009, 9 master's awarded. *Degree requirements:* For master's, thesis or alternative, written qualifying exam, student teaching experience. *Entrance requirements:* For master's, GRE, 2 letters of recommendation. Additional exam requirements/recommendations for international students: Required—TOEFL. *Application deadline:* For fall admission, 4/1 for domestic students; for spring admission, 11/1 for domestic students. Applications are processed on a rolling basis. Application fee: $45. Electronic applications accepted. *Financial support:* In 2009–10, research assistantships (averaging $12,400 per year), teaching assistantships (averaging $13,300 per year) were awarded; Federal Work-Study, scholarships/grants, and unspecified assistantships also available. Support available to part-time students. Financial award application deadline: 4/1; financial award applicants required to submit FAFSA. *Unit head:* Dr. Angela Cozart, Director, 843-953-6353, Fax: 843-953-5407, E-mail: cozarta@cofc.edu. *Application contact:* Susan Hallatt, Director of Graduate Admissions, 843-953-5614, Fax: 843-953-1434, E-mail: hallats@cofc.edu.

The College of New Jersey, Graduate Division, School of Education, Department of Elementary and Early Childhood Education, Program in Elementary Education, Ewing, NJ 08628. Offers M Ed, MAT. *Accreditation:* NCATE. Part-time programs available. *Students:* 34 full-time (24 women), 14 part-time (13 women); includes 8 minority (1 African American, 5 Asian Americans or Pacific Islanders, 2 Hispanic Americans). 88 applicants, 68% accepted. In 2009, 18 master's awarded. *Degree requirements:* For master's, comprehensive exam. *Entrance requirements:* For master's, GRE General Test, minimum GPA of 3.0 in field or 2.75 overall. Additional exam requirements/recommendations for international students: Required—TOEFL. *Application deadline:* For fall admission, 2/1 priority date for domestic students; for spring admission, 10/1 priority date for domestic students. Application fee: $70. Electronic applications accepted. *Expenses:* Tuition, state resident: part-time $573.70 per credit. Tuition, nonresident: part-time $887.75 per credit. Required fees: $140.85 per credit. One-time fee: $10 part-time. *Financial support:* Tuition waivers (partial) and unspecified assistantships available. Financial award application deadline: 5/1; financial award applicants required to submit FAFSA. *Unit head:* Dr. Brenda Leake, Coordinator, 609-771-2219, Fax: 609-637-5197. *Application contact:* Susan L. Hydro, Assistant Dean, Office of Graduate Studies, 609-771-2300, Fax: 609-637-5105, E-mail: graduate@tcnj.edu.

The College of New Rochelle, Graduate School, Division of Education, Program in Elementary Education/Early Childhood Education, New Rochelle, NY 10805-2308. Offers MS Ed. Part-time programs available. *Degree requirements:* For master's, comprehensive exam (for some programs), thesis (for some programs), practicum. *Entrance requirements:* For master's, interview, minimum GPA of 3.0 in field, 2.7 overall.

College of St. Joseph, Graduate Programs, Division of Education, Program in Elementary Education, Rutland, VT 05701-3899. Offers M Ed. Part-time and evening/weekend programs available. *Degree requirements:* For master's, comprehensive exam. *Entrance requirements:* For master's, PRAXIS I (for initial licensure), 2 letters of reference, minimum GPA of 3.0 (initial licensure) or 2.7 (nonlicensure), interview. Electronic applications accepted. *Expenses:* Tuition: Full-time $13,500; part-time $350 per credit. Required fees: $45 per term. One-time fee: $445. Tuition and fees vary according to program.

The College of Saint Rose, Graduate Studies, School of Education, Teacher Education Department, Albany, NY 12203-1419. Offers business and marketing (MS Ed); childhood education (MS Ed); curriculum and instruction (MS Ed); early childhood education (MS Ed); elementary education (K-6) (MS Ed); secondary education (MS Ed, Certificate); teacher education (MS Ed, Certificate), including bilingual pupil personnel services (Certificate), teacher education (MS Ed). Part-time and evening/weekend programs available. *Entrance requirements:* For master's, minimum undergraduate GPA of 3.0. Additional exam requirements/recommendations for international students: Required—TOEFL (minimum score 550 paper-based; 213 computer-based). Electronic applications accepted.

College of Staten Island of the City University of New York, Graduate Programs, Department of Education, Program in Childhood Education, Staten Island, NY 10314-6600. Offers MS Ed. Part-time and evening/weekend programs available. *Faculty:* 3 full-time (2 women), 8 part-time/adjunct (4 women). *Students:* 28 full-time (24 women), 244 part-time (226 women); includes 48 minority (9 African Americans, 13 Asian Americans or Pacific Islanders, 26 Hispanic

Americans). Average age 30. 107 applicants, 79% accepted, 61 enrolled. In 2009, 64 master's awarded. *Degree requirements:* For master's, research project. *Entrance requirements:* For master's, minimum GPA of 2.75, 2 letters of recommendation, letter of intent, N.Y. State Initial Certification. Additional exam requirements/recommendations for international students: Required—TOEFL (minimum score 550 paper-based; 213 computer-based; 79 iBT). *Application deadline:* For fall admission, 4/19 priority date for domestic and international students; for spring admission, 11/16 priority date for domestic and international students. Applications are processed on a rolling basis. Application fee: $125. Electronic applications accepted. *Expenses:* Tuition, state resident: full-time $7360; part-time $310 per credit. Tuition, nonresident: part-time $575 per credit. Required fees: $378; $113 per semester. *Financial support:* Career-related internships or fieldwork, Federal Work-Study, and scholarships/grants available. Support available to part-time students. Financial award applicants required to submit FAFSA. *Unit head:* Dr. Greg Seals, Coordinator, 718-982-3725, Fax: 718-982-3743, E-mail: seals@mail.csi.cuny.edu. *Application contact:* Sasha Spence, Assistant Director of Graduate Recruitment Admissions, 718-982-2699, Fax: 718-982-2500, E-mail: sasha.spence@csi.cuny.edu.

The College of William and Mary, School of Education, Program in Curriculum and Instruction, Williamsburg, VA 23187-8795. Offers elementary education (MA Ed); gifted education (MA Ed); math specialist (MA Ed); reading education (MA Ed); secondary education (MA Ed), including English education, mathematics education, modern foreign languages education, science education, social studies education; special education (MA Ed), including general curriculum, resource collaborating teaching. *Accreditation:* NCATE. Part-time programs available. *Faculty:* 18 full-time (12 women), 17 part-time/adjunct (15 women). *Students:* 54 full-time (45 women), 12 part-time (all women); includes 3 minority (2 African Americans, 1 Asian American or Pacific Islander), 2 international. Average age 27. 120 applicants, 75% accepted. In 2009, 70 master's awarded. *Degree requirements:* For master's, project. *Entrance requirements:* For master's, GRE or MAT, minimum GPA of 2.5. Additional exam requirements/recommendations for international students: Required—TOEFL. *Application deadline:* For fall admission, 1/15 for domestic and international students; for spring admission, 10/1 for domestic and international students. Application fee: $45. Electronic applications accepted. *Expenses:* Tuition, state resident: full-time $6400; part-time $315 per credit hour. Tuition, nonresident: full-time $19,720; part-time $840 per credit hour. Required fees: $4114. *Financial support:* In 2009–10, 30 students received support, including 10 research assistantships with full and partial tuition reimbursements available (averaging $5,500 per year); career-related internships or fieldwork, Federal Work-Study, institutionally sponsored loans, scholarships/grants, and unspecified assistantships also available. Financial award application deadline: 1/15; financial award applicants required to submit FAFSA. *Faculty research:* National Council of Teachers of Mathematics Standards, counseling, self-concept and self-esteem, special education, curriculum development. *Unit head:* Dr. C. Denise Johnson, Area Coordinator, 757-221-1528, E-mail: cdjohn@wm.edu. *Application contact:* Dorothy Smith Osborne, Director of Admissions, 757-221-2317, Fax: 757-221-2293, E-mail: dsosbo@wm.edu.

The Colorado College, Department of Education, Program in Elementary Education, Colorado Springs, CO 80903-3294. Offers elementary school teaching (MAT). *Faculty:* 3 full-time (2 women), 5 part-time/adjunct (4 women). *Students:* 10 full-time (9 women). Average age 28. 17 applicants, 88% accepted, 10 enrolled. In 2009, 6 master's awarded. *Degree requirements:* For master's, thesis, internship. *Entrance requirements:* For master's, PRAXIS II or PLACE Exam. *Application deadline:* For fall admission, 12/1 for domestic and international students. Applications are processed on a rolling basis. Application fee: $50. *Expenses:* Tuition: Part-time $2545 per credit. *Financial support:* In 2009–10, 6 students received support, including 8 teaching assistantships (averaging $16,000 per year); career-related internships or fieldwork, institutionally sponsored loans, health care benefits, and tuition waivers (partial) also available. Financial award application deadline: 2/15; financial award applicants required to submit FAFSA. *Unit head:* Dr. Charlotte Mendoza, Director, 719-389-6474, Fax: 719-389-6473, E-mail: cmendoza@coloradocollege.edu. *Application contact:* Debra Yazulla Mortenson, Education Services Manager, 719-389-6472, Fax: 719-389-6473, E-mail: debra.mortenson@coloradocollege.edu.

Columbia College, Graduate Programs, Department of Education, Columbia, SC 29203-5998. Offers divergent learning (M Ed). *Accreditation:* NCATE. Part-time and evening/weekend programs available. Postbaccalaureate distance learning degree programs offered (minimal on-campus study). *Faculty:* 3 full-time (1 woman), 18 part-time/adjunct (10 women). *Students:* 175 full-time (158 women), 60 part-time (37 women); includes 59 minority (57 African Americans, 2 Asian Americans or Pacific Islanders), 1 international. Average age 27. 152 applicants, 98% accepted, 135 enrolled. In 2009, 143 master's awarded. *Degree requirements:* For master's, thesis. *Entrance requirements:* For master's, GRE General Test, MAT, 2 recommendations, current South Carolina teaching certificate, minimum GPA of 3.2. *Expenses:* Contact institution. *Financial support:* Available to part-time students. Application deadline: 7/1. *Unit head:* Dr. Mary Steppling, Chair, 803-786-3782, Fax: 803-786-3034, E-mail: mstepping@colacoll.edu. *Application contact:* Carolyn Emeneker, Director of Graduate School and Evening College Admissions, 803-786-3766, Fax: 803-786-3674, E-mail: emeneker@colacoll.edu.

Columbia College Chicago, Graduate School, Department of Educational Studies, Chicago, IL 60605-1996. Offers elementary education (MAT); English (MAT); interdisciplinary arts (MAT); multicultural education (MA); urban teaching (MA). Part-time and evening/weekend programs available. *Degree requirements:* For master's, thesis, student teaching experience, 100 preclinical hours. *Entrance requirements:* For master's, supplemental recommendation form. Additional exam requirements/recommendations for international students: Required—TOEFL (minimum score 550 paper-based; 213 computer-based). Electronic applications accepted. *Expenses:* Tuition: Part-time $651 per credit hour. Required fees: $205 per semester. One-time fee: $285 part-time. Tuition and fees vary according to program.

Columbia International University, Columbia Graduate School, Columbia, SC 29230-3122. Offers Bible teaching (MABT); Christian higher education leadership (Ed D); Christian school educational leadership (Ed D); counseling (MACN); curriculum and instruction (M Ed), including Christian school guidance, English as a second language, learning disabilities, school technology; early childhood and elementary education (MAT); educational administration (M Ed); teaching English as a foreign language (Certificate); teaching English as a foreign language and intercultural studies (MATF). Part-time and evening/weekend programs available. *Degree requirements:* For master's, internships, professional project. *Entrance requirements:* For master's, Minnesota Multiphasic Personality Inventory, MAT, minimum GPA of 2.7. Additional exam requirements/recommendations for international students: Required—TOEFL. Electronic applications accepted.

Concordia University, College of Education, Portland, OR 97211-6099. Offers curriculum and instruction (elementary) (M Ed); educational administration (M Ed); elementary education (MAT); secondary education (MAT). Part-time programs available. Postbaccalaureate distance learning degree programs offered (no on-campus study). *Degree requirements:* For master's, comprehensive exam, work samples/portfolio. *Entrance requirements:* For master's, California Basic Educational Skills Test or PRAXIS I, minimum undergraduate GPA of 2.8, graduate 3.0; 2 letters of recommendation. Additional exam requirements/recommendations for international students: Required—TOEFL (minimum score 525 paper-based; 195 computer-based). Electronic applications accepted. *Faculty research:* Learner centered classroom, brain-based learning future of on-line learning.

Concordia University Chicago, College of Education, Program in Teaching, River Forest, IL 60305-1499. Offers early childhood education (MAT); elementary education (MAT); secondary education (MAT). *Degree requirements:* For master's, thesis or alternative. *Entrance requirements:* For master's, minimum GPA of 2.9. Additional exam requirements/recommendations for international students: Required—TOEFL (minimum score 550 paper-based; 195 computer-based). Electronic applications accepted.

Concordia University, Nebraska, Graduate Programs in Education, Program in Educational Administration, Seward, NE 68434-1599. Offers elementary and secondary education (M Ed); elementary education (M Ed); secondary education (M Ed). *Accreditation:* NCATE. Part-time programs available. *Degree requirements:* For master's, thesis or alternative. *Entrance requirements:* For master's, GRE, MAT, or NTE, BS in education or equivalent, minimum GPA of 3.0.

Converse College, School of Education and Graduate Studies, Program in Elementary Education, Spartanburg, SC 29302-0006. Offers M Ed, MAT. Part-time programs available. *Degree requirements:* For master's, capstone paper. *Entrance requirements:* For master's, NTE or PRAXIS II (M Ed), minimum GPA of 2.75, 2 recommendations. Electronic applications accepted.

Creighton University, Graduate School, College of Arts and Sciences, Department of Education, Program in Teaching, Omaha, NE 68178-0001. Offers elementary teaching (M Ed); secondary teaching (M Ed). Part-time and evening/weekend programs available. *Students:* 15 full-time (11 women), 18 part-time (13 women); includes 2 minority (1 American Indian/Alaska Native, 1 Asian American or Pacific Islander). Average age 26. 2 applicants, 50% accepted, 1 enrolled. In 2009, 17 master's awarded. *Entrance requirements:* For master's, 3 letters of recommendation, 2 writing samples. Additional exam requirements/recommendations for international students: Required—TOEFL (minimum score 550 paper-based; 213 computer-based; 80 iBT). *Application deadline:* For fall admission, 7/1 priority date for domestic students, 3/1 priority date for international students; for winter admission, 12/1 priority date for domestic students, 6/1 priority date for international students; for spring admission, 3/1 priority date for domestic and international students. Applications are processed on a rolling basis. Application fee: $50. Electronic applications accepted. *Expenses:* Tuition: Full-time $11,700; part-time $650 per credit hour. Required fees: $126 per semester. *Financial support:* Scholarships/grants and tuition waivers (partial) available. Support available to part-time students. Financial award applicants required to submit FAFSA. *Unit head:* Fr. Tom Simonds, Director, 402-280-3602, E-mail: thomassimonds@creighton.edu. *Application contact:* Taunya Plater, Senior Program Coordinator, 402-280-2870, Fax: 402-280-2899, E-mail: taunyaplater@creighton.edu.

Curry College, Graduate Studies, Program in Education, Milton, MA 02186-9984. Offers educational administration (M Ed); educational diagnostic assessment (Certificate); educational therapy (Certificate); elementary education (M Ed); foundations (non-license) (M Ed); learning disabilities across the lifespan (Certificate); reading (M Ed, Certificate); special education (M Ed). Part-time and evening/weekend programs available. *Faculty:* 6 full-time (4 women), 12 part-time/adjunct (9 women). *Students:* 101 part-time (82 women). Average age 37. In 2009, 25 master's awarded. *Degree requirements:* For master's, project or thesis. *Entrance requirements:* For master's, MAT or GRE, interview, recommendations, resume, written statement. Additional exam requirements/recommendations for international students: Required—TOEFL (minimum score 550 paper-based; 213 computer-based; 80 iBT). *Application deadline:* For fall admission, 8/1 priority date for domestic students, 6/1 for international students; for winter admission, 10/1 for international students; for spring admission, 1/1 for domestic students, 1/28 for international students. Applications are processed on a rolling basis. Application fee: $50. *Expenses:* Contact institution. *Financial support:* Career-related internships or fieldwork and tuition waivers (partial) available. *Faculty research:* Classroom trauma, therapeutic writing, inclusionary practices. *Unit head:* Dr. Donald Gratz, Director and Associate Professor, 617-333-2243, E-mail: dgratz0703@curry.edu. *Application contact:* John Bresnahan, Director of Graduate Enrollment and Student Services, 617-333-2243, Fax: 617-979-3535, E-mail: jbresnah0104@curry.edu.

Dallas Baptist University, Dorothy M. Bush College of Education, Teaching Program, Dallas, TX 75211-9299. Offers elementary (MAT); English as a second language (MAT); hi-level (MAT); secondary (MAT). Part-time and evening/weekend programs available. *Entrance requirements:* For master's, GRE General Test, minimum GPA of 3.0. Additional exam requirements/recommendations for international students: Required—TOEFL, IELTS. Electronic applications accepted. *Expenses:* Tuition: Full-time $10,674; part-time $593 per credit hour.

Delta State University, Graduate Programs, College of Education, Division of Teacher Education, Program in Elementary Education, Cleveland, MS 38733-0001. Offers M Ed, MAT, Ed S. *Accreditation:* NCATE. Part-time and evening/weekend programs available. *Degree requirements:* For master's, thesis optional. *Entrance requirements:* For master's, GRE General Test; for Ed S, master's degree, teaching certificate. *Expenses:* Tuition, state resident: full-time $4450; part-time $247 per credit hour. Tuition, nonresident: full-time $11,520; part-time $640 per credit hour.

Delta State University, Graduate Programs, College of Education, Thad Cochran Center for Rural School Leadership and Research, Program in Administration and Supervision, Cleveland, MS 38733-0001. Offers educational administration and supervision (Ed S); educational leadership (M Ed); elementary education (Ed S); secondary education (Ed S). *Accreditation:* NCATE. Part-time and evening/weekend programs available. *Degree requirements:* For master's, thesis optional. *Entrance requirements:* For master's, GRE General Test or MAT; for Ed S, master's degree, teaching certificate. *Expenses:* Tuition, state resident: full-time $4450; part-time $247 per credit hour. Tuition, nonresident: full-time $11,520; part-time $640 per credit hour.

Delta State University, Graduate Programs, College of Education, Thad Cochran Center for Rural School Leadership and Research, Program in Professional Studies, Cleveland, MS 38733-0001. Offers counselor education (Ed D); educational leadership (Ed D); elementary education (Ed D); higher education (Ed D). Part-time and evening/weekend programs available. *Degree requirements:* For doctorate, thesis/dissertation. *Entrance requirements:* For doctorate, GRE General Test. *Expenses:* Tuition, state resident: full-time $4450; part-time $247 per credit hour. Tuition, nonresident: full-time $11,520; part-time $640 per credit hour.

DePaul University, School of Education, Chicago, IL 60106. Offers bilingual and bicultural education (M Ed, MA); curriculum studies (M Ed, MA, Ed D); educational leadership (M Ed, MA, Ed D), including administration and supervision (M Ed, MA), Catholic school leadership (M Ed, MA), physical education (M Ed, MA); human development and learning (MA); human services and counseling (M Ed, MA), including agencies, family concerns, and higher education, elementary schools, human services management, secondary schools; reading and learning disabilities (M Ed, MA); social culture studies in education and development (M Ed, MA), including curriculum studies/development; teaching and learning (early childhood, elementary and secondary) (M Ed), including elementary education (M Ed, MA), secondary education (M Ed, MA); teaching and learning (early childhood, elementary, and secondary) (MA), including elementary education (M Ed, MA), secondary education (M Ed, MA). *Accreditation:* NCATE. Part-time and evening/weekend programs available. *Faculty:* 61 full-time (40 women), 66 part-time/adjunct (41 women). *Students:* 799 full-time (779 women), 470 part-time (365 women); includes 319 minority (153 African Americans, 3 American Indian/Alaska Native, 48 Asian Americans or Pacific Islanders, 115 Hispanic Americans), 15 international. Average age 30. 635 applicants, 74% accepted, 318 enrolled. In 2009, 604 master's, 5 doctorates awarded. *Degree requirements:* For doctorate, thesis/dissertation. *Entrance requirements:* For master's, interview, minimum GPA of 2.75, 2 letters of recommendation; for doctorate, interview, master's degree, writing sample, 3 letters of recommendation. Additional exam requirements/recommendations for international students: Required—TOEFL (minimum score 550 paper-based; 213 computer-based; 80 iBT). *Application deadline:* Applications are processed on a rolling basis. Application fee: $40. Electronic applications accepted. *Expenses:* Tuition: Full-time $37,525; part-time $620 per credit hour. *Financial support:* In 2009–10, 14 research assistantships with tuition reimbursements (averaging $5,800 per year) were awarded; career-related internships or fieldwork also available. *Faculty research:* Reflective teaching, children at risk, loss, ethnicity, urban education. Total annual research expenditures: $1.6 million. *Unit head:* Dr. Marie Donovan, Dean, 773-325-7581, Fax: 773-325-7713, E-mail: mdonovan@depaul.edu. *Application contact:* Brandon Washington, Data Project Manager, 773-325-1152, Fax: 773-325-2270, E-mail: bwashin3@depaul.edu.

DeSales University, Graduate Division, Program in Education, Center Valley, PA 18034-9568. Offers elementary education (M Ed); instructional technology for K-12 (M Ed); interdisciplinary (M Ed); mathematics (M Ed); special education (M Ed); TESOL/ESL (M Ed). Part-time and

Elementary Education

DeSales University (continued)

evening/weekend programs available. Postbaccalaureate distance learning degree programs offered (no on-campus study). *Students:* 218 part-time. *Degree requirements:* For master's, thesis project. *Entrance requirements:* For master's, teaching certificate. Additional exam requirements/recommendations for international students: Required—TOEFL. *Application deadline:* Applications are processed on a rolling basis. Application fee: $35. Electronic applications accepted. *Expenses:* Tuition: Full-time $17,500; part-time $665 per credit. Full-time tuition and fees vary according to program. Part-time tuition and fees vary according to course load. *Financial support:* Application deadline: 5/1. *Faculty research:* Effective teaching, computer interfacing in chemistry labs, computer applications to teaching, history of philosophy, aesthetics multidrug-resistant cancer. *Unit head:* Dr. Lujean Baab, Director, 610-282-1100 Ext. 1739, Fax: 610-282-3734, E-mail: lujean.baab@desales.edu. *Application contact:* Caryn Stopper, Director of Graduate Admissions, 610-282-1100 Ext. 1768, Fax: 610-282-0525, E-mail: caryn.stopper@desales.edu.

Dominican College, Division of Teacher Education, Department of Teacher Education, Orangeburg, NY 10962-1210. Offers childhood education (MS Ed); teacher of students with disabilities (MS Ed); teacher of visually impaired (MS Ed). *Accreditation:* Teacher Education Accreditation Council. Part-time and evening/weekend programs available. Postbaccalaureate distance learning degree programs offered (minimal on-campus study). *Faculty:* 2 full-time (both women), 6 part-time/adjunct (all women). *Students:* 50 part-time (42 women); includes 2 minority (both Hispanic Americans). Average age 39. In 2009, 10 master's awarded. *Degree requirements:* For master's, practicum, research project. *Entrance requirements:* For master's, interview, 3 letters of recommendation, minimum undergraduate GPA of 3.0. Additional exam requirements/recommendations for international students: Required—TOEFL (minimum score 550 paper-based; 213 computer-based). *Application deadline:* Applications are processed on a rolling basis. Application fee: $50. *Financial support:* Applicants required to submit FAFSA. *Unit head:* Dr. Rona Shaw, Program Director, 845-848-4081, Fax: 845-359-7802, E-mail: rona.shaw@dc.edu. *Application contact:* Director of Admissions, 845-848-7900, Fax: 845-365-3150, E-mail: admissions@dc.edu.

Dominican University, School of Education, River Forest, IL 60305-1099. Offers curriculum and instruction (MA Ed); early childhood education (MS); education (MAT); educational administration (MA); elementary (online) (MS); English as a second language (online) (MS); reading (online) (MS); special education (MS). Part-time and evening/weekend programs available. Postbaccalaureate distance learning degree programs offered. *Faculty:* 16 full-time (12 women), 59 part-time/adjunct (46 women). *Students:* 236 full-time (182 women), 622 part-time (509 women); includes 180 minority (54 African Americans, 3 American Indian/Alaska Native, 36 Asian Americans or Pacific Islanders, 87 Hispanic Americans), 2 international. Average age 32. In 2009, 199 master's awarded. *Entrance requirements:* For master's, Illinois certification test of basic skills. Additional exam requirements/recommendations for international students: Required—TOEFL (minimum score 550 paper-based; 213 computer-based; 79 iBT). *Application deadline:* Applications are processed on a rolling basis. Application fee: $25. *Expenses:* Contact institution. *Financial support:* Career-related internships or fieldwork, scholarships/grants, and tuition waivers (partial) available. Support available to part-time students. Financial award application deadline: 8/15; financial award applicants required to submit FAFSA. *Faculty research:* Governance of private education institutions, reading and language arts, inclusion, organizational planning, leadership and vision. *Unit head:* Dr. Colleen Reardon, Dean, 718-524-6643, Fax: 708-524-6665, E-mail: creardon@dom.edu. *Application contact:* Keven Hansen, Coordinator of Recruitment and Admissions, 708-524-6921, Fax: 708-524-6665, E-mail: educate@dom.edu.

Dowling College, Graduate Programs in Education, Oakdale, NY 11769-1999. Offers adolescence education (MS Ed), including educational administration; advanced certificate in gifted education (AC); childhood and early childhood education (MS Ed); childhood education (MS Ed); educational administration (AC, PD), including computers in education (PD), school administration and supervision (PD), school district administration (PD); educational technology specialist (AC); literacy (MS Ed); literacy/special education (MS Ed); secondary education (MS Ed); special education (MS Ed). *Accreditation:* NCATE. Part-time and evening/weekend programs available. Postbaccalaureate distance learning degree programs offered. *Faculty:* 32 full-time (18 women), 98 part-time/adjunct (59 women). *Students:* 563 full-time (393 women), 885 part-time (668 women); includes 133 minority (47 African Americans, 2 American Indian/Alaska Native, 10 Asian Americans or Pacific Islanders, 74 Hispanic Americans). Average age 32. 363 applicants, 89% accepted, 213 enrolled. In 2009, 459 master's, 85 ACs awarded. *Degree requirements:* For master's and other advanced degree, comprehensive exam. *Entrance requirements:* For master's, minimum GPA of 3.0; for other advanced degree, teaching certificate. Additional exam requirements/recommendations for international students: Required—TOEFL (minimum score 550 paper-based). *Application deadline:* For fall admission, 9/1 priority date for domestic students; for winter admission, 1/1 priority date for domestic students; for spring admission, 2/1 priority date for domestic students. Applications are processed on a rolling basis. Application fee: $50. Electronic applications accepted. *Expenses:* Tuition: Full-time $14,490; part-time $805 per credit. Required fees: $346 per term. *Financial support:* Career-related internships or fieldwork and Federal Work-Study available. Support available to part-time students. Financial award application deadline: 6/30; financial award applicants required to submit FAFSA. *Faculty research:* Natural readers, Korean styles and learning strategies, mothers of children with disabilities, computers in instruction, cultural background and organizational roadblocks to problem solving. *Unit head:* Dr. Clyde Payne, Dean of the School of Education, 631-244-3404, Fax: 631-589-6644, E-mail: paynec@dowling.edu. *Application contact:* Glenn M. Berman, Assistant Vice President for Enrollment Services/Dean of Admissions, 631-244-3357, Fax: 631-244-1059, E-mail: glenn.berman@dowling.edu.

Drury University, Graduate Programs in Education, Springfield, MO 65802. Offers elementary education (M Ed); gifted education (M Ed); human services (M Ed); instructional mathematics K-8 (M Ed); instructional technology (M Ed); middle school teaching (M Ed); secondary education (M Ed); special education (M Ed); special reading (M Ed). *Accreditation:* NCATE. Part-time and evening/weekend programs available. *Degree requirements:* For master's, thesis. *Entrance requirements:* For master's, GRE or MAT, minimum GPA of 2.75. Additional exam requirements/recommendations for international students: Required—TOEFL. Electronic applications accepted. *Faculty research:* Cultural enrichment, research skills, parental involvement relating to reading skills, reading strategies for mainstreaming children.

Duquesne University, School of Education, Department of Instruction and Leadership, Program in Elementary Education, Pittsburgh, PA 15282-0001. Offers elementary education (MS Ed); elementary education/early childhood (MS Ed). Part-time and evening/weekend programs available. *Faculty:* 5 full-time (3 women), 4 part-time/adjunct (2 women). *Students:* 54 full-time (50 women), 3 part-time (all women); includes 4 minority (2 African Americans, 2 Hispanic Americans). Average age 29. 49 applicants, 67% accepted, 19 enrolled. In 2009, 19 master's awarded. *Degree requirements:* For master's, thesis optional. *Entrance requirements:* For master's, MAT, minimum GPA of 3.0. Additional exam requirements/recommendations for international students: Required—TOEFL (minimum score 550 paper-based; 80 computer-based). *Application deadline:* For fall admission, 8/1 for domestic students; for spring admission, 12/1 for domestic students. Applications are processed on a rolling basis. Application fee: $0. Electronic applications accepted. *Expenses:* Tuition: Part-time $851 per credit. Required fees: $81 per credit. *Financial support:* Research assistantships, Federal Work-Study available. Support available to part-time students. *Unit head:* Dr. Kimberly Hyatt, Director, 412-396-4794, Fax: 412-396-5388, E-mail: hyatt@duq.edu. *Application contact:* Michael Dolinger, Director of Student and Academic Services, 412-396-6647, Fax: 412-396-5585, E-mail: dolingerm@duq.edu.

D'Youville College, Department of Education, Buffalo, NY 14201-1084. Offers elementary education (MS Ed, Teaching Certificate); secondary education (MS Ed, Teaching Certificate); special education (MS Ed). Part-time and evening/weekend programs available. *Degree requirements:* For master's, one foreign language, comprehensive exam, project or thesis. *Entrance requirements:* For master's, GRE (if GPA less than 2.75), minimum GPA of 3.0. Additional exam requirements/recommendations for international students: Required—TOEFL (minimum score 500 paper-based; 173 computer-based). Electronic applications accepted. *Faculty research:* Developmental disabilities, multiculturalism, early childhood education.

East Carolina University, Graduate School, College of Education, Department of Curriculum and Instruction, Greenville, NC 27858-4353. Offers behavior/emotional disabilities (MA Ed); elementary education (MA Ed); English education (MA Ed); learning disabilities (MA Ed); low incidence disabilities (MA Ed); mental retardation (MA Ed); middle grade education (MA Ed); reading education (MA Ed); social studies education (MA Ed). Part-time programs available. Postbaccalaureate distance learning degree programs offered. *Degree requirements:* For master's, comprehensive exam, thesis optional. *Entrance requirements:* For master's, GRE General Test or MAT, interview, bachelor's degree in related field, minimum GPA of 2.5, teaching license. Additional exam requirements/recommendations for international students: Required—TOEFL.

Eastern Connecticut State University, School of Education and Professional Studies/Graduate Division, Program in Elementary Education, Willimantic, CT 06226-2295. Offers MS. *Accreditation:* NCATE. Part-time and evening/weekend programs available. *Degree requirements:* For master's, comprehensive exam or thesis. *Entrance requirements:* For master's, PRAXIS I, minimum GPA of 2.7, teaching certificate. Additional exam requirements/recommendations for international students: Required—TOEFL (minimum score 550 paper-based; 213 computer-based).

Eastern Illinois University, Graduate School, College of Education and Professional Studies, Department of Early Childhood, Elementary and Middle Level Education, Charleston, IL 61920-3099. Offers elementary education (MS Ed). *Accreditation:* NCATE. Part-time programs available. *Faculty:* 14 full-time (6 women). In 2009, 55 master's awarded. *Degree requirements:* For master's, comprehensive exam. *Application deadline:* For fall admission, 3/31 priority date for domestic students. Applications are processed on a rolling basis. Application fee: $30. *Expenses:* Tuition, state resident: full-time $9434; part-time $239 per credit hour. Tuition, nonresident: full-time $23,774; part-time $717 per credit hour. Required fees: $802.63. *Financial support:* In 2009–10, research assistantships with tuition reimbursements (averaging $8,100 per year), 5 teaching assistantships with tuition reimbursements (averaging $8,100 per year) were awarded. *Unit head:* Dr. Joy Russell, Chairperson, 217-581-5728, E-mail: jlrussell@eiu.edu. *Application contact:* Dr. Linda Reven, Coordinator of Graduate Studies, 217-581-7883, E-mail: lmreven@eiu.edu.

Eastern Kentucky University, The Graduate School, College of Education, Department of Curriculum and Instruction, Richmond, KY 40475-3102. Offers elementary education (MA Ed), including early elementary education, reading; library science (MA Ed); music education (MA Ed); secondary and higher education (MA Ed), including secondary education; teaching (MAT). *Accreditation:* NCATE. Part-time programs available. *Degree requirements:* For master's, portfolio is part of exam. *Entrance requirements:* For master's, GRE General Test, PRAXIS II (KY), minimum GPA of 2.5. *Faculty research:* Technology in education, reading instruction, e-portfolios, induction to teacher education, dispositions of teachers.

Eastern Michigan University, Graduate School, College of Education, Department of Teacher Education, Program in K–12 Education, Ypsilanti, MI 48197. Offers curriculum and instruction (MA); elementary education (MA); K-12 education (MA); middle school education (MA); secondary school education (MA). *Accreditation:* NCATE. Part-time and evening/weekend programs available. Postbaccalaureate distance learning degree programs offered (minimal on-campus study). *Students:* 18 full-time (10 women), 103 part-time (83 women); includes 20 minority (11 African Americans, 2 American Indian/Alaska Native, 3 Asian Americans or Pacific Islanders, 4 Hispanic Americans), 1 international. Average age 36. In 2009, 10 master's awarded. *Entrance requirements:* For master's, GRE. Additional exam requirements/recommendations for international students: Required—TOEFL. *Application deadline:* Applications are processed on a rolling basis. Application fee: $35. Tuition and fees vary according to course level. *Financial support:* Fellowships, research assistantships with full tuition reimbursements, teaching assistantships with full tuition reimbursements, career-related internships or fieldwork, Federal Work-Study, institutionally sponsored loans, scholarships/grants, tuition waivers (partial), and unspecified assistantships available. Support available to part-time students. Financial award applicants required to submit FAFSA. *Unit head:* Dr. Wendy Burke, Coordinator, 734-487-3260, Fax: 734-487-2101, E-mail: wendy.burke@emich.edu. *Application contact:* Dr. Wendy Burke, Coordinator, 734-487-3260, Fax: 734-487-2101, E-mail: wendy.burke@emich.edu.

Eastern Nazarene College, Adult and Graduate Studies, Division of Education, Quincy, MA 02170. Offers early childhood education (M Ed, Certificate); elementary education (M Ed, Certificate); English as a second language (M Ed, Certificate); instructional enrichment and development (M Ed, Certificate); middle school education (M Ed, Certificate); moderate special needs education (M Ed, Certificate); principal (Certificate); program development and supervision (M Ed, Certificate); secondary education (M Ed, Certificate); special education administrator (Certificate); supervisor (Certificate); teacher of reading (M Ed, Certificate). M Ed and Certificate also available through weekend program for administration, special needs, and reading only. Part-time and evening/weekend programs available. *Entrance requirements:* Additional exam requirements/recommendations for international students: Required—TOEFL (minimum score 550 paper-based).

Eastern Oregon University, School of Education and Business, Program in Elementary Education, La Grande, OR 97850-2899. Offers MTE. Part-time programs available. Postbaccalaureate distance learning degree programs offered (minimal on-campus study). *Degree requirements:* For master's, thesis. *Entrance requirements:* For master's, NTE.

Eastern Washington University, Graduate Studies, College of Education and Human Development, Department of Education, Program in Elementary Teaching, Cheney, WA 99004-2431. Offers M Ed. *Accreditation:* NCATE. *Degree requirements:* For master's, comprehensive exam. *Entrance requirements:* For master's, minimum GPA of 3.0. *Expenses:* Tuition, state resident: full-time $7476; part-time $249 per quarter hour. Tuition, nonresident: full-time $18,030; part-time $601 per quarter hour. Required fees: $3.50 per quarter hour. $142 per quarter.

East Stroudsburg University of Pennsylvania, Graduate School, College of Education, Program in Elementary Education, East Stroudsburg, PA 18301-2999. Offers M Ed. Part-time and evening/weekend programs available. *Faculty:* 6 full-time (4 women), 1 (woman) part-time/adjunct. *Students:* 19 full-time (17 women), 51 part-time (44 women); includes 3 minority (1 African American, 2 Hispanic Americans). Average age 33. In 2009, 11 master's awarded. *Degree requirements:* For master's, comprehensive exam, professional portfolio, curriculum project or action research. *Entrance requirements:* For master's, PRAXIS/teacher certification, letter of recommendation, Pennsylvania Department of Education requirements. Additional exam requirements/recommendations for international students: Required—TOEFL (minimum score 560 paper-based; 220 computer-based; 83 iBT). *Application deadline:* For fall admission, 7/31 priority date for domestic students, 5/1 priority date for international students; for spring admission, 11/30 for domestic students, 10/1 for international students. Applications are processed on a rolling basis. Application fee: $50. *Expenses:* Tuition, state resident: full-time $9942; part-time $387 per credit. Tuition, nonresident: full-time $14,240; part-time $619 per credit. *Financial support:* In 2009–10, 16 research assistantships with full and partial tuition reimbursements (averaging $2,111 per year) were awarded; Federal Work-Study and institutionally sponsored loans also available. Financial award application deadline: 3/1; financial award applicants required to submit FAFSA. *Unit head:* Dr. Paula Kelberman, Graduate Coordinator, 570-422-3365, Fax: 570-422-3942, E-mail: pkelberman@po-box.esu.edu. *Application contact:* Kevin Quintero, Graduate Admissions Coordinator, 570-422-3890, Fax: 570-422-2711, E-mail: kquintero@po-box.esu.edu.

East Tennessee State University, School of Graduate Studies, College of Education, Department of Curriculum and Instruction, Johnson City, TN 37614. Offers 7-12 (MAT); classroom technology (M Ed); educational communication (M Ed); educational media/educational

technology (M Ed); elementary education (M Ed, MAT); K-12 (MAT); reading and storytelling (M Ed, MA); reading education (M Ed, MA); school library media (M Ed); secondary education (M Ed, MAT). *Accreditation:* NCATE. Part-time and evening/weekend programs available. *Degree requirements:* For master's, thesis (for some programs). *Entrance requirements:* For master's, GRE, minimum GPA of 3.0. Additional exam requirements/recommendations for international students: Required—TOEFL (minimum score 550 paper-based; 213 computer-based). *Faculty research:* Critical thinking, curriculum development, cultural diversity, cognitive processes, effective teaching strategies.

Edinboro University of Pennsylvania, School of Graduate Studies and Research, School of Education, Department of Elementary, Middle and Secondary Education, Edinboro, PA 16444. Offers character education (Certificate); elementary education (M Ed), including character education, early childhood education, elementary education; reading (M Ed, Certificate), including reading (M Ed), reading specialist (Certificate). Part-time and evening/weekend programs available. *Faculty:* 10 full-time (6 women), 3 part-time/adjunct (2 women). *Students:* 106 full-time (63 women), 172 part-time (126 women); includes 7 minority (4 African Americans, 3 Hispanic Americans). Average age 31. In 2009, 153 master's, 7 Certificates awarded. *Degree requirements:* For master's, comprehensive exam, thesis or alternative, project; for Certificate, thesis or alternative, exam. *Entrance requirements:* For master's and Certificate, GRE or MAT, minimum QPA of 2.5. *Application deadline:* Applications are processed on a rolling basis. Application fee: $30. Electronic applications accepted. *Expenses:* Tuition, state resident: full-time $6666; part-time $370 per credit. Tuition, nonresident: full-time $10,666; part-time $593 per credit. Required fees: $2206.28. One-time fee: $204 part-time. *Financial support:* In 2009–10, 14 research assistantships with full and partial tuition reimbursements (averaging $4,050 per year) were awarded; career-related internships or fieldwork, Federal Work-Study, scholarships/grants, and unspecified assistantships also available. Support available to part-time students. Financial award application deadline: 2/15; financial award applicants required to submit FAFSA. *Unit head:* Dr. Maureen Walcavich, Program Head, Elementary Education, 814-732-2303, E-mail: mwalcavich@edinboro.edu.

Elizabeth City State University, School of Education and Psychology, Program in Elementary Education, Elizabeth City, NC 27909-7806. Offers M Ed. *Accreditation:* NCATE. Part-time and evening/weekend programs available. *Degree requirements:* For master's, comprehensive exam, thesis. *Entrance requirements:* For master's, GRE and/or MAT, full-time teacher employment in elementary classroom. Electronic applications accepted. *Faculty research:* Diverse learners, disproportionality, inclusionary classrooms, international curriculum development.

Elms College, Division of Education, Chicopee, MA 01013-2839. Offers early childhood education (MAT); education (M Ed, CAGS); elementary education (MAT); English as a second language (MAT); reading (MAT); secondary education (MAT), including biology education, English education, Spanish education; special education (MAT). Part-time and evening/weekend programs available. *Faculty:* 12 full-time (8 women), 4 part-time/adjunct (2 women). *Students:* 17 full-time (14 women), 153 part-time (136 women); includes 5 minority (1 American Indian/Alaska Native, 4 Hispanic Americans). Average age 36. 43 applicants, 88% accepted, 37 enrolled. In 2009, 23 master's, 8 other advanced degrees awarded. *Degree requirements:* For master's, thesis (for some programs). *Entrance requirements:* For master's, Massachusetts Educators Certification Test, minimum GPA of 3.0; for CAGS, master's degree in education. Additional exam requirements/recommendations for international students: Required—TOEFL. *Application deadline:* For fall admission, 7/1 priority date for domestic students; for spring admission, 11/1 priority date for domestic students. Applications are processed on a rolling basis. Application fee: $30. *Financial support:* In 2009–10, 2 teaching assistantships with partial tuition reimbursements were awarded; tuition waivers (partial) also available. Support available to part-time students. Financial award applicants required to submit FAFSA. *Unit head:* Dr. Mary Janeczek, Director, 413-594-2761, Fax: 413-592-4871, E-mail: janeczeke@elms.edu. *Application contact:* Dana Malone, Associate Director for Graduate Studies and Continuing Education, 413-265-2445, Fax: 413-265-2459, E-mail: maloned@elms.edu.

Elon University, Program in Education, Elon, NC 27244-2010. Offers elementary education (M Ed); gifted education (M Ed); special education (M Ed). *Accreditation:* NCATE. Part-time programs available. *Faculty:* 15 full-time (11 women). *Students:* 1 (woman) full-time, 79 part-time (65 women); includes 15 minority (13 African Americans, 1 Asian American or Pacific Islander, 1 Hispanic American), 1 international. Average age 30. 57 applicants, 84% accepted, 39 enrolled. In 2009, 45 master's awarded. *Entrance requirements:* For master's, GRE, MAT. Additional exam requirements/recommendations for international students: Required—TOEFL (minimum score 550 paper-based; 213 computer-based; 79 iBT). *Application deadline:* For winter admission, 6/1 priority date for domestic students. Applications are processed on a rolling basis. Application fee: $50. Electronic applications accepted. *Expenses:* Contact institution. *Financial support:* In 2009–10, 4 students received support. Federal Work-Study and scholarships/grants available. Support available to part-time students. Financial award application deadline: 6/1; financial award applicants required to submit FAFSA. *Faculty research:* Teaching reading to low-achieving second and third graders, pre- and post-student teaching attitudes toward teaching, children's writing, whole language methodology, critical creative thinking. *Unit head:* Dr. Judith B. Howard, Director, 336-278-5885, Fax: 336-278-5919, E-mail: howardj@elon.edu. *Application contact:* Art Fadde, Director of Graduate Admissions, 800-334-8448 Ext. 3, Fax: 336-278-7699, E-mail: afadde@elon.edu.

Emmanuel College, Graduate Programs, Programs in Education, Boston, MA 02115. Offers educational leadership (CAGS); elementary education (MAT); school administration (M Ed); secondary education (MAT). Part-time and evening/weekend programs available. *Faculty:* 6 part-time/adjunct (2 women). *Students:* 6 full-time (5 women), 46 part-time (33 women); includes 8 minority (4 African Americans, 4 Hispanic Americans). Average age 33. 16 applicants, 56% accepted, 9 enrolled. In 2009, 23 master's awarded. *Entrance requirements:* For master's, interview, resume, 2 letters of recommendation, essay, bachelor's degree; for CAGS, interview, leadership statement, resume, 2 letters of recommendation. Additional exam requirements/recommendations for international students: Required—TOEFL (minimum score 600 paper-based; 250 computer-based). *Application deadline:* For fall admission, 8/15 priority date for domestic students; for spring admission, 12/8 priority date for domestic students. Applications are processed on a rolling basis. Application fee: $50. Electronic applications accepted. *Expenses:* Tuition: Part-time $665 per credit. *Faculty research:* Literature/reading, history of education, multicultural education, special education. *Unit head:* Dr. Judith Marley, Dean, Graduate and Professional Programs, 617-735-9700, Fax: 617-507-0434, E-mail: gpp@emmanuel.edu. *Application contact:* Enrollment Counselor, 617-735-9700, Fax: 617-507-0434, E-mail: gpp@emmanuel.edu.

Emporia State University, School of Graduate Studies, The Teachers College, Department of Early Childhood/Elementary Teacher Education, Program in Master Teacher, Emporia, KS 66801-5087. Offers elementary subject matter (MS); English as a second language (MS); reading (MS); secondary subject matter (MS). *Accreditation:* NCATE. Part-time programs available. *Students:* 3 full-time (all women), 87 part-time (84 women); includes 6 minority (1 African American, 1 American Indian/Alaska Native, 2 Asian Americans or Pacific Islanders, 2 Hispanic Americans). 14 applicants, 100% accepted, 12 enrolled. In 2009, 40 master's awarded. *Degree requirements:* For master's, comprehensive exam or thesis, practicum. *Entrance requirements:* For master's, GRE General Test or MAT, graduate essay exam, appropriate bachelor's degree, letters of recommendation. Additional exam requirements/recommendations for international students: Required—TOEFL (minimum score 520 paper-based; 133 computer-based; 68 iBT). *Application deadline:* For fall admission, 8/15 priority date for domestic students. Applications are processed on a rolling basis. Application fee: $30 ($75 for international students). Electronic applications accepted. *Expenses:* Tuition, state resident: full-time $4154; part-time $173 per credit hour. Tuition, nonresident: full-time $12,864; part-time $536 per credit hour. Required fees: $948; $58 per credit hour. Tuition and fees vary according to campus/location. *Financial support:* Federal Work-Study, institutionally sponsored loans, health care benefits, and unspecified assistantships available. Financial award application deadline: 3/15; financial award applicants required to submit FAFSA. *Unit head:* Dr. Jean Morrow, Chair,

620-341-5766, E-mail: jmorrow@emporia.edu. *Application contact:* Mary Sewell, Admissions Coordinator, 800-950-GRAD, Fax: 620-341-5909, E-mail: msewell@emporia.edu.

Endicott College, Van Loan School of Graduate and Professional Studies, Program in Elementary Education, Beverly, MA 01915-2096. Offers initial and professional licensure (M Ed). Part-time and evening/weekend programs available. *Degree requirements:* For master's, comprehensive exam. *Entrance requirements:* For master's, MAT or GRE, Massachusetts teaching certificate, 2 professional letters of recommendation. *Expenses:* Tuition: Part-time $389 per credit. One-time fee: $1350.

Fairfield University, Graduate School of Education and Allied Professions, Department of Curriculum and Instruction, Fairfield, CT 06824-5195. Offers bilingual education (CAS); elementary education (MA); media/educational technology (MA); secondary education (MA); teaching and foundations (MA, CAS); TESOL, foreign language and bilingual/multicultural education (MA, CAS). Part-time and evening/weekend programs available. *Degree requirements:* For master's, comprehensive exam, thesis or alternative. *Entrance requirements:* For master's, PRAXIS I (PPST), minimum QPA of 3.0, 2 recommendations, resume. Additional exam requirements/recommendations for international students: Required—TOEFL (minimum score 550 paper-based; 213 computer-based; 80 iBT). Electronic applications accepted. *Faculty research:* Urban and multicultural education; participatory action for social justice; culture and family; second language acquisition; science, technology and social education.

Fayetteville State University, Graduate School, Program in Elementary Education, Fayetteville, NC 28301-4298. Offers MA Ed. *Accreditation:* NCATE. Part-time and evening/weekend programs available. *Faculty:* 6 full-time (3 women), 1 (woman) part-time/adjunct. *Degree requirements:* For master's, comprehensive exam, internships. *Entrance requirements:* For master's, GRE or MAT, minimum GPA of 2.5, professional certification or waiver permission. *Application deadline:* For fall admission, 4/15 for domestic students; for spring admission, 10/15 for domestic students. Applications are processed on a rolling basis. Application fee: $35. Electronic applications accepted. *Faculty research:* Outdoor play, early literacy, math, professional development, accreditation. *Unit head:* Dr. Saundra Shorter, Chairperson, 910-672-1257, E-mail: sshorter@uncfsu.edu. *Application contact:* Roxie Shabazz, Associate Vice-Chancellor for Enrollment Management, 910-672-1784, Fax: 910-672-2209, E-mail: rshabazz@uncfsu.edu.

Felician College, Program in Education, Lodi, NJ 07644-2117. Offers education (MA); educational supervision (MA, PMC); elementary education (MA); principal (PMC); principal/supervision dual certification (MA); school nurse/health (MA); school nurse/health educator (Certificate); special education (MA). *Accreditation:* Teacher Education Accreditation Council. Part-time and evening/weekend programs available. *Students:* 12 full-time (9 women), 93 part-time (83 women); includes 5 African Americans, 1 Asian American or Pacific Islander, 9 Hispanic Americans, 3 international. Average age 37. 18 applicants, 50% accepted, 9 enrolled. *Degree requirements:* For master's, project. *Entrance requirements:* For master's, MAT, minimum GPA of 3.0, 3 letters of recommendation. Additional exam requirements/recommendations for international students: Recommended—TOEFL (minimum score 550 paper-based; 213 computer-based). *Application deadline:* Applications are processed on a rolling basis. Application fee: $40. *Financial support:* Federal Work-Study available. *Unit head:* Dr. Rosemarie Liebmann, Associate Dean, 201-559-3537, E-mail: liebmannr@felician.edu. *Application contact:* Dr. Wendy Lin-Cook, Director of Adult and Graduate Admission, 201-559-6077, Fax: 201-559-6138, E-mail: adultandgraduate@felician.edu.

See Close-Up on page 709.

Ferris State University, College of Education and Human Services, School of Education, Big Rapids, MI 49307. Offers administration (MSCTE); curriculum and instruction (M Ed), including administration, elementary education, experiential education, philanthropic education, reading, secondary education, special education, subject matter option; education technology (MSCTE); instructor (MSCTE); post-secondary administration (MSCTE); training and development (MSCTE). Part-time and evening/weekend programs available. Postbaccalaureate distance learning degree programs offered. *Faculty:* 12 full-time (8 women), 11 part-time/adjunct (5 women). *Students:* 19 full-time (13 women), 185 part-time (122 women); includes 24 minority (20 African Americans, 1 Asian American or Pacific Islander, 3 Hispanic Americans), 1 international. Average age 36. 37 applicants, 32% accepted, 11 enrolled. In 2009, 73 master's awarded. *Degree requirements:* For master's, thesis, research paper. *Entrance requirements:* For master's, 2 years of work experience for vocational setting, minimum GPA of 2.75. Additional exam requirements/recommendations for international students: Recommended—TOEFL (minimum score 500 paper-based; 173 computer-based; 61 iBT). *Application deadline:* For fall admission, 7/1 priority date for domestic students; for spring admission, 11/1 priority date for domestic students. Applications are processed on a rolling basis. Application fee: $30. *Financial support:* Career-related internships or fieldwork and scholarships/grants available. Support available to part-time students. Financial award applicants required to submit FAFSA. *Faculty research:* Suicide prevention, reading, women in education, special needs, administration. *Unit head:* Dr. Liza Ing, Director, 231-591-5362, Fax: 231-591-2041. *Application contact:* Kimisue Worrall, Secretary, 231-591-5361, Fax: 231-591-2043.

Fitchburg State University, Division of Graduate and Continuing Education, Program in Elementary Education, Fitchburg, MA 01420-2697. Offers M Ed. *Accreditation:* NCATE. Part-time and evening/weekend programs available. *Students:* 3 full-time (all women), 59 part-time (54 women); includes 1 minority (Hispanic American). Average age 32. 19 applicants, 100% accepted, 14 enrolled. In 2009, 28 master's awarded. *Entrance requirements:* For master's, GRE General Test or MAT, teaching certificate, letters of recommendation, resume. Additional exam requirements/recommendations for international students: Required—TOEFL (minimum score 550 paper-based; 213 computer-based; 79 iBT). *Application deadline:* Applications are processed on a rolling basis. Application fee: $25 ($50 for international students). *Expenses:* Tuition, area resident: Part-time $150 per credit. Tuition, state resident: part-time $150 per credit. Tuition, nonresident: part-time $150 per credit. Required fees: $120 per credit. *Financial support:* In 2009–10, research assistantships with partial tuition reimbursements (averaging $5,500 per year); Federal Work-Study, scholarships/grants, and unspecified assistantships also available. Support available to part-time students. Financial award application deadline: 3/1; financial award applicants required to submit FAFSA. *Unit head:* Dr. Pam Hill, Chair, 978-665-3515, Fax: 978-665-3658, E-mail: gce@fsc.edu. *Application contact:* Director of Admissions, 978-665-3144, Fax: 978-665-4540, E-mail: admissions@fsc.edu.

Florida Agricultural and Mechanical University, Division of Graduate Studies, Research, and Continuing Education, College of Education, Department of Elementary Education, Tallahassee, FL 32307-3200. Offers early childhood and elementary education (M Ed, MS Ed). *Accreditation:* NCATE. *Faculty:* 8 full-time (7 women). *Students:* 4 full-time (all women), 3 part-time (all women); all minorities (all African Americans). In 2009, 1 master's awarded. *Degree requirements:* For master's, thesis (for some programs). *Entrance requirements:* For master's, GRE General Test, minimum GPA of 3.0. Additional exam requirements/recommendations for international students: Required—TOEFL. *Application deadline:* For fall admission, 5/18 for domestic students, 12/18 for international students; for spring admission, 11/12 for domestic students, 5/12 for international students. Application fee: $20. *Unit head:* Dr. Marian Smith, Chairperson, 850-599-3397, Fax: 850-561-2211. *Application contact:* Dr. Chanta M. Haywood, Dean of Graduate Studies, Research, and Continuing Education, 850-599-3315, Fax: 850-599-3727.

Florida Atlantic University, College of Education, Department of Teaching and Learning, Boca Raton, FL 33431-0991. Offers curriculum and instruction (M Ed); elementary education (M Ed); environmental education (M Ed); reading education (M Ed); social foundations of education (M Ed). *Accreditation:* NCATE. Part-time and evening/weekend programs available. *Faculty:* 35 full-time (29 women), 92 part-time/adjunct (61 women). *Students:* 56 full-time (50 women), 134 part-time (128 women); includes 36 minority (15 African Americans, 4 Asian Americans or Pacific Islanders, 17 Hispanic Americans), 2 international. Average age 32. 162 applicants, 74% accepted, 66 enrolled. In 2009, 52 master's awarded. *Entrance requirements:* For master's, GRE General Test, minimum GPA of 3.0 in last 2 years of undergraduate course work. Additional exam requirements/recommendations for international students: Required—

Elementary Education

Florida Atlantic University *(continued)*
TOEFL. *Application deadline:* For fall admission, 7/1 for domestic students, 2/15 for international students; for spring admission, 11/1 for domestic students, 7/15 for international students. Applications are processed on a rolling basis. Application fee: $30. *Expenses:* Tuition, state resident: full-time $7055; part-time $293.94 per credit hour. Tuition, nonresident: full-time $22,096; part-time $920.66 per credit hour. *Financial support:* Fellowships with partial tuition reimbursements, research assistantships with partial tuition reimbursements, teaching assistantships with partial tuition reimbursements, career-related internships or fieldwork, scholarships/grants, and unspecified assistantships available. *Faculty research:* Technology, teaching English to speakers of other languages, math teaching, electronic portfolio assessment, global perspectives through social studies. *Unit head:* Dr. Barbara Ridener, Chairperson, 561-297-3588. *Application contact:* Dr. Barbara Ridener, Chairperson, 561-297-3588.

Florida Gulf Coast University, College of Education, Program in Elementary Education, Fort Myers, FL 33965-6565. Offers early childhood education (M Ed); elementary curriculum (M Ed); elementary education (MA). Part-time and evening/weekend programs available. Post-baccalaureate distance learning degree programs offered (minimal on-campus study). *Faculty:* 31 full-time (24 women), 39 part-time/adjunct (28 women). *Students:* 7 full-time (6 women), 1 (woman) part-time. Average age 40. 8 applicants, 25% accepted, 1 enrolled. In 2009, 4 master's awarded. *Degree requirements:* For master's, comprehensive exam, thesis or alternative, final project. *Entrance requirements:* For master's, GRE General Test, MAT, minimum GPA of 3.0. Additional exam requirements/recommendations for international students: Required—TOEFL (minimum score 550 paper-based; 213 computer-based). *Application deadline:* For fall admission, 7/1 priority date for domestic students; for spring admission, 10/15 for domestic students. Applications are processed on a rolling basis. Application fee: $30. Electronic applications accepted. *Faculty research:* Language acquisition, impact of literature on reading, action research in the classroom. *Unit head:* Dr. Patricia Wachholz, Head, 239-590-7808, Fax: 239-590-7801, E-mail: pwachhol@fgcu.edu. *Application contact:* Dr. Patricia Wachholz, Head, 239-590-7808, Fax: 239-590-7801, E-mail: pwachhol@fgcu.edu.

Florida Institute of Technology, Graduate Programs, College of Science, Department of Science and Mathematics Education, Melbourne, FL 32901-6975. Offers computer education (MS); elementary science education (M Ed); environmental education (MS); informal science education (M Ed); mathematics education (MS, Ed D, PhD, Ed S); science education (MS, Ed D, PhD, Ed S); teaching (MAT). Part-time and evening/weekend programs available. *Faculty:* 4 full-time (1 woman), 3 part-time/adjunct (2 women). *Students:* 15 full-time (9 women), 18 part-time (12 women); includes 5 minority (2 African Americans, 3 Hispanic Americans), 5 international. Average age 36. 42 applicants, 52% accepted, 7 enrolled. In 2009, 3 master's, 1 doctorate, 1 other advanced degree awarded. Terminal master's awarded for partial completion of doctoral program. *Degree requirements:* For master's, comprehensive exam (for some programs), thesis (for some programs), oral final exam; for doctorate, comprehensive exam, thesis/dissertation, oral defense of dissertation; for Ed S, comprehensive exam. *Entrance requirements:* For master's, minimum GPA of 3.0, resume, 3 letters of recommendation (elementary science education); for doctorate, minimum GPA of 3.2, resume, 3 letters of recommendation, statement of objectives, 3 years teaching experience (recommended); for Ed S, minimum GPA of 3.0, resume, 3 letters of recommendation, statement of objectives. Additional exam requirements/recommendations for international students: Required—TOEFL (minimum score 550 paper-based; 213 computer-based; 79 iBT). *Application deadline:* For fall admission, 4/1 for international students; for spring admission, 9/30 for international students. Applications are processed on a rolling basis. Application fee: $50. Electronic applications accepted. *Expenses:* Tuition: Part-time $1015 per credit. Tuition and fees vary according to campus/location and program. *Financial support:* In 2009-10, 3 students received support, including 3 teaching assistantships with full and partial tuition reimbursements available (averaging $6,212 per year); research assistantships with full and partial tuition reimbursements available, career-related internships or fieldwork, institutionally sponsored loans, tuition waivers (partial), unspecified assistantships, and tuition remissions also available. Support available to part-time students. Financial award application deadline: 3/1; financial award applicants required to submit FAFSA. *Faculty research:* Measurement and evaluation, computers in education, educational technology. Total annual research expenditures: $352,726. *Unit head:* Dr. David E. Cook, Department Head, 321-674-8126, Fax: 321-674-7598, E-mail: dcook@fit.edu. *Application contact:* Thomas M. Shea, Director of Graduate Admissions, 321-674-7577, Fax: 321-723-9468, E-mail: tshea@fit.edu.

Florida International University, College of Education, Department of Curriculum and Instruction, Program in Elementary Education; Miami, FL 33199. Offers MS, Ed D. *Accreditation:* NCATE. Part-time and evening/weekend programs available. *Entrance requirements:* For master's, GRE General Test or minimum GPA of 3.0. Additional exam requirements/recommendations for international students: Required—TOEFL. *Expenses:* Tuition, state resident: full-time $8008; part-time $4004 per year. Tuition, nonresident: full-time $20,104; part-time $10,052 per year. Required fees: $298; $149 per term. *Faculty research:* Social studies, aerospace education, teacher training.

Florida Memorial University, School of Education, Miami-Dade, FL 33054. Offers elementary education (MS); exceptional student education (MS); reading (MS). *Degree requirements:* For master's, comprehensive exam or thesis, field and clinical experiences, exit exam. *Entrance requirements:* For master's, GRE, CLAST, PRAXIS I, baccalaureate or graduate degree with minimum GPA of 3.0 in last 60 hours, 3 recommendations.

Florida State University, The Graduate School, College of Education, School of Teacher Education, Program in Elementary Education, Tallahassee, FL 32306. Offers MS, Ed D, PhD, Ed S. Part-time programs available. *Faculty:* 6 full-time (5 women), 1 (woman) part-time/adjunct. *Students:* 17 full-time (14 women), 33 part-time (27 women); includes 5 minority (1 African American, 1 Asian American or Pacific Islander, 3 Hispanic Americans). 34 applicants, 44% accepted, 10 enrolled. In 2009, 13 master's, 1 doctorate awarded. *Degree requirements:* For master's and Ed S, comprehensive exam, thesis optional; for doctorate, comprehensive exam, thesis/dissertation. *Entrance requirements:* For master's, doctorate, and Ed S, GRE General Test, minimum GPA of 3.0. Additional exam requirements/recommendations for international students: Required—TOEFL (minimum score 550 paper-based; 213 computer-based; 80 iBT); Recommended—TWE. *Application deadline:* For fall admission, 6/1 priority date for domestic and international students; for spring admission, 10/1 for domestic and international students. Applications are processed on a rolling basis. Application fee: $30. *Expenses:* Tuition, state resident: full-time $7413. Tuition, nonresident: full-time $22,567. *Financial support:* In 2009-10, 1 fellowship with full and partial tuition reimbursement, 5 teaching assistantships with full and partial tuition reimbursements were awarded; research assistantships with full and partial tuition reimbursements, career-related internships or fieldwork also available. Financial award applicants required to submit FAFSA. *Unit head:* Dr. Diana Rice, Head, 850-644-6553, Fax: 850-644-8715, E-mail: drice@coe.fsu.edu. *Application contact:* Timolin Lynette Bodison-Baker, Program Assistant, 850-644-5458, Fax: 850-644-7736, E-mail: bodison@coe.fsu.edu.

Fordham University, Graduate School of Education, Division of Curriculum and Teaching, New York, NY 10023. Offers adult education (MS, MSE); bilingual teacher education (MSE); curriculum and teaching (MSE); early childhood education (MSE); elementary education (MST); language, literacy, and learning (PhD); reading education (MSE, Adv C); secondary education (MAT, MSE); special education (MSE, Adv C); teaching English as a second language (MSE). *Accreditation:* NCATE. *Degree requirements:* For doctorate, thesis/dissertation; for Adv C, thesis. *Entrance requirements:* For doctorate, MAT, GRE General Test.

Framingham State University, Division of Graduate and Continuing Education, Program in Elementary Education, Framingham, MA 01701-9101. Offers M Ed.

Francis Marion University, Graduate Programs, School of Education, Florence, SC 29502-0547. Offers early childhood education (M Ed); elementary education (M Ed); learning disabilities (M Ed, MAT); remedial education (M Ed); secondary education (M Ed). *Accreditation:* NCATE. Part-time programs available. *Faculty:* 20 full-time (15 women). *Students:* 8 full-time

(7 women), 107 part-time (90 women); includes 33 minority (all African Americans), 1 international. Average age 34. 221 applicants, 94% accepted, 94 enrolled. In 2009, 57 degrees awarded. *Degree requirements:* For master's, comprehensive exam. *Entrance requirements:* For master's, GRE General Test, MAT, NTE, or PRAXIS II. *Application deadline:* For fall admission, 3/15 priority date for domestic students; for spring admission, 10/15 priority date for domestic students. Applications are processed on a rolling basis. Application fee: $30. *Expenses:* Tuition, state resident: full-time $8345; part-time $417.25 per semester hour. Tuition, nonresident: full-time $16,690; part-time $814.50 per semester hour. Required fees: $335; $12.25 per semester hour. $30 per semester. *Financial support:* In 2009-10, 4 research assistantships (averaging $6,000 per year) were awarded; unspecified assistantships also available. Support available to part-time students. Financial award application deadline: 3/1; financial award applicants required to submit FAFSA. *Faculty research:* Identification and alternate assessment of at-risk students. *Unit head:* Dr. James R. Faulkenberry, Dean, 843-661-1460, Fax: 843-661-4647. *Application contact:* Dr. James R. Faulkenberry, Dean, 843-661-1460, Fax: 843-661-4647.

Fresno Pacific University, Graduate Programs, School of Education, Division of Mathematics/Science/Computer Education, Program in Mathematics Education, Fresno, CA 93702-4709. Offers elementary and middle school mathematics (MA Ed); secondary school mathematics (MA Ed). Part-time and evening/weekend programs available. *Degree requirements:* For master's, thesis or alternative. *Entrance requirements:* Additional exam requirements/recommendations for international students: Required—TOEFL (minimum score 550 paper-based; 213 computer-based).

Friends University, Graduate School, Division of Science, Arts, and Education, Program in Teaching, Wichita, KS 67213. Offers elementary education (MAT); secondary education (MAT). *Accreditation:* NCATE. Evening/weekend programs available. Postbaccalaureate distance learning degree programs offered (minimal on-campus study). *Entrance requirements:* Additional exam requirements/recommendations for international students: Required—TOEFL (minimum score 560 paper-based; 220 computer-based; 83 iBT), IELTS (minimum score 6). Electronic applications accepted.

Frostburg State University, Graduate School, College of Education, Department of Educational Professions, Program in Curriculum and Instruction, Frostburg, MD 21532-1099. Offers educational technology (M Ed); elementary education (M Ed); secondary education (M Ed). Part-time and evening/weekend programs available. *Faculty:* 2. *Students:* 5 full-time (all women), 42 part-time (36 women); includes 1 minority (Hispanic American). Average age 32. 20 applicants, 75% accepted, 13 enrolled. In 2009, 8 master's awarded. *Degree requirements:* For master's, thesis or alternative. *Entrance requirements:* For master's, teaching certificate. Additional exam requirements/recommendations for international students: Required—TOEFL. *Application deadline:* For fall admission, 7/15 priority date for domestic students. Applications are processed on a rolling basis. Application fee: $30. Electronic applications accepted. *Expenses:* Tuition, state resident: full-time $5706; part-time $317 per credit hour. Tuition, nonresident: full-time $6948; part-time $386 per credit hour. Required fees: $1476; $82 per credit hour. $11 per term. One-time fee: $30 full-time. *Financial support:* In 2009-10, 2 research assistantships with full tuition reimbursements (averaging $5,000 per year) were awarded. Financial award application deadline: 4/1; financial award applicants required to submit FAFSA. *Unit head:* Dr. Doris Santamaria-Makang, Coordinator, 301-687-7018, E-mail: dsantamaria@frostburg.edu. *Application contact:* Vickie Mazer, Director, Graduate Services, 301-687-7053, Fax: 301-687-4597, E-mail: vmmazer@frostburg.edu.

Frostburg State University, Graduate School, College of Education, Department of Educational Professions, Program in Elementary Teaching, Frostburg, MD 21532-1099. Offers MAT. *Accreditation:* NCATE. *Students:* 34 full-time (26 women), 1 (woman) part-time. Average age 34. 54 applicants, 69% accepted, 34 enrolled. In 2009, 23 master's awarded. *Degree requirements:* For master's, thesis or alternative, PRAXIS II. *Entrance requirements:* For master's, PRAXIS I, entry portfolio. Additional exam requirements/recommendations for international students: Required—TOEFL. *Application deadline:* For fall admission, 7/15 priority date for domestic students. Applications are processed on a rolling basis. Application fee: $30. Electronic applications accepted. *Expenses:* Tuition, state resident: full-time $5706; part-time $317 per credit hour. Tuition, nonresident: full-time $6948; part-time $386 per credit hour. Required fees: $1476; $82 per credit hour. $11 per term. One-time fee: $30 full-time. *Financial support:* In 2009-10, 1 research assistantship with full tuition reimbursement (averaging $5,000 per year) was awarded. Financial award application deadline: 4/1; financial award applicants required to submit FAFSA. *Unit head:* Dr. Kim Rotruck, Coordinator, 240-527-2736, E-mail: krotruck@frostburg.edu. *Application contact:* Vickie Mazer, Director, Graduate Services, 301-687-7053, Fax: 301-687-4597, E-mail: vmmazer@frostburg.edu.

Gallaudet University, The Graduate School, Department of Education, Washington, DC 20002-3625. Offers early childhood education (MA, Ed S); education of deaf and hard of hearing students and multihandicapped deaf and hard of hearing students (MA, Ed S); elementary education (MA, Ed S); individualized program of study (PhD); parent/infant specialty (MA, Ed S); secondary education (MA, Ed S). *Accreditation:* NCATE. *Degree requirements:* For master's, thesis optional; for doctorate, thesis/dissertation. *Entrance requirements:* For doctorate, GRE General Test or MAT, interview. Electronic applications accepted.

Gardner-Webb University, Graduate School, School of Education, Program in Elementary Education, Boiling Springs, NC 28017. Offers MA. *Accreditation:* NCATE. Part-time and evening/weekend programs available. *Faculty:* 7 full-time (3 women), 2 part-time/adjunct (both women). *Students:* 34 part-time (31 women); includes 4 minority (3 African Americans, 1 Hispanic American). Average age 32. 12 applicants, 100% accepted, 12 enrolled. In 2009, 16 master's awarded. *Degree requirements:* For master's, comprehensive exam. *Entrance requirements:* For master's, GRE General Test or NTE, PRAXIS, minimum GPA of 2.5. *Application deadline:* For fall admission, 8/1 priority date for domestic students. Applications are processed on a rolling basis. Application fee: $25. Electronic applications accepted. *Expenses:* Tuition: Part-time $305 per credit hour. *Financial support:* Unspecified assistantships available. *Unit head:* Dr. Carrol Smith, Chair, 704-406-3913, Fax: 704-406-3921, E-mail: dsimmons@gardner-webb.edu. *Application contact:* Dr. Franki Burch, Dean, Graduate School, 704-406-4422, Fax: 704-406-4329, E-mail: gradschool@gardner-webb.edu.

The George Washington University, Graduate School of Education and Human Development, Department of Teacher Preparation and Special Education, Program in Elementary Education, Washington, DC 20052. Offers M Ed. *Accreditation:* NCATE. Part-time programs available. *Students:* 33 full-time (31 women), 12 part-time (10 women); includes 12 minority (3 African Americans, 1 American Indian/Alaska Native, 6 Asian Americans or Pacific Islanders, 2 Hispanic Americans), 1 international. Average age 28. 55 applicants, 98% accepted, 38 enrolled. In 2009, 28 master's awarded. *Degree requirements:* For master's, comprehensive exam. *Entrance requirements:* For master's, GRE General Test or MAT, minimum GPA of 2.75. *Application deadline:* For fall admission, 1/15 priority date for domestic students; for spring admission, 10/1 for domestic students. Applications are processed on a rolling basis. Application fee: $60. *Financial support:* In 2009-10, 27 students received support; fellowships, career-related internships or fieldwork, Federal Work-Study, and tuition waivers (partial) available. Financial award application deadline: 1/15; financial award applicants required to submit FAFSA. *Faculty research:* Issues in teacher training. *Unit head:* Dr. Sylven S. Beck, Director, 202-994-3365, E-mail: sbeck@gwu.edu. *Application contact:* Sarah Lang, Director of Graduate Admissions, 202-994-1447, Fax: 202-994-7207, E-mail: slang@gwu.edu.

Georgia Southern University, Jack N. Averitt College of Graduate Studies, College of Education, Department of Teaching and Learning, Program in Secondary and P-12 Education, Statesboro, GA 30460. Offers M Ed. Part-time and evening/weekend programs available. *Degree requirements:* For master's, portfolio, transition point assessments, exit assessment. *Entrance requirements:* For master's, GRE General Test or MAT, minimum cumulative GPA of 2.5. Additional exam requirements/recommendations for international students: Required—TOEFL (minimum score 550 paper-based; 213 computer-based; 80 iBT). *Application deadline:* For fall admission, 3/1 priority date for domestic and international students; for spring admission,

10/1 priority date for domestic students, 10/1 for international students. Applications are processed on a rolling basis. Application fee: $50. Electronic applications accepted. *Expenses:* Tuition, state resident: full-time $5040; part-time $210 per credit hour. Tuition, nonresident: full-time $20,136; part-time $839 per credit hour. Required fees: $1644. *Financial support:* In 2009–10, research assistantships with partial tuition reimbursements (averaging $7,200 per year), teaching assistantships with partial tuition reimbursements (averaging $7,200 per year) were awarded; career-related internships or fieldwork, Federal Work-Study, and tuition waivers (partial) also available. Support available to part-time students. Financial award application deadline: 4/15; financial award applicants required to submit FAFSA. *Unit head:* Dr. Ronnie Sheppard, Chair, 912-478-5203, Fax: 912-478-0026, E-mail: sheppard@georgiasouthern.edu. *Application contact:* Dr. Charles Ziglar, Coordinator for Graduate Student Recruitment, 912-478-5635, Fax: 912-478-0740, E-mail: gradadmissions@georgiasouthern.edu.

Grand Canyon University, College of Education, Phoenix, AZ 85017-1097. Offers curriculum and instruction (M Ed); education administration (M Ed); elementary education (M Ed); organizational leadership (Ed D); secondary education (M Ed); special education (M Ed); teaching (MA). Part-time and evening/weekend programs available. Postbaccalaureate distance learning degree programs offered (no on-campus study). *Degree requirements:* For master's, publishable research paper (M Ed), e-portfolio. *Entrance requirements:* Additional exam requirements/recommendations for international students: Required—TOEFL (minimum score 550 paper-based; 213 computer-based; 79 iBT), IELTS (minimum score 6). Electronic applications accepted.

Grand Valley State University, College of Education, Programs in General Education, Allendale, MI 49401-9403. Offers adult and higher education (M Ed); early childhood education (M Ed); educational differentiation (M Ed); educational leadership (M Ed); educational technology integration (M Ed); elementary education (M Ed); middle level education (M Ed); school library media services (M Ed); secondary level education (M Ed); teaching English to speakers of other languages (M Ed). Part-time and evening/weekend programs available. Postbaccalaureate distance learning degree programs offered (minimal on-campus study). *Faculty:* 82 full-time (42 women), 43 part-time/adjunct (25 women). *Students:* 100 full-time (53 women), 723 part-time (478 women); includes 59 minority (25 African Americans, 4 American Indian/Alaska Native, 13 Asian Americans or Pacific Islanders, 17 Hispanic Americans), 10 international. Average age 33. 237 applicants, 96% accepted, 117 enrolled. In 2009, 291 master's awarded. *Degree requirements:* For master's, thesis. *Entrance requirements:* For master's, GRE General Test or minimum GPA of 3.0. Additional exam requirements/recommendations for international students: Required—TOEFL. *Application deadline:* Applications are processed on a rolling basis. Application fee: $30. Electronic applications accepted. *Expenses:* Tuition, state resident: part-time $471 per credit hour. Tuition, nonresident: part-time $646 per credit hour. Tuition and fees vary according to course level. *Financial support:* In 2009–10, 73 students received support, including 55 fellowships (averaging $2,273 per year), 19 research assistantships with full and partial tuition reimbursements available (averaging $8,000 per year); career-related internships or fieldwork, Federal Work-Study, scholarships/grants, and unspecified assistantships also available. *Faculty research:* Effectiveness of technology in education, parental involvement, effective teaching, effective schools research. *Unit head:* Dr. Linda McCrea, Director, 616-331-2080, E-mail: mccreal@gvsu.edu. *Application contact:* Thomas Owens, Student Information and Services Center, 616-331-6282, Fax: 616-331-2000, E-mail: owenst@gvsu.edu.

Greensboro College, Program in Education, Greensboro, NC 27401-1875. Offers elementary education (M Ed); special education (M Ed). Part-time and evening/weekend programs available. *Degree requirements:* For master's, thesis. *Entrance requirements:* For master's, GRE, teacher license, 2 years of teaching experience, 2 letters of recommendation. Additional exam requirements/recommendations for international students: Required—TOEFL (minimum score 550 paper-based; 213 computer-based). Electronic applications accepted.

Greenville College, Program in Education, Greenville, IL 62246-0159. Offers education (MAT); elementary education (MAE); secondary education (MAE). *Degree requirements:* For master's, thesis (for some programs). *Entrance requirements:* For master's, GRE, Illinois Basic Skills Test, teacher certification. Electronic applications accepted.

Hampton University, Graduate College, Department of Education, Program in Elementary Education, Hampton, VA 23668. Offers MA. *Accreditation:* NCATE. Part-time and evening/weekend programs available. *Entrance requirements:* For master's, GRE General Test.

Harding University, College of Education, Searcy, AR 72149-0001. Offers advanced studies in teaching and learning (M Ed); art (MSE); behavioral science (MSE); counseling (MS, Ed S); early childhood special education (M Ed, MSE); education (MSE); educational leadership (M Ed, Ed S); elementary education (M Ed); English (MSE); family and consumer science (MSE); French (MSE); history/social science (MSE); kinesiology (MSE); math (MSE); physical science (MSE); reading (M Ed); secondary education (M Ed); Spanish (MSE); special education licensure (M Ed); teaching (MAT); teaching English as a second language (M Ed). *Accreditation:* NCATE. Part-time and evening/weekend programs available. *Faculty:* 11 full-time (4 women), 49 part-time/adjunct (26 women). *Students:* 104 full-time (85 women), 392 part-time (282 women); includes 77 minority (67 African Americans, 5 American Indian/Alaska Native, 1 Asian American or Pacific Islander, 4 Hispanic Americans), 5 international. Average age 36. 153 applicants, 92% accepted, 131 enrolled. In 2009, 153 master's, 6 other advanced degrees awarded. *Degree requirements:* For master's, comprehensive exam (for some programs), thesis optional, portfolio(s); for Ed S, comprehensive exam, portfolio, specialist project. *Entrance requirements:* For master's, GRE, MAT, PRAXIS; for Ed S, MAT or GRE. Additional exam requirements/recommendations for international students: Required—TOEFL (minimum score 550 paper-based; 79 iBT). *Application deadline:* For fall admission, 8/1 for domestic and international students; for spring admission, 1/1 for domestic and international students. Applications are processed on a rolling basis. Application fee: $35. *Expenses:* Tuition: Full-time $9720; part-time $540 per credit hour. Required fees: $22 per credit hour. Tuition and fees vary according to course load and program. *Financial support:* In 2009–10, 30 students received support. Unspecified assistantships available. *Faculty research:* Reading, comprehension, school violence, educational technology, behavior, college choice, differentiated instruction, brain-based teaching. *Unit head:* Dr. Clara Carroll, Chair, 501-279-4501, Fax: 501-279-4083, E-mail: ccarroll@harding.edu. *Application contact:* Information Contact, 501-279-4315, E-mail: gradstudiesedu@harding.edu.

High Point University, Norcross Graduate School, High Point, NC 27262-3598. Offers business administration (MBA); educational leadership (M Ed); elementary education (M Ed); history (MA); nonprofit management (MA); special education (M Ed); sport studies (MS). *Accreditation:* ACBSP; NCATE. Part-time and evening/weekend programs available. *Degree requirements:* For master's, comprehensive exam (for some programs), thesis (for some programs). *Entrance requirements:* For master's, GMAT (MBA), GRE General Test, MAT, minimum GPA of 3.0. Additional exam requirements/recommendations for international students: Required—TOEFL (minimum score 550 paper-based). Electronic applications accepted.

Hofstra University, School of Education, Health, and Human Services, Department of Counseling, Research, Special Education and Rehabilitation, Program in Special Education, Hempstead, NY 11549. Offers early childhood special education (MS Ed, Advanced Certificate); gifted education (Advanced Certificate); inclusive early childhood special education (MS Ed); inclusive elementary special education (MS Ed); inclusive secondary special education (MS Ed); literacy studies and special education (MS Ed); special education (MA, MS Ed, PD); special education assessment and diagnosis (Advanced Certificate); teaching students with severe or multiple disabilities (Advanced Certificate). Part-time and evening/weekend programs available. *Students:* 113 full-time (96 women), 105 part-time (95 women); includes 39 minority (18 African Americans, 1 American Indian/Alaska Native, 3 Asian Americans or Pacific Islanders, 17 Hispanic Americans). Average age 29. 134 applicants, 71% accepted, 74 enrolled. In 2009, 88 master's, 7 other advanced degrees awarded. *Degree requirements:* For master's, comprehensive exam (for some programs), thesis (for some programs), seminars, student teaching. *Entrance requirements:* For master's, interview, 3 letters of reference, initial/professional certification; for other advanced degree, interview, 3 letters of recommendation, resume, master's degree, certification. Additional exam requirements/recommendations for international students: Required—TOEFL (minimum score 550 paper-based; 213 computer-based; 80 iBT). *Application deadline:* Applications are processed on a rolling basis. Application fee: $60. Electronic applications accepted. *Expenses:* Tuition: Full-time $16,200; part-time $900 per credit hour. Required fees: $970; $145 per term. Tuition and fees vary according to program. *Financial support:* In 2009–10, 78 students received support, including 10 fellowships with full and partial tuition reimbursements available (averaging $2,541 per year), 4 research assistantships with full and partial tuition reimbursements available (averaging $7,210 per year); Federal Work-Study, institutionally sponsored loans, scholarships/grants, tuition waivers (full and partial), and unspecified assistantships also available. Support available to part-time students. Financial award applicants required to submit FAFSA. *Faculty research:* Inclusive schooling, autism spectrum disorders related services, cultural competency and culturally responsive instruction, co-teaching student teaching, universal design for learning. *Unit head:* Dr. George Guiliani, Director, 516-463-5143, Fax: 516-463-6184, E-mail: cprgag@hofstra.edu. *Application contact:* Carol Drummer, Dean of Graduate Admissions, 516-463-4876, Fax: 516-463-4664, E-mail: gradstudent@hofstra.edu.

Hofstra University, School of Education, Health, and Human Services, Department of Curriculum and Teaching, Program in Elementary Education, Hempstead, NY 11549. Offers MA, MS Ed. Part-time and evening/weekend programs available. *Students:* 68 full-time (59 women), 31 part-time (25 women); includes 12 minority (5 African Americans, 1 American Indian/Alaska Native, 2 Asian Americans or Pacific Islanders, 4 Hispanic Americans). Average age 29. 90 applicants, 82% accepted, 39 enrolled. In 2009, 43 master's awarded. *Degree requirements:* For master's, comprehensive exam. *Entrance requirements:* For master's, 2 letters of recommendation, teacher certification (MA), interview. Additional exam requirements/recommendations for international students: Required—TOEFL (minimum score 550 paper-based; 213 computer-based; 80 iBT). *Application deadline:* Applications are processed on a rolling basis. Application fee: $60. Electronic applications accepted. *Expenses:* Tuition: Full-time $16,200; part-time $900 per credit hour. Required fees: $970; $145 per term. Tuition and fees vary according to program. *Financial support:* In 2009–10, 46 students received support, including 6 fellowships with full and partial tuition reimbursements available (averaging $3,019 per year), 2 research assistantships with full and partial tuition reimbursements available (averaging $12,867 per year); career-related internships or fieldwork, Federal Work-Study, institutionally sponsored loans, scholarships/grants, health care benefits, tuition waivers (full and partial), and unspecified assistantships also available. Support available to part-time students. Financial award applicants required to submit FAFSA. *Faculty research:* Curriculum interaction and development; assessment; response to intervention; multiculturalism. *Unit head:* Dr. Andrea Libresco, Program Director, 516-463-5768, Fax: 516-463-6196, E-mail: catasl@hofstra.edu. *Application contact:* Carol Drummer, Dean of Graduate Admissions, 516-463-4876, Fax: 516-463-4664, E-mail: gradstudent@hofstra.edu.

Holy Family University, Graduate School, School of Education, Philadelphia, PA 19114. Offers education (M Ed); education leadership (M Ed); elementary education (M Ed); reading specialist (M Ed); secondary education (M Ed); special education (M Ed). Part-time and evening/weekend programs available. *Faculty:* 14 full-time (10 women), 42 part-time/adjunct (23 women). *Students:* 63 full-time (48 women), 608 part-time (487 women); includes 45 minority (23 African Americans, 7 Asian Americans or Pacific Islanders, 15 Hispanic Americans), 1 international. Average age 31. 202 applicants, 86% accepted, 146 enrolled. In 2009, 248 master's awarded. *Degree requirements:* For master's, thesis optional. *Entrance requirements:* For master's, GRE or MAT, interview. *Application deadline:* For fall admission, 7/1 priority date for domestic students; for winter admission, 11/1 priority date for domestic students. Applications are processed on a rolling basis. Application fee: $25. *Expenses:* Tuition: Part-time $600 per credit. Required fees: $58 per semester. *Financial support:* Research assistantships, Federal Work-Study available. Support available to part-time students. Financial award application deadline: 2/15; financial award applicants required to submit FAFSA. *Faculty research:* Cognition, developmental issues, sociological issues in education. *Unit head:* Dr. Leonard Soroka, Dean, 267-341-3565, Fax: 215-824-2438, E-mail: lsoroka@holyfamily.edu. *Application contact:* Gidget Marie Montelibano, Graduate Admissions Counselor, 267-341-3558, Fax: 215-637-1478, E-mail: gmontelibano@holyfamily.edu.

Hood College, Graduate School, Department of Education, Frederick, MD 21701-8575. Offers curriculum and instruction (MS), including early childhood education, elementary education, elementary school science and mathematics, secondary education, special education; educational leadership (MS, Certificate); reading specialization (MS). Part-time and evening/weekend programs available. *Faculty:* 4 full-time (all women), 39 part-time/adjunct (21 women). *Students:* 2 full-time (both women), 397 part-time (326 women); includes 41 minority (29 African Americans, 5 Asian Americans or Pacific Islanders, 7 Hispanic Americans). Average age 33. 100 applicants, 92% accepted, 84 enrolled. In 2009, 73 master's, 65 other advanced degrees awarded. *Degree requirements:* For master's, action research project, portfolio (reading). *Entrance requirements:* For master's, minimum GPA of 2.75, teaching certification. *Application deadline:* For fall admission, 7/15 for domestic and international students; for spring admission, 12/15 for domestic and international students. Applications are processed on a rolling basis. Application fee: $35. Electronic applications accepted. *Expenses:* Tuition: Full-time $6480; part-time $360 per credit. Required fees: $100; $50 per term. *Financial support:* Applicants required to submit FAFSA. *Faculty research:* Leadership, action research, brain research, learning styles. *Unit head:* Dr. John George, Chairperson, 301-696-3471, Fax: 301-696-3597, E-mail: george@hood.edu. *Application contact:* Dr. Allen P. Flora, Dean of Graduate School, 301-696-3811, Fax: 301-696-3597, E-mail: gofurther@hood.edu.

Howard University, School of Education, Department of Curriculum and Instruction, Program in Elementary Education, Washington, DC 20059-0002. Offers M Ed. *Accreditation:* NCATE. *Faculty:* 1 (woman) full-time, 1 part-time/adjunct (0 women). *Students:* 12 full-time (7 women), 9 part-time (8 women); includes all African Americans. Average age 28. 17 applicants, 88% accepted, 11 enrolled. In 2009, 7 master's awarded. *Degree requirements:* For master's, comprehensive exam, expository writing exam, internships, seminar paper. *Entrance requirements:* For master's, PRAXIS I, minimum GPA of 2.7. *Application deadline:* For fall admission, 2/15 priority date for domestic students; for spring admission, 11/1 for domestic students. Applications are processed on a rolling basis. Application fee: $45. Electronic applications accepted. *Financial support:* In 2009–10, 11 students received support, including 1 fellowship with full and partial tuition reimbursement available (averaging $15,000 per year), 9 research assistantships with full and partial tuition reimbursements available (averaging $13,000 per year); career-related internships or fieldwork, Federal Work-Study, scholarships/grants, and unspecified assistantships also available. Financial award application deadline: 2/15. *Unit head:* Dr. Helen Bond, Assistant Professor/Coordinator, 202-806-5299, Fax: 202-806-5297, E-mail: hbond@howard.edu. *Application contact:* June L. Harris, Administrative Assistant, Department of Curriculum and Instruction, 202-806-7343, Fax: 202-806-5297, E-mail: jlharris@howard.edu.

Hunter College of the City University of New York, Graduate School, School of Education, Department of Curriculum and Teaching and Department of Educational Foundations and Counseling Programs, Program in Elementary Education, New York, NY 10021-5085. Offers MS. *Accreditation:* NCATE. *Faculty:* 8 full-time (2 women), 24 part-time/adjunct (9 women). *Students:* 105 full-time (95 women), 368 part-time (312 women); includes 110 minority (39 African Americans, 2 American Indian/Alaska Native, 30 Asian Americans or Pacific Islanders, 39 Hispanic Americans). Average age 29. 359 applicants, 50% accepted, 122 enrolled. In 2009, 132 master's awarded. *Degree requirements:* For master's, thesis, integrative seminar, New York State Teacher Certification Exams, student teaching. *Entrance requirements:* For master's, minimum undergraduate GPA of 2.8, writing sample. Additional exam requirements/recommendations for international students: Required—TOEFL, TWE. *Application deadline:* For fall admission, 4/1 for domestic students, 2/1 for international students; for spring admission, 11/1 for domestic students, 9/1 for international students. Application fee: $125. *Expenses:* Tuition, state resident: full-time $7360; part-time $310 per credit. Required fees: $250 per semester. *Financial support:* Federal Work-Study, scholarships/grants, and tuition waivers

Elementary Education

Hunter College of the City University of New York *(continued)*
(partial) available. Support available to part-time students. *Faculty research:* Urban education, multicultural education, gifted education, educational technology, cultural cognition. *Unit head:* Dr. Patrick Burke, Education Adviser, 212-396-6043, E-mail: patrick.burke@hunter.cuny.edu. *Application contact:* William Zlata, Director for Graduate Admissions, 212-772-4482, Fax: 212-650-3336, E-mail: admissions@hunter.cuny.edu.

Idaho State University, Office of Graduate Studies, College of Education, Department of Educational Foundations, Pocatello, ID 83209-8059. Offers child and family studies (M Ed); curriculum leadership (M Ed); education (M Ed); educational administration (M Ed); educational foundations (5th Year Certificate); elementary education (M Ed), including K-12 education, literacy, secondary education. Part-time programs available. *Faculty:* 13 full-time (8 women). *Students:* 15 full-time (9 women), 100 part-time (64 women); includes 2 minority (1 African American, 1 Hispanic American), 3 international. Average age 39. In 2009, 25 master's awarded. *Degree requirements:* For master's, comprehensive exam, thesis optional, oral exam, written exam; for 5th Year Certificate, comprehensive exam, thesis (for some programs), oral exam, written exam. *Entrance requirements:* For master's, GRE General Test or MAT, minimum undergraduate GPA of 3.0; for 5th Year Certificate, GRE General Test, minimum undergraduate GPA of 3.0, master's degree. Additional exam requirements/recommendations for international students: Required—TOEFL (minimum score 550 paper-based; 213 computer-based; 80 iBT). *Application deadline:* For fall admission, 7/1 for domestic students, 6/1 for international students; for spring admission, 12/1 for domestic students, 11/1 for international students. Applications are processed on a rolling basis. Application fee: $55. Electronic applications accepted. *Expenses:* Tuition, state resident: full-time $3318; part-time $297 per credit hour. Tuition, nonresident: full-time $13,120; part-time $437 per credit hour. Required fees: $2530. Tuition and fees vary according to program. *Financial support:* Research assistantships with full and partial tuition reimbursements, teaching assistantships with full and partial tuition reimbursements, career-related internships or fieldwork, Federal Work-Study, institutionally sponsored loans, scholarships/grants, traineeships, health care benefits, tuition waivers (full and partial), and unspecified assistantships available. Support available to part-time students. Financial award application deadline: 1/1; financial award applicants required to submit FAFSA. *Faculty research:* Child and families studies; business education; special education; math, science, and technology education. *Unit head:* Dr. Beverly Ray, Chair, 208-282-4516, Fax: 208-282-3791, E-mail: raybeve@isu.edu. *Application contact:* Dr. Peter Denner, Assistant Dean, 208-282-3807, Fax: 208-282-4697, E-mail: dennpete@isu.edu.

Immaculata University, College of Graduate Studies, Program in Educational Leadership and Administration, Immaculata, PA 19345. Offers educational leadership and administration (MA, Ed D); elementary education (Certificate); school principal (Certificate); school superintendent (Certificate); secondary education (Certificate); special education (Certificate). Part-time and evening/weekend programs available. *Degree requirements:* For master's, comprehensive exam, thesis optional; for doctorate, comprehensive exam, thesis/dissertation. *Entrance requirements:* For master's, GRE or MAT, minimum GPA of 3.0; for doctorate, GRE General Test, minimum GPA of 3.5. Additional exam requirements/recommendations for international students: Required—TOEFL. *Faculty research:* Cooperative learning, school-based management, whole language, performance assessment.

Indiana State University, School of Graduate Studies, College of Education, Department of Elementary, Early and Special Education, Terre Haute, IN 47809. Offers early childhood education (M Ed); elementary education (M Ed); MA/MS. *Accreditation:* NCATE. Electronic applications accepted.

Indiana University Bloomington, School of Education, Department of Curriculum and Instruction, Bloomington, IN 47405-7000. Offers art education (MS, Ed D, PhD); curriculum studies (Ed D, PhD); elementary education (MS, Ed D, PhD, Ed S); mathematics education (MS, Ed D, PhD); science education (MS, Ed D, PhD); secondary education (MS, Ed D, PhD); social studies education (MS, PhD); special education (MS, Ed D, PhD, Ed S). *Accreditation:* NCATE. Part-time and evening/weekend programs available. *Students:* 208 full-time (155 women), 44 part-time (25 women); includes 28 minority (9 African Americans, 3 American Indian/Alaska Native, 9 Asian Americans or Pacific Islanders, 7 Hispanic Americans), 34 international. Average age 34. 100 applicants, 68% accepted, 39 enrolled. In 2009, 48 master's, 20 doctorates awarded. Terminal master's awarded for partial completion of doctoral program. *Degree requirements:* For doctorate, thesis/dissertation; for Ed S, comprehensive exam or project. *Entrance requirements:* For master's, doctorate, and Ed S, GRE General Test. *Application deadline:* For fall admission, 6/1 priority date for domestic students, 3/1 for international students; for winter admission, 11/1 priority date for domestic students; for spring admission, 9/1 for international students. Applications are processed on a rolling basis. Application fee: $55 ($65 for international students). Electronic applications accepted. *Financial support:* Fellowships with full and partial tuition reimbursements, research assistantships with full and partial tuition reimbursements, teaching assistantships with full and partial tuition reimbursements, career-related internships or fieldwork, Federal Work-Study, institutionally sponsored loans, and tuition waivers (partial) available. Support available to part-time students. *Unit head:* Cary Buzzelli, Chairperson, 812-856-8100. *Application contact:* Bobbie Partenheimer, Admissions Services Coordinator, 812-856-8127, Fax: 812-856-8333, E-mail: partenhe@indiana.edu.

Indiana University Kokomo, Division of Education, Kokomo, IN 46904-9003. Offers elementary education (MS Ed). *Accreditation:* NCATE. Part-time and evening/weekend programs available. *Faculty:* 1 full-time (0 women). *Students:* 17 part-time (13 women). Average age 34. In 2009, 6 master's awarded. *Degree requirements:* For master's, thesis optional, research project. *Entrance requirements:* For master's, GRE General Test, minimum GPA of 2.5. *Application deadline:* For fall admission, 8/1 for domestic students; for spring admission, 12/1 for domestic students. Applications are processed on a rolling basis. Application fee: $40 ($50 for international students). *Financial support:* In 2009–10, 2 fellowships (averaging $375 per year) were awarded; minority teacher scholarships also available. *Faculty research:* Reading, teaching effectiveness, portfolio, curriculum development. *Unit head:* D. Antonio Cantu, Dean, 765-455-9441, Fax: 765-455-9503. *Application contact:* Charlotte Miller, Coordinator, Educational and Student Resources, 765-455-9367, Fax: 765-455-9503, E-mail: cmiller@iuk.edu.

Indiana University Northwest, School of Education, Gary, IN 46408-1197. Offers elementary education (MS Ed); secondary education (MS Ed). *Accreditation:* NCATE. Part-time and evening/weekend programs available. *Faculty:* 5 full-time (2 women). *Students:* 35 full-time (29 women), 150 part-time (115 women); includes 83 minority (69 African Americans, 1 American Indian/Alaska Native, 13 Hispanic Americans). Average age 37. In 2009, 33 master's awarded. *Entrance requirements:* For master's, GRE General Test or MAT, minimum GPA of 3.0. *Application deadline:* For fall admission, 7/15 priority date for domestic students; for spring admission, 11/15 for domestic students. Application fee: $25. *Unit head:* Dr. Stanley E. Wigle, Dean, 219-980-6510, Fax: 219-981-4208, E-mail: amsanche@iun.edu. *Application contact:* Dr. Stanley E. Wigle, Dean, 219-980-6510, Fax: 219-981-4208, E-mail: amsanche@iun.edu.

Indiana University of Pennsylvania, School of Graduate Studies and Research, College of Education and Educational Technology, Department of Professional Studies in Education, Program in Elementary Education, Indiana, PA 15705-1087. Offers M Ed. *Accreditation:* NCATE. Part-time programs available. *Faculty:* 1 (woman) full-time. *Students:* 15 full-time (13 women), 8 part-time (6 women). Average age 30. 5 applicants, 0% accepted, 0 enrolled. In 2009, 23 master's awarded. *Degree requirements:* For master's, thesis optional. *Entrance requirements:* For master's, 2 letters of recommendation. Additional exam requirements/recommendations for international students: Required—TOEFL. *Application deadline:* For fall admission, 7/1 priority date for domestic students; for spring admission, 11/1 for domestic students. Applications are processed on a rolling basis. Application fee: $40. *Expenses:* Tuition, state resident: full-time $6666; part-time $370 per credit hour. Tuition, nonresident: full-time $10,666; part-time $593 per credit hour. Required fees: $813 per semester. *Financial support:* In 2009–10, 6 research assistantships (averaging $2,493 per year) were awarded; career-related internships or fieldwork and Federal Work-Study also available. Financial award application deadline:

3/15; financial award applicants required to submit FAFSA. *Unit head:* Dr. Mary R. Jalongo, Graduate Coordinator, 724-357-2417, E-mail: mjalongo@iup.edu. *Application contact:* Dr. Mary R. Jalongo, Graduate Coordinator, 724-357-2417, E-mail: mjalongo@iup.edu.

Indiana University–Purdue University Fort Wayne, School of Education, Department of Educational Studies, Fort Wayne, IN 46805-1499. Offers elementary education (MS Ed); secondary education (MS Ed). *Accreditation:* NCATE. Part-time programs available. *Faculty:* 15 full-time (9 women). *Students:* 2 full-time (1 woman), 48 part-time (40 women); includes 8 minority (4 African Americans, 1 Asian American or Pacific Islander, 3 Hispanic Americans). Average age 38. 22 applicants, 100% accepted, 22 enrolled. In 2009, 22 master's awarded. *Entrance requirements:* For master's, minimum GPA of 2.5. Additional exam requirements/recommendations for international students: Required—TOEFL (minimum score 550 paper-based; 213 computer-based; 77 iBT). *Application deadline:* For fall admission, 4/1 priority date for domestic and international students. Applications are processed on a rolling basis. Application fee: $55. *Expenses:* Tuition, state resident: full-time $4595; part-time $255 per credit. Tuition, nonresident: full-time $10,963; part-time $609 per credit. Required fees: $528; $29.35 per credit. Tuition and fees vary according to course load. *Financial support:* In 2009–10, 1 teaching assistantship with partial tuition reimbursement (averaging $12,740 per year) was awarded; scholarships/grants also available. Support available to part-time students. Financial award application deadline: 3/1; financial award applicants required to submit FAFSA. *Unit head:* Dr. Joe Nichols, Chair, 260-481-6445, Fax: 260-481-5408, E-mail: nicholsj@ipfw.edu. *Application contact:* Vicky L. Schmidt, Graduate Recorder, 260-481-6450, Fax: 260-481-5408, E-mail: schmidt@ipfw.edu.

Indiana University South Bend, School of Education, South Bend, IN 46634-7111. Offers counseling and human services (MS Ed); elementary education (MS Ed); secondary education (MS Ed); special education (MS Ed). *Accreditation:* NCATE. Part-time and evening/weekend programs available. *Faculty:* 21 full-time (11 women), 9 part-time/adjunct (3 women). *Students:* 72 full-time (48 women), 256 part-time (202 women); includes 36 minority (24 African Americans, 2 American Indian/Alaska Native, 1 Asian American or Pacific Islander, 9 Hispanic Americans), 9 international. Average age 36. In 2009, 103 master's awarded. *Degree requirements:* For master's, thesis or alternative, exit project. *Entrance requirements:* For master's, letters of recommendation, GRE or minimum GPA of 3.0. Additional exam requirements/recommendations for international students: Required—TOEFL. *Application deadline:* For fall admission, 7/1 for domestic students; for spring admission, 11/1 for domestic students. Applications are processed on a rolling basis. Application fee: $46 ($58 for international students). Electronic applications accepted. *Financial support:* Career-related internships or fieldwork available. Support available to part-time students. Financial award application deadline: 3/1; financial award applicants required to submit FAFSA. *Faculty research:* Professional dispositions, early childhood literacy, online learning, program assessments, problem-based learning. *Unit head:* Dr. Michael Horvath, Professor/Dean, 574-520-4339, Fax: 574-520-4550. *Application contact:* Dr. Todd Norris, Director of Education Student Services, 574-520-4845, E-mail: toanorri@iusb.edu.

Indiana University Southeast, School of Education, New Albany, IN 47150-6405. Offers counselor education (MS Ed); elementary education (MS Ed); secondary education (MS Ed). *Accreditation:* NCATE. Part-time and evening/weekend programs available. *Students:* 7 full-time (all women), 366 part-time (305 women); includes 31 minority (27 African Americans, 3 American Indian/Alaska Native, 1 Asian American or Pacific Islander), 1 international. Average age 32. In 2009, 138 master's awarded. *Entrance requirements:* For master's, minimum undergraduate GPA of 2.5, graduate 3.0. *Application deadline:* Applications are processed on a rolling basis. Application fee: $35. *Financial support:* In 2009–10, 29 students received support. Career-related internships or fieldwork, Federal Work-Study, and institutionally sponsored loans available. Support available to part-time students. Financial award applicants required to submit FAFSA. *Faculty research:* Learning styles, technology, constructivism, group process, innovative math strategies. *Unit head:* Dr. Gloria Murray, Dean, 812-941-2169, Fax: 812-941-2667, E-mail: soeinfo@ius.edu. *Application contact:* Dr. Gloria Murray, Dean, 812-941-2169, Fax: 812-941-2667, E-mail: soeinfo@ius.edu.

Inter American University of Puerto Rico, Aguadilla Campus, Graduate School, Aguadilla, PR 00605. Offers accounting (MBA); business information systems (MBA); counseling psychology with an emphasis in family (MS); criminal justice (MA); educative management and leadership (MA); elementary education (MA); finance (MBA); human resources (MBA); industrial management (MBA); marketing (MBA). Part-time and evening/weekend programs available. *Degree requirements:* For master's, comprehensive exam. *Entrance requirements:* For master's, EXADEP, 2 letters of recommendation, minimum GPA of 2.5. Electronic applications accepted.

Inter American University of Puerto Rico, Arecibo Campus, Programs in Education, Arecibo, PR 00614-4050. Offers administration and educational supervision (MA Ed); counseling and guidance (MA Ed); curriculum and teaching (MA Ed), including biology education, English as a second language, history education, math education, Spanish; elementary education (MA Ed). *Degree requirements:* For master's, comprehensive exam, thesis optional. *Entrance requirements:* For master's, GRE, EXADEP, bachelor's degree in education or teaching license (administration and supervision) or courses in education and psychology (counseling and guidance), minimum GPA of 2.5 in last 60 credits.

Inter American University of Puerto Rico, Barranquitas Campus, Program in Education, Barranquitas, PR 00794. Offers curriculum and teaching (M Ed); educational administration and supervision (MA); elementary education (M Ed); information and library service technology (M Ed). *Degree requirements:* For master's, comprehensive exam, thesis optional. *Entrance requirements:* For master's, EXADEP, letter of recommendation. Electronic applications accepted.

Inter American University of Puerto Rico, Guayama Campus, Department of Education and Social Sciences, Guayama, PR 00785. Offers early childhood education (MA); elementary education (MA). Part-time programs available. *Entrance requirements:* For master's, GRE, MAT, EXADEP, letters of recommendation, minimum GPA of 2.5. Electronic applications accepted.

Inter American University of Puerto Rico, Metropolitan Campus, Graduate Programs, Program in Elementary Education, San Juan, PR 00919-1293. Offers MA. *Degree requirements:* For master's, comprehensive exam. *Entrance requirements:* For master's, GRE or EXADEP, interview. Electronic applications accepted.

Inter American University of Puerto Rico, Ponce Campus, Graduate School, Mercedita, PR 00715-1602. Offers accounting (MBA); biology (M Ed); chemistry (M Ed); criminal justice (MA); elementary education (M Ed); English as a Second Language (M Ed); finance (MBA); history (M Ed); human resources (MBA); marketing (MBA); mathematics (M Ed); Spanish (M Ed). *Entrance requirements:* For master's, minimum GPA of 2.5.

Inter American University of Puerto Rico, San Germán Campus, Graduate Studies Center, Program in Elementary Education, San Germán, PR 00683-5008. Offers MA. Part-time and evening/weekend programs available. *Degree requirements:* For master's, comprehensive exam. *Entrance requirements:* For master's, GRE General Test or EXADEP, minimum GPA of 3.0.

Iowa State University of Science and Technology, Graduate College, College of Human Sciences, Department of Curriculum and Instruction, Ames, IA 50011. Offers curriculum and instructional technology (M Ed, MS, PhD); elementary education (M Ed, MS); historical, philosophical, and comparative studies in education (M Ed, MS); special education (M Ed, MS). *Faculty:* 26 full-time (16 women), 1 (woman) part-time/adjunct. *Students:* 51 full-time (34 women), 72 part-time (49 women); includes 11 minority (5 African Americans, 1 American Indian/Alaska Native, 4 Asian Americans or Pacific Islanders, 1 Hispanic American), 25 international. 54 applicants, 69% accepted, 25 enrolled. In 2009, 41 master's, 6 doctorates awarded. *Degree requirements:* For master's, thesis or alternative; for doctorate, thesis/dissertation. *Entrance requirements:* For doctorate, GRE General Test. Additional exam requirements/recommendations for international students: Required—TOEFL (minimum score 560 paper-based; 83 iBT) or IELTS (minimum score 6.5). *Application deadline:* For fall admission,

1/1 priority date for domestic and international students; for spring admission, 9/1 for domestic and international students. Application fee: $40 ($90 for international students). Electronic applications accepted. *Expenses:* Tuition, state resident: full-time $6716. Tuition, nonresident: full-time $8908. Tuition and fees vary according to course level, course load, program and student level. *Financial support:* In 2009–10, 21 research assistantships with full and partial tuition reimbursements (averaging $14,600 per year), 12 teaching assistantships with full and partial tuition reimbursements (averaging $14,600 per year) were awarded; fellowships, scholarships/grants, health care benefits, and unspecified assistantships also available. *Unit head:* Dr. Carl Smith, Director of Graduate Education, 515-294-0317, E-mail: cigrad@iastate.edu. *Application contact:* Dr. Patricia Leigh, Director of Graduate Education, 515-294-7021, E-mail: cigrad@iastate.edu.

Ithaca College, Division of Graduate and Professional Studies, School of Humanities and Sciences, Program in Childhood Education, Ithaca, NY 14850. Offers MS. Part-time programs available. *Faculty:* 18 full-time (7 women). *Students:* 11 full-time (10 women); includes 2 minority (both Asian Americans or Pacific Islanders). Average age 28. 24 applicants, 71% accepted, 11 enrolled. In 2009, 19 master's awarded. *Degree requirements:* For master's, thesis or alternative, student teaching. *Entrance requirements:* For master's, minimum GPA of 3.0. Additional exam requirements/recommendations for international students: Required—TOEFL (minimum score 550 paper-based; 213 computer-based; 80 iBT). *Application deadline:* For fall admission, 5/15 for domestic and international students; for spring admission, 12/1 for domestic and international students. Applications are processed on a rolling basis. Application fee: $40. Electronic applications accepted. *Expenses:* Contact institution. *Financial support:* In 2009–10, 10 students received support, including 5 teaching assistantships (averaging $6,474 per year); career-related internships or fieldwork, Federal Work-Study, scholarships/grants, and unspecified assistantships also available. Support available to part-time students. Financial award applicants required to submit CSS PROFILE or FAFSA. *Faculty research:* Bilingual education, socio-linguistic perspectives on literacy. *Unit head:* Dr. Linda Hanrahan, Chairperson, 607-274-3527, Fax: 607-274-1263, E-mail: gps@ithaca.edu. *Application contact:* Rob Gearhart, Dean, Graduate and Professional Studies, 607-274-3527, Fax: 607-274-1263, E-mail: gps@ithaca.edu.

Jackson State University, Graduate School, School of Education, Department of Curriculum and Instruction, Jackson, MS 39217. Offers early childhood education (MS Ed, Ed D); elementary education (MS Ed, Ed S). *Accreditation:* NCATE. Evening/weekend programs available. Terminal master's awarded for partial completion of doctoral program. *Degree requirements:* For master's, comprehensive exam, thesis or alternative; for doctorate, comprehensive exam, thesis/dissertation. *Entrance requirements:* For master's, GRE General Test; for doctorate, MAT, teaching experience. Additional exam requirements/recommendations for international students: Required—TOEFL.

Jacksonville State University, College of Graduate Studies and Continuing Education, College of Education and Professional Studies, Program in Elementary Education, Jacksonville, AL 36265-1602. Offers MS Ed. *Accreditation:* NCATE. Part-time and evening/weekend programs available. *Degree requirements:* For master's, comprehensive exam, thesis (for some programs). *Entrance requirements:* For master's, GRE General Test or MAT. Electronic applications accepted.

Jacksonville University, College of Arts and Sciences, School of Education, Program in Elementary Education, Jacksonville, FL 32211. Offers MAT. Part-time and evening/weekend programs available. *Degree requirements:* For master's, comprehensive exam. *Entrance requirements:* For master's, GRE General Test, minimum GPA of 3.0. Additional exam requirements/recommendations for international students: Required—TOEFL.

James Madison University, The Graduate School, College of Education, Early, Elementary, and Reading Education Department, Program in Elementary Education, Harrisonburg, VA 22807. Offers M Ed. *Students:* Average age 27. *Entrance requirements:* For master's, GRE General Test, PRAXIS II, minimum undergraduate GPA of 2.75, 2-page essay, interview. Additional exam requirements/recommendations for international students: Required—TOEFL. *Application deadline:* For fall admission, 5/1 for domestic students; for spring admission, 9/1 for domestic students. Applications are processed on a rolling basis. Application fee: $55. Electronic applications accepted. *Expenses:* Tuition, area resident: Part-time $305 per credit hour. Tuition, state resident: part-time $305 per credit hour. Tuition, nonresident: part-time $890 per credit hour. *Unit head:* Dr. Martha Ross, Academic Unit Head, 540-568-6255. *Application contact:* Lynette M. Bible, Director of Graduate Admissions, 540-568-6395, Fax: 540-568-7860, E-mail: biblelm@jmu.edu.

The Johns Hopkins University, School of Education, Department of Teacher Preparation, Baltimore, MD 21218. Offers education (MS), including educational studies; elementary education (MAT); English for speakers of other languages (MAT); K-8 mathematics lead-teacher (Certificate); K-8 science lead-teacher (Certificate); secondary education (MAT), including biology, chemistry, earth/space/environmental science, English, French, mathematics, physics, social studies, Spanish. Part-time and evening/weekend programs available. *Faculty:* 13 full-time (11 women), 35 part-time/adjunct (21 women). *Students:* 162 full-time (119 women), 347 part-time (256 women); includes 138 minority (80 African Americans, 3 American Indian/Alaska Native, 38 Asian Americans or Pacific Islanders, 17 Hispanic Americans), 3 international. Average age 27. 89 applicants, 37% accepted, 24 enrolled. In 2009, 177 master's awarded. *Degree requirements:* For master's, portfolio, PRAXIS II, internship. *Entrance requirements:* For master's, PRAXIS I, SAT, ACT, or GRE (MAT), minimum undergraduate GPA of 3.0, interview, 1 letter of recommendation, curriculum vitae/resume; for Certificate, bachelor's degree, minimum undergraduate GPA of 3.0, essay/statement of goals, interview. Additional exam requirements/recommendations for international students: Required—TOEFL (minimum score 600 paper-based; 250 computer-based; 100 iBT). *Application deadline:* For fall admission, 5/1 for international students; for spring admission, 10/15 for international students. Applications are processed on a rolling basis. Application fee: $80. Electronic applications accepted. *Financial support:* Scholarships/grants available. Support available to part-time students. Financial award application deadline: 6/1; financial award applicants required to submit FAFSA. *Faculty research:* Teacher retention; STEM education reform; alternative certification programs; school-university partnerships; urban education; action research/data-informed instruction; family engagement. *Unit head:* Dr. Francis Masci, Chair, 410-516-9774, Fax: 410-516-9770, E-mail: matjhu@jhu.edu. *Application contact:* Jennifer Shaffer, Director of Admissions, 410-516-9797, Fax: 410-516-9799, E-mail: educationinfo@jhu.edu.

Johnson & Wales University, The Alan Shawn Feinstein Graduate School, Ed D Program, Providence, RI 02903-3703. Offers higher education (Ed D); K-12 (Ed D). Part-time programs available. *Faculty:* 7 full-time (3 women), 3 part-time/adjunct (2 women). *Students:* 95 full-time (54 women); includes 3 minority (1 African American, 2 Asian Americans or Pacific Islanders). Average age 42. 27 applicants, 89% accepted, 22 enrolled. In 2009, 30 doctorates awarded. *Degree requirements:* For doctorate, thesis/dissertation. *Entrance requirements:* For doctorate, MAT, minimum GPA of 3.25. Additional exam requirements/recommendations for international students: Required—TOEFL (minimum score 550 paper-based; 210 computer-based) or IELTS recommended; Recommended—TWE. *Application deadline:* Applications are processed on a rolling basis. Application fee: $0. *Expenses:* Required fees: $340 per quarter hour. *Financial support:* Application deadline: 5/1. *Faculty research:* Site-based management, collaborative learning, technology and education, K–16 education. *Unit head:* Dr. Robert Gable, Director, 401-598-4738, Fax: 401-598-1162, E-mail: rgable@jwu.edu. *Application contact:* Dr. Allan G. Freedman, Director of Graduate Admissions, 401-598-1015, Fax: 401-598-1286, E-mail: gradadm@jwu.edu.

Jones International University, Graduate School of Education, Centennial, CO 80112. Offers adult education (M Ed); corporate training and knowledge management (M Ed); curriculum and instruction (M Ed), including elementary teacher licensure, secondary teacher licensure; e-learning technology and design (M Ed); educational leadership and administration (M Ed); educational leadership and administration: principal and administrator licensure (M Ed); elementary curriculum instruction and assessment (M Ed); higher education leadership and administration (M Ed); K-12 instructional technology (M Ed); K-12 instructional technology: teacher licensure (M Ed); secondary curriculum instruction and assessment (M Ed); technology and design (M Ed). Part-time and evening/weekend programs available. Postbaccalaureate distance learning degree programs offered (no on-campus study). *Entrance requirements:* For master's, minimum cumulative GPA of 2.5. Additional exam requirements/recommendations for international students: Recommended—TOEFL (minimum score 550 paper-based; 213 computer-based). Electronic applications accepted.

Kennesaw State University, Leland and Clarice C. Bagwell College of Education, Program in Graduate Education, Kennesaw, GA 30144-5591. Offers adolescent education (M Ed); educational leadership (M Ed); educational leadership technology (M Ed); elementary and early childhood education (M Ed); special education (M Ed); teaching English to speakers of other languages (M Ed). *Accreditation:* NCATE. Part-time programs available. *Faculty:* 60 full-time (38 women), 12 part-time/adjunct (4 women). *Students:* 140 full-time (116 women), 136 part-time (107 women); includes 51 minority (39 African Americans, 1 American Indian/Alaska Native, 3 Asian Americans or Pacific Islanders, 8 Hispanic Americans), 4 international. Average age 34. 113 applicants, 83% accepted, 69 enrolled. In 2009, 282 master's awarded. *Degree requirements:* For master's, thesis or alternative. *Entrance requirements:* For master's, GRE General Test, T-4 state certification, minimum GPA of 2.75. Additional exam requirements/recommendations for international students: Required—TOEFL (minimum score 550 paper-based; 213 computer-based; 80 iBT), IELTS (minimum score 6). *Application deadline:* For fall admission, 7/1 for domestic and international students; for spring admission, 10/1 for domestic and international students. Application fee: $60. Electronic applications accepted. *Expenses:* Tuition, state resident: full-time $2341; part-time $196 per credit hour. Tuition, nonresident: full-time $9396; part-time $783 per credit hour. Required fees: $573 per semester. *Financial support:* Federal Work-Study and unspecified assistantships available. Support available to part-time students. Financial award application deadline: 6/15; financial award applicants required to submit FAFSA. *Unit head:* Dr. Nita Paris, Associate Dean for Graduate Programs, 770-423-6636, E-mail: nparis@kennesaw.edu. *Application contact:* Alisha Bello, Administrative Coordinator, 770-423-6043, Fax: 770-420-4435, E-mail: abello1@kennesaw.edu.

Kutztown University of Pennsylvania, College of Education, Program in Elementary Education, Kutztown, PA 19530-0730. Offers early childhood education (Certificate); elementary education (M Ed, Certificate); special education (Certificate). *Accreditation:* NCATE. Part-time and evening/weekend programs available. *Faculty:* 7 full-time (all women), 2 part-time/adjunct (both women). *Students:* 25 full-time (18 women), 27 part-time (25 women); includes 2 minority (both Hispanic Americans). Average age 29. 46 applicants, 83% accepted, 15 enrolled. In 2009, 23 master's awarded. *Degree requirements:* For master's, comprehensive exam, thesis optional, comprehensive project. *Entrance requirements:* For master's, GRE General Test. Additional exam requirements/recommendations for international students: Required—TOEFL. *Application deadline:* For fall admission, 8/15 priority date for domestic and international students; for spring admission, 12/15 priority date for domestic and international students. Applications are processed on a rolling basis. Application fee: $35. Electronic applications accepted. *Expenses:* Tuition, state resident: full-time $6666; part-time $370 per credit. Tuition, nonresident: full-time $10,666; part-time $593 per credit. Required fees: $62 per credit. $60 per semester. *Financial support:* Career-related internships or fieldwork, Federal Work-Study, scholarships/grants, and unspecified assistantships available. Financial award application deadline: 3/1; financial award applicants required to submit FAFSA. *Faculty research:* Whole language, middle schools, cooperative learning discussion techniques, oral reading techniques, hemisphericity. *Unit head:* Dr. Elsa Geskus, Chairperson, 610-683-4262, Fax: 610-683-1327, E-mail: geskus@kutztown.edu. *Application contact:* Kelly D. Burr, Associate Director, Graduate Admissions, 610-683-4200, Fax: 610-683-1393, E-mail: graduate@kutztown.edu.

Lander University, School of Education, Greenwood, SC 29649-2099. Offers elementary education (M Ed); teaching (MAT). *Accreditation:* NCATE. Part-time programs available. *Degree requirements:* For master's, comprehensive exam, thesis or alternative. *Entrance requirements:* For master's, GRE General Test. Additional exam requirements/recommendations for international students: Required—TOEFL (minimum score 550 paper-based; 213 computer-based). Electronic applications accepted.

Langston University, School of Education and Behavioral Sciences, Langston, OK 73050. Offers bilingual/multicultural (M Ed); elementary education (M Ed); English as a second language (M Ed); rehabilitation counseling (M Sc); urban education (M Ed). *Accreditation:* CORE; NCATE (one or more programs are accredited). Part-time programs available. *Degree requirements:* For master's, comprehensive exam, thesis optional. *Entrance requirements:* For master's, GRE, writing skills test, minimum GPA of 2.5, 3 letters of recommendation. Additional exam requirements/recommendations for international students: Required—TOEFL, TWE. *Faculty research:* Bilingual/multicultural education, financing post-secondary education.

Lee University, Program in Education, Cleveland, TN 37320-3450. Offers classroom teaching (M Ed, Ed S); educational leadership (M Ed, Ed S); elementary/secondary education (MAT); secondary education (MAT); special education (elementary) (M Ed); special education (secondary) (M Ed, MAT); special education (severe disabilities) (M Ed). Part-time programs available. *Faculty:* 11 full-time (4 women), 3 part-time/adjunct (2 women). *Students:* 65 full-time (45 women), 140 part-time (80 women); includes 8 minority (5 African Americans, 1 American Indian/Alaska Native, 2 Hispanic Americans), 6 international. Average age 31. 4 applicants, 100% accepted, 2 enrolled. In 2009, 75 master's, 7 other advanced degrees awarded. *Degree requirements:* For master's, variable foreign language requirement, comprehensive exam, thesis, internship. *Entrance requirements:* For master's, MAT or GRE General Test, minimum GPA of 2.75, 3 letters of recommendation, interview, writing sample. Additional exam requirements/recommendations for international students: Required—TOEFL (minimum score 450 paper-based; 45 computer-based). *Application deadline:* For fall admission, 4/1 priority date for domestic students; for spring admission, 10/1 priority date for domestic students. Applications are processed on a rolling basis. Application fee: $25. *Expenses:* Tuition: Full-time $11,100; part-time $463 per credit. Required fees: $305. *Financial support:* Career-related internships or fieldwork, Federal Work-Study, institutionally sponsored loans, scholarships/grants, and unspecified assistantships available. Financial award application deadline: 3/1; financial award applicants required to submit FAFSA. *Unit head:* Dr. Gary Riggins, Director, 423-614-8193. *Application contact:* Vicki Glasscock, Graduate Admissions Director, 423-614-8059, E-mail: vglasscock@leeuniversity.edu.

Lehigh University, College of Education, Program in Teaching, Learning and Technology, Bethlehem, PA 18015. Offers elementary education with certification (M Ed); instructional technology (MS); learning sciences and technology (PhD); secondary education with certification (M Ed); teaching and learning (M Ed, MA); technology use in the schools (Graduate Certificate). Part-time programs available. *Faculty:* 7 full-time (4 women), 7 part-time/adjunct (3 women). *Students:* 48 full-time (39 women), 61 part-time (41 women); includes 11 minority (3 African Americans, 4 Asian Americans or Pacific Islanders, 4 Hispanic Americans), 5 international. Average age 31. 81 applicants, 67% accepted, 23 enrolled. In 2009, 48 master's awarded. Terminal master's awarded for partial completion of doctoral program. *Degree requirements:* For master's, comprehensive exam and dissertation (M Ed); for doctorate, comprehensive exam, thesis/dissertation. *Entrance requirements:* For master's, minimum GPA of 3.0, 2 letters of recommendation, essay, transcript; for doctorate, GRE General Test, minimum graduate GPA of 3.0, writing sample, 2 letters of recommendation, essay, transcript. Additional exam requirements/recommendations for international students: Required—TOEFL (minimum score 600 paper-based; 250 computer-based; 93 iBT). *Application deadline:* For fall admission, 2/1 for domestic and international students; for spring admission, 11/1 for domestic and international students. Applications are processed on a rolling basis. Application fee: $65. Electronic applications accepted. *Financial support:* In 2009–10, 18 students received support, including 1 fellowship with full and partial tuition reimbursement available (averaging $16,000 per year), 2 research assistantships with full and partial tuition reimbursements available (averaging $18,000 per year); career-related internships or fieldwork, institutionally sponsored loans, scholarships/grants, and tuition waivers (full and partial) also available. Financial award application deadline: 1/31. *Faculty research:* Instructional media and delivery systems,

Elementary Education

Lehigh University *(continued)*
technologies to enhance education, technical and informal education, Web-based learning. *Unit head:* Dr. MJ Bishop, Coordinator, 610-758-3235, Fax: 610-758-3243, E-mail: mjba@lehigh.edu. *Application contact:* Donna M. Johnson, Coordinator, 610-758-3231, Fax: 610-758-6223, E-mail: dmj4@lehigh.edu.

Lehman College of the City University of New York, Division of Education, Department of Early Childhood and Elementary Education, Program in Elementary Education, Bronx, NY 10468-1589. Offers MS Ed. *Accreditation:* NCATE. Part-time and evening/weekend programs available. *Degree requirements:* For master's, thesis. *Entrance requirements:* For master's, minimum GPA of 3.0. *Faculty research:* POS network, emotional and intellectual learning, realistic picture books.

Le Moyne College, Department of Education, Syracuse, NY 13214. Offers adolescent education (MS Ed, MST); adolescent education/special education (MS Ed, MST); adolescent English (grades 7-12) (MST); adolescent history (grades 7-12) (MST); childhood education (MS Ed); childhood education/special education (MS Ed); elementary education (MS Ed); general professional education (MS Ed); inclusive childhood education (MST); middle child specialist/special education (MS Ed); middle childhood specialist (MS Ed); school building leadership (MS Ed, CAS); school district business leader (MS Ed, CAS); school district leadership (MS Ed, CAS); secondary education (MS Ed); special education (MS Ed). *Accreditation:* Teacher Education Accreditation Council. Part-time and evening/weekend programs available. *Faculty:* 15 full-time (8 women), 61 part-time/adjunct (33 women). *Students:* 40 full-time (30 women), 260 part-time (180 women); includes 25 minority (11 African Americans, 3 American Indian/Alaska Native, 3 Asian Americans or Pacific Islanders, 8 Hispanic Americans). Average age 31. 168 applicants, 89% accepted, 140 enrolled. In 2009, 180 master's awarded. *Degree requirements:* For master's, thesis. *Entrance requirements:* For master's, GRE General Test, 2 letters of recommendation. Additional exam requirements/recommendations for international students: Required—TOEFL (minimum score 550 paper-based; 213 computer-based; 79 iBT). *Application deadline:* For fall admission, 4/1 priority date for domestic and international students; for spring admission, 10/1 priority date for domestic and international students. Applications are processed on a rolling basis. Application fee: $50. *Expenses:* Contact institution. *Financial support:* In 2009–10, 28 students received support. Career-related internships or fieldwork and health care benefits available. Support available to part-time students. Financial award applicants required to submit FAFSA. *Faculty research:* Recruitment/retention strategies, minority teachers, special education, multiculturalism, literacy, technology, video games learning, autism, school district organization. *Unit head:* Dr. Norbert J. Henry, Interim Chair/Director, 315-445-4376, Fax: 315-445-4744, E-mail: henry@lemoyne.edu. *Application contact:* Kristen P. Trapasso, Director of Graduate Admission, 315-445-4265, Fax: 315-445-6027, E-mail: trapaskp@lemoyne.edu.

Lesley University, School of Education, Cambridge, MA 02138-2790. Offers curriculum and instruction (M Ed, CAGS); early childhood education (M Ed); educational studies (PhD); elementary education (M Ed); individually designed (M Ed); middle school education (M Ed); moderate special needs (M Ed); reading (M Ed, CAGS); science in education (M Ed); severe special needs (M Ed); special needs (CAGS); technology in education (M Ed, CAGS). *Accreditation:* Teacher Education Accreditation Council. Part-time and evening/weekend programs available. Postbaccalaureate distance learning degree programs offered (no on-campus study). *Degree requirements:* For master's, practicum; for doctorate, thesis/dissertation. *Entrance requirements:* For doctorate, GRE General Test or MAT, interview, master's degree, resume; for CAGS, interview, master's degree. Additional exam requirements/recommendations for international students: Required—TOEFL (minimum score 550 paper-based; 213 computer-based; 80 iBT). Electronic applications accepted. *Faculty research:* Assessment in literacy, mathematics and science; autism spectrum disorders; instructional technology and online learning; multicultural education and ELL.

Lewis & Clark College, Graduate School of Education and Counseling, Department of Teacher Education, Program in Early Childhood/Elementary Education, Portland, OR 97219-7899. Offers MAT. *Accreditation:* NCATE. *Faculty:* 3 full-time (1 woman), 2 part-time/adjunct (both women). *Students:* 66 full-time (55 women), 1 part-time (0 women); includes 8 minority (1 American Indian/Alaska Native, 3 Asian Americans or Pacific Islanders, 4 Hispanic Americans), 2 international. Average age 28. 115 applicants, 89% accepted, 66 enrolled. In 2009, 61 master's awarded. *Entrance requirements:* For master's, minimum undergraduate GPA of 2.75. Candidates for admission must have a history of work, either volunteer or paid, with children in grades K-6. Additional exam requirements/recommendations for international students: Required—TOEFL (minimum score 575 paper-based; 233 computer-based). *Application deadline:* For fall admission, 12/1 priority date for domestic and international students. Application fee: $50. Electronic applications accepted. *Expenses:* Tuition: Part-time $713 per semester hour. Tuition and fees vary according to course level and campus/location. *Financial support:* In 2009–10, 64 students received support. Career-related internships or fieldwork, Federal Work-Study, institutionally sponsored loans, scholarships/grants, health care benefits, and tuition waivers (partial) available. Support available to part-time students. Financial award application deadline: 3/1; financial award applicants required to submit FAFSA. *Faculty research:* Classroom ethnography, assessing student learning, reading, moral development, language arts. *Unit head:* Dr. Vern Jones, Chair of Teacher Education Department, 503-768-6100, Fax: 503-768-6115, E-mail: lcteach@lclark.edu. *Application contact:* Becky Haas, Director of Admissions, 503-768-6200, Fax: 503-768-6205, E-mail: gseadmit@lclark.edu.

Lewis University, College of Education, Program in Elementary Education, Romeoville, IL 60446. Offers MA. *Students:* 16 full-time (12 women), 44 part-time (39 women); includes 13 minority (3 African Americans, 2 Asian Americans or Pacific Islanders, 8 Hispanic Americans). Average age 31. In 2009, 13 master's awarded. *Entrance requirements:* For master's, departmental qualifying exam, writing exam, minimum GPA of 2.75, 2 letters of recommendation, interview. Additional exam requirements/recommendations for international students: Required—TOEFL (minimum score 550 paper-based; 213 computer-based). *Application deadline:* For fall admission, 5/1 priority date for international students; for spring admission, 11/15 priority date for international students. Application fee: $40. Electronic applications accepted. *Expenses:* Tuition: Full-time $6480; part-time $720 per credit. One-time fee: $40. Tuition and fees vary according to course load, degree level and program. *Financial support:* Federal Work-Study, scholarships/grants, and unspecified assistantships available. Financial award application deadline: 5/1; financial award applicants required to submit FAFSA. *Unit head:* Dr. Edward Tatro, Program Director, 815-838-0500 Ext. 5046, E-mail: tatroed@lewisu.edu. *Application contact:* Sandy Zigrossi, Information Contact, 815-838-0500 Ext. 5398, E-mail: zigrossa@lewisu.edu.

Liberty University, School of Education, Lynchburg, VA 24502. Offers administration and supervision (M Ed); curriculum and instruction (M Ed); early childhood education (M Ed); education specialist (Ed S); educational leadership (Ed D); elementary education (M Ed); gifted education (M Ed); reading specialist (M Ed); school counseling (M Ed); secondary education (M Ed); special education (M Ed). *Accreditation:* NCATE. Part-time programs available. Postbaccalaureate distance learning degree programs offered (minimal on-campus study). *Degree requirements:* For doctorate, comprehensive exam, thesis/dissertation. *Entrance requirements:* For master's, GRE General Test or MAT (aken in or before 1999), 2 letters of recommendation, minimum undergraduate GPA of 3.0, curriculum vitae; for doctorate, GRE General Test or MAT (if taken before 1999), minimum master's GPA of 3.0, 3 years of teacher experience; for Ed S, GRE General Test or MAT (if taken before 1999), minimum master's GPA of 3.0, 3 years of teaching experience. Additional exam requirements/recommendations for international students: Required—TOEFL (minimum score 600 paper-based; 250 computer-based). Electronic applications accepted. *Expenses:* Contact institution. *Faculty research:* Self-determination, character education, bibliotherapy, learning styles, distance education.

Lincoln University, Graduate Center, Lincoln University, PA 19352. Offers administration (MSA), including finance, human resources management; early childhood education (M Ed); elementary education (M Ed); human services (M Hum Svcs); reading (MSR). Evening/weekend programs available. *Degree requirements:* For master's, thesis. *Entrance requirements:* For master's, 5 years of work experience in human services. *Faculty research:* Gerontology/minority aging, computers in composition instruction.

Lincoln University, School of Graduate Studies and Continuing Education, Jefferson City, MO 65102. Offers business administration (MBA), including accounting, entrepreneurship, management, public administration and policy; educational leadership (Ed S), including elementary leadership, secondary leadership, superintendency; guidance and counseling (M Ed), including community/agency counseling, elementary school, secondary school; history (MA); school administration and supervision (M Ed), including elementary school administration, secondary school administration, special education administration; school teaching (M Ed), including elementary school teaching, secondary school teaching; social science (MA), including history, political science, sociology; sociology (MA); sociology/criminal justice (MA). Part-time and evening/weekend programs available. *Students:* 52 full-time (27 women), 146 part-time (107 women); includes 40 minority (39 African Americans, 1 Asian American or Pacific Islander), 15 international. Average age 35. 76 applicants, 95% accepted, 46 enrolled. In 2009, 60 master's, 6 other advanced degrees awarded. *Degree requirements:* For master's and Ed S, comprehensive exam, thesis optional. *Entrance requirements:* For master's and Ed S, GRE, MAT or GMAT, minimum GPA of 2.75 in major, 2.5 overall; 3 letters of recommendation; minimum C average in English composition; personal statement of purpose. Additional exam requirements/recommendations for international students: Required—TOEFL (minimum score 500 paper-based; 173 computer-based; 61 iBT). *Application deadline:* For fall admission, 7/1 priority date for domestic and international students; for spring admission, 12/1 priority date for domestic and international students. Applications are processed on a rolling basis. Application fee: $20. *Expenses:* Tuition, state resident: full-time $4185; part-time $232.50 per credit hour. Tuition, nonresident: full-time $7767; part-time $431.50 per credit hour. Required fees: $270; $15 per credit hour. $20 per term. *Financial support:* Federal Work-Study and scholarships/grants available. Financial award application deadline: 4/1; financial award applicants required to submit FAFSA. *Faculty research:* Suicide prevention. *Unit head:* Dr. Linda S. Bickel, Dean, 573-681-5247, Fax: 573-681-5106, E-mail: gradschool@lincolnu.edu. *Application contact:* Irasema Steck, Administrative Assistant, 573-681-5247, Fax: 573-681-5106, E-mail: gradschool@lincolnu.edu.

Lock Haven University of Pennsylvania, Department of Education, Lock Haven, PA 17745-2390. Offers alternative education (M Ed); teaching and learning (M Ed). *Accreditation:* NCATE. Part-time and evening/weekend programs available. Postbaccalaureate distance learning degree programs offered. *Degree requirements:* For master's, thesis. *Entrance requirements:* For master's, minimum undergraduate GPA of 3.0. Additional exam requirements/recommendations for international students: Required—TOEFL. Electronic applications accepted. *Expenses:* Tuition, state resident: full-time $6666; part-time $370 per credit hour. Tuition, nonresident: full-time $10,666; part-time $593 per credit hour. Required fees: $1988; $112 per credit hour. One-time fee: $25. Tuition and fees vary according to course load, campus/location and program.

Long Island University at Riverhead, Education Division, Program in Childhood Education, Riverhead, NY 11901. Offers childhood education (MS Ed); elementary education (MS Ed). *Accreditation:* Teacher Education Accreditation Council. *Faculty:* 1 full-time (0 women), 11 part-time/adjunct (7 women). *Students:* 23 full-time (19 women), 25 part-time (23 women); includes 1 African American, 1 Hispanic American. Average age 30. In 2009, 22 master's awarded. *Degree requirements:* For master's, thesis. *Entrance requirements:* For master's, minimum undergraduate GPA of 2.75, on-campus writing sample. Additional exam requirements/recommendations for international students: Required—TOEFL (minimum score 550 paper-based; 250 computer-based). *Application deadline:* Applications are processed on a rolling basis. Application fee: $30. Electronic applications accepted. *Financial support:* In 2009–10, 1 research assistantship with full tuition reimbursement was awarded; scholarships/grants and unspecified assistantships also available. Support available to part-time students. Financial award applicants required to submit FAFSA. *Unit head:* Prof. David S. Schultz, Head, 631-287-8010, Fax: 631-287-8253. *Application contact:* Andrea Borra, Admissions Counselor, 631-287-8010, Fax: 631-287-8253, E-mail: andrea.borra@liu.edu.

Long Island University, Brooklyn Campus, School of Education, Department of Teaching and Learning, Program in Elementary Education, Brooklyn, NY 11201-8423. Offers MS Ed. Part-time and evening/weekend programs available. *Degree requirements:* For master's, thesis optional. *Entrance requirements:* For master's, 2 letters of recommendation. Additional exam requirements/recommendations for international students: Required—TOEFL (minimum score 500 paper-based; 173 computer-based). Electronic applications accepted.

Long Island University, C.W. Post Campus, School of Education, Department of Curriculum and Instruction, Brookville, NY 11548-1300. Offers adolescence education (MS); adolescence education: biology (MS); adolescence education: earth science (MS); adolescence education: English (MS); adolescence education: mathematics (MS); adolescence education: social studies (MS); adolescence education: Spanish (MS); art education (MS); bilingual education (MS); childhood education (MS); early childhood education (MS); middle childhood education (MS); music education (MS); teaching English to speakers of other languages (MS). Part-time and evening/weekend programs available. *Degree requirements:* For master's, comprehensive exam or thesis, student teaching. *Entrance requirements:* For master's, minimum GPA of 2.75 in major, 2.5 overall. Electronic applications accepted. *Faculty research:* Ethics and education, teaching strategies.

Long Island University, Rockland Graduate Campus, Graduate School, Program in Curriculum and Instruction, Orangeburg, NY 10962. Offers adolescence education (MS Ed); childhood education (MS). *Faculty:* 1 (woman) full-time, 8 part-time/adjunct (3 women). *Students:* 18 full-time (15 women), 46 part-time (40 women). In 2009, 35 master's awarded. *Entrance requirements:* For master's, GRE General Test. *Application deadline:* Applications are processed on a rolling basis. Application fee: $30. *Expenses:* Tuition: Part-time $930 per credit. Required fees: $200 per semester. *Financial support:* Scholarships/grants available. Support available to part-time students. Financial award applicants required to submit FAFSA. *Unit head:* Dr. Nancy T. Goldman, Program Director, 845-359-7200 Ext. 5409, Fax: 845-359-7248, E-mail: nancy.goldman@liu.edu. *Application contact:* Peter S. Reiner, Director of Admissions and Marketing, 845-359-7200, Fax: 845-359-7248, E-mail: peter.reiner@liu.edu.

Long Island University, Westchester Graduate Campus, Programs in Education-Teaching, Purchase, NY 10577. Offers early childhood education (MS Ed, Advanced Certificate); elementary education (MS Ed, Advanced Certificate); literacy education (MS Ed, Advanced Certificate); second language, TESOL, bilingual education (MS Ed, Advanced Certificate); special education and secondary education (MS Ed, Advanced Certificate). *Accreditation:* Teacher Education Accreditation Council. Part-time and evening/weekend programs available. *Degree requirements:* For master's, comprehensive exam.

Longwood University, Office of Graduate Studies, College of Education and Human Services, Farmville, VA 23909. Offers communication sciences and disorders (MS); community and college counseling (MS); curriculum and instruction specialist-elementary (MS), including mild disabilities, modern languages; curriculum and instruction specialist-secondary (MS), including English, mild disabilities, modern languages; educational leadership (MS); guidance and counseling (MS); literacy and culture (MS); school library media (MS). *Accreditation:* NCATE. Part-time and evening/weekend programs available. *Degree requirements:* For master's, comprehensive exam, thesis optional. *Entrance requirements:* For master's, GRE (communication sciences and disorders), minimum GPA of 2.75. Additional exam requirements/recommendations for international students: Required—TOEFL (minimum score 550 paper-based; 213 computer-based).

Louisiana State University and Agricultural and Mechanical College, Graduate School, College of Education, Department of Educational Theory, Policy and Practice, Baton Rouge, LA 70803. Offers counseling (M Ed, MA, Ed S); educational administration (M Ed, MA, PhD, Ed S); educational technology (MA); elementary education (M Ed); higher education (PhD);

research methodology (PhD); secondary education (M Ed). *Accreditation:* ACA (one or more programs are accredited); NCATE. Part-time and evening/weekend programs available. *Faculty:* 38 full-time (24 women). *Students:* 174 full-time (139 women), 154 part-time (129 women); includes 74 minority (66 African Americans, 3 Asian Americans or Pacific Islanders, 5 Hispanic Americans), 9 international. Average age 32. 122 applicants, 60% accepted, 48 enrolled. In 2009, 124 master's, 13 doctorates, 11 other advanced degrees awarded. Terminal master's awarded for partial completion of doctoral program. *Degree requirements:* For doctorate, thesis/dissertation; for Ed S, thesis optional. *Entrance requirements:* For master's and doctorate, GRE General Test, minimum GPA of 3.0. Additional exam requirements/recommendations for international students: Required—TOEFL (minimum score 550 paper-based; 213 computer-based; 79 iBT) or IELTS (minimum score 6.5). *Application deadline:* For fall admission, 1/25 priority date for domestic students, 5/15 for international students; for spring admission, 10/15 for international students. Applications are processed on a rolling basis. Application fee: $50 ($70 for international students). Electronic applications accepted. *Financial support:* In 2009–10, 226 students received support, including 1 fellowship (averaging $31,711 per year), 27 research assistantships with full and partial tuition reimbursements available (averaging $10,143 per year), 35 teaching assistantships with full and partial tuition reimbursements available (averaging $12,555 per year); career-related internships or fieldwork, Federal Work-Study, institutionally sponsored loans, health care benefits, and unspecified assistantships also available. Support available to part-time students. Financial award applicants required to submit FAFSA. *Faculty research:* Literary, curriculum studies, science education, K-12 leadership, higher education. Total annual research expenditures: $1.8 million. *Unit head:* Dr. Earl Cheek, Chair, 225-578-6867, Fax: 225-578-9135, E-mail: echeek@lsu.edu. *Application contact:* Dr., Graduate Coordinator, 225-578-2280, Fax: 225-578-9135.

Loyola Marymount University, School of Education, Department of Elementary and Secondary Education, Program in Elementary Education, Los Angeles, CA 90045. Offers MA. Part-time and evening/weekend programs available. *Faculty:* 6 full-time (5 women), 11 part-time/adjunct (6 women). *Students:* 87 full-time (72 women), 35 part-time (30 women); includes 67 minority (7 African Americans, 1 American Indian/Alaska Native, 17 Asian Americans or Pacific Islanders, 42 Hispanic Americans), 1 international. Average age 30. 68 applicants, 65% accepted, 33 enrolled. In 2009, 87 master's awarded. *Degree requirements:* For master's, comprehensive exam. *Entrance requirements:* For master's, CBEST, CSET, RICA, 3 letters of recommendation. Additional exam requirements/recommendations for international students: Required—TOEFL (minimum score 600 paper-based; 250 computer-based; 100 iBT). *Application deadline:* For fall admission, 6/15 for domestic students; for spring admission, 11/15 for domestic students. Application fee: $50. Electronic applications accepted. *Financial support:* In 2009–10, 83 students received support, including 1 research assistantship (averaging $2,160 per year); scholarships/grants and unspecified assistantships also available. Support available to part-time students. Financial award application deadline: 6/15; financial award applicants required to submit FAFSA. *Unit head:* Dr. Irene Oliver, Chair, 310-338-7302, E-mail: ioliver@lmu.edu. *Application contact:* Chake H. Kouyoumjian, Director, Graduate Admissions, 310-338-2721, Fax: 310-338-6086, E-mail: ckouyoum@lmu.edu.

Loyola University Chicago, School of Education, Program in Initial Teacher Preparation, Chicago, IL 60660. Offers elementary education (M Ed); math education (M Ed); reading specialist (M Ed); school technology (M Ed); science education (M Ed); secondary education (M Ed); special education (M Ed). *Accreditation:* NCATE. *Faculty:* 12 full-time (9 women), 12 part-time/adjunct (6 women). *Students:* 154. Average age 28. 125 applicants, 69% accepted, 38 enrolled. In 2009, 89 master's awarded. *Degree requirements:* For master's, comprehensive exam. *Entrance requirements:* For master's, Illinois Basic Skills Test, 3 letters of recommendation, minimum GPA of 3.0, resume. Additional exam requirements/recommendations for international students: Required—TOEFL (minimum score 550 paper-based; 213 computer-based; 79 iBT). *Application deadline:* For fall admission, 7/1 priority date for domestic and international students; for spring admission, 11/1 priority date for domestic and international students. Applications are processed on a rolling basis. Application fee: $50. Electronic applications accepted. *Expenses:* Tuition: Full-time $14,220; part-time $790 per credit hour. Required fees: $60 per semester hour. Tuition and fees vary according to program. *Financial support:* In 2009–10, 1 research assistantship with full tuition reimbursement (averaging $8,500 per year), 1 teaching assistantship were awarded. Financial award application deadline: 2/15. *Faculty research:* Positive behavior support, school reform, school improvement. *Unit head:* Dr. Dorothy Giroux, Director, 312-915-7027, E-mail: dgiroux@luc.edu. *Application contact:* Marie Rosin-Dittmar, Information Contact, 312-915-6800, E-mail: schleduc@luc.edu.

Maharishi University of Management, Graduate Studies, Department of Education, Fairfield, IA 52557. Offers teaching elementary education (MA); teaching secondary education (MA). *Degree requirements:* For master's, thesis or alternative. *Entrance requirements:* For master's, GRE, minimum GPA of 3.0. Additional exam requirements/recommendations for international students: Required—TOEFL. *Faculty research:* Unified field-based approach to education, moral climate, scientific study of teaching.

Manhattanville College, Graduate Programs, School of Education, Program in Child and Early Childhood Education, Purchase, NY 10577-2132. Offers MAT, MPS. Part-time and evening/weekend programs available. *Students:* 144 full-time (130 women), 258 part-time (236 women); includes 26 minority (9 African Americans, 3 Asian Americans or Pacific Islanders, 14 Hispanic Americans), 1 international. In 2009, 72 master's awarded. *Degree requirements:* For master's, comprehensive exam or research project, field experience. *Entrance requirements:* For master's, minimum undergraduate GPA of 3.0, 2 letters of recommendation. Additional exam requirements/recommendations for international students: Required—TOEFL. *Application deadline:* Applications are processed on a rolling basis. Application fee: $70. Electronic applications accepted. *Financial support:* Career-related internships or fieldwork, Federal Work-Study, institutionally sponsored loans, and unspecified assistantships available. Financial award applicants required to submit FAFSA. *Unit head:* Dr. Shelley Wepner, Dean, 914-323-5192, Fax: 914-694-2386, E-mail: wepners@mville.edu. *Application contact:* Jeanine Pardey-Levine, Director of Admissions, 914-323-3208, Fax: 914-694-1732, E-mail: edschool@mville.edu.

Manhattanville College, Graduate Programs, School of Education, Program in Childhood Education, Purchase, NY 10577-2132. Offers childhood and special education (MPS); childhood education (MAT); special education childhood (MPS). Part-time and evening/weekend programs available. *Students:* 67 full-time (62 women), 150 part-time (120 women); includes 6 African Americans, 3 Asian Americans or Pacific Islanders, 10 Hispanic Americans, 2 international. In 2009, 65 master's awarded. *Degree requirements:* For master's, comprehensive exam or research project, field experience. *Entrance requirements:* For master's, minimum undergraduate GPA of 3.0, 2 letters of recommendation. Additional exam requirements/recommendations for international students: Required—TOEFL. *Application deadline:* Applications are processed on a rolling basis. Application fee: $70. *Financial support:* Career-related internships or fieldwork and institutionally sponsored loans available. Support available to part-time students. Financial award applicants required to submit FAFSA. *Unit head:* Dr. Shelley Wepner, Dean, 914-323-5192, Fax: 914-694-2386, E-mail: wepners@mville.edu. *Application contact:* Jeanine Pardey-Levine, Director of Admissions, 914-323-3208, Fax: 914-694-1732, E-mail: edschool@mville.edu.

Mansfield University of Pennsylvania, Graduate Studies, Department of Education and Special Education, Mansfield, PA 16933. Offers elementary education (M Ed); secondary education (MS). *Accreditation:* NCATE (one or more programs are accredited). Part-time and evening/weekend programs available. Postbaccalaureate distance learning degree programs offered (no on-campus study). *Faculty:* 9 full-time (6 women). *Students:* 52 full-time (40 women), 56 part-time (41 women); includes 4 minority (1 African American, 1 Asian American or Pacific Islander, 2 Hispanic Americans), 2 international. Average age 29. In 2009, 56 master's awarded. *Degree requirements:* For master's, comprehensive exam, thesis optional. *Entrance requirements:* For master's, minimum GPA of 3.0. Additional exam requirements/recommendations for international students: Required—TOEFL (minimum score 550 paper-based; 220 computer-based). *Application deadline:* For fall admission, 8/1 priority date for domestic students, 8/1 for international students; for spring admission, 11/1 priority date for domestic students, 9/1 for international students. Applications are processed on a rolling basis. Application fee: $25. Electronic applications accepted. *Expenses:* Tuition, state resident: full-time $6666; part-time $370 per credit. Tuition, nonresident: full-time $10,666; part-time $593 per credit. Required fees: $1388. *Financial support:* Career-related internships or fieldwork and unspecified assistantships available. Support available to part-time students. Financial award application deadline: 5/1; financial award applicants required to submit FAFSA. *Unit head:* Dr. Jesus Lucero, Chairperson, 570-662-4791, E-mail: jlucero@mansfield.edu. *Application contact:* Christina Hale, Assistant Director of Enrollment Services/Graduate Admissions, 570-662-4812, Fax: 570-662-4121, E-mail: chale@mansfield.edu.

Marshall University, Academic Affairs Division, Graduate School of Education and Professional Development, Program in Elementary Education, Huntington, WV 25755. Offers MA. *Accreditation:* NCATE. Part-time and evening/weekend programs available. *Faculty:* 24 full-time (13 women). *Students:* 25 full-time (24 women), 106 part-time (98 women); includes 2 minority (both African Americans). Average age 33. In 2009, 23 master's awarded. *Degree requirements:* For master's, thesis optional, comprehensive or oral assessment, research project. *Entrance requirements:* For master's, GRE General Test or MAT. Application fee: $40. *Financial support:* Federal Work-Study, tuition waivers (full and partial), and unspecified assistantships available. Support available to part-time students. Financial award applicants required to submit FAFSA. *Unit head:* Dr. Calvin Meyer, Director, 304-746-1936, E-mail: meyer@marshall.edu. *Application contact:* Graduate Admissions, 304-746-1900, Fax: 304-746-1902, E-mail: services@marshall.edu.

Mary Baldwin College, Graduate Studies, Program in Teaching, Staunton, VA 24401-3610. Offers elementary education (MAT); middle grades education (MAT). *Accreditation:* Teacher Education Accreditation Council.

Marygrove College, Graduate Division, Sage Program, Detroit, MI 48221-2599. Offers M Ed. *Entrance requirements:* For master's, Michigan Teacher Test for Certification.

Marymount University, School of Education and Human Services, Program in Education, Arlington, VA 22207-4299. Offers elementary education (M Ed); English as a second language (M Ed); professional studies (M Ed); secondary education (M Ed); special education, general curriculum (M Ed). *Accreditation:* NCATE. Part-time and evening/weekend programs available. *Faculty:* 9 full-time (6 women), 9 part-time/adjunct (8 women). *Students:* 55 full-time (46 women), 117 part-time (100 women); includes 13 minority (1 African American, 4 Asian Americans or Pacific Islanders, 8 Hispanic Americans), 7 international. Average age 31. 73 applicants, 93% accepted, 55 enrolled. In 2009, 62 master's awarded. *Degree requirements:* For master's, thesis or alternative. *Entrance requirements:* For master's, GRE or MAT and PRAXIS I or SAT/ACT, 2 letters of recommendation, interview. Additional exam requirements/recommendations for international students: Required—TOEFL (minimum score 600 paper-based; 250 computer-based; 96 iBT), IELTS (minimum score 6.5). *Application deadline:* For fall admission, 7/1 for international students; for spring admission, 10/15 for international students. Applications are processed on a rolling basis. Application fee: $40. Electronic applications accepted. *Expenses:* Tuition: Full-time $13,050; part-time $725 per credit hour. Required fees: $135; $7.50 per credit hour. *Financial support:* In 2009–10, 48 students received support; research assistantships with full tuition reimbursements available, career-related internships or fieldwork, Federal Work-Study, scholarships/grants, and unspecified assistantships available. Support available to part-time students. Financial award applicants required to submit FAFSA. *Unit head:* Dr. Shelly Haser, Chair, 703-526-6855, Fax: 703-284-1631, E-mail: shelly.haser@marymount.edu. *Application contact:* Francesca Reed, Director, Graduate Admissions, 703-284-5901, Fax: 703-527-3815, E-mail: grad.admissions@marymount.edu.

Maryville University of Saint Louis, School of Education, St. Louis, MO 63141-7299. Offers art education (MA Ed); early childhood education (MA Ed); educational leadership (Ed D); educational leadership: principal certification (MA Ed); elementary education (MA Ed); elementary education/English (MA Ed); elementary education/psychology (MA Ed); environmental education (MA Ed); gifted education (MA Ed); literacy specialist (MA Ed); middle grades education (MA Ed); secondary teaching and inquiry (MA Ed); teacher as leader (MA Ed). *Accreditation:* NASAD; NCATE. Part-time and evening/weekend programs available. *Students:* 25 full-time (18 women), 198 part-time (145 women); includes 33 minority (27 African Americans, 2 American Indian/Alaska Native, 1 Asian American or Pacific Islander, 3 Hispanic Americans). Average age 36. In 2009, 61 master's, 45 doctorates awarded. *Degree requirements:* For master's, thesis, project. *Entrance requirements:* For master's and doctorate, minimum GPA of 3.0, 3 professional recommendations. Additional exam requirements/recommendations for international students: Required—TOEFL (minimum score 550 paper-based). *Application deadline:* Applications are processed on a rolling basis. Application fee: $40 ($60 for international students). Electronic applications accepted. *Expenses:* Tuition: Full-time $20,384; part-time $627.50 per credit hour. Required fees: $100 per semester. *Financial support:* Career-related internships or fieldwork, Federal Work-Study, tuition waivers (partial), and professional educator discounts available. Financial award application deadline: 3/1; financial award applicants required to submit FAFSA. *Faculty research:* Collaboration with public schools, pre-service program development, mathematics, diversity, literacy. *Unit head:* Dr. Sam Hausfather, Dean, 314-529-9466, Fax: 314-529-9921, E-mail: shausfather@maryville.edu. *Application contact:* Holly Stanwich, Graduate Admissions Coordinator, 314-529-9542, Fax: 314-529-9921, E-mail: teachered@maryville.edu.

Marywood University, Academic Affairs, Reap College of Education and Human Development, Department of Education, Program in Elementary Education, Scranton, PA 18509-1598. Offers MAT. *Accreditation:* NCATE. *Students:* 8 full-time (7 women), 9 part-time (8 women). Average age 31. In 2009, 10 master's awarded. *Entrance requirements:* Additional exam requirements/recommendations for international students: Required—TOEFL (minimum score 550 paper-based; 213 computer-based; 79 iBT). *Application deadline:* For fall admission, 4/1 priority date for domestic students, 3/31 priority date for international students; for spring admission, 11/1 priority date for domestic students, 8/31 priority date for international students. Applications are processed on a rolling basis. Application fee: $35. Electronic applications accepted. *Expenses:* Tuition: Part-time $715 per credit. Required fees: $270 per semester. Tuition and fees vary according to degree level, campus/location and program. *Financial support:* Research assistantships, career-related internships or fieldwork, scholarships/grants, and unspecified assistantships available. Support available to part-time students. Financial award application deadline: 6/30; financial award applicants required to submit FAFSA. *Unit head:* Sr. Ann Jablonski, Chair, 570-348-6211, E-mail: jablonski@marywood.edu. *Application contact:* Tammy Manka, Assistant Director of Graduate Admissions, 866-279-9663, E-mail: tmanka@marywood.edu.

McDaniel College, Graduate and Professional Studies, Program in Elementary and Secondary Education, Westminster, MD 21157-4390. Offers elementary education (MS); secondary education (MS). *Accreditation:* NCATE. Part-time and evening/weekend programs available. *Degree requirements:* For master's, comprehensive exam (for some programs), thesis optional. *Entrance requirements:* For master's, GRE General Test, MAT, or NTE/PRAXIS I, letters of reference (3). Additional exam requirements/recommendations for international students: Required—TOEFL (minimum score 213 computer-based). *Expenses:* Tuition: Part-time $325 per credit hour.

McNeese State University, Doré School of Graduate Studies, Burton College of Education, Department of Teacher Education, Program in Curriculum and Instruction, Lake Charles, LA 70609. Offers early childhood education (M Ed); elementary education (M Ed); secondary education (M Ed). Evening/weekend programs available. *Faculty:* 12 full-time (6 women). *Students:* 4 full-time (all women), 9 part-time (all women); includes 2 minority (both African Americans). In 2009, 3 master's awarded. *Entrance requirements:* For master's, GRE, teaching certificate. *Application deadline:* For fall admission, 5/15 priority date for domestic and international students; for spring admission, 10/15 priority date for domestic and international students. Applications are processed on a rolling basis. Application fee: $20 ($30 for international students). *Expenses:* Tuition, area resident: Full-time $2556. Tuition, state resident: full-time $2556. Required fees: $1031. Tuition and fees vary according to course load. *Financial*

Elementary Education

McNeese State University (continued)

support: Application deadline: 5/1. *Unit head:* Dr. Royce Zant, Head, 337-475-5404, Fax: 337-475-5398, E-mail: rzant@mcneese.edu. *Application contact:* Dr. George F. Mead, Interim Dean of Dore' School of Graduate Studies, 337-475-5396, Fax: 337-475-5397, E-mail: admissions@mcneese.edu.

McNeese State University, Doré School of Graduate Studies, Burton College of Education, Department of Teacher Education, Program in Teaching, Lake Charles, LA 70609. Offers elementary education grades 1-5 (MAT); secondary education grades 6-12 (MAT); special education—mild/moderate grades 1-12 (MAT). Evening/weekend programs available. *Faculty:* 12 full-time (6 women). *Students:* 44 full-time (37 women), 126 part-time (112 women); includes 34 minority (25 African Americans, 1 American Indian/Alaska Native, 2 Asian Americans or Pacific Islanders, 6 Hispanic Americans), 1 international. In 2009, 43 master's awarded. *Entrance requirements:* For master's, GRE, PRAXIS, 2 letters of recommendation; autobiography. *Application deadline:* For fall admission, 5/15 priority date for domestic and international students; for spring admission, 10/15 priority date for domestic and international students. Applications are processed on a rolling basis. Application fee: $20 ($30 for international students). *Expenses:* Tuition, area resident: Full-time $2556. Tuition, state resident: full-time $2556. Required fees: $1031. Tuition and fees vary according to course load. *Financial support:* Application deadline: 5/1. *Unit head:* Dr. Royce Zant, Head, 337-475-5404, Fax: 337-475-5398, E-mail: rzant@mcneese.edu. *Application contact:* Dr. George F. Mead, Interim Dean of Dore' School of Graduate Studies, 337-475-5396, Fax: 337-475-5397, E-mail: admissions@mcneese.edu.

Medaille College, Program in Education, Buffalo, NY 14214-2695. Offers adolescent education (MS Ed); curriculum and instruction (MS Ed); education preparation (MS Ed); literacy (MS Ed); special education (MS). *Accreditation:* Teacher Education Accreditation Council. Part-time and evening/weekend programs available. *Faculty:* 22 full-time (16 women), 47 part-time/adjunct (36 women). *Students:* 721 full-time (596 women), 2 part-time (both women); includes 34 minority (16 African Americans, 1 American Indian/Alaska Native, 14 Asian Americans or Pacific Islanders, 3 Hispanic Americans). Average age 26. 621 applicants, 46% accepted, 288 enrolled. In 2009, 608 master's awarded. *Degree requirements:* For master's, thesis or alternative. *Entrance requirements:* For master's, minimum undergraduate GPA of 2.7. Additional exam requirements/recommendations for international students: Required—TOEFL (minimum score 550 paper-based; 213 computer-based). *Application deadline:* For fall admission, 8/15 priority date for domestic students; for spring admission, 1/15 priority date for domestic students. Applications are processed on a rolling basis. Application fee: $35. Electronic applications accepted. *Financial support:* In 2009–10, 501 students received support. Federal Work-Study available. Financial award applicants required to submit FAFSA. *Faculty research:* Curriculum planning, truancy, tracking minority students, curriculum design, mentoring students. *Unit head:* Dr. Robert DiSibio, Director of Graduate Programs, 716-932-2548, Fax: 716-631-1380, E-mail: rdisibio@medaille.edu. *Application contact:* Jacqueline Matheny, Executive Director of Marketing and Enrollment, 716-932-2541, Fax: 716-632-1811, E-mail: jmatheny@medaille.edu.

Mercy College, School of Education, Program in Childhood Education, Grade 1-6, Dobbs Ferry, NY 10522-1189. Offers MS. Part-time and evening/weekend programs available. *Students:* 141 full-time (123 women), 286 part-time (234 women); includes 177 minority (99 African Americans, 1 American Indian/Alaska Native, 8 Asian Americans or Pacific Islanders, 69 Hispanic Americans), 1 international. Average age 33. 198 applicants, 69% accepted, 114 enrolled. In 2009, 144 master's awarded. *Degree requirements:* For master's, comprehensive exam. *Entrance requirements:* For master's, interview, resume, minimum undergraduate GPA of 3.0 (writing sample for those with GPA lower than 3.0), assessment by specific program director or designee. Additional exam requirements/recommendations for international students: Required—TOEFL (minimum score 600 paper-based; 250 computer-based; 100 iBT). *Application deadline:* For fall admission, 8/1 for international students. Applications are processed on a rolling basis. Application fee: $40. Electronic applications accepted. *Expenses:* Tuition: Full-time $13,158; part-time $731 per credit. Required fees: $500. Tuition and fees vary according to degree level and program. *Financial support:* In 2009–10, 19 students received support. Career-related internships or fieldwork, Federal Work-Study, scholarships/grants, and unspecified assistantships available. *Faculty research:* Teaching literacy, behavior management applications, assistive technology. *Unit head:* Dr. Andrew Peiser, Chairperson, 914-674-7489, Fax: 914-674-7352, E-mail: apeiser@mercy.edu. *Application contact:* Mary Ellen Hoffman, Director, Graduate Education Programs, 914-674-7334, E-mail: mhoffman@mercy.edu.

Metropolitan College of New York, Program in Childhood Education, New York, NY 10013. Offers MS. *Degree requirements:* For master's, one foreign language. *Entrance requirements:* For master's, Liberal Arts and Sciences Test (LAST) recommended, minimum GPA of 3.0, 2 letters of reference, writing sample, interview. Additional exam requirements/recommendations for international students: Required—TOEFL (minimum score 600 paper-based; 250 computer-based). *Expenses:* Contact institution. *Faculty research:* Classroom management, learner autonomy, teacher research, math and gender, intelligence.

Miami University, Graduate School, School of Education and Allied Professions, Department of Teacher Education, Oxford, OH 45056. Offers elementary education (M Ed, MAT); reading education (M Ed); secondary education (M Ed, MAT), including adolescent education (MAT), elementary mathematics education (M Ed), secondary education. Part-time programs available. *Students:* 48 full-time (31 women), 70 part-time (60 women); includes 6 minority (3 African Americans, 3 Hispanic Americans), 5 international. *Entrance requirements:* For master's, GRE (MAT), minimum undergraduate GPA of 3.0 during previous 2 years or 2.75 overall. Application fee: $50. *Expenses:* Tuition, state resident: full-time $11,280. Tuition, nonresident: full-time $24,912. Required fees: $516. *Financial support:* Fellowships with full tuition reimbursements, research assistantships, teaching assistantships, career-related internships or fieldwork, Federal Work-Study, scholarships/grants, health care benefits, tuition waivers (full), and unspecified assistantships available. Financial award application deadline: 3/1. *Unit head:* Dr. James Shiveley, Chair, 513-529-6443, Fax: 513-529-4931, E-mail: shiveljm@muohio.edu. *Application contact:* Dr. Iris Johnson, Assistant Chair and Graduate Coordinator, 513-529-6443, Fax: 513-529-4931, E-mail: johnsoid@muohio.edu.

Middle Tennessee State University, College of Graduate Studies, College of Education and Behavioral Science, Department of Elementary and Special Education, Major in Curriculum and Instruction, Murfreesboro, TN 37132. Offers early childhood education (M Ed); elementary education (M Ed, Ed S); middle school education (M Ed). *Accreditation:* NCATE. Part-time and evening/weekend programs available. Postbaccalaureate distance learning degree programs offered. *Students:* 14 full-time (12 women), 126 part-time (118 women); includes 11 minority (8 African Americans, 2 Asian Americans or Pacific Islanders, 1 Hispanic American). 39 applicants, 72% accepted. In 2009, 55 master's awarded. *Degree requirements:* For master's, comprehensive exam; for Ed S, thesis. *Entrance requirements:* For master's and Ed S, GRE, MAT or PRAXIS. Additional exam requirements/recommendations for international students: Required—TOEFL (minimum score 525 paper-based; 195 computer-based; 71 iBT) or IELTS (minimum score 6). *Application deadline:* For fall admission, 8/1 priority date for domestic students. Applications are processed on a rolling basis. Application fee: $25. Electronic applications accepted. *Expenses:* Tuition, state resident: full-time $4404. Tuition, nonresident: full-time $10,956. *Financial support:* Institutionally sponsored loans available. Support available to part-time students. Financial award application deadline: 5/1. *Unit head:* Dr. Kathy Burriss, Director, 615-898-2323, Fax: 615-898-5309, E-mail: kburriss@mtsu.edu. *Application contact:* Dr. Michael Allen, Dean and Vice Provost for Research, 615-898-2840, Fax: 615-904-8020, E-mail: mallen@mtsu.edu.

Millersville University of Pennsylvania, College of Graduate and Professional Studies, School of Education, Department of Elementary and Early Childhood Education, Program in Elementary Education, Millersville, PA 17551-0302. Offers M Ed. *Accreditation:* NCATE. Part-time and evening/weekend programs available. *Faculty:* 18 full-time (14 women), 15 part-time/adjunct (7 women). *Students:* 6 full-time (5 women), 12 part-time (10 women). Average age 32. 2 applicants, 100% accepted, 1 enrolled. In 2009, 13 master's awarded. *Degree requirements:* For master's, comprehensive exam, thesis optional. *Entrance requirements:* For master's, GRE or MAT, 3 letters of recommendation, copy of teaching certificate. Additional exam requirements/recommendations for international students: Required—TOEFL (minimum score 500 paper-based; 183 computer-based; 65 iBT) or IELTS (minimum score 6). *Application deadline:* For fall admission, 1/15 priority date for domestic and international students; for winter admission, 10/1 priority date for domestic and international students; for spring admission, 10/1 priority date for domestic and international students. Applications are processed on a rolling basis. Application fee: $40 ($50 for international students). Electronic applications accepted. *Expenses:* Tuition, state resident: full-time $6666; part-time $370 per credit. Tuition, nonresident: full-time $10,666; part-time $593 per credit. Required fees: $1578.50; $76.25 per credit. One-time fee: $60 part-time. Tuition and fees vary according to course load. *Financial support:* In 2009–10, 2 students received support, including 2 research assistantships with full tuition reimbursements available (averaging $5,000 per year); institutionally sponsored loans and unspecified assistantships also available. Support available to part-time students. Financial award application deadline: 3/15; financial award applicants required to submit FAFSA. *Faculty research:* Longitudinal study of teacher development. *Unit head:* Dr. Kazi Hossain, Coordinator, 717-871-2265, Fax: 717-871-5462, E-mail: kazi.hossain@millersville.edu. *Application contact:* Dr. Victor S. DeSantis, Dean of Graduate and Professional Studies, 717-872-3099, Fax: 717-872-3453, E-mail: victor.desantis@millersville.edu.

Mills College, Graduate Studies, School of Education, Oakland, CA 94613-1000. Offers child life in hospitals (MA); early childhood education (MA); education (MA), including art education, curriculum and instruction, elementary education, English education, foreign language education, mathematics education, science education, secondary education, social studies education, teaching; educational leadership (MA, Ed D); infant mental health (MA). Part-time and evening/weekend programs available. *Faculty:* 11 full-time (9 women), 16 part-time/adjunct (14 women). *Students:* 138 full-time (119 women), 55 part-time (48 women); includes 71 minority (34 African Americans, 19 Asian Americans or Pacific Islanders, 18 Hispanic Americans), 3 international. Average age 34. 210 applicants, 82% accepted, 93 enrolled. In 2009, 54 master's, 15 doctorates awarded. Terminal master's awarded for partial completion of doctoral program. *Degree requirements:* For master's, comprehensive exam. *Entrance requirements:* For doctorate, GRE General Test. Additional exam requirements/recommendations for international students: Required—TOEFL. *Application deadline:* For fall admission, 2/1 for domestic and international students; for spring admission, 11/1 for domestic and international students. Applications are processed on a rolling basis. Application fee: $50. Electronic applications accepted. *Expenses:* Tuition: Full-time $26,326; part-time $6584 per course. Required fees: $896. One-time fee: $896 part-time. Tuition and fees vary according to program. *Financial support:* In 2009–10, 188 students received support, including 186 fellowships (averaging $6,499 per year), 28 teaching assistantships with partial tuition reimbursements available (averaging $3,187 per year); career-related internships or fieldwork and scholarships/grants also available. Support available to part-time students. Financial award application deadline: 2/1; financial award applicants required to submit FAFSA. *Faculty research:* Child development, gender and education, public policy, cross-cultural development, development of literacy. Total annual research expenditures: $1.2 million. *Unit head:* Joseph Kahne, Chairperson, 510-430-3190, Fax: 510-430-3314, E-mail: grad-studies@mills.edu. *Application contact:* Jessica King, Graduate Admission Specialist, 510-430-3305, Fax: 510-430-2159, E-mail: grad-studies@mills.edu.

Minnesota State University Mankato, College of Graduate Studies, College of Education, Department of Elementary and Early Childhood Education, Mankato, MN 56001. Offers MS, Certificate. *Accreditation:* NCATE. Part-time programs available. *Students:* 2 full-time (1 woman), 62 part-time (59 women). *Degree requirements:* For master's, comprehensive exam, thesis or alternative. *Entrance requirements:* For master's, GRE General Test or MAT, minimum GPA of 3.0 during previous 2 years. Additional exam requirements/recommendations for international students: Required—TOEFL. *Application deadline:* For fall admission, 7/1 priority date for domestic students; for spring admission, 11/1 for domestic students. Applications are processed on a rolling basis. Application fee: $40. Electronic applications accepted. *Expenses:* Tuition, state resident: full-time $5364. Tuition, nonresident: full-time $8314. *Financial support:* Application deadline: 3/15. *Unit head:* Dr. Peggy Ballard, Graduate Coordinator, 507-389-1516. *Application contact:* 507-389-2321, E-mail: grad@mnsu.edu.

Minot State University, Graduate School, Teacher Education and Human Performance Department, Minot, ND 58707-0002. Offers elementary education (M Ed). *Accreditation:* NCATE. *Degree requirements:* For master's, thesis. *Entrance requirements:* For master's, 2 years of teaching experience, bachelor's degree in education, minimum GPA of 2.75. Additional exam requirements/recommendations for international students: Required—TOEFL. *Expenses:* Tuition, state resident: full-time $5720; part-time $283 per credit hour. Tuition, nonresident: full-time $5720; part-time $283 per credit hour. Required fees: $1034; $1034 per year. Tuition and fees vary according to course load, degree level and program. *Faculty research:* Technology, personnel-teaching efficacy, reflective teaching.

Mississippi College, Graduate School, School of Education, Department of Teacher Education and Leadership, Clinton, MS 39058. Offers art (M Ed); biological science (M Ed); business education (M Ed); computer science (M Ed); dyslexia therapy (M Ed); educational leadership (M Ed, Ed D, Ed S); elementary education (M Ed, Ed S); English (M Ed); higher education administration (MS); mathematics (M Ed); secondary education (M Ed); social studies (history) (M Ed); teaching arts (M Ed). Part-time programs available. Postbaccalaureate distance learning degree programs offered (no on-campus study). *Faculty:* 11 full-time (7 women), 13 part-time/adjunct (7 women). *Students:* 33 full-time (22 women), 282 part-time (240 women); includes 148 minority (146 African Americans, 2 American Indian/Alaska Native), 1 international. Average age 34. In 2009, 147 master's awarded. *Degree requirements:* For master's, comprehensive exam, thesis optional. *Entrance requirements:* For master's, NTE. Additional exam requirements/recommendations for international students: Recommended—IELTS. *Application deadline:* For fall admission, 8/15 priority date for domestic students. Applications are processed on a rolling basis. Application fee: $30. Electronic applications accepted. *Expenses:* Tuition: Part-time $452 per credit hour. Required fees: $101 per semester. Tuition and fees vary according to degree level, campus/location, program and student level. *Financial support:* Teaching assistantships, career-related internships or fieldwork, Federal Work-Study, scholarships/grants, and unspecified assistantships available. Support available to part-time students. Financial award applicants required to submit FAFSA. *Unit head:* Dr. Tom Williams, Chair, 601-925-3844, E-mail: twilliams@mc.edu. *Application contact:* Elnora Lewis, Secretary, 601-925-3225, Fax: 601-925-3889, E-mail: lewis09@mc.edu.

Mississippi State University, College of Education, Department of Curriculum, Instruction and Special Education, Mississippi State, MS 39762. Offers curriculum and instruction (PhD); education (Ed D, Ed S), including elementary education, secondary education, special education (Ed S); elementary education (MS, PhD); secondary education (MS, PhD); secondary teacher alternate route (MAT); special education (MS). *Accreditation:* NCATE. Part-time and evening/weekend programs available. *Faculty:* 13 full-time (11 women). *Students:* 35 full-time (33 women), 126 part-time (103 women); includes 55 minority (all African Americans). Average age 35. 80 applicants, 60% accepted, 40 enrolled. In 2009, 60 master's, 6 doctorates, 7 other advanced degrees awarded. *Degree requirements:* For master's, comprehensive exam; for doctorate, thesis/dissertation; for Ed S, comprehensive exam, thesis or alternative. *Entrance requirements:* For master's, GRE, minimum GPA of 2.75 in junior and senior year, eligibility for initial teacher certification; for doctorate, GRE, minimum graduate GPA of 3.4; for Ed S, GRE, minimum graduate GPA of 3.2. Additional exam requirements/recommendations for international students: Required—TOEFL (minimum score 600 paper-based; 250 computer-based; 100 iBT); Recommended—IELTS (minimum score 7.5). *Application deadline:* For fall admission, 3/1 priority date for domestic students, 5/1 for international students; for spring admission, 9/1 priority date for domestic students, 9/1 for international students. Applications are processed on a rolling basis. Application fee: $40. Electronic applications accepted. *Expenses:* Tuition, state resident: full-time $2575.50; part-time $286.25 per credit hour. Tuition, nonresident: full-time $6510; part-time $723.50 per credit hour. Tuition and fees vary according to course

load. *Financial support:* In 2009–10, 30 students received support, including 5 research assistantships with full and partial tuition reimbursements available (averaging $8,959 per year), 3 teaching assistantships (averaging $10,443 per year); Federal Work-Study, institutionally sponsored loans, scholarships/grants, and unspecified assistantships also available. Financial award applicants required to submit FAFSA. *Faculty research:* Early childhood education, reading, rural schools, multicultural education, use of technology in instruction. *Unit head:* Dr. Charlotte S. Burroughs, Associate Professor and Interim Head, 662-325-3747, Fax: 662-325-7857, E-mail: susie.burroughs@msstate.edu. *Application contact:* Dr. Kent Coffey, Professor and Graduate Coordinator, 662-325-2188, Fax: 662-325-7857, E-mail: kcoffey@colled.msstate.edu.

Mississippi Valley State University, Department of Education, Itta Bena, MS 38941-1400. Offers education (MAT); elementary education (MA). *Accreditation:* NCATE.

Missouri State University, Graduate College, College of Education, Department of Childhood Education and Family Studies, Program in Elementary Education, Springfield, MO 65897. Offers MS Ed. Part-time and evening/weekend programs available. Postbaccalaureate distance learning degree programs offered (minimal on-campus study). *Students:* 27 full-time (25 women), 56 part-time (51 women); includes 2 minority (1 African American, 1 Hispanic American). Average age 32. 13 applicants, 100% accepted, 4 enrolled. In 2009, 29 master's awarded. *Degree requirements:* For master's, comprehensive exam, thesis or alternative. *Entrance requirements:* For master's, GRE (if GPA less than 3.0), minimum GPA of 2.75, teaching certificate. Additional exam requirements/recommendations for international students: Required—TOEFL (minimum score 550 paper-based; 213 computer-based; 79 iBT). *Application deadline:* For fall admission, 7/20 priority date for domestic students, 5/1 for international students; for spring admission, 12/20 priority date for domestic students, 9/1 for international students. Applications are processed on a rolling basis. Application fee: $35 ($50 for international students). Electronic applications accepted. *Expenses:* Tuition, state resident: full-time $3852; part-time $214 per credit hour. Tuition, nonresident: full-time $7524; part-time $418 per credit hour. Required fees: $696; $172 per semester. Tuition and fees vary according to course level, course load, degree level and program. *Financial support:* Teaching assistantships, Federal Work-Study, institutionally sponsored loans, and scholarships/grants available. Financial award application deadline: 3/31; financial award applicants required to submit FAFSA. *Unit head:* Dr. Dale Range, Program Director, 417-836-3262, Fax: 417-836-8900, E-mail: dalerange@missouristate.edu. *Application contact:* Eric Eckert, Coordinator of Graduate Admissions and Recruitment, 417-836-5331, Fax: 417-836-6200, E-mail: ericeckert@missouristate.edu.

Missouri State University, Graduate College, College of Education, Department of Counseling, Leadership, and Special Education, Program in Educational Administration, Springfield, MO 65897. Offers educational administration (MS Ed, Ed S); elementary education (MS Ed); elementary principal (Ed S); secondary education (MS Ed); secondary principal (Ed S); superintendent (Ed S). Part-time and evening/weekend programs available. *Students:* 12 full-time (10 women), 161 part-time (98 women); includes 3 minority (1 Asian American or Pacific Islander, 2 Hispanic Americans), 3 international. Average age 36. 25 applicants, 96% accepted, 21 enrolled. In 2009, 42 master's, 23 Ed Ss awarded. *Degree requirements:* For master's and Ed S, comprehensive exam, thesis or alternative. *Entrance requirements:* For master's, minimum GPA of 2.75; for Ed S, GRE General Test, MAT, minimum GPA of 2.75. Additional exam requirements/recommendations for international students: Required—TOEFL (minimum score 550 paper-based; 213 computer-based; 79 iBT). *Application deadline:* For fall admission, 7/20 priority date for domestic students, 5/1 for international students; for spring admission, 12/20 priority date for domestic students, 9/1 for international students. Applications are processed on a rolling basis. Application fee: $35 ($50 for international students). Electronic applications accepted. *Expenses:* Tuition, state resident: full-time $3852; part-time $214 per credit hour. Tuition, nonresident: full-time $7524; part-time $418 per credit hour. Required fees: $696; $172 per semester. Tuition and fees vary according to course level, course load, degree level and program. *Financial support:* Career-related internships or fieldwork, Federal Work-Study, institutionally sponsored loans, scholarships/grants, and unspecified assistantships available. Financial award application deadline: 3/31; financial award applicants required to submit FAFSA. *Unit head:* Gerald Moseman, Graduate Program Coordinator, 417-836-5490, Fax: 417-836-4918, E-mail: geraldmoseman@missouristate.edu. *Application contact:* Eric Eckert, Coordinator of Admissions and Recruitment, 417-836-5331, Fax: 417-836-6200, E-mail: ericeckert@missouristate.edu.

Monmouth University, Graduate School, School of Education, West Long Branch, NJ 07764-1898. Offers education (M Ed); initial certification (MAT), including elementary level, K-12, secondary level; learning disabilities-teacher consultant (Certificate); principal (MS Ed); principal/school administrator (MS Ed); reading specialist (MS Ed, Certificate); school counseling (MS Ed); special education (MS Ed), including autism, learning disabilities teacher consultant, teacher of students with disabilities, teaching in inclusive settings; supervisor (Certificate); teacher of the handicapped (Certificate); teaching english to speakers of other languages (TESOL) (Certificate). *Accreditation:* NCATE. Part-time and evening/weekend programs available. *Faculty:* 20 full-time (13 women), 32 part-time/adjunct (22 women). *Students:* 182 full-time (146 women), 353 part-time (286 women); includes 40 minority (15 African Americans, 3 American Indian/Alaska Native, 5 Asian Americans or Pacific Islanders, 17 Hispanic Americans), 1 international. Average age 29. 361 applicants, 96% accepted, 176 enrolled. In 2009, 178 master's awarded. *Entrance requirements:* For master's, minimum GPA of 3.0 in major, 2.75 overall; 2 letters of recommendation (for some programs). Additional exam requirements/recommendations for international students: Required—TOEFL (minimum score 550 paper-based; 213 computer-based; 79 iBT), IELTS (minimum score 5), Michigan English Language Assessment Battery (minimum score 77), Cambridge A, B, C. *Application deadline:* For fall admission, 7/15 priority date for domestic students, 7/1 for international students; for spring admission, 11/15 priority date for domestic students, 11/1 for international students. Applications are processed on a rolling basis. Application fee: $50. Electronic applications accepted. *Expenses:* Tuition: Part-time $773 per credit. Required fees: $157 per semester. *Financial support:* In 2009–10, 326 students received support, including 211 fellowships (averaging $1,824 per year), 23 research assistantships (averaging $7,943 per year); career-related internships or fieldwork, scholarships/grants, and unspecified assistantships also available. Support available to part-time students. Financial award applicants required to submit FAFSA. *Faculty research:* Multicultural literacy, science and mathematics teaching strategies, teacher as reflective practitioner, children with disabilities, varied contexts of learning. *Unit head:* Dr. Terri Rothman, Associate Dean, 732-571-7507, Fax: 732-263-5277, E-mail: trothman@monmouth.edu. *Application contact:* Kevin Roane, Director, Office of Graduate Admission, 732-571-3452, Fax: 732-263-5123, E-mail: gradadm@monmouth.edu.

Montclair State University, The Graduate School, College of Education and Human Services, Department of Curriculum and Teaching, Montclair, NJ 07043-1624. Offers education (M Ed); educational technology (M Ed); learning disabled teacher consultant (Certificate); school library media specialist (Certificate); teaching (MAT, Certificate), including art (MAT), biological science (MAT), early childhood education (P-3) (MAT), earth science (MAT), elementary education (K-8) (MAT), English (MAT), French (MAT), health and physical education (MAT), health education (MAT), home economics (MAT), mathematics (MAT), music (MAT), physical education (MAT), physical science (MAT), social studies (MAT), Spanish (MAT), teacher of ESL (MAT), teacher of students with disabilities (MAT). Part-time and evening/weekend programs available. *Faculty:* 17 full-time (12 women), 29 part-time/adjunct (21 women). *Students:* 124 full-time (63 women), 174 part-time (126 women). Average age 31. 112 applicants, 69% accepted, 59 enrolled. In 2009, 179 master's, 2 other advanced degrees awarded. *Degree requirements:* For master's, comprehensive exam, field experience. *Entrance requirements:* For master's, GRE, 2 letters of recommendation. Additional exam requirements/recommendations for international students: Required—TOEFL (minimum score 83 computer-based), or IELTS. *Application deadline:* For fall admission, 2/15 for domestic and international students; for spring admission, 9/15 for domestic and international students. Applications are processed on a rolling basis. Application fee: $60. Electronic applications accepted. *Expenses:* Tuition, area resident: Part-time $486.74 per credit. Tuition, state resident: part-time $486.74 per credit. Tuition, nonresident:

part-time $751.34 per credit. Tuition and fees vary according to degree level and program. *Financial support:* In 2009–10, 12 research assistantships with full tuition reimbursements (averaging $7,000 per year) were awarded; Federal Work-Study, scholarships/grants, and unspecified assistantships also available. Support available to part-time students. Financial award application deadline: 3/1; financial award applicants required to submit FAFSA. *Unit head:* Dr. David Schwarzer, Chairperson, 973-655-5187. *Application contact:* Amy Aiello, Director of Graduate Admissions and Operations, 973-655-5147, Fax: 973-655-7869, E-mail: graduate.school@montclair.edu.

Montclair State University, The Graduate School, College of Education and Human Services, Department of Early Childhood, Elementary and Literacy Education, Montclair, NJ 07043-1624. Offers early childhood education and teaching students with disabilities (MAT); early childhood special education (M Ed, Certificate); early childhood/elementary education (M Ed); elementary education with disabilities (MAT); elementary school teacher (Certificate); learning disabilities (Certificate); reading (MA, Certificate); reading specialist (Certificate). Part-time and evening/weekend programs available. *Faculty:* 17 full-time (15 women), 68 part-time/adjunct (52 women). *Students:* 124 full-time (105 women), 274 part-time (257 women). Average age 31. 139 applicants, 65% accepted, 75 enrolled. In 2009, 85 master's awarded. *Degree requirements:* For master's, comprehensive exam, clinical experience, portfolio. *Entrance requirements:* For master's, GRE, 2 letters of recommendation. Additional exam requirements/recommendations for international students: Required—TOEFL (minimum score 83 computer-based), or IELTS. *Application deadline:* For fall admission, 6/1 for international students; for spring admission, 10/1 for international students. Applications are processed on a rolling basis. Application fee: $60. Electronic applications accepted. *Expenses:* Tuition, area resident: Part-time $486.74 per credit. Tuition, state resident: part-time $486.74 per credit. Tuition, nonresident: part-time $751.34 per credit. Tuition and fees vary according to degree level and program. *Financial support:* In 2009–10, 12 research assistantships with full tuition reimbursements (averaging $7,000 per year) were awarded; Federal Work-Study, scholarships/grants, and unspecified assistantships also available. Support available to part-time students. Financial award application deadline: 3/1; financial award applicants required to submit FAFSA. *Unit head:* Dr. Tina Jacobowitz, Chairperson, 973-655-7191. *Application contact:* Amy Aiello, Director of Graduate Admissions and Operations, 973-655-5147, Fax: 973-655-7869, E-mail: graduate.school@montclair.edu.

Montreat College, School of Professional and Adult Studies, Montreat, NC 28757-1267. Offers business administration (MBA); K-6 education (MA Ed). Evening/weekend programs available. Postbaccalaureate distance learning degree programs offered. *Entrance requirements:* Additional exam requirements/recommendations for international students: Required—TOEFL (minimum score 500 paper-based; 190 computer-based).

Morehead State University, Graduate Programs, College of Education, Department of Curriculum and Instruction, Morehead, KY 40351. Offers curriculum and instruction (Ed S); elementary education (MA Ed), including elementary education, international education, middle school education, reading; secondary education (MA Ed); special education (MA Ed); teaching (MAT). Part-time and evening/weekend programs available. *Faculty:* 25 full-time (17 women), 2 part-time/adjunct (1 woman). *Students:* 25 full-time (22 women), 165 part-time (139 women); includes 4 minority (1 African American, 2 American Indian/Alaska Native, 1 Hispanic American). Average age 33. 148 applicants, 68% accepted, 48 enrolled. In 2009, 178 master's awarded. *Degree requirements:* For master's, comprehensive exam, thesis optional; for Ed S, thesis, oral exam. *Entrance requirements:* For master's, GRE General Test, minimum GPA of 2.75, teaching certificate; for Ed S, GRE General Test, interview, master's degree, minimum GPA of 3.5, work experience. Additional exam requirements/recommendations for international students: Required—TOEFL (minimum score 500 paper-based; 173 computer-based). *Application deadline:* For fall admission, 8/1 priority date for domestic and international students; for spring admission, 12/1 priority date for domestic and international students. Applications are processed on a rolling basis. Application fee: $30. Electronic applications accepted. *Expenses:* Tuition, state resident: full-time $6318; part-time $351 per credit hour. Tuition, nonresident: full-time $15,804; part-time $878 per credit hour. *Financial support:* In 2009–10, 2 teaching assistantships (averaging $6,000 per year) were awarded; career-related internships or fieldwork, Federal Work-Study, and unspecified assistantships also available. Financial award application deadline: 3/15; financial award applicants required to submit FAFSA. *Faculty research:* Communicative competence of learning-disabled students, teaching social studies in elementary schools, ungraded primary school organization, study skills. *Unit head:* Dr. James Knoll, Chair, 606-783-2598, Fax: 606-783-5044, E-mail: j.knoll@moreheadstate.edu. *Application contact:* Michelle Barber, Graduate Recruitment and Retention Assistant Director, 606-783-5127, Fax: 606-783-5061, E-mail: m.barber@moreheadstate.edu.

Morehead State University, Graduate Programs, College of Education, Department of Foundational and Graduate Studies in Education, Morehead, KY 40351. Offers adult and higher education (MA, Ed S); certified professional counselor (Ed S); counseling P-12 (MA); curriculum and instruction (Ed S); educational technology (MA Ed); instructional leadership (Ed S); school administration (MA); school counseling (Ed S); teacher leader business and marketing- content (MA Ed); teacher leader business and marketing- technology (MA Ed); teacher leader educational technology (MA Ed); teacher leader English (MA Ed); teacher leader gifted educ (MA Ed); teacher leader IECE—non-certification (MA Ed); teacher leader IECE certification (MA Ed); teacher leader interdisciplinary educaction P-5 (MA Ed); teacher leader middle grades 5-9 (MA Ed); teacher leader reading/writing—non-certification (MA Ed); teacher leader reading/writing certification (MA Ed); teacher leader school communication—non-certification (MA Ed); teacher leader school communication certification (MA Ed); teacher leader social studies (MA Ed); teacher leader special education (MA Ed). *Accreditation:* NCATE. Part-time and evening/weekend programs available. *Faculty:* 20 full-time (10 women), 7 part-time/adjunct (3 women). *Students:* 26 full-time (18 women), 371 part-time (295 women); includes 11 minority (9 African Americans, 1 American Indian/Alaska Native, 1 Hispanic American). Average age 35. 201 applicants, 73% accepted, 73 enrolled. In 2009, 105 master's, 5 other advanced degrees awarded. *Degree requirements:* For master's, thesis optional, oral and/or written comprehensive exams; for Ed S, thesis, oral exam. *Entrance requirements:* For master's, GRE General Test, minimum overall undergraduate GPA of 2.5; for Ed S, GRE General Test, interview, master's degree, minimum GPA of 3.5, work experience. Additional exam requirements/recommendations for international students: Required—TOEFL (minimum score 500 paper-based; 173 computer-based). *Application deadline:* For fall admission, 8/1 priority date for domestic and international students; for spring admission, 12/1 priority date for domestic and international students. Applications are processed on a rolling basis. Application fee: $30. Electronic applications accepted. *Expenses:* Tuition, state resident: full-time $6318; part-time $351 per credit hour. Tuition, nonresident: full-time $15,804; part-time $878 per credit hour. *Financial support:* In 2009–10, 2 research assistantships (averaging $10,000 per year) were awarded; career-related internships or fieldwork, Federal Work-Study, and unspecified assistantships also available. Financial award application deadline: 3/15; financial award applicants required to submit FAFSA. *Faculty research:* Character education, school accountability, computer applications for school administrators. *Unit head:* Dr. Cathy Gunn, Dean and Professor, 606-783-2040, Fax: 606-783-5029, E-mail: c.gunn@moreheadstate.edu. *Application contact:* Michelle Barber, Graduate Recruitment and Retention Assistant Director, 606-783-5127, Fax: 606-783-5061, E-mail: m.barber@moreheadstate.edu.

Morgan State University, School of Graduate Studies, School of Education and Urban Studies, Department of Advanced Studies, Leadership and Policy, Program in Elementary and Middle School Education, Baltimore, MD 21251. Offers elementary education (MS). *Accreditation:* NCATE. Part-time and evening/weekend programs available. *Degree requirements:* For master's, comprehensive exam, thesis optional. *Faculty research:* Multicultural education, cooperative learning, psychology of cognition.

Morgan State University, School of Graduate Studies, School of Education and Urban Studies, MAT Program, Baltimore, MD 21251. Offers elementary education (MAT); high school education (MAT); middle school education (MAT). Part-time programs available. *Degree*

Elementary Education

Morgan State University (continued)
requirements: For master's, comprehensive exam. *Entrance requirements:* For master's, GRE General Test or MAT. *Faculty research:* Multicultural education, cooperative learning, psychology of cognition.

Mount Saint Mary College, Division of Education, Newburgh, NY 12550-3494. Offers adolescence and special education (MS Ed); adolescence education (MS Ed); childhood and special education (MS Ed); childhood education (MS Ed); literacy (5-12) (Advanced Certificate); literacy (birth-6) (Advanced Certificate); literacy and special education (MS Ed); literacy/childhood (MS Ed); middle school (5-6) (MS Ed); middle school (7-9) (MS Ed); special education (1-6) (MS Ed); special education (7-12) (MS Ed). *Accreditation:* NCATE. Part-time and evening/weekend programs available. *Faculty:* 15 full-time (13 women), 16 part-time/adjunct (10 women). *Students:* 76 full-time (63 women), 226 part-time (188 women); includes 27 minority (7 African Americans, 3 Asian Americans or Pacific Islanders, 17 Hispanic Americans). Average age 30. 141 applicants, 56% accepted, 44 enrolled. In 2009, 142 master's awarded. *Application deadline:* Applications are processed on a rolling basis. Application fee: $45. *Expenses:* Tuition: Full-time $13,356; part-time $742 per credit. Required fees: $50 per semester. *Financial support:* In 2009–10, 106 students received support. Unspecified assistantships available. Financial award application deadline: 4/15; financial award applicants required to submit FAFSA. *Faculty research:* Learning and teaching styles, computers in special education, language development. *Unit head:* Dr. Theresa Lewis, Coordinator, 845-569-3149, Fax: 845-569-3535, E-mail: tlewis@msmc.edu. *Application contact:* Dr. Theresa Lewis, Coordinator, 845-569-3149, Fax: 845-569-3535, E-mail: tlewis@msmc.edu.

Mount St. Mary's College, Graduate Division, Department of Education, Specialization in Elementary Education, Los Angeles, CA 90049-1599. Offers MS. *Students:* 41 full-time (34 women), 19 part-time (16 women); includes 4 African Americans, 3 Asian Americans or Pacific Islanders, 15 Hispanic Americans. Average age 34. *Degree requirements:* For master's, thesis, research project. *Entrance requirements:* For master's, MAT, minimum GPA of 3.0. *Application deadline:* For fall admission, 7/15 priority date for domestic students; for spring admission, 11/15 priority date for domestic students. Application fee: $50 ($75 for international students). *Expenses:* Tuition: Part-time $730 per unit. Part-time tuition and fees vary according to degree level and program. *Financial support:* Career-related internships or fieldwork available. Financial award application deadline: 3/15; financial award applicants required to submit FAFSA. *Unit head:* Dr. Julie Feldman-Abe, Director, 213-477-2625, E-mail: jabe@msmc.la.edu. *Application contact:* Director of Graduate Admission.

Mount Saint Vincent University, Graduate Programs, Faculty of Education, Program in Elementary Education, Halifax, NS B3M 2J6, Canada. Offers M Ed, MA Ed, MA-R. Part-time and evening/weekend programs available. Postbaccalaureate distance learning degree programs offered (minimal on-campus study). *Degree requirements:* For master's, thesis (for some programs). *Entrance requirements:* For master's, bachelor's degree in education, 1 year of teaching experience. Electronic applications accepted. *Faculty research:* Curriculum theory, mathematics education, philosophy in teacher education, science education, literacy education.

Murray State University, College of Education, Department of Early Childhood and Elementary Education, Programs in Elementary Education/Reading and Writing, Murray, KY 42071. Offers elementary education (MA Ed, Ed S); reading and writing (MA Ed). *Accreditation:* NCATE. Part-time programs available. *Degree requirements:* For master's, comprehensive exam, thesis optional; for Ed S, comprehensive exam. *Entrance requirements:* For master's, minimum GPA of 2.5 for conditional admittance, 3.0 for unconditional; for Ed S, GRE General Test or MAT. Additional exam requirements/recommendations for international students: Required—TOEFL.

National-Louis University, National College of Education, Program in Elementary Education, Chicago, IL 60603. Offers MAT. Part-time and evening/weekend programs available. *Degree requirements:* For master's, student teaching experience. *Entrance requirements:* For master's, GRE, minimum GPA of 3.0. *Expenses:* Tuition: Full-time $17,160; part-time $715 per semester hour. Tuition and fees vary according to course load, degree level, campus/location and program.

Nazareth College of Rochester, Graduate Studies, Department of Education, Program in Inclusive Education-Childhood Level, Rochester, NY 14618-3790. Offers MS Ed. *Accreditation:* Teacher Education Accreditation Council. *Entrance requirements:* For master's, minimum GPA of 3.0.

New Jersey City University, Graduate Studies and Continuing Education, Debra Cannon Partridge Wolfe College of Education, Department of Elementary and Secondary Education, Jersey City, NJ 07305-1597. Offers elementary education (MAT); secondary education (MAT). Part-time and evening/weekend programs available. *Faculty:* 6. *Students:* 16 full-time (13 women), 44 part-time (32 women); includes 16 minority (3 African Americans, 5 Asian Americans or Pacific Islanders, 8 Hispanic Americans). Average age 32. In 2009, 24 master's awarded. *Entrance requirements:* Additional exam requirements/recommendations for international students: Required—TOEFL. *Application deadline:* For fall admission, 8/1 priority date for domestic students; for spring admission, 12/1 for domestic students. Applications are processed on a rolling basis. Application fee: $0. *Expenses:* Tuition, area resident: Part-time $456.75 per credit. Tuition, nonresident: part-time $842.55 per credit. Required fees: $65 per term. *Financial support:* Teaching assistantships, career-related internships or fieldwork and unspecified assistantships available. *Unit head:* Dr. Althea Hall, Coordinator, 201-200-2101, E-mail: ahall@njcu.edu. *Application contact:* Dr. Althea Hall, Coordinator, 201-200-2101, E-mail: ahall@njcu.edu.

New York Institute of Technology, Graduate Division, School of Education, Program in Childhood Education, Old Westbury, NY 11568-8000. Offers MS. Part-time and evening/weekend programs available. Postbaccalaureate distance learning degree programs offered. *Students:* 5 full-time (4 women), 14 part-time (11 women); includes 1 Asian American or Pacific Islander, 3 Hispanic Americans. Average age 35. In 2009, 3 master's awarded. *Entrance requirements:* Additional exam requirements/recommendations for international students: Required—TOEFL (minimum score 550 paper-based; 213 computer-based). *Application deadline:* For fall admission, 7/1 priority date for domestic students; for spring admission, 12/1 priority date for domestic students. Applications are processed on a rolling basis. Application fee: $50. Electronic applications accepted. *Expenses:* Tuition: Part-time $825 per credit. *Financial support:* Research assistantships with partial tuition reimbursements, career-related internships or fieldwork, institutionally sponsored loans, and tuition waivers (full and partial) available. Support available to part-time students. Financial award applicants required to submit FAFSA. *Unit head:* Dr. Michael Uttendorfer, Dean, 516-686-7706, Fax: 516-686-7655, E-mail: muttendo@nyit.edu. *Application contact:* Dr. Jacquelyn Nealon, Vice President for Enrollment Services, 516-686-7925, Fax: 516-686-7597, E-mail: jnealon@nyit.edu.

New York University, Steinhardt School of Culture, Education, and Human Development, Department of Teaching and Learning, Program in Early Childhood and Childhood Education, New York, NY 10012-1019. Offers childhood education (MA); childhood education/special education: childhood (MA); early childhood education (MA); positions of leadership: early childhood and elementary education (PhD). *Accreditation:* Teacher Education Accreditation Council. Part-time programs available. *Students:* 40 full-time (all women), 19 part-time (all women); includes 20 minority (4 African Americans, 10 Asian Americans or Pacific Islanders, 6 Hispanic Americans), 2 international. Average age 25. 140 applicants, 72% accepted, 23 enrolled. In 2009, 47 master's awarded. *Degree requirements:* For master's, thesis (for some programs); for doctorate, thesis/dissertation. *Entrance requirements:* For doctorate, GRE General Test, interview. Additional exam requirements/recommendations for international students: Required—TOEFL. *Application deadline:* For fall admission, 12/15 priority date for domestic and international students; for spring admission, 11/1 for domestic and international students. Applications are processed on a rolling basis. Application fee: $75. Electronic applications accepted. *Expenses:* Tuition: Full-time $30,528; part-time $1272 per credit. Required fees: $2177. *Financial support:* Fellowships with full and partial tuition reimbursements, career-related internships or fieldwork, Federal Work-Study, institutionally sponsored loans, scholarships/grants, tuition waivers (partial), and unspecified assistantships available. Support available to part-time students. Financial award application deadline: 2/1; financial award applicants required to submit FAFSA. *Faculty research:* Teacher evaluation and beliefs about teaching, early literacy development, language arts, child development and education, cultural differences. *Application contact:* 212-998-5030, Fax: 212-995-4328, E-mail: steinhardt.gradadmissions@nyu.edu.

Niagara University, Graduate Division of Education, Concentration in Teacher Education, Niagara Falls, Niagara University, NY 14109. Offers early childhood and childhood education (MS Ed); middle and adolescence education (MS Ed); special education (grades 1-12) (MS Ed). *Accreditation:* NCATE. *Entrance requirements:* For master's, GRE General Test or MAT. *Expenses:* Contact institution.

North Carolina Agricultural and Technical State University, Graduate School, School of Education, Department of Curriculum and Instruction, Program in Elementary Education, Greensboro, NC 27411. Offers MA Ed. *Accreditation:* NCATE. Part-time and evening/weekend programs available. *Degree requirements:* For master's, comprehensive exam, thesis or alternative, qualifying exam. *Entrance requirements:* For master's, GRE General Test, minimum GPA of 3.0.

North Carolina Central University, Division of Academic Affairs, School of Education, Department of Curriculum, Instruction and Professional Studies, Durham, NC 27707-3129. Offers curriculum and instruction (MA), including elementary education, middle grades education. *Accreditation:* NCATE. Part-time and evening/weekend programs available. *Degree requirements:* For master's, comprehensive exam, thesis or alternative. *Entrance requirements:* For master's, minimum GPA of 3.0 in major, 2.5 overall. Additional exam requirements/recommendations for international students: Required—TOEFL. *Faculty research:* Simulation of decision-making behavior of school boards.

North Carolina State University, Graduate School, College of Education, Department of Elementary Education, Raleigh, NC 27695. Offers M Ed. *Entrance requirements:* For master's, MAT or GRE, 3 letters of reference.

Northern Arizona University, Graduate College, College of Education, Department of Teaching and Learning, Flagstaff, AZ 86011. Offers early childhood education (M Ed); elementary education—certification (M Ed); elementary education—continuing professional (M Ed); secondary education—certification (M Ed); secondary education—continuing professional (M Ed). *Faculty:* 40 full-time (32 women). *Students:* 488 full-time (397 women), 599 part-time (535 women); includes 250 minority (25 African Americans, 77 American Indian/Alaska Native, 23 Asian Americans or Pacific Islanders, 125 Hispanic Americans), 2 international. Average age 29. 271 applicants, 93% accepted, 188 enrolled. In 2009, 555 master's awarded. *Degree requirements:* For master's, comprehensive exam (for some programs), thesis (for some programs). *Entrance requirements:* For master's, minimum GPA of 3.0. Additional exam requirements/recommendations for international students: Required—TOEFL (minimum score 550 paper-based; 213 computer-based; 80 iBT), IELTS (minimum score 7), or a bachelor's degree from an English-speaking university and demonstrated proficiency. *Application deadline:* For fall admission, 2/1 for domestic students, 9/1 for international students; for spring admission, 12/1 for domestic students. Applications are processed on a rolling basis. Application fee: $65. Electronic applications accepted. *Financial support:* In 2009–10, 7 teaching assistantships with partial tuition reimbursements (averaging $10,000 per year) were awarded. Financial award application deadline: 3/30. *Unit head:* Dr. Sandra J. Stone, Chair, 928-523-6166, E-mail: sandra.stone@nau.edu. *Application contact:* Dr. Sandra J. Stone, Chair, 928-523-6166, E-mail: sandra.stone@nau.edu.

Northern Illinois University, Graduate School, College of Education, Department of Teaching and Learning, De Kalb, IL 60115-2854. Offers curriculum and instruction (MS Ed, Ed D), including curriculum leadership (Ed D), elementary education (Ed D), secondary education (Ed D); early childhood education (MS Ed); elementary education (MS Ed); special education (MS Ed). Part-time and evening/weekend programs available. *Faculty:* 22 full-time (14 women), 2 part-time/adjunct (both women). *Students:* 50 full-time (38 women), 435 part-time (344 women); includes 107 minority (16 African Americans, 1 American Indian/Alaska Native, 12 Asian Americans or Pacific Islanders, 78 Hispanic Americans), 9 international. Average age 35. 154 applicants, 53% accepted, 57 enrolled. In 2009, 142 master's, 2 doctorates awarded. *Degree requirements:* For master's, comprehensive exam, thesis optional; for doctorate, thesis/dissertation, candidacy exam, dissertation defense. *Entrance requirements:* For master's, GRE General Test or MAT, minimum undergraduate GPA of 2.75; for doctorate, GRE General Test or MAT, minimum undergraduate GPA of 2.75, graduate 3.2. Additional exam requirements/recommendations for international students: Required—TOEFL (minimum score 550 paper-based; 213 computer-based). *Application deadline:* For fall admission, 6/1 for domestic students, 5/1 for international students; for spring admission, 11/1 for domestic students, 10/1 for international students. Applications are processed on a rolling basis. Application fee: $30. Electronic applications accepted. *Expenses:* Tuition, state resident: full-time $6576; part-time $274 per credit hour. Tuition, nonresident: full-time $13,152; part-time $548 per credit hour. Required fees: $1813; $75.53 per credit hour. Part-time tuition and fees vary according to course load. *Financial support:* In 2009–10, 20 research assistantships with full tuition reimbursements were awarded; fellowships with full tuition reimbursements, teaching assistantships with full tuition reimbursements, career-related internships or fieldwork, Federal Work-Study, scholarships/grants, tuition waivers (full), and unspecified assistantships also available. Support available to part-time students. Financial award applicants required to submit FAFSA. *Faculty research:* Teacher certification, stress reduction during student teaching, teaching history, portfolios in student teaching. *Unit head:* Dr. Helen Brantley, Chair, 815-753-0327, E-mail: tedur@niu.edu. *Application contact:* Gail Myers, E-mail: gmyers@niu.edu.

Northern Michigan University, College of Graduate Studies, College of Professional Studies, School of Education, Program in Elementary Education, Marquette, MI 49855-5301. Offers MA Ed. Part-time programs available. *Degree requirements:* For master's, thesis or alternative. *Entrance requirements:* For master's, minimum GPA of 3.0. *Faculty research:* Whole language research, literature-based reading, essential elements of instruction, supervision and improvement of instruction.

Northern State University, Division of Graduate Studies in Education, Program in Teaching and Learning, Aberdeen, SD 57401-7198. Offers educational studies (MS Ed); elementary classroom teaching (MS Ed); health, physical education, and coaching (MS Ed); language and literacy (MS Ed); secondary classroom teaching (MS Ed); special education (MS Ed). *Accreditation:* NCATE. Part-time and evening/weekend programs available. *Faculty:* 10 full-time (8 women). *Students:* 23 full-time (16 women), 35 part-time (17 women); includes 2 minority (1 American Indian/Alaska Native, 1 Asian American or Pacific Islander). Average age 32. In 2009, 26 master's awarded. *Degree requirements:* For master's, thesis optional. *Entrance requirements:* For master's, minimum GPA of 2.75. Additional exam requirements/recommendations for international students: Required—TOEFL (minimum score 550 paper-based; 213 computer-based; 76 iBT). *Application deadline:* For fall admission, 8/15 priority date for domestic students; for spring admission, 12/15 for domestic students. Applications are processed on a rolling basis. Application fee: $35. Electronic applications accepted. *Financial support:* In 2009–10, 18 teaching assistantships with partial tuition reimbursements (averaging $5,558 per year) were awarded; career-related internships or fieldwork, Federal Work-Study, institutionally sponsored loans, scholarships/grants, and unspecified assistantships also available. Support available to part-time students. Financial award application deadline: 3/1; financial award applicants required to submit FAFSA. *Application contact:* Tammy K. Griffith, Program Assistant, 605-626-2558, Fax: 605-626-7190, E-mail: griffith@northern.edu.

Northwestern Oklahoma State University, School of Professional Studies, Program in Elementary Education, Alva, OK 73717-2799. Offers M Ed. *Accreditation:* NCATE. Part-time programs available. *Faculty:* 10 full-time (7 women). *Students:* 1 (woman) full-time, 4 part-time (all women); includes 1 minority (American Indian/Alaska Native). 15 applicants, 100% accepted. In 2009, 3 master's awarded. *Degree requirements:* For master's, thesis optional, portfolio.

Entrance requirements: For master's, GRE General Test or MAT, minimum GPA of 2.75. *Application deadline:* Applications are processed on a rolling basis. Application fee: $15. *Financial support:* Federal Work-Study available. Support available to part-time students. Financial award application deadline: 5/1; financial award applicants required to submit FAFSA. *Unit head:* Dr. Sue Diel, Chair, 580-327-8451. *Application contact:* Leah Haines, Coordinator of Graduate Studies, 580-327-8410, E-mail: ldhaines@nwosu.edu.

Northwestern State University of Louisiana, Graduate Studies and Research, College of Education, Program in Elementary Education, Natchitoches, LA 71497. Offers MAT. *Degree requirements:* For master's, comprehensive exam, thesis or alternative. *Entrance requirements:* For master's, GRE General Test, minimum undergraduate GPA of 2.5.

Northwestern State University of Louisiana, Graduate Studies and Research, College of Education, Programs in Education, Natchitoches, LA 71497. Offers business and distributive education (M Ed); counseling (M Ed); early childhood education (M Ed); education (M Ed); education leadership (M Ed); educational technology (M Ed); elementary teaching (M Ed); English education (M Ed); home economics education (M Ed); mathematics education (M Ed); reading (M Ed); science education (M Ed); secondary teaching (M Ed); social sciences education (M Ed). *Degree requirements:* For master's, comprehensive exam, thesis or alternative. *Entrance requirements:* For master's, GRE General Test, minimum undergraduate GPA of 2.5.

Northwestern State University of Louisiana, Graduate Studies and Research, College of Education, Programs in Educational Leadership and Instruction, Natchitoches, LA 71497. Offers counseling (Ed S); educational leadership (Ed S); educational technology (Ed S); elementary teaching (Ed S); reading (Ed S); secondary teaching (Ed S); special education (Ed S). *Entrance requirements:* For degree, GRE General Test.

Northwestern University, The Graduate School, School of Education and Social Policy, Education and Social Policy Program, Evanston, IL 60035. Offers advanced teaching (MS); elementary education and policy (MS); higher education administration (MS); secondary teaching (MS). Part-time and evening/weekend programs available. *Faculty:* 3 full-time (all women), 20 part-time/adjunct (11 women). *Students:* 64 full-time (47 women), 94 part-time (70 women); includes 27 minority (11 African Americans, 1 American Indian/Alaska Native, 9 Asian Americans or Pacific Islanders, 6 Hispanic Americans). Average age 27. 117 applicants, 63% accepted, 57 enrolled. In 2009, 82 master's awarded. *Degree requirements:* For master's, research project. *Entrance requirements:* For master's, GRE General Test, Illinois State Board of Education Basic Skills Exam (secondary and elementary), bachelor's degree. *Application deadline:* For fall admission, 7/16 for domestic students; for winter admission, 11/7 for domestic students; for spring admission, 2/15 priority date for domestic students. Applications are processed on a rolling basis. Application fee: $100. Electronic applications accepted. *Financial support:* In 2009–10, 6 students received support, including 1 fellowship with partial tuition reimbursement available (averaging $16,000 per year); career-related internships or fieldwork, Federal Work-Study, institutionally sponsored loans, scholarships/grants, tuition waivers (partial), and unspecified assistantships also available. Financial award application deadline: 1/9; financial award applicants required to submit FAFSA. *Faculty research:* Cultural context and literacy, philosophy of education and interpretive discussion, productivity, enhancing research and teaching, motivation, new and junior faculty issues, professional development for K-12 teachers to improve math and science teaching, female/underrepresented students/faculty in STEM disciplines. *Unit head:* Dr. Sophie Haroutunian-Gordon, Director and Professor, 847-467-1458, Fax: 847-467-2495, E-mail: shg@northwestern.edu. *Application contact:* Bradley Wadle, Assistant Director, 847-491-3829, Fax: 847-467-2495, E-mail: msedapply@northwestern.edu.

Northwest Missouri State University, Graduate School, College of Education and Human Services, Department of Curriculum and Instruction, Program in Teaching: Elementary Self Contained, Maryville, MO 64468-6001. Offers MS Ed. *Accreditation:* NCATE. Part-time programs available. *Faculty:* 12 full-time (all women). *Students:* 3 full-time (all women), 5 part-time (all women). 4 applicants, 75% accepted, 2 enrolled. In 2009, 2 master's awarded. *Degree requirements:* For master's, comprehensive exam. *Entrance requirements:* For master's, GRE General Test, minimum undergraduate GPA of 2.75, teaching certificate, writing sample. Additional exam requirements/recommendations for international students: Required—TOEFL (minimum score 550 paper-based; 213 computer-based). *Application deadline:* For fall admission, 7/1 for domestic and international students; for spring admission, 11/15 for domestic and international students. Applications are processed on a rolling basis. Application fee: $0 ($50 for international students). Electronic applications accepted. *Expenses:* Tuition, state resident: part-time $296.34 per credit hour. Tuition, nonresident: part-time $510.43 per credit hour. *Financial support:* Application deadline: 4/1. *Unit head:* Dr. Carolyn McCall, Director, 660-562-1236. *Application contact:* Dr. Gregory Haddock, Dean of Graduate School, 660-562-1145, Fax: 660-562-1096, E-mail: gradsch@nwmissouri.edu.

Northwest Missouri State University, Graduate School, College of Education and Human Services, Department of Educational Leadership, Program in Educational Leadership, Maryville, MO 64468-6001. Offers educational leadership: elementary (MS Ed); educational leadership: secondary (MS Ed); elementary principalship (Ed S); secondary principalship (Ed S); superintendency (Ed S). *Accreditation:* NCATE. Part-time programs available. *Faculty:* 16 full-time (6 women). *Students:* 21 full-time (13 women), 60 part-time (39 women); includes 3 minority (1 African American, 1 Asian American or Pacific Islander, 1 Hispanic American). 30 applicants, 83% accepted, 17 enrolled. In 2009, 63 master's awarded. *Degree requirements:* For master's, comprehensive exam; for Ed S, comprehensive exam, thesis. *Entrance requirements:* For master's, GRE General Test, minimum undergraduate GPA of 2.75, teaching certificate, writing sample; for Ed S, minimum graduate GPA of 3.25. Additional exam requirements/recommendations for international students: Required—TOEFL (minimum score 550 paper-based; 213 computer-based). *Application deadline:* For fall admission, 7/1 for domestic and international students; for spring admission, 11/15 for domestic and international students. Application fee: $0 ($50 for international students). *Expenses:* Tuition, state resident: part-time $296.34 per credit hour. Tuition, nonresident: part-time $510.43 per credit hour. *Financial support:* In 2009–10, 5 research assistantships with full tuition reimbursements (averaging $6,000 per year), 1 teaching assistantship with full tuition reimbursement (averaging $6,000 per year) were awarded; unspecified assistantships also available. Financial award application deadline: 4/1; financial award applicants required to submit FAFSA. *Unit head:* Dr. Joyce Piveral, Chairperson, 660-562-1231. *Application contact:* Dr. Gregory Haddock, Dean of Graduate School, 660-562-1145, Fax: 660-562-1096, E-mail: gradsch@nwmissouri.edu.

Nova Southeastern University, Fischler School of Education and Human Services, Graduate Teacher Education Program, Fort Lauderdale, FL 33314-7796. Offers athletic administration (MS); brain research (MS, Ed S); charter school education/leadership (MS); cognitive and behavioral disabilities (MS); computer science education (Ed S); computer science education (K-12) (MS); curriculum and teaching (Ed S); curriculum, instruction and technology (MS); curriculum, instruction, management and administration (Ed S); early childhood education (MS); early literacy and reading (Ed S); early literacy education (MS); education technology (MS); educational leadership (administration K–12) (MS, Ed S); educational media (Ed S); educational media (K-12) (MS); elementary education (MS, Ed S), including ESOL endorsement (MS); English education (MS, Ed S); environmental education (MS); exceptional student education (MS), including ESOL endorsement; gifted education (MS, Ed S); interdisciplinary arts education (MS); management and administration of educational programs (MS); mathematics (MS); mathematics education (Ed S); multicultural early intervention (MS); pre-kindergarten/primary (MS); preschool education (MS); reading (MS); reading and TESOL (MS); reading education (Ed S); science (MS); science education (Ed S); secondary education (MS); social studies (MS, Ed S); Spanish language (MS); special education and reading (MS); teaching and learning (MA, MS), including curriculum and instruction (MA), elementary mathematics (MA), elementary reading (MA), K-12 technology integration (MA); teaching English to speakers of other languages (MS, Ed S); technology management and administration (Ed S); urban studies education (MS). Part-time and evening/weekend programs available. Postbaccalaureate distance learning degree programs offered (minimal on-campus study). *Faculty:* 72 full-time (43 women), 385 part-time/adjunct (252 women). *Students:* 196 full-time

(175 women), 1,304 part-time (1,128 women); includes 594 minority (471 African Americans, 5 American Indian/Alaska Native, 18 Asian Americans or Pacific Islanders, 100 Hispanic Americans). Average age 37. 2,610 applicants, 72% accepted, 1352 enrolled. In 2009, 836 other advanced degrees awarded. *Degree requirements:* For master's and Ed S, thesis, practicum, internship. *Entrance requirements:* For master's, MAT, GRE, CLAST, CBEST, PRAXIS I, General Knowledge Test, minimum GPA of 2.5; for Ed S, MAT or GRE, master's degree, teaching certificate, minimum GPA of 3.0. Additional exam requirements/recommendations for international students: Required—TSE (recommended, minimum score 50); Recommended—TOEFL (minimum score 550 paper-based; 213 computer-based; 80 iBT), IELTS (minimum score 6). *Application deadline:* For fall admission, 9/25 priority date for domestic and international students; for winter admission, 2/23 priority date for domestic and international students; for spring admission, 4/25 priority date for domestic and international students. Applications are processed on a rolling basis. Application fee: $50. Electronic applications accepted. *Financial support:* Federal Work-Study available. Support available to part-time students. Financial award application deadline: 4/15; financial award applicants required to submit FAFSA. *Faculty research:* School effectiveness, critical thinking, leadership skills acquisition, child education, multicultural education. *Unit head:* Dr. Ronald Kern, Dean of Academic Affairs, 800-986-3223 Ext. 7809, Fax: 954-262-3606, E-mail: rk429@nsu.nova.edu. *Application contact:* Dr. Jennifer Quinones Nottingham, Dean of Student Affairs, 800-986-3223 Ext. 1559.

Nyack College, School of Education, Nyack, NY 10960-3698. Offers childhood education (MS); childhood special education (MS); inclusive education (MS). Part-time and evening/weekend programs available. *Degree requirements:* For master's, comprehensive exam (for some programs), thesis (for some programs), field experience. *Entrance requirements:* For master's, GRE, baccalaureate degree with minimum GPA of 3.0, evidence of initial/provisional teaching certification. Additional exam requirements/recommendations for international students: Required—TOEFL (minimum score 500 paper-based), TWE (minimum score 4). *Expenses:* Contact institution.

Occidental College, Graduate Studies, Department of Education, Program in Elementary Education, Los Angeles, CA 90041-3314. Offers liberal studies (MAT). Part-time programs available. *Degree requirements:* For master's, comprehensive exam, graduate synthesis paper. *Entrance requirements:* For master's, GRE General Test, minimum GPA of 3.0. Additional exam requirements/recommendations for international students: Required—TOEFL (minimum score 625 paper-based; 263 computer-based). *Expenses:* Contact institution.

Oklahoma City University, Petree College of Arts and Sciences, Division of Education and Kinesiology Exercise Studies, Programs in Education, Oklahoma City, OK 73106-1402. Offers applied behavioral studies (M Ed); early childhood education (M Ed); elementary education (M Ed). Part-time and evening/weekend programs available. *Faculty:* 2 full-time (1 woman), 3 part-time/adjunct (all women). *Students:* 25 full-time (20 women), 13 part-time (9 women); includes 10 minority (8 African Americans, 2 American Indian/Alaska Native), 5 international. Average age 32. 45 applicants, 78% accepted, 18 enrolled. In 2009, 12 master's awarded. *Degree requirements:* For master's, thesis optional. *Entrance requirements:* For master's, minimum GPA of 3.0. Additional exam requirements/recommendations for international students: Required—TOEFL (minimum score 550 paper-based). *Application deadline:* For fall admission, 8/20 for domestic students; for spring admission, 1/6 for domestic students. Applications are processed on a rolling basis. Application fee: $50 ($70 for international students). *Expenses:* Tuition: Full-time $15,930; part-time $885 per hour. *Financial support:* Fellowships with partial tuition reimbursements, career-related internships or fieldwork, Federal Work-Study, and tuition waivers (partial) available. Support available to part-time students. Financial award application deadline: 8/1; financial award applicants required to submit FAFSA. *Faculty research:* Adult literacy, cognition, reading strategies. *Unit head:* Dr. Lois Lawler-Brown, Chair, 405-208-5374, Fax: 405-208-6012, E-mail: llbrown@okcu.edu. *Application contact:* Michelle Lockhart, Director, Admissions, 800-633-7242, Fax: 405-208-5916, E-mail: gadmissions@okcu.edu.

Old Dominion University, Darden College of Education, Program in Elementary/Middle Education, Norfolk, VA 23529. Offers elementary education (MS Ed); instructional technology (MS Ed); library science (MS Ed); middle school education (MS Ed). *Accreditation:* NCATE. Part-time and evening/weekend programs available. Postbaccalaureate distance learning degree programs offered (no on-campus study). *Faculty:* 20 full-time (16 women), 22 part-time/adjunct (2 women). *Students:* 109 full-time (103 women), 171 part-time (148 women); includes 41 minority (22 African Americans, 1 American Indian/Alaska Native, 10 Asian Americans or Pacific Islanders, 8 Hispanic Americans). Average age 33. 191 applicants, 76% accepted, 123 enrolled. In 2009, 155 master's awarded. *Degree requirements:* For master's, comprehensive exam. *Entrance requirements:* For master's, GRE General Test or MAT; PRAXIS I, SAT or ACT, minimum GPA of 2.8. Additional exam requirements/recommendations for international students: Required—TOEFL (minimum score 600 paper-based; 250 computer-based). *Application deadline:* For fall admission, 6/1 priority date for domestic students; for winter admission, 11/1 priority date for domestic students; for spring admission, 3/1 priority date for domestic students. Applications are processed on a rolling basis. Application fee: $50. Electronic applications accepted. *Expenses:* Tuition, state resident: full-time $8112; part-time $338 per credit. Tuition, nonresident: full-time $20,256; part-time $844 per credit. Required fees: $119 per semester. One-time fee: $50. *Financial support:* In 2009–10, 180 students received support, including teaching assistantships (averaging $9,000 per year); career-related internships or fieldwork, Federal Work-Study, institutionally sponsored loans, and scholarships/grants also available. Support available to part-time students. Financial award application deadline: 2/15; financial award applicants required to submit FAFSA. *Faculty research:* Education pre-K to 6, school librarianship. *Unit head:* Dr. Charlene Fleener, Graduate Program Director, 757-683-4374, E-mail: cfleener@odu.edu. *Application contact:* Alice McAdory, Director of Admissions, 757-683-3685, Fax: 757-683-3255, E-mail: gradadmit@odu.edu.

Olivet Nazarene University, Graduate School, Division of Education, Program in Elementary Education, Bourbonnais, IL 60914. Offers MAT. *Accreditation:* NCATE. Evening/weekend programs available. *Degree requirements:* For master's, thesis or alternative.

Oregon State University, Graduate School, College of Education, Program in Elementary Education, Corvallis, OR 97331. Offers MAT. *Accreditation:* NCATE. *Students:* 55. In 2009, 51 master's awarded. *Entrance requirements:* For master's, NTE, minimum GPA of 3.0 in last 90 hours of course work. Additional exam requirements/recommendations for international students: Required—TOEFL. *Application deadline:* For fall admission, 3/1 priority date for domestic students. Applications are processed on a rolling basis. Application fee: $50. *Expenses:* Tuition, state resident: full-time $9774; part-time $362 per credit. Tuition, nonresident: full-time $15,849; part-time $587 per credit. Required fees: $1639. Full-time tuition and fees vary according to course load and program. *Financial support:* Fellowships, Federal Work-Study and institutionally sponsored loans available. Support available to part-time students. Financial award application deadline: 2/1. *Faculty research:* Kindergarten curriculum, the reading-writing connection, authentic assessment, classroom management. *Unit head:* Dr. Kenneth J. Winograd, Chair, 541-737-5988, Fax: 541-737-2040, E-mail: winograk@oregonstate.edu. *Application contact:* Dr. Kenneth J. Winograd, Chair, 541-737-5988, Fax: 541-737-2040, E-mail: winograk@oregonstate.edu.

Ottawa University, Graduate Studies-Arizona, Program in Education, Ottawa, KS 66067-3399. Offers community college counseling (MA); curriculum and instruction (MA); early childhood (MA); education intervention (MA); education leadership (MA); education technology (MA); Montessori early childhood education (MA); Montessori elementary education (MA); professional development (MA); school guidance counseling (MA); special education—cross categorical (MA). Programs offered in Mesa, Phoenix, Tempe and West Valley, AZ. *Accreditation:* NCATE. Part-time programs available. *Degree requirements:* For master's, thesis or alternative. *Entrance requirements:* For master's, minimum undergraduate GPA of 3.0, copy of current state certification or teaching license. Additional exam requirements/recommendations for international students: Required—TOEFL (minimum score 550 paper-based; 213 computer-based). Electronic applications accepted. *Expenses:* Contact institution.

Elementary Education

Our Lady of the Lake University of San Antonio, School of Professional Studies, Program in Early Elementary Education, San Antonio, TX 78207-4689. Offers M Ed. Part-time programs available. *Students:* 1 (woman) full-time, 4 part-time (3 women); all minorities (all Hispanic Americans). Average age 40. In 2009, 5 master's awarded. *Expenses:* Tuition: Full-time $12,330; part-time $685 per contact hour. Required fees: $139; $12 per contact hour. $57 per semester. Tuition and fees vary according to campus/location. *Unit head:* Dr. Cullen Grinnan, 210-434-6711 Ext. 8928, E-mail: ctgrinnan@lake.ollusa.edu. *Application contact:* Dr. Cullen Grinnan, 210-434-6711 Ext. 8928, E-mail: ctgrinnan@lake.ollusa.edu.

Our Lady of the Lake University of San Antonio, School of Professional Studies, Program in Generic Special Education, San Antonio, TX 78207-4689. Offers elementary education (M Ed). Part-time and evening/weekend programs available. *Students:* 6 full-time (5 women), 16 part-time (15 women); includes 13 minority (2 African Americans, 11 Hispanic Americans). Average age 37. In 2009, 10 master's awarded. *Degree requirements:* For master's, comprehensive exam, thesis optional, examination for the Certification of Education in Texas. *Entrance requirements:* For master's, GRE General Test or MAT, interview. Additional exam requirements/recommendations for international students: Required—TOEFL. *Application deadline:* Applications are processed on a rolling basis. Application fee: $25 ($50 for international students). Electronic applications accepted. *Expenses:* Tuition: Full-time $12,330; part-time $685 per contact hour. Required fees: $139; $12 per contact hour. $57 per semester. Tuition and fees vary according to campus/location. *Financial support:* Career-related internships or fieldwork and tuition waivers (partial) available. Financial award application deadline: 4/15. *Unit head:* Dr. Cullen Grinnan, Coordinator, 210-434-6711, E-mail: ctgrinnan@lake.ollusa.edu. *Application contact:* 210-434-6711 Ext. 2314, Fax: 210-431-4036, E-mail: gradadm@lake.ollusa.edu.

Pace University, School of Education, New York, NY 10038. Offers administration and supervision (MS Ed); adolescent education (MST); childhood education (MST); curriculum and instruction (MS); education (MST); literacy (MSE); school business management (Certificate); teaching students with disabilities (MSE); teaching visual arts (MST). *Accreditation:* NCATE. Part-time and evening/weekend programs available. *Students:* 235 full-time (177 women), 766 part-time (515 women); includes 158 minority (58 African Americans, 1 American Indian/Alaska Native, 37 Asian Americans or Pacific Islanders, 62 Hispanic Americans), 7 international. Average age 30. 332 applicants, 83% accepted, 165 enrolled. In 2009, 669 master's, 34 other advanced degrees awarded. *Degree requirements:* For master's, internship. *Entrance requirements:* For master's, interview, teaching certificate. Additional exam requirements/recommendations for international students: Required—TOEFL. *Application deadline:* For fall admission, 7/31 priority date for domestic students; for spring admission, 11/30 for domestic students. Applications are processed on a rolling basis. Application fee: $70. Electronic applications accepted. *Expenses:* Contact institution. *Financial support:* Research assistantships, career-related internships or fieldwork and Federal Work-Study available. Support available to part-time students. Financial award applicants required to submit FAFSA. *Unit head:* Dr. Harriet Feldman, Interim Dean, 212-346-1512. *Application contact:* Susan Ford-Goldschein, Director of Admissions, 212-346-1652, Fax: 212-346-1585, E-mail: gradnyc@pace.edu.

Pacific University, College of Education, Forest Grove, OR 97116-1797. Offers early childhood education (MAT); education (MAE); elementary education (MAT); high school education (MAT); middle school education (MAT); special education (MAT); visual function in learning (M Ed). *Accreditation:* NCATE. Part-time and evening/weekend programs available. *Degree requirements:* For master's, research project. *Entrance requirements:* For master's, California Basic Educational Skills Test, PRAXIS II, minimum undergraduate GPA of 2.75, 3.0 graduate. Additional exam requirements/recommendations for international students: Required—TOEFL. Electronic applications accepted. *Expenses:* Contact institution. *Faculty research:* Defining a culturally competent classroom, technology in the k-12 classroom, Socratic seminars, social studies education.

Pfeiffer University, School of Education, Misenheimer, NC 28109-0960. Offers elementary education (MS); teaching (MAT). *Accreditation:* NCATE. *Entrance requirements:* For master's, GRE, MAT, minimum GPA of 2.75.

Pittsburg State University, Graduate School, College of Education, Department of Curriculum and Instruction, Pittsburg, KS 66762. Offers classroom reading teacher (MS); early childhood education (MS); elementary education (MS); reading (MS); reading specialist (MS); secondary education (MS); teaching (MAT). *Accreditation:* NCATE. *Degree requirements:* For master's, thesis or alternative. *Entrance requirements:* For master's, GRE or MAT. *Expenses:* Tuition, state resident: full-time $4212; part-time $176 per credit. Tuition, nonresident: full-time $11,530; part-time $480 per credit. Required fees: $940; $43 per credit. Tuition and fees vary according to course level, course load, degree level, campus/location, reciprocity agreements and student level.

Plymouth State University, College of Graduate Studies, Graduate Studies in Education, Program in Elementary Education, Plymouth, NH 03264-1595. Offers M Ed. *Accreditation:* NCATE. Part-time and evening/weekend programs available. *Entrance requirements:* For master's, MAT, minimum GPA of 3.0.

Plymouth State University, College of Graduate Studies, Graduate Studies in Education, Program in K-12 Education, Plymouth, NH 03264-1595. Offers M Ed. *Accreditation:* NCATE. Part-time and evening/weekend programs available. *Degree requirements:* For master's, PRAXIS. *Entrance requirements:* For master's, MAT, minimum GPA of 3.0.

Portland State University, Graduate Studies, School of Education, Department of Curriculum and Instruction, Portland, OR 97207-0751. Offers early childhood education (MA, MS); education (M Ed, MA, MS); educational leadership: curriculum and instruction (Ed D); educational media/school librarianship (MA, MS); elementary education (M Ed, MAT, MST); reading (MA, MS); secondary education (M Ed, MAT, MST). *Accreditation:* NCATE. Part-time programs available. *Degree requirements:* For master's, comprehensive exam, thesis or alternative; for doctorate, thesis/dissertation. *Entrance requirements:* For master's, California Basic Educational Skills Test, minimum GPA of 3.0 in upper-division course work or 2.75 overall. Additional exam requirements/recommendations for international students: Required—TOEFL (minimum score 550 paper-based; 213 computer-based). *Faculty research:* Early literacy, characteristics of successful teachers of at-risk students, participation of women/minorities in technology courses, selection of cooperating teachers.

Prescott College, Graduate Programs, Program in Education, Prescott, AZ 86301. Offers early childhood education (MA); early childhood special education (MA); education (MA); elementary education (MA); environmental education leadership and administration (MA); equine-assisted experiential learning (MA); school guidance counseling (MA); secondary education (MA); special education, learning disability (MA); special education, mental retardation (MA); special education, serious emotional disability (MA); student-directed independent study (MA); sustainability education (PhD). Part-time programs available. Postbaccalaureate distance learning degree programs offered (minimal on-campus study). *Faculty:* 3 full-time (1 woman), 79 part-time/adjunct (41 women). *Students:* 75 full-time (44 women), 46 part-time (36 women); includes 18 minority (3 African Americans, 3 American Indian/Alaska Native, 4 Asian Americans or Pacific Islanders, 8 Hispanic Americans), 2 international. Average age 39. 66 applicants, 67% accepted, 31 enrolled. In 2009, 22 master's, 4 doctorates awarded. *Degree requirements:* For master's, thesis, fieldwork or internship, practicum; for doctorate, thesis/dissertation. *Entrance requirements:* For master's, 2 letters of recommendation, resume; for doctorate, 3 letters of recommendation, resume, official transcripts, personal statement, program proposal. Additional exam requirements/recommendations for international students: Required—TOEFL (minimum score 500 paper-based; 173 computer-based). *Application deadline:* For fall admission, 4/15 priority date for domestic and international students; for spring admission, 9/15 priority date for domestic and international students. Applications are processed on a rolling basis. Application fee: $40. Electronic applications accepted. *Expenses:* Tuition: Full-time $14,712; part-time $613 per credit. Required fees: $50 per term. One-time fee: $150. Tuition and fees vary according to course load and degree level. *Financial support:* Career-related internships or fieldwork and Federal Work-Study available. Financial award applicants required to submit FAFSA. *Unit head:* Noel Caniglia, Chair, 928-358-3201, Fax: 928-776-5151, E-mail: ncaniglia@prescott.edu. *Application contact:* Kerstin Alicki, Admissions Counselor, 877-412-8705, Fax: 928-277-4695, E-mail: admissions@prescott.edu.

Providence College, Graduate Studies, Department of Education, Program in Special Education, Providence, RI 02918. Offers elementary special education (M Ed), including elementary, secondary. Part-time and evening/weekend programs available. *Faculty:* 4 full-time (3 women), 39 part-time/adjunct (22 women). *Students:* 11 full-time (8 women), 38 part-time (29 women); includes 1 minority (Hispanic American). Average age 31. 14 applicants, 100% accepted. In 2009, 35 master's awarded. *Degree requirements:* For master's, comprehensive exam. *Entrance requirements:* For master's, GRE General Test. Additional exam requirements/recommendations for international students: Required—TOEFL (minimum score 550 paper-based; 213 computer-based; 80 iBT). *Application deadline:* For fall admission, 8/1 priority date for domestic and international students; for spring admission, 12/1 priority date for domestic and international students. Applications are processed on a rolling basis. Application fee: $55. *Expenses:* Tuition: Full-time $9909; part-time $367 per credit. One-time fee: $200. Tuition and fees vary according to course load and program. *Financial support:* In 2009–10, 1 research assistantship with full tuition reimbursement (averaging $8,400 per year) was awarded; career-related internships or fieldwork and unspecified assistantships also available. Support available to part-time students. Financial award application deadline: 8/1; financial award applicants required to submit FAFSA. *Unit head:* Diane LaMontagne, Director, 401-865-2912, Fax: 401-865-1147, E-mail: dlamonta@providence.edu. *Application contact:* Carol A. Daniels, Coordinator of Graduate Faculty and Administrative Services, 401-865-2247, Fax: 401-865-1147, E-mail: daniels@providence.edu.

Providence College, Graduate Studies, Department of Education, Programs in Administration, Providence, RI 02918. Offers elementary administration (M Ed); secondary administration (M Ed). Part-time and evening/weekend programs available. *Faculty:* 4 full-time (3 women), 39 part-time/adjunct (22 women). *Students:* 7 full-time (3 women), 50 part-time (23 women); includes 1 minority (African American). Average age 36. 7 applicants, 100% accepted. In 2009, 23 master's awarded. *Degree requirements:* For master's, comprehensive exam. *Entrance requirements:* For master's, GRE General Test. Additional exam requirements/recommendations for international students: Required—TOEFL (minimum score 550 paper-based; 213 computer-based; 80 iBT). *Application deadline:* For fall admission, 8/1 priority date for domestic and international students; for spring admission, 12/1 priority date for domestic and international students. Applications are processed on a rolling basis. Application fee: $55. *Expenses:* Tuition: Full-time $9909; part-time $367 per credit. One-time fee: $200. Tuition and fees vary according to course load and program. *Financial support:* In 2009–10, research assistantships with full tuition reimbursements (averaging $8,400 per year); career-related internships or fieldwork, institutionally sponsored loans, and unspecified assistantships also available. Support available to part-time students. Financial award application deadline: 8/1; financial award applicants required to submit FAFSA. *Unit head:* Francis J. Leary, Director, 401-865-2247, Fax: 401-865-1147, E-mail: fleary@providence.edu. *Application contact:* Carol A. Daniels, Coordinator of Graduate Faculty and Administrative Services, 401-865-2247, Fax: 401-865-1147, E-mail: daniels@providence.edu.

Purdue University, Graduate School, School of Education, Department of Curriculum and Instruction, West Lafayette, IN 47907. Offers agricultural and extension education (PhD, Ed S); agriculture and extension education (MS, MS Ed); art education (PhD); consumer and family sciences and extension education (MS Ed, PhD, Ed S); curriculum studies (MS Ed, PhD, Ed S); educational technology (MS Ed, PhD, Ed S); elementary education (MS Ed); foreign language education (MS Ed, PhD, Ed S); industrial technology (PhD, Ed S); language arts (MS Ed, PhD, Ed S); literacy (MS Ed, PhD, Ed S); mathematics/science education (MS, MS Ed, PhD, Ed S); social studies (MS Ed, PhD); social studies education (Ed S); vocational/industrial education (MS Ed, PhD, Ed S); vocational/technical education (MS Ed, PhD, Ed S). *Accreditation:* NCATE. Part-time and evening/weekend programs available. *Degree requirements:* For master's, thesis optional; for doctorate, thesis/dissertation, oral and written exams; for Ed S, oral presentation, project. *Entrance requirements:* For master's, GRE General Test, minimum B average; for doctorate, GRE General Test; for Ed S, GRE, minimum B average. Additional exam requirements/recommendations for international students: Required—TOEFL. Electronic applications accepted. *Faculty research:* Literacy acquisition and development, teacher beliefs and knowledge, recruitment and retention of underrepresented students, economic education, literacy discourse.

Purdue University North Central, Program in Education, Westville, IN 46391-9542. Offers elementary education (MS Ed). *Accreditation:* NCATE. Part-time and evening/weekend programs available. *Degree requirements:* For master's, one foreign language. *Entrance requirements:* For master's, GRE, minimum GPA of 3.0. Electronic applications accepted. *Faculty research:* Diversity, integration.

Queens College of the City University of New York, Division of Graduate Studies, Division of Education, Department of Elementary and Early Childhood Education, Flushing, NY 11367-1597. Offers bilingual education (MS Ed); childhood education (MA); early childhood education (MA); elementary education (MS Ed, AC); literacy (MS Ed). Part-time and evening/weekend programs available. *Faculty:* 31 full-time (25 women). *Students:* 98 full-time (88 women), 430 part-time (392 women). 436 applicants, 64% accepted, 212 enrolled. In 2009, 220 master's awarded. *Degree requirements:* For master's, research project; for AC, thesis optional. *Entrance requirements:* For master's, minimum GPA of 3.0. Additional exam requirements/recommendations for international students: Required—TOEFL. *Application deadline:* For fall admission, 4/1 for domestic students; for spring admission, 11/1 for domestic students. Applications are processed on a rolling basis. Application fee: $125. *Expenses:* Tuition, state resident: full-time $7360; part-time $310 per credit. Tuition, nonresident: part-time $575 per credit. One-time fee: $195 full-time; $145.25 part-time. *Financial support:* Career-related internships or fieldwork, Federal Work-Study, institutionally sponsored loans, and tuition waivers (partial) available. Support available to part-time students. Financial award application deadline: 4/1; financial award applicants required to submit FAFSA. *Unit head:* Dr. Myra Zarnowski, Chairperson, 718-997-5328. *Application contact:* Mario Caruso, Director of Graduate Admissions, 718-997-5200, Fax: 718-997-5193, E-mail: graduate_admissions@qc.edu.

Queens University of Charlotte, Wayland H. Cato, Jr. School of Education, Charlotte, NC 28274-0002. Offers education in literacy (M Ed); elementary education (MAT); school administration (MSA). *Accreditation:* NCATE. Part-time and evening/weekend programs available. *Degree requirements:* For master's, comprehensive exam. *Entrance requirements:* For master's, GRE General Test. *Expenses:* Contact institution.

Quinnipiac University, Division of Education, Program in Elementary Education, Hamden, CT 06518-1940. Offers MAT. *Accreditation:* NCATE. *Faculty:* 10 full-time (7 women), 5 part-time/adjunct (3 women). *Students:* 76 full-time (69 women), 1 (woman) part-time; includes 5 minority (1 African American, 2 Asian Americans or Pacific Islanders, 2 Hispanic Americans). 84 applicants, 88% accepted, 63 enrolled. In 2009, 58 master's awarded. *Entrance requirements:* For master's, PRAXIS I, minimum GPA of 2.67, interview. Additional exam requirements/recommendations for international students: Required—TOEFL (minimum score 575 paper-based; 233 computer-based; 90 iBT), IELTS (minimum score 6.5). *Application deadline:* For fall admission, 3/31 priority date for domestic students. Applications are processed on a rolling basis. Application fee: $45. Electronic applications accepted. *Expenses:* Tuition: Full-time $16,030; part-time $770 per credit. Required fees: $630; $35 per credit. *Financial support:* Career-related internships or fieldwork, scholarships/grants, and tuition waivers (partial) available. Financial award application deadline: 4/15; financial award applicants required to submit FAFSA. *Faculty research:* Multicultural and urban education, challenges of teaching diverse learners, socio-cultural nature of learning. *Unit head:* Dr. Bernadine Krawczyk, Assistant Dean, Division of Education, 203-582-3510, Fax: 203-582-3473, E-mail: bernadine.krawczyk@quinnipiac.edu. *Application contact:* Jennifer Boutin, Associate Director of Graduate Admissions, 203-582-8672, Fax: 203-582-3443, E-mail: jennifer.boutin@quinnipiac.edu.

Regent University, Graduate School, School of Education, Virginia Beach, VA 23464-9800. Offers career switcher (M Ed); Christian school program (M Ed); cross-categorical special education (M Ed); education (M Ed, Ed D); education licensure (M Ed); educational leadership (M Ed); elementary education (M Ed); individualized degree plan (M Ed); leadership in character education (M Ed); master teacher (M Ed); mathematics education (M Ed); special education leadership (Ed S); student affairs (M Ed); TESOL (M Ed). *Accreditation:* Teacher Education Accreditation Council. Part-time and evening/weekend programs available. Postbaccalaureate distance learning degree programs offered (minimal on-campus study). *Faculty:* 26 full-time (13 women), 104 part-time/adjunct (78 women). *Students:* 141 full-time (116 women), 622 part-time (488 women); includes 218 minority (186 African Americans, 1 American Indian/Alaska Native, 10 Asian Americans or Pacific Islanders, 21 Hispanic Americans), 8 international. Average age 39. 509 applicants, 60% accepted, 176 enrolled. In 2009, 212 master's, 15 doctorates awarded. *Degree requirements:* For master's, thesis or alternative; for doctorate, comprehensive exam, thesis/dissertation. *Entrance requirements:* For master's, MAT, minimum undergraduate GPA of 2.75, writing sample, resume, recommendations, interview; for doctorate, GRE, writing sample, 3 years of relevant professional experience, master's-level paper, copies of published work, resume, transcripts, interview, recommendations. Additional exam requirements/recommendations for international students: Required—TOEFL (minimum score 577 paper-based; 233 computer-based). *Application deadline:* For fall admission, 4/1 priority date for domestic students; for spring admission, 10/15 priority date for domestic students. Applications are processed on a rolling basis. Application fee: $50. Electronic applications accepted. *Expenses:* Contact institution. *Financial support:* In 2009–10, 480 students received support; fellowships, career-related internships or fieldwork, scholarships/grants, tuition waivers (full and partial), and unspecified assistantships available. Support available to part-time students. Financial award application deadline: 4/1; financial award applicants required to submit FAFSA. *Faculty research:* Character development and discipline for children, education leadership development, diversity in schools, classroom management, technology in education settings. *Unit head:* Dr. Alan A. Arroyo, Dean, 757-352-4261, Fax: 757-352-4318, E-mail: alanarr@regent.edu. *Application contact:* Matthew Chadwick, Director of Admissions, 800-373-5504, Fax: 757-352-4381, E-mail: admissions@regent.edu.

Regis College, Department of Education, Weston, MA 02493. Offers elementary teacher (MAT); reading (MAT); special education (MAT). Part-time and evening/weekend programs available. *Faculty:* 2 full-time (both women), 5 part-time/adjunct (all women). *Students:* 2 full-time (both women), 49 part-time (42 women); includes 1 minority (Asian American or Pacific Islander). Average age 36. 8 applicants, 88% accepted, 4 enrolled. In 2009, 11 master's awarded. *Degree requirements:* For master's, thesis. *Entrance requirements:* For master's, GRE or MAT. Additional exam requirements/recommendations for international students: Required—TOEFL. *Application deadline:* Applications are processed on a rolling basis. Application fee: $50. Electronic applications accepted. *Expenses:* Tuition: Full-time $29,000; part-time $800 per credit. Tuition and fees vary according to course load, degree level and program. *Financial support:* In 2009–10, 1 student received support, including 1 fellowship with full tuition reimbursement available (averaging $11,970 per year); Federal Work-Study and scholarships/grants also available. Financial award applicants required to submit FAFSA. *Faculty research:* Reflective teaching, gender-based education, integrated teaching. *Unit head:* Dr. Leona McCaughey-Oreszak, Program Director, 781-768-7421, Fax: 781-768-7159, E-mail: leona.mccaughey-oreszak@regiscollege.edu. *Application contact:* Christine Petherick, Administrative Coordinator, Graduate Admission, 866-438-7344, Fax: 781-768-7071, E-mail: christine.petherick@regiscollege.edu.

Regis University, College for Professional Studies, Program in Teacher Education, Denver, CO 80221-1099. Offers adult learning, training, and development (M Ed); curriculum, instruction, and assessment (M Ed); early childhood (M Ed); educational technology (Certificate); elementary (M Ed); ESL (M Ed); fine arts (M Ed), including arts, music; instructional technology (M Ed); professional leadership (M Ed); reading (M Ed); secondary (M Ed); self-designed (M Ed); space studies (M Ed); special education (M Ed); teacher licensure (M Ed). Program also offered in Henderson and Las Vegas (Summerlin), NV. *Accreditation:* Teacher Education Accreditation Council. Part-time and evening/weekend programs available. Postbaccalaureate distance learning degree programs offered (no on-campus study). *Degree requirements:* For master's, thesis. *Entrance requirements:* For master's, resume, minimum GPA of 2.75, criminal background check. Additional exam requirements/recommendations for international students: Required—TOEFL (minimum score 213 computer-based), TWE (minimum score 5). Electronic applications accepted. *Faculty research:* Issues of equity in the middle school classroom, professional learning communities, school reform, socialinguistic and discursive obstacles to student integration, inclusive language arts curriculum.

Rhode Island College, School of Graduate Studies, Feinstein School of Education and Human Development, Department of Elementary Education, Providence, RI 02908-1991. Offers early childhood education (M Ed); elementary education (M Ed, MAT); reading (M Ed). *Accreditation:* NCATE. Part-time and evening/weekend programs available. *Faculty:* 10 full-time (6 women), 7 part-time/adjunct (5 women). *Students:* 15 full-time (12 women), 40 part-time (all women); includes 1 minority (Asian American or Pacific Islander), 1 international. Average age 32. In 2009, 47 master's awarded. *Degree requirements:* For master's, comprehensive exam (for some programs), comprehensive assessment. *Entrance requirements:* For master's, GRE General Test or MAT, PRAXIS II (elementary content knowledge), undergraduate transcripts; minimum undergraduate GPA of 3.0; copy of teaching certificate (when applicable); 3 letters of recommendation. Additional exam requirements/recommendations for international students: Recommended—TOEFL (minimum score 550 paper-based; 213 computer-based; 79 iBT). *Application deadline:* For fall admission, 3/15 for domestic students; for spring admission, 11/1 for domestic students. Applications are processed on a rolling basis. Application fee: $50. *Expenses:* Tuition, state resident: full-time $7440; part-time $310 per credit hour. Tuition, nonresident: full-time $14,784; part-time $616 per credit hour. Required fees: $552; $20 per credit. $70 per term. *Financial support:* Teaching assistantships with full tuition reimbursements, Federal Work-Study, scholarships/grants, and health care benefits available. Support available to part-time students. Financial award application deadline: 5/15; financial award applicants required to submit FAFSA. *Unit head:* Dr. Patricia Cordeiro, Chair, 401-456-8016. *Application contact:* Graduate Studies, 401-456-8700.

Rider University, Department of Graduate Education, Leadership and Counseling, Teacher Certification Program, Lawrenceville, NJ 08648-3001. Offers business education (Certificate); elementary education (Certificate); English as a second language (Certificate); English education (Certificate); mathematics education (Certificate); preschool to grade 3 (Certificate); science education (Certificate); social studies education (Certificate); world languages (Certificate), including French, German, Spanish. Part-time programs available. *Degree requirements:* For Certificate, internship, professional portfolio. *Entrance requirements:* For degree, PRAXIS, resume. Additional exam requirements/recommendations for international students: Required—TOEFL (minimum score 550 paper-based; 213 computer-based). Electronic applications accepted. *Faculty research:* Conceptual foundations for optimal development of creativity; creative theory, cognitive processes in mathematics learning, teacher collaboration.

Rivier College, School of Graduate Studies, Department of Education, Nashua, NH 03060. Offers curriculum and instruction (M Ed); early childhood education (M Ed); educational administration (M Ed); educational studies (M Ed); elementary education (M Ed); elementary education and general special education (M Ed); emotional and behavioral disorders (M Ed); general social education (M Ed); leadership and learning (Ed D, CAGS); learning disabilities (M Ed); learning disabilities and reading (M Ed); mental health counseling (MA); reading (M Ed); school counseling (M Ed). Part-time and evening/weekend programs available. *Faculty:* 13 full-time (9 women), 38 part-time/adjunct (25 women). *Students:* 87 full-time (78 women), 293 part-time (246 women); includes 10 minority (3 African Americans, 4 Asian Americans or Pacific Islanders, 3 Hispanic Americans). Average age 38. 182 applicants, 82% accepted, 72 enrolled. In 2009, 110 master's, 18 other advanced degrees awarded. *Degree requirements:* For master's, comprehensive exam (for some programs), internships. *Entrance requirements:* For master's, GRE General Test or MAT. *Application deadline:* Applications are processed on

a rolling basis. Application fee: $25. *Expenses:* Tuition: Part-time $447 per credit. *Financial support:* Available to part-time students. Application deadline: 2/1. *Unit head:* Dr. Patricia Howson, Chairman, 603-897-8562, E-mail: phowson@rivier.edu. *Application contact:* Mathew Kittredge, Director of Graduate Admissions, 603-897-8129, Fax: 603-897-8810, E-mail: mkittredge@rivier.edu.

Rockford College, Graduate Studies, Department of Education, Program in Elementary Education, Rockford, IL 61108-2393. Offers MAT. Initial certification track available. Part-time and evening/weekend programs available. *Degree requirements:* For master's, thesis optional. *Entrance requirements:* For master's, GRE General Test, basic skills test (for students seeking certification), 3 letters of recommendation. Additional exam requirements/recommendations for international students: Required—TOEFL (minimum score 550 paper-based; 213 computer-based; 79 iBT). Electronic applications accepted.

Roger Williams University, School of Education, Program in Elementary Education, Bristol, RI 02809. Offers MAT. Part-time and evening/weekend programs available. *Degree requirements:* For master's, state-mandated exams. *Entrance requirements:* For master's, resume, 3 letters of recommendation. Additional exam requirements/recommendations for international students: Recommended—IELTS. Electronic applications accepted. *Expenses:* Contact institution. *Faculty research:* Assistive technology; standards-based curricular development; professional development strategies, instruction, and assessment.

Rollins College, Hamilton Holt School, Program in Education, Winter Park, FL 32789-4499. Offers elementary education (M Ed, MAT); secondary education (MAT), including English, mathematics, music. Part-time and evening/weekend programs available. *Faculty:* 5 full-time (3 women), 3 part-time/adjunct (2 women). *Students:* 14 full-time (11 women), 26 part-time (25 women); includes 7 minority (4 African Americans, 3 Hispanic Americans). Average age 31. 27 applicants, 100% accepted, 27 enrolled. In 2009, 10 master's awarded. *Degree requirements:* For master's, comprehensive exam. *Entrance requirements:* For master's, GRE or MAT, interview. Additional exam requirements/recommendations for international students: Required—TOEFL. *Application deadline:* For fall admission, 7/16 for domestic students; for winter admission, 12/3 for domestic students; for spring admission, 4/22 for domestic students. Applications are processed on a rolling basis. Application fee: $50. *Expenses:* Contact institution. *Financial support:* Teaching assistantships, scholarships/grants available. Support available to part-time students. *Unit head:* Dr. J. Scott Hewit, Director, 407-646-2300, E-mail: jhewit@rollins.edu. *Application contact:* Rebecca Cordray, Coordinator of Records and Registration, 407-646-1568, Fax: 407-975-6430, E-mail: rcordray@rollins.edu.

Roosevelt University, Graduate Division, College of Education, Department of Teaching and Learning, Program in Elementary Education, Chicago, IL 60605. Offers MA.

Rosemont College, Schools of Graduate and Professional Studies, Program in Curriculum and Instruction, Rosemont, PA 19010-1699. Offers elementary certification (MA). Part-time and evening/weekend programs available. *Entrance requirements:* For master's, minimum college GPA of 3.0, 3 letters of recommendation. Additional exam requirements/recommendations for international students: Required—TOEFL. Electronic applications accepted.

Rowan University, Graduate School, College of Education, Department of Teacher Education, Program in Elementary Education, Glassboro, NJ 08028-1701. Offers MST. Part-time and evening/weekend programs available. *Students:* 10 full-time (8 women); includes 4 minority (2 African Americans, 2 Asian Americans or Pacific Islanders). Average age 25. In 2009, 11 master's awarded. *Degree requirements:* For master's, thesis. *Entrance requirements:* For master's, GRE General Test, minimum GPA of 2.8, 1 year of teaching experience. Additional exam requirements/recommendations for international students: Required—TOEFL. *Application deadline:* For spring admission, 2/15 priority date for domestic students. Application fee: $50. Electronic applications accepted. *Expenses:* Tuition, state resident: full-time $10,624; part-time $590 per semester hour. Tuition, nonresident: full-time $10,624; part-time $590 per semester hour. Required fees: $2320; $125 per semester hour. *Financial support:* Career-related internships or fieldwork, scholarships/grants, health care benefits, and unspecified assistantships available. Support available to part-time students. *Unit head:* Dr. Mira Lalovic-Hand, Interim Associate Provost/Director of Graduate School, 856-256-5120, E-mail: lalovic-hand@rowan.edu. *Application contact:* Karen Haynes, Graduate Coordinator, 856-256-4052, Fax: 856-256-4436, E-mail: haynes@rowan.edu.

Rowan University, Graduate School, College of Education, Department of Teacher Education, Program in Elementary School Teaching, Glassboro, NJ 08028-1701. Offers MA. Part-time and evening/weekend programs available. *Students:* 2 part-time (both women). Average age 36. In 2009, 1 master's awarded. *Degree requirements:* For master's, thesis. *Entrance requirements:* For master's, GRE General Test, minimum GPA of 2.8, 1 year of teaching experience. Additional exam requirements/recommendations for international students: Required—TOEFL. *Application deadline:* Applications are processed on a rolling basis. Application fee: $50. Electronic applications accepted. *Expenses:* Tuition, state resident: full-time $10,624; part-time $590 per semester hour. Tuition, nonresident: full-time $10,624; part-time $590 per semester hour. Required fees: $2320; $125 per semester hour. *Financial support:* Career-related internships or fieldwork, scholarships/grants, health care benefits, and unspecified assistantships available. Support available to part-time students. *Unit head:* Dr. Mira Lalovic-Hand, Interim Associate Provost/Director of Graduate School, 856-256-5120, E-mail: lalovic-hand@rowan.edu. *Application contact:* Karen Haynes, Graduate Coordinator, 856-256-4052, Fax: 856-256-4436, E-mail: haynes@rowan.edu.

Rutgers, The State University of New Jersey, New Brunswick, Graduate School of Education, Department of Learning and Teaching, Program in Early Childhood/Elementary Education, Piscataway, NJ 08854-8097. Offers Ed M, Ed D. Part-time programs available. Terminal master's awarded for partial completion of doctoral program. *Degree requirements:* For master's, comprehensive exam (for some programs); for doctorate, thesis/dissertation, qualifying exam. *Entrance requirements:* For master's, GRE General Test, minimum GPA of 3.0; for doctorate, GRE General Test, minimum GPA of 3.5. Additional exam requirements/recommendations for international students: Required—TOEFL. Electronic applications accepted.

Sacred Heart University, Graduate Programs, College of Education and Health Professions, Isabelle Farrington School of Education, Fairfield, CT 06825-1000. Offers administration (CAS); educational technology (MAT); elementary education (MAT); reading (CAS); secondary education (MAT); teaching (CAS). Part-time and evening/weekend programs available. Postbaccalaureate distance learning degree programs offered (minimal on-campus study). *Faculty:* 23 full-time (10 women). *Students:* 377 full-time (291 women), 691 part-time (495 women); includes 63 minority (31 African Americans, 2 American Indian/Alaska Native, 8 Asian Americans or Pacific Islanders, 22 Hispanic Americans), 2 international. Average age 34. 429 applicants, 90% accepted, 338 enrolled. In 2009, 409 master's, 66 other advanced degrees awarded. *Degree requirements:* For master's, thesis or alternative. *Entrance requirements:* For master's, PRAXIS (teacher certification/MAT); for CAS, PRAXIS I. Additional exam requirements/recommendations for international students: Required—TOEFL (minimum score 550 paper-based; 213 computer-based). *Application deadline:* Applications are processed on a rolling basis. Application fee: $50 ($100 for international students). Electronic applications accepted. *Expenses:* Contact institution. *Financial support:* Teaching assistantships with partial tuition reimbursements, career-related internships or fieldwork, institutionally sponsored loans, traineeships, tuition waivers (partial), and unspecified assistantships available. Support available to part-time students. Financial award applicants required to submit FAFSA. *Faculty research:* Reading education, learning theory, teacher preparation, education of underachievers. *Unit head:* Dr. Edward Malin, Director, 203-371-7800, Fax: 203-365-7513. *Application contact:* Kathy Dilks, Assistant Dean of Graduate Admissions, 203-365-7619, Fax: 203-365-4732, E-mail: gradstudies@sacredheart.edu.

Sage Graduate School, Graduate School, School of Education, Program in Childhood Education, Troy, NY 12180-4115. Offers MS Ed. *Accreditation:* NCATE. Part-time and evening/weekend programs available. *Faculty:* 15 full-time (9 women), 19 part-time/adjunct (16 women). *Students:* 8 full-time (7 women), 20 part-time (13 women); includes 1 minority (Hispanic

Elementary Education

Sage Graduate School (continued)

American). Average age 28. 20 applicants, 55% accepted, 6 enrolled. In 2009, 13 degrees awarded. *Degree requirements:* For master's, thesis. *Entrance requirements:* For master's, minimum GPA of 2.75, resume, 2 letters of recommendation, interview, assessment of writing skills. Additional exam requirements/recommendations for international students: Required—TOEFL (minimum score 550 paper-based; 213 computer-based). *Application deadline:* Applications are processed on a rolling basis. Application fee: $40. *Expenses:* Tuition: Full-time $10,620; part-time $590 per credit hour. *Financial support:* Federal Work-Study, scholarships/grants, and unspecified assistantships available. Support available to part-time students. Financial award application deadline: 3/1; financial award applicants required to submit FAFSA. *Faculty research:* The effects of teachers' personal characteristics on the instructional process. *Unit head:* Dr. Nancy A. DeKorp, Dean, 518-244-2496, Fax: 518-244-2334, E-mail: diefew@sage.edu. *Application contact:* Wendy D. Diefendorf, Director of Graduate and Adult Admission, 518-244-2443, Fax: 518-244-6880, E-mail: diefew@sage.edu.

Sage Graduate School, Graduate School, School of Education, Program in Childhood Education/Literacy, Troy, NY 12180-4115. Offers MS. Part-time and evening/weekend programs available. *Faculty:* 15 full-time (9 women), 19 part-time/adjunct (16 women). *Students:* 5 full-time (all women), 18 part-time (16 women). Average age 27. 12 applicants, 50% accepted, 4 enrolled. In 2009, 5 master's awarded. *Degree requirements:* For master's, thesis optional. *Entrance requirements:* For master's, minimum GPA of 2.75, resume, 2 letters of recommendation, interview, assessment of writing skills. Additional exam requirements/recommendations for international students: Required—TOEFL (minimum score 550 paper-based; 213 computer-based). *Application deadline:* Applications are processed on a rolling basis. Application fee: $40. *Expenses:* Tuition: Full-time $10,620; part-time $590 per credit hour. *Financial support:* Fellowships, research assistantships, Federal Work-Study, scholarships/grants, and unspecified assistantships available. Support available to part-time students. Financial award application deadline: 3/1. *Unit head:* Ellen Adams, Assistant Professor, Education Department, 518-244-2054, E-mail: adamse@sage.edu. *Application contact:* Wendy D. Diefendorf, Director of Graduate and Adult Admission, 518-244-2443, Fax: 518-244-6880, E-mail: diefew@sage.edu.

Sage Graduate School, Graduate School, School of Education, Program in Childhood Special Education, Troy, NY 12180-4115. Offers MS Ed. *Accreditation:* NCATE. Part-time and evening/weekend programs available. *Faculty:* 15 full-time (9 women), 19 part-time/adjunct (16 women). *Students:* 19 full-time (16 women), 29 part-time (24 women); includes 2 minority (1 Asian American or Pacific Islander, 1 Hispanic American). Average age 28. 38 applicants, 55% accepted, 10 enrolled. In 2009, 15 master's awarded. *Degree requirements:* For master's, thesis optional. *Entrance requirements:* For master's, minimum GPA of 2.75, resume, 2 letters of recommendation, interview, assessment of writing skills. Additional exam requirements/recommendations for international students: Required—TOEFL (minimum score 550 paper-based; 213 computer-based). *Application deadline:* Applications are processed on a rolling basis. Application fee: $40. *Expenses:* Tuition: Full-time $10,620; part-time $590 per credit hour. *Financial support:* Fellowships, research assistantships, Federal Work-Study, scholarships/grants, and unspecified assistantships available. Support available to part-time students. Financial award application deadline: 3/1; financial award applicants required to submit FAFSA. *Faculty research:* Effective behavioral strategies for classroom instruction. *Unit head:* Dr. Nancy A. DeKorp, Interim Dean, Education, 518-244-2496, Fax: 518-244-2334, E-mail: dekorn@sage.edu. *Application contact:* Wendy D. Diefendorf, Director of Graduate and Adult Admission, 518-244-2443, Fax: 518-244-6880, E-mail: diefew@sage.edu.

Saginaw Valley State University, College of Education, Program in Elementary Classroom Teaching, University Center, MI 48710. Offers MAT. *Accreditation:* NCATE. Part-time and evening/weekend programs available. *Students:* 5 full-time (all women), 70 part-time (63 women); includes 6 minority (4 African Americans, 1 American Indian/Alaska Native, 1 Hispanic American), 3 international. Average age 33. 11 applicants, 100% accepted, 8 enrolled. In 2009, 18 master's awarded. *Degree requirements:* For master's, capstone course. *Entrance requirements:* For master's, minimum GPA of 3.0, teaching certificate. Additional exam requirements/recommendations for international students: Required—TOEFL (minimum score 525 paper-based; 197 computer-based; 71 iBT). *Application deadline:* Applications are processed on a rolling basis. Application fee: $25. Electronic applications accepted. *Financial support:* Federal Work-Study and scholarships/grants available. Support available to part-time students. Financial award applicants required to submit FAFSA. *Unit head:* Dr. Steve P. Barbus, Dean, 989-964-6067, Fax: 989-790-4385, E-mail: barbus@svsu.edu. *Application contact:* Dr. Steve P. Barbus, Dean, 989-964-6067, Fax: 989-790-4385, E-mail: barbus@svsu.edu.

Saginaw Valley State University, College of Education, Program in Natural Science Teaching, University Center, MI 48710. Offers elementary (MAT); middle school (MAT); secondary school (MAT). *Accreditation:* NCATE. Part-time and evening/weekend programs available. *Students:* 20 part-time (16 women); includes 2 minority (1 African American, 1 Hispanic American), 1 international. Average age 35. 5 applicants, 100% accepted, 3 enrolled. In 2009, 14 master's awarded. *Degree requirements:* For master's, capstone course. *Entrance requirements:* For master's, minimum GPA of 3.0, teaching certificate. Additional exam requirements/recommendations for international students: Required—TOEFL (minimum score 525 paper-based; 197 computer-based; 71 iBT). *Application deadline:* Applications are processed on a rolling basis. Application fee: $25. Electronic applications accepted. *Financial support:* Federal Work-Study and scholarships/grants available. Support available to part-time students. Financial award applicants required to submit FAFSA. *Unit head:* Dr. Steve P. Barbus, Dean, 989-964-6067, Fax: 989-790-4385, E-mail: barbus@svsu.edu. *Application contact:* Dr. Steve P. Barbus, Dean, 989-964-6067, Fax: 989-790-4385, E-mail: barbus@svsu.edu.

St. John Fisher College, Ralph C. Wilson Jr. School of Education, Program in Childhood Education/Special Education, Rochester, NY 14618-3597. Offers MS Ed. Part-time and evening/weekend programs available. *Faculty:* 3 full-time (1 woman), 1 (woman) part-time/adjunct. *Students:* 64 full-time (52 women), 4 part-time (3 women); includes 6 minority (all African Americans). Average age 28. 76 applicants, 71% accepted, 36 enrolled. In 2009, 28 master's awarded. *Degree requirements:* For master's, field experience, student teaching, LAST. *Entrance requirements:* For master's, 2 letters of recommendation, personal statement, current resume. Additional exam requirements/recommendations for international students: Required—TOEFL (minimum score 575 paper-based; 233 computer-based; 80 iBT). *Application deadline:* Applications are processed on a rolling basis. Application fee: $30. Electronic applications accepted. *Expenses:* Tuition: Part-time $680 per credit hour. Required fees: $25 per semester. Tuition and fees vary according to degree level and program. *Financial support:* In 2009–10, 65 students received support. Federal Work-Study and scholarships/grants available. Financial award applicants required to submit FAFSA. *Faculty research:* Professional development, science assessment, multi-cultural; educational technology. *Unit head:* Dr. Michelle Erklenz-Watts, Program Director, 585-385-8404, E-mail: merklenz-watts@sjfc.edu. *Application contact:* Jose Perales, Director of Graduate Admissions, 585-385-8067, E-mail: jperales@sjfc.edu.

St. John's University, The School of Education, Department of Curriculum and Instruction, Program in Childhood Education, Queens, NY 11439. Offers MS Ed. *Students:* 132 full-time (117 women), 275 part-time (239 women); includes 116 minority (47 African Americans, 16 Asian Americans or Pacific Islanders, 53 Hispanic Americans), 11 international. Average age 31. 259 applicants, 77% accepted, 121 enrolled. In 2009, 64 master's awarded. *Degree requirements:* For master's, comprehensive exam. *Entrance requirements:* For master's, minimum GPA of 3.0, qualification for New York State provisional (initial) teaching certificate. Additional exam requirements/recommendations for international students: Required—TOEFL (minimum score 500 paper-based; 173 computer-based; 61 iBT), IELTS (minimum score 5.5). *Application deadline:* For fall admission, 4/1 priority date for domestic students, 6/1 priority date for international students; for spring admission, 11/1 priority date for domestic and international students. Applications are processed on a rolling basis. Application fee: $70. Electronic applications accepted. *Expenses:* Tuition: Full-time $16,290; part-time $905 per credit. Required fees: $300; $150 per semester. Tuition and fees vary according to program. *Financial support:* Research assistantships available. *Faculty research:* Self determination in special education setting; parent, teacher, and student views on testing in elementary school. *Unit head:* Dr. Peter Quinn, Chair, 718-990-6775, Fax: 718-990-3803, E-mail: quinnp@stjohns.edu. *Application contact:* Dr. Kelly K. Ronayne, Associate Dean for Graduate Admissions, 718-990-2303, Fax: 718-990-2343, E-mail: graded@stjohns.edu.

Saint Joseph's University, College of Arts and Sciences, Department of Education, Philadelphia, PA 19131-1395. Offers educational leadership (Ed D); elementary education (MS); instructional technology (MS); organizational development and leadership (MS); professional education (MS); reading specialist (MS); secondary education (MS); special education (MS). Part-time and evening/weekend programs available. *Students:* 5 full-time (3 women), 750 part-time (561 women); includes 100 minority (76 African Americans, 1 American Indian/Alaska Native, 11 Asian Americans or Pacific Islanders, 12 Hispanic Americans), 3 international. Average age 33. In 2009, 210 master's, 14 doctorates awarded. *Entrance requirements:* For master's, 2 letters of recommendation, minimum GPA of 3.0, application, official transcripts, personal statement; for doctorate, GRE, master's degree from accredited institution, minimum graduate GPA of 3.5, computer competence, commitment to participate in cohort, interview with program director. Additional exam requirements/recommendations for international students: Required—TOEFL (minimum score 550 paper-based; 213 computer-based; 79 iBT). *Application deadline:* For fall admission, 7/15 priority date for domestic students, 4/15 for international students; for winter admission, 11/15 for domestic students, 1/15 for international students; for spring admission, 11/15 priority date for domestic students, 10/15 for international students. Applications are processed on a rolling basis. Application fee: $35. Electronic applications accepted. *Expenses:* Contact institution. *Financial support:* Unspecified assistantships available. Financial award applicants required to submit FAFSA. *Faculty research:* Early childhood course design, public education professional development. Total annual research expenditures: $91,900. *Unit head:* Dr. Teri Sosa, Director of Graduate Education, 610-660-3162, E-mail: tsosa@sju.edu. *Application contact:* Kate McConnell, Director, Graduate College of Arts and Sciences Admissions and Retention, 610-660-3184, Fax: 610-660-3230, E-mail: kate.mcconnell@sju.edu.

Saint Mary's University of Minnesota, Schools of Graduate and Professional Programs, Graduate School of Education, Instruction Program, Winona, MN 55987-1399. Offers MA, Certificate. *Unit head:* Rebecca Hopkins, Director, 507-457-6620, E-mail: rhopkins@smumn.edu. *Application contact:* Yasin Alsaidi, Director of Admissions for Graduate and Professional Programs, 612-728-5207, Fax: 612-728-5121, E-mail: yalsaidi@smumn.edu.

Saint Peter's College, Graduate Programs in Education, Program in Teaching, Jersey City, NJ 07306-5997. Offers elementary teacher (Certificate); supervisor of instruction (Certificate); teaching (MA). Part-time and evening/weekend programs available. *Degree requirements:* For master's, comprehensive exam. *Entrance requirements:* For master's, GRE or MAT. Additional exam requirements/recommendations for international students: Required—TOEFL. *Application deadline:* Applications are processed on a rolling basis. Application fee: $0. Electronic applications accepted. *Expenses:* Tuition: Part-time $971 per credit. *Financial support:* Career-related internships or fieldwork, Federal Work-Study, and institutionally sponsored loans available. *Unit head:* Dr. Anthony Sciarrillo, Chairperson, 201-761-6473, Fax: 201-435-5270. *Application contact:* Dr. Anthony Sciarrillo, Chairperson, 201-761-6473, Fax: 201-435-5270.

St. Thomas Aquinas College, Division of Teacher Education, Sparkill, NY 10976. Offers adolescence education (MST); childhood and special education (MST); childhood education (MST); educational leadership (MS Ed); reading (MS Ed, PMC); special education (MS Ed, PMC); teaching (MS Ed), including elementary education, middle school education, secondary education. *Accreditation:* NCATE. Part-time and evening/weekend programs available. *Degree requirements:* For master's, comprehensive exam, comprehensive professional portfolio; for PMC, action research project. *Entrance requirements:* For master's, New York State Qualifying Exam, GRE General Test or minimum GPA of 3.0, teaching certificate; for PMC, GRE General Test or minimum GPA of 3.0. Electronic applications accepted. *Faculty research:* Computer applications in education, adolescent special education students, literacy development, inclusive practices for special education students.

St. Thomas University, School of Leadership Studies, Institute for Education, Miami Gardens, FL 33054-6459. Offers earth/space science (Certificate); educational administration (MS, Certificate); educational leadership (Ed D); elementary education (MS); ESOL (Certificate); gifted education (Certificate); instructional technology (MS, Certificate); professional/studies (Certificate); reading (MS, Certificate); special education (MS). Part-time and evening/weekend programs available. *Degree requirements:* For master's, comprehensive exam; for doctorate, comprehensive exam, thesis/dissertation. *Entrance requirements:* For master's, interview, minimum GPA of 3.0 or GRE; for doctorate, GRE or MAT. Additional exam requirements/recommendations for international students: Required—TOEFL (minimum score 550 paper-based; 213 computer-based; 79 iBT). Electronic applications accepted.

Saint Xavier University, Graduate Studies, School of Education, Chicago, IL 60655-3105. Offers counseling (MA); counselor education (MA); curriculum and instruction (MA); early childhood education (MA); education (CAS); educational administration (MA); elementary education (MA); field-based education (MA); general educational studies (MA); individualized program (MA); learning disabilities (MA); reading (MA); secondary education (MA). *Accreditation:* NCATE. Part-time and evening/weekend programs available. *Degree requirements:* For master's, thesis or project. *Entrance requirements:* For master's, minimum GPA of 3.0. *Expenses:* Contact institution.

Salem College, Department of Education, Winston-Salem, NC 27101. Offers early education and leadership (MAT); elementary education (MAT); English as a second language (MAT); language and literacy (M Ed); middle school education (MAT); secondary education (MAT); special education (MAT). *Accreditation:* NCATE. Part-time and evening/weekend programs available. *Degree requirements:* For master's, comprehensive exam, practicum (MAT), project (M Ed), oral and written comprehensive exams. *Entrance requirements:* For master's, GRE, minimum GPA of 2.5. *Faculty research:* Content area reading strategies, literacy development, brain compatible instruction.

Salem State College, School of Graduate Studies, Program in Elementary Education, Salem, MA 01970-5353. Offers M Ed. *Accreditation:* NCATE. Part-time and evening/weekend programs available. *Students:* 23 full-time (18 women), 87 part-time (78 women). Average age 33. 26 applicants, 100% accepted, 26 enrolled. In 2009, 42 master's awarded. *Entrance requirements:* For master's, GRE or MAT. Additional exam requirements/recommendations for international students: Required—TOEFL (minimum score 550 paper-based; 80 iBT), or IELTS (minimum score 5.5). *Application deadline:* For fall admission, 5/1 for domestic students; for spring admission, 10/1 for domestic students. Applications are processed on a rolling basis. Application fee: $50. *Expenses:* Tuition, state resident: full-time $2520; part-time $275 per credit hour. Tuition, nonresident: full-time $4140; part-time $365 per credit hour. Required fees: $2430. *Financial support:* In 2009–10, 38 students received support. Career-related internships or fieldwork, Federal Work-Study, scholarships/grants, and unspecified assistantships available. Support available to part-time students. Financial award application deadline: 5/1; financial award applicants required to submit FAFSA. *Unit head:* Anneliese Worster, Coordinator, 978-542-6310, Fax: 978-542-7215, E-mail: aworster@salemstate.edu. *Application contact:* Dr. Lee A. Brossoit, Assistant Dean of Graduate Admissions, 978-542-6673, Fax: 978-542-7215, E-mail: lbrossoit@salemstate.edu.

Salem State College, School of Graduate Studies, Program in Spanish, Salem, MA 01970-5353. Offers MAT. Part-time and evening/weekend programs available. *Students:* 28 part-time (22 women); includes 1 minority (African American). Average age 32. 3 applicants, 100% accepted, 3 enrolled. In 2009, 9 master's awarded. *Entrance requirements:* For master's, GRE or MAT. Additional exam requirements/recommendations for international students: Required—TOEFL (minimum score 550 paper-based; 80 iBT), or IELTS (minimum score 5.5). *Application deadline:* For fall admission, 5/1 for domestic students; for spring admission, 10/1 for domestic students. Applications are processed on a rolling basis. Application fee: $50. *Expenses:*

Tuition, state resident: full-time $2520; part-time $275 per credit hour. Tuition, nonresident: full-time $4140; part-time $365 per credit hour. Required fees: $2430. *Financial support:* In 2009–10, 4 students received support. Career-related internships or fieldwork, Federal Work-Study, scholarships/grants, and unspecified assistantships available. Support available to part-time students. Financial award application deadline: 5/1; financial award applicants required to submit FAFSA. *Unit head:* Kristine Doll, Program Coordinator, 978-542-6321, E-mail: kdoll@salemstate.edu. *Application contact:* Dr. Lee A. Brossoit, Assistant Dean of Graduate Admissions, 978-542-6675, Fax: 978-542-7215, E-mail: lbrossoit@salemstate.edu.

Samford University, Orlean Bullard Beeson School of Education and Professional Studies, Birmingham, AL 35229. Offers early childhood education (Ed S); early childhood/elementary education (MS Ed); educational administration (Ed S); educational leadership (Ed D); elementary education (Ed S); gifted education (MS Ed); instructional leadership (MS Ed); secondary collaboration (MS Ed); M Div/MS Ed. *Accreditation:* NCATE. Part-time programs available. *Faculty:* 11 full-time (8 women), 9 part-time/adjunct (5 women). *Students:* 16 full-time (13 women), 173 part-time (131 women); includes 47 minority (46 African Americans, 1 American Indian/Alaska Native), 1 international. Average age 40. 15 applicants, 100% accepted, 15 enrolled. In 2009, 52 master's, 11 doctorates, 27 other advanced degrees awarded. *Degree requirements:* For master's, comprehensive exam; for doctorate, comprehensive exam, thesis/dissertation. *Entrance requirements:* For master's, GRE or MAT, minimum GPA of 3.0; for doctorate, minimum GPA of 3.7; for Ed S, GRE, master's degree, teaching certificate, minimum GPA of 3.25. Additional exam requirements/recommendations for international students: Required—TOEFL (minimum score 550 paper-based; 213 computer-based). *Application deadline:* Applications are processed on a rolling basis. Application fee: $25. *Expenses:* Tuition: Full-time $26,660; part-time $595 per credit hour. Required fees: $110 per semester. *Financial support:* In 2009–10, 127 students received support; research assistantships, career-related internships or fieldwork, Federal Work-Study, scholarships/grants, and tuition waivers (partial) available. Support available to part-time students. Financial award applicants required to submit FAFSA. *Faculty research:* School law, the characteristics of beginning teachers, the nature of school reform, school culture, quality improvement in education, K-12 student achievement. *Unit head:* Dr. Jean Ann Box, Dean, 205-726-2559, E-mail: jabox@samford.edu. *Application contact:* Dr. Maurice Persall, Director, Graduate Office, 205-726-2019, E-mail: jmpersal@samford.edu.

San Diego State University, Graduate and Research Affairs, College of Education, School of Teacher Education, Program in Elementary Curriculum and Instruction, San Diego, CA 92182. Offers MA. *Accreditation:* NCATE. Evening/weekend programs available. *Entrance requirements:* For master's, GRE General Test, letters of reference. Additional exam requirements/recommendations for international students: Required—TOEFL. Electronic applications accepted.

San Francisco State University, Division of Graduate Studies, College of Education, Department of Elementary Education, Program in Elementary Education, San Francisco, CA 94132-1722. Offers MA. *Accreditation:* NCATE.

San Jose State University, Graduate Studies and Research, Connie L. Lurie College of Education, Department of Elementary Education, San Jose, CA 95192-0001. Offers curriculum and instruction (MA); reading (Certificate). *Accreditation:* NCATE. *Students:* 318 full-time (270 women), 163 part-time (140 women); includes 166 minority (5 African Americans, 97 Asian Americans or Pacific Islanders, 64 Hispanic Americans), 7 international. Average age 32. 257 applicants, 87% accepted, 189 enrolled. In 2009, 40 master's awarded. *Degree requirements:* For master's, thesis or alternative. *Application deadline:* For fall admission, 6/29 for domestic students; for spring admission, 11/30 for domestic students. Applications are processed on a rolling basis. Application fee: $59. Electronic applications accepted. *Financial support:* Career-related internships or fieldwork available. Financial award applicants required to submit FAFSA. *Unit head:* Dr. Andrea Whittaker, Chair, 408-924-3751, Fax: 408-924-3775. *Application contact:* Dr. Andrea Whittaker, Chair, 408-924-3751, Fax: 408-924-3775.

Seton Hill University, Program in Elementary Education, Greensburg, PA 15601. Offers MA, Teaching Certificate. *Accreditation:* Teacher Education Accreditation Council. Part-time and evening/weekend programs available. *Faculty:* 6 full-time (3 women), 4 part-time/adjunct (2 women). *Students:* 10 full-time (6 women), 12 part-time (10 women); includes 1 minority (African American). Average age 28. 18 applicants, 83% accepted, 10 enrolled. In 2009, 3 master's awarded. *Degree requirements:* For master's, thesis optional. *Entrance requirements:* For master's, minimum GPA of 3.0. Additional exam requirements/recommendations for international students: Required—TOEFL (minimum score 600 paper-based; 250 computer-based), IELTS (minimum score 6.5). *Application deadline:* For fall admission, 8/15 priority date for domestic students; for spring admission, 12/15 for domestic students. Applications are processed on a rolling basis. Application fee: $35. Electronic applications accepted. *Expenses:* Tuition: Full-time $12,780; part-time $710 per credit. Required fees: $300; $150 per semester. Tuition and fees vary according to course load and program. *Financial support:* Scholarships/grants, tuition waivers (partial), and unspecified assistantships available. Support available to part-time students. Financial award application deadline: 8/15; financial award applicants required to submit FAFSA. *Faculty research:* Second language acquisition, curriculum development, distance education, Holocaust studies. *Unit head:* Dr. Audrey Quinlan, Director, 724-830-4734, Fax: 724-830-1294, E-mail: quinlan@setonhill.edu. *Application contact:* Laurel Pellis, Advisor, 724-838-4209, Fax: 724-830-1891, E-mail: lpellis@setonhill.edu.

Shenandoah University, School of Education and Human Development, Winchester, VA 22601-5195. Offers administrative leadership (D Ed); advanced professional teaching English to speakers of other languages (Certificate); education (MSE); elementary education (Certificate); middle school education (Certificate); organizational leadership (MS); professional studies (Certificate); professional studies (for initial teacher licensure) (Certificate); professional studies (for special education teacher licensure) (Certificate); professional studies (for VA licensure reading specialists) (Certificate); professional studies (for VA licensure) (Certificate); professional teaching English to speakers of other languages (Certificate); public management (Certificate); school reform (Certificate); secondary education (Certificate). *Accreditation:* Teacher Education Accreditation Council. Part-time and evening/weekend programs available. Post-baccalaureate distance learning degree programs offered (minimal on-campus study). *Faculty:* 13 full-time (7 women), 27 part-time/adjunct (20 women). *Students:* 11 full-time (8 women), 382 part-time (276 women); includes 35 minority (17 African Americans, 1 American Indian/Alaska Native, 6 Asian Americans or Pacific Islanders, 11 Hispanic Americans), 4 international. Average age 39. 272 applicants, 95% accepted, 218 enrolled. In 2009, 103 master's, 2 doctorates awarded. *Degree requirements:* For master's, comprehensive exam (for some programs), thesis (for some programs), internship; for doctorate, comprehensive exam, thesis/dissertation; for Certificate, full time teaching in area for 1 year. *Entrance requirements:* For master's, minimum GPA of 3.0 or satisfactory GRE, 3 letters of recommendation, valid teaching license, essay; for doctorate, minimum graduate GPA of 3.5, 3 years of teaching experience, 3 letters of recommendation, writing samples; for Certificate, minimum undergraduate GPA of 3.0, essay, 3 letters of recommendation. Additional exam requirements/recommendations for international students: Required—TOEFL (minimum score 550 paper-based; 213 computer-based; 79 iBT), IELTS (minimum score 6.5). *Application deadline:* For fall admission, 7/1 for domestic and international students; for spring admission, 10/15 for domestic and international students. Application fee: $30. Electronic applications accepted. *Expenses:* Tuition: Full-time $11,925; part-time $695 per credit. Required fees: $400 per semester. *Financial support:* Application deadline: 3/15. *Unit head:* Dr. Steven E. Humphries, Dean, 540-535-3574, E-mail: shumphri@su.edu. *Application contact:* David Anthony, Dean of Admissions, 540-665-4581, Fax: 540-665-4627, E-mail: admit@su.edu.

Shippensburg University of Pennsylvania, School of Graduate Studies, College of Education and Human Services, Department of Teacher Education, Shippensburg, PA 17257-2299. Offers curriculum and instruction (M Ed), including biology, early childhood education, elementary education, English, foreign languages, geography/earth science, history, mathematics, middle school education; reading (M Ed). *Accreditation:* NCATE. Part-time and evening/weekend programs available. *Degree requirements:* For master's, comprehensive exam (for some programs), thesis optional, practicum or internship (for some programs). *Entrance requirements:* For master's, MAT (if GPA less than 2.75), interview, 3 letters of recommendation, writing sample of teaching background and future goals. Additional exam requirements/recommendations for international students: Required—TOEFL (minimum score 560 paper-based; 220 computer-based); Recommended—IELTS (minimum score 6). Electronic applications accepted.

Siena Heights University, Graduate College, Program in Teacher Education, Concentration in Elementary Education, Adrian, MI 49221-1796. Offers elementary education/reading (MA). Part-time programs available. *Degree requirements:* For master's, thesis, presentation. *Entrance requirements:* For master's, interview, minimum GPA of 3.0.

Sierra Nevada College, Teacher Education Program, Incline Village, NV 89451. Offers elementary education (MAT); secondary education (MAT). Part-time and evening/weekend programs available. *Degree requirements:* For master's, comprehensive exam, thesis, PRAXIS I and II. *Entrance requirements:* For master's, 2 letters of recommendation, minimum GPA of 3.0.

Simmons College, College of Arts and Sciences Graduate Studies, Department of Education, Program in Teacher Preparation, Boston, MA 02115. Offers educational leadership (MS Ed); elementary education (MAT); general education (CAGS); general purposes (MS); middle school education (MAT); professional license (CAGS); professional license: elementary (MS Ed); professional license: middle/high (MS Ed); secondary education (MAT); urban education (MS Ed, CAGS). Part-time programs available. *Students:* 68 full-time (58 women), 125 part-time (113 women); includes 25 minority (10 African Americans, 3 American Indian/Alaska Native, 8 Asian Americans or Pacific Islanders, 4 Hispanic Americans). Average age 27. 115 applicants, 88% accepted, 75 enrolled. In 2009, 137 master's, 14 other advanced degrees awarded. *Degree requirements:* For master's, practicum. *Entrance requirements:* For master's, GRE General Test, MAT or Massachusetts Tests for Educator Licensure (MTEL). Additional exam requirements/recommendations for international students: Required—TOEFL (minimum score 600 paper-based; 250 computer-based; 100 iBT). *Application deadline:* For fall admission, 8/1 priority date for domestic and international students; for winter admission, 12/15 priority date for domestic and international students; for spring admission, 12/15 priority date for domestic and international students. Applications are processed on a rolling basis. Application fee: $35. Electronic applications accepted. *Expenses:* Contact institution. *Financial support:* Application deadline: 3/1. *Faculty research:* Educational psychology, mentorship with first year teachers, urban classrooms, first generation college students. *Unit head:* Gary Oakes, Director, Master of Arts in Teaching (MAT) Program, 617-521-2203, Fax: 617-521-3133. *Application contact:* Kristen Haack, Director, Graduate Studies Admission, 617-521-2917, Fax: 617-521-3058, E-mail: gsa@simmons.edu.

Sinte Gleska University, Graduate Education Program, Mission, SD 57555. Offers elementary education (M Ed). Part-time and evening/weekend programs available. *Degree requirements:* For master's, thesis. *Entrance requirements:* For master's, 2 years of experience in elementary education, minimum GPA of 2.5, South Dakota elementary education certification. *Faculty research:* American Indian graduate education, teaching of Native American students.

Slippery Rock University of Pennsylvania, Graduate Studies (Recruitment), College of Education, Department of Elementary Education and Early Childhood, Slippery Rock, PA 16057-1383. Offers reading (M Ed). *Accreditation:* NCATE. Part-time and evening/weekend programs available. *Degree requirements:* For master's, comprehensive exam (for some programs), thesis (for some programs), reflective presentation. *Entrance requirements:* For master's, GRE General Test, MAT, minimum GPA of 2.75 (3.0 for initial certification programs). Additional exam requirements/recommendations for international students: Required—TOEFL (minimum score 550 paper-based; 213 computer-based). *Application deadline:* For fall admission, 3/1 priority date for domestic students, 5/1 priority date for international students; for spring admission, 11/1 priority date for domestic students, 9/1 priority date for international students. Applications are processed on a rolling basis. Application fee: $25 ($30 for international students). Electronic applications accepted. *Expenses:* Tuition, state resident: full-time $6666; part-time $370 per credit. Tuition, nonresident: full-time $10,666; part-time $593 per credit. Required fees: $2184; $182 per credit. *Financial support:* Career-related internships or fieldwork, Federal Work-Study, scholarships/grants, and unspecified assistantships available. Support available to part-time students. Financial award application deadline: 5/1; financial award applicants required to submit FAFSA. *Unit head:* Dr. Suzanne Rose, Graduate Coordinator, 724-738-2863, Fax: 724-738-4987, E-mail: suzanne.rose@sru.edu. *Application contact:* Angela Piverotto, Interim Director of Graduate Studies, 724-738-2051, Fax: 724-738-2146, E-mail: graduate.admissions@sru.edu.

Smith College, Graduate and Special Programs, Department of Education and Child Study, Program in Elementary Education, Northampton, MA 01063. Offers MAT. Part-time programs available. *Faculty:* 6 full-time (4 women), 3 part-time/adjunct (2 women). *Students:* 13 full-time (10 women), 4 part-time (3 women); includes 2 minority (1 African American, 1 Asian American or Pacific Islander), 1 international. Average age 33. 27 applicants, 81% accepted, 14 enrolled. In 2009, 10 master's awarded. *Entrance requirements:* Additional exam requirements/recommendations for international students: Required—TOEFL (minimum score 590 paper-based; 243 computer-based; 97 iBT). *Application deadline:* For fall admission, 4/1 for domestic students, 1/15 priority date for international students; for spring admission, 12/1 for domestic students. Application fee: $60. *Financial support:* In 2009–10, 14 students received support. Career-related internships or fieldwork, institutionally sponsored loans, and scholarships/grants available. Support available to part-time students. Financial award application deadline: 1/15. *Unit head:* Alan Rudnitsky, Graduate Student Adviser, 413-585-3261, E-mail: arudnits@smith.edu. *Application contact:* Ruth Morgan, Administrative Assistant, 413-585-3050, Fax: 413-585-3054, E-mail: gradstdy@smith.edu.

Sonoma State University, School of Education, Department of Literacy Studies and Elementary Education, Rohnert Park, CA 94928-3609. Offers MA. Part-time and evening/weekend programs available. *Degree requirements:* For master's, thesis or alternative. *Entrance requirements:* For master's, GRE General Test, minimum GPA of 2.5. *Expenses:* Tuition, nonresident: full-time $11,160. Required fees: $6226. Full-time tuition and fees vary according to course load.

South Carolina State University, School of Graduate Studies, Department of Education, Orangeburg, SC 29117-0001. Offers early childhood and special education (M Ed); early childhood education (MAT); elementary education (M Ed, MAT); engineering (MAT); general science (MAT); mathematics (MAT); secondary education (M Ed), including biology education, business education, counselor education, English education, home economics education, industrial education, mathematics education, science education, social studies education; special education (M Ed), including emotionally handicapped, learning disabilities, mentally handicapped. *Accreditation:* NCATE. Part-time and evening/weekend programs available. *Degree requirements:* For master's, thesis optional, departmental qualifying exam. *Entrance requirements:* For master's, GRE General Test, NTE, interview, teaching certificate. Electronic applications accepted. *Expenses:* Tuition, state resident: part-time $470 per credit hour. Tuition, nonresident: part-time $924 per credit hour. *Faculty research:* Critical thinking, child abuse, stress, test-taking skills, conflict resolution, mainstreaming.

Southeastern Louisiana University, College of Education and Human Development, Department of Teaching and Learning, Hammond, LA 70402. Offers curriculum and instruction (M Ed); elementary education (MAT); special education (M Ed, MAT), including mild/moderate grades K-12 (MAT). *Accreditation:* NCATE. Part-time programs available. *Faculty:* 16 full-time (14 women). *Students:* 20 full-time (all women), 107 part-time (99 women); includes 18 minority (11 African Americans, 1 American Indian/Alaska Native, 1 Asian American or Pacific Islander, 5 Hispanic Americans), 1 international. Average age 35. 16 applicants, 94% accepted, 13 enrolled. In 2009, 61 master's awarded. *Degree requirements:* For master's, comprehensive exam (for some programs), portfolio. *Entrance requirements:* For master's, GRE (verbal and quantitative), PRAXIS (MAT), bachelor's degree from an accredited U.S. institution or its foreign equivalent; minimum undergraduate GPA of 2.5 on all undergraduate work attempted

Elementary Education

Southeastern Louisiana University *(continued)*
or 2.75 on all undergraduate upper-level work attempted. Additional exam requirements/recommendations for international students: Required—TOEFL (minimum score 500 paper-based; 173 computer-based; 61 iBT). *Application deadline:* For fall admission, 7/15 priority date for domestic students, 6/1 priority date for international students; for spring admission, 12/1 priority date for domestic students, 10/1 priority date for international students. Applications are processed on a rolling basis. Application fee: $20 ($30 for international students). Electronic applications accepted. *Expenses:* Tuition, state resident: full-time $3086; part-time $225 per credit hour. Tuition, nonresident: part-time $529 per credit hour. Required fees: $1195. Tuition and fees vary according to course level and course load. *Financial support:* In 2009–10, 9 students received support. Federal Work-Study, institutionally sponsored loans, and administrative assistantship available. Support available to part-time students. Financial award application deadline: 5/1; financial award applicants required to submit FAFSA. *Faculty research:* Reading, instructional methodology, science education, math education, early childhood. Total annual research expenditures: $458,029. *Unit head:* Dr. Shirley Jacob, Department Head, 985-549-2221, Fax: 985-549-5009, E-mail: sjacob@selu.edu. *Application contact:* Sandra Meyers, Graduate Admissions Analyst, 985-549-5620, Fax: 985-549-5632, E-mail: admissions@selu.edu.

Southeastern University, College of Education, Lakeland, FL 33801-6099. Offers educational leadership (M Ed); elementary education (M Ed); teaching and learning (M Ed).

Southeast Missouri State University, School of Graduate Studies, Department of Elementary, Early and Special Education, Program in Elementary Education, Cape Girardeau, MO 63701-4799. Offers MA. *Accreditation:* NCATE. Part-time and evening/weekend programs available. *Degree requirements:* For master's, thesis or alternative. *Entrance requirements:* For master's, GRE General Test, MAT or PRAXIS, minimum undergraduate GPA of 2.75. Additional exam requirements/recommendations for international students: Required—TOEFL (minimum score 550 paper-based; 213 computer-based). Recommended—IELTS (minimum score 6). Electronic applications accepted. *Expenses:* Tuition, state resident: full-time $4266; part-time $237 per credit hour. Tuition, nonresident: full-time $7506; part-time $417 per credit hour. Required fees: $427; $427.

Southern Arkansas University–Magnolia, Graduate Programs, Magnolia, AR 71753. Offers agriculture (MS); business administration (MBA); computer and information sciences (MS); counseling (MS); education (M Ed), including counseling and development, curriculum and instruction emphasis, educational administration and supervision, elementary education, middle level emphasis, reading emphasis, secondary education, TESOL emphasis; kinesiology (MS); library media and information specialist (M Ed); mental health and clinical counseling (MS); public administration (EMPA); school counseling (M Ed); teaching (MAT). *Accreditation:* NCATE. Part-time and evening/weekend programs available. *Faculty:* 43 full-time (24 women), 12 part-time/adjunct (7 women). *Students:* 116 full-time (78 women), 333 part-time (255 women); includes 105 minority (98 African Americans, 3 American Indian/Alaska Native, 3 Asian Americans or Pacific Islanders, 1 Hispanic American), 11 international. Average age 33. In 2009, 88 master's awarded. *Degree requirements:* For master's, comprehensive exam, thesis optional. *Entrance requirements:* For master's, GRE, MAT or GMAT, minimum GPA of 2.75. *Application deadline:* For fall admission, 8/15 for domestic students; for winter admission, 1/8 for domestic students; for spring admission, 1/8 for domestic students. Applications are processed on a rolling basis. Application fee: $0. *Expenses:* Tuition, state resident: full-time $3798; part-time $211 per hour. Tuition, nonresident: full-time $5580; part-time $310 per hour. Required fees: $584. *Financial support:* Career-related internships or fieldwork, Federal Work-Study, scholarships/grants, tuition waivers (full), and unspecified assistantships available. Financial award applicants required to submit FAFSA. *Faculty research:* Alternative certification for teachers, supervision of instruction, instructional leadership, counseling. *Unit head:* Dr. Kim Bloss, Dean, Graduate Studies, 870-235-4150, Fax: 870-235-5227, E-mail: kkbloss@saumag.edu. *Application contact:* Dr. Kim Bloss, Dean, Graduate Studies, 870-235-4150, Fax: 870-235-5227, E-mail: kkbloss@saumag.edu.

Southern Connecticut State University, School of Graduate Studies, School of Education, Department of Education, New Haven, CT 06515-1355. Offers classroom teacher specialist (Diploma); elementary education (MS). *Accreditation:* NCATE. Part-time and evening/weekend programs available. *Faculty:* 14 full-time, 12 part-time/adjunct. *Students:* 123 full-time (108 women), 253 part-time (211 women); includes 22 minority (10 African Americans, 1 American Indian/Alaska Native, 3 Asian Americans or Pacific Islanders, 8 Hispanic Americans). 174 applicants, 31% accepted, 41 enrolled. In 2009, 109 master's awarded. *Degree requirements:* For master's, thesis or alternative. *Entrance requirements:* For master's, interview, minimum QPA of 2.5; for Diploma, master's degree. *Application deadline:* For fall admission, 7/15 priority date for domestic students. Applications are processed on a rolling basis. Application fee: $50. Electronic applications accepted. Tuition and fees vary according to program. *Financial support:* Application deadline: 4/15. *Unit head:* Dr. Maria Diamantis, Chairperson, 203-392-6143, Fax: 203-392-6473, E-mail: diamantism1@southernct.edu. *Application contact:* Dr. Adam Goldberg, Graduate Coordinator, 203-392-6442, E-mail: goldberga2@southernct.edu.

Southern New Hampshire University, School of Education, Manchester, NH 03106-1045. Offers business education (MS); child development (M Ed); computer technology education (Certificate); curriculum and instruction (M Ed); education (M Ed, CAS); elementary education (M Ed); general special education (Certificate); school business administrator (Certificate); secondary education (M Ed); training and development (Certificate). Part-time and evening/weekend programs available. Postbaccalaureate distance learning degree programs offered (no on-campus study). *Degree requirements:* For master's, comprehensive exam (for some programs), thesis or alternative. *Entrance requirements:* For master's, PRAXIS I, minimum GPA of 2.75. Additional exam requirements/recommendations for international students: Required—TOEFL (minimum score 550 paper-based; 213 computer-based). Electronic applications accepted. *Expenses:* Contact institution.

Southern Oregon University, Graduate Studies, School of Education, Ashland, OR 97520. Offers elementary education (MA Ed, MS Ed), including classroom teacher, early childhood, handicapped learner, reading, supervision; secondary education (MA Ed, MS Ed), including classroom teacher, handicapped learner, reading, supervision; teaching (MAT). *Degree requirements:* For master's, thesis optional. *Entrance requirements:* For master's, GRE General Test, minimum GPA of 3.0. Electronic applications accepted.

Southern University and Agricultural and Mechanical College, Graduate School, College of Education, Department of Curriculum and Instruction, Baton Rouge, LA 70813. Offers elementary education (M Ed); media (M Ed); secondary education (M Ed). *Degree requirements:* For master's, comprehensive exam, thesis optional. *Entrance requirements:* For master's, GMAT or GRE General Test. Additional exam requirements/recommendations for international students: Required—TOEFL (minimum score 525 paper-based; 193 computer-based).

Southwestern Oklahoma State University, College of Professional and Graduate Studies, School of Behavioral Sciences and Education, Specialization in Elementary Education, Weatherford, OK 73096-3098. Offers M Ed. M Ed distance learning degree program offered to Oklahoma residents only. *Accreditation:* NCATE. Part-time and evening/weekend programs available. *Degree requirements:* For master's, exam. *Entrance requirements:* For master's, GRE General Test or minimum undergraduate GPA of 3.0. Additional exam requirements/recommendations for international students: Required—TOEFL.

Spalding University, Graduate Studies, College of Education, Programs in Education, Louisville, KY 40203-2188. Offers elementary school education (MAT); general education (MA); high school education (MAT); middle school education (MAT); school administration (MA); special education (learning and behavioral disorders) (MAT); student guidance counselor (MA). MAT degree programs offered for first teaching certificate/license students. *Accreditation:* NCATE. Part-time and evening/weekend programs available. *Faculty:* 6 full-time (4 women), 32 part-time/adjunct (23 women). *Students:* 125 full-time (93 women), 64 part-time (49 women); includes 53 minority (50 African Americans, 2 American Indian/Alaska Native, 1 Hispanic

American), 2 international. Average age 37. 57 applicants, 79% accepted, 41 enrolled. In 2009, 56 master's awarded. *Degree requirements:* For master's, portfolio, final project, clinical experience. *Entrance requirements:* For master's, GRE General Test or MAT, interview, recommendations, resume. Additional exam requirements/recommendations for international students: Required—TOEFL (minimum score 535 paper-based; 203 computer-based). *Application deadline:* Applications are processed on a rolling basis. Application fee: $30. Electronic applications accepted. *Expenses:* Tuition: Full-time $11,340; part-time $630 per credit hour. Tuition and fees vary according to program. *Financial support:* In 2009–10, 106 students received support, including 3 research assistantships with partial tuition reimbursements available (averaging $3,590 per year); scholarships/grants, traineeships, and unspecified assistantships also available. Financial award application deadline: 3/15; financial award applicants required to submit FAFSA. *Faculty research:* Instructional technology, achievement gap, classroom management, assessment. *Unit head:* Dr. Beverly Keepers, Dean, 502-588-7121, Fax: 502-585-7123, E-mail: bkeepers@spalding.edu. *Application contact:* Admissions Office, 502-585-7111, E-mail: admissions@spalding.edu.

Springfield College, Graduate Programs, Program in Education, Springfield, MA 01109-3797. Offers counseling and secondary education (M Ed, MS); early childhood education (M Ed, MS); education (M Ed, MS); educational administration (M Ed, MS); educational studies (M Ed, MS); elementary education (M Ed, MS); secondary education (M Ed, MS); special education (M Ed, MS). Part-time and evening/weekend programs available. *Entrance requirements:* Additional exam requirements/recommendations for international students: Required—TOEFL (minimum score 550 paper-based; 213 computer-based). Electronic applications accepted. *Expenses:* Tuition: Full-time $19,800; part-time $825 per credit hour. Required fees: $150.

Spring Hill College, Graduate Programs, Program in Education, Mobile, AL 36608-1791. Offers early childhood education (MAT, MS Ed); educational theory (MS Ed); elementary education (MAT, MS Ed); secondary education (MAT, MS Ed). Part-time programs available. *Faculty:* 3 full-time (all women), 3 part-time/adjunct (2 women). *Students:* 9 full-time (7 women), 26 part-time (21 women); includes 6 minority (5 African Americans, 1 Asian American or Pacific Islander). Average age 31. 33 applicants, 48% accepted, 9 enrolled. In 2009, 14 master's awarded. *Degree requirements:* For master's, comprehensive exam, completion of program within 6 calendar years of entrance into graduate studies at Spring Hill. *Entrance requirements:* For master's, GRE, MAT, NTE, or PRAXIS, bachelor's degree. Additional exam requirements/recommendations for international students: Required—TOEFL (minimum score 550 paper-based; 213 computer-based; 80 iBT), IELTS (minimum score 6.5). *Application deadline:* For fall admission, 8/1 priority date for domestic and international students; for spring admission, 12/1 priority date for domestic and international students. Applications are processed on a rolling basis. Application fee: $25 ($35 for international students). Electronic applications accepted. *Expenses:* Contact institution. *Financial support:* In 2009–10, 24 students received support. Career-related internships or fieldwork, institutionally sponsored loans, and scholarships/grants available. Support available to part-time students. Financial award applicants required to submit FAFSA. *Unit head:* Dr. Ann A. Adams, Chair of Teacher Education, 251-380-3479, Fax: 251-460-2184, E-mail: aadams@shc.edu. *Application contact:* Donna B. Tarasavage, Director of Marketing and Recruiting, Graduate and Continuing Studies, 251-380-3067, Fax: 251-460-2190, E-mail: dtarasavage@shc.edu.

State University of New York at Fredonia, Graduate Studies, College of Education, Program in Elementary Education, Fredonia, NY 14063-1136. Offers MS Ed. *Accreditation:* NCATE. Part-time and evening/weekend programs available. *Degree requirements:* For master's, thesis optional. *Expenses:* Tuition, state resident: full-time $8370; part-time $349 per credit. Tuition, nonresident: full-time $13,250; part-time $552 per credit. Required fees: $1289; $53.55 per credit.

State University of New York at New Paltz, Graduate School, School of Education, Department of Elementary Education, New Paltz, NY 12561. Offers childhood education (MS Ed); childhood education (1-6) (MST); literacy education (5-12) (MS Ed); literacy education (B-6) (MS Ed); literacy education and adolescence special education (MS Ed); literacy education and childhood education and childhood special education (MS Ed). *Accreditation:* NCATE. Part-time and evening/weekend programs available. *Faculty:* 7 full-time (all women), 7 part-time/adjunct (5 women). *Students:* 61 full-time (54 women), 139 part-time (126 women); includes 8 minority (1 African American, 2 American Indian/Alaska Native, 2 Asian Americans or Pacific Islanders, 3 Hispanic Americans). Average age 30. 122 applicants, 63% accepted, 63 enrolled. In 2009, 81 master's awarded. *Degree requirements:* For master's, comprehensive exam (for some programs), portfolio. *Entrance requirements:* For master's, GRE and MAT (MST), minimum GPA of 3.0 (3.2 for literacy and special education), NYS teaching certificate (MS Ed). Additional exam requirements/recommendations for international students: Required—TOEFL (minimum score 550 paper-based; 213 computer-based; 80 iBT), IELTS (minimum score 6.5). *Application deadline:* For fall admission, 4/1 for domestic and international students; for spring admission, 11/15 for domestic and international students. Application fee: $50. Electronic applications accepted. *Financial support:* Federal Work-Study and institutionally sponsored loans available. Financial award application deadline: 8/1; financial award applicants required to submit FAFSA. *Faculty research:* Multi-sensory teaching methods, volunteer tutoring programs for struggling readers, school readiness and transition, math/science/technology, university-school partnerships. *Unit head:* Dr. Aaron Isabelle, Chair, 845-257-2860, E-mail: isabella@newpaltz.edu. *Application contact:* Caroline Murphy, Graduate Admissions Advisor, 845-257-3285, Fax: 845-257-3284, E-mail: gradschool@newpaltz.edu.

State University of New York at Oswego, Graduate Studies, School of Education, Department of Curriculum and Instruction, Oswego, NY 13126. Offers art education (MAT); elementary education (MS Ed); literacy education (MS Ed); secondary education (MS Ed); special education (MS Ed). Part-time and evening/weekend programs available. *Degree requirements:* For master's, comprehensive exam (for some programs), thesis optional. *Entrance requirements:* For master's, GRE General Test, minimum GPA of 2.7, provisional teaching certificate. Additional exam requirements/recommendations for international students: Required—TOEFL (minimum score 560 paper-based; 220 computer-based). *Faculty research:* Classroom applications for microcomputers; classroom questioning, wait-time, and achievement; values clarification and academic achievement.

State University of New York at Plattsburgh, Division of Education, Health, and Human Services, Program in Teacher Education: Adolescence MST, Plattsburgh, NY 12901-2681. Offers adolescence education (MST); biology 7-12 (MST); chemistry 7-12 (MST); earth science 7-12 (MST); English 7-12 (MST); French 7-12 (MST); mathematics 7-12 (MST); physics 7-12 (MST); social studies 7-12 (MST); Spanish 7-12 (MST). *Accreditation:* Teacher Education Accreditation Council. Part-time and evening/weekend programs available. *Faculty:* 4 full-time (3 women), 2 part-time/adjunct (0 women). *Students:* 83 full-time (49 women), 5 part-time (3 women); includes 9 minority (2 African Americans, 1 American Indian/Alaska Native, 1 Asian American or Pacific Islander, 5 Hispanic Americans), 2 international. Average age 27. 72 applicants, 71% accepted, 44 enrolled. In 2009, 57 master's awarded. *Degree requirements:* For master's, portfolio. *Entrance requirements:* For master's, minimum GPA of 2.75. Additional exam requirements/recommendations for international students: Required—TOEFL (minimum score 550 paper-based; 213 computer-based; 79 iBT). *Application deadline:* For fall admission, 2/15 priority date for domestic students. Applications are processed on a rolling basis. Application fee: $75. *Expenses:* Tuition, state resident: full-time $8370; part-time $349 per credit hour. Tuition, nonresident: full-time $13,250; part-time $552 per credit hour. Required fees: $1130. *Financial support:* Application deadline: 4/15. *Unit head:* Dr. Robert Ackland, Coordinator, 518-564-5131, E-mail: acklanrt@plattsburgh.edu. *Application contact:* Marguerite Adelman, Assistant Director, Graduate Admissions, 518-564-4723, Fax: 518-564-4722, E-mail: adelmaml@plattsburgh.edu.

State University of New York at Plattsburgh, Division of Education, Health, and Human Services, Program in Teacher Education: Childhood MST, Plattsburgh, NY 12901-2681. Offers childhood education (grades 1-6) (MST). *Accreditation:* Teacher Education Accreditation Council. Part-time and evening/weekend programs available. *Faculty:* 8 full-time (6 women), 6 part-

time/adjunct (2 women). *Students:* 36 full-time (28 women), 11 part-time (10 women); includes 1 minority (African American). Average age 32. 32 applicants, 53% accepted, 13 enrolled. In 2009, 21 master's awarded. *Degree requirements:* For master's, thesis, portfolio. *Entrance requirements:* For master's, minimum GPA of 2.75. Additional exam requirements/recommendations for international students: Required—TOEFL (minimum score 550 paper-based; 213 computer-based; 79 iBT). *Application deadline:* For fall admission, 2/15 priority date for domestic students. Applications are processed on a rolling basis. Application fee: $75. *Expenses:* Tuition, state resident: full-time $8370; part-time $349 per credit hour. Tuition, nonresident: full-time $13,250; part-time $552 per credit hour. Required fees: $1130. *Financial support:* Federal Work-Study available. Support available to part-time students. Financial award application deadline: 4/15; financial award applicants required to submit FAFSA. *Unit head:* Dr. Robert Ackland, Coordinator, 518-564-5131, E-mail: acklanrt@plattsburgh.edu. *Application contact:* Marguerite Adelman, Assistant Director, Graduate Admissions, 518-564-4723, Fax: 518-564-4722, E-mail: adelmaml@plattsburgh.edu.

State University of New York College at Geneseo, Graduate Studies, School of Education, Program in Elementary Education, Geneseo, NY 14454-1401. Offers MS Ed. Part-time and evening/weekend programs available. In 2009, 4 master's awarded. *Degree requirements:* For master's, thesis optional. *Application deadline:* For fall admission, 3/1 priority date for domestic students; for spring admission, 10/1 for domestic students. Application fee: $50. *Expenses:* Tuition, state resident: full-time $8370; part-time $349 per credit hour. Tuition, nonresident: full-time $13,250; part-time $552 per credit hour. Required fees: $700.52; $29 per credit hour. *Financial support:* Scholarships/grants, health care benefits, and unspecified assistantships available. Support available to part-time students. Financial award application deadline: 4/1; financial award applicants required to submit FAFSA. *Unit head:* Dr. Osman Alawiye, Dean/Chairperson, 585-245-5560, Fax: 585-245-5220, E-mail: alawiyeo@geneseo.edu. *Application contact:* Dr. Susan Salmon, Assistant to the Dean/Graduate Liaison, 585-245-5560, Fax: 585-245-5220, E-mail: salmon@geneseo.edu.

State University of New York College at Oneonta, Graduate Education, Division of Education, Department of Elementary Education and Reading, Oneonta, NY 13820-4015. Offers childhood education (MS Ed); literacy education (MS Ed). *Accreditation:* NCATE. Part-time and evening/weekend programs available. *Entrance requirements:* For master's, GRE General Test. *Application deadline:* For fall admission, 3/25 priority date for domestic students; for spring admission, 10/1 priority date for domestic students. Applications are processed on a rolling basis. Application fee: $50. *Expenses:* Tuition, state resident: part-time $349 per credit hour. Tuition, nonresident: full-time $12,870; part-time $552 per credit hour. Required fees: $1280; $15.85 per credit hour. *Unit head:* Dr. Constance Feldt-Golden, Chair, 607-436-3176, Fax: 607-436-2554, E-mail: feldtcc@oneonta.edu. *Application contact:* Dr. Constance Feldt-Golden, Chair, 607-436-3176, Fax: 607-436-2554, E-mail: feldtcc@oneonta.edu.

State University of New York College at Potsdam, School of Education and Professional Studies, Program in Curriculum and Instruction, Potsdam, NY 13676. Offers childhood education (MST); childhood instruction (MST); curriculum and instruction (MS Ed). *Accreditation:* NCATE. Postbaccalaureate distance learning degree programs offered (minimal on-campus study). *Faculty:* 14 full-time (12 women), 8 part-time/adjunct (4 women). *Students:* 209 full-time (157 women), 55 part-time (49 women); includes 9 minority (4 African Americans, 2 American Indian/Alaska Native, 2 Asian Americans or Pacific Islanders, 1 Hispanic American), 138 international. 130 applicants, 85% accepted, 90 enrolled. In 2009, 188 master's awarded. *Degree requirements:* For master's, thesis. *Entrance requirements:* For master's, minimum GPA of 2.75 in last 60 credit hours of undergraduate study. Additional exam requirements/recommendations for international students: Required—TOEFL (minimum score 550 paper-based; 213 computer-based; 80 iBT), IELTS (minimum score 6). *Application deadline:* For fall admission, 4/1 priority date for domestic and international students; for spring admission, 10/15 priority date for domestic and international students. Applications are processed on a rolling basis. Application fee: $50. *Expenses:* Tuition, state resident: full-time $8370; part-time $349 per credit hour. Tuition, nonresident: full-time $13,250; part-time $552 per credit hour. Required fees: $942; $38.70 per credit hour. *Financial support:* Federal Work-Study, scholarships/grants, and unspecified assistantships available. Support available to part-time students. Financial award application deadline: 3/1; financial award applicants required to submit FAFSA. *Unit head:* Dr. Kathleen Valentine, Chairperson, 315-267-3314, Fax: 315-267-4802, E-mail: valentkm@potsdam.edu. *Application contact:* Peter Cutler, Graduate Admissions Counselor, 315-267-3154, Fax: 315-267-4802, E-mail: cutlerpj@potsdam.edu.

State University of New York College at Potsdam, School of Education and Professional Studies, Program in Special Education, Potsdam, NY 13676. Offers birth-grade 2 (MS Ed); grades 1-6 (MS Ed); grades 5-9 (MS Ed); grades 7-12 (MS Ed). *Accreditation:* NCATE. *Faculty:* 3 full-time (1 woman), 5 part-time/adjunct (4 women). *Students:* 19 full-time (17 women), 6 part-time (4 women); includes 2 minority (1 African American, 1 American Indian/Alaska Native). 18 applicants, 100% accepted, 16 enrolled. In 2009, 11 master's awarded. *Degree requirements:* For master's, thesis optional, culminating experience. *Entrance requirements:* For master's, minimum GPA of 3.0 in last 60 hours of undergraduate course work. Additional exam requirements/recommendations for international students: Required—TOEFL (minimum score 550 paper-based; 213 computer-based; 80 iBT), IELTS (minimum score 6). *Application deadline:* For fall admission, 4/1 priority date for domestic and international students. Applications are processed on a rolling basis. Application fee: $50. *Expenses:* Tuition, state resident: full-time $8370; part-time $349 per credit hour. Tuition, nonresident: full-time $13,250; part-time $552 per credit hour. Required fees: $942; $38.70 per credit hour. *Financial support:* Unspecified assistantships available. Financial award application deadline: 3/1; financial award applicants required to submit FAFSA. *Unit head:* Dr. Anjali Misra, Chairperson, 315-267-2764, Fax: 315-267-4802, E-mail: misraa@potsdam.edu. *Application contact:* Peter Cutler, Graduate Admissions Counselor, 315-267-3154, Fax: 315-267-4802, E-mail: cutlerpj@potsdam.edu.

Stephen F. Austin State University, Graduate School, College of Education, Department of Elementary Education, Program in Elementary Education, Nacogdoches, TX 75962. Offers M Ed. *Accreditation:* NCATE. *Degree requirements:* For master's, comprehensive exam. *Entrance requirements:* For master's, GRE General Test. Additional exam requirements/recommendations for international students: Required—TOEFL.

Sul Ross State University, Rio Grande College of Sul Ross State University, Alpine, TX 79832. Offers business administration (MBA); teacher education (M Ed), including bilingual education, counseling, educational diagnostics, elementary education, general education, reading, school administration, secondary education. Part-time and evening/weekend programs available. *Degree requirements:* For master's, thesis optional. *Entrance requirements:* For master's, GMAT or GRE General Test, minimum GPA of 2.5 in last 60 hours of undergraduate work. *Faculty research:* Drug and substance abuse counseling, U.S.-Mexico border economic development.

Sul Ross State University, School of Professional Studies, Department of Teacher Education, Program in Elementary Education, Alpine, TX 79832. Offers M Ed. Part-time and evening/weekend programs available. *Degree requirements:* For master's, thesis optional. *Entrance requirements:* For master's, GMAT or GRE General Test, minimum GPA of 2.5 in last 60 hours of undergraduate work.

Teachers College, Columbia University, Graduate Faculty of Education, Department of Curriculum and Teaching, Program in Elementary/Childhood Education, Preservice, New York, NY 10027-6696. Offers MA. *Accreditation:* NCATE. *Faculty:* 3 full-time (all women). *Students:* 3 full-time (all women), 2 part-time (1 woman); includes 2 minority (1 Asian American or Pacific Islander, 1 Hispanic American). Average age 26. *Application deadline:* For fall admission, 5/15 for domestic students; for spring admission, 12/1 for domestic students. Application fee: $65. *Financial support:* Career-related internships or fieldwork, Federal Work-Study, and tuition waivers (full and partial) available. Financial award application deadline: 2/1. *Faculty research:* Teaching of reading and writing, reforming schools, urban education, curriculum development. *Unit head:* Marjorie Siegel, Chair, 212-678-3765. *Application contact:* Peter Shon, Assistant Director of Admission, 212-678-3305, Fax: 212-678-4171, E-mail: shon@exchange.tc.columbia.edu.

Temple University, Graduate School, College of Education, Department of Curriculum, Instruction, and Technology in Education, Philadelphia, PA 19122-6096. Offers applied behavioral analysis (MS Ed); career and technical education (MS Ed); early childhood education and elementary education (MS Ed); English education (MS Ed); language arts education (Ed D); math/science education (Ed D); mathematics education (MS Ed); science education (MS Ed); second and foreign language education (MS Ed); special education (MS Ed); teaching English as a second language (MS Ed). Part-time and evening/weekend programs available. Terminal master's awarded for partial completion of doctoral program. *Degree requirements:* For master's, thesis or alternative; for doctorate, thesis/dissertation. *Entrance requirements:* For master's and doctorate, GRE General Test or MAT, minimum GPA of 3.0. Additional exam requirements/recommendations for international students: Required—TOEFL (minimum score 550 paper-based; 213 computer-based; 79 iBT). Electronic applications accepted. *Faculty research:* School improvement, problem solving, literacy, language development.

Tennessee State University, The School of Graduate Studies and Research, College of Education, Department of Teaching and Learning, Nashville, TN 37209-1561. Offers curriculum and instruction (M Ed, Ed D); elementary education (M Ed, MA Ed, Ed D); special education (M Ed, MA Ed, Ed D). *Accreditation:* NCATE. *Degree requirements:* For doctorate, thesis/dissertation. *Entrance requirements:* For master's, GRE General Test, GRE Subject Test, or MAT, minimum GPA of 2.5; for doctorate, GRE General Test, GRE Subject Test, or MAT, minimum GPA of 3.25. Electronic applications accepted. *Faculty research:* Multicultural education, teacher education reform, whole language, interactive video teaching, English as a second language.

Tennessee Technological University, Graduate School, College of Education, Department of Curriculum and Instruction, Program in Elementary Education, Cookeville, TN 38505. Offers MA, Ed S. *Accreditation:* NCATE. Part-time and evening/weekend programs available. *Faculty:* 8 full-time (2 women). *Students:* 15 full-time (all women), 7 part-time (6 women); includes 1 minority (African American). Average age 27. 26 applicants, 73% accepted, 10 enrolled. In 2009, 5 master's awarded. *Degree requirements:* For master's and Ed S, comprehensive exam, thesis or alternative. *Entrance requirements:* For master's and Ed S, MAT or GRE. Additional exam requirements/recommendations for international students: Required—TOEFL (minimum score 550 paper-based; 79 iBT), IELTS (minimum score 5.5). *Application deadline:* For fall admission, 8/1 for domestic students, 5/1 for international students; for spring admission, 12/1 for domestic students, 10/1 for international students. Application fee: $25 ($30 for international students). Electronic applications accepted. *Expenses:* Tuition, state resident: full-time $7034; part-time $368 per credit hour. *Financial support:* In 2009–10, 1 fellowship (averaging $8,000 per year), research assistantships (averaging $4,000 per year), 1 teaching assistantship (averaging $4,000 per year) were awarded; career-related internships or fieldwork also available. Financial award application deadline: 4/1. *Faculty research:* Educational television art program. *Unit head:* Dr. Matthew R. Smith, Chairperson, 931-372-3181, Fax: 931-372-6270. *Application contact:* Shelia K. Kendrick, Coordinator of Graduate Studies, 931-372-3808, Fax: 931-372-3497, E-mail: skendrick@tntech.edu.

Texas A&M University–Commerce, Graduate School, College of Education and Human Services, Department of Curriculum and Instruction, Commerce, TX 75429-3011. Offers bilingual/ESL education (M Ed, MS); early childhood education (M Ed, MS); elementary education (M Ed, MS); reading (M Ed, MS); secondary education (M Ed, MS); supervision, curriculum and instruction: elementary education (Ed D). Part-time programs available. Terminal master's awarded for partial completion of doctoral program. *Degree requirements:* For master's, comprehensive exam, thesis (for some programs); for doctorate, 2 foreign languages, thesis/dissertation, departmental qualifying exam. *Entrance requirements:* For master's and doctorate, GRE General Test. Electronic applications accepted. *Faculty research:* Literacy and learning, early childhood, preservice teacher education, technology.

Texas A&M University–Corpus Christi, Graduate Studies and Research, College of Education, Program in Elementary Education, Corpus Christi, TX 78412-5503. Offers MS. Part-time and evening/weekend programs available. *Degree requirements:* For master's, comprehensive exam, thesis (for some programs). *Entrance requirements:* For master's, GRE General Test. Additional exam requirements/recommendations for international students: Required—TOEFL. Electronic applications accepted.

Texas A&M University–Kingsville, College of Graduate Studies, College of Education, Department of Education, Program in Elementary Education, Kingsville, TX 78363. Offers MA, MS. Part-time and evening/weekend programs available. *Degree requirements:* For master's, comprehensive exam, thesis or alternative. *Entrance requirements:* For master's, GRE General Test, MAT, minimum GPA of 3.0. *Faculty research:* Strategies in elementary science, manipulatives in the classroom, latest developments.

Texas Christian University, College of Education, Program in Elementary Education, Fort Worth, TX 76129-0002. Offers M Ed. Part-time and evening/weekend programs available. *Degree requirements:* For master's, oral exams. *Entrance requirements:* Additional exam requirements/recommendations for international students: Required—TOEFL (minimum score 550 paper-based; 213 computer-based; 80 iBT). *Application deadline:* For fall admission, 7/15 for domestic and international students; for spring admission, 11/15 for domestic and international students. Applications are processed on a rolling basis. Application fee: $50. *Expenses:* Tuition: Full-time $17,640; part-time $980 per credit hour. Tuition and fees vary according to program. *Financial support:* Teaching assistantships with full tuition reimbursements, career-related internships or fieldwork and unspecified assistantships available. Financial award application deadline: 3/15; financial award applicants required to submit FAFSA. *Unit head:* Dr. Kay B. Stevens, Associate Dean, 817-257-7661, E-mail: k.stevens2@tcu.edu. *Application contact:* Robyn P. Shepheard, Academic Program Specialist, 817-257-7661, E-mail: r.shepheard@tcu.edu.

Texas Christian University, College of Education, Program in Elementary (Four-One Option), Fort Worth, TX 76129-0002. Offers M Ed. Part-time and evening/weekend programs available. *Degree requirements:* For master's, oral exams. *Entrance requirements:* Additional exam requirements/recommendations for international students: Required—TOEFL (minimum score 550 paper-based; 213 computer-based; 80 iBT). *Application deadline:* For fall admission, 7/15 for domestic and international students; for spring admission, 11/15 for domestic and international students. Applications are processed on a rolling basis. Application fee: $50. *Expenses:* Tuition: Full-time $17,640; part-time $980 per credit hour. Tuition and fees vary according to program. *Financial support:* Teaching assistantships with full tuition reimbursements, career-related internships or fieldwork and unspecified assistantships available. Financial award application deadline: 3/15; financial award applicants required to submit FAFSA. *Unit head:* Dr. Mary M. Patton, Dean, 817-257-7663, E-mail: m.patton@tcu.edu. *Application contact:* Robyn P. Shepheard, Academic Program Specialist, 817-257-7661, E-mail: r.shepheard@tcu.edu.

Texas State University–San Marcos, Graduate School, College of Education, Department of Curriculum and Instruction, Program in Elementary Education, San Marcos, TX 78666. Offers M Ed, MA. Part-time and evening/weekend programs available. *Faculty:* 23 full-time (16 women), 7 part-time/adjunct (all women). *Students:* 140 full-time (124 women), 204 part-time (191 women); includes 87 minority (11 African Americans, 1 American Indian/Alaska Native, 8 Asian Americans or Pacific Islanders, 67 Hispanic Americans), 6 international. Average age 32. 174 applicants, 95% accepted, 117 enrolled. In 2009, 117 master's awarded. *Degree requirements:* For master's, comprehensive exam, thesis (for some programs). *Entrance requirements:* For master's, minimum GPA of 2.75 in last 60 hours of course work, teaching experience. Additional exam requirements/recommendations for international students: Required—TOEFL (minimum score 550 paper-based; 213 computer-based). *Application deadline:* For fall admission, 6/15 priority date for domestic students; for spring admission, 10/15 priority date for domestic students. Applications are processed on a rolling basis.

Elementary Education

Texas State University–San Marcos (continued)
Application fee: $40 ($90 for international students). Electronic applications accepted. *Expenses:* Tuition, state resident: full-time $5784; part-time $241 per credit hour. Tuition, nonresident: full-time $13,224; part-time $551 per credit hour. Required fees: $1728; $48 per credit hour. $306. Tuition and fees vary according to course load. *Financial support:* In 2009–10, 198 students received support, including 27 research assistantships (averaging $5,768 per year); teaching assistantships, career-related internships or fieldwork, Federal Work-Study, and institutionally sponsored loans also available. Support available to part-time students. Financial award application deadline: 4/1; financial award applicants required to submit FAFSA. *Faculty research:* Bilingual, general elementary, and early childhood education; gifted and talented education. *Unit head:* Carolyn McCall, Graduate Advisor, 512-245-3701, Fax: 512-245-7911, E-mail: cm06@txstate.edu. *Application contact:* Carolyn McCall, Graduate Advisor, 512-245-3701, Fax: 512-245-7911, E-mail: cm06@txstate.edu.

Texas State University–San Marcos, Graduate School, College of Education, Department of Curriculum and Instruction, Program in Elementary Education-Bilingual/Bicultural, San Marcos, TX 78666. Offers M Ed, MA. Part-time programs available. *Students:* 4 full-time (3 women), 9 part-time (all women); all minorities (all Hispanic Americans). Average age 32. 5 applicants, 100% accepted, 4 enrolled. In 2009, 4 master's awarded. *Degree requirements:* For master's, comprehensive exam, thesis optional. *Entrance requirements:* For master's, minimum GPA of 2.75 in last 60 hours of course work, teaching experience. Additional exam requirements/recommendations for international students: Required—TOEFL (minimum score 550 paper-based; 213 computer-based). *Application deadline:* For fall admission, 6/15 priority date for domestic students; for spring admission, 10/15 priority date for domestic students. Applications are processed on a rolling basis. Application fee: $40 ($90 for international students). Electronic applications accepted. *Expenses:* Tuition, state resident: full-time $5784; part-time $241 per credit hour. Tuition, nonresident: full-time $13,224; part-time $551 per credit hour. Required fees: $1728; $48 per credit hour. $306. Tuition and fees vary according to course load. *Financial support:* In 2009–10, 11 students received support, including 1 teaching assistantship (averaging $5,076 per year); career-related internships or fieldwork, Federal Work-Study, institutionally sponsored loans, and unspecified assistantships also available. Support available to part-time students. Financial award application deadline: 4/1; financial award applicants required to submit FAFSA. *Unit head:* Carolyn McCall, Graduate Advisor, 512-245-3701, Fax: 512-245-7911, E-mail: cm06@txstate.edu. *Application contact:* Dr. J. Michael Willoughby, Dean of Graduate School, 512-245-2581, Fax: 512-245-8365, E-mail: gradcollege@txstate.edu.

Texas State University–San Marcos, Graduate School, Interdisciplinary Studies Program in Elementary Mathematics, Science, and Technology, San Marcos, TX 78666. Offers MSIS. *Students:* 1 full-time (0 women), 4 part-time (3 women). Average age 32. 1 applicant, 100% accepted, 0 enrolled. In 2009, 1 master's awarded. *Degree requirements:* For master's, comprehensive exam, thesis optional. *Entrance requirements:* For master's, minimum GPA of 2.75 in the last 60 hours of undergraduate work. Additional exam requirements/recommendations for international students: Required—TOEFL (minimum score 550 paper-based; 213 computer-based). *Application deadline:* For fall admission, 6/15 priority date for domestic students, 6/1 priority date for international students; for spring admission, 10/15 priority date for domestic students, 10/1 priority date for international students. Applications are processed on a rolling basis. Application fee: $40 ($90 for international students). Electronic applications accepted. *Expenses:* Tuition, state resident: full-time $5784; part-time $241 per credit hour. Tuition, nonresident: full-time $13,224; part-time $551 per credit hour. Required fees: $1728; $48 per credit hour. $306. Tuition and fees vary according to course load. *Financial support:* In 2009–10, 3 students received support; research assistantships, teaching assistantships available. Financial award application deadline: 4/1; financial award applicants required to submit FAFSA. *Unit head:* Dr. Sandra Mody, Acting Dean, 512-245-3360, Fax: 512-245-8095, E-mail: sw04@txstate.edu. *Application contact:* Dr. J. Michael Willoughby, Dean of Graduate School, 512-245-2581, Fax: 512-245-8365, E-mail: gradcollege@txstate.edu.

Texas Tech University, Graduate School, College of Education, Division of Curriculum and Instruction, Lubbock, TX 79409. Offers bilingual education (M Ed); curriculum and instruction (M Ed, PhD); elementary education (M Ed); language and literacy education (M Ed); secondary education (M Ed). *Accreditation:* NCATE. Part-time programs available. *Students:* 72 full-time (54 women), 109 part-time (85 women); includes 50 minority (11 African Americans, 1 American Indian/Alaska Native, 4 Asian Americans or Pacific Islanders, 34 Hispanic Americans), 11 international. Average age 35. 228 applicants, 54% accepted, 56 enrolled. In 2009, 59 master's, 5 doctorates awarded. *Degree requirements:* For master's, thesis or alternative; for doctorate, thesis/dissertation. *Entrance requirements:* For master's and doctorate, GRE General Test. Additional exam requirements/recommendations for international students: Required—TOEFL (minimum score 550 paper-based; 213 computer-based). *Application deadline:* For fall admission, 3/1 priority date for international students; for spring admission, 11/1 priority date for international students. Applications are processed on a rolling basis. Application fee: $50 ($75 for international students). Electronic applications accepted. *Expenses:* Tuition, state resident: full-time $5100; part-time $213 per credit hour. Tuition, nonresident: full-time $11,748; part-time $490 per credit hour. Required fees: $2298; $50 per credit hour. $555 per semester. *Financial support:* Research assistantships with partial tuition reimbursements, teaching assistantships with partial tuition reimbursements, career-related internships or fieldwork, Federal Work-Study, and institutionally sponsored loans available. Support available to part-time students. Financial award application deadline: 4/15; financial award applicants required to submit FAFSA. *Faculty research:* Multicultural foundations of education, teacher education, instruction and pedagogy in subject areas, curriculum theory, language and literacy. *Unit head:* Dr. Walter Smith, Chair, 806-742-1988 Ext. 437, Fax: 806-742-2179, E-mail: walter.smith@ttu.edu. *Application contact:* Dr. Walter Smith, Chair, 806-742-1988 Ext. 437, Fax: 806-742-2179, E-mail: walter.smith@ttu.edu.

Texas Woman's University, Graduate School, College of Professional Education, Department of Teacher Education, Denton, TX 76201. Offers administration (M Ed, MA); elementary education (MA); special education (M Ed, MA, PhD), including educational diagnostician (M Ed, MA); teaching (MAT); teaching, learning, and curriculum (M Ed). Part-time programs available. *Faculty:* 19 full-time (13 women), 14 part-time/adjunct (11 women). *Students:* 36 full-time (29 women), 155 part-time (135 women); includes 65 minority (31 African Americans, 1 American Indian/Alaska Native, 3 Asian Americans or Pacific Islanders, 30 Hispanic Americans), 6 international. Average age 38. 48 applicants, 90% accepted, 21 enrolled. In 2009, 52 master's, 2 doctorates awarded. Terminal master's awarded for partial completion of doctoral program. *Degree requirements:* For master's, professional paper (MEd); for doctorate, comprehensive exam, thesis/dissertation. *Entrance requirements:* For master's, minimum GPA of 3.0, 3 letters of reference, curriculum vitae, copy of certifications, teacher service record; for doctorate, minimum GPA of 3.0, 3 letters of reference, curriculum vitae, copy of certifications, teacher service record, statement of intent. Additional exam requirements/recommendations for international students: Required—TOEFL (minimum score 550 paper-based; 213 computer-based; 79 iBT). *Application deadline:* For fall admission, 7/1 priority date for domestic students, 3/1 for international students; for spring admission, 11/1 priority date for domestic students, 7/1 for international students. Applications are processed on a rolling basis. Application fee: $50. Electronic applications accepted. *Expenses:* Tuition, state resident: full-time $3564; part-time $198 per credit hour. Tuition, nonresident: full-time $8550; part-time $475 per credit hour. Required fees: $69.26 per credit hour. Tuition and fees vary according to course load. *Financial support:* In 2009–10, 47 students received support, including 5 research assistantships (averaging $10,440 per year); career-related internships or fieldwork, Federal Work-Study, institutionally sponsored loans, scholarships/grants, traineeships, health care benefits, and unspecified assistantships also available. Support available to part-time students. Financial award application deadline: 3/1; financial award applicants required to submit FAFSA. *Faculty research:* Language and literacy, classroom management, learning disabilities, staff and professional development, leadership preparation practice. *Unit head:* Dr. Jane Pemberton, Interim Chair, 940-898-2271, Fax: 940-898-2270, E-mail: jpemberton@twu.edu. *Application contact:* Samuel Wheeler, Assistant Director of Admissions, 940-898-3188, Fax: 940-898-3081, E-mail: wheelersr@twu.edu.

Towson University, College of Graduate Studies and Research, Program in Elementary Education, Towson, MD 21252-0001. Offers M Ed. *Accreditation:* NCATE. Part-time and evening/weekend programs available. *Degree requirements:* For master's, capstone project or thesis. *Entrance requirements:* For master's, minimum GPA of 3.0, bachelor's degree in education, certified in teaching or eligibility for certification. Additional exam requirements/recommendations for international students: Required—TOEFL. Electronic applications accepted. *Faculty research:* Professional development schools, values education, teacher development, reading, academic underachievement.

Trevecca Nazarene University, Graduate Division, School of Education, Major in Teaching, Nashville, TN 37210-2877. Offers teaching 7-12 (MAT); teaching K-6 (MAT). Part-time and evening/weekend programs available. *Students:* 200 full-time (149 women), 37 part-time (29 women); includes 44 minority (43 African Americans, 1 Asian American or Pacific Islander), 1 international. In 2009, 122 master's awarded. *Degree requirements:* For master's, exit assessment, student teaching. *Entrance requirements:* For master's, GRE General Test, MAT, PRAXIS I: Pre-Professional Skills Test, minimum GPA of 2.7, 2 letters of reference. Additional exam requirements/recommendations for international students: Required—TOEFL (minimum score 550 paper-based; 213 computer-based). *Application deadline:* Applications are processed on a rolling basis. Application fee: $25. *Expenses:* Contact institution. *Financial support:* Applicants required to submit FAFSA. *Unit head:* Dr. Esther Swink, Dean, School of Education/Director of Graduate Education Programs, 615-248-1201, Fax: 615-248-1597, E-mail: admissions_ged@trevecca.edu. *Application contact:* Admissions Office, 615-248-1201, Fax: 615-248-1597, E-mail: admissions_ged@trevecca.edu.

Trinity (Washington) University, School of Education, Washington, DC 20017-1094. Offers counseling (MA); early childhood education (MAT); educating for change (M Ed); educational administration (MSA); elementary education (MAT); school counseling (MA); secondary education (MAT), including English, social studies; special education (MAT); teaching English as a second language (MAT); teaching English to speakers of other languages (M Ed); the teaching of reading (M Ed). *Accreditation:* NCATE. Part-time and evening/weekend programs available. *Degree requirements:* For master's, thesis (for some programs), capstone project(s). *Entrance requirements:* For master's, PRAXIS I, minimum GPA of 2.8. Additional exam requirements/recommendations for international students: Required—TOEFL (minimum score 550 paper-based; 213 computer-based). *Faculty research:* Technology, literacy, special education, organizations, inclusion models.

Troy University, Graduate School, College of Education, Program in K–6 Elementary and Collaborative Education, Troy, AL 36082. Offers alternative K-6 elementary (MS); elementary education (Ed S); traditional K-6 elementary (MS). *Accreditation:* NCATE. Part-time and evening/weekend programs available. *Students:* 130 full-time (123 women), 155 part-time (150 women); includes 94 minority (87 African Americans, 3 American Indian/Alaska Native, 3 Asian Americans or Pacific Islanders, 1 Hispanic American). Average age 32. 147 applicants, 92% accepted. In 2009, 139 master's, 30 other advanced degrees awarded. *Degree requirements:* For master's, comprehensive exam, thesis. *Entrance requirements:* For master's, minimum GPA of 2.5; for Ed S, GRE General Test or MAT, Alabama Class A certificate or equivalent, minimum graduate GPA of 3.0. Additional exam requirements/recommendations for international students: Required—TOEFL (minimum score 523 paper-based; 193 computer-based; 70 iBT), IELTS (minimum score 6). *Application deadline:* Applications are processed on a rolling basis. Application fee: $50. Electronic applications accepted. *Financial support:* Available to part-time students. Applicants required to submit FAFSA. *Unit head:* Dr. Darrell Pearson, Interim Chair, 334-670-3444, Fax: 334-670-3474, E-mail: dpearson@troy.edu. *Application contact:* Brenda K. Campbell, Director of Graduate Admissions, 334-670-3178, Fax: 334-670-3733, E-mail: bcamp@troy.edu.

Union College, Graduate Programs, Department of Education, Program in Elementary Education, Barbourville, KY 40906-1499. Offers MA. *Degree requirements:* For master's, thesis optional. *Entrance requirements:* For master's, GRE General Test, NTE.

Union Institute & University, M Ed Program–Vermont Campus, Montpelier, VT 05602. Offers school administration (M Ed), including principalship; school counseling (M Ed); teaching (M Ed), including art, early childhood, elementary, English, math, middle schools, science, social studies, special education. *Faculty:* 3 full-time (1 woman), 23 part-time/adjunct (19 women). *Students:* 41 part-time (29 women). Average age 38. In 2009, 15 master's awarded. *Degree requirements:* For master's, thesis. *Entrance requirements:* For master's, 3 letters of reference. *Application deadline:* Applications are processed on a rolling basis. Application fee: $50. *Expenses:* Contact institution. *Financial support:* Federal Work-Study, scholarships/grants, and tuition waivers available. Financial award applicants required to submit FAFSA. *Unit head:* Dr. Arlene Sacks, Dean, Graduate Programs in Education, 305-653-6713 Ext. 2152, E-mail: arlene.sacks@myunion.edu. *Application contact:* Dr. Arlene Sacks, Dean, Graduate Programs in Education, 305-653-6713 Ext. 2152, E-mail: arlene.sacks@myunion.edu.

Universidad del Este, Graduate School, Carolina, PR 00984. Offers accounting (MBA); adult education (M Ed); agribusiness (MBA); bilingual education (M Ed); criminal justice and criminology (MA); early education (M Ed); elementary education (M Ed); human resources (MBA); information security management (MBA); information technology and Web business development (MBA); management (MBA); public policy (MPA); social work (MA), including clinical social work; special education (M Ed); strategic leadership (MBA); teaching English (M Ed); teaching Spanish (M Ed).

Université de Sherbrooke, Faculty of Education, Program in Elementary Education, Sherbrooke, QC J1K 2R1, Canada. Offers M Ed, Diploma. Part-time and evening/weekend programs available. *Degree requirements:* For master's, thesis.

University at Buffalo, the State University of New York, Graduate School, Graduate School of Education, Department of Learning and Instruction, Buffalo, NY 14260. Offers biology education (Ed M, Certificate); chemistry education (Ed M, Certificate); childhood education (Ed M); childhood education with bilingual extension (Ed M); early childhood education (Ed M); earth science education (Ed M, Certificate); elementary education (Ed D, PhD); English education (Ed M, PhD, Certificate); English for speakers of other languages (Ed M); foreign and second language education (PhD); French education (Ed M, Certificate); general education (Ed M); German education (Ed M, Certificate); gifted education (online) (Certificate); Latin education (Ed M, Certificate); literary specialist (Ed M); mathematics education (Ed M, PhD, Certificate); music education (Ed M, Certificate); physics education (Ed M, Certificate); reading education (PhD); science and the public (online) (Ed M); science education (PhD); social studies education (Ed M, Certificate); Spanish education (Ed M, Certificate); special education (PhD); teaching and leading for diversity (Certificate); teaching English to speakers of other languages (Ed M). Part-time and evening/weekend programs available. Postbaccalaureate distance learning degree programs offered (no on-campus study). *Faculty:* 34 full-time (24 women), 50 part-time/adjunct (39 women). *Students:* 332 full-time (245 women), 365 part-time (272 women); includes 50 minority (18 African Americans, 4 American Indian/Alaska Native, 10 Asian Americans or Pacific Islanders, 18 Hispanic Americans), 55 international. Average age 30. 627 applicants, 78% accepted, 286 enrolled. In 2009, 255 master's, 16 doctorates, 51 other advanced degrees awarded. *Degree requirements:* For master's, comprehensive exam; for doctorate, thesis/dissertation, research analysis exam, research experience component. *Entrance requirements:* For doctorate, GRE General Test or MAT, interview, writing sample, letters of recommendation. Additional exam requirements/recommendations for international students: Required—TOEFL (minimum score 600 paper-based; 250 computer-based; 96 iBT). *Application deadline:* For fall admission, 2/1 priority date for domestic and international students; for spring admission, 11/15 priority date for domestic students, 10/1 for international students. Applications are processed on a rolling basis. Application fee: $50. Electronic applications accepted. *Financial support:* In 2009–10, 23 fellowships with full tuition reimbursements (averaging $9,000 per year), 42 research assistantships with full tuition reimbursements (averaging $10,000 per year) were awarded; teaching assistantships with full tuition reimbursements, career-related internships or fieldwork, Federal Work-Study, institutionally sponsored loans, scholarships/grants, tuition waivers (partial), and unspecified assistantships also available. Financial award

application deadline: 2/28; financial award applicants required to submit FAFSA. *Faculty research:* Science assessment, foreign language teaching and learning, early learning, new literacies, gender and education. Total annual research expenditures: $1.8 million. *Unit head:* Dr. Suzanne Miller, Chair, 716-645-2455, Fax: 716-645-3161, E-mail: smiller@buffalo.edu. *Application contact:* Cathy Dimino, Admissions Assistant, 716-645-2110, Fax: 716-645-7937, E-mail: cadimino@buffalo.edu.

The University of Akron, Graduate School, College of Education, Department of Curricular and Instructional Studies, Program in Elementary Education, Akron, OH 44325. Offers elementary education (PhD); elementary education—literacy (MA); elementary education with licensure (MS). *Accreditation:* NCATE. *Students:* 21 full-time (20 women), 126 part-time (119 women); includes 6 minority (5 African Americans, 1 Hispanic American), 1 international. Average age 37. 46 applicants, 91% accepted, 37 enrolled. In 2009, 53 master's, 4 doctorates awarded. *Degree requirements:* For master's, comprehensive exam, thesis optional; for doctorate, variable foreign language requirement, comprehensive exam, thesis/dissertation, written and oral exams. *Entrance requirements:* For master's, minimum GPA of 2.75, letters of recommendation, competency in reading comprehension, writing, mathematics, computer literacy, Bureau of Criminal Investigation clearance; for doctorate, MAT or GRE, minimum GPA of 3.5, writing sample, letters of reference, resume, curriculum vitae, three years of teaching experience. Additional exam requirements/recommendations for international students: Required—TOEFL (minimum score 550 paper-based; 213 computer-based; 79 iBT). *Application deadline:* Applications are processed on a rolling basis. Application fee: $30 ($40 for international students). Electronic applications accepted. *Expenses:* Tuition, state resident: full-time $6570; part-time $365 per credit hour. Tuition, nonresident: full-time $11,250; part-time $625 per credit hour. *Unit head:* Dr. Bridgie Ford, Chair, 330-972-6967, E-mail: alexis2@uakron.edu. *Application contact:* Dr. Bridgie Ford, Chair, 330-972-6967, E-mail: alexis2@uakron.edu.

The University of Alabama, Graduate School, College of Education, Department of Curriculum and Instruction, Tuscaloosa, AL 35487. Offers elementary education (MA, Ed D, PhD, Ed S); secondary education (MA, Ed D, PhD, Ed S). Evening/weekend programs available. Postbaccalaureate distance learning degree programs offered (minimal on-campus study). *Faculty:* 21 full-time (14 women). *Students:* 93 full-time (63 women), 129 part-time (97 women); includes 38 minority (29 African Americans, 2 American Indian/Alaska Native, 2 Asian Americans or Pacific Islanders, 5 Hispanic Americans), 5 international. Average age 32. 140 applicants, 40% accepted, 43 enrolled. In 2009, 92 master's, 16 doctorates, 13 other advanced degrees awarded. *Degree requirements:* For master's, comprehensive exam, thesis (for some programs); for doctorate, comprehensive exam, thesis/dissertation; for Ed S, comprehensive exam, thesis optional. *Entrance requirements:* For master's, doctorate, and Ed S, MAT and/or GRE. Additional exam requirements/recommendations for international students: Recommended—TOEFL (minimum score 550 paper-based; 213 computer-based), IELTS (minimum score 6.5). *Application deadline:* For fall admission, 7/1 priority date for domestic students, 1/15 priority date for international students; for spring admission, 11/1 priority date for domestic students, 6/1 priority date for international students. Application fee: $50 ($60 for international students). Electronic applications accepted. *Expenses:* Tuition, state resident: full-time $7000. Tuition, nonresident: full-time $19,200. *Financial support:* In 2009–10, 14 students received support, including 10 research assistantships with tuition reimbursements available (averaging $9,844 per year), 4 teaching assistantships with tuition reimbursements available (averaging $9,844 per year), institutionally sponsored loans, traineeships, and unspecified assistantships also available. *Faculty research:* Teacher education, diversity, integration of curriculum, technology. Total annual research expenditures: $338,697. *Unit head:* Dr. Miguel Mantero, Chair, 205-348-1402, Fax: 205-348-9863, E-mail: mmantero@bamaed.ua.edu. *Application contact:* Dr. Miguel Mantero, Chair, 205-348-1402, Fax: 205-348-9863, E-mail: mmantero@bamaed.ua.edu.

The University of Alabama at Birmingham, College of Arts and Sciences, School of Education, Program in Elementary Education, Birmingham, AL 35294. Offers MA Ed. *Accreditation:* NCATE. *Degree requirements:* For master's, thesis optional. *Entrance requirements:* For master's, GRE General Test, MAT, or NTE, minimum GPA of 3.0. Electronic applications accepted.

University of Alaska Fairbanks, School of Education, Program in Education, Fairbanks, AK 99775. Offers curriculum and instruction (M Ed); education (M Ed); elementary education (M Ed); language and literacy (M Ed); reading (M Ed); secondary education (M Ed). *Faculty:* 23 full-time (15 women), 10 part-time/adjunct (9 women). *Students:* 35 full-time (26 women), 58 part-time (43 women); includes 25 minority (2 African Americans, 17 American Indian/Alaska Native, 4 Asian Americans or Pacific Islanders, 2 Hispanic Americans), 1 international. Average age 36. 94 applicants, 64% accepted, 42 enrolled. In 2009, 19 master's, 18 other advanced degrees awarded. *Degree requirements:* For master's, comprehensive exam, thesis, oral defense. *Entrance requirements:* Additional exam requirements/recommendations for international students: Required—TOEFL (minimum score 550 paper-based; 213 computer-based; 80 iBT). *Application deadline:* For fall admission, 5/1 for domestic students, 3/1 for international students; for spring admission, 10/15 for domestic students, 8/1 for international students. Applications are processed on a rolling basis. Application fee: $60. Electronic applications accepted. *Expenses:* Tuition, state resident: full-time $7584; part-time $316 per credit. Tuition, nonresident: full-time $15,504; part-time $646 per credit. Required fees: $23 per credit. $135 per semester. Tuition and fees vary according to course level, course load and reciprocity agreements. *Financial support:* In 2009–10, 1 teaching assistantship (averaging $11,955 per year) was awarded; fellowships, career-related internships or fieldwork, Federal Work-Study, scholarships/grants, health care benefits, and unspecified assistantships also available. Support available to part-time students. Financial award application deadline: 6/1; financial award applicants required to submit FAFSA. *Unit head:* Dr. Eric C. Madsen, Dean, 907-474-7341, Fax: 907-474-5451, E-mail: fysoed@uaf.edu. *Application contact:* Dr. Eric C. Madsen, Dean, 907-474-7341, Fax: 907-474-5451, E-mail: fysoed@uaf.edu.

University of Alaska Southeast, Graduate Programs, Program in Education, Juneau, AK 99801. Offers early childhood education (M Ed, MAT); educational technology (M Ed); elementary education (MAT); reading (M Ed); secondary education (MAT). *Accreditation:* NCATE. Part-time and evening/weekend programs available. Postbaccalaureate distance learning degree programs offered (minimal on-campus study). *Degree requirements:* For master's, comprehensive exam or project, portfolio. *Entrance requirements:* For master's, PRAXIS, minimum GPA of 3.0, writing sample, letters of recommendation. Electronic applications accepted. *Faculty research:* Applied classroom research, culturally responsive practices, action research, teaching effectiveness.

University of Alberta, Faculty of Graduate Studies and Research, Department of Elementary Education, Edmonton, AB T6G 2E1, Canada. Offers M Ed, Ed D, PhD. Part-time and evening/weekend programs available. Postbaccalaureate distance learning degree programs offered (minimal on-campus study). *Faculty:* 26 full-time (18 women). *Students:* 32 full-time (26 women), 146 part-time (121 women). Average age 38. 51 applicants, 80% accepted. In 2009, 28 master's, 11 doctorates awarded. *Degree requirements:* For master's, thesis (for some programs); for doctorate, thesis/dissertation. *Entrance requirements:* For master's and doctorate, 1 year of teaching experience, minimum GPA of 6.5 on a 9.0 scale. *Application deadline:* For fall admission, 4/1 for domestic students; for winter admission, 10/1 for domestic students; for spring admission, 4/1 for domestic students. Application fee: $0. Tuition and fees charges are reported in Canadian dollars. *Expenses:* Tuition, area resident: Full-time $4626 Canadian dollars; part-time $99.72 Canadian dollars per unit. International tuition: $8216 Canadian dollars full-time. Required fees: $3590 Canadian dollars; $99.72 Canadian dollars per unit. $215 Canadian dollars per term. *Financial support:* In 2009–10, 23 students received support, including 3 fellowships with full tuition reimbursements available, 9 research assistantships with partial tuition reimbursements available, 6 teaching assistantships with full tuition reimbursements available; career-related internships or fieldwork and scholarships/grants also available. Financial award application deadline: 6/1. *Faculty research:* Literacy education, early childhood education, teacher education, curriculum studies, instructional studies. Total annual research expenditures: $100,000. *Unit head:* Dr. Jill McClay, Graduate Coordinator, 780-492-2267, Fax: 780-492-7622. *Application contact:* Gwen Parker, Information Contact, 780-492-4273 Ext. 225, Fax: 780-492-7622, E-mail: educ.elem@ualberta.ca.

University of Arkansas, Graduate School, College of Education and Health Professions, Department of Curriculum and Instruction, Program in Elementary Education, Fayetteville, AR 72701-1201. Offers M Ed, Ed S. *Accreditation:* NCATE. *Students:* 5 full-time (4 women), 11 part-time (10 women); includes 3 minority (all African Americans), 2 international. In 2009, 7 master's awarded. Application fee: $40 ($50 for international students). *Expenses:* Tuition, state resident: full-time $7355; part-time $356.58 per hour. Tuition, nonresident: full-time $17,401; part-time $775.17 per hour. Required fees: $1203. *Financial support:* Fellowships, research assistantships, teaching assistantships, career-related internships or fieldwork and Federal Work-Study available. Support available to part-time students. Financial award application deadline: 4/1; financial award applicants required to submit FAFSA. *Unit head:* Dr. Michael Daugherty, Unit Head, 479-575-4201, E-mail: mkd03@uark.edu. *Application contact:* Dr. William McComas, Graduate Coordinator, 479-575-7525, E-mail: mccomas@uark.edu.

University of Arkansas at Pine Bluff, Program in Education, Pine Bluff, AR 71601-2799. Offers elementary education (M Ed); secondary education (M Ed), including general science, physical education, social studies. *Accreditation:* NCATE. Part-time and evening/weekend programs available. *Degree requirements:* For master's, comprehensive exam. *Entrance requirements:* For master's, GRE, minimum GPA of 2.75, NTE or Standard Arkansas Teaching Certificate. *Faculty research:* Teacher certification, accreditation, assessment, standards, portfolio development, rehabilitation, technology.

University of Bridgeport, School of Education and Human Resources, Division of Education, Program in Elementary Education, Bridgeport, CT 06604. Offers early childhood education (MS, Diploma); elementary education (MS, Diploma). Evening/weekend programs available. *Degree requirements:* For master's, final exam, final project, or thesis; for Diploma, thesis or alternative, final project. *Entrance requirements:* For master's, minimum undergraduate QPA of 2.67; for Diploma, GRE General Test or MAT, minimum graduate QPA of 3.0. Additional exam requirements/recommendations for international students: Recommended—TOEFL (minimum score 550 paper-based; 213 computer-based; 80 iBT), IELTS (minimum score 6.5). Electronic applications accepted. *Faculty research:* Self-concept, internship assessment, stress and situational development, follow-up of graduation.

University of California, Irvine, Office of Graduate Studies, Department of Education, Irvine, CA 92697. Offers educational administration (Ed D); educational administration and leadership (Ed D); elementary and secondary education (MAT). Part-time and evening/weekend programs available. *Students:* 292 full-time (210 women), 11 part-time (9 women); includes 114 minority (7 African Americans, 2 American Indian/Alaska Native, 64 Asian Americans or Pacific Islanders, 41 Hispanic Americans), 6 international. Average age 28. 523 applicants, 75% accepted, 233 enrolled. In 2009, 164 master's, 20 doctorates awarded. *Degree requirements:* For doctorate, thesis/dissertation. *Entrance requirements:* For master's, GRE, minimum GPA of 3.0; for doctorate, GRE General Test, minimum GPA of 3.0. Additional exam requirements/recommendations for international students: Required—TOEFL (minimum score 550 paper-based; 213 computer-based). *Application deadline:* For fall admission, 1/4 priority date for domestic students, 1/4 for international students. Application fee: $70 ($90 for international students). Electronic applications accepted. *Financial support:* Fellowships, research assistantships with full tuition reimbursements, institutionally sponsored loans, traineeships, health care benefits, and unspecified assistantships available. Financial award application deadline: 3/1; financial award applicants required to submit FAFSA. *Faculty research:* Education technology, learning theory, social theory, cultural diversity, postmodernism. *Unit head:* David Brant, Interim Chair, 949-824-7840, E-mail: dbrant@uci.edu. *Application contact:* Sarah K. Singh, Student Affairs Officer, 949-824-7832, Fax: 949-824-2965, E-mail: sksingh@uci.edu.

University of Central Florida, College of Education, Department of Teaching and Learning Principles, Program in Elementary Education, Orlando, FL 32816. Offers M Ed, MA. *Accreditation:* NCATE. *Students:* 45 full-time (44 women), 80 part-time (77 women); includes 19 minority (7 African Americans, 1 American Indian/Alaska Native, 3 Asian Americans or Pacific Islanders, 8 Hispanic Americans), 1 international. Average age 28. 78 applicants, 88% accepted, 44 enrolled. In 2009, 25 master's awarded. *Degree requirements:* For master's, thesis or alternative. *Application deadline:* For fall admission, 7/15 for domestic students; for spring admission, 12/15 for domestic students. Application fee: $30. Electronic applications accepted. *Expenses:* Tuition, state resident: part-time $306.31 per credit hour. Tuition, nonresident: part-time $1099.01 per credit hour. Part-time tuition and fees vary according to degree level and program. *Financial support:* In 2009–10, 3 students received support, including 1 fellowship with tuition reimbursement available (averaging $10,000 per year), 1 research assistantship with tuition reimbursement available (averaging $7,650 per year), 1 teaching assistantship (averaging $6,900 per year); career-related internships or fieldwork, Federal Work-Study, institutionally sponsored loans, tuition waivers (partial), and unspecified assistantships also available.

University of Central Florida, College of Education, Education PhD Program, Orlando, FL 32816. Offers communication sciences and disorders (PhD); counselor education (PhD); elementary education (PhD); exceptional education (PhD); higher education (PhD); hospitality education (PhD); instructional technology (PhD); mathematics education (PhD); science education (PhD); social science education (PhD). *Students:* 99 full-time (70 women), 14 part-time (9 women); includes 28 minority (17 African Americans, 2 Asian Americans or Pacific Islanders, 9 Hispanic Americans), 20 international. In 2009, 15 doctorates awarded. Application fee: $30. Electronic applications accepted. *Expenses:* Tuition, state resident: part-time $306.31 per credit hour. Tuition, nonresident: part-time $1099.01 per credit hour. Part-time tuition and fees vary according to degree level and program. *Financial support:* In 2009–10, 40 fellowships with partial tuition reimbursements (averaging $9,200 per year), 61 research assistantships with partial tuition reimbursements (averaging $7,800 per year), 18 teaching assistantships with partial tuition reimbursements (averaging $6,500 per year) were awarded. *Unit head:* Dr. B. Grant Hayes, Associate Dean, 407-823-5391, E-mail: ghayes@mail.ucf.edu. *Application contact:* Dr. B. Grant Hayes, Associate Dean, 407-823-5391, E-mail: ghayes@mail.ucf.edu.

University of Central Missouri, The Graduate School, College of Education, Warrensburg, MO 64093. Offers career and technical education administration (MS); career and technical education industry training (MS); career and technical education leadership/teaching (MS); college student personnel administration (MS); counseling (MS); curriculum and instruction (Ed S); educational leadership (Ed D); educational technology (MS); elementary education/educational foundations and literacy (MSE); elementary school administration (MSE); elementary school principalship (Ed S); human services/learning resources (Ed S); human services/professional counseling (Ed S); human services/special education (Ed S); human services/technology and occupational education (Ed S); K-12 education/educational foundations and literacy (MSE); K-12 special education (MSE); library science and information services (MS); literacy education (MSE); secondary education/educational foundations & literacy (MSE); secondary school administration (MSE); secondary school principalship (Ed S); superintendency (Ed S); teaching (MAT). Part-time programs available. Postbaccalaureate distance learning degree programs offered. *Faculty:* 42. *Students:* 123 full-time (82 women), 721 part-time (552 women); includes 58 minority (38 African Americans, 3 American Indian/Alaska Native, 6 Asian Americans or Pacific Islanders, 11 Hispanic Americans), 6 international. Average age 34. 229 applicants, 88% accepted, 190 enrolled. In 2009, 212 master's, 47 other advanced degrees awarded. *Entrance requirements:* Additional exam requirements/recommendations for international students: Required—TOEFL (minimum score 550 paper-based; 79 computer-based). *Application deadline:* For fall admission, 6/1 priority date for domestic students, 5/1 for international students; for spring admission, 10/1 priority date for domestic students, 10/1 for international students. Applications are processed on a rolling basis. Application fee: $30 ($75 for international students). Electronic applications accepted. *Expenses:* Tuition, area resident: Part-time $245.80 per credit hour. Tuition, nonresident: part-time $491.60 per credit hour. Required fees: $24.20 per credit hour. Full-time tuition and fees vary according to course load, degree level, campus/location and reciprocity agreements. *Financial support:* Research assistantships with full and partial tuition reimbursements, teaching assistantships with full and partial tuition reimbursements, career-related internships or fieldwork, Federal Work-Study, scholarships/grants, and administrative and laboratory assistantships available. Support available to part-time

Elementary Education

University of Central Missouri (continued)

students. Financial award application deadline: 3/1; financial award applicants required to submit FAFSA. *Unit head:* Dr. Michael Wright, Dean, 660-543-4272, Fax: 660-543-8753, E-mail: mwright@ucmo.edu. *Application contact:* Laurie Delap, Admissions Coordinator, 660-543-4621, Fax: 660-543-4778, E-mail: gradinfo@ucmo.edu.

University of Central Oklahoma, College of Graduate Studies and Research, College of Education, Department of Curriculum and Instruction, Program in Elementary Education, Edmond, OK 73034-5209. Offers M Ed. *Accreditation:* NCATE. Part-time programs available. *Faculty:* 7 full-time (4 women). *Students:* 7 full-time (all women), 12 part-time (10 women); includes 3 minority (1 African American, 2 Asian Americans or Pacific Islanders). Average age 31. 6 applicants, 100% accepted. In 2009, 2 master's awarded. *Entrance requirements:* For master's, GRE General Test. Additional exam requirements/recommendations for international students: Required—TOEFL (minimum score 550 paper-based; 213 computer-based). *Application deadline:* For fall admission, 7/1 for international students; for spring admission, 11/1 for international students. Applications are processed on a rolling basis. Application fee: $25. Electronic applications accepted. *Expenses:* Tuition, state resident: full-time $4128; part-time $172 per credit hour. Tuition, nonresident: full-time $10,373; part-time $432.20 per credit hour. Required fees: $433.20; $18.05 per credit hour. *Financial support:* Unspecified assistantships available. Financial award application deadline: 3/31; financial award applicants required to submit FAFSA. *Faculty research:* Science education. *Unit head:* Dr. Paulette Shreck, Adviser, 405-974-5721, E-mail: dsprung@aix1.uco.edu. *Application contact:* Dr. Richard Bernard, Dean, Graduate College, 405-974-3493, Fax: 405-974-3852, E-mail: gradcoll@uco.edu.

University of Cincinnati, Graduate School, College of Education, Criminal Justice, and Human Services, Division of Teacher Education, Program in Middle Childhood Education, Cincinnati, OH 45221. Offers M Ed. *Accreditation:* NCATE. Part-time programs available. *Degree requirements:* For master's, thesis or alternative. *Entrance requirements:* For master's, GRE General Test. Additional exam requirements/recommendations for international students: Required—TOEFL (minimum score 550 paper-based; 213 computer-based), TWE (minimum score 4.5), OEPT. Electronic applications accepted.

University of Connecticut, Graduate School, Neag School of Education, Department of Curriculum and Instruction, Program in Elementary Education, Storrs, CT 06269. Offers MA, PhD, Post-Master's Certificate. *Accreditation:* NCATE. *Faculty:* 21 full-time (11 women). *Students:* 45 full-time (43 women), 3 part-time (2 women); includes 6 minority (1 African American, 3 Asian Americans or Pacific Islanders, 2 Hispanic Americans). Average age 24. 56 applicants, 61% accepted, 31 enrolled. In 2009, 40 master's, 1 other advanced degree awarded. Terminal master's awarded for partial completion of doctoral program. *Degree requirements:* For master's, comprehensive exam, thesis or alternative; for doctorate, thesis/dissertation. *Entrance requirements:* For doctorate, GRE General Test. Additional exam requirements/recommendations for international students: Required—TOEFL (minimum score 550 paper-based; 214 computer-based). *Application deadline:* For fall admission, 2/1 priority date for domestic and international students; for spring admission, 11/1 for domestic students, 10/1 for international students. Applications are processed on a rolling basis. Application fee: $55. Electronic applications accepted. *Expenses:* Tuition, state resident: full-time $4725; part-time $525 per credit. Tuition, nonresident: full-time $12,267; part-time $1363 per credit. Required fees: $346 per semester. Tuition and fees vary according to course load. *Financial support:* In 2009–10, 1 research assistantship with full tuition reimbursement was awarded; fellowships, teaching assistantships with full tuition reimbursements, Federal Work-Study, scholarships/grants, health care benefits, and unspecified assistantships also available. Financial award application deadline: 2/1; financial award applicants required to submit FAFSA. *Unit head:* Mary Anne Doyle, Head, 860-486-2433, Fax: 860-486-0280, E-mail: mary.dolye@uconn.edu. *Application contact:* Lisa Rasicot, Graduate Coordinator, 860-486-3065, Fax: 860-486-0210, E-mail: l.rasicot@uconn.edu.

The University of Findlay, Graduate and Professional Studies, College of Education, Findlay, OH 45840-3653. Offers administration (MA Ed); early childhood (MA Ed); elementary education (MA Ed); human resource development (MA Ed); leadership (MA Ed); special education (MA Ed); technology (MA Ed); web instruction (MA Ed). *Accreditation:* NCATE. Part-time and evening/weekend programs available. *Degree requirements:* For master's, thesis, cumulative project. *Entrance requirements:* For master's, minimum undergraduate GPA of 2.75 in last 62 hours of course work. Additional exam requirements/recommendations for international students: Required—TOEFL (minimum score 550 paper-based; 213 computer-based; 80 iBT). Electronic applications accepted. *Expenses:* Contact institution. *Faculty research:* Children's literature, books and artwork, educational technology, professional development.

University of Florida, Graduate School, College of Education, School of Teaching and Learning, Gainesville, FL 32611. Offers bilingual/ESOL education (M Ed, MAE, Ed D, PhD, Ed S); curriculum and instruction (M Ed, MAE, Ed D, PhD, Ed S); early childhood education (Ed D, PhD, Ed S); elementary education (M Ed, MAE); English education (M Ed, MAE); mathematics education (M Ed, MAE); reading education (M Ed, MAE); science education (M Ed, MAE); social foundations (M Ed, MAE, Ed D, PhD); social studies education (M Ed, MAE). *Accreditation:* NCATE. *Degree requirements:* For master's, thesis optional; for doctorate, variable foreign language requirement, thesis/dissertation. *Entrance requirements:* For master's and doctorate, GRE General Test, minimum GPA of 3.0; for Ed S, GRE General Test. Additional exam requirements/recommendations for international students: Required—TOEFL (minimum score 550 paper-based; 213 computer-based). Electronic applications accepted. *Faculty research:* Teacher education, inclusive education, classroom processes, curriculum and technology.

University of Georgia, Graduate School, College of Education, Department of Elementary and Social Studies Education, Athens, GA 30602. Offers early childhood education (M Ed, MAT, PhD, Ed S), including child and family development (MAT); elementary education (PhD); middle school education (M Ed, PhD, Ed S); social studies education (M Ed, Ed D, PhD, Ed S). *Faculty:* 14 full-time (9 women). *Students:* 114 full-time (94 women), 130 part-time (112 women); includes 37 minority (20 African Americans, 1 American Indian/Alaska Native, 11 Asian Americans or Pacific Islanders, 5 Hispanic Americans), 9 international. 168 applicants, 57% accepted, 48 enrolled. In 2009, 75 master's, 9 doctorates, 12 other advanced degrees awarded. *Entrance requirements:* For master's and Ed S, GRE General Test or MAT; for doctorate, GRE General Test. *Application deadline:* For fall admission, 7/1 priority date for domestic students; for spring admission, 11/15 for domestic students. Application fee: $50. Electronic applications accepted. *Expenses:* Tuition, state resident: full-time $6000; part-time $250 per credit hour. Tuition, nonresident: full-time $20,904; part-time $871 per credit hour. Required fees: $730 per semester. *Financial support:* Fellowships, research assistantships, teaching assistantships, unspecified assistantships available. *Unit head:* Dr. Ronald L. VanSickle, Interim Head, 706-542-7265, Fax: 706-542-6506, E-mail: rvansick@uga.edu. *Application contact:* Dr. Ronald E. Butchart, Graduate Coordinator, 706-542-6490, Fax: 706-542-8996, E-mail: essegrad@uga.edu.

University of Hartford, College of Education, Nursing, and Health Professions, Program in Elementary and Special Education, West Hartford, CT 06117-1599. Offers elementary education (M Ed). *Accreditation:* NCATE. Part-time and evening/weekend programs available. *Degree requirements:* For master's, comprehensive exam. *Entrance requirements:* For master's, PRAXIS I or waiver, interview, 2 letters of recommendation. Additional exam requirements/recommendations for international students: Required—TOEFL (minimum score 550 paper-based; 213 computer-based). Electronic applications accepted.

University of Houston, College of Education, Department of Curriculum and Instruction, Houston, TX 77204. Offers art education (M Ed); bilingual education (M Ed); curriculum and instruction (M Ed, Ed D); early childhood education (M Ed); elementary education (M Ed); gifted and talented education (M Ed); instructional technology (M Ed); mathematics education (M Ed); reading and language arts education (M Ed); science education (M Ed); second language education (M Ed); secondary education (M Ed); social studies education (M Ed); teaching (M Ed). *Accreditation:* NCATE. Part-time and evening/weekend programs available. *Faculty:* 20 full-time (9 women), 22 part-time/adjunct (17 women). *Students:* 113 full-time (81 women), 195 part-time (150 women); includes 107 minority (43 African Americans, 29 Asian Americans or Pacific Islanders, 35 Hispanic Americans), 29 international. Average age 35. 150 applicants, 77% accepted, 55 enrolled. In 2009, 75 master's, 31 doctorates awarded. *Degree requirements:* For master's, comprehensive exam, thesis optional; for doctorate, comprehensive exam, thesis/dissertation. *Entrance requirements:* For master's and doctorate, GRE, minimum cumulative undergraduate GPA of 2.6. Additional exam requirements/recommendations for international students: Required—TOEFL (minimum score 550 paper-based; 79 iBT). *Application deadline:* For fall admission, 3/1 for domestic and international students; for spring admission, 10/1 for domestic and international students. Application fee: $45 ($75 for international students). Electronic applications accepted. *Expenses:* Tuition, state resident: full-time $7676; part-time $320 per credit hour. Tuition, nonresident: full-time $14,324; part-time $597 per credit hour. Required fees: $3034. *Financial support:* In 2009–10, 4 fellowships with full tuition reimbursements (averaging $9,500 per year), 6 research assistantships with full tuition reimbursements (averaging $8,800 per year), 25 teaching assistantships with full tuition reimbursements (averaging $8,800 per year) were awarded; career-related internships or fieldwork, Federal Work-Study, institutionally sponsored loans, scholarships/grants, health care benefits, and unspecified assistantships also available. Support available to part-time students. Financial award application deadline: 2/1. *Faculty research:* Teaching-learning process, instructional technology in schools, teacher education, classroom management, at-risk students. *Unit head:* Dr. Laveria Hutchison, Chairperson, 713-743-4958, Fax: 713-743-4990, E-mail: lhutchison@uh.edu. *Application contact:* Renee C. Rattelade, Executive Secretary, 713-743-4997, Fax: 713-743-4990, E-mail: rrattelade@mail.coe.uh.edu.

University of Houston–Downtown, College of Public Service, Department of Urban Education, Houston, TX 77002. Offers bilingual education (MAT); curriculum and instruction (MAT); elementary education (MAT); secondary education (MAT). Part-time and evening/weekend programs available. *Faculty:* 8 full-time (5 women). *Students:* 1 (woman) full-time, 42 part-time (34 women); includes 27 minority (15 African Americans, 3 Asian Americans or Pacific Islanders, 9 Hispanic Americans). Average age 37. 16 applicants, 100% accepted, 12 enrolled. In 2009, 17 master's awarded. *Degree requirements:* For master's, capstone course with completed project, position paper, grant proposal, empirical study, curriculum development/revision, or advanced technology project presented at annual Graduate Project Exhibition. *Entrance requirements:* For master's, GRE, personal statement, 3 recommendation forms. Additional exam requirements/recommendations for international students: Required—TOEFL (minimum score 550 paper-based; 213 computer-based; 80 iBT). *Application deadline:* For fall admission, 6/1 for domestic and international students; for spring admission, 11/1 for domestic and international students. Applications are processed on a rolling basis. Application fee: $35 ($60 for international students). Electronic applications accepted. *Expenses:* Tuition, state resident: full-time $3150; part-time $175 per credit hour. Tuition, nonresident: full-time $7506; part-time $417 per credit hour. Required fees: $908; $322 per term. *Financial support:* Scholarships/grants available. Financial award applicants required to submit FAFSA. *Unit head:* Dr. Myrna Cohen, Chair, 713-221-2759, Fax: 713-226-5294, E-mail: cohenm@uhd.edu. *Application contact:* Traneshia Parker, Assistant Director, Admissions-Graduate, International and Residency, 713-221-8093, Fax: 713-221-8157, E-mail: parkert@uhd.edu.

University of Illinois at Chicago, Graduate College, College of Education, Department of Curriculum and Instruction, Chicago, IL 60607-7128. Offers curriculum studies (PhD); educational studies (M Ed); elementary education (M Ed); literacy, language and culture (M Ed, PhD); secondary education (M Ed). Part-time and evening/weekend programs available. *Degree requirements:* For doctorate, thesis/dissertation. *Entrance requirements:* For master's, minimum GPA of 2.75; for doctorate, GRE General Test, minimum GPA of 2.75. Additional exam requirements/recommendations for international students: Required—TOEFL. Electronic applications accepted. *Faculty research:* Curriculum theory, curriculum development, research on teaching, curriculum and context, reading/literacy.

University of Indianapolis, Graduate Programs, School of Education, Indianapolis, IN 46227-3697. Offers art education (MAT); biology (MAT); chemistry (MAT); curriculum and instruction (MA); earth sciences (MAT); education (MA, MAT); educational leadership (MA); elementary education (MA); English (MAT); French (MAT); math (MAT); physical education (MAT); physics (MAT); secondary education (MA), including art education, education, English education, social studies education; social studies (MAT); Spanish (MAT). *Accreditation:* NCATE. Part-time and evening/weekend programs available. *Faculty:* 4 full-time (3 women), 3 part-time/adjunct (2 women). *Students:* 52 full-time (28 women), 110 part-time (67 women); includes 3 minority (all African Americans), 2 international. Average age 33. *Entrance requirements:* For master's, GRE Subject Test, PRAXIS I, minimum GPA of 2.5, 3 letters of recommendation, interview, writing exercise. Additional exam requirements/recommendations for international students: Required—TOEFL (minimum score 550 paper-based; 213 computer-based). *Application deadline:* Applications are processed on a rolling basis. Application fee: $50. *Financial support:* Federal Work-Study available. Financial award application deadline: 5/1; financial award applicants required to submit FAFSA. *Faculty research:* Assessment of teacher education, perceptions of prospective teachers by parents. *Unit head:* Dr. Kathy Moran, Dean, 317-788-3285, Fax: 317-788-3300, E-mail: kmoran@uindy.edu. *Application contact:* Chemain Slater, 317-788-2051, E-mail: slaterc@uindy.edu.

The University of Iowa, Graduate College, College of Education, Department of Teaching and Learning, Program in Elementary Education, Iowa City, IA 52242-1316. Offers curriculum and supervision (MA, PhD); developmental reading (MA); early childhood education and care (MA); elementary education (MA, PhD); language, literature and culture (PhD). *Degree requirements:* For master's, thesis optional, exam; for doctorate, comprehensive exam, thesis/dissertation. *Entrance requirements:* For master's and doctorate, GRE General Test, minimum GPA of 3.0. Additional exam requirements/recommendations for international students: Required—TOEFL (minimum score 550 paper-based; 213 computer-based; 81 iBT). Electronic applications accepted.

University of Louisiana at Monroe, Graduate School, College of Education and Human Development, Department of Curriculum and Instruction, Program in Curriculum and Instruction, Monroe, LA 71209-0001. Offers curriculum and instruction (Ed D); elementary education (1-5) (M Ed); reading education (K-12) (M Ed); SPED-academically gifted education (K-12) (M Ed); SPED-early intervention education (birth-3) (M Ed); SPED-educational diagnostics education (PreK-12) (M Ed). *Accreditation:* NCATE. *Faculty:* 17 full-time (all women), 2 part-time/adjunct (both women). *Students:* 15 full-time (13 women), 125 part-time (118 women); includes 38 minority (36 African Americans, 1 Asian American or Pacific Islander, 1 Hispanic American). Average age 37. In 2009, 11 master's, 4 doctorates awarded. *Degree requirements:* For master's, comprehensive exam (for some programs), thesis; for doctorate, thesis/dissertation, internships. *Entrance requirements:* For master's, GRE General Test; for doctorate, GRE General Test, minimum undergraduate GPA of 2.75, graduate 3.25. Additional exam requirements/recommendations for international students: Required—TOEFL (minimum score 500 paper-based; 173 computer-based; 61 iBT). *Application deadline:* For fall admission, 8/24 priority date for domestic students, 7/1 for international students; for winter admission, 12/14 priority date for domestic students; for spring admission, 1/19 for domestic students, 11/1 for international students. Applications are processed on a rolling basis. Application fee: $20 ($30 for international students). Electronic applications accepted. *Expenses:* Tuition, state resident: part-time $159 per credit hour. Tuition, nonresident: part-time $159 per credit hour. Required fees: $1300 per year. Tuition and fees vary according to course load. *Financial support:* In 2009–10, 8 teaching assistantships with full tuition reimbursements (averaging $2,969 per year) were awarded; career-related internships or fieldwork, Federal Work-Study, and unspecified assistantships also available. Financial award application deadline: 4/1; financial award applicants required to submit FAFSA. *Unit head:* Dr. Dorothy Schween, Coordinator, 318-342-1269, Fax: 318-342-3131, E-mail: schween@ulm.edu. *Application contact:* Whitney Sutherland, Administrative Assistant to the Department Head, 318-342-1266, Fax: 318-342-3131, E-mail: sutherland@ulm.edu.

University of Louisiana at Monroe, Graduate School, College of Education and Human Development, Department of Curriculum and Instruction, Program in Elementary Education, Monroe, LA 71209-0001. Offers elementary education (MAT); grades 1-5 (M Ed). *Accreditation:* NCATE. Part-time and evening/weekend programs available. *Faculty:* 9 full-time (8 women). *Students:* 18 full-time (15 women), 34 part-time (31 women); includes 12 minority (11 African Americans, 1 Hispanic American). Average age 30. In 2009, 19 master's awarded. *Degree requirements:* For master's, thesis optional. *Entrance requirements:* For master's, GRE General Test, minimum GPA of 2.5. Additional exam requirements/recommendations for international students: Required—TOEFL (minimum score 500 paper-based; 173 computer-based; 61 iBT). *Application deadline:* For fall admission, 8/24 for domestic students, 7/1 for international students; for winter admission, 12/14 priority date for domestic students; for spring admission, 1/19 for domestic students, 11/1 for international students. Applications are processed on a rolling basis. Application fee: $20 ($30 for international students). Electronic applications accepted. *Expenses:* Tuition, state resident: part-time $159 per credit hour. Tuition, nonresident: part-time $159 per credit hour. Required fees: $1300 per year. Tuition and fees vary according to course load. *Financial support:* Career-related internships or fieldwork, Federal Work-Study, and unspecified assistantships available. Financial award application deadline: 4/1; financial award applicants required to submit FAFSA. *Faculty research:* Student attitudes.

University of Louisville, Graduate School, College of Education and Human Development, Department of Teaching and Learning, Louisville, KY 40292-0001. Offers art education (MAT); curriculum and instruction (PhD); early elementary education (MAT); instructional technology (M Ed); interdisciplinary early childhood education (MAT); middle school education (MAT); music education (MAT); reading education (M Ed); secondary education (MAT); special education (M Ed, MAT); teacher leadership (M Ed). Part-time and evening/weekend programs available. *Faculty:* 43 full-time (33 women), 43 part-time/adjunct (36 women). *Students:* 207 full-time (144 women), 410 part-time (306 women); includes 68 minority (43 African Americans, 2 American Indian/Alaska Native, 14 Asian Americans or Pacific Islanders, 9 Hispanic Americans), 5 international. Average age 33. 216 applicants, 68% accepted, 112 enrolled. In 2009, 269 master's, 6 doctorates awarded. *Degree requirements:* For doctorate, comprehensive exam, thesis/dissertation. *Entrance requirements:* For master's, GRE General Test, PRAXIS II (for some programs); for doctorate, GRE General Test. Additional exam requirements/recommendations for international students: Required—TOEFL (minimum score 560 paper-based; 210 computer-based; 83 iBT). Application fee: $50. Electronic applications accepted. *Financial support:* In 2009–10, 172 students received support; fellowships, research assistantships, teaching assistantships, career-related internships or fieldwork, Federal Work-Study, scholarships/grants, and unspecified assistantships available. Financial award application deadline: 6/1; financial award applicants required to submit FAFSA. *Faculty research:* Assessment of cognitive and language abilities in infants and preschool children; mathematics teachers' conceptions and beliefs, effect, and understanding of mathematics; incorporating nanoscience and nanotechnology into middle and high school science classrooms; urban teacher preparation through inquiry, action and advocacy; impacts of cognitive coaching on teacher practice and student achievement. Total annual research expenditures: $3.7 million. *Unit head:* Dr. Ann E. Larson, Acting Chair, 502-852-6431, Fax: 502-852-1497, E-mail: ann@louisville.edu. *Application contact:* Libby Leggett, Director, Graduate Admissions, 502-852-3101, Fax: 502-852-6536, E-mail: gradadm@louisville.edu.

University of Maine, Graduate School, College of Education and Human Development, Program in Elementary Education, Orono, ME 04469. Offers M Ed, MAT, MS, CAS. *Accreditation:* NCATE. Part-time and evening/weekend programs available. *Students:* 12 full-time (11 women). Average age 27. 5 applicants, 20% accepted, 1 enrolled. In 2009, 11 master's awarded. *Degree requirements:* For master's, thesis or alternative. *Entrance requirements:* For master's, MAT; for CAS, MA, M Ed, or MS. Additional exam requirements/recommendations for international students: Required—TOEFL. *Application deadline:* For fall admission, 2/1 priority date for domestic students. Applications are processed on a rolling basis. Application fee: $65. Electronic applications accepted. *Financial support:* Career-related internships or fieldwork, Federal Work-Study, institutionally sponsored loans, tuition waivers (full and partial), and unspecified assistantships available. Financial award application deadline: 3/1. *Unit head:* Dr. Janet Spector, Coordinator, 207-581-2444, Fax: 207-581-2423. *Application contact:* Scott G. Delcourt, Associate Dean of the Graduate School, 207-581-3291, Fax: 207-581-3232, E-mail: graduate@maine.edu.

University of Maryland, Baltimore County, Graduate School, College of Arts, Humanities and Social Sciences, Department of Education, Program in Teaching, Baltimore, MD 21250. Offers early childhood education (MAT); elementary education (MAT); secondary education (MAT), including art, biology, chemistry, dance, earth/space science, English, foreign language, mathematics, music, physics, theatre; secondary science (MAT), including social studies. Part-time and evening/weekend programs available. *Faculty:* 24 full-time (18 women), 25 part-time/adjunct (19 women). *Students:* 52 full-time (41 women), 64 part-time (55 women); includes 20 minority (5 African Americans, 1 American Indian/Alaska Native, 10 Asian Americans or Pacific Islanders, 4 Hispanic Americans), 3 international. Average age 31. 88 applicants, 57% accepted, 39 enrolled. In 2009, 106 master's awarded. *Degree requirements:* For master's, comprehensive exam (for some programs), thesis (for some programs). *Entrance requirements:* For master's, PRAXIS I and II, minimum GPA of 3.0. Additional exam requirements/recommendations for international students: Required—TOEFL. *Application deadline:* For fall admission, 6/1 for domestic students; for spring admission, 11/1 for domestic students. Applications are processed on a rolling basis. Application fee: $50. Electronic applications accepted. *Financial support:* In 2009–10, 6 students received support, including research assistantships with full tuition reimbursements available (averaging $12,000 per year); career-related internships or fieldwork, Federal Work-Study, scholarships/grants, tuition waivers, and unspecified assistantships also available. Financial award application deadline: 3/1. *Faculty research:* STEM teacher education, culturally sensitive pedagogy, ESOL/bilingual education, early childhood education, language, literacy and culture. *Unit head:* Dr. Susan M. Blunck, Director, 410-455-2869, Fax: 410-455-3986, E-mail: blunck@umbc.edu. *Application contact:* Dr. Susan M. Blunck, Director, 410-455-2869, Fax: 410-455-3986, E-mail: blunck@umbc.edu.

University of Massachusetts Amherst, Graduate School, School of Education, Program in Education, Amherst, MA 01003. Offers bilingual, English as a second language, and multicultural education (M Ed, CAGS); child study and early education (M Ed); children, families and schools (Ed D, CAGS); early childhood and elementary teacher education (M Ed); education policy and leadership (CAGS); educational administration (M Ed, CAGS); educational policy and leadership (Ed D); higher education (M Ed, CAGS); international education (M Ed); language, literacy and culture (Ed D); learning, media and technology (M Ed, CAGS); mathematics, science, and learning technologies (Ed D); policy studies (M Ed); policy studies in education (CAGS); reading and writing (M Ed); research and evaluation methods (Ed D); school counselor education (M Ed, CAGS); school psychology (CAGS); science education (CAGS); secondary teacher education (M Ed); social justice education (M Ed, Ed D, CAGS); special education (M Ed, Ed D, CAGS). *Accreditation:* NCATE. Part-time programs available. Postbaccalaureate distance learning degree programs offered (minimal on-campus study). *Faculty:* 74 full-time (41 women). *Students:* 377 full-time (268 women), 347 part-time (232 women); includes 115 minority (59 African Americans, 2 American Indian/Alaska Native, 16 Asian Americans or Pacific Islanders, 38 Hispanic Americans), 108 international. Average age 35. 708 applicants, 68% accepted, 266 enrolled. In 2009, 183 master's, 17 doctorates awarded. Terminal master's awarded for partial completion of doctoral program. *Degree requirements:* For master's, thesis or alternative; for doctorate, comprehensive exam, thesis/dissertation. *Entrance requirements:* Additional exam requirements/recommendations for international students: Required—TOEFL (minimum score 550 paper-based; 213 computer-based; 80 iBT), IELTS (minimum score 6.5). *Application deadline:* For fall admission, 1/15 for domestic and international students. Applications are processed on a rolling basis. Application fee: $50 ($65 for international students). Electronic applications accepted. *Expenses:* Tuition, state resident: full-time $2640; part-time $110 per credit. Tuition, nonresident: full-time $9936; part-time $414 per credit. Tuition and fees vary according to course load. *Financial support:* In 2009–10, 1 fellowship with full tuition reimbursement (averaging $8,036 per year), 92 research assistantships with full tuition reimbursements (averaging $8,555 per year), 83 teaching assistantships with full tuition reimbursements (averaging $4,661 per year) were awarded; career-related internships or fieldwork, Federal Work-Study, scholarships/grants, traineeships, health care benefits, tuition waivers (full), and unspecified assistantships also available. Support available to part-time students. Financial award application deadline: 1/15. *Unit head:* Dr. Linda L. Griffin, Graduate Program Director, 413-545-6984, Fax: 413-545-2873. *Application contact:* Jean M. Ames, Supervisor of Admissions, 413-545-0722, Fax: 413-577-0010, E-mail: gradadm@grad.umass.edu.

University of Massachusetts Boston, Office of Graduate Studies, Graduate College of Education, School Organization, Curriculum and Instruction Department, Boston, MA 02125-3393. Offers education (M Ed, Ed D), including elementary and secondary education/certification (M Ed), higher education administration (Ed D), teacher certification (M Ed), urban school leadership (Ed D); educational administration (M Ed, CAGS); special education (M Ed). *Degree requirements:* For master's and CAGS, comprehensive exam; for doctorate, comprehensive exam, thesis/dissertation. *Entrance requirements:* For master's, GRE General Test or MAT; for doctorate, GRE General Test or MAT, minimum GPA of 2.75; for CAGS, minimum GPA of 2.75.

University of Massachusetts Boston, Office of Graduate Studies, Graduate College of Education, School Organization, Curriculum and Instruction Department, Program in Education, Track in Elementary and Secondary Education/Certification, Boston, MA 02125-3393. Offers M Ed. Part-time and evening/weekend programs available. *Degree requirements:* For master's, comprehensive exam, thesis optional, practicum. *Entrance requirements:* For master's, GRE General Test or MAT, minimum GPA of 3.0, 2 years of teaching experience. *Faculty research:* Anti-bias education, inclusionary curriculum and instruction, creativity and learning, science, technology and society, teaching of reading.

University of Massachusetts Dartmouth, Graduate School, School of Education, Public Policy, and Civic Engagement, Department of Teaching and Learning, North Dartmouth, MA 02747-2300. Offers elementary education (MAT, Postbaccalaureate Certificate); middle school education (MAT); principal initial licensure (Postbaccalaureate Certificate); secondary school education (MAT). *Faculty:* 7 full-time (4 women), 6 part-time/adjunct (3 women). *Students:* 53 full-time (33 women), 183 part-time (118 women); includes 16 minority (6 African Americans, 1 American Indian/Alaska Native, 2 Asian Americans or Pacific Islanders, 7 Hispanic Americans). Average age 35. 188 applicants, 75% accepted, 109 enrolled. In 2009, 34 master's, 4 other advanced degrees awarded. *Degree requirements:* For master's, thesis or alternative. *Entrance requirements:* For master's, MAT or GRE, GMAT, minimum undergraduate GPA of 2.7, teacher certification, 3 letters of recommendation. Additional exam requirements/recommendations for international students: Required—TOEFL (minimum score 500 paper-based). *Application deadline:* For fall admission, 4/20 priority date for domestic students, 2/20 for international students; for spring admission, 11/15 priority date for domestic students, 9/15 for international students. Applications are processed on a rolling basis. Application fee: $40 ($60 for international students). *Expenses:* Tuition, state resident: full-time $2071; part-time $86.29 per credit. Tuition, nonresident: full-time $8099; part-time $337.46 per credit. Required fees: $9446. Tuition and fees vary according to class time, course load and reciprocity agreements. *Financial support:* Federal Work-Study available. Financial award application deadline: 3/1. Total annual research expenditures: $1.3 million. *Unit head:* Dr. Gerard Koot, Director, 508-999-8305, Fax: 508-999-9125, E-mail: gkoot@umassd.edu. *Application contact:* Elan Turcotte-Shamski, Graduate Admissions Officer, 508-999-8604, Fax: 508-999-8183, E-mail: graduate@umassd.edu.

University of Memphis, Graduate School, College of Education, Department of Instruction and Curriculum Leadership, Memphis, TN 38152. Offers early childhood education (MAT, MS, Ed D); elementary education (MAT); instruction and curriculum (MS, Ed D); instruction design and technology (MS, Ed D); middle grades education (MAT); reading (MS, Ed D); secondary education (MAT); special education (MAT, MS, Ed D). *Accreditation:* NCATE (one or more programs are accredited). Part-time programs available. *Faculty:* 40 full-time (28 women), 20 part-time/adjunct (15 women). *Students:* 119 full-time (90 women), 631 part-time (505 women); includes 348 minority (331 African Americans, 2 American Indian/Alaska Native, 4 Asian Americans or Pacific Islanders, 11 Hispanic Americans), 7 international. Average age 34. 202 applicants, 77% accepted, 29 enrolled. In 2009, 137 master's, 10 doctorates awarded. Terminal master's awarded for partial completion of doctoral program. *Degree requirements:* For master's, comprehensive exam, thesis or alternative; for doctorate, comprehensive exam, thesis/dissertation. *Entrance requirements:* For master's, GRE General Test, minimum GPA of 2.5; for doctorate, GRE General Test, GRE Subject Test, 2 years of teaching experience. *Application deadline:* For fall admission, 8/1 for domestic students; for spring admission, 12/1 for domestic students. Applications are processed on a rolling basis. Application fee: $35 ($60 for international students). Electronic applications accepted. *Expenses:* Tuition, state resident: full-time $6246; part-time $347 per credit hour. Tuition, nonresident: full-time $15,894; part-time $883 per credit hour. Required fees: $1160. Full-time tuition and fees vary according to course load, degree level and program. *Financial support:* In 2009–10, 635 students received support; research assistantships with full tuition reimbursements available, teaching assistantships with full tuition reimbursements available, career-related internships or fieldwork, Federal Work-Study, institutionally sponsored loans, scholarships/grants, traineeships, and unspecified assistantships available. Support available to part-time students. Financial award application deadline: 2/15; financial award applicants required to submit FAFSA. *Faculty research:* Effective urban teachers, preparation and retention of urban teachers, technology utilization in schools, field-based teacher preparation programs, effective use of online instruction. *Unit head:* Dr. Sandra Cooley-Nichols, Interim Chair, 901-678-2365. *Application contact:* Dr. Sally Blake, Director of Graduate Studies, 901-678-4861.

University of Michigan–Flint, School of Education and Human Services, Department of Education, Flint, MI 48502-1950. Offers education (MA); elementary education with teaching certification (MA); literacy (K-12) (MA); special education (MA); technology in education (MA). Part-time programs available. *Faculty:* 14 full-time (12 women), 8 part-time/adjunct (4 women). *Students:* 27 full-time (24 women), 215 part-time (186 women); includes 22 minority (20 African Americans, 2 American Indian/Alaska Native). Average age 35. 63 applicants, 86% accepted, 43 enrolled. In 2009, 91 master's awarded. *Entrance requirements:* For master's, BS with minimum GPA of 3.0. Additional exam requirements/recommendations for international students: Required—TOEFL (minimum score 560 paper-based; 220 computer-based; 84 iBT), IELTS (minimum score 6.5). *Application deadline:* For fall admission, 8/1 priority date for domestic students, 5/1 priority date for international students; for winter admission, 11/15 priority date for domestic students, 9/15 priority date for international students; for spring admission, 3/15 priority date for domestic students, 1/15 priority date for international students. Application fee: $55. *Expenses:* Contact institution. *Financial support:* Federal Work-Study, scholarships/grants, and unspecified assistantships available. Support available to part-time students. Financial award application deadline: 6/1; financial award applicants required to submit FAFSA. *Unit head:* Dr. Beverly Schumer, Director, 810-424-5215, E-mail: bschumer@umflint.edu. *Application contact:* Beulah Alexander, Executive Secretary, 810-766-6879, Fax: 810-766-6891, E-mail: beulaha@umflint.edu.

University of Minnesota, Twin Cities Campus, Graduate School, College of Education and Human Development, Department of Curriculum and Instruction, Minneapolis, MN 55455-0213. Offers art education (M Ed, MA, PhD); children's literature (M Ed, MA, PhD); curriculum and instruction (MA, PhD); early childhood education (M Ed, PhD); elementary education (M Ed, MA, PhD); English education (MA, PhD); environmental education (M Ed); family education (M Ed, MA, Ed D, PhD); instructional systems and technology (M Ed, MA, PhD); language arts (MA, PhD); language immersion education (Certificate); literacy education (MA); mathematics education (MA, PhD); reading education (MA, PhD); science education (MA, PhD); second languages and cultures education (MA, PhD); social studies education (MA, PhD); teaching (M Ed), including Chinese, earth science, elementary special education, English,

Elementary Education

University of Minnesota, Twin Cities Campus *(continued)*
English as a second language, French, German, Hebrew, Japanese, life sciences, mathematics, middle school science, science, second languages and cultures, social studies, Spanish; technology enhanced learning (Certificate); writing education (M Ed, MA, PhD). *Faculty:* 34 full-time (21 women). *Students:* 436 full-time (307 women), 375 part-time (280 women); includes 80 minority (30 African Americans, 6 American Indian/Alaska Native, 33 Asian Americans or Pacific Islanders, 11 Hispanic Americans), 40 international. Average age 32. 660 applicants, 64% accepted, 379 enrolled. In 2009, 552 master's, 14 doctorates, 7 other advanced degrees awarded. *Financial support:* In 2009–10, 5 fellowships (averaging $27,000 per year), 47 research assistantships with full tuition reimbursements (averaging $25,682 per year), 60 teaching assistantships with full tuition reimbursements (averaging $29,889 per year) were awarded. *Faculty research:* Teaching and learning; quality of education; influence of cultural, linguistic, social, political, technological and economic factors on teaching, learning and educational research; relationship between educational practice and a democratic and just society. Total annual research expenditures: $1.8 million. *Unit head:* Dr. Ruth Thomas, Chair, 612-624-4772, Fax: 612-624-8277, E-mail: thoma006@umn.edu. *Application contact:* Dr. Mary Trettin, Associate Dean, 612-625-6501, Fax: 612-626-1580, E-mail: mtrettin@umn.edu.

University of Missouri, Graduate School, College of Education, Department of Learning, Teaching and Curriculum, Columbia, MO 65211. Offers agricultural education (M Ed, PhD, Ed S); art education (M Ed, PhD, Ed S); business and office education (M Ed, PhD, Ed S); early childhood education (M Ed, PhD, Ed S); elementary education (M Ed, PhD, Ed S); English education (M Ed, PhD, Ed S); foreign language education (M Ed, PhD, Ed S); health education and promotion (M Ed, PhD); learning and instruction (M Ed); marketing education (M Ed, PhD, Ed S); mathematics education (M Ed, PhD, Ed S); music education (M Ed, PhD, Ed S); reading education (M Ed, PhD, Ed S); science education (M Ed, PhD, Ed S); social studies education (M Ed, PhD, Ed S); vocational education (M Ed, PhD, Ed S). Part-time programs available. Terminal master's awarded for partial completion of doctoral program. *Degree requirements:* For doctorate, thesis/dissertation. *Entrance requirements:* For master's and Ed S, GRE General Test or MAT, minimum GPA of 3.0; for doctorate, GRE General Test, minimum GPA of 3.0. Additional exam requirements/recommendations for international students: Required—TOEFL (minimum score 600 paper-based; 250 computer-based; 100 iBT). Electronic applications accepted.

University of Missouri–St. Louis, College of Education, Division of Teaching and Learning, St. Louis, MO 63121. Offers elementary education (M Ed), including early childhood, general, reading; secondary education (M Ed), including curriculum and instruction, general, middle level education, reading, teaching English to speakers of other languages (TESOL); secondary school teaching (Certificate); special education (M Ed), including behavioral disorders, early childhood special education, general, learning disabilities, mental retardation; teaching English to speakers of other languages (Certificate). Part-time and evening/weekend programs available. *Faculty:* 36 full-time (23 women), 51 part-time/adjunct (42 women). *Students:* 123 full-time (77 women), 569 part-time (435 women); includes 137 minority (110 African Americans, 4 American Indian/Alaska Native, 10 Asian Americans or Pacific Islanders, 13 Hispanic Americans), 11 international. Average age 32. In 2009, 1,852 master's awarded. *Degree requirements:* For master's, comprehensive exam. *Entrance requirements:* Additional exam requirements/recommendations for international students: Recommended—TOEFL (minimum score 550 paper-based; 213 computer-based). *Application deadline:* For fall admission, 7/1 priority date for domestic and international students; for spring admission, 12/1 priority date for domestic and international students. Application fee: $35 ($40 for international students). Electronic applications accepted. *Expenses:* Tuition, state resident: full-time $5377; part-time $297.70 per credit hour. Tuition, nonresident: full-time $13,882; part-time $771.20 per credit hour. Required fees: $220; $12.20 per credit hour. One-time fee: $12. Tuition and fees vary according to course level, campus/location and program. *Financial support:* In 2009–10, 5 research assistantships (averaging $10,339 per year), 2 teaching assistantships (averaging $6,800 per year) were awarded. Financial award application deadline: 4/1; financial award applicants required to submit FAFSA. *Unit head:* Dr. Joseph Polman, Chair, 314-516-5791. *Application contact:* 314-516-5458, Fax: 314-516-6996, E-mail: gadadm@umsl.edu.

University of Montevallo, College of Education, Program in Elementary Education, Montevallo, AL 35115. Offers M Ed. *Accreditation:* NCATE. Part-time programs available. *Students:* 46 full-time (45 women), 33 part-time (all women); includes 11 minority (7 African Americans, 4 Asian Americans or Pacific Islanders). In 2009, 46 master's awarded. *Degree requirements:* For master's, comprehensive exam. *Entrance requirements:* For master's, GRE General Test, MAT, minimum undergraduate GPA of 2.5. Additional exam requirements/recommendations for international students: Required—TOEFL (minimum score 550 paper-based). *Application deadline:* For fall admission, 7/15 for domestic students; for spring admission, 11/15 for domestic students. Application fee: $25. *Expenses:* Tuition, state resident: full-time $5592; part-time $233 per credit. Tuition, nonresident: full-time $11,184; part-time $466 per credit hour. Required fees: $482; $241 per semester. One-time fee: $25 part-time. *Financial support:* Federal Work-Study, scholarships/grants, and unspecified assistantships available. *Application contact:* Rebecca Hartley, Coordinator for Graduate Studies, 205-665-6350, Fax: 205-665-6353, E-mail: hartleyrs@montevallo.edu.

University of Nebraska at Omaha, Graduate Studies, College of Education, Department of Teacher Education, Program in Elementary Education, Omaha, NE 68182. Offers MA, MS. *Accreditation:* NCATE. Part-time and evening/weekend programs available. *Faculty:* 10 full-time (7 women). *Students:* 4 full-time (all women), 128 part-time (121 women); includes 6 minority (3 African Americans, 3 Hispanic Americans), 2 international. Average age 31. 42 applicants, 76% accepted, 24 enrolled. In 2009, 47 master's awarded. *Degree requirements:* For master's, comprehensive exam, thesis (for some programs). *Entrance requirements:* For master's, minimum GPA of 3.0. Additional exam requirements/recommendations for international students: Required—TOEFL (minimum score 550 paper-based; 213 computer-based; 80 iBT). *Application deadline:* For fall admission, 7/1 priority date for domestic students; for spring admission, 12/1 priority date for domestic students. Applications are processed on a rolling basis. Application fee: $45. Electronic applications accepted. *Financial support:* In 2009–10, 41 students received support; fellowships, teaching assistantships, Federal Work-Study, institutionally sponsored loans, scholarships/grants, tuition waivers (full), and unspecified assistantships available. Support available to part-time students. Financial award application deadline: 3/1. *Application contact:* Dr. Wilma Kuhlman, Student Contact, 402-554-2212.

University of Nevada, Reno, Graduate School, College of Education, Department of Curriculum, Teaching and Learning, Program in Elementary Education, Reno, NV 89557. Offers M Ed, MA, MS. *Degree requirements:* For master's, thesis optional. *Entrance requirements:* For master's, GRE General Test, minimum GPA of 2.75. Additional exam requirements/recommendations for international students: Required—TOEFL (minimum score 500 paper-based; 173 computer-based; 61 iBT), IELTS (minimum score 6). Electronic applications accepted. *Faculty research:* Child development, educational trends.

University of New Hampshire, Graduate School, College of Liberal Arts, Department of Education, Program in Elementary Education, Durham, NH 03824. Offers M Ed, MAT. Part-time programs available. *Faculty:* 32 full-time. *Students:* 32 full-time (28 women), 28 part-time (26 women); includes 2 minority (1 African American, 1 Asian American or Pacific Islander). Average age 29. 29 applicants, 59% accepted, 11 enrolled. In 2009, 63 master's awarded. *Degree requirements:* For master's, thesis or alternative. *Entrance requirements:* For master's, GRE General Test. Additional exam requirements/recommendations for international students: Required—TOEFL (minimum score 550 paper-based; 213 computer-based; 80 iBT). *Application deadline:* For fall admission, 4/1 priority date for domestic students, 4/1 for international students; for spring admission, 11/1 for domestic students. Applications are processed on a rolling basis. Application fee: $65. *Expenses:* Tuition, state resident: full-time $10,380; part-time $577 per credit hour. Tuition, nonresident: full-time $24,350; part-time $1002 per credit hour.

Required fees: $1550; $387.50 per semester. Tuition and fees vary according to course load and program. *Financial support:* In 2009–10, 9 students received support, including 1 teaching assistantship; fellowships, research assistantships, career-related internships or fieldwork, Federal Work-Study, scholarships/grants, and tuition waivers (full and partial) also available. Support available to part-time students. Financial award application deadline: 2/15. *Faculty research:* Pre-service teacher education. *Unit head:* Dr. Michael D. Andrew, Coordinator, 603-862-2371, E-mail: education.department@unh.edu. *Application contact:* Dr. Michael D. Andrew, Coordinator, 603-862-2371, E-mail: education.department@unh.edu.

University of New Mexico, Graduate School, College of Education, Department of Teacher Education, Program in Elementary Education, Albuquerque, NM 87131-2039. Offers MA. Part-time programs available. *Students:* 51 full-time (42 women), 136 part-time (119 women); includes 66 minority (3 African Americans, 15 American Indian/Alaska Native, 3 Asian Americans or Pacific Islanders, 45 Hispanic Americans), 7 international. Average age 36. 45 applicants, 62% accepted, 21 enrolled. In 2009, 52 master's awarded. *Degree requirements:* For master's, comprehensive exam, thesis optional. *Entrance requirements:* For master's, minimum overall GPA of 3.0, some experience working with students, NMTA or teacher's license, 3 letters of reference, 1 letter of intent. Additional exam requirements/recommendations for international students: Required—TOEFL (minimum score 550 paper-based; 213 computer-based). *Application deadline:* For fall admission, 3/1 for domestic students; for spring admission, 10/30 for domestic students. Application fee: $50. Electronic applications accepted. *Expenses:* Tuition, state resident: full-time $2099; part-time $233.20 per credit hour. Tuition, nonresident: full-time $6650. Required fees: $25 per semester. Tuition and fees vary according to course load, program and reciprocity agreements. *Financial support:* In 2009–10, 2 teaching assistantships with partial tuition reimbursements (averaging $11,641 per year) were awarded; career-related internships or fieldwork, scholarships/grants, and unspecified assistantships also available. Financial award application deadline: 4/15; financial award applicants required to submit FAFSA. *Faculty research:* Elementary education, science education, technology education, reflective practice, teacher education. *Unit head:* Dr. Rosalita Mitchell, Chair, 505-277-9611, Fax: 505-277-0455, E-mail: ted@unm.edu. *Application contact:* Mary Francis, Administrative Assistant, 505-277-9439, Fax: 505-277-0455, E-mail: ted@unm.edu.

University of North Alabama, College of Education, Department of Elementary Education, Program in Elementary Education, Florence, AL 35632-0001. Offers MA Ed, Ed S. *Accreditation:* NCATE. Part-time and evening/weekend programs available. *Faculty:* 7 part-time/adjunct (all women). *Students:* 5 full-time (all women), 47 part-time (44 women); includes 1 minority (American Indian/Alaska Native). Average age 33. In 2009, 16 master's awarded. *Degree requirements:* For master's, comprehensive exam. *Entrance requirements:* For master's, GRE, MAT, or NTE, minimum GPA of 2.5, Alabama Class B Certificate or equivalent, teaching experience. *Application deadline:* For fall admission, 7/1 priority date for domestic students; for spring admission, 12/1 for domestic students. Applications are processed on a rolling basis. Application fee: $25. Electronic applications accepted. *Expenses:* Tuition, state resident: full-time $5040; part-time $210 per credit hour. Tuition, nonresident: full-time $10,080; part-time $420 per credit hour. Required fees: $906. *Financial support:* Federal Work-Study available. Support available to part-time students. Financial award application deadline: 4/1. *Unit head:* Dr. Linda Armstrong, Chair, 256-765-4251, Fax: 256-765-4664, E-mail: ljarmstrong@una.edu. *Application contact:* Kim Mauldin, Director of Admissions, 256-765-4608, Fax: 256-765-4960, E-mail: komauldin@una.edu.

The University of North Carolina at Charlotte, Graduate School, College of Education, Department of Reading and Elementary Education, Charlotte, NC 28223-0001. Offers elementary education (M Ed); reading, language and literacy (M Ed). Part-time and evening/weekend programs available. Postbaccalaureate distance learning degree programs offered (no on-campus study). *Faculty:* 23 full-time (13 women), 3 part-time/adjunct (2 women). *Students:* 4 full-time (all women), 64 part-time (all women); includes 4 minority (3 African Americans, 1 Hispanic American). Average age 30. 17 applicants, 94% accepted, 12 enrolled. In 2009, 18 master's awarded. *Entrance requirements:* For master's, GRE or MAT. Additional exam requirements/recommendations for international students: Required—TOEFL (minimum score 557 paper-based; 220 computer-based; 83 iBT). *Application deadline:* For fall admission, 7/1 for domestic students, 5/1 for international students; for spring admission, 11/1 for domestic students, 10/1 for international students. Applications are processed on a rolling basis. Application fee: $55. Electronic applications accepted. *Financial support:* In 2009–10, 2 students received support, including 2 teaching assistantships (averaging $24,000 per year); fellowships, research assistantships, career-related internships or fieldwork, Federal Work-Study, institutionally sponsored loans, scholarships/grants, and unspecified assistantships also available. Support available to part-time students. Financial award application deadline: 4/1; financial award applicants required to submit FAFSA. *Unit head:* Dr. Robert J. Rickelman, Chair, 704-687-8890, Fax: 704-687-3749, E-mail: rjrickel@uncc.edu. *Application contact:* Kathy B. Giddings, Director of Graduate Admissions, 704-687-5503, Fax: 704-687-3279, E-mail: gradadm@uncc.edu.

The University of North Carolina at Charlotte, Graduate School, College of Education, Program in Teacher Education, Charlotte, NC 28223-0001. Offers art education (K-12) (MAT); dance education (K-12) (MAT); elementary education (K-6) (MAT); English as a second language (K-12) (MAT); foreign language education (K-12) (MAT); general teacher education (MAT); middle grades education (6-9) (MAT); music education (K-12) (MAT); secondary education (9-12) (MAT); special education (K-12) (MAT); theatre education (K-12) (MAT). *Faculty:* 108 full-time (64 women), 16 part-time/adjunct (12 women). *Students:* 29 full-time (20 women), 229 part-time (189 women); includes 32 minority (22 African Americans, 2 American Indian/Alaska Native, 3 Asian Americans or Pacific Islanders, 5 Hispanic Americans). Average age 32. 108 applicants, 92% accepted, 85 enrolled. In 2009, 59 master's awarded. *Entrance requirements:* For master's, GRE or MAT. Additional exam requirements/recommendations for international students: Required—TOEFL (minimum score 557 paper-based; 220 computer-based; 83 iBT). *Application deadline:* For fall admission, 7/1 for domestic students, 5/1 for international students; for spring admission, 11/1 for domestic students, 10/1 for international students. Applications are processed on a rolling basis. Application fee: $55. Electronic applications accepted. *Financial support:* In 2009–10, 5 students received support, including 1 research assistantship (averaging $18,000 per year), 3 teaching assistantships (averaging $12,183 per year); career-related internships or fieldwork, Federal Work-Study, institutionally sponsored loans, scholarships/grants, and administrative assistantship also available. Support available to part-time students. Financial award application deadline: 4/1; financial award applicants required to submit FAFSA. Total annual research expenditures: $5.1 million. *Unit head:* Dr. Kimberly J. Hartman, Coordinator, 704-687-8883, Fax: 704-687-6430, E-mail: khartman@uncc.edu. *Application contact:* Kathy B. Giddings, Director of Graduate Admissions, 704-687-5503, Fax: 704-687-3279, E-mail: gradadmn@uncc.edu.

The University of North Carolina at Greensboro, Graduate School, School of Education, Department of Curriculum and Instruction, Program in Curriculum and Teaching, Greensboro, NC 27412-5001. Offers higher education (PhD); teacher education and development (PhD). *Accreditation:* NCATE. *Degree requirements:* For doctorate, comprehensive exam, thesis/dissertation. *Entrance requirements:* For doctorate, GRE General Test. Additional exam requirements/recommendations for international students: Required—TOEFL. Electronic applications accepted.

The University of North Carolina at Pembroke, Graduate Studies, School of Education, Program in Elementary Education, Pembroke, NC 28372-1510. Offers MA Ed. *Accreditation:* NCATE. Part-time and evening/weekend programs available. *Degree requirements:* For master's, comprehensive exam, thesis optional. *Entrance requirements:* For master's, GRE General Test or MAT, minimum GPA of 3.0 in major, 2.5 overall; teaching license. Additional exam requirements/recommendations for international students: Required—TOEFL.

The University of North Carolina Wilmington, School of Education, Department of Elementary, Middle Level and Literacy Education, Program in Elementary Education, Wilmington, NC

28403-3297. Offers M Ed. *Accreditation:* NCATE. Part-time and evening/weekend programs available. *Degree requirements:* For master's, comprehensive exam. *Entrance requirements:* For master's, GRE General Test, MAT, minimum B average in upper-division undergraduate course work, bachelor's degree in elementary education.

University of North Dakota, Graduate School, College of Education and Human Development, Program in Elementary Education, Grand Forks, ND 58202. Offers M Ed, MS. *Accreditation:* NCATE. Part-time programs available. Postbaccalaureate distance learning degree programs offered (minimal on-campus study). *Degree requirements:* For master's, comprehensive exam, thesis or alternative. *Entrance requirements:* For master's, minimum GPA of 3.0. Additional exam requirements/recommendations for international students: Required—TOEFL (minimum score 550 paper-based; 213 computer-based; 79 iBT), IELTS (minimum score 6.5). Electronic applications accepted. *Faculty research:* Whole language, multicultural education, child-focused learning, experiential science, cooperative learning.

University of North Dakota, Graduate School, College of Education and Human Development, Teaching and Learning Program, Grand Forks, ND 58202. Offers elementary education (Ed D, PhD); measurement and statistics (Ed D, PhD); secondary education (Ed D, PhD); special education (Ed D, PhD). *Accreditation:* NCATE. Postbaccalaureate distance learning degree programs offered (minimal on-campus study). *Degree requirements:* For doctorate, comprehensive exam, thesis/dissertation, final exam. *Entrance requirements:* For doctorate, minimum GPA of 3.5. Additional exam requirements/recommendations for international students: Required—TOEFL (minimum score 550 paper-based; 213 computer-based; 79 iBT), IELTS (minimum score 6.5). Electronic applications accepted.

University of Northern Iowa, Graduate College, College of Education, Department of Curriculum and Instruction, Program in Elementary Education, Cedar Falls, IA 50614. Offers MAE. Part-time and evening/weekend programs available. *Students:* 1 (woman) full-time, 17 part-time (16 women); includes 1 minority (African American), 1 international. 20 applicants, 70% accepted, 14 enrolled. In 2009, 1 master's awarded. *Degree requirements:* For master's, comprehensive exam, thesis or alternative. *Entrance requirements:* For master's, minimum GPA of 3.0. Additional exam requirements/recommendations for international students: Required—TOEFL (minimum score 500 paper-based; 180 computer-based; 61 iBT). *Application deadline:* For fall admission, 8/1 priority date for domestic students. Applications are processed on a rolling basis. Application fee: $30 ($50 for international students). *Financial support:* Career-related internships or fieldwork, Federal Work-Study, and tuition waivers (full and partial) available. Support available to part-time students. Financial award application deadline: 2/1. *Unit head:* Dr. Lynn E. Nielsen, Coordinator, 319-273-7759, Fax: 319-273-5886, E-mail: lynn.nielsen@uni.edu. *Application contact:* Laurie S. Russell, Record Analyst, 319-273-2623, Fax: 319-273-6792, E-mail: laurie.russell@uni.edu.

University of North Florida, College of Education and Human Services, Department of Childhood Education, Jacksonville, FL 32224. Offers literacy K-12 (M Ed); professional education—elementary ed (M Ed); TESOL K-12 (M Ed). *Accreditation:* NCATE. Part-time and evening/weekend programs available. *Faculty:* 11 full-time (8 women). *Students:* 11 full-time (all women), 22 part-time (21 women); includes 7 minority (4 African Americans, 1 Asian American or Pacific Islander, 2 Hispanic Americans). Average age 30. 17 applicants, 35% accepted, 3 enrolled. In 2009, 23 master's awarded. *Entrance requirements:* For master's, GRE General Test, minimum GPA of 3.0 in last 60 hours, 3 letters of recommendation, interview. Additional exam requirements/recommendations for international students: Required—TOEFL (minimum score 500 paper-based; 173 computer-based). *Application deadline:* For fall admission, 7/1 priority date for domestic students, 5/1 for international students; for spring admission, 11/1 priority date for domestic students, 10/1 for international students. Applications are processed on a rolling basis. Application fee: $30. Electronic applications accepted. *Expenses:* Tuition, state resident: full-time $6649.20; part-time $277.05 per credit hour. Tuition, nonresident: full-time $22,970; part-time $957.08 per credit hour. Required fees: $985; $41.03 per credit hour. *Financial support:* In 2009–10, 12 students received support. Federal Work-Study and tuition waivers (partial) available. Support available to part-time students. Financial award application deadline: 4/1; financial award applicants required to submit FAFSA. *Faculty research:* The social context of and processes in learning, inter-disciplinary instruction, cross-cultural conflict resolution, the Vygotskian perspective on literacy diagnosis and instruction, performance poetry and teaching the language arts through drama. Total annual research expenditures: $256,831. *Unit head:* Dr. Ronghua Ouyang, Chair, 904-620-2611, Fax: 904-620-1025, E-mail: ronghua.ouyang@unf.edu. *Application contact:* Dr. John Kemppainen, Director, Office of Student Services, 904-620-2530, Fax: 904-620-1135, E-mail: jkemppai@unf.edu.

University of Oklahoma, Graduate College, College of Education, Department of Instructional Leadership and Academic Curriculum, Norman, OK 73072. Offers education (Certificate); instructional leadership and academic curriculum (M Ed, PhD), including bilingual education, early childhood education, elementary education, English education, math education, reading education, science education, secondary education, social studies education. *Accreditation:* NCATE. Part-time and evening/weekend programs available. *Faculty:* 18 full-time (11 women). *Students:* 44 full-time (36 women), 117 part-time (92 women); includes 35 minority (11 African Americans, 14 American Indian/Alaska Native, 5 Asian Americans or Pacific Islanders, 5 Hispanic Americans), 2 international. 50 applicants, 84% accepted, 32 enrolled. In 2009, 31 master's, 6 doctorates awarded. Terminal master's awarded for partial completion of doctoral program. *Degree requirements:* For doctorate, thesis/dissertation. *Entrance requirements:* For master's, 12 hours of course work in education; for doctorate, GRE General Test, master's degree, minimum graduate GPA of 3.0. Additional exam requirements/recommendations for international students: Required—TOEFL (minimum score 550 paper-based; 213 computer-based). *Application deadline:* For fall admission, 6/1 priority date for domestic students, 4/1 for international students; for spring admission, 11/1 for domestic students, 9/1 for international students. Applications are processed on a rolling basis. Application fee: $40 ($90 for international students). Electronic applications accepted. *Expenses:* Tuition, state resident: full-time $3744; part-time $156 per credit hour. Tuition, nonresident: full-time $13,577; part-time $565.70 per credit hour. Required fees: $2415; $90.10 per credit hour. *Financial support:* In 2009–10, 107 students received support, including 1 research assistantship with partial tuition reimbursement available (averaging $9,630 per year), 6 teaching assistantships with partial tuition reimbursements available (averaging $10,801 per year); scholarships/grants, health care benefits, and unspecified assistantships also available. Financial award applicants required to submit FAFSA. *Faculty research:* English education, mathematics education, reading, science education, social studies education. Total annual research expenditures: $752,908. *Unit head:* Lawrence Baines, Chair, 405-325-1498, Fax: 405-325-4061, E-mail: lbaines@ou.edu. *Application contact:* Lynn Crussel, Administrative Assistant for Graduate Studies, 405-325-4843, Fax: 405-325-4061, E-mail: lcrussel@ou.edu.

University of Pennsylvania, Graduate School of Education, Division of Foundations and Practices in Education, Program in Elementary and Secondary Education, Philadelphia, PA 19104. Offers MS Ed. *Students:* 296 full-time (198 women), 130 part-time (86 women); includes 32 minority (20 African Americans, 2 American Indian/Alaska Native, 9 Asian Americans or Pacific Islanders, 1 Hispanic American), 8 international. 292 applicants, 84% accepted, 183 enrolled. In 2009, 147 master's awarded. *Degree requirements:* For master's, comprehensive exam or portfolio. *Entrance requirements:* For master's, GRE General Test, MAT. *Application deadline:* For fall admission, 12/15 priority date for domestic students. Applications are processed on a rolling basis. Application fee: $70. Electronic applications accepted. *Expenses:* Contact institution. *Financial support:* Fellowships available. Financial award applicants required to submit FAFSA.

University of Phoenix, College of Natural Sciences, College of Education, Phoenix, AZ 85034-7209. Offers administration and supervision (MAEd); adult education and training (MAEd); curriculum and instruction (MAEd); curriculum and instruction-adult education (MAEd); curriculum and instruction-computer education (MAEd); curriculum and instruction-English and language arts education (MAEd); curriculum and instruction-English as a second language (MAEd); curriculum and instruction-mathematics education (MAEd); curriculum education (MAEd); early childhood (MAEd); elementary teacher education (MAEd); secondary teacher education (MAEd); special education (MAEd); teacher leadership (MAEd). *Accreditation:* Teacher Education Accreditation Council. Evening/weekend programs available. Postbaccalaureate distance learning degree programs offered (no on-campus study). *Faculty:* 47 full-time (34 women), 844 part-time/adjunct (636 women). *Students:* 13,657 full-time (10,698 women); includes 4,000 minority (3,063 African Americans, 74 American Indian/Alaska Native, 241 Asian Americans or Pacific Islanders, 622 Hispanic Americans), 307 international. Average age 36. In 2009, 17,246 master's awarded. *Degree requirements:* For master's, thesis (for some programs). *Entrance requirements:* For master's, 3 years of work experience, minimum GPA of 2.5. Additional exam requirements/recommendations for international students: Required—TOEFL (minimum score 550 paper-based; 213 computer-based; 79 iBT). *Application deadline:* Applications are processed on a rolling basis. Application fee: $45. Electronic applications accepted. *Expenses:* Tuition: Full-time $13,272. Required fees: $660. Full-time tuition and fees vary according to course level, degree level and program. *Financial support:* Institutionally sponsored loans and scholarships/grants available. Financial award applicants required to submit FAFSA. *Unit head:* Dr. Meredith Curley, Dean/Executive Director, 480-557-1217, Fax: 480-557-1588, E-mail: meredith.curley@phoenix.edu. *Application contact:* Chair, 602-387-7000, Fax: 602-387-6020.

University of Phoenix–Bay Area Campus, The Artemis School, College of Education, Pleasanton, CA 94588-3677. Offers curriculum instruction (MA Ed); curriculum instruction—adult education (MA Ed); elementary teacher education (MA Ed); secondary teacher education (MA Ed). Evening/weekend programs available. Postbaccalaureate distance learning degree programs offered (no on-campus study). *Degree requirements:* For master's, thesis (for some programs). *Entrance requirements:* For master's, minimum undergraduate GPA of 2.5, 3 years of work experience. Additional exam requirements/recommendations for international students: Required—TOEFL (minimum score 550 paper-based; 213 computer-based; 79 iBT). Electronic applications accepted.

University of Phoenix–Central Florida Campus, The Artemis School, College of Education, Maitland, FL 32751-7057. Offers administration and supervision (MA Ed); curriculum and instruction (MA Ed); curriculum and instruction-computer education (MA Ed); curriculum and instruction-mathematics education (MA Ed); early childhood education (MA Ed); elementary teacher education (MA Ed); secondary teacher education (MA Ed). Evening/weekend programs available. *Degree requirements:* For master's, thesis (for some programs). *Entrance requirements:* For master's, 3 years of work experience, minimum undergraduate GPA of 2.5. Additional exam requirements/recommendations for international students: Required—TOEFL (minimum score 550 paper-based; 213 computer-based; 79 iBT). Electronic applications accepted.

University of Phoenix–Central Valley Campus, College of Education, Fresno, CA 93720-1562. Offers curriculum and instruction (MA Ed); curriculum and instruction-computer education (MA Ed); elementary teacher education (MA Ed); secondary teacher education (MA Ed).

University of Phoenix–Chattanooga Campus, College of Education, Chattanooga, TN 37421-3707. Offers administration and supervision (MA Ed); curriculum and instruction (MA Ed); elementary teacher education (MA Ed); secondary teacher education (MA Ed).

University of Phoenix–Denver Campus, The Artemis School, College of Education, Lone Tree, CO 80124-5453. Offers administration and supervision (MAEd); curriculum instruction (MAEd); elementary teacher education (MAEd); school counseling (MSC); secondary teacher education (MAEd). Evening/weekend programs available. *Degree requirements:* For master's, thesis (for some programs). *Entrance requirements:* For master's, minimum undergraduate GPA of 2.5, 3 years work experience. Additional exam requirements/recommendations for international students: Required—TOEFL (minimum score 550 paper-based; 213 computer-based; 79 iBT). Electronic applications accepted.

University of Phoenix–Hawaii Campus, The Artemis School, College of Education, Honolulu, HI 96813-4317. Offers administration and supervision (MA Ed); curriculum and instruction (MA Ed); elementary education (MA Ed); secondary education (MA Ed); special education (MA Ed); teacher education for elementary licensure (MA Ed). Evening/weekend programs available. *Degree requirements:* For master's, thesis (for some programs). *Entrance requirements:* For master's, minimum undergraduate GPA of 2.5, 3 years of work experience. Additional exam requirements/recommendations for international students: Required—TOEFL (minimum score 550 paper-based; 213 computer-based; 79 iBT). Electronic applications accepted.

University of Phoenix–Idaho Campus, The Artemis School, College of Education, Meridian, ID 83642-3014. Offers administration and supervision (MA Ed); curriculum and instruction (MA Ed); elementary teacher education (MA Ed); secondary teacher education (MA Ed). Evening/weekend programs available. *Degree requirements:* For master's, thesis (for some programs). *Entrance requirements:* For master's, minimum undergraduate GPA of 2.5, 3 years of work experience. Additional exam requirements/recommendations for international students: Required—TOEFL (minimum score 550 paper-based; 213 computer-based). Electronic applications accepted.

University of Phoenix–Indianapolis Campus, The Artemis School, College of Education, Indianapolis, IN 46250-932. Offers elementary teacher education (MA Ed); secondary teacher education (MA Ed).

University of Phoenix–Las Vegas Campus, The Artemis School, College of Education, Las Vegas, NV 89128. Offers administration and supervision (MA Ed); curriculum and instruction (MA Ed); school counseling (MSC); teacher education-elementary licensure (MA Ed). Evening/weekend programs available. *Degree requirements:* For master's, thesis (for some programs). *Entrance requirements:* For master's, minimum undergraduate GPA of 2.5, 3 years of work experience. Additional exam requirements/recommendations for international students: Required—TOEFL (minimum score 550 paper-based; 213 computer-based; 79 iBT). Electronic applications accepted.

University of Phoenix–Memphis Campus, College of Education, Cordova, TN 38018. Offers administration and supervision (MA Ed); curriculum and instruction (MA Ed); elementary teacher education (MA Ed); secondary teacher education (MA Ed).

University of Phoenix–Metro Detroit Campus, College of Education, Troy, MI 48098-2623. Offers administration and supervision (MA Ed); elementary teacher education (MA Ed); secondary teacher education (MA Ed); special education (MA Ed). Evening/weekend programs available. *Faculty:* 3 full-time (1 woman), 2 part-time/adjunct (both women). *Students:* 34 full-time (30 women); includes 23 minority (all African Americans). Average age 44. In 2009, 44 master's awarded. *Degree requirements:* For master's, thesis (for some programs). *Entrance requirements:* For master's, 3 years of work experience, minimum undergraduate GPA of 2.5. Additional exam requirements/recommendations for international students: Required—TOEFL (minimum score 550 paper-based; 213 computer-based; 79 iBT). *Application deadline:* Applications are processed on a rolling basis. Application fee: $45. Electronic applications accepted. *Expenses:* Tuition: Full-time $14,136. Required fees: $660. *Financial support:* Institutionally sponsored loans and scholarships/grants available. Financial award applicants required to submit FAFSA. *Unit head:* Dr. Meredith Curley, Dean/Executive Director, 480-557-1217, E-mail: meredith.curley@phoenix.edu. *Application contact:* Chair, 800-834-2438, Fax: 248-267-0147.

University of Phoenix–Nashville Campus, The Artemis School, College of Education, Nashville, TN 37214-5048. Offers administration and supervision (MA Ed); curriculum and instruction (MA Ed); elementary teacher education (MA Ed); secondary teacher education

Elementary Education

University of Phoenix–Nashville Campus *(continued)*
(MA Ed). Evening/weekend programs available. *Degree requirements:* For master's, thesis (for some programs). *Entrance requirements:* For master's, minimum undergraduate GPA of 2.5, 3 years work experience. Additional exam requirements/recommendations for international students: Required—TOEFL (minimum score 500 paper-based; 213 computer-based; 79 iBT). Electronic applications accepted.

University of Phoenix–New Mexico Campus, The Artemis School, College of Education, Albuquerque, NM 87113-1570. Offers administration and supervision (MAEd); curriculum and instruction (MAEd); elementary teacher education (MAEd); school counseling (MSC); secondary teacher education (MAEd). Evening/weekend programs available. *Degree requirements:* For master's, thesis (for some programs). *Entrance requirements:* For master's, minimum undergraduate GPA of 2.5, 3 years of work experience. Additional exam requirements/recommendations for international students: Required—TOEFL (minimum score 550 paper-based; 213 computer-based; 79 iBT). Electronic applications accepted.

University of Phoenix–Northern Nevada Campus, College of Education, Reno, NV 89521-5862. Offers administration and supervision (MA Ed); curriculum and instruction (MA Ed); elementary teacher education (MA Ed); secondary teacher education (MA Ed).

University of Phoenix–North Florida Campus, The Artemis School, College of Education, Jacksonville, FL 32216-0959. Offers administration and supervision (MA Ed); curriculum and instruction (MA Ed), including computer education, mathematics education; early childhood education (MA Ed); elementary teacher education (MA Ed); secondary teacher education (MA Ed). Evening/weekend programs available. *Degree requirements:* For master's, thesis (for some programs). *Entrance requirements:* For master's, 3 years of work experience, minimum undergraduate GPA of 2.5. Additional exam requirements/recommendations for international students: Required—TOEFL (minimum score 550 paper-based; 213 computer-based; 49 iBT). Electronic applications accepted.

University of Phoenix–Omaha Campus, College of Education, Omaha, NE 68154-5240. Offers administration and supervision (MA Ed); curriculum and instruction (MA Ed), including adult education, computer education, curriculum and instruction, English and language arts education, English as a second language, mathematics education; elementary teacher education (MA Ed); secondary teacher education (MA Ed); special education (MA Ed).

University of Phoenix–Oregon Campus, The Artemis School, College of Education, Tigard, OR 97223. Offers curriculum and instruction (MA Ed); early childhood education (MA Ed); elementary education (MA Ed), including early childhood specialization, middle level specialization; secondary education (MA Ed), including middle level specialization. Evening/weekend programs available. *Degree requirements:* For master's, thesis (for some programs). *Entrance requirements:* For master's, minimum undergraduate GPA of 2.5, 3 years work experience. Additional exam requirements/recommendations for international students: Required—TOEFL (minimum score 550 paper-based; 213 computer-based; 79 iBT). Electronic applications accepted.

University of Phoenix–Phoenix Campus, College of Social Sciences, College of Education, Phoenix, AZ 85040-1958. Offers administration and supervision (MA Ed); elementary teacher education (MA Ed); secondary teacher education (MA Ed); special education (MA Ed). Evening/weekend programs available. *Faculty:* 39 full-time (23 women), 422 part-time/adjunct (255 women). *Students:* 443 full-time (297 women); includes 79 minority (32 African Americans, 8 American Indian/Alaska Native, 8 Asian Americans or Pacific Islanders, 31 Hispanic Americans), 6 international. Average age 35. In 2009, 199 master's awarded. *Degree requirements:* For master's, thesis (for some programs). *Entrance requirements:* For master's, 3 years of work experience, minimum undergraduate GPA of 2.5. Additional exam requirements/recommendations for international students: Required—TOEFL (minimum score 550 paper-based; 213 computer-based; 79 iBT). *Application deadline:* Applications are processed on a rolling basis. Application fee: $45. Electronic applications accepted. *Expenses:* Tuition: Full-time $10,272. Required fees: $760. *Financial support:* Institutionally sponsored loans and scholarships/grants available. Financial award applicants required to submit FAFSA. *Unit head:* Dr. Meredith Curley, Dean/Executive Director, 480-557-1217, Fax: 480-557-1588, E-mail: meredith.curley@phoenix.edu. *Application contact:* College Chair, 480-804-2000.

University of Phoenix–Sacramento Valley Campus, The Artemis School, College of Education, Sacramento, CA 95833-3632. Offers adult education (MA Ed); curriculum instruction (MA Ed); elementary teacher education (MA Ed); secondary teacher education (MA Ed); teacher education (Certificate). Evening/weekend programs available. *Degree requirements:* For master's, thesis (for some programs). *Entrance requirements:* For master's, 3 years of work experience, minimum undergraduate GPA of 2.5. Additional exam requirements/recommendations for international students: Required—TOEFL (minimum score 550 paper-based; 213 computer-based; 79 iBT). Electronic applications accepted.

University of Phoenix–San Diego Campus, The Artemis School, College of Education, San Diego, CA 92123. Offers curriculum and instruction (MA Ed), including computer education, curriculum and instruction, English as a second language; elementary teacher education (MA Ed); secondary teacher education (MA Ed). Evening/weekend programs available. *Degree requirements:* For master's, thesis (for some programs). *Entrance requirements:* For master's, 3 years of work experience, minimum undergraduate GPA of 3.0. Additional exam requirements/recommendations for international students: Required—TOEFL (minimum score 550 paper-based; 213 computer-based; 79 iBT). Electronic applications accepted.

University of Phoenix–Southern Arizona Campus, The Artemis School, College of Education, Tucson, AZ 85711. Offers administration and supervision (MA Ed); adult education and training (MA Ed); curriculum instruction (MA Ed); educational counseling (MA Ed); elementary teacher education (MA Ed); school counseling (MSC); secondary teacher education (MA Ed); special education (MA Ed, Certificate). Evening/weekend programs available. *Degree requirements:* For master's, thesis (for some programs). *Entrance requirements:* For master's, minimum undergraduate GPA of 2.5, 3 years of work experience. Additional exam requirements/recommendations for international students: Required—TOEFL (minimum score 550 paper-based; 213 computer-based; 79 iBT). Electronic applications accepted.

University of Phoenix–Southern Colorado Campus, The Artemis School, College of Education, Colorado Springs, CO 80919-2335. Offers administration and supervision (MA Ed); curriculum and instruction (MA Ed); elementary teacher education (MA Ed); principal licensure certification (Certificate); school counseling (MSC); secondary teacher education (MA Ed). Evening/weekend programs available. *Degree requirements:* For master's, thesis (for some programs). *Entrance requirements:* For master's, minimum undergraduate GPA of 2.5, 3 years of work experience. Additional exam requirements/recommendations for international students: Required—TOEFL (minimum score 550 paper-based; 213 computer-based; 79 iBT). Electronic applications accepted.

University of Phoenix–South Florida Campus, The Artemis School, College of Education, Fort Lauderdale, FL 33309. Offers administration and supervision (MA Ed); curriculum and instruction (MA Ed), including computer education, curriculum and instruction, mathematics education; early childhood education (MA Ed); elementary teacher education (MA Ed); secondary teacher education (MA Ed). Evening/weekend programs available. *Degree requirements:* For master's, thesis (for some programs). *Entrance requirements:* For master's, 3 years of work experience, minimum undergraduate GPA of 2.5. Additional exam requirements/recommendations for international students: Required—TOEFL (minimum score 550 paper-based; 213 computer-based; 79 iBT). Electronic applications accepted.

University of Phoenix–Utah Campus, The Artemis School, College of Education, Salt Lake City, UT 84123-4617. Offers administration and supervision (MA Ed); curriculum and instruction (MA Ed); elementary teacher education (MA Ed); school counseling (MSC); secondary teacher education (MA Ed); special education (MA Ed). Evening/weekend programs available. *Degree requirements:* For master's, thesis (for some programs). *Entrance requirements:* For master's, minimum undergraduate GPA of 2.5, 3 years work experience. Additional exam requirements/recommendations for international students: Required—TOEFL (minimum score 550 paper-based; 213 computer-based; 79 iBT). Electronic applications accepted.

University of Phoenix–West Florida Campus, The Artemis School, College of Education, Temple Terrace, FL 33637. Offers administration and supervision (MA Ed); curriculum and instruction (MA Ed), including computer education, curriculum and instruction, mathematics education; curriculum and technology (MA Ed); early childhood education (MA Ed); elementary teacher education (MA Ed); secondary teacher education (MA Ed). Evening/weekend programs available. *Degree requirements:* For master's, thesis (for some programs). *Entrance requirements:* For master's, 3 years of work experience, minimum undergraduate GPA of 2.5. Additional exam requirements/recommendations for international students: Required—TOEFL (minimum score 550 paper-based; 213 computer-based; 79 iBT).

University of Pittsburgh, School of Education, Department of Instruction and Learning, Program in Elementary Education, Pittsburgh, PA 15260. Offers M Ed, MAT. *Students:* 76 full-time (63 women), 10 part-time (7 women); includes 5 minority (4 African Americans, 1 Hispanic American). Average age 26. 70 applicants, 84% accepted, 50 enrolled. *Degree requirements:* For master's, thesis. *Entrance requirements:* For master's, PRAXIS I. Additional exam requirements/recommendations for international students: Required—TOEFL. *Application deadline:* For fall admission, 2/1 for domestic students. Application fee: $50. Electronic applications accepted. *Expenses:* Tuition, state resident: full-time $16,402; part-time $665 per credit. Tuition, nonresident: full-time $28,694; part-time $1175 per credit. Required fees: $690; $175 per term. Tuition and fees vary according to program. *Financial support:* In 2009–10, fellowships (averaging $1,000 per year); career-related internships or fieldwork, Federal Work-Study, traineeships, and tuition waivers (partial) also available. Support available to part-time students. Financial award application deadline: 3/15; financial award applicants required to submit FAFSA. *Unit head:* Dr. Richard Donato, Chairman, 412-624-7248, Fax: 412-648-7081, E-mail: donato@pitt.edu. *Application contact:* Dr. Marjie Schermer, Graduate Enrollment Manager, 412-648-2230, Fax: 412-648-1899, E-mail: soeinfo@pitt.edu.

University of Puget Sound, Graduate Studies, School of Education, Program in Teaching, Tacoma, WA 98416. Offers elementary education (MAT); secondary education (MAT). *Accreditation:* NASM; NCATE. *Faculty:* 8 full-time (4 women), 1 (woman) part-time/adjunct. *Students:* 45 full-time (26 women); includes 9 minority (4 African Americans, 4 Asian Americans or Pacific Islanders, 1 Hispanic American). Average age 25. 70 applicants, 84% accepted, 45 enrolled. In 2009, 41 master's awarded. *Entrance requirements:* For master's, GRE General Test, WEST-B, WEST-E in content area, minimum GPA of 3.0. Additional exam requirements/recommendations for international students: Required—TOEFL (minimum score 550 paper-based; 213 computer-based; 80 iBT). *Application deadline:* For fall admission, 3/1 priority date for domestic and international students. Applications are processed on a rolling basis. Application fee: $60. Electronic applications accepted. Tuition and fees vary according to course load, degree level and program. *Financial support:* In 2009–10, 18 students received support. Career-related internships or fieldwork and scholarships/grants available. Financial award application deadline: 3/31; financial award applicants required to submit FAFSA. *Faculty research:* Math education, social studies education, professional development, international education, classroom discourse, equity education. *Unit head:* Dr. John Woodward, Dean, 253-879-3375, E-mail: woodward@pugetsound.edu. *Application contact:* Dr. George H. Mills, Vice President for Enrollment, 253-879-3211, Fax: 253-879-3993, E-mail: admission@pugetsound.edu.

University of Rhode Island, Graduate School, College of Human Science and Services, School of Education, Kingston, RI 02881. Offers adult education (MA); education (PhD); elementary education (MA); music education (MM); reading education (MA); secondary education (MA); special education (MA); MS/PhD. *Accreditation:* NCATE. Part-time and evening/weekend programs available. *Faculty:* 19 full-time (12 women), 5 part-time/adjunct (1 woman). *Students:* 44 full-time (33 women), 128 part-time (101 women); includes 14 minority (8 African Americans, 2 American Indian/Alaska Native, 2 Asian Americans or Pacific Islanders, 2 Hispanic Americans), 3 international. In 2009, 44 master's, 7 doctorates awarded. *Degree requirements:* For master's, comprehensive exam (for some programs), thesis optional; for doctorate, comprehensive exam, thesis/dissertation. *Entrance requirements:* For master's, 2 letters of recommendation; interview (for special education applicants); for doctorate, GRE, 3 letters of recommendation, resume. Additional exam requirements/recommendations for international students: Required—TOEFL (minimum score 600 paper-based; 250 computer-based; 100 iBT). *Application deadline:* For fall admission, 1/31 for international students. Application fee: $65. Electronic applications accepted. *Expenses:* Tuition, state resident: full-time $8828; part-time $490 per credit hour. Tuition, nonresident: full-time $22,100; part-time $1228 per credit hour. Required fees: $1118; $57 per semester. Tuition and fees vary according to program. *Financial support:* In 2009–10, 5 research assistantships with full and partial tuition reimbursements (averaging $11,518 per year), 3 teaching assistantships with full and partial tuition reimbursements (averaging $10,421 per year) were awarded; career-related internships or fieldwork also available. Financial award applicants required to submit FAFSA. Total annual research expenditures: $3.4 million. *Unit head:* Dr. David Byrd, Director, 401-874-5484, Fax: 401-874-5471, E-mail: dbyrd@uri.edu. *Application contact:* Dr. John Boulmetis, Coordinator of Graduate Studies, 401-874-4159, Fax: 401-874-7610, E-mail: johnb@uri.edu.

University of St. Francis, College of Education, Joliet, IL 60435-6169. Offers educational leadership (MS), including reading; elementary education certification (M Ed); reading (MS); secondary education certification (M Ed), including English education, math education, science education, social studies education; special education (M Ed); teaching and learning (MS), including character education, curriculum and instruction, differentiated instruction, technology. *Accreditation:* NCATE. Part-time and evening/weekend programs available. *Faculty:* 10 full-time (8 women), 26 part-time/adjunct (18 women). *Students:* 60 full-time (45 women), 349 part-time (283 women); includes 36 minority (10 African Americans, 2 Asian Americans or Pacific Islanders, 24 Hispanic Americans). Average age 33. 211 applicants, 65% accepted, 102 enrolled. In 2009, 174 master's awarded. *Entrance requirements:* For master's, Illinois Basic Skills Test (M Ed), teaching certificate (MS), minimum undergraduate GPA of 2.75, 2 letters of recommendation, computer competency. Additional exam requirements/recommendations for international students: Required—TOEFL (minimum score 550 paper-based; 213 computer-based). *Application deadline:* Applications are processed on a rolling basis. Application fee: $30. Electronic applications accepted. *Expenses:* Contact institution. *Financial support:* In 2009–10, 254 students received support. Federal Work-Study, scholarships/grants, tuition waivers (partial), and unspecified assistantships available. Support available to part-time students. Financial award applicants required to submit FAFSA. *Unit head:* Dr. John Gambro, Dean, 815-740-3332, Fax: 815-740-2264, E-mail: jgambro@stfrancis.edu. *Application contact:* Sandra Sloka, Director of Admissions for Graduate and Degree Completion Programs, 800-735-7500, Fax: 815-740-5032, E-mail: ssloka@stfrancis.edu.

University of St. Thomas, Graduate Studies, School of Education, Department of Teacher Education, St. Paul, MN 55105-1096. Offers curriculum and instruction (MA), including elementary, individualized, K-12, secondary; elementary (MAT); multicultural education (Certificate); reading (MA, Certificate), including elementary (MA), K-12 (MA). *Accreditation:* NCATE. Part-time and evening/weekend programs available. *Faculty:* 10 full-time (7 women), 25 part-time/adjunct (16 women). *Students:* 31 full-time (25 women), 260 part-time (195 women); includes 19 minority (6 African Americans, 7 Asian Americans or Pacific Islanders, 6 Hispanic Americans), 3 international. Average age 34. 325 applicants, 72% accepted, 225 enrolled. In 2009, 135 master's, 17 other advanced degrees awarded. *Entrance requirements:*

For master's, minimum GPA of 3.0 or MAT. Additional exam requirements/recommendations for international students: Required—TOEFL (minimum score 550 paper-based; 210 computer-based; 80 iBT). *Application deadline:* For fall admission, 6/1 for domestic students; for spring admission, 11/1 for domestic students. Applications are processed on a rolling basis. Application fee: $50. *Financial support:* Fellowships, research assistantships, institutionally sponsored loans and scholarships/grants available. Support available to part-time students. Financial award applicants required to submit FAFSA. *Unit head:* Dr. Douglas F. Warring, Department Chair, 651-962-4877, Fax: 651-962-4169, E-mail: dfwarring@stthomas.edu. *Application contact:* Kathy J. Neary, Department Assistant, 651-962-4420, Fax: 651-962-4169, E-mail: kjneary@stthomas.edu.

The University of Scranton, College of Graduate and Continuing Education, Department of Education, Program in Elementary Education, Scranton, PA 18510. Offers MS. *Accreditation:* NCATE. Part-time and evening/weekend programs available. *Students:* 8 full-time (7 women); includes 2 minority (1 African American, 1 Hispanic American). Average age 25. 5 applicants, 80% accepted. In 2009, 6 master's awarded. *Degree requirements:* For master's, comprehensive exam, capstone experience. *Entrance requirements:* For master's, minimum GPA of 2.75. Additional exam requirements/recommendations for international students: Required—TOEFL (minimum score 500 paper-based; 173 computer-based), IELTS (minimum score 5.5). *Application deadline:* Applications are processed on a rolling basis. Application fee: $0. *Financial support:* Fellowships, teaching assistantships, career-related internships or fieldwork, Federal Work-Study, and unspecified assistantships available. Support available to part-time students. Financial award application deadline: 3/1. *Unit head:* Dr. Art Chambers, Director, 570-941-4668, Fax: 570-941-5515, E-mail: stufftda@scranton.edu. *Application contact:* Joseph M. Roback, Director of Admissions, 570-941-4385, Fax: 570-941-5928, E-mail: roback_j2@scranton.edu.

University of South Alabama, Graduate School, College of Education, Department of Leadership and Teacher Education, Mobile, AL 36688-0002. Offers early childhood education (M Ed); educational administration (Ed S); educational leadership (M Ed); elementary education (M Ed); reading education (M Ed); science education (M Ed); secondary education (M Ed); special education (M Ed, Ed S). *Accreditation:* NCATE. Part-time programs available. *Degree requirements:* For master's, comprehensive exam. *Entrance requirements:* For master's, GRE General Test or MAT, minimum GPA of 3.0. *Expenses:* Tuition, state resident: part-time $218 per contact hour. Required fees: $1102 per year.

University of South Carolina, The Graduate School, College of Education, Department of Instruction and Teacher Education, Program in Elementary Education, Columbia, SC 29208. Offers MAT, Ed D, PhD. *Accreditation:* NCATE. *Degree requirements:* For master's, comprehensive exam; for doctorate, one foreign language, comprehensive exam, thesis/dissertation. *Entrance requirements:* For master's, GRE General Test, MAT, interview, letters of reference, resume; for doctorate, GRE General Test, MAT, interview, letters of reference, letters of intent, resum&e, transcript. *Faculty research:* Children's conception of science, whole language, middle school curriculum.

University of South Carolina Aiken, School of Education, Program in Elementary Education, Aiken, SC 29801-6309. Offers M Ed. *Accreditation:* NCATE. Part-time and evening/weekend programs available. *Degree requirements:* For master's, comprehensive evaluation. *Entrance requirements:* For master's, GRE General Test or MAT. Electronic applications accepted.

University of South Carolina Upstate, Graduate Programs, Spartanburg, SC 29303-4999. Offers early childhood education (M Ed); elementary education (M Ed); special education: visual impairment (M Ed). *Accreditation:* NCATE. Part-time and evening/weekend programs available. *Faculty:* 8 full-time (7 women), 4 part-time/adjunct (2 women). *Students:* 5 full-time (all women), 107 part-time (102 women). Average age 34. *Degree requirements:* For master's, professional portfolio. *Entrance requirements:* For master's, GRE General Test or MAT, interview, minimum undergraduate GPA of 2.5, teaching certificate, 2 letters of recommendation. *Application deadline:* Applications are processed on a rolling basis. Application fee: $40. *Expenses:* Tuition, state resident: full-time $9436; part-time $467 per credit hour. Tuition, nonresident: full-time $20,336; part-time $992 per credit hour. Required fees: $500. Tuition and fees vary according to course load. *Financial support:* Institutionally sponsored loans and institutional work-study available. Financial award application deadline: 7/15; financial award applicants required to submit FAFSA. *Faculty research:* Rough and tumble play, social justice education, American Indian literatures and cultures, diversity and multicultural education, science teaching strategy. *Unit head:* Dr. Rebecca L. Stevens, Director of Graduate Programs, 864-503-5521, Fax: 864-503-5574, E-mail: rstevens@uscupstate.edu. *Application contact:* Donette Stewart, Associate Vice Chancellor for Enrollment Services, 864-503-5280, E-mail: dstewart@uscupstate.edu.

The University of South Dakota, Graduate School, School of Education, Division of Curriculum and Instruction, Program in Elementary Education, Vermillion, SD 57069-2390. Offers MA. *Accreditation:* NCATE. Part-time programs available. Postbaccalaureate distance learning degree programs offered. *Degree requirements:* For master's, comprehensive exam, thesis or alternative. *Entrance requirements:* For master's, GRE General Test, MAT, minimum GPA of 2.7. Additional exam requirements/recommendations for international students: Required—TOEFL (minimum score 550 paper-based; 213 computer-based; 79 iBT). Electronic applications accepted.

University of Southern Indiana, Graduate Studies, College of Education and Human Services, Department of Teacher Education, Program in Elementary Education, Evansville, IN 47712-3590. Offers MS. *Accreditation:* NCATE. Part-time and evening/weekend programs available. *Faculty:* 7 full-time (3 women), 1 (woman) part-time/adjunct. *Students:* 75 part-time (69 women); includes 4 minority (all African Americans), 1 international. Average age 32. 33 applicants, 100% accepted, 19 enrolled. In 2009, 19 master's awarded. *Entrance requirements:* For master's, GRE General Test, NTE or PRAXIS I, minimum GPA of 3.0, teaching license. Additional exam requirements/recommendations for international students: Required—TOEFL (minimum score 550 paper-based; 213 computer-based; 79 iBT), IELTS (minimum score 6). *Application deadline:* For fall admission, 7/1 priority date for domestic students. Applications are processed on a rolling basis. Application fee: $25. Electronic applications accepted. *Expenses:* Tuition, state resident: full-time $4592; part-time $255 per credit hour. Tuition, nonresident: full-time $9060; part-time $503 per credit hour. Required fees: $220; $22.75 per term. Tuition and fees vary according to course load and reciprocity agreements. *Financial support:* In 2009–10, 21 students received support. Federal Work-Study, scholarships/grants, tuition waivers (full and partial), and unspecified assistantships available. Financial award application deadline: 3/1; financial award applicants required to submit FAFSA. *Unit head:* Dr. Vella Goebel, Coordinator, 812-461-5306, E-mail: vgoebel@usi.edu. *Application contact:* Dr. Vella Goebel, Coordinator, 812-461-5306, E-mail: vgoebel@usi.edu.

University of Southern Mississippi, Graduate School, College of Education and Psychology, Department of Curriculum, Instruction, and Special Education, Hattiesburg, MS 39406-0001. Offers alternative secondary teacher education (MAT); early childhood education (M Ed, Ed S); education of the gifted (M Ed, Ed D, PhD, Ed S); elementary education (M Ed, Ed D, PhD, Ed S); reading (M Ed, MS, Ed S); secondary education (M Ed, MS, Ed D, PhD, Ed S); special education (M Ed, Ed D, PhD, Ed S). *Faculty:* 23 full-time (17 women), 3 part-time/adjunct (2 women). *Students:* 31 full-time (26 women), 77 part-time (68 women); includes 18 minority (15 African Americans, 3 Hispanic Americans). Average age 37. 50 applicants, 52% accepted, 19 enrolled. In 2009, 43 master's, 3 doctorates, 2 other advanced degrees awarded. *Degree requirements:* For master's, comprehensive exam, thesis (for some programs); for doctorate, comprehensive exam, thesis/dissertation; for Ed S, comprehensive exam, thesis. *Entrance requirements:* For master's, GRE General Test, MAT, minimum GPA of 3.0; for doctorate, GRE General Test, minimum GPA of 3.5; for Ed S, GRE General Test, MAT, minimum GPA of 3.25. Additional exam requirements/recommendations for international students: Required—TOEFL. *Application deadline:* For fall admission, 3/1 priority date for domestic students, 3/1 for inter-

national students. Applications are processed on a rolling basis. Application fee: $35. *Expenses:* Tuition, state resident: full-time $5096; part-time $284 per hour. Tuition, nonresident: full-time $13,052; part-time $726 per hour. Required fees: $402. Tuition and fees vary according to course level and course load. *Financial support:* In 2009–10, 9 research assistantships with tuition reimbursements (averaging $18,316 per year), 2 teaching assistantships with full tuition reimbursements (averaging $8,500 per year) were awarded; Federal Work-Study, institutionally sponsored loans, and tuition waivers (partial) also available. Financial award application deadline: 3/15; financial award applicants required to submit FAFSA. *Faculty research:* Mathematical problem solving, integrative curriculum, writing process, teacher education models. Total annual research expenditures: $100,000. *Unit head:* Dr. David Daves, Chair, 601-266-4547, Fax: 601-266-4175. *Application contact:* Rachea Cawthorn, Administrative Assistant, 601-266-6987, Fax: 601-266-4548.

University of South Florida, Graduate School, College of Education–Main Campus, Department of Childhood Education, Tampa, FL 33620-9951. Offers early childhood education (M Ed, MA, PhD); elementary education (MA, MAT); reading/language arts (MA, PhD, Ed S). *Accreditation:* NCATE. Part-time and evening/weekend programs available. *Faculty:* 24 full-time (21 women), 2 part-time/adjunct (both women). *Students:* 92 full-time (84 women), 165 part-time (157 women); includes 62 minority (36 African Americans, 1 American Indian/Alaska Native, 6 Asian Americans or Pacific Islanders, 19 Hispanic Americans), 9 international. Average age 30. 192 applicants, 76% accepted, 113 enrolled. In 2009, 94 master's, 11 doctorates awarded. *Degree requirements:* For master's, comprehensive exam; for doctorate, comprehensive exam, thesis/dissertation. *Entrance requirements:* For master's, GRE (if GPA less than 3.0), minimum GPA of 3.0 in last 60 hours of course work; for doctorate, GRE General Test, minimum GPA of 3.0 undergraduate, 3.5 graduate; interview; for Ed S, GRE General Test, interview. Additional exam requirements/recommendations for international students: Required—TOEFL (minimum score 550 paper-based; 213 computer-based). *Application deadline:* For fall admission, 2/15 for domestic students, 1/2 for international students; for winter admission, 2/15 for domestic students, 1/2 for international students; for spring admission, 10/15 for domestic students, 6/1 for international students. Application fee: $30. Electronic applications accepted. *Financial support:* In 2009–10, 7 teaching assistantships with full tuition reimbursements (averaging $10,300 per year) were awarded; institutionally sponsored loans, scholarships/grants, and unspecified assistantships also available. Financial award applicants required to submit FAFSA. *Faculty research:* Evaluating interventions for struggling users, prevention and intervention services for young children at risk for behavioral and mental health challenges, preservice teacher education and young adolescent middle school experience, art and inquiry-based approaches to teaching and learning, study of children's writing development. Total annual research expenditures: $381,048. *Unit head:* Dr. Diane Yendol-Hoppey, Chairperson, 813-974-3460, Fax: 813-974-0938. *Application contact:* Dr. Diane Yendol-Hoppey, Chairperson, 813-974-3460, Fax: 813-974-0938.

The University of Tennessee, Graduate School, College of Education, Health and Human Sciences, Program in Education, Knoxville, TN 37996. Offers art education (MS); counseling education (PhD); cultural studies in education (PhD); curriculum (MS, Ed S); curriculum, educational research and evaluation (Ed D, PhD); early childhood education (PhD); early childhood special education (MS); education of deaf and hard of hearing (MS); educational administration and policy studies (Ed D, PhD); educational administration and supervision (Ed S); educational psychology (Ed D, PhD); elementary education (MS, Ed S); elementary teaching (MS); English education (MS, Ed S); exercise science (PhD); foreign language/ESL education (MS, Ed S); instructional technology (MS, Ed D, PhD, Ed S); literacy, language and ESL education (PhD); literacy, language education, and ESL education (Ed D); mathematics education (MS, Ed S); modified and comprehensive special education (MS); reading education (MS, Ed S); school counseling (Ed S); school psychology (PhD, Ed S); science education (MS, Ed S); secondary teaching (MS); social foundations (MS); social science education (MS, Ed S); socio-cultural foundations of sports and education (PhD); special education (Ed S); teacher education (Ed D, PhD). *Accreditation:* NCATE. Part-time and evening/weekend programs available. *Degree requirements:* For master's and Ed S, thesis optional; for doctorate, variable foreign language requirement, thesis/dissertation. *Entrance requirements:* For master's, minimum GPA of 2.7; for doctorate and Ed S, GRE General Test, minimum GPA of 2.7. Additional exam requirements/recommendations for international students: Required—TOEFL. Electronic applications accepted. *Expenses:* Tuition, state resident: full-time $6826; part-time $380 per semester hour. Tuition, nonresident: full-time $21,844; part-time $1147 per semester hour. Tuition and fees vary according to program.

The University of Tennessee at Chattanooga, Graduate School, College of Health, Education and Professional Studies, Graduate Studies Division of Education, Program in Education, Chattanooga, TN 37403-2598. Offers elementary education (M Ed); school leadership (M Ed, Post-Master's Certificate); secondary education (M Ed); special education (M Ed). Part-time and evening/weekend programs available. Postbaccalaureate distance learning degree programs offered (no on-campus study). *Faculty:* 10 full-time (9 women), 6 part-time/adjunct (3 women). *Students:* 124 full-time (83 women), 208 part-time (150 women); includes 42 minority (32 African Americans, 2 American Indian/Alaska Native, 3 Asian Americans or Pacific Islanders, 5 Hispanic Americans), 1 international. Average age 33. 117 applicants, 97% accepted, 80 enrolled. In 2009, 97 master's, 4 other advanced degrees awarded. *Degree requirements:* For master's, comprehensive exam (for some programs), thesis (for some programs). *Entrance requirements:* For master's and Post-Master's Certificate, PRAXIS I, minimum GPA of 2.5 overall or 3.0 in senior year. Additional exam requirements/recommendations for international students: Required—TOEFL (minimum score 550 paper-based; 213 computer-based; 79 iBT), IELTS (minimum score 6). *Application deadline:* For fall admission, 8/1 for domestic students, 6/1 for international students; for spring admission, 12/1 for domestic students, 10/1 for international students. Applications are processed on a rolling basis. Application fee: $35. Electronic applications accepted. *Expenses:* Tuition, state resident: full-time $5404; part-time $300 per credit hour. Tuition, nonresident: full-time $16,702; part-time $928 per credit hour. Required fees: $1150; $130 per credit hour. *Financial support:* In 2009–10, 8 research assistantships with full and partial tuition reimbursements (averaging $5,500 per year) were awarded; career-related internships or fieldwork, scholarships/grants, and unspecified assistantships also available. Support available to part-time students. *Faculty research:* Elementary education, community counseling, school counseling, secondary education, special education. *Unit head:* Dr. John Freeman, Department Head, 423-425-4133, Fax: 423-425-5443, E-mail: john-freeman@utc.edu. *Application contact:* Dr. Stephanie Bellar, Dean of Graduate Studies, 423-425-4666, Fax: 423-425-5223, E-mail: stephanie-bellar@utc.edu.

The University of Texas–Pan American, College of Education, Department of Curriculum and Instruction: Elementary and Secondary, Edinburg, TX 78539. Offers bilingual education (M Ed); early childhood education (M Ed); elementary education (M Ed); reading (M Ed); secondary education (M Ed). Part-time programs available. *Degree requirements:* For master's, comprehensive exam, thesis optional. *Entrance requirements:* For master's, GRE. Additional exam requirements/recommendations for international students: Required—TOEFL, IELTS. *Expenses:* Tuition, state resident: full-time $3630.60; part-time $201.70 per credit hour. Tuition, nonresident: full-time $8617; part-time $478.70 per credit hour. Required fees: $806.50. *Faculty research:* Dual language instruction, literacy and technology, teacher education in diverse populations, mathematics and science education.

University of the Cumberlands, Graduate Programs in Education, Program in Elementary Education, Williamsburg, KY 40769-1372. Offers elementary (P-5) (MA Ed, MAT); middle school (5-9) (MA Ed, MAT). Part-time and evening/weekend programs available. *Degree requirements:* For master's, comprehensive exam. *Entrance requirements:* For master's, GRE or NTE, Kentucky teaching certificate.

University of the Incarnate Word, School of Graduate Studies and Research, Dreeben School of Education, Program in Teaching, San Antonio, TX 78209-6397. Offers all-level teaching (MAT); elementary teaching (MAT); secondary teaching (MAT). Part-time and evening/

Elementary Education

University of the Incarnate Word *(continued)*
weekend programs available. *Students:* 45 part-time (38 women); includes 27 minority (7 African Americans, 20 Hispanic Americans). Average age 33. In 2009, 37 master's awarded. *Degree requirements:* For master's, internship. *Entrance requirements:* For master's, GRE, Texas Higher Education Assessment test (THEA), interview. Additional exam requirements/recommendations for international students: Required—TOEFL (minimum score 560 paper-based; 220 computer-based; 83 iBT). *Application deadline:* Applications are processed on a rolling basis. Application fee: $20. Electronic applications accepted. *Expenses:* Tuition: Full-time $12,150; part-time $675 per credit hour. Required fees: $83 per credit hour. *Financial support:* Federal Work-Study and scholarships/grants available. Financial award applicants required to submit FAFSA. *Unit head:* Dr. Elda Martinez, Director of Teacher Education, 210-832-3297, Fax: 210-829-3134, E-mail: eemartin@uiwtx.edu. *Application contact:* Andrea Cyterski-Acosta, Dean of Enrollment, 210-829-6005, Fax: 210-829-3921, E-mail: admis@uiwtx.edu.

The University of Toledo, College of Graduate Studies, College of Education, Department of Curriculum and Instruction, Program in Elementary Education, Toledo, OH 43606-3390. Offers DE, PhD. *Entrance requirements:* For doctorate, GRE, minimum undergraduate GPA of 2.7.

The University of Toledo, College of Graduate Studies, College of Education, Department of Early Childhood, Physical and Special Education, Program in Elementary Education, Toledo, OH 43606-3390. Offers Ed S.

University of Tulsa, Graduate School, College of Arts and Sciences, School of Education, Program in Education, Tulsa, OK 74104-3189. Offers education (MA); elementary certification (M Ed); secondary certification (M Ed). Part-time programs available. *Faculty:* 6 full-time (2 women), 1 (woman) part-time/adjunct. *Students:* 7 full-time (6 women), 3 part-time (1 woman); includes 1 minority (American Indian/Alaska Native), 2 international. Average age 25. 10 applicants, 100% accepted, 7 enrolled. In 2009, 4 master's awarded. *Degree requirements:* For master's, thesis optional. *Entrance requirements:* For master's, GRE General Test. Additional exam requirements/recommendations for international students: Required—TOEFL (minimum score 575 paper-based; 231 computer-based; 91 iBT), IELTS (minimum score 6.5). *Application deadline:* Applications are processed on a rolling basis. Application fee: $40. Electronic applications accepted. *Expenses:* Tuition: Full-time $16,182; part-time $899 per credit hour. Required fees: $4 per credit hour. Tuition and fees vary according to course load. *Financial support:* In 2009–10, 7 students received support, including 1 fellowship with full and partial tuition reimbursement available (averaging $11,594 per year), 6 teaching assistantships with full and partial tuition reimbursements available (averaging $10,627 per year); research assistantships with full and partial tuition reimbursements available, Federal Work-Study, scholarships/grants, health care benefits, tuition waivers (full and partial), and unspecified assistantships also available. Support available to part-time students. Financial award application deadline: 2/1; financial award applicants required to submit FAFSA. Total annual research expenditures: $5.1 million. *Unit head:* Dr. David Brown, Advisor, 918-631-2719, Fax: 918-631-2133, E-mail: david-brown@utulsa.edu. *Application contact:* Dr. David Brown, Advisor, 918-631-2719, Fax: 918-631-2133, E-mail: david-brown@utulsa.edu.

University of Utah, Graduate School, College of Education, Department of Teaching and Learning, Salt Lake City, UT 84112-1107. Offers elementary education (MAT); secondary education (MAT); teaching and learning (M Ed, M Phil, MA, MS, PhD). Part-time and evening/weekend programs available. *Faculty:* 1 (woman) full-time, 5 part-time/adjunct (all women). *Students:* 49 full-time (36 women), 27 part-time (21 women); includes 3 minority (2 Asian Americans or Pacific Islanders, 1 Hispanic American), 2 international. Average age 34. 44 applicants, 52% accepted, 19 enrolled. In 2009, 38 master's, 4 doctorates awarded. *Degree requirements:* For master's, comprehensive exam (for some programs), thesis optional; for doctorate, thesis/dissertation. *Entrance requirements:* For master's, GRE General Test or MAT, GRE Subject Test, minimum GPA of 3.0; for doctorate, GRE General Test, minimum graduate GPA of 3.5, undergraduate 3.0. Additional exam requirements/recommendations for international students: Required—TOEFL (minimum score 500 paper-based; 173 computer-based). *Application deadline:* For fall admission, 3/1 for domestic students, 4/1 for international students; for spring admission, 10/15 for domestic students, 11/1 for international students. Applications are processed on a rolling basis. Application fee: $55 ($65 for international students). *Expenses:* Tuition, state resident: full-time $4004; part-time $1674 per semester. Tuition, nonresident: full-time $14,134; part-time $5915 per semester. Required fees: $324 per semester. Tuition and fees vary according to course load, degree level and program. *Financial support:* Fellowships, research assistantships with full and partial tuition reimbursements, teaching assistantships with full and partial tuition reimbursements, career-related internships or fieldwork and tuition waivers (partial) available. Financial award application deadline: 2/1; financial award applicants required to submit FAFSA. *Faculty research:* Teacher development, teacher education, reading instruction, math instruction, technology. Total annual research expenditures: $13,727. *Unit head:* Doug Hacker, Department Chair, 801-581-5080, Fax: 801-581-3609, E-mail: douglas.hacker@utah.edu. *Application contact:* Jan Dole, Graduate Program Director, 801-587-7991, Fax: 801-581-3609, E-mail: jan.dole@utah.edu.

University of Virginia, Curry School of Education, Department of Curriculum, Instruction, and Special Education, Program in Curriculum and Instruction, Charlottesville, VA 22903. Offers curriculum and instruction (M Ed, Ed S); elementary (M Ed, Ed D); English (M Ed, Ed D); foreign language (M Ed); mathematics (M Ed, Ed D); reading (M Ed, Ed D, Ed S); science (Ed D); social studies (M Ed). *Students:* 12 full-time (8 women), 30 part-time (24 women); includes 2 minority (1 Asian American or Pacific Islander, 1 Hispanic American), 1 international. Average age 36. 55 applicants, 69% accepted, 26 enrolled. In 2009, 247 master's, 14 doctorates, 10 other advanced degrees awarded. *Degree requirements:* For master's, comprehensive exam (for some programs); for doctorate, comprehensive exam, thesis/dissertation; for Ed S, comprehensive exam. *Entrance requirements:* For master's, doctorate, and Ed S, GRE General Test, 2 letters of recommendation. Additional exam requirements/recommendations for international students: Required—TOEFL (minimum score 600 paper-based; 250 computer-based; 90 iBT), IELTS (minimum score 7). *Application deadline:* Applications are processed on a rolling basis. Application fee: $60. Electronic applications accepted. *Financial support:* Fellowships with tuition reimbursements, research assistantships with tuition reimbursements, teaching assistantships with tuition reimbursements available. Financial award application deadline: 1/5; financial award applicants required to submit FAFSA.

University of Virginia, Curry School of Education, Program in Education, Charlottesville, VA 22903. Offers administration and supervision (PhD); applied developmental science (PhD); counselor education (PhD); curriculum and instruction (PhD); early childhood-developmental risk (MT); education evaluation (PhD); educational psychology (PhD); educational research (PhD); elementary (MT, PhD); English education (MT, PhD); foreign language education (MT); higher education (PhD); instructional technology (PhD); kinesiology (MT, PhD); math education (PhD); reading education (PhD); research statistics and evaluation (PhD); school psychology (PhD); science education (PhD); social studies education (MT, PhD); special education (PhD); world languages education (MT). *Students:* 336 full-time (239 women), 88 part-time (54 women); includes 43 minority (24 African Americans, 2 American Indian/Alaska Native, 11 Asian Americans or Pacific Islanders, 6 Hispanic Americans), 18 international. Average age 27. 199 applicants, 48% accepted, 55 enrolled. In 2009, 127 master's, 52 doctorates awarded. *Degree requirements:* For master's, comprehensive exam (for some programs), field project; for doctorate, comprehensive exam, thesis/dissertation. *Entrance requirements:* For doctorate, GRE General Test. Additional exam requirements/recommendations for international students: Required—TOEFL (minimum score 600 paper-based; 250 computer-based; 90 iBT), IELTS (minimum score 7). *Application deadline:* Applications are processed on a rolling basis. Application fee: $60. Electronic applications accepted. *Financial support:* Fellowships, research assistantships, teaching assistantships available. Financial award application deadline: 1/5; financial award applicants required to submit FAFSA.

University of Washington, Tacoma, Graduate Programs, Program in Education, Tacoma, WA 98402-3100. Offers educational administrator (M Ed); K-8 teacher education (M Ed); professional certification (M Ed); secondary science (M Ed); special education (M Ed). Part-time and evening/weekend programs available. *Faculty:* 13 full-time (8 women), 9 part-time/adjunct (8 women). *Students:* 85 full-time (66 women), 118 part-time (99 women); includes 24 minority (4 African Americans, 9 Asian Americans or Pacific Islanders, 11 Hispanic Americans). Average age 33. 36 applicants, 75% accepted, 23 enrolled. In 2009, 68 master's awarded. *Entrance requirements:* For master's, official sealed transcript from every college/university attended, personal goal statement, letters of recommendation, copy of valid teaching certificate. *Application deadline:* For fall admission, 8/1 for domestic students; for winter admission, 11/1 priority date for domestic students; for spring admission, 2/1 priority date for domestic students. Applications are processed on a rolling basis. Application fee: $65. Electronic applications accepted. *Expenses:* Tuition, state resident: full-time $10,660; part-time $484 per credit. Tuition, nonresident: full-time $24,000; part-time $1119 per credit. Required fees: $150 per term. Tuition and fees vary according to course load and program. *Faculty research:* Global learning communities for English/Chinese languages, evaluation of mathematics and reading intervention programs, response to intervention, school wide behavioral and emotional support, mathematics education and culturally responsive mathematics education. *Unit head:* Dr. Karen Landenburger, Chancellor, 253-692-4430, Fax: 253-692-5612, E-mail: uwted@u.washington.edu. *Application contact:* Dr. Carla Van Rossum, Recruiter/Advisor, 253-692-4430, Fax: 253-692-5612, E-mail: uwted@u.washington.edu.

The University of West Alabama, School of Graduate Studies, College of Education, Department of Teacher Education, Program in Elementary Education, Livingston, AL 35470. Offers M Ed. *Accreditation:* NCATE. Part-time programs available. *Entrance requirements:* For master's, GRE General Test, MAT, minimum GPA of 2.75.

University of West Florida, College of Professional Studies, School of Education, Master's Program in Curriculum and Instruction, Pensacola, FL 32514-5750. Offers curriculum and instruction: special education (M Ed); elementary education (M Ed); primary education (M Ed). Part-time and evening/weekend programs available. *Students:* 12 full-time (all women), 108 part-time (96 women); includes 16 minority (11 African Americans, 2 Asian Americans or Pacific Islanders, 3 Hispanic Americans), 2 international. Average age 36. 36 applicants, 25% accepted, 9 enrolled. In 2009, 35 master's awarded. *Entrance requirements:* For master's, GRE (minimum score 450 verbal) or MAT (minimum score 396) if bachelor's GPA less than 3.0, state teaching certification; letter of intent; two professional references. Additional exam requirements/recommendations for international students: Required—TOEFL (minimum score 550 paper-based; 213 computer-based). *Application deadline:* For fall admission, 6/1 for domestic students, 5/15 for international students; for spring admission, 11/1 for domestic students, 10/1 for international students. Applications are processed on a rolling basis. Application fee: $30. *Expenses:* Tuition, state resident: full-time $4982; part-time $260 per credit hour. Tuition, nonresident: full-time $20,059; part-time $919 per credit hour. Required fees: $1247; $52 per credit hour. *Financial support:* Career-related internships or fieldwork, Federal Work-Study, scholarships/grants, and tuition waivers (partial) available. Support available to part-time students. Financial award application deadline: 4/15; financial award applicants required to submit FAFSA. *Unit head:* Dr. David Stout, Interim Chairperson, 850-474-2284, Fax: 850-474-2844. *Application contact:* Terry McCray, Assistant Director of Graduate Admissions, 850-473-7718, Fax: 850-473-7714, E-mail: gradadmissions@uwf.edu.

University of Wisconsin–Eau Claire, College of Education and Human Sciences, Program in Elementary Education, Eau Claire, WI 54702-4004. Offers MST. Part-time programs available. *Faculty:* 13 full-time (8 women). *Students:* 1 (woman) part-time. Average age 24. *Degree requirements:* For master's, thesis optional, oral exam, written exam, portfolio. *Entrance requirements:* For master's, GRE, minimum undergraduate GPA of 2.75, certification to teach. Additional exam requirements/recommendations for international students: Required—TOEFL (minimum score 550 paper-based; 213 computer-based; 79 iBT). *Application deadline:* For fall admission, 7/1 priority date for domestic students, 6/1 priority date for international students; for spring admission, 12/1 priority date for domestic students, 11/1 priority date for international students. Applications are processed on a rolling basis. Application fee: $56. Electronic applications accepted. *Expenses:* Tuition, state resident: full-time $6705.90; part-time $372.55 per credit. Tuition, nonresident: full-time $16,771; part-time $931.74 per credit. Required fees: $925.50; $51.19 per credit. One-time fee: $56. *Financial support:* In 2009–10, 1 student received support. Federal Work-Study and unspecified assistantships available. Financial award application deadline: 3/1; financial award applicants required to submit FAFSA. *Unit head:* Dr. Dwight Watson, Chair, 715-836-2013, Fax: 715-836-4868, E-mail: watsondc@uwec.edu. *Application contact:* Kristina Anderson, Director of Admissions, 715-836-5415, Fax: 715-836-2409, E-mail: admissions@uwec.edu.

University of Wisconsin–La Crosse, Office of University Graduate Studies, College of Liberal Studies, Department of Educational Studies, Program in Professional Development, La Crosse, WI 54601-3742. Offers elementary education (MEPD), including grades 1 through 6, grades 1 through 9; K–12 (MEPD); professional development (MEPD); secondary education (MEPD), including grades 6 through 12. Part-time programs available. *Faculty:* 18 part-time/adjunct (13 women). *Students:* 14 full-time (9 women), 345 part-time (275 women); includes 7 minority (2 Asian Americans or Pacific Islanders, 5 Hispanic Americans), 5 international. Average age 33. 121 applicants, 92% accepted, 75 enrolled. In 2009, 236 master's awarded. *Degree requirements:* For master's, thesis optional. *Entrance requirements:* For master's, PPST, minimum GPA of 2.85; minimum cumulative GPA of 3.0 in subject area. Additional exam requirements/recommendations for international students: Required—TOEFL (minimum score 550 paper-based; 213 computer-based; 79 iBT). *Application deadline:* Applications are processed on a rolling basis. Application fee: $56. Electronic applications accepted. *Financial support:* Research assistantships with partial tuition reimbursements, career-related internships or fieldwork, Federal Work-Study, health care benefits, unspecified assistantships, and grant-funded positions available. Support available to part-time students. Financial award application deadline: 3/15; financial award applicants required to submit FAFSA. *Unit head:* Dr. Gary Willhite, Director, 608-785-8142, E-mail: whillhite.gary@uwlax.edu. *Application contact:* Kathryn Kiefer, Associate Director of Admissions, 608-785-8939, E-mail: admissions@uwlax.edu.

University of Wisconsin–Milwaukee, Graduate School, School of Education, Department of Curriculum and Instruction, Milwaukee, WI 53201-0413. Offers curriculum planning and instruction improvement (MS); early childhood education (MS); elementary education (MS); junior high/middle school education (MS); reading education (MS); secondary education (MS); teaching in an urban setting (MS). Part-time programs available. *Faculty:* 22 full-time (17 women). *Students:* 23 full-time (14 women), 64 part-time (58 women); includes 8 minority (4 African Americans, 1 American Indian/Alaska Native, 3 Hispanic Americans), 1 international. Average age 31. 46 applicants, 57% accepted, 12 enrolled. In 2009, 28 master's awarded. *Degree requirements:* For master's, thesis or alternative. *Entrance requirements:* Additional exam requirements/recommendations for international students: Required—TOEFL (minimum score 550 paper-based; 79 iBT), IELTS (minimum score 6.5). *Application deadline:* For fall admission, 1/1 priority date for domestic students; for spring admission, 9/1 for domestic students. Applications are processed on a rolling basis. Application fee: $45 ($75 for international students). *Expenses:* Tuition, state resident: full-time $8800. Tuition, nonresident: full-time $20,760. Tuition and fees vary according to program and reciprocity agreements. *Financial support:* Career-related internships or fieldwork and unspecified assistantships available. Support available to part-time students. Financial award application deadline: 4/15. Total annual research expenditures: $65,946. *Unit head:* Hope Longwell-Grice, Chair, 414-229-4884, Fax: 414-229-5571, E-mail: hope@uwm.edu. *Application contact:* General Information Contact, 414-229-4982, Fax: 414-229-6967, E-mail: gradschool@uwm.edu.

University of Wisconsin–Platteville, School of Graduate Studies, College of Liberal Arts and Education, School of Education, Platteville, WI 53818-3099. Offers adult education (MSE); elementary education (MSE); English education (MSE); middle school education (MSE);

secondary education (MSE); vocational and technical education (MSE). *Accreditation:* NCATE. Part-time programs available. *Faculty:* 8 part-time/adjunct (3 women). *Students:* 16 full-time (12 women), 183 part-time (137 women); includes 35 minority (27 African Americans, 1 American Indian/Alaska Native, 1 Asian American or Pacific Islander, 6 Hispanic Americans), 63 international. 23 applicants, 100% accepted, 23 enrolled. In 2009, 85 master's awarded. *Degree requirements:* For master's, comprehensive exam, thesis or alternative. *Entrance requirements:* Additional exam requirements/recommendations for international students: Required—TOEFL (minimum score 500 paper-based; 173 computer-based; 61 iBT). *Application deadline:* For fall admission, 7/1 priority date for domestic students; for spring admission, 11/1 for domestic students. Applications are processed on a rolling basis. Application fee: $56. Electronic applications accepted. *Expenses:* Tuition, state resident: full-time $6706. Tuition, nonresident: full-time $16,772. *Financial support:* Research assistantships with partial tuition reimbursements, career-related internships or fieldwork, Federal Work-Study, institutionally sponsored loans, scholarships/grants, and unspecified assistantships available. Support available to part-time students. *Unit head:* Dr. Karen Stinson, Director, 608-342-1131, Fax: 608-342-1133. *Application contact:* Lisa Popp, School of Graduate Studies, 608-342-1322, Fax: 608-342-1389, E-mail: poppl@uwplatt.edu.

University of Wisconsin–River Falls, Outreach and Graduate Studies, College of Education and Professional Studies, Department of Teacher Education, River Falls, WI 54022. Offers elementary education (MSE); professional development shared inquiry communities (MSE); reading (MSE). Part-time programs available. *Degree requirements:* For master's, comprehensive exam, thesis or alternative. *Entrance requirements:* For master's, minimum GPA of 2.75. Additional exam requirements/recommendations for international students: Required—TOEFL (minimum score 500 paper-based; 65 iBT), IELTS (minimum score 5.5). Electronic applications accepted.

University of Wisconsin–Stevens Point, College of Professional Studies, School of Education, Program in Elementary Education, Stevens Point, WI 54481-3897. Offers MSE. Part-time programs available. *Students:* 1 (woman) full-time. *Degree requirements:* For master's, comprehensive exam, thesis or alternative. *Entrance requirements:* For master's, teacher certification, minimum undergraduate GPA of 3.0. Additional exam requirements/recommendations for international students: Required—TOEFL (minimum score 523 paper-based). *Application deadline:* For fall admission, 5/1 priority date for domestic students. Applications are processed on a rolling basis. Application fee: $45. *Expenses:* Tuition, state resident: full-time $7740; part-time $430 per credit hour. Tuition, nonresident: full-time $17,804; part-time $989 per credit hour. Tuition and fees vary according to course load and reciprocity agreements. *Financial support:* In 2009–10, 4 research assistantships with partial tuition reimbursements (averaging $9,807 per year) were awarded; Federal Work-Study also available. Support available to part-time students. Financial award application deadline: 5/1. *Faculty research:* Gifted education, early childhood special education, curriculum and instruction, standards-based education. *Unit head:* Dr. JoAnne Katzmarek, Associate Dean, 715-346-4430, Fax: 715-346-4846, E-mail: jkatzmar@uwsp.edu. *Application contact:* Dr. Patricia Caro, Director, 715-346-4403, Fax: 715-346-4846, E-mail: pcaro@uwsp.edu.

Utah State University, School of Graduate Studies, College of Education and Human Services, Department of Elementary Education, Logan, UT 84322. Offers M Ed, MA, MS. Part-time programs available. Postbaccalaureate distance learning degree programs offered (no on-campus study). *Degree requirements:* For master's, comprehensive exam (for some programs), thesis (for some programs). *Entrance requirements:* For master's, GRE General Test or MAT, minimum GPA of 3.0, teaching certificate, 3 recommendations, 1 year teaching department record. Additional exam requirements/recommendations for international students: Required—TOEFL. *Faculty research:* Teacher education, supervision, gifted and talented education, language arts/writing, early childhood education.

Vanderbilt University, Peabody College, Department of Teaching and Learning, Nashville, TN 37240-1001. Offers elementary education (M Ed); English language learners (M Ed); learning and instruction (M Ed); learning, diversity, and urban studies (M Ed); reading education (M Ed); secondary education (M Ed). *Accreditation:* NCATE. *Faculty:* 31 full-time (20 women), 23 part-time/adjunct (20 women). *Students:* 95 full-time (88 women), 21 part-time (6 women); includes 14 minority (6 African Americans, 4 Asian Americans or Pacific Islanders, 4 Hispanic Americans), 5 international. Average age 27. 150 applicants, 69% accepted, 59 enrolled. In 2009, 74 master's awarded. *Degree requirements:* For master's, comprehensive exam, thesis optional. *Entrance requirements:* For master's, GRE General Test, MAT. Additional exam requirements/recommendations for international students: Required—TOEFL (minimum score 550 paper-based; 213 computer-based). *Application deadline:* For fall admission, 12/31 priority date for domestic and international students; for spring admission, 11/1 priority date for domestic and international students. Applications are processed on a rolling basis. Application fee: $0. Electronic applications accepted. *Financial support:* In 2009–10, 104 students received support, including 27 research assistantships with full and partial tuition reimbursements available; fellowships with full and partial tuition reimbursements available, teaching assistantships with full and partial tuition reimbursements available, Federal Work-Study, institutionally sponsored loans, scholarships/grants, tuition waivers (partial), and unspecified assistantships also available. Support available to part-time students. Financial award application deadline: 2/1; financial award applicants required to submit FAFSA. *Faculty research:* Teaching and learning, development of mathematical and scientific knowledge, interventions to foster early literacy and numeracy, reading and writing in the digital age, teaching diverse learners. *Unit head:* Dr. David Dickinson, Acting Chair, 615-322-8100, Fax: 615-322-8999, E-mail: david.k.dickinson@vanderbilt.edu. *Application contact:* Angela Saylor, Educational Coordinator, 615-322-8092, Fax: 615-322-8999, E-mail: angela.saylor@vanderbilt.edu.

Villanova University, Graduate School of Liberal Arts and Sciences, Department of Education and Human Services, Program in Elementary Teacher Education, Villanova, PA 19085-1699. Offers MA. Part-time and evening/weekend programs available. *Students:* 5 part-time (all women). Average age 26. In 2009, 6 master's awarded. *Degree requirements:* For master's, comprehensive exam. *Entrance requirements:* For master's, GRE or MAT, minimum GPA of 3.0. *Application deadline:* For fall admission, 3/1 priority date for domestic students; for spring admission, 11/15 for domestic students. Applications are processed on a rolling basis. Application fee: $50. Electronic applications accepted. *Expenses:* Tuition: Part-time $630 per credit. Required fees: $60 per credit. Part-time tuition and fees vary according to degree level and program. *Financial support:* Career-related internships or fieldwork and Federal Work-Study available. Financial award applicants required to submit FAFSA. *Unit head:* Dr. Connie Titone, Coordinator, 610-519-4620. *Application contact:* Dr. Connie Titone, Coordinator, 610-519-4620.

Wagner College, Division of Graduate Studies, Department of Education, Program in Childhood Education, Staten Island, NY 10301-4495. Offers MS Ed. Part-time and evening/weekend programs available. *Entrance requirements:* For master's, New York State Teacher Certification Examinations (NYSTCE), Liberal Arts and Sciences Test (LAST), minimum GPA of 2.75. Additional exam requirements/recommendations for international students: Required—TOEFL (minimum score 550 paper-based; 217 computer-based). *Expenses:* Tuition: Full-time $15,570; part-time $865 per credit. Required fees: $2.

Walden University, Graduate Programs, Richard W. Riley College of Education and Leadership, Minneapolis, MN 55401. Offers administrator leadership for teaching and learning (Ed D, Ed S); curriculum, instruction, and professional development (Ed S); early childhood education (birth-grade 3) (MAT); education (MS, PhD), including adolescent literacy and technology (grades 6-12) (MS), adult education leadership (PhD), community college leadership (PhD), curriculum, instruction, and assessment, early childhood education (PhD), educational leadership (MS), educational technology (PhD), elementary reading and literacy (MS), elementary reading and mathematics (MS), emotional/behavioral disorders (K-12) (MS), general program, higher education (PhD), integrating technology in the classroom (MS), K-12 educational leadership

(PhD), learning disabilities (K-12) (MS); literacy and learning in the content areas (MS), mathematics (grades 6-8) (MS), mathematics (grades K-5) (MS), middle level education (grades 5-8) (MS), professional development (MS), science (grades K-8) (MS), self-designed (PhD), special education (PhD), special education (non-licensure) (MS), teacher leadership (grades K-12) (MS); educational leadership and administration (principal preparation) (Ed S); educational technology (Ed S); higher education and adult learning (Ed D); instructional design (Postbaccalaureate Certificate); instructional design and technology (MS), including general program (MS, PhD), online learning, training and performance improvement; special education: emotional/behavioral disorders (K-12) (MAT); special education: learning disabilities (K-12) (MAT); teacher leadership (Ed D, Ed S). Part-time and evening/weekend programs available. Postbaccalaureate distance learning degree programs offered (minimal on-campus study). *Faculty:* 54 full-time, 835 part-time/adjunct. *Students:* 13,940 full-time (11,339 women), 1,940 part-time (1,637 women); includes 4,626 minority (3,795 African Americans, 111 American Indian/Alaska Native, 199 Asian Americans or Pacific Islanders, 521 Hispanic Americans), 124 international. Average age 38. In 2009, 4,688 master's, 190 doctorates awarded. *Degree requirements:* For doctorate, thesis/dissertation (for some programs), residency; for other advanced degree, residency (for some programs). *Entrance requirements:* For master's, bachelor's degree or equivalent in related field; minimum GPA of 2.5; official transcripts; goal statement; access to computer and Internet; for doctorate, master's degree or equivalent in related field; minimum GPA of 3.0; official transcripts; three years' related professional/academic experience (preferred); access to computer and Internet; for other advanced degree, master's degree or equivalent in related field; minimum GPA of 3.0; 3 years related professional/academic experience (preferred); access to computer and Internet (Ed S). Additional exam requirements/recommendations for international students: Required—TOEFL (minimum score 550 paper-based; 213 computer-based), IELTS (minimum score 6.5), or Michigan English Language Assessment Battery (minimum score 82). *Application deadline:* Applications are processed on a rolling basis. Application fee: $50. Electronic applications accepted. *Expenses:* Tuition: Full-time $13,665; part-time $560 per credit. Required fees: $1375. Tuition and fees vary according to course load, degree level and program. *Financial support:* In 2009–10, 2,418 students received support; fellowships, Federal Work-Study, scholarships/grants, unspecified assistantships, and family tuition reduction, active duty/veteran tuition reduction, group tuition reduction, interest-free payment plans available. Support available to part-time students. Financial award applicants required to submit FAFSA. *Unit head:* Dr. Kate Steffens, Dean, 800-925-3368. *Application contact:* Jennifer Hall, Director of Enrollment, 866-4-WALDEN, E-mail: info@waldenu.edu.

Washington State University, Graduate School, College of Education, Department of Teaching and Learning, Pullman, WA 99164. Offers curriculum and instruction (Ed D, PhD); diverse languages (M Ed, MA); elementary education (M Ed, MA, MIT); exercise science (MS); literacy education (M Ed, MA, PhD); math education (PhD); secondary education (M Ed, MA). *Accreditation:* NCATE. *Degree requirements:* For master's, comprehensive exam (for some programs), thesis (for some programs), oral or written exam; for doctorate, comprehensive exam, thesis/dissertation, oral, written exam. *Entrance requirements:* For master's and doctorate, GRE General Test, minimum GPA of 3.0, 3 letters of recommendation. Additional exam requirements/recommendations for international students: Required—TOEFL. *Faculty research:* Evolution of middle school education issues in special education, computer-assisted language learning.

Washington University in St. Louis, Graduate School of Arts and Sciences, Department of Education, Program in Elementary Education, St. Louis, MO 63130-4899. Offers MA Ed. *Degree requirements:* For master's, thesis or alternative. *Entrance requirements:* For master's, GRE General Test or MAT. Electronic applications accepted.

Wayne State College, School of Education and Counseling, Department of Educational Foundations and Leadership, Program in Curriculum and Instruction, Wayne, NE 68787. Offers alternative education (MSE); business and information technology education (MSE); communication arts education (MSE); early childhood education (MSE); elementary education (MSE); English as a second language (MSE); English education (MSE); family and consumer sciences education (MSE); industrial technology and vocational education (MSE); learning communities (MSE); mathematics education (MSE); music education (MSE); science education (MSE); social science education (MSE). *Accreditation:* NCATE. Part-time and evening/weekend programs available. *Degree requirements:* For master's, comprehensive exam, thesis optional. *Entrance requirements:* For master's, GRE General Test. Additional exam requirements/recommendations for international students: Required—TOEFL (minimum score 550 paper-based; 213 computer-based).

Wayne State University, College of Education, Division of Administrative and Organizational Studies, Detroit, MI 48202. Offers administration and supervision-secondary (Ed S); college and university teaching (Certificate); curriculum and instruction (PhD); educational leadership (M Ed, Ed S); educational leadership and policy studies (Ed D, PhD); elementary education curriculum and instruction (MA, Ed S); general administration and supervision (Ed D, PhD, Ed S); higher education (Ed D, PhD); instructional technology (M Ed, Ed D, PhD, Ed S); secondary curriculum and instruction (M Ed, Ed S). *Degree requirements:* For doctorate, thesis/dissertation. *Entrance requirements:* For doctorate, interview, minimum GPA of 3.0, an autobiography or curriculum vitae; references. Additional exam requirements/recommendations for international students: Required—TOEFL (minimum score 550 paper-based; 213 computer-based), TWE (minimum score 6). Electronic applications accepted. *Faculty research:* Total quality management, participatory management, administering educational technology, school improvement, principalship.

Wayne State University, College of Education, Division of Teacher Education, Detroit, MI 48202. Offers adult and continuing education (M Ed); art education (M Ed); bilingual/bicultural education (M Ed, MAT); business education (M Ed, MAT); career and technical education (M Ed, Ed D, PhD, Ed S); curriculum and instruction (Ed D, PhD, Ed S); distributive education (M Ed, MAT); early childhood education (M Ed); elementary education (M Ed, MAT, Ed D, PhD, Ed S); elementary education curriculum and instruction (M Ed); English education (M Ed); English education-secondary (M Ed, Ed S); foreign language education (M Ed); general education (Ed D, Ed S); health occupations education (M Ed); industrial education (M Ed); mathematics education (M Ed, Ed S); pre-school and parent education (M Ed); reading (M Ed, Ed D, Ed S); reading, languages and literature (Ed D); school music-vocal (M Ed); science education (M Ed, MAT, Ed S); secondary education (MAT); secondary school reading (M Ed); social studies education (M Ed, Ed S), including education-secondary (M Ed); special education (M Ed, Ed D, PhD, Ed S); teacher education (MAT, Ed D, PhD). *Degree requirements:* For doctorate, thesis/dissertation. *Entrance requirements:* For master's, Michigan Basic Skills Test (MA in teaching), minimum GPA of 2.6; for doctorate, minimum undergraduate GPA of 3.0, graduate 3.5; interview, curriculum vitae; references. Additional exam requirements/recommendations for international students: Required—TOEFL (minimum score 550 paper-based; 213 computer-based), TWE (minimum score 6). Electronic applications accepted. *Faculty research:* Reading and writing literacy and literature.

West Chester University of Pennsylvania, Office of Graduate Studies, College of Education, Department of Early and Middle Grades, West Chester, PA 19383. Offers early childhood education (M Ed, Teaching Certificate); elementary education (M Ed). *Accreditation:* NCATE. Part-time and evening/weekend programs available. *Students:* 32 full-time (28 women), 148 part-time (132 women); includes 13 minority (6 African Americans, 4 Asian Americans or Pacific Islanders, 3 Hispanic Americans). Average age 30. 96 applicants, 96% accepted, 55 enrolled. In 2009, 67 master's awarded. *Degree requirements:* For master's, comprehensive exam, thesis optional. *Entrance requirements:* For master's, GMAT, GRE General Test, or MAT, interview, minimum GPA of 3.0. Additional exam requirements/recommendations for international students: Required—TOEFL (minimum score 550 paper-based; 213 computer-based; 80 iBT). *Application deadline:* For fall admission, 4/15 priority date for domestic students, 3/15 for international students; for spring admission, 10/15 for domestic students.

Elementary Education

West Chester University of Pennsylvania (continued)
Applications are processed on a rolling basis. Application fee: $35. Electronic applications accepted. *Expenses:* Tuition, state resident: full-time $6666; part-time $370 per credit. Tuition, nonresident: full-time $10,666; part-time $593 per credit. Required fees: $122.56 per credit. *Financial support:* In 2009–10, research assistantships with full and partial tuition reimbursements (averaging $5,000 per year); unspecified assistantships also available. Support available to part-time students. Financial award application deadline: 2/15; financial award applicants required to submit FAFSA. *Faculty research:* Cooperative learning, peer mediation in schools, creative thinking and questioning. *Unit head:* Dr. Heather Leaman, Chair, 610-738-0515, E-mail: hleaman@wcupa.edu. *Application contact:* Dr. Connie DiLucchio, Graduate Coordinator, 610-436-3323, E-mail: cdilucchio@wcupa.edu.

Western Illinois University, School of Graduate Studies, College of Education and Human Services, Department of Curriculum and Instruction, Program in Elementary Education, Macomb, IL 61455-1390. Offers MS Ed. *Accreditation:* NCATE. Part-time programs available. *Students:* 5 full-time (4 women), 99 part-time (96 women); includes 2 minority (both Hispanic Americans), 2 international. Average age 35. 14 applicants, 71% accepted. In 2009, 40 master's awarded. *Degree requirements:* For master's, thesis or alternative. *Entrance requirements:* Additional exam requirements/recommendations for international students: Required—TOEFL (minimum score 550 paper-based; 213 computer-based; 80 iBT). *Application deadline:* Applications are processed on a rolling basis. Application fee: $30. Electronic applications accepted. *Expenses:* Tuition, state resident: full-time $4486; part-time $249.21 per credit hour. Tuition, nonresident: full-time $8972; part-time $498.42 per credit hour. Required fees: $72.62 per credit hour. *Financial support:* In 2009–10, research assistantships with full tuition reimbursements (averaging $7,280 per year). Financial award applicants required to submit FAFSA. *Unit head:* Dr. Angela Ferree, Graduate Committee Chairperson, 309-298-1961. *Application contact:* Evelyn Hoing, Assistant Director of Graduate Studies, 309-298-1806, Fax: 309-298-2345, E-mail: grad-office@wiu.edu.

Western Kentucky University, Graduate Studies, College of Education and Behavioral Sciences, Department of Counseling and Student Affairs, Bowling Green, KY 42101. Offers business and marketing education (MA Ed); counseling (MA Ed); counselor education (Ed S); education and behavioral science (MA Ed); elementary education (MA Ed, Ed S); middle years education (MA Ed); secondary education (MA Ed, Ed S); student affairs (MA Ed). *Accreditation:* ACA; NCATE. Part-time and evening/weekend programs available. *Degree requirements:* For master's, comprehensive exam, thesis optional. *Entrance requirements:* For master's, GRE General Test. Additional exam requirements/recommendations for international students: Required—TOEFL (minimum score 555 paper-based; 213 computer-based; 79 iBT). *Expenses:* Tuition, state resident: full-time $4160; part-time $416 per credit hour. Tuition, nonresident: full-time $9550; part-time $506 per credit hour. Tuition and fees vary according to campus/location and reciprocity agreements. *Faculty research:* Counselor education, research for residential workers.

Western Kentucky University, Graduate Studies, College of Education and Behavioral Sciences, Department of Curriculum and Instruction, Bowling Green, KY 42101. Offers business and marketing education (MAE); elementary education (MAE, Ed S); middle grades education (MAE); secondary education (MAE, Ed S). *Degree requirements:* For master's, comprehensive exam; for Ed S, thesis. *Entrance requirements:* For master's, GRE. Additional exam requirements/recommendations for international students: Required—TOEFL (minimum score 555 paper-based; 213 computer-based; 79 iBT). *Expenses:* Tuition, state resident: full-time $4160; part-time $416 per credit hour. Tuition, nonresident: full-time $9550; part-time $506 per credit hour. Tuition and fees vary according to campus/location and reciprocity agreements.

Western New England College, School of Arts and Sciences, Program in Elementary Education, Springfield, MA 01119. Offers M Ed. Part-time and evening/weekend programs available. *Students:* 41 part-time (36 women). In 2009, 15 master's awarded. *Entrance requirements:* For master's, initial license for elementary teaching, recommendations, resume, personal statement. *Application deadline:* Applications are processed on a rolling basis. Application fee: $30. *Expenses:* Tuition: Part-time $552 per credit hour. Part-time tuition and fees vary according to program. *Financial support:* Available to part-time students. Applicants required to submit FAFSA. *Unit head:* Dr. Saeed Ghahramani, Dean, 413-782-1218, Fax: 413-796-2118, E-mail: sghahram@wnec.edu. *Application contact:* Matt Fox, Director of Recruiting and Marketing for Adult Learners, 413-782-1249, Fax: 413-782-1779, E-mail: ce@wnec.edu.

Western New Mexico University, Graduate Division, School of Education, Silver City, NM 88062-0680. Offers bilingual education (MAT); counseling (MA); educational leadership (MA); elementary education (MAT); reading (MAT); school psychology (MA); secondary education (MAT); special education (MAT); TESOL (teaching English to speakers of other languages) (MAT). *Accreditation:* NCATE. *Degree requirements:* For master's, comprehensive exam. *Entrance requirements:* For master's, GRE General Test, GRE Subject Test, minimum GPA of 3.2 in last 64 hours of undergraduate study. Additional exam requirements/recommendations for international students: Required—TOEFL (minimum score 550 paper-based; 213 computer-based). Electronic applications accepted.

Western Washington University, Graduate School, Woodring College of Education, Department of Elementary Education, Bellingham, WA 98225-5996. Offers M Ed. *Accreditation:* NCATE. Part-time programs available. *Degree requirements:* For master's, comprehensive exam, thesis optional. *Entrance requirements:* For master's, GRE General Test or MAT, minimum GPA of 3.0 in last 60 semester hours or last 90 quarter hours, elementary teaching certificate. Additional exam requirements/recommendations for international students: Required—TOEFL (minimum score 567 paper-based; 227 computer-based). Electronic applications accepted. *Faculty research:* Teacher learning through National Board certification.

Westfield State College, Division of Graduate and Continuing Education, Department of Education, Program in Elementary Education, Westfield, MA 01086. Offers M Ed. *Accreditation:* NCATE. Part-time and evening/weekend programs available. *Degree requirements:* For master's, comprehensive exam, practicum. *Entrance requirements:* For master's, GRE General Test or MAT, minimum undergraduate GPA of 2.7.

West Virginia University, College of Human Resources and Education, Department of Curriculum and Instruction-Literacy, Program in Elementary Education, Morgantown, WV 26506. Offers MA. Students enter program as undergraduates. *Accreditation:* NCATE. Part-time programs available. *Degree requirements:* For master's, thesis optional, content exams. *Entrance requirements:* For master's, minimum GPA of 2.75. Additional exam requirements/recommendations for international students: Required—TOEFL. Electronic applications accepted. *Faculty research:* Teacher education, school reform, teacher and student attitudes, curriculum development, education technology.

Wheaton College, Graduate School, Department of Education, Wheaton, IL 60187-5593. Offers elementary level (MAT); secondary level (MAT). *Accreditation:* NCATE. *Degree requirements:* For master's, thesis or alternative. *Entrance requirements:* For master's, GRE General Test. Electronic applications accepted.

Wheelock College, Graduate Programs, Division of Education, Boston, MA 02215-4176. Offers early childhood education (MS); education leadership (MS); elementary education (MS); language, literacy, and reading (MS); teaching students with moderate disabilities (MS). *Accreditation:* NCATE. Postbaccalaureate distance learning degree programs offered (minimal on-campus study). *Degree requirements:* For master's, comprehensive exam. *Entrance requirements:* Additional exam requirements/recommendations for international students: Required—TOEFL. Electronic applications accepted. *Faculty research:* Symbolic learning, emergent literacy, diversity inclusion, beginning reading language and culture, math education.

Whittier College, Graduate Programs, Department of Education and Child Development, Program in Elementary Education, Whittier, CA 90608-0634. Offers MA Ed. Part-time and evening/weekend programs available. *Degree requirements:* For master's, thesis. *Entrance requirements:* For master's, GRE General Test, MAT.

Whitworth University, School of Education, Graduate Studies in Education, Spokane, WA 99251-0001. Offers administration (M Ed); counseling (M Ed), including school counselors, social agency/church setting; elementary education (M Ed); gifted and talented (MAT); secondary education (M Ed); special education (MAT); teaching (MIT). *Accreditation:* NCATE. Part-time and evening/weekend programs available. *Degree requirements:* For master's, comprehensive exam, thesis (for some programs). *Entrance requirements:* For master's, GRE General Test, MAT. Additional exam requirements/recommendations for international students: Required—TOEFL. Tuition and fees vary according to program. *Faculty research:* Rural program development, mainstreaming, special needs learners.

Widener University, School of Human Service Professions, Center for Education, Chester, PA 19013-5792. Offers adult education (M Ed); counseling in higher education (M Ed); counselor education (M Ed); early childhood education (M Ed); educational foundations (M Ed); educational leadership (M Ed); educational psychology (M Ed); elementary education (M Ed); English and language arts (M Ed); health education (M Ed); higher education leadership (Ed D); home and school visitor (M Ed); human sexuality (M Ed); mathematics education (M Ed); middle school education (M Ed); principalship (M Ed); reading and language arts (Ed D); reading education (M Ed); school administration (Ed D); science education (M Ed); social studies education (M Ed); special education (M Ed); technology education (M Ed). *Accreditation:* NCATE. Part-time and evening/weekend programs available. *Faculty:* 34 full-time (22 women), 37 part-time/adjunct (14 women). *Students:* 203 full-time (154 women), 415 part-time (298 women); includes 50 minority (34 African Americans, 1 American Indian/Alaska Native, 5 Asian Americans or Pacific Islanders, 10 Hispanic Americans), 3 international. Average age 39. 139 applicants, 88% accepted. In 2009, 168 master's, 31 doctorates awarded. Terminal master's awarded for partial completion of doctoral program. *Degree requirements:* For doctorate, thesis/dissertation. *Entrance requirements:* For master's, minimum GPA of 2.5; for doctorate, GRE or MAT, minimum GPA of 2.0 (undergraduate), 3.5 (graduate). *Application deadline:* Applications are processed on a rolling basis. Application fee: $25 ($300 for international students). Electronic applications accepted. *Expenses:* Contact institution. *Financial support:* Career-related internships or fieldwork, tuition waivers (full and partial), and unspecified assistantships available. Support available to part-time students. Financial award application deadline: 5/1. *Faculty research:* Reading and cognition, adult education, technology education, educational leadership, special education. *Unit head:* Dr. Michael W. LeDoux, Associate Dean, 610-499-4294, Fax: 610-499-4623, E-mail: mwledoux@widener.edu. *Application contact:* Dr. Roberta D. Nolan, Director of Graduate Admissions, 610-499-4125, E-mail: rdnolan@widener.edu.

Wilkes University, College of Graduate and Professional Studies, School of Education, Wilkes-Barre, PA 18766-0002. Offers classroom technology (MS Ed); educational computing (MS Ed); educational development and strategies (MS Ed); educational leadership (MS Ed); educational technology (Ed D); elementary education (MS Ed); higher education administration (Ed D); instructional technology (MS Ed); K-12 administration (Ed D); online teaching (MS Ed); school business leadership (MS Ed); secondary education (MS Ed), including biology, chemistry, English, history; special education (MS Ed). Part-time and evening/weekend programs available. Postbaccalaureate distance learning degree programs offered (minimal on-campus study). *Students:* 89 full-time (60 women), 2,849 part-time (2,058 women); includes 52 minority (10 African Americans, 2 American Indian/Alaska Native, 13 Asian Americans or Pacific Islanders, 27 Hispanic Americans), 6 international. Average age 33. In 2009, 947 master's awarded. *Entrance requirements:* Additional exam requirements/recommendations for international students: Required—TOEFL (minimum score 500 paper-based; 173 computer-based; 79 iBT). *Application deadline:* Applications are processed on a rolling basis. Application fee: $45. *Expenses:* Contact institution. *Financial support:* Federal Work-Study and unspecified assistantships available. Financial award application deadline: 3/1; financial award applicants required to submit FAFSA. *Unit head:* Dr. Michael Speziale, Dean, 570-408-4679, Fax: 570-408-4905, E-mail: michael.speziale@wilkes.edu. *Application contact:* Kathleen Houlihan, Director of Graduate Studies, 570-408-3235, Fax: 570-408-7846, E-mail: kathleen.houlihan@wilkes.edu.

William Carey University, School of Education, Hattiesburg, MS 39401-5499. Offers art education (M Ed); art of teaching (M Ed); elementary education (M Ed, Ed S); English education (M Ed); gifted education (M Ed); history and social science (M Ed); mild/moderate disabilities (M Ed); secondary education (M Ed). Part-time programs available. *Degree requirements:* For master's, comprehensive exam. *Entrance requirements:* For master's, GRE, MAT, minimum GPA of 2.5, Class A teacher's license. Additional exam requirements/recommendations for international students: Required—TOEFL (minimum score 550 paper-based; 213 computer-based).

William Woods University, Graduate and Adult Studies, Fulton, MO 65251-1098. Offers administration (Ed S); agriculture (MBA); athletic/activities administration (M Ed); curriculum and instruction (M Ed); curriculum leadership (Ed S); elementary administration (M Ed); health management (MBA); human resources (MBA); principalship (Ed S); secondary administration (M Ed); special education director (M Ed). Evening/weekend programs available. *Degree requirements:* For master's, capstone course (MBA), action research (M Ed); for Ed S, field experience. *Entrance requirements:* For master's, 2 recommendations, resumé, BA/BS; teaching certification (M Ed); course work in economics and accounting (MBA); for Ed S, M Ed, 2 letters of recommendation, resume, teaching certification. Additional exam requirements/recommendations for international students: Required—TOEFL (minimum score 550 paper-based). Electronic applications accepted.

Wilmington University, College of Education, New Castle, DE 19720-6491. Offers applied education technology (M Ed); career and technical education (M Ed); elementary and secondary school counseling (M Ed); elementary special education (M Ed); elementary studies (M Ed); instruction: gifted and talented (M Ed); instruction: teaching and learning (M Ed); literacy (M Ed); reading (M Ed); school leadership (M Ed); secondary teaching (MAT). *Accreditation:* NCATE. Part-time and evening/weekend programs available. *Entrance requirements:* For master's, 2 letters of recommendation, interview. Additional exam requirements/recommendations for international students: Required—TOEFL (minimum score 500 paper-based; 173 computer-based). Electronic applications accepted.

Wilson College, Program in Education, Chambersburg, PA 17201-1285. Offers M Ed. Evening/weekend programs available. *Degree requirements:* For master's, project. *Entrance requirements:* For master's, PRAXIS, minimum undergraduate cumulative GPA of 3.0, 2 letters of recommendation, current certification for eligibility to teach in grades K-12, resume, personal interview. Electronic applications accepted.

Wingate University, Program in Education, Wingate, NC 28174-0159. Offers educational leadership (MA Ed); elementary education (MA Ed, MAT); physical education (MA Ed); sport administration (MA Ed). *Accreditation:* NCATE. Part-time and evening/weekend programs available. *Degree requirements:* For master's, portfolio. *Entrance requirements:* For master's, GRE General Test or MAT, teaching certificate (MA Ed).

Winston-Salem State University, Program in Elementary Education, Winston-Salem, NC 27110-0003. Offers M Ed. *Accreditation:* NCATE. Part-time and evening/weekend programs available. Postbaccalaureate distance learning degree programs offered (minimal on-campus study). *Entrance requirements:* For master's, GRE, MAT, NC teacher licensure. Electronic applications accepted. *Faculty research:* Action research on issues in elementary classroom.

Worcester State College, Graduate Studies, Department of Education, Program in Elementary Education, Worcester, MA 01602-2597. Offers M Ed. Part-time and evening/weekend programs available. *Faculty:* 9 full-time (7 women), 19 part-time/adjunct (7 women). *Students:* 3 full-time

(2 women), 26 part-time (25 women); includes 1 minority (Hispanic American). Average age 31. 13 applicants, 85% accepted, 6 enrolled. In 2009, 15 master's awarded. *Degree requirements:* For master's, comprehensive exam (for some programs), thesis optional. *Entrance requirements:* For master's, GRE General Test or MAT, elementary teaching certificate. Additional exam requirements/recommendations for international students: Required—TOEFL (minimum score 550 paper-based; 213 computer-based; 79 iBT). *Application deadline:* Applications are processed on a rolling basis. Application fee: $30. *Expenses:* Tuition, area resident: Part-time $150 per credit. Tuition, state resident: part-time $150 per credit. Tuition, nonresident: part-time $150 per credit. Required fees: $85. *Financial support:* Career-related internships or fieldwork, scholarships/grants, and unspecified assistantships available. Financial award application deadline: 3/1; financial award applicants required to submit FAFSA. *Faculty research:* Contemporary elementary education, social studies in the elementary school. *Unit head:* Dr. Elaine Tateronis, Coordinator, 508-929-8823, Fax: 508-929-8164, E-mail: etateronis@worcester.edu. *Application contact:* Nicole Brown, Assistant Dean of Graduate and Continuing Education, 508-929-8787, Fax: 508-929-8100, E-mail: nbrown@worcester.edu.

Wright State University, School of Graduate Studies, College of Education and Human Services, Department of Teacher Education, Programs in Classroom Teacher Education, Dayton, OH 45435. Offers M Ed, MA. *Accreditation:* NCATE. *Degree requirements:* For master's, thesis (for some programs). *Entrance requirements:* For master's, GRE General Test, MAT, PRAXIS II. Additional exam requirements/recommendations for international students: Required—TOEFL.

Xavier University, College of Social Sciences, Health and Education, School of Education, Department of Childhood Education and Literacy, Program in Elementary Education, Cincinnati, OH 45207. Offers M Ed. Part-time and evening/weekend programs available. *Faculty:* 1 full-time (0 women), 2 part-time/adjunct (1 woman). *Students:* 51 full-time (40 women), 54 part-time (46 women); includes 9 minority (7 African Americans, 2 Hispanic Americans). Average age 32. 43 applicants, 95% accepted, 29 enrolled. In 2009, 51 master's awarded. *Degree requirements:* For master's, comprehensive exam, research project or thesis. *Entrance requirements:* For master's, GRE or MAT. *Application deadline:* Applications are processed on a rolling basis. Application fee: $35. Electronic applications accepted. *Expenses:* Tuition: Part-time $697 per credit hour. One-time fee: $35 part-time. *Financial support:* In 2009–10, 66 students received support. Scholarships/grants available. Financial award applicants required to submit FAFSA. *Faculty research:* First-year teacher retention, teaching efficacy of science educators, adolescents' literacy practices, family resiliency, preparing culturally responsive teachers. Total annual research expenditures: $1,000. *Unit head:* Dr. Cynthia Geer, Chair, Department of Childhood Education and Literacy, 513-745-3262, Fax: 513-745-1052, E-mail: geer@xavier.edu. *Application contact:* Roger Bosse, Interim Director of Graduate Studies, 513-745-3357, Fax: 513-745-1048, E-mail: bosse@xavier.edu.

Higher Education

Abilene Christian University, Graduate School, College of Education and Human Services, Graduate Studies in Education, Program in Higher Education, Abilene, TX 79699-9100. Offers M Ed. Postbaccalaureate distance learning degree programs offered (minimal on-campus study). *Faculty:* 5 part-time/adjunct (1 woman). *Students:* 20 full-time (7 women), 41 part-time (28 women); includes 9 minority (8 African Americans, 1 Hispanic American), 2 international. 28 applicants, 68% accepted, 19 enrolled. In 2009, 8 master's awarded. *Degree requirements:* For master's, comprehensive exam. *Application deadline:* For fall admission, 4/1 priority date for domestic students; for spring admission, 11/1 for domestic students. Applications are processed on a rolling basis. Application fee: $40. Electronic applications accepted. *Expenses:* Tuition: Full-time $11,520; part-time $640 per hour. Required fees: $1090; $53.50 per hour. $10 per term. Tuition and fees vary according to program. *Financial support:* In 2009–10, 47 students received support. Application deadline: 4/1. *Unit head:* Dr. Jason Morris, Graduate Advisor, 325-674-2838, Fax: 325-674-2123, E-mail: morrisj@acu.edu. *Application contact:* William Horn, Graduate Admissions Counselor, 325-674-2656, Fax: 325-674-6717, E-mail: gradinfo@acu.edu.

Alliant International University–Irvine, Graduate School of Education, Educational Leadership Programs, Irvine, CA 92612. Offers educational administration (MA, Credential); educational leadership and management (K-12) (Ed D); higher education (Ed D); preliminary administrative services (Credential). Part-time programs available. *Entrance requirements:* For master's and doctorate, minimum GPA of 3.0, letters of recommendation. Additional exam requirements/recommendations for international students: Required—TOEFL (minimum score 550 paper-based; 213 computer-based), TWE (minimum score 5). Electronic applications accepted.

Alliant International University–Los Angeles, Graduate School of Education, Educational Leadership Programs, Alhambra, CA 91803-1360. Offers educational administration (MA); educational leadership and management (K-12) (Ed D); higher education (Ed D); preliminary administrative services (Credential). Part-time programs available. *Entrance requirements:* For master's and doctorate, minimum GPA of 3.0, letters of recommendation. Additional exam requirements/recommendations for international students: Required—TOEFL (minimum score 550 paper-based; 213 computer-based), TWE (minimum score 5).

Alliant International University–San Diego, Graduate School of Education, Educational Leadership Programs, San Diego, CA 92131-1799. Offers educational administration (MA); educational leadership and management (K-12) (Ed D); higher education (Ed D, Certificate); preliminary administrative services (Credential). Part-time programs available. *Entrance requirements:* For master's and doctorate, minimum GPA of 3.0, letters of recommendation. Additional exam requirements/recommendations for international students: Required—TOEFL (minimum score 550 paper-based; 213 computer-based), TWE (minimum score 5). Electronic applications accepted.

Alliant International University–San Francisco, Graduate School of Education, Educational Leadership Programs, San Francisco, CA 94133-1221. Offers community college administration (Ed D); educational administration (MA); educational leadership and management (K-12) (Ed D); higher education (Ed D); preliminary administrative services (Credential); university administration (Ed D). Part-time programs available. *Entrance requirements:* For master's and doctorate, minimum GPA of 3.0, letters of recommendation. Additional exam requirements/recommendations for international students: Required—TOEFL (minimum score 550 paper-based; 213 computer-based), TWE (minimum score 5). Electronic applications accepted. *Faculty research:* Leadership in higher education, community colleges.

Angelo State University, College of Graduate Studies, College of Education, Department of Curriculum and Instruction, Program in Student Development and Leadership in Higher Education, San Angelo, TX 76909. Offers M Ed. Part-time and evening/weekend programs available. *Faculty:* 17 full-time (12 women). *Students:* 6 full-time (5 women), 11 part-time (6 women); includes 2 minority (1 African American, 1 Hispanic American). Average age 32. 3 applicants, 100% accepted, 3 enrolled. In 2009, 1 master's awarded. *Degree requirements:* For master's, comprehensive exam. *Entrance requirements:* For master's, GRE General Test. Additional exam requirements/recommendations for international students: Required—TOEFL or IELTS. *Application deadline:* For fall admission, 7/15 priority date for domestic students, 6/10 for international students; for spring admission, 12/1 priority date for domestic students, 11/1 for international students. Applications are processed on a rolling basis. Application fee: $40 ($50 for international students). Electronic applications accepted. *Expenses:* Tuition, state resident: full-time $3396; part-time $142 per credit hour. Tuition, nonresident: full-time $10,152; part-time $423 per credit hour. Required fees: $1786; $36.25 per credit hour. $494 per semester. Full-time tuition and fees vary according to course load, degree level and program. *Financial support:* In 2009–10, 7 students received support. Federal Work-Study, scholarships/grants, and unspecified assistantships available. Support available to part-time students. Financial award application deadline: 3/1; financial award applicants required to submit FAFSA. *Unit head:* Dr. Alaric Williams, Graduate Advisor, 325-942-2052 Ext. 262, Fax: 325-942-2039, E-mail: alaric.williams@angelo.edu. *Application contact:* Theresa Fortin, Graduate Admissions Assistant, 325-942-2169, Fax: 325-942-2194, E-mail: theresa.fortin@angelo.edu.

Appalachian State University, Cratis D. Williams Graduate School, Department of Leadership and Educational Studies, Boone, NC 28608. Offers educational administration (Ed S); educational media (MA); higher education (MA, Ed S); library science (MLS); school administration (MSA). Part-time and evening/weekend programs available. Postbaccalaureate distance learning degree programs offered (no on-campus study). *Faculty:* 25 full-time (10 women), 28 part-time/adjunct (16 women). *Students:* 48 full-time (35 women), 474 part-time (373 women); includes 24 minority (21 African Americans, 2 Asian Americans or Pacific Islanders, 1 Hispanic American), 2 international. 229 applicants, 89% accepted, 156 enrolled. In 2009, 133 master's, 32 other advanced degrees awarded. *Degree requirements:* For master's and Ed S, comprehensive exam, thesis optional. *Entrance requirements:* For master's and Ed S, GRE or MAT, 3 letters of recommendation. Additional exam requirements/recommendations for international students: Required—TOEFL (minimum score 570 paper-based; 230 computer-based; 79 iBT), IELTS (minimum score 6.5). *Application deadline:* For fall admission, 7/1 for domestic students, 2/1 for international students; for spring admission, 11/1 for domestic students, 7/1 for international students. Applications are processed on a rolling basis. Application fee: $50. Electronic applications accepted. *Expenses:* Tuition, state resident: full-time $2960. Tuition, nonresident: full-time $14,051. Required fees: $2320. *Financial support:* In 2009–10, 10 research assistantships (averaging $8,000 per year) were awarded; career-related internships or fieldwork, scholarships/grants, and unspecified assistantships also available. Financial award application deadline: 4/1; financial award applicants required to submit FAFSA. *Faculty research:* Brain, learning and meditation; leadership of teaching and learning. Total annual research expenditures: $475,000. *Unit head:* Dr. Richard Riedl, Interim Director, 828-262-3112, E-mail: reidlr@appstate.edu. *Application contact:* Lori Dean, Graduate Student Coordinator, 828-262-6041, E-mail: deanlk@appstate.edu.

Argosy University, Atlanta, College of Education, Atlanta, GA 30328. Offers educational leadership (MAEd, Ed D, Ed S), including higher education administration (Ed D), K-12 education (Ed D); teaching and learning (MAEd, Ed D, Ed S), including education technology (Ed D), higher education (Ed D), K-12 education (Ed D).

See Close-Up on page 887.

Argosy University, Chicago, College of Education, Chicago, IL 60601. Offers adult education and training (MA Ed); community college executive leadership (Ed D); educational leadership (MA Ed, Ed D, Ed S), including district leadership (Ed D), higher education administration (Ed D), K-12 education (Ed D); instructional leadership (Ed D, Ed S), including higher education (Ed D), K-12 education (Ed D). Postbaccalaureate distance learning degree programs offered (minimal on-campus study).

See Close-Up on page 675.

Argosy University, Dallas, College of Education, Farmers Branch, TX 75244. Offers educational administration (MA Ed); educational leadership (Ed D); higher and postsecondary education (MA Ed); instructional leadership (MA Ed); school psychology (MA).

See Close-Up on page 677.

Argosy University, Denver, College of Education, Denver, CO 80231. Offers community college executive leadership (Ed D); educational leadership (MA Ed, Ed D), including higher education (Ed D), K-12 education (Ed D); instructional leadership (MA Ed, Ed D), including higher education administration (Ed D), K-12 education (Ed D).

See Close-Up on page 679.

Argosy University, Hawai'i, College of Education, Honolulu, HI 96813. Offers adult education and training (MAEd); educational leadership (Ed D), including higher education administration, K-12 education; instructional leadership (Ed D), including higher education, K-12 education; school psychology (MA).

See Close-Up on page 681.

Argosy University, Inland Empire, College of Education, San Bernardino, CA 92408. Offers community college executive leadership (Ed D); educational leadership (MA Ed, Ed D), including higher education administration (Ed D), K-12 education (Ed D); instructional leadership (MA Ed, Ed D), including higher education (Ed D), K-12 education (Ed D), multiple subject teacher preparation (MA Ed), single subject teacher preparation (MA Ed).

See Close-Up on page 889.

Argosy University, Los Angeles, College of Education, Santa Monica, CA 90045. Offers community college executive leadership (Ed D); educational leadership (MA Ed, Ed D), including higher education administration (Ed D), K-12 education (Ed D); instructional leadership (MA Ed, Ed D), including higher education (Ed D), K-12 education (Ed D), multiple subject teacher preparation (MA Ed), single subject teacher preparation (MA Ed).

See Close-Up on page 683.

Argosy University, Nashville, College of Education, Program in Educational Leadership, Nashville, TN 37214. Offers educational leadership (MA Ed, Ed S); higher education administration (Ed D); K-12 education (Ed D).

See Close-Up on page 891.

Argosy University, Nashville, College of Education, Program in Instructional Leadership, Nashville, TN 37214. Offers education technology (Ed D); higher education administration (Ed D); instructional leadership (MA Ed, Ed S); K-12 education (Ed D).

See Close-Up on page 891.

Argosy University, Orange County, College of Education, Orange, CA 92868. Offers community college executive leadership (Ed D); educational leadership (MA Ed, Ed D), including higher education administration (Ed D), K-12 education (Ed D); instructional leadership (MA Ed, Ed D), including education technology (Ed D), higher education (Ed D), K-12 education (Ed D), multiple subject teacher preparation (MA Ed), single subject teacher preparation (MA Ed).

See Close-Up on page 685.

Higher Education

Argosy University, Phoenix, College of Education, Phoenix, AZ 85021. Offers adult education and training (MA Ed); advanced educational administration (Ed D, Ed S); community college executive leadership (Ed D); educational administration (MA Ed); educational leadership (MA Ed, Ed D, Ed S), including education technology (Ed D), higher education administration (Ed D), K-12 education (Ed D); higher and postsecondary education (MA Ed); initial educational administration (Ed D, Ed S); school psychology (MA); teaching and learning (MA Ed, Ed D, Ed S), including education technology (Ed D), higher education (Ed D), K-12 education (Ed D).

See Close-Up on page 687.

Argosy University, San Diego, College of Education, San Diego, CA 92108. Offers community college executive leadership (Ed D); educational leadership (MA Ed, Ed D), including higher education administration (Ed D), K-12 education (Ed D); instructional leadership (MA Ed, Ed D), including higher education (Ed D), K-12 education (Ed D).

See Close-Up on page 691.

Argosy University, San Francisco Bay Area, College of Education, Alameda, CA 94501. Offers community college executive leadership (Ed D); educational leadership (MA Ed, Ed D), including education technology (Ed D), higher education administration (Ed D), K-12 education (Ed D); instructional leadership (MA Ed, Ed D), including education technology (Ed D), higher education (Ed D), K-12 education (Ed D), multiple subject teacher preparation (MA Ed), single subject teacher preparation (MA Ed).

See Close-Up on page 693.

Argosy University, Sarasota, College of Education, Sarasota, FL 34235. Offers community college executive leadership (Ed D); educational leadership (MA Ed, Ed D, Ed S), including higher education administration (Ed D), K-12 education (Ed D); school counseling (MA, Ed S); school psychology (MA); teaching and learning (MA Ed, Ed D, Ed S), including education technology (Ed D), higher education (Ed D), K-12 education (Ed D).

See Close-Up on page 695.

Argosy University, Schaumburg, College of Education, Schaumburg, IL 60173-5403. Offers community college executive leadership (Ed D); educational leadership (MA Ed, Ed D, Ed S), including district leadership (Ed D), higher education administration (Ed D), K-12 education (Ed D); instructional leadership (Ed D, Ed S), including higher education (Ed D), K-12 education (Ed D).

See Close-Up on page 697.

Argosy University, Seattle, College of Education, Seattle, WA 98121. Offers adult education and training (MA Ed); community college executive leadership (Ed D); educational leadership (MA Ed, Ed D), including higher education administration (Ed D), K-12 education (Ed D); higher and postsecondary education (MA Ed); instructional leadership (MA Ed, Ed D), including education technology (Ed D), higher education (Ed D), K-12 education (Ed D).

See Close-Up on page 699.

Argosy University, Tampa, College of Education, Tampa, FL 33607. Offers community college executive leadership (Ed D); educational leadership (MA Ed, Ed D, Ed S), including higher education administration (Ed D), K-12 education (Ed D); school counseling (MA); teaching and learning (MA Ed, Ed D, Ed S), including higher education (Ed D), K-12 education (Ed D).

See Close-Up on page 701.

Argosy University, Twin Cities, College of Education, Eagan, MN 55121. Offers advanced educational administration (Ed D, Ed S); educational leadership (MA Ed, Ed D, Ed S), including higher education administration (Ed D), K-12 education (Ed D); higher and postsecondary education (MA Ed); initial educational administration (Ed D, Ed S); instructional leadership (MA Ed, Ed D, Ed S), including education technology (Ed D), higher education (Ed D), K-12 education (Ed D).

See Close-Up on page 703.

Argosy University, Washington DC, College of Education, Arlington, VA 22209. Offers community college executive leadership (Ed D); educational leadership (MA Ed, Ed D, Ed S), including higher education administration (Ed D), K-12 education (Ed D); instructional leadership (MA Ed, Ed D, Ed S), including higher education (Ed D), K-12 education (Ed D).

See Close-Up on page 705.

Arizona State University, Graduate College, Mary Lou Fulton College of Education, Division of Educational Leadership and Policy Studies, Program in Higher and Post-Secondary Education, Tempe, AZ 85287. Offers M Ed. *Entrance requirements:* For master's, GRE General Test or MAT.

Auburn University, Graduate School, College of Education, Department of Curriculum and Teaching, Auburn University, AL 36849. Offers business education (M Ed, MS, PhD); early childhood education (M Ed, MS, PhD, Ed S); elementary education (M Ed, MS, PhD, Ed S); foreign languages (M Ed, MS); music education (M Ed, MS, PhD, Ed S); postsecondary education (PhD); reading education (PhD, Ed S); secondary education (M Ed, MS, PhD, Ed S), including English language arts, mathematics, science, social studies. *Accreditation:* NASM (one or more programs are accredited); NCATE. Part-time programs available. *Faculty:* 28 full-time (21 women), 8 part-time/adjunct (5 women). *Students:* 76 full-time (55 women), 186 part-time (139 women); includes 43 minority (29 African Americans, 1 American Indian/Alaska Native, 4 Asian Americans or Pacific Islanders, 9 Hispanic Americans), 4 international. Average age 33. 248 applicants, 65% accepted, 110 enrolled. In 2009, 102 master's, 12 doctorates, 6 other advanced degrees awarded. *Degree requirements:* For master's, thesis (for some programs); for doctorate, thesis/dissertation; for Ed S, field project. *Entrance requirements:* For master's, doctorate, and Ed S, GRE General Test. *Application deadline:* For fall admission, 7/7 for domestic students; for spring admission, 11/24 for domestic students. Applications are processed on a rolling basis. Application fee: $50 ($60 for international students). Electronic applications accepted. *Expenses:* Tuition, state resident: full-time $6240. Tuition, nonresident: full-time $18,720. International tuition: $18,938 full-time. Required fees: $492. Tuition and fees vary according to course load, program and reciprocity agreements. *Financial support:* Fellowships, teaching assistantships, career-related internships or fieldwork and Federal Work-Study available. Support available to part-time students. Financial award application deadline: 3/15; financial award applicants required to submit FAFSA. *Faculty research:* Emerging literacy, reading attitudes, music for at-risk youth, portfolio assessment. *Unit head:* Dr. Nancy H. Barry, Head, 334-844-4434. *Application contact:* Dr. George Flowers, Dean of the Graduate School, 334-844-2125.

Auburn University, Graduate School, College of Education, Department of Educational Foundations, Leadership, and Technology, Auburn University, AL 36849. Offers adult education (M Ed, MS, Ed D); curriculum and instruction (M Ed, MS, Ed D, Ed S); curriculum supervision (M Ed, MS, Ed D, Ed S); educational psychology (PhD); higher education administration (M Ed, MS, Ed D, Ed S); media instructional design (MS); media specialist (M Ed); school administration (M Ed, MS, Ed D, Ed S). *Accreditation:* NCATE. Part-time programs available. *Faculty:* 21 full-time (11 women), 6 part-time/adjunct (4 women). *Students:* 68 full-time (40 women), 175 part-time (103 women); includes 87 minority (84 African Americans, 1 Asian American or Pacific Islander, 2 Hispanic Americans), 8 international. Average age 37. 112 applicants, 65% accepted, 53 enrolled. In 2009, 31 master's, 12 doctorates, 1 other advanced degree awarded. *Degree requirements:* For master's, thesis (for some programs); for doctorate, thesis/dissertation; for Ed S, field project. *Entrance requirements:* For master's, doctorate, and Ed S, GRE General Test. *Application deadline:* For fall admission, 7/7 for domestic students; for spring admission, 11/24 for domestic students. Applications are processed on a rolling basis. Application fee: $50 ($60 for international students). Electronic applications accepted. *Expenses:* Tuition, state resident: full-time $6240. Tuition, nonresident: full-time $18,720. International tuition: $18,938 full-time. Required fees: $492. Tuition and fees vary according to course load, program and reciprocity agreements. *Financial support:* Teaching assistantships, Federal Work-Study available. Support available to part-time students. Financial award application deadline: 3/15; financial award applicants required to submit FAFSA. *Unit head:* Dr. Jose Llanes, Head, 334-844-4460. *Application contact:* Dr. George Flowers, Dean of the Graduate School, 334-844-4700.

Azusa Pacific University, School of Behavioral and Applied Sciences, Department of Higher Education and Organizational Leadership, Azusa, CA 91702-7000. Offers college student affairs (M Ed); higher education leadership (Ed D); leadership and organizational studies (MLOS); organizational leadership (MA).

Ball State University, Graduate School, Teachers College, Department of Educational Studies, Program in Adult Education, Muncie, IN 47306-1099. Offers adult and community education (MA); adult, community, and higher education (Ed D). *Accreditation:* NCATE. *Degree requirements:* For doctorate, thesis/dissertation. *Entrance requirements:* For doctorate, GRE General Test, minimum graduate GPA of 3.2. *Faculty research:* Community education, executive development for public services, applied gerontology.

Ball State University, Graduate School, Teachers College, Department of Educational Studies, Program in Student Affairs Administration in Higher Education, Muncie, IN 47306-1099. Offers MA. *Accreditation:* NCATE. *Entrance requirements:* For master's, GRE General Test, interview.

Barry University, School of Education, Program in Higher Education Administration, Miami Shores, FL 33161-6695. Offers MS. Part-time and evening/weekend programs available. *Degree requirements:* For master's, comprehensive exam. *Entrance requirements:* For master's, GRE General Test or MAT, minimum GPA of 3.0. Electronic applications accepted.

Barry University, School of Education, Program in Leadership and Education, Miami Shores, FL 33161-6695. Offers educational technology (PhD); exceptional student education (PhD); higher education administration (PhD); human resource development (PhD); leadership (PhD). Part-time and evening/weekend programs available. *Degree requirements:* For doctorate, thesis/dissertation. *Entrance requirements:* For doctorate, GRE General Test, minimum GPA of 3.25. Electronic applications accepted.

Bay Path College, Program in Higher Education Administration, Longmeadow, MA 01106-2292. Offers enrollment management (MS); general administration (MS); institutional advancement (MS). Postbaccalaureate distance learning degree programs offered (no on-campus study). Electronic applications accepted.

Benedictine University, Graduate Programs, Program in Higher Education and Organizational Change, Lisle, IL 60532-0900. Offers Ed D. *Students:* 41 full-time (29 women), 18 part-time (8 women); includes 19 minority (14 African Americans, 2 Asian Americans or Pacific Islanders, 3 Hispanic Americans). 64 applicants, 66% accepted, 36 enrolled. In 2009, 14 doctorates awarded. Application fee: $40. *Expenses:* Tuition: Part-time $750 per credit hour. Tuition and fees vary according to campus/location and program. *Unit head:* Dr. Donald Fouts, Director, 630-829-6343. *Application contact:* Kari Gibbons, Director, Admissions, 630-829-6200, Fax: 630-829-6584, E-mail: kgibbons@ben.edu.

Bernard M. Baruch College of the City University of New York, School of Public Affairs, Program in Higher Education Administration, New York, NY 10010-5585. Offers MS Ed. Part-time and evening/weekend programs available. *Degree requirements:* For master's, internship (for some students). *Entrance requirements:* For master's, GRE General Test. Additional exam requirements/recommendations for international students: Required—TOEFL (minimum score 625 paper-based; 263 computer-based; 106 iBT). Electronic applications accepted. *Expenses:* Contact institution.

Bethel University, Graduate School, Program in Communication, St. Paul, MN 55112-6999. Offers communication (MA); post-secondary teaching (Certificate). Part-time and evening/weekend programs available. *Faculty:* 3 full-time (1 woman), 3 part-time/adjunct (1 woman). *Students:* 47 full-time (30 women), 16 part-time (10 women); includes 3 minority (2 African Americans, 1 Asian American or Pacific Islander), 1 international. Average age 38. 28 applicants, 89% accepted, 18 enrolled. In 2009, 19 master's awarded. *Degree requirements:* For master's, comprehensive exam, thesis. *Entrance requirements:* For master's, MAT, baccalaureate degree, interview, minimum GPA of 3.0, course work in communication and statistics, references, sample of written work, interview. Additional exam requirements/recommendations for international students: Required—TOEFL (minimum score 550 paper-based; 213 computer-based; 80 iBT). *Application deadline:* For fall admission, 5/15 priority date for domestic students. Applications are processed on a rolling basis. Application fee: $25. Electronic applications accepted. *Expenses:* Tuition: Full-time $7920; part-time $440 per credit. One-time fee: $25. Tuition and fees vary according to course load, degree level and program. *Financial support:* Applicants required to submit FAFSA. *Unit head:* Dr. Lori J. Jass, Assistant Dean, 651-635-8000, Fax: 651-635-8039, E-mail: l-jass@bethel.edu. *Application contact:* Michael Price, Director of Admissions, 651-635-8000, Fax: 651-635-8004, E-mail: m-price@bethel.edu.

Boston College, Lynch Graduate School of Education, Department of Educational Administration and Higher Education, Higher Education Specialization, Chestnut Hill, MA 02467-3800. Offers MA, PhD, JD/MA, MBA/MA. *Accreditation:* Teacher Education Accreditation Council. Part-time and evening/weekend programs available. *Students:* 25 full-time (14 women), 109 part-time (75 women); includes 22 minority (5 African Americans, 13 Asian Americans or Pacific Islanders, 4 Hispanic Americans), 6 international. 250 applicants, 52% accepted, 55 enrolled. In 2009, 31 master's, 10 doctorates awarded. Terminal master's awarded for partial completion of doctoral program. *Degree requirements:* For master's, comprehensive exam; for doctorate, comprehensive exam, thesis/dissertation. *Entrance requirements:* For master's, GRE General Test or MAT; for doctorate, GRE General Test. Additional exam requirements/recommendations for international students: Required—TOEFL (minimum score 550 paper-based; 213 computer-based; 81 iBT). Application fee: $60. Electronic applications accepted. *Financial support:* Fellowships with full and partial tuition reimbursements, research assistantships with full and partial tuition reimbursements, teaching assistantships with full and partial tuition reimbursements, career-related internships or fieldwork, Federal Work-Study, scholarships/grants, traineeships, health care benefits, tuition waivers (full and partial), and unspecified assistantships available. Support available to part-time students. Financial award applicants required to submit FAFSA. *Faculty research:* Race, culture and gender in higher education; international education; college student development; Catholic higher education; organizational analysis. *Unit head:* Dr. Ana M. Martinez-Aleman, Chairperson, 617-552-1760, Fax: 617-552-0812, E-mail: ana.aleman.1@bc.edu. *Application contact:* Adam Poluzzi, Director, Graduate Admission and Financial Aid, 617-552-4214, Fax: 617-552-0398, E-mail: poluzzi@bc.edu.

Bowling Green State University, Graduate College, College of Education and Human Development, School of Leadership and Policy Studies, Program in Higher Education Administration, Bowling Green, OH 43403. Offers PhD. *Accreditation:* NCATE. Part-time programs available. *Degree requirements:* For doctorate, comprehensive exam, thesis/dissertation. *Entrance requirements:* For doctorate, GRE General Test. Additional exam requirements/recommendations for international students: Required—TOEFL. Electronic applications accepted. *Faculty research:* Adult learners, legal issues, intellectual development.

California Lutheran University, Graduate Studies, School of Education, Emphasis in Educational Leadership, Thousand Oaks, CA 91360-2787. Offers educational leadership (MA); educational leadership (k-12) (Ed D); higher education leadership (Ed D). Part-time and evening/weekend programs available. *Degree requirements:* For master's, thesis or comprehensive exam. *Entrance requirements:* For master's, GRE General Test, interview, minimum GPA of 3.0.

Higher Education

California State University, Long Beach, Graduate Studies, College of Education, Department of Advanced Studies in Education and Counseling, Master of Science in Counseling Program, Long Beach, CA 90840. Offers marriage and family therapy (MS); school counseling (MS); student development in higher education (MS). *Accreditation:* NCATE. *Students:* 139 full-time (103 women), 73 part-time (54 women); includes 137 minority (27 African Americans, 35 Asian Americans or Pacific Islanders, 75 Hispanic Americans), 5 international. Average age 30. *Degree requirements:* For master's, comprehensive exam or thesis. *Application deadline:* For fall admission, 3/1 for domestic students. Applications are processed on a rolling basis. Application fee: $55. Electronic applications accepted. *Expenses:* Required fees: $1802 per semester. Part-time tuition and fees vary according to course load. *Financial support:* Federal Work-Study, institutionally sponsored loans, and scholarships/grants available. Financial award application deadline: 3/2. *Unit head:* Dr. Jennifer Coots, Chair, 562-985-4517, Fax: 562-985-4534, E-mail: jcoots@csulb.edu. *Application contact:* Dr. Bita Ghafoori, Assistant Chair, 562-985-7864, Fax: 562-985-4534, E-mail: bghafoor@csulb.edu.

Capella University, School of Education, Minneapolis, MN 55402. Offers college teaching (Certificate); curriculum and instruction (MS, PhD); education (MS); enrollment management (MS); instructional design for online learning (MS, PhD); k-12 studies in education (MS, PhD); leadership for higher education (MS, PhD); leadership in education administration (Certificate); leadership in educational administration (MS, PhD); postsecondary and adult education (MS, PhD); professional studies in education (MS, PhD); reading and literacy (MS); training and performance improvement (MS, PhD). Part-time and evening/weekend programs available. Postbaccalaureate distance learning degree programs offered (minimal on-campus study). Terminal master's awarded for partial completion of doctoral program. *Degree requirements:* For master's, thesis optional, integrative project; for doctorate, comprehensive exam, thesis/dissertation. *Entrance requirements:* Additional exam requirements/recommendations for international students: Required—TOEFL (minimum score 550 paper-based; 213 computer-based), TWE (minimum score 4). Electronic applications accepted. *Faculty research:* Higher education administration, distance learning, adult education, training and curriculum design.

Central Michigan University, College of Graduate Studies, College of Education and Human Services, Department of Educational Leadership, Mount Pleasant, MI 48859. Offers educational leadership (MA, Ed D), including charter school leadership (Ed D), educational technology (Ed D), general educational leadership, higher education administration (Ed D), higher education leadership (Ed D), K-12 curriculum (Ed D), K-12 leadership (Ed D), student affairs administration (Ed D); general educational administration (Ed S); school principalship (MA). Part-time and evening/weekend programs available. *Degree requirements:* For master's and Ed S, thesis or alternative; for doctorate, thesis/dissertation. *Entrance requirements:* For doctorate, GRE or MAT, master's degree, minimum GPA of 3.5, 3 years of professional education experience. Electronic applications accepted. *Faculty research:* Elementary administration, secondary administration, student achievement, in-service training, internships in administration.

Chicago State University, School of Graduate and Professional Studies, College of Education, Department of Educational Leadership, Curriculum and Foundations, Program in Educational Leadership, Chicago, IL 60628. Offers educational leadership (Ed D); general administration (MA); higher education administration (MA). *Accreditation:* NCATE. *Degree requirements:* For master's, comprehensive exam, thesis optional. *Entrance requirements:* For master's, minimum GPA of 2.75.

Claremont Graduate University, Graduate Programs, School of Educational Studies, Claremont, CA 91711-6160. Offers Africana education (Certificate); education and policy (MA, PhD); higher education/student affairs (MA, PhD); human development (MA, PhD); public school administration (MA, PhD); quantitative evaluation (MA, PhD); special education (MA, PhD); teacher education (MA); teaching and learning (MA, PhD); urban leadership (PhD); MBA/PhD. Part-time programs available. *Faculty:* 18 full-time (12 women), 1 part-time/adjunct (0 women). *Students:* 279 full-time (190 women), 174 part-time (122 women); includes 196 minority (50 African Americans, 1 American Indian/Alaska Native, 37 Asian Americans or Pacific Islanders, 108 Hispanic Americans), 10 international. Average age 37. In 2009, 84 master's, 23 doctorates awarded. Terminal master's awarded for partial completion of doctoral program. *Entrance requirements:* For master's and doctorate, GRE General Test. Additional exam requirements/recommendations for international students: Required—TOEFL (minimum score 550 paper-based; 213 computer-based; 80 iBT). *Application deadline:* For fall admission, 2/1 priority date for domestic students. Applications are processed on a rolling basis. Application fee: $60. Electronic applications accepted. *Expenses:* Tuition: Full-time $35,046; part-time $1524 per credit. Required fees: $161 per semester. *Financial support:* Fellowships, research assistantships, Federal Work-Study, institutionally sponsored loans, and scholarships/grants available. Support available to part-time students. Financial award application deadline: 2/15; financial award applicants required to submit FAFSA. *Faculty research:* Education administration, K-12 and higher education, multicultural education, education policy, diversity in higher education, faculty issues. *Unit head:* Margaret Grogan, Dean, 909-621-8075, Fax: 909-621-8734, E-mail: margaret.grogan@cgu.edu.

College of Saint Elizabeth, Department of Psychology, Morristown, NJ 07960-6989. Offers counseling psychology (MA); forensic psychology (MA); student affairs in higher education (Certificate). Part-time and evening/weekend programs available. *Faculty:* 5 full-time (2 women), 10 part-time/adjunct (9 women). *Students:* 23 full-time (19 women), 73 part-time (67 women); includes 25 minority (12 African Americans, 2 Asian Americans or Pacific Islanders, 11 Hispanic Americans), 2 international. Average age 32. 104 applicants, 58% accepted, 47 enrolled. In 2009, 10 master's awarded. *Degree requirements:* For master's, thesis or alternative, portfolio. *Entrance requirements:* For master's, minimum GPA of 3.0, BA in psychology (preferred), 12 credits of course work in psychology. *Application deadline:* For fall admission, 4/14 priority date for domestic students; for spring admission, 11/15 for domestic students. Applications are processed on a rolling basis. Application fee: $35. Electronic applications accepted. *Expenses:* Tuition: Part-time $797 per credit hour. Required fees: $65 per credit hour. *Financial support:* Career-related internships or fieldwork, tuition waivers (partial), and unspecified assistantships available. Support available to part-time students. Financial award application deadline: 3/15; financial award applicants required to submit FAFSA. *Faculty research:* Family systems, dissociative identity disorder, multicultural counseling, outcomes assessment. *Unit head:* Dr. Valerie Scott, Director of the Graduate Program in Counseling Psychology, 973-290-4102, Fax: 973-290-4676, E-mail: vscott@cse.edu. *Application contact:* Donna Tatarka, Dean of Admission, 973-290-4705, Fax: 973-290-4710, E-mail: dtatarka@cse.edu.

Columbia International University, Columbia Graduate School, Columbia, SC 29230-3122. Offers Bible teaching (MABT); Christian higher education leadership (Ed D); Christian school educational leadership (Ed D); counseling (MACN); curriculum and instruction (M Ed), including Christian school guidance, English as a second language, learning disabilities, school technology; early childhood and elementary education (MAT); educational administration (M Ed); teaching English as a foreign language (Certificate); teaching English as a foreign language and intercultural studies (MATF). Part-time and evening/weekend programs available. *Degree requirements:* For master's, internships, professional project. *Entrance requirements:* For master's, Minnesota Multiphasic Personality Inventory, MAT, minimum GPA of 2.7. Additional exam requirements/recommendations for international students: Required—TOEFL. Electronic applications accepted.

Dallas Baptist University, College of Adult Education, Professional Development Program, Dallas, TX 75211-9299. Offers accounting (MA); church leadership (MA); counseling (MA); criminal justice (MA); English as a second language (MA); finance (MA); higher education (MA); leadership studies (MA); management (MA); management information systems (MA); marketing (MA); missions (MA). Part-time and evening/weekend programs available. *Entrance requirements:* For master's, minimum GPA of 3.0. Additional exam requirements/recommendations for international students: Required—TOEFL, IELTS. *Expenses:* Tuition: Full-time $10,674; part-time $593 per credit hour.

Dallas Baptist University, Gary Cook School of Leadership, Program in Education in Higher Education, Dallas, TX 75211-9299. Offers M Ed. Part-time and evening/weekend programs available. *Entrance requirements:* For master's, GRE General Test, minimum GPA of 3.0. Additional exam requirements/recommendations for international students: Required—TOEFL, IELTS. Electronic applications accepted. *Expenses:* Tuition: Full-time $10,674; part-time $593 per credit hour. *Faculty research:* Enrollment management, portfolio assessment, servant leadership.

Delta State University, Graduate Programs, College of Education, Thad Cochran Center for Rural School Leadership and Research, Program in Professional Studies, Cleveland, MS 38733-0001. Offers counselor education (Ed D); educational leadership (Ed D); elementary education (Ed D); higher education (Ed D). Part-time and evening/weekend programs available. *Degree requirements:* For doctorate, thesis/dissertation. *Entrance requirements:* For doctorate, GRE General Test. *Expenses:* Tuition, state resident: full-time $4450; part-time $247 per credit hour. Tuition, nonresident: full-time $11,520; part-time $640 per credit hour.

Drexel University, School of Education, Program in Higher Education, Philadelphia, PA 19104-2875. Offers MS. Postbaccalaureate distance learning degree programs offered (no on-campus study). *Degree requirements:* For master's, co-op experience. *Entrance requirements:* For master's, bachelor's degree from an accredited institution, minimum GPA of 3.0 or GRE. Additional exam requirements/recommendations for international students: Required—TOEFL (minimum score 550 paper-based). *Faculty research:* Governance and administration, financial management, enrollment management, institutional research, strategic planning, advancement, academic development, technology, and instruction.

Eastern Kentucky University, The Graduate School, College of Education, Department of Curriculum and Instruction, Program in Secondary and Higher Education, Richmond, KY 40475-3102. Offers secondary education (MA Ed), including agricultural education, art education, biological sciences education, business education, English education, geography education, history education, home economics education, industrial education, mathematical sciences education, physical education, school health education. *Accreditation:* NCATE. Part-time programs available. *Entrance requirements:* For master's, GRE General Test, minimum GPA of 2.5.

Fitchburg State University, Division of Graduate and Continuing Education, Program in Educational Leadership and Management, Fitchburg, MA 01420-2697. Offers educational technology (Certificate); higher education administration (CAGS); non-licensure (M Ed, CAGS); school principal (M Ed, CAGS); supervisor director (M Ed, CAGS); technology leader (M Ed, CAGS). *Accreditation:* NCATE. Part-time and evening/weekend programs available. *Students:* 29 full-time (9 women), 66 part-time (30 women); includes 2 minority (1 Asian American or Pacific Islander, 1 Hispanic American). Average age 37. 23 applicants, 100% accepted, 22 enrolled. In 2009, 17 master's, 50 CAGSs awarded. *Degree requirements:* For master's, comprehensive exam, thesis or alternative. *Entrance requirements:* For master's, GRE General Test or MAT, 3 years of teaching experience, teaching certificate, letters of recommendation, resume; for other advanced degree, master's degree, letters of recommendation, resume. Additional exam requirements/recommendations for international students: Required—TOEFL (minimum score 550 paper-based; 213 computer-based; 79 iBT). *Application deadline:* Applications are processed on a rolling basis. Application fee: $25 ($50 for international students). *Expenses:* Tuition, area resident: Part-time $150 per credit. Tuition, state resident: part-time $150 per credit. Tuition, nonresident: part-time $150 per credit. Required fees: $120 per credit. *Financial support:* In 2009–10, research assistantships with partial tuition reimbursements (averaging $5,500 per year); Federal Work-Study, scholarships/grants, and unspecified assistantships also available. Support available to part-time students. Financial award application deadline: 3/1; financial award applicants required to submit FAFSA. *Unit head:* Dr. Randy Howe, Chair, 978-665-3544, Fax: 978-665-3658, E-mail: gce@fsc.edu. *Application contact:* Director of Admissions, 978-665-3144, Fax: 978-665-4540, E-mail: admissions@fsc.edu.

Florida Atlantic University, College of Education, Department of Educational Leadership, Boca Raton, FL 33431-0991. Offers adult and community education (M Ed, PhD, Ed S); educational leadership (M Ed, PhD, Ed S); higher education (M Ed, PhD); K-12 school leadership (M Ed, PhD, Ed S). *Accreditation:* NCATE. Part-time and evening/weekend programs available. Postbaccalaureate distance learning degree programs offered (minimal on-campus study). *Faculty:* 16 full-time (8 women), 19 part-time/adjunct (10 women). *Students:* 103 full-time (63 women), 261 part-time (186 women); includes 119 minority (71 African Americans, 9 Asian Americans or Pacific Islanders, 39 Hispanic Americans), 1 international. Average age 36. 254 applicants, 57% accepted, 96 enrolled. In 2009, 123 master's, 22 doctorates awarded. *Degree requirements:* For doctorate, comprehensive exam, thesis/dissertation, departmental qualifying exam; for Ed S, departmental qualifying exam. *Entrance requirements:* For master's, GRE General Test, minimum GPA of 3.0 during previous 2 years; for doctorate, GRE General Test, minimum GPA of 3.5; for Ed S, GRE General Test. *Application deadline:* For fall admission, 7/1 for domestic students, 2/15 for international students; for spring admission, 9/15 for domestic students, 7/15 for international students. Applications are processed on a rolling basis. Application fee: $30. Electronic applications accepted. *Expenses:* Tuition, state resident: full-time $7055; part-time $293.94 per credit hour. Tuition, nonresident: full-time $22,096; part-time $920.66 per credit hour. *Financial support:* Fellowships, research assistantships, teaching assistantships, career-related internships or fieldwork and tuition waivers (partial) available. *Faculty research:* Self-directed learning, school reform issues, legal issues, mentoring, school leadership. *Unit head:* Dr. Robert Shockley, Chair, 561-297-3550, Fax: 561-297-3618, E-mail: shockley@fau.edu. *Application contact:* Catherine Politi, Senior Secretary, 561-297-3550, Fax: 561-297-3618, E-mail: edleadership@fau.edu.

Florida International University, College of Education, Department of Educational Leadership and Policy Studies, Program in Higher Education, Miami, FL 33199. Offers Ed D. Part-time and evening/weekend programs available. *Degree requirements:* For doctorate, thesis/dissertation. *Entrance requirements:* For doctorate, GRE General Test. Additional exam requirements/recommendations for international students: Required—TOEFL (minimum score 550 paper-based; 213 computer-based; 80 iBT), IELTS (minimum score 6.3). Electronic applications accepted. *Expenses:* Tuition, state resident: full-time $8008; part-time $4004 per year. Tuition, nonresident: full-time $20,104; part-time $10,052 per year. Required fees: $298; $149 per term. *Faculty research:* Access and equity in college admission, social justice, higher education law, faculty and tenure issues for individuals of color.

Florida State University, The Graduate School, College of Education, Department of Educational Leadership and Policy Studies, Program in Higher Education, Tallahassee, FL 32306. Offers MS, Ed D, PhD, Ed S. *Faculty:* 6 full-time (2 women), 2 part-time/adjunct (0 women). *Students:* 72 full-time (45 women), 26 part-time (13 women); includes 31 minority (17 African Americans, 1 American Indian/Alaska Native, 4 Asian Americans or Pacific Islanders, 9 Hispanic Americans), 3 international. 103 applicants, 65% accepted, 35 enrolled. In 2009, 4 master's, 4 doctorates awarded. Terminal master's awarded for partial completion of doctoral program. *Degree requirements:* For master's and Ed S, comprehensive exam, thesis optional; for doctorate, comprehensive exam, thesis/dissertation. *Entrance requirements:* For master's, GRE General Test, minimum GPA of 3.0; for doctorate and Ed S, GRE General Test, minimum graduate GPA of 3.0. Additional exam requirements/recommendations for international students: Required—TOEFL (minimum score 550 paper-based; 213 computer-based; 80 iBT). *Application deadline:* For fall admission, 7/1 for domestic and international students; for spring admission, 11/1 for domestic students, 11/1 priority date for international students. Application fee: $30. Electronic applications accepted. *Expenses:* Tuition, state resident: full-time $7413. Tuition, nonresident: full-time $22,567. *Financial support:* In 2009–10, 4 fellowships with full and partial tuition reimbursements were awarded; research assistantships with full and partial tuition reimbursements, teaching assistantships with full and partial tuition reimbursements, career-related internships or fieldwork, scholarships/grants, and unspecified assistantships also available. Financial award applicants required to submit FAFSA. *Faculty research:* Higher

Higher Education

Florida State University (continued)

education laws, public policy, organizational theory. *Unit head:* Dr. Shouping Hu, Associate Professor and Program Coordinator, 850-644-6777, Fax: 850-644-1258, E-mail: shu@coe.fsu.edu. *Application contact:* Jimmy Pastrano, Program Assistant, 850-644-6777, Fax: 850-644-1258, E-mail: pastrano@coe.fsu.edu.

Geneva College, Program in Higher Education, Beaver Falls, PA 15010-3599. Offers campus ministry (MA); college teaching (MA); educational leadership (MA); student affairs administration (MA). Part-time and evening/weekend programs available. Postbaccalaureate distance learning degree programs offered (minimal on-campus study). *Faculty:* 2 full-time (0 women), 4 part-time/adjunct (0 women). *Students:* 28 full-time (13 women), 37 part-time (21 women); includes 2 minority (1 African American, 1 Asian American or Pacific Islander). Average age 25. 41 applicants, 98% accepted, 19 enrolled. In 2009, 29 master's awarded. *Degree requirements:* For master's, research seminar. *Entrance requirements:* For master's, minimum GPA of 3.0, writing sample, 3 letters of recommendation. Additional exam requirements/recommendations for international students: Required—TOEFL. *Application deadline:* For fall admission, 9/1 priority date for domestic students; for winter admission, 1/2 priority date for domestic students; for spring admission, 3/11 priority date for domestic students. Applications are processed on a rolling basis. Electronic applications accepted. *Expenses:* Tuition: Full-time $11,250; part-time $625 per credit. Tuition and fees vary according to program. *Financial support:* In 2009–10, 1 research assistantship with partial tuition reimbursement (averaging $4,500 per year), 1 teaching assistantship with partial tuition reimbursement (averaging $4,500 per year) were awarded; career-related internships or fieldwork and unspecified assistantships also available. Support available to part-time students. Financial award application deadline: 9/1; financial award applicants required to submit FAFSA. *Faculty research:* Student development, learning theories, church-related higher education, assessment, organizational culture. *Unit head:* Dr. Donald Opitz, Director, 724-847-6883, Fax: 724-847-6107, E-mail: hed@geneva.edu. *Application contact:* Jerryn S. Carson, Coordinator, 724-847-6510, Fax: 724-847-6696, E-mail: hed@geneva.edu.

George Fox University, School of Education, Educational Foundations and Leadership Program, Newberg, OR 97132-2697. Offers continuing administrator license (Certificate); curriculum and instruction (M Ed); educational leadership (M Ed, Ed D); higher education (M Ed); initial administrator license (Certificate); library media (M Ed, Certificate); literacy (M Ed); reading (M Ed); secondary education (M Ed). *Accreditation:* NCATE. Part-time and evening/weekend programs available. Postbaccalaureate distance learning degree programs offered (minimal on-campus study). *Faculty:* 10 full-time (3 women), 7 part-time/adjunct (3 women). *Students:* 1 (woman) full-time, 151 part-time (101 women); includes 15 minority (1 African American, 4 American Indian/Alaska Native, 4 Asian Americans or Pacific Islanders, 6 Hispanic Americans), 1 international. Average age 40. 44 applicants, 75% accepted, 26 enrolled. In 2009, 44 master's, 27 doctorates, 82 Certificates awarded. *Degree requirements:* For master's, thesis (for some programs); for doctorate, comprehensive exam, thesis/dissertation, project. *Entrance requirements:* For master's, minimum undergraduate GPA of 3.0 during previous 2 years of course work, resume, 3 professional recommendations on university forms, copy of teaching license (if applicable); for doctorate, GRE or MAT, master's degree with minimum GPA of 3.25, 3 years of relevant professional experience, interview, personal essay, scholarly work, 3 professional recommendations on university forms along with 3 written letters of recommendation, official transcripts. Additional exam requirements/recommendations for international students: Required—TOEFL (minimum score 577 paper-based; 233 computer-based; 90 iBT). *Application deadline:* For fall admission, 7/15 for domestic and international students; for winter admission, 11/1 for domestic and international students; for spring admission, 4/1 for domestic and international students. Applications are processed on a rolling basis. Application fee: $40. Electronic applications accepted. *Expenses:* Contact institution. *Financial support:* Career-related internships or fieldwork available. Financial award applicants required to submit FAFSA. *Unit head:* Dr. Scott Headley, Chair, 503-554-2836, E-mail: sheadley@georgefox.edu. *Application contact:* Kristie DeHaven, Admissions Counselor, 800-631-0921, Fax: 503-554-3110, E-mail: edfl@georgefox.edu.

George Mason University, College of Humanities and Social Sciences, Higher Education Program, Fairfax, VA 22030. Offers college teaching (Certificate); community college education (DA Ed); higher education administration (Certificate). *Faculty:* 5 full-time (4 women). *Students:* 4 full-time (3 women), 54 part-time (33 women); includes 15 minority (11 African Americans, 3 Asian Americans or Pacific Islanders, 1 Hispanic American). Average age 48. 19 applicants, 58% accepted, 7 enrolled. In 2009, 8 doctorates, 3 Certificates awarded. *Degree requirements:* For doctorate, thesis/dissertation, internship. *Entrance requirements:* For doctorate, GRE (taken within the last 5 years), writing sample, 3 letters of recommendation, resume. Additional exam requirements/recommendations for international students: Required—TOEFL. *Application deadline:* For fall admission, 3/1 for domestic students; for spring admission, 10/15 for domestic students. Applications are processed on a rolling basis. Application fee: $75. Electronic applications accepted. *Expenses:* Tuition, state resident: full-time $7568; part-time $315.33 per credit hour. Tuition, nonresident: full-time $21,704; part-time $904.33 per credit hour. Required fees: $2184; $91 per credit hour. *Financial support:* In 2009–10, 2 students received support, including 1 research assistantship with full and partial tuition reimbursement available (averaging $6,000 per year), 1 teaching assistantship with full and partial tuition reimbursement available (averaging $985 per year); Federal Work-Study, scholarships/grants, unspecified assistantships, and health care benefits (full-time research or teaching assistantship recipients) also available. Support available to part-time students. Financial award application deadline: 3/1; financial award applicants required to submit FAFSA. *Faculty research:* Leadership, the scholarship of teaching, learning, and assessment; ethical leadership; assessment; information technology; diversity. *Unit head:* John O'Connor, Director, 703-993-2310, E-mail: joconnor@gmu.edu. *Application contact:* Nina Joshi, Administrative Coordinator, 703-993-2310, E-mail: njoshi@gmu.edu.

The George Washington University, Graduate School of Education and Human Development, Department of Educational Leadership, Program in Higher Education Administration, Washington, DC 20052. Offers MA Ed, Ed D, Ed S. *Accreditation:* NCATE. *Students:* 26 full-time (20 women), 141 part-time (90 women); includes 44 minority (30 African Americans, 2 American Indian/Alaska Native, 7 Asian Americans or Pacific Islanders, 5 Hispanic Americans), 3 international. Average age 35. 136 applicants, 90% accepted, 45 enrolled. In 2009, 25 master's, 19 doctorates, 4 other advanced degrees awarded. *Degree requirements:* For master's and Ed S, comprehensive exam; for doctorate, comprehensive exam, thesis/dissertation. *Entrance requirements:* For master's, GRE General Test or MAT, minimum GPA of 2.75; for doctorate, GRE General Test or MAT, interview, minimum GPA of 3.3; for Ed S, GRE General Test or MAT, minimum GPA of 3.3. *Application deadline:* For fall admission, 1/15 priority date for domestic students; for spring admission, 10/1 for domestic students. Applications are processed on a rolling basis. Application fee: $60. *Financial support:* In 2009–10, 17 students received support; fellowships, research assistantships, career-related internships or fieldwork, Federal Work-Study, and tuition waivers (partial) available. Financial award application deadline: 1/15; financial award applicants required to submit FAFSA. *Faculty research:* Technology in higher education administration. *Application contact:* Sarah Lang, Director of Graduate Admissions, 202-994-1447, Fax: 202-994-7207, E-mail: slang@gwu.edu.

Georgia Southern University, Jack N. Averitt College of Graduate Studies, College of Education, Department of Leadership, Technology, and Human Development, Program in Higher Education, Statesboro, GA 30460. Offers M Ed. *Accreditation:* NCATE. Part-time and evening/weekend programs available. *Students:* 15 full-time (10 women), 22 part-time (17 women); includes 14 minority (13 African Americans, 1 Hispanic American). Average age 32. 23 applicants, 78% accepted, 16 enrolled. In 2009, 15 master's awarded. *Degree requirements:* For master's, portfolio, practicum, transition point assessments. *Entrance requirements:* For master's, GRE General Test or MAT, minimum GPA of 2.5. Additional exam requirements/recommendations for international students: Required—TOEFL (minimum score 550 paper-based; 213 computer-based; 80 iBT). *Application deadline:* For fall admission, 3/1 priority date for domestic and international students; for spring admission, 10/1 priority date for domestic students, 10/1 for international students. Applications are processed on a rolling basis. Application fee: $50. Electronic applications accepted. *Expenses:* Tuition, state resident: full-time $5040; part-time $210 per credit hour. Tuition, nonresident: full-time $20,136; part-time $839 per credit hour. Required fees: $1644. *Financial support:* In 2009–10, 26 students received support, including research assistantships with partial tuition reimbursements available (averaging $7,200 per year), teaching assistantships with partial tuition reimbursements available (averaging $7,200 per year); career-related internships or fieldwork, Federal Work-Study, scholarships/grants, tuition waivers (partial), and unspecified assistantships also available. Support available to part-time students. Financial award application deadline: 4/15; financial award applicants required to submit FAFSA. *Unit head:* Dr. Brenda Marina, Coordinator, 912-478-5600, Fax: 912-478-7140, E-mail: dmarina@georgiasouthern.edu. *Application contact:* Dr. Charles Ziglar, Coordinator for Graduate Student Recruitment, 912-478-5635, Fax: 912-478-0740, E-mail: gradadmissions@georgiasouthern.edu.

Grambling State University, School of Graduate Studies and Research, College of Education, Department of Educational Leadership, Grambling, LA 71245. Offers curriculum and instruction (Ed D); developmental education (MS, Ed D), including curriculum and instruction: reading (Ed D), English (MS), guidance and counseling (MS), higher education administration (Ed D), instructional systems and technology (Ed D), mathematics (MS), reading (MS), science (MS), student development and personnel services (Ed D); educational leadership (MS, Ed D). Part-time and evening/weekend programs available. *Faculty:* 19 full-time (12 women). *Students:* 23 full-time (18 women), 84 part-time (62 women); includes 81 minority (80 African Americans, 1 Asian American or Pacific Islander), 5 international. Average age 39. 72 applicants, 75% accepted, 39 enrolled. In 2009, 5 master's, 9 doctorates awarded. *Degree requirements:* For master's, comprehensive exam, thesis (for some programs); for doctorate, comprehensive exam, thesis/dissertation. *Entrance requirements:* For master's, GRE, minimum GPA of 2.5 on last degree; for doctorate, GRE (minimum 1000, 500 on Verbal), master's degree, minimum GPA of 3.0 on last degree. Additional exam requirements/recommendations for international students: Required—TOEFL (minimum score 500 paper-based; 173 computer-based; 61 iBT). *Application deadline:* For fall admission, 7/1 for domestic and international students; for spring admission, 12/1 for domestic and international students. Applications are processed on a rolling basis. Application fee: $20 ($30 for international students). Electronic applications accepted. *Expenses:* Tuition, state resident: full-time $2610. Tuition, nonresident: full-time $2610. *Financial support:* In 2009–10, 5 research assistantships (averaging $10,948 per year) were awarded; health care benefits, tuition waivers (full), and unspecified assistantships also available. Financial award application deadline: 5/31; financial award applicants required to submit FAFSA. *Unit head:* Dr. Olatunde Ogunyemi, Director, 318-274-6105, Fax: 318-274-2799, E-mail: ogunyemio@gram.edu. *Application contact:* Laketha Richards, Administrative Assistant III, 318-274-6105, Fax: 318-274-6249, E-mail: richardsl@gram.edu.

Grand Valley State University, College of Education, Program in College Student Affairs Leadership, Allendale, MI 49401-9403. Offers M Ed. Part-time programs available. *Students:* 49 full-time (33 women), 12 part-time (11 women); includes 13 minority (7 African Americans, 2 Asian Americans or Pacific Islanders, 4 Hispanic Americans), 1 international. Average age 27. In 2009, 18 master's awarded. *Entrance requirements:* For master's, GRE General Test or minimum GPA of 3.0. *Expenses:* Tuition, state resident: part-time $471 per credit hour. Tuition, nonresident: part-time $646 per credit hour. Tuition and fees vary according to course level. *Financial support:* In 2009–10, 11 fellowships (averaging $2,462 per year), 43 research assistantships with full and partial tuition reimbursements (averaging $8,000 per year) were awarded; unspecified assistantships also available. *Faculty research:* Adult learners, diversity and multiculturalism. *Unit head:* Dr. Jay Cooper, Associate Professor of Education, 616-331-0336, E-mail: cooperj@gvsu.edu. *Application contact:* Ginger Randall, Associate Dean of Students, 616-331-3585, E-mail: randallg@gvsu.edu.

Grand Valley State University, College of Education, Program in Higher Education, Allendale, MI 49401-9403. Offers M Ed. *Expenses:* Tuition, state resident: part-time $471 per credit hour. Tuition, nonresident: part-time $646 per credit hour. Tuition and fees vary according to course level.

Grand Valley State University, College of Education, Programs in General Education, Allendale, MI 49401-9403. Offers adult and higher education (M Ed); early childhood education (M Ed); educational differentiation (M Ed); educational leadership (M Ed); educational technology integration (M Ed); elementary education (M Ed); middle level education (M Ed); school library media services (M Ed); secondary level education (M Ed); teaching English to speakers of other languages (M Ed). Part-time and evening/weekend programs available. Postbaccalaureate distance learning degree programs offered (minimal on-campus study). *Faculty:* 82 full-time (42 women), 43 part-time/adjunct (25 women). *Students:* 100 full-time (53 women), 723 part-time (478 women); includes 59 minority (25 African Americans, 4 American Indian/Alaska Native, 13 Asian Americans or Pacific Islanders, 17 Hispanic Americans), 10 international. Average age 33. 237 applicants, 96% accepted, 117 enrolled. In 2009, 291 master's awarded. *Degree requirements:* For master's, thesis. *Entrance requirements:* For master's, GRE General Test or minimum GPA of 3.0. Additional exam requirements/recommendations for international students: Required—TOEFL. *Application deadline:* Applications are processed on a rolling basis. Application fee: $30. Electronic applications accepted. *Expenses:* Tuition, state resident: part-time $471 per credit hour. Tuition, nonresident: part-time $646 per credit hour. Tuition and fees vary according to course level. *Financial support:* In 2009–10, 73 students received support, including 55 fellowships (averaging $2,273 per year), 19 research assistantships with full and partial tuition reimbursements available (averaging $8,000 per year); career-related internships or fieldwork, Federal Work-Study, scholarships/grants, and unspecified assistantships also available. *Faculty research:* Effectiveness of technology in education, parental involvement, effective teaching, effective schools research. *Unit head:* Dr. Linda McCrea, Director, 616-331-2080, E-mail: mccreal@gvsu.edu. *Application contact:* Thomas Owens, Student Information and Services Center, 616-331-6282, Fax: 616-331-2000, E-mail: owenst@gvsu.edu.

Harvard University, Graduate School of Education, Doctoral Program in Education, Cambridge, MA 02138. Offers culture, communities and education (Ed D); education policy, leadership and instructional practice (Ed D); higher education (Ed D); human development and education (Ed D); quantitative policy analysis in education (Ed D); urban superintendency (Ed D). Part-time programs available. *Faculty:* 70 full-time (33 women), 36 part-time/adjunct (20 women). *Students:* 295 full-time (198 women), 23 part-time (11 women); includes 103 minority (40 African Americans, 4 American Indian/Alaska Native, 34 Asian Americans or Pacific Islanders, 25 Hispanic Americans), 33 international. Average age 32. 551 applicants, 9% accepted, 39 enrolled. In 2009, 41 doctorates awarded. Terminal master's awarded for partial completion of doctoral program. *Degree requirements:* For doctorate, thesis/dissertation. *Entrance requirements:* For doctorate, GRE General Test, 3 letters of recommendation. Additional exam requirements/recommendations for international students: Required—TOEFL (minimum score 600 paper-based; 250 computer-based; 100 iBT), TWE (minimum score 5). *Application deadline:* For fall admission, 12/14 for domestic and international students. Application fee: $85. Electronic applications accepted. *Expenses:* Contact institution. *Financial support:* In 2009–10, 265 students received support, including 129 fellowships with full and partial tuition reimbursements available (averaging $11,142 per year), 41 research assistantships (averaging $11,990 per year), 173 teaching assistantships (averaging $9,174 per year); career-related internships or fieldwork, Federal Work-Study, institutionally sponsored loans, scholarships/grants, health care benefits, tuition waivers (full and partial), and unspecified assistantships also available. Support available to part-time students. Financial award application deadline: 2/1; financial award applicants required to submit FAFSA. *Faculty research:* Learning and development, educational leadership and organizations, education policy analysis. Total annual research expenditures: $18.1 million. *Unit head:* Dr. Shu-Ling Chen, Assistant Dean, 617-496-4406.

Application contact: Information Contact, 617-495-3414, Fax: 617-496-3577, E-mail: gseadmissions@harvard.edu.

Illinois State University, Graduate School, College of Education, Department of Curriculum and Instruction, Normal, IL 61790-2200. Offers curriculum and instruction (MS, MS Ed, Ed D); educational policies (Ed D); postsecondary education (Ed D); reading (MS Ed); supervision (Ed D). *Accreditation:* NCATE. *Degree requirements:* For master's, variable foreign language requirement, thesis or alternative; for doctorate, variable foreign language requirement, thesis/dissertation, 2 terms of residency, internship. *Entrance requirements:* For master's, GRE General Test, minimum GPA of 3.0 in last 60 hours of course work; for doctorate, GRE General Test. *Faculty research:* In-service and pre-service teacher education for teachers of English language learners; teachers for all children: developing a model for alternative, bilingual elementary certification for paraprofessionals in Illinois; Illinois Geographic Alliance, Connections Project.

Indiana State University, School of Graduate Studies, College of Education, Department of Educational Leadership, Administration, and Foundations, Terre Haute, IN 47809. Offers educational administration (PhD); leadership in higher education (PhD); school administration (Ed S); school administration and supervision (M Ed); student affairs in higher education (MS). *Accreditation:* NCATE. Part-time and evening/weekend programs available. Terminal master's awarded for partial completion of doctoral program. *Degree requirements:* For master's, thesis; for doctorate, thesis/dissertation. *Entrance requirements:* For master's, GRE General Test, minimum undergraduate GPA of 2.5; for doctorate, GRE General Test, minimum undergraduate GPA of 3.5; for Ed S, GRE General Test, minimum graduate GPA of 3.25. Electronic applications accepted.

Indiana University Bloomington, School of Education, Department of Educational Leadership and Policy Studies, Bloomington, IN 47405-7000. Offers education policy studies (PhD); educational leadership (MS, Ed D, PhD, Ed S); higher education (MS, Ed D, PhD); history and philosophy of education (MS); history of education (PhD); international and comparative education (MS, PhD); philosophy of education (PhD); student affairs administration (MS). *Accreditation:* NCATE. Part-time and evening/weekend programs available. *Faculty:* 31 full-time (16 women), 8 part-time/adjunct (4 women). *Students:* 195 full-time (120 women), 102 part-time (53 women); includes 78 minority (49 African Americans, 1 American Indian/Alaska Native, 6 Asian Americans or Pacific Islanders, 22 Hispanic Americans), 29 international. Average age 33. 331 applicants, 77% accepted, 75 enrolled. In 2009, 61 master's, 21 doctorates, 7 other advanced degrees awarded. *Degree requirements:* For master's, thesis optional; for doctorate, comprehensive exam, thesis/dissertation; for Ed S, comprehensive exam or project. *Entrance requirements:* For master's, doctorate, and Ed S, GRE General Test. Additional exam requirements/recommendations for international students: Required—TOEFL (minimum score 213 computer-based; 79 iBT). *Application deadline:* For fall admission, 1/15 priority date for domestic students, 12/1 priority date for international students; for spring admission, 9/1 priority date for domestic and international students. Applications are processed on a rolling basis. Application fee: $55 ($65 for international students). Electronic applications accepted. *Financial support:* In 2009–10, 73 students received support, including 34 fellowships with full and partial tuition reimbursements available (averaging $7,677 per year), 16 research assistantships with full and partial tuition reimbursements available (averaging $17,757 per year), 23 teaching assistantships with full and partial tuition reimbursements available (averaging $13,496 per year); career-related internships or fieldwork, Federal Work-Study, institutionally sponsored loans, and tuition waivers (full and partial) also available. Support available to part-time students. *Faculty research:* Student engagement at higher education institutions in the nation, Reading First professional development initiative, state finance policy on financial access to higher education, school reform, special needs studies. *Unit head:* Martha McCarthy, Chair, 812-856-8377. *Application contact:* Sandy Strain, Department Secretary, 812-856-8360, Fax: 812-856-8394, E-mail: strain@indiana.edu.

Indiana University of Pennsylvania, School of Graduate Studies and Research, College of Education and Educational Technology, Department of Student Affairs in Higher Education, Indiana, PA 15705-1087. Offers MA. *Accreditation:* NCATE. Part-time programs available. *Faculty:* 4 full-time (2 women). *Students:* 55 full-time (36 women), 5 part-time (2 women); includes 7 minority (4 African Americans, 1 American Indian/Alaska Native, 1 Asian American or Pacific Islander, 1 Hispanic American). Average age 24. 102 applicants, 38% accepted, 29 enrolled. In 2009, 25 master's awarded. *Degree requirements:* For master's, comprehensive exam, thesis optional. *Entrance requirements:* For master's, resume, interview, 2 letters of recommendation, writing sample. Additional exam requirements/recommendations for international students: Required—TOEFL. *Application deadline:* For fall admission, 7/1 priority date for domestic students; for spring admission, 11/1 for domestic students. Applications are processed on a rolling basis. Application fee: $40. *Expenses:* Tuition, state resident: full-time $6666; part-time $370 per credit hour. Tuition, nonresident: full-time $10,666; part-time $593 per credit hour. Required fees: $813 per semester. *Financial support:* In 2009–10, 1 fellowship (averaging $500 per year), 19 research assistantships with full and partial tuition reimbursements (averaging $5,440 per year) were awarded; career-related internships or fieldwork and Federal Work-Study also available. Support available to part-time students. Financial award application deadline: 3/15; financial award applicants required to submit FAFSA. *Unit head:* Dr. Linda W. Hall, Chairperson and Graduate Coordinator, 724-357-4535, E-mail: linda.hall@iup.edu. *Application contact:* Dr. Edward Nardi, Interim Associate Dean, 724-357-2480, Fax: 724-357-5595, E-mail: ewnardi@iup.edu.

Indiana University–Purdue University Indianapolis, School of Education, Indianapolis, IN 46202-2896. Offers computer education (Certificate); curriculum and instruction (MS); early childhood (MS); educational leadership (MS, Certificate); English as a second language (Certificate); higher education and student affairs (MS); kindergarten (Certificate); language education (MS); reading (Certificate); school counseling (MS); special education (MS, Certificate). Part-time and evening/weekend programs available. *Faculty:* 41 full-time, 80 part-time/adjunct. *Students:* 72 full-time (60 women), 427 part-time (325 women); includes 57 minority (42 African Americans, 1 American Indian/Alaska Native, 4 Asian Americans or Pacific Islanders, 10 Hispanic Americans), 5 international. Average age 32. 181 applicants, 78% accepted, 112 enrolled. In 2009, 162 master's awarded. *Degree requirements:* For master's, thesis optional. *Entrance requirements:* For master's, GRE General Test, minimum GPA of 3.0. Additional exam requirements/recommendations for international students: Required—TOEFL. *Application deadline:* For fall admission, 5/1 priority date for domestic students; for spring admission, 11/1 for domestic students. Application fee: $55 ($65 for international students). *Financial support:* In 2009–10, 2 fellowships (averaging $780 per year), 18 teaching assistantships (averaging $9,756 per year) were awarded; research assistantships with partial tuition reimbursements, Federal Work-Study, institutionally sponsored loans, scholarships/grants, and tuition waivers (partial) also available. Support available to part-time students. *Faculty research:* Teachers in the process of change, learning cycles, children's concepts of science. Total annual research expenditures: $614,458. *Unit head:* Dr. Chris Leland, Interim Executive Associate Dean, 317-274-6801, Fax: 317-274-6864. *Application contact:* Sarah Brandenburg, Graduate Advisor, 317-274-6801, Fax: 317-274-6864, E-mail: edugrad@iupui.edu.

Inter American University of Puerto Rico, Metropolitan Campus, Graduate Programs, Program in Higher Education Administration, San Juan, PR 00919-1293. Offers MA. *Degree requirements:* For master's, comprehensive exam. *Entrance requirements:* For master's, GRE or EXADEP, interview. Electronic applications accepted.

Iowa State University of Science and Technology, Graduate College, College of Human Sciences, Department of Educational Leadership and Policy Studies, Ames, IA 50011. Offers counselor education (M Ed, MS); educational administration (M Ed, MS); educational leadership (PhD); higher education (M Ed, MS); organizational learning and human resource development (M Ed, MS); research and evaluation (MS). *Faculty:* 21 full-time (10 women), 14 part-time/adjunct (8 women). *Students:* 116 full-time (68 women), 218 part-time (130 women); includes

58 minority (34 African Americans, 3 American Indian/Alaska Native, 4 Asian Americans or Pacific Islanders, 17 Hispanic Americans), 7 international. 138 applicants, 78% accepted, 74 enrolled. In 2009, 77 master's, 18 doctorates awarded. *Degree requirements:* For master's, thesis or alternative; for doctorate, thesis/dissertation. *Entrance requirements:* For doctorate, GRE General Test. Additional exam requirements/recommendations for international students: Required—TOEFL (minimum score 560 paper-based; 83 iBT) or IELTS (minimum score 6.5). *Application deadline:* For fall admission, 1/1 priority date for domestic and international students. Applications are processed on a rolling basis. Application fee: $40 ($90 for international students). Electronic applications accepted. *Expenses:* Tuition, state resident: full-time $6716. Tuition, nonresident: full-time $8908. Tuition and fees vary according to course level, course load, program and student level. *Financial support:* In 2009–10, 104 research assistantships with full and partial tuition reimbursements (averaging $13,500 per year), 2 teaching assistantships with full and partial tuition reimbursements (averaging $13,500 per year) were awarded; fellowships, scholarships/grants, health care benefits, and unspecified assistantships also available. *Unit head:* Dr. Laura Rendon, Chair, 515-294-7093, E-mail: lrendon@iastate.edu. *Application contact:* Dr. Daniel Robinson, Information Contact, 515-294-1241, E-mail: eldrshp@iastate.edu.

John Brown University, Graduate Business Division, Siloam Springs, AR 72761-2121. Offers business administration (MBA), including international business, leadership and ethics; leadership and ethics (MS), including higher education. Part-time and evening/weekend programs available. Postbaccalaureate distance learning degree programs offered (minimal on-campus study). *Faculty:* 2 full-time (0 women), 13 part-time/adjunct (6 women). *Students:* 13 full-time (6 women), 143 part-time (56 women); includes 19 minority (6 African Americans, 2 American Indian/Alaska Native, 6 Asian Americans or Pacific Islanders, 5 Hispanic Americans), 5 international. Average age 35. 94 applicants, 85% accepted, 71 enrolled. In 2009, 54 master's awarded. *Entrance requirements:* For master's, GRE General Test, MAT, minimum GPA of 3.0. Additional exam requirements/recommendations for international students: Required—TOEFL (minimum score 550 paper-based; 173 computer-based). *Application deadline:* For fall admission, 8/11 priority date for domestic students; for spring admission, 1/12 priority date for domestic students. Applications are processed on a rolling basis. Application fee: $35 ($100 for international students). Electronic applications accepted. *Expenses:* Tuition: Full-time $8100; part-time $450 per credit. *Financial support:* In 2009–10, 8 students received support, including 8 fellowships (averaging $5,500 per year); scholarships/grants, tuition waivers (full), and unspecified assistantships also available. Financial award application deadline: 3/1; financial award applicants required to submit FAFSA. *Unit head:* Dr. Joe Walenciak, Program Director, 479-524-7170, Fax: 479-524-9548. *Application contact:* Brent Young, Graduate Business Representative, 479-631-0496, E-mail: byoung@jbu.edu.

Johnson & Wales University, The Alan Shawn Feinstein Graduate School, Ed D Program, Providence, RI 02903-3703. Offers higher education (Ed D); K-12 (Ed D). Part-time programs available. *Faculty:* 7 full-time (3 women), 3 part-time/adjunct (2 women). *Students:* 95 full-time (54 women); includes 3 minority (1 African American, 2 Asian Americans or Pacific Islanders). Average age 42. 27 applicants, 89% accepted, 22 enrolled. In 2009, 30 doctorates awarded. *Degree requirements:* For doctorate, thesis/dissertation. *Entrance requirements:* For doctorate, MAT, minimum GPA of 3.25. Additional exam requirements/recommendations for international students: Required—TOEFL (minimum score 550 paper-based; 210 computer-based) or IELTS recommended; Recommended—TWE. *Application deadline:* Applications are processed on a rolling basis. Application fee: $0. *Expenses:* Required fees: $340 per quarter hour. *Financial support:* Application deadline: 5/1. *Faculty research:* Site-based management, collaborative learning, technology and education, K–16 education. *Unit head:* Dr. Robert Gable, Director, 401-598-4738, Fax: 401-598-1162, E-mail: rgable@jwu.edu. *Application contact:* Dr. Allan G. Freedman, Director of Graduate Admissions, 401-598-1015, Fax: 401-598-1286, E-mail: gradadm@jwu.edu.

Jones International University, Graduate School of Education, Centennial, CO 80112. Offers adult education (M Ed); corporate training and knowledge management (M Ed); curriculum and instruction (M Ed), including elementary teacher licensure, secondary teacher licensure; e-learning technology and design (M Ed); educational leadership and administration (M Ed); educational leadership and administration: principal and administrator licensure (M Ed); elementary curriculum instruction and assessment (M Ed); higher education leadership and administration (M Ed); K-12 instructional technology (M Ed); K-12 instructional technology: teacher licensure (M Ed); secondary curriculum instruction and assessment (M Ed); technology and design (M Ed). Part-time and evening/weekend programs available. Postbaccalaureate distance learning degree programs offered (no on-campus study). *Entrance requirements:* For master's, minimum cumulative GPA of 2.5. Additional exam requirements/recommendations for international students: Recommended—TOEFL (minimum score 550 paper-based; 213 computer-based). Electronic applications accepted.

Kansas State University, Graduate School, College of Education, Department of Special Education, Counseling and Student Affairs, Manhattan, KS 66506. Offers academic advising (MS); college student development (MS); counseling and student development (Ed D); counselor education and supervision (PhD); school counseling (MS); special education (MS, Ed D); student affairs in higher education (PhD). *Accreditation:* NCATE. Part-time programs available. *Faculty:* 10 full-time (4 women), 3 part-time/adjunct (1 woman). *Students:* 64 full-time (38 women), 256 part-time (197 women); includes 33 minority (16 African Americans, 3 American Indian/Alaska Native, 6 Asian Americans or Pacific Islanders, 8 Hispanic Americans), 2 international. Average age 36. 100 applicants, 97% accepted, 73 enrolled. In 2009, 31 master's, 5 doctorates awarded. *Degree requirements:* For master's, thesis or alternative, final written exam. *Entrance requirements:* For master's, GRE General Test or MAT, teaching experience, BS in education with minimum B average. Additional exam requirements/recommendations for international students: Required—TOEFL. *Application deadline:* For fall admission, 2/1 priority date for domestic and international students; for spring admission, 8/1 priority date for domestic and international students. Applications are processed on a rolling basis. Application fee: $40 ($55 for international students). Electronic applications accepted. *Financial support:* In 2009–10, 1 research assistantship (averaging $12,134 per year) was awarded; career-related internships or fieldwork, Federal Work-Study, institutionally sponsored loans, and scholarships/grants also available. Support available to part-time students. Financial award application deadline: 3/1; financial award applicants required to submit FAFSA. *Faculty research:* Application of principles of universal design for learning, on-line applications for supervision of practicum students, interpretation of facial expressions by students with EBD and ASD, school-wide screening techniques for behavioral concerns, field-based observation technique refinements. Total annual research expenditures: $2,948. *Unit head:* Kenneth Hughey, Head, 785-532-6445, Fax: 785-532-7304, E-mail: khughey@ksu.edu. *Application contact:* Gail Shroyer, Director, 785-532-6737, Fax: 785-532-7304, E-mail: gshroyer@ksu.edu.

Kaplan University, Davenport Campus, School of Higher Education Studies, Davenport, IA 52807-2095. Offers college administration and leadership (MS); college teaching and learning (MS); student services (MS). Part-time and evening/weekend programs available. Postbaccalaureate distance learning degree programs offered (no on-campus study). *Entrance requirements:* Additional exam requirements/recommendations for international students: Required—TOEFL (minimum score 550 paper-based; 218 computer-based; 80 iBT).

Kent State University, Graduate School of Education, Health, and Human Services, School of Foundations, Leadership and Administration, Program in Higher Education, Kent, OH 44242-0001. Offers PhD, Ed S. *Accreditation:* NCATE. Part-time and evening/weekend programs available. *Faculty:* 7 full-time (4 women), 2 part-time/adjunct (0 women). *Students:* 13 full-time (9 women), 15 part-time (8 women); includes 4 minority (2 African Americans, 1 Asian American or Pacific Islander, 1 Hispanic American), 1 international. 17 applicants, 47% accepted. In 2009, 2 doctorates awarded. *Degree requirements:* For doctorate, comprehensive exam, thesis/dissertation. *Entrance requirements:* For doctorate and Ed S, GRE General Test. Additional exam requirements/recommendations for international students: Required—TOEFL. *Application*

Higher Education

Kent State University (continued)

deadline: Applications are processed on a rolling basis. Application fee: $30. Electronic applications accepted. *Financial support:* In 2009–10, 1 fellowship with full tuition reimbursement (averaging $12,000 per year), research assistantships with full tuition reimbursements (averaging $12,000 per year), teaching assistantships with full tuition reimbursements (averaging $12,000 per year) were awarded; career-related internships or fieldwork, Federal Work-Study, institutionally sponsored loans, scholarships/grants, health care benefits, and unspecified assistantships also available. Support available to part-time students. Financial award application deadline: 4/1; financial award applicants required to submit FAFSA. *Faculty research:* Leadership, the superintendency. *Unit head:* Dr. Mark Kretovics, Coordinator, 330-672-0642, E-mail: mkretov1@kent.edu. *Application contact:* Nancy Miller, Academic Program Coordinator, Office of Graduate Student Services, 330-672-2576, Fax: 330-672-9162, E-mail: ogs@kent.edu.

Kent State University, Graduate School of Education, Health, and Human Services, School of Foundations, Leadership and Administration, Program in Higher Education and Student Personnel, Kent, OH 44242-0001. Offers M Ed, MA. *Accreditation:* NCATE. Part-time and evening/weekend programs available. *Faculty:* 7 full-time (4 women), 2 part-time/adjunct (0 women). *Students:* 66 full-time (47 women), 24 part-time (20 women); includes 7 minority (5 African Americans, 2 Hispanic Americans), 2 international. 107 applicants, 64% accepted. In 2009, 43 master's awarded. *Degree requirements:* For master's, thesis (for some programs). *Entrance requirements:* Additional exam requirements/recommendations for international students: Required—TOEFL. *Application deadline:* Applications are processed on a rolling basis. Application fee: $30. Electronic applications accepted. *Financial support:* In 2009–10, 10 research assistantships with full tuition reimbursements (averaging $8,500 per year) were awarded; teaching assistantships with full tuition reimbursements, Federal Work-Study, scholarships/grants, and unspecified assistantships also available. Financial award application deadline: 4/1; financial award applicants required to submit FAFSA. *Faculty research:* History/sociology of higher education, organization and administration in higher education. *Unit head:* Dr. Mark Kretovics, Coordinator, 330-672-0642, E-mail: mkretov1@kent.edu. *Application contact:* Nancy Miller, Academic Program Coordinator, Office of Graduate Student Services, 330-672-2576, Fax: 330-672-9162, E-mail: ogs@kent.edu.

Louisiana State University and Agricultural and Mechanical College, Graduate School, College of Education, Department of Educational Theory, Policy and Practice, Baton Rouge, LA 70803. Offers counseling (M Ed, MA, Ed S); educational administration (M Ed, MA, PhD, Ed S); educational technology (MA); elementary education (M Ed); higher education (PhD); research methodology (PhD); secondary education (M Ed). *Accreditation:* ACA (one or more programs are accredited); NCATE. Part-time and evening/weekend programs available. *Faculty:* 38 full-time (24 women). *Students:* 174 full-time (139 women), 154 part-time (129 women); includes 74 minority (66 African Americans, 3 Asian Americans or Pacific Islanders, 5 Hispanic Americans), 9 international. Average age 32. 122 applicants, 60% accepted, 48 enrolled. In 2009, 124 master's, 13 doctorates, 11 other advanced degrees awarded. Terminal master's awarded for partial completion of doctoral program. *Degree requirements:* For doctorate, thesis/dissertation; for Ed S, thesis optional. *Entrance requirements:* For master's and doctorate, GRE General Test, minimum GPA of 3.0. Additional exam requirements/recommendations for international students: Required—TOEFL (minimum score 550 paper-based; 213 computer-based; 79 iBT) or IELTS (minimum score 6.5). *Application deadline:* For fall admission, 1/25 priority date for domestic students, 5/15 for international students; for spring admission, 10/15 for international students. Applications are processed on a rolling basis. Application fee: $50 ($70 for international students). Electronic applications accepted. *Financial support:* In 2009–10, 226 students received support, including 1 fellowship (averaging $31,711 per year), 27 research assistantships with full and partial tuition reimbursements available (averaging $10,143 per year), 35 teaching assistantships with full and partial tuition reimbursements available (averaging $12,555 per year); career-related internships or fieldwork, Federal Work-Study, institutionally sponsored loans, health care benefits, and unspecified assistantships also available. Support available to part-time students. Financial award applicants required to submit FAFSA. *Faculty research:* Literary, curriculum studies, science education, K-12 leadership, higher education. Total annual research expenditures: $1.8 million. *Unit head:* Dr. Earl Cheek, Chair, 225-578-6867, Fax: 225-578-9135, E-mail: echeek@lsu.edu. *Application contact:* Dr., Graduate Coordinator, 225-578-2280, Fax: 225-578-9135.

Loyola University Chicago, School of Education, Program in Higher Education, Chicago, IL 60660. Offers M Ed, PhD. PhD offered through the Graduate School. *Accreditation:* NCATE. Part-time programs available. *Faculty:* 5 full-time (2 women), 4 part-time/adjunct (2 women). *Students:* 140. Average age 38. 138 applicants, 74% accepted, 36 enrolled. In 2009, 36 master's, 10 doctorates awarded. *Degree requirements:* For master's, comprehensive exam; for doctorate, comprehensive exam, thesis/dissertation, dissertation defense, oral candidacy exam. *Entrance requirements:* For master's, letters of recommendation, minimum GPA of 3.0, resume, transcripts; for doctorate, GMAT, GRE General Test, or MAT, 5 years of higher education work experience, interview. Additional exam requirements/recommendations for international students: Required—TOEFL (minimum score 550 paper-based; 213 computer-based; 79 iBT). *Application deadline:* For fall admission, 4/1 for domestic and international students; for winter admission, 1/1 for domestic and international students; for spring admission, 11/1 for domestic and international students. Applications are processed on a rolling basis. Application fee: $50. Electronic applications accepted. *Expenses:* Tuition: Full-time $14,220; part-time $790 per credit hour. Required fees: $60 per semester hour. Tuition and fees vary according to program. *Financial support:* In 2009–10, 4 research assistantships with full tuition reimbursements (averaging $8,500 per year) were awarded; career-related internships or fieldwork also available. Support available to part-time students. Financial award application deadline: 2/15; financial award applicants required to submit FAFSA. *Faculty research:* Church-affiliated higher education, enrollment management, academic programs, program evaluation/quality. *Unit head:* Dr. Terry E. Williams, Director, 312-915-7002, Fax: 312-915-6660, E-mail: twillia@luc.edu. *Application contact:* Marie Rosin-Dittmar, Information Contact, 312-915-6800, E-mail: schleduc@luc.edu.

Marywood University, Academic Affairs, Reap College of Education and Human Development, Department of Education, Program in Higher Education Administration, Scranton, PA 18509-1598. Offers MS. Part-time and evening/weekend programs available. *Students:* 3 full-time (2 women), 15 part-time (12 women); includes 2 minority (both Hispanic Americans). Average age 39. 6 applicants, 100% accepted. In 2009, 3 master's awarded. *Entrance requirements:* Additional exam requirements/recommendations for international students: Required—TOEFL (minimum score 550 paper-based; 213 computer-based; 79 iBT). *Application deadline:* For fall admission, 4/1 priority date for domestic students, 3/31 priority date for international students; for spring admission, 11/1 priority date for domestic students, 8/31 priority date for international students. Applications are processed on a rolling basis. Application fee: $30. Electronic applications accepted. *Expenses:* Tuition: Part-time $715 per credit. Required fees: $270 per semester. Tuition and fees vary according to degree level, campus/location and program. *Financial support:* Research assistantships with tuition reimbursements, career-related internships or fieldwork, scholarships/grants, and unspecified assistantships available. Support available to part-time students. Financial award application deadline: 6/30; financial award applicants required to submit FAFSA. *Faculty research:* Integrated thematic instruction. *Unit head:* Sr. Ann Jablonski, Chair, 570-348-6211 Ext. 2638, E-mail: jablonski@marywood.edu. *Application contact:* Tammy Manka, Assistant Director of Graduate Admissions, 570-340-6002, E-mail: tmanka@marywood.edu.

Marywood University, Academic Affairs, Reap College of Education and Human Development, Department of Human Development, Emphasis in Higher Education Administration, Scranton, PA 18509-1598. Offers PhD. *Students:* 1 full-time (0 women), 24 part-time (16 women), 1 international. Average age 37. In 2009, 2 doctorates awarded. *Entrance requirements:* Additional exam requirements/recommendations for international students: Required—TOEFL (minimum score 550 paper-based; 213 computer-based; 79 iBT). *Application deadline:* For fall admission, 1/30 for domestic and international students. Application fee: $35. Electronic applications accepted. *Expenses:* Contact institution. *Financial support:* Career-related internships or fieldwork, scholarships/grants, and unspecified assistantships available. Support available to part-time students. Financial award application deadline: 6/30; financial award applicants required to submit FAFSA. *Unit head:* Dr. Brook Cannon, Director, 570-348-6211 Ext. 2324, E-mail: cannon@marywood.edu. *Application contact:* Tammy Manka, Assistant Director of Graduate Admissions, 866-279-9663, E-mail: tmanka@marywood.edu.

McKendree University, Graduate Programs, Master of Arts in Education Program, Lebanon, IL 62254-1299. Offers certification (MA Ed); educational administration and leadership (MA Ed); educational studies (MA Ed); higher education administrative services (MA Ed); music education (MA Ed); special education (MA Ed); teacher leadership (MA Ed); transition to teaching (MA Ed). *Accreditation:* NCATE. Part-time and evening/weekend programs available. Postbaccalaureate distance learning degree programs offered (no on-campus study). *Faculty:* 18 full-time (7 women), 56 part-time/adjunct (34 women). *Students:* 107 full-time (83 women), 445 part-time (325 women); includes 41 minority (32 African Americans, 3 Asian Americans or Pacific Islanders, 6 Hispanic Americans). Average age 35. 225 applicants, 77% accepted, 129 enrolled. In 2009, 200 master's awarded. *Entrance requirements:* For master's, official transcripts from institutions attended, minimum GPA of 3.0, resume, references. Additional exam requirements/recommendations for international students: Required—TOEFL. *Application deadline:* Applications are processed on a rolling basis. Application fee: $0. Electronic applications accepted. *Expenses:* Tuition: Full-time $6300; part-time $350 per credit hour. One-time fee: $125. *Financial support:* In 2009–10, 1 student received support. Application deadline: 6/30. *Unit head:* Dr. Joseph J. Cipfl, Interim Chair of the School of Education, 618-537-6462, Fax: 618-537-6417, E-mail: jjcipfl@mckendree.edu. *Application contact:* Sabrina Storner, Director of Graduate Admission, 618-537-6477, Fax: 618-537-6410, E-mail: skstorner@mckendree.edu.

Miami University, Graduate School, School of Education and Allied Professions, Department of Educational Leadership, Oxford, OH 45056. Offers curriculum and teacher leadership (M Ed); educational administration (Ed D, PhD); school leadership (MS); student affairs in higher education (MS, PhD). *Accreditation:* NCATE. Part-time programs available. *Students:* 78 full-time (51 women), 77 part-time (53 women); includes 38 minority (30 African Americans, 1 American Indian/Alaska Native, 4 Asian Americans or Pacific Islanders, 3 Hispanic Americans), 4 international. *Entrance requirements:* For master's, MAT or GRE, minimum undergraduate GPA of 3.0 during previous 2 years or 2.75 overall; for doctorate, GRE, minimum GPA of 2.75 (undergraduate), 3.0 (graduate). Additional exam requirements/recommendations for international students: Required—TOEFL. Application fee: $50. *Expenses:* Tuition, state resident: full-time $11,280. Tuition, nonresident: full-time $24,912. Required fees: $516. *Financial support:* Fellowships with full tuition reimbursements, research assistantships with full tuition reimbursements, teaching assistantships with full tuition reimbursements, career-related internships or fieldwork, Federal Work-Study, health care benefits, tuition waivers (full), and unspecified assistantships available. Financial award application deadline: 3/1. *Unit head:* Dr. Kate Rousmaniere, Chair, 513-529-6843, Fax: 513-529-1729, E-mail: roumak@muohio.edu. *Application contact:* Dr. Denise Taliaferri Baszile, Director of Graduate Studies, 513-529-1798, E-mail: taliafda@muohio.edu.

Michigan State University, The Graduate School, College of Education, Department of Educational Administration, East Lansing, MI 48824. Offers higher, adult and lifelong education (MA, PhD); K–12 educational administration (MA, PhD, Ed S); student affairs administration (MA). Part-time programs available. *Faculty:* 20 full-time (9 women). *Students:* 158 full-time (95 women), 158 part-time (92 women); includes 59 minority (33 African Americans, 5 American Indian/Alaska Native, 11 Asian Americans or Pacific Islanders, 10 Hispanic Americans), 33 international. Average age 33. 274 applicants, 52% accepted. In 2009, 73 master's, 27 doctorates awarded. *Entrance requirements:* Additional exam requirements/recommendations for international students: Required—TOEFL. Electronic applications accepted. *Expenses:* Tuition, state resident: part-time $478.25 per credit hour. Tuition, nonresident: part-time $966.50 per credit hour. Part-time tuition and fees vary according to program. *Financial support:* In 2009–10, 51 research assistantships with tuition reimbursements (averaging $6,633 per year), 3 teaching assistantships with tuition reimbursements (averaging $6,967 per year) were awarded. Total annual research expenditures: $365,790. *Unit head:* Dr. Marilyn J. Amey, Chairperson, 517-432-1056, Fax: 517-884-1392, E-mail: amey@msu.edu. *Application contact:* Cathy Ogar, Graduate Secretary, 517-355-4537, Fax: 517-884-1392, E-mail: cogar@msu.edu.

Mississippi College, Graduate School, School of Education, Department of Teacher Education and Leadership, Clinton, MS 39058. Offers art (M Ed); biological science (M Ed); business education (M Ed); computer science (M Ed); dyslexia therapy (M Ed); educational leadership (M Ed, Ed D, Ed S); elementary education (M Ed, Ed S); English (M Ed); higher education administration (MS); mathematics (M Ed); secondary education (M Ed); social studies (history) (M Ed); teaching arts (M Ed). Part-time programs available. Postbaccalaureate distance learning degree programs offered (no on-campus study). *Faculty:* 11 full-time (7 women), 13 part-time/adjunct (7 women). *Students:* 33 full-time (22 women), 282 part-time (240 women); includes 148 minority (146 African Americans, 2 American Indian/Alaska Native), 1 international. Average age 34. In 2009, 147 master's awarded. *Degree requirements:* For master's, comprehensive exam, thesis optional. *Entrance requirements:* For master's, NTE. Additional exam requirements/recommendations for international students: Recommended—IELTS. *Application deadline:* For fall admission, 8/15 priority date for domestic students. Applications are processed on a rolling basis. Application fee: $30. Electronic applications accepted. *Expenses:* Tuition: Part-time $452 per credit hour. Required fees: $101 per semester. Tuition and fees vary according to degree level, campus/location, program and student level. *Financial support:* Teaching assistantships, career-related internships or fieldwork, Federal Work-Study, scholarships/grants, and unspecified assistantships available. Support available to part-time students. Financial award applicants required to submit FAFSA. *Unit head:* Dr. Tom Williams, Chair, 601-925-3844, E-mail: twilliams@mc.edu. *Application contact:* Elnora Lewis, Secretary, 601-925-3225, Fax: 601-925-3889, E-mail: lewis09@mc.edu.

Mississippi College, Graduate School, School of Education, Program in Higher Education Administration, Clinton, MS 39058. Offers MS. Part-time programs available. Postbaccalaureate distance learning degree programs offered (no on-campus study). *Faculty:* 4 part-time/adjunct (1 woman). *Students:* 4 full-time (2 women), 26 part-time (21 women); includes 13 minority (all African Americans). Average age 30. In 2009, 4 master's awarded. *Degree requirements:* For master's, comprehensive exam, thesis optional. *Entrance requirements:* For master's, GRE or GMAT, minimum GPA of 3.0. Additional exam requirements/recommendations for international students: Recommended—IELTS. *Application deadline:* For fall admission, 8/15 priority date for domestic students. Application fee: $30. *Expenses:* Tuition: Part-time $452 per credit hour. Required fees: $101 per semester. Tuition and fees vary according to degree level, campus/location, program and student level. *Financial support:* Teaching assistantships, career-related internships or fieldwork, Federal Work-Study, and unspecified assistantships available. Support available to part-time students. Financial award application deadline: 4/1; financial award applicants required to submit FAFSA. *Unit head:* Dr. Debbie C. Norris, Graduate Dean, 601-925-3260, Fax: 601-925-3889, E-mail: dnorris@mc.edu. *Application contact:* Elnora Lewis, Secretary, 601-925-3225, Fax: 601-925-3889, E-mail: lewis09@mc.edu.

Montana State University, College of Graduate Studies, College of Education, Health, and Human Development, Department of Education, Bozeman, MT 59717. Offers adult and higher education (Ed D); curriculum and instruction (Ed D, Ed S); education (M Ed), including adult and higher education, curriculum and instruction, educational leadership, school counseling; educational leadership (Ed D, Ed S). Part-time programs available. Postbaccalaureate distance learning degree programs offered (minimal on-campus study). *Faculty:* 22 full-time (13 women), 18 part-time/adjunct (14 women). *Students:* 15 full-time (8 women), 210 part-time (126 women); includes 29 minority (27 American Indian/Alaska Native, 1 Asian American or Pacific Islander, 1 Hispanic American), 2 international. Average age 37. 52 applicants. In 2009, 62 master's, 9 doctorates awarded. *Degree requirements:* For master's, comprehensive exam; for doctorate,

comprehensive exam, thesis/dissertation. *Entrance requirements:* For master's and doctorate, GRE General Test. Additional exam requirements/recommendations for international students: Required—TOEFL (minimum score 550 paper-based; 213 computer-based). *Application deadline:* For fall admission, 7/15 priority date for domestic students, 5/15 priority date for international students; for spring admission, 12/1 priority date for domestic students, 10/1 priority date for international students. Applications are processed on a rolling basis. Application fee: $30. Electronic applications accepted. *Expenses:* Tuition, state resident: full-time $5635; part-time $3492 per year. Tuition, nonresident: full-time $17,212; part-time $7865.10 per year. Required fees: $1441; $153.15 per credit. Tuition and fees vary according to course load and program. *Financial support:* In 2009–10, 45 students received support, including 5 teaching assistantships with tuition reimbursements available (averaging $9,000 per year); traineeships, tuition waivers (full and partial), and unspecified assistantships also available. Financial award application deadline: 3/1; financial award applicants required to submit FAFSA. *Faculty research:* Online teaching and learning, statistical strategies to course and student assessment, environmental education, copyright issues/web-based resources, multicultural education, curriculum design, preparation for North American teachers to be administrators, NCES data sets, relational trust in public school administration. Total annual research expenditures: $1.2 million. *Unit head:* Dr. Joanne Erickson, Interim Department Head, 406-994-6670, Fax: 406-994-3261, E-mail: jle@montana.edu. *Application contact:* Dr. Carl A. Fox, Vice Provost for Graduate Education, 406-994-4145, Fax: 406-994-7433, E-mail: gradstudy@montana.edu.

Morehead State University, Graduate Programs, College of Education, Department of Foundational and Graduate Studies in Education, Morehead, KY 40351. Offers adult and higher education (MA, Ed S); certified professional counselor (Ed S); counseling P-12 (MA); curriculum and instruction (Ed S); educational technology (MA Ed); instructional leadership (Ed S); school administration (MA); school counseling (Ed S); teacher leader business and marketing- content (MA Ed); teacher leader business and marketing- technology (MA Ed); teacher leader educational technology (MA Ed); teacher leader English (MA Ed); teacher leader gifted educ (MA Ed); teacher leader IECE—non-certification (MA Ed); teacher leader IECE certification (MA Ed); teacher leader interdisciplanary educaction P-5 (MA Ed); teacher leader middle grades 5-9 (MA Ed); teacher leader reading/writing—non-certification (MA Ed); teacher leader reading/writing certification (MA Ed); teacher leader school communication—non-certification (MA Ed); teacher leader school communication certification (MA Ed); teacher leader social studies (MA Ed); teacher leader special education (MA Ed). *Accreditation:* NCATE. Part-time and evening/weekend programs available. *Faculty:* 20 full-time (10 women), 7 part-time/adjunct (3 women). *Students:* 26 full-time (18 women), 371 part-time (295 women); includes 11 minority (9 African Americans, 1 American Indian/Alaska Native, 1 Hispanic American). Average age 35. 201 applicants, 73% accepted, 73 enrolled. In 2009, 105 master's, 5 other advanced degrees awarded. *Degree requirements:* For master's, thesis optional, oral and/or written comprehensive exams; for Ed S, thesis, oral exam. *Entrance requirements:* For master's, GRE General Test, minimum overall undergraduate GPA of 2.5; for Ed S, GRE General Test, interview, master's degree, minimum GPA of 3.5, work experience. Additional exam requirements/recommendations for international students: Required—TOEFL (minimum score 500 paper-based; 173 computer-based). *Application deadline:* For fall admission, 8/1 priority date for domestic and international students; for spring admission, 12/1 priority date for domestic and international students. Applications are processed on a rolling basis. Application fee: $30. Electronic applications accepted. *Expenses:* Tuition, state resident: full-time $6318; part-time $351 per credit hour. Tuition, nonresident: full-time $15,804; part-time $878 per credit hour. *Financial support:* In 2009–10, 2 research assistantships (averaging $10,000 per year) were awarded; career-related internships or fieldwork, Federal Work-Study, and unspecified assistantships also available. Financial award application deadline: 3/15; financial award applicants required to submit FAFSA. *Faculty research:* Character education, school accountability, computer applications for school administrators. *Unit head:* Dr. Cathy Gunn, Dean and Professor, 606-783-2040, Fax: 606-783-5029, E-mail: c.gunn@moreheadstate.edu. *Application contact:* Michelle Barber, Graduate Recruitment and Retention Assistant Director, 606-783-5127, Fax: 606-783-5061, E-mail: m.barber@moreheadstate.edu.

Morgan State University, School of Graduate Studies, School of Education and Urban Studies, Department of Advanced Studies, Leadership and Policy, Program in Higher Education Administration, Baltimore, MD 21251. Offers PhD. *Degree requirements:* For doctorate, comprehensive exam, thesis/dissertation. *Entrance requirements:* For doctorate, GRE General Test or MAT, minimum GPA of 3.0.

Morgan State University, School of Graduate Studies, School of Education and Urban Studies, Department of Advanced Studies, Leadership and Policy, Program in Higher Education-Community College Leadership, Baltimore, MD 21251. Offers Ed D. *Accreditation:* NCATE. Part-time and evening/weekend programs available. *Degree requirements:* For doctorate, comprehensive exam, thesis/dissertation. *Entrance requirements:* For doctorate, GRE General Test or MAT. Additional exam requirements/recommendations for international students: Required—TOEFL (minimum score 550 paper-based; 213 computer-based). *Faculty research:* Multicultural education, cooperative learning, psychology of cognition.

New England College, Program in Education, Henniker, NH 03242-3293. Offers higher education administration (MS); literacy and language arts (M Ed); meeting the needs of all learners/special education (M Ed); teacher leadership/school reform (M Ed). Part-time and evening/weekend programs available.

New York University, Steinhardt School of Culture, Education, and Human Development, Department of Administration, Leadership, and Technology, Program in Higher Education, New York, NY 10012-1019. Offers higher and postsecondary education (PhD); higher education administration (Ed D); student personnel administration in higher education (MA). *Accreditation:* Teacher Education Accreditation Council. Part-time programs available. *Students:* 43 full-time (25 women), 93 part-time (73 women); includes 41 minority (18 African Americans, 10 Asian Americans or Pacific Islanders, 13 Hispanic Americans), 3 international. Average age 32. 199 applicants, 26% accepted, 41 enrolled. In 2009, 37 master's, 9 doctorates awarded. *Degree requirements:* For master's, thesis (for some programs); for doctorate, thesis/dissertation. *Entrance requirements:* For master's, interview, 2 letters of recommendation; for doctorate, GRE General Test, interview. Additional exam requirements/recommendations for international students: Required—TOEFL. *Application deadline:* For fall admission, 12/15 priority date for domestic and international students; for spring admission, 11/1 for domestic and international students. Applications are processed on a rolling basis. Application fee: $75. Electronic applications accepted. *Expenses:* Tuition: Full-time $30,528; part-time $1272 per credit. Required fees: $2177. *Financial support:* Fellowships with full and partial tuition reimbursements, career-related internships or fieldwork, Federal Work-Study, institutionally sponsored loans, scholarships/grants, tuition waivers (partial), and unspecified assistantships available. Support available to part-time students. Financial award application deadline: 2/1; financial award applicants required to submit FAFSA. *Faculty research:* Organizational theory and culture, systemic change, leadership development, access, equity and diversity. *Unit head:* Dr. Ann Marcus, Head, 212-998-4041, Fax: 212-995-4041. *Application contact:* 212-998-5030, Fax: 212-995-4328, E-mail: steinhardt.gradadmissions@nyu.edu.

North Carolina State University, Graduate School, College of Education, Department of Adult and Higher Education, Program in Higher Education Administration, Raleigh, NC 27695. Offers M Ed, MS, Ed D. *Degree requirements:* For master's, thesis (for some programs); for doctorate, thesis/dissertation. *Entrance requirements:* For master's and doctorate, GRE General Test or MAT, minimum GPA of 3.0 in major. Electronic applications accepted.

Northeastern State University, Graduate College, College of Education, Department of Educational Foundations and Leadership, Program in Collegiate Scholarship and Services, Tahlequah, OK 74464-2399. Offers MS. Part-time and evening/weekend programs available. *Degree requirements:* For master's, thesis. *Entrance requirements:* For master's, MAT or GRE, minimum GPA of 3.0. Additional exam requirements/recommendations for international students: Required—TOEFL (minimum score 213 computer-based). Electronic applications accepted.

Northern Arizona University, Graduate College, College of Education, Department of Educational Leadership, Flagstaff, AZ 86011. Offers community college/higher education (M Ed); educational foundations (M Ed); educational leadership (M Ed, Ed D); principal (Certificate); principal K-12 (M Ed); school leadership K-12 (M Ed); superintendent (Certificate). *Faculty:* 21 full-time (11 women). *Students:* 196 full-time (128 women), 744 part-time (452 women); includes 249 minority (59 African Americans, 39 American Indian/Alaska Native, 21 Asian Americans or Pacific Islanders, 130 Hispanic Americans), 4 international. Average age 32. 267 applicants, 97% accepted, 185 enrolled. In 2009, 461 master's, 12 doctorates awarded. *Degree requirements:* For master's, comprehensive exam, thesis (for some programs); for doctorate, comprehensive exam, thesis/dissertation. *Entrance requirements:* For master's, minimum GPA of 3.0; for doctorate, GRE or MAT, minimum GPA of 3.5. Additional exam requirements/recommendations for international students: Required—TOEFL (minimum score 550 paper-based; 213 computer-based; 80 iBT), IELTS (minimum score 7), or a bachelor's degree from an English-speaking university and demonstrated proficiency. *Application deadline:* For fall admission, 2/1 priority date for domestic students, 9/15 priority date for international students; for spring admission, 12/1 for domestic students. Applications are processed on a rolling basis. Application fee: $65. Electronic applications accepted. *Financial support:* In 2009–10, 1 teaching assistantship with partial tuition reimbursement (averaging $10,000 per year) was awarded. Financial award application deadline: 3/30. *Unit head:* Dr. Michael Schwanenberger, Chair, 928-523-3202, Fax: 928-523-8950, E-mail: michael.schwanenberger@nau.edu. *Application contact:* Dr. Michael Schwanenberger, Chair, 928-523-3202, Fax: 928-523-8950, E-mail: michael.schwanenberger@nau.edu.

Northern Illinois University, Graduate School, College of Education, Department of Counseling, Adult and Higher Education, De Kalb, IL 60115-2854. Offers adult and higher education (MS Ed, Ed D); counseling (MS Ed, Ed D). *Accreditation:* ACA. Part-time and evening/weekend programs available. *Faculty:* 19 full-time (11 women), 2 part-time/adjunct (1 woman). *Students:* 119 full-time (80 women), 280 part-time (198 women); includes 126 minority (93 African Americans, 4 American Indian/Alaska Native, 8 Asian Americans or Pacific Islanders, 21 Hispanic Americans), 18 international. Average age 38. 118 applicants, 53% accepted, 45 enrolled. In 2009, 76 master's, 12 doctorates awarded. Terminal master's awarded for partial completion of doctoral program. *Degree requirements:* For master's, comprehensive exam, thesis optional; for doctorate, thesis/dissertation, candidacy exam, dissertation defense. *Entrance requirements:* For master's, GRE General Test or MAT, minimum undergraduate GPA of 2.75, interview (counseling); for doctorate, GRE General Test, minimum undergraduate GPA of 2.75, 3.2 graduate, interview (counseling). Additional exam requirements/recommendations for international students: Required—TOEFL (minimum score 550 paper-based; 213 computer-based). *Application deadline:* For fall admission, 6/1 for domestic students, 5/1 for international students; for spring admission, 11/1 for domestic students, 10/1 for international students. Applications are processed on a rolling basis. Application fee: $30. Electronic applications accepted. *Expenses:* Tuition, state resident: full-time $6576; part-time $274 per credit hour. Tuition, nonresident: full-time $13,152; part-time $548 per credit hour. Required fees: $1813; $75.53 per credit hour. Part-time tuition and fees vary according to course load. *Financial support:* In 2009–10, 1 teaching assistantship with full tuition reimbursement was awarded; fellowships with full tuition reimbursements, research assistantships with full tuition reimbursements, career-related internships or fieldwork, Federal Work-Study, scholarships/grants, tuition waivers (full), and staff assistantships also available. Support available to part-time students. Financial award applicants required to submit FAFSA. *Unit head:* Dr. Barbara Johnson, Interim Chair, 815-753-1448, E-mail: cahe@niu.edu. *Application contact:* Graduate School Office, 815-753-0395, E-mail: gradsch@niu.edu.

Northwestern University, The Graduate School, School of Education and Social Policy, Education and Social Policy Program, Evanston, IL 60035. Offers advanced teaching (MS); elementary education and policy (MS); higher education administration (MS); secondary teaching (MS). Part-time and evening/weekend programs available. *Faculty:* 3 full-time (all women), 20 part-time/adjunct (11 women). *Students:* 64 full-time (47 women), 94 part-time (70 women); includes 27 minority (11 African Americans, 1 American Indian/Alaska Native, 9 Asian Americans or Pacific Islanders, 6 Hispanic Americans). Average age 27. 117 applicants, 63% accepted, 57 enrolled. In 2009, 82 master's awarded. *Degree requirements:* For master's, research project. *Entrance requirements:* For master's, GRE General Test, Illinois State Board of Education Basic Skills Exam (secondary and elementary), bachelor's degree. *Application deadline:* For fall admission, 7/16 for domestic students; for winter admission, 11/7 for domestic students; for spring admission, 2/15 priority date for domestic students. Applications are processed on a rolling basis. Application fee: $100. Electronic applications accepted. *Financial support:* In 2009–10, 6 students received support, including 1 fellowship with partial tuition reimbursement available (averaging $16,000 per year); career-related internships or fieldwork, Federal Work-Study, institutionally sponsored loans, scholarships/grants, tuition waivers (partial), and unspecified assistantships also available. Financial award application deadline: 1/9; financial award applicants required to submit FAFSA. *Faculty research:* Cultural context and literacy, philosophy of education and interpretive discussion, productivity, enhancing research and teaching, motivation, new and junior faculty issues, professional development for K-12 teachers to improve math and science teaching, female/underrepresented students/faculty in STEM disciplines. *Unit head:* Dr. Sophie Haroutunian-Gordon, Director and Professor, 847-467-1458, Fax: 847-467-2495, E-mail: shg@northwestern.edu. *Application contact:* Bradley Wadle, Assistant Director, 847-491-3829, Fax: 847-467-2495, E-mail: msedapply@northwestern.edu.

Northwest Missouri State University, Graduate School, College of Education and Human Services, Department of Educational Leadership, Maryville, MO 64468-6001. Offers educational leadership (MS Ed, Ed S), including educational leadership: elementary (MS Ed), educational leadership: secondary (MS Ed), elementary principalship (Ed S), secondary principalship (Ed S), superintendency (Ed S); higher education leadership (MS); secondary individualized prescribed programs (MS Ed), including teacher leadership, teaching secondary. Part-time programs available. *Faculty:* 16 full-time (6 women). *Students:* 49 full-time (31 women), 197 part-time (132 women); includes 21 minority (16 African Americans, 1 American Indian/Alaska Native, 1 Asian American or Pacific Islander, 3 Hispanic Americans), 1 international. 59 applicants, 86% accepted, 37 enrolled. In 2009, 82 master's, 19 other advanced degrees awarded. *Degree requirements:* For master's, comprehensive exam; for Ed S, comprehensive exam, thesis. *Entrance requirements:* For master's, GRE General Test, minimum undergraduate GPA of 2.75, teaching certificate, writing sample; for Ed S, minimum graduate GPA of 3.25. Additional exam requirements/recommendations for international students: Required—TOEFL (minimum score 550 paper-based; 213 computer-based). *Application deadline:* For fall admission, 7/1 for domestic and international students; for spring admission, 11/15 for domestic and international students. Application fee: $0 ($50 for international students). *Expenses:* Tuition, state resident: part-time $296.34 per credit hour. Tuition, nonresident: part-time $510.43 per credit hour. *Financial support:* In 2009–10, 5 research assistantships with full tuition reimbursements (averaging $6,000 per year), 1 teaching assistantship with full tuition reimbursement (averaging $6,000 per year) were awarded; unspecified assistantships also available. Financial award application deadline: 4/1; financial award applicants required to submit FAFSA. *Unit head:* Dr. Joyce Piveral, Chairperson, 660-562-1231. *Application contact:* Dr. Gregory Haddock, Dean of Graduate School, 660-562-1145, Fax: 660-562-1096, E-mail: gradsch@nwmissouri.edu.

Nova Southeastern University, Fischler School of Education and Human Services, Program in Education, Fort Lauderdale, FL 33314-7796. Offers educational leadership (Ed D); health care education (Ed D); higher education leadership (Ed D); human services administration (Ed D); instructional leadership (Ed D); instructional technology and distance education (Ed D); organizational leadership (Ed D); special education (Ed D); speech language pathology (Ed D). Part-time and evening/weekend programs available. Postbaccalaureate distance learning degree programs offered (minimal on-campus study). *Faculty:* 88 full-time (46 women), 132 part-time/

Higher Education

Nova Southeastern University *(continued)*
adjunct (63 women). *Students:* 2,805 full-time (2,128 women), 1,411 part-time (1,081 women); includes 2,629 minority (2,034 African Americans, 19 American Indian/Alaska Native, 62 Asian Americans or Pacific Islanders, 514 Hispanic Americans), 30 international. Average age 41. 964 applicants, 69% accepted, 513 enrolled. In 2009, 445 doctorates awarded. *Degree requirements:* For doctorate, thesis/dissertation. *Entrance requirements:* For doctorate, MAT or GRE, master's degree, 2 letters of recommendation, work experience. Additional exam requirements/recommendations for international students: Required—TSE (recommended, minimum score 50); Recommended—TOEFL (minimum score 550 paper-based; 213 computer-based; 80 iBT), IELTS (minimum score 6). *Application deadline:* For fall admission, 8/20 priority date for domestic and international students; for winter admission, 12/19 priority date for domestic and international students; for spring admission, 4/26 priority date for domestic students, 4/25 priority date for international students. Applications are processed on a rolling basis. Application fee: $50. Electronic applications accepted. *Financial support:* In 2009–10, 2 fellowships with full tuition reimbursements (averaging $30,000 per year) were awarded; scholarships/grants and tuition waivers (full) also available. Support available to part-time students. Financial award application deadline: 4/15; financial award applicants required to submit FAFSA. *Unit head:* Dr. Ronald Kern, Dean of Academic Affairs, 800-986-3223 Ext. 7809, Fax: 954-262-3606, E-mail: rk429@nsu.nova.edu. *Application contact:* Dr. Jennifer Quinones Nottingham, Dean of Student Affairs, 800-986-3223 Ext. 1546.

Nova Southeastern University, Fischler School of Education and Human Services, Programs for Higher Education, Fort Lauderdale, FL 33314-7796. Offers adult education (Ed D); computing and information technology (Ed D); health care education (Ed D); higher education (Ed D); vocational, occupational and technical education (Ed D). Part-time and evening/weekend programs available. Postbaccalaureate distance learning degree programs offered (minimal on-campus study). *Faculty:* 6 full-time (3 women), 8 part-time/adjunct (2 women). *Students:* 113 full-time (81 women), 2 part-time (both women); includes 57 minority (51 African Americans, 6 Hispanic Americans). 4 applicants, 75% accepted, 3 enrolled. In 2009, 13 doctorates awarded. *Degree requirements:* For doctorate, thesis/dissertation, practicum. *Entrance requirements:* For doctorate, MAT or GRE, master's degree, work experience in field, minimum GPA of 3.0. Additional exam requirements/recommendations for international students: Required—TSE (recommended, minimum score 50); Recommended—TOEFL (minimum score 550 paper-based; 213 computer-based; 80 iBT), IELTS (minimum score 6). *Application deadline:* For fall admission, 8/11 priority date for domestic and international students; for winter admission, 12/28 priority date for domestic and international students; for spring admission, 4/22 priority date for domestic and international students. Applications are processed on a rolling basis. Application fee: $50. Electronic applications accepted. *Expenses:* Contact institution. *Financial support:* Career-related internships or fieldwork and tuition waivers (full) available. Financial award application deadline: 1/7. *Unit head:* Dr. Karen D. Bowser, Associate Dean of Doctoral Programs, 954-262-8677, Fax: 954-262-3606, E-mail: bowserk@nova.edu. *Application contact:* Dr. Jennifer Quinones Nottingham, Dean of Student Affairs, 800-986-3223 Ext. 8624, Fax: 954-262-3883, E-mail: jlquinon@nova.edu.

Oakland University, Graduate Study and Lifelong Learning, School of Education and Human Services, Department of Educational Leadership, Rochester, MI 48309-4401. Offers educational leadership (M Ed, PhD); higher education (Certificate); higher education administration (Certificate); school administration (Ed S). *Entrance requirements:* Additional exam requirements/recommendations for international students: Required—TOEFL (minimum score 550 paper-based; 213 computer-based).

Ohio University, Graduate College, College of Education, Department of Counseling and Higher Education, Athens, OH 45701-2979. Offers college student personnel (M Ed); community/agency counseling (M Ed); counselor education (PhD); higher education (PhD); rehabilitation counseling (M Ed); school counseling (M Ed). *Accreditation:* ACA; CORE. Part-time and evening/weekend programs available. *Faculty:* 12 full-time (6 women), 7 part-time/adjunct (1 woman). *Students:* 164 full-time (120 women), 51 part-time (30 women); includes 36 minority (27 African Americans, 3 American Indian/Alaska Native, 3 Asian Americans or Pacific Islanders, 3 Hispanic Americans), 9 international. 129 applicants, 58% accepted, 57 enrolled. In 2009, 60 master's, 16 doctorates awarded. *Degree requirements:* For master's, comprehensive exam (for some programs), thesis or alternative; for doctorate, comprehensive exam, thesis/dissertation. *Entrance requirements:* For master's, GRE General Test or MAT (if GPA less than 2.9), 3 letters of reference; for doctorate, GRE General Test, work experience, minimum GPA of 3.4. Additional exam requirements/recommendations for international students: Required—TOEFL (minimum score 550 paper-based; 80 iBT) or IELTS Academic (minimum score 6.5). *Application deadline:* For fall admission, 1/15 for domestic and international students. Application fee: $50 ($55 for international students). Electronic applications accepted. *Expenses:* Tuition, state resident: full-time $7839; part-time $323 per quarter hour. Tuition, nonresident: full-time $15,831; part-time $654 per quarter hour. Required fees: $2931. *Financial support:* Research assistantships with full tuition reimbursements, teaching assistantships with full tuition reimbursements, Federal Work-Study, institutionally sponsored loans, tuition waivers (partial), and unspecified assistantships available. Financial award application deadline: 1/15. *Faculty research:* Youth violence, gender studies, student affairs, chemical dependency, disabilities issues. Total annual research expenditures: $527,983. *Unit head:* Dr. Tracy Leinbaugh, Chair, 740-593-0846, Fax: 740-593-0477, E-mail: leinbaug@ohio.edu. *Application contact:* Floyd J. Doney, Director of Student Affairs, 740-593-4400, Fax: 740-593-9310, E-mail: doney@ohio.edu.

Oklahoma State University, College of Education, School of Educational Studies, Stillwater, OK 74078. Offers higher education (Ed D). Part-time programs available. *Faculty:* 29 full-time (12 women), 22 part-time/adjunct (8 women). *Students:* 51 full-time (24 women), 190 part-time (124 women); includes 38 minority (13 African Americans, 22 American Indian/Alaska Native, 3 Hispanic Americans), 27 international. Average age 37. 90 applicants, 57% accepted, 27 enrolled. In 2009, 54 master's, 14 doctorates awarded. *Degree requirements:* For master's, thesis (for some programs); for doctorate, comprehensive exam, thesis/dissertation. *Entrance requirements:* For master's and doctorate, GRE or GMAT. Additional exam requirements/recommendations for international students: Required—TOEFL (minimum score 550 paper-based; 79 iBT). *Application deadline:* For fall admission, 3/1 priority date for international students; for spring admission, 8/1 priority date for international students. Applications are processed on a rolling basis. Application fee: $40 ($75 for international students). Electronic applications accepted. *Expenses:* Tuition, state resident: full-time $3716; part-time $154.85 per credit hour. Tuition, nonresident: full-time $14,448; part-time $602 per credit hour. Required fees: $1772; $73.85 per credit hour. One-time fee: $50. Tuition and fees vary according to course load and campus/location. *Financial support:* In 2009–10, 14 research assistantships (averaging $9,237 per year), 10 teaching assistantships (averaging $8,178 per year) were awarded; career-related internships or fieldwork, Federal Work-Study, scholarships/grants, health care benefits, tuition waivers (partial), and unspecified assistantships also available. Support available to part-time students. Financial award application deadline: 3/1; financial award applicants required to submit FAFSA. *Unit head:* Dr. Bert Jacobson, Head, 405-744-6275, Fax: 405-744-7758. *Application contact:* Dr. Gordon Emslie, Dean, 405-744-6368, Fax: 405-744-0355, E-mail: grad-i@okstate.edu.

Old Dominion University, Darden College of Education, Doctoral Programs in Higher Education, Norfolk, VA 23529. Offers PhD. Part-time programs available. Postbaccalaureate distance learning degree programs offered (minimal on-campus study). *Faculty:* 3 full-time (1 woman), 10 part-time/adjunct (5 women). *Students:* 8 full-time (4 women), 14 part-time (9 women); includes 5 minority (3 African Americans, 1 American Indian/Alaska Native, 1 Asian American or Pacific Islander), 1 international. Average age 37. 13 applicants, 54% accepted, 5 enrolled. In 2009, 3 doctorates awarded. *Degree requirements:* For doctorate, comprehensive exam, thesis/dissertation. *Entrance requirements:* For doctorate, GRE, master's degree, minimum graduate GPA of 3.5. Additional exam requirements/recommendations for international students: Required—TOEFL. *Application deadline:* For spring admission, 2/1 for

domestic and international students. Application fee: $40. Electronic applications accepted. *Expenses:* Tuition, state resident: full-time $8112; part-time $338 per credit. Tuition, nonresident: full-time $20,256; part-time $844 per credit. Required fees: $119 per semester. One-time fee: $50. *Financial support:* In 2009–10, 2 fellowships with tuition reimbursements (averaging $15,000 per year), research assistantships with full tuition reimbursements (averaging $15,000 per year), 6 teaching assistantships with full tuition reimbursements (averaging $15,000 per year) were awarded; career-related internships or fieldwork, tuition waivers (full), and unspecified assistantships also available. Financial award application deadline: 2/1. *Faculty research:* Law leadership, student development, research administration, international higher education administration, academic integrity, leadership. *Unit head:* Dr. Dana D. Burnett, Graduate Program Director, 757-683-3287, Fax: 757-683-5756, E-mail: dburnett@odu.edu. *Application contact:* Alice McAdory, Director of Admissions, 757-683-3685, Fax: 757-683-3255, E-mail: gradadmit@odu.edu.

Old Dominion University, Darden College of Education, Programs in Higher Education, Norfolk, VA 23529. Offers educational leadership (MS Ed, Ed S), including higher education. Part-time programs available. *Faculty:* 3 full-time (1 woman), 10 part-time/adjunct (5 women). *Students:* 38 full-time (26 women), 10 part-time (7 women); includes 15 minority (13 African Americans, 1 Asian American or Pacific Islander, 1 Hispanic American), 2 international. Average age 26. 43 applicants, 63% accepted, 20 enrolled. In 2009, 18 master's, 1 Ed S awarded. *Degree requirements:* For master's, comprehensive exam. *Entrance requirements:* For master's, GRE or MAT, minimum undergraduate GPA of 2.8; for Ed S, GRE or MAT, 2 letters of reference, minimum GPA of 3.5, master's degree. Additional exam requirements/recommendations for international students: Required—TOEFL. *Application deadline:* For fall admission, 3/1 priority date for domestic and international students; for winter admission, 10/1 for domestic and international students; for spring admission, 3/1 for domestic and international students. Applications are processed on a rolling basis. Application fee: $40. Electronic applications accepted. *Expenses:* Tuition, state resident: full-time $8112; part-time $338 per credit. Tuition, nonresident: full-time $20,256; part-time $844 per credit. Required fees: $119 per semester. One-time fee: $50. *Financial support:* Research assistantships with partial tuition reimbursements, career-related internships or fieldwork, scholarships/grants, and unspecified assistantships available. *Faculty research:* Law leadership, student development, research administration, international higher education administration. *Unit head:* Dr. Dana D. Burnett, Graduate Program Director, 757-683-3287, Fax: 757-683-5756, E-mail: hied@odu.edu. *Application contact:* Dr. Dana D. Burnett, Graduate Program Director, 757-683-3287, Fax: 757-683-5756, E-mail: hied@odu.edu.

Oral Roberts University, School of Education, Tulsa, OK 74171. Offers Christian school administration (K-12) (MA Ed, Ed D); Christian school curriculum development (MA Ed); college and higher education administration (Ed D); public school administration (K-12) (MA Ed, Ed D); public school teaching (MA Ed). *Accreditation:* NCATE. Part-time programs available. Postbaccalaureate distance learning degree programs offered (minimal on-campus study). *Faculty:* 7 full-time (2 women), 6 part-time/adjunct (2 women). *Students:* 344 full-time (223 women); includes 117 minority (93 African Americans, 7 American Indian/Alaska Native, 11 Asian Americans or Pacific Islanders, 6 Hispanic Americans). 80 applicants, 94% accepted, 65 enrolled. In 2009, 14 master's, 4 doctorates awarded. *Degree requirements:* For master's, comprehensive exam, thesis optional; for doctorate, comprehensive exam, thesis/dissertation. *Entrance requirements:* For master's, GRE General Test or MAT, minimum GPA of 3.0; for doctorate, minimum GPA of 3.0. Additional exam requirements/recommendations for international students: Required—TOEFL (minimum score 500 paper-based; 173 computer-based). *Application deadline:* For fall admission, 1/1 for domestic and international students; for spring admission, 1/1 priority date for domestic students, 1/1 for international students. Applications are processed on a rolling basis. *Expenses:* Contact institution. *Financial support:* In 2009–10, 4 research assistantships (averaging $5,000 per year) were awarded; scholarships/grants and unspecified assistantships also available. Financial award application deadline: 6/1; financial award applicants required to submit FAFSA. *Faculty research:* Teacher effectiveness, college success in high achieving African-Americans, professional development practices. *Unit head:* Dr. Kim Boyd, Dean, 918-495-7108, E-mail: kboyd@oru.edu. *Application contact:* Lance Miller, Graduate Admissions, 918-495-6553, Fax: 918-495-6222, E-mail: gradeducation@oru.edu.

Phillips Theological Seminary, Programs in Theology, Tulsa, OK 74116. Offers administration of church agencies (M Div); campus ministry (M Div); church-related social work (M Div); college and seminary teaching (M Div); global mission work (M Div); institutional chaplaincy (M Div); ministerial vocations in Christian education (M Div); ministry (D Min), including parish ministry, pastoral counseling, practices of ministry; ministry and culture (MAMC), including Christian education, congregational leadership, history and practice of Christian spirituality, theology, ethics, and culture; ministry of music (M Div); pastoral care and counseling (M Div); pastoral ministry (M Div); theological studies (MTS). *Accreditation:* ATS. Part-time programs available. Postbaccalaureate distance learning degree programs offered (minimal on-campus study). *Degree requirements:* For master's, thesis (for some programs); for doctorate, thesis/dissertation. *Entrance requirements:* For master's, minimum GPA of 2.5; for doctorate, M Div, minimum GPA of 3.0. *Faculty research:* Biblical studies, historical studies, theology and culture, practical theology, theology and film.

Pittsburg State University, Graduate School, College of Education, Department of Special Services and Leadership Studies, Pittsburg, KS 66762. Offers community college and higher education (Ed S); educational leadership (MS), including educational technology; educational technology (MS); general school administration (Ed S); special education (MS), including behavioral disorders, learning disabilities, mentally retarded. *Degree requirements:* For master's, thesis or alternative. *Entrance requirements:* For master's, GRE General Test or MAT. *Expenses:* Tuition, state resident: full-time $4212; part-time $176 per credit. Tuition, nonresident: full-time $11,530; part-time $480 per credit. Required fees: $940; $43 per credit. Tuition and fees vary according to course level, course load, degree level, campus/location, reciprocity agreements and student level.

Portland State University, Graduate Studies, School of Education, Department of Educational Policy, Foundations, and Administrative Studies, Portland, OR 97207-0751. Offers educational leadership (MA, MS, Ed D); postsecondary, adult and continuing education (Ed D). *Accreditation:* NCATE. Part-time and evening/weekend programs available. *Degree requirements:* For master's, thesis or alternative, written exam or research project; for doctorate, comprehensive exam, thesis/dissertation. *Entrance requirements:* For master's, California Basic Educational Skills Test, minimum GPA of 3.0 in upper-division course work or 2.75 overall; for doctorate, GRE General Test or MAT. Additional exam requirements/recommendations for international students: Required—TOEFL (minimum score 550 paper-based; 213 computer-based). *Faculty research:* Leadership development and research, principals and urban schools, accelerated schools, cooperative learning, family involvement in schools.

Purdue University, Graduate School, School of Education, Department of Educational Studies, West Lafayette, IN 47907. Offers administration (MS Ed, PhD, Ed S); counseling and development (MS Ed, PhD); education of the gifted (MS Ed); educational psychology (MS Ed, PhD); foundations of education (MS Ed, PhD); higher education administration (MS Ed, PhD); special education (MS Ed, PhD). *Accreditation:* ACA (one or more programs are accredited); NCATE (one or more programs are accredited). Part-time and evening/weekend programs available. *Degree requirements:* For master's, thesis optional; for doctorate, thesis/dissertation, oral and written exams; for Ed S, oral presentation, project. *Entrance requirements:* For master's, GRE General Test, minimum undergraduate GPA of 3.0; for doctorate, GRE General Test; for Ed S, GRE, minimum B average. Additional exam requirements/recommendations for international students: Required—TOEFL. Electronic applications accepted. *Faculty research:* Motivation, learning disabilities, school learning, group processes, cognitive development.

Rowan University, Graduate School, College of Education, Department of Educational Leadership, Program in Higher Education Administration, Glassboro, NJ 08028-1701. Offers

MA. *Accreditation:* NCATE. Part-time and evening/weekend programs available. *Students:* 17 full-time (11 women), 21 part-time (16 women); includes 12 minority (10 African Americans, 2 Hispanic Americans). Average age 25. 23 applicants, 91% accepted, 14 enrolled. In 2009, 19 master's awarded. *Degree requirements:* For master's, comprehensive exam, thesis. *Entrance requirements:* For master's, GRE General Test, minimum GPA of 2.8, 2 years of teaching experience. Additional exam requirements/recommendations for international students: Required—TOEFL. *Application deadline:* Applications are processed on a rolling basis. Application fee: $50. Electronic applications accepted. *Expenses:* Tuition, state resident: full-time $10,624; part-time $590 per semester hour. Tuition, nonresident: full-time $10,624; part-time $590 per semester hour. Required fees: $2320; $125 per semester hour. *Financial support:* Career-related internships or fieldwork, scholarships/grants, health care benefits, and unspecified assistantships available. Support available to part-time students. *Unit head:* Dr. Mira Lalovic-Hand, Interim Associate Provost/Director of Graduate School, 856-256-5120, E-mail: lalovic-hand@rowan.edu. *Application contact:* Karen Haynes, Graduate Coordinator, 856-256-4052, Fax: 856-256-4436, E-mail: haynes@rowan.edu.

St. Cloud State University, School of Graduate Studies, College of Education, Department of Counselor Education, Higher Education, and Educational Psychology, Program in Higher Education Administration, St. Cloud, MN 56301-4498. Offers MS, Ed D. *Students:* 16 full-time (9 women), 52 part-time (28 women); includes 9 minority (3 African Americans, 1 American Indian/Alaska Native, 5 Asian Americans or Pacific Islanders), 9 international. 19 applicants, 100% accepted. In 2009, 7 master's awarded. Application fee: $35. *Unit head:* Dr. Christine Imbra, Head, 320-308-4909, E-mail: cmimbra@stcloudstate.edu. *Application contact:* Linda Lou Krueger, School of Graduate Studies, 320-308-2113, Fax: 320-308-5371, E-mail: lekrueger@stcloudstate.edu.

Saint Leo University, Graduate Studies in Education, Saint Leo, FL 33574-6665. Offers educational leadership (M Ed, Ed S); exceptional student education (M Ed); higher education leadership (Ed S); instructional design (MS); instructional leadership (M Ed); reading (M Ed). Part-time and evening/weekend programs available. Postbaccalaureate distance learning degree programs offered (minimal on-campus study). *Faculty:* 13 full-time (10 women), 12 part-time/adjunct (9 women). *Students:* 432 full-time (355 women), 35 part-time (24 women); includes 56 minority (40 African Americans, 2 American Indian/Alaska Native, 2 Asian Americans or Pacific Islanders, 12 Hispanic Americans), 1 international. Average age 37. In 2009, 131 master's awarded. *Degree requirements:* For master's, comprehensive exam, appropriate State of Florida Certification Tests. *Entrance requirements:* For master's, GRE (minimum score of 1000) or MAT (minimum score of 410) if undergraduate GPA for last 60 hours of coursework was below 3.0 (for M Ed), bachelor's degree from regionally-accredited college or university with minimum GPA of 3.0 for last 60 hours of coursework, 2 recommendations, resume, statement of professional goals, copy of valid teaching certificate (for M Ed); for Ed S, GRE (minimum score 1000) or MAT (minimum score 410) if undergraduate GPA for last 60 hours of coursework less than 3.0, bachelor's degree from regionally-accredited college or university with minimum GPA of 3.0 for last 60 hours of coursework, 2 recommendations, resume, valid teaching certificate. Additional exam requirements/recommendations for international students: Required—TOEFL (minimum score 550 paper-based; 213 computer-based; 80 iBT). *Application deadline:* For fall admission, 7/1 priority date for domestic students; for spring admission, 11/12 priority date for domestic students. Applications are processed on a rolling basis. Application fee: $75. Electronic applications accepted. *Expenses:* Tuition: Part-time $1767 per course. Required fees: $115 per course. *Financial support:* Career-related internships or fieldwork, Federal Work-Study, and health care benefits available. Financial award application deadline: 3/1; financial award applicants required to submit FAFSA. *Faculty research:* The role of the school leader in data analysis of student achievement, teacher recruitment, and teacher effectiveness. *Unit head:* Dr. John Smith, Director, 352-588-8309, Fax: 352-588-8861, E-mail: med@saintleo.edu. *Application contact:* Jared Welling, Director, Graduate/Weekend and Evening Admission, 800-707-8846, Fax: 352-588-7873, E-mail: grad.admissions@saintleo.edu.

Saint Louis University, Graduate School, College of Education and Public Service and Graduate School, Department of Educational Leadership and Higher Education, St. Louis, MO 63103-2097. Offers Catholic school leadership (MA); educational administration (MA, Ed D, PhD, Ed S); higher education (MA, Ed D, PhD); student personnel administration (MA). *Accreditation:* NCATE. Part-time programs available. *Degree requirements:* For master's, comprehensive written and oral exam; for doctorate, comprehensive exam, thesis/dissertation, preliminary oral and written exams. *Entrance requirements:* For master's, GRE General Test, MAT, LSAT, GMAT or MCAT, letters of recommendation, resume; for doctorate and Ed S, GRE General Test, LSAT, GMAT or MCAT, letters of recommendation, resumé, goal statement, transcripts. Additional exam requirements/recommendations for international students: Required—TOEFL (minimum score 525 paper-based; 194 computer-based). Electronic applications accepted. *Faculty research:* Superintendent of schools, school finance, school facilities, student personal administration, building leadership.

Salem State College, School of Graduate Studies, Program in Higher Education in Student Affairs, Salem, MA 01970-5353. Offers M Ed. Part-time and evening/weekend programs available. *Students:* 13 full-time (12 women), 29 part-time (19 women); includes 6 minority (3 African Americans, 3 Hispanic Americans). Average age 32. 12 applicants, 100% accepted, 12 enrolled. In 2009, 8 master's awarded. *Entrance requirements:* For master's, GRE or MAT. Additional exam requirements/recommendations for international students: Required—TOEFL (minimum score 550 paper-based; 80 iBT), or IELTS (minimum score 5.5). *Application deadline:* For fall admission, 5/1 for domestic students. Application fee: $50. *Expenses:* Tuition, state resident: full-time $2520; part-time $275 per credit hour. Tuition, nonresident: full-time $4140; part-time $365 per credit hour. Required fees: $2430. *Financial support:* In 2009–10, 22 students received support. Career-related internships or fieldwork, Federal Work-Study, scholarships/grants, and unspecified assistantships available. Support available to part-time students. Financial award application deadline: 5/1; financial award applicants required to submit FAFSA. *Unit head:* Dr. Lee A. Brossoit, Program Coordinator, 978-542-6675, E-mail: lbrossoit@salemstate.edu. *Application contact:* Dr. Lee A. Brossoit, Assistant Dean of Graduate Admissions, 978-542-6675, Fax: 978-542-7215, E-mail: lbrossoit@salemstate.edu.

San Diego State University, Graduate and Research Affairs, College of Education, Department of Administration, Rehabilitation and Post-Secondary Education, San Diego, CA 92182. Offers educational leadership in post-secondary education (MA); rehabilitation counseling (MS), including deafness. Evening/weekend programs available. Postbaccalaureate distance learning degree programs offered. *Degree requirements:* For master's, comprehensive exam (for some programs), thesis (for some programs). *Entrance requirements:* For master's, GRE General Test, letters of reference. Additional exam requirements/recommendations for international students: Required—TOEFL. Electronic applications accepted. *Faculty research:* Rehabilitation in cultural diversity, distance learning technology.

San Jose State University, Graduate Studies and Research, Connie L. Lurie College of Education, Department of Educational Leadership, San Jose, CA 95192-0001. Offers educational administration (K-12) (MA); higher education administration (MA). *Accreditation:* NCATE. *Students:* 185 full-time (128 women), 76 part-time (53 women); includes 99 minority (7 African Americans, 2 American Indian/Alaska Native, 34 Asian Americans or Pacific Islanders, 56 Hispanic Americans). Average age 38. 108 applicants, 83% accepted, 81 enrolled. In 2009, 157 master's awarded. *Degree requirements:* For master's, thesis or alternative. *Application deadline:* For fall admission, 6/29 for domestic students; for spring admission, 11/30 for domestic students. Applications are processed on a rolling basis. Application fee: $59. Electronic applications accepted. *Financial support:* Career-related internships or fieldwork available. Financial award applicants required to submit FAFSA. *Unit head:* Dr. Noni Mendoza Reis, Chair, 408-924-3616, Fax: 408-924-3713. *Application contact:* Dr. Noni Mendoza Reis, Chair, 408-924-3616, Fax: 408-924-3713.

Santa Clara University, School of Education and Counseling Psychology, Department of Education, Program in Educational Administration, Santa Clara, CA 95053. Offers educational administration (MA), including administrative services, higher education. Part-time and evening/weekend programs available. *Students:* 3 full-time (all women), 29 part-time (21 women); includes 4 minority (2 African Americans, 2 Hispanic Americans), 1 international. Average age 34. 21 applicants, 57% accepted, 11 enrolled. In 2009, 15 master's awarded. *Degree requirements:* For master's, comprehensive exam. *Entrance requirements:* For master's, GRE or MAT, minimum GPA of 3.0. Additional exam requirements/recommendations for international students: Required—TOEFL. *Application deadline:* Applications are processed on a rolling basis. *Expenses:* Contact institution. *Financial support:* Fellowships, Federal Work-Study, scholarships/grants, and traineeships available. Support available to part-time students. Financial award application deadline: 5/15; financial award applicants required to submit FAFSA. *Unit head:* Patricia DeMarlo, Director, 408-554-4696. *Application contact:* Patricia DeMarlo, Director, 408-554-4696.

Seton Hall University, College of Education and Human Services, Department of Education Leadership, Management and Policy, Program in Higher Education Administration, South Orange, NJ 07079-2697. Offers Ed D, PhD. *Accreditation:* NCATE. Part-time and evening/weekend programs available. *Faculty:* 12 full-time (4 women), 1 part-time/adjunct (0 women). *Students:* 14 full-time (8 women), 62 part-time (39 women); includes 19 minority (13 African Americans, 6 Hispanic Americans), 9 international. Average age 41. 26 applicants, 81% accepted, 16 enrolled. In 2009, 6 doctorates awarded. *Degree requirements:* For doctorate, comprehensive exam, thesis/dissertation, internship. *Entrance requirements:* For doctorate, GRE or MAT, interview, minimum GPA of 3.5. Additional exam requirements/recommendations for international students: Required—TOEFL. *Application deadline:* For fall admission, 2/1 priority date for domestic students; for spring admission, 10/1 for domestic students. Applications are processed on a rolling basis. Application fee: $50. *Financial support:* In 2009–10, 7 research assistantships with tuition reimbursements (averaging $5,000 per year) were awarded. Financial award application deadline: 2/1.

Shippensburg University of Pennsylvania, School of Graduate Studies, College of Arts and Sciences, Department of Sociology and Anthropology, Shippensburg, PA 17257-2299. Offers organizational development and leadership (MS), including business, communications, education, environmental management, higher education, historical administration, individual and organizational development, public organizations, social structures and organizations. Part-time and evening/weekend programs available. *Degree requirements:* For master's, capstone experience. *Entrance requirements:* For master's, interview (if GPA less than 2.75), resume. Additional exam requirements/recommendations for international students: Required—TOEFL (minimum score 560 paper-based; 220 computer-based); Recommended—IELTS (minimum score 6). Electronic applications accepted.

Southeast Missouri State University, School of Graduate Studies, Department of Educational Leadership and Counseling, Cape Girardeau, MO 63701-4799. Offers counseling (MA, Ed S), including counseling education (Ed S), mental health counseling (MA), school counseling (MA); educational administration (MA, Ed S); higher education (MA). *Accreditation:* NCATE. Part-time and evening/weekend programs available. Postbaccalaureate distance learning degree programs offered. *Degree requirements:* For master's, comprehensive exam, thesis or alternative, graduate paper; for Ed S, comprehensive exam. *Entrance requirements:* For master's, GRE General Test, PRAXIS or MAT, minimum undergraduate GPA of 2.75, teacher certification; for Ed S, GRE General Test, PRAXIS or MAT, minimum graduate GPA of 3.5. Additional exam requirements/recommendations for international students: Required—TOEFL (minimum score 550 paper-based; 213 computer-based). Electronic applications accepted. *Expenses:* Tuition, state resident: full-time $4266; part-time $237 per credit hour. Tuition, nonresident: full-time $7506; part-time $417 per credit hour. Required fees: $427; $427.

Southern Illinois University Carbondale, Graduate School, College of Education, Department of Educational Administration and Higher Education, Program in Higher Education, Carbondale, IL 62901-4701. Offers MS Ed. *Accreditation:* NCATE. Part-time programs available. *Degree requirements:* For master's, thesis. *Entrance requirements:* For master's, GRE General Test or MAT, minimum GPA of 2.7. Additional exam requirements/recommendations for international students: Required—TOEFL. *Faculty research:* Student affairs administration, international education, community college teaching.

Stanford University, School of Education, Program in Social Sciences, Policy, and Educational Practice, Stanford, CA 94305-9991. Offers administration and policy analysis (Ed D, PhD); anthropology of education (PhD); economics of education (PhD); educational linguistics (PhD); evaluation (MA), including interdisciplinary studies; higher education (PhD); history of education (PhD); interdisciplinary studies (PhD); international comparative education (MA, PhD); international education administration and policy analysis (MA); philosophy of education (PhD); policy analysis (MA); prospective principal's program (MA); sociology of education (PhD). *Degree requirements:* For master's, thesis (for some programs); for doctorate, thesis/dissertation. *Entrance requirements:* For master's and doctorate, GRE General Test. Electronic applications accepted. *Expenses:* Tuition: Full-time $37,380; part-time $2760 per quarter. Required fees: $501.

Syracuse University, College of Arts and Sciences, Program in College Science Teaching, Syracuse, NY 13244. Offers PhD. Part-time programs available. *Students:* 4 full-time (3 women), 5 part-time (2 women); includes 1 minority (Asian American or Pacific Islander). Average age 39. *Entrance requirements:* For doctorate, GRE General Test, GRE Subject Test. Additional exam requirements/recommendations for international students: Required—TOEFL (minimum score 100 iBT). *Application deadline:* Applications are processed on a rolling basis. Application fee: $75. Electronic applications accepted. *Expenses:* Tuition: Full-time $26,808; part-time $1117 per credit. Required fees: $1024. *Financial support:* Fellowships with full tuition reimbursements, teaching assistantships with full and partial tuition reimbursements available. Financial award application deadline: 1/1; financial award applicants required to submit FAFSA. *Unit head:* Dr. John Tillotson, Director of Graduate Studies, 315-443-9137, E-mail: jwtilot@syr.edu. *Application contact:* Cynthia Daley, Information Contact, 315-443-2586.

Syracuse University, School of Education, Program in Higher Education, Syracuse, NY 13244. Offers MS, PhD. Part-time programs available. *Students:* 24 full-time (16 women), 44 part-time (30 women); includes 5 minority (3 African Americans, 1 American Indian/Alaska Native, 1 Asian American or Pacific Islander), 3 international. Average age 32. 62 applicants, 77% accepted, 22 enrolled. In 2009, 16 master's, 2 doctorates awarded. *Degree requirements:* For master's, thesis or alternative; for doctorate, thesis/dissertation. *Entrance requirements:* For doctorate, GRE, resume, interview, writing sample, 3-5 years of experience in higher education administration. Additional exam requirements/recommendations for international students: Required—TOEFL (minimum score 100 iBT). *Application deadline:* For fall admission, 2/1 priority date for domestic and international students; for spring admission, 10/15 for domestic students, 10/15 priority date for international students. Applications are processed on a rolling basis. Application fee: $75. Electronic applications accepted. *Expenses:* Tuition: Full-time $26,808; part-time $1117 per credit. Required fees: $1024. *Financial support:* Fellowships with full tuition reimbursements, research assistantships with full tuition reimbursements, teaching assistantships with full tuition reimbursements, career-related internships or fieldwork, Federal Work-Study, and unspecified assistantships available. Support available to part-time students. Financial award application deadline: 1/1; financial award applicants required to submit FAFSA. *Faculty research:* Faculty evaluation, teaching portfolios, student culture, college student personnel development, organizational culture. *Unit head:* Dr. Catherine Engstrom, Chair, 315-443-4763, E-mail: cmengstr@syr.edu. *Application contact:* Liza Rochelson, Graduate Recruiter, School of Education, 315-443-2505, E-mail: e-gradrcrt@syr.edu.

Taylor University, Master of Arts in Higher Education Program, Upland, IN 46989-1001. Offers MA. *Accreditation:* NCATE. Part-time programs available. *Faculty:* 1 full-time (0 women),

Higher Education

Taylor University *(continued)*
5 part-time/adjunct (0 women). *Students:* 30 full-time (17 women), 2 part-time (1 woman); includes 6 minority (3 African Americans, 1 Asian American or Pacific Islander, 2 Hispanic Americans). Average age 27. 30 applicants, 70% accepted, 15 enrolled. In 2009, 17 master's awarded. *Degree requirements:* For master's, thesis. *Application deadline:* For fall admission, 2/1 for domestic students, 1/1 for international students. Applications are processed on a rolling basis. Application fee: $100. *Expenses:* Tuition: Full-time $10,800. *Financial support:* In 2009–10, 22 students received support, including 30 fellowships (averaging $5,000 per year). Financial award applicants required to submit FAFSA. *Unit head:* Dr. Tim Herrmann, Graduate Chair, 765-998-5142, E-mail: tmherrmann@taylor.edu. *Application contact:* Cindi Carder, Program Assistant, 765-998-5373, Fax: 765-998-4577, E-mail: jccarder@taylor.edu.

Teachers College, Columbia University, Graduate Faculty of Education, Department of Organization and Leadership, Program in Higher Education, New York, NY 10027-6696. Offers Ed M, MA, Ed D, PhD. *Accreditation:* NCATE. *Students:* 43 full-time (30 women), 82 part-time (66 women); includes 46 minority (15 African Americans, 12 Asian Americans or Pacific Islanders, 19 Hispanic Americans), 5 international. Average age 31. 176 applicants, 66% accepted, 46 enrolled. In 2009, 37 master's, 2 doctorates awarded. *Degree requirements:* For doctorate, variable foreign language requirement, thesis/dissertation. *Entrance requirements:* For doctorate, master's degree, 2 years of professional experience. *Application deadline:* For fall admission, 5/15 for domestic students. Application fee: $65. *Financial support:* Career-related internships or fieldwork, Federal Work-Study, institutionally sponsored loans, and tuition waivers (full and partial) available. Support available to part-time students. Financial award application deadline: 2/1. *Faculty research:* Educational leadership, general management issues, finance and planning, organizational analysis and development, higher education issues. *Unit head:* Warner Burke, Chair, 212-678-3258. *Application contact:* Debbie Lesperance, Assistant Director of Admission, 212-678-3710, Fax: 212-678-4171.

Texas A&M University–Commerce, Graduate School, College of Education and Human Services, Department of Educational Leadership, Commerce, TX 75429-3011. Offers educational administration (M Ed, Ed D); educational technology (M Ed, MS); higher education (MS, Ed D); training and development (MS). Part-time programs available. Terminal master's awarded for partial completion of doctoral program. *Degree requirements:* For master's, comprehensive exam, thesis (for some programs); for doctorate, thesis/dissertation, departmental qualifying exam. *Entrance requirements:* For master's, GRE General Test; for doctorate, GRE General Test, writing skills exam, interview. Electronic applications accepted. *Faculty research:* Property tax reform, politics of education, administrative stress.

Texas A&M University–Commerce, Graduate School, College of Education and Human Services, Department of Secondary and Higher Education, Commerce, TX 75429-3011. Offers higher education (MS), including administration, teaching; learning technology and information systems (M Ed, MS), including educational computing, library and information science, media and technology; secondary education (M Ed, MS); supervision, curriculum, and instruction (Ed D); training and development (MS). Part-time programs available. Terminal master's awarded for partial completion of doctoral program. *Degree requirements:* For master's, comprehensive exam, thesis (for some programs); for doctorate, thesis/dissertation, departmental qualifying exam. *Entrance requirements:* For master's and doctorate, GRE General Test. Electronic applications accepted. *Faculty research:* Deviance, migration.

Texas A&M University–Kingsville, College of Graduate Studies, College of Education, Department of Education, Program in Higher Education Administration Leadership, Kingsville, TX 78363. Offers PhD. *Degree requirements:* For doctorate, one foreign language, comprehensive exam, thesis/dissertation. *Entrance requirements:* For doctorate, GRE General Test, MAT, minimum GPA of 3.25.

Texas Southern University, College of Education, Department of Educational Administration and Foundation, Houston, TX 77004-4584. Offers educational administration (M Ed, Ed D). Part-time and evening/weekend programs available. *Faculty:* 11 full-time (5 women), 2 part-time/adjunct (0 women). *Students:* 37 full-time (27 women), 70 part-time (50 women); includes 97 minority (92 African Americans, 5 Hispanic Americans). Average age 38. 51 applicants, 100% accepted, 39 enrolled. In 2009, 27 master's, 5 doctorates awarded. *Degree requirements:* For master's, comprehensive exam; for doctorate, comprehensive exam, thesis/dissertation. *Entrance requirements:* For master's, GRE General Test, minimum GPA of 2.5; for doctorate, GRE General Test or MAT, master's degree, minimum B+ average. Additional exam requirements/recommendations for international students: Required—TOEFL. *Application deadline:* For fall admission, 7/1 for domestic and international students; for spring admission, 11/1 for domestic and international students. Applications are processed on a rolling basis. Application fee: $50 ($75 for international students). Electronic applications accepted. *Expenses:* Tuition, state resident: full-time $1805; part-time $100 per credit hour. Tuition, nonresident: full-time $6470; part-time $343 per credit hour. Tuition and fees vary according to course level, course load and degree level. *Financial support:* Scholarships/grants and unspecified assistantships available. Support available to part-time students. Financial award application deadline: 5/1. *Unit head:* Dr. Emmanuel Nwagwu, Chair, 713-313-1055, E-mail: nwagwu_ec@tsu.edu. *Application contact:* Dr. Gregory Maddox, Dean of the Graduate School, 713-313-7011 Ext. 4410, Fax: 713-639-1876, E-mail: maddox_gh@tsu.edu.

Texas Tech University, Graduate School, College of Education, Department of Educational Psychology and Leadership, Lubbock, TX 79409. Offers counselor education (M Ed, PhD); educational leadership (M Ed, Ed D); educational psychology (M Ed, PhD); higher education (M Ed, Ed D); higher education: higher education research (PhD); instructional technology (M Ed, Ed D); instructional technology: distance education (M Ed); special education (M Ed, Ed D). *Accreditation:* ACA; NCATE. Part-time programs available. *Students:* 137 full-time (94 women), 335 part-time (236 women); includes 90 minority (27 African Americans, 6 American Indian/Alaska Native, 3 Asian Americans or Pacific Islanders, 54 Hispanic Americans), 34 international. Average age 36. 390 applicants, 51% accepted, 90 enrolled. In 2009, 113 master's, 18 doctorates awarded. *Degree requirements:* For master's, thesis optional; for doctorate, thesis/dissertation. *Entrance requirements:* For master's and doctorate, GRE General Test. Additional exam requirements/recommendations for international students: Required—TOEFL (minimum score 550 paper-based; 213 computer-based). *Application deadline:* For fall admission, 3/1 priority date for international students; for spring admission, 11/1 priority date for international students. Applications are processed on a rolling basis. Application fee: $50 ($75 for international students). Electronic applications accepted. *Expenses:* Tuition, state resident: full-time $5100; part-time $213 per credit hour. Tuition, nonresident: full-time $11,748; part-time $490 per credit hour. Required fees: $2298; $50 per credit hour. $555 per semester. *Financial support:* Research assistantships with partial tuition reimbursements, teaching assistantships with partial tuition reimbursements, career-related internships or fieldwork, Federal Work-Study, and institutionally sponsored loans available. Support available to part-time students. Financial award application deadline: 4/15; financial award applicants required to submit FAFSA. *Faculty research:* Psychological processes of teaching and learning, teaching populations with special needs, instructional technology, educational administration in education, theories and practice in counseling and counselor education K-12 and higher. *Unit head:* Dr. William Lan, Chair, 806-742-1998 Ext. 436, Fax: 806-742-2179, E-mail: william.lan@ttu.edu. *Application contact:* Dr. Joseph G. Claudet, Graduate Adviser, 806-742-1998, Fax: 806-742-2179.

Troy University, Graduate School, College of Education, Program in Postsecondary Education, Troy, AL 36082. Offers adult education (M Ed); biology (M Ed); criminal justice (M Ed); english (M Ed); foundations of education (M Ed); general science (M Ed); higher education administration (M Ed); history (M Ed); instructional technology (M Ed); mathematics (M Ed); music industry (M Ed); physical fitness (M Ed); political science (M Ed); public administration (M Ed); social science (M Ed); teaching english (M Ed). Also offered through the University College. *Accreditation:* NCATE. Part-time and evening/weekend programs available. *Students:* 267 full-time (192 women), 381 part-time (293 women); includes 326 minority (309 African Americans, 4 American Indian/Alaska Native, 5 Asian Americans or Pacific Islanders, 8 Hispanic Americans). Average age 34. 343 applicants, 90% accepted. In 2009, 480 master's awarded. *Degree requirements:* For master's, comprehensive exam, thesis. *Entrance requirements:* For master's, MAT (minimum score 385), minimum GPA of 2.5. Additional exam requirements/recommendations for international students: Required—TOEFL (minimum score 523 paper-based; 193 computer-based; 70 iBT), IELTS, or ACT Compass ESL (minimum score 270 on Listening, Reading, and Grammar with no individual score below 85 and a minimum score of 8 out of 12 on writing test). *Application deadline:* Applications are processed on a rolling basis. Application fee: $50. Electronic applications accepted. *Financial support:* Available to part-time students. Applicants required to submit FAFSA. *Unit head:* Dr. Andrew Creamer, Chair, 334-670-3350, E-mail: drcreamer@troy.edu. *Application contact:* Brenda K. Campbell, Director of Graduate Admissions, 334-670-3178, Fax: 334-670-3733, E-mail: bcamp@troy.edu.

TUI University, College of Education, Program in Education, Cypress, CA 90630. Offers adult education (MA Ed); aviation education (MA Ed); children's literacy development (MA Ed); e-learning (MA Ed); early childhood education (MA Ed); enrollment management (MA Ed); higher education (MA Ed); teaching and instruction (MA Ed); training and development (MA Ed). Part-time and evening/weekend programs available. Postbaccalaureate distance learning degree programs offered (no on-campus study). *Degree requirements:* For master's, capstone project with integrative paper. *Entrance requirements:* For master's, minimum GPA of 2.5 (students with GPA 3.0 or greater may transfer up to 30% of graduate level credits). Additional exam requirements/recommendations for international students: Required—TOEFL (minimum score 525 paper-based). Electronic applications accepted.

TUI University, College of Education, Program in Educational Leadership, Cypress, CA 90630. Offers e-learning leadership (MA Ed, PhD); educational leadership (MA Ed); higher education leadership (PhD); K-12 leadership (PhD). Part-time and evening/weekend programs available. Postbaccalaureate distance learning degree programs offered (no on-campus study). *Degree requirements:* For doctorate, comprehensive exam, thesis/dissertation, defense of dissertation. *Entrance requirements:* For master's, minimum GPA of 2.5 (students with GPA 3.0 or greater may transfer up to 30% of graduate level credits); for doctorate, minimum GPA of 3.4, course work in research methods or statistics. Additional exam requirements/recommendations for international students: Required—TOEFL. Electronic applications accepted.

Union Institute & University, Doctor of Education Program, Cincinnati, OH 45206-1925. Offers educational leadership (Ed D); higher education (Ed D). Postbaccalaureate distance learning degree programs offered (minimal on-campus study). *Faculty:* 2 full-time (0 women), 7 part-time/adjunct (3 women). *Students:* 19 full-time (13 women); includes 5 minority (3 African Americans, 2 Hispanic Americans). Average age 49. *Application deadline:* Applications are processed on a rolling basis. Tuition and fees vary according to course load, degree level, campus/location and program. *Financial support:* Federal Work-Study and scholarships/grants available. *Unit head:* Dr. Arlene Sacks, Dean, 305-653-6713, E-mail: arlene.sacks@myunion.edu. *Application contact:* Michelle Flick, Admissions Counselor, 513-861-6400 Ext. 1225, E-mail: admissions@tui.edu.

Union University, School of Education, Jackson, TN 38305-3697. Offers education (M Ed, MA Ed); education administration generalist (Ed S); educational leadership (Ed D); educational supervision (Ed S); higher education (Ed D). M Ed also available at Germantown campus. *Accreditation:* NCATE. Part-time and evening/weekend programs available. *Degree requirements:* For master's, thesis (for some programs), capstone research course; for doctorate, comprehensive exam, thesis/dissertation; for Ed S, thesis or alternative. *Entrance requirements:* For master's, MAT, PRAXIS II or GRE, minimum GPA of 3.0, teaching license, writing sample; for doctorate, GRE, minimum graduate GPA of 3.2, writing sample; for Ed S, PRAXIS II, minimum graduate GPA of 3.2, writing sample. *Faculty research:* Mathematics education, direct instruction, language disorders and special education, brain compatible learning, empathy and school leadership.

Universidad Central del Este, Graduate School, San Pedro de Macoris, Dominican Republic. Offers administration (M Ad); dentistry (DMD); development of educational and social policies (PhD); environmental engineering (ME); financial management (M Ad); higher education (M Ed); human resources (M Ad); public health (MPH). *Entrance requirements:* For master's, letters of recommendation.

Université de Sherbrooke, Faculty of Education, Program in Postsecondary Education Training, Sherbrooke, QC J1K 2R1, Canada. Offers M Ed, Diploma. *Degree requirements:* For master's, thesis.

University at Buffalo, the State University of New York, Graduate School, Graduate School of Education, Department of Educational Leadership and Policy, Buffalo, NY 14260. Offers educational administration (Ed M, Ed D, PhD); general education (Ed M); higher education administration (Ed M, Ed D, PhD), including student affairs (Ed D); school building leadership (LIFTS) (Certificate); school business and human resource administration (Certificate); school district business leadership (LIFTS) (Certificate); school district leadership (LIFTS) (Certificate); social foundations (PhD). Part-time and evening/weekend programs available. *Faculty:* 12 full-time (6 women), 13 part-time/adjunct (7 women). *Students:* 71 full-time (53 women), 159 part-time (99 women); includes 42 minority (27 African Americans, 1 American Indian/Alaska Native, 4 Asian Americans or Pacific Islanders, 10 Hispanic Americans), 20 international. Average age 36.7. 170 applicants, 59% accepted, 65 enrolled. In 2009, 29 master's, 24 doctorates, 29 other advanced degrees awarded. *Degree requirements:* For master's, comprehensive exam (for some programs), thesis optional; for doctorate, comprehensive exam, thesis/dissertation. *Entrance requirements:* For doctorate, GRE General Test or MAT, writing sample. Additional exam requirements/recommendations for international students: Required—TOEFL (minimum score 550 paper-based; 213 computer-based; 79 iBT). *Application deadline:* For fall admission, 3/1 priority date for domestic students, 3/1 for international students; for spring admission, 11/15 priority date for domestic students, 10/1 for international students. Applications are processed on a rolling basis. Application fee: $50. Electronic applications accepted. *Financial support:* In 2009–10, 6 fellowships with full tuition reimbursements (averaging $9,000 per year), 12 research assistantships with full tuition reimbursements (averaging $9,000 per year) were awarded; career-related internships or fieldwork, Federal Work-Study, institutionally sponsored loans, health care benefits, tuition waivers (full and partial), and unspecified assistantships also available. Financial award application deadline: 3/15; financial award applicants required to submit FAFSA. *Faculty research:* College access and choice, school leadership preparation and practice, public policy, curriculum and pedagogy, comparative and international education. Total annual research expenditures: $34,848. *Unit head:* Dr. William C. Barba, Chairman, 716-645-2471, Fax: 716-645-2481, E-mail: barba@buffalo.edu. *Application contact:* Bonnie Fisher, Admissions Assistant, 716-645-2110, Fax: 716-645-7937, E-mail: brfisher@buffalo.edu.

The University of Akron, Graduate School, College of Education, Department of Educational Foundations and Leadership, Program in Higher Education Administration, Akron, OH 44325. Offers MA, MS. *Accreditation:* NCATE. *Students:* 64 full-time (46 women), 50 part-time (33 women); includes 23 minority (20 African Americans, 2 Asian Americans or Pacific Islanders, 1 Hispanic American), 3 international. Average age 35. 56 applicants, 88% accepted, 24 enrolled. In 2009, 20 master's awarded. *Degree requirements:* For master's, written comprehensive exam. *Entrance requirements:* For master's, minimum GPA of 2.75. Additional exam requirements/recommendations for international students: Required—TOEFL (minimum score 550 paper-based; 213 computer-based; 79 iBT). *Application deadline:* Applications are processed on a rolling basis. Application fee: $30 ($40 for international students). Electronic applications accepted. *Expenses:* Tuition, state resident: full-time $6570; part-time $365 per credit hour. Tuition, nonresident: full-time $11,250; part-time $625 per credit hour. *Financial support:* Fellowships, research assistantships, teaching assistantships available. *Unit head:* Dr. Sandra

Coyner, Coordinator, 330-972-5822, E-mail: scoyner@uakron.edu. *Application contact:* Dr. Sandra Coyner, Coordinator, 330-972-5822, E-mail: scoyner@uakron.edu.

The University of Alabama, Graduate School, College of Education, Department of Educational Leadership, Policy, and Technology Studies, Higher Education Administration Program, Tuscaloosa, AL 35487. Offers MA, Ed D, PhD. Evening/weekend programs available. *Faculty:* 24 full-time (12 women), 1 (woman) part-time/adjunct. *Students:* 42 full-time (24 women), 102 part-time (61 women); includes 28 minority (24 African Americans, 1 American Indian/Alaska Native, 1 Asian American or Pacific Islander, 2 Hispanic Americans), 1 international. Average age 37. 75 applicants, 48% accepted, 30 enrolled. In 2009, 12 master's, 21 doctorates awarded. Terminal master's awarded for partial completion of doctoral program. *Degree requirements:* For master's, comprehensive exam; for doctorate, comprehensive exam, thesis/dissertation. *Entrance requirements:* For master's, GRE, MAT or GMAT; for doctorate, GRE or MAT. Application fee: $50 ($60 for international students). Electronic applications accepted. *Expenses:* Tuition, state resident: full-time $7000. Tuition, nonresident: full-time $19,200. *Financial support:* In 2009–10, 5 students received support. Career-related internships or fieldwork, scholarships/grants, and unspecified assistantships available. *Unit head:* Dr. Claire H. Major, Coordinator and Associate Professor, 205-348-6871, Fax: 205-348-2161, E-mail: bea@bamaed.ua.edu. *Application contact:* Donna Smith, Administration Assistant, 205-348-6871, Fax: 205-348-2161, E-mail: dbsmith@bamaed.ua.edu.

The University of Arizona, Graduate College, College of Education, Department of Educational Policy Studies and Practice, Program in Higher Education, Tucson, AZ 85721. Offers MA, PhD. *Faculty:* 6. *Students:* 35 full-time (22 women), 60 part-time (39 women); includes 27 minority (8 African Americans, 4 American Indian/Alaska Native, 4 Asian Americans or Pacific Islanders, 11 Hispanic Americans), 10 international. Average age 36. 88 applicants, 40% accepted, 18 enrolled. In 2009, 17 master's, 9 doctorates awarded. Terminal master's awarded for partial completion of doctoral program. *Degree requirements:* For master's, comprehensive exam, thesis; for doctorate, comprehensive exam, thesis/dissertation. *Entrance requirements:* For master's and doctorate, GRE General Test or MAT, minimum undergraduate GPA of 3.0, graduate 3.5. Additional exam requirements/recommendations for international students: Required—TOEFL (minimum score 550 paper-based; 213 computer-based; 79 iBT). *Application deadline:* For fall admission, 1/15 for domestic and international students. Applications are processed on a rolling basis. Application fee: $65. Electronic applications accepted. *Expenses:* Tuition, state resident: full-time $9028. Tuition, nonresident: full-time $24,890. *Financial support:* In 2009–10, 1 research assistantship with full tuition reimbursement (averaging $12,623 per year) was awarded; career-related internships or fieldwork, scholarships/grants, health care benefits, tuition waivers (partial), and unspecified assistantships also available. Financial award application deadline: 4/30. *Faculty research:* Technology transfer, higher education policy, finance, curricular change. Total annual research expenditures: $112,593. *Unit head:* Dr. John Cheslock, Professor and Interim Department Head, 520-626-7313, Fax: 520-621-1875, E-mail: grhoades@mail.ed.arizona.edu. *Application contact:* Sara J. Kersels, Administrative Assistant, 520-626-7313, Fax: 520-621-1875, E-mail: skersels@email.arizona.edu.

University of Arkansas, Graduate School, College of Education and Health Professions, Department of Rehabilitation, Human Resources and Communication Disorders, Program in Higher Education, Fayetteville, AR 72701-1201. Offers M Ed, Ed D, Ed S. *Accreditation:* NCATE. Part-time and evening/weekend programs available. *Students:* 26 full-time (17 women), 59 part-time (34 women); includes 15 minority (11 African Americans, 1 American Indian/Alaska Native, 1 Asian American or Pacific Islander, 2 Hispanic Americans), 3 international. In 2009, 14 master's, 7 doctorates awarded. *Degree requirements:* For master's, thesis optional; for doctorate, thesis/dissertation. *Entrance requirements:* For master's, GRE General Test, MAT or minimum GPA of 3.0; for doctorate, GRE General Test or MAT. Application fee: $40 ($50 for international students). *Expenses:* Tuition, state resident: full-time $7355; part-time $356.58 per hour. Tuition, nonresident: full-time $17,401; part-time $775.17 per hour. Required fees: $1203. *Financial support:* In 2009–10, 14 research assistantships were awarded; fellowships with tuition reimbursements, teaching assistantships, career-related internships or fieldwork and Federal Work-Study also available. Support available to part-time students. Financial award application deadline: 4/1; financial award applicants required to submit FAFSA. *Unit head:* Dr. Fran Hagstrom, Department Chairperson, 479-575-4758, Fax: 479-575-2492, E-mail: fhagstr@uark.edu. *Application contact:* Dr. Brent Williams, Graduate Coordinator, 479-575-4758, E-mail: btwilli@uark.edu.

University of Arkansas at Little Rock, Graduate School, College of Education, Department of Educational Leadership, Program in Higher Education Administration, Little Rock, AR 72204-1099. Offers Ed D. *Degree requirements:* For doctorate, comprehensive exam, oral defense of dissertation, residency. *Entrance requirements:* For doctorate, GRE General Test or MAT, interview, minimum graduate GPA of 3.0, teaching certificate, work experience.

The University of British Columbia, Faculty of Education, Department of Educational Studies, Vancouver, BC V6T 1Z1, Canada. Offers adult education (M Ed, MA); adult learning and global change (M Ed); educational administration (M Ed, MA); educational leadership and policy (Ed D); educational studies (PhD); higher education (M Ed, MA); society, culture and politics in education (M Ed, MA). Part-time and evening/weekend programs available. Terminal master's awarded for partial completion of doctoral program. *Degree requirements:* For master's, thesis; for doctorate, comprehensive exam, thesis/dissertation, master's thesis. *Entrance requirements:* For master's, minimum B+ average, 4-year undergraduate degree, field-related experience; for doctorate, minimum B+ average, 4-year undergraduate degree, master's degree, field-related experience. Additional exam requirements/recommendations for international students: Required—TOEFL (600 paper; 250 computer; 100 Internet-based) or IELTS (6.5). Electronic applications accepted. *Faculty research:* Educational leadership educational administration adult education politics in education, global change and adult learning.

University of Calgary, Faculty of Graduate Studies, Faculty of Education, Graduate Division of Educational Research, Calgary, AB T2N 1N4, Canada. Offers community rehabilitation and disability studies (M Ed, M Sc, Ed D, PhD, Graduate Certificate, Graduate Diploma); curriculum, teaching and learning (M Ed, M Sc, MA, Ed D, PhD, Graduate Certificate, Graduate Diploma); educational contexts (M Ed, MA, Ed D, PhD, Graduate Certificate, Graduate Diploma); educational leadership (M Ed, MA, Ed D, PhD, Graduate Certificate, Graduate Diploma); educational technology (M Ed, M Sc, MA, Ed D, PhD, Graduate Certificate, Graduate Diploma); gifted education (M Sc, MA, Ed D, PhD, Graduate Certificate, Graduate Diploma); higher education administration (Ed D); interpretive studies in education (M Ed, M Sc, MA, Ed D, PhD, Graduate Certificate, Graduate Diploma); second language teaching (M Ed, Ed D, PhD, Graduate Certificate, Graduate Diploma); teaching English as a second language (M Ed, M Sc, MA, Ed D, PhD, Graduate Certificate, Graduate Diploma); workplace and adult learning (M Ed, MA, Ed D, PhD, Graduate Certificate, Graduate Diploma). Ed D in both higher education administration and educational leadership offered via distance delivery. Part-time and evening/weekend programs available. Postbaccalaureate distance learning degree programs offered (minimal on-campus study). *Degree requirements:* For master's, thesis (for some programs); for doctorate, thesis/dissertation, candidacy exam. *Entrance requirements:* For master's, minimum GPA of 3.0, 3 letters of reference; for doctorate, minimum GPA of 3.5, 3 letters of reference; for other advanced degree, minimum GPA of 3.0. Additional exam requirements/recommendations for international students: Required—TOEFL, IELTS. Electronic applications accepted. *Faculty research:* Curriculum, leadership, technology, contexts, gifted, second language teaching, work place and adult learning.

University of California, Riverside, Graduate Division, Graduate School of Education, Riverside, CA 92521-0102. Offers autism (M Ed); curriculum and instruction (MA, PhD); diversity and equity (M Ed); educational leadership and policy (MA, PhD); educational psychology (MA, PhD); general education (M Ed); higher education administration and policy (M Ed, PhD); leadership (M Ed); reading (M Ed); school psychology (PhD); special education (M Ed, MA, PhD). *Faculty:* 23 full-time (12 women), 12 part-time/adjunct (8 women). *Students:* 230 full-time (183 women), 6 part-time (3 women); includes 75 minority (12 African Americans, 1 American Indian/Alaska Native, 21 Asian Americans or Pacific Islanders, 41 Hispanic Americans), 6 international. Average age 32. 288 applicants, 60% accepted, 118 enrolled. In 2009, 68 master's, 13 doctorates awarded. Terminal master's awarded for partial completion of doctoral program. *Degree requirements:* For master's, comprehensive exam (for some programs), comprehensive exams or thesis (MA), case study or analytical report (M Ed); for doctorate, thesis/dissertation, written and oral qualifying exams, college teaching practicum. *Entrance requirements:* For master's, GRE General Test, GRE Subject Test, CBEST, CSET, minimum GPA of 3.2; for doctorate, GRE General Test, GRE Subject Test, master's degree (desirable), minimum GPA of 3.2. Additional exam requirements/recommendations for international students: Required—TOEFL (minimum score 550 paper-based; 213 computer-based; 80 iBT). *Application deadline:* For fall admission, 9/1 for domestic students, 4/1 for international students; for winter admission, 12/1 for domestic students, 9/1 for international students; for spring admission, 3/1 for domestic students, 10/1 for international students. Applications are processed on a rolling basis. Application fee: $70 ($85 for international students). Electronic applications accepted. *Financial support:* In 2009–10, 55 students received support, including 13 fellowships with full and partial tuition reimbursements available (averaging $26,809 per year), 21 research assistantships with full and partial tuition reimbursements available (averaging $14,238 per year), 1 teaching assistantship with full and partial tuition reimbursement available (averaging $16,638 per year); career-related internships or fieldwork, Federal Work-Study, institutionally sponsored loans, scholarships/grants, and unspecified assistantships also available. Financial award application deadline: 1/5; financial award applicants required to submit FAFSA. *Faculty research:* Responsiveness to intervention, faculty core, response to intervention of English language learners, advanced modeling techniques, study on social capital, trust, and motivation. Total annual research expenditures: $5.6 million. *Unit head:* Dr. Steven T. Bossert, Dean, 951-827-5802, Fax: 951-827-3942, E-mail: steven.bossert@ucr.edu. *Application contact:* Dr. John Wills, Graduate Advisor for Admission, 951-827-6362, Fax: 951-827-3942, E-mail: edgrad@ucr.edu.

University of Central Florida, College of Education, Education PhD Program, Orlando, FL 32816. Offers communication sciences and disorders (PhD); counselor education (PhD); elementary education (PhD); exceptional education (PhD); higher education (PhD); hospitality education (PhD); instructional technology (PhD); mathematics education (PhD); science education (PhD); social science education (PhD). *Students:* 99 full-time (70 women), 14 part-time (9 women); includes 28 minority (17 African Americans, 2 Asian Americans or Pacific Islanders, 9 Hispanic Americans), 20 international. In 2009, 15 doctorates awarded. Application fee: $30. Electronic applications accepted. *Expenses:* Tuition, state resident: part-time $306.31 per credit hour. Tuition, nonresident: part-time $1099.01 per credit hour. Part-time tuition and fees vary according to degree level and program. *Financial support:* In 2009–10, 40 fellowships with partial tuition reimbursements (averaging $9,200 per year), 61 research assistantships with partial tuition reimbursements (averaging $7,800 per year), 18 teaching assistantships with partial tuition reimbursements (averaging $6,500 per year) were awarded. *Unit head:* Dr. B. Grant Hayes, Associate Dean, 407-823-5391, E-mail: ghayes@mail.ucf.edu. *Application contact:* Dr. B. Grant Hayes, Associate Dean, 407-823-5391, E-mail: ghayes@mail.ucf.edu.

University of Central Oklahoma, College of Graduate Studies and Research, College of Education, Department of Occupational and Technical Education, Program in General Education, Edmond, OK 73034-5209. Offers M Ed. *Accreditation:* NCATE. Part-time programs available. *Faculty:* 27 full-time (18 women), 7 part-time/adjunct (3 women). *Students:* 72 full-time (52 women), 160 part-time (118 women); includes 42 minority (12 African Americans, 9 American Indian/Alaska Native, 3 Asian Americans or Pacific Islanders, 18 Hispanic Americans), 42 international. Average age 35. 39 applicants, 100% accepted. In 2009, 61 master's awarded. *Entrance requirements:* For master's, GRE General Test. Additional exam requirements/recommendations for international students: Required—TOEFL (minimum score 550 paper-based; 213 computer-based). *Application deadline:* For fall admission, 7/1 for international students; for spring admission, 11/1 for international students. Applications are processed on a rolling basis. Application fee: $25. Electronic applications accepted. *Expenses:* Tuition, state resident: full-time $4128; part-time $172 per credit hour. Tuition, nonresident: full-time $10,373; part-time $432.20 per credit hour. Required fees: $433.20; $18.05 per credit hour. *Financial support:* Application deadline: 3/31. *Faculty research:* Community college education. *Unit head:* Dr. Candy Sebert, Director, 405-974-5780. *Application contact:* Dr. Richard Bernard, Dean, Graduate College, 405-974-3493, Fax: 405-974-3852, E-mail: gradcoll@uco.edu.

University of Connecticut, Graduate School, Neag School of Education, Department of Educational Leadership, Field of Higher Education and Student Affairs, Storrs, CT 06269. Offers MA. *Accreditation:* NCATE. *Faculty:* 18 full-time (9 women). *Students:* 37 full-time (25 women); includes 12 minority (4 African Americans, 3 Asian Americans or Pacific Islanders, 5 Hispanic Americans). Average age 24. 188 applicants, 10% accepted, 14 enrolled. In 2009, 17 master's awarded. *Degree requirements:* For master's, comprehensive exam, thesis or alternative. *Entrance requirements:* Additional exam requirements/recommendations for international students: Required—TOEFL (minimum score 550 paper-based; 213 computer-based). *Application deadline:* For fall admission, 2/1 priority date for domestic and international students; for spring admission, 11/1 for domestic students, 10/1 for international students. Applications are processed on a rolling basis. Application fee: $55. Electronic applications accepted. *Expenses:* Tuition, state resident: full-time $4725; part-time $525 per credit. Tuition, nonresident: full-time $12,267; part-time $1363 per credit. Required fees: $346 per semester. Tuition and fees vary according to course load. *Financial support:* In 2009–10, 29 research assistantships with full tuition reimbursements, 8 teaching assistantships with full tuition reimbursements were awarded; fellowships, Federal Work-Study, scholarships/grants, health care benefits, and unspecified assistantships also available. Financial award application deadline: 2/1; financial award applicants required to submit FAFSA. *Unit head:* Barry G. Sheckley, Head, 860-486-2738, Fax: 860-486-4028, E-mail: barry.sheckley@uconn.edu. *Application contact:* Lisa Rasicot, Graduate Coordinator, 860-486-3065, Fax: 860-486-0210, E-mail: l.rasicot@uconn.edu.

University of Delaware, College of Human Services, Education and Public Policy and Department of Individual and Family Studies, Program in Counseling in Higher Education, Newark, DE 19716. Offers M Ed, MA. *Accreditation:* NCATE. *Degree requirements:* For master's, comprehensive exam. *Entrance requirements:* For master's, GRE (quantitative and verbal), on-campus interview, letters of recommendation. Additional exam requirements/recommendations for international students: Required—TOEFL (minimum score 600 paper-based). Electronic applications accepted. *Faculty research:* Counseling outcomes, student culture, group counseling.

University of Delaware, College of Human Services, Education and Public Policy, School of Education, Newark, DE 19716. Offers education (PhD); educational leadership (Ed D); higher education (M Ed); instruction (MI); reading (M Ed); school leadership (M Ed); school psychology (MA, Ed S); teaching English as a second language (TESL) (MA). *Accreditation:* NCATE. Part-time and evening/weekend programs available. Terminal master's awarded for partial completion of doctoral program. *Degree requirements:* For master's, comprehensive exam (for some programs), thesis (for some programs); for doctorate, comprehensive exam (for some programs), thesis/dissertation. *Entrance requirements:* For master's and doctorate, GRE, 3 letters of recommendation. Additional exam requirements/recommendations for international students: Required—TOEFL (minimum score 600 paper-based; 250 computer-based). Electronic applications accepted. *Faculty research:* Teacher education; curriculum theory and development; community based education models, educational leadership.

University of Denver, College of Education, Denver, CO 80208. Offers counseling psychology (MA, PhD); curriculum and instruction (MA, PhD, Certificate), including curriculum leadership (MA, PhD); educational administration and policy studies (Certificate); educational psychology (MA, PhD, Ed S), including child and family studies (MA, PhD), quantitative research methods (MA, PhD), school psychology (PhD, Ed S); higher education and adult studies (MA, PhD); library and information science (MLIS); library and information sciences (Certificate); school

Higher Education

University of Denver (continued)
administration (PhD). *Accreditation:* ALA; APA (one or more programs are accredited). Part-time and evening/weekend programs available. Postbaccalaureate distance learning degree programs offered (no on-campus study). *Faculty:* 33 full-time (24 women), 62 part-time/adjunct (41 women). *Students:* 384 full-time (305 women), 453 part-time (336 women); includes 164 minority (47 African Americans, 8 American Indian/Alaska Native, 14 Asian Americans or Pacific Islanders, 95 Hispanic Americans), 20 international. Average age 34. 1,065 applicants, 59% accepted, 433 enrolled. In 2009, 206 master's, 38 doctorates, 117 other advanced degrees awarded. Terminal master's awarded for partial completion of doctoral program. *Degree requirements:* For master's, comprehensive exam; for doctorate, 2 foreign languages, comprehensive exam, thesis/dissertation. *Entrance requirements:* For master's and doctorate, GRE General Test or MAT. *Application deadline:* Applications are processed on a rolling basis. Application fee: $50. Electronic applications accepted. *Expenses:* Tuition: Full-time $34,596; part-time $961 per quarter hour. Required fees: $4 per quarter hour. Tuition and fees vary according to course load, campus/location and program. *Financial support:* In 2009–10, 78 teaching assistantships with full and partial tuition reimbursements (averaging $11,700 per year) were awarded; career-related internships or fieldwork, Federal Work-Study, institutionally sponsored loans, and scholarships/grants also available. Support available to part-time students. Financial award application deadline: 3/1; financial award applicants required to submit FAFSA. *Faculty research:* Parkinson's disease, personnel training, development and assessments, gifted education, service-learning, transportation, public schools. Total annual research expenditures: $340,000. *Unit head:* Dr. Gregory M. Anderson, Dean, 303-871-3665. *Application contact:* Janet Erickson, Director of Graduate Admission, 303-871-2485, E-mail: edinfo@du.edu.

University of Florida, Graduate School, College of Education, Department of Educational Administration and Policy, Gainesville, FL 32611. Offers curriculum and instruction (Ed D, PhD); educational leadership (M Ed, MAE, Ed D, PhD, Ed S); higher education administration (Ed D, PhD, Ed S); student personnel in higher education (M Ed, MAE); PhD/JD. *Accreditation:* NCATE. *Degree requirements:* For master's, thesis optional; for doctorate, variable foreign language requirement, thesis/dissertation. *Entrance requirements:* For master's, GRE General Test, minimum GPA of 3.0, teaching experience; for doctorate and Ed S, GRE General Test, minimum GPA of 3.0. Additional exam requirements/recommendations for international students: Required—TOEFL (minimum score 550 paper-based; 213 computer-based). Electronic applications accepted. *Faculty research:* Educational finance, community education, middle school curriculum, community college administration.

University of Georgia, Graduate School, College of Education, Program in Higher Education, Athens, GA 30602. Offers PhD. *Accreditation:* NCATE. *Students:* 23 full-time (11 women), 31 part-time (15 women); includes 10 minority (9 African Americans, 1 Hispanic American), 5 international. 24 applicants, 42% accepted, 11 enrolled. In 2009, 9 doctorates awarded. *Degree requirements:* For doctorate, thesis/dissertation. *Entrance requirements:* For doctorate, GRE General Test. *Application deadline:* For fall admission, 7/1 priority date for domestic students; for spring admission, 11/15 for domestic students. Application fee: $50. Electronic applications accepted. *Expenses:* Tuition, state resident: full-time $6000; part-time $250 per credit hour. Tuition, nonresident: full-time $20,904; part-time $871 per credit hour. Required fees: $730 per semester. *Financial support:* Fellowships, research assistantships, teaching assistantships, unspecified assistantships available. *Unit head:* Dr. Libby V. Morris, Director, 706-542-3464, E-mail: lvmorris@uga.edu. *Application contact:* Dr. Christopher C. Morphew, Graduate Coordinator, 706-542-0573, E-mail: morphew@uga.edu.

University of Houston, College of Education, Department of Educational Leadership and Cultural Studies, Houston, TX 77204. Offers administration and supervison (M Ed, Ed D); higher education (M Ed); historical, social, and cultural foundations of education (M Ed). *Accreditation:* NCATE. Part-time and evening/weekend programs available. *Faculty:* 6 full-time (4 women), 3 part-time/adjunct (0 women). *Students:* 57 full-time (42 women), 113 part-time (70 women); includes 82 minority (44 African Americans, 1 American Indian/Alaska Native, 12 Asian Americans or Pacific Islanders, 25 Hispanic Americans), 4 international. Average age 35. 102 applicants, 85% accepted, 65 enrolled. In 2009, 38 master's, 8 doctorates awarded. *Degree requirements:* For master's, comprehensive exam or thesis; for doctorate, comprehensive exam, thesis/dissertation. *Entrance requirements:* For master's, GRE General Test or MAT, minimum GPA of 3.0 in last 60 hours of course work; for doctorate, GRE General Test, interview, minimum GPA of 3.0 in last 60 hours. *Application deadline:* Applications are processed on a rolling basis. Application fee: $75 for international students. Electronic applications accepted. *Expenses:* Tuition, state resident: full-time $7676; part-time $320 per credit hour. Tuition, nonresident: full-time $14,324; part-time $597 per credit hour. Required fees: $3034. *Financial support:* In 2009–10, 2 fellowships with full tuition reimbursements (averaging $9,500 per year), 2 teaching assistantships with full tuition reimbursements (averaging $9,500 per year) were awarded; career-related internships or fieldwork, Federal Work-Study, institutionally sponsored loans, scholarships/grants, health care benefits, and unspecified assistantships also available. Support available to part-time students. Financial award application deadline: 2/1; financial award applicants required to submit FAFSA. *Faculty research:* Change, supervision, multiculturalism, evaluation, policy.

University of Illinois at Urbana–Champaign, Graduate College, College of Education, Department of Educational Organization and Leadership, Champaign, IL 61820. Offers Ed M, MS, Ed D, PhD, CAS. Part-time programs available. Postbaccalaureate distance learning degree programs offered (minimal on-campus study). *Faculty:* 10 full-time (3 women), 2 part-time/adjunct (both women). *Students:* 50 full-time (33 women), 168 part-time (104 women); includes 41 minority (23 African Americans, 10 Asian Americans or Pacific Islanders, 8 Hispanic Americans), 3 international. 146 applicants, 56% accepted, 53 enrolled. In 2009, 48 master's, 12 doctorates, 3 other advanced degrees awarded. *Entrance requirements:* For master's, minimum GPA of 3.0; for doctorate, GRE General Test, minimum GPA of 3.0, writing samples, interview. Additional exam requirements/recommendations for international students: Required—TOEFL (minimum score 620 paper-based; 260 computer-based; 105 iBT). *Application deadline:* Applications are processed on a rolling basis. Application fee: $60 ($75 for international students). Electronic applications accepted. *Financial support:* In 2009–10, 5 fellowships, 18 research assistantships, 3 teaching assistantships were awarded; tuition waivers (full and partial) also available. *Unit head:* Donald Hackmann, Interim Head, 217-333-0230, Fax: 217-244-3378, E-mail: dghack@illinois.edu. *Application contact:* Laura A. Ketchum, 217-333-0807, Fax: 217-244-3378, E-mail: lirle@illinois.edu.

The University of Iowa, Graduate College, College of Education, Department of Educational Policy and Leadership Studies, Program in Higher Education, Iowa City, IA 52242-1316. Offers MA, PhD, Ed S, JD/PhD. *Degree requirements:* For master's and Ed S, exam; for doctorate, comprehensive exam, thesis/dissertation. *Entrance requirements:* For master's, doctorate, and Ed S, GRE General Test, minimum GPA of 3.0. Additional exam requirements/recommendations for international students: Required—TOEFL (minimum score 550 paper-based; 213 computer-based; 81 iBT). Electronic applications accepted.

The University of Kansas, Graduate Studies, School of Education, Department of Educational Leadership and Policy Studies, Program in Educational Policy and Leadership, Lawrence, KS 66045-3101. Offers educational administration (Ed D, PhD); foundations (PhD); higher education (Ed D, PhD); policy studies (PhD). Part-time and evening/weekend programs available. *Students:* 116 full-time (70 women), 58 part-time (32 women); includes 28 minority (12 African Americans, 4 American Indian/Alaska Native, 7 Asian Americans or Pacific Islanders, 5 Hispanic Americans), 9 international. Average age 38. 69 applicants, 68% accepted, 39 enrolled. In 2009, 11 doctorates awarded. *Degree requirements:* For doctorate, comprehensive exam, thesis/dissertation. *Entrance requirements:* For doctorate, GRE General Test, minimum graduate GPA of 3.5. Additional exam requirements/recommendations for international students: Required—TOEFL (minimum score 570 paper-based; 230 computer-based; 80 iBT). *Application*

deadline: For fall admission, 7/1 for domestic and international students; for spring admission, 11/1 for domestic and international students. Applications are processed on a rolling basis. Application fee: $45 ($55 for international students). Electronic applications accepted. *Expenses:* Tuition, state resident: full-time $6492; part-time $270.50 per credit hour. Tuition, nonresident: full-time $15,510; part-time $646.25 per credit hour. Required fees: $847; $70.56 per credit hour. Tuition and fees vary according to course load and program. *Financial support:* Fellowships, research assistantships with full and partial tuition reimbursements, teaching assistantships with full and partial tuition reimbursements, scholarships/grants and unspecified assistantships available. Financial award application deadline: 3/15. *Faculty research:* Historical and philosophical issues in education, education policy and leadership, higher education faculty, research on college students, education technology. *Unit head:* Dr. Susan Twombly, Chair, 785-864-9721, Fax: 785-864-4697, E-mail: stwombly@ku.edu. *Application contact:* Denise Brubaker, Admissions Coordinator, 785-864-4458, Fax: 785-864-4697, E-mail: elps@ku.edu.

The University of Kansas, Graduate Studies, School of Education, Department of Educational Leadership and Policy Studies, Program in Higher Education Administration, Lawrence, KS 66045-3101. Offers higher education (MS Ed). Part-time and evening/weekend programs available. *Students:* 39 full-time (22 women), 20 part-time (18 women); includes 7 minority (3 African Americans, 1 American Indian/Alaska Native, 3 Hispanic Americans), 3 international. Average age 26. 106 applicants, 34% accepted, 29 enrolled. In 2009, 33 master's awarded. *Degree requirements:* For master's, comprehensive exam. *Entrance requirements:* For master's, minimum GPA of 3.0. Additional exam requirements/recommendations for international students: Required—TOEFL (minimum score 570 paper-based; 230 computer-based; 80 iBT). *Application deadline:* For fall admission, 2/1 for domestic and international students. Application fee: $45 ($55 for international students). Electronic applications accepted. *Expenses:* Tuition, state resident: full-time $6492; part-time $270.50 per credit hour. Tuition, nonresident: full-time $15,510; part-time $646.25 per credit hour. Required fees: $847; $70.56 per credit hour. Tuition and fees vary according to course load and program. *Financial support:* Fellowships with full and partial tuition reimbursements, career-related internships or fieldwork available. Financial award application deadline: 3/15. *Faculty research:* Higher education policy, faculty issues, research on college students, financial aid, access to higher education. *Unit head:* Dr. Susan Twombly, Chair, 785-864-9721, Fax: 785-864-4697, E-mail: stwombly@ku.edu. *Application contact:* Denise Brubaker, Admissions Coordinator, 785-864-4458, Fax: 785-864-4697, E-mail: elps@ku.edu.

University of Kentucky, Graduate School, College of Education, Program in Educational Policy Studies and Evaluation, Lexington, KY 40506-0032. Offers educational policy studies and evaluation (Ed D); higher education (MS Ed, PhD). *Accreditation:* NCATE. Terminal master's awarded for partial completion of doctoral program. *Degree requirements:* For master's, comprehensive exam, thesis optional; for doctorate, comprehensive exam, thesis/dissertation. *Entrance requirements:* For master's, GRE General Test, minimum undergraduate GPA of 2.75; for doctorate, GRE General Test, minimum graduate GPA of 3.0. Additional exam requirements/recommendations for international students: Required—TOEFL (minimum score 550 paper-based; 213 computer-based). Electronic applications accepted. *Faculty research:* Studies in higher education; comparative and international education; evaluation of educational programs, policies, and reform; student, teacher, and faculty cultures; gender and education.

University of Louisville, Graduate School, College of Education and Human Development, Department of Leadership, Foundations and Human Resource Education, Louisville, KY 40292-0001. Offers educational leadership and organizational development (Ed D, PhD); higher education (MA); human resource education (MS); p-12 educational administration (M Ed, Ed S). *Accreditation:* NCATE. Part-time and evening/weekend programs available. Postbaccalaureate distance learning degree programs offered. *Faculty:* 23 full-time (11 women), 14 part-time/adjunct (7 women). *Students:* 57 full-time (37 women), 189 part-time (125 women); includes 32 minority (28 African Americans, 2 Asian Americans or Pacific Islanders, 2 Hispanic Americans), 7 international. Average age 39. 103 applicants, 63% accepted, 59 enrolled. In 2009, 35 master's, 27 doctorates, 12 other advanced degrees awarded. *Entrance requirements:* For master's, doctorate, and Ed S, GRE General Test. Additional exam requirements/recommendations for international students: Required—TOEFL (minimum score 560 paper-based; 210 computer-based; 83 iBT). *Application deadline:* Applications are processed on a rolling basis. Application fee: $50. Electronic applications accepted. *Financial support:* In 2009–10, 28 students received support; fellowships, research assistantships, teaching assistantships, career-related internships or fieldwork, Federal Work-Study, scholarships/grants, and unspecified assistantships available. Financial award application deadline: 6/1; financial award applicants required to submit FAFSA. *Faculty research:* Evaluation of programs to improve elementary and secondary education; research on organizational and human resource development; student access, retention and success in post-secondary education; educational policy analysis; multivariate quantitative research methods. Total annual research expenditures: $4.2 million. *Unit head:* Dr. Bridgette Pregliasco, Acting Chair, 502-852-6204, Fax: 502-852-4563, E-mail: bridgette.pregliasco@louisville.edu. *Application contact:* Libby Leggett, Director, Graduate Admissions, 502-852-3101, Fax: 502-852-6536, E-mail: gradadm@louisville.edu.

University of Maine, Graduate School, College of Education and Human Development, Program in Higher Education, Orono, ME 04469. Offers M Ed, MA, MS, Ed D, CAS. *Accreditation:* NCATE. Part-time and evening/weekend programs available. *Students:* 23 full-time (17 women), 16 part-time (12 women); includes 1 minority (African American), 2 international. Average age 34. 30 applicants, 50% accepted, 5 enrolled. In 2009, 10 master's, 2 doctorates awarded. *Degree requirements:* For master's, thesis or alternative. *Entrance requirements:* For master's, MAT; for doctorate, GRE General Test, MA, M Ed, or MS; for CAS, MA, M Ed, or MS. Additional exam requirements/recommendations for international students: Required—TOEFL. *Application deadline:* For fall admission, 2/1 priority date for domestic students. Applications are processed on a rolling basis. Application fee: $65. Electronic applications accepted. *Financial support:* Federal Work-Study, institutionally sponsored loans, tuition waivers (full and partial), and unspecified assistantships available. Financial award application deadline: 3/1. *Unit head:* Dr. Janet Spector, Coordinator, 207-581-2444, Fax: 207-581-2423. *Application contact:* Scott G. Delcourt, Associate Dean of the Graduate School, 207-581-3291, Fax: 207-581-3232, E-mail: graduate@maine.edu.

University of Manitoba, Faculty of Graduate Studies, Faculty of Education, Department of Educational Administration, Foundations and Psychology, Winnipeg, MB R3T 2N2, Canada. Offers adult and post-secondary education (M Ed); educational administration (M Ed); guidance and counseling (M Ed); inclusive special education (M Ed); social foundations of education (M Ed). *Degree requirements:* For master's, thesis or alternative.

University of Mary, Program in Education, Bismarck, ND 58504-9652. Offers college teaching (M Ed); curriculum, instruction and assessment (M Ed); early childhood education (M Ed); early childhood special education (M Ed); elementary education administration (M Ed); emotional disorders (M Ed); learning disabilities (M Ed); reading (M Ed); secondary education administration (M Ed); special education (M Ed); special education strategist (M Ed). Part-time programs available. *Degree requirements:* For master's, portfolio or thesis. *Entrance requirements:* For master's, interview, letters of reference. Additional exam requirements/recommendations for international students: Required—TOEFL (minimum score 550 paper-based). *Expenses:* Tuition: Full-time $10,062; part-time $430 per credit. Tuition and fees vary according to course load, degree level, program and student level. *Faculty research:* Innovative pedagogy in higher education, technology in education, content standards, children of poverty, children with diverse learning needs.

University of Maryland, College Park, Academic Affairs, College of Education, Department of Education Leadership, Higher Education and International Education, College Park, MD 20742. Offers MA, Ed D, PhD. *Faculty:* 11 full-time (6 women), 3 part-time/adjunct (1 women). *Students:* 53 full-time (40 women), 26 part-time (18 women); includes 22 minority (15 African Americans, 1 Asian American or Pacific Islander, 6 Hispanic Americans), 8 international. 245

applicants, 36% accepted, 44 enrolled. *Application deadline:* For fall admission, 12/15 for domestic students, 2/1 for international students; for spring admission, 6/1 for international students. *Expenses:* Tuition, area resident: Part-time $471 per credit hour. Tuition, state resident: part-time $471 per credit hour. Tuition, nonresident: part-time $1016 per credit hour. Required fees: $337.04 per term. *Financial support:* In 2009–10, 2 fellowships (averaging $11,756 per year), 1 research assistantship (averaging $15,349 per year), 37 teaching assistantships (averaging $15,814 per year) were awarded. Total annual research expenditures: $157,387. *Unit head:* Dr. Thomas Weible, Acting Chair, 301-405-3589, Fax: 301-405-3573, E-mail: tweible@umd.edu. *Application contact:* Dean of Graduate School, 301-405-0358.

University of Massachusetts Amherst, Graduate School, School of Education, Program in Education, Amherst, MA 01003. Offers bilingual, English as a second language, and multicultural education (M Ed, CAGS); child study and early education (M Ed); children, families and schools (Ed D, CAGS); early childhood and elementary teacher education (M Ed); education policy and leadership (CAGS); educational administration (M Ed, CAGS); educational policy and leadership (Ed D); higher education (M Ed, CAGS); international education (M Ed); language, literacy and culture (Ed D); learning, media and technology (M Ed, CAGS); mathematics, science, and learning technologies (Ed D); policy studies (M Ed); policy studies in education (CAGS); reading and writing (M Ed); research and evaluation methods (Ed D); school counselor education (M Ed, CAGS); school psychology (CAGS); science education (CAGS); secondary teacher education (M Ed); social justice education (M Ed, Ed D, CAGS); special education (M Ed, Ed D, CAGS). *Accreditation:* NCATE. Part-time programs available. Postbaccalaureate distance learning degree programs offered (minimal on-campus study). *Faculty:* 74 full-time (41 women). *Students:* 377 full-time (268 women), 347 part-time (232 women); includes 115 minority (59 African Americans, 2 American Indian/Alaska Native, 16 Asian Americans or Pacific Islanders, 38 Hispanic Americans), 108 international. Average age 35. 708 applicants, 68% accepted, 266 enrolled. In 2009, 183 master's, 17 doctorates awarded. Terminal master's awarded for partial completion of doctoral program. *Degree requirements:* For master's, thesis or alternative; for doctorate, comprehensive exam, thesis/dissertation. *Entrance requirements:* Additional exam requirements/recommendations for international students: Required—TOEFL (minimum score 550 paper-based; 213 computer-based; 80 iBT), IELTS (minimum score 6.5). *Application deadline:* For fall admission, 1/15 for domestic and international students. Applications are processed on a rolling basis. Application fee: $50 ($65 for international students). Electronic applications accepted. *Expenses:* Tuition, state resident: full-time $2640; part-time $110 per credit. Tuition, nonresident: full-time $9936; part-time $414 per credit. Tuition and fees vary according to course load. *Financial support:* In 2009–10, 1 fellowship with full tuition reimbursement (averaging $8,036 per year), 92 research assistantships with full tuition reimbursements (averaging $8,555 per year), 83 teaching assistantships with full tuition reimbursements (averaging $4,661 per year) were awarded; career-related internships or fieldwork, Federal Work-Study, scholarships/grants, traineeships, health care benefits, tuition waivers (full), and unspecified assistantships also available. Support available to part-time students. Financial award application deadline: 1/15. *Unit head:* Dr. Linda L. Griffin, Graduate Program Director, 413-545-6984, Fax: 413-545-2873. *Application contact:* Jean M. Ames, Supervisor of Admissions, 413-545-0722, Fax: 413-577-0010, E-mail: gradadm@grad.umass.edu.

University of Massachusetts Boston, Office of Graduate Studies, Graduate College of Education, School Organization, Curriculum and Instruction Department, Boston, MA 02125-3393. Offers education (M Ed, Ed D), including elementary and secondary education/certification (M Ed), higher education administration (Ed D), teacher certification (M Ed), urban school leadership (Ed D); educational administration (M Ed, CAGS); special education (M Ed). *Degree requirements:* For master's and CAGS, comprehensive exam; for doctorate, comprehensive exam, thesis/dissertation. *Entrance requirements:* For master's, GRE General Test or MAT; for doctorate, GRE General Test or MAT, minimum GPA of 2.75; for CAGS, minimum GPA of 2.75.

University of Massachusetts Boston, Office of Graduate Studies, Graduate College of Education, School Organization, Curriculum and Instruction Department, Program in Education, Track in Higher Education Administration, Boston, MA 02125-3393. Offers Ed D. Part-time and evening/weekend programs available. *Degree requirements:* For doctorate, comprehensive exam, thesis/dissertation. *Entrance requirements:* For doctorate, GRE General Test or MAT, minimum GPA of 2.75. *Faculty research:* Women, higher education and professionalization, school reform, urban classroom, higher education policy.

University of Memphis, Graduate School, College of Education, Department of Leadership, Memphis, TN 38152. Offers adult education (Ed D); educational leadership (Ed D); higher education (Ed D); leadership (MS); policy studies (Ed D); school administration and supervision (MS). *Accreditation:* NCATE. Part-time and evening/weekend programs available. Postbaccalaureate distance learning degree programs offered (minimal on-campus study). *Faculty:* 10 full-time (5 women), 9 part-time/adjunct (2 women). *Students:* 34 full-time (21 women), 115 part-time (69 women); includes 87 minority (86 African Americans, 1 Hispanic American), 1 international. Average age 40. 27 applicants, 85% accepted, 5 enrolled. In 2009, 12 master's, 13 doctorates awarded. *Degree requirements:* For master's, comprehensive exam, thesis optional; for doctorate, comprehensive exam, thesis/dissertation. *Entrance requirements:* For master's and doctorate, GRE. *Application deadline:* For fall admission, 4/1 for domestic students; for spring admission, 10/1 for domestic students. Application fee: $35 ($60 for international students). Electronic applications accepted. *Expenses:* Tuition, state resident: full-time $6246; part-time $347 per credit hour. Tuition, nonresident: full-time $15,894; part-time $883 per credit hour. Required fees: $1160. Full-time tuition and fees vary according to course load, degree level and program. *Financial support:* In 2009–10, 70 students received support; research assistantships with full tuition reimbursements available, teaching assistantships, Federal Work-Study, scholarships/grants, and unspecified assistantships available. Financial award application deadline: 2/15; financial award applicants required to submit FAFSA. *Faculty research:* School improvement, social justice, online learning, adult learning, diversity. *Unit head:* Katrina Mayer, Interim Chair, E-mail: kmeyer@memphis.edu. *Application contact:* Larry McNeal, Professor, School Administration and Supervision Programs, E-mail: lmcneal1@memphis.edu.

University of Miami, Graduate School, School of Education, Department of Educational and Psychological Studies, Program in Higher Education Administration, Coral Gables, FL 33124. Offers enrollment management (MS Ed, Certificate); higher education leadership (Ed D); student life and development (Certificate). Part-time and evening/weekend programs available. *Students:* 14 full-time (10 women), 12 part-time (8 women); includes 13 minority (3 African Americans, 10 Hispanic Americans). Average age 31. 31 applicants, 52% accepted, 13 enrolled. In 2009, 10 master's, 1 doctorate awarded. Terminal master's awarded for partial completion of doctoral program. *Degree requirements:* For master's, comprehensive exam; for doctorate, thesis/dissertation, qualifying exam. *Entrance requirements:* For master's and doctorate, GRE General Test. Additional exam requirements/recommendations for international students: Required—TOEFL (minimum score 550 paper-based; 80 iBT); Recommended—IELTS (minimum score 6.5). *Application deadline:* Applications are processed on a rolling basis. Application fee: $65. Electronic applications accepted. *Financial support:* In 2009–10, 19 students received support. Career-related internships or fieldwork, institutionally sponsored loans, scholarships/grants, health care benefits, and unspecified assistantships available. Support available to part-time students. Financial award application deadline: 3/1; financial award applicants required to submit FAFSA. *Unit head:* Dr. Carol Anne Phekoo, Lecturer and Program Director, 305-284-5013, Fax: 305-284-3003, E-mail: cphekoo@miami.edu. *Application contact:* Marissa Stevenson-Jacobs, Graduate Admissions Coordinator, 305-284-2167, Fax: 305-284-3003, E-mail: mstevenson@miami.edu.

University of Michigan, Horace H. Rackham School of Graduate Studies, School of Education, Center for the Study of Higher and Postsecondary Education, Ann Arbor, MI 48109. Offers academic affairs and student development (PhD); development (AM); higher education (AM); individually designed concentration (PhD); medical and professional education (AM); organizational behavior and management (PhD); public policy (PhD); research, evaluation, and assessment (PhD); MBA/MA; MPP/MA. Terminal master's awarded for partial completion of doctoral program. *Degree requirements:* For master's, thesis optional; for doctorate, comprehensive exam, thesis/dissertation. *Entrance requirements:* For master's and doctorate, GRE General Test. Additional exam requirements/recommendations for international students: Required—TOEFL (minimum score 600 paper-based; 250 computer-based). *Application deadline:* For fall admission, 12/1 priority date for domestic students, 12/1 for international students. Application fee: $60 ($75 for international students). Electronic applications accepted. *Expenses:* Tuition, state resident: full-time $17,286; part-time $1099 per credit hour. Tuition, nonresident: full-time $34,944; part-time $2080 per credit hour. Required fees: $95 per semester. Tuition and fees vary according to course load, degree level and program. *Financial support:* Applicants required to submit FAFSA. *Unit head:* Dr. Stephen DesJardins, Chairperson, 734-647-1981, Fax: 734-764-2510, E-mail: sdesj@umich.edu. *Application contact:* Laura Mayers, Student Services Assistant, 734-764-7563, Fax: 734-763-1495, E-mail: ed.grad.admit@umich.edu.

University of Minnesota, Twin Cities Campus, Graduate School, College of Education and Human Development, Department of Organizational Leadership, Policy and Development, Program in Higher Education, Minneapolis, MN 55455-0213. Offers MA, PhD. *Students:* 56 full-time (33 women), 98 part-time (58 women); includes 19 minority (12 African Americans, 1 American Indian/Alaska Native, 2 Asian Americans or Pacific Islanders, 4 Hispanic Americans), 16 international. Average age 38. 49 applicants, 80% accepted, 29 enrolled. In 2009, 6 master's, 7 doctorates awarded. *Application contact:* Dr. Mary Trettin, Associate Dean, 612-625-6501, Fax: 612-626-1580, E-mail: mtrettin@umn.edu.

University of Mississippi, Graduate School, School of Education, Department of Educational Leadership and Counselor Education, Oxford, University, MS 38677. Offers counselor education (M Ed, PhD, Specialist); educational leadership (PhD); educational leadership and counselor education (M Ed, MA, Ed D, Ed S); higher education/student personnel (MA). *Accreditation:* ACA; NCATE. *Faculty:* 14 full-time (5 women), 1 part-time/adjunct (0 women). *Students:* 107 full-time (83 women), 192 part-time (129 women); includes 94 minority (91 African Americans, 2 Asian Americans or Pacific Islanders, 1 Hispanic American), 7 international. In 2009, 48 master's, 13 doctorates, 18 other advanced degrees awarded. *Degree requirements:* For doctorate, thesis/dissertation. *Entrance requirements:* For master's, GRE General Test, minimum GPA of 3.0; for doctorate, GRE General Test. Additional exam requirements/recommendations for international students: Required—TOEFL. *Application deadline:* For fall admission, 4/1 for domestic students; for spring admission, 10/1 for domestic students. Applications are processed on a rolling basis. Application fee: $25. Electronic applications accepted. *Financial support:* Scholarships/grants available. Financial award application deadline: 3/1; financial award applicants required to submit FAFSA. *Unit head:* Dr. Timothy Letzring, Acting Chair, 662-915-7069, E-mail: fdl@olemiss.edu. *Application contact:* Dr. Christy M. Wyandt, Associate Dean, 662-915-7474, Fax: 662-915-7577, E-mail: cwyandt@olemiss.edu.

University of Missouri, Graduate School, College of Education, Department of Educational Leadership and Policy Analysis, Columbia, MO 65211. Offers education administration (M Ed, MA, Ed D, PhD, Ed S); higher and adult education (M Ed, MA, Ed D, PhD, Ed S). Part-time programs available. *Faculty:* 15 full-time (8 women), 5 part-time/adjunct (4 women). *Students:* 212 full-time (128 women), 160 part-time (97 women); includes 35 minority (22 African Americans, 2 American Indian/Alaska Native, 4 Asian Americans or Pacific Islanders, 7 Hispanic Americans), 12 international. Average age 39. 186 applicants, 74% accepted, 91 enrolled. In 2009, 7 master's, 19 doctorates, 7 other advanced degrees awarded. *Degree requirements:* For doctorate, variable foreign language requirement, comprehensive exam (for some programs), thesis/dissertation. *Entrance requirements:* For master's, doctorate, and Ed S, minimum GPA of 3.0. Additional exam requirements/recommendations for international students: Required—TOEFL (minimum score 500 paper-based; 173 computer-based; 61 iBT), IELTS (minimum score 5.5). *Application deadline:* For fall admission, 2/15 priority date for domestic students; for spring admission, 10/15 for domestic students. Applications are processed on a rolling basis. Application fee: $45 ($60 for international students). Electronic applications accepted. *Financial support:* In 2009–10, 2 fellowships with full tuition reimbursements, 32 research assistantships with full tuition reimbursements, 4 teaching assistantships with full tuition reimbursements were awarded; institutionally sponsored loans, scholarships/grants, health care benefits, and unspecified assistantships also available. *Faculty research:* Administrative communication and behavior, middle schools leadership, administration of special education. *Unit head:* Dr. Jay Scribner, Department Chair, E-mail: scribnerj@missouri.edu. *Application contact:* Betty Kissane, 573-882-8231, E-mail: kissaneb@missouri.edu.

University of Missouri–St. Louis, College of Education, Division of Educational Leadership and Policy Studies, St. Louis, MO 63121. Offers adult and higher education (M Ed), including adult education; educational administration (M Ed, Ed S), including community education (M Ed), elementary education (M Ed), secondary education (M Ed); institutional research (Certificate). *Accreditation:* NCATE. Part-time and evening/weekend programs available. *Faculty:* 19 full-time (8 women), 7 part-time/adjunct (4 women). *Students:* 25 full-time (21 women), 196 part-time (137 women); includes 88 minority (84 African Americans, 1 Asian American or Pacific Islander, 3 Hispanic Americans), 4 international. Average age 36. In 2009, 66 master's, 25 Certificates awarded. *Degree requirements:* For master's, comprehensive exam (for some programs). *Entrance requirements:* Additional exam requirements/recommendations for international students: Required—TOEFL (minimum score 550 paper-based; 213 computer-based). *Application deadline:* For fall admission, 7/1 priority date for domestic and international students; for spring admission, 12/1 priority date for domestic and international students. Applications are processed on a rolling basis. Application fee: $35 ($40 for international students). Electronic applications accepted. *Expenses:* Tuition, state resident: full-time $5377; part-time $297.70 per credit hour. Tuition, nonresident: full-time $13,882; part-time $771.20 per credit hour. Required fees: $220; $12.20 per credit hour. One-time fee: $12. Tuition and fees vary according to course level, campus/location and program. *Financial support:* In 2009–10, 3 research assistantships (averaging $5,133 per year) were awarded. Financial award application deadline: 4/1; financial award applicants required to submit FAFSA. *Faculty research:* Educational policy research; philosophy of education; higher, adult, and vocational education; school initiatives, change, and reform. *Unit head:* Dr. E. Paulette Savage, Chair, 514-516-5944. *Application contact:* 314-516-5458, Fax: 314-516-6996, E-mail: gradadm@umsl.edu.

University of Missouri–St. Louis, College of Education, Interdisciplinary Doctoral Programs, St. Louis, MO 63121. Offers adult and higher education (Ed D); counseling (PhD); counselor education (Ed D); educational administration (Ed D); educational leadership and policy studies (PhD); educational psychology (PhD). *Faculty:* 72 full-time (33 women). *Students:* 23 full-time (18 women), 240 part-time (159 women); includes 76 minority (61 African Americans, 2 American Indian/Alaska Native, 7 Asian Americans or Pacific Islanders, 6 Hispanic Americans), 5 international. Average age 40. In 2009, 19 doctorates awarded. *Degree requirements:* For doctorate, thesis/dissertation. *Entrance requirements:* For doctorate, GRE General Test, 3 letters of recommendation; personal interview. Additional exam requirements/recommendations for international students: Recommended—TOEFL (minimum score 550 paper-based; 230 computer-based). *Application deadline:* For fall admission, 2/15 for domestic and international students; for spring admission, 10/1 for domestic and international students. Application fee: $35 ($40 for international students). Electronic applications accepted. *Expenses:* Tuition, state resident: full-time $5377; part-time $297.70 per credit hour. Tuition, nonresident: full-time $13,882; part-time $771.20 per credit hour. Required fees: $220; $12.20 per credit hour. One-time fee: $12. Tuition and fees vary according to course level, campus/location and program. *Financial support:* In 2009–10, 15 research assistantships (averaging $12,240 per year), 8 teaching assistantships (averaging $12,240 per year) were awarded. Financial award application deadline: 4/1; financial award applicants required to submit FAFSA. *Faculty research:* Higher education law and policy, gender and higher education, student retention, lifelong learning orientation, school counselor's role in violence prevention. *Unit head:* Dr. Kathleen Haywood, Director of Graduate Studies, 314-516-5483, Fax: 314-516-5227, E-mail:

Higher Education

University of Missouri–St. Louis (continued)
kathleen_haywood@umsl.edu. *Application contact:* Dr. Kathleen Haywood, Director of Graduate Studies, 314-516-5483, Fax: 314-516-5227, E-mail: kathleen_haywood@umsl.edu.

University of New Hampshire, Graduate School, Interdisciplinary Programs, Program in College Teaching, Durham, NH 03824. Offers MST. Program offered in summer only. Part-time programs available. *Faculty:* 17 full-time (7 women). *Students:* 3 part-time (1 woman). Average age 43. 1 applicant, 100% accepted, 1 enrolled. In 2009, 3 master's awarded. *Entrance requirements:* Additional exam requirements/recommendations for international students: Required—TOEFL (minimum score 550 paper-based; 213 computer-based; 80 iBT). *Application deadline:* For fall admission, 6/1 priority date for domestic students, 4/1 for international students; for spring admission, 12/1 for domestic students. Applications are processed on a rolling basis. Application fee: $65. Electronic applications accepted. *Expenses:* Tuition, state resident: full-time $10,380; part-time $577 per credit hour. Tuition, nonresident: full-time $24,350; part-time $1002 per credit hour. Required fees: $1550; $387.50 per semester. Tuition and fees vary according to course load and program. *Financial support:* Fellowships, research assistantships, teaching assistantships available. Financial award application deadline: 2/15. *Unit head:* Dr. Harry J. Richards, Dean, 603-862-3005, Fax: 603-862-0275, E-mail: harry.richards@unh.edu. *Application contact:* Sharon Andrews, Senior Administrative Assistant, 603-862-3005, E-mail: college.teaching@unh.edu.

The University of North Carolina at Greensboro, Graduate School, School of Education, Department of Curriculum and Instruction, Program in Curriculum and Teaching, Greensboro, NC 27412-5001. Offers higher education (PhD); teacher education and development (PhD). *Accreditation:* NCATE. *Degree requirements:* For doctorate, comprehensive exam, thesis/dissertation. *Entrance requirements:* For doctorate, GRE General Test. Additional exam requirements/recommendations for international students: Required—TOEFL. Electronic applications accepted.

University of Northern Colorado, Graduate School, College of Education and Behavioral Sciences, School of Educational Research, Leadership and Technology, Program in Higher Education and Student Affairs Leadership, Greeley, CO 80639. Offers PhD. Part-time programs available. *Faculty:* 1 full-time (0 women). *Students:* 13 full-time (10 women), 20 part-time (11 women); includes 6 minority (2 African Americans, 1 American Indian/Alaska Native, 3 Hispanic Americans), 1 international. Average age 33. 14 applicants, 79% accepted, 11 enrolled. In 2009, 4 doctorates awarded. *Entrance requirements:* For doctorate, GRE General Test, transcripts, 3 letters of recommendation. *Application deadline:* Applications are processed on a rolling basis. Application fee: $50 ($60 for international students). Electronic applications accepted. *Expenses:* Tuition, state resident: full-time $5770; part-time $320.55 per credit hour. Tuition, nonresident: full-time $13,847; part-time $769.27 per credit hour. Required fees: $948.78; $52.72 per credit. *Financial support:* Research assistantships, teaching assistantships available. Financial award application deadline: 3/1; financial award applicants required to submit FAFSA. *Unit head:* Katrina Rodriguez, Program Coordinator, 970-351-2861, E-mail: hesal@unco.edu. *Application contact:* Linda Sisson, Graduate Student Admission Coordinator, 970-351-1807, Fax: 970-351-2371, E-mail: linda.sisson@unco.edu.

University of Northern Iowa, Graduate College, College of Education, Department of Educational Leadership, Counseling, and Postsecondary Education, Program in Postsecondary Education, Cedar Falls, IA 50614. Offers student affairs (MAE). *Students:* 17 full-time (14 women), 14 part-time (10 women); includes 3 minority (2 African Americans, 1 Hispanic American), 1 international. 35 applicants, 60% accepted, 11 enrolled. In 2009, 12 master's awarded. *Degree requirements:* For master's, comprehensive exam, thesis or alternative. *Entrance requirements:* For master's, minimum GPA of 3.0. Additional exam requirements/recommendations for international students: Required—TOEFL (minimum score 500 paper-based; 180 computer-based; 61 iBT). *Application deadline:* For fall admission, 8/1 priority date for domestic students. Applications are processed on a rolling basis. Application fee: $30 ($50 for international students). Electronic applications accepted. *Financial support:* Career-related internships or fieldwork, Federal Work-Study, scholarships/grants, and tuition waivers (full) available. Financial award application deadline: 2/1. *Unit head:* Dr. Michael Waggoner, Professor, 319-273-2605, Fax: 319-273-5175, E-mail: mike.waggoner@uni.edu. *Application contact:* Laurie S. Russell, Record Analyst, 319-273-2623, Fax: 319-273-6792, E-mail: laurie.russell@uni.edu.

University of North Texas, Robert B. Toulouse School of Graduate Studies, College of Education, Department of Counseling and Higher Education, Program in Higher Education, Denton, TX 76203-5017. Offers M Ed, MS, Ed D, PhD, Certificate. *Accreditation:* NCATE. Part-time and evening/weekend programs available. *Degree requirements:* For master's, internship; for doctorate, comprehensive exam, thesis/dissertation. *Entrance requirements:* For master's, GRE General Test, recommendations; for doctorate, GRE General Test, admissions exam, recommendations, interview. Additional exam requirements/recommendations for international students: Required—proof of English language proficiency required for non-native English speakers; Recommended—TOEFL (minimum score 550 paper-based; 213 computer-based; 79 iBT). Application fee: $50 ($75 for international students). *Expenses:* Tuition, state resident: full-time $4298; part-time $239 per contact hour. Tuition, nonresident: full-time $9878; part-time $549 per contact hour. Required fees: $265 per contact hour. *Financial support:* Research assistantships, career-related internships or fieldwork, Federal Work-Study, institutionally sponsored loans, scholarships/grants, and unspecified assistantships available. Financial award applicants required to submit FAFSA. *Faculty research:* Access to higher education, transfer issues, student development, community colleges, diversity in higher education.

University of Oklahoma, Graduate College, College of Education, Department of Educational Leadership and Policy Studies, Program in Adult and Higher Education, Norman, OK 73019. Offers M Ed, PhD. *Accreditation:* NCATE. Part-time and evening/weekend programs available. *Students:* 112 full-time (45 women), 91 part-time (48 women); includes 51 minority (23 African Americans, 14 American Indian/Alaska Native, 6 Asian Americans or Pacific Islanders, 8 Hispanic Americans), 7 international. 124 applicants, 85% accepted, 58 enrolled. In 2009, 51 master's, 5 doctorates awarded. Terminal master's awarded for partial completion of doctoral program. *Degree requirements:* For master's, comprehensive exam; for doctorate, variable foreign language requirement, thesis/dissertation, general exam. *Entrance requirements:* For master's, minimum GPA of 3.0 in last 60 hours of undergraduate course work; for doctorate, GRE General Test, resume, 3 letters of reference, scholarly writing sample. Additional exam requirements/recommendations for international students: Required—TOEFL (minimum score 550 paper-based; 213 computer-based). *Application deadline:* For fall admission, 6/1 for domestic students, 4/1 for international students; for spring admission, 10/1 for domestic students, 9/1 for international students. Application fee: $40 ($90 for international students). Electronic applications accepted. *Expenses:* Tuition, state resident: full-time $3744; part-time $156 per credit hour. Tuition, nonresident: full-time $13,577; part-time $565.70 per credit hour. Required fees: $2415; $90.10 per credit hour. *Financial support:* In 2009–10, 148 students received support. Career-related internships or fieldwork, traineeships, health care benefits, and unspecified assistantships available. Financial award applicants required to submit FAFSA. *Faculty research:* Diversity, leadership, intercollegiate athletics, technology in learning, democratic education. *Unit head:* David Tan, Interim Chair, 405-325-5986, Fax: 405-325-2403, E-mail: dtan@ou.edu. *Application contact:* Dr. Kathleen Rager, Program Area Coordinator, 405-325-0548, Fax: 405-325-2403, E-mail: kbrager@ou.edu.

University of Phoenix, School of Advanced Studies, Phoenix, AZ 85034-7209. Offers business administration (DBA); education (Ed D); educational leadership (Ed D), including curriculum and instruction, educational leadership, educational technology; health administration (DHA); higher education administration (PhD); industrial/organizational psychology (PhD); nursing (PhD); organizational leadership (DM), including information systems and technology, organizational leadership. Evening/weekend programs available. *Faculty:* 83 full-time (47 women), 540 part-time/adjunct (264 women). *Students:* 7,749 full-time (5,032 women); includes 3,180 minority (2,473 African Americans, 61 American Indian/Alaska Native, 221 Asian Americans or Pacific Islanders, 425 Hispanic Americans), 490 international. Average age 44. In 2009, 467 doctorates awarded. *Degree requirements:* For doctorate, thesis/dissertation. *Entrance requirements:* For doctorate, 3 letters of recommendation, minimum master's GPA of 3.0, 3 years professional work experience. Additional exam requirements/recommendations for international students: Required—TOEFL (minimum score 550 paper-based; 213 computer-based; 79 iBT). *Application deadline:* Applications are processed on a rolling basis. Application fee: $45. Electronic applications accepted. *Expenses:* Tuition: Full-time $13,272. Required fees: $660. Full-time tuition and fees vary according to course level, degree level and program. *Financial support:* Institutionally sponsored loans and scholarships/grants available. Financial award applicants required to submit FAFSA. *Unit head:* Dr. Jeremy Moreland, Dean/Executive Director, 480-557-3231, E-mail: jeremy.moreland@phoenix.edu. *Application contact:* Information Contact, 800-697-8223.

University of Pittsburgh, School of Education, Department of Administrative and Policy Studies, Program in Higher Education Management, Pittsburgh, PA 15260. Offers higher education (M Ed, Ed D). Part-time and evening/weekend programs available. *Students:* 30 full-time (18 women), 51 part-time (34 women); includes 6 minority (all African Americans), 7 international. Average age 35. 61 applicants, 85% accepted, 24 enrolled. In 2009, 14 master's, 6 doctorates awarded. *Degree requirements:* For master's, thesis; for doctorate, thesis/dissertation. *Entrance requirements:* For doctorate, GRE General Test. Additional exam requirements/recommendations for international students: Required—TOEFL (minimum score 213 computer-based; 80 iBT). *Application deadline:* For fall admission, 2/1 priority date for domestic and international students; for spring admission, 11/1 priority date for domestic students, 7/1 priority date for international students. Applications are processed on a rolling basis. Application fee: $50. Electronic applications accepted. *Expenses:* Tuition, state resident: full-time $16,402; part-time $665 per credit. Tuition, nonresident: full-time $28,694; part-time $1175 per credit. Required fees: $690; $175 per term. Tuition and fees vary according to program. *Financial support:* Fellowships, Federal Work-Study, institutionally sponsored loans, scholarships/grants, health care benefits, tuition waivers (partial), and unspecified assistantships available. Support available to part-time students. Financial award application deadline: 3/15; financial award applicants required to submit FAFSA. *Unit head:* Dr. John C. Weidman, Chair, 412-648-7114, Fax: 412-648-1784, E-mail: weidman@pitt.edu. *Application contact:* Lauren Pasquini, Enrollment Manager, 412-648-2230, Fax: 412-648-1899, E-mail: soeinfo@pitt.edu.

University of San Diego, School of Leadership and Education Sciences, Department of Leadership Studies, San Diego, CA 92110-2492. Offers higher education leadership (MA); leadership studies (MA, PhD); nonprofit leadership and management (MA, Certificate). Part-time and evening/weekend programs available. *Faculty:* 8 full-time (5 women), 13 part-time/adjunct (9 women). *Students:* 23 full-time (12 women), 189 part-time (137 women); includes 63 minority (14 African Americans, 1 American Indian/Alaska Native, 17 Asian Americans or Pacific Islanders, 31 Hispanic Americans), 4 international. Average age 35. 186 applicants, 53% accepted, 72 enrolled. In 2009, 37 master's, 9 doctorates awarded. *Degree requirements:* For master's, thesis (for some programs), portfolio; for doctorate, comprehensive exam, thesis/dissertation. *Entrance requirements:* For master's, minimum GPA of 3.0, interview; for doctorate, GRE, master's degree, minimum GPA of 3.5 (recommended), interview, writing sample, resume. Additional exam requirements/recommendations for international students: Required—TOEFL (minimum score 580 paper-based; 237 computer-based; 83 iBT), TWE. *Application deadline:* For fall admission, 3/1 for domestic and international students. Application fee: $45. Electronic applications accepted. *Expenses:* Tuition: Full-time $21,042; part-time $1169 per unit. Required fees: $224. Full-time tuition and fees vary according to course load and degree level. *Financial support:* In 2009–10, 182 students received support. Career-related internships or fieldwork, Federal Work-Study, institutionally sponsored loans, unspecified assistantships, and stipends available. Support available to part-time students. Financial award application deadline: 4/1; financial award applicants required to submit FAFSA. *Faculty research:* Educational leadership, higher education policy and relations, leadership development, nonprofits and philanthropy, peace studies. *Unit head:* Dr. Cheryl Getz, Graduate Program Director, 619-260-4289, Fax: 619-260-6835, E-mail: cgetz@sandiego.edu. *Application contact:* Dr. John Mosby, Associate Director of Graduate Admissions, 619-260-4524, Fax: 619-260-4158, E-mail: grads@sandiego.edu.

University of South Carolina, The Graduate School, College of Education, Department of Educational Leadership and Policies, Program in Higher Education and Student Affairs, Columbia, SC 29208. Offers M Ed. *Accreditation:* NCATE. Part-time programs available. *Degree requirements:* For master's, comprehensive exam, thesis (for some programs). *Entrance requirements:* For master's, GRE General Test or MAT, letters of reference. Electronic applications accepted. *Faculty research:* Minorities in higher education, community college transfer problem, federal role in educational research.

University of Southern California, Graduate School, Rossier School of Education, Doctor of Education Programs, Los Angeles, CA 90089. Offers educational psychology (Ed D); higher education administration (Ed D); K-12 leadership in urban school settings (Ed D); teacher education in multicultural societies (Ed D). Part-time and evening/weekend programs available. *Faculty:* 59 full-time (32 women), 12 part-time/adjunct (3 women). *Students:* 567 full-time (361 women), 12 part-time (6 women); includes 339 minority (73 African Americans, 11 American Indian/Alaska Native, 129 Asian Americans or Pacific Islanders, 126 Hispanic Americans), 13 international. 300 applicants, 76% accepted, 182 enrolled. In 2009, 143 doctorates awarded. *Degree requirements:* For doctorate, thesis/dissertation. *Entrance requirements:* For doctorate, GRE. Additional exam requirements/recommendations for international students: Required—TOEFL (minimum score 250 computer-based; 100 iBT). *Application deadline:* For fall admission, 1/15 priority date for domestic and international students. Application fee: $85. Electronic applications accepted. *Expenses:* Tuition: Full-time $25,980; part-time $1315 per unit. Required fees: $554. One-time fee: $35 full-time. Full-time tuition and fees vary according to degree level and program. *Financial support:* In 2009–10, 385 students received support. Scholarships/grants available. Support available to part-time students. Financial award application deadline: 5/5. *Faculty research:* Data-driven decision-making in K-12 schools and districts; examination of college and university leadership and management in U. S. and Asia; studies in facilitating student learning; organizational change and the role of leaders; leadership, diversity, learning and accountability. *Unit head:* Dr. Kathy Stowe, Executive Director/Assistant Professor of Clinical Education, 213-740-9323. *Application contact:* Carolyn Stirling, Associate Director of Recruiting and Admissions, 213-740-0224, Fax: 213-740-9433, E-mail: soeinfo@usc.edu.

University of Southern California, Graduate School, Rossier School of Education, Doctor of Philosophy in Education Programs, Los Angeles, CA 90089. Offers educational psychology (PhD); higher education administration and policy (PhD); K-12 policy and practice (PhD). *Faculty:* 20 full-time (11 women). *Students:* 23 full-time (17 women); includes 12 minority (3 African Americans, 3 Asian Americans or Pacific Islanders, 6 Hispanic Americans), 1 international. 64 applicants, 17% accepted, 5 enrolled. In 2009, 14 doctorates awarded. *Degree requirements:* For doctorate, thesis/dissertation, qualifying exam, proposal and defense. *Entrance requirements:* For doctorate, GRE. Additional exam requirements/recommendations for international students: Required—TOEFL (minimum score 250 computer-based; 100 iBT). *Application deadline:* For fall admission, 12/1 for domestic and international students. Application fee: $85. Electronic applications accepted. *Expenses:* Tuition: Full-time $25,980; part-time $1315 per unit. Required fees: $554. One-time fee: $35 full-time. Full-time tuition and fees vary according to degree level and program. *Financial support:* In 2009–10, 5 fellowships with full tuition reimbursements (averaging $29,000 per year), 23 research assistantships with full tuition reimbursements (averaging $31,000 per year) were awarded; health care benefits and full tuition coverage for all required coursework, academic stipend, awards for professional development and academic conferences also available. *Faculty research:* Diversity in higher education, organizational change, educational psychology, policy and politics of educational reform, economics of education and education policy. *Unit head:* Dianne Morris, Director, 213-740-

6303, Fax: 213-740-9433, E-mail: rsoephd@usc.edu. *Application contact:* Aba Cassell, 213-821-1517, Fax: 213-740-9433, E-mail: rossier.phd@usc.edu.

University of Southern Mississippi, Graduate School, College of Education and Psychology, Department of Educational Leadership and Research, Hattiesburg, MS 39406-0001. Offers adult education (M Ed, Ed D, PhD, Ed S); educational administration (M Ed, Ed D, PhD, Ed S); higher education (PhD). *Faculty:* 7 full-time (1 woman), 5 part-time/adjunct (1 woman). *Students:* 45 full-time (34 women), 97 part-time (66 women); includes 42 minority (40 African Americans, 1 American Indian/Alaska Native, 1 Hispanic American), 2 international. Average age 36. 54 applicants, 67% accepted, 33 enrolled. In 2009, 26 master's, 11 doctorates, 3 other advanced degrees awarded. *Degree requirements:* For master's, comprehensive exam, thesis (for some programs), internship; for doctorate, comprehensive exam, thesis/dissertation; for Ed S, comprehensive exam, thesis (for some programs). *Entrance requirements:* For master's, GRE General Test, minimum GPA of 2.75; for doctorate, GRE General Test, minimum GPA of 3.5; for Ed S, GRE General Test, minimum GPA of 3.25. Additional exam requirements/recommendations for international students: Required—TOEFL. *Application deadline:* For fall admission, 3/1 priority date for domestic students, 3/1 for international students. Applications are processed on a rolling basis. Application fee: $35. *Expenses:* Tuition, state resident: full-time $5096; part-time $284 per hour. Tuition, nonresident: full-time $13,052; part-time $726 per hour. Required fees: $402. Tuition and fees vary according to course level and course load. *Financial support:* In 2009–10, 10 research assistantships with full tuition reimbursements (averaging $8,000 per year) were awarded; teaching assistantships, career-related internships or fieldwork, Federal Work-Study, and institutionally sponsored loans also available. Financial award application deadline: 3/15; financial award applicants required to submit FAFSA. *Faculty research:* Supervision, learning styles, education finance, higher education organization. Total annual research expenditures: $88,500. *Unit head:* Dr. Gaylynn Parker, Interim Chair, 601-266-4589, Fax: 601-266-5141. *Application contact:* Shonna Breland, Manager of Graduate Admissions, 601-266-6563, Fax: 601-266-5138.

University of Southern Mississippi, Graduate School, College of Education and Psychology, Department of Educational Leadership and School Counseling, Hattiesburg, MS 39401. Offers education (M Ed), including educational administration, educational administration and supervision, school business administration, secondary administration; education (Ed S), including elementary administration, higher education administration; educational administration (M Ed); educational administration and supervision (M Ed), including educational administration; educational leadership and school counseling (Ed D, PhD). *Faculty:* 9 full-time (5 women), 3 part-time/adjunct (1 woman). *Students:* 51 full-time (32 women), 217 part-time (158 women); includes 92 minority (84 African Americans, 2 Asian Americans or Pacific Islanders, 6 Hispanic Americans), 2 international. Average age 39. 84 applicants, 57% accepted, 45 enrolled. In 2009, 68 master's, 25 doctorates, 35 other advanced degrees awarded. *Degree requirements:* For master's, internship. *Entrance requirements:* For master's, doctorate, and Ed S, GRE General Test, minimum GPA of 2.75. *Application deadline:* For fall admission, 3/1 priority date for domestic and international students. Application fee: $35. *Expenses:* Tuition, state resident: full-time $5096; part-time $284 per hour. Tuition, nonresident: full-time $13,052; part-time $726 per hour. Required fees: $402. Tuition and fees vary according to course level and course load. *Financial support:* Career-related internships or fieldwork, Federal Work-Study, and institutionally sponsored loans available. Financial award application deadline: 3/15; financial award applicants required to submit FAFSA. *Unit head:* Dr. Mary Ann Adams, Interim Chair, 601-266-4579. *Application contact:* Shonna Breland, Manager of Graduate Admissions, 601-266-6563, Fax: 601-266-5138.

University of Southern Mississippi, Graduate School, College of Education and Psychology, Department of Educational Studies and Research, Hattiesburg, MS 39406-0001. Offers adult education (Graduate Certificate); community college leadership (Graduate Certificate); counseling and personnel services (college) (M Ed); education (PhD, Ed S), including adult education, research, evaluation and statistics (PhD); education (Ed D), including educational administration, educational research; education: educational leadership and research (Ed S), including higher education administration; educational administration and supervision (M Ed); higher education administration (Ed D, PhD); institutional research (Graduate Certificate). *Faculty:* 7 full-time (1 woman), 5 part-time/adjunct (1 woman). *Students:* 45 full-time (34 women), 97 part-time (66 women); includes 42 minority (40 African Americans, 1 American Indian/Alaska Native, 1 Hispanic American), 2 international. Average age 36. 54 applicants, 67% accepted, 33 enrolled. In 2009, 26 master's, 11 doctorates, 3 other advanced degrees awarded. *Degree requirements:* For master's and other advanced degree, comprehensive exam, thesis (for some programs); for doctorate, comprehensive exam, thesis/dissertation. *Entrance requirements:* For master's, doctorate, and other advanced degree, GRE General Test, minimum GPA of 2.75. Additional exam requirements/recommendations for international students: Required—TOEFL. *Application deadline:* For fall admission, 2/1 for domestic students, 3/1 for international students. Applications are processed on a rolling basis. Application fee: $35. *Expenses:* Tuition, state resident: full-time $5096; part-time $284 per hour. Tuition, nonresident: full-time $13,052; part-time $726 per hour. Required fees: $402. Tuition and fees vary according to course level and course load. *Financial support:* Career-related internships or fieldwork, Federal Work-Study, and institutionally sponsored loans available. Financial award application deadline: 3/15; financial award applicants required to submit FAFSA. Total annual research expenditures: $88,500. *Unit head:* Dr. Thomas V. O'Brien, Chair, 601-266-6093, E-mail: thomas.obrien@usm.edu. *Application contact:* Shonna Breland, Manager of Graduate Admissions, 601-266-6563, Fax: 601-266-5138.

University of South Florida, Graduate School, College of Education–Main Campus, Department of Adult, Career and Higher Education, Tampa, FL 33620-9951. Offers adult education (MA, Ed D, PhD, Ed S); career and technical education (MA); career and workforce education (PhD); higher education/community college teaching (MA, Ed D, PhD); vocational education (Ed S). Part-time programs available. *Faculty:* 9 full-time (3 women), 4 part-time/adjunct (3 women). *Students:* 52 full-time (34 women), 211 part-time (149 women); includes 71 minority (41 African Americans, 1 American Indian/Alaska Native, 5 Asian Americans or Pacific Islanders, 24 Hispanic Americans), 6 international. Average age 30. 94 applicants, 69% accepted, 58 enrolled. In 2009, 31 master's, 11 doctorates awarded. *Degree requirements:* For master's, comprehensive exam; for doctorate, comprehensive exam, thesis/dissertation; for Ed S, comprehensive exam, thesis. *Entrance requirements:* For master's, minimum GPA of 3.0 in last 60 hours of course work; for doctorate and Ed S, GRE General Test, GRE Writing Test. Additional exam requirements/recommendations for international students: Required—TOEFL (minimum score 500 paper-based; 213 computer-based; 91 iBT). *Application deadline:* For fall admission, 2/15 for domestic students, 1/2 for international students; for spring admission, 10/15 for domestic students, 6/1 for international students. Applications are processed on a rolling basis. Application fee: $30. Electronic applications accepted. *Financial support:* Career-related internships or fieldwork, scholarships/grants, and unspecified assistantships available. Financial award applicants required to submit FAFSA. *Faculty research:* Community college leadership; integration of academic, career and technical education; competency-based education; continuing education administration; adult learning and development. Total annual research expenditures: $9,807. *Unit head:* Dr. Ann Cranston-Gingras, Chairperson, 813-974-6036, Fax: 813-974-3366, E-mail: cranston@usf.edu. *Application contact:* Dr. William Young, Program Director, 813-974-1861, Fax: 813-974-3366, E-mail: williamyoung@usf.edu.

University of the Incarnate Word, School of Graduate Studies and Research, Dreeben School of Education, Programs in Education, San Antonio, TX 78209-6397. Offers adult education (M Ed, MA); cross-cultural education (M Ed, MA); early childhood literacy (M Ed, MA); general education (M Ed, MA); Higher Education (PhD); instructional technology (M Ed, MA); international education and entrepreneurship (PhD); kinesiology (M Ed, MA); literacy (M Ed, MA); organizational leadership (PhD); organizational learning and learning (M Ed, MA); reading (M Ed, MA); special education (M Ed, MA); teacher leadership (M Ed, MA). Part-time and evening/weekend programs available. *Students:* 20 full-time (11 women), 201 part-time (122 women); includes 113 minority (29 African Americans, 2 American Indian/Alaska Native, 2 Asian Americans or Pacific Islanders, 80 Hispanic Americans), 30 international. Average age 41. In 2009, 26 master's, 19 doctorates awarded. *Degree requirements:* For master's, capstone; for doctorate, thesis/dissertation, qualifying exam. *Entrance requirements:* For master's, baccalaureate degree; minimum foundation GPA of 2.5; interview; for doctorate, master's degree; interview; supervised writing sample. Additional exam requirements/recommendations for international students: Required—TOEFL (minimum score 560 paper-based; 220 computer-based; 83 iBT). *Application deadline:* Applications are processed on a rolling basis. Application fee: $20. Electronic applications accepted. *Expenses:* Tuition: Full-time $12,150; part-time $675 per credit hour. Required fees: $83 per credit hour. *Financial support:* Federal Work-Study and scholarships/grants available. Financial award applicants required to submit FAFSA. *Unit head:* Dr. Denise Staudt, Dean, Dreeben School of Education, 210-829-2762, E-mail: staudt@uiwtx.edu. *Application contact:* Andrea Cyterski-Acosta, Dean of Enrollment, 210-829-6005, Fax: 210-829-3921, E-mail: admis@uiwtx.edu.

The University of Toledo, College of Graduate Studies, College of Education, Department of Educational Foundations and Leadership, Program in Higher Education, Toledo, OH 43606-3390. Offers ME, PhD. *Accreditation:* NCATE. *Degree requirements:* For master's, comprehensive exam, thesis or alternative; for doctorate, thesis/dissertation, comprehensive exams. *Entrance requirements:* For master's, minimum GPA of 2.7; for doctorate, GRE General Test, minimum GPA of 2.7 (undergraduate), 3.0 (graduate).

University of Virginia, Curry School of Education, Department of Leadership, Foundations and Policy, Program in Higher Education, Charlottesville, VA 22903. Offers higher education (Ed S); student affairs practice (M Ed). *Students:* 7 full-time (6 women), 8 part-time (5 women). Average age 35. 2 applicants, 50% accepted, 1 enrolled. In 2009, 15 master's, 5 doctorates awarded. *Entrance requirements:* For master's, doctorate, and Ed S, GRE General Test, 2 letters of recommendation. Additional exam requirements/recommendations for international students: Required—TOEFL (minimum score 600 paper-based; 250 computer-based; 90 iBT), IELTS (minimum score 7). *Application deadline:* Applications are processed on a rolling basis. Application fee: $60. Electronic applications accepted. *Financial support:* Fellowships, research assistantships, teaching assistantships available. Financial award applicants required to submit FAFSA. *Unit head:* Brian Pusser, Associate Professor and Director, 434-924-7782, E-mail: highered@virginia.edu. *Application contact:* Brian Pusser, Associate Professor and Director, 434-924-7782, E-mail: highered@virginia.edu.

University of Virginia, Curry School of Education, Program in Education, Charlottesville, VA 22903. Offers administration and supervision (PhD); applied developmental science (PhD); counselor education (PhD); curriculum and instruction (PhD); early childhood-developmental risk (MT); education evaluation (PhD); educational psychology (PhD); educational research (PhD); elementary (MT, PhD); English education (MT, PhD); foreign language education (MT); higher education (PhD); instructional technology (PhD); kinesiology (MT, PhD); math education (PhD); reading education (PhD); research statistics and evaluation (PhD); school psychology (PhD); science education (PhD); social studies education (MT, PhD); special education (PhD); world languages education (MT). *Students:* 336 full-time (239 women), 88 part-time (54 women); includes 43 minority (24 African Americans, 2 American Indian/Alaska Native, 11 Asian Americans or Pacific Islanders, 6 Hispanic Americans), 18 international. Average age 27. 199 applicants, 48% accepted, 55 enrolled. In 2009, 127 master's, 52 doctorates awarded. *Degree requirements:* For master's, comprehensive exam (for some programs), field project; for doctorate, comprehensive exam, thesis/dissertation. *Entrance requirements:* For doctorate, GRE General Test. Additional exam requirements/recommendations for international students: Required—TOEFL (minimum score 600 paper-based; 250 computer-based; 90 iBT), IELTS (minimum score 7). *Application deadline:* Applications are processed on a rolling basis. Application fee: $60. Electronic applications accepted. *Financial support:* Fellowships, research assistantships, teaching assistantships available. Financial award application deadline: 1/5; financial award applicants required to submit FAFSA.

University of Washington, Graduate School, College of Education, Seattle, WA 98195. Offers curriculum and instruction (M Ed, Ed D, PhD), including educational technology, general curriculum (Ed D, PhD), language, literacy, and culture, mathematics education, multicultural education, reading and language arts education (Ed D), science education, social studies education, teaching and curriculum (M Ed); educational leadership and policy studies (M Ed, Ed D, PhD), including administration (Ed D), educational policy, organization, and leadership (M Ed, PhD), higher education, leadership for learning (Ed D), social and cultural foundations of education (M Ed, PhD); educational psychology (M Ed, PhD), including educational psychology (PhD), human development and cognition (M Ed), learning sciences, measurement, statistics and research design (M Ed), school psychology (M Ed); instructional leadership (M Ed); intercollegiate athletic leadership (M Ed); special education (M Ed, Ed D, PhD), including early childhood special education (M Ed), emotional and behavioral disabilities (M Ed), learning disabilities (M Ed), low-incidence disabilities (M Ed), severe disabilities (M Ed), special education (Ed D, PhD); teacher education (MIT). *Accreditation:* APA. Part-time and evening/weekend programs available. *Degree requirements:* For master's, thesis optional; for doctorate, thesis/dissertation. *Entrance requirements:* For master's and doctorate, GRE General Test, minimum GPA of 3.0. Additional exam requirements/recommendations for international students: Required—TOEFL. Electronic applications accepted. *Faculty research:* School restructuring/effective schools, special education interventions, literacy and writing, technology, school partnerships, teacher preparation.

University of Wisconsin–Milwaukee, Graduate School, School of Education, Department of Administrative Leadership, Milwaukee, WI 53201-0413. Offers administrative leadership and supervision in education (MS); specialist in administrative leadership (Certificate); teaching and learning in higher education (Certificate). Part-time programs available. *Faculty:* 7 full-time (5 women). *Students:* 22 full-time (10 women), 102 part-time (82 women); includes 30 minority (20 African Americans, 1 American Indian/Alaska Native, 5 Asian Americans or Pacific Islanders, 4 Hispanic Americans), 2 international. Average age 36. 63 applicants, 73% accepted, 14 enrolled. In 2009, 46 master's awarded. *Degree requirements:* For master's, comprehensive exam, thesis or alternative. *Entrance requirements:* For master's, GRE General Test. Additional exam requirements/recommendations for international students: Required—TOEFL (minimum score 550 paper-based; 79 iBT), IELTS (minimum score 6.5). *Application deadline:* For fall admission, 1/1 priority date for domestic students; for spring admission, 9/1 for domestic students. Applications are processed on a rolling basis. Application fee: $45 ($75 for international students). *Expenses:* Tuition, state resident: full-time $8800. Tuition, nonresident: full-time $20,760. Tuition and fees vary according to program and reciprocity agreements. *Financial support:* Career-related internships or fieldwork and unspecified assistantships available. Support available to part-time students. Financial award application deadline: 4/15. Total annual research expenditures: $135,576. *Unit head:* Barbara J. Daley, Chair, 414-229-4740, Fax: 414-229-5300, E-mail: bdaley@uwm.edu. *Application contact:* General Information Contact, 414-229-4982, Fax: 414-229-6967, E-mail: gradschool@uwm.edu.

University of Wisconsin–Whitewater, School of Graduate Studies, College of Business and Economics, Department of Business Education, Whitewater, WI 53190-1790. Offers general business education (MS); post-secondary business education (MS); secondary business education (MS). *Accreditation:* NCATE. Part-time and evening/weekend programs available. Postbaccalaureate distance learning degree programs offered (no on-campus study). *Degree requirements:* For master's, thesis or alternative. *Entrance requirements:* For master's, interview, teaching license. Additional exam requirements/recommendations for international students: Required—TOEFL (minimum score 550 paper-based; 213 computer-based). Electronic applications accepted. *Faculty research:* Active learning and performance strategies, technology-enhanced formative assessment, computer-supported cooperative work, privacy surveillance.

University of Wisconsin–Whitewater, School of Graduate Studies, College of Education, Department of Counselor Education, Whitewater, WI 53190-1790. Offers community counseling (MS Ed); higher education (MS Ed); school counseling (MS Ed). *Accreditation:* ACA; NCATE.

Higher Education

University of Wisconsin–Whitewater (continued)

Part-time and evening/weekend programs available. *Degree requirements:* For master's, thesis or alternative. *Entrance requirements:* For master's, resume, 2 letters of reference. Additional exam requirements/recommendations for international students: Required—TOEFL (minimum score 550 paper-based; 213 computer-based). Electronic applications accepted. *Faculty research:* Alcohol and other drugs, counseling effectiveness, teacher mentoring.

Upper Iowa University, Online Master's Programs, Fayette, IA 52142-1857. Offers accounting (MBA); corporate financial management (MBA); global business (MBA); health and human services (MPA); higher education administration (MHEA); homeland security (MPA); human resources management (MBA); justice administration (MPA); organizational development (MBA); public personnel management (MPA); quality management (MBA). MBA also available at Madison, WI campus. Part-time programs available. Postbaccalaureate distance learning degree programs offered (no on-campus study). *Faculty:* 3 full-time (0 women), 66 part-time/adjunct (27 women). *Students:* 723 full-time (442 women). *Degree requirements:* For master's, research project. *Entrance requirements:* For master's, GMAT, GRE, or minimum GPA of 2.7 during last 60 hours. Additional exam requirements/recommendations for international students: Required—TOEFL (minimum score 570 paper-based; 230 computer-based). *Application deadline:* Applications are processed on a rolling basis. Application fee: $50. Electronic applications accepted. *Expenses:* Tuition: Full-time $6948; part-time $386 per credit hour. *Financial support:* Available to part-time students. Applicants required to submit FAFSA. *Faculty research:* Total quality management, CQI, teams, organization culture and climate, management. *Application contact:* David Hannum, Admissions Advisor, 800-603-3756, E-mail: hannumd@uiu.edu.

Vanderbilt University, Peabody College, Department of Leadership, Policy, and Organizations, Nashville, TN 37240-1001. Offers education policy (MPP); educational leadership and policy (Ed D); higher education (M Ed); higher education, leadership and policy (Ed D); human resource development (M Ed); international education policy and management (M Ed); organizational leadership (M Ed). Part-time and evening/weekend programs available. *Faculty:* 28 full-time (13 women), 8 part-time/adjunct (3 women). *Students:* 155 full-time (111 women), 95 part-time (52 women); includes 36 minority (27 African Americans, 6 Asian Americans or Pacific Islanders, 3 Hispanic Americans), 21 international. Average age 31. 298 applicants, 76% accepted, 94 enrolled. In 2009, 65 master's, 21 doctorates awarded. *Degree requirements:* For master's, comprehensive exam, thesis optional; for doctorate, thesis/dissertation, qualifying exams, residency. *Entrance requirements:* For master's and doctorate, GRE General Test. Additional exam requirements/recommendations for international students: Required—TOEFL (minimum score 550 paper-based; 213 computer-based). *Application deadline:* For fall admission, 12/31 priority date for domestic and international students; for spring admission, 11/1 priority date for domestic and international students. Applications are processed on a rolling basis. Application fee: $0. Electronic applications accepted. *Financial support:* In 2009–10, 155 students received support, including 3 fellowships with full and partial tuition reimbursements available, 61 research assistantships with full and partial tuition reimbursements available, 1 teaching assistantship with full and partial tuition reimbursement available; Federal Work-Study, institutionally sponsored loans, scholarships/grants, tuition waivers (partial), and unspecified assistantships also available. Support available to part-time students. Financial award application deadline: 2/1; financial award applicants required to submit FAFSA. *Faculty research:* Education and leadership policy, education finances/economics of education, higher education leadership and policy, educator pay for performance and school choice, international and comparative education and policy management. *Unit head:* Dr. Ellen B. Goldring, Chair, 615-322-8000, Fax: 615-343-7094, E-mail: ellen.b.goldring@vanderbilt.edu. *Application contact:* Rosie Moody, Educational Coordinator, 615-322-8019, Fax: 615-343-7094, E-mail: rosie.moody@vanderbilt.edu.

Villanova University, Graduate School of Liberal Arts and Sciences, Department of Education and Human Services, Program in Higher Education, Villanova, PA 19085-1699. Offers MA. Part-time and evening/weekend programs available. *Application deadline:* For fall admission, 3/1 for domestic students; for spring admission, 11/15 for domestic students. Applications are processed on a rolling basis. Electronic applications accepted. *Expenses:* Tuition: Part-time $630 per credit. Required fees: $60 per credit. Part-time tuition and fees vary according to degree level and program. *Financial support:* Applicants required to submit FAFSA. *Unit head:* Dr. Connie Titone, Chairperson, 610-519-4620. *Application contact:* Dr. Connie Titone, Chairperson, 610-519-4620.

Virginia Polytechnic Institute and State University, Graduate School, College of Liberal Arts and Human Sciences, School of Education, Department of Educational Leadership and Policy Studies, Blacksburg, VA 24061. Offers administration and supervision of special education (Ed D, PhD, Ed S); counselor education (MA, Ed D, PhD, Ed S); educational leadership (MA, Ed D, PhD); educational research and evaluation (PhD); higher education (MA Ed, PhD). *Accreditation:* ACA; NCATE. *Students:* 138 full-time (84 women), 236 part-time (160 women); includes 109 minority (1 African American, 5 American Indian/Alaska Native, 95 Asian Americans or Pacific Islanders, 8 Hispanic Americans), 12 international. Average age 39. 251 applicants, 44% accepted, 107 enrolled. In 2009, 51 master's, 45 doctorates, 10 other advanced degrees awarded. *Degree requirements:* For doctorate, comprehensive exam, thesis/dissertation. *Entrance requirements:* For master's and doctorate, GRE, GMAT. Additional exam requirements/recommendations for international students: Required—TOEFL (minimum score 550 paper-based; 213 computer-based). *Application deadline:* For fall admission, 5/15 for international students; for spring admission, 10/15 for international students. Applications are processed on a rolling basis. Application fee: $65. Electronic applications accepted. *Expenses:* Tuition, area resident: Full-time $10,228; part-time $459 per credit hour. Tuition, nonresident: Full-time $17,892; part-time $865 per credit hour. Required fees: $1966; $451 per semester. *Financial support:* Career-related internships or fieldwork, Federal Work-Study, scholarships/grants, and unspecified assistantships available. Financial award application deadline: 1/15. *Unit head:* Dr. M. David Alexander, Dean, 540-231-5642, Fax: 540-231-7845, E-mail: mdavid@vt.edu. *Application contact:* Daisy Stewart, Information Contact, 540-231-8180, Fax: 540-231-7845, E-mail: daisys@vt.edu.

Walden University, Graduate Programs, Richard W. Riley College of Education and Leadership, Minneapolis, MN 55401. Offers administrator leadership for teaching and learning (Ed D, Ed S); curriculum, instruction, and professional development (Ed S); early childhood education (birth-grade 3) (MAT); education (MS, PhD), including adolescent literacy and technology (grades 6-12) (MS), adult education leadership (PhD), community college leadership (PhD), curriculum, instruction, and assessment, early childhood education (PhD), educational leadership (MS), educational technology (PhD), elementary reading and literacy (MS), elementary reading and mathematics (MS), emotional/behavioral disorders (K-12) (MS), general program, higher education (PhD), integrating technology in the classroom (MS), K-12 educational leadership (PhD), learning disabilities (K-12) (MS), literacy and learning in the content areas (MS), mathematics (grades 6-8) (MS), mathematics (grades K-5) (MS), middle level education (grades 5-8) (MS), professional development (MS), science (grades K-8) (MS), self-designed (PhD), special education (PhD), special education (non-licensure) (MS), teacher leadership (grades K-12) (MS); educational leadership and administration (principal preparation) (Ed S); educational technology (Ed S); higher education and adult learning (Ed D); instructional design (Postbaccalaureate Certificate); instructional design and technology (MS), including general program (MS, PhD), online learning, training and performance improvement; special education: emotional/behavioral disorders (K-12) (MAT); special education: learning disabilities (K-12) (MAT); teacher leadership (Ed D, Ed S). Part-time and evening/weekend programs available. Postbaccalaureate distance learning degree programs offered (minimal on-campus study). *Faculty:* 54 full-time, 835 part-time/adjunct. *Students:* 13,940 full-time (11,339 women), 1,940 part-time (1,637 women); includes 4,626 minority (3,795 African Americans, 111 American Indian/Alaska Native, 199 Asian Americans or Pacific Islanders, 521 Hispanic Americans), 124 international. Average age 38. In 2009, 4,688 master's, 190 doctorates awarded. *Degree*

requirements: For doctorate, thesis/dissertation (for some programs), residency; for other advanced degree, residency (for some programs). *Entrance requirements:* For master's, bachelor's degree or equivalent in related field; minimum GPA of 2.5; official transcripts; goal statement; access to computer and Internet; for doctorate, master's degree or equivalent in related field; minimum GPA of 3.0; official transcripts; three years' related professional/academic experience (preferred); access to computer and Internet; for other advanced degree, master's degree or equivalent in related field; minimum GPA of 3.0; 3 years related professional/academic experience (preferred); access to computer and Internet (Ed S). Additional exam requirements/recommendations for international students: Required—TOEFL (minimum score 550 paper-based; 213 computer-based), IELTS (minimum score 6.5), or Michigan English Language Assessment Battery (minimum score 82). *Application deadline:* Applications are processed on a rolling basis. Application fee: $50. Electronic applications accepted. *Expenses:* Tuition: Full-time $13,665; part-time $560 per credit. Required fees: $1375. Tuition and fees vary according to course load, degree level and program. *Financial support:* In 2009–10, 2,418 students received support; fellowships, Federal Work-Study, scholarships/grants, unspecified assistantships, and family tuition reduction, active duty/veteran tuition reduction, group tuition reduction, interest-free payment plans available. Support available to part-time students. Financial award applicants required to submit FAFSA. *Unit head:* Dr. Kate Steffens, Dean, 800-925-3368. *Application contact:* Jennifer Hall, Director of Enrollment, 866-4-WALDEN, E-mail: info@waldenu.edu.

Washington State University, Graduate School, College of Education, Department of Educational Leadership and Counseling Psychology, Pullman, WA 99164. Offers counseling psychology (Ed M, MA, PhD, Certificate), including counseling psychology (Ed M, MA, PhD), school psychologist (Certificate); educational leadership (M Ed, MA, Ed D, PhD); educational psychology (Ed M, MA, PhD); higher education (Ed M, MA, Ed D, PhD), including higher education administration (PhD), sport management (PhD), student affairs (PhD); higher education with sport management (Ed M). *Accreditation:* NCATE. Terminal master's awarded for partial completion of doctoral program. *Degree requirements:* For master's, comprehensive exam (for some programs), thesis (for some programs), oral exam or written exam; for doctorate, comprehensive exam, thesis/dissertation, oral and written exams. *Entrance requirements:* For master's and doctorate, GRE General Test, minimum GPA of 3.0, 3 letters of recommendation. Additional exam requirements/recommendations for international students: Required—TOEFL (minimum score 550 paper-based; 213 computer-based). *Faculty research:* Attentional processes, cross cultural psychology, faculty development in higher education.

Wayland Baptist University, Graduate Programs, Program in Education, Plainview, TX 79072-6998. Offers education administration (M Ed); higher education administration (M Ed); instructional leadership (M Ed); instructional technology (M Ed); special education (M Ed). Part-time and evening/weekend programs available. Postbaccalaureate distance learning degree programs offered (no on-campus study). *Faculty:* 6 full-time (4 women). *Students:* 4 full-time (2 women), 45 part-time (26 women); includes 6 minority (3 African Americans, 3 Hispanic Americans). Average age 30. 26 applicants, 77% accepted, 9 enrolled. In 2009, 4 master's awarded. *Degree requirements:* For master's, comprehensive exam, capstone course. *Entrance requirements:* For master's, GRE, GMAT or MAT. Additional exam requirements/recommendations for international students: Required—TOEFL (minimum score 500 paper-based; 173 computer-based; 61 iBT). *Application deadline:* Applications are processed on a rolling basis. Application fee: $50. Electronic applications accepted. *Expenses:* Tuition: Full-time $5796; part-time $322 per credit hour. Required fees: $782; $9 per credit hour. $60 per semester. Tuition and fees vary according to course load and campus/location. *Financial support:* Federal Work-Study, institutionally sponsored loans, and scholarships/grants available. Support available to part-time students. Financial award application deadline: 5/1; financial award applicants required to submit FAFSA. *Unit head:* Dr. Jim Todd, Chairman, 806-291-1045, Fax: 806-291-1951. *Application contact:* Amanda Stanton, Graduate Studies, 806-291-3423, Fax: 806-291-1950, E-mail: stanton@wbu.edu.

Wayne State University, College of Education, Division of Administrative and Organizational Studies, Detroit, MI 48202. Offers administration and supervision-secondary (Ed S); college and university teaching (Certificate); curriculum and instruction (PhD); educational leadership (M Ed, Ed S); educational leadership and policy studies (Ed D, PhD); elementary education curriculum and instruction (MA, Ed S); general administration and supervision (Ed D, PhD, Ed S); higher education (Ed D, PhD); instructional technology (M Ed, Ed D, PhD, Ed S); secondary curriculum and instruction (M Ed, Ed S). *Degree requirements:* For doctorate, thesis/dissertation. *Entrance requirements:* For doctorate, interview, minimum GPA of 3.0, an autobiography or curriculum vitae; references. Additional exam requirements/recommendations for international students: Required—TOEFL (minimum score 550 paper-based; 213 computer-based), TWE (minimum score 6). Electronic applications accepted. *Faculty research:* Total quality management, participatory management, administering educational technology, school improvement, principalship.

Western Carolina University, Graduate School, College of Education and Allied Professions, Department of Educational Leadership and Foundations, Program in Community College and Higher Education, Cullowhee, NC 28723. Offers community college administration (MA Ed); community college teaching (MA Ed). *Accreditation:* NCATE. Part-time and evening/weekend programs available. Postbaccalaureate distance learning degree programs offered. *Students:* 6 full-time (5 women), 25 part-time (17 women). Average age 40. 70 applicants, 13% accepted, 5 enrolled. In 2009, 8 master's awarded. *Degree requirements:* For master's, comprehensive exam. *Entrance requirements:* For master's, GRE General Test, appropriate undergraduate degree, 3 letters of recommendation. Additional exam requirements/recommendations for international students: Required—TOEFL (minimum score 550 paper-based; 270 computer-based; 79 iBT). *Application deadline:* For fall admission, 5/1 priority date for domestic students; for spring admission, 9/1 priority date for domestic students. Applications are processed on a rolling basis. Application fee: $45. *Financial support:* In 2009–10, 1 student received support, including 1 research assistantship with full and partial tuition reimbursement available (averaging $7,000 per year); fellowships, teaching assistantships with full and partial tuition reimbursements available, career-related internships or fieldwork, institutionally sponsored loans, scholarships/grants, and unspecified assistantships also available. Financial award application deadline: 3/31; financial award applicants required to submit FAFSA. *Faculty research:* Women leaders, program evaluation, organizational culture and change, rural education, democracy in education, faculty careers and development. *Unit head:* Dr. Jacqueline Jacobs, Head, 828-227-7415, Fax: 828-227-7607, E-mail: jjacobs@email.wcu.edu. *Application contact:* Admissions Specialist for Community College and Higher Education, 828-227-7398, Fax: 828-227-7480, E-mail: jbewsey@email.wcu.edu.

Western Governors University, Teachers College, Salt Lake City, UT 84107. Offers English language learning (K-12) (MA); learning and technology (M Ed, MA); management and innovation (M Ed); mathematics education (5-12) (MA); mathematics education (5-9) (MA); mathematics education (K-6) (MA); measurement and evaluation (M Ed); science (5-12) (MA), including biology, geology; science education (5-9) (MA); teaching (MAT); technology for principals (Post-Graduate Certificate). *Accreditation:* NCATE. Part-time and evening/weekend programs available. Postbaccalaureate distance learning degree programs offered (no on-campus study). *Degree requirements:* For master's, comprehensive exam. *Entrance requirements:* Additional exam requirements/recommendations for international students: Required—TOEFL (minimum score 450 paper-based). Electronic applications accepted. *Expenses:* Contact institution.

Western Washington University, Graduate School, Woodring College of Education, Department of Educational Leadership, Program in Continuing and College Education, Bellingham, WA 98225-5996. Offers M Ed. Part-time and evening/weekend programs available. Postbaccalaureate distance learning degree programs offered (minimal on-campus study). *Degree requirements:* For master's, comprehensive exam, thesis optional. *Entrance requirements:* For master's, GRE General Test or MAT, minimum GPA of 3.0 in last 60 semester hours or last 90 quarter hours. Additional exam requirements/recommendations for international students:

Required—TOEFL (minimum score 567 paper-based; 227 computer-based). Electronic applications accepted. *Faculty research:* Transfer of learning, postsecondary faculty development, action research as professional development, literacy education in community colleges, adult education in the Middle East, distance learning tools for graduate students.

West Virginia University, College of Human Resources and Education, Department of Curriculum and Instruction-Literacy, Program in Secondary Education, Morgantown, WV 26506. Offers higher education curriculum and teaching (MA); secondary education (MA). Students enter program as undergraduates. *Accreditation:* NCATE. Part-time programs available. *Degree requirements:* For master's, thesis optional, content exams. *Entrance requirements:* For master's, minimum GPA of 2.75. Additional exam requirements/recommendations for international students: Required—TOEFL. Electronic applications accepted. *Faculty research:* Teacher education, school reform, curriculum development, education technology.

West Virginia University, College of Human Resources and Education, Department of Educational Leadership Studies, Morgantown, WV 26506. Offers educational leadership (Ed D); higher education administration (MA); public school administration (MA). *Accreditation:* NCATE. Part-time programs available. *Degree requirements:* For master's, content exams; for doctorate, comprehensive exam, thesis/dissertation. *Entrance requirements:* For master's, minimum GPA of 2.75 or MA Degree or MAT of 4107; for doctorate, GRE General Test or MAT, minimum GPA of 3.25. Additional exam requirements/recommendations for international students: Required—TOEFL. Electronic applications accepted. *Faculty research:* Evaluation, collective bargaining, educational law, international higher education, superintendency.

Wilkes University, College of Graduate and Professional Studies, School of Education, Wilkes-Barre, PA 18766-0002. Offers classroom technology (MS Ed); educational computing (MS Ed); educational development and strategies (MS Ed); educational leadership (MS Ed); educational technology (Ed D); elementary education (MS Ed); higher education administration (Ed D); instructional technology (MS Ed); K-12 administration (Ed D); online teaching (MS Ed); school business leadership (MS Ed); secondary education (MS Ed), including biology, chemistry, English, history; special education (MS Ed). Part-time and evening/weekend programs available. Postbaccalaureate distance learning degree programs offered (minimal on-campus study). *Students:* 89 full-time (60 women), 2,849 part-time (2,058 women); includes 52 minority (10 African Americans, 2 American Indian/Alaska Native, 13 Asian Americans or Pacific Islanders, 27 Hispanic Americans), 6 international. Average age 33. In 2009, 947 master's awarded. *Entrance requirements:* Additional exam requirements/recommendations for international students: Required—TOEFL (minimum score 500 paper-based; 173 computer-based; 79 iBT). *Application deadline:* Applications are processed on a rolling basis. Application fee: $45. *Expenses:* Contact institution. *Financial support:* Federal Work-Study and unspecified assistantships available. Financial award application deadline: 3/1; financial award applicants required to submit FAFSA. *Unit head:* Dr. Michael Speziale, Dean, 570-408-4679, Fax: 570-408-4905, E-mail: michael.speziale@wilkes.edu. *Application contact:* Kathleen Houlihan, Director of Graduate Studies, 570-408-3235, Fax: 570-408-7846, E-mail: kathleen.houlihan@wilkes.edu.

Wright State University, School of Graduate Studies, College of Education and Human Services, Department of Educational Leadership, Program in Advanced Educational Leadership, Dayton, OH 45435. Offers advanced curriculum and instruction (Ed S); higher education-adult education (Ed S); superintendent (Ed S). *Accreditation:* NCATE. *Degree requirements:* For Ed S, thesis. *Entrance requirements:* For degree, GRE General Test, MAT. Additional exam requirements/recommendations for international students: Required—TOEFL.

Wright State University, School of Graduate Studies, College of Education and Human Services, Department of Educational Leadership, Programs in Educational Leadership, Dayton, OH 45435. Offers curriculum and instruction: teacher leader (MA); educational administrative specialist: teacher leader (M Ed); educational administrative specialist: vocational education administration (M Ed, MA); student affairs in higher education-administration (M Ed, MA). *Accreditation:* NCATE. *Degree requirements:* For master's, thesis (for some programs). *Entrance requirements:* For master's, GRE General Test, MAT. Additional exam requirements/recommendations for international students: Required—TOEFL.

Middle School Education

Alaska Pacific University, Graduate Programs, Education Department, Program in Teaching, Anchorage, AK 99508-4672. Offers teaching (K-8) (MAT). *Degree requirements:* For master's, research project. *Entrance requirements:* For master's, GRE or MAT, PRAXIS, minimum GPA of 3.0.

Albany State University, College of Education, Program in Middle Grades Education, Albany, GA 31705-2717. Offers M Ed. *Accreditation:* NCATE. Part-time programs available. *Students:* 7 full-time (5 women), 17 part-time (15 women); includes 15 minority (14 African Americans, 1 Asian American or Pacific Islander). Average age 35. 2 applicants, 100% accepted, 2 enrolled. In 2009, 3 master's awarded. *Degree requirements:* For master's, comprehensive exam, GACE II. *Entrance requirements:* For master's, GRE General Test or MAT, GACE I, teaching certificate, 2 letters of recommendation. Additional exam requirements/recommendations for international students: Required—TOEFL. *Application deadline:* For fall admission, 11/16 for domestic and international students; for spring admission, 4/19 for domestic students, 2/19 for international students. Applications are processed on a rolling basis. Application fee: $20. Electronic applications accepted. *Expenses:* Tuition, state resident: full-time $2970; part-time $162 per credit hour. Tuition, nonresident: full-time $12,168; part-time $676 per credit hour. Required fees: $962; $75 per credit hour. *Financial support:* Application deadline: 6/30. *Unit head:* Dr. Audrey Beard, Chairperson, 229-430-4687, Fax: 229-430-4993, E-mail: audrey.beard@asurams.edu. *Application contact:* Nicole Lane, Interim Graduate Admissions Officer, 229-430-4862, Fax: 229-430-6398, E-mail: nicole.lane@asurams.edu.

American International College, School of Arts, Education and Sciences, Department of Education, Springfield, MA 01109-3189. Offers early childhood education (M Ed, CAGS); educational leadership and supervision (Ed D); elementary education (M Ed, CAGS); middle/secondary education (M Ed, CAGS); moderate disabilities (M Ed, CAGS); reading (M Ed, CAGS); school adjustment counseling (MA, CAGS); school administration (M Ed, CAGS); school guidance counseling (MA, CAGS); teaching (MA, MS); teaching and learning (Ed D). Part-time and evening/weekend programs available. Terminal master's awarded for partial completion of doctoral program. *Degree requirements:* For master's, comprehensive exam (for some programs), thesis (for some programs), practicum; for doctorate, comprehensive exam (for some programs), thesis/dissertation; for CAGS, practicum. *Entrance requirements:* For master's, minimum B- average in undergraduate course work; for doctorate, GRE General Test, interview. Additional exam requirements/recommendations for international students: Required—TOEFL. Electronic applications accepted. *Expenses:* Tuition: Full-time $12,510; part-time $695 per credit hour. Required fees: $35 per term.

Appalachian State University, Cratis D. Williams Graduate School, Department of Curriculum and Instruction, Boone, NC 28608. Offers curriculum specialist (MA); educational media (MA); elementary education (MA); middle grades education (MA), including language arts, mathematics, science, social studies. *Accreditation:* NCATE. Part-time and evening/weekend programs available. Postbaccalaureate distance learning degree programs offered (no on-campus study). *Faculty:* 32 full-time (22 women), 9 part-time/adjunct (3 women). *Students:* 16 full-time (12 women), 168 part-time (140 women); includes 2 minority (both African Americans), 1 international. 97 applicants, 99% accepted, 77 enrolled. In 2009, 78 master's awarded. *Degree requirements:* For master's, comprehensive exam, thesis or alternative. *Entrance requirements:* For master's, GRE General Test or MAT, 3 letters of recommendation. Additional exam requirements/recommendations for international students: Required—TOEFL (minimum score 570 paper-based; 230 computer-based; 79 iBT), IELTS (minimum score 6.5). *Application deadline:* For fall admission, 7/1 for domestic students, 2/1 for international students; for spring admission, 11/1 for domestic students, 7/1 for international students. Applications are processed on a rolling basis. Application fee: $50. Electronic applications accepted. *Expenses:* Tuition, state resident: full-time $2960. Tuition, nonresident: full-time $14,051. Required fees: $2320. *Financial support:* In 2009–10, 8 teaching assistantships (averaging $8,000 per year) were awarded; fellowships, research assistantships, career-related internships or fieldwork, Federal Work-Study, scholarships/grants, and unspecified assistantships also available. Financial award application deadline: 4/1; financial award applicants required to submit FAFSA. *Faculty research:* Media literacy, elementary teaching, curriculum development, online learning environments. Total annual research expenditures: $690,000. *Unit head:* Dr. Michael Jacobson, Chairperson, 828-262-2224. *Application contact:* Sandy Krause, Director of Admissions and Recruiting, 828-262-2130, Fax: 828-262-2709, E-mail: krausesl@appstate.edu.

Arkansas State University—Jonesboro, Graduate School, College of Education, Department of Teacher Education, Jonesboro, State University, AR 72467. Offers early childhood education (MSE); early childhood services (MS); middle level education (MSE); reading (MSE, SCCT). *Accreditation:* NCATE. Part-time programs available. *Faculty:* 5 full-time (4 women), 4 part-time/adjunct (3 women). *Students:* 10 full-time (all women), 87 part-time (84 women); includes 40 minority (39 African Americans, 1 American Indian/Alaska Native). Average age 35. 63 applicants, 79% accepted, 39 enrolled. In 2009, 31 master's awarded. *Degree requirements:* For master's, comprehensive exam, thesis or alternative; for SCCT, comprehensive exam. *Entrance requirements:* For master's, GRE General Test or MAT, appropriate bachelor's degree; for SCCT, GRE General Test or MAT, interview, master's degree, official transcript, immunization records. Additional exam requirements/recommendations for international students: Required—TOEFL (minimum score 550 paper-based; 213 computer-based; 79 iBT), IELTS (minimum score 6). *Application deadline:* For fall admission, 7/15 for domestic students, 7/1 for international students; for spring admission, 12/1 for domestic students, 11/13 for international students. Applications are processed on a rolling basis. Application fee: $30 ($40 for international students). Electronic applications accepted. *Expenses:* Tuition, state resident: full-time $3744; part-time $208 per credit hour. Tuition, nonresident: full-time $9540; part-time $530 per credit hour. Required fees: $896; $47 per credit hour. $25 per term. One-time fee: $50. Tuition and fees vary according to course load and program. *Financial support:* In 2009–10, 16 students received support; teaching assistantships, career-related internships or fieldwork, scholarships/grants, and unspecified assistantships available. Financial award application deadline: 7/1; financial award applicants required to submit FAFSA. *Unit head:* Dr. Dianne Lawler-Prince, Chair, 870-972-3059, Fax: 870-972-3344, E-mail: dprince@astate.edu. *Application contact:* Dr. Andrew Sustich, Dean of the Graduate School, 870-972-3029, Fax: 870-972-3857, E-mail: sustich@astate.edu.

Armstrong Atlantic State University, School of Graduate Studies, Program in Education, Savannah, GA 31419-1997. Offers adult education (M Ed); curriculum and instruction (M Ed); early childhood education (M Ed); education (M Ed); elementary education (M Ed); middle grades education (M Ed); secondary education (M Ed), including business education, English education, mathematics education, science education, social science education; special education (M Ed), including behavioral disorders, learning disabilities, speech-language pathology. *Accreditation:* NCATE. Part-time and evening/weekend programs available. Postbaccalaureate distance learning degree programs offered (minimal on-campus study). *Degree requirements:* For master's, comprehensive exam, portfolio. *Entrance requirements:* For master's, GRE General Test or MAT, minimum GPA of 2.5, letters of recommendation. Additional exam requirements/recommendations for international students: Required—TOEFL (minimum score 523 paper-based; 193 computer-based). Electronic applications accepted.

Austin College, Program in Education, Sherman, TX 75090-4400. Offers art education (MA); elementary education (MA); middle school education (MA); music education (MA); physical education and coaching (MA); secondary education (MA); theatre education (MA). Part-time programs available. *Faculty:* 5 full-time (3 women), 1 (woman) part-time/adjunct. *Students:* 29 full-time (21 women); includes 3 minority (1 Asian American or Pacific Islander, 2 Hispanic Americans). Average age 23. In 2009, 23 master's awarded. *Degree requirements:* For master's, one foreign language, thesis or alternative. *Entrance requirements:* For master's, Texas Academic Skills Program Test. *Application deadline:* For fall admission, 5/1 priority date for domestic students; for spring admission, 1/15 priority date for domestic students. Applications are processed on a rolling basis. Application fee: $35. Electronic applications accepted. *Expenses:* Tuition: Full-time $31,575. Required fees: $160. *Financial support:* Career-related internships or fieldwork, Federal Work-Study, scholarships/grants, and unspecified assistantships available. Support available to part-time students. Financial award application deadline: 4/1; financial award applicants required to submit FAFSA. *Unit head:* Dr. Barbara Sylvester, Director of Teaching Program, 903-813-2327, Fax: 903-813-2326, E-mail: bsylvester@austincollege.edu. *Application contact:* Dr. Barbara Sylvester, Director of Teaching Program, 903-813-2327, Fax: 903-813-2326, E-mail: bsylvester@austincollege.edu.

Bank Street College of Education, Graduate School, Program in Middle School Education, New York, NY 10025. Offers MS Ed. *Students:* 5 full-time (all women), 15 part-time (11 women); includes 1 minority (Hispanic American). Average age 28. 17 applicants, 76% accepted, 10 enrolled. In 2009, 10 master's awarded. *Degree requirements:* For master's, thesis. *Entrance requirements:* For master's, academic background in middle school level subjects, interview. Additional exam requirements/recommendations for international students: Required—TOEFL (minimum score 600 paper-based; 250 computer-based; 100 iBT), IELTS (minimum score 7). *Application deadline:* For fall admission, 3/1 priority date for domestic students; for spring admission, 11/1 priority date for domestic students. Applications are processed on a rolling basis. Application fee: $65. *Expenses:* Tuition: Part-time $1120 per credit. *Financial support:* Career-related internships or fieldwork, Federal Work-Study, scholarships/grants, and unspecified assistantships available. Support available to part-time students. Financial award application deadline: 4/15; financial award applicants required to submit FAFSA. *Faculty research:* Collaborative learning in middle school settings, the interdisciplinary middle school classroom, experiential learning in middle school, adolescent development. *Unit head:* Dr. Sue Ruskin-Mayher, Director, 212-875-4780, Fax: 212-875-4753, E-mail: sruskin-mayher@bankstreet.edu. *Application contact:* Ann Morgan, Director of Graduate Admissions, 212-875-4403, Fax: 212-875-4678, E-mail: amorgan@bankstreet.edu.

Bellarmine University, Annsley Frazier Thornton School of Education, Louisville, KY 40205-0671. Offers early elementary education (MA, MAT); instructional leadership and school administration/school principal (MA); learning and behavior disorders (MA); middle school

Middle School Education

Bellarmine University (continued)
education (MA, MAT); reading and writing endorsement (MA); secondary school education (MAT); Waldorf inspired curriculum (MA). *Accreditation:* NCATE. Part-time and evening/weekend programs available. *Faculty:* 16 full-time (11 women), 20 part-time/adjunct (13 women). *Students:* 67 full-time (47 women), 140 part-time (111 women); includes 14 minority (10 African Americans, 1 American Indian/Alaska Native, 3 Asian Americans or Pacific Islanders), 1 international. Average age 33. In 2009, 106 degrees awarded. *Degree requirements:* For master's, comprehensive exam, thesis (for some programs). *Entrance requirements:* For master's, GRE, baccalaureate degree from an accredited institution; minimum overall GPA of 2.75, 3.0 in major; letters of recommendation; valid Kentucky provisional or professional certificate. Additional exam requirements/recommendations for international students: Required—TOEFL (minimum score 550 paper-based; 213 computer-based; 80 iBT). *Application deadline:* Applications are processed on a rolling basis. Application fee: $25. *Expenses:* Contact institution. *Financial support:* Scholarships/grants available. Financial award applicants required to submit FAFSA. *Faculty research:* Literacy, service learning, dispositions, educational technology, special education. *Unit head:* Dr. Cindy Gnadinger, Dean, 502-452-8191, Fax: 502-452-8189, E-mail: cgnadinger@bellarmine.edu. *Application contact:* Theresa Klapheke, Administrative Director of Graduate Programs, 502-452-8271, Fax: 502-452-8002, E-mail: tklapheke@bellarmine.edu.

Belmont University, College of Arts and Sciences, School of Education, Nashville, TN 37212-3757. Offers education (M Ed); elementary education (MAT), including early childhood education, elementary education, language arts education; English (MAT); history (MAT); mathematics (MAT); middle grade education (MAT); science (MAT); secondary education (MAT); special education (MAT); sports administration (MSA). *Accreditation:* NCATE. Part-time and evening/weekend programs available. *Degree requirements:* For master's, comprehensive exam, thesis, culminating portfolio. *Entrance requirements:* For master's, MAT or GRE and/or LSAT or GMAT, minimum GPA of 2.75. Additional exam requirements/recommendations for international students: Required—TOEFL. *Expenses:* Contact institution. *Faculty research:* Improving secondary literacy, Montessori, classroom management strategies, teacher residency programs, online professional development, mentoring, leadership, sociological issues in sport, faculty development, coaching.

Berry College, Graduate Programs, Graduate Programs in Education, Program in Middle Grades Education and Reading, Mount Berry, GA 30149-0159. Offers M Ed. *Accreditation:* NCATE. Part-time programs available. *Faculty:* 13 part-time/adjunct (8 women). *Students:* 1 full-time (0 women), 35 part-time (27 women); includes 1 minority (African American). Average age 33. In 2009, 6 master's awarded. *Degree requirements:* For master's, thesis optional, oral exams. *Entrance requirements:* For master's, GRE General Test, MAT, or NTE, minimum GPA of 2.5. Additional exam requirements/recommendations for international students: Required—TOEFL (minimum score 550 paper-based; 213 computer-based). *Application deadline:* For fall admission, 5/1 for domestic and international students; for spring admission, 10/1 for domestic and international students. Applications are processed on a rolling basis. Application fee: $25 ($30 for international students). *Expenses:* Contact institution. *Financial support:* In 2009–10, 14 students received support, including 3 research assistantships with full tuition reimbursements available (averaging $3,399 per year); scholarships/grants, tuition waivers (partial), and unspecified assistantships also available. Support available to part-time students. Financial award application deadline: 4/1; financial award applicants required to submit FAFSA. *Faculty research:* Curriculum development, teacher training, pedagogy. *Unit head:* Dr. Jacqueline McDowell, 706-236-1717, Fax: 706-238-5827, E-mail: jmcdowell@berry.edu. *Application contact:* Brett Kennedy, Director of Admissions, 706-236-2215, Fax: 706-290-2178, E-mail: admissions@berry.edu.

Brenau University, Graduate Programs, School of Education, Gainesville, GA 30501. Offers early childhood (Ed S); early childhood education (M Ed, MAT); middle grades (Ed S); middle grades education (M Ed, MAT); secondary education (MAT); special education (M Ed, MAT). *Accreditation:* NCATE. Part-time and evening/weekend programs available. Postbaccalaureate distance learning degree programs offered (no on-campus study). *Faculty:* 12 full-time (7 women), 25 part-time/adjunct (21 women). *Students:* 161 full-time (146 women), 143 part-time (122 women); includes 43 minority (30 African Americans, 5 Asian Americans or Pacific Islanders, 8 Hispanic Americans), 1 international. Average age 35. 163 applicants, 34% accepted, 47 enrolled. In 2009, 154 master's, 20 other advanced degrees awarded. *Degree requirements:* For master's, thesis optional, comprehensive exam or applied research project, effective portfolio; for Ed S, applied research project. *Entrance requirements:* For master's, GRE, MAT, interview, minimum GPA of 3.0, 3 references, writing samples; for Ed S, GRE, MAT, master's degree, minimum GPA of 3.0, writing sample, letters of reference. Additional exam requirements/recommendations for international students: Required—TOEFL (minimum score 500 paper-based). *Application deadline:* Applications are processed on a rolling basis. Application fee: $35. Electronic applications accepted. *Expenses:* Contact institution. *Financial support:* In 2009–10, 2 students received support. Scholarships/grants available. Support available to part-time students. Financial award application deadline: 7/15; financial award applicants required to submit FAFSA. *Unit head:* Dr. Lora Bailey, Dean, 770-534-6220, Fax: 770-534-6221, E-mail: lbailey@brenau.edu. *Application contact:* Christina White, Dean of Admissions, 770-718-5320, Fax: 770-718-5337, E-mail: cwhite@brenau.edu.

Brooklyn College of the City University of New York, Division of Graduate Studies, School of Education, Program in Middle Childhood Education (Math), Brooklyn, NY 11210-2889. Offers MS Ed. *Students:* 1 (woman) full-time, 97 part-time (53 women); includes 47 minority (25 African Americans, 14 Asian Americans or Pacific Islanders, 8 Hispanic Americans), 2 international. Average age 30. 31 applicants, 84% accepted, 17 enrolled. In 2009, 63 master's awarded. *Entrance requirements:* For master's, LAST, 2 letters of recommendation, essay, resume. Additional exam requirements/recommendations for international students: Required—TOEFL (minimum score 500 paper-based; 173 computer-based; 61 iBT). *Application deadline:* For fall admission, 7/15 priority date for domestic students, 6/1 priority date for international students; for spring admission, 11/15 priority date for domestic students, 10/1 priority date for international students. Applications are processed on a rolling basis. Electronic applications accepted. *Expenses:* Tuition, state resident: full-time $7360; part-time $310 per credit hour. Tuition, nonresident: full-time $13,800; part-time $575 per credit hour. Required fees: $140.10 per semester. *Financial support:* Federal Work-Study, institutionally sponsored loans, and scholarships/grants available. Support available to part-time students. Financial award application deadline: 5/1; financial award applicants required to submit FAFSA. *Unit head:* Prof. Mary Chiusano, Program Head, 718-951-5214, E-mail: mchiusano@brooklyn.cuny.edu. *Application contact:* Hernan Sierra, Graduate Admissions Coordinator, 718-951-4536, Fax: 718-951-4506, E-mail: grads@brooklyn.cuny.edu.

Brooklyn College of the City University of New York, Division of Graduate Studies, School of Education, Program in Middle Childhood Education (Science), Brooklyn, NY 11210-2889. Offers biology (MA); chemistry (MA); earth science (MA); general science (MA); physics (MA). Part-time and evening/weekend programs available. *Students:* 2 full-time (both women), 80 part-time (55 women); includes 34 minority (22 African Americans, 3 Asian Americans or Pacific Islanders, 9 Hispanic Americans), 4 international. Average age 31. 43 applicants, 98% accepted, 31 enrolled. In 2009, 29 master's awarded. *Entrance requirements:* For master's, LAST, interview, previous course work in education and mathematics, resume, 2 letters of recommendation, essay. Additional exam requirements/recommendations for international students: Required—TOEFL (minimum score 500 paper-based; 173 computer-based; 61 iBT). *Application deadline:* For fall admission, 7/15 priority date for domestic students, 6/1 priority date for international students; for spring admission, 11/15 priority date for domestic students, 10/1 priority date for international students. Applications are processed on a rolling basis. Application fee: $125. Electronic applications accepted. *Expenses:* Tuition, state resident: full-time $7360; part-time $310 per credit hour. Tuition, nonresident: full-time $13,800; part-time $575 per credit hour. Required fees: $140.10 per semester. *Financial support:* Federal Work-Study, institutionally sponsored loans, and scholarships/grants available. Support available to part-time students. Financial award application deadline: 5/1; financial award applicants required to submit FAFSA. *Faculty research:* Geometric thinking, mastery of basic facts, problem-solving strategies, history of mathematics. *Unit head:* Dr. Jennifer Adams, Program Head, 718-951-5214, E-mail: jadams@brooklyn.cuny.edu. *Application contact:* Hernan Sierra, Graduate Admissions Coordinator, 718-951-4536, Fax: 718-951-4506, E-mail: grads@brooklyn.cuny.edu.

California Lutheran University, Graduate Studies, School of Education, Emphasis in Educational Leadership, Thousand Oaks, CA 91360-2787. Offers educational leadership (MA); educational leadership (k-12) (Ed D); higher education leadership (Ed D). Part-time and evening/weekend programs available. *Degree requirements:* For master's, thesis or comprehensive exam. *Entrance requirements:* For master's, GRE General Test, interview, minimum GPA of 3.0.

California State University, Bakersfield, Division of Graduate Studies, School of Natural Sciences and Mathematics, Program in Teaching Mathematics, Bakersfield, CA 93311. Offers MA. *Entrance requirements:* For master's, minimum GPA of 2.5 for last 90 quarter units.

California State University, Fullerton, Graduate Studies, College of Education, Department of Secondary Education, Fullerton, CA 92834-9480. Offers middle school mathematics (MS); secondary education (MS); teacher induction (MS). Part-time programs available. *Students:* 1 (woman) full-time, 41 part-time (33 women); includes 15 minority (1 African American, 1 American Indian/Alaska Native, 4 Asian Americans or Pacific Islanders, 9 Hispanic Americans). Average age 32. 32 applicants, 63% accepted, 17 enrolled. In 2009, 39 master's awarded. Application fee: $55. *Expenses:* Tuition, nonresident: full-time $11,160; part-time $373 per credit. Required fees: $1440 per term. Tuition and fees vary according to course load, degree level and program. *Financial support:* Career-related internships or fieldwork, Federal Work-Study, institutionally sponsored loans, and scholarships/grants available. Support available to part-time students. Financial award application deadline: 3/1; financial award applicants required to submit FAFSA. *Unit head:* Dr. Victoria Costa, Head, 657-278-7037. *Application contact:* Admissions/Applications, 657-278-2371.

California State University, Stanislaus, College of Education, Department of Teacher Education, Turlock, CA 95382. Offers curriculum and instruction (MA), including elementary education, multilingual education, reading, secondary education; education (MA); middle/junior high studies (Graduate Certificate). Part-time and evening/weekend programs available. *Degree requirements:* For master's, thesis. *Entrance requirements:* For master's, MAT or GRE, 3 letters of recommendation. Additional exam requirements/recommendations for international students: Required—TOEFL (minimum score 550 paper-based; 213 computer-based). Electronic applications accepted. *Faculty research:* Children's perspectives on historical events, method elementary schools dual language education, K-12 reading and CYRM programs.

Cambridge College, School of Education, Cambridge, MA 02138-5304. Offers autism specialist (M Ed); autism/behavior analyst (M Ed); behavior analyst (Post-Master's Certificate); behavioral management (M Ed); early childhood teacher (M Ed); education specialist in curriculum and instruction (CAGS); educational leadership (Ed D); elementary teacher (M Ed); English as a second language (M Ed, Certificate); general science (M Ed); health education, health promotion (Post-Master's Certificate); health/family and consumer sciences (M Ed); history (M Ed); individualized degree (M Ed); information technology literacy (M Ed); instructional technology (M Ed); interdisciplinary studies (M Ed); library teacher (M Ed); literacy education (M Ed); mathematics (M Ed); mathematics specialist (Certificate); middle school mathematics and science (M Ed); school administration (M Ed, CAGS); school guidance counselor (M Ed); school nurse education (M Ed); school social worker/school adjustment counselor (M Ed); special education administrator (CAGS); special education/moderate disabilities (M Ed); teaching skills and methodologies (M Ed). Part-time and evening/weekend programs available. Postbaccalaureate distance learning degree programs offered (minimal on-campus study). *Faculty:* 10 full-time (3 women), 283 part-time/adjunct (187 women). *Students:* 974 full-time (755 women), 1,071 part-time (835 women); includes 940 minority (762 African Americans, 4 American Indian/Alaska Native, 22 Asian Americans or Pacific Islanders, 152 Hispanic Americans), 28 international. Average age 39. In 2009, 866 master's, 4 doctorates, 209 CAGSs awarded. *Degree requirements:* For master's, thesis, internship/practicum (licensure program only); for doctorate, thesis/dissertation; for other advanced degree, thesis. *Entrance requirements:* For master's, interview, resume, documentation of licensure, 2 professional references; for doctorate, official transcripts, interview, resume, documentation of licensure (if any), written personal statement/essay, portfolio of scholarly and professional work, qualifying assessment, 2 professional references, health insurance, immunizations form; for other advanced degree, official transcripts, interview, resume, documentation of licensure (if any), written personal statement/essay, 2 professional references, health insurance, immunizations form. Additional exam requirements/recommendations for international students: Required—TOEFL (minimum score 550 paper-based; 213 computer-based; 79 iBT); Recommended—IELTS (minimum score 6). *Application deadline:* Applications are processed on a rolling basis. Application fee: $30. Electronic applications accepted. *Expenses:* Contact institution. *Financial support:* In 2009–10, 1,373 students received support. Career-related internships or fieldwork, Federal Work-Study, and scholarships/grants available. Financial award applicants required to submit FAFSA. *Faculty research:* Adult education, accelerated learning, mathematics education, brain compatible learning, special education and law. *Unit head:* Dr. N. Alan Sheppard, Interim Associate Dean, 617-873-0619, E-mail: alan.sheppard@cambridgecollege.edu. *Application contact:* Stephen Lyons, Director of Enrollment, Graduate and N.I.T.E. Programs, 617-868-1000, Fax: 617-349-3561, E-mail: stephen.lyons@cambridgecollege.edu.

Campbell University, Graduate and Professional Programs, School of Education, Buies Creek, NC 27506. Offers administration (MSA); community counseling (MA); elementary education (M Ed); English education (M Ed); interdisciplinary studies (M Ed); mathematics education (M Ed); middle grades education (M Ed); physical education (M Ed); school counseling (M Ed); secondary education (M Ed); social science education (M Ed). *Accreditation:* NCATE. Part-time and evening/weekend programs available. *Degree requirements:* For master's, comprehensive exam. *Entrance requirements:* For master's, GRE General Test, minimum GPA of 2.7. *Faculty research:* Spiritual values and wellness issues in counseling, stress and professional burnout among counselors, thinking strategies, leadership, adaptive technology.

Canisius College, Graduate Division, School of Education and Human Services, Department of Graduate Education, Buffalo, NY 14208-1098. Offers adolescence education (grades 7-12) (MS); childhood education (grades 1-6) (MS); college student personnel administration (MS); deaf education (MS); differentiated instruction (MS Ed); educational administration and supervision (MS); general education (MS Ed); initial teacher certification (elementary education) (MS); initial teacher certification (secondary education) (MS); literacy (MS Ed); special education (MS). *Accreditation:* NCATE. Part-time and evening/weekend programs available. *Faculty:* 22 full-time (14 women), 84 part-time/adjunct (54 women). *Students:* 409 full-time (288 women), 261 part-time (187 women); includes 29 minority (24 African Americans, 5 Hispanic Americans), 156 international. Average age 30. 518 applicants, 74% accepted, 240 enrolled. In 2009, 346 master's awarded. Application fee: $25. *Financial support:* Research assistantships with full tuition reimbursements, career-related internships or fieldwork, institutionally sponsored loans, scholarships/grants, health care benefits, tuition waivers (full and partial), and unspecified assistantships available. *Faculty research:* Autism, Asperger's disease, private higher education, reading strategies. *Unit head:* Rev. Paul Nochelski, Chair of Graduate Education and Leadership, 716-888-3297, Fax: 716-888-3299. *Application contact:* James D. Bagwell, Director of Graduate Recruitment and Admissions, 716-888-2544, Fax: 716-888-3290, E-mail: bagwellj@canisius.edu.

Capella University, School of Education, Minneapolis, MN 55402. Offers college teaching (Certificate); curriculum and instruction (MS, PhD); education (MS); enrollment management (MS); instructional design for online learning (MS, PhD); k-12 studies in education (MS, PhD); leadership for higher education (MS, PhD); leadership in education administration (Certificate);

leadership in educational administration (MS, PhD); postsecondary and adult education (MS, PhD); professional studies in education (MS, PhD); reading and literacy (MS); training and performance improvement (MS, PhD). Part-time and evening/weekend programs available. Postbaccalaureate distance learning degree programs offered (minimal on-campus study). Terminal master's awarded for partial completion of doctoral program. *Degree requirements:* For master's, thesis optional, integrative project; for doctorate, comprehensive exam, thesis/dissertation. *Entrance requirements:* Additional exam requirements/recommendations for international students: Required—TOEFL (minimum score 550 paper-based; 213 computer-based), TWE (minimum score 4). Electronic applications accepted. *Faculty research:* Higher education administration, distance learning, adult education, training and curriculum design.

Central Michigan University, College of Graduate Studies, College of Education and Human Services, Department of Teacher Education and Professional Development, Program in Middle Level Education, Mount Pleasant, MI 48859. Offers MA. Part-time and evening/weekend programs available. *Degree requirements:* For master's, thesis or alternative. *Entrance requirements:* For master's, bachelor's degree with a minimum GPA of 2.7, Michigan teaching certificate or equivalent. Electronic applications accepted.

Chicago State University, School of Graduate and Professional Studies, College of Education, Department of Reading, Elementary Education, Library Information and Media Studies, Program in Middle School Education, Chicago, IL 60628. Offers MAT.

City College of the City University of New York, Graduate School, School of Education, Department of Secondary Education, New York, NY 10031-9198. Offers adolescent mathematics education (MA, AC); English education (MA); middle school mathematics education (MS); science education (MA); social studies education (AC). *Accreditation:* NCATE. *Entrance requirements:* For master's, Liberal Arts and Sciences Test (LAST), Content Specialty Test (CST). Additional exam requirements/recommendations for international students: Required—TOEFL. *Expenses:* Tuition, state resident: part-time $310 per credit. Tuition, nonresident: part-time $575 per credit. Tuition and fees vary according to course load and program.

Clemson University, Graduate School, College of Health, Education, and Human Development, School of Education, Program in Middle Grades Education, Clemson, SC 29634. Offers MAT. *Students:* 30 full-time (18 women), 16 part-time (9 women); includes 4 minority (3 African Americans, 1 Hispanic American). Average age 32. 30 applicants, 87% accepted, 15 enrolled. In 2009, 42 master's awarded. *Entrance requirements:* For master's, GRE, PRAXIS II. Additional exam requirements/recommendations for international students: Required—TOEFL. *Application deadline:* Applications are processed on a rolling basis. Application fee: $70 ($80 for international students). Electronic applications accepted. *Expenses:* Contact institution. *Financial support:* In 2009–10, 1 student received support, including 1 research assistantship with partial tuition reimbursement available (averaging $9,083 per year); career-related internships or fieldwork, institutionally sponsored loans, scholarships/grants, health care benefits, and unspecified assistantships also available. Support available to part-time students. *Unit head:* Dr. Michael J. Padilla, Director/Associate Dean, 864-656-4444, Fax: 864-656-0311, E-mail: padilla@clemson.edu. *Application contact:* Dr. David Fleming, Graduate Coordinator, 864-656-1881, Fax: 864-656-0311, E-mail: dflemin@clemson.edu.

Cleveland State University, College of Graduate Studies, College of Education and Human Services, Department of Teacher Education, Cleveland, OH 44115. Offers art education (M Ed); early childhood education (M Ed); foreign language education (M Ed); mathematics and science education (M Ed); middle childhood education (M Ed); special education (M Ed), including mild/moderate disabilities, moderate/intensive disabilities; teaching English to speakers of other languages (M Ed). Part-time and evening/weekend programs available. *Degree requirements:* For master's, comprehensive exam (for some programs), thesis or alternative. *Entrance requirements:* For master's, GRE General Test or MAT, minimum GPA of 2.75. Additional exam requirements/recommendations for international students: Required—TOEFL (minimum score 525 paper-based; 197 computer-based), IELTS (minimum score 6). *Faculty research:* Early literacy, professional development in reading, reading recovery, dual language, induction programs.

The College at Brockport, State University of New York, School of Education and Human Services, Department of Education and Human Development, Program in Adolescence Education, Brockport, NY 14420-2997. Offers adolescence biology education (MS Ed); adolescence chemistry education (MS Ed); adolescence earth science education (MS Ed); adolescence English education (MS Ed); adolescence mathematics education (MS Ed); adolescence physics education (MS Ed); adolescence social studies education (MS Ed). *Accreditation:* NCATE. Part-time programs available. *Students:* 10 full-time (6 women), 98 part-time (60 women); includes 1 minority (African American). 15 applicants, 67% accepted, 8 enrolled. In 2009, 60 master's awarded. *Degree requirements:* For master's, thesis or alternative. *Entrance requirements:* For master's, minimum GPA of 3.0, letters of recommendation. Additional exam requirements/recommendations for international students: Required—TOEFL (minimum score 550 paper-based; 213 computer-based; 79 iBT). *Application deadline:* For fall admission, 2/15 priority date for domestic and international students; for spring admission, 9/15 priority date for domestic and international students. Application fee: $80. Electronic applications accepted. *Expenses:* Tuition, state resident: full-time $8370; part-time $349 per credit. Tuition, nonresident: full-time $13,250; part-time $522 per credit. *Financial support:* Federal Work-Study, scholarships/grants, and unspecified assistantships available. Support available to part-time students. Financial award application deadline: 3/15; financial award applicants required to submit FAFSA. *Unit head:* Dr. Sue Novinger, Chairperson, 585-395-2205, Fax: 585-395-2172, E-mail: snovinge@brockport.edu. *Application contact:* Coordinator of Certification and Graduate Advisement.

The College at Brockport, State University of New York, School of Education and Human Services, Department of Education and Human Development, Program in Alternate Adolescence Inclusive Education, Brockport, NY 14420-2997. Offers alternate adolescence English inclusive education (MS Ed); alternate adolescence mathematics inclusive education (MS Ed); alternate adolescence science inclusive education (MS Ed); alternate adolescence social studies inclusive education (MS Ed). *Students:* 25 full-time (8 women), 5 part-time (3 women). 26 applicants, 50% accepted, 11 enrolled. *Degree requirements:* For master's, thesis or alternative. *Entrance requirements:* For master's, minimum GPA of 3.0, letters of recommendation, statement of objectives, academic major (or equivalent) in program discipline. Additional exam requirements/recommendations for international students: Required—TOEFL (minimum score 550 paper-based; 213 computer-based; 79 iBT). *Application deadline:* For fall admission, 2/15 priority date for domestic and international students; for spring admission, 9/15 priority date for domestic and international students. Application fee: $80. Electronic applications accepted. *Expenses:* Tuition, state resident: full-time $8370; part-time $349 per credit. Tuition, nonresident: full-time $13,250; part-time $522 per credit. *Financial support:* Federal Work-Study, scholarships/grants, and unspecified assistantships available. Support available to part-time students. Financial award application deadline: 3/15; financial award applicants required to submit FAFSA. *Unit head:* Dr. Sue Novinger, Chairperson, 585-395-2205, E-mail: snovinge@brockport.edu. *Application contact:* Coordinator of Certification and Graduate Advisement.

College of Mount St. Joseph, Graduate Education Program, Cincinnati, OH 45233-1670. Offers adolescent young adult education (MA); art (MA); inclusive early childhood education (MA); instructional leadership (MA); middle childhood education (MA); multi-age education (MA); multicultural special education (MA); music (MA); reading (MA). *Accreditation:* Teacher Education Accreditation Council. Part-time and evening/weekend programs available. *Faculty:* 15 full-time (11 women), 9 part-time/adjunct (6 women). *Students:* 93 full-time (75 women), 99 part-time (66 women); includes 19 minority (18 African Americans, 1 American Indian/Alaska Native). Average age 34. 116 applicants, 97% accepted, 94 enrolled. In 2009, 51 master's awarded. *Degree requirements:* For master's, research project, student teaching, clinical and field-based experiences. *Entrance requirements:* For master's, GRE, PRAXIS II in teaching content area (math or science), 2 letters of recommendation, interview, resume. Additional exam requirements/recommendations for international students: Required—TOEFL (minimum score 560 paper-based; 220 computer-based; 83 iBT). *Application deadline:* Applications are processed on a rolling basis. Application fee: $50. Electronic applications accepted. *Expenses:* Tuition: Part-time $500 per hour. Required fees: $200 per year. Tuition and fees vary according to degree level and program. *Financial support:* In 2009–10, 51 students received support. Scholarships/grants available. Financial award applicants required to submit FAFSA. *Faculty research:* Foreign and second language learning problems/reading disabilities/hyperlexia, multicultural/bilingual special education, alternative educator licensure, science education, pedagogical content knowledge. *Unit head:* Dr. Mary West, Chair of Graduate Education, 513-244-3263, Fax: 513-244-4867, E-mail: mary_west@mail.msj.edu. *Application contact:* Marilyn Hoskins, Assistant Director of Graduate Recruitment, 513-244-4723, Fax: 513-244-4629, E-mail: marilyn_hoskins@mail.msj.edu.

College of Mount Saint Vincent, School of Professional and Continuing Studies, Department of Teacher Education, Riverdale, NY 10471-1093. Offers instructional technology and global perspectives (Certificate); middle level education (Certificate); multicultural studies (Certificate); urban and multicultural education (MS Ed). *Accreditation:* Teacher Education Accreditation Council. Part-time programs available. *Degree requirements:* For master's, comprehensive exam. *Entrance requirements:* For master's, interview, New York teaching certificate. Additional exam requirements/recommendations for international students: Required—TOEFL.

College of Staten Island of the City University of New York, Graduate Programs, Department of Education, Program in Special Education Middle Childhood Generalist (5-9), Staten Island, NY 10314-6600. Offers MS Ed. *Students:* 9 full-time (7 women), 4 part-time (all women); includes 4 minority (1 African American, 1 Asian American or Pacific Islander, 2 Hispanic Americans). Average age 31. 14 applicants, 93% accepted, 13 enrolled. *Expenses:* Tuition, state resident: full-time $7360; part-time $310 per credit. Tuition, nonresident: part-time $575 per credit. Required fees: $378; $113 per semester. *Financial support:* Applicants required to submit FAFSA. *Unit head:* Prof. Ed Lehner, Program Coordinator, 718-982-3728, E-mail: lehner@mail.csi.cuny.edu. *Application contact:* Sasha Spence, Assistant Director of Graduate Recruitment and Admissions, 718-982-2699, Fax: 718-982-2500, E-mail: sasha.spence@csi.cuny.edu.

Columbus State University, Graduate Studies, College of Education and Health Professions, Department of Teacher Education, Columbus, GA 31907-5645. Offers accomplished teaching (M Ed); early childhood education (M Ed, Ed S); health administration (MPA); instructional technology (MS); middle grades education (M Ed, Ed S); physical education (M Ed); secondary education (M Ed, MAT, Ed S), including English/language arts (M Ed, Ed S), general science (M Ed), mathematics (M Ed), social science (M Ed); special education (M Ed), including behavior disorders, mental retardation. *Accreditation:* NCATE. Part-time and evening/weekend programs available. Postbaccalaureate distance learning degree programs offered (minimal on-campus study). *Faculty:* 18 full-time (15 women), 14 part-time/adjunct (10 women). *Students:* 146 full-time (113 women), 312 part-time (261 women); includes 142 minority (120 African Americans, 1 American Indian/Alaska Native, 8 Asian Americans or Pacific Islanders, 13 Hispanic Americans), 2 international. Average age 31. 248 applicants, 64% accepted, 114 enrolled. In 2009, 103 master's, 22 other advanced degrees awarded. *Degree requirements:* For master's, thesis, exit exam; for Ed S, thesis or alternative. *Entrance requirements:* For master's, GRE General Test, minimum GPA of 2.75; for Ed S, GRE General Test. Additional exam requirements/recommendations for international students: Required—TOEFL (minimum score 550 paper-based; 213 computer-based; 79 iBT). *Application deadline:* For fall admission, 5/1 priority date for domestic students, 5/1 for international students; for spring admission, 11/1 for domestic and international students. Applications are processed on a rolling basis. Application fee: $30. Electronic applications accepted. *Financial support:* In 2009–10, 305 students received support, including 36 research assistantships with partial tuition reimbursements available (averaging $3,000 per year); career-related internships or fieldwork, Federal Work-Study, institutionally sponsored loans, scholarships/grants, tuition waivers (partial), and unspecified assistantships also available. Support available to part-time students. Financial award application deadline: 5/1; financial award applicants required to submit FAFSA. *Unit head:* Dr. Deborah Gober, Acting Chair, 706-568-2255, Fax: 706-568-3134, E-mail: gober_deborah@colstate.edu. *Application contact:* Katie Thornton, Graduate Admissions Specialist, 706-568-2035, Fax: 706-568-2462, E-mail: thornton_katie@colstate.edu.

Daemen College, Education Department, Amherst, NY 14226-3592. Offers adolescence education (MS); childhood education (MS); childhood special education (MS); childhood special-alternative certification (MS); early childhood special-alternative certification (MS). Part-time programs available. *Faculty:* 14 full-time (11 women), 42 part-time/adjunct (36 women). *Students:* 320 full-time (292 women), 225 part-time (202 women); includes 5 minority (3 African Americans, 1 American Indian/Alaska Native, 1 Hispanic American), 135 international. Average age 25. 331 applicants, 82% accepted, 220 enrolled. In 2009, 302 master's awarded. *Degree requirements:* For master's, comprehensive exam, thesis optional, completion of degree within 5 years. *Entrance requirements:* For master's, 2 letters of recommendation, proof of initial certificate of licensure for professional programs, resume, minimum undergraduate GPA of 3.0. Additional exam requirements/recommendations for international students: Required—TOEFL (minimum score 500 paper-based; 173 computer-based; 61 iBT). *Application deadline:* For fall admission, 3/1 priority date for domestic and international students; for spring admission, 10/1 priority date for domestic and international students. Applications are processed on a rolling basis. Application fee: $25. Electronic applications accepted. *Expenses:* Tuition: Part-time $770 per credit hour. Tuition and fees vary according to course load, program and reciprocity agreements. *Financial support:* In 2009–10, 16 students received support. Institutionally sponsored loans, scholarships/grants, and some discounted programs available. Financial award application deadline: 2/15; financial award applicants required to submit FAFSA. *Faculty research:* Transition for students with disabilities, early childhood special education, traumatic brain injury (TBI), reading assessment. *Unit head:* Dr. Mary H. Fox, Chair, 716-839-8530, Fax: 716-839-8516, E-mail: mfox@daemen.edu. *Application contact:* Scott Rowe, Associate Director of Graduate Admissions, 716-839-8225, Fax: 716-839-8229, E-mail: srowe@daemen.edu.

Dowling College, Graduate Programs in Education, Oakdale, NY 11769-1999. Offers adolescence education (MS Ed), including educational administration; advanced certificate in gifted education (AC); childhood and early childhood education (MS Ed); childhood education (MS Ed); educational administration (AC, PD), including computers in education (PD), school administration and supervision (PD), school district administration (PD); educational technology specialist (AC); literacy (MS Ed); literacy/special education (MS Ed); secondary education (MS Ed); special education (MS Ed). *Accreditation:* NCATE. Part-time and evening/weekend programs available. Postbaccalaureate distance learning degree programs offered. *Faculty:* 32 full-time (18 women), 98 part-time/adjunct (59 women). *Students:* 563 full-time (393 women), 885 part-time (668 women); includes 133 minority (47 African Americans, 2 American Indian/Alaska Native, 10 Asian Americans or Pacific Islanders, 74 Hispanic Americans). Average age 32. 363 applicants, 89% accepted, 213 enrolled. In 2009, 459 master's, 85 ACs awarded. *Degree requirements:* For master's and other advanced degree, comprehensive exam. *Entrance requirements:* For master's, minimum GPA of 3.0; for other advanced degree, teaching certificate. Additional exam requirements/recommendations for international students: Required—TOEFL (minimum score 550 paper-based). *Application deadline:* For fall admission, 9/1 priority date for domestic students; for winter admission, 1/1 priority date for domestic students; for spring admission, 2/1 priority date for domestic students. Applications are processed on a rolling basis. Application fee: $50. Electronic applications accepted. *Expenses:* Tuition: Full-time $14,490; part-time $805 per credit. Required fees: $346 per term. *Financial support:* Career-related internships or fieldwork and Federal Work-Study available. Support available to part-time students. Financial award application deadline: 6/30; financial award applicants required to submit FAFSA. *Faculty research:* Natural readers, Korean styles and learning strategies, mothers of children with disabilities, computers in instruction, cultural background and organizational roadblocks to problem solving. *Unit head:* Dr. Clyde Payne, Dean of the School of

Middle School Education

Dowling College *(continued)*

Education, 631-244-3404, Fax: 631-589-6644, E-mail: paynec@dowling.edu. *Application contact:* Glenn M. Berman, Assistant Vice President for Enrollment Services/Dean of Admissions, 631-244-3357, Fax: 631-244-1059, E-mail: glenn.berman@dowling.edu.

Drury University, Graduate Programs in Education, Springfield, MO 65802. Offers elementary education (M Ed); gifted education (M Ed); human services (M Ed); instructional mathematics K-8 (M Ed); instructional technology (M Ed); middle school teaching (M Ed); secondary education (M Ed); special education (M Ed); special reading (M Ed). *Accreditation:* NCATE. Part-time and evening/weekend programs available. *Degree requirements:* For master's, thesis. *Entrance requirements:* For master's, GRE or MAT, minimum GPA of 2.75. Additional exam requirements/recommendations for international students: Required—TOEFL. Electronic applications accepted. *Faculty research:* Cultural enrichment, research skills, parental involvement relating to reading skills, reading strategies for mainstreaming children.

East Carolina University, Graduate School, College of Education, Department of Curriculum and Instruction, Greenville, NC 27858-4353. Offers behavior/emotional disabilities (MA Ed); elementary education (MA Ed); English education (MA Ed); learning disabilities (MA Ed); low incidence disabilities (MA Ed); mental retardation (MA Ed); middle grade education (MA Ed); reading education (MA Ed); social studies education (MA Ed). Part-time programs available. Postbaccalaureate distance learning degree programs offered. *Degree requirements:* For master's, comprehensive exam, thesis optional. *Entrance requirements:* For master's, GRE General Test or MAT, interview, bachelor's degree in related field, minimum GPA of 2.5, teaching license. Additional exam requirements/recommendations for international students: Required—TOEFL.

Eastern Illinois University, Graduate School, College of Education and Professional Studies, Department of Early Childhood, Elementary and Middle Level Education, Charleston, IL 61920-3099. Offers elementary education (MS Ed). *Accreditation:* NCATE. Part-time programs available. *Faculty:* 14 full-time (6 women). In 2009, 55 master's awarded. *Degree requirements:* For master's, comprehensive exam. *Application deadline:* For fall admission, 3/31 priority date for domestic students. Applications are processed on a rolling basis. Application fee: $30. *Expenses:* Tuition, state resident: full-time $9434; part-time $239 per credit hour. Tuition, nonresident: full-time $23,774; part-time $717 per credit hour. Required fees: $802.63. *Financial support:* In 2009–10, research assistantships with tuition reimbursements (averaging $8,100 per year), 5 teaching assistantships with tuition reimbursements (averaging $8,100 per year) were awarded. *Unit head:* Dr. Joy Russell, Chairperson, 217-581-5728, E-mail: jlrussell@eiu.edu. *Application contact:* Dr. Linda Reven, Coordinator of Graduate Studies, 217-581-7883, E-mail: lmreven@eiu.edu.

Eastern Michigan University, Graduate School, College of Education, Department of Teacher Education, Program in K–12 Education, Ypsilanti, MI 48197. Offers curriculum and instruction (MA); elementary education (MA); K-12 education (MA); middle school education (MA); secondary school education (MA). *Accreditation:* NCATE. Part-time and evening/weekend programs available. Postbaccalaureate distance learning degree programs offered (minimal on-campus study). *Students:* 18 full-time (10 women), 103 part-time (83 women); includes 20 minority (11 African Americans, 2 American Indian/Alaska Native, 3 Asian Americans or Pacific Islanders, 4 Hispanic Americans), 1 international. Average age 36. In 2009, 10 master's awarded. *Entrance requirements:* For master's, GRE. Additional exam requirements/recommendations for international students: Required—TOEFL. *Application deadline:* Applications are processed on a rolling basis. Application fee: $35. Tuition and fees vary according to course level. *Financial support:* Fellowships, research assistantships with full tuition reimbursements, teaching assistantships with full tuition reimbursements, career-related internships or fieldwork, Federal Work-Study, institutionally sponsored loans, scholarships/grants, tuition waivers (partial), and unspecified assistantships available. Support available to part-time students. Financial award applicants required to submit FAFSA. *Unit head:* Dr. Wendy Burke, Coordinator, 734-487-3260, Fax: 734-487-2101, E-mail: wendy.burke@emich.edu. *Application contact:* Dr. Wendy Burke, Coordinator, 734-487-3260, Fax: 734-487-2101, E-mail: wendy.burke@emich.edu.

Eastern Nazarene College, Adult and Graduate Studies, Division of Education, Quincy, MA 02170. Offers early childhood education (M Ed, Certificate); elementary education (M Ed, Certificate); English as a second language (M Ed, Certificate); instructional enrichment and development (M Ed, Certificate); middle school education (M Ed, Certificate); moderate special needs education (M Ed, Certificate); principal (Certificate); program development and supervision (M Ed, Certificate); secondary education (M Ed, Certificate); special education administrator (Certificate); supervisor (Certificate); teacher of reading (M Ed, Certificate). M Ed and Certificate also available through weekend program for administration, special needs, and reading only. Part-time and evening/weekend programs available. *Entrance requirements:* Additional exam requirements/recommendations for international students: Required—TOEFL (minimum score 550 paper-based).

Emory University, Graduate School of Arts and Sciences, Division of Educational Studies, Atlanta, GA 30322-1100. Offers educational studies (MA, PhD, DAST); middle grades teaching (M Ed, MAT); secondary teaching (M Ed, MAT). *Accreditation:* NCATE. Terminal master's awarded for partial completion of doctoral program. *Degree requirements:* For master's, thesis; for doctorate, comprehensive exam, thesis/dissertation. *Entrance requirements:* For master's and doctorate, GRE General Test, minimum GPA of 3.0. Additional exam requirements/recommendations for international students: Required—TOEFL. Electronic applications accepted. *Faculty research:* Educational policy, educational measurement, urban and multicultural education, mathematics and science education, comparative education.

Fayetteville State University, Graduate School, Program in Middle Grades, Secondary and Special Education, Fayetteville, NC 28301-4298. Offers biology (MA Ed); history (MA Ed); mathematics (MA Ed); middle grades (MA Ed); political science (MA Ed); reading (MA Ed); sociology (MA Ed); special education (MA Ed), including behavioral-emotional handicaps, mentally handicapped, specific training disability. *Accreditation:* NCATE. Part-time and evening/weekend programs available. *Faculty:* 15 full-time (10 women), 3 part-time/adjunct (2 women). *Students:* 16 full-time (12 women), 70 part-time (57 women); includes 55 minority (50 African Americans, 1 American Indian/Alaska Native, 1 Asian American or Pacific Islander, 3 Hispanic Americans). Average age 35. 14 applicants, 100% accepted, 14 enrolled. In 2009, 32 master's awarded. *Degree requirements:* For master's, comprehensive exam, internship. *Application deadline:* For fall admission, 4/15 for domestic students; for spring admission, 10/15 for domestic students. Applications are processed on a rolling basis. Application fee: $35. Electronic applications accepted. *Unit head:* Dr. Charletta Barringer-Brown, Interim Chair, 910-672-1182, E-mail: cbarringerbrown@uncfsu.edu. *Application contact:* Roxie Shabazz, Associate Vice-Chancellor for Enrollment Management, 910-672-1784, Fax: 910-672-2209, E-mail: rshabazz@uncfsu.edu.

Fitchburg State University, Division of Graduate and Continuing Education, Program in Middle School Education, Fitchburg, MA 01420-2697. Offers M Ed. *Accreditation:* NCATE. Part-time and evening/weekend programs available. *Students:* 1 full-time (0 women), 34 part-time (27 women); includes 2 minority (1 African American, 1 Hispanic American). Average age 39. 9 applicants, 100% accepted, 9 enrolled. In 2009, 12 master's awarded. *Entrance requirements:* For master's, GRE General Test or MAT, teaching certificate. Additional exam requirements/recommendations for international students: Required—TOEFL (minimum score 550 paper-based; 213 computer-based; 79 iBT). *Application deadline:* Applications are processed on a rolling basis. Application fee: $25 ($50 for international students). *Expenses:* Tuition, area resident: Part-time $150 per credit. Tuition, state resident: part-time $150 per credit. Tuition, nonresident: part-time $150 per credit. Required fees: $120 per credit. *Financial support:* In 2009–10, research assistantships with partial tuition reimbursements (averaging $5,500 per year); Federal Work-Study, scholarships/grants, and unspecified assistantships also available.

Support available to part-time students. Financial award application deadline: 3/1; financial award applicants required to submit FAFSA. *Unit head:* Dr. Pam Hill, Chair, 978-665-3515, Fax: 978-665-3658, E-mail: gce@fsc.edu. *Application contact:* Director of Admissions, 978-665-3144, Fax: 978-665-4540, E-mail: admissions@fsc.edu.

Fresno Pacific University, Graduate Programs, School of Education, Division of Mathematics/Science/Computer Education, Program in Mathematics Education, Fresno, CA 93702-4709. Offers elementary and middle school mathematics (MA Ed); secondary school mathematics (MA Ed). Part-time and evening/weekend programs available. *Degree requirements:* For master's, thesis or alternative. *Entrance requirements:* Additional exam requirements/recommendations for international students: Required—TOEFL (minimum score 550 paper-based; 213 computer-based).

Gardner-Webb University, Graduate School, School of Education, Program in Middle Grades Education, Boiling Springs, NC 28017. Offers MA. *Accreditation:* NCATE. Part-time and evening/weekend programs available. *Faculty:* 7 full-time (3 women), 2 part-time/adjunct (both women). *Students:* 1 full-time (0 women), 8 part-time (7 women); includes 3 minority (all African Americans). Average age 38. 6 applicants, 100% accepted, 6 enrolled. In 2009, 5 master's awarded. *Degree requirements:* For master's, comprehensive exam. *Entrance requirements:* For master's, GRE General Test or NTE, PRAXIS, minimum GPA of 2.5. *Application deadline:* For fall admission, 8/1 priority date for domestic students. Applications are processed on a rolling basis. Application fee: $25. Electronic applications accepted. *Expenses:* Tuition: Part-time $305 per credit hour. *Financial support:* Unspecified assistantships available. *Unit head:* Dr. Carrol Smith, Chair, 704-406-3913, Fax: 704-406-3921, E-mail: dsimmons@gardner-webb.edu. *Application contact:* Dr. Franki Burch, Dean, Graduate School, 704-406-4422, Fax: 704-406-4329, E-mail: gradschool@gardner-webb.edu.

Georgia College & State University, Graduate School, The John H. Lounsbury College of Education, Department of Early Childhood and Middle Grades Education, Milledgeville, GA 31061. Offers early childhood education (M Ed, Ed S); middle grades education (M Ed, Ed S). *Accreditation:* NCATE. Part-time and evening/weekend programs available. *Faculty:* 20 full-time (17 women). *Students:* 7 full-time (5 women), 47 part-time (44 women); includes 10 minority (8 African Americans, 2 Hispanic Americans), 1 international. Average age 29. 57 applicants, 100% accepted, 36 enrolled. In 2009, 10 master's, 44 other advanced degrees awarded. *Degree requirements:* For master's and Ed S, comprehensive exam. *Entrance requirements:* For master's, on-site writing assessment, level 4 teaching certificate, 2 recommendations; for Ed S, on-site writing assessment, master's degree, 2 years of teaching experience, 2 professional recommendations, level 5 teacher certification. Additional exam requirements/recommendations for international students: Recommended—TOEFL (minimum score 550 paper-based; 213 computer-based; 79 iBT). *Application deadline:* For fall admission, 7/1 for domestic students; for spring admission, 11/15 for domestic students. Applications are processed on a rolling basis. Application fee: $40. Electronic applications accepted. *Expenses:* Tuition, area resident: Part-time $241 per credit hour. Tuition, state resident: full-time $4338. Tuition, nonresident: full-time $17,352; part-time $964 per credit hour. Required fees: $609 per semester. Tuition and fees vary according to course load and campus/location. *Financial support:* In 2009–10, 2 research assistantships were awarded; career-related internships or fieldwork, Federal Work-Study, and unspecified assistantships also available. Support available to part-time students. Financial award applicants required to submit FAFSA. *Unit head:* Dr. Nancy Mizelle, Chair, 478-445-5479, Fax: 478-445-6695, E-mail: nancy.mizelle@gcsu.edu. *Application contact:* Shanda Brand, Graduate Coordinator, 478-445-1383, E-mail: shanda.brand@gcsu.edu.

Georgia Southern University, Jack N. Averitt College of Graduate Studies, College of Education, Department of Teaching and Learning, Program in Middle Grades Education, Statesboro, GA 30460. Offers M Ed, MAT. *Accreditation:* NCATE. Part-time and evening/weekend programs available. *Students:* 10 full-time (7 women), 3 part-time (2 women); includes 3 minority (2 African Americans, 1 Hispanic American). Average age 27. 2 applicants, 100% accepted, 2 enrolled. In 2009, 3 master's awarded. *Degree requirements:* For master's, portfolio, transition point assessments, exit assessment. *Entrance requirements:* For master's, GRE General Test or MAT; GACE Basic Skills and Content Assessments (MAT), minimum cumulative GPA of 2.5. Additional exam requirements/recommendations for international students: Required—TOEFL (minimum score 550 paper-based; 213 computer-based; 80 iBT). *Application deadline:* For fall admission, 3/1 priority date for domestic and international students; for spring admission, 10/1 priority date for domestic students, 10/1 for international students. Applications are processed on a rolling basis. Application fee: $50. Electronic applications accepted. *Expenses:* Tuition, state resident: full-time $5040; part-time $210 per credit hour. Tuition, nonresident: full-time $20,136; part-time $839 per credit hour. Required fees: $1644. *Financial support:* In 2009–10, 8 students received support, including research assistantships with partial tuition reimbursements available (averaging $7,200 per year), teaching assistantships with partial tuition reimbursements available (averaging $7,200 per year); career-related internships or fieldwork, Federal Work-Study, and tuition waivers (partial) also available. Support available to part-time students. Financial award application deadline: 4/15; financial award applicants required to submit FAFSA. *Faculty research:* Teacher teams, gender, technology applications. *Unit head:* Dr. Ronnie Sheppard, Department Chair, 912-478-5203, Fax: 912-478-0026, E-mail: sheppard@georgiasouthern.edu. *Application contact:* Dr. Charles Ziglar, Coordinator for Graduate Student Recruitment, 912-478-5635, Fax: 912-478-0740, E-mail: gradadmissions@georgiasouthern.edu.

Georgia Southwestern State University, Graduate Studies, School of Education, Americus, GA 31709-4693. Offers early childhood education (M Ed, Ed S); health and physical education (M Ed); middle grades education (M Ed, Ed S); reading (M Ed); secondary education (M Ed); special education (M Ed). *Accreditation:* NCATE. *Degree requirements:* For master's, comprehensive exam. *Entrance requirements:* For master's, GRE General Test or MAT, minimum GPA of 2.5; for Ed S, GRE General Test or MAT, minimum graduate GPA of 3.25, M Ed from accredited college or university, 3 years teaching experience. Electronic applications accepted.

Georgia State University, College of Education, Department of Middle-Secondary Education and Instructional Technology, Program in Middle Childhood Education, Atlanta, GA 30302-3083. Offers M Ed, Ed S. *Accreditation:* NCATE. Part-time and evening/weekend programs available. *Degree requirements:* For master's, comprehensive exam; for Ed S, project/exam. *Entrance requirements:* For master's, GRE General Test, minimum GPA of 2.5; for Ed S, GRE General Test or MAT, minimum graduate GPA of 3.25.

Grand Valley State University, College of Education, Programs in General Education, Allendale, MI 49401-9403. Offers adult and higher education (M Ed); early childhood education (M Ed); educational differentiation (M Ed); educational leadership (M Ed); educational technology integration (M Ed); elementary education (M Ed); middle level education (M Ed); school library media services (M Ed); secondary level education (M Ed); teaching English to speakers of other languages (M Ed). Part-time and evening/weekend programs available. Postbaccalaureate distance learning degree programs offered (minimal on-campus study). *Faculty:* 82 full-time (42 women), 43 part-time/adjunct (25 women). *Students:* 100 full-time (53 women), 723 part-time (478 women); includes 59 minority (25 African Americans, 4 American Indian/Alaska Native, 13 Asian Americans or Pacific Islanders, 17 Hispanic Americans), 10 international. Average age 33. 237 applicants, 96% accepted, 117 enrolled. In 2009, 291 master's awarded. *Degree requirements:* For master's, thesis. *Entrance requirements:* For master's, GRE General Test or minimum GPA of 3.0. Additional exam requirements/recommendations for international students: Required—TOEFL. *Application deadline:* Applications are processed on a rolling basis. Application fee: $30. Electronic applications accepted. *Expenses:* Tuition, state resident: part-time $471 per credit hour. Tuition, nonresident: part-time $646 per credit hour. Tuition and fees vary according to course level. *Financial support:* In 2009–10, 73 students received support, including 55 fellowships (averaging $2,273 per year), 19 research assistantships with full and partial tuition reimbursements available (averaging $8,000 per year); career-related internships or fieldwork, Federal Work-Study, scholarships/grants, and unspecified assistant-

ships also available. *Faculty research:* Effectiveness of technology in education, parental involvement, effective teaching, effective schools research. *Unit head:* Dr. Linda McCrea, Director, 616-331-2080, E-mail: mccreal@gvsu.edu. *Application contact:* Thomas Owens, Student Information and Services Center, 616-331-6282, Fax: 616-331-2000, E-mail: owenst@gvsu.edu.

Hampton University, Graduate College, Department of Education, Program in Teaching, Hampton, VA 23668. Offers early childhood education (MT); middle school education (MT); music education (MT); secondary education (MT); special education (MT). *Entrance requirements:* For master's, GRE General Test.

Hebrew College, Shoolman Graduate School of Education, Newton Centre, MA 02459. Offers early childhood Jewish education (Certificate); Jewish day school education (Certificate); Jewish education (MJ Ed); Jewish family education (Certificate); Jewish special education (Certificate); Jewish youth education, informal education and camping (Certificate). Part-time and evening/weekend programs available. Postbaccalaureate distance learning degree programs offered. *Degree requirements:* For master's, one foreign language. *Entrance requirements:* For master's, GRE, interview. Additional exam requirements/recommendations for international students: Required—TOEFL.

Henderson State University, Graduate Studies, School of Education, Department of Advanced Instructional Studies, Arkadelphia, AR 71999-0001. Offers early childhood (P-4) (MSE); education (MAT); middle school (MSE); reading (MSE); special education (MSE). *Accreditation:* NCATE. Part-time programs available. *Faculty:* 7 full-time (4 women), 2 part-time/adjunct (both women). *Students:* 7 full-time (all women), 131 part-time (119 women); includes 16 minority (11 African Americans, 1 Asian American or Pacific Islander, 4 Hispanic Americans). Average age 33. 25 applicants, 100% accepted, 25 enrolled. In 2009, 53 master's awarded. *Entrance requirements:* For master's, GRE General Test or MAT, minimum GPA of 2.7, teacher certification. Additional exam requirements/recommendations for international students: Required—TOEFL (minimum score 550 paper-based; 213 computer-based); Recommended—IELTS (minimum score 6). *Application deadline:* For fall admission, 8/1 priority date for domestic students, 6/30 priority date for international students; for spring admission, 1/1 priority date for domestic students, 11/30 priority date for international students. Application fee: $25 ($75 for international students). Electronic applications accepted. *Expenses:* Tuition, state resident: full-time $3798; part-time $211 per credit hour. Tuition, nonresident: full-time $7596; part-time $422 per credit hour. Required fees: $903. *Financial support:* Research assistantships, teaching assistantships with tuition reimbursements available. *Unit head:* Dr. Gary Smithey, Chairperson, 870-230-5361, Fax: 870-230-5455, E-mail: smitheg@hsu.edu. *Application contact:* Dr. Marck L. Beggs, Graduate Dean, 870-230-5126, Fax: 870-230-5479, E-mail: beggsm@hsu.edu.

Hofstra University, School of Education, Health, and Human Services, Department of Curriculum and Teaching, Program in Middle Level Education, Hempstead, NY 11549. Offers middle school extension (grades 5-6) (Advanced Certificate); middle school extension (grades 7-9) (Advanced Certificate). Part-time and evening/weekend programs available. *Students:* 1 (woman) full-time. Average age 23. 15 applicants, 93% accepted, 0 enrolled. In 2009, 7 Advanced Certificates awarded. *Entrance requirements:* For degree, interview, teacher certificate. Additional exam requirements/recommendations for international students: Required—TOEFL (minimum score 550 paper-based; 213 computer-based; 80 iBT). *Application deadline:* Applications are processed on a rolling basis. Application fee: $60. Electronic applications accepted. *Expenses:* Tuition: Full-time $16,200; part-time $900 per credit hour. Required fees: $970; $145 per term. Tuition and fees vary according to program. *Financial support:* In 2009–10, 1 student received support; fellowships with full and partial tuition reimbursements available, research assistantships with full and partial tuition reimbursements available, Federal Work-Study, institutionally sponsored loans, scholarships/grants, and tuition waivers (full and partial) available. Support available to part-time students. Financial award applicants required to submit FAFSA. *Unit head:* Dr. Sandra L. Stacki, Director, 516-463-5783, Fax: 516-463-6196, E-mail: catsls@hofstra.edu. *Application contact:* Carol Drummer, Dean of Graduate Admissions, 516-463-4876, Fax: 516-463-4664, E-mail: gradstudent@hofstra.edu.

Hood College, Graduate School, Program in Secondary Mathematics Education, Frederick, MD 21701-8575. Offers mathematics education (MS), including high school, middle school; secondary mathematics education (Certificate). Part-time and evening/weekend programs available. *Faculty:* 1 full-time (0 women), 2 part-time/adjunct (0 women). *Students:* 32 part-time (24 women); includes 1 minority (African American). Average age 34. 8 applicants, 88% accepted, 7 enrolled. In 2009, 1 master's, 1 other advanced degree awarded. *Degree requirements:* For master's, capstone/research project. *Entrance requirements:* For master's, minimum GPA of 2.75. *Application deadline:* For fall admission, 7/15 for domestic and international students; for spring admission, 12/15 for domestic and international students. Applications are processed on a rolling basis. Application fee: $35. Electronic applications accepted. *Expenses:* Tuition: Full-time $6480; part-time $360 per credit. Required fees: $100; $50 per term. *Financial support:* Applicants required to submit FAFSA. *Unit head:* Dr. Betty Mayfield, Chairperson, 301-696-3763, E-mail: mayfield@hood.edu. *Application contact:* Dr. Allen P. Flora, Dean of Graduate School, 301-696-3811, Fax: 301-696-3597, E-mail: gofurther@hood.edu.

James Madison University, The Graduate School, College of Education, Middle, Secondary, and Mathematics Education Department, Program in Middle Education, Harrisonburg, VA 22807. Offers MAT. *Accreditation:* NCATE. Part-time and evening/weekend programs available. *Students:* Average age 27. *Entrance requirements:* For master's, GRE General Test, minimum undergraduate GPA of 2.5. Additional exam requirements/recommendations for international students: Required—TOEFL. *Application deadline:* For fall admission, 5/1 priority date for domestic students; for spring admission, 9/1 priority date for domestic students. Applications are processed on a rolling basis. Application fee: $55. Electronic applications accepted. *Expenses:* Tuition, area resident: Part-time $305 per credit hour. Tuition, state resident: part-time $305 per credit hour. Tuition, nonresident: part-time $890 per credit hour. *Financial support:* Federal Work-Study and unspecified assistantships available. Financial award application deadline: 3/1; financial award applicants required to submit FAFSA. *Unit head:* Dr. Steven L. Purcell, Academic Unit Head, 540-568-6793. *Application contact:* Lynette M. Bible, Director of Graduate Admissions, 540-568-6395, Fax: 540-568-7860, E-mail: biblelm@jmu.edu.

John Carroll University, Graduate School, Department of Education and Allied Studies, Program in School Based Middle Childhood Education, University Heights, OH 44118-4581. Offers M Ed. *Accreditation:* NCATE. *Degree requirements:* For master's, comprehensive exam. *Entrance requirements:* For master's, GRE General Test or MAT, minimum GPA of 2.75, interview. Additional exam requirements/recommendations for international students: Required—TOEFL. Electronic applications accepted.

John Carroll University, Graduate School, Program in Integrated Science, University Heights, OH 44118-4581. Offers MA. Part-time programs available. *Degree requirements:* For master's, thesis optional. *Entrance requirements:* For master's, minimum GPA of 2.5, teachers license. Electronic applications accepted.

Kennesaw State University, Leland and Clarice C. Bagwell College of Education, Program in Graduate Education, Kennesaw, GA 30144-5591. Offers adolescent education (M Ed); educational leadership (M Ed); educational leadership technology (M Ed); elementary and early childhood education (M Ed); special education (M Ed); teaching English to speakers of other languages (M Ed). *Accreditation:* NCATE. Part-time programs available. *Faculty:* 60 full-time (38 women), 12 part-time/adjunct (4 women). *Students:* 140 full-time (116 women), 136 part-time (107 women); includes 51 minority (39 African Americans, 1 American Indian/Alaska Native, 3 Asian Americans or Pacific Islanders, 8 Hispanic Americans), 4 international. Average age 34. 113 applicants, 83% accepted, 69 enrolled. In 2009, 282 master's awarded.

Degree requirements: For master's, thesis or alternative. *Entrance requirements:* For master's, GRE General Test, T-4 state certification, minimum GPA of 2.75. Additional exam requirements/recommendations for international students: Required—TOEFL (minimum score 550 paper-based; 213 computer-based; 80 iBT), IELTS (minimum score 6). *Application deadline:* For fall admission, 7/1 for domestic and international students; for spring admission, 10/1 for domestic and international students. Application fee: $60. Electronic applications accepted. *Expenses:* Tuition, state resident: full-time $2341; part-time $196 per credit hour. Tuition, nonresident: full-time $9396; part-time $783 per credit hour. Required fees: $573 per semester. *Financial support:* Federal Work-Study and unspecified assistantships available. Support available to part-time students. Financial award application deadline: 6/15; financial award applicants required to submit FAFSA. *Unit head:* Dr. Nita Paris, Associate Dean for Graduate Programs, 770-423-6636, E-mail: nparis@kennesaw.edu. *Application contact:* Alisha Bello, Administrative Coordinator, 770-423-6043, Fax: 770-420-4435, E-mail: abello1@kennesaw.edu.

Kent State University, Graduate School of Education, Health, and Human Services, School of Teaching, Learning and Curriculum Studies, Program in Junior High/Middle School, Kent, OH 44242-0001. Offers M Ed, MA. Part-time programs available. *Faculty:* 5 full-time (3 women). *Students:* 2 applicants, 0% accepted. In 2009, 2 master's awarded. *Entrance requirements:* For master's, GRE. Additional exam requirements/recommendations for international students: Required—TOEFL. *Application deadline:* Applications are processed on a rolling basis. Application fee: $30 ($60 for international students). Electronic applications accepted. *Financial support:* In 2009–10, research assistantships with full tuition reimbursements (averaging $9,000 per year); Federal Work-Study, scholarships/grants, and unspecified assistantships also available. Financial award applicants required to submit FAFSA. *Faculty research:* Middle school reform, teacher action research. *Unit head:* Dr. Bette Brooks, Coordinator, 330-672-0536, E-mail: ebrooks@kent.edu. *Application contact:* Nancy Miller, Academic Program Coordinator, Office of Graduate Student Services, 330-672-2576, Fax: 330-672-9162, E-mail: ogs@kent.edu.

LaGrange College, Graduate Programs, Department of Education, LaGrange, GA 30240-2999. Offers curriculum and instruction (M Ed); middle grades (MAT); secondary education (MAT). Part-time and evening/weekend programs available. *Degree requirements:* For master's, comprehensive exam. *Entrance requirements:* For master's, GRE, MAT, minimum GPA of 2.5. Additional exam requirements/recommendations for international students: Required—TOEFL (minimum score 550 paper-based).

Le Moyne College, Department of Education, Syracuse, NY 13214. Offers adolescent education (MS Ed, MST); adolescent education/special education (MS Ed, MST); adolescent English (grades 7-12) (MST); adolescent history (grades 7-12) (MST); childhood education (MS Ed); childhood education/special education (MS Ed); elementary education (MS Ed); general professional education (MS Ed); inclusive childhood education (MST); middle child specialist/special education (MS Ed); middle childhood specialist (MS Ed); school building leadership (MS Ed, CAS); school district business leader (MS Ed, CAS); school district leadership (MS Ed, CAS); secondary education (MS Ed); special education (MS Ed). *Accreditation:* Teacher Education Accreditation Council. Part-time and evening/weekend programs available. *Faculty:* 15 full-time (8 women), 61 part-time/adjunct (33 women). *Students:* 40 full-time (30 women), 260 part-time (180 women); includes 25 minority (11 African Americans, 3 American Indian/Alaska Native, 3 Asian Americans or Pacific Islanders, 8 Hispanic Americans). Average age 31. 168 applicants, 89% accepted, 140 enrolled. In 2009, 180 master's awarded. *Degree requirements:* For master's, thesis. *Entrance requirements:* For master's, GRE General Test, 2 letters of recommendation. Additional exam requirements/recommendations for international students: Required—TOEFL (minimum score 550 paper-based; 213 computer-based; 79 iBT). *Application deadline:* For fall admission, 4/1 priority date for domestic and international students; for spring admission, 10/1 priority date for domestic and international students. Applications are processed on a rolling basis. Application fee: $50. *Expenses:* Contact institution. *Financial support:* In 2009–10, 28 students received support. Career-related internships or fieldwork and health care benefits available. Support available to part-time students. Financial award applicants required to submit FAFSA. *Faculty research:* Recruitment/retention strategies, minority teachers, special education, multiculturalism, literacy, technology, video games learning, autism, school district organization. *Unit head:* Dr. Norbert J. Henry, Interim Chair/Director, 315-445-4376, Fax: 315-445-4744, E-mail: henry@lemoyne.edu. *Application contact:* Kristen P. Trapasso, Director of Graduate Admission, 315-445-4265, Fax: 315-445-6027, E-mail: trapaskp@lemoyne.edu.

Lesley University, School of Education, Cambridge, MA 02138-2790. Offers curriculum and instruction (M Ed, CAGS); early childhood education (M Ed); educational studies (PhD); elementary education (M Ed); individually designed (M Ed); middle school education (M Ed); moderate special needs (M Ed); reading (M Ed, CAGS); science in education (M Ed); severe special needs (M Ed); special needs (CAGS); technology in education (M Ed, CAGS). *Accreditation:* Teacher Education Accreditation Council. Part-time and evening/weekend programs available. Postbaccalaureate distance learning degree programs offered (no on-campus study). *Degree requirements:* For master's, practicum; for doctorate, thesis/dissertation. *Entrance requirements:* For doctorate, GRE General Test or MAT, interview, master's degree, resume; for CAGS, interview, master's degree. Additional exam requirements/recommendations for international students: Required—TOEFL (minimum score 550 paper-based; 213 computer-based; 80 iBT). Electronic applications accepted. *Faculty research:* Assessment in literacy, mathematics and science; autism spectrum disorders; instructional technology and online learning; multicultural education and ELL.

Lewis & Clark College, Graduate School of Education and Counseling, Department of Teacher Education, Program in Middle Level/High School Education, Portland, OR 97219-7899. Offers MAT. *Accreditation:* NCATE. *Faculty:* 4 full-time (3 women), 9 part-time/adjunct (5 women). *Students:* 71 full-time (42 women); includes 8 minority (2 African Americans, 2 American Indian/Alaska Native, 1 Asian American or Pacific Islander, 3 Hispanic Americans), 2 international. Average age 29. 123 applicants, 82% accepted, 72 enrolled. In 2009, 57 master's awarded. *Entrance requirements:* For master's, Prior experience working with children and/or youth. Minimum undergraduate GPA of 2.75. Additional exam requirements/recommendations for international students: Required—TOEFL (minimum score 575 paper-based; 233 computer-based). *Application deadline:* For fall admission, 12/1 priority date for domestic and international students. Application fee: $50. Electronic applications accepted. *Expenses:* Tuition: Part-time $713 per semester hour. Tuition and fees vary according to course level and campus/location. *Financial support:* In 2009–10, 60 students received support. Career-related internships or fieldwork, Federal Work-Study, institutionally sponsored loans, scholarships/grants, health care benefits, and tuition waivers (partial) available. Support available to part-time students. Financial award application deadline: 3/1; financial award applicants required to submit FAFSA. *Faculty research:* Classroom management, classroom assessment, science education, classroom ethnography, moral development. *Unit head:* Dr. Kimberly Campbell, Coordinator, 503-768-6108, Fax: 503-768-7715, E-mail: lcteach@lclark.edu. *Application contact:* Becky Haas, Director of Admissions, 503-768-6200, Fax: 503-768-6205, E-mail: gseadmit@lclark.edu.

Long Island University, C.W. Post Campus, School of Education, Department of Curriculum and Instruction, Brookville, NY 11548-1300. Offers adolescence education (MS); adolescence education: biology (MS); adolescence education: earth science (MS); adolescence education: English (MS); adolescence education: mathematics (MS); adolescence education: social studies (MS); adolescence education: Spanish (MS); art education (MS); bilingual education (MS); childhood education (MS); early childhood education (MS); middle childhood education (MS); music education (MS); teaching English to speakers of other languages (MS). Part-time and evening/weekend programs available. *Degree requirements:* For master's, comprehensive exam or thesis, student teaching. *Entrance requirements:* For master's, minimum GPA of 2.75 in major, 2.5 overall. Electronic applications accepted. *Faculty research:* Ethics and education, teaching strategies.

Middle School Education

Manhattanville College, Graduate Programs, School of Education, Program in Middle Childhood/Adolescence Education (Grades 5-12), Purchase, NY 10577-2132. Offers biology (MAT); biology and special education (MPS); chemistry (MAT); chemistry and special education (MPS); English (MAT); English and special education (MPS); literacy (MPS), including reading and writing; writing; literacy and special education (MPS); math (MAT); math and special education (MPS); second language (MAT), including French, Italian, Latin, Spanish; social studies (MAT); social studies and special education (MPS); special education (MPS). Part-time and evening/weekend programs available. *Students:* 52 full-time (39 women), 106 part-time (71 women); includes 8 African Americans, 3 Asian Americans or Pacific Islanders, 4 Hispanic Americans, 1 international. In 2009, 82 master's awarded. *Degree requirements:* For master's, comprehensive exam or research project, field experience. *Entrance requirements:* For master's, minimum undergraduate GPA of 3.0, 2 letters of recommendation. Additional exam requirements/recommendations for international students: Required—TOEFL. *Application deadline:* Applications are processed on a rolling basis. Application fee: $70. Electronic applications accepted. *Financial support:* Career-related internships or fieldwork, Federal Work-Study, institutionally sponsored loans, and unspecified assistantships available. Support available to part-time students. Financial award application deadline: 3/1; financial award applicants required to submit FAFSA. *Unit head:* Dr. Shelley Wepner, Dean, 914-323-5192, Fax: 914-694-2386, E-mail: wepners@mville.edu. *Application contact:* Jeanine Pardey-Levine, Director of Admissions, 914-323-3208, Fax: 914-694-1732, E-mail: edschool@mville.edu.

Mary Baldwin College, Graduate Studies, Program in Teaching, Staunton, VA 24401-3610. Offers elementary education (MAT); middle grades education (MAT). *Accreditation:* Teacher Education Accreditation Council.

Maryville University of Saint Louis, School of Education, St. Louis, MO 63141-7299. Offers art education (MA Ed); early childhood education (MA Ed); educational leadership (Ed D); educational leadership: principal certification (MA Ed); elementary education (MA Ed); elementary education/English (MA Ed); elementary education/psychology (MA Ed); environmental education (MA Ed); gifted education (MA Ed); literacy specialist (MA Ed); middle grades education (MA Ed); secondary teaching and inquiry (MA Ed); teacher as leader (MA Ed). *Accreditation:* NASAD; NCATE. Part-time and evening/weekend programs available. *Students:* 25 full-time (18 women), 198 part-time (145 women); includes 33 minority (27 African Americans, 2 American Indian/Alaska Native, 1 Asian American or Pacific Islander, 3 Hispanic Americans). Average age 36. In 2009, 61 master's, 45 doctorates awarded. *Degree requirements:* For master's, thesis, project. *Entrance requirements:* For master's and doctorate, minimum GPA of 3.0, 3 professional recommendations. Additional exam requirements/recommendations for international students: Required—TOEFL (minimum score 550 paper-based). *Application deadline:* Applications are processed on a rolling basis. Application fee: $40 ($60 for international students). Electronic applications accepted. *Expenses:* Tuition: Full-time $20,384; part-time $627.50 per credit hour. Required fees: $100 per semester. *Financial support:* Career-related internships or fieldwork, Federal Work-Study, tuition waivers (partial), and professional educator discounts available. Financial award application deadline: 3/1; financial award applicants required to submit FAFSA. *Faculty research:* Collaboration with public schools, pre-service program development, mathematics, diversity, literacy. *Unit head:* Dr. Sam Hausfather, Dean, 314-529-9466, Fax: 314-529-9921, E-mail: shausfather@maryville.edu. *Application contact:* Holly Stanwich, Graduate Admissions Coordinator, 314-529-9542, Fax: 314-529-9921, E-mail: teachered@maryville.edu.

Mercer University, Graduate Studies, Cecil B. Day Campus, Tift College of Education (Atlanta), Macon, GA 31207-0003. Offers curriculum and instruction (PhD); early childhood education (M Ed, MAT); educational leadership (PhD, Ed S); middle grades education (M Ed, MAT); reading education (M Ed); secondary education (M Ed, MAT); teacher leadership (Ed S). *Accreditation:* NCATE. Part-time and evening/weekend programs available. *Faculty:* 27 full-time (14 women), 6 part-time/adjunct (3 women). *Students:* 302 full-time (251 women), 543 part-time (430 women); includes 334 minority (311 African Americans, 1 American Indian/Alaska Native, 21 Asian Americans or Pacific Islanders, 1 Hispanic American), 7 international. Average age 34. In 2009, 195 master's, 20 doctorates awarded. *Degree requirements:* For master's and Ed S, research project; for doctorate, thesis/dissertation. *Entrance requirements:* For master's, GRE or MAT, minimum undergraduate GPA of 2.75; for doctorate, GRE; for Ed S, GRE or MAT, minimum GPA of 3.25, 3 years of teaching experience. Additional exam requirements/recommendations for international students: Required—TOEFL. *Application deadline:* For fall admission, 8/1 for domestic and international students; for spring admission, 12/1 for domestic and international students. Applications are processed on a rolling basis. Application fee: $25. *Expenses:* Contact institution. *Financial support:* Federal Work-Study available. Support available to part-time students. Financial award application deadline: 5/1. *Faculty research:* Educational computing, content area reading, concept learning, importance of play for young children, multicultural literature. *Unit head:* Dr. Carl R. Martray, Dean, 478-301-5397, Fax: 478-301-2280, E-mail: martray_cr@mercer.edu. *Application contact:* Dr. Allison Gilmore, Associate Dean for Graduate Teacher Education, 678-547-6330, Fax: 678-547-6055, E-mail: gilmore_a@mercer.edu.

Mercy College, School of Education, Program in Middle Childhood Education, Grades 5-9, Dobbs Ferry, NY 10522-1189. Offers MS. Part-time and evening/weekend programs available. *Students:* 26 full-time (20 women), 72 part-time (49 women); includes 24 African Americans, 2 Asian Americans or Pacific Islanders, 15 Hispanic Americans. Average age 33. 41 applicants, 71% accepted, 18 enrolled. In 2009, 34 master's awarded. *Entrance requirements:* For master's, interview, resume, minimum undergraduate GPA of 3.0 (writing sample for those with GPA lower than 3.0), assessment by specific program director or designee. Additional exam requirements/recommendations for international students: Required—TOEFL (minimum score 600 paper-based; 250 computer-based; 100 iBT). *Application deadline:* For fall admission, 8/1 for international students. Applications are processed on a rolling basis. Application fee: $40. Electronic applications accepted. *Expenses:* Tuition: Full-time $13,158; part-time $731 per credit. Required fees: $500. Tuition and fees vary according to degree level and program. *Financial support:* In 2009-10, 2 students received support. Career-related internships or fieldwork, Federal Work-Study, scholarships/grants, and unspecified assistantships available. Support available to part-time students. Financial award applicants required to submit FAFSA. *Faculty research:* Behavior management application, assistive technology, educational psychology. *Unit head:* Dr. Andrew Peiser, Interim Dean, School of Education, 914-674-7489, Fax: 914-674-7352, E-mail: apeiser@mercy.edu. *Application contact:* Mary Ellen Hoffman, Interim Associate Dean, 914-674-7334, E-mail: mhoffman@mercy.edu.

Middle Tennessee State University, College of Graduate Studies, College of Education and Behavioral Science, Department of Elementary and Special Education, Major in Curriculum and Instruction, Murfreesboro, TN 37132. Offers early childhood education (M Ed); elementary education (M Ed, Ed S); middle school education (M Ed). *Accreditation:* NCATE. Part-time and evening/weekend programs available. Postbaccalaureate distance learning degree programs offered. *Students:* 14 full-time (12 women), 126 part-time (118 women); includes 11 minority (8 African Americans, 2 Asian Americans or Pacific Islanders, 1 Hispanic American). 39 applicants, 72% accepted. In 2009, 55 master's awarded. *Degree requirements:* For master's, comprehensive exam; for Ed S, thesis. *Entrance requirements:* For master's and Ed S, GRE, MAT or PRAXIS. Additional exam requirements/recommendations for international students: Required—TOEFL (minimum score 525 paper-based; 195 computer-based; 71 iBT) or IELTS (minimum score 6). *Application deadline:* For fall admission, 8/1 priority date for domestic students. Applications are processed on a rolling basis. Application fee: $25. Electronic applications accepted. *Expenses:* Tuition: state resident: full-time $4404. Tuition, nonresident: full-time $10,956. *Financial support:* Institutionally sponsored loans available. Support available to part-time students. Financial award application deadline: 5/1. *Unit head:* Dr. Kathy Burriss, Director, 615-898-2323, Fax: 615-898-5309, E-mail: kburriss@mtsu.edu. *Application contact:* Dr. Michael Allen, Dean and Vice Provost for Research, 615-898-2840, Fax: 615-904-8020, E-mail: mallen@mtsu.edu.

Montclair State University, The Graduate School, College of Science and Mathematics, Department of Mathematics, Montclair, NJ 07043-1624. Offers math pedagogy (Ed D); mathematics (MS), including computer science, mathematics education, pure and applied mathematics, statistics; physical science (Certificate); teaching middle grades math (MS, Certificate). Part-time and evening/weekend programs available. *Faculty:* 30 full-time (10 women), 39 part-time/adjunct (19 women). *Students:* 15 full-time (7 women), 101 part-time (75 women). Average age 32. 55 applicants, 76% accepted, 31 enrolled. In 2009, 32 master's, 2 doctorates, 9 other advanced degrees awarded. *Degree requirements:* For master's, comprehensive exam. *Entrance requirements:* For master's, GRE General Test, 2 letters of recommendation. Additional exam requirements/recommendations for international students: Required—TOEFL (minimum score 83 computer-based), or IELTS. *Application deadline:* For fall admission, 6/1 for international students; for spring admission, 10/1 for international students. Applications are processed on a rolling basis. Application fee: $60. *Expenses:* Tuition, area resident: Part-time $486.74 per credit. Tuition, state resident: part-time $486.74 per credit. Tuition, nonresident: part-time $751.34 per credit. Tuition and fees vary according to degree level and program. *Financial support:* In 2009-10, 9 research assistantships with full tuition reimbursements (averaging $7,000 per year), 1 teaching assistantship with full tuition reimbursement (averaging $15,000 per year) were awarded; Federal Work-Study, scholarships/grants, and unspecified assistantships also available. Support available to part-time students. Financial award application deadline: 3/1; financial award applicants required to submit FAFSA. *Faculty research:* Infectious disease. *Unit head:* Dr. Helen Roberts, Chairperson, 973-655-5132. *Application contact:* Amy Aiello, Director of Graduate Admissions and Operations, 973-655-5147, Fax: 973-655-7869, E-mail: graduate.school@montclair.edu.

Morehead State University, Graduate Programs, College of Education, Department of Curriculum and Instruction, Morehead, KY 40351. Offers curriculum and instruction (Ed S); elementary education (MA Ed), including elementary education, international education, middle school education, reading; secondary education (MA Ed); special education (MA Ed); teaching (MAT). Part-time and evening/weekend programs available. *Faculty:* 25 full-time (17 women), 2 part-time/adjunct (1 woman). *Students:* 25 full-time (22 women), 165 part-time (139 women); includes 4 minority (1 African American, 2 American Indian/Alaska Native, 1 Hispanic American). Average age 33. 148 applicants, 68% accepted, 48 enrolled. In 2009, 178 master's awarded. *Degree requirements:* For master's, comprehensive exam, thesis optional; for Ed S, thesis, oral exam. *Entrance requirements:* For master's, GRE General Test, minimum GPA of 2.75, teaching certificate; for Ed S, GRE General Test, interview, master's degree, minimum GPA of 3.5, work experience. Additional exam requirements/recommendations for international students: Required—TOEFL (minimum score 500 paper-based; 173 computer-based). *Application deadline:* For fall admission, 8/1 priority date for domestic and international students; for spring admission, 12/1 priority date for domestic and international students. Applications are processed on a rolling basis. Application fee: $30. Electronic applications accepted. *Expenses:* Tuition, state resident: full-time $6318; part-time $351 per credit hour. Tuition, nonresident: full-time $15,804; part-time $878 per credit hour. *Financial support:* In 2009-10, 2 teaching assistantships (averaging $6,000 per year) were awarded; career-related internships or fieldwork, Federal Work-Study, and unspecified assistantships also available. Financial award application deadline: 3/15; financial award applicants required to submit FAFSA. *Faculty research:* Communicative competence of learning-disabled students, teaching social studies in elementary schools, ungraded primary school organization, study skills. *Unit head:* Dr. James Knoll, Chair, 606-783-2598, Fax: 606-783-5044, E-mail: j.knoll@moreheadstate.edu. *Application contact:* Michelle Barber, Graduate Recruitment and Retention Assistant Director, 606-783-5127, Fax: 606-783-5061, E-mail: m.barber@moreheadstate.edu.

Morehead State University, Graduate Programs, College of Education, Department of Foundational and Graduate Studies in Education, Morehead, KY 40351. Offers adult and higher education (MA, Ed S); certified professional counselor (Ed S); counseling P-12 (MA); curriculum and instruction (Ed S); educational technology (MA Ed); instructional leadership (Ed S); school administration (MA); school counseling (Ed S); teacher leader business and marketing- content (MA Ed); teacher leader business and marketing- technology (MA Ed); teacher leader educational technology (MA Ed); teacher leader English (MA Ed); teacher leader gifted educ (MA Ed); teacher leader IECE—non-certification (MA Ed); teacher leader IECE certification (MA Ed); teacher leader interdisciplanary educaction P-5 (MA Ed); teacher leader middle grades 5-9 (MA Ed); teacher leader reading/writing—non-certification (MA Ed); teacher leader reading/writing certification (MA Ed); teacher leader school communication—non-certification (MA Ed); teacher leader school communication certification (MA Ed); teacher leader social studies (MA Ed); teacher leader special education (MA Ed). *Accreditation:* NCATE. Part-time and evening/weekend programs available. *Faculty:* 20 full-time (10 women), 7 part-time/adjunct (3 women). *Students:* 26 full-time (18 women), 371 part-time (295 women); includes 11 minority (9 African Americans, 1 American Indian/Alaska Native, 1 Hispanic American). Average age 35. 201 applicants, 73% accepted, 73 enrolled. In 2009, 105 master's, 5 other advanced degrees awarded. *Degree requirements:* For master's, thesis optional, oral and/or written comprehensive exams; for Ed S, thesis, oral exam. *Entrance requirements:* For master's, GRE General Test, minimum overall undergraduate GPA of 2.5; for Ed S, GRE General Test, interview, master's degree, minimum GPA of 3.5, work experience. Additional exam requirements/recommendations for international students: Required—TOEFL (minimum score 500 paper-based; 173 computer-based). *Application deadline:* For fall admission, 8/1 priority date for domestic and international students; for spring admission, 12/1 priority date for domestic and international students. Applications are processed on a rolling basis. Application fee: $30. Electronic applications accepted. *Expenses:* Tuition, state resident: full-time $6318; part-time $351 per credit hour. Tuition, nonresident: full-time $15,804; part-time $878 per credit hour. *Financial support:* In 2009-10, 2 research assistantships (averaging $10,000 per year) were awarded; career-related internships or fieldwork, Federal Work-Study, and unspecified assistantships also available. Financial award application deadline: 3/15; financial award applicants required to submit FAFSA. *Faculty research:* Character education, school accountability, computer applications for school administrators. *Unit head:* Dr. Cathy Gunn, Dean and Professor, 606-783-2040, Fax: 606-783-5029, E-mail: c.gunn@moreheadstate.edu. *Application contact:* Michelle Barber, Graduate Recruitment and Retention Assistant Director, 606-783-5127, Fax: 606-783-5061, E-mail: m.barber@moreheadstate.edu.

Morehead State University, Graduate Programs, College of Education, Department of Middle Grades and Secondary Education, Morehead, KY 40351. Offers business and marketing education (MAT); English/language arts 5-9 (MAT); French (MAT); health P-12 (MAT); mathematics 5-9 (MAT); physical education P-12 (MAT); science 5-9 (MAT); secondary biology (MAT); secondary chemistry (MAT); secondary earth science (MAT); secondary English (MAT); secondary math (MAT); secondary physics (MAT); secondary social studies (MAT); social studies 5-9 (MAT); Spanish (MAT). Part-time and evening/weekend programs available. *Students:* 54 full-time (31 women), 233 part-time (142 women); includes 11 minority (5 African Americans, 1 American Indian/Alaska Native, 1 Asian American or Pacific Islander, 4 Hispanic Americans). Average age 32. 206 applicants, 71% accepted, 79 enrolled. In 2009, 101 master's awarded. *Degree requirements:* For master's, portfolio. *Entrance requirements:* For master's, GRE or PRAXIS II content exam, minimum overall undergraduate GPA of 2.5. Additional exam requirements/recommendations for international students: Required—TOEFL (minimum score 500 paper-based; 173 computer-based). *Application deadline:* For fall admission, 8/1 priority date for domestic and international students; for spring admission, 12/1 priority date for domestic and international students. Applications are processed on a rolling basis. Application fee: $30. Electronic applications accepted. *Expenses:* Tuition, state resident: full-time $6318; part-time $351 per credit hour. Tuition, nonresident: full-time $15,804; part-time $878 per credit hour. *Financial support:* In 2009-10, 1 research assistantship (averaging $10,000 per year) was awarded; career-related internships or fieldwork, Federal Work-Study, and unspecified assistantships also available. Financial award application deadline: 3/15; financial award applicants required to submit FAFSA. *Unit head:* Dr. Cathy Gunn, Dean, 606-783-2040, Fax: 606-783-5029, E-mail: c.gunn@moreheadstate.edu. *Application contact:* Michelle Barber, Graduate Recruitment and Retention Assistant Director, 606-783-5127, Fax: 606-783-5061, E-mail: m.barber@moreheadstate.edu.

Morgan State University, School of Graduate Studies, School of Education and Urban Studies, MAT Program, Baltimore, MD 21251. Offers elementary education (MAT); high school education (MAT); middle school education (MAT). Part-time programs available. *Degree requirements:* For master's, comprehensive exam. *Entrance requirements:* For master's, GRE General Test or MAT. *Faculty research:* Multicultural education, cooperative learning, psychology of cognition.

Mount Saint Mary College, Division of Education, Newburgh, NY 12550-3494. Offers adolescence and special education (MS Ed); adolescence education (MS Ed); childhood and special education (MS Ed); childhood education (MS Ed); literacy (5-12) (Advanced Certificate); literacy (birth-6) (Advanced Certificate); literacy and special education (MS Ed); literacy/childhood (MS Ed); middle school (5-6) (MS Ed); middle school (7-9) (MS Ed); special education (1-6) (MS Ed); special education (7-12) (MS Ed). *Accreditation:* NCATE. Part-time and evening/weekend programs available. *Faculty:* 15 full-time (13 women), 16 part-time/adjunct (10 women). *Students:* 76 full-time (63 women), 226 part-time (188 women); includes 27 minority (7 African Americans, 3 Asian Americans or Pacific Islanders, 17 Hispanic Americans). Average age 30. 141 applicants, 56% accepted, 44 enrolled. In 2009, 142 master's awarded. *Application deadline:* Applications are processed on a rolling basis. Application fee: $45. *Expenses:* Tuition: Full-time $13,356; part-time $742 per credit. Required fees: $50 per semester. *Financial support:* In 2009–10, 106 students received support. Unspecified assistantships available. Financial award application deadline: 4/15; financial award applicants required to submit FAFSA. *Faculty research:* Learning and teaching styles, computers in special education, language development. *Unit head:* Dr. Theresa Lewis, Coordinator, 845-569-3149, Fax: 845-569-3535, E-mail: tlewis@msmc.edu. *Application contact:* Dr. Theresa Lewis, Coordinator, 845-569-3149, Fax: 845-569-3535, E-mail: tlewis@msmc.edu.

Mount Saint Vincent University, Graduate Programs, Faculty of Education, Program in Curriculum Studies, Halifax, NS B3M 2J6, Canada. Offers education of young adolescents (M Ed, MA Ed, MA-R); general studies (M Ed, MA Ed, MA-R); teaching English as a second language (M Ed, MA Ed, MA-R). Part-time and evening/weekend programs available. Postbaccalaureate distance learning degree programs offered (minimal on-campus study). *Degree requirements:* For master's, thesis (for some programs). *Entrance requirements:* For master's, bachelor's degree in related field, minimum B average, 1 year of teaching experience. Electronic applications accepted. *Faculty research:* Science education, cultural studies, international education, curriculum development.

Murray State University, College of Education, Department of Adolescent, Career and Special Education, Program in Middle School Education, Murray, KY 42071. Offers MA Ed, Ed S. *Accreditation:* NCATE. *Degree requirements:* For master's, comprehensive exam, thesis optional. *Entrance requirements:* Additional exam requirements/recommendations for international students: Required—TOEFL.

Nazareth College of Rochester, Graduate Studies, Department of Education, Program in Inclusive Education-Adolescence Level, Rochester, NY 14618-3790. Offers MS Ed. *Accreditation:* Teacher Education Accreditation Council. *Entrance requirements:* For master's, minimum GPA of 3.0.

Niagara University, Graduate Division of Education, Concentration in Teacher Education, Niagara Falls, Niagara University, NY 14109. Offers early childhood and childhood education (MS Ed); middle and adolescence education (MS Ed); special education (grades 1-12) (MS Ed). *Accreditation:* NCATE. *Entrance requirements:* For master's, GRE General Test or MAT. *Expenses:* Contact institution.

North Carolina Central University, Division of Academic Affairs, School of Education, Department of Curriculum, Instruction and Professional Studies, Durham, NC 27707-3129. Offers curriculum and instruction (MA), including elementary education, middle grades education. *Accreditation:* NCATE. Part-time and evening/weekend programs available. *Degree requirements:* For master's, comprehensive exam, thesis or alternative. *Entrance requirements:* For master's, minimum GPA of 3.0 in major, 2.5 overall. Additional exam requirements/recommendations for international students: Required—TOEFL. *Faculty research:* Simulation of decision-making behavior of school boards.

North Carolina State University, Graduate School, College of Education, Department of Curriculum and Instruction, Program in Middle Grades Education, Raleigh, NC 27695. Offers M Ed, MS. *Accreditation:* NCATE. *Degree requirements:* For master's, thesis optional. *Entrance requirements:* For master's, GRE General Test or MAT, minimum GPA of 3.0 in major.

North Georgia College & State University, Graduate Studies, Program in Teacher Education, Dahlonega, GA 30597. Offers early childhood education (M Ed); educational leadership (Ed S); middle grades education (M Ed); secondary education (M Ed), including art education, biology education, chemistry education, English education, history education, mathematics education, physical education, science education; special education (M Ed), including interrelated special education, learning disabilities. *Accreditation:* NCATE. Part-time and evening/weekend programs available. Postbaccalaureate distance learning degree programs offered (minimal on-campus study). *Degree requirements:* For master's, comprehensive exam, thesis optional. *Entrance requirements:* For master's, GRE General Test or MAT, minimum GPA of 2.75; for Ed S, GRE General Test or MAT, 3 years of teaching experience, master's degree, minimum graduate GPA of 3.25. Electronic applications accepted. *Faculty research:* Computers and teachers' attitudes, rural versus urban teacher attitudes, teacher leadership roles, minority recruitment in teaching force.

Northwestern State University of Louisiana, Graduate Studies and Research, College of Education, Program in Middle School Education, Natchitoches, LA 71497. Offers MAT. *Degree requirements:* For master's, comprehensive exam, thesis or alternative. *Entrance requirements:* For master's, GRE General Test, minimum undergraduate GPA of 2.5.

Northwest Missouri State University, Graduate School, College of Education and Human Services, Department of Curriculum and Instruction, Program in Teaching: Middle School, Maryville, MO 64468-6001. Offers MS Ed. *Accreditation:* NCATE. *Faculty:* 12 full-time (all women). *Students:* 1 (woman) part-time. 1 applicant, 100% accepted, 0 enrolled. *Degree requirements:* For master's, comprehensive exam. *Entrance requirements:* For master's, GRE General Test, minimum undergraduate GPA of 2.75, teaching certificate, writing sample. Additional exam requirements/recommendations for international students: Required—TOEFL. *Application deadline:* For fall admission, 7/1 for domestic and international students; for spring admission, 11/15 for domestic and international students. Applications are processed on a rolling basis. Application fee: $0 ($50 for international students). *Expenses:* Tuition, state resident: part-time $296.34 per credit hour. Tuition, nonresident: part-time $510.43 per credit hour. *Financial support:* Application deadline: 4/1. *Unit head:* Pat Thompson, Director, 660-562-1775. *Application contact:* Dr. Gregory Haddock, Dean of Graduate School, 660-562-1145, Fax: 660-562-1096, E-mail: gradsch@nwmissouri.edu.

Oberlin College, Graduate Teacher Education Program, Oberlin, OH 44074. Offers early childhood education (M Ed); middle childhood education (M Ed). *Degree requirements:* For master's, comprehensive exam, portfolio. *Entrance requirements:* For master's, GRE General Test, PRAXIS II. *Faculty research:* Literacy learning, teacher education reform, program development.

The Ohio State University at Lima, Graduate Programs, Lima, OH 45804. Offers early childhood education (M Ed); education (MA); middle childhood education (M Ed); social work (MSW). *Students:* 23 full-time (18 women), 83 part-time (72 women); includes 1 minority (African American). Average age 34. *Degree requirements:* For master's, comprehensive exam (for some programs), thesis (for some programs). *Entrance requirements:* For master's, GRE, minimum GPA of 3.0. Additional exam requirements/recommendations for international students: Required—TOEFL, IELTS or Michigan English Language Assessment Battery. *Application deadline:* For fall admission, 8/15 priority date for domestic students, 7/1 priority date for international students; for winter admission, 12/1 priority date for domestic students, 11/1 priority date for international students; for spring admission, 3/1 priority date for domestic students, 2/1 priority date for international students. Applications are processed on a rolling basis. Application fee: $40 ($50 for international students). Electronic applications accepted. *Expenses:* Tuition, state resident: full-time $10,155. Tuition, nonresident: full-time $25,395. Tuition and fees vary according to course load. *Unit head:* Dr. John Snyder, Dean/Director, 419-995-8481, E-mail: snyder.4@osu.edu. *Application contact:* Graduate Admissions, 614-292-9444, Fax: 614-292-3895, E-mail: domestic.grad@osu.edu.

The Ohio State University at Marion, Graduate Programs, Marion, OH 43302-5695. Offers early childhood education (pre-K to grade 3) (M Ed); integrated teaching and learning (MA); middle childhood education (grades 4-9) (M Ed); nursing (MS, PhD); social work (MSW); MS/PhD. Part-time programs available. *Students:* 49 full-time (38 women), 34 part-time (25 women); includes 2 minority (both African Americans). Average age 31. *Degree requirements:* For master's, comprehensive exam (for some programs), thesis (for some programs). *Entrance requirements:* For master's and doctorate, GRE, minimum undergraduate GPA of 3.0. Additional exam requirements/recommendations for international students: Required—TOEFL, IELTS or Michigan English Language Assessment Battery. *Application deadline:* For fall admission, 8/15 priority date for domestic students, 7/1 priority date for international students; for winter admission, 12/1 priority date for domestic students, 11/1 priority date for international students; for spring admission, 3/1 priority date for domestic students, 2/1 priority date for international students. Applications are processed on a rolling basis. Application fee: $40 ($50 for international students). Electronic applications accepted. *Expenses:* Tuition, state resident: full-time $10,155. Tuition, nonresident: full-time $25,395. Tuition and fees vary according to course load. *Unit head:* Gregory S. Rose, Dean/Director, 740-389-6786 Ext. 6218, E-mail: rose.9@osu.edu. *Application contact:* Graduate Admissions, 614-292-9444, Fax: 614-292-3895, E-mail: domestic.grad@osu.edu.

The Ohio State University–Mansfield Campus, Graduate Programs, Mansfield, OH 44906-1599. Offers early and middle childhood education (MA); early childhood education (M Ed); middle childhood education (M Ed); social work (MSW). *Faculty:* 8 full-time (4 women). *Students:* 31 full-time (29 women), 32 part-time (29 women); includes 1 minority (Asian American or Pacific Islander), 1 international. Average age 31. *Degree requirements:* For master's, comprehensive exam (for some programs), thesis (for some programs). *Entrance requirements:* For master's, GRE, minimum GPA of 3.0. Additional exam requirements/recommendations for international students: Required—TOEFL (minimum score 550 paper-based; 213 computer-based). *Application deadline:* For fall admission, 8/15 priority date for domestic students, 7/1 priority date for international students; for winter admission, 12/1 priority date for domestic students, 11/1 priority date for international students; for spring admission, 3/1 priority date for domestic students, 2/1 priority date for international students. Applications are processed on a rolling basis. Application fee: $40 ($50 for international students). Electronic applications accepted. *Expenses:* Tuition, state resident: full-time $10,155. Tuition, nonresident: full-time $25,395. Tuition and fees vary according to course load. *Financial support:* In 2009–10, 14 students received support, including 3 teaching assistantships with full tuition reimbursements available (averaging $9,000 per year); Federal Work-Study and scholarships/grants also available. Support available to part-time students. Financial award application deadline: 7/1. *Application contact:* Graduate Admissions, 614-292-9444, Fax: 614-292-3895, E-mail: domestic.grad@osu.edu.

The Ohio State University–Newark Campus, Graduate Programs, Newark, OH 43055-1797. Offers early/middle childhood education (M Ed); integrated teaching and learning (MA); social work (MSW). *Students:* 40 full-time (36 women), 64 part-time (59 women); includes 5 minority (4 African Americans, 1 Asian American or Pacific Islander), 1 international. Average age 31. *Degree requirements:* For master's, comprehensive exam (for some programs), thesis (for some programs). *Entrance requirements:* For master's, GRE, minimum GPA of 3.0. Additional exam requirements/recommendations for international students: Required—TOEFL, IELTS or Michigan English Language Assessment Battery. *Application deadline:* For fall admission, 8/15 priority date for domestic students, 7/1 priority date for international students; for winter admission, 12/1 priority date for domestic students, 11/1 priority date for international students; for spring admission, 3/1 priority date for domestic students, 2/1 priority date for international students. Applications are processed on a rolling basis. Application fee: $40 ($50 for international students). Electronic applications accepted. *Expenses:* Tuition, state resident: full-time $10,155. Tuition, nonresident: full-time $25,395. Tuition and fees vary according to course load. *Unit head:* Dr. William L. MacDonald, Dean/Director, 740-366-9333 Ext. 330, E-mail: macdonald.24@osu.edu. *Application contact:* Graduate Admissions, 614-292-9444, Fax: 614-292-3985, E-mail: domestic.grad@osu.edu.

Ohio University, Graduate College, College of Education, Department of Teacher Education, Athens, OH 45701-2979. Offers adolescent to young adult education (M Ed); curriculum and instruction (M Ed, PhD); early childhood/special education (M Ed); intervention specialist/mild-moderate needs (M Ed); intervention specialist/moderate-intensive needs (M Ed); mathematics education (PhD); middle child education (M Ed); reading education (M Ed); social studies education (PhD). Part-time and evening/weekend programs available. *Faculty:* 21 full-time (13 women), 7 part-time/adjunct (all women). *Students:* 105 full-time (75 women), 183 part-time (161 women); includes 9 minority (5 African Americans, 3 American Indian/Alaska Native, 1 Asian American or Pacific Islander), 14 international. 190 applicants, 80% accepted, 72 enrolled. *Degree requirements:* For master's, thesis or alternative; for doctorate, comprehensive exam, thesis/dissertation. *Entrance requirements:* For master's, GRE General Test or MAT (if GPA is below 2.9); for doctorate, GRE General Test, minimum GPA of 3.4, work experience. Additional exam requirements/recommendations for international students: Required—TOEFL (minimum score 550 paper-based; 80 iBT) or IELTS Academic (minimum score 6.5). *Application deadline:* For fall admission, 5/1 priority date for domestic students, 4/1 priority date for international students; for winter admission, 11/1 priority date for domestic students, 10/1 priority date for international students; for spring admission, 2/15 priority date for domestic students, 1/1 priority date for international students. Applications are processed on a rolling basis. Application fee: $50 ($55 for international students). Electronic applications accepted. *Expenses:* Tuition, state resident: full-time $7839; part-time $323 per quarter hour. Tuition, nonresident: full-time $15,831; part-time $654 per quarter hour. Required fees: $2931. *Financial support:* Research assistantships with full tuition reimbursements, teaching assistantships with full tuition reimbursements, Federal Work-Study, institutionally sponsored loans, tuition waivers (partial), and unspecified assistantships available. Financial award application deadline: 3/1. *Faculty research:* Cognition literacy, character education, teacher's education reform, disabilities. Total annual research expenditures: $46,933. *Unit head:* Dr. John Henning, Chair, 740-597-1830, Fax: 740-593-0477, E-mail: henningj@ohio.edu. *Application contact:* Floyd J. Doney, Director of Student Affairs, 740-593-4400, Fax: 740-593-9310, E-mail: doney@ohio.edu.

Old Dominion University, Darden College of Education, Program in Elementary/Middle Education, Norfolk, VA 23529. Offers elementary education (MS Ed); instructional technology (MS Ed); library science (MS Ed); middle school education (MS Ed). *Accreditation:* NCATE. Part-time and evening/weekend programs available. Postbaccalaureate distance learning degree programs offered (no on-campus study). *Faculty:* 20 full-time (16 women), 22 part-time/adjunct (2 women). *Students:* 109 full-time (103 women), 171 part-time (148 women); includes 41 minority (22 African Americans, 1 American Indian/Alaska Native, 10 Asian Americans or Pacific Islanders, 8 Hispanic Americans). Average age 33. 191 applicants, 76% accepted, 123 enrolled. In 2009, 155 master's awarded. *Degree requirements:* For master's, comprehensive exam. *Entrance requirements:* For master's, GRE General Test or MAT; PRAXIS I, SAT or ACT, minimum GPA of 2.8. Additional exam requirements/recommendations for international students: Required—TOEFL (minimum score 600 paper-based; 250 computer-based). *Application deadline:* For fall admission, 6/1 priority date for domestic students; for winter admission, 11/1 priority date for domestic students; for spring admission, 3/1 priority date for

Middle School Education

Old Dominion University (continued)

domestic students. Applications are processed on a rolling basis. Application fee: $50. Electronic applications accepted. *Expenses:* Tuition, state resident: full-time $8112; part-time $338 per credit. Tuition, nonresident: full-time $20,256; part-time $844 per credit. Required fees: $119 per semester. One-time fee: $50. *Financial support:* In 2009–10, 180 students received support, including teaching assistantships (averaging $9,000 per year); career-related internships or fieldwork, Federal Work-Study, institutionally sponsored loans, and scholarships/grants also available. Support available to part-time students. Financial award application deadline: 2/15; financial award applicants required to submit FAFSA. *Faculty research:* Education pre-K to 6, school librarianship. *Unit head:* Dr. Charlene Fleener, Graduate Program Director, 757-683-4374, E-mail: cfleener@odu.edu. *Application contact:* Alice McAdory, Director of Admissions, 757-683-3685, Fax: 757-683-3255, E-mail: gradadmit@odu.edu.

Our Lady of the Lake University of San Antonio, School of Professional Studies, Program in Intermediate Education, San Antonio, TX 78207-4689. Offers math/science education (M Ed); professional studies (M Ed). Part-time and evening/weekend programs available. *Students:* 3 full-time (1 woman), 14 part-time (11 women); includes 11 minority (3 African Americans, 8 Hispanic Americans). Average age 36. In 2009, 4 master's awarded. *Expenses:* Tuition: Full-time $12,330; part-time $685 per contact hour. Required fees: $139; $12 per contact hour. $57 per semester. Tuition and fees vary according to campus/location. *Unit head:* Dr. Cullen Grinnen, E-mail: ctgrinnan@lake.ollusa.edu. *Application contact:* Dr. Cullen Grinnen, E-mail: ctgrinnan@lake.ollusa.edu.

Pacific University, College of Education, Forest Grove, OR 97116-1797. Offers early childhood education (MAT); education (MAE); elementary education (MAT); high school education (MAT); middle school education (MAT); special education (MAT); visual function in learning (M Ed). *Accreditation:* NCATE. Part-time and evening/weekend programs available. *Degree requirements:* For master's, research project. *Entrance requirements:* For master's, California Basic Educational Skills Test, PRAXIS II, minimum undergraduate GPA of 2.75, 3.0 graduate. Additional exam requirements/recommendations for international students: Required—TOEFL. Electronic applications accepted. *Expenses:* Contact institution. *Faculty research:* Defining a culturally competent classroom, technology in the k-12 classroom, Socratic seminars, social studies education.

Park University, College of Graduate and Professional Studies, Kansas City, MO 54105. Offers adult education (M Ed); at-risk students (M Ed); disaster and emergency management (MPA); educational administration (M Ed); entrepreneurship (MBA); general business (MBA); general education (M Ed); government/business relations (MPA); healthcare/services management (MBA, MPA); international business (MBA); K-12 certification (MAT); management information systems (MBA); management of information systems (MPA); middle school certification (MAT); multi-cultural education (M Ed); nonprofit management (MPA); public management (MPA); school law (M Ed); secondary school certification (MAT); special education (M Ed). Part-time and evening/weekend programs available. Postbaccalaureate distance learning degree programs offered (no on-campus study). *Degree requirements:* For master's, comprehensive exam, thesis (for some programs). *Entrance requirements:* For master's, GRE, GMAT, teacher certification (M Ed). Additional exam requirements/recommendations for international students: Required—TOEFL (minimum score 550 paper-based). Electronic applications accepted. *Faculty research:* Literacy, leadership, brain based research, multicultural education, diversity.

Plymouth State University, College of Graduate Studies, Graduate Studies in Education, Program in K-12 Education, Plymouth, NH 03264-1595. Offers M Ed. *Accreditation:* NCATE. Part-time and evening/weekend programs available. *Degree requirements:* For master's, PRAXIS. *Entrance requirements:* For master's, MAT, minimum GPA of 3.0.

Quinnipiac University, Division of Education, Program in Secondary Education, Hamden, CT 06518-1940. Offers biology (MAT); English (MAT); history/social studies (MAT); mathematics (MAT); Spanish (MAT). *Accreditation:* NCATE. *Faculty:* 10 full-time (7 women), 5 part-time/adjunct (3 women). *Students:* 80 full-time (56 women), 2 part-time (1 woman); includes 6 minority (2 African Americans, 2 Asian Americans or Pacific Islanders, 2 Hispanic Americans). 77 applicants, 95% accepted, 66 enrolled. In 2009, 33 master's awarded. *Entrance requirements:* For master's, PRAXIS I, minimum GPA of 2.67, interview. Additional exam requirements/recommendations for international students: Required—TOEFL (minimum score 575 paper-based; 233 computer-based; 90 iBT), IELTS (minimum score 6.5). *Application deadline:* For fall admission, 3/31 priority date for domestic students. Applications are processed on a rolling basis. Application fee: $45. Electronic applications accepted. *Expenses:* Tuition: Full-time $16,030; part-time $770 per credit. Required fees: $630; $35 per credit. *Financial support:* Career-related internships or fieldwork, scholarships/grants, and tuition waivers (partial) available. Financial award application deadline: 4/15; financial award applicants required to submit FAFSA. *Faculty research:* Multicultural and urban education, role of technology in education, challenges of teaching diverse learners, socio-cultural nature of learning. *Unit head:* Dr. Bernadine Krawczyk, Assistant Dean, Division of Education, 203-582-3510, Fax: 203-582-3473, E-mail: bernadine.krawczyk@quinnipiac.edu. *Application contact:* Jennifer Boutin, Associate Director of Graduate Admissions, 800-462-1944, Fax: 203-582-3443, E-mail: jennifer.boutin@quinnipiac.edu.

Roberts Wesleyan College, Division of Teacher Education, Rochester, NY 14624-1997. Offers adolescence education (M Ed); childhood and special education (M Ed); literacy education (M Ed); urban education (M Ed). Part-time and evening/weekend programs available. *Degree requirements:* For master's, thesis.

Saginaw Valley State University, College of Education, Program in Middle School Classroom Teaching, University Center, MI 48710. Offers MAT. *Accreditation:* NCATE. Part-time and evening/weekend programs available. *Students:* 27 part-time (23 women); includes 1 minority (Asian American or Pacific Islander). Average age 31. 2 applicants, 100% accepted, 2 enrolled. In 2009, 4 master's awarded. *Degree requirements:* For master's, capstone course. *Entrance requirements:* For master's, minimum GPA of 3.0, teaching certificate. Additional exam requirements/recommendations for international students: Required—TOEFL (minimum score 525 paper-based; 197 computer-based; 71 iBT). *Application deadline:* Applications are processed on a rolling basis. Application fee: $25. Electronic applications accepted. *Financial support:* Federal Work-Study and scholarships/grants available. Support available to part-time students. Financial award applicants required to submit FAFSA. *Faculty research:* Pre-service, middle school, secondary teacher, literacy education. *Unit head:* Dr. Steve P. Barbus, Dean, 989-964-6067, Fax: 989-790-4385, E-mail: barbus@svsu.edu. *Application contact:* Jeanne Chipman, Certification Officer, 989-964-4083, Fax: 989-964-4385, E-mail: jdc@svsu.edu.

Saginaw Valley State University, College of Education, Program in Natural Science Teaching, University Center, MI 48710. Offers elementary (MAT); middle school (MAT); secondary school (MAT). *Accreditation:* NCATE. Part-time and evening/weekend programs available. *Students:* 20 part-time (16 women); includes 2 minority (1 African American, 1 Hispanic American), 1 international. Average age 35. 5 applicants, 100% accepted, 3 enrolled. In 2009, 14 master's awarded. *Degree requirements:* For master's, capstone course. *Entrance requirements:* For master's, minimum GPA of 3.0, teaching certificate. Additional exam requirements/recommendations for international students: Required—TOEFL (minimum score 525 paper-based; 197 computer-based; 71 iBT). *Application deadline:* Applications are processed on a rolling basis. Application fee: $25. Electronic applications accepted. *Financial support:* Federal Work-Study and scholarships/grants available. Support available to part-time students. Financial award applicants required to submit FAFSA. *Unit head:* Dr. Steve P. Barbus, Dean, 989-964-6067, Fax: 989-790-4385, E-mail: barbus@svsu.edu. *Application contact:* Dr. Steve P. Barbus, Dean, 989-964-6067, Fax: 989-790-4385, E-mail: barbus@svsu.edu.

St. Bonaventure University, School of Graduate Studies, School of Education, Adolescence Education Program, St. Bonaventure, NY 14778-2284. Offers MS Ed. *Faculty:* 1 (woman) full-time, 2 part-time/adjunct (1 woman). *Students:* 9 full-time (6 women), 7 part-time (1 woman); includes 1 Hispanic American. Average age 25. 13 applicants, 85% accepted, 9 enrolled. In 2009, 11 master's awarded. *Entrance requirements:* For master's, undergraduate degree in teachable content area; minimum GPA of 3.0. Additional exam requirements/recommendations for international students: Required—TOEFL (minimum score 550 paper-based; 240 computer-based; 85 iBT). *Application deadline:* For fall admission, 4/1 priority date for domestic students, 10/15 priority date for international students. Applications are processed on a rolling basis. Application fee: $30. *Expenses:* Tuition: Full-time $11,700; part-time $650 per credit. *Financial support:* In 2009–10, 2 research assistantships were awarded. Financial award application deadline: 3/15; financial award applicants required to submit FAFSA. *Unit head:* Dr. Paula Kenneson, Coordinator, 716-375-2177, E-mail: pkenneso@sbu.edu. *Application contact:* Dr. Paula Kenneson, Coordinator, 716-375-2177, E-mail: pkenneso@sbu.edu.

St. Bonaventure University, School of Graduate Studies, School of Education, Literacy Programs, St. Bonaventure, NY 14778-2284. Offers adolescent literacy 5-12 (MS Ed); childhood literacy B-6 (MS Ed). *Accreditation:* NCATE. Part-time and evening/weekend programs available. *Faculty:* 2 full-time (1 woman), 1 (woman) part-time/adjunct. *Students:* 37 full-time (33 women), 33 part-time (31 women); includes 1 minority (Hispanic American). Average age 27. 37 applicants, 86% accepted, 26 enrolled. In 2009, 45 master's awarded. *Degree requirements:* For master's, comprehensive exam, thesis optional. *Entrance requirements:* For master's, interview, writing sample, minimum undergraduate GPA of 3.0. Additional exam requirements/recommendations for international students: Required—TOEFL. *Application deadline:* For fall admission, 8/1 for domestic students; for spring admission, 11/1 priority date for domestic students. Applications are processed on a rolling basis. Application fee: $30. Electronic applications accepted. *Expenses:* Tuition: Full-time $11,700; part-time $650 per credit. *Financial support:* In 2009–10, 9 research assistantships with full and partial tuition reimbursements were awarded; scholarships/grants also available. Support available to part-time students. Financial award application deadline: 4/15; financial award applicants required to submit FAFSA. *Faculty research:* Children's literary tastes, reading diagnosis. *Unit head:* Dr. Joseph Zimmer, Director, 716-375-2388. *Application contact:* Bruce Campbell, 716-375-2429, E-mail: gradsch@sbu.edu.

St. John Fisher College, Ralph C. Wilson Jr. School of Education, Program in Adolescence Education/Special Education, Rochester, NY 14618-3597. Offers adolescence English (MS Ed); adolescence French (MS Ed); adolescence social studies (MS Ed); adolescence Spanish (MS Ed). Part-time and evening/weekend programs available. *Faculty:* 3 full-time (1 woman), 1 (woman) part-time/adjunct. *Students:* 39 full-time (18 women), 5 part-time (2 women); includes 7 minority (1 African American, 2 American Indian/Alaska Native, 1 Asian American or Pacific Islander, 3 Hispanic Americans). Average age 28. 39 applicants, 90% accepted, 20 enrolled. In 2009, 17 master's awarded. *Degree requirements:* For master's, field experiences, student teaching, LAST. *Entrance requirements:* For master's, 2 letters of recommendation, personal statement, current resume. Additional exam requirements/recommendations for international students: Required—TOEFL (minimum score 575 paper-based; 233 computer-based; 80 iBT). *Application deadline:* Applications are processed on a rolling basis. Application fee: $30. Electronic applications accepted. *Expenses:* Tuition: Part-time $680 per credit hour. Required fees: $25 per semester. Tuition and fees vary according to degree level and program. *Financial support:* In 2009–10, 40 students received support. Federal Work-Study and scholarships/grants available. Financial award applicants required to submit FAFSA. *Faculty research:* Arts and humanities, urban schools, constructivist learning, at risk students, mentoring. *Unit head:* Dr. Russell Coward, Program Director, 585-385-8114, E-mail: rcoward@sjfc.edu. *Application contact:* Jose Perales, Director of Graduate Admissions, 585-385-8067, E-mail: jperales@sjfc.edu.

St. Thomas Aquinas College, Division of Teacher Education, Sparkill, NY 10976. Offers adolescence education (MST); childhood and special education (MST); childhood education (MST); educational leadership (MS Ed); reading (MS Ed, PMC); special education (MS Ed, PMC); teaching (MS Ed), including elementary education, middle school education, secondary education. *Accreditation:* NCATE. Part-time and evening/weekend programs available. *Degree requirements:* For master's, comprehensive exam, comprehensive professional portfolio; for PMC, action research project. *Entrance requirements:* For master's, New York State Qualifying Exam, GRE General Test or minimum GPA of 3.0, teaching certificate; for PMC, GRE General Test or minimum GPA of 3.0. Electronic applications accepted. *Faculty research:* Computer applications in education, adolescent special education students, literacy development, inclusive practices for special education students.

Salem College, Department of Education, Winston-Salem, NC 27101. Offers early education and leadership (MAT); elementary education (MAT); English as a second language (MAT); language and literacy (M Ed); middle school education (MAT); secondary education (MAT); special education (MAT). *Accreditation:* NCATE. Part-time and evening/weekend programs available. *Degree requirements:* For master's, comprehensive exam, practicum (MAT), project (M Ed), oral and written comprehensive exams. *Entrance requirements:* For master's, GRE, minimum GPA of 2.5. *Faculty research:* Content area reading strategies, literacy development, brain compatible instruction.

Salem State College, School of Graduate Studies, Program in Middle School Education, Salem, MA 01970-5353. Offers humanities (M Ed); math/science (MAT). Part-time and evening/weekend programs available. *Students:* 29 part-time (19 women). Average age 36. 8 applicants, 88% accepted, 7 enrolled. In 2009, 15 master's awarded. *Entrance requirements:* For master's, GRE or MAT. Additional exam requirements/recommendations for international students: Required—TOEFL (minimum score 550 paper-based; 80 iBT), or IELTS (minimum score 5.5). *Application deadline:* For fall admission, 5/1 for domestic students; for spring admission, 10/1 for domestic students. Applications are processed on a rolling basis. Application fee: $50. *Expenses:* Tuition, state resident: full-time $2520; part-time $275 per credit hour. Tuition, nonresident: full-time $4140; part-time $365 per credit hour. Required fees: $2430. *Financial support:* In 2009–10, 2 students received support. Career-related internships or fieldwork, Federal Work-Study, scholarships/grants, and unspecified assistantships available. Support available to part-time students. Financial award application deadline: 5/1; financial award applicants required to submit FAFSA. *Unit head:* Steve Prodanas, Program Coordinator, 978-542-6310, Fax: 978-542-7215, E-mail: spondanas@salemstate.edu. *Application contact:* Dr. Lee A. Brossoit, Assistant Dean of Graduate Admissions, 978-542-6675, Fax: 978-542-7215, E-mail: lbrossoit@salemstate.edu.

Salem State College, School of Graduate Studies, Program in Middle School General Science, Salem, MA 01970-5353. Offers MAT. Part-time and evening/weekend programs available. *Students:* 3 part-time (2 women). Average age 35. In 2009, 2 master's awarded. *Entrance requirements:* For master's, GRE or MAT. Additional exam requirements/recommendations for international students: Required—TOEFL (minimum score 550 paper-based; 80 iBT), or IELTS (minimum score 5.5). *Application deadline:* For fall admission, 5/1 for domestic students; for spring admission, 10/1 for domestic students. Applications are processed on a rolling basis. Application fee: $50. *Expenses:* Tuition, state resident: full-time $2520; part-time $275 per credit hour. Tuition, nonresident: full-time $4140; part-time $365 per credit hour. Required fees: $2430. *Financial support:* In 2009–10, 2 students received support. Career-related internships or fieldwork, Federal Work-Study, scholarships/grants, and unspecified assistantships available. Support available to part-time students. Financial award application deadline: 5/1; financial award applicants required to submit FAFSA. *Unit head:* Lindley Hanson, Program Coordinator, 978-542-6321, Fax: 978-542-7215, E-mail: lhanson@salemstate.edu. *Application contact:* Dr. Lee A. Brossoit, Assistant Dean of Graduate Admissions, 978-542-6675, Fax: 978-542-7215, E-mail: lbrossoit@salemstate.edu.

Salem State College, School of Graduate Studies, Program in Middle School Math, Salem, MA 01970-5353. Offers MAT. Part-time and evening/weekend programs available. *Students:* 21 part-time (14 women); includes 1 minority (Hispanic American). Average age 32. 10 applicants, 100% accepted, 10 enrolled. In 2009, 11 master's awarded. *Entrance requirements:*

For master's, GRE or MAT. Additional exam requirements/recommendations for international students: Required—TOEFL (minimum score 550 paper-based; 80 iBT), or IELTS (minimum score 5.5). *Application deadline:* For fall admission, 5/1 for domestic students; for spring admission, 10/1 for domestic students. Applications are processed on a rolling basis. Application fee: $50. *Expenses:* Tuition, state resident: full-time $2520; part-time $275 per credit hour. Tuition, nonresident: full-time $4140; part-time $365 per credit hour. Required fees: $2430. *Financial support:* In 2009–10, 1 student received support. Career-related internships or fieldwork, Federal Work-Study, scholarships/grants, and unspecified assistantships available. Support available to part-time students. Financial award application deadline: 5/1; financial award applicants required to submit FAFSA. *Unit head:* Jule Belock, Program Coordinator, 978-542-6321, Fax: 978-542-7215, E-mail: jbelock@salemstate.edu. *Application contact:* Dr. Lee A. Brossoit, Assistant Dean of Graduate Admissions, 978-542-6675, Fax: 978-542-7215, E-mail: lbrossoit@salemstate.edu.

Shenandoah University, School of Education and Human Development, Winchester, VA 22601-5195. Offers administrative leadership (D Ed); advanced professional teaching English to speakers of other languages (Certificate); education (MSE); elementary education (Certificate); middle school education (Certificate); organizational leadership (MS); professional studies (Certificate); professional studies (for initial teacher licensure) (Certificate); professional studies (for special education teacher licensure) (Certificate); professional studies (for VA licensure reading specialists) (Certificate); professional studies (for VA licensure) (Certificate); professional teaching English to speakers of other languages (Certificate); public management (Certificate); school reform (Certificate); secondary education (Certificate). *Accreditation:* Teacher Education Accreditation Council. Part-time and evening/weekend programs available. Postbaccalaureate distance learning degree programs offered (minimal on-campus study). *Faculty:* 13 full-time (7 women), 27 part-time/adjunct (20 women). *Students:* 11 full-time (8 women), 382 part-time (276 women); includes 35 minority (17 African Americans, 1 American Indian/Alaska Native, 6 Asian Americans or Pacific Islanders, 11 Hispanic Americans), 4 international. Average age 39. 272 applicants, 95% accepted, 218 enrolled. In 2009, 103 master's, 2 doctorates awarded. *Degree requirements:* For master's, comprehensive exam (for some programs), thesis (for some programs), internship; for doctorate, comprehensive exam, thesis/dissertation; for Certificate, full time teaching in area for 1 year. *Entrance requirements:* For master's, minimum GPA of 3.0 or satisfactory GRE, 3 letters of recommendation, valid teaching license, essay; for doctorate, minimum graduate GPA of 3.5, 3 years of teaching experience, 3 letters of recommendation, writing samples; for Certificate, minimum undergraduate GPA of 3.0, essay, 3 letters of recommendation. Additional exam requirements/recommendations for international students: Required—TOEFL (minimum score 550 paper-based; 213 computer-based; 79 iBT), IELTS (minimum score 6.5). *Application deadline:* For fall admission, 7/1 for domestic and international students; for spring admission, 10/15 for domestic and international students. Application fee: $30. Electronic applications accepted. *Expenses:* Tuition: Full-time $11,925; part-time $695 per credit. Required fees: $400 per semester. *Financial support:* Application deadline: 3/15. *Unit head:* Dr. Steven E. Humphries, Dean, 540-535-3574, E-mail: shumphri@su.edu. *Application contact:* David Anthony, Dean of Admissions, 540-665-4581, Fax: 540-665-4627, E-mail: admit@su.edu.

Shippensburg University of Pennsylvania, School of Graduate Studies, College of Education and Human Services, Department of Teacher Education, Shippensburg, PA 17257-2299. Offers curriculum and instruction (M Ed), including biology, early childhood education, elementary education, English, foreign languages, geography/earth science, history, mathematics, middle school education; reading (M Ed). *Accreditation:* NCATE. Part-time and evening/weekend programs available. *Degree requirements:* For master's, comprehensive exam (for some programs), thesis optional, practicum or internship (for some programs). *Entrance requirements:* For master's, MAT (if GPA less than 2.75), interview, 3 letters of recommendation, writing sample of teaching background and future goals. Additional exam requirements/recommendations for international students: Required—TOEFL (minimum score 560 paper-based; 220 computer-based); Recommended—IELTS (minimum score 6). Electronic applications accepted.

Siena Heights University, Graduate College, Program in Teacher Education, Concentration in Middle School Education, Adrian, MI 49221-1796. Offers MA. Part-time programs available. *Degree requirements:* For master's, thesis, presentation. *Entrance requirements:* For master's, minimum GPA of 3.0, interview.

Simmons College, College of Arts and Sciences Graduate Studies, Department of Education, Program in Teacher Preparation, Boston, MA 02115. Offers educational leadership (MS Ed); elementary education (MAT); general education (CAGS); general purposes (MS); middle school education (MAT); professional license (CAGS); professional license: elementary (MS Ed); professional license: middle/high (MS Ed); secondary education (MAT); urban education (MS Ed, CAGS). Part-time programs available. *Students:* 68 full-time (58 women), 125 part-time (113 women); includes 25 minority (10 African Americans, 3 American Indian/Alaska Native, 8 Asian Americans or Pacific Islanders, 4 Hispanic Americans). Average age 27. 115 applicants, 88% accepted, 75 enrolled. In 2009, 137 master's, 14 other advanced degrees awarded. *Degree requirements:* For master's, practicum. *Entrance requirements:* For master's, GRE General Test, MAT or Massachusetts Tests for Educator Licensure (MTEL). Additional exam requirements/recommendations for international students: Required—TOEFL (minimum score 600 paper-based; 250 computer-based; 100 iBT). *Application deadline:* For fall admission, 8/1 priority date for domestic and international students; for winter admission, 12/15 priority date for domestic and international students; for spring admission, 12/15 priority date for domestic and international students. Applications are processed on a rolling basis. Application fee: $35. Electronic applications accepted. *Expenses:* Contact institution. *Financial support:* Application deadline: 3/1. *Faculty research:* Educational psychology, mentorship with first year teachers, urban classrooms, first generation college students. *Unit head:* Gary Oakes, Director, Master of Arts in Teaching (MAT) Program, 617-521-2203, Fax: 617-521-3133. *Application contact:* Kristen Haack, Director, Graduate Studies Admission, 617-521-2917, Fax: 617-521-3058, E-mail: gsa@simmons.edu.

Smith College, Graduate and Special Programs, Department of Education and Child Study, Northampton, MA 01063. Offers education of the deaf (MED); elementary education (MAT); middle school education (MAT); secondary education (MAT), including biological sciences education, chemistry education, English education, French education, geology education, government education, history education, mathematics education, physics education, Spanish education. Part-time programs available. *Faculty:* 6 full-time (4 women), 3 part-time/adjunct (2 women). *Students:* 20 full-time (14 women), 5 part-time (3 women); includes 2 minority (1 African American, 1 Asian American or Pacific Islander), 1 international. Average age 30. 41 applicants, 88% accepted, 22 enrolled. In 2009, 19 master's awarded. *Entrance requirements:* Additional exam requirements/recommendations for international students: Required—TOEFL. *Application deadline:* For fall admission, 4/1 for domestic students, 1/15 for international students; for spring admission, 12/1 for domestic students. Application fee: $60. *Financial support:* In 2009–10, 20 students received support, including 6 teaching assistantships with full tuition reimbursements available (averaging $11,910 per year); career-related internships or fieldwork, institutionally sponsored loans, and scholarships/grants also available. Support available to part-time students. Financial award application deadline: 1/15; financial award applicants required to submit CSS PROFILE or FAFSA. *Unit head:* Alan Rudnitsky, Chair, 413-585-3261, Fax: 413-585-3268, E-mail: arudnits@smith.edu. *Application contact:* Ruth Morgan, Administrative Assistant, 413-585-3050, Fax: 413-585-3054, E-mail: gradstdy@smith.edu.

Southeast Missouri State University, School of Graduate Studies, Department of Middle and Secondary Education, Cape Girardeau, MO 63701-4799. Offers educational studies (MA); middle level education (MA). *Accreditation:* NCATE. Part-time and evening/weekend programs available. *Degree requirements:* For master's, thesis or alternative. *Entrance requirements:* For master's, GRE General Test, MAT, PRAXIS II, minimum undergraduate GPA of 2.75. Additional exam requirements/recommendations for international students: Required—TOEFL (minimum score 550 paper-based; 213 computer-based); Recommended—IELTS (minimum score 6). Electronic applications accepted. *Expenses:* Tuition, state resident: full-time $4266; part-time $237 per credit hour. Tuition, nonresident: full-time $7506; part-time $417 per credit hour. Required fees: $427; $427. *Faculty research:* Educational administration issues in K-12, leadership in educational setting, counselor education and supervision issues, rural education issues.

Southern Arkansas University–Magnolia, Graduate Programs, Magnolia, AR 71753. Offers agriculture (MS); business administration (MBA); computer and information sciences (MS); counseling (MS); education (M Ed), including counseling and development, curriculum and instruction emphasis, educational administration and supervision, elementary education, middle level emphasis, reading emphasis, secondary education, TESOL emphasis; kinesiology (MS); library media and information specialist (M Ed); mental health and clinical counseling (MS); public administration (EMPA); school counseling (M Ed); teaching (MAT). *Accreditation:* NCATE. Part-time and evening/weekend programs available. *Faculty:* 43 full-time (24 women), 12 part-time/adjunct (7 women). *Students:* 116 full-time (78 women), 333 part-time (255 women); includes 105 minority (98 African Americans, 3 American Indian/Alaska Native, 3 Asian Americans or Pacific Islanders, 1 Hispanic American), 11 international. Average age 33. In 2009, 88 master's awarded. *Degree requirements:* For master's, comprehensive exam, thesis optional. *Entrance requirements:* For master's, GRE, MAT or GMAT, minimum GPA of 2.75. *Application deadline:* For fall admission, 8/15 for domestic students; for winter admission, 1/8 for domestic students; for spring admission, 1/8 for domestic students. Applications are processed on a rolling basis. Application fee: $0. *Expenses:* Tuition, state resident: full-time $3798; part-time $211 per hour. Tuition, nonresident: full-time $5580; part-time $310 per hour. Required fees: $584. *Financial support:* Career-related internships or fieldwork, Federal Work-Study, scholarships/grants, tuition waivers (full), and unspecified assistantships available. Financial award applicants required to submit FAFSA. *Faculty research:* Alternative certification for teachers, supervision of instruction, instructional leadership, counseling. *Unit head:* Dr. Kim Bloss, Dean, Graduate Studies, 870-235-4150, Fax: 870-235-5227, E-mail: kkbloss@saumag.edu. *Application contact:* Dr. Kim Bloss, Dean, Graduate Studies, 870-235-4150, Fax: 870-235-5227, E-mail: kkbloss@saumag.edu.

Spalding University, Graduate Studies, College of Education, Programs in Education, Louisville, KY 40203-2188. Offers elementary school education (MAT); general education (MA); high school education (MAT); middle school education (MAT); school administration (MA); special education (learning and behavioral disorders) (MAT); student guidance counselor (MA). MAT degree programs offered for first teaching certificate/license students. *Accreditation:* NCATE. Part-time and evening/weekend programs available. *Faculty:* 6 full-time (4 women), 32 part-time/adjunct (23 women). *Students:* 125 full-time (93 women), 64 part-time (49 women); includes 53 minority (50 African Americans, 2 American Indian/Alaska Native, 1 Hispanic American), 2 international. Average age 37. 57 applicants, 79% accepted, 41 enrolled. In 2009, 56 master's awarded. *Degree requirements:* For master's, portfolio, final project, clinical experience. *Entrance requirements:* For master's, GRE General Test or MAT, interview, recommendations, resume. Additional exam requirements/recommendations for international students: Required—TOEFL (minimum score 535 paper-based; 203 computer-based). *Application deadline:* Applications are processed on a rolling basis. Application fee: $30. Electronic applications accepted. *Expenses:* Tuition: Full-time $11,340; part-time $630 per credit hour. Tuition and fees vary according to program. *Financial support:* In 2009–10, 106 students received support, including 3 research assistantships with partial tuition reimbursements available (averaging $3,590 per year); scholarships/grants, traineeships, and unspecified assistantships also available. Financial award application deadline: 3/15; financial award applicants required to submit FAFSA. *Faculty research:* Instructional technology, achievement gap, classroom management, assessment. *Unit head:* Dr. Beverly Keepers, Dean, 502-588-7121, Fax: 502-585-7123, E-mail: bkeepers@spalding.edu. *Application contact:* Admissions Office, 502-585-7111, E-mail: admissions@spalding.edu.

State University of New York College at Oneonta, Graduate Education, Division of Education, Department of Secondary Education, Oneonta, NY 13820-4015. Offers adolescence education (MS Ed); family and consumer science education (MS Ed). *Accreditation:* NCATE. Part-time and evening/weekend programs available. *Entrance requirements:* For master's, GRE General Test. *Application deadline:* For fall admission, 3/25 priority date for domestic students; for spring admission, 10/1 priority date for domestic students. Applications are processed on a rolling basis. Application fee: $50. *Expenses:* Tuition, state resident: part-time $349 per credit hour. Tuition, nonresident: full-time $12,870; part-time $552 per credit hour. Required fees: $1280; $15.85 per credit hour. *Unit head:* Dr. Dennis Banks, Chair, 607-436-3391, Fax: 607-436-2554, E-mail: banksdn@oneonta.edu. *Application contact:* Dr. Dennis Banks, Chair, 607-436-3391, Fax: 607-436-2554, E-mail: banksdn@oneonta.edu.

State University of New York College at Potsdam, School of Education and Professional Studies, Program in Special Education, Potsdam, NY 13676. Offers birth-grade 2 (MS Ed); grades 1-6 (MS Ed); grades 5-9 (MS Ed); grades 7-12 (MS Ed). *Accreditation:* NCATE. *Faculty:* 3 full-time (1 woman), 5 part-time/adjunct (4 women). *Students:* 19 full-time (17 women), 6 part-time (4 women); includes 2 minority (1 African American, 1 American Indian/Alaska Native). 18 applicants, 100% accepted, 16 enrolled. In 2009, 11 master's awarded. *Degree requirements:* For master's, thesis optional, culminating experience. *Entrance requirements:* For master's, minimum GPA of 3.0 in last 60 hours of undergraduate course work. Additional exam requirements/recommendations for international students: Required—TOEFL (minimum score 550 paper-based; 213 computer-based; 80 iBT), IELTS (minimum score 6). *Application deadline:* For fall admission, 4/1 priority date for domestic and international students. Applications are processed on a rolling basis. Application fee: $50. *Expenses:* Tuition, state resident: full-time $8370; part-time $349 per credit hour. Tuition, nonresident: full-time $13,250; part-time $552 per credit hour. Required fees: $942; $38.70 per credit hour. *Financial support:* Unspecified assistantships available. Financial award application deadline: 3/1; financial award applicants required to submit FAFSA. *Unit head:* Dr. Anjali Misra, Chairperson, 315-267-2764, Fax: 315-267-4802, E-mail: misraa@potsdam.edu. *Application contact:* Peter Cutler, Graduate Admissions Counselor, 315-267-3154, Fax: 315-267-4802, E-mail: cutlerpj@potsdam.edu.

Suffolk University, College of Arts and Sciences, Department of Education and Human Services, Programs in School Teaching, Boston, MA 02108-2770. Offers foundations of education (M Ed); middle school teaching (M Ed); school teaching (CAGS); secondary school teaching (M Ed). Part-time and evening/weekend programs available. *Entrance requirements:* For master's, GRE General Test, MAT, or Massachusetts Test for Educator Licensure, 2 letters of recommendation, resume. *Application deadline:* For fall admission, 6/15 priority date for domestic students, 6/15 for international students; for spring admission, 11/15 priority date for domestic students, 11/15 for international students. Applications are processed on a rolling basis. Application fee: $50. *Expenses:* Tuition: Full-time $33,000; part-time $1100 per credit. Required fees: $20. Tuition and fees vary according to program. *Financial support:* Fellowships, career-related internships or fieldwork, Federal Work-Study, and institutionally sponsored loans available. Support available to part-time students. Financial award application deadline: 4/1; financial award applicants required to submit FAFSA. *Faculty research:* Assessment systems, reflection, teamwork, learning environment. *Unit head:* Dr. Sarah M. Carroll, Graduate Program Director, 617-573-8015, Fax: 617-305-1743, E-mail: scarroll@suffolk.edu. *Application contact:* Judith Reynolds, Director of Graduate Admissions, 617-573-8302, Fax: 617-305-1733, E-mail: grad.admission@suffolk.edu.

Texas Christian University, College of Education, Program in Middle School Education (Four-One Option), Fort Worth, TX 76129-0002. Offers M Ed. Part-time and evening/weekend programs available. *Degree requirements:* For master's, oral exams. *Entrance requirements:* Additional exam requirements/recommendations for international students: Required—TOEFL (minimum score 550 paper-based; 213 computer-based; 80 iBT). *Application deadline:* For fall admission, 7/15 for domestic and international students; for spring admission, 10/15 for

Middle School Education

Texas Christian University (continued)
domestic students, 11/15 for international students. Applications are processed on a rolling basis. Application fee: $50. *Expenses:* Tuition: Full-time $17,640; part-time $980 per credit hour. Tuition and fees vary according to program. *Financial support:* Teaching assistantships with full tuition reimbursements, career-related internships or fieldwork and unspecified assistantships available. Financial award application deadline: 3/15; financial award applicants required to submit FAFSA. *Unit head:* Dr. Kay B. Stevens, Associate Dean, 817-257-7661, E-mail: k.stevens2@tcu.edu. *Application contact:* Robyn P. Shepheard, Academic Program Specialist, 817-257-7661, E-mail: r.shepheard@tcu.edu.

Tufts University, Graduate School of Arts and Sciences, Department of Education, Program in Education, Medford, MA 02155. Offers education (MS, PhD); middle and secondary education (MA, MAT); secondary education (MA). *Faculty:* 13 full-time, 9 part-time/adjunct. *Students:* 116 (84 women); includes 17 minority (7 African Americans, 1 American Indian/Alaska Native, 3 Asian Americans or Pacific Islanders, 6 Hispanic Americans), 4 international. Average age 27. 180 applicants, 83% accepted, 77 enrolled. In 2009, 74 master's, 5 doctorates awarded. *Degree requirements:* For master's, thesis optional; for doctorate, thesis/dissertation. *Entrance requirements:* For master's, GRE General Test. Additional exam requirements/recommendations for international students: Required—TOEFL (minimum score 550 paper-based; 213 computer-based; 80 iBT). *Application deadline:* For fall admission, 2/1 for domestic students, 12/15 for international students; for spring admission, 10/15 for domestic students, 9/15 for international students. Applications are processed on a rolling basis. Application fee: $75. Electronic applications accepted. *Expenses:* Tuition: Full-time $38,096; part-time $3962 per credit. Required fees: $686; $40 per year. Tuition and fees vary according to course level, course load, degree level, program and student level. *Financial support:* Teaching assistantships with full and partial tuition reimbursements, Federal Work-Study, scholarships/grants, and tuition waivers (full and partial) available. Support available to part-time students. Financial award application deadline: 2/1. *Unit head:* Barbara Brizuela, Chair, 617-627-3244, Fax: 617-627-3901. *Application contact:* Patricia Romeo, Information Contact, 617-627-3244.

Union College, Graduate Programs, Department of Education, Program in Middle Grades, Barbourville, KY 40906-1499. Offers MA. *Degree requirements:* For master's, thesis optional. *Entrance requirements:* For master's, GRE General Test, NTE.

Union Graduate College, School of Education, Schenectady, NY 12308-3107. Offers biology (MAT, MS); chemistry (MAT); Chinese (MAT); earth science (MAT); English (MAT); French (MAT); general science (MAT); German (MAT); Greek (MAT); languages (MAT); Latin (MAT); mathematics (MAT); mathematics and technology (MS); mentoring and teacher leadership (AC); middle childhood extension (AC); national board certificate and teacher leadership (AC); physical science (MS); physics (MAT); social studies (MAT); Spanish (MAT). *Accreditation:* Teacher Education Accreditation Council. *Faculty:* 3 full-time (1 woman), 39 part-time/adjunct (19 women). *Students:* 46 full-time (27 women), 45 part-time (39 women); includes 5 minority (1 Asian American or Pacific Islander, 4 Hispanic Americans), 2 international. Average age 33. 66 applicants, 73% accepted, 39 enrolled. In 2009, 44 master's awarded. *Degree requirements:* For master's, thesis or project. *Entrance requirements:* For master's, minimum GPA of 3.0, letters of recommendation. Additional exam requirements/recommendations for international students: Required—TOEFL (minimum score 550 paper-based; 213 computer-based). *Application deadline:* Applications are processed on a rolling basis. Application fee: $60. Electronic applications accepted. *Expenses:* Contact institution. *Financial support:* In 2009–10, 12 research assistantships with tuition reimbursements (averaging $3,000 per year) were awarded; Federal Work-Study, scholarships/grants, health care benefits, and tuition waivers (partial) also available. Support available to part-time students. Financial award applicants required to submit FAFSA. *Faculty research:* Transformative learning, science education, National Board Certification, teacher leadership, teacher quality. *Unit head:* Dr. Patrick Allen, Dean, 518-631-9870, Fax: 518-631-9901. *Application contact:* Christine Angley, Assistant, 518-631-9871, Fax: 518-631-9903, E-mail: angleyc@uniongraduatecollege.edu.

Union Institute & University, M Ed Program–Vermont Campus, Montpelier, VT 05602. Offers school administration (M Ed), including principalship; school counseling (M Ed); teaching (M Ed), including art, early childhood, elementary, English, math, middle schools, science, social studies, special education. *Faculty:* 3 full-time (1 woman), 23 part-time/adjunct (19 women). *Students:* 41 part-time (29 women). Average age 38. In 2009, 15 master's awarded. *Degree requirements:* For master's, thesis. *Entrance requirements:* For master's, 3 letters of reference. *Application deadline:* Applications are processed on a rolling basis. Application fee: $50. *Expenses:* Contact institution. *Financial support:* Federal Work-Study, scholarships/grants, and tuition waivers available. Financial award applicants required to submit FAFSA. *Unit head:* Dr. Arlene Sacks, Dean, Graduate Programs in Education, 305-653-6713 Ext. 2152, E-mail: arlene.sacks@myunion.edu. *Application contact:* Dr. Arlene Sacks, Dean, Graduate Programs in Education, 305-653-6713 Ext. 2152, E-mail: arlene.sacks@myunion.edu.

University of Arkansas, Graduate School, College of Education and Health Professions, Department of Curriculum and Instruction, Fayetteville, AR 72701-1201. Offers childhood education (MAT); curriculum and instruction (PhD); educational leadership (M Ed, Ed D, Ed S); educational statistics and research methods (MS, PhD); educational technology (M Ed); elementary education (M Ed, Ed S); middle-level education (MAT); secondary education (M Ed, MAT, Ed S); special education (M Ed, MAT). *Accreditation:* NCATE. *Students:* 170 full-time (129 women), 202 part-time (162 women); includes 40 minority (21 African Americans, 7 American Indian/Alaska Native, 6 Asian Americans or Pacific Islanders, 6 Hispanic Americans), 14 international. In 2009, 131 master's, 11 doctorates awarded. *Degree requirements:* For doctorate, thesis/dissertation. *Entrance requirements:* For doctorate, GRE General Test or MAT. *Application deadline:* Applications are processed on a rolling basis. Application fee: $40 ($50 for international students). *Expenses:* Tuition, state resident: full-time $7355; part-time $356.58 per hour. Tuition, nonresident: full-time $17,401; part-time $775.17 per hour. Required fees: $1203. *Financial support:* In 2009–10, 5 fellowships with tuition reimbursements, 15 research assistantships, 8 teaching assistantships were awarded; career-related internships or fieldwork and Federal Work-Study also available. Support available to part-time students. Financial award application deadline: 4/1; financial award applicants required to submit FAFSA. *Unit head:* Dr. Michael Daugherty, Department Chairperson, 479-575-4209, Fax: 479-575-5119, E-mail: mkd03@uark.edu. *Application contact:* Dr. William McComas, Graduate Coordinator, 479-575-7525, E-mail: mccomas@uark.edu.

University of Arkansas at Little Rock, Graduate School, College of Education, Department of Teacher Education, Program in Middle Childhood Education, Little Rock, AR 72204-1099. Offers M Ed.

University of Central Florida, College of Education, Department of Teaching and Learning Principles, Program in Science Education, Orlando, FL 32816. Offers biology (MA); chemistry (MA); middle school science (MA); physics (MA); science education (M Ed). *Accreditation:* NCATE. Part-time and evening/weekend programs available. *Students:* 11 full-time (6 women), 19 part-time (15 women); includes 6 minority (all Hispanic Americans). Average age 34. 12 applicants, 92% accepted, 10 enrolled. In 2009, 13 master's awarded. *Entrance requirements:* For master's, GRE General Test. Additional exam requirements/recommendations for international students: Required—TOEFL. *Application deadline:* For fall admission, 7/15 for domestic students; for spring admission, 12/1 for domestic students. Application fee: $30. Electronic applications accepted. *Expenses:* Tuition, state resident: part-time $306.31 per credit hour. Tuition, nonresident: part-time $1099.01 per credit hour. Part-time tuition and fees vary according to degree level and program. *Financial support:* Career-related internships or fieldwork, Federal Work-Study, institutionally sponsored loans, tuition waivers (partial), and unspecified assistantships available. Financial award application deadline: 3/1; financial award applicants required to submit FAFSA.

University of Dayton, Graduate School, School of Education and Allied Professions, Department of Teacher Education, Dayton, OH 45469-1300. Offers adolescent/young adult (MS Ed); art education (MS Ed); early childhood education (MS Ed); inclusive early childhood (MS Ed); interdisciplinary education (MS Ed); intervention specialist education, mild/moderate (MS Ed); literacy (MS Ed); middle childhood (MS Ed); multi-age education (MS Ed); music education (MS Ed); teacher as leader (MS Ed); technology in education (MS Ed). Part-time and evening/weekend programs available. *Faculty:* 17 full-time (13 women), 27 part-time/adjunct (21 women). *Students:* 105 full-time (76 women), 152 part-time (131 women); includes 25 minority (21 African Americans, 1 Asian American or Pacific Islander, 3 Hispanic Americans), 8 international. Average age 33. 199 applicants, 58% accepted, 48 enrolled. In 2009, 139 master's awarded. *Degree requirements:* For master's, thesis, capstone research project. *Entrance requirements:* For master's, GRE General Test, minimum GPA of 2.75. Additional exam requirements/recommendations for international students: Required—TOEFL (minimum score 550 paper-based; 213 computer-based; 80 iBT). *Application deadline:* For fall admission, 3/15 priority date for domestic students, 3/1 priority date for international students; for winter admission, 7/1 priority date for international students; for spring admission, 1/1 priority date for international students. Applications are processed on a rolling basis. Application fee: $0 ($50 for international students). Electronic applications accepted. *Expenses:* Contact institution. *Financial support:* In 2009–10, 5 research assistantships with full and partial tuition reimbursements (averaging $8,000 per year) were awarded; career-related internships or fieldwork, institutionally sponsored loans, health care benefits, and unspecified assistantships also available. Financial award applicants required to submit FAFSA. *Faculty research:* Diversity, literacy, art representation by young children, preservice teacher preparation. *Unit head:* Dr. Katie A. Kinnucan-Welsch, Chair, 937-229-3346. *Application contact:* Graduate Admissions, 937-229-4411, Fax: 937-229-4729, E-mail: gradadmission@udayton.edu.

University of Georgia, Graduate School, College of Education, Department of Elementary and Social Studies Education, Athens, GA 30602. Offers early childhood education (M Ed, MAT, PhD, Ed S), including child and family development (MAT); elementary education (PhD); middle school education (M Ed, PhD, Ed S); social studies education (M Ed, Ed D, PhD, Ed S). *Faculty:* 14 full-time (9 women). *Students:* 114 full-time (94 women), 130 part-time (112 women); includes 37 minority (20 African Americans, 1 American Indian/Alaska Native, 11 Asian Americans or Pacific Islanders, 5 Hispanic Americans), 9 international. 168 applicants, 57% accepted, 48 enrolled. In 2009, 75 master's, 9 doctorates, 12 other advanced degrees awarded. *Entrance requirements:* For master's and Ed S, GRE General Test or MAT; for doctorate, GRE General Test. *Application deadline:* For fall admission, 7/1 priority date for domestic students; for spring admission, 11/15 for domestic students. Application fee: $50. Electronic applications accepted. *Expenses:* Tuition, state resident: full-time $6000; part-time $250 per credit hour. Tuition, nonresident: full-time $20,904; part-time $871 per credit hour. Required fees: $730 per semester. *Financial support:* Fellowships, research assistantships, teaching assistantships, unspecified assistantships available. *Unit head:* Dr. Ronald L. VanSickle, Interim Head, 706-542-7265, Fax: 706-542-6506, E-mail: rvansick@uga.edu. *Application contact:* Dr. Ronald E. Butchart, Graduate Coordinator, 706-542-6490, Fax: 706-542-8996, E-mail: essegrad@uga.edu.

University of Kentucky, Graduate School, College of Education, Program in Curriculum and Instruction, Lexington, KY 40506-0032. Offers curriculum and instruction (MA Ed, Ed D); instruction and administration (Ed D); instruction system design (MS Ed); middle school education (MS Ed). *Accreditation:* NCATE. *Degree requirements:* For master's, comprehensive exam, thesis optional; for doctorate, comprehensive exam, thesis/dissertation. *Entrance requirements:* For master's, GRE General Test, minimum undergraduate GPA of 2.75; for doctorate, GRE General Test, minimum graduate GPA of 3.0. Additional exam requirements/recommendations for international students: Required—TOEFL (minimum score 550 paper-based; 213 computer-based). Electronic applications accepted. *Faculty research:* Educational reform, multicultural education, classroom instructional practices, performance based assessment, primary school programs.

University of Louisiana at Monroe, Graduate School, College of Education and Human Development, Department of Curriculum and Instruction, Program in Multiple Levels Grades K-12, Monroe, LA 71209-0001. Offers MAT. *Faculty:* 9 full-time (8 women). *Students:* 1 full-time (0 women), 3 part-time (2 women); includes 3 minority (2 African Americans, 1 Hispanic American). Average age 32. In 2009, 4 master's awarded. *Degree requirements:* For master's, thesis optional. *Entrance requirements:* For master's, GRE, PRAXIS, minimum GPA of 2.5. Additional exam requirements/recommendations for international students: Required—TOEFL (minimum score 500 paper-based; 173 computer-based; 61 iBT). *Application deadline:* For fall admission, 8/24 priority date for domestic students, 7/1 for international students; for winter admission, 12/14 priority date for domestic students; for spring admission, 1/19 priority date for domestic students, 11/1 for international students. Applications are processed on a rolling basis. Electronic applications accepted. *Expenses:* Tuition, state resident: part-time $159 per credit hour. Tuition, nonresident: part-time $159 per credit hour. Required fees: $1300 per year. Tuition and fees vary according to course load. *Financial support:* Career-related internships or fieldwork, Federal Work-Study, and unspecified assistantships available. Financial award application deadline: 4/1; financial award applicants required to submit FAFSA.

University of Louisville, Graduate School, College of Education and Human Development, Department of Teaching and Learning, Louisville, KY 40292-0001. Offers art education (MAT); curriculum and instruction (PhD); early elementary education (MAT); instructional technology (M Ed); interdisciplinary early childhood education (MAT); middle school education (MAT); music education (MAT); reading education (M Ed); secondary education (MAT); special education (M Ed, MAT); teacher leadership (M Ed). Part-time and evening/weekend programs available. *Faculty:* 43 full-time (33 women), 43 part-time/adjunct (36 women). *Students:* 207 full-time (144 women), 410 part-time (306 women); includes 68 minority (43 African Americans, 2 American Indian/Alaska Native, 14 Asian Americans or Pacific Islanders, 9 Hispanic Americans), 5 international. Average age 33. 216 applicants, 68% accepted, 112 enrolled. In 2009, 269 master's, 6 doctorates awarded. *Degree requirements:* For doctorate, comprehensive exam, thesis/dissertation. *Entrance requirements:* For master's, GRE General Test, PRAXIS II (for some programs); for doctorate, GRE General Test. Additional exam requirements/recommendations for international students: Required—TOEFL (minimum score 560 paper-based; 210 computer-based; 83 iBT). Application fee: $50. Electronic applications accepted. *Financial support:* In 2009–10, 172 students received support; fellowships, research assistantships, teaching assistantships, career-related internships or fieldwork, Federal Work-Study, scholarships/grants, and unspecified assistantships available. Financial award application deadline: 6/1; financial award applicants required to submit FAFSA. *Faculty research:* Assessment of cognitive and language abilities in infants and preschool children; mathematics teachers' conceptions and beliefs, effect, and understanding of mathematics; incorporating nanoscience and nanotechnology into middle and high school science classrooms; urban teacher preparation through inquiry, action and advocacy; impacts of cognitive coaching on teacher practice and student achievement. Total annual research expenditures: $3.7 million. *Unit head:* Dr. Ann E. Larson, Acting Chair, 502-852-6431, Fax: 502-852-1497, E-mail: ann@louisville.edu. *Application contact:* Libby Leggett, Director, Graduate Admissions, 502-852-3101, Fax: 502-852-6536, E-mail: gradadm@louisville.edu.

University of Massachusetts Dartmouth, Graduate School, School of Education, Public Policy, and Civic Engagement, Department of Teaching and Learning, North Dartmouth, MA 02747-2300. Offers elementary education (MAT, Postbaccalaureate Certificate); middle school education (MAT); principal initial licensure (Postbaccalaureate Certificate); secondary school education (MAT). *Faculty:* 7 full-time (4 women), 6 part-time/adjunct (3 women). *Students:* 53 full-time (33 women), 183 part-time (118 women); includes 16 minority (6 African Americans, 1 American Indian/Alaska Native, 2 Asian Americans or Pacific Islanders, 7 Hispanic Americans). Average age 35. 188 applicants, 75% accepted, 109 enrolled. In 2009, 34 master's, 4 other advanced degrees awarded. *Degree requirements:* For master's, thesis or alternative. *Entrance requirements:* For master's, MAT or GRE, GMAT, minimum undergraduate GPA of 2.7, teacher

certification, 3 letters of recommendation. Additional exam requirements/recommendations for international students: Required—TOEFL (minimum score 500 paper-based). *Application deadline:* For fall admission, 4/20 priority date for domestic students, 2/20 for international students; for spring admission, 11/15 priority date for domestic students, 9/15 for international students. Applications are processed on a rolling basis. Application fee: $40 ($60 for international students). *Expenses:* Tuition, state resident: full-time $2071; part-time $86.29 per credit. Tuition, nonresident: full-time $8099; part-time $337.46 per credit. Required fees: $9446. Tuition and fees vary according to class time, course load and reciprocity agreements. *Financial support:* Federal Work-Study available. Financial award application deadline: 3/1. Total annual research expenditures: $1.3 million. *Unit head:* Dr. Gerard Koot, Director, 508-999-8305, Fax: 508-999-9125, E-mail: gkoot@umassd.edu. *Application contact:* Elan Turcotte-Shamski, Graduate Admissions Officer, 508-999-8604, Fax: 508-999-8183, E-mail: graduate@umassd.edu.

University of Memphis, Graduate School, College of Education, Department of Instruction and Curriculum Leadership, Memphis, TN 38152. Offers early childhood education (MAT, MS, Ed D); elementary education (MAT); instruction and curriculum (MS, Ed D); instruction design and technology (MS, Ed D); middle grades education (MAT); reading (MS, Ed D); secondary education (MAT); special education (MAT, MS, Ed D). *Accreditation:* NCATE (one or more programs are accredited). Part-time programs available. *Faculty:* 40 full-time (28 women), 20 part-time/adjunct (15 women). *Students:* 119 full-time (90 women), 631 part-time (505 women); includes 348 minority (331 African Americans, 2 American Indian/Alaska Native, 4 Asian Americans or Pacific Islanders, 11 Hispanic Americans), 7 international. Average age 34. 202 applicants, 77% accepted, 29 enrolled. In 2009, 137 master's, 10 doctorates awarded. Terminal master's awarded for partial completion of doctoral program. *Degree requirements:* For master's, comprehensive exam, thesis or alternative; for doctorate, comprehensive exam, thesis/dissertation. *Entrance requirements:* For master's, GRE General Test, minimum GPA of 2.5; for doctorate, GRE General Test, GRE Subject Test, 2 years of teaching experience. *Application deadline:* For fall admission, 8/1 for domestic students; for spring admission, 12/1 for domestic students. Applications are processed on a rolling basis. Application fee: $35 ($60 for international students). Electronic applications accepted. *Expenses:* Tuition, state resident: full-time $6246; part-time $347 per credit hour. Tuition, nonresident: full-time $15,894; part-time $883 per credit hour. Required fees: $1160. Full-time tuition and fees vary according to course load, degree level and program. *Financial support:* In 2009–10, 635 students received support; research assistantships with full tuition reimbursements available, teaching assistantships with full tuition reimbursements available, career-related internships or fieldwork, Federal Work-Study, institutionally sponsored loans, scholarships/grants, traineeships, and unspecified assistantships available. Support available to part-time students. Financial award application deadline: 2/15; financial award applicants required to submit FAFSA. *Faculty research:* Effective urban teachers, preparation and retention of urban teachers, technology utilization in schools, field-based teacher preparation programs, effective use of online instruction. *Unit head:* Dr. Sandra Cooley-Nichols, Interim Chair, 901-678-2365. *Application contact:* Dr. Sally Blake, Director of Graduate Studies, 901-678-4861.

University of Missouri–St. Louis, College of Education, Division of Teaching and Learning, St. Louis, MO 63121. Offers elementary education (M Ed), including early childhood, general, reading; secondary education (M Ed), including curriculum and instruction, general, middle level education, reading, teaching English to speakers of other languages (TESOL); secondary school teaching (Certificate); special education (M Ed), including behavioral disorders, early childhood special education, general, learning disabilities, mental retardation; teaching English to speakers of other languages (Certificate). Part-time and evening/weekend programs available. *Faculty:* 36 full-time (23 women), 51 part-time/adjunct (42 women). *Students:* 123 full-time (77 women), 569 part-time (435 women); includes 137 minority (110 African Americans, 4 American Indian/Alaska Native, 10 Asian Americans or Pacific Islanders, 13 Hispanic Americans), 11 international. Average age 32. In 2009, 1,852 master's awarded. *Degree requirements:* For master's, comprehensive exam. *Entrance requirements:* Additional exam requirements/recommendations for international students: Recommended—TOEFL (minimum score 550 paper-based; 213 computer-based). *Application deadline:* For fall admission, 7/1 priority date for domestic and international students; for spring admission, 12/1 priority date for domestic and international students. Application fee: $35 ($40 for international students). Electronic applications accepted. *Expenses:* Tuition, state resident: full-time $5377; part-time $297.70 per credit hour. Tuition, nonresident: full-time $13,882; part-time $771.20 per credit hour. Required fees: $220; $12.20 per credit hour. One-time fee: $12. Tuition and fees vary according to course level, campus/location and program. *Financial support:* In 2009–10, 5 research assistantships (averaging $10,339 per year), 2 teaching assistantships (averaging $6,800 per year) were awarded. Financial award application deadline: 4/1; financial award applicants required to submit FAFSA. *Unit head:* Dr. Joseph Polman, Chair, 314-516-5791. *Application contact:* 314-516-5458, Fax: 314-516-6996, E-mail: gadadm@umsl.edu.

The University of North Carolina at Charlotte, Graduate School, College of Education, Department of Middle, Secondary and K-12 Education, Charlotte, NC 28223-0001. Offers middle grades and secondary education (M Ed); teaching English as a second language (M Ed). *Faculty:* 16 full-time (9 women), 5 part-time/adjunct (4 women). *Students:* 1 full-time (0 women), 39 part-time (26 women); includes 1 minority (African American). Average age 30. 6 applicants, 100% accepted, 5 enrolled. In 2009, 44 master's awarded. *Entrance requirements:* For master's, GRE or MAT. Additional exam requirements/recommendations for international students: Required—TOEFL (minimum score 557 paper-based; 220 computer-based; 83 iBT). *Application deadline:* For fall admission, 7/1 for domestic students, 5/1 for international students; for spring admission, 11/1 for domestic students, 10/1 for international students. Applications are processed on a rolling basis. Application fee: $55. Electronic applications accepted. *Financial support:* In 2009–10, 5 students received support, including 5 teaching assistantships (averaging $15,644 per year); career-related internships or fieldwork, Federal Work-Study, institutionally sponsored loans, scholarships/grants, and unspecified assistantships also available. Support available to part-time students. Financial award application deadline: 4/1; financial award applicants required to submit FAFSA. Total annual research expenditures: $65,335. *Unit head:* Melba Spooner, Chair, 704-687-8704, Fax: 704-687-6430, E-mail: mcspoone@uncc.edu. *Application contact:* Kathy B. Giddings, Director of Graduate Admissions, 704-687-5503, Fax: 704-687-3279, E-mail: gradadm@uncc.edu.

The University of North Carolina at Charlotte, Graduate School, College of Education, Program in Teacher Education, Charlotte, NC 28223-0001. Offers art education (K-12) (MAT); dance education (K-12) (MAT); elementary education (K-6) (MAT); English as a second language (K-12) (MAT); foreign language education (K-12) (MAT); general teacher education (MAT); middle grades education (6-9) (MAT); music education (K-12) (MAT); secondary education (9-12) (MAT); special education (K-12) (MAT); theatre education (K-12) (MAT). *Faculty:* 108 full-time (64 women), 16 part-time/adjunct (12 women). *Students:* 29 full-time (20 women), 229 part-time (189 women); includes 32 minority (22 African Americans, 2 American Indian/Alaska Native, 3 Asian Americans or Pacific Islanders, 5 Hispanic Americans). Average age 32. 108 applicants, 92% accepted, 85 enrolled. In 2009, 59 master's awarded. *Entrance requirements:* For master's, GRE or MAT. Additional exam requirements/recommendations for international students: Required—TOEFL (minimum score 557 paper-based; 220 computer-based; 83 iBT). *Application deadline:* For fall admission, 7/1 for domestic students, 5/1 for international students; for spring admission, 11/1 for domestic students, 10/1 for international students. Applications are processed on a rolling basis. Application fee: $55. Electronic applications accepted. *Financial support:* In 2009–10, 5 students received support, including 1 research assistantship (averaging $18,000 per year), 3 teaching assistantships (averaging $12,183 per year); career-related internships or fieldwork, Federal Work-Study, institutionally sponsored loans, scholarships/grants, and administrative assistantship also available. Support available to part-time students. Financial award application deadline: 4/1; financial award applicants required to submit FAFSA. Total annual research expenditures: $5.1 million. *Unit head:* Dr. Kimberly J. Hartman, Coordinator, 704-687-8883, Fax: 704-687-6430, E-mail: khartman@uncc.edu. *Application contact:* Kathy B. Giddings, Director of Graduate Admissions, 704-687-5503, Fax: 704-687-3279, E-mail: gradadmn@uncc.edu.

The University of North Carolina at Greensboro, Graduate School, School of Education, Department of Curriculum and Instruction, Greensboro, NC 27412-5001. Offers college teaching and adult learning (Certificate); curriculum and instruction (M Ed), including chemistry education, elementary education, English as a second language, French education, instructional technology, mathematics education, middle grades education, reading education, science education, social studies education, Spanish education; curriculum and teaching (PhD), including higher education, teacher education and development; English as a second language (Certificate); higher education (M Ed); supervision (M Ed). *Accreditation:* NCATE. Part-time programs available. *Degree requirements:* For doctorate, thesis/dissertation. *Entrance requirements:* For master's and doctorate, GRE General Test. Additional exam requirements/recommendations for international students: Required—TOEFL. Electronic applications accepted. *Faculty research:* Community college literacy program, middle school mathematics/computer mathematics.

The University of North Carolina at Pembroke, Graduate Studies, School of Education, Program in Middle Grades Education, Pembroke, NC 28372-1510. Offers MA Ed, MAT. *Accreditation:* NCATE. Part-time and evening/weekend programs available. *Degree requirements:* For master's, thesis optional. *Entrance requirements:* For master's, GRE General Test or MAT, minimum GPA of 3.0 in major, 2.5 overall. Additional exam requirements/recommendations for international students: Required—TOEFL.

The University of North Carolina Wilmington, School of Education, Department of Elementary, Middle Level and Literacy Education, Program in Middle Grades Education, Wilmington, NC 28403-3297. Offers M Ed. *Degree requirements:* For master's, comprehensive exam.

University of Northern Iowa, Graduate College, College of Education, Department of Curriculum and Instruction, Program in Middle School/Junior High Education, Cedar Falls, IA 50614. Offers MAE. *Students:* 1 applicant, 100% accepted, 0 enrolled. In 2009, 3 master's awarded. *Degree requirements:* For master's, comprehensive exam (for some programs), thesis or alternative. *Entrance requirements:* For master's, minimum GPA of 3.0. Additional exam requirements/recommendations for international students: Required—TOEFL (minimum score 500 paper-based; 180 computer-based; 61 iBT). *Application deadline:* For fall admission, 8/1 priority date for domestic students. Applications are processed on a rolling basis. Application fee: $30 ($50 for international students). Electronic applications accepted. *Financial support:* Application deadline: 2/1. *Unit head:* Dr. Jean Schneider, Coordinator, 319-273-3274, Fax: 319-273-5886, E-mail: jean.schneider@uni.edu. *Application contact:* Laurie S. Russell, Record Analyst, 319-273-2623, Fax: 319-273-6792, E-mail: laurie.russell@uni.edu.

University of Phoenix–Oregon Campus, The Artemis School, College of Education, Tigard, OR 97223. Offers curriculum and instruction (MA Ed); early childhood education (MA Ed); elementary education (MA Ed), including early childhood specialization, middle level specialization; secondary education (MA Ed), including middle level specialization. Evening/weekend programs available. *Degree requirements:* For master's, thesis (for some programs). *Entrance requirements:* For master's, minimum undergraduate GPA of 2.5, 3 years work experience. Additional exam requirements/recommendations for international students: Required—TOEFL (minimum score 550 paper-based; 213 computer-based; 79 iBT). Electronic applications accepted.

University of Southern Maine, College of Education and Human Development, Educational Leadership Program, Portland, ME 04104-9300. Offers assistant principal (Certificate); athletic administration (Certificate); educational leadership (MS Ed, CAS); middle-level education (Certificate). Part-time and evening/weekend programs available. Postbaccalaureate distance learning degree programs offered (minimal on-campus study). *Faculty:* 5 full-time (0 women), 2 part-time/adjunct (1 woman). *Students:* 15 full-time (6 women), 42 part-time (23 women); includes 1 minority (American Indian/Alaska Native). 20 applicants, 85% accepted, 10 enrolled. In 2009, 26 master's, 11 CASs awarded. *Degree requirements:* For master's, thesis or alternative, practicum, internship; for other advanced degree, thesis or alternative. *Entrance requirements:* For master's, three years of documented teaching; for other advanced degree, master's degree. Additional exam requirements/recommendations for international students: Required—TOEFL (minimum score 550 paper-based; 213 computer-based; 79 iBT). *Application deadline:* For fall admission, 5/1 priority date for domestic students; for spring admission, 10/15 priority date for domestic students. Applications are processed on a rolling basis. Application fee: $50. Electronic applications accepted. *Financial support:* Research assistantships with partial tuition reimbursements, career-related internships or fieldwork, Federal Work-Study, institutionally sponsored loans, scholarships/grants, and unspecified assistantships available. Financial award application deadline: 3/1; financial award applicants required to submit FAFSA. *Unit head:* Dr. James Curry, Chair, Professional Education Department, 270-780-5400, Fax: 270-780-5674, E-mail: jcurry@usm.maine.edu. *Application contact:* Mary Sloan, Director of Graduate Admissions, 207-780-4386, Fax: 207-780-4969, E-mail: msloan@usm.maine.edu.

University of the Cumberlands, Graduate Programs in Education, Program in Elementary Education, Williamsburg, KY 40769-1372. Offers elementary (P-5) (MA Ed, MAT); middle school (5-9) (MA Ed, MAT). Part-time and evening/weekend programs available. *Degree requirements:* For master's, comprehensive exam. *Entrance requirements:* For master's, GRE or NTE, Kentucky teaching certificate.

University of the Cumberlands, Graduate Programs in Education, Program in Middle School Education, Williamsburg, KY 40769-1372. Offers MA Ed, MAT. *Degree requirements:* For master's, comprehensive exam. *Entrance requirements:* For master's, GRE or NTE, Kentucky teaching certificate.

The University of Toledo, College of Graduate Studies, College of Education, Department of Curriculum and Instruction, Program in Middle Childhood Education, Toledo, OH 43606-3390. Offers ME.

University of Washington, Bothell, Program in Education, Bothell, WA 98011-8246. Offers leadership development for educators (M Ed); secondary/middle level endorsement (M Ed). Part-time and evening/weekend programs available. *Faculty:* 9 full-time (7 women), 1 (woman) part-time/adjunct. *Students:* 25 full-time (15 women), 118 part-time (91 women); includes 17 minority (6 African Americans, 6 Asian Americans or Pacific Islanders, 5 Hispanic Americans). Average age 34. 78 applicants, 76% accepted, 55 enrolled. In 2009, 47 master's awarded. *Degree requirements:* For master's, thesis. *Entrance requirements:* Additional exam requirements/recommendations for international students: Required—TOEFL. *Application deadline:* For fall admission, 8/14 priority date for domestic and international students; for spring admission, 2/12 priority date for domestic and international students. Applications are processed on a rolling basis. Application fee: $65. Electronic applications accepted. *Expenses:* Tuition, state resident: full-time $10,160; part-time $484 per credit hour. Tuition, nonresident: full-time $23,500; part-time $1120 per credit hour. Required fees: $567; $21.50 per credit hour. Tuition and fees vary according to course load and program. *Financial support:* Federal Work-Study and unspecified assistantships available. *Faculty research:* Multicultural education in citizenship education, intercultural education, knowledge and practice in the principalship, educational public policy, national board certification for teachers, teacher learning in literacy, technology and its impact on teaching and learning of mathematics, reading assessments, professional development in literacy education and mobility, digital media, education and class. *Unit head:* Dr. Bradley S. Portin, Director and Professor, 425-352-3482, Fax: 425-352-5234, E-mail: bportin@uwb.edu. *Application contact:* Amelia Bowers, Education Program Advisor, 425-352-5274, Fax: 425-352-5434, E-mail: abowers@uwb.edu.

University of Washington, Tacoma, Graduate Programs, Program in Education, Tacoma, WA 98402-3100. Offers educational administrator (M Ed); K-8 teacher education (M Ed); professional certification (M Ed); secondary science (M Ed); special education (M Ed). Part-time

Middle School Education

University of Washington, Tacoma *(continued)*
and evening/weekend programs available. *Faculty:* 13 full-time (8 women), 9 part-time/adjunct (8 women). *Students:* 85 full-time (66 women), 118 part-time (99 women); includes 24 minority (4 African Americans, 9 Asian Americans or Pacific Islanders, 11 Hispanic Americans). Average age 33. 36 applicants, 75% accepted, 23 enrolled. In 2009, 68 master's awarded. *Entrance requirements:* For master's, official sealed transcript from every college/university attended, personal goal statement, letters of recommendation, copy of valid teaching certificate. *Application deadline:* For fall admission, 8/1 for domestic students; for winter admission, 11/1 priority date for domestic students; for spring admission, 2/1 priority date for domestic students. Applications are processed on a rolling basis. Application fee: $65. Electronic applications accepted. *Expenses:* Tuition, state resident: full-time $10,660; part-time $484 per credit. Tuition, nonresident: full-time $24,000; part-time $1119 per credit. Required fees: $150 per term. Tuition and fees vary according to course load and program. *Faculty research:* Global learning communities for English/Chinese languages, evaluation of mathematics and reading intervention programs, response to intervention, school wide behavioral and emotional support, mathematics education and culturally responsive mathematics education. *Unit head:* Dr. Karen Landenburger, Chancellor, 253-692-4430, Fax: 253-692-5612, E-mail: uwted@u.washington.edu. *Application contact:* Dr. Carla Van Rossum, Recruiter/Advisor, 253-692-4430, Fax: 253-692-5612, E-mail: uwted@u.washington.edu.

University of West Florida, College of Professional Studies, Department of Professional and Community Leadership, Specialization in Middle and Secondary Level Education and ESOL, Pensacola, FL 32514-5750. Offers M Ed. *Accreditation:* NCATE. Part-time and evening/weekend programs available. *Students:* 10 part-time (all women). Average age 32. 1 applicant. In 2009, 30 master's awarded. *Degree requirements:* For master's, thesis or alternative. *Entrance requirements:* For master's, GRE (minimum score 450 verbal) or MAT (minimum score 396) if bachelor's GPA less than 3.0, state teaching certification; letter of intent; two professional references. Additional exam requirements/recommendations for international students: Required—TOEFL (minimum score 550 paper-based; 213 computer-based). *Application deadline:* For fall admission, 6/1 for domestic students, 5/15 for international students; for spring admission, 11/1 for domestic students, 10/1 for international students. Applications are processed on a rolling basis. Application fee: $30. *Expenses:* Tuition, state resident: full-time $4982; part-time $260 per credit hour. Tuition, nonresident: full-time $20,059; part-time $919 per credit hour. Required fees: $1247; $52 per credit hour. *Financial support:* Unspecified assistantships available. *Unit head:* Dr. David Stout, Chairperson, 850-474-2284, Fax: 850-474-2844. *Application contact:* Terry McCray, Assistant Director of Graduate Admissions, 850-473-7718, Fax: 850-473-7714, E-mail: gradadmissions@uwf.edu.

University of West Georgia, Graduate School, College of Education, Department of Curriculum and Instruction, Carrollton, GA 30118. Offers art education (M Ed); art teacher education (Ed S); biology/secondary education (Ed S); business education (M Ed, Ed S); early childhood education (M Ed, Ed S); economics/secondary teacher education (Ed S); English teacher education (Ed S); French language teacher education (Ed S); history teacher education (Ed S); mathematics teacher education (Ed S); middle grades education (M Ed, Ed S); reading education (M Ed, Ed S); science teacher education (Ed S); secondary education (M Ed, Ed S); social science teacher education (Ed S); Spanish language teacher education (Ed S). Part-time and evening/weekend programs available. *Faculty:* 18 full-time (15 women), 7 part-time/adjunct (6 women). *Students:* 119 full-time (101 women), 358 part-time (280 women); includes 109 minority (97 African Americans, 3 American Indian/Alaska Native, 2 Asian Americans or Pacific Islanders, 7 Hispanic Americans). Average age 33. 193 applicants, 82% accepted, 34 enrolled. In 2009, 109 master's, 27 Ed Ss awarded. *Degree requirements:* For master's, comprehensive exam; for Ed S, research project. *Entrance requirements:* For master's, GRE General Test or MAT, minimum GPA of 2.7; for Ed S, GRE General Test, master's degree, minimum graduate GPA of 2.7. *Application deadline:* For fall admission, 7/17 for domestic students; for spring admission, 11/20 for domestic students. Applications are processed on a rolling basis. Application fee: $30. Electronic applications accepted. *Expenses:* Tuition, state resident: full-time $2952; part-time $164 per semester hour. Tuition, nonresident: full-time $11,808; part-time $656 per semester hour. Required fees: $42.90 per semester hour. $307 per semester. Tuition and fees vary according to course load. *Financial support:* In 2009–10, 5 research assistantships with full tuition reimbursements (averaging $3,000 per year) were awarded; career-related internships or fieldwork and scholarships/grants also available. Support available to part-time students. Financial award applicants required to submit FAFSA. *Unit head:* Dr. Donna Harkins, Chair, 678-839-6066, Fax: 678-839-6559, E-mail: dharkins@westga.edu. *Application contact:* Dr. Charles W. Clark, Dean, 678-839-6508, E-mail: cclark@westga.edu.

University of Wisconsin–Milwaukee, Graduate School, School of Education, Department of Curriculum and Instruction, Milwaukee, WI 53201-0413. Offers curriculum planning and instruction improvement (MS); early childhood education (MS); elementary education (MS); junior high/middle school education (MS); reading education (MS); secondary education (MS); teaching in an urban setting (MS). Part-time programs available. *Faculty:* 22 full-time (17 women). *Students:* 23 full-time (14 women), 64 part-time (58 women); includes 8 minority (4 African Americans, 1 American Indian/Alaska Native, 3 Hispanic Americans), 1 international. Average age 31. 46 applicants, 57% accepted, 12 enrolled. In 2009, 28 master's awarded. *Degree requirements:* For master's, thesis or alternative. *Entrance requirements:* Additional exam requirements/recommendations for international students: Required—TOEFL (minimum score 550 paper-based; 79 iBT), IELTS (minimum score 6.5). *Application deadline:* For fall admission, 1/1 priority date for domestic students; for spring admission, 9/1 for domestic students. Applications are processed on a rolling basis. Application fee: $45 ($75 for international students). *Expenses:* Tuition, state resident: full-time $8800. Tuition, nonresident: full-time $20,760. Tuition and fees vary according to program and reciprocity agreements. *Financial support:* Career-related internships or fieldwork and unspecified assistantships available. Support available to part-time students. Financial award application deadline: 4/15. Total annual research expenditures: $65,946. *Unit head:* Hope Longwell-Grice, Chair, 414-229-4884, Fax: 414-229-5571, E-mail: hope@uwm.edu. *Application contact:* General Information Contact, 414-229-4982, Fax: 414-229-6967, E-mail: gradschool@uwm.edu.

University of Wisconsin–Platteville, School of Graduate Studies, College of Liberal Arts and Education, School of Education, Platteville, WI 53818-3099. Offers adult education (MSE); elementary education (MSE); English education (MSE); middle school education (MSE); secondary education (MSE); vocational and technical education (MSE). *Accreditation:* NCATE. Part-time programs available. *Faculty:* 8 part-time/adjunct (3 women). *Students:* 16 full-time (12 women), 183 part-time (137 women); includes 35 minority (27 African Americans, 1 American Indian/Alaska Native, 1 Asian American or Pacific Islander, 6 Hispanic Americans), 63 international. 23 applicants, 100% accepted, 23 enrolled. In 2009, 85 master's awarded. *Degree requirements:* For master's, comprehensive exam, thesis or alternative. *Entrance requirements:* Additional exam requirements/recommendations for international students: Required—TOEFL (minimum score 500 paper-based; 173 computer-based; 61 iBT). *Application deadline:* For fall admission, 7/1 priority date for domestic students; for spring admission, 11/1 for domestic students. Applications are processed on a rolling basis. Application fee: $56. Electronic applications accepted. *Expenses:* Tuition, state resident: full-time $6706. Tuition, nonresident: full-time $16,772. *Financial support:* Research assistantships with partial tuition reimbursements, career-related internships or fieldwork, Federal Work-Study, institutionally sponsored loans, scholarships/grants, and unspecified assistantships available. Support available to part-time students. *Unit head:* Dr. Karen Stinson, Director, 608-342-1131, Fax: 608-342-1133. *Application contact:* Lisa Popp, School of Graduate Studies, 608-342-1322, Fax: 608-342-1389, E-mail: poppl@uwplatt.edu.

Ursuline College, School of Graduate Studies, Program in Education, Pepper Pike, OH 44124-4398. Offers art education (MA); early childhood education (MA); language arts education (MA); life science education (MA); math education (MA); middle school education (MA); social studies education (MA); special education (MA). *Accreditation:* NCATE. *Faculty:* 1 (woman)

full-time, 10 part-time/adjunct (8 women). *Students:* 53 full-time (40 women), 3 part-time (all women); includes 8 minority (7 African Americans, 1 Hispanic American). Average age 34. In 2009, 11 master's awarded. *Degree requirements:* For master's, comprehensive exam. *Entrance requirements:* For master's, minimum undergraduate GPA of 3.0. Additional exam requirements/recommendations for international students: Required—TOEFL (minimum score 500 paper-based; 173 computer-based). *Application deadline:* For fall admission, 8/1 priority date for domestic students. Applications are processed on a rolling basis. Application fee: $25. *Expenses:* Contact institution. *Financial support:* Federal Work-Study available. Financial award application deadline: 3/1. *Unit head:* Karen Godenschwager Nelson, Director, 440-684-8338, Fax: 440-684-6088, E-mail: kgodenschwager@ursuline.edu. *Application contact:* Melanie Steele, Secretary, 440-646-8199, Fax: 440-684-6138, E-mail: gradsch@ursuline.edu.

Valdosta State University, Graduate School, Department of Middle, Secondary, Reading and Deaf Education, Valdosta, GA 31698. Offers middle grades education (M Ed, Ed S); secondary education (M Ed, Ed S). *Accreditation:* NCATE. Part-time and evening/weekend programs available. *Degree requirements:* For master's, thesis (for some programs), comprehensive written and/or oral exams; for Ed S, thesis. *Entrance requirements:* For master's, GRE General Test or MAT, minimum GPA of 2.5; for Ed S, GRE General Test or MAT, minimum GPA of 3.0. Additional exam requirements/recommendations for international students: Required—TOEFL (minimum score 523 paper-based; 193 computer-based). Electronic applications accepted. *Faculty research:* Distance education, learning styles, alternative assessment methods, interactive teaching strategies, learning styles of pre-service teachers.

Virginia Commonwealth University, Graduate School, School of Education, Program in Teaching and Learning, Richmond, VA 23284-9005. Offers early education (MT); middle education (MT); secondary education (MT, Certificate); special education (MT). *Accreditation:* NCATE. Part-time programs available. *Entrance requirements:* For master's, GRE General Test or MAT.

Wagner College, Division of Graduate Studies, Department of Education, Program in Adolescent Education, Staten Island, NY 10301-4495. Offers MS Ed. Part-time and evening/weekend programs available. *Entrance requirements:* For master's, Liberal Arts and Sciences Test (LAST), New York State Teacher Certification Examinations (NYSTCE), minimum GPA of 2.75. Additional exam requirements/recommendations for international students: Required—TOEFL (minimum score 550 paper-based; 217 computer-based). *Expenses:* Tuition: Full-time $15,570; part-time $865 per credit. Required fees: $2.

Wagner College, Division of Graduate Studies, Department of Education, Program in Middle Level Education (5-9), Staten Island, NY 10301-4495. Offers MS Ed. *Degree requirements:* For master's, thesis. *Entrance requirements:* For master's, minimum GPA of 2.75. Additional exam requirements/recommendations for international students: Required—TOEFL (minimum score 550 paper-based; 217 computer-based). *Expenses:* Tuition: Full-time $15,570; part-time $865 per credit. Required fees: $2.

Walden University, Graduate Programs, Richard W. Riley College of Education and Leadership, Minneapolis, MN 55401. Offers administrator leadership for teaching and learning (Ed D, Ed S); curriculum, instruction, and professional development (Ed S); early childhood education (birth-grade 3) (MAT); education (MS, PhD), including adolescent literacy and technology (grades 6-12) (MS), adult education leadership (PhD), community college leadership (PhD), curriculum, instruction, and assessment, early childhood education (PhD), educational leadership (MS), educational technology (PhD), elementary reading and literacy (MS), elementary reading and mathematics (MS), emotional/behavioral disorders (K-12) (MS), general program, higher education (PhD), integrating technology in the classroom (MS), K-12 educational leadership (PhD), learning disabilities (K-12) (MS), literacy and learning in the content areas (MS), mathematics (grades 6-8) (MS), mathematics (grades K-5) (MS), middle level education (grades 5-8) (MS), professional development (MS), science (grades K-8) (MS), self-designed (PhD), special education (PhD), special education (non-licensure) (MS), teacher leadership (grades K-12) (MS); educational leadership and administration (principal preparation) (Ed S); educational technology (Ed S); higher education and adult learning (Ed D); instructional design (Postbaccalaureate Certificate); instructional design and technology (MS), including general program (MS, PhD), online learning, training and performance improvement; special education: emotional/behavioral disorders (K-12) (MAT); special education: learning disabilities (K-12) (MAT); teacher leadership (Ed D, Ed S). Part-time and evening/weekend programs available. Postbaccalaureate distance learning degree programs offered (minimal on-campus study). *Faculty:* 54 full-time, 835 part-time/adjunct. *Students:* 13,940 full-time (11,339 women), 1,940 part-time (1,637 women); includes 4,626 minority (3,795 African Americans, 111 American Indian/Alaska Native, 199 Asian Americans or Pacific Islanders, 521 Hispanic Americans), 124 international. Average age 38. In 2009, 4,688 master's, 190 doctorates awarded. *Degree requirements:* For doctorate, thesis/dissertation (for some programs), residency; for other advanced degree, residency (for some programs). *Entrance requirements:* For master's, bachelor's degree or equivalent in related field; minimum GPA of 2.5; official transcripts; goal statement; access to computer and Internet; for doctorate, master's degree or equivalent in related field; minimum GPA of 3.0; official transcripts; three years' related professional/academic experience (preferred); access to computer and Internet; for other advanced degree, master's degree or equivalent in related field; minimum GPA of 3.0; 3 years related professional/academic experience (preferred); access to computer and Internet (Ed S). Additional exam requirements/recommendations for international students: Required—TOEFL (minimum score 550 paper-based; 213 computer-based), IELTS (minimum score 6.5), or Michigan English Language Assessment Battery (minimum score 82). *Application deadline:* Applications are processed on a rolling basis. Application fee: $50. Electronic applications accepted. *Expenses:* Tuition: Full-time $13,665; part-time $560 per credit. Required fees: $1375. Tuition and fees vary according to course load, degree level and program. *Financial support:* In 2009–10, 2,418 students received support; fellowships, Federal Work-Study, scholarships/grants, unspecified assistantships, and family tuition reduction, active duty/veteran tuition reduction, group tuition reduction, interest-free payment plans available. Support available to part-time students. Financial award applicants required to submit FAFSA. *Unit head:* Dr. Kate Steffens, Dean, 800-925-3368. *Application contact:* Jennifer Hall, Director of Enrollment, 866-4-WALDEN, E-mail: info@waldenu.edu.

Western Kentucky University, Graduate Studies, College of Education and Behavioral Sciences, Department of Counseling and Student Affairs, Bowling Green, KY 42101. Offers business and marketing education (MA Ed); counseling (MA Ed); counselor education (Ed S); education and behavioral science (MA Ed); elementary education (MA Ed, Ed S); middle years education (MA Ed); secondary education (MA Ed, Ed S); student affairs (MA Ed). *Accreditation:* ACA; NCATE. Part-time and evening/weekend programs available. *Degree requirements:* For master's, comprehensive exam, thesis optional. *Entrance requirements:* For master's, GRE General Test. Additional exam requirements/recommendations for international students: Required—TOEFL (minimum score 555 paper-based; 213 computer-based; 79 iBT). *Expenses:* Tuition, state resident: full-time $4160; part-time $416 per credit hour. Tuition, nonresident: full-time $9550; part-time $506 per credit hour. Tuition and fees vary according to campus/location and reciprocity agreements. *Faculty research:* Counselor education, research for residential workers.

Western Kentucky University, Graduate Studies, College of Education and Behavioral Sciences, Department of Curriculum and Instruction, Bowling Green, KY 42101. Offers business and marketing education (MAE); elementary education (MAE, Ed S); middle grades education (MAE); secondary education (MAE, Ed S). *Degree requirements:* For master's, comprehensive exam; for Ed S, thesis. *Entrance requirements:* For master's, GRE. Additional exam requirements/recommendations for international students: Required—TOEFL (minimum score 555 paper-based; 213 computer-based; 79 iBT). *Expenses:* Tuition, state resident: full-time $4160; part-time $416 per credit hour. Tuition, nonresident: full-time $9550; part-time $506 per credit hour. Tuition and fees vary according to campus/location and reciprocity agreements.

Widener University, School of Human Service Professions, Center for Education, Chester, PA 19013-5792. Offers adult education (M Ed); counseling in higher education (M Ed); counselor education (M Ed); early childhood education (M Ed); educational foundations (M Ed); educational leadership (M Ed); educational psychology (M Ed); elementary education (M Ed); English and language arts (M Ed); health education (M Ed); higher education leadership (Ed D); home and school visitor (M Ed); human sexuality (M Ed); mathematics education (M Ed); middle school education (M Ed); principalship (M Ed); reading and language arts (Ed D); reading education (M Ed); school administration (Ed D); science education (M Ed); social studies education (M Ed); special education (M Ed); technology education (M Ed). *Accreditation:* NCATE. Part-time and evening/weekend programs available. *Faculty:* 34 full-time (22 women), 37 part-time/adjunct (14 women). *Students:* 203 full-time (154 women), 415 part-time (298 women); includes 50 minority (34 African Americans, 1 American Indian/Alaska Native, 5 Asian Americans or Pacific Islanders, 10 Hispanic Americans), 3 international. Average age 39. 139 applicants, 88% accepted. In 2009, 168 master's, 31 doctorates awarded. Terminal master's awarded for partial completion of doctoral program. *Degree requirements:* For doctorate, thesis/dissertation. *Entrance requirements:* For master's, minimum GPA of 2.5; for doctorate, GRE or MAT, minimum GPA of 2.0 (undergraduate), 3.5 (graduate). *Application deadline:* Applications are processed on a rolling basis. Application fee: $25 ($300 for international students). Electronic applications accepted. *Expenses:* Contact institution. *Financial support:* Career-related internships or fieldwork, tuition waivers (full and partial), and unspecified assistantships available. Support available to part-time students. Financial award application deadline: 5/1. *Faculty research:* Reading and cognition, adult education, technology education, educational leadership, special education. *Unit head:* Dr. Michael W. LeDoux, Associate Dean, 610-499-4294, Fax: 610-499-4623, E-mail: mwledoux@widener.edu. *Application contact:* Dr. Roberta D. Nolan, Director of Graduate Admissions, 610-499-4125, E-mail: rdnolan@widener.edu.

Winthrop University, College of Education, Program in Middle Level Education, Rock Hill, SC 29733. Offers M Ed. *Entrance requirements:* For master's, minimum GPA of 3.0, South Carolina Class III Teaching Certificate, 2 letters of recommendation. Electronic applications accepted.

Worcester State College, Graduate Studies, Department of Education, Program in Middle School Education, Worcester, MA 01602-2597. Offers M Ed. Part-time programs available. *Faculty:* 9 full-time (7 women), 19 part-time/adjunct (7 women). *Students:* 1 (woman) full-time, 23 part-time (12 women); includes 1 minority (African American). Average age 39. 44 applicants, 75% accepted, 6 enrolled. In 2009, 17 master's awarded. *Degree requirements:* For master's, comprehensive exam (for some programs), thesis optional. *Entrance requirements:* For master's, GRE General Test or MAT. Additional exam requirements/recommendations for international students: Required—TOEFL (minimum score 550 paper-based; 213 computer-based; 79 iBT). *Application deadline:* Applications are processed on a rolling basis. Application fee: $30. *Expenses:* Tuition, area resident: Part-time $150 per credit. Tuition, state resident: part-time $150 per credit. Tuition, nonresident: part-time $150 per credit. Required fees: $85. *Financial support:* Career-related internships or fieldwork, scholarships/grants, and unspecified assistantships available. Financial award application deadline: 3/1; financial award applicants required to submit FAFSA. *Unit head:* Dr. Caroline Chiccarelli, Coordinator, 508-929-8967, Fax: 508-929-8164, E-mail: cchiccarelli@worcester.edu. *Application contact:* Nicole Brown, Assistant Dean of Graduate and Continuing Education, 508-929-8787, Fax: 508-929-8100, E-mail: nbrown@worcester.edu.

Wright State University, School of Graduate Studies, College of Education and Human Services, Department of Teacher Education, Dayton, OH 45435. Offers adolescent young adult (M Ed, MA); classroom teacher education (M Ed, MA); early childhood education (M Ed, MA); intervention specialist (M Ed, MA), including gifted educational needs, mild to moderate educational needs, moderate to intensive educational needs; middle childhood education (M Ed, MA); multi-age (M Ed, MA); workforce education (M Ed, MA), including career, technology and vocational education, computer/technology education, library/media, vocational education. *Accreditation:* NCATE. *Entrance requirements:* For master's, GRE General Test, MAT, PRAXIS II. Additional exam requirements/recommendations for international students: Required—TOEFL. *Faculty research:* Reading recovery, early kindergarten birthdays, international children's literature, discipline models, university and public schools cooperation.

Youngstown State University, Graduate School, Beeghly College of Education, Department of Teacher Education, Program in Early Childhood Education, Youngstown, OH 44555-0001. Offers MS Ed. *Accreditation:* NCATE. Part-time and evening/weekend programs available. *Degree requirements:* For master's, comprehensive exam. *Entrance requirements:* For master's, GRE, MAT, or teaching certificate; minimum GPA of 2.7. Additional exam requirements/recommendations for international students: Required—TOEFL.

Youngstown State University, Graduate School, Beeghly College of Education, Department of Teacher Education, Program in Middle Childhood Education, Youngstown, OH 44555-0001. Offers MS Ed. *Accreditation:* NCATE. Part-time and evening/weekend programs available. *Degree requirements:* For master's, comprehensive exam, thesis optional. *Entrance requirements:* For master's, GRE, MAT, or teaching certificate; minimum GPA of 2.7. Additional exam requirements/recommendations for international students: Required—TOEFL. *Faculty research:* Critical reflectivity, gender issues in classroom instruction, collaborative research and analysis, literacy methodology.

Secondary Education

Adelphi University, School of Education, Program in Adolescent Education, Garden City, NY 11530-0701. Offers MA. Part-time and evening/weekend programs available. *Students:* 46 full-time (36 women), 60 part-time (38 women); includes 13 minority (10 African Americans, 1 Asian American or Pacific Islander, 2 Hispanic Americans). Average age 27. In 2009, 99 master's awarded. *Entrance requirements:* For master's, 2 letters of recommendation, resume. Additional exam requirements/recommendations for international students: Required—TOEFL (minimum score 550 paper-based; 213 computer-based; 80 iBT). *Application deadline:* For fall admission, 4/1 for international students; for spring admission, 11/1 for international students. Applications are processed on a rolling basis. Application fee: $50. Electronic applications accepted. *Expenses:* Tuition: Full-time $28,340; part-time $830 per credit. Required fees: $600; $250 per credit. Full-time tuition and fees vary according to course load and program. *Financial support:* Fellowships, research assistantships with partial tuition reimbursements, teaching assistantships, career-related internships or fieldwork, Federal Work-Study, institutionally sponsored loans, tuition waivers (full), and unspecified assistantships available. Support available to part-time students. Financial award application deadline: 2/15; financial award applicants required to submit FAFSA. *Faculty research:* Methods to enhance the development of teaching dispositions, ethical and moral issues in education. *Unit head:* Dr. Rob Linne, Director, 516-877-4411, E-mail: linne@adelphi.edu. *Application contact:* Christine Murphy, Director of Admissions, 516-877-3050, Fax: 516-877-3039, E-mail: graduateadmissions@adelphi.edu.

Alabama Agricultural and Mechanical University, School of Graduate Studies, School of Education, Area in Secondary Education, Huntsville, AL 35811. Offers education (M Ed, Ed S); higher administration (MS). *Accreditation:* NCATE. Evening/weekend programs available. *Degree requirements:* For master's, comprehensive exam; for Ed S, thesis. *Entrance requirements:* For master's, GRE General Test. Additional exam requirements/recommendations for international students: Required—TOEFL (minimum score 500 paper-based; 173 computer-based; 61 iBT). Electronic applications accepted. *Faculty research:* World peace through education, computer-assisted instruction.

Alabama State University, School of Graduate Studies, College of Education, Department of Curriculum and Instruction, Program in Secondary Education, Montgomery, AL 36101-0271. Offers biology education (M Ed, Ed S); English/language arts (M Ed); history education (M Ed, Ed S); mathematics education (M Ed); secondary education (Ed S); social studies (Ed S). Part-time programs available. *Degree requirements:* For master's, comprehensive exam; for Ed S, comprehensive exam, thesis. *Entrance requirements:* For master's, GRE General Test, MAT, graduate writing competency test; for Ed S, graduate writing competency test, GRE, MAT. Additional exam requirements/recommendations for international students: Required—TOEFL (minimum score 500 paper-based; 173 computer-based).

Alcorn State University, School of Graduate Studies, School of Psychology and Education, Alcorn State, MS 39096-7500. Offers agricultural education (MS Ed); elementary education (MS Ed, Ed S); guidance and counseling (MS Ed); industrial education (MS Ed); secondary education (MS Ed), including health and physical education; special education (MS Ed). *Accreditation:* NCATE. *Degree requirements:* For master's, thesis optional.

American International College, School of Arts, Education and Sciences, Department of Education, Springfield, MA 01109-3189. Offers early childhood education (M Ed, CAGS); educational leadership and supervision (Ed D); elementary education (M Ed, CAGS); middle/secondary education (M Ed, CAGS); moderate disabilities (M Ed, CAGS); reading (M Ed, CAGS); school adjustment counseling (MA, CAGS); school administration (M Ed, CAGS); school guidance counseling (MA, CAGS); teaching (MA, MS); teaching and learning (Ed D). Part-time and evening/weekend programs available. Terminal master's awarded for partial completion of doctoral program. *Degree requirements:* For master's, comprehensive exam (for some programs), thesis (for some programs), practicum; for doctorate, comprehensive exam (for some programs), thesis/dissertation; for CAGS, practicum. *Entrance requirements:* For master's, minimum B- average in undergraduate course work; for doctorate, GRE General Test, interview. Additional exam requirements/recommendations for international students: Required—TOEFL. Electronic applications accepted. *Expenses:* Tuition: Full-time $12,510; part-time $695 per credit hour. Required fees: $35 per term.

American University, College of Arts and Sciences, School of Education, Teaching, and Health, Program in Secondary Teaching, Washington, DC 20016-8030. Offers MAT, Certificate. *Students:* 18 full-time (11 women), 204 part-time (135 women); includes 46 minority (25 African Americans, 8 American Indian/Alaska Native, 7 Asian Americans or Pacific Islanders, 6 Hispanic Americans). Average age 25. 160 applicants, 91% accepted, 133 enrolled. In 2009, 88 master's, 9 other advanced degrees awarded. *Degree requirements:* For master's, comprehensive exam, PRAXIS II. *Entrance requirements:* For master's, GRE General Test, PRAXIS I, minimum GPA of 3.0, 2 recommendations; for Certificate, bachelor's degree. *Application deadline:* For fall admission, 2/1 priority date for domestic students; for spring admission, 10/1 priority date for domestic students. Applications are processed on a rolling basis. Application fee: $80. *Expenses:* Tuition: Full-time $22,266; part-time $1237 per credit hour. Required fees: $430. Tuition and fees vary according to program. *Financial support:* Research assistantships with partial tuition reimbursements available. Financial award application deadline: 2/1. *Unit head:* Karen DiGiovanni, Director, Teacher Education, 202-885-3727, Fax: 202-885-1187, E-mail: digiovanni@american.edu. *Application contact:* Karen DiGiovanni, Director, Teacher Education, 202-885-3727, Fax: 202-885-1187, E-mail: digiovanni@american.edu.

Andrews University, School of Graduate Studies, School of Education, Department of Teaching, Learning, and Curriculum, Berrien Springs, MI 49104. Offers curriculum and instruction (MA, Ed D, PhD, Ed S); elementary education (MAT); reading (MA); secondary education (MAT), including biology, education, English, English as a second language, French, history, physics; special education/learning disabilities (MS); teacher education (MAT). *Students:* 12 full-time (8 women), 30 part-time (19 women); includes 17 minority (14 African Americans, 1 Asian American or Pacific Islander, 2 Hispanic Americans), 10 international. Average age 43. 28 applicants, 54% accepted, 6 enrolled. In 2009, 11 master's, 4 doctorates, 1 other advanced degree awarded. *Entrance requirements:* For master's, GRE Subject Test. Additional exam requirements/recommendations for international students: Required—TOEFL (minimum score 550 paper-based). *Application deadline:* For fall admission, 8/15 for domestic students. Applications are processed on a rolling basis. Application fee: $40. *Unit head:* Dr. Lee C. Davidson, Chair, 269-471-6364. *Application contact:* Carolyn Hurst, Supervisor of Graduate Admission, 800-253-2874, Fax: 269-471-6321, E-mail: graduate@andrews.edu.

Arcadia University, Graduate Studies, Department of Education, Glenside, PA 19038-3295. Offers art education (M Ed, MA Ed); biology education (MA Ed); chemistry education (MA Ed); child development (CAS); computer education (M Ed, CAS); computer education 7–12 (MA Ed); early childhood education (M Ed, CAS), including individualized (M Ed), master teacher (M Ed), research in child development (M Ed); educational leadership (M Ed, CAS); educational psychology (CAS); elementary education (M Ed, CAS); English education (MA Ed); environmental education (MA Ed, CAS); history education (MA Ed); language arts (M Ed, CAS); mathematics education (M Ed, MA Ed, CAS); music education (MA Ed); psychology (MA Ed); pupil personnel services (CAS); reading (M Ed, CAS); school library science (M Ed); science education (M Ed, CAS); secondary education (M Ed, CAS); special education (M Ed, Ed D, CAS); theater arts (MA Ed); written communication (MA Ed). *Accreditation:* NASAD. Part-time and evening/weekend programs available. Postbaccalaureate distance learning degree programs offered (minimal on-campus study). *Faculty:* 12 full-time (8 women), 38 part-time/adjunct (26 women). *Students:* 89 full-time (74 women), 622 part-time (487 women); includes 112 minority (94 African Americans, 9 Asian Americans or Pacific Islanders, 9 Hispanic Americans), 2 international. Average age 32. In 2009, 257 master's, 4 doctorates awarded. *Application deadline:* Applications are processed on a rolling basis. Application fee: $40. Electronic applications accepted. *Expenses:* Tuition: Full-time $30,450; part-time $620 per credit hour. Required fees: $165. Tuition and fees vary according to program. *Financial support:* Career-related internships or fieldwork, tuition waivers (partial), and unspecified assistantships available. *Unit head:* Dr. Steven P. Gulkus. *Application contact:* 215-572-2925, Fax: 215-572-2126, E-mail: grad@arcadia.edu.

Argosy University, Atlanta, College of Education, Atlanta, GA 30328. Offers educational leadership (MAEd, Ed D, Ed S), including higher education administration (Ed D), K-12 education (Ed D); teaching and learning (MAEd, Ed D, Ed S), including education technology (Ed D), higher education (Ed D), K-12 education (Ed D).

See Close-Up on page 887.

Argosy University, Chicago, College of Education, Chicago, IL 60601. Offers adult education and training (MA Ed); community college executive leadership (Ed D); educational leadership (MA Ed, Ed D, Ed S), including district leadership (Ed D), higher education administration (Ed D), K-12 education (Ed D); instructional leadership (Ed D, Ed S), including higher education

Secondary Education

Argosy University, Chicago (continued)
(Ed D), K-12 education (Ed D). Postbaccalaureate distance learning degree programs offered (minimal on-campus study).

See Close-Up on page 675.

Argosy University, Hawai'i, College of Education, Honolulu, HI 96813. Offers adult education and training (MAEd); educational leadership (Ed D), including higher education administration, K-12 education; instructional leadership (Ed D), including higher education, K-12 education; school psychology (MA).

See Close-Up on page 681.

Argosy University, Inland Empire, College of Education, San Bernardino, CA 92408. Offers community college executive leadership (Ed D); educational leadership (MA Ed, Ed D), including higher education administration (Ed D), K-12 education (Ed D); instructional leadership (MA Ed, Ed D), including higher education (Ed D), K-12 education (Ed D), multiple subject teacher preparation (MA Ed), single subject teacher preparation (MA Ed).

See Close-Up on page 889.

Argosy University, Los Angeles, College of Education, Santa Monica, CA 90045. Offers community college executive leadership (Ed D); educational leadership (MA Ed, Ed D), including higher education administration (Ed D), K-12 education (Ed D); instructional leadership (MA Ed, Ed D), including higher education (Ed D), K-12 education (Ed D), multiple subject teacher preparation (MA Ed), single subject teacher preparation (MA Ed).

See Close-Up on page 683.

Argosy University, Nashville, College of Education, Program in Educational Leadership, Nashville, TN 37214. Offers educational leadership (MA Ed, Ed S); higher education administration (Ed D); K-12 education (Ed D).

See Close-Up on page 891.

Argosy University, Nashville, College of Education, Program in Instructional Leadership, Nashville, TN 37214. Offers education technology (Ed D); higher education administration (Ed D); instructional leadership (MA Ed, Ed S); K-12 education (Ed D).

See Close-Up on page 891.

Argosy University, Orange County, College of Education, Orange, CA 92868. Offers community college executive leadership (Ed D); educational leadership (MA Ed, Ed D), including higher education administration (Ed D), K-12 education (Ed D); instructional leadership (MA Ed, Ed D), including education technology (Ed D), higher education (Ed D), K-12 education (Ed D), multiple subject teacher preparation (MA Ed), single subject teacher preparation (MA Ed).

See Close-Up on page 685.

Argosy University, Phoenix, College of Education, Phoenix, AZ 85021. Offers adult education and training (MA Ed); advanced educational administration (Ed D, Ed S); community college executive leadership (Ed D); educational administration (MA Ed); educational leadership (MA Ed, Ed D, Ed S), including education technology (Ed D), higher education administration (Ed D), K-12 education (Ed D); higher and postsecondary education (MA Ed); initial educational administration (Ed D, Ed S); school psychology (MA); teaching and learning (MA Ed, Ed D, Ed S), including education technology (Ed D), higher education (Ed D), K-12 education (Ed D).

See Close-Up on page 687.

Argosy University, San Diego, College of Education, San Diego, CA 92108. Offers community college executive leadership (Ed D); educational leadership (MA Ed, Ed D), including higher education administration (Ed D), K-12 education (Ed D); instructional leadership (MA Ed, Ed D), including higher education (Ed D), K-12 education (Ed D).

See Close-Up on page 691.

Argosy University, San Francisco Bay Area, College of Education, Alameda, CA 94501. Offers community college executive leadership (Ed D); educational leadership (MA Ed, Ed D), including education technology (Ed D), higher education administration (Ed D), K-12 education (Ed D); instructional leadership (MA Ed, Ed D), including education technology (Ed D), higher education (Ed D), K-12 education (Ed D), multiple subject teacher preparation (MA Ed), single subject teacher preparation (MA Ed).

See Close-Up on page 693.

Argosy University, Sarasota, College of Education, Sarasota, FL 34235. Offers community college executive leadership (Ed D); educational leadership (MA Ed, Ed D, Ed S), including higher education administration (Ed D), K-12 education (Ed D); school counseling (MA, Ed S); school psychology (MA); teaching and learning (MA Ed, Ed D, Ed S), including education technology (Ed D), higher education (Ed D), K-12 education (Ed D).

See Close-Up on page 695.

Argosy University, Schaumburg, College of Education, Schaumburg, IL 60173-5403. Offers community college executive leadership (Ed D); educational leadership (MA Ed, Ed D, Ed S), including district leadership (Ed D), higher education administration (Ed D), K-12 education (Ed D); instructional leadership (Ed D, Ed S), including higher education (Ed D), K-12 education (Ed D).

See Close-Up on page 697.

Argosy University, Seattle, College of Education, Seattle, WA 98121. Offers adult education and training (MA Ed); community college executive leadership (Ed D); educational leadership (MA Ed, Ed D), including higher education administration (Ed D), K-12 education (Ed D); higher and postsecondary education (MA Ed); instructional leadership (MA Ed, Ed D), including education technology (Ed D), higher education (Ed D), K-12 education (Ed D).

See Close-Up on page 699.

Argosy University, Tampa, College of Education, Tampa, FL 33607. Offers community college executive leadership (Ed D); educational leadership (MA Ed, Ed D, Ed S), including higher education administration (Ed D), K-12 education (Ed D); school counseling (MA); teaching and learning (MA Ed, Ed D, Ed S), including higher education (Ed D), K-12 education (Ed D).

See Close-Up on page 701.

Argosy University, Twin Cities, College of Education, Eagan, MN 55121. Offers advanced educational administration (Ed D, Ed S); educational leadership (MA Ed, Ed D, Ed S), including higher education administration (Ed D), K-12 education (Ed D); higher and postsecondary education (MA Ed); initial educational administration (Ed D, Ed S); instructional leadership (MA Ed, Ed D, Ed S), including education technology (Ed D), higher education (Ed D), K-12 education (Ed D).

See Close-Up on page 703.

Argosy University, Washington DC, College of Education, Arlington, VA 22209. Offers community college executive leadership (Ed D); educational leadership (MA Ed, Ed D, Ed S), including higher education administration (Ed D), K-12 education (Ed D); instructional leadership (MA Ed, Ed D, Ed S), including higher education (Ed D), K-12 education (Ed D).

See Close-Up on page 705.

Arizona State University, Graduate College, College of Teacher Education and Leadership, Tempe, AZ 85287. Offers educational administration and supervision (M Ed); elementary education (M Ed, Certificate); leadership/innovation (administration) (Ed D); leadership/innovation (teaching) (Ed D); physical education (MPE); secondary education (M Ed, Certificate); special education (M Ed). Part-time and evening/weekend programs available. *Degree requirements:* For master's, applied project or comprehensive exams; for doctorate, comprehensive exam, thesis/dissertation. *Entrance requirements:* For master's, 3 letters of recommendation, minimum undergraduate GPA of 3.0, resume; for doctorate, master's degree in education or related field, 3 professional references, resumé, graduate GPA of 3.0, 3 letters of recommendation. Additional exam requirements/recommendations for international students: Required—TOEFL (minimum score 550 paper-based; 213 computer-based; 83 iBT), IELTS (minimum score 6.5). Electronic applications accepted. *Expenses:* Contact institution. *Faculty research:* Self-regulated learning in students, collaboration and consultation skills for educators, school reform and restructuring, hands-on science and mathematics programs, educational technology.

Arkansas Tech University, Graduate College, College of Education, Russellville, AR 72801. Offers college student personnel (MS); educational leadership (M Ed, Ed S); English education (M Ed); instructional improvement (M Ed); secondary education (M Ed); teaching, learning and leadership (M Ed). *Accreditation:* NCATE. Part-time and evening/weekend programs available. Postbaccalaureate distance learning degree programs offered (no on-campus study). *Students:* 39 full-time (26 women), 246 part-time (179 women); includes 27 minority (18 African Americans, 4 American Indian/Alaska Native, 5 Hispanic Americans), 4 international. Average age 33. In 2009, 92 master's, 11 other advanced degrees awarded. *Degree requirements:* For master's, comprehensive exam, thesis optional, action research project. *Entrance requirements:* For master's, GRE General Test or MAT. Additional exam requirements/recommendations for international students: Required—TOEFL (minimum score 550 paper-based; 213 computer-based; 79 iBT), IELTS (minimum score 6). *Application deadline:* For fall admission, 3/1 priority date for domestic students, 5/1 priority date for international students; for spring admission, 10/1 priority date for domestic and international students. Applications are processed on a rolling basis. Application fee: $0 ($50 for international students). Electronic applications accepted. *Expenses:* Tuition, state resident: full-time $3438; part-time $191 per hour. Tuition, nonresident: full-time $6876; part-time $382 per hour. Required fees: $482; $9 per credit hour. $140 per semester. Tuition and fees vary according to course load. *Financial support:* In 2009–10, teaching assistantships with full tuition reimbursements (averaging $4,000 per year); research assistantships, career-related internships or fieldwork, Federal Work-Study, scholarships/grants, health care benefits, and unspecified assistantships also available. Support available to part-time students. Financial award application deadline: 4/15; financial award applicants required to submit FAFSA. *Unit head:* Dr. Eldon G. Clary, Dean, 479-968-0350, Fax: 479-968-0350, E-mail: eclary@atu.edu. *Application contact:* Dr. Mary B. Gunter, Dean of Graduate College, 479-968-0398, Fax: 479-964-0542, E-mail: graduate.school@atu.edu.

Armstrong Atlantic State University, School of Graduate Studies, Program in Education, Savannah, GA 31419-1997. Offers adult education (M Ed); curriculum and instruction (M Ed); early childhood education (M Ed); education (M Ed); elementary education (M Ed); middle grades education (M Ed); secondary education (M Ed), including business education, English education, mathematics education, science education, social science education; special education (M Ed), including behavioral disorders, learning disabilities, speech-language pathology. *Accreditation:* NCATE. Part-time and evening/weekend programs available. Postbaccalaureate distance learning degree programs offered (minimal on-campus study). *Degree requirements:* For master's, comprehensive exam, portfolio. *Entrance requirements:* For master's, GRE General Test or MAT, minimum GPA of 2.5, letters of recommendation. Additional exam requirements/recommendations for international students: Required—TOEFL (minimum score 523 paper-based; 193 computer-based). Electronic applications accepted.

Auburn University, Graduate School, College of Education, Department of Curriculum and Teaching, Auburn University, AL 36849. Offers business education (M Ed, MS, PhD); early childhood education (M Ed, MS, PhD, Ed S); elementary education (M Ed, MS, PhD, Ed S); foreign languages (M Ed, MS); music education (M Ed, MS, PhD, Ed S); postsecondary education (PhD); reading education (PhD, Ed S); secondary education (M Ed, MS, PhD, Ed S), including English language arts, mathematics, science, social studies. *Accreditation:* NASM (one or more programs are accredited); NCATE. Part-time programs available. *Faculty:* 28 full-time (21 women), 8 part-time/adjunct (5 women). *Students:* 76 full-time (55 women), 186 part-time (139 women); includes 43 minority (29 African Americans, 1 American Indian/Alaska Native, 4 Asian Americans or Pacific Islanders, 9 Hispanic Americans), 4 international. Average age 33. 248 applicants, 65% accepted, 110 enrolled. In 2009, 102 master's, 12 doctorates, 6 other advanced degrees awarded. *Degree requirements:* For master's, thesis (for some programs); for doctorate, thesis/dissertation; for Ed S, field project. *Entrance requirements:* For master's, doctorate, and Ed S, GRE General Test. *Application deadline:* For fall admission, 7/7 for domestic students; for spring admission, 11/24 for domestic students. Applications are processed on a rolling basis. Application fee: $50 ($60 for international students). Electronic applications accepted. *Expenses:* Tuition, state resident: full-time $6240. Tuition, nonresident: full-time $18,720. International tuition: $18,938 full-time. Required fees: $492. Tuition and fees vary according to course load, program and reciprocity agreements. *Financial support:* Fellowships, teaching assistantships, career-related internships or fieldwork and Federal Work-Study available. Support available to part-time students. Financial award application deadline: 3/15; financial award applicants required to submit FAFSA. *Faculty research:* Emerging literacy, reading attitudes, music for at-risk youth, portfolio assessment. *Unit head:* Dr. Nancy H. Barry, Head, 334-844-4434. *Application contact:* Dr. George Flowers, Dean of the Graduate School, 334-844-2125.

Auburn University Montgomery, School of Education, Department of Foundations, Secondary, and Physical Education, Montgomery, AL 36124-4023. Offers physical education (M Ed); secondary education (M Ed, Ed S). *Accreditation:* NCATE. Part-time and evening/weekend programs available. *Faculty:* 12 full-time (8 women), 2 part-time/adjunct (both women). *Students:* 58 full-time (43 women), 101 part-time (78 women); includes 60 minority (56 African Americans, 2 American Indian/Alaska Native, 2 Asian Americans or Pacific Islanders), 3 international. Average age 32. In 2009, 38 master's awarded. *Degree requirements:* For master's and Ed S, comprehensive exam, thesis optional. *Entrance requirements:* For master's, GRE General Test or MAT, certification, BS in teaching; for Ed S, GRE General Test or MAT, certification. *Application deadline:* Applications are processed on a rolling basis. Electronic applications accepted. *Expenses:* Tuition, state resident: full-time $2841; part-time $225 per credit hour. Tuition, nonresident: full-time $8241; part-time $675 per credit hour. Required fees: $282; $8 per hour. $45 per term. *Financial support:* In 2009–10, 3 teaching assistantships were awarded; career-related internships or fieldwork and scholarships/grants also available. Support available to part-time students. Financial award application deadline: 3/1; financial award applicants required to submit FAFSA. *Unit head:* Dr. Henry N. Williford, Head, 334-244-3548, Fax: 334-244-3547, E-mail: hwilliford@mail.aum.edu. *Application contact:* Dr. Sam Flynt, Associate Graduate Coordinator, 334-244-3270, Fax: 334-244-3835, E-mail: sflynt@mail.aum.edu.

Augusta State University, Graduate Studies, College of Education, Program in Teaching/Learning, Augusta, GA 30904-2200. Offers MAT, Ed S. *Degree requirements:* For master's, thesis, portfolio. *Entrance requirements:* For master's, GRE, MAT, minimum GPA of 2.5.

Austin College, Program in Education, Sherman, TX 75090-4400. Offers art education (MA); elementary education (MA); middle school education (MA); music education (MA); physical education and coaching (MA); secondary education (MA); theatre education (MA). Part-time programs available. *Faculty:* 5 full-time (3 women), 1 (woman) part-time/adjunct. *Students:* 29 full-time (21 women); includes 3 minority (1 Asian American or Pacific Islander, 2 Hispanic Americans). Average age 23. In 2009, 23 master's awarded. *Degree requirements:* For master's, one foreign language, thesis or alternative. *Entrance requirements:* For master's, Texas Academic Skills Program Test. *Application deadline:* For fall admission, 5/1 priority date for domestic students; for spring admission, 1/15 priority date for domestic students. Applications are processed on a rolling basis. Application fee: $35. Electronic applications accepted. *Expenses:* Tuition: Full-time $31,575. Required fees: $160. *Financial support:* Career-related internships or fieldwork, Federal Work-Study, scholarships/grants, and unspecified assistant-

ships available. Support available to part-time students. Financial award application deadline: 4/1; financial award applicants required to submit FAFSA. *Unit head:* Dr. Barbara Sylvester, Director of Teaching Program, 903-813-2327, Fax: 903-813-2326, E-mail: bsylvester@austincollege.edu. *Application contact:* Dr. Barbara Sylvester, Director of Teaching Program, 903-813-2327, Fax: 903-813-2326, E-mail: bsylvester@austincollege.edu.

Austin Peay State University, College of Graduate Studies, College of Education, Department of Educational Specialties, Clarksville, TN 37044. Offers administration and supervision (Ed S); curriculum and instruction (MA Ed); education leadership (MA Ed); elementary education (Ed S); secondary education (Ed S); special education (MA Ed). Part-time and evening/weekend programs available. Postbaccalaureate distance learning degree programs offered. *Faculty:* 7 full-time (4 women), 4 part-time/adjunct (3 women). *Students:* 17 full-time (11 women), 96 part-time (76 women); includes 20 minority (12 African Americans, 1 American Indian/Alaska Native, 7 Hispanic Americans). Average age 36. 81 applicants, 99% accepted, 45 enrolled. In 2009, 47 master's awarded. *Degree requirements:* For master's, comprehensive exam, thesis optional. *Entrance requirements:* For master's, GRE General Test, 3 letters of recommendation, minimum undergraduate GPA of 2.75. Additional exam requirements/recommendations for international students: Required—TOEFL (minimum score 500 paper-based; 173 computer-based). *Application deadline:* For fall admission, 7/27 priority date for domestic students; for spring admission, 12/17 priority date for domestic students. Applications are processed on a rolling basis. Application fee: $25. Electronic applications accepted. *Expenses:* Tuition, state resident: full-time $6160; part-time $608 per credit hour. Tuition, nonresident: full-time $17,080; part-time $854 per credit hour. Required fees: $1224; $61.20 per credit hour. *Financial support:* Career-related internships or fieldwork, Federal Work-Study, institutionally sponsored loans, scholarships/grants, and unspecified assistantships available. Support available to part-time students. Financial award application deadline: 3/1; financial award applicants required to submit FAFSA. *Unit head:* Dr. Moniqueka Gold, Chair, 931-221-7696, Fax: 931-221-1292, E-mail: goldm@apsu.edu. *Application contact:* Dr. Dixie Dennis, Dean, College of Graduate Studies, 931-221-7662, Fax: 931-221-7641, E-mail: dennisdi@apsu.edu.

Austin Peay State University, College of Graduate Studies, College of Education, Department of Teaching and Learning, Clarksville, TN 37044. Offers elementary education K-6 (MAT); reading (MA Ed); secondary education 7-12 (MAT); special education K-12 (MAT). Part-time and evening/weekend programs available. Postbaccalaureate distance learning degree programs offered. *Faculty:* 8 full-time (6 women), 3 part-time/adjunct (all women). *Students:* 91 full-time (74 women), 84 part-time (67 women); includes 14 minority (12 African Americans, 2 Asian Americans or Pacific Islanders), 1 international. Average age 32. 122 applicants, 94% accepted, 75 enrolled. In 2009, 61 master's awarded. *Degree requirements:* For master's, comprehensive exam, thesis optional. *Entrance requirements:* For master's, GRE General Test, 3 letters of recommendation, minimum undergraduate GPA of 2.75. Additional exam requirements/recommendations for international students: Required—TOEFL (minimum score 500 paper-based; 173 computer-based). *Application deadline:* For fall admission, 7/27 priority date for domestic students; for spring admission, 12/17 priority date for domestic students. Applications are processed on a rolling basis. Application fee: $25. Electronic applications accepted. *Expenses:* Tuition, state resident: full-time $6160; part-time $608 per credit hour. Tuition, nonresident: full-time $17,080; part-time $854 per credit hour. Required fees: $1224; $61.20 per credit hour. *Financial support:* Career-related internships or fieldwork, Federal Work-Study, institutionally sponsored loans, scholarships/grants, and unspecified assistantships available. Support available to part-time students. Financial award application deadline: 3/1; financial award applicants required to submit FAFSA. *Unit head:* Dr. Rebecca McMahan, Interim Chair, 931-221-7513, Fax: 931-221-1292, E-mail: mcmahanb@apsu.edu. *Application contact:* Dr. Dixie Dennis, Dean, College of Graduate Studies, 931-221-7662, Fax: 931-221-7641, E-mail: dennisdi@apsu.edu.

Ball State University, Graduate School, Teachers College, Department of Educational Studies, Program in Secondary Education, Muncie, IN 47306-1099. Offers MA. *Accreditation:* NCATE.

Belhaven University, School of Education, Jackson, MS 39202-1789. Offers elementary education (M Ed, MAT); secondary education (M Ed, MAT). Part-time and evening/weekend programs available. *Faculty:* 4 full-time (all women), 19 part-time/adjunct (10 women). *Students:* 159 full-time (132 women), 51 part-time (42 women); includes 108 African Americans, 1 American Indian/Alaska Native, 7 Hispanic Americans. Average age 34. 392 applicants, 70% accepted, 140 enrolled. In 2009, 44 master's awarded. *Degree requirements:* For master's, comprehensive exam, portfolio. *Entrance requirements:* For master's, PRAXIS I, PRAXIS II, minimum GPA of 2.8. *Application deadline:* Applications are processed on a rolling basis. Application fee: $25. Electronic applications accepted. *Expenses:* Tuition: Full-time $8730; part-time $485 per credit hour. Required fees: $1260; $70 per credit hour. Tuition and fees vary according to campus/location. *Financial support:* Federal Work-Study, scholarships/grants, tuition waivers (full), and unspecified assistantships available. Support available to part-time students. Financial award applicants required to submit FAFSA. *Unit head:* Dr. Sandra L. Rasberry, Dean, 601-968-8703, Fax: 601-974-6461, E-mail: srasberry@belhaven.edu. *Application contact:* Jenny Mixon, Director of Graduate and Online Admission, 601-968-8947, Fax: 601-968-5953, E-mail: gradadmission@belhaven.edu.

Bellarmine University, Annsley Frazier Thornton School of Education, Louisville, KY 40205-0671. Offers early elementary education (MA, MAT); instructional leadership and school administration/school principal (MA); learning and behavior disorders (MA); middle school education (MA, MAT); reading and writing endorsement (MA); secondary school education (MAT); Waldorf inspired curriculum (MA). *Accreditation:* NCATE. Part-time and evening/weekend programs available. *Faculty:* 16 full-time (11 women), 20 part-time/adjunct (13 women). *Students:* 67 full-time (47 women), 140 part-time (111 women); includes 14 minority (10 African Americans, 1 American Indian/Alaska Native, 3 Asian Americans or Pacific Islanders), 1 international. Average age 33. In 2009, 106 degrees awarded. *Degree requirements:* For master's, comprehensive exam, thesis (for some programs). *Entrance requirements:* For master's, GRE, baccalaureate degree from an accredited institution; minimum overall GPA of 2.75, 3.0 in major; letters of recommendation; valid Kentucky provisional or professional certificate. Additional exam requirements/recommendations for international students: Required—TOEFL (minimum score 550 paper-based; 213 computer-based; 80 iBT). *Application deadline:* Applications are processed on a rolling basis. Application fee: $25. *Expenses:* Contact institution. *Financial support:* Scholarships/grants available. Financial award applicants required to submit FAFSA. *Faculty research:* Literacy, service learning, dispositions, educational technology, special education. *Unit head:* Dr. Cindy Gnadinger, Dean, 502-452-8191, Fax: 502-452-8189, E-mail: cgnadinger@bellarmine.edu. *Application contact:* Theresa Klapheke, Administrative Director of Graduate Programs, 502-452-8271, Fax: 502-452-8002, E-mail: tklapheke@bellarmine.edu.

Belmont University, College of Arts and Sciences, School of Education, Nashville, TN 37212-3757. Offers education (M Ed); elementary education (MAT), including early childhood education, elementary education, language arts education; English (MAT); history (MAT); mathematics (MAT); middle grade education (MAT); science (MAT); secondary education (MAT); special education (MAT); sports administration (MSA). *Accreditation:* NCATE. Part-time and evening/weekend programs available. *Degree requirements:* For master's, comprehensive exam, thesis, culminating portfolio. *Entrance requirements:* For master's, MAT or GRE and/or LSAT or GMAT, minimum GPA of 2.75. Additional exam requirements/recommendations for international students: Required—TOEFL. *Expenses:* Contact institution. *Faculty research:* Improving secondary literacy, Montessori, classroom management strategies, teacher residency programs, online professional development, mentoring, leadership, sociological issues in sport, faculty development, coaching.

Benedictine University, Graduate Programs, Program in Education, Lisle, IL 60532-0900. Offers curriculum and instruction and collaborative teaching (M Ed); elementary education (MA Ed); leadership and administration (M Ed); reading and literacy (M Ed); secondary education (MA Ed); special education (MA Ed). Part-time and evening/weekend programs available. *Faculty:* 4 full-time (2 women), 52 part-time/adjunct (30 women). *Students:* 286 full-time (252 women), 443 part-time (349 women); includes 61 minority (22 African Americans, 11 Asian Americans or Pacific Islanders, 28 Hispanic Americans), 5 international. Average age 33. 341 applicants, 90% accepted, 264 enrolled. In 2009, 299 master's awarded. *Degree requirements:* For master's, comprehensive exam, thesis (for some programs). *Entrance requirements:* For master's, GRE or MAT. Additional exam requirements/recommendations for international students: Required—TOEFL (minimum score 550 paper-based; 213 computer-based). *Application deadline:* For fall admission, 9/1 for domestic students; for winter admission, 12/1 for domestic students; for spring admission, 2/15 for domestic students. Applications are processed on a rolling basis. Application fee: $40. Electronic applications accepted. *Expenses:* Contact institution. *Financial support:* Career-related internships or fieldwork and health care benefits available. Support available to part-time students. *Unit head:* Dr. Richard Campbell, Director, 630-829-6242, Fax: 630-960-1126, E-mail: rcampbell@ben.edu. *Application contact:* Kari Gibbons, Director, Admissions, 630-829-6200, Fax: 630-829-6584, E-mail: kgibbons@ben.edu.

Bennington College, Graduate Programs, MA in Teaching Program, Bennington, VT 05201. Offers art education (MAT); early childhood (MAT); elementary education (MAT); English education (MAT); foreign language education (MAT); k-12 education (MAT); mathematics education (MAT); music education (MAT); science education (MAT); secondary education (MAT); social studies education (MAT); theater arts (MAT). *Faculty:* 5 part-time/adjunct (3 women). *Students:* 8 full-time (5 women), 1 part-time (0 women). Average age 28. 11 applicants, 27% accepted, 1 enrolled. In 2009, 4 master's awarded. *Degree requirements:* For master's, comprehensive exam, 1 year teaching practicum, professional portfolio. *Entrance requirements:* For master's, interview. *Application deadline:* For fall admission, 3/1 for domestic students. Application fee: $60. *Expenses:* Contact institution. *Financial support:* In 2009–10, 6 students received support, including 4 fellowships (averaging $10,475 per year); scholarships/grants and unspecified assistantships also available. Financial award application deadline: 4/1; financial award applicants required to submit FAFSA. *Unit head:* Carol Meyer, Director of Programs in Teacher Education, 802-440-4375, E-mail: cmeyer@bennington.edu. *Application contact:* Nancy Pearlman, Assistant Director of Programs in Teacher Education, 802-440-4710, Fax: 802-440-4383, E-mail: npearlman@bennington.edu.

Berry College, Graduate Programs, Graduate Programs in Education, Program in Secondary Education, Mount Berry, GA 30149-0159. Offers M Ed. *Faculty:* 7 part-time/adjunct (3 women). *Students:* 1 (woman) full-time, 24 part-time (13 women); includes 2 minority (both Hispanic Americans). Average age 32. In 2009, 8 master's awarded. *Degree requirements:* For master's, thesis optional, oral exams. *Entrance requirements:* For master's, GRE General Test, MAT, or NTE, minimum GPA of 2.5. Additional exam requirements/recommendations for international students: Required—TOEFL (minimum score 550 paper-based; 213 computer-based). *Application deadline:* For fall admission, 5/1 for domestic and international students; for spring admission, 10/1 for domestic and international students. Applications are processed on a rolling basis. Application fee: $25 ($30 for international students). *Expenses:* Contact institution. *Financial support:* In 2009–10, 8 students received support, including 5 research assistantships with full tuition reimbursements available (averaging $3,461 per year); scholarships/grants, tuition waivers (partial), and unspecified assistantships also available. Support available to part-time students. Financial award application deadline: 4/1; financial award applicants required to submit FAFSA. *Faculty research:* Curriculum development, teacher training, pedagogy. *Unit head:* Dr. Jacqueline McDowell, Dean, Charter School of Education and Human Sciences, 706-236-1717, Fax: 706-238-5827, E-mail: jmcdowell@berry.edu. *Application contact:* Brett Kennedy, Director of Admissions, 706-236-2215, Fax: 706-290-2178, E-mail: admissions@berry.edu.

Bethel University, Graduate School, Department of Education, St. Paul, MN 55112-6999. Offers education K-12 (MA), including autism spectrum disorders, coordinator of work-based learning, differentiation, international baccalaureate, literacy, special education; educational administration (Ed D), including director of special education, K-12 principal license, superintendent license; literacy (Certificate); literacy education (MA); special education (MA), including autism spectrum disorders; teaching (MA). *Accreditation:* Teacher Education Accreditation Council. Evening/weekend programs available. Postbaccalaureate distance learning degree programs offered (minimal on-campus study). *Faculty:* 17 full-time (11 women), 37 part-time/adjunct (17 women). *Students:* 182 full-time (119 women), 172 part-time (120 women); includes 18 minority (2 African Americans, 1 American Indian/Alaska Native, 6 Asian Americans or Pacific Islanders, 9 Hispanic Americans), 1 international. Average age 35. 236 applicants, 79% accepted, 173 enrolled. In 2009, 51 master's, 5 doctorates awarded. *Degree requirements:* For master's, thesis, practicum; for doctorate, comprehensive exam, thesis/dissertation, internship. *Entrance requirements:* For master's, baccalaureate degree, statement of purpose essay, interview, current teaching license (if applicable), minimum GPA of 3.0, teaching experience (if applicable), letters of reference; for doctorate, MAT or GRE, minimum GPA of 3.0, letters of reference, statement of purpose essay, pre-assessment of prior experience and preparation, current license (if applicable), master's degree, interview, work experience in education. Additional exam requirements/recommendations for international students: Required—TOEFL (minimum score 550 paper-based; 213 computer-based; 80 iBT). *Application deadline:* For fall admission, 8/1 priority date for domestic students; for winter admission, 12/5 priority date for domestic students; for spring admission, 5/1 priority date for domestic students. Applications are processed on a rolling basis. Application fee: $25. Electronic applications accepted. *Expenses:* Contact institution. *Financial support:* Applicants required to submit FAFSA. *Unit head:* Dr. Judi Landrum, Assistant Dean, 651-635-8000, Fax: 651-638-8004, E-mail: j-landrum@bethel.edu. *Application contact:* Michael Price, Director of Admissions, 651-635-8000, Fax: 651-635-8004, E-mail: m-price@bethel.edu.

Bob Jones University, Graduate Programs, Greenville, SC 29614. Offers accountancy (MS); Bible (MA); Bible translation (MA); Biblical studies (Certificate); broadcast management (MS); business administration (MBA); church history (MA, PhD); church ministries (MA); church music (MM); cinema and video production (MA); counseling (MS); curriculum and instruction (Ed D); divinity (M Div); dramatic production (MA); educational leadership (MS, Ed D, Ed S); elementary education (M Ed, MAT); English (M Ed, MA, MAT); fine arts (MA); graphic design (MA); history (M Ed, MA); illustration (MA); interpretative speech (MA); mathematics (M Ed, MAT); medical missions (Certificate); ministry (MM, D Min); multi-categorical special education (M Ed, MAT); music (M Ed); New Testament interpretation (PhD); Old Testament interpretation (PhD); orchestral instrument performance (MM); organ performance (MM); pastoral studies (MA); personnel services (MS, Ed S); piano pedagogy (MM); piano performance (MM); platform arts (MA); radio and television broadcasting (MS); rhetoric and public address (MA); secondary education (M Ed); studio art (MA); teaching Bible (MA); theology (MA, PhD); voice performance (MM); youth ministries (MA); M Div/MM.

Boston College, Lynch Graduate School of Education, Department of Teacher Education/Special Education and Curriculum and Instruction, Program in Secondary Education, Chestnut Hill, MA 02467-3800. Offers biology (MST); chemistry (MST); English (MAT); French (MAT); geology (MST); history (MAT); Latin and classical humanities (MAT); mathematics (MST); physics (MST); secondary teaching (M Ed), including biology, chemistry, English, French, geology, history, Latin and classical humanities, mathematics, physics, Spanish; Spanish (MAT). *Accreditation:* Teacher Education Accreditation Council. Part-time and evening/weekend programs available. *Students:* 14 full-time (10 women), 68 part-time (37 women); includes 17 minority (9 African Americans, 3 Asian Americans or Pacific Islanders, 5 Hispanic Americans), 1 international. 252 applicants, 59% accepted, 47 enrolled. In 2009, 39 master's awarded. *Degree requirements:* For master's, comprehensive exam. *Entrance requirements:* For master's, GRE General Test or MAT. Additional exam requirements/recommendations for international students: Required—TOEFL (minimum score 550 paper-based; 213 computer-based; 81 iBT). *Application deadline:* For fall admission, 1/1 priority date for domestic students.

Secondary Education

Boston College (continued)

Application fee: $60. Electronic applications accepted. *Financial support:* Fellowships with full and partial tuition reimbursements, research assistantships with full and partial tuition reimbursements, teaching assistantships with full and partial tuition reimbursements, career-related internships or fieldwork, Federal Work-Study, institutionally sponsored loans, scholarships/grants, traineeships, health care benefits, tuition waivers (full and partial), and unspecified assistantships available. Support available to part-time students. Financial award applicants required to submit FAFSA. *Faculty research:* School reform; urban science education; teacher research; critical literacy; poverty and achievement. *Unit head:* Dr. Maria E. Brisk, Chairperson, 617-552-4216, Fax: 617-552-0812, E-mail: brisk@bc.edu. *Application contact:* Adam Poluzzi, Director, Graduate Admission and Financial Aid, 617-552-4214, Fax: 617-552-0398, E-mail: poluzzi@bc.edu.

Bowie State University, Graduate Programs, Program in Secondary Education, Bowie, MD 20715-9465. Offers M Ed. *Accreditation:* NCATE. Part-time and evening/weekend programs available. *Degree requirements:* For master's, comprehensive exam, thesis optional, research paper. *Entrance requirements:* For master's, minimum undergraduate GPA of 3.0, bachelor's degree in education, teaching certificate, teaching experience. Electronic applications accepted.

Brandeis University, Graduate School of Arts and Sciences, Teaching Program, Waltham, MA 02454-9110. Offers elementary education (public) (MAT); Jewish day school (MAT); secondary education (English, history, biology, Bible) (MAT). *Faculty:* 4 full-time (3 women), 12 part-time/adjunct (9 women). *Students:* 24 full-time (20 women), 1 part-time (0 women), 2 international. Average age 27. 61 applicants, 70% accepted, 24 enrolled. In 2009, 31 master's awarded. *Entrance requirements:* For master's, GRE General Test, 3 letters of recommendation, resume. Additional exam requirements/recommendations for international students: Required—TOEFL (minimum score 600 paper-based; 250 computer-based; 100 iBT); Recommended—IELTS (minimum score 7). *Application deadline:* For fall admission, 1/15 priority date for domestic and international students. Applications are processed on a rolling basis. Application fee: $75. Electronic applications accepted. *Expenses:* Contact institution. *Financial support:* Scholarships/grants and tuition waivers (partial) available. Financial award applicants required to submit FAFSA. *Faculty research:* Teacher education, induction, philosophy, education, democracy education, social justice. *Unit head:* Prof. Dirck Roosevelt, Director, MAT Program, 781-736-2020, Fax: 781-736-5020, E-mail: drooseve@brandeis.edu. *Application contact:* Manuel Tuan, Department Administrator, 781-736-2633, Fax: 781-736-5020, E-mail: tuan@brandeis.edu.

Brenau University, Graduate Programs, School of Education, Gainesville, GA 30501. Offers early childhood (Ed S); early childhood education (M Ed, MAT); middle grades (Ed S); middle grades education (M Ed, MAT); secondary education (MAT); special education (M Ed, MAT). *Accreditation:* NCATE. Part-time and evening/weekend programs available. Postbaccalaureate distance learning degree programs offered (no on-campus study). *Faculty:* 12 full-time (7 women), 25 part-time/adjunct (21 women). *Students:* 161 full-time (146 women), 143 part-time (122 women); includes 43 minority (30 African Americans, 5 Asian Americans or Pacific Islanders, 8 Hispanic Americans), 1 international. Average age 35. 163 applicants, 34% accepted, 47 enrolled. In 2009, 154 master's, 20 other advanced degrees awarded. *Degree requirements:* For master's, thesis optional, comprehensive exam or applied research project, effective portfolio; for Ed S, applied research project. *Entrance requirements:* For master's, GRE, MAT, interview, minimum GPA of 3.0, 3 references, writing samples; for Ed S, GRE, MAT, master's degree, minimum GPA of 3.0, writing sample, letters of reference. Additional exam requirements/recommendations for international students: Required—TOEFL (minimum score 500 paper-based). *Application deadline:* Applications are processed on a rolling basis. Application fee: $35. Electronic applications accepted. *Expenses:* Contact institution. *Financial support:* In 2009–10, 2 students received support. Scholarships/grants available. Support available to part-time students. Financial award application deadline: 7/15; financial award applicants required to submit FAFSA. *Unit head:* Dr. Lora Bailey, Dean, 770-534-6220, Fax: 770-534-6221, E-mail: lbailey@brenau.edu. *Application contact:* Christina White, Dean of Admissions, 770-718-5320, Fax: 770-718-5337, E-mail: cwhite@brenau.edu.

Bridgewater State University, School of Graduate Studies, School of Education and Allied Science, Department of Secondary Education and Professional Programs, Program in Secondary Education, Bridgewater, MA 02325-0001. Offers MAT. *Accreditation:* NCATE. Part-time and evening/weekend programs available. *Entrance requirements:* For master's, GRE General Test.

Brooklyn College of the City University of New York, Division of Graduate Studies, School of Education, Program in Adolescence Education and Special Subjects, Brooklyn, NY 11210-2889. Offers adolescence science education (MAT); art teacher (MA); biology teacher (MA); chemistry teacher (MA); earth science teacher (MAT); English teacher (MA); French teacher (MA); health and nutrition sciences: health teacher (MS Ed); mathematics teacher (MA); music education (CAS); music teacher (MA); physical education teacher (MS Ed); physics teacher (MA); social studies teacher (MA); Spanish teacher (MA). Part-time and evening/weekend programs available. *Students:* 23 full-time (15 women), 449 part-time (256 women); includes 147 minority (96 African Americans, 1 American Indian/Alaska Native, 18 Asian Americans or Pacific Islanders, 32 Hispanic Americans), 12 international. Average age 30. 251 applicants, 80% accepted, 141 enrolled. In 2009, 163 master's, 2 other advanced degrees awarded. *Degree requirements:* For master's, comprehensive exam (for some programs), thesis (for some programs). *Entrance requirements:* For master's, LAST, previous course work in education, resume, 2 letters of recommendation, essay. Additional exam requirements/recommendations for international students: Required—TOEFL (minimum score 500 paper-based; 173 computer-based; 61 iBT). *Application deadline:* For fall admission, 7/15 for domestic students, 7/1 for international students; for spring admission, 11/15 for domestic students, 10/1 for international students. Applications are processed on a rolling basis. Application fee: $125. Electronic applications accepted. *Expenses:* Tuition, state resident: full-time $7360; part-time $310 per credit hour. Tuition, nonresident: full-time $13,800; part-time $575 per credit hour. Required fees: $140.10 per semester. *Financial support:* Career-related internships or fieldwork, Federal Work-Study, institutionally sponsored loans, and scholarships/grants available. Support available to part-time students. Financial award application deadline: 5/1; financial award applicants required to submit FAFSA. *Faculty research:* Interdisciplinary education, semiotics, discourse analysis, autobiography, teacher identity. *Unit head:* Prof. Stephen Phillips, Program Head, 718-951-5214, E-mail: phillips@brooklyn.cuny.edu. *Application contact:* Hernan Sierra, Graduate Admissions Coordinator, 718-951-4536, Fax: 718-951-4506, E-mail: grads@brooklyn.cuny.edu.

Brown University, Graduate School, Department of Education, Providence, RI 02912. Offers teaching (MAT), including biology, elementary education, English, history/social studies; urban education policy (AM). *Degree requirements:* For master's, student teaching, portfolio. *Entrance requirements:* For master's, GRE General Test, letters of recommendation, interview. Electronic applications accepted.

Butler University, College of Education, Indianapolis, IN 46208-3485. Offers administration (MS); elementary education (MS); reading (MS); school counseling (MS); secondary education (MS); special education (MS). *Accreditation:* ACA; NCATE. Part-time and evening/weekend programs available. *Faculty:* 9 full-time (7 women), 7 part-time/adjunct (6 women). *Students:* 18 full-time (11 women), 137 part-time (111 women); includes 17 minority (14 African Americans, 1 American Indian/Alaska Native, 2 Asian Americans or Pacific Islanders), 9 international. Average age 31. 57 applicants, 77% accepted, 24 enrolled. In 2009, 61 master's awarded. *Entrance requirements:* For master's, GRE General Test, MAT, interview. *Application deadline:* For fall admission, 8/15 priority date for domestic students. Applications are processed on a rolling basis. Application fee: $35. Electronic applications accepted. *Financial support:* Institutionally sponsored loans available. Support available to part-time students. Financial award application deadline: 7/15; financial award applicants required to submit FAFSA. *Faculty research:* Ethics in cybercounseling, history of sports for disabled, effect of fetal alcohol syndrome on perceptual learning, reading recovery's theoretical framework in teacher education. *Unit head:* Dr. Ena Shelley, Dean, 317-940-9752, Fax: 317-940-6481. *Application contact:* Karen Farrell, Department Secretary, 317-940-9220, E-mail: kfarrell@butler.edu.

California State University, Bakersfield, Division of Graduate Studies, School of Natural Sciences and Mathematics, Program in Teaching Mathematics, Bakersfield, CA 93311. Offers MA. *Entrance requirements:* For master's, minimum GPA of 2.5 for last 90 quarter units.

California State University, Fullerton, Graduate Studies, College of Education, Department of Secondary Education, Fullerton, CA 92834-9480. Offers middle school mathematics (MS); secondary education (MS); teacher induction (MS). Part-time programs available. *Students:* 1 (woman) full-time, 41 part-time (33 women); includes 15 minority (1 African American, 1 American Indian/Alaska Native, 4 Asian Americans or Pacific Islanders, 9 Hispanic Americans). Average age 32. 32 applicants, 63% accepted, 17 enrolled. In 2009, 39 master's awarded. Application fee: $55. *Expenses:* Tuition, nonresident: full-time $11,160; part-time $373 per credit. Required fees: $1440 per term. Tuition and fees vary according to course load, degree level and program. *Financial support:* Career-related internships or fieldwork, Federal Work-Study, institutionally sponsored loans, and scholarships/grants available. Support available to part-time students. Financial award application deadline: 3/1; financial award applicants required to submit FAFSA. *Unit head:* Dr. Victoria Costa, Head, 657-278-7037. *Application contact:* Admissions/Applications, 657-278-2371.

California State University, Long Beach, Graduate Studies, College of Natural Sciences and Mathematics, Department of Mathematics and Statistics, Long Beach, CA 90840. Offers mathematics (MS), including applied mathematics, applied statistics, mathematics education for secondary school teachers. Part-time programs available. *Faculty:* 11 full-time (5 women). *Students:* 73 full-time (30 women), 90 part-time (36 women); includes 75 minority (6 African Americans, 47 Asian Americans or Pacific Islanders, 22 Hispanic Americans), 15 international. Average age 30. 123 applicants, 69% accepted, 44 enrolled. *Degree requirements:* For master's, comprehensive exam or thesis. *Application deadline:* For fall admission, 7/1 for domestic students; for spring admission, 12/1 for domestic students. Applications are processed on a rolling basis. Application fee: $55. Electronic applications accepted. *Expenses:* Required fees: $1802 per semester. Part-time tuition and fees vary according to course load. *Financial support:* Teaching assistantships, Federal Work-Study, institutionally sponsored loans, scholarships/grants, and traineeships available. Financial award application deadline: 3/2. *Faculty research:* Algebra, functional analysis, partial differential equations, operator theory, numerical analysis. *Unit head:* Dr. Robert Mena, Chair, 562-985-4721, Fax: 562-985-8227, E-mail: rmena@csulb.edu. *Application contact:* Dr. Ngo Viet, Graduate Associate Chair, 562-985-4721, Fax: 562-985-8227, E-mail: viet@csulb.edu.

California State University, Los Angeles, Graduate Studies, Charter College of Education, Division of Curriculum and Instruction, Los Angeles, CA 90032-8530. Offers elementary teaching (MA); reading (MA); secondary teaching (MA). Part-time and evening/weekend programs available. *Faculty:* 8 full-time (6 women), 7 part-time/adjunct (4 women). *Students:* 308 full-time (217 women), 297 part-time (211 women); includes 399 minority (22 African Americans, 98 Asian Americans or Pacific Islanders, 279 Hispanic Americans), 19 international. Average age 32. 53 applicants, 100% accepted, 30 enrolled. In 2009, 101 master's awarded. *Entrance requirements:* For master's, minimum GPA of 2.75 in last 90 units of course work, teaching certificate. Additional exam requirements/recommendations for international students: Required—TOEFL (minimum score 500 paper-based; 173 computer-based). *Application deadline:* For fall admission, 5/1 for domestic and international students. Applications are processed on a rolling basis. Application fee: $55. Electronic applications accepted. *Financial support:* Federal Work-Study available. Support available to part-time students. Financial award application deadline: 3/1. *Faculty research:* Media, language arts, mathematics, computers, drug-free schools. *Unit head:* Dr. Ramakrishan Menon, Chair, 323-343-4350, Fax: 323-343-5458, E-mail: rmenon@calstatela.edu. *Application contact:* Dr. Cheryl L. Ney, Associate Vice President for Academic Affairs and Dean of Graduate Studies, 323-343-3820 Ext. 3827, Fax: 323-343-5653, E-mail: cney@cslanet.calstatela.edu.

California State University, Northridge, Graduate Studies, College of Education, Department of Secondary Education, Northridge, CA 91330. Offers educational technology (MA); English education (MA); mathematics education (MA); secondary science education (MA); teaching and learning (MA). *Accreditation:* NCATE. Part-time programs available. *Faculty:* 13 full-time (7 women), 41 part-time/adjunct (20 women). *Students:* 10 full-time (6 women), 99 part-time (65 women); includes 40 minority (6 African Americans, 2 American Indian/Alaska Native, 13 Asian Americans or Pacific Islanders, 19 Hispanic Americans). Average age 34. 86 applicants, 60% accepted, 40 enrolled. *Degree requirements:* For master's, thesis optional. *Entrance requirements:* For master's, GRE General Test or minimum GPA of 3.0. Additional exam requirements/recommendations for international students: Required—TOEFL. *Application deadline:* For fall admission, 11/30 for domestic students. Application fee: $55. *Financial support:* Application deadline: 3/1. *Unit head:* Dr. Bonnie Ericson, Chair, 818-677-2580. *Application contact:* Dr. Michael Rivas, Graduate Advisor, 818-677-6792, E-mail: michael.rivas@csun.edu.

California State University, San Bernardino, Graduate Studies, College of Education, Program in Secondary Education, San Bernardino, CA 92407-2397. Offers MA. *Accreditation:* NCATE. Part-time and evening/weekend programs available. *Degree requirements:* For master's, thesis or alternative. *Entrance requirements:* For master's, GRE General Test, minimum GPA of 3.0 in education. *Application deadline:* For fall admission, 8/31 priority date for domestic students. Application fee: $55. *Financial support:* Career-related internships or fieldwork and Federal Work-Study available. Support available to part-time students. *Unit head:* Dr. Patricia Arlin, Dean, 909-537-5600, Fax: 909-537-7510, E-mail: parlin@csusb.edu. *Application contact:* Olivia Rosas, Director of Admissions, 909-537-7577, Fax: 909-537-7034, E-mail: orosas@csusb.edu.

California State University, Stanislaus, College of Education, Department of Teacher Education, Turlock, CA 95382. Offers curriculum and instruction (MA), including elementary education, multilingual education, reading, secondary education; education (MA); middle/junior high studies (Graduate Certificate). Part-time and evening/weekend programs available. *Degree requirements:* For master's, thesis. *Entrance requirements:* For master's, MAT or GRE, 3 letters of recommendation. Additional exam requirements/recommendations for international students: Required—TOEFL (minimum score 550 paper-based; 213 computer-based). Electronic applications accepted. *Faculty research:* Children's perspectives on historical events, method elementary schools dual language education, K-12 reading and CYRM programs.

California State University, Stanislaus, College of Humanities and Social Sciences, Department of History, Turlock, CA 95382. Offers history (MA); international relations (MA); secondary school teachers (MA). Part-time programs available. *Degree requirements:* For master's, one foreign language, comprehensive exam, thesis or alternative. *Entrance requirements:* For master's, GRE General Test, minimum undergraduate GPA of 3.0. Additional exam requirements/recommendations for international students: Required—TOEFL (minimum score 550 paper-based; 213 computer-based). Electronic applications accepted. *Faculty research:* History of Ancient Greece, history and ecology of the central valley, acculturation and gender.

California University of Pennsylvania, School of Graduate Studies and Research, School of Education, Department of Secondary Education, California, PA 15419-1394. Offers MAT. Part-time and evening/weekend programs available. Postbaccalaureate distance learning degree programs offered (no on-campus study). *Degree requirements:* For master's, comprehensive exam, thesis. *Entrance requirements:* For master's, PRAXIS, minimum GPA of 3.0, clearances. Additional exam requirements/recommendations for international students: Required—TOEFL (minimum score 550 paper-based; 213 computer-based; 80 iBT). Electronic applications accepted. *Faculty research:* The effectiveness of online instruction, student-centered instruction

strategies in secondary education, computer technology in education, environmental education, multi-media in education.

Campbell University, Graduate and Professional Programs, School of Education, Buies Creek, NC 27506. Offers administration (MSA); community counseling (MA); elementary education (M Ed); English education (M Ed); interdisciplinary studies (M Ed); mathematics education (M Ed); middle grades education (M Ed); physical education (M Ed); school counseling (M Ed); secondary education (M Ed); social science education (M Ed). *Accreditation:* NCATE. Part-time and evening/weekend programs available. *Degree requirements:* For master's, comprehensive exam. *Entrance requirements:* For master's, GRE General Test, minimum GPA of 2.7. *Faculty research:* Spiritual values and wellness issues in counseling, stress and professional burnout among counselors, thinking strategies, leadership, adaptive technology.

Canisius College, Graduate Division, School of Education and Human Services, Department of Graduate Education, Buffalo, NY 14208-1098. Offers adolescence education (grades 7-12) (MS); childhood education (grades 1-6) (MS); college student personnel administration (MS); deaf education (MS); differentiated instruction (MS Ed); educational administration and supervision (MS); general education (MS Ed); initial teacher certification (elementary education) (MS); initial teacher certification (secondary education) (MS); literacy (MS Ed); special education (MS). *Accreditation:* NCATE. Part-time and evening/weekend programs available. *Faculty:* 22 full-time (14 women), 84 part-time/adjunct (54 women). *Students:* 409 full-time (288 women), 261 part-time (187 women); includes 29 minority (24 African Americans, 5 Hispanic Americans), 156 international. Average age 30. 518 applicants, 74% accepted, 240 enrolled. In 2009, 346 master's awarded. Application fee: $25. *Financial support:* Research assistantships with full tuition reimbursements, career-related internships or fieldwork, institutionally sponsored loans, scholarships/grants, health care benefits, tuition waivers (full and partial), and unspecified assistantships available. *Faculty research:* Autism, Asperger's disease, private higher education, reading strategies. *Unit head:* Rev. Paul Nochelski, Chair of Graduate Education and Leadership, 716-888-3297, Fax: 716-888-3299. *Application contact:* James D. Bagwell, Director of Graduate Recruitment and Admissions, 716-888-2544, Fax: 716-888-3290, E-mail: bagwellj@canisius.edu.

Carlow University, School of Education, Program in Education, Pittsburgh, PA 15213-3165. Offers elementary education (M Ed); instructional technology specialist (M Ed); secondary education (M Ed); special education (M Ed). Part-time and evening/weekend programs available. *Entrance requirements:* For master's, resume, 3 letters of recommendation, minimum GPA of 3.0, interview. Electronic applications accepted. *Expenses:* Tuition: Full-time $11,250; part-time $625 per credit. Tuition and fees vary according to course load, degree level and program.

Carson-Newman College, Graduate Program in Education, Jefferson City, TN 37760. Offers curriculum and instruction (M Ed); educational leadership (M Ed); elementary education (MAT); school counseling (MS); secondary education (MAT); teaching English as a second language (MATESL). *Accreditation:* NCATE. Part-time and evening/weekend programs available. *Faculty:* 5 full-time (2 women), 10 part-time/adjunct (3 women). *Students:* 112 full-time (84 women), 84 part-time (52 women); includes 5 African Americans, 17 international. Average age 32. 86 applicants, 98% accepted. In 2009, 55 master's awarded. *Degree requirements:* For master's, thesis or alternative. *Entrance requirements:* For master's, NTE, minimum GPA of 3.0 in major, 2.5 overall. *Application deadline:* For fall admission, 7/15 priority date for domestic students. Applications are processed on a rolling basis. Application fee: $25 ($50 for international students). *Expenses:* Tuition: Full-time $5490; part-time $305 per semester hour. Required fees: $200. *Financial support:* In 2009–10, 41 students received support. Federal Work-Study and unspecified assistantships available. Financial award application deadline: 4/1; financial award applicants required to submit FAFSA. *Unit head:* Dr. Sharon Teets, Chair, 865-471-3461. *Application contact:* Graduate Admissions and Services Adviser, 865-471-3460, Fax: 865-471-3875.

The Catholic University of America, School of Arts and Sciences, Department of Education, Washington, DC 20064. Offers Catholic educational leadership (PhD); education (Certificate); educational psychology (PhD); learning and instruction (MA); secondary education (MA); special education (MA). *Accreditation:* NCATE. Part-time programs available. *Faculty:* 11 full-time (8 women), 3 part-time/adjunct (0 women). *Students:* 6 full-time (5 women), 56 part-time (39 women); includes 9 minority (5 African Americans, 2 Asian Americans or Pacific Islanders, 2 Hispanic Americans), 2 international. Average age 38. 54 applicants, 59% accepted, 14 enrolled. In 2009, 14 master's, 6 doctorates, 1 other advanced degree awarded. *Degree requirements:* For master's, comprehensive exam, thesis or alternative; for doctorate, comprehensive exam, thesis/dissertation. *Entrance requirements:* For master's and doctorate, GRE General Test or MAT, statement of purpose, official copies of academic transcripts, three letters of recommendation. Additional exam requirements/recommendations for international students: Required—TOEFL (minimum score 580 paper-based; 237 computer-based). *Application deadline:* For fall admission, 8/1 priority date for domestic students, 7/15 for international students; for spring admission, 12/1 priority date for domestic students, 10/15 for international students. Applications are processed on a rolling basis. Application fee: $55. Electronic applications accepted. *Expenses:* Tuition: Full-time $31,740; part-time $1245 per credit hour. Required fees: $50; $25 per semester hour. One-time fee: $425. *Financial support:* Fellowships, research assistantships, teaching assistantships, Federal Work-Study, scholarships/grants, tuition waivers (full and partial), and unspecified assistantships available. Financial award application deadline: 2/1; financial award applicants required to submit FAFSA. *Faculty research:* Catholic school issues, reflective teaching, cognitive psychology, urban education. Total annual research expenditures: $68,905. *Unit head:* Dr. Merylann J. Schuttloffel, Chair, 202-319-5805, Fax: 202-319-5815, E-mail: schuttloffel@cua.edu. *Application contact:* Julie Schwing, Director of Graduate Admissions, 202-319-5057, Fax: 202-319-6533, E-mail: cua-admissions@cua.edu.

Centenary College of Louisiana, Graduate Programs, Department of Education, Shreveport, LA 71104. Offers administration (M Ed); elementary education (MAT); secondary education (MAT); supervision of instruction (M Ed). Part-time and evening/weekend programs available. *Degree requirements:* For master's, comprehensive exam. *Entrance requirements:* For master's, GRE General Test (M Ed), PRAXIS I and PRAXIS II (MAT), teacher certification (M Ed), minimum GPA of 2.5. *Expenses:* Contact institution. *Faculty research:* Teachers as advocates for teachers, portfolio assessment, disabled readers.

Central Connecticut State University, School of Graduate Studies, School of Education and Professional Studies, Department of Teacher Education, Program in Educational Foundations Policy/Secondary Education, New Britain, CT 06050-4010. Offers MS. Part-time and evening/weekend programs available. *Students:* 23 part-time (13 women); includes 1 minority (African American). Average age 35. 7 applicants, 43% accepted, 3 enrolled. In 2009, 7 master's awarded. *Degree requirements:* For master's, comprehensive exam, thesis or alternative. *Entrance requirements:* For master's, minimum undergraduate GPA of 2.7. Additional exam requirements/recommendations for international students: Required—TOEFL. *Application deadline:* For fall admission, 7/1 for domestic students; for spring admission, 12/1 for domestic students. Applications are processed on a rolling basis. Application fee: $50. Electronic applications accepted. *Expenses:* Tuition, area resident: Full-time $4662; part-time $440 per credit. Tuition, state resident: full-time $6994; part-time $440 per credit. Tuition, nonresident: full-time $12,988; part-time $440 per credit. Required fees: $3606. One-time fee: $62 part-time. *Financial support:* Application deadline: 3/1.

Central Michigan University, College of Graduate Studies, College of Education and Human Services, Department of Teacher Education and Professional Development, Mount Pleasant, MI 48859. Offers educational technology (MA); elementary education (MA), including classroom teaching, early childhood; middle level education (MA); reading and literacy K-12 (MA); secondary education (MA). Part-time and evening/weekend programs available. *Degree requirements:* For master's, thesis or alternative. Electronic applications accepted. *Faculty*

research: Integrating literacy across the curriculum; science teaching and aesthetic learning in science; diversity education; educational technology; educational psychology and child development.

Central Michigan University, College of Graduate Studies, College of Science and Technology, Department of Chemistry, Mount Pleasant, MI 48859. Offers chemistry (MS); teaching chemistry (MA), including teaching college chemistry, teaching high school chemistry. Part-time programs available. *Degree requirements:* For master's, comprehensive exam, thesis or alternative. *Entrance requirements:* For master's, GRE. Electronic applications accepted. *Faculty research:* Analytical and organic-inorganic chemistry, biochemistry, catalysis, dendrimer and polymer studies, nanotechnology.

Chadron State College, School of Professional and Graduate Studies, Department of Education, Chadron, NE 69337. Offers business (MA Ed); community counseling (MA Ed); educational administration (MS Ed, Sp Ed); elementary education (MS Ed); history (MA Ed); language and literature (MA Ed); secondary administration (MS Ed); secondary education (MS Ed). *Accreditation:* NCATE. Part-time and evening/weekend programs available. Postbaccalaureate distance learning degree programs offered. *Degree requirements:* For master's, thesis optional. *Entrance requirements:* For master's, GRE General Test, GRE Writing Test, minimum GPA of 2.75 or 12 graduate hours at CSC with minimum GPA of 3.25. Additional exam requirements/recommendations for international students: Required—TOEFL. Electronic applications accepted. *Faculty research:* Rural education, technology, mental health.

Chapman University, Graduate Studies, College of Educational Studies, Program in Teaching: Secondary Education, Orange, CA 92866. Offers MA. Part-time and evening/weekend programs available. *Faculty:* 19 full-time (13 women), 20 part-time/adjunct (12 women). *Students:* 30 full-time (23 women), 24 part-time (15 women); includes 12 minority (1 African American, 5 Asian Americans or Pacific Islanders, 6 Hispanic Americans). Average age 27. 35 applicants, 66% accepted, 16 enrolled. In 2009, 18 master's awarded. *Degree requirements:* For master's, thesis. *Entrance requirements:* For master's, GRE General Test, MAT, or California Subject Examinations for Teachers, minimum GPA of 2.75. Additional exam requirements/recommendations for international students: Required—TOEFL (minimum score 550 paper-based). *Application deadline:* Applications are processed on a rolling basis. Application fee: $55. Electronic applications accepted. *Expenses:* Contact institution. *Financial support:* Fellowships, Federal Work-Study and scholarships/grants available. Financial award application deadline: 6/30; financial award applicants required to submit FAFSA. *Unit head:* Dr. Jan Osborn, Coordinator, 714-628-7221, E-mail: josborn@chapman.edu. *Application contact:* Rika Judd, Graduate Admission Counselor, 714-997-6786, Fax: 714-997-6713, E-mail: rjudd@chapman.edu.

Charleston Southern University, School of Education, Charleston, SC 29423-8087. Offers administration and supervision (M Ed), including elementary, secondary; elementary education (M Ed); secondary education (M Ed). *Accreditation:* NCATE. Part-time and evening/weekend programs available. *Faculty:* 4 full-time (2 women). *Students:* 70 part-time (57 women); includes 17 minority (all African Americans). Average age 34. 48 applicants, 79% accepted, 22 enrolled. In 2009, 27 master's awarded. *Degree requirements:* For master's, thesis optional. *Entrance requirements:* For master's, GRE or MAT. Additional exam requirements/recommendations for international students: Required—TOEFL (minimum score 550 paper-based; 213 computer-based; 79 iBT). *Application deadline:* Applications are processed on a rolling basis. Application fee: $30. *Expenses:* Contact institution. *Financial support:* Research assistantships with full tuition reimbursements, career-related internships or fieldwork and Federal Work-Study available. Financial award application deadline: 4/15; financial award applicants required to submit FAFSA. *Unit head:* Dr. Norma Harper, Dean, 843-863-7765, Fax: 843-863-7085, E-mail: nharper@csuniv.edu. *Application contact:* Alison Harrison, Graduate Enrollment Counselor, 843-863-7534, Fax: 843-863-7070, E-mail: aharrison@cwuniv.edu.

Chatham University, Program in Education, Pittsburgh, PA 15232-2826. Offers early childhood education (MAT); elementary education (MAT); English—secondary (MAT); environmental education (K-12) (MAT); secondary art (MAT); secondary biology education (MAT); secondary chemistry education (MAT); secondary English education (MAT); secondary math education (MAT); secondary physics education (MAT); secondary social studies education (MAT); special education (MAT). *Students:* 52 full-time (41 women), 20 part-time (16 women). Average age 30. 39 applicants, 79% accepted, 26 enrolled. In 2009, 37 master's awarded. *Degree requirements:* For master's, thesis, teaching experience. *Entrance requirements:* For master's, PRAXIS I, minimum GPA of 3.0, sample of written work, recommendation letters. Additional exam requirements/recommendations for international students: Required—TOEFL (minimum score 600 paper-based; 250 computer-based; 100 iBT), IELTS (minimum score 6.5), TWE. *Application deadline:* For fall admission, 5/1 priority date for domestic and international students; for spring admission, 10/15 priority date for domestic and international students. Applications are processed on a rolling basis. Application fee: $45. Electronic applications accepted. *Financial support:* Career-related internships or fieldwork available. Financial award applicants required to submit FAFSA. *Faculty research:* Gifted education, environmental education, technology in education, writing as learning, class size and achievement. *Unit head:* Dr. Barbara Biglan, Interim Director, 412-365-1170, E-mail: biglan@chatham.edu. *Application contact:* Dory Perry, Associate Director of Graduate Admissions, 412-365-2758, Fax: 412-365-1609, E-mail: gradadmissions@chatham.edu.

Chestnut Hill College, School of Graduate Studies, Department of Education, Program in Secondary Education, Philadelphia, PA 19118-2693. Offers M Ed. Part-time and evening/weekend programs available. *Degree requirements:* For master's, thesis optional. *Entrance requirements:* For master's, PRAXIS I or proof of teaching certification, letters of recommendation; writing sample; 6 graduate credits with B average if undergraduate GPA less than 3.0. Additional exam requirements/recommendations for international students: Required—TOEFL (minimum score 500 paper-based; 213 computer-based). *Faculty research:* Science teaching.

Chicago State University, School of Graduate and Professional Studies, College of Education, Department of Technology and Education, Chicago, IL 60628. Offers secondary education (MAT); technology and education (MS Ed). Postbaccalaureate distance learning degree programs offered. *Degree requirements:* For master's, thesis optional. *Entrance requirements:* For master's, minimum GPA of 2.75.

The Citadel, The Military College of South Carolina, Citadel Graduate College, School of Education, Program in Guidance and Counseling, Charleston, SC 29409. Offers elementary/secondary school counseling (M Ed); student affairs and college counseling (M Ed). *Accreditation:* ACA; NCATE. Part-time and evening/weekend programs available. *Faculty:* 12 full-time (7 women), 8 part-time/adjunct (5 women). *Students:* 16 full-time (15 women), 34 part-time (32 women); includes 10 minority (9 African Americans, 1 Hispanic American). Average age 29. In 2009, 16 master's awarded. *Degree requirements:* For master's, comprehensive exam, practicum or internship. *Entrance requirements:* For master's, GRE (minimum score 900) or MAT (minimum score 396), minimum undergraduate GPA of 3.0, 3 letters of reference, group admissions interview. Additional exam requirements/recommendations for international students: Required—TOEFL (minimum score 550 paper-based; 213 computer-based; 79 iBT). *Application deadline:* For fall admission, 6/1 for domestic students; for spring admission, 10/1 for domestic students. Application fee: $30. Electronic applications accepted. *Expenses:* Tuition, state resident: part-time $400 per credit hour. Tuition, nonresident: part-time $657 per credit hour. Required fees: $40 per term. *Financial support:* Career-related internships or fieldwork, health care benefits, and unspecified assistantships available. Support available to part-time students. Financial award application deadline: 7/1; financial award applicants required to submit FAFSA. *Unit head:* Dr. George T. Williams, Director, 843-953-2205, Fax: 843-953-7258, E-mail: williamsg@citadel.edu. *Application contact:* Dr. Steve A.

Secondary Education

The Citadel, The Military College of South Carolina (continued)
Nida, Associate Provost, The Citadel Graduate College, 843-953-5089, Fax: 843-953-7630, E-mail: cgc@citadel.edu.

The Citadel, The Military College of South Carolina, Citadel Graduate College, School of Education, Program in Secondary Education, Charleston, SC 29409. Offers biology (MAT); English language arts (MAT); mathematics (MAT); social studies (MAT). *Accreditation:* NCATE. Part-time and evening/weekend programs available. *Faculty:* 12 full-time (7 women), 8 part-time/adjunct (5 women). *Students:* 27 full-time (18 women), 62 part-time (37 women); includes 15 minority (11 African Americans, 2 Asian Americans or Pacific Islanders, 2 Hispanic Americans). Average age 29. In 2009, 22 master's awarded. *Degree requirements:* For master's, comprehensive exam, internship. *Entrance requirements:* For master's, GRE (minimum score 900) or MAT (minimum score 396), minimum undergraduate GPA of 2.5. Additional exam requirements/recommendations for international students: Required—TOEFL (minimum score 550 paper-based; 213 computer-based). *Application deadline:* Applications are processed on a rolling basis. Application fee: $30. Electronic applications accepted. *Expenses:* Tuition, state resident: part-time $400 per credit hour. Tuition, nonresident: part-time $657 per credit hour. Required fees: $40 per term. *Financial support:* Career-related internships or fieldwork, health care benefits, and unspecified assistantships available. Support available to part-time students. Financial award application deadline: 7/1; financial award applicants required to submit FAFSA. *Unit head:* Dr. Kathryn A. Richardson-Jones, Coordinator, 843-953-3163, Fax: 843-953-7258, E-mail: kathryn.jones@citadel.edu. *Application contact:* Dr. Steve A. Nida, Associate Provost, The Citadel Graduate College, 843-953-5089, Fax: 843-953-7630, E-mail: cgc@citadel.edu.

City College of the City University of New York, Graduate School, School of Education, Department of Secondary Education, New York, NY 10031-9198. Offers adolescent mathematics education (MA, AC); English education (MA); middle school mathematics education (MS); science education (MA); social studies education (AC). *Accreditation:* NCATE. *Entrance requirements:* For master's, Liberal Arts and Sciences Test (LAST), Content Specialty Test (CST). Additional exam requirements/recommendations for international students: Required—TOEFL. *Expenses:* Tuition, state resident: part-time $310 per credit. Tuition, nonresident: part-time $575 per credit. Tuition and fees vary according to course load and program.

Clemson University, Graduate School, College of Health, Education, and Human Development, School of Education, Program in Secondary Education, Clemson, SC 29634. Offers English (M Ed); mathematics (M Ed); natural sciences (M Ed); social studies (M Ed). *Accreditation:* NCATE. *Students:* 5 full-time (3 women), 4 part-time (2 women); includes 2 minority (1 Asian American or Pacific Islander, 1 Hispanic American), 2 international. Average age 29. 11 applicants, 82% accepted, 4 enrolled. In 2009, 2 master's awarded. *Entrance requirements:* For master's, GRE General Test, teaching certificate. Additional exam requirements/recommendations for international students: Required—TOEFL. *Application deadline:* Applications are processed on a rolling basis. Application fee: $70 ($80 for international students). Electronic applications accepted. *Expenses:* Contact institution. *Financial support:* In 2009–10, 2 students received support. Career-related internships or fieldwork, institutionally sponsored loans, scholarships/grants, health care benefits, and unspecified assistantships available. Support available to part-time students. Financial award application deadline: 6/1; financial award applicants required to submit FAFSA. *Unit head:* Dr. Michael J. Padilla, Director/Associate Dean, 864-656-4444, Fax: 864-656-0311, E-mail: padilla@clemson.edu. *Application contact:* Dr. David Fleming, Graduate Coordinator, 864-656-1881, Fax: 864-656-0311, E-mail: dflemin@clemson.edu.

Coastal Carolina University, Spadoni College of Education, Conway, SC 29528-6054. Offers education (MAT); educational leadership (M Ed); learning and teaching (M Ed); secondary education (M Ed). *Accreditation:* NCATE. Part-time and evening/weekend programs available. *Faculty:* 12 full-time (4 women), 3 part-time/adjunct (1 woman). *Students:* 66 full-time (41 women), 138 part-time (105 women); includes 29 minority (24 African Americans, 1 American Indian/Alaska Native, 2 Asian Americans or Pacific Islanders, 2 Hispanic Americans), 3 international. Average age 33. 242 applicants, 88% accepted, 150 enrolled. In 2009, 76 master's awarded. *Degree requirements:* For master's, comprehensive exam. *Entrance requirements:* For master's, GRE General Test, MAT, 2 letters of recommendation, copy of teaching credential. Additional exam requirements/recommendations for international students: Required—TOEFL (minimum score 550 paper-based; 213 computer-based; 79 iBT). *Application deadline:* For fall admission, 7/1 priority date for domestic and international students; for spring admission, 11/15 priority date for domestic and international students. Applications are processed on a rolling basis. Application fee: $45. Electronic applications accepted. *Expenses:* Tuition, state resident: full-time $9600; part-time $400 per credit hour. Tuition, nonresident: full-time $11,880; part-time $495 per credit hour. Required fees: $80; $40 per term. *Financial support:* Fellowships, research assistantships, unspecified assistantships available. Support available to part-time students. Financial award application deadline: 3/1; financial award applicants required to submit FAFSA. *Unit head:* Dr. Diane L. Mark, Dean, 843-349-2629, Fax: 843-349-2106, E-mail: dmark@coastal.edu. *Application contact:* Dr. Richard L. Johnson, Director of Graduate Studies, 843-349-2192, Fax: 843-349-6444, E-mail: rjohnson@coastal.edu.

Colgate University, Master of Arts in Teaching Program, Hamilton, NY 13346-1386. Offers adolescence education NY state certification (MAT). *Accreditation:* Teacher Education Accreditation Council. *Faculty:* 5 full-time (4 women), 3 part-time/adjunct (2 women). *Students:* 7 full-time (4 women), 2 part-time (both women); includes 1 minority (American Indian/Alaska Native), 2 international. Average age 25. 12 applicants, 67% accepted, 6 enrolled. In 2009, 5 master's awarded. *Degree requirements:* For master's, special project or thesis. *Entrance requirements:* For master's, GRE General Test. *Application deadline:* For fall admission, 2/15 for domestic students. Application fee: $50. *Expenses:* Tuition: Full-time $40,690; part-time $4521 per course. Required fees: $140 per semester. Tuition and fees vary according to course load. *Financial support:* In 2009–10, 9 students received support. Scholarships/grants and unspecified assistantships available. Financial award application deadline: 2/15; financial award applicants required to submit FAFSA. *Faculty research:* Culturally responsive teaching, comparative education, moral development in education, politics in education, educational psychology. *Unit head:* Dr. Douglas Johnson, Associate Dean of the Faculty, 315-228-7220. *Application contact:* Ginger Babich, Administrative Assistant, 315-228-7256, Fax: 315-228-7857, E-mail: gbabich@colgate.edu.

College of Mount St. Joseph, Graduate Education Program, Cincinnati, OH 45233-1670. Offers adolescent young adult education (MA); art (MA); inclusive early childhood education (MA); instructional leadership (MA); middle childhood education (MA); multi-age education (MA); multicultural special education (MA); music (MA); reading (MA). *Accreditation:* Teacher Education Accreditation Council. Part-time and evening/weekend programs available. *Faculty:* 15 full-time (11 women), 9 part-time/adjunct (6 women). *Students:* 93 full-time (75 women), 99 part-time (66 women); includes 19 minority (18 African Americans, 1 American Indian/Alaska Native). Average age 34. 116 applicants, 97% accepted, 94 enrolled. In 2009, 51 master's awarded. *Degree requirements:* For master's, research project, student teaching, clinical and field-based experiences. *Entrance requirements:* For master's, GRE, PRAXIS II in teaching content area (math or science), 2 letters of recommendation, interview, resume. Additional exam requirements/recommendations for international students: Required—TOEFL (minimum score 560 paper-based; 220 computer-based; 83 iBT). *Application deadline:* Applications are processed on a rolling basis. Application fee: $50. Electronic applications accepted. *Expenses:* Tuition: Part-time $500 per hour. Required fees: $200 per year. Tuition and fees vary according to degree level and program. *Financial support:* In 2009–10, 51 students received support. Scholarships/grants available. Financial award applicants required to submit FAFSA. *Faculty research:* Foreign and second language learning problems/reading disabilities/hyperlexia, multicultural/bilingual special education, alternative educator licensure, science education, pedagogical content knowledge. *Unit head:* Dr. Mary West, Chair of Graduate Education, 513-244-3263, Fax: 513-244-4867, E-mail: mary_west@mail.msj.edu. *Application contact:* Marilyn Hoskins, Assistant Director of Graduate Recruitment, 513-244-4723, Fax: 513-244-4629, E-mail: marilyn_hoskins@mail.msj.edu.

The College of New Jersey, Graduate Division, School of Education, Department of Educational Administration and Secondary Education, Program in Secondary Education, Ewing, NJ 08628. Offers MAT. *Students:* 31 full-time (13 women), 6 part-time (5 women); includes 7 minority (2 African Americans, 2 Asian Americans or Pacific Islanders, 3 Hispanic Americans). 59 applicants, 69% accepted. In 2009, 33 master's awarded. *Degree requirements:* For master's, comprehensive exam. *Entrance requirements:* For master's, GRE, minimum GPA of 3.0 in field or 2.75 overall. Additional exam requirements/recommendations for international students: Required—TOEFL. *Application deadline:* For fall admission, 2/1 priority date for domestic students; for spring admission, 10/1 priority date for domestic students. Application fee: $70. Electronic applications accepted. *Expenses:* Tuition, state resident: part-time $573.70 per credit. Tuition, nonresident: part-time $887.75 per credit. Required fees: $140.85 per credit. One-time fee: $10 part-time. *Financial support:* Tuition waivers (partial) and unspecified assistantships available. Financial award applicants required to submit FAFSA. *Unit head:* Dr. Ruth Palmer, Coordinator, 609-771-2803. *Application contact:* Susan L. Hydro, Assistant Dean, Office of Graduate Studies, 609-771-2300, Fax: 609-637-5105, E-mail: graduate@tcnj.edu.

College of St. Joseph, Graduate Programs, Division of Education, Program in Secondary Education, Rutland, VT 05701-3899. Offers English (M Ed); social studies (M Ed). Part-time and evening/weekend programs available. *Entrance requirements:* For master's, PRAXIS I, 2 letters of recommendation, minimum GPA of 3.0, interview. Electronic applications accepted. *Expenses:* Tuition: Full-time $13,500; part-time $350 per credit. Required fees: $45 per term. One-time fee: $445. Tuition and fees vary according to program.

The College of Saint Rose, Graduate Studies, School of Education, Teacher Education Department, Albany, NY 12203-1419. Offers business and marketing (MS Ed); childhood education (MS Ed); curriculum and instruction (MS Ed); early childhood education (MS Ed); elementary education (K-6) (MS Ed); secondary education (MS Ed, Certificate); teacher education (MS Ed, Certificate), including bilingual pupil personnel services (Certificate), teacher education (MS Ed). Part-time and evening/weekend programs available. *Entrance requirements:* For master's, minimum undergraduate GPA of 3.0. Additional exam requirements/recommendations for international students: Required—TOEFL (minimum score 550 paper-based; 213 computer-based). Electronic applications accepted.

College of Staten Island of the City University of New York, Graduate Programs, Department of Education, Program in Adolescence Education, Staten Island, NY 10314-6600. Offers MS Ed. Part-time and evening/weekend programs available. *Faculty:* 4 full-time (3 women), 4 part-time/adjunct (2 women). *Students:* 15 full-time (11 women), 157 part-time (97 women); includes 21 minority (6 African Americans, 6 Asian Americans or Pacific Islanders, 9 Hispanic Americans). Average age 29. 87 applicants, 59% accepted, 51 enrolled. In 2009, 50 master's awarded. *Degree requirements:* For master's, research project. *Entrance requirements:* For master's, minimum GPA of 2.75, 2 letters of recommendation, New York State Initial Certification at secondary (adolescence) level. Additional exam requirements/recommendations for international students: Required—TOEFL (minimum score 550 paper-based; 213 computer-based; 79 iBT). *Application deadline:* For fall admission, 4/19 priority date for domestic and international students; for spring admission, 11/16 priority date for domestic and international students. Applications are processed on a rolling basis. Application fee: $125. Electronic applications accepted. *Expenses:* Tuition, state resident: full-time $7360; part-time $310 per credit. Tuition, nonresident: part-time $575 per credit. Required fees: $378; $113 per semester. *Financial support:* In 2009–10, 4 students received support. Career-related internships or fieldwork, Federal Work-Study, and scholarships/grants available. Support available to part-time students. Financial award applicants required to submit FAFSA. *Unit head:* Dr. Eileen Donoghue, Coordinator, 718-982-3770, Fax: 718-982-3743, E-mail: eileen.donoghue@csi.cuny.edu. *Application contact:* Sasha Spence, Assistant Director of Graduate Recruitment and Admissions, 718-982-2699, Fax: 718-982-2500, E-mail: sasha.spence@csi.cuny.edu.

The College of William and Mary, School of Education, Program in Curriculum and Instruction, Williamsburg, VA 23187-8795. Offers elementary education (MA Ed); gifted education (MA Ed); math specialist (MA Ed); reading education (MA Ed); secondary education (MA Ed), including English education, mathematics education, modern foreign languages education, science education, social studies education; special education (MA Ed), including general curriculum, resource collaborating teaching. *Accreditation:* NCATE. Part-time programs available. *Faculty:* 18 full-time (12 women), 17 part-time/adjunct (15 women). *Students:* 54 full-time (45 women), 12 part-time (all women); includes 3 minority (2 African Americans, 1 Asian American or Pacific Islander), 2 international. Average age 27. 120 applicants, 75% accepted. In 2009, 70 master's awarded. *Degree requirements:* For master's, project. *Entrance requirements:* For master's, GRE or MAT, minimum GPA of 2.5. Additional exam requirements/recommendations for international students: Required—TOEFL. *Application deadline:* For fall admission, 1/15 for domestic and international students; for spring admission, 10/1 for domestic and international students. Application fee: $45. Electronic applications accepted. *Expenses:* Tuition, state resident: full-time $6400; part-time $315 per credit hour. Tuition, nonresident: full-time $19,720; part-time $840 per credit hour. Required fees: $4114. *Financial support:* In 2009–10, 30 students received support, including 10 research assistantships with full and partial tuition reimbursements available (averaging $5,500 per year); career-related internships or fieldwork, Federal Work-Study, institutionally sponsored loans, scholarships/grants, and unspecified assistantships also available. Financial award application deadline: 1/15; financial award applicants required to submit FAFSA. *Faculty research:* National Council of Teachers of Mathematics Standards, counseling, self-concept and self-esteem, special education, curriculum development. *Unit head:* Dr. C. Denise Johnson, Area Coordinator, 757-221-1528, E-mail: cdjohn@wm.edu. *Application contact:* Dorothy Smith Osborne, Director of Admissions, 757-221-2317, Fax: 757-221-2293, E-mail: dsosbo@wm.edu.

The Colorado College, Department of Education, Program in Secondary Education, Colorado Springs, CO 80903-3294. Offers art teaching (K-12) (MAT); English teaching (MAT); foreign language teaching (MAT); mathematics teaching (MAT); music teaching (MAT); science teaching (MAT); social studies teaching (MAT). *Faculty:* 3 full-time (2 women), 8 part-time/adjunct (6 women). *Students:* 15 full-time (5 women); includes 2 minority (1 American Indian/Alaska Native, 1 Asian American or Pacific Islander). Average age 27. 26 applicants, 81% accepted, 15 enrolled. In 2009, 17 master's awarded. *Degree requirements:* For master's, thesis, internship. *Entrance requirements:* For master's, PRAXIS II or PLACE Exam. *Application deadline:* For fall admission, 12/1 priority date for domestic students, 12/1 for international students. Applications are processed on a rolling basis. Application fee: $50. *Expenses:* Tuition: Part-time $2545 per credit. *Financial support:* In 2009–10, 15 students received support, including 7 teaching assistantships (averaging $16,000 per year); career-related internships or fieldwork, institutionally sponsored loans, health care benefits, and tuition waivers (partial) also available. Financial award application deadline: 2/15; financial award applicants required to submit FAFSA. *Unit head:* Mike Taber, Director, 719-389-6026, Fax: 719-389-6473, E-mail: mike.taber@coloradocollege.edu. *Application contact:* Debra Yazulla Mortenson, Education Services Manager, 719-389-6472, Fax: 719-389-6473, E-mail: debra.mortenson@coloradocollege.edu.

Columbus State University, Graduate Studies, College of Education and Health Professions, Department of Teacher Education, Columbus, GA 31907-5645. Offers accomplished teaching (M Ed); early childhood education (M Ed, Ed S); health administration (MPA); instructional technology (MS); middle grades education (M Ed, Ed S); physical education (M Ed); secondary education (M Ed, MAT, Ed S), including English/language arts (M Ed, Ed S), general science (M Ed), mathematics (M Ed), social science (M Ed); special education (M Ed), including behavior disorders, mental retardation. *Accreditation:* NCATE. Part-time and evening/weekend programs available. Postbaccalaureate distance learning degree programs offered (minimal on-campus study). *Faculty:* 18 full-time (15 women), 14 part-time/adjunct (10 women). *Students:* 146 full-time (113 women), 312 part-time (261 women); includes 142 minority (120 African Americans,

1 American Indian/Alaska Native, 8 Asian Americans or Pacific Islanders, 13 Hispanic Americans), 2 international. Average age 31. 248 applicants, 64% accepted, 114 enrolled. In 2009, 103 master's, 22 other advanced degrees awarded. *Degree requirements:* For master's, thesis, exit exam; for Ed S, thesis or alternative. *Entrance requirements:* For master's, GRE General Test, minimum GPA of 2.75; for Ed S, GRE General Test. Additional exam requirements/recommendations for international students: Required—TOEFL (minimum score 550 paper-based; 213 computer-based; 79 iBT). *Application deadline:* For fall admission, 5/1 priority date for domestic students, 5/1 for international students; for spring admission, 11/1 for domestic and international students. Applications are processed on a rolling basis. Application fee: $30. Electronic applications accepted. *Financial support:* In 2009–10, 305 students received support, including 36 research assistantships with partial tuition reimbursements available (averaging $3,000 per year); career-related internships or fieldwork, Federal Work-Study, institutionally sponsored loans, scholarships/grants, tuition waivers (partial), and unspecified assistantships also available. Support available to part-time students. Financial award application deadline: 5/1; financial award applicants required to submit FAFSA. *Unit head:* Dr. Deborah Gober, Acting Chair, 706-568-2255, Fax: 706-568-3134, E-mail: gober_deborah@colstate.edu. *Application contact:* Katie Thornton, Graduate Admissions Specialist, 706-568-2035, Fax: 706-568-2462, E-mail: thornton_katie@colstate.edu.

Concordia University, College of Education, Portland, OR 97211-6099. Offers curriculum and instruction (elementary) (M Ed); educational administration (M Ed); elementary education (MAT); secondary education (MAT). Part-time programs available. Postbaccalaureate distance learning degree programs offered (no on-campus study). *Degree requirements:* For master's, comprehensive exam, work samples/portfolio. *Entrance requirements:* For master's, California Basic Educational Skills Test or PRAXIS I, minimum undergraduate GPA of 2.8, graduate 3.0; 2 letters of recommendation. Additional exam requirements/recommendations for international students: Required—TOEFL (minimum score 525 paper-based; 195 computer-based). Electronic applications accepted. *Faculty research:* Learner centered classroom, brain-based learning future of on-line learning.

Concordia University Chicago, College of Education, Program in Teaching, River Forest, IL 60305-1499. Offers early childhood education (MAT); elementary education (MAT); secondary education (MAT). *Degree requirements:* For master's, thesis or alternative. *Entrance requirements:* For master's, minimum GPA of 2.9. Additional exam requirements/recommendations for international students: Required—TOEFL (minimum score 550 paper-based; 195 computer-based). Electronic applications accepted.

Concordia University, Nebraska, Graduate Programs in Education, Program in Educational Administration, Seward, NE 68434-1599. Offers elementary and secondary education (M Ed); elementary education (M Ed); secondary education (M Ed). *Accreditation:* NCATE. Part-time programs available. *Degree requirements:* For master's, thesis or alternative. *Entrance requirements:* For master's, GRE, MAT, or NTE, BS in education or equivalent, minimum GPA of 3.0.

Converse College, School of Education and Graduate Studies, Program in Secondary Education, Spartanburg, SC 29302-0006. Offers biology (MAT); chemistry (MAT); English (M Ed, MAT); mathematics (M Ed, MAT); natural sciences (M Ed); social sciences (M Ed, MAT). Part-time programs available. *Degree requirements:* For master's, capstone paper. *Entrance requirements:* For master's, NTE or PRAXIS II (M Ed), minimum GPA of 2.75, 2 recommendations. Electronic applications accepted.

Creighton University, Graduate School, College of Arts and Sciences, Department of Education, Program in Teaching, Omaha, NE 68178-0001. Offers elementary teaching (M Ed); secondary teaching (M Ed). Part-time and evening/weekend programs available. *Students:* 15 full-time (11 women), 18 part-time (13 women); includes 2 minority (1 American Indian/Alaska Native, 1 Asian American or Pacific Islander). Average age 26. 2 applicants, 50% accepted, 1 enrolled. In 2009, 17 master's awarded. *Entrance requirements:* For master's, 3 letters of recommendation, 2 writing samples. Additional exam requirements/recommendations for international students: Required—TOEFL (minimum score 550 paper-based; 213 computer-based; 80 iBT). *Application deadline:* For fall admission, 7/1 priority date for domestic students, 3/1 priority date for international students; for winter admission, 12/1 priority date for domestic students, 6/1 priority date for international students; for spring admission, 3/1 priority date for domestic and international students. Applications are processed on a rolling basis. Application fee: $50. Electronic applications accepted. *Expenses:* Tuition: Full-time $11,700; part-time $650 per credit hour. Required fees: $126 per semester. *Financial support:* Scholarships/grants and tuition waivers (partial) available. Support available to part-time students. Financial award applicants required to submit FAFSA. *Unit head:* Fr. Tom Simonds, Director, 402-280-3602, E-mail: thomassimonds@creighton.edu. *Application contact:* Taunya Plater, Senior Program Coordinator, 402-280-2870, Fax: 402-280-2899, E-mail: taunyaplater@creighton.edu.

Dakota Wesleyan University, Program in Education, Mitchell, SD 57301-4398. Offers curriculum and instruction (MA Ed); education (MA); educational policy and administration (MA Ed); pre K-12 principal with certification (MA Ed); secondary with certification (MA Ed). Part-time and evening/weekend programs available. *Faculty:* 12 part-time/adjunct (7 women). *Students:* 31 part-time (15 women); includes 4 African Americans. Average age 30. 9 applicants, 100% accepted, 9 enrolled. In 2009, 14 master's awarded. *Degree requirements:* For master's, comprehensive exam, thesis optional, electronic portfolio. *Entrance requirements:* For master's, minimum GPA of 2.7, elementary statistics course. Additional exam requirements/recommendations for international students: Required—TOEFL (minimum score 500 paper-based; 71 computer-based), IELTS (minimum score 6.5). *Application deadline:* For fall admission, 8/1 priority date for domestic and international students; for winter admission, 12/1 priority date for domestic students; for spring admission, 4/1 priority date for domestic students, 12/1 priority date for international students. Applications are processed on a rolling basis. Application fee: $50. Electronic applications accepted. *Expenses:* Tuition: Full-time $5400; part-time $300 per credit hour. *Faculty research:* Math, political policy, technology in the classroom. *Unit head:* Dr. Ruth Haidle, Director of Graduate Studies, 605-995-2630, Fax: 605-995-2609, E-mail: ruhaidle@dwv.edu. *Application contact:* Coordinator of Graduate Admissions, 800-333-8506, Fax: 605-995-2699, E-mail: admissions@dwv.edu.

Dallas Baptist University, Dorothy M. Bush College of Education, Teaching Program, Dallas, TX 75211-9299. Offers elementary (MAT); English as a second language (MAT); hi-level (MAT); secondary (MAT). Part-time and evening/weekend programs available. *Entrance requirements:* For master's, GRE General Test, minimum GPA of 3.0. Additional exam requirements/recommendations for international students: Required—TOEFL, IELTS. Electronic applications accepted. *Expenses:* Tuition: Full-time $10,674; part-time $593 per credit hour.

Defiance College, Program in Education, Defiance, OH 43512-1610. Offers adolescent and young adult (MA); mild and moderate intervention specialist (MA); sport science (MA). Part-time programs available. *Degree requirements:* For master's, thesis (for some programs). *Entrance requirements:* For master's, teaching certificate.

Delta State University, Graduate Programs, College of Education, Thad Cochran Center for Rural School Leadership and Research, Program in Administration and Supervision, Cleveland, MS 38733-0001. Offers educational administration and supervision (Ed S); educational leadership (M Ed); elementary education (Ed S); secondary education (Ed S). *Accreditation:* NCATE. Part-time and evening/weekend programs available. *Degree requirements:* For master's, thesis optional. *Entrance requirements:* For master's, GRE General Test or MAT; for Ed S, master's degree, teaching certificate. *Expenses:* Tuition, state resident: full-time $4450; part-time $247 per credit hour. Tuition, nonresident: full-time $11,520; part-time $640 per credit hour.

DePaul University, School of Education, Chicago, IL 60106. Offers bilingual and bicultural education (M Ed, MA); curriculum studies (M Ed, MA, Ed D); educational leadership (M Ed, MA, Ed D), including administration and supervision (M Ed, MA), Catholic school leadership (M Ed, MA), physical education (M Ed, MA); human development and learning (MA); human services and counseling (M Ed, MA), including agencies, family concerns, and higher education, elementary schools, human services management, secondary schools; reading and learning disabilities (M Ed, MA); social culture studies in education and development (M Ed, MA), including curriculum studies/development; teaching and learning (early childhood, elementary and secondary) (M Ed), including elementary education (M Ed, MA), secondary education (M Ed, MA); teaching and learning (early childhood, elementary, and secondary) (MA), including elementary education (M Ed, MA), secondary education (M Ed, MA). *Accreditation:* NCATE. Part-time and evening/weekend programs available. *Faculty:* 61 full-time (40 women), 66 part-time/adjunct (41 women). *Students:* 799 full-time (779 women), 470 part-time (365 women); includes 319 minority (153 African Americans, 3 American Indian/Alaska Native, 48 Asian Americans or Pacific Islanders, 115 Hispanic Americans), 15 international. Average age 30. 635 applicants, 74% accepted, 318 enrolled. In 2009, 604 master's, 5 doctorates awarded. *Degree requirements:* For doctorate, thesis/dissertation. *Entrance requirements:* For master's, interview, minimum GPA of 2.75, 2 letters of recommendation; for doctorate, interview, master's degree, writing sample, 3 letters of recommendation. Additional exam requirements/recommendations for international students: Required—TOEFL (minimum score 550 paper-based; 213 computer-based; 80 iBT). *Application deadline:* Applications are processed on a rolling basis. Application fee: $40. Electronic applications accepted. *Expenses:* Tuition: Full-time $37,525; part-time $620 per credit hour. *Financial support:* In 2009–10, 14 research assistantships with tuition reimbursements (averaging $5,800 per year) were awarded; career-related internships or fieldwork also available. *Faculty research:* Reflective teaching, children at risk, loss, ethnicity, urban education. Total annual research expenditures: $1.6 million. *Unit head:* Dr. Marie Donovan, Dean, 773-325-7581, Fax: 773-325-7713, E-mail: mdonovan@depaul.edu. *Application contact:* Brandon Washington, Data Project Manager, 773-325-1152, Fax: 773-325-2270, E-mail: bwashin3@depaul.edu.

Dowling College, Graduate Programs in Education, Oakdale, NY 11769-1999. Offers adolescence education (MS Ed), including educational administration; advanced certificate in gifted education (AC); childhood and early childhood education (MS Ed); childhood education (MS Ed); educational administration (AC, PD), including computers in education (PD), school administration and supervision (PD), school district administration (PD); educational technology specialist (AC); literacy (MS Ed); literacy/special education (MS Ed); secondary education (MS Ed); special education (MS Ed). *Accreditation:* NCATE. Part-time and evening/weekend programs available. Postbaccalaureate distance learning degree programs offered. *Faculty:* 32 full-time (18 women), 98 part-time/adjunct (59 women). *Students:* 563 full-time (393 women), 885 part-time (668 women); includes 133 minority (47 African Americans, 2 American Indian/Alaska Native, 10 Asian Americans or Pacific Islanders, 74 Hispanic Americans). Average age 32. 363 applicants, 89% accepted, 213 enrolled. In 2009, 459 master's, 85 ACs awarded. *Degree requirements:* For master's and other advanced degree, comprehensive exam. *Entrance requirements:* For master's, minimum GPA of 3.0; for other advanced degree, teaching certificate. Additional exam requirements/recommendations for international students: Required—TOEFL (minimum score 550 paper-based). *Application deadline:* For fall admission, 9/1 priority date for domestic students; for winter admission, 1/1 priority date for domestic students; for spring admission, 2/1 priority date for domestic students. Applications are processed on a rolling basis. Application fee: $50. Electronic applications accepted. *Expenses:* Tuition: Full-time $14,490; part-time $805 per credit. Required fees: $346 per term. *Financial support:* Career-related internships or fieldwork and Federal Work-Study available. Support available to part-time students. Financial award application deadline: 6/30; financial award applicants required to submit FAFSA. *Faculty research:* Natural readers, Korean styles and learning strategies, mothers of children with disabilities, computers in instruction, cultural background and organizational roadblocks to problem solving. *Unit head:* Dr. Clyde Payne, Dean of the School of Education, 631-244-3404, Fax: 631-589-6644, E-mail: paynec@dowling.edu. *Application contact:* Glenn M. Berman, Assistant Vice President for Enrollment Services/Dean of Admissions, 631-244-3357, Fax: 631-244-1059, E-mail: glenn.berman@dowling.edu.

Drury University, Graduate Programs in Education, Springfield, MO 65802. Offers elementary education (M Ed); gifted education (M Ed); human services (M Ed); instructional mathematics K-8 (M Ed); instructional technology (M Ed); middle school teaching (M Ed); secondary education (M Ed); special education (M Ed); special reading (M Ed). *Accreditation:* NCATE. Part-time and evening/weekend programs available. *Degree requirements:* For master's, thesis. *Entrance requirements:* For master's, GRE or MAT, minimum GPA of 2.75. Additional exam requirements/recommendations for international students: Required—TOEFL. Electronic applications accepted. *Faculty research:* Cultural enrichment, research skills, parental involvement relating to reading skills, reading strategies for mainstreaming children.

Duquesne University, School of Education, Department of Instruction and Leadership, Program in Secondary Education, Pittsburgh, PA 15282-0001. Offers secondary education (MS Ed), including biology, chemistry, English, Latin, math, physics, social studies, Spanish. Part-time and evening/weekend programs available. *Faculty:* 4 full-time (3 women), 1 part-time/adjunct (0 women). *Students:* 56 full-time (34 women), 8 part-time (3 women); includes 6 minority (3 African Americans, 2 Asian Americans or Pacific Islanders, 1 Hispanic American), 2 international. Average age 29. 69 applicants, 70% accepted, 27 enrolled. In 2009, 36 master's awarded. *Degree requirements:* For master's, thesis optional. *Entrance requirements:* For master's, MAT, minimum GPA of 3.0. Additional exam requirements/recommendations for international students: Required—TOEFL (minimum score 550 paper-based; 80 computer-based). *Application deadline:* For fall admission, 8/1 for domestic students; for spring admission, 12/1 for domestic students. Applications are processed on a rolling basis. Application fee: $0. Electronic applications accepted. *Expenses:* Tuition: Part-time $851 per credit. Required fees: $81 per credit. *Financial support:* Research assistantships, Federal Work-Study available. Support available to part-time students. *Unit head:* Dr. Melissa Boston, Assistant Professor, 412-396-6109, E-mail: bostonm@duq.edu. *Application contact:* Michael Dolinger, Director of Student and Academic Services, 412-396-6647, Fax: 412-396-5585, E-mail: dolingerm@duq.edu.

D'Youville College, Department of Education, Buffalo, NY 14201-1084. Offers elementary education (MS Ed, Teaching Certificate); secondary education (MS Ed, Teaching Certificate); special education (MS Ed). Part-time and evening/weekend programs available. *Degree requirements:* For master's, one foreign language, comprehensive exam, project or thesis. *Entrance requirements:* For master's, GRE (if GPA less than 2.75), minimum GPA of 3.0. Additional exam requirements/recommendations for international students: Required—TOEFL (minimum score 500 paper-based; 173 computer-based). Electronic applications accepted. *Faculty research:* Developmental disabilities, multiculturalism, early childhood education.

Eastern Connecticut State University, School of Education and Professional Studies/Graduate Division, Program in Secondary Education, Willimantic, CT 06226-2295. Offers MS. *Accreditation:* NCATE. Part-time and evening/weekend programs available. *Degree requirements:* For master's, comprehensive exam or thesis. *Entrance requirements:* For master's, PRAXIS I and II, minimum GPA of 2.7. Additional exam requirements/recommendations for international students: Required—TOEFL (minimum score 550 paper-based; 213 computer-based).

Eastern Kentucky University, The Graduate School, College of Education, Department of Curriculum and Instruction, Program in Secondary and Higher Education, Richmond, KY 40475-3102. Offers secondary education (MA Ed), including agricultural education, art education, biological sciences education, business education, English education, geography education, history education, home economics education, industrial education, mathematical sciences education, physical education, school health education. *Accreditation:* NCATE. Part-time programs available. *Entrance requirements:* For master's, GRE General Test, minimum GPA of 2.5.

Eastern Michigan University, Graduate School, College of Education, Department of Teacher Education, Program in K–12 Education, Ypsilanti, MI 48197. Offers curriculum and instruction (MA); elementary education (MA); K-12 education (MA); middle school education (MA); secondary school education (MA). *Accreditation:* NCATE. Part-time and evening/weekend

Secondary Education

Eastern Michigan University (continued)

programs available. Postbaccalaureate distance learning degree programs offered (minimal on-campus study). *Students:* 18 full-time (10 women), 103 part-time (83 women); includes 20 minority (11 African Americans, 2 American Indian/Alaska Native, 3 Asian Americans or Pacific Islanders, 4 Hispanic Americans), 1 international. Average age 36. In 2009, 10 master's awarded. *Entrance requirements:* For master's, GRE. Additional exam requirements/recommendations for international students: Required—TOEFL. *Application deadline:* Applications are processed on a rolling basis. Application fee: $35. Tuition and fees vary according to course level. *Financial support:* Fellowships, research assistantships with full tuition reimbursements, teaching assistantships with full tuition reimbursements, career-related internships or fieldwork, Federal Work-Study, institutionally sponsored loans, scholarships/grants, tuition waivers (partial), and unspecified assistantships available. Support available to part-time students. Financial award applicants required to submit FAFSA. *Unit head:* Dr. Wendy Burke, Coordinator, 734-487-3260, Fax: 734-487-2101, E-mail: wendy.burke@emich.edu. *Application contact:* Dr. Wendy Burke, Coordinator, 734-487-3260, Fax: 734-487-2101, E-mail: wendy.burke@emich.edu.

Eastern Nazarene College, Adult and Graduate Studies, Division of Education, Quincy, MA 02170. Offers early childhood education (M Ed, Certificate); elementary education (M Ed, Certificate); English as a second language (M Ed, Certificate); instructional enrichment and development (M Ed, Certificate); middle school education (M Ed, Certificate); moderate special needs education (M Ed, Certificate); principal (Certificate); program development and supervision (M Ed, Certificate); secondary education (M Ed, Certificate); special education administrator (Certificate); supervisor (Certificate); teacher of reading (M Ed, Certificate). M Ed and Certificate also available through weekend program for administration, special needs, and reading only. Part-time and evening/weekend programs available. *Entrance requirements:* Additional exam requirements/recommendations for international students: Required—TOEFL (minimum score 550 paper-based).

Eastern Oregon University, School of Education and Business, Program in Secondary Education, La Grande, OR 97850-2899. Offers MTE. Part-time programs available. Postbaccalaureate distance learning degree programs offered (minimal on-campus study). *Degree requirements:* For master's, thesis. *Entrance requirements:* For master's, NTE.

East Stroudsburg University of Pennsylvania, Graduate School, College of Education, Department of Professional and Secondary Education, East Stroudsburg, PA 18301-2999. Offers M Ed. *Accreditation:* NCATE. Part-time and evening/weekend programs available. *Faculty:* 10 full-time (3 women), 5 part-time/adjunct (1 woman). *Students:* 63 full-time (37 women), 160 part-time (96 women); includes 20 minority (7 African Americans, 1 American Indian/Alaska Native, 1 Asian American or Pacific Islander, 11 Hispanic Americans). Average age 33. In 2009, 42 master's awarded. *Degree requirements:* For master's, independent research problem or comprehensive assessment portfolio. *Entrance requirements:* For master's, PRAXIS/teacher certification, letter of recommendation, Pennsylvania Department of Education requirements. Additional exam requirements/recommendations for international students: Required—TOEFL (minimum score 560 paper-based; 220 computer-based; 83 iBT). *Application deadline:* For fall admission, 7/31 priority date for domestic students, 5/1 priority date for international students; for spring admission, 11/30 for domestic students, 10/1 for international students. Applications are processed on a rolling basis. Application fee: $50. *Expenses:* Tuition, state resident: full-time $9942; part-time $387 per credit. Tuition, nonresident: full-time $14,240; part-time $619 per credit. *Financial support:* In 2009–10, 16 research assistantships with full and partial tuition reimbursements (averaging $1,907 per year) were awarded; career-related internships or fieldwork, Federal Work-Study, and institutionally sponsored loans also available. Financial award application deadline: 3/1; financial award applicants required to submit FAFSA. *Unit head:* Dr. Jeffrey T. Scheetz, Graduate Coordinator, 570-422-3361, Fax: 570-422-3506, E-mail: jscheetz@po-box.esu.edu. *Application contact:* Kevin Quintero, Graduate Admissions Coordinator, 570-422-3890, Fax: 570-422-2711, E-mail: kquintero@po-box.esu.edu.

East Tennessee State University, School of Graduate Studies, College of Education, Department of Curriculum and Instruction, Johnson City, TN 37614. Offers 7-12 (MAT); classroom technology (M Ed); educational communication (M Ed); educational media/educational technology (M Ed); elementary education (M Ed, MAT); K-12 (MAT); reading and storytelling (M Ed, MA); reading education (M Ed, MA); school library media (M Ed); secondary education (M Ed, MAT). *Accreditation:* NCATE. Part-time and evening/weekend programs available. *Degree requirements:* For master's, thesis (for some programs). *Entrance requirements:* For master's, GRE, minimum GPA of 3.0. Additional exam requirements/recommendations for international students: Required—TOEFL (minimum score 550 paper-based; 213 computer-based). *Faculty research:* Critical thinking, curriculum development, cultural diversity, cognitive processes, effective teaching strategies.

Elms College, Division of Education, Chicopee, MA 01013-2839. Offers early childhood education (MAT); education (M Ed, CAGS); elementary education (MAT); English as a second language (MAT); reading (MAT); secondary education (MAT), including biology education, English education, Spanish education; special education (MAT). Part-time and evening/weekend programs available. *Faculty:* 12 full-time (8 women), 4 part-time/adjunct (2 women). *Students:* 17 full-time (14 women), 153 part-time (136 women); includes 5 minority (1 American Indian/Alaska Native, 4 Hispanic Americans). Average age 36. 43 applicants, 88% accepted, 37 enrolled. In 2009, 23 master's, 8 other advanced degrees awarded. *Degree requirements:* For master's, thesis (for some programs). *Entrance requirements:* For master's, Massachusetts Educators Certification Test, minimum GPA of 3.0; for CAGS, master's degree in education. Additional exam requirements/recommendations for international students: Required—TOEFL. *Application deadline:* For fall admission, 7/1 priority date for domestic students; for spring admission, 11/1 priority date for domestic students. Applications are processed on a rolling basis. Application fee: $30. *Financial support:* In 2009–10, 2 teaching assistantships with partial tuition reimbursements were awarded; tuition waivers (partial) also available. Support available to part-time students. Financial award applicants required to submit FAFSA. *Unit head:* Dr. Mary Janeczek, Director, 413-594-2761, Fax: 413-592-4871, E-mail: janeczeke@elms.edu. *Application contact:* Dana Malone, Associate Director for Graduate Studies and Continuing Education, 413-265-2445, Fax: 413-265-2459, E-mail: maloned@elms.edu.

Emmanuel College, Graduate Programs, Programs in Education, Boston, MA 02115. Offers educational leadership (CAGS); elementary education (MAT); school administration (M Ed); secondary education (MAT). Part-time and evening/weekend programs available. *Faculty:* 6 part-time/adjunct (2 women). *Students:* 6 full-time (5 women), 46 part-time (33 women); includes 8 minority (4 African Americans, 4 Hispanic Americans). Average age 33. 16 applicants, 56% accepted, 9 enrolled. In 2009, 23 master's awarded. *Entrance requirements:* For master's, interview, resume, 2 letters of recommendation, essay, bachelor's degree; for CAGS, interview, leadership statement, resume, 2 letters of recommendation. Additional exam requirements/recommendations for international students: Required—TOEFL (minimum score 600 paper-based; 250 computer-based). *Application deadline:* For fall admission, 8/15 priority date for domestic students; for spring admission, 12/8 priority date for domestic students. Applications are processed on a rolling basis. Application fee: $50. Electronic applications accepted. *Expenses:* Tuition: Part-time $665 per credit. *Faculty research:* Literature/reading, history of education, multicultural education, special education. *Unit head:* Dr. Judith Marley, Dean, Graduate and Professional Programs, 617-735-9700, Fax: 617-507-0434, E-mail: gpp@emmanuel.edu. *Application contact:* Enrollment Counselor, 617-735-9700, Fax: 617-507-0434, E-mail: gpp@emmanuel.edu.

Emory University, Graduate School of Arts and Sciences, Division of Educational Studies, Atlanta, GA 30322-1100. Offers educational studies (MA, PhD, DAST); middle grades teaching (M Ed, MAT); secondary teaching (M Ed, MAT). *Accreditation:* NCATE. Terminal master's awarded for partial completion of doctoral program. *Degree requirements:* For master's, thesis; for doctorate, comprehensive exam, thesis/dissertation. *Entrance requirements:* For master's and doctorate, GRE General Test, minimum GPA of 3.0. Additional exam requirements/

recommendations for international students: Required—TOEFL. Electronic applications accepted. *Faculty research:* Educational policy, educational measurement, urban and multicultural education, mathematics and science education, comparative education.

Emporia State University, School of Graduate Studies, The Teachers College, Department of Early Childhood/Elementary Teacher Education, Program in Master Teacher, Emporia, KS 66801-5087. Offers elementary subject matter (MS); English as a second language (MS); reading (MS); secondary subject matter (MS). *Accreditation:* NCATE. Part-time programs available. *Students:* 3 full-time (all women), 87 part-time (84 women); includes 6 minority (1 African American, 1 American Indian/Alaska Native, 2 Asian Americans or Pacific Islanders, 2 Hispanic Americans). 14 applicants, 100% accepted, 12 enrolled. In 2009, 40 master's awarded. *Degree requirements:* For master's, comprehensive exam or thesis, practicum. *Entrance requirements:* For master's, GRE General Test or MAT, graduate essay exam, appropriate bachelor's degree, letters of recommendation. Additional exam requirements/recommendations for international students: Required—TOEFL (minimum score 520 paper-based; 133 computer-based; 68 iBT). *Application deadline:* For fall admission, 8/15 priority date for domestic students. Applications are processed on a rolling basis. Application fee: $30 ($75 for international students). Electronic applications accepted. *Expenses:* Tuition, state resident: full-time $4154; part-time $173 per credit hour. Tuition, nonresident: full-time $12,864; part-time $536 per credit hour. Required fees: $948; $58 per credit hour. Tuition and fees vary according to campus/location. *Financial support:* Federal Work-Study, institutionally sponsored loans, health care benefits, and unspecified assistantships available. Financial award application deadline: 3/15; financial award applicants required to submit FAFSA. *Unit head:* Dr. Jean Morrow, Chair, 620-341-5766, E-mail: jmorrow@emporia.edu. *Application contact:* Mary Sewell, Admissions Coordinator, 800-950-GRAD, Fax: 620-341-5909, E-mail: msewell@emporia.edu.

Evangel University, Department of Education, Springfield, MO 65802. Offers educational leadership (M Ed); reading education (M Ed); secondary teaching (M Ed); teaching (MA). *Accreditation:* NCATE. Part-time and evening/weekend programs available. *Faculty:* 4 full-time (2 women), 5 part-time/adjunct (3 women). *Students:* 10 full-time (6 women), 40 part-time (31 women). Average age 33. 14 applicants, 86% accepted, 11 enrolled. In 2009, 23 master's awarded. *Degree requirements:* For master's, comprehensive exam, thesis optional. *Entrance requirements:* For master's, PRAXIS II (preferred) or GRE. Additional exam requirements/recommendations for international students: Required—TOEFL (minimum score 550 paper-based; 213 computer-based). *Application deadline:* For fall admission, 7/15 priority date for domestic students; for spring admission, 11/15 priority date for domestic students. Applications are processed on a rolling basis. Application fee: $25. *Financial support:* In 2009–10, 3 students received support. Career-related internships or fieldwork, institutionally sponsored loans, and scholarships/grants available. Support available to part-time students. Financial award application deadline: 3/1; financial award applicants required to submit FAFSA. *Unit head:* Dr. Colleen Hardy, Program Coordinator, 417-865-2815 Ext. 8553, E-mail: hardyc@evangel.edu. *Application contact:* Charity H. Fahlstrom, Admissions Representative, Graduate and Professional Studies, 417-865-2811 Ext. 7227, Fax: 417-865-9599.

Fairfield University, Graduate School of Education and Allied Professions, Department of Curriculum and Instruction, Fairfield, CT 06824-5195. Offers bilingual education (CAS); elementary education (MA); media/educational technology (MA); secondary education (MA); teaching and foundations (MA, CAS); TESOL, foreign language and bilingual/multicultural education (MA, CAS). Part-time and evening/weekend programs available. *Degree requirements:* For master's, comprehensive exam, thesis or alternative. *Entrance requirements:* For master's, PRAXIS I (PPST), minimum QPA of 3.0, 2 recommendations, resume. Additional exam requirements/recommendations for international students: Required—TOEFL (minimum score 550 paper-based; 213 computer-based; 80 iBT). Electronic applications accepted. *Faculty research:* Urban and multicultural education; participatory action for social justice; culture and family; second language acquisition; science, technology and social education.

Fayetteville State University, Graduate School, Program in Middle Grades, Secondary and Special Education, Fayetteville, NC 28301-4298. Offers biology (MA Ed); history (MA Ed); mathematics (MA Ed); middle grades (MA Ed); political science (MA Ed); reading (MA Ed); sociology (MA Ed); special education (MA Ed), including behavioral-emotional handicaps, mentally handicapped, specific training disability. *Accreditation:* NCATE. Part-time and evening/weekend programs available. *Faculty:* 15 full-time (10 women), 3 part-time/adjunct (2 women). *Students:* 16 full-time (12 women), 70 part-time (57 women); includes 55 minority (50 African Americans, 1 American Indian/Alaska Native, 1 Asian American or Pacific Islander, 3 Hispanic Americans). Average age 35. 14 applicants, 100% accepted, 14 enrolled. In 2009, 32 master's awarded. *Degree requirements:* For master's, comprehensive exam, internship. *Application deadline:* For fall admission, 4/15 for domestic students; for spring admission, 10/15 for domestic students. Applications are processed on a rolling basis. Application fee: $35. Electronic applications accepted. *Unit head:* Dr. Charletta Barringer-Brown, Interim Chair, 910-672-1182, E-mail: cbarringerbrown@uncfsu.edu. *Application contact:* Roxie Shabazz, Associate Vice-Chancellor for Enrollment Management, 910-672-1784, Fax: 910-672-2209, E-mail: rshabazz@uncfsu.edu.

Fitchburg State University, Division of Graduate and Continuing Education, Program in Secondary Education, Fitchburg, MA 01420-2697. Offers M Ed. *Accreditation:* NCATE. Part-time and evening/weekend programs available. *Students:* 7 full-time (5 women), 15 part-time (8 women), 1 international. Average age 35. 5 applicants, 100% accepted, 5 enrolled. In 2009, 11 master's awarded. *Entrance requirements:* For master's, GRE General Test or MAT, teaching certificate, letters of recommendation, resume. Additional exam requirements/recommendations for international students: Required—TOEFL (minimum score 550 paper-based; 213 computer-based; 79 iBT). *Application deadline:* Applications are processed on a rolling basis. Application fee: $25 ($50 for international students). *Expenses:* Tuition, area resident: Part-time $150 per credit. Tuition, state resident: part-time $150 per credit. Tuition, nonresident: part-time $150 per credit. Required fees: $120 per credit. *Financial support:* In 2009–10, research assistantships with partial tuition reimbursements (averaging $5,500 per year); Federal Work-Study, scholarships/grants, and unspecified assistantships also available. Support available to part-time students. Financial award application deadline: 3/1; financial award applicants required to submit FAFSA. *Unit head:* Dr. Nancy Kelly, Chair, 978-665-3447, Fax: 978-665-3658, E-mail: gce@fsc.edu. *Application contact:* Director of Admissions, 978-665-3144, Fax: 978-665-4540, E-mail: admissions@fsc.edu.

Florida Agricultural and Mechanical University, Division of Graduate Studies, Research, and Continuing Education, College of Education, Program in Secondary Education and Foundation, Tallahassee, FL 32307-3200. Offers biology (M Ed); chemistry (MS Ed); English (MS Ed); history (MS Ed); math (MS Ed); physics (MS Ed). *Accreditation:* NCATE. *Faculty:* 10 full-time (5 women). In 2009, 28 master's awarded. *Degree requirements:* For master's, thesis (for some programs). *Entrance requirements:* For master's, GRE General Test, minimum GPA of 3.0. Additional exam requirements/recommendations for international students: Required—TOEFL. *Application deadline:* For fall admission, 5/18 for domestic students, 12/18 for international students; for spring admission, 11/12 for domestic students, 5/12 for international students. Application fee: $20. *Unit head:* Dr. Bernadette Kelley, Chairperson, 850-599-3123. *Application contact:* Dr. Chanta M. Haywood, Dean of Graduate Studies, Research, and Continuing Education, 850-599-3315, Fax: 850-599-3727.

Fordham University, Graduate School of Education, Division of Curriculum and Teaching, New York, NY 10023. Offers adult education (MS, MSE); bilingual teacher education (MSE); curriculum and teaching (MSE); early childhood education (MSE); elementary education (MST); language, literacy, and learning (PhD); reading education (MSE, Adv C); secondary education (MAT, MSE); special education (MSE, Adv C); teaching English as a second language (MSE). *Accreditation:* NCATE. *Degree requirements:* For doctorate, thesis/dissertation; for Adv C, thesis. *Entrance requirements:* For doctorate, MAT, GRE General Test.

Francis Marion University, Graduate Programs, School of Education, Florence, SC 29502-0547. Offers early childhood education (M Ed); elementary education (M Ed); learning disabilities (M Ed, MAT); remedial education (M Ed); secondary education (M Ed). *Accreditation:*

NCATE. Part-time programs available. *Faculty:* 20 full-time (15 women). *Students:* 8 full-time (7 women), 107 part-time (90 women); includes 33 minority (all African Americans), 1 international. Average age 34. 221 applicants, 94% accepted, 94 enrolled. In 2009, 57 degrees awarded. *Degree requirements:* For master's, comprehensive exam. *Entrance requirements:* For master's, GRE General Test, MAT, NTE, or PRAXIS II. *Application deadline:* For fall admission, 3/15 priority date for domestic students; for spring admission, 10/15 priority date for domestic students. Applications are processed on a rolling basis. Application fee: $30. *Expenses:* Tuition, state resident: full-time $8345; part-time $417.25 per semester hour. Tuition, nonresident: full-time $16,690; part-time $814.50 per semester hour. Required fees: $335; $12.25 per semester hour. $30 per semester. *Financial support:* In 2009–10, 4 research assistantships (averaging $6,000 per year) were awarded; unspecified assistantships also available. Support available to part-time students. Financial award application deadline: 3/1; financial award applicants required to submit FAFSA. *Faculty research:* Identification and alternate assessment of at-risk students. *Unit head:* Dr. James R. Faulkenberry, Dean, 843-661-1460, Fax: 843-661-4647. *Application contact:* Dr. James R. Faulkenberry, Dean, 843-661-1460, Fax: 843-661-4647.

Fresno Pacific University, Graduate Programs, School of Education, Division of Mathematics/Science/Computer Education, Program in Mathematics Education, Fresno, CA 93702-4709. Offers elementary and middle school mathematics (MA Ed); secondary school mathematics (MA Ed). Part-time and evening/weekend programs available. *Degree requirements:* For master's, thesis or alternative. *Entrance requirements:* Additional exam requirements/recommendations for international students: Required—TOEFL (minimum score 550 paper-based; 213 computer-based).

Friends University, Graduate School, Division of Science, Arts, and Education, Program in Teaching, Wichita, KS 67213. Offers elementary education (MAT); secondary education (MAT). *Accreditation:* NCATE. Evening/weekend programs available. Postbaccalaureate distance learning degree programs offered (minimal on-campus study). *Entrance requirements:* Additional exam requirements/recommendations for international students: Required—TOEFL (minimum score 560 paper-based; 220 computer-based; 83 iBT), IELTS (minimum score 6). Electronic applications accepted.

Frostburg State University, Graduate School, College of Education, Department of Educational Professions, Program in Curriculum and Instruction, Frostburg, MD 21532-1099. Offers educational technology (M Ed); elementary education (M Ed); secondary education (M Ed). Part-time and evening/weekend programs available. *Faculty:* 2. *Students:* 5 full-time (all women), 42 part-time (36 women); includes 1 minority (Hispanic American). Average age 32. 20 applicants, 75% accepted, 13 enrolled. In 2009, 8 master's awarded. *Degree requirements:* For master's, thesis or alternative. *Entrance requirements:* For master's, teaching certificate. Additional exam requirements/recommendations for international students: Required—TOEFL. *Application deadline:* For fall admission, 7/15 priority date for domestic students. Applications are processed on a rolling basis. Application fee: $30. Electronic applications accepted. *Expenses:* Tuition, state resident: full-time $5706; part-time $317 per credit hour. Tuition, nonresident: full-time $6948; part-time $386 per credit hour. Required fees: $1476; $82 per credit hour. $11 per term. One-time fee: $30 full-time. *Financial support:* In 2009–10, 2 research assistantships with full tuition reimbursements (averaging $5,000 per year) were awarded. Financial award application deadline: 4/1; financial award applicants required to submit FAFSA. *Unit head:* Dr. Doris Santamaria-Makang, Coordinator, 301-687-7018, E-mail: dsantamaria@frostburg.edu. *Application contact:* Vickie Mazer, Director, Graduate Services, 301-687-7053, Fax: 301-687-4597, E-mail: vmmazer@frostburg.edu.

Frostburg State University, Graduate School, College of Education, Department of Educational Professions, Program in Secondary Teaching, Frostburg, MD 21532-1099. Offers MAT. *Faculty:* 7. *Students:* 44 full-time (32 women); includes 3 minority (1 African American, 2 Hispanic Americans). Average age 28. 63 applicants, 63% accepted, 39 enrolled. In 2009, 34 master's awarded. *Entrance requirements:* For master's, PRAXIS I, entry portfolio. Additional exam requirements/recommendations for international students: Required—TOEFL. *Expenses:* Tuition, state resident: full-time $5706; part-time $317 per credit hour. Tuition, nonresident: full-time $6948; part-time $386 per credit hour. Required fees: $1476; $82 per credit hour. $11 per term. One-time fee: $30 full-time. *Financial support:* In 2009–10, 1 research assistantship was awarded. *Unit head:* Dr. Marcia Cushall, Coordinator, 301-687-4308, E-mail: mcushall@frostburg.edu. *Application contact:* Vickie Mazer, Director, Graduate Services, 301-687-7053, Fax: 301-687-4597, E-mail: vmmazer@frostburg.edu.

Gallaudet University, The Graduate School, Department of Education, Washington, DC 20002-3625. Offers early childhood education (MA, Ed S); education of deaf and hard of hearing students and multihandicapped deaf and hard of hearing students (MA, Ed S); elementary education (MA, Ed S); individualized program of study (PhD); parent/infant specialty (MA, Ed S); secondary education (MA, Ed S). *Accreditation:* NCATE. *Degree requirements:* For master's, thesis optional; for doctorate, thesis/dissertation. *Entrance requirements:* For doctorate, GRE General Test or MAT, interview. Electronic applications accepted.

George Fox University, School of Education, Educational Foundations and Leadership Program, Newberg, OR 97132-2697. Offers continuing administrator license (Certificate); curriculum and instruction (M Ed); educational leadership (M Ed, Ed D); higher education (M Ed); initial administrator license (Certificate); library media (M Ed, Certificate); literacy (M Ed); reading (M Ed); secondary education (M Ed). *Accreditation:* NCATE. Part-time and evening/weekend programs available. Postbaccalaureate distance learning degree programs offered (minimal on-campus study). *Faculty:* 10 full-time (3 women), 7 part-time/adjunct (3 women). *Students:* 1 (woman) full-time, 151 part-time (101 women); includes 15 minority (1 African American, 4 American Indian/Alaska Native, 4 Asian Americans or Pacific Islanders, 6 Hispanic Americans), 1 international. Average age 40. 44 applicants, 75% accepted, 26 enrolled. In 2009, 44 master's, 27 doctorates, 82 Certificates awarded. *Degree requirements:* For master's, thesis (for some programs); for doctorate, comprehensive exam, thesis/dissertation, project. *Entrance requirements:* For master's, minimum undergraduate GPA of 3.0 during previous 2 years of course work, resume, 3 professional recommendations on university forms, copy of teaching license (if applicable); for doctorate, GRE or MAT, master's degree with minimum GPA of 3.25, 3 years of relevant professional experience, interview, personal essay, scholarly work, 3 professional recommendations on university forms along with 3 written letters of recommendation, official transcripts. Additional exam requirements/recommendations for international students: Required—TOEFL (minimum score 577 paper-based; 233 computer-based; 90 iBT). *Application deadline:* For fall admission, 7/15 for domestic and international students; for winter admission, 11/1 for domestic and international students; for spring admission, 4/1 for domestic and international students. Applications are processed on a rolling basis. Application fee: $40. Electronic applications accepted. *Expenses:* Contact institution. *Financial support:* Career-related internships or fieldwork available. Financial award applicants required to submit FAFSA. *Unit head:* Dr. Scott Headley, Chair, 503-554-2836, E-mail: sheadley@georgefox.edu. *Application contact:* Kristie DeHaven, Admissions Counselor, 800-631-0921, Fax: 503-554-3110, E-mail: edfl@georgefox.edu.

The George Washington University, Graduate School of Education and Human Development, Department of Teacher Preparation and Special Education, Program in Secondary Education, Washington, DC 20052. Offers M Ed. Program also offered in Arlington and Ashburn, VA. *Accreditation:* NCATE. *Students:* 43 full-time (25 women), 106 part-time (87 women); includes 33 minority (20 African Americans, 1 American Indian/Alaska Native, 6 Asian Americans or Pacific Islanders, 6 Hispanic Americans), 6 international. Average age 33. 111 applicants, 97% accepted, 67 enrolled. In 2009, 52 master's awarded. *Degree requirements:* For master's, comprehensive exam. *Entrance requirements:* For master's, GRE General Test or MAT, interview, minimum GPA of 2.75. *Application deadline:* For fall admission, 1/15 priority date for domestic students; for spring admission, 10/1 for domestic students. Applications are processed on a rolling basis. Application fee: $60. *Financial support:* Fellowships, career-related internships or fieldwork, Federal Work-Study, tuition waivers (full and partial), and stipends available. Financial award application deadline: 1/15; financial award applicants required to submit FAFSA. *Application contact:* Sarah Lang, Director of Graduate Admissions, 202-994-1447, Fax: 202-994-7207, E-mail: slang@gwu.edu.

Georgia College & State University, Graduate School, The John H. Lounsbury College of Education, Department of Foundations and Secondary Education, Milledgeville, GA 31061. Offers curriculum and instruction (Ed S), including secondary education; instructional technology (M Ed); secondary education (M Ed, MAT). *Accreditation:* NCATE. Part-time and evening/weekend programs available. *Faculty:* 13 full-time (7 women). *Students:* 127 full-time (81 women), 99 part-time (83 women); includes 39 minority (34 African Americans, 5 Hispanic Americans). Average age 32. In 2009, 104 master's awarded. *Degree requirements:* For master's and Ed S, comprehensive exam. *Entrance requirements:* For master's, on-site writing assessment, 2 letters of recommendation, level 4 teaching certificate; for Ed S, on-site writing assessment, master's degree, 2 letters of recommendation, 2 years of teaching experience, level 5 teacher certification. Additional exam requirements/recommendations for international students: Recommended—TOEFL (minimum score 550 paper-based; 213 computer-based; 79 iBT). *Application deadline:* Applications are processed on a rolling basis. Application fee: $40. Electronic applications accepted. *Expenses:* Tuition, area resident: Part-time $241 per credit hour. Tuition, state resident: full-time $4338. Tuition, nonresident: full-time $17,352; part-time $964 per credit hour. Required fees: $609 per semester. Tuition and fees vary according to course load and campus/location. *Financial support:* In 2009–10, 12 research assistantships with full tuition reimbursements were awarded; career-related internships or fieldwork and Federal Work-Study also available. Support available to part-time students. Financial award applicants required to submit FAFSA. *Unit head:* Dr. Jane Hinson, Chair, 478-445-7368, Fax: 478-445-2513, E-mail: jane.hinson@gcsu.edu. *Application contact:* Shanda Brand, Graduate Advisor, 478-445-1383, E-mail: shanda.brand@gcsu.edu.

Georgia Southern University, Jack N. Averitt College of Graduate Studies, College of Education, Department of Teaching and Learning, Program in Secondary and P-12 Education, Statesboro, GA 30460. Offers M Ed. Part-time and evening/weekend programs available. *Degree requirements:* For master's, portfolio, transition point assessments, exit assessment. *Entrance requirements:* For master's, GRE General Test or MAT, minimum cumulative GPA of 2.5. Additional exam requirements/recommendations for international students: Required—TOEFL (minimum score 550 paper-based; 213 computer-based; 80 iBT). *Application deadline:* For fall admission, 3/1 priority date for domestic and international students; for spring admission, 10/1 priority date for domestic students, 10/1 for international students. Applications are processed on a rolling basis. Application fee: $50. Electronic applications accepted. *Expenses:* Tuition, state resident: full-time $5040; part-time $210 per credit hour. Tuition, nonresident: full-time $20,136; part-time $839 per credit hour. Required fees: $1644. *Financial support:* In 2009–10, research assistantships with partial tuition reimbursements (averaging $7,200 per year), teaching assistantships with partial tuition reimbursements (averaging $7,200 per year) were awarded; career-related internships or fieldwork, Federal Work-Study, and tuition waivers (partial) also available. Support available to part-time students. Financial award application deadline: 4/15; financial award applicants required to submit FAFSA. *Unit head:* Dr. Ronnie Sheppard, Chair, 912-478-5203, Fax: 912-478-0026, E-mail: sheppard@georgiasouthern.edu. *Application contact:* Dr. Charles Ziglar, Coordinator for Graduate Student Recruitment, 912-478-5635, Fax: 912-478-0740, E-mail: gradadmissions@georgiasouthern.edu.

Georgia Southwestern State University, Graduate Studies, School of Education, Americus, GA 31709-4693. Offers early childhood education (M Ed, Ed S); health and physical education (M Ed); middle grades education (M Ed, Ed S); reading (M Ed); secondary education (M Ed); special education (M Ed). *Accreditation:* NCATE. *Degree requirements:* For master's, comprehensive exam. *Entrance requirements:* For master's, GRE General Test or MAT, minimum GPA of 2.5; for Ed S, GRE General Test or MAT, minimum graduate GPA of 3.25, M Ed from accredited college or university, 3 years teaching experience. Electronic applications accepted.

Georgia State University, College of Education, Department of Middle-Secondary Education and Instructional Technology, Programs in Secondary Education, Atlanta, GA 30302-3083. Offers art education (Ed S); English education (M Ed, Ed S); mathematics education (M Ed, PhD, Ed S); music education (PhD); science education (M Ed, PhD, Ed S); social studies education (M Ed, PhD, Ed S). *Accreditation:* NASM (one or more programs are accredited); NCATE. Part-time and evening/weekend programs available. *Degree requirements:* For master's, comprehensive exam; for doctorate, comprehensive exam, thesis/dissertation; for Ed S, project/exam. *Entrance requirements:* For master's, GRE General Test, minimum GPA of 2.5; for doctorate, GRE General Test or MAT, minimum GPA of 3.3; for Ed S, GRE General Test or MAT, minimum graduate GPA of 3.25. *Faculty research:* Women and science, problem solving in mathematics, dialects, economic education.

Grand Canyon University, College of Education, Phoenix, AZ 85017-1097. Offers curriculum and instruction (M Ed); education administration (M Ed); elementary education (M Ed); organizational leadership (Ed D); secondary education (M Ed); special education (M Ed); teaching (MA). Part-time and evening/weekend programs available. Postbaccalaureate distance learning degree programs offered (no on-campus study). *Degree requirements:* For master's, publishable research paper (M Ed), e-portfolio. *Entrance requirements:* Additional exam requirements/recommendations for international students: Required—TOEFL (minimum score 550 paper-based; 213 computer-based; 79 iBT), IELTS (minimum score 6). Electronic applications accepted.

Grand Valley State University, College of Education, Programs in General Education, Allendale, MI 49401-9403. Offers adult and higher education (M Ed); early childhood education (M Ed); educational differentiation (M Ed); educational leadership (M Ed); educational technology integration (M Ed); elementary education (M Ed); middle level education (M Ed); school library media services (M Ed); secondary level education (M Ed); teaching English to speakers of other languages (M Ed). Part-time and evening/weekend programs available. Postbaccalaureate distance learning degree programs offered (minimal on-campus study). *Faculty:* 82 full-time (42 women), 43 part-time/adjunct (25 women). *Students:* 100 full-time (53 women), 723 part-time (478 women); includes 59 minority (25 African Americans, 4 American Indian/Alaska Native, 13 Asian Americans or Pacific Islanders, 17 Hispanic Americans), 10 international. Average age 33. 237 applicants, 96% accepted, 117 enrolled. In 2009, 291 master's awarded. *Degree requirements:* For master's, thesis. *Entrance requirements:* For master's, GRE General Test or minimum GPA of 3.0. Additional exam requirements/recommendations for international students: Required—TOEFL. *Application deadline:* Applications are processed on a rolling basis. Application fee: $30. Electronic applications accepted. *Expenses:* Tuition, state resident: part-time $471 per credit hour. Tuition, nonresident: part-time $646 per credit hour. Tuition and fees vary according to course level. *Financial support:* In 2009–10, 73 students received support, including 55 fellowships (averaging $2,273 per year), 19 research assistantships with full and partial tuition reimbursements available (averaging $8,000 per year); career-related internships or fieldwork, Federal Work-Study, scholarships/grants, and unspecified assistantships also available. *Faculty research:* Effectiveness of technology in education, parental involvement, effective teaching, effective schools research. *Unit head:* Dr. Linda McCrea, Director, 616-331-2080, E-mail: mccreal@gvsu.edu. *Application contact:* Thomas Owens, Student Information and Services Center, 616-331-6282, Fax: 616-331-2000, E-mail: owenst@gvsu.edu.

Greenville College, Program in Education, Greenville, IL 62246-0159. Offers education (MAT); elementary education (MAE); secondary education (MAE). *Degree requirements:* For master's, thesis (for some programs). *Entrance requirements:* For master's, GRE, Illinois Basic Skills Test, teacher certification. Electronic applications accepted.

Hampton University, Graduate College, Department of Education, Program in Teaching, Hampton, VA 23668. Offers early childhood education (MT); middle school education (MT); music education (MT); secondary education (MT); special education (MT). *Entrance requirements:* For master's, GRE General Test.

Harding University, College of Education, Searcy, AR 72149-0001. Offers advanced studies in teaching and learning (M Ed); art (MSE); behavioral science (MSE); counseling (MS, Ed S); early childhood special education (M Ed, MSE); education (MSE); educational leadership

Secondary Education

Harding University (continued)

(M Ed, Ed S); elementary education (M Ed); English (MSE); family and consumer science (MSE); French (MSE); history/social science (MSE); kinesiology (MSE); math (MSE); physical science (MSE); reading (M Ed); secondary education (M Ed); Spanish (MSE); special education licensure (M Ed); teaching (MAT); teaching English as a second language (M Ed). *Accreditation:* NCATE. Part-time and evening/weekend programs available. *Faculty:* 11 full-time (4 women), 49 part-time/adjunct (26 women). *Students:* 104 full-time (85 women), 392 part-time (282 women); includes 77 minority (67 African Americans, 5 American Indian/Alaska Native, 1 Asian American or Pacific Islander, 4 Hispanic Americans), 5 international. Average age 36. 153 applicants, 92% accepted, 131 enrolled. In 2009, 153 master's, 6 other advanced degrees awarded. *Degree requirements:* For master's, comprehensive exam (for some programs), thesis optional, portfolio(s); for Ed S, comprehensive exam, portfolio, specialist project. *Entrance requirements:* For master's, GRE, MAT, PRAXIS; for Ed S, MAT or GRE. Additional exam requirements/recommendations for international students: Required—TOEFL (minimum score 550 paper-based; 79 iBT). *Application deadline:* For fall admission, 8/1 for domestic and international students; for spring admission, 1/1 for domestic and international students. Applications are processed on a rolling basis. Application fee: $35. *Expenses:* Tuition: Full-time $9720; part-time $540 per credit hour. Required fees: $22 per credit hour. Tuition and fees vary according to course load and program. *Financial support:* In 2009–10, 30 students received support. Unspecified assistantships available. *Faculty research:* Reading, comprehension, school violence, educational technology, behavior, college choice, differentiated instruction, brain-based teaching. *Unit head:* Dr. Clara Carroll, Chair, 501-279-4501, Fax: 501-279-4083, E-mail: ccarroll@harding.edu. *Application contact:* Information Contact, 501-279-4315, E-mail: gradstudiesedu@harding.edu.

Hawai'i Pacific University, College of Humanities and Social Sciences, Program in Secondary Education, Honolulu, HI 96813. Offers M Ed. *Faculty:* 2 full-time (both women), 1 part-time/adjunct (0 women). *Students:* 24 full-time (15 women), 48 part-time (21 women); includes 25 minority (2 African Americans, 23 Asian Americans or Pacific Islanders), 4 international. Average age 31. 35 applicants, 69% accepted, 16 enrolled. In 2009, 16 master's awarded. *Degree requirements:* For master's, thesis. *Entrance requirements:* For master's, PRAXIS I and II. Additional exam requirements/recommendations for international students: Recommended—TOEFL (minimum score 550 paper-based; 213 computer-based; 80 iBT), TWE (minimum score 5). *Application deadline:* For fall admission, 2/15 priority date for domestic students; for spring admission, 10/15 priority date for domestic students. Applications are processed on a rolling basis. Application fee: $50. Electronic applications accepted. *Expenses:* Tuition: Full-time $12,600; part-time $700 per credit hour. Tuition and fees vary according to program. *Financial support:* In 2009–10, 24 students received support. Career-related internships or fieldwork, Federal Work-Study, scholarships/grants, and unspecified assistantships available. Support available to part-time students. Financial award application deadline: 3/1. *Unit head:* Dr. Valentina Abordonado, Program Chair, 808-544-1143, Fax: 808-544-0841, E-mail: vabordonado@hpu.edu. *Application contact:* Danny Lam, Assistant Director of Graduate Admissions, 808-544-1135, Fax: 808-544-0280, E-mail: graduate@hpu.edu.

Hofstra University, School of Education, Health, and Human Services, Department of Counseling, Research, Special Education and Rehabilitation, Program in Special Education, Hempstead, NY 11549. Offers early childhood special education (MS Ed, Advanced Certificate); gifted education (Advanced Certificate); inclusive early childhood special education (MS Ed); inclusive elementary special education (MS Ed); inclusive secondary special education (MS Ed); literacy studies and special education (MS Ed); special education (MA, MS Ed, PD); special education assessment and diagnosis (Advanced Certificate); teaching students with severe or multiple disabilities (Advanced Certificate). Part-time and evening/weekend programs available. *Students:* 113 full-time (96 women), 105 part-time (95 women); includes 39 minority (18 African Americans, 1 American Indian/Alaska Native, 3 Asian Americans or Pacific Islanders, 17 Hispanic Americans). Average age 29. 134 applicants, 71% accepted, 74 enrolled. In 2009, 88 master's, 7 other advanced degrees awarded. *Degree requirements:* For master's, comprehensive exam (for some programs), thesis (for some programs), seminars, student teaching. *Entrance requirements:* For master's, interview, 3 letters of reference, initial/professional certification; for other advanced degree, interview, 3 letters of recommendation, resume, master's degree, certification. Additional exam requirements/recommendations for international students: Required—TOEFL (minimum score 550 paper-based; 213 computer-based; 80 iBT). *Application deadline:* Applications are processed on a rolling basis. Application fee: $60. Electronic applications accepted. *Expenses:* Tuition: Full-time $16,200; part-time $900 per credit hour. Required fees: $970; $145 per term. Tuition and fees vary according to program. *Financial support:* In 2009–10, 78 students received support, including 10 fellowships with full and partial tuition reimbursements available (averaging $2,541 per year), 4 research assistantships with full and partial tuition reimbursements available (averaging $7,210 per year); Federal Work-Study, institutionally sponsored loans, scholarships/grants, tuition waivers (full and partial), and unspecified assistantships also available. Support available to part-time students. Financial award applicants required to submit FAFSA. *Faculty research:* Inclusive schooling, autism spectrum disorders related services, cultural competency and culturally responsive instruction, co-teaching student teaching, universal design for learning. *Unit head:* Dr. George Guiliani, Director, 516-463-5143, Fax: 516-463-6184, E-mail: cprgag@hofstra.edu. *Application contact:* Carol Drummer, Dean of Graduate Admissions, 516-463-4876, Fax: 516-463-4664, E-mail: gradstudent@hofstra.edu.

Hofstra University, School of Education, Health, and Human Services, Department of Curriculum and Teaching, Program in Secondary Education, Hempstead, NY 11549. Offers Advanced Certificate. Part-time and evening/weekend programs available. *Students:* 4 full-time (2 women), 4 part-time (1 woman); includes 1 minority (Hispanic American). Average age 40. 5 applicants, 80% accepted, 3 enrolled. In 2009, 3 Advanced Certificates awarded. *Degree requirements:* For Advanced Certificate, 3 foreign languages, comprehensive exam (for some programs), thesis project. *Entrance requirements:* For degree, 2 letters of recommendation, interview and/or portfolio. Additional exam requirements/recommendations for international students: Required—TOEFL (minimum score 550 paper-based; 213 computer-based; 80 iBT). *Application deadline:* Applications are processed on a rolling basis. Application fee: $60. Electronic applications accepted. *Expenses:* Tuition: Full-time $16,200; part-time $900 per credit hour. Required fees: $970; $145 per term. Tuition and fees vary according to program. *Financial support:* In 2009–10, 8 students received support; fellowships with full and partial tuition reimbursements available, research assistantships with full and partial tuition reimbursements available, Federal Work-Study, institutionally sponsored loans, scholarships/grants, and tuition waivers (full and partial) available. Support available to part-time students. Financial award applicants required to submit FAFSA. *Faculty research:* Urban education, multicultural education, assessment and instruction, teaching for understanding, curriculum development. *Unit head:* Dr. Susan Zwirn, Program Director, 516-463-4976, Fax: 516-463-6196, E-mail: catsgz@hofstra.edu. *Application contact:* Carol Drummer, Dean of Graduate Admissions, 516-463-4876, Fax: 516-463-4664, E-mail: gradstudent@hofstra.edu.

Holy Family University, Graduate School, School of Education, Philadelphia, PA 19114. Offers education (M Ed); education leadership (M Ed); elementary education (M Ed); reading specialist (M Ed); secondary education (M Ed); special education (M Ed). Part-time and evening/weekend programs available. *Faculty:* 14 full-time (10 women), 42 part-time/adjunct (23 women). *Students:* 63 full-time (48 women), 608 part-time (487 women); includes 45 minority (23 African Americans, 7 Asian Americans or Pacific Islanders, 15 Hispanic Americans), 1 international. Average age 31. 202 applicants, 86% accepted, 146 enrolled. In 2009, 248 master's awarded. *Degree requirements:* For master's, thesis optional. *Entrance requirements:* For master's, GRE or MAT, interview. *Application deadline:* For fall admission, 7/1 priority date for domestic students; for winter admission, 11/1 priority date for domestic students. Applications are processed on a rolling basis. Application fee: $25. *Expenses:* Tuition: Part-time $600 per credit. Required fees: $58 per semester. *Financial support:* Research assistantships, Federal Work-Study available. Support available to part-time students. Financial award application deadline: 2/15; financial award applicants required to submit FAFSA. *Faculty research:* Cognition, developmental issues, sociological issues in education. *Unit head:* Dr. Leonard Soroka, Dean, 267-341-3565, Fax: 215-824-2438, E-mail: lsoroka@holyfanily.edu. *Application contact:* Gidget Marie Montelibano, Graduate Admissions Counselor, 267-341-3558, Fax: 215-637-1478, E-mail: gmontelibano@holyfamily.edu.

Hood College, Graduate School, Department of Education, Frederick, MD 21701-8575. Offers curriculum and instruction (MS), including early childhood education, elementary education, elementary school science and mathematics, secondary education, special education; educational leadership (MS, Certificate); reading specialization (MS). Part-time and evening/weekend programs available. *Faculty:* 4 full-time (all women), 39 part-time/adjunct (21 women). *Students:* 2 full-time (both women), 397 part-time (326 women); includes 41 minority (29 African Americans, 5 Asian Americans or Pacific Islanders, 7 Hispanic Americans). Average age 33. 100 applicants, 92% accepted, 84 enrolled. In 2009, 73 master's, 65 other advanced degrees awarded. *Degree requirements:* For master's, action research project, portfolio (reading). *Entrance requirements:* For master's, minimum GPA of 2.75, teaching certification. *Application deadline:* For fall admission, 7/15 for domestic and international students; for spring admission, 12/15 for domestic and international students. Applications are processed on a rolling basis. Application fee: $35. Electronic applications accepted. *Expenses:* Tuition: Full-time $6480; part-time $360 per credit. Required fees: $100; $50 per term. *Financial support:* Applicants required to submit FAFSA. *Faculty research:* Leadership, action research, brain research, learning styles. *Unit head:* Dr. John George, Chairperson, 301-696-3471, Fax: 301-696-3597, E-mail: george@hood.edu. *Application contact:* Dr. Allen P. Flora, Dean of Graduate School, 301-696-3811, Fax: 301-696-3597, E-mail: gofurther@hood.edu.

Hood College, Graduate School, Program in Secondary Mathematics Education, Frederick, MD 21701-8575. Offers mathematics education (MS), including high school, middle school; secondary mathematics education (Certificate). Part-time and evening/weekend programs available. *Faculty:* 1 full-time (0 women), 2 part-time/adjunct (0 women). *Students:* 32 part-time (24 women); includes 1 minority (African American). Average age 34. 8 applicants, 88% accepted, 7 enrolled. In 2009, 1 master's, 1 other advanced degree awarded. *Degree requirements:* For master's, capstone/research project. *Entrance requirements:* For master's, minimum GPA of 2.75. *Application deadline:* For fall admission, 7/15 for domestic and international students; for spring admission, 12/15 for domestic and international students. Applications are processed on a rolling basis. Application fee: $35. Electronic applications accepted. *Expenses:* Tuition: Full-time $6480; part-time $360 per credit. Required fees: $100; $50 per term. *Financial support:* Applicants required to submit FAFSA. *Unit head:* Dr. Betty Mayfield, Chairperson, 301-696-3763, E-mail: mayfield@hood.edu. *Application contact:* Dr. Allen P. Flora, Dean of Graduate School, 301-696-3811, Fax: 301-696-3597, E-mail: gofurther@hood.edu.

Howard University, School of Education, Department of Curriculum and Instruction, Program in Secondary Education, Washington, DC 20059-0002. Offers M Ed, MA, MAT, CAGS. MA offered through the Graduate School of Arts and Sciences. *Accreditation:* NCATE. *Faculty:* 2 full-time (both women), 1 (woman) part-time/adjunct. *Students:* 7 full-time (5 women), 8 part-time (6 women); all minorities (12 African Americans, 2 Asian Americans or Pacific Islanders, 1 Hispanic American). Average age 26. 6 applicants, 83% accepted, 4 enrolled. In 2009, 11 master's awarded. *Degree requirements:* For master's, comprehensive exam, thesis (for some programs), expository writing exam, internships, practicum. *Entrance requirements:* For master's, GRE General Test (MA), minimum GPA of 2.7. *Application deadline:* For fall admission, 2/15 priority date for domestic students; for spring admission, 11/1 for domestic students. Applications are processed on a rolling basis. Application fee: $45. Electronic applications accepted. *Financial support:* In 2009–10, 5 students received support, including fellowships with full and partial tuition reimbursements available (averaging $15,000 per year), 4 research assistantships with full and partial tuition reimbursements available (averaging $13,000 per year); career-related internships or fieldwork, Federal Work-Study, institutionally sponsored loans, scholarships/grants, and unspecified assistantships also available. Financial award application deadline: 2/15. *Unit head:* Dr. Vinetta C. Jones, Professor/Coordinator, 202-806-5298, E-mail: v_jones@howard.edu. *Application contact:* June L. Harris, Administrative Assistant, Department of Curriculum and Instruction, 202-806-7343, Fax: 202-806-5297, E-mail: jlharris@howard.edu.

Hunter College of the City University of New York, Graduate School, School of Arts and Sciences, Department of Mathematics and Statistics, New York, NY 10021-5085. Offers applied mathematics (MA); mathematics for secondary education (MA); pure mathematics (MA). Part-time and evening/weekend programs available. *Faculty:* 7 full-time (1 woman). *Students:* 19 full-time (7 women), 56 part-time (26 women); includes 24 minority (3 African Americans, 18 Asian Americans or Pacific Islanders, 3 Hispanic Americans). Average age 31. 43 applicants, 77% accepted, 21 enrolled. In 2009, 35 master's awarded. *Degree requirements:* For master's, one foreign language, comprehensive exam, thesis (for some programs). *Entrance requirements:* For master's, GRE General Test, 24 credits in mathematics. Additional exam requirements/recommendations for international students: Required—TOEFL. *Application deadline:* For fall admission, 4/1 for domestic students, 2/1 for international students; for spring admission, 11/1 for domestic students, 9/1 for international students. Application fee: $125. *Expenses:* Tuition, state resident: full-time $7360; part-time $310 per credit. Required fees: $250 per semester. *Financial support:* Federal Work-Study, institutionally sponsored loans, scholarships/grants, and tuition waivers (partial) available. Support available to part-time students. *Faculty research:* Data analysis, dynamical systems, computer graphics, topology, statistical decision theory. *Unit head:* Ada Peluso, Chairperson, 212-772-5300, Fax: 212-772-4858, E-mail: peluso@math.hunter.cuny.edu. *Application contact:* William Zlata, Director for Graduate Admissions, 212-772-4482, Fax: 212-650-3336, E-mail: admissions@hunter.cuny.edu.

Hunter College of the City University of New York, Graduate School, School of Education, Programs in Secondary Education, New York, NY 10021-5085. Offers biology education (MA); chemistry education (MA); earth science (MA); English education (MA); French education (MA); Italian education (MA); mathematics education (MA); physics education (MA); social studies education (MA); Spanish education (MA). *Accreditation:* NCATE. *Faculty:* 12 full-time (6 women), 57 part-time/adjunct (42 women). *Students:* 33 full-time (22 women), 312 part-time (183 women); includes 79 minority (18 African Americans, 1 American Indian/Alaska Native, 18 Asian Americans or Pacific Islanders, 42 Hispanic Americans). Average age 32. 659 applicants, 56% accepted, 226 enrolled. In 2009, 159 master's awarded. *Degree requirements:* For master's, thesis. *Entrance requirements:* Additional exam requirements/recommendations for international students: Required—TOEFL. *Application deadline:* For fall admission, 4/1 for domestic students, 2/1 for international students; for spring admission, 11/1 for domestic students, 9/1 for international students. Applications are processed on a rolling basis. Application fee: $125. *Expenses:* Tuition, state resident: full-time $7360; part-time $310 per credit. Required fees: $250 per semester. *Financial support:* Fellowships, tuition waivers (full and partial) available. Support available to part-time students. *Unit head:* Dr. Kate Garret, Coordinator, 212-772-4700, E-mail: kgarret@hunter.cuny.edu. *Application contact:* Milena Solo, Director for Graduate Admissions, 212-772-4482, Fax: 212-650-3336, E-mail: milena.solo@hunter.cuny.edu.

Idaho State University, Office of Graduate Studies, College of Education, Department of Educational Foundations, Pocatello, ID 83209-8059. Offers child and family studies (M Ed); curriculum leadership (M Ed); education (M Ed); educational administration (M Ed); educational foundations (5th Year Certificate); elementary education (M Ed), including K-12 education, literacy, secondary education. Part-time programs available. *Faculty:* 13 full-time (8 women). *Students:* 15 full-time (9 women), 100 part-time (64 women); includes 2 minority (1 African American, 1 Hispanic American), 3 international. Average age 39. In 2009, 25 master's awarded. *Degree requirements:* For master's, comprehensive exam, thesis optional, oral exam, written exam; for 5th Year Certificate, comprehensive exam, thesis (for some programs), oral exam, written exam. *Entrance requirements:* For master's, GRE General Test or MAT, minimum undergraduate GPA of 3.0; for 5th Year Certificate, GRE General Test, minimum undergraduate GPA of 3.0, master's degree. Additional exam requirements/recommendations for international students: Required—TOEFL (minimum score 550 paper-based; 213 computer-based; 80 iBT). *Application deadline:* For fall admission, 7/1 for domestic students, 6/1 for

international students; for spring admission, 12/1 for domestic students, 11/1 for international students. Applications are processed on a rolling basis. Application fee: $55. Electronic applications accepted. *Expenses:* Tuition, state resident: full-time $3318; part-time $297 per credit hour. Tuition, nonresident: full-time $13,120; part-time $437 per credit hour. Required fees: $2530. Tuition and fees vary according to program. *Financial support:* Research assistantships with full and partial tuition reimbursements, teaching assistantships with full and partial tuition reimbursements, career-related internships or fieldwork, Federal Work-Study, institutionally sponsored loans, scholarships/grants, traineeships, health care benefits, tuition waivers (full and partial), and unspecified assistantships available. Support available to part-time students. Financial award application deadline: 1/1; financial award applicants required to submit FAFSA. *Faculty research:* Child and families studies; business education; special education; math, science, and technology education. *Unit head:* Dr. Beverly Ray, Chair, 208-282-4516, Fax: 208-282-3791, E-mail: raybeve@isu.edu. *Application contact:* Dr. Peter Denner, Assistant Dean, 208-282-3807, Fax: 208-282-4697, E-mail: dennpete@isu.edu.

Immaculata University, College of Graduate Studies, Program in Educational Leadership and Administration, Immaculata, PA 19345. Offers educational leadership and administration (MA, Ed D); elementary education (Certificate); school principal (Certificate); school superintendent (Certificate); secondary education (Certificate); special education (Certificate). Part-time and evening/weekend programs available. *Degree requirements:* For master's, comprehensive exam, thesis optional; for doctorate, comprehensive exam, thesis/dissertation. *Entrance requirements:* For master's, GRE or MAT, minimum GPA of 3.0; for doctorate, GRE General Test, minimum GPA of 3.5. Additional exam requirements/recommendations for international students: Required—TOEFL. *Faculty research:* Cooperative learning, school-based management, whole language, performance assessment.

Indiana University Bloomington, School of Education, Department of Curriculum and Instruction, Bloomington, IN 47405-7000. Offers art education (MS, Ed D, PhD); curriculum studies (Ed D, PhD); elementary education (MS, Ed D, PhD, Ed S); mathematics education (MS, Ed D, PhD); science education (MS, Ed D, PhD); secondary education (MS, Ed D, PhD); social studies education (MS, PhD); special education (MS, Ed D, PhD, Ed S). *Accreditation:* NCATE. Part-time and evening/weekend programs available. *Students:* 208 full-time (155 women), 44 part-time (25 women); includes 28 minority (9 African Americans, 3 American Indian/Alaska Native, 9 Asian Americans or Pacific Islanders, 7 Hispanic Americans), 34 international. Average age 34. 100 applicants, 68% accepted, 39 enrolled. In 2009, 48 master's, 20 doctorates awarded. Terminal master's awarded for partial completion of doctoral program. *Degree requirements:* For doctorate, thesis/dissertation; for Ed S, comprehensive exam or project. *Entrance requirements:* For master's, doctorate, and Ed S, GRE General Test. *Application deadline:* For fall admission, 6/1 priority date for domestic students, 3/1 for international students; for winter admission, 11/1 priority date for domestic students; for spring admission, 9/1 for international students. Applications are processed on a rolling basis. Application fee: $55 ($65 for international students). Electronic applications accepted. *Financial support:* Fellowships with full and partial tuition reimbursements, research assistantships with full and partial tuition reimbursements, teaching assistantships with full and partial tuition reimbursements, career-related internships or fieldwork, Federal Work-Study, institutionally sponsored loans, and tuition waivers (partial) available. Support available to part-time students. *Unit head:* Cary Buzzelli, Chairperson, 812-856-8100. *Application contact:* Bobbie Partenheimer, Admissions Services Coordinator, 812-856-8127, Fax: 812-856-8333, E-mail: partenhe@indiana.edu.

Indiana University Northwest, School of Education, Gary, IN 46408-1197. Offers elementary education (MS Ed); secondary education (MS Ed). *Accreditation:* NCATE. Part-time and evening/weekend programs available. *Faculty:* 5 full-time (2 women). *Students:* 35 full-time (29 women), 150 part-time (115 women); includes 83 minority (69 African Americans, 1 American Indian/Alaska Native, 13 Hispanic Americans). Average age 37. In 2009, 33 master's awarded. *Entrance requirements:* For master's, GRE General Test or MAT, minimum GPA of 3.0. *Application deadline:* For fall admission, 7/15 priority date for domestic students; for spring admission, 11/15 for domestic students. Application fee: $25. *Unit head:* Dr. Stanley E. Wigle, Dean, 219-980-6510, Fax: 219-981-4208, E-mail: amsanche@iun.edu. *Application contact:* Dr. Stanley E. Wigle, Dean, 219-980-6510, Fax: 219-981-4208, E-mail: amsanche@iun.edu.

Indiana University–Purdue University Fort Wayne, School of Education, Department of Educational Studies, Fort Wayne, IN 46805-1499. Offers elementary education (MS Ed); secondary education (MS Ed). *Accreditation:* NCATE. Part-time programs available. *Faculty:* 15 full-time (9 women). *Students:* 2 full-time (1 woman), 48 part-time (40 women); includes 8 minority (4 African Americans, 1 Asian American or Pacific Islander, 3 Hispanic Americans). Average age 38. 22 applicants, 100% accepted, 22 enrolled. In 2009, 22 master's awarded. *Entrance requirements:* For master's, minimum GPA of 2.5. Additional exam requirements/recommendations for international students: Required—TOEFL (minimum score 550 paper-based; 213 computer-based; 77 iBT). *Application deadline:* For fall admission, 4/1 priority date for domestic and international students. Applications are processed on a rolling basis. Application fee: $55. *Expenses:* Tuition, state resident: full-time $4595; part-time $255 per credit. Tuition, nonresident: full-time $10,963; part-time $609 per credit. Required fees: $528; $29.35 per credit. Tuition and fees vary according to course load. *Financial support:* In 2009–10, 1 teaching assistantship with partial tuition reimbursement (averaging $12,740 per year) was awarded; scholarships/grants also available. Support available to part-time students. Financial award application deadline: 3/1; financial award applicants required to submit FAFSA. *Unit head:* Dr. Joe Nichols, Chair, 260-481-6445, Fax: 260-481-5408, E-mail: nicholsj@ipfw.edu. *Application contact:* Vicky L. Schmidt, Graduate Recorder, 260-481-6450, Fax: 260-481-5408, E-mail: schmidt@ipfw.edu.

Indiana University South Bend, School of Education, South Bend, IN 46634-7111. Offers counseling and human services (MS Ed); elementary education (MS Ed); secondary education (MS Ed); special education (MS Ed). *Accreditation:* NCATE. Part-time and evening/weekend programs available. *Faculty:* 21 full-time (11 women), 9 part-time/adjunct (3 women). *Students:* 72 full-time (48 women), 256 part-time (202 women); includes 36 minority (24 African Americans, 2 American Indian/Alaska Native, 1 Asian American or Pacific Islander, 9 Hispanic Americans), 9 international. Average age 36. In 2009, 103 master's awarded. *Degree requirements:* For master's, thesis or alternative, exit project. *Entrance requirements:* For master's, letters of recommendation, GRE or minimum GPA of 3.0. Additional exam requirements/recommendations for international students: Required—TOEFL. *Application deadline:* For fall admission, 7/1 for domestic students; for spring admission, 11/1 for domestic students. Applications are processed on a rolling basis. Application fee: $46 ($58 for international students). Electronic applications accepted. *Financial support:* Career-related internships or fieldwork available. Support available to part-time students. Financial award application deadline: 3/1; financial award applicants required to submit FAFSA. *Faculty research:* Professional dispositions, early childhood literacy, online learning, program assessments, problem-based learning. *Unit head:* Dr. Michael Horvath, Professor/Dean, 574-520-4339, Fax: 574-520-4550. *Application contact:* Dr. Todd Norris, Director of Education Student Services, 574-520-4845, E-mail: toanorri@iusb.edu.

Indiana University Southeast, School of Education, New Albany, IN 47150-6405. Offers counselor education (MS Ed); elementary education (MS Ed); secondary education (MS Ed). *Accreditation:* NCATE. Part-time and evening/weekend programs available. *Students:* 7 full-time (all women), 366 part-time (305 women); includes 31 minority (27 African Americans, 3 American Indian/Alaska Native, 1 Asian American or Pacific Islander), 1 international. Average age 32. In 2009, 138 master's awarded. *Entrance requirements:* For master's, minimum undergraduate GPA of 2.5, graduate 3.0. *Application deadline:* Applications are processed on a rolling basis. Application fee: $35. *Financial support:* In 2009–10, 29 students received support. Career-related internships or fieldwork, Federal Work-Study, and institutionally sponsored loans available. Support available to part-time students. Financial award applicants required to submit FAFSA. *Faculty research:* Learning styles, technology, constructivism, group process, innovative math strategies. *Unit head:* Dr. Gloria Murray, Dean, 812-941-2169, Fax: 812-941-2667, E-mail: soeinfo@ius.edu. *Application contact:* Dr. Gloria Murray, Dean, 812-941-2169, Fax: 812-941-2667, E-mail: soeinfo@ius.edu.

Ithaca College, Division of Graduate and Professional Studies, School of Humanities and Sciences, Program in Adolescent Education, Ithaca, NY 14850. Offers biology 7-12 (MAT); chemistry 7-12 (MAT); English 7-12 (MAT); French 7-12 (MAT); math 7-12 (MAT); physics 7-12 (MAT); social studies 7-12 (MAT); Spanish (MAT). Part-time programs available. *Faculty:* 18 full-time (7 women). *Students:* 15 full-time (10 women), 2 part-time (1 woman); includes 1 minority (African American). Average age 26. 31 applicants, 68% accepted, 16 enrolled. In 2009, 31 master's awarded. *Degree requirements:* For master's, thesis or alternative, student teaching. *Entrance requirements:* For master's, minimum GPA of 3.0. Additional exam requirements/recommendations for international students: Required—TOEFL (minimum score 550 paper-based; 213 computer-based; 80 iBT). *Application deadline:* For fall admission, 5/15 for domestic and international students; for spring admission, 12/1 for domestic and international students. Applications are processed on a rolling basis. Application fee: $40. Electronic applications accepted. *Expenses:* Contact institution. *Financial support:* In 2009–10, 15 students received support, including 10 teaching assistantships (averaging $6,474 per year); career-related internships or fieldwork, Federal Work-Study, scholarships/grants, and unspecified assistantships also available. Support available to part-time students. Financial award applicants required to submit CSS PROFILE or FAFSA. *Faculty research:* Bilingual education, sociolinguistic perspective on literacy. *Unit head:* Dr. Linda Hanrahan, Chairperson, 607-274-3527, Fax: 607-274-1263, E-mail: gps@ithaca.edu. *Application contact:* Rob Gearhart, Dean, Graduate and Professional Studies, 607-274-3527, Fax: 607-274-1263, E-mail: gps@ithaca.edu.

Jackson State University, Graduate School, School of Education, Department of Educational Foundations and Leadership, Jackson, MS 39217. Offers education administration (Ed S); educational administration (MS Ed, PhD); secondary education (MS Ed, Ed S), including educational technology (MS Ed). *Accreditation:* NCATE. Part-time and evening/weekend programs available. *Degree requirements:* For master's, comprehensive exam, thesis or alternative; for doctorate, comprehensive exam, thesis/dissertation; for Ed S, comprehensive exam, thesis. *Entrance requirements:* For master's, GRE General Test; for doctorate, MAT, GRE, teaching experience. Additional exam requirements/recommendations for international students: Required—TOEFL.

Jacksonville State University, College of Graduate Studies and Continuing Education, College of Education and Professional Studies, Program in Secondary Education, Jacksonville, AL 36265-1602. Offers MS Ed. *Accreditation:* NCATE. Part-time and evening/weekend programs available. *Degree requirements:* For master's, comprehensive exam, thesis (for some programs). *Entrance requirements:* For master's, GRE General Test or MAT. Electronic applications accepted.

James Madison University, The Graduate School, College of Education, Middle, Secondary, and Mathematics Education Department, Program in Secondary Education, Harrisonburg, VA 22807. Offers MAT. *Accreditation:* NCATE. Part-time and evening/weekend programs available. *Students:* Average age 27. *Entrance requirements:* For master's, GRE General Test. Additional exam requirements/recommendations for international students: Required—TOEFL. *Application deadline:* For fall admission, 5/1 priority date for domestic students; for spring admission, 9/1 priority date for domestic students. Applications are processed on a rolling basis. Application fee: $55. Electronic applications accepted. *Expenses:* Tuition, area resident: Part-time $305 per credit hour. Tuition, state resident: part-time $305 per credit hour. Tuition, nonresident: part-time $890 per credit hour. *Financial support:* Federal Work-Study and unspecified assistantships available. Financial award application deadline: 3/1; financial award applicants required to submit FAFSA. *Unit head:* Dr. Steven L. Purcell, Academic Unit Head, 540-568-6793. *Application contact:* Lynette M. Bible, Director of Graduate Admissions, 540-568-6395, Fax: 540-568-7860, E-mail: biblelm@jmu.edu.

John Carroll University, Graduate School, Department of Education and Allied Studies, Program in School Based Adolescent-Young Adult Education, University Heights, OH 44118-4581. Offers M Ed. *Degree requirements:* For master's, comprehensive exam. *Entrance requirements:* For master's, GRE General Test or MAT, minimum GPA of 2.75, interview. Electronic applications accepted.

The Johns Hopkins University, School of Education, Department of Teacher Preparation, Baltimore, MD 21218. Offers education (MS), including educational studies; elementary education (MAT); English for speakers of other languages (MAT); K-8 mathematics lead-teacher (Certificate); K-8 science lead-teacher (Certificate); secondary education (MAT), including biology, chemistry, earth/space/environmental science, English, French, mathematics, physics, social studies, Spanish. Part-time and evening/weekend programs available. *Faculty:* 13 full-time (11 women), 35 part-time/adjunct (21 women). *Students:* 162 full-time (119 women), 347 part-time (256 women); includes 138 minority (80 African Americans, 3 American Indian/Alaska Native, 38 Asian Americans or Pacific Islanders, 17 Hispanic Americans), 3 international. Average age 27. 89 applicants, 37% accepted, 24 enrolled. In 2009, 177 master's awarded. *Degree requirements:* For master's, portfolio, PRAXIS II, internship. *Entrance requirements:* For master's, PRAXIS I, SAT, ACT, or GRE (MAT), minimum undergraduate GPA of 3.0, interview, 1 letter of recommendation, curriculum vitae/resume; for Certificate, bachelor's degree, minimum undergraduate GPA of 3.0, essay/statement of goals, interview. Additional exam requirements/recommendations for international students: Required—TOEFL (minimum score 600 paper-based; 250 computer-based; 100 iBT). *Application deadline:* For fall admission, 5/1 for international students; for spring admission, 10/15 for international students. Applications are processed on a rolling basis. Application fee: $80. Electronic applications accepted. *Financial support:* Scholarships/grants available. Support available to part-time students. Financial award application deadline: 6/1; financial award applicants required to submit FAFSA. *Faculty research:* Teacher retention; STEM education reform; alternative certification programs; school-university partnerships; urban education; action research/data-informed instruction; family engagement. *Unit head:* Dr. Francis Masci, Chair, 410-516-9774, Fax: 410-516-9770, E-mail: matjhu@jhu.edu. *Application contact:* Jennifer Shaffer, Director of Admissions, 410-516-9797, Fax: 410-516-9799, E-mail: educationinfo@jhu.edu.

Johnson & Wales University, The Alan Shawn Feinstein Graduate School, Ed D Program, Providence, RI 02903-3703. Offers higher education (Ed D); K-12 (Ed D). Part-time programs available. *Faculty:* 7 full-time (3 women), 3 part-time/adjunct (2 women). *Students:* 95 full-time (54 women); includes 3 minority (1 African American, 2 Asian Americans or Pacific Islanders). Average age 42. 27 applicants, 89% accepted, 22 enrolled. In 2009, 30 doctorates awarded. *Degree requirements:* For doctorate, thesis/dissertation. *Entrance requirements:* For doctorate, MAT, minimum GPA of 3.25. Additional exam requirements/recommendations for international students: Required—TOEFL (minimum score 550 paper-based; 210 computer-based) or IELTS recommended; Recommended—TWE. *Application deadline:* Applications are processed on a rolling basis. Application fee: $0. *Expenses:* Required fees: $340 per quarter hour. *Financial support:* Application deadline: 5/1. *Faculty research:* Site-based management, collaborative learning, technology and education, K–16 education. *Unit head:* Dr. Robert Gable, Director, 401-598-4738, Fax: 401-598-1162, E-mail: rgable@jwu.edu. *Application contact:* Dr. Allan G. Freedman, Director of Graduate Admissions, 401-598-1015, Fax: 401-598-1286, E-mail: gradadm@jwu.edu.

Johnson State College, Graduate Program in Education, Program in Secondary Education, Johnson, VT 05656. Offers MA Ed, CAGS. *Entrance requirements:* Additional exam requirements/recommendations for international students: Required—TOEFL. *Expenses:* Tuition, area resident: Part-time $416 per credit. Tuition, state resident: part-time $416 per credit. Tuition, nonresident: part-time $899 per credit.

Jones International University, Graduate School of Education, Centennial, CO 80112. Offers adult education (M Ed); corporate training and knowledge management (M Ed); curriculum and instruction (M Ed), including elementary teacher licensure, secondary teacher licensure; e-learning technology and design (M Ed); educational leadership and administration (M Ed); educational leadership and administration: principal and administrator licensure (M Ed); elementary curriculum instruction and assessment (M Ed); higher education leadership and administration (M Ed); K-12 instructional technology (M Ed); K-12 instructional technology: teacher licensure (M Ed); secondary curriculum instruction and assessment (M Ed); technology

Secondary Education

Jones International University (continued)
and design (M Ed). Part-time and evening/weekend programs available. Postbaccalaureate distance learning degree programs offered (no on-campus study). *Entrance requirements:* For master's, minimum cumulative GPA of 2.5. Additional exam requirements/recommendations for international students: Recommended—TOEFL (minimum score 550 paper-based; 213 computer-based). Electronic applications accepted.

Kaplan University, Davenport Campus, School of Teacher Education, Davenport, IA 52807-2095. Offers education (M Ed); secondary education (M Ed); teaching and learning (MA); teaching literacy and language: grades 6-12 (MA); teaching literacy and language: grades K-6 (MA); teaching mathematics: grades 6-8 (MA); teaching mathematics: grades 9-12 (MA); teaching mathematics: grades K-5 (MA); teaching science: grades 6-12 (MA); teaching science: grades K-6 (MA); teaching students with special needs (MA); teaching with technology (MA). Part-time and evening/weekend programs available. Postbaccalaureate distance learning degree programs offered (no on-campus study). *Entrance requirements:* Additional exam requirements/recommendations for international students: Required—TOEFL (minimum score 550 paper-based; 218 computer-based; 80 iBT).

Kennesaw State University, Leland and Clarice C. Bagwell College of Education, Program in Teaching, Kennesaw, GA 30144-5591. Offers secondary English or mathematics (MAT); teaching English to speakers of other languages (MAT). Program offered only in summer. Part-time and evening/weekend programs available. *Students:* 120 full-time (94 women), 16 part-time (9 women); includes 23 minority (12 African Americans, 4 Asian Americans or Pacific Islanders, 7 Hispanic Americans), 1 international. Average age 33. 28 applicants, 79% accepted, 19 enrolled. In 2009, 50 master's awarded. *Entrance requirements:* For master's, GRE, GACE I (state certificate exam), minimum GPA of 2.75, 2 recommendations, resume. Additional exam requirements/recommendations for international students: Required—TOEFL (minimum score 550 paper-based; 213 computer-based; 80 iBT), IELTS (minimum score 6). *Application deadline:* For fall admission, 6/1 for domestic and international students; for spring admission, 3/1 for domestic and international students. Application fee: $60. Electronic applications accepted. *Expenses:* Tuition, state resident: full-time $2341; part-time $196 per credit hour. Tuition, nonresident: full-time $9396; part-time $783 per credit hour. Required fees: $573 per semester. *Financial support:* In 2009–10, 2 research assistantships with tuition reimbursements (averaging $4,000 per year) were awarded; unspecified assistantships also available. Financial award application deadline: 6/15; financial award applicants required to submit FAFSA. *Unit head:* Dr. Lynn Stallings, Director, 770-420-4477, E-mail: lstalling@kennesaw.edu. *Application contact:* Alisha Bello, Administrative Coordinator, 770-423-6043, Fax: 770-420-4435, E-mail: abello1@kennesaw.edu.

Kent State University, Graduate School of Education, Health, and Human Services, School of Teaching, Learning and Curriculum Studies, Program in Secondary Education, Kent, OH 44242-0001. Offers MAT. *Accreditation:* NCATE. *Faculty:* 7 full-time (3 women), 2 part-time/adjunct (0 women). *Students:* 25 full-time (19 women), 3 part-time (2 women); includes 1 minority (African American). 45 applicants, 69% accepted. In 2009, 32 master's awarded. *Degree requirements:* For master's, thesis (for some programs). *Entrance requirements:* For master's, GRE General Test. Additional exam requirements/recommendations for international students: Required—TOEFL. *Application deadline:* For spring admission, 2/1 for domestic students. Application fee: $30 ($60 for international students). Electronic applications accepted. *Financial support:* In 2009–10, research assistantships with full tuition reimbursements (averaging $9,000 per year); career-related internships or fieldwork, Federal Work-Study, institutionally sponsored loans, scholarships/grants, health care benefits, and unspecified assistantships also available. Support available to part-time students. Financial award application deadline: 4/1; financial award applicants required to submit FAFSA. *Faculty research:* Creativity in science, women in science, teaching of writing, curriculum theory, mathematical reasoning. *Unit head:* Dr. Janice Hutchison, Coordinator, 330-672-0629, E-mail: jhutchi1@kent.edu. *Application contact:* Nancy Miller, Academic Program Coordinator, Office of Graduate Student Services, 330-672-2576, Fax: 330-672-9162, E-mail: ogs@kent.edu.

Kutztown University of Pennsylvania, College of Education, Program in Secondary Education, Kutztown, PA 19530-0730. Offers biology (M Ed); curriculum and instruction (M Ed); English (M Ed); mathematics (M Ed); secondary education (Certificate); social studies (M Ed). *Accreditation:* NCATE. Part-time and evening/weekend programs available. *Faculty:* 7 full-time (4 women). *Students:* 90 full-time (45 women), 84 part-time (56 women); includes 8 minority (4 African Americans, 1 Asian American or Pacific Islander, 3 Hispanic Americans), 2 international. Average age 29. 129 applicants, 76% accepted, 31 enrolled. In 2009, 36 master's awarded. *Degree requirements:* For master's, comprehensive exam, thesis optional. *Entrance requirements:* For master's, GRE General Test. Additional exam requirements/recommendations for international students: Required—TOEFL. *Application deadline:* For fall admission, 8/15 priority date for domestic and international students; for spring admission, 12/15 priority date for domestic and international students. Applications are processed on a rolling basis. Application fee: $35. Electronic applications accepted. *Expenses:* Tuition, state resident: full-time $6666; part-time $370 per credit. Tuition, nonresident: full-time $10,666; part-time $593 per credit. Required fees: $62 per credit. $60 per semester. *Financial support:* Career-related internships or fieldwork, Federal Work-Study, scholarships/grants, and unspecified assistantships available. Financial award application deadline: 3/1; financial award applicants required to submit FAFSA. *Unit head:* Dr. Theresa Stahler, Chairperson, 610-683-4259, Fax: 610-683-1338, E-mail: stahler@kutztown.edu. *Application contact:* Kelly D. Burr, Associate Director, Graduate Admissions, 610-683-4200, Fax: 610-683-1393, E-mail: graduate@kutztown.edu.

LaGrange College, Graduate Programs, Department of Education, LaGrange, GA 30240-2999. Offers curriculum and instruction (M Ed); middle grades (MAT); secondary education (MAT). Part-time and evening/weekend programs available. *Degree requirements:* For master's, comprehensive exam. *Entrance requirements:* For master's, GRE, MAT, minimum GPA of 2.5. Additional exam requirements/recommendations for international students: Required—TOEFL (minimum score 550 paper-based).

Lee University, Program in Education, Cleveland, TN 37320-3450. Offers classroom teaching (M Ed, Ed S); educational leadership (M Ed, Ed S); elementary/secondary education (MAT); secondary education (MAT); special education (elementary) (M Ed); special education (secondary) (M Ed, MAT); special education (severe disabilities) (M Ed). Part-time programs available. *Faculty:* 11 full-time (4 women), 3 part-time/adjunct (2 women). *Students:* 65 full-time (45 women), 140 part-time (80 women); includes 8 minority (5 African Americans, 1 American Indian/Alaska Native, 2 Hispanic Americans), 6 international. Average age 31. 4 applicants, 100% accepted, 2 enrolled. In 2009, 75 master's, 7 other advanced degrees awarded. *Degree requirements:* For master's, variable foreign language requirement, comprehensive exam, thesis, internship. *Entrance requirements:* For master's, MAT or GRE General Test, minimum GPA of 2.75, 3 letters of recommendation, interview, writing sample. Additional exam requirements/recommendations for international students: Required—TOEFL (minimum score 450 paper-based; 45 computer-based). *Application deadline:* For fall admission, 4/1 priority date for domestic students; for spring admission, 10/1 priority date for domestic students. Applications are processed on a rolling basis. Application fee: $25. *Expenses:* Tuition: Full-time $11,100; part-time $463 per credit. Required fees: $305. *Financial support:* Career-related internships or fieldwork, Federal Work-Study, institutionally sponsored loans, scholarships/grants, and unspecified assistantships available. Financial award application deadline: 3/1; financial award applicants required to submit FAFSA. *Unit head:* Dr. Gary Riggins, Director, 423-614-8193. *Application contact:* Vicki Glasscock, Graduate Admissions Director, 423-614-8059, E-mail: vglasscock@leeuniversity.edu.

Lehigh University, College of Education, Program in Teaching, Learning and Technology, Bethlehem, PA 18015. Offers elementary education with certification (M Ed); instructional technology (MS); learning sciences and technology (PhD); secondary education with certification (M Ed); teaching and learning (M Ed, MA); technology use in the schools (Graduate Certificate). Part-time programs available. *Faculty:* 7 full-time (4 women), 7 part-time/adjunct (3 women). *Students:* 48 full-time (39 women), 61 part-time (41 women); includes 11 minority (3 African Americans, 4 Asian Americans or Pacific Islanders, 4 Hispanic Americans), 5 international. Average age 31. 81 applicants, 67% accepted, 23 enrolled. In 2009, 48 master's awarded. Terminal master's awarded for partial completion of doctoral program. *Degree requirements:* For master's, comprehensive exam and dissertation (M Ed); for doctorate, comprehensive exam, thesis/dissertation. *Entrance requirements:* For master's, minimum GPA of 3.0, 2 letters of recommendation, essay, transcript; for doctorate, GRE General Test, minimum graduate GPA of 3.0, writing sample, 2 letters of recommendation, essay, transcript. Additional exam requirements/recommendations for international students: Required—TOEFL (minimum score 600 paper-based; 250 computer-based; 93 iBT). *Application deadline:* For fall admission, 2/1 for domestic and international students; for spring admission, 11/1 for domestic and international students. Applications are processed on a rolling basis. Application fee: $65. Electronic applications accepted. *Financial support:* In 2009–10, 18 students received support, including 1 fellowship with full and partial tuition reimbursement available (averaging $16,000 per year), 2 research assistantships with full and partial tuition reimbursements available (averaging $18,000 per year); career-related internships or fieldwork, institutionally sponsored loans, scholarships/grants, and tuition waivers (full and partial) also available. Financial award application deadline: 1/31. *Faculty research:* Instructional media and delivery systems, technologies to enhance education, technical and informal education, Web-based learning. *Unit head:* Dr. MJ Bishop, Coordinator, 610-758-3235, Fax: 610-758-3243, E-mail: mjba@lehigh.edu. *Application contact:* Donna M. Johnson, Coordinator, 610-758-3231, Fax: 610-758-6223, E-mail: dmj4@lehigh.edu.

Le Moyne College, Department of Education, Syracuse, NY 13214. Offers adolescent education (MS Ed, MST); adolescent education/special education (MS Ed, MST); adolescent English (grades 7-12) (MST); adolescent history (grades 7-12) (MST); childhood education (MS Ed); childhood education/special education (MS Ed); elementary education (MS Ed); general professional education (MS Ed); inclusive childhood education (MST); middle child specialist/special education (MS Ed); middle childhood specialist (MS Ed); school building leadership (MS Ed, CAS); school district business leader (MS Ed, CAS); school district leadership (MS Ed, CAS); secondary education (MS Ed); special education (MS Ed). *Accreditation:* Teacher Education Accreditation Council. Part-time and evening/weekend programs available. *Faculty:* 15 full-time (8 women), 61 part-time/adjunct (33 women). *Students:* 40 full-time (30 women), 260 part-time (180 women); includes 25 minority (11 African Americans, 3 American Indian/Alaska Native, 3 Asian Americans or Pacific Islanders, 8 Hispanic Americans). Average age 31. 168 applicants, 89% accepted, 140 enrolled. In 2009, 180 master's awarded. *Degree requirements:* For master's, thesis. *Entrance requirements:* For master's, GRE General Test, 2 letters of recommendation. Additional exam requirements/recommendations for international students: Required—TOEFL (minimum score 550 paper-based; 213 computer-based; 79 iBT). *Application deadline:* For fall admission, 4/1 priority date for domestic and international students; for spring admission, 10/1 priority date for domestic and international students. Applications are processed on a rolling basis. Application fee: $50. *Expenses:* Contact institution. *Financial support:* In 2009–10, 28 students received support. Career-related internships or fieldwork and health care benefits available. Support available to part-time students. Financial award applicants required to submit FAFSA. *Faculty research:* Recruitment/retention strategies, minority teachers, special education, multiculturalism, literacy, technology, video games learning, autism, school district organization. *Unit head:* Dr. Norbert J. Henry, Interim Chair/Director, 315-445-4376, Fax: 315-445-4744, E-mail: henry@lemoyne.edu. *Application contact:* Kristen P. Trapasso, Director of Graduate Admission, 315-445-4265, Fax: 315-445-6027, E-mail: trapaskp@lemoyne.edu.

Lewis & Clark College, Graduate School of Education and Counseling, Department of Teacher Education, Program in Middle Level/High School Education, Portland, OR 97219-7899. Offers MAT. *Accreditation:* NCATE. *Faculty:* 4 full-time (3 women), 9 part-time/adjunct (5 women). *Students:* 71 full-time (42 women); includes 8 minority (2 African Americans, 2 American Indian/Alaska Native, 1 Asian American or Pacific Islander, 3 Hispanic Americans), 2 international. Average age 29. 123 applicants, 82% accepted, 72 enrolled. In 2009, 57 master's awarded. *Entrance requirements:* For master's, Prior experience working with children and/or youth. Minimum undergraduate GPA of 2.75. Additional exam requirements/recommendations for international students: Required—TOEFL (minimum score 575 paper-based; 233 computer-based). *Application deadline:* For fall admission, 12/1 priority date for domestic and international students. Application fee: $50. Electronic applications accepted. *Expenses:* Tuition: Part-time $713 per semester hour. Tuition and fees vary according to course level and campus/location. *Financial support:* In 2009–10, 60 students received support. Career-related internships or fieldwork, Federal Work-Study, institutionally sponsored loans, scholarships/grants, health care benefits, and tuition waivers (partial) available. Support available to part-time students. Financial award application deadline: 3/1; financial award applicants required to submit FAFSA. *Faculty research:* Classroom management, classroom assessment, science education, classroom ethnography, moral development. *Unit head:* Dr. Kimberly Campbell, Coordinator, 503-768-6108, Fax: 503-768-7715, E-mail: lcteach@lclark.edu. *Application contact:* Becky Haas, Director of Admissions, 503-768-6200, Fax: 503-768-6205, E-mail: gseadmit@lclark.edu.

Lewis University, College of Education, Program in Secondary Education, Romeoville, IL 60446. Offers biology (MA); chemistry (MA); English (MA); history (MA); math (MA); physics (MA); psychology and social science (MA). Part-time programs available. *Students:* 20 full-time (12 women), 24 part-time (16 women); includes 2 minority (1 African American, 1 Hispanic American). Average age 29. 39 applicants, 51% accepted, 18 enrolled. In 2009, 15 master's awarded. *Entrance requirements:* For master's, departmental qualifying exam, writing exam, minimum GPA of 2.75, 2 letters of recommendation, interview. Additional exam requirements/recommendations for international students: Required—TOEFL (minimum score 550 paper-based; 213 computer-based). *Application deadline:* For fall admission, 5/1 priority date for international students; for spring admission, 11/15 priority date for international students. Applications are processed on a rolling basis. Application fee: $40. Electronic applications accepted. *Expenses:* Tuition: Full-time $6480; part-time $720 per credit. One-time fee: $40. Tuition and fees vary according to course load, degree level and program. *Financial support:* Federal Work-Study, scholarships/grants, and unspecified assistantships available. Financial award application deadline: 5/1; financial award applicants required to submit FAFSA. *Unit head:* Dr. Dorene Huvaere, Program Director, 815-838-0500 Ext. 5885, E-mail: huvaersdo@lewisu.edu. *Application contact:* Fran Welsh, Secretary, 815-838-0500 Ext. 5880, E-mail: welshfr@lewisu.edu.

Liberty University, School of Education, Lynchburg, VA 24502. Offers administration and supervision (M Ed); curriculum and instruction (M Ed); early childhood education (M Ed); education specialist (Ed S); educational leadership (Ed D); elementary education (M Ed); gifted education (M Ed); reading specialist (M Ed); school counseling (M Ed); secondary education (M Ed); special education (M Ed). *Accreditation:* NCATE. Part-time programs available. Postbaccalaureate distance learning degree programs offered (minimal on-campus study). *Degree requirements:* For doctorate, comprehensive exam, thesis/dissertation. *Entrance requirements:* For master's, GRE General Test or MAT (aken in or before 1999), 2 letters of recommendation, minimum undergraduate GPA of 3.0, curriculum vitae; for doctorate, GRE General Test or MAT (if taken before 1999), minimum master's GPA of 3.0, 3 years of teacher experience; for Ed S, GRE General Test or MAT (if taken before 1999), minimum master's GPA of 3.0, 3 years of teaching experience. Additional exam requirements/recommendations for international students: Required—TOEFL (minimum score 600 paper-based; 250 computer-based). Electronic applications accepted. *Expenses:* Contact institution. *Faculty research:* Self-determination, character education, bibliotherapy, learning styles, distance education.

Lincoln University, School of Graduate Studies and Continuing Education, Jefferson City, MO 65102. Offers business administration (MBA), including accounting, entrepreneurship, management, public administration and policy; educational leadership (Ed S), including elementary leadership, secondary leadership, superintendency; guidance and counseling (M Ed), including community/agency counseling, elementary school, secondary school; history (MA); school administration and supervision (M Ed), including elementary school administration,

secondary school administration, special education administration; school teaching (M Ed), including elementary school teaching, secondary school teaching; social science (MA), including history, political science, sociology; sociology (MA); sociology/criminal justice (MA). Part-time and evening/weekend programs available. *Students:* 52 full-time (27 women), 146 part-time (107 women); includes 40 minority (39 African Americans, 1 Asian American or Pacific Islander), 15 international. Average age 35. 76 applicants, 95% accepted, 46 enrolled. In 2009, 60 master's, 6 other advanced degrees awarded. *Degree requirements:* For master's and Ed S, comprehensive exam, thesis optional. *Entrance requirements:* For master's and Ed S, GRE, MAT or GMAT, minimum GPA of 2.75 in major, 2.5 overall; 3 letters of recommendation; minimum C average in English composition; personal statement of purpose. Additional exam requirements/recommendations for international students: Required—TOEFL (minimum score 500 paper-based; 173 computer-based; 61 iBT). *Application deadline:* For fall admission, 7/1 priority date for domestic and international students; for spring admission, 12/1 priority date for domestic and international students. Applications are processed on a rolling basis. Application fee: $20. *Expenses:* Tuition, state resident: full-time $4185; part-time $232.50 per credit hour. Tuition, nonresident: full-time $7767; part-time $431.50 per credit hour. Required fees: $270; $15 per credit hour. $20 per term. *Financial support:* Federal Work-Study and scholarships/grants available. Financial award application deadline: 4/1; financial award applicants required to submit FAFSA. *Faculty research:* Suicide prevention. *Unit head:* Dr. Linda S. Bickel, Dean, 573-681-5247, Fax: 573-681-5106, E-mail: gradschool@lincolnu.edu. *Application contact:* Irasema Steck, Administrative Assistant, 573-681-5247, Fax: 573-681-5106, E-mail: gradschool@lincolnu.edu.

Long Island University, C.W. Post Campus, College of Liberal Arts and Sciences, Department of English, Brookville, NY 11548-1300. Offers English (MA); English for adolescence education (MS). Part-time and evening/weekend programs available. *Degree requirements:* For master's, comprehensive exam (for some programs), thesis (for some programs). *Entrance requirements:* For master's, minimum GPA of 3.5 in major, 3.0 overall; 21 credits of English. Electronic applications accepted. *Faculty research:* English Renaissance, Sinclair Lewis: The Early Years, puppetry archives, Irish-American Experiences: literature of memory, Henry James's anxiety of Poe's influence.

Long Island University, Rockland Graduate Campus, Graduate School, Program in Curriculum and Instruction, Orangeburg, NY 10962. Offers adolescence education (MS Ed); childhood education (MS). *Faculty:* 1 (woman) full-time, 8 part-time/adjunct (3 women). *Students:* 18 full-time (15 women), 46 part-time (40 women). In 2009, 35 master's awarded. *Entrance requirements:* For master's, GRE General Test. *Application deadline:* Applications are processed on a rolling basis. Application fee: $30. *Expenses:* Tuition: Part-time $930 per credit. Required fees: $200 per semester. *Financial support:* Scholarships/grants available. Support available to part-time students. Financial award applicants required to submit FAFSA. *Unit head:* Dr. Nancy T. Goldman, Program Director, 845-359-7200 Ext. 5409, Fax: 845-359-7248, E-mail: nancy.goldman@liu.edu. *Application contact:* Peter S. Reiner, Director of Admissions and Marketing, 845-359-7200, Fax: 845-359-7248, E-mail: peter.reiner@liu.edu.

Long Island University, Westchester Graduate Campus, Programs in Education-Teaching, Program in Special Education and Secondary Education, Purchase, NY 10577. Offers MS Ed, Advanced Certificate. Part-time and evening/weekend programs available.

Longwood University, Office of Graduate Studies, College of Education and Human Services, Farmville, VA 23909. Offers communication sciences and disorders (MS); community and college counseling (MS); curriculum and instruction specialist-elementary (MS), including mild disabilities, modern languages; curriculum and instruction specialist-secondary (MS), including English, mild disabilities, modern languages; educational leadership (MS); guidance and counseling (MS); literacy and culture (MS); school library media (MS). *Accreditation:* NCATE. Part-time and evening/weekend programs available. *Degree requirements:* For master's, comprehensive exam, thesis optional. *Entrance requirements:* For master's, GRE (communication sciences and disorders), minimum GPA of 2.75. Additional exam requirements/recommendations for international students: Required—TOEFL (minimum score 550 paper-based; 213 computer-based).

Louisiana State University and Agricultural and Mechanical College, Graduate School, College of Education, Department of Educational Theory, Policy and Practice, Baton Rouge, LA 70803. Offers counseling (M Ed, MA, Ed S); educational administration (M Ed, MA, PhD, Ed S); educational technology (MA); elementary education (M Ed); higher education (PhD); research methodology (PhD); secondary education (M Ed). *Accreditation:* ACA (one or more programs are accredited); NCATE. Part-time and evening/weekend programs available. *Faculty:* 38 full-time (24 women). *Students:* 174 full-time (139 women), 154 part-time (129 women); includes 74 minority (66 African Americans, 3 Asian Americans or Pacific Islanders, 5 Hispanic Americans), 9 international. Average age 32. 122 applicants, 60% accepted, 48 enrolled. In 2009, 124 master's, 13 doctorates, 11 other advanced degrees awarded. Terminal master's awarded for partial completion of doctoral program. *Degree requirements:* For doctorate, thesis/dissertation; for Ed S, thesis optional. *Entrance requirements:* For master's and doctorate, GRE General Test, minimum GPA of 3.0. Additional exam requirements/recommendations for international students: Required—TOEFL (minimum score 550 paper-based; 213 computer-based; 79 iBT) or IELTS (minimum score 6.5). *Application deadline:* For fall admission, 1/25 priority date for domestic students, 5/15 for international students; for spring admission, 10/15 for international students. Applications are processed on a rolling basis. Application fee: $50 ($70 for international students). Electronic applications accepted. *Financial support:* In 2009–10, 226 students received support, including 1 fellowship (averaging $31,711 per year), 27 research assistantships with full and partial tuition reimbursements available (averaging $10,143 per year), 35 teaching assistantships with full and partial tuition reimbursements available (averaging $12,555 per year); career-related internships or fieldwork, Federal Work-Study, institutionally sponsored loans, health care benefits, and unspecified assistantships also available. Support available to part-time students. Financial award applicants required to submit FAFSA. *Faculty research:* Literary, curriculum studies, science education, K-12 leadership, higher education. Total annual research expenditures: $1.8 million. *Unit head:* Dr. Earl Cheek, Chair, 225-578-6867, Fax: 225-578-9135, E-mail: echeek@lsu.edu. *Application contact:* Dr., Graduate Coordinator, 225-578-2280, Fax: 225-578-9135.

Louisiana Tech University, Graduate School, College of Education, Department of Curriculum, Instruction and Leadership, Ruston, LA 71272. Offers curriculum and instruction (MS, Ed D); educational leadership (Ed D); secondary education (M Ed), including business education, English education, foreign language education, health and physical education, mathematics education, science education, social studies education, speech education. *Accreditation:* NCATE. Part-time programs available. *Degree requirements:* For doctorate, thesis/dissertation. *Entrance requirements:* For master's and doctorate, GRE General Test.

Loyola Marymount University, School of Education, Department of Elementary and Secondary Education, Program in Secondary Education, Los Angeles, CA 90045. Offers MA. Part-time programs available. *Faculty:* 6 full-time (5 women), 11 part-time/adjunct (6 women). *Students:* 103 full-time (49 women), 52 part-time (36 women); includes 84 minority (15 African Americans, 22 Asian Americans or Pacific Islanders, 47 Hispanic Americans), 1 international. Average age 29. 74 applicants, 72% accepted, 47 enrolled. In 2009, 82 master's awarded. *Degree requirements:* For master's, comprehensive exam. *Entrance requirements:* For master's, CBEST, CSET, 3 letters of recommendation. Additional exam requirements/recommendations for international students: Required—TOEFL (minimum score 600 paper-based; 250 computer-based; 100 iBT). *Application deadline:* For fall admission, 6/15 for domestic students; for spring admission, 11/15 for domestic students. Application fee: $50. Electronic applications accepted. *Financial support:* In 2009–10, 99 students received support. Scholarships/grants and unspecified assistantships available. Support available to part-time students. Financial award application deadline: 6/15; financial award applicants required to submit FAFSA. *Unit head:* Dr. Irene Oliver, Chair, 310-338-7302, E-mail: ioliver@lmu.edu. *Application contact:* Chake H. Kouyoumjian, Director, Graduate Admissions, 310-338-2721, Fax: 310-338-6086, E-mail: ckouyoum@lmu.edu.

Loyola University Chicago, School of Education, Program in Initial Teacher Preparation, Chicago, IL 60660. Offers elementary education (M Ed); math education (M Ed); reading specialist (M Ed); school technology (M Ed); science education (M Ed); secondary education (M Ed); special education (M Ed). *Accreditation:* NCATE. *Faculty:* 12 full-time (9 women), 12 part-time/adjunct (6 women). *Students:* 154. Average age 28. 125 applicants, 69% accepted, 38 enrolled. In 2009, 89 master's awarded. *Degree requirements:* For master's, comprehensive exam. *Entrance requirements:* For master's, Illinois Basic Skills Test, 3 letters of recommendation, minimum GPA of 3.0, resume. Additional exam requirements/recommendations for international students: Required—TOEFL (minimum score 550 paper-based; 213 computer-based; 79 iBT). *Application deadline:* For fall admission, 7/1 priority date for domestic and international students; for spring admission, 11/1 priority date for domestic and international students. Applications are processed on a rolling basis. Application fee: $50. Electronic applications accepted. *Expenses:* Tuition: Full-time $14,220; part-time $790 per credit hour. Required fees: $60 per semester hour. Tuition and fees vary according to program. *Financial support:* In 2009–10, 1 research assistantship with full tuition reimbursement (averaging $8,500 per year), 1 teaching assistantship were awarded. Financial award application deadline: 2/15. *Faculty research:* Positive behavior support, school reform, school improvement. *Unit head:* Dr. Dorothy Giroux, Director, 312-915-7027, E-mail: dgiroux@luc.edu. *Application contact:* Marie Rosin-Dittmar, Information Contact, 312-915-6800, E-mail: schleduc@luc.edu.

Maharishi University of Management, Graduate Studies, Department of Education, Fairfield, IA 52557. Offers teaching elementary education (MA); teaching secondary education (MA). *Degree requirements:* For master's, thesis or alternative. *Entrance requirements:* For master's, GRE, minimum GPA of 3.0. Additional exam requirements/recommendations for international students: Required—TOEFL. *Faculty research:* Unified field-based approach to education, moral climate, scientific study of teaching.

Manhattanville College, Graduate Programs, School of Education, Program in Middle Childhood/Adolescence Education (Grades 5-12), Purchase, NY 10577-2132. Offers biology (MAT); biology and special education (MPS); chemistry (MAT); chemistry and special education (MPS); English (MAT); English and special education (MPS); literacy (MPS), including reading and writing, writing; literacy and special education (MPS); math (MAT); math and special education (MPS); second language (MAT), including French, Italian, Latin, Spanish; social studies (MAT); social studies and special education (MPS); special education (MPS). Part-time and evening/weekend programs available. *Students:* 52 full-time (39 women), 106 part-time (71 women); includes 8 African Americans, 3 Asian Americans or Pacific Islanders, 4 Hispanic Americans, 1 international. In 2009, 82 master's awarded. *Degree requirements:* For master's, comprehensive exam or research project, field experience. *Entrance requirements:* For master's, minimum undergraduate GPA of 3.0, 2 letters of recommendation. Additional exam requirements/recommendations for international students: Required—TOEFL. *Application deadline:* Applications are processed on a rolling basis. Application fee: $70. Electronic applications accepted. *Financial support:* Career-related internships or fieldwork, Federal Work-Study, institutionally sponsored loans, and unspecified assistantships available. Support available to part-time students. Financial award application deadline: 3/1; financial award applicants required to submit FAFSA. *Unit head:* Dr. Shelley Wepner, Dean, 914-323-5192, Fax: 914-694-2386, E-mail: wepners@mville.edu. *Application contact:* Jeanine Pardey-Levine, Director of Admissions, 914-323-3208, Fax: 914-694-1732, E-mail: edschool@mville.edu.

Mansfield University of Pennsylvania, Graduate Studies, Department of Education and Special Education, Mansfield, PA 16933. Offers elementary education (M Ed); secondary education (MS). *Accreditation:* NCATE (one or more programs are accredited). Part-time and evening/weekend programs available. Postbaccalaureate distance learning degree programs offered (no on-campus study). *Faculty:* 9 full-time (6 women). *Students:* 52 full-time (40 women), 56 part-time (41 women); includes 4 minority (1 African American, 1 Asian American or Pacific Islander, 2 Hispanic Americans), 2 international. Average age 29. In 2009, 56 master's awarded. *Degree requirements:* For master's, comprehensive exam, thesis optional. *Entrance requirements:* For master's, minimum GPA of 3.0. Additional exam requirements/recommendations for international students: Required—TOEFL (minimum score 550 paper-based; 220 computer-based). *Application deadline:* For fall admission, 8/1 priority date for domestic students, 8/1 for international students; for spring admission, 11/1 priority date for domestic students, 9/1 for international students. Applications are processed on a rolling basis. Application fee: $25. Electronic applications accepted. *Expenses:* Tuition, state resident: full-time $6666; part-time $370 per credit. Tuition, nonresident: full-time $10,666; part-time $593 per credit. Required fees: $1388. *Financial support:* Career-related internships or fieldwork and unspecified assistantships available. Support available to part-time students. Financial award application deadline: 5/1; financial award applicants required to submit FAFSA. *Unit head:* Dr. Jesus Lucero, Chairperson, 570-662-4791, E-mail: jlucero@mansfield.edu. *Application contact:* Christina Hale, Assistant Director of Enrollment Services/Graduate Admissions, 570-662-4812, Fax: 570-662-4121, E-mail: chale@mansfield.edu.

Marshall University, Academic Affairs Division, Graduate School of Education and Professional Development, Program in Secondary Education, Huntington, WV 25755. Offers MA. *Accreditation:* NCATE. Part-time and evening/weekend programs available. *Faculty:* 8 full-time (5 women). *Students:* 20 full-time (14 women), 86 part-time (61 women); includes 2 minority (both Asian Americans or Pacific Islanders). Average age 35. In 2009, 19 master's awarded. *Degree requirements:* For master's, thesis optional, comprehensive or oral assessment. *Entrance requirements:* For master's, GRE General Test or MAT. Application fee: $40. *Financial support:* Federal Work-Study, tuition waivers (full), and unspecified assistantships available. Support available to part-time students. Financial award applicants required to submit FAFSA. *Unit head:* Dr. Calvin Meyer, Director, 304-746-1936, E-mail: meyer@marshall.edu. *Application contact:* Graduate Admissions, 304-746-1900, Fax: 304-746-1902, E-mail: services@marshall.edu.

Marygrove College, Graduate Division, Sage Program, Detroit, MI 48221-2599. Offers M Ed. *Entrance requirements:* For master's, Michigan Teacher Test for Certification.

Marymount University, School of Education and Human Services, Program in Education, Arlington, VA 22207-4299. Offers elementary education (M Ed); English as a second language (M Ed); professional studies (M Ed); secondary education (M Ed); special education, general curriculum (M Ed). *Accreditation:* NCATE. Part-time and evening/weekend programs available. *Faculty:* 9 full-time (6 women), 9 part-time/adjunct (8 women). *Students:* 55 full-time (46 women), 117 part-time (100 women); includes 13 minority (1 African American, 4 Asian Americans or Pacific Islanders, 8 Hispanic Americans), 7 international. Average age 31. 73 applicants, 93% accepted, 55 enrolled. In 2009, 62 master's awarded. *Degree requirements:* For master's, thesis or alternative. *Entrance requirements:* For master's, GRE or MAT and PRAXIS I or SAT/ACT, 2 letters of recommendation, interview. Additional exam requirements/recommendations for international students: Required—TOEFL (minimum score 600 paper-based; 250 computer-based; 96 iBT), IELTS (minimum score 6.5). *Application deadline:* For fall admission, 7/1 for international students; for spring admission, 10/15 for international students. Applications are processed on a rolling basis. Application fee: $40. Electronic applications accepted. *Expenses:* Tuition: Full-time $13,050; part-time $725 per credit hour. Required fees: $135; $7.50 per credit hour. *Financial support:* In 2009–10, 48 students received support; research assistantships with full tuition reimbursements available, career-related internships or fieldwork, Federal Work-Study, scholarships/grants, and unspecified assistantships available. Support available to part-time students. Financial award applicants required to submit FAFSA. *Unit head:* Dr. Shelly Haser, Chair, 703-526-6855, Fax: 703-284-1631, E-mail: shelly.haser@marymount.edu. *Application contact:* Francesca Reed, Director, Graduate Admissions, 703-284-5901, Fax: 703-527-3815, E-mail: grad.admissions@marymount.edu.

Maryville University of Saint Louis, School of Education, St. Louis, MO 63141-7299. Offers art education (MA Ed); early childhood education (MA Ed); educational leadership (Ed D); educational leadership: principal certification (MA Ed); elementary education (MA Ed); elementary education/English (MA Ed); elementary education/psychology (MA Ed); environmental education (MA Ed); gifted education (MA Ed); literacy specialist (MA Ed); middle grades education (MA Ed);

Secondary Education

Maryville University of Saint Louis (continued)
secondary teaching and inquiry (MA Ed); teacher as leader (MA Ed). *Accreditation:* NASAD; NCATE. Part-time and evening/weekend programs available. *Students:* 25 full-time (18 women), 198 part-time (145 women); includes 33 minority (27 African Americans, 2 American Indian/Alaska Native, 1 Asian American or Pacific Islander, 3 Hispanic Americans). Average age 36. In 2009, 61 master's, 45 doctorates awarded. *Degree requirements:* For master's, thesis, project. *Entrance requirements:* For master's and doctorate, minimum GPA of 3.0, 3 professional recommendations. Additional exam requirements/recommendations for international students: Required—TOEFL (minimum score 550 paper-based). *Application deadline:* Applications are processed on a rolling basis. Application fee: $40 ($60 for international students). Electronic applications accepted. *Expenses:* Tuition: Full-time $20,384; part-time $627.50 per credit hour. Required fees: $100 per semester. *Financial support:* Career-related internships or fieldwork, Federal Work-Study, tuition waivers (partial), and professional educator discounts available. Financial award application deadline: 3/1; financial award applicants required to submit FAFSA. *Faculty research:* Collaboration with public schools, pre-service program development, mathematics, diversity, literacy. *Unit head:* Dr. Sam Hausfather, Dean, 314-529-9466, Fax: 314-529-9921, E-mail: shausfather@maryville.edu. *Application contact:* Holly Stanwich, Graduate Admissions Coordinator, 314-529-9542, Fax: 314-529-9921, E-mail: teachered@maryville.edu.

Marywood University, Academic Affairs, Reap College of Education and Human Development, Department of Education, Program in Secondary/K-12 Education, Scranton, PA 18509-1598. Offers MAT. *Students:* 22 full-time (13 women), 15 part-time (13 women); includes 2 minority (1 American Indian/Alaska Native, 1 Asian American or Pacific Islander). Average age 27. In 2009, 2 master's awarded. *Entrance requirements:* Additional exam requirements/recommendations for international students: Required—TOEFL (minimum score 550 paper-based; 213 computer-based; 79 iBT). *Application deadline:* For fall admission, 4/1 priority date for domestic students, 3/31 priority date for international students; for spring admission, 11/1 priority date for domestic students, 8/31 priority date for international students. Applications are processed on a rolling basis. Application fee: $35. Electronic applications accepted. *Expenses:* Tuition: Part-time $715 per credit. Required fees: $270 per semester. Tuition and fees vary according to degree level, campus/location and program. *Financial support:* Career-related internships or fieldwork, scholarships/grants, and unspecified assistantships available. Support available to part-time students. Financial award application deadline: 6/30; financial award applicants required to submit FAFSA. *Application contact:* Tammy Manka, Assistant Director of Graduate Admissions, 866-279-9663, E-mail: tmanka@marywood.edu.

McDaniel College, Graduate and Professional Studies, Program in Elementary and Secondary Education, Westminster, MD 21157-4390. Offers elementary education (MS); secondary education (MS). *Accreditation:* NCATE. Part-time and evening/weekend programs available. *Degree requirements:* For master's, comprehensive exam (for some programs), thesis optional. *Entrance requirements:* For master's, GRE General Test, MAT, or NTE/PRAXIS I, letters of reference (3). Additional exam requirements/recommendations for international students: Required—TOEFL (minimum score 213 computer-based). *Expenses:* Tuition: Part-time $325 per credit hour.

McNeese State University, Doré School of Graduate Studies, Burton College of Education, Department of Teacher Education, Program in Curriculum and Instruction, Lake Charles, LA 70609. Offers early childhood education (M Ed); elementary education (M Ed); secondary education (M Ed). Evening/weekend programs available. *Faculty:* 12 full-time (6 women). *Students:* 4 full-time (all women), 9 part-time (all women); includes 2 minority (both African Americans). In 2009, 3 master's awarded. *Entrance requirements:* For master's, GRE, teaching certificate. *Application deadline:* For fall admission, 5/15 priority date for domestic and international students; for spring admission, 10/15 priority date for domestic and international students. Applications are processed on a rolling basis. Application fee: $20 ($30 for international students). *Expenses:* Tuition, area resident: Full-time $2556. Tuition, state resident: full-time $2556. Required fees: $1031. Tuition and fees vary according to course load. *Financial support:* Application deadline: 5/1. *Unit head:* Dr. Royce Zant, Head, 337-475-5404, Fax: 337-475-5398, E-mail: rzant@mcneese.edu. *Application contact:* Dr. George F. Mead, Interim Dean of Dore' School of Graduate Studies, 337-475-5396, Fax: 337-475-5397, E-mail: admissions@mcneese.edu.

McNeese State University, Doré School of Graduate Studies, Burton College of Education, Department of Teacher Education, Program in Teaching, Lake Charles, LA 70609. Offers elementary education grades 1-5 (MAT); secondary education grades 6-12 (MAT); special education—mild/moderate grades 1-12 (MAT). Evening/weekend programs available. *Faculty:* 12 full-time (6 women). *Students:* 44 full-time (37 women), 126 part-time (112 women); includes 34 minority (25 African Americans, 1 American Indian/Alaska Native, 2 Asian Americans or Pacific Islanders, 6 Hispanic Americans), 1 international. In 2009, 43 master's awarded. *Entrance requirements:* For master's, GRE, PRAXIS, 2 letters of recommendation; autobiography. *Application deadline:* For fall admission, 5/15 priority date for domestic and international students; for spring admission, 10/15 priority date for domestic and international students. Applications are processed on a rolling basis. Application fee: $20 ($30 for international students). *Expenses:* Tuition, area resident: Full-time $2556. Tuition, state resident: full-time $2556. Required fees: $1031. Tuition and fees vary according to course load. *Financial support:* Application deadline: 5/1. *Unit head:* Dr. Royce Zant, Head, 337-475-5404, Fax: 337-475-5398, E-mail: rzant@mcneese.edu. *Application contact:* Dr. George F. Mead, Interim Dean of Dore' School of Graduate Studies, 337-475-5396, Fax: 337-475-5397, E-mail: admissions@mcneese.edu.

Medaille College, Program in Education, Buffalo, NY 14214-2695. Offers adolescent education (MS Ed); curriculum and instruction (MS Ed); education preparation (MS Ed); literacy (MS Ed); special education (MS). *Accreditation:* Teacher Education Accreditation Council. Part-time and evening/weekend programs available. *Faculty:* 22 full-time (16 women), 47 part-time/adjunct (36 women). *Students:* 721 full-time (596 women), 2 part-time (both women); includes 34 minority (16 African Americans, 1 American Indian/Alaska Native, 14 Asian Americans or Pacific Islanders, 3 Hispanic Americans). Average age 26. 621 applicants, 46% accepted, 288 enrolled. In 2009, 608 master's awarded. *Degree requirements:* For master's, thesis or alternative. *Entrance requirements:* For master's, minimum undergraduate GPA of 2.7. Additional exam requirements/recommendations for international students: Required—TOEFL (minimum score 550 paper-based; 213 computer-based). *Application deadline:* For fall admission, 8/15 priority date for domestic students; for spring admission, 1/15 priority date for domestic students. Applications are processed on a rolling basis. Application fee: $35. Electronic applications accepted. *Financial support:* In 2009–10, 501 students received support. Federal Work-Study available. Financial award applicants required to submit FAFSA. *Faculty research:* Curriculum planning, truancy, tracking minority students, curriculum design, mentoring students. *Unit head:* Dr. Robert DiSibio, Director of Graduate Programs, 716-932-2548, Fax: 716-631-1380, E-mail: rdisibio@medaille.edu. *Application contact:* Jacqueline Matheny, Executive Director of Marketing and Enrollment, 716-932-2541, Fax: 716-632-1811, E-mail: jmatheny@medaille.edu.

Mercer University, Graduate Studies, Cecil B. Day Campus, Tift College of Education (Atlanta), Macon, GA 31207-0003. Offers curriculum and instruction (PhD); early childhood education (M Ed, MAT); educational leadership (PhD, Ed S); middle grades education (M Ed, MAT); reading education (M Ed); secondary education (M Ed, MAT); teacher leadership (Ed S). *Accreditation:* NCATE. Part-time and evening/weekend programs available. *Faculty:* 27 full-time (14 women), 6 part-time/adjunct (3 women). *Students:* 302 full-time (251 women), 543 part-time (430 women); includes 334 minority (311 African Americans, 1 American Indian/Alaska Native, 21 Asian Americans or Pacific Islanders, 1 Hispanic American), 7 international. Average age 34. In 2009, 195 master's, 20 doctorates awarded. *Degree requirements:* For master's and Ed S, research project; for doctorate, thesis/dissertation. *Entrance requirements:* For master's, GRE or MAT, minimum undergraduate GPA of 2.75; for doctorate, GRE; for Ed S, GRE or MAT, minimum GPA of 3.25, 3 years of teaching experience. Additional exam requirements/recommendations for international students: Required—TOEFL. *Application deadline:* For fall admission, 8/1 for domestic and international students; for spring admission, 12/1 for domestic and international students. Applications are processed on a rolling basis. Application fee: $25. *Expenses:* Contact institution. *Financial support:* Federal Work-Study available. Support available to part-time students. Financial award application deadline: 5/1. *Faculty research:* Educational computing, content area reading, concept learning, importance of play for young children, multicultural literature. *Unit head:* Dr. Carl R. Martray, Dean, 478-301-5397, Fax: 478-301-2280, E-mail: martray_cr@mercer.edu. *Application contact:* Dr. Allison Gilmore, Associate Dean for Graduate Teacher Education, 678-547-6330, Fax: 678-547-6055, E-mail: gilmore_a@mercer.edu.

Mercy College, School of Education, Program in Adolescence Education, Grades 7-12, Dobbs Ferry, NY 10522-1189. Offers MS. Part-time and evening/weekend programs available. *Students:* 83 full-time (42 women), 195 part-time (111 women); includes 37 African Americans, 4 Asian Americans or Pacific Islanders, 46 Hispanic Americans. Average age 33. 141 applicants, 70% accepted, 83 enrolled. In 2009, 123 master's awarded. *Entrance requirements:* For master's, resume, interview, assessment by specific program director or designee. Additional exam requirements/recommendations for international students: Required—TOEFL (minimum score 600 paper-based; 250 computer-based; 100 iBT). *Application deadline:* For fall admission, 8/1 for international students. Applications are processed on a rolling basis. Application fee: $40. Electronic applications accepted. *Expenses:* Tuition: Full-time $13,158; part-time $731 per credit. Required fees: $500. Tuition and fees vary according to degree level and program. *Financial support:* In 2009–10, 13 students received support. Career-related internships or fieldwork, Federal Work-Study, scholarships/grants, and unspecified assistantships available. Support available to part-time students. Financial award applicants required to submit FAFSA. *Faculty research:* Teaching-learning process, adolescent development, literacy instruction. *Unit head:* Dr. Andrew Peiser, Interim Dean for the School of Education, 914-674-7489, Fax: 914-674-7352, E-mail: apeiser@mercy.edu. *Application contact:* Mary Ellen Hoffman, Interim Associate Dean, 914-674-7334, E-mail: mhoffman@mercy.edu.

Miami University, Graduate School, School of Education and Allied Professions, Department of Teacher Education, Oxford, OH 45056. Offers elementary education (M Ed, MAT); reading education (M Ed); secondary education (M Ed, MAT), including adolescent education (MAT), elementary mathematics education (M Ed), secondary education. Part-time programs available. *Students:* 48 full-time (31 women), 70 part-time (60 women); includes 6 minority (3 African Americans, 3 Hispanic Americans), 5 international. *Entrance requirements:* For master's, GRE (MAT), minimum undergraduate GPA of 3.0 during previous 2 years or 2.75 overall. Application fee: $50. *Expenses:* Tuition, state resident: full-time $11,280. Tuition, nonresident: full-time $24,912. Required fees: $516. *Financial support:* Fellowships with full tuition reimbursements, research assistantships, teaching assistantships, career-related internships or fieldwork, Federal Work-Study, scholarships/grants, health care benefits, tuition waivers (full), and unspecified assistantships available. Financial award application deadline: 3/1. *Unit head:* Dr. James Shiveley, Chair, 513-529-6443, Fax: 513-529-4931, E-mail: shiveljm@muohio.edu. *Application contact:* Dr. Iris Johnson, Assistant Chair and Graduate Coordinator, 513-529-6443, Fax: 513-529-4931, E-mail: johnsoid@muohio.edu.

Middle Tennessee State University, College of Graduate Studies, College of Education and Behavioral Science, Department of Educational Leadership, Program in Curriculum and Instruction, Murfreesboro, TN 37132. Offers curriculum and instruction (M Ed, Ed S); English as a second language (M Ed, Ed S); secondary education (M Ed); technology and curriculum design (Ed S). *Accreditation:* NCATE. Part-time and evening/weekend programs available. Postbaccalaureate distance learning degree programs offered. *Students:* 14 full-time (7 women), 277 part-time (249 women); includes 39 minority (35 African Americans, 3 Asian Americans or Pacific Islanders, 1 Hispanic American). 80 applicants, 89% accepted, 71 enrolled. In 2009, 69 master's, 40 Ed Ss awarded. *Degree requirements:* For master's, comprehensive exam. *Entrance requirements:* For master's and Ed S, GRE, MAT or PRAXIS. Additional exam requirements/recommendations for international students: Required—TOEFL (minimum score 525 paper-based; 195 computer-based; 71 iBT) or IELTS (minimum score 6). *Application deadline:* For fall admission, 6/1 for domestic and international students. Applications are processed on a rolling basis. Application fee: $25 ($30 for international students). Electronic applications accepted. *Expenses:* Tuition, state resident: full-time $4404. Tuition, nonresident: full-time $10,956. *Financial support:* Application deadline: 5/1. *Unit head:* Dr. James Huffman, Chair, 615-898-2855, Fax: 615-898-2859. *Application contact:* Dr. Michael Allen, Dean and Vice Provost for Research, 615-898-2840, Fax: 615-904-8020, E-mail: mallen@mtsu.edu.

Mills College, Graduate Studies, School of Education, Oakland, CA 94613-1000. Offers child life in hospitals (MA); early childhood education (MA); education (MA), including art education, curriculum and instruction, elementary education, English education, foreign language education, mathematics education, science education, secondary education, social studies education, teaching; educational leadership (MA, Ed D); infant mental health (MA). Part-time and evening/weekend programs available. *Faculty:* 11 full-time (9 women), 16 part-time/adjunct (14 women). *Students:* 138 full-time (119 women), 55 part-time (48 women); includes 71 minority (34 African Americans, 19 Asian Americans or Pacific Islanders, 18 Hispanic Americans), 3 international. Average age 34. 210 applicants, 82% accepted, 93 enrolled. In 2009, 54 master's, 15 doctorates awarded. Terminal master's awarded for partial completion of doctoral program. *Degree requirements:* For master's, comprehensive exam. *Entrance requirements:* For doctorate, GRE General Test. Additional exam requirements/recommendations for international students: Required—TOEFL. *Application deadline:* For fall admission, 2/1 for domestic and international students; for spring admission, 11/1 for domestic and international students. Applications are processed on a rolling basis. Application fee: $50. Electronic applications accepted. *Expenses:* Tuition: Full-time $26,326; part-time $6584 per course. Required fees: $896. One-time fee: $896 part-time. Tuition and fees vary according to program. *Financial support:* In 2009–10, 188 students received support, including 186 fellowships (averaging $6,499 per year), 28 teaching assistantships with partial tuition reimbursements available (averaging $3,187 per year); career-related internships or fieldwork and scholarships/grants also available. Support available to part-time students. Financial award application deadline: 2/1; financial award applicants required to submit FAFSA. *Faculty research:* Child development, gender and education, public policy, cross-cultural development, development of literacy. Total annual research expenditures: $1.2 million. *Unit head:* Joseph Kahne, Chairperson, 510-430-3190, Fax: 510-430-3314, E-mail: grad-studies@mills.edu. *Application contact:* Jessica King, Graduate Admission Specialist, 510-430-3305, Fax: 510-430-2159, E-mail: grad-studies@mills.edu.

Minnesota State University Mankato, College of Graduate Studies, College of Education, Department of Educational Studies: K–12 and Secondary Programs, Mankato, MN 56001. Offers curriculum and instruction (SP); educational technology (MS); library media education (MS, Certificate); teacher licensure program (MAT); teaching and learning (MS, Certificate). *Accreditation:* NCATE. *Students:* 34 full-time (23 women), 100 part-time (75 women). *Degree requirements:* For master's, comprehensive exam, thesis or alternative; for other advanced degree, comprehensive exam, thesis. *Entrance requirements:* For master's, GRE General Test or MAT, minimum GPA of 3.0 during previous 2 years; for other advanced degree, GRE, minimum GPA of 3.0. Additional exam requirements/recommendations for international students: Required—TOEFL. *Application deadline:* For fall admission, 7/1 priority date for domestic students, 5/1 for international students; for spring admission, 11/1 for domestic students, 10/1 for international students. Applications are processed on a rolling basis. Application fee: $40. Electronic applications accepted. *Expenses:* Tuition, state resident: full-time $5364. Tuition, nonresident: full-time $8314. *Financial support:* Application deadline: 3/15. *Unit head:* Dr. Kitty Foord, Chairperson, 507-389-1965. *Application contact:* 507-389-2321, E-mail: grad@mnsu.edu.

Mississippi College, Graduate School, School of Education, Department of Teacher Education and Leadership, Clinton, MS 39058. Offers art (M Ed); biological science (M Ed); business education (M Ed); computer science (M Ed); dyslexia therapy (M Ed); educational leadership (M Ed, Ed D, Ed S); elementary education (M Ed, Ed S); English (M Ed); higher education administration (MS); mathematics (M Ed); secondary education (M Ed); social studies (history) (M Ed); teaching arts (M Ed). Part-time programs available. Postbaccalaureate distance learning

degree programs offered (no on-campus study). *Faculty:* 11 full-time (7 women), 13 part-time/adjunct (7 women). *Students:* 33 full-time (22 women), 282 part-time (240 women); includes 148 minority (146 African Americans, 2 American Indian/Alaska Native), 1 international. Average age 34. In 2009, 147 master's awarded. *Degree requirements:* For master's, comprehensive exam, thesis optional. *Entrance requirements:* For master's, NTE. Additional exam requirements/recommendations for international students: Recommended—IELTS. *Application deadline:* For fall admission, 8/15 priority date for domestic students. Applications are processed on a rolling basis. Application fee: $30. Electronic applications accepted. *Expenses:* Tuition: Part-time $452 per credit hour. Required fees: $101 per semester. Tuition and fees vary according to degree level, campus/location, program and student level. *Financial support:* Teaching assistantships, career-related internships or fieldwork, Federal Work-Study, scholarships/grants, and unspecified assistantships available. Support available to part-time students. Financial award applicants required to submit FAFSA. *Unit head:* Dr. Tom Williams, Chair, 601-925-3844, E-mail: twilliams@mc.edu. *Application contact:* Elnora Lewis, Secretary, 601-925-3225, Fax: 601-925-3889, E-mail: lewis09@mc.edu.

Mississippi State University, College of Education, Department of Curriculum, Instruction and Special Education, Mississippi State, MS 39762. Offers curriculum and instruction (PhD); education (Ed D, Ed S), including elementary education, secondary education, special education (Ed S); elementary education (MS, PhD); secondary education (MS, PhD); secondary teacher alternate route (MAT); special education (MS). *Accreditation:* NCATE. Part-time and evening/weekend programs available. *Faculty:* 13 full-time (11 women). *Students:* 35 full-time (33 women), 126 part-time (103 women); includes 55 minority (all African Americans). Average age 35. 80 applicants, 60% accepted, 40 enrolled. In 2009, 60 master's, 6 doctorates, 7 other advanced degrees awarded. *Degree requirements:* For master's, comprehensive exam; for doctorate, thesis/dissertation; for Ed S, comprehensive exam, thesis or alternative. *Entrance requirements:* For master's, GRE, minimum GPA of 2.75 in junior and senior year, eligibility for initial teacher certification; for doctorate, GRE, minimum graduate GPA of 3.4; for Ed S, GRE, minimum graduate GPA of 3.2. Additional exam requirements/recommendations for international students: Required—TOEFL (minimum score 600 paper-based; 250 computer-based; 100 iBT); Recommended—IELTS (minimum score 7.5). *Application deadline:* For fall admission, 3/1 priority date for domestic students, 5/1 for international students; for spring admission, 9/1 priority date for domestic students, 9/1 for international students. Applications are processed on a rolling basis. Application fee: $40. Electronic applications accepted. *Expenses:* Tuition, state resident: full-time $2575.50; part-time $286.25 per credit hour. Tuition, nonresident: full-time $6510; part-time $723.50 per credit hour. Tuition and fees vary according to course load. *Financial support:* In 2009–10, 30 students received support, including 5 research assistantships with full and partial tuition reimbursements available (averaging $8,959 per year), 3 teaching assistantships (averaging $10,443 per year); Federal Work-Study, institutionally sponsored loans, scholarships/grants, and unspecified assistantships also available. Financial award applicants required to submit FAFSA. *Faculty research:* Early childhood education, reading, rural schools, multicultural education, use of technology in instruction. *Unit head:* Dr. Charlotte S. Burroughs, Associate Professor and Interim Head, 662-325-3747, Fax: 662-325-7857, E-mail: susie.burroughs@msstate.edu. *Application contact:* Dr. Kent Coffey, Professor and Graduate Coordinator, 662-325-2188, Fax: 662-325-7857, E-mail: kcoffey@colled.msstate.edu.

Missouri State University, Graduate College, College of Arts and Letters, Department of Art and Design, Springfield, MO 65897. Offers secondary education (MS Ed), including art. Part-time programs available. *Faculty:* 8 full-time (3 women). *Students:* 1 full-time (0 women). Average age 38. 2 applicants, 100% accepted, 1 enrolled. *Entrance requirements:* For master's, minimum GPA of 3.0, 9-12 teaching certification. Additional exam requirements/recommendations for international students: Required—TOEFL (minimum score 550 paper-based; 213 computer-based; 79 iBT). *Application deadline:* For fall admission, 7/20 priority date for domestic students, 5/1 for international students; for spring admission, 12/20 priority date for domestic students, 9/1 for international students. Applications are processed on a rolling basis. Application fee: $35 ($50 for international students). Electronic applications accepted. *Expenses:* Tuition, state resident: full-time $3852; part-time $214 per credit hour. Tuition, nonresident: full-time $7524; part-time $418 per credit hour. Required fees: $696; $172 per semester. Tuition and fees vary according to course level, course load, degree level and program. *Financial support:* Federal Work-Study and unspecified assistantships available. Financial award applicants required to submit FAFSA. *Unit head:* Wade S. Thompson, Head, 417-836-6055, E-mail: artahddesign@missouristate.edu. *Application contact:* Eric Eckert, Coordinator of Graduate Admissions and Recruitment, 417-836-5331, Fax: 417-386-6888, E-mail: ericeckert@missouristate.edu.

Missouri State University, Graduate College, College of Arts and Letters, Department of English, Springfield, MO 65897. Offers English and writing (MA); secondary education (MS Ed), including English. Part-time and evening/weekend programs available. *Faculty:* 24 full-time (15 women), 3 part-time/adjunct (0 women). *Students:* 38 full-time (29 women), 56 part-time (40 women); includes 2 minority (1 Asian American or Pacific Islander, 1 Hispanic American), 4 international. Average age 30. 39 applicants, 97% accepted, 23 enrolled. In 2009, 43 master's awarded. *Degree requirements:* For master's, one foreign language, comprehensive exam, thesis or alternative. *Entrance requirements:* For master's, GRE (MA), minimum GPA of 3.0 (MA), 9-12 teacher certification (MS Ed). Additional exam requirements/recommendations for international students: Required—TOEFL (minimum score 550 paper-based; 213 computer-based; 79 iBT). *Application deadline:* For fall admission, 7/20 for domestic students, 5/1 for international students; for spring admission, 12/20 for domestic students, 9/1 for international students. Applications are processed on a rolling basis. Application fee: $35 ($50 for international students). Electronic applications accepted. *Expenses:* Tuition, state resident: full-time $3852; part-time $214 per credit hour. Tuition, nonresident: full-time $7524; part-time $418 per credit hour. Required fees: $696; $172 per semester. Tuition and fees vary according to course level, course load, degree level and program. *Financial support:* In 2009–10, 36 teaching assistantships with full tuition reimbursements (averaging $7,340 per year) were awarded; Federal Work-Study, institutionally sponsored loans, scholarships/grants, and unspecified assistantships also available. Support available to part-time students. Financial award application deadline: 3/31; financial award applicants required to submit FAFSA. *Faculty research:* Renaissance literature, William Blake, autobiography, Georgian theatre, TESOL. *Unit head:* Dr. W. D. Blackmon, Head, 417-836-5107, Fax: 417-836-6940, E-mail: wdblackon@missouristate.edu. *Application contact:* Eric Eckert, Coordinator of Graduate Admissions and Recruitment, 417-836-5331, Fax: 417-836-6888, E-mail: ericeckert@missouristate.edu.

Missouri State University, Graduate College, College of Arts and Letters, Department of Modern and Classical Languages, Springfield, MO 65897. Offers secondary education (MS Ed), including Spanish. Part-time programs available. *Faculty:* 4 full-time (1 woman). *Students:* 1 (woman) full-time, 3 part-time (2 women); includes 1 minority (Hispanic American). Average age 37. In 2009, 1 master's awarded. *Entrance requirements:* For master's, grades 9-12 teaching certification. Additional exam requirements/recommendations for international students: Required—TOEFL (minimum score 550 paper-based; 213 computer-based; 79 iBT), IELTS (minimum score 6). *Application deadline:* For fall admission, 7/20 priority date for domestic students, 5/1 for international students; for spring admission, 12/20 priority date for domestic students, 9/1 for international students. Applications are processed on a rolling basis. Application fee: $35 ($50 for international students). Electronic applications accepted. *Expenses:* Tuition, state resident: full-time $3852; part-time $214 per credit hour. Tuition, nonresident: full-time $7524; part-time $418 per credit hour. Required fees: $696; $172 per semester. Tuition and fees vary according to course level, course load, degree level and program. *Financial support:* Federal Work-Study, scholarships/grants, and unspecified assistantships available. Financial award applicants required to submit FAFSA. *Unit head:* Dr. Madeleine Kernen, Head, 417-836-7626, E-mail: mcl@missouristate.edu. *Application contact:* Eric Eckert, Coordinator of Admissions and Recruitment, 417-836-5331, Fax: 417-836-6888, E-mail: ericeckert@missouristate.edu.

Missouri State University, Graduate College, College of Arts and Letters, Department of Music, Springfield, MO 65897. Offers music (MM), including conducting, music education, music pedagogy, music theory and composition, performance; secondary education (MS Ed), including music. *Accreditation:* NASM. Part-time programs available. *Faculty:* 24 full-time (9 women). *Students:* 13 full-time (9 women), 29 part-time (14 women); includes 1 minority (Asian American or Pacific Islander), 4 international. Average age 30. 14 applicants, 100% accepted, 8 enrolled. In 2009, 12 master's awarded. *Degree requirements:* For master's, comprehensive exam, thesis or alternative. *Entrance requirements:* For master's, GRE, interview/audition (MM), 9-12 teaching certification (MS Ed). Additional exam requirements/recommendations for international students: Required—TOEFL (minimum score 550 paper-based; 213 computer-based; 79 iBT). *Application deadline:* For fall admission, 7/20 for domestic students, 5/1 for international students; for spring admission, 12/20 for domestic students, 9/1 for international students. Applications are processed on a rolling basis. Application fee: $35 ($50 for international students). Electronic applications accepted. *Expenses:* Tuition, state resident: full-time $3852; part-time $214 per credit hour. Tuition, nonresident: full-time $7524; part-time $418 per credit hour. Required fees: $696; $172 per semester. Tuition and fees vary according to course level, course load, degree level and program. *Financial support:* In 2009–10, 10 teaching assistantships with full tuition reimbursements (averaging $7,340 per year) were awarded; Federal Work-Study, institutionally sponsored loans, scholarships/grants, tuition waivers (partial), and unspecified assistantships also available. Financial award application deadline: 3/31; financial award applicants required to submit FAFSA. *Faculty research:* Bulgarian violin literature, Ozarks fiddle music, carillon, nineteenth century piano. *Unit head:* Diane C. Strickland, Head, 417-836-4122, Fax: 417-836-7665, E-mail: music@missouristate.edu. *Application contact:* Eric Eckert, Coordinator of Graduate Admissions and Recruitment, 417-836-5331, Fax: 417-836-6888.

Missouri State University, Graduate College, College of Arts and Letters, Department of Theatre and Dance, Springfield, MO 65897. Offers secondary education (MS Ed), including speech and theatre; theatre (MA). *Accreditation:* NAST. Part-time programs available. *Faculty:* 10 full-time (6 women). *Students:* 4 full-time (1 woman), 5 part-time (all women). Average age 30. 7 applicants, 71% accepted, 4 enrolled. In 2009, 6 master's awarded. *Degree requirements:* For master's, comprehensive exam, thesis or alternative. *Entrance requirements:* For master's, minimum GPA of 3.0 (MA), 9-12 teaching certification (MS Ed). Additional exam requirements/recommendations for international students: Required—TOEFL (minimum score 550 paper-based; 213 computer-based; 79 iBT). *Application deadline:* For fall admission, 7/20 for domestic students, 5/1 for international students; for spring admission, 12/20 for domestic students, 9/1 for international students. Applications are processed on a rolling basis. Application fee: $35 ($50 for international students). Electronic applications accepted. *Expenses:* Tuition, state resident: full-time $3852; part-time $214 per credit hour. Tuition, nonresident: full-time $7524; part-time $418 per credit hour. Required fees: $696; $172 per semester. Tuition and fees vary according to course level, course load, degree level and program. *Financial support:* In 2009–10, 3 teaching assistantships with full tuition reimbursements (averaging $7,340 per year) were awarded; Federal Work-Study, institutionally sponsored loans, scholarships/grants, and unspecified assistantships also available. Financial award application deadline: 3/31; financial award applicants required to submit FAFSA. *Unit head:* Bob Willenbrink, Department Head, 417-836-4156, Fax: 417-836-4234, E-mail: rwillenbrink@missouristate.edu. *Application contact:* Eric Eckert, Coordinator of Admissions and Recruitment, 417-836-5331, Fax: 417-836-6888, E-mail: ericeckert@missouristate.edu.

Missouri State University, Graduate College, College of Business Administration, Department of Computer Information Systems, Springfield, MO 65897. Offers computer information systems (MS); secondary education (MS Ed), including business. Part-time and evening/weekend programs available. Postbaccalaureate distance learning degree programs offered (no on-campus study). *Faculty:* 13 full-time (3 women), 1 part-time/adjunct (0 women). *Students:* 34 full-time (7 women), 4 part-time (all women); includes 1 minority (Asian American or Pacific Islander), 1 international. Average age 41. 15 applicants, 100% accepted, 13 enrolled. In 2009, 16 master's awarded. *Degree requirements:* For master's, thesis optional. *Entrance requirements:* For master's, GMAT, 3 years of work experience in computer information systems, minimum GPA of 2.75 (MS), 9-12 teaching certification (MS Ed). Additional exam requirements/recommendations for international students: Required—TOEFL (minimum score 550 paper-based; 213 computer-based; 79 iBT). *Application deadline:* For fall admission, 7/20 priority date for domestic students, 5/1 for international students; for spring admission, 12/20 priority date for domestic students, 9/1 for international students. Applications are processed on a rolling basis. Application fee: $35 ($50 for international students). Electronic applications accepted. *Expenses:* Contact institution. *Financial support:* Federal Work-Study, institutionally sponsored loans, scholarships/grants, and unspecified assistantships available. Support available to part-time students. Financial award application deadline: 3/31; financial award applicants required to submit FAFSA. *Faculty research:* Decision support systems, algorithms in Visual Basic, end-user satisfaction, information security. *Unit head:* Dr. Jerry Chin, Head, 417-836-4131, Fax: 417-836-6907, E-mail: jerrychin@missouristate.edu. *Application contact:* Dr. Jerry Chin, Head, 417-836-4131, Fax: 417-836-6907, E-mail: jerrychin@missouristate.edu.

Missouri State University, Graduate College, College of Education, Department of Counseling, Leadership, and Special Education, Program in Educational Administration, Springfield, MO 65897. Offers educational administration (MS Ed, Ed S); elementary education (MS Ed); elementary principal (Ed S); secondary education (MS Ed); secondary principal (Ed S); superintendent (Ed S). Part-time and evening/weekend programs available. *Students:* 12 full-time (10 women), 161 part-time (98 women); includes 3 minority (1 Asian American or Pacific Islander, 2 Hispanic Americans), 3 international. Average age 36. 25 applicants, 96% accepted, 21 enrolled. In 2009, 42 master's, 23 Ed Ss awarded. *Degree requirements:* For master's and Ed S, comprehensive exam, thesis or alternative. *Entrance requirements:* For master's, minimum GPA of 2.75; for Ed S, GRE General Test, MAT, minimum GPA of 2.75. Additional exam requirements/recommendations for international students: Required—TOEFL (minimum score 550 paper-based; 213 computer-based; 79 iBT). *Application deadline:* For fall admission, 7/20 priority date for domestic students, 5/1 for international students; for spring admission, 12/20 priority date for domestic students, 9/1 for international students. Applications are processed on a rolling basis. Application fee: $35 ($50 for international students). Electronic applications accepted. *Expenses:* Tuition, state resident: full-time $3852; part-time $214 per credit hour. Tuition, nonresident: full-time $7524; part-time $418 per credit hour. Required fees: $696; $172 per semester. Tuition and fees vary according to course level, course load, degree level and program. *Financial support:* Career-related internships or fieldwork, Federal Work-Study, institutionally sponsored loans, scholarships/grants, and unspecified assistantships available. Financial award application deadline: 3/31; financial award applicants required to submit FAFSA. *Unit head:* Gerald Moseman, Graduate Program Coordinator, 417-836-5490, Fax: 417-836-4918, E-mail: geraldmoseman@missouristate.edu. *Application contact:* Eric Eckert, Coordinator of Admissions and Recruitment, 417-836-5331, Fax: 417-836-6200, E-mail: ericeckert@missouristate.edu.

Missouri State University, Graduate College, College of Health and Human Services, Department of Health, Physical Education, and Recreation, Springfield, MO 65897. Offers health promotion and wellness management (MS); secondary education (MS Ed), including physical education. Part-time programs available. *Faculty:* 13 full-time (5 women). *Students:* 20 full-time (10 women), 10 part-time (6 women), 1 international. Average age 27. 17 applicants, 94% accepted, 12 enrolled. In 2009, 10 master's awarded. *Degree requirements:* For master's, comprehensive exam, thesis or alternative. *Entrance requirements:* For master's, GRE (MS), minimum GPA of 2.8 (MS); 9-12 teaching certification (MS Ed). Additional exam requirements/recommendations for international students: Required—TOEFL (minimum score 550 paper-based; 213 computer-based; 79 iBT). *Application deadline:* For fall admission, 7/20 priority date for domestic students, 5/1 for international students; for spring admission, 12/20 priority date for domestic students, 9/1 for international students. Applications are processed on a rolling basis. Application fee: $35 ($50 for international students). Electronic applications accepted. *Expenses:* Tuition, state resident: full-time $3852; part-time $214 per credit hour. Tuition, nonresident: full-time $7524; part-time $418 per credit hour. Required fees: $696; $172 per semester. Tuition and fees vary according to course level, course load, degree level and program. *Financial support:* In 2009–10, 5 teaching assistantships with full tuition reimburse-

Secondary Education

Missouri State University (continued)

ments (averaging $7,340 per year) were awarded; Federal Work-Study, institutionally sponsored loans, scholarships/grants, and unspecified assistantships also available. Financial award application deadline: 3/31; financial award applicants required to submit FAFSA. *Unit head:* Dr. Sarah McCallister, Acting Head, 417-836-6582, Fax: 417-836-5371, E-mail: sarahmccallister@missouristate.edu. *Application contact:* Eric Eckert, Coordinator of Graduate Admissions and Recruitment, 417-836-5331, Fax: 417-836-6200, E-mail: ericeckert@missouristate.edu.

Missouri State University, Graduate College, College of Humanities and Public Affairs, Department of History, Springfield, MO 65897. Offers history (MA); secondary education (MS Ed), including history, social science. Part-time programs available. *Faculty:* 17 full-time (4 women). *Students:* 18 full-time (7 women), 46 part-time (17 women). Average age 33. 19 applicants, 84% accepted, 15 enrolled. In 2009, 6 master's awarded. *Degree requirements:* For master's, comprehensive exam, thesis or alternative. *Entrance requirements:* For master's, minimum GPA of 2.75, 24 hours of undergraduate course work in history (MA), 9-12 teaching certification (MS Ed). Additional exam requirements/recommendations for international students: Required—TOEFL (minimum score 550 paper-based; 213 computer-based; 79 iBT). *Application deadline:* For fall admission, 7/20 priority date for domestic students, 5/1 for international students; for spring admission, 12/20 priority date for domestic students, 9/1 for international students. Applications are processed on a rolling basis. Application fee: $35 ($50 for international students). Electronic applications accepted. *Expenses:* Tuition, state resident: full-time $3852; part-time $214 per credit hour. Tuition, nonresident: full-time $7524; part-time $418 per credit hour. Required fees: $696; $172 per semester. Tuition and fees vary according to course level, course load, degree level and program. *Financial support:* In 2009–10, 5 teaching assistantships with full tuition reimbursements (averaging $7,340 per year) were awarded; Federal Work-Study, scholarships/grants, and unspecified assistantships also available. Support available to part-time students. Financial award application deadline: 3/31; financial award applicants required to submit FAFSA. *Faculty research:* U.S. history, Native American history, Latin American history, women's history, ancient Near East. *Unit head:* Thomas S. Dicke, Head, 417-836-5511, Fax: 417-836-5523, E-mail: history@missouristate.edu. *Application contact:* Eric Eckert, Coordinator of Admissions and Recruitment, 417-836-5331, Fax: 417-836-6200, E-mail: ericeckert@missouristate.edu.

Missouri State University, Graduate College, College of Natural and Applied Sciences, Department of Agriculture, Springfield, MO 65897. Offers natural and applied science (MNAS), including agriculture (MNAS, MS Ed); plant science (MS); secondary education (MS Ed), including agriculture (MNAS, MS Ed). Part-time programs available. *Faculty:* 16 full-time (3 women). *Students:* 10 full-time (7 women), 16 part-time (10 women), 2 international. Average age 31. 7 applicants, 71% accepted, 3 enrolled. In 2009, 9 master's awarded. *Degree requirements:* For master's, comprehensive exam, thesis or alternative. *Entrance requirements:* For master's, GRE (MS plant science, MNAS), 9-12 teacher certification (MS Ed), minimum GPA of 3.0 (MS plant science, MNAS). Additional exam requirements/recommendations for international students: Required—TOEFL (minimum score 550 paper-based; 213 computer-based; 79 iBT). *Application deadline:* For fall admission, 7/20 priority date for domestic students, 5/1 for international students; for spring admission, 12/20 priority date for domestic students, 9/1 for international students. Applications are processed on a rolling basis. Application fee: $35 ($50 for international students). Electronic applications accepted. *Expenses:* Tuition, state resident: full-time $3852; part-time $214 per credit hour. Tuition, nonresident: full-time $7524; part-time $418 per credit hour. Required fees: $696; $172 per semester. Tuition and fees vary according to course level, course load, degree level and program. *Financial support:* In 2009–10, 6 research assistantships with full tuition reimbursements (averaging $8,535 per year), 6 teaching assistantships with full tuition reimbursements (averaging $8,535 per year) were awarded; Federal Work-Study, institutionally sponsored loans, scholarships/grants, and unspecified assistantships also available. Financial award application deadline: 3/31; financial award applicants required to submit FAFSA. *Faculty research:* Grapevine biotechnology, agricultural marketing, Asian elephant reproduction, poultry science, integrated pest management. *Unit head:* Dr. W. Anson Elliott, Head, 417-836-5638, E-mail: ansonelliot@missouristate.edu. *Application contact:* Eric Eckert, Coordinator of Graduate Admissions and Recruitment, 417-836-5331, Fax: 417-836-6200.

Missouri State University, Graduate College, College of Natural and Applied Sciences, Department of Biology, Springfield, MO 65897. Offers biology (MS); natural and applied science (MNAS), including biology (MNAS, MS Ed); secondary education (MS Ed), including biology (MNAS, MS Ed). *Faculty:* 18 full-time (3 women), 6 part-time/adjunct (1 woman). *Students:* 25 full-time (13 women), 22 part-time (10 women); includes 2 minority (1 American Indian/Alaska Native, 1 Asian American or Pacific Islander), 3 international. Average age 26. 17 applicants, 94% accepted, 10 enrolled. In 2009, 20 master's awarded. *Degree requirements:* For master's, comprehensive exam, thesis or alternative. *Entrance requirements:* For master's, GRE (MS, MNAS), 24 hours of course work in biology (MS); minimum GPA of 3.0 (MS, MNAS), 9-12 teacher certification (MS Ed). Additional exam requirements/recommendations for international students: Required—TOEFL (minimum score 550 paper-based; 213 computer-based; 79 iBT). *Application deadline:* For fall admission, 7/20 priority date for domestic students, 5/1 for international students; for spring admission, 12/20 priority date for domestic students, 9/1 for international students. Applications are processed on a rolling basis. Application fee: $35 ($50 for international students). Electronic applications accepted. *Expenses:* Tuition, state resident: full-time $3852; part-time $214 per credit hour. Tuition, nonresident: full-time $7524; part-time $418 per credit hour. Required fees: $696; $172 per semester. Tuition and fees vary according to course level, course load, degree level and program. *Financial support:* In 2009–10, 4 research assistantships with full tuition reimbursements (averaging $9,730 per year), 23 teaching assistantships with full tuition reimbursements (averaging $8,372 per year) were awarded; Federal Work-Study, institutionally sponsored loans, scholarships/grants, and unspecified assistantships also available. Financial award application deadline: 3/31; financial award applicants required to submit FAFSA. *Faculty research:* Hibernation physiology of bats, behavioral ecology of salamanders, mussel conservation, plant evolution and systematics, cellular/molecular mechanisms involved in migraine pathology. *Unit head:* Dr. S. Alicia Mathis, Head, 417-836-5126, Fax: 417-836-6934, E-mail: biology@missouristate.edu. *Application contact:* Dr. Eric Eckert, Coordinator of Graduate Admissions and Recruitment, 417-836-5331, Fax: 417-836-6200, E-mail: ericeckert@missouristate.edu.

Missouri State University, Graduate College, College of Natural and Applied Sciences, Department of Chemistry, Springfield, MO 65897. Offers chemistry (MS); natural and applied science (MNAS), including chemistry (MNAS, MS Ed); secondary education (MS Ed), including chemistry (MNAS, MS Ed). Part-time programs available. *Faculty:* 14 full-time (1 woman). *Students:* 7 full-time (4 women), 9 part-time (3 women), 1 international. Average age 28. 10 applicants, 90% accepted, 5 enrolled. In 2009, 3 master's awarded. *Degree requirements:* For master's, comprehensive exam, thesis. *Entrance requirements:* For master's, GRE General Test (MS, MNAS), minimum undergraduate GPA of 3.0 (MS and MNAS), 9-12 teacher certification (MS Ed). Additional exam requirements/recommendations for international students: Required—TOEFL (minimum score 550 paper-based; 213 computer-based; 79 iBT). *Application deadline:* For fall admission, 7/20 priority date for domestic students, 5/1 for international students; for spring admission, 12/20 priority date for domestic students, 9/1 for international students. Applications are processed on a rolling basis. Application fee: $35 ($50 for international students). Electronic applications accepted. *Expenses:* Tuition, state resident: full-time $3852; part-time $214 per credit hour. Tuition, nonresident: full-time $7524; part-time $418 per credit hour. Required fees: $696; $172 per semester. Tuition and fees vary according to course level, course load, degree level and program. *Financial support:* In 2009–10, 1 research assistantship with full tuition reimbursement (averaging $9,730 per year), 9 teaching assistantships with full tuition reimbursements (averaging $9,730 per year) were awarded; Federal Work-Study, institutionally sponsored loans, scholarships/grants, and unspecified assistantships also available. Financial award application deadline: 3/31; financial award applicants required to submit FAFSA. *Faculty research:* Polyethylene glycol derivatives, electrochemiluminescence of environmental systems, enzymology, environmental organic pollutants, DNA repair via NMR. *Unit head:* Dr. Alan Schick, Department Head, 417-836-5506, Fax: 417-836-5507, E-mail: chemistry@missouristate.edu. *Application contact:* Eric Eckert, Coordinator of Admissions and Recruitment, 417-836-5331, Fax: 417-836-6200, E-mail: ericeckert@missouristate.edu.

Missouri State University, Graduate College, College of Natural and Applied Sciences, Department of Fashion and Interior Design, Springfield, MO 65897. Offers secondary education (MS Ed), including consumer sciences. Part-time programs available. *Faculty:* 2 full-time (both women), 1 (woman) part-time/adjunct. *Students:* 3 part-time (all women). Average age 47. 2 applicants, 50% accepted, 0 enrolled. *Degree requirements:* For master's, comprehensive exam, thesis or alternative. *Entrance requirements:* For master's, 9-12 teaching certification (MS Ed), minimum GPA of 3.0 (MNAS). Additional exam requirements/recommendations for international students: Required—TOEFL (minimum score 550 paper-based; 213 computer-based; 79 iBT). *Application deadline:* For fall admission, 7/20 priority date for domestic students, 5/1 for international students; for spring admission, 12/20 priority date for domestic students, 9/1 for international students. Applications are processed on a rolling basis. Application fee: $35 ($50 for international students). Electronic applications accepted. *Expenses:* Tuition, state resident: full-time $3852; part-time $214 per credit hour. Tuition, nonresident: full-time $7524; part-time $418 per credit hour. Required fees: $696; $172 per semester. Tuition and fees vary according to course level, course load, degree level and program. *Financial support:* Career-related internships or fieldwork, Federal Work-Study, institutionally sponsored loans, scholarships/grants, and unspecified assistantships available. Financial award application deadline: 3/31; financial award applicants required to submit FAFSA. *Unit head:* Dr. Paula Kemp, Head, 417-836-5497, Fax: 417-836-4341, E-mail: paulakemp@missouristate.edu. *Application contact:* Eric Eckert, Coordinator of Graduate Admissions and Recruitment, 417-836-5331, Fax: 417-836-6200, E-mail: ericeckert@missouristate.edu.

Missouri State University, Graduate College, College of Natural and Applied Sciences, Department of Geography, Geology, and Planning, Springfield, MO 65897. Offers geospatial sciences (MS); natural and applied science (MNAS), including geography, geology and planning; secondary education (MS Ed), including earth science, geography. *Accreditation:* ACSP. Part-time and evening/weekend programs available. *Faculty:* 20 full-time (4 women). *Students:* 19 full-time (10 women), 12 part-time (5 women); includes 1 minority (American Indian/Alaska Native), 1 international. Average age 29. 19 applicants, 100% accepted, 13 enrolled. In 2009, 4 master's awarded. *Degree requirements:* For master's, comprehensive exam, thesis (for some programs). *Entrance requirements:* For master's, GRE General Test (MS, MNAS), minimum undergraduate GPA of 3.0 (MS, MNAS), 9-12 teacher certification (MS Ed). Additional exam requirements/recommendations for international students: Required—TOEFL (minimum score 550 paper-based; 213 computer-based; 79 iBT). *Application deadline:* For fall admission, 7/20 priority date for domestic students, 5/1 for international students; for spring admission, 12/20 priority date for domestic students, 9/1 for international students. Applications are processed on a rolling basis. Application fee: $35 ($50 for international students). Electronic applications accepted. *Expenses:* Tuition, state resident: full-time $3852; part-time $214 per credit hour. Tuition, nonresident: full-time $7524; part-time $418 per credit hour. Required fees: $696; $172 per semester. Tuition and fees vary according to course level, course load, degree level and program. *Financial support:* In 2009–10, 7 research assistantships with full tuition reimbursements (averaging $8,933 per year), 8 teaching assistantships with full tuition reimbursements (averaging $8,236 per year) were awarded; career-related internships or fieldwork, Federal Work-Study, institutionally sponsored loans, scholarships/grants, and unspecified assistantships also available. Financial award application deadline: 3/31; financial award applicants required to submit FAFSA. *Faculty research:* Stratigraphy and ancient meteorite impacts, environmental geochemistry of karst, hyperspectral image processing, water quality, small town planning. *Unit head:* Dr. Thomas Plymate, Head, 417-836-5800, Fax: 417-836-6934, E-mail: tomplymate@missouristate.edu. *Application contact:* Eric Eckert, Coordinator of Graduate Admissions and Recruitment, 417-836-5331, Fax: 417-836-6200, E-mail: ericeckert@missouristate.edu.

Missouri State University, Graduate College, College of Natural and Applied Sciences, Department of Mathematics, Springfield, MO 65897. Offers mathematics (MS); natural and applied science (MNAS), including mathematics (MNAS, MS Ed); secondary education (MS Ed), including mathematics (MNAS, MS Ed). Part-time programs available. *Faculty:* 23 full-time (5 women). *Students:* 15 full-time (1 woman), 7 part-time (1 woman), 1 international. Average age 25. 12 applicants, 100% accepted, 9 enrolled. In 2009, 4 master's awarded. *Degree requirements:* For master's, comprehensive exam, thesis or alternative. *Entrance requirements:* For master's, GRE (MS, MNAS), minimum undergraduate GPA of 3.0 (MS, MNAS), 9-12 teacher certification (MS Ed). Additional exam requirements/recommendations for international students: Required—TOEFL (minimum score 550 paper-based; 213 computer-based; 79 iBT). *Application deadline:* For fall admission, 7/20 priority date for domestic students, 5/1 for international students; for spring admission, 12/20 priority date for domestic students, 9/1 for international students. Applications are processed on a rolling basis. Application fee: $35 ($50 for international students). Electronic applications accepted. *Expenses:* Tuition, state resident: full-time $3852; part-time $214 per credit hour. Tuition, nonresident: full-time $7524; part-time $418 per credit hour. Required fees: $696; $172 per semester. Tuition and fees vary according to course level, course load, degree level and program. *Financial support:* In 2009–10, 7 teaching assistantships with full tuition reimbursements (averaging $9,730 per year) were awarded; Federal Work-Study, institutionally sponsored loans, scholarships/grants, and unspecified assistantships also available. Financial award application deadline: 3/31; financial award applicants required to submit FAFSA. *Faculty research:* Harmonic analysis, commutative algebra, number theory, K-theory, probability. *Unit head:* Dr. Yungchen Cheng, Head, 417-836-5112, Fax: 417-836-6966, E-mail: yungchencheng@missouristate.edu. *Application contact:* Eric Eckert, Coordinator of Admissions and Recruitment, 417-836-5331, Fax: 417-836-6200, E-mail: ericeckert@missouristate.edu.

Missouri State University, Graduate College, College of Natural and Applied Sciences, Department of Physics, Astronomy, and Materials Science, Springfield, MO 65897. Offers materials science (MS); physics, astronomy, and materials science (MNAS); secondary education (MS Ed), including physics. Part-time programs available. *Faculty:* 13 full-time (0 women). *Students:* 6 full-time (2 women), 7 part-time (1 woman), 3 international. Average age 31. 12 applicants, 58% accepted, 6 enrolled. In 2009, 12 master's awarded. *Degree requirements:* For master's, comprehensive exam, thesis. *Entrance requirements:* For master's, GRE (MS, MNAS), minimum undergraduate GPA of 3.0 (MS and MNAS), 9-12 teaching certification (MS Ed). Additional exam requirements/recommendations for international students: Required—TOEFL (minimum score 550 paper-based; 213 computer-based; 79 iBT). *Application deadline:* For fall admission, 7/20 priority date for domestic students, 5/1 for international students; for spring admission, 12/20 priority date for domestic students, 9/1 for international students. Applications are processed on a rolling basis. Application fee: $35 ($50 for international students). Electronic applications accepted. *Expenses:* Tuition, state resident: full-time $3852; part-time $214 per credit hour. Tuition, nonresident: full-time $7524; part-time $418 per credit hour. Required fees: $696; $172 per semester. Tuition and fees vary according to course level, course load, degree level and program. *Financial support:* In 2009–10, 8 teaching assistantships with full tuition reimbursements (averaging $8,834 per year) were awarded; research assistantships with full tuition reimbursements, Federal Work-Study, institutionally sponsored loans, scholarships/grants, and unspecified assistantships also available. Financial award application deadline: 3/31; financial award applicants required to submit FAFSA. *Faculty research:* Nanocomposites, ferroelectricity, infrared focal plane array sensors, biosensors, pulsating stars. *Unit head:* Dr. Robert Patterson, Head, 417-836-5131, Fax: 417-836-6226, E-mail: physics@missouristate.edu. *Application contact:* Eric Eckert, Coordinator of Admissions and Recruitment, 417-836-5331, Fax: 417-836-6200, E-mail: ericeckertn@missouristate.edu.

Monmouth University, Graduate School, School of Education, West Long Branch, NJ 07764-1898. Offers education (M Ed); initial certification (MAT), including elementary level, K-12, secondary level; learning disabilities-teacher consultant (Certificate); principal (MS Ed); principal/

school administrator (MS Ed); reading specialist (MS Ed, Certificate); school counseling (MS Ed); special education (MS Ed), including autism, learning disabilities teacher consultant, teacher of students with disabilities, teaching in inclusive settings; supervisor (Certificate); teacher of the handicapped (Certificate); teaching english to speakers of other languages (TESOL) (Certificate). *Accreditation:* NCATE. Part-time and evening/weekend programs available. *Faculty:* 20 full-time (13 women), 32 part-time/adjunct (22 women). *Students:* 182 full-time (146 women), 353 part-time (286 women); includes 40 minority (15 African Americans, 3 American Indian/Alaska Native, 5 Asian Americans or Pacific Islanders, 17 Hispanic Americans), 1 international. Average age 29. 361 applicants, 96% accepted, 176 enrolled. In 2009, 178 master's awarded. *Entrance requirements:* For master's, minimum GPA of 3.0 in major, 2.75 overall; 2 letters of recommendation (for some programs). Additional exam requirements/recommendations for international students: Required—TOEFL (minimum score 550 paper-based; 213 computer-based; 79 iBT), IELTS (minimum score 5), Michigan English Language Assessment Battery (minimum score 77), Cambridge A, B, C. *Application deadline:* For fall admission, 7/15 priority date for domestic students, 7/1 for international students; for spring admission, 11/15 priority date for domestic students, 11/1 for international students. Applications are processed on a rolling basis. Application fee: $50. Electronic applications accepted. *Expenses:* Tuition: Part-time $773 per credit. Required fees: $157 per semester. *Financial support:* In 2009–10, 326 students received support, including 211 fellowships (averaging $1,824 per year), 23 research assistantships (averaging $7,943 per year); career-related internships or fieldwork, scholarships/grants, and unspecified assistantships also available. Support available to part-time students. Financial award applicants required to submit FAFSA. *Faculty research:* Multicultural literacy, science and mathematics teaching strategies, teacher as reflective practitioner, children with disabilities, varied contexts of learning. *Unit head:* Dr. Terri Rothman, Associate Dean, 732-571-7507, Fax: 732-263-5277, E-mail: trothman@monmouth.edu. *Application contact:* Kevin Roane, Director, Office of Graduate Admission, 732-571-3452, Fax: 732-263-5123, E-mail: gradadm@monmouth.edu.

Montana State University Billings, College of Education, Department of Educational Theory and Practice, Option in Secondary Education, Billings, MT 59101-0298. Offers M Ed. *Accreditation:* NCATE. Part-time programs available. *Degree requirements:* For master's, professional paper or thesis. *Entrance requirements:* For master's, GRE General Test or MAT, minimum GPA of 3.0 (undergraduate), 3.25 (graduate).

Morehead State University, Graduate Programs, College of Education, Department of Curriculum and Instruction, Morehead, KY 40351. Offers curriculum and instruction (Ed S); elementary education (MA Ed), including elementary education, international education, middle school education, reading; secondary education (MA Ed); special education (MA Ed); teaching (MAT). Part-time and evening/weekend programs available. *Faculty:* 25 full-time (17 women), 2 part-time/adjunct (1 woman). *Students:* 25 full-time (22 women), 165 part-time (139 women); includes 4 minority (1 African American, 2 American Indian/Alaska Native, 1 Hispanic American). Average age 33. 148 applicants, 68% accepted, 48 enrolled. In 2009, 178 master's awarded. *Degree requirements:* For master's, comprehensive exam, thesis optional; for Ed S, thesis, oral exam. *Entrance requirements:* For master's, GRE General Test, minimum GPA of 2.75, teaching certificate; for Ed S, GRE General Test, interview, master's degree, minimum GPA of 3.5, work experience. Additional exam requirements/recommendations for international students: Required—TOEFL (minimum score 500 paper-based; 173 computer-based). *Application deadline:* For fall admission, 8/1 priority date for domestic and international students; for spring admission, 12/1 priority date for domestic and international students. Applications are processed on a rolling basis. Application fee: $30. Electronic applications accepted. *Expenses:* Tuition, state resident: full-time $6318; part-time $351 per credit hour. Tuition, nonresident: full-time $15,804; part-time $878 per credit hour. *Financial support:* In 2009–10, 2 teaching assistantships (averaging $6,000 per year) were awarded; career-related internships or fieldwork, Federal Work-Study, and unspecified assistantships also available. Financial award application deadline: 3/15; financial award applicants required to submit FAFSA. *Faculty research:* Communicative competence of learning-disabled students, teaching social studies in elementary schools, ungraded primary school organization, study skills. *Unit head:* Dr. James Knoll, Chair, 606-783-2598, Fax: 606-783-5044, E-mail: j.knoll@moreheadstate.edu. *Application contact:* Michelle Barber, Graduate Recruitment and Retention Assistant Director, 606-783-5127, Fax: 606-783-5061, E-mail: m.barber@moreheadstate.edu.

Morehead State University, Graduate Programs, College of Education, Department of Middle Grades and Secondary Education, Morehead, KY 40351. Offers business and marketing education (MAT); English/language arts 5-9 (MAT); French (MAT); health P-12 (MAT); mathematics 5-9 (MAT); physical education P-12 (MAT); science 5-9 (MAT); secondary biology (MAT); secondary chemistry (MAT); secondary earth science (MAT); secondary English (MAT); secondary math (MAT); secondary physics (MAT); secondary social studies (MAT); social studies 5-9 (MAT); Spanish (MAT). Part-time and evening/weekend programs available. *Students:* 54 full-time (31 women), 233 part-time (142 women); includes 11 minority (5 African Americans, 1 American Indian/Alaska Native, 1 Asian American or Pacific Islander, 4 Hispanic Americans). Average age 32. 206 applicants, 71% accepted, 79 enrolled. In 2009, 101 master's awarded. *Degree requirements:* For master's, portfolio. *Entrance requirements:* For master's, GRE or PRAXIS II content exam, minimum overall undergraduate GPA of 2.5. Additional exam requirements/recommendations for international students: Required—TOEFL (minimum score 500 paper-based; 173 computer-based). *Application deadline:* For fall admission, 8/1 priority date for domestic and international students; for spring admission, 12/1 priority date for domestic and international students. Applications are processed on a rolling basis. Application fee: $30. Electronic applications accepted. *Expenses:* Tuition, state resident: full-time $6318; part-time $351 per credit hour. Tuition, nonresident: full-time $15,804; part-time $878 per credit hour. *Financial support:* In 2009–10, 1 research assistantship (averaging $10,000 per year) was awarded; career-related internships or fieldwork, Federal Work-Study, and unspecified assistantships also available. Financial award application deadline: 3/15; financial award applicants required to submit FAFSA. *Unit head:* Dr. Cathy Gunn, Dean, 606-783-2040, Fax: 606-783-5029, E-mail: c.gunn@moreheadstate.edu. *Application contact:* Michelle Barber, Graduate Recruitment and Retention Assistant Director, 606-783-5127, Fax: 606-783-5061, E-mail: m.barber@moreheadstate.edu.

Morgan State University, School of Graduate Studies, School of Education and Urban Studies, MAT Program, Baltimore, MD 21251. Offers elementary education (MAT); high school education (MAT); middle school education (MAT). Part-time programs available. *Degree requirements:* For master's, comprehensive exam. *Entrance requirements:* For master's, GRE General Test or MAT. *Faculty research:* Multicultural education, cooperative learning, psychology of cognition.

Mount Saint Mary College, Division of Education, Newburgh, NY 12550-3494. Offers adolescence and special education (MS Ed); adolescence education (MS Ed); childhood and special education (MS Ed); childhood education (MS Ed); literacy (5-12) (Advanced Certificate); literacy (birth-6) (Advanced Certificate); literacy and special education (MS Ed); literacy/childhood (MS Ed); middle school (5-6) (MS Ed); middle school (7-9) (MS Ed); special education (1-6) (MS Ed); special education (7-12) (MS Ed). *Accreditation:* NCATE. Part-time and evening/weekend programs available. *Faculty:* 15 full-time (13 women), 16 part-time/adjunct (10 women). *Students:* 76 full-time (63 women), 226 part-time (188 women); includes 27 minority (7 African Americans, 3 Asian Americans or Pacific Islanders, 17 Hispanic Americans). Average age 30. 141 applicants, 56% accepted, 44 enrolled. In 2009, 142 master's awarded. *Application deadline:* Applications are processed on a rolling basis. Application fee: $45. *Expenses:* Tuition: Full-time $13,356; part-time $742 per credit. Required fees: $50 per semester. *Financial support:* In 2009–10, 106 students received support. Unspecified assistantships available. Financial award application deadline: 4/15; financial award applicants required to submit FAFSA. *Faculty research:* Learning and teaching styles, computers in special education, language development. *Unit head:* Dr. Theresa Lewis, Coordinator, 845-569-3149, Fax: 845-569-3535, E-mail: tlewis@msmc.edu. *Application contact:* Dr. Theresa Lewis, Coordinator, 845-569-3149, Fax: 845-569-3535, E-mail: tlewis@msmc.edu.

Mount St. Mary's College, Graduate Division, Department of Education, Specialization in Secondary Education, Los Angeles, CA 90049-1599. Offers MS. *Students:* 32 full-time (23

women), 18 part-time (13 women); includes 26 minority (6 African Americans, 6 Asian Americans or Pacific Islanders, 14 Hispanic Americans). Average age 36. *Degree requirements:* For master's, thesis, research project. *Entrance requirements:* For master's, MAT, minimum GPA of 3.0. *Application deadline:* For fall admission, 7/15 priority date for domestic students; for spring admission, 11/15 priority date for domestic students. Application fee: $50 ($75 for international students). *Expenses:* Tuition: Part-time $730 per unit. Part-time tuition and fees vary according to degree level and program. *Financial support:* Application deadline: 3/15. *Unit head:* Dr. Robin Gordon, Director, 213-477-2623. *Application contact:* Jessica M. Bibeau, Director of Graduate Admission, 213-477-2800 Ext. 2798, Fax: 213-477-2797, E-mail: jbibeau@msmc.la.edu.

Murray State University, College of Education, Department of Adolescent, Career and Special Education, Program in Secondary Education, Murray, KY 42071. Offers MA Ed, Ed S. *Accreditation:* NCATE. Part-time programs available. *Degree requirements:* For master's, comprehensive exam, thesis optional; for Ed S, comprehensive exam. *Entrance requirements:* Additional exam requirements/recommendations for international students: Required—TOEFL.

National-Louis University, National College of Education, Program in Secondary Education, Chicago, IL 60603. Offers MAT. *Degree requirements:* For master's, student teaching experience. *Entrance requirements:* For master's, GRE, minimum GPA of 3.0. *Expenses:* Tuition: Full-time $17,160; part-time $715 per semester hour. Tuition and fees vary according to course load, degree level, campus/location and program.

New Jersey City University, Graduate Studies and Continuing Education, Debra Cannon Partridge Wolfe College of Education, Department of Elementary and Secondary Education, Jersey City, NJ 07305-1597. Offers elementary education (MAT); secondary education (MAT). Part-time and evening/weekend programs available. *Faculty:* 6. *Students:* 16 full-time (13 women), 44 part-time (32 women); includes 16 minority (3 African Americans, 5 Asian Americans or Pacific Islanders, 8 Hispanic Americans). Average age 32. In 2009, 24 master's awarded. *Entrance requirements:* Additional exam requirements/recommendations for international students: Required—TOEFL. *Application deadline:* For fall admission, 8/1 priority date for domestic students; for spring admission, 12/1 for domestic students. Applications are processed on a rolling basis. Application fee: $0. *Expenses:* Tuition, area resident: Part-time $456.75 per credit. Tuition, nonresident: part-time $842.55 per credit. Required fees: $65 per term. *Financial support:* Teaching assistantships, career-related internships or fieldwork and unspecified assistantships available. *Unit head:* Dr. Althea Hall, Coordinator, 201-200-2101, E-mail: ahall@njcu.edu. *Application contact:* Dr. Althea Hall, Coordinator, 201-200-2101, E-mail: ahall@njcu.edu.

Niagara University, Graduate Division of Education, Concentration in Teacher Education, Niagara Falls, Niagara University, NY 14109. Offers early childhood and childhood education (MS Ed); middle and adolescence education (MS Ed); special education (grades 1-12) (MS Ed). *Accreditation:* NCATE. *Entrance requirements:* For master's, GRE General Test or MAT. *Expenses:* Contact institution.

Norfolk State University, School of Graduate Studies, School of Education, Department of Secondary Education and School Leadership, Norfolk, VA 23504. Offers principal preparation (MA); secondary education (MAT); urban education/administration (MA), including teaching. *Accreditation:* NCATE. Part-time programs available. *Entrance requirements:* For master's, GRE General Test, PRAXIS I, minimum GPA of 3.0 in major, 2.5 overall. Additional exam requirements/recommendations for international students: Required—TOEFL (minimum score 500 paper-based).

North Carolina State University, Graduate School, College of Education, Department of Curriculum and Instruction, Program in Secondary English Education, Raleigh, NC 27695. Offers M Ed, MS Ed. *Degree requirements:* For master's, thesis optional.

Northern Arizona University, Graduate College, College of Education, Department of Teaching and Learning, Flagstaff, AZ 86011. Offers early childhood education (M Ed); elementary education—certification (M Ed); elementary education—continuing professional (M Ed); secondary education—certification (M Ed); secondary education—continuing professional (M Ed). *Faculty:* 40 full-time (32 women). *Students:* 488 full-time (397 women), 599 part-time (535 women); includes 250 minority (25 African Americans, 77 American Indian/Alaska Native, 23 Asian Americans or Pacific Islanders, 125 Hispanic Americans), 2 international. Average age 29. 271 applicants, 93% accepted, 188 enrolled. In 2009, 555 master's awarded. *Degree requirements:* For master's, comprehensive exam (for some programs), thesis (for some programs). *Entrance requirements:* For master's, minimum GPA of 3.0. Additional exam requirements/recommendations for international students: Required—TOEFL (minimum score 550 paper-based; 213 computer-based; 80 iBT), IELTS (minimum score 7), or a bachelor's degree from an English-speaking university and demonstrated proficiency. *Application deadline:* For fall admission, 2/1 for domestic students, 9/1 for international students; for spring admission, 12/1 for domestic students. Applications are processed on a rolling basis. Application fee: $65. Electronic applications accepted. *Financial support:* In 2009–10, 7 teaching assistantships with partial tuition reimbursements (averaging $10,000 per year) were awarded. Financial award application deadline: 3/30. *Unit head:* Dr. Sandra J. Stone, Chair, 928-523-6166, E-mail: sandra.stone@nau.edu. *Application contact:* Dr. Sandra J. Stone, Chair, 928-523-6166, E-mail: sandra.stone@nau.edu.

Northern Illinois University, Graduate School, College of Education, Department of Teaching and Learning, De Kalb, IL 60115-2854. Offers curriculum and instruction (MS Ed, Ed D), including curriculum leadership (Ed D), elementary education (Ed D), secondary education (Ed D); early childhood education (MS Ed); elementary education (MS Ed); special education (MS Ed). Part-time and evening/weekend programs available. *Faculty:* 22 full-time (14 women), 2 part-time/adjunct (both women). *Students:* 50 full-time (38 women), 435 part-time (344 women); includes 107 minority (16 African Americans, 1 American Indian/Alaska Native, 12 Asian Americans or Pacific Islanders, 78 Hispanic Americans), 9 international. Average age 35. 154 applicants, 53% accepted, 57 enrolled. In 2009, 142 master's, 2 doctorates awarded. *Degree requirements:* For master's, comprehensive exam, thesis optional; for doctorate, thesis/dissertation, candidacy exam, dissertation defense. *Entrance requirements:* For master's, GRE General Test or MAT, minimum undergraduate GPA of 2.75; for doctorate, GRE General Test or MAT, minimum undergraduate GPA of 2.75, graduate 3.2. Additional exam requirements/recommendations for international students: Required—TOEFL (minimum score 550 paper-based; 213 computer-based). *Application deadline:* For fall admission, 6/1 for domestic students, 5/1 for international students; for spring admission, 11/1 for domestic students, 10/1 for international students. Applications are processed on a rolling basis. Application fee: $30. Electronic applications accepted. *Expenses:* Tuition, state resident: full-time $6576; part-time $274 per credit hour. Tuition, nonresident: full-time $13,152; part-time $548 per credit hour. Required fees: $1813; $75.53 per credit hour. Part-time tuition and fees vary according to course load. *Financial support:* In 2009–10, 20 research assistantships with full tuition reimbursements were awarded; fellowships with full tuition reimbursements, teaching assistantships with full tuition reimbursements, career-related internships or fieldwork, Federal Work-Study, scholarships/grants, tuition waivers (full), and unspecified assistantships also available. Support available to part-time students. Financial award applicants required to submit FAFSA. *Faculty research:* Teacher certification, stress reduction during student teaching, teaching history, portfolios in student teaching. *Unit head:* Dr. Helen Brantley, Chair, 815-753-0327, E-mail: tedur@niu.edu. *Application contact:* Gail Myers, E-mail: gmyers@niu.edu.

Northern Michigan University, College of Graduate Studies, College of Professional Studies, School of Education, Program in Secondary Education, Marquette, MI 49855-5301. Offers MA Ed. Part-time programs available. *Degree requirements:* For master's, thesis or alternative. *Entrance requirements:* For master's, minimum GPA of 3.0. *Faculty research:* Supervision and improvement of instruction.

Northern State University, Division of Graduate Studies in Education, Program in Teaching and Learning, Aberdeen, SD 57401-7198. Offers educational studies (MS Ed); elementary classroom teaching (MS Ed); health, physical education, and coaching (MS Ed); language and

Secondary Education

Northern State University (continued)
literacy (MS Ed); secondary classroom teaching (MS Ed); special education (MS Ed). *Accreditation:* NCATE. Part-time and evening/weekend programs available. *Faculty:* 10 full-time (8 women). *Students:* 23 full-time (16 women), 35 part-time (17 women); includes 2 minority (1 American Indian/Alaska Native, 1 Asian American or Pacific Islander). Average age 32. In 2009, 26 master's awarded. *Degree requirements:* For master's, thesis optional. *Entrance requirements:* For master's, minimum GPA of 2.75. Additional exam requirements/ recommendations for international students: Required—TOEFL (minimum score 550 paper-based; 213 computer-based; 76 iBT). *Application deadline:* For fall admission, 8/15 priority date for domestic students; for spring admission, 12/15 for domestic students. Applications are processed on a rolling basis. Application fee: $35. Electronic applications accepted. *Financial support:* In 2009–10, 18 teaching assistantships with partial tuition reimbursements (averaging $5,558 per year) were awarded; career-related internships or fieldwork, Federal Work-Study, institutionally sponsored loans, scholarships/grants, and unspecified assistantships also available. Support available to part-time students. Financial award application deadline: 3/1; financial award applicants required to submit FAFSA. *Application contact:* Tammy K. Griffith, Program Assistant, 605-626-2558, Fax: 605-626-7190, E-mail: griffith@northern.edu.

North Georgia College & State University, Graduate Studies, Program in Teacher Education, Dahlonega, GA 30597. Offers early childhood education (M Ed); educational leadership (Ed S); middle grades education (M Ed); secondary education (M Ed), including art education, biology education, chemistry education, English education, history education, mathematics education, physical education, science education; special education (M Ed), including interrelated special education, learning disabilities. *Accreditation:* NCATE. Part-time and evening/weekend programs available. Postbaccalaureate distance learning degree programs offered (minimal on-campus study). *Degree requirements:* For master's, comprehensive exam, thesis optional. *Entrance requirements:* For master's, GRE General Test or MAT, minimum GPA of 2.75; for Ed S, GRE General Test or MAT, 3 years of teaching experience, master's degree, minimum graduate GPA of 3.25. Electronic applications accepted. *Faculty research:* Computers and teachers' attitudes, rural versus urban teacher attitudes, teacher leadership roles, minority recruitment in teaching force.

Northwestern Oklahoma State University, School of Professional Studies, Program in Secondary Education, Alva, OK 73717-2799. Offers M Ed. *Accreditation:* NCATE. Part-time programs available. *Faculty:* 10 full-time (7 women). *Students:* 9 full-time (6 women), 52 part-time (30 women); includes 9 minority (3 African Americans, 4 American Indian/Alaska Native, 2 Hispanic Americans), 1 international. 50 applicants, 100% accepted. In 2009, 18 master's awarded. *Degree requirements:* For master's, thesis optional, portfolio. *Entrance requirements:* For master's, GRE General Test or MAT, minimum GPA of 2.75. *Application deadline:* Applications are processed on a rolling basis. Application fee: $15. *Financial support:* Federal Work-Study available. Support available to part-time students. Financial award application deadline: 5/1; financial award applicants required to submit FAFSA. *Faculty research:* Teacher education, professional school models of pedagogy, competency exams for teachers, teacher accreditation/certification. *Unit head:* Dr. Sue Diel, Chair, 580-327-8451. *Application contact:* Leah Haines, Coordinator of Graduate Studies, 580-327-8410, E-mail: ldhaines@nwosu.edu.

Northwestern State University of Louisiana, Graduate Studies and Research, College of Education, Program in Secondary Education, Natchitoches, LA 71497. Offers MAT. *Degree requirements:* For master's, comprehensive exam, thesis or alternative. *Entrance requirements:* For master's, GRE General Test, minimum undergraduate GPA of 2.5.

Northwestern State University of Louisiana, Graduate Studies and Research, College of Education, Programs in Education, Natchitoches, LA 71497. Offers business and distributive education (M Ed); counseling (M Ed); early childhood education (M Ed); education (M Ed); education leadership (M Ed); educational technology (M Ed); elementary teaching (M Ed); English education (M Ed); home economics education (M Ed); mathematics education (M Ed); reading (M Ed); science education (M Ed); secondary teaching (M Ed); social sciences education (M Ed). *Degree requirements:* For master's, comprehensive exam, thesis or alternative. *Entrance requirements:* For master's, GRE General Test, minimum undergraduate GPA of 2.5.

Northwestern State University of Louisiana, Graduate Studies and Research, College of Education, Programs in Educational Leadership and Instruction, Natchitoches, LA 71497. Offers counseling (Ed S); educational leadership (Ed S); educational technology (Ed S); elementary teaching (Ed S); reading (Ed S); secondary teaching (Ed S); special education (Ed S). *Entrance requirements:* For degree, GRE General Test.

Northwestern University, The Graduate School, School of Education and Social Policy, Education and Social Policy Program, Evanston, IL 60035. Offers advanced teaching (MS); elementary education and policy (MS); higher education administration (MS); secondary teaching (MS). Part-time and evening/weekend programs available. *Faculty:* 3 full-time (all women), 20 part-time/adjunct (11 women). *Students:* 64 full-time (47 women), 94 part-time (70 women); includes 27 minority (11 African Americans, 1 American Indian/Alaska Native, 9 Asian Americans or Pacific Islanders, 6 Hispanic Americans). Average age 27. 117 applicants, 63% accepted, 57 enrolled. In 2009, 82 master's awarded. *Degree requirements:* For master's, research project. *Entrance requirements:* For master's, GRE General Test, Illinois State Board of Education Basic Skills Exam (secondary and elementary), bachelor's degree. *Application deadline:* For fall admission, 7/16 for domestic students; for winter admission, 11/7 for domestic students; for spring admission, 2/15 priority date for domestic students. Applications are processed on a rolling basis. Application fee: $100. Electronic applications accepted. *Financial support:* In 2009–10, 6 students received support, including 1 fellowship with partial tuition reimbursement available (averaging $16,000 per year); career-related internships or fieldwork, Federal Work-Study, institutionally sponsored loans, scholarships/grants, tuition waivers (partial), and unspecified assistantships also available. Financial award application deadline: 1/9; financial award applicants required to submit FAFSA. *Faculty research:* Cultural context and literacy, philosophy of education and interpretive discussion, productivity, enhancing research and teaching, motivation, new and junior faculty issues, professional development for K-12 teachers to improve math and science teaching, female/underrepresented students/faculty in STEM disciplines. *Unit head:* Dr. Sophie Haroutunian-Gordon, Director and Professor, 847-467-1458, Fax: 847-467-2495, E-mail: shg@northwestern.edu. *Application contact:* Bradley Wadle, Assistant Director, 847-491-3829, Fax: 847-467-2495, E-mail: msedapply@northwestern.edu.

Northwest Missouri State University, Graduate School, College of Education and Human Services, Department of Educational Leadership, Program in Educational Leadership, Maryville, MO 64468-6001. Offers educational leadership: elementary (MS Ed); educational leadership: secondary (MS Ed); elementary principalship (Ed S); secondary principalship (Ed S); superintendency (Ed S). *Accreditation:* NCATE. Part-time programs available. *Faculty:* 16 full-time (6 women). *Students:* 21 full-time (13 women), 60 part-time (39 women); includes 3 minority (1 African American, 1 Asian American or Pacific Islander, 1 Hispanic American). 30 applicants, 83% accepted, 17 enrolled. In 2009, 63 master's awarded. *Degree requirements:* For master's, comprehensive exam; for Ed S, comprehensive exam, thesis. *Entrance requirements:* For master's, GRE General Test, minimum undergraduate GPA of 2.75, teaching certificate, writing sample; for Ed S, minimum graduate GPA of 3.25. Additional exam requirements/recommendations for international students: Required—TOEFL (minimum score 550 paper-based; 213 computer-based). *Application deadline:* For fall admission, 7/1 for domestic and international students; for spring admission, 11/15 for domestic and international students. Application fee: $0 ($50 for international students). *Expenses:* Tuition, state resident: part-time $296.34 per credit hour. Tuition, nonresident: part-time $510.43 per credit hour. *Financial support:* In 2009–10, 5 research assistantships with full tuition reimbursements (averaging $6,000 per year), 1 teaching assistantship with full tuition reimbursement (averaging $6,000 per year) were awarded; unspecified assistantships also available. Financial award application deadline: 4/1; financial award applicants required to submit FAFSA. *Unit head:* Dr. Joyce Piveral, Chairperson, 660-562-1231. *Application contact:* Dr. Gregory Haddock, Dean of Graduate School, 660-562-1145, Fax: 660-562-1096, E-mail: gradsch@nwmissouri.edu.

Northwest Missouri State University, Graduate School, College of Education and Human Services, Department of Educational Leadership, Program in Secondary Individualized Prescribed Programs, Maryville, MO 64468-6001. Offers teaching secondary (MS Ed). *Faculty:* 16 full-time (6 women). In 2009, 1 master's awarded. *Entrance requirements:* Additional exam requirements/recommendations for international students: Required—TOEFL (minimum score 550 paper-based; 213 computer-based). *Application deadline:* For fall admission, 7/1 for domestic and international students; for spring admission, 11/15 for domestic and international students. Application fee: $0 ($50 for international students). *Expenses:* Tuition, state resident: part-time $296.34 per credit hour. Tuition, nonresident: part-time $510.43 per credit hour. *Financial support:* Application deadline: 4/1. *Unit head:* Dr. Matt Symonds, Director, 660-562-1069. *Application contact:* Dr. Gregory Haddock, Dean of Graduate School, 660-562-1145, Fax: 660-562-1096, E-mail: gradsch@nwmissouri.edu.

Nova Southeastern University, Fischler School of Education and Human Services, Graduate Teacher Education Program, Fort Lauderdale, FL 33314-7796. Offers athletic administration (MS); brain research (MS, Ed S); charter school education/leadership (MS); cognitive and behavioral disabilities (MS); computer science education (Ed S); computer science education (K-12) (MS); curriculum and teaching (Ed S); curriculum, instruction and technology (MS); curriculum, instruction, management and administration (Ed S); early childhood education (MS); early literacy and reading (Ed S); early literacy education (MS); education technology (MS); educational leadership (administration K–12) (MS, Ed S); educational media (Ed S); educational media (K-12) (MS); elementary education (MS, Ed S), including ESOL endorsement (MS); English education (MS, Ed S); environmental education (MS); exceptional student education (MS), including ESOL endorsement; gifted education (MS, Ed S); interdisciplinary arts education (MS); management and administration of educational programs (MS); mathematics (MS); mathematics education (Ed S); multicultural early intervention (MS); pre-kindergarten/primary (MS); preschool education (MS); reading (MS); reading and TESOL (MS); reading education (Ed S); science (MS); science education (Ed S); secondary education (MS); social studies (MS, Ed S); Spanish language (MS); special education and reading (MS); teaching and learning (MA, MS), including curriculum and instruction (MA), elementary mathematics (MA), elementary reading (MA), K-12 technology integration (MA); teaching English to speakers of other languages (MS, Ed S); technology management and administration (Ed S); urban studies education (MS). Part-time and evening/weekend programs available. Postbaccalaureate distance learning degree programs offered (minimal on-campus study). *Faculty:* 72 full-time (43 women), 385 part-time/adjunct (252 women). *Students:* 196 full-time (175 women), 1,304 part-time (1,128 women); includes 594 minority (471 African Americans, 5 American Indian/Alaska Native, 18 Asian Americans or Pacific Islanders, 100 Hispanic Americans). Average age 37. 2,610 applicants, 72% accepted, 1352 enrolled. In 2009, 836 other advanced degrees awarded. *Degree requirements:* For master's and Ed S, thesis, practicum, internship. *Entrance requirements:* For master's, MAT, GRE, CLAST, CBEST, PRAXIS I, General Knowledge Test, minimum GPA of 2.5; for Ed S, MAT or GRE, master's degree, teaching certificate, minimum GPA of 3.0. Additional exam requirements/ recommendations for international students: Required—TSE (recommended, minimum score 50); Recommended—TOEFL (minimum score 550 paper-based; 213 computer-based; 80 iBT), IELTS (minimum score 6). *Application deadline:* For fall admission, 9/25 priority date for domestic and international students; for winter admission, 2/23 priority date for domestic and international students; for spring admission, 4/25 priority date for domestic and international students. Applications are processed on a rolling basis. Application fee: $50. Electronic applications accepted. *Financial support:* Federal Work-Study available. Support available to part-time students. Financial award application deadline: 4/15; financial award applicants required to submit FAFSA. *Faculty research:* School effectiveness, critical thinking, leadership skills acquisition, child education, multicultural education. *Unit head:* Dr. Ronald Kern, Dean of Academic Affairs, 800-986-3223 Ext. 7809, Fax: 954-262-3606, E-mail: rk429@nsu.nova.edu. *Application contact:* Dr. Jennifer Quinones Nottingham, Dean of Student Affairs, 800-986-3223 Ext. 1559.

Oakland University, Graduate Study and Lifelong Learning, School of Education and Human Services, Department of Teacher Development and Educational Studies, Rochester, MI 48309-4401. Offers education studies (M Ed); secondary education (MAT). *Entrance requirements:* For master's, minimum GPA of 3.0 for unconditional admission. Electronic applications accepted. *Faculty research:* Earth science for middle and high school teachers through real world connections, learning communities, content enrichment.

Occidental College, Graduate Studies, Department of Education, Program in Secondary Education, Los Angeles, CA 90041-3314. Offers English and comparative literary studies (MAT); history (MAT); life science (MAT); mathematics (MAT); physical science (MAT); social science (MAT); Spanish (MAT). Part-time programs available. *Degree requirements:* For master's, comprehensive exam, graduate synthesis paper. *Entrance requirements:* For master's, GRE General Test, minimum GPA of 3.0. Additional exam requirements/recommendations for international students: Required—TOEFL (minimum score 625 paper-based; 263 computer-based). *Expenses:* Contact institution.

Ohio University, Graduate College, College of Education, Department of Teacher Education, Athens, OH 45701-2979. Offers adolescent to young adult education (M Ed); curriculum and instruction (M Ed, PhD); early childhood/special education (M Ed); intervention specialist/mild-moderate needs (M Ed); intervention specialist/moderate-intensive needs (M Ed); mathematics education (PhD); middle child education (M Ed); reading education (M Ed); social studies education (PhD). Part-time and evening/weekend programs available. *Faculty:* 21 full-time (13 women), 7 part-time/adjunct (all women). *Students:* 105 full-time (75 women), 183 part-time (161 women); includes 9 minority (5 African Americans, 3 American Indian/Alaska Native, 1 Asian American or Pacific Islander), 14 international. 190 applicants, 80% accepted, 72 enrolled. *Degree requirements:* For master's, thesis or alternative; for doctorate, comprehensive exam, thesis/dissertation. *Entrance requirements:* For master's, GRE General Test or MAT (if GPA is below 2.9); for doctorate, GRE General Test, minimum GPA of 3.4, work experience. Additional exam requirements/recommendations for international students: Required—TOEFL (minimum score 550 paper-based; 80 iBT) or IELTS Academic (minimum score 6.5). *Application deadline:* For fall admission, 5/1 priority date for domestic students, 4/1 priority date for international students; for winter admission, 11/1 priority date for domestic students, 10/1 priority date for international students; for spring admission, 2/15 priority date for domestic students, 1/1 priority date for international students. Applications are processed on a rolling basis. Application fee: $50 ($55 for international students). Electronic applications accepted. *Expenses:* Tuition, state resident: full-time $7839; part-time $323 per quarter hour. Tuition, nonresident: full-time $15,831; part-time $654 per quarter hour. Required fees: $2931. *Financial support:* Research assistantships with full tuition reimbursements, teaching assistantships with full tuition reimbursements, Federal Work-Study, institutionally sponsored loans, tuition waivers (partial), and unspecified assistantships available. Financial award application deadline: 3/1. *Faculty research:* Cognition literacy, character education, teacher's education reform, disabilities. Total annual research expenditures: $46,933. *Unit head:* Dr. John Henning, Chair, 740-597-1830, Fax: 740-593-0477, E-mail: henningj@ohio.edu. *Application contact:* Floyd J. Doney, Director of Student Affairs, 740-593-4400, Fax: 740-593-9310, E-mail: doney@ohio.edu.

Old Dominion University, Darden College of Education, Programs in Secondary Education, Norfolk, VA 23529. Offers biology (MS Ed); chemistry (MS Ed); English (MS Ed); instructional technology (MS Ed); library science (MS Ed); secondary education (MS Ed). *Accreditation:* NCATE. Part-time and evening/weekend programs available. Postbaccalaureate distance learning degree programs offered (minimal on-campus study). *Faculty:* 20 full-time (16 women). *Students:* 74 full-time (54 women), 137 part-time (92 women); includes 41 minority (22 African Americans, 1 American Indian/Alaska Native, 11 Asian Americans or Pacific Islanders, 7 Hispanic Americans). Average age 33. 67 applicants, 79% accepted, 53 enrolled. In 2009, 131 master's awarded. *Degree requirements:* For master's, comprehensive exam, thesis. *Entrance requirements:* For master's, GRE General Test or MAT, PRAXIS I (for licensure), minimum GPA of 2.8, teaching certificate. Additional exam requirements/recommendations for international students: Required—TOEFL. *Application deadline:* For fall admission, 6/1 for domestic

and international students; for winter admission, 11/1 for domestic and international students; for spring admission, 3/1 for domestic and international students. Applications are processed on a rolling basis. Application fee: $50. Electronic applications accepted. *Expenses:* Tuition, state resident: full-time $8112; part-time $338 per credit. Tuition, nonresident: full-time $20,256; part-time $844 per credit. Required fees: $119 per semester. One-time fee: $50. *Financial support:* In 2009–10, 56 students received support, including fellowships (averaging $15,000 per year), 2 research assistantships with tuition reimbursements available (averaging $9,000 per year), 3 teaching assistantships with tuition reimbursements available (averaging $12,500 per year); career-related internships or fieldwork, Federal Work-Study, institutionally sponsored loans, scholarships/grants, and tuition waivers (partial) also available. Support available to part-time students. Financial award application deadline: 2/15; financial award applicants required to submit FAFSA. *Faculty research:* Use of technology, writing project for teachers, geography teaching, reading. *Unit head:* Dr. Robert Lucking, Graduate Program Director, 757-683-5545, Fax: 757-683-5862, E-mail: rlucking@odu.edu. *Application contact:* Dr. Robert Lucking, Graduate Program Director, 757-683-5545, Fax: 757-683-5862, E-mail: rlucking@odu.edu.

Olivet Nazarene University, Graduate School, Division of Education, Program in Secondary Education, Bourbonnais, IL 60914. Offers MAT. *Accreditation:* NCATE. Evening/weekend programs available. *Degree requirements:* For master's, thesis or alternative.

Our Lady of the Lake University of San Antonio, School of Professional Studies, Program in Secondary Education, San Antonio, TX 78207-4689. Offers M Ed. *Students:* 3 full-time (1 woman), 5 part-time (4 women); includes 4 Hispanic Americans. Average age 31. In 2009, 5 master's awarded. *Expenses:* Tuition: Full-time $12,330; part-time $685 per contact hour. Required fees: $139; $12 per contact hour. $57 per semester. Tuition and fees vary according to campus/location. *Unit head:* Dr. Suzanne Mudge, E-mail: smudge@lake.ollusa.edu. *Application contact:* Dr. Suzanne Mudge, E-mail: smudge@lake.ollusa.edu.

Pacific University, College of Education, Forest Grove, OR 97116-1797. Offers early childhood education (MAT); education (MAE); elementary education (MAT); high school education (MAT); middle school education (MAT); special education (MAT); visual function in learning (M Ed). *Accreditation:* NCATE. Part-time and evening/weekend programs available. *Degree requirements:* For master's, research project. *Entrance requirements:* For master's, California Basic Educational Skills Test, PRAXIS II, minimum undergraduate GPA of 2.75, 3.0 graduate. Additional exam requirements/recommendations for international students: Required—TOEFL. Electronic applications accepted. *Expenses:* Contact institution. *Faculty research:* Defining a culturally competent classroom, technology in the k-12 classroom, Socratic seminars, social studies education.

Park University, College of Graduate and Professional Studies, Kansas City, MO 54105. Offers adult education (M Ed); at-risk students (M Ed); disaster and emergency management (MPA); educational administration (M Ed); entrepreneurship (MBA); general business (MBA); general education (M Ed); government/business relations (MPA); healthcare/services management (MBA, MPA); international business (MBA); K-12 certification (MAT); management information systems (MBA); management of information systems (MPA); middle school certification (MAT); multi-cultural education (M Ed); nonprofit management (MPA); public management (MPA); school law (M Ed); secondary school certification (MAT); special education (M Ed). Part-time and evening/weekend programs available. Postbaccalaureate distance learning degree programs offered (no on-campus study). *Degree requirements:* For master's, comprehensive exam, thesis (for some programs). *Entrance requirements:* For master's, GRE, GMAT, teacher certification (M Ed). Additional exam requirements/recommendations for international students: Required—TOEFL (minimum score 550 paper-based). Electronic applications accepted. *Faculty research:* Literacy, leadership, brain based research, multicultural education, diversity.

Piedmont College, School of Education, Demorest, GA 30535-0010. Offers early childhood education (MA, MAT); instruction (Ed S); secondary education (MA, MAT). Part-time and evening/weekend programs available. *Degree requirements:* For master's, thesis, field experience in the teaching classroom. *Entrance requirements:* For master's, GRE General Test, MAT, minimum undergraduate GPA of 2.5; for Ed S, minimum graduate GPA of 3.5, valid teaching certificate. Additional exam requirements/recommendations for international students: Required—TOEFL (minimum score 550 paper-based; 213 computer-based).

Pittsburg State University, Graduate School, College of Education, Department of Curriculum and Instruction, Pittsburg, KS 66762. Offers classroom reading teacher (MS); early childhood education (MS); elementary education (MS); reading (MS); reading specialist (MS); secondary education (MS); teaching (MAT). *Accreditation:* NCATE. *Degree requirements:* For master's, thesis or alternative. *Entrance requirements:* For master's, GRE or MAT. *Expenses:* Tuition, state resident: full-time $4212; part-time $176 per credit. Tuition, nonresident: full-time $11,530; part-time $480 per credit. Required fees: $940; $43 per credit. Tuition and fees vary according to course level, course load, degree level, campus/location, reciprocity agreements and student level.

Plymouth State University, College of Graduate Studies, Graduate Studies in Education, Program in K-12 Education, Plymouth, NH 03264-1595. Offers M Ed. *Accreditation:* NCATE. Part-time and evening/weekend programs available. *Degree requirements:* For master's, PRAXIS. *Entrance requirements:* For master's, MAT, minimum GPA of 3.0.

Plymouth State University, College of Graduate Studies, Graduate Studies in Education, Program in Secondary Education, Plymouth, NH 03264-1595. Offers M Ed. Part-time and evening/weekend programs available. *Entrance requirements:* For master's, MAT.

Portland State University, Graduate Studies, School of Education, Department of Curriculum and Instruction, Portland, OR 97207-0751. Offers early childhood education (MA, MS); education (M Ed, MA, MS); educational leadership: curriculum and instruction (Ed D); educational media/school librarianship (MA, MS); elementary education (M Ed, MAT, MST); reading (MA, MS); secondary education (M Ed, MAT, MST). *Accreditation:* NCATE. Part-time programs available. *Degree requirements:* For master's, comprehensive exam, thesis or alternative; for doctorate, thesis/dissertation. *Entrance requirements:* For master's, California Basic Educational Skills Test, minimum GPA of 3.0 in upper-division course work or 2.75 overall. Additional exam requirements/recommendations for international students: Required—TOEFL (minimum score 550 paper-based; 213 computer-based). *Faculty research:* Early literacy, characteristics of successful teachers of at-risk students, participation of women/minorities in technology courses, selection of cooperating teachers.

Prescott College, Graduate Programs, Program in Education, Prescott, AZ 86301. Offers early childhood education (MA); early childhood special education (MA); education (MA); elementary education (MA); environmental education leadership and administration (MA); equine-assisted experiential learning (MA); school guidance counseling (MA); secondary education (MA); special education, learning disability (MA); special education, mental retardation (MA); special education, serious emotional disability (MA); student-directed independent study (MA); sustainability education (PhD). Part-time programs available. Postbaccalaureate distance learning degree programs offered (minimal on-campus study). *Faculty:* 3 full-time (1 woman), 79 part-time/adjunct (41 women). *Students:* 75 full-time (44 women), 46 part-time (36 women); includes 18 minority (3 African Americans, 3 American Indian/Alaska Native, 4 Asian Americans or Pacific Islanders, 8 Hispanic Americans), 2 international. Average age 39. 66 applicants, 67% accepted, 31 enrolled. In 2009, 22 master's, 4 doctorates awarded. *Degree requirements:* For master's, thesis, fieldwork or internship, practicum; for doctorate, thesis/dissertation. *Entrance requirements:* For master's, 2 letters of recommendation, resume; for doctorate, 3 letters of recommendation, resume, official transcripts, personal statement, program proposal. Additional exam requirements/recommendations for international students: Required—TOEFL (minimum score 500 paper-based; 173 computer-based). *Application deadline:* For fall admission, 4/15 priority date for domestic and international students; for spring admission, 9/15 priority date for domestic and international students. Applications are processed on a rolling basis. Application fee: $40. Electronic applications accepted. *Expenses:* Tuition: Full-time $14,712; part-time $613 per credit. Required fees: $50 per term. One-time fee: $150. Tuition and fees vary according to course load and degree level. *Financial support:* Career-related internships or

fieldwork and Federal Work-Study available. Financial award applicants required to submit FAFSA. *Unit head:* Noel Caniglia, Chair, 928-358-3201, Fax: 928-776-5151, E-mail: ncaniglia@prescott.edu. *Application contact:* Kerstin Alicki, Admissions Counselor, 877-412-8705, Fax: 928-277-4695, E-mail: admissions@prescott.edu.

Providence College, Graduate Studies, Department of Education, Program in Special Education, Providence, RI 02918. Offers elementary special education (M Ed), including elementary, secondary. Part-time and evening/weekend programs available. *Faculty:* 4 full-time (3 women), 39 part-time/adjunct (22 women). *Students:* 11 full-time (8 women), 38 part-time (29 women); includes 1 minority (Hispanic American). Average age 31. 14 applicants, 100% accepted. In 2009, 35 master's awarded. *Degree requirements:* For master's, comprehensive exam. *Entrance requirements:* For master's, GRE General Test. Additional exam requirements/recommendations for international students: Required—TOEFL (minimum score 550 paper-based; 213 computer-based; 80 iBT). *Application deadline:* For fall admission, 8/1 priority date for domestic and international students; for spring admission, 12/1 priority date for domestic and international students. Applications are processed on a rolling basis. Application fee: $55. *Expenses:* Tuition: Full-time $9909; part-time $367 per credit. One-time fee: $200. Tuition and fees vary according to course load and program. *Financial support:* In 2009–10, 1 research assistantship with full tuition reimbursement (averaging $8,400 per year) was awarded; career-related internships or fieldwork and unspecified assistantships also available. Support available to part-time students. Financial award application deadline: 8/1; financial award applicants required to submit FAFSA. *Unit head:* Diane LaMontagne, Director, 401-865-2912, Fax: 401-865-1147, E-mail: dlamonta@providence.edu. *Application contact:* Carol A. Daniels, Coordinator of Graduate Faculty and Administrative Services, 401-865-2247, Fax: 401-865-1147, E-mail: daniels@providence.edu.

Providence College, Graduate Studies, Department of Education, Programs in Administration, Providence, RI 02918. Offers elementary administration (M Ed); secondary administration (M Ed). Part-time and evening/weekend programs available. *Faculty:* 4 full-time (3 women), 39 part-time/adjunct (22 women). *Students:* 7 full-time (3 women), 50 part-time (23 women); includes 1 minority (African American). Average age 36. 7 applicants, 100% accepted. In 2009, 23 master's awarded. *Degree requirements:* For master's, comprehensive exam. *Entrance requirements:* For master's, GRE General Test. Additional exam requirements/recommendations for international students: Required—TOEFL (minimum score 550 paper-based; 213 computer-based; 80 iBT). *Application deadline:* For fall admission, 8/1 priority date for domestic and international students; for spring admission, 12/1 priority date for domestic and international students. Applications are processed on a rolling basis. Application fee: $55. *Expenses:* Tuition: Full-time $9909; part-time $367 per credit. One-time fee: $200. Tuition and fees vary according to course load and program. *Financial support:* In 2009–10, research assistantships with full tuition reimbursements (averaging $8,400 per year); career-related internships or fieldwork, institutionally sponsored loans, and unspecified assistantships also available. Support available to part-time students. Financial award application deadline: 8/1; financial award applicants required to submit FAFSA. *Unit head:* Francis J. Leary, Director, 401-865-2247, Fax: 401-865-1147, E-mail: fleary@providence.edu. *Application contact:* Carol A. Daniels, Coordinator of Graduate Faculty and Administrative Services, 401-865-2247, Fax: 401-865-1147, E-mail: daniels@providence.edu.

Providence College, Graduate Studies, Department of Education, Providence Alliance for Catholic Teachers (PACT) Program, Providence, RI 02918. Offers secondary education (M Ed). *Faculty:* 4 full-time (3 women), 39 part-time/adjunct (22 women). *Students:* 23 full-time (15 women). Average age 23. 74 applicants, 30% accepted. In 2009, 15 master's awarded. *Degree requirements:* For master's, comprehensive exam. *Entrance requirements:* For master's, GRE/MAT. Additional exam requirements/recommendations for international students: Required—TOEFL (minimum score 550 paper-based; 213 computer-based; 80 iBT). *Application deadline:* For fall admission, 2/1 priority date for domestic and international students. Applications are processed on a rolling basis. Application fee: $55. *Expenses:* Tuition: Full-time $9909; part-time $367 per credit. One-time fee: $200. Tuition and fees vary according to course load and program. *Financial support:* In 2009–10, teaching assistantships (averaging $14,500 per year). Financial award application deadline: 8/1; financial award applicants required to submit FAFSA. *Unit head:* Br. Patrick Carey, Director, 401-865-2657, E-mail: pcarey@providence.edu. *Application contact:* Carol A. Daniels, Coordinator of Graduate Faculty and Administrative Services, 401-865-2247, Fax: 401-865-1147, E-mail: daniels@providence.edu.

Queens College of the City University of New York, Division of Graduate Studies, Division of Education, Department of Secondary Education, Flushing, NY 11367-1597. Offers art (MS Ed); biology (MS Ed, AC); chemistry (MS Ed, AC); earth sciences (MS Ed, AC); English (MS Ed, AC); French (MS Ed, AC); Italian (MS Ed, AC); mathematics (MS Ed, AC); music (MS Ed, AC); physics (MS Ed, AC); social studies (MS Ed, AC); Spanish (MS Ed, AC). Part-time and evening/weekend programs available. *Faculty:* 22 full-time (14 women). *Students:* 86 full-time (47 women), 1,118 part-time (736 women). 591 applicants, 60% accepted, 250 enrolled. In 2009, 187 master's awarded. *Degree requirements:* For master's, research project; for AC, thesis optional. *Entrance requirements:* For master's, minimum GPA of 3.0. Additional exam requirements/recommendations for international students: Required—TOEFL. *Application deadline:* For fall admission, 4/1 for domestic students; for spring admission, 11/1 for domestic students. Applications are processed on a rolling basis. Application fee: $125. *Expenses:* Tuition, state resident: full-time $7360; part-time $310 per credit. Tuition, nonresident: part-time $575 per credit. One-time fee: $195 full-time; $145.25 part-time. *Financial support:* Career-related internships or fieldwork, Federal Work-Study, institutionally sponsored loans, and tuition waivers (partial) available. Support available to part-time students. Financial award application deadline: 4/1; financial award applicants required to submit FAFSA. *Unit head:* Dr. Eleanor Armour-Thomas, Chairperson, 718-997-5150, E-mail: armourthomas@yahoo.com. *Application contact:* Mario Caruso, Director of Graduate Admissions, 718-997-5200, Fax: 718-997-5193, E-mail: graduate_admissions@qc.edu.

Quinnipiac University, Division of Education, Program in Secondary Education, Hamden, CT 06518-1940. Offers biology (MAT); English (MAT); history/social studies (MAT); mathematics (MAT); Spanish (MAT). *Accreditation:* NCATE. *Faculty:* 10 full-time (7 women), 5 part-time/adjunct (3 women). *Students:* 80 full-time (56 women), 2 part-time (1 woman); includes 6 minority (2 African Americans, 2 Asian Americans or Pacific Islanders, 2 Hispanic Americans). 77 applicants, 95% accepted, 66 enrolled. In 2009, 33 master's awarded. *Entrance requirements:* For master's, PRAXIS I, minimum GPA of 2.67, interview. Additional exam requirements/recommendations for international students: Required—TOEFL (minimum score 575 paper-based; 233 computer-based; 90 iBT), IELTS (minimum score 6.5). *Application deadline:* For fall admission, 3/31 priority date for domestic students. Applications are processed on a rolling basis. Application fee: $45. Electronic applications accepted. *Expenses:* Tuition: Full-time $16,030; part-time $770 per credit. Required fees: $630; $35 per credit. *Financial support:* Career-related internships or fieldwork, scholarships/grants, and tuition waivers (partial) available. Financial award application deadline: 4/15; financial award applicants required to submit FAFSA. *Faculty research:* Multicultural and urban education, role of technology in education, challenges of teaching diverse learners, socio-cultural nature of learning. *Unit head:* Dr. Bernadine Krawczyk, Assistant Dean, Division of Education, 203-582-3510, Fax: 203-582-3473, E-mail: bernadine.krawczyk@quinnipiac.edu. *Application contact:* Jennifer Boutin, Associate Director of Graduate Admissions, 800-462-1944, Fax: 203-582-3443, E-mail: jennifer.boutin@quinnipiac.edu.

Regis University, College for Professional Studies, Program in Teacher Education, Denver, CO 80221-1099. Offers adult learning, training, and development (M Ed); curriculum, instruction, and assessment (M Ed); early childhood (M Ed); educational technology (Certificate); elementary (M Ed); ESL (M Ed); fine arts (M Ed), including arts, music; instructional technology (M Ed); professional leadership (M Ed); reading (M Ed); secondary (M Ed); self-designed (M Ed); space studies (M Ed); special education (M Ed); teacher licensure (M Ed). Program also offered in Henderson and Las Vegas (Summerlin), NV. *Accreditation:* Teacher Education Accreditation Council. Part-time and evening/weekend programs available. Postbaccalaureate distance learning degree programs offered (no on-campus study). *Degree requirements:* For

Secondary Education

Regis University (continued)

master's, thesis. *Entrance requirements:* For master's, resume, minimum GPA of 2.75, criminal background check. Additional exam requirements/recommendations for international students: Required—TOEFL (minimum score 213 computer-based), TWE (minimum score 5). Electronic applications accepted. *Faculty research:* Issues of equity in the middle school classroom, professional learning communities, school reform, socialinguistic and discursive obstacles to student integration, inclusive language arts curriculum.

Rhode Island College, School of Graduate Studies, Feinstein School of Education and Human Development, Department of Educational Studies, Providence, RI 02908-1991. Offers English (MAT); French (MAT); history (MAT); math (MAT); secondary education (MAT); Spanish (MAT); teaching English as a second language (M Ed); technology education (M Ed). *Accreditation:* NCATE. Part-time and evening/weekend programs available. *Faculty:* 10 full-time (5 women), 6 part-time/adjunct (5 women). *Students:* 8 full-time (all women), 56 part-time (40 women); includes 2 minority (both Hispanic Americans). Average age 35. In 2009, 28 master's awarded. *Degree requirements:* For master's, capstone or comprehensive assessment. *Entrance requirements:* For master's, GRE or MAT (for most programs), minimum undergraduate GPA of 3.0; baccalaureate degree in English, French, history, math or Spanish; evaluation of content area knowledge; 3 letters of recommendation; interview. Additional exam requirements/recommendations for international students: Recommended—TOEFL (minimum score 550 paper-based; 213 computer-based; 79 iBT). *Application deadline:* For fall admission, 3/15 for domestic students; for spring admission, 11/1 for domestic students. Applications are processed on a rolling basis. Application fee: $50. *Expenses:* Tuition, state resident: full-time $7440; part-time $310 per credit hour. Tuition, nonresident: full-time $14,784; part-time $616 per credit hour. Required fees: $552; $20 per credit. $70 per term. *Financial support:* Teaching assistantships with full tuition reimbursements, career-related internships or fieldwork, Federal Work-Study, scholarships/grants, health care benefits, and unspecified assistantships available. Support available to part-time students. Financial award application deadline: 5/15; financial award applicants required to submit FAFSA. *Faculty research:* School administration, school/college articulation. *Unit head:* Dr. Ellen Bigler, Chair, 401-456-8170. *Application contact:* Graduate Studies, 401-456-8700.

Roberts Wesleyan College, Division of Teacher Education, Rochester, NY 14624-1997. Offers adolescence education (M Ed); childhood and special education (M Ed); literacy education (M Ed); urban education (M Ed). Part-time and evening/weekend programs available. *Degree requirements:* For master's, thesis.

Rochester Institute of Technology, Graduate Enrollment Services, National Technical Institute for the Deaf, Department of Research and Teacher Education, Rochester, NY 14623-5603. Offers MS. *Accreditation:* Teacher Education Accreditation Council. *Students:* 46 full-time (34 women), 9 part-time (7 women); includes 7 minority (4 African Americans, 2 Asian Americans or Pacific Islanders, 1 Hispanic American). Average age 29. 50 applicants, 74% accepted, 33 enrolled. In 2009, 25 master's awarded. *Degree requirements:* For master's, thesis or alternative. *Entrance requirements:* For master's, minimum GPA of 3.0. Additional exam requirements/recommendations for international students: Required—TOEFL (minimum score 550 paper-based; 213 computer-based; 88 iBT), or IELTS (minimum score 6.5). *Application deadline:* For fall admission, 2/15 priority date for domestic and international students. Applications are processed on a rolling basis. Application fee: $50. Electronic applications accepted. *Expenses:* Tuition: Full-time $31,533; part-time $876 per credit hour. Required fees: $210. *Financial support:* In 2009–10, 46 students received support; fellowships with full and partial tuition reimbursements available, research assistantships with partial tuition reimbursements available, teaching assistantships with partial tuition reimbursements available, career-related internships or fieldwork, institutionally sponsored loans, scholarships/grants, and unspecified assistantships available. Support available to part-time students. Financial award applicants required to submit FAFSA. *Unit head:* Gerald Bateman, Director, 585-475-6480, Fax: 585-475-2525, E-mail: gcbnmp@rit.edu. *Application contact:* Diane Ellison, Assistant Vice President, Graduate Enrollment Services, 585-475-2229, Fax: 585-475-7164, E-mail: gradinfo@rit.edu.

Rockford College, Graduate Studies, Department of Education, Program in Secondary Education, Rockford, IL 61108-2393. Offers MAT. Secondary Education certification available in English, math, social sciences (history), and science (biology and chemistry); K-12 certification available in physical education, theatre, visual arts, and foreign language. Part-time and evening/weekend programs available. *Degree requirements:* For master's, thesis optional. *Entrance requirements:* For master's, GRE General Test, basic skills test (for students seeking certification), 3 letters of recommendation. Additional exam requirements/recommendations for international students: Required—TOEFL (minimum score 550 paper-based; 213 computer-based; 79 iBT). Electronic applications accepted.

Rollins College, Hamilton Holt School, Program in Education, Winter Park, FL 32789-4499. Offers elementary education (M Ed, MAT); secondary education (MAT), including English, mathematics, music. Part-time and evening/weekend programs available. *Faculty:* 5 full-time (3 women), 3 part-time/adjunct (2 women). *Students:* 14 full-time (11 women), 26 part-time (25 women); includes 7 minority (4 African Americans, 3 Hispanic Americans). Average age 31. 27 applicants, 100% accepted, 27 enrolled. In 2009, 10 master's awarded. *Degree requirements:* For master's, comprehensive exam. *Entrance requirements:* For master's, GRE or MAT, interview. Additional exam requirements/recommendations for international students: Required—TOEFL. *Application deadline:* For fall admission, 7/16 for domestic students; for winter admission, 12/3 for domestic students; for spring admission, 4/22 for domestic students. Applications are processed on a rolling basis. Application fee: $50. *Expenses:* Contact institution. *Financial support:* Teaching assistantships, scholarships/grants available. Support available to part-time students. *Unit head:* Dr. J. Scott Hewit, Director, 407-646-2300, E-mail: jhewit@rollins.edu. *Application contact:* Rebecca Cordray, Coordinator of Records and Registration, 407-646-1568, Fax: 407-975-6430, E-mail: rcordray@rollins.edu.

Roosevelt University, Graduate Division, College of Education, Department of Secondary Education, Chicago, IL 60605. Offers MA.

Rowan University, Graduate School, College of Education, Department of Teacher Education, Program in Secondary Education, Glassboro, NJ 08028-1701. Offers MST. *Students:* 9 full-time (4 women); includes 1 minority (Hispanic American). Average age 25. 1 applicant, 100% accepted, 0 enrolled. In 2009, 5 master's awarded. *Degree requirements:* For master's, thesis. *Entrance requirements:* For master's, GRE General Test. Additional exam requirements/recommendations for international students: Required—TOEFL. *Application deadline:* For spring admission, 2/15 priority date for domestic students. Applications are processed on a rolling basis. Application fee: $50. Electronic applications accepted. *Expenses:* Tuition, state resident: full-time $10,624; part-time $590 per semester hour. Tuition, nonresident: full-time $10,624; part-time $590 per semester hour. Required fees: $2320; $125 per semester hour. *Financial support:* Career-related internships or fieldwork, scholarships/grants, health care benefits, and unspecified assistantships available. *Unit head:* Dr. Mira Lalovic-Hand, Interim Associate Provost/Director of Graduate School, 856-256-5120, E-mail: lalovic-hand@rowan.edu. *Application contact:* Karen Haynes, Graduate Coordinator, 856-256-4052, Fax: 856-256-4436, E-mail: haynes@rowan.edu.

Sacred Heart University, Graduate Programs, College of Education and Health Professions, Isabelle Farrington School of Education, Fairfield, CT 06825-1000. Offers administration (CAS); educational technology (MAT); elementary education (MAT); reading (CAS); secondary education (MAT); teaching (CAS). Part-time and evening/weekend programs available. Postbaccalaureate distance learning degree programs offered (minimal on-campus study). *Faculty:* 23 full-time (10 women). *Students:* 377 full-time (291 women), 691 part-time (495 women); includes 63 minority (31 African Americans, 2 American Indian/Alaska Native, 8 Asian Americans or Pacific Islanders, 22 Hispanic Americans), 2 international. Average age 34. 429 applicants, 90% accepted, 338 enrolled. In 2009, 409 master's, 66 other advanced degrees awarded. *Degree requirements:* For master's, thesis or alternative. *Entrance requirements:* For master's, PRAXIS (teacher certification/MAT); for CAS, PRAXIS I. Additional exam requirements/recommendations for international students: Required—TOEFL (minimum score 550 paper-based; 213 computer-based). *Application deadline:* Applications are processed on a rolling basis. Application fee: $50 ($100 for international students). Electronic applications accepted. *Expenses:* Contact institution. *Financial support:* Teaching assistantships with partial tuition reimbursements, career-related internships or fieldwork, institutionally sponsored loans, traineeships, tuition waivers (partial), and unspecified assistantships available. Support available to part-time students. Financial award applicants required to submit FAFSA. *Faculty research:* Reading education, learning theory, teacher preparation, education of underachievers. *Unit head:* Dr. Edward Malin, Director, 203-371-7800, Fax: 203-365-7513. *Application contact:* Kathy Dilks, Assistant Dean of Graduate Admissions, 203-365-7619, Fax: 203-365-4732, E-mail: gradstudies@sacredheart.edu.

Saginaw Valley State University, College of Education, Program in Natural Science Teaching, University Center, MI 48710. Offers elementary (MAT); middle school (MAT); secondary school (MAT). *Accreditation:* NCATE. Part-time and evening/weekend programs available. *Students:* 20 part-time (16 women); includes 2 minority (1 African American, 1 Hispanic American), 1 international. Average age 35. 5 applicants, 100% accepted, 3 enrolled. In 2009, 14 master's awarded. *Degree requirements:* For master's, capstone course. *Entrance requirements:* For master's, minimum GPA of 3.0, teaching certificate. Additional exam requirements/recommendations for international students: Required—TOEFL (minimum score 525 paper-based; 197 computer-based; 71 iBT). *Application deadline:* Applications are processed on a rolling basis. Application fee: $25. Electronic applications accepted. *Financial support:* Federal Work-Study and scholarships/grants available. Support available to part-time students. Financial award applicants required to submit FAFSA. *Unit head:* Dr. Steve P. Barbus, Dean, 989-964-6067, Fax: 989-790-4385, E-mail: barbus@svsu.edu. *Application contact:* Dr. Steve P. Barbus, Dean, 989-964-6067, Fax: 989-790-4385, E-mail: barbus@svsu.edu.

Saginaw Valley State University, College of Education, Program in Secondary Classroom Teaching, University Center, MI 48710. Offers MAT. *Accreditation:* NCATE. Part-time and evening/weekend programs available. *Students:* 8 full-time (4 women), 50 part-time (25 women); includes 2 minority (1 African American, 1 Hispanic American), 1 international. Average age 32. 12 applicants, 92% accepted, 5 enrolled. In 2009, 20 master's awarded. *Degree requirements:* For master's, capstone course. *Entrance requirements:* For master's, minimum GPA of 3.0, teaching certificate. Additional exam requirements/recommendations for international students: Required—TOEFL (minimum score 525 paper-based; 197 computer-based; 71 iBT). *Application deadline:* Applications are processed on a rolling basis. Application fee: $25. Electronic applications accepted. *Financial support:* Federal Work-Study and scholarships/grants available. Support available to part-time students. Financial award applicants required to submit FAFSA. *Unit head:* Dr. Steve P. Barbus, Dean, 989-964-6067, Fax: 989-790-4385, E-mail: barbus@svsu.edu. *Application contact:* Dr. Steve P. Barbus, Dean, 989-964-6067, Fax: 989-790-4385, E-mail: barbus@svsu.edu.

St. Bonaventure University, School of Graduate Studies, School of Education, Literacy Programs, St. Bonaventure, NY 14778-2284. Offers adolescent literacy 5-12 (MS Ed); childhood literacy B-6 (MS Ed). *Accreditation:* NCATE. Part-time and evening/weekend programs available. *Faculty:* 2 full-time (1 woman), 1 (woman) part-time/adjunct. *Students:* 37 full-time (33 women), 33 part-time (31 women); includes 1 minority (Hispanic American). Average age 27. 37 applicants, 86% accepted, 26 enrolled. In 2009, 45 master's awarded. *Degree requirements:* For master's, comprehensive exam, thesis optional. *Entrance requirements:* For master's, interview, writing sample, minimum undergraduate GPA of 3.0. Additional exam requirements/recommendations for international students: Required—TOEFL. *Application deadline:* For fall admission, 8/1 for domestic students; for spring admission, 11/1 priority date for domestic students. Applications are processed on a rolling basis. Application fee: $30. Electronic applications accepted. *Expenses:* Tuition: Full-time $11,700; part-time $650 per credit. *Financial support:* In 2009–10, 9 research assistantships with full and partial tuition reimbursements were awarded; scholarships/grants also available. Support available to part-time students. Financial award application deadline: 4/15; financial award applicants required to submit FAFSA. *Faculty research:* Children's literary tastes, reading diagnosis. *Unit head:* Dr. Joseph Zimmer, Director, 716-375-2388. *Application contact:* Bruce Campbell, 716-375-2429, E-mail: gradsch@sbu.edu.

St. John's University, The School of Education, Department of Curriculum and Instruction, Program in Adolescent Education, Queens, NY 11439. Offers MS Ed. Part-time and evening/weekend programs available. *Students:* 58 full-time (26 women), 217 part-time (135 women); includes 80 minority (36 African Americans, 12 Asian Americans or Pacific Islanders, 32 Hispanic Americans), 3 international. Average age 29. 188 applicants, 84% accepted, 102 enrolled. In 2009, 100 master's awarded. *Degree requirements:* For master's, variable foreign language requirement, comprehensive exam. *Entrance requirements:* For master's, minimum GPA of 3.0, 2 letters of recommendation, qualification for the New York State provisional (initial) teaching certificate. Additional exam requirements/recommendations for international students: Required—TOEFL (minimum score 500 paper-based; 173 computer-based; 61 iBT), IELTS (minimum score 5.5). *Application deadline:* For fall admission, 4/1 priority date for domestic students, 6/1 priority date for international students; for spring admission, 11/1 priority date for domestic and international students. Applications are processed on a rolling basis. Application fee: $70. Electronic applications accepted. *Expenses:* Tuition: Full-time $16,290; part-time $905 per credit. Required fees: $300; $150 per semester. Tuition and fees vary according to program. *Financial support:* Research assistantships, career-related internships or fieldwork and scholarships/grants available. Support available to part-time students. Financial award application deadline: 3/1; financial award applicants required to submit FAFSA. *Faculty research:* Investigating self-efficacy in literacy learning, using problem solving as an approach for math learning. *Unit head:* Dr. Peter Quinn, Chair, 718-990-6775, E-mail: quinnp@stjohns.edu. *Application contact:* Dr. Kelly K. Ronayne, Associate Dean for Graduate Admissions, 718-990-2303, Fax: 718-990-2343, E-mail: graded@stjohns.edu.

Saint Joseph's University, College of Arts and Sciences, Department of Education, Philadelphia, PA 19131-1395. Offers educational leadership (Ed D); elementary education (MS); instructional technology (MS); organizational development and leadership (MS); professional education (MS); reading specialist (MS); secondary education (MS); special education (MS). Part-time and evening/weekend programs available. *Students:* 5 full-time (3 women), 750 part-time (561 women); includes 100 minority (76 African Americans, 1 American Indian/Alaska Native, 11 Asian Americans or Pacific Islanders, 12 Hispanic Americans), 3 international. Average age 33. In 2009, 210 master's, 14 doctorates awarded. *Entrance requirements:* For master's, 2 letters of recommendation, minimum GPA of 3.0, application, official transcripts, personal statement; for doctorate, GRE, master's degree from accredited institution, minimum graduate GPA of 3.5, computer competence, commitment to participate in cohort, interview with program director. Additional exam requirements/recommendations for international students: Required—TOEFL (minimum score 550 paper-based; 213 computer-based; 79 iBT). *Application deadline:* For fall admission, 7/15 priority date for domestic students, 4/15 for international students; for winter admission, 11/15 for domestic students, 1/15 for international students; for spring admission, 11/15 priority date for domestic students, 10/15 for international students. Applications are processed on a rolling basis. Application fee: $35. Electronic applications accepted. *Expenses:* Contact institution. *Financial support:* Unspecified assistantships available. Financial award applicants required to submit FAFSA. *Faculty research:* Early childhood course design, public education professional development. Total annual research expenditures: $91,900. *Unit head:* Dr. Teri Sosa, Director of Graduate Education, 610-660-3162, E-mail: tsosa@sju.edu. *Application contact:* Kate McConnell, Director, Graduate College of Arts and Sciences Admissions and Retention, 610-660-3184, Fax: 610-660-3230, E-mail: kate.mcconnell@sju.edu.

Saint Mary's University of Minnesota, Schools of Graduate and Professional Programs, Graduate School of Education, Instruction Program, Winona, MN 55987-1399. Offers MA, Certificate. *Unit head:* Rebecca Hopkins, Director, 507-457-6620, E-mail: rhopkins@smumn.edu. *Application contact:* Yasin Alsaidi, Director of Admissions for Graduate and Professional Programs, 612-728-5207, Fax: 612-728-5121, E-mail: yalsaidi@smumn.edu.

St. Thomas Aquinas College, Division of Teacher Education, Sparkill, NY 10976. Offers adolescence education (MST); childhood and special education (MST); childhood education (MST); educational leadership (MS Ed); reading (MS Ed, PMC); special education (MS Ed, PMC); teaching (MS Ed), including elementary education, middle school education, secondary education. *Accreditation:* NCATE. Part-time and evening/weekend programs available. *Degree requirements:* For master's, comprehensive exam, comprehensive professional portfolio; for PMC, action research project. *Entrance requirements:* For master's, New York State Qualifying Exam, GRE General Test or minimum GPA of 3.0, teaching certificate; for PMC, GRE General Test or minimum GPA of 3.0. Electronic applications accepted. *Faculty research:* Computer applications in education, adolescent special education students, literacy development, inclusive practices for special education students.

Saint Xavier University, Graduate Studies, School of Education, Chicago, IL 60655-3105. Offers counseling (MA); counselor education (MA); curriculum and instruction (MA); early childhood education (MA); education (CAS); educational administration (MA); elementary education (MA); field-based education (MA); general educational studies (MA); individualized program (MA); learning disabilities (MA); reading (MA); secondary education (MA). *Accreditation:* NCATE. Part-time and evening/weekend programs available. *Degree requirements:* For master's, thesis or project. *Entrance requirements:* For master's, minimum GPA of 3.0. *Expenses:* Contact institution.

Salem College, Department of Education, Winston-Salem, NC 27101. Offers early education and leadership (MAT); elementary education (MAT); English as a second language (MAT); language and literacy (M Ed); middle school education (MAT); secondary education (MAT); special education (MAT). *Accreditation:* NCATE. Part-time and evening/weekend programs available. *Degree requirements:* For master's, comprehensive exam, practicum (MAT), project (M Ed), oral and written comprehensive exams. *Entrance requirements:* For master's, GRE, minimum GPA of 2.5. *Faculty research:* Content area reading strategies, literacy development, brain compatible instruction.

Salem State College, School of Graduate Studies, Program in Secondary Education, Salem, MA 01970-5353. Offers M Ed. Part-time and evening/weekend programs available. *Students:* 1 full-time (0 women), 23 part-time (17 women); includes 1 minority (Hispanic American), 1 international. Average age 39. 5 applicants, 100% accepted, 5 enrolled. In 2009, 16 master's awarded. *Entrance requirements:* For master's, GRE or MAT. Additional exam requirements/recommendations for international students: Required—TOEFL (minimum score 550 paper-based; 80 iBT), or IELTS (minimum score 5.5). *Application deadline:* For fall admission, 5/1 for domestic students; for spring admission, 10/1 for domestic students. Applications are processed on a rolling basis. Application fee: $50. *Expenses:* Tuition, state resident: full-time $2520; part-time $275 per credit hour. Tuition, nonresident: full-time $4140; part-time $365 per credit hour. Required fees: $2430. *Financial support:* In 2009–10, 6 students received support. Career-related internships or fieldwork, Federal Work-Study, scholarships/grants, and unspecified assistantships available. Support available to part-time students. Financial award application deadline: 5/1; financial award applicants required to submit FAFSA. *Unit head:* Thomas Billings, Program Coordinator, 978-542-6310, Fax: 978-542-7215, E-mail: tbillings@salemstate.edu. *Application contact:* Dr. Lee A. Brossoit, Assistant Dean of Graduate Admissions, 978-542-6675, Fax: 978-542-7215, E-mail: lbrossoit@salemstate.edu.

Salem State College, School of Graduate Studies, Program in Spanish, Salem, MA 01970-5353. Offers MAT. Part-time and evening/weekend programs available. *Students:* 28 part-time (22 women); includes 1 minority (African American). Average age 32. 3 applicants, 100% accepted, 3 enrolled. In 2009, 9 master's awarded. *Entrance requirements:* For master's, GRE or MAT. Additional exam requirements/recommendations for international students: Required—TOEFL (minimum score 550 paper-based; 80 iBT), or IELTS (minimum score 5.5). *Application deadline:* For fall admission, 5/1 for domestic students; for spring admission, 10/1 for domestic students. Applications are processed on a rolling basis. Application fee: $50. *Expenses:* Tuition, state resident: full-time $2520; part-time $275 per credit hour. Tuition, nonresident: full-time $4140; part-time $365 per credit hour. Required fees: $2430. *Financial support:* In 2009–10, 4 students received support. Career-related internships or fieldwork, Federal Work-Study, scholarships/grants, and unspecified assistantships available. Support available to part-time students. Financial award application deadline: 5/1; financial award applicants required to submit FAFSA. *Unit head:* Kristine Doll, Program Coordinator, 978-542-6321, E-mail: kdoll@salemstate.edu. *Application contact:* Dr. Lee A. Brossoit, Assistant Dean of Graduate Admissions, 978-542-6675, Fax: 978-542-7215, E-mail: lbrossoit@salemstate.edu.

Samford University, Orlean Bullard Beeson School of Education and Professional Studies, Birmingham, AL 35229. Offers early childhood education (Ed S); early childhood/elementary education (MS Ed); educational administration (Ed S); educational leadership (Ed D); elementary education (Ed S); gifted education (MS Ed); instructional leadership (MS Ed); secondary collaboration (MS Ed); M Div/MS Ed. *Accreditation:* NCATE. Part-time programs available. *Faculty:* 11 full-time (8 women), 9 part-time/adjunct (5 women). *Students:* 16 full-time (13 women), 173 part-time (131 women); includes 47 minority (46 African Americans, 1 American Indian/Alaska Native), 1 international. Average age 40. 15 applicants, 100% accepted, 15 enrolled. In 2009, 52 master's, 11 doctorates, 27 other advanced degrees awarded. *Degree requirements:* For master's, comprehensive exam; for doctorate, comprehensive exam, thesis/dissertation. *Entrance requirements:* For master's, GRE or MAT, minimum GPA of 3.0; for doctorate, minimum GPA of 3.7; for Ed S, GRE, master's degree, teaching certificate, minimum GPA of 3.25. Additional exam requirements/recommendations for international students: Required—TOEFL (minimum score 550 paper-based; 213 computer-based). *Application deadline:* Applications are processed on a rolling basis. Application fee: $25. *Expenses:* Tuition: Full-time $26,660; part-time $595 per credit hour. Required fees: $110 per semester. *Financial support:* In 2009–10, 127 students received support; research assistantships, career-related internships or fieldwork, Federal Work-Study, scholarships/grants, and tuition waivers (partial) available. Support available to part-time students. Financial award applicants required to submit FAFSA. *Faculty research:* School law, the characteristics of beginning teachers, the nature of school reform, school culture, quality improvement in education, K-12 student achievement. *Unit head:* Dr. Jean Ann Box, Dean, 205-726-2559, E-mail: jabox@samford.edu. *Application contact:* Dr. Maurice Persall, Director, Graduate Office, 205-726-2019, E-mail: jmpersal@samford.edu.

San Diego State University, Graduate and Research Affairs, College of Education, School of Teacher Education, Program in Secondary Curriculum and Instruction, San Diego, CA 92182. Offers MA. *Accreditation:* NCATE. *Entrance requirements:* For master's, GRE General Test, letters of reference. Additional exam requirements/recommendations for international students: Required—TOEFL. Electronic applications accepted.

San Francisco State University, Division of Graduate Studies, College of Education, Department of Secondary Education, San Francisco, CA 94132-1722. Offers MA Ed. *Accreditation:* NCATE.

San Jose State University, Graduate Studies and Research, Connie L. Lurie College of Education, Department of Secondary Education, San Jose, CA 95192-0001. Offers Certificate. *Accreditation:* NCATE. Evening/weekend programs available. *Students:* 145 full-time (88 women), 61 part-time (35 women); includes 65 minority (4 African Americans, 37 Asian Americans or Pacific Islanders, 24 Hispanic Americans), 2 international. Average age 34. 229 applicants, 47% accepted, 95 enrolled. *Application deadline:* For fall admission, 6/29 for domestic students; for spring admission, 11/30 for domestic students. Applications are processed on a rolling basis. Application fee: $59. Electronic applications accepted. *Financial support:* Career-related internships or fieldwork available. Financial award applicants required to submit FAFSA. *Unit head:* Dr. Mark Felton, Chair, 408-924-3755. *Application contact:* Dr. Mark Felton, Chair, 408-924-3755.

Seattle Pacific University, Master of Arts in Teaching Program, Seattle, WA 98119-1997. Offers alternate routes to certification (Certificate); teaching (MAT). *Accreditation:* NCATE. Part-time and evening/weekend programs available. *Faculty:* 4 full-time (0 women), 3 part-time/adjunct (1 woman). *Students:* 62 full-time (44 women), 79 part-time (51 women); includes 15 minority (2 African Americans, 3 American Indian/Alaska Native, 8 Asian Americans or Pacific Islanders, 2 Hispanic Americans), 2 international. Average age 32. 78 applicants, 50% accepted, 39 enrolled. In 2009, 57 master's awarded. *Degree requirements:* For master's, field experience, internship. *Entrance requirements:* For master's, GRE General Test or MAT, minimum GPA of 3.0. *Application deadline:* For fall admission, 9/24 for domestic students; for spring admission, 4/15 for domestic students. Application fee: $50. Electronic applications accepted. *Expenses:* Contact institution. *Financial support:* In 2009–10, 108 students received support. Scholarships/grants available. Financial award applicants required to submit FAFSA. *Unit head:* Dr. Richard Schuerman, Chair, 206-281-2186, Fax: 206-281-2756. *Application contact:* The Grad Center, 206-281-2091.

Shenandoah University, School of Education and Human Development, Winchester, VA 22601-5195. Offers administrative leadership (D Ed); advanced professional teaching English to speakers of other languages (Certificate); education (MSE); elementary education (Certificate); middle school education (Certificate); organizational leadership (MS); professional studies (Certificate); professional studies (for initial teacher licensure) (Certificate); professional studies (for special education teacher licensure) (Certificate); professional studies (for VA licensure reading specialists) (Certificate); professional studies (for VA licensure) (Certificate); professional teaching English to speakers of other languages (Certificate); public management (Certificate); school reform (Certificate); secondary education (Certificate). *Accreditation:* Teacher Education Accreditation Council. Part-time and evening/weekend programs available. Post-baccalaureate distance learning degree programs offered (minimal on-campus study). *Faculty:* 13 full-time (7 women), 27 part-time/adjunct (20 women). *Students:* 11 full-time (8 women), 382 part-time (276 women); includes 35 minority (17 African Americans, 1 American Indian/Alaska Native, 6 Asian Americans or Pacific Islanders, 11 Hispanic Americans), 4 international. Average age 39. 272 applicants, 95% accepted, 218 enrolled. In 2009, 103 master's, 2 doctorates awarded. *Degree requirements:* For master's, comprehensive exam (for some programs), thesis (for some programs), internship; for doctorate, comprehensive exam, thesis/dissertation; for Certificate, full time teaching in area for 1 year. *Entrance requirements:* For master's, minimum GPA of 3.0 or satisfactory GRE, 3 letters of recommendation, valid teaching license, essay; for doctorate, minimum graduate GPA of 3.5, 3 years of teaching experience, 3 letters of recommendation, writing samples; for Certificate, minimum undergraduate GPA of 3.0, essay, 3 letters of recommendation. Additional exam requirements/recommendations for international students: Required—TOEFL (minimum score 550 paper-based; 213 computer-based; 79 iBT), IELTS (minimum score 6.5). *Application deadline:* For fall admission, 7/1 for domestic and international students; for spring admission, 10/15 for domestic and international students. Application fee: $30. Electronic applications accepted. *Expenses:* Tuition: Full-time $11,925; part-time $695 per credit. Required fees: $400 per semester. *Financial support:* Application deadline: 3/15. *Unit head:* Dr. Steven E. Humphries, Dean, 540-535-3574, E-mail: shumphri@su.edu. *Application contact:* David Anthony, Dean of Admissions, 540-665-4581, Fax: 540-665-4627, E-mail: admit@su.edu.

Siena Heights University, Graduate College, Program in Teacher Education, Concentration in Secondary Education, Adrian, MI 49221-1796. Offers secondary education/reading (MA). Part-time programs available. *Degree requirements:* For master's, thesis, presentation. *Entrance requirements:* For master's, minimum GPA of 3.0, interview.

Sierra Nevada College, Teacher Education Program, Incline Village, NV 89451. Offers elementary education (MAT); secondary education (MAT). Part-time and evening/weekend programs available. *Degree requirements:* For master's, comprehensive exam, thesis, PRAXIS I and II. *Entrance requirements:* For master's, 2 letters of recommendation, minimum GPA of 3.0.

Simmons College, College of Arts and Sciences Graduate Studies, Department of Education, Program in Teacher Preparation, Boston, MA 02115. Offers educational leadership (MS Ed); elementary education (MAT); general education (CAGS); general purposes (MS); middle school education (MAT); professional license (CAGS); professional license: elementary (MS Ed); professional license: middle/high (MS Ed); secondary education (MAT); urban education (MS Ed, CAGS). Part-time programs available. *Students:* 68 full-time (58 women), 125 part-time (113 women); includes 25 minority (10 African Americans, 3 American Indian/Alaska Native, 8 Asian Americans or Pacific Islanders, 4 Hispanic Americans). Average age 27. 115 applicants, 88% accepted, 75 enrolled. In 2009, 137 master's, 14 other advanced degrees awarded. *Degree requirements:* For master's, practicum. *Entrance requirements:* For master's, GRE General Test, MAT or Massachusetts Tests for Educator Licensure (MTEL). Additional exam requirements/recommendations for international students: Required—TOEFL (minimum score 600 paper-based; 250 computer-based; 100 iBT). *Application deadline:* For fall admission, 8/1 priority date for domestic and international students; for winter admission, 12/15 priority date for domestic and international students; for spring admission, 12/15 priority date for domestic and international students. Applications are processed on a rolling basis. Application fee: $35. Electronic applications accepted. *Expenses:* Contact institution. *Financial support:* Application deadline: 3/1. *Faculty research:* Educational psychology, mentorship with first year teachers, urban classrooms, first generation college students. *Unit head:* Gary Oakes, Director, Master of Arts in Teaching (MAT) Program, 617-521-2203, Fax: 617-521-3133. *Application contact:* Kristen Haack, Director, Graduate Studies Admission, 617-521-2917, Fax: 617-521-3058, E-mail: gsa@simmons.edu.

Simpson College, Department of Education, Indianola, IA 50125-1297. Offers secondary education (MAT). *Degree requirements:* For master's, PRAXIS II, electronic portfolio. *Entrance requirements:* For master's, bachelor's degree; minimum cumulative GPA of 2.75, 3.0 in major; 3 letters of recommendation.

Slippery Rock University of Pennsylvania, Graduate Studies (Recruitment), College of Education, Department of Secondary Education/Foundations of Education, Slippery Rock, PA 16057-1383. Offers secondary education in math/science (M Ed). *Accreditation:* NCATE. *Degree requirements:* For master's, comprehensive exam (for some programs), thesis (for some programs). *Entrance requirements:* For master's, GRE General Test, MAT, minimum GPA of 2.75 (3.0 for initial certification programs). Additional exam requirements/recommendations for international students: Required—TOEFL (minimum score 550 paper-based; 213 computer-based). *Application deadline:* For fall admission, 3/1 priority date for domestic students, 5/1 priority date for international students; for spring admission, 11/1 priority date for domestic students, 9/1 priority date for international students. Applications are processed on a rolling basis. Application fee: $25 ($30 for international students). Electronic applications accepted. *Expenses:* Tuition, state resident: full-time $6666; part-time $370 per credit. Tuition, nonresident: full-time $10,666; part-time $593 per credit. Required fees: $2184; $182 per credit. *Financial support:* Career-related internships or fieldwork, Federal Work-Study, scholarships/grants, and unspecified assistantships available. Support available to part-time students. Financial award application deadline: 5/1; financial award applicants required to submit FAFSA. *Unit head:* Dr. Jeffrey Lehman, Graduate Coordinator, 724-738-2311, Fax: 724-738-4987, E-mail: jeffrey.lehman@sru.edu. *Application contact:* Angela Piverotto, Interim Director of Graduate Studies, 724-738-2051, Fax: 724-738-2146, E-mail: graduate.admissions@sru.edu.

Smith College, Graduate and Special Programs, Department of Education and Child Study, Program in Secondary Education, Northampton, MA 01063. Offers biological sciences education (MAT); chemistry education (MAT); English education (MAT); French education (MAT); geology education (MAT); government education (MAT); history education (MAT); mathematics education (MAT); physics education (MAT); Spanish education (MAT). Part-time programs available. *Faculty:* 6 full-time (4 women), 3 part-time/adjunct (2 women). *Students:* 7 full-time (4 women), 1 part-time (0 women). Average age 25. 14 applicants, 100% accepted, 8 enrolled. In 2009, 9 master's awarded. *Entrance requirements:* Additional exam requirements/recommendations for international students: Required—TOEFL (minimum score 590 paper-based; 243 computer-based; 97 iBT). *Application deadline:* For fall admission, 4/1 for domestic students, 1/15 priority date for international students; for spring admission, 12/1 for domestic students. Application fee: $60. *Financial support:* In 2009–10, 6 students received support. Career-related internships or fieldwork, institutionally sponsored loans, and scholarships/grants available.

Secondary Education

Smith College (continued)

Support available to part-time students. Financial award application deadline: 1/15; financial award applicants required to submit CSS PROFILE or FAFSA. *Unit head:* Rosetta Cohen, Graduate Student Advisor, 413-585-3266, E-mail: rcohen@smith.edu. *Application contact:* Ruth Morgan, Administrative Assistant, 413-585-3050, Fax: 413-585-3054, E-mail: gradstdy@smith.edu.

South Carolina State University, School of Graduate Studies, Department of Education, Orangeburg, SC 29117-0001. Offers early childhood and special education (M Ed); early childhood education (MAT); elementary education (M Ed, MAT); engineering (MAT); general science (MAT); mathematics (MAT); secondary education (M Ed), including biology education, business education, counselor education, English education, home economics education, industrial education, mathematics education, science education, social studies education; special education (M Ed), including emotionally handicapped, learning disabilities, mentally handicapped. *Accreditation:* NCATE. Part-time and evening/weekend programs available. *Degree requirements:* For master's, thesis optional, departmental qualifying exam. *Entrance requirements:* For master's, GRE General Test, NTE, interview, teaching certificate. Electronic applications accepted. *Expenses:* Tuition, state resident: part-time $470 per credit hour. Tuition, nonresident: part-time $924 per credit hour. *Faculty research:* Critical thinking, child abuse, stress, test-taking skills, conflict resolution, mainstreaming.

Southeast Missouri State University, School of Graduate Studies, Department of Middle and Secondary Education, Cape Girardeau, MO 63701-4799. Offers educational studies (MA); middle level education (MA). *Accreditation:* NCATE. Part-time and evening/weekend programs available. *Degree requirements:* For master's, thesis or alternative. *Entrance requirements:* For master's, GRE General Test, MAT, PRAXIS II, minimum undergraduate GPA of 2.75. Additional exam requirements/recommendations for international students: Required—TOEFL (minimum score 550 paper-based; 213 computer-based); Recommended—IELTS (minimum score 6). Electronic applications accepted. *Expenses:* Tuition, state resident: full-time $4266; part-time $237 per credit hour. Tuition, nonresident: full-time $7506; part-time $417 per credit hour. Required fees: $427; $427. *Faculty research:* Educational administration issues in K-12, leadership in educational setting, counselor education and supervision issues, rural education issues.

Southern Arkansas University–Magnolia, Graduate Programs, Magnolia, AR 71753. Offers agriculture (MS); business administration (MBA); computer and information sciences (MS); counseling (MS); education (M Ed), including counseling and development, curriculum and instruction emphasis, educational administration and supervision, elementary education, middle level emphasis, reading emphasis, secondary education, TESOL emphasis; kinesiology (MS); library media and information specialist (M Ed); mental health and clinical counseling (MS); public administration (EMPA); school counseling (M Ed); teaching (MAT). *Accreditation:* NCATE. Part-time and evening/weekend programs available. *Faculty:* 43 full-time (24 women), 12 part-time/adjunct (7 women). *Students:* 116 full-time (78 women), 333 part-time (255 women); includes 105 minority (98 African Americans, 3 American Indian/Alaska Native, 3 Asian Americans or Pacific Islanders, 1 Hispanic American), 11 international. Average age 33. In 2009, 88 master's awarded. *Degree requirements:* For master's, comprehensive exam, thesis optional. *Entrance requirements:* For master's, GRE, MAT or GMAT, minimum GPA of 2.75. *Application deadline:* For fall admission, 8/15 for domestic students; for winter admission, 1/8 for domestic students; for spring admission, 1/8 for domestic students. Applications are processed on a rolling basis. Application fee: $0. *Expenses:* Tuition, state resident: full-time $3798; part-time $211 per hour. Tuition, nonresident: full-time $5580; part-time $310 per hour. Required fees: $584. *Financial support:* Career-related internships or fieldwork, Federal Work-Study, scholarships/grants, tuition waivers (full), and unspecified assistantships available. Financial award applicants required to submit FAFSA. *Faculty research:* Alternative certification for teachers, supervision of instruction, instructional leadership, counseling. *Unit head:* Dr. Kim Bloss, Dean, Graduate Studies, 870-235-4150, Fax: 870-235-5227, E-mail: kkbloss@saumag.edu. *Application contact:* Dr. Kim Bloss, Dean, Graduate Studies, 870-235-4150, Fax: 870-235-5227, E-mail: kkbloss@saumag.edu.

Southern Illinois University Edwardsville, Graduate Studies and Research, School of Education, Department of Curriculum and Instruction, Program in Secondary Education, Edwardsville, IL 62026-0001. Offers art (MS Ed); biology (MS Ed); chemistry (MS Ed); earth and space sciences (MS Ed); English/language arts (MS Ed); foreign languages (MS Ed); history (MS Ed); mathematics (MS Ed); physics (MS Ed). *Accreditation:* NCATE. Part-time and evening/weekend programs available. *Students:* 24 part-time (19 women); includes 2 minority (1 African American, 1 Hispanic American). Average age 26. 13 applicants, 31% accepted. In 2009, 5 master's awarded. *Degree requirements:* For master's, thesis or alternative, final exam/paper. *Entrance requirements:* Additional exam requirements/recommendations for international students: Required—TOEFL (minimum score 550 paper-based; 213 computer-based; 79 iBT), IELTS (minimum score 6.5). *Application deadline:* For fall admission, 7/23 for domestic students, 6/1 for international students; for spring admission, 12/11 for domestic students, 10/1 for international students. Applications are processed on a rolling basis. Application fee: $30. Electronic applications accepted. *Expenses:* Tuition, state resident: part-time $1252.50 per semester. Tuition, nonresident: part-time $3131.25 per semester. Required fees: $586.85 per semester. Tuition and fees vary according to course load. *Financial support:* Fellowships, research assistantships, teaching assistantships, career-related internships or fieldwork, Federal Work-Study, institutionally sponsored loans, scholarships/grants, traineeships, and unspecified assistantships available. Support available to part-time students. Financial award application deadline: 3/1; financial award applicants required to submit FAFSA. *Unit head:* Dr. Kathy Bushrow, Director, 618-650-3082, E-mail: kbushro@siue.edu. *Application contact:* Dr. Kathy Bushrow, Director, 618-650-3082, E-mail: kbushro@siue.edu.

Southern New Hampshire University, School of Education, Manchester, NH 03106-1045. Offers business education (MS); child development (M Ed); computer technology education (Certificate); curriculum and instruction (M Ed); education (M Ed, CAS); elementary education (M Ed); general special education (Certificate); school business administrator (Certificate); secondary education (M Ed); training and development (Certificate). Part-time and evening/weekend programs available. Postbaccalaureate distance learning degree programs offered (no on-campus study). *Degree requirements:* For master's, comprehensive exam (for some programs), thesis or alternative. *Entrance requirements:* For master's, PRAXIS I, minimum GPA of 2.75. Additional exam requirements/recommendations for international students: Required—TOEFL (minimum score 550 paper-based; 213 computer-based). Electronic applications accepted. *Expenses:* Contact institution.

Southern Oregon University, Graduate Studies, School of Education, Ashland, OR 97520. Offers elementary education (MA Ed, MS Ed), including classroom teacher, early childhood, handicapped learner, reading, supervision; secondary education (MA Ed, MS Ed), including classroom teacher, handicapped learner, reading, supervision; teaching (MAT). *Degree requirements:* For master's, thesis optional. *Entrance requirements:* For master's, GRE General Test, minimum GPA of 3.0. Electronic applications accepted.

Southern University and Agricultural and Mechanical College, Graduate School, College of Education, Department of Curriculum and Instruction, Baton Rouge, LA 70813. Offers elementary education (M Ed); media (M Ed); secondary education (M Ed). *Degree requirements:* For master's, comprehensive exam, thesis optional. *Entrance requirements:* For master's, GMAT or GRE General Test. Additional exam requirements/recommendations for international students: Required—TOEFL (minimum score 525 paper-based; 193 computer-based).

Southwestern Assemblies of God University, Thomas F. Harrison School of Graduate Studies, Program in Education, Waxahachie, TX 75165-5735. Offers Christian school administration (MS); curriculum development (MS); early education administration (M Ed); middle and secondary education (M Ed). *Degree requirements:* For master's, comprehensive written and oral exams. *Entrance requirements:* For master's, GRE General Test, minimum GPA of 2.5. Electronic applications accepted.

Southwestern Oklahoma State University, College of Professional and Graduate Studies, School of Behavioral Sciences and Education, Weatherford, OK 73096-3098. Offers community counseling (M Ed); early childhood education (M Ed); educational administration (M Ed); elementary education (M Ed); health sciences and microbiology (M Ed); kinesiology (M Ed); parks and recreation management (M Ed); school counseling (M Ed); school psychology (MS); school psychometry (M Ed); secondary education (M Ed); special education (M Ed). *Accreditation:* NCATE. Part-time and evening/weekend programs available. Postbaccalaureate distance learning degree programs offered (minimal on-campus study). *Degree requirements:* For master's, exam. *Entrance requirements:* For master's, GRE General Test or minimum undergraduate GPA of 3.0. Additional exam requirements/recommendations for international students: Required—TOEFL.

Spalding University, Graduate Studies, College of Education, Programs in Education, Louisville, KY 40203-2188. Offers elementary school education (MAT); general education (MA); high school education (MAT); middle school education (MAT); school administration (MA); special education (learning and behavioral disorders) (MAT); student guidance counselor (MA). MAT degree programs offered for first teaching certificate/license students. *Accreditation:* NCATE. Part-time and evening/weekend programs available. *Faculty:* 6 full-time (4 women), 32 part-time/adjunct (23 women). *Students:* 125 full-time (93 women), 64 part-time (49 women); includes 53 minority (50 African Americans, 2 American Indian/Alaska Native, 1 Hispanic American), 2 international. Average age 37. 57 applicants, 79% accepted, 41 enrolled. In 2009, 56 master's awarded. *Degree requirements:* For master's, portfolio, final project, clinical experience. *Entrance requirements:* For master's, GRE General Test or MAT, interview, recommendations, resume. Additional exam requirements/recommendations for international students: Required—TOEFL (minimum score 535 paper-based; 203 computer-based). *Application deadline:* Applications are processed on a rolling basis. Application fee: $30. Electronic applications accepted. *Expenses:* Tuition: Full-time $11,340; part-time $630 per credit hour. Tuition and fees vary according to program. *Financial support:* In 2009–10, 106 students received support, including 3 research assistantships with partial tuition reimbursements available (averaging $3,590 per year); scholarships/grants, traineeships, and unspecified assistantships also available. Financial award application deadline: 3/15; financial award applicants required to submit FAFSA. *Faculty research:* Instructional technology, achievement gap, classroom management, assessment. *Unit head:* Dr. Beverly Keepers, Dean, 502-588-7121, Fax: 502-585-7123, E-mail: bkeepers@spalding.edu. *Application contact:* Admissions Office, 502-585-7111, E-mail: admissions@spalding.edu.

Springfield College, Graduate Programs, Program in Education, Springfield, MA 01109-3797. Offers counseling and secondary education (M Ed, MS); early childhood education (M Ed, MS); education (M Ed, MS); educational administration (M Ed, MS); educational studies (M Ed, MS); elementary education (M Ed, MS); secondary education (M Ed, MS); special education (M Ed, MS). Part-time and evening/weekend programs available. *Entrance requirements:* Additional exam requirements/recommendations for international students: Required—TOEFL (minimum score 550 paper-based; 213 computer-based). Electronic applications accepted. *Expenses:* Tuition: Full-time $19,800; part-time $825 per credit hour. Required fees: $150.

Spring Hill College, Graduate Programs, Program in Education, Mobile, AL 36608-1791. Offers early childhood education (MAT, MS Ed); educational theory (MS Ed); elementary education (MAT, MS Ed); secondary education (MAT, MS Ed). Part-time programs available. *Faculty:* 3 full-time (all women), 3 part-time/adjunct (2 women). *Students:* 9 full-time (7 women), 26 part-time (21 women); includes 6 minority (5 African Americans, 1 Asian American or Pacific Islander). Average age 31. 33 applicants, 48% accepted, 9 enrolled. In 2009, 14 master's awarded. *Degree requirements:* For master's, comprehensive exam, completion of program within 6 calendar years of entrance into graduate studies at Spring Hill. *Entrance requirements:* For master's, GRE, MAT, NTE, or PRAXIS, bachelor's degree. Additional exam requirements/recommendations for international students: Required—TOEFL (minimum score 550 paper-based; 213 computer-based; 80 iBT), IELTS (minimum score 6.5). *Application deadline:* For fall admission, 8/1 priority date for domestic and international students; for spring admission, 12/1 priority date for domestic and international students. Applications are processed on a rolling basis. Application fee: $25 ($35 for international students). Electronic applications accepted. *Expenses:* Contact institution. *Financial support:* In 2009–10, 24 students received support. Career-related internships or fieldwork, institutionally sponsored loans, and scholarships/grants available. Support available to part-time students. Financial award applicants required to submit FAFSA. *Unit head:* Dr. Ann A. Adams, Chair of Teacher Education, 251-380-3479, Fax: 251-460-2184, E-mail: aadams@shc.edu. *Application contact:* Donna B. Tarasavage, Director of Marketing and Recruiting, Graduate and Continuing Studies, 251-380-3067, Fax: 251-460-2190, E-mail: dtarasavage@shc.edu.

State University of New York at Binghamton, Graduate School, School of Education, Program in Adolescence Education, Binghamton, NY 13902-6000. Offers biology education (MAT, MS Ed, MST); earth science education (MAT, MS Ed, MST); English education (MAT, MS Ed, MST); French education (MAT, MST); mathematical sciences education (MAT, MS Ed, MST); physics (MAT, MS Ed, MST); social studies (MAT, MS Ed, MST); Spanish education (MAT, MST). *Accreditation:* Teacher Education Accreditation Council. Part-time and evening/weekend programs available. *Students:* 93 full-time (37 women), 21 part-time (8 women); includes 6 minority (2 Asian Americans or Pacific Islanders, 4 Hispanic Americans), 1 international. Average age 27. 69 applicants, 81% accepted, 46 enrolled. In 2009, 53 master's awarded. *Entrance requirements:* For master's, GRE General Test. Additional exam requirements/recommendations for international students: Required—TOEFL (minimum score 550 paper-based; 213 computer-based; 80 iBT). *Application deadline:* For fall admission, 2/1 priority date for domestic and international students; for spring admission, 10/15 priority date for domestic and international students. Applications are processed on a rolling basis. Application fee: $60. Electronic applications accepted. *Financial support:* Fellowships with partial tuition reimbursements, research assistantships with full and partial tuition reimbursements, teaching assistantships with full tuition reimbursements, career-related internships or fieldwork, Federal Work-Study, institutionally sponsored loans, scholarships/grants, health care benefits, tuition waivers (full), and unspecified assistantships available. Financial award application deadline: 2/15; financial award applicants required to submit FAFSA. *Unit head:* Dr. S. G. Grant, Dean of School of Education, 607-777-7329, E-mail: sggrant@binghamton.edu. *Application contact:* Victoria Williams, Recruiting and Admissions Coordinator, 607-777-2151, Fax: 607-777-2501, E-mail: vwilliam@binghamton.edu.

State University of New York at Fredonia, Graduate Studies, College of Education, Program in Secondary Education, Fredonia, NY 14063-1136. Offers MS Ed. *Accreditation:* NCATE. Part-time and evening/weekend programs available. *Degree requirements:* For master's, thesis optional. *Expenses:* Tuition, state resident: full-time $8370; part-time $349 per credit. Tuition, nonresident: full-time $13,250; part-time $552 per credit. Required fees: $1289; $53.55 per credit.

State University of New York at New Paltz, Graduate School, School of Education, Department of Educational Studies, Program in Special Education, New Paltz, NY 12561. Offers adolescence (7-12) (MS Ed); adolescence special education and literacy education (MS Ed); childhood (1-6) (MS Ed); childhood special education and literacy education (MS Ed); early childhood (B-2) (MS Ed). *Accreditation:* NCATE. Part-time and evening/weekend programs available. *Faculty:* 5 full-time (3 women), 7 part-time/adjunct (all women). *Students:* 33 full-time (30 women), 73 part-time (58 women); includes 4 minority (1 African American, 1 American Indian/Alaska Native, 1 Asian American or Pacific Islander, 1 Hispanic American). Average age 31. 53 applicants, 45% accepted, 19 enrolled. In 2009, 48 master's awarded. *Degree requirements:* For master's, portfolio. *Entrance requirements:* For master's, minimum GPA of 3.0 (3.2 for special education and literacy programs), NYS teaching certificate. Additional exam requirements/recommendations for international students: Required—TOEFL (minimum score 550 paper-based; 213 computer-based; 80 iBT), IELTS (minimum score 6.5). *Application deadline:* For fall admission, 3/15 priority date for domestic students, 3/15 for international students; for spring admission, 11/1 for domestic and international students. Application fee: $50. Electronic applications accepted. *Financial support:* In 2009–10, 1 student received

support, including 1 fellowship (averaging $9,000 per year); career-related internships or fieldwork, Federal Work-Study, and institutionally sponsored loans also available. Financial award application deadline: 8/1; financial award applicants required to submit FAFSA. *Faculty research:* Grouping formats. *Unit head:* Dr. Spencer Salend, Coordinator, 845-257-2831, E-mail: salends@newpaltz.edu. *Application contact:* Dr. Catherine Whittaker, Coordinator, 845-257-2831, E-mail: whittakc@newpaltz.edu.

State University of New York at New Paltz, Graduate School, School of Education, Department of Secondary Education, New Paltz, NY 12561. Offers adolescence education: biology (MAT, MS Ed); adolescence education: english (MAT); adolescence education: English (MS Ed); adolescence education: social studies (MAT, MS Ed); English as a second language (MS Ed); second language education (MS Ed). *Accreditation:* NCATE. Part-time and evening/weekend programs available. *Faculty:* 9 full-time (5 women), 4 part-time/adjunct (3 women). *Students:* 86 full-time (51 women), 102 part-time (74 women); includes 22 minority (4 African Americans, 1 American Indian/Alaska Native, 3 Asian Americans or Pacific Islanders, 14 Hispanic Americans), 2 international. Average age 30. 122 applicants, 54% accepted, 53 enrolled. In 2009, 81 master's awarded. *Degree requirements:* For master's, comprehensive exam (for some programs), portfolio. *Entrance requirements:* For master's, minimum GPA of 3.0, NYS teaching certificate (MS Ed). Additional exam requirements/recommendations for international students: Required—TOEFL (minimum score 550 paper-based; 213 computer-based; 80 iBT), IELTS (minimum score 6.5). *Application deadline:* For fall admission, 3/1 priority date for domestic students, 3/1 for international students; for spring admission, 10/1 priority date for domestic students, 10/1 for international students. Application fee: $50. Electronic applications accepted. *Financial support:* In 2009–10, 4 students received support, including 3 fellowships (averaging $9,000 per year); Federal Work-Study, institutionally sponsored loans, and tuition waivers (full) also available. Financial award application deadline: 8/1; financial award applicants required to submit FAFSA. *Unit head:* Dr. Devon Duhaney, Chair, 845-257-2850, E-mail: duhaneyd@newpaltz.edu. *Application contact:* Caroline Murphy, Graduate Admissions Advisor, 845-257-3285, Fax: 845-257-3284, E-mail: gradschool@newpaltz.edu.

State University of New York at Oswego, Graduate Studies, School of Education, Department of Curriculum and Instruction, Oswego, NY 13126. Offers art education (MAT); elementary education (MS Ed); literacy education (MS Ed); secondary education (MS Ed); special education (MS Ed). Part-time and evening/weekend programs available. *Degree requirements:* For master's, comprehensive exam (for some programs), thesis optional. *Entrance requirements:* For master's, GRE General Test, minimum GPA of 2.7, provisional teaching certificate. Additional exam requirements/recommendations for international students: Required—TOEFL (minimum score 560 paper-based; 220 computer-based). *Faculty research:* Classroom applications for microcomputers; classroom questioning, wait-time, and achievement; values clarification and academic achievement.

State University of New York at Plattsburgh, Division of Education, Health, and Human Services, Program in Teacher Education: Adolescence MST, Plattsburgh, NY 12901-2681. Offers adolescence education (MST); biology 7-12 (MST); chemistry 7-12 (MST); earth science 7-12 (MST); English 7-12 (MST); French 7-12 (MST); mathematics 7-12 (MST); physics 7-12 (MST); social studies 7-12 (MST); Spanish 7-12 (MST). *Accreditation:* Teacher Education Accreditation Council. Part-time and evening/weekend programs available. *Faculty:* 4 full-time (3 women), 2 part-time/adjunct (0 women). *Students:* 83 full-time (49 women), 5 part-time (3 women); includes 9 minority (2 African Americans, 1 American Indian/Alaska Native, 1 Asian American or Pacific Islander, 5 Hispanic Americans), 2 international. Average age 27. 72 applicants, 71% accepted, 44 enrolled. In 2009, 57 master's awarded. *Degree requirements:* For master's, portfolio. *Entrance requirements:* For master's, minimum GPA of 2.75. Additional exam requirements/recommendations for international students: Required—TOEFL (minimum score 550 paper-based; 213 computer-based; 79 iBT). *Application deadline:* For fall admission, 2/15 priority date for domestic students. Applications are processed on a rolling basis. Application fee: $75. *Expenses:* Tuition, state resident: full-time $8370; part-time $349 per credit hour. Tuition, nonresident: full-time $13,250; part-time $552 per credit hour. Required fees: $1130. *Financial support:* Application deadline: 4/15. *Unit head:* Dr. Robert Ackland, Coordinator, 518-564-5131, E-mail: acklanrt@plattsburgh.edu. *Application contact:* Marguerite Adelman, Assistant Director, Graduate Admissions, 518-564-4723, Fax: 518-564-4722, E-mail: adelmaml@plattsburgh.edu.

State University of New York College at Cortland, Graduate Studies, School of Arts and Sciences, Programs in Adolescence Education, Cortland, NY 13045. Offers biology (MAT, MS Ed); chemistry (MAT, MS Ed); earth science (MAT, MS Ed); English (MS Ed); French (MS Ed); mathematics (MAT, MS Ed); physics (MAT, MS Ed); social studies (MS Ed); Spanish (MS Ed). *Accreditation:* NCATE. Part-time and evening/weekend programs available. *Degree requirements:* For master's, one foreign language, comprehensive exam (for some programs), thesis (for some programs). *Entrance requirements:* For master's, GRE General Test.

State University of New York College at Geneseo, Graduate Studies, School of Education, Program in Secondary Education, Geneseo, NY 14454-1401. Offers MS Ed. Part-time and evening/weekend programs available. *Faculty:* 14 full-time (7 women), 2 part-time/adjunct (0 women). *Students:* 4 full-time (3 women), 16 part-time (13 women). Average age 26. 17 applicants, 100% accepted, 14 enrolled. In 2009, 4 master's awarded. *Degree requirements:* For master's, thesis optional. *Application deadline:* For fall admission, 3/1 priority date for domestic students; for spring admission, 10/1 for domestic students. Application fee: $50. *Expenses:* Tuition, state resident: full-time $8370; part-time $349 per credit hour. Tuition, nonresident: full-time $13,250; part-time $552 per credit hour. Required fees: $700.52; $29 per credit hour. *Financial support:* In 2009–10, 1 student received support. Scholarships/grants, health care benefits, tuition waivers (full), and unspecified assistantships available. Support available to part-time students. Financial award application deadline: 4/1; financial award applicants required to submit FAFSA. *Unit head:* Dr. Osman Alawiye, Dean/Chairperson, 585-245-5560, Fax: 585-245-5220, E-mail: alawiyeo@geneseo.edu. *Application contact:* Dr. Susan Salmon, Assistant to the Dean/Graduate Liaison, 585-245-5560, Fax: 585-245-5220, E-mail: salmon@geneseo.edu.

State University of New York College at Oneonta, Graduate Education, Division of Education, Department of Secondary Education, Oneonta, NY 13820-4015. Offers adolescence education (MS Ed); family and consumer science education (MS Ed). *Accreditation:* NCATE. Part-time and evening/weekend programs available. *Entrance requirements:* For master's, GRE General Test. *Application deadline:* For fall admission, 3/25 priority date for domestic students; for spring admission, 10/1 priority date for domestic students. Applications are processed on a rolling basis. Application fee: $50. *Expenses:* Tuition, state resident: part-time $349 per credit hour. Tuition, nonresident: full-time $12,870; part-time $552 per credit hour. Required fees: $1280; $15.85 per credit hour. *Unit head:* Dr. Dennis Banks, Chair, 607-436-3391, Fax: 607-436-2554, E-mail: banksdn@oneonta.edu. *Application contact:* Dr. Dennis Banks, Chair, 607-436-3391, Fax: 607-436-2554, E-mail: banksdn@oneonta.edu.

State University of New York College at Potsdam, School of Education and Professional Studies, Program in Secondary Education, Potsdam, NY 13676. Offers English (MST); mathematics (with grades 5-6 extension) (MST); science (MST), including biology, chemistry, earth science, physics; Social Studies (with grades 5-6 extension) (MST). *Accreditation:* NCATE. *Faculty:* 9 full-time (3 women), 3 part-time/adjunct (2 women). *Students:* 49 full-time (27 women), 6 part-time (1 woman); includes 5 minority (3 African Americans, 2 American Indian/Alaska Native), 7 international. 13 applicants, 62% accepted, 8 enrolled. In 2009, 49 master's awarded. *Degree requirements:* For master's, thesis optional, culminating experience. *Entrance requirements:* For master's, minimum GPA of 2.75 in last 60 hours of course work (3.0 for English program). Additional exam requirements/recommendations for international students: Required—TOEFL (minimum score 550 paper-based; 213 computer-based; 80 iBT), IELTS (minimum score 6). *Application deadline:* For fall admission, 4/1 priority date for domestic and international students; for spring admission, 10/15 priority date for domestic and international students. Applications are processed on a rolling basis. Application fee: $50. *Expenses:* Tuition, state resident: full-time $8370; part-time $349 per credit hour. Tuition, nonresident: full-time $13,250; part-time $552 per credit hour. Required fees: $942; $38.70 per credit hour. *Financial support:* Fellowships, teaching assistantships, career-related internships or fieldwork, Federal Work-Study, scholarships/grants, and unspecified assistantships available. Support available to part-time students. Financial award application deadline: 3/1; financial award applicants required to submit FAFSA. *Unit head:* Dr. Peter Brouwer, Chairperson, 315-267-3018, Fax: 315-267-4802, E-mail: brouweps@potsdam.edu. *Application contact:* Peter Cutler, Graduate Admissions Counselor, 315-267-3154, Fax: 315-267-4802, E-mail: cutlerpj@potsdam.edu.

State University of New York College at Potsdam, School of Education and Professional Studies, Program in Special Education, Potsdam, NY 13676. Offers birth-grade 2 (MS Ed); grades 1-6 (MS Ed); grades 5-9 (MS Ed); grades 7-12 (MS Ed). *Accreditation:* NCATE. *Faculty:* 3 full-time (1 woman), 5 part-time/adjunct (4 women). *Students:* 19 full-time (17 women), 6 part-time (4 women); includes 2 minority (1 African American, 1 American Indian/Alaska Native). 18 applicants, 100% accepted, 16 enrolled. In 2009, 11 master's awarded. *Degree requirements:* For master's, thesis optional, culminating experience. *Entrance requirements:* For master's, minimum GPA of 3.0 in last 60 hours of undergraduate course work. Additional exam requirements/recommendations for international students: Required—TOEFL (minimum score 550 paper-based; 213 computer-based; 80 iBT), IELTS (minimum score 6). *Application deadline:* For fall admission, 4/1 priority date for domestic and international students. Applications are processed on a rolling basis. Application fee: $50. *Expenses:* Tuition, state resident: full-time $8370; part-time $349 per credit hour. Tuition, nonresident: full-time $13,250; part-time $552 per credit hour. Required fees: $942; $38.70 per credit hour. *Financial support:* Unspecified assistantships available. Financial award application deadline: 3/1; financial award applicants required to submit FAFSA. *Unit head:* Dr. Anjali Misra, Chairperson, 315-267-2764, Fax: 315-267-4802, E-mail: misraa@potsdam.edu. *Application contact:* Peter Cutler, Graduate Admissions Counselor, 315-267-3154, Fax: 315-267-4802, E-mail: cutlerpj@potsdam.edu.

Stephen F. Austin State University, Graduate School, College of Education, Department of Secondary Education and Educational Leadership, Nacogdoches, TX 75962. Offers educational leadership (Ed D); secondary education (M Ed). *Accreditation:* NCATE. *Degree requirements:* For master's, comprehensive exam; for doctorate, thesis/dissertation. *Entrance requirements:* For master's, GRE General Test; for doctorate, GRE General Test, interview, writing sample. Additional exam requirements/recommendations for international students: Required—TOEFL. Electronic applications accepted.

Suffolk University, College of Arts and Sciences, Department of Education and Human Services, Programs in School Teaching, Boston, MA 02108-2770. Offers foundations of education (M Ed); middle school teaching (M Ed); school teaching (CAGS); secondary school teaching (M Ed). Part-time and evening/weekend programs available. *Entrance requirements:* For master's, GRE General Test, MAT, or Massachusetts Test for Educator Licensure, 2 letters of recommendation, resume. *Application deadline:* For fall admission, 6/15 priority date for domestic students, 6/15 for international students; for spring admission, 11/15 priority date for domestic students, 11/15 for international students. Applications are processed on a rolling basis. Application fee: $50. *Expenses:* Tuition: Full-time $33,000; part-time $1100 per credit. Required fees: $20. Tuition and fees vary according to program. *Financial support:* Fellowships, career-related internships or fieldwork, Federal Work-Study, and institutionally sponsored loans available. Support available to part-time students. Financial award application deadline: 4/1; financial award applicants required to submit FAFSA. *Faculty research:* Assessment systems, reflection, teamwork, learning environment. *Unit head:* Dr. Sarah M. Carroll, Graduate Program Director, 617-573-8015, Fax: 617-305-1743, E-mail: scarroll@suffolk.edu. *Application contact:* Judith Reynolds, Director of Graduate Admissions, 617-573-8302, Fax: 617-305-1733, E-mail: grad.admission@suffolk.edu.

Sul Ross State University, Rio Grande College of Sul Ross State University, Alpine, TX 79832. Offers business administration (MBA); teacher education (M Ed), including bilingual education, counseling, educational diagnostics, elementary education, general education, reading, school administration, secondary education. Part-time and evening/weekend programs available. *Degree requirements:* For master's, thesis optional. *Entrance requirements:* For master's, GMAT or GRE General Test, minimum GPA of 2.5 in last 60 hours of undergraduate work. *Faculty research:* Drug and substance abuse counseling, U.S.-Mexico border economic development.

Sul Ross State University, School of Professional Studies, Department of Teacher Education, Program in Secondary Education, Alpine, TX 79832. Offers M Ed. Part-time and evening/weekend programs available. *Degree requirements:* For master's, thesis optional. *Entrance requirements:* For master's, GMAT or GRE General Test, minimum GPA of 2.5 in last 60 hours of undergraduate work.

Tarleton State University, College of Graduate Studies, College of Education, Department of Psychology and Counseling, Stephenville, TX 76402. Offers counseling and psychology (M Ed), including counseling, counseling psychology, educational psychology; educational administration (M Ed); secondary education (Certificate); special education (Certificate). Part-time and evening/weekend programs available. Postbaccalaureate distance learning degree programs offered (minimal on-campus study). *Degree requirements:* For master's, comprehensive exam, thesis optional. *Entrance requirements:* For master's, GRE General Test, minimum GPA of 3.0. Additional exam requirements/recommendations for international students: Required—TOEFL (minimum score 550 paper-based; 213 computer-based; 80 iBT). Electronic applications accepted.

Tennessee Technological University, Graduate School, College of Education, Department of Curriculum and Instruction, Program in Secondary Education, Cookeville, TN 38505. Offers MA, Ed S. *Accreditation:* NCATE. Part-time and evening/weekend programs available. *Faculty:* 7 full-time (0 women). *Students:* 31 full-time (16 women), 31 part-time (22 women); includes 6 minority (3 African Americans, 1 American Indian/Alaska Native, 1 Asian American or Pacific Islander, 1 Hispanic American). Average age 27. 42 applicants, 71% accepted, 21 enrolled. In 2009, 11 master's, 1 other advanced degree awarded. *Degree requirements:* For master's and Ed S, comprehensive exam, thesis or alternative. *Entrance requirements:* For master's and Ed S, MAT or GRE. Additional exam requirements/recommendations for international students: Required—TOEFL (minimum score 550 paper-based; 79 iBT), IELTS (minimum score 5.5). *Application deadline:* For fall admission, 8/1 for domestic students, 5/1 for international students; for spring admission, 12/1 for domestic students, 10/1 for international students. Application fee: $25 ($30 for international students). Electronic applications accepted. *Expenses:* Tuition, state resident: full-time $7034; part-time $368 per credit hour. *Financial support:* In 2009–10, 1 fellowship (averaging $8,000 per year), 1 research assistantship (averaging $4,000 per year), 1 teaching assistantship (averaging $4,000 per year) were awarded; career-related internships or fieldwork also available. Financial award application deadline: 4/1. *Unit head:* Dr. Mattew R. Smith, Chairperson, 931-372-3181, Fax: 931-372-6270. *Application contact:* Shelia K. Kendrick, Coordinator of Graduate Studies, 931-372-3808, Fax: 931-372-3497, E-mail: skendrick@tntech.edu.

Texas A&M University–Commerce, Graduate School, College of Education and Human Services, Department of Curriculum and Instruction, Commerce, TX 75429-3011. Offers bilingual/ESL education (M Ed, MS); early childhood education (M Ed, MS); elementary education (M Ed, MS); reading (M Ed, MS); secondary education (M Ed, MS); supervision, curriculum and instruction: elementary education (Ed D). Part-time programs available. Terminal master's awarded for partial completion of doctoral program. *Degree requirements:* For master's, comprehensive exam, thesis (for some programs); for doctorate, 2 foreign languages, thesis/dissertation, departmental qualifying exam. *Entrance requirements:* For master's and doctorate, GRE General Test. Electronic applications accepted. *Faculty research:* Literacy and learning, early childhood, preservice teacher education, technology.

Texas A&M University–Commerce, Graduate School, College of Education and Human Services, Department of Secondary and Higher Education, Commerce, TX 75429-3011. Offers higher education (MS), including administration, teaching; learning technology and information

Secondary Education

Texas A&M University–Commerce (continued)

systems (M Ed, MS), including educational computing, library and information science, media and technology; secondary education (M Ed, MS); supervision, curriculum, and instruction (Ed D); training and development (MS). Part-time programs available. Terminal master's awarded for partial completion of doctoral program. *Degree requirements:* For master's, comprehensive exam, thesis (for some programs); for doctorate, thesis/dissertation, departmental qualifying exam. *Entrance requirements:* For master's and doctorate, GRE General Test. Electronic applications accepted. *Faculty research:* Deviance, migration.

Texas A&M University–Corpus Christi, Graduate Studies and Research, College of Education, Program in Secondary Education, Corpus Christi, TX 78412-5503. Offers MS. Part-time and evening/weekend programs available. *Degree requirements:* For master's, comprehensive exam, thesis (for some programs). *Entrance requirements:* For master's, GRE General Test. Additional exam requirements/recommendations for international students: Required—TOEFL. Electronic applications accepted.

Texas A&M University–Kingsville, College of Graduate Studies, College of Education, Department of Education, Program in Secondary Education, Kingsville, TX 78363. Offers MA, MS. Part-time and evening/weekend programs available. *Degree requirements:* For master's, comprehensive exam, thesis or alternative, research report. *Entrance requirements:* For master's, GRE General Test, MAT, minimum GPA of 3.0. *Faculty research:* Professional development/ technology, interdisciplinary teaming, educational restructuring.

Texas Christian University, College of Education, Program in Secondary Education (Four-One Option), Fort Worth, TX 76129-0002. Offers M Ed. Part-time and evening/weekend programs available. *Degree requirements:* For master's, oral exams. *Entrance requirements:* Additional exam requirements/recommendations for international students: Required—TOEFL (minimum score 550 paper-based; 213 computer-based; 80 iBT). *Application deadline:* For fall admission, 7/15 for domestic and international students; for spring admission, 10/15 for domestic students, 11/15 for international students. Applications are processed on a rolling basis. Application fee: $50. *Expenses:* Tuition: Full-time $17,640; part-time $980 per credit hour. Tuition and fees vary according to program. *Financial support:* Teaching assistantships with full tuition reimbursements, career-related internships or fieldwork and unspecified assistantships available. Financial award application deadline: 3/15; financial award applicants required to submit FAFSA. *Unit head:* Dr. Kay M. B. Stevens, Associate Dean, 817-257-7661, E-mail: kstevens2@tcu.edu. *Application contact:* Robyn P. Shepheard, Academic Program Specialist, 817-257-7661, E-mail: r.shepheard@tcu.edu.

Texas Southern University, College of Education, Area of Curriculum and Instruction, Houston, TX 77004-4584. Offers bilingual education (M Ed); curriculum and instruction (Ed D); secondary education (M Ed). Part-time and evening/weekend programs available. *Faculty:* 7 full-time (5 women), 1 part-time/adjunct (0 women). *Students:* 20 full-time (17 women), 50 part-time (43 women); includes 66 minority (64 African Americans, 1 Asian American or Pacific Islander, 1 Hispanic American), 1 international. Average age 37. 16 applicants, 100% accepted, 9 enrolled. In 2009, 12 master's, 5 doctorates awarded. *Degree requirements:* For master's, comprehensive exam; for doctorate, comprehensive exam, thesis/dissertation. *Entrance requirements:* For master's, GRE General Test, minimum GPA of 2.5; for doctorate, GRE General Test or MAT, master's degree, minimum B+ average. Additional exam requirements/recommendations for international students: Required—TOEFL. *Application deadline:* For fall admission, 7/1 for domestic and international students; for spring admission, 11/1 for domestic and international students. Applications are processed on a rolling basis. Application fee: $50 ($75 for international students). Electronic applications accepted. *Expenses:* Tuition, state resident: full-time $1805; part-time $100 per credit hour. Tuition, nonresident: full-time $6470; part-time $343 per credit hour. Tuition and fees vary according to course level, course load and degree level. *Financial support:* In 2009–10, 1 research assistantship (averaging $3,000 per year), 1 teaching assistantship (averaging $2,000 per year) were awarded; scholarships/grants and unspecified assistantships also available. Support available to part-time students. Financial award application deadline: 5/1. *Unit head:* Dr. Cherry Gooden, Chair, 713-313-7496, Fax: 713-313-7496, E-mail: gooden_cr@tsu.edu. *Application contact:* Dr. Gregory Maddox, Interim Dean of the Graduate School, 713-313-7011 Ext. 4410, Fax: 713-639-1876, E-mail: maddox_gh@tsu.edu.

Texas State University–San Marcos, Graduate School, College of Education, Department of Curriculum and Instruction, Program in Secondary Education, San Marcos, TX 78666. Offers M Ed, MA. Part-time and evening/weekend programs available. *Faculty:* 23 full-time (16 women), 7 part-time/adjunct (all women). *Students:* 61 full-time (38 women), 68 part-time (49 women); includes 29 minority (6 African Americans, 1 American Indian/Alaska Native, 5 Asian Americans or Pacific Islanders, 17 Hispanic Americans), 1 international. Average age 32. 55 applicants, 96% accepted, 37 enrolled. In 2009, 25 master's awarded. *Degree requirements:* For master's, comprehensive exam, thesis (for some programs). *Entrance requirements:* For master's, GRE General Test, minimum GPA of 2.75 in last 60 hours of course work, teaching experience. Additional exam requirements/recommendations for international students: Required—TOEFL (minimum score 550 paper-based; 213 computer-based). *Application deadline:* For fall admission, 6/15 priority date for domestic students; for spring admission, 10/15 priority date for domestic students. Applications are processed on a rolling basis. Application fee: $40 ($90 for international students). Electronic applications accepted. *Expenses:* Tuition, state resident: full-time $5784; part-time $241 per credit hour. Tuition, nonresident: full-time $13,224; part-time $551 per credit hour. Required fees: $1728; $48 per credit hour. $306. Tuition and fees vary according to course load. *Financial support:* In 2009–10, 100 students received support, including 1 research assistantship (averaging $4,928 per year), 3 teaching assistantships (averaging $5,233 per year); career-related internships or fieldwork, Federal Work-Study, and institutionally sponsored loans also available. Support available to part-time students. Financial award application deadline: 4/1; financial award applicants required to submit FAFSA. *Faculty research:* Gifted and talented education, general secondary education, induction of first-year teachers. *Unit head:* Dr. Gene Martin, Graduate Advisor, 512-245-2157, Fax: 512-245-7911, E-mail: gm01@txstate.edu. *Application contact:* Dr. J. Michael Willoughby, Dean of Graduate School, 512-245-2581, Fax: 512-245-8365, E-mail: gradcollege@txstate.edu.

Texas Tech University, Graduate School, College of Education, Division of Curriculum and Instruction, Lubbock, TX 79409. Offers bilingual education (M Ed); curriculum and instruction (M Ed, PhD); elementary education (M Ed); language and literacy education (M Ed); secondary education (M Ed). *Accreditation:* NCATE. Part-time programs available. *Students:* 72 full-time (54 women), 109 part-time (85 women); includes 50 minority (11 African Americans, 1 American Indian/Alaska Native, 4 Asian Americans or Pacific Islanders, 34 Hispanic Americans), 11 international. Average age 35. 228 applicants, 54% accepted, 56 enrolled. In 2009, 59 master's, 5 doctorates awarded. *Degree requirements:* For master's, thesis or alternative; for doctorate, thesis/dissertation. *Entrance requirements:* For master's and doctorate, GRE General Test. Additional exam requirements/recommendations for international students: Required—TOEFL (minimum score 550 paper-based; 213 computer-based). *Application deadline:* For fall admission, 3/1 priority date for international students; for spring admission, 11/1 priority date for international students. Applications are processed on a rolling basis. Application fee: $50 ($75 for international students). Electronic applications accepted. *Expenses:* Tuition, state resident: full-time $5100; part-time $213 per credit hour. Tuition, nonresident: full-time $11,748; part-time $490 per credit hour. Required fees: $2298; $50 per credit hour. $555 per semester. *Financial support:* Research assistantships with partial tuition reimbursements, teaching assistantships with partial tuition reimbursements, career-related internships or fieldwork, Federal Work-Study, and institutionally sponsored loans available. Support available to part-time students. Financial award application deadline: 4/15; financial award applicants required to submit FAFSA. *Faculty research:* Multicultural foundations of education, teacher education, instruction and pedagogy in subject areas, curriculum theory, language and literary. *Unit head:* Dr. Walter Smith, Chair, 806-742-1988 Ext. 437, Fax: 806-742-2179, E-mail: walter.smith@ttu.edu. *Application contact:* Dr. Walter Smith, Chair, 806-742-1988 Ext. 437, Fax: 806-742-2179, E-mail: walter.smith@ttu.edu.

Towson University, College of Graduate Studies and Research, Program in Secondary Education, Towson, MD 21252-0001. Offers M Ed. *Accreditation:* NCATE. Part-time and evening/weekend programs available. *Degree requirements:* For master's, thesis optional. *Entrance requirements:* For master's, Maryland teaching certification or permission of program director, minimum GPA of 3.0. Electronic applications accepted. *Faculty research:* Assessment, learning disabilities.

Trevecca Nazarene University, Graduate Division, School of Education, Major in Teaching, Nashville, TN 37210-2877. Offers teaching 7-12 (MAT); teaching K-6 (MAT). Part-time and evening/weekend programs available. *Students:* 200 full-time (149 women), 37 part-time (29 women); includes 44 minority (43 African Americans, 1 Asian American or Pacific Islander), 1 international. In 2009, 122 master's awarded. *Degree requirements:* For master's, exit assessment, student teaching. *Entrance requirements:* For master's, GRE General Test, MAT, PRAXIS I: Pre-Professional Skills Test, minimum GPA of 2.7, 2 letters of reference. Additional exam requirements/recommendations for international students: Required—TOEFL (minimum score 550 paper-based; 213 computer-based). *Application deadline:* Applications are processed on a rolling basis. Application fee: $25. *Expenses:* Contact institution. *Financial support:* Applicants required to submit FAFSA. *Unit head:* Dr. Esther Swink, Dean, School of Education/Director of Graduate Education Programs, 615-248-1201, Fax: 615-248-1597, E-mail: admissions_ged@trevecca.edu. *Application contact:* Admissions Office, 615-248-1201, Fax: 615-248-1597, E-mail: admissions_ged@trevecca.edu.

Trinity (Washington) University, School of Education, Washington, DC 20017-1094. Offers counseling (MA); early childhood education (MAT); educating for change (M Ed); educational administration (MSA); elementary education (MAT); school counseling (MA); secondary education (MAT), including English, social studies; special education (MAT); teaching English as a second language (MAT); teaching English to speakers of other languages (M Ed); the teaching of reading (M Ed). *Accreditation:* NCATE. Part-time and evening/weekend programs available. *Degree requirements:* For master's, thesis (for some programs), capstone project(s). *Entrance requirements:* For master's, PRAXIS I, minimum GPA of 2.8. Additional exam requirements/recommendations for international students: Required—TOEFL (minimum score 550 paper-based; 213 computer-based). *Faculty research:* Technology, literacy, special education, organizations, inclusion models.

Troy University, Graduate School, College of Education, Program in Secondary Education, Troy, AL 36082. Offers 5th year biology (MS); 5th year computer science (MS); 5th year history (MS); 5th year language arts (MS); 5th year mathematics (MS); 5th year social science (MS); educationtraditional language arts (MS); traditional biology (MS); traditional computer science (MS); traditional history (MS); traditional mathematics (MS); traditional social science (MS). *Accreditation:* NCATE. Part-time and evening/weekend programs available. *Students:* 17 full-time (12 women), 25 part-time (23 women); includes 8 minority (all African Americans). Average age 27. 10 applicants, 90% accepted. In 2009, 29 master's awarded. *Degree requirements:* For master's, comprehensive exam, thesis. *Entrance requirements:* For master's, minimum GPA of 2.5. Additional exam requirements/recommendations for international students: Required—TOEFL (minimum score 523 paper-based; 193 computer-based; 70 iBT), IELTS (minimum score 6). *Application deadline:* Applications are processed on a rolling basis. Application fee: $50. Electronic applications accepted. *Financial support:* Career-related internships or fieldwork available. Support available to part-time students. Financial award applicants required to submit FAFSA. *Unit head:* Dr. Marian Parker, Coordinator, 334-670-5661, Fax: 334-670-3548, E-mail: mjparker@troy.edu. *Application contact:* Brenda K. Campbell, Director of Graduate Admissions, 334-670-3178, Fax: 334-670-3733, E-mail: bcamp@troy.edu.

Tufts University, Graduate School of Arts and Sciences, Department of Education, Program in Education, Medford, MA 02155. Offers education (MS, PhD); middle and secondary education (MA, MAT); secondary education (MA). *Faculty:* 13 full-time, 9 part-time/adjunct. *Students:* 116 (84 women); includes 17 minority (7 African Americans, 1 American Indian/Alaska Native, 3 Asian Americans or Pacific Islanders, 6 Hispanic Americans), 4 international. Average age 27. 180 applicants, 83% accepted, 77 enrolled. In 2009, 74 master's, 5 doctorates awarded. *Degree requirements:* For master's, thesis optional; for doctorate, thesis/dissertation. *Entrance requirements:* For master's, GRE General Test. Additional exam requirements/recommendations for international students: Required—TOEFL (minimum score 550 paper-based; 213 computer-based; 80 iBT). *Application deadline:* For fall admission, 2/1 for domestic students, 12/15 for international students; for spring admission, 10/15 for domestic students, 9/15 for international students. Applications are processed on a rolling basis. Application fee: $75. Electronic applications accepted. *Expenses:* Tuition: Full-time $38,096; part-time $3962 per credit. Required fees: $686; $40 per year. Tuition and fees vary according to course level, course load, degree level, program and student level. *Financial support:* Teaching assistantships with full and partial tuition reimbursements, Federal Work-Study, scholarships/grants, and tuition waivers (full and partial) available. Support available to part-time students. Financial award application deadline: 2/1. *Unit head:* Barbara Brizuela, Chair, 617-627-3244, Fax: 617-627-3901. *Application contact:* Patricia Romeo, Information Contact, 617-627-3244.

Union College, Graduate Programs, Department of Education, Program in Secondary Education, Barbourville, KY 40906-1499. Offers MA. *Degree requirements:* For master's, thesis optional. *Entrance requirements:* For master's, GRE General Test, NTE.

Universidad Adventista de las Antillas, EGECED Department, Mayagüez, PR 00681-0118. Offers curriculum and instruction (MA), including secondary biology, secondary history, secondary Spanish; education (MA), including ESL (elementary school level), ESL (high school level), school administration and supervision. *Degree requirements:* For master's, comprehensive exam (for some programs), thesis (for some programs). *Entrance requirements:* For master's, EXADEP or GRE General Test, recommendations. Application fee: $175. Electronic applications accepted. *Expenses:* Tuition: Full-time $3990; part-time $190 per credit. Required fees: $570; $190 per credit. $1375 per summer. *Financial support:* Fellowships, Federal Work-Study available. *Unit head:* Dr. Zilma Sepulveda, Director, 787-834-9595 Ext. 2282, Fax: 787-834-9595, E-mail: zsantiago@uaa.edu. *Application contact:* Prof. Evelyn del Valle, Admissions Department Director, 787-834-9595 Ext. 2261, Fax: 787-834-9597, E-mail: admissions@uaa.edu.

The University of Akron, Graduate School, College of Education, Department of Curricular and Instructional Studies, Program in Secondary Education, Akron, OH 44325. Offers secondary education (MA, PhD); secondary education with licensure (MS). *Accreditation:* NCATE. *Students:* 16 full-time (13 women), 45 part-time (28 women); includes 5 minority (all African Americans), 1 international. Average age 39. 21 applicants, 62% accepted, 9 enrolled. In 2009, 12 master's, 4 doctorates awarded. *Degree requirements:* For master's, comprehensive exam, portfolio; for doctorate, variable foreign language requirement, comprehensive exam, thesis/dissertation, written and oral exams. *Entrance requirements:* For master's, speech and hearing test, minimum GPA of 2.75, letters of recommendation, criminal background check; for doctorate, MAT or GRE, interview, minimum GPA of 3.5, writing sample, letters of reference, resume, three years of teaching experience. Additional exam requirements/recommendations for international students: Required—TOEFL (minimum score 550 paper-based; 213 computer-based; 79 iBT). *Application deadline:* For fall admission, 3/31 for domestic and international students; for spring admission, 10/31 for domestic and international students. Applications are processed on a rolling basis. Application fee: $30 ($40 for international students). Electronic applications accepted. *Expenses:* Tuition, state resident: full-time $6570; part-time $365 per credit hour. Tuition, nonresident: full-time $11,250; part-time $625 per credit hour. *Unit head:* Dr. Bridgie Ford, Chair, 330-972-6967, E-mail: alexis2@uakron.edu. *Application contact:* Dr. Bridgie Ford, Chair, 330-972-6967, E-mail: alexis2@uakron.edu.

The University of Alabama, Graduate School, College of Education, Department of Curriculum and Instruction, Tuscaloosa, AL 35487. Offers elementary education (MA, Ed D, PhD, Ed S); secondary education (MA, Ed D, PhD, Ed S). Evening/weekend programs available. Postbaccalaureate distance learning degree programs offered (minimal on-campus study). *Faculty:* 21 full-time (14 women). *Students:* 93 full-time (63 women), 129 part-time (97 women); includes 38 minority (29 African Americans, 2 American Indian/Alaska Native, 2 Asian Americans

or Pacific Islanders, 5 Hispanic Americans), 5 international. Average age 32. 140 applicants, 40% accepted, 43 enrolled. In 2009, 92 master's, 16 doctorates, 13 other advanced degrees awarded. *Degree requirements:* For master's, comprehensive exam, thesis (for some programs); for doctorate, comprehensive exam, thesis/dissertation; for Ed S, comprehensive exam, thesis optional. *Entrance requirements:* For master's, doctorate, and Ed S, MAT and/or GRE. Additional exam requirements/recommendations for international students: Recommended—TOEFL (minimum score 550 paper-based; 213 computer-based), IELTS (minimum score 6.5). *Application deadline:* For fall admission, 7/1 priority date for domestic students, 1/15 priority date for international students; for spring admission, 11/1 priority date for domestic students, 6/1 priority date for international students. Application fee: $50 ($60 for international students). Electronic applications accepted. *Expenses:* Tuition, state resident: full-time $7000. Tuition, nonresident: full-time $19,200. *Financial support:* In 2009–10, 14 students received support, including 10 research assistantships with tuition reimbursements available (averaging $9,844 per year), 4 teaching assistantships with tuition reimbursements available (averaging $9,844 per year); institutionally sponsored loans, traineeships, and unspecified assistantships also available. *Faculty research:* Teacher education, diversity, integration of curriculum, technology. Total annual research expenditures: $338,697. *Unit head:* Dr. Miguel Mantero, Chair, 205-348-1402, Fax: 205-348-9863, E-mail: mmantero@bamaed.ua.edu. *Application contact:* Dr. Miguel Mantero, Chair, 205-348-1402, Fax: 205-348-9863, E-mail: mmantero@bamaed.ua.edu.

The University of Alabama at Birmingham, College of Arts and Sciences, School of Education, Program in High School Education, Birmingham, AL 35294. Offers MA Ed. *Accreditation:* NCATE. *Degree requirements:* For master's, thesis optional. *Entrance requirements:* For master's, GRE General Test, MAT, or NTE, minimum GPA of 3.0. Electronic applications accepted. *Faculty research:* Soviet education, religious education, cultural pluralism.

University of Alaska Fairbanks, School of Education, Program in Education, Fairbanks, AK 99775. Offers curriculum and instruction (M Ed); education (M Ed); elementary education (M Ed); language and literacy (M Ed); reading (M Ed); secondary education (M Ed). *Faculty:* 23 full-time (15 women), 10 part-time/adjunct (9 women). *Students:* 35 full-time (26 women), 58 part-time (43 women); includes 25 minority (2 African Americans, 17 American Indian/Alaska Native, 4 Asian Americans or Pacific Islanders, 2 Hispanic Americans), 1 international. Average age 36. 94 applicants, 64% accepted, 42 enrolled. In 2009, 19 master's, 18 other advanced degrees awarded. *Degree requirements:* For master's, comprehensive exam, thesis, oral defense. *Entrance requirements:* Additional exam requirements/recommendations for international students: Required—TOEFL (minimum score 550 paper-based; 213 computer-based; 80 iBT). *Application deadline:* For fall admission, 5/1 for domestic students, 3/1 for international students; for spring admission, 10/15 for domestic students, 8/1 for international students. Applications are processed on a rolling basis. Application fee: $60. Electronic applications accepted. *Expenses:* Tuition, state resident: full-time $7584; part-time $316 per credit. Tuition, nonresident: full-time $15,504; part-time $646 per credit. Required fees: $23 per credit. $135 per semester. Tuition and fees vary according to course level, course load and reciprocity agreements. *Financial support:* In 2009–10, 1 teaching assistantship (averaging $11,955 per year) was awarded; fellowships, career-related internships or fieldwork, Federal Work-Study, scholarships/grants, health care benefits, and unspecified assistantships also available. Support available to part-time students. Financial award application deadline: 6/1; financial award applicants required to submit FAFSA. *Unit head:* Dr. Eric C. Madsen, Dean, 907-474-7341, Fax: 907-474-5451, E-mail: fysoed@uaf.edu. *Application contact:* Dr. Eric C. Madsen, Dean, 907-474-7341, Fax: 907-474-5451, E-mail: fysoed@uaf.edu.

University of Alaska Southeast, Graduate Programs, Program in Education, Juneau, AK 99801. Offers early childhood education (M Ed, MAT); educational technology (M Ed); elementary education (MAT); reading (M Ed); secondary education (MAT). *Accreditation:* NCATE. Part-time and evening/weekend programs available. Postbaccalaureate distance learning degree programs offered (minimal on-campus study). *Degree requirements:* For master's, comprehensive exam or project, portfolio. *Entrance requirements:* For master's, PRAXIS, minimum GPA of 3.0, writing sample, letters of recommendation. Electronic applications accepted. *Faculty research:* Applied classroom research, culturally responsive practices, action research, teaching effectiveness.

University of Alberta, Faculty of Graduate Studies and Research, Department of Secondary Education, Edmonton, AB T6G 2E1, Canada. Offers M Ed, Ed D, PhD. Part-time programs available. *Faculty:* 17 full-time (7 women). *Students:* 32 full-time (21 women), 47 part-time (22 women). 34 applicants, 88% accepted. In 2009, 5 master's, 6 doctorates awarded. *Degree requirements:* For master's, thesis or alternative, 1 year of residency; for doctorate, thesis/dissertation, 2 years of residency (PhD), 1 year of residency (Ed D). *Entrance requirements:* For master's, teaching certificate, 2 years of teaching experience; for doctorate, master's degree. *Application deadline:* For fall admission, 4/1 priority date for domestic students; for spring admission, 10/1 for domestic students. Application fee: $60. Tuition and fees charges are reported in Canadian dollars. *Expenses:* Tuition, area resident: Full-time $4626 Canadian dollars; part-time $99.72 Canadian dollars per unit. International tuition: $8216 Canadian dollars full-time. Required fees: $3590 Canadian dollars; $99.72 Canadian dollars per unit. $215 Canadian dollars per term. *Financial support:* In 2009–10, 32 students received support, including 2 fellowships, 10 research assistantships, 20 teaching assistantships; scholarships/grants and graduate teaching awards also available. Financial award application deadline: 6/1. *Faculty research:* Curriculum studies, teacher education, subject area specializations. Total annual research expenditures: $100,000. *Unit head:* Dr. D. Sumara, Graduate Coordinator, 780-492-2688, Fax: 403-492-9402, E-mail: educ.sec@ualberta.ca. *Application contact:* Barb Keppy, Graduate Secretary, 403-492-2688, Fax: 403-492-9402.

University of Arkansas, Graduate School, College of Education and Health Professions, Department of Curriculum and Instruction, Program in Secondary Education, Fayetteville, AR 72701-1201. Offers M Ed, MAT, Ed S. *Accreditation:* NCATE. *Students:* 58 full-time (36 women), 16 part-time (10 women); includes 4 minority (1 African American, 3 Hispanic Americans). In 2009, 54 master's awarded. Application fee: $40 ($50 for international students). *Expenses:* Tuition, state resident: full-time $7355; part-time $356.58 per hour. Tuition, nonresident: full-time $17,401; part-time $775.17 per hour. Required fees: $1203. *Financial support:* Fellowships with tuition reimbursements, research assistantships, teaching assistantships, career-related internships or fieldwork and Federal Work-Study available. Support available to part-time students. Financial award application deadline: 4/1; financial award applicants required to submit FAFSA. *Faculty research:* Mathematics. *Unit head:* Dr. Michael Daugherty, Unit Head, 479-575-4209, E-mail: mkd03@uark.edu. *Application contact:* Dr. William McComas, Graduate Coordinator, 479-575-7525, E-mail: mccomas@uark.edu.

University of Arkansas at Little Rock, Graduate School, College of Education, Department of Teacher Education, Program in Secondary Education, Little Rock, AR 72204-1099. Offers M Ed. *Accreditation:* NCATE. Part-time programs available. *Degree requirements:* For master's, comprehensive exam. *Entrance requirements:* For master's, interview, minimum GPA of 2.75, GRE General Test or teaching certificate.

University of Arkansas at Pine Bluff, Program in Education, Pine Bluff, AR 71601-2799. Offers elementary education (M Ed); secondary education (M Ed), including general science, physical education, social studies. *Accreditation:* NCATE. Part-time and evening/weekend programs available. *Degree requirements:* For master's, comprehensive exam. *Entrance requirements:* For master's, GRE, minimum GPA of 2.75, NTE or Standard Arkansas Teaching Certificate. *Faculty research:* Teacher certification, accreditation, assessment, standards, portfolio development, rehabilitation, technology.

University of Bridgeport, School of Education and Human Resources, Division of Education, Program in Secondary Education, Bridgeport, CT 06604. Offers computer specialist (Diploma); international education (Diploma); reading specialist (MS, Diploma); secondary education (MS, Diploma). Part-time and evening/weekend programs available. *Degree requirements:* For master's, final exam, final project, or thesis; for Diploma, thesis or alternative, final project. *Entrance requirements:* For master's, minimum undergraduate QPA of 2.67; for Diploma, minimum graduate QPA of 3.0. Additional exam requirements/recommendations for international students: Recommended—TOEFL (minimum score 550 paper-based; 213 computer-based; 80 iBT), IELTS (minimum score 6.5). Electronic applications accepted. *Faculty research:* Self-concept, internship assessment, stress and situational development, follow-up of graduation, trend analysis.

University of California, Irvine, Office of Graduate Studies, Department of Education, Irvine, CA 92697. Offers educational administration (Ed D); educational administration and leadership (Ed D); elementary and secondary education (MAT). Part-time and evening/weekend programs available. *Students:* 292 full-time (210 women), 11 part-time (9 women); includes 114 minority (7 African Americans, 2 American Indian/Alaska Native, 64 Asian Americans or Pacific Islanders, 41 Hispanic Americans), 6 international. Average age 28. 523 applicants, 75% accepted, 233 enrolled. In 2009, 164 master's, 20 doctorates awarded. *Degree requirements:* For doctorate, thesis/dissertation. *Entrance requirements:* For master's, GRE, minimum GPA of 3.0; for doctorate, GRE General Test, minimum GPA of 3.0. Additional exam requirements/recommendations for international students: Required—TOEFL (minimum score 550 paper-based; 213 computer-based). *Application deadline:* For fall admission, 1/4 priority date for domestic students, 1/4 for international students. Application fee: $70 ($90 for international students). Electronic applications accepted. *Financial support:* Fellowships, research assistantships with full tuition reimbursements, institutionally sponsored loans, traineeships, health care benefits, and unspecified assistantships available. Financial award application deadline: 3/1; financial award applicants required to submit FAFSA. *Faculty research:* Education technology, learning theory, social theory, cultural diversity, postmodernism. *Unit head:* David Brant, Interim Chair, 949-824-7840, E-mail: dbrant@uci.edu. *Application contact:* Sarah K. Singh, Student Affairs Officer, 949-824-7832, Fax: 949-824-2965, E-mail: sksingh@uci.edu.

University of Central Missouri, The Graduate School, College of Education, Warrensburg, MO 64093. Offers career and technical education administration (MS); career and technical education industry training (MS); career and technical education leadership/teaching (MS); college student personnel administration (MS); counseling (MS); curriculum and instruction (Ed S); educational leadership (Ed D); educational technology (MS); elementary education/educational foundations and literacy (MSE); elementary school administration (MSE); elementary school principalship (Ed S); human services/learning resources (Ed S); human services/professional counseling (Ed S); human services/special education (Ed S); human services/technology and occupational education (Ed S); K-12 education/educational foundations and literacy (MSE); K-12 special education (MSE); library science and information services (MS); literacy education (MSE); secondary education/educational foundations & literacy (MSE); secondary school administration (MSE); secondary school principalship (Ed S); superintendency (Ed S); teaching (MAT). Part-time programs available. Postbaccalaureate distance learning degree programs offered. *Faculty:* 42. *Students:* 123 full-time (82 women), 721 part-time (552 women); includes 58 minority (38 African Americans, 3 American Indian/Alaska Native, 6 Asian Americans or Pacific Islanders, 11 Hispanic Americans), 6 international. Average age 34. 229 applicants, 88% accepted, 190 enrolled. In 2009, 212 master's, 47 other advanced degrees awarded. *Entrance requirements:* Additional exam requirements/recommendations for international students: Required—TOEFL (minimum score 550 paper-based; 79 computer-based). *Application deadline:* For fall admission, 6/1 priority date for domestic students, 5/1 for international students; for spring admission, 10/1 priority date for domestic students, 10/1 for international students. Applications are processed on a rolling basis. Application fee: $30 ($75 for international students). Electronic applications accepted. *Expenses:* Tuition, area resident: Part-time $245.80 per credit hour. Tuition, nonresident: part-time $491.60 per credit hour. Required fees: $24.20 per credit hour. Full-time tuition and fees vary according to course load, degree level, campus/location and reciprocity agreements. *Financial support:* Research assistantships with full and partial tuition reimbursements, teaching assistantships with full and partial tuition reimbursements, career-related internships or fieldwork, Federal Work-Study, scholarships/grants, and administrative and laboratory assistantships available. Support available to part-time students. Financial award application deadline: 3/1; financial award applicants required to submit FAFSA. *Unit head:* Dr. Michael Wright, Dean, 660-543-4272, Fax: 660-543-8753, E-mail: mwright@ucmo.edu. *Application contact:* Laurie Delap, Admissions Coordinator, 660-543-4621, Fax: 660-543-4778, E-mail: gradinfo@ucmo.edu.

University of Central Oklahoma, College of Graduate Studies and Research, College of Education, Department of Professional Teacher Education, Program in Secondary Education, Edmond, OK 73034-5209. Offers M Ed. *Accreditation:* NCATE. Part-time programs available. *Faculty:* 6 full-time (4 women). *Students:* 4 full-time (2 women), 11 part-time (7 women). Average age 32. 13 applicants, 100% accepted. In 2009, 1 master's awarded. *Entrance requirements:* For master's, GRE General Test. Additional exam requirements/recommendations for international students: Required—TOEFL (minimum score 550 paper-based; 213 computer-based). *Application deadline:* For fall admission, 7/1 for international students; for spring admission, 11/1 for international students. Applications are processed on a rolling basis. Application fee: $25. Electronic applications accepted. *Expenses:* Tuition, state resident: full-time $4128; part-time $172 per credit hour. Tuition, nonresident: full-time $10,373; part-time $432.20 per credit hour. Required fees: $433.20; $18.05 per credit hour. *Financial support:* Unspecified assistantships available. Financial award application deadline: 3/31; financial award applicants required to submit FAFSA. *Unit head:* Dr. Bryan Duke, Director, 405-974-5529, Fax: 405-974-3822. *Application contact:* Dr. John Garic, Interim Dean, Graduate College, 405-974-3341, Fax: 405-974-3852, E-mail: gradcoll@ucok.edu.

University of Cincinnati, Graduate School, College of Education, Criminal Justice, and Human Services, Division of Teacher Education, Program in Secondary Education, Cincinnati, OH 45221. Offers M Ed. *Accreditation:* NCATE. Part-time programs available. *Degree requirements:* For master's, thesis or alternative. *Entrance requirements:* For master's, GRE General Test. Additional exam requirements/recommendations for international students: Required—TOEFL (minimum score 550 paper-based), TWE (minimum score 4.5), OEPT. Electronic applications accepted.

University of Connecticut, Graduate School, Neag School of Education, Department of Curriculum and Instruction, Program in Secondary Education, Storrs, CT 06269. Offers MA, PhD, Post-Master's Certificate. *Accreditation:* NCATE. *Faculty:* 26 full-time (12 women). *Students:* 1 (woman) full-time. Average age 22. 4 applicants, 0% accepted, 0 enrolled. Terminal master's awarded for partial completion of doctoral program. *Degree requirements:* For master's, comprehensive exam, thesis or alternative; for doctorate, thesis/dissertation. *Entrance requirements:* For doctorate, GRE General Test. Additional exam requirements/recommendations for international students: Required—TOEFL (minimum score 550 paper-based; 213 computer-based). *Application deadline:* For fall admission, 2/1 priority date for domestic and international students; for spring admission, 11/1 for domestic students, 10/1 for international students. Applications are processed on a rolling basis. Application fee: $55. Electronic applications accepted. *Expenses:* Tuition, state resident: full-time $4725; part-time $525 per credit. Tuition, nonresident: full-time $12,267; part-time $1363 per credit. Required fees: $346 per semester. Tuition and fees vary according to course load. *Financial support:* Fellowships, research assistantships with full tuition reimbursements, teaching assistantships with full tuition reimbursements, Federal Work-Study, scholarships/grants, health care benefits, and unspecified assistantships available. Financial award application deadline: 2/1; financial award applicants required to submit FAFSA. *Unit head:* Mary Anne Doyle, Head, 860-486-2433, Fax: 860-486-0280, E-mail: mary.dolye@uconn.edu. *Application contact:* Lisa Rasicot, Graduate Coordinator, 860-486-3065, Fax: 860-486-0210, E-mail: l.rasicot@uconn.edu.

University of Dayton, Graduate School, School of Education and Allied Professions, Department of Teacher Education, Dayton, OH 45469-1300. Offers adolescent/young adult (MS Ed); art education (MS Ed); early childhood education (MS Ed); inclusive early childhood (MS Ed); interdisciplinary education (MS Ed); intervention specialist education, mild/moderate (MS Ed); literacy (MS Ed); middle childhood (MS Ed); multi-age education (MS Ed); music education (MS Ed); teacher as leader (MS Ed); technology in education (MS Ed). Part-time and evening/weekend programs available. *Faculty:* 17 full-time (13 women), 27 part-time/adjunct (21 women). *Students:* 105 full-time (76 women), 152 part-time (131 women); includes 25 minority (21 African Americans, 1 Asian American or Pacific Islander, 3 Hispanic Americans), 8 international.

Secondary Education

University of Dayton (continued)

Average age 33. 199 applicants, 58% accepted, 48 enrolled. In 2009, 139 master's awarded. *Degree requirements:* For master's, thesis, capstone research project. *Entrance requirements:* For master's, GRE General Test, minimum GPA of 2.75. Additional exam requirements/recommendations for international students: Required—TOEFL (minimum score 550 paper-based; 213 computer-based; 80 iBT). *Application deadline:* For fall admission, 3/15 priority date for domestic students, 3/1 priority date for international students; for winter admission, 7/1 priority date for international students; for spring admission, 1/1 priority date for international students. Applications are processed on a rolling basis. Application fee: $0 ($50 for international students). Electronic applications accepted. *Expenses:* Contact institution. *Financial support:* In 2009–10, 5 research assistantships with full and partial tuition reimbursements (averaging $8,000 per year) were awarded; career-related internships or fieldwork, institutionally sponsored loans, health care benefits, and unspecified assistantships also available. Financial award applicants required to submit FAFSA. *Faculty research:* Diversity, literacy, art representation by young children, preservice teacher preparation. *Unit head:* Dr. Katie A. Kinnucan-Welsch, Chair, 937-229-3346. *Application contact:* Graduate Admissions, 937-229-4411, Fax: 937-229-4729, E-mail: gradadmission@udayton.edu.

University of Great Falls, Graduate Studies, Secondary Teaching Program, Great Falls, MT 59405. Offers MAT. Part-time programs available. Postbaccalaureate distance learning degree programs offered (no on-campus study). *Degree requirements:* For master's, comprehensive exam, thesis optional, extensive portfolio. *Entrance requirements:* For master's, GRE General Test or MAT, bachelor's degree in teaching, teaching certificate, 3 years of teaching experience, interview, 3 letters of recommendation. Additional exam requirements/recommendations for international students: Required—TOEFL (minimum score 500 paper-based; 205 computer-based). Electronic applications accepted. *Faculty research:* Gifted, curriculum design, administration.

University of Guam, Office of Graduate Studies, School of Education, Program in Secondary Education, Mangilao, GU 96923. Offers M Ed. *Degree requirements:* For master's, thesis, comprehensive oral and written exams. *Entrance requirements:* For master's, GRE General Test. Additional exam requirements/recommendations for international students: Required—TOEFL.

University of Houston, College of Education, Department of Curriculum and Instruction, Houston, TX 77204. Offers art education (M Ed); bilingual education (M Ed); curriculum and instruction (M Ed, Ed D); early childhood education (M Ed); elementary education (M Ed); gifted and talented education (M Ed); instructional technology (M Ed); mathematics education (M Ed); reading and language arts education (M Ed); science education (M Ed); second language education (M Ed); secondary education (M Ed); social studies education (M Ed); teaching (M Ed). *Accreditation:* NCATE. Part-time and evening/weekend programs available. *Faculty:* 20 full-time (9 women), 22 part-time/adjunct (17 women). *Students:* 113 full-time (81 women), 195 part-time (150 women); includes 107 minority (43 African Americans, 29 Asian Americans or Pacific Islanders, 35 Hispanic Americans), 29 international. Average age 35. 150 applicants, 77% accepted, 55 enrolled. In 2009, 75 master's, 31 doctorates awarded. *Degree requirements:* For master's, comprehensive exam, thesis optional; for doctorate, comprehensive exam, thesis/dissertation. *Entrance requirements:* For master's and doctorate, GRE, minimum cumulative undergraduate GPA of 2.6. Additional exam requirements/recommendations for international students: Required—TOEFL (minimum score 550 paper-based; 79 iBT). *Application deadline:* For fall admission, 3/1 for domestic and international students; for spring admission, 10/1 for domestic and international students. Application fee: $45 ($75 for international students). Electronic applications accepted. *Expenses:* Tuition, state resident: full-time $7676; part-time $320 per credit hour. Tuition, nonresident: full-time $14,324; part-time $597 per credit hour. Required fees: $3034. *Financial support:* In 2009–10, 4 fellowships with full tuition reimbursements (averaging $9,500 per year), 6 research assistantships with full tuition reimbursements (averaging $8,800 per year), 25 teaching assistantships with full tuition reimbursements (averaging $8,800 per year) were awarded; career-related internships or fieldwork, Federal Work-Study, institutionally sponsored loans, scholarships/grants, health care benefits, and unspecified assistantships also available. Support available to part-time students. Financial award application deadline: 2/1. *Faculty research:* Teaching-learning process, instructional technology in schools, teacher education, classroom management, at-risk students. *Unit head:* Dr. Laveria Hutchison, Chairperson, 713-743-4958, Fax: 713-743-4990, E-mail: lhutchison@uh.edu. *Application contact:* Renee C. Rattelade, Executive Secretary, 713-743-4997, Fax: 713-743-4990, E-mail: rrattelade@mail.coe.uh.edu.

University of Houston–Downtown, College of Public Service, Department of Urban Education, Houston, TX 77002. Offers bilingual education (MAT); curriculum and instruction (MAT); elementary education (MAT); secondary education (MAT). Part-time and evening/weekend programs available. *Faculty:* 8 full-time (5 women). *Students:* 1 (woman) full-time, 42 part-time (34 women); includes 27 minority (15 African Americans, 3 Asian Americans or Pacific Islanders, 9 Hispanic Americans). Average age 37. 16 applicants, 100% accepted, 12 enrolled. In 2009, 17 master's awarded. *Degree requirements:* For master's, capstone course with completed project, position paper, grant proposal, empirical study, curriculum development/revision, or advanced technology project presented at annual Graduate Project Exhibition. *Entrance requirements:* For master's, GRE, personal statement, 3 recommendation forms. Additional exam requirements/recommendations for international students: Required—TOEFL (minimum score 550 paper-based; 213 computer-based; 80 iBT). *Application deadline:* For fall admission, 6/1 for domestic and international students; for spring admission, 11/1 for domestic and international students. Applications are processed on a rolling basis. Application fee: $35 ($60 for international students). Electronic applications accepted. *Expenses:* Tuition, state resident: full-time $3150; part-time $175 per credit hour. Tuition, nonresident: full-time $7506; part-time $417 per credit hour. Required fees: $908; $322 per term. *Financial support:* Scholarships/grants available. Financial award applicants required to submit FAFSA. *Unit head:* Dr. Myrna Cohen, Chair, 713-221-2759, Fax: 713-226-5294, E-mail: cohenm@uhd.edu. *Application contact:* Traneshia Parker, Assistant Director, Admissions-Graduate, International and Residency, 713-221-8093, Fax: 713-221-8157, E-mail: parkert@uhd.edu.

University of Illinois at Chicago, Graduate College, College of Education, Department of Curriculum and Instruction, Chicago, IL 60607-7128. Offers curriculum studies (PhD); educational studies (M Ed); elementary education (M Ed); literacy, language and culture (M Ed, PhD); secondary education (M Ed). Part-time and evening/weekend programs available. *Degree requirements:* For doctorate, thesis/dissertation. *Entrance requirements:* For master's, minimum GPA of 2.75; for doctorate, GRE General Test, minimum GPA of 2.75. Additional exam requirements/recommendations for international students: Required—TOEFL. Electronic applications accepted. *Faculty research:* Curriculum theory, curriculum development, research on teaching, curriculum and context, reading/literacy.

University of Indianapolis, Graduate Programs, School of Education, Indianapolis, IN 46227-3697. Offers art education (MAT); biology (MAT); chemistry (MAT); curriculum and instruction (MA); earth sciences (MAT); education (MA, MAT); educational leadership (MA); elementary education (MA); English (MAT); French (MAT); math (MAT); physical education (MAT); physics (MAT); secondary education (MA), including art education, education, English education, social studies education; social studies (MAT); Spanish (MAT). *Accreditation:* NCATE. Part-time and evening/weekend programs available. *Faculty:* 4 full-time (3 women), 3 part-time/adjunct (2 women). *Students:* 52 full-time (28 women), 110 part-time (67 women); includes 3 minority (all African Americans), 2 international. Average age 33. *Entrance requirements:* For master's, GRE Subject Test, PRAXIS I, minimum GPA of 2.5, 3 letters of recommendation, interview, writing exercise. Additional exam requirements/recommendations for international students: Required—TOEFL (minimum score 550 paper-based; 213 computer-based). *Application deadline:* Applications are processed on a rolling basis. Application fee: $50. *Financial support:* Federal Work-Study available. Financial award application deadline: 5/1; financial award applicants required to submit FAFSA. *Faculty research:* Assessment of teacher education, perceptions of prospective teachers by parents. *Unit head:* Dr. Kathy Moran, Dean, 317-788-

3285, Fax: 317-788-3300, E-mail: kmoran@uindy.edu. *Application contact:* Chemain Slater, 317-788-2051, E-mail: slaterc@uindy.edu.

The University of Iowa, Graduate College, College of Education, Department of Teaching and Learning, Program in Secondary Education, Iowa City, IA 52242-1316. Offers art education (PhD); curriculum and supervision (PhD); curriculum supervision (MA); developmental reading (MA); English education (MA, MAT); foreign language education (MA, MAT); foreign language/ESL education (PhD); language, literature and culture (PhD); math education (PhD); mathematics education (MA); social studies (MA, PhD). *Degree requirements:* For master's, thesis optional, exam; for doctorate, comprehensive exam, thesis/dissertation. *Entrance requirements:* For master's and doctorate, GRE General Test, minimum GPA of 3.0. Additional exam requirements/recommendations for international students: Required—TOEFL (minimum score 550 paper-based; 213 computer-based; 81 iBT). Electronic applications accepted.

University of Louisiana at Monroe, Graduate School, College of Education and Human Development, Department of Curriculum and Instruction, Program in Secondary Education 6-12, Monroe, LA 71209-0001. Offers M Ed, MAT. *Accreditation:* NCATE. Part-time and evening/weekend programs available. *Faculty:* 8 full-time (6 women), 1 part-time/adjunct (0 women). *Students:* 11 full-time (7 women), 21 part-time (12 women); includes 6 African Americans, 2 international. Average age 32. In 2009, 28 master's awarded. *Entrance requirements:* For master's, GRE General Test, PRAXIS, minimum GPA of 2.5. Additional exam requirements/recommendations for international students: Required—TOEFL (minimum score 500 paper-based; 173 computer-based; 61 iBT). *Application deadline:* For fall admission, 8/24 priority date for domestic students, 7/1 for international students; for winter admission, 12/14 priority date for domestic students; for spring admission, 1/19 for domestic students, 11/1 for international students. Applications are processed on a rolling basis. Application fee: $20 ($30 for international students). Electronic applications accepted. *Expenses:* Tuition, state resident: part-time $159 per credit hour. Tuition, nonresident: part-time $159 per credit hour. Required fees: $1300 per year. Tuition and fees vary according to course load. *Financial support:* Career-related internships or fieldwork, Federal Work-Study, and unspecified assistantships available. Financial award application deadline: 4/1; financial award applicants required to submit FAFSA. *Unit head:* Dr. Dorothy Schween, Department Head, 318-342-1266, E-mail: schween@ulm.edu. *Application contact:* Dr. Dorothy Schween, Department Head, 318-342-1266, E-mail: schween@ulm.edu.

University of Louisville, Graduate School, College of Education and Human Development, Department of Teaching and Learning, Louisville, KY 40292-0001. Offers art education (MAT); curriculum and instruction (PhD); early elementary education (MAT); instructional technology (M Ed); interdisciplinary early childhood education (MAT); middle school education (MAT); music education (MAT); reading education (M Ed); secondary education (MAT); special education (M Ed, MAT); teacher leadership (M Ed). Part-time and evening/weekend programs available. *Faculty:* 43 full-time (33 women), 43 part-time/adjunct (36 women). *Students:* 207 full-time (144 women), 410 part-time (306 women); includes 68 minority (43 African Americans, 2 American Indian/Alaska Native, 14 Asian Americans or Pacific Islanders, 9 Hispanic Americans), 5 international. Average age 33. 216 applicants, 68% accepted, 112 enrolled. In 2009, 269 master's, 6 doctorates awarded. *Degree requirements:* For doctorate, comprehensive exam, thesis/dissertation. *Entrance requirements:* For master's, GRE General Test, PRAXIS II (for some programs); for doctorate, GRE General Test. Additional exam requirements/recommendations for international students: Required—TOEFL (minimum score 560 paper-based; 210 computer-based; 83 iBT). Application fee: $50. Electronic applications accepted. *Financial support:* In 2009–10, 172 students received support; fellowships, research assistantships, teaching assistantships, career-related internships or fieldwork, Federal Work-Study, scholarships/grants, and unspecified assistantships available. Financial award application deadline: 6/1; financial award applicants required to submit FAFSA. *Faculty research:* Assessment of cognitive and language abilities in infants and preschool children; mathematics teachers' conceptions and beliefs, effect, and understanding of mathematics; incorporating nanoscience and nanotechnology into middle and high school science classrooms; urban teacher preparation through inquiry, action and advocacy; impacts of cognitive coaching on teacher practice and student achievement. Total annual research expenditures: $3.7 million. *Unit head:* Dr. Ann E. Larson, Acting Chair, 502-852-6431, Fax: 502-852-1497, E-mail: ann@louisville.edu. *Application contact:* Libby Leggett, Director, Graduate Admissions, 502-852-3101, Fax: 502-852-6536, E-mail: gradadm@louisville.edu.

University of Maine, Graduate School, College of Education and Human Development, Program in Secondary Education, Orono, ME 04469. Offers M Ed, MA, MAT, MS, CAS. *Accreditation:* NCATE. Part-time and evening/weekend programs available. *Students:* 11 full-time (5 women), 1 (woman) part-time. Average age 26. 3 applicants, 33% accepted, 0 enrolled. In 2009, 7 master's awarded. *Degree requirements:* For master's, thesis or alternative. *Entrance requirements:* For master's, MAT; for CAS, MAT, MA, M Ed, or MS. Additional exam requirements/recommendations for international students: Required—TOEFL. *Application deadline:* For fall admission, 2/1 priority date for domestic students. Applications are processed on a rolling basis. Application fee: $65. Electronic applications accepted. *Financial support:* Career-related internships or fieldwork, Federal Work-Study, tuition waivers (full and partial), and unspecified assistantships available. Support available to part-time students. Financial award application deadline: 3/1. *Unit head:* Dr. Janet Spector, Coordinator, 207-581-2444, Fax: 207-581-2423. *Application contact:* Scott G. Delcourt, Associate Dean of the Graduate School, 207-581-3291, Fax: 207-581-3232, E-mail: graduate@maine.edu.

University of Maryland, Baltimore County, Graduate School, College of Arts, Humanities and Social Sciences, Department of Education, Program in Teaching, Baltimore, MD 21250. Offers early childhood education (MAT); elementary education (MAT); secondary education (MAT), including art, biology, chemistry, dance, earth/space science, English, foreign language, mathematics, music, physics, theatre; secondary science (MAT), including social studies. Part-time and evening/weekend programs available. *Faculty:* 24 full-time (18 women), 25 part-time/adjunct (19 women). *Students:* 52 full-time (41 women), 64 part-time (55 women); includes 20 minority (5 African Americans, 1 American Indian/Alaska Native, 10 Asian Americans or Pacific Islanders, 4 Hispanic Americans), 3 international. Average age 31. 88 applicants, 57% accepted, 39 enrolled. In 2009, 106 master's awarded. *Degree requirements:* For master's, comprehensive exam (for some programs), thesis (for some programs). *Entrance requirements:* For master's, PRAXIS I and II, minimum GPA of 3.0. Additional exam requirements/recommendations for international students: Required—TOEFL. *Application deadline:* For fall admission, 6/1 for domestic students; for spring admission, 11/1 for domestic students. Applications are processed on a rolling basis. Application fee: $50. Electronic applications accepted. *Financial support:* In 2009–10, 6 students received support, including research assistantships with full tuition reimbursements available (averaging $12,000 per year); career-related internships or fieldwork, Federal Work-Study, scholarships/grants, tuition waivers, and unspecified assistantships also available. Financial award application deadline: 3/1. *Faculty research:* STEM teacher education, culturally sensitive pedagogy, ESOL/bilingual education, early childhood education, language, literacy and culture. *Unit head:* Dr. Susan M. Blunck, Director, 410-455-2869, Fax: 410-455-3986, E-mail: blunck@umbc.edu. *Application contact:* Dr. Susan M. Blunck, Director, 410-455-2869, Fax: 410-455-3986, E-mail: blunck@umbc.edu.

University of Maryland, College Park, Academic Affairs, College of Education, Department of Curriculum and Instruction, College Park, MD 20742. Offers reading (M Ed, MA, PhD, CAGS); secondary education (M Ed, MA, Ed D, PhD, CAGS); teaching English to speakers of other languages (M Ed). *Accreditation:* NCATE. Part-time and evening/weekend programs available. Postbaccalaureate distance learning degree programs offered (no on-campus study). *Faculty:* 57 full-time (36 women), 35 part-time/adjunct (30 women). *Students:* 280 full-time (216 women), 181 part-time (150 women); includes 117 minority (60 African Americans, 2 American Indian/Alaska Native, 33 Asian Americans or Pacific Islanders, 22 Hispanic Americans), 51 international. 300 applicants, 40% accepted, 85 enrolled. In 2009, 143 master's, 20 doctorates awarded. *Degree requirements:* For master's, comprehensive exam, seminar paper; for doctorate, comprehensive exam, thesis/dissertation, published paper, oral exam. *Entrance requirements:* For master's, GRE General Test or MAT, minimum GPA of 3.0, 3 letters of

recommendation; for doctorate, GRE General Test or MAT, minimum undergraduate GPA of 3.0, graduate 3.5; 3 letters of recommendation. *Application deadline:* For fall admission, 1/20 priority date for domestic students, 1/20 for international students; for spring admission, 9/1 priority date for domestic students, 6/1 for international students. Applications are processed on a rolling basis. Application fee: $60. Electronic applications accepted. *Expenses:* Tuition, area resident: Part-time $471 per credit hour. Tuition, state resident: part-time $471 per credit hour. Tuition, nonresident: part-time $1016 per credit hour. Required fees: $337.04 per term. *Financial support:* In 2009–10, 19 research assistantships with tuition reimbursements (averaging $18,124 per year), 76 teaching assistantships with tuition reimbursements (averaging $17,105 per year) were awarded; fellowships, Federal Work-Study and scholarships/grants also available. Support available to part-time students. Financial award applicants required to submit FAFSA. *Faculty research:* Teacher preparation, curriculum study, inservice education. Total annual research expenditures: $3.9 million. *Unit head:* Dr. Linda M. Valli, Interim Chair, 301-405-3117, E-mail: lrv@umd.edu. *Application contact:* Dean of Graduate School, 301-405-0358.

University of Massachusetts Amherst, Graduate School, School of Education, Program in Education, Amherst, MA 01003. Offers bilingual, English as a second language, and multicultural education (M Ed, CAGS); child study and early education (M Ed); children, families and schools (Ed D, CAGS); early childhood and elementary teacher education (M Ed); education policy and leadership (CAGS); educational administration (M Ed, CAGS); educational policy and leadership (Ed D); higher education (M Ed, CAGS); international education (M Ed); language, literacy and culture (Ed D); learning, media and technology (M Ed, CAGS); mathematics, science, and learning technologies (Ed D); policy studies (M Ed); policy studies in education (CAGS); reading and writing (M Ed); research and evaluation methods (Ed D); school counselor education (M Ed, CAGS); school psychology (CAGS); science education (CAGS); secondary teacher education (M Ed); social justice education (M Ed, Ed D, CAGS); special education (M Ed, Ed D, CAGS). *Accreditation:* NCATE. Part-time programs available. Postbaccalaureate distance learning degree programs offered (minimal on-campus study). *Faculty:* 74 full-time (41 women). *Students:* 377 full-time (268 women), 347 part-time (232 women); includes 115 minority (59 African Americans, 2 American Indian/Alaska Native, 16 Asian Americans or Pacific Islanders, 38 Hispanic Americans), 108 international. Average age 35. 708 applicants, 68% accepted, 266 enrolled. In 2009, 183 master's, 17 doctorates awarded. Terminal master's awarded for partial completion of doctoral program. *Degree requirements:* For master's, thesis or alternative; for doctorate, comprehensive exam, thesis/dissertation. *Entrance requirements:* Additional exam requirements/recommendations for international students: Required—TOEFL (minimum score 550 paper-based; 213 computer-based; 80 iBT), IELTS (minimum score 6.5). *Application deadline:* For fall admission, 1/15 for domestic and international students. Applications are processed on a rolling basis. Application fee: $50 ($65 for international students). Electronic applications accepted. *Expenses:* Tuition, state resident: full-time $2640; part-time $110 per credit. Tuition, nonresident: full-time $9936; part-time $414 per credit. Tuition and fees vary according to course load. *Financial support:* In 2009–10, 1 fellowship with full tuition reimbursement (averaging $8,036 per year), 92 research assistantships with full tuition reimbursements (averaging $8,555 per year), 83 teaching assistantships with full tuition reimbursements (averaging $4,661 per year) were awarded; career-related internships or fieldwork, Federal Work-Study, scholarships/grants, traineeships, health care benefits, tuition waivers (full), and unspecified assistantships also available. Support available to part-time students. Financial award application deadline: 1/15. *Unit head:* Dr. Linda L. Griffin, Graduate Program Director, 413-545-6984, Fax: 413-545-2873. *Application contact:* Jean M. Ames, Supervisor of Admissions, 413-545-0722, Fax: 413-577-0010, E-mail: gradadm@grad.umass.edu.

University of Massachusetts Boston, Office of Graduate Studies, Graduate College of Education, School Organization, Curriculum and Instruction Department, Boston, MA 02125-3393. Offers education (M Ed, Ed D), including elementary and secondary education/certification (M Ed), higher education administration (Ed D), teacher certification (M Ed), urban school leadership (Ed D); educational administration (M Ed, CAGS); special education (M Ed). *Degree requirements:* For master's and CAGS, comprehensive exam; for doctorate, comprehensive exam, thesis/dissertation. *Entrance requirements:* For master's, GRE General Test or MAT; for doctorate, GRE General Test or MAT, minimum GPA of 2.75; for CAGS, minimum GPA of 2.75.

University of Massachusetts Boston, Office of Graduate Studies, Graduate College of Education, School Organization, Curriculum and Instruction Department, Program in Education, Track in Elementary and Secondary Education/Certification, Boston, MA 02125-3393. Offers M Ed. Part-time and evening/weekend programs available. *Degree requirements:* For master's, comprehensive exam, thesis optional, practicum. *Entrance requirements:* For master's, GRE General Test or MAT, minimum GPA of 3.0, 2 years of teaching experience. *Faculty research:* Anti-bias education, inclusionary curriculum and instruction, creativity and learning, science, technology and society, teaching of reading.

University of Massachusetts Dartmouth, Graduate School, School of Education, Public Policy, and Civic Engagement, Department of Teaching and Learning, North Dartmouth, MA 02747-2300. Offers elementary education (MAT, Postbaccalaureate Certificate); middle school education (MAT); principal initial licensure (Postbaccalaureate Certificate); secondary school education (MAT). *Faculty:* 7 full-time (4 women), 6 part-time/adjunct (3 women). *Students:* 53 full-time (33 women), 183 part-time (118 women); includes 16 minority (6 African Americans, 1 American Indian/Alaska Native, 2 Asian Americans or Pacific Islanders, 7 Hispanic Americans). Average age 35. 188 applicants, 75% accepted, 109 enrolled. In 2009, 34 master's, 4 other advanced degrees awarded. *Degree requirements:* For master's, thesis or alternative. *Entrance requirements:* For master's, MAT or GRE, GMAT, minimum undergraduate GPA of 2.7, teacher certification, 3 letters of recommendation. Additional exam requirements/recommendations for international students: Required—TOEFL (minimum score 500 paper-based). *Application deadline:* For fall admission, 4/20 priority date for domestic students, 2/20 for international students; for spring admission, 11/15 priority date for domestic students, 9/15 for international students. Applications are processed on a rolling basis. Application fee: $40 ($60 for international students). *Expenses:* Tuition, state resident: full-time $2071; part-time $86.29 per credit. Tuition, nonresident: full-time $8099; part-time $337.46 per credit. Required fees: $9446. Tuition and fees vary according to class time, course load and reciprocity agreements. *Financial support:* Federal Work-Study available. Financial award application deadline: 3/1. Total annual research expenditures: $1.3 million. *Unit head:* Dr. Gerard Koot, Director, 508-999-8305, Fax: 508-999-9125, E-mail: gkoot@umassd.edu. *Application contact:* Elan Turcotte-Shamski, Graduate Admissions Officer, 508-999-8604, Fax: 508-999-8183, E-mail: graduate@umassd.edu.

University of Memphis, Graduate School, College of Education, Department of Instruction and Curriculum Leadership, Memphis, TN 38152. Offers early childhood education (MAT, MS, Ed D); elementary education (MAT); instruction and curriculum (MS, Ed D); instruction design and technology (MS, Ed D); middle grades education (MAT); reading (MS, Ed D); secondary education (MAT); special education (MAT, MS, Ed D). *Accreditation:* NCATE (one or more programs are accredited). Part-time programs available. *Faculty:* 40 full-time (28 women), 20 part-time/adjunct (15 women). *Students:* 119 full-time (90 women), 631 part-time (505 women); includes 348 minority (331 African Americans, 2 American Indian/Alaska Native, 4 Asian Americans or Pacific Islanders, 11 Hispanic Americans), 7 international. Average age 34. 202 applicants, 77% accepted, 29 enrolled. In 2009, 137 master's, 10 doctorates awarded. Terminal master's awarded for partial completion of doctoral program. *Degree requirements:* For master's, comprehensive exam, thesis or alternative; for doctorate, comprehensive exam, thesis/dissertation. *Entrance requirements:* For master's, GRE General Test, minimum GPA of 2.5; for doctorate, GRE General Test, GRE Subject Test, 2 years of teaching experience. *Application deadline:* For fall admission, 8/1 for domestic students; for spring admission, 12/1 for domestic students. Applications are processed on a rolling basis. Application fee: $35 ($60 for international students). Electronic applications accepted. *Expenses:* Tuition, state resident: full-time $6246; part-time $347 per credit hour. Tuition, nonresident: full-time $15,894; part-time $883 per credit hour. Required fees: $1160. Full-time tuition and fees vary according to course load, degree level and program. *Financial support:* In 2009–10, 635 students received support; research assistantships with full tuition reimbursements available, teaching assistantships with full tuition reimbursements available, career-related internships or fieldwork, Federal Work-Study, institutionally sponsored loans, scholarships/grants, traineeships, and unspecified assistantships available. Support available to part-time students. Financial award application deadline: 2/15; financial award applicants required to submit FAFSA. *Faculty research:* Effective urban teachers, preparation and retention of urban teachers, technology utilization in schools, field-based teacher preparation programs, effective use of online instruction. *Unit head:* Dr. Sandra Cooley-Nichols, Interim Chair, 901-678-2365. *Application contact:* Dr. Sally Blake, Director of Graduate Studies, 901-678-4861.

University of Missouri–St. Louis, College of Education, Division of Teaching and Learning, St. Louis, MO 63121. Offers elementary education (M Ed), including early childhood, general, reading; secondary education (M Ed), including curriculum and instruction, general, middle level education, reading, teaching English to speakers of other languages (TESOL); secondary school teaching (Certificate); special education (M Ed), including behavioral disorders, early childhood special education, general, learning disabilities, mental retardation; teaching English to speakers of other languages (Certificate). Part-time and evening/weekend programs available. *Faculty:* 36 full-time (23 women), 51 part-time/adjunct (42 women). *Students:* 123 full-time (77 women), 569 part-time (435 women); includes 137 minority (110 African Americans, 4 American Indian/Alaska Native, 10 Asian Americans or Pacific Islanders, 13 Hispanic Americans), 11 international. Average age 32. In 2009, 1,852 master's awarded. *Degree requirements:* For master's, comprehensive exam. *Entrance requirements:* Additional exam requirements/recommendations for international students: Recommended—TOEFL (minimum score 550 paper-based; 213 computer-based). *Application deadline:* For fall admission, 7/1 priority date for domestic and international students; for spring admission, 12/1 priority date for domestic and international students. Application fee: $35 ($40 for international students). Electronic applications accepted. *Expenses:* Tuition, state resident: full-time $5377; part-time $297.70 per credit hour. Tuition, nonresident: full-time $13,882; part-time $771.20 per credit hour. Required fees: $220; $12.20 per credit hour. One-time fee: $12. Tuition and fees vary according to course level, campus/location and program. *Financial support:* In 2009–10, 5 research assistantships (averaging $10,339 per year), 2 teaching assistantships (averaging $6,800 per year) were awarded. Financial award application deadline: 4/1; financial award applicants required to submit FAFSA. *Unit head:* Dr. Joseph Polman, Chair, 314-516-5791. *Application contact:* 314-516-5458, Fax: 314-516-6996, E-mail: gadadm@umsl.edu.

University of Montevallo, College of Education, Program in Secondary/High School Education, Montevallo, AL 35115. Offers M Ed. *Accreditation:* NCATE. *Students:* 85 full-time (60 women), 69 part-time (39 women); includes 19 minority (13 African Americans, 1 American Indian/Alaska Native, 5 Asian Americans or Pacific Islanders), 1 international. In 2009, 55 master's awarded. *Degree requirements:* For master's, comprehensive exam. *Entrance requirements:* For master's, GRE General Test, MAT, minimum undergraduate GPA of 2.5. Additional exam requirements/recommendations for international students: Required—TOEFL (minimum score 550 paper-based). *Application deadline:* For fall admission, 7/15 for domestic students; for spring admission, 11/15 for domestic students. Application fee: $25. *Expenses:* Tuition, state resident: full-time $5592; part-time $233 per credit. Tuition, nonresident: full-time $11,184; part-time $466 per credit hour. Required fees: $482; $241 per semester. One-time fee: $25 part-time. *Financial support:* Federal Work-Study, scholarships/grants, and unspecified assistantships available. *Application contact:* Rebecca Hartley, Coordinator for Graduate Studies, 205-665-6350, Fax: 205-665-6353, E-mail: hartleyrs@montevallo.edu.

University of Nebraska at Omaha, Graduate Studies, College of Education, Department of Teacher Education, Program in Secondary Education, Omaha, NE 68182. Offers MA, MS. *Accreditation:* NCATE. Part-time and evening/weekend programs available. *Faculty:* 9 full-time (6 women). *Students:* 18 full-time (12 women), 133 part-time (95 women); includes 9 minority (2 African Americans, 7 Hispanic Americans), 2 international. Average age 33. 27 applicants, 89% accepted, 18 enrolled. In 2009, 40 master's awarded. *Degree requirements:* For master's, comprehensive exam, thesis (for some programs). *Entrance requirements:* For master's, minimum GPA of 3.0. Additional exam requirements/recommendations for international students: Required—TOEFL (minimum score 550 paper-based; 213 computer-based; 80 iBT). *Application deadline:* For fall admission, 7/1 priority date for domestic students; for spring admission, 12/1 priority date for domestic students. Applications are processed on a rolling basis. Application fee: $45. Electronic applications accepted. *Financial support:* In 2009–10, 58 students received support; fellowships, teaching assistantships with tuition reimbursements available, Federal Work-Study, institutionally sponsored loans, scholarships/grants, tuition waivers (full), and unspecified assistantships available. Support available to part-time students. Financial award application deadline: 3/1. *Application contact:* Dr. Wilma Kuhlman, Student Contact, 402-554-2212.

University of Nevada, Reno, Graduate School, College of Education, Department of Curriculum, Teaching and Learning, Program in Secondary Education, Reno, NV 89557. Offers M Ed, MA, MS. *Degree requirements:* For master's, thesis optional. *Entrance requirements:* For master's, GRE General Test, minimum GPA of 2.75. Additional exam requirements/recommendations for international students: Required—TOEFL (minimum score 500 paper-based; 173 computer-based; 61 iBT), IELTS (minimum score 6). Electronic applications accepted. *Faculty research:* Educational trends, pedagogy.

University of New Hampshire, Graduate School, College of Liberal Arts, Department of Education, Program in Secondary Education, Durham, NH 03824. Offers M Ed, MAT. Part-time programs available. *Faculty:* 32 full-time. *Students:* 36 full-time (23 women), 34 part-time (15 women); includes 2 minority (1 Asian American or Pacific Islander, 1 Hispanic American). Average age 27. 35 applicants, 86% accepted, 25 enrolled. In 2009, 34 master's awarded. *Degree requirements:* For master's, thesis or alternative. *Entrance requirements:* For master's, GRE General Test. Additional exam requirements/recommendations for international students: Required—TOEFL (minimum score 550 paper-based; 213 computer-based; 80 iBT). *Application deadline:* For fall admission, 6/1 priority date for domestic students, 4/1 for international students; for spring admission, 12/1 for domestic students. Applications are processed on a rolling basis. Application fee: $65. Electronic applications accepted. *Expenses:* Tuition, state resident: full-time $10,380; part-time $577 per credit hour. Tuition, nonresident: full-time $24,350; part-time $1002 per credit hour. Required fees: $1550; $387.50 per semester. Tuition and fees vary according to course load and program. *Financial support:* In 2009–10, 9 students received support, including 3 teaching assistantships; fellowships, research assistantships, career-related internships or fieldwork, Federal Work-Study, scholarships/grants, and tuition waivers (full and partial) also available. Support available to part-time students. Financial award application deadline: 2/15. *Faculty research:* Pre-service teacher education. *Unit head:* Dr. Michael D. Andrew, Coordinator, 603-862-2371, E-mail: education.department@unh.edu. *Application contact:* Dr. Michael D. Andrew, Coordinator, 603-862-2371, E-mail: education.department@unh.edu.

University of New Mexico, Graduate School, College of Education, Department of Teacher Education, Program in Secondary Education, Albuquerque, NM 87131-2039. Offers MA. Part-time programs available. *Faculty:* 25 full-time (21 women), 8 part-time/adjunct (7 women). *Students:* 77 full-time (46 women), 62 part-time (42 women); includes 38 minority (5 African Americans, 3 American Indian/Alaska Native, 2 Asian Americans or Pacific Islanders, 28 Hispanic Americans), 5 international. Average age 35. 47 applicants, 74% accepted, 29 enrolled. In 2009, 51 master's awarded. *Degree requirements:* For master's, comprehensive exam, thesis optional. *Entrance requirements:* For master's, minimum overall GPA of 3.0, some experience working with students, NMTA or teacher's licensure, 3 letters of reference, 1 letter of intent. Additional exam requirements/recommendations for international students: Required—TOEFL (minimum score 550 paper-based; 213 computer-based). *Application deadline:* For fall admission, 3/1 for domestic students; for spring admission, 10/1 for domestic students. Applications are processed on a rolling basis. Application fee: $50. Electronic applications accepted. *Expenses:* Tuition, state resident: full-time $2099; part-time $233.20 per credit hour. Tuition, nonresident: full-time $6650. Required fees: $25 per semester. Tuition and fees vary according to course load, program and reciprocity agreements. *Financial support:* In

Secondary Education

University of New Mexico (continued)
2009–10, 2 teaching assistantships with partial tuition reimbursements (averaging $11,641 per year) were awarded; career-related internships or fieldwork, scholarships/grants, and unspecified assistantships also available. Financial award application deadline: 4/15. *Faculty research:* Secondary education, teacher education, reflective practice, teacher leadership, student learning. *Unit head:* Dr. Rosalita Mitchell, Chair, 505-277-9611, Fax: 505-277-0455, E-mail: ted@unm.edu. *Application contact:* Robert Romero, Administrative Assistant, 505-277-0513, Fax: 505-277-0455, E-mail: ted@unm.edu.

University of North Alabama, College of Education, Department of Secondary Education, Program in Secondary Education, Florence, AL 35632-0001. Offers MA Ed. *Accreditation:* NCATE. Part-time and evening/weekend programs available. *Faculty:* 3 full-time (all women), 6 part-time/adjunct (2 women). *Students:* 67 full-time (42 women), 70 part-time (47 women); includes 16 minority (11 African Americans, 3 American Indian/Alaska Native, 1 Asian American or Pacific Islander, 1 Hispanic American). Average age 30. In 2009, 46 master's awarded. *Degree requirements:* For master's, comprehensive exam. *Entrance requirements:* For master's, GRE, MAT, or NTE, minimum GPA of 2.5, Alabama Class B Certificate or equivalent, teaching experience. *Application deadline:* For fall admission, 7/1 priority date for domestic students; for spring admission, 12/1 for domestic students. Applications are processed on a rolling basis. Application fee: $25. Electronic applications accepted. *Expenses:* Tuition, state resident: full-time $5040; part-time $210 per credit hour. Tuition, nonresident: full-time $10,080; part-time $420 per credit hour. Required fees: $906. *Financial support:* Federal Work-Study available. Support available to part-time students. Financial award application deadline: 4/1. *Unit head:* Dr. Lee Hurren, Chair, 256-765-4575, Fax: 256-765-4159, E-mail: blhurren@una.edu. *Application contact:* Kim Mauldin, Director of Admissions, 256-765-4608, Fax: 256-765-4960, E-mail: komauldin@una.edu.

The University of North Carolina at Chapel Hill, Graduate School, School of Education, Program in Secondary Education, Chapel Hill, NC 27599. Offers English (Grades 9-12) (MAT); English as a second language (MAT); French (Grades K-12) (MAT); German (Grades K-12) (MAT); Japanese (Grades K-12) (MAT); Latin (Grades 9-12) (MAT); mathematics (Grades 9-12) (MAT); music (Grades K-12) (MAT); science (Grades 9-12) (MAT); social studies (Grades 9-12) (MAT); Spanish (Grades K-12) (MAT). *Accreditation:* NCATE. *Students:* 53 full-time (35 women), 1 part-time (0 women); includes 8 minority (4 African Americans, 2 Asian Americans or Pacific Islanders, 2 Hispanic Americans), 3 international. Average age 25. 137 applicants, 77% accepted, 54 enrolled. In 2009, 39 master's awarded. *Degree requirements:* For master's, comprehensive exam. *Entrance requirements:* For master's, GRE General Test, minimum GPA of 3.0 during last 2 years of undergraduate course work. Additional exam requirements/recommendations for international students: Required—TOEFL (minimum score 550 paper-based; 79 computer-based). *Application deadline:* For fall admission, 12/15 priority date for domestic and international students. Applications are processed on a rolling basis. Application fee: $77. Electronic applications accepted. *Financial support:* Federal Work-Study available. Support available to part-time students. Financial award application deadline: 3/1; financial award applicants required to submit FAFSA. *Unit head:* Dr. James Trier, Coordinator, 919-843-4627, Fax: 919-962-1533. *Application contact:* Amy Butler, Student Services Assistant, 919-966-1346, Fax: 919-962-1533, E-mail: abutler@email.unc.edu.

The University of North Carolina at Charlotte, Graduate School, College of Education, Department of Middle, Secondary and K-12 Education, Charlotte, NC 28223-0001. Offers middle grades and secondary education (M Ed); teaching English as a second language (M Ed). *Faculty:* 16 full-time (9 women), 5 part-time/adjunct (4 women). *Students:* 1 full-time (0 women), 39 part-time (26 women); includes 1 minority (African American). Average age 30. 6 applicants, 100% accepted, 5 enrolled. In 2009, 44 master's awarded. *Entrance requirements:* For master's, GRE or MAT. Additional exam requirements/recommendations for international students: Required—TOEFL (minimum score 557 paper-based; 220 computer-based; 83 iBT). *Application deadline:* For fall admission, 7/1 for domestic students, 5/1 for international students; for spring admission, 11/1 for domestic students, 10/1 for international students. Applications are processed on a rolling basis. Application fee: $55. Electronic applications accepted. *Financial support:* In 2009–10, 5 students received support, including 5 teaching assistantships (averaging $15,644 per year); career-related internships or fieldwork, Federal Work-Study, institutionally sponsored loans, scholarships/grants, and unspecified assistantships also available. Support available to part-time students. Financial award application deadline: 4/1; financial award applicants required to submit FAFSA. Total annual research expenditures: $65,335. *Unit head:* Melba Spooner, Chair, 704-687-8704, Fax: 704-687-6430, E-mail: mcspoone@uncc.edu. *Application contact:* Kathy B. Giddings, Director of Graduate Admissions, 704-687-5503, Fax: 704-687-3279, E-mail: gradadm@uncc.edu.

The University of North Carolina at Charlotte, Graduate School, College of Education, Program in Teacher Education, Charlotte, NC 28223-0001. Offers art education (K-12) (MAT); dance education (K-12) (MAT); elementary education (K-6) (MAT); English as a second language (K-12) (MAT); foreign language education (K-12) (MAT); general teacher education (MAT); middle grades education (6-9) (MAT); music education (K-12) (MAT); secondary education (9-12) (MAT); special education (K-12) (MAT); theatre education (K-12) (MAT). *Faculty:* 108 full-time (64 women), 16 part-time/adjunct (12 women). *Students:* 29 full-time (20 women), 229 part-time (189 women); includes 32 minority (22 African Americans, 2 American Indian/Alaska Native, 3 Asian Americans or Pacific Islanders, 5 Hispanic Americans). Average age 32. 108 applicants, 92% accepted, 85 enrolled. In 2009, 59 master's awarded. *Entrance requirements:* For master's, GRE or MAT. Additional exam requirements/recommendations for international students: Required—TOEFL (minimum score 557 paper-based; 220 computer-based; 83 iBT). *Application deadline:* For fall admission, 7/1 for domestic students, 5/1 for international students; for spring admission, 11/1 for domestic students, 10/1 for international students. Applications are processed on a rolling basis. Application fee: $55. Electronic applications accepted. *Financial support:* In 2009–10, 5 students received support, including 1 research assistantship (averaging $18,000 per year), 3 teaching assistantships (averaging $12,183 per year); career-related internships or fieldwork, Federal Work-Study, institutionally sponsored loans, scholarships/grants, and administrative assistantship also available. Support available to part-time students. Financial award application deadline: 4/1; financial award applicants required to submit FAFSA. Total annual research expenditures: $5.1 million. *Unit head:* Dr. Kimberly J. Hartman, Coordinator, 704-687-8883, Fax: 704-687-6430, E-mail: khartman@uncc.edu. *Application contact:* Kathy B. Giddings, Director of Graduate Admissions, 704-687-5503, Fax: 704-687-3279, E-mail: gradadmn@uncc.edu.

University of North Dakota, Graduate School, College of Education and Human Development, Teaching and Learning Program, Grand Forks, ND 58202. Offers elementary education (Ed D, PhD); measurement and statistics (Ed D, PhD); secondary education (Ed D, PhD); special education (Ed D, PhD). *Accreditation:* NCATE. Postbaccalaureate distance learning degree programs offered (minimal on-campus study). *Degree requirements:* For doctorate, comprehensive exam, thesis/dissertation, final exam. *Entrance requirements:* For doctorate, minimum GPA of 3.5. Additional exam requirements/recommendations for international students: Required—TOEFL (minimum score 550 paper-based; 213 computer-based; 79 iBT), IELTS (minimum score 6.5). Electronic applications accepted.

University of North Florida, College of Education and Human Services, Department of Foundations and Secondary Education, Jacksonville, FL 32224. Offers adult learning (M Ed); instructional technology (M Ed); professional education (M Ed). *Accreditation:* NCATE. Part-time and evening/weekend programs available. *Faculty:* 11 full-time (5 women). *Students:* 12 full-time (8 women), 27 part-time (17 women); includes 9 minority (7 African Americans, 1 Asian American or Pacific Islander, 1 Hispanic American). Average age 37. 13 applicants, 23% accepted, 2 enrolled. In 2009, 13 master's awarded. *Entrance requirements:* For master's, GRE General Test, minimum GPA of 3.0 in last 60 hours, interview, 3 letters of recommendation. Additional exam requirements/recommendations for international students: Required—TOEFL (minimum score 500 paper-based; 173 computer-based). *Application deadline:* For fall admission, 7/1 priority date for domestic students, 5/1 for international students; for spring admission, 11/1 priority date for domestic students, 10/1 for international students. Applications are processed on a rolling basis. Application fee: $30. Electronic applications accepted. *Expenses:* Tuition, state resident: full-time $6649.20; part-time $277.05 per credit hour. Tuition, nonresident: full-time $22,970; part-time $957.08 per credit hour. Required fees: $985; $41.03 per credit hour. *Financial support:* In 2009–10, 19 students received support; teaching assistantships, career-related internships or fieldwork, Federal Work-Study, and tuition waivers (partial) available. Support available to part-time students. Financial award application deadline: 4/1; financial award applicants required to submit FAFSA. *Faculty research:* Using children's literature to enhance metalinguistic awareness, education, oral language diagnosis of middle-schoolers, science inquiry teaching and learning. Total annual research expenditures: $8,501. *Unit head:* Dr. Jeffery Cornett, Chair, 904-620-2610, Fax: 904-620-1821, E-mail: jcornett@unf.edu. *Application contact:* Dr. John Kemppainen, Director of Academic Advising, 904-620-2530, Fax: 904-620-1135, E-mail: jkemppai@unf.edu.

University of North Texas, Robert B. Toulouse School of Graduate Studies, College of Education, Department of Teacher Education and Administration, Program in Secondary Education, Denton, TX 76203. Offers M Ed, Certificate. *Accreditation:* NCATE. In 2009, 2 master's awarded. *Degree requirements:* For master's, portfolio. *Entrance requirements:* For master's, GRE General Test, resume. Additional exam requirements/recommendations for international students: Required—proof of English language proficiency required for non-native English speakers; Recommended—TOEFL (minimum score 550 paper-based; 213 computer-based; 79 iBT). *Application deadline:* Applications are processed on a rolling basis. Application fee: $50 ($75 for international students). Electronic applications accepted. *Expenses:* Tuition, state resident: full-time $4298; part-time $239 per contact hour. Tuition, nonresident: full-time $9878; part-time $549 per contact hour. Required fees: $265 per contact hour. *Financial support:* Fellowships, research assistantships, teaching assistantships, career-related internships or fieldwork, Federal Work-Study, and institutionally sponsored loans available. Financial award application deadline: 4/15; financial award applicants required to submit FAFSA. *Faculty research:* Geography instruction and digital technology, multicultural education teacher development.

University of Oklahoma, Graduate College, College of Education, Department of Instructional Leadership and Academic Curriculum, Norman, OK 73072. Offers education (Certificate); instructional leadership and academic curriculum (M Ed, PhD), including bilingual education, early childhood education, elementary education, English education, math education, reading education, science education, secondary education, social studies education. *Accreditation:* NCATE. Part-time and evening/weekend programs available. *Faculty:* 18 full-time (11 women). *Students:* 44 full-time (36 women), 117 part-time (92 women); includes 35 minority (11 African Americans, 14 American Indian/Alaska Native, 5 Asian Americans or Pacific Islanders, 5 Hispanic Americans), 2 international. 50 applicants, 84% accepted, 32 enrolled. In 2009, 31 master's, 6 doctorates awarded. Terminal master's awarded for partial completion of doctoral program. *Degree requirements:* For doctorate, thesis/dissertation. *Entrance requirements:* For master's, 12 hours of course work in education; for doctorate, GRE General Test, master's degree, minimum graduate GPA of 3.0. Additional exam requirements/recommendations for international students: Required—TOEFL (minimum score 550 paper-based; 213 computer-based). *Application deadline:* For fall admission, 6/1 priority date for domestic students, 4/1 for international students; for spring admission, 11/1 for domestic students, 9/1 for international students. Applications are processed on a rolling basis. Application fee: $40 ($90 for international students). Electronic applications accepted. *Expenses:* Tuition, state resident: full-time $3744; part-time $156 per credit hour. Tuition, nonresident: full-time $13,577; part-time $565.70 per credit hour. Required fees: $2415; $90.10 per credit hour. *Financial support:* In 2009–10, 107 students received support, including 1 research assistantship with partial tuition reimbursement available (averaging $9,630 per year), 6 teaching assistantships with partial tuition reimbursements available (averaging $10,801 per year); scholarships/grants, health care benefits, and unspecified assistantships also available. Financial award applicants required to submit FAFSA. *Faculty research:* English education, mathematics education, reading, science education, social studies education. Total annual research expenditures: $752,908. *Unit head:* Lawrence Baines, Chair, 405-325-1498, Fax: 405-325-4061, E-mail: lbaines@ou.edu. *Application contact:* Lynn Crussel, Administrative Assistant for Graduate Studies, 405-325-4843, Fax: 405-325-4061, E-mail: lcrussel@ou.edu.

University of Pennsylvania, Graduate School of Education, Division of Foundations and Practices in Education, Program in Elementary and Secondary Education, Philadelphia, PA 19104. Offers MS Ed. *Students:* 296 full-time (198 women), 130 part-time (86 women); includes 32 minority (20 African Americans, 2 American Indian/Alaska Native, 9 Asian Americans or Pacific Islanders, 1 Hispanic American), 8 international. 292 applicants, 84% accepted, 183 enrolled. In 2009, 147 master's awarded. *Degree requirements:* For master's, comprehensive exam or portfolio. *Entrance requirements:* For master's, GRE General Test, MAT. *Application deadline:* For fall admission, 12/15 priority date for domestic students. Applications are processed on a rolling basis. Application fee: $70. Electronic applications accepted. *Expenses:* Contact institution. *Financial support:* Fellowships available. Financial award applicants required to submit FAFSA.

University of Phoenix, College of Natural Sciences, College of Education, Phoenix, AZ 85034-7209. Offers administration and supervision (MAEd); adult education and training (MAEd); curriculum and instruction (MAEd); curriculum and instruction-adult education (MAEd); curriculum and instruction-computer education (MAEd); curriculum and instruction-English and language arts education (MAEd); curriculum and instruction-English as a second language (MAEd); curriculum and instruction-mathematics education (MAEd); curriculum education (MAEd); early childhood (MAEd); elementary teacher education (MAEd); secondary teacher education (MAEd); special education (MAEd); teacher leadership (MAEd). *Accreditation:* Teacher Education Accreditation Council. Evening/weekend programs available. Postbaccalaureate distance learning degree programs offered (no on-campus study). *Faculty:* 47 full-time (34 women), 844 part-time/adjunct (636 women). *Students:* 13,657 full-time (10,698 women); includes 4,000 minority (3,063 African Americans, 74 American Indian/Alaska Native, 241 Asian Americans or Pacific Islanders, 622 Hispanic Americans), 307 international. Average age 36. In 2009, 17,246 master's awarded. *Degree requirements:* For master's, thesis (for some programs). *Entrance requirements:* For master's, 3 years of work experience, minimum GPA of 2.5. Additional exam requirements/recommendations for international students: Required—TOEFL (minimum score 550 paper-based; 213 computer-based; 79 iBT). *Application deadline:* Applications are processed on a rolling basis. Application fee: $45. Electronic applications accepted. *Expenses:* Tuition: Full-time $13,272. Required fees: $660. Full-time tuition and fees vary according to course level, degree level and program. *Financial support:* Institutionally sponsored loans and scholarships/grants available. Financial award applicants required to submit FAFSA. *Unit head:* Dr. Meredith Curley, Dean/Executive Director, 480-557-1217, Fax: 480-557-1588, E-mail: meredith.curley@phoenix.edu. *Application contact:* Chair, 602-387-7000, Fax: 602-387-6020.

University of Phoenix–Bay Area Campus, The Artemis School, College of Education, Pleasanton, CA 94588-3677. Offers curriculum instruction (MA Ed); curriculum instruction—adult education (MA Ed); elementary teacher education (MA Ed); secondary teacher education (MA Ed). Evening/weekend programs available. Postbaccalaureate distance learning degree programs offered (no on-campus study). *Degree requirements:* For master's, thesis (for some programs). *Entrance requirements:* For master's, minimum undergraduate GPA of 2.5, 3 years of work experience. Additional exam requirements/recommendations for international students: Required—TOEFL (minimum score 550 paper-based; 213 computer-based; 79 iBT). Electronic applications accepted.

University of Phoenix–Central Florida Campus, The Artemis School, College of Education, Maitland, FL 32751-7057. Offers administration and supervision (MA Ed); curriculum and instruction (MA Ed); curriculum and instruction-computer education (MA Ed); curriculum and instruction-mathematics education (MA Ed); early childhood education (MA Ed); elementary teacher education (MA Ed); secondary teacher education (MA Ed). Evening/weekend programs available. *Degree requirements:* For master's, thesis (for some programs). *Entrance*

requirements: For master's, 3 years of work experience, minimum undergraduate GPA of 2.5. Additional exam requirements/recommendations for international students: Required—TOEFL (minimum score 550 paper-based; 213 computer-based; 79 iBT). Electronic applications accepted.

University of Phoenix–Central Valley Campus, College of Education, Fresno, CA 93720-1562. Offers curriculum and instruction (MA Ed); curriculum and instruction-computer education (MA Ed); elementary teacher education (MA Ed); secondary teacher education (MA Ed).

University of Phoenix–Chattanooga Campus, College of Education, Chattanooga, TN 37421-3707. Offers administration and supervision (MA Ed); curriculum and instruction (MA Ed); elementary teacher education (MA Ed); secondary teacher education (MA Ed).

University of Phoenix–Denver Campus, The Artemis School, College of Education, Lone Tree, CO 80124-5453. Offers administration and supervision (MAEd); curriculum instruction (MAEd); elementary teacher education (MAEd); school counseling (MSC); secondary teacher education (MAEd). Evening/weekend programs available. *Degree requirements:* For master's, thesis (for some programs). *Entrance requirements:* For master's, minimum undergraduate GPA of 2.5, 3 years work experience. Additional exam requirements/recommendations for international students: Required—TOEFL (minimum score 550 paper-based; 213 computer-based; 79 iBT). Electronic applications accepted.

University of Phoenix–Hawaii Campus, The Artemis School, College of Education, Honolulu, HI 96813-4317. Offers administration and supervision (MA Ed); curriculum and instruction (MA Ed); elementary education (MA Ed); secondary education (MA Ed); special education (MA Ed); teacher education for elementary licensure (MA Ed). Evening/weekend programs available. *Degree requirements:* For master's, thesis (for some programs). *Entrance requirements:* For master's, minimum undergraduate GPA of 2.5, 3 years of work experience. Additional exam requirements/recommendations for international students: Required—TOEFL (minimum score 550 paper-based; 213 computer-based; 79 iBT). Electronic applications accepted.

University of Phoenix–Idaho Campus, The Artemis School, College of Education, Meridian, ID 83642-3014. Offers administration and supervision (MA Ed); curriculum and instruction (MA Ed); elementary teacher education (MA Ed); secondary teacher education (MA Ed). Evening/weekend programs available. *Degree requirements:* For master's, thesis (for some programs). *Entrance requirements:* For master's, minimum undergraduate GPA of 2.5, 3 years of work experience. Additional exam requirements/recommendations for international students: Required—TOEFL (minimum score 550 paper-based; 213 computer-based). Electronic applications accepted.

University of Phoenix–Indianapolis Campus, The Artemis School, College of Education, Indianapolis, IN 46250-932. Offers elementary teacher education (MA Ed); secondary teacher education (MA Ed).

University of Phoenix–Memphis Campus, College of Education, Cordova, TN 38018. Offers administration and supervision (MA Ed); curriculum and instruction (MA Ed); elementary teacher education (MA Ed); secondary teacher education (MA Ed).

University of Phoenix–Metro Detroit Campus, College of Education, Troy, MI 48098-2623. Offers administration and supervision (MA Ed); elementary teacher education (MA Ed); secondary teacher education (MA Ed); special education (MA Ed). Evening/weekend programs available. *Faculty:* 3 full-time (1 woman), 2 part-time/adjunct (both women). *Students:* 34 full-time (30 women); includes 23 minority (all African Americans). Average age 44. In 2009, 44 master's awarded. *Degree requirements:* For master's, thesis (for some programs). *Entrance requirements:* For master's, 3 years of work experience, minimum undergraduate GPA of 2.5. Additional exam requirements/recommendations for international students: Required—TOEFL (minimum score 550 paper-based; 213 computer-based; 79 iBT). *Application deadline:* Applications are processed on a rolling basis. Application fee: $45. Electronic applications accepted. *Expenses:* Tuition: Full-time $14,136. Required fees: $660. *Financial support:* Institutionally sponsored loans and scholarships/grants available. Financial award applicants required to submit FAFSA. *Unit head:* Dr. Meredith Curley, Dean/Executive Director, 480-557-1217, E-mail: meredith.curley@phoenix.edu. *Application contact:* Chair, 800-834-2438, Fax: 248-267-0147.

University of Phoenix–Nashville Campus, The Artemis School, College of Education, Nashville, TN 37214-5048. Offers administration and supervision (MA Ed); curriculum and instruction (MA Ed); elementary teacher education (MA Ed); secondary teacher education (MA Ed). Evening/weekend programs available. *Degree requirements:* For master's, thesis (for some programs). *Entrance requirements:* For master's, minimum undergraduate GPA of 2.5, 3 years work experience. Additional exam requirements/recommendations for international students: Required—TOEFL (minimum score 500 paper-based; 213 computer-based; 79 iBT). Electronic applications accepted.

University of Phoenix–New Mexico Campus, The Artemis School, College of Education, Albuquerque, NM 87113-1570. Offers administration and supervision (MAEd); curriculum and instruction (MAEd); elementary teacher education (MAEd); school counseling (MSC); secondary teacher education (MAEd). Evening/weekend programs available. *Degree requirements:* For master's, thesis (for some programs). *Entrance requirements:* For master's, minimum undergraduate GPA of 2.5, 3 years of work experience. Additional exam requirements/recommendations for international students: Required—TOEFL (minimum score 550 paper-based; 213 computer-based; 79 iBT). Electronic applications accepted.

University of Phoenix–Northern Nevada Campus, College of Education, Reno, NV 89521-5862. Offers administration and supervision (MA Ed); curriculum and instruction (MA Ed); elementary teacher education (MA Ed); secondary teacher education (MA Ed).

University of Phoenix–North Florida Campus, The Artemis School, College of Education, Jacksonville, FL 32216-0959. Offers administration and supervision (MA Ed); curriculum and instruction (MA Ed), including computer education, mathematics education; early childhood education (MA Ed); elementary teacher education (MA Ed); secondary teacher education (MA Ed). Evening/weekend programs available. *Degree requirements:* For master's, thesis (for some programs). *Entrance requirements:* For master's, 3 years of work experience, minimum undergraduate GPA of 2.5. Additional exam requirements/recommendations for international students: Required—TOEFL (minimum score 550 paper-based; 213 computer-based; 49 iBT). Electronic applications accepted.

University of Phoenix–Omaha Campus, College of Education, Omaha, NE 68154-5240. Offers administration and supervision (MA Ed); curriculum and instruction (MA Ed), including adult education, computer education, curriculum and instruction, English and language arts education, English as a second language, mathematics education; elementary teacher education (MA Ed); secondary teacher education (MA Ed); special education (MA Ed).

University of Phoenix–Oregon Campus, The Artemis School, College of Education, Tigard, OR 97223. Offers curriculum and instruction (MA Ed); early childhood education (MA Ed); elementary education (MA Ed), including early childhood specialization, middle level specialization; secondary education (MA Ed), including middle level specialization. Evening/weekend programs available. *Degree requirements:* For master's, thesis (for some programs). *Entrance requirements:* For master's, minimum undergraduate GPA of 2.5, 3 years work experience. Additional exam requirements/recommendations for international students: Required—TOEFL (minimum score 550 paper-based; 213 computer-based; 79 iBT). Electronic applications accepted.

University of Phoenix–Phoenix Campus, College of Social Sciences, College of Education, Phoenix, AZ 85040-1958. Offers administration and supervision (MA Ed); elementary teacher education (MA Ed); secondary teacher education (MA Ed); special education (MA Ed). Evening/weekend programs available. *Faculty:* 39 full-time (23 women), 422 part-time/adjunct (255 women). *Students:* 443 full-time (297 women); includes 79 minority (32 African Americans, 8 American Indian/Alaska Native, 8 Asian Americans or Pacific Islanders, 31 Hispanic Americans), 6 international. Average age 35. In 2009, 199 master's awarded. *Degree requirements:* For master's, thesis (for some programs). *Entrance requirements:* For master's, 3 years of work experience, minimum undergraduate GPA of 2.5. Additional exam requirements/recommendations for international students: Required—TOEFL (minimum score 550 paper-based; 213 computer-based; 79 iBT). *Application deadline:* Applications are processed on a rolling basis. Application fee: $45. Electronic applications accepted. *Expenses:* Tuition: Full-time $10,272. Required fees: $760. *Financial support:* Institutionally sponsored loans and scholarships/grants available. Financial award applicants required to submit FAFSA. *Unit head:* Dr. Meredith Curley, Dean/Executive Director, 480-557-1217, Fax: 480-557-1588, E-mail: meredith.curley@phoenix.edu. *Application contact:* College Chair, 480-804-2000.

University of Phoenix–Sacramento Valley Campus, The Artemis School, College of Education, Sacramento, CA 95833-3632. Offers adult education (MA Ed); curriculum instruction (MA Ed); elementary teacher education (MA Ed); secondary teacher education (MA Ed); teacher education (Certificate). Evening/weekend programs available. *Degree requirements:* For master's, thesis (for some programs). *Entrance requirements:* For master's, 3 years of work experience, minimum undergraduate GPA of 2.5. Additional exam requirements/recommendations for international students: Required—TOEFL (minimum score 550 paper-based; 213 computer-based; 79 iBT). Electronic applications accepted.

University of Phoenix–San Diego Campus, The Artemis School, College of Education, San Diego, CA 92123. Offers curriculum and instruction (MA Ed), including computer education, curriculum and instruction, English as a second language; elementary teacher education (MA Ed); secondary teacher education (MA Ed). Evening/weekend programs available. *Degree requirements:* For master's, thesis (for some programs). *Entrance requirements:* For master's, 3 years of work experience, minimum undergraduate GPA of 3.0. Additional exam requirements/recommendations for international students: Required—TOEFL (minimum score 550 paper-based; 213 computer-based; 79 iBT). Electronic applications accepted.

University of Phoenix–Southern Arizona Campus, The Artemis School, College of Education, Tucson, AZ 85711. Offers administration and supervision (MA Ed); adult education and training (MA Ed); curriculum instruction (MA Ed); educational counseling (MA Ed); elementary teacher education (MA Ed); school counseling (MSC); secondary teacher education (MA Ed); special education (MA Ed, Certificate). Evening/weekend programs available. *Degree requirements:* For master's, thesis (for some programs). *Entrance requirements:* For master's, minimum undergraduate GPA of 2.5, 3 years of work experience. Additional exam requirements/recommendations for international students: Required—TOEFL (minimum score 550 paper-based; 213 computer-based; 79 iBT). Electronic applications accepted.

University of Phoenix–Southern Colorado Campus, The Artemis School, College of Education, Colorado Springs, CO 80919-2335. Offers administration and supervision (MA Ed); curriculum and instruction (MA Ed); elementary teacher education (MA Ed); principal licensure certification (Certificate); school counseling (MSC); secondary teacher education (MA Ed). Evening/weekend programs available. *Degree requirements:* For master's, thesis (for some programs). *Entrance requirements:* For master's, minimum undergraduate GPA of 2.5, 3 years of work experience. Additional exam requirements/recommendations for international students: Required—TOEFL (minimum score 550 paper-based; 213 computer-based; 79 iBT). Electronic applications accepted.

University of Phoenix–South Florida Campus, The Artemis School, College of Education, Fort Lauderdale, FL 33309. Offers administration and supervision (MA Ed); curriculum and instruction (MA Ed), including computer education, curriculum and instruction, mathematics education; early childhood education (MA Ed); elementary teacher education (MA Ed); secondary teacher education (MA Ed). Evening/weekend programs available. *Degree requirements:* For master's, thesis (for some programs). *Entrance requirements:* For master's, 3 years of work experience, minimum undergraduate GPA of 2.5. Additional exam requirements/recommendations for international students: Required—TOEFL (minimum score 550 paper-based; 213 computer-based; 79 iBT). Electronic applications accepted.

University of Phoenix–Utah Campus, The Artemis School, College of Education, Salt Lake City, UT 84123-4617. Offers administration and supervision (MA Ed); curriculum and instruction (MA Ed); elementary teacher education (MA Ed); school counseling (MSC); secondary teacher education (MA Ed); special education (MA Ed). Evening/weekend programs available. *Degree requirements:* For master's, thesis (for some programs). *Entrance requirements:* For master's, minimum undergraduate GPA of 2.5, 3 years work experience. Additional exam requirements/recommendations for international students: Required—TOEFL (minimum score 550 paper-based; 213 computer-based; 79 iBT). Electronic applications accepted.

University of Phoenix–West Florida Campus, The Artemis School, College of Education, Temple Terrace, FL 33637. Offers administration and supervision (MA Ed); curriculum and instruction (MA Ed), including computer education, curriculum and instruction, mathematics education; curriculum and technology (MA Ed); early childhood education (MA Ed); elementary teacher education (MA Ed); secondary teacher education (MA Ed). Evening/weekend programs available. *Degree requirements:* For master's, thesis (for some programs). *Entrance requirements:* For master's, 3 years of work experience, minimum undergraduate GPA of 2.5. Additional exam requirements/recommendations for international students: Required—TOEFL (minimum score 550 paper-based; 213 computer-based; 79 iBT).

University of Pittsburgh, School of Education, Department of Instruction and Learning, Program in Secondary Education, Pittsburgh, PA 15260. Offers English/communications education (M Ed, MAT); foreign languages education (M Ed, MAT); mathematics education (M Ed, MAT, Ed D); science education (M Ed, MAT, MS, Ed D); social studies education (M Ed, MAT). Part-time and evening/weekend programs available. *Students:* 170 full-time (107 women), 70 part-time (54 women); includes 19 minority (11 African Americans, 6 Asian Americans or Pacific Islanders, 2 Hispanic Americans), 10 international. Average age 29. 220 applicants, 72% accepted, 128 enrolled. In 2009, 108 master's, 5 doctorates awarded. *Degree requirements:* For master's, thesis; for doctorate, thesis/dissertation. *Entrance requirements:* For master's, PRAXIS I; for doctorate, GRE General Test. Additional exam requirements/recommendations for international students: Required—TOEFL. *Application deadline:* For fall admission, 2/1 priority date for domestic students; for spring admission, 11/15 priority date for domestic students. Applications are processed on a rolling basis. Application fee: $50. Electronic applications accepted. *Expenses:* Tuition, state resident: full-time $16,402; part-time $665 per credit. Tuition, nonresident: full-time $28,694; part-time $1175 per credit. Required fees: $690; $175 per term. Tuition and fees vary according to program. *Financial support:* Fellowships, teaching assistantships, career-related internships or fieldwork, Federal Work-Study, tuition waivers (partial), and unspecified assistantships available. Support available to part-time students. Financial award application deadline: 3/15; financial award applicants required to submit FAFSA. *Unit head:* Dr. Richard Donato, Chairman, 412-624-7248, Fax: 412-648-7081, E-mail: donato@pitt.edu. *Application contact:* Joan M. Cutone, Director, School of Education Student Service Center, 412-648-2230, Fax: 412-648-1899, E-mail: soeinfo@pitt.edu.

University of Puget Sound, Graduate Studies, School of Education, Program in Teaching, Tacoma, WA 98416. Offers elementary education (MAT); secondary education (MAT). *Accreditation:* NASM; NCATE. *Faculty:* 8 full-time (4 women), 1 (woman) part-time/adjunct. *Students:* 45 full-time (26 women); includes 9 minority (4 African Americans, 4 Asian Americans or Pacific Islanders, 1 Hispanic American). Average age 25. 70 applicants, 84% accepted, 45 enrolled. In 2009, 41 master's awarded. *Entrance requirements:* For master's, GRE General Test, WEST-B, WEST-E in content area, minimum GPA of 3.0. Additional exam requirements/recommendations for international students: Required—TOEFL (minimum score 550 paper-based; 213 computer-based; 80 iBT). *Application deadline:* For fall admission, 3/1 priority date for domestic and international students. Applications are processed on a rolling basis. Application fee: $60. Electronic applications accepted. Tuition and fees vary according to course load, degree level and program. *Financial support:* In 2009–10, 18 students received support. Career-related internships or fieldwork and scholarships/grants available. Financial award application deadline: 3/31; financial award applicants required to submit FAFSA. *Faculty*

Secondary Education

University of Puget Sound (continued)
research: Math education, social studies education, professional development, international education, classroom discourse, equity education. *Unit head:* Dr. John Woodward, Dean, 253-879-3375, E-mail: woodward@pugetsound.edu. *Application contact:* Dr. George H. Mills, Vice President for Enrollment, 253-879-3211, Fax: 253-879-3993, E-mail: admission@pugetsound.edu.

University of Rhode Island, Graduate School, College of Human Science and Services, School of Education, Kingston, RI 02881. Offers adult education (MA); education (PhD); elementary education (MA); music education (MM); reading education (MA); secondary education (MA); special education (MA); MS/PhD. *Accreditation:* NCATE. Part-time and evening/weekend programs available. *Faculty:* 19 full-time (12 women), 5 part-time/adjunct (1 woman). *Students:* 44 full-time (33 women), 128 part-time (101 women); includes 14 minority (8 African Americans, 2 American Indian/Alaska Native, 2 Asian Americans or Pacific Islanders, 2 Hispanic Americans), 3 international. In 2009, 44 master's, 7 doctorates awarded. *Degree requirements:* For master's, comprehensive exam (for some programs), thesis optional; for doctorate, comprehensive exam, thesis/dissertation. *Entrance requirements:* For master's, 2 letters of recommendation; interview (for special education applicants); for doctorate, GRE, 3 letters of recommendation, resume. Additional exam requirements/recommendations for international students: Required—TOEFL (minimum score 600 paper-based; 250 computer-based; 100 iBT). *Application deadline:* For fall admission, 1/31 for international students. Application fee: $65. Electronic applications accepted. *Expenses:* Tuition, state resident: full-time $8828; part-time $490 per credit hour. Tuition, nonresident: full-time $22,100; part-time $1228 per credit hour. Required fees: $1118; $57 per semester. Tuition and fees vary according to program. *Financial support:* In 2009–10, 5 research assistantships with full and partial tuition reimbursements (averaging $11,518 per year), 3 teaching assistantships with full and partial tuition reimbursements (averaging $10,421 per year) were awarded; career-related internships or fieldwork also available. Financial award applicants required to submit FAFSA. Total annual research expenditures: $3.4 million. *Unit head:* Dr. David Byrd, Director, 401-874-5484, Fax: 401-874-5471, E-mail: dbyrd@uri.edu. *Application contact:* Dr. John Boulmetis, Coordinator of Graduate Studies, 401-874-4159, Fax: 401-874-7610, E-mail: johnb@uri.edu.

University of St. Francis, College of Education, Joliet, IL 60435-6169. Offers educational leadership (MS), including reading; elementary education certification (M Ed); reading (MS); secondary education certification (M Ed), including English education, math education, science education, social studies education; special education (M Ed); teaching and learning (MS), including character education, curriculum and instruction, differentiated instruction, technology. *Accreditation:* NCATE. Part-time and evening/weekend programs available. *Faculty:* 10 full-time (8 women), 26 part-time/adjunct (18 women). *Students:* 60 full-time (45 women), 349 part-time (283 women); includes 36 minority (10 African Americans, 2 Asian Americans or Pacific Islanders, 24 Hispanic Americans). Average age 33. 211 applicants, 65% accepted, 102 enrolled. In 2009, 174 master's awarded. *Entrance requirements:* For master's, Illinois Basic Skills Test (M Ed), teaching certificate (MS), minimum undergraduate GPA of 2.75, 2 letters of recommendation, computer competency. Additional exam requirements/recommendations for international students: Required—TOEFL (minimum score 550 paper-based; 213 computer-based). *Application deadline:* Applications are processed on a rolling basis. Application fee: $30. Electronic applications accepted. *Expenses:* Contact institution. *Financial support:* In 2009–10, 254 students received support. Federal Work-Study, scholarships/grants, tuition waivers (partial), and unspecified assistantships available. Support available to part-time students. Financial award applicants required to submit FAFSA. *Unit head:* Dr. John Gambro, Dean, 815-740-3332, Fax: 815-740-2264, E-mail: jgambro@stfrancis.edu. *Application contact:* Sandra Sloka, Director of Admissions for Graduate and Degree Completion Programs, 800-735-7500, Fax: 815-740-5032, E-mail: ssloka@stfrancis.edu.

University of St. Thomas, Graduate Studies, School of Education, Department of Teacher Education, St. Paul, MN 55105-1096. Offers curriculum and instruction (MA), including elementary, individualized, K-12, secondary; elementary (MAT); multicultural education (Certificate); reading (MA, Certificate), including elementary (MA), K-12 (MA). *Accreditation:* NCATE. Part-time and evening/weekend programs available. *Faculty:* 10 full-time (7 women), 25 part-time/adjunct (16 women). *Students:* 31 full-time (25 women), 260 part-time (195 women); includes 19 minority (6 African Americans, 7 Asian Americans or Pacific Islanders, 6 Hispanic Americans), 3 international. Average age 34. 325 applicants, 72% accepted, 225 enrolled. In 2009, 135 master's, 17 other advanced degrees awarded. *Entrance requirements:* For master's, minimum GPA of 3.0 or MAT. Additional exam requirements/recommendations for international students: Required—TOEFL (minimum score 550 paper-based; 210 computer-based; 80 iBT). *Application deadline:* For fall admission, 6/1 for domestic students; for spring admission, 11/1 for domestic students. Applications are processed on a rolling basis. Application fee: $50. *Financial support:* Fellowships, research assistantships, institutionally sponsored loans and scholarships/grants available. Support available to part-time students. Financial award applicants required to submit FAFSA. *Unit head:* Dr. Douglas F. Warring, Department Chair, 651-962-4877, Fax: 651-962-4169, E-mail: dfwarring@stthomas.edu. *Application contact:* Kathy J. Neary, Department Assistant, 651-962-4420, Fax: 651-962-4169, E-mail: kjneary@stthomas.edu.

The University of Scranton, College of Graduate and Continuing Education, Department of Education, Program in Secondary Education, Scranton, PA 18510. Offers MS. *Accreditation:* NCATE. Part-time and evening/weekend programs available. *Students:* 23 full-time (15 women), 3 part-time (1 woman); includes 1 minority (Hispanic American), 1 international. Average age 30. 14 applicants, 93% accepted. In 2009, 6 master's awarded. *Degree requirements:* For master's, comprehensive exam, capstone experience. *Entrance requirements:* For master's, minimum GPA of 2.75. Additional exam requirements/recommendations for international students: Required—TOEFL (minimum score 500 paper-based; 173 computer-based), IELTS (minimum score 5.5). *Application deadline:* Applications are processed on a rolling basis. Application fee: $0. *Financial support:* Teaching assistantships, career-related internships or fieldwork, Federal Work-Study, and unspecified assistantships available. Support available to part-time students. Financial award application deadline: 3/1. *Unit head:* Dr. Art Chambers, Director, 570-941-4668, Fax: 570-941-5515, E-mail: chambera2@scranton.edu. *Application contact:* Joseph M. Roback, Director of Admissions, 570-941-4385, Fax: 570-941-5928, E-mail: roback j2@scranton.edu.

University of South Alabama, Graduate School, College of Education, Department of Leadership and Teacher Education, Mobile, AL 36688-0002. Offers early childhood education (M Ed); educational administration (Ed S); educational leadership (M Ed); elementary education (M Ed); reading education (M Ed); science education (M Ed); secondary education (M Ed); special education (M Ed, Ed S). *Accreditation:* NCATE. Part-time programs available. *Degree requirements:* For master's, comprehensive exam. *Entrance requirements:* For master's, GRE General Test or MAT, minimum GPA of 3.0. *Expenses:* Tuition, state resident: part-time $218 per contact hour. Required fees: $1102 per year.

University of South Carolina, The Graduate School, College of Education, Department of Instruction and Teacher Education, Program in Secondary Education, Columbia, SC 29208. Offers art education (IMA, MAT); business education (IMA, MAT); English (MAT); foreign language (MAT); health education (MAT); mathematics (MAT); science (IMA, MAT); secondary (Ed D); secondary education (MT, PhD); social studies (MAT); theatre and speech (MAT). IMA and MT offered jointly with the subject areas. *Accreditation:* NCATE. *Degree requirements:* For master's, comprehensive exam, thesis (for some programs), foreign language (MA); for doctorate, one foreign language, comprehensive exam, thesis/dissertation. *Entrance requirements:* For master's, GRE General Test or MAT, teaching certificate (IMA, M Ed), interview; for doctorate, GRE General Test or MAT, interview. *Faculty research:* Middle school programs, professional development, school collaboration.

The University of South Dakota, Graduate School, School of Education, Division of Curriculum and Instruction, Program in Secondary Education, Vermillion, SD 57069-2390. Offers MA. *Accreditation:* NCATE. Part-time programs available. Postbaccalaureate distance learning

degree programs offered. *Degree requirements:* For master's, comprehensive exam, thesis or alternative. *Entrance requirements:* For master's, GRE General Test, MAT, minimum GPA of 2.7. Additional exam requirements/recommendations for international students: Required—TOEFL (minimum score 550 paper-based; 213 computer-based; 79 iBT). Electronic applications accepted.

University of Southern Indiana, Graduate Studies, College of Education and Human Services, Department of Teacher Education, Program in Secondary Education, Evansville, IN 47712-3590. Offers MS. *Accreditation:* NCATE. Part-time and evening/weekend programs available. *Faculty:* 7 full-time (3 women), 1 (woman) part-time/adjunct. *Students:* 3 full-time (1 woman), 51 part-time (32 women); includes 2 minority (1 African American, 1 Asian American or Pacific Islander), 1 international. Average age 34. 24 applicants, 100% accepted, 18 enrolled. In 2009, 19 master's awarded. *Entrance requirements:* For master's, GRE General Test, NTE or PRAXIS I, minimum GPA of 3.0, teaching license. Additional exam requirements/recommendations for international students: Required—TOEFL (minimum score 550 paper-based; 213 computer-based; 79 iBT), IELTS (minimum score 6). *Application deadline:* For fall admission, 7/1 priority date for domestic students, 1/1 priority date for international students. Applications are processed on a rolling basis. Application fee: $25. Electronic applications accepted. *Expenses:* Tuition, state resident: full-time $4592; part-time $255 per credit hour. Tuition, nonresident: full-time $9060; part-time $503 per credit hour. Required fees: $220; $22.75 per term. Tuition and fees vary according to course load and reciprocity agreements. *Financial support:* In 2009–10, 17 students received support. Federal Work-Study, institutionally sponsored loans, scholarships/grants, tuition waivers (full and partial), and unspecified assistantships available. Financial award application deadline: 3/1; financial award applicants required to submit FAFSA. *Unit head:* Dr. Vella Goebel, Coordinator, 812-461-5306, E-mail: vgoebel@usi.edu. *Application contact:* Dr. Vella Goebel, Coordinator, 812-461-5306, E-mail: vgoebel@usi.edu.

University of Southern Mississippi, Graduate School, College of Education and Psychology, Department of Curriculum, Instruction, and Special Education, Hattiesburg, MS 39406-0001. Offers alternative secondary teacher education (MAT); early childhood education (M Ed, Ed S); education of the gifted (M Ed, Ed D, PhD, Ed S); elementary education (M Ed, Ed D, PhD, Ed S); reading (M Ed, MS, Ed S); secondary education (M Ed, MS, Ed D, PhD, Ed S); special education (M Ed, Ed D, PhD, Ed S). *Faculty:* 23 full-time (17 women), 3 part-time/adjunct (2 women). *Students:* 31 full-time (26 women), 77 part-time (68 women); includes 18 minority (15 African Americans, 3 Hispanic Americans). Average age 37. 50 applicants, 52% accepted, 19 enrolled. In 2009, 43 master's, 3 doctorates, 2 other advanced degrees awarded. *Degree requirements:* For master's, comprehensive exam, thesis (for some programs); for doctorate, comprehensive exam, thesis/dissertation; for Ed S, comprehensive exam, thesis. *Entrance requirements:* For master's, GRE General Test, MAT, minimum GPA of 3.0; for doctorate, GRE General Test, minimum GPA of 3.5; for Ed S, GRE General Test, MAT, minimum GPA of 3.25. Additional exam requirements/recommendations for international students: Required—TOEFL. *Application deadline:* For fall admission, 3/1 priority date for domestic students, 3/1 for international students. Applications are processed on a rolling basis. Application fee: $35. *Expenses:* Tuition, state resident: full-time $5096; part-time $284 per hour. Tuition, nonresident: full-time $13,052; part-time $726 per hour. Required fees: $402. Tuition and fees vary according to course level and course load. *Financial support:* In 2009–10, 9 research assistantships with tuition reimbursements (averaging $18,316 per year), 2 teaching assistantships with full tuition reimbursements (averaging $8,500 per year) were awarded; Federal Work-Study, institutionally sponsored loans, and tuition waivers (partial) also available. Financial award application deadline: 3/15; financial award applicants required to submit FAFSA. *Faculty research:* Mathematical problem solving, integrative curriculum, writing process, teacher education models. Total annual research expenditures: $100,000. *Unit head:* Dr. David Daves, Chair, 601-266-4547, Fax: 601-266-4175. *Application contact:* Rachea Cawthorn, Administrative Assistant, 601-266-6987, Fax: 601-266-4548.

University of South Florida, Graduate School, College of Education–Main Campus, Department of Secondary Education, Tampa, FL 33620-9951. Offers English education (M Ed, MA, MAT, PhD); foreign language education/ESOL (M Ed, MA, MAT); instructional technology (M Ed, PhD, Ed S); mathematics education (M Ed, MA, MAT, PhD, Ed S); science education (M Ed, MA, MAT, PhD); second language acquisition/instructional technology (PhD); secondary education (M Ed, PhD); secondary education/TESOL (M Ed); social science education (M Ed, MA, MAT); teaching and learning in the content area (PhD). *Accreditation:* NCATE. Part-time and evening/weekend programs available. *Faculty:* 28 full-time (17 women), 3 part-time/adjunct (1 woman). *Students:* 144 full-time (97 women), 322 part-time (212 women); includes 100 minority (32 African Americans, 4 American Indian/Alaska Native, 17 Asian Americans or Pacific Islanders, 47 Hispanic Americans), 25 international. Average age 30. 230 applicants, 67% accepted, 122 enrolled. In 2009, 122 master's, 14 doctorates, 1 other advanced degree awarded. *Degree requirements:* For master's, variable foreign language requirement, comprehensive exam; for doctorate, variable foreign language requirement, comprehensive exam, thesis/dissertation. *Entrance requirements:* For master's, GRE General Test or General Knowledge Test, minimum GPA of 3.0; for doctorate, GRE General Test, minimum GPA of 3.5; for Ed S, GRE General Test. Additional exam requirements/recommendations for international students: Required—TOEFL (minimum score 550 paper-based; 213 computer-based; 79 iBT). *Application deadline:* For fall admission, 2/15 for domestic students, 1/2 for international students; for spring admission, 10/15 for domestic students, 6/1 for international students. Application fee: $30. Electronic applications accepted. *Financial support:* In 2009–10, 7 students received support, including 1 research assistantship with full tuition reimbursement available (averaging $10,000 per year), 55 teaching assistantships with full and partial tuition reimbursements available (averaging $7,900 per year); scholarships/grants and unspecified assistantships also available. Financial award application deadline: 4/15; financial award applicants required to submit FAFSA. *Faculty research:* English language learners/multicultural, social science education, mathematics education, science education, instructional technology. Total annual research expenditures: $336,023. *Unit head:* Dr. Stephen Thornton, Chairperson, 813-974-3533, Fax: 813-974-3837, E-mail: thornton@usf.edu. *Application contact:* Dr. James White, Program Director, 813-974-1629, Fax: 813-974-3837, E-mail: jwhite@usf.edu.

The University of Tennessee, Graduate School, College of Education, Health and Human Sciences, Program in Education, Knoxville, TN 37996. Offers art education (MS); counseling education (PhD); cultural studies in education (PhD); curriculum (MS, Ed S); curriculum, educational research and evaluation (Ed D, PhD); early childhood education (PhD); early childhood special education (MS); education of deaf and hard of hearing (MS); educational administration and policy studies (Ed D, PhD); educational administration and supervision (Ed S); educational psychology (Ed D, PhD); elementary education (MS, Ed S); elementary teaching (MS); English education (MS, Ed S); exercise science (PhD); foreign language/ESL education (MS, Ed S); instructional technology (MS, Ed D, PhD, Ed S); literacy, language and ESL education (PhD); literacy, language education, and ESL education (Ed D); mathematics education (MS, Ed S); modified and comprehensive special education (MS); reading education (MS, Ed S); school counseling (Ed S); school psychology (PhD, Ed S); science education (MS, Ed S); secondary teaching (MS); social foundations (MS); social science education (MS, Ed S); socio-cultural foundations of sports and education (PhD); special education (Ed S); teacher education (Ed D, PhD). *Accreditation:* NCATE. Part-time and evening/weekend programs available. *Degree requirements:* For master's and Ed S, thesis optional; for doctorate, variable foreign language requirement, thesis/dissertation. *Entrance requirements:* For master's, minimum GPA of 2.7; for doctorate and Ed S, GRE General Test, minimum GPA of 2.7. Additional exam requirements/recommendations for international students: Required—TOEFL. Electronic applications accepted. *Expenses:* Tuition, state resident: full-time $6826; part-time $380 per semester hour. Tuition, nonresident: full-time $21,844; part-time $1147 per semester hour. Tuition and fees vary according to program.

The University of Tennessee at Chattanooga, Graduate School, College of Health, Education and Professional Studies, Graduate Studies Division of Education, Program in Education, Chattanooga, TN 37403-2598. Offers elementary education (M Ed); school leadership (M Ed,

Post-Master's Certificate); secondary education (M Ed); special education (M Ed). Part-time and evening/weekend programs available. Postbaccalaureate distance learning degree programs offered (no on-campus study). *Faculty:* 10 full-time (9 women), 6 part-time/adjunct (3 women). *Students:* 124 full-time (83 women), 208 part-time (150 women); includes 42 minority (32 African Americans, 2 American Indian/Alaska Native, 3 Asian Americans or Pacific Islanders, 5 Hispanic Americans), 1 international. Average age 33. 117 applicants, 97% accepted, 80 enrolled. In 2009, 97 master's, 4 other advanced degrees awarded. *Degree requirements:* For master's, comprehensive exam (for some programs), thesis (for some programs). *Entrance requirements:* For master's and Post-Master's Certificate, PRAXIS I, minimum GPA of 2.5 overall or 3.0 in senior year. Additional exam requirements/recommendations for international students: Required—TOEFL (minimum score 550 paper-based; 213 computer-based; 79 iBT), IELTS (minimum score 6). *Application deadline:* For fall admission, 8/1 for domestic students, 6/1 for international students; for spring admission, 12/1 for domestic students, 10/1 for international students. Applications are processed on a rolling basis. Application fee: $35. Electronic applications accepted. *Expenses:* Tuition, state resident: full-time $5404; part-time $300 per credit hour. Tuition, nonresident: full-time $16,702; part-time $928 per credit hour. Required fees: $1150; $130 per credit hour. *Financial support:* In 2009–10, 8 research assistantships with full and partial tuition reimbursements (averaging $5,500 per year) were awarded; career-related internships or fieldwork, scholarships/grants, and unspecified assistantships also available. Support available to part-time students. *Faculty research:* Elementary education, community counseling, school counseling, secondary education, special education. *Unit head:* Dr. John Freeman, Department Head, 423-425-4133, Fax: 423-425-5443, E-mail: john-freeman@utc.edu. *Application contact:* Dr. Stephanie Bellar, Dean of Graduate Studies, 423-425-4666, Fax: 423-425-5223, E-mail: stephanie-bellar@utc.edu.

The University of Texas–Pan American, College of Education, Department of Curriculum and Instruction: Elementary and Secondary, Edinburg, TX 78539. Offers bilingual education (M Ed); early childhood education (M Ed); elementary education (M Ed); reading (M Ed); secondary education (M Ed). Part-time programs available. *Degree requirements:* For master's, comprehensive exam, thesis optional. *Entrance requirements:* For master's, GRE. Additional exam requirements/recommendations for international students: Required—TOEFL, IELTS. *Expenses:* Tuition, state resident: full-time $3630.60; part-time $201.70 per credit hour. Tuition, nonresident: full-time $8617; part-time $478.70 per credit hour. Required fees: $806.50. *Faculty research:* Dual language instruction, literacy and technology, teacher education in diverse populations, mathematics and science education.

University of the Cumberlands, Graduate Programs in Education, Program in Secondary Education, Williamsburg, KY 40769-1372. Offers MA Ed, MAT. *Degree requirements:* For master's, comprehensive exam. *Entrance requirements:* For master's, GRE or NTE, Kentucky teaching certificate.

University of the Incarnate Word, School of Graduate Studies and Research, Dreeben School of Education, Program in Teaching, San Antonio, TX 78209-6397. Offers all-level teaching (MAT); elementary teaching (MAT); secondary teaching (MAT). Part-time and evening/weekend programs available. *Students:* 45 part-time (38 women); includes 27 minority (7 African Americans, 20 Hispanic Americans). Average age 33. In 2009, 37 master's awarded. *Degree requirements:* For master's, internship. *Entrance requirements:* For master's, GRE, Texas Higher Education Assessment test (THEA), interview. Additional exam requirements/recommendations for international students: Required—TOEFL (minimum score 560 paper-based; 220 computer-based; 83 iBT). *Application deadline:* Applications are processed on a rolling basis. Application fee: $20. Electronic applications accepted. *Expenses:* Tuition: Full-time $12,150; part-time $675 per credit hour. Required fees: $83 per credit hour. *Financial support:* Federal Work-Study and scholarships/grants available. Financial award applicants required to submit FAFSA. *Unit head:* Dr. Elda Martinez, Director of Teacher Education, 210-832-3297, Fax: 210-829-3134, E-mail: eemartin@uiwtx.edu. *Application contact:* Andrea Cyterski-Acosta, Dean of Enrollment, 210-829-6005, Fax: 210-829-3921, E-mail: admis@uiwtx.edu.

The University of Toledo, College of Graduate Studies, College of Education, Department of Curriculum and Instruction, Program in Secondary Education, Toledo, OH 43606-3390. Offers ME, DE, PhD, Ed S.

University of Tulsa, Graduate School, College of Arts and Sciences, School of Education, Program in Education, Tulsa, OK 74104-3189. Offers education (MA); elementary certification (M Ed); secondary certification (M Ed). Part-time programs available. *Faculty:* 6 full-time (2 women), 1 (woman) part-time/adjunct. *Students:* 7 full-time (6 women), 3 part-time (1 woman); includes 1 minority (American Indian/Alaska Native), 2 international. Average age 25. 10 applicants, 100% accepted, 7 enrolled. In 2009, 4 master's awarded. *Degree requirements:* For master's, thesis optional. *Entrance requirements:* For master's, GRE General Test. Additional exam requirements/recommendations for international students: Required—TOEFL (minimum score 575 paper-based; 231 computer-based; 91 iBT), IELTS (minimum score 6.5). *Application deadline:* Applications are processed on a rolling basis. Application fee: $40. Electronic applications accepted. *Expenses:* Tuition: Full-time $16,182; part-time $899 per credit hour. Required fees: $4 per credit hour. Tuition and fees vary according to course load. *Financial support:* In 2009–10, 7 students received support, including 1 fellowship with full and partial tuition reimbursement available (averaging $11,594 per year), 6 teaching assistantships with full and partial tuition reimbursements available (averaging $10,627 per year); research assistantships with full and partial tuition reimbursements available, Federal Work-Study, scholarships/grants, health care benefits, tuition waivers (full and partial), and unspecified assistantships also available. Support available to part-time students. Financial award application deadline: 2/1; financial award applicants required to submit FAFSA. Total annual research expenditures: $5.1 million. *Unit head:* Dr. David Brown, Advisor, 918-631-2719, Fax: 918-631-2133, E-mail: david-brown@utulsa.edu. *Application contact:* Dr. David Brown, Advisor, 918-631-2719, Fax: 918-631-2133, E-mail: david-brown@utulsa.edu.

University of Utah, Graduate School, College of Education, Department of Teaching and Learning, Salt Lake City, UT 84112-1107. Offers elementary education (MAT); secondary education (MAT); teaching and learning (M Ed, M Phil, MA, MS, PhD). Part-time and evening/weekend programs available. *Faculty:* 1 (woman) full-time, 5 part-time/adjunct (all women). *Students:* 49 full-time (36 women), 27 part-time (21 women); includes 3 minority (2 Asian Americans or Pacific Islanders, 1 Hispanic American), 2 international. Average age 34. 44 applicants, 52% accepted, 19 enrolled. In 2009, 38 master's, 4 doctorates awarded. *Degree requirements:* For master's, comprehensive exam (for some programs), thesis optional; for doctorate, thesis/dissertation. *Entrance requirements:* For master's, GRE General Test or MAT, GRE Subject Test, minimum GPA of 3.0; for doctorate, GRE General Test, minimum graduate GPA of 3.5, undergraduate 3.0. Additional exam requirements/recommendations for international students: Required—TOEFL (minimum score 500 paper-based; 173 computer-based). *Application deadline:* For fall admission, 3/1 for domestic students, 4/1 for international students; for spring admission, 10/15 for domestic students, 11/1 for international students. Applications are processed on a rolling basis. Application fee: $55 ($65 for international students). *Expenses:* Tuition, state resident: full-time $4004; part-time $1674 per semester. Tuition, nonresident: full-time $14,134; part-time $5915 per semester. Required fees: $324 per semester. Tuition and fees vary according to course load, degree level and program. *Financial support:* Fellowships, research assistantships with full and partial tuition reimbursements, teaching assistantships with full and partial tuition reimbursements, career-related internships or fieldwork and tuition waivers (partial) available. Financial award application deadline: 2/1; financial award applicants required to submit FAFSA. *Faculty research:* Teacher development, teacher education, reading instruction, math instruction, technology. Total annual research expenditures: $13,727. *Unit head:* Doug Hacker, Department Chair, 801-581-5080, Fax: 801-581-3609, E-mail: douglas.hacker@utah.edu. *Application contact:* Jan Dole, Graduate Program Director, 801-587-7991, Fax: 801-581-3609, E-mail: jan.dole@utah.edu.

University of Washington, Bothell, Program in Education, Bothell, WA 98011-8246. Offers leadership development for educators (M Ed); secondary/middle level endorsement (M Ed). Part-time and evening/weekend programs available. *Faculty:* 9 full-time (7 women), 1 (woman) part-time/adjunct. *Students:* 25 full-time (15 women), 118 part-time (91 women); includes 17 minority (6 African Americans, 6 Asian Americans or Pacific Islanders, 5 Hispanic Americans). Average age 34. 78 applicants, 76% accepted, 55 enrolled. In 2009, 47 master's awarded. *Degree requirements:* For master's, thesis. *Entrance requirements:* Additional exam requirements/recommendations for international students: Required—TOEFL. *Application deadline:* For fall admission, 8/14 priority date for domestic and international students; for spring admission, 2/12 priority date for domestic and international students. Applications are processed on a rolling basis. Application fee: $65. Electronic applications accepted. *Expenses:* Tuition, state resident: full-time $10,160; part-time $484 per credit hour. Tuition, nonresident: full-time $23,500; part-time $1120 per credit hour. Required fees: $567; $21.50 per credit hour. Tuition and fees vary according to course load and program. *Financial support:* Federal Work-Study and unspecified assistantships available. *Faculty research:* Multicultural education in citizenship education, intercultural education, knowledge and practice in the principalship, educational public policy, national board certification for teachers, teacher learning in literacy, technology and its impact on teaching and learning of mathematics, reading assessments, professional development in literacy education and mobility, digital media, education and class. *Unit head:* Dr. Bradley S. Portin, Director and Professor, 425-352-3482, Fax: 425-352-5234, E-mail: bportin@uwb.edu. *Application contact:* Amelia Bowers, Education Program Advisor, 425-352-5274, Fax: 425-352-5434, E-mail: abowers@uwb.edu.

University of Washington, Tacoma, Graduate Programs, Program in Education, Tacoma, WA 98402-3100. Offers educational administrator (M Ed); K-8 teacher education (M Ed); professional certification (M Ed); secondary science (M Ed); special education (M Ed). Part-time and evening/weekend programs available. *Faculty:* 13 full-time (8 women), 9 part-time/adjunct (8 women). *Students:* 85 full-time (66 women), 118 part-time (99 women); includes 24 minority (4 African Americans, 9 Asian Americans or Pacific Islanders, 11 Hispanic Americans). Average age 33. 36 applicants, 75% accepted, 23 enrolled. In 2009, 68 master's awarded. *Entrance requirements:* For master's, official sealed transcript from every college/university attended, personal goal statement, letters of recommendation, copy of valid teaching certificate. *Application deadline:* For fall admission, 8/1 for domestic students; for winter admission, 11/1 priority date for domestic students; for spring admission, 2/1 priority date for domestic students. Applications are processed on a rolling basis. Application fee: $65. Electronic applications accepted. *Expenses:* Tuition, state resident: full-time $10,660; part-time $484 per credit. Tuition, nonresident: full-time $24,000; part-time $1119 per credit. Required fees: $150 per term. Tuition and fees vary according to course load and program. *Faculty research:* Global learning communities for English/Chinese languages, evaluation of mathematics and reading intervention programs, response to intervention, school wide behavioral and emotional support, mathematics education and culturally responsive mathematics education. *Unit head:* Dr. Karen Landenburger, Chancellor, 253-692-4430, Fax: 253-692-5612, E-mail: uwted@u.washington.edu. *Application contact:* Dr. Carla Van Rossum, Recruiter/Advisor, 253-692-4430, Fax: 253-692-5612, E-mail: uwted@u.washington.edu.

The University of West Alabama, School of Graduate Studies, College of Education, Department of Teacher Education, Program in Secondary Education, Livingston, AL 35470. Offers MAT. Part-time programs available. *Entrance requirements:* For master's, GRE General Test, MAT, minimum GPA of 2.75. *Faculty research:* Integrated arts into the curriculum, moral development of children.

University of West Florida, College of Professional Studies, Department of Professional and Community Leadership, Specialization in Middle and Secondary Level Education and ESOL, Pensacola, FL 32514-5750. Offers M Ed. *Accreditation:* NCATE. Part-time and evening/weekend programs available. *Students:* 10 part-time (all women). Average age 32. 1 applicant. In 2009, 30 master's awarded. *Degree requirements:* For master's, thesis or alternative. *Entrance requirements:* For master's, GRE (minimum score 450 verbal) or MAT (minimum score 396) if bachelor's GPA less than 3.0, state teaching certification; letter of intent; two professional references. Additional exam requirements/recommendations for international students: Required—TOEFL (minimum score 550 paper-based; 213 computer-based). *Application deadline:* For fall admission, 6/1 for domestic students, 5/15 for international students; for spring admission, 11/1 for domestic students, 10/1 for international students. Applications are processed on a rolling basis. Application fee: $30. *Expenses:* Tuition, state resident: full-time $4982; part-time $260 per credit hour. Tuition, nonresident: full-time $20,059; part-time $919 per credit hour. Required fees: $1247; $52 per credit hour. *Financial support:* Unspecified assistantships available. *Unit head:* Dr. David Stout, Chairperson, 850-474-2284, Fax: 850-474-2844. *Application contact:* Terry McCray, Assistant Director of Graduate Admissions, 850-473-7718, Fax: 850-473-7714, E-mail: gradadmissions@uwf.edu.

University of West Georgia, Graduate School, College of Education, Department of Curriculum and Instruction, Carrollton, GA 30118. Offers art education (M Ed); art teacher education (Ed S); biology/secondary education (Ed S); business education (M Ed, Ed S); early childhood education (M Ed, Ed S); economics/secondary teacher education (Ed S); English teacher education (Ed S); French language teacher education (Ed S); history teacher education (Ed S); mathematics teacher education (Ed S); middle grades education (M Ed, Ed S); reading education (M Ed, Ed S); science teacher education (Ed S); secondary education (M Ed, Ed S); social science teacher education (Ed S); Spanish language teacher education (Ed S). Part-time and evening/weekend programs available. *Faculty:* 18 full-time (15 women), 7 part-time/adjunct (6 women). *Students:* 119 full-time (101 women), 358 part-time (280 women); includes 109 minority (97 African Americans, 3 American Indian/Alaska Native, 2 Asian Americans or Pacific Islanders, 7 Hispanic Americans). Average age 33. 193 applicants, 82% accepted, 34 enrolled. In 2009, 109 master's, 27 Ed Ss awarded. *Degree requirements:* For master's, comprehensive exam; for Ed S, research project. *Entrance requirements:* For master's, GRE General Test or MAT, minimum GPA of 2.7; for Ed S, GRE General Test, master's degree, minimum graduate GPA of 2.7. *Application deadline:* For fall admission, 7/17 for domestic students; for spring admission, 11/20 for domestic students. Applications are processed on a rolling basis. Application fee: $30. Electronic applications accepted. *Expenses:* Tuition, state resident: full-time $2952; part-time $164 per semester hour. Tuition, nonresident: full-time $11,808; part-time $656 per semester hour. Required fees: $42.90 per semester hour. $307 per semester. Tuition and fees vary according to course load. *Financial support:* In 2009–10, 5 research assistantships with full tuition reimbursements (averaging $3,000 per year) were awarded; career-related internships or fieldwork and scholarships/grants also available. Support available to part-time students. Financial award applicants required to submit FAFSA. *Unit head:* Dr. Donna Harkins, Chair, 678-839-6066, Fax: 678-839-6559, E-mail: dharkins@westga.edu. *Application contact:* Dr. Charles W. Clark, Dean, 678-839-6508, E-mail: cclark@westga.edu.

University of Wisconsin–Eau Claire, College of Education and Human Sciences, Program in Secondary Education, Eau Claire, WI 54702-4004. Offers English (MST); professional development (MEPD), including library science, professional educator. Part-time and evening/weekend programs available. Postbaccalaureate distance learning degree programs offered. *Faculty:* 13 full-time (8 women). *Students:* 3 full-time (2 women), 9 part-time (5 women); includes 1 minority (African American). Average age 31. 8 applicants, 50% accepted, 3 enrolled. In 2009, 14 master's awarded. *Degree requirements:* For master's, thesis optional, oral exam, portfolio, written exam. *Entrance requirements:* For master's, certification to teach, minimum GPA of 2.75. Additional exam requirements/recommendations for international students: Required—TOEFL (minimum score 550 paper-based; 213 computer-based; 79 iBT). *Application deadline:* For fall admission, 7/1 priority date for domestic students, 6/1 priority date for international students; for spring admission, 12/1 priority date for domestic students, 11/1 priority date for international students. Applications are processed on a rolling basis. Application fee: $56. Electronic applications accepted. *Expenses:* Tuition, state resident: full-time $6705.90; part-time $372.55 per credit. Tuition, nonresident: full-time $16,771; part-time $931.74 per credit. Required fees: $925.50; $51.19 per credit. One-time fee: $56. *Financial support:* In 2009–10, 6 students received support, including 4 fellowships (averaging $3,125 per year); Federal Work-Study and unspecified assistantships also available. Financial award application deadline: 3/1; financial award applicants required to submit FAFSA. *Unit head:* Dr. Dwight Watson, Chair, 715-836-2013, Fax: 715-836-4868, E-mail: watsondc@uwec.edu. *Application*

Secondary Education

University of Wisconsin–Eau Claire (continued)
contact: Kristina Anderson, Director of Admissions, 715-836-5415, Fax: 715-836-2409, E-mail: admissions@uwec.edu.

University of Wisconsin–La Crosse, Office of University Graduate Studies, College of Liberal Studies, Department of Educational Studies, Program in Professional Development, La Crosse, WI 54601-3742. Offers elementary education (MEPD), including grades 1 through 6, grades 1 through 9; K–12 (MEPD); professional development (MEPD); secondary education (MEPD), including grades 6 through 12. Part-time programs available. *Faculty:* 18 part-time/adjunct (13 women). *Students:* 14 full-time (9 women), 345 part-time (275 women); includes 7 minority (2 Asian Americans or Pacific Islanders, 5 Hispanic Americans), 5 international. Average age 33. 121 applicants, 92% accepted, 75 enrolled. In 2009, 236 master's awarded. *Degree requirements:* For master's, thesis optional. *Entrance requirements:* For master's, PPST, minimum GPA of 2.85; minimum cumulative GPA of 3.0 in subject area. Additional exam requirements/recommendations for international students: Required—TOEFL (minimum score 550 paper-based; 213 computer-based; 79 iBT). *Application deadline:* Applications are processed on a rolling basis. Application fee: $56. Electronic applications accepted. *Financial support:* Research assistantships with partial tuition reimbursements, career-related internships or fieldwork, Federal Work-Study, health care benefits, unspecified assistantships, and grant-funded positions available. Support available to part-time students. Financial award application deadline: 3/15; financial award applicants required to submit FAFSA. *Unit head:* Dr. Gary Willhite, Director, 608-785-8142, E-mail: whillhite.gary@uwlax.edu. *Application contact:* Kathryn Kiefer, Associate Director of Admissions, 608-785-8939, E-mail: admissions@uwlax.edu.

University of Wisconsin–Milwaukee, Graduate School, School of Education, Department of Curriculum and Instruction, Milwaukee, WI 53201-0413. Offers curriculum planning and instruction improvement (MS); early childhood education (MS); elementary education (MS); junior high/middle school education (MS); reading education (MS); secondary education (MS); teaching in an urban setting (MS). Part-time programs available. *Faculty:* 22 full-time (17 women). *Students:* 23 full-time (14 women), 64 part-time (58 women); includes 8 minority (4 African Americans, 1 American Indian/Alaska Native, 3 Hispanic Americans), 1 international. Average age 31. 46 applicants, 57% accepted, 12 enrolled. In 2009, 28 master's awarded. *Degree requirements:* For master's, thesis or alternative. *Entrance requirements:* Additional exam requirements/recommendations for international students: Required—TOEFL (minimum score 550 paper-based; 79 iBT), IELTS (minimum score 6.5). *Application deadline:* For fall admission, 1/1 priority date for domestic students; for spring admission, 9/1 for domestic students. Applications are processed on a rolling basis. Application fee: $45 ($75 for international students). *Expenses:* Tuition, state resident: full-time $8800. Tuition, nonresident: full-time $20,760. Tuition and fees vary according to program and reciprocity agreements. *Financial support:* Career-related internships or fieldwork and unspecified assistantships available. Support available to part-time students. Financial award application deadline: 4/15. Total annual research expenditures: $65,946. *Unit head:* Hope Longwell-Grice, Chair, 414-229-4884, Fax: 414-229-5571, E-mail: hope@uwm.edu. *Application contact:* General Information Contact, 414-229-4982, Fax: 414-229-6967, E-mail: gradschool@uwm.edu.

University of Wisconsin–Platteville, School of Graduate Studies, College of Liberal Arts and Education, School of Education, Platteville, WI 53818-3099. Offers adult education (MSE); elementary education (MSE); English education (MSE); middle school education (MSE); secondary education (MSE); vocational and technical education (MSE). *Accreditation:* NCATE. Part-time programs available. *Faculty:* 8 part-time/adjunct (3 women). *Students:* 16 full-time (12 women), 183 part-time (137 women); includes 35 minority (27 African Americans, 1 American Indian/Alaska Native, 1 Asian American or Pacific Islander, 6 Hispanic Americans), 63 international. 23 applicants, 100% accepted, 23 enrolled. In 2009, 85 master's awarded. *Degree requirements:* For master's, comprehensive exam, thesis or alternative. *Entrance requirements:* Additional exam requirements/recommendations for international students: Required—TOEFL (minimum score 500 paper-based; 173 computer-based; 61 iBT). *Application deadline:* For fall admission, 7/1 priority date for domestic students; for spring admission, 11/1 for domestic students. Applications are processed on a rolling basis. Application fee: $56. Electronic applications accepted. *Expenses:* Tuition, state resident: full-time $6706. Tuition, nonresident: full-time $16,772. *Financial support:* Research assistantships with partial tuition reimbursements, career-related internships or fieldwork, Federal Work-Study, institutionally sponsored loans, scholarships/grants, and unspecified assistantships available. Support available to part-time students. *Unit head:* Dr. Karen Stinson, Director, 608-342-1131, Fax: 608-342-1133. *Application contact:* Lisa Popp, School of Graduate Studies, 608-342-1322, Fax: 608-342-1389, E-mail: poppl@uwplatt.edu.

University of Wisconsin–Whitewater, School of Graduate Studies, College of Business and Economics, Department of Business Education, Whitewater, WI 53190-1790. Offers general business education (MS); post-secondary business education (MS); secondary business education (MS). *Accreditation:* NCATE. Part-time and evening/weekend programs available. Postbaccalaureate distance learning degree programs offered (no on-campus study). *Degree requirements:* For master's, thesis or alternative. *Entrance requirements:* For master's, interview, teaching license. Additional exam requirements/recommendations for international students: Required—TOEFL (minimum score 550 paper-based; 213 computer-based). Electronic applications accepted. *Faculty research:* Active learning and performance strategies, technology-enhanced formative assessment, computer-supported cooperative work, privacy surveillance.

Utah State University, School of Graduate Studies, College of Education and Human Services, Department of Secondary Education, Logan, UT 84322. Offers M Ed, MA, MS. Part-time and evening/weekend programs available. *Degree requirements:* For master's, thesis (for some programs). *Entrance requirements:* For master's, GRE General Test or MAT, minimum GPA of 3.0, 1 year teaching, teaching license, letters of recommendation. Additional exam requirements/recommendations for international students: Required—TOEFL. Electronic applications accepted. *Faculty research:* Character education, science education, reading/writing skills, mathematics education, pre-service teacher education.

Valdosta State University, Graduate School, Department of Middle, Secondary, Reading and Deaf Education, Valdosta, GA 31698. Offers middle grades education (M Ed, Ed S); secondary education (M Ed, Ed S). *Accreditation:* NCATE. Part-time and evening/weekend programs available. *Degree requirements:* For master's, thesis (for some programs), comprehensive written and/or oral exams; for Ed S, thesis. *Entrance requirements:* For master's, GRE General Test or MAT, minimum GPA of 2.5; for Ed S, GRE General Test or MAT, minimum GPA of 3.0. Additional exam requirements/recommendations for international students: Required—TOEFL (minimum score 523 paper-based; 193 computer-based). Electronic applications accepted. *Faculty research:* Distance education, learning styles, alternative assessment methods, interactive teaching strategies, learning styles of pre-service teachers.

Vanderbilt University, Peabody College, Department of Teaching and Learning, Nashville, TN 37240-1001. Offers elementary education (M Ed); English language learners (M Ed); learning and instruction (M Ed); learning, diversity, and urban studies (M Ed); reading education (M Ed); secondary education (M Ed). *Accreditation:* NCATE. *Faculty:* 31 full-time (20 women), 23 part-time/adjunct (20 women). *Students:* 95 full-time (88 women), 21 part-time (6 women); includes 14 minority (6 African Americans, 4 Asian Americans or Pacific Islanders, 4 Hispanic Americans), 5 international. Average age 27. 150 applicants, 69% accepted, 59 enrolled. In 2009, 74 master's awarded. *Degree requirements:* For master's, comprehensive exam, thesis optional. *Entrance requirements:* For master's, GRE General Test, MAT. Additional exam requirements/recommendations for international students: Required—TOEFL (minimum score 550 paper-based; 213 computer-based). *Application deadline:* For fall admission, 12/31 priority date for domestic and international students; for spring admission, 11/1 priority date for domestic and international students. Applications are processed on a rolling basis. Application fee: $0. Electronic applications accepted. *Financial support:* In 2009–10, 104 students received support, including 27 research assistantships with full and partial tuition reimbursements available; fellowships with full and partial tuition reimbursements available, teaching assistantships with full and partial tuition reimbursements available, Federal Work-Study, institutionally sponsored loans, scholarships/grants, tuition waivers (partial), and unspecified assistantships also available. Support available to part-time students. Financial award application deadline: 2/1; financial award applicants required to submit FAFSA. *Faculty research:* Teaching and learning, development of mathematical and scientific knowledge, interventions to foster early literacy and numeracy, reading and writing in the digital age, teaching diverse learners. *Unit head:* Dr. David Dickinson, Acting Chair, 615-322-8100, Fax: 615-322-8999, E-mail: david.k.dickinson@vanderbilt.edu. *Application contact:* Angela Saylor, Educational Coordinator, 615-322-8092, Fax: 615-322-8999, E-mail: angela.saylor@vanderbilt.edu.

Villanova University, Graduate School of Liberal Arts and Sciences, Department of Education and Human Services, Program in Secondary Teacher Education, Villanova, PA 19085-1699. Offers MA. Part-time and evening/weekend programs available. *Students:* 15 full-time (10 women), 17 part-time (10 women); includes 1 minority (Asian American or Pacific Islander). Average age 30. In 2009, 21 master's awarded. *Degree requirements:* For master's, comprehensive exam. *Entrance requirements:* For master's, GRE or MAT, minimum GPA of 3.0. *Application deadline:* For fall admission, 3/1 priority date for domestic students; for spring admission, 11/15 for domestic students. Applications are processed on a rolling basis. Application fee: $50. Electronic applications accepted. *Expenses:* Tuition: Part-time $630 per credit. Required fees: $60 per credit. Part-time tuition and fees vary according to degree level and program. *Financial support:* Career-related internships or fieldwork and Federal Work-Study available. Financial award applicants required to submit FAFSA. *Unit head:* Dr. Connie Titone, Coordinator, 610-519-4620. *Application contact:* Dr. Connie Titone, Coordinator, 610-519-4620.

Virginia Commonwealth University, Graduate School, School of Education, Program in Teaching and Learning, Richmond, VA 23284-9005. Offers early education (MT); middle education (MT); secondary education (MT, Certificate); special education (MT). *Accreditation:* NCATE. Part-time programs available. *Entrance requirements:* For master's, GRE General Test or MAT.

Wagner College, Division of Graduate Studies, Department of Education, Program in Adolescent Education, Staten Island, NY 10301-4495. Offers MS Ed. Part-time and evening/weekend programs available. *Entrance requirements:* For master's, Liberal Arts and Sciences Test (LAST), New York State Teacher Certification Examinations (NYSTCE), minimum GPA of 2.75. Additional exam requirements/recommendations for international students: Required—TOEFL (minimum score 550 paper-based; 217 computer-based). *Expenses:* Tuition: Full-time $15,570; part-time $865 per credit. Required fees: $2.

Wake Forest University, Graduate School of Arts and Sciences, Department of Education, Winston-Salem, NC 27109. Offers secondary education (MA Ed). *Accreditation:* ACA; NCATE. Part-time programs available. *Faculty:* 11 full-time (7 women), 8 part-time/adjunct (6 women). *Students:* 23 full-time (16 women), 26 part-time (21 women); includes 25 minority (11 African Americans, 2 Asian Americans or Pacific Islanders, 12 Hispanic Americans). Average age 28. 61 applicants, 52% accepted, 27 enrolled. In 2009, 32 master's awarded. *Degree requirements:* For master's, thesis optional. *Entrance requirements:* For master's, GRE General Test. Additional exam requirements/recommendations for international students: Required—TOEFL (minimum score 550 paper-based; 213 computer-based). *Application deadline:* For fall admission, 1/15 for domestic students, 1/15 priority date for international students. Application fee: $45 ($55 for international students). Electronic applications accepted. *Expenses:* Contact institution. *Financial support:* In 2009–10, 23 students received support, including 23 fellowships with full tuition reimbursements available (averaging $6,000 per year); teaching assistantships with full tuition reimbursements available, scholarships/grants and tuition waivers (full) also available. Support available to part-time students. Financial award application deadline: 2/15. *Faculty research:* Teaching and learning. *Unit head:* Dr. MaryLynn Redmond, Chair, 336-758-5341, Fax: 336-758-4591, E-mail: redmond@wfu.edu. *Application contact:* Dr. Leah McCoy, Program Director, 336-758-5998, Fax: 336-758-4591, E-mail: mccoy@wfu.edu.

Washington State University, Graduate School, College of Education, Department of Teaching and Learning, Pullman, WA 99164. Offers curriculum and instruction (Ed D, PhD); diverse languages (M Ed, MA); elementary education (M Ed, MA, MIT); exercise science (MS); literacy education (M Ed, MA, PhD); math education (PhD); secondary education (M Ed, MA). *Accreditation:* NCATE. *Degree requirements:* For master's, comprehensive exam (for some programs), thesis (for some programs), oral or written exam; for doctorate, comprehensive exam, thesis/dissertation, oral, written exam. *Entrance requirements:* For master's and doctorate, GRE General Test, minimum GPA of 3.0, 3 letters of recommendation. Additional exam requirements/recommendations for international students: Required—TOEFL. *Faculty research:* Evolution of middle school education issues in special education, computer-assisted language learning.

Washington State University Tri-Cities, Graduate Programs, Program in Education, Richland, WA 99354. Offers counseling (Ed M); educational leadership (Ed M, Ed D); literacy (Ed M); secondary certification (Ed M); teaching (MIT). Part-time programs available. *Faculty:* 24. *Students:* 11 full-time (8 women), 97 part-time (80 women); includes 17 minority (1 African American, 3 Asian Americans or Pacific Islanders, 13 Hispanic Americans). Average age 36. In 2009, 39 master's awarded. *Degree requirements:* For master's, comprehensive exam, thesis or alternative; for doctorate, comprehensive exam, thesis/dissertation. *Entrance requirements:* For master's, GRE, minimum GPA of 3.0, Working with Youth form, Character and Fitness form, 3 letters of recommendation. Additional exam requirements/recommendations for international students: Required—TOEFL. *Application deadline:* For fall admission, 1/10 priority date for domestic students, 1/10 for international students; for spring admission, 7/1 priority date for domestic students, 7/1 for international students. Applications are processed on a rolling basis. Application fee: $50. Electronic applications accepted. *Expenses:* Tuition, state resident: part-time $423 per credit. Tuition, nonresident: part-time $1032 per credit. *Financial support:* In 2009–10, 59 students received support, including research assistantships (averaging $14,634 per year), teaching assistantships (averaging $13,383 per year); Federal Work-Study, scholarships/grants, and unspecified assistantships also available. Financial award application deadline: 2/15. *Faculty research:* Multicultural counseling, socio-cultural influences in schools, diverse learners, teacher education, K-12 educational leadership. *Unit head:* Dr. Elizabeth Nagel, Director, 509-372-7398, E-mail: elizabeth_nagel@tricity.wsu.edu. *Application contact:* Helen Berry, Academic Coordinator, 800-GRADWSU, Fax: 509-372-3796, E-mail: hberry@tricity.wsu.edu.

Washington University in St. Louis, Graduate School of Arts and Sciences, Department of Education, Program in Secondary Education, St. Louis, MO 63130-4899. Offers MA Ed, MAT. *Degree requirements:* For master's, thesis or alternative. *Entrance requirements:* For master's, GRE General Test or MAT. Electronic applications accepted.

Wayne State University, College of Education, Division of Administrative and Organizational Studies, Detroit, MI 48202. Offers administration and supervision-secondary (Ed S); college and university teaching (Certificate); curriculum and instruction (PhD); educational leadership (M Ed, Ed S); educational leadership and policy studies (Ed D, PhD); elementary education curriculum and instruction (MA, Ed S); general administration and supervision (Ed D, PhD, Ed S); higher education (Ed D, PhD); instructional technology (M Ed, Ed D, PhD, Ed S); secondary curriculum and instruction (M Ed, Ed S). *Degree requirements:* For doctorate, thesis/dissertation. *Entrance requirements:* For doctorate, interview, minimum GPA of 3.0, an autobiography or curriculum vitae; references. Additional exam requirements/recommendations for international students: Required—TOEFL (minimum score 550 paper-based; 213 computer-based), TWE (minimum score 6). Electronic applications accepted. *Faculty research:* Total quality management, participatory management, administering educational technology, school improvement, principalship.

Wayne State University, College of Education, Division of Teacher Education, Detroit, MI 48202. Offers adult and continuing education (M Ed); art education (M Ed); bilingual/bicultural education (M Ed, MAT); business education (M Ed, MAT); career and technical education (M Ed, Ed D, PhD, Ed S); curriculum and instruction (Ed D, PhD, Ed S); distributive education

(M Ed, MAT); early childhood education (M Ed); elementary education (M Ed, MAT, Ed D, PhD, Ed S); elementary education curriculum and instruction (M Ed); English education (M Ed); English education-secondary (M Ed, Ed S); foreign language education (M Ed); general education (Ed D, Ed S); health occupations education (M Ed); industrial education (M Ed); mathematics education (M Ed, Ed S); pre-school and parent education (M Ed); reading (M Ed, Ed D, Ed S); reading, languages and literature (Ed D); school music-vocal (M Ed); science education (M Ed, MAT, Ed S); secondary education (MAT); secondary school reading (M Ed); social studies education (M Ed, Ed S), including education-secondary (M Ed); special education (M Ed, Ed D, PhD, Ed S); teacher education (MAT, Ed D, PhD). *Degree requirements:* For doctorate, thesis/dissertation. *Entrance requirements:* For master's, Michigan Basic Skills Test (MA in teaching), minimum GPA of 2.6; for doctorate, minimum undergraduate GPA of 3.0, graduate 3.5; interview, curriculum vitae; references. Additional exam requirements/recommendations for international students: Required—TOEFL (minimum score 550 paper-based; 213 computer-based), TWE (minimum score 6). Electronic applications accepted. *Faculty research:* Reading and writing literacy and literature.

West Chester University of Pennsylvania, Office of Graduate Studies, College of Education, Department of Professional and Secondary Education, West Chester, PA 19383. Offers education for sustainability (Certificate); entrepreneurial education (Certificate); secondary education (M Ed, Teaching Certificate); teaching and learning with technology (Certificate). Part-time and evening/weekend programs available. *Students:* 4 full-time (3 women), 39 part-time (27 women); includes 2 minority (both Asian Americans or Pacific Islanders). Average age 30. 33 applicants, 97% accepted, 16 enrolled. In 2009, 13 master's, 3 Certificates awarded. *Degree requirements:* For master's, comprehensive exam, thesis (for some programs). *Entrance requirements:* For master's, GRE or MAT, teaching certificate. Additional exam requirements/recommendations for international students: Required—TOEFL (minimum score 550 paper-based; 213 computer-based; 80 iBT). *Application deadline:* For fall admission, 4/15 priority date for domestic students, 3/15 for international students; for spring admission, 10/15 priority date for domestic students, 9/1 for international students. Applications are processed on a rolling basis. Application fee: $35. Electronic applications accepted. *Expenses:* Tuition, state resident: full-time $6666; part-time $370 per credit. Tuition, nonresident: full-time $10,666; part-time $593 per credit. Required fees: $122.56 per credit. *Financial support:* In 2009–10, research assistantships with full and partial tuition reimbursements (averaging $5,000 per year); unspecified assistantships also available. Support available to part-time students. Financial award application deadline: 2/15; financial award applicants required to submit FAFSA. *Faculty research:* Technology integration: preparing our teachers for the twenty-first century. *Unit head:* Dr. John Kinslow, Chair, 610-436-3108, E-mail: jkinslow@wcupa.edu. *Application contact:* Dr. Cynthia Haggard, Graduate Coordinator, 610-436-6934, E-mail: chaggard@wcupa.edu.

Western Connecticut State University, Division of Graduate Studies, School of Professional Studies, Department of Education and Educational Psychology, Program in Secondary Education, Danbury, CT 06810-6885. Offers biology option (MAT); mathematics option (MAT). Part-time programs available. *Students:* 18 full-time (9 women), 1 part-time (0 women); includes 1 African American. Average age 34. 30 applicants, 73% accepted, 19 enrolled. *Entrance requirements:* For master's, PRAXIS I Pre_Professional Skills Tests, PRAXIS II subject assessment(s), minimum combined undergraduate GPA of 2.8 or score rated at 35th percentile or higher on MAT. Additional exam requirements/recommendations for international students: Recommended—TOEFL (minimum score 550 paper-based; 213 computer-based; 79 iBT), IELTS (minimum score 6). *Application deadline:* For fall admission, 8/5 priority date for domestic students; for spring admission, 1/5 priority date for domestic students. Application fee: $50. *Expenses:* Tuition, state resident: full-time $5012; part-time $278 per credit hour. Tuition, nonresident: full-time $13,962; part-time $284 per credit hour. Required fees: $3886; $139 per credit hour. Full-time tuition and fees vary according to course load and program. Part-time tuition and fees vary according to course level, degree level and program. *Financial support:* Application deadline: 5/1. *Unit head:* Dr. Theresa Canada, Chairperson, Department of Education and Educational Psychology. *Application contact:* Chris Shankle, Associate Director of Graduate Studies, 203-837-9005, Fax: 203-837-8326, E-mail: shanklec@wcsu.edu.

Western Kentucky University, Graduate Studies, College of Education and Behavioral Sciences, Department of Counseling and Student Affairs, Bowling Green, KY 42101. Offers business and marketing education (MA Ed); counseling (MA Ed); counselor education (Ed S); education and behavioral science (MA Ed); elementary education (MA Ed, Ed S); middle years education (MA Ed); secondary education (MA Ed, Ed S); student affairs (MA Ed). *Accreditation:* ACA; NCATE. Part-time and evening/weekend programs available. *Degree requirements:* For master's, comprehensive exam, thesis optional. *Entrance requirements:* For master's, GRE General Test. Additional exam requirements/recommendations for international students: Required—TOEFL (minimum score 555 paper-based; 213 computer-based; 79 iBT). *Expenses:* Tuition, state resident: full-time $4160; part-time $416 per credit hour. Tuition, nonresident: full-time $9550; part-time $506 per credit hour. Tuition and fees vary according to campus/location and reciprocity agreements. *Faculty research:* Counselor education, research for residential workers.

Western Kentucky University, Graduate Studies, College of Education and Behavioral Sciences, Department of Curriculum and Instruction, Bowling Green, KY 42101. Offers business and marketing education (MAE); elementary education (MAE, Ed S); middle grades education (MAE); secondary education (MAE, Ed S). *Degree requirements:* For master's, comprehensive exam; for Ed S, thesis. *Entrance requirements:* For master's, GRE. Additional exam requirements/recommendations for international students: Required—TOEFL (minimum score 555 paper-based; 213 computer-based; 79 iBT). *Expenses:* Tuition, state resident: full-time $4160; part-time $416 per credit hour. Tuition, nonresident: full-time $9550; part-time $506 per credit hour. Tuition and fees vary according to campus/location and reciprocity agreements.

Western New Mexico University, Graduate Division, School of Education, Silver City, NM 88062-0680. Offers bilingual education (MAT); counseling (MA); educational leadership (MA); elementary education (MAT); reading (MAT); school psychology (MA); secondary education (MAT); special education (MAT); TESOL (teaching English to speakers of other languages) (MAT). *Accreditation:* NCATE. *Degree requirements:* For master's, comprehensive exam. *Entrance requirements:* For master's, GRE General Test, GRE Subject Test, minimum GPA of 3.2 in last 64 hours of undergraduate study. Additional exam requirements/recommendations for international students: Required—TOEFL (minimum score 550 paper-based; 213 computer-based). Electronic applications accepted.

Western Oregon University, Graduate Programs, College of Education, Division of Teacher Education, Program in Secondary Education, Monmouth, OR 97361-1394. Offers bilingual education (MS Ed); health (MS Ed); humanities (MAT, MS Ed); initial licensure (MAT); mathematics (MAT, MS Ed); science (MAT, MS Ed); social science (MAT, MS Ed). *Accreditation:* NCATE. Part-time and evening/weekend programs available. *Degree requirements:* For master's, thesis optional, written exam. *Entrance requirements:* For master's, minimum GPA of 3.0, teaching license. Additional exam requirements/recommendations for international students: Required—TOEFL (minimum score 550 paper-based; 213 computer-based; 79 iBT), IELTS (minimum score 6.5). *Faculty research:* Literacy, science in primary grades, geography education, retention, teacher burnout.

Western Washington University, Graduate School, Woodring College of Education, Department of Secondary Education, Bellingham, WA 98225-5996. Offers MIT. *Accreditation:* NCATE. Part-time programs available. *Degree requirements:* For master's, comprehensive exam, thesis optional. *Entrance requirements:* For master's, GRE General Test or MAT, minimum GPA of 3.0 in last 60 semester hours or last 90 quarter hours, secondary teaching certification. Additional exam requirements/recommendations for international students: Required—TOEFL (minimum score 567 paper-based; 227 computer-based). Electronic applications accepted. *Faculty research:* Service learning, controversial issues in classroom, trauma-sensitive teaching-learning, measuring a teacher's 'withitness".

Westfield State College, Division of Graduate and Continuing Education, Department of Education, Program in Secondary Education, Westfield, MA 01086. Offers M Ed. *Accreditation:*

NCATE. Part-time and evening/weekend programs available. *Degree requirements:* For master's, comprehensive exam, practicum. *Entrance requirements:* For master's, GRE General Test or MAT, minimum undergraduate GPA of 2.7.

West Virginia University, College of Human Resources and Education, Department of Curriculum and Instruction-Literacy, Program in Secondary Education, Morgantown, WV 26506. Offers higher education curriculum and teaching (MA); secondary education (MA). Students enter program as undergraduates. *Accreditation:* NCATE. Part-time programs available. *Degree requirements:* For master's, thesis optional, content exams. *Entrance requirements:* For master's, minimum GPA of 2.75. Additional exam requirements/recommendations for international students: Required—TOEFL. Electronic applications accepted. *Faculty research:* Teacher education, school reform, curriculum development, education technology.

West Virginia University, Eberly College of Arts and Sciences, Department of Mathematics, Morgantown, WV 26506. Offers applied mathematics (MS, PhD); discrete mathematics (PhD); interdisciplinary mathematics (MS); mathematics for secondary education (MS); pure mathematics (MS). Part-time programs available. Terminal master's awarded for partial completion of doctoral program. *Degree requirements:* For master's, comprehensive exam (for some programs), thesis optional; for doctorate, one foreign language, comprehensive exam, thesis/dissertation. *Entrance requirements:* For master's, GRE Subject Test (recommended), minimum GPA of 2.5; for doctorate, GRE Subject Test (recommended), master's degree in mathematics. Additional exam requirements/recommendations for international students: Required—TOEFL (paper-based 550; computer-based 213) or IELTS (paper-based 6). *Faculty research:* Combinatorics and graph theory, differential equations, applied and computational mathematics.

Wheaton College, Graduate School, Department of Education, Wheaton, IL 60187-5593. Offers elementary level (MAT); secondary level (MAT). *Accreditation:* NCATE. *Degree requirements:* For master's, thesis or alternative. *Entrance requirements:* For master's, GRE General Test. Electronic applications accepted.

Whittier College, Graduate Programs, Department of Education and Child Development, Program in Secondary Education, Whittier, CA 90608-0634. Offers MA Ed. Part-time and evening/weekend programs available. *Degree requirements:* For master's, thesis. *Entrance requirements:* For master's, GRE General Test, MAT.

Whitworth University, School of Education, Graduate Studies in Education, Spokane, WA 99251-0001. Offers administration (M Ed); counseling (M Ed), including school counselors, social agency/church setting; elementary education (M Ed); gifted and talented (MAT); secondary education (M Ed); special education (MAT); teaching (MIT). *Accreditation:* NCATE. Part-time and evening/weekend programs available. *Degree requirements:* For master's, comprehensive exam, thesis (for some programs). *Entrance requirements:* For master's, GRE General Test, MAT. Additional exam requirements/recommendations for international students: Required—TOEFL. Tuition and fees vary according to program. *Faculty research:* Rural program development, mainstreaming, special needs learners.

Wilkes University, College of Graduate and Professional Studies, School of Education, Wilkes-Barre, PA 18766-0002. Offers classroom technology (MS Ed); educational computing (MS Ed); educational development and strategies (MS Ed); educational leadership (MS Ed); educational technology (Ed D); elementary education (MS Ed); higher education administration (Ed D); instructional technology (MS Ed); K-12 administration (Ed D); online teaching (MS Ed); school business leadership (MS Ed); secondary education (MS Ed), including biology, chemistry, English, history; special education (MS Ed). Part-time and evening/weekend programs available. Postbaccalaureate distance learning degree programs offered (minimal on-campus study). *Students:* 89 full-time (60 women), 2,849 part-time (2,058 women); includes 52 minority (10 African Americans, 2 American Indian/Alaska Native, 13 Asian Americans or Pacific Islanders, 27 Hispanic Americans), 6 international. Average age 33. In 2009, 947 master's awarded. *Entrance requirements:* Additional exam requirements/recommendations for international students: Required—TOEFL (minimum score 500 paper-based; 173 computer-based; 79 iBT). *Application deadline:* Applications are processed on a rolling basis. Application fee: $45. *Expenses:* Contact institution. *Financial support:* Federal Work-Study and unspecified assistantships available. Financial award application deadline: 3/1; financial award applicants required to submit FAFSA. *Unit head:* Dr. Michael Speziale, Dean, 570-408-4679, Fax: 570-408-4905, E-mail: michael.speziale@wilkes.edu. *Application contact:* Kathleen Houlihan, Director of Graduate Studies, 570-408-3235, Fax: 570-408-7846, E-mail: kathleen.houlihan@wilkes.edu.

William Carey University, School of Education, Hattiesburg, MS 39401-5499. Offers art education (M Ed); art of teaching (M Ed); elementary education (M Ed, Ed S); English education (M Ed); gifted education (M Ed); history and social science (M Ed); mild/moderate disabilities (M Ed); secondary education (M Ed). Part-time programs available. *Degree requirements:* For master's, comprehensive exam. *Entrance requirements:* For master's, GRE, MAT, minimum GPA of 2.5, Class A teacher's license. Additional exam requirements/recommendations for international students: Required—TOEFL (minimum score 550 paper-based; 213 computer-based).

William Woods University, Graduate and Adult Studies, Fulton, MO 65251-1098. Offers administration (Ed S); agriculture (MBA); athletic/activities administration (M Ed); curriculum and instruction (M Ed); curriculum leadership (Ed S); elementary administration (M Ed); health management (MBA); human resources (MBA); principalship (Ed S); secondary administration (M Ed); special education director (M Ed). Evening/weekend programs available. *Degree requirements:* For master's, capstone course (MBA), action research (M Ed); for Ed S, field experience. *Entrance requirements:* For master's, 2 recommendations, resumé, BA/BS; teaching certification (M Ed); course work in economics and accounting (MBA); for Ed S, M Ed, 2 letters of recommendation, resume, teaching certification. Additional exam requirements/recommendations for international students: Required—TOEFL (minimum score 550 paper-based). Electronic applications accepted.

Wilmington University, College of Education, New Castle, DE 19720-6491. Offers applied education technology (M Ed); career and technical education (M Ed); elementary and secondary school counseling (M Ed); elementary special education (M Ed); elementary studies (M Ed); instruction: gifted and talented (M Ed); instruction: teaching and learning (M Ed); literacy (M Ed); reading (M Ed); school leadership (M Ed); secondary teaching (MAT). *Accreditation:* NCATE. Part-time and evening/weekend programs available. *Entrance requirements:* For master's, 2 letters of recommendation, interview. Additional exam requirements/recommendations for international students: Required—TOEFL (minimum score 500 paper-based; 173 computer-based). Electronic applications accepted.

Wilson College, Program in Education, Chambersburg, PA 17201-1285. Offers M Ed. Evening/weekend programs available. *Degree requirements:* For master's, project. *Entrance requirements:* For master's, PRAXIS, minimum undergraduate cumulative GPA of 3.0, 2 letters of recommendation, current certification for eligibility to teach in grades K-12, resume, personal interview. Electronic applications accepted.

Winthrop University, College of Education, Program in Secondary Education, Rock Hill, SC 29733. Offers M Ed, MAT. *Accreditation:* NCATE. Part-time programs available. *Entrance requirements:* For master's, PRAXIS, minimum GPA of 3.0, South Carolina Class III Teaching Certificate. Electronic applications accepted.

Worcester State College, Graduate Studies, Department of Education, Program in Secondary Education, Worcester, MA 01602-2597. Offers M Ed. Part-time programs available. *Faculty:* 9 full-time (7 women), 19 part-time/adjunct (7 women). *Students:* 6 full-time (4 women), 68 part-time (49 women); includes 6 minority (1 African American, 1 Asian American or Pacific Islander, 4 Hispanic Americans), 2 international. Average age 32. 61 applicants, 74% accepted, 23 enrolled. In 2009, 18 master's awarded. *Degree requirements:* For master's, comprehensive exam (for some programs), thesis optional. *Entrance requirements:* For master's, GRE General Test or MAT. Additional exam requirements/recommendations for international students: Required—TOEFL (minimum score 550 paper-based; 213 computer-based; 79 iBT). *Application*

Secondary Education

Worcester State College *(continued)*
deadline: Applications are processed on a rolling basis. Application fee: $30. *Expenses:* Tuition, area resident: Part-time $150 per credit. Tuition, state resident: part-time $150 per credit. Tuition, nonresident: part-time $150 per credit. Required fees: $85. *Financial support:* Career-related internships or fieldwork, scholarships/grants, and unspecified assistantships available. Financial award application deadline: 3/1; financial award applicants required to submit FAFSA. *Unit head:* Dr. Caroline Chiccarelli, Coordinator, 508-929-8967, Fax: 508-929-8164, E-mail: cchiccarelli@worcester.edu. *Application contact:* Nicole Brown, Assistant Dean of Continuing Education, 508-929-8787, Fax: 508-929-8100, E-mail: nbrown@worcester.edu.

Wright State University, School of Graduate Studies, College of Education and Human Services, Department of Teacher Education, Programs in Classroom Teacher Education, Dayton, OH 45435. Offers M Ed, MA. *Accreditation:* NCATE. *Degree requirements:* For master's, thesis (for some programs). *Entrance requirements:* For master's, GRE General Test, MAT, PRAXIS II. Additional exam requirements/recommendations for international students: Required—TOEFL.

Xavier University, College of Social Sciences, Health and Education, School of Education, Department of Secondary and Special Education, Program in Secondary Education, Cincinnati, OH 45207. Offers M Ed. Part-time and evening/weekend programs available. *Faculty:* 3 full-time (0 women), 2 part-time/adjunct (both women). *Students:* 87 full-time (56 women), 95 part-time (54 women); includes 16 minority (11 African Americans, 1 American Indian/Alaska Native, 2 Asian Americans or Pacific Islanders, 2 Hispanic Americans), 3 international. Average age 31. 61 applicants, 89% accepted, 41 enrolled. In 2009, 57 master's awarded. *Degree requirements:* For master's, comprehensive exam, thesis. *Entrance requirements:* For master's, MAT. *Expenses:* Tuition: Part-time $697 per credit hour. One-time fee: $35 part-time. *Financial support:* In 2009–10, 98 students received support. Applicants required to submit FAFSA. *Unit head:* Dr. Michael Flick, Chair, Department of Secondary and Special Education, 513-745-3225, Fax: 513-745-3410, E-mail: flick@xavier.edu. *Application contact:* Jeff Hutton, Director, 513-745-3702, Fax: 513-745-3225, E-mail: hutton@xavier.edu.

Youngstown State University, Graduate School, Beeghly College of Education, Department of Teacher Education, Program in Middle Childhood Education, Youngstown, OH 44555-0001. Offers MS Ed. *Accreditation:* NCATE. Part-time and evening/weekend programs available. *Degree requirements:* For master's, comprehensive exam, thesis optional. *Entrance requirements:* For master's, GRE, MAT, or teaching certificate; minimum GPA of 2.7. Additional exam requirements/recommendations for international students: Required—TOEFL. *Faculty research:* Critical reflectivity, gender issues in classroom instruction, collaborative research and analysis, literacy methodology.

Section 25
Special Focus

This section contains a directory of institutions offering graduate work in special focus, followed by in-depth entries submitted by institutions that chose to prepare detailed program descriptions. Additional information about programs listed in the directory but not augmented by an in-depth entry may be obtained by writing directly to the dean of a graduate school or chair of a department at the address given in the directory.

For programs offering related work, see also in this book *Administration, Instruction, and Theory; Education; Health-Related Professions; Instructional Levels; Leisure Studies and Recreation; Physical Education and Kinesiology;* and *Subject Areas.* In another guide in this series:

Graduate Programs in the Humanities, Arts & Social Sciences
See *Psychology and Counseling (School Psychology)* and *Public, Regional, and Industrial Affairs (Urban Studies)*

CONTENTS

Program Directories

Close-Ups

Education of Students with Severe/Multiple Disabilities

Cleveland State University, College of Graduate Studies, College of Education and Human Services, Department of Teacher Education, Cleveland, OH 44115. Offers art education (M Ed); early childhood education (M Ed); foreign language education (M Ed); mathematics and science education (M Ed); middle childhood education (M Ed); special education (M Ed), including mild/moderate disabilities, moderate/intensive disabilities; teaching English to speakers of other languages (M Ed). Part-time and evening/weekend programs available. *Degree requirements:* For master's, comprehensive exam (for some programs), thesis or alternative. *Entrance requirements:* For master's, GRE General Test or MAT, minimum GPA of 2.75. Additional exam requirements/recommendations for international students: Required—TOEFL (minimum score 525 paper-based; 197 computer-based), IELTS (minimum score 6). *Faculty research:* Early literacy, professional development in reading, reading recovery, dual language, induction programs.

Fresno Pacific University, Graduate Programs, School of Education, Division of Special Education, Fresno, CA 93702-4709. Offers mild/moderate (MA Ed); moderate/severe (MA Ed); physical and health impairments (MA Ed). Part-time and evening/weekend programs available. *Degree requirements:* For master's, thesis or alternative. *Entrance requirements:* Additional exam requirements/recommendations for international students: Required—TOEFL (minimum score 550 paper-based; 213 computer-based).

Gallaudet University, The Graduate School, Department of Education, Washington, DC 20002-3625. Offers early childhood education (MA, Ed S); education of deaf and hard of hearing students and multihandicapped deaf and hard of hearing students (MA, Ed S); elementary education (MA, Ed S); individualized program of study (PhD); parent/infant specialty (MA, Ed S); secondary education (MA, Ed S). *Accreditation:* NCATE. *Degree requirements:* For master's, thesis optional; for doctorate, thesis/dissertation. *Entrance requirements:* For doctorate, GRE General Test or MAT, interview. Electronic applications accepted.

Georgia State University, College of Education, Department of Educational Psychology and Special Education, Program in Multiple and Severe Disabilities, Atlanta, GA 30302-3083. Offers M Ed, MAT. *Accreditation:* NCATE. *Degree requirements:* For master's, comprehensive exam. *Entrance requirements:* For master's, GRE General Test, minimum GPA of 2.5. *Faculty research:* Cognition, discipline, curriculum development, social maladjustment.

Hunter College of the City University of New York, Graduate School, School of Education, Department of Special Education, New York, NY 10021-5085. Offers blind or visually impaired (MS Ed); deaf or hard of hearing (MS Ed); severe/multiple disabilities (MS Ed); special education (MS Ed). *Accreditation:* NCATE. *Faculty:* 13 full-time (5 women), 12 part-time/adjunct (5 women). *Students:* 107 full-time (99 women), 541 part-time (478 women); includes 133 minority (37 African Americans, 1 American Indian/Alaska Native, 23 Asian Americans or Pacific Islanders, 72 Hispanic Americans). Average age 28. 344 applicants, 66% accepted, 151 enrolled. In 2009, 138 master's awarded. *Degree requirements:* For master's, comprehensive exam, thesis, student teaching practica and clinical teaching lab courses, New York State Teacher Certification exams. *Entrance requirements:* For master's, minimum GPA of 2.8. Additional exam requirements/recommendations for international students: Required—TOEFL, TWE. *Application deadline:* For fall admission, 4/1 for domestic students, 2/1 for international students; for spring admission, 11/1 for domestic students, 9/1 for international students. Applications are processed on a rolling basis. Application fee: $50. *Expenses:* Tuition, state resident: full-time $7360; part-time $310 per credit. Required fees: $250 per semester. *Financial support:* Career-related internships or fieldwork, Federal Work-Study, institutionally sponsored loans, and tuition waivers (partial) available. Support available to part-time students. *Faculty research:* Mathematics learning disabilities; street behavior; assessment; bilingual special education; families, diversity, and disabilities. *Unit head:* Dr. Kate Garnett, Chairperson, 212-772-4700, E-mail: kgarnett@hunter.cuny.edu. *Application contact:* William Zlata, Director for Graduate Admissions, 212-772-4482, Fax: 212-650-3336, E-mail: admissions@hunter.cuny.edu.

Minot State University, Graduate School, Program in Special Education, Minot, ND 58707-0002. Offers education of the deaf (MS); learning disabilities (MS); special education strategist (MS), including early childhood special education, severe multiple handicaps. *Accreditation:* NCATE. *Degree requirements:* For master's, comprehensive exam (for some programs), thesis (for some programs). *Entrance requirements:* For master's, GRE General Test or minimum GPA of 3.0. Additional exam requirements/recommendations for international students: Required—TOEFL. *Expenses:* Tuition, state resident: full-time $5720; part-time $283 per credit hour. Tuition, nonresident: full-time $5720; part-time $283 per credit hour. Required fees: $1034; $1034 per year. Tuition and fees vary according to course load, degree level and program. *Faculty research:* Special education team diagnostic unit; individual diagnostic assessments of mentally retarded, learning-disabled, hearing-impaired, and speech-impaired youth; educational programming for the hearing impaired.

Montclair State University, The Graduate School, College of Education and Human Services, Department of Curriculum and Teaching, Montclair, NJ 07043-1624. Offers education (M Ed); educational technology (M Ed); learning disabled teacher consultant (Certificate); school library media specialist (Certificate); teaching (MAT, Certificate), including art (MAT), biological science (MAT), early childhood education (P-3) (MAT), earth science (MAT), elementary education (K-8) (MAT), English (MAT), French (MAT), health and physical education (MAT), health education (MAT), home economics (MAT), mathematics (MAT), music (MAT), physical education (MAT), physical science (MAT), social studies (MAT), Spanish (MAT), teacher of ESL (MAT), teacher of students with disabilities (MAT). Part-time and evening/weekend programs available. *Faculty:* 17 full-time (12 women), 29 part-time/adjunct (21 women). *Students:* 124 full-time (63 women), 174 part-time (126 women). Average age 31. 112 applicants, 69% accepted, 59 enrolled. In 2009, 179 master's, 2 other advanced degrees awarded. *Degree requirements:* For master's, comprehensive exam, field experience. *Entrance requirements:* For master's, GRE, 2 letters of recommendation. Additional exam requirements/recommendations for international students: Required—TOEFL (minimum score 83 computer-based), or IELTS. *Application deadline:* For fall admission, 2/15 for domestic and international students; for spring admission, 9/15 for domestic and international students. Applications are processed on a rolling basis. Application fee: $60. Electronic applications accepted. *Expenses:* Tuition, area resident: Part-time $486.74 per credit. Tuition, state resident: part-time $486.74 per credit. Tuition, nonresident: part-time $751.34 per credit. Tuition and fees vary according to degree level and program. *Financial support:* In 2009–10, 12 research assistantships with full tuition reimbursements (averaging $7,000 per year) were awarded; Federal Work-Study, scholarships/grants, and unspecified assistantships also available. Support available to part-time students. Financial award application deadline: 3/1; financial award applicants required to submit FAFSA. *Unit head:* Dr. David Schwarzer, Chairperson, 973-655-5187. *Application contact:* Amy Aiello, Director of Graduate Admissions and Operations, 973-655-5147, Fax: 973-655-7869, E-mail: graduate.school@montclair.edu.

Norfolk State University, School of Graduate Studies, School of Education, Department of Special Education, Program in Severe Disabilities, Norfolk, VA 23504. Offers MA. *Accreditation:* NCATE. Part-time programs available. *Degree requirements:* For master's, thesis or alternative. *Entrance requirements:* For master's, GRE, minimum GPA of 3.0 in major, 2.5 overall.

Syracuse University, School of Education, Program in Inclusive Special Education: Severe/Multiple Disabilities, Syracuse, NY 13244. Offers MS. Part-time programs available. *Students:* 3 full-time (all women), 3 part-time (all women); includes 1 minority (Asian American or Pacific Islander). Average age 23. 2 applicants, 100% accepted, 1 enrolled. *Entrance requirements:* For master's, provisional/initial certification. Additional exam requirements/recommendations for international students: Required—TOEFL (minimum score 100 iBT). *Application deadline:* For fall admission, 2/1 priority date for domestic and international students; for spring admission, 10/15 priority date for domestic and international students. Applications are processed on a rolling basis. Application fee: $75. Electronic applications accepted. *Expenses:* Tuition: Full-time $26,808; part-time $1117 per credit. Required fees: $1024. *Financial support:* Fellowships with tuition reimbursements, teaching assistantships with tuition reimbursements, tuition waivers (partial) available. Financial award application deadline: 1/1. *Unit head:* Dr. Beth Ferri, Program Coordinator, 315-443-1465, E-mail: baferri@syr.edu. *Application contact:* Liza Rochelson, Graduate Recruiter, School of Education, 315-443-2505, E-mail: e-gradrcrt@syr.edu.

Teachers College, Columbia University, Graduate Faculty of Education, Department of Health and Behavioral Studies, Program in Severe or Multiple Disabilities, New York, NY 10027-6696. Offers Ed M. *Students:* 1 (woman) full-time, 6 part-time (all women); includes 1 minority (African American), 1 international. Average age 25. 9 applicants, 89% accepted, 4 enrolled. In 2009, 3 master's awarded. *Application deadline:* For fall admission, 5/15 for domestic students. Application fee: $65. *Financial support:* Career-related internships or fieldwork, Federal Work-Study, institutionally sponsored loans, and tuition waivers (partial) available. Support available to part-time students. Financial award application deadline: 2/1. *Faculty research:* Reading and spelling disorders, workplace literacy, reading and writing among children and adults. *Unit head:* Dr. Chuck Basch, Chair, 212-678-3964, E-mail: ceb35@columbia.edu. *Application contact:* Director of Admissions, 212-678-3083, Fax: 212-678-4171.

University of Illinois at Urbana–Champaign, Graduate College, College of Education, Department of Special Education, Champaign, IL 61820. Offers Ed M, MS, Ed D, PhD, CAS. Part-time programs available. Postbaccalaureate distance learning degree programs offered (minimal on-campus study). *Faculty:* 12 full-time (8 women), 1 (woman) part-time/adjunct. *Students:* 49 full-time (40 women), 41 part-time (37 women); includes 12 minority (5 African Americans, 4 Asian Americans or Pacific Islanders, 3 Hispanic Americans), 9 international. 69 applicants, 42% accepted, 19 enrolled. In 2009, 21 master's, 3 doctorates, 2 other advanced degrees awarded. *Entrance requirements:* For master's and doctorate, minimum GPA of 3.0. Additional exam requirements/recommendations for international students: Required—TOEFL (minimum score 102 iBT). *Application deadline:* Applications are processed on a rolling basis. Application fee: $60 ($75 for international students). Electronic applications accepted. *Financial support:* In 2009–10, 41 fellowships, 15 research assistantships, 7 teaching assistantships were awarded; tuition waivers (full and partial) also available. *Unit head:* Michaelene Ostrosky, Interim Head, 217-333-0260, Fax: 217-333-6555, E-mail: ostrosky@illinois.edu. *Application contact:* Cheri Karrick, Office Support Assistant, 217-333-0260, Fax: 217-333-6555, E-mail: karrick@illinois.edu.

West Virginia University, College of Human Resources and Education, Department of Special Education, Morgantown, WV 26506. Offers autism spectrum disorder (5-adult) (MA); autism spectrum disorder (K-6) (MA); early intervention/early childhood special education (MA); gifted education (1-12) (MA); low vision (PreK-adult) (MA); multicategorical special education (5-adult) (MA); multicategorical special education (K-6) (MA); severe/multiple disabilities (K-adult) (MA); special education (MA, Ed D); vision impairments (PreK-adult) (MA). *Accreditation:* NCATE. Part-time and evening/weekend programs available. Postbaccalaureate distance learning degree programs offered (no on-campus study). *Degree requirements:* For master's, thesis optional; for doctorate, comprehensive exam, thesis/dissertation. *Entrance requirements:* For master's, minimum GPA of 2.75 passing scores on PRAXIS PPST; for doctorate, GRE General Test or MAT. Additional exam requirements/recommendations for international students: Required—TOEFL.

Education of the Gifted

Arkansas State University—Jonesboro, Graduate School, College of Education, Department of Educational Leadership, Curriculum, and Special Education, Jonesboro, State University, AR 72467. Offers community college administration education (SCCT); curriculum and instruction (MSE); education theory and practice (MSE); educational leadership (MSE, Ed D, Ed S), including curriculum and instruction (MSE, Ed S); special education (MSE), including gifted and talented and creative, instructional specialist 4-12, instructional specialist P-4. *Accreditation:* NCATE. Part-time programs available. Postbaccalaureate distance learning degree programs offered (no on-campus study). *Faculty:* 15 full-time (6 women), 19 part-time/adjunct (11 women). *Students:* 16 full-time (11 women), 734 part-time (606 women); includes 111 minority (96 African Americans, 4 American Indian/Alaska Native, 4 Asian Americans or Pacific Islanders, 7 Hispanic Americans), 2 international. Average age 38. 882 applicants, 70% accepted, 240 enrolled. In 2009, 80 master's, 6 doctorates, 15 other advanced degrees awarded. *Degree requirements:* For master's, comprehensive exam, thesis or alternative; for doctorate, comprehensive exam, thesis/dissertation; for other advanced degree, comprehensive exam. *Entrance requirements:* For master's, GRE General Test or MAT, appropriate bachelor's degree, letters of reference, interview; for doctorate, GRE General Test or MAT, interview, master's degree, letters of reference, official transcript, personal statement, writing sample, immunization records; for other advanced degree, GRE General Test or MAT, interview, master's degree, letters of reference, official transcript, 3 years teaching experience, mentor, teaching license, immunization records. Additional exam requirements/recommendations for international students: Required—TOEFL (minimum score 550 paper-based; 213 computer-based; 79 iBT), IELTS (minimum score 6). *Application deadline:* Applications are processed on a rolling basis. Application fee: $50. Electronic applications accepted. *Expenses:* Tuition, state resident: full-time $3744; part-time $208 per credit hour. Tuition, nonresident: full-time $9540; part-time $530 per credit hour. Required fees: $896; $47 per credit hour. $25 per term. One-time fee: $50. Tuition and fees vary according to course load and program. *Financial support:* In 2009–10, 16 students received support; fellowships, teaching assistantships, career-related internships or fieldwork, scholarships/grants, and unspecified assistantships available. Financial award application deadline: 7/1; financial award applicants required to submit FAFSA. *Unit head:* Dr. Mitchell Holifield, Chair, 870-972-3062, Fax: 870-680-8130, E-mail: hfield@astate.edu. *Application contact:* Dr. Andrew Sustich, Dean of the Graduate School, 870-972-3029, Fax: 870-972-3857, E-mail: sustich@astate.edu.

Barry University, School of Education, Program in Curriculum and Instruction, Miami Shores, FL 33161-6695. Offers accomplished teacher (Ed S); culture, language and literacy (TESOL) (PhD); curriculum evaluation and research (PhD); early childhood (Ed S); early childhood education (PhD); elementary (Ed S); elementary education (PhD); ESOL (Ed S); gifted (Ed S); Montessori (Ed S); PKP/elementary (Ed S); reading (Ed S); reading, language and cognition (PhD). *Entrance requirements:* For doctorate, GRE, minimum GPA of 3.25.

Barry University, School of Education, Program in Exceptional Student Education, Miami Shores, FL 33161-6695. Offers MS, Ed S. Part-time and evening/weekend programs available. *Degree requirements:* For master's, comprehensive exam; for Ed S, practicum. *Entrance requirements:* For master's, GRE General Test or MAT, minimum GPA of 3.0; for Ed S, GRE General Test, minimum GPA of 3.0. Electronic applications accepted.

Barry University, School of Education, Program in Leadership and Education, Miami Shores, FL 33161-6695. Offers educational technology (PhD); exceptional student education (PhD); higher education administration (PhD); human resource development (PhD); leadership (PhD). Part-time and evening/weekend programs available. *Degree requirements:* For doctorate, thesis/dissertation. *Entrance requirements:* For doctorate, GRE General Test, minimum GPA of 3.25. Electronic applications accepted.

Bowling Green State University, Graduate College, College of Education and Human Development, School of Education and Intervention Services, Intervention Services Division, Program in Special Education, Bowling Green, OH 43403. Offers assistive technology (M Ed); early childhood intervention (M Ed); gifted education (M Ed); hearing impaired intervention (M Ed); mild/moderate intervention (M Ed); moderate/intensive intervention (M Ed). *Accreditation:* NCATE. Part-time programs available. *Degree requirements:* For master's, thesis or alternative. *Entrance requirements:* For master's, GRE General Test. Additional exam requirements/recommendations for international students: Required—TOEFL. Electronic applications accepted. *Faculty research:* Reading and special populations, deafness, early childhood, gifted and talented, behavior disorders.

Carlos Albizu University, Miami Campus, Graduate Programs, Miami, FL 33172-2209. Offers clinical psychology (Psy D); entrepreneurship (MBA); exceptional student education (MS); industrial/organizational psychology (MS); marriage and family therapy (MS); mental health counseling (MS); nonprofit management (MBA); organizational management (MBA); psychology (MS); school counseling (MS); teaching English as a second language (MS). *Accreditation:* APA. Part-time and evening/weekend programs available. *Faculty:* 23 full-time (13 women), 41 part-time/adjunct (21 women). *Students:* 529 full-time (420 women), 171 part-time (139 women); includes 551 minority (55 African Americans, 1 American Indian/Alaska Native, 5 Asian Americans or Pacific Islanders, 490 Hispanic Americans). Average age 37. 278 applicants, 57% accepted, 142 enrolled. In 2009, 139 master's, 26 doctorates awarded. Terminal master's awarded for partial completion of doctoral program. *Degree requirements:* For master's, one foreign language, comprehensive exam, integrative project (MBA), research project (exceptional student education, teaching English as a second language); for doctorate, one foreign language, comprehensive exam, internship, project. *Entrance requirements:* For master's, 3 letters of recommendation, interview, minimum GPA of 3.0, resume; for doctorate, 3 letters of recommendation, minimum GPA of 3.0, resume, interview. *Application deadline:* For fall admission, 8/1 priority date for domestic students; for spring admission, 11/30 priority date for domestic students. Applications are processed on a rolling basis. Application fee: $50. Electronic applications accepted. *Expenses:* Tuition: Full-time $9090; part-time $505 per credit hour. Required fees: $298 per term. Tuition and fees vary according to course load, degree level and program. *Financial support:* In 2009–10, 127 students received support. Federal Work-Study, scholarships/grants, and tuition discounts available. Financial award application deadline: 6/1; financial award applicants required to submit FAFSA. *Faculty research:* Psychotherapy, forensic psychology, neuropsychology, marketing strategy, entrepreneurship, special education. *Unit head:* Dr. Carmen S. Roca, Chancellor, 305-593-1223 Ext. 120, Fax: 305-629-8052, E-mail: croca@albizu.edu. *Application contact:* Annalye Alonso, Secretary, 305-593-1223 Ext. 137, Fax: 305-593-1854, E-mail: aalonso@albizu.edu.

Carthage College, Division of Teacher Education, Kenosha, WI 53140. Offers classroom guidance and counseling (M Ed); creative arts (M Ed); gifted and talented children (M Ed); language arts (M Ed); modern language (M Ed); natural sciences (M Ed); reading (M Ed, Certificate); social sciences (M Ed); teacher leadership (M Ed). Part-time and evening/weekend programs available. *Degree requirements:* For master's, thesis optional. *Entrance requirements:* For master's, MAT, minimum B average, letters of reference.

The College of New Rochelle, Graduate School, Division of Education, Program in Creative Teaching and Learning, New Rochelle, NY 10805-2308. Offers MS Ed, Certificate. Part-time programs available. *Degree requirements:* For master's, practicum. *Entrance requirements:* For master's, interview, minimum GPA of 3.0 in field, 2.7 overall.

The College of William and Mary, School of Education, Program in Curriculum and Instruction, Williamsburg, VA 23187-8795. Offers elementary education (MA Ed); gifted education (MA Ed); math specialist (MA Ed); reading education (MA Ed); secondary education (MA Ed), including English education, mathematics education, modern foreign languages education, science education, social studies education; special education (MA Ed), including general curriculum, resource collaborating teaching. *Accreditation:* NCATE. Part-time programs available. *Faculty:* 18 full-time (12 women), 17 part-time/adjunct (15 women). *Students:* 54 full-time (45 women), 12 part-time (all women); includes 3 minority (2 African Americans, 1 Asian American or Pacific Islander), 2 international. Average age 27. 120 applicants, 75% accepted. In 2009, 70 master's awarded. *Degree requirements:* For master's, project. *Entrance requirements:* For master's, GRE or MAT, minimum GPA of 2.5. Additional exam requirements/recommendations for international students: Required—TOEFL. *Application deadline:* For fall admission, 1/15 for domestic and international students; for spring admission, 10/1 for domestic and international students. Application fee: $45. Electronic applications accepted. *Expenses:* Tuition, state resident: full-time $6400; part-time $315 per credit hour. Tuition, nonresident: full-time $19,720; part-time $840 per credit hour. Required fees: $4114. *Financial support:* In 2009–10, 30 students received support, including 10 research assistantships with full and partial tuition reimbursements available (averaging $5,500 per year); career-related internships or fieldwork, Federal Work-Study, institutionally sponsored loans, scholarships/grants, and unspecified assistantships also available. Financial award application deadline: 1/15; financial award applicants required to submit FAFSA. *Faculty research:* National Council of Teachers of Mathematics Standards, counseling, self-concept and self-esteem, special education, curriculum development. *Unit head:* Dr. C. Denise Johnson, Area Coordinator, 757-221-1528, E-mail: cdjohn@wm.edu. *Application contact:* Dorothy Smith Osborne, Director of Admissions, 757-221-2317, Fax: 757-221-2293, E-mail: dsosbo@wm.edu.

Converse College, School of Education and Graduate Studies, Program in Gifted Education, Spartanburg, SC 29302-0006. Offers M Ed. Part-time programs available. *Degree requirements:* For master's, capstone paper. *Entrance requirements:* For master's, NTE or PRAXIS II, minimum GPA of 2.75, teaching certificate, 2 recommendations. Electronic applications accepted. *Faculty research:* Identification of gifted minorities, arts in gifted education.

Dowling College, Graduate Programs in Education, Oakdale, NY 11769-1999. Offers adolescence education (MS Ed), including educational administration; advanced certificate in gifted education (AC); childhood and early childhood education (MS Ed); childhood education (MS Ed); educational administration (AC, PD), including computers in education (PD), school administration and supervision (PD), school district administration (PD); educational technology specialist (AC); literacy (MS Ed); literacy/special education (MS Ed); secondary education (MS Ed); special education (MS Ed). *Accreditation:* NCATE. Part-time and evening/weekend programs available. Postbaccalaureate distance learning degree programs offered. *Faculty:* 32 full-time (18 women), 98 part-time/adjunct (59 women). *Students:* 563 full-time (393 women), 885 part-time (668 women); includes 133 minority (47 African Americans, 2 American Indian/Alaska Native, 10 Asian Americans or Pacific Islanders, 74 Hispanic Americans). Average age 32. 363 applicants, 89% accepted, 213 enrolled. In 2009, 459 master's, 85 ACs awarded. *Degree requirements:* For master's and other advanced degree, comprehensive exam. *Entrance requirements:* For master's, minimum GPA of 3.0; for other advanced degree, teaching certificate. Additional exam requirements/recommendations for international students: Required—TOEFL (minimum score 550 paper-based). *Application deadline:* For fall admission, 9/1 priority date for domestic students; for winter admission, 1/1 priority date for domestic students; for spring admission, 2/1 priority date for domestic students. Applications are processed on a rolling basis. Application fee: $50. Electronic applications accepted. *Expenses:* Tuition: Full-time $14,490; part-time $805 per credit. Required fees: $346 per term. *Financial support:* Career-related internships or fieldwork and Federal Work-Study available. Support available to part-time students. Financial award application deadline: 6/30; financial award applicants required to submit FAFSA. *Faculty research:* Natural readers, Korean styles and learning strategies, mothers of children with disabilities, computers in instruction, cultural background and organizational roadblocks to problem solving. *Unit head:* Dr. Clyde Payne, Dean of the School of Education, 631-244-3404, Fax: 631-589-6644, E-mail: paynec@dowling.edu. *Application contact:* Glenn M. Berman, Assistant Vice President for Enrollment Services/Dean of Admissions, 631-244-3357, Fax: 631-244-1059, E-mail: glenn.berman@dowling.edu.

Drury University, Graduate Programs in Education, Springfield, MO 65802. Offers elementary education (M Ed); gifted education (M Ed); human services (M Ed); instructional mathematics K-8 (M Ed); instructional technology (M Ed); middle school teaching (M Ed); secondary education (M Ed); special education (M Ed); special reading (M Ed). *Accreditation:* NCATE. Part-time and evening/weekend programs available. *Degree requirements:* For master's, thesis. *Entrance requirements:* For master's, GRE or MAT, minimum GPA of 2.75. Additional exam requirements/recommendations for international students: Required—TOEFL. Electronic applications accepted. *Faculty research:* Cultural enrichment, research skills, parental involvement relating to reading skills, reading strategies for mainstreaming children.

Elon University, Program in Education, Elon, NC 27244-2010. Offers elementary education (M Ed); gifted education (M Ed); special education (M Ed). *Accreditation:* NCATE. Part-time programs available. *Faculty:* 15 full-time (11 women). *Students:* 1 (woman) full-time, 79 part-time (65 women); includes 15 minority (13 African Americans, 1 Asian American or Pacific Islander, 1 Hispanic American), 1 international. Average age 30. 57 applicants, 84% accepted, 39 enrolled. In 2009, 45 master's awarded. *Entrance requirements:* For master's, GRE, MAT. Additional exam requirements/recommendations for international students: Required—TOEFL (minimum score 550 paper-based; 213 computer-based; 79 iBT). *Application deadline:* For winter admission, 6/1 priority date for domestic students. Applications are processed on a rolling basis. Application fee: $50. Electronic applications accepted. *Expenses:* Contact institution. *Financial support:* In 2009–10, 4 students received support. Federal Work-Study and scholarships/grants available. Support available to part-time students. Financial award application deadline: 6/1; financial award applicants required to submit FAFSA. *Faculty research:* Teaching reading to low-achieving second and third graders, pre- and post-student teaching attitudes toward teaching, children's writing, whole language methodology, critical creative thinking. *Unit head:* Dr. Judith B. Howard, Director, 336-278-5885, Fax: 336-278-5919, E-mail: howardj@elon.edu. *Application contact:* Art Fadde, Director of Graduate Admissions, 800-334-8448 Ext. 3, Fax: 336-278-7699, E-mail: afadde@elon.edu.

Emporia State University, School of Graduate Studies, The Teachers College, Department of Special Education and School Counseling, Program in Special Education, Emporia, KS 66801-5087. Offers behavior disorders (MS); gifted, talented, and creative (MS); interrelated special education (MS); learning disabilities (MS); mental retardation (MS). *Accreditation:* NCATE. Part-time programs available. *Students:* 1 (woman) full-time, 179 part-time (137 women); includes 6 minority (1 African American, 1 American Indian/Alaska Native, 3 Asian Americans or Pacific Islanders, 1 Hispanic American), 1 international. 23 applicants, 96% accepted, 22 enrolled. In 2009, 39 master's awarded. *Degree requirements:* For master's, comprehensive exam or thesis, practicum. *Entrance requirements:* For master's, GRE General Test or MAT, graduate essay exam, appropriate bachelor's degree, teacher certification, letters of recommendation. Additional exam requirements/recommendations for international students: Required—TOEFL (minimum score 520 paper-based; 133 computer-based; 68 iBT). *Application deadline:* For fall admission, 8/15 priority date for domestic students. Applications are processed on a rolling basis. Application fee: $30 ($75 for international students). Electronic applications accepted. *Expenses:* Tuition, state resident: full-time $4154; part-time $173 per credit hour. Tuition, nonresident: full-time $12,864; part-time $536 per credit hour. Required fees: $948; $58 per credit hour. Tuition and fees vary according to campus/location. *Financial support:* Federal Work-Study, institutionally sponsored loans, health care benefits, and unspecified assistantships available. Financial award application deadline: 3/15; financial award applicants required to submit FAFSA. *Unit head:* Dr. Jean Morrow, Interim Chair, 620-341-5317, E-mail: jmorrow@emporia.edu. *Application contact:* Mary Sewell, Admissions Coordinator, 800-950-GRAD, Fax: 620-341-5909, E-mail: msewell@emporia.edu.

Hardin-Simmons University, Graduate School, Irvin School of Education, Department of Educational Studies, Program in Gifted Education, Abilene, TX 79698-0001. Offers M Ed. Part-time programs available. *Faculty:* 1 (woman) full-time, 1 (woman) part-time/adjunct. *Students:* 21 part-time (18 women); includes 4 minority (all Hispanic Americans). Average age 34. 6 applicants, 83% accepted, 4 enrolled. In 2009, 8 master's awarded. *Degree requirements:* For master's, comprehensive exam. *Entrance requirements:* For master's, minimum undergraduate GPA of 3.0 in major, 2.7 overall. Additional exam requirements/recommendations for international students: Required—TOEFL (minimum score 550 paper-based; 213 computer-based; 75 iBT). *Application deadline:* For fall admission, 8/15 priority date for domestic students, 4/1 for international students; for spring admission, 1/5 priority date for domestic students, 9/1 for international students. Applications are processed on a rolling basis. Application fee: $50. *Expenses:* Tuition: Full-time $11,430; part-time $635 per credit hour. Required fees: $650; $110 per semester. Tuition and fees vary according to degree level. *Financial support:* In 2009–10, 7 students received support, including 1 fellowship (averaging $2,400 per year); scholarships/grants also available. Support available to part-time students. Financial award application deadline: 6/30; financial award applicants required to submit FAFSA. *Faculty research:* Experiences of gifted learners in college, use of authentic assessment, brain research and how it works in learning, theories of multiple intelligence beyond Gardner. *Unit head:* Dr. Mary Christopher, Director, 325-670-1510, E-mail: mchris@hsutx.edu. *Application contact:* Dr. Gary Stanlake, Dean of Graduate Studies, 325-670-1298, Fax: 325-670-1564, E-mail: gradoff@hsutx.edu.

Hofstra University, School of Education, Health, and Human Services, Department of Counseling, Research, Special Education and Rehabilitation, Program in Special Education, Hempstead, NY 11549. Offers early childhood special education (MS Ed, Advanced Certificate); gifted education (Advanced Certificate); inclusive early childhood special education (MS Ed); inclusive elementary special education (MS Ed); inclusive secondary special education (MS Ed); literacy studies and special education (MS Ed); special education (MA, MS Ed, PD); special education assessment and diagnosis (Advanced Certificate); teaching students with severe or multiple disabilities (Advanced Certificate). Part-time and evening/weekend programs available. *Students:* 113 full-time (96 women), 105 part-time (95 women); includes 39 minority (18 African Americans, 1 American Indian/Alaska Native, 3 Asian Americans or Pacific Islanders, 17 Hispanic Americans). Average age 29. 134 applicants, 71% accepted, 74 enrolled. In 2009, 88 master's, 7 other advanced degrees awarded. *Degree requirements:* For master's, comprehensive exam (for some programs), thesis (for some programs), seminars, student teaching. *Entrance requirements:* For master's, interview, 3 letters of reference, initial/professional certification; for other advanced degree, interview, 3 letters of recommendation, resume, master's degree, certification. Additional exam requirements/recommendations for international students: Required—TOEFL (minimum score 550 paper-based; 213 computer-based; 80 iBT). *Application deadline:* Applications are processed on a rolling basis. Application fee: $60. Electronic applications accepted. *Expenses:* Tuition: Full-time $16,200; part-time $900 per credit hour. Required fees: $970; $145 per term. Tuition and fees vary according to program. *Financial support:* In 2009–10, 78 students received support, including 10 fellowships with full and partial tuition reimbursements available (averaging $2,541 per year), 4

Education of the Gifted

Hofstra University (continued)

research assistantships with full and partial tuition reimbursements available (averaging $7,210 per year); Federal Work-Study, institutionally sponsored loans, scholarships/grants, tuition waivers (full and partial), and unspecified assistantships also available. Support available to part-time students. Financial award applicants required to submit FAFSA. *Faculty research:* Inclusive schooling, autism spectrum disorders related services, cultural competency and culturally responsive instruction, co-teaching student teaching, universal design for learning. *Unit head:* Dr. George Guiliani, Director, 516-463-5143, Fax: 516-463-6184, E-mail: cprgag@hofstra.edu. *Application contact:* Carol Drummer, Dean of Graduate Admissions, 516-463-4876, Fax: 516-463-4664, E-mail: gradstudent@hofstra.edu.

The Johns Hopkins University, School of Education, Department of Teacher Development and Leadership, Baltimore, MD 21218-2699. Offers adolescent literacy education (Certificate); data-based decision making and organizational improvement (Certificate); education (MS), including reading, school administration and supervision, technology for educators; educational leadership for independent schools (Certificate); effective teaching of reading (Certificate); emergent literacy education (Certificate); English as a second language instruction (Certificate); gifted education (Certificate); leadership for school, family, and community collaboration (Certificate); leadership in technology integration (Certificate); school administration and supervision (Certificate); teacher development and leadership (Ed D); teacher leadership (Certificate); technology for educators (MS). Part-time and evening/weekend programs available. Postbaccalaureate distance learning degree programs offered (minimal on-campus study). *Faculty:* 8 full-time (2 women), 53 part-time/adjunct (36 women). *Students:* 17 full-time (16 women), 462 part-time (358 women); includes 117 minority (77 African Americans, 25 Asian Americans or Pacific Islanders, 15 Hispanic Americans), 11 international. Average age 33. 217 applicants, 62% accepted, 107 enrolled. In 2009, 85 master's, 2 doctorates, 181 other advanced degrees awarded. *Degree requirements:* For master's and Certificate, portfolio; for doctorate, comprehensive exam (for some programs), thesis/dissertation, portfolio or comprehensive exam. *Entrance requirements:* For master's and Certificate, bachelor's degree; minimum undergraduate GPA of 3.0; essay/statement of goals; for doctorate, GRE, essay/statement of goals; three letters of recommendation; curriculum vitae/resume; K-12 professional experience; interview; writing assessment. Additional exam requirements/recommendations for international students: Required—TOEFL (minimum score 600 paper-based; 250 computer-based; 100 iBT). *Application deadline:* For fall admission, 5/1 for international students; for spring admission, 10/15 for international students. Applications are processed on a rolling basis. Application fee: $80. Electronic applications accepted. *Financial support:* In 2009–10, 5 research assistantships, 1 teaching assistantship were awarded; scholarships/grants also available. Support available to part-time students. Financial award application deadline: 6/1; financial award applicants required to submit FAFSA. *Faculty research:* Application of psychoanalytic concepts to teaching, schools, and education reform; adolescent literacies; use of emerging technologies for teaching, learning, and school leadership; quantitative analyses of the social contexts of education; school, family, and community collaboration; program evaluation methodologies. *Unit head:* Dr. Edward Pajak, Chair, 410-516-9755, Fax: 410-516-9770, E-mail: mbuckingham@jhu.edu. *Application contact:* Jennifer Shaffer, Director of Admissions, 410-516-9797, Fax: 410-516-9799, E-mail: educationinfo@jhu.edu.

Johnson State College, Graduate Program in Education, Program in Gifted and Talented, Johnson, VT 05656. Offers MA Ed. Part-time programs available. *Degree requirements:* For master's, comprehensive exam, thesis or alternative. *Entrance requirements:* For master's, interview. Additional exam requirements/recommendations for international students: Required—TOEFL. *Expenses:* Tuition, area resident: Part-time $416 per credit. Tuition, state resident: part-time $416 per credit. Tuition, nonresident: part-time $899 per credit.

Kent State University, Graduate School of Education, Health, and Human Services, School of Lifespan Development and Educational Sciences, Program in Intervention Specialist, Kent, OH 44242-0001. Offers deaf education (M Ed, MA); early childhood intervention specialist (M Ed, MA); educational interpreter K-12 (M Ed, MA); general special education (M Ed, MA); gifted education (M Ed, MA); mild/moderate intervention (M Ed, MA); moderate/intensive intervention (M Ed, MA); transition to work (M Ed, MA). *Faculty:* 9 full-time (8 women), 17 part-time/adjunct (15 women). *Students:* 51 full-time (41 women), 63 part-time (56 women); includes 8 minority (3 African Americans, 2 Asian Americans or Pacific Islanders, 3 Hispanic Americans), 2 international. 62 applicants, 77% accepted. In 2009, 36 master's awarded. *Entrance requirements:* For master's, GRE. Application fee: $30. *Financial support:* In 2009–10, 1 research assistantship with tuition reimbursement (averaging $8,313 per year) was awarded; fellowships with tuition reimbursements, teaching assistantships with tuition reimbursements, career-related internships or fieldwork, Federal Work-Study, institutionally sponsored loans, scholarships/grants, health care benefits, and unspecified assistantships also available. Support available to part-time students. *Unit head:* Kristie Pretti-Frontczak, Coordinator, 330-672-0597, E-mail: kprettif@kent.edu. *Application contact:* Nancy Miller, Academic Program Coordinator, Office of Graduate Student Services, 330-672-2576, Fax: 330-672-9162, E-mail: ogs@kent.edu.

Liberty University, School of Education, Lynchburg, VA 24502. Offers administration and supervision (M Ed); curriculum and instruction (M Ed); early childhood education (M Ed); education specialist (Ed S); educational leadership (Ed D); elementary education (M Ed); gifted education (M Ed); reading specialist (M Ed); school counseling (M Ed); secondary education (M Ed); special education (M Ed). *Accreditation:* NCATE. Part-time programs available. Postbaccalaureate distance learning degree programs offered (minimal on-campus study). *Degree requirements:* For doctorate, comprehensive exam, thesis/dissertation. *Entrance requirements:* For master's, GRE General Test or MAT (aken in or before 1999), 2 letters of recommendation, minimum undergraduate GPA of 3.0, curriculum vitae; for doctorate, GRE General Test or MAT (if taken before 1999), minimum master's GPA of 3.0, 3 years of teacher experience; for Ed S, GRE General Test or MAT (if taken before 1999), minimum master's GPA of 3.0, 3 years of teaching experience. Additional exam requirements/recommendations for international students: Required—TOEFL (minimum score 600 paper-based; 250 computer-based). Electronic applications accepted. *Expenses:* Contact institution. *Faculty research:* Self-determination, character education, bibliotherapy, learning styles, distance education.

Lynn University, Donald and Helen Ross College of Education, Boca Raton, FL 33431-5598. Offers educational leadership (M Ed, PhD); exceptional student education (M Ed); teacher preparation (PhD). Part-time and evening/weekend programs available. *Degree requirements:* For master's, thesis (for some programs); for doctorate, thesis/dissertation, qualifying paper. *Entrance requirements:* For master's, GRE, minimum undergraduate GPA of 3.0, resume, 2 letters of recommendation; for doctorate, GRE or GMAT, minimum GPA of 3.25, resume, 2 letters of recommendation. Additional exam requirements/recommendations for international students: Required—TOEFL (minimum score 550 paper-based; 213 computer-based). *Application deadline:* Applications are processed on a rolling basis. Application fee: $50. Electronic applications accepted. *Expenses:* Tuition: Part-time $580 per credit. One-time fee: $200 part-time. Part-time tuition and fees vary according to degree level. *Financial support:* Career-related internships or fieldwork, Federal Work-Study, institutionally sponsored loans, scholarships/grants, tuition waivers (partial), and unspecified assistantships available. Support available to part-time students. Financial award application deadline: 8/1; financial award applicants required to submit FAFSA. *Faculty research:* Non-traditional education, innovative curricula, multicultural education, simulation games. *Application contact:* Dr. Larissa Baia, Assistant Director of Graduate Admissions, 561-237-7916, Fax: 561-237-7100, E-mail: lbaia@lynn.edu.

Maryville University of Saint Louis, School of Education, St. Louis, MO 63141-7299. Offers art education (MA Ed); early childhood education (MA Ed); educational leadership (Ed D); educational leadership: principal certification (MA Ed); elementary education (MA Ed); elementary education/English (MA Ed); elementary education/psychology (MA Ed); environmental education (MA Ed); gifted education (MA Ed); literacy specialist (MA Ed); middle grades education (MA Ed); secondary teaching and inquiry (MA Ed); teacher as leader (MA Ed). *Accreditation:* NASAD; NCATE. Part-time and evening/weekend programs available. *Students:* 25 full-time (18 women), 198 part-time (145 women); includes 33 minority (27 African Americans, 2 American Indian/Alaska Native, 1 Asian American or Pacific Islander, 3 Hispanic Americans). Average age 36. In 2009, 61 master's, 45 doctorates awarded. *Degree requirements:* For master's, thesis, project. *Entrance requirements:* For master's and doctorate, minimum GPA of 3.0, 3 professional recommendations. Additional exam requirements/recommendations for international students: Required—TOEFL (minimum score 550 paper-based). *Application deadline:* Applications are processed on a rolling basis. Application fee: $40 ($60 for international students). Electronic applications accepted. *Expenses:* Tuition: Full-time $20,384; part-time $627.50 per credit hour. Required fees: $100 per semester. *Financial support:* Career-related internships or fieldwork, Federal Work-Study, tuition waivers (partial), and professional educator discounts available. Financial award application deadline: 3/1; financial award applicants required to submit FAFSA. *Faculty research:* Collaboration with public schools, pre-service program development, mathematics, diversity, literacy. *Unit head:* Dr. Sam Hausfather, Dean, 314-529-9466, Fax: 314-529-9921, E-mail: shausfather@maryville.edu. *Application contact:* Holly Stanwich, Graduate Admissions Coordinator, 314-529-9542, Fax: 314-529-9921, E-mail: teachered@maryville.edu.

Millersville University of Pennsylvania, College of Graduate and Professional Studies, School of Education, Department of Elementary and Early Childhood Education, Program in Gifted Education, Millersville, PA 17551-0302. Offers M Ed. Part-time and evening/weekend programs available. *Faculty:* 18 full-time (14 women), 15 part-time/adjunct (7 women). *Students:* 2 full-time (1 woman), 10 part-time (9 women); includes 1 minority (Asian American or Pacific Islander). Average age 36. 1 applicant, 100% accepted, 0 enrolled. In 2009, 1 master's awarded. *Degree requirements:* For master's, thesis optional. *Entrance requirements:* For master's, GRE or MAT, 3 letters of recommendation, copy of teaching certificate. Additional exam requirements/recommendations for international students: Required—TOEFL (minimum score 500 paper-based; 183 computer-based; 65 iBT) or IELTS (minimum score 6). *Application deadline:* For fall admission, 1/15 priority date for domestic and international students; for winter admission, 10/1 priority date for domestic and international students; for spring admission, 10/1 priority date for domestic and international students. Applications are processed on a rolling basis. Application fee: $40 ($50 for international students). Electronic applications accepted. *Expenses:* Tuition, state resident: full-time $6666; part-time $370 per credit. Tuition, nonresident: full-time $10,666; part-time $593 per credit. Required fees: $1578.50; $76.25 per credit. One-time fee: $60 part-time. Tuition and fees vary according to course load. *Financial support:* In 2009–10, 1 student received support, including 1 research assistantship with full tuition reimbursement available (averaging $5,400 per year); institutionally sponsored loans and unspecified assistantships also available. Support available to part-time students. Financial award application deadline: 3/15; financial award applicants required to submit FAFSA. *Unit head:* Dr. Kimberly S. Heilshorn, Coordinator, 717-871-5146, E-mail: kimberly.heilshorn@millersville.edu. *Application contact:* Dr. Victor S. DeSantis, Dean of Graduate and Professional Studies, 717-872-3099, Fax: 717-872-3453, E-mail: victor.desantis@millersville.edu.

Minnesota State University Mankato, College of Graduate Studies, College of Education, Department of Special Education, Program in Talent Development and Gifted Education, Mankato, MN 56001. Offers MS, Certificate, SP. *Accreditation:* NCATE. *Degree requirements:* For master's, comprehensive exam, thesis or alternative. *Entrance requirements:* For master's, GRE General Test or MAT, minimum GPA of 3.0 during previous 2 years. Additional exam requirements/recommendations for international students: Required—TOEFL. *Application deadline:* For fall admission, 7/1 priority date for domestic students; for spring admission, 11/1 for domestic students. Applications are processed on a rolling basis. Application fee: $40. Electronic applications accepted. *Expenses:* Tuition, state resident: full-time $5364. Tuition, nonresident: full-time $8314. *Financial support:* Research assistantships, teaching assistantships available. Financial award application deadline: 3/15. *Application contact:* 507-389-2321, E-mail: grad@mnsu.edu.

Mississippi University for Women, Graduate School, College of Education and Human Sciences, Columbus, MS 39701-9998. Offers differentiated instruction (M Ed); gifted studies (M Ed); teaching (MAT). *Accreditation:* ASHA; NCATE. Part-time programs available. *Degree requirements:* For master's, comprehensive exam, thesis optional. *Entrance requirements:* For master's, GRE General Test or NTE (M Ed in gifted education or MS in speech/language pathology), MAT (M Ed in instructional management), minimum QPA of 3.0.

Morehead State University, Graduate Programs, College of Education, Department of Foundational and Graduate Studies in Education, Morehead, KY 40351. Offers adult and higher education (MA, Ed S); certified professional counselor (Ed S); counseling P-12 (MA); curriculum and instruction (Ed S); educational technology (MA Ed); instructional leadership (Ed S); school administration (MA); school counseling (Ed S); teacher leader business and marketing- content (MA Ed); teacher leader business and marketing- technology (MA Ed); teacher leader educational technology (MA Ed); teacher leader English (MA Ed); teacher leader gifted educ (MA Ed); teacher leader IECE—non-certification (MA Ed); teacher leader IECE certification (MA Ed); teacher leader interdisciplanary educaction P-5 (MA Ed); teacher leader middle grades 5-9 (MA Ed); teacher leader reading/writing—non-certification (MA Ed); teacher leader reading/writing certification (MA Ed); teacher leader school communication—non-certification (MA Ed); teacher leader school communication certification (MA Ed); teacher leader social studies (MA Ed); teacher leader special education (MA Ed). *Accreditation:* NCATE. Part-time and evening/weekend programs available. *Faculty:* 20 full-time (10 women), 7 part-time/adjunct (3 women). *Students:* 26 full-time (18 women), 371 part-time (295 women); includes 11 minority (9 African Americans, 1 American Indian/Alaska Native, 1 Hispanic American). Average age 35. 201 applicants, 73% accepted, 73 enrolled. In 2009, 105 master's, 5 other advanced degrees awarded. *Degree requirements:* For master's, thesis optional, oral and/or written comprehensive exams; for Ed S, thesis, oral exam. *Entrance requirements:* For master's, GRE General Test, minimum overall undergraduate GPA of 2.5; for Ed S, GRE General Test, interview, master's degree, minimum GPA of 3.5, work experience. Additional exam requirements/recommendations for international students: Required—TOEFL (minimum score 500 paper-based; 173 computer-based). *Application deadline:* For fall admission, 8/1 priority date for domestic and international students; for spring admission, 12/1 priority date for domestic and international students. Applications are processed on a rolling basis. Application fee: $30. Electronic applications accepted. *Expenses:* Tuition, state resident: full-time $6318; part-time $351 per credit hour. Tuition, nonresident: full-time $15,804; part-time $878 per credit hour. *Financial support:* In 2009–10, 2 research assistantships (averaging $10,000 per year) were awarded; career-related internships or fieldwork, Federal Work-Study, and unspecified assistantships also available. Financial award application deadline: 3/15; financial award applicants required to submit FAFSA. *Faculty research:* Character education, school accountability, computer applications for school administrators. *Unit head:* Dr. Cathy Gunn, Dean and Professor, 606-783-2040, Fax: 606-783-5029, E-mail: c.gunn@moreheadstate.edu. *Application contact:* Michelle Barber, Graduate Recruitment and Retention Assistant Director, 606-783-5127, Fax: 606-783-5061, E-mail: m.barber@moreheadstate.edu.

Northeastern Illinois University, Graduate College, College of Education, Department of Special Education, Program in Gifted Education, Chicago, IL 60625-4699. Offers MA. Part-time and evening/weekend programs available. *Degree requirements:* For master's, comprehensive exam, thesis or alternative. *Entrance requirements:* For master's, teaching certificate or previous course work in history or philosophy of education, minimum GPA of 2.75. Additional exam requirements/recommendations for international students: Required—TOEFL (minimum score 550 paper-based; 213 computer-based; 80 iBT). Electronic applications accepted. *Faculty research:* Effect of inclusion in public school gifted programs, social and emotional needs of gifted children, problem-based learning strategies.

Nova Southeastern University, Fischler School of Education and Human Services, Graduate Teacher Education Program, Fort Lauderdale, FL 33314-7796. Offers athletic administration (MS); brain research (MS, Ed S); charter school education/leadership (MS); cognitive and behavioral disabilities (MS); computer science education (Ed S); computer science education (K-12) (MS); curriculum and teaching (Ed S); curriculum, instruction and technology (MS);

curriculum, instruction, management and administration (Ed S); early childhood education (MS); early literacy and reading (Ed S); early literacy education (MS); education technology (MS); educational leadership (administration K–12) (MS, Ed S); educational media (Ed S); educational media (K-12) (MS); elementary education (MS, Ed S), including ESOL endorsement (MS); English education (MS, Ed S); environmental education (MS); exceptional student education (MS), including ESOL endorsement; gifted education (MS, Ed S); interdisciplinary arts education (MS); management and administration of educational programs (MS); mathematics (MS); mathematics education (Ed S); multicultural early intervention (MS); pre-kindergarten/primary (MS); preschool education (MS); reading (MS); reading and TESOL (MS); reading education (Ed S); science (MS); science education (Ed S); secondary education (MS); social studies (MS, Ed S); Spanish language (MS); special education and reading (MS); teaching and learning (MA, MS), including curriculum and instruction (MA), elementary mathematics (MA), elementary reading (MA), K-12 technology integration (MA); teaching English to speakers of other languages (MS, Ed S); technology management and administration (Ed S); urban studies education (MS). Part-time and evening/weekend programs available. Postbaccalaureate distance learning degree programs offered (minimal on-campus study). *Faculty:* 72 full-time (43 women), 385 part-time/adjunct (252 women). *Students:* 196 full-time (175 women), 1,304 part-time (1,128 women); includes 594 minority (471 African Americans, 5 American Indian/Alaska Native, 18 Asian Americans or Pacific Islanders, 100 Hispanic Americans). Average age 37. 2,610 applicants, 72% accepted, 1352 enrolled. In 2009, 836 other advanced degrees awarded. *Degree requirements:* For master's and Ed S, thesis, practicum, internship. *Entrance requirements:* For master's, MAT, GRE, CLAST, CBEST, PRAXIS I, General Knowledge Test, minimum GPA of 2.5; for Ed S, MAT or GRE, master's degree, teaching certificate, minimum GPA of 3.0. Additional exam requirements/recommendations for international students: Required—TSE (recommended, minimum score 50); Recommended—TOEFL (minimum score 550 paper-based; 213 computer-based; 80 iBT), IELTS (minimum score 6). *Application deadline:* For fall admission, 9/25 priority date for domestic and international students; for winter admission, 2/23 priority date for domestic and international students; for spring admission, 4/25 priority date for domestic and international students. Applications are processed on a rolling basis. Application fee: $50. Electronic applications accepted. *Financial support:* Federal Work-Study available. Support available to part-time students. Financial award application deadline: 4/15; financial award applicants required to submit FAFSA. *Faculty research:* School effectiveness, critical thinking, leadership skills acquisition, child education, multicultural education. *Unit head:* Dr. Ronald Kern, Dean of Academic Affairs, 800-986-3223 Ext. 7809, Fax: 954-262-3606, E-mail: rk429@nsu.nova.edu. *Application contact:* Dr. Jennifer Quinones Nottingham, Dean of Student Affairs, 800-986-3223 Ext. 1559.

Purdue University, Graduate School, School of Education, Department of Educational Studies, West Lafayette, IN 47907. Offers administration (MS Ed, PhD, Ed S); counseling and development (MS Ed, PhD); education of the gifted (MS Ed); educational psychology (MS Ed, PhD); foundations of education (MS Ed, PhD); higher education administration (MS Ed, PhD); special education (MS Ed, PhD). *Accreditation:* ACA (one or more programs are accredited); NCATE (one or more programs are accredited). Part-time and evening/weekend programs available. *Degree requirements:* For master's, thesis optional; for doctorate, thesis/dissertation, oral and written exams; for Ed S, oral presentation, project. *Entrance requirements:* For master's, GRE General Test, minimum undergraduate GPA of 3.0; for doctorate, GRE General Test; for Ed S, GRE, minimum B average. Additional exam requirements/recommendations for international students: Required—TOEFL. Electronic applications accepted. *Faculty research:* Motivation, learning disabilities, school learning, group processes, cognitive development.

Saint Leo University, Graduate Studies in Education, Saint Leo, FL 33574-6665. Offers educational leadership (M Ed, Ed S); exceptional student education (M Ed); higher education leadership (Ed S); instructional design (MS); instructional leadership (M Ed); reading (M Ed). Part-time and evening/weekend programs available. Postbaccalaureate distance learning degree programs offered (minimal on-campus study). *Faculty:* 13 full-time (10 women), 12 part-time/adjunct (9 women). *Students:* 432 full-time (355 women), 35 part-time (24 women); includes 56 minority (40 African Americans, 2 American Indian/Alaska Native, 2 Asian Americans or Pacific Islanders, 12 Hispanic Americans), 1 international. Average age 37. In 2009, 131 master's awarded. *Degree requirements:* For master's, comprehensive exam, appropriate State of Florida Certification Tests. *Entrance requirements:* For master's, GRE (minimum score of 1000) or MAT (minimum score of 410) if undergraduate GPA for last 60 hours of coursework was below 3.0 (for M Ed), bachelor's degree from regionally-accredited college or university with minimum GPA of 3.0 for last 60 hours of coursework, 2 recommendations, resume, statement of professional goals, copy of valid teaching certificate (for M Ed); for Ed S, GRE (minimum score 1000) or MAT (minimum score 410) if undergraduate GPA for last 60 hours of coursework less than 3.0, bachelor's degree from regionally-accredited college or university with minimum GPA of 3.0 for last 60 hours of coursework, 2 recommendations, resume, valid teaching certificate. Additional exam requirements/recommendations for international students: Required—TOEFL (minimum score 550 paper-based; 213 computer-based; 80 iBT). *Application deadline:* For fall admission, 7/1 priority date for domestic students; for spring admission, 11/12 priority date for domestic students. Applications are processed on a rolling basis. Application fee: $75. Electronic applications accepted. *Expenses:* Tuition: Part-time $1767 per course. Required fees: $115 per course. *Financial support:* Career-related internships or fieldwork, Federal Work-Study, and health care benefits available. Financial award application deadline: 3/1; financial award applicants required to submit FAFSA. *Faculty research:* The role of the school leader in data analysis of student achievement, teacher recruitment, and teacher effectiveness. *Unit head:* Dr. John Smith, Director, 352-588-8309, Fax: 352-588-8861, E-mail: med@saintleo.edu. *Application contact:* Jared Welling, Director, Graduate/Weekend and Evening Admission, 800-707-8846, Fax: 352-588-7873, E-mail: grad.admissions@saintleo.edu.

Saint Mary's University of Minnesota, Schools of Graduate and Professional Programs, Graduate School of Education, Education Program, Winona, MN 55987-1399. Offers education (MA); gifted and talented instruction (Certificate). *Unit head:* Claudia Risnes, Director, 612-728-5179, Fax: 612-728-5121, E-mail: crisnes@smumn.edu. *Application contact:* Yasin Alsaidi, Director of Admissions for Graduate and Professional Programs, 612-728-5207, Fax: 612-728-5121, E-mail: yalsaidi@smumn.edu.

St. Thomas University, School of Leadership Studies, Institute for Education, Miami Gardens, FL 33054-6459. Offers earth/space science (Certificate); educational administration (MS, Certificate); educational leadership (Ed D); elementary education (MS); ESOL (Certificate); gifted education (Certificate); instructional technology (MS, Certificate); professional/studies (Certificate); reading (MS, Certificate); special education (MS). Part-time and evening/weekend programs available. *Degree requirements:* For master's, comprehensive exam; for doctorate, comprehensive exam, thesis/dissertation. *Entrance requirements:* For master's, interview, minimum GPA of 3.0 or GRE; for doctorate, GRE or MAT. Additional exam requirements/recommendations for international students: Required—TOEFL (minimum score 550 paper-based; 213 computer-based; 79 iBT). Electronic applications accepted.

Samford University, Orlean Bullard Beeson School of Education and Professional Studies, Birmingham, AL 35229. Offers early childhood education (Ed S); early childhood/elementary education (MS Ed); educational administration (Ed S); educational leadership (Ed D); elementary education (Ed S); gifted education (MS Ed); instructional leadership (MS Ed); secondary collaboration (MS Ed); M Div/MS Ed. *Accreditation:* NCATE. Part-time programs available. *Faculty:* 11 full-time (8 women), 9 part-time/adjunct (5 women). *Students:* 16 full-time (13 women), 173 part-time (131 women); includes 47 minority (46 African Americans, 1 American Indian/Alaska Native), 1 international. Average age 40. 15 applicants, 100% accepted, 15 enrolled. In 2009, 52 master's, 11 doctorates, 27 other advanced degrees awarded. *Degree requirements:* For master's, comprehensive exam; for doctorate, comprehensive exam, thesis/dissertation. *Entrance requirements:* For master's, GRE or MAT, minimum GPA of 3.0; for doctorate, minimum GPA of 3.7; for Ed S, GRE, master's degree, teaching certificate, minimum GPA of 3.25. Additional exam requirements/recommendations for international students: Required—TOEFL (minimum score 550 paper-based; 213 computer-based). *Application deadline:* Applications are processed on a rolling basis. Application fee: $25. *Expenses:* Tuition: Full-time $26,660; part-time $595 per credit hour. Required fees: $110 per semester. *Financial support:* In 2009–10, 127 students received support; research assistantships, career-related internships or fieldwork, Federal Work-Study, scholarships/grants, and tuition waivers (partial) available. Support available to part-time students. Financial award applicants required to submit FAFSA. *Faculty research:* School law, the characteristics of beginning teachers, the nature of school reform, school culture, quality improvement in education, K-12 student achievement. *Unit head:* Dr. Jean Ann Box, Dean, 205-726-2559, E-mail: jabox@samford.edu. *Application contact:* Dr. Maurice Persall, Director, Graduate Office, 205-726-2019, E-mail: jmpersal@samford.edu.

Southern Methodist University, Annette Caldwell Simmons School of Education and Human Development, Department of Teaching and Learning, Dallas, TX 75275. Offers bilingual/ESL education (MBE); education (M Ed, PhD); educational preparation (Certificate); gifted and talented focus (MBE); learning therapist (Certificate). Part-time and evening/weekend programs available. *Faculty:* 16 full-time (12 women), 31 part-time/adjunct (26 women). *Students:* 28 full-time (23 women), 413 part-time (335 women); includes 125 minority (40 African Americans, 4 American Indian/Alaska Native, 14 Asian Americans or Pacific Islanders, 67 Hispanic Americans), 16 international. Average age 36. 36 applicants, 92% accepted, 29 enrolled. In 2009, 85 master's, 28 other advanced degrees awarded. Terminal master's awarded for partial completion of doctoral program. *Degree requirements:* For master's, comprehensive exam, minimum GPA of 3.0; for doctorate, thesis/dissertation, qualifying exams, major area paper, evidence of teaching competency, dissemination of research (e.g., conference presentation), professional portfolio. *Entrance requirements:* For master's, minimum GPA of 3.0 or GRE, 3 letters of recommendation; for doctorate, GRE, minimum GPA of 3.3, 3 years of full-time teaching, 3 letters of recommendation, interview. Additional exam requirements/recommendations for international students: Required—TOEFL. Application fee: $75. Electronic applications accepted. *Financial support:* In 2009–10, 31 students received support; teaching assistantships, scholarships/grants and tuition waivers available. Financial award application deadline: 5/1. *Faculty research:* Reading intervention, mathematics intervention, bilingual education, new literacies. Total annual research expenditures: $2.7 million. *Unit head:* Prof. Jill H. Allor, Associate Professor and Chair, 214-768-2346, Fax: 214-768-8700, E-mail: jallor@smu.edu. *Application contact:* Dr. Deborah Diffily, Administrative Assistant, 214-768-2346, E-mail: ddiffily@smu.edu.

Teachers College, Columbia University, Graduate Faculty of Education, Department of Curriculum and Teaching, Program in Giftedness, New York, NY 10027-6696. Offers MA, Ed D. Part-time programs available. *Faculty:* 1 full-time (0 women). *Students:* 4 full-time (all women), 5 part-time (3 women); includes 1 minority (African American). Average age 42. 7 applicants, 71% accepted, 2 enrolled. In 2009, 5 master's, 1 doctorate awarded. Terminal master's awarded for partial completion of doctoral program. *Degree requirements:* For master's, thesis or alternative; for doctorate, thesis/dissertation. *Entrance requirements:* For doctorate, GRE General Test or MAT. *Application deadline:* For fall admission, 5/15 for domestic students; for spring admission, 12/1 for domestic students. Application fee: $65. *Financial support:* Research assistantships, career-related internships or fieldwork, Federal Work-Study, institutionally sponsored loans, and tuition waivers (full and partial) available. Support available to part-time students. Financial award application deadline: 2/1. *Faculty research:* Urban and economically disadvantaged gifted children, identification issues with regard to gifted and early childhood giftedness. *Unit head:* Marjorie Siegel, Chair, 212-678-3765. *Application contact:* Peter Shon, Assistant Director of Admission, 212-678-3305, Fax: 212-678-4171, E-mail: shon@exchange.tc.columbia.edu.

Tennessee Technological University, Graduate School, College of Education, Department of Curriculum and Instruction, Program in Exceptional Learning, Cookeville, TN 38505. Offers applied behavior and learning (PhD); literacy (PhD); program planning and evaluation (PhD). *Students:* 11 full-time (10 women), 14 part-time (11 women); includes 3 minority (2 African Americans, 1 Asian American or Pacific Islander). 22 applicants, 18% accepted, 4 enrolled. In 2009, 4 doctorates awarded. *Degree requirements:* For doctorate, comprehensive exam, thesis/dissertation. *Entrance requirements:* For doctorate, GRE, minimum GPA of 3.0. Additional exam requirements/recommendations for international students: Required—TOEFL (minimum score 550 paper-based; 79 iBT), IELTS (minimum score 5.5). *Application deadline:* For fall admission, 8/1 for domestic students, 5/1 for international students; for spring admission, 12/1 for domestic students, 10/1 for international students. Application fee: $25 ($30 for international students). Electronic applications accepted. *Expenses:* Tuition, state resident: full-time $7034; part-time $368 per credit hour. *Financial support:* In 2009–10, 4 fellowships (averaging $8,000 per year), 10 research assistantships (averaging $12,000 per year), 1 teaching assistantship (averaging $12,000 per year) were awarded. Financial award application deadline: 4/1. *Unit head:* Dr. John J. Wheeler, Director, Doctoral Studies, 931-372-3078, Fax: 931-372-3517. *Application contact:* Shelia K. Kendrick, Coordinator of Graduate Studies, 931-372-3808, Fax: 931-372-3497, E-mail: skendrick@Tntech.edu.

Texas A&M University, College of Education and Human Development, Department of Educational Psychology, College Station, TX 77843. Offers counseling psychology (PhD); educational psychology (PhD); educational technology (M Ed); gifted and talented education (M Ed, MS); Hispanic bilingual education (M Ed, PhD); human learning and development (MS); intelligence, creativity, and giftedness (PhD); learning, development, and instruction (PhD); research, measurement and statistics (MS); research, measurement, and statistics (PhD); school counseling (M Ed); school psychology (PhD); special education (M Ed, PhD). *Accreditation:* APA (one or more programs are accredited). Part-time and evening/weekend programs available. Postbaccalaureate distance learning degree programs offered (no on-campus study). *Faculty:* 45. *Students:* 160 full-time (126 women), 144 part-time (118 women); includes 99 minority (25 African Americans, 13 Asian Americans or Pacific Islanders, 61 Hispanic Americans), 41 international. In 2009, 53 master's, 30 doctorates awarded. *Degree requirements:* For master's, thesis optional; for doctorate, thesis/dissertation. *Entrance requirements:* For master's and doctorate, GRE General Test. Additional exam requirements/recommendations for international students: Required—TOEFL. Application fee: $50 ($75 for international students). Electronic applications accepted. *Expenses:* Tuition, state resident: full-time $3991; part-time $221.74 per credit hour. Tuition, nonresident: full-time $9049; part-time $502.74 per credit hour. *Financial support:* In 2009–10, fellowships (averaging $12,000 per year), research assistantships (averaging $9,000 per year), teaching assistantships (averaging $9,000 per year) were awarded; career-related internships or fieldwork, institutionally sponsored loans, scholarships/grants, and unspecified assistantships also available. Financial award applicants required to submit FAFSA. *Unit head:* Dr. Victor Willson, Head, 979-845-1800. *Application contact:* Carol A. Wagner, Director of Advising, 979-845-1833, Fax: 979-862-1256, E-mail: epsyadvisor@tamu.edu.

Troy University, Graduate School, College of Education, Program in Teacher Education-Multiple Levels, Troy, AL 36082. Offers alternative 5th year art education (MS); alternative 5th year instrumental (MS); alternative 5th year physical education (MS); alternative 5th year vocal/choral (MS); traditional art education (MS); traditional gifted education (MS); traditional instrumental (MS); traditional physical education (MS); traditional reading specialist (MS); traditional vocal/choral (MS). Part-time and evening/weekend programs available. *Students:* 5 full-time (3 women), 21 part-time (12 women); includes 11 minority (9 African Americans, 1 American Indian/Alaska Native, 1 Asian American or Pacific Islander). Average age 30. 2 applicants, 50% accepted. In 2009, 8 master's awarded. *Degree requirements:* For master's, comprehensive exam, thesis. *Entrance requirements:* For master's, minimum GPA of 2.5. Additional exam requirements/recommendations for international students: Required—TOEFL (minimum score 523 paper-based; 193 computer-based; 70 iBT), IELTS (minimum score 6). *Application deadline:* Applications are processed on a rolling basis. Application fee: $50. Electronic applications accepted. *Financial support:* Available to part-time students. Applicants required to submit FAFSA. *Unit head:* Dr. Marian Parker, Coordinator, 334-670-5661, Fax: 334-670-3548, E-mail: mjparker@troy.edu. *Application contact:* Brenda K. Campbell, Director of Graduate Admissions, 334-670-3178, Fax: 334-670-3733, E-mail: bcamp@troy.edu.

Education of the Gifted

University at Buffalo, the State University of New York, Graduate School, Graduate School of Education, Department of Learning and Instruction, Buffalo, NY 14260. Offers biology education (Ed M, Certificate); chemistry education (Ed M, Certificate); childhood education (Ed M); childhood education with bilingual extension (Ed M); early childhood education (Ed M); earth science education (Ed M, Certificate); elementary education (Ed D, PhD); English education (Ed M, PhD, Certificate); English for speakers of other languages (Ed M); foreign and second language education (PhD); French education (Ed M, Certificate); general education (Ed M); German education (Ed M, Certificate); gifted education (online) (Certificate); Latin education (Ed M, Certificate); literary specialist (Ed M); mathematics education (Ed M, PhD, Certificate); music education (Ed M, Certificate); physics education (Ed M, Certificate); reading education (PhD); science and the public (online) (Ed M); science education (PhD); social studies education (Ed M, Certificate); Spanish education (Ed M, Certificate); special education (PhD); teaching and leading for diversity (Certificate); teaching English to speakers of other languages (Ed M). Part-time and evening/weekend programs available. Postbaccalaureate distance learning degree programs offered (no on-campus study). *Faculty:* 34 full-time (24 women), 50 part-time/adjunct (39 women). *Students:* 332 full-time (245 women), 365 part-time (272 women); includes 50 minority (18 African Americans, 4 American Indian/Alaska Native, 10 Asian Americans or Pacific Islanders, 18 Hispanic Americans), 55 international. Average age 30. 627 applicants, 78% accepted, 286 enrolled. In 2009, 255 master's, 16 doctorates, 51 other advanced degrees awarded. *Degree requirements:* For master's, comprehensive exam; for doctorate, thesis/dissertation, research analysis exam, research experience component. *Entrance requirements:* For doctorate, GRE General Test or MAT, interview, writing sample, letters of recommendation. Additional exam requirements/recommendations for international students: Required—TOEFL (minimum score 600 paper-based; 250 computer-based; 96 iBT). *Application deadline:* For fall admission, 2/1 priority date for domestic and international students; for spring admission, 11/15 priority date for domestic students, 10/1 for international students. Applications are processed on a rolling basis. Application fee: $50. Electronic applications accepted. *Financial support:* In 2009–10, 23 fellowships with full tuition reimbursements (averaging $9,000 per year), 42 research assistantships with full tuition reimbursements (averaging $10,000 per year) were awarded; teaching assistantships with full tuition reimbursements, career-related internships or fieldwork, Federal Work-Study, institutionally sponsored loans, scholarships/grants, tuition waivers (partial), and unspecified assistantships also available. Financial award application deadline: 2/28; financial award applicants required to submit FAFSA. *Faculty research:* Science assessment, foreign language teaching and learning, early learning, new literacies, gender and education. Total annual research expenditures: $1.8 million. *Unit head:* Dr. Suzanne Miller, Chair, 716-645-2455, Fax: 716-645-3161, E-mail: smiller@buffalo.edu. *Application contact:* Cathy Dimino, Admissions Assistant, 716-645-2110, Fax: 716-645-7937, E-mail: cadimino@buffalo.edu.

The University of Alabama, Graduate School, College of Education, Department of Special Education and Multiple Abilities, Tuscaloosa, AL 35487. Offers collaborative teacher program (M Ed, Ed S); early intervention (M Ed, Ed S); gifted education (M Ed, Ed S); multiple abilities program (M Ed); special education (Ed D, PhD). Part-time and evening/weekend programs available. *Faculty:* 11 full-time (8 women). *Students:* 20 full-time (17 women), 50 part-time (46 women); includes 13 minority (8 African Americans, 3 American Indian/Alaska Native, 2 Hispanic Americans). Average age 32. 45 applicants, 40% accepted, 13 enrolled. In 2009, 33 master's, 2 other advanced degrees awarded. Terminal master's awarded for partial completion of doctoral program. *Degree requirements:* For master's, comprehensive exam, thesis optional; for doctorate, one foreign language, comprehensive exam, thesis/dissertation. *Entrance requirements:* For master's, GRE or MAT, minimum undergraduate GPA of 3.0, teaching certificate, 3 letters of recommendation; for doctorate, GRE or MAT, 3 years of teaching experience, minimum undergraduate GPA of 3.25. Additional exam requirements/recommendations for international students: Required—TOEFL. *Application deadline:* For fall admission, 7/1 for domestic students; for spring admission, 11/1 for domestic students. Applications are processed on a rolling basis. Application fee: $50 ($60 for international students). Electronic applications accepted. *Expenses:* Tuition, state resident: full-time $7000. Tuition, nonresident: full-time $19,200. *Financial support:* In 2009–10, 8 students received support, including 4 research assistantships with tuition reimbursements available (averaging $9,000 per year), 4 teaching assistantships with tuition reimbursements available (averaging $9,000 per year); health care benefits and unspecified assistantships also available. Financial award application deadline: 7/1; financial award applicants required to submit FAFSA. *Faculty research:* Gifted education, mild disabilities, early intervention, severe disabilities. *Unit head:* James A. Siders, Associate Professor and Head, 205-348-5577, Fax: 205-348-6782, E-mail: jsiders@bama.ua.edu. *Application contact:* April Zark, Office Support, 205-348-6093, Fax: 205-348-6782, E-mail: azark@bamaed.ua.edu.

University of Arkansas at Little Rock, Graduate School, College of Education, Department of Teacher Education, Program in Teaching the Gifted and Talented, Little Rock, AR 72204-1099. Offers M Ed. *Accreditation:* NCATE. Part-time and evening/weekend programs available. *Degree requirements:* For master's, comprehensive exam. *Entrance requirements:* For master's, interview, minimum GPA of 2.75, GRE General Test or teaching certificate.

University of Calgary, Faculty of Graduate Studies, Faculty of Education, Graduate Division of Educational Research, Calgary, AB T2N 1N4, Canada. Offers community rehabilitation and disability studies (M Ed, M Sc, Ed D, PhD, Graduate Certificate, Graduate Diploma); curriculum, teaching and learning (M Ed, M Sc, MA, Ed D, PhD, Graduate Certificate, Graduate Diploma); educational contexts (M Ed, MA, Ed D, PhD, Graduate Certificate, Graduate Diploma); educational leadership (M Ed, MA, Ed D, PhD, Graduate Certificate, Graduate Diploma); educational technology (M Ed, M Sc, MA, Ed D, PhD, Graduate Certificate, Graduate Diploma); gifted education (M Sc, MA, Ed D, PhD, Graduate Certificate, Graduate Diploma); higher education administration (Ed D); interpretive studies in education (M Ed, M Sc, MA, Ed D, PhD, Graduate Certificate, Graduate Diploma); second language teaching (M Ed, Ed D, PhD, Graduate Certificate, Graduate Diploma); teaching English as a second language (M Ed, M Sc, MA, Ed D, PhD, Graduate Certificate, Graduate Diploma); workplace and adult learning (M Ed, MA, Ed D, PhD, Graduate Certificate, Graduate Diploma). Ed D in both higher education administration and educational leadership offered via distance delivery. Part-time and evening/weekend programs available. Postbaccalaureate distance learning degree programs offered (minimal on-campus study). *Degree requirements:* For master's, thesis (for some programs); for doctorate, thesis/dissertation, candidacy exam. *Entrance requirements:* For master's, minimum GPA of 3.0, 3 letters of reference; for doctorate, minimum GPA of 3.5, 3 letters of reference; for other advanced degree, minimum GPA of 3.0. Additional exam requirements/recommendations for international students: Required—TOEFL, IELTS. Electronic applications accepted. *Faculty research:* Curriculum, leadership, technology, contexts, gifted, second language teaching, work place and adult learning.

University of Central Florida, College of Education, Department of Educational Studies, Orlando, FL 32816. Offers applied learning and instruction (MA); community college education (Certificate); curriculum and instruction (Ed S); education (Ed D, PhD, Ed S); gifted education (Certificate); global and comparative education (Certificate); initial teacher professional preparation (Certificate); teacher leadership (M Ed); urban education (Certificate). *Accreditation:* NCATE. Part-time and evening/weekend programs available. *Faculty:* 18 full-time (10 women), 16 part-time/adjunct (10 women). *Students:* 155 full-time (106 women), 156 part-time (131 women); includes 80 minority (37 African Americans, 5 Asian Americans or Pacific Islanders, 38 Hispanic Americans), 22 international. Average age 36. 200 applicants, 57% accepted, 77 enrolled. In 2009, 9 master's, 34 doctorates, 17 other advanced degrees awarded. *Degree requirements:* For other advanced degree, thesis or alternative, final exam. *Entrance requirements:* For degree, GRE General Test, minimum GPA of 3.0, resume. Additional exam requirements/recommendations for international students: Required—TOEFL. *Application deadline:* For fall admission, 2/20 for domestic students; for spring admission, 9/20 for domestic students. Application fee: $30. Electronic applications accepted. *Expenses:* Tuition, state resident: part-time $306.31 per credit hour. Tuition, nonresident: part-time $1099.01 per credit hour. Part-time tuition and fees vary according to degree level and program. *Financial support:* In 2009–10, 82 students received support, including 55 fellowships with partial tuition reimbursements available (averaging $8,300 per year), 29 research assistantships with partial tuition reimbursements available (averaging $7,000 per year), 43 teaching assistantships with partial tuition reimbursements available (averaging $8,000 per year); career-related internships or fieldwork, Federal Work-Study, institutionally sponsored loans, and unspecified assistantships also available. Financial award application deadline: 3/1; financial award applicants required to submit FAFSA. *Unit head:* Dr. Karen Biraimah, Chair, 407-823-2428, E-mail: biraimah@mail.ucf.edu. *Application contact:* Dr. Karen Biraimah, Chair, 407-823-2428, E-mail: biraimah@mail.ucf.edu.

University of Connecticut, Graduate School, Neag School of Education, Department of Educational Psychology, Program in Gifted and Talented Education, Storrs, CT 06269. Offers MA, PhD, Post-Master's Certificate. *Accreditation:* NCATE. *Faculty:* 17 full-time (11 women). *Students:* 18 full-time (16 women), 58 part-time (45 women); includes 5 minority (2 African Americans, 1 Asian American or Pacific Islander, 2 Hispanic Americans), 6 international. Average age 39. 34 applicants, 21% accepted, 3 enrolled. In 2009, 26 master's, 3 doctorates awarded. Terminal master's awarded for partial completion of doctoral program. *Degree requirements:* For master's, comprehensive exam, thesis or alternative; for doctorate, thesis/dissertation. *Entrance requirements:* For master's and doctorate, GRE General Test. Additional exam requirements/recommendations for international students: Required—TOEFL (minimum score 550 paper-based; 213 computer-based). *Application deadline:* For fall admission, 2/1 priority date for domestic and international students; for spring admission, 11/1 for domestic students, 10/1 for international students. Applications are processed on a rolling basis. Application fee: $55. Electronic applications accepted. *Expenses:* Tuition, state resident: full-time $4725; part-time $525 per credit. Tuition, nonresident: full-time $12,267; part-time $1363 per credit. Required fees: $346 per semester. Tuition and fees vary according to course load. *Financial support:* In 2009–10, 13 research assistantships with full tuition reimbursements were awarded; fellowships, teaching assistantships with full tuition reimbursements, Federal Work-Study, scholarships/grants, health care benefits, and unspecified assistantships also available. Financial award application deadline: 2/1; financial award applicants required to submit FAFSA. *Unit head:* Hariharan Swaminathan, Head, 860-486-4031, Fax: 860-486-0210, E-mail: hariharan.swaminathan@uconn.edu. *Application contact:* Lisa Rasicot, Graduate Coordinator, 860-486-3065, Fax: 860-486-0210, E-mail: l.rasicot@uconn.edu.

University of Houston, College of Education, Department of Curriculum and Instruction, Houston, TX 77204. Offers art education (M Ed); bilingual education (M Ed); curriculum and instruction (M Ed, Ed D); early childhood education (M Ed); elementary education (M Ed); gifted and talented education (M Ed); instructional technology (M Ed); mathematics education (M Ed); reading and language arts education (M Ed); science education (M Ed); second language education (M Ed); secondary education (M Ed); social studies education (M Ed); teaching (M Ed). *Accreditation:* NCATE. Part-time and evening/weekend programs available. *Faculty:* 20 full-time (9 women), 22 part-time/adjunct (17 women). *Students:* 113 full-time (81 women), 195 part-time (150 women); includes 107 minority (43 African Americans, 29 Asian Americans or Pacific Islanders, 35 Hispanic Americans), 29 international. Average age 35. 150 applicants, 77% accepted, 55 enrolled. In 2009, 75 master's, 31 doctorates awarded. *Degree requirements:* For master's, comprehensive exam, thesis optional; for doctorate, comprehensive exam, thesis/dissertation. *Entrance requirements:* For master's and doctorate, GRE, minimum cumulative undergraduate GPA of 2.6. Additional exam requirements/recommendations for international students: Required—TOEFL (minimum score 550 paper-based; 79 iBT). *Application deadline:* For fall admission, 3/1 for domestic and international students; for spring admission, 10/1 for domestic and international students. Application fee: $45 ($75 for international students). Electronic applications accepted. *Expenses:* Tuition, state resident: full-time $7676; part-time $320 per credit hour. Tuition, nonresident: full-time $14,324; part-time $597 per credit hour. Required fees: $3034. *Financial support:* In 2009–10, 4 fellowships with full tuition reimbursements (averaging $9,500 per year), 6 research assistantships with full tuition reimbursements (averaging $8,800 per year), 25 teaching assistantships with full tuition reimbursements (averaging $8,800 per year) were awarded; career-related internships or fieldwork, Federal Work-Study, institutionally sponsored loans, scholarships/grants, health care benefits, and unspecified assistantships also available. Support available to part-time students. Financial award application deadline: 2/1. *Faculty research:* Teaching-learning process, instructional technology in schools, teacher education, classroom management, at-risk students. *Unit head:* Dr. Laveria Hutchison, Chairperson, 713-743-4958, Fax: 713-743-4990, E-mail: lhutchison@uh.edu. *Application contact:* Renee C. Rattelade, Executive Secretary, 713-743-4997, Fax: 713-743-4990, E-mail: rrattelade@mail.coe.uh.edu.

University of Louisiana at Lafayette, College of Education, Graduate Studies and Research in Education, Program in Education of the Gifted, Lafayette, LA 70504. Offers M Ed. *Accreditation:* NCATE. *Degree requirements:* For master's, thesis or alternative. *Entrance requirements:* For master's, GRE General Test, teaching certificate. Additional exam requirements/recommendations for international students: Required—TOEFL (minimum score 550 paper-based; 213 computer-based). Electronic applications accepted.

University of Louisiana at Monroe, Graduate School, College of Education and Human Development, Department of Curriculum and Instruction, Program in Curriculum and Instruction, Monroe, LA 71209-0001. Offers curriculum and instruction (Ed D); elementary education (1-5) (M Ed); reading education (K-12) (M Ed); SPED-academically gifted education (K-12) (M Ed); SPED-early intervention education (birth-3) (M Ed); SPED-educational diagnostics education (PreK-12) (M Ed). *Accreditation:* NCATE. *Faculty:* 17 full-time (all women), 2 part-time/adjunct (both women). *Students:* 15 full-time (13 women), 125 part-time (118 women); includes 38 minority (36 African Americans, 1 Asian American or Pacific Islander, 1 Hispanic American). Average age 37. In 2009, 11 master's, 4 doctorates awarded. *Degree requirements:* For master's, comprehensive exam (for some programs), thesis; for doctorate, thesis/dissertation, internships. *Entrance requirements:* For master's, GRE General Test; for doctorate, GRE General Test, minimum undergraduate GPA of 2.75, graduate 3.25. Additional exam requirements/recommendations for international students: Required—TOEFL (minimum score 500 paper-based; 173 computer-based; 61 iBT). *Application deadline:* For fall admission, 8/24 priority date for domestic students, 7/1 for international students; for winter admission, 12/14 priority date for domestic students; for spring admission, 1/19 for domestic students, 11/1 for international students. Applications are processed on a rolling basis. Application fee: $20 ($30 for international students). Electronic applications accepted. *Expenses:* Tuition, state resident: part-time $159 per credit hour. Tuition, nonresident: part-time $159 per credit hour. Required fees: $1300 per year. Tuition and fees vary according to course load. *Financial support:* In 2009–10, 8 teaching assistantships with full tuition reimbursements (averaging $2,969 per year) were awarded; career-related internships or fieldwork, Federal Work-Study, and unspecified assistantships also available. Financial award application deadline: 4/1; financial award applicants required to submit FAFSA. *Unit head:* Dr. Dorothy Schween, Coordinator, 318-342-1269, Fax: 318-342-3131, E-mail: schween@ulm.edu. *Application contact:* Whitney Sutherland, Administrative Assistant to the Department Head, 318-342-1266, Fax: 318-342-3131, E-mail: sutherland@ulm.edu.

University of Minnesota, Twin Cities Campus, Graduate School, College of Education and Human Development, Department of Educational Psychology, Minneapolis, MN 55455-0213. Offers counseling and student personnel psychology (MA, PhD, Ed S); early childhood education (M Ed, MA, PhD); educational psychology (PhD); psychological foundations of education (MA, PhD, Ed S); school psychology (MA, PhD, Ed S); special education (M Ed, MA, PhD, Ed S); talent development and gifted education (Certificate). *Accreditation:* APA (one or more programs are accredited). *Faculty:* 34 full-time (12 women). *Students:* 286 full-time (214 women), 93 part-time (73 women); includes 43 minority (14 African Americans, 2 American Indian/Alaska Native, 19 Asian Americans or Pacific Islanders, 8 Hispanic Americans), 50 international. Average age 31. 395 applicants, 42% accepted, 107 enrolled. In 2009, 72 master's, 30 doctorates, 17 other advanced degrees awarded. *Financial support:* In 2009–10, 20 fellowships (averaging $26,215 per year), 61 research assistantships (averaging $26,184 per year), 38 teaching assistantships (averaging $28,004 per year) were awarded. *Faculty research:* Learning, cognitive and social processes; multicultural education and counseling; measurement

and statistical processes; performance assessment; instructional design/strategies for students with special needs. Total annual research expenditures: $3 million. *Unit head:* Dr. Susan Hupp, Chair, 612-624-1003, Fax: 612-624-8241, E-mail: shupp@umn.edu. *Application contact:* Dr. Mary Trettin, Associate Dean, 612-625-6501, Fax: 612-626-1580, E-mail: mtrettin@umn.edu.

University of Missouri, Graduate School, College of Education, Department of Special Education, Columbia, MO 65211. Offers administration and supervision of special education (PhD); behavior disorders (M Ed, PhD); curriculum development of exceptional students (M Ed, PhD); early childhood special education (M Ed, PhD); general special education (M Ed, MA, PhD); learning and instruction (M Ed); learning disabilities (M Ed, PhD); mental retardation (M Ed, PhD). Part-time and evening/weekend programs available. Postbaccalaureate distance learning degree programs offered (no on-campus study). *Degree requirements:* For master's, comprehensive exam, thesis or alternative; for doctorate, comprehensive exam, thesis/dissertation. *Entrance requirements:* For master's and doctorate, GRE General Test, letters of recommendation. Additional exam requirements/recommendations for international students: Required—TOEFL (minimum score 500 paper-based; 173 computer-based; 61 iBT). Electronic applications accepted. *Faculty research:* Positive behavior support, applied behavior analysis, attention deficit disorder, pre-linguistic development, school discipline.

The University of North Carolina at Charlotte, Graduate School, College of Education, Department of Special Education and Child Development, Charlotte, NC 28223-0001. Offers special education (M Ed, PhD), including academically gifted (M Ed), behavioral—emotional handicaps (M Ed), cross-categorical disabilities (M Ed), learning disabilities (M Ed), mental handicaps (M Ed), severe and profound handicaps (M Ed). Part-time programs available. *Faculty:* 25 full-time (17 women), 5 part-time/adjunct (4 women). *Students:* 20 full-time (19 women), 141 part-time (130 women); includes 13 African Americans, 3 American Indian/Alaska Native, 2 Hispanic Americans, 2 international. Average age 35. 17 applicants, 94% accepted, 12 enrolled. In 2009, 19 master's, 22 doctorates awarded. *Degree requirements:* For doctorate, comprehensive exam, thesis/dissertation, portfolio, qualifying exam. *Entrance requirements:* For master's, GRE or MAT; for doctorate, GRE or MAT, 3 letters of reference, resume or curriculum vitae, minimum GPA of 3.5, master's degree in special education or related field, 3 years of teaching experience. Additional exam requirements/recommendations for international students: Required—TOEFL (minimum score 557 paper-based; 220 computer-based; 83 iBT), TOEFL (minimum score 550 paper-based; 220 computer-based) or Michigan English Language Assessment Battery. *Application deadline:* For fall admission, 7/15 for domestic students, 5/1 for international students; for spring admission, 11/15 for domestic students, 10/1 for international students. Application fee: $55. *Financial support:* In 2009–10, 18 students received support, including 9 research assistantships (averaging $12,299 per year), 9 teaching assistantships (averaging $14,165 per year). Financial award application deadline: 4/1; financial award applicants required to submit FAFSA. *Faculty research:* Transition to adulthood and self-determination, teaching reading and other academic skills to students with disabilities, alternate assessment, early intervention, preschool education. Total annual research expenditures: $3.2 million. *Unit head:* David Gilmore, Unit Head, 704-687-8186, Fax: 704-687-2916. *Application contact:* Kathy B. Giddings, Director of Graduate Admissions, 704-687-5503, Fax: 704-687-3279, E-mail: gradadm@uncc.edu.

University of St. Thomas, Graduate Studies, School of Education, Department of Special and Gifted Education, St. Paul, MN 55105-1096. Offers autism spectrum disorders (Certificate); autism spectrum disporders (MA); developmental disabilities (MA); director of special education (Ed S); early childhood special education (MA); gifted, creative, and talented education (MA); learning disabilities (MA); Orton-Gillingham reading (Certificate); special education (MA). *Accreditation:* NCATE. Part-time and evening/weekend programs available. *Faculty:* 7 full-time (6 women), 16 part-time/adjunct (14 women). *Students:* 25 full-time (23 women), 226 part-time (180 women); includes 16 minority (6 African Americans, 6 Asian Americans or Pacific Islanders, 4 Hispanic Americans), 3 international. Average age 34. 447 applicants, 60% accepted. In 2009, 65 master's, 65 other advanced degrees awarded. *Degree requirements:* For master's, thesis; for other advanced degree, professional portfolio. *Entrance requirements:* For master's, minimum GPA of 3.0 or MAT; for other advanced degree, MAT or minimum GPA of 2.75. Additional exam requirements/recommendations for international students: Required—TOEFL (minimum score 550 paper-based; 213 computer-based; 80 iBT). *Application deadline:* For fall admission, 6/1 priority date for domestic students; for spring admission, 11/1 priority date for domestic students. Applications are processed on a rolling basis. Application fee: $50. *Financial support:* Fellowships, research assistantships, institutionally sponsored loans and scholarships/grants available. Support available to part-time students. Financial award applicants required to submit FAFSA. *Faculty research:* Reading and math fluency, inclusion curriculum for developmental disorders, parent involvement in positive behavior supports, children's friendships, preschool inclusion. *Unit head:* Dr. Terri L. Vandercook, Chair, 651-962-4389, Fax: 651-962-4169, E-mail: tlvandercook@stthomas.edu. *Application contact:* Patricia L. Thomas, Department Assistant, 651-962-4980, Fax: 651-962-4169, E-mail: plhelland@stthomas.edu.

University of Southern Maine, College of Education and Human Development, Abilities and Disabilities Studies Program, Portland, ME 04104-9300. Offers gifted and talented (MS); self-design in special education (MS); teaching all students (MS). *Accreditation:* Teacher Education Accreditation Council. Part-time and evening/weekend programs available. *Faculty:* 2 full-time (1 woman), 1 part-time/adjunct (0 women). *Students:* 8 full-time (7 women), 31 part-time (25 women); includes 1 minority (Hispanic American). 9 applicants, 89% accepted, 5 enrolled. In 2009, 13 master's awarded. *Degree requirements:* For master's, thesis or alternative, portfolio. *Entrance requirements:* For master's, proof of teacher certification. Additional exam requirements/recommendations for international students: Required—TOEFL (minimum score 550 paper-based; 213 computer-based; 79 iBT). *Application deadline:* For fall admission, 5/1 priority date for domestic students; for spring admission, 10/15 priority date for domestic students. Applications are processed on a rolling basis. Application fee: $50. Electronic applications accepted. *Financial support:* In 2009–10, 1 student received support, including 1 research assistantship with partial tuition reimbursement available (averaging $4,500 per year); career-related internships or fieldwork, Federal Work-Study, institutionally sponsored loans, scholarships/grants, and unspecified assistantships also available. Support available to part-time students. Financial award application deadline: 3/1; financial award applicants required to submit FAFSA. *Unit head:* Dr. James Curry, Chair, Professional Education Department, 207-780-5400, Fax: 207-228-8277, E-mail: jcurry@usm.maine.edu. *Application contact:* Mary Sloan, Director of Graduate Admissions, 207-780-4386, Fax: 207-780-4969, E-mail: msloan@usm.maine.edu.

University of Southern Mississippi, Graduate School, College of Education and Psychology, Department of Curriculum, Instruction, and Special Education, Hattiesburg, MS 39406-0001. Offers alternative secondary teacher education (MAT); early childhood education (M Ed, Ed S); education of the gifted (M Ed, Ed D, PhD, Ed S); elementary education (M Ed, Ed D, PhD, Ed S); reading (M Ed, MS, Ed S); secondary education (M Ed, MS, Ed D, PhD, Ed S); special education (M Ed, Ed D, PhD, Ed S). *Faculty:* 23 full-time (17 women), 3 part-time/adjunct (2 women). *Students:* 31 full-time (26 women), 77 part-time (68 women); includes 18 minority (15 African Americans, 3 Hispanic Americans). Average age 37. 50 applicants, 52% accepted, 19 enrolled. In 2009, 43 master's, 3 doctorates, 2 other advanced degrees awarded. *Degree requirements:* For master's, comprehensive exam, thesis (for some programs); for doctorate, comprehensive exam, thesis/dissertation; for Ed S, comprehensive exam, thesis. *Entrance requirements:* For master's, GRE General Test, MAT, minimum GPA of 3.0; for doctorate, GRE General Test, minimum GPA of 3.5; for Ed S, GRE General Test, MAT, minimum GPA of 3.25. Additional exam requirements/recommendations for international students: Required—TOEFL. *Application deadline:* For fall admission, 3/1 priority date for domestic students, 3/1 for international students. Applications are processed on a rolling basis. Application fee: $35. *Expenses:* Tuition, state resident: full-time $5096; part-time $284 per hour. Tuition, nonresident: full-time $13,052; part-time $726 per hour. Required fees: $402. Tuition and fees vary according to course level and course load. *Financial support:* In 2009–10, 9 research assistantships with tuition reimbursements (averaging $18,316 per year), 2 teaching assistantships with full tuition reimbursements (averaging $8,500 per year) were awarded; Federal Work-Study, institutionally sponsored loans, and tuition waivers (partial) also available. Financial award application

deadline: 3/15; financial award applicants required to submit FAFSA. *Faculty research:* Mathematical problem solving, integrative curriculum, writing process, teacher education models. Total annual research expenditures: $100,000. *Unit head:* Dr. David Daves, Chair, 601-266-4547, Fax: 601-266-4175. *Application contact:* Rachea Cawthorn, Administrative Assistant, 601-266-6987, Fax: 601-266-4548.

University of South Florida, Graduate School, College of Education–Main Campus, Department of Special Education, Tampa, FL 33620-9951. Offers behavior disorders (MA); exceptional student education (MA, MAT); gifted education (MA); mental retardation (MA); special education (PhD); specific learning disabilities (MA). *Accreditation:* NCATE. Part-time and evening/weekend programs available. *Faculty:* 12 full-time (9 women), 2 part-time/adjunct (1 woman). *Students:* 59 full-time (48 women), 85 part-time (78 women); includes 43 minority (24 African Americans, 1 American Indian/Alaska Native, 7 Asian Americans or Pacific Islanders, 11 Hispanic Americans), 1 international. Average age 30. 73 applicants, 74% accepted, 45 enrolled. In 2009, 32 master's, 4 doctorates awarded. *Degree requirements:* For master's, comprehensive exam; for doctorate, comprehensive exam, thesis/dissertation. *Entrance requirements:* For master's, GRE General Test (if undergraduate GPA less than 3.0), minimum GPA of 3.0 in last 60 hours of course work; for doctorate, GRE General Test, minimum GPA of 3.0 undergraduate, 3.5 graduate; interview. Additional exam requirements/recommendations for international students: Required—TOEFL (minimum score 500 paper-based; 213 computer-based). *Application deadline:* For fall admission, 2/15 for domestic students, 1/2 for international students; for winter admission, 2/15 for domestic students, 1/2 for international students; for spring admission, 10/15 for domestic students, 6/1 for international students. Application fee: $30. Electronic applications accepted. *Financial support:* In 2009–10, 3 fellowships with full tuition reimbursements (averaging $10,000 per year), 4 research assistantships with full tuition reimbursements (averaging $10,000 per year), 7 teaching assistantships with full tuition reimbursements (averaging $10,000 per year) were awarded; scholarships/grants and unspecified assistantships also available. Financial award application deadline: 6/1; financial award applicants required to submit FAFSA. *Faculty research:* Instruction methods for students with learning and behavioral disabilities; teacher preparation, experiential learning, and participatory action research; public policy research; personal preparation for transitional services; case-based instruction, partnerships and mentor development; inclusion and voices of teachers and students with disabilities; narrative ethics and philosophies of research. Total annual research expenditures: $2.9 million. *Unit head:* Dr. Daphne Thomas, Chairperson, 813-974-1383, Fax: 813-974-5542, E-mail: dthomas@usf.edu. *Application contact:* Dr. Daphne Thomas, Chairperson, 813-974-1383, Fax: 813-974-5542, E-mail: dthomas@usf.edu.

The University of Texas–Pan American, College of Education, Department of Educational Psychology, Edinburg, TX 78539. Offers counseling (M Ed); educational diagnostician (M Ed); gifted education (M Ed); school psychology (MA); special education (M Ed). Part-time and evening/weekend programs available. *Degree requirements:* For master's, comprehensive exam (for some programs), thesis (for some programs). *Entrance requirements:* For master's, GRE General Test, interview. *Expenses:* Tuition, state resident: full-time $3630.60; part-time $201.70 per credit hour. Tuition, nonresident: full-time $8617; part-time $478.70 per credit hour. Required fees: $806.50. *Faculty research:* Reading instruction, assessment practice, behavior interventions consultation, mental retardation.

The University of Toledo, College of Graduate Studies, College of Education, Department of Early Childhood, Physical and Special Education, Program in Gifted and Talented, Toledo, OH 43606-3390. Offers PhD, Ed S.

University of Virginia, Curry School of Education, Department of Leadership, Foundations and Policy, Program in Educational Psychology, Charlottesville, VA 22903. Offers applied developmental science (M Ed); educational evaluation (M Ed); educational psychology (M Ed, Ed D, Ed S); educational research (Ed D); gifted education (M Ed); instructional technology (M Ed, Ed S); research statistics and evaluation (Ed D); school psychology (Ed D). *Students:* 28 full-time (22 women), 18 part-time (13 women); includes 3 minority (1 African American, 1 Asian American or Pacific Islander, 1 Hispanic American), 7 international. Average age 31. 130 applicants, 36% accepted, 31 enrolled. In 2009, 50 master's, 25 doctorates, 1 other advanced degree awarded. *Degree requirements:* For master's, comprehensive exam. *Entrance requirements:* For master's and doctorate, GRE General Test, 2 letters of recommendation. Additional exam requirements/recommendations for international students: Required—TOEFL (minimum score 600 paper-based; 250 computer-based; 90 iBT), IELTS (minimum score 7). *Application deadline:* Applications are processed on a rolling basis. Application fee: $60. Electronic applications accepted. *Financial support:* Fellowships, research assistantships, teaching assistantships available. Financial award application deadline: 1/5; financial award applicants required to submit FAFSA. *Unit head:* Jen Mashburn, Program Coordinator, E-mail: jmashburn@virginia.edu. *Application contact:* Jen Mashburn, Program Coordinator, E-mail: jmashburn@virginia.edu.

Western Washington University, Graduate School, Woodring College of Education, Department of Special Education, Bellingham, WA 98225-5996. Offers M Ed. *Accreditation:* NCATE. Part-time programs available. *Degree requirements:* For master's, comprehensive exam, thesis optional. *Entrance requirements:* For master's, GRE General Test or MAT, minimum GPA of 3.0 in last 60 semester hours or last 90 quarter hours. Additional exam requirements/recommendations for international students: Required—TOEFL (minimum score 567 paper-based; 227 computer-based). Electronic applications accepted. *Faculty research:* Applied behavioral analysis, controversial practices, infant/toddler social-emotional interventions, reflective practices in teacher education.

West Virginia University, College of Human Resources and Education, Department of Special Education, Morgantown, WV 26506. Offers autism spectrum disorder (5-adult) (MA); autism spectrum disorder (K-6) (MA); early intervention/early childhood special education (MA); gifted education (1-12) (MA); low vision (PreK-adult) (MA); multicategorical special education (5-adult) (MA); multicategorical special education (K-6) (MA); severe/multiple disabilities (K-adult) (MA); special education (MA, Ed D); vision impairments (PreK-adult) (MA). *Accreditation:* NCATE. Part-time and evening/weekend programs available. Postbaccalaureate distance learning degree programs offered (no on-campus study). *Degree requirements:* For master's, thesis optional; for doctorate, comprehensive exam, thesis/dissertation. *Entrance requirements:* For master's, minimum GPA of 2.75 passing scores on PRAXIS PPST; for doctorate, GRE General Test or MAT. Additional exam requirements/recommendations for international students: Required—TOEFL.

Whitworth University, School of Education, Graduate Studies in Education, Program in Gifted and Talented, Spokane, WA 99251-0001. Offers MAT. *Accreditation:* NCATE. Part-time and evening/weekend programs available. *Degree requirements:* For master's, comprehensive exam, thesis (for some programs). *Entrance requirements:* For master's, GRE General Test, MAT. Tuition and fees vary according to program.

Wichita State University, Graduate School, College of Education, Department of Curriculum and Instruction, Wichita, KS 67260. Offers curriculum and instruction (M Ed); special education (M Ed), including adaptive, early childhood unified, functional, gifted; teaching (MAT). *Accreditation:* NCATE. Part-time and evening/weekend programs available. *Entrance requirements:* For master's, MAT, minimum GPA of 2.75. *Expenses:* Tuition, state resident: full-time $4247; part-time $235.95 per credit hour. Tuition, nonresident: full-time $11,171; part-time $620.60 per credit hour. Required fees: $34; $3.60 per credit hour. $17 per term. Tuition and fees vary according to campus/location and program. *Unit head:* Dr. Janice Ewing, Chairperson, 316-978-3322, E-mail: janice.ewing@wichita.edu. *Application contact:* Dr. Janice Ewing, Chairperson, 316-978-3322, E-mail: janice.ewing@wichita.edu.

William Carey University, School of Education, Hattiesburg, MS 39401-5499. Offers art education (M Ed); art of teaching (M Ed); elementary education (M Ed, Ed S); English education (M Ed); gifted education (M Ed); history and social science (M Ed); mild/moderate disabilities (M Ed); secondary education (M Ed). Part-time programs available. *Degree requirements:* For master's, comprehensive exam. *Entrance requirements:* For master's, GRE, MAT, minimum

Education of the Gifted

William Carey University (continued)
GPA of 2.5, Class A teacher's license. Additional exam requirements/recommendations for international students: Required—TOEFL (minimum score 550 paper-based; 213 computer-based).

Wilmington University, College of Education, New Castle, DE 19720-6491. Offers applied education technology (M Ed); career and technical education (M Ed); elementary and secondary school counseling (M Ed); elementary special education (M Ed); elementary studies (M Ed); instruction: gifted and talented (M Ed); instruction: teaching and learning (M Ed); literacy (M Ed); reading (M Ed); school leadership (M Ed); secondary teaching (MAT). *Accreditation:* NCATE. Part-time and evening/weekend programs available. *Entrance requirements:* For master's, 2 letters of recommendation, interview. Additional exam requirements/recommendations for international students: Required—TOEFL (minimum score 500 paper-based; 173 computer-based). Electronic applications accepted.

Wright State University, School of Graduate Studies, College of Education and Human Services, Department of Teacher Education, Programs in Intervention Specialist, Dayton, OH 45435. Offers gifted educational needs (M Ed, MA); mild to moderate educational needs (M Ed, MA); moderate to intensive educational needs (M Ed, MA). *Accreditation:* NCATE. *Degree requirements:* For master's, thesis (for some programs). *Entrance requirements:* For master's, GRE General Test, MAT. Additional exam requirements/recommendations for international students: Required—TOEFL.

Youngstown State University, Graduate School, Beeghly College of Education, Department of Teacher Education, Program in Special Education, Youngstown, OH 44555-0001. Offers gifted and talented education (MS Ed); special education (MS Ed). *Accreditation:* NCATE. Part-time and evening/weekend programs available. *Degree requirements:* For master's, comprehensive exam. *Entrance requirements:* For master's, GRE, MAT, or teaching certificate; interview; minimum GPA of 2.7. Additional exam requirements/recommendations for international students: Required—TOEFL. *Faculty research:* Learning disabilities, learning styles, developing self-esteem and social skills of severe behaviorally handicapped students, inclusion.

English as a Second Language

Adelphi University, School of Education, Program in Teaching English to Speakers of Other Languages, Garden City, NY 11530-0701. Offers MA, Certificate. Part-time and evening/weekend programs available. *Students:* 11 full-time (all women), 50 part-time (42 women); includes 18 minority (3 African Americans, 4 Asian Americans or Pacific Islanders, 11 Hispanic Americans), 7 international. Average age 36. In 2009, 12 master's, 3 other advanced degrees awarded. *Entrance requirements:* For master's, 2 letters of recommendation, resume. Additional exam requirements/recommendations for international students: Required—TOEFL (minimum score 550 paper-based; 213 computer-based; 80 iBT). *Application deadline:* For fall admission, 4/1 priority date for domestic students; for spring admission, 11/1 priority date for domestic students. Applications are processed on a rolling basis. Application fee: $50. Electronic applications accepted. *Expenses:* Tuition: Full-time $28,340; part-time $830 per credit. Required fees: $600; $250 per credit. Full-time tuition and fees vary according to course load and program. *Financial support:* Fellowships, research assistantships with partial tuition reimbursements, teaching assistantships, career-related internships or fieldwork, Federal Work-Study, institutionally sponsored loans, tuition waivers (full), and unspecified assistantships available. Support available to part-time students. Financial award application deadline: 2/15; financial award applicants required to submit FAFSA. *Faculty research:* Theories of language acquisition, English as a second language in the content areas, apprenticeship in English as a second language instruction. *Unit head:* Eva Roca, Director, 516-877-4072, E-mail: rocaz@adelphi.edu. *Application contact:* Christine Murphy, Director of Admissions, 516-877-3050, Fax: 516-877-3039, E-mail: graduateadmissions@adelphi.edu.

Albright College, Department of Education—Graduate Division, Reading, PA 19612-5234. Offers early childhood education (MS); elementary education (MS); English as a second language (MA); general education (MA); special education (MS). Part-time and evening/weekend programs available. *Degree requirements:* For master's, thesis. *Entrance requirements:* For master's, GRE General Test or MAT, minimum undergraduate GPA of 3.0, 2 letters of recommendation, interview. Additional exam requirements/recommendations for international students: Recommended—TOEFL (minimum score 525 paper-based; 197 computer-based). Electronic applications accepted.

Alliant International University–Fresno, Graduate School of Education, Program in Teaching English to Speakers of Other Languages, Fresno, CA 93727. Offers MA, Ed D, Certificate. Part-time programs available. *Degree requirements:* For doctorate, thesis/dissertation. *Entrance requirements:* For master's and doctorate, minimum GPA of 3.0, letters of recommendation. Additional exam requirements/recommendations for international students: Required—TOEFL (minimum score 550 paper-based; 213 computer-based), TWE. Electronic applications accepted. *Faculty research:* Technology and second language instruction, curriculum design, sociolinguistics, TESOL teaching training, bilingualism.

Alliant International University–Irvine, Graduate School of Education, Program in Teaching English to Speakers of Other Languages, Irvine, CA 92612. Offers MA, Ed D. Part-time programs available. *Degree requirements:* For doctorate, thesis/dissertation. *Entrance requirements:* For master's and doctorate, minimum GPA of 3.0, letters of recommendation. Additional exam requirements/recommendations for international students: Required—TOEFL (minimum score 550 paper-based; 213 computer-based), TWE. Electronic applications accepted.

Alliant International University–San Diego, Graduate School of Education, Program in Teaching English to Speakers of Other Languages, San Diego, CA 92131-1799. Offers MA, Ed D, Certificate. Part-time programs available. *Degree requirements:* For doctorate, thesis/dissertation. *Entrance requirements:* For master's and doctorate, minimum GPA of 3.0, letters of recommendation. Additional exam requirements/recommendations for international students: Required—TOEFL (minimum score 550 paper-based; 213 computer-based), TWE. Electronic applications accepted.

American University, College of Arts and Sciences, Department of Language and Foreign Studies, Program in Teaching English to Speakers of Other Languages, Washington, DC 20016-8045. Offers MA, Certificate. *Students:* 16 full-time (15 women), 21 part-time (17 women); includes 3 minority (2 African Americans, 1 Asian American or Pacific Islander), 9 international. Average age 35. 32 applicants, 59% accepted, 9 enrolled. In 2009, 9 master's, 18 other advanced degrees awarded. *Degree requirements:* For master's, one foreign language, comprehensive exam, thesis or alternative, portfolio. *Entrance requirements:* For master's, GRE. Additional exam requirements/recommendations for international students: Required—TOEFL. *Application deadline:* For fall admission, 2/1 for domestic students; for spring admission, 10/1 for domestic students. Application fee: $80. *Expenses:* Tuition: Full-time $22,266; part-time $1237 per credit hour. Required fees: $430. Tuition and fees vary according to program. *Financial support:* Fellowships available. Financial award application deadline: 2/1. *Faculty research:* Language, acquisition, written language, e-mail. *Unit head:* Brock Brady, Coordinator, 202-885-1146, Fax: 202-885-1076, E-mail: bbrady@american.edu. *Application contact:* Brock Brady, Coordinator, 202-885-1146, Fax: 202-885-1076, E-mail: bbrady@american.edu.

American University, College of Arts and Sciences, School of Education, Teaching, and Health, Program in English for Speakers of Other Languages, Washington, DC 20016-8001. Offers MAT, Certificate. *Students:* 2 full-time (1 woman), 20 part-time (16 women); includes 10 minority (2 African Americans, 1 American Indian/Alaska Native, 1 Asian American or Pacific Islander, 6 Hispanic Americans), 1 international. Average age 29. 19 applicants, 84% accepted, 10 enrolled. In 2009, 13 master's, 4 other advanced degrees awarded. *Degree requirements:* For master's, comprehensive exam, PRAXIS II. *Entrance requirements:* For master's, GRE General Test, PRAXIS I, minimum GPA of 3.0, 2 recommendations; for Certificate, bachelor's degree. *Application deadline:* For fall admission, 2/1 priority date for domestic students; for spring admission, 10/1 priority date for domestic students. Application fee: $80. *Expenses:* Tuition: Full-time $22,266; part-time $1237 per credit hour. Required fees: $430. Tuition and fees vary according to program. *Financial support:* Research assistantships with partial tuition reimbursements available. Financial award application deadline: 2/1. *Unit head:* Karen DiGiovanni, Director, Teacher Education, 202-885-3727, Fax: 202-885-1187, E-mail: digiovanni@american.edu. *Application contact:* Karen DiGiovanni, Director, Teacher Education, 202-885-3727, Fax: 202-885-1187, E-mail: digiovanni@american.edu.

The American University in Cairo, Graduate Studies and Research, School of Humanities and Social Sciences, English Language Institute, Cairo, Egypt. Offers teaching English as a foreign language (MA, Diploma). Part-time programs available. *Degree requirements:* For master's, one foreign language, thesis optional. *Entrance requirements:* Additional exam requirements/recommendations for international students: Required—English entrance exam and/or TOEFL. Electronic applications accepted. *Faculty research:* Teacher education, social linguistics, teaching methodology pragmatics.

American University of Sharjah, Graduate Programs, Sharjah, United Arab Emirates. Offers business (EMBA, GEMPA, MBA); chemical engineering (MS Ch E); civil engineering (MSCE); computer engineering (MS); electrical engineering (MSEE); mechanical engineering (MSME); mechatronics engineering (MS); public administration (MPA); teaching English to speakers of other languages (MA); translation and interpreting (MA); urban planning (MUP). Part-time and evening/weekend programs available. *Faculty:* 59 full-time (4 women), 5 part-time/adjunct (1 woman). *Students:* 101 full-time (44 women), 218 part-time (95 women). Average age 27. 184 applicants, 83% accepted, 92 enrolled. In 2009, 97 master's awarded. *Entrance requirements:* For master's, GMAT (MBA). Additional exam requirements/recommendations for international students: Required—TOEFL (minimum score 550 paper-based; 213 computer-based; 80 iBT), TWE (minimum score 5). *Application deadline:* For fall admission, 7/30 priority date for domestic students, 7/15 priority date for international students; for spring admission, 12/31 priority date for domestic students, 12/16 for international students. Applications are processed on a rolling basis. Application fee: $300. Electronic applications accepted. Tuition charges are reported in United Arab Emirates dirhams. *Expenses:* Tuition: Part-time 3250 United Arab Emirates dirhams per credit hour. *Financial support:* In 2009–10, 63 students received support, including 28 research assistantships with tuition reimbursements available, 35 teaching assistantships with tuition reimbursements available. *Faculty research:* Chemical engineering, civil engineering, computer engineering, electrical engineering, linguistics, translation. *Unit head:* Ghada S. Sami, Admissions Manager, 971-65151006 Ext. 1006, Fax: 971-65151020, E-mail: graduateadmission@aus.edu. *Application contact:* Ghada S. Sami, Admissions Manager, 971-65151006 Ext. 1006, Fax: 971-65151020, E-mail: graduateadmission@aus.edu.

Anaheim University, Program in Teaching English to Speakers of Other Languages, Anaheim, CA 92806-5150. Offers MA, Certificate. Postbaccalaureate distance learning degree programs offered (no on-campus study).

Andrews University, School of Graduate Studies, School of Education, Department of Teaching, Learning, and Curriculum, Berrien Springs, MI 49104. Offers curriculum and instruction (MA, Ed D, PhD, Ed S); elementary education (MAT); reading (MA); secondary education (MAT), including biology, education, English, English as a second language, French, history, physics; special education/learning disabilities (MS); teacher education (MAT). *Students:* 12 full-time (8 women), 30 part-time (19 women); includes 17 minority (14 African Americans, 1 Asian American or Pacific Islander, 2 Hispanic Americans), 10 international. Average age 43. 28 applicants, 54% accepted, 6 enrolled. In 2009, 11 master's, 4 doctorates, 1 other advanced degree awarded. *Entrance requirements:* For master's, GRE Subject Test. Additional exam requirements/recommendations for international students: Required—TOEFL (minimum score 550 paper-based). *Application deadline:* For fall admission, 8/15 for domestic students. Applications are processed on a rolling basis. Application fee: $40. *Unit head:* Dr. Lee C. Davidson, Chair, 269-471-6364. *Application contact:* Carolyn Hurst, Supervisor of Graduate Admission, 800-253-2874, Fax: 269-471-6321, E-mail: graduate@andrews.edu.

Arizona State University, Graduate College, College of Liberal Arts and Sciences, Division of Humanities, Department of English, Tempe, AZ 85287. Offers creative writing (MFA); English (MA, PhD), including comparative literature (MA), linguistics (MA), literature, rhetoric and composition (MA), rhetoric/composition and linguistics (PhD); teaching English to speakers of other languages (MTESOL). *Degree requirements:* For doctorate, thesis/dissertation. *Entrance requirements:* For master's and doctorate, GRE.

Arkansas Tech University, Graduate College, College of Arts and Humanities, Russellville, AR 72801. Offers communication (MLA); English (M Ed, MA); fine arts (MLA); history (MA); multi-media journalism (MA); psychology (MS); social science (MLA); Spanish (MA, MLA); teaching English as a second language (MA, MLA). Part-time programs available. *Students:* 39 full-time (30 women), 80 part-time (63 women); includes 11 minority (3 African Americans, 1 American Indian/Alaska Native, 1 Asian American or Pacific Islander, 6 Hispanic Americans), 23 international. Average age 33. In 2009, 70 master's awarded. *Degree requirements:* For master's, comprehensive exam (for some programs), thesis (for some programs), project. *Entrance requirements:* For master's, GRE General Test or MAT. Additional exam requirements/recommendations for international students: Required—TOEFL (minimum score 550 paper-based; 213 computer-based; 79 iBT), IELTS (minimum score 6). *Application deadline:* For fall admission, 3/1 priority date for domestic students, 5/1 priority date for international students; for spring admission, 10/1 priority date for domestic and international students. Applications are processed on a rolling basis. Application fee: $0 ($50 for international students). Electronic applications accepted. *Expenses:* Tuition, state resident: full-time $3438; part-time $191 per hour. Tuition, nonresident: full-time $6876; part-time $382 per hour. Required fees: $482; $9 per credit hour. $140 per semester. Tuition and fees vary according to course load. *Financial support:* In 2009–10, teaching assistantships with full tuition reimbursements (averaging $4,000 per year); research assistantships, career-related internships or fieldwork, Federal Work-Study, scholarships/grants, health care benefits, and unspecified assistantships also available. Support available to part-time students. Financial award application deadline: 4/15; financial award applicants required to submit FAFSA. *Unit head:* Dr. Micheal Tarver, Dean, 479-968-0274, Fax: 479-964-0812, E-mail: mtarver@atu.edu. *Application contact:* Dr. Mary B. Gunter, Dean of Graduate College, 479-968-0398, Fax: 479-964-0542, E-mail: graduate.school@atu.edu.

Asbury University, School of Graduate and Professional Studies, Wilmore, KY 40390-1198. Offers biology: alternative certificate (MA Ed); chemistry: alternative certificate (MA Ed); English (MA Ed); English as a second language (MA Ed); ESL (MA Ed); French (MA Ed); Latin: alternative certificate (MA Ed); mathematics: alternative certificate (MA Ed); reading/writing endorsement (MA Ed); social studies (MA Ed); social work (MSW), including child and family

services; Spanish (MA Ed); special education (MA Ed); special education: alternative certificate (MA Ed); teacher as leader endorsement (MA Ed). *Accreditation:* NCATE. Part-time programs available. *Faculty:* 8 full-time (7 women), 9 part-time/adjunct (4 women). *Students:* 108 part-time (87 women); includes 8 minority (4 African Americans, 2 Asian Americans or Pacific Islanders, 2 Hispanic Americans). Average age 36. 36 applicants, 86% accepted, 24 enrolled. In 2009, 20 master's awarded. *Degree requirements:* For master's, action research project, portfolio. *Entrance requirements:* For master's, PRAXIS/NTE, minimum GPA of 2.75, letters of recommendation. Additional exam requirements/recommendations for international students: Required—TOEFL (minimum score 550 paper-based). *Application deadline:* Applications are processed on a rolling basis. Application fee: $25. Electronic applications accepted. *Financial support:* Scholarships/grants and traineeships available. Financial award applicants required to submit FAFSA. *Unit head:* Dr. Bonnie J. Banker, Dean, School of Graduate and Professional Studies, 859-858-3511 Ext. 2221, Fax: 859-858-3921, E-mail: bonnie.banker@asbury.edu. *Application contact:* Lenore A. Sweigard, Graduate Program Assistant and Certification Specialist, 859-858-3511 Ext. 2502, Fax: 859-858-3921, E-mail: graded@asbury.edu.

Avila University, School of Education, Kansas City, MO 64145-1698. Offers education (MA); English for speakers of other languages (Advanced Certificate). Part-time and evening/weekend programs available. *Faculty:* 6 full-time (4 women), 12 part-time/adjunct (9 women). *Students:* 195 full-time (148 women), 52 part-time (40 women); includes 27 minority (19 African Americans, 3 American Indian/Alaska Native, 1 Asian American or Pacific Islander, 4 Hispanic Americans). Average age 34. 289 applicants, 74% accepted, 154 enrolled. In 2009, 52 master's awarded. *Entrance requirements:* For master's, minimum GPA of 3.0, writing sample, recommendation, interview; for Advanced Certificate, foreign language. Additional exam requirements/recommendations for international students: Required—TOEFL (minimum score 580 paper-based; 237 computer-based; 92 iBT). *Application deadline:* Applications are processed on a rolling basis. Application fee: $0. Electronic applications accepted. *Expenses:* Contact institution. *Financial support:* In 2009–10, 64 students received support, including 1 research assistantship; career-related internships or fieldwork also available. Support available to part-time students. Financial award applicants required to submit FAFSA. *Unit head:* Deana Angotti, Director of Graduate Education, 816-501-2446, Fax: 816-501-2915, E-mail: deana.augotti@avila.edu. *Application contact:* Deana Angotti, Director of Graduate Education, 816-501-2446, Fax: 816-501-2915, E-mail: deana.augotti@avila.edu.

Azusa Pacific University, College of Liberal Arts and Sciences, Program in Teaching English to Speakers of Other Languages, Azusa, CA 91702-7000. Offers MA.

Azusa Pacific University, School of Education, Department of Education, Program in Language Development, Azusa, CA 91702-7000. Offers MA. *Accreditation:* NCATE. *Degree requirements:* For master's, comprehensive exam or thesis, core exams, oral presentation. *Entrance requirements:* For master's, 12 units of course work in education, minimum GPA of 3.0. *Faculty research:* Biliteracy development, home-school connections, integrated curriculum.

Ball State University, Graduate School, College of Sciences and Humanities, Department of English, Muncie, IN 47306-1099. Offers English (MA, PhD), including composition, creative writing (MA), general (MA), literature; linguistics (MA, PhD), including applied linguistics (PhD); linguistics and teaching English to speakers of other languages (MA); teaching English to speakers of other languages (MA). *Degree requirements:* For doctorate, variable foreign language requirement, thesis/dissertation. *Entrance requirements:* For master's, GRE General Test, writing sample; for doctorate, GRE General Test, GRE Subject Test, minimum graduate GPA of 3.2, writing sample. *Faculty research:* American literature; literary editing; Medieval, Renaissance, and eighteenth century British literature; rhetoric.

Barry University, School of Education, Program in Curriculum and Instruction, Miami Shores, FL 33161-6695. Offers accomplished teacher (Ed S); culture, language and literacy (TESOL) (PhD); curriculum evaluation and research (PhD); early childhood (Ed S); early childhood education (PhD); elementary (Ed S); elementary education (PhD); ESOL (Ed S); gifted (Ed S); Montessori (Ed S); PKP/elementary (Ed S); reading (Ed S); reading, language and cognition (PhD). *Entrance requirements:* For doctorate, GRE, minimum GPA of 3.25.

Barry University, School of Education, Program in Technology and TESOL, Miami Shores, FL 33161-6695. Offers MS, Ed S.

Barry University, School of Education, Program in TESOL, Miami Shores, FL 33161-6695. Offers TESOL (MS); TESOL international (MS). *Entrance requirements:* For master's, GRE or MAT.

Biola University, School of Intercultural Studies, La Mirada, CA 90639-0001. Offers applied linguistics (MA); intercultural education (PhD); intercultural studies (MAICS); missiology (D Miss); missions (MA); teaching English to speakers of other languages (MA, Certificate). Part-time and evening/weekend programs available. Terminal master's awarded for partial completion of doctoral program. *Degree requirements:* For master's, one foreign language, comprehensive exam; for doctorate, one foreign language, comprehensive exam, thesis/dissertation. *Entrance requirements:* For master's, minimum undergraduate GPA of 3.0; for doctorate, MA, 3 years of ministry experience, minimum graduate GPA of 3.3. Additional exam requirements/recommendations for international students: Required—TOEFL (minimum score 550 paper-based; 213 computer-based). Electronic applications accepted.

Bishop's University, School of Education, Sherbrooke, QC J1M 0C8, Canada. Offers advanced studies in education (Diploma); education (M Ed, MA); teaching English as a second language (Certificate). Part-time programs available. Postbaccalaureate distance learning degree programs offered (minimal on-campus study). *Degree requirements:* For master's, thesis (for some programs). *Entrance requirements:* For master's, teaching license, 2 years of teaching experience. *Faculty research:* Integration of special needs students, multigrade classes/small schools, leadership in organizational development, second language acquisition.

Boston University, School of Education, Department of Literacy and Language, Counseling and Development, Teaching of English to Speakers of Other Languages Program, Boston, MA 02215. Offers Ed M, CAGS. *Degree requirements:* For CAGS, comprehensive exam. *Entrance requirements:* For master's and CAGS, GRE General Test or MAT. Additional exam requirements/recommendations for international students: Required—TOEFL. Electronic applications accepted. *Expenses:* Tuition: Full-time $37,910; part-time $1184 per credit hour. Required fees: $386; $40 per semester. Part-time tuition and fees vary according to class time, course level, degree level and program. *Faculty research:* Second language acquisition, innovative approaches to language teaching.

Brigham Young University, Graduate Studies, College of Humanities, Department of Linguistics and English Language, Provo, UT 84602. Offers general linguistics (MA); teaching English as a second language (MA, Certificate). Part-time programs available. *Faculty:* 20 full-time (4 women). *Students:* 97 full-time (69 women); includes 33 minority (1 African American, 29 Asian Americans or Pacific Islanders, 3 Hispanic Americans). Average age 30. 69 applicants, 78% accepted, 49 enrolled. In 2009, 11 master's, 32 other advanced degrees awarded. *Degree requirements:* For master's, 2 foreign languages, thesis. *Entrance requirements:* For master's, GRE General Test, minimum GPA of 3.6 in last 60 hours of course work. Additional exam requirements/recommendations for international students: Required—TOEFL (minimum score 580 paper-based; 237 computer-based; 90 iBT), TWE. *Application deadline:* 1/15 for domestic and international students. Application fee: $50. Electronic applications accepted. *Expenses:* Tuition: Full-time $5580; part-time $301 per credit hour. Tuition and fees vary according to student's religious affiliation. *Financial support:* In 2009–10, 51 students received support, including 52 research assistantships with partial tuition reimbursements available (averaging $2,763 per year), 28 teaching assistantships with partial tuition reimbursements available (averaging $1,704 per year); fellowships with partial tuition reimbursements available, career-related internships or fieldwork, institutionally sponsored loans, scholarships/grants, tuition waivers (partial), unspecified assistantships, and student instructorships also available. Support available to part-time students. Financial award application deadline: 3/28. *Faculty research:* TESOL, second language acquisition, computational linguistics, semiotics and semantics, computer-assisted language instruction. Total annual research expenditures: $261,058. *Unit head:* Dr. William G. Eggington, Chair, 801-422-2937, Fax: 801-422-0906, E-mail: bill_eggington@byu.edu. *Application contact:* LoriAnn Spear, Secretary, 801-422-2937, Fax: 801-422-0906, E-mail: phyllis_daniel@byu.edu.

Brock University, Faculty of Graduate Studies, Faculty of Humanities, Program in Applied Linguistics, St. Catharines, ON L2S 3A1, Canada. Offers MA. Part-time programs available. *Degree requirements:* For master's, thesis optional. *Entrance requirements:* For master's, honours degree with a background in English, English linguistics, teaching English as a second language, or a comparable field. Additional exam requirements/recommendations for international students: Required—TOEFL (minimum score 630 paper-based; 267 computer-based; 109 iBT), IELTS (minimum score 8), TWE (minimum score 5.5). Electronic applications accepted. *Expenses:* Contact institution. *Faculty research:* Metalinguistic ability in subsequent language learning, language teaching methodology, forensic linguistics, philosophy of education, culturally appropriate pedagogy.

Buena Vista University, School of Education, Storm Lake, IA 50588. Offers curriculum and instruction (M Ed), including effective teaching, TESL; school guidance and counseling (MS Ed). Program offered in summer only. Part-time and evening/weekend programs available. Postbaccalaureate distance learning degree programs offered (minimal on-campus study). *Degree requirements:* For master's, thesis, fieldwork/practicum, capstone portfolio. *Entrance requirements:* For master's, Analytical Writing Assessment (in-house), minimum undergraduate GPA of 2.75. Electronic applications accepted. *Faculty research:* Reading, curriculum, educational psychology, special education.

California Baptist University, Program in English, Riverside, CA 92504-3206. Offers English pedagogy (MA); literature (MA); teaching English as a second language (TESOL) (MA). Part-time programs available. *Faculty:* 4 full-time (3 women). *Students:* 3 full-time (all women), 29 part-time (21 women); includes 3 minority (1 African American, 1 Asian American or Pacific Islander, 1 Hispanic American), 5 international. 51 applicants, 55% accepted, 12 enrolled. In 2009, 3 master's awarded. *Degree requirements:* For master's, thesis (for some programs). *Entrance requirements:* For master's, minimum undergraduate GPA of 2.75, 18 semester hours of course work in English beyond freshman level. Additional exam requirements/recommendations for international students: Required—TOEFL (minimum score 575 paper-based; 230 computer-based; 89 iBT). *Application deadline:* For fall admission, 8/1 priority date for domestic students, 7/1 for international students; for spring admission, 12/1 priority date for domestic students, 10/15 for international students. Applications are processed on a rolling basis. Application fee: $45. Electronic applications accepted. *Expenses:* Tuition: Full-time $8352; part-time $464 per semester hour. Required fees: $125 per semester. Tuition and fees vary according to course load, campus/location and program. *Financial support:* Federal Work-Study and scholarships/grants available. Support available to part-time students. Financial award applicants required to submit FAFSA. *Unit head:* Dr. Jennifer Newton, Director, 951-343-4276, Fax: 951-343-4661, E-mail: jnewton@calbaptist.edu. *Application contact:* Gail Ronveaux, Dean of Graduate Enrollment, 951-343-5045, Fax: 951-343-5095, E-mail: graduateadmissions@calbaptist.edu.

California State University, Dominguez Hills, College of Arts and Humanities, Department of English, Carson, CA 90747-0001. Offers English (MA); rhetoric and composition (Certificate); teaching English as a second language (Certificate). Part-time and evening/weekend programs available. *Faculty:* 13 full-time (5 women). *Students:* 23 full-time (14 women), 52 part-time (33 women); includes 34 minority (9 African Americans, 5 Asian Americans or Pacific Islanders, 20 Hispanic Americans), 3 international. Average age 39. 39 applicants, 79% accepted, 19 enrolled. In 2009, 20 master's awarded. *Degree requirements:* For master's, comprehensive exam (for some programs), thesis or alternative. *Entrance requirements:* For master's, minimum GPA of 3.0 in last 60 units. Additional exam requirements/recommendations for international students: Required—TOEFL (minimum score 550 paper-based; 213 computer-based). *Application deadline:* Applications are processed on a rolling basis. Application fee: $55. Electronic applications accepted. *Expenses:* Tuition, nonresident: full-time $6696; part-time $372 per unit. Required fees: $5946; $1752 per semester. *Faculty research:* Gender studies, transnationalism, discourse analysis, visual culture, Shakespeare. *Unit head:* Dr. Helen Oesterheld, Chair, 310-243-3322, E-mail: hoesterheld@csudh.edu. *Application contact:* 310-243-3600.

California State University, Fresno, Division of Graduate Studies, College of Arts and Humanities, Department of Linguistics, Fresno, CA 93740-8027. Offers linguistics (MA), including Teaching English as a second language. Part-time and evening/weekend programs available. *Degree requirements:* For master's, comprehensive exam. *Entrance requirements:* For master's, GRE General Test, minimum GPA of 3.0. Additional exam requirements/recommendations for international students: Required—TOEFL. Electronic applications accepted. *Faculty research:* Communication systems, bilingual education, animal communication, conflict resolution, literacy programs.

California State University, Fullerton, Graduate Studies, College of Humanities and Social Sciences, Department of Modern Languages and Literatures, Fullerton, CA 92834-9480. Offers French (MA); German (MA); Spanish (MA); teaching English to speakers of other languages (MS). Part-time programs available. *Students:* 40 full-time (30 women), 63 part-time (47 women); includes 49 minority (1 African American, 14 Asian Americans or Pacific Islanders, 34 Hispanic Americans), 20 international. Average age 33. 101 applicants, 52% accepted, 29 enrolled. In 2009, 37 master's awarded. *Degree requirements:* For master's, comprehensive exam, thesis or alternative. *Entrance requirements:* For master's, minimum GPA of 2.5 in last 60 hours of course work, undergraduate major in a language. Application fee: $55. *Expenses:* Tuition, nonresident: full-time $11,160; part-time $373 per credit. Required fees: $1440 per term. Tuition and fees vary according to course load, degree level and program. *Financial support:* Career-related internships or fieldwork, Federal Work-Study, institutionally sponsored loans, and scholarships/grants available. Support available to part-time students. Financial award application deadline: 3/1; financial award applicants required to submit FAFSA. *Unit head:* Dr. Janet Eyring, Chair, 657-278-3534. *Application contact:* Admissions/Applications, 657-278-2371.

California State University, Long Beach, Graduate Studies, College of Liberal Arts, Department of Linguistics, Long Beach, CA 90840. Offers general linguistics (MA); language and culture (MA); special concentration (MA); teaching English as a second language (MA). Part-time and evening/weekend programs available. *Faculty:* 12 full-time (10 women), 1 part-time/adjunct (0 women). *Students:* 33 full-time (23 women), 36 part-time (24 women); includes 20 minority (1 African American, 10 Asian Americans or Pacific Islanders, 9 Hispanic Americans), 20 international. Average age 31. 47 applicants, 62% accepted, 15 enrolled. *Degree requirements:* For master's, one foreign language, comprehensive exam, thesis optional. *Application deadline:* For fall admission, 5/1 for domestic students. Applications are processed on a rolling basis. Application fee: $55. Electronic applications accepted. *Expenses:* Required fees: $1802 per semester. Part-time tuition and fees vary according to course load. *Financial support:* Teaching assistantships, career-related internships or fieldwork, Federal Work-Study, institutionally sponsored loans, and scholarships/grants available. Financial award application deadline: 3/2. *Faculty research:* Pedagogy of language instruction, role of language in society, Khmer language instruction. *Unit head:* Dr. Malcolm Awadajin Finney, Chair, 562-985-7425, Fax: 562-985-2593, E-mail: mfinney@csulb.edu. *Application contact:* Dr. Xiaoping Liang, Graduate Advisor, 562-985-8509, Fax: 562-985-5792, E-mail: xliang@csulb.edu.

California State University, Sacramento, Graduate Studies, College of Arts and Letters, Department of English, Sacramento, CA 95819. Offers creative writing (MA); teaching English to speakers of other languages (MA). Part-time programs available. *Degree requirements:* For master's, thesis, project, or comprehensive exam; writing proficiency exam. *Entrance requirements:* For master's, portfolio (creative writing); minimum GPA of 3.0 in English, 2.75 overall during previous 2 years. Additional exam requirements/recommendations for international students: Required—TOEFL. Electronic applications accepted. *Faculty research:* Teaching composition, remedial writing.

English as a Second Language

California State University, San Bernardino, Graduate Studies, College of Education, San Bernardino, CA 92407-2397. Offers bilingual/cross-cultural education (MA); curriculum and instruction (MA); educational administration (MA); educational leadership and curriculum (Ed D); educational psychology and counseling (MA, MS), including correctional and alternative education (MA), counseling and guidance (MS), rehabilitation counseling (MA); elementary education (MA); English as a second language (MA); environmental education (MA); general education (MA); history and English for secondary teachers (MA); instructional technology (MA); reading (MA); secondary education (MA); special education and rehabilitation counseling (MA), including rehabilitation counseling, special education; teaching of science (MA); vocational and career education (MA). *Accreditation:* NCATE. Part-time and evening/weekend programs available. *Faculty:* 35 full-time (15 women), 24 part-time/adjunct (15 women). *Students:* 921 full-time (710 women), 716 part-time (490 women); includes 751 minority (137 African Americans, 12 American Indian/Alaska Native, 73 Asian Americans or Pacific Islanders, 529 Hispanic Americans), 18 international. Average age 36. 493 applicants, 86% accepted, 243 enrolled. In 2009, 370 master's awarded. *Degree requirements:* For master's, comprehensive exam (for some programs), thesis (for some programs), advancement to candidacy. *Entrance requirements:* For master's, minimum GPA of 3.0 in education. *Application deadline:* For fall admission, 8/31 priority date for domestic students. Application fee: $55. *Financial support:* Career-related internships or fieldwork and Federal Work-Study available. Support available to part-time students. *Faculty research:* Multicultural education, brain-based learning, science education, social studies/global education. *Unit head:* Dr. Patricia Arlin, Dean, 909-537-5600, Fax: 909-537-7011, E-mail: parlin@csusb.edu. *Application contact:* Olivia Rosas, Director of Admissions, 909-537-7577, Fax: 909-537-7034, E-mail: orosas@csusb.edu.

California State University, San Bernardino, Graduate Studies, College of Extended Learning, San Bernardino, CA 92407-2397. Offers executive business administration (MBA); TESOL (MA Ed). Part-time and evening/weekend programs available. *Students:* 356 full-time (268 women), 476 part-time (317 women); includes 353 minority (53 African Americans, 7 American Indian/Alaska Native, 38 Asian Americans or Pacific Islanders, 255 Hispanic Americans), 4 international. Average age 35. 745 applicants, 93% accepted, 356 enrolled. *Application deadline:* For fall admission, 8/31 for domestic students. Application fee: $55. *Financial support:* Application deadline: 3/1. *Unit head:* Dr. Tatiana Karmanova, Acting Dean, 909-537-3986, E-mail: tkarma@csusb.edu. *Application contact:* Olivia Rosas, Director of Admissions, 909-537-7577, Fax: 909-537-7034, E-mail: orosas@csusb.edu.

California State University, Stanislaus, College of Humanities and Social Sciences, Department of English, Turlock, CA 95382. Offers English (MA); literature (MA); rhetoric and teaching of writing (MA); TESOL (MA, Certificate). Part-time programs available. *Degree requirements:* For master's, one foreign language, comprehensive exam, thesis. *Entrance requirements:* For master's, GRE General Test, minimum GPA of 3.0, 2 letters of reference; for Certificate, minimum GPA of 3.0, 2 letters of reference. Additional exam requirements/recommendations for international students: Required—TOEFL (minimum score 550 paper-based; 213 computer-based), TWE (minimum score 4). Electronic applications accepted. *Faculty research:* Transnational literacies, Renaissance and Medieval literature, abolition writings and slave narratives, qualitative writing.

Cambridge College, School of Education, Cambridge, MA 02138-5304. Offers autism specialist (M Ed); autism/behavior analyst (M Ed); behavior analyst (Post-Master's Certificate); behavioral management (M Ed); early childhood teacher (M Ed); education specialist in curriculum and instruction (CAGS); educational leadership (Ed D); elementary teacher (M Ed); English as a second language (M Ed, Certificate); general science (M Ed); health education, health promotion (Post-Master's Certificate); health/family and consumer sciences (M Ed); history (M Ed); individualized degree (M Ed); information technology literacy (M Ed); instructional technology (M Ed); interdisciplinary studies (M Ed); library teacher (M Ed); literacy education (M Ed); mathematics (M Ed); mathematics specialist (Certificate); middle school mathematics and science (M Ed); school administration (M Ed, CAGS); school guidance counselor (M Ed); school nurse education (M Ed); school social worker/school adjustment counselor (M Ed); special education administrator (CAGS); special education/moderate disabilities (M Ed); teaching skills and methodologies (M Ed). Part-time and evening/weekend programs available. Post-baccalaureate distance learning degree programs offered (minimal on-campus study). *Faculty:* 10 full-time (3 women), 283 part-time/adjunct (187 women). *Students:* 974 full-time (755 women), 1,071 part-time (835 women); includes 940 minority (762 African Americans, 4 American Indian/Alaska Native, 22 Asian Americans or Pacific Islanders, 152 Hispanic Americans), 28 international. Average age 39. In 2009, 866 master's, 4 doctorates, 209 CAGSs awarded. *Degree requirements:* For master's, thesis, internship/practicum (licensure program only); for doctorate, thesis/dissertation; for other advanced degree, thesis. *Entrance requirements:* For master's, interview, resume, documentation of licensure, 2 professional references; for doctorate, official transcripts, interview, resume, documentation of licensure (if any), written personal statement/essay, portfolio of scholarly and professional work, qualifying assessment, 2 professional references, health insurance, immunizations form; for other advanced degree, official transcripts, interview, resume, documentation of licensure (if any), written personal statement/essay, 2 professional references, health insurance, immunizations form. Additional exam requirements/recommendations for international students: Required—TOEFL (minimum score 550 paper-based; 213 computer-based; 79 iBT); Recommended—IELTS (minimum score 6). *Application deadline:* Applications are processed on a rolling basis. Application fee: $30. Electronic applications accepted. *Expenses:* Contact institution. *Financial support:* In 2009–10, 1,373 students received support. Career-related internships or fieldwork, Federal Work-Study, and scholarships/grants available. Financial award applicants required to submit FAFSA. *Faculty research:* Adult education, accelerated learning, mathematics education, brain compatible learning, special education and law. *Unit head:* Dr. N. Alan Sheppard, Interim Associate Dean, 617-873-0619, E-mail: alan.sheppard@cambridgecollege.edu. *Application contact:* Stephen Lyons, Director of Enrollment, Graduate and N.I.T.E. Programs, 617-868-1000, Fax: 617-349-3561, E-mail: stephen.lyons@cambridgecollege.edu.

Cardinal Stritch University, College of Education, Department of Literacy, Milwaukee, WI 53217-3985. Offers literacy/English as a second language (MA); reading/language arts (MA); reading/learning disability (MA). *Accreditation:* NCATE. Part-time and evening/weekend programs available. *Degree requirements:* For master's, comprehensive exam, thesis, faculty recommendation, research project. *Entrance requirements:* For master's, letters of recommendation (2), minimum GPA of 2.75.

Carlos Albizu University, Miami Campus, Graduate Programs, Miami, FL 33172-2209. Offers clinical psychology (Psy D); entrepreneurship (MBA); exceptional student education (MS); industrial/organizational psychology (MS); marriage and family therapy (MS); mental health counseling (MS); nonprofit management (MBA); organizational management (MBA); psychology (MS); school counseling (MS); teaching English as a second language (MS). *Accreditation:* APA. Part-time and evening/weekend programs available. *Faculty:* 23 full-time (13 women), 41 part-time/adjunct (21 women). *Students:* 529 full-time (420 women), 171 part-time (139 women); includes 551 minority (55 African Americans, 1 American Indian/Alaska Native, 5 Asian Americans or Pacific Islanders, 490 Hispanic Americans). Average age 37. 278 applicants, 57% accepted, 142 enrolled. In 2009, 139 master's, 26 doctorates awarded. Terminal master's awarded for partial completion of doctoral program. *Degree requirements:* For master's, one foreign language, comprehensive exam, integrative project (MBA), research project (exceptional student education, teaching English as a second language); for doctorate, one foreign language, comprehensive exam, internship, project. *Entrance requirements:* For master's, 3 letters of recommendation, interview, minimum GPA of 3.0, resume; for doctorate, 3 letters of recommendation, minimum GPA of 3.0, resume, interview. *Application deadline:* For fall admission, 8/1 priority date for domestic students; for spring admission, 11/30 priority date for domestic students. Applications are processed on a rolling basis. Application fee: $50. Electronic applications accepted. *Expenses:* Tuition: Full-time $9090; part-time $505 per credit hour. Required fees: $298 per term. Tuition and fees vary according to course load, degree level and program. *Financial support:* In 2009–10, 127 students received support. Federal Work-Study, scholarships/grants, and tuition discounts available. Financial award application

deadline: 6/1; financial award applicants required to submit FAFSA. *Faculty research:* Psychotherapy, forensic psychology, neuropsychology, marketing strategy, entrepreneurship, special education. *Unit head:* Dr. Carmen S. Roca, Chancellor, 305-593-1223 Ext. 120, Fax: 305-629-8052, E-mail: croca@albizu.edu. *Application contact:* Annalye Alonso, Secretary, 305-593-1223 Ext. 137, Fax: 305-593-1854, E-mail: aalonso@albizu.edu.

Carson-Newman College, Graduate Program in Education, Jefferson City, TN 37760. Offers curriculum and instruction (M Ed); educational leadership (M Ed); elementary education (MAT); school counseling (MS); secondary education (MAT); teaching English as a second language (MATESL). *Accreditation:* NCATE. Part-time and evening/weekend programs available. *Faculty:* 5 full-time (2 women), 10 part-time/adjunct (3 women). *Students:* 112 full-time (84 women), 84 part-time (52 women); includes 5 African Americans, 17 international. Average age 32. 86 applicants, 98% accepted. In 2009, 55 master's awarded. *Degree requirements:* For master's, thesis or alternative. *Entrance requirements:* For master's, NTE, minimum GPA of 3.0 in major, 2.5 overall. *Application deadline:* For fall admission, 7/15 priority date for domestic students. Applications are processed on a rolling basis. Application fee: $25 ($50 for international students). *Expenses:* Tuition: Full-time $5490; part-time $305 per semester hour. Required fees: $200. *Financial support:* In 2009–10, 41 students received support. Federal Work-Study and unspecified assistantships available. Financial award application deadline: 4/1; financial award applicants required to submit FAFSA. *Unit head:* Dr. Sharon Teets, Chair, 865-471-3461. *Application contact:* Graduate Admissions and Services Adviser, 865-471-3460, Fax: 865-471-3875.

Central Connecticut State University, School of Graduate Studies, School of Arts and Sciences, Department of English, Program in Teaching English to Speakers of Other Languages, New Britain, CT 06050-4010. Offers MS, Certificate. Part-time and evening/weekend programs available. *Students:* 14 full-time (11 women), 22 part-time (18 women); includes 3 minority (2 Asian Americans or Pacific Islanders, 1 Hispanic American), 2 international. Average age 36. 23 applicants, 70% accepted, 13 enrolled. In 2009, 13 master's, 2 other advanced degrees awarded. *Degree requirements:* For master's, comprehensive exam, thesis or alternative; for Certificate, qualifying exam. *Entrance requirements:* For master's, 3 semester hours of study of a second language. Additional exam requirements/recommendations for international students: Required—TOEFL. *Application deadline:* For fall admission, 7/1 for domestic students; for spring admission, 12/1 for domestic students. Applications are processed on a rolling basis. Application fee: $50. Electronic applications accepted. *Expenses:* Tuition, area resident: Full-time $4662; part-time $440 per credit. Tuition, state resident: full-time $6994; part-time $440 per credit. Tuition, nonresident: full-time $12,988; part-time $440 per credit. Required fees: $3606. One-time fee: $62 part-time. *Faculty research:* Phonology, general linguistics, second language writing, East Asian languages, English language structure.

Central Michigan University, College of Graduate Studies, College of Humanities and Social and Behavioral Sciences, Department of English Language and Literature, Mount Pleasant, MI 48859. Offers English composition and communication (MA); English language and literature (MA), including children's and young adult literature, creative writing, general concentration; teaching English to speakers of other languages (TESOL) (MA). Part-time and evening/weekend programs available. *Degree requirements:* For master's, thesis or alternative. Electronic applications accepted. *Faculty research:* Composition theory, science fiction history and bibliography, children's and young adult literature, nineteenth century American literature, applied linguistics.

Central Washington University, Graduate Studies and Research, College of Arts and Humanities, Department of English, Ellensburg, WA 98926. Offers English (MA); teaching English as a second language (MA). Part-time programs available. *Faculty:* 20 full-time (11 women). *Students:* 26 full-time (18 women), 7 part-time (2 women); includes 4 minority (2 Asian Americans or Pacific Islanders, 2 Hispanic Americans). 27 applicants, 93% accepted, 25 enrolled. In 2009, 10 master's awarded. *Degree requirements:* For master's, thesis or alternative. *Entrance requirements:* For master's, GRE General Test, minimum GPA of 3.0, writing sample. Additional exam requirements/recommendations for international students: Required—TOEFL (minimum score 550 paper-based; 213 computer-based; 79 iBT). *Application deadline:* For fall admission, 2/1 priority date for domestic students; for winter admission, 10/1 for domestic students; for spring admission, 1/1 for domestic students. Applications are processed on a rolling basis. Application fee: $50. Electronic applications accepted. *Expenses:* Tuition, state resident: full-time $7353; part-time $245 per credit. Tuition, nonresident: full-time $16,383; part-time $546 per credit. Required fees: $882. Tuition and fees vary according to degree level. *Financial support:* In 2009–10, 17 teaching assistantships with partial tuition reimbursements (averaging $9,145 per year) were awarded; research assistantships with partial tuition reimbursements, Federal Work-Study, health care benefits, and unspecified assistantships also available. Financial award application deadline: 3/1; financial award applicants required to submit FAFSA. *Unit head:* Dr. George Drake, Chair, 509-963-1546, Fax: 509-963-1561, E-mail: drakeg@cwu.edu. *Application contact:* Justine Eason, Admissions Program Coordinator, 509-963-3103, Fax: 509-963-1799, E-mail: masters@cwu.edu.

Cleveland State University, College of Graduate Studies, College of Education and Human Services, Department of Teacher Education, Cleveland, OH 44115. Offers art education (M Ed); early childhood education (M Ed); foreign language education (M Ed); mathematics and science education (M Ed); middle childhood education (M Ed); special education (M Ed), including mild/moderate disabilities, moderate/intensive disabilities; teaching English to speakers of other languages (M Ed). Part-time and evening/weekend programs available. *Degree requirements:* For master's, comprehensive exam (for some programs), thesis or alternative. *Entrance requirements:* For master's, GRE General Test or MAT, minimum GPA of 2.75. Additional exam requirements/recommendations for international students: Required—TOEFL (minimum score 525 paper-based; 197 computer-based), IELTS (minimum score 6). *Faculty research:* Early literacy, professional development in reading, reading recovery, dual language, induction programs.

College of Charleston, Graduate School, School of Education, Health, and Human Performance, Program in English to Speakers of Other Languages, Charleston, SC 29424-0001. Offers Certificate. Postbaccalaureate distance learning degree programs offered (minimal on-campus study). *Entrance requirements:* Additional exam requirements/recommendations for international students: Required—TOEFL. *Application deadline:* For fall admission, 3/1 for domestic students; for spring admission, 11/1 for domestic students. Application fee: $45. Electronic applications accepted. *Unit head:* Dr. Angela Crespo Cozart, Director, 843-953-6353, E-mail: cozarta@cofc.edu. *Application contact:* Susan Hallatt, Director of Graduate Admissions, 843-953-5614, Fax: 843-953-1434, E-mail: hallatts@cofc.edu.

The College of New Jersey, Graduate Division, School of Education, Department of Special Education, Language and Literacy, Program in Teaching English as a Second Language, Ewing, NJ 08628. Offers English as a second language (M Ed); teaching English as a second language (Certificate). *Accreditation:* NCATE. Part-time programs available. *Students:* 14 full-time (12 women), 43 part-time (34 women); includes 13 minority (1 African American, 4 Asian Americans or Pacific Islanders, 8 Hispanic Americans), 5 international. 79 applicants, 76% accepted. In 2009, 16 master's, 23 Certificates awarded. *Degree requirements:* For master's, comprehensive exam. *Entrance requirements:* For master's, GRE General Test, minimum GPA of 3.0 in field or 2.75 overall. Additional exam requirements/recommendations for international students: Required—TOEFL. *Application deadline:* For fall admission, 2/1 priority date for domestic students; for spring admission, 10/1 priority date for domestic students. Application fee: $70. Electronic applications accepted. *Expenses:* Tuition, state resident: part-time $573.70 per credit. Tuition, nonresident: part-time $887.75 per credit. Required fees: $140.85 per credit. One-time fee: $10 part-time. *Financial support:* Tuition waivers (partial) and unspecified assistantships available. Financial award application deadline: 5/1; financial award applicants required to submit FAFSA. *Unit head:* Dr. Yiqiang Wu, Coordinator, 609-771-2808, E-mail: wuyiqian@tcnj.edu. *Application contact:* Susan L. Hydro, Assistant Dean, Office of Graduate Studies, 609-771-2300, Fax: 609-637-5105, E-mail: graduate@tcnj.edu.

The College of New Rochelle, Graduate School, Division of Education, Program in Teaching English as a Second Language and Multilingual/Multicultural Education, New Rochelle, NY 10805-2308. Offers bilingual education (Certificate); teaching English as a second language (MS Ed). Part-time and evening/weekend programs available. *Degree requirements:* For master's, practicum. *Entrance requirements:* For master's, interview, minimum GPA of 3.0 in field, 2.7 overall.

College of Notre Dame of Maryland, Graduate Studies, Program in Teaching English to Speakers of Other Languages, Baltimore, MD 21210-2476. Offers MA. *Accreditation:* NCATE. Part-time and evening/weekend programs available. *Entrance requirements:* Additional exam requirements/recommendations for international students: Required—TOEFL (minimum score 500 paper-based; 173 computer-based; 61 iBT). Electronic applications accepted.

College of Saint Mary, Program in Education, Omaha, NE 68106. Offers assessment leadership (MSE); English as a second language (MSE). Part-time programs available. *Entrance requirements:* For master's, technology competency test or equivalent, minimum cumulative GPA of 3.0, teaching certificate, 2 letters of reference, resume.

Columbia International University, Columbia Graduate School, Columbia, SC 29230-3122. Offers Bible teaching (MABT); Christian higher education leadership (Ed D); Christian school educational leadership (Ed D); counseling (MACN); curriculum and instruction (M Ed), including Christian school guidance, English as a second language, learning disabilities, school technology; early childhood and elementary education (MAT); educational administration (M Ed); teaching English as a foreign language (Certificate); teaching English as a foreign language and intercultural studies (MATF). Part-time and evening/weekend programs available. *Degree requirements:* For master's, internships, professional project. *Entrance requirements:* For master's, Minnesota Multiphasic Personality Inventory, MAT, minimum GPA of 2.7. Additional exam requirements/recommendations for international students: Required—TOEFL. Electronic applications accepted.

Concordia University, School of Graduate Studies, Faculty of Arts and Science, Department of Education, Program in Applied Linguistics, Montréal, QC H3G 1M8, Canada. Offers applied linguistics (MA); teaching English as a second language (Certificate).

Cornerstone University, Graduate Programs, Grand Rapids, MI 49525-5897. Offers business administration (MBA); education (MA Ed); management (MSM); teaching English to speakers of other languages (MA, Graduate Certificate). Programs also offered at Holland, Kalamazoo, and Troy, MI campuses. Part-time programs available. Postbaccalaureate distance learning degree programs offered. *Degree requirements:* For master's, comprehensive exam (for some programs), thesis (for some programs). *Entrance requirements:* For master's, minimum GPA of 2.5, 2 letters of reference. Additional exam requirements/recommendations for international students: Required—TOEFL (minimum score 575 paper-based; 235 computer-based). Electronic applications accepted.

Dallas Baptist University, College of Adult Education, Liberal Arts Program, Dallas, TX 75211-9299. Offers arts (MLA); Christian ministry (MLA); English (MLA); English as a second language (MLA); fine arts (MLA); history (MLA); missions (MLA); political science (MLA). Part-time and evening/weekend programs available. *Entrance requirements:* For master's, minimum GPA of 3.0. Additional exam requirements/recommendations for international students: Required—TOEFL. Electronic applications accepted. *Expenses:* Tuition: Full-time $10,674; part-time $593 per credit hour. *Faculty research:* Milton and seventeenth-century Puritans, inter-Biblical years, nineteenth-century literature, Latin American and Texas history.

Dallas Baptist University, College of Adult Education, Professional Development Program, Dallas, TX 75211-9299. Offers accounting (MA); church leadership (MA); counseling (MA); criminal justice (MA); English as a second language (MA); finance (MA); higher education (MA); leadership studies (MA); management (MA); management information systems (MA); marketing (MA); missions (MA). Part-time and evening/weekend programs available. *Entrance requirements:* For master's, minimum GPA of 3.0. Additional exam requirements/recommendations for international students: Required—TOEFL, IELTS. *Expenses:* Tuition: Full-time $10,674; part-time $593 per credit hour.

Dallas Baptist University, Dorothy M. Bush College of Education, Program in Reading and English as a Second Language, Dallas, TX 75211-9299. Offers English as a second language (M Ed); master reading teacher (M Ed); reading specialist (M Ed). Part-time and evening/weekend programs available. *Entrance requirements:* For master's, GRE General Test, minimum GPA of 3.0. Additional exam requirements/recommendations for international students: Required—TOEFL, IELTS. *Expenses:* Tuition: Full-time $10,674; part-time $593 per credit hour.

Dallas Baptist University, Dorothy M. Bush College of Education, Teaching Program, Dallas, TX 75211-9299. Offers elementary (MAT); English as a second language (MAT); hi-level (MAT); secondary (MAT). Part-time and evening/weekend programs available. *Entrance requirements:* For master's, GRE General Test, minimum GPA of 3.0. Additional exam requirements/recommendations for international students: Required—TOEFL, IELTS. Electronic applications accepted. *Expenses:* Tuition: Full-time $10,674; part-time $593 per credit hour.

Dallas Baptist University, Gary Cook School of Leadership, Program in Global Leadership, Dallas, TX 75211-9299. Offers business communication (MA); Christian education/missions (MA); ESL (MA); general studies (MA); global studies (MA); international business (MA); missions (MA); worship/missions (MA). Part-time and evening/weekend programs available. *Entrance requirements:* For master's, minimum GPA of 3.0. Additional exam requirements/recommendations for international students: Required—TOEFL, IELTS. *Expenses:* Tuition: Full-time $10,674; part-time $593 per credit hour.

DeSales University, Graduate Division, Program in Education, Center Valley, PA 18034-9568. Offers elementary education (M Ed); instructional technology for K-12 (M Ed); interdisciplinary (M Ed); mathematics (M Ed); special education (M Ed); TESOL/ESL (M Ed). Part-time and evening/weekend programs available. Postbaccalaureate distance learning degree programs offered (no on-campus study). *Students:* 218 part-time. *Degree requirements:* For master's, thesis project. *Entrance requirements:* For master's, teaching certificate. Additional exam requirements/recommendations for international students: Required—TOEFL. *Application deadline:* Applications are processed on a rolling basis. Application fee: $35. Electronic applications accepted. *Expenses:* Tuition: Full-time $17,500; part-time $665 per credit. Full-time tuition and fees vary according to program. Part-time tuition and fees vary according to course load. *Financial support:* Application deadline: 5/1. *Faculty research:* Effective teaching, computer interfacing in chemistry labs, computer applications to teaching, history of philosophy, aesthetics multidrug-resistant cancer. *Unit head:* Dr. Lujean Baab, Director, 610-282-1100 Ext. 1739, Fax: 610-282-3734, E-mail: lujean.baab@desales.edu. *Application contact:* Caryn Stopper, Director of Graduate Admissions, 610-282-1100 Ext. 1768, Fax: 610-282-0525, E-mail: caryn.stopper@desales.edu.

Dominican University, School of Education, River Forest, IL 60305-1099. Offers curriculum and instruction (MA Ed); early childhood education (MS); education (MAT); educational administration (MA); elementary (online) (MS); English as a second language (online) (MS); reading (online) (MS); special education (MS). Part-time and evening/weekend programs available. Postbaccalaureate distance learning degree programs offered. *Faculty:* 16 full-time (12 women), 59 part-time/adjunct (46 women). *Students:* 236 full-time (182 women), 622 part-time (509 women); includes 180 minority (54 African Americans, 3 American Indian/Alaska Native, 36 Asian Americans or Pacific Islanders, 87 Hispanic Americans), 2 international. Average age 32. In 2009, 199 master's awarded. *Entrance requirements:* For master's, Illinois certification test of basic skills. Additional exam requirements/recommendations for international students: Required—TOEFL (minimum score 550 paper-based; 213 computer-based; 79 iBT). *Application deadline:* Applications are processed on a rolling basis. Application fee: $25. *Expenses:* Contact institution. *Financial support:* Career-related internships or fieldwork, scholarships/grants, and tuition waivers (partial) available. Support available to part-time students. Financial award application deadline: 8/15; financial award applicants required to

submit FAFSA. *Faculty research:* Governance of private education institutions, reading and language arts, inclusion, organizational planning, leadership and vision. *Unit head:* Dr. Colleen Reardon, Dean, 718-524-6643, Fax: 708-524-6665, E-mail: creardon@dom.edu. *Application contact:* Keven Hansen, Coordinator of Recruitment and Admissions, 708-524-6921, Fax: 708-524-6665, E-mail: educate@dom.edu.

Drexel University, School of Education, Philadelphia, PA 19104-2875. Offers educational administration and collaborative learning (MS); educational leadership and learning technology (PhD); global and international education (MS); graduate intern teaching (Certificate); higher education (MS); instructional technology (Spt); post-bachelor's teaching (Certificate); school principal (Certificate); school superintendent (Certificate); science of instruction (MS); teaching English as a second language (Certificate); teaching, learning and curriculum (MS). Part-time and evening/weekend programs available. Postbaccalaureate distance learning degree programs offered. *Degree requirements:* For doctorate, thesis/dissertation. Electronic applications accepted. *Expenses:* Contact institution.

Duquesne University, School of Education, Department of Instruction and Leadership, Pittsburgh, PA 15282-0001. Offers early childhood education (MS Ed), including early childhood; elementary education (MS Ed), including elementary education, elementary education/early childhood; English as a second language (MS Ed); instructional technology (MS Ed, Ed D); reading and language arts (MS Ed); secondary education (MS Ed), including secondary education. Part-time and evening/weekend programs available. *Faculty:* 15 full-time (9 women), 13 part-time/adjunct (6 women). *Students:* 178 full-time (138 women), 74 part-time (50 women); includes 20 minority (11 African Americans, 5 Asian Americans or Pacific Islanders, 4 Hispanic Americans), 10 international. Average age 33. 161 applicants, 71% accepted, 68 enrolled. In 2009, 94 master's, 9 doctorates awarded. *Degree requirements:* For doctorate, thesis/dissertation. *Entrance requirements:* For master's, MAT, minimum GPA of 3.0; for doctorate, GRE General Test, MAT, interview, minimum GPA of 3.25. Additional exam requirements/recommendations for international students: Required—TOEFL (minimum score 550 paper-based; 80 computer-based). *Application deadline:* For fall admission, 8/1 priority date for domestic students; for spring admission, 12/1 priority date for domestic students. Applications are processed on a rolling basis. Electronic applications accepted. *Expenses:* Tuition: Part-time $851 per credit. Required fees: $81 per credit. *Financial support:* Research assistantships, teaching assistantships with tuition reimbursements, career-related internships or fieldwork, Federal Work-Study, and institutionally sponsored loans available. Support available to part-time students. *Unit head:* Dr. Arentha Ball, Chair, 412-396-6106, Fax: 412-396-5388, E-mail: balla@duq.edu. *Application contact:* Michael Dolinger, Director of Student and Academic Services, 412-396-6647, Fax: 412-396-5585, E-mail: dolingerm@duq.edu.

Eastern Michigan University, Graduate School, College of Arts and Sciences, Department of World Languages, Program in Teaching English to Speakers of Other Languages, Ypsilanti, MI 48197. Offers MA, Graduate Certificate. Part-time and evening/weekend programs available. Postbaccalaureate distance learning degree programs offered (minimal on-campus study). *Students:* 10 full-time (8 women), 39 part-time (34 women); includes 6 minority (2 Asian Americans or Pacific Islanders, 4 Hispanic Americans), 17 international. Average age 35. In 2009, 11 master's, 5 other advanced degrees awarded. *Degree requirements:* For master's, one foreign language. *Entrance requirements:* Additional exam requirements/recommendations for international students: Required—TOEFL. *Application deadline:* Applications are processed on a rolling basis. Application fee: $35. Tuition and fees vary according to course level. *Financial support:* Fellowships, research assistantships with full tuition reimbursements, teaching assistantships with full tuition reimbursements, career-related internships or fieldwork, Federal Work-Study, institutionally sponsored loans, scholarships/grants, tuition waivers (partial), and unspecified assistantships available. Support available to part-time students. Financial award applicants required to submit FAFSA. *Application contact:* Dr. Jo Ann Aebersold, Program Advisor, 734-487-0130, Fax: 734-487-3411, E-mail: jaebersol@emich.edu.

Eastern Nazarene College, Adult and Graduate Studies, Division of Education, Quincy, MA 02170. Offers early childhood education (M Ed, Certificate); elementary education (M Ed, Certificate); English as a second language (M Ed, Certificate); instructional enrichment and development (M Ed, Certificate); middle school education (M Ed, Certificate); moderate special needs education (M Ed, Certificate); principal (Certificate); program development and supervision (M Ed, Certificate); secondary education (M Ed, Certificate); special education administrator (Certificate); supervisor (Certificate); teacher of reading (M Ed, Certificate). M Ed and Certificate also available through weekend program for administration, special needs, and reading only. Part-time and evening/weekend programs available. *Entrance requirements:* Additional exam requirements/recommendations for international students: Required—TOEFL (minimum score 550 paper-based).

Eastern Washington University, Graduate Studies, College of Arts and Letters, Department of English, Cheney, WA 99004-2431. Offers literature (MA); rhetoric, composition, and technical communication (MA); teaching English as a second language (MA). *Degree requirements:* For master's, comprehensive exam, thesis or alternative. *Entrance requirements:* For master's, GRE General Test, minimum GPA of 3.0. *Expenses:* Tuition, state resident: full-time $7476; part-time $249 per quarter hour. Tuition, nonresident: full-time $18,030; part-time $601 per quarter hour. Required fees: $3.50 per quarter hour. $142 per quarter.

Elms College, Division of Education, Chicopee, MA 01013-2839. Offers early childhood education (MAT); education (M Ed, CAGS); elementary education (MAT); English as a second language (MAT); reading (MAT); secondary education (MAT), including biology education, English education, Spanish education; special education (MAT). Part-time and evening/weekend programs available. *Faculty:* 12 full-time (8 women), 4 part-time/adjunct (2 women). *Students:* 17 full-time (14 women), 153 part-time (136 women); includes 5 minority (1 American Indian/Alaska Native, 4 Hispanic Americans). Average age 36. 43 applicants, 88% accepted, 37 enrolled. In 2009, 23 master's, 8 other advanced degrees awarded. *Degree requirements:* For master's, thesis (for some programs). *Entrance requirements:* For master's, Massachusetts Educators Certification Test, minimum GPA of 3.0; for CAGS, master's degree in education. Additional exam requirements/recommendations for international students: Required—TOEFL. *Application deadline:* For fall admission, 7/1 priority date for domestic students; for spring admission, 11/1 priority date for domestic students. Applications are processed on a rolling basis. Application fee: $30. *Financial support:* In 2009–10, 2 teaching assistantships with partial tuition reimbursements were awarded; tuition waivers (partial) also available. Support available to part-time students. Financial award applicants required to submit FAFSA. *Unit head:* Dr. Mary Janeczek, Director, 413-594-2761, Fax: 413-592-4871, E-mail: janeczeke@elms.edu. *Application contact:* Dana Malone, Associate Director for Graduate Studies and Continuing Education, 413-265-2445, Fax: 413-265-2459, E-mail: maloned@elms.edu.

Emporia State University, School of Graduate Studies, College of Liberal Arts and Sciences, Department of English, Modern Languages and Journalism, Program in Teaching English to Speakers of Other Languages, Emporia, KS 66801-5087. Offers MA. Part-time programs available. *Students:* 5 full-time (4 women), 22 part-time (17 women); includes 2 minority (1 African American, 1 Hispanic American), 1 international. 9 applicants, 67% accepted, 4 enrolled. In 2009, 7 master's awarded. *Degree requirements:* For master's, comprehensive exam, thesis optional. *Entrance requirements:* For master's, minimum undergraduate GPA of 2.75 over last 60 hours. Additional exam requirements/recommendations for international students: Required—TOEFL (minimum score 520 paper-based; 133 computer-based; 68 iBT). *Application deadline:* For fall admission, 8/15 priority date for domestic students. Applications are processed on a rolling basis. Application fee: $30 ($75 for international students). Electronic applications accepted. *Expenses:* Tuition, state resident: full-time $4154; part-time $173 per credit hour. Tuition, nonresident: full-time $12,864; part-time $536 per credit hour. Required fees: $948; $58 per credit hour. Tuition and fees vary according to campus/location. *Financial support:* Federal Work-Study, institutionally sponsored loans, health care benefits, and unspecified assistantships available. Financial award application deadline: 2/15. *Unit head:* Dr. Abdelilah Salim Sehlaoui, Unit Head, 620-341-5237, E-mail: asehlaou@emporia.edu. *Application contact:* Mary Sewell, Admissions Coordinator, 800-950-GRAD, Fax: 620-341-5909, E-mail: msewell@emporia.edu.

English as a Second Language

Emporia State University, School of Graduate Studies, The Teachers College, Department of Early Childhood/Elementary Teacher Education, Program in Master Teacher, Emporia, KS 66801-5087. Offers elementary subject matter (MS); English as a second language (MS); reading (MS); secondary subject matter (MS). *Accreditation:* NCATE. Part-time programs available. *Students:* 3 full-time (all women), 87 part-time (84 women); includes 6 minority (1 African American, 1 American Indian/Alaska Native, 2 Asian Americans or Pacific Islanders, 2 Hispanic Americans). 14 applicants, 100% accepted, 12 enrolled. In 2009, 40 master's awarded. *Degree requirements:* For master's, comprehensive exam or thesis, practicum. *Entrance requirements:* For master's, GRE General Test or MAT, graduate essay exam, appropriate bachelor's degree, letters of recommendation. Additional exam requirements/recommendations for international students: Required—TOEFL (minimum score 520 paper-based; 133 computer-based; 68 iBT). *Application deadline:* For fall admission, 8/15 priority date for domestic students. Applications are processed on a rolling basis. Application fee: $30 ($75 for international students). Electronic applications accepted. *Expenses:* Tuition, state resident: full-time $4154; part-time $173 per credit hour. Tuition, nonresident: full-time $12,864; part-time $536 per credit hour. Required fees: $948; $58 per credit hour. Tuition and fees vary according to campus/location. *Financial support:* Federal Work-Study, institutionally sponsored loans, health care benefits, and unspecified assistantships available. Financial award application deadline: 3/15; financial award applicants required to submit FAFSA. *Unit head:* Dr. Jean Morrow, Chair, 620-341-5766, E-mail: jmorrow@emporia.edu. *Application contact:* Mary Sewell, Admissions Coordinator, 800-950-GRAD, Fax: 620-341-5909, E-mail: msewell@emporia.edu.

Erikson Institute, Academic Programs, Chicago, IL 60654. Offers administration (Certificate); bilingual/ESL (Certificate); child development (MS); early childhood education (MS); infant mental health (Certificate); infant studies (Certificate); MS/MSW. Part-time and evening/weekend programs available. *Degree requirements:* For master's, comprehensive exam, internship; for Certificate, internship. *Entrance requirements:* For master's and Certificate, minimum GPA of 2.75. Additional exam requirements/recommendations for international students: Required—TOEFL. *Faculty research:* Assessment strategies from early childhood through elementary years; language, literacy, and the arts in children's development; inclusive special education; parent-child relationships; cognitive development.

The Evergreen State College, Graduate Programs, Program in Curriculum and Instruction, Olympia, WA 98505. Offers English as a second language (M Ed); mathematics (M Ed). *Faculty:* 2 full-time (both women). *Students:* 40 part-time (30 women); includes 5 minority (1 African American, 1 American Indian/Alaska Native, 2 Asian Americans or Pacific Islanders, 1 Hispanic American). Average age 42. 23 applicants, 100% accepted, 17 enrolled. *Degree requirements:* For master's, research paper and presentation, passing score on WEST-E (math or ELL). *Entrance requirements:* For master's, bachelor's degree with 4-quarter/3-semester credits in child/adolescent development, lifespan development or another human development course covering the cognitive, affective, and psychological components of individuals; minimum GPA of 3.0 in last 90 quarter/60 semester credits; 1 year classroom teaching experience (preferred). *Application deadline:* For fall admission, 3/29 priority date for domestic and international students. Applications are processed on a rolling basis. Application fee: $50. Electronic applications accepted. *Expenses:* Contact institution. *Financial support:* In 2009–10, 1 student received support, including 1 fellowship (averaging $2,250 per year); scholarships/grants and tuition waivers (partial) also available. Financial award application deadline: 3/15; financial award applicants required to submit FAFSA. *Faculty research:* Multicultural education, bilingual education, ELL, qualitative research methodologies, critical theory, education leadership policy, math and science education. *Unit head:* Sherry Walton, Director, 360-867-6856, Fax: 360-867-6575, E-mail: adairl@evergreen.edu. *Application contact:* Lynne Adair, Program Coordinator, 360-867-6639, Fax: 360-867-6575, E-mail: adairl@evergreen.edu.

Fairfield University, Graduate School of Education and Allied Professions, Department of Curriculum and Instruction, Fairfield, CT 06824-5195. Offers bilingual education (CAS); elementary education (MA); media/educational technology (MA); secondary education (MA); teaching and foundations (MA, CAS); TESOL, foreign language and bilingual/multicultural education (MA, CAS). Part-time and evening/weekend programs available. *Degree requirements:* For master's, comprehensive exam, thesis or alternative. *Entrance requirements:* For master's, PRAXIS I (PPST), minimum QPA of 3.0, 2 recommendations, resume. Additional exam requirements/recommendations for international students: Required—TOEFL (minimum score 550 paper-based; 213 computer-based; 80 iBT). Electronic applications accepted. *Faculty research:* Urban and multicultural education; participatory action for social justice; culture and family; second language acquisition; science, technology and social education.

Florida Atlantic University, College of Education, Department of Curriculum, Culture, and Educational Inquiry, Boca Raton, FL 33431-0991. Offers curriculum and instruction (Ed D, Ed S); early childhood education (M Ed); multicultural education (M Ed); teaching English to speakers of other languages (TESOL) (M Ed). *Faculty:* 11 full-time (8 women), 17 part-time/adjunct (13 women). *Students:* 38 full-time (26 women), 124 part-time (105 women); includes 40 minority (23 African Americans, 3 Asian Americans or Pacific Islanders, 14 Hispanic Americans), 4 international. Average age 36. 84 applicants, 56% accepted, 34 enrolled. In 2009, 39 master's, 5 doctorates awarded. *Application deadline:* For fall admission, 7/1 for domestic students, 2/15 for international students; for spring admission, 11/1 for domestic students, 7/15 for international students. *Expenses:* Tuition, state resident: full-time $7055; part-time $293.94 per credit hour. Tuition, nonresident: full-time $22,096; part-time $920.66 per credit hour. *Faculty research:* Multicultural education, early intervention strategies, family literacy, religious diversity in schools, early childhood curriculum. *Unit head:* Dr. James McLaughlin, Interim Chair, 561-297-3965, E-mail: jmclau17@fau.edu. *Application contact:* Dr. Eliah Watlington, Associate Dean, 561-296-8520, Fax: 261-297-2991, E-mail: ewatling@fau.edu.

Florida International University, College of Education, Department of Curriculum and Instruction, Miami, FL 33199. Offers art education (MAT, MS, Ed D); curriculum and instruction (Ed S); curriculum development (MS); curriculum studies (PhD); early childhood education (MS, Ed D); elementary education (MS, Ed D); English education (MAT, MS, Ed D); foreign language education—teaching English to speakers of other languages (TESOL) (Certificate), including foreign language education; foreign language education- teaching English to speakers of other languages (TESOL) (MS), including teaching English; French education—initial teacher preparation (MAT); international and intercultural development education (Ed D); international and intercultural developmental education (MS); language, literacy and culture (PhD); learning technologies (MS, Ed D, PhD); mathematics education (MAT, MS, Ed D, PhD); modern language education/bilingual education (MS, Ed D); physical education (MS); reading education (MS, Ed D); science education (MAT, MS, Ed D, PhD); social studies education (MAT, MS, Ed D); Spanish education—initial teacher preparation (MAT); special education (MS). Part-time and evening/weekend programs available. *Degree requirements:* For doctorate, comprehensive exam, thesis/dissertation. *Entrance requirements:* For master's, GRE General Test, Florida General Knowledge Test or Florida College Level Academic Skills Test; for doctorate and other advanced degree, GRE General Test. Additional exam requirements/recommendations for international students: Required—TOEFL (minimum score 550 paper-based; 213 computer-based; 80 iBT), IELTS (minimum score 6.3). Electronic applications accepted. *Expenses:* Tuition, state resident: full-time $8008; part-time $4004 per year. Tuition, nonresident: full-time $20,104; part-time $10,052 per year. Required fees: $298; $149 per term.

Fordham University, Graduate School of Education, Division of Curriculum and Teaching, New York, NY 10023. Offers adult education (MS, MSE); bilingual teacher education (MSE); curriculum and teaching (MSE); early childhood education (MSE); elementary education (MST); language, literacy, and learning (PhD); reading education (MSE, Adv C); secondary education (MAT, MSE); special education (MSE, Adv C); teaching English as a second language (MSE). *Accreditation:* NCATE. *Degree requirements:* For doctorate, thesis/dissertation; for Adv C, thesis. *Entrance requirements:* For doctorate, MAT, GRE General Test.

Framingham State University, Division of Graduate and Continuing Education, Program in the Teaching of English as a Second Language, Framingham, MA 01701-9101. Offers M Ed.

Fresno Pacific University, Graduate Programs, School of Education, Division of Language, Literacy, and Culture, Program in Reading, Fresno, CA 93702-4709. Offers reading/English as a second language (MA Ed); reading/language arts (MA Ed). Part-time and evening/weekend programs available. *Degree requirements:* For master's, thesis or alternative. *Entrance requirements:* Additional exam requirements/recommendations for international students: Required—TOEFL (minimum score 550 paper-based; 213 computer-based). Electronic applications accepted.

Fresno Pacific University, Graduate Programs, School of Education, Division of Language, Literacy, and Culture, Program in Teaching English to Speakers of Other Languages, Fresno, CA 93702-4709. Offers MA. Part-time and evening/weekend programs available. *Degree requirements:* For master's, thesis. *Entrance requirements:* For master's, GMAT, MAT, GRE, interview, 2 writing samples. Additional exam requirements/recommendations for international students: Required—TOEFL (minimum score 550 paper-based; 213 computer-based). Electronic applications accepted.

Furman University, Graduate Division, Department of Education, Greenville, SC 29613. Offers curriculum and instruction (MA); early childhood education (MA); English as a second language (MA); literacy (MA); school leadership (MA); special education (MA). *Accreditation:* NCATE. Part-time programs available. Postbaccalaureate distance learning degree programs offered (minimal on-campus study). *Faculty:* 14 full-time (8 women), 10 part-time/adjunct (6 women). *Students:* 114 part-time (93 women); includes 13 minority (10 African Americans, 3 Asian Americans or Pacific Islanders). Average age 29. 24 applicants, 100% accepted, 23 enrolled. In 2009, 71 master's awarded. *Degree requirements:* For master's, comprehensive exam (for some programs), thesis or alternative. *Entrance requirements:* For master's, PRAXIS II. *Application deadline:* For fall admission, 8/1 priority date for domestic students, 7/15 priority date for international students; for spring admission, 12/1 priority date for domestic and international students. Applications are processed on a rolling basis. Application fee: $50. *Financial support:* In 2009–10, 43 students received support; fellowships, scholarships/grants available. Financial award application deadline: 5/15; financial award applicants required to submit FAFSA. *Faculty research:* Literacy, pedagogy and practice, social justice, advanced leadership, achievement in high poverty schools. *Unit head:* Dr. Nelly Hecker, Head, 864-294-3385. *Application contact:* Helen Reynolds, Department Assistant, 864-294-2213, Fax: 864-294-3579, E-mail: helen.reynolds@furman.edu.

Gannon University, School of Graduate Studies, College of Humanities, Education, and Social Sciences, School of Education, Program in English as a Second Language, Erie, PA 16541-0001. Offers Certificate. Part-time and evening/weekend programs available. *Entrance requirements:* Additional exam requirements/recommendations for international students: Required—TOEFL (minimum score 79 iBT). *Application deadline:* Applications are processed on a rolling basis. Application fee: $25. Electronic applications accepted. *Expenses:* Contact institution. *Financial support:* Application deadline: 7/1. *Unit head:* Dr. Kathleen Kingston, Director, 814-871-5626, E-mail: kingston002@gannon.edu. *Application contact:* Kara Morgan, Assistant Director of Graduate Admissions, 814-871-5831, Fax: 814-871-5827, E-mail: graduate@gannon.edu.

George Fox University, School of Education, Master of Arts in Teaching Program, Newberg, OR 97132-2697. Offers teaching (MAT); teaching plus ESOL (MAT); teaching plus ESOL/bilingual (MAT); teaching plus reading (MAT). MAT program is offered in Oregon and Idaho. Part-time and evening/weekend programs available. *Faculty:* 16 full-time (13 women), 22 part-time/adjunct (15 women). *Students:* 158 full-time (116 women), 70 part-time (49 women); includes 22 minority (1 African American, 2 American Indian/Alaska Native, 8 Asian Americans or Pacific Islanders, 11 Hispanic Americans), 1 international. Average age 32. 59 applicants, 75% accepted, 35 enrolled. In 2009, 195 master's awarded. *Entrance requirements:* For master's, CBEST or PRAXIS PPST, bachelor's degree from regionally-accredited college or university with minimum GPA of 3.0 in last two years of course work. Additional exam requirements/recommendations for international students: Required—TOEFL (minimum score 577 paper-based; 233 computer-based; 90 iBT). *Application deadline:* For fall admission, 6/1 for domestic and international students; for winter admission, 10/1 for domestic and international students; for spring admission, 2/1 for domestic and international students. Applications are processed on a rolling basis. Application fee: $40. Electronic applications accepted. *Expenses:* Contact institution. *Financial support:* In 2009–10, 20 students received support. Scholarships/grants available. Financial award application deadline: 2/1; financial award applicants required to submit FAFSA. *Unit head:* Kristin Dixon, Chair, 971-239-4934, E-mail: kdixon@georgefox.edu. *Application contact:* Beth Molzahn, Admissions Counselor, Oregon Master of Arts in Teaching Programs, 800-631-0921, Fax: 503-554-3110, E-mail: mat@georgefox.edu.

George Mason University, College of Humanities and Social Sciences, Department of English, Fairfax, VA 22030. Offers creative writing (MFA); English (MA); folklore studies (Certificate); linguistics (PhD); professional writing and rhetoric (Certificate); teaching English as a second language (Certificate). *Faculty:* 82 full-time (47 women), 48 part-time/adjunct (29 women). *Students:* 72 full-time (51 women), 228 part-time (172 women); includes 39 minority (12 African Americans, 3 American Indian/Alaska Native, 20 Asian Americans or Pacific Islanders, 4 Hispanic Americans), 10 international. Average age 31. 314 applicants, 57% accepted, 86 enrolled. In 2009, 63 master's, 12 other advanced degrees awarded. *Degree requirements:* For master's, thesis (for some programs), proficiency in a foreign language by course work or translation test. *Entrance requirements:* For master's, 30 credits in graduate English courses, minimum undergraduate GPA of 3.0, 2 letters of recommendation. Additional exam requirements/recommendations for international students: Required—TOEFL. *Application deadline:* For fall admission, 3/15 priority date for domestic students; for spring admission, 10/15 for domestic students. Application fee: $75. Electronic applications accepted. *Expenses:* Tuition, state resident: full-time $7568; part-time $315.33 per credit hour. Tuition, nonresident: full-time $21,704; part-time $904.33 per credit hour. Required fees: $2184; $91 per credit hour. *Financial support:* In 2009–10, 49 students received support, including 1 fellowship with full tuition reimbursement available (averaging $18,000 per year), 3 research assistantships with full and partial tuition reimbursements available (averaging $9,443 per year), 46 teaching assistantships with full and partial tuition reimbursements available (averaging $10,509 per year); Federal Work-Study, scholarships/grants, unspecified assistantships, and health care benefits (full-time research or teaching assistantship recipients) also available. Support available to part-time students. Financial award application deadline: 3/1; financial award applicants required to submit FAFSA. *Faculty research:* Literature, professional writing and editing, writing of fiction or poetry. Total annual research expenditures: $1.2 million. *Unit head:* Robert Matz, Chair, 703-993-1170, E-mail: rmatz@gmu.edu. *Application contact:* Denise Albanese, Graduate Director, 703-993-1175, E-mail: dalbanes@gmu.edu.

Georgetown University, Graduate School of Arts and Sciences, Department of Linguistics, Washington, DC 20057. Offers bilingual education (Certificate); language and communication (MA); linguistics (MS, PhD), including applied linguistics, computational linguistics, sociolinguistics, theoretical linguistics; teaching English as a second language (MAT, Certificate); teaching English as a second language and bilingual education (MAT). Terminal master's awarded for partial completion of doctoral program. *Degree requirements:* For master's, one foreign language, comprehensive exam, optional research project; for doctorate, 2 foreign languages, comprehensive exam, thesis/dissertation. *Entrance requirements:* For master's and doctorate, 18 undergraduate credits in a foreign language. Additional exam requirements/recommendations for international students: Required—TOEFL.

Georgia State University, College of Education, Department of Middle-Secondary Education and Instructional Technology, Program in Reading Instruction, Atlanta, GA 30302-3083. Offers reading, language and literacy (M Ed); reading, language, and literacy (PhD, Ed S); teaching English as a second language (M Ed). *Accreditation:* NCATE. Part-time and evening/weekend programs available. *Degree requirements:* For master's, comprehensive exam; for Ed S, project/exam. *Entrance requirements:* For master's, GRE General Test, minimum GPA of 2.5;

for Ed S, GRE General Test or MAT, minimum graduate GPA of 3.25. *Faculty research:* Language development, attribution theory, linguistics.

Gonzaga University, Program in Teaching English as a Second Language, Spokane, WA 99258. Offers MATESL. *Faculty:* 1 (woman) full-time. *Students:* 7 full-time (6 women), 19 part-time (15 women); includes 2 minority (1 African American, 1 Asian American or Pacific Islander), 8 international. Average age 33. In 2009, 15 master's awarded. *Application deadline:* Applications are processed on a rolling basis. Application fee: $40. Electronic applications accepted. Tuition and fees vary according to course level, course load, degree level, campus/location and program. *Unit head:* Dr. Mary Jeannot, Chairperson, 509-324-6559. *Application contact:* Julie McCulloh, Dean of Admissions, 509-323-6592, Fax: 509-323-5780, E-mail: mcculloh@gu.gonzaga.edu.

Grand Valley State University, College of Education, Programs in General Education, Allendale, MI 49401-9403. Offers adult and higher education (M Ed); early childhood education (M Ed); educational differentiation (M Ed); educational leadership (M Ed); educational technology integration (M Ed); elementary education (M Ed); middle level education (M Ed); school library media services (M Ed); secondary level education (M Ed); teaching English to speakers of other languages (M Ed). Part-time and evening/weekend programs available. Postbaccalaureate distance learning degree programs offered (minimal on-campus study). *Faculty:* 82 full-time (42 women), 43 part-time/adjunct (25 women). *Students:* 100 full-time (53 women), 723 part-time (478 women); includes 59 minority (25 African Americans, 4 American Indian/Alaska Native, 13 Asian Americans or Pacific Islanders, 17 Hispanic Americans), 10 international. Average age 33. 237 applicants, 96% accepted, 117 enrolled. In 2009, 291 master's awarded. *Degree requirements:* For master's, thesis. *Entrance requirements:* For master's, GRE General Test or minimum GPA of 3.0. Additional exam requirements/recommendations for international students: Required—TOEFL. *Application deadline:* Applications are processed on a rolling basis. Application fee: $30. Electronic applications accepted. *Expenses:* Tuition, state resident: part-time $471 per credit hour. Tuition, nonresident: part-time $646 per credit hour. Tuition and fees vary according to course level. *Financial support:* In 2009–10, 73 students received support, including 55 fellowships (averaging $2,273 per year), 19 research assistantships with full and partial tuition reimbursements available (averaging $8,000 per year); career-related internships or fieldwork, Federal Work-Study, scholarships/grants, and unspecified assistantships also available. *Faculty research:* Effectiveness of technology in education, parental involvement, effective teaching, effective schools research. *Unit head:* Dr. Linda McCrea, Director, 616-331-2080, E-mail: mccreal@gvsu.edu. *Application contact:* Thomas Owens, Student Information and Services Center, 616-331-6282, Fax: 616-331-2000, E-mail: owenst@gvsu.edu.

Greensboro College, Program in Teaching English to Speakers of Other Languages, Greensboro, NC 27401-1875. Offers MA. *Accreditation:* NCATE. Part-time and evening/weekend programs available. *Degree requirements:* For master's, thesis, portfolio. *Entrance requirements:* For master's, GRE or MAT, 2 letters of reference. Additional exam requirements/recommendations for international students: Required—TOEFL (minimum score 550 paper-based; 213 computer-based). Electronic applications accepted.

Hamline University, School of Education, St. Paul, MN 55104-1284. Offers education (MA Ed, Ed D); English as a second language (MAESL); literacy education (MALED); natural science and environmental education (MA Ed); teaching (MAT). *Accreditation:* NCATE (one or more programs are accredited). Part-time and evening/weekend programs available. *Faculty:* 27 full-time (18 women), 128 part-time/adjunct (100 women). *Students:* 324 full-time (242 women), 1,049 part-time (780 women); includes 116 minority (36 African Americans, 4 American Indian/Alaska Native, 42 Asian Americans or Pacific Islanders, 34 Hispanic Americans), 25 international. Average age 33. 501 applicants, 79% accepted, 311 enrolled. In 2009, 196 master's, 9 doctorates awarded. *Degree requirements:* For master's, thesis; for doctorate, comprehensive exam, thesis/dissertation. *Entrance requirements:* For doctorate, personal statement, master's degree, 3 years experience, letters of recommendation, writing sample, interview. Additional exam requirements/recommendations for international students: Required—TOEFL (minimum score 550 paper-based; 213 computer-based; 79 iBT), TWE (minimum score 5). *Application deadline:* Applications are processed on a rolling basis. Application fee: $0. Electronic applications accepted. *Expenses:* Tuition: Full-time $6816; part-time $426 per credit. Required fees: $6 per credit. One-time fee: $205. Tuition and fees vary according to degree level, campus/location and program. *Financial support:* In 2009–10, 8 students received support. Federal Work-Study and scholarships/grants available. Support available to part-time students. Financial award applicants required to submit FAFSA. *Faculty research:* Adult basic education, service learning, teacher dispositions, diversity, technology. *Unit head:* Dr. Sheila Wright, Dean, 651-523-2600, Fax: 651-523-2489, E-mail: swright04@hamline.edu. *Application contact:* Rae A. Lenway, Director, Graduate Recruitment and Admission, 651-523-2900, Fax: 651-523-3058, E-mail: rlenway@hamline.edu.

Harding University, College of Education, Searcy, AR 72149-0001. Offers advanced studies in teaching and learning (M Ed); art (MSE); behavioral science (MSE); counseling (MS, Ed S); early childhood special education (M Ed, MSE); education (MSE); educational leadership (M Ed, Ed S); elementary education (M Ed); English (MSE); family and consumer science (MSE); French (MSE); history/social science (MSE); kinesiology (MSE); math (MSE); physical science (MSE); reading (M Ed); secondary education (M Ed); Spanish (MSE); special education licensure (M Ed); teaching (MAT); teaching English as a second language (M Ed). *Accreditation:* NCATE. Part-time and evening/weekend programs available. *Faculty:* 11 full-time (4 women), 49 part-time/adjunct (26 women). *Students:* 104 full-time (85 women), 392 part-time (282 women); includes 77 minority (67 African Americans, 5 American Indian/Alaska Native, 1 Asian American or Pacific Islander, 4 Hispanic Americans), 5 international. Average age 36. 153 applicants, 92% accepted, 131 enrolled. In 2009, 153 master's, 6 other advanced degrees awarded. *Degree requirements:* For master's, comprehensive exam (for some programs), thesis optional, portfolio(s); for Ed S, comprehensive exam, portfolio, specialist project. *Entrance requirements:* For master's, GRE, MAT, PRAXIS; for Ed S, MAT or GRE. Additional exam requirements/recommendations for international students: Required—TOEFL (minimum score 550 paper-based; 79 iBT). *Application deadline:* For fall admission, 8/1 for domestic and international students; for spring admission, 1/1 for domestic and international students. Applications are processed on a rolling basis. Application fee: $35. *Expenses:* Tuition: Full-time $9720; part-time $540 per credit hour. Required fees: $22 per credit hour. Tuition and fees vary according to course load and program. *Financial support:* In 2009–10, 30 students received support. Unspecified assistantships available. *Faculty research:* Reading, comprehension, school violence, educational technology, behavior, college choice, differentiated instruction, brain-based teaching. *Unit head:* Dr. Clara Carroll, Chair, 501-279-4501, Fax: 501-279-4083, E-mail: ccarroll@harding.edu. *Application contact:* Information Contact, 501-279-4315, E-mail: gradstudiesedu@harding.edu.

Hawai'i Pacific University, College of Humanities and Social Sciences, Program in Teaching English as a Second Language, Honolulu, HI 96813. Offers MA. Part-time and evening/weekend programs available. *Faculty:* 7 full-time (5 women), 2 part-time/adjunct (both women). *Students:* 38 full-time (30 women), 20 part-time (14 women); includes 14 minority (1 African American, 11 Asian Americans or Pacific Islanders, 2 Hispanic Americans), 29 international. Average age 33. 32 applicants, 75% accepted, 13 enrolled. In 2009, 13 master's awarded. *Entrance requirements:* Additional exam requirements/recommendations for international students: Recommended—TOEFL (minimum score 550 paper-based; 213 computer-based; 80 iBT), TWE (minimum score 5). *Application deadline:* For fall admission, 2/15 priority date for domestic students; for spring admission, 10/15 priority date for domestic students. Applications are processed on a rolling basis. Application fee: $50. Electronic applications accepted. *Expenses:* Tuition: Full-time $12,600; part-time $700 per credit hour. Tuition and fees vary according to program. *Financial support:* In 2009–10, 23 students received support. Career-related internships or fieldwork, Federal Work-Study, scholarships/grants, and unspecified assistantships available. Support available to part-time students. Financial award application deadline: 3/1; financial award applicants required to submit FAFSA. *Unit head:* Dr. Carlos Juarez, Dean, 808-566-2493, Fax: 808-544-0834, E-mail: cjuarez@hpu.edu. *Application contact:* Danny Lam, Assistant Director of Graduate Admissions, 808-544-1135, Fax: 808-544-0280, E-mail: graduate@hpu.edu.

See Close-Up on page 1117.

Heritage University, Graduate Programs in Education, Program in Professional Studies, Toppenish, WA 98948-9599. Offers bilingual education/ESL (M Ed); biology (M Ed); English and literature (M Ed); reading/literacy (M Ed); special education (M Ed). Part-time and evening/weekend programs available. *Degree requirements:* For master's, comprehensive exam (for some programs), thesis (for some programs).

Hofstra University, School of Education, Health, and Human Services, Department of Curriculum and Teaching, Program in Foreign Language Education, Hempstead, NY 11549. Offers foreign language and TESOL (MS Ed); foreign language education (MA, MS Ed), including French, German, Russian, Spanish. Part-time and evening/weekend programs available. *Students:* 4 full-time (all women), 3 part-time (1 woman); includes 2 minority (both Hispanic Americans). Average age 29. 9 applicants, 67% accepted, 3 enrolled. In 2009, 2 master's awarded. *Degree requirements:* For master's, one foreign language. *Entrance requirements:* For master's, 2 letters of recommendation, teacher certification (MA). Additional exam requirements/recommendations for international students: Required—TOEFL (minimum score 550 paper-based; 213 computer-based; 80 iBT). *Application deadline:* Applications are processed on a rolling basis. Application fee: $60. Electronic applications accepted. *Expenses:* Tuition: Full-time $16,200; part-time $900 per credit hour. Required fees: $970; $145 per term. Tuition and fees vary according to program. *Financial support:* In 2009–10, 6 students received support, including 2 fellowships with full and partial tuition reimbursements available (averaging $2,878 per year); research assistantships with full and partial tuition reimbursements available, Federal Work-Study, institutionally sponsored loans, scholarships/grants, tuition waivers (full and partial), and unspecified assistantships also available. Support available to part-time students. Financial award applicants required to submit FAFSA. *Faculty research:* First language acquisition and second language learning; theory and practice in language teaching; technology and language teaching and learning; language and colonialism. *Unit head:* Dr. Mustapha Masrour, Program Director, 516-463-6033, Fax: 516-463-6266, E-mail: lalmzm@hofstra.edu. *Application contact:* Carol Drummer, Dean of Graduate Admissions, 516-463-4876, Fax: 516-463-4664, E-mail: gradstudent@hofstra.edu.

Hofstra University, School of Education, Health, and Human Services, Department of Curriculum and Teaching, Programs in TESL/Bilingual Education, Hempstead, NY 11549. Offers bilingual education (MA); bilingual extension education (CAS); TESOL (MS Ed, CAS). Part-time programs available. *Students:* 36 full-time (34 women), 38 part-time (35 women); includes 28 minority (7 African Americans, 3 Asian Americans or Pacific Islanders, 18 Hispanic Americans). Average age 31. 58 applicants, 74% accepted, 32 enrolled. In 2009, 24 master's, 9 other advanced degrees awarded. Terminal master's awarded for partial completion of doctoral program. *Degree requirements:* For master's, one foreign language, thesis or alternative, portfolios. *Entrance requirements:* For master's, interview, 2 letters of recommendation, teaching certificate; for CAS, 2 letters of recommendation, interview, teaching certificate, essay, proficiency in language. Additional exam requirements/recommendations for international students: Required—TOEFL (minimum score 550 paper-based; 213 computer-based; 80 iBT). *Application deadline:* Applications are processed on a rolling basis. Application fee: $60. Electronic applications accepted. *Expenses:* Tuition: Full-time $16,200; part-time $900 per credit hour. Required fees: $970; $145 per term. Tuition and fees vary according to program. *Financial support:* In 2009–10, 43 students received support, including 1 fellowship with full and partial tuition reimbursement available (averaging $3,400 per year), 1 research assistantship with full and partial tuition reimbursement available (averaging $17,682 per year); career-related internships or fieldwork, Federal Work-Study, institutionally sponsored loans, scholarships/grants, tuition waivers (full and partial), and unspecified assistantships also available. Support available to part-time students. Financial award applicants required to submit FAFSA. *Faculty research:* Innateness hypothesis, content-based ESL instruction, linking linguistic research to practice. *Unit head:* Dr. Tatiana Gordon, Director, 516-463-5170, Fax: 516-463-6196, E-mail: cattzg@hofstra.edu. *Application contact:* Carol Drummer, Dean of Graduate Admissions, 516-463-4876, Fax: 516-463-4664, E-mail: gradstudent@hofstra.edu.

Holy Names University, Graduate Division, Department of Education, Oakland, CA 94619-1699. Offers educational therapy (Certificate); level 1 education specialist mild/moderate disabilities (Credential); level 2 education specialist mild/moderate disabilities (Credential); multiple subject teaching credential (Credential); single subject teaching credential (Credential); teaching English as a second language (TESL) (M Ed); urban education: educational therapy (M Ed); urban education: K-12 education (M Ed); urban education: special education (M Ed). Part-time programs available. *Degree requirements:* For master's, comprehensive exam, research paper, thesis or project. *Entrance requirements:* For master's, minimum undergraduate GPA of 2.6 overall, 3.0 in major. Additional exam requirements/recommendations for international students: Required—TOEFL (minimum score 550 paper-based; 213 computer-based; 80 iBT). *Faculty research:* Cognitive development, language development, learning handicaps.

Houston Baptist University, College of Education and Behavioral Sciences, Programs in Education, Houston, TX 77074-3298. Offers bilingual education (M Ed); counselor education (M Ed); curriculum and instruction (M Ed); educational administration (M Ed); educational diagnostician (M Ed); reading education (M Ed). Part-time programs available. *Entrance requirements:* For master's, GRE General Test or MAT. Additional exam requirements/recommendations for international students: Required—TOEFL (minimum score 550 paper-based; 213 computer-based).

Hunter College of the City University of New York, Graduate School, School of Education, Department of Curriculum and Teaching, Program in Teaching English as a Second Language, New York, NY 10021-5085. Offers MA. *Accreditation:* NCATE. *Faculty:* 12 full-time (6 women), 57 part-time/adjunct (42 women). *Students:* 29 full-time (26 women), 171 part-time (142 women); includes 47 minority (6 African Americans, 2 American Indian/Alaska Native, 17 Asian Americans or Pacific Islanders, 22 Hispanic Americans). Average age 34. 147 applicants, 62% accepted, 66 enrolled. In 2009, 53 master's awarded. *Degree requirements:* For master's, one foreign language, thesis, comprehensive exam or essay, New York state teacher certification exams. *Entrance requirements:* For master's, minimum GPA of 2.8, 2 letters of recommendation, interview. Additional exam requirements/recommendations for international students: Required—TOEFL (minimum score 600 paper-based), TWE (minimum score 5). *Application deadline:* For fall admission, 4/1 for domestic students, 2/1 for international students; for spring admission, 11/1 for domestic students, 9/1 for international students. Applications are processed on a rolling basis. Application fee: $125. *Expenses:* Tuition, state resident: full-time $7360; part-time $310 per credit. Required fees: $250 per semester. *Financial support:* Federal Work-Study, scholarships/grants, and tuition waivers (partial) available. Support available to part-time students. *Unit head:* Dr. Bede McCormack, Coordinator, 212-777-4665, E-mail: bmccorma@hunter.cuny.edu. *Application contact:* William Zlata, Director for Graduate Admissions, 212-772-4482, Fax: 212-650-3336, E-mail: admissions@hunter.cuny.edu.

Idaho State University, Office of Graduate Studies, College of Arts and Sciences, Department of English, Pocatello, ID 83209-8056. Offers English (MA, DA); English and the teaching of English (PhD); TESOL (Post-Master's Certificate). Part-time programs available. *Faculty:* 20 full-time (7 women). *Students:* 29 full-time (16 women), 37 part-time (22 women); includes 4 minority (1 Asian American or Pacific Islander, 3 Hispanic Americans), 5 international. Average age 37. In 2009, 6 master's, 2 doctorates, 2 other advanced degrees awarded. *Degree requirements:* For master's, one foreign language, comprehensive exam, thesis optional; for doctorate, one foreign language, comprehensive exam, thesis/dissertation, 2 papers, 2 teaching internships; for Post-Master's Certificate, 6 credits of elective linguistics, practicum. *Entrance requirements:* For master's, GRE General Test (minimum 50th percentile verbal), general literature exam, minimum GPA of 3.0, 3 letters of recommendation, 5-page writing sample; for doctorate, GRE General Test, GRE Subject Test, minimum GPA of 3.5, writing examples, 3 letters of recommendation, master's degree in English; for Post-Master's Certificate, GRE (minimum 35th percentile on verbal section), bachelor's degree, minimum undergraduate GPA

English as a Second Language

Idaho State University (continued)

of 3.0 in last 2 years, 3 letters of recommendation, knowledge of second language. Additional exam requirements/recommendations for international students: Required—TOEFL (minimum score 550 paper-based; 213 computer-based; 80 iBT). *Application deadline:* For fall admission, 7/1 for domestic students, 6/1 for international students; for spring admission, 12/1 for domestic students, 11/1 for international students. Applications are processed on a rolling basis. Application fee: $55. Electronic applications accepted. *Expenses:* Tuition, state resident: full-time $3318; part-time $297 per credit hour. Tuition, nonresident: full-time $13,120; part-time $437 per credit hour. Required fees: $2530. Tuition and fees vary according to program. *Financial support:* In 2009–10, 7 fellowships with full and partial tuition reimbursements (averaging $12,282 per year), 2 research assistantships (averaging $9,401 per year), 9 teaching assistantships with full and partial tuition reimbursements (averaging $10,841 per year) were awarded; career-related internships or fieldwork, Federal Work-Study, institutionally sponsored loans, scholarships/grants, health care benefits, tuition waivers (full and partial), and unspecified assistantships also available. Support available to part-time students. Financial award application deadline: 1/1; financial award applicants required to submit FAFSA. *Faculty research:* American literature, Renaissance literature, composition and rhetoric, Intermountain West studies, ethics. *Unit head:* Dr. Margaret Johnson, Department Chair, 208-282-3207, Fax: 208-282-4472, E-mail: johnmarg@isu.edu. *Application contact:* Tami Carson, Graduate School Technical Records Specialist, 208-282-2150, Fax: 208-282-4847, E-mail: carstami@isu.edu.

Indiana State University, School of Graduate Studies, College of Arts and Sciences, Department of Languages, Literatures, and Linguistics, Terre Haute, IN 47809. Offers linguistics/teaching English as a second language (MA); TESL/TEFL (CAS). *Degree requirements:* For master's, comprehensive exam. Electronic applications accepted.

Indiana University Bloomington, University Graduate School, College of Arts and Sciences, Department of Second Language Studies, Bloomington, IN 47405-7000. Offers second language studies (MA, PhD); TESOL and applied linguistics (MA). *Faculty:* 1 (woman) full-time. *Students:* 22 full-time (19 women), 3 part-time (1 woman); includes 4 minority (1 African American, 3 Hispanic Americans), 10 international. Average age 33. 78 applicants, 38% accepted, 6 enrolled. In 2009, 6 master's awarded. Application fee: $55 ($65 for international students). *Financial support:* In 2009–10, 1 fellowship with tuition reimbursement (averaging $15,000 per year), 12 teaching assistantships with tuition reimbursements (averaging $12,750 per year) were awarded. *Unit head:* Kathleen Bardovi-Harlig, Chair, 812-855-7951, E-mail: bardovi@indiana.edu. *Application contact:* Karla Reynolds, Graduate Secretary, 812-855-7951, E-mail: kjbastin@indiana.edu.

Indiana University of Pennsylvania, School of Graduate Studies and Research, College of Humanities and Social Sciences, Department of English, Program in Composition and Teaching English to Speakers of Other Languages, Indiana, PA 15705-1087. Offers composition and teaching English to speakers of other languages (PhD); teaching English (MAT); teaching English to speakers of other languages (MA). *Faculty:* 27 full-time (15 women). *Students:* 73 full-time (48 women), 142 part-time (95 women); includes 10 minority (2 African Americans, 6 Asian Americans or Pacific Islanders, 2 Hispanic Americans), 63 international. Average age 36. 203 applicants, 36% accepted, 45 enrolled. In 2009, 20 master's, 12 doctorates awarded. *Degree requirements:* For master's, thesis optional; for doctorate, one foreign language, comprehensive exam, thesis/dissertation. *Entrance requirements:* For master's and doctorate, 2 letters of recommendation. Additional exam requirements/recommendations for international students: Required—TOEFL. *Application deadline:* For fall admission, 7/1 priority date for domestic students; for spring admission, 11/1 for domestic students. Applications are processed on a rolling basis. Application fee: $40. *Expenses:* Tuition, state resident: full-time $6666; part-time $370 per credit hour. Tuition, nonresident: full-time $10,666; part-time $593 per credit hour. Required fees: $813 per semester. *Financial support:* In 2009–10, 4 fellowships (averaging $938 per year), 22 research assistantships with full and partial tuition reimbursements (averaging $5,922 per year), 8 teaching assistantships with partial tuition reimbursements (averaging $17,498 per year) were awarded. Financial award application deadline: 3/15; financial award applicants required to submit FAFSA. *Unit head:* Dr. Ben Rafoth, Graduate Coordinator, 724-357-2272. *Application contact:* Dr. Ben Rafoth, Graduate Coordinator, 724-357-2272.

Indiana University–Purdue University Fort Wayne, College of Arts and Sciences, Department of English and Linguistics, Fort Wayne, IN 46805-1499. Offers English (MA, MAT); TENL (teaching English as a new language) (Certificate). Part-time programs available. *Faculty:* 28 full-time (14 women). *Students:* 8 full-time (5 women), 23 part-time (14 women); includes 2 minority (both Asian Americans or Pacific Islanders). Average age 35. 14 applicants, 100% accepted, 14 enrolled. In 2009, 10 master's, 2 other advanced degrees awarded. *Degree requirements:* For master's, one foreign language, thesis (for some programs), teaching certificate (MAT). *Entrance requirements:* For master's, GRE General Test, minimum GPA of 3.0, major or minor in English, 3 letters of recommendation; for Certificate, bachelor's degree with minimum GPA of 2.5. Additional exam requirements/recommendations for international students: Required—TOEFL (minimum score 600 paper-based; 260 computer-based). *Application deadline:* For fall admission, 8/1 for domestic students; for spring admission, 10/15 for domestic students. Applications are processed on a rolling basis. Application fee: $50. *Expenses:* Tuition, state resident: full-time $4595; part-time $255 per credit. Tuition, nonresident: full-time $10,963; part-time $609 per credit. Required fees: $528; $29.35 per credit. Tuition and fees vary according to course load. *Financial support:* In 2009–10, 13 teaching assistantships with partial tuition reimbursements (averaging $12,740 per year) were awarded; career-related internships or fieldwork, scholarships/grants, and unspecified assistantships also available. Support available to part-time students. Financial award application deadline: 3/1; financial award applicants required to submit FAFSA. *Faculty research:* Shakespeare, three-volume novels, poetry of Nikola Vaptsarov, philanthropy. Total annual research expenditures: $52,321. *Unit head:* Dr. Hardin Aasand, Chair and Professor, 260-481-6750, Fax: 260-481-6985, E-mail: aasandh@ipfw.edu. *Application contact:* Dr. Michael Stapleton, Graduate Program Director, 260-481-6772, Fax: 260-481-6985, E-mail: stapletm@ipfw.edu.

Indiana University–Purdue University Indianapolis, School of Education, Indianapolis, IN 46202-2896. Offers computer education (Certificate); curriculum and instruction (MS); early childhood (MS); educational leadership (MS, Certificate); English as a second language (Certificate); higher education and student affairs (MS); kindergarten (Certificate); language education (MS); reading (Certificate); school counseling (MS); special education (MS, Certificate). Part-time and evening/weekend programs available. *Faculty:* 41 full-time, 80 part-time/adjunct. *Students:* 72 full-time (60 women), 427 part-time (325 women); includes 57 minority (42 African Americans, 1 American Indian/Alaska Native, 4 Asian Americans or Pacific Islanders, 10 Hispanic Americans), 5 international. Average age 32. 181 applicants, 78% accepted, 112 enrolled. In 2009, 162 master's awarded. *Degree requirements:* For master's, thesis optional. *Entrance requirements:* For master's, GRE General Test, minimum GPA of 3.0. Additional exam requirements/recommendations for international students: Required—TOEFL. *Application deadline:* For fall admission, 5/1 priority date for domestic students; for spring admission, 11/1 for domestic students. Application fee: $55 ($65 for international students). *Financial support:* In 2009–10, 2 fellowships (averaging $780 per year), 18 teaching assistantships (averaging $9,756 per year) were awarded; research assistantships with partial tuition reimbursements, Federal Work-Study, institutionally sponsored loans, scholarships/grants, and tuition waivers (partial) also available. Support available to part-time students. *Faculty research:* Teachers in the process of change, learning cycles, children's concepts of science. Total annual research expenditures: $614,458. *Unit head:* Dr. Chris Leland, Interim Executive Associate Dean, 317-274-6801, Fax: 317-274-6864. *Application contact:* Sarah Brandenburg, Graduate Advisor, 317-274-6801, Fax: 317-274-6864, E-mail: edugrad@iupui.edu.

Inter American University of Puerto Rico, Arecibo Campus, Programs in Education, Arecibo, PR 00614-4050. Offers administration and educational supervision (MA Ed); counseling and guidance (MA Ed); curriculum and teaching (MA Ed), including biology education, English as a second language, history education, math education, Spanish; elementary education (MA Ed). *Degree requirements:* For master's, comprehensive exam, thesis optional. *Entrance requirements:* For master's, GRE, EXADEP, bachelor's degree in education or teaching license (administration and supervision) or courses in education and psychology (counseling and guidance), minimum GPA of 2.5 in last 60 credits.

Inter American University of Puerto Rico, Metropolitan Campus, Graduate Programs, Program in Teaching English as a Second Language, San Juan, PR 00919-1293. Offers MA. Part-time and evening/weekend programs available. *Degree requirements:* For master's, comprehensive exam, thesis or alternative. *Entrance requirements:* For master's, GRE General Test or EXADEP, interview, minimum GPA of 2.5. Electronic applications accepted.

Inter American University of Puerto Rico, Ponce Campus, Graduate School, Mercedita, PR 00715-1602. Offers accounting (MBA); biology (M Ed); chemistry (M Ed); criminal justice (MA); elementary education (M Ed); English as a Second Language (M Ed); finance (MBA); history (M Ed); human resources (MBA); marketing (MBA); mathematics (M Ed); Spanish (M Ed). *Entrance requirements:* For master's, minimum GPA of 2.5.

Inter American University of Puerto Rico, San Germán Campus, Graduate Studies Center, Program in Teaching English as a Second Language, San Germán, PR 00683-5008. Offers MA. Part-time and evening/weekend programs available. *Degree requirements:* For master's, comprehensive exam. *Entrance requirements:* For master's, GRE General Test or EXADEP, minimum GPA of 3.0.

The Johns Hopkins University, School of Education, Department of Teacher Development and Leadership, Baltimore, MD 21218-2699. Offers adolescent literacy education (Certificate); data-based decision making and organizational improvement (Certificate); education (MS), including reading, school administration and supervision, technology for educators; educational leadership for independent schools (Certificate); effective teaching of reading (Certificate); emergent literacy education (Certificate); English as a second language instruction (Certificate); gifted education (Certificate); leadership for school, family, and community collaboration (Certificate); leadership in technology integration (Certificate); school administration and supervision (Certificate); teacher development and leadership (Ed D); teacher leadership (Certificate); technology for educators (MS). Part-time and evening/weekend programs available. Postbaccalaureate distance learning degree programs offered (minimal on-campus study). *Faculty:* 8 full-time (2 women), 53 part-time/adjunct (36 women). *Students:* 17 full-time (16 women), 462 part-time (358 women); includes 117 minority (77 African Americans, 25 Asian Americans or Pacific Islanders, 15 Hispanic Americans), 11 international. Average age 33. 217 applicants, 62% accepted, 107 enrolled. In 2009, 85 master's, 2 doctorates, 181 other advanced degrees awarded. *Degree requirements:* For master's and Certificate, portfolio; for doctorate, comprehensive exam (for some programs), thesis/dissertation, portfolio or comprehensive exam. *Entrance requirements:* For master's and Certificate, bachelor's degree; minimum undergraduate GPA of 3.0; essay/statement of goals; for doctorate, GRE, essay/statement of goals; three letters of recommendation; curriculum vitae/resume; K-12 professional experience; interview; writing assessment. Additional exam requirements/recommendations for international students: Required—TOEFL (minimum score 600 paper-based; 250 computer-based; 100 iBT). *Application deadline:* For fall admission, 5/1 for international students; for spring admission, 10/15 for international students. Applications are processed on a rolling basis. Application fee: $80. Electronic applications accepted. *Financial support:* In 2009–10, 5 research assistantships, 1 teaching assistantship were awarded; scholarships/grants also available. Support available to part-time students. Financial award application deadline: 6/1; financial award applicants required to submit FAFSA. *Faculty research:* Application of psychoanalytic concepts to teaching, schools, and education reform; adolescent literacies; use of emerging technologies for teaching, learning, and school leadership; quantitative analyses of the social contexts of education; school, family, and community collaboration; program evaluation methodologies. *Unit head:* Dr. Edward Pajak, Chair, 410-516-9755, Fax: 410-516-9770, E-mail: mbuckingham@jhu.edu. *Application contact:* Jennifer Shaffer, Director of Admissions, 410-516-9797, Fax: 410-516-9799, E-mail: educationinfo@jhu.edu.

The Johns Hopkins University, School of Education, Department of Teacher Preparation, Baltimore, MD 21218. Offers education (MS), including educational studies; elementary education (MAT); English for speakers of other languages (MAT); K-8 mathematics lead-teacher (Certificate); K-8 science lead-teacher (Certificate); secondary education (MAT), including biology, chemistry, earth/space/environmental science, English, French, mathematics, physics, social studies, Spanish. Part-time and evening/weekend programs available. *Faculty:* 13 full-time (11 women), 35 part-time/adjunct (21 women). *Students:* 162 full-time (119 women), 347 part-time (256 women); includes 138 minority (80 African Americans, 3 American Indian/Alaska Native, 38 Asian Americans or Pacific Islanders, 17 Hispanic Americans), 3 international. Average age 27. 89 applicants, 37% accepted, 24 enrolled. In 2009, 177 master's awarded. *Degree requirements:* For master's, portfolio, PRAXIS II, internship. *Entrance requirements:* For master's, PRAXIS I, SAT, ACT, or GRE (MAT), minimum undergraduate GPA of 3.0, interview, 1 letter of recommendation, curriculum vitae/resume; for Certificate, bachelor's degree, minimum undergraduate GPA of 3.0, essay/statement of goals, interview. Additional exam requirements/recommendations for international students: Required—TOEFL (minimum score 600 paper-based; 250 computer-based; 100 iBT). *Application deadline:* For fall admission, 5/1 for international students; for spring admission, 10/15 for international students. Applications are processed on a rolling basis. Application fee: $80. Electronic applications accepted. *Financial support:* Scholarships/grants available. Support available to part-time students. Financial award application deadline: 6/1; financial award applicants required to submit FAFSA. *Faculty research:* Teacher retention; STEM education reform; alternative certification programs; school-university partnerships; urban education; action research/data-informed instruction; family engagement. *Unit head:* Dr. Francis Masci, Chair, 410-516-9774, Fax: 410-516-9770, E-mail: matjhu@jhu.edu. *Application contact:* Jennifer Shaffer, Director of Admissions, 410-516-9797, Fax: 410-516-9799, E-mail: educationinfo@jhu.edu.

Kean University, College of Education, Program in Instruction and Curriculum, Union, NJ 07083. Offers bilingual/bicultural education (MA); classroom instruction (MA); earth science (MA); mathematics/science/computer education (MA); teaching (MA); teaching English as a second language (MA); world languages (Spanish) (MA). *Accreditation:* NCATE. Part-time and evening/weekend programs available. *Faculty:* 16 full-time (7 women). *Students:* 45 full-time (34 women), 131 part-time (104 women); includes 60 minority (11 African Americans, 6 Asian Americans or Pacific Islanders, 43 Hispanic Americans), 6 international. Average age 33. 64 applicants, 94% accepted, 46 enrolled. In 2009, 58 master's awarded. *Entrance requirements:* For master's, GRE General Test or MAT, PRAXIS, minimum GPA of 3.0, 2 letters of recommendation, interview, teacher certification (for some programs). *Application deadline:* For fall admission, 5/1 for domestic students; for spring admission, 11/1 for domestic students. Application fee: $60 ($150 for international students). Electronic applications accepted. *Expenses:* Tuition, state resident: full-time $10,440; part-time $435 per credit. Tuition, nonresident: full-time $14,160; part-time $590 per credit. Required fees: $2642; $110 per credit. Part-time tuition and fees vary according to course load and degree level. *Financial support:* In 2009–10, 1 research assistantship with full tuition reimbursement (averaging $3,263 per year) was awarded; unspecified assistantships also available. *Unit head:* Dr. Thomas Walsh, Program Coordinator, 908-737-4296, E-mail: twalsh@kean.edu. *Application contact:* Ann-Marie Kay, Assistant Director of Graduate Admissions, 908-737-5922, Fax: 908-737-5965, E-mail: akay@kean.edu.

Kennesaw State University, Leland and Clarice C. Bagwell College of Education, Program in Graduate Education, Kennesaw, GA 30144-5591. Offers adolescent education (M Ed); educational leadership (M Ed); educational leadership technology (M Ed); elementary and early childhood education (M Ed); special education (M Ed); teaching English to speakers of other languages (M Ed). *Accreditation:* NCATE. Part-time programs available. *Faculty:* 60 full-time (38 women), 12 part-time/adjunct (4 women). *Students:* 140 full-time (116 women), 136 part-time (107 women); includes 51 minority (39 African Americans, 1 American Indian/Alaska Native, 3 Asian Americans or Pacific Islanders, 8 Hispanic Americans), 4 international. Average age 34. 113 applicants, 83% accepted, 69 enrolled. In 2009, 282 master's awarded. *Degree requirements:* For master's, thesis or alternative. *Entrance requirements:* For master's, GRE General Test, T-4 state certification, minimum GPA of 2.75. Additional exam requirements/

recommendations for international students: Required—TOEFL (minimum score 550 paper-based; 213 computer-based; 80 iBT), IELTS (minimum score 6). *Application deadline:* For fall admission, 7/1 for domestic and international students; for spring admission, 10/1 for domestic and international students. Application fee: $60. Electronic applications accepted. *Expenses:* Tuition, state resident: full-time $2341; part-time $196 per credit hour. Tuition, nonresident: full-time $9396; part-time $783 per credit hour. Required fees: $573 per semester. *Financial support:* Federal Work-Study and unspecified assistantships available. Support available to part-time students. Financial award application deadline: 6/15; financial award applicants required to submit FAFSA. *Unit head:* Dr. Nita Paris, Associate Dean for Graduate Programs, 770-423-6636, E-mail: nparis@kennesaw.edu. *Application contact:* Alisha Bello, Administrative Coordinator, 770-423-6043, Fax: 770-420-4435, E-mail: abello1@kennesaw.edu.

Kennesaw State University, Leland and Clarice C. Bagwell College of Education, Program in Teaching, Kennesaw, GA 30144-5591. Offers secondary English or mathematics (MAT); teaching English to speakers of other languages (MAT). Program offered only in summer. Part-time and evening/weekend programs available. *Students:* 120 full-time (94 women), 16 part-time (9 women); includes 23 minority (12 African Americans, 4 Asian Americans or Pacific Islanders, 7 Hispanic Americans), 1 international. Average age 33. 28 applicants, 79% accepted, 19 enrolled. In 2009, 50 master's awarded. *Entrance requirements:* For master's, GRE, GACE I (state certificate exam), minimum GPA of 2.75, 2 recommendations, resume. Additional exam requirements/recommendations for international students: Required—TOEFL (minimum score 550 paper-based; 213 computer-based; 80 iBT), IELTS (minimum score 6). *Application deadline:* For fall admission, 6/1 for domestic and international students; for spring admission, 3/1 for domestic and international students. Application fee: $60. Electronic applications accepted. *Expenses:* Tuition, state resident: full-time $2341; part-time $196 per credit hour. Tuition, nonresident: full-time $9396; part-time $783 per credit hour. Required fees: $573 per semester. *Financial support:* In 2009–10, 2 research assistantships with tuition reimbursements (averaging $4,000 per year) were awarded; unspecified assistantships also available. Financial award application deadline: 6/15; financial award applicants required to submit FAFSA. *Unit head:* Dr. Lynn Stallings, Director, 770-420-4477, E-mail: lstalling@kennesaw.edu. *Application contact:* Alisha Bello, Administrative Coordinator, 770-423-6043, Fax: 770-420-4435, E-mail: abello1@kennesaw.edu.

Kent State University, College of Arts and Sciences, Department of English, Kent, OH 44242-0001. Offers comparative literature (MA); creative writing (MFA); English (PhD); English for teachers (MA); literature and writing (MA); rhetoric and composition (PhD); teaching English as a second language (MA). Part-time programs available. Terminal master's awarded for partial completion of doctoral program. *Degree requirements:* For master's, one foreign language, thesis optional; for doctorate, one foreign language, thesis/dissertation, qualifying exams. *Entrance requirements:* For master's and doctorate, GRE General Test, writing sample, letters of recommendation. Additional exam requirements/recommendations for international students: Required—TOEFL (minimum score 600 paper-based). Electronic applications accepted. *Faculty research:* British and American literature, textual editing, rhetoric and composition, cultural studies, linguistic and critical theories.

Langston University, School of Education and Behavioral Sciences, Langston, OK 73050. Offers bilingual/multicultural (M Ed); elementary education (M Ed); English as a second language (M Ed); rehabilitation counseling (M Sc); urban education (M Ed). *Accreditation:* CORE; NCATE (one or more programs are accredited). Part-time programs available. *Degree requirements:* For master's, comprehensive exam, thesis optional. *Entrance requirements:* For master's, GRE, writing skills test, minimum GPA of 2.5, 3 letters of recommendation. Additional exam requirements/recommendations for international students: Required—TOEFL, TWE. *Faculty research:* Bilingual/multicultural education, financing post-secondary education.

Lehigh University, College of Education, Program in Comparative and International Education, Bethlehem, PA 18015. Offers comparative and international education (MA); globalization and educational change (M Ed); international counseling (Certificate); international development in education (Certificate); special education (Certificate); TESOL (Certificate). Part-time and evening/weekend programs available. Postbaccalaureate distance learning degree programs offered (no on-campus study). *Faculty:* 2 full-time (1 woman). *Students:* 9 full-time (6 women), 40 part-time (39 women); includes 3 minority (2 African Americans, 1 Hispanic American), 10 international. Average age 36. 46 applicants, 67% accepted, 18 enrolled. In 2009, 11 master's awarded. *Degree requirements:* For master's, thesis (MA). *Entrance requirements:* For master's, 2 letters of recommendation. Additional exam requirements/recommendations for international students: Required—TOEFL (minimum score 600 paper-based; 250 computer-based; 93 iBT). *Application deadline:* For fall admission, 5/15 for domestic and international students; for spring admission, 11/1 for domestic and international students. Applications are processed on a rolling basis. Application fee: $65. Electronic applications accepted. *Financial support:* In 2009–10, 4 students received support, including 4 research assistantships with full and partial tuition reimbursements available (averaging $13,000 per year). Financial award application deadline: 3/15. *Faculty research:* Gender equity in education, post-socialist education transformation, educational borrowing, comparing education systems, education policy and globalization. *Unit head:* Dr. Alexander W. Wiseman, Coordinator, 610-758-5740, Fax: 610-758-6223, E-mail: aww207@lehigh.edu. *Application contact:* Donna M. Johnson, Coordinator, 610-758-3231, Fax: 610-758-6223, E-mail: dmj4@lehigh.edu.

Lehman College of the City University of New York, Division of Education, Department of Middle and High School Education, Program in Teaching English to Speakers of Other Languages, Bronx, NY 10468-1589. Offers MS Ed. *Accreditation:* NCATE. *Degree requirements:* For master's, thesis. *Entrance requirements:* For master's, minimum GPA of 3.0.

Lewis University, College of Education, Program in English as a Second Language, Romeoville, IL 60446. Offers M Ed. Part-time and evening/weekend programs available. *Students:* 34 part-time (32 women); includes 4 minority (1 African American, 1 Asian American or Pacific Islander, 2 Hispanic Americans). Average age 35. 1 applicant, 100% accepted, 1 enrolled. In 2009, 9 master's awarded. *Entrance requirements:* For master's, departmental qualifying exam, writing exam, minimum GPA of 2.75, 2 letters of recommendation, interview. Additional exam requirements/recommendations for international students: Required—TOEFL (minimum score 550 paper-based; 213 computer-based). *Application deadline:* For fall admission, 5/1 priority date for international students; for spring admission, 11/15 priority date for international students. Application fee: $40. *Expenses:* Tuition: Full-time $6480; part-time $720 per credit. One-time fee: $40. Tuition and fees vary according to course load, degree level and program. *Financial support:* Federal Work-Study, scholarships/grants, and unspecified assistantships available. Financial award application deadline: 5/1; financial award applicants required to submit FAFSA. *Unit head:* Dr. Barbara Mackey, Program Director, 815-838-0500 Ext. 5962, E-mail: mackeyba@lewisu.edu. *Application contact:* Pat Levenda, Secretary, 815-838-0500 Ext. 5769, E-mail: levendpa@lewisu.edu.

Lipscomb University, Program in Education, Nashville, TN 37204-3951. Offers English language learners (MAT); instructional leadership (M Ed); instructional technology (M Ed); learning and teaching (MALT); math specialty (M Ed); school administration and supervision (M Ed); special education instruction, K-12 (MASE). *Accreditation:* NCATE. Part-time and evening/weekend programs available. *Faculty:* 4 full-time (1 woman), 12 part-time/adjunct (8 women). *Students:* 140 full-time (103 women), 200 part-time (144 women); includes 32 minority (29 African Americans, 3 Hispanic Americans). Average age 31. 206 applicants, 75% accepted. In 2009, 131 master's awarded. *Entrance requirements:* For master's, MAT or GRE General Test, 2 reference letters. Additional exam requirements/recommendations for international students: Required—TOEFL (minimum score 570 paper-based; 230 computer-based). *Application deadline:* For fall admission, 8/29 priority date for domestic students; for spring admission, 1/16 priority date for domestic students. Applications are processed on a rolling basis. Application fee: $50. *Expenses:* Tuition: Full-time $16,002; part-time $889 per credit hour. Tuition and fees vary according to program. *Financial support:* In 2009–10, 67 students received support. Federal Work-Study, tuition waivers (full), and unspecified assistantships available. Support available to part-time students. Financial award applicants required to submit FAFSA. *Faculty research:* Facilitative learning styles, leadership, student assessment, interactive multimedia inclusion. *Unit head:* Dr. Deborah Boyd, Director of M Ed Program, 615-966-6263. *Application contact:* Kristin Green, Administrative Assistant, 615-966-7628 Ext. 6081, Fax: 615-966-7628, E-mail: kristin.green@lipscomb.edu.

Long Island University, Brooklyn Campus, School of Education, Department of Teaching and Learning, Program in Teaching English to Speakers of Other Languages, Brooklyn, NY 11201-8423. Offers MS Ed. Part-time and evening/weekend programs available. *Degree requirements:* For master's, thesis optional. *Entrance requirements:* For master's, 2 letters of recommendation. Additional exam requirements/recommendations for international students: Required—TOEFL (minimum score 500 paper-based; 173 computer-based). Electronic applications accepted.

Long Island University, C.W. Post Campus, School of Education, Department of Curriculum and Instruction, Brookville, NY 11548-1300. Offers adolescence education (MS); adolescence education: biology (MS); adolescence education: earth science (MS); adolescence education: English (MS); adolescence education: mathematics (MS); adolescence education: social studies (MS); adolescence education: Spanish (MS); art education (MS); bilingual education (MS); childhood education (MS); early childhood education (MS); middle childhood education (MS); music education (MS); teaching English to speakers of other languages (MS). Part-time and evening/weekend programs available. *Degree requirements:* For master's, comprehensive exam or thesis, student teaching. *Entrance requirements:* For master's, minimum GPA of 2.75 in major, 2.5 overall. Electronic applications accepted. *Faculty research:* Ethics and education, teaching strategies.

Long Island University, Westchester Graduate Campus, Programs in Education-Teaching, Program in Second Language, TESOL, Bilingual Education, Purchase, NY 10577. Offers MS Ed, Advanced Certificate. Part-time and evening/weekend programs available.

Loyola Marymount University, School of Education, Department of Language and Culture in Education, Program in Teaching English as a Second Language, Los Angeles, CA 90045. Offers MA. Part-time and evening/weekend programs available. *Faculty:* 7 full-time (5 women), 5 part-time/adjunct (3 women). *Students:* 2 full-time (1 woman); includes 1 minority (Asian American or Pacific Islander), 1 international. Average age 36. 3 applicants, 100% accepted, 2 enrolled. *Degree requirements:* For master's, comprehensive exam. *Entrance requirements:* For master's, CBEST, CSET, CSET LOTE Test 3, RICA, 3 letters of recommendation. Additional exam requirements/recommendations for international students: Required—TOEFL (minimum score 600 paper-based; 250 computer-based; 100 iBT). *Application deadline:* For fall admission, 6/15 for domestic students; for spring admission, 11/15 for domestic students. Application fee: $50. Electronic applications accepted. *Financial support:* In 2009–10, 1 student received support. Scholarships/grants and unspecified assistantships available. Support available to part-time students. Financial award application deadline: 11/15; financial award applicants required to submit FAFSA. Total annual research expenditures: $321,465. *Unit head:* Dr. Yvette Lapayese, Chair, 310-338-3773, E-mail: ylapapes@lmu.edu. *Application contact:* Chake H. Kouyoumjian, Director, Graduate Admissions, 310-338-2721, Fax: 310-338-6086, E-mail: ckouyoum@lmu.edu.

Madonna University, Department of English, Livonia, MI 48150-1173. Offers teaching English to speakers of other languages (MATESOL). Part-time and evening/weekend programs available. *Degree requirements:* For master's, one foreign language, thesis or alternative. Electronic applications accepted.

Manhattanville College, Graduate Programs, School of Education, Program in English as a Second Language, Purchase, NY 10577-2132. Offers English as a second language (MAT); teaching English as a second language (MPS). Part-time and evening/weekend programs available. *Students:* 7 full-time (6 women), 54 part-time (48 women); includes 13 minority (all Hispanic Americans), 1 international. In 2009, 13 master's awarded. *Degree requirements:* For master's, comprehensive exam or research project, field experience. *Entrance requirements:* For master's, minimum undergraduate GPA of 3.0. Additional exam requirements/recommendations for international students: Required—TOEFL. *Application deadline:* Applications are processed on a rolling basis. Application fee: $70. Electronic applications accepted. *Financial support:* Career-related internships or fieldwork, Federal Work-Study, institutionally sponsored loans, and unspecified assistantships available. Support available to part-time students. Financial award application deadline: 3/1; financial award applicants required to submit FAFSA. *Unit head:* Dr. Shelley Wepner, Dean, 914-323-5192, Fax: 914-694-2386, E-mail: wepners@mville.edu. *Application contact:* Jeanine Pardey-Levine, Director of Admissions, 914-323-3208, Fax: 914-694-1732, E-mail: edschool@mville.edu.

Marymount University, School of Education and Human Services, Program in Education, Arlington, VA 22207-4299. Offers elementary education (M Ed); English as a second language (M Ed); professional studies (M Ed); secondary education (M Ed); special education, general curriculum (M Ed). *Accreditation:* NCATE. Part-time and evening/weekend programs available. *Faculty:* 9 full-time (6 women), 9 part-time/adjunct (8 women). *Students:* 55 full-time (46 women), 117 part-time (100 women); includes 13 minority (1 African American, 4 Asian Americans or Pacific Islanders, 8 Hispanic Americans), 7 international. Average age 31. 73 applicants, 93% accepted, 55 enrolled. In 2009, 62 master's awarded. *Degree requirements:* For master's, thesis or alternative. *Entrance requirements:* For master's, GRE or MAT and PRAXIS I or SAT/ACT, 2 letters of recommendation, interview. Additional exam requirements/recommendations for international students: Required—TOEFL (minimum score 600 paper-based; 250 computer-based; 96 iBT), IELTS (minimum score 6.5). *Application deadline:* For fall admission, 7/1 for international students; for spring admission, 10/15 for international students. Applications are processed on a rolling basis. Application fee: $40. Electronic applications accepted. *Expenses:* Tuition: Full-time $13,050; part-time $725 per credit hour. Required fees: $135; $7.50 per credit hour. *Financial support:* In 2009–10, 48 students received support; research assistantships with full tuition reimbursements available, career-related internships or fieldwork, Federal Work-Study, scholarships/grants, and unspecified assistantships available. Support available to part-time students. Financial award applicants required to submit FAFSA. *Unit head:* Dr. Shelly Haser, Chair, 703-526-6855, Fax: 703-284-1631, E-mail: shelly.haser@marymount.edu. *Application contact:* Francesca Reed, Director, Graduate Admissions, 703-284-5901, Fax: 703-527-3815, E-mail: grad.admissions@marymount.edu.

Mercy College, School of Education, Program in Teaching English to Speakers of Other Languages (TESOL), Dobbs Ferry, NY 10522-1189. Offers MS. Part-time and evening/weekend programs available. *Students:* 12 full-time (11 women), 28 part-time (26 women); includes 2 African Americans, 21 Hispanic Americans, 1 international. Average age 37. 31 applicants, 58% accepted, 13 enrolled. In 2009, 22 master's awarded. *Entrance requirements:* For master's, resume, interview, minimum undergraduate GPA of 3.0. Additional exam requirements/recommendations for international students: Required—TOEFL (minimum score 600 paper-based; 250 computer-based; 100 iBT). *Application deadline:* For fall admission, 8/1 for international students. Applications are processed on a rolling basis. Application fee: $40. Electronic applications accepted. *Expenses:* Tuition: Full-time $13,158; part-time $731 per credit. Required fees: $500. Tuition and fees vary according to degree level and program. *Financial support:* In 2009–10, 2 students received support. Career-related internships or fieldwork, Federal Work-Study, scholarships/grants, and unspecified assistantships available. Support available to part-time students. Financial award applicants required to submit FAFSA. *Faculty research:* Multicultural literature, literacy assessment, literacy acquisition. *Unit head:* Dr. Andrew Peiser, Interim Dean for the School of Education, 914-674-7489, Fax: 914-674-7352, E-mail: apeiser@mercy.edu. *Application contact:* Mary Ellen Hoffman, Interim Associate Dean, 914-674-7334, E-mail: mhoffman@mercy.edu.

Mesa State College, Center for Teacher Education, Grand Junction, CO 81501-3122. Offers educational leadership (MAEd); ESOL (MAEd). *Accreditation:* NCATE. Part-time and evening/weekend programs available. Postbaccalaureate distance learning degree programs offered (minimal on-campus study). *Faculty:* 6 full-time (3 women), 8 part-time/adjunct (3 women). *Students:* 1 (woman) full-time, 71 part-time (50 women); includes 3 Hispanic Americans.

English as a Second Language

Mesa State College (continued)
Average age 37. 11 applicants, 27% accepted, 3 enrolled. In 2009, 29 master's awarded. *Degree requirements:* For master's, capstone course. *Entrance requirements:* For master's, GRE, 2 professional letters of recommendation. Additional exam requirements/recommendations for international students: Required—TOEFL (minimum score 550 paper-based; 207 computer-based). *Application deadline:* For fall admission, 4/1 for domestic students; for spring admission, 3/31 for domestic students. Applications are processed on a rolling basis. Application fee: $50. Electronic applications accepted. *Expenses:* Tuition, state resident: full-time $5400; part-time $300 per credit hour. Tuition, nonresident: full-time $16,200; part-time $900 per credit hour. Required fees: $460; $25 per credit hour. Tuition and fees vary according to program. *Financial support:* Applicants required to submit FAFSA. *Unit head:* Valerie Dobbs, Director of Teacher Education, 970-248-1953, Fax: 970-248-1112, E-mail: vdobbs@mesastate.edu. *Application contact:* Mary Kienietz, Administrative Assistant, 970-248-1785, Fax: 970-248-1112, E-mail: mkieniet@mesastate.edu.

Michigan State University, The Graduate School, College of Arts and Letters, Department of Linguistics and Germanic, Slavic, Asian, and African Languages, East Lansing, MI 48824. Offers German studies (MA, PhD); linguistics (MA, PhD); teaching English to speakers of other languages (MA). Part-time and evening/weekend programs available. *Faculty:* 30 full-time (16 women). *Students:* 78 full-time (46 women), 20 part-time (13 women); includes 8 minority (2 African Americans, 3 American Indian/Alaska Native, 2 Asian Americans or Pacific Islanders, 1 Hispanic American), 51 international. Average age 30. 149 applicants, 38% accepted. In 2009, 24 master's awarded. *Entrance requirements:* For master's, GRE General Test, minimum GPA of 3.2 in last 2 undergraduate years, 2 years of college-level foreign language, 3 letters of recommendation, portfolio (German studies); for doctorate, GRE General Test, minimum graduate GPA of 3.5, 3 letters of recommendation, master's degree or sufficient graduate course work in linguistics or language of study, master's thesis or major research paper. Additional exam requirements/recommendations for international students: Required—TOEFL. Electronic applications accepted. *Expenses:* Tuition, state resident: part-time $478.25 per credit hour. Tuition, nonresident: part-time $966.50 per credit hour. Part-time tuition and fees vary according to program. *Financial support:* In 2009–10, 7 research assistantships with tuition reimbursements (averaging $6,071 per year), 31 teaching assistantships with tuition reimbursements (averaging $5,986 per year) were awarded. Total annual research expenditures: $351,012. *Unit head:* Dr. David K. Prestel, Chairperson, 517-353-0740, Fax: 517-432-2736, E-mail: prestel@msu.edu. *Application contact:* Julie Delgado, Graduate Studies Secretary, 517-353-0740, Fax: 517-432-2736, E-mail: delgadof@msu.edu.

MidAmerica Nazarene University, Graduate Studies in Education, Olathe, KS 66062-1899. Offers ESOL (M Ed); professional teaching (M Ed); special education (MA); technology enhanced teaching (M Ed). *Accreditation:* NCATE. Part-time and evening/weekend programs available. Postbaccalaureate distance learning degree programs offered (no on-campus study). *Faculty:* 6 full-time (2 women), 14 part-time/adjunct (8 women). *Students:* 2 full-time (1 woman), 148 part-time (120 women); includes 15 minority (7 African Americans, 3 American Indian/Alaska Native, 1 Asian American or Pacific Islander, 4 Hispanic Americans). Average age 36. In 2009, 72 master's awarded. *Degree requirements:* For master's, thesis or alternative, creative project, technology leadership practicum. *Entrance requirements:* For master's, minimum undergraduate GPA of 2.8, 2 years of teaching experience. *Application deadline:* Applications are processed on a rolling basis. Application fee: $25. *Expenses:* Contact institution. *Financial support:* Applicants required to submit FAFSA. *Unit head:* Dr. Martin Dunlap, Director, 913-971-3292, Fax: 913-971-3407, E-mail: mhdunlap@mnu.edu. *Application contact:* Glenna Murray, Administrative Assistant, 913-971-3292, Fax: 913-971-3407, E-mail: gkmurray@mnu.edu.

Middle Tennessee State University, College of Graduate Studies, College of Education and Behavioral Science, Department of Educational Leadership, Program in Curriculum and Instruction, Murfreesboro, TN 37132. Offers curriculum and instruction (M Ed, Ed S); English as a second language (M Ed, Ed S); secondary education (M Ed); technology and curriculum design (Ed S). *Accreditation:* NCATE. Part-time and evening/weekend programs available. Postbaccalaureate distance learning degree programs offered. *Students:* 14 full-time (7 women), 277 part-time (249 women); includes 39 minority (35 African Americans, 3 Asian Americans or Pacific Islanders, 1 Hispanic American). 80 applicants, 89% accepted, 71 enrolled. In 2009, 69 master's, 40 Ed Ss awarded. *Degree requirements:* For master's, comprehensive exam. *Entrance requirements:* For master's and Ed S, GRE, MAT or PRAXIS. Additional exam requirements/recommendations for international students: Required—TOEFL (minimum score 525 paper-based; 195 computer-based; 71 iBT) or IELTS (minimum score 6). *Application deadline:* For fall admission, 6/1 for domestic and international students. Applications are processed on a rolling basis. Application fee: $25 ($30 for international students). Electronic applications accepted. *Expenses:* Tuition, state resident: full-time $4404. Tuition, nonresident: full-time $10,956. *Financial support:* Application deadline: 5/1. *Unit head:* Dr. James Huffman, Chair, 615-898-2855, Fax: 615-898-2859. *Application contact:* Dr. Michael Allen, Dean and Vice Provost for Research, 615-898-2840, Fax: 615-904-8020, E-mail: mallen@mtsu.edu.

Middle Tennessee State University, College of Graduate Studies, College of Liberal Arts, Department of Foreign Languages and Literatures, Murfreesboro, TN 37132. Offers English as a second language (M Ed); foreign language (MAT). Part-time and evening/weekend programs available. Postbaccalaureate distance learning degree programs offered. *Faculty:* 14 full-time (8 women). *Students:* 5 full-time (3 women), 11 part-time (8 women); includes 3 minority (1 African American, 1 Asian American or Pacific Islander, 1 Hispanic American). Average age 30. 15 applicants, 87% accepted, 13 enrolled. In 2009, 6 master's awarded. *Degree requirements:* For master's, one foreign language, comprehensive exam. *Entrance requirements:* For master's, GRE. Additional exam requirements/recommendations for international students: Required—TOEFL (minimum score 525 paper-based; 195 computer-based; 71 iBT) or IELTS (minimum score 6). *Application deadline:* For fall admission, 6/1 for domestic and international students. Applications are processed on a rolling basis. Application fee: $25 ($30 for international students). Electronic applications accepted. *Expenses:* Tuition, state resident: full-time $4404. Tuition, nonresident: full-time $10,956. *Financial support:* In 2009–10, 15 students received support. Career-related internships or fieldwork and institutionally sponsored loans available. Support available to part-time students. Financial award application deadline: 5/1; financial award applicants required to submit FAFSA. *Faculty research:* Literature and linguistics, French literature, interactive material design, Holocaust literature, foreign language pedagogy. *Unit head:* Dr. Joan McRae, Chair, 615-898-2981, Fax: 615-898-5826, E-mail: jmcrae@mtsu.edu. *Application contact:* Dr. Michael Allen, Dean and Vice Provost for Research, 615-898-2840, Fax: 615-904-8020, E-mail: mallen@mtsu.edu.

Midwest University, Graduate Programs, Wentzville, MO 63385. Offers social work (DSW); teaching English to speakers of other languages (MA); theology (M Div, MA, D Min). Part-time programs available. Postbaccalaureate distance learning degree programs offered (minimal on-campus study). *Degree requirements:* For master's, thesis (for some programs); for doctorate, thesis/dissertation; for M Div, thesis/dissertation (for some programs). *Entrance requirements:* Additional exam requirements/recommendations for international students: Recommended—TOEFL (minimum score 550 paper-based).

Minnesota State University Mankato, College of Graduate Studies, College of Arts and Humanities, Department of English, Mankato, MN 56001. Offers creative writing (MFA); English (MAT); English studies (MA); literature (MA); teaching English as a second language (MA, Certificate); technical communication (MA, Certificate). Part-time programs available. *Students:* 54 full-time (34 women), 114 part-time (78 women). *Degree requirements:* For master's, one foreign language, comprehensive exam, thesis or alternative. *Entrance requirements:* For master's, minimum GPA of 3.0 during previous 2 years, writing sample (MFA). Additional exam requirements/recommendations for international students: Required—TOEFL. *Application deadline:* Applications are processed on a rolling basis. Application fee: $40. Electronic applications accepted. *Expenses:* Tuition, state resident: full-time $5364. Tuition, nonresident: full-time $8314. *Financial support:* Research assistantships with full tuition reimbursements, teaching assistantships with full tuition reimbursements, career-related internships or fieldwork, Federal Work-Study, and unspecified assistantships available. Financial award application deadline: 3/15; financial award applicants required to submit FAFSA. *Faculty research:* Keats and Christianity. *Unit head:* Dr. John Banschbach, Chairperson, 507-389-2117. *Application contact:* 507-389-2321, E-mail: grad@mnsu.edu.

Mississippi College, Graduate School, College of Arts and Sciences, School of Humanities and Social Sciences, Department of Modern Languages, Clinton, MS 39058. Offers teaching English to speakers of other languages (MA, MS). Part-time programs available. *Faculty:* 1 (woman) full-time. *Students:* 3 full-time (all women), 7 part-time (all women); includes 3 minority (all African Americans), 1 international. Average age 32. In 2009, 8 master's awarded. *Degree requirements:* For master's, thesis (for some programs). *Entrance requirements:* For master's, GRE or NTE. Additional exam requirements/recommendations for international students: Recommended—IELTS. *Application deadline:* For fall admission, 8/15 priority date for domestic students. Applications are processed on a rolling basis. Application fee: $30. Electronic applications accepted. *Expenses:* Tuition: Part-time $452 per credit hour. Required fees: $101 per semester. Tuition and fees vary according to degree level, campus/location, program and student level. *Financial support:* Career-related internships or fieldwork, Federal Work-Study, and unspecified assistantships available. Support available to part-time students. Financial award applicants required to submit FAFSA. *Unit head:* Dr. Deborah Pierce, Chair, 601-925-3216, E-mail: pierce@mc.edu. *Application contact:* Elnora Lewis, Secretary, 601-925-3225, Fax: 601-925-3889, E-mail: lewis09@mc.edu.

Monmouth University, Graduate School, School of Education, West Long Branch, NJ 07764-1898. Offers education (M Ed); initial certification (MAT), including elementary level, K-12, secondary level; learning disabilities-teacher consultant (Certificate); principal (MS Ed); principal/school administrator (MS Ed); reading specialist (MS Ed, Certificate); school counseling (MS Ed); special education (MS Ed), including autism, learning disabilities teacher consultant, teacher of students with disabilities, teaching in inclusive settings; supervisor (Certificate); teacher of the handicapped (Certificate); teaching english to speakers of other languages (TESOL) (Certificate). *Accreditation:* NCATE. Part-time and evening/weekend programs available. *Faculty:* 20 full-time (13 women), 32 part-time/adjunct (22 women). *Students:* 182 full-time (146 women), 353 part-time (286 women); includes 40 minority (15 African Americans, 3 American Indian/Alaska Native, 5 Asian Americans or Pacific Islanders, 17 Hispanic Americans), 1 international. Average age 29. 361 applicants, 96% accepted, 176 enrolled. In 2009, 178 master's awarded. *Entrance requirements:* For master's, minimum GPA of 3.0 in major, 2.75 overall; 2 letters of recommendation (for some programs). Additional exam requirements/recommendations for international students: Required—TOEFL (minimum score 550 paper-based; 213 computer-based; 79 iBT), IELTS (minimum score 5), Michigan English Language Assessment Battery (minimum score 77), Cambridge A, B, C. *Application deadline:* For fall admission, 7/15 priority date for domestic students, 7/1 for international students; for spring admission, 11/15 priority date for domestic students, 11/1 for international students. Applications are processed on a rolling basis. Application fee: $50. Electronic applications accepted. *Expenses:* Tuition: Part-time $773 per credit. Required fees: $157 per semester. *Financial support:* In 2009–10, 326 students received support, including 211 fellowships (averaging $1,824 per year), 23 research assistantships (averaging $7,943 per year); career-related internships or fieldwork, scholarships/grants, and unspecified assistantships also available. Support available to part-time students. Financial award applicants required to submit FAFSA. *Faculty research:* Multicultural literacy, science and mathematics teaching strategies, teacher as reflective practitioner, children with disabilities, varied contexts of learning. *Unit head:* Dr. Terri Rothman, Associate Dean, 732-571-7507, Fax: 732-263-5277, E-mail: trothman@monmouth.edu. *Application contact:* Kevin Roane, Director, Office of Graduate Admission, 732-571-3452, Fax: 732-263-5123, E-mail: gradadm@monmouth.edu.

Montclair State University, The Graduate School, College of Education and Human Services, Department of Curriculum and Teaching, Montclair, NJ 07043-1624. Offers education (M Ed); educational technology (M Ed); learning disabled teacher consultant (Certificate); school library media specialist (Certificate); teaching (MAT, Certificate), including art (MAT), biological science (MAT), early childhood education (P-3) (MAT), earth science (MAT), elementary education (K-8) (MAT), English (MAT), French (MAT), health and physical education (MAT), health education (MAT), home economics (MAT), mathematics (MAT), music (MAT), physical education (MAT), physical science (MAT), social studies (MAT), Spanish (MAT), teacher of ESL (MAT), teacher of students with disabilities (MAT). Part-time and evening/weekend programs available. *Faculty:* 17 full-time (12 women), 29 part-time/adjunct (21 women). *Students:* 124 full-time (63 women), 174 part-time (126 women). Average age 31. 112 applicants, 69% accepted, 59 enrolled. In 2009, 179 master's, 2 other advanced degrees awarded. *Degree requirements:* For master's, comprehensive exam, field experience. *Entrance requirements:* For master's, GRE, 2 letters of recommendation. Additional exam requirements/recommendations for international students: Required—TOEFL (minimum score 83 computer-based), or IELTS. *Application deadline:* For fall admission, 2/15 for domestic and international students; for spring admission, 9/15 for domestic and international students. Applications are processed on a rolling basis. Application fee: $60. Electronic applications accepted. *Expenses:* Tuition, area resident: Part-time $486.74 per credit. Tuition, state resident: part-time $486.74 per credit. Tuition, nonresident: part-time $751.34 per credit. Tuition and fees vary according to degree level and program. *Financial support:* In 2009–10, 12 research assistantships with full tuition reimbursements (averaging $7,000 per year) were awarded; Federal Work-Study, scholarships/grants, and unspecified assistantships also available. Support available to part-time students. Financial award application deadline: 3/1; financial award applicants required to submit FAFSA. *Unit head:* Dr. David Schwarzer, Chairperson, 973-655-5187. *Application contact:* Amy Aiello, Director of Graduate Admissions and Operations, 973-655-5147, Fax: 973-655-7869, E-mail: graduate.school@montclair.edu.

Montclair State University, The Graduate School, College of Humanities and Social Sciences, Department of Linguistics, Montclair, NJ 07043-1624. Offers applied linguistics (MA); teacher of English as a second language (Certificate). Part-time and evening/weekend programs available. *Faculty:* 6 full-time (5 women), 18 part-time/adjunct (17 women). *Students:* 8 full-time (6 women), 26 part-time (24 women). Average age 36. 20 applicants, 55% accepted, 8 enrolled. In 2009, 17 master's, 6 other advanced degrees awarded. *Degree requirements:* For master's, comprehensive exam. *Entrance requirements:* For master's, GRE General Test, 2 letters of recommendation. Additional exam requirements/recommendations for international students: Required—TOEFL (minimum score 83 computer-based), or IELTS. *Application deadline:* For fall admission, 6/1 for international students; for spring admission, 10/1 for international students. Applications are processed on a rolling basis. Application fee: $60. Electronic applications accepted. *Expenses:* Tuition, area resident: Part-time $486.74 per credit. Tuition, state resident: part-time $486.74 per credit. Tuition, nonresident: part-time $751.34 per credit. Tuition and fees vary according to degree level and program. *Financial support:* In 2009–10, 1 research assistantship with full tuition reimbursement (averaging $7,000 per year) was awarded; Federal Work-Study, scholarships/grants, and unspecified assistantships also available. Support available to part-time students. Financial award application deadline: 3/1; financial award applicants required to submit FAFSA. *Unit head:* Dr. Eileen Fitzpatrick, Chairperson, 973-655-4480. *Application contact:* Amy Aiello, Director of Graduate Admissions and Operations, 973-655-5147, E-mail: graduate.school@montclair.edu.

Monterey Institute of International Studies, Graduate School of Translation, Interpretation and Language Education, Program in Teaching English to Speakers of Other Languages, Monterey, CA 93940-2691. Offers MATESOL. *Students:* 43 full-time (31 women), 13 part-time (12 women); includes 12 minority (1 African American, 5 Asian Americans or Pacific Islanders, 6 Hispanic Americans), 14 international. Average age 31. In 2009, 24 master's awarded. *Degree requirements:* For master's, portfolio, oral defense. *Entrance requirements:* For master's, minimum GPA of 3.0. Additional exam requirements/recommendations for international students: Required—TOEFL (minimum score 600 paper-based; 250 computer-based; 100 iBT). *Application deadline:* For fall admission, 3/15 priority date for domestic and international students; for spring admission, 10/1 priority date for domestic and international students. Applications are processed on a rolling basis. Application fee: $50. Electronic applications accepted. *Expenses:*

Tuition: Full-time $31,000; part-time $1500 per credit. Required fees: $56. *Financial support:* Federal Work-Study and institutionally sponsored loans available. Support available to part-time students. Financial award application deadline: 3/15; financial award applicants required to submit FAFSA. *Application contact:* 831-647-4123, Fax: 831-647-6405, E-mail: admit@miis.edu.

See Close-Up on page 1119.

Mount Saint Vincent University, Graduate Programs, Faculty of Education, Program in Curriculum Studies, Halifax, NS B3M 2J6, Canada. Offers education of young adolescents (M Ed, MA Ed, MA-R); general studies (M Ed, MA Ed, MA-R); teaching English as a second language (M Ed, MA Ed, MA-R). Part-time and evening/weekend programs available. Postbaccalaureate distance learning degree programs offered (minimal on-campus study). *Degree requirements:* For master's, thesis (for some programs). *Entrance requirements:* For master's, bachelor's degree in related field, minimum B average, 1 year of teaching experience. Electronic applications accepted. *Faculty research:* Science education, cultural studies, international education, curriculum development.

Multnomah University, Multnomah Bible College Graduate Degree Programs, Portland, OR 97220-5898. Offers counseling (MA); teaching (MA); TESOL (MA). *Faculty:* 3 full-time (all women), 26 part-time/adjunct (16 women). *Students:* 45 full-time (30 women), 22 part-time (13 women); includes 10 minority (1 African American, 1 American Indian/Alaska Native, 5 Asian Americans or Pacific Islanders, 3 Hispanic Americans), 1 international. Average age 35. 56 applicants, 42 enrolled. *Degree requirements:* For master's, thesis optional. *Entrance requirements:* Additional exam requirements/recommendations for international students: Required—TOEFL (minimum score 550 paper-based; 213 computer-based). *Application deadline:* For fall admission, 7/15 for domestic and international students; for spring admission, 11/15 for domestic and international students. *Expenses:* Tuition: Full-time $10,464; part-time $436 per credit hour. *Financial support:* In 2009–10, 61 students received support. Career-related internships or fieldwork and scholarships/grants available. Support available to part-time students. Financial award application deadline: 7/1; financial award applicants required to submit FAFSA. *Unit head:* Dr. Wayne Strickland, Academic Dean, 503-251-6401. *Application contact:* Penny Rader, Seminary Admissions Counselor, 503-251-6485, Fax: 503-254-1268, E-mail: admiss@multnomah.edu.

Murray State University, College of Humanities and Fine Arts, Department of English and Philosophy, Program in Teaching English to Speakers of Other Languages, Murray, KY 42071. Offers MA. Part-time programs available. Postbaccalaureate distance learning degree programs offered (no on-campus study). *Degree requirements:* For master's, one foreign language, comprehensive exam, 12 hours for portfolio. *Entrance requirements:* For master's, minimum GPA of 2.25. Additional exam requirements/recommendations for international students: Required—TOEFL (minimum score 525 paper-based), IELTS (minimum score 5.5). *Faculty research:* Methods, integrated skills, intercultural communication, assessment.

Nazareth College of Rochester, Graduate Studies, Department of Education, Program in Teaching English to Speakers of Other Languages, Rochester, NY 14618-3790. Offers MS Ed. *Accreditation:* Teacher Education Accreditation Council. *Entrance requirements:* For master's, minimum GPA of 3.0.

New Jersey City University, Graduate Studies and Continuing Education, Debra Cannon Partridge Wolfe College of Education, Department of Educational Leadership, Jersey City, NJ 07305-1597. Offers basics and urban studies (MA); bilingual/bicultural education and English as a second language (MA); educational administration and supervision (MA). Part-time and evening/weekend programs available. *Faculty:* 3. *Students:* 27 full-time (18 women), 187 part-time (115 women); includes 77 minority (18 African Americans, 6 Asian Americans or Pacific Islanders, 53 Hispanic Americans), 16 international. Average age 34. In 2009, 121 master's awarded. *Entrance requirements:* For master's, GRE General Test or MAT. Additional exam requirements/recommendations for international students: Required—TOEFL. *Application deadline:* For fall admission, 8/1 priority date for domestic students; for spring admission, 12/1 for domestic students. Applications are processed on a rolling basis. Application fee: $0. *Expenses:* Tuition, area resident: Part-time $456.75 per credit. Tuition, nonresident: part-time $842.55 per credit. Required fees: $65 per term. *Financial support:* Fellowships, teaching assistantships, career-related internships or fieldwork and unspecified assistantships available. *Unit head:* Dr. Susan Phifer, Chairperson, 201-200-3012, E-mail: sphifer@njcu.edu. *Application contact:* Dr. Susan Phifer, Chairperson, 201-200-3012, E-mail: sphifer@njcu.edu.

Newman University, School of Education, Wichita, KS 67213-2097. Offers building leadership (MS Ed); curriculum and instruction (MS Ed), including accountability, English as a second language. *Accreditation:* NCATE. Part-time programs available. Postbaccalaureate distance learning degree programs offered (no on-campus study). *Faculty:* 3 full-time (0 women), 22 part-time/adjunct (all women). *Students:* 12 full-time (8 women), 329 part-time (263 women); includes 29 minority (5 African Americans, 2 American Indian/Alaska Native, 5 Asian Americans or Pacific Islanders, 17 Hispanic Americans), 4 international. Average age 37. 41 applicants, 76% accepted, 24 enrolled. In 2009, 57 master's awarded. *Degree requirements:* For master's, thesis optional. *Entrance requirements:* For master's, interview, minimum GPA of 3.0, writing sample, 3 letters of recommendation. Additional exam requirements/recommendations for international students: Required—TOEFL (minimum score 600 paper-based; 250 computer-based; 100 iBT). *Application deadline:* For fall admission, 8/15 priority date for domestic students, 7/15 priority date for international students; for spring admission, 1/10 priority date for domestic students, 11/15 priority date for international students. Applications are processed on a rolling basis. Application fee: $25 ($40 for international students). Electronic applications accepted. *Expenses:* Contact institution. *Financial support:* In 2009–10, 8 students received support. Federal Work-Study available. Financial award application deadline: 8/15; financial award applicants required to submit FAFSA. *Unit head:* Dr. Guy Glidden, Director, 316-942-4291 Ext. 2331, Fax: 316-942-4483, E-mail: gliddeng@newmanu.edu. *Application contact:* Linda Kay Sabala, Director of Graduate Admissions, 316-942-4291 Ext. 2230, Fax: 316-942-4483, E-mail: sabalal@newmanu.edu.

The New School: A University, The New School for General Studies, Program in Teaching English to Speakers of Other Languages, New York, NY 10011. Offers MA. Part-time and evening/weekend programs available. Postbaccalaureate distance learning degree programs offered (no on-campus study). *Students:* 6 full-time (4 women), 50 part-time (38 women); includes 10 minority (2 African Americans, 3 Asian Americans or Pacific Islanders, 5 Hispanic Americans), 4 international. Average age 38. 77 applicants, 74% accepted, 31 enrolled. In 2009, 10 master's awarded. *Entrance requirements:* Additional exam requirements/recommendations for international students: Required—TOEFL (minimum score 600 paper-based; 250 computer-based; 100 iBT), IELTS (minimum score 7), TWE. *Application deadline:* For fall admission, 6/1 priority date for domestic and international students; for spring admission, 11/1 priority date for domestic and international students. Applications are processed on a rolling basis. Application fee: $50. Electronic applications accepted. *Financial support:* Federal Work-Study, scholarships/grants, and tuition waivers available. Support available to part-time students. Financial award application deadline: 3/1; financial award applicants required to submit FAFSA. *Unit head:* Sean Conley, Interim Director, English Language Studies/Director, MATESOL Program, 212-229-5372, E-mail: conleys@newschool.edu. *Application contact:* Robert MadDonald, Director of Admissions, 212-229-5710 Ext. 3007, Fax: 212-989-3887, E-mail: macdonar@newschool.edu.

New York University, Steinhardt School of Culture, Education, and Human Development, Department of Teaching and Learning, Program in Multilingual/Multicultural Studies, New York, NY 10012-1019. Offers bilingual education (MA, PhD, Advanced Certificate); foreign language education (MA, Advanced Certificate); foreign language education/TESOL (MA); teaching English to speakers of other languages (MA, PhD, Advanced Certificate); teaching French as a foreign language (MA). *Accreditation:* Teacher Education Accreditation Council. Part-time and evening/weekend programs available. *Students:* 138 full-time (121 women), 97 part-time (78 women); includes 49 minority (4 African Americans, 25 Asian Americans or Pacific Islanders, 20 Hispanic Americans), 79 international. Average age 28. 330 applicants, 75% accepted, 88 enrolled. In 2009, 120 master's, 5 doctorates, 13 other advanced degrees awarded. *Degree requirements:* For master's, thesis (for some programs); for doctorate, thesis/dissertation. *Entrance requirements:* For doctorate, GRE General Test, interview; for Advanced Certificate, master's degree. Additional exam requirements/recommendations for international students: Required—TOEFL. *Application deadline:* For fall admission, 12/15 priority date for domestic and international students; for spring admission, 11/1 for domestic and international students. Applications are processed on a rolling basis. Application fee: $75. Electronic applications accepted. *Expenses:* Tuition: Full-time $30,528; part-time $1272 per credit. Required fees: $2177. *Financial support:* Fellowships with full and partial tuition reimbursements, career-related internships or fieldwork, Federal Work-Study, institutionally sponsored loans, scholarships/grants, and tuition waivers (partial) available. Support available to part-time students. Financial award application deadline: 2/1; financial award applicants required to submit FAFSA. *Faculty research:* Second language acquisition, cross-cultural communication, technology-enhanced language learning, language variation, action learning. *Unit head:* Dr. Miriam Eisenstein Ebsworth, Director, 212-998-5460, Fax: 212-995-4049. *Application contact:* 212-998-5030, Fax: 212-995-4328, E-mail: steinhardt.gradadmissions@nyu.edu.

Northern Arizona University, Graduate College, College of Arts and Letters, Department of English, Flagstaff, AZ 86011. Offers applied linguistics (PhD); English (MA), including creative writing, general English studies, literacy, technology and professional writing, literature, secondary English education; professional writing (Certificate); teaching English as a second language (MA, PhD, Certificate). *Faculty:* 40 full-time (24 women). *Students:* 138 full-time (92 women), 113 part-time (84 women); includes 27 minority (7 African Americans, 8 American Indian/Alaska Native, 5 Asian Americans or Pacific Islanders, 7 Hispanic Americans), 18 international. Average age 31. 189 applicants, 70% accepted, 81 enrolled. In 2009, 92 master's, 9 doctorates awarded. *Degree requirements:* For master's, comprehensive exam, thesis (for some programs), departmental qualifying exam; for doctorate, comprehensive exam, thesis/dissertation, departmental qualifying exam. *Entrance requirements:* For master's, minimum GPA of 3.0 or GRE; for doctorate, GRE General Test. Additional exam requirements/recommendations for international students: Required—TOEFL (minimum score 550 paper-based; 213 computer-based; 80 iBT), IELTS (minimum score 7), or a bachelor's degree from an English-speaking university and demonstrated proficiency. *Application deadline:* For fall admission, 2/15 priority date for domestic students, 9/1 priority date for international students; for winter admission, 4/15 priority date for domestic students; for spring admission, 11/15 priority date for domestic students. Applications are processed on a rolling basis. Application fee: $65. Electronic applications accepted. *Financial support:* In 2009–10, 63 teaching assistantships with partial tuition reimbursements (averaging $11,623 per year) were awarded; Federal Work-Study, tuition waivers (full and partial), and unspecified assistantships also available. Financial award application deadline: 3/30; financial award applicants required to submit FAFSA. *Unit head:* Dr. J. Allen Woodman, Chair, 928-523-5651, E-mail: allen.woodman@nau.edu. *Application contact:* Barbara Hanks, Secretary, 928-523-4911, E-mail: barbara.hanks@nau.edu.

Northern Arizona University, Graduate College, College of Education, Department of Educational Specialties, Flagstaff, AZ 86011. Offers autism spectrum disorders (Certificate); bilingual/multicultural education (M Ed), including bilingual education, ESL education; career and technical education (M Ed, Certificate); curriculum and instruction (Ed D); early childhood special education (M Ed); early intervention (Certificate); educational technology (M Ed, Certificate); special education (M Ed). *Faculty:* 29 full-time (16 women). *Students:* 153 full-time (118 women), 360 part-time (291 women); includes 152 minority (12 African Americans, 43 American Indian/Alaska Native, 5 Asian Americans or Pacific Islanders, 92 Hispanic Americans), 9 international. Average age 30. 215 applicants, 87% accepted, 133 enrolled. In 2009, 200 master's, 8 doctorates awarded. *Degree requirements:* For master's, comprehensive exam (for some programs), thesis (for some programs). *Entrance requirements:* For master's, minimum GPA of 3.0. Additional exam requirements/recommendations for international students: Required—TOEFL (minimum score 550 paper-based; 213 computer-based; 80 iBT), IELTS (minimum score 7), or a bachelor's degree from an English-speaking university and demonstrated proficiency. *Application deadline:* For fall admission, 2/1 for domestic students, 8/1 for international students; for spring admission, 12/1 for domestic students. Applications are processed on a rolling basis. Application fee: $65. Electronic applications accepted. *Financial support:* In 2009–10, 2 research assistantships with partial tuition reimbursements (averaging $10,000 per year), 8 teaching assistantships with partial tuition reimbursements (averaging $10,000 per year) were awarded. Financial award application deadline: 3/30. *Unit head:* Dr. Lawrence Gallagher, Chair, 928-523-5083, E-mail: lawrence.gallagher@nau.edu. *Application contact:* Dr. Lawrence Gallagher, Chair, 928-523-5083, E-mail: lawrence.gallagher@nau.edu.

Northwest Missouri State University, Graduate School, College of Education and Human Services, Department of Curriculum and Instruction, Maryville, MO 64468-6001. Offers English language learners (Certificate); reading (MS Ed); special education (MS Ed); teaching: early childhood (MS Ed); teaching: elementary self contained (MS Ed); teaching: English language learners (MS Ed); teaching: middle school (MS Ed). *Accreditation:* NCATE. Part-time programs available. *Faculty:* 12 full-time (all women). *Students:* 16 full-time (all women), 77 part-time (72 women); includes 4 minority (2 African Americans, 2 Hispanic Americans). 33 applicants, 82% accepted, 19 enrolled. In 2009, 30 master's awarded. *Degree requirements:* For master's, comprehensive exam. *Entrance requirements:* For master's, GRE General Test, minimum undergraduate GPA of 2.75, teaching certificate, writing sample. Additional exam requirements/recommendations for international students: Required—TOEFL (minimum score 550 paper-based; 213 computer-based). *Application deadline:* For fall admission, 7/1 for domestic and international students; for spring admission, 11/15 for domestic and international students. Applications are processed on a rolling basis. Application fee: $0 ($50 for international students). Electronic applications accepted. *Expenses:* Tuition, state resident: part-time $296.34 per credit hour. Tuition, nonresident: part-time $510.43 per credit hour. *Financial support:* In 2009–10, 4 research assistantships with full tuition reimbursements (averaging $6,000 per year), 7 teaching assistantships with full tuition reimbursements (averaging $6,000 per year) were awarded; unspecified assistantships also available. Financial award application deadline: 4/1; financial award applicants required to submit FAFSA. *Unit head:* Dr. Barbara Crossland, Head, 660-562-1776, E-mail: barbara@mail.nwmissouri.edu. *Application contact:* Dr. Gregory Haddock, Dean of Graduate School, 660-562-1145, Fax: 660-562-1096, E-mail: gradsch@nwmissouri.edu.

Notre Dame de Namur University, Division of Academic Affairs, College of Arts and Sciences, Department of English, Belmont, CA 94002-1908. Offers English (MA); teaching English to speakers of other languages (Certificate). Part-time and evening/weekend programs available. *Faculty:* 5 full-time (2 women), 5 part-time/adjunct (3 women). *Students:* 3 full-time (all women), 15 part-time (12 women); includes 4 minority (1 Asian American or Pacific Islander, 3 Hispanic Americans), 1 international. Average age 28. 6 applicants, 100% accepted, 4 enrolled. In 2009, 10 master's awarded. *Degree requirements:* For master's, thesis optional, exam. *Entrance requirements:* For master's, minimum GPA of 2.5, writing sample. Additional exam requirements/recommendations for international students: Required—TOEFL (minimum score 550 paper-based; 213 computer-based; 79 iBT). *Application deadline:* For fall admission, 8/1 priority date for domestic students; for spring admission, 12/1 priority date for domestic students. Applications are processed on a rolling basis. Application fee: $50 ($500 for international students). Electronic applications accepted. *Expenses:* Tuition: Part-time $720 per credit. Required fees: $35 per semester hour. *Financial support:* Career-related internships or fieldwork available. Support available to part-time students. Financial award applicants required to submit FAFSA. *Unit head:* Jacqueline Berger, Director, 650-508-3730. *Application contact:* Candace Hallmark, Associate Director of Admissions, 650-508-3592, Fax: 650-508-3426, E-mail: grad.admit@ndnu.edu.

Nova Southeastern University, Fischler School of Education and Human Services, Graduate Teacher Education Program, Fort Lauderdale, FL 33314-7796. Offers athletic administration (MS); brain research (MS, Ed S); charter school education/leadership (MS); cognitive and behavioral disabilities (MS); computer science education (Ed S); computer science education (K-12) (MS); curriculum and teaching (Ed S); curriculum, instruction and technology (MS);

English as a Second Language

Nova Southeastern University (continued)

curriculum, instruction, management and administration (Ed S); early childhood education (MS); early literacy and reading (Ed S); early literacy education (MS); education technology (MS); educational leadership (administration K–12) (MS, Ed S); educational media (Ed S); educational media (K-12) (MS); elementary education (MS, Ed S), including ESOL endorsement (MS); English education (MS, Ed S); environmental education (MS); exceptional student education (MS), including ESOL endorsement; gifted education (MS, Ed S); interdisciplinary arts education (MS); management and administration of educational programs (MS); mathematics (MS); mathematics education (Ed S); multicultural early intervention (MS); pre-kindergarten/primary (MS); preschool education (MS); reading (MS); reading and TESOL (MS); reading education (Ed S); science (MS); science education (Ed S); secondary education (MS); social studies (MS, Ed S); Spanish language (MS); special education and reading (MS); teaching and learning (MA, MS), including curriculum and instruction (MA), elementary mathematics (MA), elementary reading (MA), K-12 technology integration (MA); teaching English to speakers of other languages (MS, Ed S); technology management and administration (Ed S); urban studies education (MS). Part-time and evening/weekend programs available. Postbaccalaureate distance learning degree programs offered (minimal on-campus study). *Faculty:* 72 full-time (43 women), 385 part-time/adjunct (252 women). *Students:* 196 full-time (175 women), 1,304 part-time (1,128 women); includes 594 minority (471 African Americans, 5 American Indian/Alaska Native, 18 Asian Americans or Pacific Islanders, 100 Hispanic Americans). Average age 37. 2,610 applicants, 72% accepted, 1352 enrolled. In 2009, 836 other advanced degrees awarded. *Degree requirements:* For master's and Ed S, thesis, practicum, internship. *Entrance requirements:* For master's, MAT, GRE, CLAST, CBEST, PRAXIS I, General Knowledge Test, minimum GPA of 2.5; for Ed S, MAT or GRE, master's degree, teaching certificate, minimum GPA of 3.0. Additional exam requirements/recommendations for international students: Required—TSE (recommended, minimum score 50); Recommended—TOEFL (minimum score 550 paper-based; 213 computer-based; 80 iBT), IELTS (minimum score 6). *Application deadline:* For fall admission, 9/25 priority date for domestic and international students; for winter admission, 2/23 priority date for domestic and international students; for spring admission, 4/25 priority date for domestic and international students. Applications are processed on a rolling basis. Application fee: $50. Electronic applications accepted. *Financial support:* Federal Work-Study available. Support available to part-time students. Financial award application deadline: 4/15; financial award applicants required to submit FAFSA. *Faculty research:* School effectiveness, critical thinking, leadership skills acquisition, child education, multicultural education. *Unit head:* Dr. Ronald Kern, Dean of Academic Affairs, 800-986-3223 Ext. 7809, Fax: 954-262-3606, E-mail: rk429@nsu.nova.edu. *Application contact:* Dr. Jennifer Quinones Nottingham, Dean of Student Affairs, 800-986-3223 Ext. 1559.

Oakland University, Graduate Study and Lifelong Learning, College of Arts and Sciences, Department of Linguistics, Rochester, MI 48309-4401. Offers linguistics (MA); teaching English as a second language (Certificate). Part-time and evening/weekend programs available. *Entrance requirements:* For master's, minimum GPA of 3.0 for unconditional admission. Additional exam requirements/recommendations for international students: Required—TOEFL (minimum score 550 paper-based; 213 computer-based).

Ohio Dominican University, Graduate Programs, TESOL Program, Columbus, OH 43219-2099. Offers MA. Part-time and evening/weekend programs available. *Students:* 39 full-time (29 women), 13 part-time (12 women); includes 5 minority (3 African Americans, 2 Hispanic Americans). Average age 32. In 2009, 14 master's awarded. *Degree requirements:* For master's, thesis. *Entrance requirements:* For master's, minimum undergraduate GPA of 3.0, 3 letters of recommendation, interview. Additional exam requirements/recommendations for international students: Required—TOEFL (minimum score 550 paper-based; 213 computer-based). *Application deadline:* For fall admission, 7/15 priority date for domestic and international students; for spring admission, 12/15 priority date for domestic and international students. Applications are processed on a rolling basis. Application fee: $25. *Financial support:* Applicants required to submit FAFSA. *Unit head:* Dr. Timothy Micek, Director, 614-251-4675, E-mail: micekt@ohiodominican.edu. *Application contact:* Jill M. Westerfeld, Graduate Admissions Recruiter, 614-251-4725, Fax: 614-251-4634, E-mail: westerfj@ohiodominican.edu.

Ohio University, Graduate College, College of Arts and Sciences, Department of Linguistics, Athens, OH 45701-2979. Offers applied linguistics/TESOL (MA). Part-time programs available. *Faculty:* 9 full-time (3 women), 5 part-time/adjunct (3 women). *Students:* 37 full-time (27 women), 3 part-time (2 women); includes 2 minority (1 Asian American or Pacific Islander, 1 Hispanic American), 24 international. 53 applicants, 62% accepted, 16 enrolled. In 2009, 20 master's awarded. *Degree requirements:* For master's, one foreign language, thesis or alternative. *Entrance requirements:* For master's, minimum GPA of 3.0. Additional exam requirements/recommendations for international students: Required—TOEFL (minimum score 600 paper-based; 100 iBT) or IELTS Academic (minimum score 7). *Application deadline:* For fall admission, 2/15 priority date for domestic and international students. Application fee: $50 ($55 for international students). Electronic applications accepted. *Expenses:* Tuition, state resident: full-time $7839; part-time $323 per quarter hour. Tuition, nonresident: full-time $15,831; part-time $654 per quarter hour. Required fees: $2931. *Financial support:* In 2009–10, 2 fellowships with tuition reimbursements were awarded; research assistantships with tuition reimbursements, teaching assistantships with tuition reimbursements, Federal Work-Study, institutionally sponsored loans, tuition waivers (partial), and unspecified assistantships also available. Financial award application deadline: 2/15. *Faculty research:* Syntax, language learning, language teaching, computers for teaching, sociolinguistics. *Unit head:* Dr. Chris Thompson, Chair, E-mail: thompsoc@ohio.edu. *Application contact:* Dr. Hiroyuki Oshita, Graduate Chair, 740-593-4570, Fax: 740-593-2967, E-mail: oshita@ohio.edu.

Oklahoma City University, Petree College of Arts and Sciences, Program in Teaching English to Speakers of Other Languages, Oklahoma City, OK 73106-1402. Offers MA. Part-time and evening/weekend programs available. *Faculty:* 3 full-time (1 woman), 1 (woman) part-time/adjunct. *Students:* 44 full-time (35 women), 23 part-time (19 women); includes 5 minority (2 African Americans, 1 Asian American or Pacific Islander, 2 Hispanic Americans), 61 international. Average age 34. 57 applicants, 100% accepted, 24 enrolled. In 2009, 52 master's awarded. *Degree requirements:* For master's, comprehensive exam, thesis optional. *Entrance requirements:* For master's, minimum GPA of 3.0. Additional exam requirements/recommendations for international students: Required—TOEFL (minimum score 600 paper-based; 260 computer-based). *Application deadline:* For fall admission, 8/20 for domestic students; for spring admission, 1/6 for domestic students. Applications are processed on a rolling basis. Application fee: $50 ($70 for international students). *Expenses:* Tuition: Full-time $15,930; part-time $885 per hour. *Financial support:* Career-related internships or fieldwork, Federal Work-Study, and tuition waivers (partial) available. Support available to part-time students. Financial award application deadline: 8/1. *Faculty research:* L2 language acquisition, L2 writing language. *Unit head:* Dr. Robert Griffin, Acting Director, 405-208-5941, Fax: 405-208-6012, E-mail: rgriffin@okcu.edu. *Application contact:* Michelle Lockhart, Director, Graduate Admissions, 800-633-7242, Fax: 405-208-5916, E-mail: gadmissions@okcu.edu.

Our Lady of the Lake University of San Antonio, School of Professional Studies, Program in Curriculum and Instruction, San Antonio, TX 78207-4689. Offers bilingual (M Ed); early childhood education (M Ed); English as a second language (M Ed); integrated math teaching (M Ed); integrated science teaching (M Ed); master reading teacher (M Ed); master technology teacher (M Ed); reading specialist (M Ed). *Students:* 2 full-time (1 woman), 112 part-time (94 women); includes 64 minority (5 African Americans, 1 American Indian/Alaska Native, 1 Asian American or Pacific Islander, 57 Hispanic Americans). Average age 38. In 2009, 49 master's awarded. *Expenses:* Tuition: Full-time $12,330; part-time $685 per contact hour. Required fees: $139; $12 per contact hour. $57 per semester. Tuition and fees vary according to campus/location. *Unit head:* Dr. Cullen Grinnan, 210-434-6711 Ext. 8928, E-mail: ctgrinnan@lake.ollusa.edu. *Application contact:* Dr. Cullen Grinnan, 210-434-6711 Ext. 8928, E-mail: ctgrinnan@lake.ollusa.edu.

Pontifical Catholic University of Puerto Rico, College of Education, Program in English as a Second Language, Ponce, PR 00717-0777. Offers M Ed. *Degree requirements:* For master's, comprehensive exam, thesis (for some programs). *Entrance requirements:* For master's, GRE, 2 letters of recommendation, interview, minimum GPA of 2.75.

Portland State University, Graduate Studies, College of Liberal Arts and Sciences, Department of Applied Linguistics, Portland, OR 97207-0751. Offers teaching English to speakers of other languages (MA). Part-time programs available. *Degree requirements:* For master's, one foreign language, comprehensive exam, thesis. *Entrance requirements:* For master's, minimum GPA of 3.0 in upper-division course work or 2.75 overall, proficiency in at least 1 foreign language. Additional exam requirements/recommendations for international students: Required—TOEFL (minimum score 600 paper-based; 250 computer-based). *Faculty research:* Sociolinguistics, linguistics and cognitive science, language proficiency testing, lexical phrases and language teaching, teaching English as a second language methodology.

Providence College and Theological Seminary, Theological Seminary, Otterburne, MB R0A 1G0, Canada. Offers children's ministry (Certificate); Christian studies (MA, Certificate); counseling (MA); cross-cultural discipleship (Certificate); divinity (M Div); educational studies (MA), including counseling psychology, educational ministries, student development, teaching English to speakers of other languages, training teachers of English to speakers of other languages; global studies (MA); lay counseling (Diploma); ministry (D Min); teaching English to speakers of other languages (Certificate); theological studies (MA); training teacher of English to speakers of other languages (Certificate); youth ministry (Certificate). *Accreditation:* ATS. Part-time programs available. *Degree requirements:* For master's, variable foreign language requirement, thesis (for some programs); for doctorate, thesis/dissertation; for M Div, 2 foreign languages, comprehensive exam, thesis/dissertation (for some programs). *Entrance requirements:* Additional exam requirements/recommendations for international students: Recommended—TOEFL (minimum score 550 paper-based; 213 computer-based). *Faculty research:* Studies in Isaiah, theology of sin.

Queens College of the City University of New York, Division of Graduate Studies, Arts and Humanities Division, Department of Linguistics and Communication Disorders, Program in Teaching English to Speakers of Other Languages, Flushing, NY 11367-1597. Offers MS Ed. Part-time and evening/weekend programs available. *Faculty:* 8 full-time (5 women). *Students:* 11 full-time (8 women), 89 part-time (82 women). 110 applicants, 52% accepted, 42 enrolled. In 2009, 18 master's awarded. *Degree requirements:* For master's, thesis optional. *Entrance requirements:* For master's, minimum GPA of 3.0. Additional exam requirements/recommendations for international students: Required—TOEFL. *Application deadline:* For fall admission, 4/1 for domestic students; for spring admission, 11/1 for domestic students. Applications are processed on a rolling basis. Application fee: $125. *Expenses:* Tuition, state resident: full-time $7360; part-time $310 per credit. Tuition, nonresident: part-time $575 per credit. One-time fee: $195 full-time; $145.25 part-time. *Financial support:* Career-related internships or fieldwork, Federal Work-Study, institutionally sponsored loans, and tuition waivers (partial) available. Support available to part-time students. Financial award application deadline: 4/1; financial award applicants required to submit FAFSA. *Unit head:* Dr. Robert M. Vago, Chairperson, 718-997-2875. *Application contact:* Mario Caruso, Director of Graduate Admissions, 718-997-5200, Fax: 718-997-5193, E-mail: graduate_admissions@qc.edu.

Regent University, Graduate School, School of Education, Virginia Beach, VA 23464-9800. Offers career switcher (M Ed); Christian school program (M Ed); cross-categorical special education (M Ed); education (M Ed, Ed D); education licensure (M Ed); educational leadership (M Ed); elementary education (M Ed); individualized degree plan (M Ed); leadership in character education (M Ed); master teacher (M Ed); mathematics education (M Ed); special education leadership (Ed S); student affairs (M Ed); TESOL (M Ed). *Accreditation:* Teacher Education Accreditation Council. Part-time and evening/weekend programs available. Postbaccalaureate distance learning degree programs offered (minimal on-campus study). *Faculty:* 26 full-time (13 women), 104 part-time/adjunct (78 women). *Students:* 141 full-time (116 women), 622 part-time (488 women); includes 218 minority (186 African Americans, 1 American Indian/Alaska Native, 10 Asian Americans or Pacific Islanders, 21 Hispanic Americans), 8 international. Average age 39. 509 applicants, 60% accepted, 176 enrolled. In 2009, 212 master's, 15 doctorates awarded. *Degree requirements:* For master's, thesis or alternative; for doctorate, comprehensive exam, thesis/dissertation. *Entrance requirements:* For master's, MAT, minimum undergraduate GPA of 2.75, writing sample, resume, recommendations, interview; for doctorate, GRE, writing sample, 3 years of relevant professional experience, master's-level paper, copies of published work, resume, transcripts, interview, recommendations. Additional exam requirements/recommendations for international students: Required—TOEFL (minimum score 577 paper-based; 233 computer-based). *Application deadline:* For fall admission, 4/1 priority date for domestic students; for spring admission, 10/15 priority date for domestic students. Applications are processed on a rolling basis. Application fee: $50. Electronic applications accepted. *Expenses:* Contact institution. *Financial support:* In 2009–10, 480 students received support; fellowships, career-related internships or fieldwork, scholarships/grants, tuition waivers (full and partial), and unspecified assistantships available. Support available to part-time students. Financial award application deadline: 4/1; financial award applicants required to submit FAFSA. *Faculty research:* Character development and discipline for children, education leadership development, diversity in schools, classroom management, technology in education settings. *Unit head:* Dr. Alan A. Arroyo, Dean, 757-352-4261, Fax: 757-352-4318, E-mail: alanarr@regent.edu. *Application contact:* Matthew Chadwick, Director of Admissions, 800-373-5504, Fax: 757-352-4381, E-mail: admissions@regent.edu.

Regis University, College for Professional Studies, Program in Teacher Education, Denver, CO 80221-1099. Offers adult learning, training, and development (M Ed); curriculum, instruction, and assessment (M Ed); early childhood (M Ed); educational technology (Certificate); elementary (M Ed); ESL (M Ed); fine arts (M Ed), including arts, music; instructional technology (M Ed); professional leadership (M Ed); reading (M Ed); secondary (M Ed); self-designed (M Ed); space studies (M Ed); special education (M Ed); teacher licensure (M Ed). Program also offered in Henderson and Las Vegas (Summerlin), NV. *Accreditation:* Teacher Education Accreditation Council. Part-time and evening/weekend programs available. Postbaccalaureate distance learning degree programs offered (no on-campus study). *Degree requirements:* For master's, thesis. *Entrance requirements:* For master's, resume, minimum GPA of 2.75, criminal background check. Additional exam requirements/recommendations for international students: Required—TOEFL (minimum score 213 computer-based), TWE (minimum score 5). Electronic applications accepted. *Faculty research:* Issues of equity in the middle school classroom, professional learning communities, school reform, socialinguistic and discursive obstacles to student integration, inclusive language arts curriculum.

Rhode Island College, School of Graduate Studies, Feinstein School of Education and Human Development, Department of Educational Studies, Providence, RI 02908-1991. Offers English (MAT); French (MAT); history (MAT); math (MAT); secondary education (MAT); Spanish (MAT); teaching English as a second language (M Ed); technology education (M Ed). *Accreditation:* NCATE. Part-time and evening/weekend programs available. *Faculty:* 10 full-time (5 women), 6 part-time/adjunct (5 women). *Students:* 8 full-time (all women), 56 part-time (40 women); includes 2 minority (both Hispanic Americans). Average age 35. In 2009, 28 master's awarded. *Degree requirements:* For master's, capstone or comprehensive assessment. *Entrance requirements:* For master's, GRE or MAT (for most programs), minimum undergraduate GPA of 3.0; baccalaureate degree in English, French, history, math or Spanish; evaluation of content area knowledge; 3 letters of recommendation; interview. Additional exam requirements/recommendations for international students: Recommended—TOEFL (minimum score 550 paper-based; 213 computer-based; 79 iBT). *Application deadline:* For fall admission, 3/15 for domestic students; for spring admission, 11/1 for domestic students. Applications are processed on a rolling basis. Application fee: $50. *Expenses:* Tuition, state resident: full-time $7440; part-time $310 per credit hour. Tuition, nonresident: full-time $14,784; part-time $616 per credit hour. Required fees: $552; $20 per credit. $70 per term. *Financial support:* Teaching assistantships with full tuition reimbursements, career-related internships or fieldwork, Federal Work-Study, scholarships/grants, health care benefits, and unspecified assistantships available.

Support available to part-time students. Financial award application deadline: 5/15; financial award applicants required to submit FAFSA. *Faculty research:* School administration, school/college articulation. *Unit head:* Dr. Ellen Bigler, Chair, 401-456-8170. *Application contact:* Graduate Studies, 401-456-8700.

Rider University, Department of Graduate Education, Leadership and Counseling, Teacher Certification Program, Lawrenceville, NJ 08648-3001. Offers business education (Certificate); elementary education (Certificate); English as a second language (Certificate); English education (Certificate); mathematics education (Certificate); preschool to grade 3 (Certificate); science education (Certificate); social studies education (Certificate); world languages (Certificate), including French, German, Spanish. Part-time programs available. *Degree requirements:* For Certificate, internship, professional portfolio. *Entrance requirements:* For degree, PRAXIS, resume. Additional exam requirements/recommendations for international students: Required—TOEFL (minimum score 550 paper-based; 213 computer-based). Electronic applications accepted. *Faculty research:* Conceptual foundations for optimal development of creativity; creative theory, cognitive processes in mathematics learning, teacher collaboration.

Rowan University, Graduate School, College of Education, Department of Teacher Education, Program in ESL/Bilingual Education, Glassboro, NJ 08028-1701. Offers Graduate Certificate. Part-time and evening/weekend programs available. *Students:* 3 part-time (all women). Average age 36. 1 applicant, 100% accepted, 0 enrolled. *Entrance requirements:* Additional exam requirements/recommendations for international students: Required—TOEFL. *Application deadline:* Applications are processed on a rolling basis. Application fee: $50. Electronic applications accepted. *Expenses:* Tuition, state resident: full-time $10,624; part-time $590 per semester hour. Tuition, nonresident: full-time $10,624; part-time $590 per semester hour. Required fees: $2320; $125 per semester hour. *Financial support:* Career-related internships or fieldwork and unspecified assistantships available. Support available to part-time students. *Unit head:* Dr. Mira Lalovic-Hand, Interim Associate Provost/Director of Graduate School, 856-256-5120 Ext. 3812, E-mail: lalovic-hand@rowan.edu. *Application contact:* Karen Haynes, Graduate Coordinator, 856-256-4052, Fax: 856-256-4436, E-mail: haynes@rowan.edu.

Rutgers, The State University of New Jersey, New Brunswick, Graduate School of Education, Department of Learning and Teaching, Program in Language Education, Piscataway, NJ 08854-8097. Offers English as a second language education (Ed M); language education (Ed M, Ed D). Part-time programs available. Terminal master's awarded for partial completion of doctoral program. *Degree requirements:* For master's, comprehensive exam; for doctorate, thesis/dissertation, concept paper, qualifying exam. *Entrance requirements:* For master's, GRE General Test, minimum GPA of 3.0; for doctorate, GRE General Test, minimum GPA of 3.5. Additional exam requirements/recommendations for international students: Required—TOEFL. Electronic applications accepted. *Faculty research:* Linguistics, sociolinguistics, cross-cultural/international communication.

St. Cloud State University, School of Graduate Studies, College of Fine Arts and Humanities, Department of English, St. Cloud, MN 56301-4498. Offers English (MA, MS); teaching English as a second language (MA). Part-time programs available. *Faculty:* 35 full-time (16 women). *Students:* 58 full-time (42 women), 62 part-time (44 women); includes 10 minority (3 African Americans, 1 American Indian/Alaska Native, 5 Asian Americans or Pacific Islanders, 1 Hispanic American), 16 international. 30 applicants, 100% accepted. In 2009, 31 master's awarded. *Degree requirements:* For master's, thesis or alternative. *Entrance requirements:* For master's, GRE General Test, minimum GPA of 2.75. Additional exam requirements/recommendations for international students: Required—Michigan English Language Assessment Battery; Recommended—TOEFL (minimum score 550 paper-based; 213 computer-based), IELTS (minimum score 6.5). *Application deadline:* For fall admission, 6/1 priority date for domestic students, 4/1 for international students; for spring admission, 10/1 priority date for domestic students, 8/1 for international students. Applications are processed on a rolling basis. Application fee: $35. Electronic applications accepted. *Financial support:* Federal Work-Study, scholarships/grants, and unspecified assistantships available. Financial award application deadline: 3/1. *Unit head:* Dr. Robert Inkster, Chairperson, 320-308-3061, Fax: 320-308-5524. *Application contact:* Linda Lou Krueger, School of Graduate Studies, 320-308-2113, Fax: 320-308-5371, E-mail: lekrueger@stcloudstate.edu.

St. John's University, The School of Education, Department of Human Services and Counseling, Program in Bilingual/Multicultural Education/Teaching English to Speakers of Other Languages, Queens, NY 11439. Offers MS Ed. Part-time and evening/weekend programs available. *Students:* 35 full-time (32 women), 124 part-time (112 women); includes 59 minority (6 African Americans, 6 Asian Americans or Pacific Islanders, 47 Hispanic Americans), 7 international. Average age 31. 91 applicants, 85% accepted, 40 enrolled. In 2009, 31 master's awarded. *Degree requirements:* For master's, comprehensive exam. *Entrance requirements:* For master's, minimum GPA of 3.0, eligibility for teacher certification. Additional exam requirements/recommendations for international students: Required—TOEFL (minimum score 500 paper-based; 173 computer-based; 61 iBT), IELTS (minimum score 5.5). *Application deadline:* For fall admission, 4/1 priority date for domestic students, 6/1 priority date for international students; for spring admission, 11/1 priority date for domestic and international students. Applications are processed on a rolling basis. Application fee: $70. Electronic applications accepted. *Expenses:* Tuition: Full-time $16,290; part-time $905 per credit. Required fees: $300; $150 per semester. Tuition and fees vary according to program. *Financial support:* Research assistantships, career-related internships or fieldwork and scholarships/grants available. Support available to part-time students. Financial award application deadline: 3/1; financial award applicants required to submit FAFSA. *Faculty research:* Second language learning and academic achievement, heritage language education, assessing the progress of English language learners towards English acquisition, dual language acquisition, study of English Creoles and dialects of other Englishes. *Unit head:* Dr. Francine Guastello, Acting Chair, 718-990-1475, E-mail: guastelf@stjohns.edu. *Application contact:* Dr. Kelly K. Ronayne, Associate Dean for Graduate Admissions, 718-990-2303, Fax: 718-990-2343, E-mail: graded@stjohns.edu.

Saint Martin's University, Graduate Programs, College of Education, Lacey, WA 98503. Offers administration (M Ed); English as a second language (M Ed); guidance and counseling (M Ed); reading (M Ed); special education (M Ed); teaching (MIT); technology in education (M Ed). *Accreditation:* Teacher Education Accreditation Council. Part-time and evening/weekend programs available. *Faculty:* 13 full-time (9 women), 11 part-time/adjunct (7 women). *Students:* 61 full-time (42 women), 23 part-time (17 women); includes 7 minority (2 African Americans, 1 American Indian/Alaska Native, 3 Asian Americans or Pacific Islanders, 1 Hispanic American), 1 international. Average age 35. 26 applicants, 92% accepted, 22 enrolled. In 2009, 12 master's awarded. *Degree requirements:* For master's, comprehensive exam (for some programs), thesis or alternative, project or comprehensives. *Entrance requirements:* For master's, GRE General Test or MAT, resume. Additional exam requirements/recommendations for international students: Required—TOEFL (minimum score 560 paper-based; 220 computer-based; 83 iBT). *Application deadline:* For fall admission, 6/1 priority date for domestic and international students; for spring admission, 10/1 priority date for domestic and international students. Applications are processed on a rolling basis. Application fee: $35. *Expenses:* Tuition: Full-time $12,440; part-time $827 per credit hour. *Financial support:* In 2009–10, 62 students received support. Career-related internships or fieldwork, Federal Work-Study, institutionally sponsored loans, and unspecified assistantships available. Support available to part-time students. Financial award application deadline: 3/1; financial award applicants required to submit FAFSA. *Faculty research:* Reader's theatre and reader/writer workshops, curriculum and assessment integration, gender and equity, classroom evaluations, organizational leadership. *Unit head:* Dr. Joyce Westgard, Director, 360-438-4509, Fax: 360-438-4486, E-mail: westgard@stmartin.edu. *Application contact:* Ryan M. Smith, Administrative Assistant, 360-438-4333, Fax: 360-438-4486, E-mail: ryan.smith@stmartin.edu.

Saint Michael's College, Graduate Programs, Program in Teaching English as a Second Language, Colchester, VT 05439. Offers MATESL, Certificate. Part-time and evening/weekend programs available. *Degree requirements:* For master's, one foreign language, comprehensive exam, thesis or alternative. *Entrance requirements:* For master's, minimum GPA of 3.0. Additional exam requirements/recommendations for international students: Required—TOEFL (minimum score 550 paper-based; 213 computer-based; 80 iBT). *Faculty research:* Language teaching methodology, discourse analysis, second language acquisition, language assessment, sociolinguistics, K–12 English as a second language for children.

St. Thomas University, School of Leadership Studies, Institute for Education, Miami Gardens, FL 33054-6459. Offers earth/space science (Certificate); educational administration (MS, Certificate); educational leadership (Ed D); elementary education (MS); ESOL (Certificate); gifted education (Certificate); instructional technology (MS, Certificate); professional/studies (Certificate); reading (MS, Certificate); special education (MS). Part-time and evening/weekend programs available. *Degree requirements:* For master's, comprehensive exam; for doctorate, comprehensive exam, thesis/dissertation. *Entrance requirements:* For master's, interview, minimum GPA of 3.0 or GRE; for doctorate, GRE or MAT. Additional exam requirements/recommendations for international students: Required—TOEFL (minimum score 550 paper-based; 213 computer-based; 79 iBT). Electronic applications accepted.

Salem College, Department of Education, Winston-Salem, NC 27101. Offers early education and leadership (MAT); elementary education (MAT); English as a second language (MAT); language and literacy (M Ed); middle school education (MAT); secondary education (MAT); special education (MAT). *Accreditation:* NCATE. Part-time and evening/weekend programs available. *Degree requirements:* For master's, comprehensive exam, practicum (MAT), project (M Ed), oral and written comprehensive exams. *Entrance requirements:* For master's, GRE, minimum GPA of 2.5. *Faculty research:* Content area reading strategies, literacy development, brain compatible instruction.

Salem State College, School of Graduate Studies, Program in Teaching English as a Second Language, Salem, MA 01970-5353. Offers MAT. Part-time and evening/weekend programs available. *Students:* 9 full-time (7 women), 30 part-time (24 women); includes 1 minority (African American), 2 international. Average age 40. 15 applicants, 100% accepted, 15 enrolled. In 2009, 8 master's awarded. *Entrance requirements:* Additional exam requirements/recommendations for international students: Required—TOEFL (minimum score 550 paper-based; 80 iBT), or IELTS (minimum score 5.5). *Application deadline:* For fall admission, 5/1 for domestic students; for spring admission, 10/1 for domestic students. Applications are processed on a rolling basis. Application fee: $50. *Expenses:* Tuition, state resident: full-time $2520; part-time $275 per credit hour. Tuition, nonresident: full-time $4140; part-time $365 per credit hour. Required fees: $2430. *Financial support:* In 2009–10, 5 students received support. Career-related internships or fieldwork, Federal Work-Study, scholarships/grants, and unspecified assistantships available. Support available to part-time students. Financial award application deadline: 5/1; financial award applicants required to submit FAFSA. *Unit head:* Ellen Rintell, Program Coordinator, 978-542-6321, Fax: 978-542-7023, E-mail: erintell@salemstate.edu. *Application contact:* Dr. Lee A. Brossoit, Assistant Dean of Graduate Admissions, 978-542-6675, Fax: 978-542-7215, E-mail: lbrossoit@salemstate.edu.

Salisbury University, Graduate Division, Program in English, Salisbury, MD 21801-6837. Offers composition, language and rhetoric (MA); literature (MA); teaching English to speakers of other languages (MA). Part-time and evening/weekend programs available. *Faculty:* 11 full-time (6 women). *Students:* 17 full-time (14 women), 20 part-time (14 women); includes 2 minority (both Hispanic Americans), 1 international. Average age 28. 31 applicants, 52% accepted, 2 enrolled. In 2009, 16 master's awarded. *Degree requirements:* For master's, comprehensive exam (for some programs), thesis optional. *Entrance requirements:* For master's, GRE General Test, MAT or PRAXIS, minimum GPA of 3.0, 2 letters of recommendation. Additional exam requirements/recommendations for international students: Required—TOEFL (minimum score 550 paper-based; 213 computer-based). *Application deadline:* For fall admission, 8/1 for domestic students; for spring admission, 1/1 for domestic students. Applications are processed on a rolling basis. Application fee: $45. Electronic applications accepted. *Expenses:* Tuition, area resident: Part-time $278 per credit hour. Tuition, state resident: part-time $278 per credit hour. Tuition, nonresident: part-time $574 per credit hour. Required fees: $57 per credit hour. *Financial support:* In 2009–10, 9 students received support, including 14 teaching assistantships with full tuition reimbursements available; career-related internships or fieldwork and scholarships/grants also available. Support available to part-time students. Financial award applicants required to submit FAFSA. *Faculty research:* Shakespeare, Keats, J. D. Salinger, Samuel Johnson, post-colonial theory. *Unit head:* Dr. John D. Kalb, Director, 410-543-6049, Fax: 410-548-2142, E-mail: jdkalb@salisbury.edu. *Application contact:* Dr. John D. Kalb, Director, 410-543-6049, Fax: 410-548-2142, E-mail: jdkalb@salisbury.edu.

San Diego State University, Graduate and Research Affairs, College of Arts and Letters, Department of Linguistics and Oriental Languages, San Diego, CA 92182. Offers applied linguistics and English as a second language (CAL); computational linguistics (MA); English as a second language/applied linguistics (MA); general linguistics (MA). *Degree requirements:* For master's, one foreign language, comprehensive exam, thesis optional. *Entrance requirements:* For master's, GRE General Test, 2 letters of recommendation. Additional exam requirements/recommendations for international students: Required—TOEFL (minimum score 570 paper-based). Electronic applications accepted. *Faculty research:* Cross-cultural linguistic studies of semantics.

San Francisco State University, Division of Graduate Studies, College of Humanities, Department of English Language and Literature, Program in Teaching English to Speakers of Other Languages, San Francisco, CA 94132-1722. Offers MA. Part-time programs available. *Degree requirements:* For master's, comprehensive exam (for some programs), thesis (for some programs). Electronic applications accepted.

San Jose State University, Graduate Studies and Research, College of Humanities and the Arts, Department of Linguistics and Language Development, San Jose, CA 95192-0001. Offers computational linguistics (Certificate); linguistics (MA); teaching English to speakers of other languages (MA, Certificate). *Students:* 44 full-time (28 women), 55 part-time (44 women); includes 35 minority (25 Asian Americans or Pacific Islanders, 10 Hispanic Americans), 18 international. Average age 38. 101 applicants, 58% accepted, 26 enrolled. In 2009, 38 master's awarded. *Entrance requirements:* Additional exam requirements/recommendations for international students: Required—TOEFL (minimum score 570 paper-based; 230 computer-based). *Application deadline:* For fall admission, 6/29 for domestic students; for spring admission, 11/30 for domestic students. Applications are processed on a rolling basis. Application fee: $59. Electronic applications accepted. *Financial support:* Applicants required to submit FAFSA. *Unit head:* Dr. Manjari Ohala, Chair, 408-924-4413, Fax: 408-924-4703. *Application contact:* Dr. Manjari Ohala, Chair, 408-924-4413, Fax: 408-924-4703.

Seattle Pacific University, MA in Teaching English to Speakers of Other Languages Program, Seattle, WA 98119-1997. Offers K-12 certification (MA); teaching English to speakers of other languages (MA). Part-time programs available. *Faculty:* 1 (woman) full-time, 5 part-time/adjunct (3 women). *Students:* 4 full-time (3 women), 19 part-time (12 women); includes 1 minority (Asian American or Pacific Islander), 4 international. Average age 36. 15 applicants, 47% accepted, 7 enrolled. In 2009, 2 master's awarded. *Degree requirements:* For master's, one foreign language, practicum. *Entrance requirements:* For master's, GRE General Test or MAT, minimum GPA of 3.0 in last 45 quarter credits. Additional exam requirements/recommendations for international students: Required—TOEFL (minimum score 600 paper-based; 250 computer-based). *Application deadline:* For fall admission, 8/11 priority date for domestic students, 8/11 for international students; for winter admission, 12/1 for domestic and international students; for spring admission, 3/11 for domestic and international students. Applications are processed on a rolling basis. Application fee: $50. Electronic applications accepted. *Expenses:* Contact institution. *Financial support:* In 2009–10, 12 students received support. Career-related internships or fieldwork available. Financial award applicants required to submit FAFSA. *Faculty research:* Second language acquisition. *Unit head:* Dr. Kathryn Bartholomew, Chair, 206-281-3533, Fax: 206-281-2500. *Application contact:* The Grad Center, 206-281-2091.

English as a Second Language

Seattle University, College of Education, Program in Teaching English to Speakers of Other Languages, Seattle, WA 98122-1090. Offers M Ed, MA, Certificate. *Accreditation:* NCATE. Part-time programs available. *Degree requirements:* For master's, comprehensive exam, thesis, internship. *Entrance requirements:* For master's, GRE, MAT, or minimum GPA of 3.0. Additional exam requirements/recommendations for international students: Required—TOEFL.

Shenandoah University, School of Education and Human Development, Winchester, VA 22601-5195. Offers administrative leadership (D Ed); advanced professional teaching English to speakers of other languages (Certificate); education (MSE); elementary education (Certificate); middle school education (Certificate); organizational leadership (MS); professional studies (Certificate); professional studies (for initial teacher licensure) (Certificate); professional studies (for special education teacher licensure) (Certificate); professional studies (for VA licensure reading specialists) (Certificate); professional studies (for VA licensure) (Certificate); professional teaching English to speakers of other languages (Certificate); public management (Certificate); school reform (Certificate); secondary education (Certificate). *Accreditation:* Teacher Education Accreditation Council. Part-time and evening/weekend programs available. Postbaccalaureate distance learning degree programs offered (minimal on-campus study). *Faculty:* 13 full-time (7 women), 27 part-time/adjunct (20 women). *Students:* 11 full-time (8 women), 382 part-time (276 women); includes 35 minority (17 African Americans, 1 American Indian/Alaska Native, 6 Asian Americans or Pacific Islanders, 11 Hispanic Americans), 4 international. Average age 39. 272 applicants, 95% accepted, 218 enrolled. In 2009, 103 master's, 2 doctorates awarded. *Degree requirements:* For master's, comprehensive exam (for some programs), thesis (for some programs), internship; for doctorate, comprehensive exam, thesis/dissertation; for Certificate, full time teaching in area for 1 year. *Entrance requirements:* For master's, minimum GPA of 3.0 or satisfactory GRE, 3 letters of recommendation, valid teaching license, essay; for doctorate, minimum graduate GPA of 3.5, 3 years of teaching experience, 3 letters of recommendation, writing samples; for Certificate, minimum undergraduate GPA of 3.0, essay, 3 letters of recommendation. Additional exam requirements/recommendations for international students: Required—TOEFL (minimum score 550 paper-based; 213 computer-based; 79 iBT), IELTS (minimum score 6.5). *Application deadline:* For fall admission, 7/1 for domestic and international students; for spring admission, 10/15 for domestic and international students. Application fee: $30. Electronic applications accepted. *Expenses:* Tuition: Full-time $11,925; part-time $695 per credit. Required fees: $400 per semester. *Financial support:* Application deadline: 3/15. *Unit head:* Dr. Steven E. Humphries, Dean, 540-535-3574, E-mail: shumphri@su.edu. *Application contact:* David Anthony, Dean of Admissions, 540-665-4581, Fax: 540-665-4627, E-mail: admit@su.edu.

Simmons College, College of Arts and Sciences Graduate Studies, Department of Education, Program in Teaching English as a Second Language, Boston, MA 02115. Offers MAT, CAGS. Part-time programs available. *Students:* 10 full-time (8 women), 13 part-time (12 women); includes 2 minority (1 Asian American or Pacific Islander, 1 Hispanic American). Average age 25. 11 applicants, 82% accepted, 8 enrolled. In 2009, 11 master's awarded. *Degree requirements:* For master's, one foreign language, student teaching. *Entrance requirements:* For master's, GRE General Test, MAT, or Massachusetts Test for Education Licensure in communication and literacy, intermediate proficiency in a second language. Additional exam requirements/recommendations for international students: Required—TOEFL (minimum score 600 paper-based; 250 computer-based; 100 iBT). *Application deadline:* For fall admission, 8/1 priority date for domestic and international students; for winter admission, 12/1 priority date for domestic students, 12/15 priority date for international students; for spring admission, 5/1 priority date for domestic and international students. Applications are processed on a rolling basis. Application fee: $35. Electronic applications accepted. *Expenses:* Contact institution. *Financial support:* Application deadline: 3/1. *Faculty research:* Second language reading, the efficacy of language learning with computers. *Unit head:* Dr. Paul Abraham, Professor/Director, Master of Arts in Teaching ESL Program/Chair of the Department of Education, 617-521-2575, Fax: 617-521-3058, E-mail: paul.abraham@simmons.edu. *Application contact:* Kristen Haack, Director, Graduate Studies Admission, 617-521-2917, Fax: 617-521-3058, E-mail: gsa@simmons.edu.

Simon Fraser University, Graduate Studies, Faculty of Education, Program in Teaching English as a Second/Foreign Language, Burnaby, BC V5A 1S6, Canada. Offers M Ed. *Degree requirements:* For master's, comprehensive exam.

SIT Graduate Institute, Graduate Programs, Programs in Language Teacher Education, Brattleboro, VT 05302-0676. Offers English for speakers of other languages (MAT); French (MAT); Spanish (MAT). *Degree requirements:* For master's, one foreign language, thesis, teaching practice. *Entrance requirements:* For master's, 4 letters of reference. Additional exam requirements/recommendations for international students: Required—TOEFL.

Soka University of America, Graduate School, Aliso Viejo, CA 92656. Offers teaching Japanese as a foreign language (Certificate). Evening/weekend programs available. *Entrance requirements:* For degree, bachelor's degree with minimum GPA of 3.0, proficiency in Japanese. Additional exam requirements/recommendations for international students: Required—TOEFL (minimum score 600 paper-based; 100 iBT).

Southeast Missouri State University, School of Graduate Studies, Department of English, Cape Girardeau, MO 63701-4799. Offers English (MA); teaching English to speakers of other languages (MA). Part-time and evening/weekend programs available. Postbaccalaureate distance learning degree programs offered (no on-campus study). *Degree requirements:* For master's, comprehensive exam (for some programs), thesis or alternative. *Entrance requirements:* For master's, minimum undergraduate GPA of 2.5. Additional exam requirements/recommendations for international students: Required—TOEFL (minimum score 550 paper-based; 213 computer-based); Recommended—IELTS (minimum score 6). Electronic applications accepted. *Expenses:* Tuition, state resident: full-time $4266; part-time $237 per credit hour. Tuition, nonresident: full-time $7506; part-time $417 per credit hour. Required fees: $427; $427. *Faculty research:* Literature, writing, linguistics, education, TESOL.

Southern Arkansas University–Magnolia, Graduate Programs, Magnolia, AR 71753. Offers agriculture (MS); business administration (MBA); computer and information sciences (MS); counseling (MS); education (M Ed), including counseling and development, curriculum and instruction emphasis, educational administration and supervision, elementary education, middle level emphasis, reading emphasis, secondary education, TESOL emphasis; kinesiology (MS); library media and information specialist (M Ed); mental health and clinical counseling (MS); public administration (EMPA); school counseling (M Ed); teaching (MAT). *Accreditation:* NCATE. Part-time and evening/weekend programs available. *Faculty:* 43 full-time (24 women), 12 part-time/adjunct (7 women). *Students:* 116 full-time (78 women), 333 part-time (255 women); includes 105 minority (98 African Americans, 3 American Indian/Alaska Native, 3 Asian Americans or Pacific Islanders, 1 Hispanic American), 11 international. Average age 33. In 2009, 88 master's awarded. *Degree requirements:* For master's, comprehensive exam, thesis optional. *Entrance requirements:* For master's, GRE, MAT or GMAT, minimum GPA of 2.75. *Application deadline:* For fall admission, 8/15 for domestic students; for winter admission, 1/8 for domestic students; for spring admission, 1/8 for domestic students. Applications are processed on a rolling basis. Application fee: $0. *Expenses:* Tuition, state resident: full-time $3798; part-time $211 per hour. Tuition, nonresident: full-time $5580; part-time $310 per hour. Required fees: $584. *Financial support:* Career-related internships or fieldwork, Federal Work-Study, scholarships/grants, tuition waivers (full), and unspecified assistantships available. Financial award applicants required to submit FAFSA. *Faculty research:* Alternative certification for teachers, supervision of instruction, instructional leadership, counseling. *Unit head:* Dr. Kim Bloss, Dean, Graduate Studies, 870-235-4150, Fax: 870-235-5227, E-mail: kkbloss@saumag.edu. *Application contact:* Dr. Kim Bloss, Dean, Graduate Studies, 870-235-4150, Fax: 870-235-5227, E-mail: kkbloss@saumag.edu.

Southern Connecticut State University, School of Graduate Studies, School of Arts and Sciences, Department of Foreign Languages, New Haven, CT 06515-1355. Offers multicultural-bilingual education/teaching English to speakers of other languages (MS). Part-time and evening/weekend programs available. *Faculty:* 6 full-time. *Students:* 16 full-time (9 women), 25 part-time (22 women); includes 7 minority (1 Asian American or Pacific Islander, 6 Hispanic Americans). 5 applicants, 60% accepted, 3 enrolled. In 2009, 24 master's awarded. *Degree requirements:* For master's, one foreign language, thesis or alternative. *Entrance requirements:* For master's, interview, minimum undergraduate GPA of 2.7. *Application deadline:* For fall admission, 7/15 priority date for domestic students. Applications are processed on a rolling basis. Application fee: $50. Electronic applications accepted. Tuition and fees vary according to program. *Financial support:* Application deadline: 4/15. *Unit head:* Dr. Elena Schmitt, Chairperson, 203-392-6138, Fax: 203-392-6136, E-mail: schmitte1@southernct.edu. *Application contact:* Dr. Luisa Piemontese, Graduate Coordinator, 203-392-6751, E-mail: piemontesel1@southernct.edu.

Southern Illinois University Carbondale, Graduate School, College of Liberal Arts, Department of Applied Linguistics, Carbondale, IL 62901-4701. Offers applied linguistics (MA); teaching English to speakers of other languages (MA). *Degree requirements:* For master's, one foreign language, thesis. *Entrance requirements:* For master's, minimum GPA of 3.0. Additional exam requirements/recommendations for international students: Required—TOEFL. *Faculty research:* Theory and methods, second language acquisition, pidgin and Creole languages, cognitive grammar.

Southern Illinois University Carbondale, Graduate School, College of Liberal Arts, Program in Teaching English to Speakers of Other Languages, Carbondale, IL 62901-4701. Offers MA.

Southern Illinois University Edwardsville, Graduate Studies and Research, College of Arts and Sciences, Department of English Language and Literature, Program in Teaching English as a Second Language, Edwardsville, IL 62026-0001. Offers MA, Postbaccalaureate Certificate. Part-time and evening/weekend programs available. *Students:* 7 full-time (5 women), 15 part-time (14 women); includes 3 minority (1 Asian American or Pacific Islander, 2 Hispanic Americans), 1 international. Average age 26. 19 applicants, 47% accepted. In 2009, 3 master's awarded. *Degree requirements:* For master's, one foreign language, thesis or alternative, final exam. *Entrance requirements:* Additional exam requirements/recommendations for international students: Required—TOEFL (minimum score 550 paper-based; 213 computer-based; 79 iBT), IELTS (minimum score 6.5). *Application deadline:* For fall admission, 7/23 for domestic students, 6/1 for international students; for spring admission, 12/11 for domestic students, 10/1 for international students. Applications are processed on a rolling basis. Application fee: $30. Electronic applications accepted. *Expenses:* Tuition, state resident: part-time $1252.50 per semester. Tuition, nonresident: part-time $3131.25 per semester. Required fees: $586.85 per semester. Tuition and fees vary according to course load. *Financial support:* Fellowships with full tuition reimbursements, research assistantships with full tuition reimbursements, teaching assistantships with full tuition reimbursements, career-related internships or fieldwork, Federal Work-Study, institutionally sponsored loans, scholarships/grants, traineeships, and unspecified assistantships available. Support available to part-time students. Financial award application deadline: 3/1; financial award applicants required to submit FAFSA. *Unit head:* Dr. Joel Hardman, Director, 618-650-5978, E-mail: jhardma@siue.edu. *Application contact:* Dr. Joel Hardman, Director, 618-650-5978, E-mail: jhardma@siue.edu.

Southern New Hampshire University, School of Liberal Arts, Manchester, NH 03106-1045. Offers clinical services for adults psychiatric disabilities (Certificate); clinical services for children and adolescents with psychiatric disabilities (Certificate); clinical services for persons with co-occurring substance abuse and psychiatric disabilities (Certificate); community mental health (MS); fiction writing (MFA); non-fiction writing (MFA); teaching English as a foreign language (MS). Part-time and evening/weekend programs available. *Degree requirements:* For master's, one foreign language, thesis. *Entrance requirements:* For master's, minimum GPA of 2.75: MS-TEFL, 3.0: MFA. Additional exam requirements/recommendations for international students: Required—TOEFL (minimum score 550 paper-based; 213 computer-based; 79 iBT), IELTS (minimum score 6.5), TWE (minimum score 5). Electronic applications accepted. *Expenses:* Contact institution. *Faculty research:* Action research, state of the art practice in behavioral health services, wraparound approaches to working with youth, learning styles.

State University of New York at Fredonia, Graduate Studies, College of Education, Program in Teaching English to Speakers of Other Languages, Fredonia, NY 14063-1136. Offers MS Ed. *Expenses:* Tuition, state resident: full-time $8370; part-time $349 per credit. Tuition, nonresident: full-time $13,250; part-time $552 per credit. Required fees: $1289; $53.55 per credit.

State University of New York at New Paltz, Graduate School, School of Education, Department of Secondary Education, Program in Second Language Education, New Paltz, NY 12561. Offers MS Ed. *Accreditation:* NCATE. Part-time and evening/weekend programs available. *Faculty:* 1 full-time (0 women), 2 part-time/adjunct (1 woman). *Students:* 14 full-time (10 women), 31 part-time (27 women); includes 7 minority (all Hispanic Americans), 1 international. Average age 32. 40 applicants, 65% accepted, 24 enrolled. In 2009, 5 master's awarded. *Degree requirements:* For master's, practicum. *Entrance requirements:* For master's, minimum GPA of 3.0, 12 credits of a foreign language. Additional exam requirements/recommendations for international students: Required—TOEFL (minimum score 575 paper-based; 233 computer-based; 90 iBT). *Application deadline:* For fall admission, 4/15 priority date for domestic and international students. Application fee: $50. Electronic applications accepted. *Financial support:* In 2009–10, 4 students received support, including 1 fellowship (averaging $9,000 per year); tuition waivers (full) also available. Financial award application deadline: 8/1; financial award applicants required to submit FAFSA. *Unit head:* Prof. Vern Todd, Coordinator, 845-257-2818, E-mail: toddv@newpaltz.edu. *Application contact:* Caroline Murphy, Graduate Admissions Advisor, 845-257-3285, Fax: 845-257-3284, E-mail: gradschool@newpaltz.edu.

State University of New York College at Cortland, Graduate Studies, School of Arts and Sciences, Department of Second Language Education, Cortland, NY 13045. Offers MS Ed. *Accreditation:* NCATE.

Stony Brook University, State University of New York, Graduate School, College of Arts and Sciences, Department of Linguistics, Program in Teaching English to Speakers of Other Languages, Stony Brook, NY 11794. Offers MA. *Accreditation:* NCATE. *Students:* 32 full-time (24 women), 17 part-time (16 women); includes 8 minority (2 Asian Americans or Pacific Islanders, 6 Hispanic Americans), 5 international. Average age 30. 64 applicants, 28% accepted. In 2009, 18 master's awarded. *Application deadline:* For fall admission, 1/15 for domestic students. Application fee: $60. *Expenses:* Tuition, state resident: full-time $8370; part-time $349 per credit. Tuition, nonresident: full-time $13,250; part-time $552 per credit. Required fees: $933. *Financial support:* Fellowships, research assistantships, teaching assistantships available. *Unit head:* Dr. Robert Hoberman, Chair, 631-632-7774. *Application contact:* Michelle Carbone, 631-632-7774, Fax: 631-632-9789.

Syracuse University, School of Education, Program in Teaching English Language Learners, Syracuse, NY 13244. Offers MS. Part-time programs available. *Students:* 4 full-time (all women), 3 part-time (all women); includes 1 minority (Hispanic American). Average age 32. 8 applicants, 88% accepted, 6 enrolled. *Entrance requirements:* For master's, New York State Teacher Certification or eligibility. Additional exam requirements/recommendations for international students: Required—TOEFL (minimum score 100 iBT). *Application deadline:* For fall admission, 2/1 for domestic students, 2/1 priority date for international students. Application fee: $75. Electronic applications accepted. *Expenses:* Tuition: Full-time $26,808; part-time $1117 per credit. Required fees: $1024. *Financial support:* Fellowships with tuition reimbursements, teaching assistantships with tuition reimbursements, tuition waivers (partial) available. Financial award application deadline: 1/1; financial award applicants required to submit FAFSA. *Unit head:* Dr. Zaline Roy-Campbell, Program Coordinator, 315-443-8194, E-mail: zmroycam@syr.edu. *Application contact:* Liza Rochelson, Graduate Recruiter, School of Education, 315-443-2505, E-mail: e-gradrcrt@syr.edu.

Taylor College and Seminary, Graduate and Professional Programs, Edmonton, AB T6J 4T3, Canada. Offers Christian studies (Diploma); intercultural studies (MA, Diploma), including intercultural studies (Diploma), TESOL; theology (M Div, MTS). *Accreditation:* ATS. Part-time programs available. Postbaccalaureate distance learning degree programs offered (minimal

on-campus study). *Faculty:* 5 full-time (0 women), 5 part-time/adjunct (1 woman). *Students:* 13 full-time (4 women), 52 part-time (24 women); includes 18 minority (2 African Americans, 1 American Indian/Alaska Native, 15 Asian Americans or Pacific Islanders). Average age 38. 40 applicants, 73% accepted, 20 enrolled. In 2009, 11 first professional degrees awarded. *Degree requirements:* For master's, thesis optional. *Entrance requirements:* Additional exam requirements/recommendations for international students: Required—TOEFL (minimum score 550 paper-based; 80 iBT), IELTS (minimum score 6.5). *Application deadline:* For fall admission, 9/1 priority date for domestic and international students. Applications are processed on a rolling basis. Application fee: $35 ($70 for international students). *Financial support:* In 2009–10, 16 students received support. Career-related internships or fieldwork and scholarships/grants available. Financial award application deadline: 8/1. *Faculty research:* Biblical studies, administration and organization, world religions, ethics, missiology. *Unit head:* Dr. Joost Pikkert, Academic Dean, 780-431-5243, Fax: 780-436-9416, E-mail: joost.pikkert@taylor-edu.ca. *Application contact:* Craig Weston, Registrar and Director of Enrolment Services, 780-431-5208, Fax: 780-436-9416, E-mail: craig.weston@taylor-edu.ca.

Teachers College, Columbia University, Graduate Faculty of Education, Department of Arts and Humanities, Program in Teaching English to Speakers of Other Languages, New York, NY 10027-6696. Offers Ed M, MA, Ed D. *Accreditation:* NCATE. Part-time programs available. *Faculty:* 16 part-time/adjunct. *Students:* 21 full-time (18 women), 163 part-time (116 women); includes 33 minority (1 African American, 28 Asian Americans or Pacific Islanders, 4 Hispanic Americans), 54 international. Average age 34. 206 applicants, 48% accepted, 45 enrolled. In 2009, 70 master's, 1 doctorate awarded. *Degree requirements:* For doctorate, thesis/dissertation. *Entrance requirements:* For doctorate, MA in teaching English to speakers of other languages. Additional exam requirements/recommendations for international students: Required—TOEFL. *Application deadline:* For fall admission, 2/1 priority date for domestic students. Application fee: $65. *Financial support:* Career-related internships or fieldwork, Federal Work-Study, institutionally sponsored loans, and tuition waivers (full and partial) available. Support available to part-time students. Financial award application deadline: 2/1. *Faculty research:* Classroom-centered research, electronic media, K-12 English as a second language, second language acquisition. *Unit head:* Graeme Sullivan, Chair, 212-678-3799. *Application contact:* Mark E. Stearns, Associate Director of Admission, 212-678-3710, Fax: 212-678-4171.

Temple University, Graduate School, College of Education, Department of Curriculum, Instruction, and Technology in Education, Philadelphia, PA 19122-6096. Offers applied behavioral analysis (MS Ed); career and technical education (MS Ed); early childhood education and elementary education (MS Ed); English education (MS Ed); language arts education (Ed D); math/science education (Ed D); mathematics education (MS Ed); science education (MS Ed); second and foreign language education (MS Ed); special education (MS Ed); teaching English as a second language (MS Ed). Part-time and evening/weekend programs available. Terminal master's awarded for partial completion of doctoral program. *Degree requirements:* For master's, thesis or alternative; for doctorate, thesis/dissertation. *Entrance requirements:* For master's and doctorate, GRE General Test or MAT, minimum GPA of 3.0. Additional exam requirements/recommendations for international students: Required—TOEFL (minimum score 550 paper-based; 213 computer-based; 79 iBT). Electronic applications accepted. *Faculty research:* School improvement, problem solving, literacy, language development.

Texas A&M University–Commerce, Graduate School, College of Education and Human Services, Department of Curriculum and Instruction, Commerce, TX 75429-3011. Offers bilingual/ESL education (M Ed, MS); early childhood education (M Ed, MS); elementary education (M Ed, MS); reading (M Ed, MS); secondary education (M Ed, MS); supervision, curriculum and instruction: elementary education (Ed D). Part-time programs available. Terminal master's awarded for partial completion of doctoral program. *Degree requirements:* For master's, comprehensive exam, thesis (for some programs); for doctorate, 2 foreign languages, thesis/dissertation, departmental qualifying exam. *Entrance requirements:* For master's and doctorate, GRE General Test. Electronic applications accepted. *Faculty research:* Literacy and learning, early childhood, preservice teacher education, technology.

Texas A&M University–Kingsville, College of Graduate Studies, College of Education, Department of Education, Program in English as a Second Language, Kingsville, TX 78363. Offers M Ed. *Degree requirements:* For master's, comprehensive exam. *Entrance requirements:* For master's, GRE General Test, MAT, minimum GPA of 3.0.

Trevecca Nazarene University, Graduate Division, School of Education, Major in English Language Learners (PreK-12), Nashville, TN 37210-2877. Offers M Ed. *Accreditation:* NCATE. Part-time and evening/weekend programs available. *Students:* 29 full-time (25 women), 4 part-time (all women); includes 7 minority (4 African Americans, 3 Hispanic Americans), 1 international. In 2009, 11 master's awarded. *Degree requirements:* For master's, exit assessment. *Entrance requirements:* For master's, GRE General Test, MAT, minimum GPA of 2.7, 2 reference forms. Additional exam requirements/recommendations for international students: Required—TOEFL (minimum score 550 paper-based; 213 computer-based). *Application deadline:* Applications are processed on a rolling basis. Application fee: $25. *Expenses:* Contact institution. *Financial support:* Applicants required to submit FAFSA. *Unit head:* Dr. Esther Swink, Dean/Director of Graduate Education Programs, 615-248-1201, Fax: 615-248-1597, E-mail: admissions_ged@trevecca.edu. *Application contact:* Admissions Office, 615-248-1201, Fax: 615-248-1597, E-mail: admissions_ged@trevecca.edu.

Trinity (Washington) University, School of Education, Washington, DC 20017-1094. Offers counseling (MA); early childhood education (MAT); educating for change (M Ed); educational administration (MSA); elementary education (MAT); school counseling (MA); secondary education (MAT), including English, social studies; special education (MAT); teaching English as a second language (MAT); teaching English to speakers of other languages (M Ed); the teaching of reading (M Ed). *Accreditation:* NCATE. Part-time and evening/weekend programs available. *Degree requirements:* For master's, thesis (for some programs), capstone project(s). *Entrance requirements:* For master's, PRAXIS I, minimum GPA of 2.8. Additional exam requirements/recommendations for international students: Required—TOEFL (minimum score 550 paper-based; 213 computer-based). *Faculty research:* Technology, literacy, special education, organizations, inclusion models.

Trinity Western University, School of Graduate Studies, Program in Teaching English to Speakers of Other Languages (TESOL), Langley, BC V2Y 1Y1, Canada. Offers MA. Part-time programs available. Postbaccalaureate distance learning degree programs offered (minimal on-campus study). *Degree requirements:* For master's, project. *Entrance requirements:* For master's, minimum GPA of 3.0. Additional exam requirements/recommendations for international students: Required—TOEFL (minimum score 600 paper-based; 250 computer-based). *Faculty research:* ESL methodology, second language acquisition, computer assisted language learning.

Universidad Adventista de las Antillas, EGECED Department, Mayagüez, PR 00681-0118. Offers curriculum and instruction (MA), including secondary biology, secondary history, secondary Spanish; education (MA), including ESL (elementary school level), ESL (high school level), school administration and supervision. *Degree requirements:* For master's, comprehensive exam (for some programs), thesis (for some programs). *Entrance requirements:* For master's, EXADEP or GRE General Test, recommendations. Application fee: $175. Electronic applications accepted. *Expenses:* Tuition: Full-time $3990; part-time $190 per credit. Required fees: $570; $190 per credit. $1375 per summer. *Financial support:* Fellowships, Federal Work-Study available. *Unit head:* Dr. Zilma Sepulveda, Director, 787-834-9595 Ext. 2282, Fax: 787-834-9595, E-mail: zsantiago@uaa.edu. *Application contact:* Prof. Evelyn del Valle, Admissions Department Director, 787-834-9595 Ext. 2261, Fax: 787-834-9597, E-mail: admissions@uaa.edu.

Universidad del Este, Graduate School, Carolina, PR 00984. Offers accounting (MBA); adult education (M Ed); agribusiness (MBA); bilingual education (M Ed); criminal justice and criminology (MA); early education (M Ed); elementary education (M Ed); human resources (MBA); information security management (MBA); information technology and Web business development (MBA); management (MBA); public policy (MPA); social work (MA), including clinical social work; special education (M Ed); strategic leadership (MBA); teaching English (M Ed); teaching Spanish (M Ed).

Universidad del Turabo, Graduate Programs, Programs in Education, Program in Teaching English as a Second Language, Gurabo, PR 00778-3030. Offers M Ed. *Students:* 18 full-time (17 women), 150 part-time (130 women); includes 85 Hispanic Americans. Average age 36. 105 applicants, 97% accepted, 83 enrolled. In 2009, 108 master's awarded. *Entrance requirements:* For master's, GRE, EXADEP, interview. *Application deadline:* For fall admission, 8/5 for domestic students. Application fee: $25. *Financial support:* Institutionally sponsored loans available. *Unit head:* Angela Candelario, Dean, 787-743-7979 Ext. 4126. *Application contact:* Virginia Gonzalez, Admissions Officer, 787-746-3009.

University at Buffalo, the State University of New York, Graduate School, Graduate School of Education, Department of Learning and Instruction, Buffalo, NY 14260. Offers biology education (Ed M, Certificate); chemistry education (Ed M, Certificate); childhood education (Ed M); childhood education with bilingual extension (Ed M); early childhood education (Ed M); earth science education (Ed M, Certificate); elementary education (Ed D, PhD); English education (Ed M, PhD, Certificate); English for speakers of other languages (Ed M); foreign and second language education (PhD); French education (Ed M, Certificate); general education (Ed M); German education (Ed M, Certificate); gifted education (online) (Certificate); Latin education (Ed M, Certificate); literary specialist (Ed M); mathematics education (Ed M, PhD, Certificate); music education (Ed M, Certificate); physics education (Ed M, Certificate); reading education (PhD); science and the public (online) (Ed M); science education (PhD); social studies education (Ed M, Certificate); Spanish education (Ed M, Certificate); special education (PhD); teaching and leading for diversity (Certificate); teaching English to speakers of other languages (Ed M). Part-time and evening/weekend programs available. Postbaccalaureate distance learning degree programs offered (no on-campus study). *Faculty:* 34 full-time (24 women), 50 part-time/adjunct (39 women). *Students:* 332 full-time (245 women), 365 part-time (272 women); includes 50 minority (18 African Americans, 4 American Indian/Alaska Native, 10 Asian Americans or Pacific Islanders, 18 Hispanic Americans), 55 international. Average age 30. 627 applicants, 78% accepted, 286 enrolled. In 2009, 255 master's, 16 doctorates, 51 other advanced degrees awarded. *Degree requirements:* For master's, comprehensive exam; for doctorate, thesis/dissertation, research analysis exam, research experience component. *Entrance requirements:* For doctorate, GRE General Test or MAT, interview, writing sample, letters of recommendation. Additional exam requirements/recommendations for international students: Required—TOEFL (minimum score 600 paper-based; 250 computer-based; 96 iBT). *Application deadline:* For fall admission, 2/1 priority date for domestic and international students; for spring admission, 11/15 priority date for domestic students, 10/1 for international students. Applications are processed on a rolling basis. Application fee: $50. Electronic applications accepted. *Financial support:* In 2009–10, 23 fellowships with full tuition reimbursements (averaging $9,000 per year), 42 research assistantships with full tuition reimbursements (averaging $10,000 per year) were awarded; teaching assistantships with full tuition reimbursements, career-related internships or fieldwork, Federal Work-Study, institutionally sponsored loans, scholarships/grants, tuition waivers (partial), and unspecified assistantships also available. Financial award application deadline: 2/28; financial award applicants required to submit FAFSA. *Faculty research:* Science assessment, foreign language teaching and learning, early learning, new literacies, gender and education. Total annual research expenditures: $1.8 million. *Unit head:* Dr. Suzanne Miller, Chair, 716-645-2455, Fax: 716-645-3161, E-mail: smiller@buffalo.edu. *Application contact:* Cathy Dimino, Admissions Assistant, 716-645-2110, Fax: 716-645-7937, E-mail: cadimino@buffalo.edu.

The University of Alabama, Graduate School, College of Arts and Sciences, Department of English, Tuscaloosa, AL 35487. Offers composition and rhetoric (PhD); creative writing (MFA), including fiction, poetry; literature (MA, PhD); rhetoric and composition (MA); teaching English as a second language (MATESOL). *Faculty:* 30 full-time (12 women). *Students:* 123 full-time (71 women), 12 part-time (9 women); includes 14 minority (9 African Americans, 2 American Indian/Alaska Native, 1 Asian American or Pacific Islander, 2 Hispanic Americans), 4 international. Average age 27. 339 applicants, 17% accepted, 39 enrolled. In 2009, 31 degrees awarded. *Degree requirements:* For master's, one foreign language, comprehensive exam, thesis (for some programs); for doctorate, 2 foreign languages, comprehensive exam, thesis/dissertation. *Entrance requirements:* For master's and doctorate, GRE, minimum GPA of 3.0, critical writing sample. Additional exam requirements/recommendations for international students: Required—TOEFL. *Application deadline:* For fall admission, 1/15 priority date for domestic students, 1/15 for international students. Application fee: $50 ($60 for international students). Electronic applications accepted. *Expenses:* Tuition, state resident: full-time $7000. Tuition, nonresident: full-time $19,200. *Financial support:* In 2009–10, 7 fellowships with full tuition reimbursements (averaging $15,000 per year), 1 research assistantship (averaging $11,708 per year), 106 teaching assistantships with full tuition reimbursements (averaging $11,708 per year) were awarded; career-related internships or fieldwork, scholarships/grants, health care benefits, and unspecified assistantships also available. Financial award application deadline: 1/15. *Faculty research:* Critical theory; modern, Renaissance, and African-American literature. *Unit head:* Dr. Catherine E. Davies, Director of Graduate Studies, 205-348-8499, E-mail: cdavies@bama.ua.edu. *Application contact:* Vernita W. James, Office Assistant II, 205-348-0766, Fax: 205-348-1388, E-mail: vwjames@bama.ua.edu.

The University of Alabama in Huntsville, School of Graduate Studies, College of Liberal Arts, Department of English, Huntsville, AL 35899. Offers English (MA); teaching of English to speakers of other languages (Certificate); technical communications (Certificate). Part-time and evening/weekend programs available. *Faculty:* 14 full-time (9 women). *Students:* 14 full-time (9 women), 39 part-time (31 women); includes 11 minority (8 African Americans, 1 American Indian/Alaska Native, 2 Hispanic Americans). Average age 33. 28 applicants, 86% accepted, 17 enrolled. In 2009, 23 master's, 1 other advanced degree awarded. *Degree requirements:* For master's, one foreign language, comprehensive exam, thesis or alternative, oral and written exams. *Entrance requirements:* For master's and Certificate, GRE General Test, minimum GPA of 3.0. Additional exam requirements/recommendations for international students: Required—TOEFL (minimum score 500 paper-based; 173 computer-based; 62 iBT). *Application deadline:* For fall admission, 7/15 for domestic students, 4/1 for international students; for spring admission, 11/30 for domestic students, 9/1 for international students. Applications are processed on a rolling basis. Application fee: $40 ($50 for international students). Electronic applications accepted. *Expenses:* Tuition, state resident: part-time $355.75 per credit hour. Tuition, nonresident: part-time $847.10 per credit hour. Required fees: $210.80 per semester. Tuition and fees vary according to course load and program. *Financial support:* In 2009–10, 9 students received support, including 4 teaching assistantships with full and partial tuition reimbursements available (averaging $8,460 per year); career-related internships or fieldwork, Federal Work-Study, institutionally sponsored loans, scholarships/grants, health care benefits, tuition waivers, and unspecified assistantships also available. Support available to part-time students. Financial award application deadline: 4/1; financial award applicants required to submit FAFSA. *Faculty research:* American and British literature, linguistics, technical writing, women's studies, rhetoric. *Unit head:* Dr. Rose Norman, Chair, 256-824-6320, Fax: 256-824-6949, E-mail: normanr@uah.edu. *Application contact:* Kathy Biggs, Graduate Studies Admissions Manager, 256-824-6199, Fax: 256-824-6405, E-mail: deangrad@uah.edu.

University of Alberta, Faculty of Graduate Studies and Research, Department of Educational Psychology, Edmonton, AB T6G 2E1, Canada. Offers counseling psychology (M Ed, PhD); educational psychology (M Ed, PhD); instructional technology (M Ed); school counseling (M Ed); school psychology (M Ed, PhD); special education (M Ed, PhD); special education-deafness studies (M Ed); teaching English as a second language (M Ed). Part-time programs available. *Faculty:* 34 full-time (14 women), 12 part-time/adjunct (6 women). *Students:* 117 full-time (93 women), 173 part-time (121 women). Average age 36. 252 applicants, 34% accepted. In 2009, 30 master's, 10 doctorates awarded. *Degree requirements:* For master's, thesis optional; for doctorate, comprehensive exam, thesis/dissertation. *Entrance requirements:* For master's and

English as a Second Language

University of Alberta (continued)
doctorate, minimum GPA of 3.0. Additional exam requirements/recommendations for international students: Required—TOEFL. *Application deadline:* For fall admission, 2/1 priority date for domestic and international students. Applications are processed on a rolling basis. Tuition and fees charges are reported in Canadian dollars. *Expenses:* Tuition, area resident: Full-time $4626 Canadian dollars; part-time $99.72 Canadian dollars per unit. International tuition: $8216 Canadian dollars full-time. Required fees: $3590 Canadian dollars; $99.72 Canadian dollars per unit. $215 Canadian dollars per term. *Financial support:* In 2009–10, 10 fellowships with full tuition reimbursements (averaging $16,120 per year), 36 research assistantships with full tuition reimbursements (averaging $12,614 per year), 46 teaching assistantships with full tuition reimbursements (averaging $5,462 per year) were awarded; career-related internships or fieldwork and scholarships/grants also available. *Faculty research:* Human learning, development and assessment. *Unit head:* Dr. Linda M. McDonald, Chair, 780-492-1149, Fax: 780-492-1318, E-mail: linda.mcdonald@ualberta.ca. *Application contact:* Judy Maynes, Information Contact, 780-492-1149, Fax: 780-492-1318, E-mail: edpygrad@ualberta.ca.

The University of Arizona, Graduate College, College of Humanities, Department of English, English Language/Linguistics Program, Tucson, AZ 85721. Offers ESL (MA). *Students:* 13 full-time (11 women), 3 part-time (all women), 6 international. Average age 29. 25 applicants, 68% accepted, 9 enrolled. In 2009, 10 master's awarded. *Application deadline:* For fall admission, 1/15 priority date for domestic students, 1/15 for international students. Application fee: $75. *Expenses:* Tuition, state resident: full-time $9028. Tuition, nonresident: full-time $24,890. *Unit head:* Dr. Jun Liu, Department Head, 520-621-3287, E-mail: junliu@email.arizona.edu. *Application contact:* Marcia Marma, Graduate Secretary, 520-621-1358, Fax: 520-621-7397, E-mail: mmarma@u.arizona.edu.

The University of Arizona, Graduate College, Graduate Interdisciplinary Programs, Graduate Interdisciplinary Program in Second Language Acquisition and Teaching, Tucson, AZ 85721. Offers PhD. *Students:* 20 full-time (14 women), 43 part-time (33 women); includes 3 minority (2 African Americans, 1 Hispanic American), 32 international. Average age 36. 58 applicants, 47% accepted, 13 enrolled. In 2009, 12 doctorates awarded. *Degree requirements:* For doctorate, one foreign language, comprehensive exam, thesis/dissertation. *Entrance requirements:* For doctorate, GRE, 3 letters of recommendation, writing sample. Additional exam requirements/recommendations for international students: Required—TOEFL (minimum score 550 paper-based; 213 computer-based; 79 iBT); Recommended—TWE. *Application deadline:* For fall admission, 2/1 for domestic students, 1/15 for international students. Applications are processed on a rolling basis. Application fee: $65. Electronic applications accepted. *Expenses:* Tuition, state resident: full-time $9028. Tuition, nonresident: full-time $24,890. *Financial support:* Scholarships/grants, health care benefits, tuition waivers (full and partial), and unspecified assistantships available. Financial award application deadline: 2/1; financial award applicants required to submit FAFSA. *Unit head:* Dr. Linda Waugh, Chair, 520-621-7391, E-mail: lwaugh@u.arizona.edu. *Application contact:* Shaun O'Connor, Senior Program Coordinator, 520-621-7391, E-mail: azslat@u.arizona.edu.

University of Arkansas at Little Rock, Graduate School, College of Arts, Humanities, and Social Science, Department of International and Second Language Studies, Little Rock, AR 72204-1099. Offers second languages (MA).

The University of British Columbia, Faculty of Education, Program in Language and Literacy Education, Vancouver, BC V6T 1Z1, Canada. Offers library education (M Ed); literacy education (M Ed, MA, PhD); modern language education (M Ed, MA, PhD); teaching English as a second language (M Ed, MA, PhD). Part-time and evening/weekend programs available. *Degree requirements:* For master's, thesis (MA); for doctorate, thesis/dissertation. *Entrance requirements:* For master's and doctorate, minimum B+ average in last 2 years with minimum 2 courses at A standing. Additional exam requirements/recommendations for international students: Required—TOEFL (minimum score 580 paper-based; 237 computer-based; 92 iBT), TWE (minimum score 5). Electronic applications accepted. *Faculty research:* Language and literacy development, second language acquisition, Asia Pacific language curriculum, children's literature, whole language instruction.

University of Calgary, Faculty of Graduate Studies, Faculty of Education, Graduate Division of Educational Research, Calgary, AB T2N 1N4, Canada. Offers community rehabilitation and disability studies (M Ed, M Sc, Ed D, PhD, Graduate Certificate, Graduate Diploma); curriculum, teaching and learning (M Ed, M Sc, MA, Ed D, PhD, Graduate Certificate, Graduate Diploma); educational contexts (M Ed, MA, Ed D, PhD, Graduate Certificate, Graduate Diploma); educational leadership (M Ed, MA, Ed D, PhD, Graduate Certificate, Graduate Diploma); educational technology (M Ed, M Sc, MA, Ed D, PhD, Graduate Certificate, Graduate Diploma); gifted education (M Sc, MA, Ed D, PhD, Graduate Certificate, Graduate Diploma); higher education administration (Ed D); interpretive studies in education (M Ed, M Sc, MA, Ed D, PhD, Graduate Certificate, Graduate Diploma); second language teaching (M Ed, Ed D, PhD, Graduate Certificate, Graduate Diploma); teaching English as a second language (M Ed, M Sc, MA, Ed D, PhD, Graduate Certificate, Graduate Diploma); workplace and adult learning (M Ed, MA, Ed D, PhD, Graduate Certificate, Graduate Diploma). Ed D in both higher education administration and educational leadership offered via distance delivery. Part-time and evening/weekend programs available. Postbaccalaureate distance learning degree programs offered (minimal on-campus study). *Degree requirements:* For master's, thesis (for some programs); for doctorate, thesis/dissertation, candidacy exam. *Entrance requirements:* For master's, minimum GPA of 3.0, 3 letters of reference; for doctorate, minimum GPA of 3.5, 3 letters of reference; for other advanced degree, minimum GPA of 3.0. Additional exam requirements/recommendations for international students: Required—TOEFL, IELTS. Electronic applications accepted. *Faculty research:* Curriculum, leadership, technology, contexts, gifted, second language teaching, work place and adult learning.

University of California, Berkeley, UC Berkeley Extension, Certificate Programs in Education, Berkeley, CA 94720-1500. Offers college admissions and career planning (Certificate); teaching English as a second language (Certificate). *Unit head:* Diana Wu, Dean, 510-642-4181. *Application contact:* Education, 510-642-1171, E-mail: askeducation@unex.berkeley.edu.

University of California, Los Angeles, Graduate Division, College of Letters and Science, Department of Applied Linguistics and Teaching English as a Second Language, Los Angeles, CA 90095. Offers applied linguistics (PhD); applied linguistics and teaching English as a second language (MA); teaching English as a second language (Certificate). *Students:* 48 full-time (35 women); includes 9 minority (1 African American, 4 Asian Americans or Pacific Islanders, 4 Hispanic Americans), 21 international. Average age 34. 125 applicants, 14% accepted, 7 enrolled. In 2009, 1 master's, 11 doctorates awarded. *Degree requirements:* For master's, one foreign language, thesis; for doctorate, one foreign language, thesis/dissertation, oral and written exams. *Entrance requirements:* For master's, minimum GPA of 3.0, sample of research writing; for doctorate, minimum GPA of 3.0, MA in relevant field. *Application deadline:* For fall admission, 12/15 for domestic and international students. Application fee: $60 ($80 for international students). Electronic applications accepted. *Financial support:* In 2009–10, 33 fellowships with full and partial tuition reimbursements, 20 research assistantships with full and partial tuition reimbursements, 33 teaching assistantships with full and partial tuition reimbursements were awarded; Federal Work-Study, institutionally sponsored loans, scholarships/grants, health care benefits, tuition waivers (full and partial), and unspecified assistantships also available. Financial award application deadline: 3/1; financial award applicants required to submit FAFSA. *Unit head:* Dr. Olga Yokoyama, Chair, 310-825-4631. *Application contact:* Department Office, 310-825-4631, Fax: 310-206-4118, E-mail: jkim@humnet.ucla.edu.

University of Central Florida, College of Arts and Humanities, Department of Modern Languages and Literatures, Program in Teaching English to Speakers of Other Languages, Orlando, FL 32816. Offers MA, Certificate. *Accreditation:* NCATE. Part-time and evening/weekend programs available. *Students:* 19 full-time (13 women), 29 part-time (21 women); includes 13 minority (5 African Americans, 1 Asian American or Pacific Islander, 7 Hispanic Americans), 5 international. Average age 32. 36 applicants, 81% accepted, 18 enrolled. In 2009, 20 master's, 8 other advanced degrees awarded. *Degree requirements:* For master's, comprehensive exam, thesis or alternative. *Entrance requirements:* For master's, GRE General Test, minimum GPA of 3.0 in last 60 hours. Additional exam requirements/recommendations for international students: Required—TOEFL. *Application deadline:* For fall admission, 6/15 for domestic students; for spring admission, 11/1 for domestic students. Application fee: $30. Electronic applications accepted. *Expenses:* Tuition, state resident: part-time $306.31 per credit hour. Tuition, nonresident: part-time $1099.01 per credit hour. Part-time tuition and fees vary according to degree level and program. *Financial support:* In 2009–10, 3 students received support, including 3 teaching assistantships with partial tuition reimbursements available (averaging $6,900 per year); career-related internships or fieldwork, Federal Work-Study, institutionally sponsored loans, tuition waivers (partial), and unspecified assistantships also available. Financial award application deadline: 3/1; financial award applicants required to submit FAFSA. *Unit head:* Keith Folse. *Application contact:* Keith Folse.

University of Central Missouri, The Graduate School, College of Arts, Humanities and Social Sciences, Warrensburg, MO 64093. Offers English (MA); history (MA); mass communication (MA); music (MA); psychology (MS); speech communication (MA); teaching english as a second language (MA); theatre (MA). Part-time programs available. *Faculty:* 82. *Students:* 60 full-time (35 women), 101 part-time (61 women); includes 11 minority (5 African Americans, 3 Asian Americans or Pacific Islanders, 3 Hispanic Americans), 17 international. Average age 30. 80 applicants, 80% accepted, 58 enrolled. In 2009, 51 master's awarded. *Entrance requirements:* Additional exam requirements/recommendations for international students: Required—TOEFL (minimum score 550 paper-based; 79 computer-based). *Application deadline:* For fall admission, 6/1 priority date for domestic students, 5/1 for international students; for spring admission, 10/1 priority date for domestic students, 10/1 for international students. Applications are processed on a rolling basis. Application fee: $30 ($75 for international students). Electronic applications accepted. *Expenses:* Tuition, area resident: Part-time $245.80 per credit hour. Tuition, nonresident: part-time $491.60 per credit hour. Required fees: $24.20 per credit hour. Full-time tuition and fees vary according to course load, degree level, campus/location and reciprocity agreements. *Financial support:* Research assistantships with full and partial tuition reimbursements, teaching assistantships with full and partial tuition reimbursements, career-related internships or fieldwork, Federal Work-Study, scholarships/grants, and administrative and laboratory assistantships available. Support available to part-time students. Financial award application deadline: 3/1; financial award applicants required to submit FAFSA. *Unit head:* Dr. Gersham Nelson, Dean, 660-543-4750, Fax: 660-543-8271, E-mail: nelson@ucmo.edu. *Application contact:* Laurie Delap, Admissions Coordinator, 660-543-4621, Fax: 660-543-4778, E-mail: gradinfo@ucmo.edu.

University of Central Oklahoma, College of Graduate Studies and Research, College of Liberal Arts, Department of English, Edmond, OK 73034-5209. Offers composition skills (MA); contemporary literature (MA); creative writing (MA); teaching English as a second language (MA); traditional studies (MA). Part-time programs available. *Faculty:* 18 full-time (9 women), 5 part-time/adjunct (2 women). *Students:* 31 full-time (16 women), 57 part-time (42 women); includes 11 minority (6 African Americans, 2 Asian Americans or Pacific Islanders, 3 Hispanic Americans), 3 international. Average age 33. 25 applicants, 100% accepted. In 2009, 17 master's awarded. *Degree requirements:* For master's, one foreign language. *Entrance requirements:* For master's, 24 hours of course work in English language and literature. Additional exam requirements/recommendations for international students: Required—TOEFL (minimum score 550 paper-based; 213 computer-based). *Application deadline:* For fall admission, 7/1 for international students; for spring admission, 11/1 for international students. Applications are processed on a rolling basis. Application fee: $25. Electronic applications accepted. *Expenses:* Tuition, state resident: full-time $4128; part-time $172 per credit hour. Tuition, nonresident: full-time $10,373; part-time $432.20 per credit hour. Required fees: $433.20; $18.05 per credit hour. *Financial support:* In 2009–10, 6 teaching assistantships with partial tuition reimbursements were awarded; career-related internships or fieldwork, Federal Work-Study, and unspecified assistantships also available. Financial award application deadline: 3/31; financial award applicants required to submit FAFSA. *Faculty research:* John Milton, Harriet Beecher Stowe. *Unit head:* Dr. David Macey, Chairman, 405-974-5894, Fax: 405-974-3823. *Application contact:* Dr. Kurt Hochenauer, Director, 405-974-5607 Ext. 5607, Fax: 405-974-3823.

University of Cincinnati, Graduate School, College of Education, Criminal Justice, and Human Services, Division of Teacher Education, Program in Teaching English as a Second Language, Cincinnati, OH 45221. Offers M Ed, Ed D, Certificate. *Entrance requirements:* For master's and doctorate, GRE General Test. Additional exam requirements/recommendations for international students: Required—TOEFL (minimum score 550 paper-based; 213 computer-based), TWE (minimum score 5), Test of Spoken English (minimum score: 50).

University of Colorado Denver, College of Liberal Arts and Sciences, Department of English, Denver, CO 80217-3364. Offers applied linguistics (MA); English studies (MA); literature (MA); teaching English to speakers of other languages (Certificate); teaching of writing (MA). Part-time and evening/weekend programs available. *Students:* 12 full-time (9 women), 47 part-time (28 women); includes 3 minority (1 Asian American or Pacific Islander, 2 Hispanic Americans), 2 international. 36 applicants, 78% accepted, 19 enrolled. In 2009, 19 master's awarded. *Degree requirements:* For master's, thesis optional. *Entrance requirements:* For master's, GRE General Test, minimum GPA of 3.0. Additional exam requirements/recommendations for international students: Required—TOEFL (minimum score 550 paper-based). *Application deadline:* For fall admission, 5/25 for domestic students; for spring admission, 10/25 for domestic students. Applications are processed on a rolling basis. Application fee: $50 ($75 for international students). Electronic applications accepted. *Financial support:* Research assistantships, teaching assistantships, Federal Work-Study available. Financial award application deadline: 4/1; financial award applicants required to submit FAFSA. *Unit head:* Prof. Nancy Ciccone, Chair, 303-556-8395, Fax: 303-556-2959, E-mail: nancy.ciccone@ucdenver.edu. *Application contact:* Prof. Ian Ying, Program Advisor, 303-556-6728, Fax: 303-556-2959, E-mail: hongguang.ying@ucdenver.edu.

University of Delaware, College of Human Services, Education and Public Policy, School of Education, Newark, DE 19716. Offers education (PhD); educational leadership (Ed D); higher education (M Ed); instruction (MI); reading (M Ed); school leadership (M Ed); school psychology (MA, Ed S); teaching English as a second language (TESL) (MA). *Accreditation:* NCATE. Part-time and evening/weekend programs available. Terminal master's awarded for partial completion of doctoral program. *Degree requirements:* For master's, comprehensive exam (for some programs), thesis (for some programs); for doctorate, comprehensive exam (for some programs), thesis/dissertation. *Entrance requirements:* For master's and doctorate, GRE, 3 letters of recommendation. Additional exam requirements/recommendations for international students: Required—TOEFL (minimum score 600 paper-based; 250 computer-based). Electronic applications accepted. *Faculty research:* Teacher education; curriculum theory and development; community based education models, educational leadership.

The University of Findlay, Graduate and Professional Studies, College of Liberal Arts, Intensive English Language and Teaching English as a Second Language (TESOL) Program, Findlay, OH 45840-3653. Offers bilingual and multicultural education (MA); teaching English to speakers of other languages (MA). Part-time and evening/weekend programs available. *Degree requirements:* For master's, cumulative project. *Entrance requirements:* For master's, minimum undergraduate GPA of 2.5 in last 64 hours of course work, 3 letters of recommendation. Additional exam requirements/recommendations for international students: Required—TOEFL (minimum score 550 paper-based; 213 computer-based; 80 iBT). Electronic applications accepted.

University of Florida, Graduate School, College of Liberal Arts and Sciences, Program in Linguistics, Gainesville, FL 32611. Offers linguistics (MA, PhD); teaching English as a second language (Certificate). *Degree requirements:* For master's, one foreign language, comprehensive exam, thesis optional; for doctorate, 2 foreign languages, thesis/dissertation, qualifying exam. *Entrance requirements:* For master's and doctorate, GRE General Test, minimum GPA of 3.0.

Additional exam requirements/recommendations for international students: Required—TOEFL (minimum score 550 paper-based; 213 computer-based). Electronic applications accepted. *Faculty research:* Theoretical, applied, and descriptive linguistics.

University of Guam, Office of Graduate Studies, School of Education, Program in Teaching English to Speakers of Other Languages, Mangilao, GU 96923. Offers M Ed. *Degree requirements:* For master's, comprehensive oral and written exams, special project or thesis. *Entrance requirements:* For master's, GRE General Test. Additional exam requirements/ recommendations for international students: Required—TOEFL.

University of Hawaii at Manoa, Graduate Division, College of Language, Linguistics and Literature, Department of Second Language Studies, Honolulu, HI 96822. Offers English as a second language (MA, Graduate Certificate); second language acquisition (PhD). Part-time programs available. *Faculty:* 23 full-time (9 women), 3 part-time/adjunct (2 women). *Students:* 83 full-time (53 women), 20 part-time (12 women); includes 20 minority (1 African American, 19 Asian Americans or Pacific Islanders), 62 international. Average age 31. 129 applicants, 45% accepted, 31 enrolled. In 2009, 28 master's, 2 doctorates, 1 other advanced degree awarded. *Degree requirements:* For master's, 2 foreign languages, thesis optional; for doctorate, 2 foreign languages, comprehensive exam, thesis/dissertation. *Entrance requirements:* For master's, GRE General Test, minimum GPA of 3.0; for doctorate, GRE General Test, MA, scholarly publications. Additional exam requirements/recommendations for international students: Required—TOEFL (minimum score 600 paper-based; 250 computer-based; 100 iBT), IELTS (minimum score 7). *Application deadline:* For fall admission, 1/15 for domestic and international students; for spring admission, 9/1 for domestic and international students. Applications are processed on a rolling basis. Application fee: $60. *Expenses:* Tuition, state resident: full-time $8900; part-time $372 per credit. Tuition, nonresident: full-time $21,400; part-time $898 per credit. Required fees: $207 per semester. *Financial support:* In 2009–10, 24 fellowships (averaging $3,677 per year), 9 research assistantships (averaging $16,850 per year), 26 teaching assistantships (averaging $13,795 per year) were awarded; career-related internships or fieldwork, Federal Work-Study, institutionally sponsored loans, scholarships/grants, and tuition waivers (full and partial) also available. Financial award application deadline: 2/1; financial award applicants required to submit FAFSA. *Faculty research:* Second language use, second language analysis, second language pedagogy and testing, second language learning, qualitative and quantitative research methods for second languages. Total annual research expenditures: $360,000. *Application contact:* Thomas Hudson, Graduate Chair, 808-956-2799, Fax: 808-956-2802, E-mail: tdh@hawaii.edu.

University of Houston, College of Education, Department of Curriculum and Instruction, Houston, TX 77204. Offers art education (M Ed); bilingual education (M Ed); curriculum and instruction (M Ed, Ed D); early childhood education (M Ed); elementary education (M Ed); gifted and talented education (M Ed); instructional technology (M Ed); mathematics education (M Ed); reading and language arts education (M Ed); science education (M Ed); second language education (M Ed); secondary education (M Ed); social studies education (M Ed); teaching (M Ed). *Accreditation:* NCATE. Part-time and evening/weekend programs available. *Faculty:* 20 full-time (9 women), 22 part-time/adjunct (17 women). *Students:* 113 full-time (81 women), 195 part-time (150 women); includes 107 minority (43 African Americans, 29 Asian Americans or Pacific Islanders, 35 Hispanic Americans), 29 international. Average age 35. 150 applicants, 77% accepted, 55 enrolled. In 2009, 75 master's, 31 doctorates awarded. *Degree requirements:* For master's, comprehensive exam, thesis optional; for doctorate, comprehensive exam, thesis/dissertation. *Entrance requirements:* For master's and doctorate, GRE, minimum cumulative undergraduate GPA of 2.6. Additional exam requirements/recommendations for international students: Required—TOEFL (minimum score 550 paper-based; 79 iBT). *Application deadline:* For fall admission, 3/1 for domestic and international students; for spring admission, 10/1 for domestic and international students. Application fee: $45 ($75 for international students). Electronic applications accepted. *Expenses:* Tuition, state resident: full-time $7676; part-time $320 per credit hour. Tuition, nonresident: full-time $14,324; part-time $597 per credit hour. Required fees: $3034. *Financial support:* In 2009–10, 4 fellowships with full tuition reimbursements (averaging $9,500 per year), 6 research assistantships with full tuition reimbursements (averaging $8,800 per year), 25 teaching assistantships with full tuition reimbursements (averaging $8,800 per year) were awarded; career-related internships or fieldwork, Federal Work-Study, institutionally sponsored loans, scholarships/grants, health care benefits, and unspecified assistantships also available. Support available to part-time students. Financial award application deadline: 2/1. *Faculty research:* Teaching-learning process, instructional technology in schools, teacher education, classroom management, at-risk students. *Unit head:* Dr. Laveria Hutchison, Chairperson, 713-743-4958, Fax: 713-743-4990, E-mail: lhutchison@uh.edu. *Application contact:* Renee C. Rattelade, Executive Secretary, 713-743-4997, Fax: 713-743-4990, E-mail: rrattelade@mail.coe.uh.edu.

University of Idaho, College of Graduate Studies, College of Letters, Arts and Social Sciences, Department of English, Program in Teaching English as a Second Language, Moscow, ID 83844-2282. Offers MA. *Students:* 12 full-time, 4 part-time. In 2009, 7 master's awarded. *Entrance requirements:* For master's, minimum GPA of 2.8. *Application deadline:* For fall admission, 8/1 for domestic students; for spring admission, 12/15 for domestic students. Application fee: $55 ($60 for international students). *Expenses:* Tuition, state resident: full-time $6120. Tuition, nonresident: full-time $17,712. *Financial support:* Application deadline: 2/15. *Unit head:* Dr. Gary Williams, Chair, 208-883-6156. *Application contact:* Dr. Gary Williams, Chair, 208-883-6156.

University of Illinois at Chicago, Graduate College, College of Liberal Arts and Sciences, Department of English, Program in Linguistics, Chicago, IL 60607-7128. Offers teaching English to speakers of other languages/applied linguistics (MA). Part-time programs available. *Degree requirements:* For master's, one foreign language, comprehensive exam, thesis (for some programs). *Entrance requirements:* For master's, minimum GPA of 3.0. Additional exam requirements/recommendations for international students: Required—TOEFL. Electronic applications accepted. *Faculty research:* Second language acquisition, methodology of second language teaching, lexicography, language, sex and gender.

University of Illinois at Urbana–Champaign, Graduate College, College of Liberal Arts and Sciences, School of Literatures, Cultures and Linguistics, Department of Linguistics, Champaign, IL 61820. Offers linguistics (MA, PhD); teaching of English as a second language (MA). *Faculty:* 16 full-time (5 women). *Students:* 65 full-time (40 women), 45 part-time (36 women); includes 9 minority (1 African American, 6 Asian Americans or Pacific Islanders, 2 Hispanic Americans), 64 international. 219 applicants, 22% accepted, 35 enrolled. In 2009, 32 master's, 7 doctorates awarded. *Entrance requirements:* For master's, GRE, minimum GPA of 3.0; writing sample; for doctorate, GRE, minimum GPA of 3.5; writing sample. Additional exam requirements/recommendations for international students: Required—TOEFL (minimum score 88 iBT). *Application deadline:* Applications are processed on a rolling basis. Application fee: $60 ($75 for international students). Electronic applications accepted. *Financial support:* In 2009–10, 17 fellowships, 22 research assistantships, 74 teaching assistantships were awarded; tuition waivers (full and partial) also available. *Unit head:* Hye Suk James Yoon, Acting Head, 217-244-3055, E-mail: jyoon@illinois.edu. *Application contact:* Lynn Stanke, Office Support Specialist, 217-333-6269, Fax: 217-244-3050, E-mail: stanke@illinois.edu.

University of Manitoba, Faculty of Graduate Studies, Faculty of Education, Department of Curriculum, Teaching and Learning, Winnipeg, MB R3T 2N2, Canada. Offers language and literacy (M Ed); second language education (M Ed); studies in curriculum, teaching and learning (M Ed). *Degree requirements:* For master's, thesis or alternative.

University of Maryland, Baltimore County, Graduate School, College of Arts, Humanities and Social Sciences, Department of Education, Program in Teaching English to Speakers of Other Languages, Baltimore, MD 21250. Offers MA, Postbaccalaureate Certificate. Part-time and evening/weekend programs available. Postbaccalaureate distance learning degree programs offered (no on-campus study). *Faculty:* 4 full-time (3 women), 12 part-time/adjunct (8 women). *Students:* 19 full-time (all women), 132 part-time (121 women); includes 11 minority (2 African Americans, 3 Asian Americans or Pacific Islanders, 6 Hispanic Americans), 16 international.

Average age 36. 56 applicants, 77% accepted, 37 enrolled. In 2009, 18 master's awarded. *Degree requirements:* For master's, comprehensive exam, thesis optional, internship (for certification). *Entrance requirements:* For master's, GRE (minimum score 500 verbal), 3 letters of reference. Additional exam requirements/recommendations for international students: Required—TOEFL (minimum score 550 paper-based; 213 computer-based; 80 iBT). *Application deadline:* For fall admission, 4/15 priority date for domestic students, 3/1 priority date for international students; for spring admission, 11/30 priority date for domestic students, 10/31 priority date for international students. Application fee: $50. Electronic applications accepted. *Financial support:* In 2009–10, 6 students received support, including research assistantships with full tuition reimbursements available (averaging $12,000 per year); career-related internships or fieldwork, Federal Work-Study, scholarships/grants, and unspecified assistantships also available. Financial award application deadline: 3/1. *Faculty research:* Adult education, bilingual language learning, online instruction, English grammar, cross-culture communication. *Unit head:* Dr. John Nelson, Director, 410-455-2379, E-mail: jnelson@umbc.edu. *Application contact:* Bridget Wessel, Graduate Assistant, 410-455-3061, E-mail: esol@umbc.edu.

University of Maryland, College Park, Academic Affairs, College of Education, Department of Curriculum and Instruction, College Park, MD 20742. Offers reading (M Ed, MA, PhD, CAGS); secondary education (M Ed, MA, Ed D, PhD, CAGS); teaching English to speakers of other languages (M Ed). *Accreditation:* NCATE. Part-time and evening/weekend programs available. Postbaccalaureate distance learning degree programs offered (no on-campus study). *Faculty:* 57 full-time (36 women), 35 part-time/adjunct (30 women). *Students:* 280 full-time (216 women), 181 part-time (150 women); includes 117 minority (60 African Americans, 2 American Indian/Alaska Native, 33 Asian Americans or Pacific Islanders, 22 Hispanic Americans), 51 international. 300 applicants, 40% accepted, 85 enrolled. In 2009, 143 master's, 20 doctorates awarded. *Degree requirements:* For master's, comprehensive exam, seminar paper; for doctorate, comprehensive exam, thesis/dissertation, published paper, oral exam. *Entrance requirements:* For master's, GRE General Test or MAT, minimum GPA of 3.0, 3 letters of recommendation; for doctorate, GRE General Test or MAT, minimum undergraduate GPA of 3.0, graduate 3.5; 3 letters of recommendation. *Application deadline:* For fall admission, 1/20 priority date for domestic students, 1/20 for international students; for spring admission, 9/1 priority date for domestic students, 6/1 for international students. Applications are processed on a rolling basis. Application fee: $60. Electronic applications accepted. *Expenses:* Tuition, area resident: Part-time $471 per credit hour. Tuition, state resident: part-time $471 per credit hour. Tuition, nonresident: part-time $1016 per credit hour. Required fees: $337.04 per term. *Financial support:* In 2009–10, 19 research assistantships with tuition reimbursements (averaging $18,124 per year), 76 teaching assistantships with tuition reimbursements (averaging $17,105 per year) were awarded; fellowships, Federal Work-Study and scholarships/grants also available. Support available to part-time students. Financial award applicants required to submit FAFSA. *Faculty research:* Teacher preparation, curriculum study, inservice education. Total annual research expenditures: $3.9 million. *Unit head:* Dr. Linda M. Valli, Interim Chair, 301-405-3117, E-mail: lrv@umd.edu. *Application contact:* Dean of Graduate School, 301-405-0358.

University of Massachusetts Amherst, Graduate School, School of Education, Program in Education, Amherst, MA 01003. Offers bilingual, English as a second language, and multicultural education (M Ed, CAGS); child study and early education (M Ed); children, families and schools (Ed D, CAGS); early childhood and elementary teacher education (M Ed); education policy and leadership (CAGS); educational administration (M Ed, CAGS); educational policy and leadership (Ed D); higher education (M Ed, CAGS); international education (M Ed); language, literacy and culture (Ed D); learning, media and technology (M Ed, CAGS); mathematics, science, and learning technologies (Ed D); policy studies (M Ed); policy studies in education (CAGS); reading and writing (M Ed); research and evaluation methods (Ed D); school counselor education (M Ed, CAGS); school psychology (CAGS); science education (CAGS); secondary teacher education (M Ed); social justice education (M Ed, Ed D, CAGS); special education (M Ed, Ed D, CAGS). *Accreditation:* NCATE. Part-time programs available. Postbaccalaureate distance learning degree programs offered (minimal on-campus study). *Faculty:* 74 full-time (41 women). *Students:* 377 full-time (268 women), 347 part-time (232 women); includes 115 minority (59 African Americans, 2 American Indian/Alaska Native, 16 Asian Americans or Pacific Islanders, 38 Hispanic Americans), 108 international. Average age 35. 708 applicants, 68% accepted, 266 enrolled. In 2009, 183 master's, 17 doctorates awarded. Terminal master's awarded for partial completion of doctoral program. *Degree requirements:* For master's, thesis or alternative; for doctorate, comprehensive exam, thesis/dissertation. *Entrance requirements:* Additional exam requirements/recommendations for international students: Required—TOEFL (minimum score 550 paper-based; 213 computer-based; 80 iBT), IELTS (minimum score 6.5). *Application deadline:* For fall admission, 1/15 for domestic and international students. Applications are processed on a rolling basis. Application fee: $50 ($65 for international students). Electronic applications accepted. *Expenses:* Tuition, state resident: full-time $2640; part-time $110 per credit. Tuition, nonresident: full-time $9936; part-time $414 per credit. Tuition and fees vary according to course load. *Financial support:* In 2009–10, 1 fellowship with full tuition reimbursement (averaging $8,036 per year), 92 research assistantships with full tuition reimbursements (averaging $8,555 per year), 83 teaching assistantships with full tuition reimbursements (averaging $4,661 per year) were awarded; career-related internships or fieldwork, Federal Work-Study, scholarships/grants, traineeships, health care benefits, tuition waivers (full), and unspecified assistantships also available. Support available to part-time students. Financial award application deadline: 1/15. *Unit head:* Dr. Linda L. Griffin, Graduate Program Director, 413-545-6984, Fax: 413-545-2873. *Application contact:* Jean M. Ames, Supervisor of Admissions, 413-545-0722, Fax: 413-577-0010, E-mail: gradadm@grad.umass.edu.

University of Massachusetts Boston, Office of Graduate Studies, College of Liberal Arts, Program in Applied Linguistics, Boston, MA 02125-3393. Offers bilingual education (MA); English as a second language (MA); foreign language pedagogy (MA). Part-time and evening/weekend programs available. *Degree requirements:* For master's, one foreign language, comprehensive exam. *Entrance requirements:* For master's, minimum GPA of 2.75. *Faculty research:* Multicultural theory and curriculum development, foreign language pedagogy, language and culture, applied psycholinguistics, bilingual education.

University of Memphis, Graduate School, College of Arts and Sciences, Department of English, Memphis, TN 38152. Offers African-American literature (Graduate Certificate); applied linguistics (PhD); composition studies (PhD); creative writing (MFA); English as a second language (MA); linguistics (MA); literary and cultural studies (PhD), including African-American literature; literature (MA); professional writing (MA, PhD); teaching English as a second language (Graduate Certificate). Part-time and evening/weekend programs available. Postbaccalaureate distance learning degree programs offered (no on-campus study). *Faculty:* 31 full-time (15 women), 2 part-time/adjunct (both women). *Students:* 98 full-time (59 women), 99 part-time (66 women); includes 36 minority (28 African Americans, 5 Asian Americans or Pacific Islanders, 3 Hispanic Americans), 7 international. Average age 34. 128 applicants, 71% accepted, 29 enrolled. In 2009, 38 master's, 4 doctorates, 21 other advanced degrees awarded. Terminal master's awarded for partial completion of doctoral program. *Degree requirements:* For master's, one foreign language, comprehensive exam, thesis optional; for doctorate, 2 foreign languages, comprehensive exam, thesis/dissertation. *Entrance requirements:* For master's and doctorate, GRE. Additional exam requirements/recommendations for international students: Required—TOEFL. *Application deadline:* For fall admission, 7/1 for domestic students; for spring admission, 10/15 for domestic students. Applications are processed on a rolling basis. Application fee: $35 ($60 for international students). Electronic applications accepted. *Expenses:* Tuition, state resident: full-time $6246; part-time $347 per credit hour. Tuition, nonresident: full-time $15,894; part-time $883 per credit hour. Required fees: $1160. Full-time tuition and fees vary according to course load, degree level and program. *Financial support:* In 2009–10, 123 students received support; research assistantships with full tuition reimbursements available, teaching assistantships with full tuition reimbursements available, Federal Work-Study, scholarships/grants, and unspecified assistantships available. Financial award application deadline: 2/15; financial award applicants required to submit FAFSA. *Faculty research:* Applied linguistis, British and American literature, professional writing, composition

English as a Second Language

University of Memphis (continued)

studies. *Unit head:* Dr. Eric C. Link, Chair, 901-678-2651, Fax: 901-678-2226, E-mail: eclink@memphis.edu. *Application contact:* Dr. Verner D. Mitchell, Director, Graduate Studies, 901-678-3099, Fax: 901-678-2226, E-mail: vdmtchll@memphis.edu.

University of Michigan, Horace H. Rackham School of Graduate Studies, School of Education, Programs in Educational Studies, Ann Arbor, MI 48109. Offers cross specialization (PhD); curriculum development (MA); early childhood education (MA, PhD); educational administration and policy (MA, PhD); educational foundations and policy (MA, PhD); English education (MA); English language learning in school settings (MA); learning technologies (MA, PhD); literacy, language, and culture (MA, PhD); mathematics education (MA, PhD); postsecondary science education (MS); research methods (MA); science education (MA, PhD); social studies education (MA); teaching and teacher education (PhD); MA/Certification; MBA/MA; PhD/MA. Terminal master's awarded for partial completion of doctoral program. *Degree requirements:* For master's, thesis (for some programs); for doctorate, comprehensive exam, thesis/dissertation. *Entrance requirements:* For master's and doctorate, GRE General Test. Additional exam requirements/recommendations for international students: Required—TOEFL (minimum score 600 paper-based; 250 computer-based). *Application deadline:* For fall admission, 12/1 priority date for domestic students, 12/1 for international students. Application fee: $60 ($75 for international students). Electronic applications accepted. *Expenses:* Tuition, state resident: full-time $17,286; part-time $1099 per credit hour. Tuition, nonresident: full-time $34,944; part-time $2080 per credit hour. Required fees: $95 per semester. Tuition and fees vary according to course load, degree level and program. *Financial support:* Applicants required to submit FAFSA. *Unit head:* Dr. Addison Stone, Chairperson, 734-763-7500, Fax: 734-615-1290, E-mail: addison@umich.edu. *Application contact:* Laura Mayers, Student Services Assistant, 734-764-7563, Fax: 734-763-1495, E-mail: ed.grad.admit@umich.edu.

University of Minnesota, Twin Cities Campus, Graduate School, College of Education and Human Development, Department of Curriculum and Instruction, Program in Teaching, Minneapolis, MN 55455-0213. Offers Chinese (M Ed); earth science (M Ed); elementary special education (M Ed); English (M Ed); English as a second language (M Ed); French (M Ed); German (M Ed); Hebrew (M Ed); Japanese (M Ed); life sciences (M Ed); mathematics (M Ed); middle school science (M Ed); science (M Ed); second languages and cultures (M Ed); social studies (M Ed); Spanish (M Ed). *Students:* 263 full-time (186 women), 117 part-time (83 women); includes 32 minority (10 African Americans, 2 American Indian/Alaska Native, 17 Asian Americans or Pacific Islanders, 3 Hispanic Americans), 4 international. Average age 27. 363 applicants, 74% accepted, 259 enrolled. In 2009, 497 master's awarded. *Unit head:* Dr. Ruth Thomas, Chair, 612-624-4772, Fax: 612-624-8277, E-mail: thoma006@umn.edu. *Application contact:* Dr. Mary Trettin, Associate Dean, 612-625-6501, Fax: 612-626-1580, E-mail: mtrettin@umn.edu.

University of Minnesota, Twin Cities Campus, Graduate School, College of Liberal Arts, Institute of Linguistics, English as a Second Language, and Slavic Languages and Literatures (ILES), English as a Second Language Program, Minneapolis, MN 55455-0213. Offers MA. *Degree requirements:* For master's, one foreign language, comprehensive exam, thesis. *Entrance requirements:* For master's, GRE, 3 letters of recommendation. Additional exam requirements/recommendations for international students: Required—TOEFL (minimum score 600 paper-based; 250 computer-based). Electronic applications accepted. *Faculty research:* Second language acquisitions, communication strategies, English for specific purposes, literacy, speech act, proymatics in general, language assessment, discourse analysis, research methods.

University of Missouri–St. Louis, College of Education, Division of Teaching and Learning, St. Louis, MO 63121. Offers elementary education (M Ed), including early childhood, general, reading; secondary education (M Ed), including curriculum and instruction, general, middle level education, reading, teaching English to speakers of other languages (TESOL); secondary school teaching (Certificate); special education (M Ed), including behavioral disorders, early childhood special education, general, learning disabilities, mental retardation; teaching English to speakers of other languages (Certificate). Part-time and evening/weekend programs available. *Faculty:* 36 full-time (23 women), 51 part-time/adjunct (42 women). *Students:* 123 full-time (77 women), 569 part-time (435 women); includes 137 minority (110 African Americans, 4 American Indian/Alaska Native, 10 Asian Americans or Pacific Islanders, 13 Hispanic Americans), 11 international. Average age 32. In 2009, 1,852 master's awarded. *Degree requirements:* For master's, comprehensive exam. *Entrance requirements:* Additional exam requirements/recommendations for international students: Recommended—TOEFL (minimum score 550 paper-based; 213 computer-based). *Application deadline:* For fall admission, 7/1 priority date for domestic and international students; for spring admission, 12/1 priority date for domestic and international students. Application fee: $35 ($40 for international students). Electronic applications accepted. *Expenses:* Tuition, state resident: full-time $5377; part-time $297.70 per credit hour. Tuition, nonresident: full-time $13,882; part-time $771.20 per credit hour. Required fees: $220; $12.20 per credit hour. One-time fee: $12. Tuition and fees vary according to course level, campus/location and program. *Financial support:* In 2009–10, 5 research assistantships (averaging $10,339 per year), 2 teaching assistantships (averaging $6,800 per year) were awarded. Financial award application deadline: 4/1; financial award applicants required to submit FAFSA. *Unit head:* Dr. Joseph Polman, Chair, 314-516-5791. *Application contact:* 314-516-5458, Fax: 314-516-6996, E-mail: gadadm@umsl.edu.

University of Nebraska at Omaha, Graduate Studies, College of Arts and Sciences, Department of English, Omaha, NE 68182. Offers advanced writing (Certificate); English (MA); teaching English to speakers of other languages (Certificate); technical communication (Certificate). Part-time and evening/weekend programs available. *Faculty:* 20 full-time (10 women). *Students:* 11 full-time (4 women), 59 part-time (43 women); includes 2 minority (1 African American, 1 Asian American or Pacific Islander), 3 international. Average age 32. 40 applicants, 68% accepted, 17 enrolled. In 2009, 13 master's, 8 other advanced degrees awarded. *Degree requirements:* For master's, comprehensive exam, thesis (for some programs). *Entrance requirements:* For master's, minimum GPA of 3.0, 3 letters of recommendation, writing sample. Additional exam requirements/recommendations for international students: Required—TOEFL (minimum score 600 paper-based; 250 computer-based; 100 iBT). *Application deadline:* For fall admission, 8/1 priority date for domestic students; for spring admission, 12/1 priority date for domestic students. Applications are processed on a rolling basis. Application fee: $45. Electronic applications accepted. *Financial support:* In 2009–10, 34 students received support; fellowships, teaching assistantships with tuition reimbursements available, Federal Work-Study, institutionally sponsored loans, scholarships/grants, tuition waivers (partial), and unspecified assistantships available. Support available to part-time students. Financial award application deadline: 3/1; financial award applicants required to submit FAFSA. *Unit head:* Dr. Susan Maher, Chairperson, 402-554-3636. *Application contact:* Dr. Joan Latchaw, Student Contact, 402-554-3636.

University of Nevada, Reno, Graduate School, College of Education, Department of Educational Specialties, Program in Teaching English to Speakers of Other Languages, Reno, NV 89557. Offers MA. Terminal master's awarded for partial completion of doctoral program. *Degree requirements:* For master's, thesis optional. *Entrance requirements:* For master's, minimum GPA of 2.75. Additional exam requirements/recommendations for international students: Required—TOEFL (minimum score 500 paper-based; 173 computer-based; 61 iBT), IELTS (minimum score 6). Electronic applications accepted. *Faculty research:* Bilingualism, multicultural education.

The University of North Carolina at Chapel Hill, Graduate School, School of Education, Program in Secondary Education, Chapel Hill, NC 27599. Offers English (Grades 9-12) (MAT); English as a second language (MAT); French (Grades K-12) (MAT); German (Grades K-12) (MAT); Japanese (Grades K-12) (MAT); Latin (Grades 9-12) (MAT); mathematics (Grades 9-12) (MAT); music (Grades K-12) (MAT); science (Grades 9-12) (MAT); social studies (Grades 9-12) (MAT); Spanish (Grades K-12) (MAT). *Accreditation:* NCATE. *Students:* 53 full-time (35 women), 1 part-time (0 women); includes 8 minority (4 African Americans, 2 Asian Americans or Pacific Islanders, 2 Hispanic Americans), 3 international. Average age 25. 137 applicants, 77% accepted, 54 enrolled. In 2009, 39 master's awarded. *Degree requirements:* For master's, comprehensive exam. *Entrance requirements:* For master's, GRE General Test, minimum GPA of 3.0 during last 2 years of undergraduate course work. Additional exam requirements/recommendations for international students: Required—TOEFL (minimum score 550 paper-based; 79 computer-based). *Application deadline:* For fall admission, 12/15 priority date for domestic and international students. Applications are processed on a rolling basis. Application fee: $77. Electronic applications accepted. *Financial support:* Federal Work-Study available. Support available to part-time students. Financial award application deadline: 3/1; financial award applicants required to submit FAFSA. *Unit head:* Dr. James Trier, Coordinator, 919-843-4627, Fax: 919-962-1533. *Application contact:* Amy Butler, Student Services Assistant, 919-966-1346, Fax: 919-962-1533, E-mail: abutler@email.unc.edu.

The University of North Carolina at Charlotte, Graduate School, College of Education, Program in Teacher Education, Charlotte, NC 28223-0001. Offers art education (K-12) (MAT); dance education (K-12) (MAT); elementary education (K-6) (MAT); English as a second language (K-12) (MAT); foreign language education (K-12) (MAT); general teacher education (MAT); middle grades education (6-9) (MAT); music education (K-12) (MAT); secondary education (9-12) (MAT); special education (K-12) (MAT); theatre education (K-12) (MAT). *Faculty:* 108 full-time (64 women), 16 part-time/adjunct (12 women). *Students:* 29 full-time (20 women), 229 part-time (189 women); includes 32 minority (22 African Americans, 2 American Indian/Alaska Native, 3 Asian Americans or Pacific Islanders, 5 Hispanic Americans). Average age 32. 108 applicants, 92% accepted, 85 enrolled. In 2009, 59 master's awarded. *Entrance requirements:* For master's, GRE or MAT. Additional exam requirements/recommendations for international students: Required—TOEFL (minimum score 557 paper-based; 220 computer-based; 83 iBT). *Application deadline:* For fall admission, 7/1 for domestic students, 5/1 for international students; for spring admission, 11/1 for domestic students, 10/1 for international students. Applications are processed on a rolling basis. Application fee: $55. Electronic applications accepted. *Financial support:* In 2009–10, 5 students received support, including 1 research assistantship (averaging $18,000 per year), 3 teaching assistantships (averaging $12,183 per year); career-related internships or fieldwork, Federal Work-Study, institutionally sponsored loans, scholarships/grants, and administrative assistantship also available. Support available to part-time students. Financial award application deadline: 4/1; financial award applicants required to submit FAFSA. Total annual research expenditures: $5.1 million. *Unit head:* Dr. Kimberly J. Hartman, Coordinator, 704-687-8883, Fax: 704-687-6430, E-mail: khartman@uncc.edu. *Application contact:* Kathy B. Giddings, Director of Graduate Admissions, 704-687-5503, Fax: 704-687-3279, E-mail: gradadmn@uncc.edu.

The University of North Carolina at Greensboro, Graduate School, School of Education, Department of Curriculum and Instruction, Greensboro, NC 27412-5001. Offers college teaching and adult learning (Certificate); curriculum and instruction (M Ed), including chemistry education, elementary education, English as a second language, French education, instructional technology, mathematics education, middle grades education, reading education, science education, social studies education, Spanish education; curriculum and teaching (PhD), including higher education, teacher education and development; English as a second language (Certificate); higher education (M Ed); supervision (M Ed). *Accreditation:* NCATE. Part-time programs available. *Degree requirements:* For doctorate, thesis/dissertation. *Entrance requirements:* For master's and doctorate, GRE General Test. Additional exam requirements/recommendations for international students: Required—TOEFL. Electronic applications accepted. *Faculty research:* Community college literacy program, middle school mathematics/computer mathematics.

University of Northern Iowa, Graduate College, College of Humanities and Fine Arts, Department of English Language and Literature, Cedar Falls, IA 50614. Offers English (MA); teaching English to speakers of other languages (MA). Part-time and evening/weekend programs available. *Students:* 34 full-time (24 women), 33 part-time (27 women); includes 4 minority (2 African Americans, 1 Asian American or Pacific Islander, 1 Hispanic American), 8 international. 45 applicants, 64% accepted, 16 enrolled. In 2009, 29 master's awarded. *Degree requirements:* For master's, one foreign language, comprehensive exam, thesis or alternative, portfolio. *Entrance requirements:* For master's, minimum GPA of 3.0. Additional exam requirements/recommendations for international students: Required—TOEFL (minimum score 600 paper-based; 250 computer-based; 100 iBT). *Application deadline:* For fall admission, 8/1 priority date for domestic students. Applications are processed on a rolling basis. Application fee: $30 ($50 for international students). Electronic applications accepted. *Financial support:* Career-related internships or fieldwork, Federal Work-Study, scholarships/grants, and tuition waivers (full and partial) available. Support available to part-time students. Financial award application deadline: 2/1. *Unit head:* Dr. Jeffrey S. Copeland, Head, 319-273-3855, Fax: 319-273-5807, E-mail: jeffrey.copeland@uni.edu. *Application contact:* Laurie S. Russell, Record Analyst, 319-273-2623, Fax: 319-273-6792, E-mail: laurie.russell@uni.edu.

University of Northern Iowa, Graduate College, College of Humanities and Fine Arts, Department of Modern Languages, Program in French, Cedar Falls, IA 50614. Offers French (MA); teaching English to speakers of other languages/French (MA). Part-time and evening/weekend programs available. *Students:* 3 full-time (2 women), 3 part-time (2 women); includes 1 minority (Hispanic American), 2 international. 3 applicants, 67% accepted, 1 enrolled. In 2009, 5 master's awarded. *Degree requirements:* For master's, one foreign language, comprehensive exam, thesis or alternative. *Entrance requirements:* For master's, minimum GPA of 3.0, valid teaching license, documentation of successful teaching experience. Additional exam requirements/recommendations for international students: Required—TOEFL (minimum score 600 paper-based; 250 computer-based; 100 iBT). *Application deadline:* For fall admission, 8/1 priority date for domestic students. Applications are processed on a rolling basis. Application fee: $30 ($50 for international students). Electronic applications accepted. *Financial support:* Career-related internships or fieldwork, Federal Work-Study, and tuition waivers (full and partial) available. Support available to part-time students. Financial award application deadline: 2/1. *Unit head:* Dr. Anne Lair, Coordinator, 319-273-2183, Fax: 319-273-2848, E-mail: anne.lair@uni.edu. *Application contact:* Laurie S. Russell, Record Analyst, 319-273-2623, Fax: 319-273-6792, E-mail: laurie.russell@uni.edu.

University of Northern Iowa, Graduate College, College of Humanities and Fine Arts, Department of Modern Languages, Program in German, Cedar Falls, IA 50614. Offers German (MA); teaching English to speakers of other languages/German (MA). Part-time and evening/weekend programs available. *Students:* 4 full-time (all women), 1 part-time (0 women), 2 international. 3 applicants, 67% accepted, 2 enrolled. In 2009, 4 master's awarded. *Degree requirements:* For master's, one foreign language, comprehensive exam, thesis or alternative. *Entrance requirements:* For master's, minimum GPA of 3.0, valid teaching license, documentation of successful teaching experience. Additional exam requirements/recommendations for international students: Required—TOEFL (minimum score 600 paper-based; 250 computer-based; 100 iBT). *Application deadline:* For fall admission, 8/1 priority date for domestic students. Applications are processed on a rolling basis. Application fee: $30 ($50 for international students). *Financial support:* Career-related internships or fieldwork, Federal Work-Study, and tuition waivers (full and partial) available. Support available to part-time students. Financial award application deadline: 2/1. *Unit head:* Dr. Samuel L. Gladden, Interim Department Head/Professor, 319-273-5437, Fax: 319-273-2848, E-mail: samuel.gladden@uni.edu. *Application contact:* Laurie S. Russell, Record Analyst, 319-273-2623, Fax: 319-273-6792, E-mail: laurie.russell@uni.edu.

University of Northern Iowa, Graduate College, College of Humanities and Fine Arts, Department of Modern Languages, Program in Spanish, Cedar Falls, IA 50614. Offers Spanish (MA); teaching English to speakers of other languages/Spanish (MA). Part-time and evening/weekend programs available. *Students:* 6 full-time (4 women), 11 part-time (9 women); includes 2 minority (both Hispanic Americans), 3 international. 8 applicants, 63% accepted, 1 enrolled. In 2009, 10 master's awarded. *Degree requirements:* For master's, one foreign language, comprehensive exam, thesis or alternative. *Entrance requirements:* For master's, minimum GPA of 3.0, valid teaching license, documentation of successful teaching experience. Additional exam requirements/recommendations for international students: Required—TOEFL (minimum score 600 paper-based; 250 computer-based; 100 iBT). *Application deadline:* For fall admission,

8/1 priority date for domestic students. Applications are processed on a rolling basis. Application fee: $30 ($50 for international students). Electronic applications accepted. *Financial support:* Career-related internships or fieldwork, Federal Work-Study, and tuition waivers (full and partial) available. Support available to part-time students. Financial award application deadline: 2/1. *Unit head:* Dr. Samuel L. Gladden, Interim Department Head/Associate Professor, 319-273-5437, Fax: 319-273-2848, E-mail: samuel.gladden@uni.edu. *Application contact:* Laurie S. Russell, Record Analyst, 319-273-2623, Fax: 319-273-6792, E-mail: laurie.russell@uni.edu.

University of North Florida, College of Education and Human Services, Department of Childhood Education, Jacksonville, FL 32224. Offers literacy K-12 (M Ed); professional education—elementary ed (M Ed); TESOL K-12 (M Ed). *Accreditation:* NCATE. Part-time and evening/weekend programs available. *Faculty:* 11 full-time (8 women). *Students:* 11 full-time (all women), 22 part-time (21 women); includes 7 minority (4 African Americans, 1 Asian American or Pacific Islander, 2 Hispanic Americans). Average age 30. 17 applicants, 35% accepted, 3 enrolled. In 2009, 23 master's awarded. *Entrance requirements:* For master's, GRE General Test, minimum GPA of 3.0 in last 60 hours, 3 letters of recommendation, interview. Additional exam requirements/recommendations for international students: Required—TOEFL (minimum score 500 paper-based; 173 computer-based). *Application deadline:* For fall admission, 7/1 priority date for domestic students, 5/1 for international students; for spring admission, 11/1 priority date for domestic students, 10/1 for international students. Applications are processed on a rolling basis. Application fee: $30. Electronic applications accepted. *Expenses:* Tuition, state resident: full-time $6649.20; part-time $277.05 per credit hour. Tuition, nonresident: full-time $22,970; part-time $957.08 per credit hour. Required fees: $985; $41.03 per credit hour. *Financial support:* In 2009–10, 12 students received support. Federal Work-Study and tuition waivers (partial) available. Support available to part-time students. Financial award application deadline: 4/1; financial award applicants required to submit FAFSA. *Faculty research:* The social context of and processes in learning, inter-disciplinary instruction, cross-cultural conflict resolution, the Vygotskian perspective on literacy diagnosis and instruction, performance poetry and teaching the language arts through drama. Total annual research expenditures: $256,831. *Unit head:* Dr. Ronghua Ouyang, Chair, 904-620-2611, Fax: 904-620-1025, E-mail: ronghua.ouyang@unf.edu. *Application contact:* Dr. John Kemppainen, Director, Office of Student Services, 904-620-2530, Fax: 904-620-1135, E-mail: jkemppai@unf.edu.

University of Pennsylvania, Graduate School of Education, Division of Language in Education, Programs in Teaching English to Speakers of Other Languages and Intercultural Communication, Philadelphia, PA 19104. Offers educational linguistics (PhD); intercultural communication (MS Ed); teaching English to speakers of other languages (MS Ed). Part-time programs available. Postbaccalaureate distance learning degree programs offered (minimal on-campus study). *Students:* 82 full-time (71 women), 23 part-time (17 women); includes 3 minority (2 African Americans, 1 Asian American or Pacific Islander), 82 international. 117 applicants, 82% accepted, 61 enrolled. In 2009, 51 master's awarded. Terminal master's awarded for partial completion of doctoral program. *Degree requirements:* For master's, comprehensive exam, thesis (for some programs); for doctorate, one foreign language, thesis/dissertation, preliminary exam. *Entrance requirements:* For master's and doctorate, GRE General Test or MAT. Additional exam requirements/recommendations for international students: Required—TOEFL. *Application deadline:* For fall admission, 12/15 priority date for domestic students. Applications are processed on a rolling basis. Application fee: $70. Electronic applications accepted. *Expenses:* Contact institution. *Financial support:* Fellowships, research assistantships, institutionally sponsored loans, scholarships/grants, traineeships, health care benefits, and unspecified assistantships available. *Faculty research:* Second language acquisition, social linguistics, English as a second language.

University of Phoenix, College of Natural Sciences, College of Education, Phoenix, AZ 85034-7209. Offers administration and supervision (MAEd); adult education and training (MAEd); curriculum and instruction (MAEd); curriculum and instruction-adult education (MAEd); curriculum and instruction-computer education (MAEd); curriculum and instruction-English and language arts education (MAEd); curriculum and instruction-English as a second language (MAEd); curriculum and instruction-mathematics education (MAEd); curriculum education (MAEd); early childhood (MAEd); elementary teacher education (MAEd); secondary teacher education (MAEd); special education (MAEd); teacher leadership (MAEd). *Accreditation:* Teacher Education Accreditation Council. Evening/weekend programs available. Postbaccalaureate distance learning degree programs offered (no on-campus study). *Faculty:* 47 full-time (34 women), 844 part-time/adjunct (636 women). *Students:* 13,657 full-time (10,698 women); includes 4,000 minority (3,063 African Americans, 74 American Indian/Alaska Native, 241 Asian Americans or Pacific Islanders, 622 Hispanic Americans), 307 international. Average age 36. In 2009, 17,246 master's awarded. *Degree requirements:* For master's, thesis (for some programs). *Entrance requirements:* For master's, 3 years of work experience, minimum GPA of 2.5. Additional exam requirements/recommendations for international students: Required—TOEFL (minimum score 550 paper-based; 213 computer-based; 79 iBT). *Application deadline:* Applications are processed on a rolling basis. Application fee: $45. Electronic applications accepted. *Expenses:* Tuition: Full-time $13,272. Required fees: $660. Full-time tuition and fees vary according to course level, degree level and program. *Financial support:* Institutionally sponsored loans and scholarships/grants available. Financial award applicants required to submit FAFSA. *Unit head:* Dr. Meredith Curley, Dean/Executive Director, 480-557-1217, Fax: 480-557-1588, E-mail: meredith.curley@phoenix.edu. *Application contact:* Chair, 602-387-7000, Fax: 602-387-6020.

University of Phoenix–Omaha Campus, College of Education, Omaha, NE 68154-5240. Offers administration and supervision (MA Ed); curriculum and instruction (MA Ed), including adult education, computer education, curriculum and instruction, English and language arts education, English as a second language, mathematics education; elementary teacher education (MA Ed); secondary teacher education (MA Ed); special education (MA Ed).

University of Phoenix–San Diego Campus, The Artemis School, College of Education, San Diego, CA 92123. Offers curriculum and instruction (MA Ed), including computer education, curriculum and instruction, English as a second language; elementary teacher education (MA Ed); secondary teacher education (MA Ed). Evening/weekend programs available. *Degree requirements:* For master's, thesis (for some programs). *Entrance requirements:* For master's, 3 years of work experience, minimum undergraduate GPA of 3.0. Additional exam requirements/recommendations for international students: Required—TOEFL (minimum score 550 paper-based; 213 computer-based; 79 iBT). Electronic applications accepted.

University of Phoenix–Southern California Campus, College of Education, Costa Mesa, CA 92626. Offers administration and supervision (MA Ed); adult education and training (MA Ed); curriculum and instruction (MA Ed), including computer education, curriculum and instruction, English and language arts, English as a second language, mathematics education; early childhood education (MA Ed); special education (MA Ed); teacher leadership (MA Ed). Evening/weekend programs available. *Faculty:* 47 full-time (34 women), 844 part-time/adjunct (636 women). *Students:* 558 full-time (391 women); includes 222 minority (60 African Americans, 4 American Indian/Alaska Native, 26 Asian Americans or Pacific Islanders, 132 Hispanic Americans), 9 international. Average age 34. In 2009, 303 master's awarded. *Degree requirements:* For master's, thesis (for some programs). *Entrance requirements:* For master's, minimum undergraduate GPA of 2.5, 3 years work experience. Additional exam requirements/recommendations for international students: Required—TOEFL (minimum score 550 paper-based; 213 computer-based; 79 iBT). *Application deadline:* Applications are processed on a rolling basis. Application fee: $45. Electronic applications accepted. *Expenses:* Tuition: Full-time $15,120. Required fees: $660. *Financial support:* Institutionally sponsored loans and scholarships/grants available. Financial award applicants required to submit FAFSA. *Unit head:* Dr. Meredith Curley, Dean/Executive Director, 480-557-1217, Fax: 480-557-1588, E-mail: meredith.curley@phoenix.edu. *Application contact:* Campus College Chair, 714-378-1878, Fax: 714-378-5875.

University of Phoenix–Springfield Campus, College of Education, Springfield, MO 65804-7211. Offers administration and supervision (MA Ed); curriculum and instruction (MA Ed), including computer education, curriculum and instruction, English and language arts education, English as a second language, mathematics education; English and language arts education (MA Ed).

University of Pittsburgh, School of Arts and Sciences, TESOL—Teaching English to Speakers of Other Languages Certificate Program, Pittsburgh, PA 15260. Offers Certificate. Part-time programs available. *Faculty:* 10 full-time (4 women). *Students:* 9 full-time (7 women), 6 part-time (all women); includes 2 minority (1 African American, 1 Asian American or Pacific Islander), 4 international. Average age 28. 3 applicants, 100% accepted, 3 enrolled. In 2009, 6 Certificates awarded. *Entrance requirements:* Additional exam requirements/recommendations for international students: Required—TOEFL (minimum score 600 paper-based; 250 computer-based; 100 iBT). *Application deadline:* For winter admission, 11/15 for domestic and international students; for spring admission, 3/15 for domestic and international students. Applications are processed on a rolling basis. Application fee: $50. *Expenses:* Tuition, state resident: full-time $16,402; part-time $665 per credit. Tuition, nonresident: full-time $28,694; part-time $1175 per credit. Required fees: $690; $175 per term. Tuition and fees vary according to program. *Faculty research:* Language contact, second language acquisition, applied linguistics, sociolinguistics. *Unit head:* Dr. Alan Juffs, Chair, 412-624-5900, Fax: 412-624-6130, E-mail: juffs@pitt.edu. *Application contact:* Patricia C. Cochran, Graduate Secretary, 412-624-5900, Fax: 412-624-6130, E-mail: lingpitt@pitt.edu.

University of Puerto Rico, Río Piedras, College of Education, Program in Teaching English as a Second Language, San Juan, PR 00931-3300. Offers M Ed. Part-time programs available. *Degree requirements:* For master's, thesis. *Entrance requirements:* For master's, PAEG or GRE, minimum GPA of 3.0, letter of recommendation. *Faculty research:* Second language acquisition, bilingual education.

University of San Diego, School of Leadership and Education Sciences, Department of Learning and Teaching, San Diego, CA 92110-2492. Offers curriculum and instruction (M Ed); mathematics, science and technology education (M Ed); special education (M Ed); special education with deaf and hard of hearing (M Ed); teaching (MAT); TESOL, literacy and culture (M Ed). Part-time and evening/weekend programs available. *Faculty:* 13 full-time (9 women), 24 part-time/adjunct (21 women). *Students:* 77 full-time (63 women), 92 part-time (74 women); includes 46 minority (13 African Americans, 12 Asian Americans or Pacific Islanders, 21 Hispanic Americans), 6 international. Average age 31. 142 applicants, 75% accepted, 59 enrolled. In 2009, 64 master's awarded. *Degree requirements:* For master's, thesis (for some programs). *Entrance requirements:* For master's, minimum GPA of 3.0. Additional exam requirements/recommendations for international students: Required—TOEFL (minimum score 580 paper-based; 237 computer-based; 83 iBT), TWE. *Application deadline:* For fall admission, 7/15 for domestic and international students; for spring admission, 12/1 for domestic and international students. Applications are processed on a rolling basis. Application fee: $45. Electronic applications accepted. *Expenses:* Tuition: Full-time $21,042; part-time $1169 per unit. Required fees: $224. Full-time tuition and fees vary according to course load and degree level. *Financial support:* In 2009–10, 113 students received support. Career-related internships or fieldwork, Federal Work-Study, institutionally sponsored loans, and stipends available. Support available to part-time students. Financial award application deadline: 4/1; financial award applicants required to submit FAFSA. *Faculty research:* Action research methodology, cultural studies, instructional theories and practices, second language acquisition, school reform. *Unit head:* Dr. Judy Mantle, Director, 619-260-7879, Fax: 619-260-6835, E-mail: jmantle@sandiego.edu. *Application contact:* Dr. John Mosby, Associate Director of Graduate Admissions, 619-260-4524, Fax: 619-260-4158, E-mail: grads@sandiego.edu.

University of San Francisco, School of Education, Department of International and Multicultural Education, San Francisco, CA 94117-1080. Offers international and multicultural education (MA, Ed D); multicultural literature for children and young adults (MA); teaching English as a second language (MA). *Faculty:* 2 full-time (both women), 6 part-time/adjunct (3 women). *Students:* 31 full-time (12 women), 54 part-time (42 women). Average age 36. 191 applicants, 69% accepted, 48 enrolled. In 2009, 32 master's, 10 doctorates awarded. *Degree requirements:* For doctorate, thesis/dissertation. Application fee: $55 ($65 for international students). *Expenses:* Tuition: Full-time $19,710; part-time $1095 per unit. Part-time tuition and fees vary according to degree level, campus/location and program. *Financial support:* In 2009–10, 56 students received support; fellowships, research assistantships, teaching assistantships available. Financial award application deadline: 3/2; financial award applicants required to submit FAFSA. *Unit head:* Dr. Katz Susan, Chair, 415-422-6878. *Application contact:* Beth Teague, Associate Director of Graduate Outreach, 415-422-5467, E-mail: schoolofeducation@usfca.edu.

The University of Scranton, College of Graduate and Continuing Education, Department of Education, Program in English as a Second Language, Scranton, PA 18510. Offers MS. Part-time and evening/weekend programs available. *Students:* 2 full-time (both women), 1 international. Average age 29. 1 applicant, 100% accepted. In 2009, 1 master's awarded. *Degree requirements:* For master's, comprehensive exam, capstone experience. *Entrance requirements:* For master's, minimum GPA of 2.75. Additional exam requirements/recommendations for international students: Required—TOEFL (minimum score 500 paper-based; 173 computer-based), IELTS (minimum score 5.5). *Application deadline:* Applications are processed on a rolling basis. Application fee: $0. *Financial support:* Application deadline: 3/1. *Unit head:* Dr. Art Chambers, Director, 570-941-4668, Fax: 570-941-5515, E-mail: chambersa2@scranton.edu. *Application contact:* Joseph M. Roback, Director of Admissions, 570-941-4385, Fax: 570-941-5928, E-mail: robackj2@scranton.edu.

University of South Africa, College of Human Sciences, Pretoria, South Africa. Offers adult education (M Ed); African languages (MA, PhD); African politics (MA, PhD); Afrikaans (MA, PhD); ancient history (MA, PhD); ancient Near Eastern studies (MA, PhD); anthropology (MA, PhD); applied linguistics (MA); Arabic (MA, PhD); archaeology (MA); art history (MA); Biblical archaeology (MA); Biblical studies (M Th, D Th, PhD); Christian spirituality (M Th, D Th); church history (M Th, D Th); classical studies (MA, PhD); clinical psychology (MA); communication (MA, PhD); comparative education (M Ed, Ed D); consulting psychology (D Admin, D Com, PhD); curriculum studies (M Ed, Ed D); development studies (M Admin, MA, D Admin, PhD); didactics (M Ed, Ed D); education (M Tech); education management (M Ed, Ed D); educational psychology (M Ed); English (MA); environmental education (M Ed); French (MA, PhD); German (MA, PhD); Greek (MA); guidance and counseling (M Ed); health studies (MA, PhD), including health sciences education (MA), health services management (MA), medical and surgical nursing science (critical care general) (MA), midwifery and neonatal nursing science (MA), trauma and emergency care (MA); history (MA, PhD); history of education (Ed D); inclusive education (M Ed, Ed D); information and communications technology policy and regulation (MA); information science (MA, MIS, PhD); international politics (MA, PhD); Islamic studies (MA, PhD); Italian (MA, PhD); Judaica (MA, PhD); linguistics (MA, PhD); mathematical education (M Ed); mathematics education (MA); missiology (M Th, D Th); modern Hebrew (MA, PhD); musicology (MA, MMus, D Mus, PhD); natural science education (M Ed); New Testament (M Th, D Th); Old Testament (D Th); pastoral therapy (M Th, D Th); philosophy (MA); philosophy of education (M Ed, Ed D); politics (MA, PhD); Portuguese (MA, PhD); practical theology (M Th, D Th); psychology (MA, MS, PhD); psychology of education (M Ed, Ed D); public health (MA); religious studies (MA, D Th, PhD); Romance languages (MA); Russian (MA, PhD); Semitic languages (MA, PhD); social behavior studies in HIV/AIDS (MA); social science (mental health) (MA); social science in development studies (MA); social science in psychology (MA); social science in social work (MA); social science in sociology (MA); social work (MSW, DSW, PhD); socio-education (M Ed, Ed D); sociolinguistics (MA); sociology (MA, PhD); Spanish (MA, PhD); systematic theology (M Th, D Th); TESOL (teaching English to speakers of other languages) (MA); theological ethics (M Th, D Th); theory of literature (MA, PhD); urban ministries (D Th); urban ministry (M Th).

University of South Carolina, The Graduate School, College of Arts and Sciences, Linguistics Program, Columbia, SC 29208. Offers linguistics (MA, PhD); teaching English to speakers of other languages (Certificate). Part-time programs available. Terminal master's awarded for

English as a Second Language

University of South Carolina *(continued)*

partial completion of doctoral program. *Degree requirements:* For master's, one foreign language, comprehensive exam, thesis optional; for doctorate, 3 foreign languages, comprehensive exam, thesis/dissertation. *Entrance requirements:* For master's and Certificate, GRE General Test, minimum GPA of 3.0; for doctorate, GRE General Test, minimum GPA of 3.5. Additional exam requirements/recommendations for international students: Required—TOEFL. Electronic applications accepted. *Faculty research:* Second language acquisition, sociolinguistics, syntax, historical linguistics and phonology.

University of Southern California, Graduate School, Rossier School of Education, Master's Programs in Education, Los Angeles, CA 90089-4038. Offers marriage, family and child counseling (MMFT); postsecondary administration and student affairs [PASA] (ME); school counseling (ME); teaching (MA); teaching and teaching credential (MAT); teaching English to speakers of other languages (MAT, MS). Part-time and evening/weekend programs available. Postbaccalaureate distance learning degree programs offered (no on-campus study). *Faculty:* 26 full-time (17 women), 24 part-time/adjunct (14 women). *Students:* 579 full-time (455 women), 85 part-time (56 women); includes 302 minority (50 African Americans, 4 American Indian/Alaska Native, 110 Asian Americans or Pacific Islanders, 138 Hispanic Americans), 62 international. 1,282 applicants, 67% accepted, 484 enrolled. In 2009, 228 master's awarded. *Degree requirements:* For master's, thesis optional. *Entrance requirements:* For master's, GRE (for all programs except MAT). Additional exam requirements/recommendations for international students: Required—TOEFL (minimum score 250 computer-based; 100 iBT). Application fee: $85. Electronic applications accepted. *Expenses:* Tuition: Full-time $25,980; part-time $1315 per unit. Required fees: $554. One-time fee: $35 full-time. Full-time tuition and fees vary according to degree level and program. *Financial support:* Career-related internships or fieldwork, Federal Work-Study, scholarships/grants, traineeships, and unspecified assistantships available. Support available to part-time students. Financial award application deadline: 4/10; financial award applicants required to submit FAFSA. *Faculty research:* College access and equity; preparing teachers for culturally diverse populations; sociocultural basis of learning as mediated by instruction with focus on reading and literacy in English learners; social and political aspects of teaching and learning English; school counselor development and training. *Unit head:* Dr. Kristan Venegas, Director/Assistant Professor of Clinical Education, 213-740-3255, E-mail: rsoemast@usc.edu. *Application contact:* Michael Jackson, 213-740-0224, E-mail: soeinfo@usc.edu.

University of Southern Maine, College of Education and Human Development, Program in Literacy Education, Portland, ME 04104-9300. Offers applied literacy (MS Ed); early language and literacy (Certificate); English as a second language (MS Ed, CAS); literacy education (MS Ed, CAS, Certificate). *Accreditation:* Teacher Education Accreditation Council. Part-time and evening/weekend programs available. *Faculty:* 2 full-time (both women), 6 part-time/adjunct (4 women). *Students:* 9 full-time (8 women), 41 part-time (37 women); includes 1 minority (Hispanic American). 19 applicants, 89% accepted, 14 enrolled. In 2009, 33 master's, 8 CASs awarded. *Degree requirements:* For master's, comprehensive exam, thesis or alternative; for other advanced degree, thesis or alternative. *Entrance requirements:* For master's, teacher certification; for other advanced degree, master's degree. Additional exam requirements/recommendations for international students: Required—TOEFL (minimum score 550 paper-based; 213 computer-based; 79 iBT). *Application deadline:* For fall admission, 5/1 priority date for domestic students; for spring admission, 10/15 priority date for domestic students. Applications are processed on a rolling basis. Application fee: $50. Electronic applications accepted. *Financial support:* In 2009–10, 3 students received support, including research assistantships with tuition reimbursements available (averaging $4,500 per year); career-related internships or fieldwork, Federal Work-Study, institutionally sponsored loans, scholarships/grants, and unspecified assistantships also available. Support available to part-time students. Financial award application deadline: 3/1; financial award applicants required to submit FAFSA. *Unit head:* Dr. James Curry, Chair, Professional Education Department, 207-780-5400, Fax: 207-780-8277, E-mail: jcurry@usm.maine.edu. *Application contact:* Mary Sloan, Director of Graduate Admissions, 207-780-4386, Fax: 207-780-4969, E-mail: msloan@usm.maine.edu.

University of South Florida, Graduate School, College of Arts and Sciences, World Languages Department, Tampa, FL 33620-9951. Offers classics: Latin/Greek (MA); French (MA); linguistics (MA); linguistics: ESL (MA); Spanish (MA). Part-time and evening/weekend programs available. *Faculty:* 19 full-time (14 women), 1 part-time/adjunct (0 women). *Students:* 36 full-time (26 women), 22 part-time (16 women); includes 23 minority (5 African Americans, 3 American Indian/Alaska Native, 2 Asian Americans or Pacific Islanders, 13 Hispanic Americans), 12 international. Average age 32. 29 applicants, 52% accepted, 12 enrolled. In 2009, 18 master's awarded. *Degree requirements:* For master's, comprehensive exam, thesis. *Entrance requirements:* For master's, GRE General Test, minimum GPA of 3.0 in last 60 hours. Additional exam requirements/recommendations for international students: Required—TOEFL (minimum score 600 paper-based; 250 computer-based). *Application deadline:* For fall admission, 2/15 for domestic students, 1/2 for international students; for spring admission, 10/15 for domestic students, 6/1 for international students. Application fee: $30. Electronic applications accepted. *Financial support:* In 2009–10, teaching assistantships with tuition reimbursements (averaging $17,024 per year); tuition waivers (partial) and unspecified assistantships also available. Financial award application deadline: 6/30. *Faculty research:* Second language writing, academic literacy. Total annual research expenditures: $19,891. *Unit head:* Dr. Victor Peppard, Chairperson, 813-974-2012, Fax: 813-974-1718, E-mail: peppard@cas.usf.edu. *Application contact:* Dr. Victor Peppard, Chairperson, 813-974-2012, Fax: 813-974-1718, E-mail: peppard@cas.usf.edu.

University of South Florida, Graduate School, College of Education–Main Campus, Department of Secondary Education, Tampa, FL 33620-9951. Offers English education (M Ed, MA, MAT, PhD); foreign language education/ESOL (M Ed, MA, MAT); instructional technology (M Ed, PhD, Ed S); mathematics education (M Ed, MA, MAT, PhD, Ed S); science education (M Ed, MA, MAT, PhD); second language acquisition/instructional technology (PhD); secondary education (M Ed, PhD); secondary education/TESOL (M Ed); social science education (M Ed, MA, MAT); teaching and learning in the content area (PhD). *Accreditation:* NCATE. Part-time and evening/weekend programs available. *Faculty:* 28 full-time (17 women), 3 part-time/adjunct (1 woman). *Students:* 144 full-time (97 women), 322 part-time (212 women); includes 100 minority (32 African Americans, 4 American Indian/Alaska Native, 17 Asian Americans or Pacific Islanders, 47 Hispanic Americans), 25 international. Average age 30. 230 applicants, 67% accepted, 122 enrolled. In 2009, 122 master's, 14 doctorates, 1 other advanced degree awarded. *Degree requirements:* For master's, variable foreign language requirement, comprehensive exam; for doctorate, variable foreign language requirement, comprehensive exam, thesis/dissertation. *Entrance requirements:* For master's, GRE General Test or General Knowledge Test, minimum GPA of 3.0; for doctorate, GRE General Test, minimum GPA of 3.5; for Ed S, GRE General Test. Additional exam requirements/recommendations for international students: Required—TOEFL (minimum score 550 paper-based; 213 computer-based; 79 iBT). *Application deadline:* For fall admission, 2/15 for domestic students, 1/2 for international students; for spring admission, 10/15 for domestic students, 6/1 for international students. Application fee: $30. Electronic applications accepted. *Financial support:* In 2009–10, 7 students received support, including 1 research assistantship with full tuition reimbursement available (averaging $10,000 per year), 55 teaching assistantships with full and partial tuition reimbursements available (averaging $7,900 per year); scholarships/grants and unspecified assistantships also available. Financial award application deadline: 4/15; financial award applicants required to submit FAFSA. *Faculty research:* English language learners/multicultural, social science education, mathematics education, science education, instructional technology. Total annual research expenditures: $336,023. *Unit head:* Dr. Stephen Thornton, Chairperson, 813-974-3533, Fax: 813-974-3837, E-mail: thornton@usf.edu. *Application contact:* Dr. James White, Program Director, 813-974-1629, Fax: 813-974-3837, E-mail: jwhite@usf.edu.

The University of Tennessee, Graduate School, College of Education, Health and Human Sciences, Program in Education, Knoxville, TN 37996. Offers art education (MS); counseling education (PhD); cultural studies in education (PhD); curriculum (MS, Ed S); curriculum,

educational research and evaluation (Ed D, PhD); early childhood education (PhD); early childhood special education (MS); education of deaf and hard of hearing (MS); educational administration and policy studies (Ed D, PhD); educational administration and supervision (Ed S); educational psychology (Ed D, PhD); elementary education (MS, Ed S); elementary teaching (MS); English education (MS, Ed S); exercise science (PhD); foreign language/ESL education (MS, Ed S); instructional technology (MS, Ed D, PhD, Ed S); literacy, language and ESL education (PhD); literacy, language education, and ESL education (Ed D); mathematics education (MS, Ed S); modified and comprehensive special education (MS); reading education (MS, Ed S); school counseling (Ed S); school psychology (PhD, Ed S); science education (MS, Ed S); secondary teaching (MS); social foundations (MS); social science education (MS, Ed S); socio-cultural foundations of sports and education (PhD); special education (Ed S); teacher education (Ed D, PhD). *Accreditation:* NCATE. Part-time and evening/weekend programs available. *Degree requirements:* For master's and Ed S, thesis optional; for doctorate, variable foreign language requirement, thesis/dissertation. *Entrance requirements:* For master's, minimum GPA of 2.7; for doctorate and Ed S, GRE General Test, minimum GPA of 2.7. Additional exam requirements/recommendations for international students: Required—TOEFL. Electronic applications accepted. *Expenses:* Tuition, state resident: full-time $6826; part-time $380 per semester hour. Tuition, nonresident: full-time $21,844; part-time $1147 per semester hour. Tuition and fees vary according to program.

The University of Texas at Arlington, Graduate School, College of Liberal Arts, Department of Linguistics and TESOL, Program in Teaching English to Speakers of Other Languages, Arlington, TX 76019. Offers MA. *Accreditation:* NCATE. Part-time and evening/weekend programs available. *Students:* 2 full-time (both women), 6 part-time (3 women); includes 3 minority (2 Asian Americans or Pacific Islanders, 1 Hispanic American), 1 international. 4 applicants, 100% accepted, 0 enrolled. In 2009, 14 master's awarded. *Degree requirements:* For master's, comprehensive exam (for some programs), thesis optional. *Entrance requirements:* For master's, GRE General Test, minimum undergraduate GPA of 3.0, 6 credits of undergraduate foundation courses, the equivalent of 2 years of university level foreign language study. Additional exam requirements/recommendations for international students: Required—TOEFL (minimum score 550 paper-based; 213 computer-based). Application fee: $35 ($50 for international students). *Financial support:* In 2009–10, 3 fellowships (averaging $1,000 per year), 1 teaching assistantship were awarded. *Unit head:* Dr. Jerrold Edmonson, Chair, 817-272-3133, Fax: 817-272-2731, E-mail: jerry@uta.edu. *Application contact:* Dr. Laurel Stvan, Graduate Advisor, 817-272-3133, Fax: 817-272-2731.

The University of Texas at Brownsville, Graduate Studies, School of Education, Brownsville, TX 78520-4991. Offers bilingual education (M Ed); counseling and guidance (M Ed); curriculum and instruction (M Ed); early childhood education (M Ed); educational administration (M Ed); educational technology (M Ed); English as a second language (M Ed); reading specialist (M Ed); special education/educational diagnostician (M Ed). Part-time and evening/weekend programs available. Postbaccalaureate distance learning degree programs offered (minimal on-campus study). *Degree requirements:* For master's, thesis optional. *Entrance requirements:* For master's, GRE General Test. Additional exam requirements/recommendations for international students: Required—TOEFL.

The University of Texas at El Paso, Graduate School, College of Liberal Arts, Department of Languages and Linguistics, El Paso, TX 79968-0001. Offers linguistics (MA); Spanish (MA); teaching English to speakers of other languages (Certificate). Part-time and evening/weekend programs available. *Students:* 28 (12 women); includes 15 minority (all Hispanic Americans), 4 international. Average age 34. In 2009, 10 master's awarded. *Degree requirements:* For master's, thesis optional. *Entrance requirements:* For master's, GRE General Test, departmental exam, minimum GPA of 3.0, letters of recommendation. Additional exam requirements/recommendations for international students: Required—TOEFL; Recommended—IELTS. *Application deadline:* For fall admission, 8/1 for domestic students, 3/1 for international students; for spring admission, 11/1 for domestic students, 9/1 for international students. Applications are processed on a rolling basis. Application fee: $45 ($80 for international students). Electronic applications accepted. *Financial support:* In 2009–10, research assistantships with partial tuition reimbursements (averaging $18,625 per year), teaching assistantships with partial tuition reimbursements (averaging $14,900 per year) were awarded; fellowships with partial tuition reimbursements, institutionally sponsored loans, scholarships/grants, health care benefits, tuition waivers (partial), and unspecified assistantships also available. Support available to part-time students. Financial award application deadline: 3/15; financial award applicants required to submit FAFSA. *Unit head:* Dr. Kirsten F. Nigro, Chair, 915-747-5767, Fax: 915-747-5292, E-mail: kfnigro@utep.edu. *Application contact:* Dr. Patricia D. Witherspoon, Dean of the Graduate School, 915-747-5491, Fax: 915-747-5788, E-mail: withersp@utep.edu.

The University of Texas at San Antonio, College of Education and Human Development, Division of Bicultural-Bilingual Studies, San Antonio, TX 78249-0617. Offers bicultural-bilingual studies (MA); culture, literacy, and language (PhD); teaching English as a second language (MA). Part-time and evening/weekend programs available. *Faculty:* 13 full-time (7 women). *Students:* 48 full-time (36 women), 94 part-time (75 women); includes 108 minority (5 African Americans, 8 Asian Americans or Pacific Islanders, 95 Hispanic Americans), 10 international. Average age 35. 76 applicants, 89% accepted, 36 enrolled. In 2009, 27 master's, 3 doctorates awarded. *Degree requirements:* For master's, comprehensive exam (for some programs), thesis (for some programs); for doctorate, comprehensive exam, thesis/dissertation. *Entrance requirements:* For master's and doctorate, GRE General Test. Additional exam requirements/recommendations for international students: Required—TOEFL (minimum score 500 paper-based; 173 computer-based; 61 iBT), IELTS (minimum score 5). *Application deadline:* For fall admission, 7/1 for domestic students, 4/1 for international students; for spring admission, 11/1 for domestic students, 9/1 for international students. Applications are processed on a rolling basis. Application fee: $45 ($80 for international students). Electronic applications accepted. *Expenses:* Tuition, state resident: full-time $3975; part-time $221 per contact hour. Tuition, nonresident: full-time $13,947; part-time $775 per contact hour. Required fees: $1853. *Financial support:* In 2009–10, 24 students received support, including 2 research assistantships (averaging $11,660 per year), 9 teaching assistantships (averaging $8,439 per year); fellowships, career-related internships or fieldwork and tuition waivers also available. Support available to part-time students. *Faculty research:* Globalization, migration and immigrant education, integrating language and content in PK-12 instruction, language and cultural policies in multilingual societies, multiple literacies. *Unit head:* Dr. Robert D. Milk, Director, 210-458-4426, Fax: 210-458-5962, E-mail: rmilk@utsa.edu. *Application contact:* Dr. Dorothy A. Flannagan, Dean of the Graduate School, 210-458-4330, Fax: 210-458-4332, E-mail: dorothy.flannagan@utsa.edu.

The University of Texas of the Permian Basin, Office of Graduate Studies, School of Education, Program in Bilingual/English as a second language Education, Odessa, TX 79762-0001. Offers MA. *Degree requirements:* For master's, comprehensive exam (for some programs), thesis (for some programs). *Entrance requirements:* For master's, GRE General Test. Additional exam requirements/recommendations for international students: Required—TOEFL (minimum score 550 paper-based; 213 computer-based).

The University of Texas–Pan American, College of Arts and Humanities, Department of English, Program in English as a Second Language, Edinburg, TX 78539. Offers MA. Part-time and evening/weekend programs available. *Degree requirements:* For master's, comprehensive exam, thesis optional. *Entrance requirements:* For master's, GRE General Test, minimum GPA of 3.0. *Expenses:* Tuition, state resident: full-time $3630.60; part-time $201.70 per credit hour. Tuition, nonresident: full-time $8617; part-time $478.70 per credit hour. Required fees: $806.50. *Faculty research:* Oral versus literary culture discourse analysis, language shift among Hispanics.

University of the Southwest, Graduate Programs, Hobbs, NM 88240-9129. Offers business administration (MBA); curriculum and instruction (MSE); curriculum and instruction: bilingual (MSE); curriculum and instruction: reading (MSE); curriculum and instruction: TESOL (MSE); early childhood education (MSE); educational diagnostician (MSE); mental health counseling (MSE); school business administration (MSE); school counseling (MSE); special education

(MSE). Part-time and evening/weekend programs available. Postbaccalaureate distance learning degree programs offered (no on-campus study). *Faculty:* 10 full-time (6 women), 10 part-time/adjunct (4 women). *Students:* 112 full-time (93 women), 99 part-time (72 women). Average age 35. 94 applicants, 47% accepted, 39 enrolled. In 2009, 32 master's awarded. *Degree requirements:* For master's, comprehensive exam. *Application deadline:* For fall admission, 3/1 priority date for domestic students; for spring admission, 10/1 for domestic students. Applications are processed on a rolling basis. Application fee: $25. Electronic applications accepted. *Expenses:* Tuition: Part-time $512 per hour. Tuition and fees vary according to course load. *Financial support:* In 2009–10, 196 students received support; research assistantships with partial tuition reimbursements available, Federal Work-Study, scholarships/grants, and tuition waivers (partial) available. Support available to part-time students. Financial award application deadline: 4/1; financial award applicants required to submit FAFSA. *Unit head:* Dr. Mary Harris, Dean of Education, 575-392-6561 Ext. 1056, Fax: 575-392-6006, E-mail: mharris@usw.edu. *Application contact:* Ryanne Evans, Assistant Registrar, 575-392-6561 Ext. 1031, Fax: 575-392-6006, E-mail: revans@usw.edu.

The University of Toledo, College of Graduate Studies, College of Arts and Sciences, Department of English Language and Literature, Toledo, OH 43606-3390. Offers English as a second language (MA); literature (MA); teaching of writing (Certificate). Part-time programs available. *Degree requirements:* For master's, one foreign language. *Entrance requirements:* For master's, minimum GPA of 2.7. Electronic applications accepted. *Faculty research:* Literary criticism, linguistics, creative writing, folklore and cultural studies.

The University of Toledo, College of Graduate Studies, College of Education, Department of Curriculum and Instruction, Program in English as a Second Language, Toledo, OH 43606-3390. Offers MAE.

University of Washington, Graduate School, College of Arts and Sciences, Department of English, Seattle, WA 98195. Offers creative writing (MFA); English as a second language (MAT); English literature and language (MA, MAT, PhD). Part-time programs available. Terminal master's awarded for partial completion of doctoral program. *Degree requirements:* For master's, one foreign language, thesis (for some programs); for doctorate, one foreign language, thesis/dissertation. *Entrance requirements:* For master's, GRE General Test, GRE Subject Test (MA and MAT in English), minimum GPA of 3.0; for doctorate, GRE General Test, GRE Subject Test. Additional exam requirements/recommendations for international students: Required—TOEFL. Electronic applications accepted. *Faculty research:* English and American literature, critical theory, creative writing, language theory.

University of West Florida, College of Professional Studies, Department of Professional and Community Leadership, Specialization in Middle and Secondary Level Education and ESOL, Pensacola, FL 32514-5750. Offers M Ed. *Accreditation:* NCATE. Part-time and evening/weekend programs available. *Students:* 10 part-time (all women). Average age 32. 1 applicant. In 2009, 30 master's awarded. *Degree requirements:* For master's, thesis or alternative. *Entrance requirements:* For master's, GRE (minimum score 450 verbal) or MAT (minimum score 396) if bachelor's GPA less than 3.0, state teaching certification; letter of intent; two professional references. Additional exam requirements/recommendations for international students: Required—TOEFL (minimum score 550 paper-based; 213 computer-based). *Application deadline:* For fall admission, 6/1 for domestic students, 5/15 for international students; for spring admission, 11/1 for domestic students, 10/1 for international students. Applications are processed on a rolling basis. Application fee: $30. *Expenses:* Tuition, state resident: full-time $4982; part-time $260 per credit hour. Tuition, nonresident: full-time $20,059; part-time $919 per credit hour. Required fees: $1247; $52 per credit hour. *Financial support:* Unspecified assistantships available. *Unit head:* Dr. David Stout, Chairperson, 850-474-2284, Fax: 850-474-2844. *Application contact:* Terry McCray, Assistant Director of Graduate Admissions, 850-473-7718, Fax: 850-473-7714, E-mail: gradadmissions@uwf.edu.

University of Wisconsin–River Falls, Outreach and Graduate Studies, College of Arts and Science, Program in Teaching English to Speakers of Other Languages, River Falls, WI 54022. Offers MA.

Valley City State University, School of Education and Graduate Studies, Valley City, ND 58072. Offers English language learners (ELL) (M Ed); library and information technologies (M Ed); teaching and technology (M Ed); technology education (M Ed). *Accreditation:* NCATE. Part-time and evening/weekend programs available. Postbaccalaureate distance learning degree programs offered (no on-campus study). *Faculty:* 19 full-time (13 women), 4 part-time/adjunct (3 women). *Students:* 7 full-time (4 women), 115 part-time (73 women); includes 4 minority (1 African American, 1 American Indian/Alaska Native, 1 Asian American or Pacific Islander, 1 Hispanic American). Average age 36. 33 applicants, 97% accepted, 22 enrolled. In 2009, 22 master's awarded. *Degree requirements:* For master's, action research report, comprehensive portfolio. *Entrance requirements:* For master's, GRE, MAT, PRAXIS II or National Teaching Board for Professional Standards (if GPAless than 3.0). Additional exam requirements/recommendations for international students: Required—TOEFL (minimum score 525 paper-based; 193 computer-based). *Application deadline:* For fall admission, 5/24 priority date for domestic and international students; for winter admission, 12/11 priority date for domestic and international students; for spring admission, 4/24 priority date for domestic and international students. Applications are processed on a rolling basis. Application fee: $35. Electronic applications accepted. *Expenses:* Tuition, state resident: full-time $4266; part-time $237.40 per credit hour. Tuition, nonresident: full-time $4266; part-time $237.40 per credit hour. Required fees: $237.40 per credit hour. One-time fee: $35. *Financial support:* In 2009–10, 30 students received support. Applicants required to submit FAFSA. *Faculty research:* Academically at-risk students in higher education, communication pedagogy and technology, gender communication, computer mediated communication, creativity in music. Total annual research expenditures: $26,000. *Unit head:* Dr. Gary Thompson, Dean, 701-845-7197, E-mail: gary.thompson@vcsu.edu. *Application contact:* Misty Lindgren, 701-845-7303, Fax: 701-845-7305, E-mail: misty.lindgren@vcsu.edu.

Valparaiso University, Graduate School, Program in English Studies and Communication, Valparaiso, IN 46383. Offers English studies and communication (MA); teaching of English to speakers of other languages (TESOL) (Certificate). Part-time and evening/weekend programs available. *Students:* 31 full-time (24 women), 10 part-time (8 women), 25 international. Average age 31. In 2009, 10 master's, 10 other advanced degrees awarded. *Entrance requirements:* For master's, minimum GPA of 3.0. Additional exam requirements/recommendations for international students: Required—TOEFL (minimum score 550 paper-based; 213 computer-based; 80 iBT). *Application deadline:* Applications are processed on a rolling basis. Application fee: $30 ($50 for international students). Electronic applications accepted. *Financial support:* Available to part-time students. Applicants required to submit FAFSA. *Unit head:* Dr. David L. Rowland, Dean, Graduate Studies and Continuing Education/ Associate Provost, 219-464-5313, Fax: 219-464-5381, E-mail: david.rowland@valpo.edu. *Application contact:* Jamie Haney, Coordinator of Graduate Admission, 219-464-5313, Fax: 219-464-5381, E-mail: jamie.haney@valpo.edu.

Virginia International University, English Language Programs Department, Fairfax, VA 22030. Offers teaching English to speakers of other languages (MA, Graduate Certificate). Part-time programs available. *Faculty:* 2 full-time (both women), 1 (woman) part-time/adjunct. *Students:* 4 full-time (3 women), 3 international. 23 applicants, 17% accepted, 3 enrolled. In 2009, 1 other advanced degree awarded. *Entrance requirements:* For master's and Graduate Certificate, bachelor's degree. Additional exam requirements/recommendations for international students: Required—TOEFL (minimum score 550 paper-based; 213 computer-based; 80 iBT), IELTS (minimum score 6). *Application deadline:* For fall admission, 7/31 for domestic students, 7/3 for international students; for spring admission, 12/18 for domestic students, 11/20 for international students. Applications are processed on a rolling basis. Application fee: $100. Electronic applications accepted. *Expenses:* Tuition: Full-time $10,044; part-time $569 per credit. One-time fee: $75. Tuition and fees vary according to degree level. *Financial support:* Scholarships/grants available. Financial award application deadline: 7/1. *Unit head:* Dr. Masha Vassilieva, Chair, 703-591-7042 Ext. 324, Fax: 703-591-7046, E-mail: masha@viu.edu. *Application contact:* Emily L. Kraus, Director of Admissions, 703-591-7042 Ext. 309, E-mail: admissions@viu.edu.

Wayne State College, School of Education and Counseling, Department of Educational Foundations and Leadership, Program in Curriculum and Instruction, Wayne, NE 68787. Offers alternative education (MSE); business and information technology education (MSE); communication arts education (MSE); early childhood education (MSE); elementary education (MSE); English as a second language (MSE); English education (MSE); family and consumer sciences education (MSE); industrial technology and vocational education (MSE); learning communities (MSE); mathematics education (MSE); music education (MSE); science education (MSE); social science education (MSE). *Accreditation:* NCATE. Part-time and evening/weekend programs available. *Degree requirements:* For master's, comprehensive exam, thesis optional. *Entrance requirements:* For master's, GRE General Test. Additional exam requirements/recommendations for international students: Required—TOEFL (minimum score 550 paper-based; 213 computer-based).

Webster University, School of Education, Department of Communication Arts, Reading and Early Childhood, St. Louis, MO 63119-3194. Offers communications (MAT); early childhood education (MAT). *Entrance requirements:* For master's, minimum GPA of 2.5. Additional exam requirements/recommendations for international students: Required—TOEFL. *Expenses:* Tuition: Part-time $565 per credit hour. Tuition and fees vary according to degree level, campus/location and program.

West Chester University of Pennsylvania, Office of Graduate Studies, College of Arts and Sciences, Department of English, West Chester, PA 19383. Offers English (MA, Teaching Certificate); TESL (MA, Certificate). Part-time and evening/weekend programs available. *Students:* 15 full-time (8 women), 104 part-time (75 women); includes 16 minority (6 African Americans, 10 Asian Americans or Pacific Islanders), 3 international. Average age 31. 91 applicants, 98% accepted, 54 enrolled. In 2009, 32 master's, 2 other advanced degrees awarded. *Degree requirements:* For master's, thesis optional. *Entrance requirements:* For master's, minimum GPA of 2.8, 3 letters of recommendation, writing sample, interview, 1 foreign language (TESL programs); for other advanced degree, goals statement; one foreign language (for TESL programs). Additional exam requirements/recommendations for international students: Required—TOEFL (minimum score 550 paper-based; 213 computer-based; 80 iBT). *Application deadline:* For fall admission, 4/15 priority date for domestic students, 3/15 for international students; for spring admission, 10/15 for domestic students, 9/1 for international students. Applications are processed on a rolling basis. Application fee: $35. Electronic applications accepted. *Expenses:* Tuition, state resident: full-time $6666; part-time $370 per credit. Tuition, nonresident: full-time $10,666; part-time $593 per credit. Required fees: $122.56 per credit. *Financial support:* In 2009–10, 12 research assistantships with full and partial tuition reimbursements (averaging $5,000 per year) were awarded; unspecified assistantships also available. Support available to part-time students. Financial award application deadline: 2/15; financial award applicants required to submit FAFSA. *Faculty research:* William Smith, Sara Winnemucca Hopkins, literacy practices for students at risk. *Unit head:* Dr. Anne Herzog, Chair, 610-436-2822, E-mail: aherzog@wcupa.edu. *Application contact:* Dr. Carolyn Sorisio, Graduate Coordinator, 610-436-2745, E-mail: kfitts@wcupa.edu.

Western Carolina University, Graduate School, College of Arts and Sciences, Department of English, Cullowhee, NC 28723. Offers English (MA); teaching English as a second language or foreign language (MA). Part-time and evening/weekend programs available. *Students:* 24 full-time (15 women), 14 part-time (12 women). Average age 30. 25 applicants, 88% accepted, 14 enrolled. In 2009, 7 master's awarded. *Degree requirements:* For master's, one foreign language, comprehensive exam, thesis (for some programs). *Entrance requirements:* For master's, GRE General Test, appropriate undergraduate degree, writing sample, 3 letters of recommendation. Additional exam requirements/recommendations for international students: Required—TOEFL (minimum score 550 paper-based; 270 computer-based; 79 iBT). *Application deadline:* For fall admission, 5/1 priority date for domestic students; for spring admission, 9/1 priority date for domestic students. Applications are processed on a rolling basis. Application fee: $45. *Financial support:* In 2009–10, 13 students received support, including 7 research assistantships with full and partial tuition reimbursements available (averaging $7,429 per year), 5 teaching assistantships with full and partial tuition reimbursements available (averaging $7,500 per year); fellowships with full and partial tuition reimbursements available, career-related internships or fieldwork, institutionally sponsored loans, scholarships/grants, and unspecified assistantships also available. Financial award application deadline: 3/31; financial award applicants required to submit FAFSA. *Faculty research:* TESOL, language assessment, applied linguistics, poetry, folk and fairy tales, post World War II British literature, Appalachian and southern literature. *Unit head:* Dr. Elizabeth Addison, Head, 828-227-7264, Fax: 828-227-7266, E-mail: addisson@email.wcu.edu. *Application contact:* Admission Specialist for Department of English, 828-227-7398, Fax: 828-227-7480, E-mail: gradsch@email.wcu.edu.

Western Connecticut State University, Division of Graduate Studies, School of Arts and Sciences, Department of English, Danbury, CT 06810-6885. Offers English (MA); literature option (MA); TESOL option (MA); writing option (MA). Part-time programs available. *Faculty:* 4 full-time (3 women), 1 part-time/adjunct (0 women). *Students:* 3 full-time (2 women), 33 part-time (24 women); includes 5 minority (2 African Americans, 3 Hispanic Americans). Average age 40. 15 applicants, 73% accepted, 7 enrolled. In 2009, 6 master's awarded. *Degree requirements:* For master's, thesis (writing option), completion of program in 6 years. *Entrance requirements:* For master's, minimum GPA of 2.5, writing sample. Additional exam requirements/recommendations for international students: Recommended—TOEFL (minimum score 550 paper-based; 213 computer-based; 79 iBT), IELTS (minimum score 6). *Application deadline:* For fall admission, 8/5 priority date for domestic students; for spring admission, 1/5 priority date for domestic students. Applications are processed on a rolling basis. Application fee: $50. *Expenses:* Tuition, state resident: full-time $5012; part-time $278 per credit hour. Tuition, nonresident: full-time $13,962; part-time $284 per credit hour. Required fees: $3886; $139 per credit hour. Full-time tuition and fees vary according to course load and program. Part-time tuition and fees vary according to course level, degree level and program. *Financial support:* Application deadline: 5/1. *Unit head:* Dr. Shouhua Qi, Co-Coordinator, 203-837-9048, Fax: 203-837-8525, E-mail: qis@wcsu.edu. *Application contact:* Chris Shankle, Associate Director of Graduate Studies, 203-837-9005, Fax: 203-837-8326, E-mail: shanklec@wcsu.edu.

Western Kentucky University, Graduate Studies, Potter College of Arts and Letters, Department of English, Bowling Green, KY 42101. Offers education (MA); English (MA Ed); literature (MA), including American literature, British literature, literary theory, women writers, world literature; teaching English as a second language (MA); writing (MA). Part-time and evening/weekend programs available. *Degree requirements:* For master's, comprehensive exam, thesis optional, final exam. *Entrance requirements:* For master's, GRE General Test, minimum GPA of 2.75. Additional exam requirements/recommendations for international students: Required—TOEFL (minimum score 555 paper-based; 213 computer-based; 79 iBT). *Expenses:* Tuition, state resident: full-time $4160; part-time $416 per credit hour. Tuition, nonresident: full-time $9550; part-time $506 per credit hour. Tuition and fees vary according to campus/location and reciprocity agreements. *Faculty research:* Improving writing, linking teacher knowledge and performance, Victorian women writers, Kentucky women writers, Kentucky poets.

Western New Mexico University, Graduate Division, School of Education, Silver City, NM 88062-0680. Offers bilingual education (MAT); counseling (MA); educational leadership (MA); elementary education (MAT); reading (MAT); school psychology (MA); secondary education (MAT); special education (MAT); TESOL (teaching English to speakers of other languages) (MAT). *Accreditation:* NCATE. *Degree requirements:* For master's, comprehensive exam. *Entrance requirements:* For master's, GRE General Test, GRE Subject Test, minimum GPA of 3.2 in last 64 hours of undergraduate study. Additional exam requirements/recommendations for international students: Required—TOEFL (minimum score 550 paper-based; 213 computer-based). Electronic applications accepted.

West Virginia University, Eberly College of Arts and Sciences, Department of Foreign Languages, Morgantown, WV 26506. Offers French (MA); linguistics (MA); Spanish (MA); teaching English to speakers of other languages (MA). Part-time programs available. *Degree*

English as a Second Language

West Virginia University (continued)
requirements: For master's, one foreign language, comprehensive exam (for some programs), thesis optional. *Entrance requirements:* For master's, minimum GPA of 3.0. Electronic applications accepted. *Faculty research:* French, German, and Spanish literature; foreign language pedagogy; English as a second language; cultural studies; linguistics.

Wheaton College, Graduate School, Department of Intercultural Studies, Wheaton, IL 60187-5593. Offers evangelism (MA); intercultural studies (MA); intercultural studies/teaching English as a second language (MA); missions (MA); teaching English as a second language (Certificate). Part-time programs available. *Degree requirements:* For master's, thesis or alternative. *Entrance requirements:* For master's, GRE General Test, MAT. Electronic applications accepted.

Wright State University, School of Graduate Studies, College of Liberal Arts, Department of English Language and Literatures, Dayton, OH 45435. Offers composition and rhetoric (MA); English (MA); literature (MA); teaching English to speakers of other languages (MA). *Degree requirements:* For master's, thesis optional, portfolio. *Entrance requirements:* For master's, 20 hours in upper-level English. Additional exam requirements/recommendations for international students: Required—TOEFL. *Faculty research:* American literature, world literature in English, applied linguistics, writing theory and pedagogy.

Multilingual and Multicultural Education

Alliant International University–Irvine, Graduate School of Education, Teacher Education Programs, Irvine, CA 92612. Offers auditory oral education (Certificate); CLAD (Certificate); preliminary multiple subject (Credential); preliminary multiple subject with BCLAD (Credential); preliminary single subject (Credential); professional clear multiple subject (Credential); professional clear single subject (Credential); teaching (MA, Credential); technology and learning (MA). Part-time and evening/weekend programs available. *Entrance requirements:* For degree, California Basic Educational Skills Test, minimum GPA of 2.5. Additional exam requirements/recommendations for international students: Required—TOEFL (minimum score 550 paper-based; 213 computer-based), TWE. Electronic applications accepted.

Alliant International University–San Francisco, Graduate School of Education, Teacher Education Programs, San Francisco, CA 94133-1221. Offers auditory oral education (Certificate); CLAD (Certificate); preliminary multiple subject (Credential); preliminary multiple subject with BCLAD (Credential); preliminary single subject (Credential); professional clear multiple subject (Credential); professional clear single subject (Credential); teaching (MA). Part-time and evening/weekend programs available. *Entrance requirements:* For degree, California Basic Educational Skills Test, minimum GPA of 2.5. Additional exam requirements/recommendations for international students: Required—TOEFL (minimum score 550 paper-based; 213 computer-based), TWE.

Azusa Pacific University, School of Education, Department of Advanced Studies, Program in Curriculum and Instruction in a Multicultural Setting, Azusa, CA 91702-7000. Offers MA. *Accreditation:* NCATE. Part-time and evening/weekend programs available. *Degree requirements:* For master's, core exams, oral presentation. *Entrance requirements:* For master's, 12 units of course work in education, minimum GPA of 3.0. *Faculty research:* Diversity in teacher education programs, teacher morale, student perception of school, case study instruction.

Azusa Pacific University, School of Education, Department of Education, Program in Language Development, Azusa, CA 91702-7000. Offers MA. *Accreditation:* NCATE. *Degree requirements:* For master's, comprehensive exam or thesis, core exams, oral presentation. *Entrance requirements:* For master's, 12 units of course work in education, minimum GPA of 3.0. *Faculty research:* Biliteracy development, home-school connections, integrated curriculum.

Bank Street College of Education, Graduate School, Program in Bilingual Education, New York, NY 10025. Offers bilingual childhood special education (Ed M); bilingual early childhood general education (MS Ed); bilingual early childhood special and general education (MS Ed); bilingual early childhood special education (Ed M, MS Ed); bilingual elementary/childhood general education (MS Ed); bilingual elementary/childhood special and general education (MS Ed); bilingual elementary/childhood special education (MS Ed); bilingual middle school general education (MS Ed); bilingual middle school special and general education (MS Ed); bilingual middle school special education (Ed M, MS Ed). *Students:* 19 full-time (15 women), 27 part-time (24 women); includes 29 minority (2 African Americans, 1 American Indian/Alaska Native, 26 Hispanic Americans), 2 international. Average age 29. 25 applicants, 68% accepted, 14 enrolled. In 2009, 7 master's awarded. *Degree requirements:* For master's, thesis. *Entrance requirements:* For master's, interview, fluency in Spanish and English. Additional exam requirements/recommendations for international students: Required—TOEFL (minimum score 600 paper-based; 250 computer-based; 100 iBT), IELTS (minimum score 7). *Application deadline:* For fall admission, 3/1 priority date for domestic students; for spring admission, 11/1 priority date for domestic students. Applications are processed on a rolling basis. Application fee: $65. *Expenses:* Tuition: Part-time $1120 per credit. *Financial support:* Career-related internships or fieldwork, Federal Work-Study, scholarships/grants, and unspecified assistantships available. Support available to part-time students. Financial award application deadline: 4/15; financial award applicants required to submit FAFSA. *Faculty research:* Dual language education, language immersion, bilingual education in the urban classroom, community and school partnerships. *Unit head:* Dr. Francisco Najera, Director, 212-875-4530, Fax: 212-875-4753, E-mail: fnajera@bankstreet.edu. *Application contact:* Director of Graduate Admissions.

Belhaven University, School of Education, Jackson, MS 39202-1789. Offers elementary education (M Ed, MAT); secondary education (M Ed, MAT). Part-time and evening/weekend programs available. *Faculty:* 4 full-time (all women), 19 part-time/adjunct (10 women). *Students:* 159 full-time (132 women), 51 part-time (42 women); includes 108 African Americans, 1 American Indian/Alaska Native, 7 Hispanic Americans. Average age 34. 392 applicants, 70% accepted, 140 enrolled. In 2009, 44 master's awarded. *Degree requirements:* For master's, comprehensive exam, portfolio. *Entrance requirements:* For master's, PRAXIS I, PRAXIS II, minimum GPA of 2.8. *Application deadline:* Applications are processed on a rolling basis. Application fee: $25. Electronic applications accepted. *Expenses:* Tuition: Full-time $8730; part-time $485 per credit hour. Required fees: $1260; $70 per credit hour. Tuition and fees vary according to campus/location. *Financial support:* Federal Work-Study, scholarships/grants, tuition waivers (full), and unspecified assistantships available. Support available to part-time students. Financial award applicants required to submit FAFSA. *Unit head:* Dr. Sandra L. Rasberry, Dean, 601-968-8703, Fax: 601-974-6461, E-mail: srasberry@belhaven.edu. *Application contact:* Jenny Mixon, Director of Graduate and Online Admission, 601-968-8947, Fax: 601-968-5953, E-mail: gradadmission@belhaven.edu.

Bennington College, Graduate Programs, MA in Teaching a Second Language Program, Bennington, VT 05201. Offers education (MATSL); foreign language education (MATSL); French (MATSL); Spanish (MATSL). Part-time programs available. *Faculty:* 1 full-time (0 women), 3 part-time/adjunct (2 women). *Students:* 16 part-time (14 women); includes 3 minority (1 African American, 2 Hispanic Americans). Average age 37. 16 applicants, 63% accepted, 9 enrolled. In 2009, 6 master's awarded. *Degree requirements:* For master's, one foreign language, 2 major projects and presentations. *Entrance requirements:* For master's, Oral Proficiency Interview (OPI). Additional exam requirements/recommendations for international students: Required—TOEFL (minimum score 577 paper-based; 233 computer-based; 91 iBT). *Application deadline:* For spring admission, 4/1 priority date for domestic and international students. Applications are processed on a rolling basis. Application fee: $60. *Expenses:* Contact institution. *Financial support:* In 2009–10, 1 student received support. Scholarships/grants available. Financial award application deadline: 4/1; financial award applicants required to submit FAFSA. *Faculty research:* Acquisition, evaluation, assessment, conceptual teaching and learning content-driven communication, applied linguistics. *Unit head:* Carol Meyer, Director, 802-440-4375, E-mail: cmeyer@bennington.edu. *Application contact:* Nancy Pearlman, Assistant Director, 802-440-4710, E-mail: matsl@bennington.edu.

Boston University, School of Education, Department of Literacy and Language, Counseling and Development, Program in Bilingual Education, Boston, MA 02215. Offers Ed M, CAGS. Part-time programs available. *Degree requirements:* For CAGS, comprehensive exam. *Entrance requirements:* For master's and CAGS, GRE General Test or MAT. Additional exam requirements/recommendations for international students: Required—TOEFL. Electronic applications accepted. *Expenses:* Tuition: Full-time $37,910; part-time $1184 per credit hour. Required fees: $386; $40 per semester. Part-time tuition and fees vary according to class time, course level, degree level and program. *Faculty research:* Use of computers in second language acquisition, cross-cultural communication, reading and language development.

Brooklyn College of the City University of New York, Division of Graduate Studies, School of Education, Program in Childhood Education, Brooklyn, NY 11210-2889. Offers bilingual education (MS Ed); liberal arts (MS Ed); mathematics (MS Ed); science/environmental education (MS Ed). Part-time and evening/weekend programs available. *Students:* 14 full-time (13 women), 245 part-time (209 women); includes 129 minority (60 African Americans, 2 American Indian/Alaska Native, 20 Asian Americans or Pacific Islanders, 47 Hispanic Americans), 6 international. Average age 30. 114 applicants, 85% accepted, 65 enrolled. In 2009, 118 master's awarded. *Entrance requirements:* For master's, LAST, interview, previous course work in education, writing sample, resume, 2 letters of recommendation. Additional exam requirements/recommendations for international students: Required—TOEFL (minimum score 500 paper-based; 173 computer-based; 61 iBT). *Application deadline:* For fall admission, 3/1 priority date for domestic students, 2/1 priority date for international students; for spring admission, 11/1 priority date for domestic students, 10/1 priority date for international students. Applications are processed on a rolling basis. Application fee: $125. Electronic applications accepted. *Expenses:* Tuition, state resident: full-time $7360; part-time $310 per credit hour. Tuition, nonresident: full-time $13,800; part-time $575 per credit hour. Required fees: $140.10 per semester. *Financial support:* Career-related internships or fieldwork, Federal Work-Study, institutionally sponsored loans, and scholarships/grants available. Support available to part-time students. Financial award application deadline: 5/1; financial award applicants required to submit FAFSA. *Faculty research:* Emotional intelligence, multiculturalism, arts immersion, the Holocaust. *Unit head:* Dr. Wayne Reed; Program Head, 718-951-5214, E-mail: wreed@brooklyn.cuny.edu. *Application contact:* Hernan Sierra, Graduate Admissions Coordinator, 718-951-4536, Fax: 718-951-4506, E-mail: grads@brooklyn.cuny.edu.

Brown University, Graduate School, Center for Portuguese and Brazilian Studies, Providence, RI 02912. Offers Brazilian studies (AM); Portuguese and Brazilian studies (AM, PhD); Portuguese Bilingual Education and Cross-Cultural Studies (AM); MA/PhD. *Degree requirements:* For doctorate, thesis/dissertation.

Buffalo State College, State University of New York, The Graduate School, Faculty of Applied Science and Education, Department of Exceptional Education, Program in Teaching Bilingual Exceptional Individuals, Buffalo, NY 14222-1095. Offers MS Ed. *Accreditation:* NCATE. Part-time and evening/weekend programs available. *Degree requirements:* For master's, project. *Entrance requirements:* For master's, minimum GPA of 2.5. Additional exam requirements/recommendations for international students: Required—TOEFL (minimum score 550 paper-based; 213 computer-based).

California Baptist University, Program in Education, Riverside, CA 92504-3206. Offers cross-cultural language and academic development (MA); educational leadership (MS); educational leadership and faith-based instruction (MS); educational technology (MS); instructional computer applications (MS); reading (MS); school counseling (MS); school psychology (MS); special education (MS); special education in mild/moderate disabilities (MS); special education in moderate/severe disabilities (MS); teaching (MS); teaching and learning (MS Ed). Part-time programs available. *Faculty:* 16 full-time (9 women), 10 part-time/adjunct (all women). *Students:* 73 full-time (60 women), 368 part-time (298 women); includes 170 minority (34 African Americans, 4 American Indian/Alaska Native, 18 Asian Americans or Pacific Islanders, 114 Hispanic Americans). 266 applicants, 72% accepted, 169 enrolled. In 2009, 120 master's awarded. *Degree requirements:* For master's, comprehensive exam (for some programs), thesis optional. *Entrance requirements:* For master's, minimum undergraduate GPA of 2.75, 12 semester hours of pre-requisite course work in education. Additional exam requirements/recommendations for international students: Required—TOEFL (minimum score 575 paper-based; 230 computer-based; 89 iBT). *Application deadline:* For fall admission, 8/1 priority date for domestic students, 7/1 for international students; for spring admission, 12/1 priority date for domestic students, 10/15 priority date for international students. Applications are processed on a rolling basis. Application fee: $45. Electronic applications accepted. *Expenses:* Tuition: Full-time $8352; part-time $464 per semester hour. Required fees: $125 per semester. Tuition and fees vary according to course load, campus/location and program. *Financial support:* Career-related internships or fieldwork, Federal Work-Study, and scholarships/grants available. Support available to part-time students. Financial award applicants required to submit FAFSA. *Unit head:* Dr. Mary Crist, Dean, School of Education, 951-343-4313, Fax: 951-343-4516, E-mail: mcrist@calbaptist.edu. *Application contact:* Gail Ronveaux, Dean of Graduate Enrollment, 951-343-5045, Fax: 951-343-5095, E-mail: graduateadmissions@calbaptist.edu.

California State University, Bakersfield, Division of Graduate Studies, School of Education, Program in Bilingual/Multicultural Education, Bakersfield, CA 93311. Offers MA Ed. *Degree requirements:* For master's, one foreign language, thesis, project, or examination. *Entrance requirements:* For master's, valid basic California teaching credential.

California State University, Chico, Graduate School, College of Communication and Education, Department of Professional Studies in Education, Option in Linguistically and Culturally Diverse Learners, Chico, CA 95929-0722. Offers MA. *Entrance requirements:* Additional exam requirements/recommendations for international students: Required—TOEFL (minimum score 550 paper-based; 213 computer-based; 80 iBT), IELTS (minimum score 6.5). Electronic applications accepted.

California State University, Dominguez Hills, College of Professional Studies, School of Education, Division of Graduate Education, Program in Multicultural Education, Carson, CA 90747-0001. Offers MA. Part-time and evening/weekend programs available. *Faculty:* 2 full-time (1 woman). *Students:* 16 full-time (11 women), 43 part-time (32 women); includes 51 minority (16 African Americans, 5 Asian Americans or Pacific Islanders, 30 Hispanic Americans), 1 international. Average age 37. 34 applicants, 79% accepted, 10 enrolled. In 2009, 37 master's awarded. *Degree requirements:* For master's, comprehensive exam. *Entrance requirements:* For master's, minimum GPA of 2.75. *Application deadline:* For fall admission, 8/1 for domestic students; for spring admission, 10/1 for domestic students. Applications are processed on a rolling basis. Application fee: $55. *Expenses:* Tuition, nonresident: full-time $6696; part-time

$372 per unit. Required fees: $5946; $1752 per semester. *Faculty research:* English learning, intercultural communications. *Unit head:* Dr. Maximilian Contreras, Chairperson, 310-343-3918 Ext. 3524, E-mail: mcontreras@csudh.edu. *Application contact:* Admissions Office, 310-243-3530.

California State University, Fullerton, Graduate Studies, College of Education, Department of Elementary and Bilingual Education, Fullerton, CA 92834-9480. Offers bilingual/bicultural education (MS); elementary curriculum and instruction (MS). *Accreditation:* NCATE. Part-time programs available. *Students:* 39 full-time (36 women), 132 part-time (121 women); includes 80 minority (3 African Americans, 28 Asian Americans or Pacific Islanders, 49 Hispanic Americans), 2 international. Average age 31. 78 applicants, 76% accepted, 43 enrolled. In 2009, 78 master's awarded. *Degree requirements:* For master's, comprehensive exam, project or thesis. *Entrance requirements:* For master's, minimum GPA of 2.5, teaching certificate. Application fee: $55. *Expenses:* Tuition, nonresident: full-time $11,160; part-time $373 per credit. Required fees: $1440 per term. Tuition and fees vary according to course load, degree level and program. *Financial support:* Career-related internships or fieldwork, Federal Work-Study, institutionally sponsored loans, and scholarships/grants available. Support available to part-time students. Financial award application deadline: 3/1; financial award applicants required to submit FAFSA. *Faculty research:* Teacher training and tracking, model for improvement of teaching. *Unit head:* Dr. Karen Ivers, Chair, 657-278-2470. *Application contact:* Admissions/Applications, 657-278-2371.

California State University, Northridge, Graduate Studies, College of Education, Department of Elementary Education, Northridge, CA 91330. Offers curriculum and instruction (MA); language and literacy (MA); multilingual/multicultural education (MA); teaching and learning (MA). *Accreditation:* NCATE. Part-time and evening/weekend programs available. *Faculty:* 18 full-time (14 women), 32 part-time/adjunct (24 women). *Students:* 29 full-time (all women), 61 part-time (57 women); includes 38 minority (1 African American, 10 Asian Americans or Pacific Islanders, 27 Hispanic Americans), 1 international. Average age 31. 64 applicants, 64% accepted, 28 enrolled. *Degree requirements:* For master's, comprehensive exam. *Entrance requirements:* For master's, GRE General Test or minimum GPA of 3.0. Additional exam requirements/recommendations for international students: Required—TOEFL. *Application deadline:* For fall admission, 11/30 for domestic students. Application fee: $55. *Financial support:* Federal Work-Study available. Financial award application deadline: 3/1. *Unit head:* Dr. David Kretschmer, Chair, 818-677-2621. *Application contact:* Joyce Burstein, Graduate Coordinator, 818-677-2621 Ext. 6850, E-mail: joyce.burstein@csun.edu.

California State University, Sacramento, Graduate Studies, College of Education, Department of Bilingual/Multicultural Education, Sacramento, CA 95819. Offers MA. Part-time programs available. *Degree requirements:* For master's, thesis or alternative, writing proficiency exam. *Entrance requirements:* For master's, minimum GPA of 2.5. Additional exam requirements/recommendations for international students: Required—TOEFL. Electronic applications accepted.

California State University, San Bernardino, Graduate Studies, College of Education, Program in Bilingual/Cross-Cultural Education, San Bernardino, CA 92407-2397. Offers MA. *Accreditation:* NCATE. *Faculty:* 1 (woman) full-time. *Students:* 6 full-time (4 women), 13 part-time (10 women); all minorities (all Hispanic Americans). Average age 35. 13 applicants, 92% accepted, 4 enrolled. In 2009, 3 master's awarded. *Unit head:* Dr. Mary Jo Skillings, Chair, 909-537-5639, Fax: 909-537-5992, E-mail: maryjosk@csusb.edu. *Application contact:* Olivia Rosas, Director of Admissions, 909-537-7577, Fax: 909-537-7034, E-mail: orosas@csusb.edu.

California State University, Stanislaus, College of Education, Department of Teacher Education, Turlock, CA 95382. Offers curriculum and instruction (MA), including elementary education, multilingual education, reading, secondary education; education (MA); middle/junior high studies (Graduate Certificate). Part-time and evening/weekend programs available. *Degree requirements:* For master's, thesis. *Entrance requirements:* For master's, MAT or GRE, 3 letters of recommendation. Additional exam requirements/recommendations for international students: Required—TOEFL (minimum score 550 paper-based; 213 computer-based). Electronic applications accepted. *Faculty research:* Children's perspectives on historical events, method elementary schools dual language education, K-12 reading and CYRM programs.

Capella University, School of Human Services, Minneapolis, MN 55402. Offers addictions counseling (Certificate); counseling studies (MS, PhD); criminal justice (MS, PhD, Certificate); diversity studies (Certificate); general human services (MS, PhD); health care administration (MS, PhD, Certificate); management of nonprofit agencies (MS, PhD, Certificate); marital, couple and family counseling/therapy (MS); marriage and family services (Certificate); mental health counseling (MS); professional counseling (Certificate); social and community services (MS, PhD, Certificate). Part-time and evening/weekend programs available. Postbaccalaureate distance learning degree programs offered (minimal on-campus study). Terminal master's awarded for partial completion of doctoral program. *Degree requirements:* For master's, thesis optional, integrative project; for doctorate, comprehensive exam, thesis/dissertation. *Entrance requirements:* Additional exam requirements/recommendations for international students: Required—TOEFL (minimum score 550 paper-based; 213 computer-based), TWE (minimum score 4). Electronic applications accepted. *Faculty research:* Compulsive and addictive behaviors, substance abuse, assessment of psychopathology and neuropsychology.

Chicago State University, School of Graduate and Professional Studies, College of Education, Department of Special Education, Early Childhood Education and Bilingual Education, Program in Bilingual Education, Chicago, IL 60628. Offers M Ed. *Accreditation:* NCATE. *Degree requirements:* For master's, comprehensive exam, thesis optional. *Entrance requirements:* For master's, minimum GPA of 2.75.

City College of the City University of New York, Graduate School, School of Education, Program in Bilingual Education, New York, NY 10031-9198. Offers MS. *Accreditation:* NCATE. Part-time programs available. *Degree requirements:* For master's, thesis. *Entrance requirements:* For master's, Liberal Arts and Sciences Test (LAST), Content Specialty Test (CST). Additional exam requirements/recommendations for international students: Required—TOEFL. *Expenses:* Tuition, state resident: part-time $310 per credit. Tuition, nonresident: part-time $575 per credit. Tuition and fees vary according to course load and program.

The College at Brockport, State University of New York, School of Education and Human Services, Department of Education and Human Development, Program in Bilingual Education, Brockport, NY 14420-2997. Offers bilingual education (MS Ed). *Accreditation:* NCATE. Part-time programs available. *Students:* 7 part-time (6 women); includes 4 minority (all Hispanic Americans). 1 applicant, 0% accepted, 0 enrolled. *Degree requirements:* For master's, thesis or alternative. *Entrance requirements:* For master's, minimum GPA of 3.0, letters of recommendation, statement of objectives, demonstrated proficiency in Spanish at the advanced level, appropriate provisional or initial teaching certificate; for AGC, minimum GPA of 3.0, appropriate New York state teaching certification, demonstrated proficiency in Spanish at the advanced level. Additional exam requirements/recommendations for international students: Required—TOEFL (minimum score 550 paper-based; 213 computer-based; 79 iBT). *Application deadline:* For fall admission, 2/15 priority date for domestic and international students; for spring admission, 9/15 priority date for domestic and international students. Application fee: $80. Electronic applications accepted. *Expenses:* Tuition, state resident: full-time $8370; part-time $349 per credit. Tuition, nonresident: full-time $13,250; part-time $522 per credit. *Financial support:* Federal Work-Study, scholarships/grants, and unspecified assistantships available. Support available to part-time students. Financial award application deadline: 3/15; financial award applicants required to submit FAFSA. *Unit head:* Dr. Sue Novinger, Chairperson, 585-395-2205, Fax: 585-395-2172, E-mail: snovinge@brockport.edu. *Application contact:* Dr. Sue Novinger, Chairperson, 585-395-2205, Fax: 585-395-2172, E-mail: snovinge@brockport.edu.

College of Mount St. Joseph, Graduate Education Program, Cincinnati, OH 45233-1670. Offers adolescent young adult education (MA); art (MA); inclusive early childhood education (MA); instructional leadership (MA); middle childhood education (MA); multi-age education (MA); multicultural special education (MA); music (MA); reading (MA). *Accreditation:* Teacher

Education Accreditation Council. Part-time and evening/weekend programs available. *Faculty:* 15 full-time (11 women), 9 part-time/adjunct (6 women). *Students:* 93 full-time (75 women), 99 part-time (66 women); includes 19 minority (18 African Americans, 1 American Indian/Alaska Native). Average age 34. 116 applicants, 97% accepted, 94 enrolled. In 2009, 51 master's awarded. *Degree requirements:* For master's, research project, student teaching, clinical and field-based experiences. *Entrance requirements:* For master's, GRE, PRAXIS II in teaching content area (math or science), 2 letters of recommendation, interview, resume. Additional exam requirements/recommendations for international students: Required—TOEFL (minimum score 560 paper-based; 220 computer-based; 83 iBT). *Application deadline:* Applications are processed on a rolling basis. Application fee: $50. Electronic applications accepted. *Expenses:* Tuition: Part-time $500 per hour. Required fees: $200 per year. Tuition and fees vary according to degree level and program. *Financial support:* In 2009–10, 51 students received support. Scholarships/grants available. Financial award applicants required to submit FAFSA. *Faculty research:* Foreign and second language learning problems/reading disabilities/hyperlexia, multicultural/bilingual special education, alternative educator licensure, science education, pedagogical content knowledge. *Unit head:* Dr. Mary West, Chair of Graduate Education, 513-244-3263, Fax: 513-244-4867, E-mail: mary_west@mail.msj.edu. *Application contact:* Marilyn Hoskins, Assistant Director of Graduate Recruitment, 513-244-4723, Fax: 513-244-4629, E-mail: marilyn_hoskins@mail.msj.edu.

College of Mount Saint Vincent, School of Professional and Continuing Studies, Department of Teacher Education, Riverdale, NY 10471-1093. Offers instructional technology and global perspectives (Certificate); middle level education (Certificate); multicultural studies (Certificate); urban and multicultural education (MS Ed). *Accreditation:* Teacher Education Accreditation Council. Part-time programs available. *Degree requirements:* For master's, comprehensive exam. *Entrance requirements:* For master's, interview, New York teaching certificate. Additional exam requirements/recommendations for international students: Required—TOEFL.

The College of New Rochelle, Graduate School, Division of Education, Program in Teaching English as a Second Language and Multilingual/Multicultural Education, New Rochelle, NY 10805-2308. Offers bilingual education (Certificate); teaching English as a second language (MS Ed). Part-time and evening/weekend programs available. *Degree requirements:* For master's, practicum. *Entrance requirements:* For master's, interview, minimum GPA of 3.0 in field, 2.7 overall.

The College of Saint Rose, Graduate Studies, School of Education, Teacher Education Department, Program in Teacher Education, Albany, NY 12203-1419. Offers bilingual pupil personnel services (Certificate); teacher education (MS Ed). Part-time and evening/weekend programs available. *Degree requirements:* For master's, comprehensive exam or thesis. *Entrance requirements:* For master's, minimum undergraduate GPA of 3.0, provisional or initial certification in a teaching area. Additional exam requirements/recommendations for international students: Required—TOEFL (minimum score 550 paper-based; 213 computer-based). Electronic applications accepted.

College of Santa Fe, Department of Education, Santa Fe, NM 87505-7634. Offers at-risk youth (MA), including bilingual/multicultural education, classroom teaching, community counseling, educational administration, leadership, school counseling, self-designed program, TESOL/Multicultural; curriculum and instruction (MA); multicultural special education (MA). Part-time and evening/weekend programs available. *Entrance requirements:* For master's, minimum GPA of 3.0. *Faculty research:* Integrated curriculum, child development, brain research, learning styles, systemic issues in education.

Columbia College Chicago, Graduate School, Department of Educational Studies, Chicago, IL 60605-1996. Offers elementary education (MAT); English (MAT); interdisciplinary arts (MAT); multicultural education (MA); urban teaching (MA). Part-time and evening/weekend programs available. *Degree requirements:* For master's, thesis, student teaching experience, 100 pre-clinical hours. *Entrance requirements:* For master's, supplemental recommendation form. Additional exam requirements/recommendations for international students: Required—TOEFL (minimum score 550 paper-based; 213 computer-based). Electronic applications accepted. *Expenses:* Tuition: Part-time $651 per credit hour. Required fees: $205 per semester. One-time fee: $285 part-time. Tuition and fees vary according to program.

Columbia International University, Columbia Graduate School, Columbia, SC 29230-3122. Offers Bible teaching (MABT); Christian higher education leadership (Ed D); Christian school educational leadership (Ed D); counseling (MACN); curriculum and instruction (M Ed), including Christian school guidance, English as a second language, learning disabilities, school technology; early childhood and elementary education (MAT); educational administration (M Ed); teaching English as a foreign language (Certificate); teaching English as a foreign language and intercultural studies (MATF). Part-time and evening/weekend programs available. *Degree requirements:* For master's, internships, professional project. *Entrance requirements:* For master's, Minnesota Multiphasic Personality Inventory, MAT, minimum GPA of 2.7. Additional exam requirements/recommendations for international students: Required—TOEFL. Electronic applications accepted.

DePaul University, School of Education, Chicago, IL 60106. Offers bilingual and bicultural education (M Ed, MA); curriculum studies (M Ed, MA, Ed D); educational leadership (M Ed, MA, Ed D), including administration and supervision (M Ed, MA), Catholic school leadership (M Ed, MA), physical education (M Ed, MA); human development and learning (MA); human services and counseling (M Ed, MA), including agencies, family concerns, and higher education, elementary schools, human services management, secondary schools; reading and learning disabilities (M Ed, MA); social culture studies in education and development (M Ed, MA), including curriculum studies/development; teaching and learning (early childhood, elementary and secondary) (M Ed), including elementary education (M Ed, MA), secondary education (M Ed, MA); teaching and learning (early childhood, elementary, and secondary) (MA), including elementary education (M Ed, MA), secondary education (M Ed, MA). *Accreditation:* NCATE. Part-time and evening/weekend programs available. *Faculty:* 61 full-time (40 women), 66 part-time/adjunct (41 women). *Students:* 799 full-time (779 women), 470 part-time (365 women); includes 319 minority (153 African Americans, 3 American Indian/Alaska Native, 48 Asian Americans or Pacific Islanders, 115 Hispanic Americans), 15 international. Average age 30. 635 applicants, 74% accepted, 318 enrolled. In 2009, 604 master's, 5 doctorates awarded. *Degree requirements:* For doctorate, thesis/dissertation. *Entrance requirements:* For master's, interview, minimum GPA of 2.75, 2 letters of recommendation; for doctorate, interview, master's degree, writing sample, 3 letters of recommendation. Additional exam requirements/recommendations for international students: Required—TOEFL (minimum score 550 paper-based; 213 computer-based; 80 iBT). *Application deadline:* Applications are processed on a rolling basis. Application fee: $40. Electronic applications accepted. *Expenses:* Tuition: Full-time $37,525; part-time $620 per credit hour. *Financial support:* In 2009–10, 14 research assistantships with tuition reimbursements (averaging $5,800 per year) were awarded; career-related internships or fieldwork also available. *Faculty research:* Reflective teaching, children at risk, loss, ethnicity, urban education. Total annual research expenditures: $1.6 million. *Unit head:* Dr. Marie Donovan, Dean, 773-325-7581, Fax: 773-325-7713, E-mail: mdonovan@depaul.edu. *Application contact:* Brandon Washington, Data Project Manager, 773-325-1152, Fax: 773-325-2270, E-mail: bwashin3@depaul.edu.

Eastern Michigan University, Graduate School, College of Education, Department of Teacher Education, Ypsilanti, MI 48197. Offers culture and diversity (MA); early childhood education (MA); educational media and technology (MA, Graduate Certificate); educational psychology and assessment (MA, Graduate Certificate), including educational assessment (Graduate Certificate), educational psychology (MA); educational studies (PhD); K-12 education (MA), including curriculum and instruction, elementary education, K-12 education, middle school education, secondary school education; reading (MA); social foundations (MA). Part-time and evening/weekend programs available. Postbaccalaureate distance learning degree programs offered (minimal on-campus study). *Faculty:* 44 full-time (35 women). *Students:* 26 full-time (15 women), 455 part-time (392 women); includes 78 minority (53 African Americans, 7 American Indian/Alaska Native, 8 Asian Americans or Pacific Islanders, 10 Hispanic Americans), 3

Multilingual and Multicultural Education

Eastern Michigan University (continued)
international. Average age 34. In 2009, 145 master's, 2 other advanced degrees awarded. *Entrance requirements:* For master's, GRE. Additional exam requirements/recommendations for international students: Required—TOEFL. *Application deadline:* Applications are processed on a rolling basis. Application fee: $35. Tuition and fees vary according to course level. *Financial support:* Fellowships, research assistantships with full tuition reimbursements, teaching assistantships with full tuition reimbursements, career-related internships or fieldwork, Federal Work-Study, institutionally sponsored loans, scholarships/grants, tuition waivers (partial), and unspecified assistantships available. Support available to part-time students. Financial award applicants required to submit FAFSA. *Unit head:* Dr. Donald Bennion, Department Head, 734-487-3260, Fax: 734-487-2101, E-mail: donald.bennion@emich.edu. *Application contact:* Dr. Toni Jones, Advisor, 734-487-3260, Fax: 734-487-2101, E-mail: tjones1@emich.edu.

Eastern University, Graduate Education Programs, Program in Multicultural Education, St. Davids, PA 19087-3696. Offers M Ed. *Entrance requirements:* For master's, minimum GPA of 2.5. Additional exam requirements/recommendations for international students: Required—TOEFL.

Fairfield University, Graduate School of Education and Allied Professions, Department of Curriculum and Instruction, Fairfield, CT 06824-5195. Offers bilingual education (CAS); elementary education (MA); media/educational technology (MA); secondary education (MA); teaching and foundations (MA, CAS); TESOL, foreign language and bilingual/multicultural education (MA, CAS). Part-time and evening/weekend programs available. *Degree requirements:* For master's, comprehensive exam, thesis or alternative. *Entrance requirements:* For master's, PRAXIS I (PPST), minimum QPA of 3.0, 2 recommendations, resume. Additional exam requirements/recommendations for international students: Required—TOEFL (minimum score 550 paper-based; 213 computer-based; 80 iBT). Electronic applications accepted. *Faculty research:* Urban and multicultural education; participatory action for social justice; culture and family; second language acquisition; science, technology and social education.

Fairleigh Dickinson University, Metropolitan Campus, University College: Arts, Sciences, and Professional Studies, Peter Sammartino School of Education, Program in Multilingual Education, Teaneck, NJ 07666-1914. Offers MA. *Accreditation:* Teacher Education Accreditation Council. *Students:* 9 full-time (all women), 2 part-time (both women), 8 international. Average age 35. 11 applicants, 91% accepted, 3 enrolled. In 2009, 8 master's awarded. *Application deadline:* Applications are processed on a rolling basis. Application fee: $40. *Application contact:* Susan Brooman, University Director of Graduate Admissions, 201-692-2554, Fax: 201-692-2560, E-mail: globaleducation@fdu.edu.

Florida Atlantic University, College of Education, Department of Curriculum, Culture, and Educational Inquiry, Boca Raton, FL 33431-0991. Offers curriculum and instruction (Ed D, Ed S); early childhood education (M Ed); multicultural education (M Ed); teaching English to speakers of other languages (TESOL) (M Ed). *Faculty:* 11 full-time (8 women), 17 part-time/adjunct (13 women). *Students:* 38 full-time (26 women), 124 part-time (105 women); includes 40 minority (23 African Americans, 3 Asian Americans or Pacific Islanders, 14 Hispanic Americans), 4 international. Average age 36. 84 applicants, 56% accepted, 34 enrolled. In 2009, 39 master's, 5 doctorates awarded. *Application deadline:* For fall admission, 7/1 for domestic students, 2/15 for international students; for spring admission, 11/1 for domestic students, 7/15 for international students. *Expenses:* Tuition, state resident: full-time $7055; part-time $293.94 per credit hour. Tuition, nonresident: full-time $22,096; part-time $920.66 per credit hour. *Faculty research:* Multicultural education, early intervention strategies, family literacy, religious diversity in schools, early childhood curriculum. *Unit head:* Dr. James McLaughlin, Interim Chair, 561-297-3965, E-mail: jmclau17@fau.edu. *Application contact:* Dr. Eliah Watlington, Associate Dean, 561-296-8520, Fax: 261-297-2991, E-mail: ewatling@fau.edu.

Fordham University, Graduate School of Education, Division of Curriculum and Teaching, New York, NY 10023. Offers adult education (MS, MSE); bilingual teacher education (MSE); curriculum and teaching (MSE); early childhood education (MSE); elementary education (MST); language, literacy, and learning (PhD); reading education (MSE, Adv C); secondary education (MAT, MSE); special education (MSE, Adv C); teaching English as a second language (MSE). *Accreditation:* NCATE. *Degree requirements:* For doctorate, thesis/dissertation; for Adv C, thesis. *Entrance requirements:* For doctorate, MAT, GRE General Test.

Fresno Pacific University, Graduate Programs, School of Education, Fresno, CA 93702-4709. Offers administration (MA Ed), including administrative services; foundations, curriculum and teaching (MA Ed), including curriculum and teaching, school library and information technology; language, literacy, and culture (MA Ed), including bilingual/cross-cultural education, language development, multilingual contexts, reading; mathematics/science/computer education (MA Ed), including educational technology, integrated mathematics/science education, mathematics education; pupil personnel services (MA Ed), including school counseling, school psychology; special education (MA Ed), including mild/moderate, moderate/severe, physical and health impairments. Part-time and evening/weekend programs available. *Degree requirements:* For master's, thesis (for some programs). *Entrance requirements:* For master's, interview; GMAT, GRE, MAT, or 6 units of course work with a faculty recommendation. Additional exam requirements/recommendations for international students: Required—TOEFL (minimum score 550 paper-based; 213 computer-based). Electronic applications accepted.

Fresno Pacific University, Graduate Programs, School of Education, Division of Language, Literacy, and Culture, Program in Bilingual/Cross-Cultural Education, Fresno, CA 93702-4709. Offers MA Ed. Part-time and evening/weekend programs available. *Degree requirements:* For master's, thesis or alternative. *Entrance requirements:* Additional exam requirements/recommendations for international students: Required—TOEFL (minimum score 550 paper-based; 213 computer-based). Electronic applications accepted.

Fresno Pacific University, Graduate Programs, School of Education, Division of Language, Literacy, and Culture, Program in Literacy in Multilingual Contexts, Fresno, CA 93702-4709. Offers MA Ed. Part-time and evening/weekend programs available. *Degree requirements:* For master's, thesis or alternative. *Entrance requirements:* Additional exam requirements/recommendations for international students: Required—TOEFL (minimum score 550 paper-based; 213 computer-based). Electronic applications accepted.

George Fox University, School of Education, Master of Arts in Teaching Program, Newberg, OR 97132-2697. Offers teaching (MAT); teaching plus ESOL (MAT); teaching plus ESOL/bilingual (MAT); teaching plus reading (MAT). MAT program is offered in Oregon and Idaho. Part-time and evening/weekend programs available. *Faculty:* 16 full-time (13 women), 22 part-time/adjunct (15 women). *Students:* 158 full-time (116 women), 70 part-time (49 women); includes 22 minority (1 African American, 2 American Indian/Alaska Native, 8 Asian Americans or Pacific Islanders, 11 Hispanic Americans), 1 international. Average age 32. 59 applicants, 75% accepted, 35 enrolled. In 2009, 195 master's awarded. *Entrance requirements:* For master's, CBEST or PRAXIS PPST, bachelor's degree from regionally-accredited college or university with minimum GPA of 3.0 in last two years of course work. Additional exam requirements/recommendations for international students: Required—TOEFL (minimum score 577 paper-based; 233 computer-based; 90 iBT). *Application deadline:* For fall admission, 6/1 for domestic and international students; for winter admission, 10/1 for domestic and international students; for spring admission, 2/1 for domestic and international students. Applications are processed on a rolling basis. Application fee: $40. Electronic applications accepted. *Expenses:* Contact institution. *Financial support:* In 2009–10, 20 students received support. Scholarships/grants available. Financial award application deadline: 2/1; financial award applicants required to submit FAFSA. *Unit head:* Kristin Dixon, Chair, 971-239-4934, E-mail: kdixon@georgefox.edu. *Application contact:* Beth Molzahn, Admissions Counselor, Oregon Master of Arts in Teaching Programs, 800-631-0921, Fax: 503-554-3110, E-mail: mat@georgefox.edu.

Georgetown University, Graduate School of Arts and Sciences, Department of Linguistics, Washington, DC 20057. Offers bilingual education (Certificate); language and communication (MA); linguistics (MS, PhD), including applied linguistics, computational linguistics, sociolinguistics, theoretical linguistics; teaching English as a second language (MAT, Certificate); teaching English as a second language and bilingual education (MAT). Terminal master's awarded for partial completion of doctoral program. *Degree requirements:* For master's, one foreign language, comprehensive exam, optional research project; for doctorate, 2 foreign languages, comprehensive exam, thesis/dissertation. *Entrance requirements:* For master's and doctorate, 18 undergraduate credits in a foreign language. Additional exam requirements/recommendations for international students: Required—TOEFL.

Graduate Institute of Applied Linguistics, Graduate Programs, Dallas, TX 75236. Offers applied linguistics (MA, Certificate); language development (MA). Part-time programs available. *Degree requirements:* For master's, one foreign language, comprehensive exam (for some programs), thesis (for some programs). *Entrance requirements:* For master's, GRE. Additional exam requirements/recommendations for international students: Required—TOEFL (minimum score 577 paper-based; 233 computer-based; 90 iBT). Electronic applications accepted. *Faculty research:* Minority languages, endangered languages, language documentation.

Harvard University, Graduate School of Education, Doctoral Program in Education, Cambridge, MA 02138. Offers culture, communities and education (Ed D); education policy, leadership and instructional practice (Ed D); higher education (Ed D); human development and education (Ed D); quantitative policy analysis in education (Ed D); urban superintendency (Ed D). Part-time programs available. *Faculty:* 70 full-time (33 women), 36 part-time/adjunct (20 women). *Students:* 295 full-time (198 women), 23 part-time (11 women); includes 103 minority (40 African Americans, 4 American Indian/Alaska Native, 34 Asian Americans or Pacific Islanders, 25 Hispanic Americans), 33 international. Average age 32. 551 applicants, 9% accepted, 39 enrolled. In 2009, 41 doctorates awarded. Terminal master's awarded for partial completion of doctoral program. *Degree requirements:* For doctorate, thesis/dissertation. *Entrance requirements:* For doctorate, GRE General Test, 3 letters of recommendation. Additional exam requirements/recommendations for international students: Required—TOEFL (minimum score 600 paper-based; 250 computer-based; 100 iBT), TWE (minimum score 5). *Application deadline:* For fall admission, 12/14 for domestic and international students. Application fee: $85. Electronic applications accepted. *Expenses:* Contact institution. *Financial support:* In 2009–10, 265 students received support, including 129 fellowships with full and partial tuition reimbursements available (averaging $11,142 per year), 41 research assistantships (averaging $11,990 per year), 173 teaching assistantships (averaging $9,174 per year); career-related internships or fieldwork, Federal Work-Study, institutionally sponsored loans, scholarships/grants, health care benefits, tuition waivers (full and partial), and unspecified assistantships also available. Support available to part-time students. Financial award application deadline: 2/1; financial award applicants required to submit FAFSA. *Faculty research:* Learning and development, educational leadership and organizations, education policy analysis. Total annual research expenditures: $18.1 million. *Unit head:* Dr. Shu-Ling Chen, Assistant Dean, 617-496-4406. *Application contact:* Information Contact, 617-495-3414, Fax: 617-496-3577, E-mail: gseadmissions@harvard.edu.

Heritage University, Graduate Programs in Education, Program in Professional Studies, Toppenish, WA 98948-9599. Offers bilingual education/ESL (M Ed); biology (M Ed); English and literature (M Ed); reading/literacy (M Ed); special education (M Ed). Part-time and evening/weekend programs available. *Degree requirements:* For master's, comprehensive exam (for some programs), thesis (for some programs).

Hofstra University, School of Education, Health, and Human Services, Department of Counseling, Research, Special Education and Rehabilitation, Program in Counseling, Hempstead, NY 11549. Offers counseling (PD); mental health counseling (MA); school counselor (MS Ed); school counselor-bilingual extension (Advanced Certificate). Part-time and evening/weekend programs available. *Students:* 34 full-time (30 women), 36 part-time (33 women); includes 9 minority (3 African Americans, 3 Asian Americans or Pacific Islanders, 3 Hispanic Americans). Average age 30. 61 applicants, 64% accepted, 19 enrolled. In 2009, 29 master's, 1 other advanced degree awarded. *Degree requirements:* For master's, comprehensive exam. *Entrance requirements:* For master's, GRE General Test, interview, 3 letters of recommendation; for other advanced degree, GRE, interview, 3 letters of recommendation, essay. Additional exam requirements/recommendations for international students: Required—TOEFL (minimum score 550 paper-based; 213 computer-based; 80 iBT). *Application deadline:* Applications are processed on a rolling basis. Application fee: $60. Electronic applications accepted. *Expenses:* Tuition: Full-time $16,200; part-time $900 per credit hour. Required fees: $970; $145 per term. Tuition and fees vary according to program. *Financial support:* In 2009–10, 35 students received support, including 2 fellowships with full and partial tuition reimbursements available (averaging $3,227 per year), 2 research assistantships with full and partial tuition reimbursements available (averaging $13,558 per year); career-related internships or fieldwork, Federal Work-Study, institutionally sponsored loans, scholarships/grants, traineeships, tuition waivers (full and partial), and unspecified assistantships also available. Support available to part-time students. Financial award applicants required to submit FAFSA. *Faculty research:* Bereavement, loss and trauma counseling; CORT issues in counseling; college student development; conflict transformation; multicultural and intracultural counseling. *Unit head:* Dr. Laurie Johnson, Director, 516-463-5754, Fax: 516-463-6184, E-mail: cprlzj@hofstra.edu. *Application contact:* Carol Drummer, Dean of Graduate Admissions, 516-463-4876, Fax: 516-463-4664, E-mail: gradstudent@hofstra.edu.

Hofstra University, School of Education, Health, and Human Services, Department of Curriculum and Teaching, Program in Learning and Teaching, Hempstead, NY 11549. Offers learning and teaching (Ed D), including applied linguistics, art education, arts and humanities, early childhood education, English education, human development, math education, math, science, and technology, multicultural education, physical education, science education, social studies education, special education. Part-time and evening/weekend programs available. *Students:* 5 full-time (all women), 21 part-time (17 women); includes 2 minority (1 African American, 1 Hispanic American), 1 international. Average age 38. 22 applicants, 68% accepted, 11 enrolled. *Degree requirements:* For doctorate, comprehensive exam, thesis/dissertation. *Entrance requirements:* For doctorate, GRE, 3 letters of recommendation, interview, 2 years full-time teaching experience. Additional exam requirements/recommendations for international students: Required—TOEFL (minimum score 550 paper-based; 213 computer-based; 80 iBT). *Application deadline:* Applications are processed on a rolling basis. Application fee: $60. Electronic applications accepted. *Expenses:* Tuition: Full-time $16,200; part-time $900 per credit hour. Required fees: $970; $145 per term. Tuition and fees vary according to program. *Financial support:* In 2009–10, 24 students received support, including 20 fellowships with full and partial tuition reimbursements available (averaging $4,906 per year); research assistantships with full and partial tuition reimbursements available, Federal Work-Study, institutionally sponsored loans, scholarships/grants, and tuition waivers (full and partial) also available. Support available to part-time students. Financial award applicants required to submit FAFSA. *Faculty research:* Critical thinking, professional development, teacher quality, quantitative research. *Unit head:* Dr. Bruce A. Torff, Director, 516-463-5803, Fax: 516-463-6196, E-mail: catajs@hofstra.edu. *Application contact:* Carol Drummer, Dean of Graduate Admissions, 516-463-4876, Fax: 516-463-4664, E-mail: gradstudent@hofstra.edu.

Hofstra University, School of Education, Health, and Human Services, Department of Curriculum and Teaching, Programs in TESL/Bilingual Education, Hempstead, NY 11549. Offers bilingual education (MA); bilingual extension education (CAS); TESOL (MS Ed, CAS). Part-time programs available. *Students:* 36 full-time (34 women), 38 part-time (35 women); includes 28

minority (7 African Americans, 3 Asian Americans or Pacific Islanders, 18 Hispanic Americans). Average age 31. 58 applicants, 74% accepted, 32 enrolled. In 2009, 24 master's, 9 other advanced degrees awarded. Terminal master's awarded for partial completion of doctoral program. *Degree requirements:* For master's, one foreign language, thesis or alternative, portfolios. *Entrance requirements:* For master's, interview, 2 letters of recommendation, teaching certificate; for CAS, 2 letters of recommendation, interview, teaching certificate, essay, proficiency in language. Additional exam requirements/recommendations for international students: Required—TOEFL (minimum score 550 paper-based; 213 computer-based; 80 iBT). *Application deadline:* Applications are processed on a rolling basis. Application fee: $60. Electronic applications accepted. *Expenses:* Tuition: Full-time $16,200; part-time $900 per credit hour. Required fees: $970; $145 per term. Tuition and fees vary according to program. *Financial support:* In 2009–10, 43 students received support, including 1 fellowship with full and partial tuition reimbursement available (averaging $3,400 per year), 1 research assistantship with full and partial tuition reimbursement available (averaging $17,682 per year); career-related internships or fieldwork, Federal Work-Study, institutionally sponsored loans, scholarships/grants, tuition waivers (full and partial), and unspecified assistantships also available. Support available to part-time students. Financial award applicants required to submit FAFSA. *Faculty research:* Innateness hypothesis, content-based ESL instruction, linking linguistic research to practice. *Unit head:* Dr. Tatiana Gordon, Director, 516-463-5170, Fax: 516-463-6196, E-mail: cattzg@hofstra.edu. *Application contact:* Carol Drummer, Dean of Graduate Admissions, 516-463-4876, Fax: 516-463-4664, E-mail: gradstudent@hofstra.edu.

Howard University, School of Communications, Department of Communication and Culture, Washington, DC 20059-0002. Offers intercultural communication (MA, PhD); organizational communication (MA, PhD). Offered through the Graduate School of Arts and Sciences. Part-time programs available. Terminal master's awarded for partial completion of doctoral program. *Degree requirements:* For master's, comprehensive exam or thesis; for doctorate, one foreign language, comprehensive exam, thesis/dissertation. *Entrance requirements:* For master's, English proficiency exam, GRE General Test, minimum GPA of 3.0; for doctorate, English proficiency exam, GRE General Test, master's degree in related field, minimum GPA of 3.5. Additional exam requirements/recommendations for international students: Required—TOEFL. *Faculty research:* Media effects, black discourse, development communication, African-American organizations.

Hunter College of the City University of New York, Graduate School, School of Education, Department of Curriculum and Teaching, Program in Bilingual Education, New York, NY 10021-5085. Offers MS. *Accreditation:* NCATE. *Faculty:* 4 full-time (3 women), 7 part-time/adjunct (4 women). *Students:* 4 full-time (all women), 18 part-time (16 women); includes 9 minority (all Hispanic Americans). Average age 30. 14 applicants, 57% accepted, 5 enrolled. *Degree requirements:* For master's, one foreign language, thesis, research seminar, student teaching experience or practicum, New York State Teacher Certification Exams. *Entrance requirements:* For master's, interview, minimum GPA of 2.8, writing sample in English and Spanish. Additional exam requirements/recommendations for international students: Required—TOEFL, TWE. *Application deadline:* For fall admission, 4/1 for domestic students, 2/1 for international students; for spring admission, 11/1 for domestic students, 9/1 for international students. Applications are processed on a rolling basis. Application fee: $125. *Expenses:* Tuition, state resident: full-time $7360; part-time $310 per credit. Required fees: $250 per semester. *Financial support:* Federal Work-Study, scholarships/grants, and tuition waivers (partial) available. Support available to part-time students. *Faculty research:* Teacher effectiveness, language development, Spanish language and linguistics and multicultural education. *Unit head:* Yvonne DeGaetano, Coordinator, 212-772-4683, E-mail: ydegaetano@hunter.cuny.edu. *Application contact:* William Zlata, Director for Graduate Admissions, 212-772-4482, Fax: 212-650-3336, E-mail: admissions@hunter.cuny.edu.

Hunter College of the City University of New York, Graduate School, School of Education, Department of Educational Foundations and Counseling Programs, Programs in School Counselor, New York, NY 10021-5085. Offers school counseling (MS Ed); school counseling with bilingual extension (MS Ed). *Accreditation:* NCATE. *Faculty:* 12 full-time (6 women), 57 part-time/adjunct (42 women). *Students:* 48 full-time (43 women), 83 part-time (66 women); includes 28 minority (10 African Americans, 4 Asian Americans or Pacific Islanders, 14 Hispanic Americans). Average age 29. 295 applicants, 15% accepted, 31 enrolled. In 2009, 29 master's awarded. *Degree requirements:* For master's, thesis, internship, practicum, research seminar. *Entrance requirements:* For master's, interview, minimum GPA of 2.7. Additional exam requirements/recommendations for international students: Required—TOEFL, TWE. *Application deadline:* For fall admission, 4/1 for domestic students, 2/1 for international students; for spring admission, 11/1 for domestic students, 9/1 for international students. Applications are processed on a rolling basis. Application fee: $125. *Expenses:* Tuition, state resident: full-time $7360; part-time $310 per credit. Required fees: $250 per semester. *Financial support:* Federal Work-Study and tuition waivers (partial) available. Support available to part-time students. *Unit head:* Dr. Tamara Buckley, Coordinator, 212-772-4758, E-mail: tamara.buckley@hunter.cuny.edu. *Application contact:* William Zlata, Director for Graduate Admissions, 212-772-4482, Fax: 212-650-3336, E-mail: admissions@hunter.cuny.edu.

Immaculata University, College of Graduate Studies, Program in Cultural and Linguistic Diversity, Immaculata, PA 19345. Offers MA. Part-time and evening/weekend programs available. *Degree requirements:* For master's, one foreign language, comprehensive exam, thesis optional, professional experience. *Entrance requirements:* For master's, GRE or MAT, proficiency in Spanish or Asian language, minimum GPA of 3.0. Additional exam requirements/recommendations for international students: Required—TOEFL, IELTS. Electronic applications accepted. *Faculty research:* Cognitive learning, Caribbean literature and culture, English as a second language, teaching English to speakers of other languages.

Indiana State University, School of Graduate Studies, College of Arts and Sciences, Department of Languages, Literatures, and Linguistics, Terre Haute, IN 47809. Offers linguistics/teaching English as a second language (MA); TESL/TEFL (CAS). *Degree requirements:* For master's, comprehensive exam. Electronic applications accepted.

Indiana University Bloomington, University Graduate School, College of Arts and Sciences, Department of Second Language Studies, Bloomington, IN 47405-7000. Offers second language studies (MA, PhD); TESOL and applied linguistics (MA). *Faculty:* 1 (woman) full-time. *Students:* 22 full-time (19 women), 3 part-time (1 woman); includes 4 minority (1 African American, 3 Hispanic Americans), 10 international. Average age 33. 78 applicants, 38% accepted, 6 enrolled. In 2009, 6 master's awarded. Application fee: $55 ($65 for international students). *Financial support:* In 2009–10, 1 fellowship with tuition reimbursement (averaging $15,000 per year), 12 teaching assistantships with tuition reimbursements (averaging $12,750 per year) were awarded. *Unit head:* Kathleen Bardovi-Harlig, Chair, 812-855-7951, E-mail: bardovi@indiana.edu. *Application contact:* Karla Reynolds, Graduate Secretary, 812-855-7951, E-mail: kjbastin@indiana.edu.

Kean University, College of Education, Program in Instruction and Curriculum, Union, NJ 07083. Offers bilingual/bicultural education (MA); classroom instruction (MA); earth science (MA); mathematics/science/computer education (MA); teaching (MA); teaching English as a second language (MA); world languages (Spanish) (MA). *Accreditation:* NCATE. Part-time and evening/weekend programs available. *Faculty:* 16 full-time (7 women). *Students:* 45 full-time (34 women), 131 part-time (104 women); includes 60 minority (11 African Americans, 6 Asian Americans or Pacific Islanders, 43 Hispanic Americans), 6 international. Average age 33. 64 applicants, 94% accepted, 46 enrolled. In 2009, 58 master's awarded. *Entrance requirements:* For master's, GRE General Test or MAT, PRAXIS, minimum GPA of 3.0, 2 letters of recommendation, interview, teacher certification (for some programs). *Application deadline:* For fall admission, 5/1 for domestic students; for spring admission, 11/1 for domestic students. Application fee: $60 ($150 for international students). Electronic applications accepted. *Expenses:* Tuition, state resident: full-time $10,440; part-time $435 per credit. Tuition, nonresident: full-time $14,160; part-time $590 per credit. Required fees: $2642; $110 per credit. Part-time tuition and fees vary according to course load and degree level. *Financial support:* In 2009–10, 1 research assistantship with full tuition reimbursement (averaging $3,263 per year) was awarded; unspecified assistantships also available. *Unit head:* Dr. Thomas Walsh, Program Coordinator, 908-737-4296, E-mail: twalsh@kean.edu. *Application contact:* Ann-Marie Kay, Assistant Director of Graduate Admissions, 908-737-5922, Fax: 908-737-5965, E-mail: akay@kean.edu.

Langston University, School of Education and Behavioral Sciences, Langston, OK 73050. Offers bilingual/multicultural (M Ed); elementary education (M Ed); English as a second language (M Ed); rehabilitation counseling (M Sc); urban education (M Ed). *Accreditation:* CORE; NCATE (one or more programs are accredited). Part-time programs available. *Degree requirements:* For master's, comprehensive exam, thesis optional. *Entrance requirements:* For master's, GRE, writing skills test, minimum GPA of 2.5, 3 letters of recommendation. Additional exam requirements/recommendations for international students: Required—TOEFL, TWE. *Faculty research:* Bilingual/multicultural education, financing post-secondary education.

Lehman College of the City University of New York, Division of Education, Department of Specialized Services in Education, Bronx, NY 10468-1589. Offers guidance and counseling (MS Ed); reading teacher (MS Ed); teachers of special education (MS Ed), including bilingual special education, early special education, emotional handicaps, learning disabilities, mental retardation. Part-time and evening/weekend programs available. *Faculty research:* Battered women, whole language classrooms, parent education, mainstreaming.

Lehman College of the City University of New York, Division of Education, Department of Specialized Services in Education, Teachers of Special Education Program, Option in Bilingual Special Education, Bronx, NY 10468-1589. Offers MS Ed. *Accreditation:* NCATE. *Entrance requirements:* For master's, minimum GPA of 3.0.

Long Island University, Brooklyn Campus, School of Education, Department of Teaching and Learning, Program in Bilingual Education, Brooklyn, NY 11201-8423. Offers MS Ed. Part-time and evening/weekend programs available. *Degree requirements:* For master's, one foreign language, thesis optional. *Entrance requirements:* For master's, 2 letters of recommendation. Additional exam requirements/recommendations for international students: Required—TOEFL (minimum score 500 paper-based; 173 computer-based). Electronic applications accepted.

Long Island University, C.W. Post Campus, School of Education, Department of Curriculum and Instruction, Brookville, NY 11548-1300. Offers adolescence education (MS); adolescence education: biology (MS); adolescence education: earth science (MS); adolescence education: English (MS); adolescence education: mathematics (MS); adolescence education: social studies (MS); adolescence education: Spanish (MS); art education (MS); bilingual education (MS); childhood education (MS); early childhood education (MS); middle childhood education (MS); music education (MS); teaching English to speakers of other languages (MS). Part-time and evening/weekend programs available. *Degree requirements:* For master's, comprehensive exam or thesis, student teaching. *Entrance requirements:* For master's, minimum GPA of 2.75 in major, 2.5 overall. Electronic applications accepted. *Faculty research:* Ethics and education, teaching strategies.

Long Island University, Westchester Graduate Campus, Programs in Education-Teaching, Program in Second Language, TESOL, Bilingual Education, Purchase, NY 10577. Offers MS Ed, Advanced Certificate. Part-time and evening/weekend programs available.

Loyola Marymount University, School of Education, Department of Language and Culture in Education, Program in Bilingual Elementary Education, Los Angeles, CA 90045. Offers MA. Part-time and evening/weekend programs available. *Faculty:* 7 full-time (5 women), 5 part-time/adjunct (3 women). *Students:* 14 full-time (12 women), 3 part-time (2 women); includes 14 minority (2 African Americans, 4 Asian Americans or Pacific Islanders, 8 Hispanic Americans), 2 international. Average age 33. 7 applicants, 71% accepted, 5 enrolled. In 2009, 3 master's awarded. *Degree requirements:* For master's, comprehensive exam. *Entrance requirements:* For master's, CBEST, CSET, CSET LOTE Test 3, RICA, 3 letters of recommendation. Additional exam requirements/recommendations for international students: Required—TOEFL (minimum score 600 paper-based; 250 computer-based; 100 iBT). *Application deadline:* For fall admission, 6/15 for domestic students; for spring admission, 11/15 for domestic students. Application fee: $50. Electronic applications accepted. *Financial support:* In 2009–10, 12 students received support. Scholarships/grants and unspecified assistantships available. Support available to part-time students. Financial award application deadline: 6/15; financial award applicants required to submit FAFSA. Total annual research expenditures: $321,465. *Unit head:* Dr. Yvette Lapayese, Chair, 310-338-3773, E-mail: ylapayes@lmu.edu. *Application contact:* Chake H. Kouyoumjian, Director, Graduate Admissions, 310-338-2721, Fax: 310-338-6086, E-mail: ckouyoum@lmu.edu.

Loyola Marymount University, School of Education, Department of Language and Culture in Education, Program in Bilingual Secondary Education, Los Angeles, CA 90064. Offers MA. Part-time and evening/weekend programs available. *Faculty:* 7 full-time (5 women), 5 part-time/adjunct (3 women). *Students:* 19 full-time (17 women), 10 part-time (8 women); includes 23 minority (13 Asian Americans or Pacific Islanders, 10 Hispanic Americans), 3 international. Average age 34. 14 applicants, 79% accepted, 9 enrolled. In 2009, 3 master's awarded. *Degree requirements:* For master's, comprehensive exam. *Entrance requirements:* For master's, CBEST, CSET, CSET LOTE Test 3, RICA, language proficiency, 3 letters of recommendation. Additional exam requirements/recommendations for international students: Required—TOEFL (minimum score 600 paper-based; 250 computer-based; 100 iBT). *Application deadline:* For fall admission, 6/15 for domestic students; for spring admission, 11/15 for domestic students. Application fee: $50. Electronic applications accepted. *Financial support:* In 2009–10, 22 students received support, including 2 research assistantships (averaging $1,200 per year); scholarships/grants and unspecified assistantships also available. Support available to part-time students. Financial award application deadline: 6/15; financial award applicants required to submit FAFSA. Total annual research expenditures: $321,465. *Unit head:* Dr. Yvette Lapayese, Acting Chair, 310-338-3773, E-mail: ylapayes@lmu.edu. *Application contact:* Chake H. Kouyoumjian, Director, Graduate Admissions, 310-338-2721, Fax: 310-338-6086, E-mail: ckouyoum@lmu.edu.

Loyola Marymount University, School of Education, Department of Language and Culture in Education, Program in Biliteracy, Leadership, and Intercultural Education, Los Angeles, CA 90045. Offers MA. Part-time and evening/weekend programs available. *Faculty:* 7 full-time (5 women), 5 part-time/adjunct (3 women). *Students:* 10 full-time (all women); includes 8 minority (1 African American, 1 Asian American or Pacific Islander, 6 Hispanic Americans). Average age 30. In 2009, 11 master's awarded. *Degree requirements:* For master's, comprehensive exam. *Entrance requirements:* For master's, CBEST, CSET, CSET LOTE Test 3, RICA, language proficiency, 3 letters of recommendation. Additional exam requirements/recommendations for international students: Required—TOEFL (minimum score 600 paper-based; 250 computer-based; 100 iBT). *Application deadline:* For fall admission, 6/15 for domestic students; for spring admission, 11/15 for domestic students. Application fee: $50. Electronic applications accepted. *Financial support:* In 2009–10, 9 students received support, including 1 research assistantship (averaging $1,440 per year); scholarships/grants and unspecified assistantships also available. Support available to part-time students. Financial award application deadline: 6/15; financial award applicants required to submit FAFSA. Total annual research expenditures: $321,465. *Unit head:* Dr. Yvette Lapayese, Chair, 310-338-3773, E-mail: ylapayes@lmu.edu. *Application contact:* Chake H. Kouyoumjian, Director, Graduate Admissions, 310-338-2721, Fax: 310-338-6086, E-mail: ckouyoum@lmu.edu.

Mercy College, School of Education, Program in Bilingual Education, Dobbs Ferry, NY 10522-1189. Offers MS. Part-time and evening/weekend programs available. *Students:* 2 full-time (1 woman), 8 part-time (all women); includes 9 minority (all Hispanic Americans). Average age 37. 12 applicants, 33% accepted, 4 enrolled. In 2009, 4 master's awarded.

Multilingual and Multicultural Education

Mercy College (continued)

Entrance requirements: For master's, resume, interview by faculty advisor, minimum undergraduate GPA of 3.0. Additional exam requirements/recommendations for international students: Required—TOEFL (minimum score 600 paper-based; 250 computer-based; 100 iBT). *Application deadline:* For fall admission, 8/1 for international students. Applications are processed on a rolling basis. Application fee: $40. Electronic applications accepted. *Expenses:* Tuition: Full-time $13,158; part-time $731 per credit. Required fees: $500. Tuition and fees vary according to degree level and program. *Financial support:* Career-related internships or fieldwork, Federal Work-Study, scholarships/grants, and unspecified assistantships available. Financial award applicants required to submit FAFSA. *Faculty research:* Literacy construction, linguistics, education assessment. *Unit head:* Dr. Andrew Peiser, Interim Dean for the School of Education, 914-674-7489, Fax: 914-674-7352, E-mail: apeiser@mercy.edu. *Application contact:* Mary Ellen Hoffman, Interim Associate Dean, 914-674-7334, E-mail: mhoffman@mercy.edu.

Mercy College, School of Social and Behavioral Sciences, Dobbs Ferry, NY 10522-1189. Offers counseling (MS, Certificate), including alcohol and substance abuse counseling (Certificate), counseling (MS), family counseling (Certificate); health services management (MPA, MS); marriage and family therapy (MS); mental health counseling (MS); psychology (MS); school counseling (Certificate); school counseling and bilingual extension (Certificate); school psychology (MS). Part-time and evening/weekend programs available. Postbaccalaureate distance learning degree programs offered (minimal on-campus study). *Faculty:* 12 full-time (7 women), 38 part-time/adjunct (25 women). *Students:* 262 full-time (230 women), 379 part-time (323 women); includes 386 minority (171 African Americans, 6 American Indian/Alaska Native, 17 Asian Americans or Pacific Islanders, 192 Hispanic Americans), 9 international. Average age 35. 550 applicants, 43% accepted, 164 enrolled. In 2009, 162 master's, 14 other advanced degrees awarded. *Entrance requirements:* For master's, 2 letters of recommendation, interview, resume, essay. Additional exam requirements/recommendations for international students: Required—TOEFL (minimum score 600 paper-based; 250 computer-based; 100 iBT). *Application deadline:* For fall admission, 8/1 for international students. Applications are processed on a rolling basis. Application fee: $40. Electronic applications accepted. *Expenses:* Tuition: Full-time $13,158; part-time $731 per credit. Required fees: $500. Tuition and fees vary according to degree level and program. *Financial support:* In 2009–10, 1 student received support. Career-related internships or fieldwork, Federal Work-Study, scholarships/grants, and unspecified assistantships available. Support available to part-time students. Financial award applicants required to submit FAFSA. *Unit head:* Hind Rassam Culhane, Interim Dean, 914-674-7376, E-mail: hculhane@mercy.edu. *Application contact:* Hind Rassam Culhane, Interim Dean, 914-674-7376, E-mail: hculhane@mercy.edu.

Mercyhurst College, Graduate Program, Program in Special Education, Erie, PA 16546. Offers bilingual/bicultural special education (MS); educational leadership (Certificate); special education (MS). Part-time and evening/weekend programs available. *Degree requirements:* For master's, thesis optional. *Entrance requirements:* For master's, GRE General Test, MAT, or minimum GPA of 3.0, interview. Additional exam requirements/recommendations for international students: Required—TOEFL. Electronic applications accepted. *Faculty research:* College age learning disabled program, teacher preparation/collaboration, applied behavior analysis, special education policy issues.

Minnesota State University Mankato, College of Graduate Studies, College of Social and Behavioral Sciences, Department of Ethnic Studies, Mankato, MN 56001. Offers MS, Certificate. *Students:* 4 full-time (3 women), 9 part-time (3 women). *Application deadline:* For fall admission, 7/1 for domestic students, 5/1 for international students; for winter admission, 11/1 for domestic students; for spring admission, 10/1 for international students. Applications are processed on a rolling basis. Electronic applications accepted. *Expenses:* Tuition, state resident: full-time $5364. Tuition, nonresident: full-time $8314. *Unit head:* Dr. Wayne Allen, Graduate Coordinator, 507-389-1185. *Application contact:* Dr. Wayne Allen, Graduate Coordinator, 507-389-1185.

National University, Academic Affairs, School of Education, Department of Teacher Education, La Jolla, CA 92037-1011. Offers best practices (MA); cross-cultural teaching (M Ed); teacher leadership (MA); teaching (MA); teaching/learning in global society (MA). Part-time and evening/weekend programs available. Postbaccalaureate distance learning degree programs offered (no on-campus study). *Faculty:* 45 full-time (27 women), 293 part-time/adjunct (185 women). *Students:* 2,731 full-time (1,904 women), 4,477 part-time (3,008 women); includes 2,111 minority (481 African Americans, 35 American Indian/Alaska Native, 364 Asian Americans or Pacific Islanders, 1,231 Hispanic Americans), 10 international. Average age 35. 3,863 applicants, 100% accepted, 2916 enrolled. In 2009, 1,822 master's awarded. *Degree requirements:* For master's, thesis. *Entrance requirements:* For master's, interview, minimum GPA of 2.5. Additional exam requirements/recommendations for international students: Required—TOEFL (minimum score 550 paper-based; 213 computer-based; 79 iBT), IELTS (minimum score 6). *Application deadline:* Applications are processed on a rolling basis. Application fee: $60 ($65 for international students). Electronic applications accepted. *Expenses:* Tuition: Part-time $338 per quarter hour. *Financial support:* Career-related internships or fieldwork, institutionally sponsored loans, scholarships/grants, and tuition waivers (partial) available. Support available to part-time students. Financial award application deadline: 6/30; financial award applicants required to submit FAFSA. *Unit head:* Dr. Cynthia Schubert-Irastroza, Chair, 858-642-8320, Fax: 858-642-8724, E-mail: cshubert@nu.edu. *Application contact:* Dominick Giovanniello, Associate Regional Dean—San Diego, 800-NAT-UNIV, Fax: 858-541-7792, E-mail: dgiovann@nu.edu.

New Jersey City University, Graduate Studies and Continuing Education, Debra Cannon Partridge Wolfe College of Education, Department of Educational Leadership, Jersey City, NJ 07305-1597. Offers basics and urban studies (MA); bilingual/bicultural education and English as a second language (MA); educational administration and supervision (MA). Part-time and evening/weekend programs available. *Faculty:* 3. *Students:* 27 full-time (18 women), 187 part-time (115 women); includes 77 minority (18 African Americans, 6 Asian Americans or Pacific Islanders, 53 Hispanic Americans), 16 international. Average age 34. In 2009, 121 master's awarded. *Entrance requirements:* For master's, GRE General Test or MAT. Additional exam requirements/recommendations for international students: Required—TOEFL. *Application deadline:* For fall admission, 8/1 priority date for domestic students; for spring admission, 12/1 for domestic students. Applications are processed on a rolling basis. Application fee: $0. *Expenses:* Tuition, area resident: Part-time $456.75 per credit. Tuition, nonresident: part-time $842.55 per credit. Required fees: $65 per term. *Financial support:* Fellowships, teaching assistantships, career-related internships or fieldwork and unspecified assistantships available. *Unit head:* Dr. Susan Phifer, Chairperson, 201-200-3012, E-mail: sphifer@njcu.edu. *Application contact:* Dr. Susan Phifer, Chairperson, 201-200-3012, E-mail: sphifer@njcu.edu.

New Mexico State University, Graduate School, College of Education, Department of Special Education and Communication Disorders, Las Cruces, NM 88003-8001. Offers bilingual/multicultural special education (Ed D, PhD); communication disorders (MA); special education (MA, Ed D, PhD). *Accreditation:* ASHA (one or more programs are accredited); NCATE. Part-time and evening/weekend programs available. Postbaccalaureate distance learning degree programs offered. *Faculty:* 16 full-time (13 women), 3 part-time/adjunct (all women). *Students:* 59 full-time (56 women), 61 part-time (47 women); includes 54 minority (5 American Indian/Alaska Native, 2 Asian Americans or Pacific Islanders, 47 Hispanic Americans). Average age 34. 93 applicants, 77% accepted, 48 enrolled. In 2009, 21 master's, 1 doctorate awarded. *Degree requirements:* For master's, comprehensive exam, thesis optional; for doctorate, comprehensive exam, thesis/dissertation. *Entrance requirements:* For master's, GRE General Test or MAT. Additional exam requirements/recommendations for international students: Required—TOEFL. *Application deadline:* For fall admission, 2/1 priority date for domestic students. Applications are processed on a rolling basis. Application fee: $30 ($50 for international students). Electronic applications accepted. *Expenses:* Tuition, state resident: full-time $4080; part-time $223 per credit. Tuition, nonresident: full-time $14,256; part-time $647 per credit. Required fees: $1278; $639 per semester. *Financial support:* In 2009–10, 28 students received support, including 2 research assistantships (averaging $10,715 per year), 12 teaching assistantships (averaging $4,617 per year); fellowships, career-related internships or fieldwork, Federal Work-Study, and health care benefits also available. Support available to part-time students. Financial award application deadline: 3/1; financial award applicants required to submit FAFSA. *Faculty research:* Multicultural special education, multicultural communication disorders, mild disability, multicultural assessment, deaf education, early childhood, bilingual special education. *Unit head:* Dr. Eric Joseph Lopez, Interim Department Head, 575-646-2402, Fax: 575-646-7712, E-mail: leric@nmsu.edu. *Application contact:* Coordinator.

New York University, Steinhardt School of Culture, Education, and Human Development, Department of Humanities and Social Sciences in the Professions, Program in Sociology of Education, New York, NY 10012-1019. Offers education and social policy (MA); sociology of education (MA, PhD), including education policy (MA), social and cultural studies of education (MA). Part-time programs available. *Students:* 16 full-time (14 women), 7 part-time (4 women); includes 3 minority (1 African American, 1 American Indian/Alaska Native, 1 Hispanic American), 3 international. Average age 27. 35 applicants, 57% accepted, 6 enrolled. In 2009, 6 master's awarded. *Degree requirements:* For master's, thesis (for some programs); for doctorate, thesis/dissertation. *Entrance requirements:* For master's, letters of recommendation; for doctorate, GRE General Test, interview. Additional exam requirements/recommendations for international students: Required—TOEFL. *Application deadline:* For fall admission, 12/15 priority date for domestic and international students; for spring admission, 11/1 for domestic and international students. Applications are processed on a rolling basis. Application fee: $75. Electronic applications accepted. *Expenses:* Tuition: Full-time $30,528; part-time $1272 per credit. Required fees: $2177. *Financial support:* Fellowships with full and partial tuition reimbursements, Federal Work-Study, institutionally sponsored loans, scholarships/grants, and tuition waivers (partial) available. Support available to part-time students. Financial award application deadline: 2/1; financial award applicants required to submit FAFSA. *Faculty research:* Legal and institutional environments of schools; social inequality; high school reform and achievement; urban schooling, economics and education, educational policy . *Unit head:* Dr. Floyd M. Hammack, Program Director, 212-998-5542, Fax: 212-995-4832, E-mail: fmhl@nyu.edu. *Application contact:* 212-998-5030, Fax: 212-995-4328, E-mail: steinhardt.gradadmissions@nyu.edu.

New York University, Steinhardt School of Culture, Education, and Human Development, Department of Teaching and Learning, Program in Multilingual/Multicultural Studies, New York, NY 10012-1019. Offers bilingual education (MA, PhD, Advanced Certificate); foreign language education (MA, Advanced Certificate); foreign language education/TESOL (MA); teaching English to speakers of other languages (MA, PhD, Advanced Certificate); teaching French as a foreign language (MA). *Accreditation:* Teacher Education Accreditation Council. Part-time and evening/weekend programs available. *Students:* 138 full-time (121 women), 97 part-time (78 women); includes 49 minority (4 African Americans, 25 Asian Americans or Pacific Islanders, 20 Hispanic Americans), 79 international. Average age 28. 330 applicants, 75% accepted, 88 enrolled. In 2009, 120 master's, 5 doctorates, 13 other advanced degrees awarded. *Degree requirements:* For master's, thesis (for some programs); for doctorate, thesis/dissertation. *Entrance requirements:* For doctorate, GRE General Test, interview; for Advanced Certificate, master's degree. Additional exam requirements/recommendations for international students: Required—TOEFL. *Application deadline:* For fall admission, 12/15 priority date for domestic and international students; for spring admission, 11/1 for domestic and international students. Applications are processed on a rolling basis. Application fee: $75. Electronic applications accepted. *Expenses:* Tuition: Full-time $30,528; part-time $1272 per credit. Required fees: $2177. *Financial support:* Fellowships with full and partial tuition reimbursements, career-related internships or fieldwork, Federal Work-Study, institutionally sponsored loans, scholarships/grants, and tuition waivers (partial) available. Support available to part-time students. Financial award application deadline: 2/1; financial award applicants required to submit FAFSA. *Faculty research:* Second language acquisition, cross-cultural communication, technology-enhanced language learning, language variation, action learning. *Unit head:* Dr. Miriam Eisenstein Ebsworth, Director, 212-998-5460, Fax: 212-995-4049. *Application contact:* 212-998-5030, Fax: 212-995-4328, E-mail: steinhardt.gradadmissions@nyu.edu.

Northeastern Illinois University, Graduate College, College of Education, School of Teacher Education, Program in Bilingual/Bicultural Education, Chicago, IL 60625-4699. Offers MAT, MSI. *Entrance requirements:* For master's, GRE, ISBE, minimum GPA of 2.75. Additional exam requirements/recommendations for international students: Required—TOEFL (minimum score 550 paper-based; 213 computer-based; 80 iBT). Electronic applications accepted. *Faculty research:* Bilingual teacher preparation, linguistics and phonetics, Middle Eastern languages and cultures, TOEFL.

Northern Arizona University, Graduate College, College of Education, Department of Educational Specialties, Flagstaff, AZ 86011. Offers autism spectrum disorders (Certificate); bilingual/multicultural education (M Ed), including bilingual education, ESL education; career and technical education (M Ed, Certificate); curriculum and instruction (Ed D); early childhood special education (M Ed); early intervention (Certificate); educational technology (M Ed, Certificate); special education (M Ed). *Faculty:* 29 full-time (16 women). *Students:* 153 full-time (118 women), 360 part-time (291 women); includes 152 minority (12 African Americans, 43 American Indian/Alaska Native, 5 Asian Americans or Pacific Islanders, 92 Hispanic Americans), 9 international. Average age 30. 215 applicants, 87% accepted, 133 enrolled. In 2009, 200 master's, 8 doctorates awarded. *Degree requirements:* For master's, comprehensive exam (for some programs), thesis (for some programs). *Entrance requirements:* For master's, minimum GPA of 3.0. Additional exam requirements/recommendations for international students: Required—TOEFL (minimum score 550 paper-based; 213 computer-based; 80 iBT), IELTS (minimum score 7), or a bachelor's degree from an English-speaking university and demonstrated proficiency. *Application deadline:* For fall admission, 2/1 for domestic students, 8/1 for international students; for spring admission, 12/1 for domestic students. Applications are processed on a rolling basis. Application fee: $65. Electronic applications accepted. *Financial support:* In 2009–10, 2 research assistantships with partial tuition reimbursements (averaging $10,000 per year), 8 teaching assistantships with partial tuition reimbursements (averaging $10,000 per year) were awarded. Financial award application deadline: 3/30. *Unit head:* Dr. Lawrence Gallagher, Chair, 928-523-5083, E-mail: lawrence.gallagher@nau.edu. *Application contact:* Dr. Lawrence Gallagher, Chair, 928-523-5083, E-mail: lawrence.gallagher@nau.edu.

Nova Southeastern University, Fischler School of Education and Human Services, Graduate Teacher Education Program, Fort Lauderdale, FL 33314-7796. Offers athletic administration (MS); brain research (MS, Ed S); charter school education/leadership (MS); cognitive and behavioral disabilities (MS); computer science education (Ed S); computer science education (K-12) (MS); curriculum and teaching (Ed S); curriculum, instruction and technology (MS); curriculum, instruction, management and administration (Ed S); early childhood education (MS); early literacy and reading (Ed S); early literacy education (MS); education technology (MS); educational leadership (administration K–12) (MS, Ed S); educational media (Ed S); educational media (K-12) (MS); elementary education (MS, Ed S), including ESOL endorsement (MS); English education (MS, Ed S); environmental education (MS); exceptional student education (MS), including ESOL endorsement; gifted education (MS, Ed S); interdisciplinary arts education (MS); management and administration of educational programs (MS); mathematics (MS); mathematics education (Ed S); multicultural early intervention (MS); pre-kindergarten/primary (MS); preschool education (MS); reading (MS); reading and TESOL (MS); reading education (Ed S); science (MS); science education (Ed S); secondary education (MS); social studies (MS, Ed S); Spanish language (MS); special education and reading (MS); teaching and learning (MA, MS), including curriculum and instruction (MA), elementary mathematics (MA), elementary reading (MA), K-12 technology integration (MA); teaching English to speakers of other languages (MS, Ed S); technology management and administration (Ed S); urban studies education (MS). Part-time and evening/weekend programs available. Postbaccalaureate distance learning degree programs offered (minimal on-campus study).

Faculty: 72 full-time (43 women), 385 part-time/adjunct (252 women). *Students:* 196 full-time (175 women), 1,304 part-time (1,128 women); includes 594 minority (471 African Americans, 5 American Indian/Alaska Native, 18 Asian Americans or Pacific Islanders, 100 Hispanic Americans). Average age 37. 2,610 applicants, 72% accepted, 1352 enrolled. In 2009, 836 other advanced degrees awarded. *Degree requirements:* For master's and Ed S, thesis, practicum, internship. *Entrance requirements:* For master's, MAT, GRE, CLAST, CBEST, PRAXIS I, General Knowledge Test, minimum GPA of 2.5; for Ed S, MAT or GRE, master's degree, teaching certificate, minimum GPA of 3.0. Additional exam requirements/recommendations for international students: Required—TSE (recommended, minimum score 50); Recommended—TOEFL (minimum score 550 paper-based; 213 computer-based; 80 iBT), IELTS (minimum score 6). *Application deadline:* For fall admission, 9/25 priority date for domestic and international students; for winter admission, 2/23 priority date for domestic and international students; for spring admission, 4/25 priority date for domestic and international students. Applications are processed on a rolling basis. Application fee: $50. Electronic applications accepted. *Financial support:* Federal Work-Study available. Support available to part-time students. Financial award application deadline: 4/15; financial award applicants required to submit FAFSA. *Faculty research:* School effectiveness, critical thinking, leadership skills acquisition, child education, multicultural education. *Unit head:* Dr. Ronald Kern, Dean of Academic Affairs, 800-986-3223 Ext. 7809, Fax: 954-262-3606, E-mail: rk429@nsu.nova.edu. *Application contact:* Dr. Jennifer Quinones Nottingham, Dean of Student Affairs, 800-986-3223 Ext. 1559.

Ohio University, Graduate College, College of Education, Department of Educational Studies, Athens, OH 45701-2979. Offers computer education and technology (M Ed); cultural studies (M Ed); educational administration (M Ed, Ed D); educational research and evaluation (M Ed, PhD); instructional technology (PhD). Part-time and evening/weekend programs available. Postbaccalaureate distance learning degree programs offered (minimal on-campus study). *Faculty:* 12 full-time (6 women), 2 part-time/adjunct (0 women). *Students:* 151 full-time (95 women), 142 part-time (105 women); includes 24 minority (19 African Americans, 1 American Indian/Alaska Native, 1 Asian American or Pacific Islander, 3 Hispanic Americans), 46 international. 107 applicants, 69% accepted, 50 enrolled. In 2009, 32 master's, 19 doctorates awarded. *Degree requirements:* For master's, thesis or alternative; for doctorate, comprehensive exam, thesis/dissertation. *Entrance requirements:* For master's, GRE General Test (if GPA less than 2.9); for doctorate, GRE General Test, GRE Subject Test, minimum GPA of 2.9, work experience, 3 letters of reference, autobiography. Additional exam requirements/recommendations for international students: Required—TOEFL (minimum score 550 paper-based; 80 iBT) or IELTS Academic (minimum score 6.5). *Application deadline:* For fall admission, 3/1 priority date for domestic and international students; for winter admission, 10/1 priority date for domestic and international students; for spring admission, 1/30 priority date for domestic students, 1/1 priority date for international students. Applications are processed on a rolling basis. Application fee: $50 ($55 for international students). Electronic applications accepted. *Expenses:* Tuition, state resident: full-time $7839; part-time $323 per quarter hour. Tuition, nonresident: full-time $15,831; part-time $654 per quarter hour. Required fees: $2931. *Financial support:* Research assistantships with full tuition reimbursements, teaching assistantships with full tuition reimbursements, Federal Work-Study, institutionally sponsored loans, tuition waivers (partial), and unspecified assistantships available. Financial award application deadline: 3/1. *Faculty research:* Race, class and gender; computer programs; development and organization theory; evaluation/development of instruments, leadership. Total annual research expenditures: $158,037. *Unit head:* Dr. Gordon Brooks, Chair, 740-593-4423, Fax: 740-593-0477, E-mail: brooksg@ohio.edu. *Application contact:* Floyd J. Doney, Director of Student Affairs, 740-593-4400, Fax: 740-593-9310, E-mail: doney@ohio.edu.

Our Lady of the Lake University of San Antonio, School of Professional Studies, Program in Curriculum and Instruction, San Antonio, TX 78207-4689. Offers bilingual (M Ed); early childhood education (M Ed); English as a second language (M Ed); integrated math teaching (M Ed); integrated science teaching (M Ed); master reading teacher (M Ed); master technology teacher (M Ed); reading specialist (M Ed). *Students:* 2 full-time (1 woman), 112 part-time (94 women); includes 64 minority (5 African Americans, 1 American Indian/Alaska Native, 1 Asian American or Pacific Islander, 57 Hispanic Americans). Average age 38. In 2009, 49 master's awarded. *Expenses:* Tuition: Full-time $12,330; part-time $685 per contact hour. Required fees: $139; $12 per contact hour. $57 per semester. Tuition and fees vary according to campus/location. *Unit head:* Dr. Cullen Grinnan, 210-434-6711 Ext. 8928, E-mail: ctgrinnan@lake.ollusa.edu. *Application contact:* Dr. Cullen Grinnan, 210-434-6711 Ext. 8928, E-mail: ctgrinnan@lake.ollusa.edu.

Park University, College of Graduate and Professional Studies, Kansas City, MO 54105. Offers adult education (M Ed); at-risk students (M Ed); disaster and emergency management (MPA); educational administration (M Ed); entrepreneurship (MBA); general business (MBA); general education (M Ed); government/business relations (MPA); healthcare/services management (MBA, MPA); international business (MBA); K-12 certification (MAT); management information systems (MBA); management of information systems (MPA); middle school certification (MAT); multi-cultural education (M Ed); nonprofit management (MPA); public management (MPA); school law (M Ed); secondary school certification (MAT); special education (M Ed). Part-time and evening/weekend programs available. Postbaccalaureate distance learning degree programs offered (no on-campus study). *Degree requirements:* For master's, comprehensive exam, thesis (for some programs). *Entrance requirements:* For master's, GRE, GMAT, teacher certification (M Ed). Additional exam requirements/recommendations for international students: Required—TOEFL (minimum score 550 paper-based). Electronic applications accepted. *Faculty research:* Literacy, leadership, brain based research, multicultural education, diversity.

Queens College of the City University of New York, Division of Graduate Studies, Division of Education, Department of Elementary and Early Childhood Education, Flushing, NY 11367-1597. Offers bilingual education (MS Ed); childhood education (MA); early childhood education (MA); elementary education (MS Ed, AC); literacy (MS Ed). Part-time and evening/weekend programs available. *Faculty:* 31 full-time (25 women). *Students:* 98 full-time (88 women), 430 part-time (392 women). 436 applicants, 64% accepted, 212 enrolled. In 2009, 220 master's awarded. *Degree requirements:* For master's, research project; for AC, thesis optional. *Entrance requirements:* For master's, minimum GPA of 3.0. Additional exam requirements/recommendations for international students: Required—TOEFL. *Application deadline:* For fall admission, 4/1 for domestic students; for spring admission, 11/1 for domestic students. Applications are processed on a rolling basis. Application fee: $125. *Expenses:* Tuition, state resident: full-time $7360; part-time $310 per credit. Tuition, nonresident: part-time $575 per credit. One-time fee: $195 full-time; $145.25 part-time. *Financial support:* Career-related internships or fieldwork, Federal Work-Study, institutionally sponsored loans, and tuition waivers (partial) available. Support available to part-time students. Financial award application deadline: 4/1; financial award applicants required to submit FAFSA. *Unit head:* Dr. Myra Zarnowski, Chairperson, 718-997-5328. *Application contact:* Mario Caruso, Director of Graduate Admissions, 718-997-5200, Fax: 718-997-5193, E-mail: graduate_admissions@qc.edu.

Rowan University, Graduate School, College of Education, Department of Teacher Education, Program in ESL/Bilingual Education, Glassboro, NJ 08028-1701. Offers Graduate Certificate. Part-time and evening/weekend programs available. *Students:* 3 part-time (all women). Average age 36. 1 applicant, 100% accepted, 0 enrolled. *Entrance requirements:* Additional exam requirements/recommendations for international students: Required—TOEFL. *Application deadline:* Applications are processed on a rolling basis. Application fee: $50. Electronic applications accepted. *Expenses:* Tuition, state resident: full-time $10,624; part-time $590 per semester hour. Tuition, nonresident: full-time $10,624; part-time $590 per semester hour. Required fees: $2320; $125 per semester hour. *Financial support:* Career-related internships or fieldwork and unspecified assistantships available. Support available to part-time students. *Unit head:* Dr. Mira Lalovic-Hand, Interim Associate Provost/Director of Graduate School, 856-256-5120 Ext. 3812, E-mail: lalovic-hand@rowan.edu. *Application contact:* Karen Haynes, Graduate Coordinator, 856-256-4052, Fax: 856-256-4436, E-mail: haynes@rowan.edu.

Rutgers, The State University of New Jersey, New Brunswick, Graduate School-New Brunswick, Program in Spanish, Piscataway, NJ 08854-8097. Offers bilingualism and second language acquisition (MA, PhD); Spanish (MA, MAT, PhD); Spanish literature (MA, PhD); translation (MA). Part-time programs available. *Degree requirements:* For master's, comprehensive exam (for some programs), thesis (for some programs); for doctorate, 2 foreign languages, comprehensive exam, thesis/dissertation. *Entrance requirements:* For master's and doctorate, GRE General Test. Additional exam requirements/recommendations for international students: Required—TOEFL. Electronic applications accepted. *Faculty research:* Hispanic literature, Luso-Brazilian literature, Spanish linguistics, Spanish translation.

St. John's University, The School of Education, Department of Human Services and Counseling, Program in Bilingual/Multicultural Education/Teaching English to Speakers of Other Languages, Queens, NY 11439. Offers MS Ed. Part-time and evening/weekend programs available. *Students:* 35 full-time (32 women), 124 part-time (112 women); includes 59 minority (6 African Americans, 6 Asian Americans or Pacific Islanders, 47 Hispanic Americans), 7 international. Average age 31. 91 applicants, 85% accepted, 40 enrolled. In 2009, 31 master's awarded. *Degree requirements:* For master's, comprehensive exam. *Entrance requirements:* For master's, minimum GPA of 3.0, eligibility for teacher certification. Additional exam requirements/recommendations for international students: Required—TOEFL (minimum score 500 paper-based; 173 computer-based; 61 iBT), IELTS (minimum score 5.5). *Application deadline:* For fall admission, 4/1 priority date for domestic students, 6/1 priority date for international students; for spring admission, 11/1 priority date for domestic and international students. Applications are processed on a rolling basis. Application fee: $70. Electronic applications accepted. *Expenses:* Tuition: Full-time $16,290; part-time $905 per credit. Required fees: $300; $150 per semester. Tuition and fees vary according to program. *Financial support:* Research assistantships, career-related internships or fieldwork and scholarships/grants available. Support available to part-time students. Financial award application deadline: 3/1; financial award applicants required to submit FAFSA. *Faculty research:* Second language learning and academic achievement, heritage language education, assessing the progress of English language learners towards English acquisition, dual language acquisition, study of English Creoles and dialects of other Englishes. *Unit head:* Dr. Francine Guastello, Acting Chair, 718-990-1475, E-mail: guastelf@stjohns.edu. *Application contact:* Dr. Kelly K. Ronayne, Associate Dean for Graduate Admissions, 718-990-2303, Fax: 718-990-2343, E-mail: graded@stjohns.edu.

St. John's University, The School of Education, Department of Human Services and Counseling, Program in Bilingual School Counseling, Queens, NY 11439. Offers MS Ed, PD. Part-time and evening/weekend programs available. *Students:* 6 full-time (all women), 11 part-time (9 women); includes 12 minority (1 African American, 11 Hispanic Americans). Average age 33. 18 applicants, 78% accepted, 5 enrolled. In 2009, 8 master's awarded. *Degree requirements:* For master's, comprehensive exam. *Entrance requirements:* For master's, New York State Bilingual Assessment (BEA), minimum GPA of 3.0, 2 letters of recommendation, interview, writing sample; for PD, personal statement, official transcripts showing conferral of degree with minimum GPA of 3.0, 2 letters of recommendation, interview. Additional exam requirements/recommendations for international students: Required—TOEFL (minimum score 500 paper-based; 173 computer-based; 61 iBT), IELTS (minimum score 5.5). *Application deadline:* For fall admission, 4/1 priority date for domestic students, 6/1 priority date for international students; for spring admission, 11/1 priority date for domestic and international students. Applications are processed on a rolling basis. Application fee: $70. Electronic applications accepted. *Expenses:* Tuition: Full-time $16,290; part-time $905 per credit. Required fees: $300; $150 per semester. Tuition and fees vary according to program. *Financial support:* Research assistantships, career-related internships or fieldwork and scholarships/grants available. Support available to part-time students. Financial award application deadline: 3/1; financial award applicants required to submit FAFSA. *Faculty research:* Cross-cultural comparisons of predictors of active coping. *Unit head:* Dr. Francine Guastello, Acting Chair, 718-990-1475, E-mail: guastelf@stjohns.edu. *Application contact:* Dr. Kelly K. Ronayne, Associate Dean for Graduate Admissions, 718-990-2303, Fax: 718-990-2343, E-mail: graded@stjohns.edu.

San Diego State University, Graduate and Research Affairs, College of Education, Department of Policy Studies in Language and Cross Cultural Education, San Diego, CA 92182. Offers multi-cultural emphasis (PhD); policy studies in language and cross cultural education (MA). *Accreditation:* NCATE. *Entrance requirements:* For master's, GRE General Test, letters of reference; for doctorate, GRE General Test, 3 letters of reference, resumé. Additional exam requirements/recommendations for international students: Required—TOEFL. Electronic applications accepted.

Seton Hall University, College of Education and Human Services, Department of Educational Studies, Program in Bilingual Education, South Orange, NJ 07079-2697. Offers Ed S. *Accreditation:* NCATE. Part-time and evening/weekend programs available. *Faculty:* 2 full-time (0 women). *Students:* 2 part-time (both women). Average age 42. *Degree requirements:* For Ed S, 2 foreign languages, comprehensive exam, cumulative project. *Entrance requirements:* For degree, GRE or MAT, minimum GPA of 2.75. *Application deadline:* For fall admission, 5/1 for domestic students; for spring admission, 10/1 for domestic students. Applications are processed on a rolling basis. Application fee: $50. *Financial support:* Fellowships with full tuition reimbursements, unspecified assistantships available. Financial award application deadline: 2/1. *Faculty research:* Spanish, Mandarin and Cantonese Chinese; Japanese; Korean; school administration and supervision. *Unit head:* Dr. Juan Cobarrubias, Director, 973-761-9617, E-mail: cobarrju@shu.edu. *Application contact:* Dr. Juan Cobarrubias, Director, 973-761-9617, E-mail: cobarrju@shu.edu.

Southern Connecticut State University, School of Graduate Studies, School of Arts and Sciences, Department of Foreign Languages, New Haven, CT 06515-1355. Offers multicultural-bilingual education/teaching English to speakers of other languages (MS). Part-time and evening/weekend programs available. *Faculty:* 6 full-time. *Students:* 16 full-time (9 women), 25 part-time (22 women); includes 7 minority (1 Asian American or Pacific Islander, 6 Hispanic Americans). 5 applicants, 60% accepted, 3 enrolled. In 2009, 24 master's awarded. *Degree requirements:* For master's, one foreign language, thesis or alternative. *Entrance requirements:* For master's, interview, minimum undergraduate GPA of 2.7. *Application deadline:* For fall admission, 7/15 priority date for domestic students. Applications are processed on a rolling basis. Application fee: $50. Electronic applications accepted. Tuition and fees vary according to program. *Financial support:* Application deadline: 4/15. *Unit head:* Dr. Elena Schmitt, Chairperson, 203-392-6138, Fax: 203-392-6136, E-mail: schmitte1@southernct.edu. *Application contact:* Dr. Luisa Piemontese, Graduate Coordinator, 203-392-6751, E-mail: piemontesel1@southernct.edu.

Southern Methodist University, Annette Caldwell Simmons School of Education and Human Development, Department of Teaching and Learning, Dallas, TX 75275. Offers bilingual/ESL education (MBE); education (M Ed, PhD); educational preparation (Certificate); gifted and talented focus (MBE); learning therapist (Certificate). Part-time and evening/weekend programs available. *Faculty:* 16 full-time (12 women), 31 part-time/adjunct (26 women). *Students:* 28 full-time (23 women), 413 part-time (335 women); includes 125 minority (40 African Americans, 4 American Indian/Alaska Native, 14 Asian Americans or Pacific Islanders, 67 Hispanic Americans), 16 international. Average age 36. 36 applicants, 92% accepted, 29 enrolled. In 2009, 85 master's, 28 other advanced degrees awarded. Terminal master's awarded for partial completion of doctoral program. *Degree requirements:* For master's, comprehensive exam, minimum GPA of 3.0; for doctorate, thesis/dissertation, qualifying exams, major area paper, evidence of teaching competency, dissemination of research (e.g., conference presentation), professional portfolio. *Entrance requirements:* For master's, minimum GPA of 3.0 or GRE, 3 letters of recommendation; for doctorate, GRE, minimum GPA of 3.3, 3 years of full-time teaching, 3 letters of recommendation, interview. Additional exam requirements/recommendations for international students: Required—TOEFL. Application fee: $75. Electronic applications

Multilingual and Multicultural Education

Southern Methodist University (continued)

accepted. *Financial support:* In 2009–10, 31 students received support; teaching assistantships, scholarships/grants and tuition waivers available. Financial award application deadline: 5/1. *Faculty research:* Reading intervention, mathematics intervention, bilingual education, new literacies. Total annual research expenditures: $2.7 million. *Unit head:* Prof. Jill H. Allor, Associate Professor and Chair, 214-768-2346, Fax: 214-768-8700, E-mail: jallor@smu.edu. *Application contact:* Dr. Deborah Diffily, Administrative Assistant, 214-768-2346, E-mail: ddiffily@smu.edu.

State University of New York at New Paltz, Graduate School, School of Education, Department of Educational Studies, Program in Humanistic/Multicultural Education, New Paltz, NY 12561. Offers MPS. *Accreditation:* NCATE. Part-time and evening/weekend programs available. *Faculty:* 6 full-time (4 women), 3 part-time/adjunct (all women). *Students:* 7 full-time (5 women), 48 part-time (36 women); includes 12 minority (6 African Americans, 1 American Indian/Alaska Native, 1 Asian American or Pacific Islander, 4 Hispanic Americans). Average age 32. 24 applicants, 71% accepted, 15 enrolled. In 2009, 49 master's awarded. *Degree requirements:* For master's, portfolio. *Entrance requirements:* For master's, minimum GPA of 3.0. Additional exam requirements/recommendations for international students: Required—TOEFL (minimum score 550 paper-based; 213 computer-based; 80 iBT), IELTS (minimum score 6.5). *Application deadline:* For fall admission, 3/15 priority date for domestic students, 3/15 for international students; for spring admission, 10/15 for domestic and international students. Application fee: $50. Electronic applications accepted. *Financial support:* In 2009–10, 3 students received support, including 1 fellowship (averaging $9,000 per year); tuition waivers (full) also available. Financial award application deadline: 8/1; financial award applicants required to submit FAFSA. *Unit head:* Dr. Nancy Schniedewind, Coordinator, 845-257-2827, E-mail: schniedn@newpaltz.edu. *Application contact:* Caroline Murphy, Graduate Admissions Advisor, 845-257-3285, E-mail: gradschool@newpaltz.edu.

State University of New York College at Geneseo, Graduate Studies, School of Education, Program in Childhood Multicultural Education (1-6), Geneseo, NY 14454-1401. Offers MS Ed. Part-time and evening/weekend programs available. *Faculty:* 8 full-time (5 women), 1 part-time/adjunct (0 women). *Students:* 4 full-time (all women), 7 part-time (4 women); includes 1 minority (Asian American or Pacific Islander). Average age 32. 4 applicants, 100% accepted, 4 enrolled. *Degree requirements:* For master's, thesis optional, culiminating experience. *Application deadline:* For fall admission, 3/1 for domestic students; for spring admission, 10/1 for domestic students. Application fee: $50. *Expenses:* Tuition, state resident: full-time $8370; part-time $349 per credit hour. Tuition, nonresident: full-time $13,250; part-time $552 per credit hour. Required fees: $700.52; $29 per credit hour. *Financial support:* In 2009–10, 2 students received support. Scholarships/grants, health care benefits, tuition waivers (full), and unspecified assistantships available. Support available to part-time students. Financial award application deadline: 4/1; financial award applicants required to submit FAFSA. *Unit head:* Dr. Osman Alawiye, Dean/Chairperson, 585-245-5560, Fax: 585-245-5220, E-mail: alawiyeo@geneseo.edu. *Application contact:* Dr. Susan Salmon, Assistant to the Dean/Graduate Liaison, 585-245-5560, Fax: 585-245-5220, E-mail: salmon@geneseo.edu.

Sul Ross State University, Rio Grande College of Sul Ross State University, Alpine, TX 79832. Offers business administration (MBA); teacher education (M Ed), including bilingual education, counseling, educational diagnostics, elementary education, general education, reading, school administration, secondary education. Part-time and evening/weekend programs available. *Degree requirements:* For master's, thesis optional. *Entrance requirements:* For master's, GMAT or GRE General Test, minimum GPA of 2.5 in last 60 hours of undergraduate work. *Faculty research:* Drug and substance abuse counseling, U.S.-Mexico border economic development.

Sul Ross State University, School of Professional Studies, Department of Teacher Education, Program in Bilingual Education, Alpine, TX 79832. Offers M Ed. Part-time and evening/weekend programs available. *Degree requirements:* For master's, thesis optional. *Entrance requirements:* For master's, GMAT or GRE General Test, minimum GPA of 2.5 in last 60 hours of undergraduate work.

Teachers College, Columbia University, Graduate Faculty of Education, Department of International and Transcultural Studies, Program in Bilingual and Bicultural Education, New York, NY 10027-6696. Offers MA. *Accreditation:* NCATE. Part-time programs available. *Faculty:* 2 full-time (both women), 2 part-time/adjunct (both women). *Students:* 17 full-time (16 women), 38 part-time (32 women); includes 17 minority (9 Asian Americans or Pacific Islanders, 8 Hispanic Americans), 17 international. Average age 27. 52 applicants, 73% accepted, 23 enrolled. In 2009, 21 master's awarded. *Degree requirements:* For master's, one foreign language. *Application deadline:* For fall admission, 5/15 for domestic students. Application fee: $65. *Financial support:* Research assistantships, career-related internships or fieldwork, Federal Work-Study, institutionally sponsored loans, scholarships/grants, and tuition waivers (full and partial) available. Support available to part-time students. Financial award application deadline: 2/1. *Faculty research:* Cross-cultural research in bilingual and bicultural school settings, diversity and teacher education. *Unit head:* Dr. George Bond, Chair, 212-678-3947. *Application contact:* Deanna Ghozati, Assistant Director of Admission, 212-678-4018, Fax: 212-678-4171, E-mail: ghozati@tc.edu.

Texas A&M International University, Office of Graduate Studies and Research, College of Education, Department of Curriculum and Instruction, Laredo, TX 78041-1900. Offers bilingual education (PhD); curriculum and instruction (MS, PhD); early childhood education (PhD); reading (MS). *Faculty:* 4 full-time (3 women). *Students:* 7 full-time (3 women), 120 part-time (105 women); includes 117 minority (all Hispanic Americans), 2 international. Average age 36. 50 applicants, 64% accepted, 29 enrolled. In 2009, 34 master's awarded. *Application deadline:* For fall admission, 4/30 priority date for domestic students; for spring admission, 11/30 for domestic students. *Unit head:* Dr. Cathy Guerra, Interim Chair, 956-326-2438, E-mail: cgsakta@tamiu.edu. *Application contact:* Rosie Dickinson, Director of Admissions, 956-326-2200.

Texas A&M University, College of Education and Human Development, Department of Teaching, Learning, and Culture, College Station, TX 77843. Offers curriculum and instruction (M Ed, MS, PhD); mathematics education (M Ed, MS, PhD); multicultural/urban/ESL/international education (M Ed, MS, PhD); reading/language arts (M Ed, MS, PhD); science education (M Ed, MS, PhD); social studies education (M Ed, MS, PhD). Part-time programs available. *Faculty:* 33. *Students:* 145 full-time (113 women), 270 part-time (214 women); includes 110 minority (60 African Americans, 4 American Indian/Alaska Native, 4 Asian Americans or Pacific Islanders, 42 Hispanic Americans), 47 international. Average age 36. In 2009, 114 master's, 17 doctorates awarded. *Degree requirements:* For master's, comprehensive exam, thesis (for some programs); for doctorate, comprehensive exam, thesis/dissertation. *Entrance requirements:* For master's, GRE General Test, minimum GPA of 3.0; for doctorate, GRE General Test, 3 years of teaching experience. Additional exam requirements/recommendations for international students: Required—TOEFL (minimum score 550 paper-based; 213 computer-based). *Application deadline:* For fall admission, 1/15 priority date for domestic and international students; for spring admission, 9/15 priority date for domestic and international students. Applications are processed on a rolling basis. Application fee: $50 ($75 for international students). Electronic applications accepted. *Expenses:* Tuition, state resident: full-time $3991; part-time $221.74 per credit hour. Tuition, nonresident: full-time $9049; part-time $502.74 per credit hour. *Financial support:* In 2009–10, fellowships with partial tuition reimbursements (averaging $3,000 per year), teaching assistantships with partial tuition reimbursements (averaging $7,200 per year) were awarded; research assistantships with partial tuition reimbursements, career-related internships or fieldwork, Federal Work-Study, institutionally sponsored loans, scholarships/grants, tuition waivers (partial), and unspecified assistantships also available. Support available to part-time students. Financial award application deadline: 4/1; financial award applicants required to submit FAFSA. *Unit head:* Dr. Dennie Smith, Head, 979-845-8384, Fax: 979-845-9663, E-mail: krsmith@tamu.edu. *Application contact:* Graduate Admissions Supervisor, 979-845-8382, Fax: 979-845-9663, E-mail: krsmith@tamu.edu.

Texas A&M University–Commerce, Graduate School, College of Education and Human Services, Department of Curriculum and Instruction, Commerce, TX 75429-3011. Offers bilingual/ESL education (M Ed, MS); early childhood education (M Ed, MS); elementary education (M Ed, MS); reading (M Ed, MS); secondary education (M Ed, MS); supervision, curriculum and instruction: elementary education (Ed D). Part-time programs available. Terminal master's awarded for partial completion of doctoral program. *Degree requirements:* For master's, comprehensive exam, thesis (for some programs); for doctorate, 2 foreign languages, thesis/dissertation, departmental qualifying exam. *Entrance requirements:* For master's and doctorate, GRE General Test. Electronic applications accepted. *Faculty research:* Literacy and learning, early childhood, preservice teacher education, technology.

Texas A&M University–Kingsville, College of Graduate Studies, College of Education, Department of Bilingual Education, Kingsville, TX 78363. Offers MA, MS, Ed D. *Degree requirements:* For master's, one foreign language, comprehensive exam, thesis or alternative; for doctorate, one foreign language, comprehensive exam, thesis/dissertation. *Entrance requirements:* For master's, GRE General Test, minimum GPA of 3.0; for doctorate, GRE General Test, MAT, minimum GPA of 3.25. *Faculty research:* Language acquisition, acculturation in minority communities, English as a second language strategies.

Texas Southern University, College of Education, Area of Curriculum and Instruction, Houston, TX 77004-4584. Offers bilingual education (M Ed); curriculum and instruction (Ed D); secondary education (M Ed). Part-time and evening/weekend programs available. *Faculty:* 7 full-time (5 women), 1 part-time/adjunct (0 women). *Students:* 20 full-time (17 women), 50 part-time (43 women); includes 66 minority (64 African Americans, 1 Asian American or Pacific Islander, 1 Hispanic American), 1 international. Average age 37. 16 applicants, 100% accepted, 9 enrolled. In 2009, 12 master's, 5 doctorates awarded. *Degree requirements:* For master's, comprehensive exam; for doctorate, comprehensive exam, thesis/dissertation. *Entrance requirements:* For master's, GRE General Test, minimum GPA of 2.5; for doctorate, GRE General Test or MAT, master's degree, minimum B+ average. Additional exam requirements/recommendations for international students: Required—TOEFL. *Application deadline:* For fall admission, 7/1 for domestic and international students; for spring admission, 11/1 for domestic and international students. Applications are processed on a rolling basis. Application fee: $50 ($75 for international students). Electronic applications accepted. *Expenses:* Tuition, state resident: full-time $1805; part-time $100 per credit hour. Tuition, nonresident: full-time $6470; part-time $343 per credit hour. Tuition and fees vary according to course level, course load and degree level. *Financial support:* In 2009–10, 1 research assistantship (averaging $3,000 per year), 1 teaching assistantship (averaging $2,000 per year) were awarded; scholarships/grants and unspecified assistantships also available. Support available to part-time students. Financial award application deadline: 5/1. *Unit head:* Dr. Cherry Gooden, Chair, 713-313-7496, Fax: 713-313-7496, E-mail: gooden_cr@tsu.edu. *Application contact:* Dr. Gregory Maddox, Interim Dean of the Graduate School, 713-313-7011 Ext. 4410, Fax: 713-639-1876, E-mail: maddox_gh@tsu.edu.

Texas State University–San Marcos, Graduate School, College of Education, Department of Curriculum and Instruction, Program in Elementary Education-Bilingual/Bicultural, San Marcos, TX 78666. Offers M Ed, MA. Part-time programs available. *Students:* 4 full-time (3 women), 9 part-time (all women); all minorities (all Hispanic Americans). Average age 32. 5 applicants, 100% accepted, 4 enrolled. In 2009, 4 master's awarded. *Degree requirements:* For master's, comprehensive exam, thesis optional. *Entrance requirements:* For master's, minimum GPA of 2.75 in last 60 hours of course work, teaching experience. Additional exam requirements/recommendations for international students: Required—TOEFL (minimum score 550 paper-based; 213 computer-based). *Application deadline:* For fall admission, 6/15 priority date for domestic students; for spring admission, 10/15 priority date for domestic students. Applications are processed on a rolling basis. Application fee: $40 ($90 for international students). Electronic applications accepted. *Expenses:* Tuition, state resident: full-time $5784; part-time $241 per credit hour. Tuition, nonresident: full-time $13,224; part-time $551 per credit hour. Required fees: $1728; $48 per credit hour. $306. Tuition and fees vary according to course load. *Financial support:* In 2009–10, 11 students received support, including 1 teaching assistantship (averaging $5,076 per year); career-related internships or fieldwork, Federal Work-Study, institutionally sponsored loans, and unspecified assistantships also available. Support available to part-time students. Financial award application deadline: 4/1; financial award applicants required to submit FAFSA. *Unit head:* Carolyn McCall, Graduate Advisor, 512-245-3701, Fax: 512-245-7911, E-mail: cm06@txstate.edu. *Application contact:* Dr. J. Michael Willoughby, Dean of Graduate School, 512-245-2581, Fax: 512-245-8365, E-mail: gradcollege@txstate.edu.

Texas Tech University, Graduate School, College of Education, Division of Curriculum and Instruction, Lubbock, TX 79409. Offers bilingual education (M Ed); curriculum and instruction (M Ed, PhD); elementary education (M Ed); language and literacy education (M Ed); secondary education (M Ed). *Accreditation:* NCATE. Part-time programs available. *Students:* 72 full-time (54 women), 109 part-time (85 women); includes 50 minority (11 African Americans, 1 American Indian/Alaska Native, 4 Asian Americans or Pacific Islanders, 34 Hispanic Americans), 11 international. Average age 35. 228 applicants, 54% accepted, 56 enrolled. In 2009, 59 master's, 5 doctorates awarded. *Degree requirements:* For master's, thesis or alternative; for doctorate, thesis/dissertation. *Entrance requirements:* For master's and doctorate, GRE General Test. Additional exam requirements/recommendations for international students: Required—TOEFL (minimum score 550 paper-based; 213 computer-based). *Application deadline:* For fall admission, 3/1 priority date for international students; for spring admission, 11/1 priority date for international students. Applications are processed on a rolling basis. Application fee: $50 ($75 for international students). Electronic applications accepted. *Expenses:* Tuition, state resident: full-time $5100; part-time $213 per credit hour. Tuition, nonresident: full-time $11,748; part-time $490 per credit hour. Required fees: $2298; $50 per credit hour. $555 per semester. *Financial support:* Research assistantships with partial tuition reimbursements, teaching assistantships with partial tuition reimbursements, career-related internships or fieldwork, Federal Work-Study, and institutionally sponsored loans available. Support available to part-time students. Financial award application deadline: 4/15; financial award applicants required to submit FAFSA. *Faculty research:* Multicultural foundations of education, teacher education, instruction and pedagogy in subject areas, curriculum theory, language and literary. *Unit head:* Dr. Walter Smith, Chair, 806-742-1988 Ext. 437, Fax: 806-742-2179, E-mail: walter.smith@ttu.edu. *Application contact:* Dr. Walter Smith, Chair, 806-742-1988 Ext. 437, Fax: 806-742-2179, E-mail: walter.smith@ttu.edu.

Universidad del Este, Graduate School, Carolina, PR 00984. Offers accounting (MBA); adult education (M Ed); agribusiness (MBA); bilingual education (M Ed); criminal justice and criminology (MA); early education (M Ed); elementary education (M Ed); human resources (MBA); information security management (MBA); information technology and Web business development (MBA); management (MBA); public policy (MPA); social work (MA), including clinical social work; special education (M Ed); strategic leadership (MBA); teaching English (M Ed); teaching Spanish (M Ed).

University at Buffalo, the State University of New York, Graduate School, Graduate School of Education, Department of Learning and Instruction, Buffalo, NY 14260. Offers biology education (Ed M, Certificate); chemistry education (Ed M, Certificate); childhood education (Ed M); childhood education with bilingual extension (Ed M); early childhood education (Ed M); earth science education (Ed M, Certificate); elementary education (Ed D, PhD); English education (Ed M, PhD, Certificate); English for speakers of other languages (Ed M); foreign and second language education (PhD); French education (Ed M, Certificate); general education (Ed M); German education (Ed M, Certificate); gifted education (online) (Certificate); Latin education (Ed M, Certificate); literary specialist (Ed M); mathematics education (Ed M, PhD, Certificate); music education (Ed M, Certificate); physics education (Ed M, Certificate); reading education (PhD); science and the public (online) (Ed M); science education (PhD); social studies education

(Ed M, Certificate); Spanish education (Ed M, Certificate); special education (PhD); teaching and leading for diversity (Certificate); teaching English to speakers of other languages (Ed M). Part-time and evening/weekend programs available. Postbaccalaureate distance learning degree programs offered (no on-campus study). *Faculty:* 34 full-time (24 women), 50 part-time/adjunct (39 women). *Students:* 332 full-time (245 women), 365 part-time (272 women); includes 50 minority (18 African Americans, 4 American Indian/Alaska Native, 10 Asian Americans or Pacific Islanders, 18 Hispanic Americans), 55 international. Average age 30. 627 applicants, 78% accepted, 286 enrolled. In 2009, 255 master's, 16 doctorates, 51 other advanced degrees awarded. *Degree requirements:* For master's, comprehensive exam; for doctorate, thesis/dissertation, research analysis exam, research experience component. *Entrance requirements:* For doctorate, GRE General Test or MAT, interview, writing sample, letters of recommendation. Additional exam requirements/recommendations for international students: Required—TOEFL (minimum score 600 paper-based; 250 computer-based; 96 iBT). *Application deadline:* For fall admission, 2/1 priority date for domestic and international students; for spring admission, 11/15 priority date for domestic students, 10/1 for international students. Applications are processed on a rolling basis. Application fee: $50. Electronic applications accepted. *Financial support:* In 2009–10, 23 fellowships with full tuition reimbursements (averaging $9,000 per year), 42 research assistantships with full tuition reimbursements (averaging $10,000 per year) were awarded; teaching assistantships with full tuition reimbursements, career-related internships or fieldwork, Federal Work-Study, institutionally sponsored loans, scholarships/grants, tuition waivers (partial), and unspecified assistantships also available. Financial award application deadline: 2/28; financial award applicants required to submit FAFSA. *Faculty research:* Science assessment, foreign language teaching and learning, early learning, new literacies, gender and education. Total annual research expenditures: $1.8 million. *Unit head:* Dr. Suzanne Miller, Chair, 716-645-2455, Fax: 716-645-3161, E-mail: smiller@buffalo.edu. *Application contact:* Cathy Dimino, Admissions Assistant, 716-645-2110, Fax: 716-645-7937, E-mail: cadimino@buffalo.edu.

University of Alaska Fairbanks, College of Liberal Arts, Department of Alaska Native Studies, Fairbanks, AK 99775-6300. Offers cross cultural studies (MA). *Faculty:* 4 full-time (1 woman), 1 part-time/adjunct (0 women). *Students:* 2 full-time (1 woman), 7 part-time (5 women); includes 4 minority (all American Indian/Alaska Native). Average age 42. 5 applicants, 20% accepted, 0 enrolled. In 2009, 3 master's awarded. *Degree requirements:* For master's, comprehensive exam. *Entrance requirements:* Additional exam requirements/recommendations for international students: Required—TOEFL (minimum score 550 paper-based; 213 computer-based; 80 iBT). *Application deadline:* For fall admission, 6/1 for domestic students, 3/1 for international students; for spring admission, 10/15 for domestic students, 9/1 for international students. Applications are processed on a rolling basis. Application fee: $60. Electronic applications accepted. *Expenses:* Tuition, state resident: full-time $7584; part-time $316 per credit. Tuition, nonresident: full-time $15,504; part-time $646 per credit. Required fees: $23 per credit. $135 per semester. Tuition and fees vary according to course level, course load and reciprocity agreements. *Financial support:* In 2009–10, 1 fellowship (averaging $13,500 per year) was awarded; research assistantships, teaching assistantships, Federal Work-Study, scholarships/grants, health care benefits, and unspecified assistantships also available. Support available to part-time students. Financial award application deadline: 7/1; financial award applicants required to submit FAFSA. *Faculty research:* Alaska native literature, oral traditions, history, law and policy; Alaska native cultures, art, native American religion and philosophy. *Unit head:* Dr. James K. Ruppert, Chair, 907-474-7181, Fax: 907-474-5666, E-mail: jkruppert@alaska.edu. *Application contact:* Dr. James K. Ruppert, Chair, 907-474-7181, Fax: 907-474-5666, E-mail: jkruppert@alaska.edu.

University of Alaska Fairbanks, College of Liberal Arts, Program in Linguistics, Fairbanks, AK 99775-6280. Offers applied linguistics (MA), including language documentation, second language acquisition teacher education. Part-time programs available. *Faculty:* 3 full-time (1 woman), 1 (woman) part-time/adjunct. *Students:* 3 full-time (2 women), 25 part-time (23 women); includes 18 minority (17 American Indian/Alaska Native, 1 Asian American or Pacific Islander), 1 international. Average age 44. 6 applicants, 50% accepted, 2 enrolled. *Degree requirements:* For master's, comprehensive exam, thesis or alternative. *Entrance requirements:* Additional exam requirements/recommendations for international students: Required—TOEFL (minimum score 550 paper-based; 213 computer-based; 80 iBT). *Application deadline:* For fall admission, 6/1 for domestic students, 3/1 for international students; for spring admission, 10/15 for domestic students, 9/1 for international students. Application fee: $60. *Expenses:* Tuition, state resident: full-time $7584; part-time $316 per credit. Tuition, nonresident: full-time $15,504; part-time $646 per credit. Required fees: $23 per credit. $135 per semester. Tuition and fees vary according to course level, course load and reciprocity agreements. *Financial support:* In 2009–10, 2 research assistantships (averaging $25,033 per year), 1 teaching assistantship (averaging $9,354 per year) were awarded; fellowships, career-related internships or fieldwork, Federal Work-Study, scholarships/grants, health care benefits, and unspecified assistantships also available. Support available to part-time students. Financial award application deadline: 7/1; financial award applicants required to submit FAFSA. *Faculty research:* Second language acquisition/teaching, INUPIAQ, Athabaskan languages, language maintenance and shift, phonology, morphology. *Unit head:* Dr. Siri Tuttle, Program Head, 907-474-7876, Fax: 907-474-6586, E-mail: ffamb@uaf.edu. *Application contact:* Dr. Siri Tuttle, Program Head, 907-474-7876, Fax: 907-474-6586, E-mail: ffamb@uaf.edu.

University of Alaska Fairbanks, School of Education, Fairbanks, AK 99775. Offers counseling (M Ed), including counseling; education (M Ed, PhD), including cross-cultural education (M Ed), curriculum and instruction (M Ed), education (M Ed), elementary education (M Ed), interdisciplinary (PhD), language and literacy (M Ed), reading (M Ed), secondary education (M Ed); guidance and counseling (M Ed). *Accreditation:* NCATE. Postbaccalaureate distance learning degree programs offered. *Faculty:* 23 full-time (15 women), 10 part-time/adjunct (9 women). *Students:* 54 full-time (38 women), 103 part-time (79 women); includes 23 minority (2 African Americans, 15 American Indian/Alaska Native, 2 Asian Americans or Pacific Islanders, 4 Hispanic Americans), 1 international. Average age 37. 126 applicants, 63% accepted, 59 enrolled. In 2009, 40 master's, 18 other advanced degrees awarded. *Degree requirements:* For master's, comprehensive exam, thesis or alternative, student teaching. *Entrance requirements:* For master's, GRE General Test, PRAXIS I, PRAXIS II, writing sample, evidence of technology competence, criminal background check. Additional exam requirements/recommendations for international students: Required—TOEFL (minimum score 550 paper-based; 213 computer-based; 80 iBT). *Application deadline:* For fall admission, 3/1 for domestic and international students; for spring admission, 10/15 for domestic students, 9/1 for international students. Application fee: $60. Electronic applications accepted. *Expenses:* Tuition, state resident: full-time $7584; part-time $316 per credit. Tuition, nonresident: full-time $15,504; part-time $646 per credit. Required fees: $23 per credit. $135 per semester. Tuition and fees vary according to course level, course load and reciprocity agreements. *Financial support:* In 2009–10, 1 research assistantship (averaging $13,330 per year), 5 teaching assistantships (averaging $10,376 per year) were awarded; fellowships, career-related internships or fieldwork, Federal Work-Study, scholarships/grants, health care benefits, and unspecified assistantships also available. Support available to part-time students. Financial award application deadline: 2/15; financial award applicants required to submit FAFSA. *Faculty research:* Native ways of knowing, classroom research in methods of literacy instruction, multiple intelligence theory, geometry concept development, mathematics and science curriculum development. *Unit head:* Dr. Eric C. Madsen, Dean, 907-474-7341, Fax: 907-474-5451, E-mail: fysoed@uaf.edu. *Application contact:* Dr. Eric C. Madsen, Dean, 907-474-7341, Fax: 907-474-5451, E-mail: fysoed@uaf.edu.

University of Alberta, Faculty of Graduate Studies and Research, Facultè Saint Jean, Edmonton, AB T6G 2E1, Canada. Offers M Ed. Part-time and evening/weekend programs available. Postbaccalaureate distance learning degree programs offered (minimal on-campus study). *Faculty:* 9 full-time (7 women). *Students:* 4 full-time (2 women), 64 part-time (50 women). Average age 30. 25 applicants, 92% accepted. In 2009, 9 master's awarded. *Degree requirements:* For master's, thesis (for some programs). *Entrance requirements:* For master's,

proficiency in French, 2 years of teaching experience. *Application deadline:* Applications are processed on a rolling basis. Application fee: $0. Tuition and fees charges are reported in Canadian dollars. *Expenses:* Tuition, area resident: Full-time $4626 Canadian dollars; part-time $99.72 Canadian dollars per unit. International tuition: $8216 Canadian dollars full-time. Required fees: $3590 Canadian dollars; $99.72 Canadian dollars per unit. $215 Canadian dollars per term. *Financial support:* In 2009–10, 3 fellowships (averaging $9,000 per year), 1 research assistantship with tuition reimbursement were awarded; teaching assistantships, scholarships/grants also available. *Faculty research:* First and second language acquisition, first and second language learning through subject matter, cultural transmission. *Unit head:* Dr. M. Cavanagh, Graduate Coordinator, 780-465-8770, Fax: 403-465-8760. *Application contact:* Lise Desbiens, Department Office, 403-465-8703, Fax: 403-465-8760, E-mail: medu@ualberta.ca.

The University of Arizona, Graduate College, College of Education, Department of Teaching, Learning and Sociocultural Studies, Tucson, AZ 85721. Offers bilingual education (M Ed); bilingual/multicultural education (MA); language, reading and culture (MA, Ed D, PhD, Ed S). Part-time programs available. *Faculty:* 11. *Students:* 40 full-time (34 women), 103 part-time (80 women); includes 37 minority (3 African Americans, 11 American Indian/Alaska Native, 3 Asian Americans or Pacific Islanders, 20 Hispanic Americans), 25 international. Average age 39. 63 applicants, 71% accepted, 30 enrolled. In 2009, 17 master's, 10 doctorates awarded. Terminal master's awarded for partial completion of doctoral program. *Degree requirements:* For master's, thesis optional, thesis (MA); for doctorate, comprehensive exam, thesis/dissertation; for Ed S, thesis optional. *Entrance requirements:* For master's, 2 letters of recommendation, resume; for doctorate, GRE or MAT, 2 letters of recommendation, resume; for Ed S, GRE, MAT. Additional exam requirements/recommendations for international students: Required—TOEFL (minimum score 550 paper-based; 213 computer-based; 79 iBT). *Application deadline:* For fall admission, 2/1 for domestic and international students. Application fee: $65. Electronic applications accepted. *Expenses:* Tuition, state resident: full-time $9028. Tuition, nonresident: full-time $24,890. *Financial support:* In 2009–10, 3 research assistantships with full tuition reimbursements (averaging $12,123 per year), 12 teaching assistantships with full tuition reimbursements (averaging $12,437 per year) were awarded; career-related internships or fieldwork, scholarships/grants, health care benefits, tuition waivers (full and partial), and unspecified assistantships also available. Financial award application deadline: 3/7; financial award applicants required to submit FAFSA. *Faculty research:* Reading, Native American education, language policy, children's literature, bilingual/bicultural literacy. Total annual research expenditures: $686,878. *Unit head:* Dr. Norma E. Gonzalez, Department Head, 520-621-1311, Fax: 520-621-1853, E-mail: ngonzale@email.arizona.edu. *Application contact:* Information Contact, 520-621-1311, Fax: 520-621-1853, E-mail: lrcinfo@email.arizona.edu.

University of California, Riverside, Graduate Division, Graduate School of Education, Riverside, CA 92521-0102. Offers autism (M Ed); curriculum and instruction (MA, PhD); diversity and equity (M Ed); educational leadership and policy (MA, PhD); educational psychology (MA, PhD); general education (M Ed); higher education administration and policy (M Ed, PhD); leadership (M Ed); reading (M Ed); school psychology (PhD); special education (M Ed, MA, PhD). *Faculty:* 23 full-time (12 women), 12 part-time/adjunct (8 women). *Students:* 230 full-time (183 women), 6 part-time (3 women); includes 75 minority (12 African Americans, 1 American Indian/Alaska Native, 21 Asian Americans or Pacific Islanders, 41 Hispanic Americans), 6 international. Average age 32. 288 applicants, 60% accepted, 118 enrolled. In 2009, 68 master's, 13 doctorates awarded. Terminal master's awarded for partial completion of doctoral program. *Degree requirements:* For master's, comprehensive exam (for some programs), comprehensive exams or thesis (MA), case study or analytical report (M Ed); for doctorate, thesis/dissertation, written and oral qualifying exams, college teaching practicum. *Entrance requirements:* For master's, GRE General Test, GRE Subject Test, CBEST, CSET, minimum GPA of 3.2; for doctorate, GRE General Test, GRE Subject Test, master's degree (desirable), minimum GPA of 3.2. Additional exam requirements/recommendations for international students: Required—TOEFL (minimum score 550 paper-based; 213 computer-based; 80 iBT). *Application deadline:* For fall admission, 9/1 for domestic students, 4/1 for international students; for winter admission, 12/1 for domestic students, 9/1 for international students; for spring admission, 3/1 for domestic students, 10/1 for international students. Applications are processed on a rolling basis. Application fee: $70 ($85 for international students). Electronic applications accepted. *Financial support:* In 2009–10, 55 students received support, including 13 fellowships with full and partial tuition reimbursements available (averaging $26,809 per year), 21 research assistantships with full and partial tuition reimbursements available (averaging $14,238 per year), 1 teaching assistantship with full and partial tuition reimbursement available (averaging $16,638 per year); career-related internships or fieldwork, Federal Work-Study, institutionally sponsored loans, scholarships/grants, and unspecified assistantships also available. Financial award application deadline: 1/5; financial award applicants required to submit FAFSA. *Faculty research:* Responsiveness to intervention, faculty core, response to intervention of English language learners, advanced modeling techniques, study on social capital, trust, and motivation. Total annual research expenditures: $5.6 million. *Unit head:* Dr. Steven T. Bossert, Dean, 951-827-5802, Fax: 951-827-3942, E-mail: steven.bossert@ucr.edu. *Application contact:* Dr. John Wills, Graduate Advisor for Admission, 951-827-6362, Fax: 951-827-3942, E-mail: edgrad@ucr.edu.

University of Colorado at Boulder, Graduate School, School of Education, Division of Social Multicultural and Bilingual Foundations, Boulder, CO 80309. Offers MA, PhD. *Accreditation:* NCATE. Part-time programs available. *Students:* 59 full-time (48 women), 209 part-time (171 women); includes 63 minority (2 African Americans, 1 American Indian/Alaska Native, 13 Asian Americans or Pacific Islanders, 47 Hispanic Americans), 6 international. Average age 35. 176 applicants, 41% accepted, 36 enrolled. In 2009, 60 master's, 3 doctorates awarded. *Degree requirements:* For master's, comprehensive exam, thesis or alternative; for doctorate, one foreign language, comprehensive exam, thesis/dissertation. *Entrance requirements:* For master's, GRE General Test or MAT, minimum undergraduate GPA of 2.75; for doctorate, GRE General Test. *Application deadline:* For fall admission, 2/1 priority date for domestic students, 12/1 for international students; for spring admission, 9/1 for domestic students, 12/1 for international students. Application fee: $50 ($60 for international students). *Financial support:* In 2009–10, 41 fellowships (averaging $2,969 per year), 23 research assistantships (averaging $11,426 per year) were awarded. *Faculty research:* Bilingual education, inclusion. *Application contact:* E-mail: edadvise@colorado.edu.

University of Connecticut, Graduate School, Neag School of Education, Department of Curriculum and Instruction, Program in Bilingual and Bicultural Education, Storrs, CT 06269. Offers MA, PhD, Post-Master's Certificate. *Accreditation:* NCATE. *Faculty:* 16 full-time (11 women). *Students:* 3 full-time (all women), 18 part-time (14 women); includes 12 minority (all Hispanic Americans). Average age 37. 37 applicants, 38% accepted, 7 enrolled. In 2009, 6 master's, 2 other advanced degrees awarded. Terminal master's awarded for partial completion of doctoral program. *Degree requirements:* For master's, comprehensive exam; for doctorate, thesis/dissertation. *Entrance requirements:* For doctorate, GRE General Test. Additional exam requirements/recommendations for international students: Required—TOEFL (minimum score 550 paper-based; 213 computer-based). *Application deadline:* For fall admission, 2/1 priority date for domestic and international students; for spring admission, 11/1 for domestic students, 10/1 for international students. Applications are processed on a rolling basis. Application fee: $55. Electronic applications accepted. *Expenses:* Tuition, state resident: full-time $4725; part-time $525 per credit. Tuition, nonresident: full-time $12,267; part-time $1363 per credit. Required fees: $346 per semester. Tuition and fees vary according to course load. *Financial support:* In 2009–10, 3 research assistantships with full tuition reimbursements were awarded; fellowships, teaching assistantships with full tuition reimbursements, Federal Work-Study, scholarships/grants, health care benefits, and unspecified assistantships also available. Financial award application deadline: 2/1; financial award applicants required to submit FAFSA. *Unit head:* Mary Anne Doyle, Head, 860-486-2433, Fax: 860-486-0280, E-mail: mary.dolye@uconn.edu. *Application contact:* Lisa Rasicot, Graduate Coordinator, 860-486-3065, Fax: 860-486-0210, E-mail: l.rasicot@uconn.edu.

Multilingual and Multicultural Education

University of Delaware, College of Human Services, Education and Public Policy, School of Education, Newark, DE 19716. Offers education (PhD); educational leadership (Ed D); higher education (M Ed); instruction (MI); reading (M Ed); school leadership (M Ed); school psychology (MA, Ed S); teaching English as a second language (TESL) (MA). *Accreditation:* NCATE. Part-time and evening/weekend programs available. Terminal master's awarded for partial completion of doctoral program. *Degree requirements:* For master's, comprehensive exam (for some programs), thesis (for some programs); for doctorate, comprehensive exam (for some programs), thesis/dissertation. *Entrance requirements:* For master's and doctorate, GRE, 3 letters of recommendation. Additional exam requirements/recommendations for international students: Required—TOEFL (minimum score 600 paper-based; 250 computer-based). Electronic applications accepted. *Faculty research:* Teacher education; curriculum theory and development; community based education models, educational leadership.

The University of Findlay, Graduate and Professional Studies, College of Liberal Arts, Intensive English Language and Teaching English as a Second Language (TESOL) Program, Findlay, OH 45840-3653. Offers bilingual and multicultural education (MA); teaching English to speakers of other languages (MA). Part-time and evening/weekend programs available. *Degree requirements:* For master's, cumulative project. *Entrance requirements:* For master's, minimum undergraduate GPA of 2.5 in last 64 hours of course work, 3 letters of recommendation. Additional exam requirements/recommendations for international students: Required—TOEFL (minimum score 550 paper-based; 213 computer-based; 80 iBT). Electronic applications accepted.

University of Florida, Graduate School, College of Education, School of Teaching and Learning, Gainesville, FL 32611. Offers bilingual/ESOL education (M Ed, MAE, Ed D, PhD, Ed S); curriculum and instruction (M Ed, MAE, Ed D, PhD, Ed S); early childhood education (Ed D, PhD, Ed S); elementary education (M Ed, MAE); English education (M Ed, MAE); mathematics education (M Ed, MAE); reading education (M Ed, MAE); science education (M Ed, MAE); social foundations (M Ed, MAE, Ed D, PhD); social studies education (M Ed, MAE). *Accreditation:* NCATE. *Degree requirements:* For master's, thesis optional; for doctorate, variable foreign language requirement, thesis/dissertation. *Entrance requirements:* For master's and doctorate, GRE General Test, minimum GPA of 3.0; for Ed S, GRE General Test. Additional exam requirements/recommendations for international students: Required—TOEFL (minimum score 550 paper-based; 213 computer-based). Electronic applications accepted. *Faculty research:* Teacher education, inclusive education, classroom processes, curriculum and technology.

University of Houston, College of Education, Department of Curriculum and Instruction, Houston, TX 77204. Offers art education (M Ed); bilingual education (M Ed); curriculum and instruction (M Ed, Ed D); early childhood education (M Ed); elementary education (M Ed); gifted and talented education (M Ed); instructional technology (M Ed); mathematics education (M Ed); reading and language arts education (M Ed); science education (M Ed); second language education (M Ed); secondary education (M Ed); social studies education (M Ed); teaching (M Ed). *Accreditation:* NCATE. Part-time and evening/weekend programs available. *Faculty:* 20 full-time (9 women), 22 part-time/adjunct (17 women). *Students:* 113 full-time (81 women), 195 part-time (150 women); includes 107 minority (43 African Americans, 29 Asian Americans or Pacific Islanders, 35 Hispanic Americans), 29 international. Average age 35. 150 applicants, 77% accepted, 55 enrolled. In 2009, 75 master's, 31 doctorates awarded. *Degree requirements:* For master's, comprehensive exam, thesis optional; for doctorate, comprehensive exam, thesis/dissertation. *Entrance requirements:* For master's and doctorate, GRE, minimum cumulative undergraduate GPA of 2.6. Additional exam requirements/recommendations for international students: Required—TOEFL (minimum score 550 paper-based; 79 iBT). *Application deadline:* For fall admission, 3/1 for domestic and international students; for spring admission, 10/1 for domestic and international students. Application fee: $45 ($75 for international students). Electronic applications accepted. *Expenses:* Tuition, state resident: full-time $7676; part-time $320 per credit hour. Tuition, nonresident: full-time $14,324; part-time $597 per credit hour. Required fees: $3034. *Financial support:* In 2009–10, 4 fellowships with full tuition reimbursements (averaging $9,500 per year), 6 research assistantships with full tuition reimbursements (averaging $8,800 per year), 25 teaching assistantships with full tuition reimbursements (averaging $8,800 per year) were awarded; career-related internships or fieldwork, Federal Work-Study, institutionally sponsored loans, scholarships/grants, health care benefits, and unspecified assistantships also available. Support available to part-time students. Financial award application deadline: 2/1. *Faculty research:* Teaching-learning process, instructional technology in schools, teacher education, classroom management, at-risk students. *Unit head:* Dr. Laveria Hutchison, Chairperson, 713-743-4958, Fax: 713-743-4990, E-mail: lhutchison@uh.edu. *Application contact:* Renee C. Rattelade, Executive Secretary, 713-743-4997, Fax: 713-743-4990, E-mail: rrattelade@mail.coe.uh.edu.

University of Houston–Clear Lake, School of Education, Program in Foundations and Professional Studies, Houston, TX 77058-1098. Offers counseling (MS); instructional technology (MS); multicultural studies (MS). Part-time and evening/weekend programs available. *Degree requirements:* For master's, thesis optional. *Entrance requirements:* For master's, GRE or minimum GPA of 3.0 in last 60 hours. Additional exam requirements/recommendations for international students: Required—TOEFL (minimum score 550 paper-based; 213 computer-based). Electronic applications accepted.

University of Houston–Downtown, College of Public Service, Department of Urban Education, Houston, TX 77002. Offers bilingual education (MAT); curriculum and instruction (MAT); elementary education (MAT); secondary education (MAT). Part-time and evening/weekend programs available. *Faculty:* 8 full-time (5 women). *Students:* 1 (woman) full-time, 42 part-time (34 women); includes 27 minority (15 African Americans, 3 Asian Americans or Pacific Islanders, 9 Hispanic Americans). Average age 37. 16 applicants, 100% accepted, 12 enrolled. In 2009, 17 master's awarded. *Degree requirements:* For master's, capstone course with completed project, position paper, grant proposal, empirical study, curriculum development/revision, or advanced technology project presented at annual Graduate Project Exhibition. *Entrance requirements:* For master's, GRE, personal statement, 3 recommendation forms. Additional exam requirements/recommendations for international students: Required—TOEFL (minimum score 550 paper-based; 213 computer-based; 80 iBT). *Application deadline:* For fall admission, 6/1 for domestic and international students; for spring admission, 11/1 for domestic and international students. Applications are processed on a rolling basis. Application fee: $35 ($60 for international students). Electronic applications accepted. *Expenses:* Tuition, state resident: full-time $3150; part-time $175 per credit hour. Tuition, nonresident: full-time $7506; part-time $417 per credit hour. Required fees: $908; $322 per term. *Financial support:* Scholarships/grants available. Financial award applicants required to submit FAFSA. *Unit head:* Dr. Myrna Cohen, Chair, 713-221-2759, Fax: 713-226-5294, E-mail: cohenm@uhd.edu. *Application contact:* Traneshia Parker, Assistant Director, Admissions-Graduate, International and Residency, 713-221-8093, Fax: 713-221-8157, E-mail: parkert@uhd.edu.

University of Illinois at Chicago, Graduate College, College of Education, Department of Curriculum and Instruction, Chicago, IL 60607-7128. Offers curriculum studies (PhD); educational studies (M Ed); elementary education (M Ed); literacy, language and culture (M Ed, PhD); secondary education (M Ed). Part-time and evening/weekend programs available. *Degree requirements:* For doctorate, thesis/dissertation. *Entrance requirements:* For master's, minimum GPA of 2.75; for doctorate, GRE General Test, minimum GPA of 2.75. Additional exam requirements/recommendations for international students: Required—TOEFL. Electronic applications accepted. *Faculty research:* Curriculum theory, curriculum development, research on teaching, curriculum and context, reading/literacy.

University of La Verne, Regional Campus Administration, Graduate Credential Program in Education, California Statewide Campus, La Verne, CA 91750-4443. Offers cross cultural language and academic development (Credential); multiple subject (Credential); single subject (Credential). *Faculty:* 2 full-time (1 woman), 1 (woman) part-time/adjunct. *Students:* 101 full-time (70 women), 50 part-time (40 women); includes 45 minority (5 African Americans, 3 American Indian/Alaska Native, 5 Asian Americans or Pacific Islanders, 32 Hispanic Americans). Average age 33. *Entrance requirements:* For degree, California Basic Educational Skills Test, minimum undergraduate GPA of 2.75, 3 letters of recommendation, interview. *Application deadline:* Applications are processed on a rolling basis. Application fee: $50. *Expenses:* Contact institution. *Financial support:* Institutionally sponsored loans available. Financial award application deadline: 3/2; financial award applicants required to submit FAFSA. *Unit head:* Juline Behrens, Director, 800-695-4858 Ext. 5400, Fax: 909-981-8695, E-mail: jbehrens@laverne.edu. *Application contact:* Juline Behrens, Director, 800-695-4858 Ext. 5400, Fax: 909-981-8695, E-mail: jbehrens@laverne.edu.

University of Maryland, Baltimore County, Graduate School, College of Arts, Humanities and Social Sciences, Department of Modern Languages and Linguistics, Program in Intercultural Communication, Baltimore, MD 21250. Offers MA. Part-time and evening/weekend programs available. *Faculty:* 18 full-time (6 women), 3 part-time/adjunct (2 women). *Students:* 14 full-time (10 women), 29 part-time (20 women); includes 4 minority (1 African American, 3 Hispanic Americans), 14 international. 30 applicants, 57% accepted, 13 enrolled. In 2009, 7 master's awarded. *Degree requirements:* For master's, one foreign language, comprehensive exam (for some programs), thesis (for some programs). *Entrance requirements:* For master's, GRE General Test, minimum GPA of 3.0, 3 letters of recommendation, self-evaluation and statement of support, resume. Additional exam requirements/recommendations for international students: Required—TOEFL (minimum score 213 computer-based). *Application deadline:* For fall admission, 1/31 for domestic and international students. Application fee: $45. Electronic applications accepted. *Financial support:* In 2009–10, 8 students received support, including 5 teaching assistantships with full tuition reimbursements available (averaging $11,324 per year); tuition waivers also available. Financial award applicants required to submit FAFSA. *Faculty research:* Comparative television research–cross-cultural; cultural studies; social developments in Latin America; intercultural communication; French civilization and cultural studies; language, gender and sexuality; sociolinguistics; African linguistics; immigrants in U.S. and Latin American societies. *Unit head:* Dr. Edward Larkey, Director, 410-455-2104, Fax: 410-455-1025, E-mail: larkey@umbc.edu. *Application contact:* Dr. Edward Larkey, Director, 410-455-2104, Fax: 410-455-1025, E-mail: larkey@umbc.edu.

University of Maryland, Baltimore County, Graduate School, College of Arts, Humanities and Social Sciences, Program in Language, Literacy, and Culture, Baltimore, MD 21250. Offers PhD. Part-time and evening/weekend programs available. *Faculty:* 4 full-time (all women), 45 part-time/adjunct (26 women). *Students:* 35 full-time (27 women), 21 part-time (13 women); includes 15 minority (11 African Americans, 2 Asian Americans or Pacific Islanders, 2 Hispanic Americans), 12 international. Average age 40. 44 applicants, 23% accepted, 8 enrolled. In 2009, 7 doctorates awarded. *Degree requirements:* For doctorate, comprehensive exam, thesis/dissertation, internship. *Entrance requirements:* For doctorate, research writing sample; resume or curriculum vitae; master's degree. Additional exam requirements/recommendations for international students: Required—TOEFL (minimum score 80 iBT). *Application deadline:* For fall admission, 2/1 for domestic and international students. Application fee: $50. Electronic applications accepted. *Financial support:* In 2009–10, 5 research assistantships with full and partial tuition reimbursements (averaging $13,622 per year), 5 teaching assistantships with full and partial tuition reimbursements (averaging $13,622 per year) were awarded; fellowships, career-related internships or fieldwork, Federal Work-Study, scholarships/grants, and tuition waivers (partial) also available. Support available to part-time students. Financial award application deadline: 3/1; financial award applicants required to submit FAFSA. *Faculty research:* Public policy, educational equity, identity, intercultural communication, technology and communication. *Unit head:* Dr. Jo Ann Crandall, Director, 410-455-2313, Fax: 410-455-8947, E-mail: crandall@umbc.edu. *Application contact:* Pam Gemmill, Administrative Assistant, 410-455-2376, Fax: 410-455-8947, E-mail: llc@umbc.edu.

University of Massachusetts Amherst, Graduate School, School of Education, Program in Education, Amherst, MA 01003. Offers bilingual, English as a second language, and multicultural education (M Ed, CAGS); child study and early education (M Ed); children, families and schools (Ed D, CAGS); early childhood and elementary teacher education (M Ed); education policy and leadership (CAGS); educational administration (M Ed, CAGS); educational policy and leadership (Ed D); higher education (M Ed, CAGS); international education (M Ed); language, literacy and culture (Ed D); learning, media and technology (M Ed, CAGS); mathematics, science, and learning technologies (Ed D); policy studies (M Ed); policy studies in education (CAGS); reading and writing (M Ed); research and evaluation methods (Ed D); school counselor education (M Ed, CAGS); school psychology (CAGS); science education (CAGS); secondary teacher education (M Ed); social justice education (M Ed, Ed D, CAGS); special education (M Ed, Ed D, CAGS). *Accreditation:* NCATE. Part-time programs available. Postbaccalaureate distance learning degree programs offered (minimal on-campus study). *Faculty:* 74 full-time (41 women). *Students:* 377 full-time (268 women), 347 part-time (232 women); includes 115 minority (59 African Americans, 2 American Indian/Alaska Native, 16 Asian Americans or Pacific Islanders, 38 Hispanic Americans), 108 international. Average age 35. 708 applicants, 68% accepted, 266 enrolled. In 2009, 183 master's, 17 doctorates awarded. Terminal master's awarded for partial completion of doctoral program. *Degree requirements:* For master's, thesis or alternative; for doctorate, comprehensive exam, thesis/dissertation. *Entrance requirements:* Additional exam requirements/recommendations for international students: Required—TOEFL (minimum score 550 paper-based; 213 computer-based; 80 iBT), IELTS (minimum score 6.5). *Application deadline:* For fall admission, 1/15 for domestic and international students. Applications are processed on a rolling basis. Application fee: $50 ($65 for international students). Electronic applications accepted. *Expenses:* Tuition, state resident: full-time $2640; part-time $110 per credit. Tuition, nonresident: full-time $9936; part-time $414 per credit. Tuition and fees vary according to course load. *Financial support:* In 2009–10, 1 fellowship with full tuition reimbursement (averaging $8,036 per year), 92 research assistantships with full tuition reimbursements (averaging $8,555 per year), 83 teaching assistantships with full tuition reimbursements (averaging $4,661 per year) were awarded; career-related internships or fieldwork, Federal Work-Study, scholarships/grants, traineeships, health care benefits, tuition waivers (full), and unspecified assistantships also available. Support available to part-time students. Financial award application deadline: 1/15. *Unit head:* Dr. Linda L. Griffin, Graduate Program Director, 413-545-6984, Fax: 413-545-2873. *Application contact:* Jean M. Ames, Supervisor of Admissions, 413-545-0722, Fax: 413-577-0010, E-mail: gradadm@grad.umass.edu.

University of Massachusetts Boston, Office of Graduate Studies, College of Liberal Arts, Program in Applied Linguistics, Boston, MA 02125-3393. Offers bilingual education (MA); English as a second language (MA); foreign language pedagogy (MA). Part-time and evening/weekend programs available. *Degree requirements:* For master's, one foreign language, comprehensive exam. *Entrance requirements:* For master's, minimum GPA of 2.75. *Faculty research:* Multicultural theory and curriculum development, foreign language pedagogy, language and culture, applied psycholinguistics, bilingual education.

University of Miami, Graduate School, School of Education, Department of Teaching and Learning, Program in Teaching and Learning, Coral Gables, FL 33124. Offers language and literacy learning in multilingual settings (PhD); mathematics and science education (PhD); special education (PhD). *Students:* 30 full-time (22 women); includes 11 minority (3 African Americans, 8 Hispanic Americans), 7 international. Average age 35. 21 applicants, 43% accepted, 7 enrolled. In 2009, 5 doctorates awarded. *Degree requirements:* For doctorate, thesis/dissertation, qualifying exam. *Entrance requirements:* For doctorate, GRE General Test. Additional exam requirements/recommendations for international students: Required—TOEFL (minimum score 550 paper-based; 80 iBT); Recommended—IELTS (minimum score 6.5). *Application deadline:* For fall admission, 2/15 for domestic students, 10/15 for international students. Application fee: $65. Electronic applications accepted. *Financial support:* In 2009–10, 25 students received support. Application deadline: 3/1. *Faculty research:* Teacher education, multicultural education, technology, second language acquisition, math and science education.

Unit head: Dr. Batya Elbaum, Associate Department Chairperson, 305-284-4218, Fax: 305-284-4439, E-mail: elbaum@miami.edu. *Application contact:* Tinisha Hollinshead, Admission Coordinator, 305-284-2102, Fax: 305-284-6998, E-mail: tinisha@miami.edu.

University of Michigan, Horace H. Rackham School of Graduate Studies, School of Education, Programs in Educational Studies, Ann Arbor, MI 48109. Offers cross specialization (PhD); curriculum development (MA); early childhood education (MA, PhD); educational administration and policy (MA, PhD); educational foundations and policy (MA, PhD); English education (MA); English language learning in school settings (MA); learning technologies (MA, PhD); literacy, language, and culture (MA, PhD); mathematics education (MA, PhD); postsecondary science education (MS); research methods (MA); science education (MA, PhD); social studies education (MA); teaching and teacher education (PhD); MA/Certification; MBA/MA; PhD/MA. Terminal master's awarded for partial completion of doctoral program. *Degree requirements:* For master's, thesis (for some programs); for doctorate, comprehensive exam, thesis/dissertation. *Entrance requirements:* For master's and doctorate, GRE General Test. Additional exam requirements/recommendations for international students: Required—TOEFL (minimum score 600 paper-based; 250 computer-based). *Application deadline:* For fall admission, 12/1 priority date for domestic students, 12/1 for international students. Application fee: $60 ($75 for international students). Electronic applications accepted. *Expenses:* Tuition, state resident: full-time $17,286; part-time $1099 per credit hour. Tuition, nonresident: full-time $34,944; part-time $2080 per credit hour. Required fees: $95 per semester. Tuition and fees vary according to course load, degree level and program. *Financial support:* Applicants required to submit FAFSA. *Unit head:* Dr. Addison Stone, Chairperson, 734-763-7500, Fax: 734-615-1290, E-mail: addison@umich.edu. *Application contact:* Laura Mayers, Student Services Assistant, 734-764-7563, Fax: 734-763-1495, E-mail: ed.grad.admit@umich.edu.

University of Minnesota, Twin Cities Campus, Graduate School, College of Education and Human Development, Department of Curriculum and Instruction, Program in Teaching, Minneapolis, MN 55455-0213. Offers Chinese (M Ed); earth science (M Ed); elementary special education (M Ed); English (M Ed); English as a second language (M Ed); French (M Ed); German (M Ed); Hebrew (M Ed); Japanese (M Ed); life sciences (M Ed); mathematics (M Ed); middle school science (M Ed); science (M Ed); second languages and cultures (M Ed); social studies (M Ed); Spanish (M Ed). *Students:* 263 full-time (186 women), 117 part-time (83 women); includes 32 minority (10 African Americans, 2 American Indian/Alaska Native, 17 Asian Americans or Pacific Islanders, 3 Hispanic Americans), 4 international. Average age 27. 363 applicants, 74% accepted, 259 enrolled. In 2009, 497 master's awarded. *Unit head:* Dr. Ruth Thomas, Chair, 612-624-4772, Fax: 612-624-8277, E-mail: thoma006@umn.edu. *Application contact:* Dr. Mary Trettin, Associate Dean, 612-625-6501, Fax: 612-626-1580, E-mail: mtrettin@umn.edu.

University of New Mexico, Graduate School, College of Education, Department of Individual, Family and Community Education, Program in Multicultural Teacher and Childhood Education, Albuquerque, NM 87131-2039. Offers Ed D, PhD. *Accreditation:* NCATE. Part-time programs available. *Students:* 9 full-time (5 women), 16 part-time (11 women); includes 7 minority (1 African American, 1 American Indian/Alaska Native, 1 Asian American or Pacific Islander, 4 Hispanic Americans). Average age 48. 6 applicants, 50% accepted, 3 enrolled. *Degree requirements:* For doctorate, comprehensive exam, thesis/dissertation (for some programs). *Entrance requirements:* For doctorate, GRE, master's degree, minimum GPA of 3.0, 3 years teaching experience, 3-5 letters of reference, 1 letter of intent, professional writing sample. Additional exam requirements/recommendations for international students: Required—TOEFL (minimum score 550 paper-based; 213 computer-based). *Application deadline:* For fall admission, 3/1 priority date for domestic students, 3/1 for international students; for spring admission, 10/30 for domestic and international students. Application fee: $50. Electronic applications accepted. *Expenses:* Tuition, state resident: full-time $2099; part-time $233.20 per credit hour. Tuition, nonresident: full-time $6650. Required fees: $25 per semester. Tuition and fees vary according to course load, program and reciprocity agreements. *Financial support:* In 2009–10, 2 teaching assistantships with partial tuition reimbursements (averaging $12,805 per year) were awarded; fellowships, career-related internships or fieldwork, scholarships/grants, and unspecified assistantships also available. Financial award application deadline: 4/15; financial award applicants required to submit FAFSA. *Faculty research:* Mathematics/science/technology education, diversity, curriculum development, reflective practice, social justice, student learning, teacher education. *Unit head:* Dr. Rosalita Mitchell, Department Chair, 505-277-9611, Fax: 505-277-0455, E-mail: ted@unm.edu. *Application contact:* Robert Romero, Program Coordinator, 505-277-0513, Fax: 505-277-0455, E-mail: ted@unm.edu.

The University of North Carolina at Greensboro, Graduate School, School of Education, Department of Educational Leadership and Cultural Foundations, Greensboro, NC 27412-5001. Offers curriculum and teaching (PhD), including cultural studies; educational leadership (Ed D, Ed S); school administration (MSA). *Accreditation:* NCATE. *Degree requirements:* For doctorate, thesis/dissertation. *Entrance requirements:* For master's, doctorate, and Ed S, GRE General Test. Additional exam requirements/recommendations for international students: Required—TOEFL. Electronic applications accepted.

University of Oklahoma, Graduate College, College of Education, Department of Instructional Leadership and Academic Curriculum, Norman, OK 73072. Offers education (Certificate); instructional leadership and academic curriculum (M Ed, PhD), including bilingual education, early childhood education, elementary education, English education, math education, reading education, science education, secondary education, social studies education. *Accreditation:* NCATE. Part-time and evening/weekend programs available. *Faculty:* 18 full-time (11 women). *Students:* 44 full-time (36 women), 117 part-time (92 women); includes 35 minority (11 African Americans, 14 American Indian/Alaska Native, 5 Asian Americans or Pacific Islanders, 5 Hispanic Americans), 2 international. 50 applicants, 84% accepted, 32 enrolled. In 2009, 31 master's, 6 doctorates awarded. Terminal master's awarded for partial completion of doctoral program. *Degree requirements:* For doctorate, thesis/dissertation. *Entrance requirements:* For master's, 12 hours of course work in education; for doctorate, GRE General Test, master's degree, minimum graduate GPA of 3.0. Additional exam requirements/recommendations for international students: Required—TOEFL (minimum score 550 paper-based; 213 computer-based). *Application deadline:* For fall admission, 6/1 priority date for domestic students, 4/1 for international students; for spring admission, 11/1 for domestic students, 9/1 for international students. Applications are processed on a rolling basis. Application fee: $40 ($90 for international students). Electronic applications accepted. *Expenses:* Tuition, state resident: full-time $3744; part-time $156 per credit hour. Tuition, nonresident: full-time $13,577; part-time $565.70 per credit hour. Required fees: $2415; $90.10 per credit hour. *Financial support:* In 2009–10, 107 students received support, including 1 research assistantship with partial tuition reimbursement available (averaging $9,630 per year), 6 teaching assistantships with partial tuition reimbursements available (averaging $10,801 per year); scholarships/grants, health care benefits, and unspecified assistantships also available. Financial award applicants required to submit FAFSA. *Faculty research:* English education, mathematics education, reading, science education, social studies education. Total annual research expenditures: $752,908. *Unit head:* Lawrence Baines, Chair, 405-325-1498, Fax: 405-325-4061, E-mail: lbaines@ou.edu. *Application contact:* Lynn Crussel, Administrative Assistant for Graduate Studies, 405-325-4843, Fax: 405-325-4061, E-mail: lcrussel@ou.edu.

University of Pennsylvania, Graduate School of Education, Division of Language in Education, Program in Intercultural Communication, Philadelphia, PA 19104. Offers MS Ed, Ed D, PhD. Part-time programs available. *Students:* 49 full-time (43 women), 16 part-time (13 women); includes 6 minority (1 African American, 4 Asian Americans or Pacific Islanders, 1 Hispanic American), 24 international. 104 applicants, 76% accepted, 30 enrolled. In 2009, 17 master's, 1 doctorate awarded. *Degree requirements:* For master's, comprehensive exam, thesis; for doctorate, comprehensive exam, thesis/dissertation, oral exams. *Entrance requirements:* For master's, GRE General Test or MAT; for doctorate, GRE General Test. *Application deadline:* For fall admission, 12/15 priority date for domestic students. Applications are processed on a rolling basis. Application fee: $70. Electronic applications accepted. *Expenses:* Contact institution. *Financial support:* Career-related internships or fieldwork, Federal Work-Study, and institutionally sponsored loans available. Support available to part-time students. Financial award applicants required to submit FAFSA. *Faculty research:* Anthropology of education, history of education, bicultural education, identity and gender education.

University of Pennsylvania, Graduate School of Education, Division of Language in Education, Programs in Teaching English to Speakers of Other Languages and Intercultural Communication, Philadelphia, PA 19104. Offers educational linguistics (PhD); intercultural communication (MS Ed); teaching English to speakers of other languages (MS Ed). Part-time programs available. Postbaccalaureate distance learning degree programs offered (minimal on-campus study). *Students:* 82 full-time (71 women), 23 part-time (17 women); includes 3 minority (2 African Americans, 1 Asian American or Pacific Islander), 82 international. 117 applicants, 82% accepted, 61 enrolled. In 2009, 51 master's awarded. Terminal master's awarded for partial completion of doctoral program. *Degree requirements:* For master's, comprehensive exam, thesis (for some programs); for doctorate, one foreign language, thesis/dissertation, preliminary exam. *Entrance requirements:* For master's and doctorate, GRE General Test or MAT. Additional exam requirements/recommendations for international students: Required—TOEFL. *Application deadline:* For fall admission, 12/15 priority date for domestic students. Applications are processed on a rolling basis. Application fee: $70. Electronic applications accepted. *Expenses:* Contact institution. *Financial support:* Fellowships, research assistantships, institutionally sponsored loans, scholarships/grants, traineeships, health care benefits, and unspecified assistantships available. *Faculty research:* Second language acquisition, social linguistics, English as a second language.

University of St. Thomas, Graduate Studies, School of Education, Department of Teacher Education, St. Paul, MN 55105-1096. Offers curriculum and instruction (MA), including elementary, individualized, K-12, secondary; elementary (MAT); multicultural education (Certificate); reading (MA, Certificate), including elementary (MA), K-12 (MA). *Accreditation:* NCATE. Part-time and evening/weekend programs available. *Faculty:* 10 full-time (7 women), 25 part-time/adjunct (16 women). *Students:* 31 full-time (25 women), 260 part-time (195 women); includes 19 minority (6 African Americans, 7 Asian Americans or Pacific Islanders, 6 Hispanic Americans), 3 international. Average age 34. 325 applicants, 72% accepted, 225 enrolled. In 2009, 135 master's, 17 other advanced degrees awarded. *Entrance requirements:* For master's, minimum GPA of 3.0 or MAT. Additional exam requirements/recommendations for international students: Required—TOEFL (minimum score 550 paper-based; 210 computer-based; 80 iBT). *Application deadline:* For fall admission, 6/1 for domestic students; for spring admission, 11/1 for domestic students. Applications are processed on a rolling basis. Application fee: $50. *Financial support:* Fellowships, research assistantships, institutionally sponsored loans and scholarships/grants available. Support available to part-time students. Financial award applicants required to submit FAFSA. *Unit head:* Dr. Douglas F. Warring, Department Chair, 651-962-4877, Fax: 651-962-4169, E-mail: dfwarring@stthomas.edu. *Application contact:* Kathy J. Neary, Department Assistant, 651-962-4420, Fax: 651-962-4169, E-mail: kjneary@stthomas.edu.

University of San Francisco, School of Education, Department of International and Multicultural Education, San Francisco, CA 94117-1080. Offers international and multicultural education (MA, Ed D); multicultural literature for children and young adults (MA); teaching English as a second language (MA). *Faculty:* 2 full-time (both women), 6 part-time/adjunct (3 women). *Students:* 31 full-time (12 women), 54 part-time (42 women). Average age 36. 191 applicants, 69% accepted, 48 enrolled. In 2009, 32 master's, 10 doctorates awarded. *Degree requirements:* For doctorate, thesis/dissertation. Application fee: $55 ($65 for international students). *Expenses:* Tuition: Full-time $19,710; part-time $1095 per unit. Part-time tuition and fees vary according to degree level, campus/location and program. *Financial support:* In 2009–10, 56 students received support; fellowships, research assistantships, teaching assistantships available. Financial award application deadline: 3/2; financial award applicants required to submit FAFSA. *Unit head:* Dr. Katz Susan, Chair, 415-422-6878. *Application contact:* Beth Teague, Associate Director of Graduate Outreach, 415-422-5467, E-mail: schoolofeducation@usfca.edu.

University of Southern California, Graduate School, Rossier School of Education, Doctor of Education Programs, Los Angeles, CA 90089. Offers educational psychology (Ed D); higher education administration (Ed D); K-12 leadership in urban school settings (Ed D); teacher education in multicultural societies (Ed D). Part-time and evening/weekend programs available. *Faculty:* 59 full-time (32 women), 12 part-time/adjunct (3 women). *Students:* 567 full-time (361 women), 12 part-time (6 women); includes 339 minority (73 African Americans, 11 American Indian/Alaska Native, 129 Asian Americans or Pacific Islanders, 126 Hispanic Americans), 13 international. 300 applicants, 76% accepted, 182 enrolled. In 2009, 143 doctorates awarded. *Degree requirements:* For doctorate, thesis/dissertation. *Entrance requirements:* For doctorate, GRE. Additional exam requirements/recommendations for international students: Required—TOEFL (minimum score 250 computer-based; 100 iBT). *Application deadline:* For fall admission, 1/15 priority date for domestic and international students. Application fee: $85. Electronic applications accepted. *Expenses:* Tuition: Full-time $25,980; part-time $1315 per unit. Required fees: $554. One-time fee: $35 full-time. Full-time tuition and fees vary according to degree level and program. *Financial support:* In 2009–10, 385 students received support. Scholarships/grants available. Support available to part-time students. Financial award application deadline: 5/5. *Faculty research:* Data-driven decision-making in K-12 schools and districts; examination of college and university leadership and management in U. S. and Asia; studies in facilitating student learning; organizational change and the role of leaders; leadership, diversity, learning and accountability. *Unit head:* Dr. Kathy Stowe, Executive Director/Assistant Professor of Clinical Education, 213-740-9323. *Application contact:* Carolyn Stirling, Associate Director of Recruiting and Admissions, 213-740-0224, Fax: 213-740-9433, E-mail: soeinfo@usc.edu.

The University of Tennessee, Graduate School, College of Education, Health and Human Sciences, Program in Education, Knoxville, TN 37996. Offers art education (MS); counseling education (PhD); cultural studies in education (PhD); curriculum (MS, Ed S); curriculum, educational research and evaluation (Ed D, PhD); early childhood education (PhD); early childhood special education (MS); education of deaf and hard of hearing (MS); educational administration and policy studies (Ed D, PhD); educational administration and supervision (Ed S); educational psychology (Ed D, PhD); elementary education (MS, Ed S); elementary teaching (MS); English education (MS, Ed S); exercise science (PhD); foreign language/ESL education (MS, Ed S); instructional technology (MS, Ed D, PhD, Ed S); literacy, language and ESL education (PhD); literacy, language education, and ESL education (Ed D); mathematics education (MS, Ed S); modified and comprehensive special education (MS); reading education (MS, Ed S); school counseling (Ed S); school psychology (PhD, Ed S); science education (MS, Ed S); secondary teaching (MS); social foundations (MS); social science education (MS, Ed S); socio-cultural foundations of sports and education (PhD); special education (Ed S); teacher education (Ed D, PhD). *Accreditation:* NCATE. Part-time and evening/weekend programs available. *Degree requirements:* For master's and Ed S, thesis optional; for doctorate, variable foreign language requirement, thesis/dissertation. *Entrance requirements:* For master's, minimum GPA of 2.7; for doctorate and Ed S, GRE General Test, minimum GPA of 2.7. Additional exam requirements/recommendations for international students: Required—TOEFL. Electronic applications accepted. *Expenses:* Tuition, state resident: full-time $6826; part-time $380 per semester hour. Tuition, nonresident: full-time $21,844; part-time $1147 per semester hour. Tuition and fees vary according to program.

The University of Texas at Brownsville, Graduate Studies, School of Education, Brownsville, TX 78520-4991. Offers bilingual education (M Ed); counseling and guidance (M Ed); curriculum and instruction (M Ed); early childhood education (M Ed); educational administration (M Ed); educational technology (M Ed); English as a second language (M Ed); reading specialist (M Ed); special education/educational diagnostician (M Ed). Part-time and evening/weekend programs available. Postbaccalaureate distance learning degree programs offered (minimal

Multilingual and Multicultural Education

The University of Texas at Brownsville (continued)
on-campus study). *Degree requirements:* For master's, thesis optional. *Entrance requirements:* For master's, GRE General Test. Additional exam requirements/recommendations for international students: Required—TOEFL.

The University of Texas at El Paso, Graduate School, College of Liberal Arts, Department of English, El Paso, TX 79968-0001. Offers bilingual professional writing (Certificate); English and American literature (MA); rhetoric and composition (PhD); rhetoric and writing studies (MA); teaching English (MAT). Part-time and evening/weekend programs available. *Degree requirements:* For master's, thesis optional. *Entrance requirements:* For master's, GRE General Test, minimum GPA of 3.0. Additional exam requirements/recommendations for international students: Required—TOEFL. Electronic applications accepted. *Faculty research:* Literature, creative writing, literary theory.

The University of Texas at San Antonio, College of Education and Human Development, Division of Bicultural-Bilingual Studies, San Antonio, TX 78249-0617. Offers bicultural-bilingual studies (MA); culture, literacy, and language (PhD); teaching English as a second language (MA). Part-time and evening/weekend programs available. *Faculty:* 13 full-time (7 women). *Students:* 48 full-time (36 women), 94 part-time (75 women); includes 108 minority (5 African Americans, 8 Asian Americans or Pacific Islanders, 95 Hispanic Americans), 10 international. Average age 35. 76 applicants, 89% accepted, 36 enrolled. In 2009, 27 master's, 3 doctorates awarded. *Degree requirements:* For master's, comprehensive exam (for some programs), thesis (for some programs); for doctorate, comprehensive exam, thesis/dissertation. *Entrance requirements:* For master's and doctorate, GRE General Test. Additional exam requirements/recommendations for international students: Required—TOEFL (minimum score 500 paper-based; 173 computer-based; 61 iBT), IELTS (minimum score 5). *Application deadline:* For fall admission, 7/1 for domestic students, 4/1 for international students; for spring admission, 11/1 for domestic students, 9/1 for international students. Applications are processed on a rolling basis. Application fee: $45 ($80 for international students). Electronic applications accepted. *Expenses:* Tuition, state resident: full-time $3975; part-time $221 per contact hour. Tuition, nonresident: full-time $13,947; part-time $775 per contact hour. Required fees: $1853. *Financial support:* In 2009–10, 24 students received support, including 2 research assistantships (averaging $11,660 per year), 9 teaching assistantships (averaging $8,439 per year); fellowships, career-related internships or fieldwork and tuition waivers also available. Support available to part-time students. *Faculty research:* Globalization, migration and immigrant education, integrating language and content in PK-12 instruction, language and cultural policies in multilingual societies, multiple literacies. *Unit head:* Dr. Robert D. Milk, Director, 210-458-4426, Fax: 210-458-5962, E-mail: rmilk@utsa.edu. *Application contact:* Dr. Dorothy A. Flannagan, Dean of the Graduate School, 210-458-4330, Fax: 210-458-4332, E-mail: dorothy.flannagan@utsa.edu.

The University of Texas–Pan American, College of Education, Department of Curriculum and Instruction: Elementary and Secondary, Edinburg, TX 78539. Offers bilingual education (M Ed); early childhood education (M Ed); elementary education (M Ed); reading (M Ed); secondary education (M Ed). Part-time programs available. *Degree requirements:* For master's, comprehensive exam, thesis optional. *Entrance requirements:* For master's, GRE. Additional exam requirements/recommendations for international students: Required—TOEFL, IELTS. *Expenses:* Tuition, state resident: full-time $3630.60; part-time $201.70 per credit hour. Tuition, nonresident: full-time $8617; part-time $478.70 per credit hour. Required fees: $806.50. *Faculty research:* Dual language instruction, literacy and technology, teacher education in diverse populations, mathematics and science education.

University of the Incarnate Word, School of Graduate Studies and Research, Dreeben School of Education, Programs in Education, San Antonio, TX 78209-6397. Offers adult education (M Ed, MA); cross-cultural education (M Ed, MA); early childhood literacy (M Ed, MA); general education (M Ed, MA); Higher Education (PhD); instructional technology (M Ed, MA); international education and entrepreneurship (PhD); kinesiology (M Ed, MA); literacy (M Ed, MA); organizational leadership (PhD); organizational learning and learning (M Ed, MA); reading (M Ed, MA); special education (M Ed, MA); teacher leadership (M Ed, MA). Part-time and evening/weekend programs available. *Students:* 20 full-time (11 women), 201 part-time (122 women); includes 113 minority (29 African Americans, 2 American Indian/Alaska Native, 2 Asian Americans or Pacific Islanders, 80 Hispanic Americans), 30 international. Average age 41. In 2009, 26 master's, 19 doctorates awarded. *Degree requirements:* For master's, capstone; for doctorate, thesis/dissertation, qualifying exam. *Entrance requirements:* For master's, baccalaureate degree; minimum foundation GPA of 2.5; interview; for doctorate, master's degree; interview; supervised writing sample. Additional exam requirements/recommendations for international students: Required—TOEFL (minimum score 560 paper-based; 220 computer-based; 83 iBT). *Application deadline:* Applications are processed on a rolling basis. Application fee: $20. Electronic applications accepted. *Expenses:* Tuition: Full-time $12,150; part-time $675 per credit hour. Required fees: $83 per credit hour. *Financial support:* Federal Work-Study and scholarships/grants available. Financial award applicants required to submit FAFSA. *Unit head:* Dr. Denise Staudt, Dean, Dreeben School of Education, 210-829-2762, E-mail: staudt@uiwtx.edu. *Application contact:* Andrea Cyterski-Acosta, Dean of Enrollment, 210-829-6005, Fax: 210-829-3921, E-mail: admis@uiwtx.edu.

University of the Southwest, Graduate Programs, Hobbs, NM 88240-9129. Offers business administration (MBA); curriculum and instruction (MSE); curriculum and instruction: bilingual (MSE); curriculum and instruction: reading (MSE); curriculum and instruction: TESOL (MSE); early childhood education (MSE); educational diagnostician (MSE); mental health counseling (MSE); school business administration (MSE); school counseling (MSE); special education (MSE). Part-time and evening/weekend programs available. Postbaccalaureate distance learning degree programs offered (no on-campus study). *Faculty:* 10 full-time (6 women), 10 part-time/adjunct (4 women). *Students:* 112 full-time (93 women), 99 part-time (72 women). Average age 35. 94 applicants, 47% accepted, 39 enrolled. In 2009, 32 master's awarded. *Degree requirements:* For master's, comprehensive exam. *Application deadline:* For fall admission, 3/1 priority date for domestic students; for spring admission, 10/1 for domestic students. Applications are processed on a rolling basis. Application fee: $25. Electronic applications accepted. *Expenses:* Tuition: Part-time $512 per hour. Tuition and fees vary according to course load. *Financial support:* In 2009–10, 196 students received support; research assistantships with partial tuition reimbursements available, Federal Work-Study, scholarships/grants, and tuition waivers (partial) available. Support available to part-time students. Financial award application deadline: 4/1; financial award applicants required to submit FAFSA. *Unit head:* Dr. Mary Harris, Dean of Education, 575-392-6561 Ext. 1056, Fax: 575-392-6006, E-mail: mharris@usw.edu. *Application contact:* Ryanne Evans, Assistant Registrar, 575-392-6561 Ext. 1031, Fax: 575-392-6006, E-mail: revans@usw.edu.

University of Washington, Graduate School, College of Education, Seattle, WA 98195. Offers curriculum and instruction (M Ed, Ed D, PhD), including educational technology, general curriculum (Ed D, PhD), language, literacy, and culture, mathematics education, multicultural education, reading and language arts education (Ed D), science education, social studies education, teaching and curriculum (M Ed); educational leadership and policy studies (M Ed, Ed D, PhD), including administration (Ed D), educational policy, organization, and leadership (M Ed, PhD), higher education, leadership for learning (Ed D), social and cultural foundations of education (M Ed, PhD); educational psychology (M Ed, PhD), including educational psychology (PhD), human development and cognition (M Ed), learning sciences, measurement, statistics and research design (M Ed), school psychology (M Ed); instructional leadership (M Ed); intercollegiate athletic leadership (M Ed); special education (M Ed, Ed D, PhD), including early childhood special education (M Ed), emotional and behavioral disabilities (M Ed), learning disabilities (M Ed), low-incidence disabilities (M Ed), severe disabilities (M Ed), special education (Ed D, PhD); teacher education (MIT). *Accreditation:* APA. Part-time and evening/weekend programs available. *Degree requirements:* For master's, thesis optional; for doctorate, thesis/dissertation. *Entrance requirements:* For master's and doctorate, GRE General Test, minimum GPA of 3.0. Additional exam requirements/recommendations for international students: Required—TOEFL. Electronic applications accepted. *Faculty research:* School restructuring/effective schools, special education interventions, literacy and writing, technology, school partnerships, teacher preparation.

University of Wisconsin–Milwaukee, Graduate School, School of Education, Program in Urban Education, Milwaukee, WI 53201-0413. Offers adult and continuing education (PhD); curriculum and instruction (PhD); educational administration (PhD); educational and media technology (PhD); educational psychology (PhD); multicultural studies (PhD); social foundations of education (PhD). *Students:* 67 full-time (51 women), 44 part-time (30 women); includes 41 minority (23 African Americans, 2 American Indian/Alaska Native, 7 Asian Americans or Pacific Islanders, 9 Hispanic Americans), 4 international. Average age 41. 31 applicants, 45% accepted, 5 enrolled. In 2009, 11 doctorates awarded. *Degree requirements:* For doctorate, comprehensive exam, thesis/dissertation. *Entrance requirements:* For doctorate, GRE General Test, minimum undergraduate GPA of 2.85, graduate 3.5. Additional exam requirements/recommendations for international students: Required—TOEFL (minimum score 550 paper-based; 79 iBT), IELTS (minimum score 6.5). *Application deadline:* For fall admission, 1/1 priority date for domestic students; for spring admission, 9/1 for domestic students. Applications are processed on a rolling basis. Application fee: $45 ($75 for international students). *Expenses:* Tuition, state resident: full-time $8800. Tuition, nonresident: full-time $20,760. Tuition and fees vary according to program and reciprocity agreements. *Financial support:* Career-related internships or fieldwork and unspecified assistantships available. Support available to part-time students. Financial award application deadline: 4/15. *Unit head:* Larry Martin, Representative, 414-229-4729, Fax: 414-229-2920, E-mail: lmartin@uwm.edu. *Application contact:* General Information Contact, 414-229-4982, Fax: 414-229-6967, E-mail: gradschool@uwm.edu.

Utah State University, School of Graduate Studies, College of Humanities, Arts and Social Sciences, Department of Languages, Philosophy, and Speech Communication, Logan, UT 84322. Offers second language teaching (MSLT). *Entrance requirements:* For master's, GRE General Test or MAT, minimum GPA of 3.0. Additional exam requirements/recommendations for international students: Required—TOEFL.

Vanderbilt University, Graduate School, Program in Learning, Teaching and Diversity, Nashville, TN 37240-1001. Offers MS, PhD. *Faculty:* 25 full-time (15 women). *Students:* 45 full-time (27 women), 1 (woman) part-time; includes 4 minority (2 African Americans, 2 Asian Americans or Pacific Islanders), 4 international. Average age 34. 99 applicants, 14% accepted, 8 enrolled. In 2009, 5 doctorates awarded. *Degree requirements:* For doctorate, comprehensive exam, thesis/dissertation. *Entrance requirements:* For doctorate, GRE General Test. Additional exam requirements/recommendations for international students: Required—TOEFL (minimum score 570 paper-based; 230 computer-based; 88 iBT). *Application deadline:* For fall admission, 12/31 for domestic and international students. Application fee: $0. Electronic applications accepted. *Financial support:* Fellowships with full and partial tuition reimbursements, research assistantships with full tuition reimbursements, teaching assistantships with full tuition reimbursements, Federal Work-Study, institutionally sponsored loans, scholarships/grants, traineeships, and health care benefits available. Financial award application deadline: 1/15; financial award applicants required to submit CSS PROFILE or FAFSA. *Faculty research:* New pedagogies for math, science, and language; the support of English language learners; the uses of new technology and media in the classroom; middle school mathematics and the institutional setting of teaching. *Unit head:* David Dickinson, Interim Chair, 615-322-8100, Fax: 615-322-8999, E-mail: david.dickinson@vanderbilt.edu. *Application contact:* Rogers P. Hall, Director of Graduate Studies, 615-322-8092, Fax: 615-322-8999, E-mail: r.hall@vanderbilt.edu.

Vanderbilt University, Peabody College, Department of Teaching and Learning, Nashville, TN 37240-1001. Offers elementary education (M Ed); English language learners (M Ed); learning and instruction (M Ed); learning, diversity, and urban studies (M Ed); reading education (M Ed); secondary education (M Ed). *Accreditation:* NCATE. *Faculty:* 31 full-time (20 women), 23 part-time/adjunct (20 women). *Students:* 95 full-time (88 women), 21 part-time (6 women); includes 14 minority (6 African Americans, 4 Asian Americans or Pacific Islanders, 4 Hispanic Americans), 5 international. Average age 27. 150 applicants, 69% accepted, 59 enrolled. In 2009, 74 master's awarded. *Degree requirements:* For master's, comprehensive exam, thesis optional. *Entrance requirements:* For master's, GRE General Test, MAT. Additional exam requirements/recommendations for international students: Required—TOEFL (minimum score 550 paper-based; 213 computer-based). *Application deadline:* For fall admission, 12/31 priority date for domestic and international students; for spring admission, 11/1 priority date for domestic and international students. Applications are processed on a rolling basis. Application fee: $0. Electronic applications accepted. *Financial support:* In 2009–10, 104 students received support, including 27 research assistantships with full and partial tuition reimbursements available; fellowships with full and partial tuition reimbursements available, teaching assistantships with full and partial tuition reimbursements available, Federal Work-Study, institutionally sponsored loans, scholarships/grants, tuition waivers (partial), and unspecified assistantships also available. Support available to part-time students. Financial award application deadline: 2/1; financial award applicants required to submit FAFSA. *Faculty research:* Teaching and learning, development of mathematical and scientific knowledge, interventions to foster early literacy and numeracy, reading and writing in the digital age, teaching diverse learners. *Unit head:* Dr. David Dickinson, Acting Chair, 615-322-8100, Fax: 615-322-8999, E-mail: david.k.dickinson@vanderbilt.edu. *Application contact:* Angela Saylor, Educational Coordinator, 615-322-8092, Fax: 615-322-8999, E-mail: angela.saylor@vanderbilt.edu.

Washington State University, Graduate School, College of Education, Department of Teaching and Learning, Pullman, WA 99164. Offers curriculum and instruction (Ed D, PhD); diverse languages (M Ed, MA); elementary education (M Ed, MA, MIT); exercise science (MS); literacy education (M Ed, MA, PhD); math education (PhD); secondary education (M Ed, MA). *Accreditation:* NCATE. *Degree requirements:* For master's, comprehensive exam (for some programs), thesis (for some programs), oral or written exam; for doctorate, comprehensive exam, thesis/dissertation, oral, written exam. *Entrance requirements:* For master's and doctorate, GRE General Test, minimum GPA of 3.0, 3 letters of recommendation. Additional exam requirements/recommendations for international students: Required—TOEFL. *Faculty research:* Evolution of middle school education issues in special education, computer-assisted language learning.

Wayne State University, College of Education, Division of Teacher Education, Detroit, MI 48202. Offers adult and continuing education (M Ed); art education (M Ed); bilingual/bicultural education (M Ed, MAT); business education (M Ed, MAT); career and technical education (M Ed, Ed D, PhD, Ed S); curriculum and instruction (Ed D, PhD, Ed S); distributive education (M Ed, MAT); early childhood education (M Ed); elementary education (M Ed, MAT, Ed D, PhD, Ed S); elementary education curriculum and instruction (M Ed); English education (M Ed); English education-secondary (M Ed, Ed S); foreign language education (M Ed); general education (Ed D, Ed S); health occupations education (M Ed); industrial education (M Ed); mathematics education (M Ed, Ed S); pre-school and parent education (M Ed); reading (M Ed, Ed D, Ed S); reading, languages and literature (Ed D); school music-vocal (M Ed); science education (M Ed, MAT, Ed S); secondary education (MAT); secondary school reading (M Ed); social studies education (M Ed, Ed S), including education-secondary (M Ed); special education (M Ed, Ed D, PhD, Ed S); teacher education (MAT, Ed D, PhD). *Degree requirements:* For doctorate, thesis/dissertation. *Entrance requirements:* For master's, Michigan Basic Skills Test (MA in teaching), minimum GPA of 2.6; for doctorate, minimum undergraduate GPA of 3.0, graduate 3.5; interview, curriculum vitae; references. Additional exam requirements/recommendations for international students: Required—TOEFL (minimum score 550 paper-based; 213 computer-based), TWE (minimum score 6). Electronic applications accepted. *Faculty research:* Reading and writing literacy and literature.

Western New Mexico University, Graduate Division, School of Education, Silver City, NM 88062-0680. Offers bilingual education (MAT); counseling (MA); educational leadership (MA); elementary education (MAT); reading (MAT); school psychology (MA); secondary education (MAT); special education (MAT); TESOL (teaching English to speakers of other languages) (MAT). *Accreditation:* NCATE. *Degree requirements:* For master's, comprehensive exam. *Entrance requirements:* For master's, GRE General Test, GRE Subject Test, minimum GPA of 3.2 in last 64 hours of undergraduate study. Additional exam requirements/recommendations for international students: Required—TOEFL (minimum score 550 paper-based; 213 computer-based). Electronic applications accepted.

Western Oregon University, Graduate Programs, College of Education, Division of Teacher Education, Program in Secondary Education, Monmouth, OR 97361-1394. Offers bilingual education (MS Ed); health (MS Ed); humanities (MAT, MS Ed); initial licensure (MAT); mathematics (MAT, MS Ed); science (MAT, MS Ed); social science (MAT, MS Ed). *Accreditation:* NCATE. Part-time and evening/weekend programs available. *Degree requirements:* For master's, thesis optional, written exam. *Entrance requirements:* For master's, minimum GPA of 3.0, teaching license. Additional exam requirements/recommendations for international students: Required—TOEFL (minimum score 550 paper-based; 213 computer-based; 79 iBT), IELTS (minimum score 6.5). *Faculty research:* Literacy, science in primary grades, geography education, retention, teacher burnout.

Xavier University, College of Social Sciences, Health and Education, School of Education, Department of Childhood Education and Literacy, Program in Multicultural Literature for Children, Cincinnati, OH 45207. Offers M Ed. Part-time and evening/weekend programs available. Postbaccalaureate distance learning degree programs offered (minimal on-campus study). *Faculty:* 3 full-time (2 women), 2 part-time/adjunct (1 woman). *Students:* 5 part-time (all women); includes 1 minority (Hispanic American). Average age 38. In 2009, 3 master's awarded. *Degree requirements:* For master's, comprehensive exam. *Entrance requirements:* For master's, GRE or MAT. Additional exam requirements/recommendations for international students: Required—TOEFL. *Application deadline:* Applications are processed on a rolling basis. Application fee: $35. Electronic applications accepted. *Expenses:* Tuition: Part-time $697 per credit hour. One-time fee: $35 part-time. *Financial support:* Tuition waivers (partial) and unspecified assistantships available. Financial award applicants required to submit FAFSA. *Faculty research:* Multicultural literacy/fluency, content area literacy, early literacy development, writing/creative and across curriculum, assessment of reading abilities, multicultural literature for children and young adults. *Unit head:* Dr. Leslie Prosak-Beres, Director, 513-745-3652, Fax: 513-745-1052, E-mail: prosak-b@xavier.edu. *Application contact:* Roger Bosse, Director of Graduate Studies, 513-745-3357, Fax: 513-745-1048, E-mail: bosse@xavier.edu.

Special Education

Abilene Christian University, Graduate School, College of Education and Human Services, Graduate Studies in Education, Special Education Program, Abilene, TX 79699-9100. Offers M Ed. *Students:* 4 full-time (all women), 14 part-time (11 women); includes 2 minority (both African Americans). 26 applicants, 88% accepted, 14 enrolled. *Degree requirements:* For master's, comprehensive exam. *Application deadline:* For fall admission, 4/1 priority date for domestic students; for spring admission, 11/1 for domestic students. Applications are processed on a rolling basis. Application fee: $40 ($45 for international students). Electronic applications accepted. *Expenses:* Tuition: Full-time $11,520; part-time $640 per hour. Required fees: $1090; $53.50 per hour. $10 per term. Tuition and fees vary according to program. *Financial support:* In 2009–10, 17 students received support. Application deadline: 4/1. *Unit head:* Dr. Lloyd Goldsmith, Graduate Advisor, 325-674-2470, Fax: 325-674-2123. *Application contact:* William Horn, Graduate Admissions Counselor, 325-674-2656, Fax: 325-674-6717, E-mail: gradinfo@acu.edu.

Acadia University, Faculty of Professional Studies, School of Education, Program in Inclusive Education, Wolfville, NS B4P 2R6, Canada. Offers M Ed. Part-time and evening/weekend programs available. *Faculty:* 2 full-time (both women). *Students:* 4 full-time (2 women), 48 part-time (46 women). 71 applicants, 79% accepted. In 2009, 56 master's awarded. *Degree requirements:* For master's, thesis optional. *Entrance requirements:* For master's, bachelor's degree in education, minimum B average in undergraduate course work, course work in special education. Additional exam requirements/recommendations for international students: Required—TOEFL (minimum score 580 paper-based; 237 computer-based; 93 iBT), IELTS (minimum score 6.5). *Application deadline:* For fall admission, 3/15 priority date for domestic and international students. Application fee: $50. *Financial support:* In 2009–10, teaching assistantships (averaging $4,000 per year). Financial award application deadline: 3/15. *Faculty research:* Technology and human interaction, inclusive education and community, accommodating diversity, program evaluation. *Unit head:* Ann Vibert, Director, E-mail: ann.vibert@acadiau.ca. *Application contact:* Sheila Langille, Secretary, 902-585-1229, Fax: 902-585-1071, E-mail: sheila.langille@acadiau.ca.

Adams State College, The Graduate School, Department of Teacher Education, Program in Special Education, Alamosa, CO 81102. Offers MA. *Accreditation:* Teacher Education Accreditation Council. Part-time programs available. Postbaccalaureate distance learning degree programs offered. *Degree requirements:* For master's, practicum, qualifying exam. *Entrance requirements:* For master's, GRE General Test or MAT, minimum undergraduate GPA of 3.0.

Adelphi University, School of Education, Program in Special Education, Garden City, NY 11530-0701. Offers MS, Certificate. Part-time and evening/weekend programs available. *Students:* 49 full-time (44 women), 149 part-time (140 women); includes 56 minority (24 African Americans, 5 Asian Americans or Pacific Islanders, 27 Hispanic Americans), 2 international. Average age 31. In 2009, 38 master's, 1 other advanced degree awarded. *Entrance requirements:* For master's, 2 letters of recommendation, resume detailing paid/volunteer experience and organizational membership. Additional exam requirements/recommendations for international students: Required—TOEFL (minimum score 550 paper-based; 213 computer-based; 80 iBT). *Application deadline:* For fall admission, 4/1 for international students; for spring admission, 11/1 for international students. Electronic applications accepted. *Expenses:* Tuition: Full-time $28,340; part-time $830 per credit. Required fees: $600; $250 per credit. Full-time tuition and fees vary according to course load and program. *Financial support:* Fellowships, research assistantships with partial tuition reimbursements, teaching assistantships, career-related internships or fieldwork, Federal Work-Study, institutionally sponsored loans, tuition waivers (full), and unspecified assistantships available. Support available to part-time students. Financial award application deadline: 2/15; financial award applicants required to submit FAFSA. *Unit head:* Dr. Anne Mungai, Director, 516-877-4096, E-mail: mungai@adelphi.edu. *Application contact:* Christine Murphy, Director of Admissions, 516-877-3050, Fax: 516-877-3039, E-mail: graduateadmissions@adelphi.edu.

Alabama Agricultural and Mechanical University, School of Graduate Studies, School of Education, Department of Counseling and Special Education, Huntsville, AL 35811. Offers communicative disorders (M Ed, MS); psychology and counseling (MS, Ed S), including clinical psychology (MS), counseling and guidance, counseling psychology (MS), personnel management (MS), psychometry (MS), school psychology (MS); special education (M Ed, MS). *Accreditation:* CORE; NCATE. Part-time and evening/weekend programs available. *Degree requirements:* For master's, comprehensive exam. *Entrance requirements:* For master's, GRE General Test. Additional exam requirements/recommendations for international students: Required—TOEFL (minimum score 500 paper-based; 173 computer-based; 61 iBT). *Faculty research:* Increasing numbers of minorities in special education and speech-language pathology.

Alabama State University, School of Graduate Studies, College of Education, Department of Curriculum and Instruction, Program in Special Education, Montgomery, AL 36101-0271. Offers M Ed. Part-time programs available. *Degree requirements:* For master's, comprehensive exam. *Entrance requirements:* For master's, GRE General Test, MAT, graduate writing competency test. Additional exam requirements/recommendations for international students: Required—TOEFL (minimum score 500 paper-based; 173 computer-based).

Albany State University, College of Education, Program in Special Education, Albany, GA 31705-2717. Offers M Ed. *Accreditation:* NCATE. *Students:* 21 full-time (16 women), 33 part-time (32 women); includes 45 minority (all African Americans). Average age 36. 4 applicants, 75% accepted, 3 enrolled. In 2009, 14 master's awarded. *Degree requirements:* For master's, comprehensive exam, GACE II. *Entrance requirements:* For master's, GRE General Test or MAT, GACE I. Additional exam requirements/recommendations for international students: Required—TOEFL. *Application deadline:* For fall admission, 11/16 for domestic students, 9/16

for international students; for spring admission, 4/19 for domestic students, 2/19 for international students. Applications are processed on a rolling basis. Application fee: $20. Electronic applications accepted. *Expenses:* Tuition, state resident: full-time $2970; part-time $162 per credit hour. Tuition, nonresident: full-time $12,168; part-time $676 per credit hour. Required fees: $962; $75 per credit hour. *Financial support:* Career-related internships or fieldwork, Federal Work-Study, and scholarships/grants available. Support available to part-time students. Financial award application deadline: 6/30; financial award applicants required to submit CSS PROFILE or FAFSA. *Unit head:* Dr. Audrey Beard, Chairperson, 229-430-4687, Fax: 229-430-4993, E-mail: audrey.beard@asurams.edu. *Application contact:* Nicole Lane, Interim Graduate Admissions Officer, 229-430-4862, Fax: 229-430-6398, E-mail: nicole.lane@asurams.edu.

Albright College, Department of Education—Graduate Division, Reading, PA 19612-5234. Offers early childhood education (MS); elementary education (MS); English as a second language (MA); general education (MA); special education (MS). Part-time and evening/weekend programs available. *Degree requirements:* For master's, thesis. *Entrance requirements:* For master's, GRE General Test or MAT, minimum undergraduate GPA of 3.0, 2 letters of recommendation, interview. Additional exam requirements/recommendations for international students: Recommended—TOEFL (minimum score 525 paper-based; 197 computer-based). Electronic applications accepted.

Alcorn State University, School of Graduate Studies, School of Psychology and Education, Alcorn State, MS 39096-7500. Offers agricultural education (MS Ed); elementary education (MS Ed, Ed S); guidance and counseling (MS Ed); industrial education (MS Ed); secondary education (MS Ed), including health and physical education; special education (MS Ed). *Accreditation:* NCATE. *Degree requirements:* For master's, thesis optional.

Alliant International University–Irvine, Graduate School of Education, Teacher Education Programs, Irvine, CA 92612. Offers auditory oral education (Certificate); CLAD (Certificate); preliminary multiple subject (Credential); preliminary multiple subject with BCLAD (Credential); preliminary single subject (Credential); professional clear multiple subject (Credential); professional clear single subject (Credential); teaching (MA, Credential); technology and learning (MA). Part-time and evening/weekend programs available. *Entrance requirements:* For degree, California Basic Educational Skills Test, minimum GPA of 2.5. Additional exam requirements/recommendations for international students: Required—TOEFL (minimum score 550 paper-based; 213 computer-based), TWE. Electronic applications accepted.

Alliant International University–San Francisco, Graduate School of Education, Teacher Education Programs, San Francisco, CA 94133-1221. Offers auditory oral education (Certificate); CLAD (Certificate); preliminary multiple subject (Credential); preliminary multiple subject with BCLAD (Credential); preliminary single subject (Credential); professional clear multiple subject (Credential); professional clear single subject (Credential); teaching (MA). Part-time and evening/weekend programs available. *Entrance requirements:* For degree, California Basic Educational Skills Test, minimum GPA of 2.5. Additional exam requirements/recommendations for international students: Required—TOEFL (minimum score 550 paper-based; 213 computer-based), TWE.

American International College, School of Arts, Education and Sciences, Department of Education, Springfield, MA 01109-3189. Offers early childhood education (M Ed, CAGS); educational leadership and supervision (Ed D); elementary education (M Ed, CAGS); middle/secondary education (M Ed, CAGS); moderate disabilities (M Ed, CAGS); reading (M Ed, CAGS); school adjustment counseling (MA, CAGS); school administration (M Ed, CAGS); school guidance counseling (MA, CAGS); teaching (MA, MS); teaching and learning (Ed D). Part-time and evening/weekend programs available. Terminal master's awarded for partial completion of doctoral program. *Degree requirements:* For master's, comprehensive exam (for some programs), thesis (for some programs), practicum; for doctorate, comprehensive exam (for some programs), thesis/dissertation; for CAGS, practicum. *Entrance requirements:* For master's, minimum B- average in undergraduate course work; for doctorate, GRE General Test, interview. Additional exam requirements/recommendations for international students: Required—TOEFL. Electronic applications accepted. *Expenses:* Tuition: Full-time $12,510; part-time $695 per credit hour. Required fees: $35 per term.

American University, College of Arts and Sciences, School of Education, Teaching, and Health, Program in Special Education, Washington, DC 22016-8030. Offers special education: learning disabilities (MA). Part-time and evening/weekend programs available. *Students:* 9 full-time (all women), 14 part-time (12 women); includes 6 minority (5 African Americans, 1 Hispanic American). Average age 31. 20 applicants, 75% accepted, 13 enrolled. In 2009, 15 master's awarded. *Degree requirements:* For master's, comprehensive exam, PRAXIS II. *Entrance requirements:* For master's, GRE General Test, PRAXIS I, minimum GPA of 3.0, 2 recommendations. *Application deadline:* For fall admission, 2/1 priority date for domestic students; for spring admission, 10/1 priority date for domestic students. Applications are processed on a rolling basis. Application fee: $80. *Expenses:* Tuition: Full-time $22,266; part-time $1237 per credit hour. Required fees: $430. Tuition and fees vary according to program. *Financial support:* Fellowships with full tuition reimbursements, research assistantships, teaching assistantships, career-related internships or fieldwork, Federal Work-Study, and institutionally sponsored loans available. Support available to part-time students. Financial award application deadline: 2/1. *Unit head:* Karen DiGiovanni, Director, Teacher Education, 202-885-3727, Fax: 202-885-1187, E-mail: digiovanni@american.edu. *Application contact:* Karen DiGiovanni, Director, Teacher Education, 202-885-3727, Fax: 202-885-1187, E-mail: digiovanni@american.edu.

American University of Puerto Rico, Program in Education, Bayamón, PR 00960-2037. Offers art history (M Ed); elementary education (4-6) (M Ed); elementary education (k-3)

Special Education

American University of Puerto Rico (continued)
(M Ed); general science education (M Ed); physical education (k-12) (M Ed); special education at secondary level (transition) (M Ed). *Faculty:* 1 full-time (0 women), 22 part-time/adjunct (6 women). *Students:* 121 full-time (98 women), 64 part-time (50 women); includes all Hispanic Americans. Average age 30. 250 applicants, 80% accepted, 185 enrolled. *Entrance requirements:* For master's, EXADEP or GRE or MAT, 2 letters of recommendation, minimum GPA of 2.5. *Application deadline:* For fall admission, 8/4 for domestic students; for winter admission, 10/18 for domestic students; for spring admission, 3/22 for domestic students. Applications are processed on a rolling basis. Application fee: $50. *Application contact:* Information Contact, E-mail: oficnaadmisiones@aupr.edu.

Andrews University, School of Graduate Studies, School of Education, Department of Educational and Counseling Psychology, Program in Special Education, Berrien Springs, MI 49104. Offers MS. *Students:* 1 (woman) full-time, 2 part-time (both women), 1 international. Average age 28. 4 applicants, 75% accepted, 2 enrolled. *Entrance requirements:* Additional exam requirements/recommendations for international students: Required—TOEFL (minimum score 550 paper-based). Application fee: $40. *Unit head:* Dr. Nona Elmendorf-Steele, Dean, 269-471-6468. *Application contact:* Carolyn Hurst, Supervisor of Graduate Admission, 800-253-2874, Fax: 269-471-6321, E-mail: graduate@andrews.edu.

Andrews University, School of Graduate Studies, School of Education, Department of Teaching, Learning, and Curriculum, Berrien Springs, MI 49104. Offers curriculum and instruction (MA, Ed D, PhD, Ed S); elementary education (MAT); reading (MA); secondary education (MAT), including biology, education, English, English as a second language, French, history, physics; special education/learning disabilities (MS); teacher education (MAT). *Students:* 12 full-time (8 women), 30 part-time (19 women); includes 17 minority (14 African Americans, 1 Asian American or Pacific Islander, 2 Hispanic Americans), 10 international. Average age 43. 28 applicants, 54% accepted, 6 enrolled. In 2009, 11 master's, 4 doctorates, 1 other advanced degree awarded. *Entrance requirements:* For master's, GRE Subject Test. Additional exam requirements/recommendations for international students: Required—TOEFL (minimum score 550 paper-based). *Application deadline:* For fall admission, 8/15 for domestic students. Applications are processed on a rolling basis. Application fee: $40. *Unit head:* Dr. Lee C. Davidson, Chair, 269-471-6364. *Application contact:* Carolyn Hurst, Supervisor of Graduate Admission, 800-253-2874, Fax: 269-471-6321, E-mail: graduate@andrews.edu.

Appalachian State University, Cratis D. Williams Graduate School, Department of Language, Reading, and Exceptionalities, Boone, NC 28608. Offers reading education (MA); special education (MA); speech-language pathology (MA). *Accreditation:* ASHA. Part-time programs available. Postbaccalaureate distance learning degree programs offered (no on-campus study). *Faculty:* 37 full-time (25 women), 6 part-time/adjunct (all women). *Students:* 89 full-time (84 women), 202 part-time (192 women); includes 7 minority (3 African Americans, 1 Asian American or Pacific Islander, 3 Hispanic Americans). 291 applicants, 57% accepted, 105 enrolled. In 2009, 95 master's awarded. *Degree requirements:* For master's, comprehensive exam, thesis optional. *Entrance requirements:* For master's, GRE General Test or MAT, 3 letters of recommendation. Additional exam requirements/recommendations for international students: Required—TOEFL (minimum score 570 paper-based; 230 computer-based; 79 iBT), IELTS (minimum score 6.5). *Application deadline:* For fall admission, 7/1 for domestic students, 2/1 for international students; for spring admission, 11/1 for domestic students, 7/1 for international students. Applications are processed on a rolling basis. Application fee: $50. Electronic applications accepted. *Expenses:* Tuition, state resident: full-time $2960. Tuition, nonresident: full-time $14,051. Required fees: $2320. *Financial support:* In 2009–10, 21 research assistantships (averaging $8,000 per year) were awarded; Federal Work-Study, scholarships/grants, and unspecified assistantships also available. Financial award application deadline: 4/1; financial award applicants required to submit FAFSA. *Faculty research:* Speech pathology, special education, language arts, reading. Total annual research expenditures: $160,500. *Unit head:* Dr. Monica Lambert, Chairperson, 828-262-7173, Fax: 828-262-6767, E-mail: lambertma@appstate.edu. *Application contact:* Eveline Watts, Graduate Student Coordinator, 828-262-2182, E-mail: wattsem@appstate.edu.

Arcadia University, Graduate Studies, Department of Education, Glenside, PA 19038-3295. Offers art education (M Ed, MA Ed); biology education (MA Ed); chemistry education (MA Ed); child development (CAS); computer education (M Ed, CAS); computer education 7–12 (MA Ed); early childhood education (M Ed, CAS), including individualized (M Ed), master teacher (M Ed), research in child development (M Ed); educational leadership (M Ed, CAS); educational psychology (CAS); elementary education (M Ed, CAS); English education (MA Ed); environmental education (MA Ed, CAS); history education (MA Ed); language arts (M Ed, CAS); mathematics education (M Ed, MA Ed, CAS); music education (MA Ed); psychology (MA Ed); pupil personnel services (CAS); reading (M Ed, CAS); school library science (M Ed); science education (M Ed, CAS); secondary education (M Ed, CAS); special education (M Ed, Ed D, CAS); theater arts (MA Ed); written communication (MA Ed). *Accreditation:* NASAD. Part-time and evening/weekend programs available. Postbaccalaureate distance learning degree programs offered (minimal on-campus study). *Faculty:* 12 full-time (8 women), 38 part-time/adjunct (26 women). *Students:* 89 full-time (74 women), 622 part-time (487 women); includes 112 minority (94 African Americans, 9 Asian Americans or Pacific Islanders, 9 Hispanic Americans), 2 international. Average age 32. In 2009, 257 master's, 4 doctorates awarded. *Application deadline:* Applications are processed on a rolling basis. Application fee: $40. Electronic applications accepted. *Expenses:* Tuition: Full-time $30,450; part-time $620 per credit hour. Required fees: $165. Tuition and fees vary according to program. *Financial support:* Career-related internships or fieldwork, tuition waivers (partial), and unspecified assistantships available. *Unit head:* Dr. Steven P. Gulkus. *Application contact:* 215-572-2925, Fax: 215-572-2126, E-mail: grad@arcadia.edu.

Arizona State University, Graduate College, College of Teacher Education and Leadership, Tempe, AZ 85287. Offers educational administration and supervision (M Ed); elementary education (M Ed, Certificate); leadership/innovation (administration) (Ed D); leadership/innovation (teaching) (Ed D); physical education (MPE); secondary education (M Ed, Certificate); special education (M Ed). Part-time and evening/weekend programs available. *Degree requirements:* For master's, applied project or comprehensive exams; for doctorate, comprehensive exam, thesis/dissertation. *Entrance requirements:* For master's, 3 letters of recommendation, minimum undergraduate GPA of 3.0, resume; for doctorate, master's degree in education or related field, 3 professional references, resumé, graduate GPA of 3.0, 3 letters of recommendation. Additional exam requirements/recommendations for international students: Required—TOEFL (minimum score 550 paper-based; 213 computer-based; 83 iBT), IELTS (minimum score 6.5). Electronic applications accepted. *Expenses:* Contact institution. *Faculty research:* Self-regulated learning in students, collaboration and consultation skills for educators, school reform and restructuring, hands-on science and mathematics programs, educational technology.

Arizona State University, Graduate College, Mary Lou Fulton College of Education, Division of Curriculum and Instruction, Program in Special Education, Tempe, AZ 85287. Offers M Ed, MA. *Degree requirements:* For master's, thesis or alternative. *Entrance requirements:* For master's, GRE General Test or MAT.

Arkansas State University—Jonesboro, Graduate School, College of Education, Department of Educational Leadership, Curriculum, and Special Education, Jonesboro, State University, AR 72467. Offers community college administration education (SCCT); curriculum and instruction (MSE); education theory and practice (MSE); educational leadership (MSE, Ed D, Ed S), including curriculum and instruction (MSE, Ed S); special education (MSE), including gifted and talented and creative, instructional specialist 4-12, instructional specialist P-4. *Accreditation:* NCATE. Part-time programs available. Postbaccalaureate distance learning degree programs offered (no on-campus study). *Faculty:* 15 full-time (6 women), 19 part-time/adjunct (11 women). *Students:* 16 full-time (11 women), 734 part-time (606 women); includes 111 minority (96

African Americans, 4 American Indian/Alaska Native, 4 Asian Americans or Pacific Islanders, 7 Hispanic Americans), 2 international. Average age 38. 882 applicants, 70% accepted, 240 enrolled. In 2009, 80 master's, 6 doctorates, 15 other advanced degrees awarded. *Degree requirements:* For master's, comprehensive exam, thesis or alternative; for doctorate, comprehensive exam, thesis/dissertation; for other advanced degree, comprehensive exam. *Entrance requirements:* For master's, GRE General Test or MAT, appropriate bachelor's degree, letters of reference, interview; for doctorate, GRE General Test or MAT, interview, master's degree, letters of reference, official transcript, personal statement, writing sample, immunization records; for other advanced degree, GRE General Test or MAT, interview, master's degree, letters of reference, official transcript, 3 years teaching experience, mentor, teaching license, immunization records. Additional exam requirements/recommendations for international students: Required—TOEFL (minimum score 550 paper-based; 213 computer-based; 79 iBT), IELTS (minimum score 6). *Application deadline:* Applications are processed on a rolling basis. Application fee: $50. Electronic applications accepted. *Expenses:* Tuition, state resident: full-time $3744; part-time $208 per credit hour. Tuition, nonresident: full-time $9540; part-time $530 per credit hour. Required fees: $896; $47 per credit hour. $25 per term. One-time fee: $50. Tuition and fees vary according to course load and program. *Financial support:* In 2009–10, 16 students received support; fellowships, teaching assistantships, career-related internships or fieldwork, scholarships/grants, and unspecified assistantships available. Financial award application deadline: 7/1; financial award applicants required to submit FAFSA. *Unit head:* Dr. Mitchell Holifield, Chair, 870-972-3062, Fax: 870-680-8130, E-mail: hfield@astate.edu. *Application contact:* Dr. Andrew Sustich, Dean of the Graduate School, 870-972-3029, Fax: 870-972-3857, E-mail: sustich@astate.edu.

Armstrong Atlantic State University, School of Graduate Studies, Program in Education, Savannah, GA 31419-1997. Offers adult education (M Ed); curriculum and instruction (M Ed); early childhood education (M Ed); education (M Ed); elementary education (M Ed); middle grades education (M Ed); secondary education (M Ed), including business education, English education, mathematics education, science education, social science education; special education (M Ed), including behavioral disorders, learning disabilities, speech-language pathology. *Accreditation:* NCATE. Part-time and evening/weekend programs available. Postbaccalaureate distance learning degree programs offered (minimal on-campus study). *Degree requirements:* For master's, comprehensive exam, portfolio. *Entrance requirements:* For master's, GRE General Test or MAT, minimum GPA of 2.5, letters of recommendation. Additional exam requirements/recommendations for international students: Required—TOEFL (minimum score 523 paper-based; 193 computer-based). Electronic applications accepted.

Asbury University, School of Graduate and Professional Studies, Wilmore, KY 40390-1198. Offers biology: alternative certificate (MA Ed); chemistry: alternative certificate (MA Ed); English (MA Ed); English as a second language (MA Ed); ESL (MA Ed); French (MA Ed); Latin: alternative certificate (MA Ed); mathematics: alternative certificate (MA Ed); reading/writing endorsement (MA Ed); social studies (MA Ed); social work (MSW), including child and family services; Spanish (MA Ed); special education (MA Ed); special education: alternative certificate (MA Ed); teacher as leader endorsement (MA Ed). *Accreditation:* NCATE. Part-time programs available. *Faculty:* 8 full-time (7 women), 9 part-time/adjunct (4 women). *Students:* 108 part-time (87 women); includes 8 minority (4 African Americans, 2 Asian Americans or Pacific Islanders, 2 Hispanic Americans). Average age 36. 36 applicants, 86% accepted, 24 enrolled. In 2009, 20 master's awarded. *Degree requirements:* For master's, action research project, portfolio. *Entrance requirements:* For master's, PRAXIS/NTE, minimum GPA of 2.75, letters of recommendation. Additional exam requirements/recommendations for international students: Required—TOEFL (minimum score 550 paper-based). *Application deadline:* Applications are processed on a rolling basis. Application fee: $25. Electronic applications accepted. *Financial support:* Scholarships/grants and traineeships available. Financial award applicants required to submit FAFSA. *Unit head:* Dr. Bonnie J. Banker, Dean, School of Graduate and Professional Studies, 859-858-3511 Ext. 2221, Fax: 859-858-3921, E-mail: bonnie.banker@asbury.edu. *Application contact:* Lenore A. Sweigart, Graduate Program Assistant and Certification Specialist, 859-858-3511 Ext. 2502, Fax: 859-858-3921, E-mail: graded@asbury.edu.

Ashland University, Dwight Schar College of Education, Department of Curriculum and Instruction, Ashland, OH 44805-3702. Offers intervention specialist–mild/moderate (M Ed); intervention specialist–moderate/intensive (M Ed); literacy (M Ed); technology facilitator (M Ed). *Accreditation:* NCATE. Part-time and evening/weekend programs available. *Faculty:* 20 full-time (14 women), 83 part-time/adjunct (53 women). *Students:* 137 full-time (116 women), 309 part-time (278 women); includes 22 minority (16 African Americans, 2 American Indian/Alaska Native, 4 Hispanic Americans), 1 international. Average age 33. 160 applicants, 98% accepted, 152 enrolled. In 2009, 245 master's awarded. *Degree requirements:* For master's, thesis or alternative, internship, practicum, inquiry seminar. *Entrance requirements:* For master's, teaching certificate or license, bachelor's degree, minimum cumulative GPA of 2.75. Additional exam requirements/recommendations for international students: Required—TOEFL. *Application deadline:* For fall admission, 8/27 for domestic students; for spring admission, 1/14 for domestic students. Applications are processed on a rolling basis. Application fee: $30. Electronic applications accepted. *Financial support:* In 2009–10, 192 students received support. Institutionally sponsored loans and scholarships/grants available. Financial award application deadline: 4/15. *Faculty research:* Gender equity, postmodern children's and young adult literature, outdoor/experimental education, re-examining literature study in middle grades, morality and giftedness. *Unit head:* Dr. David J. Kommer, Chair, 419-289-5203, E-mail: dkommer@ashland.edu. *Application contact:* Dr. David J. Kommer, Chair, 419-289-5203, E-mail: dkommer@ashland.edu.

Assumption College, Graduate School, Special Education Program, Worcester, MA 01609-1296. Offers positive behavior support (CAGS); special education (MA). Part-time and evening/weekend programs available. *Faculty:* 2 full-time (both women), 2 part-time/adjunct (1 woman). *Students:* 6 full-time (all women), 22 part-time (21 women); includes 1 minority (Asian American or Pacific Islander). Average age 23. 22 applicants, 100% accepted. In 2009, 14 master's awarded. *Degree requirements:* For master's, comprehensive exam, internship, practicum. *Entrance requirements:* For master's, 3 letters of recommendation, resume; for CAGS, 3 letters of recommendation, resume, essay. Additional exam requirements/recommendations for international students: Required—TOEFL (minimum score 540 paper-based; 200 computer-based; 76 iBT), IELTS (minimum score 6). *Application deadline:* For fall admission, 6/1 priority date for domestic students, 5/1 priority date for international students; for spring admission, 11/1 priority date for domestic students, 9/1 priority date for international students. Applications are processed on a rolling basis. Application fee: $30. Electronic applications accepted. *Expenses:* Tuition: Part-time $503 per credit. Required fees: $20 per semester. One-time fee: $100 part-time. Part-time tuition and fees vary according to campus/location. *Financial support:* In 2009–10, 10 students received support; teaching assistantships with partial tuition reimbursements available, institutional discounts available. Financial award application deadline: 6/1; financial award applicants required to submit FAFSA. *Unit head:* Dr. Nanho Vander Hart, Director, 508-767-7380, Fax: 508-767-7263, E-mail: nvanderh@assumption.edu. *Application contact:* Adrian O. Dumas, Director of Graduate Enrollment Management and Services, 508-767-7365, Fax: 508-767-7030, E-mail: adumas@assumption.edu.

Auburn University, Graduate School, College of Education, Department of Special Education, Rehabilitation, Counseling and School Psychology, Auburn University, AL 36849. Offers collaborative teacher special education (M Ed, MS); early childhood special education (M Ed, MS); rehabilitation counseling (M Ed, MS, PhD). *Accreditation:* CORE; NCATE. Part-time programs available. *Faculty:* 20 full-time (13 women), 8 part-time/adjunct (6 women). *Students:* 149 full-time (117 women), 94 part-time (78 women); includes 63 minority (56 African Americans, 1 American Indian/Alaska Native, 2 Asian Americans or Pacific Islanders, 4 Hispanic Americans), 4 international. Average age 31. 226 applicants, 51% accepted, 87 enrolled. In 2009, 48 master's, 20 doctorates awarded. *Degree requirements:* For master's, thesis (for some programs); for doctorate, thesis/dissertation. *Entrance requirements:* For master's, GRE General Test; for doctorate, GRE General Test, interview. *Application deadline:* For fall admission, 7/17

for domestic students; for spring admission, 11/24 for domestic students. Applications are processed on a rolling basis. Application fee: $50 ($60 for international students). Electronic applications accepted. *Expenses:* Tuition, state resident: full-time $6240. Tuition, nonresident: full-time $18,720. International tuition: $18,938 full-time. Required fees: $492. Tuition and fees vary according to course load, program and reciprocity agreements. *Financial support:* Research assistantships, teaching assistantships, Federal Work-Study available. Support available to part-time students. Financial award application deadline: 3/15; financial award applicants required to submit FAFSA. *Faculty research:* Emotional conflict/behavior disorders, gifted and talented, learning disabilities, mental retardation, multi-handicapped. *Unit head:* Dr. Philip L. Browning, Head, 334-844-5943. *Application contact:* Dr. George Flowers, Dean of the Graduate School, 334-844-2125.

Auburn University Montgomery, School of Education, Department of Counselor, Leadership, and Special Education, Montgomery, AL 36124-4023. Offers counseling (M Ed, Ed S); education administration (M Ed, Ed S); special education (M Ed, Ed S). *Accreditation:* NCATE. Part-time and evening/weekend programs available. *Faculty:* 8 full-time (6 women), 3 part-time/adjunct (1 woman). *Students:* 30 full-time (27 women), 61 part-time (44 women); includes 61 minority (60 African Americans, 1 Hispanic American). Average age 34. In 2009, 19 master's awarded. *Degree requirements:* For master's and Ed S, comprehensive exam. *Entrance requirements:* For master's, GRE General Test or MAT, certification, BS in teaching; for Ed S, GRE General Test or MAT, certification. *Application deadline:* Applications are processed on a rolling basis. Electronic applications accepted. *Expenses:* Tuition, state resident: full-time $2841; part-time $225 per credit hour. Tuition, nonresident: full-time $8241; part-time $675 per credit hour. Required fees: $282; $8 per hour. $45 per term. *Financial support:* In 2009–10, 1 teaching assistantship was awarded; career-related internships or fieldwork and scholarships/grants also available. Support available to part-time students. Financial award application deadline: 3/1; financial award applicants required to submit FAFSA. *Unit head:* Dr. James V. Wright, Head, 334-244-3457, Fax: 334-344-3102, E-mail: jwright@mail.aum.edu. *Application contact:* Dr. Sam Flynt, Associate Graduate Coordinator, 334-244-3270, Fax: 334-244-3835, E-mail: sflynt@mail.aum.edu.

Augusta State University, Graduate Studies, College of Education, Program in Special Education, Augusta, GA 30904-2200. Offers M Ed, Ed S. *Accreditation:* NCATE. Part-time and evening/weekend programs available. *Degree requirements:* For master's, thesis, portfolio. *Entrance requirements:* For master's, GRE, MAT, minimum GPA of 2.5; for Ed S, GRE, MAT. *Faculty research:* Behavior disorders, gifted programs.

Austin Peay State University, College of Graduate Studies, College of Education, Department of Educational Specialties, Clarksville, TN 37044. Offers administration and supervision (Ed S); curriculum and instruction (MA Ed); education leadership (MA Ed); elementary education (Ed S); secondary education (Ed S); special education (MA Ed). Part-time and evening/weekend programs available. Postbaccalaureate distance learning degree programs offered. *Faculty:* 7 full-time (4 women), 4 part-time/adjunct (3 women). *Students:* 17 full-time (11 women), 96 part-time (76 women); includes 20 minority (12 African Americans, 1 American Indian/Alaska Native, 7 Hispanic Americans). Average age 36. 81 applicants, 99% accepted, 45 enrolled. In 2009, 47 master's awarded. *Degree requirements:* For master's, comprehensive exam, thesis optional. *Entrance requirements:* For master's, GRE General Test, 3 letters of recommendation, minimum undergraduate GPA of 2.75. Additional exam requirements/recommendations for international students: Required—TOEFL (minimum score 500 paper-based; 173 computer-based). *Application deadline:* For fall admission, 7/27 priority date for domestic students; for spring admission, 12/17 priority date for domestic students. Applications are processed on a rolling basis. Application fee: $25. Electronic applications accepted. *Expenses:* Tuition, state resident: full-time $6160; part-time $608 per credit hour. Tuition, nonresident: full-time $17,080; part-time $854 per credit hour. Required fees: $1224; $61.20 per credit hour. *Financial support:* Career-related internships or fieldwork, Federal Work-Study, institutionally sponsored loans, scholarships/grants, and unspecified assistantships available. Support available to part-time students. Financial award application deadline: 3/1; financial award applicants required to submit FAFSA. *Unit head:* Dr. Moniqueka Gold, Chair, 931-221-7696, Fax: 931-221-1292, E-mail: goldm@apsu.edu. *Application contact:* Dr. Dixie Dennis, Dean, College of Graduate Studies, 931-221-7662, Fax: 931-221-7641, E-mail: dennisdi@apsu.edu.

Austin Peay State University, College of Graduate Studies, College of Education, Department of Teaching and Learning, Clarksville, TN 37044. Offers elementary education K-6 (MAT); reading (MA Ed); secondary education 7-12 (MAT); special education K-12 (MAT). Part-time and evening/weekend programs available. Postbaccalaureate distance learning degree programs offered. *Faculty:* 8 full-time (6 women), 3 part-time/adjunct (all women). *Students:* 91 full-time (74 women), 84 part-time (67 women); includes 14 minority (12 African Americans, 2 Asian Americans or Pacific Islanders), 1 international. Average age 32. 122 applicants, 94% accepted, 75 enrolled. In 2009, 61 master's awarded. *Degree requirements:* For master's, comprehensive exam, thesis optional. *Entrance requirements:* For master's, GRE General Test, 3 letters of recommendation, minimum undergraduate GPA of 2.75. Additional exam requirements/recommendations for international students: Required—TOEFL (minimum score 500 paper-based; 173 computer-based). *Application deadline:* For fall admission, 7/27 priority date for domestic students; for spring admission, 12/17 priority date for domestic students. Applications are processed on a rolling basis. Application fee: $25. Electronic applications accepted. *Expenses:* Tuition, state resident: full-time $6160; part-time $608 per credit hour. Tuition, nonresident: full-time $17,080; part-time $854 per credit hour. Required fees: $1224; $61.20 per credit hour. *Financial support:* Career-related internships or fieldwork, Federal Work-Study, institutionally sponsored loans, scholarships/grants, and unspecified assistantships available. Support available to part-time students. Financial award application deadline: 3/1; financial award applicants required to submit FAFSA. *Unit head:* Dr. Rebecca McMahan, Interim Chair, 931-221-7513, Fax: 931-221-1292, E-mail: mcmahanb@apsu.edu. *Application contact:* Dr. Dixie Dennis, Dean, College of Graduate Studies, 931-221-7662, Fax: 931-221-7641, E-mail: dennisdi@apsu.edu.

Averett University, Master in Education Program, Danville, VA 24541-3692. Offers art education (M Ed); biology (M Ed); biology education (M Ed); chemistry (M Ed); chemistry education (M Ed); curriculum and instruction (M Ed); elementary education (M Ed); English (M Ed); English education (M Ed); health and physical education (M Ed); history and social studies education (M Ed); math (M Ed); mathematics education (M Ed); physical science (M Ed); reading specialization (M Ed); special education (learning disabilities specialization PK-12) (M Ed). Program also offered at Richmond, VA regional campus location. Part-time and evening/weekend programs available. *Faculty:* 4 full-time (3 women), 36 part-time/adjunct (22 women). *Students:* 182 full-time (160 women), 110 part-time (94 women); includes 113 minority (94 African Americans, 1 American Indian/Alaska Native, 7 Asian Americans or Pacific Islanders, 11 Hispanic Americans). Average age 37. 119 applicants, 99% accepted, 98 enrolled. In 2009, 92 master's awarded. *Degree requirements:* For master's, comprehensive exam, thesis optional. *Entrance requirements:* For master's, PRAXIS, GRE General Test, MAT or NTE, writing proficiency exam, 3 letters of recommendation, current teacher's licensure or eligibility for licensure, minimum undergraduate GPA of 3.0 in previous 2 years. Additional exam requirements/recommendations for international students: Required—TOEFL (minimum score 600 paper-based; 200 computer-based). *Application deadline:* Applications are processed on a rolling basis. *Expenses:* Contact institution. *Financial support:* Career-related internships or fieldwork, Federal Work-Study, and scholarships/grants available. Financial award application deadline: 4/1; financial award applicants required to submit FAFSA. *Faculty research:* Literary assessment-PreK-6, handwriting instruction and assessment-PreK-6, written language instruction and assessment-PreK-6 and special needs students learning styles, curriculum and instruction processes. *Unit head:* Dr. Lynn H. Wolf, Chair/Associate Professor/Director, 434-793-3995, Fax: 434-791-4392, E-mail: lynn.wolf@averett.edu. *Application contact:* Dr. Lynn H. Wolf, Chair/Associate Professor/Director, 434-793-3995, Fax: 434-791-4392, E-mail: lynn.wolf@averett.edu.

Azusa Pacific University, School of Education, Program in Special Education, Azusa, CA 91702-7000. Offers MA. *Accreditation:* NCATE. Part-time and evening/weekend programs available. *Degree requirements:* For master's, core exams, oral presentations. *Entrance requirements:* For master's, 12 units of course work in education, minimum GPA of 3.0.

Baldwin-Wallace College, Graduate Programs, Division of Education, Specialization in Mild/Moderate Educational Needs, Berea, OH 44017-2088. Offers MA Ed. *Accreditation:* NCATE. Part-time and evening/weekend programs available. *Students:* 39 full-time (38 women), 22 part-time (18 women); includes 7 minority (6 African Americans, 1 Hispanic American). Average age 34. 20 applicants, 70% accepted, 7 enrolled. In 2009, 22 master's awarded. *Degree requirements:* For master's, comprehensive exam. *Entrance requirements:* For master's, bachelor's degree in field, MAT or minimum GPA of 2.75. Additional exam requirements/recommendations for international students: Required—TOEFL (minimum score 523 paper-based; 193 computer-based; 70 iBT). *Application deadline:* For fall admission, 8/15 priority date for domestic students; for spring admission, 12/15 priority date for domestic students. Applications are processed on a rolling basis. Application fee: $25. Electronic applications accepted. *Expenses:* Tuition: Full-time $14,174; part-time $682 per credit. Tuition and fees vary according to program. *Financial support:* Career-related internships or fieldwork available. Support available to part-time students. Financial award application deadline: 5/1; financial award applicants required to submit FAFSA. *Faculty research:* Adult adjustment of individuals formerly identified as having mild/moderate special education needs, professional development of special educators, teacher beliefs and special education, classroom assessment practices. *Unit head:* Karen Kaye, Chair, 440-826-2168, Fax: 440-826-3779, E-mail: kkaye@bw.edu. *Application contact:* Winifred W. Gerhardt, Director of Admission for the Evening and Weekend College, 440-826-2222, Fax: 440-826-3830, E-mail: admission@bw.edu.

Ball State University, Graduate School, Teachers College, Department of Special Education, Muncie, IN 47306-1099. Offers MA, MAE, Ed D, Ed S. *Accreditation:* NCATE. *Degree requirements:* For doctorate, thesis/dissertation; for Ed S, thesis. *Entrance requirements:* For doctorate, GRE General Test, interview, minimum graduate GPA of 3.2; for Ed S, GRE General Test. *Faculty research:* Language development and utilization in the handicapped (preschool through adult).

Bank Street College of Education, Graduate School, Program in Special Education, New York, NY 10025. Offers early childhood special and general education (MS Ed); early childhood special education (Ed M, MS Ed); elementary/childhood special and general education (MS Ed); elementary/childhood special education (MS Ed); elementary/childhood special education certification (Ed M); middle school special and general education (MS Ed); middle school special education (Ed M, MS Ed). *Students:* 111 full-time (94 women), 163 part-time (150 women); includes 56 minority (22 African Americans, 16 Asian Americans or Pacific Islanders, 18 Hispanic Americans), 5 international. Average age 30. 177 applicants, 87% accepted, 109 enrolled. In 2009, 72 master's awarded. *Degree requirements:* For master's, thesis. *Entrance requirements:* For master's, interview. Additional exam requirements/recommendations for international students: Required—TOEFL (minimum score 600 paper-based; 250 computer-based; 100 iBT), IELTS (minimum score 7). *Application deadline:* For fall admission, 3/1 priority date for domestic students; for spring admission, 11/1 priority date for domestic students. Applications are processed on a rolling basis. Application fee: $65. *Expenses:* Tuition: Part-time $1120 per credit. *Financial support:* Career-related internships or fieldwork available. Financial award application deadline: 3/1; financial award applicants required to submit FAFSA. *Faculty research:* Inclusion, observation and assessment; early intervention; neurodevelopmental assessment; teaching students with disabilities. *Unit head:* Dr. Olga Romero, Chairperson, 212-875-4468, Fax: 212-875-4753, E-mail: olgar@bankstreet.edu. *Application contact:* Dr. Olga Romero, Chairperson, 212-875-4468, Fax: 212-875-4753, E-mail: olgar@bankstreet.edu.

Barry University, School of Education, Program in Education for Teachers of Students with Hearing Impairments, Miami Shores, FL 33161-6695. Offers MS.

Barry University, School of Education, Program in Exceptional Student Education, Miami Shores, FL 33161-6695. Offers MS, Ed S. Part-time and evening/weekend programs available. *Degree requirements:* For master's, comprehensive exam; for Ed S, practicum. *Entrance requirements:* For master's, GRE General Test or MAT, minimum GPA of 3.0; for Ed S, GRE General Test, minimum GPA of 3.0. Electronic applications accepted.

Barry University, School of Education, Program in Leadership and Education, Miami Shores, FL 33161-6695. Offers educational technology (PhD); exceptional student education (PhD); higher education administration (PhD); human resource development (PhD); leadership (PhD). Part-time and evening/weekend programs available. *Degree requirements:* For doctorate, thesis/dissertation. *Entrance requirements:* For doctorate, GRE General Test, minimum GPA of 3.25. Electronic applications accepted.

Bayamón Central University, Graduate Programs, Program in Education, Bayamón, PR 00960-1725. Offers administration and supervision (MA Ed); commercial education (MA Ed); education of the autistic (MA Ed); elementary education (K–3) (MA Ed); elementary education (K–6) (MA Ed); guidance and counseling (MA Ed); organizational psychology (MA); pre-elementary teacher (MA Ed); rehabilitation counseling (MA Ed); special education (MA Ed), including attention deficit disorder, learning disabilities. Part-time and evening/weekend programs available. *Degree requirements:* For master's, comprehensive exam. *Entrance requirements:* For master's, EXADEP, bachelor's degree in education or related field.

Bellarmine University, Annsley Frazier Thornton School of Education, Louisville, KY 40205-0671. Offers early elementary education (MA, MAT); instructional leadership and school administration/school principal (MA); learning and behavior disorders (MA); middle school education (MA, MAT); reading and writing endorsement (MA); secondary school education (MAT); Waldorf inspired curriculum (MA). *Accreditation:* NCATE. Part-time and evening/weekend programs available. *Faculty:* 16 full-time (11 women), 20 part-time/adjunct (13 women). *Students:* 67 full-time (47 women), 140 part-time (111 women); includes 14 minority (10 African Americans, 1 American Indian/Alaska Native, 3 Asian Americans or Pacific Islanders), 1 international. Average age 33. In 2009, 106 degrees awarded. *Degree requirements:* For master's, comprehensive exam, thesis (for some programs). *Entrance requirements:* For master's, GRE, baccalaureate degree from an accredited institution; minimum overall GPA of 2.75, 3.0 in major; letters of recommendation; valid Kentucky provisional or professional certificate. Additional exam requirements/recommendations for international students: Required—TOEFL (minimum score 550 paper-based; 213 computer-based; 80 iBT). *Application deadline:* Applications are processed on a rolling basis. Application fee: $25. *Expenses:* Contact institution. *Financial support:* Scholarships/grants available. Financial award applicants required to submit FAFSA. *Faculty research:* Literacy, service learning, dispositions, educational technology, special education. *Unit head:* Dr. Cindy Gnadinger, Dean, 502-452-8191, Fax: 502-452-8189, E-mail: cgnadinger@bellarmine.edu. *Application contact:* Theresa Klapheke, Administrative Director of Graduate Programs, 502-452-8271, Fax: 502-452-8002, E-mail: tklapheke@bellarmine.edu.

Belmont University, College of Arts and Sciences, School of Education, Nashville, TN 37212-3757. Offers education (M Ed); elementary education (MAT), including early childhood education, elementary education, language arts education; English (MAT); history (MAT); mathematics (MAT); middle grade education (MAT); science (MAT); secondary education (MAT); special education (MAT); sports administration (MSA). *Accreditation:* NCATE. Part-time and evening/weekend programs available. *Degree requirements:* For master's, comprehensive exam, thesis, culminating portfolio. *Entrance requirements:* For master's, MAT or GRE and/or LSAT or GMAT, minimum GPA of 2.75. Additional exam requirements/recommendations for international students: Required—TOEFL. *Expenses:* Contact institution. *Faculty research:* Improving secondary literacy, Montessori, classroom management strategies, teacher residency

Special Education

Belmont University (continued)
programs, online professional development, mentoring, leadership, sociological issues in sport, faculty development, coaching.

Bemidji State University, School of Graduate Studies, College of Professional Studies, Program in Special Education, Bemidji, MN 56601-2699. Offers M Sp Ed, MS. Part-time programs available. *Degree requirements:* For master's, thesis. *Entrance requirements:* For master's, letters of recommendation. Additional exam requirements/recommendations for international students: Required—TOEFL. Electronic applications accepted.

Benedictine University, Graduate Programs, Program in Education, Lisle, IL 60532-0900. Offers curriculum and instruction and collaborative teaching (M Ed); elementary education (MA Ed); leadership and administration (M Ed); reading and literacy (M Ed); secondary education (MA Ed); special education (MA Ed). Part-time and evening/weekend programs available. *Faculty:* 4 full-time (2 women), 52 part-time/adjunct (30 women). *Students:* 286 full-time (252 women), 443 part-time (349 women); includes 61 minority (22 African Americans, 11 Asian Americans or Pacific Islanders, 28 Hispanic Americans), 5 international. Average age 33. 341 applicants, 90% accepted, 264 enrolled. In 2009, 299 master's awarded. *Degree requirements:* For master's, comprehensive exam, thesis (for some programs). *Entrance requirements:* For master's, GRE or MAT. Additional exam requirements/recommendations for international students: Required—TOEFL (minimum score 550 paper-based; 213 computer-based). *Application deadline:* For fall admission, 9/1 for domestic students; for winter admission, 12/1 for domestic students; for spring admission, 2/15 for domestic students. Applications are processed on a rolling basis. Application fee: $40. Electronic applications accepted. *Expenses:* Contact institution. *Financial support:* Career-related internships or fieldwork and health care benefits available. Support available to part-time students. *Unit head:* Dr. Richard Campbell, Director, 630-829-6242, Fax: 630-960-1126, E-mail: rcampbell@ben.edu. *Application contact:* Kari Gibbons, Director, Admissions, 630-829-6200, Fax: 630-829-6584, E-mail: kgibbons@ben.edu.

Bethel University, Graduate School, Department of Education, St. Paul, MN 55112-6999. Offers education K-12 (MA), including autism spectrum disorders, coordinator of work-based learning, differentiation, international baccalaureate, literacy, special education; educational administration (Ed D), including director of special education, K-12 principal license, superintendent license; literacy (Certificate); literacy education (MA); special education (MA), including autism spectrum disorders; teaching (MA). *Accreditation:* Teacher Education Accreditation Council. Evening/weekend programs available. Postbaccalaureate distance learning degree programs offered (minimal on-campus study). *Faculty:* 17 full-time (11 women), 37 part-time/adjunct (17 women). *Students:* 182 full-time (119 women), 172 part-time (120 women); includes 18 minority (2 African Americans, 1 American Indian/Alaska Native, 6 Asian Americans or Pacific Islanders, 9 Hispanic Americans), 1 international. Average age 35. 236 applicants, 79% accepted, 173 enrolled. In 2009, 51 master's, 5 doctorates awarded. *Degree requirements:* For master's, thesis, practicum; for doctorate, comprehensive exam, thesis/dissertation, internship. *Entrance requirements:* For master's, baccalaureate degree, statement of purpose essay, interview, current teaching license (if applicable), minimum GPA of 3.0, teaching experience (if applicable), letters of reference; for doctorate, MAT or GRE, minimum GPA of 3.0, letters of reference, statement of purpose essay, pre-assessment of prior experience and preparation, current license (if applicable), master's degree, interview, work experience in education. Additional exam requirements/recommendations for international students: Required—TOEFL (minimum score 550 paper-based; 213 computer-based; 80 iBT). *Application deadline:* For fall admission, 8/1 priority date for domestic students; for winter admission, 12/5 priority date for domestic students; for spring admission, 5/1 priority date for domestic students. Applications are processed on a rolling basis. Application fee: $25. Electronic applications accepted. *Expenses:* Contact institution. *Financial support:* Applicants required to submit FAFSA. *Unit head:* Dr. Judi Landrum, Assistant Dean, 651-635-8000, Fax: 651-638-8004, E-mail: j-landrum@bethel.edu. *Application contact:* Michael Price, Director of Admissions, 651-635-8000, Fax: 651-635-8004, E-mail: m-price@bethel.edu.

Bethel University, Program in Education, McKenzie, TN 38201. Offers administration and supervision (MA Ed); biology education K8-12 (MAT); elementary education (MAT); English education K8-12 (MAT); history education K8-12 (MAT); physical education K8-12 (MAT); special education K8-12 (MAT). Part-time and evening/weekend programs available. *Degree requirements:* For master's, thesis (for some programs). *Entrance requirements:* For master's, GRE General Test or MAT, minimum undergraduate GPA of 2.5.

Bloomsburg University of Pennsylvania, School of Graduate Studies, College of Professional Studies, School of Education, Department of Exceptionality Programs, Program in Special Education, Bloomsburg, PA 17815-1301. Offers exceptionality programs (MS). *Accreditation:* NCATE. *Degree requirements:* For master's, thesis or alternative. *Entrance requirements:* For master's, teaching certificate, minimum QPA of 3.0. Additional exam requirements/recommendations for international students: Required—TOEFL (minimum score 550 paper-based; 213 computer-based; 79 iBT). Electronic applications accepted. *Faculty research:* Exceptionalities, learning disabilities, behavior disorders, gifted, early childhood.

Bob Jones University, Graduate Programs, Greenville, SC 29614. Offers accountancy (MS); Bible (MA); Bible translation (MA); Biblical studies (Certificate); broadcast management (MS); business administration (MBA); church history (MA, PhD); church ministries (MA); church music (MM); cinema and video production (MA); counseling (MS); curriculum and instruction (Ed D); divinity (M Div); dramatic production (MA); educational leadership (MS, Ed D, Ed S); elementary education (M Ed, MAT); English (M Ed, MA, MAT); fine arts (MA); graphic design (MA); history (M Ed, MA); illustration (MA); interpretative speech (MA); mathematics (M Ed, MAT); medical missions (Certificate); ministry (MM, D Min); multi-categorical special education (M Ed, MAT); music (M Ed); New Testament interpretation (PhD); Old Testament interpretation (PhD); orchestral instrument performance (MM); organ performance (MM); pastoral studies (MA); personnel services (MS, Ed S); piano pedagogy (MM); piano performance (MM); platform arts (MA); radio and television broadcasting (MS); rhetoric and public address (MA); secondary education (M Ed); studio art (MA); teaching Bible (MA); theology (MA, PhD); voice performance (MM); youth ministries (MA); M Div/MM.

Boise State University, Graduate College, College of Education, Programs in Teacher Education, Program in Special Education, Boise, ID 83725-0399. Offers M Ed, MA. *Accreditation:* NCATE. *Degree requirements:* For master's, thesis optional. *Entrance requirements:* For master's, minimum GPA of 3.0. Electronic applications accepted. *Expenses:* Tuition, state resident: full-time $3106; part-time $209 per credit. Tuition, nonresident: part-time $284 per credit.

Boston College, Lynch Graduate School of Education, Department of Teacher Education/Special Education and Curriculum and Instruction, Program in Special Needs: Moderate Disabilities, Chestnut Hill, MA 02467-3800. Offers M Ed, CAES. *Accreditation:* Teacher Education Accreditation Council. Part-time and evening/weekend programs available. *Students:* 11 full-time (9 women), 29 part-time (27 women); includes 5 minority (3 African Americans, 1 Asian American or Pacific Islander, 1 Hispanic American). 59 applicants, 69% accepted, 23 enrolled. In 2009, 21 master's awarded. *Degree requirements:* For master's and CAES, comprehensive exam. *Entrance requirements:* For master's, GRE General Test or MAT, general licensure at the elementary or secondary level; for CAES, GRE General Test or MAT. Additional exam requirements/recommendations for international students: Required—TOEFL (minimum score 550 paper-based; 213 computer-based; 81 iBT). *Application deadline:* For fall admission, 1/1 priority date for domestic students. Application fee: $60. Electronic applications accepted. *Financial support:* Fellowships with full and partial tuition reimbursements, research assistantships with full and partial tuition reimbursements, teaching assistantships with full and partial tuition reimbursements, career-related internships or fieldwork, Federal Work-Study, scholarships/grants, traineeships, health care benefits, and unspecified assistantships available. Support

available to part-time students. Financial award applicants required to submit FAFSA. *Faculty research:* Social construction of reading problems; social implications of special education; learning disabilities; emotional behavior difficulties. *Unit head:* Dr. Maria E. Brisk, Chairperson, 617-552-4216, Fax: 617-552-0812, E-mail: brisk@bc.edu. *Application contact:* Adam Poluzzi, Director, Graduate Admission and Financial Aid, 617-552-4214, Fax: 617-552-0398, E-mail: poluzzi@bc.edu.

Boston College, Lynch Graduate School of Education, Department of Teacher Education/Special Education and Curriculum and Instruction, Program in Special Needs: Severe Disabilities, Chestnut Hill, MA 02467-3800. Offers M Ed. *Accreditation:* Teacher Education Accreditation Council. Part-time and evening/weekend programs available. *Students:* 6 full-time (all women), 22 part-time (17 women); includes 3 minority (1 Asian American or Pacific Islander, 2 Hispanic Americans), 5 international. 30 applicants, 70% accepted, 15 enrolled. In 2009, 8 master's awarded. *Degree requirements:* For master's, comprehensive exam. *Entrance requirements:* For master's, GRE General Test or MAT. Additional exam requirements/recommendations for international students: Required—TOEFL (minimum score 550 paper-based; 213 computer-based; 81 iBT). *Application deadline:* For fall admission, 1/1 priority date for domestic students. Application fee: $60. Electronic applications accepted. *Financial support:* Fellowships with full and partial tuition reimbursements, research assistantships with full and partial tuition reimbursements, teaching assistantships with full and partial tuition reimbursements, career-related internships or fieldwork, Federal Work-Study, scholarships/grants, traineeships, health care benefits, tuition waivers (full and partial), and unspecified assistantships available. Support available to part-time students. Financial award applicants required to submit FAFSA. *Faculty research:* Communication and language in learners with severe and multiple disabilities; assistive technology. *Unit head:* Dr. Maria E. Brisk, Chairperson, 617-552-4216, Fax: 617-552-0812, E-mail: brisk@bc.edu. *Application contact:* Adam Poluzzi, Director, Graduate Admission and Financial Aid, 617-552-4214, Fax: 617-552-0398, E-mail: poluzzi@bc.edu.

Boston University, School of Education, Department of Curriculum and Teaching, Program in Special Education, Boston, MA 02215. Offers special education (Ed M, Ed D, CAGS), including alternative community settings (Ed D), learning and behavioral disabilities (Ed D, CAGS), severe disabilities (Ed D, CAGS), therapeutic recreation (Ed D), young children with special needs (Ed D, CAGS); MSW/Ed D; MSW/Ed M. *Degree requirements:* For master's, thesis optional; for doctorate, comprehensive exam, thesis/dissertation; for CAGS, comprehensive exam. *Entrance requirements:* For master's, doctorate, and CAGS, GRE General Test or MAT. Additional exam requirements/recommendations for international students: Required—TOEFL. Electronic applications accepted. *Expenses:* Tuition: Full-time $37,910; part-time $1184 per credit hour. Required fees: $386; $40 per semester. Part-time tuition and fees vary according to class time, course level, degree level and program.

Boston University, School of Education, Department of Literacy and Language, Counseling and Development, Program in Education of the Deaf, Boston, MA 02215. Offers Ed M, CAGS. Part-time programs available. *Degree requirements:* For CAGS, comprehensive exam. *Entrance requirements:* For master's and CAGS, GRE General Test or MAT. Additional exam requirements/recommendations for international students: Required—TOEFL. Electronic applications accepted. *Expenses:* Tuition: Full-time $37,910; part-time $1184 per credit hour. Required fees: $386; $40 per semester. Part-time tuition and fees vary according to class time, course level, degree level and program. *Faculty research:* Structure of American Sign Language, acquisition of American Sign Language, problems in educating the deaf, impact of legislation on the deaf, relations between hearing parents and deaf children.

Bowie State University, Graduate Programs, Program in Special Education, Bowie, MD 20715-9465. Offers M Ed. *Accreditation:* NCATE. Part-time and evening/weekend programs available. *Degree requirements:* For master's, comprehensive exam, thesis optional, research paper. *Entrance requirements:* For master's, teaching experience, 3 professional letters of recommendation. Electronic applications accepted.

Bowling Green State University, Graduate College, College of Education and Human Development, School of Education and Intervention Services, Intervention Services Division, Program in Special Education, Bowling Green, OH 43403. Offers assistive technology (M Ed); early childhood intervention (M Ed); gifted education (M Ed); hearing impaired intervention (M Ed); mild/moderate intervention (M Ed); moderate/intensive intervention (M Ed). *Accreditation:* NCATE. Part-time programs available. *Degree requirements:* For master's, thesis or alternative. *Entrance requirements:* For master's, GRE General Test. Additional exam requirements/recommendations for international students: Required—TOEFL. Electronic applications accepted. *Faculty research:* Reading and special populations, deafness, early childhood, gifted and talented, behavior disorders.

Brandon University, Faculty of Education, Brandon, MB R7A 6A9, Canada. Offers curriculum and instruction (M Ed, Diploma); educational administration (M Ed, Diploma); guidance and counseling (M Ed, Diploma); special education (M Ed, Diploma). *Degree requirements:* For master's, thesis. *Entrance requirements:* For master's, minimum GPA of 3.0, teaching certificate or equivalent. Additional exam requirements/recommendations for international students: Required—TOEFL. *Faculty research:* Comparative education, environmental studies, parent/school council.

Brenau University, Graduate Programs, School of Education, Gainesville, GA 30501. Offers early childhood (Ed S); early childhood education (M Ed, MAT); middle grades (Ed S); middle grades education (M Ed, MAT); secondary education (MAT); special education (M Ed, MAT). *Accreditation:* NCATE. Part-time and evening/weekend programs available. Postbaccalaureate distance learning degree programs offered (no on-campus study). *Faculty:* 12 full-time (7 women), 25 part-time/adjunct (21 women). *Students:* 161 full-time (146 women), 143 part-time (122 women); includes 43 minority (30 African Americans, 5 Asian Americans or Pacific Islanders, 8 Hispanic Americans), 1 international. Average age 35. 163 applicants, 34% accepted, 47 enrolled. In 2009, 154 master's, 20 other advanced degrees awarded. *Degree requirements:* For master's, thesis optional, comprehensive exam or applied research project, effective portfolio; for Ed S, applied research project. *Entrance requirements:* For master's, GRE, MAT, interview, minimum GPA of 3.0, 3 references, writing samples; for Ed S, GRE, MAT, master's degree, minimum GPA of 3.0, writing sample, letters of reference. Additional exam requirements/recommendations for international students: Required—TOEFL (minimum score 500 paper-based). *Application deadline:* Applications are processed on a rolling basis. Application fee: $35. Electronic applications accepted. *Expenses:* Contact institution. *Financial support:* In 2009–10, 2 students received support. Scholarships/grants available. Support available to part-time students. Financial award application deadline: 7/15; financial award applicants required to submit FAFSA. *Unit head:* Dr. Lora Bailey, Dean, 770-534-6220, Fax: 770-534-6221, E-mail: lbailey@brenau.edu. *Application contact:* Christina White, Dean of Admissions, 770-718-5320, Fax: 770-718-5337, E-mail: cwhite@brenau.edu.

Bridgewater State University, School of Graduate Studies, School of Education and Allied Science, Department of Special Education, Bridgewater, MA 02325-0001. Offers M Ed. *Accreditation:* NCATE. Part-time and evening/weekend programs available. *Entrance requirements:* For master's, GRE General Test or Massachusetts Test for Educator Licensure.

Brigham Young University, Graduate Studies, David O. McKay School of Education, Department of Counseling Psychology and Special Education, Provo, UT 84602-1001. Offers counseling psychology (PhD); school psychology (Ed S); special education (MS). *Accreditation:* NCATE. Part-time programs available. *Faculty:* 12 full-time (7 women), 13 part-time/adjunct (5 women). *Students:* 74 full-time (54 women), 15 part-time (14 women); includes 11 minority (2 African Americans, 2 American Indian/Alaska Native, 4 Asian Americans or Pacific Islanders, 3 Hispanic Americans), 10 international. Average age 31. 85 applicants, 41% accepted, 28 enrolled. In 2009, 2 master's, 4 doctorates, 10 other advanced degrees awarded. *Degree*

requirements: For master's, comprehensive exam, thesis; for doctorate, comprehensive exam, thesis/dissertation. *Entrance requirements:* For master's and doctorate, GRE General Test, minimum GPA of 3.0 in last 60 hours of undergraduate coursework. Additional exam requirements/recommendations for international students: Required—TOEFL (minimum score 580 paper-based; 237 computer-based), IELTS (minimum score 7). *Application deadline:* For fall admission, 1/15 for domestic and international students. Application fee: $50. Electronic applications accepted. *Expenses:* Tuition: Full-time $5580; part-time $301 per credit hour. Tuition and fees vary according to student's religious affiliation. *Financial support:* In 2009–10, 53 students received support, including 36 research assistantships with partial tuition reimbursements available (averaging $6,706 per year), 3 teaching assistantships with partial tuition reimbursements available (averaging $7,457 per year); career-related internships or fieldwork, institutionally sponsored loans, and tuition waivers (partial) also available. Financial award application deadline: 3/30. *Faculty research:* Gender issues in education, psychotherapy progress and outcome, behavior disorders and ABA. *Unit head:* Dr. Mary Anne Prater, Chair, 801-422-3857, Fax: 801-422-0198, E-mail: prater@byu.edu. *Application contact:* Diane E. Hancock, Department Secretary, 801-422-3859, Fax: 801-422-0198, E-mail: diane_hancock@byu.edu.

Brooklyn College of the City University of New York, Division of Graduate Studies, School of Education, Program in Special Education, Brooklyn, NY 11210-2889. Offers teacher of students with disabilities (MS Ed), including birth-grade 2, grades 1-6, grades 5-9. Part-time programs available. *Students:* 2 full-time (both women), 358 part-time (298 women); includes 160 minority (121 African Americans, 12 Asian Americans or Pacific Islanders, 27 Hispanic Americans), 8 international. Average age 31. 269 applicants, 92% accepted, 195 enrolled. In 2009, 196 master's awarded. *Entrance requirements:* For master's, LAST, interview; previous course work in education and psychology; minimum GPA of 3.0 in education, 2.8 overall; resume, 2 letters of recommendation; essay. Additional exam requirements/recommendations for international students: Required—TOEFL (minimum score 500 paper-based; 173 computer-based; 61 iBT). *Application deadline:* For fall admission, 3/1 priority date for domestic students, 2/1 priority date for international students; for spring admission, 11/1 priority date for domestic students, 10/1 priority date for international students. Applications are processed on a rolling basis. Application fee: $125. Electronic applications accepted. *Expenses:* Tuition, state resident: full-time $7360; part-time $310 per credit hour. Tuition, nonresident: full-time $13,800; part-time $575 per credit hour. Required fees: $140.10 per semester. *Financial support:* Federal Work-Study, institutionally sponsored loans, and scholarships/grants available. Support available to part-time students. Financial award application deadline: 5/1; financial award applicants required to submit FAFSA. *Faculty research:* School reform, conflict resolution, curriculum for inclusive settings, urban issues in special education. *Unit head:* Prof. Pauline Bynoe, Program Head, 718-951-5214, Fax: 718-951-4816, E-mail: pbynoe@brooklyn.cuny.edu. *Application contact:* Hernan Sierra, Graduate Admissions Coordinator, 718-951-4536, Fax: 718-951-4506, E-mail: grads@brooklyn.cuny.edu.

Buffalo State College, State University of New York, The Graduate School, Faculty of Applied Science and Education, Department of Exceptional Education, Programs in Special Education, Buffalo, NY 14222-1095. Offers special education (MS Ed); special education: adolescents (MS Ed); special education: childhood (MS Ed); special education: early childhood (MS Ed). *Accreditation:* NCATE. Part-time and evening/weekend programs available. *Degree requirements:* For master's, thesis or project. *Entrance requirements:* For master's, minimum GPA of 2.5. Additional exam requirements/recommendations for international students: Required—TOEFL (minimum score 550 paper-based; 213 computer-based).

Butler University, College of Education, Indianapolis, IN 46208-3485. Offers administration (MS); elementary education (MS); reading (MS); school counseling (MS); secondary education (MS); special education (MS). *Accreditation:* ACA; NCATE. Part-time and evening/weekend programs available. *Faculty:* 9 full-time (7 women), 7 part-time/adjunct (6 women). *Students:* 18 full-time (11 women), 137 part-time (111 women); includes 17 minority (14 African Americans, 1 American Indian/Alaska Native, 2 Asian Americans or Pacific Islanders), 9 international. Average age 31. 57 applicants, 77% accepted, 24 enrolled. In 2009, 61 master's awarded. *Entrance requirements:* For master's, GRE General Test, MAT, interview. *Application deadline:* For fall admission, 8/15 priority date for domestic students. Applications are processed on a rolling basis. Application fee: $35. Electronic applications accepted. *Financial support:* Institutionally sponsored loans available. Support available to part-time students. Financial award application deadline: 7/15; financial award applicants required to submit FAFSA. *Faculty research:* Ethics in cybercounseling, history of sports for disabled, effect of fetal alcohol syndrome on perceptual learning, reading recovery's theoretical framework in teacher education. *Unit head:* Dr. Ena Shelley, Dean, 317-940-9752, Fax: 317-940-6481. *Application contact:* Karen Farrell, Department Secretary, 317-940-9220, E-mail: kfarrell@butler.edu.

Caldwell College, Graduate Studies, Program in Special Education, Caldwell, NJ 07006-6195. Offers MA. *Accreditation:* Teacher Education Accreditation Council. *Degree requirements:* For master's, thesis. *Entrance requirements:* For master's, GRE General Test or MAT, minimum GPA of 3.0, writing sample. Additional exam requirements/recommendations for international students: Required—TOEFL (minimum score 580 paper-based; 237 computer-based). Electronic applications accepted.

California Baptist University, Program in Education, Riverside, CA 92504-3206. Offers cross-cultural language and academic development (MA); educational leadership (MS); educational leadership and faith-based instruction (MS); educational technology (MS); instructional computer applications (MS); reading (MS); school counseling (MS); school psychology (MS); special education (MS); special education in mild/moderate disabilities (MS); special education in moderate/severe disabilities (MS); teaching (MS); teaching and learning (MS Ed). Part-time programs available. *Faculty:* 16 full-time (9 women), 10 part-time/adjunct (all women). *Students:* 73 full-time (60 women), 368 part-time (298 women); includes 170 minority (34 African Americans, 4 American Indian/Alaska Native, 18 Asian Americans or Pacific Islanders, 114 Hispanic Americans). 266 applicants, 72% accepted, 169 enrolled. In 2009, 120 master's awarded. *Degree requirements:* For master's, comprehensive exam (for some programs), thesis optional. *Entrance requirements:* For master's, minimum undergraduate GPA of 2.75, 12 semester hours of pre-requisite course work in education. Additional exam requirements/recommendations for international students: Required—TOEFL (minimum score 575 paper-based; 230 computer-based; 89 iBT). *Application deadline:* For fall admission, 8/1 priority date for domestic students, 7/1 for international students; for spring admission, 12/1 priority date for domestic students, 10/15 priority date for international students. Applications are processed on a rolling basis. Application fee: $45. Electronic applications accepted. *Expenses:* Tuition: Full-time $8352; part-time $464 per semester hour. Required fees: $125 per semester. Tuition and fees vary according to course load, campus/location and program. *Financial support:* Career-related internships or fieldwork, Federal Work-Study, and scholarships/grants available. Support available to part-time students. Financial award applicants required to submit FAFSA. *Unit head:* Dr. Mary Crist, Dean, School of Education, 951-343-4313, Fax: 951-343-4516, E-mail: mcrist@calbaptist.edu. *Application contact:* Gail Ronveaux, Dean of Graduate Enrollment, 951-343-5045, Fax: 951-343-5095, E-mail: graduateadmissions@calbaptist.edu.

California Lutheran University, Graduate Studies, School of Education, Emphasis in Special Education, Thousand Oaks, CA 91360-2787. Offers MS. *Accreditation:* NCATE. Evening/weekend programs available. *Degree requirements:* For master's, thesis or comprehensive exam. *Entrance requirements:* For master's, GRE General Test, interview, minimum GPA of 3.0.

California State University, Bakersfield, Division of Graduate Studies, School of Education, Program in Special Education, Bakersfield, CA 93311. Offers MA. *Accreditation:* NCATE. *Degree requirements:* For master's, thesis or alternative, project or culminating exam. *Entrance requirements:* For master's, 3 letters of recommendation, minimum GPA of 2.67, interview.

California State University, Chico, Graduate School, College of Communication and Education, Department of Professional Studies in Education, Option in Special Education, Chico, CA 95929-0722. Offers MA. Part-time and evening/weekend programs available. *Entrance requirements:* Additional exam requirements/recommendations for international students: Required—TOEFL (minimum score 550 paper-based; 213 computer-based; 80 iBT), IELTS (minimum score 6.5). Electronic applications accepted.

California State University, Dominguez Hills, College of Professional Studies, School of Education, Division of Teacher Education, Program in Special Education, Carson, CA 90747-0001. Offers early childhood (MA); mild/moderate (MA); moderate/severe (MA). Part-time and evening/weekend programs available. *Faculty:* 10 full-time (all women), 11 part-time/adjunct (9 women). *Students:* 123 full-time (98 women), 260 part-time (193 women); includes 245 minority (107 African Americans, 3 American Indian/Alaska Native, 34 Asian Americans or Pacific Islanders, 101 Hispanic Americans), 2 international. Average age 38. 64 applicants, 73% accepted, 29 enrolled. In 2009, 55 master's awarded. *Degree requirements:* For master's, comprehensive exam, thesis or alternative. *Entrance requirements:* For master's, minimum GPA of 2.75 in last 60 units, 3 letters of recommendation. *Application deadline:* For fall admission, 6/1 for domestic students. Applications are processed on a rolling basis. Application fee: $55. *Expenses:* Tuition, nonresident: full-time $6696; part-time $372 per unit. Required fees: $5946; $1752 per semester. *Unit head:* Dr. Jamie Dote-Kwan, Coordinator, 310-243-3861, E-mail: jdotekwan@csudh.edu. *Application contact:* Admissions Office, 310-243-3530.

California State University, East Bay, Graduate Programs, College of Education and Allied Studies, Department of Educational Psychology, Special Education Program, Hayward, CA 94542-3000. Offers special education (MS), including mild/moderate, moderate/severe. *Accreditation:* NCATE. *Faculty:* 4 full-time (3 women), 1 (woman) part-time/adjunct. *Students:* 30 full-time (27 women), 8 part-time (5 women); includes 8 minority (2 African Americans, 4 Asian Americans or Pacific Islanders, 2 Hispanic Americans). Average age 41. 30 applicants, 70% accepted, 19 enrolled. In 2009, 5 master's awarded. *Degree requirements:* For master's, project or thesis. *Entrance requirements:* For master's, GRE or MAT, interview, minimum GPA of 2.5 during previous 2 years of course work. Additional exam requirements/recommendations for international students: Required—TOEFL (minimum score 550 paper-based; 213 computer-based). *Application deadline:* For fall admission, 6/30 for domestic and international students. Application fee: $55. Electronic applications accepted. *Financial support:* Career-related internships or fieldwork, Federal Work-Study, and institutionally sponsored loans available. Support available to part-time students. Financial award application deadline: 3/1; financial award applicants required to submit FAFSA. *Unit head:* Dr. Jack Davis, Chair, 510-885-3052, E-mail: jack.davis@csueastbay.edu. *Application contact:* Donna Wiley, Interim Associate Director, 510-885-2928, Fax: 510-885-4777, E-mail: donna.wiley@csueastbay.edu.

California State University, Fresno, Division of Graduate Studies, School of Education and Human Development, Department of Counseling and Special Education, Program in Special Education, Fresno, CA 93740-8027. Offers MA. *Accreditation:* NCATE. Part-time and evening/weekend programs available. *Degree requirements:* For master's, thesis or alternative. *Entrance requirements:* For master's, GRE General Test, MAT, minimum GPA of 3.0. Additional exam requirements/recommendations for international students: Required—TOEFL. Electronic applications accepted.

California State University, Fullerton, Graduate Studies, College of Education, Department of Special Education, Fullerton, CA 92834-9480. Offers MS. *Accreditation:* NCATE. Part-time programs available. *Students:* 62 full-time (53 women), 102 part-time (86 women); includes 65 minority (2 African Americans, 29 Asian Americans or Pacific Islanders, 34 Hispanic Americans), 1 international. Average age 33. 39 applicants, 36% accepted, 12 enrolled. In 2009, 78 master's awarded. *Degree requirements:* For master's, comprehensive exam, project or thesis. *Entrance requirements:* For master's, minimum GPA of 2.75. Application fee: $55. *Expenses:* Tuition, nonresident: full-time $11,160; part-time $373 per credit. Required fees: $1440 per term. Tuition and fees vary according to course load, degree level and program. *Financial support:* Career-related internships or fieldwork, Federal Work-Study, institutionally sponsored loans, and scholarships/grants available. Support available to part-time students. Financial award application deadline: 3/1; financial award applicants required to submit FAFSA. *Unit head:* Dr. Melinda Pierson, Chair, 657-278-4711. *Application contact:* Admissions/Applications, 657-278-2371.

California State University, Long Beach, Graduate Studies, College of Education, Department of Advanced Studies in Education and Counseling, Master of Science in Special Education Program, Long Beach, CA 90840. Offers MS. *Accreditation:* NCATE. *Students:* 6 full-time (5 women), 37 part-time (32 women); includes 15 minority (1 African American, 10 Asian Americans or Pacific Islanders, 4 Hispanic Americans). Average age 33. *Degree requirements:* For master's, comprehensive exam or thesis. *Entrance requirements:* For master's, GRE General Test, minimum GPA of 2.75. *Application deadline:* For fall admission, 3/1 for domestic students. Applications are processed on a rolling basis. Application fee: $55. Electronic applications accepted. *Expenses:* Required fees: $1802 per semester. Part-time tuition and fees vary according to course load. *Financial support:* Federal Work-Study, institutionally sponsored loans, and scholarships/grants available. Financial award application deadline: 3/2. *Unit head:* Dr. Jennifer Coots, Chair, 562-985-8354, Fax: 562-985-4534, E-mail: jcoots@csulb.edu. *Application contact:* Dr. Jennifer Coots, Chair, 562-985-8354, Fax: 562-985-4534, E-mail: jcoots@csulb.edu.

California State University, Los Angeles, Graduate Studies, Charter College of Education, Division of Special Education and Counseling, Los Angeles, CA 90032-8530. Offers counseling (MS), including applied behavior analysis, community college counseling, rehabilitation counseling, school counseling and school psychology; special education (MA, PhD). *Accreditation:* ACA. Part-time and evening/weekend programs available. *Faculty:* 20 full-time (15 women), 18 part-time/adjunct (10 women). *Students:* 361 full-time (288 women), 366 part-time (284 women); includes 450 minority (43 African Americans, 65 Asian Americans or Pacific Islanders, 342 Hispanic Americans), 40 international. Average age 34. 181 applicants, 99% accepted, 108 enrolled. In 2009, 143 master's awarded. *Entrance requirements:* For master's, minimum GPA of 2.75 in last 90 units of course work, teaching certificate. Additional exam requirements/recommendations for international students: Required—TOEFL (minimum score 500 paper-based; 173 computer-based). *Application deadline:* For fall admission, 5/1 for domestic and international students. Applications are processed on a rolling basis. Application fee: $55. Electronic applications accepted. *Financial support:* Career-related internships or fieldwork and Federal Work-Study available. Support available to part-time students. Financial award application deadline: 3/1. *Unit head:* Dr. Randy Campbell, Chair, 323-343-4400, Fax: 323-343-5605, E-mail: rcampbe@calstatela.edu. *Application contact:* Dr. Cheryl L. Ney, Associate Vice President for Academic Affairs and Dean of Graduate Studies, 323-343-3820, Fax: 323-343-5653, E-mail: cney@cslanet.calstatela.edu.

California State University, Northridge, Graduate Studies, College of Education, Department of Special Education, Northridge, CA 91330. Offers early childhood special education (MA); education of the deaf and hard of hearing (MA); educational therapy (MA); mild/moderate disabilities (MA); moderate/severe disabilities (MA). *Accreditation:* NCATE. *Faculty:* 15 full-time (13 women), 25 part-time/adjunct (19 women). *Students:* 34 full-time (27 women), 133 part-time (108 women); includes 53 minority (7 African Americans, 1 American Indian/Alaska Native, 16 Asian Americans or Pacific Islanders, 29 Hispanic Americans), 9 international. Average age 36. 112 applicants, 61% accepted, 43 enrolled. In 2009, 162 master's awarded. *Entrance requirements:* For master's, GRE General Test (if cumulative undergraduate GPA less than 3.0). Additional exam requirements/recommendations for international students: Required—TOEFL. *Application deadline:* For fall admission, 11/30 for domestic students. Application fee: $55. *Financial support:* Application deadline: 3/1. *Faculty research:* Teacher training, classroom aide training. *Unit head:* Dr. Nancy Burstein, Chair, 818-677-2596. *Application contact:* Dr. Ellen Schneiderman, Graduate Studies Coordinator, 818-677-2649.

Special Education

California State University, Sacramento, Graduate Studies, College of Education, Department of Special Education, Rehabilitation, and School Psychology, Sacramento, CA 95819. Offers school psychology (MS); special education (MA); vocational rehabilitation (MS). *Accreditation:* CORE. Part-time programs available. *Degree requirements:* For master's, thesis or alternative, writing proficiency exam. *Entrance requirements:* For master's, minimum GPA of 2.5. Additional exam requirements/recommendations for international students: Required—TOEFL. Electronic applications accepted.

California State University, San Bernardino, Graduate Studies, College of Education, Programs in Special Education and Rehabilitation Counseling, San Bernardino, CA 92407-2397. Offers rehabilitation counseling (MA); special education (MA). *Accreditation:* CORE; NCATE. Part-time and evening/weekend programs available. *Faculty:* 11 full-time (8 women), 9 part-time/adjunct (6 women). *Students:* 225 full-time (170 women), 67 part-time (53 women); includes 131 minority (44 African Americans, 3 American Indian/Alaska Native, 12 Asian Americans or Pacific Islanders, 72 Hispanic Americans), 2 international. Average age 39. 158 applicants, 90% accepted, 85 enrolled. In 2009, 81 master's awarded. *Degree requirements:* For master's, thesis or alternative, advancement to candidacy. *Entrance requirements:* For master's, minimum GPA of 3.0 in education. *Application deadline:* For fall admission, 8/31 priority date for domestic students. Application fee: $55. *Financial support:* Career-related internships or fieldwork and Federal Work-Study available. Support available to part-time students. *Unit head:* Dr. Ruth Ann Sandlin, Chair, 909-537-5641, Fax: 909-537-7040, E-mail: rsandlin@csusb.edu. *Application contact:* Olivia Rosas, Director of Admissions, 909-537-7577, Fax: 909-537-7034, E-mail: orosas@csusb.edu.

California State University, Stanislaus, College of Education, Department of Advanced Studies in Education, Turlock, CA 95382. Offers community college leadership (Ed D); education (MA); educational leadership (Ed D); educational technology (MA); P-12 leadership (Ed D); school administration (MA); school counseling (MA); special education (MA). Part-time and evening/weekend programs available. Postbaccalaureate distance learning degree programs offered. *Degree requirements:* For master's, thesis. *Entrance requirements:* For master's, MAT or GRE, BEST (depending on concentration), minimum GPA of 2.8, 3 letters of reference; for doctorate, GRE, 3.0 minimum GPA, 3 letters of reference and personal statement. Additional exam requirements/recommendations for international students: Required—TOEFL (minimum score 550 paper-based; 213 computer-based). *Faculty research:* Current school technology use, social aspects of technology, staff development.

California University of Pennsylvania, School of Graduate Studies and Research, School of Education, Department of Special Education, California, PA 15419-1394. Offers mentally and/or physically handicapped education (M Ed). *Accreditation:* NCATE. Part-time and evening/weekend programs available. *Degree requirements:* For master's, comprehensive exam, thesis optional. *Entrance requirements:* For master's, MAT, PRAXIS. Additional exam requirements/recommendations for international students: Required—TOEFL (minimum score 550 paper-based; 213 computer-based; 80 iBT). Electronic applications accepted. *Faculty research:* Case-based instruction, electronic performance support tools, students with disabilities, teacher preparation, No Child Left Behind.

Calvin College, Graduate Programs in Education, Grand Rapids, MI 49546-4388. Offers curriculum and instruction (M Ed); educational leadership (M Ed); learning disabilities (M Ed); literacy (M Ed). Part-time programs available. *Faculty:* 3 full-time (2 women), 4 part-time/adjunct (1 woman). *Students:* 7 full-time (6 women), 113 part-time (79 women); includes 9 minority (2 African Americans, 5 Asian Americans or Pacific Islanders, 2 Hispanic Americans). Average age 29. In 2009, 27 master's awarded. *Degree requirements:* For master's, thesis or seminar. *Entrance requirements:* For master's, teaching certificate. Additional exam requirements/recommendations for international students: Required—TOEFL (minimum score 550 paper-based; 213 computer-based). *Application deadline:* For fall admission, 8/1 priority date for domestic students, 6/1 priority date for international students; for spring admission, 1/1 priority date for domestic students, 2/1 priority date for international students. Applications are processed on a rolling basis. Application fee: $0. Electronic applications accepted. *Expenses:* Tuition: Full-time $10,080. *Financial support:* Federal Work-Study, scholarships/grants, and tuition waivers (full and partial) available. Support available to part-time students. Financial award application deadline: 4/3. *Faculty research:* Literacy, racialized gender and gendered identity, teacher learning, learning disabilities identification. *Unit head:* Dr. Debra Buursma, Graduate Program Director, 616-526-6231, Fax: 616-526-6505, E-mail: dbuursma@calvin.edu. *Application contact:* Cindi Hoekstra, Program Coordinator, 616-526-6158, Fax: 616-526-6505, E-mail: choekstr@calvin.edu.

Cambridge College, School of Education, Cambridge, MA 02138-5304. Offers autism specialist (M Ed); autism/behavior analyst (M Ed); behavior analyst (Post-Master's Certificate); behavioral management (M Ed); early childhood teacher (M Ed); education specialist in curriculum and instruction (CAGS); educational leadership (Ed D); elementary teacher (M Ed); English as a second language (M Ed, Certificate); general science (M Ed); health education, health promotion (Post-Master's Certificate); health/family and consumer sciences (M Ed); history (M Ed); individualized degree (M Ed); information technology literacy (M Ed); instructional technology (M Ed); interdisciplinary studies (M Ed); library teacher (M Ed); literacy education (M Ed); mathematics (M Ed); mathematics specialist (Certificate); middle school mathematics and science (M Ed); school administration (M Ed, CAGS); school guidance counselor (M Ed); school nurse education (M Ed); school social worker/school adjustment counselor (M Ed); special education administrator (CAGS); special education/moderate disabilities (M Ed); teaching skills and methodologies (M Ed). Part-time and evening/weekend programs available. Postbaccalaureate distance learning degree programs offered (minimal on-campus study). *Faculty:* 10 full-time (3 women), 283 part-time/adjunct (187 women). *Students:* 974 full-time (755 women), 1,071 part-time (835 women); includes 940 minority (762 African Americans, 4 American Indian/Alaska Native, 22 Asian Americans or Pacific Islanders, 152 Hispanic Americans), 28 international. Average age 39. In 2009, 866 master's, 4 doctorates, 209 CAGSs awarded. *Degree requirements:* For master's, thesis, internship/practicum (licensure program only); for doctorate, thesis/dissertation; for other advanced degree, thesis. *Entrance requirements:* For master's, interview, resume, documentation of licensure, 2 professional references; for doctorate, official transcripts, interview, resume, documentation of licensure (if any), written personal statement/essay, portfolio of scholarly and professional work, qualifying assessment, 2 professional references, health insurance, immunizations form; for other advanced degree, official transcripts, interview, resume, documentation of licensure (if any), written personal statement/essay, 2 professional references, health insurance, immunizations form. Additional exam requirements/recommendations for international students: Required—TOEFL (minimum score 550 paper-based; 213 computer-based; 79 iBT), Recommended—IELTS (minimum score 6). *Application deadline:* Applications are processed on a rolling basis. Application fee: $30. Electronic applications accepted. *Expenses:* Contact institution. *Financial support:* In 2009–10, 1,373 students received support. Career-related internships or fieldwork, Federal Work-Study, and scholarships/grants available. Financial award applicants required to submit FAFSA. *Faculty research:* Adult education, accelerated learning, mathematics education, brain compatible learning, special education and law. *Unit head:* Dr. N. Alan Sheppard, Interim Associate Dean, 617-873-0619, E-mail: alan.sheppard@cambridgecollege.edu. *Application contact:* Stephen Lyons, Director of Enrollment, Graduate and N.I.T.E. Programs, 617-868-1000, Fax: 617-349-3561, E-mail: stephen.lyons@cambridgecollege.edu.

Campbellsville University, School of Education, Campbellsville, KY 42718-2799. Offers curriculum and instruction (MAE); special education (MASE). *Accreditation:* NCATE. Part-time and evening/weekend programs available. Postbaccalaureate distance learning degree programs offered (minimal on-campus study). *Degree requirements:* For master's, thesis, research paper. *Entrance requirements:* For master's, GRE or PRAXIS, minimum undergraduate GPA of 2.75, teaching certificate, professional growth plan, letters of recommendation, disposition assessment, entrance interview. Electronic applications accepted. *Expenses:* Tuition: Full-time

$6750; part-time $375 per credit hour. *Faculty research:* Professional development, curriculum development, school governance, assessment, special education.

Canisius College, Graduate Division, School of Education and Human Services, Department of Graduate Education, Buffalo, NY 14208-1098. Offers adolescence education (grades 7-12) (MS); childhood education (grades 1-6) (MS); college student personnel administration (MS); deaf education (MS); differentiated instruction (MS Ed); educational administration and supervision (MS); general education (MS Ed); initial teacher certification (elementary education) (MS); initial teacher certification (secondary education) (MS); literacy (MS Ed); special education (MS). *Accreditation:* NCATE. Part-time and evening/weekend programs available. *Faculty:* 22 full-time (14 women), 84 part-time/adjunct (54 women). *Students:* 409 full-time (288 women), 261 part-time (187 women); includes 29 minority (24 African Americans, 5 Hispanic Americans), 156 international. Average age 30. 518 applicants, 74% accepted, 240 enrolled. In 2009, 346 master's awarded. Application fee: $25. *Financial support:* Research assistantships with full tuition reimbursements, career-related internships or fieldwork, institutionally sponsored loans, scholarships/grants, health care benefits, tuition waivers (full and partial), and unspecified assistantships available. *Faculty research:* Autism, Asperger's disease, private higher education, reading strategies. *Unit head:* Rev. Paul Nochelski, Chair of Graduate Education and Leadership, 716-888-3297, Fax: 716-888-3299. *Application contact:* James D. Bagwell, Director of Graduate Recruitment and Admissions, 716-888-2544, Fax: 716-888-3290, E-mail: bagwellj@canisius.edu.

Cardinal Stritch University, College of Education, Department of Literacy, Milwaukee, WI 53217-3985. Offers literacy/English as a second language (MA); reading/language arts (MA); reading/learning disability (MA). *Accreditation:* NCATE. Part-time and evening/weekend programs available. *Degree requirements:* For master's, comprehensive exam, thesis, faculty recommendation, research project. *Entrance requirements:* For master's, letters of recommendation (2), minimum GPA of 2.75.

Cardinal Stritch University, College of Education, Department of Special Education, Milwaukee, WI 53217-3985. Offers MA. *Accreditation:* NCATE. Part-time and evening/weekend programs available. *Degree requirements:* For master's, comprehensive exam, thesis, practica. *Entrance requirements:* For master's, letters of recommendation (2), minimum GPA of 2.75.

Caribbean University, Graduate School, Bayamón, PR 00960-0493. Offers administration and supervision (MA Ed); criminal justice (MA); curriculum and instruction (MA Ed), including elementary education, English education, history education, mathematics education, primary education, science education, Spanish education; education (PhD); gerontology (MSN); human resources (MBA); museology, archiving and art history (MA Ed); neonatal pediatrics (MSN); physical education (MA Ed); special education (MA Ed). *Entrance requirements:* For master's, interview, minimum GPA of 2.5.

Carlos Albizu University, Miami Campus, Graduate Programs, Miami, FL 33172-2209. Offers clinical psychology (Psy D); entrepreneurship (MBA); exceptional student education (MS); industrial/organizational psychology (MS); marriage and family therapy (MS); mental health counseling (MS); nonprofit management (MBA); organizational management (MBA); psychology (MS); school counseling (MS); teaching English as a second language (MS). *Accreditation:* APA. Part-time and evening/weekend programs available. *Faculty:* 23 full-time (13 women), 41 part-time/adjunct (21 women). *Students:* 529 full-time (420 women), 171 part-time (139 women); includes 551 minority (55 African Americans, 1 American Indian/Alaska Native, 5 Asian Americans or Pacific Islanders, 490 Hispanic Americans). Average age 37. 278 applicants, 57% accepted, 142 enrolled. In 2009, 139 master's, 26 doctorates awarded. Terminal master's awarded for partial completion of doctoral program. *Degree requirements:* For master's, one foreign language, comprehensive exam, integrative project (MBA), research project (exceptional student education, teaching English as a second language); for doctorate, one foreign language, comprehensive exam, internship, project. *Entrance requirements:* For master's, 3 letters of recommendation, interview, minimum GPA of 3.0, resume; for doctorate, 3 letters of recommendation, minimum GPA of 3.0, resume, interview. *Application deadline:* For fall admission, 8/1 priority date for domestic students; for spring admission, 11/30 priority date for domestic students. Applications are processed on a rolling basis. Application fee: $50. Electronic applications accepted. *Expenses:* Tuition: Full-time $9090; part-time $505 per credit hour. Required fees: $298 per term. Tuition and fees vary according to course load, degree level and program. *Financial support:* In 2009–10, 127 students received support. Federal Work-Study, scholarships/grants, and tuition discounts available. Financial award application deadline: 6/1; financial award applicants required to submit FAFSA. *Faculty research:* Psychotherapy, forensic psychology, neuropsychology, marketing strategy, entrepreneurship, special education. *Unit head:* Dr. Carmen S. Roca, Chancellor, 305-593-1223 Ext. 120, Fax: 305-629-8052, E-mail: croca@albizu.edu. *Application contact:* Annalye Alonso, Secretary, 305-593-1223 Ext. 137, Fax: 305-593-1854, E-mail: aalonso@albizu.edu.

Carlow University, School of Education, Program in Education, Pittsburgh, PA 15213-3165. Offers elementary education (M Ed); instructional technology specialist (M Ed); secondary education (M Ed); special education (M Ed). Part-time and evening/weekend programs available. *Entrance requirements:* For master's, resume, 3 letters of recommendation, minimum GPA of 3.0, interview. Electronic applications accepted. *Expenses:* Tuition: Full-time $11,250; part-time $625 per credit. Tuition and fees vary according to course load, degree level and program.

Castleton State College, Division of Graduate Studies, Department of Education, Program in Special Education, Castleton, VT 05735. Offers MA Ed, CAGS. Part-time and evening/weekend programs available. *Degree requirements:* For master's, thesis or alternative; for CAGS, publishable paper. *Entrance requirements:* For master's, GRE General Test, MAT, interview, minimum undergraduate GPA of 3.0; for CAGS, educational research, master's degree, minimum undergraduate GPA of 3.0. *Expenses:* Tuition, state resident: full-time $10,290; part-time $429 per credit. Tuition, nonresident: full-time $15,420; part-time $643 per credit. One-time fee: $200 full-time.

The Catholic University of America, School of Arts and Sciences, Department of Education, Washington, DC 20064. Offers Catholic educational leadership (PhD); education (Certificate); educational psychology (PhD); learning and instruction (MA); secondary education (MA); special education (MA). *Accreditation:* NCATE. Part-time programs available. *Faculty:* 11 full-time (8 women), 3 part-time/adjunct (0 women). *Students:* 6 full-time (5 women), 56 part-time (39 women); includes 9 minority (5 African Americans, 2 Asian Americans or Pacific Islanders, 2 Hispanic Americans), 2 international. Average age 38. 54 applicants, 59% accepted, 14 enrolled. In 2009, 14 master's, 6 doctorates, 1 other advanced degree awarded. *Degree requirements:* For master's, comprehensive exam, thesis or alternative; for doctorate, comprehensive exam, thesis/dissertation. *Entrance requirements:* For master's and doctorate, GRE General Test or MAT, statement of purpose, official copies of academic transcripts, three letters of recommendation. Additional exam requirements/recommendations for international students: Required—TOEFL (minimum score 580 paper-based; 237 computer-based). *Application deadline:* For fall admission, 8/1 priority date for domestic students, 7/15 for international students; for spring admission, 12/1 priority date for domestic students, 10/15 for international students. Applications are processed on a rolling basis. Application fee: $55. Electronic applications accepted. *Expenses:* Tuition: Full-time $31,740; part-time $1245 per credit hour. Required fees: $50; $25 per semester hour. One-time fee: $425. *Financial support:* Fellowships, research assistantships, teaching assistantships, Federal Work-Study, scholarships/grants, tuition waivers (full and partial), and unspecified assistantships available. Financial award application deadline: 2/1; financial award applicants required to submit FAFSA. *Faculty research:* Catholic school issues, reflective teaching, cognitive psychology, urban education. Total annual research expenditures: $68,905. *Unit head:* Dr. Merylann J. Schuttloffel, Chair, 202-319-5805, Fax: 202-319-5815, E-mail: schuttloffel@cua.edu. *Application contact:* Julie Schwing, Director of Graduate Admissions, 202-319-5057, Fax: 202-319-6533, E-mail: cua-admissions@cua.edu.

Centenary College, Program in Education, Hackettstown, NJ 07840-2100. Offers instructional leadership (MA); special education (MA). *Accreditation:* Teacher Education Accreditation Council. Part-time and evening/weekend programs available. Postbaccalaureate distance learning degree programs offered (minimal on-campus study). *Degree requirements:* For master's, thesis. *Entrance requirements:* For master's, interview, minimum undergraduate GPA of 2.8.

Central Connecticut State University, School of Graduate Studies, School of Education and Professional Studies, Department of Special Education, New Britain, CT 06050-4010. Offers special education (Certificate); special education for special educators (MS); special education for teachers certified in areas other than education (MS). Part-time and evening/weekend programs available. *Faculty:* 6 full-time (1 woman), 6 part-time/adjunct (4 women). *Students:* 42 full-time (33 women), 175 part-time (143 women); includes 8 minority (5 African Americans, 3 Hispanic Americans), 1 international. Average age 30. 95 applicants, 76% accepted, 64 enrolled. In 2009, 50 master's, 7 other advanced degrees awarded. *Degree requirements:* For master's, comprehensive exam, thesis or alternative; for Certificate, qualifying exam. *Entrance requirements:* For master's, minimum undergraduate GPA of 2.7, teacher certification. Additional exam requirements/recommendations for international students: Required—TOEFL. *Application deadline:* For fall admission, 7/1 for domestic students; for spring admission, 12/1 for domestic students. Applications are processed on a rolling basis. Application fee: $50. Electronic applications accepted. *Expenses:* Tuition, area resident: full-time $4662; part-time $440 per credit. Tuition, state resident: full-time $6994; part-time $440 per credit. Tuition, nonresident: full-time $12,988; part-time $440 per credit. Required fees: $3606. One-time fee: $62 part-time. *Financial support:* In 2009–10, 4 students received support, including 2 research assistantships; career-related internships or fieldwork, Federal Work-Study, scholarships/grants, and unspecified assistantships also available. Support available to part-time students. Financial award application deadline: 3/1; financial award applicants required to submit FAFSA. *Faculty research:* Learning disabilities/language development, consulting teacher practice, occupational/special education, teaching emotionally disturbed students. *Unit head:* Dr. Mitchell Beck, Chair, 860-832-2400. *Application contact:* Dr. Mitchell Beck, Chair, 860-832-2400.

Central Michigan University, College of Graduate Studies, College of Education and Human Services, Department of Counseling and Special Education, Program in Special Education, Mount Pleasant, MI 48859. Offers special education (MA), including the master teacher. Part-time programs available. *Degree requirements:* For master's, thesis or alternative. *Entrance requirements:* For master's, MAT. Electronic applications accepted. *Faculty research:* Mainstreaming, learning disabled, attention and organization disorders.

Central Washington University, Graduate Studies and Research, College of Education and Professional Studies, Department of Education, Program in Special Education, Ellensburg, WA 98926. Offers M Ed. Part-time programs available. *Faculty:* 4 full-time (3 women). *Students:* 1 (woman) full-time. 1 applicant, 100% accepted, 1 enrolled. *Degree requirements:* For master's, thesis or alternative. *Entrance requirements:* For master's, minimum GPA of 3.0. Additional exam requirements/recommendations for international students: Required—TOEFL (minimum score 550 paper-based; 213 computer-based; 79 iBT). *Application deadline:* For fall admission, 2/1 priority date for domestic students; for winter admission, 10/1 for domestic students; for spring admission, 1/1 for domestic students. Applications are processed on a rolling basis. Application fee: $50. *Expenses:* Tuition, state resident: full-time $7353; part-time $245 per credit. Tuition, nonresident: full-time $16,383; part-time $546 per credit. Required fees: $882. Tuition and fees vary according to degree level. *Financial support:* Research assistantships with full and partial tuition reimbursements, teaching assistantships with full and partial tuition reimbursements, Federal Work-Study, health care benefits, and unspecified assistantships available. Financial award application deadline: 3/1; financial award applicants required to submit FAFSA. *Unit head:* Dr. Alberta Thyfault, Co-Director, 509-963-3427, E-mail: thyfault@cwu.edu. *Application contact:* Justine Eason, Admissions Program Coordinator, 509-963-3103, Fax: 509-963-1799, E-mail: masters@cwu.edu.

Chapman University, Graduate Studies, College of Educational Studies, Program in Special Education, Orange, CA 92866. Offers administrative services (Tier I) (Credential); mild/moderate level I (Credential); mild/moderate level II (Credential); moderate/severe level I (Credential); moderate/severe level II (Credential); special education (MA). Part-time and evening/weekend programs available. *Faculty:* 24 full-time (15 women), 25 part-time/adjunct (16 women). *Students:* 22 full-time (21 women), 37 part-time (29 women); includes 21 minority (1 African American, 5 Asian Americans or Pacific Islanders, 15 Hispanic Americans), 1 international. Average age 32. 10 applicants, 90% accepted, 8 enrolled. In 2009, 18 master's awarded. *Degree requirements:* For master's, comprehensive exam, thesis optional. *Entrance requirements:* For master's, GRE General Test, MAT, or California Subject Examinations for Teachers, minimum undergraduate GPA of 2.5. Additional exam requirements/recommendations for international students: Required—TOEFL (minimum score 550 paper-based). *Application deadline:* Applications are processed on a rolling basis. Application fee: $55. Electronic applications accepted. *Expenses:* Contact institution. *Financial support:* Fellowships, Federal Work-Study and scholarships/grants available. Financial award application deadline: 6/30; financial award applicants required to submit FAFSA. *Unit head:* Dr. Dawn Hunter, Coordinator, 714-997-6781. *Application contact:* Rika Judd, Information Contact, 714-997-6786, Fax: 714-997-6713, E-mail: rjudd@chapman.edu.

Chatham University, Program in Education, Pittsburgh, PA 15232-2826. Offers early childhood education (MAT); elementary education (MAT); English—secondary (MAT); environmental education (K-12) (MAT); secondary art (MAT); secondary biology education (MAT); secondary chemistry education (MAT); secondary English education (MAT); secondary math education (MAT); secondary physics education (MAT); secondary social studies education (MAT); special education (MAT). *Students:* 52 full-time (41 women), 20 part-time (16 women). Average age 30. 39 applicants, 79% accepted, 26 enrolled. In 2009, 37 master's awarded. *Degree requirements:* For master's, thesis, teaching experience. *Entrance requirements:* For master's, PRAXIS I, minimum GPA of 3.0, sample of written work, recommendation letters. Additional exam requirements/recommendations for international students: Required—TOEFL (minimum score 600 paper-based; 250 computer-based; 100 iBT), IELTS (minimum score 6.5), TWE. *Application deadline:* For fall admission, 5/1 priority date for domestic and international students; for spring admission, 10/15 priority date for domestic and international students. Applications are processed on a rolling basis. Application fee: $45. Electronic applications accepted. *Financial support:* Career-related internships or fieldwork available. Financial award applicants required to submit FAFSA. *Faculty research:* Gifted education, environmental education, technology in education, writing as learning, class size and achievement. *Unit head:* Dr. Barbara Biglan, Interim Director, 412-365-1170, E-mail: biglan@chatham.edu. *Application contact:* Dory Perry, Associate Director of Graduate Admissions, 412-365-2758, Fax: 412-365-1609, E-mail: gradadmissions@chatham.edu.

Cheyney University of Pennsylvania, School of Education and Professional Studies, Program in Special Education, Cheyney, PA 19319. Offers M Ed, MS. *Accreditation:* NCATE. Part-time and evening/weekend programs available. *Degree requirements:* For master's, thesis or alternative. *Entrance requirements:* For master's, GRE General Test, MAT, minimum GPA of 2.75. Electronic applications accepted.

Chicago State University, School of Graduate and Professional Studies, College of Education, Department of Special Education, Early Childhood Education and Bilingual Education, Program in Special Education, Chicago, IL 60628. Offers M Ed. *Accreditation:* NCATE. *Degree requirements:* For master's, thesis optional. *Entrance requirements:* For master's, minimum GPA of 2.75. *Faculty research:* Assistive technology, teacher efficiency.

City College of the City University of New York, Graduate School, School of Education, Program in Teaching Students with Disabilities, New York, NY 10031-9198. Offers MA. *Accreditation:* NCATE. *Degree requirements:* For master's, thesis. *Entrance requirements:* For master's, Liberal Arts and Sciences Test (LAST), Content Specialty Test (CST). Additional

exam requirements/recommendations for international students: Required—TOEFL. *Expenses:* Tuition, state resident: part-time $310 per credit. Tuition, nonresident: part-time $575 per credit. Tuition and fees vary according to course load and program.

City University of Seattle, Graduate Division, Gordon Albright School of Education, Bellevue, WA 98005. Offers curriculum and instruction (M Ed); educational leadership (M Ed); educational leadership: administrator certification (Certificate); executive leadership: superintendent certification (Certificate); guidance and counseling (M Ed); leadership (M Ed); leadership and school counseling (M Ed); professional certification for teachers (Certificate); reading and literacy (M Ed); reading and literacy in education (M Ed); teacher certification (elementary K-8) (MIT); teacher certification (special education K-12) (MIT); technology, curriculum, and instruction (M Ed). Part-time and evening/weekend programs available. Postbaccalaureate distance learning degree programs offered (no on-campus study). *Entrance requirements:* Additional exam requirements/recommendations for international students: Required—TOEFL (minimum score 540 paper-based; 207 computer-based); Recommended—IELTS. Electronic applications accepted. *Expenses:* Contact institution.

Claremont Graduate University, Graduate Programs, School of Educational Studies, Claremont, CA 91711-6160. Offers Africana education (Certificate); education and policy (MA, PhD); higher education/student affairs (MA, PhD); human development (MA, PhD); public school administration (MA, PhD); quantitative evaluation (MA, PhD); special education (MA, PhD); teacher education (MA); teaching and learning (MA, PhD); urban leadership (PhD); MBA/PhD. Part-time programs available. *Faculty:* 18 full-time (12 women), 1 part-time/adjunct (0 women). *Students:* 279 full-time (190 women), 174 part-time (122 women); includes 196 minority (50 African Americans, 1 American Indian/Alaska Native, 37 Asian Americans or Pacific Islanders, 108 Hispanic Americans), 10 international. Average age 37. In 2009, 84 master's, 23 doctorates awarded. Terminal master's awarded for partial completion of doctoral program. *Entrance requirements:* For master's and doctorate, GRE General Test. Additional exam requirements/recommendations for international students: Required—TOEFL (minimum score 550 paper-based; 213 computer-based; 80 iBT). *Application deadline:* For fall admission, 2/1 priority date for domestic students. Applications are processed on a rolling basis. Application fee: $60. Electronic applications accepted. *Expenses:* Tuition: Full-time $35,046; part-time $1524 per credit. Required fees: $161 per semester. *Financial support:* Fellowships, research assistantships, Federal Work-Study, institutionally sponsored loans, and scholarships/grants available. Support available to part-time students. Financial award application deadline: 2/15; financial award applicants required to submit FAFSA. *Faculty research:* Education administration, K-12 and higher education, multicultural education, education policy, diversity in higher education, faculty issues. *Unit head:* Margaret Grogan, Dean, 909-621-8075, Fax: 909-621-8734, E-mail: margaret.grogan@cgu.edu.

Clarion University of Pennsylvania, Office of Research and Graduate Studies, College of Education and Human Services, Department of Special Education and Rehabilitative Sciences, Clarion, PA 16214. Offers rehabilitative sciences (MS); special education (MS). *Accreditation:* NCATE. Part-time programs available. *Degree requirements:* For master's, thesis or alternative. *Entrance requirements:* For master's, GRE General Test or MAT, minimum QPA of 3.0. Additional exam requirements/recommendations for international students: Required—TOEFL (minimum score 550 paper-based; 213 computer-based; 80 iBT).

Clarke College, Program in Education, Dubuque, IA 52001-3198. Offers early childhood/special education (MAE); educational administration: elementary and secondary (MAE); educational media: elementary and secondary (MAE); multi-categorical resource k-12 (MAE); multidisciplinary studies (MAE); reading: elementary (MAE); technology in education (MAE). Part-time and evening/weekend programs available. Postbaccalaureate distance learning degree programs offered (minimal on-campus study). *Faculty:* 5 full-time (all women). *Students:* 1 (woman) full-time, 45 part-time (40 women). Average age 31. 19 applicants, 74% accepted, 13 enrolled. In 2009, 11 master's awarded. *Degree requirements:* For master's, comprehensive exam, thesis optional. *Entrance requirements:* For master's, GRE General Test or MAT, minimum GPA of 2.75. *Application deadline:* Applications are processed on a rolling basis. Application fee: $25. Electronic applications accepted. *Expenses:* Tuition: Full-time $10,836; part-time $602 per credit hour. Required fees: $30 per credit hour. *Financial support:* Career-related internships or fieldwork available. Financial award applicants required to submit FAFSA. *Unit head:* Dr. Larry Bice, Chair, 319-588-6397, Fax: 319-584-8604. *Application contact:* Joan Coates, Information Contact, 563-588-6354, Fax: 563-588-6789, E-mail: graduate@clarke.edu.

Clemson University, Graduate School, College of Health, Education, and Human Development, School of Education, Program in Special Education, Clemson, SC 29634. Offers M Ed. *Accreditation:* NCATE. Part-time and evening/weekend programs available. *Students:* 12 full-time (all women), 1 (woman) part-time; includes 1 minority (Hispanic American). Average age 26. 16 applicants, 88% accepted, 10 enrolled. In 2009, 7 master's awarded. *Entrance requirements:* For master's, GRE General Test, minimum GPA of 3.0, teaching certificate. Additional exam requirements/recommendations for international students: Required—TOEFL. *Application deadline:* Applications are processed on a rolling basis. Application fee: $70 ($80 for international students). Electronic applications accepted. *Expenses:* Contact institution. *Financial support:* In 2009–10, 12 students received support, including 12 fellowships with full and partial tuition reimbursements available (averaging $2,500 per year); research assistantships with partial tuition reimbursements available, teaching assistantships with partial tuition reimbursements available, career-related internships or fieldwork, institutionally sponsored loans, scholarships/grants, health care benefits, unspecified assistantships, and stipends also available. Support available to part-time students. Financial award application deadline: 6/1; financial award applicants required to submit FAFSA. *Faculty research:* Field-based teacher training transition, assessment, national policy outcome. Total annual research expenditures: $250,000. *Unit head:* Dr. Michael Padilla, Director/Associate Dean, 864-656-4444, Fax: 864-656-0311, E-mail: padilla@clemson.edu. *Application contact:* Dr. David Fleming, Graduate Coordinator, 864-656-1881, Fax: 864-656-0311, E-mail: dflemin@clemson.edu.

Cleveland State University, College of Graduate Studies, College of Education and Human Services, Department of Teacher Education, Cleveland, OH 44115. Offers art education (M Ed); early childhood education (M Ed); foreign language education (M Ed); mathematics and science education (M Ed); middle childhood education (M Ed); special education (M Ed), including mild/moderate disabilities, moderate/intensive disabilities; teaching English to speakers of other languages (M Ed). Part-time and evening/weekend programs available. *Degree requirements:* For master's, comprehensive exam (for some programs), thesis or alternative. *Entrance requirements:* For master's, GRE General Test or MAT, minimum GPA of 2.75. Additional exam requirements/recommendations for international students: Required—TOEFL (minimum score 525 paper-based; 197 computer-based), IELTS (minimum score 6). *Faculty research:* Early literacy, professional development in reading, reading recovery, dual language, induction programs.

College of Charleston, Graduate School, School of Education, Health, and Human Performance, Department of Foundations, Secondary, and Special Education, Program in Special Education, Charleston, SC 29424-0001. Offers MAT. *Faculty:* 31 full-time (26 women), 11 part-time/adjunct (10 women). *Students:* 17 full-time (13 women), 6 part-time (all women), 1 international. Average age 30. 16 applicants, 63% accepted, 7 enrolled. In 2009, 9 master's awarded. *Entrance requirements:* For master's, GRE, minimum GPA of 2.5, 2 letters of recommendation. Additional exam requirements/recommendations for international students: Required—TOEFL. *Application deadline:* For fall admission, 4/1 for domestic students; for spring admission, 11/1 for domestic students. Application fee: $45. Electronic applications accepted. *Financial support:* Fellowships, scholarships/grants and unspecified assistantships available. *Unit head:* Dr. Angela Cozart, Director, 843-953-6353, Fax: 843-953-5407, E-mail: cozarta@cofc.edu. *Application contact:* Susan Hallatt, Director of Graduate Admissions, 843-953-5614, Fax: 843-953-1434, E-mail: hallats@cofc.edu.

Special Education

The College of New Jersey, Graduate Division, School of Education, Department of Special Education, Language and Literacy, Program in Special Education, Ewing, NJ 08628. Offers M Ed, MAT. *Accreditation:* NCATE. Part-time programs available. *Students:* 54 full-time (52 women), 62 part-time (48 women); includes 9 minority (1 African American, 6 Asian Americans or Pacific Islanders, 2 Hispanic Americans). 129 applicants, 68% accepted. In 2009, 82 master's awarded. *Degree requirements:* For master's, comprehensive exam. *Entrance requirements:* For master's, GRE General Test, minimum GPA of 3.0 in field or 2.75 overall. Additional exam requirements/recommendations for international students: Required—TOEFL. *Application deadline:* For fall admission, 2/1 priority date for domestic students; for spring admission, 10/1 priority date for domestic students. Application fee: $70. Electronic applications accepted. *Expenses:* Tuition, state resident: part-time $573.70 per credit. Tuition, nonresident: part-time $887.75 per credit. Required fees: $140.85 per credit. One-time fee: $10 part-time. *Financial support:* Tuition waivers (partial) and unspecified assistantships available. Financial award application deadline: 5/1; financial award applicants required to submit FAFSA. *Unit head:* Dr. Shridevi Rao, Coordinator, 609-771-2308. *Application contact:* Susan L. Hydro, Assistant Dean, Office of Graduate Studies, 609-771-2300, Fax: 609-637-5105, E-mail: graduate@tcnj.edu.

The College of New Jersey, Graduate Division, School of Education, Department of Special Education, Language and Literacy, Program in Special Education with Learning Disabilities, Ewing, NJ 08628. Offers Certificate. *Accreditation:* NCATE. Part-time programs available. *Students:* 2 full-time (both women), 14 part-time (12 women); includes 2 minority (1 African American, 1 Asian American or Pacific Islander), 1 international. 26 applicants, 69% accepted. In 2009, 13 Certificates awarded. *Entrance requirements:* Additional exam requirements/recommendations for international students: Required—TOEFL. *Application deadline:* For fall admission, 2/1 priority date for domestic students; for spring admission, 10/1 priority date for domestic students. Application fee: $70. Electronic applications accepted. *Expenses:* Tuition, state resident: part-time $573.70 per credit. Tuition, nonresident: part-time $887.75 per credit. Required fees: $140.85 per credit. One-time fee: $10 part-time. *Financial support:* Tuition waivers (partial) and unspecified assistantships available. Financial award application deadline: 5/1; financial award applicants required to submit FAFSA. *Unit head:* Dr. Shridevi Rao, Coordinator, 609-771-2308. *Application contact:* Susan L. Hydro, Assistant Dean, Office of Graduate Studies, 609-771-2300, Fax: 609-637-5105, E-mail: graduate@tcnj.edu.

The College of New Rochelle, Graduate School, Division of Education, Program in Special Education, New Rochelle, NY 10805-2308. Offers MS Ed. Part-time programs available. *Degree requirements:* For master's, practicum. *Entrance requirements:* For master's, interview, minimum GPA of 3.0 in field, 2.7 overall.

College of St. Joseph, Graduate Programs, Division of Education, Program in Special Education, Rutland, VT 05701-3899. Offers M Ed. Part-time and evening/weekend programs available. *Degree requirements:* For master's, comprehensive exam. *Entrance requirements:* For master's, PRAXIS I (for initial licensure), interview, 2 letters of reference, minimum GPA of 3.0 (initial licensure) or 2.7 (nonlicensure). Electronic applications accepted. *Expenses:* Tuition: Full-time $13,500; part-time $350 per credit. Required fees: $45 per term. One-time fee: $445. Tuition and fees vary according to program.

The College of Saint Rose, Graduate Studies, School of Education, Department of Literacy and Special Education, Albany, NY 12203-1419. Offers literacy: birth-grade 6 (MS Ed); literacy: grades 5-12 (MS Ed); reading (Certificate), including literacy: birth—grade 6, literacy: grades 5-12; special education (MS Ed), including adolescent education, childhood education, special education advanced study. Part-time and evening/weekend programs available. *Entrance requirements:* For master's, minimum undergraduate GPA of 3.0. Additional exam requirements/recommendations for international students: Required—TOEFL (minimum score 550 paper-based; 213 computer-based). Electronic applications accepted.

College of Santa Fe, Department of Education, Santa Fe, NM 87505-7634. Offers at-risk youth (MA), including bilingual/multicultural education, classroom teaching, community counseling, educational administration, leadership, school counseling, self-designed program, TESOL/Multicultural; curriculum and instruction (MA); multicultural special education (MA). Part-time and evening/weekend programs available. *Entrance requirements:* For master's, minimum GPA of 3.0. *Faculty research:* Integrated curriculum, child development, brain research, learning styles, systemic issues in education.

College of Staten Island of the City University of New York, Graduate Programs, Department of Education, Program in Special Education, Staten Island, NY 10314-6600. Offers MS Ed. Part-time and evening/weekend programs available. *Faculty:* 4 full-time (2 women), 3 part-time/adjunct (2 women). *Students:* 11 full-time (all women), 107 part-time (98 women); includes 16 minority (2 African Americans, 5 Asian Americans or Pacific Islanders, 9 Hispanic Americans), 3 international. Average age 29. 67 applicants, 82% accepted, 43 enrolled. In 2009, 51 master's awarded. *Degree requirements:* For master's, research project, portfolio. *Entrance requirements:* For master's, minimum GPA of 3.0, 2 letters of recommendation. Additional exam requirements/recommendations for international students: Required—TOEFL (minimum score 550 paper-based; 213 computer-based; 79 iBT). *Application deadline:* For fall admission, 4/19 priority date for domestic and international students; for spring admission, 11/16 priority date for domestic and international students. Applications are processed on a rolling basis. Application fee: $125. Electronic applications accepted. *Expenses:* Tuition, state resident: full-time $7360; part-time $310 per credit. Tuition, nonresident: part-time $575 per credit. Required fees: $378; $113 per semester. *Financial support:* In 2009–10, 1 student received support. Career-related internships or fieldwork, Federal Work-Study, institutionally sponsored loans, and scholarships/grants available. Support available to part-time students. Financial award applicants required to submit FAFSA. *Unit head:* Dr. Nelly Tournaki, Associate Professor/Coordinator, 718-982-3728, Fax: 718-982-3743, E-mail: educationmasters@mail.csi.cuny.edu. *Application contact:* Sasha Spence, Assistant Director of Graduate Recruitment and Admissions, 718-982-2699, Fax: 718-982-2500, E-mail: spence@mail.csi.cuny.edu.

College of Staten Island of the City University of New York, Graduate Programs, Department of Education, Program in Special Education Middle Childhood Generalist (5-9), Staten Island, NY 10314-6600. Offers MS Ed. *Students:* 9 full-time (7 women), 4 part-time (all women); includes 4 minority (1 African American, 1 Asian American or Pacific Islander, 2 Hispanic Americans). Average age 31. 14 applicants, 93% accepted, 13 enrolled. *Expenses:* Tuition, state resident: full-time $7360; part-time $310 per credit. Tuition, nonresident: part-time $575 per credit. Required fees: $378; $113 per semester. *Financial support:* Applicants required to submit FAFSA. *Unit head:* Prof. Ed Lehner, Program Coordinator, 718-982-3728, E-mail: lehner@mail.csi.cuny.edu. *Application contact:* Sasha Spence, Assistant Director of Graduate Recruitment and Admissions, 718-982-2699, Fax: 718-982-2500, E-mail: sasha.spence@csi.cuny.edu.

The College of William and Mary, School of Education, Program in Curriculum and Instruction, Williamsburg, VA 23187-8795. Offers elementary education (MA Ed); gifted education (MA Ed); math specialist (MA Ed); reading education (MA Ed); secondary education (MA Ed), including English education, mathematics education, modern foreign languages education, science education, social studies education; special education (MA Ed), including general curriculum, resource collaborating teaching. *Accreditation:* NCATE. Part-time programs available. *Faculty:* 18 full-time (12 women), 17 part-time/adjunct (15 women). *Students:* 54 full-time (45 women), 12 part-time (all women); includes 3 minority (2 African Americans, 1 Asian American or Pacific Islander), 2 international. Average age 27. 120 applicants, 75% accepted. In 2009, 70 master's awarded. *Degree requirements:* For master's, project. *Entrance requirements:* For master's, GRE or MAT, minimum GPA of 2.5. Additional exam requirements/recommendations for international students: Required—TOEFL. *Application deadline:* For fall admission, 1/15 for domestic and international students; for spring admission, 10/1 for domestic and international students. Application fee: $45. Electronic applications accepted. *Expenses:* Tuition, state resident: full-time $6400; part-time $315 per credit hour. Tuition, nonresident: full-time $19,720; part-time $840 per credit hour. Required fees: $4114. *Financial support:* In 2009–10, 30 students received support, including 10 research assistantships with full and partial tuition reimbursements available (averaging $5,500 per year); career-related internships or fieldwork, Federal Work-Study, institutionally sponsored loans, scholarships/grants, and unspecified assistantships also available. Financial award application deadline: 1/15; financial award applicants required to submit FAFSA. *Faculty research:* National Council of Teachers of Mathematics Standards, counseling, self-concept and self-esteem, special education, curriculum development. *Unit head:* Dr. C. Denise Johnson, Area Coordinator, 757-221-1528, E-mail: cdjohn@wm.edu. *Application contact:* Dorothy Smith Osborne, Director of Admissions, 757-221-2317, Fax: 757-221-2293, E-mail: dsosbo@wm.edu.

Colorado State University–Pueblo, College of Education, Engineering and Professional Studies, Education Program, Pueblo, CO 81001-4901. Offers art education (M Ed); foreign language education (M Ed); health and physical education (M Ed); instructional technology (M Ed); linguistically diverse education (M Ed); music education (M Ed); special education (M Ed). *Accreditation:* Teacher Education Accreditation Council. Part-time programs available. *Degree requirements:* For master's, portfolio. *Entrance requirements:* For master's, 3 recommendations, teaching license. Additional exam requirements/recommendations for international students: Required—TOEFL (minimum score 500 paper-based; 173 computer-based). Electronic applications accepted. *Faculty research:* Portfolio assessment, math education, science education.

Columbia International University, Columbia Graduate School, Columbia, SC 29230-3122. Offers Bible teaching (MABT); Christian higher education leadership (Ed D); Christian school educational leadership (Ed D); counseling (MACN); curriculum and instruction (M Ed), including Christian school guidance, English as a second language, learning disabilities, school technology; early childhood and elementary education (MAT); educational administration (M Ed); teaching English as a foreign language (Certificate); teaching English as a foreign language and intercultural studies (MATF). Part-time and evening/weekend programs available. *Degree requirements:* For master's, internships, professional project. *Entrance requirements:* For master's, Minnesota Multiphasic Personality Inventory, MAT, minimum GPA of 2.7. Additional exam requirements/recommendations for international students: Required—TOEFL. Electronic applications accepted.

Columbus State University, Graduate Studies, College of Education and Health Professions, Department of Teacher Education, Columbus, GA 31907-5645. Offers accomplished teaching (M Ed); early childhood education (M Ed, Ed S); health administration (MPA); instructional technology (MS); middle grades education (M Ed, Ed S); physical education (M Ed); secondary education (M Ed, MAT, Ed S), including English/language arts (M Ed, Ed S), general science (M Ed), mathematics (M Ed), social science (M Ed); special education (M Ed), including behavior disorders, mental retardation. *Accreditation:* NCATE. Part-time and evening/weekend programs available. Postbaccalaureate distance learning degree programs offered (minimal on-campus study). *Faculty:* 18 full-time (15 women), 14 part-time/adjunct (10 women). *Students:* 146 full-time (113 women), 312 part-time (261 women); includes 142 minority (120 African Americans, 1 American Indian/Alaska Native, 8 Asian Americans or Pacific Islanders, 13 Hispanic Americans), 2 international. Average age 31. 248 applicants, 64% accepted, 114 enrolled. In 2009, 103 master's, 22 other advanced degrees awarded. *Degree requirements:* For master's, thesis, exit exam; for Ed S, thesis or alternative. *Entrance requirements:* For master's, GRE General Test, minimum GPA of 2.75; for Ed S, GRE General Test. Additional exam requirements/recommendations for international students: Required—TOEFL (minimum score 550 paper-based; 213 computer-based; 79 iBT). *Application deadline:* For fall admission, 5/1 priority date for domestic students, 5/1 for international students; for spring admission, 11/1 for domestic and international students. Applications are processed on a rolling basis. Application fee: $30. Electronic applications accepted. *Financial support:* In 2009–10, 305 students received support, including 36 research assistantships with partial tuition reimbursements available (averaging $3,000 per year); career-related internships or fieldwork, Federal Work-Study, institutionally sponsored loans, scholarships/grants, tuition waivers (partial), and unspecified assistantships also available. Support available to part-time students. Financial award application deadline: 5/1; financial award applicants required to submit FAFSA. *Unit head:* Dr. Deborah Gober, Acting Chair, 706-568-2255, Fax: 706-568-3134, E-mail: gober_deborah@colstate.edu. *Application contact:* Katie Thornton, Graduate Admissions Specialist, 706-568-2035, Fax: 706-568-2462, E-mail: thornton_katie@colstate.edu.

Concordia University, St. Paul, College of Education, St. Paul, MN 55104-5494. Offers curriculum and instruction (MA Ed), including K-12 reading endorsement; differentiated instruction (MA Ed); early childhood education (MA Ed); educational leadership (MA Ed); family life education (MA); K-12 reading endorsement (Certificate); special education (Certificate); sports management (MA). *Accreditation:* NCATE. Evening/weekend programs available. Postbaccalaureate distance learning degree programs offered (minimal on-campus study). *Faculty:* 12 full-time (8 women), 59 part-time/adjunct (47 women). *Students:* 697 full-time (571 women), 13 part-time (12 women); includes 64 minority (31 African Americans, 1 American Indian/Alaska Native, 21 Asian Americans or Pacific Islanders, 11 Hispanic Americans), 1 international. Average age 34. In 2009, 402 master's, 29 other advanced degrees awarded. *Application deadline:* Applications are processed on a rolling basis. Application fee: $50. Electronic applications accepted. *Financial support:* Applicants required to submit FAFSA. *Unit head:* Dr. Donald Helmstetter, Dean, 651-641-8227, Fax: 651-641-8807, E-mail: helmstetter@csp.edu. *Application contact:* Kimberly Craig, Director of Graduate and Cohort Admission, 651-603-6223, Fax: 651-603-6320, E-mail: craig@csp.edu.

Concordia University Wisconsin, Graduate Programs, Department of Education, Mequon, WI 53097-2402. Offers art education (MS Ed); curriculum and instruction (MS Ed); early childhood (MS Ed); educational administration (MS Ed); environmental education (MS Ed); family studies (MS Ed); reading (MS Ed); school counseling (MS Ed); special education (MS Ed). Part-time and evening/weekend programs available. Postbaccalaureate distance learning degree programs offered (minimal on-campus study). *Degree requirements:* For master's, comprehensive exam, thesis or alternative. *Entrance requirements:* For master's, minimum GPA of 3.0, teaching license. Additional exam requirements/recommendations for international students: Required—TOEFL. *Faculty research:* Motivation, developmental learning, learning styles.

Converse College, School of Education and Graduate Studies, Program in Special Education, Spartanburg, SC 29302-0006. Offers learning disabilities (MAT); mental disabilities (MAT); special education (M Ed). Part-time programs available. *Degree requirements:* For master's, capstone paper. *Entrance requirements:* For master's, NTE or PRAXIS II (M Ed), minimum GPA of 2.75, 2 recommendations. Electronic applications accepted.

Coppin State University, Division of Graduate Studies, Division of Education, Department of Special Education, Baltimore, MD 21216-3698. Offers M Ed. Part-time and evening/weekend programs available. *Degree requirements:* For master's, exit portfolio. *Entrance requirements:* For master's, PRAXIS I, minimum GPA of 3.0, interview, writing sample, resume, references. *Faculty research:* Survey of colleges and universities in Maryland with programs for the learning disabled.

Creighton University, Graduate School, College of Arts and Sciences, Department of Education, Program in Special Populations in Education, Omaha, NE 68178-0001. Offers MS. Part-time and evening/weekend programs available. *Students:* 5 part-time (all women); includes 1 minority (Hispanic American). 3 applicants, 100% accepted, 3 enrolled. In 2009, 2 master's awarded. *Entrance requirements:* For master's, GRE, 3 letters of recommendation, resume. Additional exam requirements/recommendations for international students: Required—TOEFL (minimum score 550 paper-based; 213 computer-based; 80 iBT). *Application deadline:* For fall admission, 7/1 priority date for domestic students, 3/1 priority date for international students; for winter admission, 12/1 priority date for domestic students, 7/1 priority date for international

students; for spring admission, 4/1 priority date for domestic students, 10/1 priority date for international students. Applications are processed on a rolling basis. Application fee: $50. Electronic applications accepted. *Expenses:* Tuition: Full-time $11,700; part-time $650 per credit hour. Required fees: $126 per semester. *Financial support:* Scholarships/grants and tuition waivers (partial) available. Support available to part-time students. Financial award application deadline: 5/1; financial award applicants required to submit FAFSA. *Unit head:* Dr. Sharon Ishii-Jordan, Associate Professor of Education, 402-280-2553, E-mail: sharonishii-jordan@creighton.edu. *Application contact:* Taunya Plater, Senior Program Coordinator, 402-280-2870, Fax: 402-280-2899, E-mail: taunyaplater@creighton.edu.

Curry College, Graduate Studies, Program in Education, Milton, MA 02186-9984. Offers educational administration (M Ed); educational diagnostic assessment (Certificate); educational therapy (Certificate); elementary education (M Ed); foundations (non-license) (M Ed); learning disabilities across the lifespan (Certificate); reading (M Ed, Certificate); special education (M Ed). Part-time and evening/weekend programs available. *Faculty:* 6 full-time (4 women), 12 part-time/adjunct (9 women). *Students:* 101 part-time (82 women). Average age 37. In 2009, 25 master's awarded. *Degree requirements:* For master's, project or thesis. *Entrance requirements:* For master's, MAT or GRE, interview, recommendations, resume, written statement. Additional exam requirements/recommendations for international students: Required—TOEFL (minimum score 550 paper-based; 213 computer-based; 80 iBT). *Application deadline:* For fall admission, 8/1 priority date for domestic students, 6/1 for international students; for winter admission, 10/1 for international students; for spring admission, 1/1 for domestic students, 1/28 for international students. Applications are processed on a rolling basis. Application fee: $50. *Expenses:* Contact institution. *Financial support:* Career-related internships or fieldwork and tuition waivers (partial) available. *Faculty research:* Classroom trauma, therapeutic writing, inclusionary practices. *Unit head:* Dr. Donald Gratz, Director and Associate Professor, 617-333-2243, E-mail: dgratz0703@curry.edu. *Application contact:* John Bresnahan, Director of Graduate Enrollment and Student Services, 617-333-2243, Fax: 617-979-3535, E-mail: jbresnah0104@curry.edu.

Daemen College, Education Department, Amherst, NY 14226-3592. Offers adolescence education (MS); childhood education (MS); childhood special education (MS); childhood special-alternative certification (MS); early childhood special-alternative certification (MS). Part-time programs available. *Faculty:* 14 full-time (11 women), 42 part-time/adjunct (36 women). *Students:* 320 full-time (292 women), 225 part-time (202 women); includes 5 minority (3 African Americans, 1 American Indian/Alaska Native, 1 Hispanic American), 135 international. Average age 25. 331 applicants, 82% accepted, 220 enrolled. In 2009, 302 master's awarded. *Degree requirements:* For master's, comprehensive exam, thesis optional, completion of degree within 5 years. *Entrance requirements:* For master's, 2 letters of recommendation, proof of initial certificate of licensure for professional programs, resume, minimum undergraduate GPA of 3.0. Additional exam requirements/recommendations for international students: Required—TOEFL (minimum score 500 paper-based; 173 computer-based; 61 iBT). *Application deadline:* For fall admission, 3/1 priority date for domestic and international students; for spring admission, 10/1 priority date for domestic and international students. Applications are processed on a rolling basis. Application fee: $25. Electronic applications accepted. *Expenses:* Tuition: Part-time $770 per credit hour. Tuition and fees vary according to course load, program and reciprocity agreements. *Financial support:* In 2009–10, 16 students received support. Institutionally sponsored loans, scholarships/grants, and some discounted programs available. Financial award application deadline: 2/15; financial award applicants required to submit FAFSA. *Faculty research:* Transition for students with disabilities, early childhood special education, traumatic brain injury (TBI), reading assessment. *Unit head:* Dr. Mary H. Fox, Chair, 716-839-8530, Fax: 716-839-8516, E-mail: mfox@daemen.edu. *Application contact:* Scott Rowe, Associate Director of Graduate Admissions, 716-839-8225, Fax: 716-839-8229, E-mail: srowe@daemen.edu.

Defiance College, Program in Education, Defiance, OH 43512-1610. Offers adolescent and young adult (MA); mild and moderate intervention specialist (MA); sport science (MA). Part-time programs available. *Degree requirements:* For master's, thesis (for some programs). *Entrance requirements:* For master's, teaching certificate.

Delaware State University, Graduate Programs, College of Education, Program in Special Education, Dover, DE 19901-2277. Offers MA. Part-time and evening/weekend programs available. *Degree requirements:* For master's, comprehensive exam, thesis optional. *Entrance requirements:* For master's, GRE General Test, minimum GPA of 3.0 in field, 2.75 overall. Additional exam requirements/recommendations for international students: Required—TOEFL (minimum score 550 paper-based). Electronic applications accepted. *Faculty research:* Curriculum and instruction, distributive education.

Delta State University, Graduate Programs, College of Education, Division of Teacher Education, Program in Special Education, Cleveland, MS 38733-0001. Offers M Ed. *Accreditation:* NCATE. Part-time and evening/weekend programs available. *Degree requirements:* For master's, thesis optional, practicum. *Expenses:* Tuition, state resident: full-time $4450; part-time $247 per credit hour. Tuition, nonresident: full-time $11,520; part-time $640 per credit hour.

DePaul University, School of Education, Chicago, IL 60106. Offers bilingual and bicultural education (M Ed, MA); curriculum studies (M Ed, MA, Ed D); educational leadership (M Ed, MA, Ed D), including administration and supervision (M Ed, MA), Catholic school leadership (M Ed, MA), physical education (M Ed, MA); human development and learning (MA); human services and counseling (M Ed, MA), including agencies, family concerns, and higher education, elementary schools, human services management, secondary schools; reading and learning disabilities (M Ed, MA); social culture studies in education and development (M Ed, MA), including curriculum studies/development; teaching and learning (early childhood, elementary and secondary) (M Ed), including elementary education (M Ed, MA), secondary education (M Ed, MA); teaching and learning (early childhood, elementary, and secondary) (MA), including elementary education (M Ed, MA), secondary education (M Ed, MA). *Accreditation:* NCATE. Part-time and evening/weekend programs available. *Faculty:* 61 full-time (40 women), 66 part-time/adjunct (41 women). *Students:* 799 full-time (779 women), 470 part-time (365 women); includes 319 minority (153 African Americans, 3 American Indian/Alaska Native, 48 Asian Americans or Pacific Islanders, 115 Hispanic Americans), 15 international. Average age 30. 635 applicants, 74% accepted, 318 enrolled. In 2009, 604 master's, 5 doctorates awarded. *Degree requirements:* For doctorate, thesis/dissertation. *Entrance requirements:* For master's, interview, minimum GPA of 2.75, 2 letters of recommendation; for doctorate, interview, master's degree, writing sample, 3 letters of recommendation. Additional exam requirements/recommendations for international students: Required—TOEFL (minimum score 550 paper-based; 213 computer-based; 80 iBT). *Application deadline:* Applications are processed on a rolling basis. Application fee: $40. Electronic applications accepted. *Expenses:* Tuition: Full-time $37,525; part-time $620 per credit hour. *Financial support:* In 2009–10, 14 research assistantships with tuition reimbursements (averaging $5,800 per year) were awarded; career-related internships or fieldwork also available. *Faculty research:* Reflective teaching, children at risk, loss, ethnicity, urban education. Total annual research expenditures: $1.6 million. *Unit head:* Dr. Marie Donovan, Dean, 773-325-7581, Fax: 773-325-7713, E-mail: mdonovan@depaul.edu. *Application contact:* Brandon Washington, Data Project Manager, 773-325-1152, Fax: 773-325-2270, E-mail: bwashin3@depaul.edu.

DeSales University, Graduate Division, Program in Education, Center Valley, PA 18034-9568. Offers elementary education (M Ed); instructional technology for K-12 (M Ed); interdisciplinary (M Ed); mathematics (M Ed); special education (M Ed); TESOL/ESL (M Ed). Part-time and evening/weekend programs available. Postbaccalaureate distance learning degree programs offered (no on-campus study). *Students:* 218 part-time. *Degree requirements:* For master's, thesis project. *Entrance requirements:* For master's, teaching certificate. Additional exam requirements/recommendations for international students: Required—TOEFL. *Application deadline:* Applications are processed on a rolling basis. Application fee: $35. Electronic applications accepted. *Expenses:* Tuition: Full-time $17,500; part-time $665 per credit. Full-time tuition and fees vary according to program. Part-time tuition and fees vary according to course load. *Financial support:* Application deadline: 5/1. *Faculty research:* Effective teaching, computer interfacing in chemistry labs, computer applications to teaching, history of philosophy, aesthetics multidrug-resistant cancer. *Unit head:* Dr. Lujean Baab, Director, 610-282-1100 Ext. 1739, Fax: 610-282-3734, E-mail: lujean.baab@desales.edu. *Application contact:* Caryn Stopper, Director of Graduate Admissions, 610-282-1100 Ext. 1768, Fax: 610-282-0525, E-mail: caryn.stopper@desales.edu.

Dominican College, Division of Teacher Education, Department of Teacher Education, Orangeburg, NY 10962-1210. Offers childhood education (MS Ed); teacher of students with disabilities (MS Ed); teacher of visually impaired (MS Ed). *Accreditation:* Teacher Education Accreditation Council. Part-time and evening/weekend programs available. Postbaccalaureate distance learning degree programs offered (minimal on-campus study). *Faculty:* 2 full-time (both women), 6 part-time/adjunct (all women). *Students:* 50 part-time (42 women); includes 2 minority (both Hispanic Americans). Average age 39. In 2009, 10 master's awarded. *Degree requirements:* For master's, practicum, research project. *Entrance requirements:* For master's, interview, 3 letters of recommendation, minimum undergraduate GPA of 3.0. Additional exam requirements/recommendations for international students: Required—TOEFL (minimum score 550 paper-based; 213 computer-based). *Application deadline:* Applications are processed on a rolling basis. Application fee: $50. *Financial support:* Applicants required to submit FAFSA. *Unit head:* Dr. Rona Shaw, Program Director, 845-848-4081, Fax: 845-359-7802, E-mail: rona.shaw@dc.edu. *Application contact:* Director of Admissions, 845-848-7900, Fax: 845-365-3150, E-mail: admissions@dc.edu.

Dominican University, School of Education, River Forest, IL 60305-1099. Offers curriculum and instruction (MA Ed); early childhood education (MS); education (MAT); educational administration (MA); elementary (online) (MS); English as a second language (online) (MS); reading (online) (MS); special education (MS). Part-time and evening/weekend programs available. Postbaccalaureate distance learning degree programs offered. *Faculty:* 16 full-time (12 women), 59 part-time/adjunct (46 women). *Students:* 236 full-time (182 women), 622 part-time (509 women); includes 180 minority (54 African Americans, 3 American Indian/Alaska Native, 36 Asian Americans or Pacific Islanders, 87 Hispanic Americans), 2 international. Average age 32. In 2009, 199 master's awarded. *Entrance requirements:* For master's, Illinois certification test of basic skills. Additional exam requirements/recommendations for international students: Required—TOEFL (minimum score 550 paper-based; 213 computer-based; 79 iBT). *Application deadline:* Applications are processed on a rolling basis. Application fee: $25. *Expenses:* Contact institution. *Financial support:* Career-related internships or fieldwork, scholarships/grants, and tuition waivers (partial) available. Support available to part-time students. Financial award application deadline: 8/15; financial award applicants required to submit FAFSA. *Faculty research:* Governance of private education institutions, reading and language arts, inclusion, organizational planning, leadership and vision. *Unit head:* Dr. Colleen Reardon, Dean, 718-524-6643, Fax: 708-524-6665, E-mail: creardon@dom.edu. *Application contact:* Keven Hansen, Coordinator of Recruitment and Admissions, 708-524-6921, Fax: 708-524-6665, E-mail: educate@dom.edu.

Dominican University of California, Graduate Programs, School of Education and Counseling Psychology, Special Education Credential Program, San Rafael, CA 94901-2298. Offers Credential. *Entrance requirements:* Additional exam requirements/recommendations for international students: Required—TOEFL (minimum score 550 paper-based; 213 computer-based). Electronic applications accepted.

Dowling College, Graduate Programs in Education, Oakdale, NY 11769-1999. Offers adolescence education (MS Ed), including educational administration; advanced certificate in gifted education (AC); childhood and early childhood education (MS Ed); childhood education (MS Ed); educational administration (AC, PD), including computers in education (PD), school administration and supervision (PD), school district administration (PD); educational technology specialist (AC); literacy (MS Ed); literacy/special education (MS Ed); secondary education (MS Ed); special education (MS Ed). *Accreditation:* NCATE. Part-time and evening/weekend programs available. Postbaccalaureate distance learning degree programs offered. *Faculty:* 32 full-time (18 women), 98 part-time/adjunct (59 women). *Students:* 563 full-time (393 women), 885 part-time (668 women); includes 133 minority (47 African Americans, 2 American Indian/Alaska Native, 10 Asian Americans or Pacific Islanders, 74 Hispanic Americans). Average age 32. 363 applicants, 89% accepted, 213 enrolled. In 2009, 459 master's, 85 ACs awarded. *Degree requirements:* For master's and other advanced degree, comprehensive exam. *Entrance requirements:* For master's, minimum GPA of 3.0; for other advanced degree, teaching certificate. Additional exam requirements/recommendations for international students: Required—TOEFL (minimum score 550 paper-based). *Application deadline:* For fall admission, 9/1 priority date for domestic students; for winter admission, 1/1 priority date for domestic students; for spring admission, 2/1 priority date for domestic students. Applications are processed on a rolling basis. Application fee: $50. Electronic applications accepted. *Expenses:* Tuition: Full-time $14,490; part-time $805 per credit. Required fees: $346 per term. *Financial support:* Career-related internships or fieldwork and Federal Work-Study available. Support available to part-time students. Financial award application deadline: 6/30; financial award applicants required to submit FAFSA. *Faculty research:* Natural readers, Korean styles and learning strategies, mothers of children with disabilities, computers in instruction, cultural background and organizational roadblocks to problem solving. *Unit head:* Dr. Clyde Payne, Dean of the School of Education, 631-244-3404, Fax: 631-589-6644, E-mail: paynec@dowling.edu. *Application contact:* Glenn M. Berman, Assistant Vice President for Enrollment Services/Dean of Admissions, 631-244-3357, Fax: 631-244-1059, E-mail: glenn.berman@dowling.edu.

Drury University, Graduate Programs in Education, Springfield, MO 65802. Offers elementary education (M Ed); gifted education (M Ed); human services (M Ed); instructional mathematics K-8 (M Ed); instructional technology (M Ed); middle school teaching (M Ed); secondary education (M Ed); special education (M Ed); special reading (M Ed). *Accreditation:* NCATE. Part-time and evening/weekend programs available. *Degree requirements:* For master's, thesis. *Entrance requirements:* For master's, GRE or MAT, minimum GPA of 2.75. Additional exam requirements/recommendations for international students: Required—TOEFL. Electronic applications accepted. *Faculty research:* Cultural enrichment, research skills, parental involvement relating to reading skills, reading strategies for mainstreaming children.

Duquesne University, School of Education, Department of Counseling, Psychology, and Special Education, Program in Special Education, Pittsburgh, PA 15282-0001. Offers community mental health (MS Ed); special education (MS Ed), including special education. Part-time and evening/weekend programs available. *Faculty:* 6 full-time (all women). *Students:* 42 full-time (38 women), 7 part-time (6 women); includes 1 minority (African American). Average age 27. 20 applicants, 85% accepted, 12 enrolled. In 2009, 12 master's awarded. *Degree requirements:* For master's, thesis optional. *Entrance requirements:* For master's, MAT, minimum GPA of 3.0. Additional exam requirements/recommendations for international students: Required—TOEFL (minimum score 550 paper-based; 80 computer-based). *Application deadline:* For fall admission, 5/1 priority date for domestic students; for spring admission, 1/1 for domestic students. Applications are processed on a rolling basis. Application fee: $0. Electronic applications accepted. *Expenses:* Tuition: Part-time $851 per credit. Required fees: $81 per credit. *Financial support:* In 2009–10, 1 research assistantship was awarded. Support available to part-time students. *Unit head:* Dr. Lisa Vernon-Dotson, Assistant Professor, 412-396-1103, Fax: 412-396-1340, E-mail: vernonl@duq.edu. *Application contact:* Michael Dolinger, Director of Student and Academic Services, 412-396-6647, Fax: 412-396-5585, E-mail: dolingerm@duq.edu.

D'Youville College, Department of Education, Buffalo, NY 14201-1084. Offers elementary education (MS Ed, Teaching Certificate); secondary education (MS Ed, Teaching Certificate); special education (MS Ed). Part-time and evening/weekend programs available. *Degree*

Special Education

D'Youville College (continued)
requirements: For master's, one foreign language, comprehensive exam, project or thesis. *Entrance requirements:* For master's, GRE (if GPA less than 2.75), minimum GPA of 3.0. Additional exam requirements/recommendations for international students: Required—TOEFL (minimum score 500 paper-based; 173 computer-based). Electronic applications accepted. *Faculty research:* Developmental disabilities, multiculturalism, early childhood education.

East Carolina University, Graduate School, College of Education, Department of Curriculum and Instruction, Greenville, NC 27858-4353. Offers behavior/emotional disabilities (MA Ed); elementary education (MA Ed); English education (MA Ed); learning disabilities (MA Ed); low incidence disabilities (MA Ed); mental retardation (MA Ed); middle grade education (MA Ed); reading education (MA Ed); social studies education (MA Ed). Part-time programs available. Postbaccalaureate distance learning degree programs offered. *Degree requirements:* For master's, comprehensive exam, thesis optional. *Entrance requirements:* For master's, GRE General Test or MAT, interview, bachelor's degree in related field, minimum GPA of 2.5, teaching license. Additional exam requirements/recommendations for international students: Required—TOEFL.

Eastern Illinois University, Graduate School, College of Education and Professional Studies, Department of Special Education, Charleston, IL 61920-3099. Offers MS Ed. *Accreditation:* NCATE. Part-time programs available. *Faculty:* 4 full-time (all women). In 2009, 4 master's awarded. *Degree requirements:* For master's, comprehensive exam. *Entrance requirements:* For master's, GRE General Test or MAT. *Application deadline:* For fall admission, 3/31 priority date for domestic students. Applications are processed on a rolling basis. Application fee: $30. *Expenses:* Tuition, state resident: full-time $9434; part-time $239 per credit hour. Tuition, nonresident: full-time $23,774; part-time $717 per credit hour. Required fees: $802.63. *Financial support:* In 2009–10, research assistantships with tuition reimbursements (averaging $8,100 per year), 3 teaching assistantships with tuition reimbursements (averaging $8,100 per year) were awarded. *Unit head:* Dr. Kathlene Shank, Chairperson, 217-581-5315, E-mail: ksshank@eiu.edu. *Application contact:* Dr. Kathlene Shank, Director of Graduate Admissions, 217-581-5315, E-mail: ksshank@eiu.edu.

Eastern Kentucky University, The Graduate School, College of Education, Department of Special Education, Richmond, KY 40475-3102. Offers communication disorders (MA Ed). *Accreditation:* NCATE. Part-time programs available. *Degree requirements:* For master's, comprehensive exam. *Entrance requirements:* For master's, GRE General Test, MAT, minimum GPA of 2.5. *Faculty research:* Personnel needs in communication disorders, education needs of people who stutter, attention of special ed teacher.

Eastern Michigan University, Graduate School, College of Education, Department of Special Education, Program in Autism Spectrum Disorders, Ypsilanti, MI 48197. Offers MA. *Students:* 20 part-time (17 women). Average age 30. 27 applicants, 41% accepted, 8 enrolled. Application fee: $35. Tuition and fees vary according to course level. *Unit head:* Dr. Sally Burton-Hoyle, Coordinator, 734-487-3300, Fax: 734-487-2473, E-mail: sburtonh@emich.edu. *Application contact:* Dr. Sally Burton-Hoyle, Coordinator, 734-487-3300, Fax: 734-487-2473, E-mail: sburtonh@emich.edu.

Eastern Michigan University, Graduate School, College of Education, Department of Special Education, Program in Cognitive Impairment, Ypsilanti, MI 48197. Offers cognitive impairment (MA); mentally impaired (MA). *Students:* 24 full-time (18 women), 40 part-time (35 women); includes 4 minority (2 African Americans, 1 Asian American or Pacific Islander, 1 Hispanic American), 1 international. Average age 33. In 2009, 13 master's awarded. Tuition and fees vary according to course level. *Unit head:* Dr. Jacquelyn McGinnis, Coordinator, 734-487-3300, Fax: 734-487-2473, E-mail: jackie.mcginnis@emich.edu. *Application contact:* Dr. Kathlyn Parker, Advisor, 734-487-3300, Fax: 734-487-2473, E-mail: kathlyn.parker@emich.edu.

Eastern Michigan University, Graduate School, College of Education, Department of Special Education, Program in Emotional Impairment, Ypsilanti, MI 48197. Offers MA. *Students:* 13 full-time (8 women), 49 part-time (38 women); includes 5 minority (2 African Americans, 1 American Indian/Alaska Native, 1 Asian American or Pacific Islander, 1 Hispanic American). Average age 33. In 2009, 10 master's awarded. Application fee: $35. Tuition and fees vary according to course level. *Unit head:* Dr. Karen Carney, Coordinator, 734-487-3300, Fax: 734-487-2473, E-mail: karen.carney@emich.edu. *Application contact:* Dr. Karen Carney, Coordinator, 734-487-3300, Fax: 734-487-2473, E-mail: karen.carney@emich.edu.

Eastern Michigan University, Graduate School, College of Education, Department of Special Education, Program in Hearing Impairment, Ypsilanti, MI 48197. Offers MA. *Students:* 2 full-time (both women). Average age 30.Application fee: $35. Tuition and fees vary according to course level. *Unit head:* Linda Polter, Coordinator, 734-487-3300, Fax: 734-487-2473, E-mail: linda.polter@emich.edu. *Application contact:* Linda Polter, Coordinator, 734-487-3300, Fax: 734-487-2473, E-mail: linda.polter@emich.edu.

Eastern Michigan University, Graduate School, College of Education, Department of Special Education, Program in Learning Disabilities, Ypsilanti, MI 48197. Offers MA. *Students:* 3 full-time (2 women), 39 part-time (36 women). Average age 36. In 2009, 22 master's awarded. Application fee: $35. Tuition and fees vary according to course level. *Unit head:* Dr. Loreena Parks, Coordinator, 734-487-3300, Fax: 734-487-2473, E-mail: lparks1@emich.edu. *Application contact:* Karen Schulte, Advisor, 734-487-3300, Fax: 734-487-2473, E-mail: kschulte@emich.edu.

Eastern Michigan University, Graduate School, College of Education, Department of Special Education, Program in Physical/Other Health Impairment, Ypsilanti, MI 48197. Offers MA. *Students:* 7 part-time (5 women). Average age 42. In 2009, 1 master's awarded. Application fee: $35. Tuition and fees vary according to course level. *Unit head:* Dr. Jacquelyn McGinnis, Coordinator, 734-487-3300, Fax: 734-487-2473, E-mail: jackie.mcginnis@emich.edu. *Application contact:* Dr. Jacquelyn McGinnis, Coordinator, 734-487-3300, Fax: 734-487-2473, E-mail: jackie.mcginnis@emich.edu.

Eastern Michigan University, Graduate School, College of Education, Department of Special Education, Program in Visual Impairment, Ypsilanti, MI 48197. Offers MA. *Students:* 1 (woman) part-time, all international. Average age 35.Application fee: $35. Tuition and fees vary according to course level. *Unit head:* Dr. Alicia Li, Coordinator, 734-487-3300, Fax: 734-487-2473, E-mail: alicia.li@emich.edu. *Application contact:* Dr. Alicia Li, Coordinator, 734-487-3300, Fax: 734-487-2473, E-mail: alicia.li@emich.edu.

Eastern Michigan University, Graduate School, College of Education, Department of Special Education, Programs in Special Education, Ypsilanti, MI 48197. Offers special education (MA); special education-administration and supervision (SPA); special education-curriculum development (SPA). *Accreditation:* NCATE. Part-time and evening/weekend programs available. Postbaccalaureate distance learning degree programs offered (minimal on-campus study). *Students:* 19 full-time (17 women), 44 part-time (37 women); includes 10 minority (4 African Americans, 1 American Indian/Alaska Native, 1 Asian American or Pacific Islander, 4 Hispanic Americans). Average age 36. In 2009, 5 master's, 4 other advanced degrees awarded. *Entrance requirements:* For master's, GRE General Test. Additional exam requirements/recommendations for international students: Required—TOEFL. *Application deadline:* Applications are processed on a rolling basis. Application fee: $35. Tuition and fees vary according to course level. *Financial support:* Fellowships, research assistantships with full tuition reimbursements, teaching assistantships with full tuition reimbursements, career-related internships or fieldwork, Federal Work-Study, institutionally sponsored loans, scholarships/grants, tuition waivers (partial), and unspecified assistantships available. Support available to part-time students. Financial award applicants required to submit FAFSA. *Application contact:* Graduate Admissions, 734-487-3400, Fax: 734-487-6559, E-mail: graduate.admissions@emich.edu.

Eastern Nazarene College, Adult and Graduate Studies, Division of Education, Quincy, MA 02170. Offers early childhood education (M Ed, Certificate); elementary education (M Ed, Certificate); English as a second language (M Ed, Certificate); instructional enrichment and development (M Ed, Certificate); middle school education (M Ed, Certificate); moderate special needs education (M Ed, Certificate); principal (Certificate); program development and supervision (M Ed, Certificate); secondary education (M Ed, Certificate); special education administrator (Certificate); supervisor (Certificate); teacher of reading (M Ed, Certificate). M Ed and Certificate also available through weekend program for administration, special needs, and reading only. Part-time and evening/weekend programs available. *Entrance requirements:* Additional exam requirements/recommendations for international students: Required—TOEFL (minimum score 550 paper-based).

Eastern New Mexico University, Graduate School, College of Education and Technology, Department of Educational Studies, Program in Special Education, Portales, NM 88130. Offers M Ed, M Sp Ed. Part-time programs available. *Faculty:* 3 full-time (2 women). *Students:* 3 full-time (all women), 36 part-time (33 women); includes 8 minority (1 American Indian/Alaska Native, 7 Hispanic Americans). Average age 39. 19 applicants, 74% accepted, 13 enrolled. In 2009, 4 master's awarded. *Degree requirements:* For master's, comprehensive exam, thesis optional, minimum student teaching experience of 6 hours, special education license or course work (8 courses). *Entrance requirements:* For master's, minimum GPA of 2.8, letter of recommendation, photocopy of teaching license, writing assessment. Additional exam requirements/recommendations for international students: Required—TOEFL (minimum score 550 paper-based; 213 computer-based; 79 iBT), IELTS (minimum score 6). *Application deadline:* For fall admission, 7/20 priority date for domestic students, 6/20 priority date for international students. Applications are processed on a rolling basis. Application fee: $10. Electronic applications accepted. *Expenses:* Tuition, state resident: full-time $2922; part-time $121.75 per credit hour. Tuition, nonresident: full-time $8454; part-time $352.25 per credit hour. Required fees: $1038; $43.25 per credit hour. *Financial support:* Research assistantships, teaching assistantships, career-related internships or fieldwork and unspecified assistantships available. Support available to part-time students. Financial award applicants required to submit FAFSA. *Unit head:* Dr. Rebecca Davis, Graduate Coordinator, 575-392-6840, E-mail: rebecca.davis@enmu.edu. *Application contact:* Dr. Rebecca Davis, Graduate Coordinator, 575-392-6840, E-mail: rebecca.davis@enmu.edu.

Eastern Washington University, Graduate Studies, College of Education and Human Development, Program in Special Education, Cheney, WA 99004-2431. Offers M Ed. *Degree requirements:* For master's, comprehensive exam, thesis or alternative. *Entrance requirements:* For master's, GRE General Test, minimum GPA of 3.0. *Expenses:* Tuition, state resident: full-time $7476; part-time $249 per quarter hour. Tuition, nonresident: full-time $18,030; part-time $601 per quarter hour. Required fees: $3.50 per quarter hour. $142 per quarter.

East Stroudsburg University of Pennsylvania, Graduate School, College of Education, Department of Special Education, East Stroudsburg, PA 18301-2999. Offers M Ed. Part-time and evening/weekend programs available. *Faculty:* 6 full-time (4 women), 1 (woman) part-time/adjunct. *Students:* 23 full-time (18 women), 93 part-time (78 women); includes 8 minority (3 African Americans, 5 Hispanic Americans). Average age 33. In 2009, 35 master's awarded. *Degree requirements:* For master's, comprehensive exam. *Entrance requirements:* For master's, PRAXIS/teacher certification, letter of recommendation, Pennsylvania Department of Education requirements. Additional exam requirements/recommendations for international students: Required—TOEFL (minimum score 560 paper-based; 220 computer-based; 83 iBT). *Application deadline:* For fall admission, 7/31 priority date for domestic students, 5/1 priority date for international students; for spring admission, 11/30 for domestic students, 10/1 for international students. Applications are processed on a rolling basis. Application fee: $50. *Expenses:* Tuition, state resident: full-time $9942; part-time $387 per credit. Tuition, nonresident: full-time $14,240; part-time $619 per credit. *Financial support:* In 2009–10, 6 research assistantships with full and partial tuition reimbursements (averaging $2,294 per year) were awarded; career-related internships or fieldwork, Federal Work-Study, and institutionally sponsored loans also available. Financial award application deadline: 3/1; financial award applicants required to submit FAFSA. *Unit head:* Dr. Teri Burcroff, Graduate Coordinator, 570-422-3558, Fax: 570-422-3506, E-mail: tburcroff@po-box.esu.edu. *Application contact:* Kevin Quintero, Graduate Admissions Coordinator, 570-422-3890, Fax: 570-422-2711, E-mail: kquintero@po-box.esu.edu.

East Tennessee State University, School of Graduate Studies, College of Education, Department of Human Development and Learning, Johnson City, TN 37614. Offers advanced practitioner (M Ed); community agency counseling (M Ed, MA); comprehensive concentration (M Ed); counseling (M Ed, MA); early childhood education (M Ed, MA); early childhood general (M Ed); early childhood special education (M Ed); early childhood teaching (M Ed); elementary and secondary (school counseling) (M Ed, MA); marriage and family therapy (M Ed, MA); modified concentration (M Ed). *Accreditation:* ACA; NCATE. Part-time programs available. *Degree requirements:* For master's, comprehensive exam, thesis (for some programs). *Entrance requirements:* For master's, GRE General Test, minimum GPA of 3.0. Additional exam requirements/recommendations for international students: Required—TOEFL (minimum score 550 paper-based; 213 computer-based). *Faculty research:* Drug and alcohol abuse, marriage and family counseling, severe mental retardation, parenting of children with disabilities.

East Tennessee State University, School of Graduate Studies, College of Public and Allied Health, Department of Communicative Disorders, Johnson City, TN 37614. Offers audiology (MS, Au D); communicative disorders (MS); special education audiology pre-K-12 (MS); special education speech pathology pre-K-12 (MS); speech pathology (MS). *Accreditation:* ASHA (one or more programs are accredited). Part-time and evening/weekend programs available. *Degree requirements:* For master's, comprehensive exam, thesis or alternative. *Entrance requirements:* For master's, GRE General Test, minimum GPA of 3.0; for doctorate, GRE. Additional exam requirements/recommendations for international students: Required—TOEFL (minimum score 550 paper-based; 213 computer-based). *Faculty research:* Treatment efficacy, hearing aid trials, language development of cleft palate children, phonological processes, neurogenic disorders.

Edgewood College, Program in Education, Madison, WI 53711-1997. Offers director of instruction (Certificate); director of special education and pupil services (Certificate); education (MA Ed); educational administration (MA); educational leadership (Ed D); program coordinator (Certificate); school business administration (Certificate); school principalship K-12 (Certificate). *Accreditation:* NCATE (one or more programs are accredited). Part-time and evening/weekend programs available. *Students:* 36 full-time (21 women), 232 part-time (141 women); includes 39 minority (10 African Americans, 3 American Indian/Alaska Native, 9 Asian Americans or Pacific Islanders, 17 Hispanic Americans), 1 international. Average age 37. In 2009, 30 master's, 23 doctorates awarded. *Degree requirements:* For master's, practicum, research project. *Entrance requirements:* For master's, minimum GPA of 2.75, 2 letters of recommendation, personal statement; for doctorate, resume, 2 letters of recommendation, interview. Additional exam requirements/recommendations for international students: Required—TOEFL (minimum score 525 paper-based; 197 computer-based; 72 iBT). *Application deadline:* For fall admission, 8/24 for domestic students, 8/1 for international students; for spring admission, 1/10 for domestic students, 10/1 for international students. Applications are processed on a rolling basis. Application fee: $25. Electronic applications accepted. *Expenses:* Tuition: Part-time $688 per credit hour. *Unit head:* Dr. Jane Belmore, Interim Dean, 608-663-8336, Fax: 608-663-3291, E-mail: jbelmore@edgewood.edu. *Application contact:* Joann Eastman, Admissions Counselor, 608-663-3250, Fax: 608-663-2214, E-mail: gps@edgewood.edu.

Edinboro University of Pennsylvania, School of Graduate Studies and Research, School of Education, Department of Early Childhood and Special Education, Edinboro, PA 16444. Offers behavior management (Certificate); educational psychology (M Ed); special education (M Ed). Part-time and evening/weekend programs available. *Faculty:* 8 full-time (7 women), 5 part-

time/adjunct (3 women). *Students:* 20 full-time (15 women), 122 part-time (105 women); includes 7 minority (5 African Americans, 1 Asian American or Pacific Islander, 1 Hispanic American). Average age 31. In 2009, 16 master's, 7 Certificates awarded. *Degree requirements:* For master's, thesis or alternative, competency exam; for Certificate, thesis or alternative. *Entrance requirements:* For master's and Certificate, GRE or MAT, minimum QPA of 2.5. *Application deadline:* Applications are processed on a rolling basis. Application fee: $30. Electronic applications accepted. *Expenses:* Tuition, state resident: full-time $6666; part-time $370 per credit. Tuition, nonresident: full-time $10,666; part-time $593 per credit. Required fees: $2206.28. One-time fee: $204 part-time. *Financial support:* In 2009–10, 4 research assistantships with full and partial tuition reimbursements (averaging $4,050 per year) were awarded; career-related internships or fieldwork, Federal Work-Study, scholarships/grants, and unspecified assistantships also available. Support available to part-time students. Financial award application deadline: 2/15; financial award applicants required to submit FAFSA. *Unit head:* Dr. Edward Snyder, Program Head, Educational Psychology, 814-732-1098, E-mail: jkasper@edinboro.edu. *Application contact:* Dr. Susan Criswell, Program Head, Special Education, 814-732-2287, E-mail: scriswell@edinboro.edu.

Elmhurst College, Graduate Programs, Program in Early Childhood Special Education, Elmhurst, IL 60126-3296. Offers M Ed. Part-time and evening/weekend programs available. *Faculty:* 2 full-time (both women), 3 part-time/adjunct (all women). *Students:* 28 part-time (27 women); includes 1 minority (Asian American or Pacific Islander). Average age 26. 45 applicants, 44% accepted, 14 enrolled. In 2009, 14 master's awarded. *Entrance requirements:* For master's, 3 recommendations. Additional exam requirements/recommendations for international students: Required—TOEFL (minimum score 550 paper-based; 213 computer-based). *Application deadline:* Applications are processed on a rolling basis. Application fee: $25. Electronic applications accepted. *Expenses:* Contact institution. *Financial support:* In 2009–10, 16 students received support. Federal Work-Study and scholarships/grants available. Support available to part-time students. Financial award application deadline: 6/1; financial award applicants required to submit FAFSA. *Unit head:* Dr. Ted Lerud, Associate Dean of the Faculty, 630-617-3661, Fax: 630-617-6415, E-mail: gradadm@elmhurst.edu. *Application contact:* Elizabeth D. Kuebler, Director of Adult and Graduate Admission, 630-617-3069, Fax: 630-617-5501, E-mail: betsyk@elmhurst.edu.

Elms College, Division of Education, Chicopee, MA 01013-2839. Offers early childhood education (MAT); education (M Ed, CAGS); elementary education (MAT); English as a second language (MAT); reading (MAT); secondary education (MAT), including biology education, English education, Spanish education; special education (MAT). Part-time and evening/weekend programs available. *Faculty:* 12 full-time (8 women), 4 part-time/adjunct (2 women). *Students:* 17 full-time (14 women), 153 part-time (136 women); includes 5 minority (1 American Indian/Alaska Native, 4 Hispanic Americans). Average age 36. 43 applicants, 88% accepted, 37 enrolled. In 2009, 23 master's, 8 other advanced degrees awarded. *Degree requirements:* For master's, thesis (for some programs). *Entrance requirements:* For master's, Massachusetts Educators Certification Test, minimum GPA of 3.0; for CAGS, master's degree in education. Additional exam requirements/recommendations for international students: Required—TOEFL. *Application deadline:* For fall admission, 7/1 priority date for domestic students; for spring admission, 11/1 priority date for domestic students. Applications are processed on a rolling basis. Application fee: $30. *Financial support:* In 2009–10, 2 teaching assistantships with partial tuition reimbursements were awarded; tuition waivers (partial) also available. Support available to part-time students. Financial award applicants required to submit FAFSA. *Unit head:* Dr. Mary Janeczek, Director, 413-594-2761, Fax: 413-592-4871, E-mail: janeczeke@elms.edu. *Application contact:* Dana Malone, Associate Director for Graduate Studies and Continuing Education, 413-265-2445, Fax: 413-265-2459, E-mail: maloned@elms.edu.

Elon University, Program in Education, Elon, NC 27244-2010. Offers elementary education (M Ed); gifted education (M Ed); special education (M Ed). *Accreditation:* NCATE. Part-time programs available. *Faculty:* 15 full-time (11 women). *Students:* 1 (woman) full-time, 79 part-time (65 women); includes 15 minority (13 African Americans, 1 Asian American or Pacific Islander, 1 Hispanic American), 1 international. Average age 30. 57 applicants, 84% accepted, 39 enrolled. In 2009, 45 master's awarded. *Entrance requirements:* For master's, GRE, MAT. Additional exam requirements/recommendations for international students: Required—TOEFL (minimum score 550 paper-based; 213 computer-based; 79 iBT). *Application deadline:* For winter admission, 6/1 priority date for domestic students. Applications are processed on a rolling basis. Application fee: $50. Electronic applications accepted. *Expenses:* Contact institution. *Financial support:* In 2009–10, 4 students received support. Federal Work-Study and scholarships/grants available. Support available to part-time students. Financial award application deadline: 6/1; financial award applicants required to submit FAFSA. *Faculty research:* Teaching reading to low-achieving second and third graders, pre- and post-student teaching attitudes toward teaching, children's writing, whole language methodology, critical creative thinking. *Unit head:* Dr. Judith B. Howard, Director, 336-278-5885, Fax: 336-278-5919, E-mail: howardj@elon.edu. *Application contact:* Art Fadde, Director of Graduate Admissions, 800-334-8448 Ext. 3, Fax: 336-278-7699, E-mail: afadde@elon.edu.

Emporia State University, School of Graduate Studies, The Teachers College, Department of Early Childhood/Elementary Teacher Education, Program in Early Childhood Education, Emporia, KS 66801-5087. Offers early childhood curriculum (MS); early childhood special education (MS). *Accreditation:* NCATE. Part-time programs available. Postbaccalaureate distance learning degree programs offered. *Students:* 1 (woman) full-time, 52 part-time (all women); includes 1 minority (Hispanic American). 6 applicants, 100% accepted, 6 enrolled. In 2009, 10 master's awarded. *Degree requirements:* For master's, comprehensive exam or thesis, practicum. *Entrance requirements:* For master's, GRE General Test or MAT, graduate essay exam, appropriate bachelor's degree, letters of recommendation. Additional exam requirements/recommendations for international students: Required—TOEFL (minimum score 520 paper-based; 133 computer-based; 68 iBT). *Application deadline:* For fall admission, 8/15 priority date for domestic students. Applications are processed on a rolling basis. Application fee: $30 ($75 for international students). Electronic applications accepted. *Expenses:* Tuition, state resident: full-time $4154; part-time $173 per credit hour. Tuition, nonresident: full-time $12,864; part-time $536 per credit hour. Required fees: $948; $58 per credit hour. Tuition and fees vary according to campus/location. *Financial support:* Federal Work-Study, institutionally sponsored loans, health care benefits, and unspecified assistantships available. Financial award application deadline: 3/15; financial award applicants required to submit FAFSA. *Unit head:* Dr. Jean Morrow, Chair, 620-341-5766, E-mail: jmorrow@emporia.edu. *Application contact:* Mary Sewell, Admissions Coordinator, 800-950-GRAD, Fax: 620-341-5909, E-mail: msewell@emporia.edu.

Emporia State University, School of Graduate Studies, The Teachers College, Department of Special Education and School Counseling, Program in Special Education, Emporia, KS 66801-5087. Offers behavior disorders (MS); gifted, talented, and creative (MS); interrelated special education (MS); learning disabilities (MS); mental retardation (MS). *Accreditation:* NCATE. Part-time programs available. *Students:* 1 (woman) full-time, 179 part-time (137 women); includes 6 minority (1 African American, 1 American Indian/Alaska Native, 3 Asian Americans or Pacific Islanders, 1 Hispanic American), 1 international. 23 applicants, 96% accepted, 22 enrolled. In 2009, 39 master's awarded. *Degree requirements:* For master's, comprehensive exam or thesis, practicum. *Entrance requirements:* For master's, GRE General Test or MAT, graduate essay exam, appropriate bachelor's degree, teacher certification, letters of recommendation. Additional exam requirements/recommendations for international students: Required—TOEFL (minimum score 520 paper-based; 133 computer-based; 68 iBT). *Application deadline:* For fall admission, 8/15 priority date for domestic students. Applications are processed on a rolling basis. Application fee: $30 ($75 for international students). Electronic applications accepted. *Expenses:* Tuition, state resident: full-time $4154; part-time $173 per credit hour. Tuition, nonresident: full-time $12,864; part-time $536 per credit hour. Required fees: $948; $58 per credit hour. Tuition and fees vary according to campus/location. *Financial support:* Federal Work-Study, institutionally sponsored loans, health care benefits, and unspecified assistantships available. Financial award application deadline: 3/15; financial award applicants required to submit FAFSA. *Unit head:* Dr. Jean Morrow, Interim Chair, 620-341-5317, E-mail: jmorrow@emporia.edu. *Application contact:* Mary Sewell, Admissions Coordinator, 800-950-GRAD, Fax: 620-341-5909, E-mail: msewell@emporia.edu.

Endicott College, Van Loan School of Graduate and Professional Studies, Program in Special Education, Beverly, MA 01915-2096. Offers initial and professional licensure (M Ed). Part-time and evening/weekend programs available. *Faculty:* 2 full-time (0 women), 21 part-time/adjunct (17 women). *Students:* 37 full-time (30 women), 57 part-time (50 women). Average age 32. 50 applicants, 100% accepted, 50 enrolled. In 2009, 3 master's awarded. *Degree requirements:* For master's, comprehensive exam, practicum. *Entrance requirements:* For master's, MAT or GRE, Massachusetts teaching certificate, letters of recommendation. Additional exam requirements/recommendations for international students: Required—TOEFL. *Application deadline:* Applications are processed on a rolling basis. Application fee: $50. *Expenses:* Tuition: Part-time $389 per credit. One-time fee: $1350. *Financial support:* Career-related internships or fieldwork, Federal Work-Study, and institutionally sponsored loans available. *Faculty research:* Literacy, parent education, inclusion, school reform, technology in education. *Unit head:* Dr. John D. MacLean, Director of Licensure Programs, 978-232-2408, E-mail: jmaclean@endicott.edu. *Application contact:* Dr. John D. MacLean, Director of Licensure Programs, 978-232-2408, E-mail: jmaclean@endicott.edu.

Fairfield University, Graduate School of Education and Allied Professions, Department of Psychological and Educational Consultation, Fairfield, CT 06824-5195. Offers applied psychology (MA), including foundations of advanced psychology, human services, industrial/organizational/personnel; media/educational technology (MA); school media specialist (MA); school psychology (MA, CAS); special education (MA, CAS). Part-time and evening/weekend programs available. *Degree requirements:* For master's, comprehensive exam, thesis optional. *Entrance requirements:* For master's, PRAXIS I (PPST), minimum QPA of 3.0, 2 recommendations, resume. Additional exam requirements/recommendations for international students: Required—TOEFL (minimum score 550 paper-based; 213 computer-based; 80 iBT). Electronic applications accepted. *Faculty research:* Child neuropsychology, disabilities, effect of pre-treatment orientation on treatment, autism, technology in business and classroom, collaboration with schools, communities and industry.

Fairleigh Dickinson University, Metropolitan Campus, University College: Arts, Sciences, and Professional Studies, Peter Sammartino School of Education, Program in Learning Disabilities, Teaneck, NJ 07666-1914. Offers MA. *Accreditation:* Teacher Education Accreditation Council. *Students:* 3 full-time (2 women), 17 part-time (all women). Average age 35. 7 applicants, 100% accepted, 5 enrolled. In 2009, 3 master's awarded. *Application deadline:* Applications are processed on a rolling basis. Application fee: $40. *Application contact:* Susan Brooman, University Director of Graduate Admissions, 201-692-2554, Fax: 201-692-2560, E-mail: globaleducation@fdu.edu.

Fairmont State University, Graduate Studies, Programs in Education, Fairmont, WV 26554. Offers education (MAT); leadership studies (M Ed); online learning (M Ed); professional studies (M Ed); reading (M Ed); special education (M Ed). *Accreditation:* NCATE.

Felician College, Program in Education, Lodi, NJ 07644-2117. Offers education (MA); educational supervision (MA, PMC); elementary education (MA); principal (PMC); principal/supervision dual certification (MA); school nurse/health (MA); school nurse/health educator (Certificate); special education (MA). *Accreditation:* Teacher Education Accreditation Council. Part-time and evening/weekend programs available. *Students:* 12 full-time (9 women), 93 part-time (83 women); includes 5 African Americans, 1 Asian American or Pacific Islander, 9 Hispanic Americans, 3 international. Average age 37. 18 applicants, 50% accepted, 9 enrolled. *Degree requirements:* For master's, project. *Entrance requirements:* For master's, MAT, minimum GPA of 3.0, 3 letters of recommendation. Additional exam requirements/recommendations for international students: Recommended—TOEFL (minimum score 550 paper-based; 213 computer-based). *Application deadline:* Applications are processed on a rolling basis. Application fee: $40. *Financial support:* Federal Work-Study available. *Unit head:* Dr. Rosemarie Liebmann, Associate Dean, 201-559-3537, E-mail: liebmannr@felician.edu. *Application contact:* Dr. Wendy Lin-Cook, Director of Adult and Graduate Admission, 201-559-6077, Fax: 201-559-6138, E-mail: adultandgraduate@felician.edu.

See Close-Up on page 709.

Ferris State University, College of Education and Human Services, School of Education, Big Rapids, MI 49307. Offers administration (MSCTE); curriculum and instruction (M Ed), including administration, elementary education, experiential education, philanthropic education, reading, secondary education, special education, subject matter option; education technology (MSCTE); instructor (MSCTE); post-secondary administration (MSCTE); training and development (MSCTE). Part-time and evening/weekend programs available. Postbaccalaureate distance learning degree programs offered. *Faculty:* 12 full-time (8 women), 11 part-time/adjunct (5 women). *Students:* 19 full-time (13 women), 185 part-time (122 women); includes 24 minority (20 African Americans, 1 Asian American or Pacific Islander, 3 Hispanic Americans), 1 international. Average age 36. 37 applicants, 32% accepted, 11 enrolled. In 2009, 73 master's awarded. *Degree requirements:* For master's, thesis, research paper. *Entrance requirements:* For master's, 2 years of work experience for vocational setting, minimum GPA of 2.75. Additional exam requirements/recommendations for international students: Recommended—TOEFL (minimum score 500 paper-based; 173 computer-based; 61 iBT). *Application deadline:* For fall admission, 7/1 priority date for domestic students; for spring admission, 11/1 priority date for domestic students. Applications are processed on a rolling basis. Application fee: $30. *Financial support:* Career-related internships or fieldwork and scholarships/grants available. Support available to part-time students. Financial award applicants required to submit FAFSA. *Faculty research:* Suicide prevention, reading, women in education, special needs, administration. *Unit head:* Dr. Liza Ing, Director, 231-591-5362, Fax: 231-591-2041. *Application contact:* Kimisue Worrall, Secretary, 231-591-5361, Fax: 231-591-2043.

Fitchburg State University, Division of Graduate and Continuing Education, Program in Special Education, Fitchburg, MA 01420-2697. Offers guided studies (M Ed); reading specialist (M Ed); teaching students with moderate disabilities (M Ed); teaching students with severe disabilities (M Ed). *Accreditation:* NCATE. Part-time and evening/weekend programs available. *Students:* 31 full-time (24 women), 130 part-time (106 women); includes 4 minority (1 Asian American or Pacific Islander, 3 Hispanic Americans). Average age 36. 40 applicants, 100% accepted, 31 enrolled. In 2009, 68 master's awarded. *Degree requirements:* For master's, internship. *Entrance requirements:* For master's, GRE General Test or MAT, letters of recommendation, resume. Additional exam requirements/recommendations for international students: Required—TOEFL (minimum score 550 paper-based; 213 computer-based; 79 iBT). *Application deadline:* Applications are processed on a rolling basis. Application fee: $25 ($50 for international students). *Expenses:* Tuition, area resident: Part-time $150 per credit. Tuition, state resident: part-time $150 per credit. Tuition, nonresident: part-time $150 per credit. Required fees: $120 per credit. *Financial support:* In 2009–10, research assistantships with partial tuition reimbursements (averaging $5,500 per year); Federal Work-Study, scholarships/grants, and unspecified assistantships also available. Support available to part-time students. Financial award application deadline: 3/1; financial award applicants required to submit FAFSA. *Unit head:* Dr. Anne Howard, Chair, 978-665-3309, Fax: 978-665-3658, E-mail: gce@fsc.edu. *Application contact:* Director of Admissions, 978-665-3144, Fax: 978-665-4540, E-mail: admissions@fsc.edu.

Florida Atlantic University, College of Education, Department of Exceptional Student Education, Boca Raton, FL 33431-0991. Offers M Ed, Ed D. *Accreditation:* NCATE. Part-time and evening/weekend programs available. *Faculty:* 14 full-time (8 women), 13 part-time/adjunct (9 women). *Students:* 7 full-time (5 women), 26 part-time (23 women); includes 4 minority (1 Asian American or Pacific Islander, 3 Hispanic Americans). Average age 35. 29 applicants, 38% accepted, 4 enrolled. In 2009, 5 master's, 2 doctorates awarded. *Degree requirements:* For

Special Education

Florida Atlantic University (continued)

master's, thesis optional, internship; for doctorate, comprehensive exam, thesis/dissertation, internship. *Entrance requirements:* For master's, GRE General Test, minimum GPA of 3.0 during previous 2 years; for doctorate, GRE General Test, 3 years teaching experience, interview. *Application deadline:* For fall admission, 7/1 for domestic students, 2/15 for international students; for spring admission, 11/1 for domestic students, 7/15 for international students. Applications are processed on a rolling basis. Application fee: $30. Electronic applications accepted. *Expenses:* Tuition, state resident: full-time $7055; part-time $293.94 per credit hour. Tuition, nonresident: full-time $22,096; part-time $920.66 per credit hour. *Financial support:* Fellowships with tuition reimbursements, research assistantships with tuition reimbursements, teaching assistantships with partial tuition reimbursements, career-related internships or fieldwork, Federal Work-Study, scholarships/grants, tuition waivers (partial), and unspecified assistantships available. Support available to part-time students. Financial award applicants required to submit FAFSA. *Faculty research:* Instructional design, assessment, educational reform, behavioral research, social integration. *Unit head:* Dr. Michael P. Brady, Chairperson, 561-297-3280, Fax: 561-297-2507, E-mail: mbrady@fau.edu. *Application contact:* Dr. Eliah Watlington, Associate Dean, 561-296-8520, Fax: 261-297-2991, E-mail: ewatling@fau.edu.

Florida Gulf Coast University, College of Education, Program in Special Education, Fort Myers, FL 33965-6565. Offers behavior disorders (MA); mental retardation (MA); specific learning disabilities (MA); varying exceptionalities (MA). Part-time and evening/weekend programs available. *Faculty:* 31 full-time (24 women), 39 part-time/adjunct (28 women). *Students:* 12 full-time (10 women), 11 part-time (all women); includes 3 minority (1 African American, 1 American Indian/Alaska Native, 1 Hispanic American). Average age 30. 19 applicants, 84% accepted, 13 enrolled. In 2009, 6 master's awarded. *Degree requirements:* For master's, thesis or alternative. *Entrance requirements:* For master's, GRE General Test, MAT, minimum GPA of 3.0. Additional exam requirements/recommendations for international students: Required—TOEFL (minimum score 550 paper-based; 213 computer-based). *Application deadline:* For fall admission, 7/1 priority date for domestic students; for spring admission, 10/15 for domestic students. Applications are processed on a rolling basis. Application fee: $30. Electronic applications accepted. *Faculty research:* Inclusion, interacting with families, alternative certification. *Unit head:* Dr. Patricia Wachholz, Head, 239-590-7808, Fax: 239-590-7801, E-mail: pwachhol@fgcu.edu. *Application contact:* Dr. Patricia Wachholz, Head, 239-590-7808, Fax: 239-590-7801, E-mail: pwachhol@fgcu.edu.

Florida International University, College of Education, Department of Curriculum and Instruction, Miami, FL 33199. Offers art education (MAT, MS, Ed D); curriculum and instruction (Ed S); curriculum development (MS); curriculum studies (PhD); early childhood education (MS, Ed D); elementary education (MS, Ed D); English education (MAT, MS, Ed D); foreign language education—teaching English to speakers of other languages (TESOL) (Certificate), including foreign language education; foreign language education- teaching English to speakers of other languages (TESOL) (MS), including teaching English; French education—initial teacher preparation (MAT); international and intercultural development education (Ed D); international and intercultural developmental education (MS); language, literacy and culture (PhD); learning technologies (MS, Ed D, PhD); mathematics education (MAT, MS, Ed D, PhD); modern language education/bilingual education (MS, Ed D); physical education (MS); reading education (MS, Ed D); science education (MAT, MS, Ed D, PhD); social studies education (MAT, MS, Ed D); Spanish education—initial teacher preparation (MAT); special education (MS). Part-time and evening/weekend programs available. *Degree requirements:* For doctorate, comprehensive exam, thesis/dissertation. *Entrance requirements:* For master's, GRE General Test, Florida General Knowledge Test or Florida College Level Academic Skills Test; for doctorate and other advanced degree, GRE General Test. Additional exam requirements/recommendations for international students: Required—TOEFL (minimum score 550 paper-based; 213 computer-based; 80 iBT), IELTS (minimum score 6.3). Electronic applications accepted. *Expenses:* Tuition, state resident: full-time $8008; part-time $4004 per year. Tuition, nonresident: full-time $20,104; part-time $10,052 per year. Required fees: $298; $149 per term.

Florida International University, College of Education, Department of Educational and Psychological Studies, Program in Exceptional Student Education, Miami, FL 33199. Offers MS, Ed D. *Accreditation:* NCATE. Part-time and evening/weekend programs available. *Degree requirements:* For doctorate, comprehensive exam, thesis/dissertation, qualifying exams. *Entrance requirements:* For doctorate, GRE General Test, interview. Additional exam requirements/recommendations for international students: Required—TOEFL (minimum score 550 paper-based; 213 computer-based; 80 iBT), IELTS (minimum score 6.3). Electronic applications accepted. *Expenses:* Tuition, state resident: full-time $8008; part-time $4004 per year. Tuition, nonresident: full-time $20,104; part-time $10,052 per year. Required fees: $298; $149 per term. *Faculty research:* Handicapped adolescents and young adults, learning disabilities, mild disabilities, autism.

Florida International University, College of Education, Department of Educational and Psychological Studies, Program in Special Education, Miami, FL 33199. Offers MS. *Accreditation:* NCATE. Part-time and evening/weekend programs available. *Entrance requirements:* For master's, minimum GPA of 3.0, interview. Additional exam requirements/recommendations for international students: Required—TOEFL (minimum score 550 paper-based; 213 computer-based; 80 iBT), IELTS (minimum score 6.3). Electronic applications accepted. *Expenses:* Tuition, state resident: full-time $8008; part-time $4004 per year. Tuition, nonresident: full-time $20,104; part-time $10,052 per year. Required fees: $298; $149 per term. *Faculty research:* Reading, brain disorders, language arts.

Florida Memorial University, School of Education, Miami-Dade, FL 33054. Offers elementary education (MS); exceptional student education (MS); reading (MS). *Degree requirements:* For master's, comprehensive exam or thesis, field and clinical experiences, exit exam. *Entrance requirements:* For master's, GRE, CLAST, PRAXIS I, baccalaureate or graduate degree with minimum GPA of 3.0 in last 60 hours, 3 recommendations.

Florida State University, The Graduate School, College of Education, School of Teacher Education, Program in Special Education, Tallahassee, FL 32306. Offers emotional disturbance/learning disabilities (MS); mental retardation (MS); rehabilitation counseling (MS, PhD, Ed S); special education (PhD, Ed S); visual disabilities (MS). *Accreditation:* CORE. *Faculty:* 5 full-time (4 women), 1 (woman) part-time/adjunct. *Students:* 45 full-time (39 women), 108 part-time (103 women); includes 38 minority (27 African Americans, 6 Asian Americans or Pacific Islanders, 5 Hispanic Americans). 111 applicants, 67% accepted, 44 enrolled. In 2009, 37 master's, 3 doctorates, 1 other advanced degree awarded. *Degree requirements:* For master's, comprehensive exam, thesis optional; for doctorate, comprehensive exam, thesis/dissertation; for Ed S, comprehensive exam. *Entrance requirements:* For master's, doctorate, and Ed S, GRE General Test, minimum GPA of 3.0. Additional exam requirements/recommendations for international students: Required—TOEFL (minimum score 550 paper-based; 213 computer-based; 80 iBT); Recommended—TWE. *Application deadline:* For fall admission, 7/1 for domestic students; for spring admission, 11/1 for domestic students. Applications are processed on a rolling basis. Application fee: $20. *Expenses:* Tuition, state resident: full-time $7413. Tuition, nonresident: full-time $22,567. *Financial support:* In 2009–10, 5 research assistantships with full and partial tuition reimbursements, 7 teaching assistantships with full and partial tuition reimbursements were awarded; fellowships with full and partial tuition reimbursements, career-related internships or fieldwork and traineeships also available. Financial award applicants required to submit FAFSA. *Unit head:* Dr. Mary Frances Hanline, Chair, 850-644-4880, Fax: 850-644-8715, E-mail: hanline@mail.coe.fsu.edu. *Application contact:* Timolin Lynette Bodison-Baker, Program Assistant, 850-644-5458, Fax: 850-644-7736, E-mail: bodison@coe.fsu.edu.

Fontbonne University, Graduate Programs, Department of Communication Disorders and Deaf Education, Studies in Early Intervention in Deaf Education, St. Louis, MO 63105-3098. Offers MA. *Faculty:* 5 full-time (4 women), 4 part-time/adjunct (all women). *Students:* 9 full-time (all women), 2 part-time (both women), 2 international. Average age 28. In 2009, 8 master's

awarded. *Entrance requirements:* For master's, minimum GPA of 3.0. *Application deadline:* For fall admission, 2/1 for domestic students. Application fee: $25. *Expenses:* Tuition: Part-time $562 per credit hour. *Financial support:* Application deadline: 4/1. *Unit head:* Dr. Gale Rice, Chair, 314-889-1407, Fax: 314-719-8016, E-mail: grice@fontbonne.edu. *Application contact:* Dr. Susan Lenihan, Director, 314-889-1461, Fax: 314-719-8016, E-mail: slenihan@fontbonne.edu.

Fordham University, Graduate School of Education, Division of Curriculum and Teaching, New York, NY 10023. Offers adult education (MS, MSE); bilingual teacher education (MSE); curriculum and teaching (MSE); early childhood education (MSE); elementary education (MST); language, literacy, and learning (PhD); reading education (MSE, Adv C); secondary education (MAT, MSE); special education (MSE, Adv C); teaching English as a second language (MSE). *Accreditation:* NCATE. *Degree requirements:* For doctorate, thesis/dissertation; for Adv C, thesis. *Entrance requirements:* For doctorate, MAT, GRE General Test.

Fort Hays State University, Graduate School, College of Education and Technology, Department of Special Education, Hays, KS 67601-4099. Offers MS. *Accreditation:* NCATE. *Degree requirements:* For master's, comprehensive exam, thesis optional. *Entrance requirements:* Additional exam requirements/recommendations for international students: Required—TOEFL (minimum score 550 paper-based; 213 computer-based). Electronic applications accepted. *Faculty research:* Severe behavior disorders, early childhood language, multicultural speech.

Framingham State University, Division of Graduate and Continuing Education, Program in Special Education, Framingham, MA 01701-9101. Offers M Ed. Part-time and evening/weekend programs available. *Entrance requirements:* For master's, MAT, interview.

Francis Marion University, Graduate Programs, School of Education, Florence, SC 29502-0547. Offers early childhood education (M Ed); elementary education (M Ed); learning disabilities (M Ed, MAT); remedial education (M Ed); secondary education (M Ed). *Accreditation:* NCATE. Part-time programs available. *Faculty:* 20 full-time (15 women). *Students:* 8 full-time (7 women), 107 part-time (90 women); includes 33 minority (all African Americans), 1 international. Average age 34. 221 applicants, 94% accepted, 94 enrolled. In 2009, 57 degrees awarded. *Degree requirements:* For master's, comprehensive exam. *Entrance requirements:* For master's, GRE General Test, MAT, NTE, or PRAXIS II. *Application deadline:* For fall admission, 3/15 priority date for domestic students; for spring admission, 10/15 priority date for domestic students. Applications are processed on a rolling basis. Application fee: $30. *Expenses:* Tuition, state resident: full-time $8345; part-time $417.25 per semester hour. Tuition, nonresident: full-time $16,690; part-time $814.50 per semester hour. Required fees: $335; $12.25 per semester hour. $30 per semester. *Financial support:* In 2009–10, 4 research assistantships (averaging $6,000 per year) were awarded; unspecified assistantships also available. Support available to part-time students. Financial award application deadline: 3/1; financial award applicants required to submit FAFSA. *Faculty research:* Identification and alternate assessment of at-risk students. *Unit head:* Dr. James R. Faulkenberry, Dean, 843-661-1460, Fax: 843-661-4647. *Application contact:* Dr. James R. Faulkenberry, Dean, 843-661-1460, Fax: 843-661-4647.

Freed-Hardeman University, Program in Education, Henderson, TN 38340-2399. Offers curriculum and instruction (M Ed); school counseling (M Ed), including administration and supervision, special education; school leadership (Ed S). *Accreditation:* NCATE. Part-time and evening/weekend programs available. *Degree requirements:* For master's, comprehensive exam, thesis optional; for Ed S, thesis. *Entrance requirements:* For master's, GRE General Test or NTE; for Ed S, 3 years of teaching experience. Additional exam requirements/recommendations for international students: Required—TOEFL (minimum score 500 paper-based; 173 computer-based).

Fresno Pacific University, Graduate Programs, School of Education, Division of Special Education, Fresno, CA 93702-4709. Offers mild/moderate (MA Ed); moderate/severe (MA Ed); physical and health impairments (MA Ed). Part-time and evening/weekend programs available. *Degree requirements:* For master's, thesis or alternative. *Entrance requirements:* Additional exam requirements/recommendations for international students: Required—TOEFL (minimum score 550 paper-based; 213 computer-based).

Frostburg State University, Graduate School, College of Education, Department of Educational Professions, Program in Special Education, Frostburg, MD 21532-1099. Offers M Ed. *Accreditation:* NCATE. Part-time and evening/weekend programs available. *Faculty:* 3. *Students:* 3 full-time (all women), 33 part-time (28 women); includes 1 minority (American Indian/Alaska Native). Average age 34. 17 applicants, 82% accepted, 11 enrolled. In 2009, 14 master's awarded. *Degree requirements:* For master's, thesis or alternative, PRAXIS II (special education section). *Entrance requirements:* For master's, teaching certificate. Additional exam requirements/recommendations for international students: Required—TOEFL. *Application deadline:* For fall admission, 7/15 priority date for domestic students. Applications are processed on a rolling basis. Application fee: $30. Electronic applications accepted. *Expenses:* Tuition, state resident: full-time $5706; part-time $317 per credit hour. Tuition, nonresident: full-time $6948; part-time $386 per credit hour. Required fees: $1476; $82 per credit hour. $11 per term. One-time fee: $30 full-time. *Financial support:* In 2009–10, 1 research assistantship with full tuition reimbursement (averaging $5,000 per year) was awarded. Financial award application deadline: 4/1; financial award applicants required to submit FAFSA. *Unit head:* Oma Gail Simmons, Coordinator, 301-687-4244, E-mail: osimmons@frostburg.edu. *Application contact:* Vickie Mazer, Director, Graduate Services, 301-687-7053, Fax: 301-687-4597, E-mail: vmmazer@frostburg.edu.

Furman University, Graduate Division, Department of Education, Greenville, SC 29613. Offers curriculum and instruction (MA); early childhood education (MA); English as a second language (MA); literacy (MA); school leadership (MA); special education (MA). *Accreditation:* NCATE. Part-time programs available. Postbaccalaureate distance learning degree programs offered (minimal on-campus study). *Faculty:* 14 full-time (8 women), 10 part-time/adjunct (6 women). *Students:* 114 part-time (93 women); includes 13 minority (10 African Americans, 3 Asian Americans or Pacific Islanders). Average age 29. 24 applicants, 100% accepted, 23 enrolled. In 2009, 71 master's awarded. *Degree requirements:* For master's, comprehensive exam (for some programs), thesis or alternative. *Entrance requirements:* For master's, PRAXIS II. *Application deadline:* For fall admission, 8/1 priority date for domestic students, 7/15 priority date for international students; for spring admission, 12/1 priority date for domestic and international students. Applications are processed on a rolling basis. Application fee: $50. *Financial support:* In 2009–10, 43 students received support; fellowships, scholarships/grants available. Financial award application deadline: 5/15; financial award applicants required to submit FAFSA. *Faculty research:* Literacy, pedagogy and practice, social justice, advanced leadership, achievement in high poverty schools. *Unit head:* Dr. Nelly Hecker, Head, 864-294-3385. *Application contact:* Helen Reynolds, Department Assistant, 864-294-2213, Fax: 864-294-3579, E-mail: helen.reynolds@furman.edu.

Gallaudet University, The Graduate School, Department of Administration and Supervision, Washington, DC 20002-3625. Offers administration (MS); administration and supervision (PhD); change leadership on deaf education (Ed S); leadership (Certificate); management (Certificate); special education administration (PhD). *Degree requirements:* For master's, thesis optional; for doctorate, 2 foreign languages, thesis/dissertation; for other advanced degree, 2 foreign languages, thesis (for some programs). *Entrance requirements:* For master's, GRE General Test or MAT; for doctorate, GRE General Test or MAT, interview. Electronic applications accepted.

Gallaudet University, The Graduate School, Department of Education, Washington, DC 20002-3625. Offers early childhood education (MA, Ed S); education of deaf and hard of hearing students and multihandicapped deaf and hard of hearing students (MA, Ed S); elementary education (MA, Ed S); individualized program of study (PhD); parent/infant specialty

(MA, Ed S); secondary education (MA, Ed S). *Accreditation:* NCATE. *Degree requirements:* For master's, thesis optional; for doctorate, thesis/dissertation. *Entrance requirements:* For doctorate, GRE General Test or MAT, interview. Electronic applications accepted.

Gallaudet University, The Graduate School, Department of Educational Foundations and Research, Washington, DC 20002-3625. Offers international development (MA, Certificate). *Accreditation:* NCATE. *Degree requirements:* For Certificate, thesis optional. *Entrance requirements:* For degree, GRE General Test or MAT. Electronic applications accepted.

Geneva College, Program in Special Education, Beaver Falls, PA 15010-3599. Offers M Ed. Part-time and evening/weekend programs available. *Faculty:* 4 full-time (all women). *Students:* 4 full-time (all women), 8 part-time (7 women); includes 1 minority (Hispanic American). 4 applicants, 100% accepted, 4 enrolled. In 2009, 5 master's awarded. *Entrance requirements:* For master's, resume, letters of recommendation, proof of certification. Additional exam requirements/recommendations for international students: Required—TOEFL. *Application deadline:* For fall admission, 3/1 priority date for domestic students; for spring admission, 11/1 priority date for domestic students. Applications are processed on a rolling basis. Application fee: $0. Electronic applications accepted. *Expenses:* Tuition: Full-time $11,250; part-time $625 per credit. Tuition and fees vary according to program. *Financial support:* Applicants required to submit FAFSA. *Unit head:* Dr. Karen Schmalz, Program Head, 724-847-6125, E-mail: kschmalz@geneva.edu. *Application contact:* Lori Hartge, Graduate Student Support Specialist, 724-847-6571, E-mail: speced@geneva.edu.

George Mason University, College of Education and Human Development, Programs in Curriculum and Instruction, Fairfax, VA 22030. Offers curriculum and instruction (M Ed); special education (M Ed). Part-time and evening/weekend programs available. *Faculty:* 88 full-time (64 women), 120 part-time/adjunct (93 women). *Students:* 190 full-time (150 women), 836 part-time (694 women); includes 100 minority (25 African Americans, 1 American Indian/Alaska Native, 29 Asian Americans or Pacific Islanders, 45 Hispanic Americans), 50 international. Average age 31. 627 applicants, 76% accepted, 389 enrolled. In 2009, 383 master's awarded. *Degree requirements:* For master's, comprehensive exam, thesis (for some programs). *Entrance requirements:* For master's, PRAXIS I, PRAXIS II, Virginia Communication and Literacy Assessment Test (VCLA), minimum GPA of 3.0 in last 60 hours, licensed as teacher or educational administrator, 3 recommendation letters, interview. Additional exam requirements/recommendations for international students: Required—TOEFL. *Application deadline:* For fall admission, 5/1 for domestic students; for spring admission, 11/1 for domestic students. Applications are processed on a rolling basis. Application fee: $75. Electronic applications accepted. *Expenses:* Tuition, state resident: full-time $7568; part-time $315.33 per credit hour. Tuition, nonresident: full-time $21,704; part-time $904.33 per credit hour. Required fees: $2184; $91 per credit hour. *Financial support:* In 2009–10, 4 students received support, including 3 research assistantships with full and partial tuition reimbursements available (averaging $8,940 per year), 1 teaching assistantship with full and partial tuition reimbursement available (averaging $2,080 per year); Federal Work-Study, scholarships/grants, unspecified assistantships, and health care benefits (full-time research or teaching assistantship recipients) also available. Support available to part-time students. Financial award application deadline: 3/1; financial award applicants required to submit FAFSA. *Unit head:* Martin E. Ford, Acting Dean, College of Education and Human Development, 703-993-2004, E-mail: mford@gmu.edu. *Application contact:* Information Contact.

Georgetown College, Department of Education, Georgetown, KY 40324-1696. Offers reading and writing (MA Ed); special education (MA Ed); teaching (MA Ed). *Accreditation:* NCATE. Part-time programs available. *Degree requirements:* For master's, portfolio. *Entrance requirements:* For master's, teaching certificate, minimum GPA of 2.7 or GRE General Test.

The George Washington University, Graduate School of Education and Human Development, Department of Teacher Preparation and Special Education, Program in Early Childhood Special Education, Washington, DC 20052. Offers MA Ed. *Accreditation:* NCATE. *Students:* 12 full-time (all women), 38 part-time (31 women); includes 17 minority (10 African Americans, 4 Asian Americans or Pacific Islanders, 3 Hispanic Americans), 2 international. Average age 29. 28 applicants, 93% accepted, 16 enrolled. In 2009, 25 master's awarded. *Degree requirements:* For master's, comprehensive exam. *Entrance requirements:* For master's, GRE General Test or MAT, minimum GPA of 2.75. *Application deadline:* For fall admission, 1/15 priority date for domestic students; for spring admission, 10/1 for domestic students. Applications are processed on a rolling basis. Application fee: $60. *Financial support:* In 2009–10, 19 students received support; fellowships, career-related internships or fieldwork, Federal Work-Study, and tuition waivers (full) available. Financial award application deadline: 1/15; financial award applicants required to submit FAFSA. *Faculty research:* Computer-assisted instruction and learning, disabled learner assessment of preschool, handicapped children. *Unit head:* Dr. Marian H. Jarrett, Faculty Coordinator, 202-994-1509, E-mail: mjarrett@gwu.edu. *Application contact:* Sarah Lang, Director of Graduate Admissions, 202-994-1447, Fax: 202-994-7207, E-mail: slang@gwu.edu.

The George Washington University, Graduate School of Education and Human Development, Department of Teacher Preparation and Special Education, Program in Special Education, Washington, DC 20052. Offers Ed D, Ed S. *Accreditation:* NCATE. *Students:* 19 full-time (17 women), 47 part-time (41 women); includes 23 minority (17 African Americans, 3 Asian Americans or Pacific Islanders, 3 Hispanic Americans), 2 international. Average age 39. 45 applicants, 84% accepted, 22 enrolled. In 2009, 7 doctorates, 12 other advanced degrees awarded. *Degree requirements:* For doctorate, comprehensive exam, thesis/dissertation; for Ed S, comprehensive exam. *Entrance requirements:* For doctorate and Ed S, GRE General Test or MAT, interview, minimum GPA of 3.3. *Application deadline:* For fall admission, 1/15 priority date for domestic students; for spring admission, 10/1 for domestic students. Applications are processed on a rolling basis. Application fee: $60. *Financial support:* In 2009–10, 46 students received support; fellowships, research assistantships, career-related internships or fieldwork, Federal Work-Study, and tuition waivers (partial) available. Financial award application deadline: 1/15; financial award applicants required to submit FAFSA. *Unit head:* Dr. Carol Kochhar, Faculty Coordinator, 202-994-6170, E-mail: kochhar@gwu.edu. *Application contact:* Sarah Lang, Director of Graduate Admissions, 202-994-1447, Fax: 202-994-7207, E-mail: slang@gwu.edu.

The George Washington University, Graduate School of Education and Human Development, Department of Teacher Preparation and Special Education, Program in Special Education for Children with Emotional and Behavioral Disabilities, Washington, DC 20052. Offers MA Ed. *Accreditation:* NCATE. *Students:* 29 full-time (22 women), 16 part-time (8 women); includes 19 minority (14 African Americans, 2 American Indian/Alaska Native, 2 Asian Americans or Pacific Islanders, 1 Hispanic American), 1 international. Average age 30. 44 applicants, 89% accepted, 32 enrolled. In 2009, 33 master's awarded. *Degree requirements:* For master's, comprehensive exam. *Entrance requirements:* For master's, GRE General Test or MAT, interview, minimum GPA of 2.75. *Application deadline:* For fall admission, 1/15 priority date for domestic students; for spring admission, 10/1 for domestic students. Applications are processed on a rolling basis. Application fee: $60. *Financial support:* In 2009–10, 19 students received support; fellowships, career-related internships or fieldwork and Federal Work-Study available. Financial award application deadline: 1/15; financial award applicants required to submit FAFSA. *Faculty research:* Action research on the act of teaching emotionally disturbed students, teacher training. *Unit head:* Elisabeth Rice, Program Coordinator, 202-994-1535, E-mail: ehess@gwu.edu. *Application contact:* Sarah Lang, Director of Admission, 202-994-1447, Fax: 202-994-7207, E-mail: slang@gwu.edu.

The George Washington University, Graduate School of Education and Human Development, Department of Teacher Preparation and Special Education, Program in Transition Special Education, Washington, DC 20052. Offers MA Ed, Certificate. *Accreditation:* NCATE. Evening/weekend programs available. *Students:* 21 full-time (19 women), 90 part-time (68 women); includes 41 minority (28 African Americans, 3 American Indian/Alaska Native, 5 Asian Americans or Pacific Islanders, 5 Hispanic Americans), 5 international. Average age 35. 20 applicants, 100% accepted, 9 enrolled. In 2009, 7 master's, 19 Certificates awarded. *Degree requirements:* For master's, comprehensive exam. *Entrance requirements:* For master's, GRE General Test or MAT, interview, minimum GPA of 2.75. *Application deadline:* For fall admission, 1/15 priority date for domestic students; for spring admission, 10/1 for domestic students. Applications are processed on a rolling basis. Application fee: $60. *Financial support:* In 2009–10, 21 students received support; fellowships, research assistantships, career-related internships or fieldwork, Federal Work-Study, tuition waivers (full and partial), and stipends available. Financial award application deadline: 1/15. *Faculty research:* Computer applications for transition, transition follow-up research, curriculum-based vocational assessment, traumatic brain injury. *Unit head:* Dr. Lynda West, Coordinator, 202-994-1533, E-mail: lwest@gwu.edu. *Application contact:* Sarah Lang, Director of Graduate Admissions, 202-994-1447, Fax: 202-994-7207, E-mail: slang@gwu.edu.

Georgia College & State University, Graduate School, The John H. Lounsbury College of Education, Department of Special Education and Educational Leadership, Program in Special Education, Milledgeville, GA 31061. Offers M Ed, MAT, Ed S. *Accreditation:* NCATE. Part-time and evening/weekend programs available. *Students:* 36 full-time (29 women), 2 part-time (both women); includes 13 minority (all African Americans). Average age 35. 6 applicants, 100% accepted, 0 enrolled. In 2009, 14 master's awarded. *Degree requirements:* For master's, comprehensive exam. *Entrance requirements:* For master's, on-site writing exam; for Ed S, on-site writing exam, 2 years of teaching experience, minimum GPA of 3.25. Additional exam requirements/recommendations for international students: Required—TOEFL (minimum score 550 paper-based; 213 computer-based; 79 iBT). *Application deadline:* Applications are processed on a rolling basis. Application fee: $4. Electronic applications accepted. *Expenses:* Tuition, area resident: Part-time $241 per credit hour. Tuition, state resident: full-time $4338. Tuition, nonresident: full-time $17,352; part-time $964 per credit hour. Required fees: $609 per semester. Tuition and fees vary according to course load and campus/location. *Financial support:* In 2009–10, 2 research assistantships with full tuition reimbursements were awarded; career-related internships or fieldwork, Federal Work-Study, and unspecified assistantships also available. Support available to part-time students. *Unit head:* Dr. Craig Smith, Chair, 478-445-4577, E-mail: craig.smith@gcsu.edu. *Application contact:* Shanda Brand, Graduate Coordinator, 478-445-1383, E-mail: shanda.brand@gcsu.edu.

Georgia Southern University, Jack N. Averitt College of Graduate Studies, College of Education, Department of Teaching and Learning, Program in Special Education, Statesboro, GA 30460. Offers M Ed, MAT. *Accreditation:* NCATE. Part-time and evening/weekend programs available. *Students:* 10 full-time (7 women), 2 part-time (both women), 1 international. Average age 31. 3 applicants, 100% accepted, 2 enrolled. In 2009, 9 master's awarded. *Degree requirements:* For master's, portfolio, transition point assessments, exit assessment. *Entrance requirements:* For master's, GRE General Test or MAT; GACE Special Skills and Content Assessments (MAT), minimum cumulative GPA of 2.5. Additional exam requirements/recommendations for international students: Required—TOEFL (minimum score 550 paper-based; 213 computer-based; 80 iBT). *Application deadline:* For fall admission, 3/1 priority date for domestic and international students; for spring admission, 10/1 priority date for domestic students, 10/1 for international students. Applications are processed on a rolling basis. Application fee: $50. Electronic applications accepted. *Expenses:* Tuition, state resident: full-time $5040; part-time $210 per credit hour. Tuition, nonresident: full-time $20,136; part-time $839 per credit hour. Required fees: $1644. *Financial support:* In 2009–10, 10 students received support, including research assistantships with partial tuition reimbursements available (averaging $7,200 per year), teaching assistantships with partial tuition reimbursements available (averaging $7,200 per year); career-related internships or fieldwork, Federal Work-Study, scholarships/grants, tuition waivers (partial), and unspecified assistantships also available. Support available to part-time students. Financial award application deadline: 4/15; financial award applicants required to submit FAFSA. *Faculty research:* Learning disorders, behavior disorders, education of the mentally retarded. *Unit head:* Dr. Ronnie Sheppard, Department Chair, 912-478-5203, Fax: 912-478-0026, E-mail: sheppard@georgiasouthern.edu. *Application contact:* Dr. Charles Ziglar, Coordinator for Graduate Student Recruitment, 912-478-5635, Fax: 912-478-0740, E-mail: gradadmissions@georgiasouthern.edu.

Georgia Southwestern State University, Graduate Studies, School of Education, Americus, GA 31709-4693. Offers early childhood education (M Ed, Ed S); health and physical education (M Ed); middle grades education (M Ed, Ed S); reading (M Ed); secondary education (M Ed); special education (M Ed). *Accreditation:* NCATE. *Degree requirements:* For master's, comprehensive exam. *Entrance requirements:* For master's, GRE General Test or MAT, minimum GPA of 2.5; for Ed S, GRE General Test or MAT, minimum graduate GPA of 3.25, M Ed from accredited college or university, 3 years teaching experience. Electronic applications accepted.

Georgia State University, College of Education, Department of Educational Psychology and Special Education, Program in Behavior and Learning Disabilities, Atlanta, GA 30302-3083. Offers M Ed. *Accreditation:* NCATE. *Entrance requirements:* For master's, GRE General Test, minimum GPA of 2.5. *Faculty research:* Inclusion, behavior management, basic teaching strategies.

Georgia State University, College of Education, Department of Educational Psychology and Special Education, Program in Communication Disorders, Atlanta, GA 30302-3083. Offers M Ed. *Accreditation:* ASHA; NCATE. *Degree requirements:* For master's, portfolio. *Entrance requirements:* For master's, GRE General Test, minimum GPA of 2.5, 2 letters of recommendation. *Faculty research:* Language development, adult language disorders, voice disorders.

Georgia State University, College of Education, Department of Educational Psychology and Special Education, Program in Education of Students with Exceptionalities, Atlanta, GA 30302-3083. Offers PhD. *Accreditation:* NCATE. *Degree requirements:* For doctorate, comprehensive exam, thesis/dissertation. *Entrance requirements:* For doctorate, GRE General Test, minimum GPA of 3.3. *Faculty research:* Literacy, behavior management, juvenile justice.

Gonzaga University, School of Education, Program in Special Education, Spokane, WA 99258. Offers MES. *Accreditation:* NCATE. *Faculty:* 4 full-time (1 woman), 3 part-time/adjunct (all women). *Students:* 5 full-time (all women), 9 part-time (7 women). Average age 34. In 2009, 3 master's awarded. *Degree requirements:* For master's, comprehensive exam. *Entrance requirements:* For master's, GRE General Test or MAT, minimum B average in undergraduate course work. Additional exam requirements/recommendations for international students: Required—TOEFL. *Application deadline:* For fall admission, 7/20 priority date for domestic students; for spring admission, 11/1 for domestic students. Applications are processed on a rolling basis. Application fee: $50. Tuition and fees vary according to course level, course load, degree level, campus/location and program. *Financial support:* Teaching assistantships available. Support available to part-time students. Financial award application deadline: 3/1. *Unit head:* Dr. Thomas F. McLaughlin, Chairman, 509-328-4220 Ext. 3508. *Application contact:* Julie McCulloh, Dean of Admissions, 509-323-6592, Fax: 509-323-5780, E-mail: mcculloh@gu.gonzaga.edu.

Governors State University, College of Education, Program in Multi-Categorical Special Education, University Park, IL 60466-0975. Offers MA. *Accreditation:* NCATE. Part-time and evening/weekend programs available. *Degree requirements:* For master's, comprehensive exam, practicum. *Entrance requirements:* For master's, minimum GPA of 2.75 in last 60 hours of undergraduate course work, minimum graduate GPA of 3.0.

Graceland University, Gleazer School of Education, Lamoni, IA 50140. Offers collaborative learning and teaching (M Ed); differentiated instruction (M Ed); instructional leadership (M Ed); mild/moderate special education (M Ed); quality schools (M Ed); technology integration (M Ed). *Accreditation:* NCATE. Part-time and evening/weekend programs available. Postbaccalaureate

Special Education

Graceland University (continued)
distance learning degree programs offered (no on-campus study). *Faculty:* 8 full-time (7 women), 25 part-time/adjunct (14 women). *Students:* 505 full-time (406 women); includes 18 minority (6 African Americans, 3 American Indian/Alaska Native, 4 Asian Americans or Pacific Islanders, 5 Hispanic Americans), 7 international. Average age 36. 167 applicants, 100% accepted, 160 enrolled. In 2009, 277 master's awarded. *Degree requirements:* For master's, action research project. *Entrance requirements:* For master's, minimum GPA of 3.0, teaching certificate, current teaching contract. *Application deadline:* For fall admission, 7/15 for domestic students; for winter admission, 10/15 for domestic students; for spring admission, 1/15 priority date for domestic students. Application fee: $50. Electronic applications accepted. *Expenses:* Tuition: Full-time $7110; part-time $395 per semester hour. Required fees: $1110; $185 per course. *Financial support:* In 2009–10, 437 students received support. Institutionally sponsored loans and scholarships/grants available. Financial award application deadline: 12/15; financial award applicants required to submit FAFSA. *Unit head:* Dr. Nancy Halferty, Dean, 641-784-5000 Ext. 5251, E-mail: halferty@graceland.edu. *Application contact:* Cathy Porter, Program Consultant, 816-833-0524 Ext. 4516, E-mail: cgporter@graceland.edu.

Grand Canyon University, College of Education, Phoenix, AZ 85017-1097. Offers curriculum and instruction (M Ed); education administration (M Ed); elementary education (M Ed); organizational leadership (Ed D); secondary education (M Ed); special education (M Ed); teaching (MA). Part-time and evening/weekend programs available. Postbaccalaureate distance learning degree programs offered (no on-campus study). *Degree requirements:* For master's, publishable research paper (M Ed), e-portfolio. *Entrance requirements:* Additional exam requirements/recommendations for international students: Required—TOEFL (minimum score 550 paper-based; 213 computer-based; 79 iBT), IELTS (minimum score 6). Electronic applications accepted.

Grand Valley State University, College of Education, Program in Special Education, Allendale, MI 49401-9403. Offers cognitive impairment (M Ed); early childhood developmental delay (M Ed); emotional impairment (M Ed); learning disabilities (M Ed); special education endorsements (M Ed). *Accreditation:* NCATE. Part-time and evening/weekend programs available. *Faculty:* 10 full-time (6 women), 6 part-time/adjunct (3 women). *Students:* 19 full-time (all women), 234 part-time (206 women); includes 17 minority (10 African Americans, 1 American Indian/Alaska Native, 4 Asian Americans or Pacific Islanders, 2 Hispanic Americans). Average age 35. 42 applicants, 100% accepted, 32 enrolled. In 2009, 63 master's awarded. *Degree requirements:* For master's, thesis. *Entrance requirements:* For master's, GRE General Test or minimum GPA of 3.0. Additional exam requirements/recommendations for international students: Required—TOEFL. *Application deadline:* Applications are processed on a rolling basis. Application fee: $30. Electronic applications accepted. *Expenses:* Tuition, state resident: part-time $471 per credit hour. Tuition, nonresident: part-time $646 per credit hour. Tuition and fees vary according to course level. *Financial support:* In 2009–10, 30 students received support, including 30 fellowships (averaging $2,168 per year); career-related internships or fieldwork, Federal Work-Study, scholarships/grants, and unspecified assistantships also available. *Faculty research:* Evaluation of special education program effects, adaptive behavior assessment, language development, writing disorders, comparative effects of presentation methods. *Unit head:* Dr. Sandy Miller, Director, 616-331-3344. *Application contact:* Thomas Owens, Student Information and Services Center, 616-331-6282, Fax: 616-331-2000, E-mail: owenst@gvsu.edu.

Greensboro College, Program in Education, Greensboro, NC 27401-1875. Offers elementary education (M Ed); special education (M Ed). Part-time and evening/weekend programs available. *Degree requirements:* For master's, thesis. *Entrance requirements:* For master's, GRE, teacher license, 2 years of teaching experience, 2 letters of recommendation. Additional exam requirements/recommendations for international students: Required—TOEFL (minimum score 550 paper-based; 213 computer-based). Electronic applications accepted.

Gwynedd-Mercy College, School of Education, Gwynedd Valley, PA 19437-0901. Offers educational administration (MS); master teacher (MS); reading (MS); school counseling (MS); special education (MS). Part-time and evening/weekend programs available. *Degree requirements:* For master's, thesis, internship, practicum. *Entrance requirements:* For master's, GRE or MAT; PRAXIS I Test, minimum GPA of 3.0. *Faculty research:* Learning and the brain, reading literacy, ethics and moral judgment, leadership, teaching and multicultural education.

Hampton University, Graduate College, Department of Education, Program in Special Education, Hampton, VA 23668. Offers MA. *Accreditation:* NCATE. Part-time and evening/weekend programs available. *Entrance requirements:* For master's, GRE General Test.

Hampton University, Graduate College, Department of Education, Program in Teaching, Hampton, VA 23668. Offers early childhood education (MT); middle school education (MT); music education (MT); secondary education (MT); special education (MT). *Entrance requirements:* For master's, GRE General Test.

Harding University, College of Education, Searcy, AR 72149-0001. Offers advanced studies in teaching and learning (M Ed); art (MSE); behavioral science (MSE); counseling (MS, Ed S); early childhood special education (M Ed, MSE); education (MSE); educational leadership (M Ed, Ed S); elementary education (M Ed); English (MSE); family and consumer science (MSE); French (MSE); history/social science (MSE); kinesiology (MSE); math (MSE); physical science (MSE); reading (M Ed); secondary education (M Ed); Spanish (MSE); special education licensure (M Ed); teaching (MAT); teaching English as a second language (M Ed). *Accreditation:* NCATE. Part-time and evening/weekend programs available. *Faculty:* 11 full-time (4 women), 49 part-time/adjunct (26 women). *Students:* 104 full-time (85 women), 392 part-time (282 women); includes 77 minority (67 African Americans, 5 American Indian/Alaska Native, 1 Asian American or Pacific Islander, 4 Hispanic Americans), 5 international. Average age 36. 153 applicants, 92% accepted, 131 enrolled. In 2009, 153 master's, 6 other advanced degrees awarded. *Degree requirements:* For master's, comprehensive exam (for some programs), thesis optional, portfolio(s); for Ed S, comprehensive exam, portfolio, specialist project. *Entrance requirements:* For master's, GRE, MAT, PRAXIS; for Ed S, MAT or GRE. Additional exam requirements/recommendations for international students: Required—TOEFL (minimum score 550 paper-based; 79 iBT). *Application deadline:* For fall admission, 8/1 for domestic and international students; for spring admission, 1/1 for domestic and international students. Applications are processed on a rolling basis. Application fee: $35. *Expenses:* Tuition: Full-time $9720; part-time $540 per credit hour. Required fees: $22 per credit hour. Tuition and fees vary according to course load and program. *Financial support:* In 2009–10, 30 students received support. Unspecified assistantships available. *Faculty research:* Reading, comprehension, school violence, educational technology, behavior, college choice, differentiated instruction, brain-based teaching. *Unit head:* Dr. Clara Carroll, Chair, 501-279-4501, Fax: 501-279-4083, E-mail: ccarroll@harding.edu. *Application contact:* Information Contact, 501-279-4315, E-mail: gradstudiesedu@harding.edu.

Hebrew College, Shoolman Graduate School of Education, Newton Centre, MA 02459. Offers early childhood Jewish education (Certificate); Jewish day school education (Certificate); Jewish education (MJ Ed); Jewish family education (Certificate); Jewish special education (Certificate); Jewish youth education, informal education and camping (Certificate). Part-time and evening/weekend programs available. Postbaccalaureate distance learning degree programs offered. *Degree requirements:* For master's, one foreign language. *Entrance requirements:* For master's, GRE, interview. Additional exam requirements/recommendations for international students: Required—TOEFL.

Henderson State University, Graduate Studies, School of Education, Department of Advanced Instructional Studies, Arkadelphia, AR 71999-0001. Offers early childhood (P-4) (MSE); education (MAT); middle school (MSE); reading (MSE); special education (MSE). *Accreditation:* NCATE. Part-time programs available. *Faculty:* 7 full-time (4 women), 2 part-time/adjunct (both women). *Students:* 7 full-time (all women), 131 part-time (119 women); includes 16 minority (11 African Americans, 1 Asian American or Pacific Islander, 4 Hispanic Americans). Average age 33. 25 applicants, 100% accepted, 25 enrolled. In 2009, 53 master's awarded. *Entrance requirements:* For master's, GRE General Test or MAT, minimum GPA of 2.7, teacher certification. Additional exam requirements/recommendations for international students: Required—TOEFL (minimum score 550 paper-based; 213 computer-based); Recommended—IELTS (minimum score 6). *Application deadline:* For fall admission, 8/1 priority date for domestic students, 6/30 priority date for international students; for spring admission, 1/1 priority date for domestic students, 11/30 priority date for international students. Application fee: $25 ($75 for international students). Electronic applications accepted. *Expenses:* Tuition, state resident: full-time $3798; part-time $211 per credit hour. Tuition, nonresident: full-time $7596; part-time $422 per credit hour. Required fees: $903. *Financial support:* Research assistantships, teaching assistantships with tuition reimbursements available. *Unit head:* Dr. Gary Smithey, Chairperson, 870-230-5361, Fax: 870-230-5455, E-mail: smitheg@hsu.edu. *Application contact:* Dr. Marck L. Beggs, Graduate Dean, 870-230-5126, Fax: 870-230-5479, E-mail: beggsm@hsu.edu.

Heritage University, Graduate Programs in Education, Program in Professional Studies, Toppenish, WA 98948-9599. Offers bilingual education/ESL (M Ed); biology (M Ed); English and literature (M Ed); reading/literacy (M Ed); special education (M Ed). Part-time and evening/weekend programs available. *Degree requirements:* For master's, comprehensive exam (for some programs), thesis (for some programs).

High Point University, Norcross Graduate School, High Point, NC 27262-3598. Offers business administration (MBA); educational leadership (M Ed); elementary education (M Ed); history (MA); nonprofit management (MA); special education (M Ed); sport studies (MS). *Accreditation:* ACBSP; NCATE. Part-time and evening/weekend programs available. *Degree requirements:* For master's, comprehensive exam (for some programs), thesis (for some programs). *Entrance requirements:* For master's, GMAT (MBA), GRE General Test, MAT, minimum GPA of 3.0. Additional exam requirements/recommendations for international students: Required—TOEFL (minimum score 550 paper-based). Electronic applications accepted.

Hofstra University, School of Education, Health, and Human Services, Department of Counseling, Research, Special Education and Rehabilitation, Program in Special Education, Hempstead, NY 11549. Offers early childhood special education (MS Ed, Advanced Certificate); gifted education (Advanced Certificate); inclusive early childhood special education (MS Ed); inclusive elementary special education (MS Ed); inclusive secondary special education (MS Ed); literacy studies and special education (MS Ed); special education (MA, MS Ed, PD); special education assessment and diagnosis (Advanced Certificate); teaching students with severe or multiple disabilities (Advanced Certificate). Part-time and evening/weekend programs available. *Students:* 113 full-time (96 women), 105 part-time (95 women); includes 39 minority (18 African Americans, 1 American Indian/Alaska Native, 3 Asian Americans or Pacific Islanders, 17 Hispanic Americans). Average age 29. 134 applicants, 71% accepted, 74 enrolled. In 2009, 88 master's, 7 other advanced degrees awarded. *Degree requirements:* For master's, comprehensive exam (for some programs), thesis (for some programs), seminars, student teaching. *Entrance requirements:* For master's, interview, 3 letters of reference, initial/professional certification; for other advanced degree, interview, 3 letters of recommendation, resume, master's degree, certification. Additional exam requirements/recommendations for international students: Required—TOEFL (minimum score 550 paper-based; 213 computer-based; 80 iBT). *Application deadline:* Applications are processed on a rolling basis. Application fee: $60. Electronic applications accepted. *Expenses:* Tuition: Full-time $16,200; part-time $900 per credit hour. Required fees: $970; $145 per term. Tuition and fees vary according to program. *Financial support:* In 2009–10, 78 students received support, including 10 fellowships with full and partial tuition reimbursements available (averaging $2,541 per year), 4 research assistantships with full and partial tuition reimbursements available (averaging $7,210 per year); Federal Work-Study, institutionally sponsored loans, scholarships/grants, tuition waivers (full and partial), and unspecified assistantships also available. Support available to part-time students. Financial award applicants required to submit FAFSA. *Faculty research:* Inclusive schooling, autism spectrum disorders related services, cultural competency and culturally responsive instruction, co-teaching student teaching, universal design for learning. *Unit head:* Dr. George Guiliani, Director, 516-463-5143, Fax: 516-463-6184, E-mail: cprgag@hofstra.edu. *Application contact:* Carol Drummer, Dean of Graduate Admissions, 516-463-4876, Fax: 516-463-4664, E-mail: gradstudent@hofstra.edu.

Hofstra University, School of Education, Health, and Human Services, Department of Curriculum and Teaching, Program in Learning and Teaching, Hempstead, NY 11549. Offers learning and teaching (Ed D), including applied linguistics, art education, arts and humanities, early childhood education, English education, human development, math education, math, science, and technology, multicultural education, physical education, science education, social studies education, special education. Part-time and evening/weekend programs available. *Students:* 5 full-time (all women), 21 part-time (17 women); includes 2 minority (1 African American, 1 Hispanic American), 1 international. Average age 38. 22 applicants, 68% accepted, 11 enrolled. *Degree requirements:* For doctorate, comprehensive exam, thesis/dissertation. *Entrance requirements:* For doctorate, GRE, 3 letters of recommendation, interview, 2 years full-time teaching experience. Additional exam requirements/recommendations for international students: Required—TOEFL (minimum score 550 paper-based; 213 computer-based; 80 iBT). *Application deadline:* Applications are processed on a rolling basis. Application fee: $60. Electronic applications accepted. *Expenses:* Tuition: Full-time $16,200; part-time $900 per credit hour. Required fees: $970; $145 per term. Tuition and fees vary according to program. *Financial support:* In 2009–10, 24 students received support, including 20 fellowships with full and partial tuition reimbursements available (averaging $4,906 per year); research assistantships with full and partial tuition reimbursements available, Federal Work-Study, institutionally sponsored loans, scholarships/grants, and tuition waivers (full and partial) also available. Support available to part-time students. Financial award applicants required to submit FAFSA. *Faculty research:* Critical thinking, professional development, teacher quality, quantitative research. *Unit head:* Dr. Bruce A. Torff, Director, 516-463-5803, Fax: 516-463-6196, E-mail: catajs@hofstra.edu. *Application contact:* Carol Drummer, Dean of Graduate Admissions, 516-463-4876, Fax: 516-463-4664, E-mail: gradstudent@hofstra.edu.

Holy Family University, Graduate School, School of Education, Philadelphia, PA 19114. Offers education (M Ed); education leadership (M Ed); elementary education (M Ed); reading specialist (M Ed); secondary education (M Ed); special education (M Ed). Part-time and evening/weekend programs available. *Faculty:* 14 full-time (10 women), 42 part-time/adjunct (23 women). *Students:* 63 full-time (48 women), 608 part-time (487 women); includes 45 minority (23 African Americans, 7 Asian Americans or Pacific Islanders, 15 Hispanic Americans), 1 international. Average age 31. 202 applicants, 86% accepted, 146 enrolled. In 2009, 248 master's awarded. *Degree requirements:* For master's, thesis optional. *Entrance requirements:* For master's, GRE or MAT, interview. *Application deadline:* For fall admission, 7/1 priority date for domestic students; for winter admission, 11/1 priority date for domestic students. Applications are processed on a rolling basis. Application fee: $25. *Expenses:* Tuition: Part-time $600 per credit. Required fees: $58 per semester. *Financial support:* Research assistantships, Federal Work-Study available. Support available to part-time students. Financial award application deadline: 2/15; financial award applicants required to submit FAFSA. *Faculty research:* Cognition, developmental issues, sociological issues in education. *Unit head:* Dr. Leonard Soroka, Dean, 267-341-3565, Fax: 215-824-2438, E-mail: lsoroka@holyfanily.edu. *Application contact:* Gidget Marie Montelibano, Graduate Admissions Counselor, 267-341-3558, Fax: 215-637-1478, E-mail: gmontelibano@holyfamily.edu.

Holy Names University, Graduate Division, Department of Education, Oakland, CA 94619-1699. Offers educational therapy (Certificate); level 1 education specialist mild/moderate disabilities (Credential); level 2 education specialist mild/moderate disabilities (Credential); multiple subject teaching credential (Credential); single subject teaching credential (Credential); teaching English as a second language (TESL) (M Ed); urban education: educational therapy (M Ed); urban education: K-12 education (M Ed); urban education: special education (M Ed).

Part-time programs available. *Degree requirements:* For master's, comprehensive exam, research paper, thesis or project. *Entrance requirements:* For master's, minimum undergraduate GPA of 2.6 overall, 3.0 in major. Additional exam requirements/recommendations for international students: Required—TOEFL (minimum score 550 paper-based; 213 computer-based; 80 iBT). *Faculty research:* Cognitive development, language development, learning handicaps.

Hood College, Graduate School, Department of Education, Frederick, MD 21701-8575. Offers curriculum and instruction (MS), including early childhood education, elementary education, elementary school science and mathematics, secondary education, special education; educational leadership (MS, Certificate); reading specialization (MS). Part-time and evening/weekend programs available. *Faculty:* 4 full-time (all women), 39 part-time/adjunct (21 women). *Students:* 2 full-time (both women), 397 part-time (326 women); includes 41 minority (29 African Americans, 5 Asian Americans or Pacific Islanders, 7 Hispanic Americans). Average age 33. 100 applicants, 92% accepted, 84 enrolled. In 2009, 73 master's, 65 other advanced degrees awarded. *Degree requirements:* For master's, action research project, portfolio (reading). *Entrance requirements:* For master's, minimum GPA of 2.75, teaching certification. *Application deadline:* For fall admission, 7/15 for domestic and international students; for spring admission, 12/15 for domestic and international students. Applications are processed on a rolling basis. Application fee: $35. Electronic applications accepted. *Expenses:* Tuition: Full-time $6480; part-time $360 per credit. Required fees: $100; $50 per term. *Financial support:* Applicants required to submit FAFSA. *Faculty research:* Leadership, action research, brain research, learning styles. *Unit head:* Dr. John George, Chairperson, 301-696-3471, Fax: 301-696-3597, E-mail: george@hood.edu. *Application contact:* Dr. Allen P. Flora, Dean of Graduate School, 301-696-3811, Fax: 301-696-3597, E-mail: gofurther@hood.edu.

Howard University, School of Education, Department of Curriculum and Instruction, Program in Special Education, Washington, DC 20059-0002. Offers M Ed, MA, CAGS. MA offered through the Graduate School of Arts and Sciences. *Accreditation:* NCATE. Part-time programs available. *Faculty:* 2 full-time (1 woman). *Students:* 5 full-time (3 women), 3 part-time (1 woman); all minorities (all African Americans). Average age 29. 7 applicants, 57% accepted, 3 enrolled. In 2009, 2 master's awarded. *Degree requirements:* For master's, comprehensive exam, thesis (for some programs), expository writing exam, internships, practicum. *Entrance requirements:* For master's, GRE General Test (MA), minimum GPA of 2.7. *Application deadline:* For fall admission, 2/15 priority date for domestic students; for spring admission, 11/1 for domestic students. Applications are processed on a rolling basis. Application fee: $45. Electronic applications accepted. *Financial support:* In 2009–10, 4 students received support, including 1 fellowship with full and partial tuition reimbursement available (averaging $15,000 per year), 3 research assistantships with full and partial tuition reimbursements available (averaging $13,000 per year); career-related internships or fieldwork, Federal Work-Study, institutionally sponsored loans, scholarships/grants, and unspecified assistantships also available. Financial award application deadline: 2/15. *Unit head:* Dr. Wilfred A. Johnson, Associate Professor/Coordinator, 202-806-7339, Fax: 202-806-5297, E-mail: wajohnson@howard.edu. *Application contact:* June L. Harris, Administrative Assistant, Department of Curriculum and Instruction, 202-806-7343, Fax: 202-806-5297, E-mail: jlharris@howard.edu.

Hunter College of the City University of New York, Graduate School, School of Education, Department of Special Education, New York, NY 10021-5085. Offers blind or visually impaired (MS Ed); deaf or hard of hearing (MS Ed); severe/multiple disabilities (MS Ed); special education (MS Ed). *Accreditation:* NCATE. *Faculty:* 13 full-time (5 women), 12 part-time/adjunct (5 women). *Students:* 107 full-time (99 women), 541 part-time (478 women); includes 133 minority (37 African Americans, 1 American Indian/Alaska Native, 23 Asian Americans or Pacific Islanders, 72 Hispanic Americans). Average age 28. 344 applicants, 66% accepted, 151 enrolled. In 2009, 138 master's awarded. *Degree requirements:* For master's, comprehensive exam, thesis, student teaching practica and clinical teaching lab courses, New York State Teacher Certification exams. *Entrance requirements:* For master's, minimum GPA of 2.8. Additional exam requirements/recommendations for international students: Required—TOEFL, TWE. *Application deadline:* For fall admission, 4/1 for domestic students, 2/1 for international students; for spring admission, 11/1 for domestic students, 9/1 for international students. Applications are processed on a rolling basis. Application fee: $50. *Expenses:* Tuition, state resident: full-time $7360; part-time $310 per credit. Required fees: $250 per semester. *Financial support:* Career-related internships or fieldwork, Federal Work-Study, institutionally sponsored loans, and tuition waivers (partial) available. Support available to part-time students. *Faculty research:* Mathematics learning disabilities; street behavior; assessment; bilingual special education; families, diversity, and disabilities. *Unit head:* Dr. Kate Garnett, Chairperson, 212-772-4700, E-mail: kgarnett@hunter.cuny.edu. *Application contact:* William Zlata, Director for Graduate Admissions, 212-772-4482, Fax: 212-650-3336, E-mail: admissions@hunter.cuny.edu.

Hunter College of the City University of New York, Graduate School, Schools of the Health Professions, School of Health Sciences, Communication Sciences Program, New York, NY 10021-5085. Offers audiology (MS); speech language pathology (MS); teacher of speech and hearing handicapped (MS). *Accreditation:* ASHA. Part-time programs available. *Degree requirements:* For master's, comprehensive exam (for some programs), NTE, research project. *Entrance requirements:* For master's, GRE, letters of reference. Additional exam requirements/recommendations for international students: Required—TOEFL. *Expenses:* Tuition, state resident: full-time $7360; part-time $310 per credit. Required fees: $250 per semester. *Faculty research:* Aging and communication disorders, fluency, speech science, diagnostic audiology, amplification.

Idaho State University, Office of Graduate Studies, College of Education, Department of Educational Learning and Development, Pocatello, ID 83209-8059. Offers human exceptionality (M Ed); school psychology (Ed S); special education (Ed S). Part-time programs available. *Faculty:* 3 full-time (1 woman). *Students:* 18 full-time (13 women), 7 part-time (6 women); includes 1 minority (American Indian/Alaska Native), 1 international. Average age 34. In 2009, 6 master's, 11 Ed Ss awarded. *Degree requirements:* For master's, comprehensive exam, thesis (for some programs), oral thesis defense or written comprehensive exam and oral exam; for Ed S, comprehensive exam, thesis (for some programs), oral exam, specialist paper or portfolio. *Entrance requirements:* For master's, GRE or MAT, minimum undergraduate GPA of 3.0, bachelor's degree, professional experience in an educational context; for Ed S, GRE or MAT, master's degree in related field. Additional exam requirements/recommendations for international students: Required—TOEFL (minimum score 550 paper-based; 213 computer-based; 80 iBT). *Application deadline:* For fall admission, 7/1 for domestic students, 6/1 for international students; for spring admission, 12/1 for domestic students, 11/1 for international students. Applications are processed on a rolling basis. Application fee: $55. Electronic applications accepted. *Expenses:* Tuition, state resident: full-time $3318; part-time $297 per credit hour. Tuition, nonresident: full-time $13,120; part-time $437 per credit hour. Required fees: $2530. Tuition and fees vary according to program. *Financial support:* Teaching assistantships with full and partial tuition reimbursements, career-related internships or fieldwork, Federal Work-Study, institutionally sponsored loans, scholarships/grants, health care benefits, and unspecified assistantships available. Support available to part-time students. Financial award application deadline: 1/1; financial award applicants required to submit FAFSA. *Faculty research:* Literacy, school psychology, special education. *Unit head:* Dr. David Mercaldo, Interim Chairman, 208-282-5188, Fax: 208-282-4697, E-mail: mercdavi@isu.edu. *Application contact:* Dr. Peter Denner, Assistant Dean, 208-282-3807, Fax: 208-282-4697, E-mail: dennpete@isu.edu.

Idaho State University, Office of Graduate Studies, Kasiska College of Health Professions, Department of Communication Sciences and Disorders and Education of the Deaf, Pocatello, ID 83209-8116. Offers audiology (MS, Au D); communication sciences and disorders (Postbaccalaureate Certificate); communication sciences and disorders and education of the deaf (Certificate); deaf education (MS); speech language pathology (MS). *Accreditation:* ASHA (one or more programs are accredited). Part-time programs available. *Faculty:* 5 full-time (1 woman). *Students:* 89 full-time (78 women), 32 part-time (27 women); includes 6 minority (1 African American, 1 American Indian/Alaska Native, 4 Asian Americans or Pacific Islanders), 3 international. Average age 30. In 2009, 26 master's, 4 doctorates awarded. *Degree requirements:* For master's, thesis optional, written and oral comprehensive exams; for doctorate, comprehensive exam, thesis/dissertation optional, externship, 1 year full time clinical practicum, 3rd year spent in Boise. *Entrance requirements:* For master's, GRE General Test, minimum GPA of 3.0, 3 letters of recommendation; for doctorate, GRE General Test (at least 2 scores minimum 40th percentile), minimum GPA of 3.0, 3 letters of recommendation, bachelor's degree. Additional exam requirements/recommendations for international students: Required—TOEFL (minimum score 600 paper-based; 250 computer-based; 80 iBT). *Application deadline:* For fall admission, 7/1 for domestic students, 6/1 for international students; for spring admission, 12/1 for domestic students, 11/1 for international students. Applications are processed on a rolling basis. Application fee: $55. Electronic applications accepted. *Expenses:* Tuition, state resident: full-time $3318; part-time $297 per credit hour. Tuition, nonresident: full-time $13,120; part-time $437 per credit hour. Required fees: $2530. Tuition and fees vary according to program. *Financial support:* In 2009–10, 8 teaching assistantships with full and partial tuition reimbursements (averaging $10,841 per year) were awarded; career-related internships or fieldwork, Federal Work-Study, institutionally sponsored loans, scholarships/grants, health care benefits, tuition waivers (full and partial), and unspecified assistantships also available. Support available to part-time students. Financial award application deadline: 1/1; financial award applicants required to submit FAFSA. *Faculty research:* Neurogenic disorders, central auditory processing disorders, vestibular disorders, cochlear implants, language disorders, professional burnout, swallowing disorders. *Unit head:* Dr. Kathleen Kangas, Interim Chairman, 208-282-4196, Fax: 208-282-4571, E-mail: kangkath@isu.edu. *Application contact:* Tami Carson, Graduate School Technical Records Specialist, 208-282-2150, Fax: 208-282-4847, E-mail: carstami@isu.edu.

Illinois State University, Graduate School, College of Education, Department of Special Education, Normal, IL 61790-2200. Offers MS, MS Ed, Ed D. *Accreditation:* NCATE. *Degree requirements:* For doctorate, thesis/dissertation, 2 terms of residency. *Entrance requirements:* For master's, GRE General Test, minimum GPA of 3.0 in last 60 hours; for doctorate, GRE General Test. *Faculty research:* Center for adult learning leadership, promoting a learning community, autism spectrum professional development and technical assistance project, preparing qualified personnel to provide early intervention for children who are deaf.

Immaculata University, College of Graduate Studies, Program in Educational Leadership and Administration, Immaculata, PA 19345. Offers educational leadership and administration (MA, Ed D); elementary education (Certificate); school principal (Certificate); school superintendent (Certificate); secondary education (Certificate); special education (Certificate). Part-time and evening/weekend programs available. *Degree requirements:* For master's, comprehensive exam, thesis optional; for doctorate, comprehensive exam, thesis/dissertation. *Entrance requirements:* For master's, GRE or MAT, minimum GPA of 3.0; for doctorate, GRE General Test, minimum GPA of 3.5. Additional exam requirements/recommendations for international students: Required—TOEFL. *Faculty research:* Cooperative learning, school-based management, whole language, performance assessment.

Indiana University Bloomington, School of Education, Department of Curriculum and Instruction, Bloomington, IN 47405-7000. Offers art education (MS, Ed D, PhD); curriculum studies (Ed D, PhD); elementary education (MS, Ed D, PhD, Ed S); mathematics education (MS, Ed D, PhD); science education (MS, Ed D, PhD); secondary education (MS, Ed D, PhD); social studies education (MS, PhD); special education (MS, Ed D, PhD, Ed S). *Accreditation:* NCATE. Part-time and evening/weekend programs available. *Students:* 208 full-time (155 women), 44 part-time (25 women); includes 28 minority (9 African Americans, 3 American Indian/Alaska Native, 9 Asian Americans or Pacific Islanders, 7 Hispanic Americans), 34 international. Average age 34. 100 applicants, 68% accepted, 39 enrolled. In 2009, 48 master's, 20 doctorates awarded. Terminal master's awarded for partial completion of doctoral program. *Degree requirements:* For doctorate, thesis/dissertation; for Ed S, comprehensive exam or project. *Entrance requirements:* For master's, doctorate, and Ed S, GRE General Test. *Application deadline:* For fall admission, 6/1 priority date for domestic students, 3/1 for international students; for winter admission, 11/1 priority date for domestic students; for spring admission, 9/1 for international students. Applications are processed on a rolling basis. Application fee: $55 ($65 for international students). Electronic applications accepted. *Financial support:* Fellowships with full and partial tuition reimbursements, research assistantships with full and partial tuition reimbursements, teaching assistantships with full and partial tuition reimbursements, career-related internships or fieldwork, Federal Work-Study, institutionally sponsored loans, and tuition waivers (partial) available. Support available to part-time students. *Unit head:* Cary Buzzelli, Chairperson, 812-856-8100. *Application contact:* Bobbie Partenheimer, Admissions Services Coordinator, 812-856-8127, Fax: 812-856-8333, E-mail: partenhe@indiana.edu.

Indiana University of Pennsylvania, School of Graduate Studies and Research, College of Education and Educational Technology, Department of Special Education and Clinical Services, Program in Education of Exceptional Persons, Indiana, PA 15705-1087. Offers M Ed. *Accreditation:* NCATE. *Faculty:* 11 full-time (7 women). *Students:* 3 full-time (1 woman), 13 part-time (all women), 1 international. Average age 28. 12 applicants, 42% accepted, 4 enrolled. In 2009, 12 master's awarded. *Degree requirements:* For master's, comprehensive exam, thesis optional. *Entrance requirements:* For master's, 2 letters of recommendation. Additional exam requirements/recommendations for international students: Required—TOEFL. *Application deadline:* For fall admission, 3/1 priority date for domestic students; for spring admission, 7/1 for domestic students. Applications are processed on a rolling basis. Application fee: $40. *Expenses:* Tuition, state resident: full-time $6666; part-time $370 per credit hour. Tuition, nonresident: full-time $10,666; part-time $593 per credit hour. Required fees: $813 per semester. *Financial support:* In 2009–10, 2 research assistantships with full and partial tuition reimbursements (averaging $5,440 per year) were awarded; career-related internships or fieldwork and Federal Work-Study also available. Support available to part-time students. Financial award application deadline: 3/15; financial award applicants required to submit FAFSA. *Unit head:* Dr. Becky Knickelbein, Graduate Coordinator, 724-357-5680, E-mail: becky.knickelbein@iup.edu. *Application contact:* Dr. Edward Nardi, Interim Associate Dean, 724-357-2480, Fax: 724-357-5595, E-mail: ewnardi@iup.edu.

Indiana University–Purdue University Fort Wayne, School of Education, Department of Professional Studies, Fort Wayne, IN 46805-1499. Offers counseling education (MS Ed); educational leadership (MS Ed); marriage and family therapy (MS Ed); school counseling (MS Ed); special education (MS Ed, Certificate). Part-time programs available. *Faculty:* 10 full-time (5 women). *Students:* 2 full-time (both women), 159 part-time (120 women); includes 19 minority (12 African Americans, 1 Asian American or Pacific Islander, 6 Hispanic Americans). Average age 35. 47 applicants, 98% accepted, 38 enrolled. In 2009, 64 master's awarded. *Degree requirements:* For master's, comprehensive exam, practicum, internship, portfolio. *Entrance requirements:* For master's, minimum GPA of 2.5. Additional exam requirements/recommendations for international students: Required—TOEFL (minimum score 550 paper-based; 213 computer-based; 77 iBT). *Application deadline:* For fall admission, 4/1 priority date for domestic and international students. Applications are processed on a rolling basis. Application fee: $55. *Expenses:* Tuition, state resident: full-time $4595; part-time $255 per credit. Tuition, nonresident: full-time $10,963; part-time $609 per credit. Required fees: $528; $29.35 per credit. Tuition and fees vary according to course load. *Financial support:* In 2009–10, 1 teaching assistantship with partial tuition reimbursement (averaging $12,740 per year) was awarded; research assistantships with partial tuition reimbursements, scholarships/grants also available. Support available to part-time students. Financial award application deadline: 3/1; financial award applicants required to submit FAFSA. *Unit head:* Dr. James Burg, Interim Chair, 260-481-5406, Fax: 260-481-5408, E-mail: burgj@ipfw.edu. *Application contact:* Vicky L. Schmidt, Graduate Recorder, 260-481-6450, Fax: 260-481-5408, E-mail: schmidt@ipfw.edu.

Indiana University–Purdue University Indianapolis, School of Education, Indianapolis, IN 46202-2896. Offers computer education (Certificate); curriculum and instruction (MS); early

Special Education

Indiana University–Purdue University Indianapolis (continued)
childhood (MS); educational leadership (MS, Certificate); English as a second language (Certificate); higher education and student affairs (MS); kindergarten (Certificate); language education (MS); reading (Certificate); school counseling (MS); special education (MS, Certificate). Part-time and evening/weekend programs available. *Faculty:* 41 full-time, 80 part-time/adjunct. *Students:* 72 full-time (60 women), 427 part-time (325 women); includes 57 minority (42 African Americans, 1 American Indian/Alaska Native, 4 Asian Americans or Pacific Islanders, 10 Hispanic Americans), 5 international. Average age 32. 181 applicants, 78% accepted, 112 enrolled. In 2009, 162 master's awarded. *Degree requirements:* For master's, thesis optional. *Entrance requirements:* For master's, GRE General Test, minimum GPA of 3.0. Additional exam requirements/recommendations for international students: Required—TOEFL. *Application deadline:* For fall admission, 5/1 priority date for domestic students; for spring admission, 11/1 for domestic students. Application fee: $55 ($65 for international students). *Financial support:* In 2009–10, 2 fellowships (averaging $780 per year), 18 teaching assistantships (averaging $9,756 per year) were awarded; research assistantships with partial tuition reimbursements, Federal Work-Study, institutionally sponsored loans, scholarships/grants, and tuition waivers (partial) also available. Support available to part-time students. *Faculty research:* Teachers in the process of change, learning cycles, children's concepts of science. Total annual research expenditures: $614,458. *Unit head:* Dr. Chris Leland, Interim Executive Associate Dean, 317-274-6801, Fax: 317-274-6864. *Application contact:* Sarah Brandenburg, Graduate Advisor, 317-274-6801, Fax: 317-274-6864, E-mail: edugrad@iupui.edu.

Indiana University South Bend, School of Education, South Bend, IN 46634-7111. Offers counseling and human services (MS Ed); elementary education (MS Ed); secondary education (MS Ed); special education (MS Ed). *Accreditation:* NCATE. Part-time and evening/weekend programs available. *Faculty:* 21 full-time (11 women), 9 part-time/adjunct (3 women). *Students:* 72 full-time (48 women), 256 part-time (202 women); includes 36 minority (24 African Americans, 2 American Indian/Alaska Native, 1 Asian American or Pacific Islander, 9 Hispanic Americans), 9 international. Average age 36. In 2009, 103 master's awarded. *Degree requirements:* For master's, thesis or alternative, exit project. *Entrance requirements:* For master's, letters of recommendation, GRE or minimum GPA of 3.0. Additional exam requirements/recommendations for international students: Required—TOEFL. *Application deadline:* For fall admission, 7/1 for domestic students; for spring admission, 11/1 for domestic students. Applications are processed on a rolling basis. Application fee: $46 ($58 for international students). Electronic applications accepted. *Financial support:* Career-related internships or fieldwork available. Support available to part-time students. Financial award application deadline: 3/1; financial award applicants required to submit FAFSA. *Faculty research:* Professional dispositions, early childhood literacy, online learning, program assessments, problem-based learning. *Unit head:* Dr. Michael Horvath, Professor/Dean, 574-520-4339, Fax: 574-520-4550. *Application contact:* Dr. Todd Norris, Director of Education Student Services, 574-520-4845, E-mail: toanorri@iusb.edu.

Inter American University of Puerto Rico, Metropolitan Campus, Graduate Programs, Program in Special Education, San Juan, PR 00919-1293. Offers MA. *Degree requirements:* For master's, comprehensive exam. *Entrance requirements:* For master's, GRE or EXADEP, interview. Electronic applications accepted.

Inter American University of Puerto Rico, San Germán Campus, Graduate Studies Center, Program in Special Education, San Germán, PR 00683-5008. Offers MA. Part-time and evening/weekend programs available. *Degree requirements:* For master's, comprehensive exam. *Entrance requirements:* For master's, GRE General Test or EXADEP, minimum GPA of 3.0.

Iowa State University of Science and Technology, Graduate College, College of Human Sciences, Department of Curriculum and Instruction, Ames, IA 50011. Offers curriculum and instructional technology (M Ed, MS, PhD); elementary education (M Ed, MS); historical, philosophical, and comparative studies in education (M Ed, MS); special education (M Ed, MS). *Faculty:* 26 full-time (16 women), 1 (woman) part-time/adjunct. *Students:* 51 full-time (34 women), 72 part-time (49 women); includes 11 minority (5 African Americans, 1 American Indian/Alaska Native, 4 Asian Americans or Pacific Islanders, 1 Hispanic American), 25 international. 54 applicants, 69% accepted, 25 enrolled. In 2009, 41 master's, 6 doctorates awarded. *Degree requirements:* For master's, thesis or alternative; for doctorate, thesis/dissertation. *Entrance requirements:* For doctorate, GRE General Test. Additional exam requirements/recommendations for international students: Required—TOEFL (minimum score 560 paper-based; 83 iBT) or IELTS (minimum score 6.5). *Application deadline:* For fall admission, 1/1 priority date for domestic and international students; for spring admission, 9/1 for domestic and international students. Application fee: $40 ($90 for international students). Electronic applications accepted. *Expenses:* Tuition, state resident: full-time $6716. Tuition, nonresident: full-time $8908. Tuition and fees vary according to course level, course load, program and student level. *Financial support:* In 2009–10, 21 research assistantships with full and partial tuition reimbursements (averaging $14,600 per year), 12 teaching assistantships with full and partial tuition reimbursements (averaging $14,600 per year) were awarded; fellowships, scholarships/grants, health care benefits, and unspecified assistantships also available. *Unit head:* Dr. Carl Smith, Director of Graduate Education, 515-294-0317, E-mail: cigrad@iastate.edu. *Application contact:* Dr. Patricia Leigh, Director of Graduate Education, 515-294-7021, E-mail: cigrad@iastate.edu.

Jackson State University, Graduate School, School of Education, Department of Special Education and Rehabilitative Services, Jackson, MS 39217. Offers rehabilitative counseling service (MS Ed); special education (MS Ed, Ed S). *Accreditation:* NCATE. Evening/weekend programs available. *Degree requirements:* For master's, comprehensive exam, thesis or alternative. *Entrance requirements:* For master's, GRE General Test. Additional exam requirements/recommendations for international students: Required—TOEFL.

Jacksonville State University, College of Graduate Studies and Continuing Education, College of Education and Professional Studies, Program in Special Education, Jacksonville, AL 36265-1602. Offers MS Ed. *Accreditation:* NCATE. *Degree requirements:* For master's, comprehensive exam, thesis (for some programs). *Entrance requirements:* For master's, GRE General Test or MAT. Electronic applications accepted.

James Madison University, The Graduate School, College of Education, Exceptional Education Department, Program in Exceptional Education, Harrisonburg, VA 22807. Offers M Ed. *Accreditation:* NCATE. Part-time programs available. *Students:* 23 full-time (22 women), 8 part-time (7 women); includes 1 minority (Hispanic American). Average age 27. In 2009, 34 master's awarded. *Entrance requirements:* For master's, GRE General Test or PRAXIS, minimum undergraduate GPA of 2.75, resume. Additional exam requirements/recommendations for international students: Required—TOEFL. *Application deadline:* For fall admission, 5/1 priority date for domestic students; for spring admission, 9/1 priority date for domestic students. Applications are processed on a rolling basis. Application fee: $55. Electronic applications accepted. *Expenses:* Tuition, area resident: Part-time $305 per credit hour. Tuition, state resident: part-time $305 per credit hour. Tuition, nonresident: part-time $890 per credit hour. *Financial support:* In 2009–10, 8 students received support. Federal Work-Study and unspecified assistantships available. Financial award application deadline: 3/1; financial award applicants required to submit FAFSA. *Unit head:* Dr. Laura Desportes, Academic Unit Head, 540-568-6193. *Application contact:* Lynette M. Bible, Director of Graduate Admissions, 540-568-6395, Fax: 540-568-7860, E-mail: biblelm@jmu.edu.

The Johns Hopkins University, School of Education, Department of Special Education, Baltimore, MD 21218. Offers advanced methods for differentiated instruction and inclusive education (Certificate); assistive technology (Certificate); early intervention/preschool special education specialist (Certificate); education of students with autism and other pervasive developmental disorders (Certificate); education of students with severe disabilities (Certificate); special education (MS, Ed D, CAGS), including early childhood special education (MS), general special education studies (MS), mild to moderate disabilities (MS), severe disabilities (MS), technology in special education (MS). *Accreditation:* NCATE. Part-time and evening/weekend programs available. Postbaccalaureate distance learning degree programs offered (minimal on-campus study). *Faculty:* 6 full-time (5 women), 21 part-time/adjunct (18 women). *Students:* 19 full-time (18 women), 270 part-time (243 women); includes 45 minority (35 African Americans, 6 Asian Americans or Pacific Islanders, 4 Hispanic Americans), 10 international. Average age 31. 114 applicants, 56% accepted, 46 enrolled. In 2009, 88 master's, 34 other advanced degrees awarded. *Degree requirements:* For master's, internships, professional portfolio, and PRAXIS II (for licensure); for doctorate, comprehensive exam, thesis/dissertation. *Entrance requirements:* For master's, PRAXIS I, SAT, ACT, or GRE, minimum undergraduate GPA of 3.0, 2 letters of recommendation (for cohort programs); for doctorate, GRE, degree in special education (or related field); minimum GPA of 3.0 in all prior academic work; 3 letters of recommendation; curriculum vitae/resume; professional experience; for other advanced degree, minimum undergraduate GPA of 3.0, master's degree (for CAGS). Additional exam requirements/recommendations for international students: Required—TOEFL (minimum score 600 paper-based; 250 computer-based; 100 iBT). *Application deadline:* For fall admission, 5/1 for international students; for spring admission, 10/15 for international students. Applications are processed on a rolling basis. Application fee: $80. Electronic applications accepted. *Financial support:* In 2009–10, 9 fellowships were awarded; scholarships/grants also available. Support available to part-time students. Financial award application deadline: 6/1; financial award applicants required to submit FAFSA. *Faculty research:* Alternative licensure programs for special educators; collaborative programming; data-based decision making and knowledge management as keys to school reform; parent training; natural environment teaching (NET). *Unit head:* Dr. Laurie U. deBettencourt, Chair, 301-294-7054, Fax: 410-516-8474, E-mail: specialed@jhu.edu. *Application contact:* Jennifer Shaffer, Director of Admissions, 410-516-9797, Fax: 410-516-9799, E-mail: educationinfo@jhu.edu.

Johnson State College, Graduate Program in Education, Program in Special Education, Johnson, VT 05656. Offers MA Ed. Part-time programs available. *Degree requirements:* For master's, comprehensive exam, thesis or alternative. *Entrance requirements:* For master's, interview. Additional exam requirements/recommendations for international students: Required—TOEFL. *Expenses:* Tuition, area resident: Part-time $416 per credit. Tuition, state resident: part-time $416 per credit. Tuition, nonresident: part-time $899 per credit.

Kansas State University, Graduate School, College of Education, Department of Special Education, Counseling and Student Affairs, Manhattan, KS 66506. Offers academic advising (MS); college student development (MS); counseling and student development (Ed D); counselor education and supervision (PhD); school counseling (MS); special education (MS, Ed D); student affairs in higher education (PhD). *Accreditation:* NCATE. Part-time programs available. *Faculty:* 10 full-time (4 women), 3 part-time/adjunct (1 woman). *Students:* 64 full-time (38 women), 256 part-time (197 women); includes 33 minority (16 African Americans, 3 American Indian/Alaska Native, 6 Asian Americans or Pacific Islanders, 8 Hispanic Americans), 2 international. Average age 36. 100 applicants, 97% accepted, 73 enrolled. In 2009, 31 master's, 5 doctorates awarded. *Degree requirements:* For master's, thesis or alternative, final written exam. *Entrance requirements:* For master's, GRE General Test or MAT, teaching experience, BS in education with minimum B average. Additional exam requirements/recommendations for international students: Required—TOEFL. *Application deadline:* For fall admission, 2/1 priority date for domestic and international students; for spring admission, 8/1 priority date for domestic and international students. Applications are processed on a rolling basis. Application fee: $40 ($55 for international students). Electronic applications accepted. *Financial support:* In 2009–10, 1 research assistantship (averaging $12,134 per year) was awarded; career-related internships or fieldwork, Federal Work-Study, institutionally sponsored loans, and scholarships/grants also available. Support available to part-time students. Financial award application deadline: 3/1; financial award applicants required to submit FAFSA. *Faculty research:* Application of principles of universal design for learning, on-line applications for supervision of practicum students, interpretation of facial expressions by students with EBD and ASD, school-wide screening techniques for behavioral concerns, field-based observation technique refinements. Total annual research expenditures: $2,948. *Unit head:* Kenneth Hughey, Head, 785-532-6445, Fax: 785-532-7304, E-mail: khughey@ksu.edu. *Application contact:* Gail Shroyer, Director, 785-532-6737, Fax: 785-532-7304, E-mail: gshroyer@ksu.edu.

Kaplan University, Davenport Campus, School of Teacher Education, Davenport, IA 52807-2095. Offers education (M Ed); secondary education (M Ed); teaching and learning (MA); teaching literacy and language: grades 6-12 (MA); teaching literacy and language: grades K-6 (MA); teaching mathematics: grades 6-8 (MA); teaching mathematics: grades 9-12 (MA); teaching mathematics: grades K-5 (MA); teaching science: grades 6-12 (MA); teaching science: grades K-6 (MA); teaching students with special needs (MA); teaching with technology (MA). Part-time and evening/weekend programs available. Postbaccalaureate distance learning degree programs offered (no on-campus study). *Entrance requirements:* Additional exam requirements/recommendations for international students: Required—TOEFL (minimum score 550 paper-based; 218 computer-based; 80 iBT).

Kean University, College of Education, Program in Special Education, Union, NJ 07083. Offers high incidence disabilities (MA); low incidence disabilities (MA). *Accreditation:* NCATE. Part-time and evening/weekend programs available. *Faculty:* 15 full-time (13 women). *Students:* 23 full-time (20 women), 342 part-time (280 women); includes 79 minority (43 African Americans, 11 Asian Americans or Pacific Islanders, 25 Hispanic Americans). Average age 34. 147 applicants, 99% accepted, 121 enrolled. In 2009, 54 master's awarded. *Degree requirements:* For master's, comprehensive exam, thesis, portfolio. *Entrance requirements:* For master's, GRE General Test or MAT, minimum GPA of 3.0, teaching certificate, 2 letters of recommendation, interview. *Application deadline:* For fall admission, 5/1 for domestic students; for spring admission, 11/1 for domestic students. Application fee: $60 ($150 for international students). Electronic applications accepted. *Expenses:* Tuition, state resident: full-time $10,440; part-time $435 per credit. Tuition, nonresident: full-time $14,160; part-time $590 per credit. Required fees: $2642; $110 per credit. Part-time tuition and fees vary according to course load and degree level. *Financial support:* In 2009–10, research assistantships with full tuition reimbursements (averaging $3,263 per year); unspecified assistantships also available. *Unit head:* Dr. Beverly Kling, Program Coordinator, 908-737-3850, E-mail: bkling@kean.edu. *Application contact:* Ann-Marie Kay, Assistant Director of Graduate Admissions, 908-737-5922, Fax: 908-737-5965, E-mail: akay@kean.edu.

Keene State College, School of Professional and Graduate Studies, Keene, NH 03435. Offers curriculum and instruction (M Ed); education leadership (PMC); educational leadership (M Ed); school counselor (M Ed, PMC); special education (M Ed); teacher certification (Post-baccalaureate Certificate). *Accreditation:* NCATE. Part-time and evening/weekend programs available. *Faculty:* 21 full-time (13 women), 14 part-time/adjunct (13 women). *Students:* 8 full-time (5 women), 80 part-time (56 women); includes 1 Asian American or Pacific Islander, 1 Hispanic American, 1 international. Average age 34. 94 applicants, 80% accepted, 62 enrolled. In 2009, 55 master's, 10 other advanced degrees awarded. *Entrance requirements:* For master's, PRAXIS I, resume; minimum GPA of 2.5. Additional exam requirements/recommendations for international students: Required—TOEFL (minimum score 550 paper-based; 173 computer-based; 61 iBT). *Application deadline:* For fall admission, 4/1 for domestic students; for spring admission, 12/1 for domestic students. Application fee: $40. *Expenses:* Tuition, state resident: part-time $320 per credit. Tuition, nonresident: part-time $350 per credit. Required fees: $92 per credit. $10 per term. Tuition and fees vary according to course load. *Financial support:* Research assistantships, career-related internships or fieldwork, Federal Work-Study, institutionally sponsored loans, and unspecified assistantships available. Support available to part-time students. Financial award application deadline: 3/1; financial award applicants required to submit FAFSA. *Unit head:* Dr. Melinda Treadwell, Dean, 603-358-2220. *Application contact:* Peggy Richmond, Director of Admissions, 603-358-2276, Fax: 603-358-2767, E-mail: admissions@keene.edu.

Kennesaw State University, Leland and Clarice C. Bagwell College of Education, Program in Graduate Education, Kennesaw, GA 30144-5591. Offers adolescent education (M Ed); educational leadership (M Ed); educational leadership technology (M Ed); elementary and early childhood education (M Ed); special education (M Ed); teaching English to speakers of other languages (M Ed). *Accreditation:* NCATE. Part-time programs available. *Faculty:* 60 full-time (38 women), 12 part-time/adjunct (4 women). *Students:* 140 full-time (116 women), 136 part-time (107 women); includes 51 minority (39 African Americans, 1 American Indian/Alaska Native, 3 Asian Americans or Pacific Islanders, 8 Hispanic Americans), 4 international. Average age 34. 113 applicants, 83% accepted, 69 enrolled. In 2009, 282 master's awarded. *Degree requirements:* For master's, thesis or alternative. *Entrance requirements:* For master's, GRE General Test, T-4 state certification, minimum GPA of 2.75. Additional exam requirements/recommendations for international students: Required—TOEFL (minimum score 550 paper-based; 213 computer-based; 80 iBT), IELTS (minimum score 6). *Application deadline:* For fall admission, 7/1 for domestic and international students; for spring admission, 10/1 for domestic and international students. Application fee: $60. Electronic applications accepted. *Expenses:* Tuition, state resident: full-time $2341; part-time $196 per credit hour. Tuition, nonresident: full-time $9396; part-time $783 per credit hour. Required fees: $573 per semester. *Financial support:* Federal Work-Study and unspecified assistantships available. Support available to part-time students. Financial award application deadline: 6/15; financial award applicants required to submit FAFSA. *Unit head:* Dr. Nita Paris, Associate Dean for Graduate Programs, 770-423-6636, E-mail: nparis@kennesaw.edu. *Application contact:* Alisha Bello, Administrative Coordinator, 770-423-6043, Fax: 770-420-4435, E-mail: abello1@kennesaw.edu.

Kent State University, Graduate School of Education, Health, and Human Services, School of Lifespan Development and Educational Sciences, Program in Intervention Specialist, Kent, OH 44242-0001. Offers deaf education (M Ed, MA); early childhood intervention specialist (M Ed, MA); educational interpreter K-12 (M Ed, MA); general special education (M Ed, MA); gifted education (M Ed, MA); mild/moderate intervention (M Ed, MA); moderate/intensive intervention (M Ed, MA); transition to work (M Ed, MA). *Faculty:* 9 full-time (8 women), 17 part-time/adjunct (15 women). *Students:* 51 full-time (41 women), 63 part-time (56 women); includes 8 minority (3 African Americans, 2 Asian Americans or Pacific Islanders, 3 Hispanic Americans), 2 international. 62 applicants, 77% accepted. In 2009, 36 master's awarded. *Entrance requirements:* For master's, GRE. Application fee: $30. *Financial support:* In 2009–10, 1 research assistantship with tuition reimbursement (averaging $8,313 per year) was awarded; fellowships with tuition reimbursements, teaching assistantships with tuition reimbursements, career-related internships or fieldwork, Federal Work-Study, institutionally sponsored loans, scholarships/grants, health care benefits, and unspecified assistantships also available. Support available to part-time students. *Unit head:* Kristie Pretti-Frontczak, Coordinator, 330-672-0597, E-mail: kprettif@kent.edu. *Application contact:* Nancy Miller, Academic Program Coordinator, Office of Graduate Student Services, 330-672-2576, Fax: 330-672-9162, E-mail: ogs@kent.edu.

Kent State University, Graduate School of Education, Health, and Human Services, School of Lifespan Development and Educational Sciences, Program in Special Education, Kent, OH 44242-0001. Offers PhD, Ed S. *Accreditation:* NCATE. *Faculty:* 9 full-time (8 women), 17 part-time/adjunct (15 women). *Students:* 16 full-time (15 women), 11 part-time (7 women). 11 applicants, 64% accepted. In 2009, 8 doctorates, 1 other advanced degree awarded. *Degree requirements:* For doctorate, comprehensive exam, thesis/dissertation. *Entrance requirements:* For doctorate and Ed S, GRE General Test. Additional exam requirements/recommendations for international students: Required—TOEFL. *Application deadline:* Applications are processed on a rolling basis. Application fee: $30. Electronic applications accepted. *Financial support:* In 2009–10, fellowships with full tuition reimbursements (averaging $11,000 per year), 4 research assistantships with full tuition reimbursements (averaging $8,313 per year), 4 teaching assistantships with full tuition reimbursements (averaging $11,000 per year) were awarded; career-related internships or fieldwork, Federal Work-Study, institutionally sponsored loans, scholarships/grants, health care benefits, and unspecified assistantships also available. Support available to part-time students. Financial award application deadline: 4/1; financial award applicants required to submit FAFSA. *Faculty research:* Social/emotional needs of gifted, inclusion transition services, early intervention/ecobehavioral assessments, applied behavioral analysis. *Unit head:* Kristie Pretti-Frontczak, Coordinator, 330-672-0597, E-mail: kprettif@kent.edu. *Application contact:* Nancy Miller, Academic Program Coordinator, Office of Graduate Student Services, 330-672-2576, Fax: 330-672-9162, E-mail: ogs@kent.edu.

Kentucky State University, College of Professional Studies, Frankfort, KY 40601. Offers business administration (MBA), including accounting, finance, management, marketing; public administration (MPA), including human resource management, international administration and development, management information systems, nonprofit management; special education (MA). Part-time and evening/weekend programs available. Postbaccalaureate distance learning degree programs offered (minimal on-campus study). *Faculty:* 11 full-time (3 women), 2 part-time/adjunct (both women). *Students:* 79 full-time (51 women), 66 part-time (34 women); includes 88 minority (85 African Americans, 2 Asian Americans or Pacific Islanders, 1 Hispanic American), 4 international. Average age 34. 92 applicants, 75% accepted, 52 enrolled. In 2009, 32 master's awarded. *Degree requirements:* For master's, comprehensive exam, thesis optional. *Entrance requirements:* For master's, GMAT, GRE. Additional exam requirements/recommendations for international students: Required—TOEFL (minimum score 525 paper-based; 173 computer-based). *Application deadline:* For fall admission, 7/1 priority date for domestic students, 4/15 priority date for international students; for spring admission, 11/15 priority date for domestic students, 8/1 priority date for international students. Applications are processed on a rolling basis. Application fee: $30 ($100 for international students). Electronic applications accepted. *Expenses:* Tuition, state resident: full-time $5634; part-time $313 per credit hour. Tuition, nonresident: full-time $14,598; part-time $811 per credit hour. Required fees: $450; $25 per credit hour. *Financial support:* In 2009–10, 113 students received support, including 4 research assistantships (averaging $14,035 per year); career-related internships or fieldwork, scholarships/grants, tuition waivers (partial), and unspecified assistantships also available. Financial award application deadline: 4/15; financial award applicants required to submit FAFSA. *Unit head:* Dr. Gashaw Lake, Dean, College of Professional Studies, 502-597-6105, Fax: 502-597-6715, E-mail: gashaw.lake@kysu.edu. *Application contact:* Cedric Cunningham, Administrative Assistant, Office of Graduate Studies, 502-597-6536, E-mail: cedric.cunningham@kysu.edu.

Kutztown University of Pennsylvania, College of Education, Program in Elementary Education, Kutztown, PA 19530-0730. Offers early childhood education (Certificate); elementary education (M Ed, Certificate); special education (Certificate). *Accreditation:* NCATE. Part-time and evening/weekend programs available. *Faculty:* 7 full-time (all women), 2 part-time/adjunct (both women). *Students:* 25 full-time (18 women), 27 part-time (25 women); includes 2 minority (both Hispanic Americans). Average age 29. 46 applicants, 83% accepted, 15 enrolled. In 2009, 23 master's awarded. *Degree requirements:* For master's, comprehensive exam, thesis optional, comprehensive project. *Entrance requirements:* For master's, GRE General Test. Additional exam requirements/recommendations for international students: Required—TOEFL. *Application deadline:* For fall admission, 8/15 priority date for domestic and international students; for spring admission, 12/15 priority date for domestic and international students. Applications are processed on a rolling basis. Application fee: $35. Electronic applications accepted. *Expenses:* Tuition, state resident: full-time $6666; part-time $370 per credit. Tuition, nonresident: full-time $10,666; part-time $593 per credit. Required fees: $62 per credit. $60 per semester. *Financial support:* Career-related internships or fieldwork, Federal Work-Study, scholarships/grants, and unspecified assistantships available. Financial award application deadline: 3/1; financial award applicants required to submit FAFSA. *Faculty research:* Whole language, middle schools, cooperative learning discussion techniques, oral reading techniques, hemisphericity. *Unit head:* Dr. Elsa Geskus, Chairperson, 610-683-4262, Fax: 610-683-1327, E-mail: geskus@kutztown.edu. *Application contact:* Kelly D. Burr, Associate Director, Graduate Admissions, 610-683-4200, Fax: 610-683-1393, E-mail: graduate@kutztown.edu.

Lamar University, College of Graduate Studies, College of Fine Arts and Communication, Department of Deaf Studies and Deaf Education, Beaumont, TX 77710. Offers MS, Ed D. *Accreditation:* ASHA. Part-time and evening/weekend programs available. *Faculty:* 6 full-time (5 women). *Students:* 26 full-time (20 women), 25 part-time (18 women); includes 10 minority (6 African Americans, 1 Asian American or Pacific Islander, 3 Hispanic Americans), 1 international. Average age 35. 46 applicants, 52% accepted, 14 enrolled. In 2009, 10 master's awarded. *Degree requirements:* For master's, thesis optional; for doctorate, thesis/dissertation. *Entrance requirements:* For master's, GRE General Test, performance IQ score of 115 (for deaf students), minimum GPA of 2.5; for doctorate, GRE General Test, performance IQ score of 115 (for deaf students). Additional exam requirements/recommendations for international students: Required—TOEFL. *Application deadline:* For fall admission, 8/1 priority date for domestic students; for spring admission, 12/1 for domestic students. Applications are processed on a rolling basis. Application fee: $25 ($50 for international students). *Financial support:* In 2009–10, 43 fellowships were awarded; research assistantships. Financial award application deadline: 4/1. *Faculty research:* Multicultural and deaf teacher training, central auditory processing, voice sign language. *Unit head:* Dr. Gabriel A. Martin, Chair, 409-880-8175, Fax: 409-880-2265. *Application contact:* Debbie Piper, Coordinator of Graduate Admissions, 409-880-8356, Fax: 409-880-8414, E-mail: gradmissions@hal.lamar.edu.

Lancaster Bible College & Graduate School, Graduate School, Lancaster, PA 17601-5036. Offers Bible (MA); consulting resource teacher (M Ed); counseling (MA); ministry (MA); school counseling (M Ed). Part-time and evening/weekend programs available. *Degree requirements:* For master's, comprehensive exam (for some programs), thesis (for some programs). *Entrance requirements:* For master's, bachelor's degree with a minimum of 30 credits of course work in Bible, minimum undergraduate GPA of 3.0, interview. Additional exam requirements/recommendations for international students: Required—TOEFL.

Lee University, Program in Education, Cleveland, TN 37320-3450. Offers classroom teaching (M Ed, Ed S); educational leadership (M Ed, Ed S); elementary/secondary education (MAT); secondary education (MAT); special education (elementary) (M Ed); special education (secondary) (M Ed, MAT); special education (severe disabilities) (M Ed). Part-time programs available. *Faculty:* 11 full-time (4 women), 3 part-time/adjunct (2 women). *Students:* 65 full-time (45 women), 140 part-time (80 women); includes 8 minority (5 African Americans, 1 American Indian/Alaska Native, 2 Hispanic Americans), 6 international. Average age 31. 4 applicants, 100% accepted, 2 enrolled. In 2009, 75 master's, 7 other advanced degrees awarded. *Degree requirements:* For master's, variable foreign language requirement, comprehensive exam, thesis, internship. *Entrance requirements:* For master's, MAT or GRE General Test, minimum GPA of 2.75, 3 letters of recommendation, interview, writing sample. Additional exam requirements/recommendations for international students: Required—TOEFL (minimum score 450 paper-based; 45 computer-based). *Application deadline:* For fall admission, 4/1 priority date for domestic students; for spring admission, 10/1 priority date for domestic students. Applications are processed on a rolling basis. Application fee: $25. *Expenses:* Tuition: Full-time $11,100; part-time $463 per credit. Required fees: $305. *Financial support:* Career-related internships or fieldwork, Federal Work-Study, institutionally sponsored loans, scholarships/grants, and unspecified assistantships available. Financial award application deadline: 3/1; financial award applicants required to submit FAFSA. *Unit head:* Dr. Gary Riggins, Director, 423-614-8193. *Application contact:* Vicki Glasscock, Graduate Admissions Director, 423-614-8059, E-mail: vglasscock@leeuniversity.edu.

Lehigh University, College of Education, Program in Comparative and International Education, Bethlehem, PA 18015. Offers comparative and international education (MA); globalization and educational change (M Ed); international counseling (Certificate); international development in education (Certificate); special education (Certificate); TESOL (Certificate). Part-time and evening/weekend programs available. Postbaccalaureate distance learning degree programs offered (no on-campus study). *Faculty:* 2 full-time (1 woman). *Students:* 9 full-time (6 women), 40 part-time (39 women); includes 3 minority (2 African Americans, 1 Hispanic American), 10 international. Average age 36. 46 applicants, 67% accepted, 18 enrolled. In 2009, 11 master's awarded. *Degree requirements:* For master's, thesis (MA). *Entrance requirements:* For master's, 2 letters of recommendation. Additional exam requirements/recommendations for international students: Required—TOEFL (minimum score 600 paper-based; 250 computer-based; 93 iBT). *Application deadline:* For fall admission, 5/15 for domestic and international students; for spring admission, 11/1 for domestic and international students. Applications are processed on a rolling basis. Application fee: $65. Electronic applications accepted. *Financial support:* In 2009–10, 4 students received support, including 4 research assistantships with full and partial tuition reimbursements available (averaging $13,000 per year). Financial award application deadline: 3/15. *Faculty research:* Gender equity in education, post-socialist education transformation, educational borrowing, comparing education systems, education policy and globalization. *Unit head:* Dr. Alexander W. Wiseman, Coordinator, 610-758-5740, Fax: 610-758-6223, E-mail: aww207@lehigh.edu. *Application contact:* Donna M. Johnson, Coordinator, 610-758-3231, Fax: 610-758-6223, E-mail: dmj4@lehigh.edu.

Lehigh University, College of Education, Program in Educational Leadership, Bethlehem, PA 18015. Offers educational leadership (M Ed, Ed D); principal certification K-12 (Certificate); pupil services (Certificate); special education (Certificate); superintendant certification (Certificate); supervisor of curriculum and instruction (Certificate); supervisor of pupil services (Certificate); MBA/M Ed. Part-time and evening/weekend programs available. Postbaccalaureate distance learning degree programs offered (minimal on-campus study). *Faculty:* 7 full-time (2 women), 16 part-time/adjunct (9 women). *Students:* 12 full-time (6 women), 174 part-time (102 women); includes 8 minority (4 African Americans, 1 Asian American or Pacific Islander, 3 Hispanic Americans), 20 international. Average age 37. 55 applicants, 73% accepted, 34 enrolled. In 2009, 39 master's, 4 doctorates awarded. *Degree requirements:* For doctorate, comprehensive exam, thesis/dissertation. *Entrance requirements:* For master's, minimum GPA of 3.0; for doctorate, GRE General Test or MAT, minimum graduate GPA of 3.6, 2 letters of recommendation, essay, transcript; for Certificate, minimum undergraduate GPA of 3.0. Additional exam requirements/recommendations for international students: Required—TOEFL (minimum score 600 paper-based; 250 computer-based; 93 iBT). *Application deadline:* For fall admission, 1/15 for domestic and international students; for spring admission, 11/1 for domestic and international students. Applications are processed on a rolling basis. Application fee: $65. Electronic applications accepted. *Financial support:* In 2009–10, 2 students received support, including 2 research assistantships with full and partial tuition reimbursements available (averaging $13,000 per year); fellowships with full and partial tuition reimbursements available, teaching assistantships with full and partial tuition reimbursements available, career-related internships or fieldwork, Federal Work-Study, institutionally sponsored loans, scholarships/grants, and tuition waivers (full and partial) also available. Financial award application deadline: 1/31. *Faculty research:* School finance and law, supervision of instruction, middle-level education, organizational change, leadership preparation and development, international school leadership, urban school leadership. *Unit head:* Dr. George P. White, Coordinator, 610-758-3250, Fax: 610-758-3227, E-mail: gpw1@lehigh.edu. *Application contact:* Donna M. Johnson, Coordinator, 610-758-3231, Fax: 610-758-6223, E-mail: dmj4@lehigh.edu.

Lehigh University, College of Education, Program in Special Education, Bethlehem, PA 18015. Offers M Ed, PhD, Certificate. Part-time and evening/weekend programs available. *Faculty:* 4 full-time (all women), 6 part-time/adjunct (5 women). *Students:* 11 full-time (10 women), 70 part-time (60 women); includes 6 minority (3 African Americans, 2 Asian Americans or Pacific Islanders, 1 Hispanic American), 4 international. Average age 30. 47 applicants, 81% accepted, 26 enrolled. In 2009, 31 master's, 2 doctorates awarded. *Degree requirements:* For master's, comprehensive exam, thesis; for doctorate, comprehensive exam, thesis/dissertation. *Entrance requirements:* For master's, minimum GPA of 3.0, 2 letters of recommendation; for doctorate, GRE General Test, minimum GPA of 3.5, essay, 3 letters of recommendation, transcripts. Additional exam requirements/recommendations for international students: Required—TOEFL (minimum score 600 paper-based; 250 computer-based; 85 iBT). *Application deadline:* For fall admission, 2/1 for domestic and international students;

Special Education

Lehigh University (continued)

for winter admission, 5/15 for domestic and international students. Application fee: $65. Electronic applications accepted. *Financial support:* In 2009–10, 28 students received support, including 23 research assistantships with full and partial tuition reimbursements available (averaging $15,500 per year); career-related internships or fieldwork, Federal Work-Study, institutionally sponsored loans, scholarships/grants, tuition waivers (full and partial), and field-based positions also available. Financial award application deadline: 1/31. *Faculty research:* Developmental disabilities, language, literacy, emotional and behavioral disorders. *Unit head:* Dr. Lee Kern, Coordinator, 610-758-3256, Fax: 610-758-6223, E-mail: lek6@lehigh.edu. *Application contact:* Sharon Y. Warden, Coordinator, 610-758-3256, Fax: 610-758-6223, E-mail: sy00@lehigh.edu.

Lehman College of the City University of New York, Division of Education, Department of Specialized Services in Education, Bronx, NY 10468-1589. Offers guidance and counseling (MS Ed); reading teacher (MS Ed); teachers of special education (MS Ed), including bilingual special education, early special education, emotional handicaps, learning disabilities, mental retardation. Part-time and evening/weekend programs available. *Faculty research:* Battered women, whole language classrooms, parent education, mainstreaming.

Lehman College of the City University of New York, Division of Education, Department of Specialized Services in Education, Teachers of Special Education Program, Option in Bilingual Special Education, Bronx, NY 10468-1589. Offers MS Ed. *Accreditation:* NCATE. *Entrance requirements:* For master's, minimum GPA of 3.0.

Lehman College of the City University of New York, Division of Education, Department of Specialized Services in Education, Teachers of Special Education Program, Option in Early Special Education, Bronx, NY 10468-1589. Offers MS Ed. *Accreditation:* NCATE. *Entrance requirements:* For master's, minimum GPA of 3.0.

Lehman College of the City University of New York, Division of Education, Department of Specialized Services in Education, Teachers of Special Education Program, Option in Emotional Handicaps, Bronx, NY 10468-1589. Offers MS Ed. *Accreditation:* NCATE. Part-time and evening/weekend programs available. *Entrance requirements:* For master's, minimum GPA of 2.7. *Faculty research:* Behavioral disorders, self-evaluation, applied behavior analysis.

Lehman College of the City University of New York, Division of Education, Department of Specialized Services in Education, Teachers of Special Education Program, Option in Learning Disabilities, Bronx, NY 10468-1589. Offers MS Ed. *Accreditation:* NCATE. Part-time and evening/weekend programs available. *Entrance requirements:* For master's, interview, minimum GPA of 2.7. *Faculty research:* Emergent literacy, language-based classrooms, primary and secondary social contexts of language and literacy, innovative in-service education models, adult literacy.

Lehman College of the City University of New York, Division of Education, Department of Specialized Services in Education, Teachers of Special Education Program, Option in Mental Retardation, Bronx, NY 10468-1589. Offers MS Ed. *Accreditation:* NCATE. Part-time and evening/weekend programs available. *Entrance requirements:* For master's, minimum GPA of 2.7. *Faculty research:* Conductive education, homeless infants and their families, infant stimulation, hospitalizing infants with AIDS, legislation PL99-457.

Le Moyne College, Department of Education, Syracuse, NY 13214. Offers adolescent education (MS Ed, MST); adolescent education/special education (MS Ed, MST); adolescent English (grades 7-12) (MST); adolescent history (grades 7-12) (MST); childhood education (MS Ed); childhood education/special education (MS Ed); elementary education (MS Ed); general professional education (MS Ed); inclusive childhood education (MST); middle child specialist/special education (MS Ed); middle childhood specialist (MS Ed); school building leadership (MS Ed, CAS); school district business leader (MS Ed, CAS); school district leadership (MS Ed, CAS); secondary education (MS Ed); special education (MS Ed). *Accreditation:* Teacher Education Accreditation Council. Part-time and evening/weekend programs available. *Faculty:* 15 full-time (8 women), 61 part-time/adjunct (33 women). *Students:* 40 full-time (30 women), 260 part-time (180 women); includes 25 minority (11 African Americans, 3 American Indian/Alaska Native, 3 Asian Americans or Pacific Islanders, 8 Hispanic Americans). Average age 31. 168 applicants, 89% accepted, 140 enrolled. In 2009, 180 master's awarded. *Degree requirements:* For master's, thesis. *Entrance requirements:* For master's, GRE General Test, 2 letters of recommendation. Additional exam requirements/recommendations for international students: Required—TOEFL (minimum score 550 paper-based; 213 computer-based; 79 iBT). *Application deadline:* For fall admission, 4/1 priority date for domestic and international students; for spring admission, 10/1 priority date for domestic and international students. Applications are processed on a rolling basis. Application fee: $50. *Expenses:* Contact institution. *Financial support:* In 2009–10, 28 students received support. Career-related internships or fieldwork and health care benefits available. Support available to part-time students. Financial award applicants required to submit FAFSA. *Faculty research:* Recruitment/retention strategies, minority teachers, special education, multiculturalism, literacy, technology, video games learning, autism, school district organization. *Unit head:* Dr. Norbert J. Henry, Interim Chair/Director, 315-445-4376, Fax: 315-445-4744, E-mail: henry@lemoyne.edu. *Application contact:* Kristen P. Trapasso, Director of Graduate Admission, 315-445-4265, Fax: 315-445-6027, E-mail: trapaskp@lemoyne.edu.

Lesley University, School of Education, Cambridge, MA 02138-2790. Offers curriculum and instruction (M Ed, CAGS); early childhood education (M Ed); educational studies (PhD); elementary education (M Ed); individually designed (M Ed); middle school education (M Ed); moderate special needs (M Ed); reading (M Ed, CAGS); science in education (M Ed); severe special needs (M Ed); special needs (CAGS); technology in education (M Ed, CAGS). *Accreditation:* Teacher Education Accreditation Council. Part-time and evening/weekend programs available. Postbaccalaureate distance learning degree programs offered (no on-campus study). *Degree requirements:* For master's, practicum; for doctorate, thesis/dissertation. *Entrance requirements:* For doctorate, GRE General Test or MAT, interview, master's degree, resume; for CAGS, interview, master's degree. Additional exam requirements/recommendations for international students: Required—TOEFL (minimum score 550 paper-based; 213 computer-based; 80 iBT). Electronic applications accepted. *Faculty research:* Assessment in literacy, mathematics and science; autism spectrum disorders; instructional technology and online learning; multicultural education and ELL.

Lewis & Clark College, Graduate School of Education and Counseling, Department of Teacher Education, Program in Special Education, Portland, OR 97219-7899. Offers M Ed. *Accreditation:* NCATE. Part-time and evening/weekend programs available. *Faculty:* 1 (woman) full-time, 2 part-time/adjunct (both women). *Students:* 14 part-time (12 women). Average age 41. 14 applicants, 100% accepted, 9 enrolled. In 2009, 4 master's awarded. *Entrance requirements:* For master's, minimum GPA of 2.75. Additional exam requirements/recommendations for international students: Required—TOEFL (minimum score 575 paper-based; 233 computer-based). *Application deadline:* Applications are processed on a rolling basis. Application fee: $50. Electronic applications accepted. *Expenses:* Tuition: Part-time $713 per semester hour. Tuition and fees vary according to course level and campus/location. *Financial support:* In 2009–10, 14 students received support. Career-related internships or fieldwork, Federal Work-Study, institutionally sponsored loans, scholarships/grants, health care benefits, and tuition waivers (partial) available. Support available to part-time students. Financial award application deadline: 3/1; financial award applicants required to submit FAFSA. *Unit head:* Christine Moore, Program Coordinator, 503-768-6128, E-mail: cmoore@lclark.edu. *Application contact:* Becky Haas, Director of Admissions, 503-768-6200, Fax: 503-768-6205, E-mail: gseadmit@lclark.edu.

Lewis University, College of Education, Program in Special Education, Romeoville, IL 60446. Offers MA. *Students:* 41 full-time (30 women), 19 part-time (15 women); includes 9 minority (5

African Americans, 1 Asian American or Pacific Islander, 3 Hispanic Americans). Average age 31. In 2009, 33 master's awarded. *Entrance requirements:* For master's, departmental qualifying exam, writing exam, minimum GPA of 2.75, 2 letters of recommendation, interview. Additional exam requirements/recommendations for international students: Required—TOEFL (minimum score 550 paper-based; 213 computer-based). *Application deadline:* For fall admission, 5/1 priority date for international students; for spring admission, 11/15 priority date for international students. Applications are processed on a rolling basis. Application fee: $40. Electronic applications accepted. *Expenses:* Tuition: Full-time $6480; part-time $720 per credit. One-time fee: $40. Tuition and fees vary according to course load, degree level and program. *Financial support:* Federal Work-Study, scholarships/grants, and unspecified assistantships available. Financial award application deadline: 5/1; financial award applicants required to submit FAFSA. *Unit head:* Dr. Christy Roberts, Director, 815-838-0500 Ext. 5317, E-mail: robertch@lewisu.edu. *Application contact:* Fran Welsh, Secretary, 815-838-0500 Ext. 5880, E-mail: welshfr@lewisu.edu.

Liberty University, School of Education, Lynchburg, VA 24502. Offers administration and supervision (M Ed); curriculum and instruction (M Ed); early childhood education (M Ed); education specialist (Ed S); educational leadership (Ed D); elementary education (M Ed); gifted education (M Ed); reading specialist (M Ed); school counseling (M Ed); secondary education (M Ed); special education (M Ed). *Accreditation:* NCATE. Part-time programs available. Postbaccalaureate distance learning degree programs offered (minimal on-campus study). *Degree requirements:* For doctorate, comprehensive exam, thesis/dissertation. *Entrance requirements:* For master's, GRE General Test or MAT (aken in or before 1999), 2 letters of recommendation, minimum undergraduate GPA of 3.0, curriculum vitae; for doctorate, GRE General Test or MAT (if taken before 1999), minimum master's GPA of 3.0, 3 years of teacher experience; for Ed S, GRE General Test or MAT (if taken before 1999), minimum master's GPA of 3.0, 3 years of teaching experience. Additional exam requirements/recommendations for international students: Required—TOEFL (minimum score 600 paper-based; 250 computer-based). Electronic applications accepted. *Expenses:* Contact institution. *Faculty research:* Self-determination, character education, bibliotherapy, learning styles, distance education.

Lincoln University, School of Graduate Studies and Continuing Education, Jefferson City, MO 65102. Offers business administration (MBA), including accounting, entrepreneurship, management, public administration and policy; educational leadership (Ed S), including elementary leadership, secondary leadership, superintendency; guidance and counseling (M Ed), including community/agency counseling, elementary school, secondary school; history (MA); school administration and supervision (M Ed), including elementary school administration, secondary school administration, special education administration; school teaching (M Ed), including elementary school teaching, secondary school teaching; social science (MA), including history, political science, sociology; sociology (MA); sociology/criminal justice (MA). Part-time and evening/weekend programs available. *Students:* 52 full-time (27 women), 146 part-time (107 women); includes 40 minority (39 African Americans, 1 Asian American or Pacific Islander), 15 international. Average age 35. 76 applicants, 95% accepted, 46 enrolled. In 2009, 60 master's, 6 other advanced degrees awarded. *Degree requirements:* For master's and Ed S, comprehensive exam, thesis optional. *Entrance requirements:* For master's and Ed S, GRE, MAT or GMAT, minimum GPA of 2.75 in major, 2.5 overall; 3 letters of recommendation; minimum C average in English composition; personal statement of purpose. Additional exam requirements/recommendations for international students: Required—TOEFL (minimum score 500 paper-based; 173 computer-based; 61 iBT). *Application deadline:* For fall admission, 7/1 priority date for domestic and international students; for spring admission, 12/1 priority date for domestic and international students. Applications are processed on a rolling basis. Application fee: $20. *Expenses:* Tuition, state resident: full-time $4185; part-time $232.50 per credit hour. Tuition, nonresident: full-time $7767; part-time $431.50 per credit hour. Required fees: $270; $15 per credit hour. $20 per term. *Financial support:* Federal Work-Study and scholarships/grants available. Financial award application deadline: 4/1; financial award applicants required to submit FAFSA. *Faculty research:* Suicide prevention. *Unit head:* Dr. Linda S. Bickel, Dean, 573-681-5247, Fax: 573-681-5106, E-mail: gradschool@lincolnu.edu. *Application contact:* Irasema Steck, Administrative Assistant, 573-681-5247, Fax: 573-681-5106, E-mail: gradschool@lincolnu.edu.

Lipscomb University, Program in Education, Nashville, TN 37204-3951. Offers English language learners (MAT); instructional leadership (M Ed); instructional technology (M Ed); learning and teaching (MALT); math specialty (M Ed); school administration and supervision (M Ed); special education instruction, K-12 (MASE). *Accreditation:* NCATE. Part-time and evening/weekend programs available. *Faculty:* 4 full-time (1 woman), 12 part-time/adjunct (8 women). *Students:* 140 full-time (103 women), 200 part-time (144 women); includes 32 minority (29 African Americans, 3 Hispanic Americans). Average age 31. 206 applicants, 75% accepted. In 2009, 131 master's awarded. *Entrance requirements:* For master's, MAT or GRE General Test, 2 reference letters. Additional exam requirements/recommendations for international students: Required—TOEFL (minimum score 570 paper-based; 230 computer-based). *Application deadline:* For fall admission, 8/29 priority date for domestic students; for spring admission, 1/16 priority date for domestic students. Applications are processed on a rolling basis. Application fee: $50. *Expenses:* Tuition: Full-time $16,002; part-time $889 per credit hour. Tuition and fees vary according to program. *Financial support:* In 2009–10, 67 students received support. Federal Work-Study, tuition waivers (full), and unspecified assistantships available. Support available to part-time students. Financial award applicants required to submit FAFSA. *Faculty research:* Facilitative learning styles, leadership, student assessment, interactive multimedia inclusion. *Unit head:* Dr. Deborah Boyd, Director of M Ed Program, 615-966-6263. *Application contact:* Kristin Green, Administrative Assistant, 615-966-7628 Ext. 6081, Fax: 615-966-7628, E-mail: kristin.green@lipscomb.edu.

Long Island University at Riverhead, Education Division, Program in Teaching Students with Disabilities, Riverhead, NY 11901. Offers MS Ed. *Faculty:* 1 full-time (0 women), 11 part-time/adjunct (7 women). *Students:* 5 full-time (all women), 24 part-time (22 women). Average age 31. In 2009, 3 master's awarded. *Degree requirements:* For master's, thesis. *Entrance requirements:* For master's, minimum GPA of 2.75, New York state teacher certification, interview, writing sample. Additional exam requirements/recommendations for international students: Required—TOEFL (minimum score 550 paper-based; 250 computer-based). *Application deadline:* Applications are processed on a rolling basis. Electronic applications accepted. *Financial support:* In 2009–10, 21 students received support, including 1 research assistantship with full tuition reimbursement available. Financial award applicants required to submit FAFSA. *Unit head:* Dr. Sanja Cale, Unit Head, 631-287-8010, Fax: 631-287-8130, E-mail: sanja.cale@liu.edu. *Application contact:* Andrea Borra, Admissions Counselor, 631-287-8010 Ext. 8326, Fax: 631-287-8253, E-mail: andrea.borra@liu.edu.

Long Island University, Brentwood Campus, School of Education, Brentwood, NY 11717. Offers childhood education (MS); early childhood education (MS); literacy (MS); mental health counseling (MS); school counseling (MS); special education (MS). Part-time and evening/weekend programs available.

Long Island University, Brooklyn Campus, School of Education, Department of Teaching and Learning, Program in Special Education, Brooklyn, NY 11201-8423. Offers MS Ed. Part-time and evening/weekend programs available. *Degree requirements:* For master's, thesis optional. *Entrance requirements:* For master's, 2 letters of recommendation. Additional exam requirements/recommendations for international students: Required—TOEFL (minimum score 500 paper-based; 173 computer-based). Electronic applications accepted.

Long Island University, C.W. Post Campus, School of Education, Department of Special Education and Literacy, Brookville, NY 11548-1300. Offers childhood education/literacy (MS); childhood education/special education (MS); literacy (MS Ed); special education (MS Ed). *Accreditation:* Teacher Education Accreditation Council. Part-time and evening/weekend programs available. *Degree requirements:* For master's, research project, comprehensive

exam or thesis. *Entrance requirements:* For master's, interview; minimum GPA of 2.75 in major, 2.5 overall. Electronic applications accepted. *Faculty research:* Autism, mainstreaming, robotics and microcomputers in special education, transition from school to work.

Long Island University, Rockland Graduate Campus, Graduate School, Programs in Special Education and Literacy, Orangeburg, NY 10962. Offers childhood/literacy (MS); childhood/ special education (MS); literacy (MS Ed); special education (MS Ed); special education autism (MS Ed). Part-time programs available. *Faculty:* 1 (woman) full-time, 10 part-time/adjunct (6 women). *Students:* 30 full-time (25 women), 130 part-time (114 women). In 2009, 81 master's awarded. *Application deadline:* Applications are processed on a rolling basis. Application fee: $30. *Expenses:* Tuition: Part-time $930 per credit. Required fees: $200 per semester. *Financial support:* Applicants required to submit FAFSA. *Unit head:* Prof. Elaine B. Geller, Program Director, 845-359-7200 Ext. 5407, Fax: 845-359-7248, E-mail: elaineb.geller@liu.edu. *Application contact:* Peter S. Reiner, Director of Admissions and Marketing, 845-359-7200, Fax: 845-359-7248, E-mail: peter.reiner@liu.edu.

Long Island University, Westchester Graduate Campus, Programs in Education-Teaching, Program in Special Education and Secondary Education, Purchase, NY 10577. Offers MS Ed, Advanced Certificate. Part-time and evening/weekend programs available.

Longwood University, Office of Graduate Studies, College of Education and Human Services, Farmville, VA 23909. Offers communication sciences and disorders (MS); community and college counseling (MS); curriculum and instruction specialist-elementary (MS), including mild disabilities, modern languages; curriculum and instruction specialist-secondary (MS), including English, mild disabilities, modern languages; educational leadership (MS); guidance and counseling (MS); literacy and culture (MS); school library media (MS). *Accreditation:* NCATE. Part-time and evening/weekend programs available. *Degree requirements:* For master's, comprehensive exam, thesis optional. *Entrance requirements:* For master's, GRE (communication sciences and disorders), minimum GPA of 2.75. Additional exam requirements/ recommendations for international students: Required—TOEFL (minimum score 550 paper-based; 213 computer-based).

Loras College, Graduate Division, Program in Education with an Emphasis in Special Education, Dubuque, IA 52004-0178. Offers instructional strategist I K-6 and 7-12 (MA). Part-time and evening/weekend programs available. *Degree requirements:* For master's, comprehensive exam, thesis optional. *Entrance requirements:* For master's, minimum cumulative undergraduate GPA of 3.0.

Louisiana Tech University, Graduate School, College of Education, Department of Behavioral Sciences and Psychology, Ruston, LA 71272. Offers counseling (MA); counseling psychology (PhD); industrial/organizational psychology (MA); special education (MA). *Accreditation:* APA (one or more programs are accredited). Part-time programs available. *Degree requirements:* For master's, thesis or alternative; for doctorate, thesis/dissertation. *Entrance requirements:* For master's and doctorate, GRE General Test.

Loyola Marymount University, School of Education, Department of Educational Support Services, Program in Special Education, Los Angeles, CA 90045. Offers MA. Part-time and evening/weekend programs available. *Faculty:* 9 full-time (6 women), 22 part-time/adjunct (19 women). *Students:* 78 full-time (61 women), 7 part-time (5 women); includes 38 minority (18 African Americans, 3 Asian Americans or Pacific Islanders, 17 Hispanic Americans). Average age 27. 49 applicants, 88% accepted, 43 enrolled. In 2009, 27 master's awarded. *Degree requirements:* For master's, comprehensive exam. *Entrance requirements:* For master's, CBEST, CSET, RICA, 3 letters of recommendation. Additional exam requirements/recommendations for international students: Required—TOEFL (minimum score 600 paper-based; 250 computer-based; 100 iBT). *Application deadline:* For fall admission, 6/15 for domestic students; for spring admission, 11/15 for domestic students. Application fee: $50. Electronic applications accepted. *Financial support:* In 2009–10, 57 students received support. Scholarships/grants and unspecified assistantships available. Support available to part-time students. Financial award application deadline: 6/15; financial award applicants required to submit FAFSA. Total annual research expenditures: $5,922. *Unit head:* Dr. Tom Batsis, Chair, 310-338-7303, E-mail: tbatsis@lmu.edu. *Application contact:* Chake H. Kouyoumjian, Director, Graduate Admissions, 310-338-2721, Fax: 310-338-6086, E-mail: ckouyoum@lmu.edu.

Loyola University Chicago, School of Education, Program in Initial Teacher Preparation, Chicago, IL 60660. Offers elementary education (M Ed); math education (M Ed); reading specialist (M Ed); school technology (M Ed); science education (M Ed); secondary education (M Ed); special education (M Ed). *Accreditation:* NCATE. *Faculty:* 12 full-time (9 women), 12 part-time/adjunct (6 women). *Students:* 154. Average age 28. 125 applicants, 69% accepted, 38 enrolled. In 2009, 89 master's awarded. *Degree requirements:* For master's, comprehensive exam. *Entrance requirements:* For master's, Illinois Basic Skills Test, 3 letters of recommendation, minimum GPA of 3.0, resume. Additional exam requirements/recommendations for international students: Required—TOEFL (minimum score 550 paper-based; 213 computer-based; 79 iBT). *Application deadline:* For fall admission, 7/1 priority date for domestic and international students; for spring admission, 11/1 priority date for domestic and international students. Applications are processed on a rolling basis. Application fee: $50. Electronic applications accepted. *Expenses:* Tuition: Full-time $14,220; part-time $790 per credit hour. Required fees: $60 per semester hour. Tuition and fees vary according to program. *Financial support:* In 2009–10, 1 research assistantship with full tuition reimbursement (averaging $8,500 per year), 1 teaching assistantship were awarded. Financial award application deadline: 2/15. *Faculty research:* Positive behavior support, school reform, school improvement. *Unit head:* Dr. Dorothy Giroux, Director, 312-915-7027, E-mail: dgiroux@luc.edu. *Application contact:* Marie Rosin-Dittmar, Information Contact, 312-915-6800, E-mail: schleduc@luc.edu.

Loyola University Maryland, Graduate Programs, College of Arts and Sciences, Department of Education, Program in Special Education, Baltimore, MD 21210-2699. Offers M Ed, CAS. *Accreditation:* NCATE. Part-time and evening/weekend programs available. *Entrance requirements:* For master's and CAS, GRE General Test, GRE Subject Test (recommended). Additional exam requirements/recommendations for international students: Required—TOEFL (minimum score 550 paper-based; 213 computer-based).

Lynchburg College, Graduate Studies, School of Education and Human Development, Lynchburg, VA 24501-3199. Offers community counseling (M Ed); counselor education (M Ed), including community counseling; curriculum and instruction (M Ed); educational leadership (M Ed); English education (M Ed); reading (M Ed); school counseling (M Ed); science education (M Ed); special education (M Ed), including autism spectrum disorder, early childhood special education, mental retardation, teaching children with learning disabilities, teaching the emotionally disturbed. Part-time and evening/weekend programs available. *Degree requirements:* For master's, comprehensive exam. *Entrance requirements:* For master's, GRE, minimum undergraduate GPA of 3.0. Additional exam requirements/recommendations for international students: Required—TOEFL. *Expenses:* Tuition: Full-time $7020; part-time $390 per credit hour.

Lyndon State College, Graduate Programs in Education, Department of Education, Lyndonville, VT 05851-0919. Offers curriculum and instruction (M Ed); reading specialist (M Ed); special education (M Ed); teaching and counseling (M Ed). Part-time and evening/weekend programs available. *Degree requirements:* For master's, exam or major field project. *Entrance requirements:* Additional exam requirements/recommendations for international students: Recommended—TOEFL (minimum score 500 paper-based; 173 computer-based).

Lynn University, Donald and Helen Ross College of Education, Boca Raton, FL 33431-5598. Offers educational leadership (M Ed, PhD); exceptional student education (M Ed); teacher preparation (PhD). Part-time and evening/weekend programs available. *Degree requirements:* For master's, thesis (for some programs); for doctorate, thesis/dissertation, qualifying paper. *Entrance requirements:* For master's, GRE, minimum undergraduate GPA of 3.0, resume, 2 letters of recommendation; for doctorate, GRE or GMAT, minimum GPA of 3.25, resume, 2 letters of recommendation. Additional exam requirements/recommendations for international students: Required—TOEFL (minimum score 550 paper-based; 213 computer-based). *Application deadline:* Applications are processed on a rolling basis. Application fee: $50. Electronic applications accepted. *Expenses:* Tuition: Part-time $580 per credit. One-time fee: $200 part-time. Part-time tuition and fees vary according to degree level. *Financial support:* Career-related internships or fieldwork, Federal Work-Study, institutionally sponsored loans, scholarships/grants, tuition waivers (partial), and unspecified assistantships available. Support available to part-time students. Financial award application deadline: 8/1; financial award applicants required to submit FAFSA. *Faculty research:* Non-traditional education, innovative curricula, multicultural education, simulation games. *Application contact:* Dr. Larissa Baia, Assistant Director of Graduate Admissions, 561-237-7916, Fax: 561-237-7100, E-mail: lbaia@lynn.edu.

Madonna University, Programs in Education, Livonia, MI 48150-1173. Offers Catholic school leadership (MSA); educational leadership (MSA); learning disabilities (MAT); literacy education (MAT); teaching and learning (MAT). *Accreditation:* NCATE. Part-time and evening/weekend programs available. *Degree requirements:* For master's, thesis or alternative. Electronic applications accepted.

Malone University, Graduate Program in Education, Canton, OH 44709. Offers curriculum and instruction (MA); curriculum, instruction, and professional development (MA); instructional technology (MA); intervention specialist (MA); reading (MA). Part-time and evening/weekend programs available. *Faculty:* 7 full-time (4 women), 7 part-time/adjunct (5 women). *Students:* 2 full-time (1 woman), 64 part-time (55 women); includes 1 minority (African American). Average age 34. In 2009, 27 master's awarded. *Degree requirements:* For master's, research project. *Entrance requirements:* For master's, minimum GPA of 3.0, teaching license. Additional exam requirements/recommendations for international students: Required—TOEFL (minimum score 550 paper-based; 213 computer-based; 79 iBT). *Application deadline:* Applications are processed on a rolling basis. Application fee: $25. *Expenses:* Tuition: Part-time $450 per semester hour. *Financial support:* Tuition waivers (partial) available. Support available to part-time students. Financial award application deadline: 6/30. *Faculty research:* The Bible as children's literature, special needs students and literacy development, middle level education, school/university partnerships and professional development, child/adolescent literature and popular culture. *Unit head:* Dr. Alice E. Christie, Director, 330-478-8541, Fax: 330-471-8563, E-mail: achristie@malone.edu. *Application contact:* David L. Kleffman, Assistant Director of Enrollment, 330-471-8447, Fax: 330-471-8343, E-mail: dkleffman@malone.edu.

Manhattan College, Graduate Division, School of Education, Program in Special Education, Riverdale, NY 10471. Offers 5 year dual childhood/special education (MS Ed); dual childhood/ special education (MS Ed); special education (MS Ed). Part-time and evening/weekend programs available. *Degree requirements:* For master's, thesis, internship. *Entrance requirements:* For master's, minimum GPA of 3.0, NYSTE Last Test. Additional exam requirements/ recommendations for international students: Required—TOEFL (minimum score 550 paper-based). *Expenses:* Contact institution. *Faculty research:* Adapted physical education.

Manhattanville College, Graduate Programs, School of Education, Program in Childhood Education, Purchase, NY 10577-2132. Offers childhood and special education (MPS); childhood education (MAT); special education childhood (MPS). Part-time and evening/weekend programs available. *Students:* 67 full-time (62 women), 150 part-time (120 women); includes 6 African Americans, 3 Asian Americans or Pacific Islanders, 10 Hispanic Americans, 2 international. In 2009, 65 master's awarded. *Degree requirements:* For master's, comprehensive exam or research project, field experience. *Entrance requirements:* For master's, minimum undergraduate GPA of 3.0, 2 letters of recommendation. Additional exam requirements/recommendations for international students: Required—TOEFL. *Application deadline:* Applications are processed on a rolling basis. Application fee: $70. *Financial support:* Career-related internships or fieldwork and institutionally sponsored loans available. Support available to part-time students. Financial award applicants required to submit FAFSA. *Unit head:* Dr. Shelley Wepner, Dean, 914-323-5192, Fax: 914-694-2386, E-mail: wepners@mville.edu. *Application contact:* Jeanine Pardey-Levine, Director of Admissions, 914-323-3208, Fax: 914-694-1732, E-mail: edschool@mville.edu.

Manhattanville College, Graduate Programs, School of Education, Program in Early Childhood Education, Purchase, NY 10577-2132. Offers childhood and early childhood education (MAT); early childhood education (birth-grade 2) (MAT); literacy (birth-grade 6) (MPS), including reading, writing; literacy (birth-grade 6) and special education (grades 1-6) (MPS); special education (birth-grade 2) (MPS); special education (birth-grade 6) (MPS). Part-time and evening/ weekend programs available. *Students:* 43 full-time (42 women), 62 part-time (59 women); includes 1 African American, 1 Asian American or Pacific Islander, 7 Hispanic Americans. In 2009, 5 master's awarded. *Degree requirements:* For master's, comprehensive exam or research project, field experience. *Entrance requirements:* For master's, minimum undergraduate GPA of 3.0, 2 letters of recommendation. Additional exam requirements/recommendations for international students: Required—TOEFL. *Application deadline:* Applications are processed on a rolling basis. Application fee: $70. Electronic applications accepted. *Financial support:* Career-related internships or fieldwork and institutionally sponsored loans available. Support available to part-time students. *Unit head:* Dr. Shelley Wepner, Dean, 914-323-5192, Fax: 914-694-2386, E-mail: wepners@mville.edu. *Application contact:* Jeanine Pardey-Levine, Director of Admissions, 914-323-3208, Fax: 914-694-1732, E-mail: edschool@mville.edu.

Manhattanville College, Graduate Programs, School of Education, Program in Middle Childhood/Adolescence Education (Grades 5-12), Purchase, NY 10577-2132. Offers biology (MAT); biology and special education (MPS); chemistry (MAT); chemistry and special education (MPS); English (MAT); English and special education (MPS); literacy (MPS), including reading and writing, writing; literacy and special education (MPS); math (MAT); math and special education (MPS); second language (MAT), including French, Italian, Latin, Spanish; social studies (MAT); social studies and special education (MPS); special education (MPS). Part-time and evening/weekend programs available. *Students:* 52 full-time (39 women), 106 part-time (71 women); includes 8 African Americans, 3 Asian Americans or Pacific Islanders, 4 Hispanic Americans, 1 international. In 2009, 82 master's awarded. *Degree requirements:* For master's, comprehensive exam or research project, field experience. *Entrance requirements:* For master's, minimum undergraduate GPA of 3.0, 2 letters of recommendation. Additional exam requirements/ recommendations for international students: Required—TOEFL. *Application deadline:* Applications are processed on a rolling basis. Application fee: $70. Electronic applications accepted. *Financial support:* Career-related internships or fieldwork, Federal Work-Study, institutionally sponsored loans, and unspecified assistantships available. Support available to part-time students. Financial award application deadline: 3/1; financial award applicants required to submit FAFSA. *Unit head:* Dr. Shelley Wepner, Dean, 914-323-5192, Fax: 914-694-2386, E-mail: wepners@mville.edu. *Application contact:* Jeanine Pardey-Levine, Director of Admissions, 914-323-3208, Fax: 914-694-1732, E-mail: edschool@mville.edu.

Marshall University, Academic Affairs Division, Graduate School of Education and Professional Development, Program in Special Education, Huntington, WV 25755. Offers MA. *Accreditation:* NCATE. Part-time and evening/weekend programs available. *Faculty:* 6 full-time (3 women), 18 part-time/adjunct (16 women). *Students:* 71 full-time (54 women), 226 part-time (184 women); includes 9 minority (7 African Americans, 2 American Indian/Alaska Native), 1 international. Average age 36. In 2009, 82 master's awarded. *Degree requirements:* For master's, thesis optional, comprehensive or oral assessment, research project. *Entrance requirements:* For master's, GRE General Test or MAT, minimum GPA of 3.0. Application fee: $40. *Financial support:* Federal Work-Study, tuition waivers (full), and unspecified assistantships available. Support available to part-time students. Financial award applicants required to submit FAFSA. *Faculty research:* Teaching the severely handicapped, career/vocational

Special Education

Marshall University (continued)
education, education of the gifted. *Unit head:* Dr. Mike Sullivan, Director, 304-746-2076, E-mail: msullivan@marshall.edu. *Application contact:* Information Contact, 304-746-1900, Fax: 304-746-1902, E-mail: services@marshall.edu.

Martin Luther College, Graduate Studies, New Ulm, MN 56073. Offers instruction (MS Ed); leadership (MS Ed); special education (MS Ed). Part-time programs available. Postbaccalaureate distance learning degree programs offered. *Degree requirements:* For master's, capstone project or comprehensive exam. *Entrance requirements:* For master's, undergraduate degree in education from an accredited college or university, minimum undergraduate GPA of 3.0. Electronic applications accepted.

Marymount University, School of Education and Human Services, Program in Education, Arlington, VA 22207-4299. Offers elementary education (M Ed); English as a second language (M Ed); professional studies (M Ed); secondary education (M Ed); special education, general curriculum (M Ed). *Accreditation:* NCATE. Part-time and evening/weekend programs available. *Faculty:* 9 full-time (6 women), 9 part-time/adjunct (8 women). *Students:* 55 full-time (46 women), 117 part-time (100 women); includes 13 minority (1 African American, 4 Asian Americans or Pacific Islanders, 8 Hispanic Americans), 7 international. Average age 31. 73 applicants, 93% accepted, 55 enrolled. In 2009, 62 master's awarded. *Degree requirements:* For master's, thesis or alternative. *Entrance requirements:* For master's, GRE or MAT and PRAXIS I or SAT/ACT, 2 letters of recommendation, interview. Additional exam requirements/recommendations for international students: Required—TOEFL (minimum score 600 paper-based; 250 computer-based; 96 iBT), IELTS (minimum score 6.5). *Application deadline:* For fall admission, 7/1 for international students; for spring admission, 10/15 for international students. Applications are processed on a rolling basis. Application fee: $40. Electronic applications accepted. *Expenses:* Tuition: Full-time $13,050; part-time $725 per credit hour. Required fees: $135; $7.50 per credit hour. *Financial support:* In 2009–10, 48 students received support; research assistantships with full tuition reimbursements available, career-related internships or fieldwork, Federal Work-Study, scholarships/grants, and unspecified assistantships available. Support available to part-time students. Financial award applicants required to submit FAFSA. *Unit head:* Dr. Shelly Haser, Chair, 703-526-6855, Fax: 703-284-1631, E-mail: shelly.haser@marymount.edu. *Application contact:* Francesca Reed, Director, Graduate Admissions, 703-284-5901, Fax: 703-527-3815, E-mail: grad.admissions@marymount.edu.

Marywood University, Academic Affairs, Reap College of Education and Human Development, Department of Special Education, Program in Special Education, Scranton, PA 18509-1598. Offers MS. *Accreditation:* NCATE. *Students:* 2 full-time (both women), 23 part-time (21 women); includes 1 minority (African American). Average age 32. In 2009, 6 master's awarded. *Entrance requirements:* Additional exam requirements/recommendations for international students: Required—TOEFL (minimum score 550 paper-based; 213 computer-based; 79 iBT). *Application deadline:* For fall admission, 4/1 priority date for domestic students, 3/31 priority date for international students; for spring admission, 11/1 priority date for domestic students, 8/30 priority date for international students. Applications are processed on a rolling basis. Application fee: $35. Electronic applications accepted. *Expenses:* Tuition: Part-time $715 per credit. Required fees: $270 per semester. Tuition and fees vary according to degree level, campus/location and program. *Financial support:* Career-related internships or fieldwork, scholarships/grants, and unspecified assistantships available. Support available to part-time students. Financial award application deadline: 6/30; financial award applicants required to submit FAFSA. *Application contact:* Tammy Manka, Assistant Director of Graduate Admissions, 866-279-9663, E-mail: tmanka@marywood.edu.

Marywood University, Academic Affairs, Reap College of Education and Human Development, Department of Special Education, Program in Special Education Administration and Supervision, Scranton, PA 18509-1598. Offers MS. *Accreditation:* NCATE. *Students:* 2 part-time (both women). Average age 31. In 2009, 3 master's awarded. *Entrance requirements:* Additional exam requirements/recommendations for international students: Required—TOEFL (minimum score 550 paper-based; 213 computer-based; 79 iBT). *Application deadline:* For fall admission, 4/1 priority date for domestic students, 3/31 priority date for international students; for spring admission, 11/1 priority date for domestic students, 8/31 priority date for international students. Applications are processed on a rolling basis. Application fee: $35. Electronic applications accepted. *Expenses:* Tuition: Part-time $715 per credit. Required fees: $270 per semester. Tuition and fees vary according to degree level, campus/location and program. *Financial support:* Career-related internships or fieldwork, scholarships/grants, and unspecified assistantships available. Support available to part-time students. Financial award application deadline: 6/30; financial award applicants required to submit FAFSA. *Application contact:* Tammy Manka, Assistant Director of Graduate Admissions, 866-279-9663, E-mail: tmanka@marywood.edu.

Massachusetts College of Liberal Arts, Program in Education, North Adams, MA 01247-4100. Offers curriculum (M Ed); educational administration (M Ed); reading (M Ed); special education (M Ed). Part-time and evening/weekend programs available. *Degree requirements:* For master's, thesis. *Entrance requirements:* For master's, writing sample. *Faculty research:* Anxiety, methodology, mainstreaming.

McDaniel College, Graduate and Professional Studies, Program in Education of the Deaf, Westminster, MD 21157-4390. Offers MS. *Accreditation:* NCATE. Part-time programs available. *Degree requirements:* For master's, comprehensive exam, thesis optional. *Entrance requirements:* For master's, American Sign Language Proficiency Interview (ASLPI). Additional exam requirements/recommendations for international students: Required—TOEFL (minimum score 213 computer-based), English Proficiency Essay. *Expenses:* Tuition: Part-time $325 per credit hour. *Faculty research:* Mainstreaming of multihandicapped children.

McDaniel College, Graduate and Professional Studies, Program in Human Services Management in Special Education, Westminster, MD 21157-4390. Offers MS. *Accreditation:* NCATE. Evening/weekend programs available. *Degree requirements:* For master's, internship. *Entrance requirements:* For master's, letters of reference (3). Additional exam requirements/recommendations for international students: Required—TOEFL (minimum score 213 computer-based). *Expenses:* Tuition: Part-time $325 per credit hour.

McDaniel College, Graduate and Professional Studies, Program in Special Education, Westminster, MD 21157-4390. Offers MS. *Accreditation:* NCATE. Part-time and evening/weekend programs available. *Degree requirements:* For master's, comprehensive exam, thesis optional. *Entrance requirements:* For master's, GRE General Test, MAT, or NTE/PRAXIS I, letters of reference (3). Additional exam requirements/recommendations for international students: Required—TOEFL (minimum score 213 computer-based). *Expenses:* Tuition: Part-time $325 per credit hour.

McKendree University, Graduate Programs, Master of Arts in Education Program, Lebanon, IL 62254-1299. Offers certification (MA Ed); educational administration and leadership (MA Ed); educational studies (MA Ed); higher education administrative services (MA Ed); music education (MA Ed); special education (MA Ed); teacher leadership (MA Ed); transition to teaching (MA Ed). *Accreditation:* NCATE. Part-time and evening/weekend programs available. Postbaccalaureate distance learning degree programs offered (no on-campus study). *Faculty:* 18 full-time (7 women), 56 part-time/adjunct (34 women). *Students:* 107 full-time (83 women), 445 part-time (325 women); includes 41 minority (32 African Americans, 3 Asian Americans or Pacific Islanders, 6 Hispanic Americans). Average age 35. 225 applicants, 77% accepted, 129 enrolled. In 2009, 200 master's awarded. *Entrance requirements:* For master's, official transcripts from institutions attended, minimum GPA of 3.0, resume, references. Additional exam requirements/recommendations for international students: Required—TOEFL. *Application deadline:* Applications are processed on a rolling basis. Application fee: $0. Electronic applications accepted. *Expenses:* Tuition: Full-time $6300; part-time $350 per credit hour. One-time fee: $125. *Financial support:* In 2009–10, 1 student received support. Application deadline: 6/30. *Unit head:* Dr. Joseph J. Cipfl, Interim Chair of the School of Education, 618-537-6462, Fax: 618-537-6417, E-mail: jjcipfl@mckendree.edu. *Application contact:* Sabrina Storner, Director of Graduate Admission, 618-537-6477, Fax: 618-537-6410, E-mail: skstorner@mckendree.edu.

McNeese State University, Doré School of Graduate Studies, Burton College of Education, Department of Teacher Education, Program in Special Education Mild/Moderate Grades 1-12, Lake Charles, LA 70609. Offers M Ed. *Faculty:* 12 full-time (6 women). *Students:* 4 part-time (all women). *Entrance requirements:* For master's, GRE, teaching certificate. *Application deadline:* For fall admission, 5/15 priority date for domestic and international students; for spring admission, 10/15 priority date for domestic and international students. Applications are processed on a rolling basis. Application fee: $20 ($30 for international students). *Expenses:* Tuition, area resident: Full-time $2556. Tuition, state resident: full-time $2556. Required fees: $1031. Tuition and fees vary according to course load. *Financial support:* Application deadline: 5/1. *Unit head:* Dr. Royce Zant, Head, 337-475-5404, Fax: 337-475-5398, E-mail: rzant@mcneese.edu. *Application contact:* Dr. George F. Mead, Interim Dean of Dore' School of Graduate Studies, 337-475-5396, Fax: 337-475-5397, E-mail: admissions@mcneese.edu.

McNeese State University, Doré School of Graduate Studies, Burton College of Education, Department of Teacher Education, Program in Teaching, Lake Charles, LA 70609. Offers elementary education grades 1-5 (MAT); secondary education grades 6-12 (MAT); special education—mild/moderate grades 1-12 (MAT). Evening/weekend programs available. *Faculty:* 12 full-time (6 women). *Students:* 44 full-time (37 women), 126 part-time (112 women); includes 34 minority (25 African Americans, 1 American Indian/Alaska Native, 2 Asian Americans or Pacific Islanders, 6 Hispanic Americans), 1 international. In 2009, 43 master's awarded. *Entrance requirements:* For master's, GRE, PRAXIS, 2 letters of recommendation; autobiography. *Application deadline:* For fall admission, 5/15 priority date for domestic and international students; for spring admission, 10/15 priority date for domestic and international students. Applications are processed on a rolling basis. Application fee: $20 ($30 for international students). *Expenses:* Tuition, area resident: Full-time $2556. Tuition, state resident: full-time $2556. Required fees: $1031. Tuition and fees vary according to course load. *Financial support:* Application deadline: 5/1. *Unit head:* Dr. Royce Zant, Head, 337-475-5404, Fax: 337-475-5398, E-mail: rzant@mcneese.edu. *Application contact:* Dr. George F. Mead, Interim Dean of Dore' School of Graduate Studies, 337-475-5396, Fax: 337-475-5397, E-mail: admissions@mcneese.edu.

Medaille College, Program in Education, Buffalo, NY 14214-2695. Offers adolescent education (MS Ed); curriculum and instruction (MS Ed); education preparation (MS Ed); literacy (MS Ed); special education (MS). *Accreditation:* Teacher Education Accreditation Council. Part-time and evening/weekend programs available. *Faculty:* 22 full-time (16 women), 47 part-time/adjunct (36 women). *Students:* 721 full-time (596 women), 2 part-time (both women); includes 34 minority (16 African Americans, 1 American Indian/Alaska Native, 14 Asian Americans or Pacific Islanders, 3 Hispanic Americans). Average age 26. 621 applicants, 46% accepted, 288 enrolled. In 2009, 608 master's awarded. *Degree requirements:* For master's, thesis or alternative. *Entrance requirements:* For master's, minimum undergraduate GPA of 2.7. Additional exam requirements/recommendations for international students: Required—TOEFL (minimum score 550 paper-based; 213 computer-based). *Application deadline:* For fall admission, 8/15 priority date for domestic students; for spring admission, 1/15 priority date for domestic students. Applications are processed on a rolling basis. Application fee: $35. Electronic applications accepted. *Financial support:* In 2009–10, 501 students received support. Federal Work-Study available. Financial award applicants required to submit FAFSA. *Faculty research:* Curriculum planning, truancy, tracking minority students, curriculum design, mentoring students. *Unit head:* Dr. Robert DiSibio, Director of Graduate Programs, 716-932-2548, Fax: 716-631-1380, E-mail: rdisibio@medaille.edu. *Application contact:* Jacqueline Matheny, Executive Director of Marketing and Enrollment, 716-932-2541, Fax: 716-632-1811, E-mail: jmatheny@medaille.edu.

Mercy College, School of Education, Dobbs Ferry, NY 10522-1189. Offers adolescence education, grades 7-12 (MS); applied behavior analysis (Post Master's Certificate); bilingual education (MS); childhood education, grade 1-6 (MS); early childhood education, birth-grade 2 (MS); early childhood education/students with disabilities (MS); individualized certification plan for teachers (ICPT) (MS); middle childhood education, grades 5-9 (MS); school building leadership (MS, Advanced Certificate); teaching English to speakers of other languages (TESOL) (MS); teaching literacy (MS); teaching literacy, birth-6 (MS); teaching literacy/birth-grade 12 (MS); teaching literacy/grades 5-12 (MS); urban education (MS). *Faculty:* 55 full-time (37 women), 78 part-time/adjunct (47 women). *Students:* 538 full-time (455 women), 1,298 part-time (1,029 women); includes 699 minority (336 African Americans, 3 American Indian/Alaska Native, 30 Asian Americans or Pacific Islanders, 330 Hispanic Americans), 4 international. Average age 33. 779 applicants, 73% accepted, 465 enrolled. In 2009, 870 master's, 5 other advanced degrees awarded. *Degree requirements:* For master's, thesis. *Entrance requirements:* For master's, interview, resume, minimum undergraduate GPA of 3.0. Additional exam requirements/recommendations for international students: Required—TOEFL (minimum score 600 paper-based; 250 computer-based; 100 iBT). *Application deadline:* For fall admission, 8/1 for international students. Applications are processed on a rolling basis. Application fee: $40. Electronic applications accepted. *Expenses:* Contact institution. *Financial support:* In 2009–10, 161 students received support. Career-related internships or fieldwork, Federal Work-Study, scholarships/grants, and unspecified assistantships available. Support available to part-time students. Financial award applicants required to submit FAFSA. *Faculty research:* Teaching, literacy, educational evaluation. *Unit head:* Dr. Andrew Peiser, Interim Dean for the School of Education, 914-674-7489, E-mail: apeiser@mercy.edu. *Application contact:* Mary Ellen Hoffman, Interim Associate Dean, 914-674-7334, E-mail: mehoffman@mercy.edu.

Mercyhurst College, Graduate Program, Program in Special Education, Erie, PA 16546. Offers bilingual/bicultural special education (MS); educational leadership (Certificate); special education (MS). Part-time and evening/weekend programs available. *Degree requirements:* For master's, thesis optional. *Entrance requirements:* For master's, GRE General Test, MAT, or minimum GPA of 3.0, interview. Additional exam requirements/recommendations for international students: Required—TOEFL. Electronic applications accepted. *Faculty research:* College age learning disabled program, teacher preparation/collaboration, applied behavior analysis, special education policy issues.

Miami University, Graduate School, School of Education and Allied Professions, Department of Educational Psychology, Oxford, OH 45056. Offers educational psychology (M Ed); instructional design and technology (M Ed, MA); school psychology (MS, Ed S); special education (M Ed). *Accreditation:* NCATE. *Students:* 39 full-time (34 women), 42 part-time (39 women); includes 5 minority (2 African Americans, 2 Asian Americans or Pacific Islanders, 1 Hispanic American), 9 international. *Entrance requirements:* For master's, GRE General Test or MAT, minimum undergraduate GPA of 3.0 during previous 2 years or 2.75 overall; for Ed S, GRE General Test or MAT. Additional exam requirements/recommendations for international students: Required—TOEFL. Application fee: $50. *Expenses:* Tuition, state resident: full-time $11,280. Tuition, nonresident: full-time $24,912. Required fees: $516. *Financial support:* Fellowships with full tuition reimbursements, research assistantships with full tuition reimbursements, teaching assistantships with full tuition reimbursements, career-related internships or fieldwork, Federal Work-Study, health care benefits, tuition waivers (full), and unspecified assistantships available. Financial award application deadline: 3/1. *Unit head:* Dr. Nelda Cambron-McCabe, Chair, 513-529-6836, Fax: 513-529-6621, E-mail: edp@muohio.edu. *Application contact:* Dr. Nelda Cambron-McCabe, Chair, 513-529-6836, Fax: 513-529-6621, E-mail: edp@muohio.edu.

Michigan State University, The Graduate School, College of Education, Department of Counseling, Educational Psychology and Special Education, East Lansing, MI 48824. Offers counseling (MA); educational psychology and educational technology (PhD); educational technology (MA); measurement and quantitative methods (PhD); rehabilitation counseling (MA); rehabilitation counselor education (PhD); school psychology (MA, PhD, Ed S); special

education (MA, PhD). *Accreditation:* APA (one or more programs are accredited); CORE (one or more programs are accredited). Part-time programs available. *Faculty:* 35 full-time (13 women). *Students:* 217 full-time (154 women), 144 part-time (107 women); includes 48 minority (25 African Americans, 13 Asian Americans or Pacific Islanders, 10 Hispanic Americans), 71 international. Average age 32. 238 applicants, 46% accepted. In 2009, 117 master's, 36 doctorates awarded. *Entrance requirements:* Additional exam requirements/recommendations for international students: Required—TOEFL. Electronic applications accepted. *Expenses:* Tuition, state resident: part-time $478.25 per credit hour. Tuition, nonresident: part-time $966.50 per credit hour. Part-time tuition and fees vary according to program. *Financial support:* In 2009–10, 71 research assistantships with tuition reimbursements (averaging $6,836 per year), 74 teaching assistantships with tuition reimbursements (averaging $6,858 per year) were awarded. Total annual research expenditures: $2.3 million. *Unit head:* Dr. Richard S. Prawat, Chairperson, 517-353-6417, Fax: 517-353-6393, E-mail: rsprawat@msu.edu. *Application contact:* Kathy Dimoff, Graduate Admissions Coordinator, 517-355-6683, Fax: 517-353-6393, E-mail: dimoff@msu.edu.

MidAmerica Nazarene University, Graduate Studies in Education, Olathe, KS 66062-1899. Offers ESOL (M Ed); professional teaching (M Ed); special education (MA); technology enhanced teaching (M Ed). *Accreditation:* NCATE. Part-time and evening/weekend programs available. Postbaccalaureate distance learning degree programs offered (no on-campus study). *Faculty:* 6 full-time (2 women), 14 part-time/adjunct (8 women). *Students:* 2 full-time (1 woman), 148 part-time (120 women); includes 15 minority (7 African Americans, 3 American Indian/Alaska Native, 1 Asian American or Pacific Islander, 4 Hispanic Americans). Average age 36. In 2009, 72 master's awarded. *Degree requirements:* For master's, thesis or alternative, creative project, technology leadership practicum. *Entrance requirements:* For master's, minimum undergraduate GPA of 2.8, 2 years of teaching experience. *Application deadline:* Applications are processed on a rolling basis. Application fee: $25. *Expenses:* Contact institution. *Financial support:* Applicants required to submit FAFSA. *Unit head:* Dr. Martin Dunlap, Director, 913-971-3292, Fax: 913-971-3407, E-mail: mhdunlap@mnu.edu. *Application contact:* Glenna Murray, Administrative Assistant, 913-971-3292, Fax: 913-971-3407, E-mail: gkmurray@mnu.edu.

Middle Tennessee State University, College of Graduate Studies, College of Education and Behavioral Science, Department of Elementary and Special Education, Major in Special Education, Murfreesboro, TN 37132. Offers M Ed. *Accreditation:* NCATE. Part-time and evening/weekend programs available. Postbaccalaureate distance learning degree programs offered. *Students:* 1 (woman) full-time, 26 part-time (23 women); includes 1 minority (African American). 16 applicants, 50% accepted, 8 enrolled. In 2009, 17 master's awarded. *Degree requirements:* For master's, comprehensive exam. *Entrance requirements:* For master's, GRE, MAT or PRAXIS. Additional exam requirements/recommendations for international students: Required—TOEFL (minimum score 525 paper-based; 195 computer-based; 71 iBT) or IELTS (minimum score 6). *Application deadline:* For fall admission, 6/1 for domestic and international students. Applications are processed on a rolling basis. Application fee: $25 ($30 for international students). Electronic applications accepted. *Expenses:* Tuition, state resident: full-time $4404. Tuition, nonresident: full-time $10,956. *Financial support:* Institutionally sponsored loans available. Support available to part-time students. Financial award application deadline: 5/1. *Unit head:* Dr. Connie Jones, Chair, 615-898-2680, Fax: 615-898-5309, E-mail: cojones@mtsu.edu. *Application contact:* Dr. Michael Allen, Dean and Vice Provost for Research, 615-898-2840, Fax: 615-904-8020, E-mail: mallen@mtsu.edu.

Middle Tennessee State University, College of Graduate Studies, College of Education and Behavioral Science, Tennessee Center for the Study and Treatment of Dyslexia, Murfreesboro, TN 37132. Offers Graduate Certificate. Part-time and evening/weekend programs available. Postbaccalaureate distance learning degree programs offered. *Faculty:* 1 full-time (0 women), 2 part-time/adjunct (both women). *Students:* 3 part-time (all women). Average age 33. *Entrance requirements:* Additional exam requirements/recommendations for international students: Required—TOEFL (minimum score 525 paper-based; 195 computer-based; 71 iBT) or IELTS (minimum score 6). *Application deadline:* For fall admission, 6/1 for domestic and international students. Applications are processed on a rolling basis. Application fee: $25 ($30 for international students). *Expenses:* Tuition, state resident: full-time $4404. Tuition, nonresident: full-time $10,956. *Financial support:* In 2009–10, 3 students received support. Institutionally sponsored loans available. Support available to part-time students. Financial award application deadline: 5/1. *Unit head:* Dr. Diane Sawyer, Director, 615-898-5642. *Application contact:* Dr. Michael Allen, Dean and Vice Provost for Research, 615-898-2840, Fax: 615-904-8020, E-mail: mallen@mtsu.edu.

Midwestern State University, Graduate Studies, College of Education, Program in Special Education, Wichita Falls, TX 76308. Offers M Ed. Part-time and evening/weekend programs available. *Degree requirements:* For master's, comprehensive exam. *Entrance requirements:* For master's, GRE General Test, MAT, or GMAT, Texas teacher certificate or equivalent GPA of 3.0 in previous education courses. Additional exam requirements/recommendations for international students: Required—TOEFL (minimum score 550 paper-based; 213 computer-based). Electronic applications accepted. *Expenses:* Tuition, state resident: full-time $1620; part-time $90 per credit hour. Tuition, nonresident: full-time $2160; part-time $120 per credit hour. International tuition: $7506 full-time. Required fees: $3068.80; $145.60 per credit hour. $179 per semester. *Faculty research:* Fragile-X syndrome, phenylketonuria and other causes of handicapping conditions.

Millersville University of Pennsylvania, College of Graduate and Professional Studies, School of Education, Department of Special Education, Millersville, PA 17551-0302. Offers M Ed. *Accreditation:* NCATE. Part-time and evening/weekend programs available. *Faculty:* 8 full-time (6 women), 4 part-time/adjunct (2 women). *Students:* 5 full-time (all women), 18 part-time (16 women). Average age 29. 7 applicants, 71% accepted, 3 enrolled. In 2009, 8 master's awarded. *Degree requirements:* For master's, thesis optional. *Entrance requirements:* For master's, GRE or MAT, 3 letters of recommendation. Additional exam requirements/recommendations for international students: Required—TOEFL (minimum score 550 paper-based; 183 computer-based; 65 iBT) or IELTS (minimum score 6). *Application deadline:* For fall admission, 1/15 for domestic and international students; for winter admission, 10/1 for domestic and international students; for spring admission, 10/1 for domestic and international students. Application fee: $40 ($50 for international students). Electronic applications accepted. *Expenses:* Tuition, state resident: full-time $6666; part-time $370 per credit. Tuition, nonresident: full-time $10,666; part-time $593 per credit. Required fees: $1578.50; $76.25 per credit. One-time fee: $60 part-time. Tuition and fees vary according to course load. *Financial support:* In 2009–10, 2 students received support, including 2 research assistantships with full tuition reimbursements available (averaging $5,200 per year); institutionally sponsored loans and unspecified assistantships also available. Support available to part-time students. Financial award application deadline: 3/15; financial award applicants required to submit FAFSA. *Unit head:* Dr. Elba I. Rohena, Chair, 717-872-3671, Fax: 717-871-5754, E-mail: elba.rohena@millersville.edu. *Application contact:* Dr. Victor S. DeSantis, Dean of Graduate and Professional Studies, 717-872-3099, Fax: 717-872-3453, E-mail: victor.desantis@millersville.edu.

Minnesota State University Mankato, College of Graduate Studies, College of Education, Department of Special Education, Mankato, MN 56001. Offers emotional/behavioral disorders (MS, Certificate); learning disabilities (MS, Certificate); talent development and gifted education (MS, Certificate, SP). *Accreditation:* NCATE. Part-time programs available. Postbaccalaureate distance learning degree programs offered. *Students:* 10 full-time (8 women), 111 part-time (89 women). *Degree requirements:* For master's, comprehensive exam, thesis or alternative. *Entrance requirements:* For master's, Council for Exceptional Children pre-program assessment, minimum GPA of 3.2 during previous 2 years. Additional exam requirements/recommendations for international students: Required—TOEFL. *Application deadline:* For fall admission, 7/1 priority date for domestic students; for spring admission, 11/1 for domestic students. Applications are processed on a rolling basis. Application fee: $40. Electronic applications accepted. *Expenses:* Tuition, state resident: full-time $5364. Tuition, nonresident: full-time $8314. *Financial*

support: Research assistantships, teaching assistantships with full tuition reimbursements, career-related internships or fieldwork, Federal Work-Study, and institutionally sponsored loans available. Support available to part-time students. Financial award application deadline: 3/15; financial award applicants required to submit FAFSA. *Unit head:* Dr. Andrew Johnson, Chair, 507-389-5660. *Application contact:* 507-389-2321, E-mail: grad@mnsu.edu.

Minnesota State University Moorhead, Graduate Studies, College of Education and Human Services, Program in Special Education, Moorhead, MN 56563-0002. Offers MS. *Accreditation:* NCATE. Part-time and evening/weekend programs available. *Degree requirements:* For master's, comprehensive exam, final oral exam, project or thesis. *Entrance requirements:* For master's, MAT, 1 year teaching experience or bachelor's degree in education, minimum GPA of 3.0. Additional exam requirements/recommendations for international students: Required—TOEFL (minimum score 550 paper-based; 213 computer-based). Electronic applications accepted.

Minot State University, Graduate School, Program in Special Education, Minot, ND 58707-0002. Offers education of the deaf (MS); learning disabilities (MS); special education strategist (MS), including early childhood special education, severe multiple handicaps. *Accreditation:* NCATE. *Degree requirements:* For master's, comprehensive exam (for some programs), thesis (for some programs). *Entrance requirements:* For master's, GRE General Test or minimum GPA of 3.0. Additional exam requirements/recommendations for international students: Required—TOEFL. *Expenses:* Tuition, state resident: full-time $5720; part-time $283 per credit hour. Tuition, nonresident: full-time $5720; part-time $283 per credit hour. Required fees: $1034; $1034 per year. Tuition and fees vary according to course load, degree level and program. *Faculty research:* Special education team diagnostic unit; individual diagnostic assessments of mentally retarded, learning-disabled, hearing-impaired, and speech-impaired youth; educational programming for the hearing impaired.

Mississippi College, Graduate School, School of Education, Department of Teacher Education and Leadership, Clinton, MS 39058. Offers art (M Ed); biological science (M Ed); business education (M Ed); computer science (M Ed); dyslexia therapy (M Ed); educational leadership (M Ed, Ed D, Ed S); elementary education (M Ed, Ed S); English (M Ed); higher education administration (MS); mathematics (M Ed); secondary education (M Ed); social studies (history) (M Ed); teaching arts (M Ed). Part-time programs available. Postbaccalaureate distance learning degree programs offered (no on-campus study). *Faculty:* 11 full-time (7 women), 13 part-time/adjunct (7 women). *Students:* 33 full-time (22 women), 282 part-time (240 women); includes 148 minority (146 African Americans, 2 American Indian/Alaska Native), 1 international. Average age 34. In 2009, 147 master's awarded. *Degree requirements:* For master's, comprehensive exam, thesis optional. *Entrance requirements:* For master's, NTE. Additional exam requirements/recommendations for international students: Recommended—IELTS. *Application deadline:* For fall admission, 8/15 priority date for domestic students. Applications are processed on a rolling basis. Application fee: $30. Electronic applications accepted. *Expenses:* Tuition: Part-time $452 per credit hour. Required fees: $101 per semester. Tuition and fees vary according to degree level, campus/location, program and student level. *Financial support:* Teaching assistantships, career-related internships or fieldwork, Federal Work-Study, scholarships/grants, and unspecified assistantships available. Support available to part-time students. Financial award applicants required to submit FAFSA. *Unit head:* Dr. Tom Williams, Chair, 601-925-3844, E-mail: twilliams@mc.edu. *Application contact:* Elnora Lewis, Secretary, 601-925-3225, Fax: 601-925-3889, E-mail: lewis09@mc.edu.

Mississippi State University, College of Education, Department of Counseling and Educational Psychology, Mississippi State, MS 39762. Offers college/postsecondary student counseling and personnel services (PhD); counselor education (MS); counselor education/student counseling and guidance services (PhD); education (Ed S), including counselor education, school psychology; educational psychology (MS, PhD). *Accreditation:* ACA (one or more programs are accredited); APA; CORE (one or more programs are accredited); NCATE. Part-time programs available. Postbaccalaureate distance learning degree programs offered (minimal on-campus study). *Faculty:* 14 full-time (10 women), 1 (woman) part-time/adjunct. *Students:* 116 full-time (95 women), 99 part-time (84 women); includes 63 minority (57 African Americans, 2 American Indian/Alaska Native, 2 Asian Americans or Pacific Islanders, 2 Hispanic Americans), 3 international. Average age 32. 154 applicants, 62% accepted, 69 enrolled. In 2009, 56 master's, 9 doctorates, 17 other advanced degrees awarded. Terminal master's awarded for partial completion of doctoral program. *Degree requirements:* For master's, comprehensive exam, thesis optional; for doctorate, thesis/dissertation, comprehensive oral and written exam. *Entrance requirements:* For master's, GRE, minimum QPA of 3.0; for doctorate, GRE, interview, minimum GPA of 3.4; for Ed S, GRE, MS in counseling or related field. Additional exam requirements/recommendations for international students: Required—TOEFL (minimum score 475 paper-based; 153 computer-based; 53 iBT); Recommended—IELTS (minimum score 4.5). *Application deadline:* For fall admission, 2/1 priority date for domestic and international students. Applications are processed on a rolling basis. Application fee: $40. Electronic applications accepted. *Expenses:* Tuition, state resident: full-time $2575.50; part-time $286.25 per credit hour. Tuition, nonresident: full-time $6510; part-time $723.50 per credit hour. Tuition and fees vary according to course load. *Financial support:* In 2009–10, 4 teaching assistantships with full tuition reimbursements (averaging $8,603 per year) were awarded; career-related internships or fieldwork, Federal Work-Study, institutionally sponsored loans, and unspecified assistantships also available. Financial award application deadline: 2/1; financial award applicants required to submit FAFSA. *Faculty research:* HIV-AIDS in college population, substance abuse in youth and college students, ADHD and conduct disorders in youth, assessment and identification of early childhood disabilities, assessment and vocational transition of the disabled. *Unit head:* Dr. Daniel Wong, Professor/Head, 662-325-7928, Fax: 662-325-3263, E-mail: dwong@colled.msstate.edu. *Application contact:* Dr. Tony Doggett, Associate Professor and Graduate Coordinator, 662-325-3312, Fax: 662-325-3263, E-mail: tdoggett@colled.msstate.edu.

Mississippi State University, College of Education, Department of Curriculum, Instruction and Special Education, Mississippi State, MS 39762. Offers curriculum and instruction (PhD); education (Ed D, Ed S), including elementary education, secondary education, special education (Ed S); elementary education (MS, PhD); secondary education (MS, PhD); secondary teacher alternate route (MAT); special education (MS). *Accreditation:* NCATE. Part-time and evening/weekend programs available. *Faculty:* 13 full-time (11 women). *Students:* 35 full-time (33 women), 126 part-time (103 women); includes 55 minority (all African Americans). Average age 35. 80 applicants, 60% accepted, 40 enrolled. In 2009, 60 master's, 6 doctorates, 7 other advanced degrees awarded. *Degree requirements:* For master's, comprehensive exam; for doctorate, thesis/dissertation; for Ed S, comprehensive exam, thesis or alternative. *Entrance requirements:* For master's, GRE, minimum GPA of 2.75 in junior and senior year, eligibility for initial teacher certification; for doctorate, GRE, minimum graduate GPA of 3.4; for Ed S, GRE, minimum graduate GPA of 3.2. Additional exam requirements/recommendations for international students: Required—TOEFL (minimum score 600 paper-based; 250 computer-based; 100 iBT); Recommended—IELTS (minimum score 7.5). *Application deadline:* For fall admission, 3/1 priority date for domestic students, 5/1 for international students; for spring admission, 9/1 priority date for domestic students, 9/1 for international students. Applications are processed on a rolling basis. Application fee: $40. Electronic applications accepted. *Expenses:* Tuition, state resident: full-time $2575.50; part-time $286.25 per credit hour. Tuition, nonresident: full-time $6510; part-time $723.50 per credit hour. Tuition and fees vary according to course load. *Financial support:* In 2009–10, 30 students received support, including 5 research assistantships with full and partial tuition reimbursements available (averaging $8,959 per year), 3 teaching assistantships (averaging $10,443 per year); Federal Work-Study, institutionally sponsored loans, scholarships/grants, and unspecified assistantships also available. Financial award applicants required to submit FAFSA. *Faculty research:* Early childhood education, reading, rural schools, multicultural education, use of technology in instruction. *Unit head:* Dr. Charlotte S. Burroughs, Associate Professor and Interim Head, 662-325-3747, Fax: 662-325-7857, E-mail: susie.burroughs@msstate.edu. *Application contact:* Dr. Kent Coffey, Professor and Graduate Coordinator, 662-325-2188, Fax: 662-325-7857, E-mail: kcoffey@colled.msstate.edu.

Special Education

Missouri State University, Graduate College, College of Education, Department of Counseling, Leadership, and Special Education, Program in Special Education, Springfield, MO 65897. Offers special education (MS Ed), including alternative certification, developmental disabilities, mild to moderate disabilities, orientation and mobility, visual impairment. Part-time and evening/weekend programs available. *Students:* 5 full-time (all women), 106 part-time (89 women); includes 7 minority (6 African Americans, 1 Asian American or Pacific Islander). Average age 37. 13 applicants, 100% accepted, 10 enrolled. In 2009, 24 master's awarded. *Degree requirements:* For master's, comprehensive exam, thesis or alternative. *Entrance requirements:* For master's, GRE or minimum GPA of 3.0, teaching certificate. Additional exam requirements/recommendations for international students: Required—TOEFL (minimum score 550 paper-based; 213 computer-based; 79 iBT). *Application deadline:* For fall admission, 7/20 for domestic students, 5/1 for international students; for spring admission, 12/20 for domestic students, 9/1 for international students. Applications are processed on a rolling basis. Application fee: $35 ($50 for international students). Electronic applications accepted. *Expenses:* Tuition, state resident: full-time $3852; part-time $214 per credit hour. Tuition, nonresident: full-time $7524; part-time $418 per credit hour. Required fees: $696; $172 per semester. Tuition and fees vary according to course level, course load, degree level and program. *Financial support:* Federal Work-Study, institutionally sponsored loans, scholarships/grants, and unspecified assistantships available. Financial award application deadline: 3/31; financial award applicants required to submit FAFSA. *Unit head:* Dr. Tamara Arthaud, Department Head, 417-836-5449, Fax: 417-836-4918, E-mail: clse@missouristate.edu. *Application contact:* Eric Eckert, Coordinator of Graduate Admissions and Recruitment, 417-836-5331, Fax: 417-836-6888, E-mail: ericeckert@missouristate.edu.

Missouri State University, Graduate College, College of Health and Human Services, Department of Communication Sciences and Disorders, Springfield, MO 65897. Offers audiology (Au D); communication sciences and disorders (MS), including education of deaf/hard of hearing, speech-language pathology. *Accreditation:* ASHA (one or more programs are accredited). *Faculty:* 18 full-time (12 women). *Students:* 100 full-time (89 women), 3 part-time (all women); includes 1 minority (Hispanic American), 4 international. Average age 26. 72 applicants, 69% accepted, 25 enrolled. In 2009, 31 master's, 5 doctorates awarded. *Degree requirements:* For master's, comprehensive exam, thesis or alternative; for doctorate, comprehensive exam, thesis/dissertation or alternative, clinical externship. *Entrance requirements:* For master's and doctorate, GRE, minimum GPA of 3.0. Additional exam requirements/recommendations for international students: Required—TOEFL (minimum score 550 paper-based; 213 computer-based; 79 iBT). *Application deadline:* For fall admission, 2/1 for domestic and international students. Application fee: $35 ($50 for international students). Electronic applications accepted. *Expenses:* Tuition, state resident: full-time $3852; part-time $214 per credit hour. Tuition, nonresident: full-time $7524; part-time $418 per credit hour. Required fees: $696; $172 per semester. Tuition and fees vary according to course level, course load, degree level and program. *Financial support:* Career-related internships or fieldwork, Federal Work-Study, scholarships/grants, and unspecified assistantships available. Support available to part-time students. Financial award application deadline: 3/31; financial award applicants required to submit FAFSA. *Faculty research:* Dysphagia, phonological intervention, elderly adult aural rehabilitation, vestibular disorders. *Unit head:* Dr. Neil DiSarno, Head, 417-836-5368, Fax: 417-836-4242, E-mail: neildisarno@missouristate.edu. *Application contact:* Eric Eckert, Coordinator of Admissions and Recruitment, 417-836-5331, Fax: 417-836-6200, E-mail: ericeckert@missouristate.edu.

Monmouth University, Graduate School, School of Education, West Long Branch, NJ 07764-1898. Offers education (M Ed); initial certification (MAT), including elementary level, K-12, secondary level; learning disabilities-teacher consultant (Certificate); principal (MS Ed); principal/school administrator (MS Ed); reading specialist (MS Ed, Certificate); school counseling (MS Ed); special education (MS Ed), including autism, learning disabilities teacher consultant, teacher of students with disabilities, teaching in inclusive settings; supervisor (Certificate); teacher of the handicapped (Certificate); teaching english to speakers of other languages (TESOL) (Certificate). *Accreditation:* NCATE. Part-time and evening/weekend programs available. *Faculty:* 20 full-time (13 women), 32 part-time/adjunct (22 women). *Students:* 182 full-time (146 women), 353 part-time (286 women); includes 40 minority (15 African Americans, 3 American Indian/Alaska Native, 5 Asian Americans or Pacific Islanders, 17 Hispanic Americans), 1 international. Average age 29. 361 applicants, 96% accepted, 176 enrolled. In 2009, 178 master's awarded. *Entrance requirements:* For master's, minimum GPA of 3.0 in major, 2.75 overall; 2 letters of recommendation (for some programs). Additional exam requirements/recommendations for international students: Required—TOEFL (minimum score 550 paper-based; 213 computer-based; 79 iBT), IELTS (minimum score 5), Michigan English Language Assessment Battery (minimum score 77), Cambridge A, B, C. *Application deadline:* For fall admission, 7/15 priority date for domestic students, 7/1 for international students; for spring admission, 11/15 priority date for domestic students, 11/1 for international students. Applications are processed on a rolling basis. Application fee: $50. Electronic applications accepted. *Expenses:* Tuition: Part-time $773 per credit. Required fees: $157 per semester. *Financial support:* In 2009–10, 326 students received support, including 211 fellowships (averaging $1,824 per year), 23 research assistantships (averaging $7,943 per year); career-related internships or fieldwork, scholarships/grants, and unspecified assistantships also available. Support available to part-time students. Financial award applicants required to submit FAFSA. *Faculty research:* Multicultural literacy, science and mathematics teaching strategies, teacher as reflective practitioner, children with disabilities, varied contexts of learning. *Unit head:* Dr. Terri Rothman, Associate Dean, 732-571-7507, Fax: 732-263-5277, E-mail: trothman@monmouth.edu. *Application contact:* Kevin Roane, Director, Office of Graduate Admission, 732-571-3452, Fax: 732-263-5123, E-mail: gradadm@monmouth.edu.

Montana State University Billings, College of Education, Department of Special Education, Counseling, Reading and Early Childhood, Program in Special Education, Billings, MT 59101-0298. Offers advanced studies (MS Sp Ed); special education generalist (MS Sp Ed). *Accreditation:* NCATE. Part-time programs available. *Degree requirements:* For master's, thesis or professional paper and/or field experience. *Entrance requirements:* For master's, GRE General Test or MAT, minimum GPA of 3.0 (undergraduate), 3.25 (graduate).

Montclair State University, The Graduate School, College of Education and Human Services, Department of Curriculum and Teaching, Montclair, NJ 07043-1624. Offers education (M Ed); educational technology (M Ed); learning disabled teacher consultant (Certificate); school library media specialist (Certificate); teaching (MAT, Certificate), including art (MAT), biological science (MAT), early childhood education (P-3) (MAT), earth science (MAT), elementary education (K-8) (MAT), English (MAT), French (MAT), health and physical education (MAT), health education (MAT), home economics (MAT), mathematics (MAT), music (MAT), physical education (MAT), physical science (MAT), social studies (MAT), Spanish (MAT), teacher of ESL (MAT), teacher of students with disabilities (MAT). Part-time and evening/weekend programs available. *Faculty:* 17 full-time (12 women), 29 part-time/adjunct (21 women). *Students:* 124 full-time (63 women), 174 part-time (126 women). Average age 31. 112 applicants, 69% accepted, 59 enrolled. In 2009, 179 master's, 2 other advanced degrees awarded. *Degree requirements:* For master's, comprehensive exam, field experience. *Entrance requirements:* For master's, GRE, 2 letters of recommendation. Additional exam requirements/recommendations for international students: Required—TOEFL (minimum score 83 computer-based), or IELTS. *Application deadline:* For fall admission, 2/15 for domestic and international students; for spring admission, 9/15 for domestic and international students. Applications are processed on a rolling basis. Application fee: $60. Electronic applications accepted. *Expenses:* Tuition, area resident: Part-time $486.74 per credit. Tuition, state resident: part-time $486.74 per credit. Tuition, nonresident: part-time $751.34 per credit. Tuition and fees vary according to degree level and program. *Financial support:* In 2009–10, 12 research assistantships with full tuition reimbursements (averaging $7,000 per year) were awarded; Federal Work-Study, scholarships/grants, and unspecified assistantships also available. Support available to part-time students. Financial award application deadline: 3/1; financial award applicants required to submit FAFSA. *Unit head:* Dr. David Schwarzer, Chairperson, 973-655-5187. *Application contact:* Amy Aiello, Director of Graduate Admissions and Operations, 973-655-5147, Fax: 973-655-7869, E-mail: graduate.school@montclair.edu.

Montclair State University, The Graduate School, College of Education and Human Services, Department of Early Childhood, Elementary and Literacy Education, Montclair, NJ 07043-1624. Offers early childhood education and teaching students with disabilities (MAT); early childhood special education (M Ed, Certificate); early childhood/elementary education (M Ed); elementary education with disabilities (MAT); elementary school teacher (Certificate); learning disabilities (Certificate); reading (MA, Certificate); reading specialist (Certificate). Part-time and evening/weekend programs available. *Faculty:* 17 full-time (15 women), 68 part-time/adjunct (52 women). *Students:* 124 full-time (105 women), 274 part-time (257 women). Average age 31. 139 applicants, 65% accepted, 75 enrolled. In 2009, 85 master's awarded. *Degree requirements:* For master's, comprehensive exam, clinical experience, portfolio. *Entrance requirements:* For master's, GRE, 2 letters of recommendation. Additional exam requirements/recommendations for international students: Required—TOEFL (minimum score 83 computer-based), or IELTS. *Application deadline:* For fall admission, 6/1 for international students; for spring admission, 10/1 for international students. Applications are processed on a rolling basis. Application fee: $60. Electronic applications accepted. *Expenses:* Tuition, area resident: Part-time $486.74 per credit. Tuition, state resident: part-time $486.74 per credit. Tuition, nonresident: part-time $751.34 per credit. Tuition and fees vary according to degree level and program. *Financial support:* In 2009–10, 12 research assistantships with full tuition reimbursements (averaging $7,000 per year) were awarded; Federal Work-Study, scholarships/grants, and unspecified assistantships also available. Support available to part-time students. Financial award application deadline: 3/1; financial award applicants required to submit FAFSA. *Unit head:* Dr. Tina Jacobowitz, Chairperson, 973-655-7191. *Application contact:* Amy Aiello, Director of Graduate Admissions and Operations, 973-655-5147, Fax: 973-655-7869, E-mail: graduate.school@montclair.edu.

Morehead State University, Graduate Programs, College of Education, Department of Curriculum and Instruction, Morehead, KY 40351. Offers curriculum and instruction (Ed S); elementary education (MA Ed), including elementary education, international education, middle school education, reading; secondary education (MA Ed); special education (MA Ed); teaching (MAT). Part-time and evening/weekend programs available. *Faculty:* 25 full-time (17 women), 2 part-time/adjunct (1 woman). *Students:* 25 full-time (22 women), 165 part-time (139 women); includes 4 minority (1 African American, 2 American Indian/Alaska Native, 1 Hispanic American). Average age 33. 148 applicants, 68% accepted, 48 enrolled. In 2009, 178 master's awarded. *Degree requirements:* For master's, comprehensive exam, thesis optional; for Ed S, thesis, oral exam. *Entrance requirements:* For master's, GRE General Test, minimum GPA of 2.75, teaching certificate; for Ed S, GRE General Test, interview, master's degree, minimum GPA of 3.5, work experience. Additional exam requirements/recommendations for international students: Required—TOEFL (minimum score 500 paper-based; 173 computer-based). *Application deadline:* For fall admission, 8/1 priority date for domestic and international students; for spring admission, 12/1 priority date for domestic and international students. Applications are processed on a rolling basis. Application fee: $30. Electronic applications accepted. *Expenses:* Tuition, state resident: full-time $6318; part-time $351 per credit hour. Tuition, nonresident: full-time $15,804; part-time $878 per credit hour. *Financial support:* In 2009–10, 2 teaching assistantships (averaging $6,000 per year) were awarded; career-related internships or fieldwork, Federal Work-Study, and unspecified assistantships also available. Financial award application deadline: 3/15; financial award applicants required to submit FAFSA. *Faculty research:* Communicative competence of learning-disabled students, teaching social studies in elementary schools, ungraded primary school organization, study skills. *Unit head:* Dr. James Knoll, Chair, 606-783-2598, Fax: 606-783-5044, E-mail: j.knoll@moreheadstate.edu. *Application contact:* Michelle Barber, Graduate Recruitment and Retention Assistant Director, 606-783-5127, Fax: 606-783-5061, E-mail: m.barber@moreheadstate.edu.

Morehead State University, Graduate Programs, College of Education, Department of Early Childhood, Elementary and Special Education, Morehead, KY 40351. Offers learning and behavioral disorders P-12 (MAT); moderate and severe disabilities P-12 (MAT). Part-time and evening/weekend programs available. *Faculty:* 22 full-time (15 women), 3 part-time/adjunct (1 woman). *Students:* 22 full-time (21 women), 12 part-time (11 women); includes 1 African American. Average age 34. 38 applicants, 50% accepted, 5 enrolled. In 2009, 47 master's awarded. *Degree requirements:* For master's, thesis. *Entrance requirements:* For master's, GRE or PRAXIS II content exam, minimum overall undergraduate GPA of 2.5. Additional exam requirements/recommendations for international students: Required—TOEFL (minimum score 500 paper-based; 173 computer-based). *Application deadline:* For fall admission, 8/1 priority date for domestic and international students; for spring admission, 12/1 priority date for domestic and international students. Applications are processed on a rolling basis. Application fee: $30. Electronic applications accepted. *Expenses:* Tuition, state resident: full-time $6318; part-time $351 per credit hour. Tuition, nonresident: full-time $15,804; part-time $878 per credit hour. *Financial support:* In 2009–10, 2 teaching assistantships (averaging $10,000 per year) were awarded; career-related internships or fieldwork, Federal Work-Study, and unspecified assistantships also available. Financial award application deadline: 3/15; financial award applicants required to submit FAFSA. *Unit head:* Dr. James Knoll, Chair, 606-783-2857, E-mail: j.knoll@moreheadstate.edu. *Application contact:* Michelle Barber, Graduate Recruitment and Retention Assistant Director, 606-783-5127, Fax: 606-783-5061, E-mail: m.barber@moreheadstate.edu.

Morehead State University, Graduate Programs, College of Education, Department of Foundational and Graduate Studies in Education, Morehead, KY 40351. Offers adult and higher education (MA, Ed S); certified professional counselor (Ed S); counseling P-12 (MA); curriculum and instruction (Ed S); educational technology (MA Ed); instructional leadership (Ed S); school administration (MA); school counseling (Ed S); teacher leader business and marketing- content (MA Ed); teacher leader business and marketing- technology (MA Ed); teacher leader educational technology (MA Ed); teacher leader English (MA Ed); teacher leader gifted educ (MA Ed); teacher leader IECE—non-certification (MA Ed); teacher leader IECE certification (MA Ed); teacher leader interdisciplinary educaction P-5 (MA Ed); teacher leader middle grades 5-9 (MA Ed); teacher leader reading/writing—non-certification (MA Ed); teacher leader reading/writing certification (MA Ed); teacher leader school communication—non-certification (MA Ed); teacher leader school communication certification (MA Ed); teacher leader social studies (MA Ed); teacher leader special education (MA Ed). *Accreditation:* NCATE. Part-time and evening/weekend programs available. *Faculty:* 20 full-time (10 women), 7 part-time/adjunct (3 women). *Students:* 26 full-time (18 women), 371 part-time (295 women); includes 11 minority (9 African Americans, 1 American Indian/Alaska Native, 1 Hispanic American). Average age 35. 201 applicants, 73% accepted, 73 enrolled. In 2009, 105 master's, 5 other advanced degrees awarded. *Degree requirements:* For master's, thesis optional, oral and/or written comprehensive exams; for Ed S, thesis, oral exam. *Entrance requirements:* For master's, GRE General Test, minimum overall undergraduate GPA of 2.5; for Ed S, GRE General Test, interview, master's degree, minimum GPA of 3.5, work experience. Additional exam requirements/recommendations for international students: Required—TOEFL (minimum score 500 paper-based; 173 computer-based). *Application deadline:* For fall admission, 8/1 priority date for domestic and international students; for spring admission, 12/1 priority date for domestic and international students. Applications are processed on a rolling basis. Application fee: $30. Electronic applications accepted. *Expenses:* Tuition, state resident: full-time $6318; part-time $351 per credit hour. Tuition, nonresident: full-time $15,804; part-time $878 per credit hour. *Financial support:* In 2009–10, 2 research assistantships (averaging $10,000 per year) were awarded; career-related internships or fieldwork, Federal Work-Study, and unspecified assistantships also available. Financial award application deadline: 3/15; financial award applicants required to submit FAFSA. *Faculty research:* Character education, school accountability, computer applications for school administrators. *Unit head:* Dr. Cathy Gunn, Dean and Professor, 606-783-2040, Fax: 606-783-5029, E-mail: c.gunn@moreheadstate.edu. *Application contact:* Michelle Barber, Graduate Recruitment and Retention Assistant Director, 606-783-5127, Fax: 606-783-5061, E-mail: m.barber@moreheadstate.edu.

Morningside College, Graduate Division, Department of Education, Sioux City, IA 51106. Offers professional educator (MAT); special education: instructional strategist I: mild/moderate elementary (K-6) (MAT); special education: instructional strategist II-mild/moderate secondary (7-12) (MAT); special education: K-12 instructional strategist II-behavior disorders/learning disabilities (MAT); special education: K-12 instructional strategist II-mental disabilities (MAT). Part-time and evening/weekend programs available. *Entrance requirements:* For master's, MAT, writing sample.

Mount Mercy College, Program in Education, Cedar Rapids, IA 52402-4797. Offers reading (MA Ed); special education (MA Ed). *Entrance requirements:* For master's, minimum cumulative GPA of 3.0, 2 letters of recommendation, resume, valid teaching license. Additional exam requirements/recommendations for international students: Required—TOEFL (minimum score 570 paper-based; 88 iBT). Electronic applications accepted.

Mount Saint Mary College, Division of Education, Newburgh, NY 12550-3494. Offers adolescence and special education (MS Ed); adolescence education (MS Ed); childhood and special education (MS Ed); childhood education (MS Ed); literacy (5-12) (Advanced Certificate); literacy (birth-6) (Advanced Certificate); literacy and special education (MS Ed); literacy/childhood (MS Ed); middle school (5-6) (MS Ed); middle school (7-9) (MS Ed); special education (1-6) (MS Ed); special education (7-12) (MS Ed). *Accreditation:* NCATE. Part-time and evening/weekend programs available. *Faculty:* 15 full-time (13 women), 16 part-time/adjunct (10 women). *Students:* 76 full-time (63 women), 226 part-time (188 women); includes 27 minority (7 African Americans, 3 Asian Americans or Pacific Islanders, 17 Hispanic Americans). Average age 30. 141 applicants, 56% accepted, 44 enrolled. In 2009, 142 master's awarded. *Application deadline:* Applications are processed on a rolling basis. Application fee: $45. *Expenses:* Tuition: Full-time $13,356; part-time $742 per credit. Required fees: $50 per semester. *Financial support:* In 2009–10, 106 students received support. Unspecified assistantships available. Financial award application deadline: 4/15; financial award applicants required to submit FAFSA. *Faculty research:* Learning and teaching styles, computers in special education, language development. *Unit head:* Dr. Theresa Lewis, Coordinator, 845-569-3149, Fax: 845-569-3535, E-mail: tlewis@msmc.edu. *Application contact:* Dr. Theresa Lewis, Coordinator, 845-569-3149, Fax: 845-569-3535, E-mail: tlewis@msmc.edu.

Mount St. Mary's College, Graduate Division, Department of Education, Specialization in Special Education, Los Angeles, CA 90049-1599. Offers MS. Part-time and evening/weekend programs available. *Students:* 13 full-time (8 women), 8 part-time (7 women); includes 5 minority (all Hispanic Americans). Average age 49. In 2009, 5 master's awarded. *Degree requirements:* For master's, thesis, research project. *Entrance requirements:* For master's, MAT, minimum GPA of 3.0. *Application deadline:* For fall admission, 7/15 priority date for domestic students; for spring admission, 11/15 priority date for domestic students. Application fee: $50 ($75 for international students). *Expenses:* Tuition: Part-time $730 per unit. Part-time tuition and fees vary according to degree level and program. *Financial support:* Institutionally sponsored loans and tuition waivers (partial) available. Support available to part-time students. Financial award application deadline: 3/15; financial award applicants required to submit FAFSA. *Unit head:* Dr. Anne Wilcoxen, Chair, 213-477-2622. *Application contact:* Jessica M. Bibeau, Director of Graduate Admission, 213-477-2800 Ext. 2798, Fax: 213-477-2797, E-mail: jbibeau@msmc.la.edu.

Mount Saint Vincent University, Graduate Programs, Faculty of Education, Program in Educational Psychology, Halifax, NS B3M 2J6, Canada. Offers education of the blind or visually impaired (M Ed, MA Ed); education of the deaf or hard of hearing (M Ed, MA Ed); educational psychology (MA-R); human relations (M Ed, MA Ed). Part-time and evening/weekend programs available. Postbaccalaureate distance learning degree programs offered (minimal on-campus study). *Degree requirements:* For master's, thesis (for some programs). *Entrance requirements:* For master's, bachelor's degree in related field, 1 year of teaching experience. Electronic applications accepted. *Faculty research:* Personality measurement, values reasoning, aggression and sexuality, power and control, quantitative and qualitative research methodologies.

Murray State University, College of Education, Department of Adolescent, Career and Special Education, Program in Special Education, Murray, KY 42071. Offers advanced learning behavior disorders (MA Ed); learning disabilities (MA Ed); moderate/severe disorders (MA Ed). *Accreditation:* NCATE. Part-time and evening/weekend programs available. *Degree requirements:* For master's, thesis optional, portfolio. *Entrance requirements:* For master's, GRE General Test or MAT, teacher certification. Additional exam requirements/recommendations for international students: Required—TOEFL. *Faculty research:* Attention Deficit Hyperactivity Disorder, assistive technology.

National-Louis University, National College of Education, Programs in Special Education, Chicago, IL 60603. Offers general special education (M Ed, MAT, CAS); learning disabilities (M Ed, CAS); learning disabilities/behavior disorders (M Ed, MAT, CAS). Part-time and evening/weekend programs available. *Degree requirements:* For master's, thesis (for some programs), practicum; for CAS, practicum. *Entrance requirements:* For master's, MAT or GRE, minimum GPA of 3.0; for CAS, master's degree, teaching certificate. *Expenses:* Tuition: Full-time $17,160; part-time $715 per semester hour. Tuition and fees vary according to course load, degree level, campus/location and program.

National University, Academic Affairs, School of Education, Department of Special Education, La Jolla, CA 92037-1011. Offers deaf and hard-of-hearing education (MS); juvenile justice special education (MS); special education (MS). Part-time and evening/weekend programs available. Postbaccalaureate distance learning degree programs offered (no on-campus study). *Degree requirements:* For master's, thesis (for some programs). *Entrance requirements:* For master's, interview, minimum GPA of 2.5. Additional exam requirements/recommendations for international students: Required—TOEFL (minimum score 550 paper-based; 213 computer-based; 79 iBT), IELTS (minimum score 6). *Application deadline:* Applications are processed on a rolling basis. Application fee: $60 ($65 for international students). Electronic applications accepted. *Expenses:* Tuition: Part-time $338 per quarter hour. *Financial support:* Career-related internships or fieldwork, institutionally sponsored loans, scholarships/grants, and tuition waivers (partial) available. Support available to part-time students. Financial award application deadline: 6/30; financial award applicants required to submit FAFSA. *Unit head:* Dr. Britt Ferguson, Department Chair, 858-642-8346, Fax: 858-642-8729, E-mail: mferguson@nu.edu. *Application contact:* Dr. Britt Ferguson, Department Chair, 858-642-8346, Fax: 858-642-8729, E-mail: mferguson@nu.edu.

New England College, Program in Education, Henniker, NH 03242-3293. Offers higher education administration (MS); literacy and language arts (M Ed); meeting the needs of all learners/special education (M Ed); teacher leadership/school reform (M Ed). Part-time and evening/weekend programs available.

New Jersey City University, Graduate Studies and Continuing Education, Debra Cannon Partridge Wolfe College of Education, Department of Special Education, Jersey City, NJ 07305-1597. Offers MA. Part-time and evening/weekend programs available. *Faculty:* 8. *Students:* 10 full-time (all women), 97 part-time (73 women); includes 15 minority (8 African Americans, 1 Asian American or Pacific Islander, 6 Hispanic Americans), 2 international. Average age 34. In 2009, 53 master's awarded. *Entrance requirements:* For master's, GRE General Test or MAT. Additional exam requirements/recommendations for international students: Required—TOEFL. *Application deadline:* For fall admission, 8/1 priority date for domestic students; for spring admission, 12/1 for domestic students. Applications are processed on a rolling basis. Application fee: $0. *Expenses:* Tuition, area resident: Part-time $456.75 per credit. Tuition, nonresident: part-time $842.55 per credit. Required fees: $65 per term. *Financial support:* Unspecified assistantships available. *Faculty research:* Mainstreaming the handicapped child and the autistic child. *Unit head:* Dr. Carol Fleres, Chairperson, 201-200-3023, E-mail: cfleres@njcu.edu. *Application contact:* Dr. Carol Fleres, Chairperson, 201-200-3023, E-mail: cfleres@njcu.edu.

New Mexico Highlands University, Graduate Studies, School of Education, Las Vegas, NM 87701. Offers curriculum and instruction (MA); education (MA), including counseling, school counseling; educational leadership (MA); exercise and sport sciences (MA), including human performance and sport, sports administration, teacher education; guidance and counseling (MA), including professional counseling, rehabilitation counseling, school counseling; special education (MA), including). Part-time programs available. *Degree requirements:* For master's, comprehensive exam, thesis or alternative. *Entrance requirements:* For master's, minimum undergraduate GPA of 3.0. Additional exam requirements/recommendations for international students: Required—TOEFL (minimum score 540 paper-based; 207 computer-based). *Faculty research:* Teaching the United States Constitution, middle school curriculum, integrated computer applications for pre-service classroom teachers, adolescent literacy, narrative cognitive modes in NM multicultural setting.

New Mexico State University, Graduate School, College of Education, Department of Special Education and Communication Disorders, Las Cruces, NM 88003-8001. Offers bilingual/multicultural special education (Ed D, PhD); communication disorders (MA); special education (MA, Ed D, PhD). *Accreditation:* ASHA (one or more programs are accredited); NCATE. Part-time and evening/weekend programs available. Postbaccalaureate distance learning degree programs offered. *Faculty:* 16 full-time (13 women), 3 part-time/adjunct (all women). *Students:* 59 full-time (56 women), 61 part-time (47 women); includes 54 minority (5 American Indian/Alaska Native, 2 Asian Americans or Pacific Islanders, 47 Hispanic Americans). Average age 34. 93 applicants, 77% accepted, 48 enrolled. In 2009, 21 master's, 1 doctorate awarded. *Degree requirements:* For master's, comprehensive exam, thesis optional; for doctorate, comprehensive exam, thesis/dissertation. *Entrance requirements:* For master's, GRE General Test or MAT. Additional exam requirements/recommendations for international students: Required—TOEFL. *Application deadline:* For fall admission, 2/1 priority date for domestic students. Applications are processed on a rolling basis. Application fee: $30 ($50 for international students). Electronic applications accepted. *Expenses:* Tuition, state resident: full-time $4080; part-time $223 per credit. Tuition, nonresident: full-time $14,256; part-time $647 per credit. Required fees: $1278; $639 per semester. *Financial support:* In 2009–10, 28 students received support, including 2 research assistantships (averaging $10,715 per year), 12 teaching assistantships (averaging $4,617 per year); fellowships, career-related internships or fieldwork, Federal Work-Study, and health care benefits also available. Support available to part-time students. Financial award application deadline: 3/1; financial award applicants required to submit FAFSA. *Faculty research:* Multicultural special education, multicultural communication disorders, mild disability, multicultural assessment, deaf education, early childhood, bilingual special education. *Unit head:* Dr. Eric Joseph Lopez, Interim Department Head, 575-646-2402, Fax: 575-646-7712, E-mail: leric@nmsu.edu. *Application contact:* Coordinator.

New York University, Steinhardt School of Culture, Education, and Human Development, Department of Teaching and Learning, Program in Early Childhood and Childhood Education, New York, NY 10012-1019. Offers childhood education (MA); childhood education/special education: childhood (MA); early childhood education (MA); positions of leadership: early childhood and elementary education (PhD). *Accreditation:* Teacher Education Accreditation Council. Part-time programs available. *Students:* 40 full-time (all women), 19 part-time (all women); includes 20 minority (4 African Americans, 10 Asian Americans or Pacific Islanders, 6 Hispanic Americans), 2 international. Average age 25. 140 applicants, 72% accepted, 23 enrolled. In 2009, 47 master's awarded. *Degree requirements:* For master's, thesis (for some programs); for doctorate, thesis/dissertation. *Entrance requirements:* For doctorate, GRE General Test, interview. Additional exam requirements/recommendations for international students: Required—TOEFL. *Application deadline:* For fall admission, 12/15 priority date for domestic and international students; for spring admission, 11/1 for domestic and international students. Applications are processed on a rolling basis. Application fee: $75. Electronic applications accepted. *Expenses:* Tuition: Full-time $30,528; part-time $1272 per credit. Required fees: $2177. *Financial support:* Fellowships with full and partial tuition reimbursements, career-related internships or fieldwork, Federal Work-Study, institutionally sponsored loans, scholarships/grants, tuition waivers (partial), and unspecified assistantships available. Support available to part-time students. Financial award application deadline: 2/1; financial award applicants required to submit FAFSA. *Faculty research:* Teacher evaluation and beliefs about teaching, early literacy development, language arts, child development and education, cultural differences. *Application contact:* 212-998-5030, Fax: 212-995-4328, E-mail: steinhardt.gradadmissions@nyu.edu.

New York University, Steinhardt School of Culture, Education, and Human Development, Department of Teaching and Learning, Program in Special Education, New York, NY 10012-1019. Offers childhood special education (MA); early childhood special education (MA). *Accreditation:* Teacher Education Accreditation Council. Part-time programs available. *Students:* 81 full-time (77 women), 18 part-time (15 women); includes 18 minority (3 African Americans, 11 Asian Americans or Pacific Islanders, 4 Hispanic Americans), 5 international. Average age 25. 112 applicants, 74% accepted, 34 enrolled. In 2009, 73 master's awarded. *Degree requirements:* For master's, thesis (for some programs). *Entrance requirements:* Additional exam requirements/recommendations for international students: Required—TOEFL. *Application deadline:* For fall admission, 12/15 priority date for domestic and international students. Applications are processed on a rolling basis. Application fee: $75. Electronic applications accepted. *Expenses:* Tuition: Full-time $30,528; part-time $1272 per credit. Required fees: $2177. *Financial support:* Career-related internships or fieldwork, Federal Work-Study, institutionally sponsored loans, scholarships/grants, and tuition waivers (partial) available. Support available to part-time students. Financial award application deadline: 2/1; financial award applicants required to submit FAFSA. *Faculty research:* Special education referrals, attention deficit disorders in children, mainstreaming, curriculum-based assessment and program implementation, special education policy. *Application contact:* 212-998-5030, Fax: 212-995-4328, E-mail: steinhardt.gradadmissions@nyu.edu.

Niagara University, Graduate Division of Education, Concentration in Teacher Education, Niagara Falls, Niagara University, NY 14109. Offers early childhood and childhood education (MS Ed); middle and adolescence education (MS Ed); special education (grades 1-12) (MS Ed). *Accreditation:* NCATE. *Entrance requirements:* For master's, GRE General Test or MAT. *Expenses:* Contact institution.

Norfolk State University, School of Graduate Studies, School of Education, Department of Special Education, Norfolk, VA 23504. Offers severe disabilities (MA). *Accreditation:* NCATE. Part-time programs available. *Degree requirements:* For master's, thesis or alternative. *Entrance requirements:* For master's, minimum GPA of 3.0 in major, 2.5 overall.

North Carolina Central University, Division of Academic Affairs, School of Education, Special Education Program, Durham, NC 27707-3129. Offers M Ed, MAT. *Accreditation:* NCATE. Part-time and evening/weekend programs available. *Degree requirements:* For master's, comprehensive exam, thesis or alternative. *Entrance requirements:* For master's, GRE, minimum GPA of 3.0 in major, 2.5 overall. Additional exam requirements/recommendations for international students: Required—TOEFL. *Faculty research:* Vocational programs for special needs learners.

North Carolina State University, Graduate School, College of Education, Department of Curriculum and Instruction, Program in Special Education, Raleigh, NC 27695. Offers M Ed, MS. *Accreditation:* NCATE. *Degree requirements:* For master's, thesis optional. *Entrance requirements:* For master's, GRE General Test and MAT, minimum GPA of 3.0 in major. Electronic applications accepted. *Faculty research:* Nature of disabilities, intervention research.

Special Education

Northeastern Illinois University, Graduate College, College of Education, Department of Special Education, Program in Special Education, Chicago, IL 60625-4699. Offers early childhood special education (MA); educating children with behavior disorders (MA); educating individuals with mental retardation (MA); teaching children with learning disabilities (MA). Part-time and evening/weekend programs available. *Degree requirements:* For master's, thesis optional, project. *Entrance requirements:* For master's, minimum GPA of 2.75; previous course work in history or philosophy of education or teaching certificate. Additional exam requirements/recommendations for international students: Required—TOEFL (minimum score 550 paper-based; 213 computer-based; 80 iBT). Electronic applications accepted. *Faculty research:* Bilingual special education, use of technology in the classroom, teachers' attitudes toward inclusion, standards for special education teachers.

Northern Arizona University, Graduate College, College of Education, Department of Educational Specialties, Flagstaff, AZ 86011. Offers autism spectrum disorders (Certificate); bilingual/multicultural education (M Ed), including bilingual education, ESL education; career and technical education (M Ed, Certificate); curriculum and instruction (Ed D); early childhood special education (M Ed); early intervention (Certificate); educational technology (M Ed, Certificate); special education (M Ed). *Faculty:* 29 full-time (16 women). *Students:* 153 full-time (118 women), 360 part-time (291 women); includes 152 minority (12 African Americans, 43 American Indian/Alaska Native, 5 Asian Americans or Pacific Islanders, 92 Hispanic Americans), 9 international. Average age 30. 215 applicants, 87% accepted, 133 enrolled. In 2009, 200 master's, 8 doctorates awarded. *Degree requirements:* For master's, comprehensive exam (for some programs), thesis (for some programs). *Entrance requirements:* For master's, minimum GPA of 3.0. Additional exam requirements/recommendations for international students: Required—TOEFL (minimum score 550 paper-based; 213 computer-based; 80 iBT), IELTS (minimum score 7), or a bachelor's degree from an English-speaking university and demonstrated proficiency. *Application deadline:* For fall admission, 2/1 for domestic students, 8/1 for international students; for spring admission, 12/1 for domestic students. Applications are processed on a rolling basis. Application fee: $65. Electronic applications accepted. *Financial support:* In 2009–10, 2 research assistantships with partial tuition reimbursements (averaging $10,000 per year), 8 teaching assistantships with partial tuition reimbursements (averaging $10,000 per year) were awarded. Financial award application deadline: 3/30. *Unit head:* Dr. Lawrence Gallagher, Chair, 928-523-5083, E-mail: lawrence.gallagher@nau.edu. *Application contact:* Dr. Lawrence Gallagher, Chair, 928-523-5083, E-mail: lawrence.gallagher@nau.edu.

Northern Illinois University, Graduate School, College of Education, Department of Teaching and Learning, De Kalb, IL 60115-2854. Offers curriculum and instruction (MS Ed, Ed D), including curriculum leadership (Ed D), elementary education (Ed D), secondary education (Ed D); early childhood education (MS Ed); elementary education (MS Ed); special education (MS Ed). Part-time and evening/weekend programs available. *Faculty:* 22 full-time (14 women), 2 part-time/adjunct (both women). *Students:* 50 full-time (38 women), 435 part-time (344 women); includes 107 minority (16 African Americans, 1 American Indian/Alaska Native, 12 Asian Americans or Pacific Islanders, 78 Hispanic Americans), 9 international. Average age 35. 154 applicants, 53% accepted, 57 enrolled. In 2009, 142 master's, 2 doctorates awarded. *Degree requirements:* For master's, comprehensive exam, thesis optional; for doctorate, thesis/dissertation, candidacy exam, dissertation defense. *Entrance requirements:* For master's, GRE General Test or MAT, minimum undergraduate GPA of 2.75; for doctorate, GRE General Test or MAT, minimum undergraduate GPA of 2.75, graduate 3.2. Additional exam requirements/recommendations for international students: Required—TOEFL (minimum score 550 paper-based; 213 computer-based). *Application deadline:* For fall admission, 6/1 for domestic students, 5/1 for international students; for spring admission, 11/1 for domestic students, 10/1 for international students. Applications are processed on a rolling basis. Application fee: $30. Electronic applications accepted. *Expenses:* Tuition, state resident: full-time $6576; part-time $274 per credit hour. Tuition, nonresident: full-time $13,152; part-time $548 per credit hour. Required fees: $1813; $75.53 per credit hour. Part-time tuition and fees vary according to course load. *Financial support:* In 2009–10, 20 research assistantships with full tuition reimbursements were awarded; fellowships with full tuition reimbursements, teaching assistantships with full tuition reimbursements, career-related internships or fieldwork, Federal Work-Study, scholarships/grants, tuition waivers (full), and unspecified assistantships also available. Support available to part-time students. Financial award applicants required to submit FAFSA. *Faculty research:* Teacher certification, stress reduction during student teaching, teaching history, portfolios in student teaching. *Unit head:* Dr. Helen Brantley, Chair, 815-753-0327, E-mail: tedur@niu.edu. *Application contact:* Gail Myers, E-mail: gmyers@niu.edu.

Northern Kentucky University, Office of Graduate Programs, College of Education and Human Services, Program in Teaching, Highland Heights, KY 41099. Offers school superintendent (Certificate); special education (Certificate); teaching (MA). Part-time programs available. *Students:* 4 full-time (2 women), 70 part-time (42 women); includes 3 minority (1 Asian American or Pacific Islander, 2 Hispanic Americans). Average age 32. 110 applicants, 36% accepted, 37 enrolled. In 2009, 45 master's awarded. *Degree requirements:* For master's, comprehensive exam, thesis optional, portfolio, student teaching or internship. *Entrance requirements:* For master's, GRE, PRAXIS II, minimum GPA of 2.5, 3 letters of recommendation, criminal background check (state and federal), resume, letter to the reviewer, interview. Additional exam requirements/recommendations for international students: Required—TOEFL (minimum score 550 paper-based; 213 computer-based; 79 iBT); Recommended—IELTS (minimum score 6.5). *Application deadline:* For fall admission, 6/1 priority date for domestic and international students; for spring admission, 10/1 priority date for international students. Application fee: $40. Electronic applications accepted. *Expenses:* Tuition, state resident: full-time $6912; part-time $384 per credit hour. Tuition, nonresident: full-time $12,150; part-time $675 per credit hour. Tuition and fees vary according to course load, program and reciprocity agreements. *Financial support:* Unspecified assistantships available. Financial award applicants required to submit FAFSA. *Faculty research:* Middle grades students, secondary students, rural classrooms, urban classrooms, teacher preparation. *Unit head:* Department Chair, 859-572-5942, Fax: 859-572-6623. *Application contact:* Melissa Decker, Alternative Certification Coordinator, 859-572-6330, Fax: 859-572-1384, E-mail: deckerm@nku.edu.

Northern Michigan University, College of Graduate Studies, College of Professional Studies, School of Education, Program in Learning Disabilities, Marquette, MI 49855-5301. Offers MA Ed. Part-time programs available. Postbaccalaureate distance learning degree programs offered. *Degree requirements:* For master's, thesis or alternative. *Entrance requirements:* For master's, GRE General Test, minimum GPA of 3.0. *Faculty research:* Interdisciplinary approaches to learning disabilities, neurological bases for cognitive processing of information.

Northern State University, Division of Graduate Studies in Education, Program in Teaching and Learning, Aberdeen, SD 57401-7198. Offers educational studies (MS Ed); elementary classroom teaching (MS Ed); health, physical education, and coaching (MS Ed); language and literacy (MS Ed); secondary classroom teaching (MS Ed); special education (MS Ed). *Accreditation:* NCATE. Part-time and evening/weekend programs available. *Faculty:* 10 full-time (8 women). *Students:* 23 full-time (16 women), 35 part-time (17 women); includes 2 minority (1 American Indian/Alaska Native, 1 Asian American or Pacific Islander). Average age 32. In 2009, 26 master's awarded. *Degree requirements:* For master's, thesis optional. *Entrance requirements:* For master's, minimum GPA of 2.75. Additional exam requirements/recommendations for international students: Required—TOEFL (minimum score 550 paper-based; 213 computer-based; 76 iBT). *Application deadline:* For fall admission, 8/15 priority date for domestic students; for spring admission, 12/15 for domestic students. Applications are processed on a rolling basis. Application fee: $35. Electronic applications accepted. *Financial support:* In 2009–10, 18 teaching assistantships with partial tuition reimbursements (averaging $5,558 per year) were awarded; career-related internships or fieldwork, Federal Work-Study, institutionally sponsored loans, scholarships/grants, and unspecified assistantships also available. Support available to part-time students. Financial award application deadline: 3/1; financial award applicants required to submit FAFSA. *Application contact:* Tammy K. Griffith, Program Assistant, 605-626-2558, Fax: 605-626-7190, E-mail: griffith@northern.edu.

North Georgia College & State University, Graduate Studies, Program in Teacher Education, Dahlonega, GA 30597. Offers early childhood education (M Ed); educational leadership (Ed S); middle grades education (M Ed); secondary education (M Ed), including art education, biology education, chemistry education, English education, history education, mathematics education, physical education, science education; special education (M Ed), including interrelated special education, learning disabilities. *Accreditation:* NCATE. Part-time and evening/weekend programs available. Postbaccalaureate distance learning degree programs offered (minimal on-campus study). *Degree requirements:* For master's, comprehensive exam, thesis optional. *Entrance requirements:* For master's, GRE General Test or MAT, minimum GPA of 2.75; for Ed S, GRE General Test or MAT, 3 years of teaching experience, master's degree, minimum graduate GPA of 3.25. Electronic applications accepted. *Faculty research:* Computers and teachers' attitudes, rural versus urban teacher attitudes, teacher leadership roles, minority recruitment in teaching force.

Northwestern State University of Louisiana, Graduate Studies and Research, College of Education, Program in Special Education, Natchitoches, LA 71497. Offers MA.

Northwestern State University of Louisiana, Graduate Studies and Research, College of Education, Program in Student Personnel Services, Natchitoches, LA 71497. Offers counseling and guidance (M Ed, Ed S); special education (M Ed, Ed S); student personnel services (MA). *Accreditation:* NCATE (one or more programs are accredited). *Degree requirements:* For master's, comprehensive exam, thesis or alternative. *Entrance requirements:* For master's, GRE General Test, GRE Subject Test, minimum undergraduate GPA of 2.5.

Northwestern State University of Louisiana, Graduate Studies and Research, College of Education, Programs in Educational Leadership and Instruction, Natchitoches, LA 71497. Offers counseling (Ed S); educational leadership (Ed S); educational technology (Ed S); elementary teaching (Ed S); reading (Ed S); secondary teaching (Ed S); special education (Ed S). *Entrance requirements:* For degree, GRE General Test.

Northwestern University, The Graduate School, School of Communication, The Roxelyn and Richard Pepper Department of Communication Sciences and Disorders, Program in Learning Disabilities, Evanston, IL 60208. Offers MA, PhD. Admissions and degrees offered through The Graduate School. Part-time programs available. Terminal master's awarded for partial completion of doctoral program. *Degree requirements:* For master's, comprehensive exam, thesis optional; for doctorate, pre-dissertation research project, qualifying exam. *Entrance requirements:* For master's and doctorate, GRE General Test, letters of recommendation. Additional exam requirements/recommendations for international students: Required—TOEFL. *Faculty research:* Reading and writing disabilities, inter-relations of oral and written language, social context of atypical development, attention deficit disorder, neuroscience of learning disorders.

See Close-Up on page 1427.

Northwestern University, The Graduate School, School of Communication, The Roxelyn and Richard Pepper Department of Communication Sciences and Disorders, Program in Speech and Language Pathology and Learning Disabilities, Evanston, IL 60208. Offers MA. Admissions and degree offered through The Graduate School. *Accreditation:* ASHA. *Degree requirements:* For master's, thesis optional, seminar paper. *Entrance requirements:* For master's, GRE General Test, letters of recommendation. Additional exam requirements/recommendations for international students: Required—TOEFL. *Faculty research:* Language and cognitive development, phonological and reading development.

See Close-Up on page 1427.

Northwest Missouri State University, Graduate School, College of Education and Human Services, Department of Curriculum and Instruction, Program in Special Education, Maryville, MO 64468-6001. Offers MS Ed. *Faculty:* 12 full-time (all women). *Students:* 2 full-time (both women), 15 part-time (12 women); includes 1 minority (African American). 8 applicants, 75% accepted, 3 enrolled. In 2009, 7 master's awarded. *Entrance requirements:* For master's, GRE General Test, minimum GPA of 2.75, teaching certificate. Additional exam requirements/recommendations for international students: Required—TOEFL (minimum score 550 paper-based; 213 computer-based). *Application deadline:* For fall admission, 7/1 for domestic and international students; for spring admission, 11/15 for domestic and international students. Application fee: $0 ($50 for international students). *Expenses:* Tuition, state resident: part-time $296.34 per credit hour. Tuition, nonresident: part-time $510.43 per credit hour. *Financial support:* Application deadline: 4/1. *Unit head:* Dr. Shirley Steffens, Head, 660-562-1443. *Application contact:* Dr. Gregory Haddock, Dean of Graduate School, 660-562-1145, Fax: 660-562-1096, E-mail: gradsch@nwmissouri.edu.

Northwest Nazarene University, Graduate Studies, Program in Teacher Education, Nampa, ID 83686-5897. Offers curriculum and instruction (M Ed); educational leadership (M Ed); exceptional child (M Ed); reading education (M Ed); school counseling (M Ed). *Accreditation:* ACA; NCATE. Part-time programs available. *Degree requirements:* For master's, comprehensive exam (for some programs), action research project. *Entrance requirements:* For master's, minimum undergraduate GPA of 2.8 overall or 3.0 during final 30 semester credits. *Faculty research:* Action research, cooperative learning, accountability, institutional accreditation.

Notre Dame College, Graduate Studies, South Euclid, OH 44121-4293. Offers accounting (Certificate); creative critical thinking (M Ed); financial services management (Certificate); information systems (Certificate); learning disabilities (M Ed); management (Certificate); paralegal (Certificate); pastoral ministry (Certificate); reading (M Ed); teacher education (Certificate). Part-time and evening/weekend programs available. *Degree requirements:* For master's, thesis. *Entrance requirements:* For master's, GRE General Test, MAT, minimum GPA of 2.75, valid teaching certificate. *Faculty research:* Cognitive psychology, teaching critical thinking in the classroom.

Notre Dame de Namur University, Division of Academic Affairs, School of Education and Leadership, Program in Special Education, Belmont, CA 94002-1908. Offers education specialist level I credential (Certificate); education specialist level II credential (Certificate); special education (MA). In 2009, 12 master's, 20 other advanced degrees awarded. *Degree requirements:* For master's, thesis. *Entrance requirements:* For master's, interview, minimum GPA of 2.5. Additional exam requirements/recommendations for international students: Required—TOEFL (minimum score 550 paper-based; 213 computer-based; 79 iBT). *Application deadline:* For fall admission, 8/1 priority date for domestic students; for spring admission, 12/1 priority date for domestic students. Applications are processed on a rolling basis. Application fee: $60. Electronic applications accepted. *Expenses:* Tuition: Part-time $720 per credit. Required fees: $35 per semester hour. *Financial support:* Career-related internships or fieldwork available. Support available to part-time students. Financial award applicants required to submit FAFSA. *Unit head:* Dr. Nicole Ofiesh, Director, 650-508-3627, E-mail: nofiesh@ndnu.edu. *Application contact:* Candace Hallmark, Associate Director of Admissions, 650-508-3529, Fax: 650-508-3426, E-mail: grad.admit@ndnu.edu.

Nova Southeastern University, Fischler School of Education and Human Services, Graduate Teacher Education Program, Fort Lauderdale, FL 33314-7796. Offers athletic administration (MS); brain research (MS, Ed S); charter school education/leadership (MS); cognitive and behavioral disabilities (MS); computer science education (Ed S); computer science education (K-12) (MS); curriculum and teaching (Ed S); curriculum, instruction and technology (MS); curriculum, instruction, management and administration (Ed S); early childhood education (MS); early literacy and reading (Ed S); early literacy education (MS); education technology (MS); educational leadership (administration K–12) (MS, Ed S); educational media (Ed S); educational media (K-12) (MS); elementary education (MS, Ed S), including ESOL endorsement (MS); English education (MS, Ed S); environmental education (MS); exceptional student education (MS), including ESOL endorsement; gifted education (MS, Ed S); interdisciplinary

arts education (MS); management and administration of educational programs (MS); mathematics (MS); mathematics education (Ed S); multicultural early intervention (MS); pre-kindergarten/primary (MS); preschool education (MS); reading (MS); reading and TESOL (MS); reading education (Ed S); science (MS); science education (Ed S); secondary education (MS); social studies (MS, Ed S); Spanish language (MS); special education and reading (MS); teaching and learning (MA, MS), including curriculum and instruction (MA), elementary mathematics (MA), elementary reading (MA), K-12 technology integration (MA); teaching English to speakers of other languages (MS, Ed S); technology management and administration (Ed S); urban studies education (MS). Part-time and evening/weekend programs available. Postbaccalaureate distance learning degree programs offered (minimal on-campus study). *Faculty:* 72 full-time (43 women), 385 part-time/adjunct (252 women). *Students:* 196 full-time (175 women), 1,304 part-time (1,128 women); includes 594 minority (471 African Americans, 5 American Indian/Alaska Native, 18 Asian Americans or Pacific Islanders, 100 Hispanic Americans). Average age 37. 2,610 applicants, 72% accepted, 1352 enrolled. In 2009, 836 other advanced degrees awarded. *Degree requirements:* For master's and Ed S, thesis, practicum, internship. *Entrance requirements:* For master's, MAT, GRE, CLAST, CBEST, PRAXIS I, General Knowledge Test, minimum GPA of 2.5; for Ed S, MAT or GRE, master's degree, teaching certificate, minimum GPA of 3.0. Additional exam requirements/recommendations for international students: Required—TSE (recommended, minimum score 50); Recommended—TOEFL (minimum score 550 paper-based; 213 computer-based; 80 iBT), IELTS (minimum score 6). *Application deadline:* For fall admission, 9/25 priority date for domestic and international students; for winter admission, 2/23 priority date for domestic and international students; for spring admission, 4/25 priority date for domestic and international students. Applications are processed on a rolling basis. Application fee: $50. Electronic applications accepted. *Financial support:* Federal Work-Study available. Support available to part-time students. Financial award application deadline: 4/15; financial award applicants required to submit FAFSA. *Faculty research:* School effectiveness, critical thinking, leadership skills acquisition, child education, multicultural education. *Unit head:* Dr. Ronald Kern, Dean of Academic Affairs, 800-986-3223 Ext. 7809, Fax: 954-262-3606, E-mail: rk429@nsu.nova.edu. *Application contact:* Dr. Jennifer Quinones Nottingham, Dean of Student Affairs, 800-986-3223 Ext. 1559.

Nova Southeastern University, Fischler School of Education and Human Services, Program in Education, Fort Lauderdale, FL 33314-7796. Offers educational leadership (Ed D); health care education (Ed D); higher education leadership (Ed D); human services administration (Ed D); instructional leadership (Ed D); instructional technology and distance education (Ed D); organizational leadership (Ed D); special education (Ed D); speech language pathology (Ed D). Part-time and evening/weekend programs available. Postbaccalaureate distance learning degree programs offered (minimal on-campus study). *Faculty:* 88 full-time (46 women), 132 part-time/adjunct (63 women). *Students:* 2,805 full-time (2,128 women), 1,411 part-time (1,081 women); includes 2,629 minority (2,034 African Americans, 19 American Indian/Alaska Native, 62 Asian Americans or Pacific Islanders, 514 Hispanic Americans), 30 international. Average age 41. 964 applicants, 69% accepted, 513 enrolled. In 2009, 445 doctorates awarded. *Degree requirements:* For doctorate, thesis/dissertation. *Entrance requirements:* For doctorate, MAT or GRE, master's degree, 2 letters of recommendation, work experience. Additional exam requirements/recommendations for international students: Required—TSE (recommended, minimum score 50); Recommended—TOEFL (minimum score 550 paper-based; 213 computer-based; 80 iBT), IELTS (minimum score 6). *Application deadline:* For fall admission, 8/20 priority date for domestic and international students; for winter admission, 12/19 priority date for domestic and international students; for spring admission, 4/26 priority date for domestic students, 4/25 priority date for international students. Applications are processed on a rolling basis. Application fee: $50. Electronic applications accepted. *Financial support:* In 2009–10, 2 fellowships with full tuition reimbursements (averaging $30,000 per year) were awarded; scholarships/grants and tuition waivers (full) also available. Support available to part-time students. Financial award application deadline: 4/15; financial award applicants required to submit FAFSA. *Unit head:* Dr. Ronald Kern, Dean of Academic Affairs, 800-986-3223 Ext. 7809, Fax: 954-262-3606, E-mail: rk429@nsu.nova.edu. *Application contact:* Dr. Jennifer Quinones Nottingham, Dean of Student Affairs, 800-986-3223 Ext. 1546.

Nyack College, School of Education, Nyack, NY 10960-3698. Offers childhood education (MS); childhood special education (MS); inclusive education (MS). Part-time and evening/weekend programs available. *Degree requirements:* For master's, comprehensive exam (for some programs), thesis (for some programs), field experience. *Entrance requirements:* For master's, GRE, baccalaureate degree with minimum GPA of 3.0, evidence of initial/provisional teaching certification. Additional exam requirements/recommendations for international students: Required—TOEFL (minimum score 500 paper-based), TWE (minimum score 4). *Expenses:* Contact institution.

Oakland University, Graduate Study and Lifelong Learning, School of Education and Human Services, Department of Human Development and Child Studies, Program in Special Education, Rochester, MI 48309-4401. Offers M Ed, Certificate. *Accreditation:* Teacher Education Accreditation Council. *Entrance requirements:* For master's, minimum GPA of 3.0 for unconditional admission, interview. Additional exam requirements/recommendations for international students: Required—TOEFL (minimum score 550 paper-based; 213 computer-based). Electronic applications accepted.

Ohio University, Graduate College, College of Education, Department of Teacher Education, Athens, OH 45701-2979. Offers adolescent to young adult education (M Ed); curriculum and instruction (M Ed, PhD); early childhood/special education (M Ed); intervention specialist/mild-moderate needs (M Ed); intervention specialist/moderate-intensive needs (M Ed); mathematics education (PhD); middle child education (M Ed); reading education (M Ed); social studies education (PhD). Part-time and evening/weekend programs available. *Faculty:* 21 full-time (13 women), 7 part-time/adjunct (all women). *Students:* 105 full-time (75 women), 183 part-time (161 women); includes 9 minority (5 African Americans, 3 American Indian/Alaska Native, 1 Asian American or Pacific Islander), 14 international. 190 applicants, 80% accepted, 72 enrolled. *Degree requirements:* For master's, thesis or alternative; for doctorate, comprehensive exam, thesis/dissertation. *Entrance requirements:* For master's, GRE General Test or MAT (if GPA is below 2.9); for doctorate, GRE General Test, minimum GPA of 3.4, work experience. Additional exam requirements/recommendations for international students: Required—TOEFL (minimum score 550 paper-based; 80 iBT) or IELTS Academic (minimum score 6.5). *Application deadline:* For fall admission, 5/1 priority date for domestic students, 4/1 priority date for international students; for winter admission, 11/1 priority date for domestic students, 10/1 priority date for international students; for spring admission, 2/15 priority date for domestic students, 1/1 priority date for international students. Applications are processed on a rolling basis. Application fee: $50 ($55 for international students). Electronic applications accepted. *Expenses:* Tuition, state resident: full-time $7839; part-time $323 per quarter hour. Tuition, nonresident: full-time $15,831; part-time $654 per quarter hour. Required fees: $2931. *Financial support:* Research assistantships with full tuition reimbursements, teaching assistantships with full tuition reimbursements, Federal Work-Study, institutionally sponsored loans, tuition waivers (partial), and unspecified assistantships available. Financial award application deadline: 3/1. *Faculty research:* Cognition literacy, character education, teacher's education reform, disabilities. Total annual research expenditures: $46,933. *Unit head:* Dr. John Henning, Chair, 740-597-1830, Fax: 740-593-0477, E-mail: henningj@ohio.edu. *Application contact:* Floyd J. Doney, Director of Student Affairs, 740-593-4400, Fax: 740-593-9310, E-mail: doney@ohio.edu.

Old Dominion University, Darden College of Education, Program in Special Education, Norfolk, VA 23529. Offers MS Ed, PhD. *Accreditation:* NCATE. Part-time and evening/weekend programs available. Postbaccalaureate distance learning degree programs offered (no on-campus study). *Faculty:* 12 full-time (9 women), 6 part-time/adjunct (4 women). *Students:* 23 full-time (20 women), 113 part-time (97 women); includes 14 minority (9 African Americans, 1 American Indian/Alaska Native, 4 Asian Americans or Pacific Islanders), 1 international. Average age 34. 78 applicants, 85% accepted, 61 enrolled. In 2009, 69 master's, 2 doctorates awarded. *Degree requirements:* For master's, comprehensive exam, thesis or alternative; for doctorate, comprehensive exam, thesis/dissertation. *Entrance requirements:* For master's, GRE General Test or MAT, PRAXIS I, minimum GPA of 2.8; for doctorate, GRE. Additional exam requirements/recommendations for international students: Recommended—TOEFL (minimum score 550 paper-based; 213 computer-based). *Application deadline:* For fall admission, 6/1 priority date for domestic and international students; for winter admission, 11/1 priority date for domestic and international students; for spring admission, 3/1 priority date for domestic and international students. Applications are processed on a rolling basis. Application fee: $50. Electronic applications accepted. *Expenses:* Tuition, state resident: full-time $8112; part-time $338 per credit. Tuition, nonresident: full-time $20,256; part-time $844 per credit. Required fees: $119 per semester. One-time fee: $50. *Financial support:* In 2009–10, 70 students received support, including 1 fellowship (averaging $15,000 per year), 2 teaching assistantships with tuition reimbursements available (averaging $15,000 per year); research assistantships with tuition reimbursements available, career-related internships or fieldwork, scholarships/grants, tuition waivers (partial), and unspecified assistantships also available. Financial award application deadline: 2/15; financial award applicants required to submit FAFSA. *Faculty research:* Inclusion, clinical practice, infant and preschool handicapped, distance learning. Total annual research expenditures: $3.6 million. *Unit head:* Dr. Cheryl S. Baker, Graduate Program Director, 757-683-4383, Fax: 757-683-4129, E-mail: csbaker@odu.edu. *Application contact:* Alice McAdory, Director of Admissions, 757-683-3685, Fax: 757-683-3255, E-mail: gradadmit@odu.edu.

Ottawa University, Graduate Studies-Arizona, Program in Education, Ottawa, KS 66067-3399. Offers community college counseling (MA); curriculum and instruction (MA); early childhood (MA); education intervention (MA); education leadership (MA); education technology (MA); Montessori early childhood education (MA); Montessori elementary education (MA); professional development (MA); school guidance counseling (MA); special education—cross categorical (MA). Programs offered in Mesa, Phoenix, Tempe and West Valley, AZ. *Accreditation:* NCATE. Part-time programs available. *Degree requirements:* For master's, thesis or alternative. *Entrance requirements:* For master's, minimum undergraduate GPA of 3.0, copy of current state certification or teaching license. Additional exam requirements/recommendations for international students: Required—TOEFL (minimum score 550 paper-based; 213 computer-based). Electronic applications accepted. *Expenses:* Contact institution.

Our Lady of the Lake University of San Antonio, School of Professional Studies, Program in Generic Special Education, San Antonio, TX 78207-4689. Offers elementary education (M Ed). Part-time and evening/weekend programs available. *Students:* 6 full-time (5 women), 16 part-time (15 women); includes 13 minority (2 African Americans, 11 Hispanic Americans). Average age 37. In 2009, 10 master's awarded. *Degree requirements:* For master's, comprehensive exam, thesis optional, examination for the Certification of Education in Texas. *Entrance requirements:* For master's, GRE General Test or MAT, interview. Additional exam requirements/recommendations for international students: Required—TOEFL. *Application deadline:* Applications are processed on a rolling basis. Application fee: $25 ($50 for international students). Electronic applications accepted. *Expenses:* Tuition: Full-time $12,330; part-time $685 per contact hour. Required fees: $139; $12 per contact hour. $57 per semester. Tuition and fees vary according to campus/location. *Financial support:* Career-related internships or fieldwork and tuition waivers (partial) available. Financial award application deadline: 4/15. *Unit head:* Dr. Cullen Grinnan, Coordinator, 210-434-6711, E-mail: ctgrinnan@lake.ollusa.edu. *Application contact:* 210-434-6711 Ext. 2314, Fax: 210-431-4036, E-mail: gradadm@lake.ollusa.edu.

Pace University, School of Education, New York, NY 10038. Offers administration and supervision (MS Ed); adolescent education (MST); childhood education (MST); curriculum and instruction (MS); education (MST); literacy (MSE); school business management (Certificate); teaching students with disabilities (MSE); teaching visual arts (MST). *Accreditation:* NCATE. Part-time and evening/weekend programs available. *Students:* 235 full-time (177 women), 766 part-time (515 women); includes 158 minority (58 African Americans, 1 American Indian/Alaska Native, 37 Asian Americans or Pacific Islanders, 62 Hispanic Americans), 7 international. Average age 30. 332 applicants, 83% accepted, 165 enrolled. In 2009, 669 master's, 34 other advanced degrees awarded. *Degree requirements:* For master's, internship. *Entrance requirements:* For master's, interview, teaching certificate. Additional exam requirements/recommendations for international students: Required—TOEFL. *Application deadline:* For fall admission, 7/31 priority date for domestic students; for spring admission, 11/30 for domestic students. Applications are processed on a rolling basis. Application fee: $70. Electronic applications accepted. *Expenses:* Contact institution. *Financial support:* Research assistantships, career-related internships or fieldwork and Federal Work-Study available. Support available to part-time students. Financial award applicants required to submit FAFSA. *Unit head:* Dr. Harriet Feldman, Interim Dean, 212-346-1512. *Application contact:* Susan Ford-Goldschein, Director of Admissions, 212-346-1652, Fax: 212-346-1585, E-mail: gradnyc@pace.edu.

Pacific University, College of Education, Forest Grove, OR 97116-1797. Offers early childhood education (MAT); education (MAE); elementary education (MAT); high school education (MAT); middle school education (MAT); special education (MAT); visual function in learning (M Ed). *Accreditation:* NCATE. Part-time and evening/weekend programs available. *Degree requirements:* For master's, research project. *Entrance requirements:* For master's, California Basic Educational Skills Test, PRAXIS II, minimum undergraduate GPA of 2.75, 3.0 graduate. Additional exam requirements/recommendations for international students: Required—TOEFL. Electronic applications accepted. *Expenses:* Contact institution. *Faculty research:* Defining a culturally competent classroom, technology in the k-12 classroom, Socratic seminars, social studies education.

Park University, College of Graduate and Professional Studies, Kansas City, MO 54105. Offers adult education (M Ed); at-risk students (M Ed); disaster and emergency management (MPA); educational administration (M Ed); entrepreneurship (MBA); general business (MBA); general education (M Ed); government/business relations (MPA); healthcare/services management (MBA, MPA); international business (MBA); K-12 certification (MAT); management information systems (MBA); management of information systems (MPA); middle school certification (MAT); multi-cultural education (M Ed); nonprofit management (MPA); public management (MPA); school law (M Ed); secondary school certification (MAT); special education (M Ed). Part-time and evening/weekend programs available. Postbaccalaureate distance learning degree programs offered (no on-campus study). *Degree requirements:* For master's, comprehensive exam, thesis (for some programs). *Entrance requirements:* For master's, GRE, GMAT, teacher certification (M Ed). Additional exam requirements/recommendations for international students: Required—TOEFL (minimum score 550 paper-based). Electronic applications accepted. *Faculty research:* Literacy, leadership, brain based research, multicultural education, diversity.

Penn State University Park, Graduate School, College of Education, Department of Educational and School Psychology and Special Education, State College, University Park, PA 16802-1503. Offers M Ed, MS, PhD.

Pittsburg State University, Graduate School, College of Education, Department of Special Services and Leadership Studies, Program in Special Education, Pittsburg, KS 66762. Offers behavioral disorders (MS); learning disabilities (MS); mentally retarded (MS). *Accreditation:* NCATE. *Degree requirements:* For master's, thesis or alternative. *Entrance requirements:* For master's, GRE General Test or MAT. *Expenses:* Tuition, state resident: full-time $4212; part-time $176 per credit. Tuition, nonresident: full-time $11,530; part-time $480 per credit. Required fees: $940; $43 per credit. Tuition and fees vary according to course level, course load, degree level, campus/location, reciprocity agreements and student level.

Plymouth State University, College of Graduate Studies, Graduate Studies in Education, Plymouth, NH 03264-1595. Offers athletic training (M Ed, MS); counselor education (M Ed); education (CAGS); educational leadership (M Ed); elementary education (M Ed); English education (M Ed); health education (M Ed); k-12 education (M Ed); learning, leadership and

Special Education

Plymouth State University (continued)

community (Ed D); mathematics education (M Ed); reading and writing specialist (M Ed); science (MS), including applied meteorology, environmental science and policy, science education; secondary education (M Ed); special education administration (M Ed); special education k-12 (M Ed); teaching (MAT). *Accreditation:* NCATE (one or more programs are accredited). Part-time and evening/weekend programs available. Postbaccalaureate distance learning degree programs offered (minimal on-campus study). *Entrance requirements:* For master's, MAT or other standardized exam, minimum GPA of 3.0. Additional exam requirements/recommendations for international students: Required—TOEFL (minimum score 550 paper-based). *Expenses:* Contact institution. *Faculty research:* Special education, technology, math and science methodology.

Portland State University, Graduate Studies, School of Education, Department of Special Education and Counselor Education, Portland, OR 97207-0751. Offers counselor education (MA, MS); special and counselor education (Ed D); special education (MA, MS). *Accreditation:* ACA (one or more programs are accredited). Part-time and evening/weekend programs available. *Degree requirements:* For master's, thesis or alternative. *Entrance requirements:* For master's, California Basic Educational Skills Test, minimum GPA of 3.0 in upper-division course work or 2.75 overall. Additional exam requirements/recommendations for international students: Required—TOEFL (minimum score 550 paper-based; 213 computer-based). *Faculty research:* Transition of students with disabilities, functional curriculum, supported/inclusive education, leisure/recreation, autism.

Prairie View A&M University, College of Education, Department of Curriculum and Instruction, Prairie View, TX 77446-0519. Offers curriculum and instruction (M Ed, MS Ed); special education (M Ed, MS Ed). *Accreditation:* NCATE. Part-time and evening/weekend programs available. *Faculty:* 7 full-time (4 women), 1 (woman) part-time/adjunct. *Students:* 20 full-time (18 women), 117 part-time (82 women); includes 113 African Americans, 3 international. Average age 36. 119 applicants, 87% accepted, 96 enrolled. In 2009, 51 master's awarded. *Degree requirements:* For master's, thesis optional. *Entrance requirements:* For master's, GRE, minimum GPA of 2.5, 3 references. *Application deadline:* For fall admission, 7/1 priority date for domestic students; for winter admission, 3/1 priority date for domestic students; for spring admission, 11/1 priority date for domestic students. Applications are processed on a rolling basis. Application fee: $50. Electronic applications accepted. *Expenses:* Tuition, state resident: full-time $2200. Tuition, nonresident: full-time $5600. Required fees: $1720. Tuition and fees vary according to course load. *Financial support:* In 2009–10, 1 research assistantship with tuition reimbursement (averaging $18,000 per year) was awarded; fellowships with tuition reimbursements, teaching assistantships, career-related internships or fieldwork, institutionally sponsored loans, scholarships/grants, health care benefits, tuition waivers (full and partial), and unspecified assistantships also available. Support available to part-time students. Financial award application deadline: 4/1. *Faculty research:* Metacognitive strategies, emotionally disturbed, language arts, teachers recruit, diversity, recruitment, retention, school collaboration. Total annual research expenditures: $25,000. *Unit head:* Dr. Edward Mason, Head, 936-261-3403, Fax: 936-261-3419, E-mail: elmason@pvamu.edu.

Pratt Institute, School of Art and Design, Programs in Creative Arts Therapy, Brooklyn, NY 11205-3899. Offers art therapy and creativity development (MPS); art therapy-special education (MPS); dance/movement therapy (MS). *Accreditation:* NASAD (one or more programs are accredited). Part-time programs available. *Faculty:* 3 full-time (all women), 19 part-time/adjunct (16 women). *Students:* 105 full-time (102 women), 4 part-time (all women); includes 19 minority (6 African Americans, 3 Asian Americans or Pacific Islanders, 10 Hispanic Americans), 6 international. Average age 30. 197 applicants, 90% accepted, 33 enrolled. In 2009, 30 master's awarded. *Degree requirements:* For master's, thesis. *Entrance requirements:* For master's, letters of recommendation, portfolio. Additional exam requirements/recommendations for international students: Required—TOEFL (minimum score 600 paper-based; 250 computer-based; 100 iBT). *Application deadline:* For fall admission, 1/5 for domestic and international students; for spring admission, 10/1 for domestic and international students. Applications are processed on a rolling basis. Application fee: $50 ($90 for international students). Electronic applications accepted. *Expenses:* Tuition: Full-time $22,734. Required fees: $1280. *Financial support:* Career-related internships or fieldwork, Federal Work-Study, institutionally sponsored loans, scholarships/grants, health care benefits, tuition waivers (full), and unspecified assistantships available. Support available to part-time students. Financial award application deadline: 2/1; financial award applicants required to submit FAFSA. *Faculty research:* Psychology and aesthetic interaction, art therapy and AIDS, art therapy and autism, art diagnosis. *Unit head:* Jean Davis, Chairperson, 718-636-3428, E-mail: jdavis@pratt.edu. *Application contact:* Young Hah, Director of Graduate Admissions, 718-636-3683, Fax: 718-399-4242, E-mail: yhah@pratt.edu.

Prescott College, Graduate Programs, Program in Education, Prescott, AZ 86301. Offers early childhood education (MA); early childhood special education (MA); education (MA); elementary education (MA); environmental education leadership and administration (MA); equine-assisted experiential learning (MA); school guidance counseling (MA); secondary education (MA); special education, learning disability (MA); special education, mental retardation (MA); special education, serious emotional disability (MA); student-directed independent study (MA); sustainability education (PhD). Part-time programs available. Postbaccalaureate distance learning degree programs offered (minimal on-campus study). *Faculty:* 3 full-time (1 woman), 79 part-time/adjunct (41 women). *Students:* 75 full-time (44 women), 46 part-time (36 women); includes 18 minority (3 African Americans, 3 American Indian/Alaska Native, 4 Asian Americans or Pacific Islanders, 8 Hispanic Americans), 2 international. Average age 39. 66 applicants, 67% accepted, 31 enrolled. In 2009, 22 master's, 4 doctorates awarded. *Degree requirements:* For master's, thesis, fieldwork or internship, practicum; for doctorate, thesis/dissertation. *Entrance requirements:* For master's, 2 letters of recommendation, resume; for doctorate, 3 letters of recommendation, resume, official transcripts, personal statement, program proposal. Additional exam requirements/recommendations for international students: Required—TOEFL (minimum score 500 paper-based; 173 computer-based). *Application deadline:* For fall admission, 4/15 priority date for domestic and international students; for spring admission, 9/15 priority date for domestic and international students. Applications are processed on a rolling basis. Application fee: $40. Electronic applications accepted. *Expenses:* Tuition: Full-time $14,712; part-time $613 per credit. Required fees: $50 per term. One-time fee: $150. Tuition and fees vary according to course load and degree level. *Financial support:* Career-related internships or fieldwork and Federal Work-Study available. Financial award applicants required to submit FAFSA. *Unit head:* Noel Caniglia, Chair, 928-358-3201, Fax: 928-776-5151, E-mail: ncaniglia@prescott.edu. *Application contact:* Kerstin Alicki, Admissions Counselor, 877-412-8705, Fax: 928-277-4695, E-mail: admissions@prescott.edu.

Providence College, Graduate Studies, Department of Education, Program in Special Education, Providence, RI 02918. Offers elementary special education (M Ed), including elementary, secondary. Part-time and evening/weekend programs available. *Faculty:* 4 full-time (3 women), 39 part-time/adjunct (22 women). *Students:* 11 full-time (8 women), 38 part-time (29 women); includes 1 minority (Hispanic American). Average age 31. 14 applicants, 100% accepted. In 2009, 35 master's awarded. *Degree requirements:* For master's, comprehensive exam. *Entrance requirements:* For master's, GRE General Test. Additional exam requirements/recommendations for international students: Required—TOEFL (minimum score 550 paper-based; 213 computer-based; 80 iBT). *Application deadline:* For fall admission, 8/1 priority date for domestic and international students; for spring admission, 12/1 priority date for domestic and international students. Applications are processed on a rolling basis. Application fee: $55. *Expenses:* Tuition: Full-time $9909; part-time $367 per credit. One-time fee: $200. Tuition and fees vary according to course load and program. *Financial support:* In 2009–10, 1 research assistantship with full tuition reimbursement (averaging $8,400 per year) was awarded; career-related internships or fieldwork and unspecified assistantships also available. Support available to part-time students. Financial award application deadline: 8/1; financial award applicants

required to submit FAFSA. *Unit head:* Diane LaMontagne, Director, 401-865-2912, Fax: 401-865-1147, E-mail: dlamonta@providence.edu. *Application contact:* Carol A. Daniels, Coordinator of Graduate Faculty and Administrative Services, 401-865-2247, Fax: 401-865-1147, E-mail: daniels@providence.edu.

Purdue University, Graduate School, School of Education, Department of Educational Studies, West Lafayette, IN 47907. Offers administration (MS Ed, PhD, Ed S); counseling and development (MS Ed, PhD); education of the gifted (MS Ed); educational psychology (MS Ed, PhD); foundations of education (MS Ed, PhD); higher education administration (MS Ed, PhD); special education (MS Ed, PhD). *Accreditation:* ACA (one or more programs are accredited); NCATE (one or more programs are accredited). Part-time and evening/weekend programs available. *Degree requirements:* For master's, thesis optional; for doctorate, thesis/dissertation, oral and written exams; for Ed S, oral presentation, project. *Entrance requirements:* For master's, GRE General Test, minimum undergraduate GPA of 3.0; for doctorate, GRE General Test; for Ed S, GRE, minimum B average. Additional exam requirements/recommendations for international students: Required—TOEFL. Electronic applications accepted. *Faculty research:* Motivation, learning disabilities, school learning, group processes, cognitive development.

Purdue University Calumet, Graduate School, School of Education, Program in Special Education, Hammond, IN 46323-2094. Offers MS Ed.

Queens College of the City University of New York, Division of Graduate Studies, Division of Education, Department of Educational and Community Programs, Program in Special Education, Flushing, NY 11367-1597. Offers MS Ed. Part-time programs available. *Faculty:* 5 full-time (3 women). *Students:* 2 full-time (both women), 379 part-time (321 women). 255 applicants, 82% accepted, 181 enrolled. In 2009, 161 master's awarded. *Degree requirements:* For master's, research project. *Entrance requirements:* For master's, minimum GPA of 3.0. Additional exam requirements/recommendations for international students: Required—TOEFL. *Application deadline:* For fall admission, 4/1 for domestic students; for spring admission, 11/1 for domestic students. Applications are processed on a rolling basis. Application fee: $125. *Expenses:* Tuition, state resident: full-time $7360; part-time $310 per credit. Tuition, nonresident: part-time $575 per credit. One-time fee: $195 full-time; $145.25 part-time. *Financial support:* Career-related internships or fieldwork, Federal Work-Study, institutionally sponsored loans, and tuition waivers (partial) available. Support available to part-time students. Financial award application deadline: 4/1; financial award applicants required to submit FAFSA. *Unit head:* Dr. Craig Michaels, Coordinator/Graduate Adviser, 718-997-5266. *Application contact:* Mario Caruso, Director of Graduate Admissions, 718-997-5200, Fax: 718-997-5193, E-mail: graduate_admissions@qc.edu.

Quincy University, Program in Education, Quincy, IL 62301-2699. Offers curriculum and instruction (MS Ed); leadership (MRS); reading education (MS Ed); school administration (MS Ed); special education (MS Ed); teaching certification (MS Ed). Part-time programs available. Postbaccalaureate distance learning degree programs offered. *Faculty:* 3 full-time (2 women), 19 part-time/adjunct (16 women). *Students:* 328 full-time (222 women), 88 part-time (57 women); includes 60 African Americans, 9 Asian Americans or Pacific Islanders, 69 Hispanic Americans. In 2009, 10 master's awarded. *Degree requirements:* For master's, thesis. *Entrance requirements:* For master's, MAT or GRE. Additional exam requirements/recommendations for international students: Required—TOEFL. *Application deadline:* Applications are processed on a rolling basis. Application fee: $25. Electronic applications accepted. *Expenses:* Tuition: Full-time $8400; part-time $350 per credit hour. Required fees: $360; $15 per credit hour. Tuition and fees vary according to course load, campus/location and program. *Financial support:* Available to part-time students. Applicants required to submit FAFSA. *Unit head:* Dot Nelson, Director, 217-228-5432 Ext. 3111, E-mail: nelsodo@quincy.edu. *Application contact:* Jennifer O'Donnell, Coordinator of Adult Studies, 217-228-5404, Fax: 217-228-5479, E-mail: admissions@quincy.edu.

Radford University, College of Graduate and Professional Studies, College of Education and Human Development, School of Teacher Education and Leadership, Program in Special Education, Radford, VA 24142. Offers deaf and hard of hearing (MS); early childhood special education (MS); high incidence disabilities (MS); severe disabilities (MS). *Accreditation:* NCATE. Part-time and evening/weekend programs available. *Faculty:* 8 full-time (7 women), 20 part-time/adjunct (14 women). *Students:* 27 full-time (23 women), 46 part-time (36 women); includes 5 minority (3 African Americans, 1 Asian American or Pacific Islander, 1 Hispanic American). Average age 33. 28 applicants, 93% accepted, 22 enrolled. In 2009, 25 master's awarded. *Degree requirements:* For master's, comprehensive exam. *Entrance requirements:* For master's, Virginia Communication and Literacy Assessment (VCLA), GRE, minimum GPA of 2.75, 3 letters of reference, resume. Additional exam requirements/recommendations for international students: Required—TOEFL (minimum score 550 paper-based; 213 computer-based; 79 iBT). *Application deadline:* For fall admission, 12/1 for international students; for spring admission, 7/1 for international students. Applications are processed on a rolling basis. Application fee: $50. Electronic applications accepted. *Expenses:* Tuition, state resident: full-time $5086; part-time $211 per credit hour. Tuition, nonresident: full-time $12,608; part-time $525 per credit hour. Required fees: $2508; $105 per credit hour. *Financial support:* In 2009–10, 10 students received support, including 4 research assistantships with partial tuition reimbursements available (averaging $8,000 per year); career-related internships or fieldwork, Federal Work-Study, institutionally sponsored loans, scholarships/grants, and unspecified assistantships also available. Financial award application deadline: 3/1; financial award applicants required to submit FAFSA. *Unit head:* Dr. Debora Bays, Coordinator, 540-831-5190, Fax: 540-831-5059, E-mail: dbays@radford.edu. *Application contact:* Graduate Admissions, 540-831-5431, Fax: 540-831-6061, E-mail: gradcollege@radford.edu.

Randolph College, Programs in Education, Lynchburg, VA 24503. Offers curriculum and instruction (MAT); special education-learning disabilities (M Ed, MAT). *Accreditation:* Teacher Education Accreditation Council. *Entrance requirements:* For master's, minimum GPA of 3.0 in prerequisite education coursework, 2.7 in major or field of interest (MAT); teaching license (M Ed); 2 recommendations; interview.

Regent University, Graduate School, School of Education, Virginia Beach, VA 23464-9800. Offers career switcher (M Ed); Christian school program (M Ed); cross-categorical special education (M Ed); education (M Ed, Ed D); education licensure (M Ed); educational leadership (M Ed); elementary education (M Ed); individualized degree plan (M Ed); leadership in character education (M Ed); master teacher (M Ed); mathematics education (M Ed); special education leadership (Ed S); student affairs (M Ed); TESOL (M Ed). *Accreditation:* Teacher Education Accreditation Council. Part-time and evening/weekend programs available. Postbaccalaureate distance learning degree programs offered (minimal on-campus study). *Faculty:* 26 full-time (13 women), 104 part-time/adjunct (78 women). *Students:* 141 full-time (116 women), 622 part-time (488 women); includes 218 minority (186 African Americans, 1 American Indian/Alaska Native, 10 Asian Americans or Pacific Islanders, 21 Hispanic Americans), 8 international. Average age 39. 509 applicants, 60% accepted, 176 enrolled. In 2009, 212 master's, 15 doctorates awarded. *Degree requirements:* For master's, thesis or alternative; for doctorate, comprehensive exam, thesis/dissertation. *Entrance requirements:* For master's, MAT, minimum undergraduate GPA of 2.75, writing sample, resume, recommendations, interview; for doctorate, GRE, writing sample, 3 years of relevant professional experience, master's-level paper, copies of published work, resume, transcripts, interview, recommendations. Additional exam requirements/recommendations for international students: Required—TOEFL (minimum score 577 paper-based; 233 computer-based). *Application deadline:* For fall admission, 4/1 priority date for domestic students; for spring admission, 10/15 priority date for domestic students. Applications are processed on a rolling basis. Application fee: $50. Electronic applications accepted. *Expenses:* Contact institution. *Financial support:* In 2009–10, 480 students received support; fellowships, career-related internships or fieldwork, scholarships/grants, tuition waivers (full and partial), and unspecified assistantships available. Support available to part-time students. Financial award application deadline: 4/1; financial award applicants required to

submit FAFSA. *Faculty research:* Character development and discipline for children, education leadership development, diversity in schools, classroom management, technology in education settings. *Unit head:* Dr. Alan A. Arroyo, Dean, 757-352-4261, Fax: 757-352-4318, E-mail: alanarr@regent.edu. *Application contact:* Matthew Chadwick, Director of Admissions, 800-373-5504, Fax: 757-352-4381, E-mail: admissions@regent.edu.

Regis College, Department of Education, Weston, MA 02493. Offers elementary teacher (MAT); reading (MAT); special education (MAT). Part-time and evening/weekend programs available. *Faculty:* 2 full-time (both women), 5 part-time/adjunct (all women). *Students:* 2 full-time (both women), 49 part-time (42 women); includes 1 minority (Asian American or Pacific Islander). Average age 36. 8 applicants, 88% accepted, 4 enrolled. In 2009, 11 master's awarded. *Degree requirements:* For master's, thesis. *Entrance requirements:* For master's, GRE or MAT. Additional exam requirements/recommendations for international students: Required—TOEFL. *Application deadline:* Applications are processed on a rolling basis. Application fee: $50. Electronic applications accepted. *Expenses:* Tuition: Full-time $29,000; part-time $800 per credit. Tuition and fees vary according to course load, degree level and program. *Financial support:* In 2009–10, 1 student received support, including 1 fellowship with full tuition reimbursement available (averaging $11,970 per year); Federal Work-Study and scholarships/grants also available. Financial award applicants required to submit FAFSA. *Faculty research:* Reflective teaching, gender-based education, integrated teaching. *Unit head:* Dr. Leona McCaughey-Oreszak, Program Director, 781-768-7421, Fax: 781-768-7159, E-mail: leona.mccaughey-oreszak@regiscollege.edu. *Application contact:* Christine Petherick, Administrative Coordinator, Graduate Admission, 866-438-7344, Fax: 781-768-7071, E-mail: christine.petherick@regiscollege.edu.

Regis University, College for Professional Studies, Program in Teacher Education, Denver, CO 80221-1099. Offers adult learning, training, and development (M Ed); curriculum, instruction, and assessment (M Ed); early childhood (M Ed); educational technology (Certificate); elementary (M Ed); ESL (M Ed); fine arts (M Ed), including arts, music; instructional technology (M Ed); professional leadership (M Ed); reading (M Ed); secondary (M Ed); self-designed (M Ed); space studies (M Ed); special education (M Ed); teacher licensure (M Ed). Program also offered in Henderson and Las Vegas (Summerlin), NV. *Accreditation:* Teacher Education Accreditation Council. Part-time and evening/weekend programs available. Postbaccalaureate distance learning degree programs offered (no on-campus study). *Degree requirements:* For master's, thesis. *Entrance requirements:* For master's, resume, minimum GPA of 2.75, criminal background check. Additional exam requirements/recommendations for international students: Required—TOEFL (minimum score 213 computer-based), TWE (minimum score 5). Electronic applications accepted. *Faculty research:* Issues of equity in the middle school classroom, professional learning communities, school reform, socialinguistic and discursive obstacles to student integration, inclusive language arts curriculum.

Rhode Island College, School of Graduate Studies, Feinstein School of Education and Human Development, Department of Special Education, Providence, RI 02908-1991. Offers M Ed, CAGS. *Accreditation:* NCATE. Part-time and evening/weekend programs available. *Faculty:* 7 full-time (4 women), 3 part-time/adjunct (1 woman). *Students:* 10 full-time (all women), 54 part-time (48 women); includes 1 minority (Hispanic American), 1 international. Average age 33. In 2009, 30 master's awarded. *Degree requirements:* For master's, comprehensive assessment/assignment. *Entrance requirements:* For master's, GRE General Test or MAT, undergraduate transcripts; minimum undergraduate GPA of 3.0; copy of teaching certificate (when applicable); 3 letters of recommendation; for CAGS, GRE or MAT, master's degree or equivalent, teaching certificate, 3 letters of recommendation, interview. Additional exam requirements/recommendations for international students: Recommended—TOEFL (minimum score 550 paper-based; 213 computer-based; 79 iBT). *Application deadline:* For fall admission, 3/15 for domestic students; for spring admission, 11/1 for domestic students. Applications are processed on a rolling basis. Application fee: $50. *Expenses:* Tuition, state resident: full-time $7440; part-time $310 per credit hour. Tuition, nonresident: full-time $14,784; part-time $616 per credit hour. Required fees: $552; $20 per credit. $70 per term. *Financial support:* Teaching assistantships with full tuition reimbursements, career-related internships or fieldwork, Federal Work-Study, scholarships/grants, health care benefits, and unspecified assistantships available. Support available to part-time students. Financial award application deadline: 5/15; financial award applicants required to submit FAFSA. *Faculty research:* Early detection, handicapped infants. *Unit head:* Dr. Susan Dell, Chair, 401-456-8557. *Application contact:* Graduate Studies, 401-456-8700.

Rider University, Department of Graduate Education, Leadership and Counseling, Program in Special Education, Lawrenceville, NJ 08648-3001. Offers alternative route in special education (Certificate); special education (MA); teacher of students with disabilities (Certificate); teacher of the handicapped (Certificate). Part-time and evening/weekend programs available. *Degree requirements:* For master's, comprehensive exam. *Entrance requirements:* For master's, letters of reference, resume, NJ teaching license, interview. Additional exam requirements/recommendations for international students: Required—TOEFL (minimum score 550 paper-based; 213 computer-based). Electronic applications accepted. *Faculty research:* Collaboration/inclusive, practice, service learning, transition.

Rivier College, School of Graduate Studies, Department of Education, Nashua, NH 03060. Offers curriculum and instruction (M Ed); early childhood education (M Ed); educational administration (M Ed); educational studies (M Ed); elementary education (M Ed); elementary education and general special education (M Ed); emotional and behavioral disorders (M Ed); general social education (M Ed); leadership and learning (Ed D, CAGS); learning disabilities (M Ed); learning disabilities and reading (M Ed); mental health counseling (MA); reading (M Ed); school counseling (M Ed). Part-time and evening/weekend programs available. *Faculty:* 13 full-time (9 women), 38 part-time/adjunct (25 women). *Students:* 87 full-time (78 women), 293 part-time (246 women); includes 10 minority (3 African Americans, 4 Asian Americans or Pacific Islanders, 3 Hispanic Americans). Average age 38. 182 applicants, 82% accepted, 72 enrolled. In 2009, 110 master's, 18 other advanced degrees awarded. *Degree requirements:* For master's, comprehensive exam (for some programs), internships. *Entrance requirements:* For master's, GRE General Test or MAT. *Application deadline:* Applications are processed on a rolling basis. Application fee: $25. *Expenses:* Tuition: Part-time $447 per credit. *Financial support:* Available to part-time students. Application deadline: 2/1. *Unit head:* Dr. Patricia Howson, Chairman, 603-897-8562, E-mail: phowson@rivier.edu. *Application contact:* Mathew Kittredge, Director of Graduate Admissions, 603-897-8129, Fax: 603-897-8810, E-mail: mkittredge@rivier.edu.

Roberts Wesleyan College, Division of Teacher Education, Rochester, NY 14624-1997. Offers adolescence education (M Ed); childhood and special education (M Ed); literacy education (M Ed); urban education (M Ed). Part-time and evening/weekend programs available. *Degree requirements:* For master's, thesis.

Rochester Institute of Technology, Graduate Enrollment Services, National Technical Institute for the Deaf, Department of Research and Teacher Education, Rochester, NY 14623-5603. Offers MS. *Accreditation:* Teacher Education Accreditation Council. *Students:* 46 full-time (34 women), 9 part-time (7 women); includes 7 minority (4 African Americans, 2 Asian Americans or Pacific Islanders, 1 Hispanic American). Average age 29. 50 applicants, 74% accepted, 33 enrolled. In 2009, 25 master's awarded. *Degree requirements:* For master's, thesis or alternative. *Entrance requirements:* For master's, minimum GPA of 3.0. Additional exam requirements/recommendations for international students: Required—TOEFL (minimum score 550 paper-based; 213 computer-based; 88 iBT), or IELTS (minimum score 6.5). *Application deadline:* For fall admission, 2/15 priority date for domestic and international students. Applications are processed on a rolling basis. Application fee: $50. Electronic applications accepted. *Expenses:* Tuition: Full-time $31,533; part-time $876 per credit hour. Required fees: $210. *Financial support:* In 2009–10, 46 students received support; fellowships with full and partial tuition reimbursements available, research assistantships with partial tuition reimbursements available,

teaching assistantships with partial tuition reimbursements available, career-related internships or fieldwork, institutionally sponsored loans, scholarships/grants, and unspecified assistantships available. Support available to part-time students. Financial award applicants required to submit FAFSA. *Unit head:* Gerald Bateman, Director, 585-475-6480, Fax: 585-475-2525, E-mail: gcbnmp@rit.edu. *Application contact:* Diane Ellison, Assistant Vice President, Graduate Enrollment Services, 585-475-2229, Fax: 585-475-7164, E-mail: gradinfo@rit.edu.

Rockford College, Graduate Studies, Department of Education, Program in Special Education, Rockford, IL 61108-2393. Offers MAT. Students may earn a Learning Behavior Specialist I (LBSI) certificate. Part-time and evening/weekend programs available. *Degree requirements:* For master's, thesis optional. *Entrance requirements:* For master's, GRE General Test, 3 letters of recommendation. Additional exam requirements/recommendations for international students: Required—TOEFL (minimum score 550 paper-based; 213 computer-based; 79 iBT). Electronic applications accepted.

Roosevelt University, Graduate Division, College of Education, Department of Teaching and Learning, Program in Special Education, Chicago, IL 60605. Offers MA.

Rowan University, Graduate School, College of Education, Department of Special Educational Services/Instruction, Program in Learning Disabilities, Glassboro, NJ 08028-1701. Offers MA. *Accreditation:* NCATE. Part-time and evening/weekend programs available. *Students:* 2 full-time (both women), 97 part-time (84 women); includes 6 minority (4 African Americans, 1 Asian American or Pacific Islander, 1 Hispanic American). Average age 35. 24 applicants, 96% accepted, 16 enrolled. In 2009, 9 master's awarded. *Degree requirements:* For master's, comprehensive exam, thesis. *Entrance requirements:* For master's, GRE General Test, minimum GPA of 2.8, 1 year of teaching experience. Additional exam requirements/recommendations for international students: Required—TOEFL. *Application deadline:* Applications are processed on a rolling basis. Application fee: $50. Electronic applications accepted. *Expenses:* Tuition, state resident: full-time $10,624; part-time $590 per semester hour. Tuition, nonresident: full-time $10,624; part-time $590 per semester hour. Required fees: $2320; $125 per semester hour. *Financial support:* Career-related internships or fieldwork, scholarships/grants, health care benefits, and unspecified assistantships available. Support available to part-time students. *Unit head:* Dr. Mira Lalovic-Hand, Interim Associate Provost/Director of Graduate School, 856-256-5120, E-mail: lalovic-hand@rowan.edu. *Application contact:* Karen Haynes, Graduate Coordinator, 856-256-4052, Fax: 856-256-4436, E-mail: haynes@rowan.edu.

Rowan University, Graduate School, College of Education, Department of Special Educational Services/Instruction, Program in Special Education, Glassboro, NJ 08028-1701. Offers MA. *Accreditation:* NCATE. Part-time and evening/weekend programs available. *Students:* 1 (woman) full-time, 14 part-time (10 women); includes 2 minority (both African Americans). Average age 35. 3 applicants, 100% accepted, 2 enrolled. In 2009, 10 master's awarded. *Degree requirements:* For master's, comprehensive exam, thesis. *Entrance requirements:* For master's, GRE General Test, minimum GPA of 2.8. Additional exam requirements/recommendations for international students: Required—TOEFL. *Application deadline:* Applications are processed on a rolling basis. Application fee: $50. Electronic applications accepted. *Expenses:* Tuition, state resident: full-time $10,624; part-time $590 per semester hour. Tuition, nonresident: full-time $10,624; part-time $590 per semester hour. Required fees: $2320; $125 per semester hour. *Financial support:* Career-related internships or fieldwork, Federal Work-Study, scholarships/grants, health care benefits, and unspecified assistantships available. *Unit head:* Dr. Mira Lalovic-Hand, Interim Associate Provost/Director of Graduate School, 856-256-5120, E-mail: lalovic-hand@rowan.edu. *Application contact:* Karen Haynes, Graduate Coordinator, 856-256-4052, E-mail: haynes@rowan.edu.

Rutgers, The State University of New Jersey, New Brunswick, Graduate School of Education, Department of Educational Psychology, Program in Special Education, Piscataway, NJ 08854-8097. Offers Ed M, Ed D. Part-time and evening/weekend programs available. *Degree requirements:* For doctorate, thesis/dissertation, residency. *Entrance requirements:* For master's, GRE General Test, 3 letters of recommendation; for doctorate, GRE General Test, 3 letters of recommendation, masters degree. Additional exam requirements/recommendations for international students: Required—TOEFL (minimum score 550 paper-based; 233 computer-based; 83 iBT). Electronic applications accepted. *Faculty research:* Pre- and in-service teacher education, teacher development, inclusion, early identification and intervention of reading disabilities, special education law and social policy.

Sage Graduate School, Graduate School, School of Education, Program in Childhood Special Education, Troy, NY 12180-4115. Offers MS Ed. *Accreditation:* NCATE. Part-time and evening/weekend programs available. *Faculty:* 15 full-time (9 women), 19 part-time/adjunct (16 women). *Students:* 19 full-time (16 women), 29 part-time (24 women); includes 2 minority (1 Asian American or Pacific Islander, 1 Hispanic American). Average age 28. 38 applicants, 55% accepted, 10 enrolled. In 2009, 15 master's awarded. *Degree requirements:* For master's, thesis optional. *Entrance requirements:* For master's, minimum GPA of 2.75, resume, 2 letters of recommendation, interview, assessment of writing skills. Additional exam requirements/recommendations for international students: Required—TOEFL (minimum score 550 paper-based; 213 computer-based). *Application deadline:* Applications are processed on a rolling basis. Application fee: $40. *Expenses:* Tuition: Full-time $10,620; part-time $590 per credit hour. *Financial support:* Fellowships, research assistantships, Federal Work-Study, scholarships/grants, and unspecified assistantships available. Support available to part-time students. Financial award application deadline: 3/1; financial award applicants required to submit FAFSA. *Faculty research:* Effective behavioral strategies for classroom instruction. *Unit head:* Dr. Nancy A. DeKorp, Interim Dean, Education, 518-244-2496, Fax: 518-244-2334, E-mail: dekorn@sage.edu. *Application contact:* Wendy D. Diefendorf, Director of Graduate and Adult Admission, 518-244-2443, Fax: 518-244-6880, E-mail: diefew@sage.edu.

Sage Graduate School, Graduate School, School of Education, Program in Literacy/Childhood Special Education, Troy, NY 12180-4115. Offers MS Ed. *Accreditation:* NCATE. Part-time and evening/weekend programs available. *Faculty:* 15 full-time (9 women), 19 part-time/adjunct (16 women). *Students:* 3 full-time (all women), 13 part-time (12 women); includes 1 minority (Hispanic American). Average age 27. 8 applicants. In 2009, 6 master's awarded. *Entrance requirements:* For master's, minimum GPA of 2.75, resume, 2 letters of recommendation, interview with advisor, assessment of writing skills. Additional exam requirements/recommendations for international students: Required—TOEFL (minimum score 550 paper-based; 213 computer-based). *Application deadline:* Applications are processed on a rolling basis. Application fee: $40. *Expenses:* Tuition: Full-time $10,620; part-time $590 per credit hour. *Financial support:* Fellowships, research assistantships, Federal Work-Study, scholarships/grants, and unspecified assistantships available. Support available to part-time students. Financial award application deadline: 3/1; financial award applicants required to submit FAFSA. *Faculty research:* Commonalities in the roles of reading specialists and resource/consultant teachers. *Unit head:* Michelle Reilly, Director, 518-244-4539, Fax: 518-244-2334, E-mail: reillm@sage.edu. *Application contact:* Wendy D. Diefendorf, Director of Graduate and Adult Admission, 518-244-2443, Fax: 518-244-6880, E-mail: diefew@sage.edu.

Saginaw Valley State University, College of Education, Program in Learning and Behavioral Disorders, University Center, MI 48710. Offers MAT. *Accreditation:* NCATE. *Students:* 1 (woman) full-time, 15 part-time (9 women). Average age 41. In 2009, 21 master's awarded. *Degree requirements:* For master's, practicum. *Entrance requirements:* For master's, minimum GPA of 3.0, teaching certificate. Additional exam requirements/recommendations for international students: Required—TOEFL (minimum score 525 paper-based; 197 computer-based; 71 iBT). *Application deadline:* Applications are processed on a rolling basis. Application fee: $25. Electronic applications accepted. *Financial support:* Federal Work-Study and scholarships/grants available. Support available to part-time students. Financial award applicants required to submit FAFSA. *Unit head:* Dr. Steve P. Barbus, Dean, 989-964-6067, Fax: 989-790-4385,

Special Education

Saginaw Valley State University (continued)
E-mail: barbus@svsu.edu. *Application contact:* Dr. Steve P. Barbus, Dean, 989-964-6067, Fax: 989-790-4385, E-mail: barbus@svsu.edu.

Saginaw Valley State University, College of Education, Program in Special Education, University Center, MI 48710. Offers MAT. Part-time and evening/weekend programs available. *Students:* 27 full-time (23 women), 281 part-time (229 women); includes 12 minority (4 African Americans, 1 American Indian/Alaska Native, 7 Hispanic Americans), 3 international. Average age 34. 63 applicants, 98% accepted, 41 enrolled. In 2009, 80 master's awarded. *Degree requirements:* For master's, capstone course. *Entrance requirements:* For master's, minimum GPA of 3.0. Additional exam requirements/recommendations for international students: Required—TOEFL (minimum score 525 paper-based; 197 computer-based; 71 iBT). *Application deadline:* Applications are processed on a rolling basis. Application fee: $25. Electronic applications accepted. *Financial support:* Federal Work-Study and scholarships/grants available. Support available to part-time students. Financial award applicants required to submit FAFSA. *Application contact:* Kathy Lopez, Certification Officer, 989-964-4661, Fax: 989-964-4385, E-mail: klopez@svsu.edu.

St. Ambrose University, College of Education and Health Sciences, Program in Education, Davenport, IA 52803-2898. Offers special education (M Ed); teaching (M Ed). *Accreditation:* Teacher Education Accreditation Council. Part-time and evening/weekend programs available. Postbaccalaureate distance learning degree programs offered (no on-campus study). *Faculty:* 3 full-time (0 women), 4 part-time/adjunct (3 women). *Students:* 7 full-time (6 women), 35 part-time (29 women); includes 1 minority (Hispanic American). Average age 39. 20 applicants, 100% accepted, 20 enrolled. In 2009, 24 master's awarded. *Degree requirements:* For master's, comprehensive exam. *Entrance requirements:* For master's, GRE General Test or MAT, minimum GPA of 2.75. Additional exam requirements/recommendations for international students: Required—TOEFL. *Application deadline:* For fall admission, 8/15 priority date for domestic students; for spring admission, 11/1 for domestic students. Applications are processed on a rolling basis. Application fee: $25. Electronic applications accepted. *Expenses:* Tuition: Part-time $702 per credit hour. Tuition and fees vary according to degree level, program and reciprocity agreements. *Financial support:* In 2009–10, 23 students received support, including 1 research assistantship with partial tuition reimbursement available (averaging $3,600 per year); career-related internships or fieldwork, scholarships/grants, tuition waivers (full and partial), and unspecified assistantships also available. Financial award application deadline: 3/15; financial award applicants required to submit FAFSA. *Faculty research:* Disabilities and postsecondary career avenues, self-determination. *Unit head:* Marguerite K. Woods, Head, 563-388-7653, Fax: 563-388-7662, E-mail: woodsmargueritek@sau.edu. *Application contact:* Penny L. McCulloch, Administrative Assistant, 563-322-1034, Fax: 563-388-7662, E-mail: mccullochpennyl@sau.edu.

St. Bonaventure University, School of Graduate Studies, School of Education, Program in Advanced Inclusive Processes, St. Bonaventure, NY 14778-2284. Offers MS Ed. Part-time and evening/weekend programs available. *Students:* 25 full-time (20 women), 5 part-time (all women); includes 1 African American. Average age 25. 20 applicants, 80% accepted, 13 enrolled. In 2009, 17 master's awarded. *Entrance requirements:* For master's, minimum undergraduate GPA of 3.0, interview, writing sample. Additional exam requirements/recommendations for international students: Required—TOEFL. *Application deadline:* For fall admission, 7/1 priority date for domestic students; for spring admission, 11/15 priority date for domestic students. Applications are processed on a rolling basis. Application fee: $30. *Expenses:* Tuition: Full-time $11,700; part-time $650 per credit. *Financial support:* In 2009–10, 4 research assistantships with full and partial tuition reimbursements were awarded; scholarships/grants also available. Support available to part-time students. Financial award application deadline: 4/15; financial award applicants required to submit FAFSA. *Unit head:* Dr. Rene Wroblewksi, Coordinator, 716-375-4078, E-mail: rwroblew@sbu.edu. *Application contact:* Bruce Campbell, Director of Graduate Admissions, 716-375-2429, E-mail: gradsch@sbu.edu.

St. Cloud State University, School of Graduate Studies, College of Education, Department of Special Education, St. Cloud, MN 56301-4498. Offers educable mentally handicapped (MS); emotionally disturbed (MS); gifted and talented (MS); learning disabled (MS); special education (MS); trainable mentally retarded (MS). *Accreditation:* NCATE. *Faculty:* 11 full-time (6 women), 5 part-time/adjunct (4 women). *Students:* 48 full-time (43 women), 142 part-time (119 women); includes 9 minority (5 African Americans, 2 American Indian/Alaska Native, 1 Asian American or Pacific Islander, 1 Hispanic American), 1 international. 13 applicants, 100% accepted. In 2009, 31 master's awarded. *Degree requirements:* For master's, thesis or alternative. *Entrance requirements:* For master's, GRE General Test, minimum GPA of 2.75. Additional exam requirements/recommendations for international students: Required—Michigan English Language Assessment Battery; Recommended—TOEFL (minimum score 550 paper-based; 213 computer-based), IELTS (minimum score 6.5). *Application deadline:* For fall admission, 6/1 priority date for domestic students, 4/1 for international students; for spring admission, 10/1 priority date for domestic students, 8/1 for international students. Applications are processed on a rolling basis. Application fee: $35. Electronic applications accepted. *Financial support:* Federal Work-Study, scholarships/grants, and unspecified assistantships available. Financial award application deadline: 3/1. *Unit head:* Dr. Adory Beutel, Chairperson, 320-308-2041, E-mail: abeutel@stcloudstate.edu. *Application contact:* Linda Lou Krueger, School of Graduate Studies, 320-308-2113, Fax: 320-308-5371, E-mail: lekrueger@stcloudstate.edu.

St. John Fisher College, Ralph C. Wilson Jr. School of Education, Program in Adolescence Education/Special Education, Rochester, NY 14618-3597. Offers adolescence English (MS Ed); adolescence French (MS Ed); adolescence social studies (MS Ed); adolescence Spanish (MS Ed). Part-time and evening/weekend programs available. *Faculty:* 3 full-time (1 woman), 1 (woman) part-time/adjunct. *Students:* 39 full-time (18 women), 5 part-time (2 women); includes 7 minority (1 African American, 2 American Indian/Alaska Native, 1 Asian American or Pacific Islander, 3 Hispanic Americans). Average age 28. 39 applicants, 90% accepted, 20 enrolled. In 2009, 17 master's awarded. *Degree requirements:* For master's, field experiences, student teaching, LAST. *Entrance requirements:* For master's, 2 letters of recommendation, personal statement, current resume. Additional exam requirements/recommendations for international students: Required—TOEFL (minimum score 575 paper-based; 233 computer-based; 80 iBT). *Application deadline:* Applications are processed on a rolling basis. Application fee: $30. Electronic applications accepted. *Expenses:* Tuition: Part-time $680 per credit hour. Required fees: $25 per semester. Tuition and fees vary according to degree level and program. *Financial support:* In 2009–10, 40 students received support. Federal Work-Study and scholarships/grants available. Financial award applicants required to submit FAFSA. *Faculty research:* Arts and humanities, urban schools, constructivist learning, at risk students, mentoring. *Unit head:* Dr. Russell Coward, Program Director, 585-385-8114, E-mail: rcoward@sjfc.edu. *Application contact:* Jose Perales, Director of Graduate Admissions, 585-385-8067, E-mail: jperales@sjfc.edu.

St. John Fisher College, Ralph C. Wilson Jr. School of Education, Program in Childhood Education/Special Education, Rochester, NY 14618-3597. Offers MS Ed. Part-time and evening/weekend programs available. *Faculty:* 3 full-time (1 woman), 1 (woman) part-time/adjunct. *Students:* 64 full-time (52 women), 4 part-time (3 women); includes 6 minority (all African Americans). Average age 28. 76 applicants, 71% accepted, 36 enrolled. In 2009, 28 master's awarded. *Degree requirements:* For master's, field experience, student teaching, LAST. *Entrance requirements:* For master's, 2 letters of recommendation, personal statement, current resume. Additional exam requirements/recommendations for international students: Required—TOEFL (minimum score 575 paper-based; 233 computer-based; 80 iBT). *Application deadline:* Applications are processed on a rolling basis. Application fee: $30. Electronic applications accepted. *Expenses:* Tuition: Part-time $680 per credit hour. Required fees: $25 per semester. Tuition and fees vary according to degree level and program. *Financial support:* In 2009–10, 65 students received support. Federal Work-Study and scholarships/grants available. Financial award applicants required to submit FAFSA. *Faculty research:* Professional development, science assessment, multi-cultural; educational technology. *Unit head:* Dr. Michelle Erklenz-Watts, Program Director, 585-385-8404, E-mail: merklenz-watts@sjfc.edu. *Application contact:* Jose Perales, Director of Graduate Admissions, 585-385-8067, E-mail: jperales@sjfc.edu.

St. John Fisher College, Ralph C. Wilson Jr. School of Education, Program in Special Education, Rochester, NY 14618-3597. Offers MS, Certificate. Part-time and evening/weekend programs available. *Faculty:* 5 full-time (3 women), 5 part-time/adjunct (4 women). *Students:* 16 full-time (12 women), 45 part-time (29 women); includes 5 minority (3 African Americans, 2 Hispanic Americans). Average age 27. 44 applicants, 93% accepted, 32 enrolled. In 2009, 23 master's awarded. *Degree requirements:* For master's, student teaching, practicum, LAST; for Certificate, practicum. *Entrance requirements:* For master's, teaching certification, 2 letters of recommendation, personal statement, current resume; for Certificate, minimum GPA of 3.0, 2 letters of reference, personal statement, teaching certification. Additional exam requirements/recommendations for international students: Required—TOEFL (minimum score 575 paper-based; 233 computer-based; 80 iBT). *Application deadline:* Applications are processed on a rolling basis. Application fee: $30. Electronic applications accepted. *Expenses:* Tuition: Part-time $680 per credit hour. Required fees: $25 per semester. Tuition and fees vary according to degree level and program. *Financial support:* In 2009–10, 48 students received support. Federal Work-Study and scholarships/grants available. Financial award applicants required to submit FAFSA. *Faculty research:* Inclusion, assistive technology, inquiry-based learning, gifted students, equity in education. *Unit head:* Dr. Susan Schultz, Program Director, 585-385-7296, E-mail: sschultz@sjfc.edu. *Application contact:* Jose Perales, Director of Graduate Admissions, 585-585-8067, E-mail: jperales@sjfc.edu.

St. John's University, The School of Education, Department of Human Services and Counseling, Program in Teaching Children with Disabilities in Childhood Education, Queens, NY 11439. Offers MS Ed. Part-time and evening/weekend programs available. *Students:* 15 full-time (12 women), 18 part-time (14 women); includes 7 minority (3 African Americans, 1 Asian American or Pacific Islander, 3 Hispanic Americans). Average age 28. 28 applicants, 89% accepted, 16 enrolled. In 2009, 21 master's awarded. *Degree requirements:* For master's, comprehensive exam. *Entrance requirements:* For master's, minimum GPA of 3.0, rudimentary computer proficiency. Additional exam requirements/recommendations for international students: Required—TOEFL (minimum score 500 paper-based; 173 computer-based; 61 iBT), IELTS (minimum score 5.5). *Application deadline:* For fall admission, 4/1 priority date for domestic students, 6/1 priority date for international students; for spring admission, 11/1 priority date for domestic and international students. Applications are processed on a rolling basis. Application fee: $70. Electronic applications accepted. *Expenses:* Tuition: Full-time $16,290; part-time $905 per credit. Required fees: $300; $150 per semester. Tuition and fees vary according to program. *Financial support:* Research assistantships available. *Faculty research:* Demographics in special education, literacy skill development in special populations, effects of distance learning in teacher training programs. *Unit head:* Dr. Francine Guastello, Acting Chair, 718-990-1475, E-mail: guastelf@stjohns.edu. *Application contact:* Dr. Kelly K. Ronayne, Associate Dean for Graduate Admissions, 718-990-2303, Fax: 718-990-2343, E-mail: graded@stjohns.edu.

Saint Joseph College, Department of Education, West Hartford, CT 06117-2700. Offers education (MA); special education (MA). Part-time and evening/weekend programs available. *Students:* 72 full-time (67 women), 299 part-time (267 women); includes 25 minority (14 African Americans, 6 Asian Americans or Pacific Islanders, 5 Hispanic Americans), 1 international. *Degree requirements:* For master's, comprehensive exam, thesis or alternative. *Entrance requirements:* For master's, 2 letters of recommendation. *Application deadline:* Applications are processed on a rolling basis. Application fee: $50. Electronic applications accepted. *Expenses:* Tuition: Part-time $595 per credit. Required fees: $30 per credit. Tuition and fees vary according to program. *Financial support:* Career-related internships or fieldwork and unspecified assistantships available. Support available to part-time students. Financial award applicants required to submit FAFSA. *Application contact:* Graduate Admissions Office, 860-231-5261, E-mail: graduate@sjc.edu.

St. Joseph's College, Long Island Campus, Program in Infant/Toddler Early Childhood Special Education, Patchogue, NY 11772-2399. Offers MA. Part-time and evening/weekend programs available. *Degree requirements:* For master's, thesis, full-time practicum experience. *Entrance requirements:* For master's, 1 course in child development, 2 courses in special education, minimum undergraduate GPA of 3.0, New York state teaching certificate, interview. Additional exam requirements/recommendations for international students: Required—TOEFL (minimum score 550 paper-based; 213 computer-based).

St. Joseph's College, New York, Graduate Programs, Program in Education, Field of Infant/Toddler Early Childhood Special Education, Brooklyn, NY 11205-3688. Offers MA.

St. Joseph's College, New York, Graduate Programs, Program in Education, Field of Special Education, Brooklyn, NY 11205-3688. Offers severe and multiple disabilities (MA).

Saint Joseph's University, College of Arts and Sciences, Department of Education, Philadelphia, PA 19131-1395. Offers educational leadership (Ed D); elementary education (MS); instructional technology (MS); organizational development and leadership (MS); professional education (MS); reading specialist (MS); secondary education (MS); special education (MS). Part-time and evening/weekend programs available. *Students:* 5 full-time (3 women), 750 part-time (561 women); includes 100 minority (76 African Americans, 1 American Indian/Alaska Native, 11 Asian Americans or Pacific Islanders, 12 Hispanic Americans), 3 international. Average age 33. In 2009, 210 master's, 14 doctorates awarded. *Entrance requirements:* For master's, 2 letters of recommendation, minimum GPA of 3.0, application, official transcripts, personal statement; for doctorate, GRE, master's degree from accredited institution, minimum graduate GPA of 3.5, computer competence, commitment to participate in cohort, interview with program director. Additional exam requirements/recommendations for international students: Required—TOEFL (minimum score 550 paper-based; 213 computer-based; 79 iBT). *Application deadline:* For fall admission, 7/15 priority date for domestic students, 4/15 for international students; for winter admission, 11/15 for domestic students, 1/15 for international students; for spring admission, 11/15 priority date for domestic students, 10/15 for international students. Applications are processed on a rolling basis. Application fee: $35. Electronic applications accepted. *Expenses:* Contact institution. *Financial support:* Unspecified assistantships available. Financial award applicants required to submit FAFSA. *Faculty research:* Early childhood course design, public education professional development. Total annual research expenditures: $91,900. *Unit head:* Dr. Teri Sosa, Director of Graduate Education, 610-660-3162, E-mail: tsosa@sju.edu. *Application contact:* Kate McConnell, Director, Graduate College of Arts and Sciences Admissions and Retention, 610-660-3184, Fax: 610-660-3230, E-mail: kate.mcconnell@sju.edu.

Saint Louis University, Graduate School, College of Education and Public Service and Graduate School, Department of Educational Studies, St. Louis, MO 63103-2097. Offers curriculum and instruction (MA, Ed D, PhD); educational foundations (MA, Ed D, PhD); special education (MA); teaching (MAT). *Accreditation:* NCATE. Part-time programs available. *Degree requirements:* For master's, comprehensive exam; for doctorate, comprehensive exam, thesis/dissertation, preliminary oral and written exams. *Entrance requirements:* For master's, GRE General Test or MAT, letters of recommendation, resume; for doctorate, GRE General Test, letters of recommendation, resumé, goal statement, transcripts. Additional exam requirements/recommendations for international students: Required—TOEFL (minimum score 525 paper-based; 194 computer-based). Electronic applications accepted. *Faculty research:* Teacher preparation, multicultural issues, children with special needs, qualitative research in education, inclusion.

Saint Martin's University, Graduate Programs, College of Education, Lacey, WA 98503. Offers administration (M Ed); English as a second language (M Ed); guidance and counseling

(M Ed); reading (M Ed); special education (M Ed); teaching (MIT); technology in education (M Ed). *Accreditation:* Teacher Education Accreditation Council. Part-time and evening/weekend programs available. *Faculty:* 13 full-time (9 women), 11 part-time/adjunct (7 women). *Students:* 61 full-time (42 women), 23 part-time (17 women); includes 7 minority (2 African Americans, 1 American Indian/Alaska Native, 3 Asian Americans or Pacific Islanders, 1 Hispanic American), 1 international. Average age 35. 26 applicants, 92% accepted, 22 enrolled. In 2009, 12 master's awarded. *Degree requirements:* For master's, comprehensive exam (for some programs), thesis or alternative, project or comprehensives. *Entrance requirements:* For master's, GRE General Test or MAT, resume. Additional exam requirements/recommendations for international students: Required—TOEFL (minimum score 560 paper-based; 220 computer-based; 83 iBT). *Application deadline:* For fall admission, 6/1 priority date for domestic and international students; for spring admission, 10/1 priority date for domestic and international students. Applications are processed on a rolling basis. Application fee: $35. *Expenses:* Tuition: Full-time $12,440; part-time $827 per credit hour. *Financial support:* In 2009–10, 62 students received support. Career-related internships or fieldwork, Federal Work-Study, institutionally sponsored loans, and unspecified assistantships available. Support available to part-time students. Financial award application deadline: 3/1; financial award applicants required to submit FAFSA. *Faculty research:* Reader's theatre and reader/writer workshops, curriculum and assessment integration, gender and equity, classroom evaluations, organizational leadership. *Unit head:* Dr. Joyce Westgard, Director, 360-438-4509, Fax: 360-438-4486, E-mail: westgard@ stmartin.edu. *Application contact:* Ryan M. Smith, Administrative Assistant, 360-438-4333, Fax: 360-438-4486, E-mail: ryan.smith@stmartin.edu.

Saint Mary's College of California, Kalmanovitz School of Education, Program in Special Education, Moraga, CA 94556. Offers M Ed, MA. Part-time programs available. *Faculty:* 2 full-time (1 woman), 2 part-time/adjunct (both women). *Students:* 10 full-time (8 women), 15 part-time (9 women). Average age 37. 12 applicants, 100% accepted, 12 enrolled. *Degree requirements:* For master's, thesis or alternative. *Entrance requirements:* For master's, writing proficiency exam, interview, minimum GPA of 3.0, teaching experience. *Application deadline:* Applications are processed on a rolling basis. Application fee: $50. *Expenses:* Tuition: Full-time $35,087; part-time $956 per credit hour. One-time fee: $50 full-time. Part-time tuition and fees vary according to course level, course load, degree level, campus/location and program. *Financial support:* Scholarships/grants and tuition waivers (partial) available. Support available to part-time students. Financial award application deadline: 2/15. *Faculty research:* Consultation model, impact of gifted model on special education. *Unit head:* E. Gail Kirby, Director, 925-631-8177, Fax: 925-376-8379, E-mail: egki@stmarys-ca.edu. *Application contact:* Jane Joyce, Coordinator, Recruitment and Admissions, 925-631-4700, Fax: 925-376-8379, E-mail: soereq@ stmarys-ca.edu.

Saint Mary's University of Minnesota, Schools of Graduate and Professional Programs, Graduate School of Education, Educational Administration Program, Winona, MN 55987-1399. Offers educational administration (Certificate, Ed S), including director of special education, K-12 principal, superintendent. *Unit head:* Dr. William Bjorum, Director, 612-728-5126, Fax: 612-728-5121, E-mail: wbjorum@smumn.edu. *Application contact:* Yasin Alsaidi, Director of Admissions for Graduate and Professional Programs, 612-728-5207, Fax: 612-728-5121, E-mail: yalsaidi@smumn.edu.

Saint Mary's University of Minnesota, Schools of Graduate and Professional Programs, Graduate School of Education, Special Education Program, Winona, MN 55987-1399. Offers behavioral disorders (Certificate); learning disabilities (Certificate); special education (MA). *Unit head:* Dr. Kathy Ryan, Director, 507-457-6611, E-mail: kryan@smumn.edu. *Application contact:* Jami Spitzer, 507-457-7500, E-mail: jspitzer@smumn.edu.

Saint Michael's College, Graduate Programs, Program in Education, Colchester, VT 05439. Offers administration (M Ed, CAGS); arts in education (CAGS); curriculum and instruction (M Ed, CAGS); information technology (CAGS); reading (M Ed); special education (M Ed, CAGS); technology (M Ed). Part-time and evening/weekend programs available. *Degree requirements:* For master's, thesis. *Entrance requirements:* For master's, minimum GPA of 3.0. Electronic applications accepted. *Faculty research:* Integrative curriculum, moral and spiritual dimensions of education, learning styles, multiple intelligences, integrating technology into the curriculum.

Saint Peter's College, Graduate Programs in Education, Program in Special Education, Jersey City, NJ 07306-5997. Offers special education (MA), including applied behavior analysis, literacy. *Degree requirements:* For master's, comprehensive exam. *Entrance requirements:* Additional exam requirements/recommendations for international students: Required—TOEFL. *Application deadline:* Applications are processed on a rolling basis. Electronic applications accepted. *Expenses:* Tuition: Part-time $971 per credit. *Financial support:* Career-related internships or fieldwork, Federal Work-Study, and institutionally sponsored loans available. *Unit head:* Dr. Anthony Sciarrillo, Chairperson, 201-761-6473, Fax: 201-435-5270. *Application contact:* Dr. Anthony Sciarrillo, Chairperson, 201-761-6473, Fax: 201-435-5270.

St. Thomas Aquinas College, Division of Teacher Education, Sparkill, NY 10976. Offers adolescence education (MST); childhood and special education (MST); childhood education (MST); educational leadership (MS Ed); reading (MS Ed, PMC); special education (MS Ed, PMC); teaching (MS Ed), including elementary education, middle school education, secondary education. *Accreditation:* NCATE. Part-time and evening/weekend programs available. *Degree requirements:* For master's, comprehensive exam, comprehensive professional portfolio; for PMC, action research project. *Entrance requirements:* For master's, New York State Qualifying Exam, GRE General Test or minimum GPA of 3.0, teaching certificate; for PMC, GRE General Test or minimum GPA of 3.0. Electronic applications accepted. *Faculty research:* Computer applications in education, adolescent special education students, literacy development, inclusive practices for special education students.

St. Thomas University, School of Leadership Studies, Institute for Education, Miami Gardens, FL 33054-6459. Offers earth/space science (Certificate); educational administration (MS, Certificate); educational leadership (Ed D); elementary education (MS); ESOL (Certificate); gifted education (Certificate); instructional technology (MS, Certificate); professional/studies (Certificate); reading (MS, Certificate); special education (MS). Part-time and evening/weekend programs available. *Degree requirements:* For master's, comprehensive exam; for doctorate, comprehensive exam, thesis/dissertation. *Entrance requirements:* For master's, interview, minimum GPA of 3.0 or GRE; for doctorate, GRE or MAT. Additional exam requirements/recommendations for international students: Required—TOEFL (minimum score 550 paper-based; 213 computer-based; 79 iBT). Electronic applications accepted.

Saint Vincent College, Program in Education, Latrobe, PA 15650-2690. Offers curriculum and instruction (MS); environmental education (MS); library media management (MS); school administration (MS); special education (MS). Part-time and evening/weekend programs available. *Degree requirements:* For master's, comprehensive exam. *Entrance requirements:* For master's, GRE (if undergraduate GPA less than 3.0). Additional exam requirements/recommendations for international students: Required—TOEFL (minimum score 550 paper-based; 213 computer-based). *Faculty research:* Assessment and instructional technology.

Saint Xavier University, Graduate Studies, School of Education, Chicago, IL 60655-3105. Offers counseling (MA); counselor education (MA); curriculum and instruction (MA); early childhood education (MA); education (CAS); educational administration (MA); elementary education (MA); field-based education (MA); general educational studies (MA); individualized program (MA); learning disabilities (MA); reading (MA); secondary education (MA). *Accreditation:* NCATE. Part-time and evening/weekend programs available. *Degree requirements:* For master's, thesis or project. *Entrance requirements:* For master's, minimum GPA of 3.0. *Expenses:* Contact institution.

Salem College, Department of Education, Winston-Salem, NC 27101. Offers early education and leadership (MAT); elementary education (MAT); English as a second language (MAT); language and literacy (M Ed); middle school education (MAT); secondary education (MAT); special education (MAT). *Accreditation:* NCATE. Part-time and evening/weekend programs available. *Degree requirements:* For master's, comprehensive exam, practicum (MAT), project (M Ed), oral and written comprehensive exams. *Entrance requirements:* For master's, GRE, minimum GPA of 2.5. *Faculty research:* Content area reading strategies, literacy development, brain compatible instruction.

Salem State College, School of Graduate Studies, Program in Special Education, Salem, MA 01970-5353. Offers M Ed. *Accreditation:* NCATE. Part-time and evening/weekend programs available. *Students:* 10 full-time (8 women), 128 part-time (109 women); includes 2 minority (1 African American, 1 Hispanic American). Average age 35. 11 applicants, 100% accepted, 11 enrolled. In 2009, 67 master's awarded. *Entrance requirements:* For master's, GRE, MAT. Additional exam requirements/recommendations for international students: Required—TOEFL (minimum score 550 paper-based; 80 iBT), or IELTS (minimum score 5.5). *Application deadline:* For fall admission, 5/1 for domestic students; for spring admission, 10/1 for domestic students. Applications are processed on a rolling basis. Application fee: $50. *Expenses:* Tuition, state resident: full-time $2520; part-time $275 per credit hour. Tuition, nonresident: full-time $4140; part-time $365 per credit hour. Required fees: $2430. *Financial support:* In 2009–10, 29 students received support. Career-related internships or fieldwork, Federal Work-Study, scholarships/grants, and unspecified assistantships available. Support available to part-time students. Financial award application deadline: 5/1; financial award applicants required to submit FAFSA. *Unit head:* Dr. Vicki Gallagher, Coordinator, 978-542-6322, Fax: 978-542-7215, E-mail: vgallagher@salemstate.edu. *Application contact:* Dr. Lee A. Brossoit, Assistant Dean of Graduate Admissions, 978-542-6675, Fax: 978-542-7215, E-mail: lbrossoit@salemstate.edu.

Salus University, Graduate Studies in Vision Impairment and Audiology, Elkins Park, PA 19027-1598. Offers education of children and youth with visual and multiple impairments (M Ed, Certificate); low vision rehabilitation (MS, Certificate); orientation and mobility therapy (MS, Certificate); vision rehabilitation therapy (MS, Certificate); OD/MS. Part-time programs available. Postbaccalaureate distance learning degree programs offered. *Faculty:* 8 full-time (7 women), 1 (woman) part-time/adjunct. *Students:* 4 full-time (all women), 64 part-time (58 women); includes 7 minority (5 African Americans, 1 American Indian/Alaska Native, 1 Hispanic American). Average age 37. In 2009, 14 master's, 12 other advanced degrees awarded. *Entrance requirements:* For master's, GRE or MAT, letters of reference (3), interviews (2). Additional exam requirements/recommendations for international students: Required—TOEFL, TWE. *Application deadline:* For fall admission, 6/1 for domestic students. Applications are processed on a rolling basis. *Expenses:* Contact institution. *Financial support:* Federal Work-Study and scholarships/grants available. Financial award applicants required to submit FAFSA. *Faculty research:* Knowledge utilization, technology transfer. *Unit head:* Dr. Audrey Smith, Associate Dean, 215-780-1361, Fax: 215-780-1357, E-mail: ASmith@Salus.edu. *Application contact:* Dr. Audrey Smith, Associate Dean, 215-780-1361, Fax: 215-780-1357, E-mail: ASmith@ Salus.edu.

Sam Houston State University, College of Education and Applied Science, Department of Language, Literacy, and Special Populations, Huntsville, TX 77341. Offers reading (M Ed, MA, Ed D); special education (M Ed, MA). Part-time and evening/weekend programs available. *Faculty:* 15 full-time (12 women), 1 (woman) part-time/adjunct. *Students:* 2 full-time (both women), 135 part-time (129 women); includes 32 minority (15 African Americans, 1 Asian American or Pacific Islander, 16 Hispanic Americans), 3 international. Average age 36. 55 applicants, 98% accepted, 37 enrolled. In 2009, 24 master's, 1 doctorate awarded. *Entrance requirements:* For master's, GRE General Test, minimum GPA of 2.5. Additional exam requirements/recommendations for international students: Required—TOEFL (minimum score 550 paper-based; 213 computer-based; 79 iBT). *Application deadline:* For fall admission, 8/1 for domestic students; for spring admission, 12/1 for domestic students. Application fee: $20. *Expenses:* Tuition, state resident: full-time $3690; part-time $205 per credit hour. Tuition, nonresident: full-time $8676; part-time $482 per credit hour. Required fees: $1474. Tuition and fees vary according to course load and campus/location. *Financial support:* Teaching assistantships available. Financial award application deadline: 5/31; financial award applicants required to submit FAFSA. *Unit head:* Dr. Sharon Lynch, Chair, 936-294-1122, Fax: 936-294-1131, E-mail: edu_sal@shsu.edu. *Application contact:* Molly Doughtie, Advisor, 936-294-1105, E-mail: edu_mxd@shsu.edu.

San Diego State University, Graduate and Research Affairs, College of Education, Department of Administration, Rehabilitation and Post-Secondary Education, San Diego, CA 92182. Offers educational leadership in post-secondary education (MA); rehabilitation counseling (MS), including deafness. Evening/weekend programs available. Postbaccalaureate distance learning degree programs offered. *Degree requirements:* For master's, comprehensive exam (for some programs), thesis (for some programs). *Entrance requirements:* For master's, GRE General Test, letters of reference. Additional exam requirements/recommendations for international students: Required—TOEFL. Electronic applications accepted. *Faculty research:* Rehabilitation in cultural diversity, distance learning technology.

San Diego State University, Graduate and Research Affairs, College of Education, Department of Special Education, San Diego, CA 92182. Offers MA. *Accreditation:* NCATE. Evening/weekend programs available. *Entrance requirements:* For master's, GRE General Test, letters of reference. Additional exam requirements/recommendations for international students: Required—TOEFL. Electronic applications accepted.

San Francisco State University, Division of Graduate Studies, College of Education, Department of Special Education, San Francisco, CA 94132-1722. Offers communicative disorders (MS); special education (MA, PhD, AC). *Accreditation:* NCATE.

San Jose State University, Graduate Studies and Research, Connie L. Lurie College of Education, Department of Special Education, San Jose, CA 95192-0001. Offers MA. *Accreditation:* NCATE. Evening/weekend programs available. *Students:* 90 full-time (75 women), 132 part-time (111 women); includes 61 minority (7 African Americans, 29 Asian Americans or Pacific Islanders, 25 Hispanic Americans), 5 international. Average age 36. 143 applicants, 50% accepted, 59 enrolled. In 2009, 14 master's awarded. *Application deadline:* For fall admission, 6/29 for domestic students; for spring admission, 11/30 for domestic students. Applications are processed on a rolling basis. Application fee: $59. Electronic applications accepted. *Financial support:* Career-related internships or fieldwork available. Financial award applicants required to submit FAFSA. *Unit head:* Dr. Chris Hagie, Chair, 408-924-3700, Fax: 408-924-3701. *Application contact:* Dr. Chris Hagie, Chair, 408-924-3700, Fax: 408-924-3701.

Santa Clara University, School of Education and Counseling Psychology, Department of Education, Program in Special Education, Santa Clara, CA 95053. Offers early childhood special education (Certificate); special education (MA), including early childhood education, mild moderate disabilities. Part-time and evening/weekend programs available. *Students:* 8 full-time (7 women), 71 part-time (63 women); includes 24 minority (1 African American, 15 Asian Americans or Pacific Islanders, 8 Hispanic Americans), 3 international. Average age 39. 48 applicants, 85% accepted, 39 enrolled. In 2009, 11 master's, 28 other advanced degrees awarded. *Degree requirements:* For master's, comprehensive exam. *Entrance requirements:* For master's, GRE or MAT, minimum GPA of 3.0. Additional exam requirements/recommendations for international students: Required—TOEFL. *Application deadline:* Applications are processed on a rolling basis. *Expenses:* Contact institution. *Financial support:* Fellowships, Federal Work-Study, institutionally sponsored loans, and scholarships/grants available. Support available to part-time students. Financial award application deadline: 5/15; financial award applicants required to submit FAFSA. *Unit head:* Dr. Ruth E. Cook, Interim Chair, 408-554-4119. *Application contact:* Dr. Ruth E. Cook, Interim Chair, 408-554-4119.

Special Education

Seattle University, College of Education, Program in Special Education, Seattle, WA 98122-1090. Offers M Ed, MA, Certificate. *Entrance requirements:* For master's, GRE, MAT or minimum GPA of 3.0, 1 year K-12 teaching experience; for Certificate, master's degree, minimum GPA of 3.0, 1 year K-12 teaching experience.

Seton Hill University, Program in Special Education, Greensburg, PA 15601. Offers MA, Teaching Certificate. Part-time and evening/weekend programs available. *Faculty:* 5 full-time (2 women), 5 part-time/adjunct (4 women). *Students:* 21 full-time (16 women), 18 part-time (16 women); includes 3 minority (1 African American, 1 American Indian/Alaska Native, 1 Hispanic American), 1 international. Average age 30. 14 applicants, 93% accepted, 11 enrolled. In 2009, 3 master's awarded. *Degree requirements:* For master's, thesis optional. *Entrance requirements:* For master's, minimum GPA of 3.0. Additional exam requirements/recommendations for international students: Required—TOEFL (minimum score 600 paper-based; 250 computer-based), IELTS (minimum score 6.5). *Application deadline:* For fall admission, 8/15 priority date for domestic students; for spring admission, 12/15 for domestic students. Applications are processed on a rolling basis. Application fee: $35. Electronic applications accepted. *Expenses:* Tuition: Full-time $12,780; part-time $710 per credit. Required fees: $300; $150 per semester. Tuition and fees vary according to course load and program. *Financial support:* Scholarships/grants, tuition waivers (partial), and unspecified assistantships available. Support available to part-time students. Financial award application deadline: 8/15; financial award applicants required to submit FAFSA. *Faculty research:* Experiential learning environments, instructional technologies, reading methods. *Unit head:* Dr. Sondra Lettrich, Director, 724-830-1010, Fax: 724-830-1294, E-mail: lettrich@setonhill.edu. *Application contact:* Laurel Pellis, Advisor, 724-838-4209, Fax: 724-830-1891, E-mail: lpellis@setonhill.edu.

Shenandoah University, School of Education and Human Development, Winchester, VA 22601-5195. Offers administrative leadership (D Ed); advanced professional teaching English to speakers of other languages (Certificate); education (MSE); elementary education (Certificate); middle school education (Certificate); organizational leadership (MS); professional studies (Certificate); professional studies (for initial teacher licensure) (Certificate); professional studies (for special education teacher licensure) (Certificate); professional studies (for VA licensure reading specialists) (Certificate); professional studies (for VA licensure) (Certificate); professional teaching English to speakers of other languages (Certificate); public management (Certificate); school reform (Certificate); secondary education (Certificate). *Accreditation:* Teacher Education Accreditation Council. Part-time and evening/weekend programs available. Post-baccalaureate distance learning degree programs offered (minimal on-campus study). *Faculty:* 13 full-time (7 women), 27 part-time/adjunct (20 women). *Students:* 11 full-time (8 women), 382 part-time (276 women); includes 35 minority (17 African Americans, 1 American Indian/Alaska Native, 6 Asian Americans or Pacific Islanders, 11 Hispanic Americans), 4 international. Average age 39. 272 applicants, 95% accepted, 218 enrolled. In 2009, 103 master's, 2 doctorates awarded. *Degree requirements:* For master's, comprehensive exam (for some programs), thesis (for some programs), internship; for doctorate, comprehensive exam, thesis/dissertation; for Certificate, full time teaching in area for 1 year. *Entrance requirements:* For master's, minimum GPA of 3.0 or satisfactory GRE, 3 letters of recommendation, valid teaching license, essay; for doctorate, minimum graduate GPA of 3.5, 3 years of teaching experience, 3 letters of recommendation, writing samples; for Certificate, minimum undergraduate GPA of 3.0, essay, 3 letters of recommendation. Additional exam requirements/recommendations for international students: Required—TOEFL (minimum score 550 paper-based; 213 computer-based; 79 iBT), IELTS (minimum score 6.5). *Application deadline:* For fall admission, 7/1 for domestic and international students; for spring admission, 10/15 for domestic and international students. Application fee: $30. Electronic applications accepted. *Expenses:* Tuition: Full-time $11,925; part-time $695 per credit. Required fees: $400 per semester. *Financial support:* Application deadline: 3/15. *Unit head:* Dr. Steven E. Humphries, Dean, 540-535-3574, E-mail: shumphri@su.edu. *Application contact:* David Anthony, Dean of Admissions, 540-665-4581, Fax: 540-665-4627, E-mail: admit@su.edu.

Shippensburg University of Pennsylvania, School of Graduate Studies, College of Education and Human Services, Department of Educational Leadership and Special Education, Shippensburg, PA 17257-2299. Offers school administration principal K-12 (M Ed); special education (M Ed), including behavior disorders, comprehensive, learning disabilities, mental retardation. *Accreditation:* NCATE. Part-time and evening/weekend programs available. *Degree requirements:* For master's, candidacy, thesis, or practicum. *Entrance requirements:* For master's, instructional or educational specialist certificate; 2 letters of reference; 2 years of successful teaching experience; interview and GRE or MAT (if GPA is less than 2.75). Additional exam requirements/recommendations for international students: Required—TOEFL (minimum score 560 paper-based; 220 computer-based); Recommended—IELTS (minimum score 6). Electronic applications accepted.

Silver Lake College, Division of Graduate Studies, Program in Special Education, Manitowoc, WI 54220-9319. Offers MASE. Part-time and evening/weekend programs available. *Faculty:* 1 (woman) full-time, 6 part-time/adjunct (all women). *Students:* 9 part-time (all women). Average age 40. *Entrance requirements:* Additional exam requirements/recommendations for international students: Required—TOEFL. *Application deadline:* For fall admission, 8/1 for domestic students; for spring admission, 12/1 for domestic students. Applications are processed on a rolling basis. Application fee: $50. Electronic applications accepted. *Expenses:* Tuition: Full-time $7380; part-time $410 per credit. Required fees: $10 per term. Part-time tuition and fees vary according to course load. *Financial support:* Federal Work-Study and scholarships/grants available. Support available to part-time students. Financial award applicants required to submit FAFSA. *Unit head:* Sr. Mary Karen Oudeans, Director, 920-686-6157, Fax: 920-684-7082. *Application contact:* Jamie Grant, Associate Director of Admissions, 800-236-4752 Ext. 186, Fax: 920-686-6322, E-mail: jgrant@silver.sl.edu.

Simmons College, College of Arts and Sciences Graduate Studies, Department of Education, Program in Special Education, Boston, MA 02115. Offers applied behavior analysis (PhD); assistive technology (MS Ed, Ed S); behavioral education (MS Ed, Ed S); health professions education (PhD); language and literacy (MS Ed, Ed S); moderate disabilities (Ed S); moderate special needs (MS Ed); severe disabilities (Ed S); severe special needs (MS Ed); special education administration (MS Ed, PhD, Ed S). Part-time and evening/weekend programs available. *Students:* 45 full-time (40 women), 316 part-time (271 women); includes 19 minority (7 African Americans, 1 American Indian/Alaska Native, 7 Asian Americans or Pacific Islanders, 4 Hispanic Americans), 2 international. 95 applicants, 89% accepted, 65 enrolled. In 2009, 145 master's awarded. *Degree requirements:* For master's, student teaching. *Entrance requirements:* For doctorate, GRE, research proposal, interview, BCBA credential. Additional exam requirements/recommendations for international students: Required—TOEFL (minimum score 600 paper-based; 250 computer-based; 100 iBT). *Application deadline:* For fall admission, 8/1 priority date for domestic and international students; for winter admission, 12/15 priority date for domestic students; for spring admission, 12/15 priority date for domestic and international students. Applications are processed on a rolling basis. Application fee: $35. Electronic applications accepted. *Expenses:* Contact institution. *Financial support:* Application deadline: 3/1. *Faculty research:* Development and application of the IEP for teachers, assistive technology, language-based disabilities, applied behavior analysis, communication challenges between general and special education teachers. *Unit head:* Paul Abraham, Chair, Department of Education, 617-521-2575, E-mail: paul.abraham@simmons.edu. *Application contact:* Kristen Haack, Director, Graduate Studies Admission, 617-521-2917, Fax: 617-521-3058, E-mail: gsa@simmons.edu.

Slippery Rock University of Pennsylvania, Graduate Studies (Recruitment), College of Education, Department of Special Education, Slippery Rock, PA 16057-1383. Offers master teacher (M Ed); supervision (M Ed). *Accreditation:* NCATE. Part-time and evening/weekend programs available. *Degree requirements:* For master's, comprehensive exam (for some programs), thesis (for some programs), portfolio presentation. *Entrance requirements:* For master's, GRE General Test, MAT, minimum GPA of 2.75 (3.0 for initial certification). Additional

exam requirements/recommendations for international students: Required—TOEFL (minimum score 550 paper-based; 213 computer-based). *Application deadline:* For fall admission, 3/1 priority date for domestic students, 5/1 priority date for international students; for spring admission, 11/1 priority date for domestic students, 9/1 priority date for international students. Applications are processed on a rolling basis. Application fee: $25 ($30 for international students). Electronic applications accepted. *Expenses:* Tuition, state resident: full-time $6666; part-time $370 per credit. Tuition, nonresident: full-time $10,666; part-time $593 per credit. Required fees: $2184; $182 per credit. *Financial support:* Career-related internships or fieldwork, Federal Work-Study, scholarships/grants, and unspecified assistantships available. Support available to part-time students. Financial award application deadline: 5/1; financial award applicants required to submit FAFSA. *Faculty research:* In-service teacher education, contemporary issues in special education, education for developmentally disabled, educational assessment. *Unit head:* Dr. Dennis Fair, Graduate Coordinator, 724-738-2614, Fax: 724-738-4395, E-mail: dennis.fair@sru.edu. *Application contact:* Angela Piverotto, Interim Director of Graduate Studies, 724-738-2051, Fax: 724-738-2146, E-mail: graduate.admissions@sru.edu.

Smith College, Graduate and Special Programs, Department of Education and Child Study, Program in the Education of the Deaf, Northampton, MA 01063. Offers MED. Part-time programs available. *Students:* 12 full-time (11 women), 2 part-time (both women); includes 2 minority (1 Asian American or Pacific Islander, 1 Hispanic American). Average age 31. 30 applicants, 53% accepted, 13 enrolled. In 2009, 10 master's awarded. *Entrance requirements:* For master's, GRE General Test or MAT. Additional exam requirements/recommendations for international students: Required—TOEFL (minimum score 590 paper-based; 243 computer-based; 97 iBT). *Application deadline:* For fall admission, 4/1 for domestic students, 1/15 for international students. Applications are processed on a rolling basis. Application fee: $60. *Financial support:* In 2009–10, 14 students received support. Career-related internships or fieldwork, institutionally sponsored loans, scholarships/grants, and tuition waivers (full) available. Support available to part-time students. Financial award application deadline: 1/15; financial award applicants required to submit CSS PROFILE or FAFSA. *Unit head:* Janice Gatty, Acting Director, 413-585-3258, Fax: 413-585-3268, E-mail: jgatty@smith.edu. *Application contact:* Ruth Morgan, Administrative Assistant, 413-585-3050, Fax: 413-585-3054, E-mail: gradstdy@smith.edu.

Sonoma State University, School of Education, Department of Educational Leadership and Special Education, Rohnert Park, CA 94928-3609. Offers educational leadership (MA); special education (MA). Part-time and evening/weekend programs available. *Degree requirements:* For master's, thesis or alternative. *Entrance requirements:* For master's, GRE General Test, minimum GPA of 2.5. *Expenses:* Tuition, nonresident: full-time $11,160. Required fees: $6226. Full-time tuition and fees vary according to course load.

South Carolina State University, School of Graduate Studies, Department of Education, Orangeburg, SC 29117-0001. Offers early childhood and special education (M Ed); early childhood education (MAT); elementary education (M Ed, MAT); engineering (MAT); general science (MAT); mathematics (MAT); secondary education (M Ed), including biology education, business education, counselor education, English education, home economics education, industrial education, mathematics education, science education, social studies education; special education (M Ed), including emotionally handicapped, learning disabilities, mentally handicapped. *Accreditation:* NCATE. Part-time and evening/weekend programs available. *Degree requirements:* For master's, thesis optional, departmental qualifying exam. *Entrance requirements:* For master's, GRE General Test, NTE, interview, teaching certificate. Electronic applications accepted. *Expenses:* Tuition, state resident: part-time $470 per credit hour. Tuition, nonresident: part-time $924 per credit hour. *Faculty research:* Critical thinking, child abuse, stress, test-taking skills, conflict resolution, mainstreaming.

Southeastern Louisiana University, College of Education and Human Development, Department of Teaching and Learning, Hammond, LA 70402. Offers curriculum and instruction (M Ed); elementary education (MAT); special education (M Ed, MAT), including mild/moderate grades K-12 (MAT). *Accreditation:* NCATE. Part-time programs available. *Faculty:* 16 full-time (14 women). *Students:* 20 full-time (all women), 107 part-time (99 women); includes 18 minority (11 African Americans, 1 American Indian/Alaska Native, 1 Asian American or Pacific Islander, 5 Hispanic Americans), 1 international. Average age 35. 16 applicants, 94% accepted, 13 enrolled. In 2009, 61 master's awarded. *Degree requirements:* For master's, comprehensive exam (for some programs), portfolio. *Entrance requirements:* For master's, GRE (verbal and quantitative), PRAXIS (MAT), bachelor's degree from an accredited U.S. institution or its foreign equivalent; minimum undergraduate GPA of 2.5 on all undergraduate work attempted or 2.75 on all undergraduate upper-level work attempted. Additional exam requirements/recommendations for international students: Required—TOEFL (minimum score 500 paper-based; 173 computer-based; 61 iBT). *Application deadline:* For fall admission, 7/15 priority date for domestic students, 6/1 priority date for international students; for spring admission, 12/1 priority date for domestic students, 10/1 priority date for international students. Applications are processed on a rolling basis. Application fee: $20 ($30 for international students). Electronic applications accepted. *Expenses:* Tuition, state resident: full-time $3086; part-time $225 per credit hour. Tuition, nonresident: part-time $529 per credit hour. Required fees: $1195. Tuition and fees vary according to course level and course load. *Financial support:* In 2009–10, 9 students received support. Federal Work-Study, institutionally sponsored loans, and administrative assistantship available. Support available to part-time students. Financial award application deadline: 5/1; financial award applicants required to submit FAFSA. *Faculty research:* Reading, instructional methodology, science education, math education, early childhood. Total annual research expenditures: $458,029. *Unit head:* Dr. Shirley Jacob, Department Head, 985-549-2221, Fax: 985-549-5009, E-mail: sjacob@selu.edu. *Application contact:* Sandra Meyers, Graduate Admissions Analyst, 985-549-5620, Fax: 985-549-5632, E-mail: admissions@selu.edu.

Southeastern Louisiana University, College of Nursing and Health Sciences, Department of Communication Sciences and Disorders, Hammond, LA 70402. Offers MS. *Accreditation:* ASHA; NCATE. *Faculty:* 10 full-time (9 women). *Students:* 41 full-time (39 women), 19 part-time (all women); includes 3 minority (1 African American, 1 Asian American or Pacific Islander, 1 Hispanic American). Average age 27. 37 applicants, 97% accepted, 21 enrolled. In 2009, 14 master's awarded. *Degree requirements:* For master's, comprehensive exam (for some programs), thesis optional. *Entrance requirements:* For master's, GRE (verbal and quantitative), 3 letters of reference. Additional exam requirements/recommendations for international students: Required—TOEFL (minimum score 500 paper-based; 173 computer-based; 61 iBT). *Application deadline:* For fall admission, 7/15 priority date for domestic students, 6/1 priority date for international students; for spring admission, 12/1 priority date for domestic students, 10/1 priority date for international students. Applications are processed on a rolling basis. Application fee: $20 ($30 for international students). Electronic applications accepted. *Expenses:* Tuition, state resident: full-time $3086; part-time $225 per credit hour. Tuition, nonresident: part-time $529 per credit hour. Required fees: $1195. Tuition and fees vary according to course level and course load. *Financial support:* In 2009–10, 2 students received support. Federal Work-Study, institutionally sponsored loans, scholarships/grants, and administrative assistantships available. Support available to part-time students. Financial award application deadline: 5/1; financial award applicants required to submit FAFSA. *Faculty research:* Conversational analysis in standard and communication disordered population, educational needs of children with cochlear implants, autism, acoustic characteristics of American English linguistics stress patterns, languages disorders and literacy. *Unit head:* Dr. Paula Currie, Department Head, 985-549-2214, Fax: 985-549-5030, E-mail: pcurrie@selu.edu. *Application contact:* Sandra Meyers, Graduate Admissions Analyst, 985-549-5620, Fax: 985-549-5632, E-mail: admissions@selu.edu.

Southeast Missouri State University, School of Graduate Studies, Department of Elementary, Early and Special Education, Program in Exceptional Child Education, Cape Girardeau, MO 63701-4799. Offers MA. *Accreditation:* NCATE. Part-time and evening/weekend programs

available. *Degree requirements:* For master's, thesis or alternative. *Entrance requirements:* For master's, GRE General Test, MAT or PRAXIS, minimum undergraduate GPA of 2.75. Additional exam requirements/recommendations for international students: Required—TOEFL (minimum score 550 paper-based; 213 computer-based); Recommended—IELTS (minimum score 6). Electronic applications accepted. *Expenses:* Tuition, state resident: full-time $4266; part-time $237 per credit hour. Tuition, nonresident: full-time $7506; part-time $417 per credit hour. Required fees: $427; $427.

Southern Connecticut State University, School of Graduate Studies, School of Education, Department of Special Education, New Haven, CT 06515-1355. Offers MS Ed, Diploma. Part-time and evening/weekend programs available. *Faculty:* 12 full-time, 9 part-time/adjunct. *Students:* 64 full-time (47 women), 260 part-time (225 women); includes 22 minority (13 African Americans, 2 Asian Americans or Pacific Islanders, 7 Hispanic Americans). 160 applicants, 49% accepted, 60 enrolled. In 2009, 110 master's, 5 Diplomas awarded. *Degree requirements:* For master's, thesis or alternative. *Entrance requirements:* For master's, interview; for Diploma, 3 years of teaching experience, master's degree, teacher certification, interview. *Application deadline:* For fall admission, 7/15 for domestic students. Applications are processed on a rolling basis. Application fee: $50. Electronic applications accepted. Tuition and fees vary according to program. *Financial support:* Career-related internships or fieldwork available. Financial award application deadline: 4/15; financial award applicants required to submit FAFSA. *Unit head:* Dr. Deborah Newton, Chairperson, 203-392-5941, Fax: 203-392-5927, E-mail: newtond2@southernct.edu. *Application contact:* Dr. Ruth Eren, Graduate Coordinator, 203-392-5647, Fax: 203-392-5927, E-mail: erenr1@southernct.edu.

Southern Illinois University Carbondale, Graduate School, College of Education, Department of Educational Psychology and Special Education, Program in Special Education, Carbondale, IL 62901-4701. Offers MS Ed. *Accreditation:* NCATE. Part-time programs available. *Degree requirements:* For master's, thesis. *Entrance requirements:* For master's, GRE General Test, minimum GPA of 2.7. Additional exam requirements/recommendations for international students: Required—TOEFL. *Faculty research:* Applied and action research; scientific methods used to evaluate effectiveness of products and programs for the handicapped; scientific methods used to develop generalizations about instructional, motivational, and learning processes of the handicapped.

Southern Illinois University Edwardsville, Graduate Studies and Research, School of Education, Department of Special Education and Communication Disorders, Program in Special Education, Edwardsville, IL 62026-0001. Offers MS Ed, Post-Master's Certificate. Part-time and evening/weekend programs available. *Students:* 1 (woman) full-time, 48 part-time (44 women); includes 4 minority (1 Asian American or Pacific Islander, 3 Hispanic Americans). Average age 26. 23 applicants, 78% accepted. In 2009, 12 master's awarded. *Degree requirements:* For master's, thesis or alternative, final exam. *Entrance requirements:* Additional exam requirements/recommendations for international students: Required—TOEFL (minimum score 550 paper-based; 213 computer-based; 79 iBT), IELTS (minimum score 6.5). *Application deadline:* For fall admission, 7/23 for domestic students, 6/1 for international students; for spring admission, 12/11 for domestic students, 10/1 for international students. Applications are processed on a rolling basis. Application fee: $30. Electronic applications accepted. *Expenses:* Tuition, state resident: part-time $1252.50 per semester. Tuition, nonresident: part-time $3131.25 per semester. Required fees: $586.85 per semester. Tuition and fees vary according to course load. *Financial support:* Fellowships, research assistantships, teaching assistantships, career-related internships or fieldwork, Federal Work-Study, institutionally sponsored loans, scholarships/grants, traineeships, and unspecified assistantships available. Support available to part-time students. Financial award application deadline: 3/1; financial award applicants required to submit FAFSA. *Unit head:* Dr. Allison Fahsl, Director, 618-650-3488, E-mail: afahsl@siue.edu. *Application contact:* Dr. Allison Fahsl, Director, 618-650-3488, E-mail: afahsl@siue.edu.

Southern New Hampshire University, School of Education, Manchester, NH 03106-1045. Offers business education (MS); child development (M Ed); computer technology education (Certificate); curriculum and instruction (M Ed); education (M Ed, CAS); elementary education (M Ed); general special education (Certificate); school business administrator (Certificate); secondary education (M Ed); training and development (Certificate). Part-time and evening/weekend programs available. Postbaccalaureate distance learning degree programs offered (no on-campus study). *Degree requirements:* For master's, comprehensive exam (for some programs), thesis or alternative. *Entrance requirements:* For master's, PRAXIS I, minimum GPA of 2.75. Additional exam requirements/recommendations for international students: Required—TOEFL (minimum score 550 paper-based; 213 computer-based). Electronic applications accepted. *Expenses:* Contact institution.

Southern Oregon University, Graduate Studies, School of Education, Ashland, OR 97520. Offers elementary education (MA Ed, MS Ed), including classroom teacher, early childhood, handicapped learner, reading, supervision; secondary education (MA Ed, MS Ed), including classroom teacher, handicapped learner, reading, supervision; teaching (MAT). *Degree requirements:* For master's, thesis optional. *Entrance requirements:* For master's, GRE General Test, minimum GPA of 3.0. Electronic applications accepted.

Southern University and Agricultural and Mechanical College, Graduate School and College of Education, Department of Special Education, Baton Rouge, LA 70813. Offers M Ed, PhD. *Accreditation:* NCATE. Part-time and evening/weekend programs available. *Degree requirements:* For master's, comprehensive exam, thesis optional; for doctorate, thesis/dissertation, comprehensive qualifying exam, oral defense of dissertation. *Entrance requirements:* For master's, GMAT or GRE General Test, PRAXIS; for doctorate, GRE General Test, PRAXIS, letters of recommendation, 2 years experience (individuals with disabilities). Additional exam requirements/recommendations for international students: Required—TOEFL. *Faculty research:* Classroom discipline/management, minority students in gifted/special education, learning styles/brain hemisphericity, school violence and prevention, certifications for special education teachers.

Southwestern College, Education Programs, Winfield, KS 67156-2499. Offers curriculum and instruction (M Ed); special education (M Ed); teaching (MA). *Accreditation:* NCATE. Part-time and evening/weekend programs available. Postbaccalaureate distance learning degree programs offered (minimal on-campus study). *Faculty:* 2 full-time (1 woman), 14 part-time/adjunct (12 women). *Students:* 1 (woman) full-time, 112 part-time (88 women); includes 9 minority (2 African Americans, 1 American Indian/Alaska Native, 3 Asian Americans or Pacific Islanders, 3 Hispanic Americans), 2 international. Average age 37. 50 applicants, 98% accepted, 46 enrolled. In 2009, 18 master's awarded. *Degree requirements:* For master's, practicum, portfolio. *Entrance requirements:* For master's, baccalaureate degree, minimum GPA of 2.5, valid teaching certificate (for special education). Additional exam requirements/recommendations for international students: Required—TOEFL (minimum score 550 paper-based; 213 computer-based). *Application deadline:* For fall admission, 8/1 for domestic students; for spring admission, 12/1 for domestic students. Applications are processed on a rolling basis. Application fee: $0. Electronic applications accepted. *Expenses:* Contact institution. *Financial support:* In 2009–10, 77 students received support. Federal Work-Study, tuition waivers (partial), and unspecified assistantships available. Financial award application deadline: 4/1; financial award applicants required to submit FAFSA. *Unit head:* Dr. David Hofmeister, Director of Teacher Education, 800-846-1543 Ext. 6115, Fax: 620-229-6341, E-mail: david.hofmeister@sckans.edu. *Application contact:* Lindy Kralicek, Education Program Representative, 888-684-5335 Ext. 130, Fax: 316-688-5218, E-mail: lindy.kralicek@sckans.edu.

Southwestern Oklahoma State University, College of Professional and Graduate Studies, School of Behavioral Sciences and Education, Specialization in Special Education, Weatherford, OK 73096-3098. Offers M Ed. M Ed distance learning degree program offered to Oklahoma residents only. *Accreditation:* NCATE. Part-time and evening/weekend programs available. *Degree requirements:* For master's, exam. *Entrance requirements:* For master's, GRE General Test or minimum undergraduate GPA of 3.0. Additional exam requirements/recommendations for international students: Required—TOEFL.

Southwest Minnesota State University, Department of Education, Marshall, MN 56258. Offers education (MS); special education (MS). Part-time and evening/weekend programs available. Postbaccalaureate distance learning degree programs offered (no on-campus study). *Faculty:* 12 full-time (8 women), 11 part-time/adjunct (5 women). *Students:* 317 full-time (233 women), 95 part-time (71 women); includes 11 minority (4 African Americans, 2 Asian Americans or Pacific Islanders, 5 Hispanic Americans), 2 international. Average age 30. In 2009, 101 master's awarded. *Entrance requirements:* Additional exam requirements/recommendations for international students: Required—TOEFL or IELTS. *Application deadline:* For fall admission, 8/28 for domestic students, 6/15 for international students; for spring admission, 1/15 for domestic students, 12/15 for international students. Applications are processed on a rolling basis. Application fee: $20. *Expenses:* Tuition, state resident: full-time $5487; part-time $304.85 per credit. Tuition, nonresident: full-time $5487; part-time $304.85 per credit. Required fees: $680; $37.76 per credit. Tuition and fees vary according to course load and reciprocity agreements. *Financial support:* Institutionally sponsored loans and unspecified assistantships available. Support available to part-time students. Financial award application deadline: 3/1; financial award applicants required to submit FAFSA. *Unit head:* Dr. Donna Burgraff, Dean of Business, Education and Professional Studies, 507-537-6218, E-mail: donna.burgraff@smsu.edu. *Application contact:* CoriAnn Dahlager, Graduate Office Coordinator, 507-537-6819, E-mail: coriann.dahlager@smsu.edu.

Spalding University, Graduate Studies, College of Education, Programs in Education, Louisville, KY 40203-2188. Offers elementary school education (MAT); general education (MA); high school education (MAT); middle school education (MAT); school administration (MA); special education (learning and behavioral disorders) (MAT); student guidance counselor (MA). MAT degree programs offered for first teaching certificate/license students. *Accreditation:* NCATE. Part-time and evening/weekend programs available. *Faculty:* 6 full-time (4 women), 32 part-time/adjunct (23 women). *Students:* 125 full-time (93 women), 64 part-time (49 women); includes 53 minority (50 African Americans, 2 American Indian/Alaska Native, 1 Hispanic American), 2 international. Average age 37. 57 applicants, 79% accepted, 41 enrolled. In 2009, 56 master's awarded. *Degree requirements:* For master's, portfolio, final project, clinical experience. *Entrance requirements:* For master's, GRE General Test or MAT, interview, recommendations, resume. Additional exam requirements/recommendations for international students: Required—TOEFL (minimum score 535 paper-based; 203 computer-based). *Application deadline:* Applications are processed on a rolling basis. Application fee: $30. Electronic applications accepted. *Expenses:* Tuition: Full-time $11,340; part-time $630 per credit hour. Tuition and fees vary according to program. *Financial support:* In 2009–10, 106 students received support, including 3 research assistantships with partial tuition reimbursements available (averaging $3,590 per year); scholarships/grants, traineeships, and unspecified assistantships also available. Financial award application deadline: 3/15; financial award applicants required to submit FAFSA. *Faculty research:* Instructional technology, achievement gap, classroom management, assessment. *Unit head:* Dr. Beverly Keepers, Dean, 502-588-7121, Fax: 502-585-7123, E-mail: bkeepers@spalding.edu. *Application contact:* Admissions Office, 502-585-7111, E-mail: admissions@spalding.edu.

Spring Arbor University, School of Education, Spring Arbor, MI 49283-9799. Offers education (MAE); special education (MSE). *Accreditation:* NCATE. Part-time programs available. *Faculty:* 8 full-time (5 women), 4 part-time/adjunct (1 woman). *Students:* 28 full-time (all women), 129 part-time (109 women); includes 12 minority (7 African Americans, 2 Asian Americans or Pacific Islanders, 3 Hispanic Americans), 1 international. Average age 38. In 2009, 69 master's awarded. *Degree requirements:* For master's, thesis. *Entrance requirements:* For master's, GRE if GPA is below 2.5, writing sample, 2 professional letters of recommendation. Additional exam requirements/recommendations for international students: Required—TOEFL (minimum score 550 paper-based; 220 computer-based). *Application deadline:* For fall admission, 9/1 priority date for domestic students; for winter admission, 2/1 priority date for domestic students; for spring admission, 2/1 priority date for domestic students. Applications are processed on a rolling basis. Application fee: $40. Electronic applications accepted. *Expenses:* Tuition: Full-time $5400; part-time $450 per credit hour. Required fees: $240; $150 per year. Tuition and fees vary according to course load and program. *Financial support:* Applicants required to submit FAFSA. *Unit head:* Dr. Linda Sherrill, Dean, 517-750-1200 Ext. 1562, Fax: 517-750-6629, E-mail: lsherril@arbor.edu. *Application contact:* Terri Reeves, Coordinator of Graduate Recruitment, 517-750-6554, Fax: 517-750-6629, E-mail: treeves@arbor.edu.

Springfield College, Graduate Programs, Program in Education, Springfield, MA 01109-3797. Offers counseling and secondary education (M Ed, MS); early childhood education (M Ed, MS); education (M Ed, MS); educational administration (M Ed, MS); educational studies (M Ed, MS); elementary education (M Ed, MS); secondary education (M Ed, MS); special education (M Ed, MS). Part-time and evening/weekend programs available. *Entrance requirements:* Additional exam requirements/recommendations for international students: Required—TOEFL (minimum score 550 paper-based; 213 computer-based). Electronic applications accepted. *Expenses:* Tuition: Full-time $19,800; part-time $825 per credit hour. Required fees: $150.

State University of New York at Binghamton, Graduate School, School of Education, Program in Special Education, Binghamton, NY 13902-6000. Offers MS Ed. *Accreditation:* Teacher Education Accreditation Council. Part-time and evening/weekend programs available. *Students:* 13 full-time (12 women), 25 part-time (19 women). Average age 28. 16 applicants, 81% accepted, 11 enrolled. In 2009, 12 master's awarded. *Entrance requirements:* For master's, GRE General Test. Additional exam requirements/recommendations for international students: Required—TOEFL (minimum score 550 paper-based; 213 computer-based; 80 iBT). *Application deadline:* For fall admission, 2/1 priority date for domestic and international students; for spring admission, 10/15 priority date for domestic and international students. Applications are processed on a rolling basis. Application fee: $60. Electronic applications accepted. *Financial support:* Fellowships, research assistantships, teaching assistantships with full tuition reimbursements, career-related internships or fieldwork, Federal Work-Study, institutionally sponsored loans, and unspecified assistantships available. Support available to part-time students. Financial award application deadline: 2/15. *Unit head:* Dr. Beverly Rainforth, Coordinator, 607-777-2277, E-mail: bevrain@binghamton.edu. *Application contact:* Victoria Williams, Recruiting and Admissions Coordinator, 607-777-2151, Fax: 607-777-2501, E-mail: vwilliam@binghamton.edu.

State University of New York at New Paltz, Graduate School, School of Education, Department of Educational Studies, Program in Special Education, New Paltz, NY 12561. Offers adolescence (7-12) (MS Ed); adolescence special education and literacy education (MS Ed); childhood (1-6) (MS Ed); childhood special education and literacy education (MS Ed); early childhood (B-2) (MS Ed). *Accreditation:* NCATE. Part-time and evening/weekend programs available. *Faculty:* 5 full-time (3 women), 7 part-time/adjunct (all women). *Students:* 33 full-time (30 women), 73 part-time (58 women); includes 4 minority (1 African American, 1 American Indian/Alaska Native, 1 Asian American or Pacific Islander, 1 Hispanic American). Average age 31. 53 applicants, 45% accepted, 19 enrolled. In 2009, 48 master's awarded. *Degree requirements:* For master's, portfolio. *Entrance requirements:* For master's, minimum GPA of 3.0 (3.2 for special education and literacy programs), NYS teaching certificate. Additional exam requirements/recommendations for international students: Required—TOEFL (minimum score 550 paper-based; 213 computer-based; 80 iBT), IELTS (minimum score 6.5). *Application deadline:* For fall admission, 3/15 priority date for domestic students, 3/15 for international students; for spring admission, 11/1 for domestic and international students. Application fee: $50. Electronic applications accepted. *Financial support:* In 2009–10, 1 student received support, including 1 fellowship (averaging $9,000 per year); career-related internships or fieldwork, Federal Work-Study, and institutionally sponsored loans also available. Financial award application deadline: 8/1; financial award applicants required to submit FAFSA. *Faculty research:* Grouping formats. *Unit head:* Dr. Spencer Salend, Coordinator, 845-257-2831,

Special Education

State University of New York at New Paltz (continued)
E-mail: salends@newpaltz.edu. *Application contact:* Dr. Catherine Whittaker, Coordinator, 845-257-2831, E-mail: whittakc@newpaltz.edu.

State University of New York at New Paltz, Graduate School, School of Education, Department of Elementary Education, New Paltz, NY 12561. Offers childhood education (MS Ed); childhood education (1-6) (MST); literacy education (5-12) (MS Ed); literacy education (B-6) (MS Ed); literacy education and adolescence special education (MS Ed); literacy education and childhood education and childhood special education (MS Ed). *Accreditation:* NCATE. Part-time and evening/weekend programs available. *Faculty:* 7 full-time (all women), 7 part-time/adjunct (5 women). *Students:* 61 full-time (54 women), 139 part-time (126 women); includes 8 minority (1 African American, 2 American Indian/Alaska Native, 2 Asian Americans or Pacific Islanders, 3 Hispanic Americans). Average age 30. 122 applicants, 63% accepted, 63 enrolled. In 2009, 81 master's awarded. *Degree requirements:* For master's, comprehensive exam (for some programs), portfolio. *Entrance requirements:* For master's, GRE and MAT (MST), minimum GPA of 3.0 (3.2 for literacy and special education), NYS teaching certificate (MS Ed). Additional exam requirements/recommendations for international students: Required—TOEFL (minimum score 550 paper-based; 213 computer-based; 80 iBT), IELTS (minimum score 6.5). *Application deadline:* For fall admission, 4/1 for domestic and international students; for spring admission, 11/15 for domestic and international students. Application fee: $50. Electronic applications accepted. *Financial support:* Federal Work-Study and institutionally sponsored loans available. Financial award application deadline: 8/1; financial award applicants required to submit FAFSA. *Faculty research:* Multi-sensory teaching methods, volunteer tutoring programs for struggling readers, school readiness and transition, math/science/technology, university-school partnerships. *Unit head:* Dr. Aaron Isabelle, Chair, 845-257-2860, E-mail: isabella@newpaltz.edu. *Application contact:* Caroline Murphy, Graduate Admissions Advisor, 845-257-3285, Fax: 845-257-3284, E-mail: gradschool@newpaltz.edu.

State University of New York at Oswego, Graduate Studies, School of Education, Department of Curriculum and Instruction, Oswego, NY 13126. Offers art education (MAT); elementary education (MS Ed); literacy education (MS Ed); secondary education (MS Ed); special education (MS Ed). Part-time and evening/weekend programs available. *Degree requirements:* For master's, comprehensive exam (for some programs), thesis optional. *Entrance requirements:* For master's, GRE General Test, minimum GPA of 2.7, provisional teaching certificate. Additional exam requirements/recommendations for international students: Required—TOEFL (minimum score 560 paper-based; 220 computer-based). *Faculty research:* Classroom applications for microcomputers; classroom questioning, wait-time, and achievement; values clarification and academic achievement.

State University of New York at Plattsburgh, Division of Education, Health, and Human Services, Program in Teacher Education: Special Education, Plattsburgh, NY 12901-2681. Offers birth to grade 2 (MS Ed); grades 1 to 6 (MS Ed); grades 7 to 12 (MS Ed). *Accreditation:* Teacher Education Accreditation Council. Part-time and evening/weekend programs available. *Faculty:* 7 full-time (4 women), 3 part-time/adjunct (2 women). *Students:* 20 full-time (18 women), 16 part-time (13 women). Average age 26. 22 applicants, 95% accepted, 16 enrolled. In 2009, 18 master's awarded. *Degree requirements:* For master's, thesis, portfolio. *Entrance requirements:* For master's, minimum GPA of 2.75. Additional exam requirements/recommendations for international students: Required—TOEFL (minimum score 550 paper-based; 213 computer-based; 79 iBT). *Application deadline:* For fall admission, 2/15 priority date for domestic students; for spring admission, 10/15 priority date for domestic students. Applications are processed on a rolling basis. Application fee: $75. *Expenses:* Tuition, state resident: full-time $8370; part-time $349 per credit hour. Tuition, nonresident: full-time $13,250; part-time $552 per credit hour. Required fees: $1130. *Financial support:* Federal Work-Study available. Support available to part-time students. Financial award application deadline: 4/15; financial award applicants required to submit FAFSA. *Faculty research:* Inclusion behavior management technology, applied behavior analysis. *Unit head:* Dr. Heidi Schnackenberg, Coordinator, 518-564-5143, E-mail: schnachl@plattsburgh.edu. *Application contact:* Marguerite Adelman, Assistant Director, Graduate Admissions, 518-564-4723, Fax: 518-564-4722, E-mail: adelmaml@plattsburgh.edu.

State University of New York College at Cortland, Graduate Studies, School of Education, Programs in Teaching Students with Disabilities, Cortland, NY 13045. Offers MS Ed. *Accreditation:* NCATE. Part-time and evening/weekend programs available. *Degree requirements:* For master's, one foreign language, comprehensive exam, thesis (for some programs). *Entrance requirements:* For master's, provisional certification. Additional exam requirements/recommendations for international students: Required—TOEFL.

State University of New York College at Oneonta, Graduate Education, Division of Education, Oneonta, NY 13820-4015. Offers educational psychology and counseling (MS Ed, CAS), including school counselor K-12; educational technology specialist (MS Ed); elementary education and reading (MS Ed), including childhood education, literacy education; secondary education (MS Ed), including adolescence education, family and consumer science education; special education (MS Ed), including adolescence, childhood. *Accreditation:* NCATE. Part-time and evening/weekend programs available. *Students:* 16 full-time (10 women), 66 part-time (39 women). Average age 25. 80 applicants, 94% accepted, 75 enrolled. In 2009, 18 master's awarded. *Entrance requirements:* For master's, GRE General Test. *Application deadline:* For fall admission, 3/25 priority date for domestic students; for spring admission, 10/1 priority date for domestic students. Applications are processed on a rolling basis. Application fee: $50. *Expenses:* Tuition, state resident: part-time $349 per credit hour. Tuition, nonresident: full-time $12,870; part-time $552 per credit hour. Required fees: $1280; $15.85 per credit hour. *Unit head:* Dr. Joanne Curran, Associate Dean, 607-436-2541, Fax: 607-436-2554, E-mail: curranjm@oneonta.edu. *Application contact:* Dean, 607-436-2523, Fax: 607-436-3084, E-mail: gradoffice@oneonta.edu.

State University of New York College at Potsdam, School of Education and Professional Studies, Program in Special Education, Potsdam, NY 13676. Offers birth-grade 2 (MS Ed); grades 1-6 (MS Ed); grades 5-9 (MS Ed); grades 7-12 (MS Ed). *Accreditation:* NCATE. *Faculty:* 3 full-time (1 woman), 5 part-time/adjunct (4 women). *Students:* 19 full-time (17 women), 6 part-time (4 women); includes 2 minority (1 African American, 1 American Indian/Alaska Native). 18 applicants, 100% accepted, 16 enrolled. In 2009, 11 master's awarded. *Degree requirements:* For master's, thesis optional, culminating experience. *Entrance requirements:* For master's, minimum GPA of 3.0 in last 60 hours of undergraduate course work. Additional exam requirements/recommendations for international students: Required—TOEFL (minimum score 550 paper-based; 213 computer-based; 80 iBT), IELTS (minimum score 6). *Application deadline:* For fall admission, 4/1 priority date for domestic and international students. Applications are processed on a rolling basis. Application fee: $50. *Expenses:* Tuition, state resident: full-time $8370; part-time $349 per credit hour. Tuition, nonresident: full-time $13,250; part-time $552 per credit hour. Required fees: $942; $38.70 per credit hour. *Financial support:* Unspecified assistantships available. Financial award application deadline: 3/1; financial award applicants required to submit FAFSA. *Unit head:* Dr. Anjali Misra, Chairperson, 315-267-2764, Fax: 315-267-4802, E-mail: misraa@potsdam.edu. *Application contact:* Peter Cutler, Graduate Admissions Counselor, 315-267-3154, Fax: 315-267-4802, E-mail: cutlerpj@potsdam.edu.

Stephen F. Austin State University, Graduate School, College of Education, Department of Human Services, Nacogdoches, TX 75962. Offers counseling (MA); school psychology (MA); special education (M Ed); speech pathology (MS). *Accreditation:* ACA (one or more programs are accredited); ASHA (one or more programs are accredited); CORE; NCATE. *Degree requirements:* For master's, comprehensive exam, thesis (for some programs). *Entrance requirements:* For master's, GRE General Test, minimum GPA of 2.8. Additional exam requirements/recommendations for international students: Required—TOEFL.

Syracuse University, School of Education, Program in Early Childhood Special Education, Syracuse, NY 13244. Offers MS. Part-time programs available. *Students:* 18 full-time (17 women), 16 part-time (15 women); includes 10 minority (6 African Americans, 1 American Indian/Alaska Native, 2 Asian Americans or Pacific Islanders, 1 Hispanic American). Average age 33. 21 applicants, 81% accepted, 8 enrolled. In 2009, 16 master's awarded. *Entrance requirements:* For master's, interview. Additional exam requirements/recommendations for international students: Required—TOEFL (minimum score 100 iBT). *Application deadline:* For fall admission, 2/1 for domestic students, 2/1 priority date for international students; for spring admission, 10/15 priority date for domestic and international students. Applications are processed on a rolling basis. Application fee: $75. Electronic applications accepted. *Expenses:* Tuition: Full-time $26,808; part-time $1117 per credit. Required fees: $1024. *Financial support:* Fellowships with tuition reimbursements, teaching assistantships with tuition reimbursements available. Financial award application deadline: 1/1; financial award applicants required to submit FAFSA. *Unit head:* Dr. Gail Ensher, Director, 315-443-9650. *Application contact:* Liza Rochelson, Graduate Recruiter, School of Education, 315-443-2505, E-mail: e-gradrcrt@syr.edu.

Syracuse University, School of Education, Program in Inclusive Special Education (grades 1-6), Syracuse, NY 13244. Offers MS. Part-time programs available. *Students:* 7 full-time (6 women), 1 part-time (0 women); includes 1 minority (Asian American or Pacific Islander). Average age 25. 6 applicants, 100% accepted, 5 enrolled. In 2009, 11 master's awarded. *Degree requirements:* For master's, thesis or alternative. *Entrance requirements:* For master's, provisional/initial certification. Additional exam requirements/recommendations for international students: Required—TOEFL (minimum score 100 iBT). *Application deadline:* For fall admission, 2/1 priority date for domestic and international students; for spring admission, 10/15 priority date for domestic and international students. Applications are processed on a rolling basis. Application fee: $75. Electronic applications accepted. *Expenses:* Tuition: Full-time $26,808; part-time $1117 per credit. Required fees: $1024. *Financial support:* Fellowships with tuition reimbursements, teaching assistantships with tuition reimbursements available. Financial award application deadline: 1/1; financial award applicants required to submit FAFSA. *Unit head:* Dr. Corinne Smith, Program Coordinator, 315-443-9321, E-mail: crsmith@syr.edu. *Application contact:* Liza Rochelson, Graduate Recruiter, School of Education, 315-443-2505, E-mail: e-gradrcrt@syr.edu.

Syracuse University, School of Education, Program in Inclusive Special Education (grades 7-12), Syracuse, NY 13244. Offers MS. Part-time programs available. *Students:* 2 full-time (0 women), 1 (woman) part-time; includes 1 minority (African American). Average age 23. 4 applicants, 75% accepted, 1 enrolled. In 2009, 6 master's awarded. *Degree requirements:* For master's, thesis or alternative. *Entrance requirements:* For master's, provisional/initial certification. Additional exam requirements/recommendations for international students: Required—TOEFL (minimum score 100 iBT). *Application deadline:* For fall admission, 2/1 priority date for domestic and international students; for spring admission, 10/15 priority date for domestic and international students. Applications are processed on a rolling basis. Application fee: $75. Electronic applications accepted. *Expenses:* Tuition: Full-time $26,808; part-time $1117 per credit. Required fees: $1024. *Financial support:* Fellowships with tuition reimbursements, teaching assistantships with tuition reimbursements, tuition waivers (partial) available. Financial award application deadline: 1/1; financial award applicants required to submit FAFSA. *Unit head:* Dr. Beth Ferri, Program Director, 315-443-1465, E-mail: baferri@syr.edu. *Application contact:* Liza Rochelson, Graduate Recruiter, School of Education, 315-443-2505, E-mail: e-gradrcrt@syr.edu.

Syracuse University, School of Education, Program in Inclusive Special Education: Severe/Multiple Disabilities, Syracuse, NY 13244. Offers MS. Part-time programs available. *Students:* 3 full-time (all women), 3 part-time (all women); includes 1 minority (Asian American or Pacific Islander). Average age 23. 2 applicants, 100% accepted, 1 enrolled. *Entrance requirements:* For master's, provisional/initial certification. Additional exam requirements/recommendations for international students: Required—TOEFL (minimum score 100 iBT). *Application deadline:* For fall admission, 2/1 priority date for domestic and international students; for spring admission, 10/15 priority date for domestic and international students. Applications are processed on a rolling basis. Application fee: $75. Electronic applications accepted. *Expenses:* Tuition: Full-time $26,808; part-time $1117 per credit. Required fees: $1024. *Financial support:* Fellowships with tuition reimbursements, teaching assistantships with tuition reimbursements, tuition waivers (partial) available. Financial award application deadline: 1/1. *Unit head:* Dr. Beth Ferri, Program Coordinator, 315-443-1465, E-mail: baferri@syr.edu. *Application contact:* Liza Rochelson, Graduate Recruiter, School of Education, 315-443-2505, E-mail: e-gradrcrt@syr.edu.

Syracuse University, School of Education, Program in Special Education, Syracuse, NY 13244. Offers PhD. Part-time and evening/weekend programs available. *Students:* 11 full-time (all women), 10 part-time (9 women); includes 3 minority (1 African American, 1 American Indian/Alaska Native, 1 Asian American or Pacific Islander), 5 international. Average age 39. 8 applicants, 13% accepted, 1 enrolled. *Degree requirements:* For doctorate, thesis/dissertation. *Entrance requirements:* For doctorate, GRE General Test, interview, writing sample. Additional exam requirements/recommendations for international students: Required—TOEFL (minimum score 100 iBT). *Application deadline:* For fall admission, 2/1 priority date for domestic and international students; for spring admission, 10/15 priority date for domestic and international students. Applications are processed on a rolling basis. Application fee: $75. Electronic applications accepted. *Expenses:* Tuition: Full-time $26,808; part-time $1117 per credit. Required fees: $1024. *Financial support:* Fellowships with tuition reimbursements, research assistantships with tuition reimbursements, teaching assistantships with tuition reimbursements, institutionally sponsored loans, health care benefits, and tuition waivers (full and partial) available. Financial award application deadline: 1/1. *Faculty research:* Aggression, inclusive education, autistic children, validation of social skills, cooperative learning in the heterogeneous classroom. *Unit head:* Dr. Beth Ferri, Program Director, 315-443-1465. *Application contact:* Liza Rochelson, Graduate Recruiter, School of Education, 315-443-2505, E-mail: e-gradrcrt@syr.edu.

Tarleton State University, College of Graduate Studies, College of Education, Department of Psychology and Counseling, Stephenville, TX 76402. Offers counseling and psychology (M Ed), including counseling, counseling psychology, educational psychology; educational administration (M Ed); secondary education (Certificate); special education (Certificate). Part-time and evening/weekend programs available. Postbaccalaureate distance learning degree programs offered (minimal on-campus study). *Degree requirements:* For master's, comprehensive exam, thesis optional. *Entrance requirements:* For master's, GRE General Test, minimum GPA of 3.0. Additional exam requirements/recommendations for international students: Required—TOEFL (minimum score 550 paper-based; 213 computer-based; 80 iBT). Electronic applications accepted.

Teachers College, Columbia University, Graduate Faculty of Education, Department of Curriculum and Teaching, Program in Dual Certificate Childhood/Disabilities, New York, NY 10027-6696. Offers Certificate. *Students:* 7 full-time (all women), 41 part-time (39 women); includes 13 minority (5 African Americans, 7 Asian Americans or Pacific Islanders, 1 Hispanic American), 6 international. Average age 30. 32 applicants, 59% accepted, 6 enrolled. Application fee: $65. *Unit head:* Marjorie Siegel, Chair, 212-678-3765. *Application contact:* Peter Shon, Assistant Director of Admission, 212-678-3305, Fax: 212-678-4171, E-mail: shon@exchange.tc.columbia.edu.

Teachers College, Columbia University, Graduate Faculty of Education, Department of Curriculum and Teaching, Program in Early Childhood Special Education, New York, NY 10027-6696. Offers Ed M, MA. *Accreditation:* NCATE. Evening/weekend programs available. *Faculty:* 1 (woman) full-time. *Students:* 36 full-time (34 women), 130 part-time (118 women); includes 42 minority (11 African Americans, 20 Asian Americans or Pacific Islanders, 11 Hispanic Americans), 16 international. Average age 26. 254 applicants, 56% accepted, 55 enrolled. In 2009, 78 master's awarded. *Application deadline:* For fall admission, 5/15 for

domestic students; for spring admission, 12/1 for domestic students. Application fee: $65. *Financial support:* Research assistantships, teaching assistantships, career-related internships or fieldwork, Federal Work-Study, institutionally sponsored loans, and tuition waivers (full and partial) available. Support available to part-time students. Financial award application deadline: 2/1. *Faculty research:* Curriculum development, infants, urban education, visually impaired infants. *Unit head:* Marjorie Siegel, Chair, 212-678-3765. *Application contact:* Peter Shon, Assistant Director of Admission, 212-678-3305, Fax: 212-678-4171, E-mail: shon@exchange.tc.columbia.edu.

Teachers College, Columbia University, Graduate Faculty of Education, Department of Curriculum and Teaching, Program in Learning Disabilities, New York, NY 10027-6696. Offers Ed M, MA, Ed D. *Accreditation:* NCATE. *Faculty:* 1 (woman) full-time. *Students:* 1 (woman) full-time. Average age 38. *Degree requirements:* For doctorate, thesis/dissertation. *Entrance requirements:* For doctorate, GRE General Test or MAT. *Application deadline:* For fall admission, 5/15 for domestic students; for spring admission, 12/1 for domestic students. Application fee: $75. *Financial support:* Fellowships, teaching assistantships, career-related internships or fieldwork, Federal Work-Study, institutionally sponsored loans, and tuition waivers (full and partial) available. Support available to part-time students. Financial award application deadline: 2/1. *Faculty research:* Reading and mathematics disorders in students with learning disabilities, special education curriculum development. *Unit head:* Marjorie Siegel, Chair, 212-678-3765. *Application contact:* Peter Shon, Assistant Director of Admission, 212-678-3305, Fax: 212-678-4171, E-mail: shon@exchange.tc.columbia.edu.

Teachers College, Columbia University, Graduate Faculty of Education, Department of Health and Behavioral Studies, Program in Behavioral Disorders, New York, NY 10027-6696. Offers MA, Ed D, PhD. Part-time programs available. *Students:* 2 full-time (both women), 12 part-time (11 women); includes 1 minority (Hispanic American), 4 international. Average age 30. Terminal master's awarded for partial completion of doctoral program. *Degree requirements:* For doctorate, thesis/dissertation. *Application deadline:* For fall admission, 5/15 for domestic students; for spring admission, 12/1 for domestic students. Application fee: $65. *Financial support:* Fellowships, research assistantships, career-related internships or fieldwork, Federal Work-Study, institutionally sponsored loans, and tuition waivers (full and partial) available. Support available to part-time students. Financial award application deadline: 2/1. *Faculty research:* Functional analysis of behavior, comprehensive analysis, comprehensive application of behavior analysis to schooling. *Unit head:* Dr. Chuck Basch, Chair, 212-678-3964, E-mail: ceb35@columbia.edu. *Application contact:* Peter Shon, Assistant Director of Admission, 212-678-3305, Fax: 212-678-4171, E-mail: shon@exchange.tc.columbia.edu.

Teachers College, Columbia University, Graduate Faculty of Education, Department of Health and Behavioral Studies, Program in Blind and Visual Impairment, New York, NY 10027-6696. Offers MA, Ed D. *Students:* 4 part-time (all women); includes 1 minority (African American), 1 international. Average age 39. 5 applicants, 60% accepted, 1 enrolled. In 2009, 2 master's awarded. *Degree requirements:* For doctorate, thesis/dissertation. *Application deadline:* For fall admission, 5/15 for domestic students; for spring admission, 12/1 for domestic students. Application fee: $65. *Financial support:* Career-related internships or fieldwork, Federal Work-Study, institutionally sponsored loans, and tuition waivers (full and partial) available. Support available to part-time students. Financial award application deadline: 2/1. *Faculty research:* Cross-modality transfer, issues in early childhood. *Unit head:* Dr. Chuck Basch, Chair, 212-678-3964, E-mail: ceb35@columbia.edu. *Application contact:* Peter Shon, Assistant Director of Admission, 212-678-3305, Fax: 212-678-4171, E-mail: shon@exchange.tc.columbia.edu.

Teachers College, Columbia University, Graduate Faculty of Education, Department of Health and Behavioral Studies, Program in Hearing Impairment, New York, NY 10027-6696. Offers MA, Ed D. *Faculty:* 1 full-time (0 women), 2 part-time/adjunct. *Students:* 10 full-time (all women), 16 part-time (15 women); includes 3 minority (1 African American, 2 Asian Americans or Pacific Islanders), 1 international. Average age 27. 16 applicants, 94% accepted, 10 enrolled. In 2009, 23 master's awarded. *Degree requirements:* For doctorate, thesis/dissertation. *Application deadline:* For fall admission, 5/15 for domestic students; for spring admission, 12/1 for domestic students. Application fee: $65. *Financial support:* Fellowships, career-related internships or fieldwork, Federal Work-Study, institutionally sponsored loans, and tuition waivers (full and partial) available. Support available to part-time students. Financial award application deadline: 2/1. *Faculty research:* Language development, reading/writing, cognitive abilities, text analysis, auditory streaming. *Unit head:* Dr. Chuck Basch, Chair, 212-678-3964, E-mail: ceb35@columbia.edu. *Application contact:* Peter Shon, Assistant Director of Admission, 212-678-3305, Fax: 212-678-4171, E-mail: shon@exchange.tc.columbia.edu.

Teachers College, Columbia University, Graduate Faculty of Education, Department of Health and Behavioral Studies, Program in Mental Retardation, New York, NY 10027-6696. Offers MA, Ed D, PhD. Part-time programs available. *Faculty:* 1 (woman) full-time, 2 part-time/adjunct. *Students:* 1 (woman) full-time, 7 part-time (6 women), 1 international. Average age 27. 51 applicants, 61% accepted. In 2009, 7 degrees awarded. Terminal master's awarded for partial completion of doctoral program. *Degree requirements:* For doctorate, thesis/dissertation. *Application deadline:* For fall admission, 5/15 for domestic students; for spring admission, 12/1 for domestic students. Application fee: $65. *Financial support:* Fellowships, research assistantships, teaching assistantships, career-related internships or fieldwork, Federal Work-Study, institutionally sponsored loans, and tuition waivers (full and partial) available. Support available to part-time students. Financial award application deadline: 2/1. *Faculty research:* Information processing, memory comprehension and problem-solving issues related to mental retardation, transition issues, cognition and comprehension. *Unit head:* Dr. Chuck Basch, Chair, 212-678-3964, E-mail: ceb35@columbia.edu. *Application contact:* Peter Shon, Assistant Director of Admission, 212-678-3305, Fax: 212-678-4171, E-mail: shon@exchange.tc.columbia.edu.

Teachers College, Columbia University, Graduate Faculty of Education, Department of Health and Behavioral Studies, Program in Physical Disabilities, New York, NY 10027-6696. Offers MA, Ed D, PhD. Part-time and evening/weekend programs available. *Students:* 5 part-time (all women). Average age 35. 1 applicant, 0% accepted, 0 enrolled. In 2009, 1 doctorate awarded. *Degree requirements:* For doctorate, variable foreign language requirement, thesis/dissertation. *Entrance requirements:* For doctorate, GRE General Test or MAT. *Application deadline:* For fall admission, 5/15 priority date for domestic students; for spring admission, 12/1 for domestic students. Applications are processed on a rolling basis. Application fee: $65. *Financial support:* Fellowships, teaching assistantships, career-related internships or fieldwork, Federal Work-Study, institutionally sponsored loans, and tuition waivers (full and partial) available. Support available to part-time students. Financial award application deadline: 2/1. *Faculty research:* Students with traumatic brain injury, health impairments, learning disabilities. *Unit head:* Dr. Chuck Basch, Chair, 212-678-3964, E-mail: ceb35@columbia.edu. *Application contact:* Peter Shon, Assistant Director of Admission, 212-678-3305, Fax: 212-678-4171, E-mail: shon@exchange.tc.columbia.edu.

Teachers College, Columbia University, Graduate Faculty of Education, Department of Health and Behavioral Studies, Program in Research in Special Education, New York, NY 10027-6696. Offers Ed D. *Accreditation:* NCATE. *Students:* 2 part-time (both women), 1 international. Average age 35. *Degree requirements:* For doctorate, thesis/dissertation. *Application deadline:* For fall admission, 5/15 for domestic students. Application fee: $75. *Financial support:* Career-related internships or fieldwork, Federal Work-Study, institutionally sponsored loans, and tuition waivers (full and partial) available. Support available to part-time students. Financial award application deadline: 2/1. *Unit head:* Dr. Chuck Basch, Chair, 212-678-3964, E-mail: ceb35@columbia.edu. *Application contact:* Peter Shon, Assistant Director of Admission, 212-678-3305, Fax: 212-678-4171, E-mail: shon@exchange.tc.columbia.edu.

Teachers College, Columbia University, Graduate Faculty of Education, Department of Health and Behavioral Studies, Program in Severe or Multiple Disabilities, New York, NY

10027-6696. Offers Ed M. *Students:* 1 (woman) full-time, 6 part-time (all women); includes 1 minority (African American), 1 international. Average age 25. 9 applicants, 89% accepted, 4 enrolled. In 2009, 3 master's awarded. *Application deadline:* For fall admission, 5/15 for domestic students. Application fee: $65. *Financial support:* Career-related internships or fieldwork, Federal Work-Study, institutionally sponsored loans, and tuition waivers (partial) available. Support available to part-time students. Financial award application deadline: 2/1. *Faculty research:* Reading and spelling disorders, workplace literacy, reading and writing among children and adults. *Unit head:* Dr. Chuck Basch, Chair, 212-678-3964, E-mail: ceb35@columbia.edu. *Application contact:* Director of Admissions, 212-678-3083, Fax: 212-678-4171.

Teachers College, Columbia University, Graduate Faculty of Education, Department of Health and Behavioral Studies, Program in Special Education, New York, NY 10027-6696. Offers Ed M, MA, Ed D. *Accreditation:* NCATE. Part-time and evening/weekend programs available. *Faculty:* 1 full-time (0 women), 3 part-time/adjunct. *Students:* 8 part-time (7 women); includes 1 minority (African American). Average age 40. 6 applicants, 0% accepted, 0 enrolled. In 2009, 1 master's, 1 doctorate awarded. Terminal master's awarded for partial completion of doctoral program. *Application deadline:* For fall admission, 5/15 for domestic students; for spring admission, 12/1 for domestic students. Application fee: $65. *Financial support:* Career-related internships or fieldwork, Federal Work-Study, institutionally sponsored loans, and tuition waivers (full and partial) available. Support available to part-time students. Financial award application deadline: 2/1. *Unit head:* Dr. Chuck Basch, Chair, 212-678-3964, E-mail: ceb35@columbia.edu. *Application contact:* Peter Shon, Assistant Director of Admission, 212-678-3305, Fax: 212-678-4171, E-mail: shon@exchange.tc.columbia.edu.

Teachers College, Columbia University, Graduate Faculty of Education, Department of Health and Behavioral Studies, Program in Teaching of Sign Language, New York, NY 10027-6696. Offers MA. *Accreditation:* NCATE. *Students:* 3 full-time (all women), 6 part-time (4 women); includes 1 minority (Hispanic American). Average age 25. 6 applicants, 83% accepted, 3 enrolled. In 2009, 7 master's awarded. Application fee: $65. *Unit head:* Dr. Chuck Basch, Chair, 212-678-3964, E-mail: ceb35@columbia.edu. *Application contact:* Peter Shon, Assistant Director of Admission, 212-678-3305, Fax: 212-678-4171, E-mail: shon@exchange.tc.columbia.edu.

Teachers College, Columbia University, Graduate Faculty of Education, Program in Administration and Supervision in Special Education, New York, NY 10027-6696. Offers Ed M, MA, Ed D, PhD. *Accreditation:* NCATE. *Students:* 1 (woman) full-time, 7 part-time (5 women); includes 1 minority (Asian American or Pacific Islander), 1 international. Average age 31. 3 applicants, 0% accepted, 0 enrolled. In 2009, 3 master's, 7 doctorates awarded. *Degree requirements:* For doctorate, thesis/dissertation. *Application deadline:* For fall admission, 5/15 for domestic students. Application fee: $65. *Financial support:* Career-related internships or fieldwork, Federal Work-Study, institutionally sponsored loans, and tuition waivers (full and partial) available. Support available to part-time students. Financial award application deadline: 2/1. *Faculty research:* Cognition and comprehension, disability studies, self-determination, literacy development. *Unit head:* Susan Furhman, President, 212-678-3050. *Application contact:* Ursula Felton, Office of Admissions, 212-678-3710, Fax: 212-678-4171.

Temple University, Graduate School, College of Education, Department of Curriculum, Instruction, and Technology in Education, Philadelphia, PA 19122-6096. Offers applied behavioral analysis (MS Ed); career and technical education (MS Ed); early childhood education and elementary education (MS Ed); English education (MS Ed); language arts education (Ed D); math/science education (Ed D); mathematics education (MS Ed); science education (MS Ed); second and foreign language education (MS Ed); special education (MS Ed); teaching English as a second language (MS Ed). Part-time and evening/weekend programs available. Terminal master's awarded for partial completion of doctoral program. *Degree requirements:* For master's, thesis or alternative; for doctorate, thesis/dissertation. *Entrance requirements:* For master's and doctorate, GRE General Test or MAT, minimum GPA of 3.0. Additional exam requirements/recommendations for international students: Required—TOEFL (minimum score 550 paper-based; 213 computer-based; 79 iBT). Electronic applications accepted. *Faculty research:* School improvement, problem solving, literacy, language development.

Tennessee State University, The School of Graduate Studies and Research, College of Education, Department of Teaching and Learning, Nashville, TN 37209-1561. Offers curriculum and instruction (M Ed, Ed D); elementary education (M Ed, MA Ed, Ed D); special education (M Ed, MA Ed, Ed D). *Accreditation:* NCATE. *Degree requirements:* For doctorate, thesis/dissertation. *Entrance requirements:* For master's, GRE General Test, GRE Subject Test, or MAT, minimum GPA of 2.5; for doctorate, GRE General Test, GRE Subject Test, or MAT, minimum GPA of 3.25. Electronic applications accepted. *Faculty research:* Multicultural education, teacher education reform, whole language, interactive video teaching, English as a second language.

Tennessee Technological University, Graduate School, College of Education, Department of Curriculum and Instruction, Program in Special Education, Cookeville, TN 38505. Offers MA, Ed S. *Accreditation:* NCATE. Part-time programs available. *Faculty:* 6 full-time (3 women). *Students:* 11 full-time (6 women), 20 part-time (16 women); includes 4 minority (2 African Americans, 2 Hispanic Americans). Average age 27. 29 applicants, 72% accepted, 13 enrolled. In 2009, 11 master's, 1 other advanced degree awarded. *Degree requirements:* For master's and Ed S, comprehensive exam, thesis or alternative. *Entrance requirements:* For master's and Ed S, MAT or GRE. Additional exam requirements/recommendations for international students: Required—TOEFL (minimum score 550 paper-based; 79 iBT), IELTS (minimum score 5.5). *Application deadline:* For fall admission, 8/1 for domestic students, 5/1 for international students; for spring admission, 12/1 for domestic students, 10/1 for international students. Application fee: $25 ($30 for international students). Electronic applications accepted. *Expenses:* Tuition, state resident: full-time $7034; part-time $368 per credit hour. *Financial support:* In 2009–10, fellowships (averaging $8,000 per year), research assistantships (averaging $5,000 per year), 2 teaching assistantships (averaging $4,000 per year) were awarded; career-related internships or fieldwork also available. Financial award application deadline: 4/1. *Unit head:* Dr. Matthew R. Smith, Chairperson, 931-372-3181, Fax: 931-372-6270. *Application contact:* Shelia K. Kendrick, Coordinator of Graduate Studies, 931-372-3808, Fax: 931-372-3497, E-mail: skendrick@tntech.edu.

Texas A&M International University, Office of Graduate Studies and Research, Department of Professional Programs, Laredo, TX 78041-1900. Offers educational administration (MS Ed); generic special education (MS Ed); school counseling (MS). *Faculty:* 9 full-time (3 women), 2 part-time/adjunct (1 woman). *Students:* 15 full-time (9 women), 152 part-time (120 women); includes 162 minority (1 African American, 161 Hispanic Americans). Average age 34. 59 applicants. In 2009, 74 master's awarded. *Application deadline:* For fall admission, 4/30 priority date for domestic students; for spring admission, 11/30 priority date for domestic students. *Financial support:* In 2009–10, 62 students received support, including 1 research assistantship. *Unit head:* Dr. Randel Brown, Interim Chair, 956-326-2679, E-mail: brown@tamiu.edu. *Application contact:* Rosie Dickinson, Director of Admissions, 956-326-2200.

Texas A&M University, College of Education and Human Development, Department of Educational Psychology, College Station, TX 77843. Offers counseling psychology (PhD); educational psychology (PhD); educational technology (M Ed); gifted and talented education (M Ed, MS); Hispanic bilingual education (M Ed, PhD); human learning and development (MS); intelligence, creativity, and giftedness (PhD); learning, development, and instruction (PhD); research, measurement and statistics (MS); research, measurement, and statistics (PhD); school counseling (M Ed); school psychology (PhD); special education (M Ed, PhD). *Accreditation:* APA (one or more programs are accredited). Part-time and evening/weekend programs available. Postbaccalaureate distance learning degree programs offered (no on-campus study). *Faculty:* 45. *Students:* 160 full-time (126 women), 144 part-time (118 women); includes 99 minority (25 African Americans, 13 Asian Americans or Pacific Islanders,

Special Education

Texas A&M University (continued)
61 Hispanic Americans), 41 international. In 2009, 53 master's, 30 doctorates awarded. *Degree requirements:* For master's, thesis optional; for doctorate, thesis/dissertation. *Entrance requirements:* For master's and doctorate, GRE General Test. Additional exam requirements/recommendations for international students: Required—TOEFL. Application fee: $50 ($75 for international students). Electronic applications accepted. *Expenses:* Tuition, state resident: full-time $3991; part-time $221.74 per credit hour. Tuition, nonresident: full-time $9049; part-time $502.74 per credit hour. *Financial support:* In 2009–10, fellowships (averaging $12,000 per year), research assistantships (averaging $9,000 per year), teaching assistantships (averaging $9,000 per year) were awarded; career-related internships or fieldwork, institutionally sponsored loans, scholarships/grants, and unspecified assistantships also available. Financial award applicants required to submit FAFSA. *Unit head:* Dr. Victor Willson, Head, 979-845-1800. *Application contact:* Carol A. Wagner, Director of Advising, 979-845-1833, Fax: 979-862-1256, E-mail: epsyadvisor@tamu.edu.

Texas A&M University–Commerce, Graduate School, College of Education and Human Services, Department of Psychology and Special Education, Commerce, TX 75429-3011. Offers cognition and instruction (PhD); psychology (MA, MS); special education (M Ed, MA, MS). Part-time programs available. Terminal master's awarded for partial completion of doctoral program. *Degree requirements:* For master's, comprehensive exam, thesis (for some programs); for doctorate, thesis/dissertation, departmental qualifying exam. *Entrance requirements:* For master's, GRE General Test; for doctorate, GRE General Test, 3 letters of recommendation. Electronic applications accepted. *Faculty research:* Human learning, study skills, multicultural bilingual, diversity and special education, educationally handicapped.

Texas A&M University–Corpus Christi, Graduate Studies and Research, College of Education, Program in Special Education, Corpus Christi, TX 78412-5503. Offers MS. Part-time and evening/weekend programs available. *Degree requirements:* For master's, comprehensive exam, thesis (for some programs). *Entrance requirements:* For master's, GRE General Test. Additional exam requirements/recommendations for international students: Required—TOEFL. Electronic applications accepted.

Texas A&M University–Kingsville, College of Graduate Studies, College of Education, Department of Education, Program in Special Education, Kingsville, TX 78363. Offers M Ed. Part-time and evening/weekend programs available. *Degree requirements:* For master's, comprehensive exam, mini-thesis. *Entrance requirements:* For master's, GRE General Test, MAT, minimum GPA of 3.0. *Faculty research:* Training for trainers of the disabled.

Texas A&M University–Texarkana, Graduate Studies and Research, College of Education and Liberal Arts, Texarkana, TX 75505-5518. Offers adult education (MS); curriculum and instruction (M Ed); education (MS); educational administration (M Ed); English (MA); instructional technology (MS); interdisciplinary studies (MA, MS); special education (MS). Part-time and evening/weekend programs available. *Degree requirements:* For master's, comprehensive exam (for some programs), thesis optional. *Entrance requirements:* For master's, minimum GPA of 2.5 on last 60 hours of bachelor's degree. Additional exam requirements/recommendations for international students: Required—TOEFL. Electronic applications accepted.

Texas Christian University, College of Education, Program in Special Education, Fort Worth, TX 76129-0002. Offers M Ed. Part-time and evening/weekend programs available. *Degree requirements:* For master's, oral exams. *Entrance requirements:* Additional exam requirements/recommendations for international students: Required—TOEFL (minimum score 550 paper-based; 213 computer-based; 80 iBT). *Application deadline:* For fall admission, 7/15 for domestic and international students; for spring admission, 11/15 for domestic and international students. Applications are processed on a rolling basis. Application fee: $50. *Expenses:* Tuition: Full-time $17,640; part-time $980 per credit hour. Tuition and fees vary according to program. *Financial support:* Teaching assistantships with full tuition reimbursements, career-related internships or fieldwork and unspecified assistantships available. Financial award application deadline: 3/15; financial award applicants required to submit FAFSA. *Unit head:* Dr. Kay B. Stevens, Associate Dean, 817-257-7661, E-mail: k.stevens2@tcu.edu. *Application contact:* Robyn P. Shepheard, Academic Program Specialist, 817-257-7661, E-mail: r.shepheard@tcu.edu.

Texas Christian University, College of Education, Program in Special Education (Four-One Option), Fort Worth, TX 76129-0002. Offers M Ed. Part-time and evening/weekend programs available. *Degree requirements:* For master's, oral exams. *Entrance requirements:* Additional exam requirements/recommendations for international students: Required—TOEFL (minimum score 550 paper-based; 213 computer-based; 80 iBT). *Application deadline:* For fall admission, 7/15 for domestic and international students; for spring admission, 11/15 for domestic and international students. Applications are processed on a rolling basis. Application fee: $50. *Expenses:* Tuition: Full-time $17,640; part-time $980 per credit hour. Tuition and fees vary according to program. *Financial support:* Teaching assistantships with full tuition reimbursements, career-related internships or fieldwork and unspecified assistantships available. Financial award application deadline: 3/15; financial award applicants required to submit FAFSA. *Unit head:* Dr. Kay B. Stevens, Associate Dean, 817-257-7661, E-mail: k.stevens2@tcu.edu. *Application contact:* Robyn P. Shepheard, Academic Program Specialist, 817-257-7661, E-mail: r.shepheard@tcu.edu.

Texas State University–San Marcos, Graduate School, College of Education, Department of Curriculum and Instruction, Program in Special Education, San Marcos, TX 78666. Offers M Ed. Part-time programs available. *Faculty:* 5 full-time (4 women), 2 part-time/adjunct (both women). *Students:* 28 full-time (23 women), 36 part-time (33 women); includes 14 minority (2 African Americans, 1 American Indian/Alaska Native, 11 Hispanic Americans), 1 international. Average age 31. 18 applicants, 94% accepted, 12 enrolled. In 2009, 13 master's awarded. *Degree requirements:* For master's, comprehensive exam. *Entrance requirements:* For master's, GRE General Test, minimum GPA of 2.75 in last 60 hour of course work, teaching experience. Additional exam requirements/recommendations for international students: Required—TOEFL (minimum score 550 paper-based; 213 computer-based). *Application deadline:* For fall admission, 6/15 priority date for domestic students; for spring admission, 10/15 priority date for domestic students. Applications are processed on a rolling basis. Application fee: $40 ($90 for international students). Electronic applications accepted. *Expenses:* Tuition, state resident: full-time $5784; part-time $241 per credit hour. Tuition, nonresident: full-time $13,224; part-time $551 per credit hour. Required fees: $1728; $48 per credit hour. $306. Tuition and fees vary according to course load. *Financial support:* In 2009–10, 46 students received support, including 2 research assistantships (averaging $3,143 per year), 2 teaching assistantships (averaging $5,076 per year); fellowships, career-related internships or fieldwork, Federal Work-Study, and institutionally sponsored loans also available. Support available to part-time students. Financial award application deadline: 4/1; financial award applicants required to submit FAFSA. *Faculty research:* Educational diagnostics; generic, severely handicapped, emotionally disturbed, autistic education. *Unit head:* Dr. Larry J. Wheeler, Graduate Adviser, 512-245-2157, Fax: 512-245-7911, E-mail: lw06@txstate.edu. *Application contact:* Dr. J. Michael Willoughby, Dean of Graduate School, 512-245-2581, Fax: 512-245-8365, E-mail: gradcollege@txstate.edu.

Texas Tech University, Graduate School, College of Education, Department of Educational Psychology and Leadership, Lubbock, TX 79409. Offers counselor education (M Ed, PhD); educational leadership (M Ed, Ed D); educational psychology (M Ed, PhD); higher education (M Ed, Ed D); higher education: higher education research (PhD); instructional technology (M Ed, Ed D); instructional technology: distance education (M Ed); special education (M Ed, Ed D). *Accreditation:* ACA; NCATE. Part-time programs available. *Students:* 137 full-time (94 women), 335 part-time (236 women); includes 90 minority (27 African Americans, 6 American Indian/Alaska Native, 3 Asian Americans or Pacific Islanders, 54 Hispanic Americans), 34 international. Average age 36. 390 applicants, 51% accepted, 90 enrolled. In 2009, 113 master's, 18 doctorates awarded. *Degree requirements:* For master's, thesis optional; for doctorate, thesis/dissertation. *Entrance requirements:* For master's and doctorate, GRE General Test. Additional exam requirements/recommendations for international students: Required—TOEFL (minimum score 550 paper-based; 213 computer-based). *Application deadline:* For fall admission, 3/1 priority date for international students; for spring admission, 11/1 priority date for international students. Applications are processed on a rolling basis. Application fee: $50 ($75 for international students). Electronic applications accepted. *Expenses:* Tuition, state resident: full-time $5100; part-time $213 per credit hour. Tuition, nonresident: full-time $11,748; part-time $490 per credit hour. Required fees: $2298; $50 per credit hour. $555 per semester. *Financial support:* Research assistantships with partial tuition reimbursements, teaching assistantships with partial tuition reimbursements, career-related internships or fieldwork, Federal Work-Study, and institutionally sponsored loans available. Support available to part-time students. Financial award application deadline: 4/15; financial award applicants required to submit FAFSA. *Faculty research:* Psychological processes of teaching and learning, teaching populations with special needs, instructional technology, educational administration in education, theories and practice in counseling and counselor education K-12 and higher. *Unit head:* Dr. William Lan, Chair, 806-742-1998 Ext. 436, Fax: 806-742-2179, E-mail: william.lan@ttu.edu. *Application contact:* Dr. Joseph G. Claudet, Graduate Adviser, 806-742-1998, Fax: 806-742-2179.

Texas Woman's University, Graduate School, College of Professional Education, Department of Teacher Education, Denton, TX 76201. Offers administration (M Ed, MA); elementary education (MA); special education (M Ed, MA, PhD), including educational diagnostician (M Ed, MA); teaching (MAT); teaching, learning, and curriculum (M Ed). Part-time programs available. *Faculty:* 19 full-time (13 women), 14 part-time/adjunct (11 women). *Students:* 36 full-time (29 women), 155 part-time (135 women); includes 65 minority (31 African Americans, 1 American Indian/Alaska Native, 3 Asian Americans or Pacific Islanders, 30 Hispanic Americans), 6 international. Average age 38. 48 applicants, 90% accepted, 21 enrolled. In 2009, 52 master's, 2 doctorates awarded. Terminal master's awarded for partial completion of doctoral program. *Degree requirements:* For master's, professional paper (MEd); for doctorate, comprehensive exam, thesis/dissertation. *Entrance requirements:* For master's, minimum GPA of 3.0, 3 letters of reference, curriculum vitae, copy of certifications, teacher service record; for doctorate, minimum GPA of 3.0, 3 letters of reference, curriculum vitae, copy of certifications, teacher service record, statement of intent. Additional exam requirements/recommendations for international students: Required—TOEFL (minimum score 550 paper-based; 213 computer-based; 79 iBT). *Application deadline:* For fall admission, 7/1 priority date for domestic students, 3/1 for international students; for spring admission, 11/1 priority date for domestic students, 7/1 for international students. Applications are processed on a rolling basis. Application fee: $50. Electronic applications accepted. *Expenses:* Tuition, state resident: full-time $3564; part-time $198 per credit hour. Tuition, nonresident: full-time $8550; part-time $475 per credit hour. Required fees: $69.26 per credit hour. Tuition and fees vary according to course load. *Financial support:* In 2009–10, 47 students received support, including 5 research assistantships (averaging $10,440 per year); career-related internships or fieldwork, Federal Work-Study, institutionally sponsored loans, scholarships/grants, traineeships, health care benefits, and unspecified assistantships also available. Support available to part-time students. Financial award application deadline: 3/1; financial award applicants required to submit FAFSA. *Faculty research:* Language and literacy, classroom management, learning disabilities, staff and professional development, leadership preparation practice. *Unit head:* Dr. Jane Pemberton, Interim Chair, 940-898-2271, Fax: 940-898-2270, E-mail: jpemberton@twu.edu. *Application contact:* Samuel Wheeler, Assistant Director of Admissions, 940-898-3188, Fax: 940-898-3081, E-mail: wheelersr@twu.edu.

Towson University, College of Graduate Studies and Research, Program in Special Education, Towson, MD 21252-0001. Offers special education leadership (M Ed). *Accreditation:* NCATE. Part-time and evening/weekend programs available. *Degree requirements:* For master's, thesis optional. *Entrance requirements:* For master's, letter of recommendation, professional teacher certification, minimum GPA of 3.0. Additional exam requirements/recommendations for international students: Required—TOEFL (minimum score 550 paper-based). Electronic applications accepted. *Faculty research:* Parent involvement, transition to adulthood, cultural diversity in special education.

Trinity Baptist College, Graduate Programs, Jacksonville, FL 32221. Offers Bible (M Ed); Christian school administration (M Ed); classroom practices (M Ed); ministry (M Min); special education (M Ed). Postbaccalaureate distance learning degree programs offered. *Entrance requirements:* For master's, GRE (M Ed), 2 letters of recommendation; minimum GPA of 2.5 (M Min) or 3.0 (M Ed); computer proficiency.

Trinity (Washington) University, School of Education, Washington, DC 20017-1094. Offers counseling (MA); early childhood education (MAT); educating for change (M Ed); educational administration (MSA); elementary education (MAT); school counseling (MA); secondary education (MAT), including English, social studies; special education (MAT); teaching English as a second language (MAT); teaching English to speakers of other languages (M Ed); the teaching of reading (M Ed). *Accreditation:* NCATE. Part-time and evening/weekend programs available. *Degree requirements:* For master's, thesis (for some programs), capstone project(s). *Entrance requirements:* For master's, PRAXIS I, minimum GPA of 2.8. Additional exam requirements/recommendations for international students: Required—TOEFL (minimum score 550 paper-based; 213 computer-based). *Faculty research:* Technology, literacy, special education, organizations, inclusion models.

Union College, Graduate Programs, Department of Education, Program in Special Education, Barbourville, KY 40906-1499. Offers MA. *Degree requirements:* For master's, thesis optional. *Entrance requirements:* For master's, GRE General Test, NTE.

Union Institute & University, Education Programs–Florida Center, North Miami Beach, FL 33162. Offers educational leadership (M Ed, Ed S); exceptional student education (M Ed, Ed S); guidance and counseling (M Ed, Ed S); reading (M Ed, Ed S). *Faculty:* 3 full-time (1 woman), 23 part-time/adjunct (19 women). *Students:* 32 full-time (21 women); includes 23 minority (21 African Americans, 2 Hispanic Americans). Average age 37. In 2009, 8 master's, 3 Ed Ss awarded. *Degree requirements:* For master's, thesis or alternative, portfolio. *Entrance requirements:* For master's, letters of recommendation. *Application deadline:* Applications are processed on a rolling basis. Application fee: $50. *Expenses:* Contact institution. *Financial support:* Federal Work-Study, scholarships/grants, and tuition waivers (partial) available. Financial award applicants required to submit FAFSA. *Unit head:* Dr. Arlene Sacks, Dean, 305-653-6713 Ext. 2152, E-mail: arlene.sacks@myunion.edu. *Application contact:* Josefina Rosario, Admissions Counselor, 305-653-6713 Ext. 2172, E-mail: admissions@tui.edu.

Union Institute & University, M Ed Program–Vermont Campus, Montpelier, VT 05602. Offers school administration (M Ed), including principalship; school counseling (M Ed); teaching (M Ed), including art, early childhood, elementary, English, math, middle schools, science, social studies, special education. *Faculty:* 3 full-time (1 woman), 23 part-time/adjunct (19 women). *Students:* 41 part-time (29 women). Average age 38. In 2009, 15 master's awarded. *Degree requirements:* For master's, thesis. *Entrance requirements:* For master's, 3 letters of reference. *Application deadline:* Applications are processed on a rolling basis. Application fee: $50. *Expenses:* Contact institution. *Financial support:* Federal Work-Study, scholarships/grants, and tuition waivers available. Financial award applicants required to submit FAFSA. *Unit head:* Dr. Arlene Sacks, Dean, Graduate Programs in Education, 305-653-6713 Ext. 2152, E-mail: arlene.sacks@myunion.edu. *Application contact:* Dr. Arlene Sacks, Dean, Graduate Programs in Education, 305-653-6713 Ext. 2152, E-mail: arlene.sacks@myunion.edu.

Universidad del Este, Graduate School, Carolina, PR 00984. Offers accounting (MBA); adult education (M Ed); agribusiness (MBA); bilingual education (M Ed); criminal justice and criminology (MA); early education (M Ed); elementary education (M Ed); human resources (MBA); information security management (MBA); information technology and Web business development (MBA); management (MBA); public policy (MPA); social work (MA), including

clinical social work; special education (M Ed); strategic leadership (MBA); teaching English (M Ed); teaching Spanish (M Ed).

Universidad del Turabo, Graduate Programs, Programs in Education, Program in Special Education, Gurabo, PR 00778-3030. Offers M Ed. *Faculty:* 3 full-time (1 woman), 13 part-time/adjunct (8 women). *Students:* 18 full-time (15 women), 52 part-time (48 women); includes 64 Hispanic Americans. Average age 34. 22 applicants, 86% accepted, 13 enrolled. In 2009, 45 master's awarded. *Entrance requirements:* For master's, GRE, EXADEP, interview. *Application deadline:* For fall admission, 8/5 for domestic students. Application fee: $25. *Financial support:* Institutionally sponsored loans available. *Unit head:* Angela Candelario, Dean, 787-743-7979 Ext. 4126. *Application contact:* Virginia Gonzalez, Admissions Officer, 787-746-3009.

Universidad Iberoamericana, Graduate School, Santo Domingo D.N., Dominican Republic. Offers advertising management (MM); business (MBA); constitutional law (MA); dentistry (DMD); educational management (MA); integrated marketing communication (MA); psychopedagogical intervention (M Ed); strategic management of human talent (MM).

Universidad Metropolitana, Graduate Programs in Education, Program in Special Education, San Juan, PR 00928-1150. Offers M Ed. *Degree requirements:* For master's, thesis or alternative. Electronic applications accepted.

Université de Sherbrooke, Faculty of Education, Program in Special Education, Sherbrooke, QC J1K 2R1, Canada. Offers M Ed, Diploma. Part-time and evening/weekend programs available. *Degree requirements:* For master's, thesis.

University at Albany, State University of New York, School of Education, Department of Educational and Counseling Psychology, Program in Special Education, Albany, NY 12222-0001. Offers MS. *Entrance requirements:* Additional exam requirements/recommendations for international students: Required—TOEFL (minimum score 550 paper-based; 213 computer-based). Electronic applications accepted.

University at Buffalo, the State University of New York, Graduate School, Graduate School of Education, Department of Learning and Instruction, Buffalo, NY 14260. Offers biology education (Ed M, Certificate); chemistry education (Ed M, Certificate); childhood education (Ed M); childhood education with bilingual extension (Ed M); early childhood education (Ed M); earth science education (Ed M, Certificate); elementary education (Ed D, PhD); English education (Ed M, PhD, Certificate); English for speakers of other languages (Ed M); foreign and second language education (PhD); French education (Ed M, Certificate); general education (Ed M); German education (Ed M, Certificate); gifted education (online) (Certificate); Latin education (Ed M, Certificate); literary specialist (Ed M); mathematics education (Ed M, PhD, Certificate); music education (Ed M, Certificate); physics education (Ed M, Certificate); reading education (PhD); science and the public (online) (Ed M); science education (PhD); social studies education (Ed M, Certificate); Spanish education (Ed M, Certificate); special education (PhD); teaching and leading for diversity (Certificate); teaching English to speakers of other languages (Ed M). Part-time and evening/weekend programs available. Postbaccalaureate distance learning degree programs offered (no on-campus study). *Faculty:* 34 full-time (24 women), 50 part-time/adjunct (39 women). *Students:* 332 full-time (245 women), 365 part-time (272 women); includes 50 minority (18 African Americans, 4 American Indian/Alaska Native, 10 Asian Americans or Pacific Islanders, 18 Hispanic Americans), 55 international. Average age 30. 627 applicants, 78% accepted, 286 enrolled. In 2009, 255 master's, 16 doctorates, 51 other advanced degrees awarded. *Degree requirements:* For master's, comprehensive exam; for doctorate, thesis/dissertation, research analysis exam, research experience component. *Entrance requirements:* For doctorate, GRE General Test or MAT, interview, writing sample, letters of recommendation. Additional exam requirements/recommendations for international students: Required—TOEFL (minimum score 600 paper-based; 250 computer-based; 96 iBT). *Application deadline:* For fall admission, 2/1 priority date for domestic and international students; for spring admission, 11/15 priority date for domestic students, 10/1 for international students. Applications are processed on a rolling basis. Application fee: $50. Electronic applications accepted. *Financial support:* In 2009–10, 23 fellowships with full tuition reimbursements (averaging $9,000 per year), 42 research assistantships with full tuition reimbursements (averaging $10,000 per year) were awarded; teaching assistantships with full tuition reimbursements, career-related internships or fieldwork, Federal Work-Study, institutionally sponsored loans, scholarships/grants, tuition waivers (partial), and unspecified assistantships also available. Financial award application deadline: 2/28; financial award applicants required to submit FAFSA. *Faculty research:* Science assessment, foreign language teaching and learning, early learning, new literacies, gender and education. Total annual research expenditures: $1.8 million. *Unit head:* Dr. Suzanne Miller, Chair, 716-645-2455, Fax: 716-645-3161, E-mail: smiller@buffalo.edu. *Application contact:* Cathy Dimino, Admissions Assistant, 716-645-2110, Fax: 716-645-7937, E-mail: cadimino@buffalo.edu.

The University of Akron, Graduate School, College of Education, Department of Curricular and Instructional Studies, Program in Special Education, Akron, OH 44325. Offers MA, MS. *Accreditation:* NCATE. *Students:* 51 full-time (43 women), 112 part-time (89 women); includes 11 minority (10 African Americans, 1 Asian American or Pacific Islander), 3 international. Average age 36. 56 applicants, 41% accepted, 16 enrolled. In 2009, 36 master's awarded. *Degree requirements:* For master's, comprehensive exam. *Entrance requirements:* For master's, speech and hearing test, minimum GPA of 2.75, letters of recommendation, criminal background check, computer literacy, valid teaching license. Additional exam requirements/recommendations for international students: Required—TOEFL (minimum score 550 paper-based; 213 computer-based; 79 iBT). *Application deadline:* Applications are processed on a rolling basis. Application fee: $30 ($40 for international students). Electronic applications accepted. *Expenses:* Tuition, state resident: full-time $6570; part-time $365 per credit hour. Tuition, nonresident: full-time $11,250; part-time $625 per credit hour. *Unit head:* Dr. Bridgie Ford, Chair, 330-972-6967, E-mail: alexis2@uakron.edu. *Application contact:* Dr. Bridgie Ford, Chair, 330-972-6967, E-mail: alexis2@uakron.edu.

The University of Alabama, Graduate School, College of Education, Department of Special Education and Multiple Abilities, Tuscaloosa, AL 35487. Offers collaborative teacher program (M Ed, Ed S); early intervention (M Ed, Ed S); gifted education (M Ed, Ed S); multiple abilities program (M Ed); special education (Ed D, PhD). Part-time and evening/weekend programs available. *Faculty:* 11 full-time (8 women). *Students:* 20 full-time (17 women), 50 part-time (46 women); includes 13 minority (8 African Americans, 3 American Indian/Alaska Native, 2 Hispanic Americans). Average age 32. 45 applicants, 40% accepted, 13 enrolled. In 2009, 33 master's, 2 other advanced degrees awarded. Terminal master's awarded for partial completion of doctoral program. *Degree requirements:* For master's, comprehensive exam, thesis optional; for doctorate, one foreign language, comprehensive exam, thesis/dissertation. *Entrance requirements:* For master's, GRE or MAT, minimum undergraduate GPA of 3.0, teaching certificate, 3 letters of recommendation; for doctorate, GRE or MAT, 3 years of teaching experience, minimum undergraduate GPA of 3.25. Additional exam requirements/recommendations for international students: Required—TOEFL. *Application deadline:* For fall admission, 7/1 for domestic students; for spring admission, 11/1 for domestic students. Applications are processed on a rolling basis. Application fee: $50 ($60 for international students). Electronic applications accepted. *Expenses:* Tuition, state resident: full-time $7000. Tuition, nonresident: full-time $19,200. *Financial support:* In 2009–10, 8 students received support, including 4 research assistantships with tuition reimbursements available (averaging $9,000 per year), 4 teaching assistantships with tuition reimbursements available (averaging $9,000 per year); health care benefits and unspecified assistantships also available. Financial award application deadline: 7/1; financial award applicants required to submit FAFSA. *Faculty research:* Gifted education, mild disabilities, early intervention, severe disabilities. *Unit head:* James A. Siders, Associate Professor and Head, 205-348-5577, Fax: 205-348-6782, E-mail: jsiders@bama.ua.edu. *Application contact:* April Zark, Office Support, 205-348-6093, Fax: 205-348-6782, E-mail: azark@bamaed.ua.edu.

The University of Alabama at Birmingham, College of Arts and Sciences, School of Education, Program in Special Education, Birmingham, AL 35294. Offers MA Ed. *Accreditation:* NCATE. *Degree requirements:* For master's, thesis optional. *Entrance requirements:* For master's, GRE General Test or NTE, minimum GPA of 3.0. Electronic applications accepted.

University of Alaska Anchorage, College of Education, Program in Special Education, Anchorage, AK 99508. Offers early childhood special education (M Ed); special education (M Ed, Certificate). Part-time programs available. *Degree requirements:* For master's, comprehensive exam (for some programs), thesis or alternative. *Entrance requirements:* For master's, GRE or MAT, interview, minimum GPA of 2.75. Additional exam requirements/recommendations for international students: Required—TOEFL (minimum score 550 paper-based; 213 computer-based). *Faculty research:* Mild disabilities, substance abuse issues for educators, partnerships to improve at-risk youth, analysis of planning models for teachers in special education.

University of Alberta, Faculty of Graduate Studies and Research, Department of Educational Psychology, Edmonton, AB T6G 2E1, Canada. Offers counseling psychology (M Ed, PhD); educational psychology (M Ed, PhD); instructional technology (M Ed); school counseling (M Ed); school psychology (M Ed, PhD); special education (M Ed, PhD); special education-deafness studies (M Ed); teaching English as a second language (M Ed). Part-time programs available. *Faculty:* 34 full-time (14 women), 12 part-time/adjunct (6 women). *Students:* 117 full-time (93 women), 173 part-time (121 women). Average age 36. 252 applicants, 34% accepted. In 2009, 30 master's, 10 doctorates awarded. *Degree requirements:* For master's, thesis optional; for doctorate, comprehensive exam, thesis/dissertation. *Entrance requirements:* For master's and doctorate, minimum GPA of 3.0. Additional exam requirements/recommendations for international students: Required—TOEFL. *Application deadline:* For fall admission, 2/1 priority date for domestic and international students. Applications are processed on a rolling basis. Tuition and fees charges are reported in Canadian dollars. *Expenses:* Tuition, area resident: Full-time $4626 Canadian dollars; part-time $99.72 Canadian dollars per unit. International tuition: $8216 Canadian dollars full-time. Required fees: $3590 Canadian dollars; $99.72 Canadian dollars per unit. $215 Canadian dollars per term. *Financial support:* In 2009–10, 10 fellowships with full tuition reimbursements (averaging $16,120 per year), 36 research assistantships with full tuition reimbursements (averaging $12,614 per year), 46 teaching assistantships with full tuition reimbursements (averaging $5,462 per year) were awarded; career-related internships or fieldwork and scholarships/grants also available. *Faculty research:* Human learning, development and assessment. *Unit head:* Dr. Linda M. McDonald, Chair, 780-492-1149, Fax: 780-492-1318, E-mail: linda.mcdonald@ualberta.ca. *Application contact:* Judy Maynes, Information Contact, 780-492-1149, Fax: 780-492-1318, E-mail: edpygrad@ualberta.ca.

University of Arkansas, Graduate School, College of Education and Health Professions, Department of Curriculum and Instruction, Program in Special Education, Fayetteville, AR 72701-1201. Offers M Ed, MAT. *Accreditation:* NCATE. Part-time and evening/weekend programs available. Postbaccalaureate distance learning degree programs offered (no on-campus study). *Students:* 5 full-time (1 woman), 71 part-time (61 women); includes 13 minority (8 African Americans, 4 American Indian/Alaska Native, 1 Asian American or Pacific Islander). In 2009, 4 master's awarded. *Entrance requirements:* For master's, GRE General Test or MAT. Application fee: $40 ($50 for international students). *Expenses:* Tuition, state resident: full-time $7355; part-time $356.58 per hour. Tuition, nonresident: full-time $17,401; part-time $775.17 per hour. Required fees: $1203. *Financial support:* Fellowships, research assistantships, teaching assistantships, career-related internships or fieldwork and Federal Work-Study available. Support available to part-time students. Financial award application deadline: 4/1; financial award applicants required to submit FAFSA. *Unit head:* Dr. Michael Daugherty, Unit Head, 479-575-4209, E-mail: mkd03@uark.edu. *Application contact:* Dr. William McComas, Graduate Coordinator, 479-575-7525, E-mail: mccomas@uark.edu.

University of Arkansas at Little Rock, Graduate School, College of Education, Department of Counseling and Rehabilitation Education, Little Rock, AR 72204-1099. Offers adult education (M Ed); counselor education (M Ed), including school counseling; orientation and mobility of the blind (Graduate Certificate); rehabilitation counseling (MA, Graduate Certificate); rehabilitation of the blind (MA). *Accreditation:* CORE; NCATE. Part-time programs available. *Entrance requirements:* For master's, interview, minimum GPA of 2.75. *Faculty research:* Low vision, orientation and mobility instruction.

University of Arkansas at Little Rock, Graduate School, College of Education, Department of Teacher Education, Program in Special Education, Little Rock, AR 72204-1099. Offers teaching deaf and hard of hearing (M Ed); teaching the visually impaired (M Ed). *Accreditation:* NCATE. Part-time and evening/weekend programs available. *Degree requirements:* For master's, comprehensive exam, portfolio or thesis. *Entrance requirements:* For master's, interview, minimum GPA of 2.75, GRE General Test or teaching certificate.

The University of British Columbia, Faculty of Education, Department of Educational and Counseling Psychology, and Special Education, Vancouver, BC V6T 1Z1, Canada. Offers counseling psychology (M Ed, MA, PhD); development, learning and culture (PhD); guidance studies (Diploma); human development, learning and culture (M Ed, MA); measurement and evaluation and research methodology (M Ed); measurement, evaluation and research methodology (MA); measurement, evaluation, and research methodology (PhD); school psychology (M Ed, MA, PhD); special education (M Ed, MA, PhD, Diploma). Part-time programs available. *Degree requirements:* For master's, thesis (for some programs); for doctorate, comprehensive exam, thesis/dissertation. *Entrance requirements:* For master's, GRE General Test (counseling psychology MA); for doctorate, GRE General Test. Additional exam requirements/recommendations for international students: Required—TOEFL. Electronic applications accepted. *Faculty research:* Women, family, social problems, career transition, stress and coping problems.

University of Calgary, Faculty of Graduate Studies, Faculty of Education, Division of Applied Psychology, Calgary, AB T2N 1N4, Canada. Offers counseling psychology (M Ed, M Sc, PhD); human development and learning (M Ed, M Sc, PhD); school psychology (M Ed, M Sc, PhD); special education (M Ed, M Sc, PhD). Part-time programs available. *Degree requirements:* For master's, thesis (for some programs), final oral exam; for doctorate, thesis/dissertation, candidacy exam, final oral exam. *Entrance requirements:* For master's, minimum GPA of 3.0, 3 letters of reference; for doctorate, minimum GPA of 3.5, 3 letters of reference. *Faculty research:* Counselor education, family life studies, learning and cognition.

University of California, Berkeley, Graduate Division, School of Education, Program in Special Education, Berkeley, CA 94720-1500. Offers PhD. Applicants must apply to both the University of California, Berkeley and San Francisco State University. *Students:* 17 full-time (14 women). Average age 34. 17 applicants, 3 enrolled. In 2009, 3 doctorates awarded. *Degree requirements:* For doctorate, thesis/dissertation, oral qualifying exam. *Entrance requirements:* For doctorate, GRE General Test, minimum undergraduate GPA of 3.0 during last 2 years, 3 letters of recommendation. *Application deadline:* For fall admission, 12/1 for domestic students. Application fee: $70 ($90 for international students). Electronic applications accepted. *Financial support:* Fellowships, unspecified assistantships available. *Unit head:* Dr. P. David Pearson, Coordinator, 510-642-3726, E-mail: gsedeansoffice@lists.berkeley.edu. *Application contact:* Admissions Office, 510-642-0841, Fax: 510-642-4808, E-mail: gse_info@berkeley.edu.

University of California, Berkeley, Graduate Division, School of Education, Programs in Education, Berkeley, CA 94720-1500. Offers development in mathematics and science (MA); education in mathematics, science, and technology (MA, PhD); human development and education (MA, PhD); special education (PhD); MA/Credential; Ph D/Credential; PhD/MA. *Students:* 374 full-time (270 women). Average age 33. 674 applicants, 111 enrolled. In 2009, 120 master's, 25 doctorates awarded. Terminal master's awarded for partial completion of

Special Education

University of California, Berkeley (continued)
doctoral program. *Degree requirements:* For master's, exam or thesis; for doctorate, thesis/dissertation, oral qualifying exam. *Entrance requirements:* For master's and doctorate, GRE General Test, minimum GPA of 3.0 during last 2 years of undergraduate course work. *Application deadline:* For fall admission, 12/1 for domestic students. Application fee: $70 ($90 for international students). Electronic applications accepted. *Financial support:* Fellowships, research assistantships, teaching assistantships, unspecified assistantships available. *Faculty research:* Human development, social and moral educational psychology, developmental teacher preparation. *Unit head:* Prof. P. David Pearson, Dean, 510-642-3726, E-mail: gsedeansoffice@lists.berkeley.edu. *Application contact:* Admissions Office, 510-642-0841, Fax: 510-642-4808, E-mail: gse_info@uclink.berkeley.edu.

University of California, Los Angeles, Graduate Division, Graduate School of Education and Information Studies, Program in Special Education, Los Angeles, CA 90095. Offers PhD. *Degree requirements:* For doctorate, thesis/dissertation, oral and written qualifying exams. *Entrance requirements:* For doctorate, GRE General Test, minimum undergraduate GPA of 3.0. Additional exam requirements/recommendations for international students: Required—TOEFL (minimum score 560 paper-based; 220 computer-based; 87 iBT). Electronic applications accepted.

University of California, Riverside, Graduate Division, Graduate School of Education, Riverside, CA 92521-0102. Offers autism (M Ed); curriculum and instruction (MA, PhD); diversity and equity (M Ed); educational leadership and policy (MA, PhD); educational psychology (MA, PhD); general education (M Ed); higher education administration and policy (M Ed, PhD); leadership (M Ed); reading (M Ed); school psychology (PhD); special education (M Ed, MA, PhD). *Faculty:* 23 full-time (12 women), 12 part-time/adjunct (8 women). *Students:* 230 full-time (183 women), 6 part-time (3 women); includes 75 minority (12 African Americans, 1 American Indian/Alaska Native, 21 Asian Americans or Pacific Islanders, 41 Hispanic Americans), 6 international. Average age 32. 288 applicants, 60% accepted, 118 enrolled. In 2009, 68 master's, 13 doctorates awarded. Terminal master's awarded for partial completion of doctoral program. *Degree requirements:* For master's, comprehensive exam (for some programs), comprehensive exams or thesis (MA), case study or analytical report (M Ed); for doctorate, thesis/dissertation, written and oral qualifying exams, college teaching practicum. *Entrance requirements:* For master's, GRE General Test, GRE Subject Test, CBEST, CSET, minimum GPA of 3.2; for doctorate, GRE General Test, GRE Subject Test, master's degree (desirable), minimum GPA of 3.2. Additional exam requirements/recommendations for international students: Required—TOEFL (minimum score 550 paper-based; 213 computer-based; 80 iBT). *Application deadline:* For fall admission, 9/1 for domestic students, 4/1 for international students; for winter admission, 12/1 for domestic students, 9/1 for international students; for spring admission, 3/1 for domestic students, 10/1 for international students. Applications are processed on a rolling basis. Application fee: $70 ($85 for international students). Electronic applications accepted. *Financial support:* In 2009–10, 55 students received support, including 13 fellowships with full and partial tuition reimbursements available (averaging $26,809 per year), 21 research assistantships with full and partial tuition reimbursements available (averaging $14,238 per year), 1 teaching assistantship with full and partial tuition reimbursement available (averaging $16,638 per year); career-related internships or fieldwork, Federal Work-Study, institutionally sponsored loans, scholarships/grants, and unspecified assistantships also available. Financial award application deadline: 1/5; financial award applicants required to submit FAFSA. *Faculty research:* Responsiveness to intervention, faculty core, response to intervention of English language learners, advanced modeling techniques, study on social capital, trust, and motivation. Total annual research expenditures: $5.6 million. *Unit head:* Dr. Steven T. Bossert, Dean, 951-827-5802, Fax: 951-827-3942, E-mail: steven.bossert@ucr.edu. *Application contact:* Dr. John Wills, Graduate Advisor for Admission, 951-827-6362, Fax: 951-827-3942, E-mail: edgrad@ucr.edu.

University of California, Santa Barbara, Graduate Division, Gevirtz Graduate School of Education, Santa Barbara, CA 93106-9490. Offers counseling, clinical and school psychology (PhD), including clinical psychology, counseling psychology, school psychology; education (M Ed, MA, PhD), including child and adolescent development (MA, PhD), cultural perspectives and comparative education (MA, PhD), educational leadership and organizations (MA, PhD), research methodology (MA, PhD), special education disabilities and risk studies (MA), special education, disabilities and risk studies (PhD), teaching (M Ed), teaching and learning (MA, PhD); educational leadership (Ed D); school psychology (M Ed); MA/PhD. *Accreditation:* APA (one or more programs are accredited). Postbaccalaureate distance learning degree programs offered (minimal on-campus study). *Faculty:* 42 full-time (20 women), 10 part-time/adjunct (4 women). *Students:* 390 full-time (303 women); includes 149 minority (14 African Americans, 3 American Indian/Alaska Native, 57 Asian Americans or Pacific Islanders, 75 Hispanic Americans), 16 international. Average age 31. 717 applicants, 40% accepted, 170 enrolled. In 2009, 140 master's, 46 doctorates awarded. Terminal master's awarded for partial completion of doctoral program. *Degree requirements:* For master's, comprehensive exam (for some programs), thesis (for some programs); for doctorate, comprehensive exam (for some programs), thesis/dissertation, qualifying exam. *Entrance requirements:* For master's, GRE, 3 letters of recommendation, resume/curriculum vitae; for doctorate, GRE, 3 letters of recommendation, statement of purpose, personal achievements/contributions statement, resume/curriculum vitae, transcripts for post-secondary institutions attended. Additional exam requirements/recommendations for international students: Required—TOEFL (minimum score 550 paper-based; 213 computer-based; 80 iBT) or IELTS (minimum score 7). Application fee: $70 ($90 for international students). Electronic applications accepted. *Financial support:* In 2009–10, 253 students received support, including 206 fellowships with full and partial tuition reimbursements available (averaging $5,000 per year), 62 research assistantships with full and partial tuition reimbursements available (averaging $6,200 per year), 87 teaching assistantships with partial tuition reimbursements available (averaging $6,500 per year); career-related internships or fieldwork, Federal Work-Study, institutionally sponsored loans, scholarships/grants, traineeships, health care benefits, and unspecified assistantships also available. Financial award applicants required to submit FAFSA. *Faculty research:* Professional development, early childhood development, school violence, literacy, science/math initiative. Total annual research expenditures: $4.4 million. *Unit head:* Dr. Jane Conoley, Chair, 805-893-2185, E-mail: jane-conoley@education.ucsb.edu. *Application contact:* Kathryn Marie Tucciarone, Student Affairs Officer, 805-893-2137, E-mail: katiet@education.ucsb.edu.

University of Central Arkansas, Graduate School, College of Education, Department of Early Childhood and Special Education, Program in Special Education, Conway, AR 72035-0001. Offers collaborative instructional specialist (ages 0–8) (MSE); collaborative instructional specialist (grades 4–12) (MSE). *Accreditation:* NCATE. *Students:* 1 full-time (0 women), 40 part-time (33 women); includes 3 minority (all African Americans). Average age 39. 9 applicants, 100% accepted, 7 enrolled. In 2009, 22 master's awarded. *Degree requirements:* For master's, comprehensive exam, thesis optional. *Entrance requirements:* For master's, GRE General Test, minimum GPA of 2.7. Additional exam requirements/recommendations for international students: Required—TOEFL (minimum score 550 paper-based; 213 computer-based). *Application deadline:* For fall admission, 3/1 priority date for domestic and international students; for spring admission, 10/1 priority date for domestic and international students. Applications are processed on a rolling basis. Application fee: $25 ($50 for international students). *Expenses:* Tuition, state resident: full-time $5136; part-time $214 per credit hour. Required fees: $379.50; $127 per term. Tuition and fees vary according to course level, course load and campus/location. *Financial support:* Federal Work-Study, scholarships/grants, tuition waivers (partial), and unspecified assistantships available. Financial award application deadline: 2/15; financial award applicants required to submit FAFSA. *Unit head:* Dr. David Naylor, Coordinator, 501-450-3171, Fax: 501-450-5457, E-mail: davidn@uca.edu. *Application contact:* Dr. Janet Filer, Coordinator, 501-450-3171, Fax: 501-450-5457.

University of Central Florida, College of Education, Department of Child, Family and Community Sciences, Program in Exceptional Student Education, Orlando, FL 32816. Offers autism spectrum disorders (Certificate); exceptional student education (M Ed, MA); severe or profound disabilities (Certificate); special education (Certificate). *Accreditation:* NCATE. Part-time and evening/weekend programs available. *Students:* 52 full-time (45 women), 207 part-time (192 women); includes 58 minority (30 African Americans, 4 Asian Americans or Pacific Islanders, 24 Hispanic Americans), 7 international. Average age 36. 154 applicants, 88% accepted, 93 enrolled. In 2009, 49 master's, 71 other advanced degrees awarded. *Degree requirements:* For master's, thesis or alternative, research project. *Entrance requirements:* For master's, GRE General Test. Additional exam requirements/recommendations for international students: Required—TOEFL. *Application deadline:* For fall admission, 7/15 for domestic students; for spring admission, 12/1 for domestic students. Application fee: $30. Electronic applications accepted. *Expenses:* Tuition, state resident: part-time $306.31 per credit hour. Tuition, nonresident: part-time $1099.01 per credit hour. Part-time tuition and fees vary according to degree level and program. *Financial support:* Fellowships with partial tuition reimbursements, research assistantships with partial tuition reimbursements, teaching assistantships with partial tuition reimbursements, career-related internships or fieldwork, Federal Work-Study, institutionally sponsored loans, tuition waivers (partial), and unspecified assistantships available. Financial award application deadline: 3/1; financial award applicants required to submit FAFSA.

University of Central Florida, College of Education, Education PhD Program, Orlando, FL 32816. Offers communication sciences and disorders (PhD); counselor education (PhD); elementary education (PhD); exceptional education (PhD); higher education (PhD); hospitality education (PhD); instructional technology (PhD); mathematics education (PhD); science education (PhD); social science education (PhD). *Students:* 99 full-time (70 women), 14 part-time (9 women); includes 28 minority (17 African Americans, 2 Asian Americans or Pacific Islanders, 9 Hispanic Americans), 20 international. In 2009, 15 doctorates awarded. Application fee: $30. Electronic applications accepted. *Expenses:* Tuition, state resident: part-time $306.31 per credit hour. Tuition, nonresident: part-time $1099.01 per credit hour. Part-time tuition and fees vary according to degree level and program. *Financial support:* In 2009–10, 40 fellowships with partial tuition reimbursements (averaging $9,200 per year), 61 research assistantships with partial tuition reimbursements (averaging $7,800 per year), 18 teaching assistantships with partial tuition reimbursements (averaging $6,500 per year) were awarded. *Unit head:* Dr. B. Grant Hayes, Associate Dean, 407-823-5391, E-mail: ghayes@mail.ucf.edu. *Application contact:* Dr. B. Grant Hayes, Associate Dean, 407-823-5391, E-mail: ghayes@mail.ucf.edu.

University of Central Missouri, The Graduate School, College of Education, Warrensburg, MO 64093. Offers career and technical education administration (MS); career and technical education industry training (MS); career and technical education leadership/teaching (MS); college student personnel administration (MS); counseling (MS); curriculum and instruction (Ed S); educational leadership (Ed D); educational technology (MS); elementary education/educational foundations and literacy (MSE); elementary school administration (MSE); elementary school principalship (Ed S); human services/learning resources (Ed S); human services/professional counseling (Ed S); human services/special education (Ed S); human services/technology and occupational education (Ed S); K-12 education/educational foundations and literacy (MSE); K-12 special education (MSE); library science and information services (MS); literacy education (MSE); secondary education/educational foundations & literacy (MSE); secondary school administration (MSE); secondary school principalship (Ed S); superintendency (Ed S); teaching (MAT). Part-time programs available. Postbaccalaureate distance learning degree programs offered. *Faculty:* 42. *Students:* 123 full-time (82 women), 721 part-time (552 women); includes 58 minority (38 African Americans, 3 American Indian/Alaska Native, 6 Asian Americans or Pacific Islanders, 11 Hispanic Americans), 6 international. Average age 34. 229 applicants, 88% accepted, 190 enrolled. In 2009, 212 master's, 47 other advanced degrees awarded. *Entrance requirements:* Additional exam requirements/recommendations for international students: Required—TOEFL (minimum score 550 paper-based; 79 computer-based). *Application deadline:* For fall admission, 6/1 priority date for domestic students, 5/1 for international students; for spring admission, 10/1 priority date for domestic students, 10/1 for international students. Applications are processed on a rolling basis. Application fee: $30 ($75 for international students). Electronic applications accepted. *Expenses:* Tuition, area resident: Part-time $245.80 per credit hour. Tuition, nonresident: part-time $491.60 per credit hour. Required fees: $24.20 per credit hour. Full-time tuition and fees vary according to course load, degree level, campus/location and reciprocity agreements. *Financial support:* Research assistantships with full and partial tuition reimbursements, teaching assistantships with full and partial tuition reimbursements, career-related internships or fieldwork, Federal Work-Study, scholarships/grants, and administrative and laboratory assistantships available. Support available to part-time students. Financial award application deadline: 3/1; financial award applicants required to submit FAFSA. *Unit head:* Dr. Michael Wright, Dean, 660-543-4272, Fax: 660-543-8753, E-mail: mwright@ucmo.edu. *Application contact:* Laurie Delap, Admissions Coordinator, 660-543-4621, Fax: 660-543-4778, E-mail: gradinfo@ucmo.edu.

University of Central Oklahoma, College of Graduate Studies and Research, College of Education, Department of Special Services, Program in Special Education, Edmond, OK 73034-5209. Offers M Ed. *Accreditation:* NCATE. Part-time programs available. *Faculty:* 9 full-time (5 women), 6 part-time/adjunct (5 women). *Students:* 6 full-time (5 women), 16 part-time (14 women); includes 6 minority (5 African Americans, 1 American Indian/Alaska Native). Average age 36. 10 applicants, 100% accepted. In 2009, 5 master's awarded. *Entrance requirements:* For master's, GRE General Test. Additional exam requirements/recommendations for international students: Required—TOEFL (minimum score 550 paper-based; 213 computer-based). *Application deadline:* For fall admission, 7/1 for international students; for spring admission, 11/1 for international students. Applications are processed on a rolling basis. Application fee: $25. Electronic applications accepted. *Expenses:* Tuition, state resident: full-time $4128; part-time $172 per credit hour. Tuition, nonresident: full-time $10,373; part-time $432.20 per credit hour. Required fees: $433.20; $18.05 per credit hour. *Financial support:* Unspecified assistantships available. Financial award application deadline: 3/31; financial award applicants required to submit FAFSA. *Unit head:* Dr. Charolette Myles-Nixon, Director, 405-974-5281. *Application contact:* Dr. John Garic, Interim Dean, Graduate College, 405-974-3341, Fax: 405-974-3852, E-mail: gradcoll@ucok.edu.

University of Cincinnati, Graduate School, College of Education, Criminal Justice, and Human Services, Division of Teacher Education, Program in Special Education, Cincinnati, OH 45221. Offers M Ed, Ed D. *Accreditation:* NCATE. Part-time programs available. *Degree requirements:* For master's, thesis or alternative; for doctorate, thesis/dissertation. *Entrance requirements:* For master's, GRE General Test; for doctorate, GRE General Test, GRE Subject Test. Additional exam requirements/recommendations for international students: Required—TOEFL (minimum score 550 paper-based; 213 computer-based), TWE (minimum score 4.5), OEPT. Electronic applications accepted.

University of Colorado at Colorado Springs, Graduate School, College of Education, Colorado Springs, CO 80933-7150. Offers counseling and human services (MA); curriculum and instruction (MA); educational administration (MA); educational leadership (MA, PhD); special education (MA). *Accreditation:* ACA; NCATE. Part-time and evening/weekend programs available. Postbaccalaureate distance learning degree programs offered (minimal on-campus study). *Faculty:* 23 full-time (15 women), 11 part-time/adjunct (8 women). *Students:* 317 full-time (243 women), 160 part-time (132 women); includes 81 minority (23 African Americans, 3 American Indian/Alaska Native, 13 Asian Americans or Pacific Islanders, 42 Hispanic Americans), 2 international. Average age 36. 375 applicants, 94% accepted, 254 enrolled. In 2009, 203 master's awarded. *Degree requirements:* For master's, comprehensive exam, thesis or alternative, microcomputer proficiency; for doctorate, comprehensive exam, research lab. *Entrance requirements:* For master's, GRE General Test, MAT. *Application deadline:* For fall admission, 6/15 for domestic students; for spring admission, 10/15 for domestic students. Applications are processed on a rolling basis. Application fee: $60 ($75 for international students). *Expenses:* Tuition, state resident: full-time $8922; part-time $639 per credit hour. Tuition, nonresident: full-time $19,372; part-time $1154 per credit hour. Tuition and fees vary according to course level, course load, degree level, program, reciprocity agreements and

student level. *Financial support:* Fellowships, career-related internships or fieldwork, Federal Work-Study, and scholarships/grants available. Support available to part-time students. Financial award application deadline: 3/1; financial award applicants required to submit FAFSA. *Faculty research:* Job training for special populations, materials development for classroom. Total annual research expenditures: $1.4 million. *Unit head:* Dr. LaVonne Neal, Dean, 719-255-4111, Fax: 719-262-4110, E-mail: lneal@uccs.edu. *Application contact:* Melissa Schecter, Student Services Manager, 719-255-4526, Fax: 719-255-4110, E-mail: mschedte@uccs.edu.

University of Colorado Denver, School of Education and Human Development, Early Childhood Education Program, Denver, CO 80217-3364. Offers early childhood education/special education (MA). *Accreditation:* NCATE. Part-time and evening/weekend programs available. *Students:* 53 full-time (45 women), 109 part-time (98 women); includes 19 minority (4 African Americans, 5 Asian Americans or Pacific Islanders, 10 Hispanic Americans), 7 international. 93 applicants, 63% accepted, 48 enrolled. In 2009, 46 master's awarded. *Degree requirements:* For master's, comprehensive exam, thesis optional. *Entrance requirements:* For master's, GRE, minimum GPA of 2.75 or MAT. Additional exam requirements/recommendations for international students: Required—TOEFL (minimum score 525 paper-based; 197 computer-based). *Application deadline:* For fall admission, 4/15 for domestic students; for spring admission, 9/15 for domestic students. Applications are processed on a rolling basis. Application fee: $50 ($75 for international students). Electronic applications accepted. *Financial support:* Research assistantships, teaching assistantships, Federal Work-Study available. Financial award application deadline: 4/1; financial award applicants required to submit FAFSA. *Faculty research:* Early childhood growth and development, faculty development, adult learning, gender and equity issues, research methodology. *Unit head:* William Goodwin, Area Coordinator, 303-315-6323, E-mail: bill.goodwin@ucdenver.edu. *Application contact:* Meredith Lopez, Academic Advisor, 303-315-4980, Fax: 303-315-6311, E-mail: meredith.lopez@ucdenver.edu.

University of Connecticut, Graduate School, Neag School of Education, Department of Educational Psychology, Program in Special Education, Storrs, CT 06269. Offers MA, PhD, Post-Master's Certificate. *Accreditation:* NCATE. *Faculty:* 20 full-time (9 women). *Students:* 34 full-time (31 women), 10 part-time (6 women); includes 2 minority (1 American Indian/Alaska Native, 1 Hispanic American). Average age 31. 62 applicants, 34% accepted, 19 enrolled. In 2009, 22 master's, 1 other advanced degree awarded. Terminal master's awarded for partial completion of doctoral program. *Degree requirements:* For master's, comprehensive exam, thesis or alternative; for doctorate, thesis/dissertation. *Entrance requirements:* For doctorate, GRE General Test. Additional exam requirements/recommendations for international students: Required—TOEFL (minimum score 550 paper-based; 213 computer-based). *Application deadline:* For fall admission, 2/1 priority date for domestic and international students; for spring admission, 11/1 for domestic students, 10/1 for international students. Applications are processed on a rolling basis. Application fee: $55. Electronic applications accepted. *Expenses:* Tuition, state resident: full-time $4725; part-time $525 per credit. Tuition, nonresident: full-time $12,267; part-time $1363 per credit. Required fees: $346 per semester. Tuition and fees vary according to course load. *Financial support:* In 2009–10, 13 research assistantships with full tuition reimbursements were awarded; fellowships, teaching assistantships with full tuition reimbursements, Federal Work-Study, scholarships/grants, health care benefits, and unspecified assistantships also available. Financial award application deadline: 2/1; financial award applicants required to submit FAFSA. *Unit head:* Hariharan Swaminathan, Head, 860-486-4031, Fax: 860-486-0210, E-mail: hariharan.swaminathan@uconn.edu. *Application contact:* Cheryl Lowe, Program Assistant, 860-486-4031, Fax: 860-486-0180, E-mail: cheryl.lowe@uconn.edu.

University of Dayton, Graduate School, School of Education and Allied Professions, Department of Teacher Education, Dayton, OH 45469-1300. Offers adolescent/young adult (MS Ed); art education (MS Ed); early childhood education (MS Ed); inclusive early childhood (MS Ed); interdisciplinary education (MS Ed); intervention specialist education, mild/moderate (MS Ed); literacy (MS Ed); middle childhood (MS Ed); multi-age education (MS Ed); music education (MS Ed); teacher as leader (MS Ed); technology in education (MS Ed). Part-time and evening/weekend programs available. *Faculty:* 17 full-time (13 women), 27 part-time/adjunct (21 women). *Students:* 105 full-time (76 women), 152 part-time (131 women); includes 25 minority (21 African Americans, 1 Asian American or Pacific Islander, 3 Hispanic Americans), 8 international. Average age 33. 199 applicants, 58% accepted, 48 enrolled. In 2009, 139 master's awarded. *Degree requirements:* For master's, thesis, capstone research project. *Entrance requirements:* For master's, GRE General Test, minimum GPA of 2.75. Additional exam requirements/recommendations for international students: Required—TOEFL (minimum score 550 paper-based; 213 computer-based; 80 iBT). *Application deadline:* For fall admission, 3/15 priority date for domestic students, 3/1 priority date for international students; for winter admission, 7/1 priority date for international students; for spring admission, 1/1 priority date for international students. Applications are processed on a rolling basis. Application fee: $0 ($50 for international students). Electronic applications accepted. *Expenses:* Contact institution. *Financial support:* In 2009–10, 5 research assistantships with full and partial tuition reimbursements (averaging $8,000 per year) were awarded; career-related internships or fieldwork, institutionally sponsored loans, health care benefits, and unspecified assistantships also available. Financial award applicants required to submit FAFSA. *Faculty research:* Diversity, literacy, art representation by young children, preservice teacher preparation. *Unit head:* Dr. Katie A. Kinnucan-Welsch, Chair, 937-229-3346. *Application contact:* Graduate Admissions, 937-229-4411, Fax: 937-229-4729, E-mail: gradadmission@udayton.edu.

University of Detroit Mercy, College of Liberal Arts and Education, Department of Education, Program in Special Education, Detroit, MI 48221. Offers emotionally impaired (MA); learning disabilities (MA). Part-time programs available. *Degree requirements:* For master's, thesis or alternative, practicum. *Entrance requirements:* For master's, minimum GPA of 2.75. *Faculty research:* Emerging roles of special education, inclusionary education, high potential underachievers in secondary schools.

The University of Findlay, Graduate and Professional Studies, College of Education, Findlay, OH 45840-3653. Offers administration (MA Ed); early childhood (MA Ed); elementary education (MA Ed); human resource development (MA Ed); leadership (MA Ed); special education (MA Ed); technology (MA Ed); web instruction (MA Ed). *Accreditation:* NCATE. Part-time and evening/weekend programs available. *Degree requirements:* For master's, thesis, cumulative project. *Entrance requirements:* For master's, minimum undergraduate GPA of 2.75 in last 62 hours of course work. Additional exam requirements/recommendations for international students: Required—TOEFL (minimum score 550 paper-based; 213 computer-based; 80 iBT). Electronic applications accepted. *Expenses:* Contact institution. *Faculty research:* Children's literature, books and artwork, educational technology, professional development.

University of Florida, Graduate School, College of Education, Department of Special Education, Gainesville, FL 32611. Offers M Ed, MAE, Ed D, PhD, Ed S. *Accreditation:* NCATE. *Degree requirements:* For master's, thesis (MAE); for doctorate, variable foreign language requirement, thesis/dissertation. *Entrance requirements:* For master's and doctorate, GRE General Test, minimum GPA of 3.0; for Ed S, GRE General Test. Additional exam requirements/recommendations for international students: Required—TOEFL (minimum score 550 paper-based; 213 computer-based). Electronic applications accepted. *Faculty research:* Teacher attrition, school restructuring, Latino families.

University of Georgia, Graduate School, College of Education, Department of Communication Sciences and Special Education, Athens, GA 30602. Offers communication science and disorders (M Ed, MA, PhD, Ed S); special education (M Ed, Ed D, PhD, Ed S). *Accreditation:* ASHA (one or more programs are accredited). *Faculty:* 13 full-time (7 women). *Students:* 77 full-time (72 women), 33 part-time (31 women); includes 20 minority (6 African Americans, 1 American Indian/Alaska Native, 9 Asian Americans or Pacific Islanders, 4 Hispanic Americans), 1 international. Average age 24. 190 applicants, 50% accepted, 42 enrolled. In 2009, 31 master's, 2 doctorates, 4 other advanced degrees awarded. Terminal master's awarded for partial completion of doctoral program. *Degree requirements:* For master's, comprehensive exam (for some programs), thesis (for some programs); for doctorate, thesis/dissertation. *Entrance requirements:* For master's, doctorate, and Ed S, GRE General Test. Additional exam requirements/recommendations for international students: Required—TOEFL. *Application deadline:* For fall admission, 7/1 priority date for domestic students; for spring admission, 11/15 for domestic students. Application fee: $50. Electronic applications accepted. *Expenses:* Tuition, state resident: full-time $6000; part-time $250 per credit hour. Tuition, nonresident: full-time $20,904; part-time $871 per credit hour. Required fees: $730 per semester. *Financial support:* Fellowships, research assistantships, teaching assistantships, unspecified assistantships available. *Unit head:* Dr. Anne C. Bothe, Interim Head, 706-542-0436, Fax: 706-542-5348, E-mail: abothe@uga.edu. *Application contact:* Dr. Rebecca S. Marshall, Graduate Coordinator, 706-542-0737, E-mail: rshisler@uga.edu.

University of Guam, Office of Graduate Studies, School of Education, Program in Special Education, Mangilao, GU 96923. Offers M Ed. *Degree requirements:* For master's, comprehensive oral and written exams, special project or thesis. *Entrance requirements:* For master's, GRE General Test. Additional exam requirements/recommendations for international students: Required—TOEFL. *Faculty research:* Mainstreaming, multiculturalism.

University of Hawaii at Manoa, Graduate Division, College of Education, Department of Special Education, Honolulu, HI 96822. Offers M Ed. *Accreditation:* NCATE. Part-time programs available. *Faculty:* 12 full-time (7 women), 3 part-time/adjunct (all women). *Students:* 140 full-time (111 women), 44 part-time (26 women); includes 94 minority (6 African Americans, 83 Asian Americans or Pacific Islanders, 5 Hispanic Americans), 3 international. Average age 33. 135 applicants, 76% accepted, 87 enrolled. In 2009, 42 master's awarded. *Degree requirements:* For master's, thesis optional. *Entrance requirements:* For master's, GRE General Test, interview, minimum GPA of 3.0. Additional exam requirements/recommendations for international students: Required—TOEFL (minimum score 580 paper-based; 237 computer-based; 92 iBT), IELTS (minimum score 5). *Application deadline:* For fall admission, 3/1 for domestic and international students; for spring admission, 10/1 for domestic and international students. Application fee: $60. *Expenses:* Tuition, state resident: full-time $8900; part-time $372 per credit. Tuition, nonresident: full-time $21,400; part-time $898 per credit. Required fees: $207 per semester. *Financial support:* In 2009–10, 5 students received support, including 12 fellowships (averaging $2,637 per year), 2 research assistantships (averaging $16,527 per year); teaching assistantships, career-related internships or fieldwork, institutionally sponsored loans, and tuition waivers (full and partial) also available. Support available to part-time students. Financial award application deadline: 3/1. *Faculty research:* Mild/moderate/severe disabilities, early childhood interventions, inclusion, transition. Total annual research expenditures: $400,000. *Application contact:* Amelia Jenkins, Chair, 808-956-8450, Fax: 808-956-4345, E-mail: amelia@hawaii.edu.

University of Hawaii at Manoa, Graduate Division, College of Education, Doctorate in Education Program, Honolulu, HI 96822. Offers curriculum and instruction (PhD); educational administration (PhD); educational foundations (PhD); educational policy studies (PhD); educational technology (PhD); exceptionalities (PhD); kinesiology (PhD). Part-time and evening/weekend programs available. *Faculty:* 65 full-time (40 women), 28 part-time/adjunct (17 women). *Students:* 74 full-time (44 women), 119 part-time (77 women); includes 101 minority (5 African Americans, 2 American Indian/Alaska Native, 86 Asian Americans or Pacific Islanders, 8 Hispanic Americans), 17 international. Average age 38. 98 applicants, 53% accepted, 35 enrolled. In 2009, 11 doctorates awarded. *Degree requirements:* For doctorate, thesis/dissertation. *Entrance requirements:* For doctorate, GRE General Test, sample of written work. Additional exam requirements/recommendations for international students: Required—TOEFL (minimum score 600 paper-based; 250 computer-based; 100 iBT), IELTS (minimum score 7). *Application deadline:* For fall admission, 2/1 for domestic students, 1/15 for international students. Application fee: $50. *Expenses:* Tuition, state resident: full-time $8900; part-time $372 per credit. Tuition, nonresident: full-time $21,400; part-time $898 per credit. Required fees: $207 per semester. *Financial support:* In 2009–10, 1 student received support, including 11 fellowships (averaging $4,147 per year), 17 research assistantships (averaging $17,392 per year), 4 teaching assistantships (averaging $14,670 per year); career-related internships or fieldwork, Federal Work-Study, and tuition waivers (full and partial) also available. *Application contact:* Dr. Helen Slaughter, Chairperson, 808-956-7913, Fax: 808-956-9905, E-mail: slaughte@hawaii.edu.

University of Houston, College of Education, Department of Educational Psychology, Houston, TX 77204. Offers counseling (M Ed); counseling psychology (PhD); educational psychology (M Ed); school psychology (PhD); school psychology and individual differences (PhD); special education (M Ed, Ed D). *Accreditation:* NCATE. Part-time and evening/weekend programs available. *Faculty:* 21 full-time (11 women), 12 part-time/adjunct (8 women). *Students:* 121 full-time (103 women), 123 part-time (106 women); includes 86 minority (23 African Americans, 3 American Indian/Alaska Native, 24 Asian Americans or Pacific Islanders, 36 Hispanic Americans), 11 international. Average age 30. 139 applicants, 52% accepted, 38 enrolled. In 2009, 32 master's, 16 doctorates awarded. *Degree requirements:* For master's, comprehensive exam or thesis; for doctorate, comprehensive exam, thesis/dissertation. *Entrance requirements:* For master's, GRE, recommendations, curriculum vitae/resume; for doctorate, GRE, recommendations, curriculum vitae/resume, goal statement, writing sample. Additional exam requirements/recommendations for international students: Required—TOEFL. *Application deadline:* For fall admission, 12/1 for domestic and international students; for spring admission, 9/15 for domestic and international students. Application fee: $45 ($75 for international students). *Expenses:* Tuition, state resident: full-time $7676; part-time $320 per credit hour. Tuition, nonresident: full-time $14,324; part-time $597 per credit hour. Required fees: $3034. *Financial support:* In 2009–10, 2 fellowships with full tuition reimbursements (averaging $9,500 per year), 2 research assistantships with full tuition reimbursements (averaging $10,225 per year), 46 teaching assistantships with full tuition reimbursements (averaging $10,225 per year) were awarded; career-related internships or fieldwork, Federal Work-Study, institutionally sponsored loans, scholarships/grants, health care benefits, and unspecified assistantships also available. Support available to part-time students. Financial award application deadline: 2/1. *Faculty research:* Evidence-based assessment and intervention, multicultural issues in psychology, social and cultural context of learning, systemic barriers to college, motivational aspects of self-regulated learning. *Unit head:* Dr. Tom Kubiszyn, Chairperson, 713-743-9865, Fax: 713-743-4996, E-mail: tkubiszyn@uh.edu. *Application contact:* Kimberly A. Zainfeld, Academic Advisor, 713-743-9830, Fax: 713-743-4996, E-mail: kzainfeld@uh.edu.

University of Houston–Victoria, School of Education and Human Development, Victoria, TX 77901-4450. Offers administration and supervision (M Ed); counseling (M Ed); curriculum and instruction (M Ed); special education (M Ed). Part-time and evening/weekend programs available. Postbaccalaureate distance learning degree programs offered. *Degree requirements:* For master's, comprehensive exam, project or thesis. *Entrance requirements:* For master's, GRE General Test. Additional exam requirements/recommendations for international students: Required—TOEFL. Electronic applications accepted. *Faculty research:* Reading and language arts education, evaluation and diagnosis of special children's abilities.

University of Idaho, College of Graduate Studies, College of Education, Department of Counseling and School Psychology, Special Education, and Educational Leadership, Program in Special Education, Moscow, ID 83844-2282. Offers M Ed. *Accreditation:* NCATE. *Students:* 6 full-time, 12 part-time. In 2009, 4 master's awarded. *Entrance requirements:* For master's, minimum GPA of 2.8. *Application deadline:* For fall admission, 8/1 for domestic students; for spring admission, 12/15 for domestic students. Application fee: $55 ($60 for international students). *Expenses:* Tuition, state resident: full-time $6120. Tuition, nonresident: full-time $17,712. *Financial support:* Research assistantships, teaching assistantships available. Financial award application deadline: 2/15. *Unit head:* Dr. Russell A. Joki, Interim Chair, 208-885-4047. *Application contact:* Dr. Russell A. Joki, Interim Chair, 208-885-4047.

University of Illinois at Chicago, Graduate College, College of Education, Department of Special Education, Chicago, IL 60607-7128. Offers M Ed, PhD. Part-time programs available.

Special Education

University of Illinois at Chicago (continued)
Terminal master's awarded for partial completion of doctoral program. *Degree requirements:* For doctorate, thesis/dissertation. *Entrance requirements:* For master's, minimum GPA of 2.75; for doctorate, GRE General Test, minimum GPA of 2.75. Additional exam requirements/ recommendations for international students: Required—TOEFL. Electronic applications accepted. *Faculty research:* Teaching and learning for special learners, individual differences.

University of Illinois at Urbana–Champaign, Graduate College, College of Education, Department of Special Education, Champaign, IL 61820. Offers Ed M, MS, Ed D, PhD, CAS. Part-time programs available. Postbaccalaureate distance learning degree programs offered (minimal on-campus study). *Faculty:* 12 full-time (8 women), 1 (woman) part-time/adjunct. *Students:* 49 full-time (40 women), 41 part-time (37 women); includes 12 minority (5 African Americans, 4 Asian Americans or Pacific Islanders, 3 Hispanic Americans), 9 international. 69 applicants, 42% accepted, 19 enrolled. In 2009, 21 master's, 3 doctorates, 2 other advanced degrees awarded. *Entrance requirements:* For master's and doctorate, minimum GPA of 3.0. Additional exam requirements/recommendations for international students: Required—TOEFL (minimum score 102 iBT). *Application deadline:* Applications are processed on a rolling basis. Application fee: $60 ($75 for international students). Electronic applications accepted. *Financial support:* In 2009–10, 41 fellowships, 15 research assistantships, 7 teaching assistantships were awarded; tuition waivers (full and partial) also available. *Unit head:* Michaelene Ostrosky, Interim Head, 217-333-0260, Fax: 217-333-6555, E-mail: ostrosky@illinois.edu. *Application contact:* Cheri Karrick, Office Support Assistant, 217-333-0260, Fax: 217-333-6555, E-mail: karrick@illinois.edu.

The University of Iowa, Graduate College, College of Education, Department of Teaching and Learning, Program in Special Education, Iowa City, IA 52242-1316. Offers MA, PhD. *Degree requirements:* For master's, thesis optional, exam; for doctorate, comprehensive exam, thesis/dissertation. *Entrance requirements:* For master's and doctorate, GRE General Test, minimum GPA of 3.0. Additional exam requirements/recommendations for international students: Required—TOEFL (minimum score 550 paper-based; 213 computer-based; 81 iBT). Electronic applications accepted.

The University of Kansas, Graduate Studies, School of Education, Department of Special Education, Lawrence, KS 66045. Offers MS Ed, Ed D, PhD. Offered jointly with the Kansas City campus. *Accreditation:* NCATE. Part-time programs available. *Faculty:* 19 full-time (9 women). *Students:* 118 full-time (110 women), 129 part-time (106 women); includes 21 minority (3 African Americans, 2 American Indian/Alaska Native, 7 Asian Americans or Pacific Islanders, 9 Hispanic Americans), 24 international. Average age 33. 119 applicants, 76% accepted, 79 enrolled. In 2009, 58 master's, 12 doctorates awarded. *Degree requirements:* For master's, project, thesis or capstone; for doctorate, comprehensive exam, thesis/dissertation. *Entrance requirements:* For master's, minimum GPA of 3.0; for doctorate, GRE General Test, master's degree. Additional exam requirements/recommendations for international students: Required—TOEFL (minimum score 57 computer-based; 23 iBT). *Application deadline:* For fall admission, 3/15 for domestic and international students; for spring admission, 10/15 for domestic and international students. Application fee: $45 ($55 for international students). Electronic applications accepted. *Expenses:* Tuition, state resident: full-time $6492; part-time $270.50 per credit hour. Tuition, nonresident: full-time $15,510; part-time $646.25 per credit hour. Required fees: $847; $70.56 per credit hour. Tuition and fees vary according to course load and program. *Financial support:* Fellowships with full and partial tuition reimbursements, research assistantships with full and partial tuition reimbursements, teaching assistantships with full and partial tuition reimbursements, Federal Work-Study, scholarships/grants, and unspecified assistantships available. Support available to part-time students. Financial award applicants required to submit FAFSA. *Faculty research:* Autism spectrum disorders, LD research, leadership development, qualitative research and evaluation. *Unit head:* Chriss Walther-Thomas, Chair, 785-864-4954, Fax: 785-864-4149, E-mail: chrisswt@ku.edu. *Application contact:* Sherrie Saathoff, Admissions and Recruitment, 785-864-0556, Fax: 785-864-4149, E-mail: ssaathoff@ku.edu.

University of Kentucky, Graduate School, College of Education, Program in Special Education, Lexington, KY 40506-0032. Offers early childhood special education (MS Ed); rehabilitation counseling (MRC); special education (MS Ed); special education leadership personnel preparation (Ed D). *Accreditation:* CORE; NCATE. Terminal master's awarded for partial completion of doctoral program. *Degree requirements:* For master's, comprehensive exam, thesis optional; for doctorate, comprehensive exam, thesis/dissertation. *Entrance requirements:* For master's, GRE General Test, minimum undergraduate GPA of 2.75; for doctorate, GRE General Test, minimum graduate GPA of 3.0. Additional exam requirements/recommendations for international students: Required—TOEFL (minimum score 550 paper-based; 213 computer-based). Electronic applications accepted. *Faculty research:* Applied behavior analysis applications in special education, single subject research design in classroom settings, transition research across life span, rural special education personnel.

University of La Verne, College of Education and Organizational Leadership, Master's Program in Education, La Verne, CA 91750-4443. Offers advanced teaching skills (M Ed); education (special emphasis) (M Ed). Part-time programs available. *Faculty:* 19 full-time (14 women), 35 part-time/adjunct (27 women). *Students:* 28 full-time (22 women), 133 part-time (106 women); includes 78 minority (11 African Americans, 4 American Indian/Alaska Native, 5 Asian Americans or Pacific Islanders, 58 Hispanic Americans). Average age 32. In 2009, 49 master's awarded. *Degree requirements:* For master's, thesis optional. *Entrance requirements:* For master's, California Basic Educational Skills Test, interview, writing sample, minimum GPA of 3.0, 3 letters of recommendation. Additional exam requirements/recommendations for international students: Required—TOEFL (minimum score 550 paper-based; 213 computer-based). *Application deadline:* Applications are processed on a rolling basis. Application fee: $50. *Expenses:* Contact institution. *Financial support:* Institutionally sponsored loans and unspecified assistantships available. Financial award application deadline: 3/2; financial award applicants required to submit FAFSA. *Unit head:* Valerie Beltran, Chair, 909-593-3511 Ext. 4659, E-mail: vbeltran@laverne.edu. *Application contact:* Christy Ranells, Program and Admission Specialist, 909-593-3511 Ext. 4644, Fax: 909-392-2761, E-mail: cranells@ulv.edu.

University of Louisville, Graduate School, College of Education and Human Development, Department of Teaching and Learning, Louisville, KY 40292-0001. Offers art education (MAT); curriculum and instruction (PhD); early elementary education (MAT); instructional technology (M Ed); interdisciplinary early childhood education (MAT); middle school education (MAT); music education (MAT); reading education (M Ed); secondary education (MAT); special education (M Ed, MAT); teacher leadership (M Ed). Part-time and evening/weekend programs available. *Faculty:* 43 full-time (33 women), 43 part-time/adjunct (36 women). *Students:* 207 full-time (144 women), 410 part-time (306 women); includes 68 minority (43 African Americans, 2 American Indian/Alaska Native, 14 Asian Americans or Pacific Islanders, 9 Hispanic Americans), 5 international. Average age 33. 216 applicants, 68% accepted, 112 enrolled. In 2009, 269 master's, 6 doctorates awarded. *Degree requirements:* For doctorate, comprehensive exam, thesis/dissertation. *Entrance requirements:* For master's, GRE General Test, PRAXIS II (for some programs); for doctorate, GRE General Test. Additional exam requirements/ recommendations for international students: Required—TOEFL (minimum score 560 paper-based; 210 computer-based; 83 iBT). Application fee: $50. Electronic applications accepted. *Financial support:* In 2009–10, 172 students received support; fellowships, research assistantships, teaching assistantships, career-related internships or fieldwork, Federal Work-Study, scholarships/grants, and unspecified assistantships available. Financial award application deadline: 6/1; financial award applicants required to submit FAFSA. *Faculty research:* Assessment of cognitive and language abilities in infants and preschool children; mathematics teachers' conceptions and beliefs, effect, and understanding of mathematics; incorporating nanoscience and nanotechnology into middle and high school science classrooms; urban teacher preparation through inquiry, action and advocacy; impacts of cognitive coaching on teacher practice and student achievement. Total annual research expenditures: $3.7 million. *Unit head:* Dr. Ann E. Larson, Acting Chair, 502-852-6431, Fax: 502-852-1497, E-mail: ann@louisville.edu. *Application contact:* Libby Leggett, Director, Graduate Admissions, 502-852-3101, Fax: 502-852-6536, E-mail: gradadm@louisville.edu.

University of Maine, Graduate School, College of Education and Human Development, Program in Special Education, Orono, ME 04469. Offers M Ed, CAS. *Accreditation:* NCATE. Part-time and evening/weekend programs available. *Students:* 21 full-time (18 women), 51 part-time (48 women); includes 1 minority (American Indian/Alaska Native). Average age 40. 37 applicants, 78% accepted, 26 enrolled. In 2009, 31 master's, 1 CAS awarded. *Degree requirements:* For master's, thesis or alternative. *Entrance requirements:* For master's, MAT; for CAS, MA, M Ed, or MS. Additional exam requirements/recommendations for international students: Required—TOEFL. *Application deadline:* For fall admission, 2/1 priority date for domestic students. Applications are processed on a rolling basis. Application fee: $65. Electronic applications accepted. *Financial support:* Career-related internships or fieldwork and tuition waivers (full and partial) available. Support available to part-time students. Financial award application deadline: 3/1. *Unit head:* Dr. Janet Spector, Coordinator, 207-581-2444, Fax: 207-581-2423. *Application contact:* Scott G. Delcourt, Associate Dean of the Graduate School, 207-581-3291, Fax: 207-581-3232, E-mail: graduate@maine.edu.

University of Manitoba, Faculty of Graduate Studies, Faculty of Education, Department of Educational Administration, Foundations and Psychology, Winnipeg, MB R3T 2N2, Canada. Offers adult and post-secondary education (M Ed); educational administration (M Ed); guidance and counseling (M Ed); inclusive special education (M Ed); social foundations of education (M Ed). *Degree requirements:* For master's, thesis or alternative.

University of Mary, Program in Education, Bismarck, ND 58504-9652. Offers college teaching (M Ed); curriculum, instruction and assessment (M Ed); early childhood education (M Ed); early childhood special education (M Ed); elementary education administration (M Ed); emotional disorders (M Ed); learning disabilities (M Ed); reading (M Ed); secondary education administration (M Ed); special education (M Ed); special education strategist (M Ed). Part-time programs available. *Degree requirements:* For master's, portfolio or thesis. *Entrance requirements:* For master's, interview, letters of reference. Additional exam requirements/recommendations for international students: Required—TOEFL (minimum score 550 paper-based). *Expenses:* Tuition: Full-time $10,062; part-time $430 per credit. Tuition and fees vary according to course load, degree level, program and student level. *Faculty research:* Innovative pedagogy in higher education, technology in education, content standards, children of poverty, children with diverse learning needs.

University of Maryland, College Park, Academic Affairs, College of Education, Department of Special Education, College Park, MD 20742. Offers M Ed, MA, PhD, CAGS. *Accreditation:* NCATE. Part-time and evening/weekend programs available. *Faculty:* 22 full-time (18 women), 18 part-time/adjunct (17 women). *Students:* 103 full-time (91 women), 42 part-time (34 women); includes 35 minority (22 African Americans, 2 American Indian/Alaska Native, 8 Asian Americans or Pacific Islanders, 3 Hispanic Americans), 6 international. 123 applicants, 53% accepted, 59 enrolled. In 2009, 56 master's, 4 doctorates awarded. *Degree requirements:* For master's, thesis (for some programs); for doctorate, thesis/dissertation, 1 year residency. *Entrance requirements:* For master's, GRE General Test or MAT, minimum GPA of 3.0, 3 letters of recommendation; for doctorate, GRE General Test or MAT, minimum undergraduate GPA of 3.0, graduate 3.5; 3 letters of recommendation. *Application deadline:* For fall admission, 5/1 priority date for domestic students, 2/1 for international students; for spring admission, 10/1 priority date for domestic students, 6/1 for international students. Applications are processed on a rolling basis. Application fee: $60. Electronic applications accepted. *Expenses:* Tuition, area resident: Part-time $471 per credit hour. Tuition, state resident: part-time $471 per credit hour. Tuition, nonresident: part-time $1016 per credit hour. Required fees: $337.04 per term. *Financial support:* In 2009–10, 28 fellowships with full and partial tuition reimbursements (averaging $22,056 per year), 4 research assistantships with tuition reimbursements (averaging $15,346 per year), 4 teaching assistantships with tuition reimbursements (averaging $16,255 per year) were awarded; career-related internships or fieldwork, Federal Work-Study, and scholarships/grants also available. Support available to part-time students. Financial award applicants required to submit FAFSA. *Faculty research:* Educational diagnosis and prescription, mental retardation, severely/profoundly handicapped. Total annual research expenditures: $4.2 million. *Unit head:* Dr. Philip J. Burke, Chairman, 301-405-6514, Fax: 301-314-9158, E-mail: pjburke@umd.edu. *Application contact:* Dean of Graduate School, 301-405-0358.

University of Maryland Eastern Shore, Graduate Programs, Department of Education, Program in Special Education, Princess Anne, MD 21853-1299. Offers M Ed. *Accreditation:* NCATE. *Degree requirements:* For master's, comprehensive exam, seminar paper, internship. *Entrance requirements:* For master's, PRAXIS I, interview, minimum GPA of 3.0. Additional exam requirements/recommendations for international students: Required—TOEFL (minimum score 213 computer-based; 80 iBT). Electronic applications accepted.

University of Massachusetts Amherst, Graduate School, School of Education, Program in Education, Amherst, MA 01003. Offers bilingual, English as a second language, and multicultural education (M Ed, CAGS); child study and early education (M Ed); children, families and schools (Ed D, CAGS); early childhood and elementary teacher education (M Ed); education policy and leadership (CAGS); educational administration (M Ed, CAGS); educational policy and leadership (Ed D); higher education (M Ed, CAGS); international education (M Ed); language, literacy and culture (Ed D); learning, media and technology (M Ed, CAGS); mathematics, science, and learning technologies (Ed D); policy studies (M Ed); policy studies in education (CAGS); reading and writing (M Ed); research and evaluation methods (Ed D); school counselor education (M Ed, CAGS); school psychology (CAGS); science education (CAGS); secondary teacher education (M Ed); social justice education (M Ed, Ed D, CAGS); special education (M Ed, Ed D, CAGS). *Accreditation:* NCATE. Part-time programs available. Postbaccalaureate distance learning degree programs offered (minimal on-campus study). *Faculty:* 74 full-time (41 women). *Students:* 377 full-time (268 women), 347 part-time (232 women); includes 115 minority (59 African Americans, 2 American Indian/Alaska Native, 16 Asian Americans or Pacific Islanders, 38 Hispanic Americans), 108 international. Average age 35. 708 applicants, 68% accepted, 266 enrolled. In 2009, 183 master's, 17 doctorates awarded. Terminal master's awarded for partial completion of doctoral program. *Degree requirements:* For master's, thesis or alternative; for doctorate, comprehensive exam, thesis/dissertation. *Entrance requirements:* Additional exam requirements/recommendations for international students: Required—TOEFL (minimum score 550 paper-based; 213 computer-based; 80 iBT), IELTS (minimum score 6.5). *Application deadline:* For fall admission, 1/15 for domestic and international students. Applications are processed on a rolling basis. Application fee: $50 ($65 for international students). Electronic applications accepted. *Expenses:* Tuition, state resident: full-time $2640; part-time $110 per credit. Tuition, nonresident: full-time $9936; part-time $414 per credit. Tuition and fees vary according to course load. *Financial support:* In 2009–10, 1 fellowship with full tuition reimbursement (averaging $8,036 per year), 92 research assistantships with full tuition reimbursements (averaging $8,555 per year), 83 teaching assistantships with full tuition reimbursements (averaging $4,661 per year) were awarded; career-related internships or fieldwork, Federal Work-Study, scholarships/grants, traineeships, health care benefits, tuition waivers (full), and unspecified assistantships also available. Support available to part-time students. Financial award application deadline: 1/15. *Unit head:* Dr. Linda L. Griffin, Graduate Program Director, 413-545-6984, Fax: 413-545-2873. *Application contact:* Jean M. Ames, Supervisor of Admissions, 413-545-0722, Fax: 413-577-0010, E-mail: gradadm@grad.umass.edu.

University of Massachusetts Boston, Office of Graduate Studies, Graduate College of Education, School Organization, Curriculum and Instruction Department, Program in Special Education, Boston, MA 02125-3393. Offers M Ed. Part-time and evening/weekend programs available. *Degree requirements:* For master's, comprehensive exam, practicum. *Entrance*

requirements: For master's, GRE General Test or MAT, minimum GPA of 2.75. *Faculty research:* Inclusionary learning, cross-cultural special needs, special education restructuring.

University of Memphis, Graduate School, College of Education, Department of Instruction and Curriculum Leadership, Memphis, TN 38152. Offers early childhood education (MAT, MS, Ed D); elementary education (MAT); instruction and curriculum (MS, Ed D); instruction design and technology (MS, Ed D); middle grades education (MAT); reading (MS, Ed D); secondary education (MAT); special education (MAT, MS, Ed D). *Accreditation:* NCATE (one or more programs are accredited). Part-time programs available. *Faculty:* 40 full-time (28 women), 20 part-time/adjunct (15 women). *Students:* 119 full-time (90 women), 631 part-time (505 women); includes 348 minority (331 African Americans, 2 American Indian/Alaska Native, 4 Asian Americans or Pacific Islanders, 11 Hispanic Americans), 7 international. Average age 34. 202 applicants, 77% accepted, 29 enrolled. In 2009, 137 master's, 10 doctorates awarded. Terminal master's awarded for partial completion of doctoral program. *Degree requirements:* For master's, comprehensive exam, thesis or alternative; for doctorate, comprehensive exam, thesis/dissertation. *Entrance requirements:* For master's, GRE General Test, minimum GPA of 2.5; for doctorate, GRE General Test, GRE Subject Test, 2 years of teaching experience. *Application deadline:* For fall admission, 8/1 for domestic students; for spring admission, 12/1 for domestic students. Applications are processed on a rolling basis. Application fee: $35 ($60 for international students). Electronic applications accepted. *Expenses:* Tuition, state resident: full-time $6246; part-time $347 per credit hour. Tuition, nonresident: full-time $15,894; part-time $883 per credit hour. Required fees: $1160. Full-time tuition and fees vary according to course load, degree level and program. *Financial support:* In 2009–10, 635 students received support; research assistantships with full tuition reimbursements available, teaching assistantships with full tuition reimbursements available, career-related internships or fieldwork, Federal Work-Study, institutionally sponsored loans, scholarships/grants, traineeships, and unspecified assistantships available. Support available to part-time students. Financial award application deadline: 2/15; financial award applicants required to submit FAFSA. *Faculty research:* Effective urban teachers, preparation and retention of urban teachers, technology utilization in schools, field-based teacher preparation programs, effective use of online instruction. *Unit head:* Dr. Sandra Cooley-Nichols, Interim Chair, 901-678-2365. *Application contact:* Dr. Sally Blake, Director of Graduate Studies, 901-678-4861.

University of Miami, Graduate School, School of Education, Department of Teaching and Learning, Program in Teaching and Learning, Coral Gables, FL 33124. Offers language and literacy learning in multilingual settings (PhD); mathematics and science education (PhD); special education (PhD). *Students:* 30 full-time (22 women); includes 11 minority (3 African Americans, 8 Hispanic Americans), 7 international. Average age 35. 21 applicants, 43% accepted, 7 enrolled. In 2009, 5 doctorates awarded. *Degree requirements:* For doctorate, thesis/dissertation, qualifying exam. *Entrance requirements:* For doctorate, GRE General Test. Additional exam requirements/recommendations for international students: Required—TOEFL (minimum score 550 paper-based; 80 iBT); Recommended—IELTS (minimum score 6.5). *Application deadline:* For fall admission, 2/15 for domestic students, 10/15 for international students. Application fee: $65. Electronic applications accepted. *Financial support:* In 2009–10, 25 students received support. Application deadline: 3/1. *Faculty research:* Teacher education, multicultural education, technology, second language acquisition, math and science education. *Unit head:* Dr. Batya Elbaum, Associate Department Chairperson, 305-284-4218, Fax: 305-284-4439, E-mail: elbaum@miami.edu. *Application contact:* Tinisha Hollinshead, Admission Coordinator, 305-284-2102, Fax: 305-284-6998, E-mail: tinisha@miami.edu.

University of Michigan–Dearborn, School of Education, Doctoral Program in Education, Dearborn, MI 48126. Offers curriculum and practice (Ed D); educational leadership (Ed D); educational psychology/special education (Ed D); metropolitan education (Ed D). Part-time and evening/weekend programs available. *Faculty:* 7 full-time (4 women). *Students:* 1 (woman) full-time, 17 part-time (9 women); includes 5 minority (3 African Americans, 1 Asian American or Pacific Islander, 1 Hispanic American). Average age 46. 62 applicants, 31% accepted, 18 enrolled. *Degree requirements:* For doctorate, comprehensive exam, thesis/dissertation. *Entrance requirements:* For doctorate, GRE (taken within the last 5 years), master's degree with minimum GPA of 3.3, 3 letters of recommendation (1 from faculty), 3 yearsprofessional and/or teaching experience. Additional exam requirements/recommendations for international students: Required—TOEFL (minimum score 550 paper-based), Test of Spoken English (TES). *Application deadline:* For fall admission, 3/1 for domestic and international students. Application fee: $60. *Expenses:* Tuition, state resident: part-time $504.10 per credit hour. Tuition, nonresident: part-time $957.90 per credit hour. *Faculty research:* Educational leadership, metropolitan education, curriculum and practice, educational psychology, special education, assessment. *Unit head:* Gail Luera, Associate Dean/Interim Coordinator, 313-593-5098, E-mail: grl@umich.edu. *Application contact:* Catherine Parkins, Customer Service Assistant, 313-583-6349, Fax: 313-593-4748, E-mail: cparkins@umd.umich.edu.

University of Michigan–Dearborn, School of Education, Programs in Special Education, Dearborn, MI 48126. Offers emotional impairments endorsement (M Ed); inclusion specialist (M Ed); learning disabilities endorsement (M Ed). Part-time and evening/weekend programs available. Postbaccalaureate distance learning degree programs offered (minimal on-campus study). *Faculty:* 4 full-time (all women), 5 part-time/adjunct (1 woman). *Students:* 10 full-time (8 women), 181 part-time (160 women); includes 20 minority (11 African Americans, 4 Asian Americans or Pacific Islanders, 5 Hispanic Americans). Average age 35. 44 applicants, 100% accepted, 44 enrolled. In 2009, 98 master's awarded. *Entrance requirements:* For master's, minimum GPA of 3.0, Michigan teaching certificate (for learning disabilities and emotional impairments endorsements); statement of purpose; 3 letters of recommendations. Additional exam requirements/recommendations for international students: Required—TOEFL, TWE. *Application deadline:* For fall admission, 9/5 priority date for domestic students, 8/3 for international students; for winter admission, 12/22 for domestic students, 1/4 for international students; for spring admission, 5/5 for domestic students, 3/4 for international students. Applications are processed on a rolling basis. Application fee: $60. *Expenses:* Tuition, state resident: part-time $504.10 per credit hour. Tuition, nonresident: part-time $957.90 per credit hour. *Financial support:* Career-related internships or fieldwork and Federal Work-Study available. Support available to part-time students. Financial award application deadline: 4/1; financial award applicants required to submit FAFSA. *Unit head:* Dr. Belinda Lazarus, Program Coordinator, 313-436-9136, Fax: 313-593-4748, E-mail: blazarus@umd.umich.edu. *Application contact:* Elizabeth M. Morden, Graduate Secretary, 313-436-9135, Fax: 313-593-4748, E-mail: emorden@umd.umich.edu.

University of Michigan–Flint, School of Education and Human Services, Department of Education, Flint, MI 48502-1950. Offers education (MA); elementary education with teaching certification (MA); literacy (K-12) (MA); special education (MA); technology in education (MA). Part-time programs available. *Faculty:* 14 full-time (12 women), 8 part-time/adjunct (4 women). *Students:* 27 full-time (24 women), 215 part-time (186 women); includes 22 minority (20 African Americans, 2 American Indian/Alaska Native). Average age 35. 63 applicants, 86% accepted, 43 enrolled. In 2009, 91 master's awarded. *Entrance requirements:* For master's, BS with minimum GPA of 3.0. Additional exam requirements/recommendations for international students: Required—TOEFL (minimum score 560 paper-based; 220 computer-based; 84 iBT), IELTS (minimum score 6.5). *Application deadline:* For fall admission, 8/1 priority date for domestic students, 5/1 priority date for international students; for winter admission, 11/15 priority date for domestic students, 9/15 priority date for international students; for spring admission, 3/15 priority date for domestic students, 1/15 priority date for international students. Application fee: $55. *Expenses:* Contact institution. *Financial support:* Federal Work-Study, scholarships/grants, and unspecified assistantships available. Support available to part-time students. Financial award application deadline: 6/1; financial award applicants required to submit FAFSA. *Unit head:* Dr. Beverly Schumer, Director, 810-424-5215, E-mail: bschumer@umflint.edu. *Application contact:* Beulah Alexander, Executive Secretary, 810-766-6879, Fax: 810-766-6891, E-mail: beulaha@umflint.edu.

University of Minnesota, Twin Cities Campus, Graduate School, College of Education and Human Development, Department of Curriculum and Instruction, Program in Teaching, Minneapolis, MN 55455-0213. Offers Chinese (M Ed); earth science (M Ed); elementary special education (M Ed); English (M Ed); English as a second language (M Ed); French (M Ed); German (M Ed); Hebrew (M Ed); Japanese (M Ed); life sciences (M Ed); mathematics (M Ed); middle school science (M Ed); science (M Ed); second languages and cultures (M Ed); social studies (M Ed); Spanish (M Ed). *Students:* 263 full-time (186 women), 117 part-time (83 women); includes 32 minority (10 African Americans, 2 American Indian/Alaska Native, 17 Asian Americans or Pacific Islanders, 3 Hispanic Americans), 4 international. Average age 27. 363 applicants, 74% accepted, 259 enrolled. In 2009, 497 master's awarded. *Unit head:* Dr. Ruth Thomas, Chair, 612-624-4772, Fax: 612-624-8277, E-mail: thoma006@umn.edu. *Application contact:* Dr. Mary Trettin, Associate Dean, 612-625-6501, Fax: 612-626-1580, E-mail: mtrettin@umn.edu.

University of Minnesota, Twin Cities Campus, Graduate School, College of Education and Human Development, Department of Educational Psychology, Program in Special Education, Minneapolis, MN 55455-0213. Offers M Ed, MA, PhD, Ed S. *Students:* 83 full-time (66 women), 33 part-time (29 women); includes 11 minority (4 African Americans, 5 Asian Americans or Pacific Islanders, 2 Hispanic Americans), 6 international. Average age 32. 104 applicants, 59% accepted, 49 enrolled. In 2009, 29 master's, 7 doctorates, 16 other advanced degrees awarded. *Unit head:* Dr. Susan Hupp, Chair, 612-624-1003, Fax: 612-624-8241, E-mail: shupp@umn.edu. *Application contact:* Dr. Mary Trettin, Associate Dean, 612-625-6501, Fax: 612-626-1580, E-mail: mtrettin@umn.edu.

University of Missouri, Graduate School, College of Education, Department of Special Education, Columbia, MO 65211. Offers administration and supervision of special education (PhD); behavior disorders (M Ed, PhD); curriculum development of exceptional students (M Ed, PhD); early childhood special education (M Ed, PhD); general special education (M Ed, MA, PhD); learning and instruction (M Ed); learning disabilities (M Ed, PhD); mental retardation (M Ed, PhD). Part-time and evening/weekend programs available. Postbaccalaureate distance learning degree programs offered (no on-campus study). *Degree requirements:* For master's, comprehensive exam, thesis or alternative; for doctorate, comprehensive exam, thesis/dissertation. *Entrance requirements:* For master's and doctorate, GRE General Test, letters of recommendation. Additional exam requirements/recommendations for international students: Required—TOEFL (minimum score 500 paper-based; 173 computer-based; 61 iBT). Electronic applications accepted. *Faculty research:* Positive behavior support, applied behavior analysis, attention deficit disorder, pre-linguistic development, school discipline.

University of Missouri–Kansas City, School of Education, Kansas City, MO 64110-2499. Offers administration (Ed D); counseling and guidance (MA, Ed S); counseling psychology (PhD); curriculum and instruction (MA, Ed S); education (PhD); educational administration (Ed S); reading education (MA, Ed S); special education (MA). PhD with concentration in education (interdisciplinary) is offered through the School of Graduate Studies. *Accreditation:* NCATE. Part-time and evening/weekend programs available. *Faculty:* 62 full-time (52 women), 45 part-time/adjunct (34 women). *Students:* 207 full-time (154 women), 401 part-time (290 women); includes 142 minority (107 African Americans, 14 Asian Americans or Pacific Islanders, 21 Hispanic Americans), 18 international. Average age 34. 294 applicants, 61% accepted, 150 enrolled. In 2009, 184 master's, 9 doctorates, 49 other advanced degrees awarded. *Degree requirements:* For doctorate, thesis/dissertation, internship, practicum. *Entrance requirements:* For master's, GRE, minimum GPA of 2.75, 2 letters of reference, written statement of purpose; for doctorate, GRE, minimum GPA of 3.0; for Ed S, minimum GPA of 3.0. Additional exam requirements/recommendations for international students: Required—TOEFL (minimum score 550 paper-based; 213 computer-based; 80 iBT). *Application deadline:* For fall admission, 4/1 priority date for domestic and international students; for spring admission, 11/1 priority date for domestic and international students. Applications are processed on a rolling basis. Application fee: $45 ($50 for international students). *Expenses:* Tuition, state resident: full-time $5378; part-time $299 per credit hour. Tuition, nonresident: full-time $13,881; part-time $771 per credit hour. Required fees: $641; $71 per credit hour. Tuition and fees vary according to course load and program. *Financial support:* In 2009–10, 19 research assistantships with partial tuition reimbursements (averaging $9,821 per year) were awarded; career-related internships or fieldwork, Federal Work-Study, institutionally sponsored loans, and tuition waivers (full and partial) also available. Support available to part-time students. Financial award application deadline: 3/1; financial award applicants required to submit FAFSA. *Faculty research:* Urban education, inquiry-based field study, theories of counseling and psychotherapy, school literacy, educational technology. Total annual research expenditures: $2.9 million. *Unit head:* Dr. Wanda Blanchett, Dean, 816-235-2234, Fax: 816-235-5270, E-mail: education@umkc.edu. *Application contact:* Erica Hernandez-Scott, Student Recruiter, 816-235-1295, Fax: 816-235-5270, E-mail: hernandeze@umkc.edu.

University of Missouri–St. Louis, College of Education, Division of Teaching and Learning, St. Louis, MO 63121. Offers elementary education (M Ed), including early childhood, general, reading; secondary education (M Ed), including curriculum and instruction, general, middle level education, reading, teaching English to speakers of other languages (TESOL); secondary school teaching (Certificate); special education (M Ed), including behavioral disorders, early childhood special education, general, learning disabilities, mental retardation; teaching English to speakers of other languages (Certificate). Part-time and evening/weekend programs available. *Faculty:* 36 full-time (23 women), 51 part-time/adjunct (42 women). *Students:* 123 full-time (77 women), 569 part-time (435 women); includes 137 minority (110 African Americans, 4 American Indian/Alaska Native, 10 Asian Americans or Pacific Islanders, 13 Hispanic Americans), 11 international. Average age 32. In 2009, 1,852 master's awarded. *Degree requirements:* For master's, comprehensive exam. *Entrance requirements:* Additional exam requirements/recommendations for international students: Recommended—TOEFL (minimum score 550 paper-based; 213 computer-based). *Application deadline:* For fall admission, 7/1 priority date for domestic and international students; for spring admission, 12/1 priority date for domestic and international students. Application fee: $35 ($40 for international students). Electronic applications accepted. *Expenses:* Tuition, state resident: full-time $5377; part-time $297.70 per credit hour. Tuition, nonresident: full-time $13,882; part-time $771.20 per credit hour. Required fees: $220; $12.20 per credit hour. One-time fee: $12. Tuition and fees vary according to course level, campus/location and program. *Financial support:* In 2009–10, 5 research assistantships (averaging $10,339 per year), 2 teaching assistantships (averaging $6,800 per year) were awarded. Financial award application deadline: 4/1; financial award applicants required to submit FAFSA. *Unit head:* Dr. Joseph Polman, Chair, 314-516-5791. *Application contact:* 314-516-5458, Fax: 314-516-6996, E-mail: gadadm@umsl.edu.

University of Nebraska at Kearney, College of Graduate Study, College of Education, Department of Teacher Education, Kearney, NE 68849-0001. Offers curriculum and instruction (MS Ed); instructional technology (MS Ed); reading education (MA Ed); special education (MA Ed). Part-time and evening/weekend programs available. *Degree requirements:* For master's, comprehensive exam, thesis optional. *Entrance requirements:* For master's, portfolio or GRE. Additional exam requirements/recommendations for international students: Required—TOEFL (minimum score 550 paper-based; 213 computer-based). Electronic applications accepted.

University of Nebraska at Omaha, Graduate Studies, College of Education, Department of Special Education and Communication Disorders, Omaha, NE 68182. Offers special education (MS); speech-language pathology (MA, MS). *Accreditation:* ASHA (one or more programs are accredited); NCATE. Part-time and evening/weekend programs available. *Faculty:* 10 full-time (6 women). *Students:* 34 full-time (32 women), 64 part-time (52 women); includes 5 minority (1 African American, 2 American Indian/Alaska Native, 1 Asian American or Pacific Islander, 1 Hispanic American), 1 international. Average age 30. 101 applicants, 49% accepted, 17 enrolled. In 2009, 26 master's awarded. *Degree requirements:* For master's, comprehensive exam, thesis (for some programs). *Entrance requirements:* For master's, GRE General Test or

Special Education

University of Nebraska at Omaha (continued)
MAT, minimum GPA of 3.0. Additional exam requirements/recommendations for international students: Required—TOEFL (minimum score 500 paper-based; 173 computer-based; 61 iBT). *Application deadline:* For fall admission, 2/1 for domestic students; for spring admission, 9/1 for domestic students. Applications are processed on a rolling basis. Application fee: $45. Electronic applications accepted. *Financial support:* In 2009–10, 64 students received support; fellowships, research assistantships with tuition reimbursements available, career-related internships or fieldwork, Federal Work-Study, institutionally sponsored loans, scholarships/grants, tuition waivers (partial), and unspecified assistantships available. Support available to part-time students. Financial award application deadline: 3/1; financial award applicants required to submit FAFSA. *Unit head:* Dr. Mary Friehe, Chairperson, 402-554-2201. *Application contact:* Dr. Mary Friehe, Chairperson, 402-554-2201.

University of Nebraska–Lincoln, Graduate College, College of Education and Human Sciences, Department of Special Education and Communication Disorders, Program in Special Education, Lincoln, NE 68588. Offers special education (M Ed). *Accreditation:* NCATE. *Degree requirements:* For master's, thesis optional. *Entrance requirements:* For master's, GRE. Additional exam requirements/recommendations for international students: Required—TOEFL (minimum score 500 paper-based; 173 computer-based). Electronic applications accepted.

University of Nebraska–Lincoln, Graduate College, College of Education and Human Sciences, Department of Teaching, Learning and Teacher Education, Lincoln, NE 68588. Offers adult and continuing education (MA); educational studies (Ed D, PhD), including special education (Ed D); teaching, learning and teacher education (M Ed, MA, MST, Ed D, PhD); vocational and adult education (M Ed, MA). *Accreditation:* NCATE. *Degree requirements:* For master's, thesis optional. *Entrance requirements:* Additional exam requirements/recommendations for international students: Required—TOEFL (minimum score 550 paper-based; 213 computer-based). Electronic applications accepted. *Faculty research:* Teacher education, instructional leadership, literacy education, technology, improvement of school curriculum.

University of Nevada, Las Vegas, Graduate College, College of Education, Department of Special Education, Las Vegas, NV 89154-3014. Offers early childhood education (M Ed); special education (MS, Ed D, PhD, Ed S). *Accreditation:* NCATE. Part-time and evening/weekend programs available. *Faculty:* 15 full-time (10 women), 12 part-time/adjunct (all women). *Students:* 203 full-time (168 women), 116 part-time (98 women); includes 79 minority (31 African Americans, 2 American Indian/Alaska Native, 19 Asian Americans or Pacific Islanders, 27 Hispanic Americans), 7 international. Average age 38. 144 applicants, 88% accepted, 105 enrolled. In 2009, 168 master's, 8 doctorates, 2 other advanced degrees awarded. *Degree requirements:* For master's, comprehensive exam (for some programs), thesis (for some programs), comprehensive portfolio (M Ed); for doctorate, comprehensive exam, thesis/dissertation. *Entrance requirements:* For doctorate and Ed S, GRE General Test. Additional exam requirements/recommendations for international students: Required—TOEFL (minimum score 550 paper-based; 213 computer-based; 80 iBT), IELTS (minimum score 7). *Application deadline:* For fall admission, 3/1 priority date for domestic and international students; for spring admission, 9/1 priority date for domestic and international students. Applications are processed on a rolling basis. Application fee: $60 ($95 for international students). Electronic applications accepted. *Financial support:* In 2009–10, 22 students received support, including 14 research assistantships with partial tuition reimbursements available (averaging $10,000 per year), 8 teaching assistantships with partial tuition reimbursements available (averaging $12,318 per year); institutionally sponsored loans, scholarships/grants, health care benefits, and unspecified assistantships also available. Financial award application deadline: 3/1. *Faculty research:* Autism, early childhood education, special education reneralist, early childhood special education, mental retardation. *Unit head:* Dr. Tom Pierce, Chair/ Professor, 702-895-3205, Fax: 702-895-0984, E-mail: tom.pierce@unlv.edu. *Application contact:* Graduate College Admissions Evaluator, 702-895-3320, Fax: 702-895-4180, E-mail: gradcollege@unlv.edu.

University of Nevada, Reno, Graduate School, College of Education, Department of Curriculum, Teaching and Learning, Reno, NV 89557. Offers curriculum and instruction (PhD); curriculum, teaching and learning (Ed D, PhD); elementary education (M Ed, MA, MS); secondary education (M Ed, MA, MS); special education and disability studies (PhD). *Degree requirements:* For master's, thesis optional; for doctorate, thesis/dissertation. *Entrance requirements:* For master's, GRE General Test, minimum GPA of 2.75; for doctorate, GRE General Test, minimum GPA of 3.0. Additional exam requirements/recommendations for international students: Required—TOEFL (minimum score 500 paper-based; 173 computer-based; 61 iBT), IELTS (minimum score 6). Electronic applications accepted. *Faculty research:* Education, curricula, pedagogy.

University of Nevada, Reno, Graduate School, College of Education, Department of Educational Specialties, Program in Special Education, Reno, NV 89557. Offers M Ed, MA, MS, Ed D, PhD. Terminal master's awarded for partial completion of doctoral program. *Degree requirements:* For master's, thesis optional; for doctorate, thesis/dissertation. *Entrance requirements:* For master's, minimum GPA of 2.75; for doctorate, GRE General Test, minimum GPA of 3.0. Additional exam requirements/recommendations for international students: Required—TOEFL (minimum score 500 paper-based; 173 computer-based; 61 iBT), IELTS (minimum score 6). Electronic applications accepted. *Faculty research:* Learning disabilities, equity and diversity in educational settings.

University of New Hampshire, Graduate School, College of Liberal Arts, Department of Education, Program in Early Childhood Education, Durham, NH 03824. Offers early childhood education (M Ed); special needs (M Ed). Part-time programs available. *Faculty:* 32 full-time. *Students:* 9 full-time (8 women), 8 part-time (7 women). Average age 31. 11 applicants, 91% accepted, 6 enrolled. In 2009, 13 master's awarded. *Degree requirements:* For master's, thesis or alternative. *Entrance requirements:* For master's, GRE General Test. Additional exam requirements/recommendations for international students: Required—TOEFL (minimum score 550 paper-based; 213 computer-based; 80 iBT). *Application deadline:* For fall admission, 2/1 priority date for domestic students, 2/1 for international students; for spring admission, 12/1 for domestic students. Applications are processed on a rolling basis. Application fee: $65. Electronic applications accepted. *Expenses:* Tuition, state resident: full-time $10,380; part-time $577 per credit hour. Tuition, nonresident: full-time $24,350; part-time $1002 per credit hour. Required fees: $1550; $387.50 per semester. Tuition and fees vary according to course load and program. *Financial support:* In 2009–10, 12 students received support; fellowships, research assistantships, teaching assistantships, career-related internships or fieldwork, Federal Work-Study, scholarships/grants, and tuition waivers (full and partial) available. Support available to part-time students. Financial award application deadline: 2/15. *Faculty research:* Young children with special needs. *Unit head:* Dr. Todd Demitchell, Coordinator, 603-862-5043, E-mail: education.department@unh.edu. *Application contact:* Dr. Todd Demitchell, Coordinator, 603-862-5043, E-mail: education.department@unh.edu.

University of New Hampshire, Graduate School, College of Liberal Arts, Department of Education, Program in Special Education, Durham, NH 03824. Offers M Ed, Postbaccalaureate Certificate. Part-time programs available. *Faculty:* 32 full-time. *Students:* 7 full-time (all women), 23 part-time (19 women). Average age 41. 14 applicants, 79% accepted, 9 enrolled. In 2009, 8 master's, 2 other advanced degrees awarded. *Degree requirements:* For master's, thesis or alternative. *Entrance requirements:* For master's, GRE General Test. Additional exam requirements/recommendations for international students: Required—TOEFL (minimum score 550 paper-based; 213 computer-based; 80 iBT). *Application deadline:* For fall admission, 6/1 priority date for domestic students, 4/1 for international students; for spring admission, 12/1 for domestic students. Applications are processed on a rolling basis. Application fee: $65. Electronic applications accepted. *Expenses:* Tuition, state resident: full-time $10,380; part-time $577 per credit hour. Tuition, nonresident: full-time $24,350; part-time $1002 per credit hour. Required fees: $1550; $387.50 per semester. Tuition and fees vary according to course load and program. *Financial support:* In 2009–10, 3 students received support; fellowships, research assistantships, teaching assistantships, career-related internships or fieldwork, Federal Work-Study, scholarships/grants, and tuition waivers (full and partial) available. Support available to part-time students. Financial award application deadline: 2/15. *Unit head:* Dr. Georgia Kerns, Coordinator, 603-862-3446, E-mail: education.department@unh.edu. *Application contact:* Dr. Georgia Kerns, Coordinator, 603-862-3446, E-mail: education.department@unh.edu.

University of New Mexico, Graduate School, College of Education, Department of Educational Specialties, Program in Intensive Social, Language and Behavioral Needs, Albuquerque, NM 87131-2039. Offers Graduate Certificate. Part-time and evening/weekend programs available. *Students:* 1 (woman) full-time, 6 part-time (all women); includes 2 minority (1 African American, 1 Hispanic American), 1 international. Average age 48. 1 applicant, 100% accepted, 1 enrolled. *Entrance requirements:* Additional exam requirements/recommendations for international students: Required—TOEFL (minimum score 550 paper-based; 213 computer-based). *Application deadline:* For fall admission, 3/31 priority date for domestic students, 3/1 for international students; for spring admission, 9/30 priority date for domestic students, 8/1 for international students. Applications are processed on a rolling basis. Application fee: $50. Electronic applications accepted. *Expenses:* Tuition, state resident: full-time $2099; part-time $233.20 per credit hour. Tuition, nonresident: full-time $6650. Required fees: $25 per semester. Tuition and fees vary according to course load, program and reciprocity agreements. *Financial support:* Application deadline: 3/1. *Unit head:* Ruth Luckasson, Chair, 505-266-6510, Fax: 505-277-6929, E-mail: ruthl@unm.edu. *Application contact:* Jo Sanchez, Information Contact, 505-277-5018, Fax: 505-277-8679, E-mail: jsanchez@unm.edu.

University of New Mexico, Graduate School, College of Education, Department of Educational Specialties, Program in Special Education, Albuquerque, NM 87131-2039. Offers MA, Ed D, PhD, EDSPC. *Accreditation:* NCATE. Part-time and evening/weekend programs available. *Faculty:* 16 full-time (15 women), 9 part-time/adjunct (7 women). *Students:* 42 full-time (31 women), 144 part-time (115 women); includes 63 minority (10 African Americans, 9 American Indian/Alaska Native, 3 Asian Americans or Pacific Islanders, 41 Hispanic Americans), 13 international. Average age 38. 50 applicants, 56% accepted, 25 enrolled. In 2009, 47 master's, 2 doctorates awarded. *Degree requirements:* For master's, comprehensive exam, thesis optional; for doctorate, comprehensive exam, thesis/dissertation, screening, proposal hearing. *Entrance requirements:* For master's, minimum GPA of 3.2; for doctorate, minimum GPA of 3.2, 2 years of relevant experience; for EDSPC, special education degree, 2 years of teaching experience with people with disabilities, writing sample, minimum GPA of 3.2. *Application deadline:* For fall admission, 3/31 priority date for domestic students; for spring admission, 9/30 priority date for domestic students. Applications are processed on a rolling basis. Application fee: $50. Electronic applications accepted. *Expenses:* Tuition, state resident: full-time $2099; part-time $233.20 per credit hour. Tuition, nonresident: full-time $6650. Required fees: $25 per semester. Tuition and fees vary according to course load, program and reciprocity agreements. *Financial support:* In 2009–10, 64 students received support, including 12 fellowships (averaging $17,250 per year), 2 research assistantships with tuition reimbursements available (averaging $17,250 per year), 8 teaching assistantships with tuition reimbursements available (averaging $17,250 per year); career-related internships or fieldwork, Federal Work-Study, scholarships/grants, traineeships, health care benefits, unspecified assistantships, and stipends also available. Support available to part-time students. Financial award application deadline: 3/1; financial award applicants required to submit FAFSA. *Faculty research:* Mathematics instruction, bilingual special education, inclusive education, autism, reading instruction for students with cognitive disabilities, alternative assessment, human rights and disability, applied behavior analysis, bilingualism, language and literacy, mathematics, science instruction, special education. *Unit head:* Prof. Ruth Luckasson, Chair, 505-277-6510, Fax: 505-277-6929, E-mail: luckasson@unm.edu. *Application contact:* Jo Sanchez, Information Contact, 505-277-5018, Fax: 505-277-8679, E-mail: jsanchez@unm.edu.

University of New Orleans, Graduate School, College of Education and Human Development, Department of Special Education, New Orleans, LA 70148. Offers M Ed, PhD, GCE. *Accreditation:* NCATE. Evening/weekend programs available. *Degree requirements:* For doctorate, variable foreign language requirement, thesis/dissertation. *Entrance requirements:* For master's, GRE General Test; for doctorate, GRE General Test, GRE Subject Test. Additional exam requirements/recommendations for international students: Required—TOEFL (minimum score 550 paper-based; 213 computer-based; 79 iBT). Electronic applications accepted. *Faculty research:* Inclusion, transition, early childhood, mild/moderate, severe/profound.

University of North Alabama, College of Education, Department of Elementary Education, Collaborative Teacher Special Education Program, Florence, AL 35632-0001. Offers learning disabilities (MA Ed); mentally retarded (MA Ed); mild learning handicapped (MA Ed). *Accreditation:* NCATE. Part-time and evening/weekend programs available. *Faculty:* 1 (woman) part-time/adjunct. *Students:* 4 full-time (all women), 21 part-time (15 women); includes 2 minority (1 African American, 1 American Indian/Alaska Native). Average age 33. In 2009, 4 master's awarded. *Degree requirements:* For master's, comprehensive exam. *Entrance requirements:* For master's, GRE, MAT, or NTE, minimum GPA of 2.5, Alabama Class B Certificate or equivalent, teaching experience. *Application deadline:* For fall admission, 7/1 priority date for domestic students; for spring admission, 12/1 for domestic students. Applications are processed on a rolling basis. Application fee: $25. Electronic applications accepted. *Expenses:* Tuition, state resident: full-time $5040; part-time $210 per credit hour. Tuition, nonresident: full-time $10,080; part-time $420 per credit hour. Required fees: $906. *Financial support:* Federal Work-Study available. Support available to part-time students. Financial award application deadline: 4/1. *Unit head:* Dr. Linda Armstrong, Chair, 256-765-4251, Fax: 256-765-4664, E-mail: ljarmstrong@una.edu. *Application contact:* Kim Mauldin, Director of Admissions, 256-765-4608, Fax: 256-765-4960, E-mail: komauldin@una.edu.

The University of North Carolina at Charlotte, Graduate School, College of Education, Department of Special Education and Child Development, Charlotte, NC 28223-0001. Offers special education (M Ed, PhD), including academically gifted (M Ed), behavioral—emotional handicaps (M Ed), cross-categorical disabilities (M Ed), learning disabilities (M Ed), mental handicaps (M Ed), severe and profound handicaps (M Ed). Part-time programs available. *Faculty:* 25 full-time (17 women), 5 part-time/adjunct (4 women). *Students:* 20 full-time (19 women), 141 part-time (130 women); includes 13 African Americans, 3 American Indian/Alaska Native, 2 Hispanic Americans, 2 international. Average age 35. 17 applicants, 94% accepted, 12 enrolled. In 2009, 19 master's, 22 doctorates awarded. *Degree requirements:* For doctorate, comprehensive exam, thesis/dissertation, portfolio, qualifying exam. *Entrance requirements:* For master's, GRE or MAT; for doctorate, GRE or MAT, 3 letters of reference, resume or curriculum vitae, minimum GPA of 3.5, master's degree in special education or related field, 3 years of teaching experience. Additional exam requirements/recommendations for international students: Required—TOEFL (minimum score 557 paper-based; 220 computer-based; 83 iBT), TOEFL (minimum score 550 paper-based; 220 computer-based) or Michigan English Language Assessment Battery. *Application deadline:* For fall admission, 7/15 for domestic students, 5/1 for international students; for spring admission, 11/15 for domestic students, 10/1 for international students. Application fee: $55. *Financial support:* In 2009–10, 18 students received support, including 9 research assistantships (averaging $12,299 per year), 9 teaching assistantships (averaging $14,165 per year). Financial award application deadline: 4/1; financial award applicants required to submit FAFSA. *Faculty research:* Transition to adulthood and self-determination, teaching reading and other academic skills to students with disabilities, alternate assessment, early intervention, preschool education. Total annual research expenditures: $3.2 million. *Unit head:* David Gilmore, Unit Head, 704-687-8186, Fax: 704-687-2916. *Application contact:* Kathy B. Giddings, Director of Graduate Admissions, 704-687-5503, Fax: 704-687-3279, E-mail: gradadm@uncc.edu.

The University of North Carolina at Charlotte, Graduate School, College of Education, Program in Teacher Education, Charlotte, NC 28223-0001. Offers art education (K-12) (MAT); dance education (K-12) (MAT); elementary education (K-6) (MAT); English as a second language (K-12) (MAT); foreign language education (K-12) (MAT); general teacher education (MAT); middle grades education (6-9) (MAT); music education (K-12) (MAT); secondary education (9-12) (MAT); special education (K-12) (MAT); theatre education (K-12) (MAT). *Faculty:* 108 full-time (64 women), 16 part-time/adjunct (12 women). *Students:* 29 full-time (20 women), 229

part-time (189 women); includes 32 minority (22 African Americans, 2 American Indian/Alaska Native, 3 Asian Americans or Pacific Islanders, 5 Hispanic Americans). Average age 32. 108 applicants, 92% accepted, 85 enrolled. In 2009, 59 master's awarded. *Entrance requirements:* For master's, GRE or MAT. Additional exam requirements/recommendations for international students: Required—TOEFL (minimum score 557 paper-based; 220 computer-based; 83 iBT). *Application deadline:* For fall admission, 7/1 for domestic students, 5/1 for international students; for spring admission, 11/1 for domestic students, 10/1 for international students. Applications are processed on a rolling basis. Application fee: $55. Electronic applications accepted. *Financial support:* In 2009–10, 5 students received support, including 1 research assistantship (averaging $18,000 per year), 3 teaching assistantships (averaging $12,183 per year); career-related internships or fieldwork, Federal Work-Study, institutionally sponsored loans, scholarships/grants, and administrative assistantship also available. Support available to part-time students. Financial award application deadline: 4/1; financial award applicants required to submit FAFSA. Total annual research expenditures: $5.1 million. *Unit head:* Dr. Kimberly J. Hartman, Coordinator, 704-687-8883, Fax: 704-687-6430, E-mail: khartman@uncc.edu. *Application contact:* Kathy B. Giddings, Director of Graduate Admissions, 704-687-5503, Fax: 704-687-3279, E-mail: gradadmn@uncc.edu.

The University of North Carolina at Greensboro, Graduate School, School of Education, Department of Specialized Education Services, Greensboro, NC 27412-5001. Offers cross-categorical special education (M Ed); interdisciplinary studies in special education (M Ed); leadership early care and education (Certificate); special education (M Ed, PhD). *Degree requirements:* For master's, thesis or alternative. *Entrance requirements:* For master's, GRE General Test. Additional exam requirements/recommendations for international students: Required—TOEFL. Electronic applications accepted.

University of North Dakota, Graduate School, College of Education and Human Development, Program in Special Education, Grand Forks, ND 58202. Offers M Ed, MS. *Accreditation:* NCATE. Part-time programs available. Postbaccalaureate distance learning degree programs offered (minimal on-campus study). *Degree requirements:* For master's, comprehensive exam, thesis or alternative. *Entrance requirements:* For master's, minimum GPA of 3.0. Additional exam requirements/recommendations for international students: Required—TOEFL (minimum score 550 paper-based; 213 computer-based; 79 iBT), IELTS (minimum score 6.5). Electronic applications accepted. *Faculty research:* Visual, emotional, and mental disabilities; early childhood.

University of North Dakota, Graduate School, College of Education and Human Development, Teaching and Learning Program, Grand Forks, ND 58202. Offers elementary education (Ed D, PhD); measurement and statistics (Ed D, PhD); secondary education (Ed D, PhD); special education (Ed D, PhD). *Accreditation:* NCATE. Postbaccalaureate distance learning degree programs offered (minimal on-campus study). *Degree requirements:* For doctorate, comprehensive exam, thesis/dissertation, final exam. *Entrance requirements:* For doctorate, minimum GPA of 3.5. Additional exam requirements/recommendations for international students: Required—TOEFL (minimum score 550 paper-based; 213 computer-based; 79 iBT), IELTS (minimum score 6.5). Electronic applications accepted.

University of Northern Colorado, Graduate School, College of Education and Behavioral Sciences, School of Special Education, Program in Special Education, Greeley, CO 80639. Offers MA, Ed D. *Accreditation:* NCATE. Part-time and evening/weekend programs available. Postbaccalaureate distance learning degree programs offered (no on-campus study). *Faculty:* 15 full-time (8 women). *Students:* 62 full-time (52 women), 146 part-time (130 women); includes 7 minority (1 African American, 1 Asian American or Pacific Islander, 5 Hispanic Americans), 15 international. Average age 35. 139 applicants, 94% accepted, 56 enrolled. In 2009, 80 master's, 2 doctorates awarded. *Degree requirements:* For master's, comprehensive exam, thesis or alternative; for doctorate, comprehensive exam, thesis/dissertation. *Entrance requirements:* For master's, letters of recommendation, interview; for doctorate, GRE General Test, resume. *Application deadline:* Applications are processed on a rolling basis. Application fee: $50 ($60 for international students). Electronic applications accepted. *Expenses:* Tuition, state resident: full-time $5770; part-time $320.55 per credit hour. Tuition, nonresident: full-time $13,847; part-time $769.27 per credit hour. Required fees: $948.78; $52.72 per credit. *Financial support:* Fellowships, research assistantships, teaching assistantships, unspecified assistantships available. Financial award application deadline: 3/1; financial award applicants required to submit FAFSA. *Unit head:* Dr. Harvey Rude, Director, 970-351-2691, Fax: 970-351-1061. *Application contact:* Linda Sisson, Graduate Student Admission Coordinator, 970-351-1807, Fax: 970-351-2371, E-mail: linda.sisson@unco.edu.

University of Northern Iowa, Graduate College, College of Education, Department of Special Education, Cedar Falls, IA 50614. Offers MAE, Ed D. Part-time and evening/weekend programs available. *Students:* 13 full-time (12 women), 34 part-time (33 women), 1 international. 14 applicants, 64% accepted, 8 enrolled. In 2009, 8 master's, 1 doctorate awarded. *Degree requirements:* For master's, comprehensive exam (for some programs), thesis or alternative; for doctorate, thesis/dissertation. *Entrance requirements:* For master's, minimum GPA of 3.0; for doctorate, GRE, minimum GPA of 3.5. Additional exam requirements/recommendations for international students: Required—TOEFL (minimum score 500 paper-based; 180 computer-based; 61 iBT). *Application deadline:* For fall admission, 8/1 priority date for domestic students. Applications are processed on a rolling basis. Application fee: $30 ($50 for international students). Electronic applications accepted. *Financial support:* Career-related internships or fieldwork, Federal Work-Study, scholarships/grants, and tuition waivers (full and partial) available. Support available to part-time students. Financial award application deadline: 2/1. *Unit head:* Dr. Frank Kohler, Interim Head, 319-273-7484, Fax: 319-273-7852, E-mail: frank.kohler@uni.edu. *Application contact:* Laurie S. Russell, Record Analyst, 319-273-2623, Fax: 319-273-6792, E-mail: laurie.russell@uni.edu.

University of North Florida, College of Education and Human Services, Department of Exceptional Student and Deaf Education, Jacksonville, FL 32224. Offers American sign language/English interpreting (M Ed); applied behavior analysis (M Ed); deaf education (M Ed); disability services (M Ed); exceptional student education (M Ed). *Accreditation:* NCATE. Part-time and evening/weekend programs available. *Faculty:* 11 full-time (9 women). *Students:* 34 full-time (all women), 33 part-time (28 women); includes 8 minority (2 African Americans, 3 Asian Americans or Pacific Islanders, 3 Hispanic Americans). Average age 31. 23 applicants, 61% accepted, 8 enrolled. In 2009, 34 master's awarded. *Entrance requirements:* For master's, GRE General Test, minimum GPA of 3.0 in last 60 hours, interview, 3 letters of recommendation. Additional exam requirements/recommendations for international students: Required—TOEFL (minimum score 500 paper-based; 173 computer-based). *Application deadline:* For fall admission, 7/1 priority date for domestic students, 5/1 for international students; for spring admission, 11/1 priority date for domestic students, 10/1 for international students. Applications are processed on a rolling basis. Application fee: $30. Electronic applications accepted. *Expenses:* Tuition, state resident: full-time $6649.20; part-time $277.05 per credit hour. Tuition, nonresident: full-time $22,970; part-time $957.08 per credit hour. Required fees: $985; $41.03 per credit hour. *Financial support:* In 2009–10, 40 students received support; research assistantships, teaching assistantships, career-related internships or fieldwork, Federal Work-Study, and tuition waivers (partial) available. Support available to part-time students. Financial award application deadline: 4/1; financial award applicants required to submit FAFSA. *Faculty research:* Transition, integrating technology into teacher education, written language development, professional school development, learning strategies. Total annual research expenditures: $1 million. *Unit head:* Dr. Karen Patterson, Chair, 904-620-2930, Fax: 904-620-3895, E-mail: karen.patterson@unf.edu. *Application contact:* Kiersten Jarvis, Graduate Admissions Coordinator, 904-620-2530, Fax: 904-620-1135, E-mail: kiersten.jarvis@unf.edu.

University of North Texas, Robert B. Toulouse School of Graduate Studies, College of Education, Department of Educational Psychology, Program in Special Education, Denton, TX 76203. Offers alternative initial certification (Certificate); autism intervention (M Ed); behavioral specialist (Certificate); EC-12 generalist certification (M Ed); emotional/behavioral disorders (M Ed); gifted education (Certificate); special education (M Ed, PhD, Certificate); teaching

students with traumatic brain injury (Certificate); transition (M Ed); transition specialist (Certificate); traumatic brain injury (M Ed). *Accreditation:* NCATE. *Degree requirements:* For master's, comprehensive exam (for some programs); for doctorate, one foreign language, comprehensive exam, thesis/dissertation, internship. *Entrance requirements:* For master's, GRE General Test, bachelor's degree; minimum GPA of 2.8, 3.0 in last 60 undergraduate hours; 2 letters of reference; resume or curriculum vitae; personal statement; for doctorate, GRE General Test, admissions exam, master's degree, minimum GPA of 3.0, 3 years teaching experience, 2 letters of reference, resume or curriculum vitae, personal statement, letter of intent; for Certificate, letter of intent. Additional exam requirements/recommendations for international students: Recommended—TOEFL (minimum score 550 paper-based; 213 computer-based). *Application deadline:* Applications are processed on a rolling basis. Application fee: $50 ($75 for international students). Electronic applications accepted. *Expenses:* Tuition, state resident: full-time $4298; part-time $239 per contact hour. Tuition, nonresident: full-time $9878; part-time $549 per contact hour. Required fees: $265 per contact hour. *Financial support:* Fellowships, research assistantships, teaching assistantships, career-related internships or fieldwork, Federal Work-Study, and institutionally sponsored loans available. *Faculty research:* Autism, behavior disorders, learning disabilities, transition, teacher preparation, severe disabilities, families of students with disabilities. Total annual research expenditures: $2.4 million. *Application contact:* Graduate Advisor, 940-565-2000, Fax: 940-565-2185, E-mail: bullock@unt.edu.

University of Oklahoma, Graduate College, College of Education, Department of Educational Psychology, Program in Special Education, Norman, OK 73019. Offers M Ed, PhD. *Accreditation:* NCATE. Part-time and evening/weekend programs available. *Students:* 16 full-time (14 women), 31 part-time (26 women); includes 13 minority (7 African Americans, 4 American Indian/Alaska Native, 1 Asian American or Pacific Islander, 1 Hispanic American), 4 international. 7 applicants, 71% accepted, 4 enrolled. In 2009, 7 master's, 2 doctorates awarded. Terminal master's awarded for partial completion of doctoral program. *Degree requirements:* For master's, thesis optional; for doctorate, variable foreign language requirement, thesis/dissertation. *Entrance requirements:* For master's, minimum GPA of 3.0; for doctorate, GRE General Test, master's degree, minimum graduate GPA of 3.0. Additional exam requirements/recommendations for international students: Required—TOEFL (minimum score 550 paper-based; 213 computer-based). *Application deadline:* For fall admission, 4/1 for domestic and international students; for spring admission, 11/1 for domestic students, 9/1 for international students. Applications are processed on a rolling basis. Application fee: $40 ($90 for international students). Electronic applications accepted. *Expenses:* Tuition, state resident: full-time $3744; part-time $156 per credit hour. Tuition, nonresident: full-time $13,577; part-time $565.70 per credit hour. Required fees: $2415; $90.10 per credit hour. *Financial support:* In 2009–10, 16 students received support. Career-related internships or fieldwork, Federal Work-Study, institutionally sponsored loans, scholarships/grants, health care benefits, and unspecified assistantships available. Support available to part-time students. Financial award applicants required to submit FAFSA. *Unit head:* Dr. Terri K. Debacker, Chair, 405-325-1068, Fax: 405-325-6655, E-mail: debacker@ou.edu. *Application contact:* Rashida Y. Douglas, Graduate Programs Officer, 405-325-4525, Fax: 405-325-6655, E-mail: ryd618@ou.edu.

University of Oklahoma Health Sciences Center, Graduate College, College of Allied Health, Department of Communication Sciences and Disorders, Oklahoma City, OK 73190. Offers audiology (MS, Au D, PhD); communication sciences and disorders (Certificate), including reading, speech-language pathology; education of the deaf (MS); speech-language pathology (MS, PhD). *Accreditation:* ASHA (one or more programs are accredited). Part-time programs available. *Faculty:* 13 full-time (10 women), 2 part-time/adjunct (1 woman). *Students:* 67 full-time (66 women), 4 part-time (3 women); includes 10 minority (8 American Indian/Alaska Native, 1 Asian American or Pacific Islander, 1 Hispanic American). Average age 25. 92 applicants, 49% accepted, 25 enrolled. In 2009, 24 master's, 7 doctorates awarded. Terminal master's awarded for partial completion of doctoral program. *Degree requirements:* For master's, comprehensive exam, thesis optional; for doctorate, one foreign language, comprehensive exam, thesis/dissertation. *Entrance requirements:* For master's and doctorate, GRE General Test, 3 letters of recommendation. Additional exam requirements/recommendations for international students: Required—TOEFL (minimum score 550 paper-based). *Application deadline:* For fall admission, 2/1 for domestic students. Applications are processed on a rolling basis. Application fee: $50. *Expenses:* Tuition, state resident: full-time $3120; part-time $156 per credit hour. Tuition, nonresident: full-time $11,314; part-time $409.70 per credit hour. Required fees: $1471; $51.20 per credit hour. $223.25 per term. *Financial support:* In 2009–10, 8 research assistantships (averaging $16,000 per year) were awarded; fellowships, career-related internships or fieldwork, Federal Work-Study, institutionally sponsored loans, and traineeships also available. Support available to part-time students. *Faculty research:* Event-related potentials, cleft palate, fluency disorders, language disorders, hearing and speech science. *Unit head:* Dr. Stephen Painton, Chair, 405-271-4214, E-mail: stephen-painton@ouhsc.edu. *Application contact:* Dr. Sarah Christman, Graduate Liaison, 405-271-4214, Fax: 405-271-1153, E-mail: sarah-christman@ouhsc.edu.

University of Phoenix, College of Natural Sciences, College of Education, Phoenix, AZ 85034-7209. Offers administration and supervision (MAEd); adult education and training (MAEd); curriculum and instruction (MAEd); curriculum and instruction-adult education (MAEd); curriculum and instruction-computer education (MAEd); curriculum and instruction-English and language arts education (MAEd); curriculum and instruction-English as a second language (MAEd); curriculum and instruction-mathematics education (MAEd); curriculum education (MAEd); early childhood (MAEd); elementary teacher education (MAEd); secondary teacher education (MAEd); special education (MAEd); teacher leadership (MAEd). *Accreditation:* Teacher Education Accreditation Council. Evening/weekend programs available. Postbaccalaureate distance learning degree programs offered (no on-campus study). *Faculty:* 47 full-time (34 women), 844 part-time/adjunct (636 women). *Students:* 13,657 full-time (10,698 women); includes 4,000 minority (3,063 African Americans, 74 American Indian/Alaska Native, 241 Asian Americans or Pacific Islanders, 622 Hispanic Americans), 307 international. Average age 36. In 2009, 17,246 master's awarded. *Degree requirements:* For master's, thesis (for some programs). *Entrance requirements:* For master's, 3 years of work experience, minimum GPA of 2.5. Additional exam requirements/recommendations for international students: Required—TOEFL (minimum score 550 paper-based; 213 computer-based; 79 iBT). *Application deadline:* Applications are processed on a rolling basis. Application fee: $45. Electronic applications accepted. *Expenses:* Tuition: Full-time $13,272. Required fees: $660. Full-time tuition and fees vary according to course level, degree level and program. *Financial support:* Institutionally sponsored loans and scholarships/grants available. Financial award applicants required to submit FAFSA. *Unit head:* Dr. Meredith Curley, Dean/Executive Director, 480-557-1217, Fax: 480-557-1588, E-mail: meredith.curley@phoenix.edu. *Application contact:* Chair, 602-387-7000, Fax: 602-387-6020.

University of Phoenix–Hawaii Campus, The Artemis School, College of Education, Honolulu, HI 96813-4317. Offers administration and supervision (MA Ed); curriculum and instruction (MA Ed); elementary education (MA Ed); secondary education (MA Ed); special education (MA Ed); teacher education for elementary licensure (MA Ed). Evening/weekend programs available. *Degree requirements:* For master's, thesis (for some programs). *Entrance requirements:* For master's, minimum undergraduate GPA of 2.5, 3 years of work experience. Additional exam requirements/recommendations for international students: Required—TOEFL (minimum score 550 paper-based; 213 computer-based; 79 iBT). Electronic applications accepted.

University of Phoenix–Metro Detroit Campus, College of Education, Troy, MI 48098-2623. Offers administration and supervision (MA Ed); elementary teacher education (MA Ed); secondary teacher education (MA Ed); special education (MA Ed). Evening/weekend programs available. *Faculty:* 3 full-time (1 woman), 2 part-time/adjunct (both women). *Students:* 34 full-time (30 women); includes 23 minority (all African Americans). Average age 44. In 2009, 44 master's awarded. *Degree requirements:* For master's, thesis (for some programs). *Entrance requirements:* For master's, 3 years of work experience, minimum undergraduate GPA of 2.5.

Special Education

University of Phoenix–Metro Detroit Campus (continued)
Additional exam requirements/recommendations for international students: Required—TOEFL (minimum score 550 paper-based; 213 computer-based; 79 iBT). *Application deadline:* Applications are processed on a rolling basis. Application fee: $45. Electronic applications accepted. *Expenses:* Tuition: Full-time $14,136. Required fees: $660. *Financial support:* Institutionally sponsored loans and scholarships/grants available. Financial award applicants required to submit FAFSA. *Unit head:* Dr. Meredith Curley, Dean/Executive Director, 480-557-1217, E-mail: meredith.curley@phoenix.edu. *Application contact:* Chair, 800-834-2438, Fax: 248-267-0147.

University of Phoenix–Omaha Campus, College of Education, Omaha, NE 68154-5240. Offers administration and supervision (MA Ed); curriculum and instruction (MA Ed), including adult education, computer education, curriculum and instruction, English and language arts education, English as a second language, mathematics education; elementary teacher education (MA Ed); secondary teacher education (MA Ed); special education (MA Ed).

University of Phoenix–Phoenix Campus, College of Social Sciences, College of Education, Phoenix, AZ 85040-1958. Offers administration and supervision (MA Ed); elementary teacher education (MA Ed); secondary teacher education (MA Ed); special education (MA Ed). Evening/weekend programs available. *Faculty:* 39 full-time (23 women), 422 part-time/adjunct (255 women). *Students:* 443 full-time (297 women); includes 79 minority (32 African Americans, 8 American Indian/Alaska Native, 8 Asian Americans or Pacific Islanders, 31 Hispanic Americans), 6 international. Average age 35. In 2009, 199 master's awarded. *Degree requirements:* For master's, thesis (for some programs). *Entrance requirements:* For master's, 3 years of work experience, minimum undergraduate GPA of 2.5. Additional exam requirements/recommendations for international students: Required—TOEFL (minimum score 550 paper-based; 213 computer-based; 79 iBT). *Application deadline:* Applications are processed on a rolling basis. Application fee: $45. Electronic applications accepted. *Expenses:* Tuition: Full-time $10,272. Required fees: $760. *Financial support:* Institutionally sponsored loans and scholarships/grants available. Financial award applicants required to submit FAFSA. *Unit head:* Dr. Meredith Curley, Dean/Executive Director, 480-557-1217, Fax: 480-557-1588, E-mail: meredith.curley@phoenix.edu. *Application contact:* College Chair, 480-804-2000.

University of Phoenix–Southern Arizona Campus, The Artemis School, College of Education, Tucson, AZ 85711. Offers administration and supervision (MA Ed); adult education and training (MA Ed); curriculum instruction (MA Ed); educational counseling (MA Ed); elementary teacher education (MA Ed); school counseling (MSC); secondary teacher education (MA Ed); special education (MA Ed, Certificate). Evening/weekend programs available. *Degree requirements:* For master's, thesis (for some programs). *Entrance requirements:* For master's, minimum undergraduate GPA of 2.5, 3 years of work experience. Additional exam requirements/recommendations for international students: Required—TOEFL (minimum score 550 paper-based; 213 computer-based; 79 iBT). Electronic applications accepted.

University of Phoenix–Southern California Campus, College of Education, Costa Mesa, CA 92626. Offers administration and supervision (MA Ed); adult education and training (MA Ed); curriculum and instruction (MA Ed), including computer education, curriculum and instruction, English and language arts, English as a second language, mathematics education; early childhood education (MA Ed); special education (MA Ed); teacher leadership (MA Ed). Evening/weekend programs available. *Faculty:* 47 full-time (34 women), 844 part-time/adjunct (636 women). *Students:* 558 full-time (391 women); includes 222 minority (60 African Americans, 4 American Indian/Alaska Native, 26 Asian Americans or Pacific Islanders, 132 Hispanic Americans), 9 international. Average age 34. In 2009, 303 master's awarded. *Degree requirements:* For master's, thesis (for some programs). *Entrance requirements:* For master's, minimum undergraduate GPA of 2.5, 3 years work experience. Additional exam requirements/recommendations for international students: Required—TOEFL (minimum score 550 paper-based; 213 computer-based; 79 iBT). *Application deadline:* Applications are processed on a rolling basis. Application fee: $45. Electronic applications accepted. *Expenses:* Tuition: Full-time $15,120. Required fees: $660. *Financial support:* Institutionally sponsored loans and scholarships/grants available. Financial award applicants required to submit FAFSA. *Unit head:* Dr. Meredith Curley, Dean/Executive Director, 480-557-1217, Fax: 480-557-1588, E-mail: meredith.curley@phoenix.edu. *Application contact:* Campus College Chair, 714-378-1878, Fax: 714-378-5875.

University of Phoenix–Utah Campus, The Artemis School, College of Education, Salt Lake City, UT 84123-4617. Offers administration and supervision (MA Ed); curriculum and instruction (MA Ed); elementary teacher education (MA Ed); school counseling (MSC); secondary teacher education (MA Ed); special education (MA Ed). Evening/weekend programs available. *Degree requirements:* For master's, thesis (for some programs). *Entrance requirements:* For master's, minimum undergraduate GPA of 2.5, 3 years work experience. Additional exam requirements/recommendations for international students: Required—TOEFL (minimum score 550 paper-based; 213 computer-based; 79 iBT). Electronic applications accepted.

University of Pittsburgh, School of Education, Department of Instruction and Learning, Program in Special Education, Pittsburgh, PA 15260. Offers early education of disabled students (M Ed); education of students with mental and physical disabilities (M Ed); general special education (M Ed); special education (Ed D, PhD); vision studies (M Ed). Part-time and evening/weekend programs available. *Students:* 66 full-time (60 women), 102 part-time (86 women); includes 11 minority (8 African Americans, 1 American Indian/Alaska Native, 1 Asian American or Pacific Islander, 1 Hispanic American), 1 international. Average age 32. 89 applicants, 76% accepted, 56 enrolled. In 2009, 49 master's, 2 doctorates awarded. *Degree requirements:* For master's, thesis; for doctorate, thesis/dissertation. *Entrance requirements:* For master's, PRAXIS I; for doctorate, GRE General Test. Additional exam requirements/recommendations for international students: Required—TOEFL. *Application deadline:* For fall admission, 2/1 priority date for domestic students; for spring admission, 11/1 priority date for domestic students. Applications are processed on a rolling basis. Application fee: $50. *Expenses:* Tuition, state resident: full-time $16,402; part-time $665 per credit. Tuition, nonresident: full-time $28,694; part-time $1175 per credit. Required fees: $690; $175 per term. Tuition and fees vary according to program. *Financial support:* Research assistantships, teaching assistantships, career-related internships or fieldwork, Federal Work-Study, and tuition waivers (partial) available. Support available to part-time students. Financial award application deadline: 3/15; financial award applicants required to submit FAFSA. *Unit head:* Dr. Richard Donato, Chairman, 412-624-7248, Fax: 412-648-7081, E-mail: donato@pitt.edu. *Application contact:* Lauren Pasquini, Graduate Enrollment Manager, 412-648-2230, Fax: 412-648-1899, E-mail: soeinfo@pitt.edu.

University of Puerto Rico, Medical Sciences Campus, Graduate School of Public Health, Program in Developmental Disabilities-Early Intervention, San Juan, PR 00936-5067. Offers Certificate. Part-time and evening/weekend programs available.

University of Puerto Rico, Río Piedras, College of Education, Graduate Program in Special Education, San Juan, PR 00931-3300. Offers M Ed. *Degree requirements:* For master's, thesis. *Entrance requirements:* For master's, GRE or PAEG, interview, minimum GPA of 3.0, letter of recommendation.

University of Rhode Island, Graduate School, College of Human Science and Services, School of Education, Kingston, RI 02881. Offers adult education (MA); education (PhD); elementary education (MA); music education (MM); reading education (MA); secondary education (MA); special education (MA); MS/PhD. *Accreditation:* NCATE. Part-time and evening/weekend programs available. *Faculty:* 19 full-time (12 women), 5 part-time/adjunct (1 woman). *Students:* 44 full-time (33 women), 128 part-time (101 women); includes 14 minority (8 African Americans, 2 American Indian/Alaska Native, 2 Asian Americans or Pacific Islanders, 2 Hispanic Americans), 3 international. In 2009, 44 master's, 7 doctorates awarded. *Degree requirements:* For master's, comprehensive exam (for some programs), thesis optional; for doctorate, comprehensive exam, thesis/dissertation. *Entrance requirements:* For master's, 2 letters of recommendation; interview (for special education applicants); for doctorate, GRE, 3 letters of recommendation, resume. Additional exam requirements/recommendations for international students: Required—TOEFL (minimum score 600 paper-based; 250 computer-based; 100 iBT). *Application deadline:* For fall admission, 1/31 for international students. Application fee: $65. Electronic applications accepted. *Expenses:* Tuition, state resident: full-time $8828; part-time $490 per credit hour. Tuition, nonresident: full-time $22,100; part-time $1228 per credit hour. Required fees: $1118; $57 per semester. Tuition and fees vary according to program. *Financial support:* In 2009–10, 5 research assistantships with full and partial tuition reimbursements (averaging $11,518 per year), 3 teaching assistantships with full and partial tuition reimbursements (averaging $10,421 per year) were awarded; career-related internships or fieldwork also available. Financial award applicants required to submit FAFSA. Total annual research expenditures: $3.4 million. *Unit head:* Dr. David Byrd, Director, 401-874-5484, Fax: 401-874-5471, E-mail: dbyrd@uri.edu. *Application contact:* Dr. John Boulmetis, Coordinator of Graduate Studies, 401-874-4159, Fax: 401-874-7610, E-mail: johnb@uri.edu.

University of Rio Grande, Graduate School, Rio Grande, OH 45674. Offers classroom teaching (M Ed), including fine arts, learning disabilities, mathematics, reading education. *Accreditation:* NCATE. Part-time and evening/weekend programs available. *Degree requirements:* For master's, final research project, portfolio. *Entrance requirements:* For master's, minimum GPA of 2.7 in major, 2.5 overall. Additional exam requirements/recommendations for international students: Required—TOEFL. *Faculty research:* Interagency collaboration, reading and mathematics, learning styles, college access, literacy.

University of St. Francis, College of Education, Joliet, IL 60435-6169. Offers educational leadership (MS), including reading; elementary education certification (M Ed); reading (MS); secondary education certification (M Ed), including English education, math education, science education, social studies education; special education (M Ed); teaching and learning (MS), including character education, curriculum and instruction, differentiated instruction, technology. *Accreditation:* NCATE. Part-time and evening/weekend programs available. *Faculty:* 10 full-time (8 women), 26 part-time/adjunct (18 women). *Students:* 60 full-time (45 women), 349 part-time (283 women); includes 36 minority (10 African Americans, 2 Asian Americans or Pacific Islanders, 24 Hispanic Americans). Average age 33. 211 applicants, 65% accepted, 102 enrolled. In 2009, 174 master's awarded. *Entrance requirements:* For master's, Illinois Basic Skills Test (M Ed), teaching certificate (MS), minimum undergraduate GPA of 2.75, 2 letters of recommendation, computer competency. Additional exam requirements/recommendations for international students: Required—TOEFL (minimum score 550 paper-based; 213 computer-based). *Application deadline:* Applications are processed on a rolling basis. Application fee: $30. Electronic applications accepted. *Expenses:* Contact institution. *Financial support:* In 2009–10, 254 students received support. Federal Work-Study, scholarships/grants, tuition waivers (partial), and unspecified assistantships available. Support available to part-time students. Financial award applicants required to submit FAFSA. *Unit head:* Dr. John Gambro, Dean, 815-740-3332, Fax: 815-740-2264, E-mail: jgambro@stfrancis.edu. *Application contact:* Sandra Sloka, Director of Admissions for Graduate and Degree Completion Programs, 800-735-7500, Fax: 815-740-5032, E-mail: ssloka@stfrancis.edu.

University of Saint Francis, Graduate School, Department of Education, Fort Wayne, IN 46808-3994. Offers special education (MS Ed). *Accreditation:* NCATE. Part-time and evening/weekend programs available. *Entrance requirements:* For master's, MAT, minimum GPA of 2.5.

University of Saint Mary, Graduate Programs, Program in Special Education, Leavenworth, KS 66048-5082. Offers MA. Part-time and evening/weekend programs available.

University of St. Thomas, Graduate Studies, School of Education, Department of Special and Gifted Education, St. Paul, MN 55105-1096. Offers autism spectrum disorders (Certificate); autism spectrum disporders (MA); developmental disabilities (MA); director of special education (Ed S); early childhood special education (MA); gifted, creative, and talented education (MA); learning disabilities (MA); Orton-Gillingham reading (Certificate); special education (MA). *Accreditation:* NCATE. Part-time and evening/weekend programs available. *Faculty:* 7 full-time (6 women), 16 part-time/adjunct (14 women). *Students:* 25 full-time (23 women), 226 part-time (180 women); includes 16 minority (6 African Americans, 6 Asian Americans or Pacific Islanders, 4 Hispanic Americans), 3 international. Average age 34. 447 applicants, 60% accepted. In 2009, 65 master's, 65 other advanced degrees awarded. *Degree requirements:* For master's, thesis; for other advanced degree, professional portfolio. *Entrance requirements:* For master's, minimum GPA of 3.0 or MAT; for other advanced degree, MAT or minimum GPA of 2.75. Additional exam requirements/recommendations for international students: Required—TOEFL (minimum score 550 paper-based; 213 computer-based; 80 iBT). *Application deadline:* For fall admission, 6/1 priority date for domestic students; for spring admission, 11/1 priority date for domestic students. Applications are processed on a rolling basis. Application fee: $50. *Financial support:* Fellowships, research assistantships, institutionally sponsored loans and scholarships/grants available. Support available to part-time students. Financial award applicants required to submit FAFSA. *Faculty research:* Reading and math fluency, inclusion curriculum for developmental disorders, parent involvement in positive behavior supports, children's friendships, preschool inclusion. *Unit head:* Dr. Terri L. Vandercook, Chair, 651-962-4389, Fax: 651-962-4169, E-mail: tlvandercook@stthomas.edu. *Application contact:* Patricia L. Thomas, Department Assistant, 651-962-4980, Fax: 651-962-4169, E-mail: plhelland@stthomas.edu.

University of San Diego, School of Leadership and Education Sciences, Department of Learning and Teaching, San Diego, CA 92110-2492. Offers curriculum and instruction (M Ed); mathematics, science and technology education (M Ed); special education (M Ed); special education with deaf and hard of hearing (M Ed); teaching (MAT); TESOL, literacy and culture (M Ed). Part-time and evening/weekend programs available. *Faculty:* 13 full-time (9 women), 24 part-time/adjunct (21 women). *Students:* 77 full-time (63 women), 92 part-time (74 women); includes 46 minority (13 African Americans, 12 Asian Americans or Pacific Islanders, 21 Hispanic Americans), 6 international. Average age 31. 142 applicants, 75% accepted, 59 enrolled. In 2009, 64 master's awarded. *Degree requirements:* For master's, thesis (for some programs). *Entrance requirements:* For master's, minimum GPA of 3.0. Additional exam requirements/recommendations for international students: Required—TOEFL (minimum score 580 paper-based; 237 computer-based; 83 iBT), TWE. *Application deadline:* For fall admission, 7/15 for domestic and international students; for spring admission, 12/1 for domestic and international students. Applications are processed on a rolling basis. Application fee: $45. Electronic applications accepted. *Expenses:* Tuition: Full-time $21,042; part-time $1169 per unit. Required fees: $224. Full-time tuition and fees vary according to course load and degree level. *Financial support:* In 2009–10, 113 students received support. Career-related internships or fieldwork, Federal Work-Study, institutionally sponsored loans, and stipends available. Support available to part-time students. Financial award application deadline: 4/1; financial award applicants required to submit FAFSA. *Faculty research:* Action research methodology, cultural studies, instructional theories and practices, second language acquisition, school reform. *Unit head:* Dr. Judy Mantle, Director, 619-260-7879, Fax: 619-260-6835, E-mail: jmantle@sandiego.edu. *Application contact:* Dr. John Mosby, Associate Director of Graduate Admissions, 619-260-4524, Fax: 619-260-4158, E-mail: grads@sandiego.edu.

University of Saskatchewan, College of Graduate Studies and Research, College of Education, Department of Educational Psychology and Special Education, Saskatoon, SK S7N 5A2, Canada. Offers M Ed, PhD, Diploma. *Faculty:* 20. *Students:* 69. In 2009, 13 master's awarded. *Degree requirements:* For master's, thesis (for some programs); for doctorate, comprehensive exam (for some programs), thesis/dissertation. *Entrance requirements:* Additional exam requirements/recommendations for international students: Required—TOEFL (minimum score 80 iBT); Recommended—IELTS (minimum score 6.5). *Application deadline:* For fall admission, 7/1 priority date for domestic students. Applications are processed on a rolling basis. Application fee: $75. Electronic applications accepted. Tuition and fees charges are reported in Canadian dollars. *Expenses:* Tuition, area resident: Full-time $3000 Canadian dollars; part-time $500 Canadian dollars per term. Required fees: $700 Canadian dollars; $100 Canadian dollars per term. *Financial support:* Fellowships, research assistantships, teaching assistantships available. Financial award application deadline: 1/31. *Unit head:* Dr. David Mykota, Head, 306-966-5246, Fax: 306-966-7719, E-mail: david.mykota@usask.ca. *Application contact:* Dr. Laure-Ann Hellsten, Graduate Chair, 306-966-7728, Fax: 306-966-7719, E-mail: laurie.hellsten@usask.ca.

The University of Scranton, College of Graduate and Continuing Education, Department of Education, Program in Special Education, Scranton, PA 18510. Offers MS. Part-time and evening/weekend programs available. *Students:* 8 full-time (6 women), 1 (woman) part-time. Average age 25. 3 applicants, 100% accepted. In 2009, 7 master's awarded. *Degree requirements:* For master's, comprehensive exam, capstone experience. *Entrance requirements:* For master's, minimum GPA of 2.75. Additional exam requirements/recommendations for international students: Required—TOEFL (minimum score 500 paper-based; 173 computer-based), IELTS (minimum score 5.5). Application fee: $0. *Financial support:* Unspecified assistantships available. *Unit head:* Dr. Art Chambers, Director, 570-941-4668, Fax: 570-941-5515, E-mail: chambersa2@scranton.edu. *Application contact:* Joseph M. Roback, Director of Admissions, 570-941-4385, Fax: 570-941-5928, E-mail: robackj2@scranton.edu.

University of South Alabama, Graduate School, College of Education, Department of Leadership and Teacher Education, Mobile, AL 36688-0002. Offers early childhood education (M Ed); educational administration (Ed S); educational leadership (M Ed); elementary education (M Ed); reading education (M Ed); science education (M Ed); secondary education (M Ed); special education (M Ed, Ed S). *Accreditation:* NCATE. Part-time programs available. *Degree requirements:* For master's, comprehensive exam. *Entrance requirements:* For master's, GRE General Test or MAT, minimum GPA of 3.0. *Expenses:* Tuition, state resident: part-time $218 per contact hour. Required fees: $1102 per year.

University of South Carolina, The Graduate School, College of Education, Department of Educational Studies, Program in Special Education, Columbia, SC 29208. Offers M Ed, MAT, PhD. *Accreditation:* NCATE. Part-time programs available. *Degree requirements:* For master's, comprehensive exam; for doctorate, one foreign language, comprehensive exam, thesis/dissertation. *Entrance requirements:* For master's, GRE General Test, MAT, interview, sample of written work; for doctorate, GRE General Test or MAT, interview, sample of written work. *Faculty research:* Strategy training, transition, technology, rural special education, behavior management.

University of South Carolina Upstate, Graduate Programs, Spartanburg, SC 29303-4999. Offers early childhood education (M Ed); elementary education (M Ed); special education: visual impairment (M Ed). *Accreditation:* NCATE. Part-time and evening/weekend programs available. *Faculty:* 8 full-time (7 women), 4 part-time/adjunct (2 women). *Students:* 5 full-time (all women), 107 part-time (102 women). Average age 34. *Degree requirements:* For master's, professional portfolio. *Entrance requirements:* For master's, GRE General Test or MAT, interview, minimum undergraduate GPA of 2.5, teaching certificate, 2 letters of recommendation. *Application deadline:* Applications are processed on a rolling basis. Application fee: $40. *Expenses:* Tuition, state resident: full-time $9436; part-time $467 per credit hour. Tuition, nonresident: full-time $20,336; part-time $992 per credit hour. Required fees: $500. Tuition and fees vary according to course load. *Financial support:* Institutionally sponsored loans and institutional work-study available. Financial award application deadline: 7/15; financial award applicants required to submit FAFSA. *Faculty research:* Rough and tumble play, social justice education, American Indian literatures and cultures, diversity and multicultural education, science teaching strategy. *Unit head:* Dr. Rebecca L. Stevens, Director of Graduate Programs, 864-503-5521, Fax: 864-503-5574, E-mail: rstevens@uscupstate.edu. *Application contact:* Donette Stewart, Associate Vice Chancellor for Enrollment Services, 864-503-5280, E-mail: dstewart@uscupstate.edu.

The University of South Dakota, Graduate School, School of Education, Division of Curriculum and Instruction, Program in Special Education, Vermillion, SD 57069-2390. Offers MA. *Accreditation:* NCATE. Part-time programs available. Postbaccalaureate distance learning degree programs offered. *Degree requirements:* For master's, comprehensive exam, thesis or alternative. *Entrance requirements:* For master's, GRE General Test, MAT, minimum GPA of 2.7. Additional exam requirements/recommendations for international students: Required—TOEFL (minimum score 550 paper-based; 213 computer-based; 79 iBT). Electronic applications accepted.

University of Southern Maine, College of Education and Human Development, Abilities and Disabilities Studies Program, Portland, ME 04104-9300. Offers gifted and talented (MS); self-design in special education (MS); teaching all students (MS). *Accreditation:* Teacher Education Accreditation Council. Part-time and evening/weekend programs available. *Faculty:* 2 full-time (1 woman), 1 part-time/adjunct (0 women). *Students:* 8 full-time (7 women), 31 part-time (25 women); includes 1 minority (Hispanic American). 9 applicants, 89% accepted, 5 enrolled. In 2009, 13 master's awarded. *Degree requirements:* For master's, thesis or alternative, portfolio. *Entrance requirements:* For master's, proof of teacher certification. Additional exam requirements/recommendations for international students: Required—TOEFL (minimum score 550 paper-based; 213 computer-based; 79 iBT). *Application deadline:* For fall admission, 5/1 priority date for domestic students; for spring admission, 10/15 priority date for domestic students. Applications are processed on a rolling basis. Application fee: $50. Electronic applications accepted. *Financial support:* In 2009–10, 1 student received support, including 1 research assistantship with partial tuition reimbursement available (averaging $4,500 per year); career-related internships or fieldwork, Federal Work-Study, institutionally sponsored loans, scholarships/grants, and unspecified assistantships also available. Support available to part-time students. Financial award application deadline: 3/1; financial award applicants required to submit FAFSA. *Unit head:* Dr. James Curry, Chair, Professional Education Department, 207-780-5400, Fax: 207-228-8277, E-mail: jcurry@usm.maine.edu. *Application contact:* Mary Sloan, Director of Graduate Admissions, 207-780-4386, Fax: 207-780-4969, E-mail: msloan@usm.maine.edu.

University of Southern Mississippi, Graduate School, College of Education and Psychology, Department of Curriculum, Instruction, and Special Education, Hattiesburg, MS 39406-0001. Offers alternative secondary teacher education (MAT); early childhood education (M Ed, Ed S); education of the gifted (M Ed, Ed D, PhD, Ed S); elementary education (M Ed, Ed D, PhD, Ed S); reading (M Ed, MS, Ed S); secondary education (M Ed, MS, Ed D, PhD, Ed S); special education (M Ed, Ed D, PhD, Ed S). *Faculty:* 23 full-time (17 women), 3 part-time/adjunct (2 women). *Students:* 31 full-time (26 women), 77 part-time (68 women); includes 18 minority (15 African Americans, 3 Hispanic Americans). Average age 37. 50 applicants, 52% accepted, 19 enrolled. In 2009, 43 master's, 3 doctorates, 2 other advanced degrees awarded. *Degree requirements:* For master's, comprehensive exam, thesis (for some programs); for doctorate, comprehensive exam, thesis/dissertation; for Ed S, comprehensive exam, thesis. *Entrance requirements:* For master's, GRE General Test, MAT, minimum GPA of 3.0; for doctorate, GRE General Test, minimum GPA of 3.5; for Ed S, GRE General Test, MAT, minimum GPA of 3.25. Additional exam requirements/recommendations for international students: Required—TOEFL. *Application deadline:* For fall admission, 3/1 priority date for domestic students, 3/1 for international students. Applications are processed on a rolling basis. Application fee: $35. *Expenses:* Tuition, state resident: full-time $5096; part-time $284 per hour. Tuition, nonresident: full-time $13,052; part-time $726 per hour. Required fees: $402. Tuition and fees vary according to course level and course load. *Financial support:* In 2009–10, 9 research assistantships with tuition reimbursements (averaging $18,316 per year), 2 teaching assistantships with full tuition reimbursements (averaging $8,500 per year) were awarded; Federal Work-Study, institutionally sponsored loans, and tuition waivers (partial) also available. Financial award application deadline: 3/15; financial award applicants required to submit FAFSA. *Faculty research:* Mathematical problem solving, integrative curriculum, writing process, teacher education models. Total annual research expenditures: $100,000. *Unit head:* Dr. David Daves, Chair, 601-266-4547, Fax: 601-266-4175. *Application contact:* Rachea Cawthorn, Administrative Assistant, 601-266-6987, Fax: 601-266-4548.

University of South Florida, Graduate School, College of Education–Main Campus, Department of Special Education, Tampa, FL 33620-9951. Offers behavior disorders (MA); exceptional student education (MA, MAT); gifted education (MA); mental retardation (MA); special education (PhD); specific learning disabilities (MA). *Accreditation:* NCATE. Part-time and evening/weekend programs available. *Faculty:* 12 full-time (9 women), 2 part-time/adjunct (1 woman). *Students:* 59 full-time (48 women), 85 part-time (78 women); includes 43 minority (24 African Americans, 1 American Indian/Alaska Native, 7 Asian Americans or Pacific Islanders, 11 Hispanic Americans), 1 international. Average age 30. 73 applicants, 74% accepted, 45 enrolled. In 2009, 32 master's, 4 doctorates awarded. *Degree requirements:* For master's, comprehensive exam; for doctorate, comprehensive exam, thesis/dissertation. *Entrance requirements:* For master's, GRE General Test (if undergraduate GPA less than 3.0), minimum GPA of 3.0 in last 60 hours of course work; for doctorate, GRE General Test, minimum GPA of 3.0 undergraduate, 3.5 graduate; interview. Additional exam requirements/recommendations for international students: Required—TOEFL (minimum score 500 paper-based; 213 computer-based). *Application deadline:* For fall admission, 2/15 for domestic students, 1/2 for international students; for winter admission, 2/15 for domestic students, 1/2 for international students; for spring admission, 10/15 for domestic students, 6/1 for international students. Application fee: $30. Electronic applications accepted. *Financial support:* In 2009–10, 3 fellowships with full tuition reimbursements (averaging $10,000 per year), 4 research assistantships with full tuition reimbursements (averaging $10,000 per year), 7 teaching assistantships with full tuition reimbursements (averaging $10,000 per year) were awarded; scholarships/grants and unspecified assistantships also available. Financial award application deadline: 6/1; financial award applicants required to submit FAFSA. *Faculty research:* Instruction methods for students with learning and behavioral disabilities; teacher preparation, experiential learning, and participatory action research; public policy research; personal preparation for transitional services; case-based instruction, partnerships and mentor development; inclusion and voices of teachers and students with disabilities; narrative ethics and philosophies of research. Total annual research expenditures: $2.9 million. *Unit head:* Dr. Daphne Thomas, Chairperson, 813-974-1383, Fax: 813-974-5542, E-mail: dthomas@usf.edu. *Application contact:* Dr. Daphne Thomas, Chairperson, 813-974-1383, Fax: 813-974-5542, E-mail: dthomas@usf.edu.

The University of Tennessee, Graduate School, College of Education, Health and Human Sciences, Program in Education, Knoxville, TN 37996. Offers art education (MS); counseling education (PhD); cultural studies in education (PhD); curriculum (MS, Ed S); curriculum, educational research and evaluation (Ed D, PhD); early childhood education (PhD); early childhood special education (MS); education of deaf and hard of hearing (MS); educational administration and policy studies (Ed D, PhD); educational administration and supervision (Ed S); educational psychology (Ed D, PhD); elementary education (MS, Ed S); elementary teaching (MS); English education (MS, Ed S); exercise science (PhD); foreign language/ESL education (MS, Ed S); instructional technology (MS, Ed D, PhD, Ed S); literacy, language and ESL education (PhD); literacy, language education, and ESL education (Ed D); mathematics education (MS, Ed S); modified and comprehensive special education (MS); reading education (MS, Ed S); school counseling (Ed S); school psychology (PhD, Ed S); science education (MS, Ed S); secondary teaching (MS); social foundations (MS); social science education (MS, Ed S); socio-cultural foundations of sports and education (PhD); special education (Ed S); teacher education (Ed D, PhD). *Accreditation:* NCATE. Part-time and evening/weekend programs available. *Degree requirements:* For master's and Ed S, thesis optional; for doctorate, variable foreign language requirement, thesis/dissertation. *Entrance requirements:* For master's, minimum GPA of 2.7; for doctorate and Ed S, GRE General Test, minimum GPA of 2.7. Additional exam requirements/recommendations for international students: Required—TOEFL. Electronic applications accepted. *Expenses:* Tuition, state resident: full-time $6826; part-time $380 per semester hour. Tuition, nonresident: full-time $21,844; part-time $1147 per semester hour. Tuition and fees vary according to program.

The University of Tennessee at Chattanooga, Graduate School, College of Health, Education and Professional Studies, Graduate Studies Division of Education, Program in Education, Chattanooga, TN 37403-2598. Offers elementary education (M Ed); school leadership (M Ed, Post-Master's Certificate); secondary education (M Ed); special education (M Ed). Part-time and evening/weekend programs available. Postbaccalaureate distance learning degree programs offered (no on-campus study). *Faculty:* 10 full-time (9 women), 6 part-time/adjunct (3 women). *Students:* 124 full-time (83 women), 208 part-time (150 women); includes 42 minority (32 African Americans, 2 American Indian/Alaska Native, 3 Asian Americans or Pacific Islanders, 5 Hispanic Americans), 1 international. Average age 33. 117 applicants, 97% accepted, 80 enrolled. In 2009, 97 master's, 4 other advanced degrees awarded. *Degree requirements:* For master's, comprehensive exam (for some programs), thesis (for some programs). *Entrance requirements:* For master's and Post-Master's Certificate, PRAXIS I, minimum GPA of 2.5 overall or 3.0 in senior year. Additional exam requirements/recommendations for international students: Required—TOEFL (minimum score 550 paper-based; 213 computer-based; 79 iBT), IELTS (minimum score 6). *Application deadline:* For fall admission, 8/1 for domestic students, 6/1 for international students; for spring admission, 12/1 for domestic students, 10/1 for international students. Applications are processed on a rolling basis. Application fee: $35. Electronic applications accepted. *Expenses:* Tuition, state resident: full-time $5404; part-time $300 per credit hour. Tuition, nonresident: full-time $16,702; part-time $928 per credit hour. Required fees: $1150; $130 per credit hour. *Financial support:* In 2009–10, 8 research assistantships with full and partial tuition reimbursements (averaging $5,500 per year) were awarded; career-related internships or fieldwork, scholarships/grants, and unspecified assistantships also available. Support available to part-time students. *Faculty research:* Elementary education, community counseling, school counseling, secondary education, special education. *Unit head:* Dr. John Freeman, Department Head, 423-425-4133, Fax: 423-425-5443, E-mail: john-freeman@utc.edu. *Application contact:* Dr. Stephanie Bellar, Dean of Graduate Studies, 423-425-4666, Fax: 423-425-5223, E-mail: stephanie-bellar@utc.edu.

The University of Texas at Austin, Graduate School, College of Education, Department of Special Education, Austin, TX 78712-1111. Offers M Ed, MA, Ed D, PhD. *Accreditation:* CORE. Part-time and evening/weekend programs available. Postbaccalaureate distance learning degree programs offered (no on-campus study). *Degree requirements:* For master's, thesis or alternative; for doctorate, thesis/dissertation. *Entrance requirements:* For master's and doctorate, GRE General Test. *Faculty research:* Anchored instruction, reading disabilities, multicultural/bilingual.

The University of Texas at Brownsville, Graduate Studies, School of Education, Brownsville, TX 78520-4991. Offers bilingual education (M Ed); counseling and guidance (M Ed); curriculum and instruction (M Ed); early childhood education (M Ed); educational administration (M Ed); educational technology (M Ed); English as a second language (M Ed); reading specialist (M Ed); special education/educational diagnostician (M Ed). Part-time and evening/weekend programs available. Postbaccalaureate distance learning degree programs offered (minimal on-campus study). *Degree requirements:* For master's, thesis optional. *Entrance requirements:* For master's, GRE General Test. Additional exam requirements/recommendations for international students: Required—TOEFL.

The University of Texas at El Paso, Graduate School, College of Education, Department of Educational Psychology and Special Services, El Paso, TX 79968-0001. Offers educational diagnostics (M Ed); guidance and counseling (M Ed); special education (M Ed). Part-time and evening/weekend programs available. *Degree requirements:* For master's, thesis optional. *Entrance requirements:* For master's, minimum graduate GPA of 3.0. Additional exam requirements/recommendations for international students: Required—TOEFL. Electronic applications accepted.

The University of Texas at San Antonio, College of Education and Human Development, Department of Interdisciplinary Learning and Teaching, San Antonio, TX 78249-0617. Offers curriculum and instruction (MA); early childhood education (MA); instructional technology (MA); reading (MA); special education (MA). Part-time and evening/weekend programs available. *Faculty:* 28 full-time (24 women), 1 part-time/adjunct (0 women). *Students:* 103 full-time (83 women), 317 part-time (253 women); includes 227 minority (36 African Americans, 11 Asian Americans or Pacific Islanders, 180 Hispanic Americans), 17 international. Average age 33. 212 applicants, 90% accepted, 140 enrolled. In 2009, 74 master's awarded. *Degree requirements:* For master's, comprehensive exam (for some programs), thesis (for some programs). *Entrance requirements:* For master's, GRE General Test, minimum GPA of 3.0. Additional exam requirements/recommendations for international students: Required—TOEFL (minimum score 500 paper-based; 173 computer-based; 61 iBT), IELTS (minimum score 5). *Application deadline:* For fall admission, 7/1 for domestic students, 4/1 for international students;

Special Education

The University of Texas at San Antonio (continued)

for spring admission, 11/1 for domestic students, 9/1 for international students. Applications are processed on a rolling basis. Application fee: $45 ($80 for international students). Electronic applications accepted. *Expenses:* Tuition, state resident: full-time $3975; part-time $221 per contact hour. Tuition, nonresident: full-time $13,947; part-time $775 per contact hour. Required fees: $1853. *Financial support:* In 2009–10, 76 students received support, including 25 research assistantships (averaging $11,599 per year), 4 teaching assistantships (averaging $8,800 per year); scholarships/grants, tuition waivers, and unspecified assistantships also available. Support available to part-time students. *Faculty research:* Adult education; early childhood education; literacy; special education; science, technology, engineering and math fields. Total annual research expenditures: $57,097. *Unit head:* Dr. Belinda B. Flores, Chair, 210-458-5969, Fax: 210-458-7281, E-mail: belinda.flores@utsa.edu. *Application contact:* Mari Cortez, Graduate Advisor, 210-458-4414, E-mail: mari.cortez@utsa.edu.

The University of Texas at Tyler, College of Education and Psychology, School of Education, Tyler, TX 75799-0001. Offers early childhood education (M Ed, MA); reading (M Ed, MA); special education (M Ed, MA). Part-time and evening/weekend programs available. *Faculty:* 18 full-time (8 women). *Students:* 4 full-time (3 women), 30 part-time (all women); includes 4 minority (3 African Americans, 1 Hispanic American), 2 international. Average age 37. 13 applicants, 100% accepted, 6 enrolled. In 2009, 14 master's awarded. *Degree requirements:* For master's, comprehensive exam, thesis (for some programs), research project. *Entrance requirements:* For master's, GRE General Test. Additional exam requirements/recommendations for international students: Required—TOEFL (minimum score 79 computer-based). *Application deadline:* For fall admission, 8/17 priority date for domestic students, 7/1 priority date for international students; for spring admission, 12/21 priority date for domestic students, 11/1 priority date for international students. Applications are processed on a rolling basis. Application fee: $25 ($50 for international students). Electronic applications accepted. *Expenses:* Tuition, state resident: part-time $665 per semester hour. Tuition, nonresident: part-time $942 per semester hour. Part-time tuition and fees vary according to degree level and program. *Financial support:* In 2009–10, 2 research assistantships (averaging $12,000 per year) were awarded; scholarships/grants also available. Financial award application deadline: 7/1. *Faculty research:* Improving quality in childcare settings, play and creativity, teacher interactions, effects of modeling on early childhood teachers, biofeedback, literacy instruction. *Unit head:* Dr. Kathy L. Morrison, Interim Director, 903-566-7016, Fax: 903-565-5560, E-mail: kmorrison@uttyler.edu. *Application contact:* Dr. Kathy Morrison, Program Director for Curriculum and Instruction and Early Childhood, 903-566-7016, Fax: 903-565-5560, E-mail: kmorrison@uttyler.edu.

The University of Texas of the Permian Basin, Office of Graduate Studies, School of Education, Program in Special Education, Odessa, TX 79762-0001. Offers MA. *Degree requirements:* For master's, comprehensive exam (for some programs), thesis (for some programs). *Entrance requirements:* For master's, GRE General Test. Additional exam requirements/recommendations for international students: Required—TOEFL (minimum score 550 paper-based; 213 computer-based).

The University of Texas–Pan American, College of Education, Department of Educational Psychology, Edinburg, TX 78539. Offers counseling (M Ed); educational diagnostician (M Ed); gifted education (M Ed); school psychology (MA); special education (M Ed). Part-time and evening/weekend programs available. *Degree requirements:* For master's, comprehensive exam (for some programs), thesis (for some programs). *Entrance requirements:* For master's, GRE General Test, interview. *Expenses:* Tuition, state resident: full-time $3630.60; part-time $201.70 per credit hour. Tuition, nonresident: full-time $8617; part-time $478.70 per credit hour. Required fees: $806.50. *Faculty research:* Reading instruction, assessment practice, behavior interventions consultation, mental retardation.

University of the Cumberlands, Graduate Programs in Education, Program in Special Education, Williamsburg, KY 40769-1372. Offers MA Ed, MAT. Evening/weekend programs available. *Degree requirements:* For master's, comprehensive exam. *Entrance requirements:* For master's, GRE or NTE, Kentucky teaching certificate.

University of the District of Columbia, College of Arts and Sciences, Department of Education, Program in Special Education, Washington, DC 20008-1175. Offers MA. *Accreditation:* NCATE. Part-time programs available. *Students:* 4 full-time (3 women), 1 part-time (0 women); all minorities (all African Americans). 16 applicants, 75% accepted. *Application deadline:* For fall admission, 6/15 priority date for domestic students; for spring admission, 11/1 for domestic students. Applications are processed on a rolling basis. Application fee: $20. *Expenses:* Tuition, state resident: full-time $7580. Tuition, nonresident: full-time $14,580. Required fees: $620. *Financial support:* Fellowships, research assistantships available. *Unit head:* Dr. Arlene King Berry, Professor, 202-274-7401. *Application contact:* Ann Marie Waterman, Associate Vice President for Admission, Recruitment and Financial Aid, 202-274-6069.

University of the Incarnate Word, School of Graduate Studies and Research, Dreeben School of Education, Programs in Education, San Antonio, TX 78209-6397. Offers adult education (M Ed, MA); cross-cultural education (M Ed, MA); early childhood literacy (M Ed, MA); general education (M Ed, MA); Higher Education (PhD); instructional technology (M Ed, MA); international education and entrepreneurship (PhD); kinesiology (M Ed, MA); literacy (M Ed, MA); organizational leadership (PhD); organizational learning and learning (M Ed, MA); reading (M Ed, MA); special education (M Ed, MA); teacher leadership (M Ed, MA). Part-time and evening/weekend programs available. *Students:* 20 full-time (11 women), 201 part-time (122 women); includes 113 minority (29 African Americans, 2 American Indian/Alaska Native, 2 Asian Americans or Pacific Islanders, 80 Hispanic Americans), 30 international. Average age 41. In 2009, 26 master's, 19 doctorates awarded. *Degree requirements:* For master's, capstone; for doctorate, thesis/dissertation, qualifying exam. *Entrance requirements:* For master's, baccalaureate degree; minimum foundation GPA of 2.5; interview; for doctorate, master's degree; interview; supervised writing sample. Additional exam requirements/recommendations for international students: Required—TOEFL (minimum score 560 paper-based; 220 computer-based; 83 iBT). *Application deadline:* Applications are processed on a rolling basis. Application fee: $20. Electronic applications accepted. *Expenses:* Tuition: Full-time $12,150; part-time $675 per credit hour. Required fees: $83 per credit hour. *Financial support:* Federal Work-Study and scholarships/grants available. Financial award applicants required to submit FAFSA. *Unit head:* Dr. Denise Staudt, Dean, Dreeben School of Education, 210-829-2762, E-mail: staudt@uiwtx.edu. *Application contact:* Andrea Cyterski-Acosta, Dean of Enrollment, 210-829-6005, Fax: 210-829-3921, E-mail: admis@uiwtx.edu.

University of the Pacific, School of Education, Department of Curriculum and Instruction, Stockton, CA 95211-0197. Offers curriculum and instruction (M Ed, MA, Ed D); education (M Ed); special education (MA). *Accreditation:* NCATE. *Faculty:* 11 full-time (7 women), 2 part-time/adjunct (1 woman). *Students:* 24 full-time (18 women), 115 part-time (81 women); includes 52 minority (10 African Americans, 1 American Indian/Alaska Native, 32 Asian Americans or Pacific Islanders, 9 Hispanic Americans), 1 international. Average age 36. 93 applicants, 84% accepted, 52 enrolled. In 2009, 21 master's awarded. *Degree requirements:* For master's, thesis (for some programs). *Entrance requirements:* For master's, GRE General Test. Additional exam requirements/recommendations for international students: Required—TOEFL (minimum score 475 paper-based; 150 computer-based). *Application deadline:* For fall admission, 3/1 priority date for domestic students; for spring admission, 10/1 priority date for domestic students. Applications are processed on a rolling basis. Application fee: $75. *Financial support:* In 2009–10, 7 teaching assistantships were awarded. Financial award application deadline: 3/1; financial award applicants required to submit FAFSA. *Unit head:* Dr. Marilyn Draheim, Chairperson, 209-946-2685, E-mail: mdraheim@pacific.edu. *Application contact:* Office of Graduate Admissions, 209-946-2344.

University of the Southwest, Graduate Programs, Hobbs, NM 88240-9129. Offers business administration (MBA); curriculum and instruction (MSE); curriculum and instruction: bilingual (MSE); curriculum and instruction: reading (MSE); curriculum and instruction: TESOL (MSE); early childhood education (MSE); educational diagnostician (MSE); mental health counseling

(MSE); school business administration (MSE); school counseling (MSE); special education (MSE). Part-time and evening/weekend programs available. Postbaccalaureate distance learning degree programs offered (no on-campus study). *Faculty:* 10 full-time (6 women), 10 part-time/adjunct (4 women). *Students:* 112 full-time (93 women), 99 part-time (72 women). Average age 35. 94 applicants, 47% accepted, 39 enrolled. In 2009, 32 master's awarded. *Degree requirements:* For master's, comprehensive exam. *Application deadline:* For fall admission, 3/1 priority date for domestic students; for spring admission, 10/1 for domestic students. Applications are processed on a rolling basis. Application fee: $25. Electronic applications accepted. *Expenses:* Tuition: Part-time $512 per hour. Tuition and fees vary according to course load. *Financial support:* In 2009–10, 196 students received support; research assistantships with partial tuition reimbursements available, Federal Work-Study, scholarships/grants, and tuition waivers (partial) available. Support available to part-time students. Financial award application deadline: 4/1; financial award applicants required to submit FAFSA. *Unit head:* Dr. Mary Harris, Dean of Education, 575-392-6561 Ext. 1056, Fax: 575-392-6006, E-mail: mharris@usw.edu. *Application contact:* Ryanne Evans, Assistant Registrar, 575-392-6561 Ext. 1031, Fax: 575-392-6006, E-mail: revans@usw.edu.

The University of Toledo, College of Graduate Studies, College of Education, Department of Early Childhood, Physical and Special Education, Program in Special Education, Toledo, OH 43606-3390. Offers ME, DE, PhD, Ed S.

University of Utah, Graduate School, College of Education, Department of Special Education, Salt Lake City, UT 84112. Offers early childhood hearing impairments (M Ed, MS); early childhood special education (M Ed, PhD); early childhood vision impairments (M Ed, MS); hearing impairments (M Ed, MS); mild/moderate disabilities (M Ed, MS, PhD); professional practice (M Ed); research in special education (MS); severe disabilities (M Ed, MS, PhD); vision impairments (M Ed). Part-time and evening/weekend programs available. Post-baccalaureate distance learning degree programs offered (no on-campus study). *Faculty:* 17 full-time (12 women), 7 part-time/adjunct (5 women). *Students:* 41 full-time (40 women), 20 part-time (16 women); includes 5 minority (1 African American, 2 American Indian/Alaska Native, 2 Hispanic Americans), 3 international. Average age 35. 34 applicants, 65% accepted, 11 enrolled. In 2009, 27 master's, 2 doctorates awarded. Terminal master's awarded for partial completion of doctoral program. *Degree requirements:* For master's, comprehensive exam, thesis (for some programs), qualifying exam; for doctorate, thesis/dissertation, qualifying exam. *Entrance requirements:* For master's, GRE or Analytical/Writing portion of GRE plus PRAXIS I; Basic Skills Test, minimum GPA of 3.0; for doctorate, GRE General Test (minimum score: Verbal-600; Quantitative-600; Analytical/Writing-4), minimum GPA of 3.0, 3.5 (recommended). Additional exam requirements/recommendations for international students: Required—TOEFL (minimum score 600 paper-based; 250 computer-based; 100 iBT). *Application deadline:* For fall admission, 3/1 for domestic and international students; for spring admission, 11/1 for domestic and international students. Application fee: $55 ($65 for international students). *Expenses:* Contact institution. *Financial support:* In 2009–10, 44 students received support, including 44 fellowships with full and partial tuition reimbursements available (averaging $8,800 per year), 1 research assistantship (averaging $4,500 per year), 3 teaching assistantships (averaging $3,000 per year); career-related internships or fieldwork and scholarships/grants also available. Support available to part-time students. Financial award application deadline: 3/1; financial award applicants required to submit FAFSA. *Faculty research:* Inclusive education, positive behavior support, reading, instruction and intervention strategies. *Unit head:* Dr. Andrea P. McDonnell, Chair, 801-581-8121, Fax: 801-585-6476, E-mail: andrea.mcdonnell@utah.edu. *Application contact:* Patty Davis, Academic Advisor, 801-581-4764, Fax: 801-585-6476, E-mail: patty.davis@utah.edu.

University of Vermont, Graduate College, College of Education and Social Services, Department of Education, Program in Special Education, Burlington, VT 05405. Offers M Ed. *Accreditation:* NCATE. *Students:* 38 (27 women); includes 1 minority (Asian American or Pacific Islander). 34 applicants, 88% accepted, 19 enrolled. In 2009, 16 master's awarded. *Degree requirements:* For master's, thesis or alternative. *Entrance requirements:* Additional exam requirements/recommendations for international students: Required—TOEFL (minimum score 550 paper-based; 213 computer-based; 80 iBT). *Application deadline:* For fall admission, 3/15 priority date for domestic students. Applications are processed on a rolling basis. Application fee: $40. Electronic applications accepted. *Expenses:* Tuition, state resident: part-time $508 per credit hour. Tuition, nonresident: part-time $1281 per credit hour. *Financial support:* Research assistantships, teaching assistantships, career-related internships or fieldwork available. Financial award application deadline: 3/1. *Unit head:* W. Williams, Coordinator, 802-656-2936. *Application contact:* W. Williams, Coordinator, 802-656-2936.

University of Victoria, Faculty of Graduate Studies, Faculty of Education, Department of Educational Psychology and Leadership Studies, Victoria, BC V8W 2Y2, Canada. Offers aboriginal communities counseling (M Ed); counseling (M Ed, MA); educational psychology (M Ed, MA, PhD), including counseling psychology (M Ed, MA), leadership studies (PhD), learning and development (MA, PhD), measurement and evaluation, special education (M Ed, MA); leadership studies (M Ed, MA). Part-time programs available. *Degree requirements:* For master's, thesis (for some programs), comprehensive exam (M Ed); for doctorate, comprehensive exam, thesis/dissertation, candidacy exam. *Entrance requirements:* For master's, 2 years of work experience in a relevant field; for doctorate, GRE, 2 years of work experience in a relevant field, minimum B average. Additional exam requirements/recommendations for international students: Required—TOEFL (minimum score 575 paper-based; 233 computer-based), IELTS (minimum score 7). *Faculty research:* Learning and development (child, adolescent and adult), special education and exceptional children.

University of Virginia, Curry School of Education, Department of Curriculum, Instruction, and Special Education, Program in Special Education, Charlottesville, VA 22903. Offers M Ed, Ed D, Ed S. *Accreditation:* Teacher Education Accreditation Council. *Students:* 4 part-time (all women). Average age 35. 8 applicants, 50% accepted, 3 enrolled. In 2009, 38 master's, 4 doctorates awarded. *Entrance requirements:* For master's, doctorate, and Ed S, GRE General Test, 2 letters of recommendation. Additional exam requirements/recommendations for international students: Required—TOEFL (minimum score 600 paper-based; 250 computer-based; 90 iBT), IELTS (minimum score 7). *Application deadline:* Applications are processed on a rolling basis. Application fee: $60. Electronic applications accepted. *Financial support:* Applicants required to submit FAFSA. *Unit head:* Paige C. Pullen, Program Coordinator. *Application contact:* Paige C. Pullen, Program Coordinator.

University of Virginia, Curry School of Education, Program in Education, Charlottesville, VA 22903. Offers administration and supervision (PhD); applied developmental science (PhD); counselor education (PhD); curriculum and instruction (PhD); early childhood-developmental risk (MT); education evaluation (PhD); educational psychology (PhD); educational research (PhD); elementary (MT, PhD); English education (MT, PhD); foreign language education (MT); higher education (PhD); instructional technology (PhD); kinesiology (MT, PhD); math education (PhD); reading education (PhD); research statistics and evaluation (PhD); school psychology (PhD); science education (PhD); social studies education (MT, PhD); special education (PhD); world languages education (MT). *Students:* 336 full-time (239 women), 88 part-time (54 women); includes 43 minority (24 African Americans, 2 American Indian/Alaska Native, 11 Asian Americans or Pacific Islanders, 6 Hispanic Americans), 18 international. Average age 27. 199 applicants, 48% accepted, 55 enrolled. In 2009, 127 master's, 52 doctorates awarded. *Degree requirements:* For master's, comprehensive exam (for some programs), field project; for doctorate, comprehensive exam, thesis/dissertation. *Entrance requirements:* For doctorate, GRE General Test. Additional exam requirements/recommendations for international students: Required—TOEFL (minimum score 600 paper-based; 250 computer-based; 90 iBT), IELTS (minimum score 7). *Application deadline:* Applications are processed on a rolling basis. Application fee: $60. Electronic applications accepted. *Financial support:* Fellowships, research assistantships, teaching assistantships available. Financial award application deadline: 1/5; financial award applicants required to submit FAFSA.

University of Washington, Graduate School, College of Education, Program in Special Education, Seattle, WA 98195. Offers early childhood special education (M Ed); emotional and

behavioral disabilities (M Ed); learning disabilities (M Ed); low-incidence disabilities (M Ed); severe disabilities (M Ed); special education (Ed D, PhD). *Degree requirements:* For master's, thesis optional; for doctorate, thesis/dissertation. *Entrance requirements:* For master's and doctorate, GRE General Test, minimum GPA of 3.0. Additional exam requirements/recommendations for international students: Required—TOEFL.

University of Washington, Tacoma, Graduate Programs, Program in Education, Tacoma, WA 98402-3100. Offers educational administrator (M Ed); K-8 teacher education (M Ed); professional certification (M Ed); secondary science (M Ed); special education (M Ed). Part-time and evening/weekend programs available. *Faculty:* 13 full-time (8 women), 9 part-time/adjunct (8 women). *Students:* 85 full-time (66 women), 118 part-time (99 women); includes 24 minority (4 African Americans, 9 Asian Americans or Pacific Islanders, 11 Hispanic Americans). Average age 33. 36 applicants, 75% accepted, 23 enrolled. In 2009, 68 master's awarded. *Entrance requirements:* For master's, official sealed transcript from every college/university attended, personal goal statement, letters of recommendation, copy of valid teaching certificate. *Application deadline:* For fall admission, 8/1 for domestic students; for winter admission, 11/1 priority date for domestic students; for spring admission, 2/1 priority date for domestic students. Applications are processed on a rolling basis. Application fee: $65. Electronic applications accepted. *Expenses:* Tuition, state resident: full-time $10,660; part-time $484 per credit. Tuition, nonresident: full-time $24,000; part-time $1119 per credit. Required fees: $150 per term. Tuition and fees vary according to course load and program. *Faculty research:* Global learning communities for English/Chinese languages, evaluation of mathematics and reading intervention programs, response to intervention, school wide behavioral and emotional support, mathematics education and culturally responsive mathematics education. *Unit head:* Dr. Karen Landenburger, Chancellor, 253-692-4430, Fax: 253-692-5612, E-mail: uwted@u.washington.edu. *Application contact:* Dr. Carla Van Rossum, Recruiter/Advisor, 253-692-4430, Fax: 253-692-5612, E-mail: uwted@u.washington.edu.

The University of West Alabama, School of Graduate Studies, College of Education, Department of Teacher Education, Program in Special Education, Livingston, AL 35470. Offers M Ed. *Accreditation:* NCATE. Part-time programs available. *Entrance requirements:* For master's, GRE General Test, MAT, minimum GPA of 2.75. *Faculty research:* Learning strategies/reading; imagine, discuss, and decide; transition; at-risk students.

The University of Western Ontario, Faculty of Graduate Studies, Social Sciences Division, Faculty of Education, Program in Educational Studies, London, ON N6A 5B8, Canada. Offers curriculum studies (M Ed); educational policy studies (M Ed); educational psychology/special education (M Ed). Part-time programs available. *Faculty research:* Reflective practice, gender and schooling, feminist pedagogy, narrative inquiry, second language, multiculturalism in Canada, education and law.

University of West Florida, College of Professional Studies, School of Education, Master's Program in Curriculum and Instruction, Pensacola, FL 32514-5750. Offers curriculum and instruction: special education (M Ed); elementary education (M Ed); primary education (M Ed). Part-time and evening/weekend programs available. *Students:* 12 full-time (all women), 108 part-time (96 women); includes 16 minority (11 African Americans, 2 Asian Americans or Pacific Islanders, 3 Hispanic Americans), 2 international. Average age 36. 36 applicants, 25% accepted, 9 enrolled. In 2009, 35 master's awarded. *Entrance requirements:* For master's, GRE (minimum score 450 verbal) or MAT (minimum score 396) if bachelor's GPA less than 3.0, state teaching certification; letter of intent; two professional references. Additional exam requirements/recommendations for international students: Required—TOEFL (minimum score 550 paper-based; 213 computer-based). *Application deadline:* For fall admission, 6/1 for domestic students, 5/15 for international students; for spring admission, 11/1 for domestic students, 10/1 for international students. Applications are processed on a rolling basis. Application fee: $30. *Expenses:* Tuition, state resident: full-time $4982; part-time $260 per credit hour. Tuition, nonresident: full-time $20,059; part-time $919 per credit hour. Required fees: $1247; $52 per credit hour. *Financial support:* Career-related internships or fieldwork, Federal Work-Study, scholarships/grants, and tuition waivers (partial) available. Support available to part-time students. Financial award application deadline: 4/15; financial award applicants required to submit FAFSA. *Unit head:* Dr. David Stout, Interim Chairperson, 850-474-2284, Fax: 850-474-2844. *Application contact:* Terry McCray, Assistant Director of Graduate Admissions, 850-473-7718, Fax: 850-473-7714, E-mail: gradadmissions@uwf.edu.

University of West Florida, College of Professional Studies, School of Education, Program in Exceptional Student Education, Pensacola, FL 32514-5750. Offers clinical teaching (MA), including emotionally handicapped, learning disabled, mentally handicapped; habilitative science (MA). *Accreditation:* NCATE. Part-time and evening/weekend programs available. *Students:* 8 full-time (all women), 32 part-time (29 women); includes 9 minority (5 African Americans, 2 Asian Americans or Pacific Islanders, 2 Hispanic Americans). Average age 34. 24 applicants, 67% accepted, 12 enrolled. In 2009, 20 master's awarded. *Entrance requirements:* For master's, GRE (minimum score 450 verbal) or MAT (minimum score 396) if bachelor's GPA less than 3.0, state teaching certification; letter of intent; two professional references. Additional exam requirements/recommendations for international students: Required—TOEFL (minimum score 550 paper-based; 213 computer-based). *Application deadline:* For fall admission, 6/1 for domestic students, 5/15 for international students; for spring admission, 11/1 for domestic students, 10/1 for international students. Applications are processed on a rolling basis. Application fee: $30. *Expenses:* Tuition, state resident: full-time $4982; part-time $260 per credit hour. Tuition, nonresident: full-time $20,059; part-time $919 per credit hour. Required fees: $1247; $52 per credit hour. *Financial support:* Unspecified assistantships available. Financial award application deadline: 4/15; financial award applicants required to submit FAFSA. *Faculty research:* Memory, semantic structure, remedial programming. *Unit head:* Dr. David Stout, Chairperson, 850-474-2284, Fax: 850-474-2844. *Application contact:* Terry McCray, Assistant Director of Graduate Admissions, 850-473-7718, Fax: 850-473-7714, E-mail: gradadmissions@uwf.edu.

University of West Georgia, Graduate School, College of Education, Department of Special Education and Speech-Language Pathology, Carrollton, GA 30118. Offers special education-general (M Ed, Ed S); speech-language pathology (M Ed). *Accreditation:* ASHA; NCATE. Part-time and evening/weekend programs available. *Faculty:* 8 full-time (6 women), 2 part-time/adjunct (both women). *Students:* 68 full-time (63 women), 222 part-time (190 women); includes 98 minority (93 African Americans, 5 Hispanic Americans), 2 international. Average age 36. 184 applicants, 48% accepted, 48 enrolled. In 2009, 42 master's, 20 Ed Ss awarded. *Degree requirements:* For Ed S, research project. *Entrance requirements:* For master's, GRE General Test, minimum GPA of 3.0 in speech-language pathology, 2.7 overall; for Ed S, GRE General Test, master's degree, minimum graduate GPA of 3.4. *Application deadline:* For fall admission, 7/17 for domestic students; for spring admission, 11/20 for domestic students. Applications are processed on a rolling basis. Application fee: $30. Electronic applications accepted. *Expenses:* Tuition, state resident: full-time $2952; part-time $164 per semester hour. Tuition, nonresident: full-time $11,808; part-time $656 per semester hour. Required fees: $42.90 per semester hour. $307 per semester. Tuition and fees vary according to course load. *Financial support:* In 2009–10, 4 research assistantships with full tuition reimbursements (averaging $12,000 per year) were awarded; career-related internships or fieldwork, scholarships/grants, and unspecified assistantships also available. Support available to part-time students. Financial award applicants required to submit FAFSA. *Faculty research:* Mentoring, inclusion, learning strategies, scaffolding strategies, applied behavior analysis. *Unit head:* Dr. John von Eschenbach, Interim Chair, 678-839-6149, Fax: 678-839-6162, E-mail: johnvone@westga.edu. *Application contact:* Dr. Charles W. Clark, Dean, 678-839-6508, E-mail: cclark@westga.edu.

University of Wisconsin–Eau Claire, College of Education and Human Sciences, Program in Special Education, Eau Claire, WI 54702-4004. Offers MSE. Part-time programs available. *Faculty:* 7 full-time (4 women). *Students:* 12 part-time (11 women). Average age 33. 4 applicants, 75% accepted, 3 enrolled. In 2009, 7 master's awarded. *Degree requirements:* For master's, comprehensive exam, thesis optional, written or oral exam with thesis, public forum presentation. *Entrance requirements:* For master's, minimum GPA of 2.75. Additional exam requirements/recommendations for international students: Required—TOEFL (minimum score 550 paper-based; 213 computer-based; 79 iBT). *Application deadline:* For fall admission, 7/1 priority date for domestic students, 6/1 priority date for international students; for spring admission, 12/1 priority date for domestic students, 11/1 priority date for international students. Applications are processed on a rolling basis. Application fee: $56. Electronic applications accepted. *Expenses:* Tuition, state resident: full-time $6705.90; part-time $372.55 per credit. Tuition, nonresident: full-time $16,771; part-time $931.74 per credit. Required fees: $925.50; $51.19 per credit. One-time fee: $56. *Financial support:* In 2009–10, 5 students received support. Federal Work-Study and unspecified assistantships available. Financial award application deadline: 3/1; financial award applicants required to submit FAFSA. *Unit head:* Dr. Rosemary Battalio, Chair, 715-836-5352, Fax: 715-836-3162, E-mail: battalrl@uwec.edu. *Application contact:* Kristina Anderson, Director of Admissions, 715-836-5415, Fax: 715-836-2409, E-mail: admissions@uwec.edu.

University of Wisconsin–La Crosse, Office of University Graduate Studies, College of Liberal Studies, Department of Educational Studies, Program in Special Education, La Crosse, WI 54601-3742. Offers emotional disturbance (MS Ed); learning disabilities (MS Ed). Part-time programs available. *Students:* 10 full-time (6 women), 15 part-time (11 women); includes 1 minority (Asian American or Pacific Islander). Average age 34. 15 applicants, 67% accepted, 6 enrolled. In 2009, 7 master's awarded. *Degree requirements:* For master's, thesis optional. *Entrance requirements:* For master's, GRE General Test, minimum undergraduate GPA of 3.0, 3 letters of recommendation. Additional exam requirements/recommendations for international students: Required—TOEFL (minimum score 550 paper-based; 213 computer-based; 79 iBT). *Application deadline:* Applications are processed on a rolling basis. Application fee: $56. Electronic applications accepted. *Financial support:* Research assistantships, career-related internships or fieldwork, health care benefits, and unspecified assistantships available. Financial award application deadline: 3/15; financial award applicants required to submit FAFSA. *Unit head:* Dr. Carol Angell, Director, 608-785-8135, E-mail: angell.caro@uwlax.edu. *Application contact:* Kathryn Kiefer, Associate Director of Admissions, 608-785-8939, E-mail: admissions@uwlax.edu.

University of Wisconsin–La Crosse, Office of University Graduate Studies, College of Science and Health, Department of Exercise and Sport Science, La Crosse, WI 54601-3742. Offers clinical exercise physiology (MS); human performance (MS), including athletic training, human performance; physical education teaching (MS); special/adapted physical education (MS); sport administration (MS). Part-time and evening/weekend programs available. *Faculty:* 20 full-time (6 women). *Students:* 71 full-time (41 women), 52 part-time (28 women); includes 4 minority (2 African Americans, 2 Hispanic Americans), 4 international. Average age 27. 143 applicants, 51% accepted, 54 enrolled. In 2009, 71 master's awarded. *Entrance requirements:* For master's, minimum GPA of 3.0 during previous 2 years, 2.85 overall. Additional exam requirements/recommendations for international students: Required—TOEFL (minimum score 550 paper-based; 213 computer-based; 79 iBT). Application fee: $56. Electronic applications accepted. *Financial support:* In 2009–10, 23 research assistantships (averaging $6,778 per year) were awarded; career-related internships or fieldwork, Federal Work-Study, institutionally sponsored loans, scholarships/grants, traineeships, health care benefits, tuition waivers (full and partial), unspecified assistantships, and grant-funded positions also available. Support available to part-time students. Financial award application deadline: 3/15; financial award applicants required to submit FAFSA. *Unit head:* Dr. Patrick DiRocco, Chair, 608-785-8173, Fax: 608-785-6520, E-mail: dirocco.patr@uwlax.edu. *Application contact:* Kathryn Kiefer, Director of Admissions, 608-785-8939, E-mail: admissions@uwlax.edu.

University of Wisconsin–Madison, Graduate School, School of Education, Department of Rehabilitation Psychology and Special Education, Program in Special Education, Madison, WI 53706-1380. Offers MA, MS, PhD. *Degree requirements:* For doctorate, thesis/dissertation. *Application deadline:* For fall admission, 3/15 for domestic and international students; for spring admission, 10/15 for domestic and international students. Application fee: $56. Electronic applications accepted. *Expenses:* Tuition, state resident: part-time $594 per credit. Tuition, nonresident: part-time $1504 per credit. Required fees: $65 per credit. Tuition and fees vary according to course load, program and reciprocity agreements. *Financial support:* Fellowships with full tuition reimbursements, research assistantships with full tuition reimbursements, teaching assistantships with full tuition reimbursements, project assistantships available. *Unit head:* Dr. David Rosenthal, Chair, 608-262-5860. *Application contact:* Dr. David Rosenthal, Chair, 608-262-5860.

University of Wisconsin–Milwaukee, Graduate School, School of Education, Department of Exceptional Education, Milwaukee, WI 53201-0413. Offers assistive technology and accessible design (Certificate); exceptional education (MS). Part-time programs available. *Faculty:* 12 full-time (10 women). *Students:* 28 full-time (19 women), 52 part-time (47 women); includes 19 minority (12 African Americans, 2 Asian Americans or Pacific Islanders, 5 Hispanic Americans). Average age 33. 21 applicants, 52% accepted, 7 enrolled. In 2009, 25 master's awarded. *Degree requirements:* For master's, thesis. *Entrance requirements:* Additional exam requirements/recommendations for international students: Required—TOEFL (minimum score 550 paper-based; 79 iBT), IELTS (minimum score 6.5). *Application deadline:* For fall admission, 1/1 priority date for domestic students; for spring admission, 9/1 for domestic students. Applications are processed on a rolling basis. Application fee: $45 ($75 for international students). *Expenses:* Tuition, state resident: full-time $8800. Tuition, nonresident: full-time $20,760. Tuition and fees vary according to program and reciprocity agreements. *Financial support:* Career-related internships or fieldwork and unspecified assistantships available. Support available to part-time students. Financial award application deadline: 4/15. *Faculty research:* Emotional disturbance, hearing impairment, learning disabilities, mental retardation. Total annual research expenditures: $88,956. *Unit head:* Dr. Karen C. Stoiber, Training Director, 414-229-6841, E-mail: kstoiber@uwm.edu. *Application contact:* General Information Contact, 414-229-4982, Fax: 414-229-6967, E-mail: gradschool@uwm.edu.

University of Wisconsin–Oshkosh, The Office of Graduate Studies, College of Education and Human Services, Department of Special Education, Oshkosh, WI 54901. Offers cross-categorical (MSE); early childhood: exceptional education needs (MSE); non-licensure (MSE). Part-time and evening/weekend programs available. *Degree requirements:* For master's, comprehensive exam (for some programs), thesis or alternative, field report. *Entrance requirements:* For master's, interview, minimum GPA of 3.0, teaching license, letters of recommendation. Additional exam requirements/recommendations for international students: Required—TOEFL (minimum score 550 paper-based; 213 computer-based; 79 iBT). Electronic applications accepted. *Faculty research:* Private agency contributions to the disabled, graduation requirements for exceptional education needs students, direct instruction in spelling for learning disabled, effects of behavioral parent training, secondary education programming issues.

University of Wisconsin–Stevens Point, College of Professional Studies, School of Education, Program in Education—General/Special, Stevens Point, WI 54481-3897. Offers MSE. Part-time programs available. *Degree requirements:* For master's, comprehensive exam, thesis or alternative. *Entrance requirements:* For master's, minimum undergraduate GPA of 3.0, 2 years teaching experience, letters of recommendation, teacher certification. *Application deadline:* For fall admission, 5/1 priority date for domestic students. Applications are processed on a rolling basis. Application fee: $45. *Expenses:* Tuition, state resident: full-time $7740; part-time $430 per credit hour. Tuition, nonresident: full-time $17,804; part-time $989 per credit hour. Tuition and fees vary according to course load and reciprocity agreements. *Financial support:* In 2009–10, 4 research assistantships with partial tuition reimbursements (averaging $9,807 per year) were awarded; Federal Work-Study also available. Support available to part-time students. Financial award application deadline: 5/1; financial award applicants required to submit FAFSA. *Faculty research:* Curriculum and instruction, early childhood special education, standards-based education. *Unit head:* Dr. JoAnne Katzmarek, Associate Dean, 715-346-4430, Fax: 715-346-4846, E-mail: jkatzmar@uwsp.edu. *Application contact:* Dr. Patricia Caro, Director, 715-346-4403, Fax: 715-346-4846, E-mail: pcaro@uwsp.edu.

Special Education

University of Wisconsin–Superior, Graduate Division, Department of Teacher Education, Program in Special Education, Superior, WI 54880-4500. Offers emotional/behavior disabilities (MSE); learning disabilities (MSE). Part-time and evening/weekend programs available. Post-baccalaureate distance learning degree programs offered (minimal on-campus study). *Faculty:* 2 full-time (both women). *Students:* 1 (woman) full-time, 60 part-time (40 women); includes 1 minority (American Indian/Alaska Native). 11 applicants, 100% accepted. In 2009, 14 master's awarded. *Degree requirements:* For master's, research project. *Entrance requirements:* For master's, minimum GPA of 2.75, teaching certificate. *Application deadline:* For fall admission, 4/1 priority date for domestic students; for spring admission, 10/15 priority date for domestic students. Applications are processed on a rolling basis. Application fee: $45. *Financial support:* Career-related internships or fieldwork, Federal Work-Study, institutionally sponsored loans, and tuition waivers (partial) available. Support available to part-time students. Financial award application deadline: 4/15; financial award applicants required to submit FAFSA. *Unit head:* Dr. Jennifer Christensen, Coordinator, 715-394-8144, E-mail: jchris27@uwsuper.edu. *Application contact:* Sandy Wallgren, Program Assistant/Status Examiner, 715-394-8295, Fax: 715-394-8146, E-mail: gradstudy@uwsuper.edu.

University of Wisconsin–Whitewater, School of Graduate Studies, College of Education, Department of Special Education, Whitewater, WI 53190-1790. Offers MS Ed. *Accreditation:* NCATE. Part-time and evening/weekend programs available. Postbaccalaureate distance learning degree programs offered (no on-campus study). *Degree requirements:* For master's, thesis or alternative. *Entrance requirements:* Additional exam requirements/recommendations for international students: Required—TOEFL (minimum score 550 paper-based; 213 computer-based). Electronic applications accepted. *Faculty research:* Language ability, cultural interaction with disability, juvenile corrections, early childhood programming and childcare issues.

University of Wyoming, College of Education, Department of Special Education, Laramie, WY 82070. Offers MA, PhD, Ed S. *Degree requirements:* For master's, comprehensive exam, thesis. *Entrance requirements:* For master's, GRE, 2 years teaching experience, 3 letters of recommendation, writing sample. *Faculty research:* Self-determination; transition; digital learning; severe disabilities; response to intervention.

Ursuline College, School of Graduate Studies, Program in Education, Pepper Pike, OH 44124-4398. Offers art education (MA); early childhood education (MA); language arts education (MA); life science education (MA); math education (MA); middle school education (MA); social studies education (MA); special education (MA). *Accreditation:* NCATE. *Faculty:* 1 (woman) full-time, 10 part-time/adjunct (8 women). *Students:* 53 full-time (40 women), 3 part-time (all women); includes 8 minority (7 African Americans, 1 Hispanic American). Average age 34. In 2009, 11 master's awarded. *Degree requirements:* For master's, comprehensive exam. *Entrance requirements:* For master's, minimum undergraduate GPA of 3.0. Additional exam requirements/recommendations for international students: Required—TOEFL (minimum score 500 paper-based; 173 computer-based). *Application deadline:* For fall admission, 8/1 priority date for domestic students. Applications are processed on a rolling basis. Application fee: $25. *Expenses:* Contact institution. *Financial support:* Federal Work-Study available. Financial award application deadline: 3/1. *Unit head:* Karen Godenschwager Nelson, Director, 440-684-8338, Fax: 440-684-6088, E-mail: kgodenschwager@ursuline.edu. *Application contact:* Melanie Steele, Secretary, 440-646-8199, Fax: 440-684-6138, E-mail: gradsch@ursuline.edu.

Utah State University, School of Graduate Studies, College of Education and Human Services, Department of Special Education and Rehabilitation, Logan, UT 84322. Offers disability disciplines (PhD); rehabilitation counselor education (MRC); special education (M Ed, MS, Ed S). *Accreditation:* NCATE (one or more programs are accredited). Part-time programs available. Postbaccalaureate distance learning degree programs offered (minimal on-campus study). *Degree requirements:* For master's, thesis (for some programs), internships (for some programs); for doctorate, comprehensive exam, thesis/dissertation. *Entrance requirements:* For master's and doctorate, GRE General Test, minimum GPA of 3.0. Additional exam requirements/recommendations for international students: Required—TOEFL (minimum score 550 paper-based; 213 computer-based). Electronic applications accepted. *Faculty research:* Applied behavior analysis, effective instructional practices, early childhood teacher training research, distance education, multicultural rehabilitation.

Valdosta State University, Graduate School, Department of Early Childhood and Special Education, Valdosta, GA 31698. Offers special education (M Ed, Ed S). *Accreditation:* ASHA (one or more programs are accredited); NCATE. Part-time and evening/weekend programs available. *Degree requirements:* For master's, thesis (for some programs), comprehensive written and/or oral exams; for Ed S, thesis. *Entrance requirements:* For master's, GRE General Test or MAT, minimum GPA of 2.5; for Ed S, GRE General Test or MAT, minimum GPA of 3.0. Additional exam requirements/recommendations for international students: Required—TOEFL (minimum score 523 paper-based; 193 computer-based). Electronic applications accepted.

Vanderbilt University, Peabody College, Department of Special Education, Nashville, TN 37240-1001. Offers M Ed. *Accreditation:* NCATE. *Faculty:* 30 full-time (18 women), 6 part-time/adjunct (5 women). *Students:* 70 full-time (65 women), 20 part-time (19 women); includes 2 minority (both Asian Americans or Pacific Islanders), 5 international. Average age 28. 86 applicants, 70% accepted, 40 enrolled. In 2009, 46 master's awarded. *Degree requirements:* For master's, comprehensive exam, thesis optional. *Entrance requirements:* For master's, GRE General Test, MAT. Additional exam requirements/recommendations for international students: Required—TOEFL (minimum score 550 paper-based; 213 computer-based). *Application deadline:* For fall admission, 12/31 priority date for domestic and international students; for spring admission, 11/1 priority date for domestic and international students. Applications are processed on a rolling basis. Application fee: $0. Electronic applications accepted. *Financial support:* In 2009–10, 87 students received support, including 64 research assistantships with full and partial tuition reimbursements available; fellowships with full and partial tuition reimbursements available, teaching assistantships with full and partial tuition reimbursements available, Federal Work-Study, institutionally sponsored loans, scholarships/grants, traineeships, health care benefits, tuition waivers (partial), and unspecified assistantships also available. Support available to part-time students. Financial award application deadline: 2/1; financial award applicants required to submit CSS PROFILE or FAFSA. *Faculty research:* Learning disabilities, autism, behavioral disorders; at risk students; attention deficit hyperactivity disorder. *Unit head:* Dr. Mark Wolery, Chair, 615-322-8150, Fax: 615-343-1570, E-mail: mark.wolery@vanderbilt.edu. *Application contact:* Jennifer M. Hinton, Administrative Assistant, 615-322-8195, Fax: 615-343-1570, E-mail: jennifer.m.hinton@vanderbilt.edu.

Vanderbilt University, School of Medicine, Department of Hearing and Speech Sciences, Nashville, TN 37240-1001. Offers audiology (Au D, PhD); education of the deaf (MED); hearing and speech sciences (MS); speech-language-pathology (MS). *Degree requirements:* For master's, thesis optional; for doctorate, thesis/dissertation, final and qualifying exams. *Entrance requirements:* For master's and doctorate, GRE General Test. Additional exam requirements/recommendations for international students: Required—TOEFL. Electronic applications accepted. *Faculty research:* Audiology, speech-language pathology, child language.

Virginia Commonwealth University, Graduate School, School of Education, Doctoral Program in Education, Special Education and Disability Leadership Track, Richmond, VA 23284-9005. Offers PhD.

Virginia Commonwealth University, Graduate School, School of Education, Program in Adult and Organizational Learning, Richmond, VA 23284-9005. Offers adult literacy (M Ed); adults with disabilities (M Ed); human resource development (M Ed). *Accreditation:* NCATE. Part-time programs available. *Entrance requirements:* For master's, GRE General Test or MAT. *Faculty research:* Adult development and learning, program planning and evaluation.

Virginia Commonwealth University, Graduate School, School of Education, Program in Special Education, Richmond, VA 23284-9005. Offers early childhood (M Ed); emotionally disturbed (M Ed, MT); learning disabilities (M Ed); mentally retarded (M Ed, MT); severely/profoundly handicapped (M Ed). *Accreditation:* NCATE. *Degree requirements:* For master's, comprehensive exam. *Entrance requirements:* For master's, GRE General Test or MAT.

Virginia Polytechnic Institute and State University, Graduate School, College of Liberal Arts and Human Sciences, School of Education, Department of Educational Leadership and Policy Studies, Program in Administration and Supervision of Special Education, Blacksburg, VA 24061. Offers Ed D, PhD, Ed S. *Accreditation:* NCATE. Postbaccalaureate distance learning degree programs offered (minimal on-campus study). *Degree requirements:* For doctorate, thesis/dissertation, internship. *Entrance requirements:* For doctorate and Ed S, GRE General Test, teaching experience. Additional exam requirements/recommendations for international students: Required—TOEFL. Electronic applications accepted. *Expenses:* Tuition, area resident: Full-time $10,228; part-time $459 per credit hour. Tuition, nonresident: full-time $17,892; part-time $865 per credit hour. Required fees: $1966; $451 per semester.

Walden University, Graduate Programs, Richard W. Riley College of Education and Leadership, Minneapolis, MN 55401. Offers administrator leadership for teaching and learning (Ed D, Ed S); curriculum, instruction, and professional development (Ed S); early childhood education (birth-grade 3) (MAT); education (MS, PhD), including adolescent literacy and technology (grades 6-12) (MS); adult education leadership (PhD), community college leadership (PhD), curriculum, instruction, and assessment, early childhood education (PhD), educational leadership (MS), educational technology (PhD), elementary reading and literacy (MS), elementary reading and mathematics (MS), emotional/behavioral disorders (K-12) (MS), general program, higher education (PhD), integrating technology in the classroom (MS), K-12 educational leadership (PhD), learning disabilities (K-12) (MS), literacy and learning in the content areas (MS), mathematics (grades 6-8) (MS), mathematics (grades K-5) (MS), middle level education (grades 5-8) (MS), professional development (MS), science (grades K-8) (MS), self-designed (PhD), special education (PhD), special education (non-licensure) (MS), teacher leadership (grades K-12) (MS); educational leadership and administration (principal preparation) (Ed S); educational technology (Ed S); higher education and adult learning (Ed D); instructional design (Postbaccalaureate Certificate); instructional design and technology (MS), including general program (MS, PhD), online learning, training and performance improvement; special education: emotional/behavioral disorders (K-12) (MAT); special education: learning disabilities (K-12) (MAT); teacher leadership (Ed D, Ed S). Part-time and evening/weekend programs available. Postbaccalaureate distance learning degree programs offered (minimal on-campus study). *Faculty:* 54 full-time, 835 part-time/adjunct. *Students:* 13,940 full-time (11,339 women), 1,940 part-time (1,637 women); includes 4,626 minority (3,795 African Americans, 111 American Indian/Alaska Native, 199 Asian Americans or Pacific Islanders, 521 Hispanic Americans), 124 international. Average age 38. In 2009, 4,688 master's, 190 doctorates awarded. *Degree requirements:* For doctorate, thesis/dissertation (for some programs), residency; for other advanced degree, residency (for some programs). *Entrance requirements:* For master's, bachelor's degree or equivalent in related field; minimum GPA of 2.5; official transcripts; goal statement; access to computer and Internet; for doctorate, master's degree or equivalent in related field; minimum GPA of 3.0; official transcripts; three years' related professional/academic experience (preferred); access to computer and Internet; for other advanced degree, master's degree or equivalent in related field; minimum GPA of 3.0; 3 years related professional/academic experience (preferred); access to computer and Internet (Ed S). Additional exam requirements/recommendations for international students: Required—TOEFL (minimum score 550 paper-based; 213 computer-based), IELTS (minimum score 6.5), or Michigan English Language Assessment Battery (minimum score 82). *Application deadline:* Applications are processed on a rolling basis. Application fee: $50. Electronic applications accepted. *Expenses:* Tuition: Full-time $13,665; part-time $560 per credit. Required fees: $1375. Tuition and fees vary according to course load, degree level and program. *Financial support:* In 2009–10, 2,418 students received support; fellowships, Federal Work-Study, scholarships/grants, unspecified assistantships, and family tuition reduction, active duty/veteran tuition reduction, group tuition reduction, interest-free payment plans available. Support available to part-time students. Financial award applicants required to submit FAFSA. *Unit head:* Dr. Kate Steffens, Dean, 800-925-3368. *Application contact:* Jennifer Hall, Director of Enrollment, 866-4-WALDEN, E-mail: info@waldenu.edu.

Walla Walla University, Graduate School, School of Education and Psychology, College Place, WA 99324-1198. Offers counseling psychology (MA); curriculum and instruction (M Ed, MA, MAT); educational leadership (M Ed, MA, MAT); literacy instruction (M Ed, MA, MAT); students at risk (M Ed, MA, MAT); teaching (MAT). Part-time programs available. *Faculty:* 7 full-time (3 women), 1 part-time/adjunct (0 women). *Students:* 32 full-time (14 women), 9 part-time (7 women); includes 5 minority (1 African American, 1 American Indian/Alaska Native, 2 Asian Americans or Pacific Islanders, 1 Hispanic American). Average age 30. 41 applicants, 80% accepted, 21 enrolled. In 2009, 29 master's awarded. *Entrance requirements:* For master's, GRE General Test, minimum GPA of 2.75. Additional exam requirements/recommendations for international students: Required—TOEFL (minimum score 550 paper-based; 213 computer-based; 79 iBT). *Application deadline:* For fall admission, 4/1 priority date for domestic students. Applications are processed on a rolling basis. Application fee: $50. Electronic applications accepted. *Expenses:* Tuition: Full-time $19,929. *Financial support:* In 2009–10, 29 students received support; research assistantships, teaching assistantships, Federal Work-Study and tuition waivers (partial) available. Support available to part-time students. Financial award application deadline: 4/1; financial award applicants required to submit FAFSA. *Faculty research:* Admissions/retention, instructional psychology, moral development, teaching of reading. *Unit head:* Dr. Julian Melgosa, Dean, 509-527-2272, Fax: 509-527-2248, E-mail: julian.melgosa@wallawalla.edu. *Application contact:* Dr. Joe G. Galusha, Dean of Graduate Studies, 509-527-2421, Fax: 509-527-2237, E-mail: joe.galusha@wallawalla.edu.

Washburn University, College of Arts and Sciences, Department of Education, Program in Special Education, Topeka, KS 66621. Offers M Ed. *Accreditation:* NCATE. *Degree requirements:* For master's, portfolio. *Entrance requirements:* For master's, GRE General Test, MAT, minimum GPA of 3.0 during previous 2 years.

Washington University in St. Louis, School of Medicine, Program in Audiology and Communication Sciences, St. Louis, MO 63110. Offers audiology (Au D); deaf education (MS); speech and hearing sciences (PhD). *Accreditation:* ASHA (one or more programs are accredited). *Faculty:* 22 full-time (12 women), 18 part-time/adjunct (12 women). *Students:* 74 full-time (72 women). Average age 24. 117 applicants, 21% accepted, 24 enrolled. In 2009, 14 master's, 9 doctorates awarded. *Degree requirements:* For master's, comprehensive exam, thesis, independent study project, oral exam; for doctorate, comprehensive exam, thesis/dissertation, capstone project, comprehensive exam. *Entrance requirements:* For master's, GRE General Test, minimum B average in undergraduate course work; for doctorate, GRE General Test, minimum B average. Additional exam requirements/recommendations for international students: Required—TOEFL (minimum score 600 paper-based; 250 computer-based; 100 iBT). *Application deadline:* For fall admission, 2/15 for domestic and international students. Application fee: $50 ($75 for international students). Electronic applications accepted. *Expenses:* Contact institution. *Financial support:* In 2009–10, 74 fellowships with tuition reimbursements were awarded; research assistantships with tuition reimbursements, teaching assistantships with tuition reimbursements, career-related internships or fieldwork, Federal Work-Study, institutionally sponsored loans, scholarships/grants, traineeships, health care benefits, tuition waivers (partial), and unspecified assistantships also available. Financial award application deadline: 2/15; financial award applicants required to submit FAFSA. *Faculty research:* Audiology, deaf education, speech and hearing sciences, hearing aids and cochlear implants, sensory neuroscience. *Unit head:* Dr. William W. Clark, Program Director, 314-747-0104, Fax: 314-747-0105. *Application contact:* Elizabeth A. Elliott, Manager, Financial Operations and Admissions, 314-747-0104, Fax: 314-747-0105, E-mail: elliottb@wustl.edu.

Wayland Baptist University, Graduate Programs, Program in Education, Plainview, TX 79072-6998. Offers education administration (M Ed); higher education administration (M Ed); instructional leadership (M Ed); instructional technology (M Ed); special education (M Ed). Part-time and evening/weekend programs available. Postbaccalaureate distance learning degree programs offered (no on-campus study). *Faculty:* 6 full-time (4 women). *Students:* 4 full-time (2 women), 45 part-time (26 women); includes 6 minority (3 African Americans, 3 Hispanic

Americans). Average age 30. 26 applicants, 77% accepted, 9 enrolled. In 2009, 4 master's awarded. *Degree requirements:* For master's, comprehensive exam, capstone course. *Entrance requirements:* For master's, GRE, GMAT or MAT. Additional exam requirements/recommendations for international students: Required—TOEFL (minimum score 500 paper-based; 173 computer-based; 61 iBT). *Application deadline:* Applications are processed on a rolling basis. Application fee: $50. Electronic applications accepted. *Expenses:* Tuition: Full-time $5796; part-time $322 per credit hour. Required fees: $782; $9 per credit hour. $60 per semester. Tuition and fees vary according to course load and campus/location. *Financial support:* Federal Work-Study, institutionally sponsored loans, and scholarships/grants available. Support available to part-time students. Financial award application deadline: 5/1; financial award applicants required to submit FAFSA. *Unit head:* Dr. Jim Todd, Chairman, 806-291-1045, Fax: 806-291-1951. *Application contact:* Amanda Stanton, Graduate Studies, 806-291-3423, Fax: 806-291-1950, E-mail: stanton@wbu.edu.

Waynesburg University, Graduate and Professional Studies, Waynesburg, PA 15370-1222. Offers business (MBA), including finance, health systems, human resources, leadership, market development; counseling (MA), including addictions counseling, clinical mental health; education (MAT); nursing (MSN), including administration, education, informatics, palliative care; nursing practice (DNP); special education (M Ed); technology (M Ed); MSN/MBA. *Accreditation:* AACN. Part-time and evening/weekend programs available. *Faculty:* 11 full-time (5 women), 136 part-time/adjunct (80 women). *Students:* 116 full-time (85 women), 984 part-time (682 women). 711 applicants, 80% accepted, 485 enrolled. In 2009, 320 master's, 41 doctorates awarded. *Degree requirements:* For doctorate, thesis/dissertation. *Entrance requirements:* Additional exam requirements/recommendations for international students: Required—TOEFL. *Application deadline:* For fall admission, 8/1 priority date for domestic students. Applications are processed on a rolling basis. Electronic applications accepted. *Expenses:* Tuition: Part-time $520 per credit. *Financial support:* Available to part-time students. Application deadline: 5/1. *Unit head:* David Mariner, Dean, 724-743-4420, Fax: 724-743-4425, E-mail: dmariner@waynesburg.edu. *Application contact:* Michael Bednarski, Director of Admissions, 724-743-4420, Fax: 724-743-4425, E-mail: mbednars@waynesburg.edu.

Wayne State College, School of Education and Counseling, Department of Counseling and Special Education, Program in Special Education, Wayne, NE 68787. Offers MSE. *Accreditation:* NCATE. Part-time and evening/weekend programs available. *Degree requirements:* For master's, comprehensive exam, thesis. *Entrance requirements:* For master's, GRE General Test, minimum GPA of 3.0. Additional exam requirements/recommendations for international students: Required—TOEFL (minimum score 550 paper-based; 213 computer-based). Electronic applications accepted.

Wayne State University, College of Education, Division of Teacher Education, Detroit, MI 48202. Offers adult and continuing education (M Ed); art education (M Ed); bilingual/bicultural education (M Ed, MAT); business education (M Ed, MAT); career and technical education (M Ed, Ed D, PhD, Ed S); curriculum and instruction (Ed D, PhD, Ed S); distributive education (M Ed, MAT); early childhood education (M Ed); elementary education (M Ed, MAT, Ed D, PhD, Ed S); elementary education curriculum and instruction (M Ed); English education (M Ed); English education-secondary (M Ed, Ed S); foreign language education (M Ed); general education (Ed D, Ed S); health occupations education (M Ed); industrial education (M Ed); mathematics education (M Ed, Ed S); pre-school and parent education (M Ed); reading (M Ed, Ed D, Ed S); reading, languages and literature (Ed D); school music-vocal (M Ed); science education (M Ed, MAT, Ed S); secondary education (MAT); secondary school reading (M Ed); social studies education (M Ed, Ed S), including education-secondary (M Ed); special education (M Ed, Ed D, PhD, Ed S); teacher education (MAT, Ed D, PhD). *Degree requirements:* For doctorate, thesis/dissertation. *Entrance requirements:* For master's, Michigan Basic Skills Test (MA in teaching), minimum GPA of 2.6; for doctorate, minimum undergraduate GPA of 3.0, graduate 3.5; interview, curriculum vitae; references. Additional exam requirements/recommendations for international students: Required—TOEFL (minimum score 550 paper-based; 213 computer-based), TWE (minimum score 6). Electronic applications accepted. *Faculty research:* Reading and writing literacy and literature.

Webster University, School of Education, Department of Multidisciplinary Studies, St. Louis, MO 63119-3194. Offers administrative leadership (Ed S); education leadership (Ed S); educational technology (MAT); mathematics (MAT); multidisciplinary studies (MAT); school systems, superintendency and leadership (Ed S); social science (MAT); special education (MAT). Part-time programs available. *Entrance requirements:* For master's, minimum GPA of 2.5. Additional exam requirements/recommendations for international students: Required—TOEFL. *Expenses:* Tuition: Part-time $565 per credit hour. Tuition and fees vary according to degree level, campus/location and program.

West Chester University of Pennsylvania, Office of Graduate Studies, College of Education, Department of Special Education, West Chester, PA 19383. Offers autism (Certificate); special education (M Ed, Teaching Certificate). *Accreditation:* NCATE. Part-time and evening/weekend programs available. *Students:* 6 full-time (all women), 93 part-time (83 women); includes 10 minority (5 African Americans, 2 Asian Americans or Pacific Islanders, 3 Hispanic Americans), 1 international. Average age 30. 89 applicants, 99% accepted, 58 enrolled. In 2009, 24 master's, 10 Certificates awarded. *Degree requirements:* For master's, thesis optional. *Entrance requirements:* For master's, GMAT, GRE General Test, or MAT, interview, minimum GPA of 2.8. Additional exam requirements/recommendations for international students: Required—TOEFL (minimum score 550 paper-based; 213 computer-based; 80 iBT). *Application deadline:* For fall admission, 4/15 priority date for domestic students, 3/15 for international students; for spring admission, 10/15 for domestic students, 9/1 for international students. Applications are processed on a rolling basis. Application fee: $35. Electronic applications accepted. *Expenses:* Tuition, state resident: full-time $6666; part-time $370 per credit. Tuition, nonresident: full-time $10,666; part-time $593 per credit. Required fees: $122.56 per credit. *Financial support:* In 2009–10, research assistantships with full and partial tuition reimbursements (averaging $5,000 per year); unspecified assistantships also available. Support available to part-time students. Financial award application deadline: 2/15; financial award applicants required to submit FAFSA. *Faculty research:* Developing online instruction for children with disabilities. *Unit head:* Dr. Michael Bell, Chair, 610-436-3067, E-mail: mbell@wcupa.edu. *Application contact:* Dr. Vicki McGinley, Graduate Coordinator, 610-436-1060, E-mail: vmcginley@wcupa.edu.

Western Connecticut State University, Division of Graduate Studies, School of Professional Studies, Department of Education and Educational Psychology, Special Education Option, Danbury, CT 06810-6885. Offers MS. Part-time programs available. *Students:* 2 full-time (both women), 37 part-time (25 women). Average age 30. 23 applicants, 70% accepted, 12 enrolled. In 2009, 14 master's awarded. *Degree requirements:* For master's, thesis or research project. *Entrance requirements:* For master's, minimum GPA of 2.8, teaching certificate. Additional exam requirements/recommendations for international students: Recommended—TOEFL (minimum score 550 paper-based; 213 computer-based; 79 iBT), IELTS (minimum score 6). *Application deadline:* For fall admission, 8/5 priority date for domestic students; for spring admission, 1/5 priority date for domestic students. Applications are processed on a rolling basis. Application fee: $50. *Expenses:* Tuition, state resident: full-time $5012; part-time $278 per credit hour. Tuition, nonresident: full-time $13,962; part-time $284 per credit hour. Required fees: $3886; $139 per credit hour. Full-time tuition and fees vary according to course load and program. Part-time tuition and fees vary according to course level, degree level and program. *Financial support:* In 2009–10, 1 student received support. Scholarships/grants available. Financial award application deadline: 5/1; financial award applicants required to submit FAFSA. *Unit head:* Dr. Theresa Canada, Chairperson, Department of Education and Educational Psychology, 203-837-8509, Fax: 203-837-8413, E-mail: canadat@wcsu.edu. *Application contact:* Chris Shankle, Associate Director of Graduate Studies, 203-837-9005, Fax: 203-837-8326, E-mail: shanklec@wcsu.edu.

Western Illinois University, School of Graduate Studies, College of Education and Human Services, Department of Special Education, Macomb, IL 61455-1390. Offers MS Ed. *Accreditation:* NCATE. Part-time programs available. *Students:* 1 (woman) full-time, 34 part-time (28 women); includes 2 minority (1 African American, 1 Hispanic American). Average age 36. 8 applicants, 63% accepted. In 2009, 9 master's awarded. *Degree requirements:* For master's, comprehensive exam, thesis or alternative. *Entrance requirements:* For master's, teacher certification. Additional exam requirements/recommendations for international students: Required—TOEFL (minimum score 550 paper-based; 213 computer-based; 80 iBT). *Application deadline:* Applications are processed on a rolling basis. Application fee: $30. Electronic applications accepted. *Expenses:* Tuition, state resident: full-time $4486; part-time $249.21 per credit hour. Tuition, nonresident: full-time $8972; part-time $498.42 per credit hour. Required fees: $72.62 per credit hour. *Financial support:* Research assistantships with full tuition reimbursements available. Financial award applicants required to submit FAFSA. *Unit head:* Dr. Darlos Mummert, Interim Chairperson, 309-298-1909. *Application contact:* Evelyn Hoing, Assistant Director of Graduate Studies, 309-298-1806, Fax: 309-298-2345, E-mail: grad-office@wiu.edu.

Western Kentucky University, Graduate Studies, College of Education and Behavioral Sciences, Department of Special Instructional Programs, Bowling Green, KY 42101. Offers exceptional child education (MAE); interdisciplinary early child education (MAE); library media education (MS); literacy (MAE). Part-time and evening/weekend programs available. Postbaccalaureate distance learning degree programs offered (minimal on-campus study). *Degree requirements:* For master's, comprehensive exam. *Entrance requirements:* For master's, GRE General Test. Additional exam requirements/recommendations for international students: Required—TOEFL (minimum score 555 paper-based; 213 computer-based; 79 iBT). *Expenses:* Tuition, state resident: full-time $4160; part-time $416 per credit hour. Tuition, nonresident: full-time $9550; part-time $506 per credit hour. Tuition and fees vary according to campus/location and reciprocity agreements. *Faculty research:* Teacher preparation in moderate/severe disabilities.

Western Michigan University, Graduate College, College of Education, Department of Special Education and Literacy Studies, Kalamazoo, MI 49008. Offers literacy studies (MA); special education (MA, Ed D); teaching children with visual impairments (MA). *Unit head:* Dan Morgan, Chair, 269-387-2968. *Application contact:* Admissions and Orientation, 269-387-2000, Fax: 269-387-2355.

Western New Mexico University, Graduate Division, School of Education, Silver City, NM 88062-0680. Offers bilingual education (MAT); counseling (MA); educational leadership (MA); elementary education (MAT); reading (MAT); school psychology (MA); secondary education (MAT); special education (MAT); TESOL (teaching English to speakers of other languages) (MAT). *Accreditation:* NCATE. *Degree requirements:* For master's, comprehensive exam. *Entrance requirements:* For master's, GRE General Test, GRE Subject Test, minimum GPA of 3.2 in last 64 hours of undergraduate study. Additional exam requirements/recommendations for international students: Required—TOEFL (minimum score 550 paper-based; 213 computer-based). Electronic applications accepted.

Western Oregon University, Graduate Programs, College of Education, Division of Special Education, Program in Deaf Education, Monmouth, OR 97361-1394. Offers MS Ed. *Accreditation:* NCATE. Part-time and evening/weekend programs available. *Degree requirements:* For master's, thesis, portfolio. *Entrance requirements:* For master's, California Basic Educational Skills Test or PRAXIS, GRE General Test or MAT, interview, minimum GPA of 3.0, teaching license. Additional exam requirements/recommendations for international students: Required—TOEFL (minimum score 550 paper-based; 213 computer-based; 79 iBT), IELTS (minimum score 6.5). *Faculty research:* Effects of infant massage on the interactions between high-risk infants and their caregivers, work sample methodology.

Western Oregon University, Graduate Programs, College of Education, Division of Special Education, Special Education Program, Monmouth, OR 97361-1394. Offers MS Ed. Part-time and evening/weekend programs available. *Degree requirements:* For master's, comprehensive exam (for some programs), thesis optional, oral exam, portfolio, written exam. *Entrance requirements:* For master's, California Basic Educational Skills Test or PRAXIS, GRE General Test or MAT, interview, minimum GPA of 3.0, teaching license. Additional exam requirements/recommendations for international students: Required—TOEFL (minimum score 550 paper-based; 213 computer-based; 79 iBT), IELTS (minimum score 6.5). *Faculty research:* Interpreter teacher training, hearing disabilities, mental retardation.

Westfield State College, Division of Graduate and Continuing Education, Department of Education, Program in Special Education, Westfield, MA 01086. Offers M Ed. *Accreditation:* NCATE. Part-time and evening/weekend programs available. *Degree requirements:* For master's, comprehensive exam, practicum. *Entrance requirements:* For master's, GRE General Test or MAT, minimum undergraduate GPA of 2.7.

West Texas A&M University, College of Education and Social Sciences, Division of Education, Program in Special Education, Canyon, TX 79016-0001. Offers M Ed. *Degree requirements:* For master's, comprehensive exam, thesis optional. *Entrance requirements:* For master's, GRE, standard classroom teaching certificate. Additional exam requirements/recommendations for international students: Required—TOEFL.

West Virginia University, College of Human Resources and Education, Department of Curriculum and Instruction-Literacy, Morgantown, WV 26506. Offers curriculum and instruction (Ed D); elementary education (MA); reading (MA); secondary education (MA), including higher education curriculum and teaching, secondary education; special education (Ed D), including special education. *Accreditation:* NCATE. Part-time and evening/weekend programs available. *Degree requirements:* For doctorate, comprehensive exam, thesis/dissertation. *Entrance requirements:* For master's, minimum GPA of 2.75; for doctorate, GRE General Test or MAT, 3 letters of recommendation, curriculum vitae. Additional exam requirements/recommendations for international students: Required—TOEFL. *Faculty research:* Teacher education, curriculum development, educational technology, curriculum assessment.

West Virginia University, College of Human Resources and Education, Department of Special Education, Morgantown, WV 26506. Offers autism spectrum disorder (5-adult) (MA); autism spectrum disorder (K-6) (MA); early intervention/early childhood special education (MA); gifted education (1-12) (MA); low vision (PreK-adult) (MA); multicategorical special education (5-adult) (MA); multicategorical special education (K-6) (MA); severe/multiple disabilities (K-adult) (MA); special education (MA, Ed D); vision impairments (PreK-adult) (MA). *Accreditation:* NCATE. Part-time and evening/weekend programs available. Postbaccalaureate distance learning degree programs offered (no on-campus study). *Degree requirements:* For master's, thesis optional; for doctorate, comprehensive exam, thesis/dissertation. *Entrance requirements:* For master's, minimum GPA of 2.75 passing scores on PRAXIS PPST; for doctorate, GRE General Test or MAT. Additional exam requirements/recommendations for international students: Required—TOEFL.

Wheelock College, Graduate Programs, Division of Education, Boston, MA 02215-4176. Offers early childhood education (MS); education leadership (MS); elementary education (MS); language, literacy, and reading (MS); teaching students with moderate disabilities (MS). *Accreditation:* NCATE. Postbaccalaureate distance learning degree programs offered (minimal on-campus study). *Degree requirements:* For master's, comprehensive exam. *Entrance requirements:* Additional exam requirements/recommendations for international students: Required—TOEFL. Electronic applications accepted. *Faculty research:* Symbolic learning, emergent literacy, diversity inclusion, beginning reading language and culture, math education.

Whitworth University, School of Education, Graduate Studies in Education, Program in Special Education, Spokane, WA 99251-0001. Offers MAT. *Accreditation:* NCATE. Part-time and evening/weekend programs available. *Degree requirements:* For master's, comprehensive exam, internship, practicum, research project, or thesis. *Entrance requirements:* For master's, GRE General Test, MAT. Additional exam requirements/recommendations for international students: Required—TOEFL. Tuition and fees vary according to program.

Wichita State University, Graduate School, College of Education, Department of Curriculum and Instruction, Wichita, KS 67260. Offers curriculum and instruction (M Ed); special education

Special Education

Wichita State University (continued)
(M Ed), including adaptive, early childhood unified, functional, gifted; teaching (MAT). *Accreditation:* NCATE. Part-time and evening/weekend programs available. *Entrance requirements:* For master's, MAT, minimum GPA of 2.75. *Expenses:* Tuition, state resident: full-time $4247; part-time $235.95 per credit hour. Tuition, nonresident: full-time $11,171; part-time $620.60 per credit hour. Required fees: $34; $3.60 per credit hour. $17 per term. Tuition and fees vary according to campus/location and program. *Unit head:* Dr. Janice Ewing, Chairperson, 316-978-3322, E-mail: janice.ewing@wichita.edu. *Application contact:* Dr. Janice Ewing, Chairperson, 316-978-3322, E-mail: janice.ewing@wichita.edu.

Widener University, School of Human Service Professions, Center for Education, Chester, PA 19013-5792. Offers adult education (M Ed); counseling in higher education (M Ed); counselor education (M Ed); early childhood education (M Ed); educational foundations (M Ed); educational leadership (M Ed); educational psychology (M Ed); elementary education (M Ed); English and language arts (M Ed); health education (M Ed); higher education leadership (Ed D); home and school visitor (M Ed); human sexuality (M Ed); mathematics education (M Ed); middle school education (M Ed); principalship (M Ed); reading and language arts (Ed D); reading education (M Ed); school administration (Ed D); science education (M Ed); social studies education (M Ed); special education (M Ed); technology education (M Ed). *Accreditation:* NCATE. Part-time and evening/weekend programs available. *Faculty:* 34 full-time (22 women), 37 part-time/adjunct (14 women). *Students:* 203 full-time (154 women), 415 part-time (298 women); includes 50 minority (34 African Americans, 1 American Indian/Alaska Native, 5 Asian Americans or Pacific Islanders, 10 Hispanic Americans), 3 international. Average age 39. 139 applicants, 88% accepted. In 2009, 168 master's, 31 doctorates awarded. Terminal master's awarded for partial completion of doctoral program. *Degree requirements:* For doctorate, thesis/dissertation. *Entrance requirements:* For master's, minimum GPA of 2.5; for doctorate, GRE or MAT, minimum GPA of 2.0 (undergraduate), 3.5 (graduate). *Application deadline:* Applications are processed on a rolling basis. Application fee: $25 ($300 for international students). Electronic applications accepted. *Expenses:* Contact institution. *Financial support:* Career-related internships or fieldwork, tuition waivers (full and partial), and unspecified assistantships available. Support available to part-time students. Financial award application deadline: 5/1. *Faculty research:* Reading and cognition, adult education, technology education, educational leadership, special education. *Unit head:* Dr. Michael W. LeDoux, Associate Dean, 610-499-4294, Fax: 610-499-4623, E-mail: mwledoux@widener.edu. *Application contact:* Dr. Roberta D. Nolan, Director of Graduate Admissions, 610-499-4125, E-mail: rdnolan@widener.edu.

Wilkes University, College of Graduate and Professional Studies, School of Education, Wilkes-Barre, PA 18766-0002. Offers classroom technology (MS Ed); educational computing (MS Ed); educational development and strategies (MS Ed); educational leadership (MS Ed); educational technology (Ed D); elementary education (MS Ed); higher education administration (Ed D); instructional technology (MS Ed); K-12 administration (Ed D); online teaching (MS Ed); school business leadership (MS Ed); secondary education (MS Ed), including biology, chemistry, English, history; special education (MS Ed). Part-time and evening/weekend programs available. Postbaccalaureate distance learning degree programs offered (minimal on-campus study). *Students:* 89 full-time (60 women), 2,849 part-time (2,058 women); includes 52 minority (10 African Americans, 2 American Indian/Alaska Native, 13 Asian Americans or Pacific Islanders, 27 Hispanic Americans), 6 international. Average age 33. In 2009, 947 master's awarded. *Entrance requirements:* Additional exam requirements/recommendations for international students: Required—TOEFL (minimum score 500 paper-based; 173 computer-based; 79 iBT). *Application deadline:* Applications are processed on a rolling basis. Application fee: $45. *Expenses:* Contact institution. *Financial support:* Federal Work-Study and unspecified assistantships available. Financial award application deadline: 3/1; financial award applicants required to submit FAFSA. *Unit head:* Dr. Michael Speziale, Dean, 570-408-4679, Fax: 570-408-4905, E-mail: michael.speziale@wilkes.edu. *Application contact:* Kathleen Houlihan, Director of Graduate Studies, 570-408-3235, Fax: 570-408-7846, E-mail: kathleen.houlihan@wilkes.edu.

William Carey University, School of Education, Hattiesburg, MS 39401-5499. Offers art education (M Ed); art of teaching (M Ed); elementary education (M Ed, Ed S); English education (M Ed); gifted education (M Ed); history and social science (M Ed); mild/moderate disabilities (M Ed); secondary education (M Ed). Part-time programs available. *Degree requirements:* For master's, comprehensive exam. *Entrance requirements:* For master's, GRE, MAT, minimum GPA of 2.5, Class A teacher's license. Additional exam requirements/recommendations for international students: Required—TOEFL (minimum score 550 paper-based; 213 computer-based).

William Paterson University of New Jersey, College of Education, Department of Special Education and Counseling Services, Wayne, NJ 07470-8420. Offers counseling services (M Ed); special education (M Ed). *Accreditation:* NCATE. *Students:* 30 full-time (26 women), 178 part-time (156 women); includes 15 minority (5 African Americans, 1 American Indian/Alaska Native, 2 Asian Americans or Pacific Islanders, 7 Hispanic Americans). In 2009, 62 master's awarded. *Degree requirements:* For master's, comprehensive exam, thesis. *Entrance requirements:* For master's, GRE General Test, MAT, minimum GPA of 2.75, teaching certificate. *Application deadline:* Applications are processed on a rolling basis. Application fee: $50. Electronic applications accepted. *Financial support:* Research assistantships with full tuition reimbursements, career-related internships or fieldwork and unspecified assistantships available. Support available to part-time students. Financial award application deadline: 4/1; financial award applicants required to submit FAFSA. *Unit head:* Dr. Peter Griswold, Graduate Program Director, 973-720-3761. *Application contact:* Danielle Liautaud, Director, 973-720-3579, Fax: 973-720-2035, E-mail: liautaudd@wpunj.edu.

William Woods University, Graduate and Adult Studies, Fulton, MO 65251-1098. Offers administration (Ed S); agriculture (MBA); athletic/activities administration (M Ed); curriculum and instruction (M Ed); curriculum leadership (Ed S); elementary administration (M Ed); health management (MBA); human resources (MBA); principalship (Ed S); secondary administration (M Ed); special education director (M Ed). Evening/weekend programs available. *Degree requirements:* For master's, capstone course (MBA), action research (M Ed); for Ed S, field experience. *Entrance requirements:* For master's, 2 recommendations, resumé, BA/BS; teaching certification (M Ed); course work in economics and accounting (MBA); for Ed S, M Ed, 2 letters of recommendation, resume, teaching certification. Additional exam requirements/recommendations for international students: Required—TOEFL (minimum score 550 paper-based). Electronic applications accepted.

Wilmington College, Department of Education, Wilmington, OH 45177. Offers reading (M Ed); special education (M Ed). Part-time programs available. *Degree requirements:* For master's, comprehensive exam. *Entrance requirements:* For master's, GRE or MAT, minimum GPA of 3.0, 2 letters of recommendation. Additional exam requirements/recommendations for international students: Required—TOEFL. *Faculty research:* Reading instruction, special education practices, conflict resolution in the schools, models of higher education for teachers.

Wilmington University, College of Education, New Castle, DE 19720-6491. Offers applied education technology (M Ed); career and technical education (M Ed); elementary and secondary school counseling (M Ed); elementary special education (M Ed); elementary studies (M Ed); instruction: gifted and talented (M Ed); instruction: teaching and learning (M Ed); literacy (M Ed); reading (M Ed); school leadership (M Ed); secondary teaching (MAT). *Accreditation:* NCATE. Part-time and evening/weekend programs available. *Entrance requirements:* For master's, 2 letters of recommendation, interview. Additional exam requirements/recommendations for international students: Required—TOEFL (minimum score 500 paper-based; 173 computer-based). Electronic applications accepted.

Winona State University, College of Education, Department of Special Education, Winona, MN 55987-5838. Offers special education (MS), including developmental disabilities, learning disabilities. Part-time and evening/weekend programs available. *Degree requirements:* For master's, comprehensive exam, thesis.

Winthrop University, College of Education, Program in Special Education, Rock Hill, SC 29733. Offers M Ed. *Accreditation:* NCATE. Part-time programs available. *Entrance requirements:* For master's, PRAXIS, South Carolina Class III Teaching Certificate, sample of written work. Electronic applications accepted.

Worcester State College, Graduate Studies, Department of Education, Program in Moderate Special Needs, Worcester, MA 01602-2597. Offers M Ed. Part-time and evening/weekend programs available. *Faculty:* 9 full-time (7 women), 19 part-time/adjunct (7 women). *Students:* 23 part-time (21 women). Average age 35. 47 applicants, 70% accepted, 8 enrolled. In 2009, 7 master's awarded. *Degree requirements:* For master's, comprehensive exam (for some programs), thesis optional. *Entrance requirements:* For master's, GRE General Test or MAT, teaching certificate. Additional exam requirements/recommendations for international students: Required—TOEFL (minimum score 550 paper-based; 213 computer-based; 79 iBT). *Application deadline:* Applications are processed on a rolling basis. Application fee: $30. *Expenses:* Tuition, area resident: Part-time $150 per credit. Tuition, state resident: part-time $150 per credit. Tuition, nonresident: part-time $150 per credit. Required fees: $85. *Financial support:* Career-related internships or fieldwork, scholarships/grants, and unspecified assistantships available. Financial award application deadline: 3/1; financial award applicants required to submit FAFSA. *Unit head:* Dr. Sue Fan Foo, Coordinator, 508-929-8071, Fax: 508-929-8164, E-mail: sfoo@worcester.edu. *Application contact:* Nicole Brown, Assistant Dean of Graduate and Continuing Education, 508-929-8787, Fax: 508-929-8100, E-mail: nbrown@worcester.edu.

Wright State University, School of Graduate Studies, College of Education and Human Services, Department of Teacher Education, Programs in Intervention Specialist, Dayton, OH 45435. Offers gifted educational needs (M Ed, MA); mild to moderate educational needs (M Ed, MA); moderate to intensive educational needs (M Ed, MA). *Accreditation:* NCATE. *Degree requirements:* For master's, thesis (for some programs). *Entrance requirements:* For master's, GRE General Test, MAT. Additional exam requirements/recommendations for international students: Required—TOEFL.

Xavier University, College of Social Sciences, Health and Education, School of Education, Department of Secondary and Special Education, Program in Special Education, Cincinnati, OH 45207. Offers M Ed. Part-time programs available. *Faculty:* 2 full-time (both women), 21 part-time/adjunct (14 women). *Students:* 39 full-time (30 women), 102 part-time (85 women); includes 20 minority (17 African Americans, 1 Asian American or Pacific Islander, 2 Hispanic Americans). Average age 32. 37 applicants, 97% accepted, 24 enrolled. In 2009, 53 master's awarded. *Degree requirements:* For master's, comprehensive exam, presentation of research. *Entrance requirements:* For master's, MAT, GRE. Application fee: $35. *Expenses:* Tuition: Part-time $697 per credit hour. One-time fee: $35 part-time. *Financial support:* In 2009–10, 106 students received support. Applicants required to submit FAFSA. *Faculty research:* Autism, collaboration of general education and special education, mental health/special education, training criminal justice personnel in special education, technology and learning. *Unit head:* Dr. Michael Flick, Chair, 513-745-3225, Fax: 513-745-3410, E-mail: flick@xavier.edu. *Application contact:* Dr. Sharon Merrill, Director, 513-745-1078, Fax: 513-745-2920, E-mail: merrill@xavier.edu.

Youngstown State University, Graduate School, Beeghly College of Education, Department of Teacher Education, Program in Special Education, Youngstown, OH 44555-0001. Offers gifted and talented education (MS Ed); special education (MS Ed). *Accreditation:* NCATE. Part-time and evening/weekend programs available. *Degree requirements:* For master's, comprehensive exam. *Entrance requirements:* For master's, GRE, MAT, or teaching certificate; interview; minimum GPA of 2.7. Additional exam requirements/recommendations for international students: Required—TOEFL. *Faculty research:* Learning disabilities, learning styles, developing self-esteem and social skills of severe behaviorally handicapped students, inclusion.

Urban Education

Alvernia University, Graduate Studies, Program in Education, Reading, PA 19607-1799. Offers urban education (M Ed). Part-time and evening/weekend programs available. *Degree requirements:* For master's, thesis optional. *Entrance requirements:* For master's, GRE or MAT (alumni excluded). Electronic applications accepted.

Brown University, Graduate School, Department of Education, Program in Urban Education Policy, Providence, RI 02912. Offers AM. *Faculty:* 5 full-time (3 women), 4 part-time/adjunct (2 women). *Students:* 22 full-time (18 women); includes 4 African Americans, 2 Asian Americans or Pacific Islanders, 3 Hispanic Americans. 75 applicants, 64% accepted, 22 enrolled. In 2009, 1 master's awarded. *Entrance requirements:* For master's, GRE General Test, official transcripts, 3 letters of recommendation. Additional exam requirements/recommendations for international students: Required—TOEFL. *Application deadline:* For fall admission, 1/15 priority date for domestic students. Application fee: $75. Electronic applications accepted. *Financial support:* In 2009–10, 20 students received support, including 2 fellowships with full tuition reimbursements available (averaging $46,000 per year), 6 research assistantships with partial tuition reimbursements available (averaging $9,200 per year), 4 teaching assistantships (averaging $1,000 per year); scholarships/grants and tuition waivers (full and partial) also available. Financial award application deadline: 1/15; financial award applicants required to submit FAFSA. *Faculty research:* Mayoral control of school systems. Total annual research expenditures: $6 million. *Unit head:* Dr. Wong Kenneth, Director of Urban Education Policy Program, 401-863-2407, Fax: 401-863-1276, E-mail: kenneth_wong@brown.edu. *Application contact:* Ann D'Abrosca, Assistant Director, 401-863-3983, Fax: 401-863-1276, E-mail: ann_dabrosca@brown.edu.

Cardinal Stritch University, College of Education, Department of Education, Milwaukee, WI 53217-3985. Offers education (ME); educational leadership (MS); leadership for the advancement of learning and service (Ed D, PhD); teaching (MAT); urban education (MA). *Accreditation:* NCATE. Evening/weekend programs available. *Degree requirements:* For master's, comprehensive exam, thesis (for some programs), research project, faculty recommendation; for doctorate, thesis/dissertation, practica, field experience. *Entrance requirements:* For master's, letters of recommendation (3), minimum GPA of 3.0; for doctorate, minimum GPA of 3.5 in master's coursework, letters of recommendation (3).

Claremont Graduate University, Graduate Programs, School of Educational Studies, Claremont, CA 91711-6160. Offers Africana education (Certificate); education and policy (MA, PhD); higher education/student affairs (MA, PhD); human development (MA, PhD); public school administration (MA, PhD); quantitative evaluation (MA, PhD); special education (MA, PhD); teacher education (MA); teaching and learning (MA, PhD); urban leadership (PhD); MBA/PhD. Part-time programs available. *Faculty:* 18 full-time (12 women), 1 part-time/adjunct (0 women). *Students:* 279 full-time (190 women), 174 part-time (122 women); includes 196 minority (50 African Americans, 1 American Indian/Alaska Native, 37 Asian Americans or

Pacific Islanders, 108 Hispanic Americans), 10 international. Average age 37. In 2009, 84 master's, 23 doctorates awarded. Terminal master's awarded for partial completion of doctoral program. *Entrance requirements:* For master's and doctorate, GRE General Test. Additional exam requirements/recommendations for international students: Required—TOEFL (minimum score 550 paper-based; 213 computer-based; 80 iBT). *Application deadline:* For fall admission, 2/1 priority date for domestic students. Applications are processed on a rolling basis. Application fee: $60. Electronic applications accepted. *Expenses:* Tuition: Full-time $35,046; part-time $1524 per credit. Required fees: $161 per semester. *Financial support:* Fellowships, research assistantships, Federal Work-Study, institutionally sponsored loans, and scholarships/grants available. Support available to part-time students. Financial award application deadline: 2/15; financial award applicants required to submit FAFSA. *Faculty research:* Education administration, K-12 and higher education, multicultural education, education policy, diversity in higher education, faculty issues. *Unit head:* Margaret Grogan, Dean, 909-621-8075, Fax: 909-621-8734, E-mail: margaret.grogan@cgu.edu.

Cleveland State University, College of Graduate Studies, College of Education and Human Services, Program in Urban Education, Cleveland, OH 44115. Offers counseling (PhD); counseling psychology (PhD); leadership and lifelong learning (PhD); learning and development (PhD); policy studies (PhD); school administration (PhD). Part-time programs available. *Degree requirements:* For doctorate, one foreign language, comprehensive exam, thesis/dissertation. *Entrance requirements:* For doctorate, GRE General Test, minimum graduate GPA of 3.25. Additional exam requirements/recommendations for international students: Required—TOEFL (minimum score 525 paper-based; 197 computer-based), IELTS (minimum score 6). *Faculty research:* Equity issues (race, ethnicity, and gender), education development consequences for special needs of urban populations, urban education programming, counseling the violent or aggressive adolescent.

College of Mount Saint Vincent, School of Professional and Continuing Studies, Department of Teacher Education, Riverdale, NY 10471-1093. Offers instructional technology and global perspectives (Certificate); middle level education (Certificate); multicultural studies (Certificate); urban and multicultural education (MS Ed). *Accreditation:* Teacher Education Accreditation Council. Part-time programs available. *Degree requirements:* For master's, comprehensive exam. *Entrance requirements:* For master's, interview, New York teaching certificate. Additional exam requirements/recommendations for international students: Required—TOEFL.

Columbia College Chicago, Graduate School, Department of Educational Studies, Chicago, IL 60605-1996. Offers elementary education (MAT); English (MAT); interdisciplinary arts (MAT); multicultural education (MA); urban teaching (MA). Part-time and evening/weekend programs available. *Degree requirements:* For master's, thesis, student teaching experience, 100 pre-clinical hours. *Entrance requirements:* For master's, supplemental recommendation form. Additional exam requirements/recommendations for international students: Required—TOEFL (minimum score 550 paper-based; 213 computer-based). Electronic applications accepted. *Expenses:* Tuition: Part-time $651 per credit hour. Required fees: $205 per semester. One-time fee: $285 part-time. Tuition and fees vary according to program.

DePaul University, School of Education, Chicago, IL 60106. Offers bilingual and bicultural education (M Ed, MA); curriculum studies (M Ed, MA, Ed D); educational leadership (M Ed, MA, Ed D), including administration and supervision (M Ed, MA), Catholic school leadership (M Ed, MA), physical education (M Ed, MA); human development and learning (MA); human services and counseling (M Ed, MA), including agencies, family concerns, and higher education, elementary schools, human services management, secondary schools; reading and learning disabilities (M Ed, MA); social culture studies in education and development (M Ed, MA), including curriculum studies/development; teaching and learning (early childhood, elementary and secondary) (M Ed), including elementary education (M Ed, MA), secondary education (M Ed, MA); teaching and learning (early childhood, elementary, and secondary) (MA), including elementary education (M Ed, MA), secondary education (M Ed, MA). *Accreditation:* NCATE. Part-time and evening/weekend programs available. *Faculty:* 61 full-time (40 women), 66 part-time/adjunct (41 women). *Students:* 799 full-time (779 women), 470 part-time (365 women); includes 319 minority (153 African Americans, 3 American Indian/Alaska Native, 48 Asian Americans or Pacific Islanders, 115 Hispanic Americans), 15 international. Average age 30. 635 applicants, 74% accepted, 318 enrolled. In 2009, 604 master's, 5 doctorates awarded. *Degree requirements:* For doctorate, thesis/dissertation. *Entrance requirements:* For master's, interview, minimum GPA of 2.75, 2 letters of recommendation; for doctorate, interview, master's degree, writing sample, 3 letters of recommendation. Additional exam requirements/recommendations for international students: Required—TOEFL (minimum score 550 paper-based; 213 computer-based; 80 iBT). *Application deadline:* Applications are processed on a rolling basis. Application fee: $40. Electronic applications accepted. *Expenses:* Tuition: Full-time $37,525; part-time $620 per credit hour. *Financial support:* In 2009–10, 14 research assistantships with tuition reimbursements (averaging $5,800 per year) were awarded; career-related internships or fieldwork also available. *Faculty research:* Reflective teaching, children at risk, loss, ethnicity, urban education. Total annual research expenditures: $1.6 million. *Unit head:* Dr. Marie Donovan, Dean, 773-325-7581, Fax: 773-325-7713, E-mail: mdonovan@depaul.edu. *Application contact:* Brandon Washington, Data Project Manager, 773-325-1152, Fax: 773-325-2270, E-mail: bwashin3@depaul.edu.

Florida International University, College of Education, Department of Educational Leadership and Policy Studies, Program in Urban Education, Miami, FL 33199. Offers MS. *Accreditation:* NCATE. Part-time and evening/weekend programs available. *Entrance requirements:* For master's, minimum undergraduate GPA of 3.0 in last 60 credits. Additional exam requirements/recommendations for international students: Required—TOEFL (minimum score 550 paper-based; 213 computer-based; 80 iBT), IELTS (minimum score 6.3). Electronic applications accepted. *Expenses:* Tuition, state resident: full-time $8008; part-time $4004 per year. Tuition, nonresident: full-time $20,104; part-time $10,052 per year. Required fees: $298; $149 per term. *Faculty research:* Urban education, literacy.

Graduate School and University Center of the City University of New York, Graduate Studies, Program in Urban Education, New York, NY 10016-4039. Offers PhD. *Students:* 105 full-time (73 women), 15 part-time (7 women); includes 17 African Americans, 8 Asian Americans or Pacific Islanders, 20 Hispanic Americans, 3 international. Average age 40. 87 applicants, 28% accepted, 17 enrolled. In 2009, 13 doctorates awarded. *Entrance requirements:* For doctorate, GRE General Test. Additional exam requirements/recommendations for international students: Required—TOEFL. *Application deadline:* For fall admission, 1/15 for domestic students. Application fee: $125. Electronic applications accepted. *Financial support:* In 2009–10, 75 students received support, including 72 fellowships, 1 teaching assistantship. *Unit head:* Dr. Philip Anderson, Executive Officer, 212-817-8281, Fax: 212-817-1515, E-mail: panderson@gc.cuny.edu. *Application contact:* Les Gribben, Director of Admissions, 212-817-7470, Fax: 212-817-1624, E-mail: lgribben@gc.cuny.edu.

Harvard University, Graduate School of Education, Doctoral Program in Education, Cambridge, MA 02138. Offers culture, communities and education (Ed D); education policy, leadership and instructional practice (Ed D); higher education (Ed D); human development and education (Ed D); quantitative policy analysis in education (Ed D); urban superintendency (Ed D). Part-time programs available. *Faculty:* 70 full-time (33 women), 36 part-time/adjunct (20 women). *Students:* 295 full-time (198 women), 23 part-time (11 women); includes 103 minority (40 African Americans, 4 American Indian/Alaska Native, 34 Asian Americans or Pacific Islanders, 25 Hispanic Americans), 33 international. Average age 32. 551 applicants, 9% accepted, 39 enrolled. In 2009, 41 doctorates awarded. Terminal master's awarded for partial completion of doctoral program. *Degree requirements:* For doctorate, thesis/dissertation. *Entrance requirements:* For doctorate, GRE General Test, 3 letters of recommendation. Additional exam requirements/recommendations for international students: Required—TOEFL (minimum score 600 paper-based; 250 computer-based; 100 iBT), TWE (minimum score 5). *Application deadline:* For fall admission, 12/14 for domestic and international students. Application fee: $85. Electronic applications accepted. *Expenses:* Contact institution. *Financial support:* In 2009–10, 265 students received support, including 129 fellowships with full and partial tuition reimbursements available (averaging $11,142 per year), 41 research assistantships (averaging $11,990 per year), 173 teaching assistantships (averaging $9,174 per year); career-related internships or fieldwork, Federal Work-Study, institutionally sponsored loans, scholarships/grants, health care benefits, tuition waivers (full and partial), and unspecified assistantships also available. Support available to part-time students. Financial award application deadline: 2/1; financial award applicants required to submit FAFSA. *Faculty research:* Learning and development, educational leadership and organizations, education policy analysis. Total annual research expenditures: $18.1 million. *Unit head:* Dr. Shu-Ling Chen, Assistant Dean, 617-496-4406. *Application contact:* Information Contact, 617-495-3414, Fax: 617-496-3577, E-mail: gseadmissions@harvard.edu.

Holy Names University, Graduate Division, Department of Education, Oakland, CA 94619-1699. Offers educational therapy (Certificate); level 1 education specialist mild/moderate disabilities (Credential); level 2 education specialist mild/moderate disabilities (Credential); multiple subject teaching credential (Credential); single subject teaching credential (Credential); teaching English as a second language (TESL) (M Ed); urban education: educational therapy (M Ed); urban education: K-12 education (M Ed); urban education: special education (M Ed). Part-time programs available. *Degree requirements:* For master's, comprehensive exam, research paper, thesis or project. *Entrance requirements:* For master's, minimum undergraduate GPA of 2.6 overall, 3.0 in major. Additional exam requirements/recommendations for international students: Required—TOEFL (minimum score 550 paper-based; 213 computer-based; 80 iBT). *Faculty research:* Cognitive development, language development, learning handicaps.

The Johns Hopkins University, School of Education, Department of Interdisciplinary Studies in Education, Baltimore, MD 21218. Offers earth/space science (Certificate); education (MS), including educational studies; mind, brain, and teaching (Certificate); teaching the adult learner (Certificate); urban education (Certificate). Part-time and evening/weekend programs available. Postbaccalaureate distance learning degree programs offered (minimal on-campus study). *Faculty:* 2 full-time (1 woman), 6 part-time/adjunct (5 women). *Students:* 8 full-time (7 women), 171 part-time (150 women); includes 44 minority (29 African Americans, 1 American Indian/Alaska Native, 11 Asian Americans or Pacific Islanders, 3 Hispanic Americans), 7 international. Average age 34. 77 applicants, 68% accepted, 39 enrolled. In 2009, 69 master's, 17 other advanced degrees awarded. *Degree requirements:* For master's, capstone course. *Entrance requirements:* For master's and Certificate, minimum undergraduate GPA of 3.0. Additional exam requirements/recommendations for international students: Required—TOEFL (minimum score 600 paper-based; 250 computer-based; 100 iBT). *Application deadline:* For fall admission, 5/1 for international students; for spring admission, 10/15 for international students. Applications are processed on a rolling basis. Application fee: $80. Electronic applications accepted. *Financial support:* Scholarships/grants available. Support available to part-time students. Financial award application deadline: 6/1; financial award applicants required to submit FAFSA. *Faculty research:* Neuro-education; urban school reform; leadership development; teacher leadership; charter schools; techniques for teaching reading to adolescents with delayed reading skills; school culture. *Unit head:* Dr. Mariale Hardiman, Assistant Dean and Chair, 410-516-8225, Fax: 410-516-3939, E-mail: mclean@jhu.edu. *Application contact:* Jennifer Shaffer, Director of Admissions, 410-516-9797, Fax: 410-516-9799, E-mail: educationinfo@jhu.edu.

Kean University, Nathan Weiss Graduate College, Program in Urban Leadership, Union, NJ 07083. Offers Ed D. Evening/weekend programs available. *Faculty:* 7 full-time (2 women). *Students:* 33 part-time (20 women); includes 21 minority (17 African Americans, 4 Hispanic Americans). Average age 43. 28 applicants, 61% accepted, 16 enrolled. *Degree requirements:* For doctorate, comprehensive exam, thesis/dissertation. *Entrance requirements:* For doctorate, GRE General Test, GRE Subject Test in psychology (taken within the last 5 years), master's degree from an accredited college, minimum GPA of 3.0 in last degree attained (lower GPAs may be considered), substantial experience working in education or family support agencies, 2 letters of recommendation. *Application deadline:* For fall admission, 1/30 for domestic students. Application fee: $60 ($150 for international students). Electronic applications accepted. *Expenses:* Contact institution. *Financial support:* Research assistantships, unspecified assistantships available. *Unit head:* Dr. Columbus Salley, Program Director, 908-737-5978, E-mail: csalley@kean.edu. *Application contact:* Steven Koch, Pre-Admissions Coordinator, 908-737-5924, Fax: 908-737-5965, E-mail: skoch@kean.edu.

Langston University, School of Education and Behavioral Sciences, Langston, OK 73050. Offers bilingual/multicultural (M Ed); elementary education (M Ed); English as a second language (M Ed); rehabilitation counseling (M Sc); urban education (M Ed). *Accreditation:* CORE; NCATE (one or more programs are accredited). Part-time programs available. *Degree requirements:* For master's, comprehensive exam, thesis optional. *Entrance requirements:* For master's, GRE, writing skills test, minimum GPA of 2.5, 3 letters of recommendation. Additional exam requirements/recommendations for international students: Required—TOEFL, TWE. *Faculty research:* Bilingual/multicultural education, financing post-secondary education.

Loyola Marymount University, School of Education, Department of Specialized Programs in Urban Education, Program in Urban Education, Los Angeles, CA 90045. Offers MA. *Faculty:* 6 full-time (4 women), 5 part-time/adjunct (1 woman). *Students:* 120 full-time (91 women), 1 (woman) part-time; includes 43 minority (4 African Americans, 9 Asian Americans or Pacific Islanders, 30 Hispanic Americans), 1 international. Average age 23. 52 applicants, 100% accepted, 48 enrolled. *Entrance requirements:* For master's, letters of recommendation. Additional exam requirements/recommendations for international students: Required—TOEFL (minimum score 600 paper-based; 250 computer-based; 100 iBT). *Application deadline:* For fall admission, 6/15 for domestic students; for spring admission, 11/15 for domestic students. Application fee: $50. Electronic applications accepted. *Financial support:* In 2009–10, 121 students received support, including 1 research assistantship (averaging $1,150 per year); scholarships/grants and unspecified assistantships also available. Support available to part-time students. Financial award applicants required to submit FAFSA. Total annual research expenditures: $1.3 million. *Unit head:* Dr. Edmundo Litton, Chair, 310-338-1859, E-mail: elitton@lmu.edu. *Application contact:* Chake H. Kouyoumjian, Director, Graduate Admissions, 310-338-2721, Fax: 310-338-6086, E-mail: ckouyoum@lmu.edu.

Marygrove College, Graduate Division, Griot Program, Detroit, MI 48221-2599. Offers M Ed.

Mercy College, School of Education, Program in Urban Education, Dobbs Ferry, NY 10522-1189. Offers MS. Part-time and evening/weekend programs available. *Students:* 135 part-time (107 women); includes 24 African Americans, 1 Asian American or Pacific Islander, 36 Hispanic Americans. Average age 30. 1 applicant, 0% accepted, 0 enrolled. In 2009, 190 master's awarded. *Entrance requirements:* For master's, appropriate New York State Teacher Examinations, including the Liberal Arts and Sciences Test (LAST) and the Content Specialty Test (CST), undergraduate transcript listing conferred bachelor's degree with major in a liberal arts and sciences subject or an interdisciplinary field. Additional exam requirements/recommendations for international students: Required—TOEFL (minimum score 600 paper-based; 250 computer-based; 100 iBT). *Application deadline:* For fall admission, 8/1 for international students. Applications are processed on a rolling basis. Application fee: $40. Electronic applications accepted. *Expenses:* Tuition: Full-time $13,158; part-time $731 per credit. Required fees: $500. Tuition and fees vary according to degree level and program. *Financial support:* Career-related internships or fieldwork, Federal Work-Study, scholarships/grants, and unspecified assistantships available. Support available to part-time students. Financial award applicants required to submit FAFSA. *Unit head:* Dr. Howard Miller, Director, Mercy College Teaching Fellows Program, 718-678-8962, E-mail: hmiller@mercy.edu. *Application contact:* Mary Ellen Hoffman, Interim Associate Dean, 914-674-7334, E-mail: mhoffman@mercy.edu.

Morgan State University, School of Graduate Studies, School of Education and Urban Studies, Department of Advanced Studies, Leadership and Policy, Baltimore, MD 21251. Offers educational administration and supervision (MS); elementary and middle school education (MS), including elementary education; higher education administration (PhD); higher education-community college leadership (Ed D); mathematics education (MS, Ed D); science education (MS, Ed D); urban educational leadership (Ed D). *Accreditation:* NCATE. Part-time and evening/

Urban Education

Morgan State University (continued)

weekend programs available. *Entrance requirements:* Additional exam requirements/recommendations for international students: Required—TOEFL. *Faculty research:* Multicultural education, cooperative learning, psychology of cognition.

New Jersey City University, Graduate Studies and Continuing Education, Debra Cannon Partridge Wolfe College of Education, Department of Educational Leadership, Jersey City, NJ 07305-1597. Offers basics and urban studies (MA); bilingual/bicultural education and English as a second language (MA); educational administration and supervision (MA). Part-time and evening/weekend programs available. *Faculty:* 3. *Students:* 27 full-time (18 women), 187 part-time (115 women); includes 77 minority (18 African Americans, 6 Asian Americans or Pacific Islanders, 53 Hispanic Americans), 16 international. Average age 34. In 2009, 121 master's awarded. *Entrance requirements:* For master's, GRE General Test or MAT. Additional exam requirements/recommendations for international students: Required—TOEFL. *Application deadline:* For fall admission, 8/1 priority date for domestic students; for spring admission, 12/1 for domestic students. Applications are processed on a rolling basis. Application fee: $0. *Expenses:* Tuition, area resident: Part-time $456.75 per credit. Tuition, nonresident: part-time $842.55 per credit. Required fees: $65 per term. *Financial support:* Fellowships, teaching assistantships, career-related internships or fieldwork and unspecified assistantships available. *Unit head:* Dr. Susan Phifer, Chairperson, 201-200-3012, E-mail: sphifer@njcu.edu. *Application contact:* Dr. Susan Phifer, Chairperson, 201-200-3012, E-mail: sphifer@njcu.edu.

Norfolk State University, School of Graduate Studies, School of Education, Department of Secondary Education and School Leadership, Program in Urban Education/Administration, Norfolk, VA 23504. Offers teaching (MA). *Accreditation:* NCATE. Part-time programs available. *Entrance requirements:* For master's, GRE General Test, PRAXIS I, minimum GPA of 3.0 in major, 2.5 overall.

Northeastern Illinois University, Graduate College, College of Education, Department of Educational Leadership and Development, Program in Inner City Studies, Chicago, IL 60625-4699. Offers MA. Part-time and evening/weekend programs available. *Degree requirements:* For master's, comprehensive exam, thesis or alternative. *Entrance requirements:* For master's, minimum GPA of 2.75. Additional exam requirements/recommendations for international students: Required—TOEFL (minimum score 550 paper-based; 213 computer-based; 80 iBT). Electronic applications accepted.

Nova Southeastern University, Fischler School of Education and Human Services, Graduate Teacher Education Program, Fort Lauderdale, FL 33314-7796. Offers athletic administration (MS); brain research (MS, Ed S); charter school education/leadership (MS); cognitive and behavioral disabilities (MS); computer science education (Ed S); computer science education (K-12) (MS); curriculum and teaching (Ed S); curriculum, instruction and technology (MS); curriculum, instruction, management and administration (Ed S); early childhood education (MS); early literacy and reading (Ed S); early literacy education (MS); education technology (MS); educational leadership (administration K–12) (MS, Ed S); educational media (Ed S); educational media (K-12) (MS); elementary education (MS, Ed S), including ESOL endorsement (MS); English education (MS, Ed S); environmental education (MS); exceptional student education (MS), including ESOL endorsement; gifted education (MS, Ed S); interdisciplinary arts education (MS); management and administration of educational programs (MS); mathematics (MS); mathematics education (Ed S); multicultural early intervention (MS); pre-kindergarten/primary (MS); preschool education (MS); reading (MS); reading and TESOL (MS); reading education (Ed S); science (MS); science education (Ed S); secondary education (MS); social studies (MS, Ed S); Spanish language (MS); special education and reading (MS); teaching and learning (MA, MS), including curriculum and instruction (MA), elementary mathematics (MA), elementary reading (MA), K-12 technology integration (MA); teaching English to speakers of other languages (MS, Ed S); technology management and administration (Ed S); urban studies education (MS). Part-time and evening/weekend programs available. Postbaccalaureate distance learning degree programs offered (minimal on-campus study). *Faculty:* 72 full-time (43 women), 385 part-time/adjunct (252 women). *Students:* 196 full-time (175 women), 1,304 part-time (1,128 women); includes 594 minority (471 African Americans, 5 American Indian/Alaska Native, 18 Asian Americans or Pacific Islanders, 100 Hispanic Americans). Average age 37. 2,610 applicants, 72% accepted, 1352 enrolled. In 2009, 836 other advanced degrees awarded. *Degree requirements:* For master's and Ed S, thesis, practicum, internship. *Entrance requirements:* For master's, MAT, GRE, CLAST, CBEST, PRAXIS I, General Knowledge Test, minimum GPA of 2.5; for Ed S, MAT or GRE, master's degree, teaching certificate, minimum GPA of 3.0. Additional exam requirements/recommendations for international students: Required—TSE (recommended, minimum score 50); Recommended—TOEFL (minimum score 550 paper-based; 213 computer-based; 80 iBT), IELTS (minimum score 6). *Application deadline:* For fall admission, 9/25 priority date for domestic and international students; for winter admission, 2/23 priority date for domestic and international students; for spring admission, 4/25 priority date for domestic and international students. Applications are processed on a rolling basis. Application fee: $50. Electronic applications accepted. *Financial support:* Federal Work-Study available. Support available to part-time students. Financial award application deadline: 4/15; financial award applicants required to submit FAFSA. *Faculty research:* School effectiveness, critical thinking, leadership skills acquisition, child education, multicultural education. *Unit head:* Dr. Ronald Kern, Dean of Academic Affairs, 800-986-3223 Ext. 7809, Fax: 954-262-3606, E-mail: rk429@nsu.nova.edu. *Application contact:* Dr. Jennifer Quinones Nottingham, Dean of Student Affairs, 800-986-3223 Ext. 1559.

Roberts Wesleyan College, Division of Teacher Education, Rochester, NY 14624-1997. Offers adolescence education (M Ed); childhood and special education (M Ed); literacy education (M Ed); urban education (M Ed). Part-time and evening/weekend programs available. *Degree requirements:* For master's, thesis.

Simmons College, College of Arts and Sciences Graduate Studies, Department of Education, Program in Teacher Preparation, Boston, MA 02115. Offers educational leadership (MS Ed); elementary education (MAT); general education (CAGS); general purposes (MS); middle school education (MAT); professional license (CAGS); professional license: elementary (MS Ed); professional license: middle/high (MS Ed); secondary education (MAT); urban education (MS Ed, CAGS). Part-time programs available. *Students:* 68 full-time (58 women), 125 part-time (113 women); includes 25 minority (10 African Americans, 3 American Indian/Alaska Native, 8 Asian Americans or Pacific Islanders, 4 Hispanic Americans). Average age 27. 115 applicants, 88% accepted, 75 enrolled. In 2009, 137 master's, 14 other advanced degrees awarded. *Degree requirements:* For master's, practicum. *Entrance requirements:* For master's, GRE General Test, MAT or Massachusetts Tests for Educator Licensure (MTEL). Additional exam requirements/recommendations for international students: Required—TOEFL (minimum score 600 paper-based; 250 computer-based; 100 iBT). *Application deadline:* For fall admission, 8/1 priority date for domestic and international students; for winter admission, 12/15 priority date for domestic and international students; for spring admission, 12/15 priority date for domestic and international students. Applications are processed on a rolling basis. Application fee: $35. Electronic applications accepted. *Expenses:* Contact institution. *Financial support:* Application deadline: 3/1. *Faculty research:* Educational psychology, mentorship with first year teachers, urban classrooms, first generation college students. *Unit head:* Gary Oakes, Director, Master of Arts in Teaching (MAT) Program, 617-521-2203, Fax: 617-521-3133. *Application contact:* Kristen Haack, Director, Graduate Studies Admission, 617-521-2917, Fax: 617-521-3058, E-mail: gsa@simmons.edu.

Sojourner-Douglass College, Graduate Program, Baltimore, MD 21205-1814. Offers human services (MASS); public administration (MASS); urban education (reading) (MASS). Part-time and evening/weekend programs available. *Degree requirements:* For master's, comprehensive exam, written proposal oral defense. *Entrance requirements:* For master's, Graduate Examination.

Teachers College, Columbia University, Graduate Faculty of Education, Department of Organization and Leadership, Urban Education Leaders Program, New York, NY 10027-6696. Offers Ed D.

Temple University, Graduate School, College of Education, Department of Educational Leadership and Policy Studies, Philadelphia, PA 19122-6096. Offers educational administration (Ed M, Ed D); urban education (Ed M, Ed D). Part-time and evening/weekend programs available. Terminal master's awarded for partial completion of doctoral program. *Degree requirements:* For master's, comprehensive exam, thesis or alternative; for doctorate, thesis/dissertation, preliminary exam. *Entrance requirements:* For master's and doctorate, GRE General Test or MAT, minimum GPA of 3.0. Additional exam requirements/recommendations for international students: Required—TOEFL (minimum score 550 paper-based; 213 computer-based; 79 iBT). Electronic applications accepted. *Faculty research:* Women in education, school effectiveness, financial policy, school improvement in city schools, nongraded schools.

Texas A&M University, College of Education and Human Development, Department of Teaching, Learning, and Culture, College Station, TX 77843. Offers curriculum and instruction (M Ed, MS, PhD); mathematics education (M Ed, MS, PhD); multicultural/urban/ESL/international education (M Ed, MS, PhD); reading/language arts (M Ed, MS, PhD); science education (M Ed, MS, PhD); social studies education (M Ed, MS, PhD). Part-time programs available. *Faculty:* 33. *Students:* 145 full-time (113 women), 270 part-time (214 women); includes 110 minority (60 African Americans, 4 American Indian/Alaska Native, 4 Asian Americans or Pacific Islanders, 42 Hispanic Americans), 47 international. Average age 36. In 2009, 114 master's, 17 doctorates awarded. *Degree requirements:* For master's, comprehensive exam, thesis (for some programs); for doctorate, comprehensive exam, thesis/dissertation. *Entrance requirements:* For master's, GRE General Test, minimum GPA of 3.0; for doctorate, GRE General Test, 3 years of teaching experience. Additional exam requirements/recommendations for international students: Required—TOEFL (minimum score 550 paper-based; 213 computer-based). *Application deadline:* For fall admission, 1/15 priority date for domestic and international students; for spring admission, 9/15 priority date for domestic and international students. Applications are processed on a rolling basis. Application fee: $50 ($75 for international students). Electronic applications accepted. *Expenses:* Tuition, state resident: full-time $3991; part-time $221.74 per credit hour. Tuition, nonresident: full-time $9049; part-time $502.74 per credit hour. *Financial support:* In 2009–10, fellowships with partial tuition reimbursements (averaging $3,000 per year), teaching assistantships with partial tuition reimbursements (averaging $7,200 per year) were awarded; research assistantships with partial tuition reimbursements, career-related internships or fieldwork, Federal Work-Study, institutionally sponsored loans, scholarships/grants, tuition waivers (partial), and unspecified assistantships also available. Support available to part-time students. Financial award application deadline: 4/1; financial award applicants required to submit FAFSA. *Unit head:* Dr. Dennie Smith, Head, 979-845-8384, Fax: 979-845-9663, E-mail: krsmith@tamu.edu. *Application contact:* Graduate Admissions Supervisor, 979-845-8382, Fax: 979-845-9663, E-mail: krsmith@tamu.edu.

University of Central Florida, College of Education, Department of Educational Studies, Orlando, FL 32816. Offers applied learning and instruction (MA); community college education (Certificate); curriculum and instruction (Ed S); education (Ed D, PhD, Ed S); gifted education (Certificate); global and comparative education (Certificate); initial teacher professional preparation (Certificate); teacher leadership (M Ed); urban education (Certificate). *Accreditation:* NCATE. Part-time and evening/weekend programs available. *Faculty:* 18 full-time (10 women), 16 part-time/adjunct (10 women). *Students:* 155 full-time (106 women), 156 part-time (131 women); includes 80 minority (37 African Americans, 5 Asian Americans or Pacific Islanders, 38 Hispanic Americans), 22 international. Average age 36. 200 applicants, 57% accepted, 77 enrolled. In 2009, 9 master's, 34 doctorates, 17 other advanced degrees awarded. *Degree requirements:* For other advanced degree, thesis or alternative, final exam. *Entrance requirements:* For degree, GRE General Test, minimum GPA of 3.0, resume. Additional exam requirements/recommendations for international students: Required—TOEFL. *Application deadline:* For fall admission, 2/20 for domestic students; for spring admission, 9/20 for domestic students. Application fee: $30. Electronic applications accepted. *Expenses:* Tuition, state resident: part-time $306.31 per credit hour. Tuition, nonresident: part-time $1099.01 per credit hour. Part-time tuition and fees vary according to degree level and program. *Financial support:* In 2009–10, 82 students received support, including 55 fellowships with partial tuition reimbursements available (averaging $8,300 per year), 29 research assistantships with partial tuition reimbursements available (averaging $7,000 per year), 43 teaching assistantships with partial tuition reimbursements available (averaging $8,000 per year); career-related internships or fieldwork, Federal Work-Study, institutionally sponsored loans, and unspecified assistantships also available. Financial award application deadline: 3/1; financial award applicants required to submit FAFSA. *Unit head:* Dr. Karen Biraimah, Chair, 407-823-2428, E-mail: biraimah@mail.ucf.edu. *Application contact:* Dr. Karen Biraimah, Chair, 407-823-2428, E-mail: biraimah@mail.ucf.edu.

University of Houston–Downtown, College of Public Service, Department of Urban Education, Houston, TX 77002. Offers bilingual education (MAT); curriculum and instruction (MAT); elementary education (MAT); secondary education (MAT). Part-time and evening/weekend programs available. *Faculty:* 8 full-time (5 women). *Students:* 1 (woman) full-time, 42 part-time (34 women); includes 27 minority (15 African Americans, 3 Asian Americans or Pacific Islanders, 9 Hispanic Americans). Average age 37. 16 applicants, 100% accepted, 12 enrolled. In 2009, 17 master's awarded. *Degree requirements:* For master's, capstone course with completed project, position paper, grant proposal, empirical study, curriculum development/revision, or advanced technology project presented at annual Graduate Project Exhibition. *Entrance requirements:* For master's, GRE, personal statement, 3 recommendation forms. Additional exam requirements/recommendations for international students: Required—TOEFL (minimum score 550 paper-based; 213 computer-based; 80 iBT). *Application deadline:* For fall admission, 6/1 for domestic and international students; for spring admission, 11/1 for domestic and international students. Applications are processed on a rolling basis. Application fee: $35 ($60 for international students). Electronic applications accepted. *Expenses:* Tuition, state resident: full-time $3150; part-time $175 per credit hour. Tuition, nonresident: full-time $7506; part-time $417 per credit hour. Required fees: $908; $322 per term. *Financial support:* Scholarships/grants available. Financial award applicants required to submit FAFSA. *Unit head:* Dr. Myrna Cohen, Chair, 713-221-2759, Fax: 713-226-5294, E-mail: cohenm@uhd.edu. *Application contact:* Traneshia Parker, Assistant Director, Admissions-Graduate, International and Residency, 713-221-8093, Fax: 713-221-8157, E-mail: parkert@uhd.edu.

University of Illinois at Chicago, Graduate College, College of Education, Department of Educational Policy Studies, Chicago, IL 60607-7128. Offers policy studies (M Ed); policy studies in urban education (PhD); urban education leadership (Ed D).

University of Massachusetts Boston, Office of Graduate Studies, Graduate College of Education, School Organization, Curriculum and Instruction Department, Boston, MA 02125-3393. Offers education (M Ed, Ed D), including elementary and secondary education/certification (M Ed), higher education administration (Ed D), teacher certification (M Ed), urban school leadership (Ed D); educational administration (M Ed, CAGS); special education (M Ed). *Degree requirements:* For master's and CAGS, comprehensive exam; for doctorate, comprehensive exam, thesis/dissertation. *Entrance requirements:* For master's, GRE General Test or MAT; for doctorate, GRE General Test or MAT, minimum GPA of 2.75; for CAGS, minimum GPA of 2.75.

University of Massachusetts Boston, Office of Graduate Studies, Graduate College of Education, School Organization, Curriculum and Instruction Department, Program in Education, Track in Urban School Leadership, Boston, MA 02125-3393. Offers Ed D. Part-time and evening/weekend programs available. *Degree requirements:* For doctorate, comprehensive exam, thesis/dissertation. *Entrance requirements:* For doctorate, GRE General Test or MAT, minimum GPA of 2.75. *Faculty research:* School reform, race and culture in schools, race and higher education, language, literacy and writing.

University of Michigan–Dearborn, School of Education, Doctoral Program in Education, Dearborn, MI 48126. Offers curriculum and practice (Ed D); educational leadership (Ed D);

educational psychology/special education (Ed D); metropolitan education (Ed D). Part-time and evening/weekend programs available. *Faculty:* 7 full-time (4 women). *Students:* 1 (woman) full-time, 17 part-time (9 women); includes 5 minority (3 African Americans, 1 Asian American or Pacific Islander, 1 Hispanic American). Average age 46. 62 applicants, 31% accepted, 18 enrolled. *Degree requirements:* For doctorate, comprehensive exam, thesis/dissertation. *Entrance requirements:* For doctorate, GRE (taken within the last 5 years), master's degree with minimum GPA of 3.3, 3 letters of recommendation (1 from faculty), 3 yearsprofessional and/or teaching experience. Additional exam requirements/recommendations for international students: Required—TOEFL (minimum score 550 paper-based), Test of Spoken English (TES). *Application deadline:* For fall admission, 3/1 for domestic and international students. Application fee: $60. *Expenses:* Tuition, state resident: part-time $504.10 per credit hour. Tuition, nonresident: part-time $957.90 per credit hour. *Faculty research:* Educational leadership, metropolitan education, curriculum and practice, educational psychology, special education, assessment. *Unit head:* Gail Luera, Associate Dean/Interim Coordinator, 313-593-5098, E-mail: grl@umich.edu. *Application contact:* Catherine Parkins, Customer Service Assistant, 313-583-6349, Fax: 313-593-4748, E-mail: cparkins@umd.umich.edu.

University of Nebraska at Omaha, Graduate Studies, College of Education, Department of Teacher Education, Omaha, NE 68182. Offers elementary education (MA, MS); instruction in urban schools (Certificate); instructional technology (Certificate); reading education (MS); secondary education (MA, MS). Part-time and evening/weekend programs available. *Faculty:* 25 full-time (15 women). *Students:* 24 full-time (18 women), 330 part-time (284 women); includes 17 minority (6 African Americans, 11 Hispanic Americans), 4 international. Average age 33. 81 applicants, 83% accepted, 51 enrolled. In 2009, 110 master's, 7 other advanced degrees awarded. *Degree requirements:* For master's, comprehensive exam, thesis (for some programs). *Entrance requirements:* For master's, minimum GPA of 3.0. Additional exam requirements/recommendations for international students: Required—TOEFL (minimum score 550 paper-based; 213 computer-based). *Application deadline:* For fall admission, 7/1 priority date for domestic students; for spring admission, 12/1 priority date for domestic students. Applications are processed on a rolling basis. Application fee: $45. Electronic applications accepted. *Financial support:* In 2009–10, 114 students received support; fellowships, teaching assistantships with tuition reimbursements available, Federal Work-Study, institutionally sponsored loans, scholarships/grants, tuition waivers (partial), and unspecified assistantships available. Support available to part-time students. Financial award application deadline: 3/1; financial award applicants required to submit FAFSA. *Unit head:* Dr. Lana Danielson, Advisor, 402-554-2212. *Application contact:* Dr. Wilma Kuhlman, Student Contact, 402-554-2212.

University of Southern California, Graduate School, Rossier School of Education, Doctor of Education Programs, Los Angeles, CA 90089. Offers educational psychology (Ed D); higher education administration (Ed D); K-12 leadership in urban school settings (Ed D); teacher education in multicultural societies (Ed D). Part-time and evening/weekend programs available. *Faculty:* 59 full-time (32 women), 12 part-time/adjunct (3 women). *Students:* 567 full-time (361 women), 12 part-time (6 women); includes 339 minority (73 African Americans, 11 American Indian/Alaska Native, 129 Asian Americans or Pacific Islanders, 126 Hispanic Americans), 13 international. 300 applicants, 76% accepted, 182 enrolled. In 2009, 143 doctorates awarded. *Degree requirements:* For doctorate, thesis/dissertation. *Entrance requirements:* For doctorate, GRE. Additional exam requirements/recommendations for international students: Required—TOEFL (minimum score 250 computer-based; 100 iBT). *Application deadline:* For fall admission, 1/15 priority date for domestic and international students. Application fee: $85. Electronic applications accepted. *Expenses:* Tuition: Full-time $25,980; part-time $1315 per unit. Required fees: $554. One-time fee: $35 full-time. Full-time tuition and fees vary according to degree level and program. *Financial support:* In 2009–10, 385 students received support. Scholarships/grants available. Support available to part-time students. Financial award application deadline: 5/5. *Faculty research:* Data-driven decision-making in K-12 schools and districts; examination of college and university leadership and management in U. S. and Asia; studies in facilitating student learning; organizational change and the role of leaders; leadership, diversity, learning and accountability. *Unit head:* Dr. Kathy Stowe, Executive Director/Assistant Professor of Clinical Education, 213-740-9323. *Application contact:* Carolyn Stirling, Associate Director of Recruiting and Admissions, 213-740-0224, Fax: 213-740-9433, E-mail: soeinfo@usc.edu.

University of Wisconsin–Milwaukee, Graduate School, School of Education, Department of Curriculum and Instruction, Milwaukee, WI 53201-0413. Offers curriculum planning and instruction improvement (MS); early childhood education (MS); elementary education (MS); junior high/middle school education (MS); reading education (MS); secondary education (MS); teaching in an urban setting (MS). Part-time programs available. *Faculty:* 22 full-time (17

women). *Students:* 23 full-time (14 women), 64 part-time (58 women); includes 8 minority (4 African Americans, 1 American Indian/Alaska Native, 3 Hispanic Americans), 1 international. Average age 41. 46 applicants, 57% accepted, 12 enrolled. In 2009, 28 master's awarded. *Degree requirements:* For master's, thesis or alternative. *Entrance requirements:* Additional exam requirements/recommendations for international students: Required—TOEFL (minimum score 550 paper-based; 79 iBT), IELTS (minimum score 6.5). *Application deadline:* For fall admission, 1/1 priority date for domestic students; for spring admission, 9/1 for domestic students. Applications are processed on a rolling basis. Application fee: $45 ($75 for international students). *Expenses:* Tuition, state resident: full-time $8800. Tuition, nonresident: full-time $20,760. Tuition and fees vary according to program and reciprocity agreements. *Financial support:* Career-related internships or fieldwork and unspecified assistantships available. Support available to part-time students. Financial award application deadline: 4/15. Total annual research expenditures: $65,946. *Unit head:* Hope Longwell-Grice, Chair, 414-229-4884, Fax: 414-229-5571, E-mail: hope@uwm.edu. *Application contact:* General Information Contact, 414-229-4982, Fax: 414-229-6967, E-mail: gradschool@uwm.edu.

University of Wisconsin–Milwaukee, Graduate School, School of Education, Program in Urban Education, Milwaukee, WI 53201-0413. Offers adult and continuing education (PhD); curriculum and instruction (PhD); educational administration (PhD); educational and media technology (PhD); educational psychology (PhD); multicultural studies (PhD); social foundations of education (PhD). *Students:* 67 full-time (51 women), 44 part-time (30 women); includes 41 minority (23 African Americans, 2 American Indian/Alaska Native, 7 Asian Americans or Pacific Islanders, 9 Hispanic Americans), 4 international. Average age 41. 31 applicants, 45% accepted, 5 enrolled. In 2009, 11 doctorates awarded. *Degree requirements:* For doctorate, comprehensive exam, thesis/dissertation. *Entrance requirements:* For doctorate, GRE General Test, minimum undergraduate GPA of 2.85, graduate 3.5. Additional exam requirements/recommendations for international students: Required—TOEFL (minimum score 550 paper-based; 79 iBT), IELTS (minimum score 6.5). *Application deadline:* For fall admission, 1/1 priority date for domestic students; for spring admission, 9/1 for domestic students. Applications are processed on a rolling basis. Application fee: $45 ($75 for international students). *Expenses:* Tuition, state resident: full-time $8800. Tuition, nonresident: full-time $20,760. Tuition and fees vary according to program and reciprocity agreements. *Financial support:* Career-related internships or fieldwork and unspecified assistantships available. Support available to part-time students. Financial award application deadline: 4/15. *Unit head:* Larry Martin, Representative, 414-229-4729, Fax: 414-229-2920, E-mail: lmartin@uwm.edu. *Application contact:* General Information Contact, 414-229-4982, Fax: 414-229-6967, E-mail: gradschool@uwm.edu.

Vanderbilt University, Peabody College, Department of Teaching and Learning, Nashville, TN 37240-1001. Offers elementary education (M Ed); English language learners (M Ed); learning and instruction (M Ed); learning, diversity, and urban studies (M Ed); reading education (M Ed); secondary education (M Ed). *Accreditation:* NCATE. *Faculty:* 31 full-time (20 women), 23 part-time/adjunct (20 women). *Students:* 95 full-time (88 women), 21 part-time (6 women); includes 14 minority (6 African Americans, 4 Asian Americans or Pacific Islanders, 4 Hispanic Americans), 5 international. Average age 27. 150 applicants, 69% accepted, 59 enrolled. In 2009, 74 master's awarded. *Degree requirements:* For master's, comprehensive exam, thesis optional. *Entrance requirements:* For master's, GRE General Test, MAT. Additional exam requirements/recommendations for international students: Required—TOEFL (minimum score 550 paper-based; 213 computer-based). *Application deadline:* For fall admission, 12/31 priority date for domestic and international students; for spring admission, 11/1 priority date for domestic and international students. Applications are processed on a rolling basis. Application fee: $0. Electronic applications accepted. *Financial support:* In 2009–10, 104 students received support, including 27 research assistantships with full and partial tuition reimbursements available; fellowships with full and partial tuition reimbursements available, teaching assistantships with full and partial tuition reimbursements available, Federal Work-Study, institutionally sponsored loans, scholarships/grants, tuition waivers (partial), and unspecified assistantships also available. Support available to part-time students. Financial award application deadline: 2/1; financial award applicants required to submit FAFSA. *Faculty research:* Teaching and learning, development of mathematical and scientific knowledge, interventions to foster early literacy and numeracy, reading and writing in the digital age, teaching diverse learners. *Unit head:* Dr. David Dickinson, Acting Chair, 615-322-8100, Fax: 615-322-8999, E-mail: david.k.dickinson@vanderbilt.edu. *Application contact:* Angela Saylor, Educational Coordinator, 615-322-8092, Fax: 615-322-8999, E-mail: angela.saylor@vanderbilt.edu.

Virginia Commonwealth University, Graduate School, School of Education, Doctoral Program in Education, Urban Services Leadership Track, Richmond, VA 23284-9005. Offers PhD.

HAWAI'I PACIFIC UNIVERSITY

Teaching English as a Second Language

Programs of Study
Hawai'i Pacific University's (HPU's) Master of Arts in Teaching English as a Second Language (M.A.T.E.S.L.) focuses on practical, hands-on education that teaches graduates the essential skills they need to become successful educators. By learning about the current theories, methods, and materials, M.A.T.E.S.L. graduates are prepared and ready to teach English as a second language in the classroom.

The M.A.T.E.S.L. features a solid curriculum in three types of courses. Linguistic theory courses taught from an applied viewpoint help the M.A.T.E.S.L. student better understand languages in general and English in particular. The second type is pedagogy courses, which present a range of current approaches, designs, and procedures for teaching language in a wide variety of contexts. In these classes, teaching demonstrations and videotaped peer practice sessions are used extensively. The third type, two practicum courses, allows future teachers to observe master teachers, serve with them in the classroom as assistants, and assume full class responsibility as practice teachers. The capstone activity synthesizes several semesters of classroom study and practicum training. Students have three options for this completion requirement: a portfolio, a comprehensive exam, or an extensive in-service project.

The M.A.T.E.S.L. requires a minimum of 37 semester hours of graduate work: 24 semester hours of core courses, 12 semester hours of electives, and 1 semester hour for a capstone activity.

Research Facilities
To support graduate studies, HPU's Meader and Atherton Libraries offer more than 110,000 bound volumes, 350,000 microfiche items, and periodical subscriptions to 1,500 print titles and 30,000 electronic journals. Databases of public and state university libraries, legislative information, and business-oriented statistical data are also available in the library or online. Students can access HPU's library databases, course information, their academic information, and an e-mail account through Pipeline, the university's internal Web site for students. The University's accessible on-campus computer center houses more than 100 computers with specialized software to support graduate academic programs. HPU also provides free Wi-Fi so students can have wireless access to Pipeline resources anywhere on campus using laptops. A significant number of online courses are available. Students are encouraged to prepare papers for publication in the *TESL Working Paper Series*, an in-house journal, which displays the best scholarly work from the University's student body.

Financial Aid
The University participates in all federal financial aid programs designated for graduate students. These programs provide aid in the form of subsidized (need-based) and unsubsidized (non-need-based) Federal Stafford Student Loans. Through these loans, funds may be available to cover the student's entire cost of education. To apply for aid, students must submit the Free Application for Federal Student Aid (FAFSA) beginning January 1. Mailing of student award letters usually begins by the end of March. The University also offers several institutional scholarships to new full-time, degree-seeking students. The Graduate Trustee Scholarship provides $6000 for two semesters, the Graduate Dean Scholarship provides $4000 for two semesters, and the Graduate Kokua Scholarship provides $2000 for two semesters. Priority consideration is given to those students who apply by the deadline.

Cost of Study
Tuition for graduate students enrolled in fall and spring semesters is determined on a per-credit basis; full-time status for a graduate student is 9 credits. Tuition for the optional winter and summer sessions is also determined on a per-credit basis. The estimated minimum funds needed for a nine-month academic year (September to May) based on 2010–11 school year expenses is $26,459. For the 2010–11 academic year, full-time tuition is $12,600 for most graduate degree programs, including the M.A.T.E.S.L. program. Books, supplies, and transportation cost $1885, and health insurance costs $880.

Living and Housing Costs
Most graduate students live in off-campus housing. The cost of living in off-campus apartments is approximately $11,094 for a double-occupancy room.

Student Group
University enrollment currently stands at more than 8,200. HPU is one of the most culturally diverse universities in America with students from all 50 U.S. states and more than 100 countries.

Location
Hawai'i Pacific University combines the excitement of an urban, downtown campus with the serenity of a residential campus. The main campus is ideally located in downtown Honolulu, the business and financial center of the Pacific. The downtown campus comprises six buildings in the center of Honolulu's business district and is home to the College of Business Administration and the College of Humanities and Social Sciences. Eight miles away, situated on 135 acres in Kaneohe, the windward Hawai'i Loa campus is the site of the College of Nursing and Health Sciences and the College of Natural and Computational Sciences. HPU is affiliated with the Oceanic Institute, an applied aquaculture research facility located on a 56-acre site at Makapu'u Point on the windward coast of Oahu, Hawaii. Students can conveniently travel between the three sites using the HPU shuttle service. There are also eight military campus programs located at Pearl Harbor, Barbers Point, Hickam Air Force Base, Schofield Barracks, Fort Shafter, Tripler Army Medical Center, Kaneohe Marine Corps Air Station, and Camp Smith.

The University
HPU is a private, nonprofit university with approximately 8,200 students. Founded in 1965, HPU prides itself on maintaining strong academic programs, small class sizes, individual attention to students, and a diverse faculty and student population. HPU is recognized as a "Best in the West" college by the Princeton Review and a "Best Buy" by *Barron's* business magazine. HPU offers more than fifty acclaimed undergraduate programs and thirteen distinguished graduate programs. The University has a faculty of more than 500, a student-faculty ratio of 15:1, and an average class size of less than 20. A wide range of counseling and other student support services are available. There are more than seventy student organizations on campus, including the Graduate Student Organization. M.A.T.E.S.L. students usually join the student club called Intercultural Teachers Organization (ITO), which sponsors many professional and social events throughout the year.

Applying
Students must have a baccalaureate degree from an accredited college or university in the United States or an equivalent degree from another country. Applicants should complete and forward a graduate admissions application, send in the $50 nonrefundable application fee, have official transcripts sent from all colleges or universities previously attended, and forward two letters of recommendation. A personal statement about the applicant's academic and career goals is required; submitting a resume is optional. Applicants who have taken the Graduate Record Examination (GRE) should have their scores sent directly to the Graduate Admissions Office. International students should submit scores of a recognized English proficiency test such as TOEFL. Admissions decisions are made on a rolling basis. Applicants are notified between one and two weeks after all documents have been submitted. Applicants are encouraged to submit their applications online.

Correspondence and Information
Graduate Admissions
Hawai'i Pacific University
1164 Bishop Street, #911
Honolulu, Hawai'i 96813

Phone: 808-544-1135
      866-GRAD-HPU (toll-free)
Fax: 808-544-0280
E-mail: graduate@hpu.edu
Web site: http://www.hpu.edu/hpumatesl

Hawai'i Pacific University

THE FACULTY

Kenneth Cook, Professor of Linguistics; Ph.D., California, San Diego.
Barbara Hannum, Assistant Professor of English (ESL); M.A., Hawai'i at Manoa.
Jean Kirschenmann, Assistant Professor of English (ESL); M.A., Hawai'i at Manoa.
Edward F. Klein, Professor of Applied Linguistics; Ph.D., Hawai'i at Manoa.
Candis Lee, Assistant Professor of English (ESL); Ed.D., USC.
Sandra McKay, Professor of Linguistics; Ph.D., Minnesota.
Hanh T. Nguyen, Assistant Professor of Applied Linguistics; Ph.D., Wisconsin–Madison.
Catherine Sajna, Assistant Professor of English; M.A., Hawai'i at Manoa.

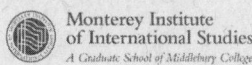
Monterey Institute
of International Studies
A Graduate School of Middlebury College

MONTEREY INSTITUTE OF INTERNATIONAL STUDIES
Language Education

Programs of Study	The Master of Arts (M.A.) degrees in teaching English to speakers of other languages (TESOL) and teaching a foreign language (TFL) combine strong academic preparation with practical training in language pedagogy. These M.A. programs offer courses in applied linguistics, pedagogical theory and practice, sociolinguistics, and second language acquisition as well as research design for behavioral scientists.
	The Peace Corps Master's International (PCMI) program provides two semesters of on-campus study toward an M.A. in TESOL before two years of service in the Peace Corps in a related overseas assignment. After successful completion of Peace Corps service, volunteers return to the Institute, and receive partial scholarships for the final semester of study in the M.A. in TESOL program.
	The School also offers several professional certificate programs. The 17-credit Language Program Administration (LPA) certificate prepares graduates to administer language programs. The Computer-Assisted Language Learning (CALL) certificate includes 12 credits of course work and enables graduates to manage and develop the curriculum for language-learning programs utilizing computer technology. In addition, 17-credit certificates in TESOL or TFL are available as stand-alone certificates for those who wish to focus solely on practical issues in language education. All certificate programs may be completed in conjunction with the M.A. in TESOL or TFL degree. In addition, LPA and CALL online courses can be completed by qualified language educators from anywhere in the world.
	The Monterey Institute also offers intensive English as a Second Language (ESL) or multiple foreign languages. For detailed information about the foreign language programs, send an e-mail to silp@miis.edu. For information about the ESL program, send an e-mail to english@miis.edu.
Research Facilities	The Institute's specialized international library has a collection of more than 100,000 volumes, maintains 600 print periodicals, the interlibrary loan service with Online Computer Library Center gives students access to millions of volumes, and is the largest international consortium of libraries in the world.
	The William Tell Coleman Library includes 100,000 volumes, more than 600 print periodicals, over 500 print and digital online databases. There are also about thirty-five newspaper subscriptions. The library subscribes to over 50 research databases, e-journals, and e-book collections. One third of the collection is in languages other than English.
	Innovative and challenging curricula at the Institute require appropriate facilities and cutting-edge technology. Classrooms vary in size from large halls where plenary sessions (often with simultaneous interpretation included) can be held to smaller classrooms and labs befitting seminar-style classes for 5 to 15 students.
	The Max Kade Language and Technology Center is a fully equipped language-learning center. It provides multimedia classrooms and conference rooms with state-of-the-art technology, including a multimedia resource center and the campus Teaching and Learning Collaborative. In addition to numerous computer labs, the entire campus has wireless access. Every student is encouraged to have a personal laptop computer adapted for wireless connectivity.
Financial Aid	Candidates with a minimum grade point average of 3.3 on a 4.0 scale (or the equivalent) are considered for scholarships that range from $4000 to $15,000 per year. Veterans of military service or orphans/dependants of veterans may be eligible for veteran's benefits. Other scholarships may be awarded by outside foundations.
	Under the Federal Stafford Loan program, students may borrow up to $8500 in subsidized loans or $20,500 in unsubsidized loans, less any subsidized amount. Graduate PLUS Loans cover the cost of college minus other financial aid resources. The Federal Work-Study Program allows students to work up to $3000 per academic year, working a maximum of 20 hours per week.
Cost of Study	Tuition and estimated fees for 2010–11 are $32,056.
Living and Housing Costs	Estimated variable expenses for the cost of books, supplies, housing, food, local transportation, personal expenses, and health insurance are $17,792.
Student Group	Institute enrollment is approximately of 800 students. About a third of the students are from outside the U.S., with citizenship represented from more than sixty different countries. Roughly 90 percent of the American students on campus have worked or studied abroad. There are more than fifty native languages spoken on campus as well. Language classes are offered in English, Spanish, Arabic, French, Russian, Japanese, and Chinese (Mandarin).
Student Outcomes	Graduates of the TESOL and TFL programs work all over the U.S. and in more than sixty-five countries around the world. They teach in universities and colleges, public and private schools, community programs, private language schools, and government-sponsored educational programs. They take leadership roles in language assessment, program administration, teacher education, and curriculum development. Prominent employers include Kanda University of International Studies; Copenhagen Business School; English Language Fellows; Fulbright; Defense Language Institute; Santa Barbara City College; Cushing Academy; National Geography; Santa Catalina School; Alaska State Mentor Project; MIT; and Iowa State, Michigan State, and Stanford Universities. Students have interned in Bolivia, China, Japan, Mexico, the United States, Vietnam, and many other locations worldwide.
	A dedicated career staff works closely with students to develop internships and assist in seeking employment opportunities in the U.S. and other countries. Advisers meet the needs and interests of students through individual academic and career advising throughout the program.
Location	The Monterey Institute is situated in one of the most spectacular natural environments in the world. The Monterey Peninsula is 130 miles south of San Francisco on California's central coast, surrounded by ocean and mountains. Silicon Valley is only a short drive away. With a population of 100,000, the area combines a variety of rich cultural resources and agricultural activities.
The Institute	Established in 1955 with summer classes in language and culture, the Monterey Institute of Foreign Studies was the first institute dedicated to the then-revolutionary concept that a "living" language should be taught as such: French in French, Russian in Russian, etc. Year-round degree programs began in 1961. By 1979, the Institute had grown to international distinction and was renamed the Monterey Institute of International Studies.
	In 2010, the Monterey Institute became an official graduate school of Middlebury College. Founded in 1800, Middlebury is one the country's top liberal arts colleges. It offers its students a broad curriculum, embracing the arts, humanities, literature, foreign languages, social sciences, and natural sciences. The integration with Middlebuy College further enriches the Institute's ability to prepare students for professional careers by creating a bicoastal presence and an expanded global network.
Applying	Applicants to the master's programs in the Graduate School of Language and Educational Linguistics must have a U.S. bachelor's degree or the equivalent. The program has start dates in September and February, but applications may be submitted all year round. There are priority deadlines for merit scholarship consideration, so students should visit the Institute's Web site at http://www.miis.edu for complete information on admission requirements and scholarship deadlines. Applications must be received at least one month prior to the applicant's proposed semester of enrollment or three months in advance for international students residing in their home countries.
Correspondence and Information	Admissions Office Monterey Institute of International Studies 460 Pierce Street Monterey, California 93940 Phone: 831-647-4123 800-824-7235 (toll-free in the United States) Fax: 831-647-6405 E-mail: admit@miis.edu Web site: http://www.miis.edu

Monterey Institute of International Studies

THE FACULTY AND THEIR RESEARCH

TESOL/TFL Faculty

The TESOL/TFL staff is made up of 7 full-time members and several adjunct faculty members who bring a combination of distinguished academic credentials and significant professional experience to their respective fields. Although the primary emphasis is placed on teaching, faculty members are expected and encouraged to maintain research agendas and to publish or consult in their fields. The full-time members of the TESOL/TFL faculty and their current research interests are listed below.

Kathleen M. Bailey, Professor and Language Program Administration Adviser; Ph.D., UCLA. Educational research, assessment, teacher education, language program administration.

Lynn M. Goldstein, Professor; Ed.D., Columbia Teachers College. Sociolinguistics, English discourse and grammar, applied linguistics research, composition, second language acquisition, writing for publication.

John Hedgcock, Professor; Ph.D., USC. Applied linguistics, pedagogical grammar, second language acquisition, teacher education, composition, literacy education.

Renee Jourdenais, Dean; Ph.D., Georgetown. Second language acquisition, sociolinguistics, applied linguistics research, language assessment, pedagogy, psycholinguistics.

Peter Shaw, Professor; Ph.D., USC. Content-based instruction, curriculum theory, practicum, authentic assessment, discourse analysis, language teaching and pedagogy, critical pedagogy, cooperative learning.

Jean Turner, Professor; Ph.D., UCLA. Language testing, program evaluation, research design and statistics, second language acquisition.

Leo van Lier, Professor; Ph.D., Lancaster (England). Educational linguistics, second language acquisition, contrastive studies, computer-assisted language learning and instruction, discourse analysis, bilingual education.

Language Studies Program Heads

Language Studies faculty members combine their diverse international experiences and professional expertise to teach language courses to students in all Monterey Institute graduate programs, with advanced instruction in six languages. They are complemented by a staff of adjunct and visiting professors, each with extensive backgrounds in linguistics, business language, political science, and environmental issues. The language faculty members offer unique perspectives and develop practical exercises for advancing foreign language acquisition.

Abdelilah Bouasria, Visiting Professor; Ph.D., American. Political science.

Kelley Calvert, Assistant Professor; M.A., Monterey Institute. English for academic purposes.

Edgar Coly, Assistant Professor; Ph.D., Colorado at Boulder. African politics and cultures, Africa in the arena of globalization, contemporary France, francophone literature, twentieth-century French literature, postmodernism and postcolonial theory.

Jin huei Dai, Assistant Professor and Chinese Program Head; Ph.D., LSU. Cognitive linguistics, Chinese cognition linguistics, Chinese as a heritage language, Chinese and Taiwanese popular culture, discourse analysis, linguistic anthropology.

Michel Gueldry, Associate Professor and French Program Head; Ph.D., Toulouse. French politics, business, and history; French language, cinema, and civilization; Western Europe; European Union, European integration, transatlantic relations, language pedagogy, and content-based instruction.

Lisa Leopold, Assistant Professor; M.A., Illinois at Urbana-Champaign. English for academic purposes.

Naoko Matsuo, Assistant Professor and Japanese Program Head; M.A., Monterey Institute. Applied linguistics.

Lama Nassif, Visiting Professor and Arabic Program Head; M.A., Monterey Institute. Applied linguistics.

Pablo Oliva, Assistant Professor and Spanish Program Head; Ph.D. candidate, Nebrija (Madrid). Latin American culture and society, applied linguistics, teaching Spanish language.

Vicki Porras, Visiting Professor; M.A., Maryland. Spanish language and culture, pedagogy, business Spanish, second language acquisition.

Jon M. Strolle, Professor; Ph.D., Wisconsin–Madison. Language policy, federal language issues, rhetoric of negotiation, education policy, Spain, Mexico.

Anna Vassilieva, Associate Professor and Russian Program Head; Ph.D., Russian Diplomatic Academy. Political science.

Section 26
Subject Areas

This section contains a directory of institutions offering graduate work in subject areas, followed by in-depth entries submitted by institutions that chose to prepare detailed program descriptions. Additional information about programs listed in the directory but not augmented by an in-depth entry may be obtained by writing directly to the dean of a graduate school or chair of a department at the address given in the directory.

For programs offering related work, see also in this book *Administration, Instruction, and Theory; Business Administration and Management; Education; Health-Related Professions; Instructional Levels; Leisure Studies and Recreation; Physical Education and Kinesiology;* and *Special Focus.* In the other guides in this series:

Graduate Programs in the Humanities, Arts & Social Sciences
See *Art and Art History; Family and Consumer Sciences; Language and Literature; Performing Arts; Psychology and Counseling (School Psychology); Public, Regional, and Industrial Affairs (Urban Studies); Religious Studies;* and *Social Sciences*

Graduate Programs in the Physical Sciences, Mathematics, Agricultural Sciences, the Environment & Natural Resources
See *Mathematical Sciences*

Graduate Programs in Engineering & Applied Sciences
See *Computer Science and Information Technology*

CONTENTS

Program Directories

Close-Ups

See also:

Agricultural Education

Alcorn State University, School of Graduate Studies, School of Psychology and Education, Alcorn State, MS 39096-7500. Offers agricultural education (MS Ed); elementary education (MS Ed, Ed S); guidance and counseling (MS Ed); industrial education (MS Ed); secondary education (MS Ed), including health and physical education; special education (MS Ed). *Accreditation:* NCATE. *Degree requirements:* For master's, thesis optional.

Arkansas State University—Jonesboro, Graduate School, College of Agriculture and Technology, Jonesboro, State University, AR 72467. Offers agricultural education (MSA, SCCT); agriculture (MSA); vocational-technical administration (MS, SCCT). Part-time programs available. *Faculty:* 8 full-time (0 women), 3 part-time/adjunct (1 woman). *Students:* 7 full-time (1 woman), 24 part-time (14 women); includes 3 minority (all African Americans), 10 international. Average age 28. 19 applicants, 74% accepted, 11 enrolled. In 2009, 10 master's awarded. *Degree requirements:* For master's, comprehensive exam, thesis or alternative; for SCCT, comprehensive exam. *Entrance requirements:* For master's, GRE General Test or MAT, appropriate bachelor's degree; for SCCT, GRE General Test or MAT, interview, master's degree, official transcript, immunization records. Additional exam requirements/recommendations for international students: Required—TOEFL (minimum score 550 paper-based; 213 computer-based; 79 iBT), IELTS (minimum score 6). *Application deadline:* For fall admission, 7/15 for domestic students, 7/1 for international students; for spring admission, 12/1 for domestic students, 11/13 for international students. Applications are processed on a rolling basis. Application fee: $30 ($40 for international students). Electronic applications accepted. *Expenses:* Tuition, state resident: full-time $3744; part-time $208 per credit hour. Tuition, nonresident: full-time $9540; part-time $530 per credit hour. Required fees: $896; $47 per credit hour. $25 per term. One-time fee: $50. Tuition and fees vary according to course load and program. *Financial support:* In 2009–10, 8 students received support; teaching assistantships, career-related internships or fieldwork, scholarships/grants, and unspecified assistantships available. Financial award application deadline: 7/1; financial award applicants required to submit FAFSA. *Unit head:* Dr. Gregory Phillips, Dean, 870-972-2085, Fax: 870-972-3885, E-mail: gphillips@astate.edu. *Application contact:* Dr. Andrew Sustich, Dean of the Graduate School, 870-972-3029, Fax: 870-972-3857, E-mail: sustich@astate.edu.

Clemson University, Graduate School, College of Agriculture, Forestry and Life Sciences, Department of Agricultural and Biological Engineering, Program in Agricultural Education, Clemson, SC 29634. Offers M Ag Ed. *Accreditation:* NCATE. Part-time programs available. *Students:* 12 full-time (6 women), 5 part-time (4 women). Average age 25. 11 applicants, 91% accepted, 9 enrolled. In 2009, 5 master's awarded. *Entrance requirements:* For master's, GRE General Test. Additional exam requirements/recommendations for international students: Required—TOEFL. *Application deadline:* For fall admission, 3/15 for domestic students; for spring admission, 11/1 for domestic students. Application fee: $70 ($80 for international students). Electronic applications accepted. *Expenses:* Tuition, state resident: full-time $8684; part-time $528 per credit hour. Tuition, nonresident: full-time $15,330; part-time $1078 per credit hour. Required fees: $736; $37 per semester. Part-time tuition and fees vary according to course load and program. *Financial support:* In 2009–10, 8 students received support, including 2 research assistantships with partial tuition reimbursements available (averaging $9,000 per year), 5 teaching assistantships with partial tuition reimbursements available (averaging $9,360 per year); career-related internships or fieldwork, institutionally sponsored loans, scholarships/grants, health care benefits, and unspecified assistantships also available. Support available to part-time students. Financial award application deadline: 4/1; financial award applicants required to submit FAFSA. *Faculty research:* Adaptation and change, curriculum assessment and innovation, career development, adult and extension education, technology transfer. *Unit head:* Dr. Young Jo Han, Chair, 864-656-3250, Fax: 864-656-0338, E-mail: yhan@clemson.edu. *Application contact:* Dr. Tom Dobbins, Coordinator, 864-656-3834, Fax: 864-656-5675, E-mail: tdbbns@clemson.edu.

Cornell University, Graduate School, Graduate Fields of Agriculture and Life Sciences, Field of Education, Ithaca, NY 14853-0001. Offers agricultural education (MAT); biology (7-12) (MAT); chemistry (7-12) (MAT); curriculum and instruction (MPS, MS, PhD); earth science (7-12) (MAT); extension, and adult education (MPS, MS, PhD); mathematics (7-12) (MAT); physics (7-12) (MAT). *Faculty:* 26 full-time (9 women). *Students:* 65 full-time (50 women); includes 15 minority (4 African Americans, 7 Asian Americans or Pacific Islanders, 4 Hispanic Americans), 2 international. Average age 34. 96 applicants, 33% accepted, 21 enrolled. In 2009, 27 master's, 2 doctorates awarded. Terminal master's awarded for partial completion of doctoral program. *Degree requirements:* For master's, thesis (MS); for doctorate, comprehensive exam, thesis/dissertation. *Entrance requirements:* For master's and doctorate, GRE General Test, sample of written work (recommended), 2 letters of recommendation. Additional exam requirements/recommendations for international students: Required—TOEFL (minimum score 550 paper-based; 213 computer-based; 77 iBT). *Application deadline:* For fall admission, 2/15 for domestic students. Application fee: $70. Electronic applications accepted. *Expenses:* Tuition: Full-time $29,500. Required fees: $70. Full-time tuition and fees vary according to degree level, program and student level. *Financial support:* In 2009–10, 33 students received support, including 3 fellowships with full tuition reimbursements available, 5 teaching assistantships with full tuition reimbursements available; research assistantships with full tuition reimbursements available, institutionally sponsored loans, scholarships/grants, health care benefits, tuition waivers (full and partial), and unspecified assistantships also available. Financial award applicants required to submit FAFSA. *Faculty research:* Moral development and professional ethics; public issues education and community development; socio/political issues in public education; teacher education and curriculum in agricultural science, and mathematics; extension research. *Unit head:* Director of Graduate Studies, 607-255-4278, Fax: 607-255-7905. *Application contact:* Graduate Field Assistant, 607-255-4278, Fax: 607-255-7905, E-mail: rh22@cornell.edu.

Eastern Kentucky University, The Graduate School, College of Education, Department of Curriculum and Instruction, Program in Secondary and Higher Education, Richmond, KY 40475-3102. Offers secondary education (MA Ed), including agricultural education, art education, biological sciences education, business education, English education, geography education, history education, home economics education, industrial education, mathematical sciences education, physical education, school health education. *Accreditation:* NCATE. Part-time programs available. *Entrance requirements:* For master's, GRE General Test, minimum GPA of 2.5.

Iowa State University of Science and Technology, Graduate College, College of Agriculture, Department of Agricultural Education and Studies, Ames, IA 50011. Offers MS, PhD. Post-baccalaureate distance learning degree programs offered (minimal on-campus study). *Faculty:* 10 full-time (1 woman). *Students:* 14 full-time (8 women), 19 part-time (9 women); includes 2 minority (both African Americans), 2 international. 21 applicants, 76% accepted, 13 enrolled. In 2009, 9 master's, 3 doctorates awarded. *Degree requirements:* For master's, thesis or alternative; for doctorate, thesis/dissertation. *Entrance requirements:* For master's and doctorate, resume. Additional exam requirements/recommendations for international students: Required—TOEFL (minimum score 550 paper-based; 79 iBT) or IELTS (minimum score 6.5). *Application deadline:* For fall admission, 3/15 priority date for domestic and international students; for spring admission, 10/15 priority date for domestic and international students. Applications are processed on a rolling basis. Application fee: $40 ($90 for international students). Electronic applications accepted. *Expenses:* Tuition, state resident: full-time $6716. Tuition, nonresident: full-time $8908. Tuition and fees vary according to course level, course load, program and student level. *Financial support:* In 2009–10, 8 research assistantships with full and partial tuition reimbursements (averaging $13,500 per year), 1 teaching assistantship with full and partial tuition reimbursement (averaging $15,120 per year) were awarded; fellowships, scholarships/grants, health care benefits, and unspecified assistantships also available. *Faculty research:* Agricultural extension education, teaching, learning processes, distance education, international education, adult education. *Unit head:* Dr. W. Wade Miller, Interim Chair, 515-294-0896, E-mail: agedsinfo@iastate.edu. *Application contact:* Dr. Greg Miller, Director of Graduate Education, 515-294-2583, E-mail: agedsinfo@iastate.edu.

Louisiana State University and Agricultural and Mechanical College, Graduate School, College of Agriculture, School of Human Resource Education and Workforce Development, Baton Rouge, LA 70803. Offers agriculture and extension education and youth development (MS, PhD); career and technical education (MS, PhD); comprehensive vocational education (MS, PhD); extension and international education (MS, PhD); human resource and leadership development (MS, PhD); industrial education (MS); vocational agriculture education (MS, PhD); vocational business education (MS); vocational home economics education (MS). *Accreditation:* NCATE. Part-time programs available. *Faculty:* 11 full-time (5 women), 2 part-time/adjunct (both women). *Students:* 39 full-time (22 women), 75 part-time (51 women); includes 14 African Americans, 1 Asian American or Pacific Islander, 2 Hispanic Americans, 7 international. Average age 37. 40 applicants, 93% accepted, 18 enrolled. In 2009, 16 master's, 13 doctorates awarded. Terminal master's awarded for partial completion of doctoral program. *Degree requirements:* For master's, thesis (for some programs); for doctorate, thesis/dissertation. *Entrance requirements:* For master's and doctorate, GRE General Test, minimum GPA of 3.0. Additional exam requirements/recommendations for international students: Required—TOEFL (minimum score 550 paper-based; 213 computer-based; 79 iBT) or IELTS (minimum score 6.5). *Application deadline:* For fall admission, 1/25 priority date for domestic students, 5/15 for international students; for spring admission, 10/15 for international students. Applications are processed on a rolling basis. Application fee: $50 ($70 for international students). Electronic applications accepted. *Financial support:* In 2009–10, 63 students received support, including 3 fellowships with full and partial tuition reimbursements available (averaging $24,885 per year), 5 research assistantships with full and partial tuition reimbursements available (averaging $14,440 per year), 4 teaching assistantships with partial tuition reimbursements available (averaging $13,750 per year); career-related internships or fieldwork, Federal Work-Study, institutionally sponsored loans, health care benefits, tuition waivers (full and partial), and unspecified assistantships also available. Financial award application deadline: 3/1; financial award applicants required to submit FAFSA. *Faculty research:* Adult education, history and philosophy of vocational education, curriculum and instruction, career decision making. Total annual research expenditures: $21,538. *Unit head:* Dr. Michael F. Burnett, Director, 225-578-5748, Fax: 225-578-2526, E-mail: vocbur@lsu.edu. *Application contact:* Paula Beecher, Recruiting Coordinator, 225-578-2468, E-mail: pbeeche@lsu.edu.

Mississippi State University, College of Agriculture and Life Sciences, School of Human Sciences, Mississippi State, MS 39762. Offers agricultural sciences (PhD), including agriculture and extension education; agriculture and extension education (MS). *Accreditation:* NCATE (one or more programs are accredited). Part-time programs available. *Faculty:* 13 full-time (8 women). *Students:* 9 full-time (6 women), 42 part-time (24 women); includes 12 minority (all African Americans). Average age 33. 23 applicants, 78% accepted, 17 enrolled. In 2009, 11 master's, 3 doctorates awarded. *Degree requirements:* For master's, thesis optional, comprehensive oral or written exam. *Entrance requirements:* For master's, GRE, minimum GPA of 2.75 in last 4 semesters of course work; for doctorate, minimum GPA of 3.0 on prior graduate work. Additional exam requirements/recommendations for international students: Required—TOEFL (minimum score 475 paper-based; 153 computer-based; 53 iBT); Recommended—IELTS (minimum score 4.5). *Application deadline:* For fall admission, 7/1 for domestic students, 5/1 for international students; for spring admission, 11/1 for domestic students, 9/1 for international students. Applications are processed on a rolling basis. Application fee: $40. Electronic applications accepted. *Expenses:* Tuition, state resident: full-time $2575.50; part-time $286.25 per credit hour. Tuition, nonresident: full-time $6510; part-time $723.50 per credit hour. Tuition and fees vary according to course load. *Financial support:* In 2009–10, 2 research assistantships (averaging $8,351 per year), 5 teaching assistantships with full tuition reimbursements (averaging $9,081 per year) were awarded; Federal Work-Study, institutionally sponsored loans, and unspecified assistantships also available. Financial award application deadline: 4/1; financial award applicants required to submit FAFSA. *Faculty research:* Animal welfare, agroscience, information technology, learning styles, problem solving. *Unit head:* Dr. Gary Jackson, Director, 662-325-8593, E-mail: gjackson@humansci.msstate.edu. *Application contact:* Dr. Jacquelyn Deeds, Professor and Graduate Coordinator, 662-325-7834, E-mail: jdeeds@ais.msstate.edu.

Missouri State University, Graduate College, College of Natural and Applied Sciences, Department of Agriculture, Springfield, MO 65897. Offers natural and applied science (MNAS), including agriculture (MNAS, MS Ed); plant science (MS); secondary education (MS Ed), including agriculture (MNAS, MS Ed). Part-time programs available. *Faculty:* 16 full-time (3 women). *Students:* 10 full-time (7 women), 16 part-time (10 women), 2 international. Average age 31. 7 applicants, 71% accepted, 3 enrolled. In 2009, 9 master's awarded. *Degree requirements:* For master's, comprehensive exam, thesis or alternative. *Entrance requirements:* For master's, GRE (MS plant science, MNAS), 9-12 teacher certification (MS Ed), minimum GPA of 3.0 (MS plant science, MNAS). Additional exam requirements/recommendations for international students: Required—TOEFL (minimum score 550 paper-based; 213 computer-based; 79 iBT). *Application deadline:* For fall admission, 7/20 priority date for domestic students, 5/1 for international students; for spring admission, 12/20 priority date for domestic students, 9/1 for international students. Applications are processed on a rolling basis. Application fee: $35 ($50 for international students). Electronic applications accepted. *Expenses:* Tuition, state resident: full-time $3852; part-time $214 per credit hour. Tuition, nonresident: full-time $7524; part-time $418 per credit hour. Required fees: $696; $172 per semester. Tuition and fees vary according to course level, course load, degree level and program. *Financial support:* In 2009–10, 6 research assistantships with full tuition reimbursements (averaging $8,535 per year), 6 teaching assistantships with full tuition reimbursements (averaging $8,535 per year) were awarded; Federal Work-Study, institutionally sponsored loans, scholarships/grants, and unspecified assistantships also available. Financial award application deadline: 3/31; financial award applicants required to submit FAFSA. *Faculty research:* Grapevine biotechnology, agricultural marketing, Asian elephant reproduction, poultry science, integrated pest management. *Unit head:* Dr. W. Anson Elliott, Head, 417-836-5638, E-mail: ansonelliot@missouristate.edu. *Application contact:* Eric Eckert, Coordinator of Graduate Admissions and Recruitment, 417-836-5331, Fax: 417-836-6200.

Montana State University, College of Graduate Studies, College of Agriculture, Division of Agricultural Education, Bozeman, MT 59717. Offers MS. Part-time programs available. Post-baccalaureate distance learning degree programs offered (minimal on-campus study). *Faculty:* 24 full-time (5 women), 4 part-time/adjunct (3 women). *Students:* 11 full-time (5 women), 12 part-time (5 women), 2 international. Average age 27. 23 applicants, 65% accepted, 9 enrolled. In 2009, 9 master's awarded. *Degree requirements:* For master's, comprehensive exam. *Entrance requirements:* For master's, GRE General Test. Additional exam requirements/recommendations for international students: Required—TOEFL (minimum score 550 paper-based; 213 computer-based). *Application deadline:* For fall admission, 7/15 priority date for domestic students, 5/15 priority date for international students; for spring admission, 12/1 priority date for domestic students, 10/1 priority date for international students. Applications are processed on a rolling basis. Application fee: $30. Electronic applications accepted. *Expenses:* Tuition, state resident: full-time $5635; part-time $3492 per year. Tuition, nonresident: full-time $17,212; part-time $7865.10 per year. Required fees: $1441; $153.15 per credit. Tuition and fees vary according to course load and program. *Financial support:* In 2009–10, 14 students received support, including 5 research assistantships with full and partial tuition reimbursements available (averaging $12,000 per year), 9 teaching assistantships with full and partial tuition reimbursements available (averaging $12,000 per year); tuition waivers (partial) and unspecified assistantships also available. Financial award application deadline: 3/1; financial award applicants required to submit FAFSA. *Faculty research:* Extension systems, youth leadership, agricultural, adult and youth education in agriculture, international agricultural education, enzymology of vitamins, coenzymes and metal ions, steroid metabolism, protein structure, impact of wolves on big game hunting demand, prescription drug price dispersion in heterogeneous markets, divorce risk and the labor force participation of women with and

without children, the economics of terraces in the Peruvian Andes. Total annual research expenditures: $1.1 million. *Unit head:* Dr. Jeffrey S. Jacobsen, Dean, 406-994-7060, Fax: 406-994-3933, E-mail: jefj@montana.edu. *Application contact:* Dr. Carl A. Fox, Vice Provost for Graduate Education, 406-994-4145, Fax: 406-994-7433, E-mail: gradstudy@montana.edu.

Murray State University, School of Agriculture, Murray, KY 42071. Offers agriculture (MS); agriculture education (MS). Evening/weekend programs available. Postbaccalaureate distance learning degree programs offered (minimal on-campus study). *Degree requirements:* For master's, comprehensive exam, thesis (for some programs). *Entrance requirements:* Additional exam requirements/recommendations for international students: Required—TOEFL. *Faculty research:* Ultrasound in beef, corn and soybean research, tobacco research.

New Mexico State University, Graduate School, College of Agricultural, Consumer and Environmental Sciences, Department of Agricultural and Extension Education, Las Cruces, NM 88003-8001. Offers MA. *Accreditation:* NCATE. Part-time and evening/weekend programs available. Postbaccalaureate distance learning degree programs offered (minimal on-campus study). *Faculty:* 3 full-time (2 women). *Students:* 13 full-time (7 women), 23 part-time (13 women); includes 10 minority (1 American Indian/Alaska Native, 9 Hispanic Americans), 1 international. Average age 30. 21 applicants, 100% accepted, 19 enrolled. In 2009, 14 master's awarded. *Degree requirements:* For master's, comprehensive exam, thesis or creative component. *Entrance requirements:* For master's, 3 letters of recommendation. Additional exam requirements/recommendations for international students: Required—TOEFL, Language Proficiency Exam. *Application deadline:* For fall admission, 7/1 priority date for domestic and international students; for spring admission, 11/1 priority date for domestic and international students. Applications are processed on a rolling basis. Application fee: $30 ($50 for international students). Electronic applications accepted. *Expenses:* Tuition, state resident: full-time $4080; part-time $223 per credit. Tuition, nonresident: full-time $14,256; part-time $647 per credit. Required fees: $1278; $639 per semester. *Financial support:* In 2009–10, 2 research assistantships (averaging $9,875 per year), 4 teaching assistantships (averaging $13,025 per year) were awarded; career-related internships or fieldwork, Federal Work-Study, institutionally sponsored loans, scholarships/grants, health care benefits, and unspecified assistantships also available. Financial award application deadline: 3/1. *Faculty research:* Secondary agricultural education programs, teaching and learning, agricultural technology and safety, volunteer programs, youth leadership development, agricultural development. *Unit head:* Dr. Cynda Clary, Head, 575-646-4511, Fax: 575-646-4082, E-mail: cclary@nmsu.edu. *Application contact:* Dr. Brenda S. Seevers, Professor, 575-646-4511, Fax: 575-646-4082, E-mail: bseevers@nmsu.edu.

North Carolina Agricultural and Technical State University, Graduate School, School of Agriculture and Environmental Sciences, Department of Agribusiness, Applied Economics, and Agriscience Education, Greensboro, NC 27411. Offers agricultural economics (MS); agricultural education (MS). *Accreditation:* NCATE. Part-time and evening/weekend programs available. *Degree requirements:* For master's, comprehensive exam, thesis or alternative, qualifying exam. *Entrance requirements:* For master's, GRE General Test, minimum GPA of 3.0. *Faculty research:* Aid for small farmers, agricultural technology resources, labor force mobility, agrology.

North Carolina State University, Graduate School, College of Agriculture and Life Sciences, Department of Agricultural and Extension Education, Program in Agricultural Education, Raleigh, NC 27695. Offers MAE, MS, Certificate. Postbaccalaureate distance learning degree programs offered. *Degree requirements:* For master's, thesis optional. *Entrance requirements:* For master's, GRE or MAT. Electronic applications accepted. *Faculty research:* Instructional methodology, distance education, leadership development, foundations, curriculum development.

North Dakota State University, College of Graduate and Interdisciplinary Studies, College of Human Development and Education, School of Education, Program in Agricultural Education, Fargo, ND 58108. Offers agricultural education (M Ed, MS); agricultural extension education (MS). *Accreditation:* NCATE. Part-time programs available. *Faculty:* 2 part-time/adjunct (1 woman). *Students:* 40 full-time (25 women), 101 part-time (70 women); includes 15 minority (4 African Americans, 7 American Indian/Alaska Native, 2 Asian Americans or Pacific Islanders, 2 Hispanic Americans), 6 international. Average age 32. In 2009, 21 master's awarded. *Degree requirements:* For master's, comprehensive exam, thesis or alternative. *Entrance requirements:* Additional exam requirements/recommendations for international students: Required—TOEFL (minimum score 525 paper-based; 197 computer-based; 71 iBT). *Application deadline:* Applications are processed on a rolling basis. Application fee: $45 ($60 for international students). *Financial support:* Research assistantships, career-related internships or fieldwork, Federal Work-Study, institutionally sponsored loans, and tuition waivers (full) available. Financial award application deadline: 4/15. *Faculty research:* Vocational and cooperative extension education, rural leadership, rural education, international extension. *Unit head:* Dr. William Martin, Chair, 701-231-7202, Fax: 701-231-7416, E-mail: william.martin@ndsu.edu. *Application contact:* Dr. Brent Young, Assistant Professor, 701-231-7439, Fax: 701-231-9685, E-mail: brent.young@ndsu.edu.

Northwest Missouri State University, Graduate School, Melvin and Valorie Booth College of Business and Professional Studies, Department of Agriculture, Maryville, MO 64468-6001. Offers agricultural economics (MBA); agriculture (MS); teaching agriculture (MS Ed). Part-time programs available. *Faculty:* 7 full-time (2 women). *Students:* 8 full-time (3 women), 4 part-time (1 woman), 2 international. 10 applicants, 80% accepted, 5 enrolled. In 2009, 3 master's awarded. *Degree requirements:* For master's, comprehensive exam, thesis (for some programs). *Entrance requirements:* For master's, GRE General Test, minimum undergraduate GPA of 2.5, writing sample. Additional exam requirements/recommendations for international students: Required—TOEFL (minimum score 550 paper-based; 213 computer-based). *Application deadline:* For fall admission, 7/1 for domestic and international students; for spring admission, 11/15 for domestic and international students. Applications are processed on a rolling basis. Application fee: $0 ($50 for international students). *Expenses:* Tuition, state resident: part-time $296.34 per credit hour. Tuition, nonresident: part-time $510.43 per credit hour. *Financial support:* In 2009–10, 3 research assistantships with full tuition reimbursements (averaging $6,000 per year), 2 teaching assistantships with full tuition reimbursements (averaging $6,000 per year) were awarded; unspecified assistantships also available. Financial award application deadline: 4/1; financial award applicants required to submit FAFSA. *Unit head:* Dr. Arley Larson, Chairperson, 660-562-1161. *Application contact:* Dr. Gregory Haddock, Dean of Graduate School, 660-562-1145, Fax: 660-562-1096, E-mail: gradsch@nwmissouri.edu.

The Ohio State University, Graduate School, College of Food, Agricultural, and Environmental Sciences, Department of Human and Community Resource Development, Program in Agricultural and Extension Education, Columbus, OH 43210. Offers M Ed, MS, PhD. *Expenses:* Tuition, state resident: full-time $10,683. Tuition, nonresident: full-time $25,923. Tuition and fees vary according to course load and program.

Oklahoma State University, College of Agricultural Science and Natural Resources, Department of Agricultural Education, Communications and Leadership, Stillwater, OK 74078. Offers M Ag, MS, PhD. Postbaccalaureate distance learning degree programs offered. *Faculty:* 12 full-time (5 women), 1 part-time/adjunct (0 women). *Students:* 20 full-time (11 women), 34 part-time (23 women); includes 7 minority (1 African American, 6 American Indian/Alaska Native), 7 international. Average age 32. 60 applicants, 65% accepted, 29 enrolled. In 2009, 18 master's, 6 doctorates awarded. *Degree requirements:* For master's, thesis (for some programs), thesis or report; for doctorate, comprehensive exam, thesis/dissertation. *Entrance requirements:* For master's and doctorate, GRE or GMAT. Additional exam requirements/recommendations for international students: Required—TOEFL (minimum score 550 paper-based; 79 iBT). *Application deadline:* For fall admission, 3/1 priority date for international students; for spring admission, 8/1 priority date for international students. Applications are processed on a rolling basis. Application fee: $40 ($75 for international students). Electronic applications accepted. *Expenses:* Tuition, state resident: full-time $3716; part-time $154.85 per credit hour. Tuition, nonresident: full-time $14,448; part-time $602 per credit hour. Required fees: $1772; $73.85 per credit hour. One-time fee: $50. Tuition and fees vary according to course load and campus/location. *Financial support:* In 2009–10, 2 research assistantships (averaging $11,748 per year), 7 teaching assistantships (averaging $15,022 per year) were awarded; career-related internships or fieldwork, Federal Work-Study, scholarships/grants, health care benefits, tuition waivers (partial), and unspecified assistantships also available. Support available to part-time students. Financial award application deadline: 3/1; financial award applicants required to submit FAFSA. *Faculty research:* Teaching and learning about and in agriculture, agriculture teacher evaluation, evaluation of information dissemination delivery methods, agricultural literacy curriculum model development, distance education delivery methods. *Unit head:* Dr. James Key, Interim Head, 405-744-8885, Fax: 405-744-5176. *Application contact:* Dr. Gordon Emslie, Dean, 405-744-6368, Fax: 405-744-0355, E-mail: grad-i@okstate.edu.

Oregon State University, Graduate School, College of Agricultural Sciences, Department of Agricultural Education, Corvallis, OR 97331. Offers M Agr, MAIS, MAT, MS. Part-time programs available. *Students:* 9 full-time (5 women); includes 1 minority (Hispanic American). Average age 33. In 2009, 9 master's awarded. *Degree requirements:* For master's, thesis (for some programs). *Entrance requirements:* For master's, GRE General Test, minimum GPA of 3.0 in last 90 hours of course work. Additional exam requirements/recommendations for international students: Required—TOEFL. *Application deadline:* Applications are processed on a rolling basis. Application fee: $50. *Expenses:* Tuition, state resident: full-time $9774; part-time $362 per credit. Tuition, nonresident: full-time $15,849; part-time $587 per credit. Required fees: $1639. Full-time tuition and fees vary according to course load and program. *Financial support:* Fellowships, research assistantships, teaching assistantships, career-related internships or fieldwork, Federal Work-Study, and institutionally sponsored loans available. Support available to part-time students. Financial award application deadline: 2/1. *Faculty research:* Curriculum development and vocational education program evaluation, agricultural extension education. *Unit head:* Dr. Greg Thompson, Department Head, 541-737-1337, Fax: 541-737-3178. *Application contact:* Dr. Stella Coakley, Associate Dean, 541-737-5264, Fax: 541-737-3178, E-mail: stella.coakley@oregonstate.edu.

Penn State University Park, Graduate School, College of Agricultural Sciences, Department of Agricultural and Extension Education, State College, University Park, PA 16802-1503. Offers M Ed, MS, PhD.

Purdue University, Graduate School, College of Agriculture, Department of Youth Development and Agricultural Education, West Lafayette, IN 47907. Offers MA, PhD. *Entrance requirements:* For master's, writing sample; for doctorate, GRE, writing sample. Additional exam requirements/recommendations for international students: Required—TOEFL, GRE; Recommended—TWE. Electronic applications accepted.

Purdue University, Graduate School, School of Education, Department of Curriculum and Instruction, West Lafayette, IN 47907. Offers agricultural and extension education (PhD, Ed S); agriculture and extension education (MS, MS Ed); art education (PhD); consumer and family sciences and extension education (MS Ed, PhD, Ed S); curriculum studies (MS Ed, PhD, Ed S); educational technology (MS Ed, PhD, Ed S); elementary education (MS Ed); foreign language education (MS Ed, PhD, Ed S); industrial technology (PhD, Ed S); language arts (MS Ed, PhD, Ed S); literacy (MS Ed, PhD, Ed S); mathematics/science education (MS, MS Ed, PhD, Ed S); social studies (MS Ed, PhD); social studies education (Ed S); vocational/industrial education (MS Ed, PhD, Ed S); vocational/technical education (MS Ed, PhD, Ed S). *Accreditation:* NCATE. Part-time and evening/weekend programs available. *Degree requirements:* For master's, thesis optional; for doctorate, thesis/dissertation, oral and written exams; for Ed S, oral presentation, project. *Entrance requirements:* For master's, GRE General Test, minimum B average; for doctorate, GRE General Test; for Ed S, GRE, minimum B average. Additional exam requirements/recommendations for international students: Required—TOEFL. Electronic applications accepted. *Faculty research:* Literacy acquisition and development, teacher beliefs and knowledge, recruitment and retention of underrepresented students, economic education, literacy discourse.

State University of New York at Oswego, Graduate Studies, School of Education, Department of Vocational Teacher Preparation, Oswego, NY 13126. Offers agriculture (MS Ed); business and marketing (MS Ed); family and consumer sciences (MS Ed); health careers (MS Ed); technical education (MS Ed); trade education (MS Ed). *Accreditation:* NCATE. Part-time and evening/weekend programs available. *Degree requirements:* For master's, thesis or alternative. *Entrance requirements:* Additional exam requirements/recommendations for international students: Required—TOEFL (minimum score 560 paper-based; 220 computer-based).

Stephen F. Austin State University, Graduate School, College of Forestry and Agriculture, Department of Agriculture, Nacogdoches, TX 75962. Offers MS. *Accreditation:* NCATE. *Degree requirements:* For master's, comprehensive exam, thesis (for some programs). *Entrance requirements:* For master's, GRE General Test, minimum GPA of 2.8 in last half of major, 2.5 overall. Additional exam requirements/recommendations for international students: Required—TOEFL (minimum score 550 paper-based; 213 computer-based). *Faculty research:* Asian vegetables, soil fertility, animal breeding, animal nutrition.

Tarleton State University, College of Graduate Studies, College of Agriculture and Human Sciences, Department of Agricultural Services and Development, Stephenville, TX 76402. Offers agriculture education (MS). Part-time and evening/weekend programs available. Postbaccalaureate distance learning degree programs offered (minimal on-campus study). *Degree requirements:* For master's, comprehensive exam. *Entrance requirements:* For master's, GRE General Test, minimum GPA of 3.0. Additional exam requirements/recommendations for international students: Required—TOEFL (minimum score 550 paper-based; 213 computer-based; 80 iBT). Electronic applications accepted.

Texas A&M University, College of Agriculture and Life Sciences, Department of Agricultural Leadership, Education and Communications, College Station, TX 77843. Offers agricultural education (M Ed, MS, Ed D, PhD); agriculture (M Agr). Part-time programs available. Postbaccalaureate distance learning degree programs offered (no on-campus study). *Faculty:* 22. *Students:* 62 full-time (37 women), 76 part-time (35 women); includes 23 minority (11 African Americans, 1 Asian American or Pacific Islander, 11 Hispanic Americans), 8 international. Average age 27. In 2009, 25 master's, 7 doctorates awarded. Terminal master's awarded for partial completion of doctoral program. *Degree requirements:* For master's, comprehensive exam, thesis (for some programs); for doctorate, comprehensive exam, thesis/dissertation. *Entrance requirements:* For master's, GRE General Test, letters of reference, curriculum vitae; for doctorate, GRE General Test, 3 years of professional experience, letters of reference, curriculum vitae. Additional exam requirements/recommendations for international students: Required—TOEFL. *Application deadline:* For fall admission, 3/15 priority date for domestic students; for spring admission, 10/15 for domestic students. Application fee: $50 ($75 for international students). Electronic applications accepted. *Expenses:* Tuition, state resident: full-time $3991; part-time $221.74 per credit hour. Tuition, nonresident: full-time $9049; part-time $502.74 per credit hour. *Financial support:* In 2009–10, fellowships with partial tuition reimbursements (averaging $12,000 per year), research assistantships with partial tuition reimbursements (averaging $12,000 per year), teaching assistantships with partial tuition reimbursements (averaging $12,000 per year) were awarded; career-related internships or fieldwork, institutionally sponsored loans, scholarships/grants, tuition waivers (partial), and unspecified assistantships also available. Financial award application deadline: 3/15; financial award applicants required to submit FAFSA. *Faculty research:* Planning and needs assessment, instructional design, delivery strategies, evaluation and accountability, distance education. *Unit head:* John Elliot, Head, 979-845-0139, E-mail: jelliot@tamu.edu. *Application contact:* Diann Dillingham, Graduate Program Coordinator, 979-845-2952, Fax: 979-845-6296, E-mail: dillingham@tamu.edu.

Texas A&M University–Commerce, Graduate School, College of Arts and Sciences, Department of Agriculture, Commerce, TX 75429-3011. Offers agricultural education (M Ed, MS); agricultural sciences (M Ed, MS). Part-time programs available. *Degree requirements:* For master's, comprehensive exam, thesis (for some programs). *Entrance requirements:* For master's, GRE General Test. Electronic applications accepted. *Faculty research:* Soil conservation, retention.

Agricultural Education

Texas A&M University–Kingsville, College of Graduate Studies, College of Agriculture and Home Economics, Program in Agricultural Education, Kingsville, TX 78363. Offers MS. *Degree requirements:* For master's, comprehensive exam, thesis or alternative. *Entrance requirements:* For master's, GRE General Test, minimum GPA of 3.0. Additional exam requirements/recommendations for international students: Required—TOEFL.

Texas State University–San Marcos, Graduate School, College of Applied Arts, Department of Agriculture, San Marcos, TX 78666. Offers M Ed. Part-time and evening/weekend programs available. *Faculty:* 2 full-time (1 woman). *Students:* 12 full-time (6 women), 10 part-time (4 women); includes 1 American Indian/Alaska Native, 1 Hispanic American, 2 international. Average age 27. 12 applicants, 92% accepted, 8 enrolled. In 2009, 5 master's awarded. *Degree requirements:* For master's, comprehensive exam, thesis (for some programs). *Entrance requirements:* For master's, minimum GPA of 2.75 in last 60 hours of course work, 3 letters of reference (2 from academia). Additional exam requirements/recommendations for international students: Required—TOEFL (minimum score 550 paper-based; 213 computer-based). *Application deadline:* For fall admission, 6/15 priority date for domestic students; for spring admission, 10/15 priority date for domestic students. Applications are processed on a rolling basis. Application fee: $40 ($90 for international students). Electronic applications accepted. *Expenses:* Tuition, state resident: full-time $5784; part-time $241 per credit hour. Tuition, nonresident: full-time $13,224; part-time $551 per credit hour. Required fees: $1728; $48 per credit hour. $306. Tuition and fees vary according to course load. *Financial support:* In 2009–10, 16 students received support, including 5 research assistantships (averaging $5,423 per year), 1 teaching assistantship (averaging $4,658 per year); career-related internships or fieldwork, Federal Work-Study, and institutionally sponsored loans also available. Support available to part-time students. Financial award application deadline: 4/1; financial award applicants required to submit FAFSA. *Faculty research:* ALKA-VITA benefits, FenBendazole Med, diversity of USDA jobs. Total annual research expenditures: $50,261. *Unit head:* Dr. C. Reed Richardson, Chair, 512-245-2130, Fax: 512-245-3320, E-mail: cr36@txstate.edu. *Application contact:* Dr. Tina Cade, Graduate Adviser, 512-245-3324, Fax: 512-245-3320, E-mail: tc10@txstate.edu.

Texas Tech University, Graduate School, College of Agricultural Sciences and Natural Resources, Department of Agricultural Education and Communications, Lubbock, TX 79409. Offers agricultural communication (MS); agricultural education (MS, Ed D). Part-time programs available. *Faculty:* 7 full-time (2 women). *Students:* 32 full-time (22 women), 46 part-time (19 women); includes 9 minority (4 African Americans, 2 American Indian/Alaska Native, 3 Hispanic Americans), 4 international. Average age 32. 68 applicants, 76% accepted, 28 enrolled. In 2009, 21 master's, 2 doctorates awarded. *Degree requirements:* For master's, thesis or alternative; for doctorate, thesis/dissertation. *Entrance requirements:* For master's, GRE General Test. Additional exam requirements/recommendations for international students: Required—TOEFL (minimum score 550 paper-based; 213 computer-based). *Application deadline:* For fall admission, 3/1 priority date for international students; for spring admission, 11/1 priority date for international students. Applications are processed on a rolling basis. Application fee: $50 ($75 for international students). Electronic applications accepted. *Expenses:* Tuition, state resident: full-time $5100; part-time $213 per credit hour. Tuition, nonresident: full-time $11,748; part-time $490 per credit hour. Required fees: $2298; $50 per credit hour. $555 per semester. *Financial support:* In 2009–10, 7 research assistantships with partial tuition reimbursements (averaging $17,100 per year), 1 teaching assistantship with partial tuition reimbursement (averaging $10,379 per year) were awarded; Federal Work-Study and institutionally sponsored loans also available. Support available to part-time students. Financial award application deadline: 4/15; financial award applicants required to submit FAFSA. *Faculty research:* Planning needs assessment, learner-centered instructional design, program delivery, evaluation accountability, research measurement and analysis. Total annual research expenditures: $117,710. *Unit head:* Dr. Matt Baker, Chairman, 806-742-2816, Fax: 806-742-2880, E-mail: matt.baker@ttu.edu. *Application contact:* Dr. David Doerfert, Graduate Adviser, 806-742-2816, Fax: 806-742-2880, E-mail: david.doerfert@ttu.edu.

The University of Arizona, Graduate College, College of Agriculture and Life Sciences, Department of Agricultural Education, Tucson, AZ 85721. Offers M Ag Ed, MS. *Faculty:* 1. *Students:* 8 full-time (6 women), 9 part-time (6 women); includes 3 minority (2 Asian Americans or Pacific Islanders, 1 Hispanic American), 1 international. Average age 33. 15 applicants, 100% accepted, 11 enrolled. In 2009, 13 master's awarded. *Degree requirements:* For master's, thesis. *Entrance requirements:* For master's, teaching/extension experience or equivalent, minimum GPA of 3.0, 2 letters of recommendation. Additional exam requirements/recommendations for international students: Required—TOEFL. *Application deadline:* For fall admission, 6/1 for domestic students, 2/1 for international students. Applications are processed on a rolling basis. Application fee: $75. Electronic applications accepted. *Expenses:* Tuition, state resident: full-time $9028. Tuition, nonresident: full-time $24,890. *Financial support:* In 2009–10, 5 students received support, including 3 teaching assistantships with full and partial tuition reimbursements available (averaging $14,982 per year); fellowships, research assistantships, career-related internships or fieldwork, scholarships/grants, health care benefits, tuition waivers (full), and unspecified assistantships also available. *Faculty research:* Career placement, learning styles, noise impact on learning, computer technology, vocational education. Total annual research expenditures: $533,182. *Unit head:* Dr. Jack F. Elliot, Head, 520-621-7173, Fax: 520-621-9889, E-mail: elliot@ag.arizona.edu. *Application contact:* Glen Miller, 520-940-3716, Fax: 520-621-9889, E-mail: vamiller@ag.arizona.edu.

University of Arkansas, Graduate School, Dale Bumpers College of Agricultural, Food and Life Sciences, Department of Agricultural and Extension Education, Program in Agricultural and Extension Education, Fayetteville, AR 72701-1201. Offers MS. Part-time programs available. Postbaccalaureate distance learning degree programs offered (minimal on-campus study). *Students:* 3 full-time (1 woman), 8 part-time (3 women); includes 1 minority (African American). In 2009, 4 master's awarded. *Degree requirements:* For master's, thesis optional. Application fee: $40 ($50 for international students). *Expenses:* Tuition, state resident: full-time $7355; part-time $356.58 per hour. Tuition, nonresident: full-time $17,401; part-time $775.17 per hour. Required fees: $1203. *Financial support:* In 2009–10, 2 research assistantships were awarded; fellowships, teaching assistantships also available. Financial award application deadline: 4/1. *Unit head:* Dr. George Wardlow, Graduate Coordinator, 479-575-2035, E-mail: wardlow@uark.edu. *Application contact:* Dr. Donald M. Johnson, Graduate Coordinator, 479-575-2039, E-mail: dmjohnso@uark.edu.

University of Connecticut, Graduate School, Neag School of Education, Department of Curriculum and Instruction, Storrs, CT 06269. Offers agriculture (MA), including agriculture education; agriculture education (PhD, Post-Master's Certificate); bilingual and bicultural education (MA, PhD, Post-Master's Certificate); elementary education (MA, PhD, Post-Master's Certificate); English education (MA, PhD, Post-Master's Certificate); history and social sciences education (MA, PhD, Post-Master's Certificate); mathematics education (MA, PhD, Post-Master's Certificate); reading education (MA, PhD, Post-Master's Certificate); science education (MA, PhD); secondary education (MA, PhD, Post-Master's Certificate); world languages education (MA, PhD, Post-Master's Certificate). *Accreditation:* NCATE. *Faculty:* 28 full-time (13 women). *Students:* 168 full-time (129 women), 60 part-time (49 women); includes 35 minority (4 African Americans, 6 Asian Americans or Pacific Islanders, 25 Hispanic Americans), 2 international. Average age 29. 280 applicants, 26% accepted, 58 enrolled. In 2009, 147 master's, 4 doctorates, 12 other advanced degrees awarded. Terminal master's awarded for partial completion of doctoral program. *Degree requirements:* For master's, comprehensive exam, thesis or alternative; for doctorate, thesis/dissertation. *Entrance requirements:* For doctorate, GRE General Test. Additional exam requirements/recommendations for international students: Required—TOEFL (minimum score 550 paper-based; 213 computer-based). *Application deadline:* For fall admission, 2/1 priority date for domestic and international students; for spring admission, 11/1 for domestic students, 10/1 for international students. Applications are processed on a rolling basis. Application fee: $55. Electronic applications accepted. *Expenses:* Tuition, state resident: full-time $4725; part-time $525 per credit. Tuition, nonresident: full-time $12,267; part-time $1363 per credit. Required fees: $346 per semester. Tuition and fees vary according to course load. *Financial support:* In 2009–10, 11 research assistantships with full tuition reimbursements, 6 teaching assistantships with full tuition reimbursements were awarded; fellowships, Federal Work-Study, scholarships/grants, health care benefits, and unspecified assistantships also available. Financial award application deadline: 2/1; financial award applicants required to submit FAFSA. *Unit head:* Mary Anne Doyle, Head, 860-486-2433, Fax: 860-486-0280, E-mail: mary.dolye@uconn.edu. *Application contact:* Lisa Rasicot, Graduate Coordinator, 860-486-3065, Fax: 860-486-0210, E-mail: l.rasicot@uconn.edu.

University of Delaware, College of Agriculture and Natural Resources, Agricultural Education Program, Newark, DE 19716. Offers MA.

University of Delaware, College of Agriculture and Natural Resources, Department of Food and Resource Economics, Newark, DE 19716. Offers agricultural economics (MS); agriculture and technical education (MA); bioresources engineering (MS). Part-time programs available. *Degree requirements:* For master's, thesis. *Entrance requirements:* For master's, GRE General Test, 3 letters of recommendation. Additional exam requirements/recommendations for international students: Required—TOEFL (minimum score 550 paper-based; 213 computer-based). Electronic applications accepted. *Faculty research:* Experimental economics, environmental and resource economics, land use, law and economics.

University of Florida, Graduate School, College of Agricultural and Life Sciences, Department of Agricultural Education and Communication, Gainesville, FL 32611. Offers MS, PhD. *Degree requirements:* For master's, thesis optional. *Entrance requirements:* For master's, GRE General Test, minimum GPA of 3.0; for doctorate, GRE General Test. Additional exam requirements/recommendations for international students: Required—TOEFL. Electronic applications accepted. *Faculty research:* Cooperative extension service, including home economics, agriculture, 4-H, foods, housing, and nutrition.

University of Georgia, Graduate School, College of Agricultural and Environmental Sciences, Department of Agricultural Leadership, Education, and Communication, Athens, GA 30602. Offers MA Ext, MAL. *Faculty:* 8 full-time (3 women). *Students:* 16 full-time (9 women), 28 part-time (15 women); includes 4 minority (3 African Americans, 1 Asian American or Pacific Islander). Average age 25. 20 applicants, 80% accepted, 15 enrolled. In 2009, 11 master's awarded. *Degree requirements:* For master's, comprehensive exam, thesis optional. *Entrance requirements:* For master's, GRE General Test. *Application deadline:* For fall admission, 7/1 priority date for domestic students; for spring admission, 11/15 for domestic students. Application fee: $50. Electronic applications accepted. *Expenses:* Tuition, state resident: full-time $6000; part-time $250 per credit hour. Tuition, nonresident: full-time $20,904; part-time $871 per credit hour. Required fees: $730 per semester. *Financial support:* In 2009–10, 2 teaching assistantships were awarded; fellowships, research assistantships, unspecified assistantships also available. *Unit head:* Dr. Ray V. Herren, Interim Head, 706-542-3898, Fax: 706-542-0262, E-mail: rherren@uga.edu. *Application contact:* Dr. Dennis Duncan, Graduate Coordinator, 706-542-1204, Fax: 706-542-0262, E-mail: dwd@uga.edu.

University of Idaho, College of Graduate Studies, College of Agricultural and Life Sciences, Department of Agricultural and Extension Education, Moscow, ID 83844-2282. Offers agricultural education (MS). *Accreditation:* NCATE. *Faculty:* 4 full-time. *Students:* 4 full-time, 4 part-time. In 2009, 2 master's awarded. *Entrance requirements:* For master's, minimum GPA of 2.8. *Application deadline:* For fall admission, 8/1 for domestic students; for spring admission, 12/15 for domestic students. Application fee: $55 ($60 for international students). *Expenses:* Tuition, state resident: full-time $6120. Tuition, nonresident: full-time $17,712. *Financial support:* Application deadline: 2/15. *Unit head:* Dr. James Joseph Connors, Head, 208-885-6358. *Application contact:* Dr. James Joseph Connors, Head, 208-885-6358.

University of Illinois at Urbana–Champaign, Graduate College, College of Agricultural, Consumer and Environmental Sciences, Department of Human and Community Development, Champaign, IL 61820. Offers agricultural education (MS); human and community development (MS, PhD); MS/MSW. *Faculty:* 16 full-time (10 women), 1 part-time/adjunct (0 women). *Students:* 31 full-time (26 women), 3 part-time (2 women); includes 9 minority (4 African Americans, 5 Asian Americans or Pacific Islanders), 3 international. 30 applicants, 37% accepted, 10 enrolled. In 2009, 18 master's, 1 doctorate awarded. *Entrance requirements:* For master's and doctorate, GRE, minimum GPA of 3.0. Additional exam requirements/recommendations for international students: Required—TOEFL (minimum score 550 paper-based; 213 computer-based; 79 iBT). *Application deadline:* Applications are processed on a rolling basis. Application fee: $60 ($75 for international students). Electronic applications accepted. *Financial support:* In 2009–10, 12 fellowships, 18 research assistantships, 19 teaching assistantships were awarded; tuition waivers (full and partial) also available. *Unit head:* Robert Hughes, Head, 217-333-3790, Fax: 217-244-7877, E-mail: hughesro@illinois.edu. *Application contact:* Leann Topol, Clerk, 217-333-3869, Fax: 217-244-7877, E-mail: ltopol@illinois.edu.

University of Minnesota, Twin Cities Campus, Graduate School, College of Education and Human Development, Department of Organizational Leadership, Policy and Development, Program in Agricultural, Food and Environmental Education, Minneapolis, MN 55455-0213. Offers M Ed, MA, Ed D, PhD. *Students:* 4 full-time (3 women), 5 part-time (4 women). Average age 29. 1 applicant, 100% accepted, 1 enrolled. In 2009, 11 master's awarded. *Application contact:* Dr. Mary Trettin, Associate Dean, 612-625-6501, Fax: 612-626-1580, E-mail: trettin@umn.edu.

University of Missouri, Graduate School, College of Agriculture, Food and Natural Resources, Department of Agricultural Education, Columbia, MO 65211. Offers MS, PhD. *Faculty:* 6 full-time (1 woman). *Students:* 9 full-time (5 women), 21 part-time (12 women). Average age 31. 12 applicants, 83% accepted, 5 enrolled. In 2009, 3 master's, 1 doctorate awarded. *Degree requirements:* For doctorate, comprehensive exam, thesis/dissertation. *Entrance requirements:* For master's, minimum GPA of 3.0 for last 60 hours of undergraduate coursework; for doctorate, GRE (minimum score of 1000 verbal and comprehensive preferred), minimum GPA of 3.5 on prior graduate course work; minimum of 3 years full-time appropriate teaching or other professional experience; correspondence with one department faculty member in proposed area of concentration. Additional exam requirements/recommendations for international students: Required—TOEFL (minimum score 550 paper-based; 80 iBT). Application fee: $45 ($60 for international students). Electronic applications accepted. *Financial support:* Research assistantships with tuition reimbursements, teaching assistantships with tuition reimbursements available. *Unit head:* Dr. Rob Terry, Department Chair, E-mail: terryh@missouri.edu. *Application contact:* Dr. Rob Terry, Department Chair, E-mail: terryh@missouri.edu.

University of Missouri, Graduate School, College of Education, Department of Learning, Teaching and Curriculum, Columbia, MO 65211. Offers agricultural education (M Ed, PhD, Ed S); art education (M Ed, PhD, Ed S); business and office education (M Ed, PhD, Ed S); early childhood education (M Ed, PhD, Ed S); elementary education (M Ed, PhD, Ed S); English education (M Ed, PhD, Ed S); foreign language education (M Ed, PhD, Ed S); health education and promotion (M Ed, PhD); learning and instruction (M Ed); marketing education (M Ed, PhD, Ed S); mathematics education (M Ed, PhD, Ed S); music education (M Ed, PhD, Ed S); reading education (M Ed, PhD, Ed S); science education (M Ed, PhD, Ed S); social studies education (M Ed, PhD, Ed S); vocational education (M Ed, PhD, Ed S). Part-time programs available. Terminal master's awarded for partial completion of doctoral program. *Degree requirements:* For doctorate, thesis/dissertation. *Entrance requirements:* For master's and Ed S, GRE General Test or MAT, minimum GPA of 3.0; for doctorate, GRE General Test, minimum GPA of 3.0. Additional exam requirements/recommendations for international students: Required—TOEFL (minimum score 600 paper-based; 250 computer-based; 100 iBT). Electronic applications accepted.

University of Nebraska–Lincoln, Graduate College, College of Agricultural Sciences and Natural Resources, Department of Agricultural Leadership, Education and Communication, Lincoln, NE 68588. Offers distance education specialization (MS); leadership development (MS); leadership education (MS); nutrition outreach education specialization (MS); teaching and extension education specialization (MS). *Degree requirements:* For master's, thesis optional. *Entrance requirements:* For master's, resume. Additional exam requirements/recommendations

for international students: Required—TOEFL (minimum score 550 paper-based; 213 computer-based). Electronic applications accepted. *Faculty research:* Teaching and instruction, extension education, leadership and human resource development, international agricultural education.

University of Puerto Rico, Mayagüez Campus, Graduate Studies, College of Agricultural Sciences, Department of Agricultural Education, Mayagüez, PR 00681-9000. Offers agricultural education (MS); agricultural extension (MS). Part-time programs available. *Degree requirements:* For master's, comprehensive exam, thesis. *Entrance requirements:* For master's, BA in home economics; BS in agricultural education, agriculture, home economics, or equivalent. *Faculty research:* Curricular development and supervision, youth education, rural sociology.

The University of Tennessee, Graduate School, College of Agricultural Sciences and Natural Resources, Department of Agricultural Economics, Knoxville, TN 37996. Offers agricultural education (MS); agricultural extension education (MS). *Accreditation:* NCATE. Part-time programs available. Postbaccalaureate distance learning degree programs offered (minimal on-campus study). *Degree requirements:* For master's, thesis or alternative. *Entrance requirements:* For master's, minimum GPA of 2.7. Additional exam requirements/recommendations for international students: Required—TOEFL. Electronic applications accepted. *Expenses:* Tuition, state resident: full-time $6826; part-time $380 per semester hour. Tuition, nonresident: full-time $21,844; part-time $1147 per semester hour. Tuition and fees vary according to program.

University of Wisconsin–River Falls, Outreach and Graduate Studies, College of Agriculture, Food, and Environmental Sciences, Department of Agricultural Education, River Falls, WI 54022. Offers MS. Part-time programs available. *Degree requirements:* For master's, comprehensive exam, thesis (for some programs). *Entrance requirements:* For master's, minimum GPA of 2.75. Additional exam requirements/recommendations for international students: Required—TOEFL (minimum score 500 paper-based; 65 iBT), IELTS (minimum score 5.5). Electronic applications accepted.

Utah State University, School of Graduate Studies, College of Agriculture, Department of Agricultural Systems Technology and Education, Logan, UT 84322. Offers agricultural systems technology (MS), including agricultural extension education, agricultural mechanization, international agricultural extension, secondary and postsecondary agricultural education; family and consumer sciences education (MS). Part-time programs available. Postbaccalaureate distance learning degree programs offered (minimal on-campus study). *Degree requirements:* For master's, comprehensive exam (for some programs), thesis (for some programs). *Entrance requirements:* For master's, GRE General Test, MAT, BS in agricultural education, agricultural extension, or related agricultural or science discipline; minimum GPA of 3.0. Additional exam requirements/recommendations for international students: Required—TOEFL. *Faculty research:* Extension and adult education; structures and environment; low-input agriculture; farm safety, systems, and mechanizations.

Virginia Polytechnic Institute and State University, Graduate School, College of Agriculture and Life Sciences, Department of Agricultural Extension Education, Blacksburg, VA 24061. Offers MS, PhD. *Faculty:* 10 full-time (5 women). *Students:* 18 full-time (14 women), 2 part-time (1 woman); includes 2 minority (1 Asian American or Pacific Islander, 1 Hispanic American). Average age 33. 7 applicants, 57% accepted, 4 enrolled. In 2009, 1 master's awarded. *Entrance requirements:* For master's and doctorate, GRE, GMAT. Additional exam requirements/recommendations for international students: Required—TOEFL (minimum score 550 paper-based; 213 computer-based). *Application deadline:* For fall admission, 5/15 for international students; for spring admission, 10/15 for international students. Applications are processed on a rolling basis. Application fee: $65. Electronic applications accepted. *Expenses:* Tuition, area resident: Full-time $10,228; part-time $459 per credit hour. Tuition, nonresident: full-time $17,892; part-time $865 per credit hour. Required fees: $1966; $451 per semester. *Financial support:* In 2009–10, 1 research assistantship with full tuition reimbursement (averaging $14,068 per year), 1 teaching assistantship with full tuition reimbursement (averaging $26,748 per year) were awarded; career-related internships or fieldwork, Federal Work-Study, scholarships/grants, and unspecified assistantships also available. Financial award application deadline: 1/15. Total annual research expenditures: $567,456. *Unit head:* Dr. Rick D. Rudd, Dean, 540-231-6836, Fax: 540-231-5182, E-mail: rrudd@vt.edu. *Application contact:* Donna Moore, Information Contact, 540-231-5717, Fax: 540-231-3824, E-mail: mooredm@vt.edu.

West Virginia University, Davis College of Agriculture, Forestry and Consumer Sciences, Division of Resource Management and Sustainable Development, Program in Agricultural and Extension Education, Morgantown, WV 26506. Offers agricultural and extension education (MS, PhD); teaching vocational-agriculture (MS). *Accreditation:* NCATE. Part-time programs available. *Degree requirements:* For master's, thesis. *Entrance requirements:* For master's, GRE General Test, minimum GPA of 2.75. Additional exam requirements/recommendations for international students: Required—TOEFL. *Faculty research:* Program development in vocational agriculture, agricultural extension, supervised experience programs, leadership development.

Art Education

Adelphi University, School of Education, Program in Art Education, Garden City, NY 11530-0701. Offers MA. Part-time programs available. *Students:* 6 full-time (5 women), 21 part-time (20 women); includes 1 minority (Asian American or Pacific Islander). Average age 26. *Entrance requirements:* For master's, 2 letters of recommendation, visual arts portfolio. Additional exam requirements/recommendations for international students: Required—TOEFL (minimum score 550 paper-based; 213 computer-based; 80 iBT). *Application deadline:* For fall admission, 4/1 for international students; for spring admission, 11/1 for international students. Application fee: $50. Electronic applications accepted. *Expenses:* Tuition: Full-time $28,340; part-time $830 per credit. Required fees: $600; $250 per credit. Full-time tuition and fees vary according to course load and program. *Financial support:* Fellowships, research assistantships with partial tuition reimbursements, teaching assistantships, career-related internships or fieldwork, Federal Work-Study, institutionally sponsored loans, tuition waivers (full), and unspecified assistantships available. Support available to part-time students. Financial award application deadline: 2/15; financial award applicants required to submit FAFSA. *Unit head:* Perry E. Greene, Coordinator, 516-877-4041, E-mail: greene@adelphi.edu. *Application contact:* Christine Murphy, Director of Admissions, 516-877-3050, Fax: 516-877-3039, E-mail: graduateadmissions@adelphi.edu.

American University of Puerto Rico, Program in Education, Bayamón, PR 00960-2037. Offers art history (M Ed); elementary education (4-6) (M Ed); elementary education (k-3) (M Ed); general science education (M Ed); physical education (k-12) (M Ed); special education at secondary level (transition) (M Ed). *Faculty:* 1 full-time (0 women), 22 part-time/adjunct (6 women). *Students:* 121 full-time (98 women), 64 part-time (50 women); includes all Hispanic Americans. Average age 30. 250 applicants, 80% accepted, 185 enrolled. *Entrance requirements:* For master's, EXADEP or GRE or MAT, 2 letters of recommendation, minimum GPA of 2.5. *Application deadline:* For fall admission, 8/4 for domestic students; for winter admission, 10/18 for domestic students; for spring admission, 3/22 for domestic students. Applications are processed on a rolling basis. Application fee: $50. *Application contact:* Information Contact, E-mail: oficnaadmisiones@aupr.edu.

Anna Maria College, Graduate Division, Program in Visual Arts, Paxton, MA 01612. Offers art and visual art (MA); teacher of visual art (M Ed). Part-time and evening/weekend programs available. *Degree requirements:* For master's, thesis. *Entrance requirements:* For master's, minimum GPA of 2.7, undergraduate major in art, portfolio. Additional exam requirements/recommendations for international students: Required—TOEFL (minimum score 500 paper-based). Electronic applications accepted.

Arcadia University, Graduate Studies, Department of Education, Glenside, PA 19038-3295. Offers art education (M Ed, MA Ed); biology education (MA Ed); chemistry education (MA Ed); child development (CAS); computer education (M Ed, CAS); computer education 7–12 (MA Ed); early childhood education (M Ed, CAS), including individualized (M Ed), master teacher (M Ed), research in child development (M Ed); educational leadership (M Ed, CAS); educational psychology (CAS); elementary education (M Ed, CAS); English education (MA Ed); environmental education (MA Ed, CAS); history education (MA Ed); language arts (M Ed, CAS); mathematics education (M Ed, MA Ed, CAS); music education (MA Ed); psychology (MA Ed); pupil personnel services (CAS); reading (M Ed, CAS); school library science (M Ed); science education (M Ed, CAS); secondary education (M Ed, CAS); special education (M Ed, Ed D, CAS); theater arts (MA Ed); written communication (MA Ed). *Accreditation:* NASAD. Part-time and evening/weekend programs available. Postbaccalaureate distance learning degree programs offered (minimal on-campus study). *Faculty:* 12 full-time (8 women), 38 part-time/adjunct (26 women). *Students:* 89 full-time (74 women), 622 part-time (487 women); includes 112 minority (94 African Americans, 9 Asian Americans or Pacific Islanders, 9 Hispanic Americans), 2 international. Average age 32. In 2009, 257 master's, 4 doctorates awarded. *Application deadline:* Applications are processed on a rolling basis. Application fee: $40. Electronic applications accepted. *Expenses:* Tuition: Full-time $30,450; part-time $620 per credit hour. Required fees: $165. Tuition and fees vary according to program. *Financial support:* Career-related internships or fieldwork, tuition waivers (partial), and unspecified assistantships available. *Unit head:* Dr. Steven P. Gulkus. *Application contact:* 215-572-2925, Fax: 215-572-2126, E-mail: grad@arcadia.edu.

Art Academy of Cincinnati, Program in Art Education, Cincinnati, OH 45202. Offers MAAE. Offered during summer only. *Accreditation:* NASAD. Part-time programs available. *Degree requirements:* For master's, thesis, portfolio/exhibit. *Entrance requirements:* For master's, 2 letters of recommendation, portfolio, state teaching license. Additional exam requirements/recommendations for international students: Required—TOEFL (minimum score 550 paper-based; 213 computer-based; 80 iBT). Electronic applications accepted.

Austin College, Program in Education, Sherman, TX 75090-4400. Offers art education (MA); elementary education (MA); middle school education (MA); music education (MA); physical education and coaching (MA); secondary education (MA); theatre education (MA). Part-time programs available. *Faculty:* 5 full-time (3 women), 1 (woman) part-time/adjunct. *Students:* 29 full-time (21 women); includes 3 minority (1 Asian American or Pacific Islander, 2 Hispanic Americans). Average age 23. In 2009, 23 master's awarded. *Degree requirements:* For master's, one foreign language, thesis or alternative. *Entrance requirements:* For master's, Texas Academic Skills Program Test. *Application deadline:* For fall admission, 5/1 priority date for domestic students; for spring admission, 1/15 priority date for domestic students. Applications are processed on a rolling basis. Application fee: $35. Electronic applications accepted. *Expenses:* Tuition: Full-time $31,575. Required fees: $160. *Financial support:* Career-related internships or fieldwork, Federal Work-Study, scholarships/grants, and unspecified assistantships available. Support available to part-time students. Financial award application deadline: 4/1; financial award applicants required to submit FAFSA. *Unit head:* Dr. Barbara Sylvester, Director of Teaching Program, 903-813-2327, Fax: 903-813-2326, E-mail: bsylvester@austincollege.edu. *Application contact:* Dr. Barbara Sylvester, Director of Teaching Program, 903-813-2327, Fax: 903-813-2326, E-mail: bsylvester@austincollege.edu.

Averett University, Master in Education Program, Danville, VA 24541-3692. Offers art education (M Ed); biology (M Ed); biology education (M Ed); chemistry (M Ed); chemistry education (M Ed); curriculum and instruction (M Ed); elementary education (M Ed); English (M Ed); English education (M Ed); health and physical education (M Ed); history and social studies education (M Ed); math (M Ed); mathematics education (M Ed); physical science (M Ed); reading specialization (M Ed); special education (learning disabilities specialization PK-12) (M Ed). Program also offered at Richmond, VA regional campus location. Part-time and evening/weekend programs available. *Faculty:* 4 full-time (3 women), 36 part-time/adjunct (22 women). *Students:* 182 full-time (160 women), 110 part-time (94 women); includes 113 minority (94 African Americans, 1 American Indian/Alaska Native, 7 Asian Americans or Pacific Islanders, 11 Hispanic Americans). Average age 37. 119 applicants, 99% accepted, 98 enrolled. In 2009, 92 master's awarded. *Degree requirements:* For master's, comprehensive exam, thesis optional. *Entrance requirements:* For master's, PRAXIS, GRE General Test, MAT or NTE, writing proficiency exam, 3 letters of recommendation, current teacher's licensure or eligibility for licensure, minimum undergraduate GPA of 3.0 in previous 2 years. Additional exam requirements/recommendations for international students: Required—TOEFL (minimum score 600 paper-based; 200 computer-based). *Application deadline:* Applications are processed on a rolling basis. *Expenses:* Contact institution. *Financial support:* Career-related internships or fieldwork, Federal Work-Study, and scholarships/grants available. Financial award application deadline: 4/1; financial award applicants required to submit FAFSA. *Faculty research:* Literary assessment-PreK-6, handwriting instruction and assessment-PreK-6, written language instruction and assessment-PreK-6 and special needs students learning styles, curriculum and instruction processes. *Unit head:* Dr. Lynn H. Wolf, Chair/Associate Professor/Director, 434-793-3995, Fax: 434-791-4392, E-mail: lynn.wolf@averett.edu. *Application contact:* Dr. Lynn H. Wolf, Chair/Associate Professor/Director, 434-793-3995, Fax: 434-791-4392, E-mail: lynn.wolf@averett.edu.

Ball State University, Graduate School, College of Fine Arts, Department of Art, Muncie, IN 47306-1099. Offers art (MA); art education (MA, MAE). *Accreditation:* NASAD.

Bennington College, Graduate Programs, MA in Teaching Program, Bennington, VT 05201. Offers art education (MAT); early childhood (MAT); elementary education (MAT); English education (MAT); foreign language education (MAT); k-12 education (MAT); mathematics education (MAT); music education (MAT); science education (MAT); secondary education (MAT); social studies education (MAT); theater arts (MAT). *Faculty:* 5 part-time/adjunct (3 women). *Students:* 8 full-time (5 women), 1 part-time (0 women). Average age 28. 11 applicants, 27% accepted, 1 enrolled. In 2009, 4 master's awarded. *Degree requirements:* For master's, comprehensive exam, 1 year teaching practicum, professional portfolio. *Entrance requirements:* For master's, interview. *Application deadline:* For fall admission, 3/1 for domestic students. Application fee: $60. *Expenses:* Contact institution. *Financial support:* In 2009–10, 6 students received support, including 4 fellowships (averaging $10,475 per year); scholarships/grants and unspecified assistantships also available. Financial award application deadline: 4/1; financial award applicants required to submit FAFSA. *Unit head:* Carol Meyer, Director of Programs in Teacher Education, 802-440-4375, E-mail: cmeyer@bennington.edu. *Application contact:* Nancy Pearlman, Assistant Director of Programs in Teacher Education, 802-440-4710, Fax: 802-440-4383, E-mail: npearlman@bennington.edu.

Boise State University, Graduate College, College of Arts and Sciences, Department of Art, Program in Art Education, Boise, ID 83725-0399. Offers MA. *Accreditation:* NASAD; NCATE. Part-time programs available. *Degree requirements:* For master's, thesis optional. *Entrance requirements:* For master's, minimum GPA of 3.0, portfolio. Additional exam requirements/recommendations for international students: Required—TOEFL (minimum score 587 paper-

Art Education

Boise State University (continued)

based; 240 computer-based). Electronic applications accepted. *Expenses:* Tuition, state resident: full-time $3106; part-time $209 per credit. Tuition, nonresident: part-time $284 per credit.

Boston University, College of Fine Arts, School of Visual Arts, Program in Art Education, Boston, MA 02215. Offers MA. *Students:* 15 full-time (12 women), 1 part-time (0 women), 1 international. Average age 30. 10 applicants, 50% accepted, 4 enrolled. In 2009, 7 master's awarded. *Entrance requirements:* For master's, portfolio. Additional exam requirements/recommendations for international students: Required—TOEFL. *Application deadline:* For fall admission, 2/15 priority date for domestic students, 2/1 for international students. Applications are processed on a rolling basis. Application fee: $65. *Expenses:* Tuition: Full-time $37,910; part-time $1184 per credit hour. Required fees: $386; $40 per semester. Part-time tuition and fees vary according to class time, course level, degree level and program. *Financial support:* Fellowships, teaching assistantships available. Financial award application deadline: 2/15. *Unit head:* Barry Shauck, Assistant Professor, 617-353-3371, E-mail: bshauck@bu.edu. *Application contact:* Mark Krone, Manager, Graduate Admissions, 617-353-3350, E-mail: arts@bu.edu.

Boston University, College of Fine Arts, School of Visual Arts, Program in Studio Teaching, Boston, MA 02215. Offers MA. *Students:* 8 full-time (6 women), 1 (woman) part-time. Average age 28. 19 applicants, 84% accepted, 9 enrolled. *Entrance requirements:* For master's, portfolio. Additional exam requirements/recommendations for international students: Required—TOEFL. *Application deadline:* For fall admission, 2/15 priority date for domestic and international students. Applications are processed on a rolling basis. Application fee: $70. *Expenses:* Tuition: Full-time $37,910; part-time $1184 per credit hour. Required fees: $386; $40 per semester. Part-time tuition and fees vary according to class time, course level, degree level and program. *Financial support:* Fellowships, teaching assistantships available. Financial award application deadline: 2/15. *Unit head:* Barry Shauck, Assistant Professor, 617-353-3371, E-mail: bshauck@bu.edu. *Application contact:* Mark Krone, Manager, Graduate Admissions, 617-353-3350, E-mail: arts@bu.edu.

Bowling Green State University, Graduate College, College of Arts and Sciences, School of Art, Bowling Green, OH 43403. Offers 2-D studio art (MA, MFA); 3-D studio art (MA, MFA); art education (MA); art history (MA); computer art (MA); design (MFA); digital arts (MFA); graphics (MFA). *Accreditation:* NASAD. Part-time programs available. *Degree requirements:* For master's, thesis or alternative, final exhibit (MFA). *Entrance requirements:* For master's, GRE General Test (MA), slide portfolio (15-20 slides). Additional exam requirements/recommendations for international students: Required—TOEFL. Electronic applications accepted. *Faculty research:* Computer animation and virtual reality, Spanish still-life painting from 1600 to 1800, art and psychotherapy, Japanese wood-firing techniques in ceramics, non-toxic printmaking technologies.

Bridgewater State University, School of Graduate Studies, School of Arts and Sciences, Department of Art, Bridgewater, MA 02325-0001. Offers MAT. Part-time and evening/weekend programs available. *Degree requirements:* For master's, comprehensive exam. *Entrance requirements:* For master's, GRE General Test.

Brigham Young University, Graduate Studies, College of Fine Arts and Communications, Department of Visual Arts, Provo, UT 84602-6414. Offers art education (MA); art history (MA); studio art (MFA). Art education applications accepted biennially. *Accreditation:* NASAD. *Faculty:* 24 full-time (7 women), 2 part-time/adjunct (1 woman). *Students:* 33 full-time (22 women); includes 4 minority (all Asian Americans or Pacific Islanders). Average age 26. 32 applicants, 38% accepted, 11 enrolled. In 2009, 9 master's awarded. *Degree requirements:* For master's, one foreign language, thesis (art history), selected project (MFA), curriculum project (art education). *Entrance requirements:* For master's, GRE (art history), minimum GPA of 3.0 (MFA, MA in art education), 3.3 (MA in art history), portfolio in slide form (MFA), writing samples (MA in art education, art history). Additional exam requirements/recommendations for international students: Required—TOEFL (minimum score 500 paper-based). *Application deadline:* For fall admission, 2/1 for domestic and international students. Application fee: $50. Electronic applications accepted. *Expenses:* Tuition: Full-time $5580; part-time $301 per credit hour. Tuition and fees vary according to student's religious affiliation. *Financial support:* In 2009–10, 27 students received support; research assistantships, teaching assistantships with partial tuition reimbursements available, scholarships/grants and tuition waivers (partial) available. Financial award application deadline: 2/1. *Faculty research:* Methodology-standards-assessment, medieval architecture, classical/Islamic eighteenth and nineteenth century art, Netherlandish art, contemporary art. Total annual research expenditures: $83,932. *Unit head:* Prof. Linda A. Reynolds, Chair, 801-422-4429, Fax: 801-422-0695, E-mail: sullivan@byu.edu. *Application contact:* Sharon Lyn Heelis, Secretary, 801-422-4429, Fax: 801-422-0695, E-mail: sharon_heelis@byu.edu.

Brooklyn College of the City University of New York, Division of Graduate Studies, School of Education, Program in Adolescence Education and Special Subjects, Brooklyn, NY 11210-2889. Offers adolescence science education (MAT); art teacher (MA); biology teacher (MA); chemistry teacher (MA); earth science teacher (MAT); English teacher (MA); French teacher (MA); health and nutrition sciences: health teacher (MS Ed); mathematics teacher (MA); music education (CAS); music teacher (MA); physical education teacher (MS Ed); physics teacher (MA); social studies teacher (MA); Spanish teacher (MA). Part-time and evening/weekend programs available. *Students:* 23 full-time (15 women), 449 part-time (256 women); includes 147 minority (96 African Americans, 1 American Indian/Alaska Native, 18 Asian Americans or Pacific Islanders, 32 Hispanic Americans), 12 international. Average age 30. 251 applicants, 80% accepted, 141 enrolled. In 2009, 163 master's, 2 other advanced degrees awarded. *Degree requirements:* For master's, comprehensive exam (for some programs), thesis (for some programs). *Entrance requirements:* For master's, LAST, previous course work in education, resume, 2 letters of recommendation, essay. Additional exam requirements/recommendations for international students: Required—TOEFL (minimum score 500 paper-based; 173 computer-based; 61 iBT). *Application deadline:* For fall admission, 7/15 for domestic students, 7/1 for international students; for spring admission, 11/15 for domestic students, 10/1 for international students. Applications are processed on a rolling basis. Application fee: $125. Electronic applications accepted. *Expenses:* Tuition, state resident: full-time $7360; part-time $310 per credit hour. Tuition, nonresident: full-time $13,800; part-time $575 per credit hour. Required fees: $140.10 per semester. *Financial support:* Career-related internships or fieldwork, Federal Work-Study, institutionally sponsored loans, and scholarships/grants available. Support available to part-time students. Financial award application deadline: 5/1; financial award applicants required to submit FAFSA. *Faculty research:* Interdisciplinary education, semiotics, discourse analysis, autobiography, teacher identity. *Unit head:* Prof. Stephen Phillips, Program Head, 718-951-5214, E-mail: phillips@brooklyn.cuny.edu. *Application contact:* Herman Sierra, Graduate Admissions Coordinator, 718-951-4536, Fax: 718-951-4506, E-mail: grads@brooklyn.cuny.edu.

Buffalo State College, State University of New York, The Graduate School, Faculty of Arts and Humanities, Department of Art Education, Buffalo, NY 14222-1095. Offers MS Ed. *Accreditation:* NASAD; NCATE. Part-time and evening/weekend programs available. *Degree requirements:* For master's, thesis or alternative, project. *Entrance requirements:* For master's, New York teaching certificate, interview, minimum GPA of 3.0. Additional exam requirements/recommendations for international students: Required—TOEFL (minimum score 550 paper-based; 213 computer-based).

California State University, Long Beach, Graduate Studies, College of the Arts, Department of Art, Long Beach, CA 90840. Offers art education (MA); art history (MA); studio art (MA, MFA). *Accreditation:* NASAD. Part-time programs available. *Faculty:* 81 full-time (49 women), 1 (woman) part-time/adjunct. *Students:* 84 full-time (54 women), 44 part-time (31 women); includes 35 minority (2 American Indian/Alaska Native, 16 Asian Americans or Pacific Islanders, 17 Hispanic Americans), 5 international. Average age 34. 183 applicants, 37% accepted, 43 enrolled. *Degree requirements:* For master's, thesis (for some programs). *Entrance requirements:* For master's, minimum GPA of 3.0 in last 60 hours. *Application deadline:* For fall admission, 7/1 for domestic students; for spring admission, 12/1 for domestic students. Applications are processed on a rolling basis. Application fee: $55. Electronic applications accepted. *Expenses:* Required fees: $1802 per semester. Part-time tuition and fees vary according to course load. *Financial support:* Federal Work-Study, institutionally sponsored loans, and scholarships/grants available. Financial award application deadline: 3/2. *Unit head:* Prof. David Hadlock, Chair, 562-985-7908, Fax: 562-985-1650, E-mail: dhadlock@csulb.edu. *Application contact:* Margaret Black, Graduate Advisor, 562-985-7910, Fax: 562-985-1650.

California State University, Los Angeles, Graduate Studies, College of Arts and Letters, Department of Art, Los Angeles, CA 90032-8530. Offers art (MA), including art education, art history, art therapy, ceramics, metals, and textiles, design (MA, MFA), painting, sculpture, and graphic arts, photography; fine arts (MFA), including crafts, design (MA, MFA), studio arts. *Accreditation:* NASAD (one or more programs are accredited). Part-time and evening/weekend programs available. *Faculty:* 12 full-time (6 women), 1 part-time/adjunct (0 women). *Students:* 28 full-time (21 women), 40 part-time (28 women); includes 22 minority (1 African American, 6 Asian Americans or Pacific Islanders, 15 Hispanic Americans), 9 international. Average age 37. 30 applicants, 100% accepted, 12 enrolled. In 2009, 17 master's awarded. *Degree requirements:* For master's, comprehensive exam, project or thesis. *Entrance requirements:* For master's, portfolio. Additional exam requirements/recommendations for international students: Required—TOEFL (minimum score 500 paper-based; 173 computer-based). *Application deadline:* For fall admission, 5/1 for domestic and international students. Applications are processed on a rolling basis. Application fee: $55. Electronic applications accepted. *Financial support:* Federal Work-Study available. Support available to part-time students. Financial award application deadline: 3/1. *Faculty research:* The artist and the book, conceptual art, ceramic processes, computer graphics, architectural graphics. *Unit head:* Dr. Abbas Daneshvari, Chair, 323-343-4010, Fax: 323-343-4045, E-mail: adanesh@calstatela.edu. *Application contact:* Dr. Cheryl L. Ney, Associate Vice President for Academic Affairs and Dean of Graduate Studies, 323-343-3820, Fax: 323-343-5653, E-mail: cney@cslanet.calstatela.edu.

California State University, Northridge, Graduate Studies, College of Arts, Media, and Communication, Department of Art, Northridge, CA 91330. Offers art education (MA); art history (MA); studio art (MA, MFA); visual communications (MA, MFA). *Accreditation:* NASAD. *Faculty:* 22 full-time (12 women), 42 part-time/adjunct (16 women). *Students:* 27 full-time (21 women), 29 part-time (23 women); includes 14 minority (2 African Americans, 1 American Indian/Alaska Native, 6 Asian Americans or Pacific Islanders, 5 Hispanic Americans), 3 international. Average age 35. 84 applicants, 29% accepted, 14 enrolled. In 2009, 29 master's awarded. *Application deadline:* For fall admission, 11/30 for domestic students. Application fee: $55. *Financial support:* Application deadline: 3/1. *Unit head:* Prof. Edward Alfano, Chair, 818-677-2242, E-mail: art.dept@csun.edu. *Application contact:* Prof. Edward Alfano, Chair, 818-677-2242, E-mail: art.dept@csun.edu.

Cape Breton University, School of Education, Health, and Wellness, Sydney, NS B1P 6L2, Canada. Offers educational counseling (Diploma); educational curriculum (Diploma); educational studies in arts education (Certificate); educational technology (Diploma). Part-time and evening/weekend programs available. Postbaccalaureate distance learning degree programs offered (no on-campus study). *Faculty:* 15 part-time/adjunct (5 women). *Students:* 171 part-time (103 women). Average age 30. *Application deadline:* For fall admission, 8/1 priority date for domestic students. Applications are processed on a rolling basis. Application fee: $50. Electronic applications accepted. *Unit head:* Susan Basso, Coordinator of the Education Program, 902-563-1651, Fax: 902-563-1861. *Application contact:* Terry MacDonald, Coordinator, Teacher Education Program, 902-563-1647, Fax: 902-563-1449, E-mail: terry_macdonald@cbu.ca.

Carlow University, School of Education, Program in Art Education, Pittsburgh, PA 15213-3165. Offers M Ed. Part-time and evening/weekend programs available. *Degree requirements:* For master's, thesis or alternative. *Entrance requirements:* Additional exam requirements/recommendations for international students: Required—TOEFL (minimum score 550 paper-based; 213 computer-based). Electronic applications accepted. *Expenses:* Tuition: Full-time $11,250; part-time $625 per credit. Tuition and fees vary according to course load, degree level and program.

Carthage College, Division of Teacher Education, Kenosha, WI 53140. Offers classroom guidance and counseling (M Ed); creative arts (M Ed); gifted and talented children (M Ed); language arts (M Ed); modern language (M Ed); natural sciences (M Ed); reading (M Ed, Certificate); social sciences (M Ed); teacher leadership (M Ed). Part-time and evening/weekend programs available. *Degree requirements:* For master's, thesis optional. *Entrance requirements:* For master's, MAT, minimum B average, letters of reference.

Case Western Reserve University, School of Graduate Studies, Department of Art History and Art, Program in Art Education, Cleveland, OH 44106. Offers MA. *Accreditation:* Teacher Education Accreditation Council. Part-time programs available. *Faculty:* 12 part-time/adjunct (7 women). *Students:* 7 full-time (5 women), 1 (woman) part-time; includes 1 minority (African American). Average age 32. 14 applicants, 71% accepted, 4 enrolled. In 2009, 5 master's awarded. *Degree requirements:* For master's, thesis, art exhibit. *Entrance requirements:* For master's, NTE, interview, portfolio. Additional exam requirements/recommendations for international students: Required—TOEFL (minimum score 550 paper-based; 213 computer-based; 79 iBT). *Application deadline:* For fall admission, 3/11 for domestic students; for spring admission, 11/1 for domestic students. Applications are processed on a rolling basis. Application fee: $50. Electronic applications accepted. *Faculty research:* Visual and aesthetic education, ethnographic arts, multiculturalism. *Unit head:* Tim Shuckerow, Director, 216-368-2714, Fax: 216-368-2715, E-mail: txs10@po.cwru.edu. *Application contact:* Debby Tenenbaum, Assistant, 216-368-4118, Fax: 216-368-4681, E-mail: deborah.tenenbaum@case.edu.

Central Connecticut State University, School of Graduate Studies, School of Arts and Sciences, Department of Art, New Britain, CT 06050-4010. Offers art education (MS, Certificate). Part-time and evening/weekend programs available. *Faculty:* 13 full-time (5 women), 13 part-time/adjunct (7 women). *Students:* 15 full-time (11 women), 16 part-time (13 women); includes 1 minority (African American). Average age 31. 34 applicants, 53% accepted, 13 enrolled. In 2009, 6 master's, 8 other advanced degrees awarded. *Degree requirements:* For master's, thesis or alternative, exhibit or special project; for Certificate, qualifying exam. *Entrance requirements:* For master's, portfolio. Additional exam requirements/recommendations for international students: Required—TOEFL. *Application deadline:* For fall admission, 7/1 for domestic students; for spring admission, 12/1 for domestic students. Applications are processed on a rolling basis. Application fee: $50. Electronic applications accepted. *Expenses:* Tuition, area resident: Full-time $4662; part-time $440 per credit. Tuition, state resident: full-time $6994; part-time $440 per credit. Tuition, nonresident: full-time $12,988; part-time $440 per credit. Required fees: $3606. One-time fee: $62 part-time. *Financial support:* In 2009–10, 6 students received support, including 3 research assistantships; career-related internships or fieldwork, Federal Work-Study, scholarships/grants, and unspecified assistantships also available. Support available to part-time students. Financial award application deadline: 3/1; financial award applicants required to submit FAFSA. *Faculty research:* Visual arts. *Unit head:* Dr. Cora Marshall, Chair, 860-832-2620. *Application contact:* Dr. Cora Marshall, Chair, 860-832-2620.

Chatham University, Program in Education, Pittsburgh, PA 15232-2826. Offers early childhood education (MAT); elementary education (MAT); English—secondary (MAT); environmental education (K-12) (MAT); secondary art (MAT); secondary biology education (MAT); secondary chemistry education (MAT); secondary English education (MAT); secondary math education (MAT); secondary physics education (MAT); secondary social studies education (MAT); special education (MAT). *Students:* 52 full-time (41 women), 20 part-time (16 women). Average age 30. 39 applicants, 79% accepted, 26 enrolled. In 2009, 37 master's awarded. *Degree requirements:* For master's, thesis, teaching experience. *Entrance requirements:* For master's, PRAXIS I, minimum GPA of 3.0, sample of written work, recommendation letters. Additional exam requirements/recommendations for international students: Required—TOEFL (minimum score 600 paper-based; 250 computer-based; 100 iBT), IELTS (minimum score 6.5), TWE. *Application deadline:* For fall admission, 5/1 priority date for domestic and international students; for spring admission, 10/15 priority date for domestic and international students. Applications are processed on a rolling basis. Application fee: $45. Electronic applications accepted.

Financial support: Career-related internships or fieldwork available. Financial award applicants required to submit FAFSA. *Faculty research:* Gifted education, environmental education, technology in education, writing as learning, class size and achievement. *Unit head:* Dr. Barbara Biglan, Interim Director, 412-365-1170, E-mail: biglan@chatham.edu. *Application contact:* Dory Perry, Associate Director of Graduate Admissions, 412-365-2758, Fax: 412-365-1609, E-mail: gradadmissions@chatham.edu.

Christopher Newport University, Graduate Studies, Department of Teacher Preparation, Newport News, VA 23606-2998. Offers art (PK-12) (MAT); biology (6-12) (MAT); computer science (6-12) (MAT); elementary (PK-6) (MAT); English (6-12) (MAT); French (PK-12) (MAT); history and social science (6-12) (MAT); mathematics (6-12) (MAT); music (PK-12) (MAT), including choral, instrumental; physics (6-12) (MAT); Spanish (PK-12) (MAT). Part-time and evening/weekend programs available. *Faculty:* 24 full-time (13 women), 4 part-time/adjunct (2 women). *Students:* 76 full-time (66 women), 12 part-time (10 women); includes 3 minority (2 African Americans, 1 Hispanic American). Average age 24. 3 applicants, 100% accepted, 2 enrolled. In 2009, 58 master's awarded. *Degree requirements:* For master's, comprehensive exam, thesis or alternative. *Entrance requirements:* For master's, PRAXIS I, minimum GPA of 3.0. Additional exam requirements/recommendations for international students: Required—TOEFL (minimum score 580 paper-based; 237 computer-based; 92 iBT). *Application deadline:* For fall admission, 8/15 for domestic students, 4/1 for international students; for spring admission, 10/15 for domestic students, 10/1 for international students. Applications are processed on a rolling basis. Application fee: $45. Electronic applications accepted. *Expenses:* Tuition, area resident: Part-time $384 per credit hour. Tuition, state resident: part-time $384 per credit hour. Tuition, nonresident: part-time $701 per credit hour. *Financial support:* In 2009–10, 3 research assistantships with full and partial tuition reimbursements (averaging $2,000 per year) were awarded; career-related internships or fieldwork, Federal Work-Study, and unspecified assistantships also available. Support available to part-time students. Financial award application deadline: 3/1; financial award applicants required to submit FAFSA. *Faculty research:* Early literacy development, instructional innovations, professional teaching standards, multicultural issues, aesthetic education. *Unit head:* Dr. Marsha Sprague, Director, 757-594-7388, Fax: 757-594-7803, E-mail: msprague@cnu.edu. *Application contact:* Lyn Sawyer, Associate Director, Graduate Admissions, 757-594-7544, Fax: 757-594-7649, E-mail: gradstdy@cnu.edu.

Cleveland State University, College of Graduate Studies, College of Education and Human Services, Department of Teacher Education, Cleveland, OH 44115. Offers art education (M Ed); early childhood education (M Ed); foreign language education (M Ed); mathematics and science education (M Ed); middle childhood education (M Ed); special education (M Ed), including mild/moderate disabilities, moderate/intensive disabilities; teaching English to speakers of other languages (M Ed). Part-time and evening/weekend programs available. *Degree requirements:* For master's, comprehensive exam (for some programs), thesis or alternative. *Entrance requirements:* For master's, GRE General Test or MAT, minimum GPA of 2.75. Additional exam requirements/recommendations for international students: Required—TOEFL (minimum score 525 paper-based; 197 computer-based), IELTS (minimum score 6). *Faculty research:* Early literacy, professional development in reading, reading recovery, dual language, induction programs.

Cleveland State University, College of Graduate Studies, College of Liberal Arts and Social Sciences, Department of Art, Cleveland, OH 44115. Offers art education (M Ed); art history (MA).

College of Mount St. Joseph, Graduate Education Program, Cincinnati, OH 45233-1670. Offers adolescent young adult education (MA); art (MA); inclusive early childhood education (MA); instructional leadership (MA); middle childhood education (MA); multi-age education (MA); multicultural special education (MA); music (MA); reading (MA). *Accreditation:* Teacher Education Accreditation Council. Part-time and evening/weekend programs available. *Faculty:* 15 full-time (11 women), 9 part-time/adjunct (6 women). *Students:* 93 full-time (75 women), 99 part-time (66 women); includes 19 minority (18 African Americans, 1 American Indian/Alaska Native). Average age 34. 116 applicants, 97% accepted, 94 enrolled. In 2009, 51 master's awarded. *Degree requirements:* For master's, research project, student teaching, clinical and field-based experiences. *Entrance requirements:* For master's, GRE, PRAXIS II in teaching content area (math or science), 2 letters of recommendation, interview, resume. Additional exam requirements/recommendations for international students: Required—TOEFL (minimum score 560 paper-based; 220 computer-based; 83 iBT). *Application deadline:* Applications are processed on a rolling basis. Application fee: $50. Electronic applications accepted. *Expenses:* Tuition: Part-time $500 per hour. Required fees: $200 per year. Tuition and fees vary according to degree level and program. *Financial support:* In 2009–10, 51 students received support. Scholarships/grants available. Financial award applicants required to submit FAFSA. *Faculty research:* Foreign and second language learning problems/reading disabilities/hyperlexia, multicultural/bilingual special education, alternative educator licensure, science education, pedagogical content knowledge. *Unit head:* Dr. Mary West, Chair of Graduate Education, 513-244-3263, Fax: 513-244-4867, E-mail: mary_west@mail.msj.edu. *Application contact:* Marilyn Hoskins, Assistant Director of Graduate Recruitment, 513-244-4723, Fax: 513-244-4629, E-mail: marilyn_hoskins@mail.msj.edu.

The College of New Rochelle, Graduate School, Division of Art and Communication Studies, Program in Art Education, New Rochelle, NY 10805-2308. Offers MA. Part-time and evening/weekend programs available. *Degree requirements:* For master's, thesis. *Entrance requirements:* For master's, interview, minimum GPA of 3.0 in field, 2.7 overall, portfolio, 36 credits of course work in studio art. *Faculty research:* Developmental stages in art, assessment and evaluation, curriculum development, multicultural education, art museum education.

The College of Saint Rose, Graduate Studies, School of Arts and Humanities, Center for Art and Design, Albany, NY 12203-1419. Offers art education (MS Ed, Certificate). *Accreditation:* NASAD; NCATE. Part-time and evening/weekend programs available. *Degree requirements:* For master's, final project. *Entrance requirements:* For master's, minimum undergraduate GPA of 3.0, art portfolio, undergraduate art degree; for Certificate, minimum undergraduate GPA of 3.0, slide portfolio. Additional exam requirements/recommendations for international students: Required—TOEFL (minimum score 550 paper-based; 213 computer-based). Electronic applications accepted.

The Colorado College, Department of Education, Program in Secondary Education, Colorado Springs, CO 80903-3294. Offers art teaching (K-12) (MAT); English teaching (MAT); foreign language teaching (MAT); mathematics teaching (MAT); music teaching (MAT); science teaching (MAT); social studies teaching (MAT). *Faculty:* 3 full-time (2 women), 8 part-time/adjunct (6 women). *Students:* 15 full-time (5 women); includes 2 minority (1 American Indian/Alaska Native, 1 Asian American or Pacific Islander). Average age 27. 26 applicants, 81% accepted, 15 enrolled. In 2009, 17 master's awarded. *Degree requirements:* For master's, thesis, internship. *Entrance requirements:* For master's, PRAXIS II or PLACE Exam. *Application deadline:* For fall admission, 12/1 priority date for domestic students, 12/1 for international students. Applications are processed on a rolling basis. Application fee: $50. *Expenses:* Tuition: Part-time $2545 per credit. *Financial support:* In 2009–10, 15 students received support, including 7 teaching assistantships (averaging $16,000 per year); career-related internships or fieldwork, institutionally sponsored loans, health care benefits, and tuition waivers (partial) also available. Financial award application deadline: 2/15; financial award applicants required to submit FAFSA. *Unit head:* Mike Taber, Director, 719-389-6026, Fax: 719-389-6473, E-mail: mike.taber@coloradocollege.edu. *Application contact:* Debra Yazulla Mortenson, Education Services Manager, 719-389-6472, Fax: 719-389-6473, E-mail: debra.mortenson@coloradocollege.edu.

Colorado State University–Pueblo, College of Education, Engineering and Professional Studies, Education Program, Pueblo, CO 81001-4901. Offers art education (M Ed); foreign language education (M Ed); health and physical education (M Ed); instructional technology (M Ed); linguistically diverse education (M Ed); music education (M Ed); special education (M Ed). *Accreditation:* Teacher Education Accreditation Council. Part-time programs available. *Degree requirements:* For master's, portfolio. *Entrance requirements:* For master's, 3 recommendations, teaching license. Additional exam requirements/recommendations for international students: Required—TOEFL (minimum score 500 paper-based; 173 computer-based). Electronic applications accepted. *Faculty research:* Portfolio assessment, math education, science education.

Columbus State University, Graduate Studies, College of the Arts, Program in Art Education, Columbus, GA 31907-5645. Offers M Ed. *Accreditation:* NASAD; NCATE. Part-time and evening/weekend programs available. *Faculty:* 1 (woman) full-time. *Students:* 2 full-time (1 woman), 3 part-time (2 women). Average age 39. 6 applicants, 83% accepted, 1 enrolled. In 2009, 3 master's awarded. *Degree requirements:* For master's, exhibit. *Entrance requirements:* For master's, GRE General Test, minimum GPA of 2.75. Additional exam requirements/recommendations for international students: Required—TOEFL (minimum score 550 paper-based; 213 computer-based; 79 iBT). *Application deadline:* For fall admission, 5/1 priority date for domestic students, 5/1 for international students; for spring admission, 11/1 for domestic and international students. Applications are processed on a rolling basis. Application fee: $30. Electronic applications accepted. *Financial support:* In 2009–10, 2 students received support; research assistantships, career-related internships or fieldwork, Federal Work-Study, institutionally sponsored loans, scholarships/grants, tuition waivers (partial), and unspecified assistantships available. Support available to part-time students. Financial award application deadline: 5/1; financial award applicants required to submit FAFSA. *Unit head:* Prof. Joe Sanders, Acting Chair, 706-507-8302, E-mail: wertz_orion@colstate.edu. *Application contact:* Katie Thornton, Graduate Admissions Specialist, 706-568-2035, Fax: 706-568-2462, E-mail: thornton_katie@colstate.edu.

Concordia University, School of Graduate Studies, Faculty of Fine Arts, Department of Art Education, Montréal, QC H3G 1M8, Canada. Offers art education (MA, PhD), including art in education (MA). *Degree requirements:* For master's, thesis (for some programs), practicum; for doctorate, comprehensive exam, thesis/dissertation. *Entrance requirements:* For master's, teaching experience; for doctorate, teaching or related professional experience. *Faculty research:* Vernacular culture, museum education, psychotic art, adults and families.

Concordia University Wisconsin, Graduate Programs, Department of Education, Mequon, WI 53097-2402. Offers art education (MS Ed); curriculum and instruction (MS Ed); early childhood (MS Ed); educational administration (MS Ed); environmental education (MS Ed); family studies (MS Ed); reading (MS Ed); school counseling (MS Ed); special education (MS Ed). Part-time and evening/weekend programs available. Postbaccalaureate distance learning degree programs offered (minimal on-campus study). *Degree requirements:* For master's, comprehensive exam, thesis or alternative. *Entrance requirements:* For master's, minimum GPA of 3.0, teaching license. Additional exam requirements/recommendations for international students: Required—TOEFL. *Faculty research:* Motivation, developmental learning, learning styles.

Converse College, School of Education and Graduate Studies, Spartanburg, SC 29302-0006. Offers art education (M Ed); early childhood education (MAT); education (Ed S), including administration and supervision, curriculum and instruction, marriage and family therapy; elementary education (M Ed, MAT); gifted education (M Ed); leadership (M Ed); liberal arts (MLA), including English (M Ed, MAT, MLA), history, political science; secondary education (M Ed, MAT), including biology (MAT), chemistry (MAT), English (M Ed, MAT, MLA), mathematics, natural sciences (M Ed), social sciences; special education (M Ed, MAT), including learning disabilities (MAT), mental disabilities (MAT), special education (M Ed). *Accreditation:* NCATE. Part-time and evening/weekend programs available. *Entrance requirements:* For master's, PRAXIS II (M Ed), minimum GPA of 2.75; for Ed S, GRE or MAT, minimum GPA of 3.0. Electronic applications accepted. *Faculty research:* Motivation, classroom management, predictors of success in classroom teaching, sex equity in public education, gifted research.

Corcoran College of Art and Design, Graduate Programs, Washington, DC 20006-4804. Offers art education (MAT); history of decorative arts (MA); interior design (MA). *Accreditation:* NASAD. Part-time programs available. *Entrance requirements:* Additional exam requirements/recommendations for international students: Required—TOEFL.

Delaware State University, Graduate Programs, College of Education, Program in Art Education, Dover, DE 19901-2277. Offers MA. *Entrance requirements:* Additional exam requirements/recommendations for international students: Required—TOEFL (minimum score 550 paper-based). Electronic applications accepted.

Eastern Illinois University, Graduate School, College of Arts and Humanities, Department of Art, Charleston, IL 61920-3099. Offers art (MA); art education (MA). *Accreditation:* NASAD. *Faculty:* 18 full-time (7 women). *Students:* 11 applicants, 64% accepted. In 2009, 7 master's awarded. *Degree requirements:* For master's, thesis or alternative, portfolio. *Application deadline:* For fall admission, 3/31 priority date for domestic students. Applications are processed on a rolling basis. Application fee: $30. *Expenses:* Tuition, state resident: full-time $9434; part-time $239 per credit hour. Tuition, nonresident: full-time $23,774; part-time $717 per credit hour. Required fees: $802.63. *Financial support:* In 2009–10, research assistantships with tuition reimbursements (averaging $7,200 per year), 6 teaching assistantships with tuition reimbursements (averaging $7,200 per year) were awarded. *Unit head:* Glenn Hild, Chairperson, 217-581-3410. *Application contact:* Chris Kahler, Coordinator, 217-581-6259, E-mail: cbkahler@eiu.edu.

Eastern Kentucky University, The Graduate School, College of Education, Department of Curriculum and Instruction, Program in Secondary and Higher Education, Richmond, KY 40475-3102. Offers secondary education (MA Ed), including agricultural education, art education, biological sciences education, business education, English education, geography education, history education, home economics education, industrial education, mathematical sciences education, physical education, school health education. *Accreditation:* NCATE. Part-time programs available. *Entrance requirements:* For master's, GRE General Test, minimum GPA of 2.5.

Eastern Michigan University, Graduate School, College of Arts and Sciences, Department of Art, Program in Art Education, Ypsilanti, MI 48197. Offers MA. Part-time and evening/weekend programs available. Postbaccalaureate distance learning degree programs offered (minimal on-campus study). *Students:* 4 part-time (all women). Average age 36. 2 applicants, 50% accepted, 1 enrolled. In 2009, 3 master's awarded. *Entrance requirements:* Additional exam requirements/recommendations for international students: Required—TOEFL. *Application deadline:* Applications are processed on a rolling basis. Tuition and fees vary according to course level. *Financial support:* Fellowships with tuition reimbursements, research assistantships with full tuition reimbursements, teaching assistantships with full tuition reimbursements, career-related internships or fieldwork, Federal Work-Study, institutionally sponsored loans, scholarships/grants, and unspecified assistantships available. Support available to part-time students. Financial award applicants required to submit FAFSA. *Unit head:* Prof. Christopher Bocklage, Graduate Coordinator, 734-487-1268, Fax: 734-487-2324, E-mail: christopher.bocklage@emich.edu. *Application contact:* Prof. Christopher Bocklage, Graduate Coordinator, 734-487-1268, Fax: 734-487-2324, E-mail: christopher.bocklage@emich.edu.

East Tennessee State University, School of Graduate Studies, College of Arts and Sciences, Department of Art and Design, Johnson City, TN 37614. Offers art education (MA); art history (MA); studio art (MA, MFA). *Accreditation:* NASAD. *Degree requirements:* For master's, thesis, exhibit, oral exam (MFA). *Entrance requirements:* For master's, GRE General Test, portfolio (MFA), bachelor's degree in art, minimum GPA of 3.0. Additional exam requirements/recommendations for international students: Required—TOEFL (minimum score 550 paper-based; 213 computer-based). *Faculty research:* History of sculpture, art and senior citizens, encaustic paintings, digital media in art history.

Endicott College, Van Loan School of Graduate and Professional Studies, Program in Arts and Learning, Beverly, MA 01915-2096. Offers M Ed. Part-time and evening/weekend programs available. Postbaccalaureate distance learning degree programs offered (minimal on-campus study). *Faculty:* 1 (woman) full-time, 8 part-time/adjunct (5 women). *Students:* 3 full-time (2 women), 19 part-time (17 women). Average age 38. 8 applicants, 100% accepted, 8 enrolled. In 2009, 5 master's awarded. *Degree requirements:* For master's, portfolio, written integrative

Art Education

Endicott College (continued)

paper, major presentation. *Entrance requirements:* For master's, MAT or GRE. Additional exam requirements/recommendations for international students: Required—TOEFL. *Application deadline:* Applications are processed on a rolling basis. Application fee: $50. *Expenses:* Contact institution. *Financial support:* Available to part-time students. *Faculty research:* Linkage of creative processes to effective teaching and learning. *Unit head:* Enid E. Larsen, Assistant Dean of Academic Programs, 978-232-2198, Fax: 978-232-3000, E-mail: elarsen@endicott.edu. *Application contact:* Enid E. Larsen, Assistant Dean of Academic Programs, 978-232-2198, Fax: 978-232-3000, E-mail: elarsen@endicott.edu.

Fitchburg State University, Division of Graduate and Continuing Education, Program in Arts Education, Fitchburg, MA 01420-2697. Offers arts education (M Ed); fine arts director (Certificate). *Accreditation:* NCATE. Part-time and evening/weekend programs available. *Students:* 1 (woman) full-time, 10 part-time (6 women); includes 1 African American. Average age 38. 3 applicants, 100% accepted, 2 enrolled. In 2009, 5 master's awarded. *Entrance requirements:* For master's, GRE General Test or MAT, letters of recommendation, resume. Additional exam requirements/recommendations for international students: Required—TOEFL (minimum score 550 paper-based; 213 computer-based; 79 iBT). *Application deadline:* Applications are processed on a rolling basis. Application fee: $25 ($50 for international students). *Expenses:* Tuition, area resident: Part-time $150 per credit. Tuition, state resident: part-time $150 per credit. Tuition, nonresident: part-time $150 per credit. Required fees: $120 per credit. *Financial support:* In 2009–10, research assistantships with partial tuition reimbursements (averaging $5,500 per year); Federal Work-Study, scholarships/grants, and unspecified assistantships also available. Support available to part-time students. Financial award application deadline: 3/1; financial award applicants required to submit FAFSA. *Unit head:* Dr. Harry Semerjian, Chair, 978-665-3279, Fax: 978-665-3658, E-mail: gce@fsc.edu. *Application contact:* Director of Admissions, 978-665-3144, Fax: 978-665-4540, E-mail: admissions@fsc.edu.

Florida Atlantic University, Dorothy F. Schmidt College of Arts and Letters, Department of Visual Arts and Art History, Boca Raton, FL 33431-0991. Offers art education (MAT); ceramics (MFA); computer art (MFA); graphic design (MFA); painting (MFA). *Faculty:* 23 full-time (12 women), 17 part-time/adjunct (11 women). *Students:* 15 full-time (11 women), 11 part-time (6 women); includes 7 minority (1 African American, 6 Hispanic Americans), 3 international. Average age 31. 19 applicants, 21% accepted, 0 enrolled. In 2009, 5 master's awarded. *Degree requirements:* For master's, one foreign language, project. *Entrance requirements:* For master's, GRE General Test, minimum GPA of 3.0 during last 60 hours of course work, slide portfolio. *Application deadline:* For fall admission, 2/21 for domestic and international students; for spring admission, 10/1 for domestic and international students. Application fee: $30. Electronic applications accepted. *Expenses:* Tuition, state resident: full-time $7055; part-time $293.94 per credit hour. Tuition, nonresident: full-time $22,096; part-time $920.66 per credit hour. *Financial support:* Research assistantships with full tuition reimbursements, teaching assistantships with full tuition reimbursements, career-related internships or fieldwork, Federal Work-Study, and institutionally sponsored loans available. Financial award applicants required to submit FAFSA. *Faculty research:* Painting, ceramics (traditional and non-traditional), installation, video and interactive sculpture. *Unit head:* Dr. Linda Johnson, Chair, 561-297-3870, Fax: 561-297-3078, E-mail: ljohnson@fau.edu. *Application contact:* James A. Novak, Associate Professor/Graduate Coordinator/Advisor, 561-297-2430, Fax: 561-297-3078, E-mail: jnovak@fau.edu.

Florida International University, College of Education, Department of Curriculum and Instruction, Program in Art Education, Miami, FL 33199. Offers MAT, MS, Ed D. *Accreditation:* NCATE. Part-time and evening/weekend programs available. *Entrance requirements:* Additional exam requirements/recommendations for international students: Required—TOEFL (minimum score 550 paper-based; 213 computer-based; 80 iBT), IELTS (minimum score 6.3). Electronic applications accepted. *Expenses:* Tuition, state resident: full-time $8008; part-time $4004 per year. Tuition, nonresident: full-time $20,104; part-time $10,052 per year. Required fees: $298; $149 per term. *Faculty research:* Elementary art, macramé, stained glass works, watercolors.

Florida State University, The Graduate School, College of Visual Arts, Theatre and Dance, Department of Art Education, Tallahassee, FL 32306. Offers MA, MS, Ed D, PhD, Ed S. *Accreditation:* NASAD (one or more programs are accredited). Part-time programs available. *Faculty:* 6 full-time (4 women), 5 part-time/adjunct (all women). *Students:* 66 full-time (60 women), 15 part-time (10 women); includes 27 minority (6 African Americans, 15 Asian Americans or Pacific Islanders, 6 Hispanic Americans). Average age 33. 73 applicants, 75% accepted, 32 enrolled. In 2009, 22 master's, 10 doctorates awarded. *Degree requirements:* For master's, thesis (for some programs); for doctorate, thesis/dissertation. *Entrance requirements:* For master's, GRE (1000 minimum), minimum GPA of 3.0 in last 2 years; for doctorate, GRE (1000 minimum), minimum GPA of 3.5. Additional exam requirements/recommendations for international students: Required—TOEFL (minimum score 550 paper-based; 213 computer-based; 80 iBT). *Application deadline:* For fall admission, 3/1 priority date for domestic and international students; for spring admission, 10/15 priority date for domestic and international students. Applications are processed on a rolling basis. Application fee: $30. Electronic applications accepted. *Expenses:* Tuition, state resident: full-time $7413. Tuition, nonresident: full-time $22,567. *Financial support:* In 2009–10, 27 students received support, including 20 research assistantships with full tuition reimbursements available (averaging $3,200 per year), 7 teaching assistantships with full tuition reimbursements available (averaging $8,500 per year); fellowships, career-related internships or fieldwork, Federal Work-Study, and scholarships/grants also available. Financial award applicants required to submit FAFSA. *Faculty research:* Teaching and learning in art, museum education, art therapy, arts administration, discipline-based art education. Total annual research expenditures: $110,000. *Unit head:* Dr. David E. Gussak, Chairman, 850-665-5663, Fax: 850-644-5067, E-mail: dgussak@fsu.edu. *Application contact:* Susan Messersmith, Academic Support Assistant, 850-644-5473, Fax: 850-644-6067, E-mail: smessersmith@fsu.edu.

George Mason University, College of Visual and Performing Arts, Program in Visual Technologies, Fairfax, VA 22030. Offers art and visual technology (MA, MFA); art education (MAT); graphic design (MA). *Faculty:* 21 full-time (11 women), 31 part-time/adjunct (18 women). *Students:* 20 full-time (14 women), 18 part-time (14 women); includes 6 minority (1 African American, 2 Asian Americans or Pacific Islanders, 3 Hispanic Americans), 1 international. Average age 32. 46 applicants, 48% accepted, 17 enrolled. In 2009, 10 master's awarded. *Degree requirements:* For master's, thesis, apprenticeship in business; dissertation or project. *Entrance requirements:* For master's, BA or BFA, portfolio, resume, 3 letters of reference. Additional exam requirements/recommendations for international students: Required—TOEFL. *Application deadline:* For fall admission, 1/15 for domestic students. Application fee: $75. Electronic applications accepted. *Expenses:* Tuition, state resident: full-time $7568; part-time $315.33 per credit hour. Tuition, nonresident: full-time $21,704; part-time $904.33 per credit hour. Required fees: $2184; $91 per credit hour. *Financial support:* Teaching assistantships, career-related internships or fieldwork, Federal Work-Study, unspecified assistantships, and health care benefits (full-time research or teaching assistantship recipients) available. Support available to part-time students. Financial award application deadline: 3/1; financial award applicants required to submit FAFSA. *Faculty research:* Digital arts, painting, photography, print-making, sculpture; combined art forms in in-disciplinary projects including installation, performance, publishing, time or writing based; combined creative and critical approaches. *Unit head:* Dr. Scott M. Martin, Director, 703-993-4574, Fax: 703-993-8995, E-mail: smartin4@gmu.edu. *Application contact:* Dr. Scott M. Martin, Director, 703-993-4574, Fax: 703-993-8995, E-mail: smartin4@gmu.edu.

Georgia Southern University, Jack N. Averitt College of Graduate Studies, College of Education, Department of Teaching and Learning, Program in Art Education, Statesboro, GA 30460. Offers M Ed, MAT. *Accreditation:* NASAD (one or more programs are accredited); NCATE (one or more programs are accredited). Part-time and evening/weekend programs available. *Students:* 2 full-time (both women), 3 part-time (all women). Average age 31. In 2009, 5 master's awarded. *Degree requirements:* For master's, transition point assessment.

Entrance requirements: For master's, GRE General Test or MAT, GACE Basic Skills and Content Assessments, minimum cumulative GPA of 2.5. Additional exam requirements/recommendations for international students: Required—TOEFL (minimum score 550 paper-based; 213 computer-based; 80 iBT). *Application deadline:* For fall admission, 3/1 priority date for domestic and international students; for spring admission, 10/1 priority date for domestic students, 10/1 for international students. Applications are processed on a rolling basis. Application fee: $50. Electronic applications accepted. *Expenses:* Tuition, state resident: full-time $5040; part-time $210 per credit hour. Tuition, nonresident: full-time $20,136; part-time $839 per credit hour. Required fees: $1644. *Financial support:* In 2009–10, 4 students received support, including research assistantships with partial tuition reimbursements available (averaging $7,200 per year), teaching assistantships with partial tuition reimbursements available (averaging $7,200 per year); career-related internships or fieldwork, Federal Work-Study, scholarships/grants, tuition waivers (partial), and unspecified assistantships also available. Support available to part-time students. Financial award application deadline: 4/15; financial award applicants required to submit FAFSA. *Unit head:* Ronnie Sheppard, Department Chair, 912-478-0198, Fax: 912-478-0026, E-mail: sheppard@georgiasouthern.edu. *Application contact:* Dr. Charles Ziglar, Coordinator for Graduate Student Recruitment, 912-478-5635, Fax: 912-478-0740, E-mail: gradadmissions@georgiasouthern.edu.

Georgia State University, College of Arts and Sciences, Ernest G. Welch School of Art and Design, Program in Art Education, Atlanta, GA 30302-3083. Offers MA Ed. *Accreditation:* NASAD. Part-time programs available. *Degree requirements:* For master's, thesis. *Entrance requirements:* For master's, GRE General Test or MAT, portfolio. Additional exam requirements/recommendations for international students: Required—TOEFL (minimum score 550 paper-based; 213 computer-based). Electronic applications accepted. *Faculty research:* Art–maturing adults, computer instruction in art, intercultural thematic art education.

Georgia State University, College of Education, Department of Middle-Secondary Education and Instructional Technology, Programs in Secondary Education, Atlanta, GA 30302-3083. Offers art education (Ed S); English education (M Ed, Ed S); mathematics education (M Ed, PhD, Ed S); music education (PhD); science education (M Ed, PhD, Ed S);* social studies education (M Ed, PhD, Ed S). *Accreditation:* NASM (one or more programs are accredited); NCATE. Part-time and evening/weekend programs available. *Degree requirements:* For master's, comprehensive exam; for doctorate, comprehensive exam, thesis/dissertation; for Ed S, project/exam. *Entrance requirements:* For master's, GRE General Test, minimum GPA of 2.5; for doctorate, GRE General Test or MAT, minimum GPA of 3.3; for Ed S, GRE General Test or MAT, minimum graduate GPA of 3.25. *Faculty research:* Women and science, problem solving in mathematics, dialects, economic education.

Harding University, College of Education, Searcy, AR 72149-0001. Offers advanced studies in teaching and learning (M Ed); art (MSE); behavioral science (MSE); counseling (MS, Ed S); early childhood special education (M Ed, MSE); education (MSE); educational leadership (M Ed, Ed S); elementary education (M Ed); English (MSE); family and consumer science (MSE); French (MSE); history/social science (MSE); kinesiology (MSE); math (MSE); physical science (MSE); reading (M Ed); secondary education (M Ed); Spanish (MSE); special education licensure (M Ed); teaching (MAT); teaching English as a second language (M Ed). *Accreditation:* NCATE. Part-time and evening/weekend programs available. *Faculty:* 11 full-time (4 women), 49 part-time/adjunct (26 women). *Students:* 104 full-time (85 women), 392 part-time (282 women); includes 77 minority (67 African Americans, 5 American Indian/Alaska Native, 1 Asian American or Pacific Islander, 4 Hispanic Americans), 5 international. Average age 36. 153 applicants, 92% accepted, 131 enrolled. In 2009, 153 master's, 6 other advanced degrees awarded. *Degree requirements:* For master's, comprehensive exam (for some programs), thesis optional, portfolio(s); for Ed S, comprehensive exam, portfolio, specialist project. *Entrance requirements:* For master's, GRE, MAT, PRAXIS; for Ed S, MAT or GRE. Additional exam requirements/recommendations for international students: Required—TOEFL (minimum score 550 paper-based; 79 iBT). *Application deadline:* For fall admission, 8/1 for domestic and international students; for spring admission, 1/1 for domestic and international students. Applications are processed on a rolling basis. Application fee: $35. *Expenses:* Tuition: Full-time $9720; part-time $540 per credit hour. Required fees: $22 per credit hour. Tuition and fees vary according to course load and program. *Financial support:* In 2009–10, 30 students received support. Unspecified assistantships available. *Faculty research:* Reading, comprehension, school violence, educational technology, behavior, college choice, differentiated instruction, brain-based teaching. *Unit head:* Dr. Clara Carroll, Chair, 501-279-4501, Fax: 501-279-4083, E-mail: ccarroll@harding.edu. *Application contact:* Information Contact, 501-279-4315, E-mail: gradstudiesedu@harding.edu.

Harvard University, Graduate School of Education, Master's Programs in Education, Cambridge, MA 02138. Offers arts in education (Ed M); education policy and management (Ed M); higher education (Ed M); human development and psychology (Ed M); international education policy (Ed M); language and literacy (Ed M); learning and teaching (Ed M); mid-career mathematics and science (teaching certificate) (Ed M); mind brain and education (Ed M); risk and prevention (Ed M); school leadership (Ed M); special studies (Ed M); teaching and curriculum (teaching certificate) (Ed M); technology innovation and education (Ed M). Part-time programs available. *Faculty:* 70 full-time (33 women), 36 part-time/adjunct (20 women). *Students:* 598 full-time (448 women), 76 part-time (60 women); includes 132 minority (40 African Americans, 2 American Indian/Alaska Native, 58 Asian Americans or Pacific Islanders, 32 Hispanic Americans), 103 international. Average age 28. 1,574 applicants, 58% accepted, 640 enrolled. In 2009, 556 master's awarded. *Entrance requirements:* For master's, GRE General Test, 3 letters of recommendation. Additional exam requirements/recommendations for international students: Required—TOEFL (minimum score 600 paper-based; 250 computer-based; 100 iBT), TWE (minimum score 5). *Application deadline:* For fall admission, 1/4 for domestic and international students. Application fee: $85. Electronic applications accepted. *Expenses:* Contact institution. *Financial support:* In 2009–10, 424 students received support, including 25 fellowships with full and partial tuition reimbursements available (averaging $15,890 per year); career-related internships or fieldwork, Federal Work-Study, institutionally sponsored loans, scholarships/grants, health care benefits, tuition waivers (full and partial), and unspecified assistantships also available. Support available to part-time students. Financial award application deadline: 2/1; financial award applicants required to submit FAFSA. *Faculty research:* Learning and development, educational leadership and organizations, educational policy analysis. Total annual research expenditures: $18.1 million. *Unit head:* Jennifer L. Petrallia, Assistant Dean, 617-495-8445. *Application contact:* Information Contact, 617-495-3414, Fax: 617-496-3577, E-mail: gseadmissions@harvard.edu.

Hofstra University, School of Education, Health, and Human Services, Department of Curriculum and Teaching, Program in Fine Arts Education, Hempstead, NY 11549. Offers MA, MS Ed. Part-time and evening/weekend programs available. *Students:* 27 full-time (25 women), 9 part-time (7 women); includes 1 minority (Hispanic American). Average age 29. 28 applicants, 89% accepted, 16 enrolled. In 2009, 10 master's awarded. *Degree requirements:* For master's, one foreign language, thesis or alternative, teaching portfolio. *Entrance requirements:* For master's, 2 letters of recommendation, portfolio, teacher certification (MA). Additional exam requirements/recommendations for international students: Required—TOEFL (minimum score 550 paper-based; 213 computer-based; 80 iBT). *Application deadline:* Applications are processed on a rolling basis. Application fee: $60. Electronic applications accepted. *Expenses:* Tuition: Full-time $16,200; part-time $900 per credit hour. Required fees: $970; $145 per term. Tuition and fees vary according to program. *Financial support:* In 2009–10, 24 students received support, including 3 fellowships with full and partial tuition reimbursements available (averaging $2,868 per year); research assistantships with full and partial tuition reimbursements available, Federal Work-Study, institutionally sponsored loans, scholarships/grants, tuition waivers (full and partial), and unspecified assistantships also available. Support available to part-time students. Financial award applicants required to submit FAFSA. *Faculty research:* Art education and interdisciplinary curricula, teacher/artist role in identity issues, early childhood art education, marginalization of the arts in education, gender issues. *Unit head:* Dr. Susan G. Zwirn, Program Director, 516-463-4976, Fax: 516-463-6196, E-mail: catsgz@hofstra.edu. *Application*

contact: Carol Drummer, Dean of Graduate Admissions, 516-463-4876, Fax: 516-463-4664, E-mail: gradstudent@hofstra.edu.

Hofstra University, School of Education, Health, and Human Services, Department of Curriculum and Teaching, Program in Learning and Teaching, Hempstead, NY 11549. Offers learning and teaching (Ed D), including applied linguistics, art education, arts and humanities, early childhood education, English education, human development, math education, math, science, and technology, multicultural education, physical education, science education, social studies education, special education. Part-time and evening/weekend programs available. *Students:* 5 full-time (all women), 21 part-time (17 women); includes 2 minority (1 African American, 1 Hispanic American), 1 international. Average age 38. 22 applicants, 68% accepted, 11 enrolled. *Degree requirements:* For doctorate, comprehensive exam, thesis/dissertation. *Entrance requirements:* For doctorate, GRE, 3 letters of recommendation, interview, 2 years full-time teaching experience. Additional exam requirements/recommendations for international students: Required—TOEFL (minimum score 550 paper-based; 213 computer-based; 80 iBT). *Application deadline:* Applications are processed on a rolling basis. Application fee: $60. Electronic applications accepted. *Expenses:* Tuition: Full-time $16,200; part-time $900 per credit hour. Required fees: $970; $145 per term. Tuition and fees vary according to program. *Financial support:* In 2009–10, 24 students received support, including 20 fellowships with full and partial tuition reimbursements available (averaging $4,906 per year); research assistantships with full and partial tuition reimbursements available, Federal Work-Study, institutionally sponsored loans, scholarships/grants, and tuition waivers (full and partial) also available. Support available to part-time students. Financial award applicants required to submit FAFSA. *Faculty research:* Critical thinking, professional development, teacher quality, quantitative research. *Unit head:* Dr. Bruce A. Torff, Director, 516-463-5803, Fax: 516-463-6196, E-mail: catajs@hofstra.edu. *Application contact:* Carol Drummer, Dean of Graduate Admissions, 516-463-4876, Fax: 516-463-4664, E-mail: gradstudent@hofstra.edu.

Indiana University Bloomington, School of Education, Department of Curriculum and Instruction, Bloomington, IN 47405-7000. Offers art education (MS, Ed D, PhD); curriculum studies (Ed D, PhD); elementary education (MS, Ed D, PhD, Ed S); mathematics education (MS, Ed D, PhD); science education (MS, Ed D, PhD); secondary education (MS, Ed D, PhD); social studies education (MS, PhD); special education (MS, Ed D, PhD, Ed S). *Accreditation:* NCATE. Part-time and evening/weekend programs available. *Students:* 208 full-time (155 women), 44 part-time (25 women); includes 28 minority (9 African Americans, 3 American Indian/Alaska Native, 9 Asian Americans or Pacific Islanders, 7 Hispanic Americans), 34 international. Average age 34. 100 applicants, 68% accepted, 39 enrolled. In 2009, 48 master's, 20 doctorates awarded. Terminal master's awarded for partial completion of doctoral program. *Degree requirements:* For doctorate, thesis/dissertation; for Ed S, comprehensive exam or project. *Entrance requirements:* For master's, doctorate, and Ed S, GRE General Test. *Application deadline:* For fall admission, 6/1 priority date for domestic students, 3/1 for international students; for winter admission, 11/1 priority date for domestic students; for spring admission, 9/1 for international students. Applications are processed on a rolling basis. Application fee: $55 ($65 for international students). Electronic applications accepted. *Financial support:* Fellowships with full and partial tuition reimbursements, research assistantships with full and partial tuition reimbursements, teaching assistantships with full and partial tuition reimbursements, career-related internships or fieldwork, Federal Work-Study, institutionally sponsored loans, and tuition waivers (partial) available. Support available to part-time students. *Unit head:* Cary Buzzelli, Chairperson, 812-856-8100. *Application contact:* Bobbie Partenheimer, Admissions Services Coordinator, 812-856-8127, Fax: 812-856-8333, E-mail: partenhe@indiana.edu.

Indiana University–Purdue University Indianapolis, Herron School of Art and Design, Indianapolis, IN 46202-2896. Offers art education (MAE); furniture design (MFA); printmaking (MFA); sculpture (MFA); visual communication (MFA). Part-time and evening/weekend programs available. *Faculty:* 2 full-time (both women). *Students:* 36 full-time (21 women), 11 part-time (all women); includes 6 minority (2 Asian Americans or Pacific Islanders, 4 Hispanic Americans), 6 international. Average age 31. 60 applicants, 60% accepted, 20 enrolled. In 2009, 1 master's awarded. *Entrance requirements:* For master's, portfolio, 44 hours of course work in art history and studio art. *Application deadline:* For fall admission, 6/1 priority date for domestic students, 3/15 priority date for international students; for spring admission, 11/1 priority date for domestic students, 10/15 priority date for international students. Applications are processed on a rolling basis. Application fee: $55 ($65 for international students). Electronic applications accepted. *Financial support:* Career-related internships or fieldwork, Federal Work-Study, institutionally sponsored loans, scholarships/grants, and tuition waivers (partial) available. Support available to part-time students. Total annual research expenditures: $6,097. *Unit head:* Valerie Eickmeier, Dean, 317-278-9470, Fax: 317-278-9471, E-mail: herron@iupui.edu. *Application contact:* Herron Student Services Office, 317-378-9400, E-mail: herrart@iupui.edu.

Indiana University South Bend, School of the Arts, South Bend, IN 46634-7111. Offers music (MM); studio teaching (MM). Part-time programs available. *Faculty:* 1 full-time (0 women). *Students:* 10 full-time (8 women), 2 part-time (1 woman); includes 1 minority (African American), 7 international. Average age 29. In 2009, 7 master's awarded. *Entrance requirements:* For master's, performance audition. *Application deadline:* For fall admission, 7/1 priority date for domestic students; for spring admission, 11/1 for domestic students. Applications are processed on a rolling basis. Application fee: $46 ($58 for international students). *Financial support:* In 2009–10, 4 fellowships (averaging $2,855 per year), 1 teaching assistantship (averaging $1,320 per year) were awarded; Federal Work-Study also available. Support available to part-time students. Financial award application deadline: 3/1; financial award applicants required to submit FAFSA. *Faculty research:* Orchestral conducting. *Unit head:* Dr. Thomas Miller, Dean, 574-520-4301, Fax: 574-520-4317, E-mail: messelst@iusb.edu. *Application contact:* Dr. Thomas Miller, Dean, 574-520-4301, Fax: 574-520-4317, E-mail: messelst@iusb.edu.

James Madison University, The Graduate School, College of Visual and Performing Arts, School of Art and Art History, Harrisonburg, VA 22807. Offers art education (MA); art history (MA); ceramics (MFA); drawing/painting (MFA); metal/jewelry (MFA); photography (MFA); printmaking (MFA); sculpture (MFA); studio art (MA); weaving/fibers (MFA). *Accreditation:* NASAD. Part-time programs available. *Faculty:* 11 full-time (6 women), 1 (woman) part-time/adjunct. *Students:* 10 full-time (8 women); includes 1 minority (African American). Average age 27. In 2009, 4 master's awarded. *Degree requirements:* For master's, thesis (for some programs). *Entrance requirements:* For master's, GRE General Test, language exam in French or German, portfolio, 3 letters of recommendation, research paper. Additional exam requirements/recommendations for international students: Required—TOEFL. *Application deadline:* For fall admission, 2/15 priority date for domestic students, 2/15 for international students; for spring admission, 10/15 priority date for domestic students, 10/15 for international students. Applications are processed on a rolling basis. Application fee: $55. Electronic applications accepted. *Expenses:* Tuition, area resident: Part-time $305 per credit hour. Tuition, state resident: part-time $305 per credit hour. Tuition, nonresident: part-time $890 per credit hour. *Financial support:* In 2009–10, 8 students received support, including 3 teaching assistantships with full tuition reimbursements available (averaging $8,664 per year); Federal Work-Study also available. Financial award application deadline: 3/1; financial award applicants required to submit FAFSA. *Unit head:* Leslie M. Bellavance, Academic Unit head, 540-568-6216. *Application contact:* Lynette M. Bible, Director of Graduate Admissions, 540-568-6395, Fax: 540-568-7860, E-mail: biblelm@jmu.edu.

Kean University, College of Visual and Performing Arts, Program in Fine Arts Education, Union, NJ 07083. Offers certification (MA); studio/research (MA); supervision (MA). *Accreditation:* NASAD. Part-time and evening/weekend programs available. *Faculty:* 14 full-time (5 women). *Students:* 13 full-time (9 women), 35 part-time (25 women); includes 4 minority (2 African Americans, 1 Asian American or Pacific Islander, 1 Hispanic American), 1 international. Average age 38. 19 applicants, 100% accepted, 11 enrolled. In 2009, 19 master's awarded. *Degree requirements:* For master's, thesis or alternative, exhibition, 3 years teaching experience (supervision), PRAXIS and fieldwork (certification). *Entrance requirements:* For master's, GRE General Test or MAT, portfolio, minimum GPA of 2.75, interview, 2 letters of recommendation,

official transcripts form all institutions attended. *Application deadline:* For fall admission, 5/1 for domestic students; for spring admission, 11/1 for domestic students. Application fee: $60 ($150 for international students). Electronic applications accepted. *Expenses:* Tuition, state resident: full-time $10,440; part-time $435 per credit. Tuition, nonresident: full-time $14,160; part-time $590 per credit. Required fees: $2642; $110 per credit. Part-time tuition and fees vary according to course load and degree level. *Financial support:* In 2009–10, 3 research assistantships with full tuition reimbursements (averaging $3,263 per year) were awarded; unspecified assistantships also available. *Unit head:* Dr. Joseph Amorino, Program Coordinator, 908-737-4403, E-mail: jamorino@kean.edu. *Application contact:* Steven Koch, Pre-Admissions Coordinator, 908-737-5924, Fax: 908-737-5965, E-mail: skoch@kean.edu.

Kent State University, College of the Arts, School of Art, Kent, OH 44242-0001. Offers art education (MA); art history (MA); crafts (MA, MFA), including ceramics (MA), glass, jewelry/metals, textiles/art; fine art (MA, MFA), including drawing/painting, printmaking, sculpture. *Accreditation:* NASAD (one or more programs are accredited). *Degree requirements:* For master's, one foreign language, thesis. *Entrance requirements:* For master's, undergraduate degree in proposed area of study (for fine arts and crafts programs); minimum overall GPA of 2.75 (3.0 for art major); 3 letters of recommendation; portfolio (15-20 slides for MA, 20-25 for MFA). Additional exam requirements/recommendations for international students: Required—TOEFL. Electronic applications accepted.

Kutztown University of Pennsylvania, College of Visual and Performing Arts, Program in Art Education, Kutztown, PA 19530-0730. Offers M Ed, Certificate. *Accreditation:* NASAD; NCATE. Part-time programs available. *Faculty:* 12 full-time (6 women). *Students:* 25 full-time (19 women), 57 part-time (46 women); includes 3 minority (1 African American, 1 Asian American or Pacific Islander, 1 Hispanic American). Average age 30. 45 applicants, 93% accepted, 18 enrolled. In 2009, 17 master's awarded. *Degree requirements:* For master's, comprehensive exam, thesis optional. *Entrance requirements:* For master's, GRE, teacher certification. Additional exam requirements/recommendations for international students: Required—TOEFL. *Application deadline:* For fall admission, 8/15 priority date for domestic and international students; for spring admission, 12/15 priority date for domestic and international students. Applications are processed on a rolling basis. Application fee: $35. Electronic applications accepted. *Expenses:* Tuition, state resident: full-time $6666; part-time $370 per credit. Tuition, nonresident: full-time $10,666; part-time $593 per credit. Required fees: $62 per credit. $60 per semester. *Financial support:* Career-related internships or fieldwork, Federal Work-Study, scholarships/grants, and unspecified assistantships available. Financial award application deadline: 3/1; financial award applicants required to submit FAFSA. *Faculty research:* Teaching of art history, child development in art, aesthetics and criticism curriculum, multicultural education, assessment in art. *Unit head:* Dr. John White, Chairperson, 610-683-4520, Fax: 610-683-4502, E-mail: white@kutztown.edu. *Application contact:* Kelly D. Burr, Associate Director, Graduate Admissions, 610-683-4200, Fax: 610-683-1393, E-mail: graduate@kutztown.edu.

Lesley University, Graduate School of Arts and Social Sciences, Cambridge, MA 02138-2790. Offers clinical mental health counseling (MA), including expressive therapies counseling, holistic counseling, school and community counseling; counseling psychology (MA, CAGS), including professional counseling (MA), school counseling (MA); creative arts in learning (CAGS); creative writing (MFA); ecological teaching and learning (MS); environmental education (MS); expressive therapies (MA, PhD, CAGS), including art (MA), dance (MA), expressive therapies, music (MA); independent studies (CAGS); independent study (MA); intercultural relations (MA, CAGS); interdisciplinary studies (MA), including individualized studies, integrative holistic health, women's studies; urban environmental leadership (MA); visual arts (MFA). Part-time and evening/weekend programs available. Postbaccalaureate distance learning degree programs offered (minimal on-campus study). *Degree requirements:* For master's, internship, practicum, thesis (expressive therapies); for doctorate, thesis/dissertation, arts apprenticeship, field placement; for CAGS, thesis, internship (counseling psychology, expressive therapies). *Entrance requirements:* For master's, MAT (counseling psychology), interview, writing samples, art portfolio; for doctorate, GRE or MAT; for CAGS, interview, master's degree. Additional exam requirements/recommendations for international students: Required—TOEFL (minimum score 550 paper-based; 213 computer-based; 80 iBT). Electronic applications accepted. *Faculty research:* Psychotherapy and culture; psychotherapy and psychological trauma; women's issues in art, teaching and psychotherapy; community based art, psycho-spiritual inquiry.

Long Island University, C.W. Post Campus, School of Education, Department of Curriculum and Instruction, Brookville, NY 11548-1300. Offers adolescence education (MS); adolescence education: biology (MS); adolescence education: earth science (MS); adolescence education: English (MS); adolescence education: mathematics (MS); adolescence education: social studies (MS); adolescence education: Spanish (MS); art education (MS); bilingual education (MS); childhood education (MS); early childhood education (MS); middle childhood education (MS); music education (MS); teaching English to speakers of other languages (MS). Part-time and evening/weekend programs available. *Degree requirements:* For master's, comprehensive exam or thesis, student teaching. *Entrance requirements:* For master's, minimum GPA of 2.75 in major, 2.5 overall. Electronic applications accepted. *Faculty research:* Ethics and education, teaching strategies.

Long Island University, C.W. Post Campus, School of Visual and Performing Arts, Department of Art, Brookville, NY 11548-1300. Offers art (MA); art education (MS); clinical art therapy (MA); fine art and design (MFA). Part-time and evening/weekend programs available. *Degree requirements:* For master's, thesis. Electronic applications accepted. *Faculty research:* Painting, sculpture, installation, computers, video.

Manhattanville College, Graduate Programs, School of Education, Program in Visual Arts Education, Purchase, NY 10577-2132. Offers MAT. Part-time and evening/weekend programs available. *Students:* 19 full-time (17 women), 33 part-time (28 women); includes 4 minority (all Hispanic Americans). In 2009, 7 master's awarded. *Entrance requirements:* Additional exam requirements/recommendations for international students: Required—TOEFL. *Application deadline:* Applications are processed on a rolling basis. Application fee: $70. Electronic applications accepted. *Financial support:* Career-related internships or fieldwork, Federal Work-Study, institutionally sponsored loans, scholarships/grants, and unspecified assistantships available. Support available to part-time students. Financial award application deadline: 3/1; financial award applicants required to submit FAFSA. *Unit head:* Alyce Ware Poli, Director of Admissions, 914-323-5941, Fax: 914-694-1732, E-mail: edschool@mville.edu. *Application contact:* Jeanine Pardey-Levine, Director of Admissions, 914-323-3208, Fax: 914-694-1732, E-mail: edschool@mville.edu.

Mansfield University of Pennsylvania, Graduate Studies, Department of Art, Mansfield, PA 16933. Offers art education (M Ed). Part-time programs available. *Faculty:* 1 (woman) full-time, 1 (woman) part-time/adjunct. *Students:* 8 full-time (6 women), 17 part-time (all women). Average age 34. In 2009, 6 master's awarded. *Degree requirements:* For master's, thesis optional. *Entrance requirements:* For master's, minimum GPA of 3.0, portfolio. Additional exam requirements/recommendations for international students: Required—TOEFL (minimum score 550 paper-based; 230 computer-based). *Application deadline:* For fall admission, 8/1 priority date for domestic students, 6/1 for international students. Applications are processed on a rolling basis. Electronic applications accepted. *Expenses:* Tuition, state resident: full-time $6666; part-time $370 per credit. Tuition, nonresident: full-time $10,666; part-time $593 per credit. Required fees: $1388. *Financial support:* Unspecified assistantships available. Support available to part-time students. Financial award application deadline: 5/1; financial award applicants required to submit FAFSA. *Unit head:* Dr. Martha Whitehouse, Chairperson, 570-662-4503, E-mail: mwhiteho@mansfield.edu. *Application contact:* Christina Hale, Assistant Director of Enrollment Management/Graduate Admissions, 570-662-4812, Fax: 570-662-4121, E-mail: chale@mansfield.edu.

Maryland Institute College of Art, Graduate Studies, Program in Art Education, Baltimore, MD 21217. Offers MA, MAT. MA program offered in summer only. *Accreditation:* NASAD. Part-time programs available. *Faculty:* 8 full-time (all women), 10 part-time/adjunct (7 women). *Students:* 27 full-time (22 women), 17 part-time (14 women); includes 10 minority (5 African

Maryland Institute College of Art (continued)

Americans, 1 Asian American or Pacific Islander, 4 Hispanic Americans). Average age 27. In 2009, 27 master's awarded. *Degree requirements:* For master's, thesis, seminar. *Entrance requirements:* For master's, portfolio, 40 studio credits, 6 credits in art history. Additional exam requirements/recommendations for international students: Required—TOEFL (minimum score 550 paper-based; 213 computer-based; 80 iBT). *Application deadline:* For fall admission, 1/15 for domestic and international students. Application fee: $60. *Expenses:* Tuition: Full-time $33,000; part-time $1375 per credit hour. Required fees: $1090; $545 per semester. *Financial support:* In 2009–10, 40 students received support, including 3 fellowships (averaging $17,274 per year); teaching assistantships, career-related internships or fieldwork and scholarships/grants also available. Financial award application deadline: 3/1; financial award applicants required to submit FAFSA. *Unit head:* Dr. Karen Carroll, Dean, 410-225-2297, Fax: 410-225-2257. *Application contact:* Scott G. Kelly, Associate Dean of Graduate Admission, 410-225-2256, Fax: 410-225-2408, E-mail: graduate@mica.edu.

Maryville University of Saint Louis, School of Education, St. Louis, MO 63141-7299. Offers art education (MA Ed); early childhood education (MA Ed); educational leadership (Ed D); educational leadership: principal certification (MA Ed); elementary education (MA Ed); elementary education/English (MA Ed); elementary education/psychology (MA Ed); environmental education (MA Ed); gifted education (MA Ed); literacy specialist (MA Ed); middle grades education (MA Ed); secondary teaching and inquiry (MA Ed); teacher as leader (MA Ed). *Accreditation:* NASAD; NCATE. Part-time and evening/weekend programs available. *Students:* 25 full-time (18 women), 198 part-time (145 women); includes 33 minority (27 African Americans, 2 American Indian/Alaska Native, 1 Asian American or Pacific Islander, 3 Hispanic Americans). Average age 36. In 2009, 61 master's, 45 doctorates awarded. *Degree requirements:* For master's, thesis, project. *Entrance requirements:* For master's and doctorate, minimum GPA of 3.0, 3 professional recommendations. Additional exam requirements/recommendations for international students: Required—TOEFL (minimum score 550 paper-based). *Application deadline:* Applications are processed on a rolling basis. Application fee: $40 ($60 for international students). Electronic applications accepted. *Expenses:* Tuition: Full-time $20,384; part-time $627.50 per credit hour. Required fees: $100 per semester. *Financial support:* Career-related internships or fieldwork, Federal Work-Study, tuition waivers (partial), and professional educator discounts available. Financial award application deadline: 3/1; financial award applicants required to submit FAFSA. *Faculty research:* Collaboration with public schools, pre-service program development, mathematics, diversity, literacy. *Unit head:* Dr. Sam Hausfather, Dean, 314-529-9466, Fax: 314-529-9921, E-mail: shausfather@maryville.edu. *Application contact:* Holly Stanwich, Graduate Admissions Coordinator, 314-529-9542, Fax: 314-529-9921, E-mail: teachered@maryville.edu.

Marywood University, Academic Affairs, Insalaco College of Creative and Performing Arts, Art Department, Program in Art Education, Scranton, PA 18509-1598. Offers MA. *Accreditation:* NASAD; NCATE. *Students:* 1 full-time (0 women), 8 part-time (7 women). Average age 29. In 2009, 4 master's awarded. *Entrance requirements:* Additional exam requirements/recommendations for international students: Required—TOEFL (minimum score 550 paper-based; 213 computer-based; 79 iBT). *Application deadline:* For fall admission, 4/1 priority date for domestic students, 3/31 priority date for international students; for spring admission, 11/1 priority date for domestic students, 8/31 priority date for international students. Applications are processed on a rolling basis. Application fee: $35. Electronic applications accepted. *Expenses:* Tuition: Part-time $715 per credit. Required fees: $270 per semester. Tuition and fees vary according to degree level, campus/location and program. *Financial support:* Career-related internships or fieldwork, scholarships/grants, and unspecified assistantships available. Support available to part-time students. Financial award application deadline: 6/30; financial award applicants required to submit FAFSA. *Faculty research:* Current trends in art education, color theories, research in Mariology. *Application contact:* Tammy Manka, Assistant Director of Graduate Admissions, 866-279-9663, E-mail: tmanka@marywood.edu.

Massachusetts College of Art and Design, Graduate Programs, Program in Art Education, Boston, MA 02115-5882. Offers MAT, MSAE. *Accreditation:* NASAD. Part-time programs available. *Faculty:* 7 full-time (3 women), 6 part-time/adjunct (5 women). *Students:* 19 part-time (14 women); includes 1 minority (Hispanic American), 1 international. Average age 36. 9 applicants, 89% accepted, 7 enrolled. In 2009, 8 master's awarded. *Degree requirements:* For master's, thesis (for some programs), exhibition. *Entrance requirements:* For master's, portfolio, resume, writing sample, letters of reference, interview. Additional exam requirements/recommendations for international students: Required—TOEFL (minimum score 563 paper-based; 223 computer-based; 85 iBT); Recommended—IELTS (minimum score 6.5). *Application deadline:* For fall admission, 1/15 for domestic and international students; for winter admission, 11/1 for international students; for spring admission, 11/1 for domestic students. Application fee: $75. Electronic applications accepted. *Expenses:* Contact institution. *Financial support:* Research assistantships, teaching assistantships, career-related internships or fieldwork, Federal Work-Study, and clerical/technical assistantships available. Support available to part-time students. Financial award application deadline: 3/1; financial award applicants required to submit FAFSA. *Faculty research:* Museum education, history of visual arts education, teaching studio art K–12. *Unit head:* George Creamer, Dean of Graduate Programs, 617-879-7525. *Application contact:* George Creamer, Dean of Graduate Programs, 617-879-7525.

Memphis College of Art, Graduate Programs, Program in Art Education, Memphis, TN 38104-2764. Offers MA, MAT. Part-time and evening/weekend programs available. *Faculty:* 25 full-time (13 women), 8 part-time/adjunct (6 women). *Students:* 1 (woman) full-time, 70 part-time (47 women); includes 18 minority (14 African Americans, 3 Asian Americans or Pacific Islanders, 1 Hispanic American), 1 international. Average age 32. 24 applicants, 100% accepted, 24 enrolled. In 2009, 9 degrees awarded. *Degree requirements:* For master's, thesis. *Entrance requirements:* For master's, portfolio, resume, interview. Additional exam requirements/recommendations for international students: Required—TOEFL (minimum score 525 paper-based; 195 computer-based). *Application deadline:* For fall admission, 3/1 for domestic and international students; for spring admission, 11/1 for domestic and international students. Applications are processed on a rolling basis. Application fee: $50. Electronic applications accepted. *Expenses:* Tuition: Full-time $23,000; part-time $958 per credit hour. Required fees: $600; $200 per course. Tuition and fees vary according to program. *Financial support:* In 2009–10, 71 students received support. Federal Work-Study and scholarships/grants available. Support available to part-time students. Financial award application deadline: 8/1; financial award applicants required to submit FAFSA. *Unit head:* Dr. Catherine Wilson, Director of Graduate Education Programs, 901-272-5100, Fax: 901-272-5158, E-mail: cwilson@mca.edu. *Application contact:* Annette Moore, Dean of Admissions, 901-272-5151, Fax: 901-272-5158, E-mail: amoore@mca.edu.

Messiah College, Program in Art Education, Grantham, PA 17027. Offers MA. Part-time programs available. *Degree requirements:* For master's, capstone project (exhibition or thesis). *Application deadline:* Applications are processed on a rolling basis. Application fee: $30. Electronic applications accepted. *Expenses:* Tuition: Part-time $518 per credit hour. *Financial support:* Applicants required to submit FAFSA. *Unit head:* Dr. Gene VanDyke, Program Coordinator, 717-796-1800 Ext. 6726, Fax: 717-691-2386, E-mail: gvandyke@messiah.edu. *Application contact:* Dr. Gene VanDyke, Program Coordinator, 717-796-1800 Ext. 6726, Fax: 717-691-2386, E-mail: gvandyke@messiah.edu.

Miami University, Graduate School, School of Fine Arts, Department of Art, Oxford, OH 45056. Offers art education (MA); studio art (MFA). *Accreditation:* NASAD (one or more programs are accredited). *Students:* 14 full-time (10 women), 1 (woman) part-time; includes 1 minority (Asian American or Pacific Islander). *Entrance requirements:* For master's, minimum undergraduate GPA of 3.0 during previous 2 years or 2.75 overall. Application fee: $50. *Expenses:* Tuition, state resident: full-time $11,280. Tuition, nonresident: full-time $24,912. Required fees: $516. *Financial support:* Fellowships with full tuition reimbursements, research assistantships, teaching assistantships, Federal Work-Study, health care benefits, tuition waivers (full), and unspecified assistantships available. Financial award application deadline: 3/1. *Unit head:* Dr. Dele Jegede, Chair, 513-529-2900. *Application contact:* Ellen Price, Professor/Graduate Director, 513-529-7128, E-mail: priceej@muohio.edu.

Millersville University of Pennsylvania, College of Graduate and Professional Studies, School of Humanities and Social Sciences, Department of Art, Millersville, PA 17551-0302. Offers M Ed. *Accreditation:* NASAD; NCATE. Part-time programs available. *Faculty:* 14 full-time (9 women), 3 part-time/adjunct (1 woman). *Students:* 5 full-time (all women), 10 part-time (8 women). Average age 29. 6 applicants, 100% accepted, 4 enrolled. In 2009, 7 master's awarded. *Degree requirements:* For master's, comprehensive exam, thesis optional. *Entrance requirements:* For master's, GRE or MAT, 3 letters of recommendation, interview (in-person), portfolio. Additional exam requirements/recommendations for international students: Required—TOEFL (minimum score 500 paper-based; 183 computer-based; 65 iBT) or IELTS (minimum score 6). *Application deadline:* For fall admission, 1/15 priority date for domestic and international students; for winter admission, 10/1 priority date for domestic and international students; for spring admission, 10/1 priority date for domestic and international students. Applications are processed on a rolling basis. Application fee: $40 ($50 for international students). Electronic applications accepted. *Expenses:* Tuition, state resident: full-time $6666; part-time $370 per credit. Tuition, nonresident: full-time $10,666; part-time $593 per credit. Required fees: $1578.50; $76.25 per credit. One-time fee: $60 part-time. Tuition and fees vary according to course load. *Financial support:* In 2009–10, 2 students received support, including 2 research assistantships with full tuition reimbursements available (averaging $5,000 per year); institutionally sponsored loans and unspecified assistantships also available. Support available to part-time students. Financial award application deadline: 3/15; financial award applicants required to submit FAFSA. *Unit head:* Dr. Jeri L. Robinson-Lawrence, Chair, 717-871-2194, Fax: 717-871-2004, E-mail: jeri.robinson@millersville.edu. *Application contact:* Dr. Victor S. DeSantis, Dean of Graduate and Professional Studies, 717-872-3099, Fax: 717-872-3453, E-mail: victor.desantis@millersville.edu.

Mills College, Graduate Studies, School of Education, Oakland, CA 94613-1000. Offers child life in hospitals (MA); early childhood education (MA); education (MA), including art education, curriculum and instruction, elementary education, English education, foreign language education, mathematics education, science education, secondary education, social studies education, teaching; educational leadership (MA, Ed D); infant mental health (MA). Part-time and evening/weekend programs available. *Faculty:* 11 full-time (9 women), 16 part-time/adjunct (14 women). *Students:* 138 full-time (119 women), 55 part-time (48 women); includes 71 minority (34 African Americans, 19 Asian Americans or Pacific Islanders, 18 Hispanic Americans), 3 international. Average age 34. 210 applicants, 82% accepted, 93 enrolled. In 2009, 54 master's, 15 doctorates awarded. Terminal master's awarded for partial completion of doctoral program. *Degree requirements:* For master's, comprehensive exam. *Entrance requirements:* For doctorate, GRE General Test. Additional exam requirements/recommendations for international students: Required—TOEFL. *Application deadline:* For fall admission, 2/1 for domestic and international students; for spring admission, 11/1 for domestic and international students. Applications are processed on a rolling basis. Application fee: $50. Electronic applications accepted. *Expenses:* Tuition: Full-time $26,326; part-time $6584 per course. Required fees: $896. One-time fee: $896 part-time. Tuition and fees vary according to program. *Financial support:* In 2009–10, 188 students received support, including 186 fellowships (averaging $6,499 per year), 28 teaching assistantships with partial tuition reimbursements available (averaging $3,187 per year); career-related internships or fieldwork and scholarships/grants also available. Support available to part-time students. Financial award application deadline: 2/1; financial award applicants required to submit FAFSA. *Faculty research:* Child development, gender and education, public policy, cross-cultural development, development of literacy. Total annual research expenditures: $1.2 million. *Unit head:* Joseph Kahne, Chairperson, 510-430-3190, Fax: 510-430-3314, E-mail: grad-studies@mills.edu. *Application contact:* Jessica King, Graduate Admission Specialist, 510-430-3305, Fax: 510-430-2159, E-mail: grad-studies@mills.edu.

Minnesota State University Mankato, College of Graduate Studies, College of Arts and Humanities, Department of Art, Mankato, MN 56001. Offers art education (MS); studio art (MA); teaching art (MAT). *Accreditation:* NASAD (one or more programs are accredited). Part-time programs available. *Students:* 5 full-time (2 women), 8 part-time (3 women). *Degree requirements:* For master's, one foreign language, comprehensive exam, thesis or alternative. *Entrance requirements:* For master's, minimum GPA of 3.0 during previous 2 years, portfolio (MA). Additional exam requirements/recommendations for international students: Required—TOEFL. *Application deadline:* For fall admission, 7/1 priority date for domestic students, 5/1 for international students; for spring admission, 11/1 for domestic students, 10/1 for international students. Applications are processed on a rolling basis. Application fee: $40. Electronic applications accepted. *Expenses:* Tuition, state resident: full-time $5364. Tuition, nonresident: full-time $8314. *Financial support:* Research assistantships, teaching assistantships with full tuition reimbursements, unspecified assistantships available. Financial award application deadline: 3/15; financial award applicants required to submit FAFSA. *Faculty research:* Photographic documentation. *Unit head:* Brian Frink, Graduate Coordinator, 507-389-6412. *Application contact:* 507-389-2321, E-mail: grad@mnsu.edu.

Mississippi College, Graduate School, School of Education, Department of Teacher Education and Leadership, Clinton, MS 39058. Offers art (M Ed); biological science (M Ed); business education (M Ed); computer science (M Ed); dyslexia therapy (M Ed); educational leadership (M Ed, Ed D, Ed S); elementary education (M Ed, Ed S); English (M Ed); higher education administration (MS); mathematics (M Ed); secondary education (M Ed); social studies (history) (M Ed); teaching arts (M Ed). Part-time programs available. Postbaccalaureate distance learning degree programs offered (no on-campus study). *Faculty:* 11 full-time (7 women), 13 part-time/adjunct (7 women). *Students:* 33 full-time (22 women), 282 part-time (240 women); includes 148 minority (146 African Americans, 2 American Indian/Alaska Native), 1 international. Average age 34. In 2009, 147 master's awarded. *Degree requirements:* For master's, comprehensive exam, thesis optional. *Entrance requirements:* For master's, NTE. Additional exam requirements/recommendations for international students: Recommended—IELTS. *Application deadline:* For fall admission, 8/15 priority date for domestic students. Applications are processed on a rolling basis. Application fee: $30. Electronic applications accepted. *Expenses:* Tuition: Part-time $452 per credit hour. Required fees: $101 per semester. Tuition and fees vary according to degree level, campus/location, program and student level. *Financial support:* Teaching assistantships, career-related internships or fieldwork, Federal Work-Study, scholarships/grants, and unspecified assistantships available. Support available to part-time students. Financial award applicants required to submit FAFSA. *Unit head:* Dr. Tom Williams, Chair, 601-925-3844, E-mail: twilliams@mc.edu. *Application contact:* Elnora Lewis, Secretary, 601-925-3225, Fax: 601-925-3889, E-mail: lewis09@mc.edu.

Missouri State University, Graduate College, College of Arts and Letters, Department of Art and Design, Springfield, MO 65897. Offers secondary education (MS Ed), including art. Part-time programs available. *Faculty:* 8 full-time (3 women). *Students:* 1 full-time (0 women). Average age 38. 2 applicants, 100% accepted, 1 enrolled. *Entrance requirements:* For master's, minimum GPA of 3.0, 9-12 teaching certification. Additional exam requirements/recommendations for international students: Required—TOEFL (minimum score 550 paper-based; 213 computer-based; 79 iBT). *Application deadline:* For fall admission, 7/20 priority date for domestic students, 5/1 for international students; for spring admission, 12/20 priority date for domestic students, 9/1 for international students. Applications are processed on a rolling basis. Application fee: $35 ($50 for international students). Electronic applications accepted. *Expenses:* Tuition, state resident: full-time $3852; part-time $214 per credit hour. Tuition, nonresident: full-time $7524; part-time $418 per credit hour. Required fees: $696; $172 per semester. Tuition and fees vary according to course level, course load, degree level and program. *Financial support:* Federal Work-Study and unspecified assistantships available. Financial award applicants required to submit FAFSA. *Unit head:* Wade S. Thompson, Head, 417-836-6055, E-mail: artanddesign@missouristate.edu. *Application contact:* Eric Eckert, Coordinator of Graduate Admissions and Recruitment, 417-836-5331, Fax: 417-386-6888, E-mail: ericeckert@missouristate.edu.

Montclair State University, The Graduate School, College of Education and Human Services, Department of Curriculum and Teaching, Montclair, NJ 07043-1624. Offers education (M Ed);

educational technology (M Ed); learning disabled teacher consultant (Certificate); school library media specialist (Certificate); teaching (MAT, Certificate), including art (MAT), biological science (MAT), early childhood education (P-3) (MAT), earth science (MAT), elementary education (K-8) (MAT), English (MAT), French (MAT), health and physical education (MAT), health education (MAT), home economics (MAT), mathematics (MAT), music (MAT), physical education (MAT), physical science (MAT), social studies (MAT), Spanish (MAT), teacher of ESL (MAT), teacher of students with disabilities (MAT). Part-time and evening/weekend programs available. *Faculty:* 17 full-time (12 women), 29 part-time/adjunct (21 women). *Students:* 124 full-time (63 women), 174 part-time (126 women). Average age 31. 112 applicants, 69% accepted, 59 enrolled. In 2009, 179 master's, 2 other advanced degrees awarded. *Degree requirements:* For master's, comprehensive exam, field experience. *Entrance requirements:* For master's, GRE, 2 letters of recommendation. Additional exam requirements/recommendations for international students: Required—TOEFL (minimum score 83 computer-based), or IELTS. *Application deadline:* For fall admission, 2/15 for domestic and international students; for spring admission, 9/15 for domestic and international students. Applications are processed on a rolling basis. Application fee: $60. Electronic applications accepted. *Expenses:* Tuition, area resident: Part-time $486.74 per credit. Tuition, state resident: part-time $486.74 per credit. Tuition, nonresident: part-time $751.34 per credit. Tuition and fees vary according to degree level and program. *Financial support:* In 2009–10, 12 research assistantships with full tuition reimbursements (averaging $7,000 per year) were awarded; Federal Work-Study, scholarships/grants, and unspecified assistantships also available. Support available to part-time students. Financial award application deadline: 3/1; financial award applicants required to submit FAFSA. *Unit head:* Dr. David Schwarzer, Chairperson, 973-655-5187. *Application contact:* Amy Aiello, Director of Graduate Admissions and Operations, 973-655-5147, Fax: 973-655-7869, E-mail: graduate.school@montclair.edu.

Montclair State University, The Graduate School, School of the Arts, Department of Art and Design, Montclair, NJ 07043-1624. Offers art education (MA, Certificate); art history (MA); studio arts (MA, MFA). *Accreditation:* NASAD (one or more programs are accredited). Part-time and evening/weekend programs available. *Faculty:* 26 full-time (11 women), 4 part-time/adjunct (2 women). *Students:* 30 full-time (19 women), 29 part-time (24 women). Average age 32. 53 applicants, 58% accepted, 20 enrolled. In 2009, 22 master's awarded. *Degree requirements:* For master's, project. *Entrance requirements:* For master's, GRE General Test or MAT (MA), portfolio, undergraduate degree in fine arts or equivalent, 2 letters of recommendation, teaching certificate (art education). Additional exam requirements/recommendations for international students: Required—TOEFL (minimum score 83 computer-based), or IELTS. *Application deadline:* For fall admission, 2/1 for domestic and international students. Applications are processed on a rolling basis. Application fee: $60. Electronic applications accepted. *Expenses:* Tuition, area resident: Part-time $486.74 per credit. Tuition, state resident: part-time $486.74 per credit. Tuition, nonresident: part-time $751.34 per credit. Tuition and fees vary according to degree level and program. *Financial support:* In 2009–10, 7 research assistantships with full tuition reimbursements (averaging $7,000 per year) were awarded; Federal Work-Study, scholarships/grants, and unspecified assistantships also available. Support available to part-time students. Financial award application deadline: 3/1; financial award applicants required to submit FAFSA. *Unit head:* Dr. Scott Gordley, Chairperson, 973-655-7295. *Application contact:* Amy Aiello, Director of Graduate Admissions and Operations, 973-655-5147, E-mail: graduate.school@montclair.edu.

Moore College of Art & Design, Program in Art Education, Philadelphia, PA 19103. Offers MA. Part-time programs available. *Degree requirements:* For master's, thesis, field practicum. *Entrance requirements:* For master's, minimum GPA of 3.0, on-site interview, portfolio, 3 letters of recommendation, resume.

Morehead State University, Graduate Programs, Caudill College of Arts, Humanities and Social Sciences, Department of Art and Design, Morehead, KY 40351. Offers art education (MA); graphic design (MA); studio art (MA). Part-time and evening/weekend programs available. *Faculty:* 9 full-time (3 women), 2 part-time/adjunct (1 woman). *Students:* 9 full-time (4 women), 3 part-time (2 women). Average age 31. 5 applicants, 60% accepted, 3 enrolled. In 2009, 7 master's awarded. *Degree requirements:* For master's, comprehensive exam, thesis (for some programs), oral exam during exhibition. *Entrance requirements:* For master's, GRE General Test, minimum undergraduate GPA of 3.0 in major, 2.5 overall; portfolio; bachelor's degree in art. Additional exam requirements/recommendations for international students: Required—TOEFL (minimum score 500 paper-based; 173 computer-based). *Application deadline:* For fall admission, 8/1 priority date for domestic and international students; for spring admission, 12/1 priority date for domestic and international students. Applications are processed on a rolling basis. Application fee: $30. Electronic applications accepted. *Expenses:* Tuition, state resident: full-time $6318; part-time $351 per credit hour. Tuition, nonresident: full-time $15,804; part-time $878 per credit hour. *Financial support:* In 2009–10, 3 research assistantships (averaging $10,000 per year), 2 teaching assistantships (averaging $10,000 per year) were awarded; career-related internships or fieldwork, Federal Work-Study, and unspecified assistantships also available. Financial award application deadline: 3/15; financial award applicants required to submit FAFSA. *Faculty research:* Computer art, painting, drawing, ceramics, photography. *Unit head:* Robert Franzini, Chair, 606-783-2193, Fax: 606-783-5048, E-mail: r.franzi@moreheadstate.edu. *Application contact:* Michelle Barber, Graduate Recruitment and Retention Assistant Director, 606-783-5127, Fax: 606-783-5061, E-mail: m.barber@moreheadstate.edu.

Nazareth College of Rochester, Graduate Studies, Department of Art, Program in Art Education, Rochester, NY 14618-3790. Offers MS Ed. *Accreditation:* Teacher Education Accreditation Council. Part-time and evening/weekend programs available. *Entrance requirements:* For master's, minimum GPA of 3.0, portfolio review.

New Jersey City University, Graduate Studies and Continuing Education, William J. Maxwell College of Arts and Sciences, Department of Art, Jersey City, NJ 07305-1597. Offers art (MFA); art education (MA); studio art (MFA). *Accreditation:* NASAD. Part-time and evening/weekend programs available. *Faculty:* 6. *Students:* 6 full-time (3 women), 5 part-time (4 women); includes 2 minority (1 African American, 1 American Indian/Alaska Native). Average age 33. In 2009, 1 master's awarded. *Degree requirements:* For master's, thesis or alternative, exhibit. *Entrance requirements:* For master's, GRE General Test or MAT, portfolio. Additional exam requirements/recommendations for international students: Required—TOEFL. *Application deadline:* For fall admission, 8/1 priority date for domestic students; for spring admission, 12/1 for domestic students. Applications are processed on a rolling basis. Application fee: $0. *Expenses:* Tuition, area resident: Part-time $456.75 per credit. Tuition, nonresident: part-time $842.55 per credit. Required fees: $65 per term. *Financial support:* Unspecified assistantships available. *Unit head:* Dr. Herbert Rosenberg, Chairperson, 201-200-2367. *Application contact:* Dr. Herbert Rosenberg, Chairperson, 201-200-2367.

New York University, Steinhardt School of Culture, Education, and Human Development, Department of Art and Art Professions, Program in Art Education, New York, NY 10003-5799. Offers MA. *Accreditation:* Teacher Education Accreditation Council. Part-time programs available. *Students:* 28 full-time (22 women), 9 part-time (all women); includes 4 minority (2 African Americans, 1 Asian American or Pacific Islander, 1 Hispanic American), 2 international. Average age 29. 52 applicants, 67% accepted, 15 enrolled. In 2009, 14 master's awarded. *Degree requirements:* For master's, thesis (for some programs). *Entrance requirements:* For master's, portfolio. Additional exam requirements/recommendations for international students: Required—TOEFL. *Application deadline:* For fall admission, 12/15 priority date for domestic and international students. Applications are processed on a rolling basis. Application fee: $75. Electronic applications accepted. *Expenses:* Tuition: Full-time $30,528; part-time $1272 per credit. Required fees: $2177. *Financial support:* Fellowships with full and partial tuition reimbursements, career-related internships or fieldwork, Federal Work-Study, institutionally sponsored loans, and tuition waivers (partial) available. Support available to part-time students. Financial award application deadline: 2/1; financial award applicants required to submit FAFSA. *Faculty research:* Multicultural aesthetic inquiry, urban art education, feminism, equity and social justice. *Unit head:* Dr. Dipti Desai, Director, 212-998-9022, Fax: 212-995-4320, E-mail: dd25@nyu.edu. *Application contact:* 212-998-5030, Fax: 212-995-4328, E-mail: steinhardt.gradadmissions@nyu.edu.

North Carolina Agricultural and Technical State University, Graduate School, College of Arts and Sciences, Department of Visual and Performing Arts, Greensboro, NC 27411. Offers art education (MS). *Accreditation:* NCATE. Part-time and evening/weekend programs available. *Degree requirements:* For master's, comprehensive exam, thesis or alternative, qualifying exam. *Entrance requirements:* For master's, GRE General Test, minimum GPA of 2.6.

North Georgia College & State University, Graduate Studies, Program in Teacher Education, Dahlonega, GA 30597. Offers early childhood education (M Ed); educational leadership (Ed S); middle grades education (M Ed); secondary education (M Ed), including art education, biology education, chemistry education, English education, history education, mathematics education, physical education, science education; special education (M Ed), including interrelated special education, learning disabilities. *Accreditation:* NCATE. Part-time and evening/weekend programs available. Postbaccalaureate distance learning degree programs offered (minimal on-campus study). *Degree requirements:* For master's, comprehensive exam, thesis optional. *Entrance requirements:* For master's, GRE General Test or MAT, minimum GPA of 2.75; for Ed S, GRE General Test or MAT, 3 years of teaching experience, master's degree, minimum graduate GPA of 3.25. Electronic applications accepted. *Faculty research:* Computers and teachers' attitudes, rural versus urban teacher attitudes, teacher leadership roles, minority recruitment in teaching force.

Nova Southeastern University, Fischler School of Education and Human Services, Graduate Teacher Education Program, Fort Lauderdale, FL 33314-7796. Offers athletic administration (MS); brain research (MS, Ed S); charter school education/leadership (MS); cognitive and behavioral disabilities (MS); computer science education (Ed S); computer science education (K-12) (MS); curriculum and teaching (Ed S); curriculum, instruction and technology (MS); curriculum, instruction, management and administration (Ed S); early childhood education (MS); early literacy and reading (Ed S); early literacy education (MS); education technology (MS); educational leadership (administration K–12) (MS, Ed S); educational media (Ed S); educational media (K-12) (MS); elementary education (MS, Ed S), including ESOL endorsement (MS); English education (MS, Ed S); environmental education (MS); exceptional student education (MS), including ESOL endorsement; gifted education (MS, Ed S); interdisciplinary arts education (MS); management and administration of educational programs (MS); mathematics (MS); mathematics education (Ed S); multicultural early intervention (MS); pre-kindergarten/primary (MS); preschool education (MS); reading (MS); reading and TESOL (MS); reading education (Ed S); science (MS); science education (Ed S); secondary education (MS); social studies (MS, Ed S); Spanish language (MS); special education and reading (MS); teaching and learning (MA, MS), including curriculum and instruction (MA), elementary mathematics (MA), elementary reading (MA), K-12 technology integration (MA); teaching English to speakers of other languages (MS, Ed S); technology management and administration (Ed S); urban studies education (MS). Part-time and evening/weekend programs available. Postbaccalaureate distance learning degree programs offered (minimal on-campus study). *Faculty:* 72 full-time (43 women), 385 part-time/adjunct (252 women). *Students:* 196 full-time (175 women), 1,304 part-time (1,128 women); includes 594 minority (471 African Americans, 5 American Indian/Alaska Native, 18 Asian Americans or Pacific Islanders, 100 Hispanic Americans). Average age 37. 2,610 applicants, 72% accepted, 1352 enrolled. In 2009, 836 other advanced degrees awarded. *Degree requirements:* For master's and Ed S, thesis, practicum, internship. *Entrance requirements:* For master's, MAT, GRE, CLAST, CBEST, PRAXIS I, General Knowledge Test, minimum GPA of 2.5; for Ed S, MAT or GRE, master's degree, teaching certificate, minimum GPA of 3.0. Additional exam requirements/recommendations for international students: Required—TSE (recommended, minimum score 50); Recommended—TOEFL (minimum score 550 paper-based; 213 computer-based; 80 iBT), IELTS (minimum score 6). *Application deadline:* For fall admission, 9/25 priority date for domestic and international students; for winter admission, 2/23 priority date for domestic and international students; for spring admission, 4/25 priority date for domestic and international students. Applications are processed on a rolling basis. Application fee: $50. Electronic applications accepted. *Financial support:* Federal Work-Study available. Support available to part-time students. Financial award application deadline: 4/15; financial award applicants required to submit FAFSA. *Faculty research:* School effectiveness, critical thinking, leadership skills acquisition, child education, multicultural education. *Unit head:* Dr. Ronald Kern, Dean of Academic Affairs, 800-986-3223 Ext. 7809, Fax: 954-262-3606, E-mail: rk429@nsu.nova.edu. *Application contact:* Dr. Jennifer Quinones Nottingham, Dean of Student Affairs, 800-986-3223 Ext. 1559.

The Ohio State University, Graduate School, College of the Arts, Department of Art Education, Columbus, OH 43210. Offers art education (MA, PhD); arts policy and administration (MA). *Accreditation:* NASAD; NCATE. *Faculty:* 20. *Students:* 63 full-time (51 women), 65 part-time (53 women); includes 5 minority (4 African Americans, 1 Asian American or Pacific Islander), 15 international. Average age 32. In 2009, 39 master's, 9 doctorates awarded. *Degree requirements:* For master's, thesis; for doctorate, thesis/dissertation. *Entrance requirements:* For master's and doctorate, GRE General Test. Additional exam requirements/recommendations for international students: Recommended—TOEFL (minimum score 600 paper-based; 250 computer-based). *Application deadline:* For fall admission, 8/15 priority date for domestic students, 7/1 priority date for international students; for winter admission, 12/1 priority date for domestic students, 11/1 priority date for international students; for spring admission, 3/1 priority date for domestic students, 2/1 priority date for international students. Applications are processed on a rolling basis. Application fee: $40 ($50 for international students). Electronic applications accepted. *Expenses:* Tuition, state resident: full-time $10,683. Tuition, nonresident: full-time $25,923. Tuition and fees vary according to course load and program. *Financial support:* Fellowships, research assistantships, teaching assistantships, career-related internships or fieldwork, Federal Work-Study, institutionally sponsored loans, and unspecified assistantships available. Support available to part-time students. Financial award applicants required to submit FAFSA. *Unit head:* Pheoris West, Graduate Studies Committee Chair, E-mail: west.1@osu.edu. *Application contact:* 614-292-9444, Fax: 614-688-3895, E-mail: domestic.grad@osu.edu.

Pace University, School of Education, New York, NY 10038. Offers administration and supervision (MS Ed); adolescent education (MST); childhood education (MST); curriculum and instruction (MS); education (MST); literacy (MSE); school business management (Certificate); teaching students with disabilities (MSE); teaching visual arts (MST). *Accreditation:* NCATE. Part-time and evening/weekend programs available. *Students:* 235 full-time (177 women), 766 part-time (515 women); includes 158 minority (58 African Americans, 1 American Indian/Alaska Native, 37 Asian Americans or Pacific Islanders, 62 Hispanic Americans), 7 international. Average age 30. 332 applicants, 83% accepted, 165 enrolled. In 2009, 669 master's, 34 other advanced degrees awarded. *Degree requirements:* For master's, internship. *Entrance requirements:* For master's, interview, teaching certificate. Additional exam requirements/recommendations for international students: Required—TOEFL. *Application deadline:* For fall admission, 7/31 priority date for domestic students; for spring admission, 11/30 for domestic students. Applications are processed on a rolling basis. Application fee: $70. Electronic applications accepted. *Expenses:* Contact institution. *Financial support:* Research assistantships, career-related internships or fieldwork and Federal Work-Study available. Support available to part-time students. Financial award applicants required to submit FAFSA. *Unit head:* Dr. Harriet Feldman, Interim Dean, 212-346-1512. *Application contact:* Susan Ford-Goldschein, Director of Admissions, 212-346-1652, Fax: 212-346-1585, E-mail: gradnyc@pace.edu.

Pittsburg State University, Graduate School, College of Arts and Sciences, Department of Art, Pittsburg, KS 66762. Offers art education (MA); studio art (MA). *Degree requirements:* For master's, thesis or alternative. *Expenses:* Tuition, state resident: full-time $4212; part-time $176 per credit. Tuition, nonresident: full-time $11,530; part-time $480 per credit. Required fees: $940; $43 per credit. Tuition and fees vary according to course level, course load, degree level, campus/location, reciprocity agreements and student level.

Pratt Institute, School of Art and Design, Program in Art and Design Education, Brooklyn, NY 11205-3899. Offers MS, Adv C. *Accreditation:* NASAD. Part-time programs available. *Faculty:* 1 (woman) full-time, 15 part-time/adjunct (13 women). *Students:* 24 full-time (22 women), 9

Art Education

Pratt Institute (continued)
part-time (6 women); includes 4 minority (2 Asian Americans or Pacific Islanders, 2 Hispanic Americans), 1 international. Average age 31. 54 applicants, 81% accepted, 14 enrolled. In 2009, 10 master's, 2 other advanced degrees awarded. *Degree requirements:* For master's, thesis. *Entrance requirements:* Additional exam requirements/recommendations for international students: Required—TOEFL (minimum score 600 paper-based; 250 computer-based; 100 iBT). *Application deadline:* For fall admission, 1/5 for domestic and international students; for spring admission, 10/1 for domestic and international students. Application fee: $50 ($90 for international students). *Expenses:* Tuition: Full-time $22,734. Required fees: $1280. *Financial support:* Career-related internships or fieldwork, Federal Work-Study, institutionally sponsored loans, scholarships/grants, health care benefits, and unspecified assistantships available. Support available to part-time students. Financial award application deadline: 2/1; financial award applicants required to submit FAFSA. *Unit head:* Dr. Amy Brook Snider, Chairperson, 718-636-3637, E-mail: absnider@pratt.edu. *Application contact:* Young Hah, Director of Graduate Admissions, 718-636-3683, Fax: 718-399-4242, E-mail: yhah@pratt.edu.

Purdue University, Graduate School, School of Education, Department of Curriculum and Instruction, West Lafayette, IN 47907. Offers agricultural and extension education (PhD, Ed S); agriculture and extension education (MS, MS Ed); art education (PhD); consumer and family sciences and extension education (MS Ed, PhD, Ed S); curriculum studies (MS Ed, PhD, Ed S); educational technology (MS Ed, PhD, Ed S); elementary education (MS Ed); foreign language education (MS Ed, PhD, Ed S); industrial technology (PhD, Ed S); language arts (MS Ed, PhD, Ed S); literacy (MS Ed, PhD, Ed S); mathematics/science education (MS, MS Ed, PhD, Ed S); social studies (MS Ed, PhD); social studies education (Ed S); vocational/industrial education (MS Ed, PhD, Ed S); vocational/technical education (MS Ed, PhD, Ed S). *Accreditation:* NCATE. Part-time and evening/weekend programs available. *Degree requirements:* For master's, thesis optional; for doctorate, thesis/dissertation, oral and written exams; for Ed S, oral presentation, project. *Entrance requirements:* For master's, GRE General Test, minimum B average; for doctorate, GRE General Test; for Ed S, GRE, minimum B average. Additional exam requirements/recommendations for international students: Required—TOEFL. Electronic applications accepted. *Faculty research:* Literacy acquisition and development, teacher beliefs and knowledge, recruitment and retention of underrepresented students, economic education, literacy discourse.

Queens College of the City University of New York, Division of Graduate Studies, Division of Education, Department of Secondary Education, Flushing, NY 11367-1597. Offers art (MS Ed); biology (MS Ed, AC); chemistry (MS Ed, AC); earth sciences (MS Ed, AC); English (MS Ed, AC); French (MS Ed, AC); Italian (MS Ed, AC); mathematics (MS Ed, AC); music (MS Ed, AC); physics (MS Ed, AC); social studies (MS Ed, AC); Spanish (MS Ed, AC). Part-time and evening/weekend programs available. *Faculty:* 22 full-time (14 women). *Students:* 86 full-time (47 women), 1,118 part-time (736 women). 591 applicants, 60% accepted, 250 enrolled. In 2009, 187 master's awarded. *Degree requirements:* For master's, research project; for AC, thesis optional. *Entrance requirements:* For master's, minimum GPA of 3.0. Additional exam requirements/recommendations for international students: Required—TOEFL. *Application deadline:* For fall admission, 4/1 for domestic students; for spring admission, 11/1 for domestic students. Applications are processed on a rolling basis. Application fee: $125. *Expenses:* Tuition, state resident: full-time $7360; part-time $310 per credit. Tuition, nonresident: part-time $575 per credit. One-time fee: $195 full-time; $145.25 part-time. *Financial support:* Career-related internships or fieldwork, Federal Work-Study, institutionally sponsored loans, and tuition waivers (partial) available. Support available to part-time students. Financial award application deadline: 4/1; financial award applicants required to submit FAFSA. *Unit head:* Dr. Eleanor Armour-Thomas, Chairperson, 718-997-5150, E-mail: armourthomas@yahoo.com. *Application contact:* Mario Caruso, Director of Graduate Admissions, 718-997-5200, Fax: 718-997-5193, E-mail: graduate_admissions@qc.edu.

Rhode Island College, School of Graduate Studies, Faculty of Arts and Sciences, Department of Art, Providence, RI 02908-1991. Offers art education (MA, MAT); media studies (MA). *Accreditation:* NASAD (one or more programs are accredited). Part-time and evening/weekend programs available. *Faculty:* 4 full-time (1 woman). *Students:* 9 full-time (5 women), 15 part-time (9 women). Average age 36. In 2009, 3 master's awarded. *Degree requirements:* For master's, thesis. *Entrance requirements:* For master's, GRE General Test or MAT, portfolio (MA), 3 letters of recommendation, interview. Additional exam requirements/recommendations for international students: Recommended—TOEFL (minimum score 550 paper-based; 213 computer-based; 79 iBT). *Application deadline:* For fall admission, 4/1 for domestic students; for spring admission, 11/1 for domestic students. Applications are processed on a rolling basis. Application fee: $50. *Expenses:* Tuition, state resident: full-time $7440; part-time $310 per credit hour. Tuition, nonresident: full-time $14,784; part-time $616 per credit hour. Required fees: $552; $20 per credit. $70 per term. *Financial support:* Teaching assistantships with full tuition reimbursements, career-related internships or fieldwork, Federal Work-Study, scholarships/grants, health care benefits, and unspecified assistantships available. Support available to part-time students. Financial award application deadline: 5/15; financial award applicants required to submit FAFSA. *Unit head:* Prof. Nancy Bockbrader, Chair, 401-456-8054. *Application contact:* Graduate Studies, 401-456-8700.

Rhode Island School of Design, Graduate Studies, Program in Art Education, Providence, RI 02903-2784. Offers MA, MAT. *Accreditation:* NASAD. *Degree requirements:* For master's, thesis, exhibit. *Entrance requirements:* For master's, portfolio, letters of recommendation. Additional exam requirements/recommendations for international students: Required—TOEFL (minimum score 580 paper-based; 237 computer-based), IELTS (minimum score 6.5).

Rochester Institute of Technology, Graduate Enrollment Services, College of Imaging Arts and Sciences, School of Art, Program in Visual Art, Rochester, NY 14623-5603. Offers MST. *Accreditation:* NASAD; Teacher Education Accreditation Council. *Students:* 14 full-time (13 women), 1 part-time (0 women). Average age 27. 30 applicants, 67% accepted. In 2009, 15 master's awarded. *Entrance requirements:* For master's, portfolio, minimum GPA of 3.0. Additional exam requirements/recommendations for international students: Required—TOEFL (minimum score 550 paper-based; 230 computer-based; 79 iBT), or IELTS (minimum score 6.5). *Application deadline:* For fall admission, 2/15 priority date for domestic and international students. Applications are processed on a rolling basis. Application fee: $50. Electronic applications accepted. *Expenses:* Tuition: Full-time $31,533; part-time $876 per credit hour. Required fees: $210. *Financial support:* In 2009–10, 12 students received support. Career-related internships or fieldwork, institutionally sponsored loans, and scholarships/grants available. Financial award application deadline: 8/30; financial award applicants required to submit FAFSA. *Unit head:* Don Arday, Administrative Chair, 585-475-7562, Fax: 585-475-6344, E-mail: facpgd@rit.edu. *Application contact:* Diane Ellison, Assistant Vice President, Graduate Enrollment Services, 585-475-2229, Fax: 585-475-7164, E-mail: gradinfo@rit.edu.

Sage Graduate School, Graduate School, School of Education, Program in Teaching, Troy, NY 12180-4115. Offers art education (MAT); English (MAT); mathematics (MAT); social studies (MAT). Part-time and evening/weekend programs available. *Faculty:* 15 full-time (9 women), 19 part-time/adjunct (16 women). *Students:* 32 full-time (25 women), 39 part-time (27 women); includes 4 minority (all Asian Americans or Pacific Islanders). Average age 27. 47 applicants, 55% accepted, 19 enrolled. In 2009, 36 master's awarded. *Entrance requirements:* For master's, minimum undergraduate GPA of 2.75 overall, 3.0 in content area; current resume; 2 letters of recommendation; assessment of writing skills. Additional exam requirements/recommendations for international students: Required—TOEFL (minimum score 550 paper-based; 213 computer-based). *Application deadline:* For fall admission, 8/1 for domestic students. Applications are processed on a rolling basis. Application fee: $40. *Expenses:* Tuition: Full-time $10,620; part-time $590 per credit hour. *Financial support:* Fellowships, research assistantships, Federal Work-Study, scholarships/grants, and unspecified assistantships available. Support available to part-time students. Financial award application deadline: 3/1; financial award applicants required to submit FAFSA. *Unit head:* Kelly Jones, Director, 518-244-2433. *Application contact:* Wendy D. Diefendorf, Director of Graduate and Adult Admission, 518-244-2443, Fax: 518-244-6880, E-mail: diefew@sage.edu.

Saint Michael's College, Graduate Programs, Program in Education, Colchester, VT 05439. Offers administration (M Ed, CAGS); arts in education (CAGS); curriculum and instruction (M Ed, CAGS); information technology (CAGS); reading (M Ed); special education (M Ed, CAGS); technology (M Ed). Part-time and evening/weekend programs available. *Degree requirements:* For master's, thesis. *Entrance requirements:* For master's, minimum GPA of 3.0. Electronic applications accepted. *Faculty research:* Integrative curriculum, moral and spiritual dimensions of education, learning styles, multiple intelligences, integrating technology into the curriculum.

Salem State College, School of Graduate Studies, Program in Art, Salem, MA 01970-5353. Offers MAT. *Accreditation:* NASAD. Part-time and evening/weekend programs available. *Students:* 3 full-time (2 women), 14 part-time (11 women). Average age 35. 7 applicants, 100% accepted, 7 enrolled. In 2009, 3 master's awarded. *Entrance requirements:* For master's, GRE or MAT. Additional exam requirements/recommendations for international students: Required—TOEFL (minimum score 550 paper-based; 80 iBT), or IELTS (minimum score 5.5). *Application deadline:* For fall admission, 5/1 for domestic and international students; for spring admission, 10/1 for domestic and international students. Application fee: $50. *Expenses:* Tuition, state resident: full-time $2520; part-time $275 per credit hour. Tuition, nonresident: full-time $4140; part-time $365 per credit hour. Required fees: $2430. *Financial support:* In 2009–10, 2 students received support. Career-related internships or fieldwork, Federal Work-Study, scholarships/grants, and unspecified assistantships available. Support available to part-time students. Financial award application deadline: 5/1; financial award applicants required to submit FAFSA. *Unit head:* Marie Meegan, Program Coordinator, 978-542-6321, E-mail: mmeegan@salemstate.edu. *Application contact:* Dr. Lee A. Brossoit, Assistant Dean of Graduate Admissions, 978-542-6673, Fax: 978-542-7215, E-mail: lbrossoit@salemstate.edu.

School of the Art Institute of Chicago, Graduate Division, Program in Art Education and Art Teaching, Chicago, IL 60603-3103. Offers MAAE, MAT. *Accreditation:* NASAD. *Entrance requirements:* Additional exam requirements/recommendations for international students: Required—TOEFL, IELTS.

School of Visual Arts, Graduate Programs, Art Education Department, New York, NY 10010-3994. Offers MAT. *Entrance requirements:* For master's, portfolio. Additional exam requirements/recommendations for international students: Required—TOEFL (minimum score 550 paper-based; 213 computer-based; 79 iBT). Electronic applications accepted.

School of Visual Arts, Graduate Programs, Program in Art Criticism and Writing, New York, NY 10010-3994. Offers MFA. *Degree requirements:* For master's, thesis. *Entrance requirements:* For master's, writing sample, letters of recommendation. Additional exam requirements/recommendations for international students: Required—TOEFL (minimum score 550 paper-based; 213 computer-based; 79 iBT). Electronic applications accepted.

Simon Fraser University, Graduate Studies, Faculty of Education, Program in Arts Education, Burnaby, BC V5A 1S6, Canada. Offers M Ed, MA, PhD. *Degree requirements:* For master's, comprehensive exam or thesis; for doctorate, comprehensive exam, thesis/dissertation.

Southern Connecticut State University, School of Graduate Studies, School of Arts and Sciences, Department of Art, New Haven, CT 06515-1355. Offers art education (MS). Part-time and evening/weekend programs available. *Faculty:* 5 full-time, 5 part-time/adjunct. *Students:* 22 full-time (20 women), 50 part-time (44 women); includes 1 minority (Asian American or Pacific Islander). 29 applicants, 69% accepted, 16 enrolled. In 2009, 14 master's awarded. *Degree requirements:* For master's, thesis or alternative. *Entrance requirements:* For master's, interview. *Application deadline:* For fall admission, 5/1 priority date for domestic students; for spring admission, 12/1 priority date for domestic students. Applications are processed on a rolling basis. Application fee: $50. Electronic applications accepted. Tuition and fees vary according to program. *Financial support:* Application deadline: 4/15. *Unit head:* Mitchell Bills, Chairperson, 203-392-6649, Fax: 203-392-6658, E-mail: billsm1@southernct.edu. *Application contact:* Dr. Jessie Whitehead, Graduate Coordinator, 203-392-8913, Fax: 203-392-6658, E-mail: whiteheadj3@southernct.edu.

Southern Illinois University Edwardsville, Graduate Studies and Research, School of Education, Department of Curriculum and Instruction, Program in Secondary Education, Edwardsville, IL 62026-0001. Offers art (MS Ed); biology (MS Ed); chemistry (MS Ed); earth and space sciences (MS Ed); English/language arts (MS Ed); foreign languages (MS Ed); history (MS Ed); mathematics (MS Ed); physics (MS Ed). *Accreditation:* NCATE. Part-time and evening/weekend programs available. *Students:* 24 part-time (19 women); includes 2 minority (1 African American, 1 Hispanic American). Average age 26. 13 applicants, 31% accepted. In 2009, 5 master's awarded. *Degree requirements:* For master's, thesis or alternative, final exam/paper. *Entrance requirements:* Additional exam requirements/recommendations for international students: Required—TOEFL (minimum score 550 paper-based; 213 computer-based; 79 iBT), IELTS (minimum score 6.5). *Application deadline:* For fall admission, 7/23 for domestic students, 6/1 for international students; for spring admission, 12/11 for domestic students, 10/1 for international students. Applications are processed on a rolling basis. Application fee: $30. Electronic applications accepted. *Expenses:* Tuition, state resident: part-time $1252.50 per semester. Tuition, nonresident: part-time $3131.25 per semester. Required fees: $586.85 per semester. Tuition and fees vary according to course load. *Financial support:* Fellowships, research assistantships, teaching assistantships, career-related internships or fieldwork, Federal Work-Study, institutionally sponsored loans, scholarships/grants, traineeships, and unspecified assistantships available. Support available to part-time students. Financial award application deadline: 3/1; financial award applicants required to submit FAFSA. *Unit head:* Dr. Kathy Bushrow, Director, 618-650-3082, E-mail: kbushro@siue.edu. *Application contact:* Dr. Kathy Bushrow, Director, 618-650-3082, E-mail: kbushro@siue.edu.

Southwestern Oklahoma State University, College of Arts and Sciences, Department of Art, Weatherford, OK 73096-3098. Offers art education (M Ed). Part-time programs available. *Degree requirements:* For master's, exam. *Entrance requirements:* For master's, GRE General Test or minimum undergraduate GPA of 3.0. Additional exam requirements/recommendations for international students: Required—TOEFL.

Stanford University, School of Education, Program in Curriculum Studies and Teacher Education, Stanford, CA 94305-9991. Offers art education (MA, PhD); dance education (MA); English education (MA, PhD); general curriculum studies (MA, PhD); mathematics education (MA, PhD); science education (MA, PhD); social studies education (PhD); teacher education (MA, PhD). *Degree requirements:* For master's, thesis (for some programs); for doctorate, thesis/dissertation. *Entrance requirements:* For master's and doctorate, GRE General Test. Electronic applications accepted. *Expenses:* Tuition: Full-time $37,380; part-time $2760 per quarter. Required fees: $501.

State University of New York at New Paltz, Graduate School, School of Fine and Performing Arts, Department of Art Education, New Paltz, NY 12561. Offers visual arts education (MS Ed). *Accreditation:* NASAD. Part-time and evening/weekend programs available. *Faculty:* 3 full-time (all women). *Students:* 29 part-time (25 women); includes 2 minority (1 African American, 1 Asian American or Pacific Islander). Average age 29. 7 applicants, 43% accepted, 3 enrolled. In 2009, 5 master's awarded. *Degree requirements:* For master's, thesis, portfolio. *Entrance requirements:* For master's, NYS art education teaching certificate, minimum GPA of 3.0, portfolio. Additional exam requirements/recommendations for international students: Required—TOEFL (minimum score 550 paper-based; 213 computer-based; 80 iBT), IELTS (minimum score 6.5). *Application deadline:* For fall admission, 4/15 for domestic and international students. Application fee: $50. Electronic applications accepted. *Financial support:* In 2009–10, 2 students received support, including 2 research assistantships with partial tuition reimbursements available (averaging $5,000 per year). *Unit head:* Prof. Margaret Johnson, Director, 845-257-3850, E-mail: johnsonm@newpaltz.edu. *Application contact:* Caroline Murphy, Graduate Admissions Advisor, 845-257-3285, E-mail: gradschool@newpaltz.edu.

State University of New York at Oswego, Graduate Studies, School of Education, Department of Curriculum and Instruction, Oswego, NY 13126. Offers art education (MAT); elementary education (MS Ed); literacy education (MS Ed); secondary education (MS Ed); special education (MS Ed). Part-time and evening/weekend programs available. *Degree requirements:* For master's, comprehensive exam (for some programs), thesis optional. *Entrance requirements:* For master's, GRE General Test, minimum GPA of 2.7, provisional teaching certificate. Additional exam requirements/recommendations for international students: Required—TOEFL (minimum score 560 paper-based; 220 computer-based). *Faculty research:* Classroom applications for microcomputers; classroom questioning, wait-time, and achievement; values clarification and academic achievement.

Sul Ross State University, School of Arts and Sciences, Department of Fine Arts and Communication, Alpine, TX 79832. Offers art education (M Ed); art history (M Ed); studio art (M Ed), including ceramics, design, drawing, jewelry, painting, printmaking, sculpture, weaving. Part-time programs available. *Degree requirements:* For master's, oral or written exam. *Entrance requirements:* For master's, GRE General Test, minimum GPA of 2.5 in last 60 hours of undergraduate work. *Faculty research:* Ceramic sculpture, watercolor, wood sculpture, rock art.

Syracuse University, School of Education, Program in Art Education, Syracuse, NY 13244. Offers art education (CAS); art education/professional certification (MS); art education: preparation (MS). Part-time and evening/weekend programs available. *Students:* 12 full-time (11 women), 3 part-time (2 women). Average age 24. 14 applicants, 93% accepted, 5 enrolled. In 2009, 9 master's awarded. *Degree requirements:* For master's, thesis or alternative. *Entrance requirements:* For master's, interview. Additional exam requirements/recommendations for international students: Required—TOEFL (minimum score 100 iBT). *Application deadline:* For fall admission, 2/1 priority date for domestic and international students; for spring admission, 10/15 priority date for domestic and international students. Applications are processed on a rolling basis. Application fee: $75. Electronic applications accepted. *Expenses:* Tuition: Full-time $26,808; part-time $1117 per credit. Required fees: $1024. *Financial support:* Fellowships with tuition reimbursements, teaching assistantships with tuition reimbursements available. *Unit head:* Dr. James Haywood Rolling, Chair, 315-443-2355. *Application contact:* Liza Rochelson, Graduate Recruiter, School of Education, 315-443-2505, E-mail: e-gradrcrt@syr.edu.

Teachers College, Columbia University, Graduate Faculty of Education, Department of Arts and Humanities, Program in Art and Art Education, New York, NY 10027-6696. Offers Ed M, MA, Ed D, Ed DCT. *Accreditation:* NCATE. Part-time and evening/weekend programs available. *Faculty:* 4 full-time (2 women). *Students:* 25 full-time (23 women), 140 part-time (116 women); includes 32 minority (2 African Americans, 19 Asian Americans or Pacific Islanders, 11 Hispanic Americans), 19 international. Average age 35. 71 applicants, 72% accepted, 31 enrolled. In 2009, 42 master's, 9 doctorates awarded. Terminal master's awarded for partial completion of doctoral program. *Degree requirements:* For doctorate, variable foreign language requirement, thesis/dissertation. *Entrance requirements:* For doctorate, portfolio. *Application deadline:* For fall admission, 5/15 for domestic students; for spring admission, 12/1 for domestic students. Application fee: $65. *Financial support:* Research assistantships, teaching assistantships, career-related internships or fieldwork, Federal Work-Study, institutionally sponsored loans, and tuition waivers (full and partial) available. Support available to part-time students. Financial award application deadline: 2/1. *Faculty research:* Technology and creativity with respect to pedagogy and curriculum, artistic-aesthetic development in children and adolescents. *Unit head:* Graeme Sullivan, Chair, 212-678-3799. *Application contact:* Mark E. Stearns, Associate Director of Admission, 212-678-3710, Fax: 212-678-4171.

Temple University, Graduate School, Tyler School of Art, Department of Art and Art Education, Philadelphia, PA 19122-6096. Offers Ed M. *Degree requirements:* For master's, paper, portfolio review. *Entrance requirements:* For master's, GRE or MAT, minimum GPA of 3.0, slide portfolio, 40 credits in studio art, 9 credits in art history. Additional exam requirements/recommendations for international students: Required—TOEFL (minimum score 550 paper-based; 213 computer-based; 79 iBT). Electronic applications accepted.

Texas Tech University, Graduate School, College of Visual and Performing Arts, School of Art, Lubbock, TX 79409. Offers art (MFA); art education (MAE); fine arts-art (PhD). *Accreditation:* NASAD (one or more programs are accredited). Part-time programs available. *Faculty:* 22 full-time (11 women). *Students:* 45 full-time (14 women), 25 part-time (20 women); includes 9 minority (1 African American, 2 American Indian/Alaska Native, 6 Hispanic Americans), 10 international. Average age 34. 91 applicants, 42% accepted, 20 enrolled. In 2009, 12 master's, 2 doctorates awarded. *Degree requirements:* For master's, thesis (for some programs); for doctorate, thesis/dissertation. *Entrance requirements:* For master's and doctorate, GRE General Test. Additional exam requirements/recommendations for international students: Required—TOEFL (minimum score 550 paper-based; 213 computer-based). *Application deadline:* For fall admission, 3/1 priority date for international students; for spring admission, 11/1 priority date for international students. Applications are processed on a rolling basis. Application fee: $50 ($75 for international students). Electronic applications accepted. *Expenses:* Tuition, state resident: full-time $5100; part-time $213 per credit hour. Tuition, nonresident: full-time $11,748; part-time $490 per credit hour. Required fees: $2298; $50 per credit hour. $555 per semester. *Financial support:* In 2009–10, 18 teaching assistantships with partial tuition reimbursements (averaging $8,730 per year) were awarded; research assistantships with partial tuition reimbursements, career-related internships or fieldwork, Federal Work-Study, and institutionally sponsored loans also available. Support available to part-time students. Financial award application deadline: 4/15; financial award applicants required to submit FAFSA. *Faculty research:* Studio, art history, art education. *Unit head:* Prof. Tina Fuentes, Director, 806-742-3825 Ext. 223, Fax: 806-742-1971, E-mail: tina.fuentes@ttu.edu. *Application contact:* Sang-Mi Yoo, Graduate Advisor, 806-742-3825 Ext. 244, Fax: 806-742-1971, E-mail: sang-mi.yoo@ttu.edu.

Towson University, College of Graduate Studies and Research, Arts Integration Institute, Towson, MD 21252-0001. Offers Certificate.

Towson University, College of Graduate Studies and Research, Program in Art Education, Towson, MD 21252-0001. Offers M Ed. *Accreditation:* NCATE. Part-time and evening/weekend programs available. *Degree requirements:* For master's, thesis optional, research project. *Entrance requirements:* For master's, bachelor's degree/certification in art education, minimum GPA of 3.0 or certified public school teacher with evidence of undergraduate coursework. Electronic applications accepted.

Troy University, Graduate School, College of Education, Program in Teacher Education-Multiple Levels, Troy, AL 36082. Offers alternative 5th year art education (MS); alternative 5th year instrumental (MS); alternative 5th year physical education (MS); alternative 5th year vocal/choral (MS); traditional art education (MS); traditional gifted education (MS); traditional instrumental (MS); traditional physical education (MS); traditional reading specialist (MS); traditional vocal/choral (MS). Part-time and evening/weekend programs available. *Students:* 5 full-time (3 women), 21 part-time (12 women); includes 11 minority (9 African Americans, 1 American Indian/Alaska Native, 1 Asian American or Pacific Islander). Average age 30. 2 applicants, 50% accepted. In 2009, 8 master's awarded. *Degree requirements:* For master's, comprehensive exam, thesis. *Entrance requirements:* For master's, minimum GPA of 2.5. Additional exam requirements/recommendations for international students: Required—TOEFL (minimum score 523 paper-based; 193 computer-based; 70 iBT), IELTS (minimum score 6). *Application deadline:* Applications are processed on a rolling basis. Application fee: $50. Electronic applications accepted. *Financial support:* Available to part-time students. Applicants required to submit FAFSA. *Unit head:* Dr. Marian Parker, Coordinator, 334-670-5661, Fax: 334-670-3548, E-mail: mjparker@troy.edu. *Application contact:* Brenda K. Campbell, Director of Graduate Admissions, 334-670-3178, Fax: 334-670-3733, E-mail: bcamp@troy.edu.

Union Institute & University, M Ed Program–Vermont Campus, Montpelier, VT 05602. Offers school administration (M Ed), including principalship; school counseling (M Ed); teaching (M Ed), including art, early childhood, elementary, English, math, middle schools, science, social studies, special education. *Faculty:* 3 full-time (1 woman), 23 part-time/adjunct (19 women). *Students:* 41 part-time (29 women). Average age 38. In 2009, 15 master's awarded. *Degree requirements:* For master's, thesis. *Entrance requirements:* For master's, 3 letters of reference. *Application deadline:* Applications are processed on a rolling basis. Application fee: $50. *Expenses:* Contact institution. *Financial support:* Federal Work-Study, scholarships/grants, and tuition waivers available. Financial award applicants required to submit FAFSA. *Unit head:* Dr. Arlene Sacks, Dean, Graduate Programs in Education, 305-653-6713 Ext. 2152, E-mail: arlene.sacks@myunion.edu. *Application contact:* Dr. Arlene Sacks, Dean, Graduate Programs in Education, 305-653-6713 Ext. 2152, E-mail: arlene.sacks@myunion.edu.

The University of Alabama at Birmingham, College of Arts and Sciences, School of Education, Program in Arts Education, Birmingham, AL 35294. Offers MA Ed. *Accreditation:* NCATE. *Degree requirements:* For master's, thesis optional. *Entrance requirements:* For master's, GRE General Test, MAT, or NTE, minimum GPA of 3.0. Electronic applications accepted.

The University of Arizona, Graduate College, College of Fine Arts, School of Art, Program in Art Education, Tucson, AZ 85721. Offers MA. *Accreditation:* NASAD. *Students:* 11 full-time (10 women), 12 part-time (9 women); includes 2 minority (1 Asian American or Pacific Islander, 1 Hispanic American). Average age 32. 21 applicants, 81% accepted, 12 enrolled. In 2009, 7 master's awarded. *Degree requirements:* For master's, thesis. *Entrance requirements:* For master's, portfolio, resume, autobiography, 3 letters of reference, writing sample. Additional exam requirements/recommendations for international students: Required—TOEFL (minimum score 550 paper-based; 213 computer-based; 79 iBT). *Application deadline:* For fall admission, 2/1 for domestic students, 12/1 for international students; for spring admission, 10/1 for domestic students, 9/1 for international students. Applications are processed on a rolling basis. Application fee: $75. Electronic applications accepted. *Expenses:* Tuition, state resident: full-time $9028. Tuition, nonresident: full-time $24,890. *Financial support:* Career-related internships or fieldwork, Federal Work-Study, institutionally sponsored loans, scholarships/grants, tuition waivers (full and partial), and unspecified assistantships available. Support available to part-time students. Financial award application deadline: 4/1; financial award applicants required to submit FAFSA. *Faculty research:* Artistic styles, visual perception, integration of arts into elementary curricula, aesthetics of the vanishing roadsides of America. *Unit head:* Dr. Lynn Beudert, Chair, 520-626-7639, Fax: 520-621-2955, E-mail: lynng@email.arizona.edu. *Application contact:* Megan Bartel, Graduate Coordinator, 520-621-8518, E-mail: mbartel@email.arizona.edu.

University of Arkansas at Little Rock, Graduate School, College of Arts, Humanities, and Social Science, Department of Art, Little Rock, AR 72204-1099. Offers art education (MA); art history (MA); studio art (MA). *Accreditation:* NASAD. Part-time programs available. *Degree requirements:* For master's, 4 foreign languages, oral exam, oral defense of thesis or exhibit. *Entrance requirements:* For master's, portfolio review or term paper evaluation, minimum GPA of 2.7.

The University of British Columbia, Faculty of Education, Department of Curriculum and Pedagogy, Vancouver, BC V6T 1Z4, Canada. Offers art education (M Ed, MA); business education (MA); curriculum studies (M Ed, MA, PhD); home economics education (M Ed, MA); math education (M Ed, MA); music education (M Ed, MA); physical education (M Ed, MA); science education (M Ed, MA); social studies education (M Ed, MA); technology studies education (M Ed, MA). Part-time programs available. *Degree requirements:* For master's, thesis (MA); for doctorate, comprehensive exam, thesis/dissertation. *Entrance requirements:* Additional exam requirements/recommendations for international students: Required—TOEFL (minimum score 580 paper-based; 237 computer-based; 92 iBT). Electronic applications accepted. *Expenses:* Contact institution. *Faculty research:* School subjects, teaching and learning.

University of Central Florida, College of Education, Department of Teaching and Learning Principles, Program in Art Education, Orlando, FL 32816. Offers M Ed, MA. *Accreditation:* NCATE. Part-time and evening/weekend programs available. *Students:* 7 full-time (5 women), 13 part-time (11 women); includes 2 minority (1 African American, 1 Hispanic American). Average age 29. 21 applicants, 86% accepted, 12 enrolled. In 2009, 6 master's awarded. *Degree requirements:* For master's, thesis or alternative, research report, internship (MA). *Entrance requirements:* Additional exam requirements/recommendations for international students: Required—TOEFL. *Application deadline:* For fall admission, 7/15 for domestic students; for spring admission, 12/1 for domestic students. Application fee: $30. Electronic applications accepted. *Expenses:* Tuition, state resident: part-time $306.31 per credit hour. Tuition, nonresident: part-time $1099.01 per credit hour. Part-time tuition and fees vary according to degree level and program. *Financial support:* Fellowships with partial tuition reimbursements, research assistantships with tuition reimbursements, teaching assistantships with partial tuition reimbursements, career-related internships or fieldwork, Federal Work-Study, institutionally sponsored loans, tuition waivers (partial), and unspecified assistantships available. Financial award application deadline: 3/1; financial award applicants required to submit FAFSA.

University of Cincinnati, Graduate School, College of Design, Architecture, Art, and Planning, School of Art, Program in Art Education, Cincinnati, OH 45221. Offers MA. *Accreditation:* NASAD; NCATE. *Entrance requirements:* For master's, MAT. Electronic applications accepted.

University of Dayton, Graduate School, School of Education and Allied Professions, Department of Teacher Education, Dayton, OH 45469-1300. Offers adolescent/young adult (MS Ed); art education (MS Ed); early childhood education (MS Ed); inclusive early childhood (MS Ed); interdisciplinary education (MS Ed); intervention specialist education, mild/moderate (MS Ed); literacy (MS Ed); middle childhood (MS Ed); multi-age education (MS Ed); music education (MS Ed); teacher as leader (MS Ed); technology in education (MS Ed). Part-time and evening/weekend programs available. *Faculty:* 17 full-time (13 women), 27 part-time/adjunct (21 women). *Students:* 105 full-time (76 women), 152 part-time (131 women); includes 25 minority (21 African Americans, 1 Asian American or Pacific Islander, 3 Hispanic Americans), 8 international. Average age 33. 199 applicants, 58% accepted, 48 enrolled. In 2009, 139 master's awarded. *Degree requirements:* For master's, thesis, capstone research project. *Entrance requirements:* For master's, GRE General Test, minimum GPA of 2.75. Additional exam requirements/recommendations for international students: Required—TOEFL (minimum score 550 paper-based; 213 computer-based; 80 iBT). *Application deadline:* For fall admission, 3/15 priority date for domestic students, 3/1 priority date for international students; for winter admission, 7/1 priority date for international students; for spring admission, 1/1 priority date for international students. Applications are processed on a rolling basis. Application fee: $0 ($50 for international students). Electronic applications accepted. *Expenses:* Contact institution. *Financial support:* In 2009–10, 5 research assistantships with full and partial tuition reimbursements (averaging $8,000 per year) were awarded; career-related internships or fieldwork, institutionally sponsored loans, health care benefits, and unspecified assistantships also available. Financial award applicants required to submit FAFSA. *Faculty research:* Diversity, literacy, art representation by young children, preservice teacher preparation. *Unit head:* Dr. Katie A. Kinnucan-Welsch, Chair, 937-229-3346. *Application contact:* Graduate Admissions, 937-229-4411, Fax: 937-229-4729, E-mail: gradadmission@udayton.edu.

University of Florida, Graduate School, College of Fine Arts, School of Art and Art History, Gainesville, FL 32611. Offers art (MFA), including ceramics, creative photography, drawing, electronic intermedia, graphic design, painting, printmaking, sculpture; art education (MA); art history (MA, PhD); digital arts and sciences (MA); museology (museum studies) (MA). *Accreditation:* NASAD. *Degree requirements:* For master's, variable foreign language requirement, project or thesis (MFA). *Entrance requirements:* For master's, portfolio (MFA), writing sample (MA), GRE General Test or minimum GPA of 3.0. Additional exam requirements/recommendations for international students: Required—TOEFL (minimum score 550 paper-based; 213 computer-based). Electronic applications accepted. *Faculty research:* Studio production, art historical studies of style context.

University of Georgia, Graduate School, College of Education, Program in Art Education, Athens, GA 30602. Offers MA Ed, Ed D, PhD, Ed S. *Accreditation:* NASAD; NCATE. *Students:* 16 full-time (13 women), 10 part-time (all women); includes 1 minority (Asian American or

Art Education

University of Georgia (continued)

Pacific Islander), 3 international. 14 applicants, 71% accepted, 10 enrolled. In 2009, 6 master's awarded. *Degree requirements:* For doctorate, thesis/dissertation. *Entrance requirements:* For master's, GRE General Test, MAT; for doctorate, GRE General Test; for Ed S, GRE General Test or MAT. *Application deadline:* For fall admission, 7/1 priority date for domestic students; for spring admission, 11/15 for domestic students. Application fee: $50. Electronic applications accepted. *Expenses:* Tuition, state resident: full-time $6000; part-time $250 per credit hour. Tuition, nonresident: full-time $20,904; part-time $871 per credit hour. Required fees: $730 per semester. *Financial support:* Fellowships, research assistantships, teaching assistantships, unspecified assistantships available.

University of Houston, College of Education, Department of Curriculum and Instruction, Houston, TX 77204. Offers art education (M Ed); bilingual education (M Ed); curriculum and instruction (M Ed, Ed D); early childhood education (M Ed); elementary education (M Ed); gifted and talented education (M Ed); instructional technology (M Ed); mathematics education (M Ed); reading and language arts education (M Ed); science education (M Ed); second language education (M Ed); secondary education (M Ed); social studies education (M Ed); teaching (M Ed). *Accreditation:* NCATE. Part-time and evening/weekend programs available. *Faculty:* 20 full-time (9 women), 22 part-time/adjunct (17 women). *Students:* 113 full-time (81 women), 195 part-time (150 women); includes 107 minority (43 African Americans, 29 Asian Americans or Pacific Islanders, 35 Hispanic Americans), 29 international. Average age 35. 150 applicants, 77% accepted, 55 enrolled. In 2009, 75 master's, 31 doctorates awarded. *Degree requirements:* For master's, comprehensive exam, thesis optional; for doctorate, comprehensive exam, thesis/dissertation. *Entrance requirements:* For master's and doctorate, GRE, minimum cumulative undergraduate GPA of 2.6. Additional exam requirements/recommendations for international students: Required—TOEFL (minimum score 550 paper-based; 79 iBT). *Application deadline:* For fall admission, 3/1 for domestic and international students; for spring admission, 10/1 for domestic and international students. Application fee: $45 ($75 for international students). Electronic applications accepted. *Expenses:* Tuition, state resident: full-time $7676; part-time $320 per credit hour. Tuition, nonresident: full-time $14,324; part-time $597 per credit hour. Required fees: $3034. *Financial support:* In 2009–10, 4 fellowships with full tuition reimbursements (averaging $9,500 per year), 6 research assistantships with full tuition reimbursements (averaging $8,800 per year), 25 teaching assistantships with full tuition reimbursements (averaging $8,800 per year) were awarded; career-related internships or fieldwork, Federal Work-Study, institutionally sponsored loans, scholarships/grants, health care benefits, and unspecified assistantships also available. Support available to part-time students. Financial award application deadline: 2/1. *Faculty research:* Teaching-learning process, instructional technology in schools, teacher education, classroom management, at-risk students. *Unit head:* Dr. Laveria Hutchison, Chairperson, 713-743-4958, Fax: 713-743-4990, E-mail: lhutchison@uh.edu. *Application contact:* Renee C. Rattelade, Executive Secretary, 713-743-4997, Fax: 713-743-4990, E-mail: rrattelade@mail.coe.uh.edu.

University of Idaho, College of Graduate Studies, College of Art and Architecture, Department of Art and Design, Moscow, ID 83844-2282. Offers art (MAT, MFA). *Accreditation:* NASAD. *Faculty:* 4 full-time. *Students:* 16 full-time, 11 part-time. In 2009, 4 master's awarded. *Degree requirements:* For master's, thesis (for some programs). *Entrance requirements:* For master's, minimum GPA of 2.8. *Application deadline:* For fall admission, 8/1 for domestic students; for spring admission, 12/15 for domestic students. Application fee: $55 ($60 for international students). *Expenses:* Tuition, state resident: full-time $6120. Tuition, nonresident: full-time $17,712. *Financial support:* Research assistantships, teaching assistantships available. Financial award application deadline: 2/15. *Faculty research:* Information design. *Unit head:* William Woolston, Chair, 208-885-7837. *Application contact:* William Woolston, Chair, 208-885-7837.

University of Illinois at Urbana–Champaign, Graduate College, College of Fine and Applied Arts, School of Art and Design, Program in Art Education, Champaign, IL 61820. Offers Ed M, MA, PhD. *Accreditation:* NASAD. *Students:* 21 full-time (18 women), 3 part-time (2 women); includes 3 minority (all Asian Americans or Pacific Islanders), 4 international. 26 applicants, 23% accepted, 5 enrolled. In 2009, 6 master's, 6 doctorates awarded. *Entrance requirements:* For master's, minimum GPA of 3.0. Additional exam requirements/recommendations for international students: Required—TOEFL (minimum score 550 paper-based; 213 computer-based; 79 iBT). *Application deadline:* Applications are processed on a rolling basis. Application fee: $60 ($75 for international students). Electronic applications accepted. *Financial support:* Fellowships, research assistantships, teaching assistantships, tuition waivers (full and partial) available. *Unit head:* Joseph Squier, Chair, 217-333-0855, Fax: 217-244-7688, E-mail: squier@illinois.edu. *Application contact:* Marsha Biddle, Coordinator of Graduate Academic Affairs, 217-333-0642, Fax: 217-244-7688, E-mail: mbiddle@illinois.edu.

University of Indianapolis, Graduate Programs, School of Education, Indianapolis, IN 46227-3697. Offers art education (MAT); biology (MAT); chemistry (MAT); curriculum and instruction (MA); earth sciences (MAT); education (MA, MAT); educational leadership (MA); elementary education (MA); English (MAT); French (MAT); math (MAT); physical education (MAT); physics (MAT); secondary education (MA), including art education, education, English education, social studies education; social studies (MAT); Spanish (MAT). *Accreditation:* NCATE. Part-time and evening/weekend programs available. *Faculty:* 4 full-time (3 women), 3 part-time/adjunct (2 women). *Students:* 52 full-time (28 women), 110 part-time (67 women); includes 3 minority (all African Americans), 2 international. Average age 33. *Entrance requirements:* For master's, GRE Subject Test, PRAXIS I, minimum GPA of 2.5, 3 letters of recommendation, interview, writing exercise. Additional exam requirements/recommendations for international students: Required—TOEFL (minimum score 550 paper-based; 213 computer-based). *Application deadline:* Applications are processed on a rolling basis. Application fee: $50. *Financial support:* Federal Work-Study available. Financial award application deadline: 5/1; financial award applicants required to submit FAFSA. *Faculty research:* Assessment of teacher education, perceptions of prospective teachers by parents. *Unit head:* Dr. Kathy Moran, Dean, 317-788-3285, Fax: 317-788-3300, E-mail: kmoran@uindy.edu. *Application contact:* Chemain Slater, 317-788-2051, E-mail: slaterc@uindy.edu.

The University of Iowa, Graduate College, College of Education, Department of Teaching and Learning, Program in Secondary Education, Iowa City, IA 52242-1316. Offers art education (PhD); curriculum and supervision (PhD); curriculum supervision (MA); developmental reading (MA); English education (MA, MAT); foreign language education (MA, MAT); foreign language/ESL education (PhD); language, literature and culture (PhD); math education (PhD); mathematics education (MA); social studies (MA, PhD). *Degree requirements:* For master's, thesis optional, exam; for doctorate, comprehensive exam, thesis/dissertation. *Entrance requirements:* For master's and doctorate, GRE General Test, minimum GPA of 3.0. Additional exam requirements/recommendations for international students: Required—TOEFL (minimum score 550 paper-based; 213 computer-based; 81 iBT). Electronic applications accepted.

The University of Kansas, Graduate Studies, College of Liberal Arts and Sciences, Department of Visual Art, Program in Visual Art Education, Lawrence, KS 66045. Offers MA. Part-time programs available. *Faculty:* 3 full-time (2 women). *Students:* 12 full-time (11 women), 8 part-time (all women); includes 2 minority (1 African American, 1 Asian American or Pacific Islander). Average age 26. 18 applicants, 83% accepted, 13 enrolled. In 2009, 2 master's awarded. *Degree requirements:* For master's, thesis or alternative. *Entrance requirements:* For master's, portfolio, 3 letters of recommendation, minimum GPA of 3.0. Additional exam requirements/recommendations for international students: Required—TOEFL (minimum score 570 paper-based; 230 computer-based) or IELTS (minimum score 6.5). *Application deadline:* For fall admission, 5/1 for domestic and international students; for spring admission, 10/15 for domestic and international students. Application fee: $45 ($55 for international students). Electronic applications accepted. *Expenses:* Tuition, state resident: full-time $6492; part-time $270.50 per credit hour. Tuition, nonresident: full-time $15,510; part-time $646.25 per credit hour. Required fees: $847; $70.56 per credit hour. Tuition and fees vary according to course load and program. *Financial support:* Teaching assistantships with full tuition reimbursements, Federal Work-Study, scholarships/grants, and unspecified assistantships available. Financial

award application deadline: 5/1. *Faculty research:* Museum education, art educator education. *Unit head:* Prof. Dawn Marie Guernsey, Chairperson, 785-864-4401, E-mail: guernsey@ku.edu. *Application contact:* Tanya E. Hartman, Director, 785-864-2957, Fax: 785-864-4404, E-mail: thartman@ku.edu.

University of Kentucky, Graduate School, College of Fine Arts, Program in Art Education, Lexington, KY 40506-0032. Offers MA. *Degree requirements:* For master's, comprehensive exam, thesis optional. *Entrance requirements:* For master's, GRE General Test, minimum undergraduate GPA of 2.75. Additional exam requirements/recommendations for international students: Required—TOEFL (minimum score 550 paper-based; 213 computer-based). Electronic applications accepted. *Faculty research:* Multicultural art education, women's issues in art education, lifelong learning in the arts, the artist-teacher, art teaching as a form of art, place and art, children's home art and creativity as a basis for school art instruction.

University of Louisville, Graduate School, College of Education and Human Development, Department of Teaching and Learning, Louisville, KY 40292-0001. Offers art education (MAT); curriculum and instruction (PhD); early elementary education (MAT); instructional technology (M Ed); interdisciplinary early childhood education (MAT); middle school education (MAT); music education (MAT); reading education (M Ed); secondary education (MAT); special education (M Ed, MAT); teacher leadership (M Ed). Part-time and evening/weekend programs available. *Faculty:* 43 full-time (33 women), 43 part-time/adjunct (36 women). *Students:* 207 full-time (144 women), 410 part-time (306 women); includes 68 minority (43 African Americans, 2 American Indian/Alaska Native, 14 Asian Americans or Pacific Islanders, 9 Hispanic Americans), 5 international. Average age 33. 216 applicants, 68% accepted, 112 enrolled. In 2009, 269 master's, 6 doctorates awarded. *Degree requirements:* For doctorate, comprehensive exam, thesis/dissertation. *Entrance requirements:* For master's, GRE General Test, PRAXIS II (for some programs); for doctorate, GRE General Test. Additional exam requirements/recommendations for international students: Required—TOEFL (minimum score 560 paper-based; 210 computer-based; 83 iBT). Application fee: $50. Electronic applications accepted. *Financial support:* In 2009–10, 172 students received support; fellowships, research assistantships, teaching assistantships, career-related internships or fieldwork, Federal Work-Study, scholarships/grants, and unspecified assistantships available. Financial award application deadline: 6/1; financial award applicants required to submit FAFSA. *Faculty research:* Assessment of cognitive and language abilities in infants and preschool children; mathematics teachers' conceptions and beliefs, effect, and understanding of mathematics; incorporating nanoscience and nanotechnology into middle and high school science classrooms; urban teacher preparation through inquiry, action and advocacy; impacts of cognitive coaching on teacher practice and student achievement. Total annual research expenditures: $3.7 million. *Unit head:* Dr. Ann E. Larson, Acting Chair, 502-852-6431, Fax: 502-852-1497, E-mail: ann@louisville.edu. *Application contact:* Libby Leggett, Director, Graduate Admissions, 502-852-3101, Fax: 502-852-6536, E-mail: gradadm@louisville.edu.

University of Maryland, Baltimore County, Graduate School, College of Arts, Humanities and Social Sciences, Department of Education, Program in Teaching, Baltimore, MD 21250. Offers early childhood education (MAT); elementary education (MAT); secondary education (MAT), including art, biology, chemistry, dance, earth/space science, English, foreign language, mathematics, music, physics, theatre; secondary science (MAT), including social studies. Part-time and evening/weekend programs available. *Faculty:* 24 full-time (18 women), 25 part-time/adjunct (19 women). *Students:* 52 full-time (41 women), 64 part-time (55 women); includes 20 minority (5 African Americans, 1 American Indian/Alaska Native, 10 Asian Americans or Pacific Islanders, 4 Hispanic Americans), 3 international. Average age 31. 88 applicants, 57% accepted, 39 enrolled. In 2009, 106 master's awarded. *Degree requirements:* For master's, comprehensive exam (for some programs), thesis (for some programs). *Entrance requirements:* For master's, PRAXIS I and II, minimum GPA of 3.0. Additional exam requirements/recommendations for international students: Required—TOEFL. *Application deadline:* For fall admission, 6/1 for domestic students; for spring admission, 11/1 for domestic students. Applications are processed on a rolling basis. Application fee: $50. Electronic applications accepted. *Financial support:* In 2009–10, 6 students received support, including research assistantships with full tuition reimbursements available (averaging $12,000 per year); career-related internships or fieldwork, Federal Work-Study, scholarships/grants, tuition waivers, and unspecified assistantships also available. Financial award application deadline: 3/1. *Faculty research:* STEM teacher education, culturally sensitive pedagogy, ESOL/bilingual education, early childhood education, language, literacy and culture. *Unit head:* Dr. Susan M. Blunck, Director, 410-455-2869, Fax: 410-455-3986, E-mail: blunck@umbc.edu. *Application contact:* Dr. Susan M. Blunck, Director, 410-455-2869, Fax: 410-455-3986, E-mail: blunck@umbc.edu.

University of Massachusetts Amherst, Graduate School, College of Humanities and Fine Arts, Department of Art, Programs in Art, Amherst, MA 01003. Offers art education (MA); studio art (MFA). Part-time programs available. *Students:* 20 full-time (14 women), 17 part-time (16 women); includes 3 minority (2 Asian Americans or Pacific Islanders, 1 Hispanic American), 2 international. Average age 31. 72 applicants, 26% accepted, 14 enrolled. In 2009, 12 master's awarded. *Degree requirements:* For master's, thesis (for some programs). *Entrance requirements:* For master's, portfolio. Additional exam requirements/recommendations for international students: Required—TOEFL (minimum score 530 paper-based; 213 computer-based; 80 iBT), IELTS (minimum score 6.5). *Application deadline:* For fall admission, 2/1 for domestic and international students. Applications are processed on a rolling basis. Application fee: $50 ($65 for international students). Electronic applications accepted. *Expenses:* Tuition, state resident: full-time $2640; part-time $110 per credit. Tuition, nonresident: full-time $9936; part-time $414 per credit. Tuition and fees vary according to course load. *Financial support:* In 2009–10, 1 fellowship with full tuition reimbursement (averaging $3,629 per year), 1 research assistantship with full tuition reimbursement (averaging $2,903 per year), 27 teaching assistantships with full tuition reimbursements (averaging $5,943 per year) were awarded; career-related internships or fieldwork, Federal Work-Study, scholarships/grants, traineeships, health care benefits, tuition waivers (full), and unspecified assistantships also available. Support available to part-time students. Financial award application deadline: 2/1. *Unit head:* Dr. Shona M. Macdonald, Graduate Program Director, 413-545-6937, Fax: 413-545-3929. *Application contact:* Jean M. Ames, Supervisor of Admissions, 413-545-0722, Fax: 413-577-0100, E-mail: gradadm@grad.umass.edu.

University of Massachusetts Dartmouth, Graduate School, College of Visual and Performing Arts, Program in Art Education, North Dartmouth, MA 02747-2300. Offers MAE. *Accreditation:* NASAD. Part-time programs available. *Faculty:* 4 full-time (3 women), 1 (woman) part-time/adjunct. *Students:* 11 full-time (10 women), 30 part-time (24 women); includes 2 minority (both Hispanic Americans), 1 international. Average age 31. 18 applicants, 100% accepted, 16 enrolled. In 2009, 4 master's awarded. *Degree requirements:* For master's, thesis or alternative. *Entrance requirements:* For master's, Massachusetts Tests for Educator Licensure (MTEL), interview, portfolio, minimum GPA of 2.75, 3 letters of recommendation. Additional exam requirements/recommendations for international students: Required—TOEFL (minimum score 500 paper-based). *Application deadline:* For fall admission, 3/15 priority date for domestic students, 1/15 priority date for international students; for spring admission, 11/15 priority date for domestic students, 9/15 priority date for international students. Applications are processed on a rolling basis. Application fee: $40 ($60 for international students). Electronic applications accepted. *Expenses:* Tuition, state resident: full-time $2071; part-time $86.29 per credit. Tuition, nonresident: full-time $8099; part-time $337.46 per credit. Required fees: $9446. Tuition and fees vary according to class time, course load and reciprocity agreements. *Financial support:* In 2009–10, 1 teaching assistantship with full tuition reimbursement (averaging $4,000 per year) was awarded; research assistantships, Federal Work-Study and unspecified assistantships also available. Financial award application deadline: 3/1; financial award applicants required to submit FAFSA. *Faculty research:* Creative art, in-service and pre-service teachers, virtual reality technology,watercolors. *Unit head:* Dr. Cathy Smilan, Director, 508-910-6594, Fax: 508-999-8901, E-mail: csmilan@umassd.edu. *Application contact:* Elan Turcotte-Shamski, Graduate Admissions Officer, 508-999-8604, Fax: 508-999-8183, E-mail: graduate@umassd.edu.

University of Minnesota, Twin Cities Campus, Graduate School, College of Education and Human Development, Department of Curriculum and Instruction, Minneapolis, MN 55455-

0213. Offers art education (M Ed, MA, PhD); children's literature (M Ed, MA, PhD); curriculum and instruction (MA, PhD); early childhood education (M Ed, PhD); elementary education (M Ed, MA, PhD); English education (MA, PhD); environmental education (M Ed); family education (M Ed, MA, Ed D, PhD); instructional systems and technology (M Ed, MA, PhD); language arts (MA, PhD); language immersion education (Certificate); literacy education (MA); mathematics education (MA, PhD); reading education (MA, PhD); science education (MA, PhD); second languages and cultures education (MA, PhD); social studies education (MA, PhD); teaching (M Ed), including Chinese, earth science, elementary special education, English, English as a second language, French, German, Hebrew, Japanese, life sciences, mathematics, middle school science, science, second languages and cultures, social studies, Spanish; technology enhanced learning (Certificate); writing education (M Ed, MA, PhD). *Faculty:* 34 full-time (21 women). *Students:* 436 full-time (307 women), 375 part-time (280 women); includes 80 minority (30 African Americans, 6 American Indian/Alaska Native, 33 Asian Americans or Pacific Islanders, 11 Hispanic Americans), 40 international. Average age 32. 660 applicants, 64% accepted, 379 enrolled. In 2009, 552 master's, 14 doctorates, 7 other advanced degrees awarded. *Financial support:* In 2009–10, 5 fellowships (averaging $27,000 per year), 47 research assistantships with full tuition reimbursements (averaging $25,682 per year), 60 teaching assistantships with full tuition reimbursements (averaging $29,889 per year) were awarded. *Faculty research:* Teaching and learning; quality of education; influence of cultural, linguistic, social, political, technological and economic factors on teaching, learning and educational research; relationship between educational practice and a democratic and just society. Total annual research expenditures: $1.8 million. *Unit head:* Dr. Ruth Thomas, Chair, 612-624-4772, Fax: 612-624-8277, E-mail: thoma006@umn.edu. *Application contact:* Dr. Mary Trettin, Associate Dean, 612-625-6501, Fax: 612-626-1580, E-mail: mtrettin@umn.edu.

University of Mississippi, Graduate School, College of Liberal Arts, Department of Art, Oxford, University, MS 38677. Offers art education (MA); art history (MA); fine arts (MFA). *Accreditation:* NASAD (one or more programs are accredited). Part-time programs available. *Students:* 9 full-time (3 women), 1 international. In 2009, 6 master's awarded. *Degree requirements:* For master's, thesis (for some programs). *Entrance requirements:* For master's, GRE General Test, minimum GPA of 3.0. Additional exam requirements/recommendations for international students: Required—TOEFL. *Application deadline:* For fall admission, 3/1 for domestic students; for spring admission, 10/1 for domestic students. Applications are processed on a rolling basis. Application fee: $25. Electronic applications accepted. *Financial support:* Fellowships, scholarships/grants and unspecified assistantships available. Financial award application deadline: 3/1; financial award applicants required to submit FAFSA. *Unit head:* Dr. Sheri Fleck Reith, Chair, 662-915-7193, Fax: 662-915-5013, E-mail: art@olemiss.edu. *Application contact:* Dr. Christy M. Wyandt, Associate Dean, 662-915-7474, Fax: 662-915-7577, E-mail: cwyandt@olemiss.edu.

University of Missouri, Graduate School, College of Education, Department of Learning, Teaching and Curriculum, Columbia, MO 65211. Offers agricultural education (M Ed, PhD, Ed S); art education (M Ed, PhD, Ed S); business and office education (M Ed, PhD, Ed S); early childhood education (M Ed, PhD, Ed S); elementary education (M Ed, PhD, Ed S); English education (M Ed, PhD, Ed S); foreign language education (M Ed, PhD, Ed S); health education and promotion (M Ed, PhD); learning and instruction (M Ed); marketing education (M Ed, PhD, Ed S); mathematics education (M Ed, PhD, Ed S); music education (M Ed, PhD, Ed S); reading education (M Ed, PhD, Ed S); science education (M Ed, PhD, Ed S); social studies education (M Ed, PhD, Ed S); vocational education (M Ed, PhD, Ed S). Part-time programs available. Terminal master's awarded for partial completion of doctoral program. *Degree requirements:* For doctorate, thesis/dissertation. *Entrance requirements:* For master's and Ed S, GRE General Test or MAT, minimum GPA of 3.0; for doctorate, GRE General Test, minimum GPA of 3.0. Additional exam requirements/recommendations for international students: Required—TOEFL (minimum score 600 paper-based; 250 computer-based; 100 iBT). Electronic applications accepted.

University of Nebraska at Kearney, College of Graduate Study, College of Fine Arts and Humanities, Department of Art, Kearney, NE 68849-0001. Offers art education (MA Ed). *Accreditation:* NCATE. Part-time and evening/weekend programs available. *Degree requirements:* For master's, thesis optional. *Entrance requirements:* For master's, slide portfolio. Additional exam requirements/recommendations for international students: Required—TOEFL (minimum score 550 paper-based; 213 computer-based). Electronic applications accepted. *Faculty research:* Fibers, art education, kiln design construction and low-fire glaze.

University of New Mexico, Graduate School, College of Education, Department of Educational Specialties, Program in Art Education, Albuquerque, NM 87131-2039. Offers MA. *Accreditation:* NCATE. Part-time and evening/weekend programs available. *Students:* 19 full-time (15 women), 22 part-time (18 women); includes 6 minority (1 American Indian/Alaska Native, 5 Hispanic Americans), 2 international. Average age 38. 17 applicants, 94% accepted, 11 enrolled. In 2009, 12 master's awarded. *Degree requirements:* For master's, comprehensive exam, thesis optional, participation in art exhibit. *Entrance requirements:* Additional exam requirements/recommendations for international students: Required—TOEFL. *Application deadline:* For fall admission, 3/30 for domestic students; for spring admission, 10/30 for domestic students. Application fee: $50. Electronic applications accepted. *Expenses:* Tuition, state resident: full-time $2099; part-time $233.20 per credit hour. Tuition, nonresident: full-time $6650. Required fees: $25 per semester. Tuition and fees vary according to course load, program and reciprocity agreements. *Financial support:* In 2009–10, 30 students received support, including 1 research assistantship with full tuition reimbursement available (averaging $12,500 per year); teaching assistantships, Federal Work-Study, institutionally sponsored loans, scholarships/grants, and unspecified assistantships also available. Financial award application deadline: 3/1; financial award applicants required to submit FAFSA. *Faculty research:* Studio in art education, visual culture, curricular issues regarding gender and sexual identity, archetypal thought in art education, teacher preparation. *Unit head:* Prof. Ruth Luckasson, Chair, 505-277-6510, Fax: 505-277-0576, E-mail: luckasson@unm.edu. *Application contact:* Dolores Mendoza, Information Contact, 505-277-4112, Fax: 505-277-0576, E-mail: arted@unm.edu.

The University of North Carolina at Charlotte, Graduate School, College of Education, Program in Teacher Education, Charlotte, NC 28223-0001. Offers art education (K-12) (MAT); dance education (K-12) (MAT); elementary education (K-6) (MAT); English as a second language (K-12) (MAT); foreign language education (K-12) (MAT); general teacher education (MAT); middle grades education (6-9) (MAT); music education (K-12) (MAT); secondary education (9-12) (MAT); special education (K-12) (MAT); theatre education (K-12) (MAT). *Faculty:* 108 full-time (64 women), 16 part-time/adjunct (12 women). *Students:* 29 full-time (20 women), 229 part-time (189 women); includes 32 minority (22 African Americans, 2 American Indian/Alaska Native, 3 Asian Americans or Pacific Islanders, 5 Hispanic Americans). Average age 32. 108 applicants, 92% accepted, 85 enrolled. In 2009, 59 master's awarded. *Entrance requirements:* For master's, GRE or MAT. Additional exam requirements/recommendations for international students: Required—TOEFL (minimum score 557 paper-based; 220 computer-based; 83 iBT). *Application deadline:* For fall admission, 7/1 for domestic students, 5/1 for international students; for spring admission, 11/1 for domestic students, 10/1 for international students. Applications are processed on a rolling basis. Application fee: $55. Electronic applications accepted. *Financial support:* In 2009–10, 5 students received support, including 1 research assistantship (averaging $18,000 per year), 3 teaching assistantships (averaging $12,183 per year); career-related internships or fieldwork, Federal Work-Study, institutionally sponsored loans, scholarships/grants, and administrative assistantship also available. Support available to part-time students. Financial award application deadline: 4/1; financial award applicants required to submit FAFSA. Total annual research expenditures: $5.1 million. *Unit head:* Dr. Kimberly J. Hartman, Coordinator, 704-687-8883, Fax: 704-687-6430, E-mail: khartman@uncc.edu. *Application contact:* Kathy B. Giddings, Director of Graduate Admissions, 704-687-5503, Fax: 704-687-3279, E-mail: gradadmn@uncc.edu.

The University of North Carolina at Pembroke, Graduate Studies, Department of Art, Pembroke, NC 28372-1510. Offers art education (MA, MAT). Part-time and evening/weekend programs available. *Degree requirements:* For master's, comprehensive exam, capstone show. *Entrance requirements:* For master's, GRE or MAT, minimum GPA of 3.0 in major or 2.5 overall. Additional exam requirements/recommendations for international students: Required—TOEFL. *Expenses:* Contact institution.

University of Northern Iowa, Graduate College, College of Humanities and Fine Arts, Department of Art, Cedar Falls, IA 50614. Offers art (MA); art education (MA). *Accreditation:* NASAD. Part-time and evening/weekend programs available. *Students:* 2 full-time (0 women), 5 part-time (4 women); includes 2 minority (both Hispanic Americans). 1 applicant, 100% accepted, 1 enrolled. In 2009, 3 master's awarded. *Degree requirements:* For master's, comprehensive exam (for some programs), thesis or alternative. *Entrance requirements:* For master's, minimum GPA of 3.0, portfolio. Additional exam requirements/recommendations for international students: Required—TOEFL (minimum score 500 paper-based; 180 computer-based; 61 iBT). *Application deadline:* For fall admission, 8/1 priority date for domestic students. Applications are processed on a rolling basis. Application fee: $30 ($50 for international students). Electronic applications accepted. *Financial support:* Career-related internships or fieldwork, Federal Work-Study, scholarships/grants, and tuition waivers (full and partial) available. Support available to part-time students. Financial award application deadline: 2/1. *Unit head:* Dr. Jeffery Byrd, Department Head/Professor, 319-273-2077, Fax: 319-273-7333, E-mail: jeffery.byrd@uni.edu. *Application contact:* Laurie S. Russell, Record Analyst, 319-273-2623, Fax: 319-273-6792, E-mail: laurie.russell@uni.edu.

University of North Texas, Robert B. Toulouse School of Graduate Studies, College of Visual Arts and Design, Department of Art Education and Art History, Denton, TX 76203. Offers art education (MA, PhD); art history (MA); art museum education (Certificate); arts leadership (Certificate). Part-time and evening/weekend programs available. *Degree requirements:* For master's, one foreign language, comprehensive exam (for some programs), thesis (for some programs); for doctorate, comprehensive exam, thesis/dissertation. *Entrance requirements:* For master's, GRE, writing sample, statement of purpose; for doctorate, GRE, master's degree in art education, writing sample, slides, statement of purpose. Additional exam requirements/recommendations for international students: Required—proof of English language proficiency required for non-native English speakers; Recommended—TOEFL (minimum score 550 paper-based; 213 computer-based; 79 iBT). Application fee: $50 ($75 for international students). *Expenses:* Tuition, state resident: full-time $4298; part-time $239 per contact hour. Tuition, nonresident: full-time $9878; part-time $549 per contact hour. Required fees: $265 per contact hour. *Financial support:* Fellowships with partial tuition reimbursements, research assistantships with partial tuition reimbursements, teaching assistantships with partial tuition reimbursements, Federal Work-Study, scholarships/grants, health care benefits, and unspecified assistantships available. Support available to part-time students. Financial award applicants required to submit FAFSA. *Faculty research:* Aesthetics, visual culture, arts leadership, British art, Latin American art, French art, Indian art, contemporary Arab art.

University of Rio Grande, Graduate School, Rio Grande, OH 45674. Offers classroom teaching (M Ed), including fine arts, learning disabilities, mathematics, reading education. *Accreditation:* NCATE. Part-time and evening/weekend programs available. *Degree requirements:* For master's, final research project, portfolio. *Entrance requirements:* For master's, minimum GPA of 2.7 in major, 2.5 overall. Additional exam requirements/recommendations for international students: Required—TOEFL. *Faculty research:* Interagency collaboration, reading and mathematics, learning styles, college access, literacy.

University of South Carolina, The Graduate School, College of Arts and Sciences, Department of Art, Program in Art Education, Columbia, SC 29208. Offers IMA, MA, MAT. IMA and MAT offered in cooperation with the College of Education. *Accreditation:* NCATE. *Degree requirements:* For master's, comprehensive exam, thesis (for some programs). *Entrance requirements:* For master's, GRE General Test or MAT, portfolio. Additional exam requirements/recommendations for international students: Required—TOEFL. Electronic applications accepted. *Faculty research:* Teaching art at the primary and secondary levels of education.

University of South Carolina, The Graduate School, College of Education, Department of Instruction and Teacher Education, Program in Secondary Education, Columbia, SC 29208. Offers art education (IMA, MAT); business education (IMA, MAT); English (MAT); foreign language (MAT); health education (MAT); mathematics (MAT); science (IMA, MAT); secondary (Ed D); secondary education (MT, PhD); social studies (MAT); theatre and speech (MAT). IMA and MT offered jointly with the subject areas. *Accreditation:* NCATE. *Degree requirements:* For master's, comprehensive exam, thesis (for some programs), foreign language (MA); for doctorate, one foreign language, comprehensive exam, thesis/dissertation. *Entrance requirements:* For master's, GRE General Test or MAT, teaching certificate (IMA, M Ed), interview; for doctorate, GRE General Test or MAT, interview. *Faculty research:* Middle school programs, professional development, school collaboration.

University of Southern Mississippi, Graduate School, College of Arts and Letters, Department of Art and Design, Hattiesburg, MS 39406-0001. Offers art education (MAE). *Accreditation:* NASAD. *Faculty:* 8 full-time (4 women). *Students:* 2 full-time (both women), 5 part-time (4 women); includes 1 minority (African American). Average age 38. 2 applicants, 50% accepted, 1 enrolled. In 2009, 1 master's awarded. *Degree requirements:* For master's, comprehensive exam, project. *Entrance requirements:* For master's, GRE General Test, BFA, minimum GPA of 3.0, portfolio. Additional exam requirements/recommendations for international students: Required—TOEFL. *Application deadline:* For fall admission, 3/1 priority date for domestic students, 3/1 for international students. Applications are processed on a rolling basis. Application fee: $35. *Expenses:* Tuition, state resident: full-time $5096; part-time $284 per hour. Tuition, nonresident: full-time $13,052; part-time $726 per hour. Required fees: $402. Tuition and fees vary according to course level and course load. *Financial support:* In 2009–10, 2 research assistantships with full tuition reimbursements (averaging $8,000 per year), 2 teaching assistantships with full tuition reimbursements (averaging $7,000 per year) were awarded; career-related internships or fieldwork, Federal Work-Study, scholarships/grants, and unspecified assistantships also available. Financial award application deadline: 3/15; financial award applicants required to submit FAFSA. *Unit head:* William Baggett, Chair, 601-266-4972, Fax: 601-266-6379, E-mail: graduate.studies@usm.edu. *Application contact:* Shonna Breland, Manager of Graduate Admissions, 601-266-4369, Fax: 601-266-5138, E-mail: graduatestudies@usm.edu.

The University of Tennessee, Graduate School, College of Education, Health and Human Sciences, Program in Education, Knoxville, TN 37996. Offers art education (MS); counseling education (PhD); cultural studies in education (PhD); curriculum (MS, Ed S); curriculum, educational research and evaluation (Ed D, PhD); early childhood education (PhD); early childhood special education (MS); education of deaf and hard of hearing (MS); educational administration and policy studies (Ed D, PhD); educational administration and supervision (Ed S); educational psychology (Ed D, PhD); elementary education (MS, Ed S); elementary teaching (MS); English education (MS, Ed S); exercise science (PhD); foreign language/ESL education (MS, Ed S); instructional technology (MS, Ed D, PhD, Ed S); literacy, language and ESL education (PhD); literacy, language education, and ESL education (Ed D); mathematics education (MS, Ed S); modified and comprehensive special education (MS); reading education (MS, Ed S); school counseling (Ed S); school psychology (PhD, Ed S); science education (MS, Ed S); secondary teaching (MS); social foundations (MS); social science education (MS, Ed S); socio-cultural foundations of sports and education (PhD); special education (Ed S); teacher education (Ed D, PhD). *Accreditation:* NCATE. Part-time and evening/weekend programs available. *Degree requirements:* For master's and Ed S, thesis optional; for doctorate, variable foreign language requirement, thesis/dissertation. *Entrance requirements:* For master's, minimum GPA of 2.7; for doctorate and Ed S, GRE General Test, minimum GPA of 2.7. Additional exam requirements/recommendations for international students: Required—TOEFL. Electronic applications accepted. *Expenses:* Tuition, state resident: full-time $6826; part-time $380 per semester hour. Tuition, nonresident: full-time $21,844; part-time $1147 per semester hour. Tuition and fees vary according to program.

The University of Texas at Austin, Graduate School, College of Fine Arts, Department of Art and Art History, Program in Art Education, Austin, TX 78712-1111. Offers MA. *Accreditation:*

Art Education

The University of Texas at Austin *(continued)*
NASAD. Part-time programs available. *Degree requirements:* For master's, thesis, oral and written exam. *Entrance requirements:* For master's, GRE General Test, 2 samples of written work, 10 slides of art work. Electronic applications accepted. *Faculty research:* Museum education; community-based, environmental, and multicultural art education; interdisciplinary art education, elementary and secondary art education.

The University of Texas at El Paso, Graduate School, College of Liberal Arts, Department of Art, El Paso, TX 79968-0001. Offers art education (MA); studio art (MA). Part-time and evening/weekend programs available. *Students:* 12 (8 women); includes 9 minority (all Hispanic Americans), 2 international. Average age 34. In 2009, 1 master's awarded. *Degree requirements:* For master's, thesis optional. *Entrance requirements:* For master's, minimum GPA of 3.0, digital portfolio, letters of recommendation. Additional exam requirements/recommendations for international students: Required—TOEFL; Recommended—IELTS. *Application deadline:* For fall admission, 8/1 priority date for domestic students, 3/1 for international students; for spring admission, 11/1 priority date for domestic students, 9/1 for international students. Applications are processed on a rolling basis. Application fee: $45 ($80 for international students). Electronic applications accepted. *Financial support:* In 2009–10, research assistantships with partial tuition reimbursements (averaging $18,625 per year), teaching assistantships with partial tuition reimbursements (averaging $14,900 per year) were awarded; fellowships with partial tuition reimbursements, institutionally sponsored loans, scholarships/grants, health care benefits, tuition waivers (partial), and unspecified assistantships also available. Support available to part-time students. Financial award application deadline: 3/15; financial award applicants required to submit FAFSA. *Unit head:* Dr. J. Quinnan, Chair, 915-747-5181, Fax: 915-747-6749, E-mail: jquinnan@utep.edu. *Application contact:* Dr. Patricia D. Witherspoon, Dean of the Graduate School, 915-747-5491, Fax: 915-747-5788, E-mail: withersp@utep.edu.

The University of the Arts, College of Art and Design, Department of Art Education, Philadelphia, PA 19102-4944. Offers art education (MA); visual arts (MAT). *Accreditation:* NASAD (one or more programs are accredited). Part-time programs available. *Degree requirements:* For master's, thesis (for some programs), student teaching experience (MAT). *Entrance requirements:* For master's, portfolio, 45 credits of studio work (MAT), 12 credits of art history (MAT), BFA or BA in art. Additional exam requirements/recommendations for international students: Required—TOEFL (minimum score 550 paper-based; 213 computer-based). *Faculty research:* Using technology and visual arts concepts to develop critical and creative thinking skills.

The University of Toledo, College of Graduate Studies, College of Education, Department of Curriculum and Instruction, Program in Art Education, Toledo, OH 43606-3390. Offers ME. *Accreditation:* NASAD.

University of Utah, Graduate School, College of Fine Arts, Department of Art and Art History, Salt Lake City, UT 84112-0380. Offers art history (MA); ceramics (MFA); community-based art education (MFA); drawing (MFA); graphic design (MFA); painting (MFA); photography/digital imaging (MFA); printmaking (MFA); sculpture/intermedia (MFA). *Faculty:* 24 full-time (11 women). *Students:* 20 full-time (15 women), 2 part-time (both women), 1 international. Average age 31. 59 applicants, 24% accepted, 9 enrolled. In 2009, 11 master's awarded. *Degree requirements:* For master's, variable foreign language requirement, comprehensive exam (for some programs), thesis or alternative, exhibit and final project paper (for MFA). *Entrance requirements:* For master's, CD portfolio (MFA), writing sample (MA), curriculum vitae, letters of recommendation. Additional exam requirements/recommendations for international students: Required—TOEFL (minimum score 575 paper-based; 183 computer-based; 75 iBT). *Application deadline:* For fall admission, 1/2 priority date for domestic and international students. Application fee: $55 ($65 for international students). Electronic applications accepted. *Expenses:* Tuition, state resident: full-time $4004; part-time $1674 per semester. Tuition, nonresident: full-time $14,134; part-time $5915 per semester. Required fees: $324 per semester. Tuition and fees vary according to course load, degree level and program. *Financial support:* In 2009–10, 2 fellowships, 6 research assistantships with partial tuition reimbursements, 34 teaching assistantships with partial tuition reimbursements were awarded; Federal Work-Study, institutionally sponsored loans, scholarships/grants, tuition waivers (partial), unspecified assistantships, and stipends also available. Financial award application deadline: 1/2; financial award applicants required to submit FAFSA. *Faculty research:* Studio art, European art history, Asian art history, Latin American art history, twentieth century/contemporary art history. Total annual research expenditures: $8,748. *Unit head:* Dr. Elizabeth A. Peterson, Chair, 801-581-7012, Fax: 801-585-6171, E-mail: elizabeth.peterson@art.utah.edu. *Application contact:* Prof. John O'Connell, Director of Graduate Studies, 801-581-8677, Fax: 801-585-6171, E-mail: j.oconnell@utah.edu.

University of Victoria, Faculty of Graduate Studies, Faculty of Education, Department of Curriculum and Instruction, Victoria, BC V8W 2Y2, Canada. Offers art education (M Ed, PhD); curriculum studies (M Ed, MA, PhD); early childhood education (M Ed, PhD); educational studies (PhD); language and literacy (M Ed, MA, PhD); mathematics (M Ed, MA, PhD); music education (M Ed, MA, PhD); science (M Ed, MA, PhD); social studies (M Ed, MA); social, cultural and foundational studies (MA, PhD); technology and environmental education (PhD). Part-time programs available. *Degree requirements:* For master's, thesis, project (M Ed); for doctorate, comprehensive exam, thesis/dissertation. *Entrance requirements:* For master's, minimum B average. Additional exam requirements/recommendations for international students: Required—TOEFL (minimum score 575 paper-based; 233 computer-based), IELTS (minimum score 7). Electronic applications accepted. *Faculty research:* Elementary and secondary English, language arts, curriculum theory and practice, educational media and technology, educational administration and leadership, history and philosophy of education.

University of West Georgia, Graduate School, College of Education, Department of Curriculum and Instruction, Carrollton, GA 30118. Offers art education (M Ed); art teacher education (Ed S); biology/secondary education (Ed S); business education (M Ed, Ed S); early childhood education (M Ed, Ed S); economics/secondary teacher education (Ed S); English teacher education (Ed S); French language teacher education (Ed S); history teacher education (Ed S); mathematics teacher education (Ed S); middle grades education (M Ed, Ed S); reading education (M Ed, Ed S); science teacher education (Ed S); secondary education (M Ed, Ed S); social science teacher education (Ed S); Spanish language teacher education (Ed S). Part-time and evening/weekend programs available. *Faculty:* 18 full-time (15 women), 7 part-time/adjunct (6 women). *Students:* 119 full-time (101 women), 358 part-time (280 women); includes 109 minority (97 African Americans, 3 American Indian/Alaska Native, 2 Asian Americans or Pacific Islanders, 7 Hispanic Americans). Average age 33. 193 applicants, 82% accepted, 34 enrolled. In 2009, 109 master's, 27 Ed Ss awarded. *Degree requirements:* For master's, comprehensive exam; for Ed S, research project. *Entrance requirements:* For master's, GRE General Test or MAT, minimum GPA of 2.7; for Ed S, GRE General Test, master's degree, minimum graduate GPA of 2.7. *Application deadline:* For fall admission, 7/17 for domestic students; for spring admission, 11/20 for domestic students. Applications are processed on a rolling basis. Application fee: $30. Electronic applications accepted. *Expenses:* Tuition, state resident: full-time $2952; part-time $164 per semester hour. Tuition, nonresident: full-time $11,808; part-time $656 per semester hour. Required fees: $42.90 per semester hour; $307 per semester. Tuition and fees vary according to course load. *Financial support:* In 2009–10, 5 research assistantships with full tuition reimbursements (averaging $3,000 per year) were awarded; career-related internships or fieldwork and scholarships/grants also available. Support available to part-time students. Financial award applicants required to submit FAFSA. *Unit head:* Dr. Donna Harkins, Chair, 678-839-6066, Fax: 678-839-6559, E-mail: dharkins@westga.edu. *Application contact:* Dr. Charles W. Clark, Dean, 678-839-6508, E-mail: cclark@westga.edu.

University of Wisconsin–Madison, Graduate School, School of Education, Department of Art and Department of Curriculum and Instruction, Program in Art Education, Madison, WI 53706-1380. Offers MA. *Accreditation:* NASAD. *Application deadline:* For fall admission, 1/10 for domestic students; for spring admission, 11/15 for domestic students. Application fee: $56. *Expenses:* Tuition, state resident: part-time $594 per credit. Tuition, nonresident: part-time $1504 per credit. Required fees: $65 per credit. Tuition and fees vary according to course load,

program and reciprocity agreements. *Financial support:* Fellowships with full tuition reimbursements, research assistantships with full tuition reimbursements, teaching assistantships with full tuition reimbursements, project assistantships available. *Unit head:* Tom Loeser, Chair, 608-262-1662. *Application contact:* Tom Loeser, Chair, 608-262-1662.

University of Wisconsin–Madison, Graduate School, School of Education, Department of Curriculum and Instruction, Madison, WI 53706-1380. Offers art education (MA); curriculum and instruction (MS, PhD); education and mathematics (MA); French education (MA); German education (MA); music education (MS); science education (MS); Spanish education (MA). *Accreditation:* NASM (one or more programs are accredited). *Degree requirements:* For doctorate, thesis/dissertation. Application fee: $56. *Expenses:* Tuition, state resident: part-time $594 per credit. Tuition, nonresident: part-time $1504 per credit. Required fees: $65 per credit. Tuition and fees vary according to course load, program and reciprocity agreements. *Financial support:* Project assistantships available. *Unit head:* Dr. Gloria Ladson-Billings, Chair, 608-262-4000. *Application contact:* Dr. Gloria Ladson-Billings, Chair, 608-262-4000.

University of Wisconsin–Milwaukee, Graduate School, Peck School of the Arts, Department of Art, Milwaukee, WI 53201-0413. Offers art (MA, MFA); art education (MA, MFA, MS). Part-time programs available. *Faculty:* 22 full-time (15 women). *Students:* 20 full-time (12 women), 3 part-time (2 women); includes 1 minority (Asian American or Pacific Islander), 1 international. Average age 34. 36 applicants, 36% accepted, 8 enrolled. In 2009, 10 master's awarded. *Degree requirements:* For master's, comprehensive exam, thesis or alternative. *Entrance requirements:* For master's, portfolio. Additional exam requirements/recommendations for international students: Required—TOEFL (minimum score 550 paper-based; 79 iBT), IELTS (minimum score 6.5). *Application deadline:* For fall admission, 1/1 priority date for domestic students; for spring admission, 9/1 for domestic students. Applications are processed on a rolling basis. Application fee: $45 ($75 for international students). *Expenses:* Tuition, state resident: full-time $8800. Tuition, nonresident: full-time $20,760. Tuition and fees vary according to program and reciprocity agreements. *Financial support:* In 2009–10, 7 teaching assistantships were awarded; career-related internships or fieldwork and unspecified assistantships also available. Support available to part-time students. Financial award application deadline: 4/15. *Unit head:* Denis Sargent, Representative, 414-229-6053, E-mail: artgrado@uwm.edu. *Application contact:* General Information Contact, 414-229-4982, Fax: 414-229-6967, E-mail: gradschool@uwm.edu.

University of Wisconsin–Superior, Graduate Division, Department of Visual Arts, Superior, WI 54880-4500. Offers art education (MA); art history (MA); art therapy (MA); studio arts (MA). Part-time programs available. *Faculty:* 7 full-time (1 woman), 1 (woman) part-time/adjunct. *Students:* 12 full-time (8 women), 18 part-time (15 women); includes 1 minority (American Indian/Alaska Native), 2 international. 14 applicants, 100% accepted. In 2009, 7 master's awarded. *Degree requirements:* For master's, comprehensive exam, exhibit. *Entrance requirements:* For master's, minimum GPA of 2.75, portfolio. *Application deadline:* For fall admission, 4/1 priority date for domestic students; for spring admission, 10/15 priority date for domestic students. Applications are processed on a rolling basis. Application fee: $45. *Financial support:* Career-related internships or fieldwork, Federal Work-Study, scholarships/grants, and tuition waivers (partial) available. Support available to part-time students. Financial award application deadline: 4/15; financial award applicants required to submit FAFSA. *Unit head:* Tim Cleary, Coordinator, 715-394-8398. *Application contact:* Sandy Wallgren, Program Assistant/Status Examiner, 715-394-8295, Fax: 715-394-8146, E-mail: gradstudy@uwsuper.edu.

Ursuline College, School of Graduate Studies, Program in Education, Pepper Pike, OH 44124-4398. Offers art education (MA); early childhood education (MA); language arts education (MA); life science education (MA); math education (MA); middle school education (MA); social studies education (MA); special education (MA). *Accreditation:* NCATE. *Faculty:* 1 (woman) full-time, 10 part-time/adjunct (8 women). *Students:* 53 full-time (40 women), 3 part-time (all women); includes 8 minority (7 African Americans, 1 Hispanic American). Average age 34. In 2009, 11 master's awarded. *Degree requirements:* For master's, comprehensive exam. *Entrance requirements:* For master's, minimum undergraduate GPA of 3.0. Additional exam requirements/recommendations for international students: Required—TOEFL (minimum score 500 paper-based; 173 computer-based). *Application deadline:* For fall admission, 8/1 priority date for domestic students. Applications are processed on a rolling basis. Application fee: $25. *Expenses:* Contact institution. *Financial support:* Federal Work-Study available. Financial award application deadline: 3/1. *Unit head:* Karen Godenschwager Nelson, Director, 440-684-8338, Fax: 440-684-6088, E-mail: kgodenschwager@ursuline.edu. *Application contact:* Melanie Steele, Secretary, 440-646-8199, Fax: 440-684-6138, E-mail: gradsch@ursuline.edu.

Virginia Commonwealth University, Graduate School, School of the Arts, Department of Art Education, Richmond, VA 23284-9005. Offers MAE. *Accreditation:* NASAD. *Degree requirements:* For master's, thesis optional. *Entrance requirements:* For master's, portfolio. *Faculty research:* Teaching methods.

Wayne State University, College of Education, Division of Teacher Education, Detroit, MI 48202. Offers adult and continuing education (M Ed); art education (M Ed); bilingual/bicultural education (M Ed, MAT); business education (M Ed, MAT); career and technical education (M Ed, Ed D, PhD, Ed S); curriculum and instruction (Ed D, PhD, Ed S); distributive education (M Ed, MAT); early childhood education (M Ed); elementary education (M Ed, MAT, Ed D, PhD, Ed S); elementary education curriculum and instruction (M Ed); English education (M Ed); English education-secondary (M Ed, Ed S); foreign language education (M Ed); general education (Ed D, Ed S); health occupations education (M Ed); industrial education (M Ed); mathematics education (M Ed, Ed S); pre-school and parent education (M Ed); reading (M Ed, Ed D, Ed S); reading, languages and literature (Ed D); school music-vocal (M Ed); science education (M Ed, MAT, Ed S); secondary education (MAT); secondary school reading (M Ed); social studies education (M Ed, Ed S), including education-secondary (M Ed); special education (M Ed, Ed D, PhD, Ed S); teacher education (MAT, Ed D, PhD). *Degree requirements:* For doctorate, thesis/dissertation. *Entrance requirements:* For master's, Michigan Basic Skills Test (MA in teaching), minimum GPA of 2.6; for doctorate, minimum undergraduate GPA of 3.0, graduate 3.5; interview, curriculum vitae; references. Additional exam requirements/recommendations for international students: Required—TOEFL (minimum score 550 paper-based; 213 computer-based), TWE (minimum score 6). Electronic applications accepted. *Faculty research:* Reading and writing literacy and literature.

Western Kentucky University, Graduate Studies, Potter College of Arts and Letters, Department of Art, Bowling Green, KY 42101. Offers art education (MA Ed). *Accreditation:* NASAD; NCATE. Part-time and evening/weekend programs available. *Degree requirements:* For master's, comprehensive exam, final exam. *Entrance requirements:* For master's, GRE General Test, minimum GPA of 2.75. Additional exam requirements/recommendations for international students: Required—TOEFL (minimum score 555 paper-based; 213 computer-based; 79 iBT). *Expenses:* Tuition, state resident: full-time $4160; part-time $416 per credit hour. Tuition, nonresident: full-time $9550; part-time $506 per credit hour. Tuition and fees vary according to campus/location and reciprocity agreements. *Faculty research:* Nineteenth century Kentucky women artists.

Western Michigan University, Graduate College, College of Fine Arts, Gwen Frostic School of Art, Kalamazoo, MI 49008. Offers art education (MA); studio art (MFA). *Accreditation:* NASAD (one or more programs are accredited). *Faculty:* 27 full-time (10 women). *Students:* 4 full-time (2 women), 3 part-time (1 woman). 17 applicants, 35% accepted, 0 enrolled. In 2009, 5 master's awarded. *Degree requirements:* For master's, thesis or alternative. *Application deadline:* For fall admission, 2/15 priority date for domestic students. Applications are processed on a rolling basis. Application fee: $25. *Financial support:* Fellowships, research assistantships, teaching assistantships, Federal Work-Study available. Financial award application deadline: 2/15; financial award applicants required to submit FAFSA. *Application contact:* Admissions and Orientation, 269-387-2000, Fax: 269-387-2355.

West Virginia University, College of Creative Arts, Division of Art and Design, Morgantown, WV 26506. Offers art education (MA); art history (MA); ceramics (MFA); graphic design (MFA);

painting (MFA); printmaking (MFA); sculpture (MFA); studio art (MA). *Accreditation:* NASAD. *Degree requirements:* For master's, thesis, exhibit. *Entrance requirements:* For master's, minimum GPA of 2.75, portfolio. Additional exam requirements/recommendations for international students: Required—TOEFL. *Expenses:* Contact institution. *Faculty research:* Medieval art history.

William Carey University, School of Education, Hattiesburg, MS 39401-5499. Offers art education (M Ed); art of teaching (M Ed); elementary education (M Ed, Ed S); English education (M Ed); gifted education (M Ed); history and social science (M Ed); mild/moderate disabilities (M Ed); secondary education (M Ed). Part-time programs available. *Degree requirements:* For master's, comprehensive exam. *Entrance requirements:* For master's, GRE, MAT, minimum

GPA of 2.5, Class A teacher's license. Additional exam requirements/recommendations for international students: Required—TOEFL (minimum score 550 paper-based; 213 computer-based).

Winthrop University, College of Visual and Performing Arts, Department of Art, Rock Hill, SC 29733. Offers art (MFA); art administration (MA); art education (MA). *Accreditation:* NASAD. Part-time programs available. *Degree requirements:* For master's, thesis, documented exhibit, oral exam. *Entrance requirements:* For master's, GRE General Test or MAT, PRAXIS (MA), minimum GPA of 3.0, resume, slide portfolio, teaching certificate (MA). Electronic applications accepted.

Business Education

Arkansas State University—Jonesboro, Graduate School, College of Business, Department of Computer and Information Technology, Jonesboro, State University, AR 72467. Offers business technology education (MSE); information systems and e-commerce (MS). Part-time programs available. *Faculty:* 11 full-time (2 women). *Students:* 6 full-time (2 women), 23 part-time (17 women); includes 9 minority (all African Americans), 3 international. Average age 35. 11 applicants, 82% accepted, 9 enrolled. In 2009, 17 master's awarded. *Degree requirements:* For master's, comprehensive exam, thesis or alternative. *Entrance requirements:* For master's, GRE General Test or MAT, appropriate bachelor's degree, official transcript, immunization records. Additional exam requirements/recommendations for international students: Required—TOEFL (minimum score 550 paper-based; 213 computer-based; 79 iBT), IELTS (minimum score 6). *Application deadline:* For fall admission, 7/15 for domestic students, 7/1 for international students; for spring admission, 12/1 for domestic students, 11/13 for international students. Applications are processed on a rolling basis. Application fee: $30 ($40 for international students). Electronic applications accepted. *Expenses:* Contact institution. *Financial support:* In 2009–10, 4 students received support. Career-related internships or fieldwork and unspecified assistantships available. Financial award application deadline: 7/1; financial award applicants required to submit FAFSA. *Unit head:* Dr. John Robertson, Chair, 870-972-3416, Fax: 870-972-3417, E-mail: jfrobert@astate.edu. *Application contact:* Dr. Andrew Sustich, Dean of the Graduate School, 870-972-3029, Fax: 870-972-3857, E-mail: sustich@astate.edu.

Arkansas State University—Jonesboro, Graduate School, College of Business, Department of Management and Marketing, Jonesboro, State University, AR 72467. Offers business administration education (SCCT); business technology education (SCCT). *Accreditation:* NCATE. Part-time programs available. *Faculty:* 8 full-time (3 women). *Students:* 2 part-time (1 woman); includes 1 minority (Asian American or Pacific Islander). Average age 30. *Degree requirements:* For SCCT, comprehensive exam. *Entrance requirements:* For degree, GRE General Test or MAT, interview, master's degree, official transcript, immunization records. Additional exam requirements/recommendations for international students: Required—TOEFL (minimum score 550 paper-based; 213 computer-based; 79 iBT), IELTS (minimum score 6). *Application deadline:* For fall admission, 7/15 for domestic students, 7/1 for international students; for spring admission, 12/1 for domestic students, 11/13 for international students. Applications are processed on a rolling basis. Application fee: $30 ($40 for international students). Electronic applications accepted. *Expenses:* Contact institution. *Financial support:* Career-related internships or fieldwork, scholarships/grants, and unspecified assistantships available. Financial award application deadline: 7/1; financial award applicants required to submit FAFSA. *Unit head:* Dr. Gail Hudson, Chair, 870-972-3430, Fax: 870-972-3833, E-mail: ghud@astate.edu. *Application contact:* Dr. Andrew Sustich, Dean of the Graduate School, 870-972-3029, Fax: 870-972-3857, E-mail: sustich@astate.edu.

Armstrong Atlantic State University, School of Graduate Studies, Program in Education, Savannah, GA 31419-1997. Offers adult education (M Ed); curriculum and instruction (M Ed); early childhood education (M Ed); education (M Ed); elementary education (M Ed); middle grades education (M Ed); secondary education (M Ed), including business education, English education, mathematics education, science education, social science education; special education (M Ed), including behavioral disorders, learning disabilities, speech-language pathology. *Accreditation:* NCATE. Part-time and evening/weekend programs available. Post-baccalaureate distance learning degree programs offered (minimal on-campus study). *Degree requirements:* For master's, comprehensive exam, portfolio. *Entrance requirements:* For master's, GRE General Test or MAT, minimum GPA of 2.5, letters of recommendation. Additional exam requirements/recommendations for international students: Required—TOEFL (minimum score 523 paper-based; 193 computer-based). Electronic applications accepted.

Auburn University, Graduate School, College of Education, Department of Curriculum and Teaching, Auburn University, AL 36849. Offers business education (M Ed, MS, PhD); early childhood education (M Ed, MS, PhD, Ed S); elementary education (M Ed, MS, PhD, Ed S); foreign languages (M Ed, MS); music education (M Ed, MS, PhD, Ed S); postsecondary education (PhD); reading education (PhD, Ed S); secondary education (M Ed, MS, PhD, Ed S), including English language arts, mathematics, science, social studies. *Accreditation:* NASM (one or more programs are accredited); NCATE. Part-time programs available. *Faculty:* 28 full-time (21 women), 8 part-time/adjunct (5 women). *Students:* 76 full-time (55 women), 186 part-time (139 women); includes 43 minority (29 African Americans, 1 American Indian/Alaska Native, 4 Asian Americans or Pacific Islanders, 9 Hispanic Americans), 4 international. Average age 33. 248 applicants, 65% accepted, 110 enrolled. In 2009, 102 master's, 12 doctorates, 6 other advanced degrees awarded. *Degree requirements:* For master's, thesis (for some programs); for doctorate, thesis/dissertation; for Ed S, field project. *Entrance requirements:* For master's, doctorate, and Ed S, GRE General Test. *Application deadline:* For fall admission, 7/7 for domestic students; for spring admission, 11/24 for domestic students. Applications are processed on a rolling basis. Application fee: $50 ($60 for international students). Electronic applications accepted. *Expenses:* Tuition, state resident: full-time $6240. Tuition, nonresident: full-time $18,720. International tuition: $18,938 full-time. Required fees: $492. Tuition and fees vary according to course load, program and reciprocity agreements. *Financial support:* Fellowships, teaching assistantships, career-related internships or fieldwork and Federal Work-Study available. Support available to part-time students. Financial award application deadline: 3/15; financial award applicants required to submit FAFSA. *Faculty research:* Emerging literacy, reading attitudes, music for at-risk youth, portfolio assessment. *Unit head:* Dr. Nancy H. Barry, Head, 334-844-4434. *Application contact:* Dr. George Flowers, Dean of the Graduate School, 334-844-2125.

Ball State University, Graduate School, Miller College of Business, Department of Information Systems and Operations Management, Muncie, IN 47306-1099. Offers business education (MAE). *Accreditation:* NCATE. *Entrance requirements:* For master's, GMAT.

Bloomsburg University of Pennsylvania, School of Graduate Studies, College of Business, Department of Business Education and Business Information Systems, Program in Business Education, Bloomsburg, PA 17815-1301. Offers M Ed. *Degree requirements:* For master's, thesis optional. *Entrance requirements:* For master's, GRE General Test, minimum QPA of 3.0, 2 letters of recommendation. Additional exam requirements/recommendations for international students: Required—TOEFL. Electronic applications accepted. *Faculty research:* Records and information management, training and development, ergonomics, office technology, telecommunications.

Bowling Green State University, Graduate College, College of Education and Human Development, School of Education and Intervention Services, Teaching and Learning Division,

Department of Business Education, Bowling Green, OH 43403. Offers M Ed. *Accreditation:* NCATE. Part-time programs available. *Degree requirements:* For master's, thesis or alternative. *Entrance requirements:* For master's, GRE General Test. Additional exam requirements/recommendations for international students: Required—TOEFL. Electronic applications accepted. *Faculty research:* School to work, workforce education, marketing education, contextual teaching and learning.

Buffalo State College, State University of New York, The Graduate School, Faculty of Applied Science and Education, Department of Business Studies, Buffalo, NY 14222-1095. Offers business and marketing education (MS Ed). Part-time and evening/weekend programs available. *Degree requirements:* For master's, thesis or alternative, project. *Entrance requirements:* For master's, minimum GPA of 2.5, New York teaching certificate.

Central Connecticut State University, School of Graduate Studies, School of Business, Program in Business Education, New Britain, CT 06050-4010. Offers MS, Certificate. Part-time and evening/weekend programs available. *Students:* 3 full-time (all women), 2 part-time (both women). Average age 38. In 2009, 3 master's awarded. *Degree requirements:* For master's, comprehensive exam, thesis or alternative; for Certificate, qualifying exam. *Entrance requirements:* For master's, bachelor's degree in business or equivalent, minimum GPA of 2.7. Additional exam requirements/recommendations for international students: Required—TOEFL. *Application deadline:* For fall admission, 7/1 for domestic students; for spring admission, 12/1 for domestic students. Applications are processed on a rolling basis. Application fee: $50. Electronic applications accepted. *Expenses:* Tuition, area resident: Full-time $4662; part-time $440 per credit. Tuition, state resident: full-time $6994; part-time $440 per credit. Tuition, nonresident: full-time $12,988; part-time $440 per credit. Required fees: $3606. One-time fee: $62 part-time. *Financial support:* Application deadline: 3/1. *Faculty research:* Marketing education, office systems education, accounting education for secondary schools. *Unit head:* Dr. George Claffey, Coordinator, 860-832-2509. *Application contact:* Dr. George Claffey, Coordinator, 860-832-2509.

Chadron State College, School of Professional and Graduate Studies, Department of Education, Chadron, NE 69337. Offers business (MA Ed); community counseling (MA Ed); educational administration (MS Ed, Sp Ed); elementary education (MS Ed); history (MA Ed); language and literature (MA Ed); secondary administration (MS Ed); secondary education (MS Ed). *Accreditation:* NCATE. Part-time and evening/weekend programs available. Postbaccalaureate distance learning degree programs offered. *Degree requirements:* For master's, thesis optional. *Entrance requirements:* For master's, GRE General Test, GRE Writing Test, minimum GPA of 2.75 or 12 graduate hours at CSC with minimum GPA of 3.25. Additional exam requirements/recommendations for international students: Required—TOEFL. Electronic applications accepted. *Faculty research:* Rural education, technology, mental health.

The College of Saint Rose, Graduate Studies, School of Education, Teacher Education Department, Albany, NY 12203-1419. Offers business and marketing (MS Ed); childhood education (MS Ed); curriculum and instruction (MS Ed); early childhood education (MS Ed); elementary education (K-6) (MS Ed); secondary education (MS Ed, Certificate); teacher education (MS Ed, Certificate), including bilingual pupil personnel services (Certificate), teacher education (MS Ed). Part-time and evening/weekend programs available. *Entrance requirements:* For master's, minimum undergraduate GPA of 3.0. Additional exam requirements/recommendations for international students: Required—TOEFL (minimum score 550 paper-based; 213 computer-based). Electronic applications accepted.

Eastern Kentucky University, The Graduate School, College of Education, Department of Curriculum and Instruction, Program in Secondary and Higher Education, Richmond, KY 40475-3102. Offers secondary education (MA Ed), including agricultural education, art education, biological sciences education, business education, English education, geography education, history education, home economics education, industrial education, mathematical sciences education, physical education, school health education. *Accreditation:* NCATE. Part-time programs available. *Entrance requirements:* For master's, GRE General Test, minimum GPA of 2.5.

Emporia State University, School of Graduate Studies, School of Business, Department of Business Administration and Education, Program in Business Education, Emporia, KS 66801-5087. Offers MS. Part-time and evening/weekend programs available. Postbaccalaureate distance learning degree programs offered (no on-campus study). *Students:* 21 part-time (13 women); includes 1 minority (American Indian/Alaska Native). 6 applicants, 83% accepted, 1 enrolled. In 2009, 7 master's awarded. *Entrance requirements:* For master's, GRE, 15 undergraduate credits in business; minimum undergraduate GPA of 2.7 over last 60 hours. Additional exam requirements/recommendations for international students: Required—TOEFL (minimum score 520 paper-based; 133 computer-based; 68 iBT). *Application deadline:* For fall admission, 8/15 priority date for domestic students. Applications are processed on a rolling basis. Application fee: $30 ($75 for international students). Electronic applications accepted. *Expenses:* Tuition, state resident: full-time $4154; part-time $173 per credit hour. Tuition, nonresident: full-time $12,864; part-time $536 per credit hour. Required fees: $948; $58 per credit hour. Tuition and fees vary according to campus/location. *Financial support:* Career-related internships or fieldwork, institutionally sponsored loans, health care benefits, and unspecified assistantships available. Financial award application deadline: 3/15; financial award applicants required to submit FAFSA. *Unit head:* Dr. Jack Sterrett, Chair, 620-341-5345, Fax: 620-341-6345, E-mail: jsterret@emporia.edu. *Application contact:* Dr. Nancy Hite, Information Contact, 620-341-5345, Fax: 620-341-6345, E-mail: nhite@emporia.edu.

Florida Agricultural and Mechanical University, Division of Graduate Studies, Research, and Continuing Education, College of Education, Department of Vocational Education, Tallahassee, FL 32307-3200. Offers business education (MBE); industrial education (M Ed, MS Ed). *Accreditation:* NCATE. *Faculty:* 2 full-time (both women). *Students:* 7 full-time (6 women); all minorities (all African Americans). *Degree requirements:* For master's, thesis (for some programs). *Entrance requirements:* For master's, GRE General Test, minimum GPA of 3.0. Additional exam requirements/recommendations for international students: Required—TOEFL. *Application deadline:* For fall admission, 5/18 for domestic students, 12/18 for international students; for spring admission, 11/12 for domestic students, 5/12 for international students. Application fee: $20. *Unit head:* Dr. Mary Young, Chairperson, 850-599-3061. *Application contact:* Dr. Chanta M. Haywood, Dean of Graduate Studies, Research, and Continuing Education, 850-599-3315, Fax: 850-599-3727.

Business Education

Georgia Southern University, Jack N. Averitt College of Graduate Studies, College of Education, Department of Teaching and Learning, Program in Business Education, Statesboro, GA 30460. Offers M Ed, MAT. *Accreditation:* NCATE. Part-time and evening/weekend programs available. *Students:* 7 full-time (4 women), 3 part-time (2 women); includes 2 minority (both African Americans). Average age 33. 1 applicant, 100% accepted, 1 enrolled. In 2009, 4 master's awarded. *Degree requirements:* For master's, transition point assessments. *Entrance requirements:* For master's, GRE General Test or MAT, GACE Basic Skills and Content Assessments, minimum cumulative GPA of 2.5. Additional exam requirements/recommendations for international students: Required—TOEFL (minimum score 550 paper-based; 213 computer-based; 80 iBT). *Application deadline:* For fall admission, 3/1 priority date for domestic and international students; for spring admission, 10/1 priority date for domestic students, 10/1 for international students. Applications are processed on a rolling basis. Application fee: $50. Electronic applications accepted. *Expenses:* Tuition, state resident: full-time $5040; part-time $210 per credit hour. Tuition, nonresident: full-time $20,136; part-time $839 per credit hour. Required fees: $1644. *Financial support:* In 2009–10, 7 students received support, including research assistantships with partial tuition reimbursements available (averaging $7,200 per year), teaching assistantships with partial tuition reimbursements available (averaging $7,200 per year); Federal Work-Study, scholarships/grants, tuition waivers (partial), and unspecified assistantships also available. Support available to part-time students. Financial award application deadline: 4/15; financial award applicants required to submit FAFSA. *Faculty research:* Technology applications. *Unit head:* Dr. Ronnie Sheppard, Department Chair, 912-478-5203, Fax: 912-478-0026, E-mail: sheppard@georgiasouthern.edu. *Application contact:* Dr. Charles Ziglar, Coordinator for Graduate Student Recruitment, 912-478-5635, Fax: 912-478-0740, E-mail: gradadmissions@georgiasouthern.edu.

Hofstra University, School of Education, Health, and Human Services, Department of Curriculum and Teaching, Program in Business Education, Hempstead, NY 11549. Offers MS Ed. Part-time programs available. *Students:* 25 full-time (16 women), 16 part-time (13 women); includes 5 minority (3 African Americans, 1 Asian American or Pacific Islander, 1 Hispanic American). Average age 30. 24 applicants, 100% accepted, 14 enrolled. In 2009, 14 master's awarded. *Degree requirements:* For master's, one foreign language, electronic portfolio, student teaching. *Entrance requirements:* For master's, 2 letters of recommendation, BBA. Additional exam requirements/recommendations for international students: Required—TOEFL (minimum score 550 paper-based; 213 computer-based; 80 iBT). *Application deadline:* Applications are processed on a rolling basis. Application fee: $60. Electronic applications accepted. *Expenses:* Tuition: Full-time $16,200; part-time $900 per credit hour. Required fees: $970; $145 per term. Tuition and fees vary according to program. *Financial support:* In 2009–10, 27 students received support, including 2 fellowships with full and partial tuition reimbursements available (averaging $2,000 per year); research assistantships with full and partial tuition reimbursements available, Federal Work-Study, institutionally sponsored loans, scholarships/grants, tuition waivers (full and partial), and unspecified assistantships also available. Support available to part-time students. Financial award applicants required to submit FAFSA. *Faculty research:* Business curriculum, business ethics. *Unit head:* Dr. Marsha W. Iverson, Program Director, 516-463-5768, Fax: 516-463-6196, E-mail: catmwi@hofstra.edu. *Application contact:* Carol Drummer, Dean of Graduate Admissions, 516-463-4876, Fax: 516-463-4664, E-mail: gradstudent@hofstra.edu.

Inter American University of Puerto Rico, Metropolitan Campus, Graduate Programs, Program in Commerical Education, San Juan, PR 00919-1293. Offers MA.

Inter American University of Puerto Rico, San Germán Campus, Graduate Studies Center, Program in Business Education, San Germán, PR 00683-5008. Offers MA. Part-time and evening/weekend programs available. *Degree requirements:* For master's, comprehensive exam. *Entrance requirements:* For master's, GRE General Test or EXADEP, minimum GPA of 3.0.

International College of the Cayman Islands, Graduate Program in Management, Newlands, Cayman Islands. Offers business administration (MBA); management (MS), including education, human resources. Part-time and evening/weekend programs available. *Degree requirements:* For master's, comprehensive exam. *Faculty research:* International human resources administration.

Lehman College of the City University of New York, Division of Education, Department of Middle and High School Education, Program in Business Education, Bronx, NY 10468-1589. Offers MS Ed. *Accreditation:* NCATE. Part-time and evening/weekend programs available. *Degree requirements:* For master's, thesis. *Entrance requirements:* For master's, minimum GPA of 2.7.

Louisiana State University and Agricultural and Mechanical College, Graduate School, College of Agriculture, School of Human Resource Education and Workforce Development, Baton Rouge, LA 70803. Offers agriculture and extension education and youth development (MS, PhD); career and technical education (MS, PhD); comprehensive vocational education (MS, PhD); extension and international education (MS, PhD); human resource and leadership development (MS, PhD); industrial education (MS); vocational agriculture education (MS, PhD); vocational business education (MS); vocational home economics education (MS). *Accreditation:* NCATE. Part-time programs available. *Faculty:* 11 full-time (5 women), 2 part-time/adjunct (both women). *Students:* 39 full-time (22 women), 75 part-time (51 women); includes 14 African Americans, 1 Asian American or Pacific Islander, 2 Hispanic Americans, 7 international. Average age 37. 40 applicants, 93% accepted, 18 enrolled. In 2009, 16 master's, 13 doctorates awarded. Terminal master's awarded for partial completion of doctoral program. *Degree requirements:* For master's, thesis (for some programs); for doctorate, thesis/dissertation. *Entrance requirements:* For master's and doctorate, GRE General Test, minimum GPA of 3.0. Additional exam requirements/recommendations for international students: Required—TOEFL (minimum score 550 paper-based; 213 computer-based; 79 iBT) or IELTS (minimum score 6.5). *Application deadline:* For fall admission, 1/25 priority date for domestic students, 5/15 for international students; for spring admission, 10/15 for international students. Applications are processed on a rolling basis. Application fee: $50 ($70 for international students). Electronic applications accepted. *Financial support:* In 2009–10, 63 students received support, including 3 fellowships with full and partial tuition reimbursements available (averaging $24,885 per year), 5 research assistantships with full and partial tuition reimbursements available (averaging $14,440 per year), 4 teaching assistantships with partial tuition reimbursements available (averaging $13,750 per year); career-related internships or fieldwork, Federal Work-Study, institutionally sponsored loans, health care benefits, tuition waivers (full and partial), and unspecified assistantships also available. Financial award application deadline: 3/1; financial award applicants required to submit FAFSA. *Faculty research:* Adult education, history and philosophy of vocational education, curriculum and instruction, career decision making. Total annual research expenditures: $21,538. *Unit head:* Dr. Michael F. Burnett, Director, 225-578-5748, Fax: 225-578-2526, E-mail: vocbur@lsu.edu. *Application contact:* Paula Beecher, Recruiting Coordinator, 225-578-2468, E-mail: pbeeche@lsu.edu.

Louisiana Tech University, Graduate School, College of Education, Department of Curriculum, Instruction and Leadership, Ruston, LA 71272. Offers curriculum and instruction (MS, Ed D); educational leadership (Ed D); secondary education (M Ed), including business education, English education, foreign language education, health and physical education, mathematics education, science education, social studies education, speech education. *Accreditation:* NCATE. Part-time programs available. *Degree requirements:* For doctorate, thesis/dissertation. *Entrance requirements:* For master's and doctorate, GRE General Test.

Maryville University of Saint Louis, The John E. Simon School of Business, St. Louis, MO 63141-7299. Offers accounting (MBA, PGC); business studies (PGC); internet marketing (MBA, PGC); management (MBA, PGC); marketing (MBA, PGC). *Accreditation:* ACBSP. Part-time and evening/weekend programs available. *Students:* 17 full-time (9 women), 133 part-time (70 women); includes 14 minority (6 African Americans, 1 American Indian/Alaska Native, 3 Asian Americans or Pacific Islanders, 4 Hispanic Americans), 4 international. Average age 30. In 2009, 68 master's awarded. *Entrance requirements:* For master's, GMAT (unless applicant possesses undergraduate business degree with minimum cumulative GPA of 3.0, or has completed master's degree from accredited university, or has completed one early access course prior to undergraduate degree). Additional exam requirements/recommendations for international students: Required—TOEFL (minimum score 550 paper-based). *Application deadline:* Applications are processed on a rolling basis. Application fee: $40 ($60 for international students). Electronic applications accepted. *Expenses:* Tuition: Full-time $20,384; part-time $627.50 per credit hour. Required fees: $100 per semester. *Financial support:* Career-related internships or fieldwork, Federal Work-Study, tuition waivers (partial), and campus employment available. Financial award application deadline: 3/1; financial award applicants required to submit FAFSA. *Faculty research:* International business, e-marketing, strategic planning, interpersonal management skills, financial analysis. *Unit head:* Dr. Pamela Horwitz, Dean, 314-529-9418, Fax: 314-529-9975, E-mail: horwitz@maryville.edu. *Application contact:* Kathy Dougherty, Director of MBA Admissions and Enrollment, 314-529-9382, Fax: 314-529-9975, E-mail: business@maryville.edu.

Middle Tennessee State University, College of Graduate Studies, Jennings A. Jones College of Business, Department of Business Communication and Entrepreneurship, Murfreesboro, TN 37132. Offers business education (MBE). Part-time and evening/weekend programs available. Postbaccalaureate distance learning degree programs offered. *Faculty:* 6 full-time (3 women). *Students:* 12 full-time (8 women), 38 part-time (27 women); includes 14 minority (all African Americans). Average age 29. 21 applicants, 76% accepted, 16 enrolled. In 2009, 17 master's awarded. *Degree requirements:* For master's, comprehensive exam. *Entrance requirements:* For master's, GRE or MAT. Additional exam requirements/recommendations for international students: Required—TOEFL (minimum score 525 paper-based; 195 computer-based; 71 iBT) or IELTS (minimum score 6). *Application deadline:* For fall admission, 6/1 for domestic and international students. Applications are processed on a rolling basis. Application fee: $25 ($30 for international students). Electronic applications accepted. *Expenses:* Tuition, state resident: full-time $4404. Tuition, nonresident: full-time $10,956. *Financial support:* In 2009–10, 10 students received support. Institutionally sponsored loans available. Support available to part-time students. Financial award application deadline: 5/1. *Faculty research:* Entrepreneurship, business and organizational communication, corporate training and development, teaching and assessment methods, administrative support personality. *Unit head:* Dr. Stephen D. Lewis, Chair, 615-898-2902, Fax: 615-898-5439. *Application contact:* Dr. Michael Allen, Dean and Vice Provost for Research, 615-898-2840, Fax: 615-904-8020, E-mail: mallen@mtsu.edu.

Mississippi College, Graduate School, School of Business, Clinton, MS 39058. Offers accounting (Certificate); business administration (MBA), including accounting; business education (M Ed); finance (MBA, Certificate); JD/MBA. *Accreditation:* ACBSP. Part-time and evening/weekend programs available. *Faculty:* 12 full-time (2 women), 5 part-time/adjunct (1 woman). *Students:* 101 full-time (41 women), 144 part-time (75 women); includes 41 minority (37 African Americans, 3 Asian Americans or Pacific Islanders, 1 Hispanic American), 78 international. Average age 28. In 2009, 90 master's awarded. *Degree requirements:* For master's, comprehensive exam, thesis optional. *Entrance requirements:* For master's, GMAT, minimum GPA of 2.5, 24 hours of undergraduate course work in business. Additional exam requirements/recommendations for international students: Recommended—IELTS. *Application deadline:* For fall admission, 8/15 priority date for domestic students. Applications are processed on a rolling basis. Application fee: $30. Electronic applications accepted. *Expenses:* Tuition: Part-time $452 per credit hour. Required fees: $101 per semester. Tuition and fees vary according to degree level, campus/location, program and student level. *Financial support:* Federal Work-Study and unspecified assistantships available. Support available to part-time students. Financial award application deadline: 4/1; financial award applicants required to submit FAFSA. *Unit head:* Dr. Marcelo Eduardo, Dean, 601-925-3420, E-mail: eduardo@mc.edu. *Application contact:* Elnora Lewis, Secretary, 601-925-3225, Fax: 601-925-3889, E-mail: lewis09@mc.edu.

Mississippi College, Graduate School, School of Education, Department of Teacher Education and Leadership, Clinton, MS 39058. Offers art (M Ed); biological science (M Ed); business education (M Ed); computer science (M Ed); dyslexia therapy (M Ed); educational leadership (M Ed, Ed D, Ed S); elementary education (M Ed, Ed S); English (M Ed); higher education administration (MS); mathematics (M Ed); secondary education (M Ed); social studies (history) (M Ed); teaching arts (M Ed). Part-time programs available. Postbaccalaureate distance learning degree programs offered (no on-campus study). *Faculty:* 11 full-time (7 women), 13 part-time/adjunct (7 women). *Students:* 33 full-time (22 women), 282 part-time (240 women); includes 148 minority (146 African Americans, 2 American Indian/Alaska Native), 1 international. Average age 34. In 2009, 147 master's awarded. *Degree requirements:* For master's, comprehensive exam, thesis optional. *Entrance requirements:* For master's, NTE. Additional exam requirements/recommendations for international students: Recommended—IELTS. *Application deadline:* For fall admission, 8/15 priority date for domestic students. Applications are processed on a rolling basis. Application fee: $30. Electronic applications accepted. *Expenses:* Tuition: Part-time $452 per credit hour. Required fees: $101 per semester. Tuition and fees vary according to degree level, campus/location, program and student level. *Financial support:* Teaching assistantships, career-related internships or fieldwork, Federal Work-Study, scholarships/grants, and unspecified assistantships also available. Support available to part-time students. Financial award applicants required to submit FAFSA. *Unit head:* Dr. Tom Williams, Chair, 601-925-3844, E-mail: twilliams@mc.edu. *Application contact:* Elnora Lewis, Secretary, 601-925-3225, Fax: 601-925-3889, E-mail: lewis09@mc.edu.

Morehead State University, Graduate Programs, College of Education, Department of Foundational and Graduate Studies in Education, Morehead, KY 40351. Offers adult and higher education (MA, Ed S); certified professional counselor (Ed S); counseling P-12 (MA); curriculum and instruction (Ed S); educational technology (MA Ed); instructional leadership (Ed S); school administration (MA); school counseling (Ed S); teacher leader business and marketing- content (MA Ed); teacher leader business and marketing- technology (MA Ed); teacher leader educational technology (MA Ed); teacher leader English (MA Ed); teacher leader gifted educ (MA Ed); teacher leader IECE—non-certification (MA Ed); teacher leader IECE certification (MA Ed); teacher leader interdisciplinary educaction P-5 (MA Ed); teacher leader middle grades 5-9 (MA Ed); teacher leader reading/writing—non-certification (MA Ed); teacher leader reading/writing certification (MA Ed); teacher leader school communication—non-certification (MA Ed); teacher leader school communication certification (MA Ed); teacher leader social studies (MA Ed); teacher leader special education (MA Ed). *Accreditation:* NCATE. Part-time and evening/weekend programs available. *Faculty:* 20 full-time (10 women), 7 part-time/adjunct (3 women). *Students:* 26 full-time (18 women), 371 part-time (295 women); includes 11 minority (9 African Americans, 1 American Indian/Alaska Native, 1 Hispanic American). Average age 35. 201 applicants, 73% accepted, 73 enrolled. In 2009, 105 master's, 5 other advanced degrees awarded. *Degree requirements:* For master's, thesis optional, oral and/or written comprehensive exams; for Ed S, thesis, oral exam. *Entrance requirements:* For master's, GRE General Test, minimum overall undergraduate GPA of 2.5; for Ed S, GRE General Test, interview, master's degree, minimum GPA of 3.5, work experience. Additional exam requirements/recommendations for international students: Required—TOEFL (minimum score 500 paper-based; 173 computer-based). *Application deadline:* For fall admission, 8/1 priority date for domestic and international students; for spring admission, 12/1 priority date for domestic and international students. Applications are processed on a rolling basis. Application fee: $30. Electronic applications accepted. *Expenses:* Tuition, state resident: full-time $6318; part-time $351 per credit hour. Tuition, nonresident: full-time $15,804; part-time $878 per credit hour. *Financial support:* In 2009–10, 2 research assistantships (averaging $10,000 per year) were awarded; career-related internships or fieldwork, Federal Work-Study, and unspecified assistantships also available. Financial award application deadline: 3/15; financial award applicants required to submit FAFSA. *Faculty research:* Character education, school accountability, computer applications for school administrators. *Unit head:* Dr. Cathy Gunn, Dean and Professor, 606-783-2040, Fax: 606-783-5029, E-mail: c.gunn@moreheadstate.edu. *Application contact:* Michelle Barber, Graduate Recruitment and Retention Assistant Director, 606-783-5127, Fax: 606-783-5061, E-mail: m.barber@moreheadstate.edu.

Morehead State University, Graduate Programs, College of Education, Department of Middle Grades and Secondary Education, Morehead, KY 40351. Offers business and marketing education (MAT); English/language arts 5-9 (MAT); French (MAT); health P-12 (MAT); mathematics 5-9 (MAT); physical education P-12 (MAT); science 5-9 (MAT); secondary biology (MAT); secondary chemistry (MAT); secondary earth science (MAT); secondary English (MAT); secondary math (MAT); secondary physics (MAT); secondary social studies (MAT); social studies 5-9 (MAT); Spanish (MAT). Part-time and evening/weekend programs available. *Students:* 54 full-time (31 women), 233 part-time (142 women); includes 11 minority (5 African Americans, 1 American Indian/Alaska Native, 1 Asian American or Pacific Islander, 4 Hispanic Americans). Average age 32. 206 applicants, 71% accepted, 79 enrolled. In 2009, 101 master's awarded. *Degree requirements:* For master's, portfolio. *Entrance requirements:* For master's, GRE or PRAXIS II content exam, minimum overall undergraduate GPA of 2.5. Additional exam requirements/recommendations for international students: Required—TOEFL (minimum score 500 paper-based; 173 computer-based). *Application deadline:* For fall admission, 8/1 priority date for domestic and international students; for spring admission, 12/1 priority date for domestic and international students. Applications are processed on a rolling basis. Application fee: $30. Electronic applications accepted. *Expenses:* Tuition, state resident: full-time $6318; part-time $351 per credit hour. Tuition, nonresident: full-time $15,804; part-time $878 per credit hour. *Financial support:* In 2009–10, 1 research assistantship (averaging $10,000 per year) was awarded; career-related internships or fieldwork, Federal Work-Study, and unspecified assistantships also available. Financial award application deadline: 3/15; financial award applicants required to submit FAFSA. *Unit head:* Dr. Cathy Gunn, Dean, 606-783-2040, Fax: 606-783-5029, E-mail: c.gunn@moreheadstate.edu. *Application contact:* Michelle Barber, Graduate Recruitment and Retention Assistant Director, 606-783-5127, Fax: 606-783-5061, E-mail: m.barber@moreheadstate.edu.

Nazareth College of Rochester, Graduate Studies, Department of Business, Program in Business Education, Rochester, NY 14618-3790. Offers MS Ed. Part-time and evening/weekend programs available. *Entrance requirements:* For master's, minimum GPA of 3.0.

New York University, Steinhardt School of Culture, Education, and Human Development, Department of Administration, Leadership, and Technology, Program in Business Education, New York, NY 10012-1019. Offers business education (Advanced Certificate); business education in higher education (MA); workplace learning (Advanced Certificate). *Accreditation:* Teacher Education Accreditation Council. Part-time programs available. *Students:* 8 full-time (7 women), 29 part-time (23 women); includes 14 minority (4 African Americans, 2 Asian Americans or Pacific Islanders, 8 Hispanic Americans), 4 international. Average age 35. 16 applicants, 44% accepted, 5 enrolled. In 2009, 8 master's, 1 other advanced degree awarded. *Degree requirements:* For master's, thesis (for some programs). *Entrance requirements:* For degree, master's degree. Additional exam requirements/recommendations for international students: Required—TOEFL. *Application deadline:* For fall admission, 12/15 priority date for domestic and international students; for spring admission, 11/1 for domestic and international students. Applications are processed on a rolling basis. Application fee: $75. Electronic applications accepted. *Expenses:* Tuition: Full-time $30,528; part-time $1272 per credit. Required fees: $2177. *Financial support:* Fellowships with full and partial tuition reimbursements, career-related internships or fieldwork, Federal Work-Study, institutionally sponsored loans, scholarships/grants, tuition waivers (partial), and unspecified assistantships available. Support available to part-time students. Financial award application deadline: 2/1; financial award applicants required to submit FAFSA. *Faculty research:* Applications of technology to instruction, workplace and corporate education, adult learning. *Unit head:* Dr. Bridget N. O'Connor, Director, 212-998-5488, Fax: 212-995-4041, E-mail: bridget.oconnor@nyu.edu. *Application contact:* 212-998-5030, Fax: 212-995-4328, E-mail: steinhardt.gradadmissions@nyu.edu.

North Carolina State University, Graduate School, College of Education, Department of Curriculum and Instruction, Program in Business and Marketing Education, Raleigh, NC 27695. Offers M Ed, MS. *Entrance requirements:* For master's, MAT or GRE, minimum GPA of 3.0, teaching license, 3 letters of reference.

Northwestern State University of Louisiana, Graduate Studies and Research, College of Education, Programs in Education, Natchitoches, LA 71497. Offers business and distributive education (M Ed); counseling (M Ed); early childhood education (M Ed); education (M Ed); education leadership (M Ed); educational technology (M Ed); elementary teaching (M Ed); English education (M Ed); home economics education (M Ed); mathematics education (M Ed); reading (M Ed); science education (M Ed); secondary teaching (M Ed); social sciences education (M Ed). *Degree requirements:* For master's, comprehensive exam, thesis or alternative. *Entrance requirements:* For master's, GRE General Test, minimum undergraduate GPA of 2.5.

Old Dominion University, Darden College of Education, Programs in Occupational and Technical Studies, Norfolk, VA 23529. Offers business and industry training (MS); career and technical education (MS, PhD); community college teaching (MS); human resources training (PhD); technology education (PhD). *Accreditation:* NCATE (one or more programs are accredited). Part-time and evening/weekend programs available. Postbaccalaureate distance learning degree programs offered (minimal on-campus study). *Faculty:* 6 full-time (1 woman), 8 part-time/adjunct (3 women). *Students:* 17 full-time (12 women), 67 part-time (39 women); includes 21 minority (17 African Americans, 1 Asian American or Pacific Islander, 3 Hispanic Americans), 2 international. Average age 41. 44 applicants, 95% accepted, 37 enrolled. In 2009, 18 master's, 7 doctorates awarded. *Degree requirements:* For master's, comprehensive exam, thesis optional, writing exam, candidacy exam; for doctorate, comprehensive exam, thesis/dissertation, writing exam, candidacy exam. *Entrance requirements:* For master's, GRE General Test or MAT, minimum GPA of 2.8, 2 letters of reference; for doctorate, GRE, minimum GPA of 3.0, 3 letters of reference. Additional exam requirements/recommendations for international students: Required—TOEFL. *Application deadline:* For fall admission, 6/1 priority date for domestic students, 6/1 for international students; for winter admission, 11/1 priority date for domestic students, 11/1 for international students; for spring admission, 3/1 priority date for domestic students, 3/1 for international students. Applications are processed on a rolling basis. Application fee: $40. Electronic applications accepted. *Expenses:* Tuition, state resident: full-time $8112; part-time $338 per credit. Tuition, nonresident: full-time $20,256; part-time $844 per credit. Required fees: $119 per semester. One-time fee: $50. *Financial support:* In 2009–10, 19 students received support, including 1 fellowship with full tuition reimbursement available (averaging $15,000 per year), 2 research assistantships with partial tuition reimbursements available (averaging $9,000 per year), 4 teaching assistantships with partial tuition reimbursements available (averaging $15,000 per year); career-related internships or fieldwork, scholarships/grants, tuition waivers (partial), and unspecified assistantships also available. Support available to part-time students. Financial award application deadline: 2/15; financial award applicants required to submit FAFSA. *Faculty research:* Training and development, marketing, technology, special populations, support of academic subjects. Total annual research expenditures: $799,773. *Unit head:* Dr. John M. Ritz, Graduate Program Director, 757-683-4305, Fax: 757-683-5227, E-mail: jritz@odu.edu. *Application contact:* Dr. John M. Ritz, Graduate Program Director, 757-683-4305, Fax: 757-683-5227, E-mail: jritz@odu.edu.

Pontifical Catholic University of Puerto Rico, College of Education, Doctoral Program in Business Teacher Education, Ponce, PR 00717-0777. Offers PhD. *Degree requirements:* For doctorate, thesis/dissertation. *Entrance requirements:* For doctorate, EXADEP, GRE General Test or MAT, 3 letters of recommendation.

Pontifical Catholic University of Puerto Rico, College of Education, Master's Program in Business Teacher Education, Ponce, PR 00717-0777. Offers M Ed. *Degree requirements:* For master's, comprehensive exam, thesis (for some programs). *Entrance requirements:* For master's, GRE, 2 letters of recommendation, interview, minimum GPA of 2.75.

Rider University, Department of Graduate Education, Leadership and Counseling, Teacher Certification Program, Lawrenceville, NJ 08648-3001. Offers business education (Certificate); elementary education (Certificate); English as a second language (Certificate); English education (Certificate); mathematics education (Certificate); preschool to grade 3 (Certificate); science education (Certificate); social studies education (Certificate); world languages (Certificate), including French, German, Spanish. Part-time programs available. *Degree requirements:* For Certificate, internship, professional portfolio. *Entrance requirements:* For degree, PRAXIS, resume. Additional exam requirements/recommendations for international students: Required—TOEFL (minimum score 550 paper-based; 213 computer-based). Electronic applications accepted. *Faculty research:* Conceptual foundations for optimal development of creativity; creative theory, cognitive processes in mathematics learning, teacher collaboration.

Robert Morris University, Graduate Studies, School of Education and Social Sciences, Moon Township, PA 15108-1189. Offers business education (MS); education (Postbaccalaureate Certificate); instructional leadership (MS); instructional management and leadership (PhD). *Accreditation:* Teacher Education Accreditation Council. Part-time and evening/weekend programs available. *Faculty:* 14 full-time (3 women), 11 part-time/adjunct (6 women). *Students:* 353 part-time (229 women); includes 24 minority (21 African Americans, 1 Asian American or Pacific Islander, 2 Hispanic Americans), 1 international. Average age 31. 117 applicants, 96% accepted, 79 enrolled. In 2009, 79 master's, 14 doctorates, 97 other advanced degrees awarded. *Degree requirements:* For doctorate, thesis/dissertation. *Entrance requirements:* Additional exam requirements/recommendations for international students: Required—TOEFL (minimum score 550 paper-based; 213 computer-based; 79 iBT). *Application deadline:* For fall admission, 7/1 priority date for domestic and international students; for spring admission, 11/1 priority date for domestic and international students. Applications are processed on a rolling basis. Application fee: $35. Electronic applications accepted. *Expenses:* Contact institution. *Unit head:* Dr. John E. Graham, Dean, 412-397-3228, Fax: 412-397-2524, E-mail: graham@rmu.edu. *Application contact:* Debra Roach, Assistant Dean, Graduate Admissions, 412-397-5200, Fax: 412-397-2425, E-mail: graduateadmissions@rmu.edu.

South Carolina State University, School of Graduate Studies, Department of Education, Orangeburg, SC 29117-0001. Offers early childhood and special education (M Ed); early childhood education (MAT); elementary education (M Ed, MAT); engineering (MAT); general science (MAT); mathematics (MAT); secondary education (M Ed), including biology education, business education, counselor education, English education, home economics education, industrial education, mathematics education, science education, social studies education; special education (M Ed), including emotionally handicapped, learning disabilities, mentally handicapped. *Accreditation:* NCATE. Part-time and evening/weekend programs available. *Degree requirements:* For master's, thesis optional, departmental qualifying exam. *Entrance requirements:* For master's, GRE General Test, NTE, interview, teaching certificate. Electronic applications accepted. *Expenses:* Tuition, state resident: part-time $470 per credit hour. Tuition, nonresident: part-time $924 per credit hour. *Faculty research:* Critical thinking, child abuse, stress, test-taking skills, conflict resolution, mainstreaming.

Southern New Hampshire University, School of Education, Manchester, NH 03106-1045. Offers business education (MS); child development (M Ed); computer technology education (Certificate); curriculum and instruction (M Ed); education (M Ed, CAS); elementary education (M Ed); general special education (Certificate); school business administrator (Certificate); secondary education (M Ed); training and development (Certificate). Part-time and evening/weekend programs available. Postbaccalaureate distance learning degree programs offered (no on-campus study). *Degree requirements:* For master's, comprehensive exam (for some programs), thesis or alternative. *Entrance requirements:* For master's, PRAXIS I, minimum GPA of 2.75. Additional exam requirements/recommendations for international students: Required—TOEFL (minimum score 550 paper-based; 213 computer-based). Electronic applications accepted. *Expenses:* Contact institution.

State University of New York at Oswego, Graduate Studies, School of Education, Department of Vocational Teacher Preparation, Oswego, NY 13126. Offers agriculture (MS Ed); business and marketing (MS Ed); family and consumer sciences (MS Ed); health careers (MS Ed); technical education (MS Ed); trade education (MS Ed). *Accreditation:* NCATE. Part-time and evening/weekend programs available. *Degree requirements:* For master's, thesis or alternative. *Entrance requirements:* Additional exam requirements/recommendations for international students: Required—TOEFL (minimum score 560 paper-based; 220 computer-based).

Thomas College, Graduate School, Programs in Business, Waterville, ME 04901-5097. Offers business (MBA); computer technology education (MS); education (MS); human resource management (MBA). Part-time and evening/weekend programs available. *Entrance requirements:* For master's, GMAT, GRE, MAT or minimum GPA of 3.3 in first 3 graduate-level courses.

The University of British Columbia, Faculty of Education, Department of Curriculum and Pedagogy, Vancouver, BC V6T 1Z4, Canada. Offers art education (M Ed, MA); business education (MA); curriculum studies (M Ed, MA, PhD); home economics education (M Ed, MA); math education (M Ed, MA); music education (M Ed, MA); physical education (M Ed, MA); science education (M Ed, MA); social studies education (M Ed, MA); technology studies education (M Ed, MA). Part-time programs available. *Degree requirements:* For master's, thesis (MA); for doctorate, comprehensive exam, thesis/dissertation. *Entrance requirements:* Additional exam requirements/recommendations for international students: Required—TOEFL (minimum score 580 paper-based; 237 computer-based; 92 iBT). Electronic applications accepted. *Expenses:* Contact institution. *Faculty research:* School subjects, teaching and learning.

University of Delaware, Alfred Lerner College of Business and Economics, Department of Economics, Newark, DE 19716. Offers economics (MA, MS, PhD); economics for entrepreneurship and educators (MA); MA/MBA. Part-time programs available. *Degree requirements:* For master's, comprehensive exam, thesis (for some programs), mathematics review exam, research project; for doctorate, comprehensive exam, thesis/dissertation, field exam. *Entrance requirements:* For master's, GMAT or GRE General Test, minimum GPA of 2.5; for doctorate, GRE General Test, minimum GPA of 3.5 in graduate economics course work. Additional exam requirements/recommendations for international students: Required—TOEFL (minimum score 550 paper-based; 225 computer-based). Electronic applications accepted. *Faculty research:* Applied quantitative economics, industrial organization, resource economics, monetary economics, labor economics.

University of Minnesota, Twin Cities Campus, Graduate School, College of Education and Human Development, Department of Organizational Leadership, Policy and Development, Program in Business and Industry Education, Minneapolis, MN 55455-0213. Offers M Ed, MA, Ed D, PhD. *Students:* 19 full-time (9 women), 14 part-time (3 women); includes 5 minority (2 African Americans, 3 Asian Americans or Pacific Islanders), 1 international. Average age 34. 22 applicants, 77% accepted, 15 enrolled. In 2009, 33 master's awarded. *Application contact:* Dr. Mary Trettin, Associate Dean, 612-625-6501, Fax: 612-626-1580, E-mail: mtrettin@umn.edu.

University of Missouri, Graduate School, College of Education, Department of Learning, Teaching and Curriculum, Columbia, MO 65211. Offers agricultural education (M Ed, PhD, Ed S); art education (M Ed, PhD, Ed S); business and office education (M Ed, PhD, Ed S); early childhood education (M Ed, PhD, Ed S); elementary education (M Ed, PhD, Ed S); English education (M Ed, PhD, Ed S); foreign language education (M Ed, PhD, Ed S); health education and promotion (M Ed, PhD); learning and instruction (M Ed); marketing education (M Ed, PhD, Ed S); mathematics education (M Ed, PhD, Ed S); music education (M Ed, PhD, Ed S); reading education (M Ed, PhD, Ed S); science education (M Ed, PhD, Ed S); social studies education (M Ed, PhD, Ed S); vocational education (M Ed, PhD, Ed S). Part-time programs available. Terminal master's awarded for partial completion of doctoral program. *Degree requirements:* For doctorate, thesis/dissertation. *Entrance requirements:* For master's and Ed S, GRE General Test or MAT, minimum GPA of 3.0; for doctorate, GRE General Test, minimum GPA of 3.0. Additional exam requirements/recommendations for international students: Required—TOEFL (minimum score 600 paper-based; 250 computer-based; 100 iBT). Electronic applications accepted.

University of St. Francis, College of Business and Health Administration, School of Professional Studies, Joliet, IL 60435-6169. Offers training and development (MS). *Accreditation:* ACBSP. Part-time and evening/weekend programs available. Postbaccalaureate distance

Business Education

University of St. Francis (continued)
learning degree programs offered (no on-campus study). *Faculty:* 2 full-time (1 woman), 4 part-time/adjunct (1 woman). *Students:* 10 full-time (9 women), 46 part-time (43 women); includes 16 minority (14 African Americans, 2 Asian Americans or Pacific Islanders). Average age 41. 48 applicants, 69% accepted, 25 enrolled. In 2009, 29 master's awarded. *Entrance requirements:* For master's, minimum undergraduate GPA of 2.75, computer competency, 2 letters of recommendation, 2 years of work experience. Additional exam requirements/recommendations for international students: Required—TOEFL (minimum score 550 paper-based; 213 computer-based). *Application deadline:* Applications are processed on a rolling basis. Application fee: $30. Electronic applications accepted. *Expenses:* Contact institution. *Financial support:* In 2009–10, 31 students received support. Tuition waivers (partial) available. Support available to part-time students. Financial award applicants required to submit FAFSA. *Unit head:* Dr. Michael LaRocco, Dean, 815-740-5025, Fax: 815-774-2920, E-mail: mlarocco@stfrancis.edu. *Application contact:* Sandra Sloka, Director of Admissions for Graduate and Degree Completion Programs, 800-735-7500, Fax: 815-740-5032, E-mail: ssloka@stfrancis.edu.

University of South Carolina, The Graduate School, College of Education, Department of Instruction and Teacher Education, Program in Secondary Education, Columbia, SC 29208. Offers art education (IMA, MAT); business education (IMA, MAT); English (MAT); foreign language (MAT); health education (MAT); mathematics (MAT); science (IMA, MAT); secondary (Ed D); secondary education (MT, PhD); social studies (MAT); theatre and speech (MAT). IMA and MT offered jointly with the subject areas. *Accreditation:* NCATE. *Degree requirements:* For master's, comprehensive exam, thesis (for some programs), foreign language (MA); for doctorate, one foreign language, comprehensive exam, thesis/dissertation. *Entrance requirements:* For master's, GRE General Test or MAT, teaching certificate (IMA, M Ed), interview; for doctorate, GRE General Test or MAT, interview. *Faculty research:* Middle school programs, professional development, school collaboration.

The University of Toledo, College of Graduate Studies, College of Education, Department of Curriculum and Instruction, Program in Education and Economics, Toledo, OH 43606-3390. Offers MAE.

University of Washington, Graduate School, Michael G. Foster School of Business, Seattle, WA 98195-3200. Offers auditing and assurance (MP Acc); business (PhD); business administration (evening) (MBA); business administration (full-time) (MBA); executive business administration (MBA); global business administration (MBA); global executive business administration (MBA); taxation (MP Acc); technology management (MBA); JD/MBA; MBA/MAIS; MBA/MHA. *Accreditation:* AACSB. Part-time and evening/weekend programs available. Terminal master's awarded for partial completion of doctoral program. *Degree requirements:* For doctorate, comprehensive exam, thesis/dissertation. *Entrance requirements:* For master's, GMAT; for doctorate, GMAT, GRE. Additional exam requirements/recommendations for international students: Required—TOEFL (minimum score 600 paper-based; 250 computer-based). Electronic applications accepted. *Expenses:* Contact institution. *Faculty research:* Finance, marketing, organizational behavior, information technology, strategy.

University of West Georgia, Graduate School, College of Education, Department of Curriculum and Instruction, Carrollton, GA 30118. Offers art education (M Ed); art teacher education (Ed S); biology/secondary education (Ed S); business education (M Ed, Ed S); early childhood education (M Ed, Ed S); economics/secondary teacher education (Ed S); English teacher education (Ed S); French language teacher education (Ed S); history teacher education (Ed S); mathematics teacher education (Ed S); middle grades education (M Ed, Ed S); reading education (M Ed, Ed S); science teacher education (Ed S); secondary education (M Ed, Ed S); social science teacher education (Ed S); Spanish language teacher education (Ed S). Part-time and evening/weekend programs available. *Faculty:* 18 full-time (15 women), 7 part-time/adjunct (6 women). *Students:* 119 full-time (101 women), 358 part-time (280 women); includes 109 minority (97 African Americans, 3 American Indian/Alaska Native, 2 Asian Americans or Pacific Islanders, 7 Hispanic Americans). Average age 33. 193 applicants, 82% accepted, 34 enrolled. In 2009, 109 master's, 27 Ed Ss awarded. *Degree requirements:* For master's, comprehensive exam; for Ed S, research project. *Entrance requirements:* For master's, GRE General Test or MAT, minimum GPA of 2.7; for Ed S, GRE General Test, master's degree, minimum graduate GPA of 2.7. *Application deadline:* For fall admission, 7/17 for domestic students; for spring admission, 11/20 for domestic students. Applications are processed on a rolling basis. Application fee: $30. Electronic applications accepted. *Expenses:* Tuition, state resident: full-time $2952; part-time $164 per semester hour. Tuition, nonresident: full-time $11,808; part-time $656 per semester hour. Required fees: $42.90 per semester hour. $307 per semester. Tuition and fees vary according to course load. *Financial support:* In 2009–10, 5 research assistantships with full tuition reimbursements (averaging $3,000 per year) were awarded; career-related internships or fieldwork and scholarships/grants also available. Support available to part-time students. Financial award applicants required to submit FAFSA. *Unit head:* Dr. Donna Harkins, Chair, 678-839-6066, Fax: 678-839-6559, E-mail: dharkins@westga.edu. *Application contact:* Dr. Charles W. Clark, Dean, 678-839-6508, E-mail: cclark@westga.edu.

University of Wisconsin–Whitewater, School of Graduate Studies, College of Business and Economics, Department of Business Education, Whitewater, WI 53190-1790. Offers general business education (MS); post-secondary business education (MS); secondary business education (MS). *Accreditation:* NCATE. Part-time and evening/weekend programs available. Postbaccalaureate distance learning degree programs offered (no on-campus study). *Degree requirements:* For master's, thesis or alternative. *Entrance requirements:* For master's, interview, teaching license. Additional exam requirements/recommendations for international students: Required—TOEFL (minimum score 550 paper-based; 213 computer-based). Electronic applications accepted. *Faculty research:* Active learning and performance strategies, technology-enhanced formative assessment, computer-supported cooperative work, privacy surveillance.

Utah State University, School of Graduate Studies, College of Business, Department of Business Information Systems, Logan, UT 84322. Offers business education (MS); business information systems (MS); business information systems and education (Ed D); education (PhD). Part-time programs available. Terminal master's awarded for partial completion of doctoral program. *Degree requirements:* For master's, thesis optional; for doctorate, thesis/dissertation. *Entrance requirements:* For master's, GMAT, minimum GPA of 3.2; for doctorate, GRE General Test, minimum GPA of 3.0. Additional exam requirements/recommendations for international students: Required—TOEFL. *Faculty research:* Oral and written communication, methods of teaching, CASE tools, object-oriented programming, decision support systems.

Utah State University, School of Graduate Studies, College of Education and Human Services, Doctoral Program in Education, Logan, UT 84322. Offers business information systems (Ed D, PhD); curriculum and instruction (Ed D, PhD); research and evaluation (PhD). *Degree requirements:* For doctorate, comprehensive exam, thesis/dissertation. *Entrance requirements:* For doctorate, GRE General Test, minimum GPA of 3.0, master's degree. Additional exam requirements/recommendations for international students: Required—TOEFL. Electronic applications accepted. *Faculty research:* Language and literacy development, math and science education, instructional technology, hearing problems/deafness, domestic violence and animal abuse.

Wayne State College, School of Education and Counseling, Department of Educational Foundations and Leadership, Program in Curriculum and Instruction, Wayne, NE 68787. Offers alternative education (MSE); business and information technology education (MSE); communication arts education (MSE); early childhood education (MSE); elementary education (MSE); English as a second language (MSE); English education (MSE); family and consumer sciences education (MSE); industrial technology and vocational education (MSE); learning communities (MSE); mathematics education (MSE); music education (MSE); science education (MSE); social science education (MSE). *Accreditation:* NCATE. Part-time and evening/weekend programs available. *Degree requirements:* For master's, comprehensive exam, thesis optional. *Entrance requirements:* For master's, GRE General Test. Additional exam requirements/recommendations for international students: Required—TOEFL (minimum score 550 paper-based; 213 computer-based).

Wayne State University, College of Education, Division of Teacher Education, Detroit, MI 48202. Offers adult and continuing education (M Ed); art education (M Ed); bilingual/bicultural education (M Ed, MAT); business education (M Ed, MAT); career and technical education (M Ed, Ed D, PhD, Ed S); curriculum and instruction (Ed D, PhD, Ed S); distributive education (M Ed, MAT); early childhood education (M Ed); elementary education (M Ed, MAT, Ed D, PhD, Ed S); elementary education curriculum and instruction (M Ed); English education (M Ed); English education-secondary (M Ed, Ed S); foreign language education (M Ed); general education (Ed D, Ed S); health occupations education (M Ed); industrial education (M Ed); mathematics education (M Ed, Ed S); pre-school and parent education (M Ed); reading (M Ed, Ed D, Ed S); reading, languages and literature (Ed D); school music-vocal (M Ed); science education (M Ed, MAT, Ed S); secondary education (MAT); secondary school reading (M Ed); social studies education (M Ed, Ed S), including education-secondary (M Ed); special education (M Ed, Ed D, PhD, Ed S); teacher education (MAT, Ed D, PhD). *Degree requirements:* For doctorate, thesis/dissertation. *Entrance requirements:* For master's, Michigan Basic Skills Test (MA in teaching), minimum GPA of 2.6; for doctorate, minimum undergraduate GPA of 3.0, graduate 3.5; interview, curriculum vitae; references. Additional exam requirements/recommendations for international students: Required—TOEFL (minimum score 550 paper-based; 213 computer-based), TWE (minimum score 6). Electronic applications accepted. *Faculty research:* Reading and writing literacy and literature.

Western Kentucky University, Graduate Studies, College of Education and Behavioral Sciences, Department of Counseling and Student Affairs, Bowling Green, KY 42101. Offers business and marketing education (MA Ed); counseling (MA Ed); counselor education (Ed S); education and behavioral science (MA Ed); elementary education (MA Ed, Ed S); middle years education (MA Ed); secondary education (MA Ed, Ed S); student affairs (MA Ed). *Accreditation:* ACA; NCATE. Part-time and evening/weekend programs available. *Degree requirements:* For master's, comprehensive exam, thesis optional. *Entrance requirements:* For master's, GRE General Test. Additional exam requirements/recommendations for international students: Required—TOEFL (minimum score 555 paper-based; 213 computer-based; 79 iBT). *Expenses:* Tuition, state resident: full-time $4160; part-time $416 per credit hour. Tuition, nonresident: full-time $9550; part-time $506 per credit hour. Tuition and fees vary according to campus/location and reciprocity agreements. *Faculty research:* Counselor education, research for residential workers.

Western Kentucky University, Graduate Studies, College of Education and Behavioral Sciences, Department of Curriculum and Instruction, Bowling Green, KY 42101. Offers business and marketing education (MAE); elementary education (MAE, Ed S); middle grades education (MAE); secondary education (MAE, Ed S). *Degree requirements:* For master's, comprehensive exam; for Ed S, thesis. *Entrance requirements:* For master's, GRE. Additional exam requirements/recommendations for international students: Required—TOEFL (minimum score 555 paper-based; 213 computer-based; 79 iBT). *Expenses:* Tuition, state resident: full-time $4160; part-time $416 per credit hour. Tuition, nonresident: full-time $9550; part-time $506 per credit hour. Tuition and fees vary according to campus/location and reciprocity agreements.

Wright State University, School of Graduate Studies, College of Education and Human Services, Department of Teacher Education, Programs in Workforce Education, Dayton, OH 45435. Offers career, technology and vocational education (M Ed, MA); computer/technology education (M Ed, MA); library/media (M Ed, MA); vocational education (M Ed, MA). *Accreditation:* NCATE. *Degree requirements:* For master's, thesis (for some programs). *Entrance requirements:* For master's, GRE General Test, MAT. Additional exam requirements/recommendations for international students: Required—TOEFL.

Computer Education

Arcadia University, Graduate Studies, Department of Education, Glenside, PA 19038-3295. Offers art education (M Ed, MA Ed); biology education (MA Ed); chemistry education (MA Ed); child development (CAS); computer education (M Ed, CAS); computer education 7–12 (MA Ed); early childhood education (M Ed, CAS), including individualized (M Ed), master teacher (M Ed), research in child development (M Ed); educational leadership (M Ed, CAS); educational psychology (CAS); elementary education (M Ed, CAS); English education (MA Ed); environmental education (MA Ed, CAS); history education (MA Ed); language arts (M Ed, CAS); mathematics education (M Ed, MA Ed, CAS); music education (MA Ed); psychology (MA Ed); pupil personnel services (CAS); reading (M Ed, CAS); school library science (M Ed); science education (M Ed, CAS); secondary education (M Ed, CAS); special education (M Ed, Ed D, CAS); theater arts (MA Ed); written communication (MA Ed). *Accreditation:* NASAD. Part-time and evening/weekend programs available. Postbaccalaureate distance learning degree programs offered (minimal on-campus study). *Faculty:* 12 full-time (8 women), 38 part-time/adjunct (26 women). *Students:* 89 full-time (74 women), 622 part-time (487 women); includes 112 minority (94 African Americans, 9 Asian Americans or Pacific Islanders, 9 Hispanic Americans), 2 international. Average age 32. In 2009, 257 master's, 4 doctorates awarded. *Application deadline:* Applications are processed on a rolling basis. Application fee: $40. Electronic applications accepted. *Expenses:* Tuition: Full-time $30,450; part-time $620 per credit hour. Required fees: $165. Tuition and fees vary according to program. *Financial support:* Career-related internships or fieldwork, tuition waivers (partial), and unspecified assistantships available. *Unit head:* Dr. Steven P. Gulkus. *Application contact:* 215-572-2925, Fax: 215-572-2126, E-mail: grad@arcadia.edu.

California State University, Dominguez Hills, College of Professional Studies, School of Education, Division of Graduate Education, Program in Technology-Based Education, Carson, CA 90747-0001. Offers MA, Certificate. Part-time and evening/weekend programs available. *Faculty:* 2 full-time (1 woman). *Students:* 15 full-time (9 women), 50 part-time (26 women); includes 31 minority (8 African Americans, 7 Asian Americans or Pacific Islanders, 16 Hispanic Americans), 2 international. Average age 41. 27 applicants, 96% accepted, 16 enrolled. In 2009, 51 master's awarded. *Degree requirements:* For master's, comprehensive exam, thesis or alternative. *Entrance requirements:* For master's, minimum GPA of 2.75. *Application deadline:* For fall admission, 6/1 for domestic students. Application fee: $55. *Expenses:* Tuition, nonresident: full-time $6696; part-time $372 per unit. Required fees: $5946; $1752 per semester. *Faculty research:* Media literacy, assistive technology. *Unit head:* Dr. Peter Desberg, Unit Head, E-mail: pdesberg@csudh.edu. *Application contact:* Admissions Office, 310-243-3530.

Cardinal Stritch University, College of Education, Department of Educational Computing, Milwaukee, WI 53217-3985. Offers instructional technology (ME, MS). Part-time and evening/weekend programs available. *Degree requirements:* For master's, comprehensive exam, thesis,

faculty recommendation. *Entrance requirements:* For master's, letters of recommendation (2), minimum GPA of 2.75.

Christopher Newport University, Graduate Studies, Department of Teacher Preparation, Newport News, VA 23606-2998. Offers art (PK-12) (MAT); biology (6-12) (MAT); computer science (6-12) (MAT); elementary (PK-6) (MAT); English (6-12) (MAT); French (PK-12) (MAT); history and social science (6-12) (MAT); mathematics (6-12) (MAT); music (PK-12) (MAT), including choral, instrumental; physics (6-12) (MAT); Spanish (PK-12) (MAT). Part-time and evening/weekend programs available. *Faculty:* 24 full-time (13 women), 4 part-time/adjunct (2 women). *Students:* 76 full-time (66 women), 12 part-time (10 women); includes 3 minority (2 African Americans, 1 Hispanic American). Average age 24. 3 applicants, 100% accepted, 2 enrolled. In 2009, 58 master's awarded. *Degree requirements:* For master's, comprehensive exam, thesis or alternative. *Entrance requirements:* For master's, PRAXIS I, minimum GPA of 3.0. Additional exam requirements/recommendations for international students: Required—TOEFL (minimum score 580 paper-based; 237 computer-based; 92 iBT). *Application deadline:* For fall admission, 8/15 for domestic students, 4/1 for international students; for spring admission, 10/15 for domestic students, 10/1 for international students. Applications are processed on a rolling basis. Application fee: $45. Electronic applications accepted. *Expenses:* Tuition, area resident: Part-time $384 per credit hour. Tuition, state resident: part-time $384 per credit hour. Tuition, nonresident: part-time $701 per credit hour. *Financial support:* In 2009–10, 3 research assistantships with full and partial tuition reimbursements (averaging $2,000 per year) were awarded; career-related internships or fieldwork, Federal Work-Study, and unspecified assistantships also available. Support available to part-time students. Financial award application deadline: 3/1; financial award applicants required to submit FAFSA. *Faculty research:* Early literacy development, instructional innovations, professional teaching standards, multicultural issues, aesthetic education. *Unit head:* Dr. Marsha Sprague, Director, 757-594-7388, Fax: 757-594-7803, E-mail: msprague@cnu.edu. *Application contact:* Lyn Sawyer, Associate Director, Graduate Admissions, 757-594-7544, Fax: 757-594-7649, E-mail: gradstdy@cnu.edu.

Eastern Washington University, Graduate Studies, College of Science, Health and Engineering, Department of Computer Science, Cheney, WA 99004-2431. Offers computer and technology-supported education (M Ed); computer science (MS). *Accreditation:* NCATE. Part-time programs available. *Degree requirements:* For master's, comprehensive exam, thesis or alternative. *Entrance requirements:* For master's, minimum GPA of 3.0. *Expenses:* Tuition, state resident: full-time $7476; part-time $249 per quarter hour. Tuition, nonresident: full-time $18,030; part-time $601 per quarter hour. Required fees: $3.50 per quarter hour. $142 per quarter.

Florida Institute of Technology, Graduate Programs, College of Science, Department of Science and Mathematics Education, Melbourne, FL 32901-6975. Offers computer education (MS); elementary science education (M Ed); environmental education (MS); informal science education (M Ed); mathematics education (MS, Ed D, PhD, Ed S); science education (MS, Ed D, PhD, Ed S); teaching (MAT). Part-time and evening/weekend programs available. *Faculty:* 4 full-time (1 woman), 3 part-time/adjunct (2 women). *Students:* 15 full-time (9 women), 18 part-time (12 women); includes 5 minority (2 African Americans, 3 Hispanic Americans), 5 international. Average age 36. 42 applicants, 52% accepted, 7 enrolled. In 2009, 3 master's, 1 doctorate, 1 other advanced degree awarded. Terminal master's awarded for partial completion of doctoral program. *Degree requirements:* For master's, comprehensive exam (for some programs), thesis (for some programs), oral final exam; for doctorate, comprehensive exam, thesis/dissertation, oral defense of dissertation; for Ed S, comprehensive exam. *Entrance requirements:* For master's, minimum GPA of 3.0, resume, 3 letters of recommendation (elementary science education); for doctorate, minimum GPA of 3.2, resume, 3 letters of recommendation, statement of objectives, 3 years teaching experience (recommended); for Ed S, minimum GPA of 3.0, resume, 3 letters of recommendation, statement of objectives. Additional exam requirements/recommendations for international students: Required—TOEFL (minimum score 550 paper-based; 213 computer-based; 79 iBT). *Application deadline:* For fall admission, 4/1 for international students; for spring admission, 9/30 for international students. Applications are processed on a rolling basis. Application fee: $50. Electronic applications accepted. *Expenses:* Tuition: Part-time $1015 per credit. Tuition and fees vary according to campus/location and program. *Financial support:* In 2009–10, 3 students received support, including 3 teaching assistantships with full and partial tuition reimbursements available (averaging $6,212 per year); research assistantships with full and partial tuition reimbursements available, career-related internships or fieldwork, institutionally sponsored loans, tuition waivers (partial), unspecified assistantships, and tuition remissions also available. Support available to part-time students. Financial award application deadline: 3/1; financial award applicants required to submit FAFSA. *Faculty research:* Measurement and evaluation, computers in education, educational technology. Total annual research expenditures: $352,726. *Unit head:* Dr. David E. Cook, Department Head, 321-674-8126, Fax: 321-674-7598, E-mail: dcook@fit.edu. *Application contact:* Thomas M. Shea, Director of Graduate Admissions, 321-674-7577, Fax: 321-723-9468, E-mail: tshea@fit.edu.

Fontbonne University, Graduate Programs, Department of Mathematics and Computer Science, St. Louis, MO 63105-3098. Offers computer education (MS). Part-time and evening/weekend programs available. Postbaccalaureate distance learning degree programs offered (no on-campus study). *Faculty:* 1 (woman) full-time, 4 part-time/adjunct (2 women). *Students:* 48 part-time (38 women); includes 14 minority (13 African Americans, 1 Hispanic American). Average age 38. In 2009, 14 master's awarded. *Degree requirements:* For master's, thesis optional. *Entrance requirements:* For master's, minimum GPA of 3.0. *Application deadline:* For fall admission, 8/1 priority date for domestic students; for spring admission, 12/15 for domestic students. Applications are processed on a rolling basis. Application fee: $25. *Expenses:* Tuition: Part-time $562 per credit hour. *Financial support:* Available to part-time students. Application deadline: 4/1. *Unit head:* Dr. Elizabeth Newton, Chairperson, 314-719-8096, Fax: 314-889-1401, E-mail: bnewton@fontbonne.edu. *Application contact:* Dr. Mary Abkemeier, Director, 314-889-1497, Fax: 314-889-1451, E-mail: mabkemei@fontbonne.edu.

Indiana University–Purdue University Indianapolis, School of Education, Indianapolis, IN 46202-2896. Offers computer education (Certificate); curriculum and instruction (MS); early childhood (MS); educational leadership (MS, Certificate); English as a second language (Certificate); higher education and student affairs (MS); kindergarten (Certificate); language education (MS); reading (Certificate); school counseling (MS); special education (MS, Certificate). Part-time and evening/weekend programs available. *Faculty:* 41 full-time, 80 part-time/adjunct. *Students:* 72 full-time (60 women), 427 part-time (325 women); includes 57 minority (42 African Americans, 1 American Indian/Alaska Native, 4 Asian Americans or Pacific Islanders, 10 Hispanic Americans), 5 international. Average age 32. 181 applicants, 78% accepted, 112 enrolled. In 2009, 162 master's awarded. *Degree requirements:* For master's, thesis optional. *Entrance requirements:* For master's, GRE General Test, minimum GPA of 3.0. Additional exam requirements/recommendations for international students: Required—TOEFL. *Application deadline:* For fall admission, 5/1 priority date for domestic students; for spring admission, 11/1 for domestic students. Application fee: $55 ($65 for international students). *Financial support:* In 2009–10, 2 fellowships (averaging $780 per year), 18 teaching assistantships (averaging $9,756 per year) were awarded; research assistantships with partial tuition reimbursements, Federal Work-Study, institutionally sponsored loans, scholarships/grants, and tuition waivers (partial) also available. Support available to part-time students. *Faculty research:* Teachers in the process of change, learning cycles, children's concepts of science. Total annual research expenditures: $614,458. *Unit head:* Dr. Chris Leland, Interim Executive Associate Dean, 317-274-6801, Fax: 317-274-6864. *Application contact:* Sarah Brandenburg, Graduate Advisor, 317-274-6801, Fax: 317-274-6864, E-mail: edugrad@iupui.edu.

Jacksonville University, College of Arts and Sciences, School of Education, Program in Computer Sciences, Jacksonville, FL 32211. Offers MAT. Part-time and evening/weekend programs available. *Degree requirements:* For master's, comprehensive exam. *Entrance requirements:* For master's, GRE General Test, minimum GPA of 3.0. Additional exam requirements/recommendations for international students: Required—TOEFL.

Kean University, College of Natural, Applied and Health Sciences, Program in Mathematics Education, Union, NJ 07083. Offers computer applications (MA); supervision of math education (MA); teaching of math (MA). Part-time and evening/weekend programs available. *Faculty:* 13 full-time (4 women). *Students:* 5 full-time (4 women), 5 part-time (1 woman); includes 4 minority (2 Asian Americans or Pacific Islanders, 2 Hispanic Americans), 1 international. Average age 31. 5 applicants, 80% accepted, 4 enrolled. In 2009, 5 master's awarded. *Degree requirements:* For master's, comprehensive exam, thesis. *Entrance requirements:* For master's, GRE General Test, minimum GPA of 3.0, undergraduate major or strong minor in math, 2 letters of recommendation, interview. *Application deadline:* For fall admission, 5/1 for domestic students; for spring admission, 11/1 for domestic students. Application fee: $60 ($150 for international students). Electronic applications accepted. *Expenses:* Tuition, state resident: full-time $10,440; part-time $435 per credit. Tuition, nonresident: full-time $14,160; part-time $590 per credit. Required fees: $2642; $110 per credit. Part-time tuition and fees vary according to course load and degree level. *Financial support:* In 2009–10, 2 research assistantships with full tuition reimbursements (averaging $3,263 per year) were awarded; unspecified assistantships also available. *Unit head:* Dr. Revathi Narasimhan, Program Coordinator, 908-737-3700, E-mail: rnarasim@kean.edu. *Application contact:* Reenat Hasan, Pre-Admissions Coordinator, 908-737-5923, Fax: 908-737-5965, E-mail: rhasan@exchange.kean.edu.

Kent State University, Graduate School of Education, Health, and Human Services, School of Lifespan Development and Educational Sciences, Program in Instructional Technology, Kent, OH 44242-0001. Offers computer technology (M Ed, MA); general instructional technology (M Ed, MA); library media (M Ed, MA). *Accreditation:* NCATE. *Faculty:* 7 full-time (3 women), 1 (woman) part-time/adjunct. *Students:* 16 full-time (13 women), 53 part-time (39 women); includes 3 minority (all African Americans). 22 applicants, 77% accepted. In 2009, 20 master's awarded. *Degree requirements:* For master's, thesis (for some programs). *Entrance requirements:* For master's, GRE General Test. Additional exam requirements/recommendations for international students: Required—TOEFL. *Application deadline:* Applications are processed on a rolling basis. Application fee: $30. *Financial support:* In 2009–10, 2 research assistantships with full tuition reimbursements (averaging $8,313 per year) were awarded; fellowships with full tuition reimbursements, teaching assistantships with full tuition reimbursements, Federal Work-Study, scholarships/grants, and unspecified assistantships also available. Financial award application deadline: 4/1; financial award applicants required to submit FAFSA. *Faculty research:* Cooperative learning, aesthetics, computers in schools. *Unit head:* Dr. Drew Tiene, Coordinator, 330-672-0607, E-mail: dtiene@kent.edu. *Application contact:* Nancy Miller, Academic Program Coordinator, Office of Graduate Student Services, 330-672-2576, Fax: 330-672-9162, E-mail: ogs@kent.edu.

Lesley University, School of Education, Cambridge, MA 02138-2790. Offers curriculum and instruction (M Ed, CAGS); early childhood education (M Ed); educational studies (PhD); elementary education (M Ed); individually designed (M Ed); middle school education (M Ed); moderate special needs (M Ed); reading (M Ed, CAGS); science in education (M Ed); severe special needs (M Ed); special needs (CAGS); technology in education (M Ed, CAGS). *Accreditation:* Teacher Education Accreditation Council. Part-time and evening/weekend programs available. Postbaccalaureate distance learning degree programs offered (no on-campus study). *Degree requirements:* For master's, practicum; for doctorate, thesis/dissertation. *Entrance requirements:* For doctorate, GRE General Test or MAT, interview, master's degree, resume; for CAGS, interview, master's degree. Additional exam requirements/recommendations for international students: Required—TOEFL (minimum score 550 paper-based; 213 computer-based; 80 iBT). Electronic applications accepted. *Faculty research:* Assessment in literacy, mathematics and science; autism spectrum disorders; instructional technology and online learning; multicultural education and ELL.

Long Island University, C.W. Post Campus, College of Information and Computer Science, Department of Computer Science/Management Engineering, Brookville, NY 11548-1300. Offers information systems (MS); information technology education (MS); management engineering (MS). Part-time and evening/weekend programs available. *Degree requirements:* For master's, comprehensive exam, thesis or alternative. *Entrance requirements:* For master's, bachelor's degree in science, mathematics, or engineering; minimum GPA of 2.5. Additional exam requirements/recommendations for international students: Required—TOEFL (minimum score 500 paper-based; 173 computer-based). Electronic applications accepted. *Faculty research:* Inductive music learning, re-engineering business process, technology and ethics.

Marlboro College, Graduate School, Program in Teaching with Technology, Marlboro, VT 05344. Offers MAT. Part-time and evening/weekend programs available. Postbaccalaureate distance learning degree programs offered (minimal on-campus study). *Faculty:* 7 part-time/adjunct (5 women). *Students:* 6 full-time (3 women), 4 part-time (2 women). Average age 38. 5 applicants, 100% accepted, 5 enrolled. In 2009, 4 master's awarded. *Degree requirements:* For master's, capstone project. *Entrance requirements:* For master's, 2 letters of recommendation. *Application deadline:* Applications are processed on a rolling basis. Application fee: $0. Electronic applications accepted. *Expenses:* Tuition: Full-time $9520; part-time $680 per credit. Tuition and fees vary according to course load and program. *Financial support:* Available to part-time students. Applicants required to submit FAFSA. *Application contact:* Joe Heslin, Associate Director of Admissions, 802-258-9209, Fax: 802-258-9201, E-mail: jheslin@gradcenter.marlboro.edu.

Mississippi College, Graduate School, School of Education, Department of Teacher Education and Leadership, Clinton, MS 39058. Offers art (M Ed); biological science (M Ed); business education (M Ed); computer science (M Ed); dyslexia therapy (M Ed); educational leadership (M Ed, Ed D, Ed S); elementary education (M Ed, Ed S); English (M Ed); higher education administration (MS); mathematics (M Ed); secondary education (M Ed); social studies (history) (M Ed); teaching arts (M Ed). Part-time programs available. Postbaccalaureate distance learning degree programs offered (no on-campus study). *Faculty:* 11 full-time (7 women), 13 part-time/adjunct (7 women). *Students:* 33 full-time (22 women), 282 part-time (240 women); includes 148 minority (146 African Americans, 2 American Indian/Alaska Native), 1 international. Average age 34. In 2009, 147 master's awarded. *Degree requirements:* For master's, comprehensive exam, thesis optional. *Entrance requirements:* For master's, NTE. Additional exam requirements/recommendations for international students: Recommended—IELTS. *Application deadline:* For fall admission, 8/15 priority date for domestic students. Applications are processed on a rolling basis. Application fee: $30. Electronic applications accepted. *Expenses:* Tuition: Part-time $452 per credit hour. Required fees: $101 per semester. Tuition and fees vary according to degree level, campus/location, program and student level. *Financial support:* Teaching assistantships, career-related internships or fieldwork, Federal Work-Study, scholarships/grants, and unspecified assistantships available. Support available to part-time students. Financial award applicants required to submit FAFSA. *Unit head:* Dr. Tom Williams, Chair, 601-925-3844, E-mail: twilliams@mc.edu. *Application contact:* Elnora Lewis, Secretary, 601-925-3225, Fax: 601-925-3889, E-mail: lewis09@mc.edu.

Nova Southeastern University, Fischler School of Education and Human Services, Graduate Teacher Education Program, Fort Lauderdale, FL 33314-7796. Offers athletic administration (MS); brain research (MS, Ed S); charter school education/leadership (MS); cognitive and behavioral disabilities (MS); computer science education (Ed S); computer science education (K-12) (MS); curriculum and teaching (Ed S); curriculum, instruction and technology (MS); curriculum, instruction, management and administration (Ed S); early childhood education (MS); early literacy and reading (Ed S); early literacy education (MS); education technology (MS); educational leadership (administration K–12) (MS, Ed S); educational media (Ed S); educational media (K-12) (MS); elementary education (MS, Ed S), including ESOL endorsement (MS); English education (MS, Ed S); environmental education (MS); exceptional student education (MS), including ESOL endorsement; gifted education (MS, Ed S); interdisciplinary arts education (MS); management and administration of educational programs (MS); mathematics (MS); mathematics education (Ed S); multicultural early intervention (MS); pre-kindergarten/primary (MS); preschool education (MS); reading (MS); reading and TESOL (MS); reading education (Ed S); science (MS); science education (Ed S); secondary education (MS); social studies (MS, Ed S); Spanish language (MS); special education and reading (MS);

Computer Education

Nova Southeastern University (continued)

teaching and learning (MA, MS), including curriculum and instruction (MA), elementary mathematics (MA), elementary reading (MA), K-12 technology integration (MA); teaching English to speakers of other languages (MS, Ed S); technology management and administration (Ed S); urban studies education (MS). Part-time and evening/weekend programs available. Postbaccalaureate distance learning degree programs offered (minimal on-campus study). *Faculty:* 72 full-time (43 women), 385 part-time/adjunct (252 women). *Students:* 196 full-time (175 women), 1,304 part-time (1,128 women); includes 594 minority (471 African Americans, 5 American Indian/Alaska Native, 18 Asian Americans or Pacific Islanders, 100 Hispanic Americans). Average age 37. 2,610 applicants, 72% accepted, 1352 enrolled. In 2009, 836 other advanced degrees awarded. *Degree requirements:* For master's and Ed S, thesis, practicum, internship. *Entrance requirements:* For master's, MAT, GRE, CLAST, CBEST, PRAXIS I, General Knowledge Test, minimum GPA of 2.5; for Ed S, MAT or GRE, master's degree, teaching certificate, minimum GPA of 3.0. Additional exam requirements/recommendations for international students: Required—TSE (recommended, minimum score 50); Recommended—TOEFL (minimum score 550 paper-based; 213 computer-based; 80 iBT), IELTS (minimum score 6). *Application deadline:* For fall admission, 9/25 priority date for domestic and international students; for winter admission, 2/23 priority date for domestic and international students; for spring admission, 4/25 priority date for domestic and international students. Applications are processed on a rolling basis. Application fee: $50. Electronic applications accepted. *Financial support:* Federal Work-Study available. Support available to part-time students. Financial award application deadline: 4/15; financial award applicants required to submit FAFSA. *Faculty research:* School effectiveness, critical thinking, leadership skills acquisition, child education, multicultural education. *Unit head:* Dr. Ronald Kern, Dean of Academic Affairs, 800-986-3223 Ext. 7809, Fax: 954-262-3606, E-mail: rk429@nsu.nova.edu. *Application contact:* Dr. Jennifer Quinones Nottingham, Dean of Student Affairs, 800-986-3223 Ext. 1559.

Nova Southeastern University, Fischler School of Education and Human Services, Programs for Higher Education, Fort Lauderdale, FL 33314-7796. Offers adult education (Ed D); computing and information technology (Ed D); health care education (Ed D); higher education (Ed D); vocational, occupational and technical education (Ed D). Part-time and evening/weekend programs available. Postbaccalaureate distance learning degree programs offered (minimal on-campus study). *Faculty:* 6 full-time (3 women), 8 part-time/adjunct (2 women). *Students:* 113 full-time (81 women), 2 part-time (both women); includes 57 minority (51 African Americans, 6 Hispanic Americans). 4 applicants, 75% accepted, 3 enrolled. In 2009, 13 doctorates awarded. *Degree requirements:* For doctorate, thesis/dissertation, practicum. *Entrance requirements:* For doctorate, MAT or GRE, master's degree, work experience in field, minimum GPA of 3.0. Additional exam requirements/recommendations for international students: Required—TSE (recommended, minimum score 50); Recommended—TOEFL (minimum score 550 paper-based; 213 computer-based; 80 iBT), IELTS (minimum score 6). *Application deadline:* For fall admission, 8/11 priority date for domestic and international students; for winter admission, 12/28 priority date for domestic and international students; for spring admission, 4/22 priority date for domestic and international students. Applications are processed on a rolling basis. Application fee: $50. Electronic applications accepted. *Expenses:* Contact institution. *Financial support:* Career-related internships or fieldwork and tuition waivers (full) available. Financial award application deadline: 1/7. *Unit head:* Dr. Karen D. Bowser, Associate Dean of Doctoral Programs, 954-262-8677, Fax: 954-262-3606, E-mail: bowserk@nova.edu. *Application contact:* Dr. Jennifer Quinones Nottingham, Dean of Student Affairs, 800-986-3223 Ext. 8624, Fax: 954-262-3883, E-mail: jlquinon@nova.edu.

Ohio University, Graduate College, College of Education, Department of Educational Studies, Athens, OH 45701-2979. Offers computer education and technology (M Ed); cultural studies (M Ed); educational administration (M Ed, Ed D); educational research and evaluation (M Ed, PhD); instructional technology (PhD). Part-time and evening/weekend programs available. Postbaccalaureate distance learning degree programs offered (minimal on-campus study). *Faculty:* 12 full-time (6 women), 2 part-time/adjunct (0 women). *Students:* 151 full-time (95 women), 142 part-time (105 women); includes 24 minority (19 African Americans, 1 American Indian/Alaska Native, 1 Asian American or Pacific Islander, 3 Hispanic Americans), 46 international. 107 applicants, 69% accepted, 50 enrolled. In 2009, 32 master's, 19 doctorates awarded. *Degree requirements:* For master's, thesis or alternative; for doctorate, comprehensive exam, thesis/dissertation. *Entrance requirements:* For master's, GRE General Test (if GPA less than 2.9); for doctorate, GRE General Test, GRE Subject Test, minimum GPA of 2.9, work experience, 3 letters of reference, autobiography. Additional exam requirements/recommendations for international students: Required—TOEFL (minimum score 550 paper-based; 80 iBT) or IELTS Academic (minimum score 6.5). *Application deadline:* For fall admission, 3/1 priority date for domestic and international students; for winter admission, 10/1 priority date for domestic and international students; for spring admission, 1/30 priority date for domestic students, 1/1 priority date for international students. Applications are processed on a rolling basis. Application fee: $50 ($55 for international students). Electronic applications accepted. *Expenses:* Tuition, state resident: full-time $7839; part-time $323 per quarter hour. Tuition, nonresident: full-time $15,831; part-time $654 per quarter hour. Required fees: $2931. *Financial support:* Research assistantships with full tuition reimbursements, teaching assistantships with full tuition reimbursements, Federal Work-Study, institutionally sponsored loans, tuition waivers (partial), and unspecified assistantships available. Financial award application deadline: 3/1. *Faculty research:* Race, class and gender; computer programs; development and organization theory; evaluation/development of instruments, leadership. Total annual research expenditures: $158,037. *Unit head:* Dr. Gordon Brooks, Chair, 740-593-4423, Fax: 740-593-0477, E-mail: brooksg@ohio.edu. *Application contact:* Floyd J. Doney, Director of Student Affairs, 740-593-4400, Fax: 740-593-9310, E-mail: doney@ohio.edu.

Southern New Hampshire University, School of Education, Manchester, NH 03106-1045. Offers business education (MS); child development (M Ed); computer technology education (Certificate); curriculum and instruction (M Ed); education (M Ed, CAS); elementary education (M Ed); general special education (Certificate); school business administrator (Certificate); secondary education (M Ed); training and development (Certificate). Part-time and evening/weekend programs available. Postbaccalaureate distance learning degree programs offered (no on-campus study). *Degree requirements:* For master's, comprehensive exam (for some programs), thesis or alternative. *Entrance requirements:* For master's, PRAXIS I, minimum GPA of 2.75. Additional exam requirements/recommendations for international students: Required—TOEFL (minimum score 550 paper-based; 213 computer-based). Electronic applications accepted. *Expenses:* Contact institution.

Stanford University, School of Education, Program in Cross-Area Specializations, Stanford, CA 94305-9991. Offers learning, design, and technology (MA, PhD); symbolic systems in education (PhD). *Degree requirements:* For doctorate, thesis/dissertation. Electronic applications accepted. *Expenses:* Tuition: Full-time $37,380; part-time $2760 per quarter. Required fees: $501.

State University of New York College at Potsdam, School of Education and Professional Studies, Program in Information and Communication Technology, Potsdam, NY 13676. Offers educational technology specialist (MS Ed); human performance technology (MS Ed); information technology (MS Ed); organizational leadership (MS Ed); technology educator (MS Ed). Part-time and evening/weekend programs available. Postbaccalaureate distance learning degree programs offered. *Faculty:* 4 full-time (1 woman), 2 part-time/adjunct (1 woman). *Students:* 22 full-time (12 women), 28 part-time (17 women); includes 4 minority (3 African Americans, 1 Asian American or Pacific Islander), 7 international. 28 applicants, 100% accepted, 20 enrolled. In 2009, 21 master's awarded. *Degree requirements:* For master's, thesis optional, culminating experience. *Entrance requirements:* For master's, minimum GPA of 2.75 in last 60 hours of course work. Additional exam requirements/recommendations for international students: Required—TOEFL (minimum score 550 paper-based; 213 computer-based; 80 iBT), IELTS (minimum score 6). *Application deadline:* For fall admission, 4/1 priority date for domestic and international students; for spring admission, 10/15 priority date for domestic and international students. Applications are processed on a rolling basis. Application fee: $50. *Expenses:* Tuition, state resident: full-time $8370; part-time $349 per credit hour. Tuition, nonresident: full-time $13,250; part-time $552 per credit hour. Required fees: $942; $38.70 per credit hour. *Financial support:* In 2009–10, 1 student received support; fellowships, teaching assistantships, career-related internships or fieldwork, Federal Work-Study, scholarships/grants, and unspecified assistantships available. Support available to part-time students. Financial award application deadline: 3/1; financial award applicants required to submit FAFSA. *Unit head:* Dr. Anthony Betrus, Chairperson, 315-267-2535, Fax: 315-267-4802, E-mail: betrusak@potsdam.edu. *Application contact:* Peter Cutler, Graduate Admissions Counselor, 315-267-3154, Fax: 315-267-4802, E-mail: cutlerpj@potsdam.edu.

Stony Brook University, State University of New York, Graduate School, College of Engineering and Applied Sciences, Department of Technology and Society, Program in Educational Technology, Stony Brook, NY 11794. Offers MS. *Accreditation:* NCATE. *Application deadline:* For fall admission, 5/1 for domestic students; for spring admission, 11/1 for domestic students. Electronic applications accepted. *Expenses:* Tuition, state resident: full-time $8370; part-time $349 per credit. Tuition, nonresident: full-time $13,250; part-time $552 per credit. Required fees: $933. *Financial support:* Research assistantships, teaching assistantships available. *Unit head:* David Ferguson, Chair, 631-632-8770, E-mail: david.ferguson@stonybrook.edu. *Application contact:* Sheldon Reaven, 631-632-8770, E-mail: sheldon.raven@sunysb.edu.

Teachers College, Columbia University, Graduate Faculty of Education, Department of Math, Science and Technology, Program in Computing in Education, New York, NY 10027-6696. Offers MA. *Accreditation:* NCATE. Part-time and evening/weekend programs available. *Faculty:* 1 full-time (0 women), 8 part-time/adjunct. *Students:* 6 full-time (3 women), 46 part-time (30 women); includes 20 minority (11 African Americans, 7 Asian Americans or Pacific Islanders, 2 Hispanic Americans), 3 international. Average age 36. 21 applicants, 86% accepted, 15 enrolled. In 2009, 17 master's awarded. *Application deadline:* For fall admission, 5/15 for domestic students; for spring admission, 12/1 for domestic students. Application fee: $65. *Financial support:* Career-related internships or fieldwork, Federal Work-Study, institutionally sponsored loans, and tuition waivers (full and partial) available. Support available to part-time students. Financial award application deadline: 2/1. *Faculty research:* Visual and interactive learning, global curriculum, cognition and learning. *Unit head:* Dr. O. Roger Anderson, Chair, 212-678-3405. *Application contact:* Deanna Ghozati, Assistant Director of Admission, 212-678-4018, Fax: 212-678-4171, E-mail: ghozati@tc.edu.

Thomas College, Graduate School, Programs in Business, Waterville, ME 04901-5097. Offers business (MBA); computer technology education (MS); education (MS); human resource management (MBA). Part-time and evening/weekend programs available. *Entrance requirements:* For master's, GMAT, GRE, MAT or minimum GPA of 3.3 in first 3 graduate-level courses.

Troy University, Graduate School, College of Education, Program in Secondary Education, Troy, AL 36082. Offers 5th year biology (MS); 5th year computer science (MS); 5th year history (MS); 5th year language arts (MS); 5th year mathematics (MS); 5th year social science (MS); educationtraditional language arts (MS); traditional biology (MS); traditional computer science (MS); traditional history (MS); traditional mathematics (MS); traditional social science (MS). *Accreditation:* NCATE. Part-time and evening/weekend programs available. *Students:* 17 full-time (12 women), 25 part-time (23 women); includes 8 minority (all African Americans). Average age 27. 10 applicants, 90% accepted. In 2009, 29 master's awarded. *Degree requirements:* For master's, comprehensive exam, thesis. *Entrance requirements:* For master's, minimum GPA of 2.5. Additional exam requirements/recommendations for international students: Required—TOEFL (minimum score 523 paper-based; 193 computer-based; 70 iBT), IELTS (minimum score 6). *Application deadline:* Applications are processed on a rolling basis. Application fee: $50. Electronic applications accepted. *Financial support:* Career-related internships or fieldwork available. Support available to part-time students. Financial award applicants required to submit FAFSA. *Unit head:* Dr. Marian Parker, Coordinator, 334-670-5661, Fax: 334-670-3548, E-mail: mjparker@troy.edu. *Application contact:* Brenda K. Campbell, Director of Graduate Admissions, 334-670-3178, Fax: 334-670-3733, E-mail: bcamp@troy.edu.

University of Bridgeport, School of Education and Human Resources, Division of Education, Program in Secondary Education, Bridgeport, CT 06604. Offers computer specialist (Diploma); international education (Diploma); reading specialist (MS, Diploma); secondary education (MS, Diploma). Part-time and evening/weekend programs available. *Degree requirements:* For master's, final exam, final project, or thesis; for Diploma, thesis or alternative, final project. *Entrance requirements:* For master's, minimum undergraduate QPA of 2.67; for Diploma, minimum graduate QPA of 3.0. Additional exam requirements/recommendations for international students: Recommended—TOEFL (minimum score 550 paper-based; 213 computer-based; 80 iBT), IELTS (minimum score 6.5). Electronic applications accepted. *Faculty research:* Self-concept, internship assessment, stress and situational development, follow-up of graduation, trend analysis.

University of Central Oklahoma, College of Graduate Studies and Research, College of Mathematics and Science, Department of Mathematics and Statistics, Edmond, OK 73034-5209. Offers applied mathematical sciences (MS), including computer science, mathematics, mathematics/computer science teaching, statistics. Part-time programs available. *Faculty:* 6 full-time (2 women). *Students:* 14 full-time (3 women), 13 part-time (5 women); includes 2 minority (1 American Indian/Alaska Native, 1 Asian American or Pacific Islander), 10 international. Average age 31. 14 applicants, 100% accepted. In 2009, 9 master's awarded. *Degree requirements:* For master's, thesis. *Entrance requirements:* Additional exam requirements/recommendations for international students: Required—TOEFL (minimum score 550 paper-based; 213 computer-based). *Application deadline:* For fall admission, 7/1 for international students; for spring admission, 11/1 for international students. Applications are processed on a rolling basis. Application fee: $25. Electronic applications accepted. *Expenses:* Tuition, state resident: full-time $4128; part-time $172 per credit hour. Tuition, nonresident: full-time $10,373; part-time $432.20 per credit hour. Required fees: $433.20; $18.05 per credit hour. *Financial support:* Federal Work-Study and unspecified assistantships available. Financial award application deadline: 3/31; financial award applicants required to submit FAFSA. *Faculty research:* Curvature, FAA, math education. *Unit head:* Dr. Charlotte Simmons, Chairperson, 405-974-5294. *Application contact:* Dr. Richard Bernard, Adviser, 405-974-3493, Fax: 405-974-3824, E-mail: jyates@aix1.uco.edu.

University of Detroit Mercy, College of Engineering and Science, Department of Mathematics and Computer Science, Detroit, MI 48221. Offers computer science (MSCS), including computer systems applications, software engineering; computer science education (MATM); mathematics education (MATM). Evening/weekend programs available. *Entrance requirements:* For master's, minimum GPA of 3.0.

University of Michigan, Horace H. Rackham School of Graduate Studies, School of Education, Programs in Educational Studies, Ann Arbor, MI 48109. Offers cross specialization (PhD); curriculum development (MA); early childhood education (MA, PhD); educational administration and policy (MA, PhD); educational foundations and policy (MA, PhD); English education (MA); English language learning in school settings (MA); learning technologies (MA, PhD); literacy, language, and culture (MA, PhD); mathematics education (MA, PhD); postsecondary science education (MS); research methods (MA); science education (MA, PhD); social studies education (MA); teaching and teacher education (PhD); MA/Certification; MBA/MA; PhD/MA. Terminal master's awarded for partial completion of doctoral program. *Degree requirements:* For master's, thesis (for some programs); for doctorate, comprehensive exam, thesis/dissertation. *Entrance requirements:* For master's and doctorate, GRE General Test. Additional exam requirements/recommendations for international students: Required—TOEFL (minimum score 600 paper-based; 250 computer-based). *Application deadline:* For fall admission, 12/1 priority date for domestic students, 12/1 for international students. Application fee: $60 ($75 for international students). Electronic applications accepted. *Expenses:* Tuition, state resident: full-time $17,286; part-time $1099 per credit hour. Tuition, nonresident: full-time $34,944; part-time $2080 per credit hour. Required fees: $95 per semester. Tuition and fees vary according to course load,

degree level and program. *Financial support:* Applicants required to submit FAFSA. *Unit head:* Dr. Addison Stone, Chairperson, 734-763-7500, Fax: 734-615-1290, E-mail: addison@umich.edu. *Application contact:* Laura Mayers, Student Services Assistant, 734-764-7563, Fax: 734-763-1495, E-mail: ed.grad.admit@umich.edu.

University of North Texas, College of Information, Department of Learning Technologies, Program in Computer Education and Cognitive Systems, Denton, TX 76203. Offers MS. *Accreditation:* NCATE. *Entrance requirements:* For master's, GRE General Test. Additional exam requirements/recommendations for international students: Required—proof of English language proficiency required for non-native English speakers; Recommended—TOEFL (minimum score 550 paper-based; 213 computer-based). *Application deadline:* Applications are processed on a rolling basis. Application fee: $50 ($75 for international students). Electronic applications accepted. *Expenses:* Tuition, state resident: full-time $4298; part-time $239 per contact hour. Tuition, nonresident: full-time $9878; part-time $549 per contact hour. Required fees: $265 per contact hour. *Financial support:* Fellowships, research assistantships, teaching assistantships, career-related internships or fieldwork, Federal Work-Study, and institutionally sponsored loans available. Financial award application deadline: 4/1; financial award applicants required to submit FAFSA. *Application contact:* Graduate Adviser, 940-565-2057, Fax: 940-565-2185.

University of North Texas, College of Information, Department of Library and Information Sciences, Denton, TX 76203-5017. Offers information science (MS, PhD); learning technologies (M Ed, Ed D), including applied technology, training and development (M Ed), computer education and cognitive systems, educational computing; library science (MS). *Accreditation:* ALA (one or more programs are accredited). Part-time and evening/weekend programs available. *Degree requirements:* For master's, comprehensive exam; for doctorate, comprehensive exam, thesis/dissertation. *Entrance requirements:* For master's, GRE General Test, MAT; for doctorate, GRE General Test. Additional exam requirements/recommendations for international students: Required—proof of English language proficiency required for non-native English speakers; Recommended—TOEFL (minimum score 550 paper-based; 213 computer-based; 79 iBT). *Application deadline:* Applications are processed on a rolling basis. Application fee: $50 ($75 for international students). Electronic applications accepted. *Expenses:* Tuition, state resident: full-time $4298; part-time $239 per contact hour. Tuition, nonresident: full-time $9878; part-time $549 per contact hour. Required fees: $265 per contact hour. *Financial support:* Fellowships, research assistantships, teaching assistantships, career-related internships or fieldwork, Federal Work-Study, institutionally sponsored loans, scholarships/grants, health care benefits, and library assistantships available. Financial award application deadline: 4/1; financial award applicants required to submit FAFSA. *Faculty research:* Information resources and services, information management and retrieval, computer-based information systems, human information behavior. *Application contact:* Graduate Academic Counselor, 940-369-2873, Fax: 940-565-3101.

University of Phoenix, College of Natural Sciences, College of Education, Phoenix, AZ 85034-7209. Offers administration and supervision (MAEd); adult education and training (MAEd); curriculum and instruction (MAEd); curriculum and instruction-adult education (MAEd); curriculum and instruction-computer education (MAEd); curriculum and instruction-English and language arts education (MAEd); curriculum and instruction-English as a second language (MAEd); curriculum and instruction-mathematics education (MAEd); curriculum education (MAEd); early childhood (MAEd); elementary teacher education (MAEd); secondary teacher education (MAEd); special education (MAEd); teacher leadership (MAEd). *Accreditation:* Teacher Education Accreditation Council. Evening/weekend programs available. Postbaccalaureate distance learning degree programs offered (no on-campus study). *Faculty:* 47 full-time (34 women), 844 part-time/adjunct (636 women). *Students:* 13,657 full-time (10,698 women); includes 4,000 minority (3,063 African Americans, 74 American Indian/Alaska Native, 241 Asian Americans or Pacific Islanders, 622 Hispanic Americans), 307 international. Average age 36. In 2009, 17,246 master's awarded. *Degree requirements:* For master's, thesis (for some programs). *Entrance requirements:* For master's, 3 years of work experience, minimum GPA of 2.5. Additional exam requirements/recommendations for international students: Required—TOEFL (minimum score 550 paper-based; 213 computer-based; 79 iBT). *Application deadline:* Applications are processed on a rolling basis. Application fee: $45. Electronic applications accepted. *Expenses:* Tuition: Full-time $13,272. Required fees: $660. Full-time tuition and fees vary according to course level, degree level and program. *Financial support:* Institutionally sponsored loans and scholarships/grants available. Financial award applicants required to submit FAFSA. *Unit head:* Dr. Meredith Curley, Dean/Executive Director, 480-557-1217, Fax: 480-557-1588, E-mail: meredith.curley@phoenix.edu. *Application contact:* Chair, 602-387-7000, Fax: 602-387-6020.

University of Phoenix–Central Florida Campus, The Artemis School, College of Education, Maitland, FL 32751-7057. Offers administration and supervision (MA Ed); curriculum and instruction (MA Ed); curriculum and instruction-computer education (MA Ed); curriculum and instruction-mathematics education (MA Ed); early childhood education (MA Ed); elementary teacher education (MA Ed); secondary teacher education (MA Ed). Evening/weekend programs available. *Degree requirements:* For master's, thesis (for some programs). *Entrance requirements:* For master's, 3 years of work experience, minimum undergraduate GPA of 2.5. Additional exam requirements/recommendations for international students: Required—TOEFL (minimum score 550 paper-based; 213 computer-based; 79 iBT). Electronic applications accepted.

University of Phoenix–Central Valley Campus, College of Education, Fresno, CA 93720-1562. Offers curriculum and instruction (MA Ed); curriculum and instruction-computer education (MA Ed); elementary teacher education (MA Ed); secondary teacher education (MA Ed).

University of Phoenix–North Florida Campus, The Artemis School, College of Education, Jacksonville, FL 32216-0959. Offers administration and supervision (MA Ed); curriculum and instruction (MA Ed), including computer education, mathematics education; early childhood education (MA Ed); elementary teacher education (MA Ed); secondary teacher education (MA Ed). Evening/weekend programs available. *Degree requirements:* For master's, thesis (for some programs). *Entrance requirements:* For master's, 3 years of work experience, minimum undergraduate GPA of 2.5. Additional exam requirements/recommendations for international students: Required—TOEFL (minimum score 550 paper-based; 213 computer-based; 49 iBT). Electronic applications accepted.

University of Phoenix–Omaha Campus, College of Education, Omaha, NE 68154-5240. Offers administration and supervision (MA Ed); curriculum and instruction (MA Ed), including adult education, computer education, curriculum and instruction, English and language arts education, English as a second language, mathematics education; elementary teacher education (MA Ed); secondary teacher education (MA Ed); special education (MA Ed).

University of Phoenix–San Diego Campus, The Artemis School, College of Education, San Diego, CA 92123. Offers curriculum and instruction (MA Ed), including computer education, curriculum and instruction, English as a second language; elementary teacher education (MA Ed); secondary teacher education (MA Ed). Evening/weekend programs available. *Degree requirements:* For master's, thesis (for some programs). *Entrance requirements:* For master's, 3 years of work experience, minimum undergraduate GPA of 3.0. Additional exam requirements/recommendations for international students: Required—TOEFL (minimum score 550 paper-based; 213 computer-based; 79 iBT). Electronic applications accepted.

University of Phoenix–Southern California Campus, College of Education, Costa Mesa, CA 92626. Offers administration and supervision (MA Ed); adult education and training (MA Ed); curriculum and instruction (MA Ed), including computer education, curriculum and instruction, English and language arts, English as a second language, mathematics education; early childhood education (MA Ed); special education (MA Ed); teacher leadership (MA Ed). Evening/weekend programs available. *Faculty:* 47 full-time (34 women), 844 part-time/adjunct (636 women). *Students:* 558 full-time (391 women); includes 222 minority (60 African Americans, 4 American Indian/Alaska Native, 26 Asian Americans or Pacific Islanders, 132 Hispanic Americans), 9 international. Average age 34. In 2009, 303 master's awarded. *Degree requirements:* For master's, thesis (for some programs). *Entrance requirements:* For master's, minimum undergraduate GPA of 2.5, 3 years work experience. Additional exam requirements/recommendations for international students: Required—TOEFL (minimum score 550 paper-based; 213 computer-based; 79 iBT). *Application deadline:* Applications are processed on a rolling basis. Application fee: $45. Electronic applications accepted. *Expenses:* Tuition: Full-time $15,120. Required fees: $660. *Financial support:* Institutionally sponsored loans and scholarships/grants available. Financial award applicants required to submit FAFSA. *Unit head:* Dr. Meredith Curley, Dean/Executive Director, 480-557-1217, Fax: 480-557-1588, E-mail: meredith.curley@phoenix.edu. *Application contact:* Campus College Chair, 714-378-1878, Fax: 714-378-5875.

University of Phoenix–South Florida Campus, The Artemis School, College of Education, Fort Lauderdale, FL 33309. Offers administration and supervision (MA Ed); curriculum and instruction (MA Ed), including computer education, curriculum and instruction, mathematics education; early childhood education (MA Ed); elementary teacher education (MA Ed); secondary teacher education (MA Ed). Evening/weekend programs available. *Degree requirements:* For master's, thesis (for some programs). *Entrance requirements:* For master's, 3 years of work experience, minimum undergraduate GPA of 2.5. Additional exam requirements/recommendations for international students: Required—TOEFL (minimum score 550 paper-based; 213 computer-based; 79 iBT). Electronic applications accepted.

University of Phoenix–Springfield Campus, College of Education, Springfield, MO 65804-7211. Offers administration and supervision (MA Ed); curriculum and instruction (MA Ed), including computer education, curriculum and instruction, English and language arts education, English as a second language, mathematics education; English and language arts education (MA Ed).

University of Phoenix–Vancouver Campus, The Artemis School, College of Education, Burnaby, BC V5C 6G9, Canada. Offers administration and supervision (MA Ed); curriculum and instruction (MA Ed), including computer education, curriculum and instruction. Evening/weekend programs available. *Degree requirements:* For master's, thesis (for some programs). *Entrance requirements:* For master's, minimum undergraduate GPA of 2.5, 3 years work experience. Additional exam requirements/recommendations for international students: Required—TOEFL (minimum score 550 paper-based; 213 computer-based; 79 iBT). Electronic applications accepted.

University of Phoenix–West Florida Campus, The Artemis School, College of Education, Temple Terrace, FL 33637. Offers administration and supervision (MA Ed); curriculum and instruction (MA Ed), including computer education, curriculum and instruction, mathematics education; curriculum and technology (MA Ed); early childhood education (MA Ed); elementary teacher education (MA Ed); secondary teacher education (MA Ed). Evening/weekend programs available. *Degree requirements:* For master's, thesis (for some programs). *Entrance requirements:* For master's, 3 years of work experience, minimum undergraduate GPA of 2.5. Additional exam requirements/recommendations for international students: Required—TOEFL (minimum score 550 paper-based; 213 computer-based; 79 iBT).

Wilkes University, College of Graduate and Professional Studies, School of Education, Wilkes-Barre, PA 18766-0002. Offers classroom technology (MS Ed); educational computing (MS Ed); educational development and strategies (MS Ed); educational leadership (MS Ed); educational technology (Ed D); elementary education (MS Ed); higher education administration (Ed D); instructional technology (MS Ed); K-12 administration (Ed D); online teaching (MS Ed); school business leadership (MS Ed); secondary education (MS Ed), including biology, chemistry, English, history; special education (MS Ed). Part-time and evening/weekend programs available. Postbaccalaureate distance learning degree programs offered (minimal on-campus study). *Students:* 89 full-time (60 women), 2,849 part-time (2,058 women); includes 52 minority (10 African Americans, 2 American Indian/Alaska Native, 13 Asian Americans or Pacific Islanders, 27 Hispanic Americans), 6 international. Average age 33. In 2009, 947 master's awarded. *Entrance requirements:* Additional exam requirements/recommendations for international students: Required—TOEFL (minimum score 500 paper-based; 173 computer-based; 79 iBT). *Application deadline:* Applications are processed on a rolling basis. Application fee: $45. *Expenses:* Contact institution. *Financial support:* Federal Work-Study and unspecified assistantships available. Financial award application deadline: 3/1; financial award applicants required to submit FAFSA. *Unit head:* Dr. Michael Speziale, Dean, 570-408-4679, Fax: 570-408-4905, E-mail: michael.speziale@wilkes.edu. *Application contact:* Kathleen Houlihan, Director of Graduate Studies, 570-408-3235, Fax: 570-408-7846, E-mail: kathleen.houlihan@wilkes.edu.

Wright State University, School of Graduate Studies, College of Education and Human Services, Department of Teacher Education, Programs in Workforce Education, Dayton, OH 45435. Offers career, technology and vocational education (M Ed, MA); computer/technology education (M Ed, MA); library/media (M Ed, MA); vocational education (M Ed, MA). *Accreditation:* NCATE. *Degree requirements:* For master's, thesis (for some programs). *Entrance requirements:* For master's, GRE General Test, MAT. Additional exam requirements/recommendations for international students: Required—TOEFL.

Counselor Education

Acadia University, Faculty of Professional Studies, School of Education, Program in Counseling, Wolfville, NS B4P 2R6, Canada. Offers M Ed. Part-time and evening/weekend programs available. *Faculty:* 4 full-time (2 women). *Students:* 20 full-time (17 women), 76 part-time (60 women). 99 applicants, 65% accepted. In 2009, 32 master's awarded. *Degree requirements:* For master's, thesis optional. *Entrance requirements:* For master's, B Ed, minimum B average in undergraduate course work, 2 years of teaching or related experience. Additional exam requirements/recommendations for international students: Required—TOEFL (minimum score 580 paper-based; 237 computer-based; 93 iBT), IELTS (minimum score 6.5). *Application deadline:* For fall admission, 2/1 for domestic and international students. Application fee: $50. *Financial support:* Teaching assistantships available. Financial award application deadline: 2/1. *Faculty research:* Computer-assisted supervision, rural/remote school counseling, non-custodial fathers, spirituality, counseling relationships. *Unit head:* Ann Vibert, Director, E-mail: ann.vibert@acadiau.ca. *Application contact:* Sheila Langille, Secretary, 902-585-1229, Fax: 902-585-1071, E-mail: sheila.langille@acadiau.ca.

Adams State College, The Graduate School, Department of Counselor Education, Alamosa, CO 81102. Offers counseling (MA). *Accreditation:* ACA. Part-time programs available. *Degree requirements:* For master's, internship, qualifying exam. *Entrance requirements:* For master's, GRE General Test or MAT, minimum undergraduate GPA of 2.75.

Counselor Education

Adler Graduate School, Program in Adlerian Studies, Richfield, MN 55423. Offers art therapy specialization (MA); clinical counseling track (MA); coaching and consulting in organizations (Certificate); management consulting and organizational leadership (MA); marriage and family track (MA); non-clinical Adlerian studies track (MA); personal and professional life coaching (Certificate); school counseling (MA). Part-time and evening/weekend programs available. *Degree requirements:* For master's, thesis or alternative, 500-700 hour internship (depending on license choice). *Entrance requirements:* For master's, minimum undergraduate GPA of 3.0, 12 credits of course work in psychology or related field.

Alabama Agricultural and Mechanical University, School of Graduate Studies, School of Education, Department of Counseling and Special Education, Huntsville, AL 35811. Offers communicative disorders (M Ed, MS); psychology and counseling (MS, Ed S), including clinical psychology (MS), counseling and guidance, counseling psychology (MS), personnel management (MS), psychometry (MS), school psychology (MS); special education (M Ed, MS). *Accreditation:* CORE; NCATE. Part-time and evening/weekend programs available. *Degree requirements:* For master's, comprehensive exam. *Entrance requirements:* For master's, GRE General Test. Additional exam requirements/recommendations for international students: Required—TOEFL (minimum score 500 paper-based; 173 computer-based; 61 iBT). *Faculty research:* Increasing numbers of minorities in special education and speech-language pathology.

Alabama State University, School of Graduate Studies, College of Education, Department of Instructional Support, Program in Guidance and Counseling, Montgomery, AL 36101-0271. Offers general counseling (MS, Ed S); school counseling (M Ed, Ed S). Part-time programs available. *Degree requirements:* For master's, comprehensive exam; for Ed S, comprehensive exam, thesis. *Entrance requirements:* For master's, GRE General Test, MAT, graduate writing competency test; for Ed S, graduate writing competency test, GRE, MAT. Additional exam requirements/recommendations for international students: Required—TOEFL (minimum score 500 paper-based; 173 computer-based). *Faculty research:* Enhancing self-concept, drug abuse education and training, comparison of group techniques, collaborative counseling.

Albany State University, College of Education, Program in School Counseling, Albany, GA 31705-2717. Offers M Ed. Evening/weekend programs available. *Students:* 15 full-time (11 women), 45 part-time (36 women); includes 51 minority (50 African Americans, 1 Asian American or Pacific Islander). Average age 35. 11 applicants, 91% accepted, 9 enrolled. In 2009, 15 master's awarded. *Degree requirements:* For master's, comprehensive exam, clinical experience. *Entrance requirements:* For master's, GRE General Test, MAT, GACE, master's degree. Additional exam requirements/recommendations for international students: Required—TOEFL. *Application deadline:* For fall admission, 11/16 for domestic students, 9/16 for international students; for spring admission, 4/19 for domestic students, 2/19 for international students. Applications are processed on a rolling basis. Application fee: $20. Electronic applications accepted. *Expenses:* Tuition, state resident: full-time $2970; part-time $162 per credit hour. Tuition, nonresident: full-time $12,168; part-time $676 per credit hour. Required fees: $962; $75 per credit hour. *Financial support:* Application deadline: 6/30. *Faculty research:* Multicultural issues in counseling and disability. *Unit head:* Dr. Deborah Bembry, Chair, 229-430-4715, Fax: 229-430-4993, E-mail: deborah.bembry@asurams.edu. *Application contact:* Nicole Lane, Interim Graduate Admissions Officer, 229-430-4862, Fax: 229-430-6398, E-mail: nicole.lane@asurams.edu.

Alcorn State University, School of Graduate Studies, School of Psychology and Education, Alcorn State, MS 39096-7500. Offers agricultural education (MS Ed); elementary education (MS Ed, Ed S); guidance and counseling (MS Ed); industrial education (MS Ed); secondary education (MS Ed), including health and physical education; special education (MS Ed). *Accreditation:* NCATE. *Degree requirements:* For master's, thesis optional.

Alfred University, Graduate School, Program in School Psychology, Alfred, NY 14802-1205. Offers school counseling (MS Ed, CAS); school psychology (MA, Psy D, CAS). *Accreditation:* APA. *Degree requirements:* For master's, internship; for doctorate, thesis/dissertation, internship. *Entrance requirements:* For master's and doctorate, GRE General Test. Additional exam requirements/recommendations for international students: Required—TOEFL (minimum score 590 paper-based; 243 computer-based; 90 iBT); Recommended—IELTS (minimum score 6.5). Electronic applications accepted. *Expenses:* Tuition: Full-time $33,296; part-time $708 per credit hour. Required fees: $880; $144 per year. Full-time tuition and fees vary according to program. *Faculty research:* Family processes, alternative assessment approaches, behavior disorders in children, parent involvement, school psychology training issues.

American International College, School of Arts, Education and Sciences, Department of Education, Springfield, MA 01109-3189. Offers early childhood education (M Ed, CAGS); educational leadership and supervision (Ed D); elementary education (M Ed, CAGS); middle/secondary education (M Ed, CAGS); moderate disabilities (M Ed, CAGS); reading (M Ed, CAGS); school adjustment counseling (MA, CAGS); school administration (M Ed, CAGS); school guidance counseling (MA, CAGS); teaching (MA, MS); teaching and learning (Ed D). Part-time and evening/weekend programs available. Terminal master's awarded for partial completion of doctoral program. *Degree requirements:* For master's, comprehensive exam (for some programs), thesis (for some programs), practicum; for doctorate, comprehensive exam (for some programs), thesis/dissertation; for CAGS, practicum. *Entrance requirements:* For master's, minimum B- average in undergraduate course work; for doctorate, GRE General Test, interview. Additional exam requirements/recommendations for international students: Required—TOEFL. Electronic applications accepted. *Expenses:* Tuition: Full-time $12,510; part-time $695 per credit hour. Required fees: $35 per term.

Angelo State University, College of Graduate Studies, College of Education, Department of Curriculum and Instruction, Program in Guidance and Counseling, San Angelo, TX 76909. Offers M Ed. Part-time and evening/weekend programs available. *Faculty:* 17 full-time (12 women). *Students:* 8 full-time (6 women), 44 part-time (41 women); includes 11 minority (1 African American, 10 Hispanic Americans). Average age 36. 17 applicants, 100% accepted, 14 enrolled. In 2009, 14 master's awarded. *Degree requirements:* For master's, comprehensive exam. *Entrance requirements:* For master's, GRE General Test. Additional exam requirements/recommendations for international students: Required—TOEFL or IELTS. *Application deadline:* For fall admission, 7/15 priority date for domestic students, 6/10 for international students; for spring admission, 12/1 priority date for domestic students, 11/1 for international students. Applications are processed on a rolling basis. Application fee: $40 ($50 for international students). Electronic applications accepted. *Expenses:* Tuition, state resident: full-time $3396; part-time $142 per credit hour. Tuition, nonresident: full-time $10,152; part-time $423 per credit hour. Required fees: $1786; $36.25 per credit hour. $494 per semester. Full-time tuition and fees vary according to course load, degree level and program. *Financial support:* In 2009–10, 19 students received support. Career-related internships or fieldwork, Federal Work-Study, scholarships/grants, and unspecified assistantships available. Support available to part-time students. Financial award application deadline: 3/1; financial award applicants required to submit FAFSA. *Unit head:* Dr. Mary McGlamery, Graduate Advisor, 325-942-2052 Ext. 262, Fax: 325-942-2039, E-mail: mary.mcglamery@angelo.edu. *Application contact:* Theresa Fortin, Graduate Admissions Assistant, 325-942-2169, Fax: 325-942-2194, E-mail: theresa.fortin@angelo.edu.

Appalachian State University, Cratis D. Williams Graduate School, Department of Human Development and Psychological Counseling, Boone, NC 28608. Offers college student development (MA); community counseling (MA); marriage and family therapy (MA); school counseling (MA). *Accreditation:* AAMFT/COAMFTE; ACA; NCATE. Part-time programs available. *Faculty:* 15 full-time (5 women), 21 part-time/adjunct (14 women). *Students:* 98 full-time (95 women), 32 part-time (25 women); includes 8 minority (5 African Americans, 2 Asian Americans or Pacific Islanders, 1 Hispanic American), 1 international. 149 applicants, 54% accepted, 59 enrolled. In 2009, 78 master's awarded. *Degree requirements:* For master's, comprehensive exam (for some programs), thesis optional, internships. *Entrance requirements:* For master's, GRE General Test, 3 letters of recommendation. Additional exam requirements/recommendations for international students: Required—TOEFL (minimum score 570 paper-based; 230 computer-based; 79 iBT), IELTS (minimum score 6.5). *Application deadline:* For fall admission, 2/1 priority date for domestic students, 2/1 for international students; for spring admission, 2/1 for international students. Applications are processed on a rolling basis. Application fee: $50. Electronic applications accepted. *Expenses:* Tuition, state resident: full-time $2960. Tuition, nonresident: full-time $14,051. Required fees: $2320. *Financial support:* In 2009–10, 20 research assistantships (averaging $8,000 per year), 7 teaching assistantships (averaging $8,000 per year) were awarded; fellowships, career-related internships or fieldwork, Federal Work-Study, scholarships/grants, and unspecified assistantships also available. Financial award application deadline: 4/1; financial award applicants required to submit FAFSA. *Faculty research:* Multicultural counseling, addictions counseling, play therapy, expressive arts, child and adolescent therapy, sexual abuse counseling. *Unit head:* Dr. Lee Baruth, Chairman, 828-262-2055, E-mail: baruthlg@appstate.edu. *Application contact:* Sandy Krause, Director of Admissions and Recruiting, 828-262-2130, Fax: 828-262-2709, E-mail: krausesl@appstate.edu.

Argosy University, Atlanta, College of Psychology and Behavioral Sciences, Atlanta, GA 30328. Offers clinical psychology (MA, Psy D, Postdoctoral Respecialization Certificate), including child and family psychology (Psy D), general adult clinical (Psy D), health psychology (Psy D), neuropsychology/geropsychology (Psy D); community counseling (MA), including marriage and family therapy; counselor education and supervision (Ed D); forensic psychology (MA); industrial organizational psychology (MA); marriage and family therapy (Certificate); sport-exercise psychology (MA). *Accreditation:* APA.

Argosy University, Chicago, College of Psychology and Behavioral Sciences, Program in Counseling Psychology, Chicago, IL 60601. Offers counselor education and supervision (Ed D). Postbaccalaureate distance learning degree programs offered (minimal on-campus study).

Argosy University, Dallas, College of Psychology and Behavioral Sciences, Program in Counselor Education and Supervision, Farmers Branch, TX 75244. Offers Ed D.

Argosy University, Denver, College of Psychology and Behavioral Sciences, Denver, CO 80231. Offers clinical mental health counseling (MA); clinical psychology (MA, Psy D); counseling psychology (Ed D); counselor education and supervision (Ed D); forensic psychology (MA); industrial organizational psychology (MA); marriage and family therapy (MA, DMFT).

Argosy University, Nashville, College of Psychology and Behavioral Sciences, Program in Counselor Education and Supervision, Nashville, TN 37214. Offers Ed D.

Argosy University, Salt Lake City, College of Psychology and Behavioral Sciences, Draper, UT 84020. Offers counseling psychology (Ed D); counselor education and supervision (Ed D); forensic psychology (MA); marriage and family therapy (MA, DMFT); mental health counseling (MA).

Argosy University, Sarasota, College of Education, Sarasota, FL 34235. Offers community college executive leadership (Ed D); educational leadership (MA Ed, Ed D, Ed S), including higher education administration (Ed D), K-12 education (Ed D); school counseling (MA, Ed S); school psychology (MA); teaching and learning (MA Ed, Ed D, Ed S), including education technology (Ed D), higher education (Ed D), K-12 education (Ed D).

See Close-Up on page 695.

Argosy University, Sarasota, College of Psychology and Behavioral Sciences, Sarasota, FL 34235. Offers community counseling (MA); counseling psychology (Ed D); counselor education and supervision (Ed D); forensic psychology (MA); marriage and family therapy (MA); mental health counseling (MA); pastoral community counseling (Ed D).

Argosy University, Schaumburg, College of Psychology and Behavioral Sciences, Schaumburg, IL 60173-5403. Offers clinical health psychology (Post-Graduate Certificate); clinical psychology (MA, Psy D), including child and family psychology (Psy D), clinical health psychology (Psy D), diversity and multicultural psychology (Psy D), forensic psychology (Psy D), neuropsychology (Psy D); community counseling (MA); counseling psychology (Ed D), including counselor education and supervision; counselor education and supervision (Ed D); forensic psychology (Post-Graduate Certificate); industrial organizational psychology (MA). *Accreditation:* ACA; APA.

Argosy University, Tampa, College of Education, Tampa, FL 33607. Offers community college executive leadership (Ed D); educational leadership (MA Ed, Ed D, Ed S), including higher education administration (Ed D), K-12 education (Ed D); school counseling (MA); teaching and learning (MA Ed, Ed D, Ed S), including higher education (Ed D), K-12 education (Ed D).

See Close-Up on page 701.

Argosy University, Tampa, College of Psychology and Behavioral Sciences, Tampa, FL 33607. Offers clinical psychology (MA, Psy D), including clinical psychology; counselor education and supervision (Ed D); industrial organizational psychology (MA); marriage and family therapy (MA); mental health counseling (MA).

Argosy University, Washington DC, College of Psychology and Behavioral Sciences, Arlington, VA 22209. Offers clinical psychology (MA, Psy D), including child and family psychology (Psy D), diversity and multicultural psychology (Psy D), forensic psychology (Psy D), health and neuropsychology (Psy D); community counseling (MA); counseling psychology (Ed D), including counselor education and supervision; counselor education and supervision (Ed D); forensic psychology (MA). *Accreditation:* APA.

Arizona State University, Graduate College, Mary Lou Fulton College of Education, Division of Psychology in Education, Program in Counseling, Tempe, AZ 85287. Offers M Ed, MC. *Accreditation:* ACA (one or more programs are accredited). *Degree requirements:* For master's, thesis or alternative. *Entrance requirements:* For master's, GRE General Test or MAT.

Arkansas State University—Jonesboro, Graduate School, College of Education, Department of Psychology and Counseling, Jonesboro, State University, AR 72467. Offers college student personnel services (MS); counselor education (Ed S), including college student personnel services, psychoeducational diagnosis, school counseling; rehabilitation counseling (MRC); school counseling (MSE); student affairs (Certificate). *Accreditation:* ACA (one or more programs are accredited); CORE (one or more programs are accredited); NCATE. Part-time programs available. *Faculty:* 11 full-time (6 women), 6 part-time/adjunct (2 women). *Students:* 49 full-time (37 women), 100 part-time (81 women); includes 32 minority (31 African Americans, 1 American Indian/Alaska Native), 1 international. Average age 32. 70 applicants, 46% accepted, 30 enrolled. In 2009, 23 master's, 11 other advanced degrees awarded. *Degree requirements:* For master's and other advanced degree, comprehensive exam, thesis or alternative. *Entrance requirements:* For master's, GRE General Test or MAT (MSE), appropriate bachelor's degree, interview, letters of reference; for other advanced degree, GRE General Test, interview, master's degree, letters of reference, official transcript, personal statement, immunization records. Additional exam requirements/recommendations for international students: Required—TOEFL (minimum score 550 paper-based; 213 computer-based; 79 iBT), IELTS (minimum score 6). *Application deadline:* For fall admission, 7/15 for domestic students, 7/1 for international students; for spring admission, 12/1 for domestic students, 11/13 for international students. Applications are processed on a rolling basis. Application fee: $30 ($40 for international students). Electronic applications accepted. *Expenses:* Tuition, state resident: full-time $3744; part-time $208 per credit hour. Tuition, nonresident: full-time $9540; part-time $530 per credit hour. Required fees: $896; $47 per credit hour. $25 per term. One-time fee: $50. Tuition and fees vary according to course load and program. *Financial support:* In 2009–10, 24 students received support; teaching assistantships, career-related internships or fieldwork, scholarships/grants, and unspecified assistantships available. Financial award application deadline: 7/1; financial award applicants required to submit FAFSA. *Unit head:* Dr. Loretta McGregor, Chair, 870-972-3064, Fax: 870-972-3962, E-mail: lmcgregor@astate.edu. *Application contact:* Dr. Andrew Sustich, Dean of the Graduate School, 870-972-3029, Fax: 870-972-3857, E-mail: sustich@astate.edu.

Ashland Theological Seminary, Graduate Programs, Ashland, OH 44805. Offers biblical and theological studies (MA, MAR), including New Testament (MA), Old Testament (MA); Christian ministry (MAPT); Christian studies (Diploma); clinical counseling (michigan) (MAC); clinical

counsseling (Ohio) (MACC), including anabaptism, pietism; historical studies (MA), including church history; ministry (D Min); pastoral ministry (M Div); theological studies (MA). *Accreditation:* ATS. Part-time programs available. *Faculty:* 23 full-time (7 women), 74 part-time/adjunct (28 women). *Students:* 663 full-time (343 women), 124 part-time (65 women); includes 312 minority (289 African Americans, 3 American Indian/Alaska Native, 8 Asian Americans or Pacific Islanders, 12 Hispanic Americans), 25 international. Average age 43. 173 applicants, 87% accepted, 142 enrolled. In 2009, 34 first professional degrees, 102 master's, 17 doctorates, 2 other advanced degrees awarded. *Degree requirements:* For master's, 2 foreign languages, comprehensive exam (for some programs), thesis (for some programs); for doctorate, thesis/dissertation; for M Div, 2 foreign languages, comprehensive exam (for some programs). *Entrance requirements:* For M Div, minimum GPA of 2.75; for master's, minimum undergraduate GPA of 2.75; for doctorate, M Div, minimum undergraduate GPA of 3.0. Additional exam requirements/recommendations for international students: Required—TOEFL (minimum score 500 paper-based; 65 computer-based; 173 iBT). *Application deadline:* For fall admission, 8/30 for domestic students. Applications are processed on a rolling basis. Application fee: $30. Electronic applications accepted. *Expenses:* Tuition: Full-time $10,476; part-time $345 per credit hour. Required fees: $180; $15 per course. Part-time tuition and fees vary according to course load. *Financial support:* In 2009–10, 311 students received support, including 17 teaching assistantships; research assistantships, career-related internships or fieldwork, institutionally sponsored loans, scholarships/grants, and unspecified assistantships also available. Support available to part-time students. Financial award application deadline: 5/15; financial award applicants required to submit FAFSA. *Faculty research:* Semitic languages and linguistics, rhetorical and social-scientific criticism, Anabaptist studies, inner spiritual healing, African-American clergy in film and literature. *Unit head:* Dr. John C. Shultz, President, 419-289-5160, Fax: 419-289-5969, E-mail: jshultz@ashland.edu. *Application contact:* Glenn Black, Director of Enrollment Management, 419-289-5151, Fax: 419-289-5969, E-mail: gblack@ashland.edu.

Athabasca University, Graduate Centre for Applied Psychology, Athabasca, AB T9S 3A3, Canada. Offers art therapy (MC); career counseling (MC); counseling (Advanced Certificate); counseling psychology (MC); school counseling (MC). *Faculty:* 5 full-time (2 women). *Students:* 210 part-time. Average age 35. 117 applicants, 15 enrolled. In 2009, 36 master's, 1 Advanced Certificate awarded. *Application deadline:* For fall admission, 3/1 for domestic and international students. Application fee: $80. *Expenses:* Tuition: Part-time $16,500 per degree program. Required fees: $200 per year. One-time fee: $80 part-time. *Unit head:* Dr. Trevor Gilbert, Chair, 866-242-8768, Fax: 780-675-6186, E-mail: trevorg@athabascau.ca. *Application contact:* Information Contact, 800-788-9041, Fax: 780-675-6437.

Auburn University Montgomery, School of Education, Department of Counselor, Leadership, and Special Education, Montgomery, AL 36124-4023. Offers counseling (M Ed, Ed S); education administration (M Ed, Ed S); special education (M Ed, Ed S). *Accreditation:* NCATE. Part-time and evening/weekend programs available. *Faculty:* 8 full-time (6 women), 3 part-time/adjunct (1 woman). *Students:* 30 full-time (27 women), 61 part-time (44 women); includes 61 minority (60 African Americans, 1 Hispanic American). Average age 34. In 2009, 19 master's awarded. *Degree requirements:* For master's and Ed S, comprehensive exam. *Entrance requirements:* For master's, GRE General Test or MAT, certification, BS in teaching; for Ed S, GRE General Test or MAT, certification. *Application deadline:* Applications are processed on a rolling basis. Electronic applications accepted. *Expenses:* Tuition, state resident: full-time $2841; part-time $225 per credit hour. Tuition, nonresident: full-time $8241; part-time $675 per credit hour. Required fees: $282; $8 per hour. $45 per term. *Financial support:* In 2009–10, 1 teaching assistantship was awarded; career-related internships or fieldwork and scholarships/grants also available. Support available to part-time students. Financial award application deadline: 3/1; financial award applicants required to submit FAFSA. *Unit head:* Dr. James V. Wright, Head, 334-244-3457, Fax: 334-344-3102, E-mail: jwright@mail.aum.edu. *Application contact:* Dr. Sam Flynt, Associate Graduate Coordinator, 334-244-3270, Fax: 334-244-3835, E-mail: sflynt@mail.aum.edu.

Augusta State University, Graduate Studies, College of Education, Program in Counseling/Guidance, Augusta, GA 30904-2200. Offers M Ed. *Accreditation:* ACA; NCATE. Part-time and evening/weekend programs available. *Degree requirements:* For master's, comprehensive exam, portfolio. *Entrance requirements:* For master's, GRE, MAT, minimum GPA of 2.5. *Faculty research:* Counseling for AIDS patients, counseling for drug and alcohol abuse.

Austin Peay State University, College of Graduate Studies, College of Behavioral and Health Sciences, Department of Psychology, Clarksville, TN 37044. Offers counseling (MS); counseling and guidance (Ed S); psychology (MA). Part-time programs available. Postbaccalaureate distance learning degree programs offered (no on-campus study). *Faculty:* 12 full-time (7 women), 1 (woman) part-time/adjunct. *Students:* 56 full-time (45 women), 27 part-time (21 women); includes 13 minority (8 African Americans, 1 Asian American or Pacific Islander, 4 Hispanic Americans), 1 international. Average age 29. 47 applicants, 96% accepted, 32 enrolled. In 2009, 23 master's awarded. *Degree requirements:* For master's, comprehensive exam, thesis (for some programs). *Entrance requirements:* For master's, GRE General Test, minimum undergraduate GPA of 2.5, 3 letters of recommendation, bachelor's degree. Additional exam requirements/recommendations for international students: Required—TOEFL (minimum score 500 paper-based; 173 computer-based). *Application deadline:* For fall admission, 3/27 priority date for domestic students; for spring admission, 11/1 priority date for domestic students. Applications are processed on a rolling basis. Application fee: $25. Electronic applications accepted. *Expenses:* Tuition, state resident: full-time $6160; part-time $608 per credit hour. Tuition, nonresident: full-time $17,080; part-time $854 per credit hour. Required fees: $1224; $61.20 per credit hour. *Financial support:* In 2009–10, 12 students received support, including 12 research assistantships with full tuition reimbursements available (averaging $5,184 per year); career-related internships or fieldwork, Federal Work-Study, institutionally sponsored loans, scholarships/grants, and unspecified assistantships also available. Support available to part-time students. Financial award application deadline: 3/1; financial award applicants required to submit FAFSA. *Unit head:* Dr. Samuel Fung, Chair, 931-221-7233, Fax: 931-221-6267, E-mail: fungs@apsu.edu. *Application contact:* Dr. Dixie Dennis, Dean, College of Graduate Studies, 931-221-7662, Fax: 931-221-7641, E-mail: dennisdi@apsu.edu.

Azusa Pacific University, School of Education, Department of School Counseling and School Psychology, Program in Educational Counseling, Azusa, CA 91702-7000. Offers MA.

Baptist Bible College of Pennsylvania, Graduate School, Clarks Summit, PA 18411-1297. Offers Bible (MA); biblical ministries (MS); Christian school education (MS); counseling (MS). Part-time and evening/weekend programs available. Postbaccalaureate distance learning degree programs offered (no on-campus study). *Faculty:* 2 full-time (0 women), 1 part-time/adjunct (0 women). *Students:* 12 full-time (7 women), 61 part-time (40 women); includes 3 minority (all African Americans), 1 international. Average age 31. In 2009, 13 master's awarded. *Entrance requirements:* Additional exam requirements/recommendations for international students: Required—TOEFL (minimum score 500 paper-based; 173 computer-based). *Application deadline:* Applications are processed on a rolling basis. Application fee: $30. *Financial support:* In 2009–10, 43 students received support. Institutionally sponsored loans and scholarships/grants available. Financial award application deadline: 8/20; financial award applicants required to submit FAFSA. *Unit head:* Dr. James Lytle, Provost, 570-586-2400 Ext. 9222, Fax: 570-586-1753. *Application contact:* Drew Whipple, Assistant Director of Enrollment, 570-585-9370, Fax: 570-585-9299, E-mail: gradadmissions@bbc.edu.

Barry University, School of Education, Program in Counseling, Miami Shores, FL 33161-6695. Offers MS, PhD, Ed S. *Accreditation:* ACA. Part-time and evening/weekend programs available. *Degree requirements:* For master's, comprehensive exam. *Entrance requirements:* For master's, GRE General Test or MAT, minimum GPA of 3.0; for doctorate, GRE, minimum GPA of 3.25; for Ed S, GRE General Test, minimum GPA of 3.0.

Barry University, School of Education, Program in Mental Health Counseling, Miami Shores, FL 33161-6695. Offers MS, Ed S. *Accreditation:* ACA. Part-time and evening/weekend programs available. *Degree requirements:* For master's, comprehensive exam, scholarly paper; for Ed S, comprehensive exam. *Entrance requirements:* For master's, GRE General Test or MAT, minimum GPA of 3.0; for Ed S, GRE General Test, minimum GPA of 3.0. Electronic applications accepted.

Barry University, School of Education, Program in School Counseling, Miami Shores, FL 33161-6695. Offers MS, Ed S. *Accreditation:* ACA (one or more programs are accredited). Part-time and evening/weekend programs available. *Degree requirements:* For master's, comprehensive exam, scholarly paper; for Ed S, comprehensive exam. *Entrance requirements:* For master's, GRE General Test or MAT, minimum GPA of 3.0; for Ed S, GRE General Test, minimum GPA of 3.0. Electronic applications accepted.

Bayamón Central University, Graduate Programs, Program in Education, Bayamón, PR 00960-1725. Offers administration and supervision (MA Ed); commercial education (MA Ed); education of the autistic (MA Ed); elementary education (K–3) (MA Ed); elementary education (K–6) (MA Ed); guidance and counseling (MA Ed); organizational psychology (MA); pre-elementary teacher (MA Ed); rehabilitation counseling (MA Ed); special education (MA Ed), including attention deficit disorder, learning disabilities. Part-time and evening/weekend programs available. *Degree requirements:* For master's, comprehensive exam. *Entrance requirements:* For master's, EXADEP, bachelor's degree in education or related field.

Bellevue University, Graduate School, Bellevue, NE 68005-3098. Offers acquisition and contract management (MS); business administration (MBA); clinical counseling (MS); computer information systems (MS); healthcare administration (MA, MHA, MS), including healthcare administration (MHA), human services (MA, MS); human capital management (MS, PhD); instructional design and development (MS); leadership (MA); management (MA); management information systems (MS); organizational performance (MS); public administration (MPA); public health (MPH); security management (MS). Part-time and evening/weekend programs available. Postbaccalaureate distance learning degree programs offered (no on-campus study). *Degree requirements:* For master's, thesis or project. *Entrance requirements:* For master's, minimum GPA of 2.5 in last 60 hours. Additional exam requirements/recommendations for international students: Required—TOEFL (minimum score 538 paper-based; 200 computer-based).

Bloomsburg University of Pennsylvania, School of Graduate Studies, College of Professional Studies, School of Education, Department of Educational Studies and Secondary Education, Program in Guidance Counseling and Student Affairs, Bloomsburg, PA 17815-1301. Offers M Ed. *Entrance requirements:* For master's, GRE, 3 letters of recommendation, resume.

Bob Jones University, Graduate Programs, Greenville, SC 29614. Offers accountancy (MS); Bible (MA); Bible translation (MA); Biblical studies (Certificate); broadcast management (MS); business administration (MBA); church history (MA, PhD); church ministries (MA); church music (MM); cinema and video production (MA); counseling (MS); curriculum and instruction (Ed D); divinity (M Div); dramatic production (MA); educational leadership (MS, Ed D, Ed S); elementary education (M Ed, MAT); English (M Ed, MA, MAT); fine arts (MA); graphic design (MA); history (M Ed, MA); illustration (MA); interpretative speech (MA); mathematics (M Ed, MAT); medical missions (Certificate); ministry (MM, D Min); multi-categorical special education (M Ed, MAT); music (M Ed); New Testament interpretation (PhD); Old Testament interpretation (PhD); orchestral instrument performance (MM); organ performance (MM); pastoral studies (MA); personnel services (MS, Ed S); piano pedagogy (MM); piano performance (MM); platform arts (MA); radio and television broadcasting (MS); rhetoric and public address (MA); secondary education (M Ed); studio art (MA); teaching Bible (MA); theology (MA, PhD); voice performance (MM); youth ministries (MA); M Div/MM.

Boise State University, Graduate College, College of Education, Department of Counselor Education, Program in Counseling, Boise, ID 83725-0399. Offers MA. *Accreditation:* ACA; NCATE. *Entrance requirements:* For master's, minimum GPA of 3.0. Electronic applications accepted. *Expenses:* Tuition, state resident: full-time $3106; part-time $209 per credit. Tuition, nonresident: part-time $284 per credit.

Boston University, School of Education, Department of Literacy and Language, Counseling and Development, Program in Counseling, Boston, MA 02215. Offers Ed M, CAGS. *Degree requirements:* For master's, thesis optional; for CAGS, comprehensive exam. *Entrance requirements:* For master's and CAGS, GRE General Test or MAT. Additional exam requirements/recommendations for international students: Required—TOEFL. Electronic applications accepted. *Expenses:* Tuition: Full-time $37,910; part-time $1184 per credit hour. Required fees: $386; $40 per semester. Part-time tuition and fees vary according to class time, course level, degree level and program.

Bowie State University, Graduate Programs, Program in Guidance and Counseling, Bowie, MD 20715-9465. Offers M Ed. Part-time and evening/weekend programs available. *Degree requirements:* For master's, comprehensive exam, thesis optional, research paper. *Entrance requirements:* For master's, teaching experience, minimum GPA of 2.5, 3 recommendations. Electronic applications accepted.

Bowling Green State University, Graduate College, College of Education and Human Development, School of Education and Intervention Services, Intervention Services Division, Program in Counseling, Bowling Green, OH 43403. Offers mental health counseling (MA); school counseling (M Ed). *Accreditation:* NCATE. Part-time programs available. *Degree requirements:* For master's, thesis or alternative. *Entrance requirements:* For master's, GRE General Test. Additional exam requirements/recommendations for international students: Required—TOEFL. Electronic applications accepted. *Faculty research:* Perfectionism, multi-cultural counseling, suicide, ethics and legal issues related to counseling, play therapy.

Bradley University, Graduate School, College of Education and Health Sciences, Department of Educational Leadership and Human Development, Peoria, IL 61625-0002. Offers human development counseling (MA), including community and agency counseling, school counseling; leadership in educational administration (MA); leadership in human service administration (MA). *Accreditation:* ACA; NCATE. Part-time and evening/weekend programs available. *Degree requirements:* For master's, comprehensive exam, thesis optional. *Entrance requirements:* For master's, GRE General Test or MAT, interview, 3 letters of recommendation. Additional exam requirements/recommendations for international students: Required—TOEFL (minimum score 550 paper-based; 213 computer-based; 79 iBT).

Brandon University, Faculty of Education, Brandon, MB R7A 6A9, Canada. Offers curriculum and instruction (M Ed, Diploma); educational administration (M Ed, Diploma); guidance and counseling (M Ed, Diploma); special education (M Ed, Diploma). *Degree requirements:* For master's, thesis. *Entrance requirements:* For master's, minimum GPA of 3.0, teaching certificate or equivalent. Additional exam requirements/recommendations for international students: Required—TOEFL. *Faculty research:* Comparative education, environmental studies, parent/school council.

Bridgewater State University, School of Graduate Studies, School of Education and Allied Science, Department of Secondary Education and Professional Programs, Program in Counseling, Bridgewater, MA 02325-0001. Offers M Ed, CAGS. *Accreditation:* ACA; NCATE. Part-time and evening/weekend programs available. *Entrance requirements:* For master's, GRE General Test.

Brooklyn College of the City University of New York, Division of Graduate Studies, School of Education, Program in School Counseling, Brooklyn, NY 11210-2889. Offers MS Ed, CAS. Part-time programs available. *Students:* 72 full-time (60 women), 78 part-time (64 women); includes 87 minority (57 African Americans, 10 Asian Americans or Pacific Islanders, 20 Hispanic Americans), 3 international. Average age 29. 175 applicants, 57% accepted, 63 enrolled. In 2009, 28 master's, 12 CASs awarded. *Degree requirements:* For master's, comprehensive exam, internship. *Entrance requirements:* For master's, interview, 2 letters of recommendation, resume, essay, supplemental application; for CAS, master's degree. Additional exam requirements/recommendations for international students: Required—TOEFL (minimum

Counselor Education

Brooklyn College of the City University of New York *(continued)*
score 500 paper-based; 173 computer-based; 61 iBT). *Application deadline:* For fall admission, 3/1 priority date for domestic students, 2/1 priority date for international students. Applications are processed on a rolling basis. Application fee: $125. Electronic applications accepted. *Expenses:* Tuition, state resident: full-time $7360; part-time $310 per credit hour. Tuition, nonresident: full-time $13,800; part-time $575 per credit hour. Required fees: $140.10 per semester. *Financial support:* Career-related internships or fieldwork, Federal Work-Study, institutionally sponsored loans, and scholarships/grants available. Support available to part-time students. Financial award application deadline: 5/1; financial award applicants required to submit FAFSA. *Faculty research:* Urban school counseling, parent involvement, multicultural competence and counselor training. *Unit head:* Prof. David Forbes, Program Head, 718-951-5938, Fax: 718-951-4816, E-mail: dforbes@brooklyn.cuny.edu. *Application contact:* Hernan Sierra, Graduate Admissions Coordinator, 718-951-4536, Fax: 718-951-4506, E-mail: grads@brooklyn.cuny.edu.

Bucknell University, Graduate Studies, College of Arts and Sciences, Department of Education, Specialization in Elementary and Secondary Counseling, Lewisburg, PA 17837. Offers MA, MS Ed. *Degree requirements:* For master's, thesis or alternative. *Entrance requirements:* For master's, GRE General Test, minimum GPA of 2.8. Additional exam requirements/ recommendations for international students: Required—TOEFL.

Buena Vista University, School of Education, Storm Lake, IA 50588. Offers curriculum and instruction (M Ed), including effective teaching, TESL; school guidance and counseling (MS Ed). Program offered in summer only. Part-time and evening/weekend programs available. Post-baccalaureate distance learning degree programs offered (minimal on-campus study). *Degree requirements:* For master's, thesis, fieldwork/practicum, capstone portfolio. *Entrance requirements:* For master's, Analytical Writing Assessment (in-house), minimum undergraduate GPA of 2.75. Electronic applications accepted. *Faculty research:* Reading, curriculum, educational psychology, special education.

Butler University, College of Education, Indianapolis, IN 46208-3485. Offers administration (MS); elementary education (MS); reading (MS); school counseling (MS); secondary education (MS); special education (MS). *Accreditation:* ACA; NCATE. Part-time and evening/weekend programs available. *Faculty:* 9 full-time (7 women), 7 part-time/adjunct (6 women). *Students:* 18 full-time (11 women), 137 part-time (111 women); includes 17 minority (14 African Americans, 1 American Indian/Alaska Native, 2 Asian Americans or Pacific Islanders), 9 international. Average age 31. 57 applicants, 77% accepted, 24 enrolled. In 2009, 61 master's awarded. *Entrance requirements:* For master's, GRE General Test, MAT, interview. *Application deadline:* For fall admission, 8/15 priority date for domestic students. Applications are processed on a rolling basis. Application fee: $35. Electronic applications accepted. *Financial support:* Institutionally sponsored loans available. Support available to part-time students. Financial award application deadline: 7/15; financial award applicants required to submit FAFSA. *Faculty research:* Ethics in cybercounseling, history of sports for disabled, effect of fetal alcohol syndrome on perceptual learning, reading recovery's theoretical framework in teacher education. *Unit head:* Dr. Ena Shelley, Dean, 317-940-9752, Fax: 317-940-6481. *Application contact:* Karen Farrell, Department Secretary, 317-940-9220, E-mail: kfarrell@butler.edu.

Caldwell College, Graduate Studies, Program in Counseling Psychology, Caldwell, NJ 07006-6195. Offers art therapy (MA); counseling psychology (MA); school counseling (MA). Part-time and evening/weekend programs available. *Degree requirements:* For master's, comprehensive exam, practicum. *Entrance requirements:* For master's, GRE General Test, minimum GPA of 3.0. Additional exam requirements/recommendations for international students: Required—TOEFL (minimum score 580 paper-based; 237 computer-based). Electronic applications accepted.

California Baptist University, Program in Education, Riverside, CA 92504-3206. Offers cross-cultural language and academic development (MA); educational leadership (MS); educational leadership and faith-based instruction (MS); educational technology (MS); instructional computer applications (MS); reading (MS); school counseling (MS); school psychology (MS); special education (MS); special education in mild/moderate disabilities (MS); special education in moderate/severe disabilities (MS); teaching (MS); teaching and learning (MS Ed). Part-time programs available. *Faculty:* 16 full-time (9 women), 10 part-time/adjunct (all women). *Students:* 73 full-time (60 women), 368 part-time (298 women); includes 170 minority (34 African Americans, 4 American Indian/Alaska Native, 18 Asian Americans or Pacific Islanders, 114 Hispanic Americans). 266 applicants, 72% accepted, 169 enrolled. In 2009, 120 master's awarded. *Degree requirements:* For master's, comprehensive exam (for some programs), thesis optional. *Entrance requirements:* For master's, minimum undergraduate GPA of 2.75, 12 semester hours of pre-requisite course work in education. Additional exam requirements/recommendations for international students: Required—TOEFL (minimum score 575 paper-based; 230 computer-based; 89 iBT). *Application deadline:* For fall admission, 8/1 priority date for domestic students, 7/1 for international students; for spring admission, 12/1 priority date for domestic students, 10/15 priority date for international students. Applications are processed on a rolling basis. Application fee: $45. Electronic applications accepted. *Expenses:* Tuition: Full-time $8352; part-time $464 per semester hour. Required fees: $125 per semester. Tuition and fees vary according to course load, campus/location and program. *Financial support:* Career-related internships or fieldwork, Federal Work-Study, and scholarships/grants available. Support available to part-time students. Financial award applicants required to submit FAFSA. *Unit head:* Dr. Mary Crist, Dean, School of Education, 951-343-4313, Fax: 951-343-4516, E-mail: mcrist@calbaptist.edu. *Application contact:* Gail Ronveaux, Dean of Graduate Enrollment, 951-343-5045, Fax: 951-343-5095, E-mail: graduateadmissions@calbaptist.edu.

California Lutheran University, Graduate Studies, School of Education, Emphasis in Counseling and Guidance, Thousand Oaks, CA 91360-2787. Offers MS. Part-time and evening/weekend programs available. *Degree requirements:* For master's, thesis or comprehensive exam. *Entrance requirements:* For master's, GRE General Test, interview, minimum GPA of 3.0.

California State University, Bakersfield, Division of Graduate Studies, School of Education, Program in Counseling, Bakersfield, CA 93311. Offers school counseling (MS); student affairs (MS). *Accreditation:* NCATE. *Degree requirements:* For master's, thesis or alternative, culminating projects. *Entrance requirements:* For master's, CBEST (school counseling).

California State University, Dominguez Hills, College of Professional Studies, School of Education, Division of Graduate Education, Program in Counseling, Carson, CA 90747-0001. Offers MA. Part-time and evening/weekend programs available. *Faculty:* 4 full-time (all women), 6 part-time/adjunct (4 women). *Students:* 118 full-time (95 women), 58 part-time (51 women); includes 133 minority (32 African Americans, 18 Asian Americans or Pacific Islanders, 83 Hispanic Americans), 2 international. Average age 32. 108 applicants, 46% accepted, 32 enrolled. In 2009, 43 master's awarded. *Degree requirements:* For master's, comprehensive exam. *Entrance requirements:* For master's, minimum GPA of 3.0. *Application deadline:* For fall admission, 4/1 for domestic students; for spring admission, 10/1 for domestic students. Applications are processed on a rolling basis. Application fee: $55. *Expenses:* Tuition, nonresident: full-time $6696; part-time $372 per unit. Required fees: $5946; $1752 per semester. *Faculty research:* Social development. *Unit head:* Dr. Adriean Mancillas, Associate Professor, 310-243-2680, E-mail: amancillas@csudh.edu. *Application contact:* Admissions Office, 310-243-3530.

California State University, East Bay, Graduate Programs, College of Education and Allied Studies, Department of Educational Psychology, Counseling Program, Hayward, CA 94542-3000. Offers MS. *Accreditation:* NCATE. *Faculty:* 11 full-time (6 women), 1 part-time/adjunct (0 women). *Students:* 130 full-time (109 women); includes 49 minority (12 African Americans, 1 American Indian/Alaska Native, 22 Asian Americans or Pacific Islanders, 14 Hispanic Americans), 1 international. Average age 31. 189 applicants, 42% accepted, 70 enrolled. In 2009, 63 master's awarded. *Degree requirements:* For master's, comprehensive exam, project or thesis.

Entrance requirements: For master's, GRE or MAT, interview, minimum GPA of 2.5 during previous 2 years of course work. Additional exam requirements/recommendations for international students: Required—TOEFL (minimum score 550 paper-based; 213 computer-based). *Application deadline:* For fall admission, 6/30 for domestic and international students. Application fee: $55. Electronic applications accepted. *Financial support:* Career-related internships or fieldwork, Federal Work-Study, and institutionally sponsored loans available. Support available to part-time students. Financial award application deadline: 3/1; financial award applicants required to submit FAFSA. *Unit head:* Dr. Rolla Lewis, Graduate Advisor, 510-885-3011, Fax: 510-885-2915, E-mail: rolla.lewis@csueastbay.edu. *Application contact:* Donna Wiley, Interim Associate Director, 510-885-2928, Fax: 510-885-4777, E-mail: donna.wiley@csueastbay.edu.

California State University, Fresno, Division of Graduate Studies, School of Education and Human Development, Department of Counseling and Special Education, Program in Counseling and Student Services, Fresno, CA 93740-8027. Offers MS. *Accreditation:* NCATE. Part-time and evening/weekend programs available. *Degree requirements:* For master's, thesis or alternative. *Entrance requirements:* For master's, GRE General Test, MAT, minimum GPA of 3.0. Additional exam requirements/recommendations for international students: Required—TOEFL. Electronic applications accepted.

California State University, Fullerton, Graduate Studies, College of Health and Human Development, Department of Counseling, Fullerton, CA 92834-9480. Offers MS. *Accreditation:* ACA; NCATE. Part-time programs available. *Students:* 120 full-time (104 women), 81 part-time (65 women); includes 71 minority (3 African Americans, 2 American Indian/Alaska Native, 25 Asian Americans or Pacific Islanders, 41 Hispanic Americans), 9 international. Average age 32. 216 applicants, 26% accepted, 54 enrolled. In 2009, 65 master's awarded. *Degree requirements:* For master's, comprehensive exam, project or thesis. *Entrance requirements:* For master's, minimum GPA of 3.0 in behavioral science and for undergraduate degree. Application fee: $55. *Expenses:* Tuition, nonresident: full-time $11,160; part-time $373 per credit. Required fees: $1440 per term. Tuition and fees vary according to course load, degree level and program. *Financial support:* Career-related internships or fieldwork, Federal Work-Study, institutionally sponsored loans, and scholarships/grants available. Support available to part-time students. Financial award application deadline: 3/1; financial award applicants required to submit FAFSA. *Unit head:* Dr. Jeffrey Kottler, Chair, 657-278-7537. *Application contact:* Admissions/Applications, 657-278-2371.

California State University, Long Beach, Graduate Studies, College of Education, Department of Advanced Studies in Education and Counseling, Master of Science in Counseling Program, Long Beach, CA 90840. Offers marriage and family therapy (MS); school counseling (MS); student development in higher education (MS). *Accreditation:* NCATE. *Students:* 139 full-time (103 women), 73 part-time (54 women); includes 137 minority (27 African Americans, 35 Asian Americans or Pacific Islanders, 75 Hispanic Americans), 5 international. Average age 30. *Degree requirements:* For master's, comprehensive exam or thesis. *Application deadline:* For fall admission, 3/1 for domestic students. Applications are processed on a rolling basis. Application fee: $55. Electronic applications accepted. *Expenses:* Required fees: $1802 per semester. Part-time tuition and fees vary according to course load. *Financial support:* Federal Work-Study, institutionally sponsored loans, and scholarships/grants available. Financial award application deadline: 3/2. *Unit head:* Dr. Jennifer Coots, Chair, 562-985-4517, Fax: 562-985-4534, E-mail: jcoots@csulb.edu. *Application contact:* Dr. Bita Ghafoori, Assistant Chair, 562-985-7864, Fax: 562-985-4534, E-mail: bghafoor@csulb.edu.

California State University, Los Angeles, Graduate Studies, Charter College of Education, Division of Special Education and Counseling, Los Angeles, CA 90032-8530. Offers counseling (MS), including applied behavior analysis, community college counseling, rehabilitation counseling, school counseling and school psychology; special education (MA, PhD). *Accreditation:* ACA. Part-time and evening/weekend programs available. *Faculty:* 20 full-time (15 women), 18 part-time/adjunct (10 women). *Students:* 361 full-time (288 women), 366 part-time (284 women); includes 450 minority (43 African Americans, 65 Asian Americans or Pacific Islanders, 342 Hispanic Americans), 40 international. Average age 34. 181 applicants, 99% accepted, 108 enrolled. In 2009, 143 master's awarded. *Entrance requirements:* For master's, minimum GPA of 2.75 in last 90 units of course work, teaching certificate. Additional exam requirements/recommendations for international students: Required—TOEFL (minimum score 500 paper-based; 173 computer-based). *Application deadline:* For fall admission, 5/1 for domestic and international students. Applications are processed on a rolling basis. Application fee: $55. Electronic applications accepted. *Financial support:* Career-related internships or fieldwork and Federal Work-Study available. Support available to part-time students. Financial award application deadline: 3/1. *Unit head:* Dr. Randy Campbell, Chair, 323-343-4400, Fax: 323-343-5605, E-mail: rcampbe@calstatela.edu. *Application contact:* Dr. Cheryl L. Ney, Associate Vice President for Academic Affairs and Dean of Graduate Studies, 323-343-3820, Fax: 323-343-5653, E-mail: cney@cslanet.calstatela.edu.

California State University, Northridge, Graduate Studies, College of Education, Department of Educational Psychology and Counseling, Northridge, CA 91330. Offers counseling (MS), including career counseling, college counseling and student services, marriage and family therapy, school counseling, school psychology; educational psychology (MA Ed), including development, learning, and instruction, early childhood education. *Accreditation:* ACA (one or more programs are accredited); NCATE. Part-time and evening/weekend programs available. *Faculty:* 19 full-time (11 women), 42 part-time/adjunct (26 women). *Students:* 341 full-time (301 women), 135 part-time (121 women); includes 21 African Americans, 31 Asian Americans or Pacific Islanders, 149 Hispanic Americans, 11 international. Average age 31. 498 applicants, 39% accepted, 167 enrolled. In 2009, 119 master's awarded. *Entrance requirements:* For master's, GRE General Test or minimum GPA of 3.0. Additional exam requirements/recommendations for international students: Required—TOEFL. *Application deadline:* For fall admission, 11/30 for domestic students. Application fee: $55. *Financial support:* Scholarships/grants available. Support available to part-time students. Financial award application deadline: 3/1. *Unit head:* Dr. Shari Tarver-Behring, Chair, 818-677-2599. *Application contact:* Dr. Shari Tarver-Behring, Chair, 818-677-2599.

California State University, Sacramento, Graduate Studies, College of Education, Department of Counselor Education, Sacramento, CA 95819. Offers career counseling (MS); generic counseling (MS); guidance (MA); school counseling (MS). *Accreditation:* ACA. *Degree requirements:* For master's, thesis or alternative, writing proficiency exam. *Entrance requirements:* For master's, minimum GPA of 2.5. Additional exam requirements/recommendations for international students: Required—TOEFL. Electronic applications accepted.

California State University, San Bernardino, Graduate Studies, College of Education, Program in Educational Psychology and Counseling, San Bernardino, CA 92407-2397. Offers correctional and alternative education (MA); counseling and guidance (MS); rehabilitation counseling (MA). *Accreditation:* NCATE. Part-time and evening/weekend programs available. *Faculty:* 7 full-time (3 women), 4 part-time/adjunct (1 woman). *Students:* 110 full-time (95 women), 5 part-time (all women); includes 73 minority (12 African Americans, 4 Asian Americans or Pacific Islanders, 57 Hispanic Americans). Average age 32. 25 applicants, 80% accepted, 9 enrolled. In 2009, 34 master's awarded. *Degree requirements:* For master's, comprehensive exam, thesis or alternative, counselor preparation comprehensive examination. *Entrance requirements:* For master's, minimum GPA of 3.0 in education. *Application deadline:* For fall admission, 8/31 priority date for domestic students. Application fee: $55. *Financial support:* Career-related internships or fieldwork and Federal Work-Study available. Support available to part-time students. *Unit head:* Dr. Ruth Ann Sandlin, Chair, 909-537-5641, Fax: 909-537-7040, E-mail: rsandlin@csusb.edu. *Application contact:* Olivia Rosas, Director of Admissions, 909-537-7577, Fax: 909-537-7034, E-mail: orosas@csusb.edu.

California State University, Stanislaus, College of Education, Department of Advanced Studies in Education, Turlock, CA 95382. Offers community college leadership (Ed D); education (MA); educational leadership (Ed D); educational technology (MA); P-12 leadership (Ed D); school administration (MA); school counseling (MA); special education (MA). Part-time and

evening/weekend programs available. Postbaccalaureate distance learning degree programs offered. *Degree requirements:* For master's, thesis. *Entrance requirements:* For master's, MAT or GRE, BEST (depending on concentration), minimum GPA of 2.8, 3 letters of reference; for doctorate, GRE, 3.0 minimum GPA, 3 letters of reference and personal statement. Additional exam requirements/recommendations for international students: Required—TOEFL (minimum score 550 paper-based; 213 computer-based). *Faculty research:* Current school technology use, social aspects of technology, staff development.

California State University, Stanislaus, College of Human and Health Sciences, Department of Psychology, Turlock, CA 95382. Offers behavior analysis (MS); child development (Graduate Certificate); counseling (MS); psychology (MA, MS). Part-time programs available. *Degree requirements:* For master's, thesis. *Entrance requirements:* For master's, GRE General Test, minimum GPA of 3.0, 3 letters of reference. Additional exam requirements/recommendations for international students: Required—TOEFL (minimum score 550 paper-based; 213 computer-based). Electronic applications accepted. *Faculty research:* Hedonic tone judgement, syntax and autism, early literacy assessment and native and non-native languages.

California University of Pennsylvania, School of Graduate Studies and Research, School of Education, Department of Counselor Education and Services, California, PA 15419-1394. Offers guidance and counseling (M Ed, MS). *Accreditation:* ACA; NCATE. Part-time and evening/weekend programs available. *Degree requirements:* For master's, comprehensive exam, thesis optional. *Entrance requirements:* For master's, MAT, minimum GPA of 3.0, resume, letters of reference. Additional exam requirements/recommendations for international students: Required—TOEFL (minimum score 550 paper-based; 213 computer-based; 80 iBT). Electronic applications accepted. *Faculty research:* Mind-body theories and practice, grief issues, career development, supervision, sports counseling.

Cambridge College, School of Education, Cambridge, MA 02138-5304. Offers autism specialist (M Ed); autism/behavior analyst (M Ed); behavior analyst (Post-Master's Certificate); behavioral management (M Ed); early childhood teacher (M Ed); education specialist in curriculum and instruction (CAGS); educational leadership (Ed D); elementary teacher (M Ed); English as a second language (M Ed, Certificate); general science (M Ed); health education, health promotion (Post-Master's Certificate); health/family and consumer sciences (M Ed); history (M Ed); individualized degree (M Ed); information technology literacy (M Ed); instructional technology (M Ed); interdisciplinary studies (M Ed); library teacher (M Ed); literacy education (M Ed); mathematics (M Ed); mathematics specialist (Certificate); middle school mathematics and science (M Ed); school administration (M Ed, CAGS); school guidance counselor (M Ed); school nurse education (M Ed); school social worker/school adjustment counselor (M Ed); special education administrator (CAGS); special education/moderate disabilities (M Ed); teaching skills and methodologies (M Ed). Part-time and evening/weekend programs available. Postbaccalaureate distance learning degree programs offered (minimal on-campus study). *Faculty:* 10 full-time (3 women), 283 part-time/adjunct (187 women). *Students:* 974 full-time (755 women), 1,071 part-time (835 women); includes 940 minority (762 African Americans, 4 American Indian/Alaska Native, 22 Asian Americans or Pacific Islanders, 152 Hispanic Americans), 28 international. Average age 39. In 2009, 866 master's, 4 doctorates, 209 CAGSs awarded. *Degree requirements:* For master's, thesis, internship/practicum (licensure program only); for doctorate, thesis/dissertation; for other advanced degree, thesis. *Entrance requirements:* For master's, interview, resume, documentation of licensure, 2 professional references; for doctorate, official transcripts, interview, resume, documentation of licensure (if any), written personal statement/essay, portfolio of scholarly and professional work, qualifying assessment, 2 professional references, health insurance, immunizations form; for other advanced degree, official transcripts, interview, resume, documentation of licensure (if any), written personal statement/essay, 2 professional references, health insurance, immunizations form. Additional exam requirements/recommendations for international students: Required—TOEFL (minimum score 550 paper-based; 213 computer-based; 79 iBT); Recommended—IELTS (minimum score 6). *Application deadline:* Applications are processed on a rolling basis. Application fee: $30. Electronic applications accepted. *Expenses:* Contact institution. *Financial support:* In 2009–10, 1,373 students received support. Career-related internships or fieldwork, Federal Work-Study, and scholarships/grants available. Financial award applicants required to submit FAFSA. *Faculty research:* Adult education, accelerated learning, mathematics education, brain compatible learning, special education and law. *Unit head:* Dr. N. Alan Sheppard, Interim Associate Dean, 617-873-0619, E-mail: alan.sheppard@cambridgecollege.edu. *Application contact:* Stephen Lyons, Director of Enrollment, Graduate and N.I.T.E. Programs, 617-868-1000, Fax: 617-349-3561, E-mail: stephen.lyons@cambridgecollege.edu.

Cambridge College, School of Psychology and Counseling, Cambridge, MA 02138-5304. Offers addiction counseling (M Ed); alcohol & drug counseling (Certificate); counseling psychology (M Ed, CAGS); counseling psychology: forensic counseling (M Ed); marriage and family therapy (M Ed); mental health and addiction counseling (M Ed); mental health counseling (M Ed); mental health counseling for school guidance counselors (Post Master's Certificate); psychological studies (M Ed); school adjustment and mental health counseling (M Ed); school adjustment, mental health and addiction counseling (M Ed); school guidance counselor (M Ed); trauma studies (Certificate). Part-time and evening/weekend programs available. *Faculty:* 5 full-time (2 women), 87 part-time/adjunct (50 women). *Students:* 501 full-time (395 women), 307 part-time (245 women); includes 382 minority (295 African Americans, 2 American Indian/Alaska Native, 6 Asian Americans or Pacific Islanders, 79 Hispanic Americans), 4 international. Average age 38. In 2009, 237 master's, 15 CAGSs awarded. *Degree requirements:* For master's, thesis, practicum/internship; for other advanced degree, thesis, practicum/Internship. *Entrance requirements:* For master's, resume, 2 professional references; for other advanced degree, official transcripts, documents for transfer credit evaluation, resume, written personal statement/essay, 2 professional references, health insurance, immunizations form. Additional exam requirements/recommendations for international students: Required—TOEFL (minimum score 550 paper-based; 213 computer-based; 79 iBT); Recommended—IELTS (minimum score 6). *Application deadline:* Applications are processed on a rolling basis. Application fee: $30. Electronic applications accepted. *Expenses:* Contact institution. *Financial support:* In 2009–10, 686 students received support. Career-related internships or fieldwork, Federal Work-Study, and scholarships/grants available. Financial award applicants required to submit FAFSA. *Unit head:* Dr. Niti Seth, Dean, 617-873-0208, Fax: 617-349-3561, E-mail: nseth@cambridgecollege.edu. *Application contact:* Stephen Lyons, Director of Enrollment, Graduate and N.I.T.E. Programs, 617-868-1000, Fax: 617-349-3561, E-mail: stephen.lyons@cambridgecollege.edu.

Campbell University, Graduate and Professional Programs, School of Education, Buies Creek, NC 27506. Offers administration (MSA); community counseling (MA); elementary education (M Ed); English education (M Ed); interdisciplinary studies (M Ed); mathematics education (M Ed); middle grades education (M Ed); physical education (M Ed); school counseling (M Ed); secondary education (M Ed); social science education (M Ed). *Accreditation:* NCATE. Part-time and evening/weekend programs available. *Degree requirements:* For master's, comprehensive exam. *Entrance requirements:* For master's, GRE General Test, minimum GPA of 2.7. *Faculty research:* Spiritual values and wellness issues in counseling, stress and professional burnout among counselors, thinking strategies, leadership, adaptive technology.

Canisius College, Graduate Division, School of Education and Human Services, Department of Counseling and Human Services, Buffalo, NY 14208-1098. Offers community mental health counseling (MS); general counseling (MS); school counseling (MS). *Accreditation:* ACA. Part-time and evening/weekend programs available. *Faculty:* 5 full-time (3 women), 6 part-time/adjunct (2 women). *Students:* 110 full-time (89 women), 62 part-time (56 women); includes 23 minority (18 African Americans, 2 Asian Americans or Pacific Islanders, 3 Hispanic Americans), 3 international. Average age 30. 106 applicants, 84% accepted, 43 enrolled. In 2009, 51 master's awarded. *Degree requirements:* For master's, thesis, research project. *Entrance requirements:* For master's, interview, minimum GPA of 2.5. *Application deadline:* Applications are processed on a rolling basis. Application fee: $25. Electronic applications accepted. *Financial support:* In 2009–10, 2 research assistantships with partial tuition reimbursements (averaging $8,500 per year) were awarded; career-related internships or fieldwork, Federal Work-Study, institutionally

sponsored loans, health care benefits, and unspecified assistantships also available. Support available to part-time students. Financial award applicants required to submit FAFSA. *Faculty research:* Positive psychology, wellness, school violence prevention, chronic pain. *Unit head:* Dr. David L. Farrugia, Chairman, 716-888-2393, Fax: 716-888-3290, E-mail: farrugia@canisius.edu. *Application contact:* James D. Bagwell, Director of Graduate Recruitment and Admissions, 716-888-2544, Fax: 716-888-3290, E-mail: bagwellj@canisius.edu.

Cape Breton University, School of Education, Health, and Wellness, Sydney, NS B1P 6L2, Canada. Offers educational counseling (Diploma); educational curriculum (Diploma); educational studies in arts education (Certificate); educational technology (Diploma). Part-time and evening/weekend programs available. Postbaccalaureate distance learning degree programs offered (no on-campus study). *Faculty:* 15 part-time/adjunct (5 women). *Students:* 171 part-time (103 women). Average age 30. *Application deadline:* For fall admission, 8/1 priority date for domestic students. Applications are processed on a rolling basis. Application fee: $50. Electronic applications accepted. *Unit head:* Susan Basso, Coordinator of the Education Program, 902-563-1651, Fax: 902-563-1861. *Application contact:* Terry MacDonald, Coordinator, Teacher Education Program, 902-563-1647, Fax: 902-563-1449, E-mail: terry_macdonald@cbu.ca.

Carlow University, School for Social Change, Pittsburgh, PA 15213-3165. Offers professional counseling (MS); professional counseling: school counseling (MS); professional leadership: management for nonprofit organizations (MS); professional leadership: organizational influence and policy (MS); professional leadership: training and development (MS). Part-time and evening/weekend programs available. *Entrance requirements:* Additional exam requirements/recommendations for international students: Required—TOEFL (minimum score 550 paper-based; 213 computer-based). Electronic applications accepted. *Expenses:* Tuition: Full-time $11,250; part-time $625 per credit. Tuition and fees vary according to course load, degree level and program. *Faculty research:* Gender and leadership, cross cultural communications and leadership, organizational culture.

Carson-Newman College, Graduate Program in Education, Jefferson City, TN 37760. Offers curriculum and instruction (M Ed); educational leadership (M Ed); elementary education (MAT); school counseling (MS); secondary education (MAT); teaching English as a second language (MATESL). *Accreditation:* NCATE. Part-time and evening/weekend programs available. *Faculty:* 5 full-time (2 women), 10 part-time/adjunct (3 women). *Students:* 112 full-time (84 women), 84 part-time (52 women); includes 5 African Americans, 17 international. Average age 32. 86 applicants, 98% accepted. In 2009, 55 master's awarded. *Degree requirements:* For master's, thesis or alternative. *Entrance requirements:* For master's, NTE, minimum GPA of 3.0 in major, 2.5 overall. *Application deadline:* For fall admission, 7/15 priority date for domestic students. Applications are processed on a rolling basis. Application fee: $25 ($50 for international students). *Expenses:* Tuition: Full-time $5490; part-time $305 per semester hour. Required fees: $200. *Financial support:* In 2009–10, 41 students received support. Federal Work-Study and unspecified assistantships available. Financial award application deadline: 4/1; financial award applicants required to submit FAFSA. *Unit head:* Dr. Sharon Teets, Chair, 865-471-3461. *Application contact:* Graduate Admissions and Services Adviser, 865-471-3460, Fax: 865-471-3875.

Carthage College, Division of Teacher Education, Kenosha, WI 53140. Offers classroom guidance and counseling (M Ed); creative arts (M Ed); gifted and talented children (M Ed); language arts (M Ed); modern language (M Ed); natural sciences (M Ed); reading (M Ed, Certificate); social sciences (M Ed); teacher leadership (M Ed). Part-time and evening/weekend programs available. *Degree requirements:* For master's, thesis optional. *Entrance requirements:* For master's, MAT, minimum B average, letters of reference.

Central Connecticut State University, School of Graduate Studies, School of Education and Professional Studies, Department of Counseling and Family Therapy, New Britain, CT 06050-4010. Offers marriage and family therapy (MS); professional counseling (MS, Certificate); school counseling (MS); student development in higher education (MS). *Accreditation:* AAMFT/COAMFTE. Part-time and evening/weekend programs available. *Faculty:* 8 full-time (5 women), 14 part-time/adjunct (9 women). *Students:* 117 full-time (97 women), 189 part-time (159 women); includes 52 minority (27 African Americans, 3 American Indian/Alaska Native, 3 Asian Americans or Pacific Islanders, 19 Hispanic Americans), 4 international. Average age 33. 249 applicants, 39% accepted, 84 enrolled. In 2009, 78 master's awarded. *Degree requirements:* For master's, comprehensive exam, thesis or alternative; for Certificate, qualifying exam. *Entrance requirements:* For master's, minimum undergraduate GPA of 2.7. Additional exam requirements/recommendations for international students: Required—TOEFL. *Application deadline:* For fall admission, 5/1 for domestic students. Applications are processed on a rolling basis. Application fee: $50. Electronic applications accepted. *Expenses:* Tuition, area resident: Full-time $4662; part-time $440 per credit. Tuition, state resident: full-time $6994; part-time $440 per credit. Tuition, nonresident: full-time $12,988; part-time $440 per credit. Required fees: $3606. One-time fee: $62 part-time. *Financial support:* In 2009–10, 29 students received support, including 22 research assistantships; career-related internships or fieldwork, Federal Work-Study, scholarships/grants, and unspecified assistantships also available. Support available to part-time students. Financial award application deadline: 3/1; financial award applicants required to submit FAFSA. *Faculty research:* Elementary/secondary school counseling, marriage/family therapy, rehabilitation counseling, counseling in higher educational settings. *Unit head:* Dr. Connie Tait, Chair, 860-832-2154. *Application contact:* Dr. Connie Tait, Chair, 860-832-2154.

Central Methodist University, College of Graduate and Extended Studies, Fayette, MO 65248-1198. Offers clinical counseling (MS); clinical nurse leader (MSN); education (M Ed). Part-time and evening/weekend programs available. Postbaccalaureate distance learning degree programs offered (no on-campus study). *Degree requirements:* For master's, thesis. *Entrance requirements:* For master's, GRE General Test, minimum GPA of 2.75. Electronic applications accepted.

Central Michigan University, Central Michigan University Off-Campus Programs, Program in Counseling, Mount Pleasant, MI 48859. Offers professional counseling (MA); school counseling (MA). Part-time and evening/weekend programs available. *Entrance requirements:* For master's, MAT, minimum GPA of 2.7. Additional exam requirements/recommendations for international students: Required—TOEFL. Electronic applications accepted. *Financial support:* Scholarships/grants available. Support available to part-time students. *Unit head:* Dr. Suzanne Shellady, Chair, 989-774-3507, E-mail: shell1sm@cmich.edu. *Application contact:* 877-268-4636, E-mail: cmuoffcampus@cmich.edu.

Central Michigan University, College of Graduate Studies, College of Education and Human Services, Department of Counseling and Special Education, Program in Counseling, Mount Pleasant, MI 48859. Offers counseling (MA), including professional counseling, school counseling. Part-time programs available. *Degree requirements:* For master's, thesis or alternative. *Entrance requirements:* For master's, MAT, Michigan teaching certificate. Electronic applications accepted. *Faculty research:* School counseling, professional counseling.

Central Washington University, Graduate Studies and Research, College of the Sciences, Department of Psychology, Program in School Counseling, Ellensburg, WA 98926. Offers M Ed. *Faculty:* 32 full-time (16 women). *Students:* 11 full-time (9 women), 2 part-time (1 woman); includes 1 minority (Hispanic American). In 2009, 4 master's awarded. *Degree requirements:* For master's, thesis, internship. *Entrance requirements:* For master's, GRE General Test, minimum GPA of 3.0. Additional exam requirements/recommendations for international students: Required—TOEFL (minimum score 550 paper-based; 213 computer-based; 79 iBT). *Application deadline:* For fall admission, 2/1 priority date for domestic students. Applications are processed on a rolling basis. Application fee: $50. Electronic applications accepted. *Expenses:* Tuition, state resident: full-time $7353; part-time $245 per credit. Tuition, nonresident: full-time $16,383; part-time $546 per credit. Required fees: $882. Tuition and fees vary according to degree level. *Financial support:* Research assistantships with full and partial tuition reimbursements, career-related internships or fieldwork, Federal Work-Study, health care benefits, and unspecified assistantships available. Financial award application deadline:

Counselor Education

Central Washington University (continued)

3/1. *Unit head:* Dr. Gene Johnson, Chair, 509-963-2381, E-mail: johnsong@cwu.edu. *Application contact:* Justine Eason, Admissions Program Coordinator, 509-963-3103, Fax: 509-963-1799, E-mail: masters@cwu.edu.

Chadron State College, School of Professional and Graduate Studies, Department of Education, Chadron, NE 69337. Offers business (MA Ed); community counseling (MA Ed); educational administration (MS Ed, Sp Ed); elementary education (MS Ed); history (MA Ed); language and literature (MA Ed); secondary administration (MS Ed); secondary education (MS Ed). *Accreditation:* NCATE. Part-time and evening/weekend programs available. Postbaccalaureate distance learning degree programs offered. *Degree requirements:* For master's, thesis optional. *Entrance requirements:* For master's, GRE General Test, GRE Writing Test, minimum GPA of 2.75 or 12 graduate hours at CSC with minimum GPA of 3.25. Additional exam requirements/recommendations for international students: Required—TOEFL. Electronic applications accepted. *Faculty research:* Rural education, technology, mental health.

Chapman University, Graduate Studies, College of Educational Studies, Program in School Counseling, Orange, CA 92866. Offers school counseling (MA). Part-time and evening/weekend programs available. *Faculty:* 24 full-time (15 women), 25 part-time/adjunct (16 women). *Students:* 33 full-time (29 women), 11 part-time (all women); includes 16 minority (4 Asian Americans or Pacific Islanders, 12 Hispanic Americans). Average age 29. 41 applicants, 46% accepted, 15 enrolled. In 2009, 13 master's awarded. *Degree requirements:* For master's, comprehensive exam. *Entrance requirements:* For master's, GRE General Test, MAT, or California Subject Examinations for Teachers, minimum undergraduate GPA of 2.75. Additional exam requirements/recommendations for international students: Required—TOEFL (minimum score 550 paper-based). *Application deadline:* Applications are processed on a rolling basis. Application fee: $55. Electronic applications accepted. *Expenses:* Contact institution. *Financial support:* Fellowships, Federal Work-Study and scholarships/grants available. Financial award application deadline: 6/30; financial award applicants required to submit FAFSA. *Unit head:* Dr. Michael Hass, Coordinator, 714-997-6781, E-mail: hass@chapman.edu. *Application contact:* Rika Judd, Information Contact, 714-997-6786, Fax: 714-997-6713, E-mail: rjudd@chapman.edu.

The Chicago School of Professional Psychology, Program in Clinical Psychology, Chicago, IL 60610. Offers applied behavior analysis (MA); clinical psychology (Psy D); counseling (MA). *Students:* 341 full-time (268 women), 10 part-time (7 women); includes 52 minority (22 African Americans, 2 American Indian/Alaska Native, 15 Asian Americans or Pacific Islanders, 13 Hispanic Americans), 16 international. 452 applicants, 54% accepted, 106 enrolled. In 2009, 71 doctorates awarded. *Degree requirements:* For master's, thesis (for some programs); for doctorate, comprehensive exam, thesis/dissertation. *Entrance requirements:* For master's, minimum undergraduate GPA of 3.0, 1 course in psychology, 1 course in either statistics or research methods; for doctorate, GRE, 18 hours of psychology credit (including courses in statistics, normal psychology and human development); minimum GPA of 3.2. Additional exam requirements/recommendations for international students: Required—TOEFL. Electronic applications accepted. *Financial support:* In 2009–10, fellowships with partial tuition reimbursements (averaging $10,000 per year), research assistantships (averaging $6,000 per year), teaching assistantships (averaging $6,000 per year) were awarded; Federal Work-Study, institutionally sponsored loans, and scholarships/grants also available. Financial award application deadline: 3/1; financial award applicants required to submit FAFSA. *Unit head:* Dr. James Galezewski, Department Chair, 312-467-2169, E-mail: jgalezewski@thechicagoschool.edu. *Application contact:* Andrea Schmoyer, Director of Admission, 312-329-6666, Fax: 312-644-3333, E-mail: admissions@thechicagoschool.edu.

Chicago State University, School of Graduate and Professional Studies, College of Arts and Sciences, Department of Psychology, Chicago, IL 60628. Offers counseling (MA). *Accreditation:* ACA; NCATE. *Degree requirements:* For master's, comprehensive exam, thesis optional. *Entrance requirements:* For master's, minimum GPA of 2.75.

The Citadel, The Military College of South Carolina, Citadel Graduate College, Department of Psychology, Charleston, SC 29409. Offers psychology (MA), including clinical counseling; school psychology (Ed S), including school psychology. Part-time and evening/weekend programs available. *Faculty:* 10 full-time (3 women), 2 part-time/adjunct (1 woman). *Students:* 69 full-time (58 women), 62 part-time (56 women); includes 7 minority (4 African Americans, 1 Asian American or Pacific Islander, 2 Hispanic Americans), 1 international. Average age 27. In 2009, 16 master's, 14 other advanced degrees awarded. *Degree requirements:* For master's, comprehensive exam, thesis optional; for Ed S, comprehensive exam, thesis, internship. *Entrance requirements:* For master's, GRE (minimum score 1000) or MAT (minimum score 410), minimum undergraduate GPA of 3.0; 2 letters of reference; for Ed S, GRE (minimum 1000) or MAT with prior permission (minimum 410), minimum undergraduate or graduate GPA of 3.0; 2 letters of reference. Additional exam requirements/recommendations for international students: Required—TOEFL (minimum score 550 paper-based; 213 computer-based). *Application deadline:* For fall admission, 3/15 for domestic students. Application fee: $30. Electronic applications accepted. *Expenses:* Tuition, state resident: part-time $400 per credit hour. Tuition, nonresident: part-time $657 per credit hour. Required fees: $40 per term. *Financial support:* Research assistantships, career-related internships or fieldwork, health care benefits, and unspecified assistantships available. Support available to part-time students. Financial award application deadline: 7/1; financial award applicants required to submit FAFSA. *Faculty research:* Ostracism and social exclusion, bullying, social concerns of special-needs children, childhood obesity, phantom limb pain, validation of psychological tests, perfectionism, school-based interventions with at-risk children. *Unit head:* Dr. P. Michael Politano, Department Head, 843-953-5230, Fax: 843-953-6797, E-mail: politanom@citadel.edu. *Application contact:* Dr. William G. Johnson, Program Director, 843-953-6827, Fax: 843-953-6769, E-mail: will.johnson@citadel.edu.

The Citadel, The Military College of South Carolina, Citadel Graduate College, School of Education, Program in Guidance and Counseling, Charleston, SC 29409. Offers elementary/secondary school counseling (M Ed); student affairs and college counseling (M Ed). *Accreditation:* ACA; NCATE. Part-time and evening/weekend programs available. *Faculty:* 12 full-time (7 women), 8 part-time/adjunct (5 women). *Students:* 16 full-time (15 women), 34 part-time (32 women); includes 10 minority (9 African Americans, 1 Hispanic American). Average age 29. In 2009, 16 master's awarded. *Degree requirements:* For master's, comprehensive exam, practicum or internship. *Entrance requirements:* For master's, GRE (minimum score 900) or MAT (minimum score 396), minimum undergraduate GPA of 3.0, 3 letters of reference, group admissions interview. Additional exam requirements/recommendations for international students: Required—TOEFL (minimum score 550 paper-based; 213 computer-based; 79 iBT). *Application deadline:* For fall admission, 6/1 for domestic students; for spring admission, 10/1 for domestic students. Application fee: $30. Electronic applications accepted. *Expenses:* Tuition, state resident: part-time $400 per credit hour. Tuition, nonresident: part-time $657 per credit hour. Required fees: $40 per term. *Financial support:* Career-related internships or fieldwork, health care benefits, and unspecified assistantships available. Support available to part-time students. Financial award application deadline: 7/1; financial award applicants required to submit FAFSA. *Unit head:* Dr. George T. Williams, Director, 843-953-2205, Fax: 843-953-7258, E-mail: williamsg@citadel.edu. *Application contact:* Dr. Steve A. Nida, Associate Provost, The Citadel Graduate College, 843-953-5089, Fax: 843-953-7630, E-mail: cgc@citadel.edu.

Clark Atlanta University, School of Education, Department of Counseling and Psychological Studies, Atlanta, GA 30314. Offers MA. Part-time programs available. *Faculty:* 5 full-time (4 women). *Students:* 18 full-time (13 women), 28 part-time (22 women); includes 43 minority (42 African Americans, 1 Hispanic American), 1 international. Average age 28. 31 applicants, 81% accepted, 11 enrolled. In 2009, 10 master's awarded. *Degree requirements:* For master's, comprehensive exam. *Entrance requirements:* For master's, GRE General Test, minimum undergraduate GPA of 2.6. Additional exam requirements/recommendations for international students: Required—TOEFL (minimum score 500 paper-based; 173 computer-based). *Application deadline:* For fall admission, 4/1 for domestic and international students; for spring admission, 11/1 for domestic and international students. Applications are processed on a rolling basis. Application fee: $40 ($55 for international students). Electronic applications accepted. *Expenses:* Tuition: Full-time $12,240; part-time $680 per credit hour. Required fees: $710; $355 per semester. *Financial support:* Career-related internships or fieldwork, Federal Work-Study, scholarships/grants, and unspecified assistantships available. Support available to part-time students. Financial award application deadline: 4/30; financial award applicants required to submit FAFSA. *Unit head:* Dr. Jill Thompson, Chairperson, 404-880-7519, E-mail: jthompson@cau.edu. *Application contact:* Michelle Clark-Davis, Graduate Program Admissions, 404-880-6605, E-mail: cauadmissions@cau.edu.

Clemson University, Graduate School, College of Health, Education, and Human Development, School of Education, Program in Counselor Education, Clemson, SC 29634. Offers clinical mental health counseling (M Ed); community counseling (M Ed); school counseling (M Ed); student affairs (M Ed). *Accreditation:* ACA; NCATE. *Students:* 118 full-time (92 women), 55 part-time (45 women); includes 16 minority (11 African Americans, 2 Asian Americans or Pacific Islanders, 3 Hispanic Americans), 1 international. Average age 28. 194 applicants, 59% accepted, 50 enrolled. In 2009, 65 master's awarded. *Entrance requirements:* For master's, GRE General Test. Additional exam requirements/recommendations for international students: Required—TOEFL. *Application deadline:* For fall admission, 2/1 for domestic students; for spring admission, 10/1 for domestic students. Applications are processed on a rolling basis. Application fee: $70 ($80 for international students). Electronic applications accepted. *Expenses:* Contact institution. *Financial support:* In 2009–10, 63 students received support, including 9 research assistantships with partial tuition reimbursements available (averaging $10,221 per year), 4 teaching assistantships with partial tuition reimbursements available (averaging $11,750 per year); career-related internships or fieldwork, institutionally sponsored loans, scholarships/grants, health care benefits, and unspecified assistantships also available. Support available to part-time students. Financial award application deadline: 6/1; financial award applicants required to submit FAFSA. *Unit head:* Dr. Michael J. Padilla, Director/Associate Dean, 864-656-4444, Fax: 864-656-0311, E-mail: padilla@clemson.edu. *Application contact:* Dr. David Fleming, Graduate Coordinator, 864-656-1881, Fax: 864-656-0311, E-mail: dflemin@clemson.edu.

Cleveland State University, College of Graduate Studies, College of Education and Human Services, Department of Counseling, Administration, Supervision and Adult Learning (CASAL), Cleveland, OH 44115. Offers accelerated degree in adult learning and development (M Ed); adult learning and development (M Ed); chemical dependency counseling (Certificate); community agency counseling (M Ed); counseling and pupil personnel administration (Ed S); early childhood mental health counseling (Certificate); educational administration and supervision (M Ed); school administration (Ed S); school counseling (M Ed). *Accreditation:* ACA (one or more programs are accredited). Part-time and evening/weekend programs available. *Degree requirements:* For master's, comprehensive exam (for some programs), thesis optional; for other advanced degree, comprehensive exam, thesis optional, internship. *Entrance requirements:* For master's, GRE General Test or MAT, letter of recommendation, minimum GPA of 2.75. Additional exam requirements/recommendations for international students: Required—TOEFL (minimum score 525 paper-based; 197 computer-based), IELTS (minimum score 6). Electronic applications accepted. *Faculty research:* Education law, career development, women in school administration, psychopharmacology, counseling and spirituality.

Cleveland State University, College of Graduate Studies, College of Education and Human Services, Program in Urban Education, Cleveland, OH 44115. Offers counseling (PhD); counseling psychology (PhD); leadership and lifelong learning (PhD); learning and development (PhD); policy studies (PhD); school administration (PhD). Part-time programs available. *Degree requirements:* For doctorate, one foreign language, comprehensive exam, thesis/dissertation. *Entrance requirements:* For doctorate, GRE General Test, minimum graduate GPA of 3.25. Additional exam requirements/recommendations for international students: Required—TOEFL (minimum score 525 paper-based; 197 computer-based), IELTS (minimum score 6). *Faculty research:* Equity issues (race, ethnicity, and gender), education development consequences for special needs of urban populations, urban education programming, counseling the violent or aggressive adolescent.

The College at Brockport, State University of New York, School of Education and Human Services, Department of Counselor Education, Brockport, NY 14420-2997. Offers college counseling (MS Ed); mental health counseling (MS); school counseling (MS Ed, CAS). *Accreditation:* ACA (one or more programs are accredited). Part-time programs available. *Students:* 29 full-time (18 women), 53 part-time (35 women); includes 19 minority (14 African Americans, 1 Asian American or Pacific Islander, 4 Hispanic Americans). 73 applicants, 25% accepted, 18 enrolled. In 2009, 14 master's, 4 other advanced degrees awarded. *Degree requirements:* For master's, thesis, internship, project. *Entrance requirements:* For master's, group interview, letters of recommendation, facilitation score, written objectives and focused answers; for CAS, master's degree, New York state school counselor certificate. Additional exam requirements/recommendations for international students: Required—TOEFL (minimum score 550 paper-based; 213 computer-based; 79 iBT). *Application deadline:* For fall admission, 2/1 priority date for domestic and international students; for spring admission, 9/1 priority date for domestic and international students. Application fee: $80. Electronic applications accepted. *Expenses:* Tuition, state resident: full-time $8370; part-time $349 per credit. Tuition, nonresident: full-time $13,250; part-time $522 per credit. *Financial support:* In 2009–10, 1 teaching assistantship with full tuition reimbursement (averaging $6,000 per year) was awarded; Federal Work-Study, scholarships/grants, and unspecified assistantships also available. Support available to part-time students. Financial award application deadline: 3/15; financial award applicants required to submit FAFSA. *Faculty research:* Gender and diversity issues; counseling outcomes; spirituality; school, college and mental health counseling; obesity. *Unit head:* Dr. Thomas J. Hernandez, Chairperson, 585-395-2258, Fax: 585-395-2366, E-mail: thernandez@brockport.edu. *Application contact:* Dr. Thomas J. Hernandez, Chairperson, 585-395-2258, Fax: 585-395-2366, E-mail: thernandez@brockport.edu.

The College of New Jersey, Graduate Division, School of Education, Department of Counselor Education, Program in Community Counseling: Human Services Specialization, Ewing, NJ 08628. Offers MA. *Accreditation:* ACA. Part-time programs available. *Students:* 10 full-time (7 women), 11 part-time (all women); includes 3 minority (1 African American, 2 Hispanic Americans). 28 applicants, 57% accepted. In 2009, 10 master's awarded. *Degree requirements:* For master's, comprehensive exam. *Entrance requirements:* For master's, GRE General Test, minimum GPA of 3.0 in field or 2.75 overall, interview. Additional exam requirements/recommendations for international students: Required—TOEFL. *Application deadline:* For fall admission, 2/1 for domestic students; for spring admission, 10/1 for domestic students. Application fee: $70. Electronic applications accepted. *Expenses:* Tuition, state resident: part-time $573.70 per credit. Tuition, nonresident: part-time $887.75 per credit. Required fees: $140.85 per credit. One-time fee: $10 part-time. *Financial support:* Tuition waivers (partial) and unspecified assistantships available. Financial award application deadline: 5/1; financial award applicants required to submit FAFSA. *Unit head:* Dr. Atsuko Seto, Coordinator, 609-771-2478, Fax: 609-637-5166, E-mail: seto@tcnj.edu. *Application contact:* Susan L. Hydrq, Assistant Dean, Office of Graduate Studies, 609-771-2300, Fax: 609-637-5105, E-mail: graduate@tcnj.edu.

The College of New Jersey, Graduate Division, School of Education, Department of Counselor Education, Program in School Counseling, Ewing, NJ 08628. Offers MA. *Accreditation:* ACA; NCATE. Part-time programs available. *Students:* 46 full-time (41 women), 34 part-time (32 women); includes 7 minority (4 African Americans, 2 Asian Americans or Pacific Islanders, 1 Hispanic American), 1 international. 144 applicants, 67% accepted. In 2009, 38 master's awarded. *Degree requirements:* For master's, comprehensive exam. *Entrance requirements:* For master's, GRE General Test, minimum GPA of 3.0 in field or 2.75 overall, interview. Additional exam requirements/recommendations for international students: Required—TOEFL. *Application deadline:* For fall admission, 2/1 for domestic students; for spring admission, 10/1 for domestic students. Application fee: $70. Electronic applications accepted. *Expenses:* Tuition, state resident: part-time $573.70 per credit. Tuition, nonresident: part-time $887.75 per credit.

Required fees: $140.85 per credit. One-time fee: $10 part-time. *Financial support:* Tuition waivers (partial) and unspecified assistantships available. Financial award application deadline: 5/1; financial award applicants required to submit FAFSA. *Unit head:* Dr. MaryLou Ramsey, Coordinator, 609-771-3033, Fax: 609-637-5166, E-mail: ramsey@tcnj.edu. *Application contact:* Susan L. Hydro, Assistant Dean, Office of Graduate Studies, 609-771-2300, Fax: 609-637-5105, E-mail: graduate@tcnj.edu.

College of St. Joseph, Graduate Programs, Division of Psychology and Human Services, Rutland, VT 05701-3899. Offers alcohol and substance abuse counseling (MS); clinical mental health counseling (MS); clinical psychology (MS); community counseling (MS); school guidance counseling (MS). Part-time and evening/weekend programs available. *Degree requirements:* For master's, comprehensive exam, thesis. *Entrance requirements:* For master's, 2 letters of reference, interview. Electronic applications accepted. *Expenses:* Tuition: Full-time $13,500; part-time $350 per credit. Required fees: $45 per term. One-time fee: $445. Tuition and fees vary according to program.

The College of Saint Rose, Graduate Studies, School of Education, Department of Counseling and Educational Administration, Program in Counseling, Albany, NY 12203-1419. Offers college student personnel (MS Ed); community counseling (MS Ed); school counseling (MS Ed). *Accreditation:* NCATE. Part-time and evening/weekend programs available. *Degree requirements:* For master's, comprehensive exam or thesis. *Entrance requirements:* For master's, interview, minimum undergraduate GPA of 3.0, 9 hours of psychology coursework. Additional exam requirements/recommendations for international students: Required—TOEFL (minimum score 550 paper-based; 213 computer-based). Electronic applications accepted.

College of Santa Fe, Department of Education, Santa Fe, NM 87505-7634. Offers at-risk youth (MA), including bilingual/multicultural education, classroom teaching, community counseling, educational administration, leadership, school counseling, self-designed program, TESOL/Multicultural; curriculum and instruction (MA); multicultural special education (MA). Part-time and evening/weekend programs available. *Entrance requirements:* For master's, minimum GPA of 3.0. *Faculty research:* Integrated curriculum, child development, brain research, learning styles, systemic issues in education.

The College of William and Mary, School of Education, Program in Counselor Education, Williamsburg, VA 23187-8795. Offers community and addictions counseling (M Ed); community counseling (M Ed); counselor education (PhD); family counseling (M Ed); school counseling (M Ed). *Accreditation:* ACA; NCATE. Part-time and evening/weekend programs available. *Faculty:* 6 full-time (3 women), 6 part-time/adjunct (all women). *Students:* 60 full-time (48 women), 7 part-time (5 women); includes 14 minority (11 African Americans, 1 American Indian/Alaska Native, 2 Asian Americans or Pacific Islanders), 1 international. Average age 30. 126 applicants, 52% accepted, 36 enrolled. In 2009, 28 master's, 6 doctorates awarded. *Degree requirements:* For doctorate, comprehensive exam, thesis/dissertation. *Entrance requirements:* For master's, GRE, minimum GPA of 2.5; for doctorate, GRE, minimum GPA of 3.5. Additional exam requirements/recommendations for international students: Required—TOEFL. *Application deadline:* For fall admission, 1/15 for domestic and international students. Application fee: $45. Electronic applications accepted. *Expenses:* Tuition, state resident: full-time $6400; part-time $315 per credit hour. Tuition, nonresident: full-time $19,720; part-time $840 per credit hour. Required fees: $4114. *Financial support:* In 2009–10, 45 students received support, including 1 fellowship with full tuition reimbursement available (averaging $20,000 per year), 36 research assistantships with full tuition reimbursements available (averaging $11,000 per year); career-related internships or fieldwork, Federal Work-Study, institutionally sponsored loans, scholarships/grants, and unspecified assistantships also available. Financial award application deadline: 1/15; financial award applicants required to submit FAFSA. *Faculty research:* Sexuality, multicultural education, substance abuse, transpersonal psychology. *Unit head:* Dr. Charles McAdams, Area Coordinator, 757-221-2338, E-mail: crmcad@wm.edu. *Application contact:* Dorothy Smith Osborne, Director of Admissions, 757-221-2317, Fax: 757-221-2293, E-mail: dsosbo@wm.edu.

Colorado State University, Graduate School, College of Applied Human Sciences, School of Education, Fort Collins, CO 80523-1588. Offers adult education and training (M Ed); community college leadership (PhD); counseling and career development (M Ed); education and human resource studies (M Ed, PhD); educational leadership (M Ed, PhD); interdisciplinary studies (PhD); organizational performance and change (M Ed, PhD); student affairs in higher education (MS). *Accreditation:* ACA; Teacher Education Accreditation Council. Part-time and evening/weekend programs available. *Faculty:* 21 full-time (10 women). *Students:* 195 full-time (132 women), 469 part-time (292 women); includes 114 minority (31 African Americans, 12 American Indian/Alaska Native, 22 Asian Americans or Pacific Islanders, 49 Hispanic Americans), 24 international. Average age 38. 451 applicants, 41% accepted, 141 enrolled. In 2009, 175 master's, 54 doctorates awarded. *Degree requirements:* For master's, comprehensive exam (for some programs), thesis optional; for doctorate, comprehensive exam, thesis/dissertation, minimum of 60 credits. *Entrance requirements:* For master's, GRE, minimum undergraduate GPA of 3.0, 3 letters of recommendation, curriculum vitae/resume; for doctorate, minimum GPA of 3.0, 3 letters of recommendation, curriculum vitae. Additional exam requirements/recommendations for international students: Required—TOEFL (minimum score 550 paper-based; 213 computer-based). *Application deadline:* For fall admission, 3/15 for domestic and international students; for spring admission, 11/1 for domestic students, 10/1 for international students. Applications are processed on a rolling basis. Application fee: $50. Electronic applications accepted. *Expenses:* Tuition, state resident: full-time $6434; part-time $359.10 per credit. Tuition, nonresident: full-time $18,116; part-time $1006.45 per credit. Required fees: $1496; $83 per credit. *Financial support:* In 2009–10, 8 students received support, including 3 research assistantships with full tuition reimbursements available (averaging $13,790 per year), 5 teaching assistantships with full tuition reimbursements available (averaging $10,253 per year); fellowships, Federal Work-Study, scholarships/grants, and unspecified assistantships also available. Financial award applicants required to submit FAFSA. *Faculty research:* Innovative instruction, diverse learners, transition, scientifically-based evaluation methods, leadership and organizational development. Total annual research expenditures: $655,700. *Unit head:* Dr. Carole Makela, Interim Director, 970-491-6317, Fax: 970-491-1317, E-mail: carole.makela@colostate.edu. *Application contact:* Dr. Sharon Anderson, Director of Graduate Programs, 970-491-6861, Fax: 970-491-1317, E-mail: sharon.anderson@colostate.edu.

Columbia International University, Columbia Graduate School, Columbia, SC 29230-3122. Offers Bible teaching (MABT); Christian higher education leadership (Ed D); Christian school educational leadership (Ed D); counseling (MACN); curriculum and instruction (M Ed), including Christian school guidance, English as a second language, learning disabilities, school technology; early childhood and elementary education (MAT); educational administration (M Ed); teaching English as a foreign language (Certificate); teaching English as a foreign language and intercultural studies (MATF). Part-time and evening/weekend programs available. *Degree requirements:* For master's, internships, professional project. *Entrance requirements:* For master's, Minnesota Multiphasic Personality Inventory, MAT, minimum GPA of 2.7. Additional exam requirements/recommendations for international students: Required—TOEFL. Electronic applications accepted.

Columbus State University, Graduate Studies, College of Education and Health Professions, Department of Counseling, Foundations, and Leadership, Columbus, GA 31907-5645. Offers community counseling (MS); curriculum and leadership (Ed D); educational leadership (M Ed, Ed S); school counseling (M Ed). *Accreditation:* ACA; NCATE. Part-time and evening/weekend programs available. Postbaccalaureate distance learning degree programs offered (minimal on-campus study). *Faculty:* 11 full-time (3 women), 7 part-time/adjunct (3 women). *Students:* 92 full-time (65 women), 110 part-time (88 women); includes 68 minority (62 African Americans, 1 American Indian/Alaska Native, 1 Asian American or Pacific Islander, 4 Hispanic Americans), 1 international. Average age 35. 134 applicants, 65% accepted, 61 enrolled. In 2009, 32 master's, 34 other advanced degrees awarded. *Degree requirements:* For master's, thesis, exit exam; for Ed S, thesis or alternative. *Entrance requirements:* For master's, GRE General Test, minimum GPA of 2.75; for doctorate, minimum graduate GPA of 3.5, four years of

professional service; for Ed S, GRE General Test. Additional exam requirements/recommendations for international students: Required—TOEFL (minimum score 550 paper-based; 213 computer-based; 79 iBT). *Application deadline:* For fall admission, 5/1 priority date for domestic students, 5/1 for international students; for spring admission, 11/1 for domestic and international students. Applications are processed on a rolling basis. Application fee: $30. Electronic applications accepted. *Financial support:* In 2009–10, 110 students received support, including 7 research assistantships with partial tuition reimbursements available (averaging $3,000 per year); career-related internships or fieldwork, Federal Work-Study, institutionally sponsored loans, scholarships/grants, tuition waivers (partial), and unspecified assistantships also available. Support available to part-time students. Financial award application deadline: 5/1; financial award applicants required to submit FAFSA. *Unit head:* Dr. Paul Tom Hackett, Chair, 706-568-5061, Fax: 706-569-3134, E-mail: hackett_paul@colstate.edu. *Application contact:* Katie Thornton, Graduate Admissions Specialist, 706-568-2035, Fax: 706-568-2462, E-mail: thornton_katie@colstate.edu.

Concordia University Chicago, College of Graduate and Innovative Programs, Program in School Counseling, River Forest, IL 60305-1499. Offers MA, CAS. *Accreditation:* ACA (one or more programs are accredited); NCATE. Part-time and evening/weekend programs available. *Degree requirements:* For master's, comprehensive exam, thesis optional; for CAS, thesis, final project. *Entrance requirements:* For master's, minimum GPA of 2.9; for CAS, master's degree. Additional exam requirements/recommendations for international students: Required—TOEFL (minimum score 550 paper-based; 195 computer-based). Electronic applications accepted. *Faculty research:* Development of comprehensive school counseling education, training of school counselors for parochial schools.

Concordia University Wisconsin, Graduate Programs, Department of Education, Mequon, WI 53097-2402. Offers art education (MS Ed); curriculum and instruction (MS Ed); early childhood (MS Ed); educational administration (MS Ed); environmental education (MS Ed); family studies (MS Ed); reading (MS Ed); school counseling (MS Ed); special education (MS Ed). Part-time and evening/weekend programs available. Postbaccalaureate distance learning degree programs offered (minimal on-campus study). *Degree requirements:* For master's, comprehensive exam, thesis or alternative. *Entrance requirements:* For master's, minimum GPA of 3.0, teaching license. Additional exam requirements/recommendations for international students: Required—TOEFL. *Faculty research:* Motivation, developmental learning, learning styles.

Creighton University, Graduate School, College of Arts and Sciences, Department of Education, Program in Counselor Education, Omaha, NE 68178-0001. Offers college student affairs (MS); community counseling (MS); elementary school guidance (MS); secondary school guidance (MS). Part-time and evening/weekend programs available. *Faculty:* 13 full-time (8 women). *Students:* 1 full-time (0 women), 42 part-time (33 women); includes 8 minority (3 African Americans, 1 American Indian/Alaska Native, 2 Asian Americans or Pacific Islanders, 2 Hispanic Americans), 4 international. Average age 32. 10 applicants, 60% accepted, 6 enrolled. In 2009, 18 master's awarded. *Entrance requirements:* For master's, GRE General Test, resume, 3 letters of recommendation. Additional exam requirements/recommendations for international students: Required—TOEFL (minimum score 550 paper-based; 213 computer-based; 80 iBT). *Application deadline:* For fall admission, 7/1 for domestic students, 3/1 for international students; for winter admission, 10/1 for domestic students, 7/1 for international students; for spring admission, 3/1 for domestic students, 9/1 for international students. Applications are processed on a rolling basis. Application fee: $50. Electronic applications accepted. *Expenses:* Tuition: Full-time $11,700; part-time $650 per credit hour. Required fees: $126 per semester. *Financial support:* Scholarships/grants available. Support available to part-time students. Financial award applicants required to submit FAFSA. *Unit head:* Dr. Debra L. Ponec, Associate Professor of Education, 402-280-2557, E-mail: dlponec@creighton.edu. *Application contact:* Taunya Plater, Senior Program Coordinator, 402-280-2870, Fax: 402-280-2899, E-mail: taunyaplater@creighton.edu.

Dallas Baptist University, Dorothy M. Bush College of Education, Program in School Counseling, Dallas, TX 75211-9299. Offers M Ed. Part-time and evening/weekend programs available. *Entrance requirements:* For master's, GRE General Test, minimum GPA of 3.0. Additional exam requirements/recommendations for international students: Required—TOEFL, IELTS. Electronic applications accepted. *Expenses:* Tuition: Full-time $10,674; part-time $593 per credit hour.

Delta State University, Graduate Programs, College of Education, Division of Counselor Education and Psychology, Cleveland, MS 38733-0001. Offers counseling (M Ed). *Accreditation:* ACA; NCATE. Part-time and evening/weekend programs available. *Degree requirements:* For master's, thesis optional, practicum. Electronic applications accepted. *Expenses:* Tuition, state resident: full-time $4450; part-time $247 per credit hour. Tuition, nonresident: full-time $11,520; part-time $640 per credit hour.

Delta State University, Graduate Programs, College of Education, Thad Cochran Center for Rural School Leadership and Research, Program in Professional Studies, Cleveland, MS 38733-0001. Offers counselor education (Ed D); educational leadership (Ed D); elementary education (Ed D); higher education (Ed D). Part-time and evening/weekend programs available. *Degree requirements:* For doctorate, thesis/dissertation. *Entrance requirements:* For doctorate, GRE General Test. *Expenses:* Tuition, state resident: full-time $4450; part-time $247 per credit hour. Tuition, nonresident: full-time $11,520; part-time $640 per credit hour.

DePaul University, School of Education, Chicago, IL 60106. Offers bilingual and bicultural education (M Ed, MA); curriculum studies (M Ed, MA, Ed D); educational leadership (M Ed, MA, Ed D), including administration and supervision (M Ed, MA), Catholic school leadership (M Ed, MA), physical education (M Ed, MA); human development and learning (MA); human services and counseling (M Ed, MA), including agencies, family concerns, and higher education, elementary schools, human services management, secondary schools; reading and learning disabilities (M Ed, MA); social culture studies in education and development (M Ed, MA), including curriculum studies/development; teaching and learning (early childhood, elementary and secondary) (M Ed), including elementary education (M Ed, MA), secondary education (M Ed, MA); teaching and learning (early childhood, elementary, and secondary) (MA), including elementary education (M Ed, MA), secondary education (M Ed, MA). *Accreditation:* NCATE. Part-time and evening/weekend programs available. *Faculty:* 61 full-time (40 women), 66 part-time/adjunct (41 women). *Students:* 799 full-time (779 women), 470 part-time (365 women); includes 319 minority (153 African Americans, 3 American Indian/Alaska Native, 48 Asian Americans or Pacific Islanders, 115 Hispanic Americans), 15 international. Average age 30. 635 applicants, 74% accepted, 318 enrolled. In 2009, 604 master's, 5 doctorates awarded. *Degree requirements:* For doctorate, thesis/dissertation. *Entrance requirements:* For master's, interview, minimum GPA of 2.75, 2 letters of recommendation; for doctorate, interview, master's degree, writing sample, 3 letters of recommendation. Additional exam requirements/recommendations for international students: Required—TOEFL (minimum score 550 paper-based; 213 computer-based; 80 iBT). *Application deadline:* Applications are processed on a rolling basis. Application fee: $40. Electronic applications accepted. *Expenses:* Tuition: Full-time $37,525; part-time $620 per credit hour. *Financial support:* In 2009–10, 14 research assistantships with tuition reimbursements (averaging $5,800 per year) were awarded; career-related internships or fieldwork also available. *Faculty research:* Reflective teaching, children at risk, loss, ethnicity, urban education. Total annual research expenditures: $1.6 million. *Unit head:* Dr. Marie Donovan, Dean, 773-325-7581, Fax: 773-325-7713, E-mail: mdonovan@depaul.edu. *Application contact:* Brandon Washington, Data Project Manager, 773-325-1152, Fax: 773-325-2270, E-mail: bwashin3@depaul.edu.

Doane College, Program in Counseling, Crete, NE 68333-2430. Offers MAC. Evening/weekend programs available. *Faculty:* 2 full-time (0 women), 11 part-time/adjunct (6 women). *Students:* 135 full-time (109 women), 23 part-time (19 women); includes 12 minority (4 African Americans, 1 American Indian/Alaska Native, 1 Asian American or Pacific Islander, 6 Hispanic Americans). Average age 34. In 2009, 25 master's awarded. *Degree requirements:* For master's, thesis. *Entrance requirements:* For master's, minimum GPA of 3.0. *Application deadline:* Applications are processed on a rolling basis. Application fee: $25. *Expenses:*

Counselor Education

Doane College *(continued)*

Contact institution. *Financial support:* Unspecified assistantships available. Financial award application deadline: 6/1; financial award applicants required to submit FAFSA. *Unit head:* Thomas Gilligan, Dean, 402-466-4774, Fax: 402-466-4228, E-mail: tom.gilligan@doane.edu. *Application contact:* Wilma Daddario, Assistant Dean, 402-466-4774, Fax: 404-466-4228, E-mail: wilma.daddario@doane.edu.

Duquesne University, School of Education, Department of Counseling, Psychology, and Special Education, Program in Counselor Education, Pittsburgh, PA 15282-0001. Offers community counseling (MS Ed); counselor education and supervision (Ed D); marriage and family therapy (MS Ed); school counseling (MS Ed). *Accreditation:* ACA (one or more programs are accredited). Part-time and evening/weekend programs available. *Faculty:* 10 full-time (3 women), 4 part-time/adjunct (2 women). *Students:* 173 full-time (132 women), 17 part-time (10 women); includes 26 minority (19 African Americans, 5 Asian Americans or Pacific Islanders, 2 Hispanic Americans), 4 international. Average age 35. 176 applicants, 43% accepted, 51 enrolled. In 2009, 51 master's, 5 doctorates awarded. *Degree requirements:* For master's, thesis optional; for doctorate, thesis/dissertation. *Entrance requirements:* For master's, MAT, minimum GPA of 3.0; for doctorate, GRE General Test, MAT, minimum GPA of 3.25, 5 years of professional experience. Additional exam requirements/recommendations for international students: Required—TOEFL. *Application deadline:* For fall admission, 8/1 for domestic students; for spring admission, 12/1 for domestic students. Applications are processed on a rolling basis. Application fee: $0. Electronic applications accepted. *Expenses:* Tuition: Part-time $851 per credit. Required fees: $81 per credit. *Financial support:* Research assistantships, teaching assistantships, Federal Work-Study available. Support available to part-time students. *Unit head:* Dr. Maura Krushinski, Director, 412-396-4026, Fax: 412-396-1340, E-mail: krushinski@duq.edu. *Application contact:* Michael Dolinger, Director of Student and Academic Services, 412-396-6647, Fax: 412-396-5585, E-mail: dolingerm@duq.edu.

East Carolina University, Graduate School, College of Education, Department of Counselor and Adult Education, Greenville, NC 27858-4353. Offers adult education (MA Ed); counselor education (MS, Ed S). *Accreditation:* NCATE. Part-time and evening/weekend programs available. *Degree requirements:* For master's, comprehensive exam, thesis optional. *Entrance requirements:* For master's, GRE General Test or MAT, interview, minimum GPA of 2.5, bachelor's degree in related field, teaching license (MA Ed). Additional exam requirements/ recommendations for international students: Required—TOEFL.

East Central University, School of Graduate Studies, Department of Human Resources, Ada, OK 74820-6899. Offers administration (MSHR); counseling (MSHR); criminal justice (MSHR); rehabilitation counseling (MSHR). *Accreditation:* CORE. Part-time and evening/weekend programs available. *Degree requirements:* For master's, thesis optional. *Entrance requirements:* For master's, GRE General Test, MAT, minimum GPA of 2.5. Electronic applications accepted.

Eastern Illinois University, Graduate School, College of Education and Professional Studies, Department of Counseling and Student Development, Charleston, IL 61920-3099. Offers clinical counseling (MS); college student affairs (MS); school counseling (MS). *Accreditation:* ACA; NCATE. Part-time and evening/weekend programs available. *Faculty:* 8 full-time (2 women). In 2009, 61 master's awarded. *Degree requirements:* For master's, comprehensive exam. *Entrance requirements:* For master's, GRE General Test or MAT. *Application deadline:* For fall admission, 3/31 priority date for domestic students. Applications are processed on a rolling basis. Application fee: $30. *Expenses:* Tuition, state resident: full-time $9434; part-time $239 per credit hour. Tuition, nonresident: full-time $23,774; part-time $717 per credit hour. Required fees: $802.63. *Financial support:* In 2009–10, research assistantships with tuition reimbursements (averaging $8,100 per year), 4 teaching assistantships with tuition reimbursements (averaging $8,100 per year) were awarded. *Unit head:* Dr. Rick Roberts, Chairperson, 217-581-2400, Fax: 217-581-7417, E-mail: rlroberts@eiu.edu. *Application contact:* Bill Elliott, Director of Graduate Admissions, 217-581-7489, Fax: 217-581-6020, E-mail: wjelliott@eiu.edu.

Eastern Kentucky University, The Graduate School, College of Education, Department of Counseling and Educational Leadership, Richmond, KY 40475-3102. Offers human services (MA); instructional leadership (MA Ed); mental health counseling (MA); school counseling (MA Ed). *Accreditation:* ACA (one or more programs are accredited); NCATE. Part-time programs available. Postbaccalaureate distance learning degree programs offered. *Entrance requirements:* For master's, GRE General Test, minimum GPA of 2.5.

Eastern Michigan University, Graduate School, College of Education, Department of Leadership and Counseling, Programs in Counseling, Ypsilanti, MI 48197. Offers college counseling (MA); community counseling (MA); helping interventions in a multicultural society (Graduate Certificate); school counseling (MA); school counselor (MA); school counselor licensure (Post Master's Certificate). Part-time and evening/weekend programs available. *Students:* 17 full-time (14 women), 108 part-time (93 women); includes 31 minority (25 African Americans, 2 American Indian/Alaska Native, 2 Asian Americans or Pacific Islanders, 2 Hispanic Americans), 2 international. Average age 33. In 2009, 28 master's, 1 other advanced degree awarded. *Degree requirements:* For master's, comprehensive exam, internship. *Entrance requirements:* Additional exam requirements/recommendations for international students: Required—TOEFL. *Application deadline:* For fall admission, 5/1 for domestic and international students; for winter admission, 9/15 for domestic and international students; for spring admission, 2/10 for domestic and international students. Applications are processed on a rolling basis. Application fee: $35. Tuition and fees vary according to course level. *Financial support:* Fellowships, research assistantships with full tuition reimbursements, teaching assistantships with full tuition reimbursements, career-related internships or fieldwork, Federal Work-Study, institutionally sponsored loans, scholarships/grants, tuition waivers (partial), and unspecified assistantships available. Support available to part-time students. Financial award applicants required to submit FAFSA. *Application contact:* Dr. Dibya Choudhuri, Advisor, 734-487-0255, Fax: 734-487-4608, E-mail: dibya.chouduri@emich.edu.

Eastern New Mexico University, Graduate School, College of Education and Technology, Department of Educational Studies, Program in Counseling, Portales, NM 88130. Offers MA. Part-time programs available. *Faculty:* 2 full-time (both women), 1 (woman) part-time/adjunct. *Students:* 2 full-time (1 woman), 41 part-time (35 women); includes 17 minority (2 African Americans, 1 American Indian/Alaska Native, 1 Asian American or Pacific Islander, 13 Hispanic Americans). Average age 35. 18 applicants, 56% accepted, 9 enrolled. In 2009, 14 master's awarded. *Degree requirements:* For master's, comprehensive exam (for some programs), thesis optional, counselor preparation comprehensive examination, 600-hour internship. *Entrance requirements:* For master's, minimum GPA of 3.0, 3 letters of recommendation, interview. Additional exam requirements/recommendations for international students: Required—TOEFL (minimum score 550 paper-based; 213 computer-based; 79 iBT), IELTS (minimum score 6). *Application deadline:* For fall admission, 7/20 priority date for domestic students; 6/20 priority date for international students. Applications are processed on a rolling basis. Application fee: $10. Electronic applications accepted. *Expenses:* Tuition, state resident: full-time $2922; part-time $121.75 per credit hour. Tuition, nonresident: full-time $8454; part-time $352.25 per credit hour. Required fees: $1038; $43.25 per credit hour. *Financial support:* In 2009–10, 3 research assistantships with partial tuition reimbursements (averaging $8,500 per year) were awarded; teaching assistantships, career-related internships or fieldwork, tuition waivers (partial), and unspecified assistantships also available. Support available to part-time students. Financial award applicants required to submit FAFSA. *Unit head:* Dr. Penny Sanders, Graduate Coordinator, 575-562-2169, E-mail: penny.sanders@enmu.edu. *Application contact:* Dr. Penny Sanders, Graduate Coordinator, 575-562-2169, E-mail: penny.sanders@enmu.edu.

Eastern New Mexico University, Graduate School, College of Education and Technology, Department of Educational Studies, Program in School Counseling, Portales, NM 88130. Offers M Ed. Part-time and evening/weekend programs available. *Faculty:* 2 full-time (both women), 1 (woman) part-time/adjunct. *Students:* 2 full-time (both women), 17 part-time (15 women); includes 5 minority (2 African Americans, 3 Hispanic Americans). Average age 30. 5

applicants, 60% accepted, 3 enrolled. In 2009, 4 master's awarded. *Degree requirements:* For master's, comprehensive exam (for some programs), thesis optional. *Entrance requirements:* For master's, minimum GPA of 3.0. Additional exam requirements/recommendations for international students: Required—TOEFL (minimum score 550 paper-based; 213 computer-based; 79 iBT), IELTS (minimum score 6). *Application deadline:* For fall admission, 7/20 priority date for domestic students, 6/20 priority date for international students. Applications are processed on a rolling basis. Application fee: $10. Electronic applications accepted. *Expenses:* Tuition, state resident: full-time $2922; part-time $121.75 per credit hour. Tuition, nonresident: full-time $8454; part-time $352.25 per credit hour. Required fees: $1038; $43.25 per credit hour. *Financial support:* Career-related internships or fieldwork and unspecified assistantships available. Support available to part-time students. Financial award applicants required to submit FAFSA. *Unit head:* Dr. Penny Sanders, Graduate Coordinator, 575-562-2169, E-mail: penny.sanders@enmu.edu. *Application contact:* Dr. Penny Sanders, Graduate Coordinator, 575-562-2169, E-mail: penny.sanders@enmu.edu.

Eastern University, Department of Counseling Psychology, Program in School Counseling, St. Davids, PA 19087-3696. Offers MA, Certificate. *Degree requirements:* For master's, internship. *Entrance requirements:* For master's, minimum GPA of 2.5. Additional exam requirements/recommendations for international students: Required—TOEFL.

Eastern Washington University, Graduate Studies, College of Education and Human Development, Program in School Counseling, Cheney, WA 99004-2431. Offers applied psychology (MS); school counseling (MS). *Accreditation:* ACA; NCATE. *Degree requirements:* For master's, comprehensive exam, thesis or alternative. *Entrance requirements:* For master's, GRE General Test, minimum GPA of 3.0. *Expenses:* Tuition, state resident: full-time $7476; part-time $249 per quarter hour. Tuition, nonresident: full-time $18,030; part-time $601 per quarter hour. Required fees: $3.50 per quarter hour. $142 per quarter.

East Tennessee State University, School of Graduate Studies, College of Education, Department of Human Development and Learning, Johnson City, TN 37614. Offers advanced practitioner (M Ed); community agency counseling (M Ed, MA); comprehensive concentration (M Ed); counseling (M Ed, MA); early childhood education (M Ed, MA); early childhood general (M Ed); early childhood special education (M Ed); early childhood teaching (M Ed); elementary and secondary (school counseling) (M Ed, MA); marriage and family therapy (M Ed, MA); modified concentration (M Ed). *Accreditation:* ACA; NCATE. Part-time programs available. *Degree requirements:* For master's, comprehensive exam, thesis (for some programs). *Entrance requirements:* For master's, GRE General Test, minimum GPA of 3.0. Additional exam requirements/recommendations for international students: Required—TOEFL (minimum score 550 paper-based; 213 computer-based). *Faculty research:* Drug and alcohol abuse, marriage and family counseling, severe mental retardation, parenting of children with disabilities.

Edinboro University of Pennsylvania, School of Graduate Studies and Research, School of Education, Department of Early Childhood and Special Education, Edinboro, PA 16444. Offers behavior management (Certificate); educational psychology (M Ed); special education (M Ed). Part-time and evening/weekend programs available. *Faculty:* 8 full-time (7 women), 5 part-time/adjunct (3 women). *Students:* 20 full-time (15 women), 122 part-time (105 women); includes 7 minority (5 African Americans, 1 Asian American or Pacific Islander, 1 Hispanic American). Average age 31. In 2009, 16 master's, 7 Certificates awarded. *Degree requirements:* For master's, thesis or alternative, competency exam; for Certificate, thesis or alternative. *Entrance requirements:* For master's and Certificate, GRE or MAT, minimum QPA of 2.5. *Application deadline:* Applications are processed on a rolling basis. Application fee: $30. Electronic applications accepted. *Expenses:* Tuition, state resident: full-time $6666; part-time $370 per credit. Tuition, nonresident: full-time $10,666; part-time $593 per credit. Required fees: $2206.28. One-time fee: $204 part-time. *Financial support:* In 2009–10, 4 research assistantships with full and partial tuition reimbursements (averaging $4,050 per year) were awarded; career-related internships or fieldwork, Federal Work-Study, scholarships/grants, and unspecified assistantships also available. Support available to part-time students. Financial award application deadline: 2/15; financial award applicants required to submit FAFSA. *Unit head:* Dr. Edward Snyder, Program Head, Educational Psychology, 814-732-1098, E-mail: jkasper@edinboro.edu. *Application contact:* Dr. Susan Criswell, Program Head, Special Education, 814-732-2287, E-mail: scriswell@edinboro.edu.

Emporia State University, School of Graduate Studies, The Teachers College, Department of Special Education and School Counseling, Program in School Counseling, Emporia, KS 66801-5087. Offers MS. *Accreditation:* ACA; NCATE. Part-time programs available. *Students:* 12 full-time (11 women), 72 part-time (65 women); includes 5 minority (2 African Americans, 1 Asian American or Pacific Islander, 2 Hispanic Americans). 10 applicants, 90% accepted, 9 enrolled. In 2009, 23 master's awarded. *Degree requirements:* For master's, comprehensive exam or thesis, practicum. *Entrance requirements:* For master's, GRE or MAT, graduate essay exam, appropriate bachelor's degree, interview, letters of recommendation. *Application deadline:* For fall admission, 8/15 priority date for domestic students. Applications are processed on a rolling basis. Application fee: $30 ($75 for international students). Electronic applications accepted. *Expenses:* Tuition, state resident: full-time $4154; part-time $173 per credit hour. Tuition, nonresident: full-time $12,864; part-time $536 per credit hour. Required fees: $948; $58 per credit hour. Tuition and fees vary according to campus/location. *Financial support:* Career-related internships or fieldwork, Federal Work-Study, institutionally sponsored loans, health care benefits, and unspecified assistantships available. Financial award application deadline: 3/15; financial award applicants required to submit FAFSA. *Unit head:* Dr. Jean Morrow, Interim Chair, 620-341-5220, E-mail: jmorrow@emporia.edu. *Application contact:* Dr. Jean Morrow, Interim Chair, 620-341-5220, E-mail: jmorrow@emporia.edu.

Evangel University, School Counseling Program, Springfield, MO 65802. Offers MS. Part-time programs available. *Faculty:* 2 full-time (both women), 3 part-time/adjunct (2 women). *Students:* 10 full-time (9 women), 61 part-time (48 women). Average age 32. 17 applicants, 94% accepted, 14 enrolled. In 2009, 9 master's awarded. *Degree requirements:* For master's, comprehensive exam (for some programs), thesis or alternative. *Entrance requirements:* For master's, MAT (preferred) or GRE, teaching certificate. Additional exam requirements/recommendations for international students: Required—TOEFL (minimum score 550 paper-based; 213 computer-based). *Application deadline:* For fall admission, 7/15 priority date for domestic and international students; for spring admission, 11/15 priority date for domestic and international students. Applications are processed on a rolling basis. Application fee: $25. Electronic applications accepted. *Financial support:* In 2009–10, 2 students received support. Career-related internships or fieldwork, scholarships/grants, and unspecified assistantships available. Support available to part-time students. Financial award application deadline: 3/1; financial award applicants required to submit FAFSA. *Unit head:* Debbie Bicket, Chair, 417-865-2815 Ext. 8567, Fax: 417-575-5484, E-mail: bicketd@evangel.edu. *Application contact:* Charity H. Fahlstrom, Admissions Representative, Graduate and Professional Studies, 417-865-2815 Ext. 7227, Fax: 417-575-5484, E-mail: fahlstromc@evangel.edu.

Fairfield University, Graduate School of Education and Allied Professions, Department of Counselor Education, Fairfield, CT 06824-5195. Offers community counseling (MA, CAS); school counseling (MA, CAS). *Accreditation:* ACA (one or more programs are accredited). Part-time and evening/weekend programs available. *Degree requirements:* For master's, comprehensive exam, thesis or alternative. *Entrance requirements:* For master's, PRAXIS I (PPST), minimum QPA of 3.0, 2 recommendations, resume. Additional exam requirements/recommendations for international students: Required—TOEFL (minimum score 550 paper-based; 213 computer-based; 80 iBT). Electronic applications accepted. *Faculty research:* Corrective feedback in group setting, applying group concepts to teaching counselor education curriculum, assessment and program evaluation, spirituality and counseling, clinical supervision, developmental school counseling, wellness and multicultural counseling.

Fitchburg State University, Division of Graduate and Continuing Education, Programs in Counseling, Fitchburg, MA 01420-2697. Offers elementary school guidance counseling (MS); mental health counseling (MS); secondary school guidance counseling (MS). *Accreditation:* NCATE. Part-time and evening/weekend programs available. *Students:* 15 full-time (all women),

57 part-time (50 women); includes 6 minority (1 African American, 1 American Indian/Alaska Native, 1 Asian American or Pacific Islander, 3 Hispanic Americans). Average age 32. 16 applicants, 88% accepted, 11 enrolled. In 2009, 23 master's awarded. *Entrance requirements:* For master's, GRE General Test or MAT, letters of recommendation, resume. Additional exam requirements/recommendations for international students: Required—TOEFL (minimum score 550 paper-based; 213 computer-based; 79 iBT). *Application deadline:* Applications are processed on a rolling basis. Application fee: $25 ($50 for international students). *Expenses:* Tuition, area resident: Part-time $150 per credit. Tuition, state resident: part-time $150 per credit. Tuition, nonresident: part-time $150 per credit. Required fees: $120 per credit. *Financial support:* In 2009–10, research assistantships with partial tuition reimbursements (averaging $5,500 per year); Federal Work-Study, scholarships/grants, and unspecified assistantships also available. Support available to part-time students. Financial award application deadline: 3/1; financial award applicants required to submit FAFSA. *Unit head:* Dr. John Hancock, Chair, 978-665-3604, Fax: 978-665-3658, E-mail: gce@fsc.edu. *Application contact:* Director of Admissions, 978-665-3144, Fax: 978-665-4540, E-mail: admissions@fsc.edu.

Florida Agricultural and Mechanical University, Division of Graduate Studies, Research, and Continuing Education, College of Education, Department of Educational Leadership and Human Services, Tallahassee, FL 32307-3200. Offers administration and supervision (M Ed, MS Ed, PhD); adult education (M Ed, MS Ed); educational leadership (PhD); guidance and counseling (M Ed, MS Ed). *Accreditation:* NCATE. *Faculty:* 15 full-time (8 women). *Students:* 58 full-time (31 women), 43 part-time (32 women); includes 94 minority (93 African Americans, 1 Asian American or Pacific Islander), 5 international. In 2009, 24 master's, 5 doctorates awarded. *Degree requirements:* For master's, thesis (for some programs); for doctorate, thesis/dissertation. *Entrance requirements:* For master's, GRE General Test, minimum GPA of 3.0. Additional exam requirements/recommendations for international students: Required—TOEFL. *Application deadline:* For fall admission, 5/18 for domestic students, 12/18 for international students; for spring admission, 11/12 for domestic students, 5/12 for international students. Application fee: $20. *Unit head:* Dr. Warren Hope, Interim Chairperson, 850-599-3191, Fax: 850-561-2211. *Application contact:* Dr. Chanta M. Haywood, Dean of Graduate Studies, Research, and Continuing Education, 850-599-3315, Fax: 850-599-3727.

Florida Atlantic University, College of Education, Department of Counselor Education, Boca Raton, FL 33431-0991. Offers counselor education (M Ed, PhD, Ed S); marriage and family therapy (Ed S); mental health counseling (M Ed, Ed S); rehabilitation counseling (M Ed); school counseling (M Ed, Ed S). *Accreditation:* ACA; NCATE. Part-time and evening/weekend programs available. *Faculty:* 7 full-time (2 women), 6 part-time/adjunct (5 women). *Students:* 65 full-time (52 women), 95 part-time (83 women); includes 59 minority (19 African Americans, 5 Asian Americans or Pacific Islanders, 35 Hispanic Americans), 2 international. Average age 33. 109 applicants, 40% accepted, 27 enrolled. In 2009, 54 master's, 2 doctorates awarded. *Degree requirements:* For Ed S, departmental qualifying exam. *Entrance requirements:* For master's, GRE General Test, minimum GPA of 3.0 during previous 2 years; for Ed S, GRE General Test, minimum graduate GPA of 3.25. Additional exam requirements/recommendations for international students: Required—TOEFL. *Application deadline:* For fall admission, 3/1 for domestic students, 2/1 for international students; for spring admission, 9/15 for domestic students, 7/1 for international students. Applications are processed on a rolling basis. Application fee: $30. *Expenses:* Tuition, state resident: full-time $7055; part-time $293.94 per credit hour. Tuition, nonresident: full-time $22,096; part-time $920.66 per credit hour. *Financial support:* Research assistantships with partial tuition reimbursements, teaching assistantships, career-related internships or fieldwork, scholarships/grants, and unspecified assistantships available. *Faculty research:* Brief therapy, psychological type, marriage and family counseling, international programs, integrated services. *Unit head:* Dr. Irene Johnson, Chair, 561-297-2136, Fax: 561-297-2309. *Application contact:* Susan Foley, Senior Secretary, 561-297-3602, Fax: 561-297-2309, E-mail: cnslred@fau.edu.

Florida Gulf Coast University, College of Education, Program in Counseling, Fort Myers, FL 33965-6565. Offers MA. *Accreditation:* ACA. Part-time and evening/weekend programs available. *Faculty:* 31 full-time (23 women), 41 part-time/adjunct (29 women). *Students:* 43 full-time (42 women), 17 part-time (13 women); includes 9 minority (1 African American, 8 Hispanic Americans), 1 international. Average age 31. 44 applicants, 57% accepted, 0 enrolled. In 2009, 12 master's awarded. *Degree requirements:* For master's, thesis or alternative. *Entrance requirements:* For master's, GRE General Test, MAT, minimum GPA of 3.0. Additional exam requirements/recommendations for international students: Required—TOEFL (minimum score 550 paper-based; 213 computer-based). *Application deadline:* For fall admission, 7/1 priority date for domestic students; for spring admission, 10/15 for domestic students. Applications are processed on a rolling basis. Application fee: $30. Electronic applications accepted. *Faculty research:* Sexuality, confidentiality, school counselor roles, distance learning, exceptional students. *Unit head:* Dr. Pat Wachholz, Associate Dean, 239-590-7808, Fax: 239-590-7801, E-mail: wachhol@fgcu.edu. *Application contact:* Dr. Pat Wachholz, Associate Dean, 239-590-7808, Fax: 239-590-7801, E-mail: wachhol@fgcu.edu.

Florida International University, College of Education, Department of Educational and Psychological Studies, Program in Counselor Education, Miami, FL 33199. Offers mental health counseling (MS); rehabilitation counseling (MS); school counseling (MS). *Accreditation:* ACA; NCATE. Part-time and evening/weekend programs available. *Entrance requirements:* For master's, General Knowledge test, College Level Academic Skills Test, GRE General Test or PRAXIS (school counseling track), minimum GPA of 3.0, interview. Additional exam requirements/recommendations for international students: Required—TOEFL (minimum score 550 paper-based; 213 computer-based; 80 iBT), IELTS (minimum score 6.3). Electronic applications accepted. *Expenses:* Tuition, state resident: full-time $8008; part-time $4004 per year. Tuition, nonresident: full-time $20,104; part-time $10,052 per year. Required fees: $298; $149 per term.

Florida State University, The Graduate School, College of Education, Department of Educational Psychology and Learning Systems, Tallahassee, FL 32306. Offers counseling/school psychology (PhD); educational psychology (MS, PhD, Ed S), including learning and cognition, sports psychology (MS, PhD); instructional systems (MS, PhD, Ed S), including instructional systems, open and distance learning (MS), performance improvement and human resources (MS); measurement and statistics (MS, PhD, Ed S); mental health counseling (PhD); psychological services (MS, PhD, Ed S); school psychology (MS, Ed S); MS/Ed S. *Faculty:* 19 full-time (8 women), 9 part-time/adjunct (3 women). *Students:* 231 full-time (166 women), 109 part-time (73 women); includes 77 minority (41 African Americans, 2 American Indian/Alaska Native, 14 Asian Americans or Pacific Islanders, 20 Hispanic Americans), 59 international. 205 applicants, 47% accepted, 53 enrolled. In 2009, 70 master's, 26 doctorates, 28 other advanced degrees awarded. *Degree requirements:* For master's and Ed S, comprehensive exam, thesis optional; for doctorate, comprehensive exam, thesis/dissertation. *Entrance requirements:* For master's, doctorate, and Ed S, GRE General Test, minimum GPA of 3.0. Additional exam requirements/recommendations for international students: Required—TOEFL (minimum score 550 paper-based; 213 computer-based; 80 iBT); Recommended—TWE. *Application deadline:* For fall admission, 6/1 priority date for domestic and international students; for spring admission, 10/1 for domestic and international students. Applications are processed on a rolling basis. Application fee: $30. *Expenses:* Tuition, state resident: full-time $7413. Tuition, nonresident: full-time $22,567. *Financial support:* In 2009–10, 6 fellowships with full tuition reimbursements, 45 research assistantships with full and partial tuition reimbursements, 30 teaching assistantships with full and partial tuition reimbursements were awarded; career-related internships or fieldwork and Federal Work-Study also available. Financial award applicants required to submit FAFSA. *Faculty research:* Educational technology, giftedness in children, instructional design, measurement and evaluation. *Unit head:* Dr. Betsy Becker, Chair, 850-644-8794, Fax: 850-644-8776, E-mail: bbecker@fsu.edu. *Application contact:* Sally Gadson, Program Assistant, 850-644-8046, Fax: 850-644-5067, E-mail: gadson@coe.fsu.edu.

Fordham University, Graduate School of Education, Division of Psychological and Educational Services, New York, NY 10023. Offers counseling and personnel services (MSE, Adv C); counseling psychology (PhD); educational psychology (MSE, PhD); school psychology (PhD); urban and urban bilingual school psychology (Adv C). *Accreditation:* APA (one or more programs are accredited); NCATE. *Degree requirements:* For doctorate, thesis/dissertation. *Entrance requirements:* For doctorate, GRE General Test.

Fort Hays State University, Graduate School, College of Education and Technology, Department of Educational Administration and Counseling, Program in Counseling, Hays, KS 67601-4099. Offers MS. *Accreditation:* NCATE. Part-time programs available. *Degree requirements:* For master's, comprehensive exam, thesis or alternative. *Entrance requirements:* For master's, GRE General Test or MAT, minimum undergraduate GPA of 3.0 in last 60 hours. Additional exam requirements/recommendations for international students: Required—TOEFL (minimum score 550 paper-based; 213 computer-based). Electronic applications accepted. *Faculty research:* Career education, evaluation and plans, counseling the disabled, marriage and family parenting, underemployment and work in the family.

Fort Valley State University, College of Graduate Studies and Extended Education, Department of Counseling Psychology, Fort Valley, GA 31030. Offers guidance and counseling (Ed S); mental health counseling (MS); rehabilitation counseling (MS). Part-time programs available. *Degree requirements:* For master's, comprehensive exam (for some programs), thesis optional. *Entrance requirements:* For master's and Ed S, GRE General Test or MAT.

Freed-Hardeman University, Program in Counseling, Henderson, TN 38340-2399. Offers MS. Part-time and evening/weekend programs available. *Degree requirements:* For master's, comprehensive exam, practicum. *Entrance requirements:* For master's, GRE General Test or MAT. Additional exam requirements/recommendations for international students: Required—TOEFL (minimum score 500 paper-based; 173 computer-based).

Freed-Hardeman University, Program in Education, Henderson, TN 38340-2399. Offers curriculum and instruction (M Ed); school counseling (M Ed), including administration and supervision, special education; school leadership (Ed S). *Accreditation:* NCATE. Part-time and evening/weekend programs available. *Degree requirements:* For master's, comprehensive exam, thesis optional; for Ed S, thesis. *Entrance requirements:* For master's, GRE General Test or NTE; for Ed S, 3 years of teaching experience. Additional exam requirements/recommendations for international students: Required—TOEFL (minimum score 500 paper-based; 173 computer-based).

Fresno Pacific University, Graduate Programs, School of Education, Fresno, CA 93702-4709. Offers administration (MA Ed), including administrative services; foundations, curriculum and teaching (MA Ed), including curriculum and teaching, school library and information technology; language, literacy, and culture (MA Ed), including bilingual/cross-cultural education, language development, multilingual contexts, reading; mathematics/science/computer education (MA Ed), including educational technology, integrated mathematics/science education, mathematics education; pupil personnel services (MA Ed), including school counseling, school psychology; special education (MA Ed), including mild/moderate, moderate/severe, physical and health impairments. Part-time and evening/weekend programs available. *Degree requirements:* For master's, thesis (for some programs). *Entrance requirements:* For master's, interview; GMAT, GRE, MAT, or 6 units of course work with a faculty recommendation. Additional exam requirements/recommendations for international students: Required—TOEFL (minimum score 550 paper-based; 213 computer-based). Electronic applications accepted.

Fresno Pacific University, Graduate Programs, School of Education, Division of Pupil Personnel Services, Program in School Counseling, Fresno, CA 93702-4709. Offers MA Ed. Part-time and evening/weekend programs available. *Degree requirements:* For master's, thesis or alternative. *Entrance requirements:* Additional exam requirements/recommendations for international students: Required—TOEFL (minimum score 550 paper-based; 213 computer-based).

Frostburg State University, Graduate School, College of Education, Department of Educational Professions, Program in School Counseling, Frostburg, MD 21532-1099. Offers M Ed. *Accreditation:* NCATE. Part-time and evening/weekend programs available. *Faculty:* 2. *Students:* 18 full-time (17 women), 6 part-time (5 women); includes 2 minority (both African Americans). Average age 27. 20 applicants, 65% accepted, 12 enrolled. In 2009, 7 master's awarded. *Degree requirements:* For master's, comprehensive exam, thesis or alternative. *Entrance requirements:* For master's, GRE General Test or MAT, interview. Additional exam requirements/recommendations for international students: Required—TOEFL. *Application deadline:* For fall admission, 7/15 priority date for domestic students. Applications are processed on a rolling basis. Application fee: $30. Electronic applications accepted. *Expenses:* Tuition, state resident: full-time $5706; part-time $317 per credit hour. Tuition, nonresident: full-time $6948; part-time $386 per credit hour. Required fees: $1476; $82 per credit hour. $11 per term. One-time fee: $30 full-time. *Financial support:* In 2009–10, 2 research assistantships with full tuition reimbursements (averaging $5,000 per year) were awarded; career-related internships or fieldwork also available. Financial award application deadline: 4/1; financial award applicants required to submit FAFSA. *Unit head:* Dr. Mikal Crawford, Coordinator, 301-687-4294, E-mail: mcrawford@frostburg.edu. *Application contact:* Vickie Mazer, Director, Graduate Services, 301-687-7053, Fax: 301-687-4597, E-mail: vmmazer@frostburg.edu.

Gallaudet University, The Graduate School, Department of Counseling, Washington, DC 20002-3625. Offers mental health counseling (MA); school counseling (MA). *Accreditation:* ACA; NCATE. *Degree requirements:* For master's, thesis optional. *Entrance requirements:* For master's, GRE General Test or MAT. Electronic applications accepted.

Gannon University, School of Graduate Studies, College of Humanities, Education, and Social Sciences, School of Humanities, Program in Advanced Counselor Studies, Erie, PA 16541-0001. Offers Certificate. *Accreditation:* ACA. Part-time and evening/weekend programs available. *Students:* 1 (woman) part-time. Average age 32. 2 applicants, 100% accepted, 0 enrolled. *Entrance requirements:* For degree, master's degree in counseling or related field. Additional exam requirements/recommendations for international students: Required—TOEFL (minimum score 79 iBT). *Application deadline:* Applications are processed on a rolling basis. Application fee: $25. Electronic applications accepted. *Expenses:* Tuition: Full-time $13,590; part-time $755 per credit. Required fees: $524; $17 per credit. Tuition and fees vary according to course load, degree level, campus/location and program. *Financial support:* Scholarships/grants available. Financial award application deadline: 7/1; financial award applicants required to submit FAFSA. *Unit head:* Dr. David Tobin, Director, 814-871-7537, E-mail: tobin001@gannon.edu. *Application contact:* Kara Morgan, Assistant Director of Graduate Admissions, 814-871-5831, Fax: 814-871-5827, E-mail: graduate@gannon.edu.

Gannon University, School of Graduate Studies, College of Humanities, Education, and Social Sciences, School of Humanities, Program in Community Counseling, Erie, PA 16541-0001. Offers MS, Certificate. *Accreditation:* ACA. Part-time and evening/weekend programs available. *Students:* 18 full-time (14 women), 21 part-time (17 women); includes 2 minority (1 African American, 1 Asian American or Pacific Islander). Average age 28. 29 applicants, 62% accepted, 0 enrolled. In 2009, 16 master's awarded. *Degree requirements:* For master's, comprehensive exam. *Entrance requirements:* For master's, bachelor's degree, minimum QPA of 3.0. Additional exam requirements/recommendations for international students: Required—TOEFL (minimum score 79 iBT). *Application deadline:* Applications are processed on a rolling basis. Application fee: $25. Electronic applications accepted. *Expenses:* Tuition: Full-time $13,590; part-time $755 per credit. Required fees: $524; $17 per credit. Tuition and fees vary according to course load, degree level, campus/location and program. *Financial support:* Career-related internships or fieldwork, Federal Work-Study, scholarships/grants, and unspecified assistantships available. Financial award application deadline: 7/1; financial award applicants required to submit FAFSA. *Unit head:* Dr. David Tobin, Director, 814-871-7537, E-mail: tobin001@gannon.edu. *Application contact:* Kara Morgan, Assistant Director of Graduate Admissions, 814-871-5831, Fax: 814-871-5827, E-mail: graduate@gannon.edu.

Gannon University, School of Graduate Studies, College of Humanities, Education, and Social Sciences, School of Humanities, Program in School Counselor Preparation, Erie, PA 16541-0001. Offers Certificate. *Accreditation:* ACA. Part-time and evening/weekend programs

Counselor Education

Gannon University (continued)

available. *Entrance requirements:* Additional exam requirements/recommendations for international students: Required—TOEFL (minimum score 500 paper-based; 173 computer-based). *Application deadline:* Applications are processed on a rolling basis. Application fee: $25. Electronic applications accepted. *Expenses:* Tuition: Full-time $13,590; part-time $755 per credit. Required fees: $524; $17 per credit. Tuition and fees vary according to course load, degree level, campus/location and program. *Financial support:* Application deadline: 7/1. *Unit head:* Dr. David Tobin, Director, 814-871-7537, E-mail: tobin001@gannon.edu. *Application contact:* Kara Morgan, Assistant Director of Graduate Admissions, 814-871-5831, Fax: 814-871-5827, E-mail: graduate@gannon.edu.

Geneva College, Program in Counseling, Beaver Falls, PA 15010-3599. Offers marriage and family (MA); mental health (MA); school counseling (MA). *Accreditation:* ACA. Part-time and evening/weekend programs available. *Faculty:* 5 full-time (2 women), 2 part-time/adjunct (1 woman). *Students:* 28 full-time (21 women), 21 part-time (17 women); includes 6 minority (5 African Americans, 1 Asian American or Pacific Islander). Average age 26. 32 applicants, 97% accepted, 18 enrolled. In 2009, 11 master's awarded. *Degree requirements:* For master's, comprehensive exam, internship. *Entrance requirements:* For master's, GRE General Test or MAT, minimum GPA of 3.0 (preferred), letters of recommendation, faith statement. Additional exam requirements/recommendations for international students: Required—TOEFL. *Application deadline:* For fall admission, 7/1 priority date for domestic students; for spring admission, 11/1 priority date for domestic students. Applications are processed on a rolling basis. Application fee: $50 ($100 for international students). Electronic applications accepted. *Expenses:* Tuition: Full-time $11,250; part-time $625 per credit. Tuition and fees vary according to program. *Financial support:* In 2009–10, 8 teaching assistantships (averaging $3,500 per year) were awarded; career-related internships or fieldwork and unspecified assistantships also available. Financial award applicants required to submit FAFSA. *Unit head:* Dr. Carol Luce, Director, 724-847-6622, Fax: 724-847-6101, E-mail: cbluce@geneva.edu. *Application contact:* JoAnn Westover, Graduate Program Manager, 724-847-6697, E-mail: counseling@geneva.edu.

George Fox University, School of Education, Graduate Department of Counseling, Newberg, OR 97132-2697. Offers counseling (MA); marriage and family therapy (MA, Certificate); mental health trauma (Certificate); school counseling (MA, Certificate); school psychology (Certificate, Ed S). Part-time programs available. *Faculty:* 9 full-time (3 women), 7 part-time/adjunct (5 women). *Students:* 100 full-time (77 women), 122 part-time (103 women); includes 24 minority (7 African Americans, 4 American Indian/Alaska Native, 9 Asian Americans or Pacific Islanders, 4 Hispanic Americans). Average age 36. 102 applicants, 75% accepted, 59 enrolled. In 2009, 61 master's, 2 other advanced degrees awarded. *Degree requirements:* For master's, clinical project. *Entrance requirements:* For master's, MAT or GRE, bachelor's degree from regionally-accredited college or university, minimum cumulative GPA of 3.0, 1 professional and 1 academic reference, resume, on-campus interview. Additional exam requirements/recommendations for international students: Required—TOEFL (minimum score 577 paper-based; 233 computer-based; 90 iBT). *Application deadline:* For fall admission, 5/30 for domestic and international students; for winter admission, 11/1 for domestic and international students; for spring admission, 2/28 for domestic and international students. Applications are processed on a rolling basis. Application fee: $40. Electronic applications accepted. *Expenses:* Contact institution. *Financial support:* Career-related internships or fieldwork available. *Unit head:* Dr. Richard Shaw, Associate Professor of Marriage and Family Therapy/Chair, 503-554-6142, E-mail: rshaw@georgefox.edu. *Application contact:* Kathy Grant, Admissions Counselor, 800-493-4937, Fax: 503-554-6111, E-mail: counseling@georgefox.edu.

George Mason University, College of Education and Human Development, Program in Counseling and Development, Fairfax, VA 22030. Offers M Ed, PhD. *Accreditation:* NCATE. Part-time and evening/weekend programs available. *Faculty:* 88 full-time (64 women), 120 part-time/adjunct (93 women). *Students:* 47 full-time (42 women), 109 part-time (96 women); includes 43 minority (19 African Americans, 10 Asian Americans or Pacific Islanders, 14 Hispanic Americans), 3 international. Average age 30. 110 applicants, 38% accepted, 22 enrolled. In 2009, 39 master's awarded. *Degree requirements:* For master's, thesis (for some programs). *Entrance requirements:* For master's, minimum undergraduate GPA of 3.0, 3 letters of recommendation, 12 credits of undergraduate work, 1000 hours of counseling or counseling experience; for doctorate, GRE, bachelor's and master's degrees from regionally-accredited institutions, transcripts, goal statement, 3 letters of recommendation, 3 years work experience in field of education. Additional exam requirements/recommendations for international students: Required—TOEFL. *Application deadline:* For fall admission, 2/1 for domestic and international students; for spring admission, 10/1 for domestic and international students. Application fee: $75. Electronic applications accepted. *Expenses:* Tuition, state resident: full-time $7568; part-time $315.33 per credit hour. Tuition, nonresident: full-time $21,704; part-time $904.33 per credit hour. Required fees: $2184; $91 per credit hour. *Financial support:* In 2009–10, 2 students received support, including 2 research assistantships with full and partial tuition reimbursements available (averaging $10,368 per year); career-related internships or fieldwork, Federal Work-Study, unspecified assistantships, and health care benefits (full-time research or teaching assistantship recipients) also available. Support available to part-time students. Financial award application deadline: 3/1; financial award applicants required to submit FAFSA. *Faculty research:* Leadership, multiculturalism, social justice, and advocacy; global well-being; social psychological, physical, and spiritual health of individuals, families, communities, and organizations. *Unit head:* Dr. Carol Kaffenberger, Coordinator, 703-993-3161, Fax: 703-993-2013. *Application contact:* Regine Talleyrand, Coordinator, 703-993-4419, E-mail: rtalleyr@gmu.edu.

The George Washington University, Graduate School of Education and Human Development, Department of Counseling/Human and Organizational Studies, Program in Counseling, Washington, DC 20052. Offers PhD, Ed S. *Accreditation:* ACA (one or more programs are accredited); NCATE. Part-time and evening/weekend programs available. *Students:* 9 part-time (8 women); includes 1 minority (African American). Average age 40. 11 applicants, 100% accepted. In 2009, 1 other advanced degree awarded. *Degree requirements:* For doctorate, comprehensive exam, thesis/dissertation; for Ed S, comprehensive exam. *Entrance requirements:* For doctorate, GRE General Test, interview, minimum GPA of 3.3; for Ed S, GRE General Test or MAT, minimum GPA of 3.3. *Application deadline:* For fall admission, 1/15 priority date for domestic students; for spring admission, 10/1 for domestic students. Applications are processed on a rolling basis. Application fee: $60. *Financial support:* Fellowships, research assistantships, teaching assistantships, career-related internships or fieldwork, Federal Work-Study, and tuition waivers (partial) available. Financial award application deadline: 1/15; financial award applicants required to submit FAFSA. *Faculty research:* Values in counseling, religion and counseling. *Unit head:* Dr. Pat Schwallie-Giddis, Director, 202-994-6856, E-mail: drpat@gwu.edu. *Application contact:* Sarah Lang, Director of Graduate Admissions, 202-994-1447, Fax: 202-994-7207, E-mail: slang@gwu.edu.

The George Washington University, Graduate School of Education and Human Development, Department of Counseling/Human and Organizational Studies, Programs in Counseling: School, Community and Rehabilitation, Washington, DC 20052. Offers community counseling (MA Ed); rehabilitation counseling (MA Ed); school counseling (MA Ed). School counseling program also offered in Alexandria, VA. *Accreditation:* ACA; CORE; NCATE. *Students:* 72 full-time (63 women), 67 part-time (53 women); includes 33 minority (22 African Americans, 2 American Indian/Alaska Native, 5 Asian Americans or Pacific Islanders, 4 Hispanic Americans), 4 international. Average age 33. 104 applicants, 94% accepted, 51 enrolled. In 2009, 93 master's awarded. *Degree requirements:* For master's, comprehensive exam. *Entrance requirements:* For master's, GRE General Test or MAT, minimum GPA of 2.75. *Application deadline:* For fall admission, 1/15 priority date for domestic students; for spring admission, 10/1 for domestic students. Applications are processed on a rolling basis. Application fee: $60. *Financial support:* In 2009–10, 27 students received support; fellowships, research assistantships, teaching assistantships, career-related internships or fieldwork, Federal Work-Study, and tuition waivers (full and partial) available. *Faculty research:* Adjustment to disability, head injury rehabilitation, cross-cultural counseling. *Application contact:* Sarah Lang, Director of Graduate Admissions, 202-994-1447, Fax: 202-994-7207, E-mail: slang@gwu.edu.

Georgia Southern University, Jack N. Averitt College of Graduate Studies, College of Education, Department of Leadership, Technology, and Human Development, Program in Counselor Education, Statesboro, GA 30460. Offers M Ed, Ed S. *Accreditation:* ACA; NCATE. Part-time and evening/weekend programs available. *Students:* 47 full-time (44 women), 57 part-time (49 women); includes 39 minority (all African Americans), 2 international. Average age 31. 27 applicants, 96% accepted, 21 enrolled. In 2009, 22 master's, 7 Ed Ss awarded. *Degree requirements:* For master's, comprehensive exam, transition point assessmenrts; for Ed S, comprehensive exam. *Entrance requirements:* For master's, GRE General Test or MAT, minimum GPA of 2.5, letters of recommendation, interview; for Ed S, GRE General Test or MAT, minimum graduate GPA of 3.25, letters of recommendation. Additional exam requirements/recommendations for international students: Required—TOEFL (minimum score 550 paper-based; 213 computer-based; 80 iBT). *Application deadline:* For fall admission, 3/15 for domestic and international students; for spring admission, 10/15 for domestic students, 10/1 for international students. Applications are processed on a rolling basis. Application fee: $50. Electronic applications accepted. *Expenses:* Tuition, state resident: full-time $5040; part-time $210 per credit hour. Tuition, nonresident: full-time $20,136; part-time $839 per credit hour. Required fees: $1644. *Financial support:* In 2009–10, 78 students received support, including research assistantships with partial tuition reimbursements available (averaging $7,200 per year), teaching assistantships with partial tuition reimbursements available (averaging $7,200 per year); career-related internships or fieldwork, Federal Work-Study, scholarships/grants, tuition waivers (partial), and unspecified assistantships also available. Support available to part-time students. Financial award application deadline: 4/15; financial award applicants required to submit FAFSA. *Faculty research:* School counseling, test development, gender equity, career counseling. *Unit head:* Dr. Leon Spencer, Coordinator, 912-478-5917, Fax: 912-478-7104, E-mail: lespence@georgiasouthern.edu. *Application contact:* Dr. Charles Ziglar, Coordinator for Graduate Student Recruitment, 912-478-5635, Fax: 912-478-0740, E-mail: gradadmissions@georgiasouthern.edu.

Georgia State University, College of Education, Department of Counseling and Psychological Services, Program in Professional Counseling, Atlanta, GA 30302-3083. Offers counseling psychology (PhD); counselor education and practice (PhD); professional counseling (MS, Ed S). *Accreditation:* ACA (one or more programs are accredited); APA (one or more programs are accredited). *Degree requirements:* For master's, comprehensive exam; for doctorate, comprehensive exam, thesis/dissertation. *Entrance requirements:* For master's, GRE General Test, minimum GPA of 2.5; for doctorate, GRE General Test, minimum GPA of 3.3; for Ed S, GRE General Test, minimum graduate GPA of 3.25. *Faculty research:* Dropout prevention, school reform, school violence, lifestyle correlates, stress management.

Georgia State University, College of Education, Department of Counseling and Psychological Services, Program in School Counseling, Atlanta, GA 30302-3083. Offers M Ed, Ed S. *Accreditation:* ACA (one or more programs are accredited); NCATE. *Degree requirements:* For master's, comprehensive exam. *Entrance requirements:* For master's, GRE General Test, minimum GPA of 2.5; for Ed S, GRE General Test, minimum graduate GPA of 3.25. *Faculty research:* School reform, play therapy and counseling through play, school violence, school consolation.

Grambling State University, School of Graduate Studies and Research, College of Education, Department of Educational Leadership, Grambling, LA 71245. Offers curriculum and instruction (Ed D); developmental education (MS, Ed D), including curriculum and instruction: reading (Ed D), English (MS), guidance and counseling (MS), higher education administration (Ed D), instructional systems and technology (Ed D), mathematics (MS), reading (MS), science (MS), student development and personnel services (Ed D); educational leadership (MS, Ed D). Part-time and evening/weekend programs available. *Faculty:* 19 full-time (12 women). *Students:* 23 full-time (18 women), 84 part-time (62 women); includes 81 minority (80 African Americans, 1 Asian American or Pacific Islander), 5 international. Average age 39. 72 applicants, 75% accepted, 39 enrolled. In 2009, 5 master's, 9 doctorates awarded. *Degree requirements:* For master's, comprehensive exam, thesis (for some programs); for doctorate, comprehensive exam, thesis/dissertation. *Entrance requirements:* For master's, GRE, minimum GPA of 2.5 on last degree; for doctorate, GRE (minimum 1000, 500 on Verbal), master's degree, minimum GPA of 3.0 on last degree. Additional exam requirements/recommendations for international students: Required—TOEFL (minimum score 500 paper-based; 173 computer-based; 61 iBT). *Application deadline:* For fall admission, 7/1 for domestic and international students; for spring admission, 12/1 for domestic and international students. Applications are processed on a rolling basis. Application fee: $20 ($30 for international students). Electronic applications accepted. *Expenses:* Tuition, state resident: full-time $2610. Tuition, nonresident: full-time $2610. *Financial support:* In 2009–10, 5 research assistantships (averaging $10,948 per year) were awarded; health care benefits, tuition waivers (full), and unspecified assistantships also available. Financial award application deadline: 5/31; financial award applicants required to submit FAFSA. *Unit head:* Dr. Olatunde Ogunyemi, Director, 318-274-6105, Fax: 318-274-2799, E-mail: ogunyemio@gram.edu. *Application contact:* Laketha Richards, Administrative Assistant III, 318-274-6105, Fax: 318-274-6249, E-mail: richardsl@gram.edu.

Grand Canyon University, College of Nursing and Health Sciences, Phoenix, AZ 85017-1097. Offers addiction counseling (MS); nursing (MS), including adult clinical nurse specialist, family nurse practitioner, nursing education, nursing leadership in health care system; professional counseling (MS). Part-time and evening/weekend programs available. Postbaccalaureate distance learning degree programs offered (no on-campus study). *Entrance requirements:* Additional exam requirements/recommendations for international students: Required—TOEFL (minimum score 575 paper-based; 233 computer-based; 90 iBT), IELTS (minimum score 7).

Gwynedd-Mercy College, School of Education, Gwynedd Valley, PA 19437-0901. Offers educational administration (MS); master teacher (MS); reading (MS); school counseling (MS); special education (MS). Part-time and evening/weekend programs available. *Degree requirements:* For master's, thesis, internship, practicum. *Entrance requirements:* For master's, GRE or MAT; PRAXIS I Test, minimum GPA of 3.0. *Faculty research:* Learning and the brain, reading literacy, ethics and moral judgment, leadership, teaching and multicultural education.

Hampton University, Graduate College, Department of Education, Program in Counseling, Hampton, VA 23668. Offers college student development (MA); community agency counseling (MA); pastoral counseling (MA); school counseling (MA). *Accreditation:* NCATE. Part-time and evening/weekend programs available. *Entrance requirements:* For master's, GRE General Test.

Harding University, College of Education, Searcy, AR 72149-0001. Offers advanced studies in teaching and learning (M Ed); art (MSE); behavioral science (MSE); counseling (MS, Ed S); early childhood special education (M Ed, MSE); education (MSE); educational leadership (M Ed, Ed S); elementary education (M Ed); English (MSE); family and consumer science (MSE); French (MSE); history/social science (MSE); kinesiology (MSE); math (MSE); physical science (MSE); reading (M Ed); secondary education (M Ed); Spanish (MSE); special education licensure (M Ed); teaching (MAT); teaching English as a second language (M Ed). *Accreditation:* NCATE. Part-time and evening/weekend programs available. *Faculty:* 11 full-time (4 women), 49 part-time/adjunct (26 women). *Students:* 104 full-time (85 women), 392 part-time (282 women); includes 77 minority (67 African Americans, 5 American Indian/Alaska Native, 1 Asian American or Pacific Islander, 4 Hispanic Americans), 5 international. Average age 36. 153 applicants, 92% accepted, 131 enrolled. In 2009, 153 master's, 6 other advanced degrees awarded. *Degree requirements:* For master's, comprehensive exam (for some programs), thesis optional, portfolio(s); for Ed S, comprehensive exam, portfolio, specialist project. *Entrance requirements:* For master's, GRE, MAT, PRAXIS; for Ed S, MAT or GRE. Additional exam requirements/recommendations for international students: Required—TOEFL (minimum score 550 paper-based; 79 iBT). *Application deadline:* For fall admission, 8/1 for domestic and international students; for spring admission, 1/1 for domestic and international students. Applications are processed on a rolling basis. Application fee: $35. *Expenses:* Tuition: Full-time $9720; part-time $540 per credit hour. Required fees: $22 per credit hour. Tuition and fees vary

according to course load and program. *Financial support:* In 2009–10, 30 students received support. Unspecified assistantships available. *Faculty research:* Reading, comprehension, school violence, educational technology, behavior, college choice, differentiated instruction, brain-based teaching. *Unit head:* Dr. Clara Carroll, Chair, 501-279-4501, Fax: 501-279-4083, E-mail: ccarroll@harding.edu. *Application contact:* Information Contact, 501-279-4315, E-mail: gradstudiesedu@harding.edu.

Hardin-Simmons University, Graduate School, Irvin School of Education, Department of Counseling and Human Development, Abilene, TX 79698-0001. Offers M Ed. Part-time programs available. *Faculty:* 3 full-time (1 woman), 3 part-time/adjunct (all women). *Students:* 30 full-time (22 women), 15 part-time (12 women); includes 8 minority (2 African Americans, 6 Hispanic Americans). Average age 29. 20 applicants, 90% accepted, 15 enrolled. In 2009, 30 master's awarded. *Degree requirements:* For master's, comprehensive exam, practicum. *Entrance requirements:* For master's, minimum undergraduate GPA of 3.0 in major, 2.7 overall; interview; 3 letters of recommendation; resume. Additional exam requirements/recommendations for international students: Required—TOEFL (minimum score 550 paper-based; 213 computer-based; 75 iBT). *Application deadline:* For fall admission, 8/15 priority date for domestic students, 4/1 for international students; for spring admission, 1/5 priority date for domestic students, 9/1 for international students. Applications are processed on a rolling basis. Application fee: $50. *Expenses:* Tuition: Full-time $11,430; part-time $635 per credit hour. Required fees: $650; $110 per semester. Tuition and fees vary according to degree level. *Financial support:* In 2009–10, 27 students received support, including 2 fellowships (averaging $2,100 per year); career-related internships or fieldwork and scholarships/grants also available. Support available to part-time students. Financial award application deadline: 6/30; financial award applicants required to submit FAFSA. *Unit head:* Dr. Robert Barnes, Head, 325-670-1451, Fax: 325-670-5859, E-mail: rbarnes@hsutx.edu. *Application contact:* Dr. Gary Stanlake, Dean of Graduate Studies, 325-670-1298, Fax: 325-670-1564, E-mail: gradoff@hsutx.edu.

Henderson State University, Graduate Studies, School of Education, Department of Counselor Education, Arkadelphia, AR 71999-0001. Offers clinical mental health counseling (MSE); elementary school counseling (MSE); secondary school counseling (MSE). *Accreditation:* ACA; NCATE. Part-time programs available. *Entrance requirements:* For master's, GRE General Test or MAT, letters of recommendation, minimum GPA of 2.7, teacher certification. Additional exam requirements/recommendations for international students: Required—TOEFL (minimum score 550 paper-based; 213 computer-based); Recommended—IELTS (minimum score 6). *Application deadline:* For fall admission, 8/1 priority date for domestic students, 6/30 priority date for international students; for spring admission, 1/1 priority date for domestic students, 11/30 priority date for international students. Application fee: $25 ($75 for international students). Electronic applications accepted. *Expenses:* Tuition, state resident: full-time $3798; part-time $211 per credit hour. Tuition, nonresident: full-time $7596; part-time $422 per credit hour. Required fees: $903. *Financial support:* Teaching assistantships with tuition reimbursements available. *Unit head:* Dr. Blair Olson, Chairperson, 870-230-5395, Fax: 870-230-5459, E-mail: olsonb@hsu.edu. *Application contact:* Dr. Marck L. Beggs, Graduate Dean, 870-230-5126, Fax: 870-230-5479, E-mail: beggsm@hsu.edu.

Heritage University, Graduate Programs in Education, Program in Counseling, Toppenish, WA 98948-9599. Offers M Ed. Part-time programs available. *Degree requirements:* For master's, comprehensive exam. *Entrance requirements:* For master's, interview, letters of recommendation, at least 9 semester-credits of behavioral sciences.

Hofstra University, School of Education, Health, and Human Services, Department of Counseling, Research, Special Education and Rehabilitation, Program in Counseling, Hempstead, NY 11549. Offers counseling (PD); mental health counseling (MA); school counselor (MS Ed); school counselor-bilingual extension (Advanced Certificate). Part-time and evening/weekend programs available. *Students:* 34 full-time (30 women), 36 part-time (33 women); includes 9 minority (3 African Americans, 3 Asian Americans or Pacific Islanders, 3 Hispanic Americans). Average age 30. 61 applicants, 64% accepted, 19 enrolled. In 2009, 29 master's, 1 other advanced degree awarded. *Degree requirements:* For master's, comprehensive exam. *Entrance requirements:* For master's, GRE General Test, interview, 3 letters of recommendation; for other advanced degree, GRE, interview, 3 letters of recommendation, essay. Additional exam requirements/recommendations for international students: Required—TOEFL (minimum score 550 paper-based; 213 computer-based; 80 iBT). *Application deadline:* Applications are processed on a rolling basis. Application fee: $60. Electronic applications accepted. *Expenses:* Tuition: Full-time $16,200; part-time $900 per credit hour. Required fees: $970; $145 per term. Tuition and fees vary according to program. *Financial support:* In 2009–10, 35 students received support, including 2 fellowships with full and partial tuition reimbursements available (averaging $3,227 per year), 2 research assistantships with full and partial tuition reimbursements available (averaging $13,558 per year); career-related internships or fieldwork, Federal Work-Study, institutionally sponsored loans, scholarships/grants, traineeships, tuition waivers (full and partial), and unspecified assistantships also available. Support available to part-time students. Financial award applicants required to submit FAFSA. *Faculty research:* Bereavement, loss and trauma counseling; CORT issues in counseling; college student development; conflict transformation; multicultural and intracultural counseling. *Unit head:* Dr. Laurie Johnson, Director, 516-463-5754, Fax: 516-463-6184, E-mail: cprlzj@hofstra.edu. *Application contact:* Carol Drummer, Dean of Graduate Admissions, 516-463-4876, Fax: 516-463-4664, E-mail: gradstudent@hofstra.edu.

Houston Baptist University, College of Education and Behavioral Sciences, Programs in Education, Houston, TX 77074-3298. Offers bilingual education (M Ed); counselor education (M Ed); curriculum and instruction (M Ed); educational administration (M Ed); educational diagnostician (M Ed); reading education (M Ed). Part-time programs available. *Entrance requirements:* For master's, GRE General Test or MAT. Additional exam requirements/recommendations for international students: Required—TOEFL (minimum score 550 paper-based; 213 computer-based).

Howard University, School of Education, Department of Human Development and Psychoeducational Studies, Program in Counseling and Guidance, Washington, DC 20059-0002. Offers M Ed, MA, CAGS. MA offered through the Graduate School of Arts and Sciences. *Accreditation:* NCATE. Part-time programs available. *Faculty:* 2 full-time (1 woman), 1 (woman) part-time/adjunct. *Students:* 4 full-time (all women), 2 part-time (both women); includes 4 minority (all African Americans), 1 international. Average age 30. 12 applicants, 83% accepted. In 2009, 5 master's awarded. *Entrance requirements:* For degree, GRE General Test, minimum graduate GPA of 3.0. *Application deadline:* For fall admission, 2/15 priority date for domestic students; for spring admission, 11/1 for domestic students. Applications are processed on a rolling basis. Application fee: $45. Electronic applications accepted. *Financial support:* In 2009–10, 1 student received support, including fellowships with full and partial tuition reimbursements available (averaging $15,000 per year), 1 research assistantship with full and partial tuition reimbursement available (averaging $4,583 per year); career-related internships or fieldwork, Federal Work-Study, institutionally sponsored loans, scholarships/grants, and unspecified assistantships also available. Financial award application deadline: 2/15. *Faculty research:* Law and forensic evaluation, juvenile justice, ethics, clinical assessment, personality disorders, substance abuse. *Unit head:* Dr. Mercedes Ebanks, Assistant Professor/Coordinator, Master's Programs, 202-806-5780, Fax: 202-806-5205, E-mail: mebanks@howard.edu. *Application contact:* Frazier Tate-Jackson, Administration Assistant, Department of Human Development and Psychoeducational Studies, 202-806-7350, Fax: 202-806-5205, E-mail: fjackson@howard.edu.

Hunter College of the City University of New York, Graduate School, School of Education, Department of Educational Foundations and Counseling Programs, Programs in School Counselor, New York, NY 10021-5085. Offers school counseling (MS Ed); school counseling with bilingual extension (MS Ed). *Accreditation:* NCATE. *Faculty:* 12 full-time (6 women), 57 part-time/adjunct (42 women). *Students:* 48 full-time (43 women), 83 part-time (66 women); includes 28 minority (10 African Americans, 4 Asian Americans or Pacific Islanders, 14 Hispanic Americans). Average age 29. 295 applicants, 15% accepted, 31 enrolled. In 2009, 29 master's

awarded. *Degree requirements:* For master's, thesis, internship, practicum, research seminar. *Entrance requirements:* For master's, interview, minimum GPA of 2.7. Additional exam requirements/recommendations for international students: Required—TOEFL, TWE. *Application deadline:* For fall admission, 4/1 for domestic students, 2/1 for international students; for spring admission, 11/1 for domestic students, 9/1 for international students. Applications are processed on a rolling basis. Application fee: $125. *Expenses:* Tuition, state resident: full-time $7360; part-time $310 per credit. Required fees: $250 per semester. *Financial support:* Federal Work-Study and tuition waivers (partial) available. Support available to part-time students. *Unit head:* Dr. Tamara Buckley, Coordinator, 212-772-4758, E-mail: tamara.buckley@hunter.cuny.edu. *Application contact:* William Zlata, Director for Graduate Admissions, 212-772-4482, Fax: 212-650-3336, E-mail: admissions@hunter.cuny.edu.

Husson University, School of Graduate and Professional Studies, Program in School Counseling, Bangor, ME 04401-2999. Offers MS.

Idaho State University, Office of Graduate Studies, Kasiska College of Health Professions, Department of Counseling, Pocatello, ID 83209-8120. Offers counseling (M Coun, Ed S), including marriage and family counseling (M Coun), mental health counseling (M Coun), school counseling (M Coun), student affairs and college counseling (M Coun); counselor education and counseling (PhD). *Accreditation:* ACA (one or more programs are accredited). Part-time programs available. *Faculty:* 7 full-time (4 women). *Students:* 72 full-time (52 women), 29 part-time (18 women); includes 11 minority (2 African Americans, 1 American Indian/Alaska Native, 2 Asian Americans or Pacific Islanders, 6 Hispanic Americans). Average age 32. In 2009, 25 master's, 5 doctorates, 1 other advanced degree awarded. *Degree requirements:* For master's, comprehensive exam, thesis, 4 semesters resident graduate study, practicum/internship; for doctorate, comprehensive exam, thesis/dissertation, 3 semesters internship, 4 consecutive semesters doctoral-level study on campus; for Ed S, comprehensive exam, thesis, case studies, oral exam. *Entrance requirements:* For master's, GRE General Test, MAT, minimum GPA of 3.0, bachelors degree, interview, 3 letters of recommendation; for doctorate, GRE General Test, MAT, minimum graduate GPA of 3.0, resume, interview, counseling license, master's degree; for Ed S, GRE General Test, minimum graduate GPA of 3.0, master's degree in counseling, 3 letters of recommendation, 2 years work experience. Additional exam requirements/recommendations for international students: Required—TOEFL (minimum score 600 paper-based; 213 computer-based; 80 iBT). *Application deadline:* For fall admission, 7/1 for domestic students, 6/1 for international students; for spring admission, 12/1 for domestic students, 11/1 for international students. Applications are processed on a rolling basis. Application fee: $55. Electronic applications accepted. *Expenses:* Tuition, state resident: full-time $3318; part-time $297 per credit hour. Tuition, nonresident: full-time $13,120; part-time $437 per credit hour. Required fees: $2530. Tuition and fees vary according to program. *Financial support:* In 2009–10, 12 teaching assistantships with full and partial tuition reimbursements (averaging $10,841 per year) were awarded; career-related internships or fieldwork, Federal Work-Study, institutionally sponsored loans, scholarships/grants, traineeships, health care benefits, tuition waivers (full and partial), and unspecified assistantships also available. Support available to part-time students. Financial award application deadline: 1/1; financial award applicants required to submit FAFSA. *Faculty research:* Group counseling, multicultural counseling, family counseling, child therapy, supervision. *Unit head:* Dr. Nicole Hill, Interim Chair, 208-282-3663, Fax: 208-282-2583, E-mail: hillnico@isu.edu. *Application contact:* Tami Carson, Graduate School Technical Records Specialist, 208-282-2150, Fax: 208-282-4847, E-mail: carstami@isu.edu.

Immaculata University, College of Graduate Studies, Department of Psychology, Immaculata, PA 19345. Offers clinical psychology (Psy D); counseling psychology (MA, Certificate), including school guidance counselor (Certificate), school psychologist (Certificate). *Accreditation:* APA. Part-time and evening/weekend programs available. *Degree requirements:* For master's, comprehensive exam, thesis optional; for doctorate, comprehensive exam, thesis/dissertation. *Entrance requirements:* For master's, GRE General Test or MAT, minimum GPA of 3.0; for doctorate, GRE General Test, minimum GPA of 3.5. Additional exam requirements/recommendations for international students: Required—TOEFL, IELTS. *Faculty research:* Supervision ethics, psychology of teaching, gender.

Indiana State University, School of Graduate Studies, College of Education, Department of Communication Disorders, Counseling and School and Educational Psychology, Terre Haute, IN 47809. Offers counseling psychology (MS, PhD); counselor education (PhD); mental health counseling (MS); school counseling (M Ed); school psychology (PhD, Ed S); MA/MS. *Accreditation:* ACA; NCATE. Part-time and evening/weekend programs available. *Degree requirements:* For master's, thesis optional; for doctorate, thesis/dissertation, research tools proficiency tests. *Entrance requirements:* For master's, GRE General Test or MAT, minimum undergraduate GPA of 2.75; for doctorate, GRE General Test, master's degree, minimum undergraduate GPA of 3.5. Electronic applications accepted. *Faculty research:* Vocational development supervision.

Indiana University Bloomington, School of Education, Department of Counseling and Educational Psychology, Bloomington, IN 47405-1006. Offers counseling (MS, PhD, Ed S); counseling psychology (PhD); counselor education (MS, Ed S); educational psychology (MS, PhD); inquiry methodology (PhD); learning and developmental sciences (MS, PhD); school psychology (PhD, Ed S). *Accreditation:* ACA (one or more programs are accredited); APA (one or more programs are accredited); NCATE. *Faculty:* 32 full-time (13 women), 20 part-time/adjunct (10 women). *Students:* 218 full-time (165 women), 34 part-time (29 women); includes 45 minority (19 African Americans, 2 American Indian/Alaska Native, 12 Asian Americans or Pacific Islanders, 12 Hispanic Americans), 42 international. Average age 30. 348 applicants, 41% accepted, 53 enrolled. In 2009, 57 master's, 21 doctorates, 22 other advanced degrees awarded. Terminal master's awarded for partial completion of doctoral program. *Degree requirements:* For master's, thesis optional; for doctorate, thesis/dissertation; for Ed S, comprehensive exam or project. *Entrance requirements:* For master's, doctorate, and Ed S, GRE General Test. Additional exam requirements/recommendations for international students: Required—TOEFL. *Application deadline:* Applications are processed on a rolling basis. Application fee: $55 ($65 for international students). Electronic applications accepted. *Financial support:* In 2009–10, 58 students received support, including 7 fellowships with partial tuition reimbursements available (averaging $15,000 per year), 15 research assistantships with partial tuition reimbursements available (averaging $12,000 per year), 36 teaching assistantships with partial tuition reimbursements available (averaging $14,280 per year); career-related internships or fieldwork, Federal Work-Study, institutionally sponsored loans, scholarships/grants, and unspecified assistantships also available. Support available to part-time students. Financial award application deadline: 1/1; financial award applicants required to submit FAFSA. *Faculty research:* Counseling psychology, inquiry methodology, school psychology, learning sciences, human development, educational psychology. *Unit head:* Dr. Joyce Alexander, Chairperson, 812-856-8300, Fax: 812-856-8333, E-mail: cep@indiana.edu. *Application contact:* Jessica Durnal, Student Services Specialist, 812-856-8300, Fax: 812-856-8333, E-mail: cep@indiana.edu.

Indiana University of Pennsylvania, School of Graduate Studies and Research, College of Education and Educational Technology, Department of Counseling, Indiana, PA 15705-1087. Offers community counseling (MA); counselor education (M Ed). *Accreditation:* ACA; NCATE. Part-time and evening/weekend programs available. *Faculty:* 11 full-time (9 women). *Students:* 48 full-time (40 women), 120 part-time (103 women); includes 15 minority (14 African Americans, 1 Hispanic American), 1 international. Average age 31. 226 applicants, 27% accepted, 51 enrolled. In 2009, 62 master's awarded. *Degree requirements:* For master's, thesis optional. *Entrance requirements:* For master's, 2 letters of recommendation. Additional exam requirements/recommendations for international students: Required—TOEFL. *Application deadline:* For fall admission, 7/1 priority date for domestic students; for spring admission, 11/1 for domestic students. Applications are processed on a rolling basis. Application fee: $40. *Expenses:* Tuition, state resident: full-time $6666; part-time $370 per credit hour. Tuition, nonresident: full-time $10,666; part-time $593 per credit hour. Required fees: $813 per semester. *Financial support:* In 2009–10, 14 research assistantships with full and partial tuition reimbursements

Counselor Education

Indiana University of Pennsylvania (continued)
(averaging $5,354 per year) were awarded; fellowships, career-related internships or fieldwork and Federal Work-Study also available. Support available to part-time students. Financial award application deadline: 3/15; financial award applicants required to submit FAFSA. *Unit head:* Dr. Claire Dandeneau, Chairperson/Graduate Coordinator, 724-357-2306, E-mail: candean@iup.edu. *Application contact:* Dr. Edward Nardi, Associate Dean, 724-357-2480, Fax: 724-357-5595, E-mail: ewnardi@iup.edu.

Indiana University–Purdue University Fort Wayne, School of Education, Department of Professional Studies, Fort Wayne, IN 46805-1499. Offers counseling education (MS Ed); educational leadership (MS Ed); marriage and family therapy (MS Ed); school counseling (MS Ed); special education (MS Ed, Certificate). Part-time programs available. *Faculty:* 10 full-time (5 women). *Students:* 2 full-time (both women), 159 part-time (120 women); includes 19 minority (12 African Americans, 1 Asian American or Pacific Islander, 6 Hispanic Americans). Average age 35. 47 applicants, 98% accepted, 38 enrolled. In 2009, 64 master's awarded. *Degree requirements:* For master's, comprehensive exam, practicum, internship, portfolio. *Entrance requirements:* For master's, minimum GPA of 2.5. Additional exam requirements/recommendations for international students: Required—TOEFL (minimum score 550 paper-based; 213 computer-based; 77 iBT). *Application deadline:* For fall admission, 4/1 priority date for domestic and international students. Applications are processed on a rolling basis. Application fee: $55. *Expenses:* Tuition, state resident: full-time $4595; part-time $255 per credit. Tuition, nonresident: full-time $10,963; part-time $609 per credit. Required fees: $528; $29.35 per credit. Tuition and fees vary according to course load. *Financial support:* In 2009–10, 1 teaching assistantship with partial tuition reimbursement (averaging $12,740 per year) was awarded; research assistantships with partial tuition reimbursements, scholarships/grants also available. Support available to part-time students. Financial award application deadline: 3/1; financial award applicants required to submit FAFSA. *Unit head:* Dr. James Burg, Interim Chair, 260-481-5406, Fax: 260-481-5408, E-mail: burgj@ipfw.edu. *Application contact:* Vicky L. Schmidt, Graduate Recorder, 260-481-6450, Fax: 260-481-5408, E-mail: schmidt@ipfw.edu.

Indiana University–Purdue University Indianapolis, School of Education, Indianapolis, IN 46202-2896. Offers computer education (Certificate); curriculum and instruction (MS); early childhood (MS); educational leadership (MS, Certificate); English as a second language (Certificate); higher education and student affairs (MS); kindergarten (Certificate); language education (MS); reading (Certificate); school counseling (MS); special education (MS, Certificate). Part-time and evening/weekend programs available. *Faculty:* 41 full-time, 80 part-time/adjunct. *Students:* 72 full-time (60 women), 427 part-time (325 women); includes 57 minority (42 African Americans, 1 American Indian/Alaska Native, 4 Asian Americans or Pacific Islanders, 10 Hispanic Americans), 5 international. Average age 32. 181 applicants, 78% accepted, 112 enrolled. In 2009, 162 master's awarded. *Degree requirements:* For master's, thesis optional. *Entrance requirements:* For master's, GRE General Test, minimum GPA of 3.0. Additional exam requirements/recommendations for international students: Required—TOEFL. *Application deadline:* For fall admission, 5/1 priority date for domestic students; for spring admission, 11/1 for domestic students. Application fee: $55 ($65 for international students). *Financial support:* In 2009–10, 2 fellowships (averaging $780 per year), 18 teaching assistantships (averaging $9,756 per year) were awarded; research assistantships with partial tuition reimbursements, Federal Work-Study, institutionally sponsored loans, scholarships/grants, and tuition waivers (partial) also available. Support available to part-time students. *Faculty research:* Teachers in the process of change, learning cycles, children's concepts of science. Total annual research expenditures: $614,458. *Unit head:* Dr. Chris Leland, Interim Executive Associate Dean, 317-274-6801, Fax: 317-274-6864. *Application contact:* Sarah Brandenburg, Graduate Advisor, 317-274-6801, Fax: 317-274-6864, E-mail: edugrad@iupui.edu.

Indiana University South Bend, School of Education, South Bend, IN 46634-7111. Offers counseling and human services (MS Ed); elementary education (MS Ed); secondary education (MS Ed); special education (MS Ed). *Accreditation:* NCATE. Part-time and evening/weekend programs available. *Faculty:* 21 full-time (11 women), 9 part-time/adjunct (3 women). *Students:* 72 full-time (48 women), 256 part-time (202 women); includes 36 minority (24 African Americans, 2 American Indian/Alaska Native, 1 Asian American or Pacific Islander, 9 Hispanic Americans), 9 international. Average age 36. In 2009, 103 master's awarded. *Degree requirements:* For master's, thesis or alternative, exit project. *Entrance requirements:* For master's, letters of recommendation, GRE or minimum GPA of 3.0. Additional exam requirements/recommendations for international students: Required—TOEFL. *Application deadline:* For fall admission, 7/1 for domestic students; for spring admission, 11/1 for domestic students. Applications are processed on a rolling basis. Application fee: $46 ($58 for international students). Electronic applications accepted. *Financial support:* Career-related internships or fieldwork available. Support available to part-time students. Financial award application deadline: 3/1; financial award applicants required to submit FAFSA. *Faculty research:* Professional dispositions, early childhood literacy, online learning, program assessments, problem-based learning. *Unit head:* Dr. Michael Horvath, Professor/Dean, 574-520-4339, Fax: 574-520-4550. *Application contact:* Dr. Todd Norris, Director of Education Student Services, 574-520-4845, E-mail: toanorri@iusb.edu.

Indiana University Southeast, School of Education, New Albany, IN 47150-6405. Offers counselor education (MS Ed); elementary education (MS Ed); secondary education (MS Ed). *Accreditation:* NCATE. Part-time and evening/weekend programs available. *Students:* 7 full-time (all women), 366 part-time (305 women); includes 31 minority (27 African Americans, 3 American Indian/Alaska Native, 1 Asian American or Pacific Islander), 1 international. Average age 32. In 2009, 138 master's awarded. *Entrance requirements:* For master's, minimum undergraduate GPA of 2.5, graduate 3.0. *Application deadline:* Applications are processed on a rolling basis. Application fee: $35. *Financial support:* In 2009–10, 29 students received support. Career-related internships or fieldwork, Federal Work-Study, and institutionally sponsored loans available. Support available to part-time students. Financial award applicants required to submit FAFSA. *Faculty research:* Learning styles, technology, constructivism, group process, innovative math strategies. *Unit head:* Dr. Gloria Murray, Dean, 812-941-2169, Fax: 812-941-2667, E-mail: soeinfo@ius.edu. *Application contact:* Dr. Gloria Murray, Dean, 812-941-2169, Fax: 812-941-2667, E-mail: soeinfo@ius.edu.

Indiana Wesleyan University, College of Graduate Studies, Graduate Studies in Counseling, Marion, IN 46953. Offers addictions counseling (MS); community counseling (MS); marriage and family counseling (MS); school counseling (MS). *Accreditation:* ACA. Part-time programs available. *Degree requirements:* For master's, thesis or alternative. *Entrance requirements:* For master's, GRE General Test. Additional exam requirements/recommendations for international students: Required—TOEFL. Electronic applications accepted. *Expenses:* Contact institution. *Faculty research:* Community counseling, multicultural counseling, addictions.

Inter American University of Puerto Rico, Arecibo Campus, Programs in Education, Arecibo, PR 00614-4050. Offers administration and educational supervision (MA Ed); counseling and guidance (MA Ed); curriculum and teaching (MA Ed), including biology education, English as a second language, history education, math education, Spanish; elementary education (MA Ed). *Degree requirements:* For master's, comprehensive exam, thesis optional. *Entrance requirements:* For master's, GRE, EXADEP, bachelor's degree in education or teaching license (administration and supervision) or courses in education and psychology (counseling and guidance), minimum GPA of 2.5 in last 60 credits.

Inter American University of Puerto Rico, Metropolitan Campus, Graduate Programs, Program in Education, San Juan, PR 00919-1293. Offers curriculum and instruction (Ed D); educational administration (Ed D); guidance and counseling (MA, Ed D); special education administration (Ed D). *Degree requirements:* For doctorate, comprehensive exam, thesis/dissertation. *Entrance requirements:* For doctorate, GRE, MAT, or EXADEP. Electronic applications accepted.

Inter American University of Puerto Rico, San Germán Campus, Graduate Studies Center, Program in Guidance and Counseling, San Germán, PR 00683-5008. Offers MA, Ed D. Part-time and evening/weekend programs available. *Degree requirements:* For master's, comprehensive exam. *Entrance requirements:* For master's, GRE General Test or EXADEP, minimum GPA of 3.0.

Iowa State University of Science and Technology, Graduate College, College of Human Sciences, Department of Educational Leadership and Policy Studies, Ames, IA 50011. Offers counselor education (M Ed, MS); educational administration (M Ed, MS); educational leadership (PhD); higher education (M Ed, MS); organizational learning and human resource development (M Ed, MS); research and evaluation (MS). *Faculty:* 21 full-time (10 women), 14 part-time/adjunct (8 women). *Students:* 116 full-time (68 women), 218 part-time (130 women); includes 58 minority (34 African Americans, 3 American Indian/Alaska Native, 4 Asian Americans or Pacific Islanders, 17 Hispanic Americans), 7 international. 138 applicants, 78% accepted, 74 enrolled. In 2009, 77 master's, 18 doctorates awarded. *Degree requirements:* For master's, thesis or alternative; for doctorate, thesis/dissertation. *Entrance requirements:* For doctorate, GRE General Test. Additional exam requirements/recommendations for international students: Required—TOEFL (minimum score 560 paper-based; 83 iBT) or IELTS (minimum score 6.5). *Application deadline:* For fall admission, 1/1 priority date for domestic and international students. Applications are processed on a rolling basis. Application fee: $40 ($90 for international students). Electronic applications accepted. *Expenses:* Tuition, state resident: full-time $6716. Tuition, nonresident: full-time $8908. Tuition and fees vary according to course level, course load, program and student level. *Financial support:* In 2009–10, 104 research assistantships with full and partial tuition reimbursements (averaging $13,500 per year), 2 teaching assistantships with full and partial tuition reimbursements (averaging $13,500 per year) were awarded; fellowships, scholarships/grants, health care benefits, and unspecified assistantships also available. *Unit head:* Dr. Laura Rendon, Chair, 515-294-7093, E-mail: lrendon@iastate.edu. *Application contact:* Dr. Daniel Robinson, Information Contact, 515-294-1241, E-mail: eldrshp@iastate.edu.

Jackson State University, Graduate School, School of Education, Department of Counseling and Human Resource Education, Jackson, MS 39217. Offers community and agency counseling (MS); guidance and counseling (MS, MS Ed, Ed S); rehabilitative counseling (MS Ed). *Accreditation:* ACA; CORE (one or more programs are accredited); NCATE. Part-time and evening/weekend programs available. *Degree requirements:* For master's, comprehensive exam, thesis. *Entrance requirements:* For master's, GRE General Test. Additional exam requirements/recommendations for international students: Required—TOEFL.

Jacksonville State University, College of Graduate Studies and Continuing Education, College of Education and Professional Studies, Program in Guidance and Counseling, Jacksonville, AL 36265-1602. Offers MS. *Accreditation:* NCATE. Part-time and evening/weekend programs available. *Degree requirements:* For master's, comprehensive exam, thesis (for some programs). *Entrance requirements:* For master's, GRE General Test or MAT. Electronic applications accepted.

John Brown University, Graduate Counseling Division, Siloam Springs, AR 72761-2121. Offers community counseling (MS); marriage and family therapy (MS); school counseling (MS). *Accreditation:* NCATE. Part-time and evening/weekend programs available. *Faculty:* 7 full-time (1 woman), 4 part-time/adjunct (0 women). *Students:* 72 full-time (55 women), 65 part-time (47 women); includes 10 minority (5 African Americans, 3 American Indian/Alaska Native, 1 Asian American or Pacific Islander, 1 Hispanic American), 1 international. Average age 33. 64 applicants, 86% accepted, 38 enrolled. In 2009, 55 master's awarded. *Degree requirements:* For master's, practica or internships. *Entrance requirements:* For master's, GRE General Test, MAT, minimum GPA of 3.0. Additional exam requirements/recommendations for international students: Required—TOEFL (minimum score 550 paper-based; 173 computer-based). *Application deadline:* For fall admission, 8/11 priority date for domestic students; for spring admission, 1/12 for domestic students. Applications are processed on a rolling basis. Application fee: $35 ($100 for international students). Electronic applications accepted. *Expenses:* Tuition: Full-time $8100; part-time $450 per credit. *Financial support:* In 2009–10, 3 students received support, including 3 research assistantships (averaging $6,210 per year); scholarships/grants, tuition waivers (full), and unspecified assistantships also available. Financial award application deadline: 3/1; financial award applicants required to submit FAFSA. *Unit head:* Dr. John V. Carmack, Program Director, 479-524-7460, Fax: 479-524-9548, E-mail: jcarmack@jbu.edu. *Application contact:* Lynne Jackson, Graduate Admissions Representative—Counseling, 479-524-7425, E-mail: ljackson@jbu.edu.

John Carroll University, Graduate School, Department of Education and Allied Studies, Program in School Counseling, University Heights, OH 44118-4581. Offers M Ed, MA. *Accreditation:* ACA; NCATE. Part-time and evening/weekend programs available. *Degree requirements:* For master's, comprehensive exam, research essay or thesis (MA only). *Entrance requirements:* For master's, GRE General Test or MAT, minimum GPA of 2.75, interview. Additional exam requirements/recommendations for international students: Required—TOEFL. Electronic applications accepted.

John Carroll University, Graduate School, Program in Community Counseling, University Heights, OH 44118-4581. Offers clinical counseling (Certificate); community counseling (MA). *Accreditation:* ACA. Part-time and evening/weekend programs available. *Degree requirements:* For master's, comprehensive exam, internship, practicum. *Entrance requirements:* For master's, MAT or GRE, minimum GPA of 2.75, statement of volunteer experience, interview, 12-18 hours social science course work, survey. Additional exam requirements/recommendations for international students: Required—TOEFL. Electronic applications accepted. *Faculty research:* Child and adolescent development, HIV, hypnosis, wellness, women's issues.

The Johns Hopkins University, School of Education, Department of Counseling and Human Services, Baltimore, MD 21218. Offers clinical community counseling (Certificate); clinical supervision (Certificate); counseling (MS, CAGS), including clinical community counseling (MS), school counseling (MS); play therapy (Certificate). Part-time and evening/weekend programs available. *Faculty:* 4 full-time (2 women), 36 part-time/adjunct (20 women). *Students:* 69 full-time (64 women), 316 part-time (275 women); includes 104 minority (75 African Americans, 12 Asian Americans or Pacific Islanders, 17 Hispanic Americans), 8 international. Average age 32. 186 applicants, 57% accepted, 72 enrolled. In 2009, 115 master's, 28 other advanced degrees awarded. *Degree requirements:* For master's, comprehensive exam. *Entrance requirements:* For master's, bachelor's degree, minimum undergraduate GPA of 3.0, 3 letters of recommendation, curriculum vitae/resume, group interview; for other advanced degree, master's degree, minimum undergraduate GPA of 3.0, 3 letters of recommendation, curriculum vitae/resume, interview. Additional exam requirements/recommendations for international students: Required—TOEFL (minimum score 600 paper-based; 250 computer-based; 100 iBT). *Application deadline:* For fall admission, 3/1 for domestic students, 5/1 for international students; for spring admission, 10/1 for domestic students, 10/15 for international students. Applications are processed on a rolling basis. Application fee: $80. Electronic applications accepted. *Financial support:* Scholarships/grants available. Support available to part-time students. Financial award application deadline: 6/1; financial award applicants required to submit FAFSA. *Faculty research:* College access of low-income students and students-of-color; multicultural counseling training; domestic violence, resilience, and traumatic stress; application of behaviorally-based and ethical practices to criminal justice setting and systems. *Unit head:* Dr. Cheryl Holcomb-McCoy, Chair, 410-516-7928, Fax: 410-516-3939, E-mail: counseling@jhu.edu. *Application contact:* Jennifer Shaffer, Director of Admissions, 410-516-9797 Ext. 410, Fax: 410-516-9799, E-mail: educationinfo@jhu.edu.

Johnson State College, Program in Counseling, Johnson, VT 05656. Offers MA. Part-time programs available. *Degree requirements:* For master's, comprehensive exam. *Entrance requirements:* For master's, interview. *Expenses:* Tuition, area resident: Part-time $416 per credit. Tuition, state resident: part-time $416 per credit. Tuition, nonresident: part-time $899 per credit.

Kansas State University, Graduate School, College of Education, Department of Special Education, Counseling and Student Affairs, Manhattan, KS 66506. Offers academic advising (MS); college student development (MS); counseling and student development (Ed D); counselor

education and supervision (PhD); school counseling (MS); special education (MS, Ed D); student affairs in higher education (PhD). *Accreditation:* NCATE. Part-time programs available. *Faculty:* 10 full-time (4 women), 3 part-time/adjunct (1 woman). *Students:* 64 full-time (38 women), 256 part-time (197 women); includes 33 minority (16 African Americans, 3 American Indian/Alaska Native, 6 Asian Americans or Pacific Islanders, 8 Hispanic Americans), 2 international. Average age 36. 100 applicants, 97% accepted, 73 enrolled. In 2009, 31 master's, 5 doctorates awarded. *Degree requirements:* For master's, thesis or alternative, final written exam. *Entrance requirements:* For master's, GRE General Test or MAT, teaching experience, BS in education with minimum B average. Additional exam requirements/recommendations for international students: Required—TOEFL. *Application deadline:* For fall admission, 2/1 priority date for domestic and international students; for spring admission, 8/1 priority date for domestic and international students. Applications are processed on a rolling basis. Application fee: $40 ($55 for international students). Electronic applications accepted. *Financial support:* In 2009–10, 1 research assistantship (averaging $12,134 per year) was awarded; career-related internships or fieldwork, Federal Work-Study, institutionally sponsored loans, and scholarships/grants also available. Support available to part-time students. Financial award application deadline: 3/1; financial award applicants required to submit FAFSA. *Faculty research:* Application of principles of universal design for learning, on-line applications for supervision of practicum students, interpretation of facial expressions by students with EBD and ASD, school-wide screening techniques for behavioral concerns, field-based observation technique refinements. Total annual research expenditures: $2,948. *Unit head:* Kenneth Hughey, Head, 785-532-6445, Fax: 785-532-7304, E-mail: khughey@ksu.edu. *Application contact:* Gail Shroyer, Director, 785-532-6737, Fax: 785-532-7304, E-mail: gshroyer@ksu.edu.

Kean University, College of Education, Program in Counselor Education, Union, NJ 07083. Offers alcohol and drug abuse counseling (MA); business and industry counseling (MA); community/agency counseling (MA); school counseling (MA). *Accreditation:* ACA; NCATE. Part-time programs available. *Faculty:* 5 full-time (3 women). *Students:* 61 full-time (56 women), 184 part-time (162 women); includes 74 minority (41 African Americans, 3 Asian Americans or Pacific Islanders, 30 Hispanic Americans). Average age 32. 153 applicants, 89% accepted, 73 enrolled. In 2009, 64 master's awarded. *Degree requirements:* For master's, comprehensive exam, thesis, practicum, internship. *Entrance requirements:* For master's, GRE General Test or MAT, minimum GPA of 3.0, 2 letters of recommendation, interview, initial teacher certification (school counseling). *Application deadline:* For fall admission, 5/1 for domestic students; for spring admission, 11/1 for domestic students. Application fee: $60 ($150 for international students). Electronic applications accepted. *Expenses:* Tuition, state resident: full-time $10,440; part-time $435 per credit. Tuition, nonresident: full-time $14,160; part-time $590 per credit. Required fees: $2642; $110 per credit. Part-time tuition and fees vary according to course load and degree level. *Financial support:* In 2009–10, 2 research assistantships with full tuition reimbursements (averaging $3,263 per year) were awarded; unspecified assistantships also available. *Unit head:* Dr. J. Barry Mascari, Program Coordinator, 908-737-3863, E-mail: jmascari@kean.edu. *Application contact:* Steven Koch, Pre-Admissions Coordinator, 908-737-5924, Fax: 908-737-5965, E-mail: skoch@kean.edu.

Keene State College, School of Professional and Graduate Studies, Keene, NH 03435. Offers curriculum and instruction (M Ed); education leadership (PMC); educational leadership (M Ed); school counselor (M Ed, PMC); special education (M Ed); teacher certification (Post-baccalaureate Certificate). *Accreditation:* NCATE. Part-time and evening/weekend programs available. *Faculty:* 21 full-time (13 women), 14 part-time/adjunct (13 women). *Students:* 8 full-time (5 women), 80 part-time (56 women); includes 1 Asian American or Pacific Islander, 1 Hispanic American, 1 international. Average age 34. 94 applicants, 80% accepted, 62 enrolled. In 2009, 55 master's, 10 other advanced degrees awarded. *Entrance requirements:* For master's, PRAXIS I, resume; minimum GPA of 2.5. Additional exam requirements/recommendations for international students: Required—TOEFL (minimum score 550 paper-based; 173 computer-based; 61 iBT). *Application deadline:* For fall admission, 4/1 for domestic students; for spring admission, 12/1 for domestic students. Application fee: $40. *Expenses:* Tuition, state resident: part-time $320 per credit. Tuition, nonresident: part-time $350 per credit. Required fees: $92 per credit. $10 per term. Tuition and fees vary according to course load. *Financial support:* Research assistantships, career-related internships or fieldwork, Federal Work-Study, institutionally sponsored loans, and unspecified assistantships available. Support available to part-time students. Financial award application deadline: 3/1; financial award applicants required to submit FAFSA. *Unit head:* Dr. Melinda Treadwell, Dean, 603-358-2220. *Application contact:* Peggy Richmond, Director of Admissions, 603-358-2276, Fax: 603-358-2767, E-mail: admissions@keene.edu.

Kent State University, Graduate School of Education, Health, and Human Services, School of Lifespan Development and Educational Sciences, Program in Counseling, Kent, OH 44242-0001. Offers Ed S. *Accreditation:* ACA. *Faculty:* 8 full-time (4 women), 16 part-time/adjunct (11 women). *Students:* 6 part-time (all women); includes 1 minority (African American). 3 applicants, 67% accepted. In 2009, 5 Ed Ss awarded. *Entrance requirements:* Additional exam requirements/recommendations for international students: Required—TOEFL. *Application deadline:* Applications are processed on a rolling basis. Application fee: $30. Electronic applications accepted. *Financial support:* In 2009–10, research assistantships (averaging $8,313 per year); Federal Work-Study, scholarships/grants, and unspecified assistantships also available. *Unit head:* Dr. Jason McGlothlin, Coordinator, 330-672-0716, E-mail: jmcgloth@kent.edu. *Application contact:* Nancy Miller, Academic Program Coordinator, Office of Graduate Student Services, 330-672-2576, Fax: 330-672-9162, E-mail: ogs@kent.edu.

Kent State University, Graduate School of Education, Health, and Human Services, School of Lifespan Development and Educational Sciences, Program in Counseling and Human Development Services, Kent, OH 44242-0001. Offers PhD. *Accreditation:* ACA; NCATE. *Faculty:* 8 full-time (4 women), 16 part-time/adjunct (11 women). *Students:* 49 full-time (39 women), 12 part-time (9 women); includes 12 minority (9 African Americans, 2 Asian Americans or Pacific Islanders, 1 Hispanic American). 23 applicants, 57% accepted. In 2009, 6 doctorates awarded. *Degree requirements:* For doctorate, comprehensive exam, thesis/dissertation. *Entrance requirements:* For doctorate, GRE General Test. Additional exam requirements/recommendations for international students: Required—TOEFL. *Application deadline:* For fall admission, 2/15 for domestic students. Application fee: $30. Electronic applications accepted. *Financial support:* In 2009–10, 12 fellowships with full tuition reimbursements (averaging $11,000 per year), research assistantships with full tuition reimbursements (averaging $11,000 per year), teaching assistantships with full tuition reimbursements (averaging $11,000 per year) were awarded; career-related internships or fieldwork, Federal Work-Study, institutionally sponsored loans, scholarships/grants, health care benefits, and unspecified assistantships also available. Support available to part-time students. Financial award application deadline: 4/1; financial award applicants required to submit FAFSA. *Faculty research:* Family/child therapy, clinical supervision, group work, experiential training methods. *Unit head:* Dr. John L. West, Coordinator, 330-672-0713, Fax: 330-672-5396, E-mail: jwest@kent.edu. *Application contact:* Nancy Miller, Academic Program Coordinator, Office of Graduate Student Services, 330-672-2576, Fax: 330-672-9162, E-mail: ogs@kent.edu.

Kent State University, Graduate School of Education, Health, and Human Services, School of Lifespan Development and Educational Sciences, Program in School Counseling, Kent, OH 44242-0001. Offers M Ed, MA. *Accreditation:* ACA; NCATE. *Faculty:* 8 full-time (4 women), 16 part-time/adjunct (11 women). *Students:* 38 full-time (34 women), 62 part-time (48 women); includes 12 minority (9 African Americans, 2 Asian Americans or Pacific Islanders, 1 Hispanic American). 50 applicants, 64% accepted. In 2009, 20 master's awarded. *Degree requirements:* For master's, thesis (for some programs). *Entrance requirements:* Additional exam requirements/recommendations for international students: Required—TOEFL. *Application deadline:* For fall admission, 6/1 for domestic students; for spring admission, 10/1 for domestic students. Application fee: $30. Electronic applications accepted. *Financial support:* In 2009–10, 1 research assistantship with full tuition reimbursement (averaging $8,313 per year) was awarded; Federal Work-Study, scholarships/grants, and unspecified assistantships also available. Financial award application deadline: 4/1; financial award applicants required to submit FAFSA. *Faculty research:* Appraisal, diagnosis, group work. *Unit head:* Dr. Jason McGlothlin, Coordinator, 330-672-0716, E-mail: jmcgloth@kent.edu. *Application contact:* Nancy Miller, Academic Program Coordinator, Office of Graduate Student Services, 330-672-2576, Fax: 330-672-9162, E-mail: ogs@kent.edu.

Kutztown University of Pennsylvania, College of Education, Program in Guidance and Counseling, Kutztown, PA 19530-0730. Offers counselor education (M Ed), including elementary counseling, secondary counseling. *Accreditation:* NCATE. Part-time and evening/weekend programs available. *Faculty:* 2 full-time (both women). *Students:* 34 full-time (25 women), 67 part-time (52 women); includes 7 minority (3 African Americans, 4 Hispanic Americans). Average age 27. 42 applicants, 55% accepted, 13 enrolled. In 2009, 29 master's awarded. *Degree requirements:* For master's, comprehensive exam, thesis optional. *Entrance requirements:* For master's, GRE General Test, interview. Additional exam requirements/recommendations for international students: Required—TOEFL. *Application deadline:* For fall admission, 2/1 for domestic and international students; for spring admission, 8/1 for domestic and international students. Application fee: $35. Electronic applications accepted. *Expenses:* Tuition, state resident: full-time $6666; part-time $370 per credit. Tuition, nonresident: full-time $10,666; part-time $593 per credit. Required fees: $62 per credit. $60 per semester. *Financial support:* Career-related internships or fieldwork, Federal Work-Study, scholarships/grants, and unspecified assistantships available. Financial award application deadline: 3/1; financial award applicants required to submit FAFSA. *Faculty research:* Family addictions, family roles. *Unit head:* Dr. Deborah Barlieb, Chairperson, 610-683-4204, Fax: 610-683-1585, E-mail: barlieb@kutztown.edu. *Application contact:* Kelly D. Burr, Associate Director, Graduate Admissions, 610-683-4200, Fax: 610-683-1393, E-mail: graduate@kutztown.edu.

Lakeland College, Graduate Studies Division, Program in Counseling, Sheboygan, WI 53082-0359. Offers MA.

Lamar University, College of Graduate Studies, College of Education and Human Development, Department of Educational Leadership, Beaumont, TX 77710. Offers counseling and development (M Ed, Certificate); education administration (M Ed); educational leadership (DE); principal (Certificate); school superintendent (Certificate); supervision (M Ed); technology application (Certificate). Part-time and evening/weekend programs available. *Faculty:* 14 full-time (7 women), 7 part-time/adjunct (2 women). *Students:* 14 full-time (8 women), 2,827 part-time (1,986 women); includes 798 minority (340 African Americans, 20 American Indian/Alaska Native, 31 Asian Americans or Pacific Islanders, 407 Hispanic Americans). Average age 40. 2,662 applicants, 75% accepted, 332 enrolled. In 2009, 199 master's, 21 doctorates awarded. Terminal master's awarded for partial completion of doctoral program. *Degree requirements:* For master's, comprehensive exam, thesis optional; for doctorate, thesis/dissertation. *Entrance requirements:* For master's, GRE General Test, minimum GPA of 2.5; for doctorate, GRE. Additional exam requirements/recommendations for international students: Required—TOEFL. *Application deadline:* For fall admission, 8/1 priority date for domestic students; for spring admission, 12/1 priority date for domestic students. Applications are processed on a rolling basis. Application fee: $25 ($50 for international students). *Financial support:* In 2009–10, 3 fellowships (averaging $20,000 per year), 1 research assistantship with tuition reimbursement (averaging $6,500 per year) were awarded; teaching assistantships with tuition reimbursements, career-related internships or fieldwork and scholarships/grants also available. Support available to part-time students. Financial award application deadline: 4/1. *Faculty research:* School dropouts, suicide prevention in public school students, school climate and gifted performance, teacher evaluation. *Unit head:* Dr. Carolyn Crawford, Chair, 409-880-8689, Fax: 409-880-8685. *Application contact:* Dr. Carolyn Crawford, Chair, 409-880-8689, Fax: 409-880-8685.

Lancaster Bible College & Graduate School, Graduate School, Lancaster, PA 17601-5036. Offers Bible (MA); consulting resource teacher (M Ed); counseling (MA); ministry (MA); school counseling (M Ed). Part-time and evening/weekend programs available. *Degree requirements:* For master's, comprehensive exam (for some programs), thesis (for some programs). *Entrance requirements:* For master's, bachelor's degree with a minimum of 30 credits of course work in Bible, minimum undergraduate GPA of 3.0, interview. Additional exam requirements/recommendations for international students: Required—TOEFL.

La Sierra University, School of Education, Department of School Psychology and Counseling, Riverside, CA 92515. Offers counseling (MA); educational psychology (Ed S); school psychology (Ed S). Part-time and evening/weekend programs available. *Degree requirements:* For master's, thesis optional; for Ed S, practicum (educational psychology). *Entrance requirements:* For master's, California Basic Educational Skills Test, NTE, minimum GPA of 3.0; for Ed S, minimum GPA of 3.3. *Faculty research:* Equivalent score scales, self perception.

Lee University, Graduate Studies in Counseling, Cleveland, TN 37320-3450. Offers mental health counseling (MS); school counseling (MS). Part-time programs available. *Faculty:* 6 full-time (2 women), 7 part-time/adjunct (4 women). *Students:* 64 full-time (55 women), 28 part-time (26 women); includes 10 minority (1 African American, 4 American Indian/Alaska Native, 3 Asian Americans or Pacific Islanders, 2 Hispanic Americans), 1 international. Average age 26. 66 applicants, 95% accepted, 52 enrolled. In 2009, 24 master's awarded. *Degree requirements:* For master's, variable foreign language requirement, comprehensive exam, thesis, internship. *Entrance requirements:* For master's, GRE General Test or MAT, minimum undergraduate GPA of 3.0, 3 letters of recommendation, interview. Additional exam requirements/recommendations for international students: Required—TOEFL (minimum score 450 paper-based; 45 computer-based). *Application deadline:* For fall admission, 4/1 priority date for domestic and international students; for spring admission, 10/1 priority date for domestic and international students. Applications are processed on a rolling basis. Application fee: $25. *Expenses:* Tuition: Full-time $11,100; part-time $463 per credit. Required fees: $305. *Financial support:* Teaching assistantships, career-related internships or fieldwork, Federal Work-Study, institutionally sponsored loans, scholarships/grants, and unspecified assistantships available. Financial award application deadline: 3/1; financial award applicants required to submit FAFSA. *Unit head:* Dr. Trevor Milliron, Director, 423-614-8126, Fax: 423-614-8129, E-mail: tmilliron@leeuniversity.edu. *Application contact:* Vicki Glasscock, Graduate Admissions Director, 423-614-8059, E-mail: vglasscock@leeuniversity.edu.

Lehigh University, College of Education, Program in Comparative and International Education, Bethlehem, PA 18015. Offers comparative and international education (MA); globalization and educational change (M Ed); international counseling (Certificate); international development in education (Certificate); special education (Certificate); TESOL (Certificate). Part-time and evening/weekend programs available. Postbaccalaureate distance learning degree programs offered (no on-campus study). *Faculty:* 2 full-time (1 woman). *Students:* 9 full-time (6 women), 40 part-time (39 women); includes 3 minority (2 African Americans, 1 Hispanic American), 10 international. Average age 36. 46 applicants, 67% accepted, 18 enrolled. In 2009, 11 master's awarded. *Degree requirements:* For master's, thesis (MA). *Entrance requirements:* For master's, 2 letters of recommendation. Additional exam requirements/recommendations for international students: Required—TOEFL (minimum score 600 paper-based; 250 computer-based; 93 iBT). *Application deadline:* For fall admission, 5/15 for domestic and international students; for spring admission, 11/1 for domestic and international students. Applications are processed on a rolling basis. Application fee: $65. Electronic applications accepted. *Financial support:* In 2009–10, 4 students received support, including 4 research assistantships with full and partial tuition reimbursements available (averaging $13,000 per year). Financial award application deadline: 3/15. *Faculty research:* Gender equity in education, post-socialist education transformation, educational borrowing, comparing education systems, education policy and globalization. *Unit head:* Dr. Alexander W. Wiseman, Coordinator, 610-758-5740, Fax: 610-758-6223, E-mail: aww207@lehigh.edu. *Application contact:* Donna M. Johnson, Coordinator, 610-758-3231, Fax: 610-758-6223, E-mail: dmj4@lehigh.edu.

Lehigh University, College of Education, Program in Counseling Psychology, Bethlehem, PA 18015. Offers counseling and human services (M Ed); counseling psychology (PhD); elementary counseling with certification (M Ed); international counseling (Certificate); international counseling with certification (M Ed); secondary school counseling (M Ed). *Accreditation:* APA (one or

Counselor Education

Lehigh University (continued)
more programs are accredited). Part-time and evening/weekend programs available. Post-baccalaureate distance learning degree programs offered (minimal on-campus study). *Faculty:* 6 full-time (4 women), 10 part-time/adjunct (5 women). *Students:* 40 full-time (33 women), 37 part-time (32 women); includes 13 minority (7 African Americans, 1 American Indian/Alaska Native, 3 Asian Americans or Pacific Islanders, 2 Hispanic Americans), 4 international. Average age 29. 194 applicants, 24% accepted, 17 enrolled. In 2009, 34 master's, 3 doctorates awarded. *Degree requirements:* For doctorate, comprehensive exam, thesis/dissertation. *Entrance requirements:* For master's, minimum GPA of 3.0, 2 letters of recommendation, essay, transcript; for doctorate, GRE General Test (Verbal and Quantitative), 2 letters of recommendation, supplemental application, transcript, essay; for Certificate, minimum GPA of 3.0. Additional exam requirements/recommendations for international students: Required—TOEFL (minimum score 600 paper-based; 250 computer-based; 93 iBT). *Application deadline:* For fall admission, 11/15 for domestic and international students; for winter admission, 2/1 for international students. Application fee: $65. Electronic applications accepted. *Financial support:* In 2009–10, 11 students received support, including 2 fellowships with full and partial tuition reimbursements available (averaging $24,000 per year), 2 research assistantships with full and partial tuition reimbursements available (averaging $13,000 per year); career-related internships or fieldwork, Federal Work-Study, institutionally sponsored loans, scholarships/grants, and tuition waivers (full and partial) also available. Financial award application deadline: 1/31; financial award applicants required to submit FAFSA. *Faculty research:* Supervision, violence prevention, multicultural training and counseling, career development and health interventions. *Unit head:* Dr. Arpana Inman, Coordinator, 610-758-4443, Fax: 610-758-3227, E-mail: agi2@lehigh.edu. *Application contact:* Donna M. Johnson, Coordinator, 610-758-3231, Fax: 610-758-6223, E-mail: dmj4@lehigh.edu.

Lehman College of the City University of New York, Division of Education, Department of Specialized Services in Education, Program in Guidance and Counseling, Bronx, NY 10468-1589. Offers MS Ed. *Accreditation:* ACA; NCATE. Part-time and evening/weekend programs available. *Degree requirements:* For master's, thesis. *Entrance requirements:* For master's, minimum GPA of 2.7. *Faculty research:* Crisis intervention, domestic violence, alcohol abuse, gender issues.

Lenoir-Rhyne University, Graduate Programs, School of Counseling and Human Services, Program in School Counseling, Hickory, NC 28601. Offers MA. Part-time and evening/weekend programs available. *Degree requirements:* For master's, comprehensive exam, thesis optional. *Entrance requirements:* For master's, GRE General Test, minimum undergraduate GPA of 2.7, graduate 3.0; writing sample. Additional exam requirements/recommendations for international students: Required—TOEFL (minimum score 600 paper-based). Electronic applications accepted.

Lenoir-Rhyne University, Graduate Programs, School of Counseling and Human Services, Programs in Counseling, Hickory, NC 28601. Offers agency counseling (MA); community counseling (MA). Part-time and evening/weekend programs available. *Degree requirements:* For master's, comprehensive exam, thesis optional. *Entrance requirements:* For master's, GRE General Test, writing sample, minimum undergraduate GPA of 2.7, minimum graduate GPA of 3.0. Additional exam requirements/recommendations for international students: Required—TOEFL (minimum score 600 paper-based). Electronic applications accepted.

Lewis University, College of Arts and Sciences, Program in School Counseling and Guidance, Romeoville, IL 60446. Offers MA. Part-time and evening/weekend programs available. *Faculty:* 5 full-time (3 women), 10 part-time/adjunct (6 women). *Students:* 89 full-time (68 women), 120 part-time (99 women); includes 60 minority (44 African Americans, 6 Asian Americans or Pacific Islanders, 10 Hispanic Americans). Average age 30. In 2009, 53 master's awarded. *Degree requirements:* For master's, comprehensive exam. *Entrance requirements:* For master's, letters of recommendation, interview, minimum GPA of 2.75. Additional exam requirements/recommendations for international students: Required—TOEFL (minimum score 550 paper-based; 213 computer-based). *Application deadline:* For fall admission, 5/1 priority date for international students; for spring admission, 11/15 priority date for international students. Applications are processed on a rolling basis. Application fee: $40. Electronic applications accepted. *Expenses:* Tuition: Full-time $6480; part-time $720 per credit. One-time fee: $40. Tuition and fees vary according to course load, degree level and program. *Financial support:* Federal Work-Study, scholarships/grants, tuition waivers (full and partial), and unspecified assistantships available. Financial award application deadline: 5/1; financial award applicants required to submit FAFSA. *Unit head:* Dr. Judith Zito, Director, 815-838-0500 Ext. 5971, E-mail: zitoju@lewisu.edu. *Application contact:* Nancy Hanley, Information Contact, 815-838-0500 Ext. 5604, E-mail: hanleyna@lewisu.edu.

Liberty University, School of Education, Lynchburg, VA 24502. Offers administration and supervision (M Ed); curriculum and instruction (M Ed); early childhood education (M Ed); education specialist (Ed S); educational leadership (Ed D); elementary education (M Ed); gifted education (M Ed); reading specialist (M Ed); school counseling (M Ed); secondary education (M Ed); special education (M Ed). *Accreditation:* NCATE. Part-time programs available. Postbaccalaureate distance learning degree programs offered (minimal on-campus study). *Degree requirements:* For doctorate, comprehensive exam, thesis/dissertation. *Entrance requirements:* For master's, GRE General Test or MAT (aken in or before 1999), 2 letters of recommendation, minimum undergraduate GPA of 3.0, curriculum vitae; for doctorate, GRE General Test or MAT (if taken before 1999), minimum master's GPA of 3.0, 3 years of teacher experience; for Ed S, GRE General Test or MAT (if taken before 1999), minimum master's GPA of 3.0, 3 years of teaching experience. Additional exam requirements/recommendations for international students: Required—TOEFL (minimum score 600 paper-based; 250 computer-based). Electronic applications accepted. *Expenses:* Contact institution. *Faculty research:* Self-determination, character education, bibliotherapy, learning styles, distance education.

Lincoln Memorial University, Carter and Moyers School of Education, Harrogate, TN 37752-1901. Offers administration and supervision (M Ed, Ed S); counseling and guidance (M Ed); curriculum and instruction (M Ed, Ed S); English (M Ed). Part-time and evening/weekend programs available. Postbaccalaureate distance learning degree programs offered. *Faculty:* 31 full-time (13 women), 22 part-time/adjunct (11 women). *Students:* 190 full-time (151 women), 1,299 part-time (959 women); includes 144 minority (128 African Americans, 1 American Indian/Alaska Native, 5 Asian Americans or Pacific Islanders, 10 Hispanic Americans), 4 international. 1,562 applicants, 96% accepted, 1489 enrolled. In 2009, 173 master's, 901 Ed Ss awarded. *Degree requirements:* For master's, comprehensive exam, thesis optional; for Ed S, comprehensive exam. *Entrance requirements:* For master's, PRAXIS, NTE, GRE, MAT, letters of recommendation; for Ed S, graduate transcripts. *Application deadline:* For fall admission, 8/10 for domestic and international students; for spring admission, 1/10 for domestic and international students. Application fee: $25. *Expenses:* Tuition: Full-time $11,700; part-time $390 per hour. *Financial support:* In 2009–10, 973 students received support. Career-related internships or fieldwork, health care benefits, and unspecified assistantships available. Support available to part-time students. Financial award application deadline: 4/1; financial award applicants required to submit FAFSA. *Faculty research:* Brain compatible teaching and learning; poverty in Appalachia; leadership for change; ethics, moral responsibility and social justice; human and organizational learning. *Unit head:* Dr. David Hand, Dean, 423-869-6259, Fax: 423-869-6261, E-mail: david.hand@lmunet.edu. *Application contact:* Terri Knuckles, Office Manager, Graduate Education, 423-869-6223, Fax: 423-869-6261, E-mail: terri.knuckles@lmunet.edu.

Lincoln University, School of Graduate Studies and Continuing Education, Jefferson City, MO 65102. Offers business administration (MBA), including accounting, entrepreneurship, management, public administration and policy; educational leadership (Ed S), including elementary leadership, secondary leadership, superintendency; guidance and counseling (M Ed), including community/agency counseling, elementary school, secondary school; history (MA); school administration and supervision (M Ed), including elementary school administration, secondary school administration, special education administration; school teaching (M Ed), including elementary school teaching, secondary school teaching; social science (MA), including history, political science, sociology; sociology (MA); sociology/criminal justice (MA). Part-time and evening/weekend programs available. *Students:* 52 full-time (27 women), 146 part-time (107 women); includes 40 minority (39 African Americans, 1 Asian American or Pacific Islander), 15 international. Average age 35. 76 applicants, 95% accepted, 46 enrolled. In 2009, 60 master's, 6 other advanced degrees awarded. *Degree requirements:* For master's and Ed S, comprehensive exam, thesis optional. *Entrance requirements:* For master's and Ed S, GRE, MAT or GMAT, minimum GPA of 2.75 in major, 2.5 overall; 3 letters of recommendation; minimum C average in English composition; personal statement of purpose. Additional exam requirements/recommendations for international students: Required—TOEFL (minimum score 500 paper-based; 173 computer-based; 61 iBT). *Application deadline:* For fall admission, 7/1 priority date for domestic and international students; for spring admission, 12/1 priority date for domestic and international students. Applications are processed on a rolling basis. Application fee: $20. *Expenses:* Tuition, state resident: full-time $4185; part-time $232.50 per credit hour. Tuition, nonresident: full-time $7767; part-time $431.50 per credit hour. Required fees: $270; $15 per credit hour. $20 per term. *Financial support:* Federal Work-Study and scholarships/grants available. Financial award application deadline: 4/1; financial award applicants required to submit FAFSA. *Faculty research:* Suicide prevention. *Unit head:* Dr. Linda S. Bickel, Dean, 573-681-5247, Fax: 573-681-5106, E-mail: gradschool@lincolnu.edu. *Application contact:* Irasema Steck, Administrative Assistant, 573-681-5247, Fax: 573-681-5106, E-mail: gradschool@lincolnu.edu.

Loma Linda University, School of Science and Technology, Department of Counseling and Family Science, Loma Linda, CA 92350. Offers MA, MS, DMFT, PhD, Certificate, MA/Certificate. *Degree requirements:* For master's, comprehensive exam, thesis optional; for doctorate, comprehensive exam, thesis/dissertation (for some programs). *Entrance requirements:* For master's, minimum GPA of 3.0; for doctorate, GRE. Additional exam requirements/recommendations for international students: Required—TOEFL (minimum score 550 paper-based; 213 computer-based), MTELP. Electronic applications accepted.

Long Island University at Riverhead, Education Division, Riverhead, NY 11901. Offers applied behavior analysis (Advanced Certificate); childhood education (MS Ed), including childhood education, elementary education; literacy education (MS Ed); teaching students with disabilities (MS Ed). *Accreditation:* Teacher Education Accreditation Council. Part-time and evening/weekend programs available. *Faculty:* 1 full-time (0 women), 11 part-time/adjunct (7 women). *Students:* 29 full-time (25 women), 90 part-time (82 women). Average age 30. 48 applicants, 69% accepted, 33 enrolled. In 2009, 38 master's awarded. *Degree requirements:* For master's, thesis (for some programs); for Advanced Certificate, comprehensive exam (for some programs). *Entrance requirements:* For master's, minimum GPA of 2.75, writing sample, letter of reference, interview, official college transcripts. Additional exam requirements/recommendations for international students: Required—TOEFL (minimum score 550 paper-based; 250 computer-based). *Application deadline:* Applications are processed on a rolling basis. Electronic applications accepted. *Financial support:* In 2009–10, 105 students received support. Scholarships/grants and tuition waivers (partial) available. Support available to part-time students. Financial award applicants required to submit FAFSA. *Unit head:* Dr. R. Lawrence McCann, Director, 631-287-8211, E-mail: admissions@southampton.liu.edu. *Application contact:* Andrea Borra, Director of Graduate Admissions and Program Administration, 631-287-8010 Ext. 8326, Fax: 631-287-8253, E-mail: andrea.borra@liu.edu.

Long Island University, Brentwood Campus, School of Education, Brentwood, NY 11717. Offers childhood education (MS); early childhood education (MS); literacy (MS); mental health counseling (MS); school counseling (MS); special education (MS). Part-time and evening/weekend programs available.

Long Island University, Brooklyn Campus, School of Education, Department of Human Development and Leadership, Program in Counseling and Development, Brooklyn, NY 11201-8423. Offers MS, MS Ed, Certificate. *Degree requirements:* For master's, thesis optional. *Entrance requirements:* For master's, 2 letters of recommendation. Additional exam requirements/recommendations for international students: Required—TOEFL (minimum score 500 paper-based; 173 computer-based).

Long Island University, C.W. Post Campus, School of Education, Department of Counseling and Development, Brookville, NY 11548-1300. Offers mental health counseling (MS); school counseling (MS). *Accreditation:* ACA. Part-time and evening/weekend programs available. *Degree requirements:* For master's, comprehensive exam or thesis, internship. *Entrance requirements:* For master's, interview, minimum GPA of 3.0. Electronic applications accepted. *Faculty research:* Community prevention programs, youth gang violence, community mental health counseling.

Long Island University, Rockland Graduate Campus, Graduate School, Program in Counseling and Development, Orangeburg, NY 10962. Offers mental health counseling (MS); school counselor (MS). *Faculty:* 2 full-time (both women), 7 part-time/adjunct (3 women). *Students:* 18 full-time (12 women), 60 part-time (51 women). In 2009, 25 master's awarded. *Application deadline:* Applications are processed on a rolling basis. Application fee: $30. *Expenses:* Tuition: Part-time $930 per credit. Required fees: $200 per semester. *Financial support:* Applicants required to submit FAFSA. *Unit head:* Dr. Linda Rosen, Program Director, 845-359-7200 Ext. 5406, Fax: 845-359-7248, E-mail: kathleen.keefe-cooperman@liu.edu. *Application contact:* Peter S. Reiner, Director of Admissions and Marketing, 845-359-7200, Fax: 845-359-7248, E-mail: peter.reiner@liu.edu.

Long Island University, Westchester Graduate Campus, Programs in Education-School Counselor and School Psychology, Purchase, NY 10577. Offers school counselor (MS Ed); school psychologist (MS Ed). Part-time and evening/weekend programs available.

Longwood University, Office of Graduate Studies, College of Education and Human Services, Farmville, VA 23909. Offers communication sciences and disorders (MS); community and college counseling (MS); curriculum and instruction specialist-elementary (MS), including mild disabilities, modern languages; curriculum and instruction specialist-secondary (MS), including English, mild disabilities, modern languages; educational leadership (MS); guidance and counseling (MS); literacy and culture (MS); school library media (MS). *Accreditation:* NCATE. Part-time and evening/weekend programs available. *Degree requirements:* For master's, comprehensive exam, thesis optional. *Entrance requirements:* For master's, GRE (communication sciences and disorders), minimum GPA of 2.75. Additional exam requirements/recommendations for international students: Required—TOEFL (minimum score 550 paper-based; 213 computer-based).

Louisiana State University and Agricultural and Mechanical College, Graduate School, College of Education, Department of Educational Theory, Policy and Practice, Baton Rouge, LA 70803. Offers counseling (M Ed, MA, Ed S); educational administration (M Ed, MA, PhD, Ed S); educational technology (MA); elementary education (M Ed); higher education (PhD); research methodology (PhD); secondary education (M Ed). *Accreditation:* ACA (one or more programs are accredited); NCATE. Part-time and evening/weekend programs available. *Faculty:* 38 full-time (24 women). *Students:* 174 full-time (139 women), 154 part-time (129 women); includes 74 minority (66 African Americans, 3 Asian Americans or Pacific Islanders, 5 Hispanic Americans), 9 international. Average age 32. 122 applicants, 60% accepted, 48 enrolled. In 2009, 124 master's, 13 doctorates, 11 other advanced degrees awarded. Terminal master's awarded for partial completion of doctoral program. *Degree requirements:* For doctorate, thesis/dissertation; for Ed S, thesis optional. *Entrance requirements:* For master's and doctorate, GRE General Test, minimum GPA of 3.0. Additional exam requirements/recommendations for international students: Required—TOEFL (minimum score 550 paper-based; 213 computer-based; 79 iBT) or IELTS (minimum score 6.5). *Application deadline:* For fall admission, 1/25 priority date for domestic students, 5/15 for international students; for spring admission, 10/15 for international students. Applications are processed on a rolling basis. Application fee: $50 ($70 for international students). Electronic applications accepted. *Financial support:* In 2009–10, 226 students received support, including 1 fellowship (averaging $31,711 per year), 27 research

assistantships with full and partial tuition reimbursements available (averaging $10,143 per year), 35 teaching assistantships with full and partial tuition reimbursements available (averaging $12,555 per year); career-related internships or fieldwork, Federal Work-Study, institutionally sponsored loans, health care benefits, and unspecified assistantships also available. Support available to part-time students. Financial award applicants required to submit FAFSA. *Faculty research:* Literary, curriculum studies, science education, K-12 leadership, higher education. Total annual research expenditures: $1.8 million. *Unit head:* Dr. Earl Cheek, Chair, 225-578-6867, Fax: 225-578-9135, E-mail: echeek@lsu.edu. *Application contact:* Dr., Graduate Coordinator, 225-578-2280, Fax: 225-578-9135.

Louisiana Tech University, Graduate School, College of Education, Department of Behavioral Sciences and Psychology, Ruston, LA 71272. Offers counseling (MA); counseling psychology (PhD); industrial/organizational psychology (MA); special education (MA). *Accreditation:* APA (one or more programs are accredited). Part-time programs available. *Degree requirements:* For master's, thesis or alternative; for doctorate, thesis/dissertation. *Entrance requirements:* For master's and doctorate, GRE General Test.

Loyola Marymount University, School of Education, Department of Educational Support Services, Program in Counseling, Los Angeles, CA 90045. Offers MA. Part-time programs available. *Faculty:* 9 full-time (6 women), 22 part-time/adjunct (19 women). *Students:* 120 full-time (106 women), 11 part-time (8 women); includes 82 minority (18 African Americans, 10 Asian Americans or Pacific Islanders, 54 Hispanic Americans), 3 international. Average age 27. 81 applicants, 81% accepted, 55 enrolled. In 2009, 35 master's awarded. *Degree requirements:* For master's, comprehensive exam. *Entrance requirements:* For master's, CBEST, 2 letters of recommendation. Additional exam requirements/recommendations for international students: Required—TOEFL (minimum score 600 paper-based; 250 computer-based; 100 iBT). *Application deadline:* For fall admission, 6/15 for domestic students; for spring admission, 11/15 for domestic students. Application fee: $50. Electronic applications accepted. *Financial support:* In 2009–10, 66 students received support, including 2 research assistantships (averaging $1,400 per year); scholarships/grants and unspecified assistantships also available. Support available to part-time students. Financial award application deadline: 6/15; financial award applicants required to submit FAFSA. Total annual research expenditures: $5,922. *Unit head:* Dr. Tom Batsis, Chair, 310-338-7303, E-mail: tbatsis@lmu.edu. *Application contact:* Chake H. Kouyoumjian, Associate Dean of Graduate Studies, 310-338-2721, Fax: 310-338-6086, E-mail: ckouyoum@lmu.edu.

Loyola Marymount University, School of Education, Department of Educational Support Services, Program in Guidance and Counseling, Los Angeles, CA 90045. Offers MA. Part-time programs available. *Faculty:* 9 full-time (6 women), 22 part-time/adjunct (19 women). *Students:* 16 full-time (12 women), 4 part-time (3 women); includes 13 minority (3 African Americans, 4 Asian Americans or Pacific Islanders, 6 Hispanic Americans). Average age 27. 10 applicants, 90% accepted, 9 enrolled. In 2009, 10 master's awarded. *Degree requirements:* For master's, comprehensive exam. *Entrance requirements:* For master's, CBEST, 2 letters of recommendation. Additional exam requirements/recommendations for international students: Required—TOEFL (minimum score 600 paper-based; 250 computer-based; 100 iBT). *Application deadline:* For fall admission, 6/15 for domestic students; for spring admission, 11/15 for domestic students. Application fee: $50. Electronic applications accepted. *Financial support:* In 2009–10, 8 students received support, including 1 research assistantship (averaging $594 per year); scholarships/grants and unspecified assistantships also available. Support available to part-time students. Total annual research expenditures: $5,922. *Unit head:* Dr. Tom Batsis, Chair, 310-338-7303, E-mail: tbatsis@lmu.edu. *Application contact:* Chake H. Kouyoumjian, Associate Dean of Graduate Studies, 310-338-2721, Fax: 310-338-6086, E-mail: ckouyoum@lmu.edu.

Loyola University Chicago, School of Education, Program in Community Counseling, Chicago, IL 60660. Offers M Ed, MA. MA offered through the Graduate School. Part-time programs available. *Faculty:* 5 full-time (4 women), 4 part-time/adjunct (2 women). *Students:* 31. Average age 25. 68 applicants, 65% accepted, 13 enrolled. In 2009, 11 master's awarded. *Degree requirements:* For master's, comprehensive exam. *Entrance requirements:* For master's, GRE General Test, minimum GPA of 3.0, letters of recommendation, resume. Additional exam requirements/recommendations for international students: Required—TOEFL (minimum score 550 paper-based; 213 computer-based; 80 iBT). *Application deadline:* For fall admission, 2/15 for domestic and international students. Application fee: $50. Electronic applications accepted. *Expenses:* Tuition: Full-time $14,220; part-time $790 per credit hour. Required fees: $60 per semester hour. Tuition and fees vary according to program. *Financial support:* Fellowships with full tuition reimbursements, research assistantships with full tuition reimbursements, teaching assistantships with full tuition reimbursements, career-related internships or fieldwork and Federal Work-Study available. Financial award application deadline: 2/15; financial award applicants required to submit FAFSA. *Faculty research:* Career development, prevention, group counseling, family therapy, multicultural counseling. *Unit head:* Dr. Steve Brown, Director, 312-915-6311, E-mail: sbrown@luc.edu. *Application contact:* Marie Rosin-Dittmar, Information Contact, 312-915-6800, E-mail: schleduc@luc.edu.

Loyola University Chicago, School of Education, Program in School Counseling, Chicago, IL 60660. Offers M Ed, Certificate. *Accreditation:* NCATE. *Faculty:* 5 full-time (4 women), 4 part-time/adjunct (2 women). *Students:* 29. Average age 25. 57 applicants, 53% accepted, 5 enrolled. In 2009, 19 master's awarded. *Degree requirements:* For master's, comprehensive exam. *Entrance requirements:* For master's, GRE General Test, minimum GPA of 3.0, letters of recommendation, resume. Additional exam requirements/recommendations for international students: Required—TOEFL (minimum score 550 paper-based; 213 computer-based; 79 iBT). *Application deadline:* For fall admission, 2/15 for domestic and international students. Application fee: $50. Electronic applications accepted. *Expenses:* Tuition: Full-time $14,220; part-time $790 per credit hour. Required fees: $60 per semester hour. Tuition and fees vary according to program. *Financial support:* Career-related internships or fieldwork and Federal Work-Study available. Financial award application deadline: 2/15; financial award applicants required to submit FAFSA. *Faculty research:* Career development, group counseling, family therapy, child and adolescent development, multicultural counseling. *Unit head:* Dr. Steve Brown, Director, 312-915-6311, E-mail: sbrown@luc.edu. *Application contact:* Marie Rosin-Dittmar, Information Contact, 312-915-6800, E-mail: schleduc@luc.edu.

Loyola University Maryland, Graduate Programs, College of Arts and Sciences, Department of Education, Program in School Counseling, Baltimore, MD 21210-2699. Offers M Ed, CAS. *Accreditation:* ACA; NCATE. Part-time and evening/weekend programs available. *Entrance requirements:* For master's and CAS, GRE General Test, GRE Subject Test (recommended). Additional exam requirements/recommendations for international students: Required—TOEFL (minimum score 550 paper-based; 213 computer-based).

Loyola University New Orleans, College of Social Sciences, Department of Counseling, Program in Counseling, New Orleans, LA 70118-6195. Offers MS. *Accreditation:* ACA. Part-time and evening/weekend programs available. *Students:* 31 full-time (25 women), 20 part-time (18 women); includes 17 minority (14 African Americans, 1 American Indian/Alaska Native, 1 Asian American or Pacific Islander, 1 Hispanic American). Average age 30. 34 applicants, 65% accepted, 19 enrolled. In 2009, 23 master's awarded. *Degree requirements:* For master's, comprehensive exam. *Entrance requirements:* For master's, GRE, MAT (recommended), interview, letters of recommendation, writing sample, resume, work experience. Additional exam requirements/recommendations for international students: Required—TOEFL (minimum score 550 paper-based; 213 computer-based). *Application deadline:* For fall admission, 8/1 priority date for domestic and international students; for spring admission, 1/5 priority date for domestic and international students. Applications are processed on a rolling basis. Application fee: $20. Electronic applications accepted. *Expenses:* Contact institution. *Financial support:* Research assistantships, career-related internships or fieldwork and Federal Work-Study available. Support available to part-time students. Financial award application deadline: 5/1; financial award applicants required to submit FAFSA. *Faculty research:* Counseling theory, spirituality issues, group counseling, multicultural applications. *Unit head:* Le Anne Steen, Chair, 504-864-7855, Fax: 504-864-7844, E-mail: lsteen@loyno.edu. *Application contact:* 800-4LOYOLA, Fax: 504-865-3383, E-mail: admit@loyno.edu.

Lynchburg College, Graduate Studies, School of Education and Human Development, Lynchburg, VA 24501-3199. Offers community counseling (M Ed); counselor education (M Ed), including community counseling; curriculum and instruction (M Ed); educational leadership (M Ed); English education (M Ed); reading (M Ed); school counseling (M Ed); science education (M Ed); special education (M Ed), including autism spectrum disorder, early childhood special education, mental retardation, teaching children with learning disabilities, teaching the emotionally disturbed. Part-time and evening/weekend programs available. *Degree requirements:* For master's, comprehensive exam. *Entrance requirements:* For master's, GRE, minimum undergraduate GPA of 3.0. Additional exam requirements/recommendations for international students: Required—TOEFL. *Expenses:* Tuition: Full-time $7020; part-time $390 per credit hour.

Lyndon State College, Graduate Programs in Education, Department of Education, Lyndonville, VT 05851-0919. Offers curriculum and instruction (M Ed); reading specialist (M Ed); special education (M Ed); teaching and counseling (M Ed). Part-time and evening/weekend programs available. *Degree requirements:* For master's, exam or major field project. *Entrance requirements:* Additional exam requirements/recommendations for international students: Recommended—TOEFL (minimum score 500 paper-based; 173 computer-based).

Malone University, Graduate Program in Counselor and Guidance Education, Canton, OH 44709. Offers clinical counseling (MA); school counseling (MA). Part-time and evening/weekend programs available. *Faculty:* 4 full-time (3 women), 5 part-time/adjunct (2 women). *Students:* 33 full-time (26 women), 109 part-time (90 women); includes 19 minority (all African Americans). Average age 33. In 2009, 29 master's awarded. *Entrance requirements:* For master's, minimum undergraduate GPA of 3.0. Additional exam requirements/recommendations for international students: Required—TOEFL (minimum score 550 paper-based; 213 computer-based; 79 iBT). *Application deadline:* Applications are processed on a rolling basis. Application fee: $25. *Expenses:* Tuition: Part-time $450 per semester hour. *Financial support:* Tuition waivers (partial) available. Support available to part-time students. Financial award application deadline: 6/30. *Faculty research:* Self-care for students in counseling programs, spiritual experiences of adolescents, stages of faith development related to grief/loss, school counseling competencies, multicultural issues in counseling. *Unit head:* Dr. Brock M. Reiman, Director, 330-471-8404, Fax: 330-471-8343, E-mail: breiman@malone.edu. *Application contact:* David L. Kleffman, Assistant Director of Enrollment, 330-471-8447, Fax: 330-471-8343, E-mail: dkleffman@malone.edu.

Manhattan College, Graduate Division, School of Education, Program in Counseling, Riverdale, NY 10471. Offers counseling (Diploma); mental health counseling (MA); school counseling (MA). Part-time and evening/weekend programs available. *Degree requirements:* For master's, thesis, internship. *Entrance requirements:* For master's, minimum GPA of 3.0. *Faculty research:* Cognition, family counseling.

Marshall University, Academic Affairs Division, Graduate School of Education and Professional Development, Program in Counseling, Huntington, WV 25755. Offers MA, Ed S. *Accreditation:* NCATE. Part-time and evening/weekend programs available. *Faculty:* 7 full-time (4 women), 20 part-time/adjunct (9 women). *Students:* 133 full-time (108 women), 88 part-time (72 women); includes 13 minority (10 African Americans, 3 Hispanic Americans), 1 international. Average age 33. In 2009, 73 master's awarded. *Degree requirements:* For master's, thesis optional, comprehensive or oral assessment. *Entrance requirements:* For master's, GRE General Test, MAT. Application fee: $40. *Financial support:* Career-related internships or fieldwork, Federal Work-Study, tuition waivers (full), and unspecified assistantships available. Support available to part-time students. Financial award applicants required to submit FAFSA. *Unit head:* Dr. Michael Burton, Director, 304-746-1928, E-mail: mburton@marshall.edu. *Application contact:* Information Contact, 304-746-1900, Fax: 304-746-1902, E-mail: services@marshall.edu.

Marymount University, School of Education and Human Services, Program in School Counseling, Arlington, VA 22207-4299. Offers MA. *Accreditation:* ACA. Part-time programs available. *Students:* 23 full-time (21 women), 14 part-time (all women); includes 7 minority (2 African Americans, 1 American Indian/Alaska Native, 2 Asian Americans or Pacific Islanders, 2 Hispanic Americans). Average age 28. 37 applicants, 62% accepted, 15 enrolled. In 2009, 16 master's awarded. *Entrance requirements:* For master's, GRE, 2 letters of recommendation, interview, resume. Additional exam requirements/recommendations for international students: Required—TOEFL (minimum score 600 paper-based; 250 computer-based; 96 iBT), IELTS (minimum score 6.5). *Application deadline:* For fall admission, 1/15 for domestic and international students. Applications are processed on a rolling basis. Application fee: $40. Electronic applications accepted. *Expenses:* Tuition: Full-time $13,050; part-time $725 per credit hour. Required fees: $135; $7.50 per credit hour. *Financial support:* Research assistantships with full tuition reimbursements, career-related internships or fieldwork, Federal Work-Study, scholarships/grants, and unspecified assistantships available. Support available to part-time students. Financial award applicants required to submit FAFSA. *Unit head:* Dr. Michele Garofalo, Director, 703-284-3822, Fax: 703-284-5708, E-mail: michele.garofalo@marymount.edu. *Application contact:* Francesca Reed, Director, Graduate Admissions, 703-284-5901, Fax: 703-527-3815, E-mail: grad.admissions@marymount.edu.

Marywood University, Academic Affairs, Reap College of Education and Human Development, Department of Psychology and Counseling, Program in Counseling, Scranton, PA 18509-1598. Offers Post-Master's Certificate. *Students:* 1 (woman) part-time. Average age 52. *Entrance requirements:* Additional exam requirements/recommendations for international students: Required—TOEFL (minimum score 550 paper-based; 213 computer-based; 79 iBT). *Application deadline:* For fall admission, 4/1 for domestic students, 3/31 for international students; for spring admission, 11/1 for domestic students, 8/31 for international students. Applications are processed on a rolling basis. Application fee: $35. Electronic applications accepted. *Expenses:* Tuition: Part-time $715 per credit. Required fees: $270 per semester. Tuition and fees vary according to degree level, campus/location and program. *Financial support:* Career-related internships or fieldwork, scholarships/grants, and unspecified assistantships available. Support available to part-time students. Financial award application deadline: 6/30; financial award applicants required to submit FAFSA. *Application contact:* Tammy Manka, Assistant Director of Graduate Admissions, 866-279-9663, E-mail: tmanka@marywood.edu.

Marywood University, Academic Affairs, Reap College of Education and Human Development, Department of Psychology and Counseling, Program in Counselor Education–Elementary, Scranton, PA 18509-1598. Offers MS. *Students:* 5 full-time (all women), 6 part-time (5 women); includes 1 minority (Hispanic American). Average age 26. In 2009, 3 master's awarded. *Entrance requirements:* Additional exam requirements/recommendations for international students: Required—TOEFL (minimum score 550 paper-based; 213 computer-based; 79 iBT). *Application deadline:* For fall admission, 4/1 priority date for domestic students, 3/31 priority date for international students; for spring admission, 11/1 priority date for domestic students, 8/31 priority date for international students. Applications are processed on a rolling basis. Application fee: $35. Electronic applications accepted. *Expenses:* Tuition: Part-time $715 per credit. Required fees: $270 per semester. Tuition and fees vary according to degree level, campus/location and program. *Financial support:* Career-related internships or fieldwork, scholarships/grants, and unspecified assistantships available. Support available to part-time students. Financial award application deadline: 6/30; financial award applicants required to submit FAFSA. *Unit head:* Dr. John Lemoncelli, Director, 570-348-6211 Ext. 2317, E-mail: lemoncelli@marywood.edu. *Application contact:* Tammy Manka, Assistant Director of Graduate Admissions, 866-279-9663, E-mail: tmanka@marywood.edu.

Marywood University, Academic Affairs, Reap College of Education and Human Development, Department of Psychology and Counseling, Program in Counselor Education–Secondary, Scranton, PA 18509-1598. Offers MS. *Students:* 13 full-time (12 women), 11 part-time (10 women); includes 2 minority (1 African American, 1 Hispanic American). Average age 26. 11

Counselor Education

Marywood University *(continued)*

applicants, 91% accepted. In 2009, 4 master's awarded. *Entrance requirements:* Additional exam requirements/recommendations for international students: Required—TOEFL (minimum score 550 paper-based; 213 computer-based; 79 iBT). *Application deadline:* For fall admission, 4/1 priority date for domestic students, 3/31 priority date for international students; for spring admission, 11/1 priority date for domestic students, 8/31 priority date for international students. Applications are processed on a rolling basis. Application fee: $35. Electronic applications accepted. *Expenses:* Tuition: Part-time $715 per credit. Required fees: $270 per semester. Tuition and fees vary according to degree level, campus/location and program. *Financial support:* Career-related internships or fieldwork, scholarships/grants, and unspecified assistantships available. Support available to part-time students. Financial award application deadline: 6/30; financial award applicants required to submit FAFSA. *Unit head:* Dr. John Lemoncelli, Director, 570-348-6211 Ext. 2317, E-mail: lemoncelli@marywood.edu. *Application contact:* Tammy Manka, Assistant Director of Graduate Admissions, 866-279-9663, E-mail: tmanka@marywood.edu.

McDaniel College, Graduate and Professional Studies, Program in Guidance and Counseling, Westminster, MD 21157-4390. Offers MS. Part-time and evening/weekend programs available. *Degree requirements:* For master's, comprehensive exam, thesis optional, internship. *Entrance requirements:* For master's, GRE General Test, MAT, or NTE/PRAXIS I, letters of reference (3). Additional exam requirements/recommendations for international students: Required—TOEFL (minimum score 213 computer-based). *Expenses:* Tuition: Part-time $325 per credit hour.

McNeese State University, Doré School of Graduate Studies, Burton College of Education, Department of Teacher Education, Program in School Counseling, Lake Charles, LA 70609. Offers M Ed. *Accreditation:* NCATE. Evening/weekend programs available. *Faculty:* 2 full-time (both women). *Students:* 7 full-time (all women), 20 part-time (18 women); includes 7 minority (all African Americans). In 2009, 6 master's awarded. *Entrance requirements:* For master's, GRE, 18 hours in professional education. *Application deadline:* For fall admission, 5/15 priority date for domestic and international students; for spring admission, 10/15 priority date for domestic and international students. Applications are processed on a rolling basis. Application fee: $20 ($30 for international students). *Expenses:* Tuition, area resident: Full-time $2556. Tuition, state resident: full-time $2556. Required fees: $1031. Tuition and fees vary according to course load. *Financial support:* Application deadline: 5/1. *Unit head:* Dr. Royce Zant, Head, 337-475-5404, Fax: 337-475-5398, E-mail: rzant@mcneese.edu. *Application contact:* Dr. George F. Mead, Interim Dean of Dore' School of Graduate Studies, 337-475-5396, Fax: 337-475-5397, E-mail: admissions@mcneese.edu.

Mercy College, School of Education, Program in Applied Behavior Analysis, Dobbs Ferry, NY 10522-1189. Offers Post Master's Certificate. *Students:* 11 part-time (9 women); includes 2 African Americans, 1 Hispanic American. Average age 36. 16 applicants, 63% accepted, 3 enrolled. *Entrance requirements:* For degree, master's degree. Additional exam requirements/recommendations for international students: Required—TOEFL (minimum score 600 paper-based; 250 computer-based; 100 iBT). *Application deadline:* For fall admission, 8/1 for international students. Applications are processed on a rolling basis. Application fee: $40. Electronic applications accepted. *Expenses:* Tuition: Full-time $13,158; part-time $731 per credit. Required fees: $500. Tuition and fees vary according to degree level and program. *Unit head:* Dr. Andrew Peiser, Chairperson, 914-674-7489, Fax: 914-674-7352, E-mail: apeiser@mercy.edu. *Application contact:* Mary Ellen Hoffman, Director, Graduate Education Programs, 914-674-7334, E-mail: mhoffman@mercy.edu.

Mercy College, School of Social and Behavioral Sciences, Dobbs Ferry, NY 10522-1189. Offers counseling (MS, Certificate), including alcohol and substance abuse counseling (Certificate), counseling (MS), family counseling (Certificate); health services management (MPA, MS); marriage and family therapy (MS); mental health counseling (MS); psychology (MS); school counseling (Certificate); school counseling and bilingual extension (Certificate); school psychology (MS). Part-time and evening/weekend programs available. Postbaccalaureate distance learning degree programs offered (minimal on-campus study). *Faculty:* 12 full-time (7 women), 38 part-time/adjunct (25 women). *Students:* 262 full-time (230 women), 379 part-time (323 women); includes 386 minority (171 African Americans, 6 American Indian/Alaska Native, 17 Asian Americans or Pacific Islanders, 192 Hispanic Americans), 9 international. Average age 35. 550 applicants, 43% accepted, 164 enrolled. In 2009, 162 master's, 14 other advanced degrees awarded. *Entrance requirements:* For master's, 2 letters of recommendation, interview, resume, essay. Additional exam requirements/recommendations for international students: Required—TOEFL (minimum score 600 paper-based; 250 computer-based; 100 iBT). *Application deadline:* For fall admission, 8/1 for international students. Applications are processed on a rolling basis. Application fee: $40. Electronic applications accepted. *Expenses:* Tuition: Full-time $13,158; part-time $731 per credit. Required fees: $500. Tuition and fees vary according to degree level and program. *Financial support:* In 2009–10, 1 student received support. Career-related internships or fieldwork, Federal Work-Study, scholarships/grants, and unspecified assistantships available. Support available to part-time students. Financial award applicants required to submit FAFSA. *Unit head:* Hind Rassam Culhane, Interim Dean, 914-674-7376, E-mail: hculhane@mercy.edu. *Application contact:* Hind Rassam Culhane, Interim Dean, 914-674-7376, E-mail: hculhane@mercy.edu.

Messiah College, Program in Counseling, Grantham, PA 17027. Offers counseling (CAGS); marriage, couple, and family counseling (MAC); mental health counseling (MAC); school counseling (MAC). Part-time programs available. *Entrance requirements:* For master's, minimum undergraduate cumulative GPA of 3.0, 2 recommendations, resume or curriculum vitae, interview; for CAGS, bachelor's degree, minimum undergraduate cumulative GPA of 3.0, essay, two recommendations, resume or curriculum vitae, interview. *Application deadline:* Applications are processed on a rolling basis. Application fee: $30. Electronic applications accepted. *Expenses:* Tuition: Part-time $518 per credit hour. *Financial support:* Applicants required to submit FAFSA. *Unit head:* Dr. John Addleman, Director, 717-796-1800 Ext. 2980, Fax: 717-691-2386, E-mail: jaddlemn@messiah.edu. *Application contact:* Dr. John Addleman, Director, 717-796-1800 Ext. 2980, Fax: 717-691-2386, E-mail: jaddlemn@messiah.edu.

Michigan State University, The Graduate School, College of Education, Department of Counseling, Educational Psychology and Special Education, East Lansing, MI 48824. Offers counseling (MA); educational psychology and educational technology (PhD); educational technology (MA); measurement and quantitative methods (PhD); rehabilitation counseling (MA); rehabilitation counselor education (PhD); school psychology (MA, PhD, Ed S); special education (MA, PhD). *Accreditation:* APA (one or more programs are accredited); CORE (one or more programs are accredited). Part-time programs available. *Faculty:* 35 full-time (13 women). *Students:* 217 full-time (154 women), 144 part-time (107 women); includes 48 minority (25 African Americans, 13 Asian Americans or Pacific Islanders, 10 Hispanic Americans), 71 international. Average age 32. 238 applicants, 46% accepted. In 2009, 117 master's, 36 doctorates awarded. *Entrance requirements:* Additional exam requirements/recommendations for international students: Required—TOEFL. Electronic applications accepted. *Expenses:* Tuition, state resident: part-time $478.25 per credit hour. Tuition, nonresident: part-time $966.50 per credit hour. Part-time tuition and fees vary according to program. *Financial support:* In 2009–10, 71 research assistantships with tuition reimbursements (averaging $6,836 per year), 74 teaching assistantships with tuition reimbursements (averaging $6,858 per year) were awarded. Total annual research expenditures: $2.3 million. *Unit head:* Dr. Richard S. Prawat, Chairperson, 517-353-6417, Fax: 517-353-6393, E-mail: rsprawat@msu.edu. *Application contact:* Kathy Dimoff, Graduate Admissions Coordinator, 517-355-6683, Fax: 517-353-6393, E-mail: dimoff@msu.edu.

Middle Tennessee State University, College of Graduate Studies, College of Education and Behavioral Science, Department of Psychology, Program in Professional Counseling, Murfreesboro, TN 37132. Offers curriculum and instruction (Ed S), including school psychology; mental health counseling (M Ed); school counseling (M Ed). *Accreditation:* ACA; NCATE. Part-time and evening/weekend programs available. Postbaccalaureate distance learning degree

programs offered. *Students:* 66 part-time (57 women); includes 6 minority (5 African Americans, 1 Asian American or Pacific Islander). 35 applicants, 69% accepted, 24 enrolled. In 2009, 27 master's, 7 Ed Ss awarded. *Degree requirements:* For master's, comprehensive exam. *Entrance requirements:* For master's, GRE or MAT. Additional exam requirements/recommendations for international students: Required—TOEFL (minimum score 525 paper-based; 195 computer-based; 71 iBT) or IELTS (minimum score 6). *Application deadline:* For fall admission, 6/1 for domestic and international students. Applications are processed on a rolling basis. Application fee: $25 ($30 for international students). Electronic applications accepted. *Expenses:* Tuition, state resident: full-time $4404. Tuition, nonresident: full-time $10,956. *Financial support:* Application deadline: 5/1. *Application contact:* Dr. Michael Allen, Dean and Vice Provost for Research, 615-898-2840, Fax: 615-904-8020, E-mail: mallen@mtsu.edu.

Midwestern State University, Graduate Studies, College of Education, Program in Counseling, Wichita Falls, TX 76308. Offers general counseling (MA); human resource development (MA); school counseling (M Ed); training and development (MA). Part-time and evening/weekend programs available. *Degree requirements:* For master's, comprehensive exam, thesis (for some programs). *Entrance requirements:* For master's, GRE General Test, MAT, or GMAT, valid teaching certificate (M Ed). Additional exam requirements/recommendations for international students: Required—TOEFL (minimum score 550 paper-based; 213 computer-based). Electronic applications accepted. *Expenses:* Tuition, state resident: full-time $1620; part-time $90 per credit hour. Tuition, nonresident: full-time $2160; part-time $120 per credit hour. International tuition: $7506 full-time. Required fees: $3068.80; $145.60 per credit hour. $179 per semester.

Minnesota State University Mankato, College of Graduate Studies, College of Education, Department of Counseling and Student Personnel, Mankato, MN 56001. Offers college student affairs (MS); counselor education and supervision (Ed D); marriage and family counseling (Certificate); professional community counseling (MS); professional school counseling (MS). *Accreditation:* ACA (one or more programs are accredited); NCATE. *Students:* 67 full-time (57 women), 41 part-time (32 women). *Degree requirements:* For master's, comprehensive exam, thesis or alternative. *Entrance requirements:* For master's, GRE General Test or MAT (if GPA less than 3.0 for last 2 years), minimum GPA of 3.0 during previous 2 years, 3 letters of reference. Additional exam requirements/recommendations for international students: Required—TOEFL. *Application deadline:* For fall admission, 1/15 priority date for domestic students. Applications are processed on a rolling basis. Application fee: $40. Electronic applications accepted. *Expenses:* Tuition, state resident: full-time $5364. Tuition, nonresident: full-time $8314. *Financial support:* Research assistantships with full tuition reimbursements, teaching assistantships with full tuition reimbursements, career-related internships or fieldwork, Federal Work-Study, institutionally sponsored loans, and unspecified assistantships available. Support available to part-time students. Financial award application deadline: 3/15; financial award applicants required to submit FAFSA. *Unit head:* Dr. Jacqueline Lewis, Chairperson, 507-389-5658. *Application contact:* 507-389-2321, E-mail: grad@mnsu.edu.

Minnesota State University Moorhead, Graduate Studies, College of Education and Human Services, Program in Counseling and Student Affairs, Moorhead, MN 56563-0002. Offers MS. *Accreditation:* ACA; NCATE. Part-time and evening/weekend programs available. *Degree requirements:* For master's, comprehensive exam, final oral exam, internship, project or thesis. *Entrance requirements:* For master's, GRE or MAT, interview, 3 letters of recommendation, minimum GPA of 3.0. Additional exam requirements/recommendations for international students: Required—TOEFL (minimum score 550 paper-based; 213 computer-based). Electronic applications accepted.

Mississippi College, Graduate School, School of Education, Department of Psychology and Counseling, Clinton, MS 39058. Offers counseling (Ed S); marriage and family counseling (MS); mental health counseling (MS); school counseling (M Ed). Part-time programs available. *Faculty:* 8 full-time (3 women), 5 part-time/adjunct (2 women). *Students:* 60 full-time (54 women), 70 part-time (63 women); includes 64 minority (63 African Americans, 1 American Indian/Alaska Native), 3 international. Average age 31. In 2009, 38 master's awarded. *Degree requirements:* For master's and Ed S, comprehensive exam, thesis optional. *Entrance requirements:* For master's, GRE or NTE. Additional exam requirements/recommendations for international students: Recommended—IELTS. *Application deadline:* For fall admission, 6/1 for domestic students; for spring admission, 9/1 for domestic students. Application fee: $30. Electronic applications accepted. *Expenses:* Tuition: Part-time $452 per credit hour. Required fees: $101 per semester. Tuition and fees vary according to degree level, campus/location, program and student level. *Financial support:* Career-related internships or fieldwork, Federal Work-Study, and unspecified assistantships available. Support available to part-time students. Financial award applicants required to submit FAFSA. *Unit head:* Dr. Buddy Wagner, Interim Chair, 601-925-3354, E-mail: bwagner@mc.edu. *Application contact:* Elnora Lewis, Secretary, 601-925-3225, Fax: 601-925-3889, E-mail: lewis09@mc.edu.

Mississippi State University, College of Education, Department of Counseling and Educational Psychology, Mississippi State, MS 39762. Offers college/postsecondary student counseling and personnel services (PhD); counselor education (MS); counselor education/student counseling and guidance services (PhD); education (Ed S), including counselor education, school psychology; educational psychology (MS, PhD). *Accreditation:* ACA (one or more programs are accredited); APA; CORE (one or more programs are accredited); NCATE. Part-time programs available. Postbaccalaureate distance learning degree programs offered (minimal on-campus study). *Faculty:* 14 full-time (10 women), 1 (woman) part-time/adjunct. *Students:* 116 full-time (95 women), 99 part-time (84 women); includes 63 minority (57 African Americans, 2 American Indian/Alaska Native, 2 Asian Americans or Pacific Islanders, 2 Hispanic Americans), 3 international. Average age 32. 154 applicants, 62% accepted, 69 enrolled. In 2009, 56 master's, 9 doctorates, 17 other advanced degrees awarded. Terminal master's awarded for partial completion of doctoral program. *Degree requirements:* For master's, comprehensive exam, thesis optional; for doctorate, thesis/dissertation, comprehensive oral and written exam. *Entrance requirements:* For master's, GRE, minimum QPA of 3.0; for doctorate, GRE, interview, minimum GPA of 3.4; for Ed S, GRE, MS in counseling or related field. Additional exam requirements/recommendations for international students: Required—TOEFL (minimum score 475 paper-based; 153 computer-based; 53 iBT); Recommended—IELTS (minimum score 4.5). *Application deadline:* For fall admission, 2/1 priority date for domestic and international students. Applications are processed on a rolling basis. Application fee: $40. Electronic applications accepted. *Expenses:* Tuition, state resident: full-time $2575.50; part-time $286.25 per credit hour. Tuition, nonresident: full-time $6510; part-time $723.50 per credit hour. Tuition and fees vary according to course load. *Financial support:* In 2009–10, 4 teaching assistantships with full tuition reimbursements (averaging $8,603 per year) were awarded; career-related internships or fieldwork, Federal Work-Study, institutionally sponsored loans, and unspecified assistantships also available. Financial award application deadline: 2/1; financial award applicants required to submit FAFSA. *Faculty research:* HIV-AIDS in college population, substance abuse in youth and college students, ADHD and conduct disorders in youth, assessment and identification of early childhood disabilities, assessment and vocational transition of the disabled. *Unit head:* Dr. Daniel Wong, Professor/Head, 662-325-7928, Fax: 662-325-3263, E-mail: dwong@colled.msstate.edu. *Application contact:* Dr. Tony Doggett, Associate Professor and Graduate Coordinator, 662-325-3312, Fax: 662-325-3263, E-mail: tdoggett@colled.msstate.edu.

Missouri Baptist University, Graduate Programs, St. Louis, MO 63141-8660. Offers business administration (MBA); Christian ministries (MACM); counseling (MAC); education (MSE); education administration (MEA); educational leadership (MSE, Ed S); teaching (MAT).

Missouri State University, Graduate College, College of Education, Department of Counseling, Leadership, and Special Education, Program in Counseling, Springfield, MO 65897. Offers counseling (MS), including community agency counseling, elementary school counseling, secondary school counseling. Part-time and evening/weekend programs available. *Students:* 47 full-time (36 women), 87 part-time (71 women); includes 3 minority (2 African Americans, 1 Hispanic American), 2 international. Average age 33. 11 applicants, 100% accepted, 11

enrolled. In 2009, 42 master's awarded. *Degree requirements:* For master's, comprehensive exam, thesis or alternative. *Entrance requirements:* For master's, GRE or MAT, minimum GPA of 2.75. Additional exam requirements/recommendations for international students: Required—TOEFL (minimum score 550 paper-based; 213 computer-based; 79 iBT). *Application deadline:* For fall admission, 2/1 priority date for domestic students, 1/1 priority date for international students; for spring admission, 10/1 priority date for domestic students, 9/1 priority date for international students. Application fee: $35 ($50 for international students). Electronic applications accepted. *Expenses:* Tuition, state resident: full-time $3852; part-time $214 per credit hour. Tuition, nonresident: full-time $7524; part-time $418 per credit hour. Required fees: $696; $172 per semester. Tuition and fees vary according to course level, course load, degree level and program. *Financial support:* In 2009–10, 2 teaching assistantships with full tuition reimbursements (averaging $7,340 per year) were awarded; Federal Work-Study, institutionally sponsored loans, scholarships/grants, and unspecified assistantships also available. Financial award application deadline: 3/31; financial award applicants required to submit FAFSA. *Unit head:* Dr. Tamara Arthaud, Acting Department Head, 417-836-5449, Fax: 417-836-4918, E-mail: clse@missouristate.edu. *Application contact:* Eric Eckert, Coordinator of Admissions and Recruitment, 417-836-5331, Fax: 417-836-6888, E-mail: ericeckert@missouristate.edu.

Montana State University, College of Graduate Studies, College of Education, Health, and Human Development, Department of Health and Human Development, Bozeman, MT 59717. Offers health and human development (MS), including counseling, exercise and nutrition sciences, family and consumer sciences, family financial planning, health promotion and education. *Accreditation:* ACA. Part-time programs available. Postbaccalaureate distance learning degree programs offered (no on-campus study). *Faculty:* 27 full-time (18 women), 7 part-time/adjunct (6 women). *Students:* 54 full-time (47 women), 18 part-time (15 women); includes 1 minority (Hispanic American). Average age 30. 32 applicants, 34% accepted, 10 enrolled. In 2009, 26 master's awarded. *Degree requirements:* For master's, comprehensive exam. *Entrance requirements:* For master's, GRE General Test. Additional exam requirements/recommendations for international students: Required—TOEFL (minimum score 550 paper-based; 213 computer-based). *Application deadline:* For fall admission, 7/15 priority date for domestic students, 5/15 priority date for international students; for spring admission, 12/1 priority date for domestic students, 10/1 priority date for international students. Applications are processed on a rolling basis. Application fee: $30. Electronic applications accepted. *Expenses:* Tuition, state resident: full-time $5635; part-time $3492 per year. Tuition, nonresident: full-time $17,212; part-time $7865.10 per year. Required fees: $1441; $153.15 per credit. Tuition and fees vary according to course load and program. *Financial support:* In 2009–10, 24 students received support, including 7 research assistantships (averaging $1,000 per year), 17 teaching assistantships with full tuition reimbursements available (averaging $8,000 per year). Financial award application deadline: 3/1; financial award applicants required to submit FAFSA. *Faculty research:* Gait analysis, cancer prevention, obesity prevention, energy expenditure, decision making. Total annual research expenditures: $2.8 million. *Unit head:* Dr. Tim Dunnagan, Head, 404-994-3242, Fax: 404-994-2013, E-mail: dunnagan@montana.edu. *Application contact:* Dr. Carl Fox.

Montana State University Billings, College of Education, Department of Special Education, Counseling, Reading and Early Childhood, Option in School Counseling, Billings, MT 59101-0298. Offers M Ed. *Accreditation:* NCATE. Part-time programs available. *Degree requirements:* For master's, thesis or professional paper and/or field experience. *Entrance requirements:* For master's, GRE General Test or MAT, minimum GPA of 3.0 (undergraduate), 3.25 (graduate).

Montana State University–Northern, College of Education and Graduate Programs, Option in Counselor Education, Havre, MT 59501-7751. Offers M Ed. Part-time and evening/weekend programs available. *Degree requirements:* For master's, comprehensive exam, thesis optional, oral exams. *Entrance requirements:* For master's, GRE General Test or MAT, minimum GPA of 3.0. Electronic applications accepted.

Montclair State University, The Graduate School, College of Education and Human Services, Department of Counseling, Human Development, and Educational Leadership, Montclair, NJ 07043-1624. Offers administration and supervision (MA), including administration and supervision, educator/trainer; advanced counseling (Certificate); counseling and guidance (MA), including addictions counseling, community counseling, student affairs; counselor education (PhD); principal (Certificate); school administrator (Certificate); school business administrator (Certificate); school counselor (Certificate); substance awareness coordinator (Certificate). *Accreditation:* NCATE. Part-time and evening/weekend programs available. *Faculty:* 17 full-time (12 women), 13 part-time/adjunct (7 women). *Students:* 161 full-time (126 women), 425 part-time (325 women). Average age 33. 269 applicants, 55% accepted, 125 enrolled. In 2009, 91 master's awarded. *Degree requirements:* For master's, comprehensive exam, thesis or alternative; for doctorate, comprehensive exam, thesis/dissertation. *Entrance requirements:* For master's, GRE General Test, interview, 2 letters of recommendation; for doctorate, GRE General Test, interview, 3 letters of recommendation. Additional exam requirements/recommendations for international students: Required—TOEFL (minimum score 83 computer-based), or IELTS. *Application deadline:* For fall admission, 6/1 for international students; for spring admission, 10/1 for international students. Applications are processed on a rolling basis. Application fee: $60. Electronic applications accepted. *Expenses:* Tuition, area resident: Part-time $486.74 per credit. Tuition, state resident: part-time $486.74 per credit. Tuition, nonresident: part-time $751.34 per credit. Tuition and fees vary according to degree level and program. *Financial support:* In 2009–10, 28 research assistantships with full tuition reimbursements (averaging $7,000 per year), 2 teaching assistantships (averaging $15,000 per year) were awarded; Federal Work-Study, scholarships/grants, and unspecified assistantships also available. Support available to part-time students. Financial award application deadline: 3/1; financial award applicants required to submit FAFSA. *Faculty research:* K-12 education, data collection. *Unit head:* Dr. Larry Burlew, Chairperson, 973-655-7611. *Application contact:* Amy Aiello, Director of Graduate Admissions and Operations, 973-655-5147, Fax: 973-655-7869, E-mail: graduate.school@montclair.edu.

Morehead State University, Graduate Programs, College of Education, Department of Foundational and Graduate Studies in Education, Morehead, KY 40351. Offers adult and higher education (MA, Ed S); certified professional counselor (Ed S); counseling P-12 (MA); curriculum and instruction (Ed S); educational technology (MA Ed); instructional leadership (Ed S); school administration (MA); school counseling (Ed S); teacher leader business and marketing- content (MA Ed); teacher leader business and marketing- technology (MA Ed); teacher leader educational technology (MA Ed); teacher leader English (MA Ed); teacher leader gifted educ (MA Ed); teacher leader IECE—non-certification (MA Ed); teacher leader IECE certification (MA Ed); teacher leader interdisciplanary educaction P-5 (MA Ed); teacher leader middle grades 5-9 (MA Ed); teacher leader reading/writing—non-certification (MA Ed); teacher leader reading/writing certification (MA Ed); teacher leader school communication—non-certification (MA Ed); teacher leader school communication certification (MA Ed); teacher leader social studies (MA Ed); teacher leader special education (MA Ed). *Accreditation:* NCATE. Part-time and evening/weekend programs available. *Faculty:* 20 full-time (10 women), 7 part-time/adjunct (3 women). *Students:* 26 full-time (18 women), 371 part-time (295 women); includes 11 minority (9 African Americans, 1 American Indian/Alaska Native, 1 Hispanic American). Average age 35. 201 applicants, 73% accepted, 73 enrolled. In 2009, 105 master's, 5 other advanced degrees awarded. *Degree requirements:* For master's, thesis optional, oral and/or written comprehensive exams; for Ed S, thesis, oral exam. *Entrance requirements:* For master's, GRE General Test, minimum overall undergraduate GPA of 2.5; for Ed S, GRE General Test, interview, master's degree, minimum GPA of 3.5, work experience. Additional exam requirements/recommendations for international students: Required—TOEFL (minimum score 500 paper-based; 173 computer-based). *Application deadline:* For fall admission, 8/1 priority date for domestic and international students; for spring admission, 12/1 priority date for domestic and international students. Applications are processed on a rolling basis. Application fee: $30. Electronic applications accepted. *Expenses:* Tuition, state resident: full-time $6318; part-time $351 per credit hour. Tuition, nonresident: full-time $15,804; part-time $878 per credit hour. *Financial support:* In 2009–10, 2 research assistantships (averaging $10,000 per year)

were awarded; career-related internships or fieldwork, Federal Work-Study, and unspecified assistantships also available. Financial award application deadline: 3/15; financial award applicants required to submit FAFSA. *Faculty research:* Character education, school accountability, computer applications for school administrators. *Unit head:* Dr. Cathy Gunn, Dean and Professor, 606-783-2040, Fax: 606-783-5029, E-mail: c.gunn@moreheadstate.edu. *Application contact:* Michelle Barber, Graduate Recruitment and Retention Assistant Director, 606-783-5127, Fax: 606-783-5061, E-mail: m.barber@moreheadstate.edu.

Mount Mary College, Graduate Programs, Program in Community Counseling, Milwaukee, WI 53222-4597. Offers community counseling (MS); pastoral counseling (MS); school counseling (MS). Part-time and evening/weekend programs available. *Faculty:* 2 full-time (both women), 8 part-time/adjunct (4 women). *Students:* 69 full-time (68 women), 23 part-time (all women); includes 25 minority (21 African Americans, 1 American Indian/Alaska Native, 3 Hispanic Americans). Average age 34. 68 applicants, 56% accepted, 28 enrolled. In 2009, 20 master's awarded. *Degree requirements:* For master's, comprehensive exam, thesis or alternative. *Entrance requirements:* For master's, minimum GPA of 3.0. Additional exam requirements/recommendations for international students: Required—TOEFL (minimum score 500 paper-based; 173 computer-based). *Application deadline:* For fall admission, 8/1 priority date for domestic and international students; for spring admission, 12/1 priority date for domestic and international students. Application fee: $35 ($100 for international students). *Expenses:* Tuition: Part-time $595 per credit. Tuition and fees vary according to program. *Financial support:* Career-related internships or fieldwork and Federal Work-Study available. Support available to part-time students. Financial award application deadline: 5/1; financial award applicants required to submit FAFSA. *Faculty research:* Cognitive behavioral interventions for depression, eating disorders and compliance. *Unit head:* Carrie King, Graduate Program Director, 414-258-4810 Ext. 318, E-mail: kingc@mtmary.edu. *Application contact:* Carrie King, Graduate Program Director, 414-258-4810 Ext. 318, E-mail: kingc@mtmary.edu.

Multnomah University, Multnomah Bible College Graduate Degree Programs, Portland, OR 97220-5898. Offers counseling (MA); teaching (MA); TESOL (MA). *Faculty:* 3 full-time (all women), 26 part-time/adjunct (16 women). *Students:* 45 full-time (30 women), 22 part-time (13 women); includes 10 minority (1 African American, 1 American Indian/Alaska Native, 5 Asian Americans or Pacific Islanders, 3 Hispanic Americans), 1 international. Average age 35. 56 applicants, 42 enrolled. *Degree requirements:* For master's, thesis optional. *Entrance requirements:* Additional exam requirements/recommendations for international students: Required—TOEFL (minimum score 550 paper-based; 213 computer-based). *Application deadline:* For fall admission, 7/15 for domestic and international students; for spring admission, 11/15 for domestic and international students. *Expenses:* Tuition: Full-time $10,464; part-time $436 per credit hour. *Financial support:* In 2009–10, 61 students received support. Career-related internships or fieldwork and scholarships/grants available. Support available to part-time students. Financial award application deadline: 7/1; financial award applicants required to submit FAFSA. *Unit head:* Dr. Wayne Strickland, Academic Dean, 503-251-6401. *Application contact:* Penny Rader, Seminary Admissions Counselor, 503-251-6485, Fax: 503-254-1268, E-mail: admiss@multnomah.edu.

Murray State University, College of Education, Department of Educational Studies, Leadership and Counseling, Program in Community and Agency Counseling, Murray, KY 42071. Offers Ed S. *Accreditation:* NCATE. Part-time programs available. *Degree requirements:* For Ed S, comprehensive exam, thesis. *Entrance requirements:* For degree, GRE General Test. Additional exam requirements/recommendations for international students: Required—TOEFL.

Murray State University, College of Education, Department of Educational Studies, Leadership and Counseling, Programs in School Guidance and Counseling, Murray, KY 42071. Offers MA Ed, Ed S. *Accreditation:* NCATE. Part-time programs available. *Degree requirements:* For master's, comprehensive exam, thesis (for some programs), portfolio; for Ed S, comprehensive exam, portfolio. *Entrance requirements:* For master's, GRE General Test or MAT. Additional exam requirements/recommendations for international students: Required—TOEFL.

Naropa University, Graduate Programs, Program in Transpersonal Counseling Psychology, Concentration in Counseling Psychology, Boulder, CO 80302-6697. Offers MA. *Degree requirements:* For master's, internships. *Entrance requirements:* For master's, in-person interview; course work in psychology, resume, 3 letters of recommendation. Additional exam requirements/recommendations for international students: Required—TOEFL (minimum score 600 paper-based; 250 computer-based). Electronic applications accepted.

National-Louis University, College of Arts and Sciences, Department of Counseling and Human Services, Chicago, IL 60603. Offers community counseling (MS); school counseling (MS). Part-time programs available. *Degree requirements:* For master's, internship. *Entrance requirements:* For master's, GRE General Test, MAT, or Watson-Glaser Critical Thinking Appraisal, interview, minimum GPA of 3.0. *Expenses:* Tuition: Full-time $17,160; part-time $715 per semester hour. Tuition and fees vary according to course load, degree level, campus/location and program. *Faculty research:* Religion and aging, drug abuse prevention, hunger, homelessness, multicultural diversity.

National University, Academic Affairs, School of Education, Department of School Counseling and Psychology, La Jolla, CA 92037-1011. Offers educational counseling (MS); school psychology (MS). Part-time and evening/weekend programs available. Postbaccalaureate distance learning degree programs offered (no on-campus study). *Faculty:* 12 full-time (5 women), 82 part-time/adjunct (49 women). *Students:* 657 full-time (529 women), 565 part-time (451 women); includes 556 minority (131 African Americans, 6 American Indian/Alaska Native, 89 Asian Americans or Pacific Islanders, 330 Hispanic Americans), 1 international. Average age 34. 566 applicants, 100% accepted, 366 enrolled. In 2009, 121 master's awarded. *Degree requirements:* For master's, thesis (for some programs). *Entrance requirements:* For master's, interview, minimum GPA of 2.5. Additional exam requirements/recommendations for international students: Required—TOEFL (minimum score 550 paper-based; 213 computer-based; 79 iBT), IELTS (minimum score 6). *Application deadline:* Applications are processed on a rolling basis. Application fee: $60 ($65 for international students). Electronic applications accepted. *Expenses:* Tuition: Part-time $338 per quarter hour. *Financial support:* Career-related internships or fieldwork, institutionally sponsored loans, scholarships/grants, and tuition waivers (partial) available. Support available to part-time students. Financial award application deadline: 6/30; financial award applicants required to submit FAFSA. *Unit head:* Dr. Susan Eldred, Chair, 858-642-8372, Fax: 858-642-8724, E-mail: seldred@nu.edu. *Application contact:* Dominick Giovanniello, Associate Regional Dean—San Diego, 800-NAT-UNIV, Fax: 858-541-7792, E-mail: dgiovann@nu.edu.

New Mexico Highlands University, Graduate Studies, School of Education, Las Vegas, NM 87701. Offers curriculum and instruction (MA); education (MA), including counseling, school counseling; educational leadership (MA); exercise and sport sciences (MA), including human performance and sport, sports administration, teacher education; guidance and counseling (MA), including professional counseling, rehabilitation counseling, school counseling; special education (MA), including). Part-time programs available. *Degree requirements:* For master's, comprehensive exam, thesis or alternative. *Entrance requirements:* For master's, minimum undergraduate GPA of 3.0. Additional exam requirements/recommendations for international students: Required—TOEFL (minimum score 540 paper-based; 207 computer-based). *Faculty research:* Teaching the United States Constitution, middle school curriculum, integrated computer applications for pre-service classroom teachers, adolescent literacy, narrative cognitive modes in NM multicultural setting.

New Mexico State University, Graduate School, College of Education, Department of Counseling and Educational Psychology, Las Cruces, NM 88003-8001. Offers counseling and guidance (MA); counseling psychology (PhD); school psychology (Ed S). *Accreditation:* ACA; APA (one or more programs are accredited); NCATE. Part-time programs available. *Faculty:* 12 full-time (8 women), 4 part-time/adjunct (2 women). *Students:* 70 full-time (52 women), 34 part-time (27 women); includes 52 minority (3 African Americans, 2 American Indian/Alaska Native, 1 Asian American or Pacific Islander, 46 Hispanic Americans), 2 international. Average

Counselor Education

New Mexico State University *(continued)*
age 32. 111 applicants, 88% accepted, 35 enrolled. In 2009, 13 master's, 3 doctorates, 5 other advanced degrees awarded. *Degree requirements:* For master's, comprehensive exam, thesis optional, internship; for doctorate, comprehensive exam, thesis/dissertation, internship; for Ed S, thesis or alternative, internship. *Entrance requirements:* For master's, doctorate, and Ed S, GRE General Test, minimum GPA of 3.0. *Application deadline:* For fall admission, 12/15 for domestic students; for spring admission, 4/1 priority date for domestic students. Application fee: $30 ($50 for international students). Electronic applications accepted. *Expenses:* Tuition, state resident: full-time $4080; part-time $223 per credit. Tuition, nonresident: full-time $14,256; part-time $647 per credit. Required fees: $1278; $639 per semester. *Financial support:* In 2009–10, 13 research assistantships with partial tuition reimbursements (averaging $8,108 per year), 32 teaching assistantships with partial tuition reimbursements (averaging $8,239 per year) were awarded; fellowships with partial tuition reimbursements, career-related internships or fieldwork, Federal Work-Study, institutionally sponsored loans, scholarships/grants, traineeships, health care benefits, and unspecified assistantships also available. Support available to part-time students. Financial award application deadline: 4/1. *Faculty research:* Multicultural counseling, integrative health psychology group, career development school counseling. *Unit head:* Dr. Michael Waldo, Head, 575-646-2121, Fax: 575-646-8035, E-mail: miwaldo@nmsu.edu. *Application contact:* Elena Luna, Coordinator, 575-646-3498, Fax: 575-646-7721, E-mail: rosluna@nmsu.edu.

New York Institute of Technology, Graduate Division, School of Education, Program in School Counseling, Old Westbury, NY 11568-8000. Offers MS. *Students:* 83 part-time (66 women); includes 18 minority (10 African Americans, 6 Asian Americans or Pacific Islanders, 2 Hispanic Americans), 2 international. Average age 33. In 2009, 22 master's awarded. *Degree requirements:* For master's, internship. *Entrance requirements:* For master's, minimum GPA of 3.0, interview, 3 letters of reference. Additional exam requirements/recommendations for international students: Required—TOEFL (minimum score 550 paper-based; 213 computer-based). *Application deadline:* For fall admission, 7/1 priority date for domestic students; for spring admission, 12/1 priority date for domestic students. Applications are processed on a rolling basis. Application fee: $50. Electronic applications accepted. *Expenses:* Tuition: Part-time $825 per credit. *Financial support:* Research assistantships available. *Unit head:* Dr. Carol Dahir, Coordinator, 516-686-7616, Fax: 516-686-7655, E-mail: cdahir@nyit.edu. *Application contact:* Dr. Jacquelyn Nealon, Vice President for Enrollment Services, 516-686-7925, Fax: 516-686-7597, E-mail: jnealon@nyit.edu.

New York University, Steinhardt School of Culture, Education, and Human Development, Department of Applied Psychology, Program in Counselor Education, New York, NY 10012-1019. Offers counseling and guidance (MA, Advanced Certificate), including bilingual school counseling (MA), school counseling (MA); counseling for mental health and wellness (MA); counseling psychology (PhD). *Accreditation:* APA (one or more programs are accredited). Part-time programs available. *Students:* 123 full-time (89 women), 77 part-time (60 women); includes 72 minority (24 African Americans, 1 American Indian/Alaska Native, 24 Asian Americans or Pacific Islanders, 23 Hispanic Americans), 20 international. Average age 30. 769 applicants, 27% accepted, 80 enrolled. In 2009, 80 master's, 6 doctorates awarded. *Degree requirements:* For master's, thesis (for some programs); for doctorate, thesis/dissertation. *Entrance requirements:* For doctorate, GRE General Test, interview. Additional exam requirements/recommendations for international students: Required—TOEFL. *Application deadline:* For fall admission, 12/15 priority date for domestic and international students. Applications are processed on a rolling basis. Application fee: $75. Electronic applications accepted. *Expenses:* Tuition: Full-time $30,528; part-time $1272 per credit. Required fees: $2177. *Financial support:* Fellowships with full and partial tuition reimbursements, research assistantships, teaching assistantships with partial tuition reimbursements, career-related internships or fieldwork, Federal Work-Study, institutionally sponsored loans, scholarships/grants, tuition waivers (partial), and unspecified assistantships available. Support available to part-time students. Financial award application deadline: 2/1; financial award applicants required to submit FAFSA. *Faculty research:* Cross-cultural counseling; group dynamics; culture, race and ethnicity; religiosity and psychological development; well-being and mental health. *Application contact:* 212-998-5030, Fax: 212-995-4328, E-mail: steinhardt.gradadmissions@nyu.edu.

Niagara University, Graduate Division of Education, Concentration in Mental Health Counseling, Niagara Falls, Niagara University, NY 14109. Offers MS, Certificate. *Entrance requirements:* For master's, GRE General Test or MAT. *Expenses:* Contact institution.

Niagara University, Graduate Division of Education, Concentration in School Counseling, Niagara Falls, Niagara University, NY 14109. Offers MS Ed, Certificate. *Accreditation:* NCATE. Part-time and evening/weekend programs available. *Entrance requirements:* For master's, GRE General Test or MAT; for Certificate, GRE General Test, GRE Subject Test or MAT. *Expenses:* Contact institution.

Nicholls State University, Graduate Studies, College of Education, Department of Teacher Education, Thibodaux, LA 70310. Offers administration and supervision (M Ed); counselor education (M Ed); curriculum and instruction (M Ed). *Accreditation:* NCATE. Part-time and evening/weekend programs available. *Degree requirements:* For master's, comprehensive exam, portfolio. *Entrance requirements:* For master's, GRE General Test, teaching license. Electronic applications accepted.

North Carolina Agricultural and Technical State University, Graduate School, School of Education, Department of Human Development and Services, Greensboro, NC 27411. Offers adult education (MS); counselor education (MS); human resources-agency counseling (MS); human resources-rehabilitation counseling (MS); leadership studies (PhD); school administration (MS). *Accreditation:* ACA. Part-time and evening/weekend programs available. *Degree requirements:* For master's, comprehensive exam, thesis, qualifying exam. *Entrance requirements:* For master's, GRE General Test, minimum GPA of 3.0.

North Carolina Central University, Division of Academic Affairs, School of Education, Department of Counselor Education, Durham, NC 27707-3129. Offers career counseling (MA); community agency counseling (MA); school counseling (MA). *Accreditation:* ACA; NCATE. Part-time and evening/weekend programs available. *Degree requirements:* For master's, comprehensive exam, thesis or alternative. *Entrance requirements:* For master's, GRE, minimum GPA of 3.0 in major, 2.5 overall. Additional exam requirements/recommendations for international students: Required—TOEFL. *Faculty research:* Becoming a leader, skill building in academia.

North Carolina State University, Graduate School, College of Education, Department of Curriculum and Instruction, Program in Counselor Education, Raleigh, NC 27695. Offers M Ed, MS, PhD. *Accreditation:* ACA. *Degree requirements:* For master's, thesis (for some programs). *Entrance requirements:* For master's, GRE or MAT. Electronic applications accepted. *Faculty research:* Career development, retention of at-risk students in higher education, psychosocial development, multicultural issues, cognitive-developmental interventions.

North Dakota State University, College of Graduate and Interdisciplinary Studies, College of Human Development and Education, School of Education, Program in Counseling, Fargo, ND 58108. Offers M Ed, MS, PhD. *Accreditation:* ACA; NCATE. Part-time programs available. Postbaccalaureate distance learning degree programs offered (minimal on-campus study). *Faculty:* 5 full-time (3 women), 1 (woman) part-time/adjunct. *Students:* 31 full-time (30 women), 14 part-time (13 women); includes 1 minority (African American), 3 international. Average age 35. 35 applicants, 54% accepted, 19 enrolled. In 2009, 23 master's awarded. *Degree requirements:* For master's, comprehensive exam, thesis or alternative; for doctorate, comprehensive exam, thesis/dissertation. *Entrance requirements:* For master's, GRE, MAT, interview. Additional exam requirements/recommendations for international students: Required—TOEFL. *Application deadline:* For fall admission, 2/15 for domestic students. Applications are processed on a rolling basis. Application fee: $45 ($60 for international students). *Financial support:* Teaching assistantships, career-related internships or fieldwork, Federal Work-Study, institutionally sponsored loans, and tuition waivers (full) available. Financial award application

deadline: 4/15. *Faculty research:* Supervision, program assessment, multicultural issues. *Unit head:* Dr. Robert Nielsen, Coordinator, 701-231-7202, Fax: 701-231-7416, E-mail: robert.nielsen@ndsu.edu. *Application contact:* Dr. Robert Nielsen, Coordinator, 701-231-7202, Fax: 701-231-7416, E-mail: robert.nielsen@ndsu.edu.

Northeastern Illinois University, Graduate College, College of Education, Department of Counselor Education, Chicago, IL 60625-4699. Offers guidance and counseling (MA), including career development, community and family counseling, elementary school counseling, secondary school counseling. *Accreditation:* ACA. Part-time and evening/weekend programs available. *Degree requirements:* For master's, comprehensive exam, thesis or alternative, internship, practicum. *Entrance requirements:* For master's, GRE, minimum GPA of 2.75, workshop. Additional exam requirements/recommendations for international students: Required—TOEFL (minimum score 550 paper-based; 213 computer-based; 80 iBT). Electronic applications accepted. *Faculty research:* Psychological factors of the visually impaired, reclaiming self through art, ego development, multicultural counseling, family therapy.

Northeastern State University, Graduate College, College of Education, Department of Psychology and Counseling, Program in School Counseling, Tahlequah, OK 74464-2399. Offers M Ed. Part-time and evening/weekend programs available. *Degree requirements:* For master's, thesis or alternative, innovative project or research paper, written and oral exams. *Entrance requirements:* For master's, MAT or GRE, minimum GPA of 2.5. Additional exam requirements/recommendations for international students: Required—TOEFL (minimum score 213 computer-based). Electronic applications accepted.

Northeastern University, Bouvé College of Health Sciences Graduate School, Department of Counseling and Applied Educational Psychology, Program in College Student Development and Counseling, Boston, MA 02115-5096. Offers MS, CAGS. Part-time and evening/weekend programs available. *Faculty:* 1 (woman) full-time, 4 part-time/adjunct (all women). *Students:* 35 full-time (29 women), 4 part-time (all women); includes 6 minority (3 African Americans, 2 Asian Americans or Pacific Islanders, 1 Hispanic American). 71 applicants, 72% accepted, 25 enrolled. In 2009, 17 master's awarded. *Entrance requirements:* For master's, GRE General Test or MAT. Additional exam requirements/recommendations for international students: Required—TOEFL (minimum score 100 iBT). *Application deadline:* For fall admission, 8/1 for domestic students; for spring admission, 12/1 for domestic students. Applications are processed on a rolling basis. Application fee: $50. Electronic applications accepted. *Financial support:* Career-related internships or fieldwork, Federal Work-Study, scholarships/grants, tuition waivers (partial), and unspecified assistantships available. Support available to part-time students. Financial award application deadline: 3/1; financial award applicants required to submit FAFSA. *Unit head:* Prof. Vanessa Johnson, Director, 617-373-4634, E-mail: v.johnson@neu.edu. *Application contact:* Margaret Schnabel, Director of Graduate Admissions, 617-373-2708, E-mail: bouvegrad@neu.edu.

Northern Arizona University, Graduate College, College of Education, Department of Educational Psychology, Flagstaff, AZ 86011. Offers counseling (MA); educational psychology (PhD), including counseling psychology, learning and instruction, school psychology; human relations (M Ed); school counseling (M Ed); school psychology (MA, Certificate); student affairs (M Ed). Part-time programs available. Postbaccalaureate distance learning degree programs offered. *Faculty:* 20 full-time (10 women). *Students:* 200 full-time (151 women), 241 part-time (189 women); includes 165 minority (28 African Americans, 21 American Indian/Alaska Native, 7 Asian Americans or Pacific Islanders, 109 Hispanic Americans), 1 international. In 2009, 167 master's, 7 doctorates awarded. Terminal master's awarded for partial completion of doctoral program. *Median time to degree:* Of those who began their doctoral program in fall 2001, 75% received their degree in 8 years or less. *Degree requirements:* For master's, internship (for some programs); for doctorate, comprehensive exam, thesis/dissertation, internship. *Entrance requirements:* Additional exam requirements/recommendations for international students: Required—TOEFL (minimum score 550 paper-based; 213 computer-based; 80 iBT), IELTS (minimum score 7), or a bachelor's degree from an English-speaking university and demonstrated proficiency. *Application deadline:* For fall admission, 9/15 for domestic students; for spring admission, 1/15 for domestic students. Application fee: $65. Electronic applications accepted. *Financial support:* In 2009–10, 20 students received support, including 2 research assistantships with partial tuition reimbursements available, 12 teaching assistantships with partial tuition reimbursements available; career-related internships or fieldwork, Federal Work-Study, scholarships/grants, health care benefits, tuition waivers (full and partial), and unspecified assistantships also available. Support available to part-time students. Financial award applicants required to submit FAFSA. *Unit head:* Dr. Kathy Bohan, Chair, 928-523-0362, E-mail: kathy.bohan@nau.edu. *Application contact:* Shirley Robinson, Director of Graduate Admissions, 928-523-4348, Fax: 928-523-8950, E-mail: graduate.college@nau.edu.

Northern Illinois University, Graduate School, College of Education, Department of Counseling, Adult and Higher Education, De Kalb, IL 60115-2854. Offers adult and higher education (MS Ed, Ed D); counseling (MS Ed, Ed D). *Accreditation:* ACA. Part-time and evening/weekend programs available. *Faculty:* 19 full-time (11 women), 2 part-time/adjunct (1 woman). *Students:* 119 full-time (80 women), 280 part-time (198 women); includes 126 minority (93 African Americans, 4 American Indian/Alaska Native, 8 Asian Americans or Pacific Islanders, 21 Hispanic Americans), 18 international. Average age 38. 118 applicants, 53% accepted, 45 enrolled. In 2009, 76 master's, 12 doctorates awarded. Terminal master's awarded for partial completion of doctoral program. *Degree requirements:* For master's, comprehensive exam, thesis optional; for doctorate, thesis/dissertation, candidacy exam, dissertation defense. *Entrance requirements:* For master's, GRE General Test or MAT, minimum undergraduate GPA of 2.75, interview (counseling); for doctorate, GRE General Test, minimum undergraduate GPA of 2.75, 3.2 graduate, interview (counseling). Additional exam requirements/recommendations for international students: Required—TOEFL (minimum score 550 paper-based; 213 computer-based). *Application deadline:* For fall admission, 6/1 for domestic students, 5/1 for international students; for spring admission, 11/1 for domestic students, 10/1 for international students. Applications are processed on a rolling basis. Application fee: $30. Electronic applications accepted. *Expenses:* Tuition, state resident: full-time $6576; part-time $274 per credit hour. Tuition, nonresident: full-time $13,152; part-time $548 per credit hour. Required fees: $1813; $75.53 per credit hour. Part-time tuition and fees vary according to course load. *Financial support:* In 2009–10, 1 teaching assistantship with full tuition reimbursement was awarded; fellowships with full tuition reimbursements, research assistantships with full tuition reimbursements, career-related internships or fieldwork, Federal Work-Study, scholarships/grants, tuition waivers (full), and staff assistantships also available. Support available to part-time students. Financial award applicants required to submit FAFSA. *Unit head:* Dr. Barbara Johnson, Interim Chair, 815-753-1448, E-mail: cahe@niu.edu. *Application contact:* Graduate School Office, 815-753-0395, E-mail: gradsch@niu.edu.

Northern Kentucky University, Office of Graduate Programs, College of Education and Human Services, Program in School Counseling, Highland Heights, KY 41099. Offers MA. Part-time and evening/weekend programs available. *Students:* 14 full-time (all women), 24 part-time (22 women), 1 international. Average age 29. 29 applicants, 59% accepted, 16 enrolled. In 2009, 26 master's awarded. *Degree requirements:* For master's, portfolio, practicum, internship. *Entrance requirements:* For master's, GRE, interview, 3 letters of recommendation, minimum GPA of 2.75, criminal background check (state and federal). Additional exam requirements/recommendations for international students: Required—TOEFL (minimum score 550 paper-based; 213 computer-based; 79 iBT); Recommended—IELTS (minimum score 6.5). *Application deadline:* For fall admission, 8/1 priority date for domestic students, 6/1 priority date for international students; for spring admission, 12/1 priority date for domestic students, 10/1 priority date for international students. Applications are processed on a rolling basis. Application fee: $40. Electronic applications accepted. *Expenses:* Tuition, state resident: full-time $6912; part-time $384 per credit hour. Tuition, nonresident: full-time $12,150; part-time $675 per credit hour. Tuition and fees vary according to course load, program and reciprocity agreements. *Financial support:* Unspecified assistantships available. Financial award applicants required to submit FAFSA. *Unit head:* Dr. Rochelle Dunn, Program Coordinator, 859-572-

1920, Fax: 859-572-6592, E-mail: dunnrl@nku.edu. *Application contact:* Dr. Peg Griffin, Director of Graduate Programs, 859-572-6934, Fax: 859-572-6670, E-mail: griffinp@nku.edu.

Northern Michigan University, College of Graduate Studies, College of Professional Studies, School of Education, Program in School Guidance Counseling, Marquette, MI 49855-5301. Offers MA Ed.

Northern State University, Division of Graduate Studies in Education, Program in Guidance and Counseling, Aberdeen, SD 57401-7198. Offers MS Ed. *Accreditation:* NCATE. Part-time and evening/weekend programs available. *Faculty:* 3 full-time (all women). *Students:* 15 full-time (10 women), 30 part-time (26 women); includes 2 minority (both American Indian/Alaska Native). Average age 32. In 2009, 22 master's awarded. *Degree requirements:* For master's, thesis optional. *Entrance requirements:* For master's, minimum GPA of 2.75. Additional exam requirements/recommendations for international students: Required—TOEFL (minimum score 550 paper-based; 213 computer-based; 78 iBT). *Application deadline:* For fall admission, 8/15 priority date for domestic students; for spring admission, 12/15 for domestic students. Applications are processed on a rolling basis. Application fee: $35. Electronic applications accepted. *Financial support:* In 2009–10, 7 teaching assistantships with partial tuition reimbursements (averaging $5,558 per year) were awarded; career-related internships or fieldwork, Federal Work-Study, institutionally sponsored loans, scholarships/grants, and unspecified assistantships also available. Support available to part-time students. Financial award application deadline: 3/1; financial award applicants required to submit FAFSA. *Unit head:* Dr. Robin Rosenthal, Head, 605-626-2558, Fax: 605-626-7190, E-mail: rrosenthal@northern.edu. *Application contact:* Tammy K. Griffith, Program Assistant, 605-626-2558, Fax: 605-626-7190, E-mail: griffith@northern.edu.

Northwest Christian University, School of Education and Counseling, Eugene, OR 97401-3745. Offers community counseling (MA); education (M Ed); school counseling (MA). Part-time and evening/weekend programs available. *Faculty:* 6 full-time (3 women). *Students:* 68 full-time, 14 part-time. 68 applicants, 78% accepted, 43 enrolled. *Entrance requirements:* For master's, MAT, interview, minimum GPA of 3.0. *Application deadline:* For fall admission, 3/15 priority date for domestic students. Applications are processed on a rolling basis. Application fee: $50. Electronic applications accepted. *Expenses:* Tuition: Full-time $9900; part-time $550 per credit hour. Tuition and fees vary according to program. *Financial support:* Scholarships/grants available. *Unit head:* Jim Howard, Dean, 541-684-7262, Fax: 541-684-7310, E-mail: jhoward@northwestchristian.edu. *Application contact:* Kathy Wilson, Assistant Director of Admission, Graduate and Professional Studies, 541-684-7326, Fax: 541-684-7333, E-mail: kwilson@northwestchristian.edu.

Northwestern Oklahoma State University, School of Professional Studies, Program in School Counseling, Alva, OK 73717-2799. Offers M Ed. *Accreditation:* NCATE. Part-time programs available. *Faculty:* 5 full-time (4 women). *Students:* 19 part-time (17 women); includes 3 minority (1 American Indian/Alaska Native, 2 Hispanic Americans). 12 applicants, 100% accepted. In 2009, 11 master's awarded. *Degree requirements:* For master's, thesis optional, portfolio. *Entrance requirements:* For master's, GRE General Test or MAT, minimum GPA of 2.75. *Application deadline:* Applications are processed on a rolling basis. Application fee: $15. *Financial support:* Federal Work-Study available. Support available to part-time students. Financial award application deadline: 5/1; financial award applicants required to submit FAFSA. *Unit head:* Dr. Sue Diel, Chair, 580-327-8451. *Application contact:* Leah Haines, Coordinator of Graduate Studies, 580-327-8410, E-mail: ldhaines@nwosu.edu.

Northwestern State University of Louisiana, Graduate Studies and Research, College of Education, Program in School Counseling, Natchitoches, LA 71497. Offers MA.

Northwestern State University of Louisiana, Graduate Studies and Research, College of Education, Program in Student Personnel Services, Natchitoches, LA 71497. Offers counseling and guidance (M Ed, Ed S); special education (M Ed, Ed S); student personnel services (MA). *Accreditation:* NCATE (one or more programs are accredited). *Degree requirements:* For master's, comprehensive exam, thesis or alternative. *Entrance requirements:* For master's, GRE General Test, GRE Subject Test, minimum undergraduate GPA of 2.5.

Northwestern State University of Louisiana, Graduate Studies and Research, College of Education, Programs in Education, Natchitoches, LA 71497. Offers business and distributive education (M Ed); counseling (M Ed); early childhood education (M Ed); education (M Ed); education leadership (M Ed); educational technology (M Ed); elementary teaching (M Ed); English education (M Ed); home economics education (M Ed); mathematics education (M Ed); reading (M Ed); science education (M Ed); secondary teaching (M Ed); social sciences education (M Ed). *Degree requirements:* For master's, comprehensive exam, thesis or alternative. *Entrance requirements:* For master's, GRE General Test, minimum undergraduate GPA of 2.5.

Northwestern State University of Louisiana, Graduate Studies and Research, College of Education, Programs in Educational Leadership and Instruction, Natchitoches, LA 71497. Offers counseling (Ed S); educational leadership (Ed S); educational technology (Ed S); elementary teaching (Ed S); reading (Ed S); secondary teaching (Ed S); special education (Ed S). *Entrance requirements:* For degree, GRE General Test.

Northwest Missouri State University, Graduate School, College of Education and Human Services, Department of Psychology and Sociology, Program in Guidance and Counseling, Maryville, MO 64468-6001. Offers MS Ed. *Accreditation:* NCATE. *Faculty:* 8 full-time (6 women). *Students:* 6 full-time (5 women), 28 part-time (25 women); includes 1 minority (Asian American or Pacific Islander). 25 applicants, 80% accepted, 15 enrolled. In 2009, 8 master's awarded. *Degree requirements:* For master's, comprehensive exam, thesis. *Entrance requirements:* For master's, GRE General Test, teaching certificate; 2 years of experience; minimum undergraduate GPA of 2.5, 3.0 in major; writing sample. Additional exam requirements/recommendations for international students: Required—TOEFL (minimum score 550 paper-based; 213 computer-based). *Application deadline:* For fall admission, 3/1 for domestic and international students. Applications are processed on a rolling basis. Application fee: $0 ($50 for international students). *Expenses:* Tuition, state resident: part-time $296.34 per credit hour. Tuition, nonresident: part-time $510.43 per credit hour. *Financial support:* In 2009–10, 4 research assistantships with full tuition reimbursements (averaging $6,000 per year) were awarded. Financial award application deadline: 4/1; financial award applicants required to submit FAFSA. *Application contact:* Dr. Gregory Haddock, Dean of Graduate School, 660-562-1145, Fax: 660-562-1096, E-mail: gradsch@nwmissouri.edu.

Northwest Nazarene University, Graduate Studies, Program in Counselor Education, Nampa, ID 83686-5897. Offers community counseling (MS); marriage and family counseling (MS); school counseling (MS).

Northwest Nazarene University, Graduate Studies, Program in Teacher Education, Nampa, ID 83686-5897. Offers curriculum and instruction (M Ed); educational leadership (M Ed); exceptional child (M Ed); reading education (M Ed); school counseling (M Ed). *Accreditation:* ACA; NCATE. Part-time programs available. *Degree requirements:* For master's, comprehensive exam (for some programs), action research project. *Entrance requirements:* For master's, minimum undergraduate GPA of 2.8 overall or 3.0 during final 30 semester credits. *Faculty research:* Action research, cooperative learning, accountability, institutional accreditation.

Nova Southeastern University, Center for Psychological Studies, Master's Programs in Counseling, Mental Health, School Guidance, and Clinical Pharmacology, Fort Lauderdale, FL 33314-7796. Offers clinical pharmacology (MS); mental health counseling (MS); school guidance and counseling (MS). Part-time and evening/weekend programs available. *Faculty:* 7 full-time (2 women), 27 part-time/adjunct (8 women). *Students:* 270 full-time (238 women), 586 part-time (521 women); includes 417 minority (186 African Americans, 14 Asian Americans or Pacific Islanders, 217 Hispanic Americans), 23 international. 562 applicants, 65% accepted, 262 enrolled. In 2009, 232 master's awarded. *Degree requirements:* For master's, comprehensive exam, 3 practica. *Entrance requirements:* Additional exam requirements/recommendations for international students: Required—TOEFL (minimum score 550 paper-based; 213 computer-based). *Application deadline:* For fall admission, 7/29 for domestic students; for winter admission, 11/29 for domestic students; for spring admission, 3/29 for domestic students. Applications are processed on a rolling basis. Application fee: $50. Electronic applications accepted. *Financial support:* Career-related internships or fieldwork, Federal Work-Study, and institutionally sponsored loans available. Financial award application deadline: 4/1. *Faculty research:* Clinical and child clinical psychology, geriatrics, interpersonal violence. *Unit head:* Karen S. Grosby, Dean, 954-262-5701, Fax: 954-262-3859. *Application contact:* Carlos Perez, Enrollment Management, 954-262-5790, Fax: 954-262-3893, E-mail: cpsinfo@cps.nova.edu.

Ohio University, Graduate College, College of Education, Department of Counseling and Higher Education, Athens, OH 45701-2979. Offers college student personnel (M Ed); community/agency counseling (M Ed); counselor education (PhD); higher education (PhD); rehabilitation counseling (M Ed); school counseling (M Ed). *Accreditation:* ACA; CORE. Part-time and evening/weekend programs available. *Faculty:* 12 full-time (6 women), 7 part-time/adjunct (1 woman). *Students:* 164 full-time (120 women), 51 part-time (30 women); includes 36 minority (27 African Americans, 3 American Indian/Alaska Native, 3 Asian Americans or Pacific Islanders, 3 Hispanic Americans), 9 international. 129 applicants, 58% accepted, 57 enrolled. In 2009, 60 master's, 16 doctorates awarded. *Degree requirements:* For master's, comprehensive exam (for some programs), thesis or alternative; for doctorate, comprehensive exam, thesis/dissertation. *Entrance requirements:* For master's, GRE General Test or MAT (if GPA less than 2.9), 3 letters of reference; for doctorate, GRE General Test, work experience, minimum GPA of 3.4. Additional exam requirements/recommendations for international students: Required—TOEFL (minimum score 550 paper-based; 80 iBT) or IELTS Academic (minimum score 6.5). *Application deadline:* For fall admission, 1/15 for domestic and international students. Application fee: $50 ($55 for international students). Electronic applications accepted. *Expenses:* Tuition, state resident: full-time $7839; part-time $323 per quarter hour. Tuition, nonresident: full-time $15,831; part-time $654 per quarter hour. Required fees: $2931. *Financial support:* Research assistantships with full tuition reimbursements, teaching assistantships with full tuition reimbursements, Federal Work-Study, institutionally sponsored loans, tuition waivers (partial), and unspecified assistantships available. Financial award application deadline: 1/15. *Faculty research:* Youth violence, gender studies, student affairs, chemical dependency, disabilities issues. Total annual research expenditures: $527,983. *Unit head:* Dr. Tracy Leinbaugh, Chair, 740-593-0846, Fax: 740-593-0477, E-mail: leinbaug@ohio.edu. *Application contact:* Floyd J. Doney, Director of Student Affairs, 740-593-4400, Fax: 740-593-9310, E-mail: doney@ohio.edu.

Old Dominion University, Darden College of Education, Counseling Program, Norfolk, VA 23529. Offers MS Ed, PhD, Ed S. *Accreditation:* ACA. Part-time and evening/weekend programs available. *Faculty:* 10 full-time (5 women), 5 part-time/adjunct (3 women). *Students:* 131 full-time (114 women), 69 part-time (63 women); includes 47 minority (41 African Americans, 3 Asian Americans or Pacific Islanders, 3 Hispanic Americans), 4 international. Average age 30. 100 applicants, 55% accepted, 45 enrolled. In 2009, 36 master's, 11 doctorates, 3 other advanced degrees awarded. *Degree requirements:* For master's and Ed S, comprehensive exam; for doctorate, comprehensive exam, thesis/dissertation. *Entrance requirements:* For master's, GRE General Test, 3 letters of recommendation, resume; for doctorate, GRE General Test, 3 letters of recommendation, resume, interview, essay; for Ed S, GRE General Test, 3 letters of recommendation, resume, essay. Additional exam requirements/recommendations for international students: Required—TOEFL. *Application deadline:* For fall admission, 2/1 for domestic students; for winter admission, 10/1 for domestic students; for spring admission, 10/1 for domestic students. Application fee: $40. Electronic applications accepted. *Expenses:* Tuition, state resident: full-time $8112; part-time $338 per credit. Tuition, nonresident: full-time $20,256; part-time $844 per credit. Required fees: $119 per semester. One-time fee: $50. *Financial support:* In 2009–10, 125 students received support, including 2 fellowships with full tuition reimbursements available (averaging $15,000 per year), 20 research assistantships with partial tuition reimbursements available (averaging $10,000 per year), 14 teaching assistantships with full tuition reimbursements available (averaging $15,000 per year); career-related internships or fieldwork, Federal Work-Study, institutionally sponsored loans, scholarships/grants, traineeships, tuition waivers (partial), and unspecified assistantships also available. Support available to part-time students. Financial award applicants required to submit FAFSA. *Faculty research:* Group counseling, counselor education, career counseling, spirituality and counseling, school counseling, GLBT counseling, legal and ethical issues. Total annual research expenditures: $75,000. *Unit head:* Dr. Danica Hays, Department Chair, 757-683-6692, Fax: 757-683-5756, E-mail: dhays@odu.edu. *Application contact:* Rebecca Michel, Admissions Graduate Assistant, 757-683-3326, Fax: 757-683-3255, E-mail: rmichel@odu.edu.

Oregon State University, Graduate School, College of Education, Program in Counseling, Corvallis, OR 97331. Offers MS, PhD. *Accreditation:* ACA (one or more programs are accredited); NCATE. *Students:* 11 full-time (9 women), 62 part-time (47 women); includes 17 minority (3 African Americans, 1 American Indian/Alaska Native, 3 Asian Americans or Pacific Islanders, 10 Hispanic Americans), 3 international. Average age 36. In 2009, 42 master's, 6 doctorates awarded. *Degree requirements:* For master's, thesis or alternative; for doctorate, one foreign language, thesis/dissertation. *Entrance requirements:* For master's, minimum GPA of 3.0 in last 90 hours; for doctorate, GRE or MAT, master's degree, minimum GPA of 3.0 in last 90 hours of course work, 2 years of teaching experience. Additional exam requirements/recommendations for international students: Required—TOEFL. *Application deadline:* For fall admission, 2/1 for domestic students. Applications are processed on a rolling basis. Application fee: $50. *Expenses:* Tuition, state resident: full-time $9774; part-time $362 per credit. Tuition, nonresident: full-time $15,849; part-time $587 per credit. Required fees: $1639. Full-time tuition and fees vary according to course load and program. *Financial support:* Teaching assistantships, career-related internships or fieldwork, Federal Work-Study, and institutionally sponsored loans available. Support available to part-time students. Financial award application deadline: 2/1. *Faculty research:* Counseling and guidance improvement in social services agencies, elementary and secondary schools. *Unit head:* Dr. Cass Dykeman, Chair, 541-737-8204, Fax: 541-737-2040, E-mail: dykeman@onid.orst.edu. *Application contact:* Dr. Cass Dykeman, Chair, 541-737-8204, Fax: 541-737-2040, E-mail: dykeman@onid.orst.edu.

Ottawa University, Graduate Studies-Arizona, Program in Education, Ottawa, KS 66067-3399. Offers community college counseling (MA); curriculum and instruction (MA); early childhood (MA); education intervention (MA); education leadership (MA); education technology (MA); Montessori early childhood education (MA); Montessori elementary education (MA); professional development (MA); school guidance counseling (MA); special education—cross categorical (MA). Programs offered in Mesa, Phoenix, Tempe and West Valley, AZ. *Accreditation:* NCATE. Part-time programs available. *Degree requirements:* For master's, thesis or alternative. *Entrance requirements:* For master's, minimum undergraduate GPA of 3.0, copy of current state certification or teaching license. Additional exam requirements/recommendations for international students: Required—TOEFL (minimum score 550 paper-based; 213 computer-based). Electronic applications accepted. *Expenses:* Contact institution.

Our Lady of Holy Cross College, Program in Education and Counseling, New Orleans, LA 70131-7399. Offers administration and supervision (M Ed); curriculum and instruction (M Ed); marriage and family counseling (MA); school counseling (M Ed, MA). *Accreditation:* ACA; NCATE. Part-time and evening/weekend programs available. *Degree requirements:* For master's, thesis. *Entrance requirements:* For master's, GRE General Test, minimum GPA of 2.7.

Our Lady of the Lake University of San Antonio, School of Professional Studies, Program in School Counseling, San Antonio, TX 78207-4689. Offers M Ed. Part-time and evening/weekend programs available. *Students:* 2 full-time (both women), 19 part-time (18 women); includes 10 minority (1 African American, 9 Hispanic Americans). Average age 35. In 2009, 6 master's awarded. *Degree requirements:* For master's, comprehensive exam, thesis optional, practicum. *Entrance requirements:* For master's, GRE General Test or MAT, interview. Additional exam requirements/recommendations for international students: Required—TOEFL. *Application deadline:* Applications are processed on a rolling basis. Application fee: $25 ($50 for international students). Electronic applications accepted. *Expenses:* Tuition: Full-time $12,330; part-time $685 per contact hour. Required fees: $139; $12 per contact hour. $57 per semester. Tuition and fees vary according to campus/location. *Financial support:* Application deadline:

Counselor Education

Our Lady of the Lake University of San Antonio *(continued)*
4/15. *Unit head:* Dr. Joan Biever, Chair, 210-434-6711, E-mail: secs@lake.ollusa.edu. *Application contact:* 210-434-6711 Ext. 2314, Fax: 210-431-4036, E-mail: gradadm@lake.ollusa.edu.

Palm Beach Atlantic University, School of Education and Behavioral Studies, West Palm Beach, FL 33416-4708. Offers counseling psychology (MSCP), including addictions/mental health, marriage and family therapy, mental health counseling, school guidance counseling. Part-time and evening/weekend programs available. *Faculty:* 16 full-time (8 women), 2 part-time/adjunct (0 women). *Students:* 230 full-time (193 women), 74 part-time (63 women); includes 109 minority (70 African Americans, 1 Asian American or Pacific Islander, 38 Hispanic Americans), 8 international. Average age 35. 136 applicants, 70% accepted, 88 enrolled. In 2009, 86 master's awarded. *Entrance requirements:* For master's, GRE, minimum GPA of 3.0. Additional exam requirements/recommendations for international students: Required—TOEFL (minimum score 550 paper-based; 213 computer-based). *Application deadline:* For fall admission, 7/15 priority date for domestic students; for spring admission, 11/15 priority date for domestic students. Applications are processed on a rolling basis. Application fee: $45. Electronic applications accepted. *Expenses:* Tuition: Full-time $8010; part-time $445 per credit hour. Required fees: $99 per semester. Tuition and fees vary according to course load and degree level. *Financial support:* Applicants required to submit FAFSA. *Unit head:* Dr. Lisa Stubbs, Program Director, 561-803-2286. *Application contact:* Graduate Admissions, 888-468-6722, Fax: 561-803-2115, E-mail: grad@pba.edu.

Penn State University Park, Graduate School, College of Education, Department of Counselor Education, Counseling Psychology and Rehabilitation Services, State College, University Park, PA 16802-1503. Offers M Ed, MS, D Ed, PhD. *Accreditation:* ACA (one or more programs are accredited); APA (one or more programs are accredited); NCATE.

Phillips Graduate Institute, Programs in Marriage and Family Therapy, School Counseling and School Psychology, Encino, CA 91316-1509. Offers marital and family therapy (MA); organizational consulting (MA); school counseling (MA). Evening/weekend programs available. *Degree requirements:* For master's, comprehensive exam, thesis. *Entrance requirements:* For master's, minimum GPA of 2.5. *Faculty research:* Integration of interpersonal psychological theory, systems approach, firsthand experiential learning.

Pittsburg State University, Graduate School, College of Education, Department of Psychology and Counseling, Program in Counselor Education, Pittsburg, KS 66762. Offers community counseling (MS); school counseling (MS). *Accreditation:* ACA; NCATE. *Degree requirements:* For master's, thesis or alternative. *Entrance requirements:* For master's, GRE General Test, minimum GPA of 2.8. *Expenses:* Tuition, state resident: full-time $4212; part-time $176 per credit. Tuition, nonresident: full-time $11,530; part-time $480 per credit. Required fees: $940; $43 per credit. Tuition and fees vary according to course level, course load, degree level, campus/location, reciprocity agreements and student level.

Plymouth State University, College of Graduate Studies, Graduate Studies in Education, Program in Counselor Education, Plymouth, NH 03264-1595. Offers M Ed. *Accreditation:* ACA; NCATE. Part-time and evening/weekend programs available. *Degree requirements:* For master's, PRAXIS I. *Entrance requirements:* For master's, MAT, minimum GPA of 3.0.

Pontifical Catholic University of Puerto Rico, College of Education, Program in Counselor Education, Ponce, PR 00717-0777. Offers M Ed. *Degree requirements:* For master's, comprehensive exam, thesis (for some programs). *Entrance requirements:* For master's, GRE, 2 letters of recommendation, interview, minimum GPA of 2.75.

Portland State University, Graduate Studies, School of Education, Department of Special Education and Counselor Education, Portland, OR 97207-0751. Offers counselor education (MA, MS); special and counselor education (Ed D); special education (MA, MS). *Accreditation:* ACA (one or more programs are accredited). Part-time and evening/weekend programs available. *Degree requirements:* For master's, thesis or alternative. *Entrance requirements:* For master's, California Basic Educational Skills Test, minimum GPA of 3.0 in upper-division course work or 2.75 overall. Additional exam requirements/recommendations for international students: Required—TOEFL (minimum score 550 paper-based; 213 computer-based). *Faculty research:* Transition of students with disabilities, functional curriculum, supported/inclusive education, leisure/recreation, autism.

Prairie View A&M University, College of Education, Department of Educational Leadership and Counseling, Prairie View, TX 77446-0519. Offers counseling (MA, MS Ed); educational administration (M Ed, MS Ed); educational leadership (PhD). *Accreditation:* NCATE. Part-time and evening/weekend programs available. *Faculty:* 21 full-time (8 women), 32 part-time/adjunct (13 women). *Students:* 84 full-time (65 women), 1,102 part-time (865 women); includes 1,033 minority (989 African Americans, 2 American Indian/Alaska Native, 3 Asian Americans or Pacific Islanders, 39 Hispanic Americans), 6 international. Average age 34. 1,341 applicants, 100% accepted. In 2009, 439 master's, 17 doctorates awarded. *Degree requirements:* For master's, thesis optional; for doctorate, comprehensive exam, thesis/dissertation. *Entrance requirements:* For master's, GRE General Test, 3 letters of reference, minimum undergraduate GPA of 2.5; for doctorate, GRE General Test, 3 letters of reference. Additional exam requirements/recommendations for international students: Required—TOEFL (minimum score 550 paper-based). *Application deadline:* For fall admission, 7/1 priority date for domestic students, 6/1 for international students; for spring admission, 11/1 priority date for domestic students, 10/1 for international students. Applications are processed on a rolling basis. Application fee: $50. Electronic applications accepted. *Expenses:* Tuition, state resident: full-time $2200. Tuition, nonresident: full-time $5600. Required fees: $1720. Tuition and fees vary according to course load. *Financial support:* In 2009–10, 600 students received support. Career-related internships or fieldwork available. Support available to part-time students. Financial award application deadline: 4/1; financial award applicants required to submit FAFSA. *Faculty research:* Mentoring, personality assessment, holistic/humanistic education. *Unit head:* Dr. Pamela Barber-Freeman, Interim Head, 936-261-3530, Fax: 936-261-3617. *Application contact:* Dr. Pamela Barber-Freeman, Interim Head, 936-261-3530, Fax: 936-261-3617.

Prescott College, Graduate Programs, Program in Education, Prescott, AZ 86301. Offers early childhood education (MA); early childhood special education (MA); education (MA); elementary education (MA); environmental education leadership and administration (MA); equine-assisted experiential learning (MA); school guidance counseling (MA); secondary education (MA); special education, learning disability (MA); special education, mental retardation (MA); special education, serious emotional disability (MA); student-directed independent study (MA); sustainability education (PhD). Part-time programs available. Postbaccalaureate distance learning degree programs offered (minimal on-campus study). *Faculty:* 3 full-time (1 woman), 79 part-time/adjunct (41 women). *Students:* 75 full-time (44 women), 46 part-time (36 women); includes 18 minority (3 African Americans, 3 American Indian/Alaska Native, 4 Asian Americans or Pacific Islanders, 8 Hispanic Americans), 2 international. Average age 39. 66 applicants, 67% accepted, 31 enrolled. In 2009, 22 master's, 4 doctorates awarded. *Degree requirements:* For master's, thesis, fieldwork or internship, practicum; for doctorate, thesis/dissertation. *Entrance requirements:* For master's, 2 letters of recommendation, resume; for doctorate, 3 letters of recommendation, resume, official transcripts, personal statement, program proposal. Additional exam requirements/recommendations for international students: Required—TOEFL (minimum score 500 paper-based; 173 computer-based). *Application deadline:* For fall admission, 4/15 priority date for domestic and international students; for spring admission, 9/15 priority date for domestic and international students. Applications are processed on a rolling basis. Application fee: $40. Electronic applications accepted. *Expenses:* Tuition: Full-time $14,712; part-time $613 per credit. Required fees: $50 per term. One-time fee: $150. Tuition and fees vary according to course load and degree level. *Financial support:* Career-related internships or fieldwork and Federal Work-Study available. Financial award applicants required to submit FAFSA. *Unit head:* Noel Caniglia, Chair, 928-358-3201, Fax: 928-776-5151, E-mail: ncaniglia@prescott.edu. *Application contact:* Kerstin Alicki, Admissions Counselor, 877-412-8705, Fax: 928-277-4695, E-mail: admissions@prescott.edu.

Providence College, Graduate Studies, Department of Education, Program in Counseling, Providence, RI 02918. Offers M Ed. Part-time and evening/weekend programs available. *Faculty:* 4 full-time (3 women), 39 part-time/adjunct (22 women). *Students:* 27 full-time (23 women), 55 part-time (45 women); includes 3 minority (1 African American, 1 American Indian/Alaska Native, 1 Hispanic American), 2 international. Average age 32. 15 applicants, 100% accepted. In 2009, 40 master's awarded. *Degree requirements:* For master's, comprehensive exam. *Entrance requirements:* For master's, GRE General Test. Additional exam requirements/recommendations for international students: Required—TOEFL (minimum score 550 paper-based; 213 computer-based; 80 iBT). *Application deadline:* For fall admission, 8/1 priority date for domestic and international students; for spring admission, 12/1 priority date for domestic and international students. Applications are processed on a rolling basis. Application fee: $55. *Expenses:* Tuition: Full-time $9909; part-time $367 per credit. One-time fee: $200. Tuition and fees vary according to course load and program. *Financial support:* In 2009–10, 12 research assistantships with full tuition reimbursements (averaging $8,400 per year) were awarded; career-related internships or fieldwork, institutionally sponsored loans, and unspecified assistantships also available. Support available to part-time students. Financial award application deadline: 8/1; financial award applicants required to submit FAFSA. *Unit head:* Alexander J. Freda, Director, 401-865-2247, Fax: 401-865-1147, E-mail: afreda@providence.edu. *Application contact:* Carol A. Daniels, Coordinator of Graduate Faculty and Administrative Services, 401-865-2247, Fax: 401-865-1147, E-mail: daniels@providence.edu.

Purdue University, Graduate School, School of Education, Department of Educational Studies, West Lafayette, IN 47907. Offers administration (MS Ed, PhD, Ed S); counseling and development (MS Ed, PhD); education of the gifted (MS Ed); educational psychology (MS Ed, PhD); foundations of education (MS Ed, PhD); higher education administration (MS Ed, PhD); special education (MS Ed, PhD). *Accreditation:* ACA (one or more programs are accredited); NCATE (one or more programs are accredited). Part-time and evening/weekend programs available. *Degree requirements:* For master's, thesis optional; for doctorate, thesis/dissertation, oral and written exams; for Ed S, oral presentation, project. *Entrance requirements:* For master's, GRE General Test, minimum undergraduate GPA of 3.0; for doctorate, GRE General Test; for Ed S, GRE, minimum B average. Additional exam requirements/recommendations for international students: Required—TOEFL. Electronic applications accepted. *Faculty research:* Motivation, learning disabilities, school learning, group processes, cognitive development.

Purdue University Calumet, Graduate School, School of Education, Program in Counseling, Hammond, IN 46323-2094. Offers human services (MS Ed); mental health counseling (MS Ed); school counseling (MS Ed). *Entrance requirements:* Additional exam requirements/recommendations for international students: Required—TOEFL.

Queens College of the City University of New York, Division of Graduate Studies, Division of Education, Department of Educational and Community Programs, Program in Counselor Education, Flushing, NY 11367-1597. Offers MS Ed. Part-time programs available. *Faculty:* 3 full-time (1 woman). *Students:* 38 full-time (32 women), 34 part-time (31 women). 165 applicants, 26% accepted, 32 enrolled. In 2009, 30 master's awarded. *Degree requirements:* For master's, research project. *Entrance requirements:* For master's, minimum GPA of 3.0. Additional exam requirements/recommendations for international students: Required—TOEFL. *Application deadline:* For fall admission, 4/1 for domestic students; for spring admission, 11/1 for domestic students. Applications are processed on a rolling basis. Application fee: $125. *Expenses:* Tuition, state resident: full-time $7360; part-time $310 per credit. Tuition, nonresident: part-time $575 per credit. One-time fee: $195 full-time; $145.25 part-time. *Financial support:* Career-related internships or fieldwork, Federal Work-Study, institutionally sponsored loans, and tuition waivers (partial) available. Support available to part-time students. Financial award application deadline: 4/1; financial award applicants required to submit FAFSA. *Unit head:* Dr. John Pellitteri, Coordinator and Graduate Adviser, 718-997-5246, E-mail: john_pellitteri@qc.edu. *Application contact:* Mario Caruso, Director of Graduate Admissions, 718-997-5200, Fax: 718-997-5193, E-mail: graduate_admissions@qc.edu.

Quincy University, Program in Counseling, Quincy, IL 62301-2699. Offers clinical mental health counseling (MS Ed); school counseling (MS Ed). Part-time and evening/weekend programs available. *Faculty:* 2 full-time (0 women), 1 part-time/adjunct (0 women). *Students:* 10 full-time (8 women), 21 part-time (16 women); includes 2 African Americans. In 2009, 12 master's awarded. *Degree requirements:* For master's, comprehensive exam, practicum, internship. *Entrance requirements:* For master's, MAT or GRE. Additional exam requirements/recommendations for international students: Required—TOEFL. *Application deadline:* Applications are processed on a rolling basis. Application fee: $25. Electronic applications accepted. *Expenses:* Tuition: Full-time $8400; part-time $350 per credit hour. Required fees: $360; $15 per credit hour. Tuition and fees vary according to course load, campus/location and program. *Financial support:* Available to part-time students. Applicants required to submit FAFSA. *Unit head:* Dr. Kenneth Oliver, Director, 217-228-5432 Ext. 3113, E-mail: oliveke@quincy.edu. *Application contact:* Jennifer O'Donnell, Coordinator of Adult Studies, 217-228-5404, Fax: 217-228-5479, E-mail: admissions@quincy.edu.

Radford University, College of Graduate and Professional Studies, College of Education and Human Development, Department of Counselor Education, Radford, VA 24142. Offers community counseling (MS); school counseling (MS); student affairs—administration (MS); student affairs—counseling (MS). *Accreditation:* ACA; NCATE. Part-time and evening/weekend programs available. *Faculty:* 7 full-time (4 women), 20 part-time/adjunct (13 women). *Students:* 62 full-time (50 women), 60 part-time (50 women); includes 11 minority (8 African Americans, 1 American Indian/Alaska Native, 1 Asian American or Pacific Islander, 1 Hispanic American). Average age 29. 85 applicants, 88% accepted, 38 enrolled. In 2009, 53 master's awarded. *Degree requirements:* For master's, comprehensive exam, thesis optional. *Entrance requirements:* For master's, GRE or MAT, minimum GPA of 2.75, 3 letters of reference. Additional exam requirements/recommendations for international students: Required—TOEFL (minimum score 550 paper-based; 213 computer-based; 79 iBT). *Application deadline:* For fall admission, 4/15 priority date for domestic students, 12/1 for international students. Applications are processed on a rolling basis. Application fee: $50. Electronic applications accepted. *Expenses:* Tuition, state resident: full-time $5086; part-time $211 per credit hour. Tuition, nonresident: full-time $12,608; part-time $525 per credit hour. Required fees: $2508; $105 per credit hour. *Financial support:* In 2009–10, 27 students received support, including 11 research assistantships with partial tuition reimbursements available (averaging $8,000 per year), 9 teaching assistantships with partial tuition reimbursements available (averaging $8,700 per year); career-related internships or fieldwork, Federal Work-Study, institutionally sponsored loans, scholarships/grants, and unspecified assistantships also available. Financial award application deadline: 3/1; financial award applicants required to submit FAFSA. *Unit head:* Dr. Alan Forrest, Chair, 540-831-5487, Fax: 540-831-6755, E-mail: aforrest@radford.edu. *Application contact:* Graduate Admissions, 540-831-5431, Fax: 540-831-6061, E-mail: gradcollege@radford.edu.

Regent University, Graduate School, School of Psychology and Counseling, Virginia Beach, VA 23464-9800. Offers clinical psychology (MA, Psy D); counseling (MA), including community counseling, human services counseling, school counseling; counseling studies (CAGS); counselor education and supervision (PhD); M Div/MA; M Ed/MA; MBA/MA. PhD program offered online only. *Accreditation:* ACA; APA (one or more programs are accredited). Part-time and evening/weekend programs available. Postbaccalaureate distance learning degree programs offered (minimal on-campus study). *Faculty:* 24 full-time (12 women), 19 part-time/adjunct (12 women). *Students:* 209 full-time (171 women), 189 part-time (137 women); includes 107 minority (92 African Americans, 4 Asian Americans or Pacific Islanders, 11 Hispanic Americans), 14 international. Average age 34. 417 applicants, 50% accepted, 104 enrolled. In 2009, 108 master's, 40 doctorates awarded. *Degree requirements:* For master's, thesis or alternative, internship, practicum, written competency exam; for doctorate, thesis/dissertation or alternative. *Entrance requirements:* For master's, GRE General Test including writing exam, minimum undergraduate GPA of 2.75, 3 recommendations, resume, transcripts, writing sample; for doctorate, GRE General Test including writing exam, GRE Subject Test, minimum undergraduate GPA of 3.0, 3.5 (PhD), 10-15 minute VHS tape demonstrating counseling skills, writing sample, 3 recommendations, resume. Additional exam requirements/recommendations for

international students: Required—TOEFL (minimum score 577 paper-based; 233 computer-based). *Application deadline:* For fall admission, 4/1 priority date for domestic students; for spring admission, 11/1 priority date for domestic students. Applications are processed on a rolling basis. Application fee: $50. Electronic applications accepted. *Expenses:* Contact institution. *Financial support:* In 2009–10, 368 students received support; research assistantships with full and partial tuition reimbursements available, teaching assistantships with full and partial tuition reimbursements available, career-related internships or fieldwork, scholarships/grants, and tuition waivers (full and partial) available. Support available to part-time students. Financial award application deadline: 9/1; financial award applicants required to submit FAFSA. *Faculty research:* Marriage enrichment, AIDS counseling, troubled youth, faith and learning, trauma. *Unit head:* Dr. William Hathaway, Acting Dean, 757-352-4294, Fax: 757-352-4282, E-mail: willhat@regent.edu. *Application contact:* Matthew Chadwick, Director of Admissions, 800-373-5504, Fax: 757-352-4381, E-mail: admissions@regent.edu.

Rhode Island College, School of Graduate Studies, Feinstein School of Education and Human Development, Department of Counseling, Educational Leadership, and School Psychology, Providence, RI 02908-1991. Offers counseling (MA); educational leadership (M Ed); school administration (M Ed); school counseling (CAGS). *Accreditation:* NCATE. Part-time and evening/weekend programs available. *Faculty:* 10 full-time (5 women), 9 part-time/adjunct (5 women). *Students:* 39 full-time (30 women), 108 part-time (79 women); includes 7 minority (3 African Americans, 3 Asian Americans or Pacific Islanders, 1 Hispanic American). Average age 35. In 2009, 39 master's, 34 other advanced degrees awarded. *Degree requirements:* For master's and CAGS, comprehensive exam (for some programs), thesis (for some programs). *Entrance requirements:* For master's, GRE General Test or MAT, undergraduate transcripts; minimum undergraduate GPA of 3.0; for CAGS, GRE or MAT (for most programs), undergraduate transcripts; minimum undergraduate GPA of 3.0; copy of teaching certificate (when applicable); 3 letters of recommendation; current resume. Additional exam requirements/recommendations for international students: Recommended—TOEFL (minimum score 550 paper-based; 213 computer-based; 79 iBT). *Application deadline:* For fall admission, 3/15 for domestic students; for spring admission, 11/1 for domestic students. Applications are processed on a rolling basis. Application fee: $50. *Expenses:* Tuition, state resident: full-time $7440; part-time $310 per credit hour. Tuition, nonresident: full-time $14,784; part-time $616 per credit hour. Required fees: $552; $20 per credit. $70 per term. *Financial support:* Teaching assistantships with full tuition reimbursements, career-related internships or fieldwork, Federal Work-Study, scholarships/grants, health care benefits, and unspecified assistantships available. Support available to part-time students. Financial award application deadline: 5/15; financial award applicants required to submit FAFSA. *Unit head:* Dr. Monica Darcy, Chair, 401-456-8023. *Application contact:* Graduate Studies, 401-456-8700.

Rider University, Department of Graduate Education, Leadership and Counseling, Program in Counseling Services, Lawrenceville, NJ 08648-3001. Offers counseling services (MA, Ed S); director of school counseling (Certificate); school counseling services (Certificate). *Accreditation:* ACA; NCATE. Part-time and evening/weekend programs available. *Degree requirements:* For master's, comprehensive exam, research project; for other advanced degree, specialty seminar. *Entrance requirements:* For master's, GRE or MAT, interview, resume, 2 letters of recommendation; for other advanced degree, GRE or MAT, interview, professional experience, 2 letters of recommendation. Additional exam requirements/recommendations for international students: Required—TOEFL (minimum score 550 paper-based; 213 computer-based). Electronic applications accepted. *Faculty research:* Diversity in counseling.

Rivier College, School of Graduate Studies, Department of Education, Nashua, NH 03060. Offers curriculum and instruction (M Ed); early childhood education (M Ed); educational administration (M Ed); educational studies (M Ed); elementary education (M Ed); elementary education and general special education (M Ed); emotional and behavioral disorders (M Ed); general social education (M Ed); leadership and learning (Ed D, CAGS); learning disabilities (M Ed); learning disabilities and reading (M Ed); mental health counseling (MA); reading (M Ed); school counseling (M Ed). Part-time and evening/weekend programs available. *Faculty:* 13 full-time (9 women), 38 part-time/adjunct (25 women). *Students:* 87 full-time (78 women), 293 part-time (246 women); includes 10 minority (3 African Americans, 4 Asian Americans or Pacific Islanders, 3 Hispanic Americans). Average age 38. 182 applicants, 82% accepted, 72 enrolled. In 2009, 110 master's, 18 other advanced degrees awarded. *Degree requirements:* For master's, comprehensive exam (for some programs), internships. *Entrance requirements:* For master's, GRE General Test or MAT. *Application deadline:* Applications are processed on a rolling basis. Application fee: $25. *Expenses:* Tuition: Part-time $447 per credit. *Financial support:* Available to part-time students. Application deadline: 2/1. *Unit head:* Dr. Patricia Howson, Chairman, 603-897-8562, E-mail: phowson@rivier.edu. *Application contact:* Mathew Kittredge, Director of Graduate Admissions, 603-897-8129, Fax: 603-897-8810, E-mail: mkittredge@rivier.edu.

Roberts Wesleyan College, Division of Social Sciences, Rochester, NY 14624-1997. Offers counseling in ministry (MA); school counseling (MS); school psychology (MS).

Rollins College, Hamilton Holt School, Program in Counseling, Winter Park, FL 32789-4499. Offers mental health counseling (MA). *Accreditation:* ACA. Part-time and evening/weekend programs available. *Faculty:* 4 full-time (3 women), 3 part-time/adjunct (2 women). *Students:* 48 full-time (40 women), 33 part-time (28 women); includes 15 minority (6 African Americans, 1 American Indian/Alaska Native, 2 Asian Americans or Pacific Islanders, 6 Hispanic Americans). Average age 30. 54 applicants, 85% accepted, 30 enrolled. In 2009, 29 master's awarded. *Degree requirements:* For master's, comprehensive exam. *Entrance requirements:* For master's, GRE General Test or MAT, interview. Additional exam requirements/recommendations for international students: Required—TOEFL. *Application deadline:* For fall admission, 4/1 for domestic students. Application fee: $50. *Expenses:* Contact institution. *Financial support:* In 2009–10, 2 teaching assistantships were awarded; scholarships/grants also available. Support available to part-time students. *Unit head:* Dr. Alicia Homrich, Director, 407-646-2307, E-mail: ahomrich@rollins.edu. *Application contact:* Rebecca Cordray, Coordinator of Records and Registration, 407-646-1568, Fax: 407-975-6430, E-mail: rcordray@rollins.edu.

Roosevelt University, Graduate Division, College of Education, Program in Counseling and Human Services, Chicago, IL 60605. Offers MA. *Accreditation:* ACA.

Rosemont College, Schools of Graduate and Professional Studies, Program in Counseling Psychology, Rosemont, PA 19010-1699. Offers human services (MA); school counseling (MA). Part-time and evening/weekend programs available. *Degree requirements:* For master's, thesis or alternative, practicum. *Entrance requirements:* For master's, minimum undergraduate GPA of 3.0, 3 letters of recommendation. Additional exam requirements/recommendations for international students: Required—TOEFL. Electronic applications accepted. *Expenses:* Contact institution. *Faculty research:* Addictions counseling.

Rowan University, Graduate School, College of Education, Department of Special Educational Services/Instruction, Program in Counseling in Educational Settings, Glassboro, NJ 08028-1701. Offers MA. Part-time and evening/weekend programs available. *Students:* 36 full-time (31 women), 39 part-time (31 women); includes 13 minority (8 African Americans, 5 Hispanic Americans). Average age 29. 31 applicants, 68% accepted, 18 enrolled. In 2009, 31 master's awarded. *Degree requirements:* For master's, thesis. *Entrance requirements:* For master's, GRE General Test, minimum GPA of 2.8, 1 year of teaching experience. Additional exam requirements/recommendations for international students: Required—TOEFL. *Application deadline:* For fall admission, 10/15 priority date for domestic students; for spring admission, 2/15 priority date for domestic students. Applications are processed on a rolling basis. Application fee: $50. Electronic applications accepted. *Expenses:* Tuition, state resident: full-time $10,624; part-time $590 per semester hour. Tuition, nonresident: full-time $10,624; part-time $590 per semester hour. Required fees: $2320; $125 per semester hour. *Financial support:* Career-related internships or fieldwork, scholarships/grants, health care benefits, and unspecified assistantships available. Support available to part-time students. *Unit head:* Dr. Mira Lalovic-Hand, Interim Associate Provost/Director of Graduate School, 856-256-5120, E-mail: lalovic-hand@rowan.edu. *Application contact:* Karen Haynes, Graduate Coordinator, 856-256-4052, Fax: 856-256-4436, E-mail: haynes@rowan.edu.

Sage Graduate School, Graduate School, School of Education, Program in Applied Behavior Analysis and Autism, Troy, NY 12180-4115. Offers MS. Part-time and evening/weekend programs available. *Faculty:* 15 full-time (9 women), 19 part-time/adjunct (16 women). *Students:* 57 part-time (51 women); includes 6 minority (2 Asian Americans or Pacific Islanders, 4 Hispanic Americans). Average age 31. 143 applicants, 41% accepted, 41 enrolled. *Entrance requirements:* Additional exam requirements/recommendations for international students: Required—TOEFL (minimum score 550 paper-based; 213 computer-based). *Application deadline:* Applications are processed on a rolling basis. Application fee: $40. *Expenses:* Tuition: Full-time $10,620; part-time $590 per credit hour. *Financial support:* Federal Work-Study, scholarships/grants, tuition waivers (partial), and unspecified assistantships available. Support available to part-time students. Financial award applicants required to submit FAFSA. *Unit head:* Dr. Thomas Zane, Director, Center for Applied Behavior Analysis, 518-244-2494, Fax: 518-244-2334, E-mail: caba@sage.edu. *Application contact:* Wendy D. Diefendorf, Director of Graduate and Adult Admission, 518-244-2443, Fax: 518-244-6880, E-mail: diefew@sage.edu.

Sage Graduate School, Graduate School, School of Education, Program in Guidance and Counseling, Troy, NY 12180-4115. Offers MS, Post Master's Certificate. *Accreditation:* NCATE. Part-time and evening/weekend programs available. *Faculty:* 15 full-time (9 women), 19 part-time/adjunct (16 women). *Students:* 56 full-time (43 women), 14 part-time (13 women); includes 6 minority (2 African Americans, 4 Hispanic Americans). Average age 26. 47 applicants, 55% accepted, 20 enrolled. In 2009, 33 master's awarded. *Entrance requirements:* For master's, minimum GPA of 2.75, current resume, essay, official transcripts, 2 letters of recommendation. Additional exam requirements/recommendations for international students: Required—TOEFL (minimum score 550 paper-based; 213 computer-based). *Application deadline:* Applications are processed on a rolling basis. Application fee: $40. *Expenses:* Tuition: Full-time $10,620; part-time $590 per credit hour. *Financial support:* Fellowships, research assistantships, Federal Work-Study, scholarships/grants, and unspecified assistantships available. Support available to part-time students. Financial award application deadline: 3/1; financial award applicants required to submit FAFSA. *Faculty research:* Roles and responsibilities of guidance personnel, projections of need for guidance counselors. *Unit head:* Dr. Laurae Coburn, Director, 518-244-2401, Fax: 518-244-2334, E-mail: wartil@sage.edu. *Application contact:* Wendy D. Diefendorf, Director of Graduate and Adult Admission, 518-244-2443, Fax: 518-244-6880, E-mail: diefew@sage.edu.

St. Bonaventure University, School of Graduate Studies, School of Education, Program in Counselor Education, St. Bonaventure, NY 14778-2284. Offers community mental health counseling (MS Ed); school counseling (MS Ed); school counselor (Adv C). *Accreditation:* ACA. Part-time and evening/weekend programs available. *Faculty:* 7 full-time (2 women), 6 part-time/adjunct (2 women). *Students:* 80 full-time (65 women), 31 part-time (20 women); includes 7 minority (3 African Americans, 1 American Indian/Alaska Native, 3 Hispanic Americans), 1 international. Average age 30. 116 applicants, 65% accepted, 51 enrolled. In 2009, 36 master's, 5 Adv Cs awarded. *Degree requirements:* For master's, comprehensive exam, thesis optional. *Entrance requirements:* For master's, interview, writing sample, minimum undergraduate GPA of 3.0. Additional exam requirements/recommendations for international students: Required—TOEFL (minimum score 550 paper-based; 240 computer-based; 95 iBT). *Application deadline:* For fall admission, 8/1 priority date for domestic students, 12/15 for international students; for spring admission, 10/15 priority date for domestic students, 3/15 for international students. Applications are processed on a rolling basis. Application fee: $30. *Expenses:* Tuition: Full-time $11,700; part-time $650 per credit. *Financial support:* In 2009–10, 7 students received support, including 9 research assistantships with full and partial tuition reimbursements available; career-related internships or fieldwork and scholarships/grants also available. Support available to part-time students. Financial award application deadline: 4/15; financial award applicants required to submit FAFSA. *Faculty research:* Parent education, learning disabilities, stress management, cyber bullying. *Unit head:* Dr. Craig Zuckerman, Director, 716-375-2374, Fax: 716-375-2360, E-mail: czuck@sbu.edu. *Application contact:* Bruce Campbell, Director of Graduate Admissions, 716-375-2429, E-mail: gradsch@sbu.edu.

St. Cloud State University, School of Graduate Studies, College of Education, Department of Counselor Education, Higher Education, and Educational Psychology, Program in College Counseling and Student Development, St. Cloud, MN 56301-4498. Offers MS. *Faculty:* 12 full-time (5 women). *Students:* 25 full-time (18 women), 11 part-time (8 women); includes 2 minority (both Asian Americans or Pacific Islanders), 3 international. 15 applicants, 93% accepted. In 2009, 10 master's awarded. *Degree requirements:* For master's, comprehensive exam, thesis or alternative. *Entrance requirements:* For master's, GRE General Test, minimum GPA of 2.75. Additional exam requirements/recommendations for international students: Required—Michigan English Language Assessment Battery; Recommended—TOEFL (minimum score 550 paper-based; 213 computer-based), IELTS (minimum score 6.5). *Application deadline:* For fall admission, 3/1 for domestic and international students. Application fee: $35. Electronic applications accepted. *Financial support:* Federal Work-Study, scholarships/grants, and unspecified assistantships available. Financial award application deadline: 3/1. *Unit head:* Dr. Dan Macari, Coordinator, 320-308-1044, E-mail: dpmacari@stcloudstate.edu. *Application contact:* Linda Lou Krueger, School of Graduate Studies, 320-308-2113, Fax: 320-308-5371, E-mail: lekrueger@stcloudstate.edu.

St. Cloud State University, School of Graduate Studies, College of Education, Department of Counselor Education, Higher Education, and Educational Psychology, Program in School Counseling, St. Cloud, MN 56301-4498. Offers MS. *Accreditation:* ACA; NCATE. *Faculty:* 12 full-time (5 women). *Students:* 19 full-time (16 women), 20 part-time (16 women); includes 1 minority (American Indian/Alaska Native), 1 international. 27 applicants, 59% accepted. *Degree requirements:* For master's, comprehensive exam (for some programs), thesis or alternative. *Entrance requirements:* For master's, GRE General Test, minimum GPA of 2.75. Additional exam requirements/recommendations for international students: Required—Michigan English Language Assessment Battery; Recommended—TOEFL (minimum score 550 paper-based; 213 computer-based), IELTS. *Application deadline:* For fall admission, 3/1 for domestic and international students. Application fee: $35. Electronic applications accepted. *Financial support:* Career-related internships or fieldwork, Federal Work-Study, scholarships/grants, and unspecified assistantships available. Financial award application deadline: 3/1. *Unit head:* Dr. William Lepkowski, Coordinator, 320-308-5280, E-mail: wjlepkowski@stcloudstate.edu. *Application contact:* Linda Lou Krueger, School of Graduate Studies, 320-308-2113, Fax: 320-308-5371, E-mail: lekrueger@stcloudstate.edu.

St. John's University, The School of Education, Department of Human Services and Counseling, Program in Bilingual School Counseling, Queens, NY 11439. Offers MS Ed, PD. Part-time and evening/weekend programs available. *Students:* 6 full-time (all women), 11 part-time (9 women); includes 12 minority (1 African American, 11 Hispanic Americans). Average age 33. 18 applicants, 78% accepted, 5 enrolled. In 2009, 8 master's awarded. *Degree requirements:* For master's, comprehensive exam. *Entrance requirements:* For master's, New York State Bilingual Assessment (BEA), minimum GPA of 3.0, 2 letters of recommendation, interview, writing sample; for PD, personal statement, official transcripts showing conferral of degree with minimum GPA of 3.0, 2 letters of recommendation, interview. Additional exam requirements/recommendations for international students: Required—TOEFL (minimum score 500 paper-based; 173 computer-based; 61 iBT), IELTS (minimum score 5.5). *Application deadline:* For fall admission, 4/1 priority date for domestic students, 6/1 priority date for international students; for spring admission, 11/1 priority date for domestic and international students. Applications are processed on a rolling basis. Application fee: $70. Electronic applications accepted. *Expenses:* Tuition: Full-time $16,290; part-time $905 per credit. Required fees: $300; $150 per semester. Tuition and fees vary according to program. *Financial support:* Research assistantships, career-related internships or fieldwork and scholarships/grants available. Support available to part-time students. Financial award application deadline: 3/1; financial award applicants required to submit FAFSA. *Faculty research:* Cross-cultural comparisons of predictors of active coping. *Unit head:* Dr. Francine Guastello, Acting Chair,

Counselor Education

St. John's University (continued)

718-990-1475, E-mail: guastelf@stjohns.edu. *Application contact:* Dr. Kelly K. Ronayne, Associate Dean for Graduate Admissions, 718-990-2303, Fax: 718-990-2343, E-mail: graded@stjohns.edu.

St. John's University, The School of Education, Department of Human Services and Counseling, Program in Mental Health Counseling, Queens, NY 11439. Offers MS Ed. Part-time and evening/weekend programs available. *Students:* 27 full-time (23 women), 16 part-time (14 women); includes 14 minority (3 African Americans, 3 Asian Americans or Pacific Islanders, 8 Hispanic Americans), 1 international. Average age 26. 54 applicants, 74% accepted, 26 enrolled. *Degree requirements:* For master's, internship. *Entrance requirements:* For master's, minimum GPA of 3.0, 2 letters of recommendation, interview, writing sample. Additional exam requirements/recommendations for international students: Required—TOEFL (minimum score 500 paper-based; 173 computer-based; 61 iBT), IELTS (minimum score 5.5). *Application deadline:* For fall admission, 4/1 priority date for domestic students, 6/1 priority date for international students; for spring admission, 11/1 priority date for domestic and international students. Applications are processed on a rolling basis. Application fee: $70. Electronic applications accepted. *Expenses:* Tuition: Full-time $16,290; part-time $905 per credit. Required fees: $300; $150 per semester. Tuition and fees vary according to program. *Financial support:* Research assistantships, career-related internships or fieldwork available. Support available to part-time students. Financial award application deadline: 3/1; financial award applicants required to submit FAFSA. *Unit head:* Dr. Francine Guastello, Acting Chair, 718-990-1475, Fax: 718-990-1614, E-mail: guastelf@stjohns.edu. *Application contact:* Dr. Kelly K. Ronayne, Associate Dean for Graduate Admissions, 718-990-2303, Fax: 718-990-2343, E-mail: graded@stjohns.edu.

St. John's University, The School of Education, Department of Human Services and Counseling, Program in School Counseling, Queens, NY 11439. Offers MS Ed, PD. *Accreditation:* ACA (one or more programs are accredited). Part-time and evening/weekend programs available. *Students:* 55 full-time (49 women), 65 part-time (52 women); includes 33 minority (13 African Americans, 12 Asian Americans or Pacific Islanders, 8 Hispanic Americans), 3 international. Average age 28. 95 applicants, 71% accepted, 36 enrolled. In 2009, 23 master's, 1 other advanced degree awarded. *Degree requirements:* For master's, comprehensive exam. *Entrance requirements:* For master's, New York State Bilingual Assessment (BEA), minimum GPA of 3.0, 2 letters of recommendation, interview, writing sample; for PD, personal statement, official transcript showing minimum GPA of 3.0, 2 letters of recommendation, interview. Additional exam requirements/recommendations for international students: Required—TOEFL (minimum score 500 paper-based; 173 computer-based; 61 iBT), IELTS (minimum score 5.5). *Application deadline:* For fall admission, 4/1 priority date for domestic students, 6/1 priority date for international students; for spring admission, 11/1 priority date for domestic and international students. Applications are processed on a rolling basis. Application fee: $70. Electronic applications accepted. *Expenses:* Tuition: Full-time $16,290; part-time $905 per credit. Required fees: $300; $150 per semester. Tuition and fees vary according to program. *Financial support:* Research assistantships, career-related internships or fieldwork available. Support available to part-time students. Financial award application deadline: 3/1; financial award applicants required to submit FAFSA. *Faculty research:* Counseling/client engagement; counseling accountability; pipe-line mentoring from grade 4 to college; stress, coping and resilience for children and adults; helping parents deal with aggressive children; effects of bullying and cyber bullying with adolescents; creative connections through the arts. *Unit head:* Dr. Francine Guastello, Acting Chair, 718-990-1475, E-mail: guastelf@stjohns.edu. *Application contact:* Dr. Kelly K. Ronayne, Associate Dean for Graduate Admissions, 718-990-2303, Fax: 718-990-2343, E-mail: graded@stjohns.edu.

Saint Joseph College, Department of Counselor Education, West Hartford, CT 06117-2700. Offers community counseling (MA); school counseling (MA). Part-time and evening/weekend programs available. *Students:* 42 full-time (37 women), 94 part-time (83 women); includes 20 minority (16 African Americans, 4 Hispanic Americans). *Degree requirements:* For master's, comprehensive exam, thesis optional. *Entrance requirements:* For master's, 2 letters of recommendation. *Application deadline:* Applications are processed on a rolling basis. Application fee: $50. Electronic applications accepted. *Expenses:* Tuition: Part-time $595 per credit. Required fees: $30 per credit. Tuition and fees vary according to program. *Financial support:* Career-related internships or fieldwork and unspecified assistantships available. Support available to part-time students. Financial award applicants required to submit FAFSA. *Application contact:* Graduate Admissions Office, 860-231-5261, E-mail: graduate@sjc.edu.

St. Lawrence University, Department of Education, Program in Counseling and Human Development, Canton, NY 13617-1455. Offers mental health counseling (MS); school counseling (M Ed, CAS). Part-time and evening/weekend programs available. *Entrance requirements:* For master's, GRE General Test. *Faculty research:* Defense mechanisms and mediation.

Saint Louis University, Graduate School, College of Education and Public Service and Graduate School, Department of Counseling and Family Therapy, St. Louis, MO 63103-2097. Offers counseling and family therapy (PhD); human development counseling (MA); marriage and family therapy (Certificate); school counseling (MA, MA-R). *Accreditation:* AAMFT; NCATE. Part-time programs available. *Degree requirements:* For master's, comprehensive exam, thesis (for some programs); for doctorate, comprehensive exam, thesis/dissertation, preliminary oral and written exams. *Entrance requirements:* For master's, GRE General Test, letters of recommendation, resume; for doctorate, GRE General Test, letters of recommendation, resumé, transcripts, goal statement. Additional exam requirements/recommendations for international students: Required—TOEFL (minimum score 550 paper-based; 213 computer-based). Electronic applications accepted. *Faculty research:* Medical family therapy/collaborative health care multicultural counseling, mental health needs of diverse, minority, or Immigrant/refugee populations, divorce, aging families.

Saint Martin's University, Graduate Programs, College of Education, Lacey, WA 98503. Offers administration (M Ed); English as a second language (M Ed); guidance and counseling (M Ed); reading (M Ed); special education (M Ed); teaching (MIT); technology in education (M Ed). *Accreditation:* Teacher Education Accreditation Council. Part-time and evening/weekend programs available. *Faculty:* 13 full-time (9 women), 11 part-time/adjunct (7 women). *Students:* 61 full-time (42 women), 23 part-time (17 women); includes 7 minority (2 African Americans, 1 American Indian/Alaska Native, 3 Asian Americans or Pacific Islanders, 1 Hispanic American), 1 international. Average age 35. 26 applicants, 92% accepted, 22 enrolled. In 2009, 12 master's awarded. *Degree requirements:* For master's, comprehensive exam (for some programs), thesis or alternative, project or comprehensives. *Entrance requirements:* For master's, GRE General Test or MAT, resume. Additional exam requirements/recommendations for international students: Required—TOEFL (minimum score 560 paper-based; 220 computer-based; 83 iBT). *Application deadline:* For fall admission, 6/1 priority date for domestic and international students; for spring admission, 10/1 priority date for domestic and international students. Applications are processed on a rolling basis. Application fee: $35. *Expenses:* Tuition: Full-time $12,440; part-time $827 per credit hour. *Financial support:* In 2009–10, 62 students received support. Career-related internships or fieldwork, Federal Work-Study, institutionally sponsored loans, and unspecified assistantships available. Support available to part-time students. Financial award application deadline: 3/1; financial award applicants required to submit FAFSA. *Faculty research:* Reader's theatre and reader/writer workshops, curriculum and assessment integration, gender and equity, classroom evaluations, organizational leadership. *Unit head:* Dr. Joyce Westgard, Director, 360-438-4509, Fax: 360-438-4486, E-mail: westgard@stmartin.edu. *Application contact:* Ryan M. Smith, Administrative Assistant, 360-438-4333, Fax: 360-438-4486, E-mail: ryan.smith@stmartin.edu.

Saint Mary's College of California, Kalmanovitz School of Education, Program in Counseling, Moraga, CA 94556. Offers general counseling (MA); marital and family therapy (MA); school counseling (MA). Part-time and evening/weekend programs available. *Faculty:* 6 full-time (5 women), 16 part-time/adjunct (13 women). *Students:* 68 full-time (55 women), 133 part-time (106 women); includes 42 minority (13 African Americans, 1 American Indian/Alaska Native, 10 Asian Americans or Pacific Islanders, 18 Hispanic Americans), 7 international. Average age

35. In 2009, 48 master's awarded. *Degree requirements:* For master's, thesis or alternative. *Entrance requirements:* For master's, interview, minimum GPA of 3.0. *Application deadline:* Applications are processed on a rolling basis. Application fee: $50. *Expenses:* Tuition: Full-time $35,087; part-time $956 per credit hour. One-time fee: $50 full-time. Part-time tuition and fees vary according to course level, course load, degree level, campus/location and program. *Financial support:* In 2009–10, 5 students received support. Career-related internships or fieldwork and Federal Work-Study available. Support available to part-time students. Financial award application deadline: 2/15; financial award applicants required to submit FAFSA. *Faculty research:* Counselor training effectiveness, multicultural development, empathy, the interface of spirituality and psychotherapy, gender issues. *Unit head:* Dr. Laura Heid, Director, 925-631-4293, Fax: 925-376-8379, E-mail: lheid@stmarys.ca.edu. *Application contact:* Jane Joyce, Coordinator, Recruitment and Admissions, 925-631-4700, Fax: 925-376-8379, E-mail: soereq@stmarys-ca.edu.

St. Mary's University, Graduate School, Department of Counseling and Human Services, Program in Counseling Education and Supervision, San Antonio, TX 78228-8507. Offers PhD. *Accreditation:* ACA. Part-time programs available. *Degree requirements:* For doctorate, comprehensive exam, thesis/dissertation. *Entrance requirements:* For doctorate, GRE, master's degree, work experience, letters of recommendation. Additional exam requirements/recommendations for international students: Required—TOEFL (minimum score 550 paper-based; 213 computer-based; 80 iBT). Electronic applications accepted. *Expenses:* Tuition: Full-time $8004. Required fees: $536. One-time fee: $5 full-time. Full-time tuition and fees vary according to program.

St. Thomas University, Biscayne College, Department of Social Sciences and Counseling, Program in Guidance and Counseling, Miami Gardens, FL 33054-6459. Offers MS, Post-Master's Certificate. Part-time and evening/weekend programs available. *Degree requirements:* For master's, comprehensive exam. *Entrance requirements:* For master's, interview, minimum GPA of 3.0 or GRE. Additional exam requirements/recommendations for international students: Required—TOEFL (minimum score 550 paper-based; 213 computer-based; 79 iBT). Electronic applications accepted.

Saint Xavier University, Graduate Studies, School of Education, Program in Counseling, Chicago, IL 60655-3105. Offers MA. *Degree requirements:* For master's, practicum, internship. *Entrance requirements:* For master's, 3 letters of recommendation, interview. Additional exam requirements/recommendations for international students: Required—TOEFL. Electronic applications accepted. *Expenses:* Tuition: Part-time $743 per credit hour. Required fees: $135 per semester.

Salem State College, School of Graduate Studies, Program in School Counseling, Salem, MA 01970-5353. Offers M Ed. *Accreditation:* NCATE. Part-time and evening/weekend programs available. *Students:* 32 full-time (23 women), 22 part-time (17 women); includes 3 minority (1 African American, 2 Hispanic Americans). Average age 32. 15 applicants, 100% accepted, 15 enrolled. In 2009, 14 master's awarded. *Entrance requirements:* For master's, GRE or MAT. Additional exam requirements/recommendations for international students: Required—TOEFL (minimum score 550 paper-based; 80 iBT), or IELTS (minimum score 5.5). *Application deadline:* For fall admission, 5/1 for domestic students; for spring admission, 10/1 for domestic students. Applications are processed on a rolling basis. Application fee: $50. *Expenses:* Tuition, state resident: full-time $2520; part-time $275 per credit hour. Tuition, nonresident: full-time $4140; part-time $365 per credit hour. Required fees: $2430. *Financial support:* In 2009–10, 33 students received support. Career-related internships or fieldwork, Federal Work-Study, scholarships/grants, and unspecified assistantships available. Support available to part-time students. Financial award application deadline: 5/1; financial award applicants required to submit FAFSA. *Unit head:* Mary Ni, Program Coordinator, 978-542-6310, Fax: 978-542-6596, E-mail: mni@salemstate.edu. *Application contact:* Dr. Lee Brossoit, Assistant Dean of Graduate Admissions, 978-542-6675, Fax: 978-542-7215, E-mail: lbrossoit@salemstate.edu.

Sam Houston State University, College of Education and Applied Science, Department of Educational Leadership and Counseling, Huntsville, TX 77341. Offers administration (M Ed, MA); counseling (M Ed, MA); counselor education (MA, PhD); educational leadership (Ed D); instructional leadership (M Ed, MA). Part-time programs available. *Faculty:* 31 full-time (20 women), 8 part-time/adjunct (6 women). *Students:* 91 full-time (73 women), 581 part-time (464 women); includes 214 minority (107 African Americans, 2 American Indian/Alaska Native, 7 Asian Americans or Pacific Islanders, 98 Hispanic Americans), 10 international. Average age 36. 231 applicants, 91% accepted, 164 enrolled. In 2009, 280 master's, 16 doctorates awarded. *Entrance requirements:* For master's, GRE General Test. Additional exam requirements/recommendations for international students: Required—TOEFL (minimum score 550 paper-based; 213 computer-based; 79 iBT). *Application deadline:* For fall admission, 8/1 for domestic students; for spring admission, 12/1 for domestic students. Application fee: $20. *Expenses:* Tuition, state resident: full-time $3690; part-time $205 per credit hour. Tuition, nonresident: full-time $8676; part-time $482 per credit hour. Required fees: $1474. Tuition and fees vary according to course load and campus/location. *Financial support:* Career-related internships or fieldwork, Federal Work-Study, and institutionally sponsored loans available. Support available to part-time students. Financial award application deadline: 5/31; financial award applicants required to submit FAFSA. *Unit head:* Dr. Beverly Irby, Chair, 936-294-1134, Fax: 936-294-3886, E-mail: edu_bid@shsu.edu. *Application contact:* Dr. Stacey Edmondson, Advisor, 936-294-1752, E-mail: sedmonson@shsu.edu.

San Diego State University, Graduate and Research Affairs, College of Education, Department of Counseling and School Psychology, San Diego, CA 92182. Offers MS. *Accreditation:* NCATE. Evening/weekend programs available. *Degree requirements:* For master's, comprehensive exam (for some programs), thesis (for some programs). *Entrance requirements:* For master's, GRE General Test, interview, letters of reference. Additional exam requirements/recommendations for international students: Required—TOEFL. Electronic applications accepted. *Faculty research:* Multicultural and cross-cultural counseling and training, AIDS counseling.

San Jose State University, Graduate Studies and Research, Connie L. Lurie College of Education, Department of Counselor Education, San Jose, CA 95192-0001. Offers MA. *Accreditation:* NCATE. Evening/weekend programs available. *Students:* 176 full-time (136 women), 73 part-time (57 women); includes 153 minority (19 African Americans, 35 Asian Americans or Pacific Islanders, 99 Hispanic Americans), 5 international. Average age 30. 135 applicants, 53% accepted, 51 enrolled. In 2009, 122 master's awarded. *Degree requirements:* For master's, thesis or alternative. *Application deadline:* For fall admission, 6/29 for domestic students; for spring admission, 11/30 for domestic students. Applications are processed on a rolling basis. Application fee: $59. Electronic applications accepted. *Financial support:* Career-related internships or fieldwork available. Financial award applicants required to submit FAFSA. *Unit head:* Dr. Xiaolu Hu, Chair, 408-924-3668, Fax: 408-924-3713. *Application contact:* Dr. Xiaolu Hu, Chair, 408-924-3668, Fax: 408-924-3713.

Santa Clara University, School of Education and Counseling Psychology, Department of Counseling Psychology, Program in Counseling, Santa Clara, CA 95053. Offers counseling (MA), including career development, correctional psychology, health psychology, Latino counseling. Part-time and evening/weekend programs available. *Students:* 2 full-time (both women), 17 part-time (14 women); includes 4 minority (1 African American, 2 Asian Americans or Pacific Islanders, 1 Hispanic American), 2 international. Average age 33. 6 applicants, 50% accepted, 0 enrolled. In 2009, 10 master's awarded. *Degree requirements:* For master's, comprehensive exam, thesis optional. *Entrance requirements:* For master's, GRE or MAT, minimum GPA of 3.0, 1 year of related experience. Additional exam requirements/recommendations for international students: Required—TOEFL. *Application deadline:* Applications are processed on a rolling basis. *Expenses:* Contact institution. *Financial support:* Fellowships, career-related internships or fieldwork, Federal Work-Study, institutionally sponsored loans, and scholarships/grants available. Support available to part-time students. Financial award application deadline: 5/15; financial award applicants required to submit FAFSA.

Seattle Pacific University, M Ed/PhD School Counseling Program, Seattle, WA 98119-1997. Offers M Ed, PhD, Certificate. *Accreditation:* NCATE. Part-time programs available. *Faculty:* 2 full-time (both women). *Students:* 31 full-time (30 women), 30 part-time (28 women); includes 6 minority (1 African American, 1 American Indian/Alaska Native, 3 Asian Americans or Pacific Islanders, 1 Hispanic American), 1 international. Average age 29. 57 applicants, 23% accepted, 13 enrolled. In 2009, 10 master's awarded. *Degree requirements:* For master's, year long internship. *Entrance requirements:* For master's, GRE General Test or MAT, minimum GPA of 3.0. *Application deadline:* For fall admission, 7/1 priority date for domestic students; for spring admission, 3/1 priority date for domestic students. Application fee: $50. Electronic applications accepted. *Expenses:* Contact institution. *Financial support:* In 2009–10, 50 students received support. Scholarships/grants available. Financial award applicants required to submit FAFSA. *Unit head:* Dr. Cher Edwards, Chair, 206-281-2286, Fax: 206-281-2756. *Application contact:* The Grad Center, 206-281-2091.

Seattle University, College of Education, Program in Counseling and School Psychology, Seattle, WA 98122-1090. Offers MA, Certificate, Ed S. *Accreditation:* NCATE. Part-time and evening/weekend programs available. *Degree requirements:* For master's, comprehensive exam. *Entrance requirements:* For master's, interview; GRE, MAT, or minimum GPA of 3.0; related work experience. Additional exam requirements/recommendations for international students: Required—TOEFL.

Shippensburg University of Pennsylvania, School of Graduate Studies, College of Education and Human Services, Department of Counseling, Shippensburg, PA 17257-2299. Offers Adlerian studies (Certificate); advanced study in counseling (Certificate); alcohol and drug counseling (Certificate); counseling (M Ed, MS), including college counseling (MS), community counseling (MS), elementary school counseling, mental health counseling (MS), secondary school counseling (MS), student personnel services (MS); couple and family counseling (Certificate). *Accreditation:* ACA (one or more programs are accredited); NCATE. Part-time and evening/weekend programs available. *Degree requirements:* For master's, fieldwork, research project, internship, candidacy. *Entrance requirements:* For master's, GRE or MAT (community, mental health, student personnel, and college counseling applicants if GPA is less than 2.75), minimum GPA of 2.75 (3.0 for M Ed), interview, resume, 3 letters of recommendation, supplemental data forms, one year of relevant work experience, on-campus interview. Additional exam requirements/recommendations for international students: Required—TOEFL (minimum score 560 paper-based; 220 computer-based); Recommended—IELTS (minimum score 6). Electronic applications accepted.

Simmons College, College of Arts and Sciences Graduate Studies, Department of Education, Program in Special Education, Boston, MA 02115. Offers applied behavior analysis (PhD); assistive technology (MS Ed, Ed S); behavioral education (MS Ed, Ed S); health professions education (PhD); language and literacy (MS Ed, Ed S); moderate disabilities (Ed S); moderate special needs (MS Ed); severe disabilities (Ed S); severe special needs (MS Ed); special education administration (MS Ed, PhD, Ed S). Part-time and evening/weekend programs available. *Students:* 45 full-time (40 women), 316 part-time (271 women); includes 19 minority (7 African Americans, 1 American Indian/Alaska Native, 7 Asian Americans or Pacific Islanders, 4 Hispanic Americans), 2 international. 95 applicants, 89% accepted, 65 enrolled. In 2009, 145 master's awarded. *Degree requirements:* For master's, student teaching. *Entrance requirements:* For doctorate, GRE, research proposal, interview, BCBA credential. Additional exam requirements/recommendations for international students: Required—TOEFL (minimum score 600 paper-based; 250 computer-based; 100 iBT). *Application deadline:* For fall admission, 8/1 priority date for domestic and international students; for winter admission, 12/15 priority date for domestic students; for spring admission, 12/15 priority date for domestic and international students. Applications are processed on a rolling basis. Application fee: $35. Electronic applications accepted. *Expenses:* Contact institution. *Financial support:* Application deadline: 3/1. *Faculty research:* Development and application of the IEP for teachers, assistive technology, language-based disabilities, applied behavior analysis, communication challenges between general and special education teachers. *Unit head:* Paul Abraham, Chair, Department of Education, 617-521-2575, E-mail: paul.abraham@simmons.edu. *Application contact:* Kristen Haack, Director, Graduate Studies Admission, 617-521-2917, Fax: 617-521-3058, E-mail: gsa@simmons.edu.

Simon Fraser University, Graduate Studies, Faculty of Education, Program in Counseling Psychology, Burnaby, BC V5A 1S6, Canada. Offers M Ed, MA. *Degree requirements:* For master's, project or thesis. *Entrance requirements:* For master's, minimum GPA of 3.0. Additional exam requirements/recommendations for international students: Required—TOEFL or IELTS.

Slippery Rock University of Pennsylvania, Graduate Studies (Recruitment), College of Education, Department of Counseling and Development, Slippery Rock, PA 16057-1383. Offers community counseling (MA), including addiction, adult, child and adolescent; elementary guidance and counseling (M Ed); secondary guidance and counseling (M Ed); student personnel (MA). *Accreditation:* ACA (one or more programs are accredited); NCATE. Part-time and evening/weekend programs available. *Degree requirements:* For master's, thesis (for some programs), oral comprehensive exam. *Entrance requirements:* For master's, GRE General Test, MAT, minimum GPA of 2.75. Additional exam requirements/recommendations for international students: Required—TOEFL (minimum score 550 paper-based; 213 computer-based). *Application deadline:* For fall admission, 3/1 priority date for domestic students, 5/1 priority date for international students; for spring admission, 11/1 priority date for domestic students, 9/1 priority date for international students. Applications are processed on a rolling basis. Application fee: $25 ($30 for international students). Electronic applications accepted. *Expenses:* Tuition, state resident: full-time $6666; part-time $370 per credit. Tuition, nonresident: full-time $10,666; part-time $593 per credit. Required fees: $2184; $182 per credit. *Financial support:* Career-related internships or fieldwork, Federal Work-Study, scholarships/grants, and unspecified assistantships available. Support available to part-time students. Financial award application deadline: 5/1; financial award applicants required to submit FAFSA. *Unit head:* Dr. Jared Colbert, Graduate Coordinator, 724-738-2272, Fax: 724-738-2880, E-mail: jared.kolbert@sru.edu. *Application contact:* Angela Piverotto, Interim Director of Graduate Studies, 724-738-2051, Fax: 724-738-2146, E-mail: graduate.admissions@sru.edu.

Sonoma State University, School of Social Sciences, Department of Counseling, Rohnert Park, CA 94928. Offers counseling (MA); marriage, family, and child counseling (MA); pupil personnel services (MA). *Accreditation:* ACA. Part-time programs available. *Faculty:* 2 full-time (1 woman), 8 part-time/adjunct (5 women). *Students:* 58 full-time (42 women), 26 part-time (22 women); includes 8 minority (1 American Indian/Alaska Native, 1 Asian American or Pacific Islander, 6 Hispanic Americans), 1 international. Average age 33. 148 applicants, 28% accepted, 13 enrolled. In 2009, 40 master's awarded. *Degree requirements:* For master's, internship. *Entrance requirements:* For master's, minimum GPA of 3.0. Additional exam requirements/recommendations for international students: Required—TOEFL (minimum score 500 paper-based; 173 computer-based). *Application deadline:* For fall admission, 11/30 for domestic students. Application fee: $55. *Expenses:* Tuition, nonresident: full-time $11,160. Required fees: $6226. Full-time tuition and fees vary according to course load. *Financial support:* Career-related internships or fieldwork available. Financial award application deadline: 3/2; financial award applicants required to submit FAFSA. *Unit head:* Jaymala Madathil, Program Coordinator, 707-664-4067, E-mail: jaymala.madathil@sonoma.edu. *Application contact:* Stephanie Wilkinson, Administrative Analyst, 707-664-2544, Fax: 707-664-2038, E-mail: stephanie.wilkinson@sonoma.edu.

South Carolina State University, School of Graduate Studies, Department of Education, Orangeburg, SC 29117-0001. Offers early childhood and special education (M Ed); early childhood education (MAT); elementary education (M Ed, MAT); engineering (MAT); general science (MAT); mathematics (MAT); secondary education (M Ed), including biology education, business education, counselor education, English education, home economics education, industrial education, mathematics education, science education, social studies education; special education (M Ed), including emotionally handicapped, learning disabilities, mentally handicapped. *Accreditation:* NCATE. Part-time and evening/weekend programs available. *Degree requirements:* For master's, thesis optional, departmental qualifying exam. *Entrance requirements:* For master's, GRE General Test, NTE, interview, teaching certificate. Electronic applications accepted. *Expenses:* Tuition, state resident: part-time $470 per credit hour. Tuition, nonresident: part-time $924 per credit hour. *Faculty research:* Critical thinking, child abuse, stress, test-taking skills, conflict resolution, mainstreaming.

South Carolina State University, School of Graduate Studies, Department of Human Services, Orangeburg, SC 29117-0001. Offers elementary counselor education (M Ed); rehabilitation counseling (MA); secondary counselor education (M Ed). *Accreditation:* CORE. Part-time and evening/weekend programs available. *Degree requirements:* For master's, comprehensive exam (for some programs), departmental qualifying exam, internship. *Entrance requirements:* For master's, GRE, MAT, minimum GPA of 2.7. Electronic applications accepted. *Expenses:* Tuition, state resident: part-time $470 per credit hour. Tuition, nonresident: part-time $924 per credit hour. *Faculty research:* Handicap, disability, rehabilitation evaluation, vocation.

South Dakota State University, Graduate School, College of Education and Human Sciences, Department of Counseling and Human Resource Development, Brookings, SD 57007. Offers MS. *Accreditation:* ACA; NCATE. Part-time and evening/weekend programs available. *Degree requirements:* For master's, comprehensive exam, thesis (for some programs), oral exams. *Entrance requirements:* For master's, minimum GPA of 2.75. Additional exam requirements/recommendations for international students: Required—TOEFL (minimum score 525 paper-based; 197 computer-based; 71 iBT). *Faculty research:* Rural mental health, family issues, character education, student affairs, solution focused therapy.

Southeastern Louisiana University, College of Education and Human Development, Department of Counseling and Human Development, Hammond, LA 70402. Offers counselor education (M Ed), including community counseling, marriage and family therapy, school counseling, substance abuse counseling. *Accreditation:* ACA; NCATE. Part-time programs available. *Faculty:* 7 full-time (5 women), 1 part-time/adjunct (0 women). *Students:* 58 full-time (54 women), 45 part-time (41 women); includes 16 minority (15 African Americans, 1 Hispanic American). Average age 29. 38 applicants, 100% accepted, 23 enrolled. In 2009, 23 master's awarded. *Degree requirements:* For master's, comprehensive exam, thesis optional. *Entrance requirements:* For master's, GRE (verbal and quantitative). Additional exam requirements/recommendations for international students: Required—TOEFL (minimum score 500 paper-based; 173 computer-based; 61 iBT). *Application deadline:* For fall admission, 7/15 priority date for domestic students, 6/1 priority date for international students; for spring admission, 12/1 priority date for domestic students, 10/1 priority date for international students. Applications are processed on a rolling basis. Application fee: $20 ($30 for international students). Electronic applications accepted. *Expenses:* Tuition, state resident: full-time $3086; part-time $225 per credit hour. Tuition, nonresident: part-time $529 per credit hour. Required fees: $1195. Tuition and fees vary according to course level and course load. *Financial support:* In 2009–10, 6 students received support. Career-related internships or fieldwork, Federal Work-Study, institutionally sponsored loans, and administrative assistantships available. Support available to part-time students. Financial award application deadline: 5/1; financial award applicants required to submit FAFSA. *Faculty research:* Marriage counseling, family of origin, counselor training, substance abuse counseling, childhood and adolescent obesity. *Unit head:* Dr. June Williams, Interim Department Head, 985-549-2309, Fax: 985-549-3758, E-mail: jwilliams@selu.edu. *Application contact:* Sandra Meyers, Graduate Admissions Analyst, 985-549-2066, Fax: 985-549-5632, E-mail: admissions@selu.edu.

Southeastern Oklahoma State University, School of Behavioral Sciences, Durant, OK 74701-0609. Offers community counseling (MBS). Part-time and evening/weekend programs available. *Faculty:* 10 full-time (3 women). *Students:* 23 full-time (18 women), 18 part-time (14 women); includes 14 minority (2 African Americans, 10 American Indian/Alaska Native, 1 Asian American or Pacific Islander, 1 Hispanic American), 2 international. Average age 35. 11 applicants, 100% accepted, 11 enrolled. *Degree requirements:* For master's, thesis optional. *Entrance requirements:* For master's, GRE General Test, minimum GPA of 3.0 in last 60 hours or 2.75 overall. Additional exam requirements/recommendations for international students: Required—TOEFL (minimum score 550 paper-based; 213 computer-based). *Application deadline:* For fall admission, 8/1 for domestic students, 6/1 for international students; for spring admission, 1/5 for domestic students, 11/1 for international students. Application fee: $20 ($55 for international students). Electronic applications accepted. *Financial support:* Fellowships, research assistantships, teaching assistantships, Federal Work-Study available. Support available to part-time students. Financial award application deadline: 6/15. *Unit head:* Dr. Kimberly Donovan, Program Coordinator, 580-745-2312, E-mail: kdonovan@se.edu. *Application contact:* Carrie Williamson, Graduate Secretary, 580-745-2200, Fax: 580-745-7474, E-mail: cwilliamson@se.edu.

Southeastern Oklahoma State University, School of Education, Durant, OK 74701-0609. Offers math specialist (M Ed); reading specialist (M Ed); school administration (M Ed); school counseling (M Ed). *Accreditation:* NCATE. Part-time and evening/weekend programs available. *Faculty:* 52 full-time (19 women), 1 (woman) part-time/adjunct. *Students:* 14 full-time (11 women), 73 part-time (58 women); includes 22 minority (4 African Americans, 17 American Indian/Alaska Native, 1 Hispanic American). Average age 32. 18 applicants, 100% accepted, 18 enrolled. *Degree requirements:* For master's, comprehensive exam, thesis optional, portfolio (M Ed). *Entrance requirements:* For master's, GRE General Test (MBS), minimum GPA of 3.0 in last 60 hours or 2.75 overall. Additional exam requirements/recommendations for international students: Required—TOEFL (minimum score 550 paper-based; 213 computer-based). *Application deadline:* For fall admission, 8/1 for domestic students, 6/1 for international students; for spring admission, 1/5 for domestic students, 11/1 for international students. Application fee: $20 ($55 for international students). Electronic applications accepted. *Financial support:* In 2009–10, 1 teaching assistantship with full tuition reimbursement (averaging $5,000 per year) was awarded; Federal Work-Study, institutionally sponsored loans, and tuition waivers (partial) also available. Support available to part-time students. Financial award application deadline: 6/15; financial award applicants required to submit FAFSA. *Unit head:* Dr. Melanie Price, Chair, 580-745-2602, Fax: 580-745-7474, E-mail: mprice@se.edu. *Application contact:* Carrie Williamson, Graduate Secretary, 580-745-2200, Fax: 580-745-7474, E-mail: cwilliamson@se.edu.

Southeastern University, Department of Behavioral and Social Sciences, Lakeland, FL 33801-6099. Offers human services (MA); professional counseling (MS); school counseling (MS). Evening/weekend programs available.

Southeast Missouri State University, School of Graduate Studies, Department of Educational Leadership and Counseling, Counseling Program, Cape Girardeau, MO 63701-4799. Offers counseling education (Ed S); mental health counseling (MA); school counseling (MA), including elementary counseling, secondary counseling. *Accreditation:* ACA; NCATE. Part-time and evening/weekend programs available. *Degree requirements:* For master's, comprehensive exam, thesis optional, portfolio, oral exam; for Ed S, oral exam. *Entrance requirements:* For master's, GRE General Test, MAT, minimum undergraduate GPA of 3.0; for Ed S, GRE General Test or MAT, minimum graduate GPA of 3.5. Additional exam requirements/recommendations for international students: Required—TOEFL (minimum score 550 paper-based; 213 computer-based); Recommended—IELTS (minimum score 6). Electronic applications accepted. *Expenses:* Tuition, state resident: full-time $4266; part-time $237 per credit hour. Tuition, nonresident: full-time $7506; part-time $417 per credit hour. Required fees: $427; $427. *Faculty research:* Counselor development, cognitive development of counselors, counselor supervision, issues in school counseling, issues in mental health counseling.

Southern Adventist University, School of Education and Psychology, Collegedale, TN 37315-0370. Offers clinical mental health counseling (MS); inclusive education (MS Ed); instructional leadership (MS Ed); literacy education (MS Ed); outdoor teacher education (MS Ed); school counseling (MS). *Accreditation:* NCATE. Part-time and evening/weekend programs available. *Faculty:* 4 full-time (2 women), 8 part-time/adjunct (5 women). *Students:* 33 full-time (15 women), 17 part-time (13 women); includes 16 minority (7 African Americans, 9 Hispanic Americans). Average age 30. In 2009, 23 master's awarded. *Degree requirements:* For

Counselor Education

Southern Adventist University *(continued)*

master's, comprehensive exam (for some programs), thesis optional, position paper (MS), portfolio (MS Ed in outdoor teacher education). *Entrance requirements:* For master's, interview (MS); 9 semester hours of upper division course work in psychology or related field, including 1 course in psychology research or statistics; 9 semester hours of education (MS Ed). Additional exam requirements/recommendations for international students: Required—TOEFL (minimum score 600 paper-based; 250 computer-based; 100 iBT). *Application deadline:* For fall admission, 7/1 priority date for domestic students, 6/1 priority date for international students; for winter admission, 11/1 priority date for domestic students, 10/1 priority date for international students; for spring admission, 4/1 priority date for domestic students, 3/1 priority date for international students. Applications are processed on a rolling basis. Application fee: $25. Electronic applications accepted. *Expenses:* Tuition: Full-time $13,149; part-time $487 per credit hour. *Financial support:* In 2009–10, 7 students received support, including 1 research assistantship with full tuition reimbursement available (averaging $15,000 per year), 5 teaching assistantships with full tuition reimbursements available (averaging $15,000 per year); career-related internships or fieldwork, scholarships/grants, tuition waivers (partial), and unspecified assistantships also available. Support available to part-time students. Financial award application deadline: 4/1; financial award applicants required to submit FAFSA. *Unit head:* Dr. Wesley Taylor, Dean, 423-236-2444, Fax: 423-236-1765, E-mail: jwtv@southern.edu. *Application contact:* Mikhaile Spence, Information Contact, 423-236-2496, Fax: 423-236-1765, E-mail: maspence@southern.edu.

Southern Arkansas University–Magnolia, Graduate Programs, Magnolia, AR 71753. Offers agriculture (MS); business administration (MBA); computer and information sciences (MS); counseling (MS); education (M Ed), including counseling and development, curriculum and instruction emphasis, educational administration and supervision, elementary education, middle level emphasis, reading emphasis, secondary education, TESOL emphasis; kinesiology (MS); library media and information specialist (M Ed); mental health and clinical counseling (MS); public administration (EMPA); school counseling (M Ed); teaching (MAT). *Accreditation:* NCATE. Part-time and evening/weekend programs available. *Faculty:* 43 full-time (24 women), 12 part-time/adjunct (7 women). *Students:* 116 full-time (78 women), 333 part-time (255 women); includes 105 minority (98 African Americans, 3 American Indian/Alaska Native, 3 Asian Americans or Pacific Islanders, 1 Hispanic American), 11 international. Average age 33. In 2009, 88 master's awarded. *Degree requirements:* For master's, comprehensive exam, thesis optional. *Entrance requirements:* For master's, GRE, MAT or GMAT, minimum GPA of 2.75. *Application deadline:* For fall admission, 8/15 for domestic students; for winter admission, 1/8 for domestic students; for spring admission, 1/8 for domestic students. Applications are processed on a rolling basis. Application fee: $0. *Expenses:* Tuition: state resident: full-time $3798; part-time $211 per hour. Tuition, nonresident: full-time $5580; part-time $310 per hour. Required fees: $584. *Financial support:* Career-related internships or fieldwork, Federal Work-Study, scholarships/grants, tuition waivers (full), and unspecified assistantships available. Financial award applicants required to submit FAFSA. *Faculty research:* Alternative certification for teachers, supervision of instruction, instructional leadership, counseling. *Unit head:* Dr. Kim Bloss, Dean, Graduate Studies, 870-235-4150, Fax: 870-235-5227, E-mail: kkbloss@saumag.edu. *Application contact:* Dr. Kim Bloss, Dean, Graduate Studies, 870-235-4150, Fax: 870-235-5227, E-mail: kkbloss@saumag.edu.

Southern Connecticut State University, School of Graduate Studies, School of Education, Department of Counseling and School Psychology, New Haven, CT 06515-1355. Offers community counseling (MS); counseling (Diploma); school counseling (MS); school psychology (MS, Diploma). *Accreditation:* ACA (one or more programs are accredited); NCATE. *Faculty:* 8 full-time, 10 part-time/adjunct. *Students:* 87 full-time (74 women), 77 part-time (67 women); includes 24 minority (18 African Americans, 6 Hispanic Americans), 3 international. 179 applicants, 27% accepted, 45 enrolled. In 2009, 44 master's, 12 other advanced degrees awarded. *Degree requirements:* For master's, comprehensive exam. *Entrance requirements:* For master's, interview, previous course work in behavioral sciences, minimum QPA of 2.7. *Application deadline:* For fall admission, 1/15 for domestic students; for spring admission, 10/15 for domestic students. Application fee: $50. Electronic applications accepted. Tuition and fees vary according to program. *Financial support:* Teaching assistantships, career-related internships or fieldwork available. Financial award application deadline: 4/15; financial award applicants required to submit FAFSA. *Unit head:* Dr. Patricia DeBarbieri, Chairperson, 203-392-5483, E-mail: debarbierip1@southernct.edu. *Application contact:* Dr. Louisa Foss, Graduate Coordinator, Clinical Mental Health Counseling, 203-392-5154, E-mail: fossl1@southernct.edu.

Southern Illinois University Carbondale, Graduate School, College of Education, Department of Educational Psychology and Special Education, Program in Educational Psychology, Carbondale, IL 62901-4701. Offers counselor education (MS Ed, PhD); educational psychology (PhD); human learning and development (MS Ed); measurement and statistics (PhD). *Accreditation:* NCATE. *Degree requirements:* For master's, thesis; for doctorate, thesis/dissertation. *Entrance requirements:* For master's, GRE General Test, minimum GPA of 2.7; for doctorate, minimum GPA of 3.25. Additional exam requirements/recommendations for international students: Required—TOEFL. *Faculty research:* Career development, problem solving, learning and instruction, cognitive development, family assessment.

Southern Methodist University, Annette Caldwell Simmons School of Education and Human Development, Department of Dispute Resolution and Counseling, Dallas, TX 75275. Offers counseling (MS); dispute resolution (MA, Certificate). Part-time programs available. *Faculty:* 6 full-time (2 women), 24 part-time/adjunct (11 women). *Students:* 5 full-time (all women), 207 part-time (165 women); includes 43 minority (18 African Americans, 8 Asian Americans or Pacific Islanders, 17 Hispanic Americans), 6 international. Average age 33. 103 applicants, 50% accepted, 46 enrolled. In 2009, 62 master's, 10 other advanced degrees awarded. *Degree requirements:* For master's, practica experience, 2 internships (counseling). *Entrance requirements:* For master's, minimum undergraduate GPA of 2.75 (for dispute resolution), 3.0 (for counseling); 3 letters of recommendation. Additional exam requirements/recommendations for international students: Required—TOEFL. *Application deadline:* For fall admission, 5/1 for domestic students; for spring admission, 12/1 for domestic students. Applications are processed on a rolling basis. Application fee: $75. Electronic applications accepted. *Unit head:* Dr. Tony Picchioni, Department Chair, 972-473-3408, Fax: 972-473-3425. *Application contact:* Cynthia McIntyre, Program Manager, 972-473-3431, Fax: 972-473-3425, E-mail: adr@smu.edu or counselingmaster@smu.edu.

Southern University and Agricultural and Mechanical College, Graduate School, College of Education, Department of Behavioral Studies and Educational Leadership, Baton Rouge, LA 70813. Offers administration and supervision (M Ed); counselor education (MA); educational leadership (M Ed); mental health counseling (MA). *Accreditation:* ACA; NCATE. *Degree requirements:* For master's, comprehensive exam, thesis optional. *Entrance requirements:* For master's, GRE General Test. Additional exam requirements/recommendations for international students: Required—TOEFL (minimum score 525 paper-based; 193 computer-based). *Faculty research:* Mental health, computer assisted programs, families relations, head start improvements, careers.

Southwestern Oklahoma State University, College of Professional and Graduate Studies, School of Behavioral Sciences and Education, Specialization in Community Counseling, Weatherford, OK 73096-3098. Offers M Ed. M Ed distance learning degree program offered to Oklahoma residents only. *Accreditation:* NCATE. Part-time and evening/weekend programs available. Postbaccalaureate distance learning degree programs offered (minimal on-campus study). *Degree requirements:* For master's, exam. *Entrance requirements:* For master's, GRE General Test or minimum undergraduate GPA of 3.0. Additional exam requirements/recommendations for international students: Required—TOEFL.

Southwestern Oklahoma State University, College of Professional and Graduate Studies, School of Behavioral Sciences and Education, Specialization in School Counseling, Weatherford, OK 73096-3098. Offers M Ed. M Ed distance learning degree program offered to Oklahoma residents only. *Accreditation:* NCATE. Part-time and evening/weekend programs available. Postbaccalaureate distance learning degree programs offered (minimal on-campus study). *Degree requirements:* For master's, exam. *Entrance requirements:* For master's, GRE General Test or minimum undergraduate GPA of 3.0, portfolio. Additional exam requirements/recommendations for international students: Required—TOEFL.

Spalding University, Graduate Studies, College of Education, Programs in Education, Louisville, KY 40203-2188. Offers elementary school education (MAT); general education (MA); high school education (MAT); middle school education (MAT); school administration (MA); special education (learning and behavioral disorders) (MAT); student guidance counselor (MA). MAT degree programs offered for first teaching certificate/license students. *Accreditation:* NCATE. Part-time and evening/weekend programs available. *Faculty:* 6 full-time (4 women), 32 part-time/adjunct (23 women). *Students:* 125 full-time (93 women), 64 part-time (49 women); includes 53 minority (50 African Americans, 2 American Indian/Alaska Native, 1 Hispanic American), 2 international. Average age 37. 57 applicants, 79% accepted, 41 enrolled. In 2009, 56 master's awarded. *Degree requirements:* For master's, portfolio, final project, clinical experience. *Entrance requirements:* For master's, GRE General Test or MAT, interview, recommendations, resume. Additional exam requirements/recommendations for international students: Required—TOEFL (minimum score 535 paper-based; 203 computer-based). *Application deadline:* Applications are processed on a rolling basis. Application fee: $30. Electronic applications accepted. *Expenses:* Tuition: Full-time $11,340; part-time $630 per credit hour. Tuition and fees vary according to program. *Financial support:* In 2009–10, 106 students received support, including 3 research assistantships with partial tuition reimbursements available (averaging $3,590 per year); scholarships/grants, traineeships, and unspecified assistantships also available. Financial award application deadline: 3/15; financial award applicants required to submit FAFSA. *Faculty research:* Instructional technology, achievement gap, classroom management, assessment. *Unit head:* Dr. Beverly Keepers, Dean, 502-588-7121, Fax: 502-585-7123, E-mail: bkeepers@spalding.edu. *Application contact:* Admissions Office, 502-585-7111, E-mail: admissions@spalding.edu.

Spalding University, Graduate Studies, College of Social Sciences and Humanities, Program in Applied Behavior Analysis, Louisville, KY 40203-2188. Offers MA. *Faculty:* 2 full-time (0 women), 3 part-time/adjunct (0 women). *Students:* 21 full-time (19 women), 3 part-time (2 women); includes 2 minority (1 African American, 1 Hispanic American). Average age 32. 28 applicants, 93% accepted. *Entrance requirements:* For master's, GRE, 12 hours in psychology (developmental, research methods, learning, behavioral modifications, applied behavioral analysis), letters of recommendation, writing sample. Additional exam requirements/recommendations for international students: Required—TOEFL (minimum score 535 paper-based; 203 computer-based). *Application deadline:* For fall admission, 2/15 for domestic students. Application fee: $30. *Expenses:* Tuition: Full-time $11,340; part-time $630 per credit hour. Tuition and fees vary according to program. *Financial support:* In 2009–10, 15 students received support, including 2 research assistantships (averaging $4,260 per year); unspecified assistantships also available. Financial award application deadline: 3/15; financial award applicants required to submit FAFSA. *Unit head:* Dr. Nicholas Weatherly, Program Director, 502-585-9111 Ext. 2750, E-mail: nweatherly@spalding.edu. *Application contact:* Debbie Pierce, Admissions Office, 502-585-7111 Ext. 2698, E-mail: dpierce@spalding.edu.

Springfield College, Graduate Programs, Program in Education, Springfield, MA 01109-3797. Offers counseling and secondary education (M Ed, MS); early childhood education (M Ed, MS); education (M Ed, MS); educational administration (M Ed, MS); educational studies (M Ed, MS); elementary education (M Ed, MS); secondary education (M Ed, MS); special education (M Ed, MS). Part-time and evening/weekend programs available. *Entrance requirements:* Additional exam requirements/recommendations for international students: Required—TOEFL (minimum score 550 paper-based; 213 computer-based). Electronic applications accepted. *Expenses:* Tuition: Full-time $19,800; part-time $825 per credit hour. Required fees: $150.

Springfield College, Graduate Programs, Programs in Psychology and Counseling, Springfield, MA 01109-3797. Offers athletic counseling (M Ed, MS, CAGS); industrial/organizational psychology (M Ed, MS, CAGS); marriage and family therapy (M Ed, MS, CAGS); mental health counseling (M Ed, MS, CAGS); school guidance and counseling (M Ed, MS, CAGS); student personnel in higher education (M Ed, MS, CAGS). Part-time programs available. *Degree requirements:* For master's, research project, portfolio. *Entrance requirements:* Additional exam requirements/recommendations for international students: Required—TOEFL (minimum score 550 paper-based; 213 computer-based). Electronic applications accepted. *Expenses:* Tuition: Full-time $19,800; part-time $825 per credit hour. Required fees: $150.

State University of New York at New Paltz, Graduate School, School of Liberal Arts and Sciences, Department of Psychology, New Paltz, NY 12561. Offers mental health counseling (MS); psychology (MA); school counseling (MS). Part-time and evening/weekend programs available. *Faculty:* 11 full-time (8 women), 1 (woman) part-time/adjunct. *Students:* 40 full-time (33 women), 11 part-time (7 women); includes 3 minority (1 African American, 1 Asian American or Pacific Islander, 1 Hispanic American), 3 international. Average age 26. 113 applicants, 44% accepted, 33 enrolled. In 2009, 24 master's awarded. *Degree requirements:* For master's, comprehensive exam, thesis. *Entrance requirements:* For master's, GRE General Test, minimum GPA of 3.0. Additional exam requirements/recommendations for international students: Required—TOEFL (minimum score 550 paper-based; 213 computer-based; 80 iBT), IELTS (minimum score 6.5). *Application deadline:* For fall admission, 1/20 priority date for domestic and international students; for spring admission, 11/15 for domestic and international students. Application fee: $50. Electronic applications accepted. *Financial support:* In 2009–10, 7 students received support, including 6 teaching assistantships with partial tuition reimbursements available (averaging $5,000 per year); career-related internships or fieldwork, Federal Work-Study, institutionally sponsored loans, traineeships, tuition waivers (full), and unspecified assistantships also available. Financial award application deadline: 8/1; financial award applicants required to submit FAFSA. *Faculty research:* Disaster mental health, women's objectification, mate selection, cultural psychology, achievement motivation. *Unit head:* Dr. Glenn Geher, Chair, 845-257-3091, E-mail: geherg@newpaltz.edu. *Application contact:* Dr. Jonathan Raskin, Coordinator, 845-257-3471, E-mail: raskinj@newpaltz.edu.

State University of New York at Plattsburgh, Division of Education, Health, and Human Services, Department of Counselor Education, Plattsburgh, NY 12901-2681. Offers college/agency counseling (MS), including mental health counseling, student affairs professional practice; school counselor (MS Ed, CAS). *Accreditation:* ACA (one or more programs are accredited); Teacher Education Accreditation Council. Part-time programs available. *Faculty:* 6 full-time (2 women), 3 part-time/adjunct (2 women). *Students:* 55 full-time (45 women), 15 part-time (12 women); includes 6 minority (3 African Americans, 1 American Indian/Alaska Native, 1 Asian American or Pacific Islander, 1 Hispanic American). Average age 29. 44 applicants, 68% accepted, 20 enrolled. In 2009, 25 master's, 14 other advanced degrees awarded. *Degree requirements:* For master's, comprehensive exam, thesis optional, portfolio; for CAS, comprehensive exam, thesis optional. *Entrance requirements:* For master's, GRE General Test or MAT, minimum GPA of 2.8. Additional exam requirements/recommendations for international students: Required—TOEFL (minimum score 550 paper-based; 213 computer-based; 79 iBT). *Application deadline:* For fall admission, 2/15 priority date for domestic students; for spring admission, 10/15 priority date for domestic students. Applications are processed on a rolling basis. Application fee: $75. *Expenses:* Tuition, state resident: full-time $8370; part-time $349 per credit hour. Tuition, nonresident: full-time $13,250; part-time $552 per credit hour. Required fees: $1130. *Financial support:* Research assistantships, teaching assistantships, career-related internships or fieldwork, Federal Work-Study, and administrative assistantships, editorial assistantships available. Support available to part-time students. Financial award application deadline: 4/15; financial award applicants required to submit FAFSA. *Faculty research:* Campus violence, program accreditation, substance abuse, vocational assessment, group counseling, divorce. *Unit head:* Dr. Stephen Saiz, Coordinator, 518-564-4170. *Application contact:* Marguerite Adelman, Assistant Director, Graduate Admissions, 518-564-4723, Fax: 518-564-4722, E-mail: adelmaml@plattsburgh.edu.

State University of New York College at Oneonta, Graduate Education, Division of Education, Department of Educational Psychology and Counseling, Oneonta, NY 13820-4015. Offers

school counselor K-12 (MS Ed, CAS). *Accreditation:* NCATE. Part-time and evening/weekend programs available. *Students:* 23 full-time (18 women), 17 part-time (11 women). Average age 28. 30 applicants, 50% accepted, 15 enrolled. In 2009, 10 master's, 2 CASs awarded. *Degree requirements:* For master's, comprehensive exam. *Entrance requirements:* For master's, GRE General Test. *Application deadline:* For fall admission, 3/1 for domestic students. Application fee: $50. *Expenses:* Tuition, state resident: part-time $349 per credit hour. Tuition, nonresident: full-time $12,870; part-time $552 per credit hour. Required fees: $1280; $15.85 per credit hour. *Unit head:* Dr. Anuradhaa Shastri, Chair, 607-436-3554, Fax: 607-436-3799, E-mail: shastra@oneonta.edu. *Application contact:* Dean, 607-436-2523, Fax: 607-436-3084, E-mail: gradoffice@oneonta.edu.

Stephen F. Austin State University, Graduate School, College of Education, Department of Human Services, Nacogdoches, TX 75962. Offers counseling (MA); school psychology (MA); special education (M Ed); speech pathology (MS). *Accreditation:* ACA (one or more programs are accredited); ASHA (one or more programs are accredited); CORE; NCATE. *Degree requirements:* For master's, comprehensive exam, thesis (for some programs). *Entrance requirements:* For master's, GRE General Test, minimum GPA of 2.8. Additional exam requirements/recommendations for international students: Required—TOEFL.

Stephens College, Division of Graduate and Continuing Studies, Programs in Counseling, Columbia, MO 65215-0002. Offers counseling (M Ed), including marriage and family therapy, professional counseling, school counseling. Part-time and evening/weekend programs available. *Faculty:* 1 (woman) full-time, 11 part-time/adjunct (10 women). *Students:* 130 full-time (116 women), 32 part-time (28 women); includes 16 minority (13 African Americans, 2 Asian Americans or Pacific Islanders, 1 Hispanic American). Average age 33. 47 applicants, 68% accepted, 28 enrolled. In 2009, 35 master's awarded. *Degree requirements:* For master's, thesis. *Entrance requirements:* For master's, minimum GPA of 3.0 in last 60 hours. Additional exam requirements/recommendations for international students: Required—TOEFL (minimum score 213 computer-based). *Application deadline:* For fall admission, 7/25 priority date for domestic and international students; for winter admission, 12/1 priority date for domestic and international students; for spring admission, 4/25 priority date for domestic and international students. Applications are processed on a rolling basis. Application fee: $40. Electronic applications accepted. *Expenses:* Tuition: Part-time $350 per credit. Required fees: $25 per credit. *Financial support:* In 2009–10, 70 students received support. Scholarships/grants and unspecified assistantships available. Financial award application deadline: 12/5; financial award applicants required to submit FAFSA. *Unit head:* Dr. Linda Thompson, Program Chair, 800-388-7579. *Application contact:* Meredith Julian, Assistant Director of Marketing and Recruitment, 800-388-7579, E-mail: online@stephens.edu.

Stetson University, College of Arts and Sciences, Division of Education, Department of Counselor Education, DeLand, FL 32723. Offers marriage and family therapy (MS); mental health counseling (MS); school guidance and family consultation (MS). *Accreditation:* ACA. Evening/weekend programs available. *Students:* 66 full-time (59 women), 12 part-time (11 women); includes 19 minority (9 African Americans, 2 American Indian/Alaska Native, 8 Hispanic Americans), 2 international. Average age 32. In 2009, 28 master's awarded. *Entrance requirements:* For master's, GRE General Test. *Application deadline:* For fall admission, 3/1 priority date for domestic students; for spring admission, 11/1 for domestic students. Applications are processed on a rolling basis. Application fee: $25. Tuition and fees vary according to course load, campus/location and program. *Unit head:* Dr. Brigid Noonan-Klima, Chair, 386-822-8992. *Application contact:* Diana Belian, Office of Graduate Studies, 386-822-7075, Fax: 386-822-7388, E-mail: dbelian@stetson.edu.

Suffolk University, College of Arts and Sciences, Department of Education and Human Services, Program in School Counseling, Boston, MA 02108-2770. Offers M Ed, CAGS. Part-time and evening/weekend programs available. *Entrance requirements:* For master's, GRE General Test, MAT or Massachusetts Test for Educator Licensure (MTEL), 2 letters of recommendation, resume. *Application deadline:* For fall admission, 6/15 priority date for domestic students, 6/15 for international students; for spring admission, 11/15 priority date for domestic students, 11/15 for international students. Applications are processed on a rolling basis. Application fee: $50. *Expenses:* Tuition: Full-time $33,000; part-time $1100 per credit. Required fees: $20. Tuition and fees vary according to program. *Financial support:* Fellowships, career-related internships or fieldwork, Federal Work-Study, and institutionally sponsored loans available. Support available to part-time students. Financial award application deadline: 4/1; financial award applicants required to submit FAFSA. *Faculty research:* School counseling, mental health counseling, human resources. *Unit head:* Dr. Timothy A. Poynton, Graduate Program Director, 617-994-6454, Fax: 617-305-1743, E-mail: tpoynton@suffolk.edu. *Application contact:* Judith Reynolds, Director of Graduate Admissions, 617-573-8302, Fax: 617-305-1733, E-mail: grad.admission@suffolk.edu.

Sul Ross State University, Rio Grande College of Sul Ross State University, Alpine, TX 79832. Offers business administration (MBA); teacher education (M Ed), including bilingual education, counseling, educational diagnostics, elementary education, general education, reading, school administration, secondary education. Part-time and evening/weekend programs available. *Degree requirements:* For master's, thesis optional. *Entrance requirements:* For master's, GMAT or GRE General Test, minimum GPA of 2.5 in last 60 hours of undergraduate work. *Faculty research:* Drug and substance abuse counseling, U.S.-Mexico border economic development.

Sul Ross State University, School of Professional Studies, Department of Teacher Education, Program in Counseling, Alpine, TX 79832. Offers M Ed. Part-time and evening/weekend programs available. *Degree requirements:* For master's, thesis optional. *Entrance requirements:* For master's, GMAT or GRE General Test, minimum GPA of 2.5 in last 60 hours of undergraduate work. *Faculty research:* Input variable effects on EXCET for graduate students.

Syracuse University, School of Education, Program in Counselor Education, Syracuse, NY 13244. Offers PhD. *Accreditation:* ACA. Part-time programs available. *Students:* 9 full-time (7 women), 5 part-time (2 women); includes 2 minority (both African Americans), 3 international. Average age 36. 9 applicants, 56% accepted, 3 enrolled. In 2009, 4 doctorates awarded. *Degree requirements:* For doctorate, thesis/dissertation. *Entrance requirements:* For doctorate, GRE, MS. Additional exam requirements/recommendations for international students: Required—TOEFL (minimum score 100 iBT). *Application deadline:* For fall admission, 1/1 priority date for domestic and international students; for spring admission, 10/15 priority date for domestic and international students. Applications are processed on a rolling basis. Application fee: $75. Electronic applications accepted. *Expenses:* Tuition: Full-time $26,808; part-time $1117 per credit. Required fees: $1024. *Financial support:* Fellowships with full tuition reimbursements, teaching assistantships with full tuition reimbursements available. Financial award application deadline: 1/1; financial award applicants required to submit FAFSA. *Unit head:* Dr. Janine Bernard, Chair, 315-443-5266, Fax: 315-443-5732, E-mail: bernard@syr.edu. *Application contact:* Liza Rochelson, Graduate Recruiter, School of Education, 315-443-2505, E-mail: e-gradrcrt@syr.edu.

Syracuse University, School of Education, Program in Educational Technology, Syracuse, NY 13244. Offers CAS. *Accreditation:* ACA. Part-time programs available. *Students:* 1 (woman) part-time; minority (African American). Average age 47. In 2009, 1 CAS awarded. *Degree requirements:* For CAS, thesis or alternative. *Entrance requirements:* Additional exam requirements/recommendations for international students: Required—TOEFL (minimum score 100 iBT). *Application deadline:* For fall admission, 2/1 priority date for domestic and international students; for spring admission, 10/15 priority date for domestic and international students. Applications are processed on a rolling basis. Application fee: $75. Electronic applications accepted. *Expenses:* Tuition: Full-time $26,808; part-time $1117 per credit. Required fees: $1024. *Financial support:* Fellowships, research assistantships, teaching assistantships available. Financial award application deadline: 1/1. *Faculty research:* Academics and athletics, drug free schools, group counseling, prejudice prevention, culture-centered counseling. *Unit head:* Dr. Janine Bernard, Chair, 315-443-5266, Fax: 315-443-5732, E-mail: bernard@syr.edu. *Application contact:* Liza Rochelson, Graduate Recruiter, School of Education, 315-443-2505, E-mail: e-gradrcrt@syr.edu.

Syracuse University, School of Education, Program in Student Affairs Counseling, Syracuse, NY 13244. Offers MS. *Students:* 2 full-time (1 woman), 2 part-time (both women). Average age 26. 7 applicants, 57% accepted, 1 enrolled. In 2009, 3 master's awarded. *Entrance requirements:* For master's, GRE General Test or MAT, interview. Additional exam requirements/recommendations for international students: Required—TOEFL (minimum score 100 iBT). *Application deadline:* For fall admission, 2/1 for domestic students, 2/1 priority date for international students; for spring admission, 10/15 for domestic students, 10/15 priority date for international students. Applications are processed on a rolling basis. Application fee: $75. Electronic applications accepted. *Expenses:* Tuition: Full-time $26,808; part-time $1117 per credit. Required fees: $1024. *Financial support:* Fellowships with tuition reimbursements, teaching assistantships with tuition reimbursements, tuition waivers (partial) available. Financial award application deadline: 1/1; financial award applicants required to submit FAFSA. *Unit head:* Dr. Dennis Gilbride, Chair, 315-443-2266, E-mail: ddgilbr@syr.edu. *Application contact:* Liza Rochelson, Graduate Recruiter, School of Education, 315-443-2505, E-mail: e-gradrcrt@syr.edu.

Tarleton State University, College of Graduate Studies, College of Education, Department of Psychology and Counseling, Stephenville, TX 76402. Offers counseling and psychology (M Ed), including counseling, counseling psychology, educational psychology; educational administration (M Ed); secondary education (Certificate); special education (Certificate). Part-time and evening/weekend programs available. Postbaccalaureate distance learning degree programs offered (minimal on-campus study). *Degree requirements:* For master's, comprehensive exam, thesis optional. *Entrance requirements:* For master's, GRE General Test, minimum GPA of 3.0. Additional exam requirements/recommendations for international students: Required—TOEFL (minimum score 550 paper-based; 213 computer-based; 80 iBT). Electronic applications accepted.

Teachers College, Columbia University, Graduate Faculty of Education, Department of Health and Behavioral Studies, Program in Applied Behavior Analysis, New York, NY 10027-6696. Offers MA, Ed D, PhD.

Teachers College, Columbia University, Graduate Faculty of Education, Department of Health and Behavioral Studies, Program in Guidance and Rehabilitation, New York, NY 10027-6696. Offers MA.

Tennessee State University, The School of Graduate Studies and Research, College of Education, Department of Psychology, Nashville, TN 37209-1561. Offers counseling and guidance (MS), including counseling, elementary school counseling, organizational counseling, secondary school counseling; counseling psychology (PhD); psychology (MS, PhD); school psychology (MS, PhD). *Accreditation:* APA. *Degree requirements:* For doctorate, thesis/dissertation (for some programs). *Entrance requirements:* For master's, GRE General Test or MAT; for doctorate, GRE General Test or MAT, minimum GPA of 3.25, work experience. Electronic applications accepted.

Texas A&M International University, Office of Graduate Studies and Research, Department of Professional Programs, Laredo, TX 78041-1900. Offers educational administration (MS Ed); generic special education (MS Ed); school counseling (MS). *Faculty:* 9 full-time (3 women), 2 part-time/adjunct (1 woman). *Students:* 15 full-time (9 women), 152 part-time (120 women); includes 162 minority (1 African American, 161 Hispanic Americans). Average age 34. 59 applicants. In 2009, 74 master's awarded. *Application deadline:* For fall admission, 4/30 priority date for domestic students; for spring admission, 11/30 priority date for domestic students. *Financial support:* In 2009–10, 62 students received support, including 1 research assistantship. *Unit head:* Dr. Randel Brown, Interim Chair, 956-326-2679, E-mail: brown@tamiu.edu. *Application contact:* Rosie Dickinson, Director of Admissions, 956-326-2200.

Texas A&M University, College of Education and Human Development, Department of Educational Psychology, College Station, TX 77843. Offers counseling psychology (PhD); educational psychology (PhD); educational technology (M Ed); gifted and talented education (M Ed, MS); Hispanic bilingual education (M Ed, PhD); human learning and development (MS); intelligence, creativity, and giftedness (PhD); learning, development, and instruction (PhD); research, measurement and statistics (MS); research, measurement, and statistics (PhD); school counseling (M Ed); school psychology (PhD); special education (M Ed, PhD). *Accreditation:* APA (one or more programs are accredited). Part-time and evening/weekend programs available. Postbaccalaureate distance learning degree programs offered (no on-campus study). *Faculty:* 45. *Students:* 160 full-time (126 women), 144 part-time (118 women); includes 99 minority (25 African Americans, 13 Asian Americans or Pacific Islanders, 61 Hispanic Americans), 41 international. In 2009, 53 master's, 30 doctorates awarded. *Degree requirements:* For master's, thesis optional; for doctorate, thesis/dissertation. *Entrance requirements:* For master's and doctorate, GRE General Test. Additional exam requirements/recommendations for international students: Required—TOEFL. Application fee: $50 ($75 for international students). Electronic applications accepted. *Expenses:* Tuition, state resident: full-time $3991; part-time $221.74 per credit hour. Tuition, nonresident: full-time $9049; part-time $502.74 per credit hour. *Financial support:* In 2009–10, fellowships (averaging $12,000 per year), research assistantships (averaging $9,000 per year), teaching assistantships (averaging $9,000 per year) were awarded; career-related internships or fieldwork, institutionally sponsored loans, scholarships/grants, and unspecified assistantships also available. Financial award applicants required to submit FAFSA. *Unit head:* Dr. Victor Willson, Head, 979-845-1800. *Application contact:* Carol A. Wagner, Director of Advising, 979-845-1833, Fax: 979-862-1256, E-mail: epsyadvisor@tamu.edu.

Texas A&M University–Commerce, Graduate School, College of Education and Human Services, Department of Counseling, Commerce, TX 75429-3011. Offers M Ed, MS, PhD. *Accreditation:* ACA (one or more programs are accredited). Part-time programs available. Terminal master's awarded for partial completion of doctoral program. *Degree requirements:* For master's, comprehensive exam, thesis (for some programs); for doctorate, thesis/dissertation, departmental qualifying exam. *Entrance requirements:* For master's and doctorate, GRE General Test. *Faculty research:* Emergency responders, efficacy and effect of web-based instruction, family violence, play therapy.

Texas A&M University–Corpus Christi, Graduate Studies and Research, College of Education, Programs in Counseling, Corpus Christi, TX 78412-5503. Offers counseling (MS); counselor education (PhD). *Accreditation:* ACA. Part-time and evening/weekend programs available. *Degree requirements:* For master's, comprehensive exam, thesis (for some programs). *Entrance requirements:* For master's, GRE General Test. Additional exam requirements/recommendations for international students: Required—TOEFL. Electronic applications accepted.

Texas A&M University–Kingsville, College of Graduate Studies, College of Education, Department of Education, Program in Guidance and Counseling, Kingsville, TX 78363. Offers MA, MS. Part-time and evening/weekend programs available. *Degree requirements:* For master's, comprehensive exam, mini-thesis. *Entrance requirements:* For master's, GRE General Test, MAT, minimum GPA of 3.0. *Faculty research:* Diagnostician requirements for certification, teaching methods for adult learner.

Texas Christian University, College of Education, Program in Counseling, Fort Worth, TX 76129-0002. Offers counseling (M Ed); LPC (Certificate); school counseling (Certificate). Part-time and evening/weekend programs available. *Degree requirements:* For master's, oral exams. *Entrance requirements:* Additional exam requirements/recommendations for international students: Required—TOEFL (minimum score 550 paper-based; 213 computer-based; 80 iBT). *Application deadline:* For fall admission, 7/15 for domestic and international students; for spring admission, 11/15 for domestic and international students. Applications are processed on a rolling basis. Application fee: $50. *Expenses:* Tuition: Full-time $17,640; part-time $980 per credit hour. Tuition and fees vary according to program. *Financial support:* Teaching assistantships with full tuition reimbursements, career-related internships or fieldwork and

Counselor Education

Texas Christian University (continued)

unspecified assistantships available. Financial award application deadline: 3/15; financial award applicants required to submit FAFSA. *Unit head:* Dr. Kay B. Stevens, Associate Dean, 817-257-7661, E-mail: k.stevens2@tcu.edu. *Application contact:* Robyn P. Shepheard, Academic Program Specialist, 817-257-7661, E-mail: r.shepheard@tcu.edu.

Texas Southern University, College of Education, Department of Counselor Education, Houston, TX 77004-4584. Offers counseling (M Ed); counselor education (Ed D). Part-time and evening/weekend programs available. *Faculty:* 1 full-time (0 women). *Students:* 55 full-time (46 women), 83 part-time (72 women); includes 117 minority (109 African Americans, 2 Asian Americans or Pacific Islanders, 6 Hispanic Americans). Average age 36. 49 applicants, 90% accepted, 39 enrolled. In 2009, 23 master's, 3 doctorates awarded. *Degree requirements:* For master's, one foreign language, comprehensive exam; for doctorate, comprehensive exam, thesis/dissertation. *Entrance requirements:* For master's, GRE General Test, minimum GPA of 2.5; for doctorate, GRE General Test or MAT, master's degree, minimum B+ average. Additional exam requirements/recommendations for international students: Required—TOEFL. *Application deadline:* For fall admission, 7/1 priority date for domestic students, 7/1 for international students; for spring admission, 11/1 priority date for domestic students, 11/1 for international students. Applications are processed on a rolling basis. Application fee: $50 ($75 for international students). Electronic applications accepted. *Expenses:* Tuition, state resident: full-time $1805; part-time $100 per credit hour. Tuition, nonresident: full-time $6470; part-time $343 per credit hour. Tuition and fees vary according to course level, course load and degree level. *Financial support:* In 2009–10, 1 research assistantship (averaging $10,000 per year), 1 teaching assistantship (averaging $13,500 per year) were awarded; scholarships/grants and unspecified assistantships also available. Support available to part-time students. Financial award application deadline: 5/1. *Faculty research:* Clinical and urban psychology. *Unit head:* Dr. Shanna Broussard, Chair, 713-313-1052, Fax: 713-313-7481, E-mail: broussard_sl@tsu.edu. *Application contact:* Dr. Gregory Maddox, Interim Dean of the Graduate School, 713-313-7011 Ext. 4410, Fax: 713-639-1876, E-mail: maddox_gh@tsu.edu.

Texas State University–San Marcos, Graduate School, College of Education, Department of Counseling, Leadership, Adult Education, and School Psychology, Program in Counseling and Guidance, San Marcos, TX 78666. Offers M Ed. *Accreditation:* ACA. Part-time and evening/weekend programs available. *Faculty:* 13 full-time (8 women), 12 part-time/adjunct (7 women). *Students:* 31 full-time (26 women), 53 part-time (50 women); includes 29 minority (5 African Americans, 24 Hispanic Americans). Average age 30. 37 applicants, 54% accepted, 17 enrolled. In 2009, 30 master's awarded. *Degree requirements:* For master's, comprehensive exam, thesis (for some programs). *Entrance requirements:* For master's, GRE General Test, minimum GPA of 3.0 in last 60 hours of course work. Additional exam requirements/recommendations for international students: Required—TOEFL (minimum score 550 paper-based; 213 computer-based). *Application deadline:* For fall admission, 4/15 for domestic students, 3/15 for international students; for spring admission, 10/1 for domestic and international students. Applications are processed on a rolling basis. Application fee: $40 ($90 for international students). Electronic applications accepted. *Expenses:* Tuition, state resident: full-time $5784; part-time $241 per credit hour. Tuition, nonresident: full-time $13,224; part-time $551 per credit hour. Required fees: $1728; $48 per credit hour. $306. Tuition and fees vary according to course load. *Financial support:* In 2009–10, 50 students received support, including 14 research assistantships (averaging $4,965 per year), 1 teaching assistantship (averaging $5,076 per year); career-related internships or fieldwork, Federal Work-Study, and institutionally sponsored loans also available. Support available to part-time students. Financial award application deadline: 4/1; financial award applicants required to submit FAFSA. *Faculty research:* Visiting teachers. *Unit head:* Dr. Colleen Connolly, Graduate Advisor, 512-245-2676, Fax: 512-245-8872, E-mail: cc32@txstate.edu. *Application contact:* Dr. J. Michael Willoughby, Dean of Graduate School, 512-245-2581, Fax: 512-245-8365, E-mail: gradcollege@txstate.edu.

Texas State University–San Marcos, Graduate School, College of Education, Department of Counseling, Leadership, Adult Education, and School Psychology, Program in Professional Counseling, San Marcos, TX 78666. Offers MA. *Accreditation:* ACA. Part-time programs available. *Faculty:* 13 full-time (8 women), 11 part-time/adjunct (7 women). *Students:* 53 full-time (50 women), 112 part-time (99 women); includes 30 minority (4 African Americans, 4 Asian Americans or Pacific Islanders, 22 Hispanic Americans). Average age 31. 59 applicants, 31% accepted, 6 enrolled. In 2009, 24 master's awarded. *Degree requirements:* For master's, comprehensive exam, internship. *Entrance requirements:* For master's, GRE General Test, minimum GPA of 3.0 in last 60 hours. Additional exam requirements/recommendations for international students: Required—TOEFL (minimum score 550 paper-based; 213 computer-based). *Application deadline:* For fall admission, 4/15 for domestic and international students; for spring admission, 10/1 for domestic and international students. Applications are processed on a rolling basis. Application fee: $40 ($90 for international students). Electronic applications accepted. *Expenses:* Tuition, state resident: full-time $5784; part-time $241 per credit hour. Tuition, nonresident: full-time $13,224; part-time $551 per credit hour. Required fees: $1728; $48 per credit hour. $306. Tuition and fees vary according to course load. *Financial support:* In 2009–10, 110 students received support, including 3 research assistantships (averaging $5,491 per year), 8 teaching assistantships (averaging $3,213 per year); Federal Work-Study and institutionally sponsored loans also available. Support available to part-time students. Financial award application deadline: 4/1; financial award applicants required to submit FAFSA. *Unit head:* Dr. Linda Homeyer, Graduate Advisor, 512-245-2575, Fax: 512-245-8872, E-mail: lh10@txstate.edu. *Application contact:* Dr. Linda Homeyer, Graduate Advisor, 512-245-2575, Fax: 512-245-8872, E-mail: lh10@txstate.edu.

Texas Tech University, Graduate School, College of Education, Department of Educational Psychology and Leadership, Lubbock, TX 79409. Offers counselor education (M Ed, PhD); educational leadership (M Ed, Ed D); educational psychology (M Ed, PhD); higher education (M Ed, Ed D); higher education: higher education research (PhD); instructional technology (M Ed, Ed D); instructional technology: distance education (M Ed); special education (M Ed, Ed D). *Accreditation:* ACA; NCATE. Part-time programs available. *Students:* 137 full-time (94 women), 335 part-time (236 women); includes 90 minority (27 African Americans, 6 American Indian/Alaska Native, 3 Asian Americans or Pacific Islanders, 54 Hispanic Americans), 34 international. Average age 36. 390 applicants, 51% accepted, 90 enrolled. In 2009, 113 master's, 18 doctorates awarded. *Degree requirements:* For master's, thesis optional; for doctorate, thesis/dissertation. *Entrance requirements:* For master's and doctorate, GRE General Test. Additional exam requirements/recommendations for international students: Required—TOEFL (minimum score 550 paper-based; 213 computer-based). *Application deadline:* For fall admission, 3/1 priority date for international students; for spring admission, 11/1 priority date for international students. Applications are processed on a rolling basis. Application fee: $50 ($75 for international students). Electronic applications accepted. *Expenses:* Tuition, state resident: full-time $5100; part-time $213 per credit hour. Tuition, nonresident: full-time $11,748; part-time $490 per credit hour. Required fees: $2298; $50 per credit hour. $555 per semester. *Financial support:* Research assistantships with partial tuition reimbursements, teaching assistantships with partial tuition reimbursements, career-related internships or fieldwork, Federal Work-Study, and institutionally sponsored loans available. Support available to part-time students. Financial award application deadline: 4/15; financial award applicants required to submit FAFSA. *Faculty research:* Psychological processes of teaching and learning, teaching populations with special needs, instructional technology, educational administration in education, theories and practice in counseling and counselor education K-12 and higher. *Unit head:* Dr. William Lan, Chair, 806-742-1998 Ext. 436, Fax: 806-742-2179, E-mail: william.lan@ttu.edu. *Application contact:* Dr. Joseph G. Claudet, Graduate Adviser, 806-742-1998, Fax: 806-742-2179.

Texas Wesleyan University, Graduate Programs, Programs in Education, Fort Worth, TX 76105-1536. Offers education (M Ed, Ed D); marraige and family therapy (MSMFT); professional counseling (MA); school counseling (MS). Part-time and evening/weekend programs available. Postbaccalaureate distance learning degree programs offered (no on-campus study). *Faculty:* 11 full-time (7 women), 3 part-time/adjunct (2 women). *Students:* 56 full-time (47

women), 208 part-time (174 women); includes 102 minority (54 African Americans, 2 American Indian/Alaska Native, 3 Asian Americans or Pacific Islanders, 43 Hispanic Americans), 4 international. Average age 36. 102 applicants, 77% accepted, 66 enrolled. In 2009, 179 master's awarded. *Entrance requirements:* For master's, GRE General Test, minimum GPA of 3.0 in final 60 hours of undergraduate course work, interview. *Application deadline:* For fall admission, 6/15 priority date for domestic students; for spring admission, 10/15 priority date for domestic students. Applications are processed on a rolling basis. Application fee: $40 ($50 for international students). Tuition and fees vary according to degree level. *Financial support:* Career-related internships or fieldwork, Federal Work-Study, scholarships/grants, and tuition waivers (full and partial) available. Support available to part-time students. Financial award application deadline: 3/15; financial award applicants required to submit FAFSA. *Faculty research:* Teacher effectiveness, bilingual education, analytic teaching. *Unit head:* Dr. Carlos Martinez, Dean, School of Education, 817-531-4940, Fax: 817-531-4943. *Application contact:* DeTrae Warren, Graduate Admission Recruiter, 817-531-4931, Fax: 817-531-4935, E-mail: dwarren@txwes.edu.

Texas Woman's University, Graduate School, College of Professional Education, Department of Family Sciences, Denton, TX 76201. Offers child development (MS, PhD); counseling and development (MS); early childhood education (M Ed, MA, MS, Ed D); family studies (MS, PhD); family therapy (MS, PhD). *Accreditation:* ACA (one or more programs are accredited). Part-time and evening/weekend programs available. *Faculty:* 25 full-time (21 women), 4 part-time/adjunct (all women). *Students:* 111 full-time (105 women), 294 part-time (269 women); includes 149 minority (99 African Americans, 3 American Indian/Alaska Native, 7 Asian Americans or Pacific Islanders, 40 Hispanic Americans), 22 international. Average age 36. 179 applicants, 86% accepted, 72 enrolled. In 2009, 86 master's, 22 doctorates awarded. Terminal master's awarded for partial completion of doctoral program. *Degree requirements:* For master's, portfolio; for doctorate, comprehensive exam, thesis/dissertation. *Entrance requirements:* For master's, interview, letter of intent, curriculum vitae; for doctorate, interview, minimum GPA of 3.5 in last 60 hours of course work. Additional exam requirements/recommendations for international students: Required—TOEFL (minimum score 550 paper-based; 213 computer-based; 79 iBT). *Application deadline:* For fall admission, 2/15 priority date for domestic students, 3/1 for international students; for spring admission, 9/15 priority date for domestic students, 8/1 for international students. Applications are processed on a rolling basis. Application fee: $50. Electronic applications accepted. *Expenses:* Tuition, state resident: full-time $3564; part-time $198 per credit hour. Tuition, nonresident: full-time $8550; part-time $475 per credit hour. Required fees: $69.26 per credit hour. Tuition and fees vary according to course load. *Financial support:* In 2009–10, 96 students received support, including 13 research assistantships (averaging $10,746 per year), 7 teaching assistantships (averaging $10,746 per year); career-related internships or fieldwork, Federal Work-Study, institutionally sponsored loans, scholarships/grants, traineeships, health care benefits, and unspecified assistantships also available. Support available to part-time students. Financial award application deadline: 3/1; financial award applicants required to submit FAFSA. *Faculty research:* Parenting/parent education, distance education, play therapy, family sexuality, diversity, ANTHEM healthy marriages initiative. *Unit head:* Dr. Larry LeFlore, Chair, 940-898-2685, Fax: 940-898-2676, E-mail: famsci@twu.edu. *Application contact:* Samuel Wheeler, Assistant Director of Admissions, 940-898-3188, Fax: 940-898-3081, E-mail: wheelersr@twu.edu.

Trevecca Nazarene University, Graduate Division, Graduate Psychology Programs, Major in Clinical Counseling, Nashville, TN 37210-2877. Offers Ed D. Evening/weekend programs available. *Students:* 36 full-time (24 women), 5 part-time (all women); includes 9 African Americans. Average age 40. *Degree requirements:* For doctorate, comprehensive exam, thesis/dissertation. *Entrance requirements:* For doctorate, GRE, minimum GPA of 3.25; 3 recommendation forms; 400-word letter of intent; interview. Additional exam requirements/recommendations for international students: Required—TOEFL (minimum score 550 paper-based; 213 computer-based). *Application deadline:* Applications are processed on a rolling basis. Application fee: $50. *Expenses:* Contact institution. *Financial support:* Applicants required to submit FAFSA. *Unit head:* Dr. Peter Wilson, Director, 615-248-1384, Fax: 615-248-1662, E-mail: pwilson@trevecca.edu. *Application contact:* Heather Ambrefe, Department Secretary, 615-248-1384, Fax: 615-248-1662, E-mail: admissions_psy@trevecca.edu.

Trevecca Nazarene University, Graduate Division, Graduate Psychology Programs, Major in Counseling, Nashville, TN 37210-2877. Offers MA. Part-time and evening/weekend programs available. *Students:* 98 full-time (78 women), 27 part-time (18 women); includes 21 minority (19 African Americans, 2 Hispanic Americans), 1 international. In 2009, 36 master's awarded. *Degree requirements:* For master's, comprehensive exam, practicum. *Entrance requirements:* For master's, GRE General Test or MAT, minimum GPA of 2.7, 2 reference assessment forms. Additional exam requirements/recommendations for international students: Required—TOEFL (minimum score 550 paper-based; 213 computer-based). *Application deadline:* Applications are processed on a rolling basis. Application fee: $25. *Expenses:* Contact institution. *Financial support:* Career-related internships or fieldwork available. Financial award applicants required to submit FAFSA. *Unit head:* Dr. Peter Wilson, Director of Graduate Psychology Program, 615-248-1384, Fax: 615-248-1662, E-mail: admissions_psy@trevecca.edu. *Application contact:* Heather Ambrefe, Department Secretary, 615-248-1384, Fax: 615-248-1662, E-mail: admissions_psy@trevecca.edu.

Trinity (Washington) University, School of Education, Washington, DC 20017-1094. Offers counseling (MA); early childhood education (MAT); educating for change (M Ed); educational administration (MSA); elementary education (MAT); school counseling (MA); secondary education (MAT), including English, social studies; special education (MAT); teaching English as a second language (MAT); teaching English to speakers of other languages (M Ed); the teaching of reading (M Ed). *Accreditation:* NCATE. Part-time and evening/weekend programs available. *Degree requirements:* For master's, thesis (for some programs), capstone project(s). *Entrance requirements:* For master's, PRAXIS I, minimum GPA of 2.8. Additional exam requirements/recommendations for international students: Required—TOEFL (minimum score 550 paper-based; 213 computer-based). *Faculty research:* Technology, literacy, special education, organizations, inclusion models.

Troy University, Graduate School, College of Education, Program in Counseling and Psychology, Troy, AL 36082. Offers agency counsleing (Ed S); clinical mental health (MS); community counseling (MS, Ed S); corrections counseling (MS); rehabilitation counseling (MS); school psychology (MS, Ed S); school psychometry (MS); social service counseling (MS); student affairs counseling (MS); substance abuse counseling (MS). *Accreditation:* ACA; CORE; NCATE. Part-time and evening/weekend programs available. *Students:* 375 full-time (302 women), 753 part-time (642 women); includes 664 minority (610 African Americans, 8 American Indian/Alaska Native, 9 Asian Americans or Pacific Islanders, 37 Hispanic Americans). Average age 33. 493 applicants, 92% accepted. In 2009, 102 master's, 191 other advanced degrees awarded. *Degree requirements:* For master's, comprehensive exam, thesis. *Entrance requirements:* For master's, MAT, minimum GPA of 2.5. Additional exam requirements/recommendations for international students: Required—TOEFL (minimum score 523 paper-based; 193 computer-based; 70 iBT), IELTS (minimum score 6). *Application deadline:* Applications are processed on a rolling basis. Application fee: $50. Electronic applications accepted. *Unit head:* Dr. Andrew Creamer, Chair, 334-670-3350, Fax: 334-670-32961, E-mail: drcreamer@troy.edu. *Application contact:* Brenda K. Campbell, Director of Graduate Admissions, 334-670-3178, Fax: 334-670-3733, E-mail: bcamp@troy.edu.

Troy University, Graduate School, College of Education, Program in School Counseling, Troy, AL 36082. Offers school counseling (Ed S). *Accreditation:* ACA; CORE; NCATE. Part-time and evening/weekend programs available. *Students:* 32 full-time (26 women), 99 part-time (90 women); includes 102 minority (99 African Americans, 2 American Indian/Alaska Native, 1 Hispanic American). Average age 35. 58 applicants, 90% accepted. In 2009, 8 Ed Ss awarded. *Entrance requirements:* Additional exam requirements/recommendations for international students: Required—TOEFL (minimum score 523 paper-based; 193 computer-based; 70 iBT), IELTS. *Application deadline:* Applications are processed on a rolling basis. Application fee: $50. Electronic applications accepted. *Unit head:* Dr. Andrew Creamer, Chair, 334-670-3350,

Fax: 334-670-32961, E-mail: drcreamer@troy.edu. *Application contact:* Brenda K. Campbell, Director of Graduate Admissions, 334-670-3178, Fax: 334-670-3733, E-mail: bcamp@troy.edu.

Union Institute & University, Education Programs–Florida Center, North Miami Beach, FL 33162. Offers educational leadership (M Ed, Ed S); exceptional student education (M Ed, Ed S); guidance and counseling (M Ed, Ed S); reading (M Ed, Ed S). *Faculty:* 3 full-time (1 woman), 23 part-time/adjunct (19 women). *Students:* 32 full-time (21 women); includes 23 minority (21 African Americans, 2 Hispanic Americans). Average age 37. In 2009, 8 master's, 3 Ed Ss awarded. *Degree requirements:* For master's, thesis or alternative, portfolio. *Entrance requirements:* For master's, letters of recommendation. *Application deadline:* Applications are processed on a rolling basis. Application fee: $50. *Expenses:* Contact institution. *Financial support:* Federal Work-Study, scholarships/grants, and tuition waivers (partial) available. Financial award applicants required to submit FAFSA. *Unit head:* Dr. Arlene Sacks, Dean, 305-653-6713 Ext. 2152, E-mail: arlene.sacks@myunion.edu. *Application contact:* Josefina Rosario, Admissions Counselor, 305-653-6713 Ext. 2172, E-mail: admissions@tui.edu.

Union Institute & University, M Ed Program–Vermont Campus, Montpelier, VT 05602. Offers school administration (M Ed), including principalship; school counseling (M Ed); teaching (M Ed), including art, early childhood, elementary, English, math, middle schools, science, social studies, special education. *Faculty:* 3 full-time (1 woman), 23 part-time/adjunct (19 women). *Students:* 41 part-time (29 women). Average age 38. In 2009, 15 master's awarded. *Degree requirements:* For master's, thesis. *Entrance requirements:* For master's, 3 letters of reference. *Application deadline:* Applications are processed on a rolling basis. Application fee: $50. *Expenses:* Contact institution. *Financial support:* Federal Work-Study, scholarships/grants, and tuition waivers available. Financial award applicants required to submit FAFSA. *Unit head:* Dr. Arlene Sacks, Dean, Graduate Programs in Education, 305-653-6713 Ext. 2152, E-mail: arlene.sacks@myunion.edu. *Application contact:* Dr. Arlene Sacks, Dean, Graduate Programs in Education, 305-653-6713 Ext. 2152, E-mail: arlene.sacks@myunion.edu.

Universidad del Turabo, Graduate Programs, Programs in Education, Program in Guidance Counseling, Gurabo, PR 00778-3030. Offers M Ed. *Students:* 82 full-time (70 women), 46 part-time (37 women); includes 116 Hispanic Americans. Average age 33. 72 applicants, 93% accepted, 51 enrolled. In 2009, 87 master's awarded. *Unit head:* Angela Candelario, Dean, 787-743-7979 Ext. 4126. *Application contact:* Virginia Gonzalez, Admissions Officer, 787-746-3009.

Université de Moncton, Faculty of Education, Graduate Studies in Education, Moncton, NB E1A 3E9, Canada. Offers educational psychology (M Ed, MA Ed); guidance (M Ed, MA Ed); school administration (M Ed, MA Ed); teaching (M Ed, MA Ed). Part-time programs available. *Degree requirements:* For master's, proficiency in English and French. *Entrance requirements:* For master's, minimum GPA of 3.0. *Faculty research:* Guidance, ethnolinguistic vitality, children's rights, ecological education, entrepreneurship.

Université Laval, Faculty of Education, Department of Foundations and Interventions in Education, Programs in Orientation Sciences, Québec, QC G1K 7P4, Canada. Offers MA, PhD. Terminal master's awarded for partial completion of doctoral program. *Degree requirements:* For master's, thesis (for some programs); for doctorate, comprehensive exam, thesis/dissertation. *Entrance requirements:* For master's, English test (comprehension of written English), knowledge of French; for doctorate, oral exam (subject of thesis), knowledge of French and English. Electronic applications accepted. *Faculty research:* Counseling psychology, psychological education, vocational guidance, growth and development.

University at Albany, State University of New York, School of Education, Department of Educational and Counseling Psychology, Albany, NY 12222-0001. Offers counseling psychology (MS, PhD, CAS); educational psychology (Ed D); educational psychology and statistics (MS); measurements and evaluation (Ed D); rehabilitation counseling (MS), including counseling psychology; school counselor (CAS); school psychology (Psy D, CAS); special education (MS); statistics and research design (Ed D). *Accreditation:* APA (one or more programs are accredited). Evening/weekend programs available. *Degree requirements:* For doctorate, thesis/dissertation. *Entrance requirements:* For doctorate, GRE General Test. Additional exam requirements/recommendations for international students: Required—TOEFL (minimum score 550 paper-based; 213 computer-based). Electronic applications accepted.

University at Buffalo, the State University of New York, Graduate School, Graduate School of Education, Department of Counseling, School, and Educational Psychology, Buffalo, NY 14260. Offers counseling/school psychology (PhD); counselor education (PhD); educational psychology (MA, PhD); general education (Ed M); mental health counseling (MS); rehabilitation counseling (MS); school counseling (Ed M, Certificate); Singapore school counseling (Ed M). *Accreditation:* CORE (one or more programs are accredited). Postbaccalaureate distance learning degree programs offered (no on-campus study). *Faculty:* 17 full-time (8 women), 36 part-time/adjunct (28 women). *Students:* 152 full-time (125 women), 127 part-time (97 women); includes 33 minority (22 African Americans, 2 American Indian/Alaska Native, 3 Asian Americans or Pacific Islanders, 6 Hispanic Americans), 27 international. Average age 30. 396 applicants, 41% accepted, 119 enrolled. In 2009, 60 master's, 12 doctorates, 24 other advanced degrees awarded. *Degree requirements:* For master's, comprehensive exam (for some programs), thesis (for some programs); for doctorate, comprehensive exam, thesis/dissertation. *Entrance requirements:* For master's and doctorate, GRE General Test, interview, letters of reference. Additional exam requirements/recommendations for international students: Required—TOEFL (minimum score 79 iBT). *Application deadline:* For fall admission, 2/1 priority date for domestic and international students. Application fee: $50. Electronic applications accepted. *Financial support:* In 2009–10, 14 fellowships with full tuition reimbursements (averaging $9,000 per year), 28 research assistantships with full tuition reimbursements (averaging $9,000 per year) were awarded; teaching assistantships with tuition reimbursements, career-related internships or fieldwork, Federal Work-Study, institutionally sponsored loans, and unspecified assistantships also available. Financial award application deadline: 2/1; financial award applicants required to submit FAFSA. *Faculty research:* Multicultural counseling, class size effects, good work in counseling, eating disorders, outcome assessment, change agents and therapeutic factors in group counseling. Total annual research expenditures: $3.7 million. *Unit head:* Dr. Timothy Janikowski, Chair, 716-645-2484, Fax: 716-645-6616, E-mail: tjanikow@buffalo.edu. *Application contact:* Rochelle Cohen, Admissions Assistant, 716-645-2110, Fax: 716-645-7937, E-mail: recohen@buffalo.edu.

The University of Akron, Graduate School, College of Education, Department of Counseling, Program in Community Counseling, Akron, OH 44325. Offers MA, MS. *Accreditation:* ACA; NCATE. *Students:* 46 full-time (39 women), 25 part-time (20 women); includes 8 African Americans, 2 international. Average age 29. 40 applicants, 38% accepted, 11 enrolled. In 2009, 13 master's awarded. *Degree requirements:* For master's, comprehensive exam. *Entrance requirements:* For master's, minimum GPA of 2.75, interview, letters of recommendation, supplemental form. Additional exam requirements/recommendations for international students: Required—TOEFL (minimum score 550 paper-based; 213 computer-based; 79 iBT). *Application deadline:* Applications are processed on a rolling basis. Application fee: $30 ($40 for international students). Electronic applications accepted. *Expenses:* Tuition, state resident: full-time $6570; part-time $365 per credit hour. Tuition, nonresident: full-time $11,250; part-time $625 per credit hour. *Unit head:* Dr. Robert Schwartz, Coordinator, 330-972-8155, E-mail: rcs@uakron.edu. *Application contact:* Dr. Robert Schwartz, Coordinator, 330-972-8155, E-mail: rcs@uakron.edu.

The University of Akron, Graduate School, College of Education, Department of Counseling, Program in Counselor Education and Supervision, Akron, OH 44325. Offers PhD. *Accreditation:* ACA. *Students:* 12 full-time (7 women), 18 part-time (15 women); includes 9 minority (all African Americans), 1 international. Average age 40. 9 applicants, 44% accepted, 3 enrolled. In 2009, 5 doctorates awarded. *Degree requirements:* For doctorate, comprehensive exam, thesis/dissertation, written and oral exams. *Entrance requirements:* For doctorate, GRE, interview, minimum GPA of 3.25, letters of recommendation. Additional exam requirements/recommendations for international students: Required—TOEFL (minimum score 550 paper-based; 213 computer-based; 79 iBT). *Application deadline:* For fall admission, 1/15 for domestic students, 1/5 for international students. Application fee: $30 ($40 for international students). Electronic applications accepted. *Expenses:* Tuition, state resident: full-time $6570; part-time $365 per credit hour. Tuition, nonresident: full-time $11,250; part-time $625 per credit hour. *Unit head:* Dr. Cynthia Reynolds, Coordinator, 330-972-6748, E-mail: creynol@uakron.edu. *Application contact:* Dr. Cynthia Reynolds, Coordinator, 330-972-6748, E-mail: creynol@uakron.edu.

The University of Akron, Graduate School, College of Education, Department of Counseling, Program in School Counseling, Akron, OH 44325. Offers MA, MS. *Accreditation:* ACA; NCATE. *Students:* 31 full-time (28 women), 52 part-time (41 women); includes 9 minority (7 African Americans, 1 Asian American or Pacific Islander, 1 Hispanic American), 1 international. Average age 32. 23 applicants, 57% accepted, 9 enrolled. In 2009, 13 master's awarded. *Degree requirements:* For master's, comprehensive exam. *Entrance requirements:* For master's, minimum GPA of 2.75, interview, letters of recommendation, supplemental form, Bureau of Criminal Investigation clearanace. Additional exam requirements/recommendations for international students: Required—TOEFL (minimum score 550 paper-based; 213 computer-based; 79 iBT). *Application deadline:* For fall admission, 3/15 for domestic and international students; for spring admission, 10/1 for domestic and international students. Application fee: $30 ($40 for international students). Electronic applications accepted. *Expenses:* Tuition, state resident: full-time $6570; part-time $365 per credit hour. Tuition, nonresident: full-time $11,250; part-time $625 per credit hour. *Unit head:* Dr. Cynthia Reynolds, Coordinator, 330-972-6748, E-mail: creynol@uakron.edu. *Application contact:* Dr. Cynthia Reynolds, Coordinator, 330-972-6748, E-mail: creynol@uakron.edu.

The University of Alabama, Graduate School, College of Education, Department of Educational Studies in Psychology, Research Methodology and Counseling, Tuscaloosa, AL 35487. Offers MA, Ed D, PhD, Ed S. *Accreditation:* ACA (one or more programs are accredited); CORE; NCATE. Part-time programs available. *Faculty:* 18 full-time (9 women). *Students:* 67 full-time (54 women), 81 part-time (70 women); includes 36 minority (30 African Americans, 2 Asian Americans or Pacific Islanders, 4 Hispanic Americans), 8 international. Average age 32. 162 applicants, 35% accepted, 31 enrolled. In 2009, 22 master's, 8 doctorates, 14 other advanced degrees awarded. *Degree requirements:* For master's, comprehensive exam, thesis optional; for doctorate, comprehensive exam, thesis/dissertation; for Ed S, comprehensive exam. *Entrance requirements:* For master's and doctorate, GRE General Test, MAT, or NTE, minimum GPA of 3.0; for Ed S, minimum GPA of 3.0 during previous 2 years. Additional exam requirements/recommendations for international students: Required—TOEFL (minimum score 550 paper-based; 213 computer-based), IELTS (minimum score 6.5). *Application deadline:* For fall admission, 7/1 for domestic students; for spring admission, 11/1 for domestic students. Applications are processed on a rolling basis. Application fee: $50 ($60 for international students). Electronic applications accepted. *Expenses:* Tuition, state resident: full-time $7000. Tuition, nonresident: full-time $19,200. *Financial support:* Research assistantships with tuition reimbursements, teaching assistantships with tuition reimbursements, career-related internships or fieldwork available. Financial award application deadline: 7/14; financial award applicants required to submit FAFSA. *Faculty research:* Moral development, positive psychology, children's fears, digital storytelling. *Unit head:* Dr. Rick House, Department Head, 205-348-0283. *Application contact:* Marie S. Marshall, Office Associate II, 205-348-8362, Fax: 205-348-0683, E-mail: mmarshal@bamaed.ua.edu.

The University of Alabama at Birmingham, College of Arts and Sciences, School of Education, Program in Counseling, Birmingham, AL 35294. Offers MA. *Accreditation:* CORE; NCATE. *Degree requirements:* For master's, thesis optional. *Entrance requirements:* For master's, GRE General Test, MAT, or NTE, minimum GPA of 3.0. Electronic applications accepted.

University of Alaska Anchorage, College of Education, Program in Counseling and Guidance, Anchorage, AK 99508. Offers M Ed. Part-time programs available. *Entrance requirements:* For master's, GRE or MAT, interview, resume. Additional exam requirements/recommendations for international students: Required—TOEFL (minimum score 550 paper-based; 213 computer-based).

University of Alaska Fairbanks, School of Education, Program in Counseling, Fairbanks, AK 99775-7520. Offers counseling (M Ed), including community counseling, school counseling. *Students:* 17 full-time (12 women), 45 part-time (36 women); includes 6 minority (2 African Americans, 1 American Indian/Alaska Native, 1 Asian American or Pacific Islander, 2 Hispanic Americans). Average age 36. 52 applicants, 63% accepted, 29 enrolled. In 2009, 21 master's awarded. *Degree requirements:* For master's, comprehensive exam, thesis, oral defense. *Entrance requirements:* For master's, 1 year teaching or administrative experience. *Application deadline:* For fall admission, 6/1 for domestic students, 3/1 for international students; for spring admission, 10/15 for domestic students, 9/1 for international students. Applications are processed on a rolling basis. Application fee: $60. Electronic applications accepted. *Expenses:* Tuition, state resident: full-time $7584; part-time $316 per credit. Tuition, nonresident: full-time $15,504; part-time $646 per credit. Required fees: $23 per credit. $135 per semester. Tuition and fees vary according to course level, course load and reciprocity agreements. *Financial support:* In 2009–10, 4 teaching assistantships (averaging $13,067 per year) were awarded; fellowships, career-related internships or fieldwork, Federal Work-Study, scholarships/grants, health care benefits, and unspecified assistantships also available. Support available to part-time students. Financial award application deadline: 7/1; financial award applicants required to submit FAFSA. *Unit head:* Dr. Eric C. Madsen, Dean, 907-474-7341, Fax: 907-474-5451, E-mail: fysoed@uaf.edu. *Application contact:* Dr. Eric C. Madsen, Dean, 907-474-7341, Fax: 907-474-5451, E-mail: fysoed@uaf.edu.

University of Alberta, Faculty of Graduate Studies and Research, Department of Educational Psychology, Edmonton, AB T6G 2E1, Canada. Offers counseling psychology (M Ed, PhD); educational psychology (M Ed, PhD); instructional technology (M Ed); school counseling (M Ed); school psychology (M Ed, PhD); special education (M Ed, PhD); special education-deafness studies (M Ed); teaching English as a second language (M Ed). Part-time programs available. *Faculty:* 34 full-time (14 women), 12 part-time/adjunct (6 women). *Students:* 117 full-time (93 women), 173 part-time (121 women). Average age 36. 252 applicants, 34% accepted. In 2009, 30 master's, 10 doctorates awarded. *Degree requirements:* For master's, thesis optional; for doctorate, comprehensive exam, thesis/dissertation. *Entrance requirements:* For master's and doctorate, minimum GPA of 3.0. Additional exam requirements/recommendations for international students: Required—TOEFL. *Application deadline:* For fall admission, 2/1 priority date for domestic and international students. Applications are processed on a rolling basis. Tuition and fees charges are reported in Canadian dollars. *Expenses:* Tuition, area resident: Full-time $4626 Canadian dollars; part-time $99.72 Canadian dollars per unit. International tuition: $8216 Canadian dollars full-time. Required fees: $3590 Canadian dollars; $99.72 Canadian dollars per unit. $215 Canadian dollars per term. *Financial support:* In 2009–10, 10 fellowships with full tuition reimbursements (averaging $16,120 per year), 36 research assistantships with full tuition reimbursements (averaging $12,614 per year), 46 teaching assistantships with full tuition reimbursements (averaging $5,462 per year) were awarded; career-related internships or fieldwork and scholarships/grants also available. *Faculty research:* Human learning, development and assessment. *Unit head:* Dr. Linda M. McDonald, Chair, 780-492-1149, Fax: 780-492-1318, E-mail: linda.mcdonald@ualberta.ca. *Application contact:* Judy Maynes, Information Contact, 780-492-1149, Fax: 780-492-1318, E-mail: edpygrad@ualberta.ca.

University of Arkansas, Graduate School, College of Education and Health Professions, Department of Rehabilitation, Human Resources and Communication Disorders, Program in Counseling, Fayetteville, AR 72701-1201. Offers MS, PhD, Ed S. *Accreditation:* ACA; NCATE. Part-time and evening/weekend programs available. *Students:* 30 full-time (24 women), 36 part-time (28 women); includes 14 minority (6 African Americans, 4 American Indian/Alaska Native, 3 Asian Americans or Pacific Islanders, 1 Hispanic American), 2 international. In 2009, 11 master's, 1 doctorate awarded. *Degree requirements:* For master's, thesis optional; for doctorate, thesis/dissertation. *Entrance requirements:* For master's, GRE General Test or

Counselor Education

University of Arkansas *(continued)*
MAT; for doctorate, GRE General Test. *Application deadline:* For fall admission, 3/15 for domestic students; for spring admission, 10/15 for domestic students. Application fee: $40 ($50 for international students). *Expenses:* Tuition, state resident: full-time $7355; part-time $356.58 per hour. Tuition, nonresident: full-time $17,401; part-time $775.17 per hour. Required fees: $1203. *Financial support:* In 2009–10, 3 fellowships with tuition reimbursements, 2 research assistantships were awarded; teaching assistantships, career-related internships or fieldwork and Federal Work-Study also available. Support available to part-time students. Financial award application deadline: 4/1; financial award applicants required to submit FAFSA. *Unit head:* Dr. Fran Hagstrom, Unit Head, 479-575-4758, E-mail: fhagstr@uark.edu. *Application contact:* Dr. Brent Williams, Graduate Coordinator, 479-575-4758, E-mail: btwilli@uark.edu.

University of Arkansas at Little Rock, Graduate School, College of Education, Department of Counseling and Rehabilitation Education, Program in Counselor Education, Little Rock, AR 72204-1099. Offers school counseling (M Ed). Part-time and evening/weekend programs available. *Degree requirements:* For master's, comprehensive exam, portfolio or thesis. *Entrance requirements:* For master's, GRE General Test, minimum GPA of 2.75, teaching certificate.

University of Central Arkansas, Graduate School, College of Education, Department of Leadership Studies, Program in School Counseling, Conway, AR 72035-0001. Offers elementary school counseling (MS); secondary school counseling (MS). *Accreditation:* NCATE. Part-time programs available. *Students:* 3 full-time (all women), 16 part-time (14 women); includes 5 minority (all African Americans). Average age 33. 4 applicants, 100% accepted, 3 enrolled. In 2009, 6 master's awarded. *Degree requirements:* For master's, comprehensive exam, thesis optional. *Entrance requirements:* For master's, GRE General Test, minimum GPA of 2.7. Additional exam requirements/recommendations for international students: Required—TOEFL (minimum score 550 paper-based; 213 computer-based). *Application deadline:* For fall admission, 3/1 priority date for domestic and international students; for spring admission, 10/1 priority date for domestic and international students. Applications are processed on a rolling basis. Application fee: $25 ($50 for international students). *Expenses:* Tuition, state resident: full-time $5136; part-time $214 per credit hour. Required fees: $379.50; $127 per term. Tuition and fees vary according to course level, course load and campus/location. *Financial support:* Career-related internships or fieldwork, scholarships/grants, and unspecified assistantships available. Financial award application deadline: 2/15; financial award applicants required to submit FAFSA. *Unit head:* Dr. Terry Smith, Associate Professor, 501-450-3193, Fax: 501-450-5424, E-mail: terrys@uca.edu. *Application contact:* Patti Hornor, Administrative Assistant, 501-450-5063, Fax: 501-450-5678, E-mail: pattih@uca.edu.

University of Central Florida, College of Education, Department of Child, Family and Community Sciences, Program in Counselor Education, Orlando, FL 32816. Offers mental health counseling (MA); school counseling (M Ed, MA, Ed S). *Accreditation:* ACA. Part-time and evening/weekend programs available. *Students:* 90 full-time (72 women), 60 part-time (49 women); includes 32 minority (15 African Americans, 2 American Indian/Alaska Native, 15 Hispanic Americans), 3 international. Average age 28. 127 applicants, 49% accepted, 39 enrolled. In 2009, 54 master's, 23 other advanced degrees awarded. *Degree requirements:* For master's, comprehensive exam, thesis or alternative. *Entrance requirements:* For master's, GRE General Test, interview, minimum GPA of 3.0. Additional exam requirements/recommendations for international students: Required—TOEFL. *Application deadline:* For fall admission, 2/1 for domestic students; for spring admission, 9/1 for domestic students. Application fee: $30. Electronic applications accepted. *Expenses:* Tuition, state resident: part-time $306.31 per credit hour. Tuition, nonresident: part-time $1099.01 per credit hour. Part-time tuition and fees vary according to degree level and program. *Financial support:* In 2009–10, 16 students received support, including 9 fellowships with partial tuition reimbursements available (averaging $2,300 per year), 7 research assistantships with partial tuition reimbursements available (averaging $5,900 per year), 3 teaching assistantships with partial tuition reimbursements available (averaging $6,700 per year); career-related internships or fieldwork, Federal Work-Study, institutionally sponsored loans, tuition waivers (partial), and unspecified assistantships also available. Financial award application deadline: 3/1; financial award applicants required to submit FAFSA.

University of Central Florida, College of Education, Education PhD Program, Orlando, FL 32816. Offers communication sciences and disorders (PhD); counselor education (PhD); elementary education (PhD); exceptional education (PhD); higher education (PhD); hospitality education (PhD); instructional technology (PhD); mathematics education (PhD); science education (PhD); social science education (PhD). *Students:* 99 full-time (70 women), 14 part-time (9 women); includes 28 minority (17 African Americans, 2 Asian Americans or Pacific Islanders, 9 Hispanic Americans), 20 international. In 2009, 15 doctorates awarded. Application fee: $30. Electronic applications accepted. *Expenses:* Tuition, state resident: part-time $306.31 per credit hour. Tuition, nonresident: part-time $1099.01 per credit hour. Part-time tuition and fees vary according to degree level and program. *Financial support:* In 2009–10, 40 fellowships with partial tuition reimbursements (averaging $9,200 per year), 61 research assistantships with partial tuition reimbursements (averaging $7,800 per year), 18 teaching assistantships with partial tuition reimbursements (averaging $6,500 per year) were awarded. *Unit head:* Dr. B. Grant Hayes, Associate Dean, 407-823-5391, E-mail: ghayes@mail.ucf.edu. *Application contact:* Dr. B. Grant Hayes, Associate Dean, 407-823-5391, E-mail: ghayes@mail.ucf.edu.

University of Central Missouri, The Graduate School, College of Education, Warrensburg, MO 64093. Offers career and technical education administration (MS); career and technical education industry training (MS); career and technical education leadership/teaching (MS); college student personnel administration (MS); counseling (MS); curriculum and instruction (Ed S); educational leadership (Ed D); educational technology (MS); elementary education/educational foundations and literacy (MSE); elementary school administration (MSE); elementary school principalship (Ed S); human services/learning resources (Ed S); human services/professional counseling (Ed S); human services/special education (Ed S); human services/technology and occupational education (Ed S); K-12 education/educational foundations and literacy (MSE); K-12 special education (MSE); library science and information services (MS); literacy education (MSE); secondary education/educational foundations & literacy (MSE); secondary school administration (MSE); secondary school principalship (Ed S); superintendency (Ed S); teaching (MAT). Part-time programs available. Postbaccalaureate distance learning degree programs offered. *Faculty:* 42. *Students:* 123 full-time (82 women), 721 part-time (552 women); includes 58 minority (38 African Americans, 3 American Indian/Alaska Native, 6 Asian Americans or Pacific Islanders, 11 Hispanic Americans), 6 international. Average age 34. 229 applicants, 88% accepted, 190 enrolled. In 2009, 212 master's, 47 other advanced degrees awarded. *Entrance requirements:* Additional exam requirements/recommendations for international students: Required—TOEFL (minimum score 550 paper-based; 79 computer-based). *Application deadline:* For fall admission, 6/1 priority date for domestic students, 5/1 for international students; for spring admission, 10/1 priority date for domestic students, 10/1 for international students. Applications are processed on a rolling basis. Application fee: $30 ($75 for international students). Electronic applications accepted. *Expenses:* Tuition, area resident: Part-time $245.80 per credit hour. Tuition, nonresident: part-time $491.60 per credit hour. Required fees: $24.20 per credit hour. Full-time tuition and fees vary according to course load, degree level, campus/location and reciprocity agreements. *Financial support:* Research assistantships with full and partial tuition reimbursements, teaching assistantships with full and partial tuition reimbursements, career-related internships or fieldwork, Federal Work-Study, scholarships/grants, and administrative and laboratory assistantships available. Support available to part-time students. Financial award application deadline: 3/1; financial award applicants required to submit FAFSA. *Unit head:* Dr. Michael Wright, Dean, 660-543-4272, Fax: 660-543-8753, E-mail: mwright@ucmo.edu. *Application contact:* Laurie Delap, Admissions Coordinator, 660-543-4621, Fax: 660-543-4778, E-mail: gradinfo@ucmo.edu.

University of Central Oklahoma, College of Graduate Studies and Research, College of Education, Department of Advanced Professional Services, Program in Guidance and Counseling, Edmond, OK 73034-5209. Offers M Ed. *Accreditation:* NCATE. Part-time programs

available. *Faculty:* 3 full-time (all women), 2 part-time/adjunct (1 woman). *Students:* 17 full-time (14 women), 52 part-time (49 women); includes 10 minority (4 African Americans, 2 American Indian/Alaska Native, 4 Hispanic Americans). Average age 32. 26 applicants, 100% accepted. In 2009, 20 master's awarded. *Entrance requirements:* For master's, GRE General Test. Additional exam requirements/recommendations for international students: Required—TOEFL (minimum score 550 paper-based; 213 computer-based). *Application deadline:* For fall admission, 7/1 for international students; for spring admission, 11/1 for international students. Applications are processed on a rolling basis. Application fee: $25. Electronic applications accepted. *Expenses:* Tuition, state resident: full-time $4128; part-time $172 per credit hour. Tuition, nonresident: full-time $10,373; part-time $432.20 per credit hour. Required fees: $433.20; $18.05 per credit hour. *Financial support:* Career-related internships or fieldwork available. Financial award application deadline: 3/31; financial award applicants required to submit FAFSA. *Unit head:* Dr. Pat Couts, Director, 405-974-5888, E-mail: chandler@aix1.uco.edu. *Application contact:* Dr. Richard Bernard, Dean, Graduate College, 405-974-3493, Fax: 405-974-3852, E-mail: gradcoll@uco.edu.

University of Cincinnati, Graduate School, College of Education, Criminal Justice, and Human Services, Division of Human Services, Program in Counseling, Cincinnati, OH 45221. Offers counseling (Ed D); counselor education (CAGS); mental health (MA); school counseling (M Ed). *Accreditation:* ACA (one or more programs are accredited); NCATE. Part-time programs available. Terminal master's awarded for partial completion of doctoral program. *Degree requirements:* For master's, comprehensive exam; for doctorate, comprehensive exam, thesis/dissertation. *Entrance requirements:* For master's, GRE General Test, interview; for doctorate, GRE General Test, GRE Subject Test, interview. Additional exam requirements/recommendations for international students: Required—TOEFL (minimum score 620 paper-based), OEPT. Electronic applications accepted. *Faculty research:* Group work, career development, ecology, prevention, multicultural.

University of Colorado at Colorado Springs, Graduate School, College of Education, Colorado Springs, CO 80933-7150. Offers counseling and human services (MA); curriculum and instruction (MA); educational administration (MA); educational leadership (MA, PhD); special education (MA). *Accreditation:* ACA; NCATE. Part-time and evening/weekend programs available. Postbaccalaureate distance learning degree programs offered (minimal on-campus study). *Faculty:* 23 full-time (15 women), 11 part-time/adjunct (8 women). *Students:* 317 full-time (243 women), 160 part-time (132 women); includes 81 minority (23 African Americans, 3 American Indian/Alaska Native, 13 Asian Americans or Pacific Islanders, 42 Hispanic Americans), 2 international. Average age 36. 375 applicants, 94% accepted, 254 enrolled. In 2009, 203 master's awarded. *Degree requirements:* For master's, comprehensive exam, thesis or alternative, microcomputer proficiency; for doctorate, comprehensive exam, research lab. *Entrance requirements:* For master's, GRE General Test, MAT. *Application deadline:* For fall admission, 6/15 for domestic students; for spring admission, 10/15 for domestic students. Applications are processed on a rolling basis. Application fee: $60 ($75 for international students). *Expenses:* Tuition, state resident: full-time $8922; part-time $639 per credit hour. Tuition, nonresident: full-time $19,372; part-time $1154 per credit hour. Tuition and fees vary according to course level, course load, degree level, program, reciprocity agreements and student level. *Financial support:* Fellowships, career-related internships or fieldwork, Federal Work-Study, and scholarships/grants available. Support available to part-time students. Financial award application deadline: 3/1; financial award applicants required to submit FAFSA. *Faculty research:* Job training for special populations, materials development for classroom. Total annual research expenditures: $1.4 million. *Unit head:* Dr. LaVonne Neal, Dean, 719-255-4111, Fax: 719-262-4110, E-mail: lneal@uccs.edu. *Application contact:* Melissa Schecter, Student Services Manager, 719-255-4526, Fax: 719-255-4110, E-mail: mschedte@uccs.edu.

University of Colorado Denver, School of Education and Human Development, Program in Counseling Psychology and Counselor Education, Denver, CO 80217-3364. Offers MA, Ed S. *Accreditation:* ACA (one or more programs are accredited); NCATE. Part-time and evening/weekend programs available. *Students:* 110 full-time (97 women), 198 part-time (175 women); includes 35 minority (6 African Americans, 3 American Indian/Alaska Native, 9 Asian Americans or Pacific Islanders, 17 Hispanic Americans), 6 international. 86 applicants, 40% accepted, 17 enrolled. In 2009, 122 master's, 7 other advanced degrees awarded. *Degree requirements:* For master's, comprehensive exam, thesis optional. *Entrance requirements:* For master's, GRE or MAT, minimum GPA of 2.75, 4 letters of recommendation, interview, resume. Additional exam requirements/recommendations for international students: Required—TOEFL (minimum score 525 paper-based; 197 computer-based). *Application deadline:* For fall admission, 2/15 for domestic students; for spring admission, 9/15 for domestic students. Applications are processed on a rolling basis. Application fee: $50 ($75 for international students). Electronic applications accepted. *Financial support:* Research assistantships, teaching assistantships, Federal Work-Study available. Financial award application deadline: 4/1; financial award applicants required to submit FAFSA. *Faculty research:* Spiritual issues in counseling, multi-cultural and diversity issues in counseling, adolescent suicide, career development. *Unit head:* Dr. Marsha Wiggins-Frame, Division Coordinator, 303-315-6332, E-mail: marsha.wiggins@ucdenver.edu. *Application contact:* Lori Sisneros, Student Services Coordinator, 303-315-4979, Fax: 303-315-6311, E-mail: lori.sisneros@ucdenver.edu.

University of Connecticut, Graduate School, Neag School of Education, Department of Educational Psychology, Program in Counseling Psychology, Storrs, CT 06269. Offers counseling psychology (PhD); school counseling (MA, Post-Master's Certificate). *Accreditation:* ACA. *Faculty:* 15 full-time (6 women). *Students:* 38 full-time (31 women), 14 part-time (9 women); includes 9 minority (6 African Americans, 3 Hispanic Americans), 4 international. Average age 29. 63 applicants, 35% accepted, 9 enrolled. In 2009, 13 master's, 2 doctorates, 1 other advanced degree awarded. Terminal master's awarded for partial completion of doctoral program. *Degree requirements:* For master's, comprehensive exam, thesis or alternative; for doctorate, thesis/dissertation. *Entrance requirements:* For doctorate, GRE General Test. Additional exam requirements/recommendations for international students: Required—TOEFL (minimum score 550 paper-based; 213 computer-based). *Application deadline:* For fall admission, 2/1 priority date for domestic and international students; for spring admission, 11/1 for domestic students, 10/1 for international students. Applications are processed on a rolling basis. Application fee: $55. Electronic applications accepted. *Expenses:* Tuition, state resident: full-time $4725; part-time $525 per credit. Tuition, nonresident: full-time $12,267; part-time $1363 per credit. Required fees: $346 per semester. Tuition and fees vary according to course load. *Financial support:* In 2009–10, 15 research assistantships with full tuition reimbursements, 2 teaching assistantships with full tuition reimbursements were awarded; fellowships, Federal Work-Study, scholarships/grants, health care benefits, and unspecified assistantships also available. Financial award application deadline: 2/1; financial award applicants required to submit FAFSA. *Unit head:* Hariharan Swaminathan, Head, 860-486-4031, Fax: 860-486-0210, E-mail: hariharan.swaminathan@uconn.edu. *Application contact:* Cheryl Lowe, Program Assistant, 860-486-4031, Fax: 860-486-0180, E-mail: cheryl.lowe@uconn.edu.

University of Dayton, Graduate School, School of Education and Allied Professions, Department of Counselor Education and Human Services, Dayton, OH 45469-1300. Offers college student personnel (MS Ed); community counseling (MS Ed); higher education administration (MS Ed); human services (MS Ed); school counseling (MS Ed); school psychology (MS Ed, Ed S); teacher as child/youth development specialist (MS Ed). *Accreditation:* NCATE. Part-time and evening/weekend programs available. *Faculty:* 11 full-time (8 women), 33 part-time/adjunct (22 women). *Students:* 254 full-time (207 women), 207 part-time (180 women); includes 76 minority (69 African Americans, 3 Asian Americans or Pacific Islanders, 4 Hispanic Americans), 2 international. Average age 32. 359 applicants, 47% accepted, 114 enrolled. In 2009, 163 master's, 11 Ed Ss awarded. *Degree requirements:* For master's, comprehensive exam (for some programs), thesis (for some programs), exit exam. *Entrance requirements:* For master's, MAT or GRE (if GPA less than 2.75), interview, writing sample. Additional exam requirements/recommendations for international students: Required—TOEFL (minimum score 550 paper-based; 213 computer-based; 80 iBT). *Application deadline:* For fall admission, 4/10 for domestic students, 3/1 priority date for international students; for winter admission, 9/10 for domestic

students, 7/1 priority date for international students; for spring admission, 1/10 for domestic students, 1/1 priority date for international students. Applications are processed on a rolling basis. Application fee: $0 ($50 for international students). Electronic applications accepted. *Expenses:* Tuition: Full-time $8412; part-time $701 per credit hour. Required fees: $325; $65 per course. $25 per semester. Tuition and fees vary according to course load, degree level and program. *Financial support:* In 2009–10, 7 research assistantships with full tuition reimbursements (averaging $8,000 per year), 1 teaching assistantship with full tuition reimbursement (averaging $8,000 per year) were awarded; career-related internships or fieldwork, institutionally sponsored loans, health care benefits, and unspecified assistantships also available. Financial award applicants required to submit FAFSA. *Faculty research:* Anger as part of the grief process, inclusion of children with severe disabilities, comparisons of school counselors in Bosnia and the U. S., graduate and professional student socialization, use of cohort groups in doctoral programs, bullying in schools, impact of space on learning, sophomore experience. *Unit head:* Dr. Alan Demmitt, Chairperson, 937-229-3644, Fax: 937-229-1055. *Application contact:* Graduate Admissions, 937-229-4411, Fax: 937-229-4729, E-mail: gradadmission@udayton.edu.

University of Detroit Mercy, College of Liberal Arts and Education, Department of Counseling and Addiction Studies, Program in Counseling, Detroit, MI 48221. Offers addiction counseling (MA); community counseling (MA); school counseling (MA). *Accreditation:* ACA. Part-time and evening/weekend programs available. *Degree requirements:* For master's, thesis or alternative. *Entrance requirements:* For master's, minimum GPA of 2.75.

University of Florida, Graduate School, College of Education, Department of Counselor Education, Gainesville, FL 32611. Offers marriage and family counseling (M Ed, MAE, Ed D, PhD, Ed S); mental health counseling (M Ed, MAE, Ed D, PhD, Ed S); school counseling and guidance (M Ed, MAE, Ed D, PhD, Ed S). *Accreditation:* ACA (one or more programs are accredited); NCATE. Part-time programs available. Terminal master's awarded for partial completion of doctoral program. *Degree requirements:* For master's, thesis optional; for doctorate, thesis/dissertation. *Entrance requirements:* For master's and doctorate, GRE General Test, minimum GPA of 3.0 (undergraduate), 3.5 (graduate); for Ed S, GRE General Test. Additional exam requirements/recommendations for international students: Required—TOEFL (minimum score 550 paper-based; 213 computer-based). Electronic applications accepted.

University of Georgia, Graduate School, College of Education, Department of Counseling and Human Development Services, Athens, GA 30602. Offers college student affairs administration (M Ed, PhD); counseling and student personnel (PhD); counseling psychology (PhD); professional counseling (M Ed); professional school counseling (Ed S); recreation and leisure studies (M Ed, MA, PhD). *Accreditation:* ACA (one or more programs are accredited); APA (one or more programs are accredited); NCATE. *Faculty:* 22 full-time (13 women). *Students:* 147 full-time (102 women), 56 part-time (30 women); includes 45 minority (36 African Americans, 5 Asian Americans or Pacific Islanders, 4 Hispanic Americans), 1 international. 278 applicants, 27% accepted, 69 enrolled. In 2009, 49 master's, 13 doctorates, 4 other advanced degrees awarded. *Degree requirements:* For master's, thesis (MA); for doctorate, variable foreign language requirement, thesis/dissertation. *Entrance requirements:* For master's, GRE General Test or MAT; for doctorate, GRE General Test. *Application deadline:* For fall admission, 7/1 priority date for domestic students; for spring admission, 11/15 for domestic students. Application fee: $50. Electronic applications accepted. *Expenses:* Tuition, state resident: full-time $6000; part-time $250 per credit hour. Tuition, nonresident: full-time $20,904; part-time $871 per credit hour. Required fees: $730 per semester. *Financial support:* Fellowships, research assistantships, teaching assistantships, unspecified assistantships available. *Unit head:* Dr. Rosemary E. Phelps, Head, 706-542-4221, Fax: 706-542-4130, E-mail: rephelps@uga.edu. *Application contact:* Dr. Georgia B. Calhoun, Graduate Coordinator, 706-542-4103, Fax: 706-542-4130, E-mail: gcalhoun@uga.edu.

University of Guam, Office of Graduate Studies, School of Education, Program in Counseling, Mangilao, GU 96923. Offers MA. *Degree requirements:* For master's, comprehensive oral and written exams, special project or thesis. *Entrance requirements:* For master's, GRE General Test. Additional exam requirements/recommendations for international students: Required—TOEFL. *Faculty research:* Drugs in the local schools, standardized teaching procedures in the elementary school, how to address the dropout problems.

University of Hartford, College of Education, Nursing, and Health Professions, Program in Counseling, West Hartford, CT 06117-1599. Offers M Ed, MS, Sixth Year Certificate. *Accreditation:* NCATE. Part-time and evening/weekend programs available. *Degree requirements:* For master's and Sixth Year Certificate, comprehensive exam. *Entrance requirements:* For master's, GRE General Test or MAT, PRAXIS I or waiver, interview, 2 letters of recommendation; for Sixth Year Certificate, GRE General Test or MAT, PRAXIS I or waiver, interview. Additional exam requirements/recommendations for international students: Required—TOEFL (minimum score 550 paper-based; 213 computer-based). Electronic applications accepted.

University of Houston–Clear Lake, School of Education, Program in Foundations and Professional Studies, Houston, TX 77058-1098. Offers counseling (MS); instructional technology (MS); multicultural studies (MS). Part-time and evening/weekend programs available. *Degree requirements:* For master's, thesis optional. *Entrance requirements:* For master's, GRE or minimum GPA of 3.0 in last 60 hours. Additional exam requirements/recommendations for international students: Required—TOEFL (minimum score 550 paper-based; 213 computer-based). Electronic applications accepted.

University of Houston–Victoria, School of Education and Human Development, Victoria, TX 77901-4450. Offers administration and supervision (M Ed); counseling (M Ed); curriculum and instruction (M Ed); special education (M Ed). Part-time and evening/weekend programs available. Postbaccalaureate distance learning degree programs offered. *Degree requirements:* For master's, comprehensive exam, project or thesis. *Entrance requirements:* For master's, GRE General Test. Additional exam requirements/recommendations for international students: Required—TOEFL. Electronic applications accepted. *Faculty research:* Reading and language arts education, evaluation and diagnosis of special children's abilities.

University of Idaho, College of Graduate Studies, College of Education, Department of Counseling and School Psychology, Special Education, and Educational Leadership, Program in Counseling and Human Services, Moscow, ID 83844-2282. Offers M Ed, MS. *Accreditation:* ACA (one or more programs are accredited); CORE. *Students:* 33 full-time, 9 part-time. In 2009, 9 master's awarded. *Entrance requirements:* For master's, minimum GPA of 2.8. Application fee: $55 ($60 for international students). *Expenses:* Tuition, state resident: full-time $6120. Tuition, nonresident: full-time $17,712. *Financial support:* Teaching assistantships available. *Unit head:* Dr. Russell A. Joki, Chair, 208-364-4099, E-mail: rjoki@uidaho.edu. *Application contact:* Dr. Russell A. Joki, Chair, 208-364-4099, E-mail: rjoki@uidaho.edu.

University of Illinois at Urbana–Champaign, Graduate College, College of Education, Department of Educational Psychology, Champaign, IL 61820. Offers Ed M, MA, MS, PhD, CAS. *Accreditation:* APA (one or more programs are accredited). Part-time programs available. Postbaccalaureate distance learning degree programs offered. *Faculty:* 19 full-time (11 women). *Students:* 72 full-time (51 women), 73 part-time (53 women); includes 32 minority (15 African Americans, 6 Asian Americans or Pacific Islanders, 11 Hispanic Americans), 37 international. 159 applicants, 25% accepted, 28 enrolled. In 2009, 36 master's, 23 doctorates awarded. *Entrance requirements:* For master's, minimum GPA of 3.5; for doctorate, GRE General Test, minimum GPA of 3.5. Additional exam requirements/recommendations for international students: Required—TOEFL (minimum score 610 paper-based; 253 computer-based; 102 iBT). *Application deadline:* Applications are processed on a rolling basis. Application fee: $60 ($75 for international students). Electronic applications accepted. *Financial support:* In 2009–10, 7 fellowships, 39 research assistantships, 40 teaching assistantships were awarded; tuition waivers (full and partial) also available. *Unit head:* Thomas A. Schwandt, Chair, 217-333-5350, Fax: 217-244-7620, E-mail: tschwand@illinois.edu. *Application contact:* Helen N. Katz, Office Support Specialist, 217-333-5242, Fax: 217-244-7620, E-mail: hnkatz@illinois.edu.

The University of Iowa, Graduate College, College of Education, Department of Counseling, Rehabilitation, and Student Development, Iowa City, IA 52242-1316. Offers administration and research (PhD); community/rehabilitation counseling (MA); counselor education and supervision (PhD); rehabilitation counselor education (PhD); school counseling (MA); student development (MA, PhD). *Accreditation:* ACA (one or more programs are accredited); CORE (one or more programs are accredited). *Degree requirements:* For master's, thesis optional, exam; for doctorate, comprehensive exam, thesis/dissertation. *Entrance requirements:* For master's and doctorate, GRE General Test, minimum GPA of 3.0. Additional exam requirements/recommendations for international students: Required—TOEFL (minimum score 550 paper-based; 213 computer-based; 81 iBT). Electronic applications accepted.

University of La Verne, College of Education and Organizational Leadership, Program in School Counseling, La Verne, CA 91750-4443. Offers pupil personnel services (Credential); school counseling (MS). Part-time programs available. *Faculty:* 18 full-time (14 women), 35 part-time/adjunct (27 women). *Students:* 24 full-time (18 women), 84 part-time (72 women); includes 57 minority (14 African Americans, 2 Asian Americans or Pacific Islanders, 41 Hispanic Americans). Average age 31. In 2009, 202 master's awarded. *Degree requirements:* For master's, thesis optional. *Entrance requirements:* For master's, California Basic Educational Skills Test, minimum undergraduate GPA of 2.75, graduate 3.0; interview; 1 year's experience working with children; 3 letters of reference. Additional exam requirements/recommendations for international students: Required—TOEFL (minimum score 550 paper-based; 213 computer-based). *Application deadline:* Applications are processed on a rolling basis. Application fee: $50. *Expenses:* Contact institution. *Financial support:* Institutionally sponsored loans and unspecified assistantships available. Financial award application deadline: 3/2; financial award applicants required to submit FAFSA. *Unit head:* Dr. Laurie Schroeder, Chairperson, 909-593-3511 Ext. 4653, E-mail: lschroeder3@laverne.edu. *Application contact:* Christy Ranells, Admissions Information Specialist, 909-593-3511 Ext. 4644, Fax: 909-392-2761, E-mail: cranells@laverne.edu.

University of La Verne, Regional Campus Administration, Master's Programs in Education, California Statewide Campus, La Verne, CA 91750-4443. Offers educational management (M Ed), including preliminary administrative services credential; multiple or single subject teaching credential (M Ed); school counseling (MS), including public personnel services credential. *Faculty:* 3 full-time (1 woman), 97 part-time/adjunct (58 women). *Students:* 145 full-time (117 women), 174 part-time (139 women); includes 165 minority (31 African Americans, 2 American Indian/Alaska Native, 12 Asian Americans or Pacific Islanders, 120 Hispanic Americans). Average age 34. In 2009, 208 master's awarded. *Entrance requirements:* For master's, California Basic Educational Skills Test, 3 letters of recommendation, teaching credential. *Application deadline:* Applications are processed on a rolling basis. Application fee: $50. *Expenses:* Contact institution. *Financial support:* Fellowships, institutionally sponsored loans available. Financial award application deadline: 3/2; financial award applicants required to submit FAFSA. *Unit head:* Juline Behrens, Director, 800-695-4858 Ext. 5400, Fax: 909-981-8695, E-mail: jbehrens@laverne.edu. *Application contact:* Juline Behrens, Director, 800-695-4858 Ext. 5400, Fax: 909-981-8695, E-mail: jbehrens@laverne.edu.

University of Louisiana at Lafayette, Department of Counselor Education, Lafayette, LA 70504. Offers MS. *Entrance requirements:* For master's, GRE General Test, minimum GPA of 2.75. Additional exam requirements/recommendations for international students: Required—TOEFL (minimum score 550 paper-based; 213 computer-based). Electronic applications accepted.

University of Louisiana at Monroe, Graduate School, College of Education and Human Development, Department of Educational Leadership and Counseling, Program in Counseling, Monroe, LA 71209-0001. Offers M Ed. *Accreditation:* ACA; NCATE. Part-time and evening/weekend programs available. *Faculty:* 2 full-time (both women). *Students:* 16 full-time (14 women), 19 part-time (15 women); includes 18 minority (17 African Americans, 1 Asian American or Pacific Islander). Average age 34. In 2009, 7 master's awarded. *Degree requirements:* For master's, comprehensive exam, thesis. *Entrance requirements:* For master's, GRE General Test, minimum GPA of 2.8 in last 60 hours. Additional exam requirements/recommendations for international students: Required—TOEFL (minimum score 500 paper-based; 173 computer-based; 61 iBT). *Application deadline:* For fall admission, 8/24 priority date for domestic students, 7/1 for international students; for winter admission, 12/14 priority date for domestic students; for spring admission, 1/19 for domestic students, 11/1 for international students. Applications are processed on a rolling basis. Application fee: $20 ($30 for international students). Electronic applications accepted. *Expenses:* Tuition, state resident: part-time $159 per credit hour. Tuition, nonresident: part-time $159 per credit hour. Required fees: $1300 per year. Tuition and fees vary according to course load. *Financial support:* In 2009–10, 1 research assistantship with full and partial tuition reimbursement (averaging $2,500 per year) was awarded; career-related internships or fieldwork, Federal Work-Study, and unspecified assistantships also available. Financial award application deadline: 4/1; financial award applicants required to submit FAFSA. *Unit head:* Dr. Pamela Newman, Department Head, 318-342-1246, E-mail: pnewman@ulm.edu. *Application contact:* Dr. Pamela Newman, Department Head, 318-342-1246, E-mail: pnewman@ulm.edu.

University of Louisville, Graduate School, College of Education and Human Development, Department of Educational and Counseling Psychology, Louisville, KY 40292-0001. Offers counseling and personnel services (M Ed, PhD). *Accreditation:* APA; NCATE. Part-time and evening/weekend programs available. *Faculty:* 16 full-time (8 women), 8 part-time/adjunct (5 women). *Students:* 184 full-time (146 women), 105 part-time (83 women); includes 54 minority (49 African Americans, 3 Asian Americans or Pacific Islanders, 2 Hispanic Americans), 1 international. Average age 31. 241 applicants, 41% accepted, 73 enrolled. In 2009, 58 master's, 9 doctorates awarded. *Degree requirements:* For doctorate, comprehensive exam, thesis/dissertation. *Entrance requirements:* For master's and doctorate, GRE General Test. Additional exam requirements/recommendations for international students: Required—TOEFL (minimum score 560 paper-based; 210 computer-based; 83 iBT). Application fee: $50. Electronic applications accepted. *Financial support:* In 2009–10, 51 students received support; fellowships, research assistantships, teaching assistantships, career-related internships or fieldwork, Federal Work-Study, scholarships/grants, and unspecified assistantships available. Financial award application deadline: 6/1; financial award applicants required to submit FAFSA. *Faculty research:* Temperament, psychological development, classroom processes, school outcomes, adolescent and adult development issues/prevention and treatment, multicultural counseling, spirituality, therapeutic outcomes, college student success, college student affairs administration, career development. Total annual research expenditures: $17,276. *Unit head:* Dr. Linda T. Shapiro, Acting Chair, 502-852-5716, Fax: 502-852-0629, E-mail: linda.shapiro@louisville.edu. *Application contact:* Libby Leggett, Director, Graduate Admissions, 502-852-3101, Fax: 502-852-6536, E-mail: gradadm@louisville.edu.

University of Maine, Graduate School, College of Education and Human Development, Program in Counselor Education, Orono, ME 04469. Offers M Ed, MA, MS, Ed D, CAS. *Accreditation:* NCATE. Part-time and evening/weekend programs available. *Students:* 69 full-time (56 women), 46 part-time (39 women); includes 3 minority (1 African American, 2 American Indian/Alaska Native). Average age 36. 45 applicants, 80% accepted, 21 enrolled. In 2009, 27 master's, 1 doctorate, 3 other advanced degrees awarded. *Degree requirements:* For master's, thesis or alternative. *Entrance requirements:* For master's, MAT; for doctorate, GRE General Test, MA, M Ed or MS; for CAS, MA, M Ed, or MS. Additional exam requirements/recommendations for international students: Required—TOEFL. *Application deadline:* For fall admission, 2/1 priority date for domestic students. Applications are processed on a rolling basis. Application fee: $65. Electronic applications accepted. *Financial support:* Career-related internships or fieldwork, Federal Work-Study, institutionally sponsored loans, tuition waivers (full and partial), and unspecified assistantships available. Financial award application deadline: 3/1. *Unit head:* Dr. Sandra Caron, Coordinator, 207-581-2444, Fax: 207-581-2423. *Application contact:* Scott G. Delcourt, Associate Dean of the Graduate School, 207-581-3291, Fax: 207-581-3232, E-mail: graduate@maine.edu.

Counselor Education

University of Manitoba, Faculty of Graduate Studies, Faculty of Education, Department of Educational Administration, Foundations and Psychology, Winnipeg, MB R3T 2N2, Canada. Offers adult and post-secondary education (M Ed); educational administration (M Ed); guidance and counseling (M Ed); inclusive special education (M Ed); social foundations of education (M Ed). *Degree requirements:* For master's, thesis or alternative.

University of Mary Hardin-Baylor, Graduate Studies in Counseling and Psychology, Belton, TX 76513. Offers community counseling (MA); marriage and family Christian counseling (MA); psychology and counseling (MA); school counseling and psychology (MA). Part-time and evening/weekend programs available. *Degree requirements:* For master's, comprehensive exam. *Entrance requirements:* For master's, GRE General Test, minimum GPA of 3.0 in last 60 hours or 2.75 overall. Electronic applications accepted.

University of Maryland, College Park, Academic Affairs, College of Education, Department of Counseling and Personnel Services, College Park, MD 20742. Offers college student personnel (M Ed, MA); college student personnel administration (PhD); community counseling (CAGS); community/career counseling (M Ed, MA); counseling and personnel services (M Ed, MA, PhD), including art therapy (M Ed), college student personnel (M Ed), counseling and personnel services (PhD), counseling psychology (M Ed), mental health counseling (M Ed), school counseling (M Ed); counseling psychology (PhD); counselor education (PhD); rehabilitation counseling (M Ed, MA, AGSC); school counseling (M Ed, MA); school psychology (M Ed, MA, PhD). *Accreditation:* ACA (one or more programs are accredited); APA (one or more programs are accredited); CORE (one or more programs are accredited); NCATE. Part-time and evening/weekend programs available. Postbaccalaureate distance learning degree programs offered (no on-campus study). *Faculty:* 34 full-time (21 women), 8 part-time/adjunct (6 women). *Students:* 152 full-time (117 women), 25 part-time (18 women); includes 67 minority (32 African Americans, 2 American Indian/Alaska Native, 20 Asian Americans or Pacific Islanders, 13 Hispanic Americans), 16 international. 319 applicants, 15% accepted, 32 enrolled. In 2009, 24 master's, 15 doctorates, 4 other advanced degrees awarded. *Degree requirements:* For master's, thesis (for some programs); for doctorate, thesis/dissertation. *Entrance requirements:* For master's, GRE General Test or MAT, minimum GPA of 3.0, 3 letters of recommendation; for doctorate, GRE General Test or MAT, minimum GPA of 3.5, 3 letters of recommendation. Additional exam requirements/recommendations for international students: Required—TOEFL. *Application deadline:* For fall admission, 12/15 for domestic and international students; for spring admission, 10/1 for domestic students, 6/1 for international students. Applications are processed on a rolling basis. Application fee: $60. Electronic applications accepted. *Expenses:* Tuition, area resident: Part-time $471 per credit hour. Tuition, state resident: part-time $471 per credit hour. Tuition, nonresident: part-time $1016 per credit hour. Required fees: $337.04 per term. *Financial support:* In 2009–10, 4 fellowships with partial tuition reimbursements (averaging $10,402 per year), 8 research assistantships (averaging $16,454 per year), 93 teaching assistantships with tuition reimbursements (averaging $16,109 per year) were awarded; career-related internships or fieldwork, Federal Work-Study, and scholarships/grants also available. Support available to part-time students. Financial award applicants required to submit FAFSA. *Faculty research:* Educational psychology, counseling, health. Total annual research expenditures: $1.5 million. *Unit head:* Dr. Dennis Kivlighan, Chair, 301-405-2858, E-mail: dennisk@umd.edu. *Application contact:* Dean of Graduate School, 301-405-0358.

University of Maryland Eastern Shore, Graduate Programs, Department of Education, Program in Guidance and Counseling, Princess Anne, MD 21853-1299. Offers M Ed. Evening/weekend programs available. *Degree requirements:* For master's, comprehensive exam, practicum, seminar paper. *Entrance requirements:* For master's, interview, minimum GPA of 3.0. Additional exam requirements/recommendations for international students: Required—TOEFL (minimum score 213 computer-based; 80 iBT). Electronic applications accepted.

University of Massachusetts Amherst, Graduate School, School of Education, Program in Education, Amherst, MA 01003. Offers bilingual, English as a second language, and multicultural education (M Ed, CAGS); child study and early education (M Ed); children, families and schools (Ed D, CAGS); early childhood and elementary teacher education (M Ed); education policy and leadership (CAGS); educational administration (M Ed, CAGS); educational policy and leadership (Ed D); higher education (M Ed, CAGS); international education (M Ed); language, literacy and culture (Ed D); learning, media and technology (M Ed, CAGS); mathematics, science, and learning technologies (Ed D); policy studies (M Ed); policy studies in education (CAGS); reading and writing (M Ed); research and evaluation methods (Ed D); school counselor education (M Ed, CAGS); school psychology (CAGS); science education (CAGS); secondary teacher education (M Ed); social justice education (M Ed, Ed D, CAGS); special education (M Ed, Ed D, CAGS). *Accreditation:* NCATE. Part-time programs available. Postbaccalaureate distance learning degree programs offered (minimal on-campus study). *Faculty:* 74 full-time (41 women). *Students:* 377 full-time (268 women), 347 part-time (232 women); includes 115 minority (59 African Americans, 2 American Indian/Alaska Native, 16 Asian Americans or Pacific Islanders, 38 Hispanic Americans), 108 international. Average age 35. 708 applicants, 68% accepted, 266 enrolled. In 2009, 183 master's, 17 doctorates awarded. Terminal master's awarded for partial completion of doctoral program. *Degree requirements:* For master's, thesis or alternative; for doctorate, comprehensive exam, thesis/dissertation. *Entrance requirements:* Additional exam requirements/recommendations for international students: Required—TOEFL (minimum score 550 paper-based; 213 computer-based; 80 iBT), IELTS (minimum score 6.5). *Application deadline:* For fall admission, 1/15 for domestic and international students. Applications are processed on a rolling basis. Application fee: $50 ($65 for international students). Electronic applications accepted. *Expenses:* Tuition, state resident: full-time $2640; part-time $110 per credit. Tuition, nonresident: full-time $9936; part-time $414 per credit. Tuition and fees vary according to course load. *Financial support:* In 2009–10, 1 fellowship with full tuition reimbursement (averaging $8,036 per year), 92 research assistantships with full tuition reimbursements (averaging $8,555 per year), 83 teaching assistantships with full tuition reimbursements (averaging $4,661 per year) were awarded; career-related internships or fieldwork, Federal Work-Study, scholarships/grants, traineeships, health care benefits, tuition waivers (full), and unspecified assistantships also available. Support available to part-time students. Financial award application deadline: 1/15. *Unit head:* Dr. Linda L. Griffin, Graduate Program Director, 413-545-6984, Fax: 413-545-2873. *Application contact:* Jean M. Ames, Supervisor of Admissions, 413-545-0722, Fax: 413-577-0010, E-mail: gradadm@grad.umass.edu.

University of Massachusetts Boston, Office of Graduate Studies, Graduate College of Education, Counseling and School Psychology Department, Program in School Guidance Counseling, Boston, MA 02125-3393. Offers M Ed, CAGS.

University of Memphis, Graduate School, College of Education, Department of Counseling, Educational Psychology and Research, Memphis, TN 38152. Offers counseling (MS, Ed D), including community counseling (MS), rehabilitation counseling (MS), school counseling (MS); counseling psychology (PhD); educational psychology and research (MS, PhD), including educational psychology, educational research. *Accreditation:* ACA (one or more programs are accredited); APA (one or more programs are accredited); CORE (one or more programs are accredited); NCATE. *Faculty:* 26 full-time (13 women), 9 part-time/adjunct (5 women). *Students:* 95 full-time (73 women), 104 part-time (81 women); includes 62 minority (56 African Americans, 3 American Indian/Alaska Native, 1 Asian American or Pacific Islander, 2 Hispanic Americans), 5 international. Average age 33. 118 applicants, 63% accepted, 36 enrolled. In 2009, 46 master's, 14 doctorates awarded. *Degree requirements:* For master's, comprehensive exam, thesis or alternative; for doctorate, comprehensive exam, thesis/dissertation. *Entrance requirements:* For master's, GRE General Test or MAT, minimum GPA of 2.5; for doctorate, GRE General Test. *Application deadline:* For fall admission, 10/1 for domestic students; for spring admission, 4/1 for domestic students. Application fee: $35 ($60 for international students). *Expenses:* Tuition, state resident: full-time $6246; part-time $347 per credit hour. Tuition, nonresident: full-time $15,894; part-time $883 per credit hour. Required fees: $1160. Full-time tuition and fees vary according to course load, degree level and program. *Financial support:* In 2009–10, 130 students received support; fellowships with full tuition reimbursements available, research assistantships with full tuition reimbursements available, teaching assistantships with full tuition reimbursements available, career-related internships or fieldwork, Federal Work-Study, scholarships/grants, and unspecified assistantships available. Financial award application deadline: 2/15; financial award applicants required to submit FAFSA. *Faculty research:* Anger management, aging and disability, supervision, multicultural counseling. *Unit head:* Dr. Douglas C. Strohmer, Chair, 901-678-2841, Fax: 901-678-5114. *Application contact:* Dr. Ernest A. Rakow, Associate Dean of Administration and Graduate Programs, 901-678-2399, Fax: 901-678-4778.

University of Miami, Graduate School, School of Education, Department of Educational and Psychological Studies, Program in Counseling, Coral Gables, FL 33124. Offers bilingual and bicultural counseling (Certificate); counseling and research (MS Ed); marriage and family therapy (MS Ed); mental health counseling (MS Ed). Part-time and evening/weekend programs available. *Students:* 49 full-time (44 women), 15 part-time (13 women); includes 26 minority (2 African Americans, 1 American Indian/Alaska Native, 1 Asian American or Pacific Islander, 22 Hispanic Americans), 5 international. Average age 26. 82 applicants, 61% accepted, 24 enrolled. In 2009, 15 master's awarded. *Degree requirements:* For master's, comprehensive exam, personal growth experience. *Entrance requirements:* For master's, GRE General Test. Additional exam requirements/recommendations for international students: Required—TOEFL (minimum score 550 paper-based; 80 iBT); Recommended—IELTS (minimum score 6.5). *Application deadline:* Applications are processed on a rolling basis. Application fee: $65. Electronic applications accepted. *Financial support:* In 2009–10, 38 students received support. Career-related internships or fieldwork, institutionally sponsored loans, scholarships/grants, and unspecified assistantships available. Support available to part-time students. Financial award application deadline: 3/1; financial award applicants required to submit FAFSA. *Faculty research:* Cocaine recidivism, HIV, non-traditional families, health psychology, diversity. *Unit head:* Dr. Stephanie Schmitz, Assistant Clinical Professor and Program Director, 305-284-4829, Fax: 305-284-3003, E-mail: sschmitz@miami.edu. *Application contact:* Marissa Stevenson-Jacobs, Graduate Admissions Coordinator, 305-284-2167, Fax: 305-284-3003, E-mail: mstevenson@miami.edu.

University of Minnesota, Twin Cities Campus, Graduate School, College of Education and Human Development, Department of Educational Psychology, Program in Counseling and Student Personnel Psychology, Minneapolis, MN 55455-0213. Offers MA, PhD, Ed S. *Students:* 99 full-time (74 women), 15 part-time (12 women); includes 18 minority (6 African Americans, 1 American Indian/Alaska Native, 9 Asian Americans or Pacific Islanders, 2 Hispanic Americans), 20 international. Average age 28. 171 applicants, 37% accepted, 38 enrolled. In 2009, 32 master's, 9 doctorates awarded. *Unit head:* Dr. Susan Hupp, Chair, 612-624-1003, Fax: 612-624-8241, E-mail: shupp@umn.edu. *Application contact:* Dr. Mary Trettin, Associate Dean, 612-625-6501, Fax: 612-626-1580, E-mail: mtrettin@umn.edu.

University of Mississippi, Graduate School, School of Education, Department of Educational Leadership and Counselor Education, Oxford, University, MS 38677. Offers counselor education (M Ed, PhD, Specialist); educational leadership (PhD); educational leadership and counselor education (M Ed, MA, Ed D, Ed S); higher education/student personnel (MA). *Accreditation:* ACA; NCATE. *Faculty:* 14 full-time (5 women), 1 part-time/adjunct (0 women). *Students:* 107 full-time (83 women), 192 part-time (129 women); includes 94 minority (91 African Americans, 2 Asian Americans or Pacific Islanders, 1 Hispanic American), 7 international. In 2009, 48 master's, 13 doctorates, 18 other advanced degrees awarded. *Degree requirements:* For doctorate, thesis/dissertation. *Entrance requirements:* For master's, GRE General Test, minimum GPA of 3.0; for doctorate, GRE General Test. Additional exam requirements/recommendations for international students: Required—TOEFL. *Application deadline:* For fall admission, 4/1 for domestic students; for spring admission, 10/1 for domestic students. Applications are processed on a rolling basis. Application fee: $25. Electronic applications accepted. *Financial support:* Scholarships/grants available. Financial award application deadline: 3/1; financial award applicants required to submit FAFSA. *Unit head:* Dr. Timothy Letzring, Acting Chair, 662-915-7069, E-mail: fdl@olemiss.edu. *Application contact:* Dr. Christy M. Wyandt, Associate Dean, 662-915-7474, Fax: 662-915-7577, E-mail: cwyandt@olemiss.edu.

University of Missouri–St. Louis, College of Education, Division of Counseling, St. Louis, MO 63121. Offers community counseling (M Ed); elementary school counseling (M Ed); secondary school counseling (M Ed). *Accreditation:* ACA; NCATE. Part-time and evening/weekend programs available. *Faculty:* 7 full-time (3 women), 11 part-time/adjunct (7 women). *Students:* 57 full-time (47 women), 152 part-time (128 women); includes 33 minority (27 African Americans, 1 American Indian/Alaska Native, 2 Asian Americans or Pacific Islanders, 3 Hispanic Americans), 8 international. Average age 31. 92 applicants, 59% accepted, 34 enrolled. In 2009, 63 master's awarded. *Degree requirements:* For master's, comprehensive exam. *Entrance requirements:* For master's, 3 letters of recommendation. Additional exam requirements/recommendations for international students: Required—TOEFL (minimum score 550 paper-based; 213 computer-based). *Application deadline:* For fall admission, 6/1 for domestic and international students; for spring admission, 10/1 for domestic and international students. Application fee: $35 ($40 for international students). Electronic applications accepted. *Expenses:* Tuition, state resident: full-time $5377; part-time $297.70 per credit hour. Tuition, nonresident: full-time $13,882; part-time $771.20 per credit hour. Required fees: $220; $12.20 per credit hour. One-time fee: $12. Tuition and fees vary according to course level, campus/location and program. *Financial support:* Application deadline: 4/1. *Faculty research:* Vocational interests, self-concept, decision-making factors, developmental differences. *Unit head:* Dr. Mark Pope, Chair, 314-516-5782. *Application contact:* 314-516-5458, Fax: 314-516-6996, E-mail: gradadm@umsl.edu.

University of Missouri–St. Louis, College of Education, Interdisciplinary Doctoral Programs, St. Louis, MO 63121. Offers adult and higher education (Ed D); counseling (PhD); counselor education (Ed D); educational administration (Ed D); educational leadership and policy studies (PhD); educational psychology (PhD). *Faculty:* 72 full-time (33 women). *Students:* 23 full-time (18 women), 240 part-time (159 women); includes 76 minority (61 African Americans, 2 American Indian/Alaska Native, 7 Asian Americans or Pacific Islanders, 6 Hispanic Americans), 5 international. Average age 40. In 2009, 19 doctorates awarded. *Degree requirements:* For doctorate, thesis/dissertation. *Entrance requirements:* For doctorate, GRE General Test, 3 letters of recommendation; personal interview. Additional exam requirements/recommendations for international students: Recommended—TOEFL (minimum score 550 paper-based; 230 computer-based). *Application deadline:* For fall admission, 2/15 for domestic and international students; for spring admission, 10/1 for domestic and international students. Application fee: $35 ($40 for international students). Electronic applications accepted. *Expenses:* Tuition, state resident: full-time $5377; part-time $297.70 per credit hour. Tuition, nonresident: full-time $13,882; part-time $771.20 per credit hour. Required fees: $220; $12.20 per credit hour. One-time fee: $12. Tuition and fees vary according to course level, campus/location and program. *Financial support:* In 2009–10, 15 research assistantships (averaging $12,240 per year), 8 teaching assistantships (averaging $12,240 per year) were awarded. Financial award application deadline: 4/1; financial award applicants required to submit FAFSA. *Faculty research:* Higher education law and policy, gender and higher education, student retention, lifelong learning orientation, school counselor's role in violence prevention. *Unit head:* Dr. Kathleen Haywood, Director of Graduate Studies, 314-516-5483, Fax: 314-516-5227, E-mail: kathleen_haywood@umsl.edu. *Application contact:* Dr. Kathleen Haywood, Director of Graduate Studies, 314-516-5483, Fax: 314-516-5227, E-mail: kathleen_haywood@umsl.edu.

The University of Montana, Graduate School, School of Education, Department of Educational Leadership and Counseling, Program in Counselor Education, Missoula, MT 59812-0002. Offers counselor education (Ed S); counselor education and supervision (Ed D); mental health counseling (MA); school counseling (MA). *Accreditation:* ACA. *Degree requirements:* For doctorate, thesis/dissertation. *Entrance requirements:* For master's, doctorate, and Ed S, GRE General Test. Additional exam requirements/recommendations for international students: Required—TOEFL.

University of Montevallo, College of Education, Program in Counseling, Montevallo, AL 35115. Offers community counseling (M Ed); marriage and family (M Ed); school counseling

(M Ed). *Accreditation:* ACA; NCATE. Part-time and evening/weekend programs available. *Students:* 36 full-time (32 women), 46 part-time (41 women); includes 14 minority (12 African Americans, 1 Asian American or Pacific Islander, 1 Hispanic American), 2 international. In 2009, 14 master's awarded. *Entrance requirements:* For master's, GRE General Test or MAT, minimum undergraduate GPA of 2.75 in last 60 hours or 2.5 overall, interview. Additional exam requirements/recommendations for international students: Required—TOEFL (minimum score 550 paper-based). *Application deadline:* For fall admission, 7/15 for domestic students; for spring admission, 11/15 for domestic students. Application fee: $25. *Expenses:* Tuition, state resident: full-time $5592; part-time $233 per credit. Tuition, nonresident: full-time $11,184; part-time $466 per credit hour. Required fees: $482; $241 per semester. One-time fee: $25 part-time. *Financial support:* Federal Work-Study, scholarships/grants, and unspecified assistantships available. *Unit head:* Dr. Leland Doebler, Chair, 205-665-6380. *Application contact:* Dr. Leland Doebler, Chair, 205-665-6380.

University of Nebraska at Kearney, College of Graduate Study, College of Education, Department of Counseling and School Psychology, Kearney, NE 68849-0001. Offers counseling (MS Ed, Ed S); school psychology (Ed S). *Accreditation:* ACA; NCATE. Part-time and evening/weekend programs available. *Degree requirements:* For master's, thesis optional; for Ed S, thesis. *Entrance requirements:* For master's and Ed S, interview. Additional exam requirements/recommendations for international students: Required—TOEFL (minimum score 550 paper-based; 213 computer-based). Electronic applications accepted. *Faculty research:* Multicultural counseling and diversity issues, team decision making, adult development, women's issues, brief therapy.

University of Nebraska at Omaha, Graduate Studies, College of Education, Department of Counseling, Omaha, NE 68182. Offers community counseling (MA, MS); counseling gerontology (MA, MS); school counseling (MA, MS); student affairs practice in higher education (MA, MS). *Accreditation:* ACA (one or more programs are accredited); NCATE. Part-time and evening/weekend programs available. *Faculty:* 5 full-time (1 woman). *Students:* 34 full-time (28 women), 152 part-time (128 women); includes 14 minority (10 African Americans, 1 Asian American or Pacific Islander, 3 Hispanic Americans). Average age 29. 50 applicants, 38% accepted, 13 enrolled. In 2009, 46 master's awarded. *Degree requirements:* For master's, comprehensive exam, thesis (for some programs). *Entrance requirements:* For master's, GRE General Test, MAT, department test, interview, minimum GPA of 3.0. Additional exam requirements/recommendations for international students: Required—TOEFL (minimum score 550 paper-based; 213 computer-based; 80 iBT). *Application deadline:* For fall admission, 3/1 for domestic students; for spring admission, 10/1 for domestic students. Applications are processed on a rolling basis. Application fee: $45. Electronic applications accepted. *Financial support:* In 2009–10, 79 students received support, including 2 research assistantships with tuition reimbursements available; fellowships, Federal Work-Study, institutionally sponsored loans, scholarships/grants, tuition waivers (partial), and unspecified assistantships also available. Support available to part-time students. Financial award application deadline: 3/1; financial award applicants required to submit FAFSA. *Unit head:* Dr. Jeanette Seaberry, Chairperson, 402-554-2727. *Application contact:* Penny Harmoney, Director, Graduate Studies, 402-554-2341, Fax: 402-554-3143, E-mail: graduate@unomaha.edu.

University of Nevada, Las Vegas, Graduate College, College of Education, Department of Counselor Education, Las Vegas, NV 89154-3066. Offers addiction studies (Advanced Certificate); community mental health (MS); rehabilitation counseling (Advanced Certificate); school counseling (M Ed). *Faculty:* 7 full-time (2 women), 10 part-time/adjunct (7 women). *Students:* 47 full-time (39 women), 37 part-time (31 women); includes 14 minority (3 African Americans, 1 Asian American or Pacific Islander, 10 Hispanic Americans). Average age 32. 97 applicants, 95% accepted, 57 enrolled. In 2009, 19 master's awarded. *Degree requirements:* For master's, comprehensive exam (for some programs), thesis (for some programs); for Advanced Certificate, thesis (for some programs). *Entrance requirements:* Additional exam requirements/recommendations for international students: Required—TOEFL (minimum score 550 paper-based; 213 computer-based; 80 iBT), IELTS (minimum score 7). *Application deadline:* For fall admission, 2/1 priority date for domestic and international students. Applications are processed on a rolling basis. Application fee: $60 ($95 for international students). Electronic applications accepted. *Financial support:* In 2009–10, 10 students received support, including 6 research assistantships with partial tuition reimbursements available (averaging $10,000 per year), 4 teaching assistantships with partial tuition reimbursements available (averaging $10,000 per year); institutionally sponsored loans, scholarships/grants, health care benefits, and unspecified assistantships also available. Financial award application deadline: 3/1. *Faculty research:* Social justice and multicultural competencies for counselors, therapeutic storytelling and bibliotherapy, school counselor education pedagogy, counseling program evaluation, addictions prevention and related trauma. *Unit head:* Dr. Dale Pehrsson, Chair/ Associate Professor, 702-895-5994, Fax: 702-895-5550, E-mail: dale.pehrsson@unlv.edu. *Application contact:* Graduate College Admissions Evaluator, 702-895-3320, Fax: 702-895-4180, E-mail: gradcollege@unlv.edu.

University of Nevada, Reno, Graduate School, College of Education, Department of Counseling and Educational Psychology, Reno, NV 89557. Offers M Ed, MA, MS, Ed D, PhD, Ed S. *Accreditation:* ACA (one or more programs are accredited); NCATE. Terminal master's awarded for partial completion of doctoral program. *Degree requirements:* For master's, comprehensive exam, thesis optional; for doctorate, comprehensive exam, thesis/dissertation, qualifying exam. *Entrance requirements:* For master's, GRE, minimum GPA of 2.75; for doctorate, GRE, minimum GPA of 3.0. Additional exam requirements/recommendations for international students: Required—TOEFL (minimum score 500 paper-based; 173 computer-based; 61 iBT), IELTS (minimum score 6). Electronic applications accepted. *Faculty research:* Marriage and family counseling, substance abuse attitudes of teachers, current supply of counseling educators, HIV-positive services for patients, family counseling for youth at risk.

University of New Hampshire, Center for Graduate and Professional Studies, Manchester, NH 03101. Offers business administration (MBA); counseling (M Ed); education (M Ed, MAT); educational administration and supervision (M Ed, CAGS); industrial statistics (Certificate); public administration (MPA); public health (MPH, Certificate); social work (MSW). Part-time and evening/weekend programs available. *Students:* 86 full-time (57 women), 150 part-time (87 women); includes 13 minority (3 African Americans, 6 Asian Americans or Pacific Islanders, 4 Hispanic Americans), 7 international. 127 applicants, 73% accepted, 60 enrolled. In 2009, 81 master's, 5 other advanced degrees awarded. *Degree requirements:* For master's, thesis or alternative. *Entrance requirements:* Additional exam requirements/recommendations for international students: Required—TOEFL (minimum score 550 paper-based; 213 computer-based; 80 iBT), TOEIC, TSE. *Application deadline:* For fall admission, 6/1 for domestic students, 4/1 for international students; for spring admission, 12/1 for domestic students. Applications are processed on a rolling basis. Application fee: $65. Electronic applications accepted. *Expenses:* Tuition, state resident: full-time $10,380; part-time $577 per credit hour. Tuition, nonresident: full-time $24,350; part-time $1002 per credit hour. Required fees: $1550; $387.50 per semester. Tuition and fees vary according to course load and program. *Financial support:* In 2009–10, 20 students received support, including 1 fellowship, 1 teaching assistantship; research assistantships, Federal Work-Study, scholarships/grants, health care benefits, and unspecified assistantships also available. Support available to part-time students. Financial award application deadline: 3/1; financial award applicants required to submit FAFSA. *Unit head:* Kate Ferreira, Director, 603-641-4313, E-mail: unhm.gradcenter@unh.edu. *Application contact:* Graduate Admissions Office, 603-862-3000, Fax: 603-862-0275, E-mail: grad.school@unh.edu.

University of New Hampshire, Graduate School, College of Liberal Arts, Department of Education, Program in Counseling, Durham, NH 03824. Offers M Ed, MA. Part-time programs available. *Faculty:* 32 full-time. *Students:* 26 full-time (19 women), 49 part-time (40 women); includes 1 minority (Hispanic American). Average age 35. 35 applicants, 77% accepted, 16 enrolled. In 2009, 32 master's awarded. *Degree requirements:* For master's, thesis (for some programs). *Entrance requirements:* For master's, GRE General Test. Additional exam requirements/recommendations for international students: Required—TOEFL (minimum score 550 paper-based; 213 computer-based; 80 iBT). *Application deadline:* For fall admission, 2/1 priority date for domestic students, 2/1 for international students; for spring admission, 12/1 for domestic students. Applications are processed on a rolling basis. Application fee: $65. Electronic applications accepted. *Expenses:* Tuition, state resident: full-time $10,380; part-time $577 per credit hour. Tuition, nonresident: full-time $24,350; part-time $1002 per credit hour. Required fees: $1550; $387.50 per semester. Tuition and fees vary according to course load and program. *Financial support:* In 2009–10, 35 students received support, including 3 teaching assistantships; fellowships, research assistantships, career-related internships or fieldwork, Federal Work-Study, scholarships/grants, and tuition waivers (full and partial) also available. Support available to part-time students. Financial award application deadline: 2/15. *Faculty research:* Generic approach to counseling. *Unit head:* Dr. Todd Demitchell, Chair, 603-862-3736, E-mail: education.department@unh.edu. *Application contact:* Lisa Wilder, 603-862-2310, E-mail: ducation.department@unh.edu.

University of New Mexico, Graduate School, College of Education, Department of Individual, Family and Community Education, Program in Counselor Education, Albuquerque, NM 87131-2039. Offers MA, PhD. *Accreditation:* ACA (one or more programs are accredited); NCATE. Part-time programs available. *Students:* 58 full-time (50 women), 43 part-time (33 women); includes 41 minority (3 African Americans, 10 American Indian/Alaska Native, 2 Asian Americans or Pacific Islanders, 26 Hispanic Americans), 5 international. Average age 36. 78 applicants, 24% accepted, 13 enrolled. In 2009, 11 master's, 1 doctorate awarded. *Degree requirements:* For master's, comprehensive exam; for doctorate, comprehensive exam, thesis/dissertation. *Entrance requirements:* For master's, 3 letters of recommendation, personal statement, departmental application; for doctorate, GRE General Test, 3 letters of recommendation, writing sample, personal statement, departmental application. Additional exam requirements/recommendations for international students: Required—TOEFL. *Application deadline:* For fall admission, 2/15 for domestic and international students; for spring admission, 9/15 for domestic and international students. Application fee: $50. Electronic applications accepted. *Expenses:* Tuition, state resident: full-time $2099; part-time $233.20 per credit hour. Tuition, nonresident: full-time $6650. Required fees: $25 per semester. Tuition and fees vary according to course load, program and reciprocity agreements. *Financial support:* In 2009–10, 38 students received support; teaching assistantships with full and partial tuition reimbursements available, unspecified assistantships available. Financial award application deadline: 3/1; financial award applicants required to submit FAFSA. *Faculty research:* Crisis and trauma, ethics, supervision, multiculturalism. *Unit head:* Program Coordinator, 505-277-4535, Fax: 505-277-8361, E-mail: divbse@unm.edu. *Application contact:* Cynthia Salas, Department Administrator, 505-277-4535, Fax: 505-277-8361, E-mail: divbse@unm.edu.

University of New Orleans, Graduate School, College of Education and Human Development, Department of Educational Leadership, Counseling, and Foundations, Program in Counselor Education, New Orleans, LA 70148. Offers M Ed, PhD, GCE. *Accreditation:* ACA (one or more programs are accredited); NCATE. Evening/weekend programs available. Terminal master's awarded for partial completion of doctoral program. *Degree requirements:* For master's, thesis (for some programs); for doctorate, variable foreign language requirement, thesis/dissertation. *Entrance requirements:* For master's and doctorate, GRE General Test. Additional exam requirements/recommendations for international students: Required—TOEFL (minimum score 550 paper-based; 213 computer-based; 79 iBT). Electronic applications accepted.

University of North Alabama, College of Education, Department of Counselor Education, Florence, AL 35632-0001. Offers counseling (MA Ed); non-school-based counseling (MA); non-school-based teaching (MA). *Accreditation:* ACA; NCATE. Part-time and evening/weekend programs available. *Faculty:* 2 full-time (both women), 2 part-time/adjunct (1 woman). *Students:* 15 full-time (13 women), 33 part-time (26 women); includes 5 minority (4 African Americans, 1 Hispanic American). Average age 31. In 2009, 30 master's awarded. *Degree requirements:* For master's, comprehensive exam. *Entrance requirements:* For master's, GRE, MAT, or NTE, minimum GPA of 2.5, Alabama Class B Certificate or equivalent, teaching experience. *Application deadline:* For fall admission, 7/1 priority date for domestic students; for spring admission, 12/1 for domestic students. Applications are processed on a rolling basis. Application fee: $25. Electronic applications accepted. *Expenses:* Tuition, state resident: full-time $5040; part-time $210 per credit hour. Tuition, nonresident: full-time $10,080; part-time $420 per credit hour. Required fees: $906. *Financial support:* Federal Work-Study available. Support available to part-time students. Financial award application deadline: 4/1. *Unit head:* Dr. Paul Baird, Chair, 256-765-4763, Fax: 256-765-4159, E-mail: jpbaird@una.edu. *Application contact:* Kim Mauldin, Director of Admissions, 256-765-4608, Fax: 256-765-4960, E-mail: komauldin@una.edu.

The University of North Carolina at Chapel Hill, Graduate School, School of Education, Program in School Counseling, Chapel Hill, NC 27599. Offers M Ed. *Accreditation:* ACA; NCATE. *Degree requirements:* For master's, comprehensive exam. *Entrance requirements:* For master's, GRE General Test, minimum GPA of 3.0 during last 2 years of undergraduate course work. Additional exam requirements/recommendations for international students: Required—TOEFL (minimum score 550 paper-based; 213 computer-based). Electronic applications accepted. *Faculty research:* Career counseling, development and assessment, multicultural counseling, measurement.

The University of North Carolina at Charlotte, Graduate School, College of Education, Department of Counseling, Charlotte, NC 28223-0001. Offers counseling (MA, PhD), including community and school counseling (MA), counseling (PhD). *Accreditation:* ACA. Part-time and evening/weekend programs available. Postbaccalaureate distance learning degree programs offered (no on-campus study). *Faculty:* 12 full-time (7 women). *Students:* 110 full-time (91 women), 100 part-time (87 women); includes 36 African Americans, 2 Asian Americans or Pacific Islanders, 7 Hispanic Americans, 3 international. Average age 32. 123 applicants, 58% accepted, 68 enrolled. In 2009, 52 master's, 5 doctorates awarded. Terminal master's awarded for partial completion of doctoral program. *Degree requirements:* For master's, thesis; for doctorate, thesis/dissertation. *Entrance requirements:* For master's, GRE or MAT. Additional exam requirements/recommendations for international students: Required—TOEFL (minimum score 557 paper-based; 220 computer-based; 83 iBT). *Application deadline:* For fall admission, 7/1 for domestic students, 5/1 for international students; for spring admission, 11/1 for domestic students, 10/1 for international students. Applications are processed on a rolling basis. Application fee: $55. Electronic applications accepted. *Financial support:* In 2009–10, 9 students received support, including 1 research assistantship (averaging $6,000 per year), 8 teaching assistantships (averaging $5,625 per year); career-related internships or fieldwork, Federal Work-Study, institutionally sponsored loans, scholarships/grants, and unspecified assistantships also available. Support available to part-time students. Financial award application deadline: 4/1; financial award applicants required to submit FAFSA. Total annual research expenditures: $6,427. *Unit head:* Dr. Susan R. Furr, Chair, 704-687-8967, Fax: 704-687-1013, E-mail: srfurr@uncc.edu. *Application contact:* Kathy B. Giddings, Director of Graduate Admissions, 704-687-5503, Fax: 704-687-3279, E-mail: gradadm@uncc.edu.

The University of North Carolina at Greensboro, Graduate School, School of Education, Department of Counseling and Educational Development, Greensboro, NC 27412-5001. Offers advanced school counseling (PMC); counseling and counselor education (PhD); counseling and educational development (MS); couple and family counseling (PMC); school counseling (PMC); MS/Ed S. *Accreditation:* ACA (one or more programs are accredited); NCATE. *Degree requirements:* For master's, comprehensive exam, practicum, internship; for doctorate, comprehensive exam, thesis/dissertation. *Entrance requirements:* For master's, doctorate, and PMC, GRE General Test. Additional exam requirements/recommendations for international students: Required—TOEFL. Electronic applications accepted. *Faculty research:* Gerontology, invitational theory, career development, marriage and family therapy, drug and alcohol abuse prevention.

The University of North Carolina at Pembroke, Graduate Studies, Department of Psychology and Counseling, Program in Service Agency Counseling, Pembroke, NC 28372-1510. Offers MA. Part-time and evening/weekend programs available. *Degree requirements:* For master's, comprehensive exam, thesis optional. *Entrance requirements:* For master's, GRE General

Counselor Education

The University of North Carolina at Pembroke *(continued)*
Test or MAT, minimum GPA of 3.0 in major, 2.5 overall. Additional exam requirements/recommendations for international students: Required—TOEFL.

The University of North Carolina at Pembroke, Graduate Studies, School of Education, Program in School Counseling, Pembroke, NC 28372-1510. Offers MA Ed. *Accreditation:* NCATE. Part-time and evening/weekend programs available. *Degree requirements:* For master's, comprehensive exam, thesis optional. *Entrance requirements:* For master's, GRE General Test or MAT, minimum GPA of 3.0 in major, 2.5 overall. Additional exam requirements/recommendations for international students: Required—TOEFL.

University of Northern Colorado, Graduate School, College of Education and Behavioral Sciences, School of Applied Psychology and Counselor Education, Program in Clinical Counseling, Greeley, CO 80639. Offers MA. Part-time programs available. *Faculty:* 16 full-time (10 women). *Students:* 63 full-time (52 women), 15 part-time (11 women); includes 6 minority (1 African American, 5 Hispanic Americans), 1 international. Average age 31. 69 applicants, 81% accepted, 25 enrolled. In 2009, 41 master's awarded. *Application deadline:* Applications are processed on a rolling basis. Application fee: $50 ($60 for international students). Electronic applications accepted. *Expenses:* Tuition, state resident: full-time $5770; part-time $320.55 per credit hour. Tuition, nonresident: full-time $13,847; part-time $769.27 per credit hour. Required fees: $948.78; $52.72 per credit. *Financial support:* Application deadline: 3/1. *Unit head:* Heather Helm, Program Coordinator, 970-351-2731, Fax: 970-351-2625. *Application contact:* Linda Sisson, Graduate Student Admission Coordinator, 970-351-1807, Fax: 970-351-2371, E-mail: linda.sisson@unco.edu.

University of Northern Colorado, Graduate School, College of Education and Behavioral Sciences, School of Applied Psychology and Counselor Education, Program in Counselor Education and Supervision, Greeley, CO 80639. Offers PhD. *Accreditation:* ACA. Part-time programs available. *Faculty:* 4 full-time (3 women). *Students:* 10 full-time (6 women), 8 part-time (4 women); includes 4 minority (1 African American, 1 American Indian/Alaska Native, 1 Asian American or Pacific Islander, 1 Hispanic American). Average age 36. 11 applicants, 82% accepted, 6 enrolled. In 2009, 1 doctorate awarded. *Degree requirements:* For doctorate, comprehensive exam, thesis/dissertation. *Entrance requirements:* For doctorate, GRE General Test, 3 letters of recommendation. *Application deadline:* For fall admission, 1/1 for domestic and international students. Application fee: $50 ($60 for international students). *Expenses:* Tuition, state resident: full-time $5770; part-time $320.55 per credit hour. Tuition, nonresident: full-time $13,847; part-time $769.27 per credit hour. Required fees: $948.78; $52.72 per credit. *Financial support:* Fellowships, research assistantships, teaching assistantships available. Financial award application deadline: 3/1; financial award applicants required to submit FAFSA. *Unit head:* Dr. Jennifer Murdock, Program Coordinator, 970-351-2544, Fax: 970-351-2625. *Application contact:* Linda Sisson, Graduate Student Admission Coordinator, 970-351-1807, Fax: 970-351-2371, E-mail: linda.sisson@unco.edu.

University of Northern Colorado, Graduate School, College of Education and Behavioral Sciences, School of Applied Psychology and Counselor Education, Program in School Counseling, Greeley, CO 80639. Offers MA. Part-time programs available. *Faculty:* 16 full-time (10 women). *Students:* 19 full-time (16 women), 6 part-time (5 women); includes 4 minority (1 American Indian/Alaska Native, 3 Hispanic Americans). Average age 30. 29 applicants, 90% accepted, 10 enrolled. In 2009, 11 master's awarded. *Application deadline:* Applications are processed on a rolling basis. Application fee: $50 ($60 for international students). Electronic applications accepted. *Expenses:* Tuition, state resident: full-time $5770; part-time $320.55 per credit hour. Tuition, nonresident: full-time $13,847; part-time $769.27 per credit hour. Required fees: $948.78; $52.72 per credit. *Financial support:* Application deadline: 3/1. *Unit head:* Heather Helm, Program Coordinator, 970-351-2731. *Application contact:* Linda Sisson, Graduate Student Admission Coordinator, 970-351-1807, Fax: 970-351-2371, E-mail: linda.sisson@unco.edu.

University of Northern Iowa, Graduate College, College of Education, Department of Educational Leadership, Counseling, and Postsecondary Education, Program in Counseling, Cedar Falls, IA 50614. Offers counseling (MA, Ed D); school counseling (MAE). *Accreditation:* ACA (one or more programs are accredited). Part-time and evening/weekend programs available. *Students:* 62 full-time (48 women), 21 part-time (19 women); includes 6 minority (3 African Americans, 1 Asian American or Pacific Islander, 2 Hispanic Americans), 1 international. 63 applicants, 41% accepted, 23 enrolled. In 2009, 17 master's awarded. *Degree requirements:* For master's, comprehensive exam, thesis or alternative. *Entrance requirements:* For master's, minimum GPA of 3.0; for doctorate, minimum GPA of 3.5, master's degree. Additional exam requirements/recommendations for international students: Required—TOEFL (minimum score 500 paper-based; 180 computer-based; 61 iBT). *Application deadline:* For fall admission, 8/1 priority date for domestic students. Applications are processed on a rolling basis. Application fee: $30 ($50 for international students). Electronic applications accepted. *Financial support:* Career-related internships or fieldwork, Federal Work-Study, and tuition waivers (full and partial) available. Support available to part-time students. Financial award application deadline: 2/1. *Unit head:* Dr. Jan Bartlett, Coordinator, 319-273-7979, Fax: 319-273-5175, E-mail: jan.bartlett@uni.edu. *Application contact:* Laurie S. Russell, Record Analyst, 319-273-2623, Fax: 319-273-6792, E-mail: laurie.russell@uni.edu.

University of North Florida, College of Education and Human Services, Department of Leadership, Counseling and Instructional Technology, Program in Counselor Education, Jacksonville, FL 32224. Offers mental health counseling (M Ed); school counseling (M Ed). *Accreditation:* ACA; NCATE. Part-time and evening/weekend programs available. *Faculty:* 18 full-time (11 women). *Students:* 19 full-time (15 women), 22 part-time (19 women); includes 11 minority (8 African Americans, 2 Asian Americans or Pacific Islanders, 1 Hispanic American). Average age 29. 6 applicants, 33% accepted, 0 enrolled. In 2009, 30 master's awarded. *Entrance requirements:* For master's, GRE General Test, minimum GPA of 3.0 in last 60 hours, 3 letters of recommendation, portfolio, interview, writing sample. Additional exam requirements/recommendations for international students: Required—TOEFL (minimum score 500 paper-based; 173 computer-based). *Application deadline:* For fall admission, 5/15 for domestic students, 4/23 for international students; for spring admission, 9/26 for domestic students. Application fee: $30. Electronic applications accepted. *Expenses:* Tuition, state resident: full-time $6649.20; part-time $277.05 per credit hour. Tuition, nonresident: full-time $22,970; part-time $957.08 per credit hour. Required fees: $985; $41.03 per credit hour. *Financial support:* In 2009–10, 30 students received support, including 3 research assistantships (averaging $3,600 per year); career-related internships or fieldwork, Federal Work-Study, and tuition waivers (partial) also available. Support available to part-time students. Financial award application deadline: 4/1; financial award applicants required to submit FAFSA. *Unit head:* Dr. Edgar N. Jackson, Chair, 904-620-2990, Fax: 904-620-2982, E-mail: newton.jackson@unf.edu. *Application contact:* Kiersten Jarvis, Graduate Admissions Coordinator, 904-620-1360, Fax: 904-620-1362, E-mail: kiersten.jarvis@unf.edu.

University of North Texas, Robert B. Toulouse School of Graduate Studies, College of Education, Department of Counseling and Higher Education, Program in Counseling, Denton, TX 76203-5017. Offers adolescent counseling (Certificate); adult counseling (Certificate); child counseling/play therapy (Certificate); college/university counseling (Certificate); community college counseling (MS); community counseling (Certificate); counseling (PhD); couple/family counseling (Certificate); elementary school counseling (M Ed, MS); group counseling (Certificate); secondary school counseling (M Ed); university counseling (M Ed). *Accreditation:* NCATE. Part-time and evening/weekend programs available. *Degree requirements:* For master's, comprehensive exam (for some programs), 600 hour internship; for doctorate, comprehensive exam, thesis/dissertation. *Entrance requirements:* For master's, GRE General Test, 3 recommendations, group interview, writing sample; for doctorate, GRE General Test, admissions exam, 3 recommendations, group interview. Additional exam requirements/recommendations for international students: Required—proof of English language proficiency required for non-native English speakers; Recommended—TOEFL (minimum score 550 paper-based; 213 computer-based). *Application deadline:* Applications are processed on a rolling basis. Application

fee: $50 ($75 for international students). Electronic applications accepted. *Expenses:* Tuition, state resident: full-time $4298; part-time $239 per contact hour. Tuition, nonresident: full-time $9878; part-time $549 per contact hour. Required fees: $265 per contact hour. *Financial support:* Research assistantships, teaching assistantships, career-related internships or fieldwork, Federal Work-Study, institutionally sponsored loans, scholarships/grants, and unspecified assistantships available. *Faculty research:* Play therapy, school counseling, suicide prevention, animal-assisted therapy, transpersonal counseling. *Application contact:* Administrative Assistant, 940-565-2910, Fax: 940-565-2905, E-mail: janet.rogers@unt.edu.

University of Oklahoma, Graduate College, College of Education, Department of Educational Psychology, Program in School Counseling, Norman, OK 73019. Offers M Ed. *Students:* 1 full-time (0 women). In 2009, 22 master's awarded. Terminal master's awarded for partial completion of doctoral program. *Degree requirements:* For master's, comprehensive exam. *Entrance requirements:* For master's, GRE General Test, minimum GPA of 3.0. Additional exam requirements/recommendations for international students: Required—TOEFL (minimum score 550 paper-based; 213 computer-based). *Application deadline:* For fall admission, 1/31 for domestic students, 4/1 for international students; for spring admission, 11/1 for domestic students, 9/1 for international students. Applications are processed on a rolling basis. Application fee: $40 ($90 for international students). Electronic applications accepted. *Expenses:* Tuition, state resident: full-time $3744; part-time $156 per credit hour. Tuition, nonresident: full-time $13,577; part-time $565.70 per credit hour. Required fees: $2415; $90.10 per credit hour. *Financial support:* In 2009–10, 1 student received support. Institutionally sponsored loans, scholarships/grants, health care benefits, and unspecified assistantships available. Financial award application deadline: 3/1; financial award applicants required to submit FAFSA. *Faculty research:* Marriage and family dynamics, multi-cultural and cross-cultural counseling, small group intervention, career development, counseling, process/outcome, at-risk/delinquent youth, women's issues. *Unit head:* Dr. Terri K. Debacker, Chair, 405-325-1068, Fax: 405-325-6655, E-mail: debacker@ou.edu. *Application contact:* Rindi Ledo, Graduate Programs Officer, 405-325-4525, Fax: 405-325-6655, E-mail: gpoedpsych@ou.edu.

University of Phoenix–New Mexico Campus, The Artemis School, College of Education, Albuquerque, NM 87113-1570. Offers administration and supervision (MAEd); curriculum and instruction (MAEd); elementary teacher education (MAEd); school counseling (MSC); secondary teacher education (MAEd). Evening/weekend programs available. *Degree requirements:* For master's, thesis (for some programs). *Entrance requirements:* For master's, minimum undergraduate GPA of 2.5, 3 years of work experience. Additional exam requirements/recommendations for international students: Required—TOEFL (minimum score 550 paper-based; 213 computer-based; 79 iBT). Electronic applications accepted.

University of Phoenix–Southern Arizona Campus, The Artemis School, College of Education, Tucson, AZ 85711. Offers administration and supervision (MA Ed); adult education and training (MA Ed); curriculum instruction (MA Ed); educational counseling (MA Ed); elementary teacher education (MA Ed); school counseling (MSC); secondary teacher education (MA Ed); special education (MA Ed, Certificate). Evening/weekend programs available. *Degree requirements:* For master's, thesis (for some programs). *Entrance requirements:* For master's, minimum undergraduate GPA of 2.5, 3 years of work experience. Additional exam requirements/recommendations for international students: Required—TOEFL (minimum score 550 paper-based; 213 computer-based; 79 iBT). Electronic applications accepted.

University of Puerto Rico, Río Piedras, College of Education, Program in Guidance and Counseling, San Juan, PR 00931-3300. Offers M Ed, Ed D. Part-time programs available. *Degree requirements:* For master's, thesis; for doctorate, thesis/dissertation, internship. *Entrance requirements:* For master's, PAEG or GRE, interview, minimum GPA of 3.0, letter of recommendation; for doctorate, GRE or PAEG, master's degree, minimum GPA of 3.0, letter of recommendation (2), interview.

University of Puget Sound, Graduate Studies, School of Education, Program in Counseling, Tacoma, WA 98416. Offers mental health counseling (M Ed); pastoral counseling (M Ed); school counseling (M Ed). *Accreditation:* NCATE. Part-time programs available. *Faculty:* 2 full-time (both women). *Students:* 1 (woman) full-time, 26 part-time (20 women); includes 4 minority (1 African American, 3 Hispanic Americans). Average age 32. 25 applicants, 56% accepted, 11 enrolled. In 2009, 10 master's awarded. *Entrance requirements:* For master's, GRE General Test, minimum GPA of 3.0. Additional exam requirements/recommendations for international students: Required—TOEFL (minimum score 550 paper-based; 213 computer-based; 80 iBT). *Application deadline:* For fall admission, 3/1 priority date for domestic and international students. Applications are processed on a rolling basis. Application fee: $60. Electronic applications accepted. *Expenses:* Contact institution. *Financial support:* Teaching assistantships, career-related internships or fieldwork available. Financial award application deadline: 3/31; financial award applicants required to submit FAFSA. *Faculty research:* Cross-role professional preparation, suicide prevention. *Unit head:* Dr. John Woodward, Dean, 253-879-3375, E-mail: woodward@pugetsound.edu. *Application contact:* Dr. George H. Mills, Vice President for Enrollment, 253-879-3211, Fax: 253-879-3993, E-mail: admission@pugetsound.edu.

University of Saint Francis, Graduate School, Department of Psychology and Counseling, Fort Wayne, IN 46808-3994. Offers general psychology (MS); mental health counseling (MS); pastoral counseling (MS); school counseling (MS Ed). Part-time and evening/weekend programs available. *Entrance requirements:* For master's, interview, minimum undergraduate GPA of 3.0.

University of San Diego, School of Leadership and Education Sciences, Program in Counseling, San Diego, CA 92110-2492. Offers clinical mental health counseling (MA); school counseling (MA). Part-time and evening/weekend programs available. *Faculty:* 6 full-time (2 women), 7 part-time/adjunct (6 women). *Students:* 84 full-time (74 women), 25 part-time (20 women); includes 45 minority (4 African Americans, 16 Asian Americans or Pacific Islanders, 25 Hispanic Americans), 1 international. Average age 27. 132 applicants, 70% accepted, 54 enrolled. In 2009, 36 master's awarded. *Degree requirements:* For master's, comprehensive exam. *Entrance requirements:* For master's, minimum GPA of 3.0, interview with faculty member. Additional exam requirements/recommendations for international students: Required—TOEFL (minimum score 580 paper-based; 237 computer-based; 83 iBT), TWE. *Application deadline:* For fall admission, 3/1 priority date for domestic students, 3/1 for international students. Application fee: $45. Electronic applications accepted. *Expenses:* Tuition: Full-time $21,042; part-time $1169 per unit. Required fees: $224. Full-time tuition and fees vary according to course load and degree level. *Financial support:* In 2009–10, 102 students received support. Career-related internships or fieldwork, Federal Work-Study, institutionally sponsored loans, unspecified assistantships, and stipends available. Support available to part-time students. Financial award application deadline: 4/1; financial award applicants required to submit FAFSA. *Faculty research:* Action research, forensic psychology, lifespan and career development, multicultural counseling, school counseling. *Unit head:* Dr. Lonnie Rowell, Graduate Program Co-Director, 619-260-4212, Fax: 619-260-8095. *Application contact:* Dr. John Mosby, Associate Director of Graduate Admissions, 619-260-4524, Fax: 619-260-4158, E-mail: grads@sandiego.edu.

University of San Francisco, School of Education, Department of Counseling Psychology, San Francisco, CA 94117-1080. Offers counseling (MA), including educational counseling, life transitions counseling, marital and family therapy; counseling psychology (Ed D). *Faculty:* 7 full-time (3 women), 37 part-time/adjunct (26 women). *Students:* 277 full-time (228 women), 9 part-time (7 women); includes 97 minority (16 African Americans, 1 American Indian/Alaska Native, 35 Asian Americans or Pacific Islanders, 45 Hispanic Americans), 8 international. Average age 31. 354 applicants, 66% accepted, 132 enrolled. In 2009, 150 master's awarded. *Degree requirements:* For doctorate, thesis/dissertation. *Entrance requirements:* For doctorate, GRE General Test. Application fee: $55 ($65 for international students). *Expenses:* Tuition: Full-time $19,710; part-time $1095 per unit. Part-time tuition and fees vary according to degree level, campus/location and program. *Financial support:* In 2009–10, 227 students received support; fellowships, research assistantships, teaching assistantships available. Financial award

application deadline: 3/2; financial award applicants required to submit FAFSA. *Unit head:* Dr. Brian Gerrard, Chair, 415-422-6868. *Application contact:* Beth Teague, Associate Director of Graduate Outreach, 415-422-5467, E-mail: schoolofeducation@usfca.edu.

The University of Scranton, College of Graduate and Continuing Education, Department of Counseling and Human Services, Program in School Counseling, Scranton, PA 18510. Offers MS. *Accreditation:* ACA; NCATE. Part-time and evening/weekend programs available. *Students:* 51 full-time (40 women), 13 part-time (9 women); includes 4 minority (1 African American, 3 Hispanic Americans). Average age 27. 57 applicants, 53% accepted. In 2009, 29 master's awarded. *Degree requirements:* For master's, comprehensive exam, capstone experience. *Entrance requirements:* For master's, minimum GPA of 2.75. Additional exam requirements/recommendations for international students: Required—TOEFL (minimum score 500 paper-based; 173 computer-based), IELTS (minimum score 5.5). *Application deadline:* For fall admission, 3/1 for domestic students. Application fee: $0. *Financial support:* Teaching assistantships, career-related internships or fieldwork and Federal Work-Study available. Support available to part-time students. Financial award application deadline: 3/1. *Unit head:* Dr. Lee Ann M. Eschbach, Co Director, 570-941-6299, Fax: 570-941-4201, E-mail: eschbach@scranton.edu. *Application contact:* Joseph M. Roback, Director of Admissions, 570-941-4385, Fax: 570-941-5928, E-mail: robackj2@scranton.edu.

University of South Africa, College of Human Sciences, Pretoria, South Africa. Offers adult education (M Ed); African languages (MA, PhD); African politics (MA, PhD); Afrikaans (MA, PhD); ancient history (MA, PhD); ancient Near Eastern studies (MA, PhD); anthropology (MA, PhD); applied linguistics (MA); Arabic (MA, PhD); archaeology (MA); art history (MA); Biblical archaeology (MA); Biblical studies (M Th, D Th, PhD); Christian spirituality (M Th, D Th); church history (M Th, D Th); classical studies (MA, PhD); clinical psychology (MA); communication (MA, PhD); comparative education (M Ed, Ed D); consulting psychology (D Admin, D Com, PhD); curriculum studies (M Ed, Ed D); development studies (M Admin, MA, D Admin, PhD); didactics (M Ed, Ed D); education (M Tech); education management (M Ed, Ed D); educational psychology (M Ed); English (MA); environmental education (M Ed); French (MA, PhD); German (MA, PhD); Greek (MA); guidance and counseling (M Ed); health studies (MA, PhD), including health sciences education (MA), health services management (MA), medical and surgical nursing science (critical care general) (MA), midwifery and neonatal nursing science (MA), trauma and emergency care (MA); history (MA, PhD); history of education (Ed D); inclusive education (M Ed, Ed D); information and communications technology policy and regulation (MA); information science (MA, MIS, PhD); international politics (MA, PhD); Islamic studies (MA, PhD); Italian (MA, PhD); Judaica (MA, PhD); linguistics (MA, PhD); mathematical education (M Ed); mathematics education (MA); missiology (M Th, D Th); modern Hebrew (MA, PhD); musicology (MA, MMus, D Mus, PhD); natural science education (M Ed); New Testament (M Th, D Th); Old Testament (D Th); pastoral therapy (M Th, D Th); philosophy (MA); philosophy of education (M Ed, Ed D); politics (MA, PhD); Portuguese (MA, PhD); practical theology (M Th, D Th); psychology (MA, MS, PhD); psychology of education (M Ed, Ed D); public health (MA); religious studies (MA, D Th, PhD); Romance languages (MA); Russian (MA, PhD); Semitic languages (MA, PhD); social behavior studies in HIV/AIDS (MA); social science (mental health) (MA); social science in development studies (MA); social science in psychology (MA); social science in social work (MA); social science in sociology (MA); social work (MSW, DSW, PhD); socio-education (M Ed, Ed D); sociolinguistics (MA); sociology (MA, PhD); Spanish (MA, PhD); systematic theology (M Th, D Th); TESOL (teaching English to speakers of other languages) (MA); theological ethics (M Th, D Th); theory of literature (MA, PhD); urban ministries (D Th); urban ministry (M Th).

University of South Alabama, Graduate School, College of Education, Department of Professional Studies, Mobile, AL 36688-0002. Offers community counseling (MS); educational media (M Ed, MS); instructional design and development (MS, PhD); rehabilitation counseling (MS); school counseling (M Ed); school psychometry (M Ed). *Accreditation:* NCATE. Part-time programs available. *Degree requirements:* For master's, comprehensive exam. *Entrance requirements:* For master's, GRE General Test or MAT, minimum GPA of 3.0. *Expenses:* Tuition, state resident: part-time $218 per contact hour. Required fees: $1102 per year. *Faculty research:* Agency counseling, rehabilitation counseling, school psychometry.

University of South Carolina, The Graduate School, College of Education, Department of Educational Studies, Program in Counseling Education, Columbia, SC 29208. Offers PhD, Ed S. *Accreditation:* ACA (one or more programs are accredited); NCATE. Part-time programs available. *Degree requirements:* For doctorate, one foreign language, comprehensive exam, thesis/dissertation; for Ed S, comprehensive exam. *Entrance requirements:* For doctorate, GRE General Test or MAT, interview, resume, references; for Ed S, GRE General Test or MAT, interview, resum&e, transcripts, letter of intent, references. Electronic applications accepted. *Faculty research:* Multicultural counseling, children's fears, career development, family counseling.

The University of South Dakota, Graduate School, School of Education, Division of Counseling and Psychology in Education, Vermillion, SD 57069-2390. Offers MA, PhD, Ed S. *Accreditation:* ACA (one or more programs are accredited); NCATE. Part-time programs available. *Degree requirements:* For master's and Ed S, comprehensive exam, thesis or alternative; for doctorate, comprehensive exam, thesis/dissertation. *Entrance requirements:* For master's and doctorate, GRE General Test, minimum GPA of 3.0. Additional exam requirements/recommendations for international students: Required—TOEFL (minimum score 550 paper-based; 213 computer-based; 79 iBT). Electronic applications accepted.

University of Southern California, Graduate School, Rossier School of Education, Master's Programs in Education, Los Angeles, CA 90089-4038. Offers marriage, family and child counseling (MMFT); postsecondary administration and student affairs [PASA] (ME); school counseling (ME); teaching (MA); teaching and teaching credential (MAT); teaching English to speakers of other languages (MAT, MS). Part-time and evening/weekend programs available. Postbaccalaureate distance learning degree programs offered (no on-campus study). *Faculty:* 26 full-time (17 women), 24 part-time/adjunct (14 women). *Students:* 579 full-time (455 women), 85 part-time (56 women); includes 302 minority (50 African Americans, 4 American Indian/Alaska Native, 110 Asian Americans or Pacific Islanders, 138 Hispanic Americans), 62 international. 1,282 applicants, 67% accepted, 484 enrolled. In 2009, 228 master's awarded. *Degree requirements:* For master's, thesis optional. *Entrance requirements:* For master's, GRE (for all programs except MAT). Additional exam requirements/recommendations for international students: Required—TOEFL (minimum score 250 computer-based; 100 iBT). Application fee: $85. Electronic applications accepted. *Expenses:* Tuition: Full-time $25,980; part-time $1315 per unit. Required fees: $554. One-time fee: $35 full-time. Full-time tuition and fees vary according to degree level and program. *Financial support:* Career-related internships or fieldwork, Federal Work-Study, scholarships/grants, traineeships, and unspecified assistantships available. Support available to part-time students. Financial award application deadline: 4/10; financial award applicants required to submit FAFSA. *Faculty research:* College access and equity; preparing teachers for culturally diverse populations; sociocultural basis of learning as mediated by instruction with focus on reading and literacy in English learners; social and political aspects of teaching and learning English; school counselor development and training. *Unit head:* Dr. Kristan Venegas, Director/Assistant Professor of Clinical Education, 213-740-3255, E-mail: rsoemast@usc.edu. *Application contact:* Michael Jackson, 213-740-0224, E-mail: soeinfo@usc.edu.

University of Southern Maine, College of Education and Human Development, Program in Counselor Education, Portland, ME 04104-9300. Offers clinical mental health (MS); counseling (CAS); mental health rehabilitation technician/community (Certificate); rehabilitation counseling (MS); school counseling (MS). *Accreditation:* ACA (one or more programs are accredited); CORE; Teacher Education Accreditation Council. Part-time and evening/weekend programs available. *Faculty:* 8 full-time (4 women), 2 part-time/adjunct (1 woman). *Students:* 110 full-time (83 women), 33 part-time (23 women); includes 5 minority (1 African American, 1 American Indian/Alaska Native, 3 Hispanic Americans). 79 applicants, 72% accepted, 44 enrolled. In 2009, 37 master's, 2 other advanced degrees awarded. *Degree requirements:* For master's, comprehensive exam, thesis or alternative; for other advanced degree, thesis or alternative. *Entrance requirements:* For master's, GRE General Test or MAT, interview; for other advanced degree, master's degree. Additional exam requirements/recommendations for international students: Required—TOEFL (minimum score 550 paper-based; 213 computer-based; 79 iBT). *Application deadline:* For fall admission, 11/15 for domestic students. Application fee: $50. Electronic applications accepted. *Financial support:* In 2009–10, 12 students received support, including 3 research assistantships with partial tuition reimbursements available (averaging $4,500 per year); career-related internships or fieldwork, Federal Work-Study, institutionally sponsored loans, scholarships/grants, and unspecified assistantships also available. Support available to part-time students. Financial award application deadline: 3/1; financial award applicants required to submit FAFSA. *Faculty research:* Counselor licensure. *Unit head:* Dr. E. Michael Brady, Chair, Human Resource Development Department, 207-780-5316, Fax: 207-780-5043, E-mail: mbrady@usm.maine.edu. *Application contact:* Mary Sloan, Director of Graduate Admissions, 207-780-4386, Fax: 207-780-4969, E-mail: msloan@usm.maine.edu.

University of Southern Mississippi, Graduate School, College of Education and Psychology, Department of Educational Leadership and School Counseling, Hattiesburg, MS 39401. Offers education (M Ed), including educational administration, educational administration and supervision, school business administration, secondary administration; education (Ed S), including elementary administration, higher education administration; educational administration (M Ed); educational administration and supervision (M Ed), including educational administration; educational leadership and school counseling (Ed D, PhD). *Faculty:* 9 full-time (5 women), 3 part-time/adjunct (1 woman). *Students:* 51 full-time (32 women), 217 part-time (158 women); includes 92 minority (84 African Americans, 2 Asian Americans or Pacific Islanders, 6 Hispanic Americans), 2 international. Average age 39. 84 applicants, 57% accepted, 45 enrolled. In 2009, 68 master's, 25 doctorates, 35 other advanced degrees awarded. *Degree requirements:* For master's, internship. *Entrance requirements:* For master's, doctorate, and Ed S, GRE General Test, minimum GPA of 2.75. *Application deadline:* For fall admission, 3/1 priority date for domestic and international students. Application fee: $35. *Expenses:* Tuition, state resident: full-time $5096; part-time $284 per hour. Tuition, nonresident: full-time $13,052; part-time $726 per hour. Required fees: $402. Tuition and fees vary according to course level and course load. *Financial support:* Career-related internships or fieldwork, Federal Work-Study, and institutionally sponsored loans available. Financial award application deadline: 3/15; financial award applicants required to submit FAFSA. *Unit head:* Dr. Mary Ann Adams, Interim Chair, 601-266-4579. *Application contact:* Shonna Breland, Manager of Graduate Admissions, 601-266-6563, Fax: 601-266-5138.

University of Southern Mississippi, Graduate School, College of Education and Psychology, Department of Educational Studies and Research, Hattiesburg, MS 39406-0001. Offers adult education (Graduate Certificate); community college leadership (Graduate Certificate); counseling and personnel services (college) (M Ed); education (PhD, Ed S), including adult education, research, evaluation and statistics (PhD); education (Ed D), including educational administration, educational research; education: educational leadership and research (Ed S), including higher education administration; educational administration and supervision (M Ed); higher education administration (Ed D, PhD); institutional research (Graduate Certificate). *Faculty:* 7 full-time (1 woman), 5 part-time/adjunct (1 woman). *Students:* 45 full-time (34 women), 97 part-time (66 women); includes 42 minority (40 African Americans, 1 American Indian/Alaska Native, 1 Hispanic American), 2 international. Average age 36. 54 applicants, 67% accepted, 33 enrolled. In 2009, 26 master's, 11 doctorates, 3 other advanced degrees awarded. *Degree requirements:* For master's and other advanced degree, comprehensive exam, thesis (for some programs); for doctorate, comprehensive exam, thesis/dissertation. *Entrance requirements:* For master's, doctorate, and other advanced degree, GRE General Test, minimum GPA of 2.75. Additional exam requirements/recommendations for international students: Required—TOEFL. *Application deadline:* For fall admission, 2/1 for domestic students, 3/1 for international students. Applications are processed on a rolling basis. Application fee: $35. *Expenses:* Tuition, state resident: full-time $5096; part-time $284 per hour. Tuition, nonresident: full-time $13,052; part-time $726 per hour. Required fees: $402. Tuition and fees vary according to course level and course load. *Financial support:* Career-related internships or fieldwork, Federal Work-Study, and institutionally sponsored loans available. Financial award application deadline: 3/15; financial award applicants required to submit FAFSA. Total annual research expenditures: $88,500. *Unit head:* Dr. Thomas V. O'Brien, Chair, 601-266-6093, E-mail: thomas.obrien@usm.edu. *Application contact:* Shonna Breland, Manager of Graduate Admissions, 601-266-6563, Fax: 601-266-5138.

University of South Florida, Graduate School, College of Behavioral and Community Sciences, Program in Applied Behavior Analysis, Tampa, FL 33620-9951. Offers MA. *Students:* 24 full-time (22 women), 29 part-time (27 women); includes 18 minority (3 African Americans, 2 Asian Americans or Pacific Islanders, 13 Hispanic Americans). Average age 32. 79 applicants, 37% accepted, 21 enrolled. In 2009, 9 master's awarded. *Degree requirements:* For master's, comprehensive exam, thesis. *Entrance requirements:* For master's, GRE General Test, minimum GPA of 3.0 in last 60 hours of coursework. Additional exam requirements/recommendations for international students: Required—TOEFL (minimum score 550 paper-based; 213 computer-based). *Application deadline:* For fall admission, 2/15 for domestic students, 1/2 for international students. Application fee: $30. *Financial support:* Unspecified assistantships available. Financial award application deadline: 4/3. *Unit head:* Dr. Raymond G. Miltenberger, Director, 813-974-5079, Fax: 813-974-6115, E-mail: rmiltenberger@fmhi.usf.edu. *Application contact:* Dr. Raymond G. Miltenberger, Director, 813-974-5079, Fax: 813-974-6115, E-mail: rmiltenberger@fmhi.usf.edu.

University of South Florida, Graduate School, College of Education–Main Campus, Department of Psychological and Social Foundations of Education, Tampa, FL 33620-9951. Offers college student affairs (M Ed); counselor education (MA, PhD, Ed S); interdisciplinary (PhD, Ed S); school psychology (PhD, Ed S). Part-time and evening/weekend programs available. *Faculty:* 22 full-time (13 women), 6 part-time/adjunct (4 women). *Students:* 154 full-time (123 women), 88 part-time (69 women); includes 62 minority (28 African Americans, 8 Asian Americans or Pacific Islanders, 26 Hispanic Americans), 7 international. Average age 30. 260 applicants, 43% accepted, 97 enrolled. In 2009, 41 master's, 7 doctorates, 5 other advanced degrees awarded. *Degree requirements:* For master's, comprehensive exam, thesis (for some programs); for doctorate, comprehensive exam, thesis/dissertation. *Entrance requirements:* For master's, GRE General Test, minimum GPA of 3.5 in last 60 hours of course work; for doctorate, GRE General Test, MAT, minimum GPA of 3.5 in last 60 hours of course work; for Ed S, GRE General Test. Additional exam requirements/recommendations for international students: Required—TOEFL (minimum score 550 paper-based; 213 computer-based; 79 iBT). *Application deadline:* For fall admission, 1/1 for domestic and international students. Application fee: $30. Electronic applications accepted. *Financial support:* In 2009–10, 47 students received support, including 6 fellowships with full tuition reimbursements available (averaging $10,000 per year), 21 teaching assistantships with full tuition reimbursements available (averaging $10,200 per year); career-related internships or fieldwork, scholarships/grants, and unspecified assistantships also available. Financial award application deadline: 1/1; financial award applicants required to submit CSS PROFILE. *Faculty research:* College student affairs, counselor education, educational psychology, school psychology, social foundations. Total annual research expenditures: $4.2 million. *Unit head:* Dr. Herbert Exum, Chairperson, 813-974-8395, Fax: 813-974-5814, E-mail: exum@tempest.coedu.usf.edu. *Application contact:* Dr. Kathy Bradley, Program Director, School Psychology, 813-974-9486, Fax: 813-974-5814, E-mail: kbradley@usf.edu.

The University of Tennessee, Graduate School, College of Education, Health and Human Sciences, Department of Educational Psychology and Counseling, Knoxville, TN 37996. Offers adult education (MS); applied educational psychology (MS); collaborative learning (Ed D); college student personnel (MS); mental health counseling (MS); rehabilitation counseling (MS); school counseling (MS). *Accreditation:* ACA (one or more programs are accredited); CORE (one or more programs are accredited); NCATE. Part-time and evening/weekend programs available. *Degree requirements:* For master's, thesis optional. *Entrance requirements:*

Counselor Education

The University of Tennessee (continued)

For master's, GRE General Test, minimum GPA of 2.7. Additional exam requirements/recommendations for international students: Required—TOEFL. Electronic applications accepted. *Expenses:* Tuition, state resident: full-time $6826; part-time $380 per semester hour. Tuition, nonresident: full-time $21,844; part-time $1147 per semester hour. Tuition and fees vary according to program.

The University of Tennessee, Graduate School, College of Education, Health and Human Sciences, Program in Education, Knoxville, TN 37996. Offers art education (MS); counseling education (PhD); cultural studies in education (PhD); curriculum (MS, Ed S); curriculum, educational research and evaluation (Ed D, PhD); early childhood education (PhD); early childhood special education (MS); education of deaf and hard of hearing (MS); educational administration and policy studies (Ed D, PhD); educational administration and supervision (Ed S); educational psychology (Ed D, PhD); elementary education (MS, Ed S); elementary teaching (MS); English education (MS, Ed S); exercise science (PhD); foreign language/ESL education (MS, Ed S); instructional technology (MS, Ed D, PhD, Ed S); literacy, language and ESL education (PhD); literacy, language education, and ESL education (Ed D); mathematics education (MS, Ed S); modified and comprehensive special education (MS); reading education (MS, Ed S); school counseling (Ed S); school psychology (PhD, Ed S); science education (MS, Ed S); secondary teaching (MS); social foundations (MS); social science education (MS, Ed S); socio-cultural foundations of sports and education (PhD); special education (Ed S); teacher education (Ed D, PhD). *Accreditation:* NCATE. Part-time and evening/weekend programs available. *Degree requirements:* For master's and Ed S, thesis optional; for doctorate, variable foreign language requirement, thesis/dissertation. *Entrance requirements:* For master's, minimum GPA of 2.7; for doctorate and Ed S, GRE General Test, minimum GPA of 2.7. Additional exam requirements/recommendations for international students: Required—TOEFL. Electronic applications accepted. *Expenses:* Tuition, state resident: full-time $6826; part-time $380 per semester hour. Tuition, nonresident: full-time $21,844; part-time $1147 per semester hour. Tuition and fees vary according to program.

The University of Tennessee at Chattanooga, Graduate School, College of Health, Education and Professional Studies, Graduate Studies Division of Education, Program in Counseling, Chattanooga, TN 37403. Offers community counseling (M Ed); school counseling (M Ed). *Faculty:* 3 full-time (all women). *Students:* 26 full-time (24 women), 29 part-time (25 women); includes 13 minority (11 African Americans, 2 Hispanic Americans). Average age 29. 36 applicants, 69% accepted, 13 enrolled. In 2009, 10 master's awarded. *Degree requirements:* For master's, comprehensive exam. *Entrance requirements:* For master's, MAT or GRE. Additional exam requirements/recommendations for international students: Required—TOEFL (minimum score 550 paper-based; 213 computer-based; 79 iBT), IELTS (minimum score 6). *Application deadline:* For fall admission, 8/1 for domestic students, 6/1 for international students; for spring admission, 12/1 for domestic students, 10/1 for international students. Applications are processed on a rolling basis. Application fee: $35. Electronic applications accepted. *Expenses:* Tuition, state resident: full-time $5404; part-time $300 per credit hour. Tuition, nonresident: full-time $16,702; part-time $928 per credit hour. Required fees: $1150; $130 per credit hour. *Financial support:* In 2009–10, 4 research assistantships with full and partial tuition reimbursements (averaging $5,500 per year) were awarded; career-related internships or fieldwork, scholarships/grants, and unspecified assistantships also available. Support available to part-time students. *Faculty research:* Play therapy; clinical supervision; technology in marital infidelity; female inmates and recidivism; grief, loss and trauma in children. *Unit head:* Dr. John Freeman, Head, 423-425-4133, Fax: 423-425-5380, E-mail: john-freeman@utc.edu. *Application contact:* Dr. Stephanie Bellar, Dean of Graduate Studies, 423-425-4666, Fax: 423-425-5223, E-mail: stephanie-bellar@utc.edu.

The University of Tennessee at Martin, Graduate Programs, College of Education and Behavioral Sciences, Program in Counseling, Martin, TN 38238. Offers community counseling (MS Ed); school counseling (MS Ed). *Accreditation:* NCATE. Part-time programs available. Postbaccalaureate distance learning degree programs offered. *Students:* 53 (47 women). 57 applicants, 47% accepted, 20 enrolled. In 2009, 16 master's awarded. *Degree requirements:* For master's, comprehensive exam. *Entrance requirements:* For master's, GRE General Test, minimum GPA of 2.5, resume, letters of reference. Additional exam requirements/recommendations for international students: Required—TOEFL (minimum score 525 paper-based; 197 computer-based; 71 iBT). *Application deadline:* For fall admission, 8/1 priority date for domestic students, 7/15 priority date for international students; for spring admission, 12/15 priority date for domestic students, 12/1 priority date for international students. Applications are processed on a rolling basis. Application fee: $30 ($130 for international students). Electronic applications accepted. *Expenses:* Tuition, state resident: full-time $6660; part-time $372 per hour. Tuition, nonresident: full-time $18,000; part-time $1005 per hour. *Financial support:* Scholarships/grants and unspecified assistantships available. Support available to part-time students. Financial award application deadline: 2/15; financial award applicants required to submit FAFSA. *Unit head:* Staci H. Fuqua, Staff Assistant, 731-881-7163, Fax: 731-881-7975, E-mail: sfuqua@utm.edu. *Application contact:* Linda S. Arant, Student Services Specialist, 731-881-7012, Fax: 731-881-7499, E-mail: larant@utm.edu.

The University of Texas at Austin, Graduate School, College of Education, Department of Educational Psychology, Austin, TX 78712-1111. Offers academic educational psychology (M Ed, MA); counseling psychology (PhD); counselor education (M Ed); human development and culture (PhD); learning, cognition and instruction (PhD); quantitative methods (PhD); school psychology (PhD). *Accreditation:* APA (one or more programs are accredited). *Degree requirements:* For master's, thesis optional; for doctorate, thesis/dissertation. *Entrance requirements:* For master's and doctorate, GRE General Test, 3 letters of recommendation. Additional exam requirements/recommendations for international students: Required—TOEFL.

The University of Texas at Brownsville, Graduate Studies, School of Education, Brownsville, TX 78520-4991. Offers bilingual education (M Ed); counseling and guidance (M Ed); curriculum and instruction (M Ed); early childhood education (M Ed); educational administration (M Ed); educational technology (M Ed); English as a second language (M Ed); reading specialist (M Ed); special education/educational diagnostician (M Ed). Part-time and evening/weekend programs available. Postbaccalaureate distance learning degree programs offered (minimal on-campus study). *Degree requirements:* For master's, thesis optional. *Entrance requirements:* For master's, GRE General Test. Additional exam requirements/recommendations for international students: Required—TOEFL.

The University of Texas at El Paso, Graduate School, College of Education, Department of Educational Psychology and Special Services, El Paso, TX 79968-0001. Offers educational diagnostics (M Ed); guidance and counseling (M Ed); special education (M Ed). Part-time and evening/weekend programs available. *Degree requirements:* For master's, thesis optional. *Entrance requirements:* For master's, minimum graduate GPA of 3.0. Additional exam requirements/recommendations for international students: Required—TOEFL. Electronic applications accepted.

The University of Texas at San Antonio, College of Education and Human Development, Department of Counseling, San Antonio, TX 78249-0617. Offers counseling (MA); counselor education and supervision (PhD). Part-time and evening/weekend programs available. *Faculty:* 18 full-time (7 women), 3 part-time/adjunct (2 women). *Students:* 117 full-time (93 women), 234 part-time (199 women); includes 199 minority (27 African Americans, 2 American Indian/Alaska Native, 7 Asian Americans or Pacific Islanders, 163 Hispanic Americans), 3 international. Average age 33. 147 applicants, 91% accepted, 106 enrolled. In 2009, 113 master's, 4 doctorates awarded. *Degree requirements:* For master's, comprehensive exam (for some programs), thesis (for some programs); for doctorate, comprehensive exam (for some programs), thesis/dissertation (for some programs). *Entrance requirements:* Additional exam requirements/recommendations for international students: Required—TOEFL (minimum score 500 paper-based; 173 computer-based; 61 iBT). *Application deadline:* For fall admission, 7/1 for domestic students, 4/1 for international students; for spring admission, 10/1 for domestic students, 9/1 for international students. Applications are processed on a rolling basis. Application fee: $45 ($80 for international students). Electronic applications accepted. *Expenses:* Tuition, state resident: full-time $3975; part-time $221 per contact hour. Tuition, nonresident: full-time $13,947; part-time $775 per contact hour. Required fees: $1853. *Financial support:* In 2009–10, 15 students received support, including 40 research assistantships (averaging $11,804 per year), 1 teaching assistantship (averaging $4,600 per year); tuition waivers (partial) also available. *Faculty research:* Community-based counseling research, counselor education and supervision, geriatric counseling, mentoring, substance abuse counseling. Total annual research expenditures: $46,982. *Unit head:* Dr. Thelma Duffey, Chair, 210-458-2600, Fax: 210-458-2605, E-mail: thelma.duffey@utsa.edu. *Application contact:* Dr. Dorothy A. Flannagan, Dean of the Graduate School, 210-458-4330, Fax: 210-458-4332, E-mail: dorothy.flannagan@utsa.edu.

The University of Texas of the Permian Basin, Office of Graduate Studies, School of Education, Program in Counseling, Odessa, TX 79762-0001. Offers MA. *Degree requirements:* For master's, comprehensive exam (for some programs), thesis (for some programs). *Entrance requirements:* For master's, GRE General Test. Additional exam requirements/recommendations for international students: Required—TOEFL (minimum score 550 paper-based; 213 computer-based).

The University of Texas–Pan American, College of Education, Department of Educational Psychology, Edinburg, TX 78539. Offers counseling (M Ed); educational diagnostician (M Ed); gifted education (M Ed); school psychology (MA); special education (M Ed). Part-time and evening/weekend programs available. *Degree requirements:* For master's, comprehensive exam (for some programs), thesis (for some programs). *Entrance requirements:* For master's, GRE General Test, interview. *Expenses:* Tuition, state resident: full-time $3630.60; part-time $201.70 per credit hour. Tuition, nonresident: full-time $8617; part-time $478.70 per credit hour. Required fees: $806.50. *Faculty research:* Reading instruction, assessment practice, behavior interventions consultation, mental retardation.

University of the District of Columbia, College of Arts and Sciences, Department of Psychology and Counseling, Washington, DC 20008-1175. Offers clinical psychology (MS); counseling (MS). *Students:* 7 full-time (5 women), 15 part-time (12 women); includes 16 minority (all African Americans). Average age 31. In 2009, 11 master's awarded. *Degree requirements:* For master's, comprehensive exam, thesis optional, seminar paper. *Entrance requirements:* For master's, GRE General Test, writing proficiency exam. *Application deadline:* For fall admission, 6/15 priority date for domestic students; for spring admission, 11/1 for domestic students. Applications are processed on a rolling basis. Application fee: $75 ($100 for international students). *Expenses:* Tuition, state resident: full-time $7580. Tuition, nonresident: full-time $14,580. Required fees: $620. *Unit head:* Dr. Eugene Johnson, Chairperson, 202-274-7406. *Application contact:* Ann Marie Waterman, Associate Vice President of Admission, Recruitment and Financial Aid, 202-274-6069.

University of the Southwest, Graduate Programs, Hobbs, NM 88240-9129. Offers business administration (MBA); curriculum and instruction (MSE); curriculum and instruction: bilingual (MSE); curriculum and instruction: reading (MSE); curriculum and instruction: TESOL (MSE); early childhood education (MSE); educational diagnostician (MSE); mental health counseling (MSE); school business administration (MSE); school counseling (MSE); special education (MSE). Part-time and evening/weekend programs available. Postbaccalaureate distance learning degree programs offered (no on-campus study). *Faculty:* 10 full-time (6 women), 10 part-time/adjunct (4 women). *Students:* 112 full-time (93 women), 99 part-time (72 women). Average age 35. 94 applicants, 47% accepted, 39 enrolled. In 2009, 32 master's awarded. *Degree requirements:* For master's, comprehensive exam. *Application deadline:* For fall admission, 3/1 priority date for domestic students; for spring admission, 10/1 for domestic students. Applications are processed on a rolling basis. Application fee: $25. Electronic applications accepted. *Expenses:* Tuition: Part-time $512 per hour. Tuition and fees vary according to course load. *Financial support:* In 2009–10, 196 students received support; research assistantships with partial tuition reimbursements available, Federal Work-Study, scholarships/grants, and tuition waivers (partial) available. Support available to part-time students. Financial award application deadline: 4/1; financial award applicants required to submit FAFSA. *Unit head:* Dr. Mary Harris, Dean of Education, 575-392-6561 Ext. 1056, Fax: 575-392-6006, E-mail: mharris@usw.edu. *Application contact:* Ryanne Evans, Assistant Registrar, 575-392-6561 Ext. 1031, Fax: 575-392-6006, E-mail: revans@usw.edu.

The University of Toledo, College of Graduate Studies, College of Health Science and Human Service, Division of Human Services, Toledo, OH 43606-3390. Offers counselor education and school psychology (MA, PhD, Ed S), including counselor education, guidance/counselor education (PhD), school psychology (MA, Ed S); criminal justice (MA, Certificate), including criminal justice (MA), juvenile justice (Certificate), severe behavioral spectrum (Certificate); health and rehabilitative services (MA), including speech language pathology; health education (PhD); kinesiology (MSX, PhD), including exercise science; recreation and leisure (MA); social work (MSW); speech-language pathology (MA).

The University of Toledo, College of Graduate Studies, College of Health Science and Human Service, Division of Human Services, Department of Counselor Education and School Psychology, Program in Counselor Education, Toledo, OH 43606-3390. Offers community counseling (MA); counselor education (Ed S); counselor education and supervision (PhD).

The University of Toledo, College of Graduate Studies, College of Health Science and Human Service, Division of Human Services, Department of Counselor Education and School Psychology, Program in School Psychology, Toledo, OH 43606-3390. Offers school counseling (MA); school psychology (Ed S). *Entrance requirements:* For master's, GRE.

University of Utah, Graduate School, College of Education, Department of Educational Psychology, Salt Lake City, UT 84112. Offers counseling psychology (PhD); educational psychology (MA); instructional design and educational technology (M Ed); learning and cognition (MS, PhD); professional counseling (MS); professional psychology (M Ed); reading and literacy (M Ed, PhD); school counseling (M Ed, MS); school psychology (MS, PhD); statistics (M Stat). *Accreditation:* APA (one or more programs are accredited). Evening/weekend programs available. Postbaccalaureate distance learning degree programs offered (minimal on-campus study). *Faculty:* 21 full-time (11 women), 8 part-time/adjunct (5 women). *Students:* 92 full-time (67 women), 74 part-time (43 women); includes 16 minority (4 Asian Americans or Pacific Islanders, 12 Hispanic Americans), 2 international. Average age 33. 177 applicants, 34% accepted, 50 enrolled. In 2009, 44 master's, 9 doctorates awarded. *Degree requirements:* For master's, variable foreign language requirement, comprehensive exam, thesis (for some programs); for doctorate, variable foreign language requirement, thesis/dissertation, oral exam. *Entrance requirements:* For master's and doctorate, GRE General Test, minimum GPA of 3.0. Additional exam requirements/recommendations for international students: Required—TOEFL (minimum score 500 paper-based; 173 computer-based). *Application deadline:* For fall admission, 4/1 for domestic and international students; for spring admission, 11/1 for domestic and international students. Application fee: $55 ($65 for international students). *Expenses:* Tuition, state resident: full-time $4004; part-time $1674 per semester. Tuition, nonresident: full-time $14,134; part-time $5915 per semester. Required fees: $324 per semester. Tuition and fees vary according to course load, degree level and program. *Financial support:* In 2009–10, 55 students received support, including 20 fellowships with full tuition reimbursements available (averaging $11,000 per year), 5 research assistantships with full tuition reimbursements available (averaging $11,000 per year), 32 teaching assistantships with full and partial tuition reimbursements available (averaging $11,000 per year); career-related internships or fieldwork, Federal Work-Study, institutionally sponsored loans, scholarships/grants, and unspecified assistantships also available. Financial award application deadline: 2/1; financial award applicants required to submit FAFSA. *Faculty research:* Autism, computer technology and instruction, cognitive behavior, aging, group counseling. Total annual research expenditures: $151,911. *Unit head:* Dr. Elaine Clark, Chair, 801-581-7148, Fax: 801-581-5566, E-mail: clark@ed.utah.edu. *Application contact:* Jenna Atkinson, Academic Program Specialist, 801-581-7148, Fax: 801-581-5566, E-mail: jenna.atkinson@utah.edu.

University of Vermont, Graduate College, College of Education and Social Services, Department of Integrated Professional Studies, Counseling Program, Burlington, VT 05405. Offers MS. *Accreditation:* ACA; NCATE. *Faculty:* 3 full-time (2 women), 6 part-time/adjunct (2 women). *Students:* 42 (36 women); includes 3 minority (2 American Indian/Alaska Native, 1 Asian American or Pacific Islander), 2 international. 46 applicants, 67% accepted, 13 enrolled. In 2009, 14 master's awarded. *Entrance requirements:* For master's, GRE General Test, resume. Additional exam requirements/recommendations for international students: Required—TOEFL (minimum score 550 paper-based; 213 computer-based; 80 iBT). *Application deadline:* For fall admission, 2/1 priority date for domestic students. Applications are processed on a rolling basis. Application fee: $40. Electronic applications accepted. *Expenses:* Tuition, state resident: part-time $508 per credit hour. Tuition, nonresident: part-time $1281 per credit hour. *Financial support:* Fellowships, research assistantships, teaching assistantships available. Financial award application deadline: 2/1. *Faculty research:* Women and tenure, counseling children and adolescents. *Unit head:* Anne Geroski, Coordinator, 802-656-3888, Fax: 802-656-3173. *Application contact:* Anne Geroski, Coordinator, 802-656-3888, Fax: 802-656-3173.

University of Victoria, Faculty of Graduate Studies, Faculty of Education, Department of Educational Psychology and Leadership Studies, Victoria, BC V8W 2Y2, Canada. Offers aboriginal communities counseling (M Ed); counseling (M Ed, MA); educational psychology (M Ed, MA, PhD), including counseling psychology (M Ed, MA), leadership studies (PhD), learning and development (MA, PhD), measurement and evaluation, special education (M Ed, MA); leadership studies (M Ed, MA). Part-time programs available. *Degree requirements:* For master's, thesis (for some programs), comprehensive exam (M Ed); for doctorate, comprehensive exam, thesis/dissertation, candidacy exam. *Entrance requirements:* For master's, 2 years of work experience in a relevant field; for doctorate, GRE, 2 years of work experience in a relevant field, minimum B average. Additional exam requirements/recommendations for international students: Required—TOEFL (minimum score 575 paper-based; 233 computer-based), IELTS (minimum score 7). *Faculty research:* Learning and development (child, adolescent and adult), special education and exceptional children.

University of Virginia, Curry School of Education, Department of Human Services, Program in Counselor Education, Charlottesville, VA 22903. Offers M Ed, Ed S. *Accreditation:* ACA (one or more programs are accredited). *Students:* 14 full-time (all women), 2 part-time (1 woman); includes 3 minority (2 African Americans, 1 Hispanic American). Average age 25. 43 applicants, 49% accepted, 10 enrolled. In 2009, 25 master's, 10 Ed Ss awarded. *Entrance requirements:* For master's, GRE General Test, 2 letters of recommendation; for Ed S, GRE General Test. Additional exam requirements/recommendations for international students: Required—TOEFL (minimum score 600 paper-based; 250 computer-based; 90 iBT), IELTS. *Application deadline:* For fall admission, 1/5 for domestic and international students. Applications are processed on a rolling basis. Application fee: $60. Electronic applications accepted. *Financial support:* Applicants required to submit FAFSA. *Unit head:* Harriet Glossof, Associate Professor/Doctoral Program Coordinator, E-mail: hlg2n@virginia.edu. *Application contact:* Harriet Glossof, Associate Professor/Doctoral Program Coordinator, E-mail: hlg2n@virginia.edu.

University of Virginia, Curry School of Education, Program in Education, Charlottesville, VA 22903. Offers administration and supervision (PhD); applied developmental science (PhD); counselor education (PhD); curriculum and instruction (PhD); early childhood-developmental risk (MT); education evaluation (PhD); educational psychology (PhD); educational research (PhD); elementary (MT, PhD); English education (MT, PhD); foreign language education (MT); higher education (PhD); instructional technology (PhD); kinesiology (MT, PhD); math education (PhD); reading education (PhD); research statistics and evaluation (PhD); school psychology (PhD); science education (PhD); social studies education (MT, PhD); special education (PhD); world languages education (MT). *Students:* 336 full-time (239 women), 88 part-time (54 women); includes 43 minority (24 African Americans, 2 American Indian/Alaska Native, 11 Asian Americans or Pacific Islanders, 6 Hispanic Americans), 18 international. Average age 27. 199 applicants, 48% accepted, 55 enrolled. In 2009, 127 master's, 52 doctorates awarded. *Degree requirements:* For master's, comprehensive exam (for some programs), field project; for doctorate, comprehensive exam, thesis/dissertation. *Entrance requirements:* For doctorate, GRE General Test. Additional exam requirements/recommendations for international students: Required—TOEFL (minimum score 600 paper-based; 250 computer-based; 90 iBT), IELTS (minimum score 7). *Application deadline:* Applications are processed on a rolling basis. Application fee: $60. Electronic applications accepted. *Financial support:* Fellowships, research assistantships, teaching assistantships available. Financial award application deadline: 1/5; financial award applicants required to submit FAFSA.

The University of West Alabama, School of Graduate Studies, College of Education, Department of Teacher Education, Program in Guidance and Counseling, Livingston, AL 35470. Offers continuing education (MSCE); guidance and counseling (M Ed). *Accreditation:* NCATE. Part-time and evening/weekend programs available. *Entrance requirements:* For master's, GRE General Test, MAT, minimum GPA of 2.75.

University of West Florida, College of Professional Studies, Department of Professional and Community Leadership, Program in College Student Personnel Administration, Pensacola, FL 32514-5750. Offers college personnel administration (M Ed); guidance and counseling (M Ed). Part-time and evening/weekend programs available. *Students:* 16 full-time (10 women), 29 part-time (25 women); includes 11 minority (8 African Americans, 3 Hispanic Americans). Average age 29. 13 applicants, 92% accepted, 11 enrolled. In 2009, 8 master's awarded. *Degree requirements:* For master's, internship. *Entrance requirements:* For master's, GRE General Test, minimum GPA of 3.0. Additional exam requirements/recommendations for international students: Required—TOEFL (minimum score 550 paper-based; 213 computer-based). *Application deadline:* For fall admission, 6/1 for domestic students, 5/15 for international students; for spring admission, 11/1 for domestic students, 10/1 for international students. Application fee: $30. *Expenses:* Tuition, state resident: full-time $4982; part-time $260 per credit hour. Tuition, nonresident: full-time $20,059; part-time $919 per credit hour. Required fees: $1247; $52 per credit hour. *Financial support:* Application deadline: 4/15. *Unit head:* Dr. Thomas J. Kramer, Chairperson, 850-474-2949, Fax: 850-857-6288. *Application contact:* Terry McCray, Assistant Director of Graduate Admissions, 850-473-7718, Fax: 850-473-7714, E-mail: gradadmissions@uwf.edu.

University of West Georgia, Graduate School, College of Education, Department of Counseling and Educational Psychology, Carrollton, GA 30118. Offers professional counseling (M Ed, Certificate, Ed S); professional counseling and supervision (Ed D). *Accreditation:* ACA; NCATE. Part-time programs available. *Faculty:* 10 full-time (7 women). *Students:* 52 full-time (44 women), 97 part-time (82 women); includes 38 minority (32 African Americans, 1 American Indian/Alaska Native, 5 Hispanic Americans), 1 international. Average age 33. 78 applicants, 55% accepted, 19 enrolled. In 2009, 44 master's, 14 Certificates awarded. *Degree requirements:* For master's, comprehensive exam; for doctorate, thesis/dissertation; for other advanced degree, comprehensive exam, research project. *Entrance requirements:* For master's, GRE General Test, minimum GPA of 2.7, interview, letter of reference; for doctorate, GRE General Test, Ed S, interview, letters of reference; for other advanced degree, GRE General Test, master's degree, minimum graduate GPA of 3.25, letter of reference. Additional exam requirements/recommendations for international students: Required—TOEFL. *Application deadline:* For fall admission, 7/17 for domestic students; for spring admission, 11/20 for domestic students. Applications are processed on a rolling basis. Application fee: $30. Electronic applications accepted. *Expenses:* Tuition, state resident: full-time $2952; part-time $164 per semester hour. Tuition, nonresident: full-time $11,808; part-time $656 per semester hour. Required fees: $42.90 per semester hour. $307 per semester. Tuition and fees vary according to course load. *Financial support:* In 2009–10, 4 students received support, including 3 research assistantships with full tuition reimbursements available (averaging $4,000 per year); career-related internships or fieldwork, scholarships/grants, and unspecified assistantships also available. Support available to part-time students. Financial award application deadline: 7/1; financial award applicants required to submit FAFSA. *Faculty research:* Academic and career development counseling, professional and ethical issues, transforming school counseling. *Unit head:* Dr. Rebecca Stanard, Interim Chair, 678-839-6554, Fax: 678-839-6098, E-mail: rstanard@westga.edu. *Application contact:* Dr. Charles W. Clark, Dean, 678-839-6508, E-mail: cclark@westga.edu.

University of Wisconsin–Madison, Graduate School, School of Education, Department of Counseling Psychology, Program in Counseling, Madison, WI 53706-1380. Offers MS. *Entrance requirements:* For master's, GRE General Test. *Application deadline:* For fall admission, 12/15 for domestic and international students. Application fee: $56. Electronic applications accepted. *Expenses:* Tuition, state resident: part-time $594 per credit. Tuition, nonresident: part-time $1504 per credit. Required fees: $65 per credit. Tuition and fees vary according to course load, program and reciprocity agreements. *Financial support:* Fellowships with full tuition reimbursements, research assistantships with full tuition reimbursements, teaching assistantships with full tuition reimbursements, project assistantships available. *Unit head:* Dr. Bruce Wampold, Chair, 608-262-0461. *Application contact:* Dr. Bruce Wampold, Chair, 608-262-0461.

University of Wisconsin–Milwaukee, Graduate School, School of Education, Department of Educational Psychology, Milwaukee, WI 53201-0413. Offers counseling (school, community) (MS); counseling psychology (PhD); learning and development (MS); research methodology (MS, PhD); school psychology (PhD). *Accreditation:* APA. Part-time programs available. *Faculty:* 22 full-time (14 women). *Students:* 124 full-time (107 women), 47 part-time (35 women); includes 20 minority (10 African Americans, 4 Asian Americans or Pacific Islanders, 6 Hispanic Americans), 2 international. Average age 30. 263 applicants, 52% accepted, 51 enrolled. In 2009, 55 master's, 13 doctorates awarded. *Degree requirements:* For master's, comprehensive exam, thesis; for doctorate, thesis/dissertation. *Entrance requirements:* For master's, minimum GPA of 3.0; for doctorate, GRE General Test, minimum GPA of 3.0. Additional exam requirements/recommendations for international students: Required—TOEFL (minimum score 550 paper-based; 79 iBT), IELTS (minimum score 6.5). *Application deadline:* For fall admission, 1/1 priority date for domestic students; for spring admission, 9/1 for domestic students. Applications are processed on a rolling basis. Application fee: $45 ($75 for international students). *Expenses:* Tuition, state resident: full-time $8800. Tuition, nonresident: full-time $20,760. Tuition and fees vary according to program and reciprocity agreements. *Financial support:* In 2009–10, 9 teaching assistantships were awarded; career-related internships or fieldwork and unspecified assistantships also available. Support available to part-time students. Financial award application deadline: 4/15. Total annual research expenditures: $1.3 million. *Unit head:* Bo Zhang, Graduate Program Representative, 414-229-5742, Fax: 414-229-4939, E-mail: boz@uwm.edu. *Application contact:* General Information Contact, 414-229-4982, Fax: 414-229-6967, E-mail: gradschool@uwm.edu.

University of Wisconsin–Oshkosh, The Office of Graduate Studies, College of Education and Human Services, Department of Professional Counseling, Oshkosh, WI 54901. Offers counseling (MSE). *Accreditation:* ACA. Part-time and evening/weekend programs available. *Degree requirements:* For master's, thesis optional, practicum. *Entrance requirements:* For master's, MAT, interview, minimum GPA of 3.0, letters of recommendation. Additional exam requirements/recommendations for international students: Required—TOEFL (minimum score 550 paper-based; 213 computer-based; 79 iBT). Electronic applications accepted. *Faculty research:* Gender issues, grief and loss, addictions, career development, close relationships.

University of Wisconsin–Platteville, School of Graduate Studies, College of Liberal Arts and Education, Counselor Education Program, Platteville, WI 53818-3099. Offers MSE. *Accreditation:* NCATE. Part-time programs available. *Faculty:* 5 full-time (2 women). *Students:* 42 full-time (34 women), 19 part-time (13 women); includes 1 minority (Hispanic American), 2 international. 11 applicants, 100% accepted, 11 enrolled. In 2009, 23 master's awarded. *Degree requirements:* For master's, comprehensive exam, thesis or alternative. *Entrance requirements:* Additional exam requirements/recommendations for international students: Required—TOEFL (minimum score 500 paper-based; 173 computer-based; 61 iBT). *Application deadline:* For fall admission, 7/1 priority date for domestic students; for spring admission, 11/1 for domestic students. Applications are processed on a rolling basis. Application fee: $56. Electronic applications accepted. *Expenses:* Tuition, state resident: full-time $6706. Tuition, nonresident: full-time $16,772. *Financial support:* Research assistantships with partial tuition reimbursements, career-related internships or fieldwork, Federal Work-Study, institutionally sponsored loans, scholarships/grants, and unspecified assistantships available. Support available to part-time students. *Unit head:* Dr. Dominic Barraclough, Coordinator, 608-342-1252, Fax: 608-342-1986, E-mail: barracld@uwplatt.edu. *Application contact:* Lisa Popp, School of Graduate Studies, 608-342-1322, Fax: 608-342-1389, E-mail: poppl@uwplatt.edu.

University of Wisconsin–River Falls, Outreach and Graduate Studies, College of Education and Professional Studies, Department of Counseling and School Psychology, River Falls, WI 54022. Offers counseling (MSE); school psychology (MSE, Ed S). Part-time programs available. *Entrance requirements:* For master's, minimum GPA of 2.75, resume, 3 letters of reference, vita. Additional exam requirements/recommendations for international students: Required—TOEFL (minimum score 500 paper-based; 65 iBT), IELTS (minimum score 5.5). Electronic applications accepted.

University of Wisconsin–Stevens Point, College of Professional Studies, School of Education, Program in Guidance and Counseling, Stevens Point, WI 54481-3897. Offers MSE. *Degree requirements:* For master's, comprehensive exam, thesis or alternative. *Application deadline:* Applications are processed on a rolling basis. Application fee: $45. *Expenses:* Tuition, state resident: full-time $7740; part-time $430 per credit hour. Tuition, nonresident: full-time $17,804; part-time $989 per credit hour. Tuition and fees vary according to course load and reciprocity agreements. *Financial support:* Application deadline: 5/1. *Unit head:* Dr. JoAnne Katzmarek, Associate Dean, 715-346-4430, Fax: 715-346-4846, E-mail: jkatzmar@uwsp.edu. *Application contact:* Dr. Patricia Caro, Director, 715-346-4403, Fax: 715-346-4846, E-mail: pcaro@uwsp.edu.

University of Wisconsin–Superior, Graduate Division, Department of Counseling and Psychological Professions, Superior, WI 54880-4500. Offers community counseling (MSE); human relations (MSE); school counseling (MSE). Part-time and evening/weekend programs available. *Faculty:* 3 full-time (1 woman), 4 part-time/adjunct (all women). *Students:* 34 full-time (23 women), 69 part-time (51 women); includes 10 minority (4 African Americans, 4 American Indian/Alaska Native, 2 Asian Americans or Pacific Islanders), 3 international. Average age 27. 19 applicants, 100% accepted. In 2009, 24 master's awarded. *Degree requirements:* For master's, position paper, practicum. *Entrance requirements:* For master's, GRE and/or MAT, minimum GPA of 2.75. *Application deadline:* For fall admission, 4/1 priority date for domestic students; for spring admission, 10/15 priority date for domestic students. Applications are processed on a rolling basis. Application fee: $45. Electronic applications accepted. *Financial support:* In 2009–10, 10 fellowships with partial tuition reimbursements (averaging $6,500 per year), 2 research assistantships with partial tuition reimbursements (averaging $5,000 per year) were awarded; career-related internships or fieldwork, Federal Work-Study, institutionally sponsored loans, scholarships/grants, traineeships, and tuition waivers (partial) also available. Support available to part-time students. Financial award application deadline: 4/15; financial award applicants required to submit FAFSA. *Faculty research:* Women and power, intrafamily dynamics. *Unit head:* Terri Kronzer, Chairperson, 715-394-8506. *Application contact:* Sandy Wallgren, Program Assistant/Status Examiner, 715-394-8295, Fax: 715-394-8146, E-mail: gradstudy@uwsuper.edu.

University of Wisconsin–Whitewater, School of Graduate Studies, College of Education, Department of Counselor Education, Whitewater, WI 53190-1790. Offers community counseling (MS Ed); higher education (MS Ed); school counseling (MS Ed). *Accreditation:* ACA; NCATE. Part-time and evening/weekend programs available. *Degree requirements:* For master's, thesis or alternative. *Entrance requirements:* For master's, resume, 2 letters of reference. Additional exam requirements/recommendations for international students: Required—TOEFL (minimum score 550 paper-based; 213 computer-based). Electronic applications accepted. *Faculty research:* Alcohol and other drugs, counseling effectiveness, teacher mentoring.

University of Wyoming, College of Education, Department of Counselor Education, Laramie, WY 82070. Offers community mental health (MS); counselor education and supervision (PhD);

Counselor Education

University of Wyoming *(continued)*
school counseling (MS); student affairs (MS). *Accreditation:* ACA (one or more programs are accredited). *Degree requirements:* For master's, comprehensive exam (for some programs), thesis optional; for doctorate, thesis/dissertation, video demonstration. *Entrance requirements:* For master's, interview, background check; for doctorate, video tape session, interview, writing sample, master's degree, background check. Additional exam requirements/recommendations for international students: Required—TOEFL. *Faculty research:* Wyoming SAGE photovoice project; accountable school counseling programs; GLBT issues; addictions; play therapy-early childhood mental health.

Utah State University, School of Graduate Studies, College of Education and Human Services, Department of Psychology, Logan, UT 84322. Offers clinical/counseling/school psychology (PhD); research and evaluation methodology (PhD); school counseling (MS); school psychology (MS). *Accreditation:* APA (one or more programs are accredited). Part-time and evening/weekend programs available. Postbaccalaureate distance learning degree programs offered (no on-campus study). Terminal master's awarded for partial completion of doctoral program. *Degree requirements:* For master's, thesis (for some programs); for doctorate, thesis/dissertation. *Entrance requirements:* For master's, GRE General Test (school psychology), MAT (school counseling), minimum GPA of 3.5; for doctorate, GRE General Test, minimum GPA of 3.5. Additional exam requirements/recommendations for international students: Required—TOEFL. *Faculty research:* Hearing loss detection in infancy, ADHD, eating disorders, domestic violence, neuropsychology, bilingual/Spanish speaking students/parents.

Valdosta State University, Graduate School, Department of Psychology and Counseling, Valdosta, GA 31698. Offers clinical/counseling psychology (MS); industrial/organizational psychology (MS); school counseling (M Ed, Ed S); school psychology (Ed S). Part-time and evening/weekend programs available. *Degree requirements:* For master's, thesis or alternative, comprehensive written and/or oral exams; for Ed S, thesis. *Entrance requirements:* For master's and Ed S, GRE General Test or MAT. Additional exam requirements/recommendations for international students: Required—TOEFL (minimum score 523 paper-based; 193 computer-based). Electronic applications accepted. *Faculty research:* Using Bender-Gestalt to predict graphomotor dimensions of the draw-a-person test, neurobehavioral hemispheric dominance.

Vanderbilt University, Peabody College, Department of Human and Organizational Development, Nashville, TN 37240-1001. Offers community development and action (M Ed); human development counseling (M Ed). *Accreditation:* ACA; NCATE. Part-time programs available. *Faculty:* 29 full-time (14 women), 27 part-time/adjunct (19 women). *Students:* 88 full-time (82 women), 7 part-time (all women); includes 16 minority (11 African Americans, 1 Asian American or Pacific Islander, 4 Hispanic Americans), 1 international. Average age 27. 141 applicants, 57% accepted, 56 enrolled. In 2009, 31 master's awarded. *Degree requirements:* For master's, comprehensive exam, thesis optional. *Entrance requirements:* For master's, GRE General Test, MAT. Additional exam requirements/recommendations for international students: Required—TOEFL (minimum score 550 paper-based; 213 computer-based). *Application deadline:* For fall admission, 12/31 priority date for domestic and international students; for spring admission, 11/1 priority date for domestic and international students. Applications are processed on a rolling basis. Application fee: $0. Electronic applications accepted. *Financial support:* In 2009–10, 86 students received support, including 31 research assistantships with full and partial tuition reimbursements available, 20 teaching assistantships with full and partial tuition reimbursements available; fellowships with full and partial tuition reimbursements available, Federal Work-Study, institutionally sponsored loans, scholarships/grants, tuition waivers (partial), and unspecified assistantships also available. Support available to part-time students. Financial award application deadline: 2/1; financial award applicants required to submit FAFSA. *Faculty research:* Community psychology, community development and urban policy, counseling and mental health services, organizational development and institutional change; youth physical and behavioral health in schools and communities. *Unit head:* Dr. Marybeth Shinn, Chair, 615-322-6881, Fax: 615-322-1141, E-mail: marybeth.shinn@vanderbilt.edu. *Application contact:* Sherrie Lane, Office Assistant, 615-322-8484, Fax: 615-322-1141, E-mail: sherrie.a.lane@vanderbilt.edu.

Villanova University, Graduate School of Liberal Arts and Sciences, Department of Education and Human Services, Program in Community Counseling, Villanova, PA 19085-1699. Offers counseling and human relations (MS). Part-time and evening/weekend programs available. *Students:* 22 full-time (20 women), 14 part-time (12 women); includes 5 minority (1 African American, 1 Asian American or Pacific Islander, 3 Hispanic Americans). Average age 31. In 2009, 12 master's awarded. *Degree requirements:* For master's, comprehensive exam. *Entrance requirements:* For master's, GRE or MAT, minimum GPA of 3.0. Additional exam requirements/recommendations for international students: Required—TOEFL. *Application deadline:* For fall admission, 3/1 priority date for domestic and international students; for spring admission, 11/15 for domestic and international students. Applications are processed on a rolling basis. Application fee: $50. Electronic applications accepted. *Expenses:* Tuition: Part-time $630 per credit. Required fees: $60 per credit. Part-time tuition and fees vary according to degree level and program. *Financial support:* Applicants required to submit FAFSA. *Unit head:* Dr. Connie M. Titon, Director, 610-519-4620. *Application contact:* Dean, Graduate School of Liberal Arts and Sciences.

Villanova University, Graduate School of Liberal Arts and Sciences, Department of Education and Human Services, Program in Elementary School Counseling, Villanova, PA 19085-1699. Offers counseling and human relations (MS). Part-time and evening/weekend programs available. *Students:* 8 full-time (all women), 8 part-time (all women); includes 1 minority (Hispanic American). Average age 27. In 2009, 10 master's awarded. *Degree requirements:* For master's, comprehensive exam. *Entrance requirements:* For master's, GRE or MAT, minimum GPA of 3.0. *Application deadline:* For fall admission, 3/1 priority date for domestic students; for spring admission, 11/15 for domestic students. Applications are processed on a rolling basis. Application fee: $50. Electronic applications accepted. *Expenses:* Tuition: Part-time $630 per credit. Required fees: $60 per credit. Part-time tuition and fees vary according to degree level and program. *Financial support:* Career-related internships or fieldwork and Federal Work-Study available. Financial award applicants required to submit FAFSA. *Unit head:* Dr. Connie Titone, Chair, 610-519-4620. *Application contact:* Dr. Connie Titone, Chair, 610-519-4620.

Villanova University, Graduate School of Liberal Arts and Sciences, Department of Education and Human Services, Program in Secondary School Counseling, Villanova, PA 19085-1699. Offers counseling and human relations (MS). *Students:* 23 full-time (21 women), 31 part-time (23 women); includes 5 minority (2 African Americans, 1 Asian American or Pacific Islander, 2 Hispanic Americans). Average age 28. In 2009, 20 master's awarded. *Degree requirements:* For master's, comprehensive exam. *Entrance requirements:* For master's, GRE or MAT, minimum GPA of 3.0. *Application deadline:* For fall admission, 3/1 priority date for domestic students; for spring admission, 11/15 for domestic students. Applications are processed on a rolling basis. Application fee: $50. Electronic applications accepted. *Expenses:* Tuition: Part-time $630 per credit. Required fees: $60 per credit. Part-time tuition and fees vary according to degree level and program. *Financial support:* Applicants required to submit FAFSA. *Unit head:* Dr. Kenneth M. Davis, Director, 610-519-4634. *Application contact:* Dr. Kenneth M. Davis, Director, 610-519-4634.

Virginia Commonwealth University, Graduate School, School of Education, Program in Counselor Education, Richmond, VA 23284-9005. Offers M Ed. *Accreditation:* ACA; NCATE. *Entrance requirements:* For master's, GRE General Test or MAT.

Virginia Polytechnic Institute and State University, Graduate School, College of Liberal Arts and Human Sciences, School of Education, Department of Educational Leadership and Policy Studies, Program in Counselor Education, Blacksburg, VA 24061. Offers MA Ed, Ed D, PhD, Ed S. *Accreditation:* ACA. *Expenses:* Tuition, area resident: Full-time $10,228; part-time $459 per credit hour. Tuition, nonresident: full-time $17,892; part-time $865 per credit hour. Required fees: $1966; $451 per semester.

Wake Forest University, Graduate School of Arts and Sciences, Counseling Program, Winston-Salem, NC 27109. Offers MA, M Div/MA. *Accreditation:* ACA. *Entrance requirements:* For master's, GRE General Test. Additional exam requirements/recommendations for international students: Required—TOEFL (minimum score 213 computer-based; 79 iBT). Electronic applications accepted.

Walden University, Graduate Programs, School of Counseling and Social Service, Minneapolis, MN 55401. Offers counselor education and supervision (PhD), including consultation, counseling and social change, forensic mental health counseling, general program, nonprofit management and leadership, trauma and crisis; human services (PhD), including clinical social work, counseling, criminal justice, family studies and intervention strategies, general program, human services administration, self-designed, social policy analysis and planning; marriage, couple, and family counseling (MS), including forensic counseling, trauma and crisis counseling; mental health counseling (MS), including forensic counseling. Part-time and evening/weekend programs available. Postbaccalaureate distance learning degree programs offered (minimal on-campus study). *Faculty:* 13 full-time, 78 part-time/adjunct. *Students:* 1,932 full-time (1,624 women), 210 part-time (181 women); includes 945 minority (817 African Americans, 24 American Indian/Alaska Native, 24 Asian Americans or Pacific Islanders, 80 Hispanic Americans), 34 international. Average age 39. In 2009, 55 master's, 5 doctorates awarded. *Degree requirements:* For master's, residency (for some programs); for doctorate, thesis/dissertation, residency. *Entrance requirements:* For master's, bachelor's degree or equivalent in related field, minimum GPA of 2.5; for doctorate, master's degree or equivalent in related field; minimum GPA of 3.0; official transcripts; three years' related professional/academic experience (preferred); access to computer and Internet. Additional exam requirements/recommendations for international students: Required—TOEFL (minimum score 550 paper-based; 213 computer-based), IELTS (minimum score 6.5), or Michigan English Language Assessment Battery (minimum score 82). *Application deadline:* Applications are processed on a rolling basis. Application fee: $50. Electronic applications accepted. *Expenses:* Tuition: Full-time $13,665; part-time $560 per credit. Required fees: $1375. Tuition and fees vary according to course load, degree level and program. *Financial support:* In 2009–10, 200 students received support; fellowships, Federal Work-Study, scholarships/grants, unspecified assistantships, and family tuition reduction, active duty/veteran tuition reduction, group tuition reduction, interest-free payment plans available. Support available to part-time students. Financial award applicants required to submit FAFSA. *Unit head:* Dr. Savitri Dixon-Saxon, Associate Dean, 800-925-3368. *Application contact:* Jennifer Hall, Director of Enrollment, 866-4-WALDEN, E-mail: info@waldenu.edu.

Walsh University, Graduate Studies, Program in Counseling and Human Development, North Canton, OH 44720-3396. Offers mental health counseling (MA); school counseling (MA). *Accreditation:* ACA. Part-time and evening/weekend programs available. *Faculty:* 5 full-time (4 women), 3 part-time/adjunct (all women). *Students:* 32 full-time (23 women), 50 part-time (42 women); includes 5 minority (3 African Americans, 1 American Indian/Alaska Native, 1 Hispanic American), 3 international. Average age 31. 36 applicants, 61% accepted, 19 enrolled. In 2009, 30 master's awarded. *Degree requirements:* For master's, comprehensive exam, internship, practicum. *Entrance requirements:* For master's, GRE General Test, MAT, interview, minimum GPA of 3.0, writing sample, reference forms, moral affidavit. Additional exam requirements/recommendations for international students: Required—TOEFL (minimum score 500 paper-based; 173 computer-based; 61 iBT). *Application deadline:* For fall admission, 7/15 priority date for domestic students. Applications are processed on a rolling basis. Application fee: $25. Electronic applications accepted. *Expenses:* Tuition: Full-time $9630; part-time $535 per credit hour. Tuition and fees vary according to course load and program. *Financial support:* In 2009–10, 79 students received support, including 12 research assistantships with tuition reimbursements available (averaging $6,020 per year); tuition waivers (partial) and tuition discounts also available. Financial award application deadline: 12/31. *Faculty research:* Mind-body connections in trauma and trauma counseling, grief/loss issues regarding counselor training, supervision, family counseling and counselor education, refugee mental health, grief counseling and grief counseling training. *Unit head:* Dr. Linda Barclay, Program Director, 330-490-7264, Fax: 330-490-7323, E-mail: lbarclay@walsh.edu. *Application contact:* Stephanie Wheeler, Director of Graduate and Transfer Admissions, 330-490-7181, Fax: 330-490-7165, E-mail: swheeler@walsh.edu.

Washington State University Tri-Cities, Graduate Programs, Program in Education, Richland, WA 99354. Offers counseling (Ed M); educational leadership (Ed M, Ed D); literacy (Ed M); secondary certification (Ed M); teaching (MIT). Part-time programs available. *Faculty:* 24. *Students:* 11 full-time (8 women), 97 part-time (80 women); includes 17 minority (1 African American, 3 Asian Americans or Pacific Islanders, 13 Hispanic Americans). Average age 36. In 2009, 39 master's awarded. *Degree requirements:* For master's, comprehensive exam, thesis or alternative; for doctorate, comprehensive exam, thesis/dissertation. *Entrance requirements:* For master's, GRE, minimum GPA of 3.0, Working with Youth form, Character and Fitness form, 3 letters of recommendation. Additional exam requirements/recommendations for international students: Required—TOEFL. *Application deadline:* For fall admission, 1/10 priority date for domestic students, 1/10 for international students; for spring admission, 7/1 priority date for domestic students, 7/1 for international students. Applications are processed on a rolling basis. Application fee: $50. Electronic applications accepted. *Expenses:* Tuition, state resident: part-time $423 per credit. Tuition, nonresident: part-time $1032 per credit. *Financial support:* In 2009–10, 59 students received support, including research assistantships (averaging $14,634 per year), teaching assistantships (averaging $13,383 per year); Federal Work-Study, scholarships/grants, and unspecified assistantships also available. Financial award application deadline: 2/15. *Faculty research:* Multicultural counseling, socio-cultural influences in schools, diverse learners, teacher education, K-12 educational leadership. *Unit head:* Dr. Elizabeth Nagel, Director, 509-372-7398, E-mail: elizabeth_nagel@tricity.wsu.edu. *Application contact:* Helen Berry, Academic Coordinator, 800-GRADWSU, Fax: 509-372-3796, E-mail: hberry@tricity.wsu.edu.

Wayne State College, School of Education and Counseling, Department of Counseling and Special Education, Program in Guidance and Counseling, Wayne, NE 68787. Offers counseling (MSE); counselor education (MSE); school counseling (MSE). *Accreditation:* NCATE. Part-time and evening/weekend programs available. *Degree requirements:* For master's, comprehensive exam, thesis optional. *Entrance requirements:* For master's, GRE General Test, minimum GPA of 3.0. Additional exam requirements/recommendations for international students: Required—TOEFL (minimum score 550 paper-based; 213 computer-based). Electronic applications accepted.

Wayne State University, College of Education, Division of Theoretical and Behavioral Foundations, Detroit, MI 48202. Offers counseling (M Ed, MA, Ed D, PhD, Ed S); education evaluation and research (M Ed, Ed D, PhD); educational psychology (M Ed, Ed D, PhD, Ed S); educational sociology (M Ed, Ed D, PhD, Ed S); history and philosophy of education (M Ed, Ed D, PhD); rehabilitation counseling and community inclusion (MA, Ed S); school and community psychology (MA, Ed S); school clinical psychology (Ed S). *Accreditation:* ACA (one or more programs are accredited); CORE (one or more programs are accredited). Evening/weekend programs available. *Degree requirements:* For doctorate, thesis/dissertation. *Entrance requirements:* For master's, GRE; for doctorate, GRE, interview, minimum GPA of 3.0, curriculum vitae, references. Additional exam requirements/recommendations for international students: Required—TOEFL (minimum score 550 paper-based; 213 computer-based), TWE (minimum score 6). Electronic applications accepted. *Faculty research:* Adolescents at risk, supervision of counseling.

West Chester University of Pennsylvania, Office of Graduate Studies, College of Education, Department of Counselor Education, West Chester, PA 19383. Offers counseling (Teaching Certificate); elementary school counseling (M Ed); higher education counseling (MS); professional counselor license preparation (Certificate); secondary school counseling (M Ed). *Accreditation:* ACA; NCATE. Part-time and evening/weekend programs available. *Students:* 43 full-time (37 women), 189 part-time (156 women); includes 32 minority (25 African Americans, 1 American Indian/Alaska Native, 1 Asian American or Pacific Islander, 5 Hispanic Americans), 1 international. Average age 27. 141 applicants, 93% accepted, 83 enrolled. In 2009, 75

master's, 9 other advanced degrees awarded. *Degree requirements:* For master's, comprehensive exam. *Entrance requirements:* For master's, GRE or MAT, interview, minimum GPA of 3.0, three letters of reference . Additional exam requirements/recommendations for international students: Required—TOEFL (minimum score 550 paper-based; 213 computer-based; 80 iBT). *Application deadline:* For fall admission, 4/15 priority date for domestic students, 3/15 for international students; for spring admission, 10/15 for domestic students, 9/1 for international students. Applications are processed on a rolling basis. Application fee: $35. Electronic applications accepted. *Expenses:* Tuition, state resident: full-time $6666; part-time $370 per credit. Tuition, nonresident: full-time $10,666; part-time $593 per credit. Required fees: $122.56 per credit. *Financial support:* In 2009–10, 29 research assistantships with full and partial tuition reimbursements (averaging $5,000 per year) were awarded; unspecified assistantships also available. Support available to part-time students. Financial award application deadline: 2/15; financial award applicants required to submit FAFSA. *Faculty research:* Teacher and student cognition, adolescent cognitive development. *Unit head:* Dr. Naijian Zhang, Chair, 610-436-2559, E-mail: nzhang@wcupa.edu. *Application contact:* Dr. Matthew Snyder, Graduate Coordinator, 610-436-2559, E-mail: msnyder@wcupa.edu.

Western Carolina University, Graduate School, College of Education and Allied Professions, Department of Human Services, Cullowhee, NC 28723. Offers counseling (M Ed, MA Ed, MS), including community counseling (M Ed, MS), school counseling (MA Ed); human resources (MS). *Accreditation:* ACA (one or more programs are accredited). Part-time and evening/weekend programs available. Postbaccalaureate distance learning degree programs offered. *Students:* 73 full-time (58 women), 116 part-time (80 women). Average age 33. 136 applicants, 77% accepted, 79 enrolled. In 2009, 46 master's awarded. *Degree requirements:* For master's, comprehensive exam, thesis or alternative. *Entrance requirements:* For master's, GRE General Test, appropriate undergraduate degree with minimum GPA of 3.0, 3 recommendations, writing sample, resume. Additional exam requirements/recommendations for international students: Required—TOEFL (minimum score 550 paper-based; 270 computer-based; 79 iBT). *Application deadline:* For fall admission, 2/1 for domestic students. Applications are processed on a rolling basis. Application fee: $45. *Financial support:* In 2009–10, 33 students received support, including 25 research assistantships with full and partial tuition reimbursements available (averaging $6,880 per year), 8 teaching assistantships with full and partial tuition reimbursements available (averaging $7,000 per year); fellowships, career-related internships or fieldwork, institutionally sponsored loans, scholarships/grants, and unspecified assistantships also available. Financial award application deadline: 3/31; financial award applicants required to submit FAFSA. *Faculty research:* Marital and family development, spirituality in counseling, home school law, sexuality education, employee recruitment/retention. *Unit head:* Dr. Lisa Bloom, Head, 828-227-7310, E-mail: bloom@email.wcu.edu. *Application contact:* Admissions Specialist for Human Services, 828-227-7398, Fax: 828-227-7480, E-mail: gradsch@email.wcu.edu.

Western Connecticut State University, Division of Graduate Studies, School of Professional Studies, Department of Education and Educational Psychology, Program in Guidance and Counseling, Danbury, CT 06810-6885. Offers MS. Part-time programs available. *Students:* 1 (woman) part-time. Average age 47. *Entrance requirements:* Additional exam requirements/recommendations for international students: Recommended—TOEFL (minimum score 550 paper-based; 213 computer-based; 79 iBT), IELTS (minimum score 6). *Application deadline:* For fall admission, 8/5 priority date for domestic students; for spring admission, 1/5 priority date for domestic students. Applications are processed on a rolling basis. Application fee: $50. *Expenses:* Tuition, state resident: full-time $5012; part-time $278 per credit hour. Tuition, nonresident: full-time $13,962; part-time $284 per credit hour. Required fees: $3886; $139 per credit hour. Full-time tuition and fees vary according to course load and program. Part-time tuition and fees vary according to course level, degree level and program. *Financial support:* Application deadline: 5/1. *Unit head:* Dr. Theresa Canada, Chairperson, Department of Education and Educational Psychology. *Application contact:* Chris Shankle, Associate Director of Graduate Studies, 203-837-9005, Fax: 203-837-8326, E-mail: shanklec@wcsu.edu.

Western Connecticut State University, Division of Graduate Studies, School of Professional Studies, Department of Education and Educational Psychology, Program in School Counseling, Danbury, CT 06810-6885. Offers MS. *Accreditation:* ACA. Part-time programs available. *Students:* 8 full-time (7 women), 43 part-time (37 women); includes 3 minority (1 African American, 1 American Indian/Alaska Native, 1 Asian American or Pacific Islander). Average age 30. 39 applicants, 69% accepted, 16 enrolled. In 2009, 15 master's awarded. *Degree requirements:* For master's, practicum, internship, completion of program in 6 years. *Entrance requirements:* For master's, PRAXIS I, minimum GPA of 2.8, 3 letters of reference, essay, 6 hours of psychology. Additional exam requirements/recommendations for international students: Recommended—TOEFL (minimum score 550 paper-based; 213 computer-based; 79 iBT), IELTS (minimum score 6). *Application deadline:* For fall admission, 8/5 priority date for domestic students; for spring admission, 1/5 priority date for domestic students. Applications are processed on a rolling basis. Application fee: $50. *Expenses:* Tuition, state resident: full-time $5012; part-time $278 per credit hour. Tuition, nonresident: full-time $13,962; part-time $284 per credit hour. Required fees: $3886; $139 per credit hour. Full-time tuition and fees vary according to course load and program. Part-time tuition and fees vary according to course level, degree level and program. *Financial support:* Application deadline: 5/1. *Unit head:* Dr. Aram Aslanian, Coordinator, 203-837-8512, Fax: 203-837-8413, E-mail: aslaniana@wcsu.edu. *Application contact:* Chris Shankle, Associate Director of Graduate Studies, 203-837-9005, Fax: 203-837-8326, E-mail: shanklec@wcsu.edu.

Western Illinois University, School of Graduate Studies, College of Education and Human Services, Department of Counselor Education, Macomb, IL 61455-1390. Offers counseling (MS Ed). *Accreditation:* ACA. Part-time programs available. *Students:* 35 full-time (28 women), 67 part-time (51 women); includes 14 minority (8 African Americans, 6 Hispanic Americans), 1 international. Average age 31. 38 applicants, 34% accepted. In 2009, 26 master's awarded. *Degree requirements:* For master's, thesis or alternative. *Entrance requirements:* For master's, interview. Additional exam requirements/recommendations for international students: Required—TOEFL (minimum score 550 paper-based; 213 computer-based; 80 iBT). *Application deadline:* Applications are processed on a rolling basis. Application fee: $30. Electronic applications accepted. *Expenses:* Tuition, state resident: full-time $4486; part-time $249.21 per credit hour. Tuition, nonresident: full-time $8972; part-time $498.42 per credit hour. Required fees: $72.62 per credit hour. *Financial support:* In 2009–10, 13 students received support, including 13 research assistantships with full tuition reimbursements available (averaging $7,280 per year). Financial award applicants required to submit FAFSA. *Unit head:* Dr. Frank Main, Chairperson, 309-762-9481. *Application contact:* Evelyn Hoing, Assistant Director of Graduate Studies, 309-298-1806, Fax: 309-298-2345, E-mail: grad-office@wiu.edu.

Western Kentucky University, Graduate Studies, College of Education and Behavioral Sciences, Department of Counseling and Student Affairs, Bowling Green, KY 42101. Offers business and marketing education (MA Ed); counseling (MA Ed); counselor education (Ed S); education and behavioral science (MA Ed); elementary education (MA Ed, Ed S); middle years education (MA Ed); secondary education (MA Ed, Ed S); student affairs (MA Ed). *Accreditation:* ACA; NCATE. Part-time and evening/weekend programs available. *Degree requirements:* For master's, comprehensive exam, thesis optional. *Entrance requirements:* For master's, GRE General Test. Additional exam requirements/recommendations for international students: Required—TOEFL (minimum score 555 paper-based; 213 computer-based; 79 iBT). *Expenses:* Tuition, state resident: full-time $4160; part-time $416 per credit hour. Tuition, nonresident: full-time $9550; part-time $506 per credit hour. Tuition and fees vary according to campus/location and reciprocity agreements. *Faculty research:* Counselor education, research for residential workers.

Western Michigan University, Graduate College, College of Education, Department of Counselor Education and Counseling Psychology, Kalamazoo, MI 49008. Offers counseling psychology (MA, PhD); counselor education (MA, PhD); human resources development (MA). *Accreditation:* ACA (one or more programs are accredited); APA (one or more programs are accredited); CORE; NCATE. *Faculty:* 19 full-time (5 women). *Students:* 328 full-time (258 women), 201 part-time (158 women); includes 57 minority (45 African Americans, 2 American Indian/Alaska Native, 4 Asian Americans or Pacific Islanders, 6 Hispanic Americans), 19 international. 294 applicants, 81% accepted, 101 enrolled. In 2009, 108 master's, 13 doctorates awarded. *Degree requirements:* For doctorate, thesis/dissertation, oral exams. *Entrance requirements:* For doctorate, GRE General Test. *Application deadline:* For fall admission, 1/15 for domestic students. Applications are processed on a rolling basis. Application fee: $25. *Financial support:* Fellowships, research assistantships, teaching assistantships, Federal Work-Study available. Financial award application deadline: 2/15; financial award applicants required to submit FAFSA. *Unit head:* Patrick Munley, Chair, 269-387-5120. *Application contact:* Admissions and Orientation, 269-387-2000, Fax: 269-387-2355.

Western New Mexico University, Graduate Division, School of Education, Silver City, NM 88062-0680. Offers bilingual education (MAT); counseling (MA); educational leadership (MA); elementary education (MAT); reading (MAT); school psychology (MA); secondary education (MAT); special education (MAT); TESOL (teaching English to speakers of other languages) (MAT). *Accreditation:* NCATE. *Degree requirements:* For master's, comprehensive exam. *Entrance requirements:* For master's, GRE General Test, GRE Subject Test, minimum GPA of 3.2 in last 64 hours of undergraduate study. Additional exam requirements/recommendations for international students: Required—TOEFL (minimum score 550 paper-based; 213 computer-based). Electronic applications accepted.

Western Washington University, Graduate School, College of Humanities and Social Sciences, Department of Psychology, Program in School Counseling, Bellingham, WA 98225-5996. Offers M Ed. *Accreditation:* ACA. *Degree requirements:* For master's, comprehensive exam. *Entrance requirements:* For master's, GRE General Test, minimum GPA of 3.0 in last 60 semester hours or last 90 quarter hours. Additional exam requirements/recommendations for international students: Required—TOEFL (minimum score 567 paper-based; 227 computer-based). Electronic applications accepted.

Westfield State College, Division of Graduate and Continuing Education, Department of Psychology, Westfield, MA 01086. Offers applied behavior analysis (MA); mental health counseling (MA); school guidance (MA). Part-time and evening/weekend programs available. *Degree requirements:* For master's, comprehensive exam. *Entrance requirements:* For master's, GRE General Test, MAT, minimum undergraduate GPA of 2.7.

Westminster College, Programs in Education, Program in Guidance and Counseling, New Wilmington, PA 16172-0001. Offers M Ed, Certificate. Part-time and evening/weekend programs available. *Degree requirements:* For master's, comprehensive exam. *Entrance requirements:* For master's, minimum GPA of 3.0.

West Texas A&M University, College of Education and Social Sciences, Division of Education, Program in Counseling Education, Canyon, TX 79016-0001. Offers M Ed. Part-time and evening/weekend programs available. *Degree requirements:* For master's, comprehensive exam, thesis or alternative. *Entrance requirements:* For master's, GRE General Test, interview. Additional exam requirements/recommendations for international students: Required—TOEFL (minimum score 550 paper-based). Electronic applications accepted. *Faculty research:* Reducing the somatoform patient's reliance on primary care through cognitive-relational group therapy, determining effects of premarital sex.

West Texas A&M University, College of Education and Social Sciences, Division of Education, Program in Professional Counseling, Canyon, TX 79016-0001. Offers MA. Part-time programs available. *Degree requirements:* For master's, comprehensive exam. *Entrance requirements:* For master's, GRE General Test, interview, 12 semester hours in education and/or psychology, approval from the Counselor Admissions Committee. Additional exam requirements/recommendations for international students: Required—TOEFL (minimum score 550 paper-based). Electronic applications accepted.

West Virginia University, College of Human Resources and Education, Department of Counseling, Rehabilitation Counseling, and Counseling Psychology, Program in Counseling, Morgantown, WV 26506. Offers MA. *Accreditation:* ACA; APA. *Degree requirements:* For master's, content exams. *Entrance requirements:* For master's, GRE General Test, minimum GPA of 2.8, interview 2.8. Additional exam requirements/recommendations for international students: Required—TOEFL (minimum score 550 paper-based; 213 computer-based; 65 iBT). Electronic applications accepted. *Faculty research:* Career development and placement, family therapy, conflict resolution, interviewing technique, multicultural counseling.

Whitworth University, School of Education, Graduate Studies in Education, Program in Counseling, Spokane, WA 99251-0001. Offers school counselors (M Ed); social agency/church setting (M Ed). *Accreditation:* NCATE. Part-time and evening/weekend programs available. *Degree requirements:* For master's, comprehensive exam, internship, practicum, research project, or thesis. *Entrance requirements:* For master's, GRE General Test, MAT. Tuition and fees vary according to program. *Faculty research:* Church counseling service support.

Wichita State University, Graduate School, College of Education, Department of Counseling, Educational and School Psychology, Wichita, KS 67260. Offers counseling (M Ed); educational psychology (M Ed); school psychology (Ed S). *Accreditation:* NCATE. Part-time and evening/weekend programs available. *Expenses:* Tuition, state resident: full-time $4247; part-time $235.95 per credit hour. Tuition, nonresident: full-time $11,171; part-time $620.60 per credit hour. Required fees: $34; $3.60 per credit hour. $17 per term. Tuition and fees vary according to campus/location and program. *Unit head:* Dr. Marlene Schommer-Aikins, Chairperson, 316-978-3326, Fax: 316-978-3102, E-mail: marlene.schommer-aikins@wichita.edu. *Application contact:* Dr. Marlene Schommer-Aikins, Chairperson, 316-978-3326, Fax: 316-978-3102, E-mail: marlene.schommer-aikins@wichita.edu.

Widener University, School of Human Service Professions, Center for Education, Chester, PA 19013-5792. Offers adult education (M Ed); counseling in higher education (M Ed); counselor education (M Ed); early childhood education (M Ed); educational foundations (M Ed); educational leadership (M Ed); educational psychology (M Ed); elementary education (M Ed); English and language arts (M Ed); health education (M Ed); higher education leadership (Ed D); home and school visitor (M Ed); human sexuality (M Ed); mathematics education (M Ed); middle school education (M Ed); principalship (M Ed); reading and language arts (Ed D); reading education (M Ed); school administration (Ed D); science education (M Ed); social studies education (M Ed); special education (M Ed); technology education (M Ed). *Accreditation:* NCATE. Part-time and evening/weekend programs available. *Faculty:* 34 full-time (22 women), 37 part-time/adjunct (14 women). *Students:* 203 full-time (154 women), 415 part-time (298 women); includes 50 minority (34 African Americans, 1 American Indian/Alaska Native, 5 Asian Americans or Pacific Islanders, 10 Hispanic Americans), 3 international. Average age 39. 139 applicants, 88% accepted. In 2009, 168 master's, 31 doctorates awarded. Terminal master's awarded for partial completion of doctoral program. *Degree requirements:* For doctorate, thesis/dissertation. *Entrance requirements:* For master's, minimum GPA of 2.5; for doctorate, GRE or MAT, minimum GPA of 2.0 (undergraduate), 3.5 (graduate). *Application deadline:* Applications are processed on a rolling basis. Application fee: $25 ($300 for international students). Electronic applications accepted. *Expenses:* Contact institution. *Financial support:* Career-related internships or fieldwork, tuition waivers (full and partial), and unspecified assistantships available. Support available to part-time students. Financial award application deadline: 5/1. *Faculty research:* Reading and cognition, adult education, technology education, educational leadership, special education. *Unit head:* Dr. Michael W. LeDoux, Associate Dean, 610-499-4294, Fax: 610-499-4623, E-mail: mwledoux@widener.edu. *Application contact:* Dr. Roberta D. Nolan, Director of Graduate Admissions, 610-499-4125, E-mail: rdnolan@widener.edu.

William Paterson University of New Jersey, College of Education, Department of Special Education and Counseling Services, Wayne, NJ 07470-8420. Offers counseling services (M Ed); special education (M Ed). *Accreditation:* NCATE. *Students:* 30 full-time (26 women), 178 part-time (156 women); includes 15 minority (5 African Americans, 1 American Indian/Alaska Native, 2 Asian Americans or Pacific Islanders, 7 Hispanic Americans). In 2009, 62

Counselor Education

William Paterson University of New Jersey (continued)
master's awarded. *Degree requirements:* For master's, comprehensive exam, thesis. *Entrance requirements:* For master's, GRE General Test, MAT, minimum GPA of 2.75, teaching certificate. *Application deadline:* Applications are processed on a rolling basis. Application fee: $50. Electronic applications accepted. *Financial support:* Research assistantships with full tuition reimbursements, career-related internships or fieldwork and unspecified assistantships available. Support available to part-time students. Financial award application deadline: 4/1; financial award applicants required to submit FAFSA. *Unit head:* Dr. Peter Griswold, Graduate Program Director, 973-720-3761. *Application contact:* Danielle Liautaud, Director, 973-720-3579, Fax: 973-720-2035, E-mail: liautaudd@wpunj.edu.

Wilmington University, College of Education, New Castle, DE 19720-6491. Offers applied education technology (M Ed); career and technical education (M Ed); elementary and secondary school counseling (M Ed); elementary special education (M Ed); elementary studies (M Ed); instruction: gifted and talented (M Ed); instruction: teaching and learning (M Ed); literacy (M Ed); reading (M Ed); school leadership (M Ed); secondary teaching (MAT). *Accreditation:* NCATE. Part-time and evening/weekend programs available. *Entrance requirements:* For master's, 2 letters of recommendation, interview. Additional exam requirements/recommendations for international students: Required—TOEFL (minimum score 500 paper-based; 173 computer-based). Electronic applications accepted.

Winona State University, College of Education, Counselor Education Department, Winona, MN 55987-5838. Offers community counseling (MS); professional development (MS); school counseling (MS). *Accreditation:* ACA; NCATE. Part-time and evening/weekend programs available. *Degree requirements:* For master's, thesis or alternative. *Entrance requirements:* For master's, letters of reference, interview, group activity, on-site writing. Electronic applications accepted.

Winthrop University, College of Education, Program in Counseling and Development, Rock Hill, SC 29733. Offers agency counseling (M Ed); school counseling (M Ed). *Accreditation:* ACA; NCATE. Part-time programs available. *Degree requirements:* For master's, comprehensive exam. *Entrance requirements:* For master's, GRE General Test or MAT, interview. Electronic applications accepted.

Wright State University, School of Graduate Studies, College of Education and Human Services, Department of Human Services, Programs in Counseling, Dayton, OH 45435. Offers counseling (MA, MS), including business and industrial management, community counseling, exceptional children, marriage and family, mental health counseling; pupil personnel services (M Ed, MA), including school counseling. *Accreditation:* ACA (one or more programs are accredited); NCATE. *Degree requirements:* For master's, comprehensive exam, thesis (for some programs). *Entrance requirements:* For master's, GRE General Test, MAT, interview. Additional exam requirements/recommendations for international students: Required—TOEFL.

Xavier University, College of Social Sciences, Health and Education, School of Education, Department of School and Community Counseling, Master of Arts in Community Counseling, Cincinnati, OH 45207. Offers MA. *Accreditation:* ACA. Part-time programs available. *Faculty:* 5 full-time (2 women), 6 part-time/adjunct (2 women). *Students:* 43 full-time (31 women), 40 part-time (35 women); includes 16 minority (15 African Americans, 1 Hispanic American), 1 international. Average age 34. 18 applicants, 67% accepted, 10 enrolled. In 2009, 30 master's awarded. *Degree requirements:* For master's, internship. *Entrance requirements:* For master's, MAT or GRE, minimum GPA of 3.0, letters of recommendation, resume. Additional exam requirements/recommendations for international students: Required—TOEFL (minimum score 550 paper-based; 213 computer-based; 79 iBT). *Application deadline:* For fall admission, 4/1 priority date for domestic and international students; for spring admission, 10/1 priority date for domestic and international students. Application fee: $35. Electronic applications accepted. *Expenses:* Tuition: Part-time $697 per credit hour. One-time fee: $35 part-time. *Financial support:* In 2009–10, 46 students received support. Tuition waivers (partial) and unspecified assistantships available. Financial award applicants required to submit FAFSA. *Faculty research:* Supervision, ethics, consultation, assessment. *Unit head:* Dr. Brent Richardson, Chair, 513-745-4294, Fax: 513-745-2920, E-mail: richardb@xavier.edu. *Application contact:* Dr. Brent Richardson, Chair, 513-745-4294, Fax: 513-745-2920, E-mail: richardb@xavier.edu.

Xavier University, College of Social Sciences, Health and Education, School of Education, Department of School and Community Counseling, Master of Arts in School Counseling, Cincinnati, OH 45207. Offers MA. *Accreditation:* ACA. Part-time and evening/weekend programs available. *Faculty:* 5 full-time (2 women), 6 part-time/adjunct (2 women). *Students:* 8 full-time (7 women), 75 part-time (67 women); includes 7 minority (2 African Americans, 5 Hispanic Americans). Average age 31. 15 applicants, 67% accepted, 9 enrolled. In 2009, 21 master's awarded. *Degree requirements:* For master's, internship. *Entrance requirements:* For master's, MAT or GRE, minimum GPA of 3.0, letters of recommendation, resume. Additional exam requirements/recommendations for international students: Required—TOEFL (minimum score 550 paper-based; 213 computer-based; 79 iBT). *Application deadline:* For fall admission, 4/1 priority date for domestic and international students; for spring admission, 10/1 priority date for domestic and international students. Application fee: $35. Electronic applications accepted. *Expenses:* Tuition: Part-time $697 per credit hour. One-time fee: $35 part-time. *Financial support:* In 2009–10, 54 students received support. Tuition waivers (partial) and unspecified assistantships available. Financial award applicants required to submit FAFSA. *Faculty research:* Supervision, ethics, consultation, assessment. *Unit head:* Dr. Brent Richardson, Chair, 513-745-4294, Fax: 513-745-2920, E-mail: richardb@xavier.edu. *Application contact:* Dr. Brent Richardson, Chair, 513-745-4294, Fax: 513-745-2920, E-mail: richardb@xavier.edu.

Xavier University of Louisiana, Graduate School, Programs in Education, New Orleans, LA 70125-1098. Offers curriculum and instruction (MA); education administration and supervision (MA); guidance and counseling (MA). *Accreditation:* NCATE. Part-time and evening/weekend programs available. *Degree requirements:* For master's, comprehensive exam, thesis or alternative. *Entrance requirements:* For master's, GRE General Test, MAT, minimum GPA of 2.5. Additional exam requirements/recommendations for international students: Required—TOEFL.

Youngstown State University, Graduate School, Beeghly College of Education, Department of Counseling, Youngstown, OH 44555-0001. Offers community counseling (MS Ed); school counseling (MS Ed). *Accreditation:* ACA; NCATE. Part-time and evening/weekend programs available. *Degree requirements:* For master's, comprehensive exam. *Entrance requirements:* For master's, MAT, interview, minimum GPA of 2.7. Additional exam requirements/recommendations for international students: Required—TOEFL. *Faculty research:* Suicide, euthanasia, ethical issues, marriage and family.

Developmental Education

Eastern Michigan University, Graduate School, College of Education, Department of Teacher Education, Programs in Educational Psychology and Assessment, Ypsilanti, MI 48197. Offers educational assessment (Graduate Certificate); educational psychology (MA), including development/personality, research and assessment, research and evaluation, the developing learner. *Accreditation:* NCATE. Part-time and evening/weekend programs available. Postbaccalaureate distance learning degree programs offered (minimal on-campus study). *Students:* 17 part-time (14 women); includes 1 minority (African American). Average age 34. In 2009, 2 master's awarded. *Degree requirements:* For master's, thesis or alternative. *Entrance requirements:* For master's, GRE. Additional exam requirements/recommendations for international students: Required—TOEFL. *Application deadline:* Applications are processed on a rolling basis. Application fee: $35. Tuition and fees vary according to course level. *Financial support:* Fellowships, research assistantships with full tuition reimbursements, teaching assistantships with full tuition reimbursements, career-related internships or fieldwork, Federal Work-Study, institutionally sponsored loans, scholarships/grants, tuition waivers (partial), and unspecified assistantships available. Support available to part-time students. Financial award applicants required to submit FAFSA. *Unit head:* Dr. Rob Carpenter, Coordinator, 734-487-3260, Fax: 734-487-2101, E-mail: rcarpen1@emich.edu. *Application contact:* Dr. Rob Carpenter, Coordinator, 734-487-3260, Fax: 734-487-2101, E-mail: rcarpen1@emich.edu.

Edinboro University of Pennsylvania, School of Graduate Studies and Research, School of Education, Department of Elementary, Middle and Secondary Education, Edinboro, PA 16444. Offers character education (Certificate); elementary education (M Ed), including character education, early childhood education, elementary education; reading (M Ed, Certificate), including reading (M Ed), reading specialist (Certificate). Part-time and evening/weekend programs available. *Faculty:* 10 full-time (6 women), 3 part-time/adjunct (2 women). *Students:* 106 full-time (63 women), 172 part-time (126 women); includes 7 minority (4 African Americans, 3 Hispanic Americans). Average age 31. In 2009, 153 master's, 7 Certificates awarded. *Degree requirements:* For master's, comprehensive exam, thesis or alternative, project; for Certificate, thesis or alternative, exam. *Entrance requirements:* For master's and Certificate, GRE or MAT, minimum QPA of 2.5. *Application deadline:* Applications are processed on a rolling basis. Application fee: $30. Electronic applications accepted. *Expenses:* Tuition, state resident: full-time $6666; part-time $370 per credit. Tuition, nonresident: full-time $10,666; part-time $593 per credit. Required fees: $2206.28. One-time fee: $204 part-time. *Financial support:* In 2009–10, 14 research assistantships with full and partial tuition reimbursements (averaging $4,050 per year) were awarded; career-related internships or fieldwork, Federal Work-Study, scholarships/grants, and unspecified assistantships also available. Support available to part-time students. Financial award application deadline: 2/15; financial award applicants required to submit FAFSA. *Unit head:* Dr. Maureen Walcavich, Program Head, Elementary Education, 814-732-2303, E-mail: mwalcavich@edinboro.edu.

Ferris State University, College of Education and Human Services, School of Education, Big Rapids, MI 49307. Offers administration (MSCTE); curriculum and instruction (M Ed), including administration, elementary education, experiential education, philanthropic education, reading, secondary education, special education, subject matter option; education technology (MSCTE); instructor (MSCTE); post-secondary administration (MSCTE); training and development (MSCTE). Part-time and evening/weekend programs available. Postbaccalaureate distance learning degree programs offered. *Faculty:* 12 full-time (8 women), 11 part-time/adjunct (5 women). *Students:* 19 full-time (13 women), 185 part-time (122 women); includes 24 minority (20 African Americans, 1 Asian American or Pacific Islander, 3 Hispanic Americans), 1 international. Average age 36. 37 applicants, 32% accepted, 11 enrolled. In 2009, 73 master's awarded. *Degree requirements:* For master's, thesis, research paper. *Entrance requirements:* For master's, 2 years of work experience for vocational setting, minimum GPA of 2.75. Additional exam requirements/recommendations for international students: Recommended—TOEFL (minimum score 500 paper-based; 173 computer-based; 61 iBT). *Application deadline:* For fall admission, 7/1 priority date for domestic students; for spring admission, 11/1 priority date for domestic students. Applications are processed on a rolling basis. Application fee: $30. *Financial support:* Career-related internships or fieldwork and scholarships/grants available. Support available to part-time students. Financial award applicants required to submit FAFSA. *Faculty research:* Suicide prevention, reading, women in education, special needs, administration. *Unit head:* Dr. Liza Ing, Director, 231-591-5362, Fax: 231-591-2041. *Application contact:* Kimisue Worrall, Secretary, 231-591-5361, Fax: 231-591-2043.

Grambling State University, School of Graduate Studies and Research, College of Education, Department of Educational Leadership, Grambling, LA 71245. Offers curriculum and instruction (Ed D); developmental education (MS, Ed D), including curriculum and instruction: reading (Ed D), English (MS), guidance and counseling (MS), higher education administration (Ed D), instructional systems and technology (Ed D), mathematics (MS), reading (MS), science (MS), student development and personnel services (Ed D); educational leadership (MS, Ed D). Part-time and evening/weekend programs available. *Faculty:* 19 full-time (12 women). *Students:* 23 full-time (18 women), 84 part-time (62 women); includes 81 minority (80 African Americans, 1 Asian American or Pacific Islander), 5 international. Average age 39. 72 applicants, 75% accepted, 39 enrolled. In 2009, 5 master's, 9 doctorates awarded. *Degree requirements:* For master's, comprehensive exam, thesis (for some programs); for doctorate, comprehensive exam, thesis/dissertation. *Entrance requirements:* For master's, GRE, minimum GPA of 2.5 on last degree; for doctorate, GRE (minimum 1000, 500 on Verbal), master's degree, minimum GPA of 3.0 on last degree. Additional exam requirements/recommendations for international students: Required—TOEFL (minimum score 500 paper-based; 173 computer-based; 61 iBT). *Application deadline:* For fall admission, 7/1 for domestic and international students; for spring admission, 12/1 for domestic and international students. Applications are processed on a rolling basis. Application fee: $20 ($30 for international students). Electronic applications accepted. *Expenses:* Tuition, state resident: full-time $2610. Tuition, nonresident: full-time $2610. *Financial support:* In 2009–10, 5 research assistantships (averaging $10,948 per year) were awarded; health care benefits, tuition waivers (full), and unspecified assistantships also available. Financial award application deadline: 5/31; financial award applicants required to submit FAFSA. *Unit head:* Dr. Olatunde Ogunyemi, Director, 318-274-6105, Fax: 318-274-2799, E-mail: ogunyemio@gram.edu. *Application contact:* Laketha Richards, Administrative Assistant III, 318-274-6105, Fax: 318-274-6249, E-mail: richardsl@gram.edu.

Instituto Tecnológico y de Estudios Superiores de Monterrey, Campus Ciudad Obregón, Programs in Education, Program in Cognitive Development, Ciudad Obregón, Mexico. Offers ME.

National-Louis University, College of Arts and Sciences, Division of Language and Academic Development, Program in Adult Literacy and Developmental Studies, Chicago, IL 60603. Offers M Ed, Certificate. Part-time and evening/weekend programs available. *Entrance requirements:* For master's, GRE General Test, MAT, or Watson-Glaser Critical Thinking Appraisal, interview, minimum GPA of 3.0; for Certificate, GRE, MAT, or Watson-Glaser Critical Thinking Appraisal, interview, minimum GPA of 3.0. *Expenses:* Tuition: Full-time $17,160; part-time $715 per semester hour. Tuition and fees vary according to course load, degree level, campus/location and program. *Faculty research:* Adult learning and development, learner-centered development, political and social foundations, reading development, curricular processes.

North Carolina State University, Graduate School, College of Education, Department of Adult and Higher Education, Program in Training and Development, Raleigh, NC 27695. Offers M Ed, Ed D, Certificate. Postbaccalaureate distance learning degree programs offered. *Degree requirements:* For master's, thesis optional. *Entrance requirements:* For master's, GRE General Test or MAT, minimum GPA of 3.0 in major. Electronic applications accepted.

Rutgers, The State University of New Jersey, New Brunswick, Graduate School of Education, Department of Educational Psychology, Program in Learning, Cognition and Development,

Piscataway, NJ 08854-8097. Offers Ed M. Part-time and evening/weekend programs available. *Entrance requirements:* For master's, GRE General Test, 3 letters of recommendation. Additional exam requirements/recommendations for international students: Required—TOEFL (minimum score 550 paper-based; 233 computer-based; 83 iBT). Electronic applications accepted. *Faculty research:* Cognitive development, gender roles, cognition and instruction, peer learning, infancy and early childhood.

Texas State University–San Marcos, Graduate School, College of Education, Department of Counseling, Leadership, Adult Education, and School Psychology, Program in Developmental and Adult Education, San Marcos, TX 78666. Offers adult, professional, and community education (PhD); developmental and adult education (MA). Part-time programs available. *Faculty:* 16 full-time (6 women). *Students:* 13 full-time (7 women), 71 part-time (23 women); includes 40 minority (14 African Americans, 4 Asian Americans or Pacific Islanders, 22 Hispanic Americans). Average age 44. 51 applicants, 29% accepted, 11 enrolled. In 2009, 3 master's, 5 doctorates awarded. *Degree requirements:* For master's, comprehensive exam, thesis, internship. *Entrance requirements:* For master's, minimum GPA of 2.75 in last 60 hours of course work. Additional exam requirements/recommendations for international students: Required—TOEFL (minimum score 550 paper-based; 213 computer-based). *Application deadline:* For fall admission, 6/15 for domestic students, 6/1 for international students; for spring admission, 10/1 for domestic and international students. Applications are processed on a rolling basis. Application fee: $40 ($90 for international students). Electronic applications accepted. *Expenses:* Tuition, state resident: full-time $5784; part-time $241 per credit hour. Tuition, nonresident: full-time $13,224; part-time $551 per credit hour. Required fees: $1728; $48 per credit hour. $306. Tuition and fees vary according to course load. *Financial support:* In 2009–10, 8 students received support, including 3 research assistantships (averaging $8,129 per year), 5 teaching assistantships (averaging $7,811 per year); career-related internships or fieldwork, Federal Work-Study, and institutionally sponsored loans also available. Support available to part-time students. Financial award application deadline: 4/1; financial award applicants required to submit FAFSA. *Unit head:* Dr. Jovita Ross-Gordan, Graduate Advisor, 512-245-3083, Fax: 512-245-8872. *Application contact:* Dr. J. Michael Willoughby, Dean of Graduate School, 512-245-2581, Fax: 512-245-8365, E-mail: gradcollege@txstate.edu.

The University of Iowa, Graduate College, College of Education, Department of Teaching and Learning, Program in Elementary Education, Iowa City, IA 52242-1316. Offers curriculum and supervision (MA, PhD); developmental reading (MA); early childhood education and care (MA); elementary education (MA, PhD); language, literature and culture (PhD). *Degree requirements:* For master's, thesis optional, exam; for doctorate, comprehensive exam, thesis/dissertation. *Entrance requirements:* For master's and doctorate, GRE General Test, minimum GPA of 3.0. Additional exam requirements/recommendations for international students: Required—TOEFL (minimum score 550 paper-based; 213 computer-based; 81 iBT). Electronic applications accepted.

The University of Iowa, Graduate College, College of Education, Department of Teaching and Learning, Program in Secondary Education, Iowa City, IA 52242-1316. Offers art education (PhD); curriculum and supervision (PhD); curriculum supervision (MA); developmental reading (MA); English education (MA, MAT); foreign language education (MA, MAT); foreign language/ESL education (PhD); language, literature and culture (PhD); math education (PhD); mathematics education (MA); social studies (MA, PhD). *Degree requirements:* For master's, thesis optional, exam; for doctorate, comprehensive exam, thesis/dissertation. *Entrance requirements:* For master's and doctorate, GRE General Test, minimum GPA of 3.0. Additional exam requirements/recommendations for international students: Required—TOEFL (minimum score 550 paper-based; 213 computer-based; 81 iBT). Electronic applications accepted.

English Education

Alabama State University, School of Graduate Studies, College of Education, Department of Curriculum and Instruction, Program in Secondary Education, Montgomery, AL 36101-0271. Offers biology education (M Ed, Ed S); English/language arts (M Ed); history education (M Ed, Ed S); mathematics education (M Ed); secondary education (Ed S); social studies (Ed S). Part-time programs available. *Degree requirements:* For master's, comprehensive exam; for Ed S, comprehensive exam, thesis. *Entrance requirements:* For master's, GRE General Test, MAT, graduate writing competency test; for Ed S, graduate writing competency test, GRE, MAT. Additional exam requirements/recommendations for international students: Required—TOEFL (minimum score 500 paper-based; 173 computer-based).

Albany State University, College of Arts and Humanities, Program in English Education, Albany, GA 31705-2717. Offers M Ed. *Accreditation:* NCATE. Part-time programs available. *Degree requirements:* For master's, comprehensive exam, GACE II. *Entrance requirements:* For master's, GRE or MAT, undergraduate degree in English education, or the equivalent, from accredited college. Additional exam requirements/recommendations for international students: Required—TOEFL. *Application deadline:* For fall admission, 11/16 for domestic students, 9/16 for international students; for spring admission, 4/19 for domestic students, 2/19 for international students. Applications are processed on a rolling basis. Application fee: $20. Electronic applications accepted. *Expenses:* Tuition, state resident: full-time $2970; part-time $162 per credit hour. Tuition, nonresident: full-time $12,168; part-time $676 per credit hour. Required fees: $962; $75 per credit hour. *Financial support:* Application deadline: 6/30. *Faculty research:* African American Literature, American literature, rhetoric and composition. *Unit head:* Dr. James Hill, Chair, 229-430-4833, Fax: 229-430-4296, E-mail: james.hilll@asurams.edu. *Application contact:* Nicole Lane, Interim Graduate Admissions Officer, 229-430-4862, Fax: 229-430-6398, E-mail: nicole.lane@asurams.edu.

Andrews University, School of Graduate Studies, College of Arts and Sciences, Department of English, Berrien Springs, MI 49104. Offers MA, MAT. Part-time programs available. *Faculty:* 10 full-time (4 women), 3 part-time/adjunct (2 women). *Students:* 12 full-time (6 women), 6 part-time (3 women); includes 4 minority (1 African American, 2 Asian Americans or Pacific Islanders, 1 Hispanic American), 3 international. Average age 34. 11 applicants, 45% accepted, 2 enrolled. In 2009, 1 master's awarded. *Degree requirements:* For master's, one foreign language, thesis optional. *Entrance requirements:* For master's, GRE Subject Test. Additional exam requirements/recommendations for international students: Required—TOEFL (minimum score 550 paper-based). *Application deadline:* For fall admission, 8/15 for domestic students. Applications are processed on a rolling basis. Application fee: $40. *Financial support:* Fellowships, research assistantships, teaching assistantships, career-related internships or fieldwork and Federal Work-Study available. *Faculty research:* Christianity and literature, Victorian literature, social linguistics, rhetoric, American literature. *Unit head:* Dr. Douglas Jones, Chairperson, 269-471-3298. *Application contact:* Carolyn Hurst, Supervisor of Graduate Admission, 800-253-2874, Fax: 269-471-6321, E-mail: graduate@andrews.edu.

Andrews University, School of Graduate Studies, School of Education, Department of Teaching, Learning, and Curriculum, Berrien Springs, MI 49104. Offers curriculum and instruction (MA, Ed D, PhD, Ed S); elementary education (MAT); reading (MA); secondary education (MAT), including biology, education, English, English as a second language, French, history, physics; special education/learning disabilities (MS); teacher education (MAT). *Students:* 12 full-time (8 women), 30 part-time (19 women); includes 17 minority (14 African Americans, 1 Asian American or Pacific Islander, 2 Hispanic Americans), 10 international. Average age 43. 28 applicants, 54% accepted, 6 enrolled. In 2009, 11 master's, 4 doctorates, 1 other advanced degree awarded. *Entrance requirements:* For master's, GRE Subject Test. Additional exam requirements/recommendations for international students: Required—TOEFL (minimum score 550 paper-based). *Application deadline:* For fall admission, 8/15 for domestic students. Applications are processed on a rolling basis. Application fee: $40. *Unit head:* Dr. Lee C. Davidson, Chair, 269-471-6364. *Application contact:* Carolyn Hurst, Supervisor of Graduate Admission, 800-253-2874, Fax: 269-471-6321, E-mail: graduate@andrews.edu.

Anna Maria College, Graduate Division, Program in Education, Paxton, MA 01612. Offers early childhood education (M Ed); education (CAGS); elementary education (M Ed); English language arts (M Ed); visual arts (M Ed). Part-time and evening/weekend programs available. *Entrance requirements:* For master's, bachelor's degree in liberal arts or sciences, minimum GPA of 3.0. Additional exam requirements/recommendations for international students: Required—TOEFL (minimum score 500 paper-based). Electronic applications accepted.

Appalachian State University, Cratis D. Williams Graduate School, Department of Curriculum and Instruction, Boone, NC 28608. Offers curriculum specialist (MA); educational media (MA); elementary education (MA); middle grades education (MA), including language arts, mathematics, science, social studies. *Accreditation:* NCATE. Part-time and evening/weekend programs available. Postbaccalaureate distance learning degree programs offered (no on-campus study). *Faculty:* 32 full-time (22 women), 9 part-time/adjunct (3 women). *Students:* 16 full-time (12 women), 168 part-time (140 women); includes 2 minority (both African Americans), 1 international. 97 applicants, 99% accepted, 77 enrolled. In 2009, 78 master's awarded. *Degree requirements:* For master's, comprehensive exam, thesis or alternative. *Entrance requirements:* For master's, GRE General Test or MAT, 3 letters of recommendation. Additional exam requirements/recommendations for international students: Required—TOEFL (minimum score 570 paper-based; 230 computer-based; 79 iBT), IELTS (minimum score 6.5). *Application deadline:* For fall admission, 7/1 for domestic students, 2/1 for international students; for spring admission, 11/1 for domestic students, 7/1 for international students. Applications are processed on a rolling basis. Application fee: $50. Electronic applications accepted. *Expenses:* Tuition, state resident: full-time $2960. Tuition, nonresident: full-time $14,051. Required fees: $2320. *Financial support:* In 2009–10, 8 teaching assistantships (averaging $8,000 per year) were awarded; fellowships, research assistantships, career-related internships or fieldwork, Federal Work-Study, scholarships/grants, and unspecified assistantships also available. Financial award application deadline: 4/1; financial award applicants required to submit FAFSA. *Faculty research:* Media literacy, elementary teaching, curriculum development, online learning environments. Total annual research expenditures: $690,000. *Unit head:* Dr. Michael Jacobson, Chairperson, 828-262-2224. *Application contact:* Sandy Krause, Director of Admissions and Recruiting, 828-262-2130, Fax: 828-262-2709, E-mail: krausesl@appstate.edu.

Appalachian State University, Cratis D. Williams Graduate School, Department of English, Boone, NC 28608. Offers English (MA); English education (MA). Part-time programs available. Postbaccalaureate distance learning degree programs offered (no on-campus study). *Faculty:* 37 full-time (18 women). *Students:* 14 full-time (9 women), 14 part-time (7 women); includes 1 minority (African American), 1 international. 21 applicants, 86% accepted, 11 enrolled. In 2009, 16 master's awarded. *Degree requirements:* For master's, one foreign language, comprehensive exam, thesis (for some programs). *Entrance requirements:* For master's, GRE General Test, 3 letters of recommendation. Additional exam requirements/recommendations for international students: Required—TOEFL (minimum score 570 paper-based; 230 computer-based; 79 iBT), IELTS (minimum score 6.5). *Application deadline:* For fall admission, 7/1 for domestic students, 2/1 for international students; for spring admission, 11/1 for domestic students, 7/1 for international students. Applications are processed on a rolling basis. Application fee: $50. Electronic applications accepted. *Expenses:* Tuition, state resident: full-time $2960. Tuition, nonresident: full-time $14,051. Required fees: $2320. *Financial support:* In 2009–10, 10 research assistantships (averaging $8,000 per year), 12 teaching assistantships (averaging $8,000 per year) were awarded; fellowships, career-related internships or fieldwork, Federal Work-Study, scholarships/grants, and unspecified assistantships also available. Financial award application deadline: 4/1; financial award applicants required to submit FAFSA. *Faculty research:* Contemporary Irish literature, Romantic psychology, cultural practices of everyday life, Gullah linguistics, Renaissance women's writing. Total annual research expenditures: $15,000. *Unit head:* Dr. James Ivory, Chair, 828-262-3098, E-mail: ivoryjm@appstate.edu. *Application contact:* Dr. Colin Ramsey, Graduate Program Director, 828-262-7390, E-mail: ramseyct@appstate.edu.

Arcadia University, Graduate Studies, Department of Education, Glenside, PA 19038-3295. Offers art education (M Ed, MA Ed); biology education (MA Ed); chemistry education (MA Ed); child development (CAS); computer education (M Ed, CAS); computer education 7–12 (MA Ed); early childhood education (M Ed, CAS), including individualized (M Ed), master teacher (M Ed), research in child development (M Ed); educational leadership (M Ed, CAS); educational psychology (CAS); elementary education (M Ed, CAS); English education (MA Ed); environmental education (MA Ed, CAS); history education (MA Ed); language arts (M Ed, CAS); mathematics education (M Ed, MA Ed, CAS); music education (MA Ed); psychology (MA Ed); pupil personnel services (CAS); reading (M Ed, CAS); school library science (M Ed); science education (M Ed, CAS); secondary education (M Ed, CAS); special education (M Ed, Ed D, CAS); theater arts (MA Ed); written communication (MA Ed). *Accreditation:* NASAD. Part-time and evening/weekend programs available. Postbaccalaureate distance learning degree programs offered (minimal on-campus study). *Faculty:* 12 full-time (8 women), 38 part-time/adjunct (26 women). *Students:* 89 full-time (74 women), 622 part-time (487 women); includes 112 minority (94 African Americans, 9 Asian Americans or Pacific Islanders, 9 Hispanic Americans), 2 international. Average age 32. In 2009, 257 master's, 4 doctorates awarded. *Application deadline:* Applications are processed on a rolling basis. Application fee: $40. Electronic applications accepted. *Expenses:* Tuition: Full-time $30,450; part-time $620 per credit hour. Required fees: $165. Tuition and fees vary according to program. *Financial support:* Career-related internships or fieldwork, tuition waivers (partial), and unspecified assistantships available. *Unit head:* Dr. Steven P. Gulkus. *Application contact:* 215-572-2925, Fax: 215-572-2126, E-mail: grad@arcadia.edu.

Arkansas State University—Jonesboro, Graduate School, College of Humanities and Social Sciences, Department of English and Philosophy, Jonesboro, State University, AR 72467. Offers English (MA); English education (MSE, SCCT). Part-time programs available. *Faculty:* 14 full-time (4 women). *Students:* 13 full-time (9 women), 14 part-time (5 women); includes 1 minority (African American), 8 international. Average age 29. 23 applicants, 91% accepted, 14 enrolled. In 2009, 10 master's awarded. *Degree requirements:* For master's, variable foreign language requirement, comprehensive exam, thesis or alternative; for SCCT, comprehensive exam. *Entrance requirements:* For master's, GRE General Test or MAT, preliminary exam, appropriate bachelor's degree, official transcript, valid teaching certificate (for MSE), immunization records; for SCCT, GRE General Test or MAT, interview, master's degree, official transcript, immunization records. Additional exam requirements/recommendations for international students: Required—TOEFL (minimum score 550 paper-based; 213 computer-based; 79 iBT), IELTS (minimum score 6). *Application deadline:* For fall admission, 4/7 for domestic and international students; for spring admission, 11/7 for domestic and international students. Applications are processed on a rolling basis. Application fee: $30 ($40 for international students). Electronic applications accepted. *Expenses:* Tuition, state resident: full-time $3744; part-time $208 per credit hour. Tuition, nonresident: full-time $9540; part-time $530 per credit hour. Required fees:

English Education

Arkansas State University—Jonesboro (continued)

$896; $47 per credit hour. $25 per term. One-time fee: $50. Tuition and fees vary according to course load and program. *Financial support:* In 2009–10, 12 students received support; teaching assistantships, career-related internships or fieldwork, scholarships/grants, and unspecified assistantships available. Financial award application deadline: 7/1; financial award applicants required to submit FAFSA. *Unit head:* Dr. Jerry Ball, Interim Chair, 870-972-3043, Fax: 870-972-3045, E-mail: jball@astate.edu. *Application contact:* Dr. Andrew Sustich, Dean of the Graduate School, 870-972-3029, Fax: 870-972-3857, E-mail: sustich@astate.edu.

Arkansas Tech University, Graduate College, College of Arts and Humanities, Russellville, AR 72801. Offers communication (MLA); English (M Ed, MA); fine arts (MLA); history (MA); multi-media journalism (MA); psychology (MS); social science (MLA); Spanish (MA, MLA); teaching English as a second language (MA, MLA). Part-time programs available. *Students:* 39 full-time (30 women), 80 part-time (63 women); includes 11 minority (3 African Americans, 1 American Indian/Alaska Native, 1 Asian American or Pacific Islander, 6 Hispanic Americans), 23 international. Average age 33. In 2009, 70 master's awarded. *Degree requirements:* For master's, comprehensive exam (for some programs), thesis (for some programs), project. *Entrance requirements:* For master's, GRE General Test or MAT. Additional exam requirements/recommendations for international students: Required—TOEFL (minimum score 550 paper-based; 213 computer-based; 79 iBT), IELTS (minimum score 6). *Application deadline:* For fall admission, 3/1 priority date for domestic students, 5/1 priority date for international students; for spring admission, 10/1 priority date for domestic and international students. Applications are processed on a rolling basis. Application fee: $0 ($50 for international students). Electronic applications accepted. *Expenses:* Tuition, state resident: full-time $3438; part-time $191 per hour. Tuition, nonresident: full-time $6876; part-time $382 per hour. Required fees: $482; $9 per credit hour. $140 per semester. Tuition and fees vary according to course load. *Financial support:* In 2009–10, teaching assistantships with full tuition reimbursements (averaging $4,000 per year); research assistantships, career-related internships or fieldwork, Federal Work-Study, scholarships/grants, health care benefits, and unspecified assistantships also available. Support available to part-time students. Financial award application deadline: 4/15; financial award applicants required to submit FAFSA. *Unit head:* Dr. Micheal Tarver, Dean, 479-968-0274, Fax: 479-964-0812, E-mail: mtarver@atu.edu. *Application contact:* Dr. Mary B. Gunter, Dean of Graduate College, 479-968-0398, Fax: 479-964-0542, E-mail: graduate.school@atu.edu.

Arkansas Tech University, Graduate College, College of Education, Russellville, AR 72801. Offers college student personnel (MS); educational leadership (M Ed, Ed S); English education (M Ed); instructional improvement (M Ed); secondary education (M Ed); teaching, learning and leadership (M Ed). *Accreditation:* NCATE. Part-time and evening/weekend programs available. Postbaccalaureate distance learning degree programs offered (no on-campus study). *Students:* 39 full-time (26 women), 246 part-time (179 women); includes 27 minority (18 African Americans, 4 American Indian/Alaska Native, 5 Hispanic Americans), 4 international. Average age 33. In 2009, 92 master's, 11 other advanced degrees awarded. *Degree requirements:* For master's, comprehensive exam, thesis optional, action research project. *Entrance requirements:* For master's, GRE General Test or MAT. Additional exam requirements/recommendations for international students: Required—TOEFL (minimum score 550 paper-based; 213 computer-based; 79 iBT), IELTS (minimum score 6). *Application deadline:* For fall admission, 3/1 priority date for domestic students, 5/1 priority date for international students; for spring admission, 10/1 priority date for domestic and international students. Applications are processed on a rolling basis. Application fee: $0 ($50 for international students). Electronic applications accepted. *Expenses:* Tuition, state resident: full-time $3438; part-time $191 per hour. Tuition, nonresident: full-time $6876; part-time $382 per hour. Required fees: $482; $9 per credit hour. $140 per semester. Tuition and fees vary according to course load. *Financial support:* In 2009–10, teaching assistantships with full tuition reimbursements (averaging $4,000 per year); research assistantships, career-related internships or fieldwork, Federal Work-Study, scholarships/grants, health care benefits, and unspecified assistantships also available. Support available to part-time students. Financial award application deadline: 4/15; financial award applicants required to submit FAFSA. *Unit head:* Dr. Eldon G. Clary, Dean, 479-968-0350, Fax: 479-968-0350, E-mail: eclary@atu.edu. *Application contact:* Dr. Mary B. Gunter, Dean of Graduate College, 479-968-0398, Fax: 479-964-0542, E-mail: graduate.school@atu.edu.

Armstrong Atlantic State University, School of Graduate Studies, Program in Education, Savannah, GA 31419-1997. Offers adult education (M Ed); curriculum and instruction (M Ed); early childhood education (M Ed); education (M Ed); elementary education (M Ed); middle grades education (M Ed); secondary education (M Ed), including business education, English education, mathematics education, science education, social science education; special education (M Ed), including behavioral disorders, learning disabilities, speech-language pathology. *Accreditation:* NCATE. Part-time and evening/weekend programs available. Post-baccalaureate distance learning degree programs offered (minimal on-campus study). *Degree requirements:* For master's, comprehensive exam, portfolio. *Entrance requirements:* For master's, GRE General Test or MAT, minimum GPA of 2.5, letters of recommendation. Additional exam requirements/recommendations for international students: Required—TOEFL (minimum score 523 paper-based; 193 computer-based). Electronic applications accepted.

Auburn University, Graduate School, College of Education, Department of Curriculum and Teaching, Auburn University, AL 36849. Offers business education (M Ed, MS, PhD); early childhood education (M Ed, MS, PhD, Ed S); elementary education (M Ed, MS, PhD, Ed S); foreign languages (M Ed, MS); music education (M Ed, MS, PhD, Ed S); postsecondary education (PhD); reading education (PhD, Ed S); secondary education (M Ed, MS, PhD, Ed S), including English language arts, mathematics, science, social studies. *Accreditation:* NASM (one or more programs are accredited); NCATE. Part-time programs available. *Faculty:* 28 full-time (21 women), 8 part-time/adjunct (5 women). *Students:* 76 full-time (55 women), 186 part-time (139 women); includes 43 minority (29 African Americans, 1 American Indian/Alaska Native, 4 Asian Americans or Pacific Islanders, 9 Hispanic Americans), 4 international. Average age 33. 248 applicants, 65% accepted, 110 enrolled. In 2009, 102 master's, 12 doctorates, 6 other advanced degrees awarded. *Degree requirements:* For master's, thesis (for some programs); for doctorate, thesis/dissertation; for Ed S, field project. *Entrance requirements:* For master's, doctorate, and Ed S, GRE General Test. *Application deadline:* For fall admission, 7/7 for domestic students; for spring admission, 11/24 for domestic students. Applications are processed on a rolling basis. Application fee: $50 ($60 for international students). Electronic applications accepted. *Expenses:* Tuition, state resident: full-time $6240. Tuition, nonresident: full-time $18,720. International tuition: $18,938 full-time. Required fees: $492. Tuition and fees vary according to course load, program and reciprocity agreements. *Financial support:* Fellowships, teaching assistantships, career-related internships or fieldwork and Federal Work-Study available. Support available to part-time students. Financial award application deadline: 3/15; financial award applicants required to submit FAFSA. *Faculty research:* Emerging literacy, reading attitudes, music for at-risk youth, portfolio assessment. *Unit head:* Dr. Nancy H. Barry, Head, 334-844-4434. *Application contact:* Dr. George Flowers, Dean of the Graduate School, 334-844-2125.

Averett University, Master in Education Program, Danville, VA 24541-3692. Offers art education (M Ed); biology (M Ed); biology education (M Ed); chemistry (M Ed); chemistry education (M Ed); curriculum and instruction (M Ed); elementary education (M Ed); English (M Ed); English education (M Ed); health and physical education (M Ed); history and social studies education (M Ed); math (M Ed); mathematics education (M Ed); physical science (M Ed); reading specialization (M Ed); special education (learning disabilities specialization PK-12) (M Ed). Program also offered at Richmond, VA regional campus location. Part-time and evening/weekend programs available. *Faculty:* 4 full-time (3 women), 36 part-time/adjunct (22 women). *Students:* 182 full-time (160 women), 110 part-time (94 women); includes 113 minority (94 African Americans, 1 American Indian/Alaska Native, 7 Asian Americans or Pacific Islanders, 11 Hispanic Americans). Average age 37. 119 applicants, 99% accepted, 98 enrolled. In 2009, 92 master's awarded. *Degree requirements:* For master's, comprehensive exam, thesis optional. *Entrance requirements:* For master's, PRAXIS, GRE General Test, MAT or NTE, writing

proficiency exam, 3 letters of recommendation, current teacher's licensure or eligibility for licensure, minimum undergraduate GPA of 3.0 in previous 2 years. Additional exam requirements/recommendations for international students: Required—TOEFL (minimum score 600 paper-based; 200 computer-based). *Application deadline:* Applications are processed on a rolling basis. *Expenses:* Contact institution. *Financial support:* Career-related internships or fieldwork, Federal Work-Study, and scholarships/grants available. Financial award application deadline: 4/1; financial award applicants required to submit FAFSA. *Faculty research:* Literary assessment-PreK-6, handwriting instruction and assessment-PreK-6, written language instruction and assessment-PreK-6 and special needs students learning styles, curriculum and instruction processes. *Unit head:* Dr. Lynn H. Wolf, Chair/Associate Professor/Director, 434-793-3995, Fax: 434-791-4392, E-mail: lynn.wolf@averett.edu. *Application contact:* Dr. Lynn H. Wolf, Chair/Associate Professor/Director, 434-793-3995, Fax: 434-791-4392, E-mail: lynn.wolf@averett.edu.

Belmont University, College of Arts and Sciences, School of Education, Nashville, TN 37212-3757. Offers education (M Ed); elementary education (MAT), including early childhood education, elementary education, language arts education; English (MAT); history (MAT); mathematics (MAT); middle grade education (MAT); science (MAT); secondary education (MAT); special education (MAT); sports administration (MSA). *Accreditation:* NCATE. Part-time and evening/weekend programs available. *Degree requirements:* For master's, comprehensive exam, thesis, culminating portfolio. *Entrance requirements:* For master's, MAT or GRE and/or LSAT or GMAT, minimum GPA of 2.75. Additional exam requirements/recommendations for international students: Required—TOEFL. *Expenses:* Contact institution. *Faculty research:* Improving secondary literacy, Montessori, classroom management strategies, teacher residency programs, online professional development, mentoring, leadership, sociological issues in sport, faculty development, coaching.

Bennington College, Graduate Programs, MA in Teaching Program, Bennington, VT 05201. Offers art education (MAT); early childhood (MAT); elementary education (MAT); English education (MAT); foreign language education (MAT); k-12 education (MAT); mathematics education (MAT); music education (MAT); science education (MAT); secondary education (MAT); social studies education (MAT); theater arts (MAT). *Faculty:* 5 part-time/adjunct (3 women). *Students:* 8 full-time (5 women), 1 part-time (0 women). Average age 28. 11 applicants, 27% accepted, 1 enrolled. In 2009, 4 master's awarded. *Degree requirements:* For master's, comprehensive exam, 1 year teaching practicum, professional portfolio. *Entrance requirements:* For master's, interview. *Application deadline:* For fall admission, 3/1 for domestic students. Application fee: $60. *Expenses:* Contact institution. *Financial support:* In 2009–10, 6 students received support, including 4 fellowships (averaging $10,475 per year); scholarships/grants and unspecified assistantships also available. Financial award application deadline: 4/1; financial award applicants required to submit FAFSA. *Unit head:* Carol Meyer, Director of Programs in Teacher Education, 802-440-4375, E-mail: cmeyer@bennington.edu. *Application contact:* Nancy Pearlman, Assistant Director of Programs in Teacher Education, 802-440-4710, Fax: 802-440-4383, E-mail: npearlman@bennington.edu.

Bethel University, Program in Education, McKenzie, TN 38201. Offers administration and supervision (MA Ed); biology education K8-12 (MAT); elementary education (MAT); English education K8-12 (MAT); history education K8-12 (MAT); physical education K8-12 (MAT); special education K8-12 (MAT). Part-time and evening/weekend programs available. *Degree requirements:* For master's, thesis (for some programs). *Entrance requirements:* For master's, GRE General Test or MAT, minimum undergraduate GPA of 2.5.

Bob Jones University, Graduate Programs, Greenville, SC 29614. Offers accountancy (MS); Bible (MA); Bible translation (MA); Biblical studies (Certificate); broadcast management (MS); business administration (MBA); church history (MA, PhD); church ministries (MA); church music (MM); cinema and video production (MA); counseling (MS); curriculum and instruction (Ed D); divinity (M Div); dramatic production (MA); educational leadership (MS, Ed D, Ed S); elementary education (M Ed, MAT); English (M Ed, MA, MAT); fine arts (MA); graphic design (MA); history (M Ed, MA); illustration (MA); interpretative speech (MA); mathematics (M Ed, MAT); medical missions (Certificate); ministry (MM, D Min); multi-categorical special education (M Ed, MAT); music (M Ed); New Testament interpretation (PhD); Old Testament interpretation (PhD); orchestral instrument performance (MM); organ performance (MM); pastoral studies (MA); personnel services (MS, Ed S); piano pedagogy (MM); piano performance (MM); platform arts (MA); radio and television broadcasting (MS); rhetoric and public address (MA); secondary education (M Ed); studio art (MA); teaching Bible (MA); theology (MA, PhD); voice performance (MM); youth ministries (MA); M Div/MM.

Boston College, Lynch Graduate School of Education, Department of Teacher Education/Special Education and Curriculum and Instruction, Program in Secondary Education, Chestnut Hill, MA 02467-3800. Offers biology (MST); chemistry (MST); English (MAT); French (MAT); geology (MST); history (MAT); Latin and classical humanities (MAT); mathematics (MST); physics (MST); secondary teaching (M.Ed), including biology, chemistry, English, French, geology, history, Latin and classical humanities, mathematics, physics, Spanish; Spanish (MAT). *Accreditation:* Teacher Education Accreditation Council. Part-time and evening/weekend programs available. *Students:* 14 full-time (10 women), 68 part-time (37 women); includes 17 minority (9 African Americans, 3 Asian Americans or Pacific Islanders, 5 Hispanic Americans), 1 international. 252 applicants, 59% accepted, 47 enrolled. In 2009, 39 master's awarded. *Degree requirements:* For master's, comprehensive exam. *Entrance requirements:* For master's, GRE General Test or MAT. Additional exam requirements/recommendations for international students: Required—TOEFL (minimum score 550 paper-based; 213 computer-based; 81 iBT). *Application deadline:* For fall admission, 1/1 priority date for domestic students. Application fee: $60. Electronic applications accepted. *Financial support:* Fellowships with full and partial tuition reimbursements, research assistantships with full and partial tuition reimbursements, teaching assistantships with full and partial tuition reimbursements, career-related internships or fieldwork, Federal Work-Study, institutionally sponsored loans, scholarships/grants, traineeships, health care benefits, tuition waivers (full and partial), and unspecified assistantships available. Support available to part-time students. Financial award applicants required to submit FAFSA. *Faculty research:* School reform; urban science education; teacher research; critical literacy; poverty and achievement. *Unit head:* Dr. Maria E. Brisk, Chairperson, 617-552-4216, Fax: 617-552-0812, E-mail: brisk@bc.edu. *Application contact:* Adam Poluzzi, Director, Graduate Admission and Financial Aid, 617-552-4214, Fax: 617-552-0398, E-mail: poluzzi@bc.edu.

Boston University, School of Education, Department of Curriculum and Teaching, Programs in English and Language Arts Education, Boston, MA 02215. Offers Ed M, CAGS. *Degree requirements:* For master's, thesis optional; for CAGS, comprehensive exam. *Entrance requirements:* For master's and CAGS, GRE General Test or MAT. Additional exam requirements/recommendations for international students: Required—TOEFL. Electronic applications accepted. *Expenses:* Tuition: Full-time $37,910; part-time $1184 per credit hour. Required fees: $386; $40 per semester. Part-time tuition and fees vary according to class time, course level, degree level and program.

Brooklyn College of the City University of New York, Division of Graduate Studies, School of Education, Program in Adolescence Education and Special Subjects, Brooklyn, NY 11210-2889. Offers adolescence science education (MAT); art teacher (MA); biology teacher (MA); chemistry teacher (MA); earth science teacher (MAT); English teacher (MA); French teacher (MA); health and nutrition sciences: health teacher (MS Ed); mathematics teacher (MA); music education (CAS); music teacher (MA); physical education teacher (MS Ed); physics teacher (MA); social studies teacher (MA); Spanish teacher (MA). Part-time and evening/weekend programs available. *Students:* 23 full-time (15 women), 449 part-time (256 women); includes 147 minority (96 African Americans, 1 American Indian/Alaska Native, 18 Asian Americans or Pacific Islanders, 32 Hispanic Americans), 12 international. Average age 30. 251 applicants, 80% accepted, 141 enrolled. In 2009, 163 master's, 2 other advanced degrees awarded. *Degree requirements:* For master's, comprehensive exam (for some programs), thesis (for some programs). *Entrance requirements:* For master's, LAST, previous course work in education,

resume, 2 letters of recommendation, essay. Additional exam requirements/recommendations for international students: Required—TOEFL (minimum score 500 paper-based; 173 computer-based; 61 iBT). *Application deadline:* For fall admission, 7/15 for domestic students, 7/1 for international students; for spring admission, 11/15 for domestic students, 10/1 for international students. Applications are processed on a rolling basis. Application fee: $125. Electronic applications accepted. *Expenses:* Tuition, state resident: full-time $7360; part-time $310 per credit hour. Tuition, nonresident: full-time $13,800; part-time $575 per credit hour. Required fees: $140.10 per semester. *Financial support:* Career-related internships or fieldwork, Federal Work-Study, institutionally sponsored loans, and scholarships/grants available. Support available to part-time students. Financial award application deadline: 5/1; financial award applicants required to submit FAFSA. *Faculty research:* Interdisciplinary education, semiotics, discourse analysis, autobiography, teacher identity. *Unit head:* Prof. Stephen Phillips, Program Head, 718-951-5214, E-mail: phillips@brooklyn.cuny.edu. *Application contact:* Hernan Sierra, Graduate Admissions Coordinator, 718-951-4536, Fax: 718-951-4506, E-mail: grads@brooklyn.cuny.edu.

Brown University, Graduate School, Department of Education, Program in Teaching, Providence, RI 02912. Offers biology (MAT); elementary education (MAT); English (MAT); history/social studies (MAT). *Faculty:* 4 full-time (3 women), 6 part-time/adjunct (all women). *Students:* 27 full-time (21 women); includes 3 minority (2 African Americans, 1 Asian American or Pacific Islander). Average age 26. 94 applicants, 62% accepted, 27 enrolled. In 2009, 21 master's awarded. *Degree requirements:* For master's, student teaching, portfolio. *Entrance requirements:* For master's, GRE General Test, transcript, personal statement, letters of recommendation, interview, writing sample (English applicants only). Additional exam requirements/recommendations for international students: Required—TOEFL (minimum score 577 paper-based; 90 computer-based). *Application deadline:* For winter admission, 1/15 for domestic students. Application fee: $75. Electronic applications accepted. *Financial support:* In 2009-10, 23 students received support, including 4 fellowships; Federal Work-Study, institutionally sponsored loans, scholarships/grants, tuition waivers (partial), and proctorships also available. Financial award application deadline: 2/1; financial award applicants required to submit FAFSA. *Faculty research:* Literacy, biodiversity, English language learners, diversity, special education. *Unit head:* Laura Snyder, Director of Graduate Study for the MAT. *Application contact:* Carin Algava, Assistant Director, 401-863-3364, Fax: 401-863-1276, E-mail: carin_algava@brown.edu.

Buffalo State College, State University of New York, The Graduate School, Faculty of Arts and Humanities, Department of English, Buffalo, NY 14222-1095. Offers English (MA); secondary education (MS Ed), including English. Part-time and evening/weekend programs available. *Degree requirements:* For master's, thesis or project, 1 foreign language (MS Ed). *Entrance requirements:* For master's, minimum GPA of 2.75, 36 hours in English, New York teaching certificate (MS Ed). Additional exam requirements/recommendations for international students: Required—TOEFL (minimum score 550 paper-based; 213 computer-based).

California Baptist University, Program in English, Riverside, CA 92504-3206. Offers English pedagogy (MA); literature (MA); teaching English as a second language (TESOL) (MA). Part-time programs available. *Faculty:* 4 full-time (3 women). *Students:* 3 full-time (all women), 29 part-time (21 women); includes 3 minority (1 African American, 1 Asian American or Pacific Islander, 1 Hispanic American), 5 international. 51 applicants, 55% accepted, 12 enrolled. In 2009, 3 master's awarded. *Degree requirements:* For master's, thesis (for some programs). *Entrance requirements:* For master's, minimum undergraduate GPA of 2.75, 18 semester hours of course work in English beyond freshman level. Additional exam requirements/recommendations for international students: Required—TOEFL (minimum score 575 paper-based; 230 computer-based; 89 iBT). *Application deadline:* For fall admission, 8/1 priority date for domestic students, 7/1 for international students; for spring admission, 12/1 priority date for domestic students, 10/15 for international students. Applications are processed on a rolling basis. Application fee: $45. Electronic applications accepted. *Expenses:* Tuition: Full-time $8352; part-time $464 per semester hour. Required fees: $125 per semester. Tuition and fees vary according to course load, campus/location and program. *Financial support:* Federal Work-Study and scholarships/grants available. Support available to part-time students. Financial award applicants required to submit FAFSA. *Unit head:* Dr. Jennifer Newton, Director, 951-343-4276, Fax: 951-343-4661, E-mail: jnewton@calbaptist.edu. *Application contact:* Gail Ronveaux, Dean of Graduate Enrollment, 951-343-5045, Fax: 951-343-5095, E-mail: graduateadmissions@calbaptist.edu.

California State University, Northridge, Graduate Studies, College of Education, Department of Secondary Education, Northridge, CA 91330. Offers educational technology (MA); English education (MA); mathematics education (MA); secondary science education (MA); teaching and learning (MA). *Accreditation:* NCATE. Part-time programs available. *Faculty:* 13 full-time (7 women), 41 part-time/adjunct (20 women). *Students:* 10 full-time (6 women), 99 part-time (65 women); includes 40 minority (6 African Americans, 2 American Indian/Alaska Native, 13 Asian Americans or Pacific Islanders, 19 Hispanic Americans). Average age 34. 86 applicants, 60% accepted, 40 enrolled. *Degree requirements:* For master's, thesis optional. *Entrance requirements:* For master's, GRE General Test or minimum GPA of 3.0. Additional exam requirements/recommendations for international students: Required—TOEFL. *Application deadline:* For fall admission, 11/30 for domestic students. Application fee: $55. *Financial support:* Application deadline: 3/1. *Unit head:* Dr. Bonnie Ericson, Chair, 818-677-2580. *Application contact:* Dr. Michael Rivas, Graduate Advisor, 818-677-6792, E-mail: michael.rivas@csun.edu.

California State University, San Bernardino, Graduate Studies, College of Education, San Bernardino, CA 92407-2397. Offers bilingual/cross-cultural education (MA); curriculum and instruction (MA); educational administration (MA); educational leadership and curriculum (Ed D); educational psychology and counseling (MA, MS), including correctional and alternative education (MA), counseling and guidance (MS), rehabilitation counseling (MA); elementary education (MA); English as a second language (MA); environmental education (MA); general education (MA); history and English for secondary teachers (MA); instructional technology (MA); reading (MA); secondary education (MA); special education and rehabilitation counseling (MA), including rehabilitation counseling, special education; teaching of science (MA); vocational and career education (MA). *Accreditation:* NCATE. Part-time and evening/weekend programs available. *Faculty:* 35 full-time (15 women), 24 part-time/adjunct (15 women). *Students:* 921 full-time (710 women), 716 part-time (490 women); includes 751 minority (137 African Americans, 12 American Indian/Alaska Native, 73 Asian Americans or Pacific Islanders, 529 Hispanic Americans), 18 international. Average age 36. 493 applicants, 86% accepted, 243 enrolled. In 2009, 370 master's awarded. *Degree requirements:* For master's, comprehensive exam (for some programs), thesis (for some programs), advancement to candidacy. *Entrance requirements:* For master's, minimum GPA of 3.0 in education. *Application deadline:* For fall admission, 8/31 priority date for domestic students. Application fee: $55. *Financial support:* Career-related internships or fieldwork and Federal Work-Study available. Support available to part-time students. *Faculty research:* Multicultural education, brain-based learning, science education, social studies/global education. *Unit head:* Dr. Patricia Arlin, Dean, 909-537-5600, Fax: 909-537-7011, E-mail: parlin@csusb.edu. *Application contact:* Olivia Rosas, Director of Admissions, 909-537-7577, Fax: 909-537-7034, E-mail: orosas@csusb.edu.

Campbell University, Graduate and Professional Programs, School of Education, Buies Creek, NC 27506. Offers administration (MSA); community counseling (MA); elementary education (M Ed); English education (M Ed); interdisciplinary studies (M Ed); mathematics education (M Ed); middle grades education (M Ed); physical education (M Ed); school counseling (M Ed); secondary education (M Ed); social science education (M Ed). *Accreditation:* NCATE. Part-time and evening/weekend programs available. *Degree requirements:* For master's, comprehensive exam. *Entrance requirements:* For master's, GRE General Test, minimum GPA of 2.7. *Faculty research:* Spiritual values and wellness issues in counseling, stress and professional burnout among counselors, thinking strategies, leadership, adaptive technology.

Caribbean University, Graduate School, Bayamón, PR 00960-0493. Offers administration and supervision (MA Ed); criminal justice (MA); curriculum and instruction (MA Ed), including

elementary education, English education, history education, mathematics education, primary education, science education, Spanish education; education (PhD); gerontology (MSN); human resources (MBA); museology, archiving and art history (MA Ed); neonatal pediatrics (MSN); physical education (MA Ed); special education (MA Ed). *Entrance requirements:* For master's, interview, minimum GPA of 2.5.

Carthage College, Division of Teacher Education, Kenosha, WI 53140. Offers classroom guidance and counseling (M Ed); creative arts (M Ed); gifted and talented children (M Ed); language arts (M Ed); modern language (M Ed); natural sciences (M Ed); reading (M Ed, Certificate); social sciences (M Ed); teacher leadership (M Ed). Part-time and evening/weekend programs available. *Degree requirements:* For master's, thesis optional. *Entrance requirements:* For master's, MAT, minimum B average, letters of reference.

Chadron State College, School of Professional and Graduate Studies, Department of Education, Chadron, NE 69337. Offers business (MA Ed); community counseling (MA Ed); educational administration (MS Ed, Sp Ed); elementary education (MS Ed); history (MA Ed); language and literature (MA Ed); secondary administration (MS Ed); secondary education (MS Ed). *Accreditation:* NCATE. Part-time and evening/weekend programs available. Postbaccalaureate distance learning degree programs offered. *Degree requirements:* For master's, thesis optional. *Entrance requirements:* For master's, GRE General Test, GRE Writing Test, minimum GPA of 2.75 or 12 graduate hours at CSC with minimum GPA of 3.25. Additional exam requirements/recommendations for international students: Required—TOEFL. Electronic applications accepted. *Faculty research:* Rural education, technology, mental health.

Chatham University, Program in Education, Pittsburgh, PA 15232-2826. Offers early childhood education (MAT); elementary education (MAT); English—secondary (MAT); environmental education (K-12) (MAT); secondary art (MAT); secondary biology education (MAT); secondary chemistry education (MAT); secondary English education (MAT); secondary math education (MAT); secondary physics education (MAT); secondary social studies education (MAT); special education (MAT). *Students:* 52 full-time (41 women), 20 part-time (16 women). Average age 30. 39 applicants, 79% accepted, 26 enrolled. In 2009, 37 master's awarded. *Degree requirements:* For master's, thesis, teaching experience. *Entrance requirements:* For master's, PRAXIS I, minimum GPA of 3.0, sample of written work, recommendation letters. Additional exam requirements/recommendations for international students: Required—TOEFL (minimum score 600 paper-based; 250 computer-based; 100 iBT), IELTS (minimum score 6.5), TWE. *Application deadline:* For fall admission, 5/1 priority date for domestic and international students; for spring admission, 10/15 priority date for domestic and international students. Applications are processed on a rolling basis. Application fee: $45. Electronic applications accepted. *Financial support:* Career-related internships or fieldwork available. Financial award applicants required to submit FAFSA. *Faculty research:* Gifted education, environmental education, technology in education, writing as learning, class size and achievement. *Unit head:* Dr. Barbara Biglan, Interim Director, 412-365-1170, E-mail: biglan@chatham.edu. *Application contact:* Dory Perry, Associate Director of Graduate Admissions, 412-365-2758, Fax: 412-365-1609, E-mail: gradadmissions@chatham.edu.

Christopher Newport University, Graduate Studies, Department of Teacher Preparation, Newport News, VA 23606-2998. Offers art (PK-12) (MAT); biology (6-12) (MAT); computer science (6-12) (MAT); elementary (PK-6) (MAT); English (6-12) (MAT); French (PK-12) (MAT); history and social science (6-12) (MAT); mathematics (6-12) (MAT); music (PK-12) (MAT), including choral, instrumental; physics (6-12) (MAT); Spanish (PK-12) (MAT). Part-time and evening/weekend programs available. *Faculty:* 24 full-time (13 women), 4 part-time/adjunct (2 women). *Students:* 76 full-time (66 women), 12 part-time (10 women); includes 3 minority (2 African Americans, 1 Hispanic American). Average age 24. 3 applicants, 100% accepted, 2 enrolled. In 2009, 58 master's awarded. *Degree requirements:* For master's, comprehensive exam, thesis or alternative. *Entrance requirements:* For master's, PRAXIS I, minimum GPA of 3.0. Additional exam requirements/recommendations for international students: Required—TOEFL (minimum score 580 paper-based; 237 computer-based; 92 iBT). *Application deadline:* For fall admission, 8/15 for domestic students, 4/1 for international students; for spring admission, 10/15 for domestic students, 10/1 for international students. Applications are processed on a rolling basis. Application fee: $45. Electronic applications accepted. *Expenses:* Tuition, area resident: Part-time $384 per credit hour. Tuition, state resident: part-time $384 per credit hour. Tuition, nonresident: part-time $701 per credit hour. *Financial support:* In 2009-10, 3 research assistantships with full and partial tuition reimbursements (averaging $2,000 per year) were awarded; career-related internships or fieldwork, Federal Work-Study, and unspecified assistantships also available. Support available to part-time students. Financial award application deadline: 3/1; financial award applicants required to submit FAFSA. *Faculty research:* Early literacy development, instructional innovations, professional teaching standards, multicultural issues, aesthetic education. *Unit head:* Dr. Marsha Sprague, Director, 757-594-7388, Fax: 757-594-7803, E-mail: msprague@cnu.edu. *Application contact:* Lyn Sawyer, Associate Director, Graduate Admissions, 757-594-7544, Fax: 757-594-7649, E-mail: gradstdy@cnu.edu.

The Citadel, The Military College of South Carolina, Citadel Graduate College, School of Education, Program in Secondary Education, Charleston, SC 29409. Offers biology (MAT); English language arts (MAT); mathematics (MAT); social studies (MAT). *Accreditation:* NCATE. Part-time and evening/weekend programs available. *Faculty:* 12 full-time (7 women), 8 part-time/adjunct (5 women). *Students:* 27 full-time (18 women), 62 part-time (37 women); includes 15 minority (11 African Americans, 2 Asian Americans or Pacific Islanders, 2 Hispanic Americans). Average age 29. In 2009, 22 master's awarded. *Degree requirements:* For master's, comprehensive exam, internship. *Entrance requirements:* For master's, GRE (minimum score 900) or MAT (minimum score 396), minimum undergraduate GPA of 2.5. Additional exam requirements/recommendations for international students: Required—TOEFL (minimum score 550 paper-based; 213 computer-based). *Application deadline:* Applications are processed on a rolling basis. Application fee: $30. Electronic applications accepted. *Expenses:* Tuition, state resident: part-time $400 per credit hour. Tuition, nonresident: part-time $657 per credit hour. Required fees: $40 per term. *Financial support:* Career-related internships or fieldwork, health care benefits, and unspecified assistantships available. Support available to part-time students. Financial award application deadline: 7/1; financial award applicants required to submit FAFSA. *Unit head:* Dr. Kathryn A. Richardson-Jones, Coordinator, 843-953-3163, Fax: 843-953-7258, E-mail: kathryn.jones@citadel.edu. *Application contact:* Dr. Steve A. Nida, Associate Provost, The Citadel Graduate College, 843-953-5089, Fax: 843-953-7630, E-mail: cgc@citadel.edu.

City College of the City University of New York, Graduate School, School of Education, Department of Secondary Education, New York, NY 10031-9198. Offers adolescent mathematics education (MA, AC); English education (MA); middle school mathematics education (MS); science education (MA); social studies education (AC). *Accreditation:* NCATE. *Entrance requirements:* For master's, Liberal Arts and Sciences Test (LAST), Content Specialty Test (CST). Additional exam requirements/recommendations for international students: Required—TOEFL. *Expenses:* Tuition, state resident: part-time $310 per credit. Tuition, nonresident: part-time $575 per credit. Tuition and fees vary according to course load and program.

Clarion University of Pennsylvania, Office of Research and Graduate Studies, College of Education and Human Services, Department of Education, Program in Education, Clarion, PA 16214. Offers curriculum and instruction (M Ed); early childhood (M Ed); English (M Ed); history (M Ed); literacy (M Ed); science (M Ed); technology (M Ed). *Accreditation:* NCATE. Part-time programs available. *Degree requirements:* For master's, comprehensive exam, thesis or alternative. *Entrance requirements:* For master's, minimum QPA of 3.0, teacher certification. Additional exam requirements/recommendations for international students: Required—TOEFL (minimum score 550 paper-based; 213 computer-based; 80 iBT). Electronic applications accepted.

Clayton State University, School of Graduate Studies, Program in Education, Morrow, GA 30260-0285. Offers English (MAT); mathematics (MAT). *Accreditation:* NCATE. *Students:* 6 full-time (3 women), 2 part-time (1 woman); includes 2 African Americans, 1 international. Average age 24. 16 applicants, 56% accepted, 7 enrolled. *Application deadline:* For fall admission, 7/15 for domestic students, 5/1 for international students; for spring admission,

English Education

Clayton State University (continued)

4/15 for domestic students, 2/1 for international students. Application fee: $50. *Unit head:* Dr. Ruth Caillouet, Program Coordinator, Master of Arts in Teaching English, 678-466-4735, Fax: 678-466-4899, E-mail: ruthcaillouet@clayton.edu. *Application contact:* Melanie Nolan, Administrative Assistant, Master of Arts in Teaching English, 678-466-4735, Fax: 678-466-4899, E-mail: melanienolan@clayton.edu.

Clemson University, Graduate School, College of Health, Education, and Human Development, School of Education, Program in Secondary Education, Clemson, SC 29634. Offers English (M Ed); mathematics (M Ed); natural sciences (M Ed); social studies (M Ed). *Accreditation:* NCATE. *Students:* 5 full-time (3 women), 4 part-time (2 women); includes 2 minority (1 Asian American or Pacific Islander, 1 Hispanic American), 2 international. Average age 29. 11 applicants, 82% accepted, 4 enrolled. In 2009, 2 master's awarded. *Entrance requirements:* For master's, GRE General Test, teaching certificate. Additional exam requirements/recommendations for international students: Required—TOEFL. *Application deadline:* Applications are processed on a rolling basis. Application fee: $70 ($80 for international students). Electronic applications accepted. *Expenses:* Contact institution. *Financial support:* In 2009–10, 2 students received support. Career-related internships or fieldwork, institutionally sponsored loans, scholarships/grants, health care benefits, and unspecified assistantships available. Support available to part-time students. Financial award application deadline: 6/1; financial award applicants required to submit FAFSA. *Unit head:* Dr. Michael J. Padilla, Director/Associate Dean, 864-656-4444, Fax: 864-656-0311, E-mail: padilla@clemson.edu. *Application contact:* Dr. David Fleming, Graduate Coordinator, 864-656-1881, Fax: 864-656-0311, E-mail: dflemin@clemson.edu.

The College at Brockport, State University of New York, School of Education and Human Services, Department of Education and Human Development, Program in Adolescence Education, Brockport, NY 14420-2997. Offers adolescence biology education (MS Ed); adolescence chemistry education (MS Ed); adolescence earth science education (MS Ed); adolescence English education (MS Ed); adolescence mathematics education (MS Ed); adolescence physics education (MS Ed); adolescence social studies education (MS Ed). *Accreditation:* NCATE. Part-time programs available. *Students:* 10 full-time (6 women), 98 part-time (60 women); includes 1 minority (African American). 15 applicants, 67% accepted, 8 enrolled. In 2009, 60 master's awarded. *Degree requirements:* For master's, thesis or alternative. *Entrance requirements:* For master's, minimum GPA of 3.0, letters of recommendation. Additional exam requirements/recommendations for international students: Required—TOEFL (minimum score 550 paper-based; 213 computer-based; 79 iBT). *Application deadline:* For fall admission, 2/15 priority date for domestic and international students; for spring admission, 9/15 priority date for domestic and international students. Application fee: $80. Electronic applications accepted. *Expenses:* Tuition, state resident: full-time $8370; part-time $349 per credit. Tuition, nonresident: full-time $13,250; part-time $522 per credit. *Financial support:* Federal Work-Study, scholarships/grants, and unspecified assistantships available. Support available to part-time students. Financial award application deadline: 3/15; financial award applicants required to submit FAFSA. *Unit head:* Dr. Sue Novinger, Chairperson, 585-395-2205, Fax: 585-395-2172, E-mail: snovinge@brockport.edu. *Application contact:* Coordinator of Certification and Graduate Advisement.

The College at Brockport, State University of New York, School of Education and Human Services, Department of Education and Human Development, Program in Alternate Adolescence Inclusive Education, Brockport, NY 14420-2997. Offers alternate adolescence English inclusive education (MS Ed); alternate adolescence mathematics inclusive education (MS Ed); alternate adolescence science inclusive education (MS Ed); alternate adolescence social studies inclusive education (MS Ed). *Students:* 25 full-time (8 women), 5 part-time (3 women). 26 applicants, 50% accepted, 11 enrolled. *Degree requirements:* For master's, thesis or alternative. *Entrance requirements:* For master's, minimum GPA of 3.0, letters of recommendation, statement of objectives, academic major (or equivalent) in program discipline. Additional exam requirements/recommendations for international students: Required—TOEFL (minimum score 550 paper-based; 213 computer-based; 79 iBT). *Application deadline:* For fall admission, 2/15 priority date for domestic and international students; for spring admission, 9/15 priority date for domestic and international students. Application fee: $80. Electronic applications accepted. *Expenses:* Tuition, state resident: full-time $8370; part-time $349 per credit. Tuition, nonresident: full-time $13,250; part-time $522 per credit. *Financial support:* Federal Work-Study, scholarships/grants, and unspecified assistantships available. Support available to part-time students. Financial award application deadline: 3/15; financial award applicants required to submit FAFSA. *Unit head:* Dr. Sue Novinger, Chairperson, 585-395-2205, E-mail: snovinge@brockport.edu. *Application contact:* Coordinator of Certification and Graduate Advisement.

College of St. Joseph, Graduate Programs, Division of Education, Program in Secondary Education, Rutland, VT 05701-3899. Offers English (M Ed); social studies (M Ed). Part-time and evening/weekend programs available. *Entrance requirements:* For master's, PRAXIS I, 2 letters of recommendation, minimum GPA of 3.0, interview. Electronic applications accepted. *Expenses:* Tuition: Full-time $13,500; part-time $350 per credit. Required fees: $45 per term. One-time fee: $445. Tuition and fees vary according to program.

The College of William and Mary, School of Education, Program in Curriculum and Instruction, Williamsburg, VA 23187-8795. Offers elementary education (MA Ed); gifted education (MA Ed); math specialist (MA Ed); reading education (MA Ed); secondary education (MA Ed), including English education, mathematics education, modern foreign languages education, science education, social studies education; special education (MA Ed), including general curriculum, resource collaborating teaching. *Accreditation:* NCATE. Part-time programs available. *Faculty:* 18 full-time (12 women), 17 part-time/adjunct (15 women). *Students:* 54 full-time (45 women), 12 part-time (all women); includes 3 minority (2 African Americans, 1 Asian American or Pacific Islander), 2 international. Average age 27. 120 applicants, 75% accepted. In 2009, 70 master's awarded. *Degree requirements:* For master's, project. *Entrance requirements:* For master's, GRE or MAT, minimum GPA of 2.5. Additional exam requirements/recommendations for international students: Required—TOEFL. *Application deadline:* For fall admission, 1/15 for domestic and international students; for spring admission, 10/1 for domestic and international students. Application fee: $45. Electronic applications accepted. *Expenses:* Tuition, state resident: full-time $6400; part-time $315 per credit hour. Tuition, nonresident: full-time $19,720; part-time $840 per credit hour. Required fees: $4114. *Financial support:* In 2009–10, 30 students received support, including 10 research assistantships with full and partial tuition reimbursements available (averaging $5,500 per year); career-related internships or fieldwork, Federal Work-Study, institutionally sponsored loans, scholarships/grants, and unspecified assistantships also available. Financial award application deadline: 1/15; financial award applicants required to submit FAFSA. *Faculty research:* National Council of Teachers of Mathematics Standards, counseling, self-concept and self-esteem, special education, curriculum development. *Unit head:* Dr. C. Denise Johnson, Area Coordinator, 757-221-1528, E-mail: cdjohn@wm.edu. *Application contact:* Dorothy Smith Osborne, Director of Admissions, 757-221-2317, Fax: 757-221-2293, E-mail: dsosbo@wm.edu.

The Colorado College, Department of Education, Program in Secondary Education, Colorado Springs, CO 80903-3294. Offers art teaching (K-12) (MAT); English teaching (MAT); foreign language teaching (MAT); mathematics teaching (MAT); music teaching (MAT); science teaching (MAT); social studies teaching (MAT). *Faculty:* 3 full-time (2 women), 8 part-time/adjunct (6 women). *Students:* 15 full-time (5 women); includes 2 minority (1 American Indian/Alaska Native, 1 Asian American or Pacific Islander). Average age 27. 26 applicants, 81% accepted, 15 enrolled. In 2009, 17 master's awarded. *Degree requirements:* For master's, thesis, internship. *Entrance requirements:* For master's, PRAXIS II or PLACE Exam. *Application deadline:* For fall admission, 12/1 priority date for domestic students, 12/1 for international students. Applications are processed on a rolling basis. Application fee: $50. *Expenses:* Tuition: Part-time $2545 per credit. *Financial support:* In 2009–10, 15 students received support, including 7 teaching assistantships (averaging $16,000 per year); career-related internships or fieldwork, institutionally sponsored loans, health care benefits, and tuition waivers (partial) also available. Financial award application deadline: 2/15; financial award applicants required to submit FAFSA. *Unit head:* Mike Taber, Director, 719-389-6026, Fax: 719-389-6473, E-mail: mike.taber@coloradocollege.edu. *Application contact:* Debra Yazulla Mortenson, Education Services Manager, 719-389-6472, Fax: 719-389-6473, E-mail: debra.mortenson@coloradocollege.edu.

Columbia College Chicago, Graduate School, Department of Educational Studies, Chicago, IL 60605-1996. Offers elementary education (MAT); English (MAT); interdisciplinary arts (MAT); multicultural education (MA); urban teaching (MA). Part-time and evening/weekend programs available. *Degree requirements:* For master's, thesis, student teaching experience, 100 pre-clinical hours. *Entrance requirements:* For master's, supplemental recommendation form. Additional exam requirements/recommendations for international students: Required—TOEFL (minimum score 550 paper-based; 213 computer-based). Electronic applications accepted. *Expenses:* Tuition: Part-time $651 per credit hour. Required fees: $205 per semester. One-time fee: $285 part-time. Tuition and fees vary according to program.

Columbus State University, Graduate Studies, College of Education and Health Professions, Department of Teacher Education, Columbus, GA 31907-5645. Offers accomplished teaching (M Ed); early childhood education (M Ed, Ed S); health administration (MPA); instructional technology (MS); middle grades education (M Ed, Ed S); physical education (M Ed); secondary education (M Ed, MAT, Ed S), including English/language arts (M Ed, Ed S), general science (M Ed), mathematics (M Ed), social science (M Ed); special education (M Ed), including behavior disorders, mental retardation. *Accreditation:* NCATE. Part-time and evening/weekend programs available. Postbaccalaureate distance learning degree programs offered (minimal on-campus study). *Faculty:* 18 full-time (15 women), 14 part-time/adjunct (10 women). *Students:* 146 full-time (113 women), 312 part-time (261 women); includes 142 minority (120 African Americans, 1 American Indian/Alaska Native, 8 Asian Americans or Pacific Islanders, 13 Hispanic Americans), 2 international. Average age 31. 248 applicants, 64% accepted, 114 enrolled. In 2009, 103 master's, 22 other advanced degrees awarded. *Degree requirements:* For master's, thesis, exit exam; for Ed S, thesis or alternative. *Entrance requirements:* For master's, GRE General Test, minimum GPA of 2.75; for Ed S, GRE General Test. Additional exam requirements/recommendations for international students: Required—TOEFL (minimum score 550 paper-based; 213 computer-based; 79 iBT). *Application deadline:* For fall admission, 5/1 priority date for domestic students, 5/1 for international students; for spring admission, 11/1 for domestic and international students. Applications are processed on a rolling basis. Application fee: $30. Electronic applications accepted. *Financial support:* In 2009–10, 305 students received support, including 36 research assistantships with partial tuition reimbursements available (averaging $3,000 per year); career-related internships or fieldwork, Federal Work-Study, institutionally sponsored loans, scholarships/grants, tuition waivers (partial), and unspecified assistantships also available. Support available to part-time students. Financial award application deadline: 5/1; financial award applicants required to submit FAFSA. *Unit head:* Dr. Deborah Gober, Acting Chair, 706-568-2255, Fax: 706-568-3134, E-mail: gober_deborah@colstate.edu. *Application contact:* Katie Thornton, Graduate Admissions Specialist, 706-568-2035, Fax: 706-568-2462, E-mail: thornton_katie@colstate.edu.

Converse College, School of Education and Graduate Studies, Program in Secondary Education, Spartanburg, SC 29302-0006. Offers biology (MAT); chemistry (MAT); English (M Ed, MAT); mathematics (M Ed, MAT); natural sciences (M Ed); social sciences (M Ed, MAT). Part-time programs available. *Degree requirements:* For master's, capstone paper. *Entrance requirements:* For master's, NTE or PRAXIS II (M Ed), minimum GPA of 2.75, 2 recommendations. Electronic applications accepted.

Delta State University, Graduate Programs, College of Arts and Sciences, Division of Languages and Literature, Cleveland, MS 38733-0001. Offers English education (M Ed). Part-time programs available. *Degree requirements:* For master's, thesis or alternative. *Expenses:* Tuition, state resident: full-time $4450; part-time $247 per credit hour. Tuition, nonresident: full-time $11,520; part-time $640 per credit hour.

Duquesne University, School of Education, Department of Instruction and Leadership, Program in Secondary Education, Pittsburgh, PA 15282-0001. Offers secondary education (MS Ed), including biology, chemistry, English, Latin, math, physics, social studies, Spanish. Part-time and evening/weekend programs available. *Faculty:* 4 full-time (3 women), 1 part-time/adjunct (0 women). *Students:* 56 full-time (34 women), 8 part-time (3 women); includes 6 minority (3 African Americans, 2 Asian Americans or Pacific Islanders, 1 Hispanic American), 2 international. Average age 29. 69 applicants, 70% accepted, 27 enrolled. In 2009, 36 master's awarded. *Degree requirements:* For master's, thesis optional. *Entrance requirements:* For master's, MAT, minimum GPA of 3.0. Additional exam requirements/recommendations for international students: Required—TOEFL (minimum score 550 paper-based; 80 computer-based). *Application deadline:* For fall admission, 8/1 for domestic students; for spring admission, 12/1 for domestic students. Applications are processed on a rolling basis. Application fee: $0. Electronic applications accepted. *Expenses:* Tuition: Part-time $851 per credit. Required fees: $81 per credit. *Financial support:* Research assistantships, Federal Work-Study available. Support available to part-time students. *Unit head:* Dr. Melissa Boston, Assistant Professor, 412-396-6109, E-mail: bostonm@duq.edu. *Application contact:* Michael Dolinger, Director of Student and Academic Services, 412-396-6647, Fax: 412-396-5585, E-mail: dolingerm@duq.edu.

East Carolina University, Graduate School, College of Education, Department of Curriculum and Instruction, Greenville, NC 27858-4353. Offers behavior/emotional disabilities (MA Ed); elementary education (MA Ed); English education (MA Ed); learning disabilities (MA Ed); low incidence disabilities (MA Ed); mental retardation (MA Ed); middle grade education (MA Ed); reading education (MA Ed); social studies education (MA Ed). Part-time programs available. Postbaccalaureate distance learning degree programs offered. *Degree requirements:* For master's, comprehensive exam, thesis optional. *Entrance requirements:* For master's, GRE General Test or MAT, interview, bachelor's degree in related field, minimum GPA of 2.5, teaching license. Additional exam requirements/recommendations for international students: Required—TOEFL.

Eastern Kentucky University, The Graduate School, College of Education, Department of Curriculum and Instruction, Program in Secondary and Higher Education, Richmond, KY 40475-3102. Offers secondary education (MA Ed), including agricultural education, art education, biological sciences education, business education, English education, geography education, history education, home economics education, industrial education, mathematical sciences education, physical education, school health education. *Accreditation:* NCATE. Part-time programs available. *Entrance requirements:* For master's, GRE General Test, minimum GPA of 2.5.

Eastern Michigan University, Graduate School, College of Arts and Sciences, Department of English Language and Literature, Program in English Studies for Teachers, Ypsilanti, MI 48197. Offers MA. Part-time and evening/weekend programs available. *Students:* 14 part-time (9 women). Average age 32. *Entrance requirements:* Additional exam requirements/recommendations for international students: Required—TOEFL. Tuition and fees vary according to course level. *Financial support:* Research assistantships with full tuition reimbursements, teaching assistantships with full tuition reimbursements, career-related internships or fieldwork, Federal Work-Study, institutionally sponsored loans, scholarships/grants, and unspecified assistantships available. Support available to part-time students. *Unit head:* Dr. Rebecca Sipes, Department Head, 734-487-4220, Fax: 734-487-9744. *Application contact:* Prof. Cathy Fleischer, Advisor, 734-487-0151, Fax: 734-487-9744, E-mail: cathy.fleischer@emich.edu.

Eastern Michigan University, Graduate School, College of Arts and Sciences, Department of English Language and Literature, Program in Teaching of Writing, Ypsilanti, MI 48197. Offers MA, Graduate Certificate. *Students:* 1 (woman) full-time. Average age 29. In 2009, 2 other advanced degrees awarded. Application fee: $35. Tuition and fees vary according to course level. *Unit head:* Dr. Rebecca Sipe, Department Head, 734-487-4220, Fax: 734-483-9744, E-mail: rebecca.sipe@emich.edu. *Application contact:* Dr. Cheryl Cassidy, Program Advisor, 734-487-0150, Fax: 734-483-9744, E-mail: cheryl.cassidy@emich.edu.

Elms College, Division of Education, Chicopee, MA 01013-2839. Offers early childhood education (MAT); education (M Ed, CAGS); elementary education (MAT); English as a second language (MAT); reading (MAT); secondary education (MAT), including biology education, English education, Spanish education; special education (MAT). Part-time and evening/weekend programs available. *Faculty:* 12 full-time (8 women), 4 part-time/adjunct (2 women). *Students:* 17 full-time (14 women), 153 part-time (136 women); includes 5 minority (1 American Indian/Alaska Native, 4 Hispanic Americans). Average age 36. 43 applicants, 88% accepted, 37 enrolled. In 2009, 23 master's, 8 other advanced degrees awarded. *Degree requirements:* For master's, thesis (for some programs). *Entrance requirements:* For master's, Massachusetts Educators Certification Test, minimum GPA of 3.0; for CAGS, master's degree in education. Additional exam requirements/recommendations for international students: Required—TOEFL. *Application deadline:* For fall admission, 7/1 priority date for domestic students; for spring admission, 11/1 priority date for domestic students. Applications are processed on a rolling basis. Application fee: $30. *Financial support:* In 2009–10, 2 teaching assistantships with partial tuition reimbursements were awarded; tuition waivers (partial) also available. Support available to part-time students. Financial award applicants required to submit FAFSA. *Unit head:* Dr. Mary Janeczek, Director, 413-594-2761, Fax: 413-592-4871, E-mail: janeczeke@elms.edu. *Application contact:* Dana Malone, Associate Director for Graduate Studies and Continuing Education, 413-265-2445, Fax: 413-265-2459, E-mail: maloned@elms.edu.

Fitchburg State University, Division of Graduate and Continuing Education, Programs in English and Teaching English (Secondary Level), Fitchburg, MA 01420-2697. Offers MA, MAT, Certificate. *Accreditation:* NCATE. Part-time and evening/weekend programs available. *Students:* 1 full-time (0 women), 30 part-time (20 women). Average age 34. 13 applicants, 100% accepted, 10 enrolled. In 2009, 14 master's awarded. *Entrance requirements:* For master's, GRE General Test or MAT, letters of recommendation, resume. Additional exam requirements/recommendations for international students: Required—TOEFL (minimum score 550 paper-based; 213 computer-based; 79 iBT). *Application deadline:* Applications are processed on a rolling basis. Application fee: $25 ($50 for international students). *Expenses:* Tuition, area resident: Part-time $150 per credit. Tuition, state resident: part-time $150 per credit. Tuition, nonresident: part-time $150 per credit. Required fees: $120 per credit. *Financial support:* In 2009–10, research assistantships with partial tuition reimbursements (averaging $5,500 per year); Federal Work-Study, scholarships/grants, and unspecified assistantships also available. Support available to part-time students. Financial award application deadline: 3/1; financial award applicants required to submit FAFSA. *Unit head:* Dr. Chola Chisunka, Chair, 978-665-3445, Fax: 978-665-3658, E-mail: gce@fsc.edu. *Application contact:* Director of Admissions, 978-665-3144, Fax: 978-665-4540, E-mail: admissions@fsc.edu.

Florida Agricultural and Mechanical University, Division of Graduate Studies, Research, and Continuing Education, College of Education, Program in Secondary Education and Foundation, Tallahassee, FL 32307-3200. Offers biology (M Ed); chemistry (MS Ed); English (MS Ed); history (MS Ed); math (MS Ed); physics (MS Ed). *Accreditation:* NCATE. *Faculty:* 10 full-time (5 women). In 2009, 28 master's awarded. *Degree requirements:* For master's, thesis (for some programs). *Entrance requirements:* For master's, GRE General Test, minimum GPA of 3.0. Additional exam requirements/recommendations for international students: Required—TOEFL. *Application deadline:* For fall admission, 5/18 for domestic students, 12/18 for international students; for spring admission, 11/12 for domestic students, 5/12 for international students. Application fee: $20. *Unit head:* Dr. Bernadette Kelley, Chairperson, 850-599-3123. *Application contact:* Dr. Chanta M. Haywood, Dean of Graduate Studies, Research, and Continuing Education, 850-599-3315, Fax: 850-599-3727.

Florida Atlantic University, Dorothy F. Schmidt College of Arts and Letters, Department of English, Boca Raton, FL 33431-0991. Offers British and American literature (MA); creative nonfiction (MFA); creative writing (MA); fiction (MFA); multicultural literatures and literacies (MA); poetry (MFA); science fiction and fantasy (MA); teaching English (MAT). Part-time programs available. *Faculty:* 49 full-time (24 women), 17 part-time/adjunct (7 women). *Students:* 63 full-time (36 women), 28 part-time (21 women); includes 22 minority (6 African Americans, 2 American Indian/Alaska Native, 2 Asian Americans or Pacific Islanders, 12 Hispanic Americans), 1 international. Average age 31. 70 applicants, 54% accepted, 16 enrolled. In 2009, 21 master's awarded. *Degree requirements:* For master's, one foreign language, thesis. *Entrance requirements:* For master's, GRE General Test, minimum GPA of 3.0, writing samples, 2 letters of recommendation. *Application deadline:* For fall admission, 3/1 for domestic students, 2/15 for international students; for spring admission, 11/1 for domestic students, 7/15 for international students. Applications are processed on a rolling basis. Application fee: $30. Electronic applications accepted. *Expenses:* Tuition, state resident: full-time $7055; part-time $293.94 per credit hour. Tuition, nonresident: full-time $22,096; part-time $920.66 per credit hour. *Financial support:* Fellowships, teaching assistantships with partial tuition reimbursements, Federal Work-Study and tuition waivers available. Support available to part-time students. Financial award application deadline: 3/1. *Faculty research:* African-American writers, critical theory, British-American, Asian-American. *Unit head:* Dr. Wenying Xu, Chair, 561-297-2065, Fax: 561-297-3807, E-mail: wxu@fau.edu. *Application contact:* Dr. Andrew Furman, Director of Graduate Studies, 561-297-3835, Fax: 561-297-3807, E-mail: afurman@fau.edu.

Florida Gulf Coast University, College of Education, Program in Curriculum and Instruction, Fort Myers, FL 33965-6565. Offers educational technology (M Ed, MA); English education (M Ed). Part-time and evening/weekend programs available. Postbaccalaureate distance learning degree programs offered (minimal on-campus study). *Faculty:* 31 full-time (23 women), 41 part-time/adjunct (29 women). *Students:* 54 full-time (42 women), 4 part-time (3 women); includes 7 minority (1 African American, 1 Asian American or Pacific Islander, 5 Hispanic Americans). Average age 35. 20 applicants, 70% accepted, 0 enrolled. In 2009, 8 master's awarded. *Degree requirements:* For master's, final project or portfolio. *Entrance requirements:* For master's, GRE General Test, MAT, minimum undergraduate GPA of 3.0 in last 2 years. Additional exam requirements/recommendations for international students: Required—TOEFL (minimum score 550 paper-based; 213 computer-based). *Application deadline:* For fall admission, 7/1 priority date for domestic students; for spring admission, 10/15 for domestic students. Applications are processed on a rolling basis. Application fee: $30. Electronic applications accepted. *Faculty research:* Internet in schools, technology in pre-service and in-service teacher training. *Unit head:* Dr. Pat Wachholz, Associate Dean, 239-590-7808, Fax: 239-590-7801, E-mail: wachhol@fgcu.edu. *Application contact:* Dr. Pat Wachholz, Associate Dean, 239-590-7808, Fax: 239-590-7801, E-mail: wachhol@fgcu.edu.

Florida International University, College of Education, Department of Curriculum and Instruction, Program in English Education, Miami, FL 33199. Offers MAT, MS, Ed D. *Accreditation:* NCATE. Part-time and evening/weekend programs available. *Entrance requirements:* For master's, GRE General Test, minimum GPA of 3.0; for doctorate, GRE General Test. Additional exam requirements/recommendations for international students: Required—TOEFL (minimum score 550 paper-based; 213 computer-based; 80 iBT), IELTS (minimum score 6.3). *Expenses:* Tuition, state resident: full-time $8008; part-time $4004 per year. Tuition, nonresident: full-time $20,104; part-time $10,052 per year. Required fees: $298; $149 per term.

Florida State University, The Graduate School, College of Education, School of Teacher Education, Program in English Education, Tallahassee, FL 32306. Offers MS, PhD, Ed S. Part-time programs available. *Faculty:* 3 full-time (all women), 1 (woman) part-time/adjunct. *Students:* 6 full-time (all women), 17 part-time (13 women); includes 8 minority (5 African Americans, 3 Hispanic Americans). 19 applicants, 58% accepted, 10 enrolled. In 2009, 12 degrees awarded. *Degree requirements:* For master's and Ed S, comprehensive exam, thesis optional; for doctorate, comprehensive exam, thesis/dissertation. *Entrance requirements:* For master's, doctorate, and Ed S, GRE General Test, minimum GPA of 3.0. Additional exam requirements/recommendations for international students: Required—TOEFL (minimum score 550 paper-based; 213 computer-based; 80 iBT). *Application deadline:* For fall admission, 6/1 priority date for domestic students, 6/1 for international students; for spring admission, 10/1 for domestic students, 10/10 for international students. Applications are processed on a rolling basis. Application fee: $30. *Expenses:* Tuition, state resident: full-time $7413. Tuition, nonresident: full-time $22,567. *Financial support:* Fellowships with full and partial tuition reimbursements, research assistantships with full and partial tuition reimbursements, teaching assistantships with full and partial tuition reimbursements available. Financial award applicants required to submit FAFSA. *Faculty research:* Teaching literacies in today's English classroom, technologies for today's student and teacher, young adult literature as art and in the curriculum, adolescent literacy, reading across all subject areas. *Unit head:* Dr. Shelbie Witte, Head, 850-644-6553, Fax: 850-644-1880, E-mail: witte@fsu.edu. *Application contact:* Amy McKnight, Office Manager, 850-644-7810, Fax: 850-644-1880, E-mail: amcknight@coe.fsu.edu.

Framingham State University, Division of Graduate and Continuing Education, Program in English, Framingham, MA 01701-9101. Offers M Ed.

Gardner-Webb University, Graduate School, Department of English, Boiling Springs, NC 28017. Offers English (MA); English education (MA). Part-time and evening/weekend programs available. *Faculty:* 2 full-time (both women), 1 (woman) part-time/adjunct. *Students:* 10 part-time (8 women); includes 3 minority (all African Americans). Average age 35. 4 applicants, 100% accepted, 4 enrolled. In 2009, 1 master's awarded. *Degree requirements:* For master's, comprehensive exam. *Entrance requirements:* For master's, GRE General Test, MAT, or NTE; PRAXIS, minimum GPA of 2.5. *Application deadline:* For fall admission, 8/1 priority date for domestic students. Applications are processed on a rolling basis. Application fee: $25. Electronic applications accepted. *Expenses:* Tuition: Part-time $305 per credit hour. *Financial support:* Unspecified assistantships available. *Unit head:* Dr. June Hobbs, Chair, 704-406-4412, Fax: 704-406-3921, E-mail: jhobbs@gardner-webb.edu. *Application contact:* Dr. Franki Burch, Dean, Graduate School, 704-406-4724, Fax: 704-406-4329, E-mail: gradschool@gardner-webb.edu.

Georgia Southern University, Jack N. Averitt College of Graduate Studies, College of Education, Department of Teaching and Learning, Program in English Education, Statesboro, GA 30460. Offers M Ed, MAT. *Accreditation:* NCATE. Part-time and evening/weekend programs available. *Students:* 9 full-time (6 women), 2 part-time (1 woman). Average age 27. 2 applicants, 100% accepted, 2 enrolled. In 2009, 5 master's awarded. *Degree requirements:* For master's, portfolio, transition point assessments, exit assessment. *Entrance requirements:* For master's, GRE General Test or MAT; GACE Basic Skills and Content Assessments (MAT), minimum cumulative GPA of 2.5. Additional exam requirements/recommendations for international students: Required—TOEFL (minimum score 550 paper-based; 213 computer-based; 80 iBT). *Application deadline:* For fall admission, 3/1 priority date for domestic and international students; for spring admission, 10/1 priority date for domestic students, 10/1 for international students. Applications are processed on a rolling basis. Application fee: $30 ($50 for international students). Electronic applications accepted. *Expenses:* Tuition, state resident: full-time $5040; part-time $210 per credit hour. Tuition, nonresident: full-time $20,136; part-time $839 per credit hour. Required fees: $1644. *Financial support:* In 2009–10, 10 students received support, including research assistantships with partial tuition reimbursements available (averaging $7,200 per year), teaching assistantships with partial tuition reimbursements available (averaging $7,200 per year); Federal Work-Study, scholarships/grants, tuition waivers (partial), and unspecified assistantships also available. Support available to part-time students. Financial award application deadline: 4/15; financial award applicants required to submit FAFSA. *Faculty research:* Literacy for at-risk students. *Unit head:* Dr. Ronnie Sheppard, Assistant Professor, 912-478-5203, Fax: 912-478-0026, E-mail: sheppard@georgiasouthern.edu. *Application contact:* Dr. Charles Ziglar, Coordinator for Graduate Student Recruitment, 912-478-5635, Fax: 912-478-0740, E-mail: gradadmissions@georgiasouthern.edu.

Georgia State University, College of Education, Department of Middle-Secondary Education and Instructional Technology, Programs in Secondary Education, Atlanta, GA 30302-3083. Offers art education (Ed S); English education (M Ed, Ed S); mathematics education (M Ed, PhD, Ed S); music education (PhD); science education (M Ed, PhD, Ed S); social studies education (M Ed, PhD, Ed S). *Accreditation:* NASM (one or more programs are accredited); NCATE. Part-time and evening/weekend programs available. *Degree requirements:* For master's, comprehensive exam; for doctorate, comprehensive exam, thesis/dissertation; for Ed S, project/exam. *Entrance requirements:* For master's, GRE General Test, minimum GPA of 2.5; for doctorate, GRE General Test or MAT, minimum GPA of 3.3; for Ed S, GRE General Test or MAT, minimum graduate GPA of 3.25. *Faculty research:* Women and science, problem solving in mathematics, dialects, economic education.

Grand Valley State University, College of Education, Program in Reading and Language Arts, Allendale, MI 49401-9403. Offers M Ed. *Accreditation:* NCATE. Part-time and evening/weekend programs available. *Faculty:* 5 full-time (4 women), 2 part-time/adjunct (both women). *Students:* 3 full-time (all women), 183 part-time (182 women); includes 6 minority (2 African Americans, 2 Asian Americans or Pacific Islanders, 2 Hispanic Americans). Average age 31. 29 applicants, 100% accepted, 21 enrolled. In 2009, 42 master's awarded. *Degree requirements:* For master's, thesis. *Entrance requirements:* For master's, GRE General Test or minimum GPA of 3.0. Additional exam requirements/recommendations for international students: Required—TOEFL. *Application deadline:* Applications are processed on a rolling basis. Application fee: $30. Electronic applications accepted. *Expenses:* Tuition, state resident: part-time $471 per credit hour. Tuition, nonresident: part-time $646 per credit hour. Tuition and fees vary according to course level. *Financial support:* In 2009–10, 16 students received support, including 15 fellowships (averaging $1,733 per year), 1 research assistantship with full and partial tuition reimbursement available (averaging $8,000 per year); career-related internships or fieldwork, Federal Work-Study, scholarships/grants, and unspecified assistantships also available. *Faculty research:* Culture of literacy, literacy acquisition, assessment, content area literacy, writing pedagogy. *Unit head:* Dr. Nancy Patterson, Director, 616-331-6226, E-mail: patterson@gvsu.edu. *Application contact:* Stephen Worst, 616-331-6831, Fax: 616-331-6217, E-mail: busmando@gvsu.edu.

Harding University, College of Education, Searcy, AR 72149-0001. Offers advanced studies in teaching and learning (M Ed); art (MSE); behavioral science (MSE); counseling (MS, Ed S); early childhood special education (M Ed, MSE); education (MSE); educational leadership (M Ed, Ed S); elementary education (M Ed); English (MSE); family and consumer science (MSE); French (MSE); history/social science (MSE); kinesiology (MSE); math (MSE); physical science (MSE); reading (M Ed); secondary education (M Ed); Spanish (MSE); special education licensure (M Ed); teaching (MAT); teaching English as a second language (M Ed). *Accreditation:* NCATE. Part-time and evening/weekend programs available. *Faculty:* 11 full-time (4 women), 49 part-time/adjunct (26 women). *Students:* 104 full-time (85 women), 392 part-time (282 women); includes 77 minority (67 African Americans, 5 American Indian/Alaska Native, 1 Asian American or Pacific Islander, 4 Hispanic Americans), 5 international. Average age 36. 153 applicants, 92% accepted, 131 enrolled. In 2009, 153 master's, 6 other advanced degrees awarded. *Degree requirements:* For master's, comprehensive exam (for some programs), thesis optional, portfolio(s); for Ed S, comprehensive exam, portfolio, specialist project. *Entrance requirements:* For master's, GRE, MAT, PRAXIS; for Ed S, MAT or GRE. Additional exam requirements/recommendations for international students: Required—TOEFL (minimum score 550 paper-based; 79 iBT). *Application deadline:* For fall admission, 8/1 for domestic and international students; for spring admission, 1/1 for domestic and international students. Applications are processed on a rolling basis. Application fee: $35. *Expenses:* Tuition: Full-time $9720; part-time $540 per credit hour. Required fees: $22 per credit hour. Tuition and fees vary according to course load and program. *Financial support:* In 2009–10, 30 students received support. Unspecified assistantships available. *Faculty research:* Reading, comprehension, school violence, educational technology, behavior, college choice, differentiated instruction, brain-based teaching. *Unit head:* Dr. Clara Carroll, Chair, 501-279-4501, Fax: 501-279-4083, E-mail: ccarroll@harding.edu. *Application contact:* Information Contact, 501-279-4315, E-mail: gradstudiesedu@harding.edu.

Hofstra University, School of Education, Health, and Human Services, Department of Curriculum and Teaching, Program in English Education, Hempstead, NY 11549. Offers MA, MS Ed. Part-time and evening/weekend programs available. *Students:* 22 full-time (16 women), 10 part-time (5 women); includes 1 minority (Asian American or Pacific Islander). Average age 27. 33 applicants, 85% accepted, 14 enrolled. In 2009, 9 master's awarded. *Degree requirements:* For master's, fieldwork, electronic portfolio, and curriculum project (MA). *Entrance*

English Education

Hofstra University (continued)

requirements: For master's, 2 letters of recommendation, teacher certification (MA). Additional exam requirements/recommendations for international students: Required—TOEFL (minimum score 550 paper-based; 213 computer-based; 80 iBT). *Application deadline:* Applications are processed on a rolling basis. Application fee: $60. Electronic applications accepted. *Expenses:* Tuition: Full-time $16,200; part-time $900 per credit hour. Required fees: $970; $145 per term. Tuition and fees vary according to program. *Financial support:* In 2009–10, 16 students received support, including 3 fellowships with full and partial tuition reimbursements available (averaging $3,666 per year), 1 research assistantship with full and partial tuition reimbursement available (averaging $6,574 per year); Federal Work-Study, institutionally sponsored loans, scholarships/grants, tuition waivers (full and partial), and unspecified assistantships also available. Support available to part-time students. Financial award applicants required to submit FAFSA. *Faculty research:* Reading and writing across the curriculum, multicultural/immigrant literature, curriculum and instruction, enhancing instruction with technology, differentiated learning for students with special needs. *Unit head:* Dr. Maureen O. Murphy, Program Director, 516-463-6775, Fax: 516-463-6169, E-mail: catmom@hofstra.edu. *Application contact:* Carol Drummer, Dean of Graduate Admissions, 516-463-4876, Fax: 516-463-4664, E-mail: gradstudent@hofstra.edu.

Hofstra University, School of Education, Health, and Human Services, Department of Curriculum and Teaching, Program in Learning and Teaching, Hempstead, NY 11549. Offers learning and teaching (Ed D), including applied linguistics, art education, arts and humanities, early childhood education, English education, human development, math education, math, science, and technology, multicultural education, physical education, science education, social studies education, special education. Part-time and evening/weekend programs available. *Students:* 5 full-time (all women), 21 part-time (17 women); includes 2 minority (1 African American, 1 Hispanic American), 1 international. Average age 38. 22 applicants, 68% accepted, 11 enrolled. *Degree requirements:* For doctorate, comprehensive exam, thesis/dissertation. *Entrance requirements:* For doctorate, GRE, 3 letters of recommendation, interview, 2 years full-time teaching experience. Additional exam requirements/recommendations for international students: Required—TOEFL (minimum score 550 paper-based; 213 computer-based; 80 iBT). *Application deadline:* Applications are processed on a rolling basis. Application fee: $60. Electronic applications accepted. *Expenses:* Tuition: Full-time $16,200; part-time $900 per credit hour. Required fees: $970; $145 per term. Tuition and fees vary according to program. *Financial support:* In 2009–10, 24 students received support, including 20 fellowships with full and partial tuition reimbursements available (averaging $4,906 per year); research assistantships with full and partial tuition reimbursements available, Federal Work-Study, institutionally sponsored loans, scholarships/grants, and tuition waivers (full and partial) also available. Support available to part-time students. Financial award applicants required to submit FAFSA. *Faculty research:* Critical thinking, professional development, teacher quality, quantitative research. *Unit head:* Dr. Bruce A. Torff, Director, 516-463-5803, Fax: 516-463-6196, E-mail: catajs@hofstra.edu. *Application contact:* Carol Drummer, Dean of Graduate Admissions, 516-463-4876, Fax: 516-463-4664, E-mail: gradstudent@hofstra.edu.

Humboldt State University, Graduate Studies, College of Arts, Humanities, and Social Sciences, Department of English, Arcata, CA 95521-8299. Offers English (MA), including international program, literature, teaching of writing. *Students:* 19 full-time (13 women), 6 part-time (5 women); includes 1 minority (Hispanic American). Average age 32. 20 applicants, 55% accepted, 9 enrolled. In 2009, 15 master's awarded. *Degree requirements:* For master's, one foreign language, thesis or alternative, qualifying exam. *Entrance requirements:* For master's, GRE, minimum GPA of 3.0, 3 letters of recommendation, sample of writing. Additional exam requirements/recommendations for international students: Required—TOEFL (minimum score 500 paper-based; 173 computer-based). *Application deadline:* For fall admission, 3/1 for domestic students; for spring admission, 11/1 for domestic students. Applications are processed on a rolling basis. Application fee: $55. *Expenses:* Tuition, nonresident: full-time $8928. Required fees: $6102. Tuition and fees vary according to program. *Financial support:* Teaching assistantships, career-related internships or fieldwork, Federal Work-Study, and institutionally sponsored loans available. Financial award application deadline: 3/1; financial award applicants required to submit FAFSA. *Faculty research:* Teaching of writing, literature. *Unit head:* Dr. Susan Bennett, Chair, 707-826-3758, Fax: 707-826-5939, E-mail: sgb1@humboldt.edu. *Application contact:* Dr. Michael S. Eldridge, Graduate Coordinator, 707-826-5906, Fax: 707-826-5939, E-mail: me2@humboldt.edu.

Hunter College of the City University of New York, Graduate School, School of Arts and Sciences, Department of English, New York, NY 10021-5085. Offers British and American literature (MA); creative writing (MFA), including creative writing, fiction, nonfiction, poetry; English education (MA). Part-time and evening/weekend programs available. *Faculty:* 24 full-time (10 women), 3 part-time/adjunct (2 women). *Students:* 12 full-time (11 women), 93 part-time (71 women); includes 10 minority (7 African Americans, 1 Asian American or Pacific Islander, 2 Hispanic Americans). Average age 32. 573 applicants, 11% accepted, 38 enrolled. In 2009, 33 master's awarded. *Entrance requirements:* Additional exam requirements/recommendations for international students: Required—TOEFL. *Application deadline:* For fall admission, 4/1 for domestic students, 2/1 for international students; for spring admission, 11/1 for domestic students, 9/1 for international students. Application fee: $125. *Expenses:* Tuition, state resident: full-time $7360; part-time $310 per credit. Required fees: $250 per semester. *Financial support:* Fellowships, Federal Work-Study and tuition waivers (partial) available. Support available to part-time students. *Faculty research:* Medieval, early modern, late century, Asian American, post-colonial literatures. *Unit head:* Dr. Christina Leon-Alfar, Chair, 212-772-5187, Fax: 212-772-5411, E-mail: calfar@hunter.cuny.edu. *Application contact:* Sarah Chinn, Adviser, 212-772-5187, E-mail: gradenghish@hunter.cuny.edu.

Hunter College of the City University of New York, Graduate School, School of Education, Programs in Secondary Education, Concentration in English Education, New York, NY 10021-5085. Offers MA. *Accreditation:* NCATE. *Faculty:* 24 full-time (10 women), 3 part-time/adjunct (2 women). *Students:* 8 full-time (6 women), 61 part-time (39 women); includes 18 minority (7 African Americans, 2 Asian Americans or Pacific Islanders, 9 Hispanic Americans). Average age 31. 90 applicants, 37% accepted, 13 enrolled. In 2009, 26 master's awarded. *Degree requirements:* For master's, thesis, professional teaching portfolio, New York State Teacher Certification Exam, research project. *Entrance requirements:* For master's, minimum GPA of 2.8, 2 letters of reference, minimum of 21 credits in English. Additional exam requirements/recommendations for international students: Required—TOEFL, TWE. *Application deadline:* For fall admission, 4/1 for domestic students, 2/1 for international students; for spring admission, 11/1 for domestic students, 9/1 for international students. Applications are processed on a rolling basis. Application fee: $125. *Expenses:* Tuition, state resident: full-time $7360; part-time $310 per credit. Required fees: $250 per semester. *Financial support:* Federal Work-Study and tuition waivers (partial) available. Support available to part-time students. *Unit head:* Sema Brainin, Education Adviser, 212-772-4773, E-mail: sbrainin@hunter.cuny.edu. *Application contact:* Marlene Hennessey, English Department Advisor, 212-772-4773, E-mail: mhenness@hunter.cuny.edu.

Indiana State University, School of Graduate Studies, College of Arts and Sciences, Department of English, Terre Haute, IN 47809. Offers English teaching (MA); history (MA); literature (MA). Part-time and evening/weekend programs available. *Degree requirements:* For master's, one foreign language, thesis optional. *Entrance requirements:* For master's, minimum GPA of 2.75 in all English courses above freshman level. Additional exam requirements/recommendations for international students: Required—TOEFL (minimum score 550 paper-based). Electronic applications accepted.

Indiana University of Pennsylvania, School of Graduate Studies and Research, College of Humanities and Social Sciences, Department of English, Program in Composition and Teaching English to Speakers of Other Languages, Indiana, PA 15705-1087. Offers composition and teaching English to speakers of other languages (PhD); teaching English (MAT); teaching English to speakers of other languages (MA). *Faculty:* 27 full-time (15 women). *Students:* 73 full-time (48 women), 142 part-time (95 women); includes 10 minority (2 African Americans, 6 Asian Americans or Pacific Islanders, 2 Hispanic Americans), 63 international. Average age 36. 203 applicants, 36% accepted, 45 enrolled. In 2009, 20 master's, 12 doctorates awarded. *Degree requirements:* For master's, thesis optional; for doctorate, one foreign language, comprehensive exam, thesis/dissertation. *Entrance requirements:* For master's and doctorate, 2 letters of recommendation. Additional exam requirements/recommendations for international students: Required—TOEFL. *Application deadline:* For fall admission, 7/1 priority date for domestic students; for spring admission, 11/1 for domestic students. Applications are processed on a rolling basis. Application fee: $40. *Expenses:* Tuition, state resident: full-time $6666; part-time $370 per credit hour. Tuition, nonresident: full-time $10,666; part-time $593 per credit hour. Required fees: $813 per semester. *Financial support:* In 2009–10, 4 fellowships (averaging $938 per year), 22 research assistantships with full and partial tuition reimbursements (averaging $5,922 per year), 8 teaching assistantships with partial tuition reimbursements (averaging $17,498 per year) were awarded. Financial award application deadline: 3/15; financial award applicants required to submit FAFSA. *Unit head:* Dr. Ben Rafoth, Graduate Coordinator, 724-357-2272. *Application contact:* Dr. Ben Rafoth, Graduate Coordinator, 724-357-2272.

Indiana University–Purdue University Fort Wayne, College of Arts and Sciences, Department of English and Linguistics, Fort Wayne, IN 46805-1499. Offers English (MA, MAT); TENL (teaching English as a new language) (Certificate). Part-time programs available. *Faculty:* 28 full-time (14 women). *Students:* 8 full-time (5 women), 23 part-time (14 women); includes 2 minority (both Asian Americans or Pacific Islanders). Average age 35. 14 applicants, 100% accepted, 14 enrolled. In 2009, 10 master's, 2 other advanced degrees awarded. *Degree requirements:* For master's, one foreign language, thesis (for some programs), teaching certificate (MAT). *Entrance requirements:* For master's, GRE General Test, minimum GPA of 3.0, major or minor in English, 3 letters of recommendation; for Certificate, bachelor's degree with minimum GPA of 2.5. Additional exam requirements/recommendations for international students: Required—TOEFL (minimum score 600 paper-based; 260 computer-based). *Application deadline:* For fall admission, 8/1 for domestic students; for spring admission, 10/15 for domestic students. Applications are processed on a rolling basis. Application fee: $50. *Expenses:* Tuition, state resident: full-time $4595; part-time $255 per credit. Tuition, nonresident: full-time $10,963; part-time $609 per credit. Required fees: $528; $29.35 per credit. Tuition and fees vary according to course load. *Financial support:* In 2009–10, 13 teaching assistantships with partial tuition reimbursements (averaging $12,740 per year) were awarded; career-related internships or fieldwork, scholarships/grants, and unspecified assistantships also available. Support available to part-time students. Financial award application deadline: 3/1; financial award applicants required to submit FAFSA. *Faculty research:* Shakespeare, three-volume novels, poetry of Nikola Vaptsarov, philanthropy. Total annual research expenditures: $52,321. *Unit head:* Dr. Hardin Aasand, Chair and Professor, 260-481-6750, Fax: 260-481-6985, E-mail: aasandh@ipfw.edu. *Application contact:* Dr. Michael Stapleton, Graduate Program Director, 260-481-6772, Fax: 260-481-6985, E-mail: stapletm@ipfw.edu.

Indiana University–Purdue University Indianapolis, School of Liberal Arts, Department of English, Indianapolis, IN 46202-2896. Offers English (MA); teaching English (MA). *Faculty:* 20 full-time (8 women). *Students:* 22 full-time (17 women), 27 part-time (19 women); includes 4 minority (1 American Indian/Alaska Native, 3 Asian Americans or Pacific Islanders), 1 international. Average age 34. 21 applicants, 90% accepted, 6 enrolled. In 2009, 10 master's awarded. *Entrance requirements:* For master's, GRE. Application fee: $55 ($65 for international students). *Financial support:* In 2009–10, 2 fellowships (averaging $10,000 per year), 12 teaching assistantships (averaging $7,103 per year) were awarded; research assistantships, career-related internships or fieldwork also available. *Unit head:* Susanmarie Harrington, Chair, 317-278-1153. *Application contact:* Susanmarie Harrington, Chair, 317-278-1153.

Iona College, School of Arts and Science, Program in Education, New Rochelle, NY 10801-1890. Offers biology education (MS Ed, MST); educational leadership (MS Ed); English education (MS Ed, MST); literacy education (MS Ed); mathematics education (MS Ed, MST); social studies education (MS Ed, MST); Spanish education (MS Ed, MST); teaching in childhood education (MST). *Accreditation:* NCATE. Part-time and evening/weekend programs available. *Faculty:* 24 full-time (13 women), 16 part-time/adjunct (10 women). *Students:* 41 full-time (35 women), 118 part-time (87 women); includes 15 minority (5 African Americans, 1 Asian American or Pacific Islander, 9 Hispanic Americans). Average age 28. 91 applicants, 67% accepted, 41 enrolled. In 2009, 61 master's awarded. *Degree requirements:* For master's, thesis or alternative. *Entrance requirements:* For master's, minimum GPA of 2.5 (MST), New York teaching certificate (MS Ed). Additional exam requirements/recommendations for international students: Required—TOEFL (minimum score 550 paper-based; 213 computer-based). *Application deadline:* Applications are processed on a rolling basis. Application fee: $50. Electronic applications accepted. *Expenses:* Tuition: Part-time $830 per credit. *Financial support:* Unspecified assistantships available. Support available to part-time students. Financial award application deadline: 4/15; financial award applicants required to submit FAFSA. *Faculty research:* Reading/writing, educational technology, administration, early literacy assessment, literacy development. *Unit head:* Dr. Catherine O'Callaghan, Chair, 914-633-2210, Fax: 914-633-2608, E-mail: cocallaghan@iona.edu. *Application contact:* Veronica Jarek-Prinz, Director of Graduate Admissions, 914-633-2420, Fax: 914-633-2277, E-mail: vjarekprinz@iona.edu.

Ithaca College, Division of Graduate and Professional Studies, School of Humanities and Sciences, Program in Adolescent Education, Ithaca, NY 14850. Offers biology 7-12 (MAT); chemistry 7-12 (MAT); English 7-12 (MAT); French 7-12 (MAT); math 7-12 (MAT); physics 7-12 (MAT); social studies 7-12 (MAT); Spanish (MAT). Part-time programs available. *Faculty:* 18 full-time (7 women). *Students:* 15 full-time (10 women), 2 part-time (1 woman); includes 1 minority (African American). Average age 26. 31 applicants, 68% accepted, 16 enrolled. In 2009, 31 master's awarded. *Degree requirements:* For master's, thesis or alternative, student teaching. *Entrance requirements:* For master's, minimum GPA of 3.0. Additional exam requirements/recommendations for international students: Required—TOEFL (minimum score 550 paper-based; 213 computer-based; 80 iBT). *Application deadline:* For fall admission, 5/15 for domestic and international students; for spring admission, 12/1 for domestic and international students. Applications are processed on a rolling basis. Application fee: $40. Electronic applications accepted. *Expenses:* Contact institution. *Financial support:* In 2009–10, 15 students received support, including 10 teaching assistantships (averaging $6,474 per year); career-related internships or fieldwork, Federal Work-Study, scholarships/grants, and unspecified assistantships also available. Support available to part-time students. Financial award applicants required to submit CSS PROFILE or FAFSA. *Faculty research:* Bilingual education, sociolinguistic perspective on literacy. *Unit head:* Dr. Linda Hanrahan, Chairperson, 607-274-3527, Fax: 607-274-1263, E-mail: gps@ithaca.edu. *Application contact:* Rob Gearhart, Dean, Graduate and Professional Studies, 607-274-3527, Fax: 607-274-1263, E-mail: gps@ithaca.edu.

Jackson State University, Graduate School, School of Liberal Arts, Department of English and Modern Foreign Languages, Jackson, MS 39217. Offers English (MA); teaching English (MAT). Part-time and evening/weekend programs available. *Degree requirements:* For master's, comprehensive exam, thesis or alternative. *Entrance requirements:* For master's, GRE General Test. Additional exam requirements/recommendations for international students: Required—TOEFL.

The Johns Hopkins University, School of Education, Department of Teacher Preparation, Baltimore, MD 21218. Offers education (MS), including educational studies; elementary education (MAT); English for speakers of other languages (MAT); K-8 mathematics lead-teacher (Certificate); K-8 science lead-teacher (Certificate); secondary education (MAT), including biology, chemistry, earth/space/environmental science, English, French, mathematics, physics, social studies, Spanish. Part-time and evening/weekend programs available. *Faculty:* 13 full-time (11 women), 35 part-time/adjunct (21 women). *Students:* 162 full-time (119 women), 347 part-time (256 women); includes 138 minority (80 African Americans, 3 American Indian/Alaska Native, 38 Asian Americans or Pacific Islanders, 17 Hispanic Americans), 3 international. Average age 27. 89 applicants, 37% accepted, 24 enrolled. In 2009, 177 master's awarded. *Degree requirements:* For master's, portfolio, PRAXIS II, internship. *Entrance requirements:* For master's, PRAXIS I, SAT, ACT, or GRE (MAT), minimum undergraduate GPA of 3.0,

interview, 1 letter of recommendation, curriculum vitae/resume; for Certificate, bachelor's degree, minimum undergraduate GPA of 3.0, essay/statement of goals, interview. Additional exam requirements/recommendations for international students: Required—TOEFL (minimum score 600 paper-based; 250 computer-based; 100 iBT). *Application deadline:* For fall admission, 5/1 for international students; for spring admission, 10/15 for international students. Applications are processed on a rolling basis. Application fee: $80. Electronic applications accepted. *Financial support:* Scholarships/grants available. Support available to part-time students. Financial award application deadline: 6/1; financial award applicants required to submit FAFSA. *Faculty research:* Teacher retention; STEM education reform; alternative certification programs; school-university partnerships; urban education; action research/data-informed instruction; family engagement. *Unit head:* Dr. Francis Masci, Chair, 410-516-9774, Fax: 410-516-9770, E-mail: matjhu@jhu.edu. *Application contact:* Jennifer Shaffer, Director of Admissions, 410-516-9797, Fax: 410-516-9799, E-mail: educationinfo@jhu.edu.

Kennesaw State University, Leland and Clarice C. Bagwell College of Education, Program in Teaching, Kennesaw, GA 30144-5591. Offers secondary English or mathematics (MAT); teaching English to speakers of other languages (MAT). Program offered only in summer. Part-time and evening/weekend programs available. *Students:* 120 full-time (94 women), 16 part-time (9 women); includes 23 minority (12 African Americans, 4 Asian Americans or Pacific Islanders, 7 Hispanic Americans), 1 international. Average age 33. 28 applicants, 79% accepted, 19 enrolled. In 2009, 50 master's awarded. *Entrance requirements:* For master's, GRE, GACE I (state certificate exam), minimum GPA of 2.75, 2 recommendations, resume. Additional exam requirements/recommendations for international students: Required—TOEFL (minimum score 550 paper-based; 213 computer-based; 80 iBT), IELTS (minimum score 6). *Application deadline:* For fall admission, 6/1 for domestic and international students; for spring admission, 3/1 for domestic and international students. Application fee: $60. Electronic applications accepted. *Expenses:* Tuition, state resident: full-time $2341; part-time $196 per credit hour. Tuition, nonresident: full-time $9396; part-time $783 per credit hour. Required fees: $573 per semester. *Financial support:* In 2009–10, 2 research assistantships with tuition reimbursements (averaging $4,000 per year) were awarded; unspecified assistantships also available. Financial award application deadline: 6/15; financial award applicants required to submit FAFSA. *Unit head:* Dr. Lynn Stallings, Director, 770-420-4477, E-mail: lstalling@kennesaw.edu. *Application contact:* Alisha Bello, Administrative Coordinator, 770-423-6043, Fax: 770-420-4435, E-mail: abello1@kennesaw.edu.

Kent State University, College of Arts and Sciences, Department of English, Kent, OH 44242-0001. Offers comparative literature (MA); creative writing (MFA); English (PhD); English for teachers (MA); literature and writing (MA); rhetoric and composition (PhD); teaching English as a second language (MA). Part-time programs available. Terminal master's awarded for partial completion of doctoral program. *Degree requirements:* For master's, one foreign language, thesis optional; for doctorate, one foreign language, thesis/dissertation, qualifying exams. *Entrance requirements:* For master's and doctorate, GRE General Test, writing sample, letters of recommendation. Additional exam requirements/recommendations for international students: Required—TOEFL (minimum score 600 paper-based). Electronic applications accepted. *Faculty research:* British and American literature, textual editing, rhetoric and composition, cultural studies, linguistic and critical theories.

Kutztown University of Pennsylvania, College of Education, Program in Secondary Education, Kutztown, PA 19530-0730. Offers biology (M Ed); curriculum and instruction (M Ed); English (M Ed); mathematics (M Ed); secondary education (Certificate); social studies (M Ed). *Accreditation:* NCATE. Part-time and evening/weekend programs available. *Faculty:* 7 full-time (4 women). *Students:* 90 full-time (45 women), 84 part-time (56 women); includes 8 minority (4 African Americans, 1 Asian American or Pacific Islander, 3 Hispanic Americans), 2 international. Average age 29. 129 applicants, 76% accepted, 31 enrolled. In 2009, 36 master's awarded. *Degree requirements:* For master's, comprehensive exam, thesis optional. *Entrance requirements:* For master's, GRE General Test. Additional exam requirements/recommendations for international students: Required—TOEFL. *Application deadline:* For fall admission, 8/15 priority date for domestic and international students; for spring admission, 12/15 priority date for domestic and international students. Applications are processed on a rolling basis. Application fee: $35. Electronic applications accepted. *Expenses:* Tuition, state resident: full-time $6666; part-time $370 per credit. Tuition, nonresident: full-time $10,666; part-time $593 per credit. Required fees: $62 per credit. $60 per semester. *Financial support:* Career-related internships or fieldwork, Federal Work-Study, scholarships/grants, and unspecified assistantships available. Financial award application deadline: 3/1; financial award applicants required to submit FAFSA. *Unit head:* Dr. Theresa Stahler, Chairperson, 610-683-4259, Fax: 610-683-1338, E-mail: stahler@kutztown.edu. *Application contact:* Kelly D. Burr, Associate Director, Graduate Admissions, 610-683-4200, Fax: 610-683-1393, E-mail: graduate@kutztown.edu.

Lehman College of the City University of New York, Division of Education, Department of Middle and High School Education, Program in English Education, Bronx, NY 10468-1589. Offers MS Ed. *Accreditation:* NCATE. *Entrance requirements:* For master's, minimum GPA of 3.0 in English, 2.8 overall; teaching certificate.

Le Moyne College, Department of Education, Syracuse, NY 13214. Offers adolescent education (MS Ed, MST); adolescent education/special education (MS Ed, MST); adolescent English (grades 7-12) (MST); adolescent history (grades 7-12) (MST); childhood education (MS Ed); childhood education/special education (MS Ed); elementary education (MS Ed); general professional education (MS Ed); inclusive childhood education (MST); middle child specialist/special education (MS Ed); middle childhood specialist (MS Ed); school building leadership (MS Ed, CAS); school district business leader (MS Ed, CAS); school district leadership (MS Ed, CAS); secondary education (MS Ed); special education (MS Ed). *Accreditation:* Teacher Education Accreditation Council. Part-time and evening/weekend programs available. *Faculty:* 15 full-time (8 women), 61 part-time/adjunct (33 women). *Students:* 40 full-time (30 women), 260 part-time (180 women); includes 25 minority (11 African Americans, 3 American Indian/Alaska Native, 3 Asian Americans or Pacific Islanders, 8 Hispanic Americans). Average age 31. 168 applicants, 89% accepted, 140 enrolled. In 2009, 180 master's awarded. *Degree requirements:* For master's, thesis. *Entrance requirements:* For master's, GRE General Test, 2 letters of recommendation. Additional exam requirements/recommendations for international students: Required—TOEFL (minimum score 550 paper-based; 213 computer-based; 79 iBT). *Application deadline:* For fall admission, 4/1 priority date for domestic and international students; for spring admission, 10/1 priority date for domestic and international students. Applications are processed on a rolling basis. Application fee: $50. *Expenses:* Contact institution. *Financial support:* In 2009–10, 28 students received support. Career-related internships or fieldwork and health care benefits available. Support available to part-time students. Financial award applicants required to submit FAFSA. *Faculty research:* Recruitment/retention strategies, minority teachers, special education, multiculturalism, literacy, technology, video games learning, autism, school district organization. *Unit head:* Dr. Norbert J. Henry, Interim Chair/Director, 315-445-4376, Fax: 315-445-4744, E-mail: henry@lemoyne.edu. *Application contact:* Kristen P. Trapasso, Director of Graduate Admission, 315-445-4265, Fax: 315-445-6027, E-mail: trapaskp@lemoyne.edu.

Lincoln Memorial University, Carter and Moyers School of Education, Harrogate, TN 37752-1901. Offers administration and supervision (M Ed, Ed S); counseling and guidance (M Ed); curriculum and instruction (M Ed, Ed S); English (M Ed). Part-time and evening/weekend programs available. Postbaccalaureate distance learning degree programs offered. *Faculty:* 31 full-time (13 women), 22 part-time/adjunct (11 women). *Students:* 190 full-time (151 women), 1,299 part-time (959 women); includes 144 minority (128 African Americans, 1 American Indian/Alaska Native, 5 Asian Americans or Pacific Islanders, 10 Hispanic Americans), 4 international. 1,562 applicants, 96% accepted, 1489 enrolled. In 2009, 173 master's, 901 Ed Ss awarded. *Degree requirements:* For master's, comprehensive exam, thesis optional; for Ed S, comprehensive exam. *Entrance requirements:* For master's, PRAXIS, NTE, GRE, MAT, letters of recommendation; for Ed S, graduate transcripts. *Application deadline:* For fall admission, 8/10 for domestic and international students; for spring admission, 1/10 for domestic and international students. Application fee: $25. *Expenses:* Tuition: Full-time $11,700; part-time

$390 per hour. *Financial support:* In 2009–10, 973 students received support. Career-related internships or fieldwork, health care benefits, and unspecified assistantships available. Support available to part-time students. Financial award application deadline: 4/1; financial award applicants required to submit FAFSA. *Faculty research:* Brain compatible teaching and learning; poverty in Appalachia; leadership for change; ethics, moral responsibility and social justice; human and organizational learning. *Unit head:* Dr. David Hand, Dean, 423-869-6259, Fax: 423-869-6261, E-mail: david.hand@lmunet.edu. *Application contact:* Terri Knuckles, Office Manager, Graduate Education, 423-869-6223, Fax: 423-869-6261, E-mail: terri.knuckles@lmunet.edu.

Long Island University, Brooklyn Campus, Richard L. Conolly College of Liberal Arts and Sciences, Department of English, Brooklyn, NY 11201-8423. Offers creative writing (MFA); literature (MA); professional writing (MA); writing and rhetoric (MA). Part-time and evening/weekend programs available. *Degree requirements:* For master's, thesis or alternative. *Entrance requirements:* For master's, 2 letters of recommendation (at least 1 from a former professor or teacher). Additional exam requirements/recommendations for international students: Required—TOEFL (minimum score 550 paper-based; 173 computer-based). Electronic applications accepted.

Long Island University, C.W. Post Campus, School of Education, Department of Curriculum and Instruction, Brookville, NY 11548-1300. Offers adolescence education (MS); adolescence education: biology (MS); adolescence education: earth science (MS); adolescence education: English (MS); adolescence education: mathematics (MS); adolescence education: social studies (MS); adolescence education: Spanish (MS); art education (MS); bilingual education (MS); childhood education (MS); early childhood education (MS); middle childhood education (MS); music education (MS); teaching English to speakers of other languages (MS). Part-time and evening/weekend programs available. *Degree requirements:* For master's, comprehensive exam or thesis, student teaching. *Entrance requirements:* For master's, minimum GPA of 2.75 in major, 2.5 overall. Electronic applications accepted. *Faculty research:* Ethics and education, teaching strategies.

Longwood University, Office of Graduate Studies, College of Education and Human Services, Farmville, VA 23909. Offers communication sciences and disorders (MS); community and college counseling (MS); curriculum and instruction specialist-elementary (MS), including mild disabilities, modern languages; curriculum and instruction specialist-secondary (MS), including English, mild disabilities, modern languages; educational leadership (MS); guidance and counseling (MS); literacy and culture (MS); school library media (MS). *Accreditation:* NCATE. Part-time and evening/weekend programs available. *Degree requirements:* For master's, comprehensive exam, thesis optional. *Entrance requirements:* For master's, GRE (communication sciences and disorders), minimum GPA of 2.75. Additional exam requirements/recommendations for international students: Required—TOEFL (minimum score 550 paper-based; 213 computer-based).

Longwood University, Office of Graduate Studies, Department of English and Modern Languages, Farmville, VA 23909. Offers 6-12 initial teaching/licensure (MA); creative writing (MA); English education and writing (MA); literature (MA). Part-time programs available. *Degree requirements:* For master's, comprehensive exam (for some programs), thesis (for some programs). *Entrance requirements:* For master's, minimum GPA of 2.75. Additional exam requirements/recommendations for international students: Required—TOEFL (minimum score 550 paper-based; 213 computer-based).

Louisiana Tech University, Graduate School, College of Education, Department of Curriculum, Instruction and Leadership, Ruston, LA 71272. Offers curriculum and instruction (MS, Ed D); educational leadership (Ed D); secondary education (M Ed), including business education, English education, foreign language education, health and physical education, mathematics education, science education, social studies education, speech education. *Accreditation:* NCATE. Part-time programs available. *Degree requirements:* For doctorate, thesis/dissertation. *Entrance requirements:* For master's and doctorate, GRE General Test.

Lynchburg College, Graduate Studies, School of Education and Human Development, Program in English Education, Lynchburg, VA 24501-3199. Offers M Ed. *Expenses:* Tuition: Full-time $7020; part-time $390 per credit hour.

Manhattanville College, Graduate Programs, School of Education, Program in Middle Childhood/Adolescence Education (Grades 5-12), Purchase, NY 10577-2132. Offers biology (MAT); biology and special education (MPS); chemistry (MAT); chemistry and special education (MPS); English (MAT); English and special education (MPS); literacy (MPS), including reading and writing, writing; literacy and special education (MPS); math (MAT); math and special education (MPS); second language (MAT), including French, Italian, Latin, Spanish; social studies (MAT); social studies and special education (MPS); special education (MPS). Part-time and evening/weekend programs available. *Students:* 52 full-time (39 women), 106 part-time (71 women); includes 8 African Americans, 3 Asian Americans or Pacific Islanders, 4 Hispanic Americans, 1 international. In 2009, 82 master's awarded. *Degree requirements:* For master's, comprehensive exam or research project, field experience. *Entrance requirements:* For master's, minimum undergraduate GPA of 3.0, 2 letters of recommendation. Additional exam requirements/recommendations for international students: Required—TOEFL. *Application deadline:* Applications are processed on a rolling basis. Application fee: $70. Electronic applications accepted. *Financial support:* Career-related internships or fieldwork, Federal Work-Study, institutionally sponsored loans, and unspecified assistantships available. Support available to part-time students. Financial award application deadline: 3/1; financial award applicants required to submit FAFSA. *Unit head:* Dr. Shelley Wepner, Dean, 914-323-5192, Fax: 914-694-2386, E-mail: wepners@mville.edu. *Application contact:* Jeanine Pardey-Levine, Director of Admissions, 914-323-3208, Fax: 914-694-1732, E-mail: edschool@mville.edu.

Maryville University of Saint Louis, School of Education, St. Louis, MO 63141-7299. Offers art education (MA Ed); early childhood education (MA Ed); educational leadership (Ed D); educational leadership: principal certification (MA Ed); elementary education (MA Ed); elementary education/English (MA Ed); elementary education/psychology (MA Ed); environmental education (MA Ed); gifted education (MA Ed); literacy specialist (MA Ed); middle grades education (MA Ed); secondary teaching and inquiry (MA Ed); teacher as leader (MA Ed). *Accreditation:* NASAD; NCATE. Part-time and evening/weekend programs available. *Students:* 25 full-time (18 women), 198 part-time (145 women); includes 33 minority (27 African Americans, 2 American Indian/Alaska Native, 1 Asian American or Pacific Islander, 3 Hispanic Americans). Average age 36. In 2009, 61 master's, 45 doctorates awarded. *Degree requirements:* For master's, thesis, project. *Entrance requirements:* For master's and doctorate, minimum GPA of 3.0, 3 professional recommendations. Additional exam requirements/recommendations for international students: Required—TOEFL (minimum score 550 paper-based). *Application deadline:* Applications are processed on a rolling basis. Application fee: $40 ($60 for international students). Electronic applications accepted. *Expenses:* Tuition: Full-time $20,384; part-time $627.50 per credit hour. Required fees: $100 per semester. *Financial support:* Career-related internships or fieldwork, Federal Work-Study, tuition waivers (partial), and professional educator discounts available. Financial award application deadline: 3/1; financial award applicants required to submit FAFSA. *Faculty research:* Collaboration with public schools, pre-service program development, mathematics, diversity, literacy. *Unit head:* Dr. Sam Hausfather, Dean, 314-529-9466, Fax: 314-529-9921, E-mail: shausfather@maryville.edu. *Application contact:* Holly Stanwich, Graduate Admissions Coordinator, 314-529-9542, Fax: 314-529-9921, E-mail: teachered@maryville.edu.

Millersville University of Pennsylvania, College of Graduate and Professional Studies, School of Humanities and Social Sciences, Department of English, Millersville, PA 17551-0302. Offers English (MA); English education (M Ed). Part-time programs available. *Faculty:* 24 full-time (13 women), 12 part-time/adjunct (8 women). *Students:* 13 full-time (9 women), 23 part-time (12 women); includes 4 minority (3 African Americans, 1 Asian American or Pacific Islander). Average age 31. 16 applicants, 94% accepted, 10 enrolled. In 2009, 11 master's awarded. *Degree requirements:* For master's, one foreign language, thesis optional. *Entrance*

English Education

Millersville University of Pennsylvania (continued)
requirements: For master's, GRE or MAT, 3 letters of recommendation. Additional exam requirements/recommendations for international students: Required—TOEFL (minimum score 500 paper-based; 183 computer-based; 65 iBT) or IELTS (minimum score 6). *Application deadline:* For fall admission, 1/15 priority date for domestic and international students; for winter admission, 10/1 priority date for domestic and international students; for spring admission, 10/1 priority date for domestic and international students. Applications are processed on a rolling basis. Application fee: $40 ($50 for international students). Electronic applications accepted. *Expenses:* Tuition, state resident: full-time $6666; part-time $370 per credit. Tuition, nonresident: full-time $10,666; part-time $593 per credit. Required fees: $1578.50; $76.25 per credit. One-time fee: $60 part-time. Tuition and fees vary according to course load. *Financial support:* In 2009–10, 10 students received support, including 10 research assistantships with full and partial tuition reimbursements available (averaging $3,890 per year); institutionally sponsored loans and unspecified assistantships also available. Support available to part-time students. Financial award application deadline: 3/15; financial award applicants required to submit FAFSA. *Faculty research:* Comparative literatures, writing studies, linguistics, film studies, curriculum and instruction/educational pedagogy. *Unit head:* Dr. Beverly Schneller, Chair, 717-871-2342, Fax: 717-871-2446, E-mail: beverly.schneller@millersville.edu. *Application contact:* Dr. Victor S. DeSantis, Dean of Graduate and Professional Studies, 717-872-3099, Fax: 717-872-3453, E-mail: victor.desantis@millersville.edu.

Mills College, Graduate Studies, School of Education, Oakland, CA 94613-1000. Offers child life in hospitals (MA); early childhood education (MA); education (MA), including art education, curriculum and instruction, elementary education, English education, foreign language education, mathematics education, science education, secondary education, social studies education, teaching; educational leadership (MA, Ed D); infant mental health (MA). Part-time and evening/weekend programs available. *Faculty:* 11 full-time (9 women), 16 part-time/adjunct (14 women). *Students:* 138 full-time (119 women), 55 part-time (48 women); includes 71 minority (34 African Americans, 19 Asian Americans or Pacific Islanders, 18 Hispanic Americans), 3 international. Average age 34. 210 applicants, 82% accepted, 93 enrolled. In 2009, 54 master's, 15 doctorates awarded. Terminal master's awarded for partial completion of doctoral program. *Degree requirements:* For master's, comprehensive exam. *Entrance requirements:* For doctorate, GRE General Test. Additional exam requirements/recommendations for international students: Required—TOEFL. *Application deadline:* For fall admission, 2/1 for domestic and international students; for spring admission, 11/1 for domestic and international students. Applications are processed on a rolling basis. Application fee: $50. Electronic applications accepted. *Expenses:* Tuition: Full-time $26,326; part-time $6584 per course. Required fees: $896. One-time fee: $896 part-time. Tuition and fees vary according to program. *Financial support:* In 2009–10, 188 students received support, including 186 fellowships (averaging $6,499 per year), 28 teaching assistantships with partial tuition reimbursements available (averaging $3,187 per year); career-related internships or fieldwork and scholarships/grants also available. Support available to part-time students. Financial award application deadline: 2/1; financial award applicants required to submit FAFSA. *Faculty research:* Child development, gender and education, public policy, cross-cultural development, development of literacy. Total annual research expenditures: $1.2 million. *Unit head:* Joseph Kahne, Chairperson, 510-430-3190, Fax: 510-430-3314, E-mail: grad-studies@mills.edu. *Application contact:* Jessica King, Graduate Admission Specialist, 510-430-3305, Fax: 510-430-2159, E-mail: grad-studies@mills.edu.

Minnesota State University Mankato, College of Graduate Studies, College of Arts and Humanities, Department of English, Mankato, MN 56001. Offers creative writing (MFA); English (MAT); English studies (MA); literature (MA); teaching English as a second language (MA, Certificate); technical communication (MA, Certificate). Part-time programs available. *Students:* 54 full-time (34 women), 114 part-time (78 women). *Degree requirements:* For master's, one foreign language, comprehensive exam, thesis or alternative. *Entrance requirements:* For master's, minimum GPA of 3.0 during previous 2 years, writing sample (MFA). Additional exam requirements/recommendations for international students: Required—TOEFL. *Application deadline:* Applications are processed on a rolling basis. Application fee: $40. Electronic applications accepted. *Expenses:* Tuition, state resident: full-time $5364. Tuition, nonresident: full-time $8314. *Financial support:* Research assistantships with full tuition reimbursements, teaching assistantships with full tuition reimbursements, career-related internships or fieldwork, Federal Work-Study, and unspecified assistantships available. Financial award application deadline: 3/15; financial award applicants required to submit FAFSA. *Faculty research:* Keats and Christianity. *Unit head:* Dr. John Banschbach, Chairperson, 507-389-2117. *Application contact:* 507-389-2321, E-mail: grad@mnsu.edu.

Mississippi College, Graduate School, School of Education, Department of Teacher Education and Leadership, Clinton, MS 39058. Offers art (M Ed); biological science (M Ed); business education (M Ed); computer science (M Ed); dyslexia therapy (M Ed); educational leadership (M Ed, Ed D, Ed S); elementary education (M Ed, Ed S); English (M Ed); higher education administration (MS); mathematics (M Ed); secondary education (M Ed); social studies (history) (M Ed); teaching arts (M Ed). Part-time programs available. Postbaccalaureate distance learning degree programs offered (no on-campus study). *Faculty:* 11 full-time (7 women), 13 part-time/adjunct (7 women). *Students:* 33 full-time (22 women), 282 part-time (240 women); includes 148 minority (146 African Americans, 2 American Indian/Alaska Native), 1 international. Average age 34. In 2009, 147 master's awarded. *Degree requirements:* For master's, comprehensive exam, thesis optional. *Entrance requirements:* For master's, NTE. Additional exam requirements/recommendations for international students: Recommended—IELTS. *Application deadline:* For fall admission, 8/15 priority date for domestic students. Applications are processed on a rolling basis. Application fee: $30. Electronic applications accepted. *Expenses:* Tuition: Part-time $452 per credit hour. Required fees: $101 per semester. Tuition and fees vary according to degree level, campus/location, program and student level. *Financial support:* Teaching assistantships, career-related internships or fieldwork, Federal Work-Study, scholarships/grants, and unspecified assistantships available. Support available to part-time students. Financial award applicants required to submit FAFSA. *Unit head:* Dr. Tom Williams, Chair, 601-925-3844, E-mail: twilliams@mc.edu. *Application contact:* Elnora Lewis, Secretary, 601-925-3225, Fax: 601-925-3889, E-mail: lewis09@mc.edu.

Montclair State University, The Graduate School, College of Education and Human Services, Department of Curriculum and Teaching, Montclair, NJ 07043-1624. Offers education (M Ed); educational technology (M Ed); learning disabled teacher consultant (Certificate); school library media specialist (Certificate); teaching (MAT, Certificate), including art (MAT), biological science (MAT), early childhood education (P-3) (MAT), earth science (MAT), elementary education (K-8) (MAT), English (MAT), French (MAT), health and physical education (MAT), health education (MAT), home economics (MAT), mathematics (MAT), music (MAT), physical education (MAT), physical science (MAT), social studies (MAT), Spanish (MAT), teacher of ESL (MAT), teacher of students with disabilities (MAT). Part-time and evening/weekend programs available. *Faculty:* 17 full-time (12 women), 29 part-time/adjunct (21 women). *Students:* 124 full-time (63 women), 174 part-time (126 women). Average age 31. 112 applicants, 69% accepted, 59 enrolled. In 2009, 179 master's, 2 other advanced degrees awarded. *Degree requirements:* For master's, comprehensive exam, field experience. *Entrance requirements:* For master's, GRE, 2 letters of recommendation. Additional exam requirements/recommendations for international students: Required—TOEFL (minimum score 83 computer-based), or IELTS. *Application deadline:* For fall admission, 2/15 for domestic and international students; for spring admission, 9/15 for domestic and international students. Applications are processed on a rolling basis. Application fee: $60. Electronic applications accepted. *Expenses:* Tuition, area resident: Part-time $486.74 per credit. Tuition, state resident: part-time $486.74 per credit. Tuition, nonresident: part-time $751.34 per credit. Tuition and fees vary according to degree level and program. *Financial support:* In 2009–10, 12 research assistantships with full tuition reimbursements (averaging $7,000 per year) were awarded; Federal Work-Study, scholarships/grants, and unspecified assistantships also available. Support available to part-time students. Financial award application deadline: 3/1; financial award applicants required to submit FAFSA. *Unit head:* Dr. David Schwarzer, Chairperson, 973-655-5187. *Application contact:* Amy Aiello, Director of Graduate Admissions and Operations, 973-655-5147, Fax: 973-655-7869, E-mail: graduate.school@montclair.edu.

Morehead State University, Graduate Programs, College of Education, Department of Foundational and Graduate Studies in Education, Morehead, KY 40351. Offers adult and higher education (MA, Ed S); certified professional counselor (Ed S); counseling P-12 (MA); curriculum and instruction (Ed S); educational technology (MA Ed); instructional leadership (Ed S); school administration (MA); school counseling (Ed S); teacher leader business and marketing- content (MA Ed); teacher leader business and marketing- technology (MA Ed); teacher leader educational technology (MA Ed); teacher leader English (MA Ed); teacher leader gifted educ (MA Ed); teacher leader IECE—non-certification (MA Ed); teacher leader IECE certification (MA Ed); teacher leader interdisciplanary educaction P-5 (MA Ed); teacher leader middle grades 5-9 (MA Ed); teacher leader reading/writing—non-certification (MA Ed); teacher leader reading/writing certification (MA Ed); teacher leader school communication—non-certification (MA Ed); teacher leader school communication certification (MA Ed); teacher leader social studies (MA Ed); teacher leader special education (MA Ed). *Accreditation:* NCATE. Part-time and evening/weekend programs available. *Faculty:* 20 full-time (10 women), 7 part-time/adjunct (3 women). *Students:* 26 full-time (18 women), 371 part-time (295 women); includes 11 minority (9 African Americans, 1 American Indian/Alaska Native, 1 Hispanic American). Average age 35. 201 applicants, 73% accepted, 73 enrolled. In 2009, 105 master's, 5 other advanced degrees awarded. *Degree requirements:* For master's, thesis optional, oral and/or written comprehensive exams; for Ed S, thesis, oral exam. *Entrance requirements:* For master's, GRE General Test, minimum overall undergraduate GPA of 2.5; for Ed S, GRE General Test, interview, master's degree, minimum GPA of 3.5, work experience. Additional exam requirements/recommendations for international students: Required—TOEFL (minimum score 500 paper-based; 173 computer-based). *Application deadline:* For fall admission, 8/1 priority date for domestic and international students; for spring admission, 12/1 priority date for domestic and international students. Applications are processed on a rolling basis. Application fee: $30. Electronic applications accepted. *Expenses:* Tuition, state resident: full-time $6318; part-time $351 per credit hour. Tuition, nonresident: full-time $15,804; part-time $878 per credit hour. *Financial support:* In 2009–10, 2 research assistantships (averaging $10,000 per year) were awarded; career-related internships or fieldwork, Federal Work-Study, and unspecified assistantships also available. Financial award application deadline: 3/15; financial award applicants required to submit FAFSA. *Faculty research:* Character education, school accountability, computer applications for school administrators. *Unit head:* Dr. Cathy Gunn, Dean and Professor, 606-783-2040, Fax: 606-783-5029, E-mail: c.gunn@moreheadstate.edu. *Application contact:* Michelle Barber, Graduate Recruitment and Retention Assistant Director, 606-783-5127, Fax: 606-783-5061, E-mail: m.barber@moreheadstate.edu.

Morehead State University, Graduate Programs, College of Education, Department of Middle Grades and Secondary Education, Morehead, KY 40351. Offers business and marketing education (MAT); English/language arts 5-9 (MAT); French (MAT); health P-12 (MAT); mathematics 5-9 (MAT); physical education P-12 (MAT); science 5-9 (MAT); secondary biology (MAT); secondary chemistry (MAT); secondary earth science (MAT); secondary English (MAT); secondary math (MAT); secondary physics (MAT); secondary social studies (MAT); social studies 5-9 (MAT); Spanish (MAT). Part-time and evening/weekend programs available. *Students:* 54 full-time (31 women), 233 part-time (142 women); includes 11 minority (5 African Americans, 1 American Indian/Alaska Native, 1 Asian American or Pacific Islander, 4 Hispanic Americans). Average age 32. 206 applicants, 71% accepted, 79 enrolled. In 2009, 101 master's awarded. *Degree requirements:* For master's, portfolio. *Entrance requirements:* For master's, GRE or PRAXIS II content exam, minimum overall undergraduate GPA of 2.5. Additional exam requirements/recommendations for international students: Required—TOEFL (minimum score 500 paper-based; 173 computer-based). *Application deadline:* For fall admission, 8/1 priority date for domestic and international students; for spring admission, 12/1 priority date for domestic and international students. Applications are processed on a rolling basis. Application fee: $30. Electronic applications accepted. *Expenses:* Tuition, state resident: full-time $6318; part-time $351 per credit hour. Tuition, nonresident: full-time $15,804; part-time $878 per credit hour. *Financial support:* In 2009–10, 1 research assistantship (averaging $10,000 per year) was awarded; career-related internships or fieldwork, Federal Work-Study, and unspecified assistantships also available. Financial award application deadline: 3/15; financial award applicants required to submit FAFSA. *Unit head:* Dr. Cathy Gunn, Dean, 606-783-2040, Fax: 606-783-5029, E-mail: c.gunn@moreheadstate.edu. *Application contact:* Michelle Barber, Graduate Recruitment and Retention Assistant Director, 606-783-5127, Fax: 606-783-5061, E-mail: m.barber@moreheadstate.edu.

National-Louis University, National College of Education, Programs in Reading and Language, Chicago, IL 60603. Offers language and literacy (M Ed, MS Ed, CAS); reading recovery (CAS); reading specialist (M Ed, MS Ed, CAS). Part-time and evening/weekend programs available. *Degree requirements:* For master's, thesis (for some programs). *Entrance requirements:* For master's, MAT or GRE, minimum GPA of 3.0, teaching certificate; for CAS, master's degree, teaching certificate. *Expenses:* Tuition: Full-time $17,160; part-time $715 per semester hour. Tuition and fees vary according to course load, degree level, campus/location and program.

New York University, Steinhardt School of Culture, Education, and Human Development, Department of Music and Performing Arts Professions, Program in Educational Theatre, New York, NY 10012-1019. Offers dual degree: educational theatre and social studies (MA); educational theatre (Ed D, PhD, Advanced Certificate); educational theatre for colleges and communities (MA); educational theatre with English 7-12 (MA); teaching educational theatre, all grades (MA). Part-time programs available. *Students:* 78 full-time (64 women), 65 part-time (43 women); includes 24 minority (10 African Americans, 1 American Indian/Alaska Native, 4 Asian Americans or Pacific Islanders, 9 Hispanic Americans), 7 international. Average age 30. 104 applicants, 84% accepted, 58 enrolled. In 2009, 74 master's, 2 doctorates awarded. *Degree requirements:* For master's, thesis (for some programs); for doctorate, thesis/dissertation. *Entrance requirements:* For master's, audition; for doctorate, GRE General Test, interview; for Advanced Certificate, master's degree. Additional exam requirements/recommendations for international students: Required—TOEFL. *Application deadline:* For fall admission, 12/15 priority date for domestic and international students; for spring admission, 11/1 for domestic and international students. Applications are processed on a rolling basis. Application fee: $75. Electronic applications accepted. *Expenses:* Tuition: Full-time $30,528; part-time $1272 per credit. Required fees: $2177. *Financial support:* Teaching assistantships with partial tuition reimbursements, career-related internships or fieldwork, Federal Work-Study, institutionally sponsored loans, and scholarships/grants available. Support available to part-time students. Financial award application deadline: 2/1; financial award applicants required to submit FAFSA. *Faculty research:* Theatre for young audiences, drama in education, applied theatre, arts education assessment, reflective praxis. *Unit head:* Dr. Philip Taylor, Director, 212-998-5424, Fax: 212-995-4043. *Application contact:* 212-998-5030, Fax: 212-995-4328, E-mail: steinhardt.gradadmissions@nyu.edu.

New York University, Steinhardt School of Culture, Education, and Human Development, Department of Teaching and Learning, Program in English Education, New York, NY 10012-1019. Offers secondary and college (PhD), including applied linguistics, comparative education, curriculum, literature and reading, media education; teachers of English 7-12 (MA); teachers of English language and literature in college (Advanced Certificate). *Accreditation:* Teacher Education Accreditation Council. Part-time programs available. *Students:* 36 full-time (30 women), 30 part-time (25 women); includes 11 minority (4 African Americans, 3 Asian Americans or Pacific Islanders, 4 Hispanic Americans), 2 international. Average age 26. 91 applicants, 80% accepted, 21 enrolled. In 2009, 27 master's, 6 doctorates, 1 other advanced degree awarded. *Degree requirements:* For master's, thesis (for some programs); for doctorate, thesis/dissertation. *Entrance requirements:* For doctorate, GRE General Test, interview; for Advanced Certificate, master's degree. Additional exam requirements/recommendations for international students: Required—TOEFL. *Application deadline:* For fall admission, 12/15 priority date for domestic and international students; for spring admission, 11/1 for domestic and international students. Applications are processed on a rolling basis. Application fee: $75.

Electronic applications accepted. *Expenses:* Tuition: Full-time $30,528; part-time $1272 per credit. Required fees: $2177. *Financial support:* Fellowships with full and partial tuition reimbursements, teaching assistantships with full and partial tuition reimbursements, career-related internships or fieldwork, Federal Work-Study, institutionally sponsored loans, scholarships/grants, tuition waivers (partial), and unspecified assistantships available. Support available to part-time students. Financial award application deadline: 2/1; financial award applicants required to submit FAFSA. *Faculty research:* Making meaning of literature, teaching of literature, urban adolescent literacy and equity, literacy development and globalization, digital media and literacy. *Unit head:* Director, 212-998-5460, Fax: 212-995-4049. *Application contact:* 212-998-5030, Fax: 212-995-4328, E-mail: steinhardt.gradadmissions@nyu.edu.

North Carolina Agricultural and Technical State University, Graduate School, College of Arts and Sciences, Department of English, Greensboro, NC 27411. Offers English (MA); English and Afro-American literature (MA); English education (MS). Part-time and evening/weekend programs available. *Degree requirements:* For master's, comprehensive exam, qualifying exam. *Entrance requirements:* For master's, GRE General Test, minimum GPA of 3.0.

North Carolina State University, Graduate School, College of Education, Department of Curriculum and Instruction, Program in Secondary English Education, Raleigh, NC 27695. Offers M Ed, MS Ed. *Degree requirements:* For master's, thesis optional.

Northeastern Illinois University, Graduate College, College of Education, School of Teacher Education, Program in Instruction, Chicago, IL 60625-4699. Offers language arts (MSI). *Degree requirements:* For master's, 2 research papers, oral exam. *Entrance requirements:* For master's, minimum GPA of 2.75; previous course work in English, linguistics, or speech; teaching certificate. Additional exam requirements/recommendations for international students: Required—TOEFL (minimum score 550 paper-based; 213 computer-based; 80 iBT). Electronic applications accepted. *Faculty research:* Emergent literacy, literature-based literacy instruction, drama and literature in the classroom, curriculum integration, standards-based assessment, integrating technology.

Northeastern Illinois University, Graduate College, College of Education, School of Teacher Education, Program in Teaching, Chicago, IL 60625-4699. Offers language arts (MAT). *Accreditation:* NCATE. *Degree requirements:* For master's, 2 research papers, oral exam. *Entrance requirements:* For master's, ISBE, minimum GPA of 2.75; previous course work in English, speech, drama, or linguistics. Additional exam requirements/recommendations for international students: Required—TOEFL (minimum score 550 paper-based; 213 computer-based; 80 iBT). Electronic applications accepted. *Faculty research:* Emergent literacy, literature-based literacy, drama and literature in the classroom, curriculum integration, standards-based assessment.

Northern Arizona University, Graduate College, College of Arts and Letters, Department of English, Flagstaff, AZ 86011. Offers applied linguistics (PhD); English (MA), including creative writing, general English studies, literacy, technology and professional writing, literature, secondary English education; professional writing (Certificate); teaching English as a second language (MA, PhD, Certificate). *Faculty:* 40 full-time (24 women). *Students:* 138 full-time (92 women), 113 part-time (84 women); includes 27 minority (7 African Americans, 8 American Indian/Alaska Native, 5 Asian Americans or Pacific Islanders, 7 Hispanic Americans), 18 international. Average age 31. 189 applicants, 70% accepted, 81 enrolled. In 2009, 92 master's, 9 doctorates awarded. *Degree requirements:* For master's, comprehensive exam, thesis (for some programs), departmental qualifying exam; for doctorate, comprehensive exam, thesis/dissertation, departmental qualifying exam. *Entrance requirements:* For master's, minimum GPA of 3.0 or GRE; for doctorate, GRE General Test. Additional exam requirements/recommendations for international students: Required—TOEFL (minimum score 550 paper-based; 213 computer-based; 80 iBT), IELTS (minimum score 7), or a bachelor's degree from an English-speaking university and demonstrated proficiency. *Application deadline:* For fall admission, 2/15 priority date for domestic students, 9/1 priority date for international students; for winter admission, 4/15 priority date for domestic students; for spring admission, 11/15 priority date for domestic students. Applications are processed on a rolling basis. Application fee: $65. Electronic applications accepted. *Financial support:* In 2009–10, 63 teaching assistantships with partial tuition reimbursements (averaging $11,623 per year) were awarded; Federal Work-Study, tuition waivers (full and partial), and unspecified assistantships also available. Financial award application deadline: 3/30; financial award applicants required to submit FAFSA. *Unit head:* Dr. J. Allen Woodman, Chair, 928-523-5651, E-mail: allen.woodman@nau.edu. *Application contact:* Barbara Hanks, Secretary, 928-523-4911, E-mail: barbara.hanks@nau.edu.

Northern State University, Division of Graduate Studies in Education, Program in Teaching and Learning, Aberdeen, SD 57401-7198. Offers educational studies (MS Ed); elementary classroom teaching (MS Ed); health, physical education, and coaching (MS Ed); language and literacy (MS Ed); secondary classroom teaching (MS Ed); special education (MS Ed). *Accreditation:* NCATE. Part-time and evening/weekend programs available. *Faculty:* 10 full-time (8 women). *Students:* 23 full-time (16 women), 35 part-time (17 women); includes 2 minority (1 American Indian/Alaska Native, 1 Asian American or Pacific Islander). Average age 32. In 2009, 26 master's awarded. *Degree requirements:* For master's, thesis optional. *Entrance requirements:* For master's, minimum GPA of 2.75. Additional exam requirements/recommendations for international students: Required—TOEFL (minimum score 550 paper-based; 213 computer-based; 76 iBT). *Application deadline:* For fall admission, 8/15 priority date for domestic students; for spring admission, 12/15 for domestic students. Applications are processed on a rolling basis. Application fee: $35. Electronic applications accepted. *Financial support:* In 2009–10, 18 teaching assistantships with partial tuition reimbursements (averaging $5,558 per year) were awarded; career-related internships or fieldwork, Federal Work-Study, institutionally sponsored loans, scholarships/grants, and unspecified assistantships also available. Support available to part-time students. Financial award application deadline: 3/1; financial award applicants required to submit FAFSA. *Application contact:* Tammy K. Griffith, Program Assistant, 605-626-2558, Fax: 605-626-7190, E-mail: griffith@northern.edu.

North Georgia College & State University, Graduate Studies, Program in Teacher Education, Dahlonega, GA 30597. Offers early childhood education (M Ed); educational leadership (Ed S); middle grades education (M Ed); secondary education (M Ed), including art education, biology education, chemistry education, English education, history education, mathematics education, physical education, science education; special education (M Ed), including interrelated special education, learning disabilities. *Accreditation:* NCATE. Part-time and evening/weekend programs available. Postbaccalaureate distance learning degree programs offered (minimal on-campus study). *Degree requirements:* For master's, comprehensive exam, thesis optional. *Entrance requirements:* For master's, GRE General Test or MAT, minimum GPA of 2.75; for Ed S, GRE General Test or MAT, 3 years of teaching experience, master's degree, minimum graduate GPA of 3.25. Electronic applications accepted. *Faculty research:* Computers and teachers' attitudes, rural versus urban teacher attitudes, teacher leadership roles, minority recruitment in teaching force.

Northwestern State University of Louisiana, Graduate Studies and Research, College of Education, Programs in Education, Natchitoches, LA 71497. Offers business and distributive education (M Ed); counseling (M Ed); early childhood education (M Ed); education (M Ed); education leadership (M Ed); educational technology (M Ed); elementary teaching (M Ed); English education (M Ed); home economics education (M Ed); mathematics education (M Ed); reading (M Ed); science education (M Ed); secondary teaching (M Ed); social sciences education (M Ed). *Degree requirements:* For master's, comprehensive exam, thesis or alternative. *Entrance requirements:* For master's, GRE General Test, minimum undergraduate GPA of 2.5.

Northwest Missouri State University, Graduate School, College of Arts and Sciences, Department of English, Maryville, MO 64468-6001. Offers English (MA); English with speech emphasis (MA); teaching English (option 1) (MS Ed); teaching English with speech emphasis (MS Ed). Part-time programs available. *Faculty:* 8 full-time (2 women). *Students:* 11 full-time (6 women), 4 part-time (3 women). 9 applicants, 67% accepted, 4 enrolled. In 2009, 3 master's awarded. *Degree requirements:* For master's, comprehensive exam, thesis optional. *Entrance requirements:* For master's, GRE General Test, minimum undergraduate GPA of 2.5, writing sample. Additional exam requirements/recommendations for international students: Required—TOEFL (minimum score 550 paper-based; 213 computer-based). *Application deadline:* For fall admission, 7/1 for domestic and international students; for spring admission, 11/15 for domestic and international students. Applications are processed on a rolling basis. Application fee: $0 ($50 for international students). *Expenses:* Tuition, state resident: part-time $296.34 per credit hour. Tuition, nonresident: part-time $510.43 per credit hour. *Financial support:* In 2009–10, 5 teaching assistantships with full tuition reimbursements (averaging $6,000 per year) were awarded. Financial award application deadline: 4/1; financial award applicants required to submit FAFSA. *Unit head:* Dr. Beth Richards, Chairperson, 660-562-1745. *Application contact:* Dr. Gregory Haddock, Dean of Graduate School, 660-562-1145, Fax: 660-562-1096, E-mail: gradsch@nwmissouri.edu.

Nova Southeastern University, Fischler School of Education and Human Services, Graduate Teacher Education Program, Fort Lauderdale, FL 33314-7796. Offers athletic administration (MS); brain research (MS, Ed S); charter school education/leadership (MS); cognitive and behavioral disabilities (MS); computer science education (Ed S); computer science education (K-12) (MS); curriculum and teaching (Ed S); curriculum, instruction and technology (MS); curriculum, instruction, management and administration (Ed S); early childhood education (MS); early literacy and reading (Ed S); early literacy education (MS); education technology (MS); educational leadership (administration K–12) (MS, Ed S); educational media (Ed S); educational media (K-12) (MS); elementary education (MS, Ed S), including ESOL endorsement (MS); English education (MS, Ed S); environmental education (MS); exceptional student education (MS), including ESOL endorsement; gifted education (MS, Ed S); interdisciplinary arts education (MS); management and administration of educational programs (MS); mathematics (MS); mathematics education (Ed S); multicultural early intervention (MS); pre-kindergarten/primary (MS); preschool education (MS); reading (MS); reading and TESOL (MS); reading education (Ed S); science (MS); science education (Ed S); secondary education (MS); social studies (MS, Ed S); Spanish language (MS); special education and reading (MS); teaching and learning (MA, MS), including curriculum and instruction (MA), elementary mathematics (MA), elementary reading (MA), K-12 technology integration (MA); teaching English to speakers of other languages (MS, Ed S); technology management and administration (Ed S); urban studies education (MS). Part-time and evening/weekend programs available. Postbaccalaureate distance learning degree programs offered (minimal on-campus study). *Faculty:* 72 full-time (43 women), 385 part-time/adjunct (252 women). *Students:* 196 full-time (175 women), 1,304 part-time (1,128 women); includes 594 minority (471 African Americans, 5 American Indian/Alaska Native, 18 Asian Americans or Pacific Islanders, 100 Hispanic Americans). Average age 37. 2,610 applicants, 72% accepted, 1352 enrolled. In 2009, 836 other advanced degrees awarded. *Degree requirements:* For master's and Ed S, thesis, practicum, internship. *Entrance requirements:* For master's, MAT, GRE, CLAST, CBEST, PRAXIS I, General Knowledge Test, minimum GPA of 2.5; for Ed S, MAT or GRE, master's degree, teaching certificate, minimum GPA of 3.0. Additional exam requirements/recommendations for international students: Required—TSE (recommended, minimum score 50); Recommended—TOEFL (minimum score 550 paper-based; 213 computer-based; 80 iBT), IELTS (minimum score 6). *Application deadline:* For fall admission, 9/25 priority date for domestic and international students; for winter admission, 2/23 priority date for domestic and international students; for spring admission, 4/25 priority date for domestic and international students. Applications are processed on a rolling basis. Application fee: $50. Electronic applications accepted. *Financial support:* Federal Work-Study available. Support available to part-time students. Financial award application deadline: 4/15; financial award applicants required to submit FAFSA. *Faculty research:* School effectiveness, critical thinking, leadership skills acquisition, child education, multicultural education. *Unit head:* Dr. Ronald Kern, Dean of Academic Affairs, 800-986-3223 Ext. 7809, Fax: 954-262-3606, E-mail: rk429@nsu.nova.edu. *Application contact:* Dr. Jennifer Quinones Nottingham, Dean of Student Affairs, 800-986-3223 Ext. 1559.

Occidental College, Graduate Studies, Department of Education, Program in Secondary Education, Los Angeles, CA 90041-3314. Offers English and comparative literary studies (MAT); history (MAT); life science (MAT); mathematics (MAT); physical science (MAT); social science (MAT); Spanish (MAT). Part-time programs available. *Degree requirements:* For master's, comprehensive exam, graduate synthesis paper. *Entrance requirements:* For master's, GRE General Test, minimum GPA of 3.0. Additional exam requirements/recommendations for international students: Required—TOEFL (minimum score 625 paper-based; 263 computer-based). *Expenses:* Contact institution.

Our Lady of the Lake University of San Antonio, College of Arts and Sciences, Program in English, San Antonio, TX 78207-4689. Offers communication arts (MA); English and literature (MA); English education (MA); writing (MA). Part-time and evening/weekend programs available. *Students:* 9 full-time (5 women), 15 part-time (14 women); includes 16 minority (all Hispanic Americans). Average age 31. In 2009, 15 master's awarded. *Degree requirements:* For master's, comprehensive exam, thesis optional. *Entrance requirements:* For master's, GRE General Test or MAT, minimum GPA of 3.0 in last 60 hours, 2.5 overall. Additional exam requirements/recommendations for international students: Required—TOEFL. *Application deadline:* Applications are processed on a rolling basis. Application fee: $25 ($50 for international students). Electronic applications accepted. *Expenses:* Tuition: Full-time $12,330; part-time $685 per contact hour. Required fees: $139; $12 per contact hour. $57 per semester. Tuition and fees vary according to campus/location. *Financial support:* Research assistantships, teaching assistantships, career-related internships or fieldwork, Federal Work-Study, institutionally sponsored loans, and tuition waivers (partial) available. Financial award application deadline: 4/15. *Faculty research:* Writing theory and research, contemporary Southern literature, popular culture, poetry, literature of the Southwest. *Unit head:* Dr. Michael Lueker, Chair, 210-434-6711 Ext. 2242, E-mail: luekm@lake.ollusa.edu. *Application contact:* 210-434-6711, Fax: 210-431-4036, E-mail: gradadm@lake.ollusa.edu.

Plymouth State University, College of Graduate Studies, Graduate Studies in Education, Program in English Education, Plymouth, NH 03264-1595. Offers M Ed. Part-time and evening/weekend programs available. *Entrance requirements:* For master's, MAT.

Purdue University, Graduate School, School of Education, Department of Curriculum and Instruction, West Lafayette, IN 47907. Offers agricultural and extension education (PhD, Ed S); agriculture and extension education (MS, MS Ed); art education (PhD); consumer and family sciences and extension education (MS Ed, PhD, Ed S); curriculum studies (MS Ed, PhD, Ed S); educational technology (MS Ed, PhD, Ed S); elementary education (MS Ed); foreign language education (MS Ed, PhD, Ed S); industrial technology (PhD, Ed S); language arts (MS Ed, PhD, Ed S); literacy (MS Ed, PhD, Ed S); mathematics/science education (MS, MS Ed, PhD, Ed S); social studies (MS Ed, PhD); social studies education (Ed S); vocational/industrial education (MS Ed, PhD, Ed S); vocational/technical education (MS Ed, PhD, Ed S). *Accreditation:* NCATE. Part-time and evening/weekend programs available. *Degree requirements:* For master's, thesis optional; for doctorate, thesis/dissertation, oral and written exams; for Ed S, oral presentation, project. *Entrance requirements:* For master's, GRE General Test, minimum B average; for doctorate, GRE General Test; for Ed S, GRE, minimum B average. Additional exam requirements/recommendations for international students: Required—TOEFL. Electronic applications accepted. *Faculty research:* Literacy acquisition and development, teacher beliefs and knowledge, recruitment and retention of underrepresented students, economic education, literacy discourse.

Queens College of the City University of New York, Division of Graduate Studies, Division of Education, Department of Secondary Education, Flushing, NY 11367-1597. Offers art (MS Ed); biology (MS Ed, AC); chemistry (MS Ed, AC); earth sciences (MS Ed, AC); English (MS Ed, AC); French (MS Ed, AC); Italian (MS Ed, AC); mathematics (MS Ed, AC); music (MS Ed, AC); physics (MS Ed, AC); social studies (MS Ed, AC); Spanish (MS Ed, AC). Part-time and evening/weekend programs available. *Faculty:* 22 full-time (14 women). *Students:* 86 full-time (47 women), 1,118 part-time (736 women). 591 applicants, 60% accepted, 250

English Education

Queens College of the City University of New York (continued)
enrolled. In 2009, 187 master's awarded. *Degree requirements:* For master's, research project; for AC, thesis optional. *Entrance requirements:* For master's, minimum GPA of 3.0. Additional exam requirements/recommendations for international students: Required—TOEFL. *Application deadline:* For fall admission, 4/1 for domestic students; for spring admission, 11/1 for domestic students. Applications are processed on a rolling basis. Application fee: $125. *Expenses:* Tuition, state resident: full-time $7360; part-time $310 per credit. Tuition, nonresident: part-time $575 per credit. One-time fee: $195 full-time; $145.25 part-time. *Financial support:* Career-related internships or fieldwork, Federal Work-Study, institutionally sponsored loans, and tuition waivers (partial) available. Support available to part-time students. Financial award application deadline: 4/1; financial award applicants required to submit FAFSA. *Unit head:* Dr. Eleanor Armour-Thomas, Chairperson, 718-997-5150, E-mail: armourthomas@yahoo.com. *Application contact:* Mario Caruso, Director of Graduate Admissions, 718-997-5200, Fax: 718-997-5193, E-mail: graduate_admissions@qc.edu.

Quinnipiac University, Division of Education, Program in Secondary Education, Hamden, CT 06518-1940. Offers biology (MAT); English (MAT); history/social studies (MAT); mathematics (MAT); Spanish (MAT). *Accreditation:* NCATE. *Faculty:* 10 full-time (7 women), 5 part-time/adjunct (3 women). *Students:* 80 full-time (56 women), 2 part-time (1 woman); includes 6 minority (2 African Americans, 2 Asian Americans or Pacific Islanders, 2 Hispanic Americans). 77 applicants, 95% accepted, 66 enrolled. In 2009, 33 master's awarded. *Entrance requirements:* For master's, PRAXIS I, minimum GPA of 2.67, interview. Additional exam requirements/recommendations for international students: Required—TOEFL (minimum score 575 paper-based; 233 computer-based; 90 iBT), IELTS (minimum score 6.5). *Application deadline:* For fall admission, 3/31 priority date for domestic students. Applications are processed on a rolling basis. Application fee: $45. Electronic applications accepted. *Expenses:* Tuition: Full-time $16,030; part-time $770 per credit. Required fees: $630; $35 per credit. *Financial support:* Career-related internships or fieldwork, scholarships/grants, and tuition waivers (partial) available. Financial award application deadline: 4/15; financial award applicants required to submit FAFSA. *Faculty research:* Multicultural and urban education, role of technology in education, challenges of teaching diverse learners, socio-cultural nature of learning. *Unit head:* Dr. Bernadine Krawczyk, Assistant Dean, Division of Education, 203-582-3510, Fax: 203-582-3473, E-mail: bernadine.krawczyk@quinnipiac.edu. *Application contact:* Jennifer Boutin, Associate Director of Graduate Admissions, 800-462-1944, Fax: 203-582-3443, E-mail: jennifer.boutin@quinnipiac.edu.

Rhode Island College, School of Graduate Studies, Feinstein School of Education and Human Development, Department of Educational Studies, Providence, RI 02908-1991. Offers English (MAT); French (MAT); history (MAT); math (MAT); secondary education (MAT); Spanish (MAT); teaching English as a second language (M Ed); technology education (M Ed). *Accreditation:* NCATE. Part-time and evening/weekend programs available. *Faculty:* 10 full-time (5 women), 6 part-time/adjunct (5 women). *Students:* 8 full-time (all women), 56 part-time (40 women); includes 2 minority (both Hispanic Americans). Average age 35. In 2009, 28 master's awarded. *Degree requirements:* For master's, capstone or comprehensive assessment. *Entrance requirements:* For master's, GRE or MAT (for most programs), minimum undergraduate GPA of 3.0; baccalaureate degree in English, French, history, math or Spanish; evaluation of content area knowledge; 3 letters of recommendation; interview. Additional exam requirements/recommendations for international students: Recommended—TOEFL (minimum score 550 paper-based; 213 computer-based; 79 iBT). *Application deadline:* For fall admission, 3/15 for domestic students; for spring admission, 11/1 for domestic students. Applications are processed on a rolling basis. Application fee: $50. *Expenses:* Tuition, state resident: full-time $7440; part-time $310 per credit hour. Tuition, nonresident: full-time $14,784; part-time $616 per credit hour. Required fees: $552; $20 per credit. $70 per term. *Financial support:* Teaching assistantships with full tuition reimbursements, career-related internships or fieldwork, Federal Work-Study, scholarships/grants, health care benefits, and unspecified assistantships available. Support available to part-time students. Financial award application deadline: 5/15; financial award applicants required to submit FAFSA. *Faculty research:* School administration, school/college articulation. *Unit head:* Dr. Ellen Bigler, Chair, 401-456-8170. *Application contact:* Graduate Studies, 401-456-8700.

Rider University, Department of Graduate Education, Leadership and Counseling, Teacher Certification Program, Lawrenceville, NJ 08648-3001. Offers business education (Certificate); elementary education (Certificate); English as a second language (Certificate); English education (Certificate); mathematics education (Certificate); preschool to grade 3 (Certificate); science education (Certificate); social studies education (Certificate); world languages (Certificate), including French, German, Spanish. Part-time programs available. *Degree requirements:* For Certificate, internship, professional portfolio. *Entrance requirements:* For degree, PRAXIS, resume. Additional exam requirements/recommendations for international students: Required—TOEFL (minimum score 550 paper-based; 213 computer-based). Electronic applications accepted. *Faculty research:* Conceptual foundations for optimal development of creativity; creative theory, cognitive processes in mathematics learning, teacher collaboration.

Rollins College, Hamilton Holt School, Program in Education, Winter Park, FL 32789-4499. Offers elementary education (M Ed, MAT); secondary education (MAT), including English, mathematics, music. Part-time and evening/weekend programs available. *Faculty:* 5 full-time (3 women), 3 part-time/adjunct (2 women). *Students:* 14 full-time (11 women), 26 part-time (25 women); includes 7 minority (4 African Americans, 3 Hispanic Americans). Average age 31. 27 applicants, 100% accepted, 27 enrolled. In 2009, 10 master's awarded. *Degree requirements:* For master's, comprehensive exam. *Entrance requirements:* For master's, GRE or MAT, interview. Additional exam requirements/recommendations for international students: Required—TOEFL. *Application deadline:* For fall admission, 7/16 for domestic students; for winter admission, 12/3 for domestic students; for spring admission, 4/22 for domestic students. Applications are processed on a rolling basis. Application fee: $50. *Expenses:* Contact institution. *Financial support:* Teaching assistantships, scholarships/grants available. Support available to part-time students. *Unit head:* Dr. J. Scott Hewit, Director, 407-646-2300, E-mail: jhewit@rollins.edu. *Application contact:* Rebecca Cordray, Coordinator of Records and Registration, 407-646-1568, Fax: 407-975-6430, E-mail: rcordray@rollins.edu.

Rutgers, The State University of New Jersey, New Brunswick, Graduate School of Education, Department of Learning and Teaching, Program in English Education, Piscataway, NJ 08854-8097. Offers Ed M. Part-time programs available. *Degree requirements:* For master's, comprehensive exam or paper. *Entrance requirements:* For master's, GRE General Test, minimum GPA of 3.0. Additional exam requirements/recommendations for international students: Required—TOEFL. Electronic applications accepted.

Sage Graduate School, Graduate School, School of Education, Program in Teaching, Troy, NY 12180-4115. Offers art education (MAT); English (MAT); mathematics (MAT); social studies (MAT). Part-time and evening/weekend programs available. *Faculty:* 15 full-time (9 women), 19 part-time/adjunct (16 women). *Students:* 32 full-time (25 women), 39 part-time (27 women); includes 4 minority (all Asian Americans or Pacific Islanders). Average age 27. 47 applicants, 55% accepted, 19 enrolled. In 2009, 36 master's awarded. *Entrance requirements:* For master's, minimum undergraduate GPA of 2.75 overall, 3.0 in content area; current resume; 2 letters of recommendation; assessment of writing skills. Additional exam requirements/recommendations for international students: Required—TOEFL (minimum score 550 paper-based; 213 computer-based). *Application deadline:* For fall admission, 8/1 for domestic students. Applications are processed on a rolling basis. Application fee: $40. *Expenses:* Tuition: Full-time $10,620; part-time $590 per credit hour. *Financial support:* Fellowships, research assistantships, Federal Work-Study, scholarships/grants, and unspecified assistantships available. Support available to part-time students. Financial award application deadline: 3/1; financial award applicants required to submit FAFSA. *Unit head:* Kelly Jones, Director, 518-244-2433. *Application contact:* Wendy D. Diefendorf, Director of Graduate and Adult Admission, 518-244-2443, Fax: 518-244-6880, E-mail: diefew@sage.edu.

St. John Fisher College, Ralph C. Wilson Jr. School of Education, Program in Adolescence Education/Special Education, Rochester, NY 14618-3597. Offers adolescence English (MS Ed); adolescence French (MS Ed); adolescence social studies (MS Ed); adolescence Spanish (MS Ed). Part-time and evening/weekend programs available. *Faculty:* 3 full-time (1 woman), 1 (woman) part-time/adjunct. *Students:* 39 full-time (18 women), 5 part-time (2 women); includes 7 minority (1 African American, 2 American Indian/Alaska Native, 1 Asian American or Pacific Islander, 3 Hispanic Americans). Average age 28. 39 applicants, 90% accepted, 20 enrolled. In 2009, 17 master's awarded. *Degree requirements:* For master's, field experiences, student teaching, LAST. *Entrance requirements:* For master's, 2 letters of recommendation, personal statement, current resume. Additional exam requirements/recommendations for international students: Required—TOEFL (minimum score 575 paper-based; 233 computer-based; 80 iBT). *Application deadline:* Applications are processed on a rolling basis. Application fee: $30. Electronic applications accepted. *Expenses:* Tuition: Part-time $680 per credit hour. Required fees: $25 per semester. Tuition and fees vary according to degree level and program. *Financial support:* In 2009–10, 40 students received support. Federal Work-Study and scholarships/grants available. Financial award applicants required to submit FAFSA. *Faculty research:* Arts and humanities, urban schools, constructivist learning, at risk students, mentoring. *Unit head:* Dr. Russell Coward, Program Director, 585-385-8114, E-mail: rcoward@sjfc.edu. *Application contact:* Jose Perales, Director of Graduate Admissions, 585-385-8067, E-mail: jperales@sjfc.edu.

Salem State College, School of Graduate Studies, Program in English, Salem, MA 01970-5353. Offers English (MA, MAT, MA/MAT); MA/MAT. Part-time and evening/weekend programs available. *Students:* 12 full-time (8 women), 61 part-time (47 women); includes 2 minority (1 African American, 1 Asian American or Pacific Islander). Average age 34. 14 applicants, 93% accepted, 13 enrolled. In 2009, 28 master's awarded. *Entrance requirements:* For master's, GRE or MAT. Additional exam requirements/recommendations for international students: Required—TOEFL (minimum score 550 paper-based; 80 iBT), or IELTS (minimum score 5.5). *Application deadline:* For fall admission, 5/1 for domestic students; for spring admission, 10/1 for domestic students. Applications are processed on a rolling basis. Application fee: $50. *Expenses:* Tuition, state resident: full-time $2520; part-time $275 per credit hour. Tuition, nonresident: full-time $4140; part-time $365 per credit hour. Required fees: $2430. *Financial support:* In 2009–10, 27 students received support. Career-related internships or fieldwork, Federal Work-Study, scholarships/grants, and unspecified assistantships available. Support available to part-time students. Financial award application deadline: 5/1; financial award applicants required to submit FAFSA. *Unit head:* Lisa Mulman, Coordinator, 978-542-6321, E-mail: lmulman@salemstate.edu. *Application contact:* Dr. Lee A. Brossoit, Assistant Dean of Graduate Admissions, 978-542-6673, Fax: 978-542-7215, E-mail: lbrossoit@salemstate.edu.

San Francisco State University, Division of Graduate Studies, College of Education, Department of Elementary Education, Program in Language and Literacy Education, San Francisco, CA 94132-1722. Offers MA.

San Francisco State University, Division of Graduate Studies, College of Humanities, Department of English Language and Literature, San Francisco, CA 94132-1722. Offers composition (MA, Certificate); linguistics (MA); literature (MA); teaching composition (Certificate); teaching English to speakers of other languages (MA); teaching post-secondary reading (Certificate). Part-time programs available.

Shippensburg University of Pennsylvania, School of Graduate Studies, College of Education and Human Services, Department of Teacher Education, Shippensburg, PA 17257-2299. Offers curriculum and instruction (M Ed), including biology, early childhood education, elementary education, English, foreign languages, geography/earth science, history, mathematics, middle school education; reading (M Ed). *Accreditation:* NCATE. Part-time and evening/weekend programs available. *Degree requirements:* For master's, comprehensive exam (for some programs), thesis optional, practicum or internship (for some programs). *Entrance requirements:* For master's, MAT (if GPA less than 2.75), interview, 3 letters of recommendation, writing sample of teaching background and future goals. Additional exam requirements/recommendations for international students: Required—TOEFL (minimum score 560 paper-based; 220 computer-based); Recommended—IELTS (minimum score 6). Electronic applications accepted.

Smith College, Graduate and Special Programs, Department of Education and Child Study, Program in Secondary Education, Northampton, MA 01063. Offers biological sciences education (MAT); chemistry education (MAT); English education (MAT); French education (MAT); geology education (MAT); government education (MAT); history education (MAT); mathematics education (MAT); physics education (MAT); Spanish education (MAT). Part-time programs available. *Faculty:* 6 full-time (4 women), 3 part-time/adjunct (2 women). *Students:* 7 full-time (4 women), 1 part-time (0 women). Average age 25. 14 applicants, 100% accepted, 8 enrolled. In 2009, 9 master's awarded. *Entrance requirements:* Additional exam requirements/recommendations for international students: Required—TOEFL (minimum score 590 paper-based; 243 computer-based; 97 iBT). *Application deadline:* For fall admission, 4/1 for domestic students, 1/15 priority date for international students; for spring admission, 12/1 for domestic students. Application fee: $60. *Financial support:* In 2009–10, 6 students received support. Career-related internships or fieldwork, institutionally sponsored loans, and scholarships/grants available. Support available to part-time students. Financial award application deadline: 1/15; financial award applicants required to submit CSS PROFILE or FAFSA. *Unit head:* Rosetta Cohen, Graduate Student Advisor, 413-585-3266, E-mail: rcohen@smith.edu. *Application contact:* Ruth Morgan, Administrative Assistant, 413-585-3050, Fax: 413-585-3054, E-mail: gradstdy@smith.edu.

Smith College, Graduate and Special Programs, Department of English Language and Literature, Northampton, MA 01063. Offers MAT. Part-time programs available. *Faculty:* 20 full-time (8 women). *Students:* 2 full-time (1 woman). Average age 23. 4 applicants, 100% accepted, 2 enrolled. In 2009, 4 master's awarded. *Entrance requirements:* Additional exam requirements/recommendations for international students: Required—TOEFL (minimum score 590 paper-based; 243 computer-based; 97 iBT). *Application deadline:* For fall admission, 1/15 for domestic and international students; for spring admission, 12/1 for domestic students. Application fee: $60. *Financial support:* In 2009–10, 2 students received support. Career-related internships or fieldwork, institutionally sponsored loans, and scholarships/grants available. Support available to part-time students. Financial award application deadline: 1/15; financial award applicants required to submit CSS PROFILE or FAFSA. *Unit head:* Ambreen Hai, Graduate Adviser, 413-585-3311, E-mail: ahai@smith.edu. *Application contact:* Ruth Morgan, Administrative Assistant, 413-585-3050, Fax: 413-585-3054, E-mail: gradstdy@smith.edu.

South Carolina State University, School of Graduate Studies, Department of Education, Orangeburg, SC 29117-0001. Offers early childhood and special education (M Ed); early childhood education (MAT); elementary education (M Ed, MAT); engineering (MAT); general science (MAT); mathematics (MAT); secondary education (M Ed), including biology education, business education, counselor education, English education, home economics education, industrial education, mathematics education, science education, social studies education; special education (M Ed), including emotionally handicapped, learning disabilities, mentally handicapped. *Accreditation:* NCATE. Part-time and evening/weekend programs available. *Degree requirements:* For master's, thesis optional, departmental qualifying exam. *Entrance requirements:* For master's, GRE General Test, NTE, interview, teaching certificate. Electronic applications accepted. *Expenses:* Tuition, state resident: part-time $470 per credit hour. Tuition, nonresident: part-time $924 per credit hour. *Faculty research:* Critical thinking, child abuse, stress, test-taking skills, conflict resolution, mainstreaming.

Southeastern Louisiana University, College of Arts, Humanities and Social Sciences, Department of English, Hammond, LA 70402. Offers creative writing (MA); language and literacy (MA); professional writing (MA). Part-time and evening/weekend programs available. *Faculty:* 15 full-time (7 women), 1 (woman) part-time/adjunct. *Students:* 27 full-time (15 women), 22 part-time (15 women); includes 4 minority (3 African Americans, 1 Asian American or Pacific Islander). Average age 29. 16 applicants, 94% accepted, 11 enrolled. In 2009, 12

master's awarded. *Degree requirements:* For master's, one foreign language, comprehensive exam, thesis optional. *Entrance requirements:* For master's, GRE General Test (850 or better), 24 undergraduate credit hours in English, minimum GPA of 2.5. Additional exam requirements/recommendations for international students: Required—TOEFL (minimum score 500 paper-based; 173 computer-based; 61 iBT). *Application deadline:* For fall admission, 7/15 priority date for domestic students, 6/1 priority date for international students; for spring admission, 12/1 priority date for domestic students, 10/1 priority date for international students. Applications are processed on a rolling basis. Application fee: $20 ($30 for international students). Electronic applications accepted. *Expenses:* Tuition, state resident: full-time $3086; part-time $225 per credit hour. Tuition, nonresident: part-time $529 per credit hour. Required fees: $1195. Tuition and fees vary according to course level and course load. *Financial support:* In 2009–10, 11 students received support, including 1 fellowship (averaging $13,050 per year), 9 research assistantships (averaging $8,078 per year), 1 teaching assistantship (averaging $6,700 per year); career-related internships or fieldwork, Federal Work-Study, institutionally sponsored loans, scholarships/grants, and administrative assistantships also available. Support available to part-time students. Financial award application deadline: 5/1; financial award applicants required to submit FAFSA. *Faculty research:* Composition/rhetoric, professional and technical writing, film and performance studies, literary criticism, creative writing. Total annual research expenditures: $34,307. *Unit head:* Dr. David Hanson, Department Head, 985-549-2100, Fax: 985-549-5021, E-mail: dhanson@selu.edu. *Application contact:* Sandra Meyers, Graduate Admissions Analyst, 985-549-5620, Fax: 985-549-5632, E-mail: admissions@selu.edu.

Southern Illinois University Edwardsville, Graduate Studies and Research, College of Arts and Sciences, Department of English Language and Literature, Program in Teaching of Writing, Edwardsville, IL 62026-0001. Offers MA, Postbaccalaureate Certificate. Part-time and evening/weekend programs available. *Students:* 3 full-time (2 women), 16 part-time (15 women); includes 3 minority (all African Americans). Average age 26. In 2009, 5 master's, 1 other advanced degree awarded. *Degree requirements:* For master's, thesis or alternative, final exam. *Entrance requirements:* Additional exam requirements/recommendations for international students: Required—TOEFL (minimum score 550 paper-based; 213 computer-based; 79 iBT), IELTS (minimum score 6.5). *Application deadline:* For fall admission, 7/23 for domestic students, 6/1 for international students; for spring admission, 12/11 for domestic students, 10/1 for international students. Applications are processed on a rolling basis. Application fee: $30. Electronic applications accepted. *Expenses:* Tuition, state resident: part-time $1252.50 per semester. Tuition, nonresident: part-time $3131.25 per semester. Required fees: $586.85 per semester. Tuition and fees vary according to course load. *Financial support:* Fellowships with full tuition reimbursements, research assistantships with full tuition reimbursements, teaching assistantships with full tuition reimbursements, Federal Work-Study, institutionally sponsored loans, scholarships/grants, traineeships, and unspecified assistantships available. Support available to part-time students. Financial award application deadline: 3/1; financial award applicants required to submit FAFSA. *Unit head:* Dr. Joel Hardman, Director, 618-650-5978, E-mail: jhardma@siue.edu. *Application contact:* Dr. Joel Hardman, Director, 618-650-5978, E-mail: jhardma@siue.edu.

Southern Illinois University Edwardsville, Graduate Studies and Research, School of Education, Department of Curriculum and Instruction, Program in Secondary Education, Edwardsville, IL 62026-0001. Offers art (MS Ed); biology (MS Ed); chemistry (MS Ed); earth and space sciences (MS Ed); English/language arts (MS Ed); foreign languages (MS Ed); history (MS Ed); mathematics (MS Ed); physics (MS Ed). *Accreditation:* NCATE. Part-time and evening/weekend programs available. *Students:* 24 part-time (19 women); includes 2 minority (1 African American, 1 Hispanic American). Average age 26. 13 applicants, 31% accepted. In 2009, 5 master's awarded. *Degree requirements:* For master's, thesis or alternative, final exam/paper. *Entrance requirements:* Additional exam requirements/recommendations for international students: Required—TOEFL (minimum score 550 paper-based; 213 computer-based; 79 iBT), IELTS (minimum score 6.5). *Application deadline:* For fall admission, 7/23 for domestic students, 6/1 for international students; for spring admission, 12/11 for domestic students, 10/1 for international students. Applications are processed on a rolling basis. Application fee: $30. Electronic applications accepted. *Expenses:* Tuition, state resident: part-time $1252.50 per semester. Tuition, nonresident: part-time $3131.25 per semester. Required fees: $586.85 per semester. Tuition and fees vary according to course load. *Financial support:* Fellowships, research assistantships, teaching assistantships, career-related internships or fieldwork, Federal Work-Study, institutionally sponsored loans, scholarships/grants, traineeships, and unspecified assistantships available. Support available to part-time students. Financial award application deadline: 3/1; financial award applicants required to submit FAFSA. *Unit head:* Dr. Kathy Bushrow, Director, 618-650-3082, E-mail: kbushro@siue.edu. *Application contact:* Dr. Kathy Bushrow, Director, 618-650-3082, E-mail: kbushro@siue.edu.

Southwestern Oklahoma State University, College of Arts and Sciences, Specialization in English, Weatherford, OK 73096-3098. Offers M Ed. M Ed distance learning degree program offered to Oklahoma residents only. *Accreditation:* NCATE. Part-time programs available. *Degree requirements:* For master's, exam. *Entrance requirements:* For master's, GRE General Test or minimum undergraduate GPA of 3.0. Additional exam requirements/recommendations for international students: Required—TOEFL.

Stanford University, School of Education, Program in Curriculum Studies and Teacher Education, Stanford, CA 94305-9991. Offers art education (MA, PhD); dance education (MA); English education (MA, PhD); general curriculum studies (MA, PhD); mathematics education (MA, PhD); science education (MA, PhD); social studies education (PhD); teacher education (MA, PhD). *Degree requirements:* For master's, thesis (for some programs); for doctorate, thesis/dissertation. *Entrance requirements:* For master's and doctorate, GRE General Test. Electronic applications accepted. *Expenses:* Tuition: Full-time $37,380; part-time $2760 per quarter. Required fees: $501.

Stanford University, School of Education, Teacher Education Program, Stanford, CA 94305-9991. Offers English education (MA); languages education (MA); mathematics education (MA); science education (MA); social studies education (MA). *Degree requirements:* For master's, thesis. *Entrance requirements:* For master's, GRE General Test. Electronic applications accepted. *Expenses:* Tuition: Full-time $37,380; part-time $2760 per quarter. Required fees: $501.

State University of New York at Binghamton, Graduate School, School of Education, Program in Adolescence Education, Binghamton, NY 13902-6000. Offers biology education (MAT, MS Ed, MST); earth science education (MAT, MS Ed, MST); English education (MAT, MS Ed, MST); French education (MAT, MST); mathematical sciences education (MAT, MS Ed, MST); physics (MAT, MS Ed, MST); social studies (MAT, MS Ed, MST); Spanish education (MAT, MST). *Accreditation:* Teacher Education Accreditation Council. Part-time and evening/weekend programs available. *Students:* 93 full-time (37 women), 21 part-time (8 women); includes 6 minority (2 Asian Americans or Pacific Islanders, 4 Hispanic Americans), 1 international. Average age 27. 69 applicants, 81% accepted, 46 enrolled. In 2009, 53 master's awarded. *Entrance requirements:* For master's, GRE General Test. Additional exam requirements/recommendations for international students: Required—TOEFL (minimum score 550 paper-based; 213 computer-based; 80 iBT). *Application deadline:* For fall admission, 2/1 priority date for domestic and international students; for spring admission, 10/15 priority date for domestic and international students. Applications are processed on a rolling basis. Application fee: $60. Electronic applications accepted. *Financial support:* Fellowships with partial tuition reimbursements, research assistantships with full and partial tuition reimbursements, teaching assistantships with full tuition reimbursements, career-related internships or fieldwork, Federal Work-Study, institutionally sponsored loans, scholarships/grants, health care benefits, tuition waivers (full), and unspecified assistantships available. Financial award application deadline: 2/15; financial award applicants required to submit FAFSA. *Unit head:* Dr. S. G. Grant, Dean of School of Education, 607-777-7329, E-mail: sggrant@binghamton.edu. *Application contact:* Victoria Williams, Recruiting and Admissions Coordinator, 607-777-2151, Fax: 607-777-2501, E-mail: vwilliam@binghamton.edu.

State University of New York at New Paltz, Graduate School, School of Education, Department of Secondary Education, New Paltz, NY 12561. Offers adolescence education: biology (MAT, MS Ed); adolescence education: english (MAT); adolescence education: English (MS Ed); adolescence education: social studies (MAT, MS Ed); English as a second language (MS Ed); second language education (MS Ed). *Accreditation:* NCATE. Part-time and evening/weekend programs available. *Faculty:* 9 full-time (5 women), 4 part-time/adjunct (3 women). *Students:* 86 full-time (51 women), 102 part-time (74 women); includes 22 minority (4 African Americans, 1 American Indian/Alaska Native, 3 Asian Americans or Pacific Islanders, 14 Hispanic Americans), 2 international. Average age 30. 122 applicants, 54% accepted, 53 enrolled. In 2009, 81 master's awarded. *Degree requirements:* For master's, comprehensive exam (for some programs), portfolio. *Entrance requirements:* For master's, minimum GPA of 3.0, NYS teaching certificate (MS Ed). Additional exam requirements/recommendations for international students: Required—TOEFL (minimum score 550 paper-based; 213 computer-based; 80 iBT), IELTS (minimum score 6.5). *Application deadline:* For fall admission, 3/1 priority date for domestic students, 3/1 for international students; for spring admission, 10/1 priority date for domestic students, 10/1 for international students. Application fee: $50. Electronic applications accepted. *Financial support:* In 2009–10, 4 students received support, including 3 fellowships (averaging $9,000 per year); Federal Work-Study, institutionally sponsored loans, and tuition waivers (full) also available. Financial award application deadline: 8/1; financial award applicants required to submit FAFSA. *Unit head:* Dr. Devon Duhaney, Chair, 845-257-2850, E-mail: duhaneyd@newpaltz.edu. *Application contact:* Caroline Murphy, Graduate Admissions Advisor, 845-257-3285, Fax: 845-257-3284, E-mail: gradschool@newpaltz.edu.

State University of New York at Plattsburgh, Division of Education, Health, and Human Services, Program in Teacher Education: Adolescence MST, Plattsburgh, NY 12901-2681. Offers adolescence education (MST); biology 7-12 (MST); chemistry 7-12 (MST); earth science 7-12 (MST); English 7-12 (MST); French 7-12 (MST); mathematics 7-12 (MST); physics 7-12 (MST); social studies 7-12 (MST); Spanish 7-12 (MST). *Accreditation:* Teacher Education Accreditation Council. Part-time and evening/weekend programs available. *Faculty:* 4 full-time (3 women), 2 part-time/adjunct (0 women). *Students:* 83 full-time (49 women), 5 part-time (3 women); includes 9 minority (2 African Americans, 1 American Indian/Alaska Native, 1 Asian American or Pacific Islander, 5 Hispanic Americans), 2 international. Average age 27. 72 applicants, 71% accepted, 44 enrolled. In 2009, 57 master's awarded. *Degree requirements:* For master's, portfolio. *Entrance requirements:* For master's, minimum GPA of 2.75. Additional exam requirements/recommendations for international students: Required—TOEFL (minimum score 550 paper-based; 213 computer-based; 79 iBT). *Application deadline:* For fall admission, 2/15 priority date for domestic students. Applications are processed on a rolling basis. Application fee: $75. *Expenses:* Tuition, state resident: full-time $8370; part-time $349 per credit hour. Tuition, nonresident: full-time $13,250; part-time $552 per credit hour. Required fees: $1130. *Financial support:* Application deadline: 4/15. *Unit head:* Dr. Robert Ackland, Coordinator, 518-564-5131, E-mail: acklanrt@plattsburgh.edu. *Application contact:* Marguerite Adelman, Assistant Director, Graduate Admissions, 518-564-4723, Fax: 518-564-4722, E-mail: adelmaml@plattsburgh.edu.

State University of New York College at Cortland, Graduate Studies, School of Arts and Sciences, Programs in Adolescence Education, Cortland, NY 13045. Offers biology (MAT, MS Ed); chemistry (MAT, MS Ed); earth science (MAT, MS Ed); English (MS Ed); French (MS Ed); mathematics (MAT, MS Ed); physics (MAT, MS Ed); social studies (MAT, MS Ed); Spanish (MS Ed). *Accreditation:* NCATE. Part-time and evening/weekend programs available. *Degree requirements:* For master's, one foreign language, comprehensive exam (for some programs), thesis (for some programs). *Entrance requirements:* For master's, GRE General Test.

Stony Brook University, State University of New York, Graduate School, College of Arts and Sciences, Department of English, Stony Brook, NY 11794. Offers composition studies (Certificate); English (MA, PhD); English education (MAT). MAT offered through the School of Professional Development. Evening/weekend programs available. *Faculty:* 25 full-time (10 women), 1 part-time/adjunct (0 women). *Students:* 77 full-time (46 women), 23 part-time (18 women); includes 12 minority (5 African Americans, 3 Asian Americans or Pacific Islanders, 4 Hispanic Americans), 5 international. Average age 32. 154 applicants, 23% accepted. In 2009, 16 master's, 7 doctorates awarded. Terminal master's awarded for partial completion of doctoral program. *Degree requirements:* For doctorate, thesis/dissertation. *Entrance requirements:* For master's and doctorate, GRE General Test. Additional exam requirements/recommendations for international students: Required—TOEFL. *Application deadline:* For fall admission, 1/15 for domestic students. Application fee: $60. *Expenses:* Tuition, state resident: full-time $8370; part-time $349 per credit. Tuition, nonresident: full-time $13,250; part-time $552 per credit. Required fees: $933. *Financial support:* In 2009–10, 42 teaching assistantships were awarded; fellowships, research assistantships also available. *Faculty research:* American literature, British literature, literary critical theory, rhetoric and composition theory, women's studies. *Unit head:* Dr. Stephen Spector, Chair, 631-632-7420, Fax: 631-632-7568. *Application contact:* Dr. Helen M. Cooper, Director, 631-632-7784, Fax: 631-632-7568, E-mail: hcooper@notes.cc.sunysb.edu.

Stony Brook University, State University of New York, School of Professional Development, Stony Brook, NY 11794. Offers biology-grade 7-12 (MAT); chemistry-grade 7-12 (MAT); coaching (Graduate Certificate); computer integrated engineering (Graduate Certificate); earth science-grade 7-12 (MAT); educational computing (Graduate Certificate); educational leadership (Advanced Certificate); English-grade 7-12 (MAT); environmental management (Graduate Certificate); environmental/occupational health and safety (Graduate Certificate); French-grade 7-12 (MAT); German-grade 7-12 (MAT); human resource management (Graduate Certificate); information systems management (Graduate Certificate); Italian-grade 7-12 (MAT); liberal studies (MA); mathematics-grade 7-12 (MAT); operation research (Graduate Certificate); physics-grade 7-12 (MAT); school administration and supervision (Graduate Certificate); school building leadership (Graduate Certificate); school district administration (Graduate Certificate); school district business leadership (Advanced Certificate); school district leadership (Graduate Certificate); social science and the professions (MPS), including environmental waste management, human resource management; social studies-grade 7-12 (MAT); Spanish-grade 7-12 (MAT); waste management (Graduate Certificate). Part-time and evening/weekend programs available. Postbaccalaureate distance learning degree programs offered. *Faculty:* 5 full-time (3 women), 131 part-time/adjunct (53 women). *Students:* 317 full-time (187 women), 1,200 part-time (773 women); includes 187 minority (77 African Americans, 2 American Indian/Alaska Native, 22 Asian Americans or Pacific Islanders, 86 Hispanic Americans), 11 international. Average age 28. In 2009, 597 master's, 234 other advanced degrees awarded. *Degree requirements:* For master's, one foreign language, thesis or alternative. *Application deadline:* Applications are processed on a rolling basis. Application fee: $62. *Expenses:* Tuition, state resident: full-time $8370; part-time $349 per credit. Tuition, nonresident: full-time $13,250; part-time $552 per credit. Required fees: $933. *Financial support:* Fellowships, research assistantships, teaching assistantships, career-related internships or fieldwork available. Support available to part-time students. *Unit head:* Dr. Paul J. Edelson, Dean, 631-632-7052, Fax: 631-632-9046, E-mail: paul.edelson@stonybrook.edu. *Application contact:* Dr. Paul J. Edelson, Dean, 631-632-7052, Fax: 631-632-9046, E-mail: paul.edelson@stonybrook.edu.

Syracuse University, School of Education, Program in English Education, Syracuse, NY 13244. Offers PhD. Part-time programs available. *Students:* 1 full-time (0 women), 3 part-time (all women), 1 international. Average age 39. *Degree requirements:* For doctorate, thesis/dissertation. *Entrance requirements:* For doctorate, GRE. Additional exam requirements/recommendations for international students: Required—TOEFL (minimum score 100 iBT). *Application deadline:* For fall admission, 2/1 priority date for domestic and international students; for spring admission, 10/15 priority date for domestic and international students. Applications are processed on a rolling basis. Application fee: $75. Electronic applications accepted. *Expenses:* Tuition: Full-time $26,808; part-time $1117 per credit. Required fees: $1024. *Financial support:* Fellowships with full tuition reimbursements, teaching assistantships with full tuition reimbursements available. Financial award application deadline: 1/1; financial award applicants required to submit FAFSA. *Unit head:* Dr. Kathy Hinchman, Program Coordinator, 315-443-

English Education

Syracuse University (continued)

4757, E-mail: kahinchm@syr.edu. *Application contact:* Liza Rochelson, Graduate Recruiter, School of Education, 315-443-2505, E-mail: e-gradrcrt@syr.edu.

Syracuse University, School of Education, Program in English Education: Preparation 7-12, Syracuse, NY 13244. Offers MS. Part-time programs available. *Students:* 14 full-time (10 women); includes 2 minority (1 African American, 1 Hispanic American). Average age 27. 14 applicants, 86% accepted, 5 enrolled. In 2009, 5 master's awarded. *Degree requirements:* For master's, thesis or alternative. *Entrance requirements:* Additional exam requirements/recommendations for international students: Required—TOEFL (minimum score 100 iBT). *Application deadline:* For fall admission, 2/1 priority date for domestic and international students; for spring admission, 10/15 priority date for domestic and international students. Applications are processed on a rolling basis. Application fee: $75. Electronic applications accepted. *Expenses:* Tuition: Full-time $26,808; part-time $1117 per credit. Required fees: $1024. *Financial support:* Fellowships with full and partial tuition reimbursements, teaching assistantships with full and partial tuition reimbursements, tuition waivers (partial) available. Financial award application deadline: 1/1. *Unit head:* Dr. Kelly Chandler-Olcott, Director, 315-443-5183, E-mail: kpchandl@syr.edu. *Application contact:* Liza Rochelson, Graduate Recruiter, School of Education, 315-443-2505, E-mail: e-gradrcrt@syr.edu.

Teachers College, Columbia University, Graduate Faculty of Education, Department of Arts and Humanities, Program in Teaching of English and English Education, New York, NY 10027-6696. Offers Ed M, MA, Ed D, PhD. *Accreditation:* NCATE. Part-time and evening/weekend programs available. *Faculty:* 5 full-time (all women). *Students:* 88 full-time (71 women), 122 part-time (95 women); includes 36 minority (12 African Americans, 14 Asian Americans or Pacific Islanders, 10 Hispanic Americans), 7 international. Average age 29. 129 applicants, 81% accepted, 47 enrolled. In 2009, 90 master's, 4 doctorates awarded. Terminal master's awarded for partial completion of doctoral program. *Degree requirements:* For doctorate, 2 foreign languages, thesis/dissertation. *Application deadline:* For fall admission, 5/15 for domestic students; for spring admission, 12/1 for domestic students. Application fee: $65. *Financial support:* Fellowships, research assistantships, teaching assistantships, career-related internships or fieldwork, Federal Work-Study, institutionally sponsored loans, and tuition waivers (full and partial) available. Support available to part-time students. Financial award application deadline: 2/1. *Faculty research:* Teaching of writing and reading, language and curriculum, literacy and health, narrative and action research. *Unit head:* Graeme Sullivan, Chair, 212-678-3799. *Application contact:* Mark E. Stearns, Associate Director of Admission, 212-678-3710, Fax: 212-678-4171.

Temple University, Graduate School, College of Education, Department of Curriculum, Instruction, and Technology in Education, Philadelphia, PA 19122-6096. Offers applied behavioral analysis (MS Ed); career and technical education (MS Ed); early childhood education and elementary education (MS Ed); English education (MS Ed); language arts education (Ed D); math/science education (Ed D); mathematics education (MS Ed); science education (MS Ed); second and foreign language education (MS Ed); special education (MS Ed); teaching English as a second language (MS Ed). Part-time and evening/weekend programs available. Terminal master's awarded for partial completion of doctoral program. *Degree requirements:* For master's, thesis or alternative; for doctorate, thesis/dissertation. *Entrance requirements:* For master's and doctorate, GRE General Test or MAT, minimum GPA of 3.0. Additional exam requirements/recommendations for international students: Required—TOEFL (minimum score 550 paper-based; 213 computer-based; 79 iBT). Electronic applications accepted. *Faculty research:* School improvement, problem solving, literacy, language development.

Texas A&M University, College of Education and Human Development, Department of Teaching, Learning, and Culture, College Station, TX 77843. Offers curriculum and instruction (M Ed, MS, PhD); mathematics education (M Ed, MS, PhD); multicultural/urban/ESL/international education (M Ed, MS, PhD); reading/language arts (M Ed, MS, PhD); science education (M Ed, MS, PhD); social studies education (M Ed, MS, PhD). Part-time programs available. *Faculty:* 33. *Students:* 145 full-time (113 women), 270 part-time (214 women); includes 110 minority (60 African Americans, 4 American Indian/Alaska Native, 4 Asian Americans or Pacific Islanders, 42 Hispanic Americans), 47 international. Average age 36. In 2009, 114 master's, 17 doctorates awarded. *Degree requirements:* For master's, comprehensive exam, thesis (for some programs); for doctorate, comprehensive exam, thesis/dissertation. *Entrance requirements:* For master's, GRE General Test, minimum GPA of 3.0; for doctorate, GRE General Test, 3 years of teaching experience. Additional exam requirements/recommendations for international students: Required—TOEFL (minimum score 550 paper-based; 213 computer-based). *Application deadline:* For fall admission, 1/15 priority date for domestic and international students; for spring admission, 9/15 priority date for domestic and international students. Applications are processed on a rolling basis. Application fee: $50 ($75 for international students). Electronic applications accepted. *Expenses:* Tuition, state resident: full-time $3991; part-time $221.74 per credit hour. Tuition, nonresident: full-time $9049; part-time $502.74 per credit hour. *Financial support:* In 2009–10, fellowships with partial tuition reimbursements (averaging $3,000 per year), teaching assistantships with partial tuition reimbursements (averaging $7,200 per year) were awarded; research assistantships with partial tuition reimbursements, career-related internships or fieldwork, Federal Work-Study, institutionally sponsored loans, scholarships/grants, tuition waivers (partial), and unspecified assistantships also available. Support available to part-time students. Financial award application deadline: 4/1; financial award applicants required to submit FAFSA. *Unit head:* Dr. Dennie Smith, Head, 979-845-8384, Fax: 979-845-9663, E-mail: krsmith@tamu.edu. *Application contact:* Graduate Admissions Supervisor, 979-845-8382, Fax: 979-845-9663, E-mail: krsmith@tamu.edu.

Texas A&M University–Commerce, Graduate School, College of Arts and Sciences, Department of Literature and Languages, Commerce, TX 75429-3011. Offers college teaching of English (PhD); English (MA, MS); Spanish (MA). Part-time programs available. Terminal master's awarded for partial completion of doctoral program. *Degree requirements:* For master's, comprehensive exam, thesis (for some programs); for doctorate, one foreign language, thesis/dissertation, departmental qualifying exam. *Entrance requirements:* For master's and doctorate, GRE General Test. Electronic applications accepted. *Faculty research:* Latino literature, American film studies, ethnographic research, Willa Carter.

Texas Tech University, Graduate School, College of Education, Division of Curriculum and Instruction, Lubbock, TX 79409. Offers bilingual education (M Ed); curriculum and instruction (M Ed, PhD); elementary education (M Ed); language and literacy education (M Ed); secondary education (M Ed). *Accreditation:* NCATE. Part-time programs available. *Students:* 72 full-time (54 women), 109 part-time (85 women); includes 50 minority (11 African Americans, 1 American Indian/Alaska Native, 4 Asian Americans or Pacific Islanders, 34 Hispanic Americans), 11 international. Average age 35. 228 applicants, 54% accepted, 56 enrolled. In 2009, 59 master's, 5 doctorates awarded. *Degree requirements:* For master's, thesis or alternative; for doctorate, thesis/dissertation. *Entrance requirements:* For master's and doctorate, GRE General Test. Additional exam requirements/recommendations for international students: Required—TOEFL (minimum score 550 paper-based; 213 computer-based). *Application deadline:* For fall admission, 3/1 priority date for international students; for spring admission, 11/1 priority date for international students. Applications are processed on a rolling basis. Application fee: $50 ($75 for international students). Electronic applications accepted. *Expenses:* Tuition, state resident: full-time $5100; part-time $213 per credit hour. Tuition, nonresident: full-time $11,748; part-time $490 per credit hour. Required fees: $2298; $50 per credit hour. $555 per semester. *Financial support:* Research assistantships with partial tuition reimbursements, teaching assistantships with partial tuition reimbursements, career-related internships or fieldwork, Federal Work-Study, and institutionally sponsored loans available. Support available to part-time students. Financial award application deadline: 4/15; financial award applicants required to submit FAFSA. *Faculty research:* Multicultural foundations of education, teacher education, instruction and pedagogy in subject areas, curriculum theory, language and literacy. *Unit head:* Dr. Walter Smith, Chair, 806-742-1988 Ext. 437, Fax: 806-742-2179, E-mail: walter.smith@ttu.edu. *Application contact:* Dr. Walter Smith, Chair, 806-742-1988 Ext. 437, Fax: 806-742-2179, E-mail: walter.smith@ttu.edu.

Trinity (Washington) University, School of Education, Washington, DC 20017-1094. Offers counseling (MA); early childhood education (MAT); educating for change (M Ed); educational administration (MSA); elementary education (MAT); school counseling (MA); secondary education (MAT), including English, social studies; special education (MAT); teaching English as a second language (MAT); teaching English to speakers of other languages (M Ed); the teaching of reading (M Ed). *Accreditation:* NCATE. Part-time and evening/weekend programs available. *Degree requirements:* For master's, thesis (for some programs), capstone project(s). *Entrance requirements:* For master's, PRAXIS I, minimum GPA of 2.8. Additional exam requirements/recommendations for international students: Required—TOEFL (minimum score 550 paper-based; 213 computer-based). *Faculty research:* Technology, literacy, special education, organizations, inclusion models.

Troy University, Graduate School, College of Education, Program in Postsecondary Education, Troy, AL 36082. Offers adult education (M Ed); biology (M Ed); criminal justice (M Ed); english (M Ed); foundations of education (M Ed); general science (M Ed); higher education administration (M Ed); history (M Ed); instructional technology (M Ed); mathematics (M Ed); music industry (M Ed); physical fitness (M Ed); political science (M Ed); public administration (M Ed); social science (M Ed); teaching english (M Ed). Also offered through the University College. *Accreditation:* NCATE. Part-time and evening/weekend programs available. *Students:* 267 full-time (192 women), 381 part-time (293 women); includes 326 minority (309 African Americans, 4 American Indian/Alaska Native, 5 Asian Americans or Pacific Islanders, 8 Hispanic Americans). Average age 34. 343 applicants, 90% accepted. In 2009, 480 master's awarded. *Degree requirements:* For master's, comprehensive exam, thesis. *Entrance requirements:* For master's, MAT (minimum score 385), minimum GPA of 2.5. Additional exam requirements/recommendations for international students: Required—TOEFL (minimum score 523 paper-based; 193 computer-based; 70 iBT), IELTS, or ACT Compass ESL (minimum score 270 on Listening, Reading, and Grammar with no individual score below 85 and a minimum score of 8 out of 12 on writing test). *Application deadline:* Applications are processed on a rolling basis. Application fee: $50. Electronic applications accepted. *Financial support:* Available to part-time students. Applicants required to submit FAFSA. *Unit head:* Dr. Andrew Creamer, Chair, 334-670-3350, E-mail: drcreamer@troy.edu. *Application contact:* Brenda K. Campbell, Director of Graduate Admissions, 334-670-3178, Fax: 334-670-3733, E-mail: bcamp@troy.edu.

Union Graduate College, School of Education, Schenectady, NY 12308-3107. Offers biology (MAT, MS); chemistry (MAT); Chinese (MAT); earth science (MAT); English (MAT); French (MAT); general science (MAT); German (MAT); Greek (MAT); languages (MAT); Latin (MAT); mathematics (MAT); mathematics and technology (MS); mentoring and teacher leadership (AC); middle childhood extension (AC); national board certificate and teacher leadership (AC); physical science (MS); physics (MAT); social studies (MAT); Spanish (MAT). *Accreditation:* Teacher Education Accreditation Council. *Faculty:* 3 full-time (1 woman), 39 part-time/adjunct (19 women). *Students:* 46 full-time (27 women), 45 part-time (39 women); includes 5 minority (1 Asian American or Pacific Islander, 4 Hispanic Americans), 2 international. Average age 33. 66 applicants, 73% accepted, 39 enrolled. In 2009, 44 master's awarded. *Degree requirements:* For master's, thesis or project. *Entrance requirements:* For master's, minimum GPA of 3.0, letters of recommendation. Additional exam requirements/recommendations for international students: Required—TOEFL (minimum score 550 paper-based; 213 computer-based). *Application deadline:* Applications are processed on a rolling basis. Application fee: $60. Electronic applications accepted. *Expenses:* Contact institution. *Financial support:* In 2009–10, 12 research assistantships with tuition reimbursements (averaging $3,000 per year) were awarded; Federal Work-Study, scholarships/grants, health care benefits, and tuition waivers (partial) also available. Support available to part-time students. Financial award applicants required to submit FAFSA. *Faculty research:* Transformative learning, science education, National Board Certification, teacher leadership, teacher quality. *Unit head:* Dr. Patrick Allen, Dean, 518-631-9870, Fax: 518-631-9901. *Application contact:* Christine Angley, Assistant, 518-631-9871, Fax: 518-631-9903, E-mail: angleyc@uniongraduatecollege.edu.

Union Institute & University, M Ed Program–Vermont Campus, Montpelier, VT 05602. Offers school administration (M Ed), including principalship; school counseling (M Ed); teaching (M Ed), including art, early childhood, elementary, English, math, middle schools, science, social studies, special education. *Faculty:* 3 full-time (1 woman), 23 part-time/adjunct (19 women). *Students:* 41 part-time (29 women). Average age 38. In 2009, 15 master's awarded. *Degree requirements:* For master's, thesis. *Entrance requirements:* For master's, 3 letters of reference. *Application deadline:* Applications are processed on a rolling basis. Application fee: $50. *Expenses:* Contact institution. *Financial support:* Federal Work-Study, scholarships/grants, and tuition waivers available. Financial award applicants required to submit FAFSA. *Unit head:* Dr. Arlene Sacks, Dean, Graduate Programs in Education, 305-653-6713 Ext. 2152, E-mail: arlene.sacks@myunion.edu. *Application contact:* Dr. Arlene Sacks, Dean, Graduate Programs in Education, 305-653-6713 Ext. 2152, E-mail: arlene.sacks@myunion.edu.

University at Buffalo, the State University of New York, Graduate School, Graduate School of Education, Department of Learning and Instruction, Buffalo, NY 14260. Offers biology education (Ed M, Certificate); chemistry education (Ed M, Certificate); childhood education (Ed M); childhood education with bilingual extension (Ed M); early childhood education (Ed M); earth science education (Ed M, Certificate); elementary education (Ed D, PhD); English education (Ed M, PhD, Certificate); English for speakers of other languages (Ed M); foreign and second language education (PhD); French education (Ed M, Certificate); general education (Ed M); German education (Ed M, Certificate); gifted education (online) (Certificate); Latin education (Ed M, Certificate); literary specialist (Ed M); mathematics education (Ed M, PhD, Certificate); music education (Ed M, Certificate); physics education (Ed M, Certificate); reading education (PhD); science and the public (online) (Ed M); science education (PhD); social studies education (Ed M, Certificate); Spanish education (Ed M, Certificate); special education (PhD); teaching and leading for diversity (Certificate); teaching English to speakers of other languages (Ed M). Part-time and evening/weekend programs available. Postbaccalaureate distance learning degree programs offered (no on-campus study). *Faculty:* 34 full-time (24 women), 50 part-time/adjunct (39 women). *Students:* 332 full-time (245 women), 365 part-time (272 women); includes 50 minority (18 African Americans, 4 American Indian/Alaska Native, 10 Asian Americans or Pacific Islanders, 18 Hispanic Americans), 55 international. Average age 30. 627 applicants, 78% accepted, 286 enrolled. In 2009, 255 master's, 16 doctorates, 51 other advanced degrees awarded. *Degree requirements:* For master's, comprehensive exam; for doctorate, thesis/dissertation, research analysis exam, research experience component. *Entrance requirements:* For doctorate, GRE General Test or MAT, interview, writing sample, letters of recommendation. Additional exam requirements/recommendations for international students: Required—TOEFL (minimum score 600 paper-based; 250 computer-based; 96 iBT). *Application deadline:* For fall admission, 2/1 priority date for domestic and international students; for spring admission, 11/15 priority date for domestic students, 10/1 for international students. Applications are processed on a rolling basis. Application fee: $50. Electronic applications accepted. *Financial support:* In 2009–10, 23 fellowships with full tuition reimbursements (averaging $9,000 per year), 42 research assistantships with full tuition reimbursements (averaging $10,000 per year) were awarded; teaching assistantships with full tuition reimbursements, career-related internships or fieldwork, Federal Work-Study, institutionally sponsored loans, scholarships/grants, tuition waivers (partial), and unspecified assistantships also available. Financial award application deadline: 2/28; financial award applicants required to submit FAFSA. *Faculty research:* Science assessment, foreign language teaching and learning, early learning, new literacies, gender and education. Total annual research expenditures: $1.8 million. *Unit head:* Dr. Suzanne Miller, Chair, 716-645-2455, Fax: 716-645-3161, E-mail: smiller@buffalo.edu. *Application contact:* Cathy Dimino, Admissions Assistant, 716-645-2110, Fax: 716-645-7937, E-mail: cadimino@buffalo.edu.

University of Alaska Fairbanks, School of Education, Program in Education, Fairbanks, AK 99775. Offers curriculum and instruction (M Ed); education (M Ed); elementary education (M Ed); language and literacy (M Ed); reading (M Ed); secondary education (M Ed). *Faculty:*

23 full-time (15 women), 10 part-time/adjunct (9 women). *Students:* 35 full-time (26 women), 58 part-time (43 women); includes 25 minority (2 African Americans, 17 American Indian/Alaska Native, 4 Asian Americans or Pacific Islanders, 2 Hispanic Americans), 1 international. Average age 36. 94 applicants, 64% accepted, 42 enrolled. In 2009, 19 master's, 18 other advanced degrees awarded. *Degree requirements:* For master's, comprehensive exam, thesis, oral defense. *Entrance requirements:* Additional exam requirements/recommendations for international students: Required—TOEFL (minimum score 550 paper-based; 213 computer-based; 80 iBT). *Application deadline:* For fall admission, 5/1 for domestic students, 3/1 for international students; for spring admission, 10/15 for domestic students, 8/1 for international students. Applications are processed on a rolling basis. Application fee: $60. Electronic applications accepted. *Expenses:* Tuition, state resident: full-time $7584; part-time $316 per credit. Tuition, nonresident: full-time $15,504; part-time $646 per credit. Required fees: $23 per credit. $135 per semester. Tuition and fees vary according to course level, course load and reciprocity agreements. *Financial support:* In 2009–10, 1 teaching assistantship (averaging $11,955 per year) was awarded; fellowships, career-related internships or fieldwork, Federal Work-Study, scholarships/grants, health care benefits, and unspecified assistantships also available. Support available to part-time students. Financial award application deadline: 6/1; financial award applicants required to submit FAFSA. *Unit head:* Dr. Eric C. Madsen, Dean, 907-474-7341, Fax: 907-474-5451, E-mail: fysoed@uaf.edu. *Application contact:* Dr. Eric C. Madsen, Dean, 907-474-7341, Fax: 907-474-5451, E-mail: fysoed@uaf.edu.

The University of Arizona, Graduate College, College of Humanities, Department of English, Rhetoric, Composition and the Teaching of English Program, Tucson, AZ 85721. Offers PhD. *Students:* 8 full-time (7 women), 45 part-time (37 women); includes 3 minority (1 American Indian/Alaska Native, 2 Hispanic Americans), 2 international. Average age 34. 41 applicants, 15% accepted, 6 enrolled. In 2009, 17 doctorates awarded. *Degree requirements:* For doctorate, one foreign language, comprehensive exam, thesis/dissertation. *Entrance requirements:* For doctorate, GRE General Test, 3 letters of recommendation, writing sample. Additional exam requirements/recommendations for international students: Required—TOEFL (minimum score 550 paper-based; 213 computer-based; 79 iBT). *Application deadline:* Applications are processed on a rolling basis. Application fee: $75. Electronic applications accepted. *Expenses:* Tuition, state resident: full-time $9028. Tuition, nonresident: full-time $24,890. *Unit head:* Theresa Enos, Director, 520-621-3255, Fax: 520-621-7397, E-mail: enos@u.arizona.edu. *Application contact:* Alison Miller, Program Assistant, 520-621-7213, Fax: 520-621-7397, E-mail: admiller@u.arizona.edu.

University of Central Florida, College of Education, Department of Teaching and Learning Principles, Program in English Language Arts Education, Orlando, FL 32816. Offers M Ed, MA. *Accreditation:* NCATE. Part-time and evening/weekend programs available. *Students:* 13 full-time (11 women), 24 part-time (18 women); includes 7 minority (2 African Americans, 2 Asian Americans or Pacific Islanders, 3 Hispanic Americans), 2 international. Average age 30. 32 applicants, 69% accepted, 17 enrolled. In 2009, 16 master's awarded. *Degree requirements:* For master's, thesis or alternative, research project. *Entrance requirements:* For master's, GRE General Test. Additional exam requirements/recommendations for international students: Required—TOEFL. *Application deadline:* For fall admission, 7/15 for domestic students; for spring admission, 12/1 for domestic students. Application fee: $30. Electronic applications accepted. *Expenses:* Tuition, state resident: part-time $306.31 per credit hour. Tuition, nonresident: part-time $1099.01 per credit hour. Part-time tuition and fees vary according to degree level and program. *Financial support:* In 2009–10, 1 student received support, including 1 research assistantship with partial tuition reimbursement available (averaging $7,600 per year); fellowships with partial tuition reimbursements available, teaching assistantships with partial tuition reimbursements available, career-related internships or fieldwork, Federal Work-Study, institutionally sponsored loans, tuition waivers (partial), and unspecified assistantships also available. Financial award application deadline: 3/1; financial award applicants required to submit FAFSA.

University of Colorado Denver, College of Liberal Arts and Sciences, Department of English, Denver, CO 80217-3364. Offers applied linguistics (MA); English studies (MA); literature (MA); teaching English to speakers of other languages (Certificate); teaching of writing (MA). Part-time and evening/weekend programs available. *Students:* 12 full-time (9 women), 47 part-time (28 women); includes 3 minority (1 Asian American or Pacific Islander, 2 Hispanic Americans), 2 international. 36 applicants, 78% accepted, 19 enrolled. In 2009, 19 master's awarded. *Degree requirements:* For master's, thesis optional. *Entrance requirements:* For master's, GRE General Test, minimum GPA of 3.0. Additional exam requirements/recommendations for international students: Required—TOEFL (minimum score 550 paper-based). *Application deadline:* For fall admission, 5/25 for domestic students; for spring admission, 10/25 for domestic students. Applications are processed on a rolling basis. Application fee: $50 ($75 for international students). Electronic applications accepted. *Financial support:* Research assistantships, teaching assistantships, Federal Work-Study available. Financial award application deadline: 4/1; financial award applicants required to submit FAFSA. *Unit head:* Prof. Nancy Ciccone, Chair, 303-556-8395, Fax: 303-556-2959, E-mail: nancy.ciccone@ucdenver.edu. *Application contact:* Prof. Ian Ying, Program Advisor, 303-556-6728, Fax: 303-556-2959, E-mail: hongguang.ying@ucdenver.edu.

University of Connecticut, Graduate School, Neag School of Education, Department of Curriculum and Instruction, Program in English Education, Storrs, CT 06269. Offers MA, PhD, Post-Master's Certificate. *Accreditation:* NCATE. *Faculty:* 15 full-time (10 women). *Students:* 27 full-time (20 women), 1 (woman) part-time; includes 3 minority (all Hispanic Americans). Average age 26. 48 applicants, 10% accepted, 5 enrolled. In 2009, 32 master's awarded. Terminal master's awarded for partial completion of doctoral program. *Degree requirements:* For master's, comprehensive exam, thesis or alternative; for doctorate, thesis/dissertation. *Entrance requirements:* For doctorate, GRE General Test. Additional exam requirements/recommendations for international students: Required—TOEFL (minimum score 550 paper-based; 213 computer-based). *Application deadline:* For fall admission, 2/1 priority date for domestic and international students; for spring admission, 11/1 for domestic students, 10/1 for international students. Applications are processed on a rolling basis. Application fee: $55. Electronic applications accepted. *Expenses:* Tuition, state resident: full-time $4725; part-time $525 per credit. Tuition, nonresident: full-time $12,267; part-time $1363 per credit. Required fees: $346 per semester. Tuition and fees vary according to course load. *Financial support:* In 2009–10, 1 teaching assistantship with full tuition reimbursement was awarded; research assistantships with full tuition reimbursements, Federal Work-Study, scholarships/grants, health care benefits, and unspecified assistantships also available. Financial award application deadline: 2/1; financial award applicants required to submit FAFSA. *Unit head:* Mary Anne Doyle, Head, 860-486-2433, Fax: 860-486-0280, E-mail: mary.dolye@uconn.edu. *Application contact:* Lisa Rasicot, Graduate Coordinator, 860-486-3065, Fax: 860-486-0210, E-mail: l.rasicot@uconn.edu.

University of Florida, Graduate School, College of Education, School of Teaching and Learning, Gainesville, FL 32611. Offers bilingual/ESOL education (M Ed, MAE, Ed D, PhD, Ed S); curriculum and instruction (M Ed, MAE, Ed D, PhD, Ed S); early childhood education (Ed D, PhD, Ed S); elementary education (M Ed, MAE); English education (M Ed, MAE); mathematics education (M Ed, MAE); reading education (M Ed, MAE); science education (M Ed, MAE); social foundations (M Ed, MAE, Ed D, PhD); social studies education (M Ed, MAE). *Accreditation:* NCATE. *Degree requirements:* For master's, thesis optional; for doctorate, variable foreign language requirement, thesis/dissertation. *Entrance requirements:* For master's and doctorate, GRE General Test, minimum GPA of 3.0; for Ed S, GRE General Test. Additional exam requirements/recommendations for international students: Required—TOEFL (minimum score 550 paper-based; 213 computer-based). Electronic applications accepted. *Faculty research:* Teacher education, inclusive education, classroom processes, curriculum and technology.

University of Georgia, Graduate School, College of Education, Department of Language and Literacy Education, Athens, GA 30602. Offers English education (M Ed, Ed S); language and literacy education (PhD); reading education (M Ed, Ed D, Ed S); teaching additional languages (M Ed, Ed S). *Accreditation:* NCATE. *Faculty:* 18 full-time (12 women). *Students:* 85 full-time

(64 women), 112 part-time (98 women); includes 24 minority (12 African Americans, 3 Asian Americans or Pacific Islanders, 9 Hispanic Americans), 19 international. 110 applicants, 47% accepted, 47 enrolled. In 2009, 45 master's, 8 doctorates, 15 other advanced degrees awarded. *Degree requirements:* For doctorate, variable foreign language requirement. *Entrance requirements:* For master's and Ed S, GRE General Test or MAT; for doctorate, GRE General Test. Additional exam requirements/recommendations for international students: Required—TOEFL (minimum score 550 paper-based; 213 computer-based). *Application deadline:* For fall admission, 7/1 priority date for domestic students; for spring admission, 11/15 for domestic students. Application fee: $50. Electronic applications accepted. *Expenses:* Tuition, state resident: full-time $6000; part-time $250 per credit hour. Tuition, nonresident: full-time $20,904; part-time $871 per credit hour. Required fees: $730 per semester. *Faculty research:* Comprehension, critical literacy, literacy and technology, vocabulary instruction, content area reading. *Unit head:* Dr. Mark A. Faust, Head, 706-542-4515, Fax: 706-542-4509, E-mail: mfaust@uga.edu. *Application contact:* Dr. Elizabeth St. Pierre, Graduate Coordinator, 706-542-4526, E-mail: stpierre@uga.edu.

University of Illinois at Chicago, Graduate College, College of Liberal Arts and Sciences, Department of English, Chicago, IL 60607-7128. Offers English (MA, PhD), including creative writing (PhD), English education (MA), English studies, writing (MA); linguistics (MA), including teaching English to speakers of other languages/applied linguistics. Part-time and evening/weekend programs available. *Degree requirements:* For doctorate, variable foreign language requirement, thesis/dissertation, written and oral exams. *Entrance requirements:* For master's, GRE General Test, GRE Subject Test; for doctorate, GRE General Test, GRE Subject Test, minimum GPA of 2.0. Additional exam requirements/recommendations for international students: Required—TOEFL. Electronic applications accepted. *Faculty research:* Literary history and theory.

University of Indianapolis, Graduate Programs, School of Education, Indianapolis, IN 46227-3697. Offers art education (MAT); biology (MAT); chemistry (MAT); curriculum and instruction (MA); earth sciences (MAT); education (MA, MAT); educational leadership (MA); elementary education (MA); English (MAT); French (MAT); math (MAT); physical education (MAT); physics (MAT); secondary education (MA), including art education, education, English education, social studies education; social studies (MAT); Spanish (MAT). *Accreditation:* NCATE. Part-time and evening/weekend programs available. *Faculty:* 4 full-time (3 women), 3 part-time/adjunct (2 women). *Students:* 52 full-time (28 women), 110 part-time (67 women); includes 3 minority (all African Americans), 2 international. Average age 33. *Entrance requirements:* For master's, GRE Subject Test, PRAXIS I, minimum GPA of 2.5, 3 letters of recommendation, interview, writing exercise. Additional exam requirements/recommendations for international students: Required—TOEFL (minimum score 550 paper-based; 213 computer-based). *Application deadline:* Applications are processed on a rolling basis. Application fee: $50. *Financial support:* Federal Work-Study available. Financial award application deadline: 5/1; financial award applicants required to submit FAFSA. *Faculty research:* Assessment of teacher education, perceptions of prospective teachers by parents. *Unit head:* Dr. Kathy Moran, Dean, 317-788-3285, Fax: 317-788-3300, E-mail: kmoran@uindy.edu. *Application contact:* Chemain Slater, 317-788-2051, E-mail: slaterc@uindy.edu.

The University of Iowa, Graduate College, College of Education, Department of Teaching and Learning, Program in Elementary Education, Iowa City, IA 52242-1316. Offers curriculum and supervision (MA, PhD); developmental reading (MA); early childhood education and care (MA); elementary education (MA, PhD); language, literature and culture (PhD). *Degree requirements:* For master's, thesis optional, exam; for doctorate, comprehensive exam, thesis/dissertation. *Entrance requirements:* For master's and doctorate, GRE General Test, minimum GPA of 3.0. Additional exam requirements/recommendations for international students: Required—TOEFL (minimum score 550 paper-based; 213 computer-based; 81 iBT). Electronic applications accepted.

The University of Iowa, Graduate College, College of Education, Department of Teaching and Learning, Program in Secondary Education, Iowa City, IA 52242-1316. Offers art education (PhD); curriculum and supervision (PhD); curriculum supervision (MA); developmental reading (MA); English education (MA, MAT); foreign language education (MA, MAT); foreign language/ESL education (PhD); language, literature and culture (PhD); math education (PhD); mathematics education (MA); social studies (MA, PhD). *Degree requirements:* For master's, thesis optional, exam; for doctorate, comprehensive exam, thesis/dissertation. *Entrance requirements:* For master's and doctorate, GRE General Test, minimum GPA of 3.0. Additional exam requirements/recommendations for international students: Required—TOEFL (minimum score 550 paper-based; 213 computer-based; 81 iBT). Electronic applications accepted.

University of Manitoba, Faculty of Graduate Studies, Faculty of Education, Department of Curriculum, Teaching and Learning, Winnipeg, MB R3T 2N2, Canada. Offers language and literacy (M Ed); second language education (M Ed); studies in curriculum, teaching and learning (M Ed). *Degree requirements:* For master's, thesis or alternative.

University of Maryland, Baltimore County, Graduate School, College of Arts, Humanities and Social Sciences, Department of Education, Program in Teaching, Baltimore, MD 21250. Offers early childhood education (MAT); elementary education (MAT); secondary education (MAT), including art, biology, chemistry, dance, earth/space science, English, foreign language, mathematics, music, physics, theatre; secondary science (MAT), including social studies. Part-time and evening/weekend programs available. *Faculty:* 24 full-time (18 women), 25 part-time/adjunct (19 women). *Students:* 52 full-time (41 women), 64 part-time (55 women); includes 20 minority (5 African Americans, 1 American Indian/Alaska Native, 10 Asian Americans or Pacific Islanders, 4 Hispanic Americans), 3 international. Average age 31. 88 applicants, 57% accepted, 39 enrolled. In 2009, 106 master's awarded. *Degree requirements:* For master's, comprehensive exam (for some programs), thesis (for some programs). *Entrance requirements:* For master's, PRAXIS I and II, minimum GPA of 3.0. Additional exam requirements/recommendations for international students: Required—TOEFL. *Application deadline:* For fall admission, 6/1 for domestic students; for spring admission, 11/1 for domestic students. Applications are processed on a rolling basis. Application fee: $50. Electronic applications accepted. *Financial support:* In 2009–10, 6 students received support, including research assistantships with full tuition reimbursements available (averaging $12,000 per year); career-related internships or fieldwork, Federal Work-Study, scholarships/grants, tuition waivers, and unspecified assistantships also available. Financial award application deadline: 3/1. *Faculty research:* STEM teacher education, culturally sensitive pedagogy, ESOL/bilingual education, early childhood education, language, literacy and culture. *Unit head:* Dr. Susan M. Blunck, Director, 410-455-2869, Fax: 410-455-3986, E-mail: blunck@umbc.edu. *Application contact:* Dr. Susan M. Blunck, Director, 410-455-2869, Fax: 410-455-3986, E-mail: blunck@umbc.edu.

University of Michigan, Horace H. Rackham School of Graduate Studies, Joint Program in English and Education, Ann Arbor, MI 48109. Offers PhD. *Faculty:* 26 full-time (18 women). *Students:* 26 full-time (18 women); includes 2 minority (both African Americans), 2 international. Average age 31. 40 applicants, 20% accepted, 5 enrolled. In 2009, 2 doctorates awarded. *Degree requirements:* For doctorate, one foreign language, comprehensive exam, thesis/dissertation, 3 preliminary exams, oral defense of dissertation. *Entrance requirements:* For doctorate, GRE General Test, master's degree, teaching experience. Additional exam requirements/recommendations for international students: Required—TOEFL (minimum score 620 paper-based; 260 computer-based). *Application deadline:* For fall admission, 1/15 for domestic and international students. Application fee: $60 ($75 for international students). Electronic applications accepted. *Expenses:* Tuition, state resident: full-time $17,286; part-time $1099 per credit hour. Tuition, nonresident: full-time $34,944; part-time $2080 per credit hour. Required fees: $95 per semester. Tuition and fees vary according to course load, degree level and program. *Financial support:* In 2009–10, 26 students received support, including 7 fellowships with full tuition reimbursements available, 4 research assistantships with full tuition reimbursements available, 39 teaching assistantships with full tuition reimbursements available; health care benefits also available. *Faculty research:* Literacy, teacher education, discourse analysis, rhetoric and composition studies. *Unit head:* Dr. Anne Ruggles Gere, Co-Chair,

English Education

University of Michigan (continued)

734-763-6643, Fax: 734-615-6524, E-mail: argere@umich.edu. *Application contact:* Jeanie Mahoney Laubenthal, Program Assistant, 734-763-6643, Fax: 734-615-6524, E-mail: laubenth@umich.edu.

University of Michigan, Horace H. Rackham School of Graduate Studies, School of Education, Programs in Educational Studies, Ann Arbor, MI 48109. Offers cross specialization (PhD); curriculum development (MA); early childhood education (MA, PhD); educational administration and policy (MA, PhD); educational foundations and policy (MA, PhD); English education (MA); English language learning in school settings (MA); learning technologies (MA, PhD); literacy, language, and culture (MA, PhD); mathematics education (MA, PhD); postsecondary science education (MS); research methods (MA); science education (MA, PhD); social studies education (MA); teaching and teacher education (PhD); MA/Certification; MBA/MA; PhD/MA. Terminal master's awarded for partial completion of doctoral program. *Degree requirements:* For master's, thesis (for some programs); for doctorate, comprehensive exam, thesis/dissertation. *Entrance requirements:* For master's and doctorate, GRE General Test. Additional exam requirements/recommendations for international students: Required—TOEFL (minimum score 600 paper-based; 250 computer-based). *Application deadline:* For fall admission, 12/1 priority date for domestic students, 12/1 for international students. Application fee: $60 ($75 for international students). Electronic applications accepted. *Expenses:* Tuition, state resident: full-time $17,286; part-time $1099 per credit hour. Tuition, nonresident: full-time $34,944; part-time $2080 per credit hour. Required fees: $95 per semester. Tuition and fees vary according to course load, degree level and program. *Financial support:* Applicants required to submit FAFSA. *Unit head:* Dr. Addison Stone, Chairperson, 734-763-7500, Fax: 734-615-1290, E-mail: addison@umich.edu. *Application contact:* Laura Mayers, Student Services Assistant, 734-764-7563, Fax: 734-763-1495, E-mail: ed.grad.admit@umich.edu.

University of Minnesota, Twin Cities Campus, Graduate School, College of Education and Human Development, Department of Curriculum and Instruction, Program in Teaching, Minneapolis, MN 55455-0213. Offers Chinese (M Ed); earth science (M Ed); elementary special education (M Ed); English (M Ed); English as a second language (M Ed); French (M Ed); German (M Ed); Hebrew (M Ed); Japanese (M Ed); life sciences (M Ed); mathematics (M Ed); middle school science (M Ed); science (M Ed); second languages and cultures (M Ed); social studies (M Ed); Spanish (M Ed). *Students:* 263 full-time (186 women), 117 part-time (83 women); includes 32 minority (10 African Americans, 2 American Indian/Alaska Native, 17 Asian Americans or Pacific Islanders, 3 Hispanic Americans), 4 international. Average age 27. 363 applicants, 74% accepted, 259 enrolled. In 2009, 497 master's awarded. *Unit head:* Dr. Ruth Thomas, Chair, 612-624-4772, Fax: 612-624-8277, E-mail: thoma006@umn.edu. *Application contact:* Dr. Mary Trettin, Associate Dean, 612-625-6501, Fax: 612-626-1580, E-mail: mtrettin@umn.edu.

University of Missouri, Graduate School, College of Education, Department of Learning, Teaching and Curriculum, Columbia, MO 65211. Offers agricultural education (M Ed, PhD, Ed S); art education (M Ed, PhD, Ed S); business and office education (M Ed, PhD, Ed S); early childhood education (M Ed, PhD, Ed S); elementary education (M Ed, PhD, Ed S); English education (M Ed, PhD, Ed S); foreign language education (M Ed, PhD, Ed S); health education and promotion (M Ed, PhD); learning and instruction (M Ed); marketing education (M Ed, PhD, Ed S); mathematics education (M Ed, PhD, Ed S); music education (M Ed, PhD, Ed S); reading education (M Ed, PhD, Ed S); science education (M Ed, PhD, Ed S); social studies education (M Ed, PhD, Ed S); vocational education (M Ed, PhD, Ed S). Part-time programs available. Terminal master's awarded for partial completion of doctoral program. *Degree requirements:* For doctorate, thesis/dissertation. *Entrance requirements:* For master's and Ed S, GRE General Test or MAT, minimum GPA of 3.0; for doctorate, GRE General Test, minimum GPA of 3.0. Additional exam requirements/recommendations for international students: Required—TOEFL (minimum score 600 paper-based; 250 computer-based; 100 iBT). Electronic applications accepted.

The University of Montana, Graduate School, College of Arts and Sciences, Department of English, Program in Teaching, Missoula, MT 59812-0002. Offers MA. *Entrance requirements:* For master's, GRE General Test, sample of written work.

University of New Hampshire, Graduate School, College of Liberal Arts, Department of English, Durham, NH 03824. Offers English (MFA, PhD); English education (MST); language and linguistics (MA); literature (MA); writing (MA). Part-time programs available. *Faculty:* 35 full-time (18 women). *Students:* 54 full-time (33 women), 64 part-time (40 women); includes 5 minority (1 African American, 2 American Indian/Alaska Native, 2 Hispanic Americans), 5 international. Average age 34. 279 applicants, 43% accepted, 38 enrolled. In 2009, 32 master's, 5 doctorates awarded. *Degree requirements:* For master's, one foreign language; for doctorate, 2 foreign languages, thesis/dissertation. *Entrance requirements:* For master's, GRE General Test, sample of written work; for doctorate, GRE General Test, GRE Subject Test, sample of written work. Additional exam requirements/recommendations for international students: Required—TOEFL (minimum score 550 paper-based; 213 computer-based; 80 iBT). *Application deadline:* For fall admission, 6/1 priority date for domestic students, 2/15 for international students; for spring admission, 12/1 for domestic students. Applications are processed on a rolling basis. Application fee: $65. Electronic applications accepted. *Expenses:* Tuition, state resident: full-time $10,380; part-time $577 per credit hour. Tuition, nonresident: full-time $24,350; part-time $1002 per credit hour. Required fees: $1550; $387.50 per semester. Tuition and fees vary according to course load and program. *Financial support:* In 2009–10, 57 students received support, including 4 fellowships, 46 teaching assistantships; research assistantships, career-related internships or fieldwork, Federal Work-Study, scholarships/grants, and tuition waivers (full and partial) also available. Support available to part-time students. Financial award application deadline: 2/15. *Unit head:* Dr. Andrew Merton, Chairperson, 603-862-3963. *Application contact:* Jamie Auger, Administrative Assistant, 603-862-3963, E-mail: engl.grad@unh.edu.

The University of North Carolina at Chapel Hill, Graduate School, School of Education, Program in Secondary Education, Chapel Hill, NC 27599. Offers English (Grades 9-12) (MAT); English as a second language (MAT); French (Grades K-12) (MAT); German (Grades K-12) (MAT); Japanese (Grades K-12) (MAT); Latin (Grades 9-12) (MAT); mathematics (Grades 9-12) (MAT); music (Grades K-12) (MAT); science (Grades 9-12) (MAT); social studies (Grades 9-12) (MAT); Spanish (Grades K-12) (MAT). *Accreditation:* NCATE. *Students:* 53 full-time (35 women), 1 part-time (0 women); includes 8 minority (4 African Americans, 2 Asian Americans or Pacific Islanders, 2 Hispanic Americans), 3 international. Average age 25. 137 applicants, 77% accepted, 54 enrolled. In 2009, 39 master's awarded. *Degree requirements:* For master's, comprehensive exam. *Entrance requirements:* For master's, GRE General Test, minimum GPA of 3.0 during last 2 years of undergraduate course work. Additional exam requirements/recommendations for international students: Required—TOEFL (minimum score 550 paper-based; 79 computer-based). *Application deadline:* For fall admission, 12/15 priority date for domestic and international students. Applications are processed on a rolling basis. Application fee: $77. Electronic applications accepted. *Financial support:* Federal Work-Study available. Support available to part-time students. Financial award application deadline: 3/1; financial award applicants required to submit FAFSA. *Unit head:* Dr. James Trier, Coordinator, 919-843-4627, Fax: 919-962-1533. *Application contact:* Amy Butler, Student Services Assistant, 919-966-1346, Fax: 919-962-1533, E-mail: abutler@email.unc.edu.

The University of North Carolina at Charlotte, Graduate School, College of Arts and Sciences, Department of English, Program in English Education, Charlotte, NC 28223-0001. Offers MA. Part-time and evening/weekend programs available. *Faculty:* 16 full-time (9 women), 5 part-time/adjunct (4 women). *Students:* 1 (woman) full-time, 6 part-time (4 women). Average age 30. 4 applicants, 50% accepted, 2 enrolled. In 2009, 1 master's awarded. *Degree requirements:* For master's, thesis. *Entrance requirements:* For master's, GRE General Test or MAT, minimum GPA of 2.75. Additional exam requirements/recommendations for international students: Required—TOEFL (minimum score 557 paper-based; 220 computer-based; 83 iBT). *Application deadline:* For fall admission, 7/15 for domestic students, 5/1 for international students; for spring admission, 11/15 for domestic students, 10/1 for international students. Application fee: $55. *Financial support:* Career-related internships or fieldwork, Federal Work-Study, institutionally sponsored loans, scholarships/grants, and unspecified assistantships available. Support available to part-time students. Financial award application deadline: 4/1; financial award applicants required to submit FAFSA. *Unit head:* Dr. Lillian Brannon, Coordinator, 704-687-3220, Fax: 704-687-6430, E-mail: lbrannon@uncc.edu. *Application contact:* Kathy B. Giddings, Director of Graduate Admissions, 704-687-5503, Fax: 704-687-3279, E-mail: gradadm@uncc.edu.

The University of North Carolina at Greensboro, Graduate School, College of Arts and Sciences, Department of English, Program in English, Greensboro, NC 27412-5001. Offers American literature (PhD); English (M Ed, MA); English literature (PhD); rhetoric and composition (PhD). *Degree requirements:* For master's, comprehensive exam, thesis or alternative; for doctorate, variable foreign language requirement, thesis/dissertation, preliminary exam. *Entrance requirements:* For master's, GRE General Test, GRE Subject Test, minimum GPA of 3.0; for doctorate, GRE General Test, GRE Subject Test, critical writing sample, minimum GPA of 3.0. Additional exam requirements/recommendations for international students: Required—TOEFL. Electronic applications accepted.

The University of North Carolina at Pembroke, Graduate Studies, Department of English, Theater and Languages, Program in English Education, Pembroke, NC 28372-1510. Offers MA, MAT. *Accreditation:* NCATE. Part-time and evening/weekend programs available. *Degree requirements:* For master's, comprehensive exam, thesis optional. *Entrance requirements:* For master's, GRE, MAT, or NTE, minimum GPA of 3.0 in major or 2.5 overall. Additional exam requirements/recommendations for international students: Required—TOEFL.

University of Oklahoma, Graduate College, College of Education, Department of Instructional Leadership and Academic Curriculum, Norman, OK 73072. Offers education (Certificate); instructional leadership and academic curriculum (M Ed, PhD), including bilingual education, early childhood education, elementary education, English education, math education, reading education, science education, secondary education, social studies education. *Accreditation:* NCATE. Part-time and evening/weekend programs available. *Faculty:* 18 full-time (11 women). *Students:* 44 full-time (36 women), 117 part-time (92 women); includes 35 minority (11 African Americans, 14 American Indian/Alaska Native, 5 Asian Americans or Pacific Islanders, 5 Hispanic Americans), 2 international. 50 applicants, 84% accepted, 32 enrolled. In 2009, 31 master's, 6 doctorates awarded. Terminal master's awarded for partial completion of doctoral program. *Degree requirements:* For doctorate, thesis/dissertation. *Entrance requirements:* For master's, 12 hours of course work in education; for doctorate, GRE General Test, master's degree, minimum graduate GPA of 3.0. Additional exam requirements/recommendations for international students: Required—TOEFL (minimum score 550 paper-based; 213 computer-based). *Application deadline:* For fall admission, 6/1 priority date for domestic students, 4/1 for international students; for spring admission, 11/1 for domestic students, 9/1 for international students. Applications are processed on a rolling basis. Application fee: $40 ($90 for international students). Electronic applications accepted. *Expenses:* Tuition, state resident: full-time $3744; part-time $156 per credit hour. Tuition, nonresident: full-time $13,577; part-time $565.70 per credit hour. Required fees: $2415; $90.10 per credit hour. *Financial support:* In 2009–10, 107 students received support, including 1 research assistantship with partial tuition reimbursement available (averaging $9,630 per year), 6 teaching assistantships with partial tuition reimbursements available (averaging $10,801 per year); scholarships/grants, health care benefits, and unspecified assistantships also available. Financial award applicants required to submit FAFSA. *Faculty research:* English education, mathematics education, reading, science education, social studies education. Total annual research expenditures: $752,908. *Unit head:* Lawrence Baines, Chair, 405-325-1498, Fax: 405-325-4061, E-mail: lbaines@ou.edu. *Application contact:* Lynn Crussel, Administrative Assistant for Graduate Studies, 405-325-4843, Fax: 405-325-4061, E-mail: lcrussel@ou.edu.

University of Phoenix, College of Natural Sciences, College of Education, Phoenix, AZ 85034-7209. Offers administration and supervision (MAEd); adult education and training (MAEd); curriculum and instruction (MAEd); curriculum and instruction-adult education (MAEd); curriculum and instruction-computer education (MAEd); curriculum and instruction-English and language arts education (MAEd); curriculum and instruction-English as a second language (MAEd); curriculum and instruction-mathematics education (MAEd); curriculum education (MAEd); early childhood (MAEd); elementary teacher education (MAEd); secondary teacher education (MAEd); special education (MAEd); teacher leadership (MAEd). *Accreditation:* Teacher Education Accreditation Council. Evening/weekend programs available. Postbaccalaureate distance learning degree programs offered (no on-campus study). *Faculty:* 47 full-time (34 women), 844 part-time/adjunct (636 women). *Students:* 13,657 full-time (10,698 women); includes 4,000 minority (3,063 African Americans, 74 American Indian/Alaska Native, 241 Asian Americans or Pacific Islanders, 622 Hispanic Americans), 307 international. Average age 36. In 2009, 17,246 master's awarded. *Degree requirements:* For master's, thesis (for some programs). *Entrance requirements:* For master's, 3 years of work experience, minimum GPA of 2.5. Additional exam requirements/recommendations for international students: Required—TOEFL (minimum score 550 paper-based; 213 computer-based; 79 iBT). *Application deadline:* Applications are processed on a rolling basis. Application fee: $45. Electronic applications accepted. *Expenses:* Tuition: Full-time $13,272. Required fees: $660. Full-time tuition and fees vary according to course level, degree level and program. *Financial support:* Institutionally sponsored loans and scholarships/grants available. Financial award applicants required to submit FAFSA. *Unit head:* Dr. Meredith Curley, Dean/Executive Director, 480-557-1217, Fax: 480-557-1588, E-mail: meredith.curley@phoenix.edu. *Application contact:* Chair, 602-387-7000, Fax: 602-387-6020.

University of Phoenix–Omaha Campus, College of Education, Omaha, NE 68154-5240. Offers administration and supervision (MA Ed); curriculum and instruction (MA Ed), including adult education, computer education, curriculum and instruction, English and language arts education, English as a second language, mathematics education; elementary teacher education (MA Ed); secondary teacher education (MA Ed); special education (MA Ed).

University of Phoenix–Southern California Campus, College of Education, Costa Mesa, CA 92626. Offers administration and supervision (MA Ed); adult education and training (MA Ed); curriculum and instruction (MA Ed), including computer education, curriculum and instruction, English and language arts, English as a second language, mathematics education; early childhood education (MA Ed); special education (MA Ed); teacher leadership (MA Ed). Evening/weekend programs available. *Faculty:* 47 full-time (34 women), 844 part-time/adjunct (636 women). *Students:* 558 full-time (391 women); includes 222 minority (60 African Americans, 4 American Indian/Alaska Native, 26 Asian Americans or Pacific Islanders, 132 Hispanic Americans), 9 international. Average age 34. In 2009, 303 master's awarded. *Degree requirements:* For master's, thesis (for some programs). *Entrance requirements:* For master's, minimum undergraduate GPA of 2.5, 3 years work experience. Additional exam requirements/recommendations for international students: Required—TOEFL (minimum score 550 paper-based; 213 computer-based; 79 iBT). *Application deadline:* Applications are processed on a rolling basis. Application fee: $45. Electronic applications accepted. *Expenses:* Tuition: Full-time $15,120. Required fees: $660. *Financial support:* Institutionally sponsored loans and scholarships/grants available. Financial award applicants required to submit FAFSA. *Unit head:* Dr. Meredith Curley, Dean/Executive Director, 480-557-1217, Fax: 480-557-1588, E-mail: meredith.curley@phoenix.edu. *Application contact:* Campus College Chair, 714-378-1878, Fax: 714-378-5875.

University of Phoenix–Springfield Campus, College of Education, Springfield, MO 65804-7211. Offers administration and supervision (MA Ed); curriculum and instruction (MA Ed), including computer education, curriculum and instruction, English and language arts education, English as a second language, mathematics education; English and language arts education (MA Ed).

University of Pittsburgh, School of Education, Department of Instruction and Learning, Program in Secondary Education, Pittsburgh, PA 15260. Offers English/communications

education (M Ed, MAT); foreign languages education (M Ed, MAT); mathematics education (M Ed, MAT, Ed D); science education (M Ed, MAT, MS, Ed D); social studies education (M Ed, MAT). Part-time and evening/weekend programs available. *Students:* 170 full-time (107 women), 70 part-time (54 women); includes 19 minority (11 African Americans, 6 Asian Americans or Pacific Islanders, 2 Hispanic Americans), 10 international. Average age 29. 220 applicants, 72% accepted, 128 enrolled. In 2009, 108 master's, 5 doctorates awarded. *Degree requirements:* For master's, thesis; for doctorate, thesis/dissertation. *Entrance requirements:* For master's, PRAXIS I; for doctorate, GRE General Test. Additional exam requirements/recommendations for international students: Required—TOEFL. *Application deadline:* For fall admission, 2/1 priority date for domestic students; for spring admission, 11/15 priority date for domestic students. Applications are processed on a rolling basis. Application fee: $50. Electronic applications accepted. *Expenses:* Tuition, state resident: full-time $16,402; part-time $665 per credit. Tuition, nonresident: full-time $28,694; part-time $1175 per credit. Required fees: $690; $175 per term. Tuition and fees vary according to program. *Financial support:* Fellowships, teaching assistantships, career-related internships or fieldwork, Federal Work-Study, tuition waivers (partial), and unspecified assistantships available. Support available to part-time students. Financial award application deadline: 3/15; financial award applicants required to submit FAFSA. *Unit head:* Dr. Richard Donato, Chairman, 412-624-7248, Fax: 412-648-7081, E-mail: donato@pitt.edu. *Application contact:* Joan M. Cutone, Director, School of Education Student Service Center, 412-648-2230, Fax: 412-648-1899, E-mail: soeinfo@pitt.edu.

University of Puerto Rico, Mayagüez Campus, Graduate Studies, College of Arts and Sciences, Department of English, Mayagüez, PR 00681-9000. Offers English education (MA). Part-time programs available. *Degree requirements:* For master's, comprehensive exam, thesis optional. *Entrance requirements:* For master's, course work in linguistics or language, American literature, British literature, and structure/grammar or syntax. *Faculty research:* Teaching English as a second language, linguistics, American literature, British literature.

University of St. Francis, College of Education, Joliet, IL 60435-6169. Offers educational leadership (MS), including reading; elementary education certification (M Ed); reading (MS); secondary education certification (M Ed), including English education, math education, science education, social studies education; special education (M Ed); teaching and learning (MS), including character education, curriculum and instruction, differentiated instruction, technology. *Accreditation:* NCATE. Part-time and evening/weekend programs available. *Faculty:* 10 full-time (8 women), 26 part-time/adjunct (18 women). *Students:* 60 full-time (45 women), 349 part-time (283 women); includes 36 minority (10 African Americans, 2 Asian Americans or Pacific Islanders, 24 Hispanic Americans). Average age 33. 211 applicants, 65% accepted, 102 enrolled. In 2009, 174 master's awarded. *Entrance requirements:* For master's, Illinois Basic Skills Test (M Ed), teaching certificate (MS), minimum undergraduate GPA of 2.75, 2 letters of recommendation, computer competency. Additional exam requirements/recommendations for international students: Required—TOEFL (minimum score 550 paper-based; 213 computer-based). *Application deadline:* Applications are processed on a rolling basis. Application fee: $30. Electronic applications accepted. *Expenses:* Contact institution. *Financial support:* In 2009–10, 254 students received support. Federal Work-Study, scholarships/grants, tuition waivers (partial), and unspecified assistantships available. Support available to part-time students. Financial award applicants required to submit FAFSA. *Unit head:* Dr. John Gambro, Dean, 815-740-3332, Fax: 815-740-2264, E-mail: jgambro@stfrancis.edu. *Application contact:* Sandra Sloka, Director of Admissions for Graduate and Degree Completion Programs, 800-735-7500, Fax: 815-740-5032, E-mail: ssloka@stfrancis.edu.

University of South Carolina, The Graduate School, College of Arts and Sciences, Department of English Language and Literature, Columbia, SC 29208. Offers creative writing (MFA); English (MA, PhD); English education (MAT); MLIS/MA. MAT offered in cooperation with the College of Education. Part-time programs available. *Degree requirements:* For master's, one foreign language, comprehensive exam, thesis; for doctorate, 2 foreign languages, comprehensive exam, thesis/dissertation. *Entrance requirements:* For master's, GRE General Test (MFA), GRE Subject Test (MA, MAT), sample of written work; for doctorate, GRE General Test, GRE Subject Test, sample of written work. Additional exam requirements/recommendations for international students: Required—TOEFL. Electronic applications accepted. *Faculty research:* American literature, British literature, composition and rhetoric, linguistics, speech communication.

University of South Carolina, The Graduate School, College of Education, Department of Instruction and Teacher Education, Program in Secondary Education, Columbia, SC 29208. Offers art education (IMA, MAT); business education (IMA, MAT); English (MAT); foreign language (MAT); health education (MAT); mathematics (MAT); science (IMA, MAT); secondary (Ed D); secondary education (MT, PhD); social studies (MAT); theatre and speech (MAT). IMA and MT offered jointly with the subject areas. *Accreditation:* NCATE. *Degree requirements:* For master's, comprehensive exam, thesis (for some programs), foreign language (MA); for doctorate, one foreign language, comprehensive exam, thesis/dissertation. *Entrance requirements:* For master's, GRE General Test or MAT, teaching certificate (IMA, M Ed), interview; for doctorate, GRE General Test or MAT, interview. *Faculty research:* Middle school programs, professional development, school collaboration.

University of South Florida, Graduate School, College of Education–Main Campus, Department of Secondary Education, Tampa, FL 33620-9951. Offers English education (M Ed, MA, MAT, PhD); foreign language education/ESOL (M Ed, MA, MAT); instructional technology (M Ed, PhD, Ed S); mathematics education (M Ed, MA, MAT, PhD, Ed S); science education (M Ed, MA, MAT, PhD); second language acquisition/instructional technology (PhD); secondary education (M Ed, PhD); secondary education/TESOL (M Ed); social science education (M Ed, MA, MAT); teaching and learning in the content area (PhD). *Accreditation:* NCATE. Part-time and evening/weekend programs available. *Faculty:* 28 full-time (17 women), 3 part-time/adjunct (1 woman). *Students:* 144 full-time (97 women), 322 part-time (212 women); includes 100 minority (32 African Americans, 4 American Indian/Alaska Native, 17 Asian Americans or Pacific Islanders, 47 Hispanic Americans), 25 international. Average age 30. 230 applicants, 67% accepted, 122 enrolled. In 2009, 122 master's, 14 doctorates, 1 other advanced degree awarded. *Degree requirements:* For master's, variable foreign language requirement, comprehensive exam; for doctorate, variable foreign language requirement, comprehensive exam, thesis/dissertation. *Entrance requirements:* For master's, GRE General Test or General Knowledge Test, minimum GPA of 3.0; for doctorate, GRE General Test, minimum GPA of 3.5; for Ed S, GRE General Test. Additional exam requirements/recommendations for international students: Required—TOEFL (minimum score 550 paper-based; 213 computer-based; 79 iBT). *Application deadline:* For fall admission, 2/15 for domestic students, 1/2 for international students; for spring admission, 10/15 for domestic students, 6/1 for international students. Application fee: $30. Electronic applications accepted. *Financial support:* In 2009–10, 7 students received support, including 1 research assistantship with full tuition reimbursement available (averaging $10,000 per year), 55 teaching assistantships with full and partial tuition reimbursements available (averaging $7,900 per year); scholarships/grants and unspecified assistantships also available. Financial award application deadline: 4/15; financial award applicants required to submit FAFSA. *Faculty research:* English language learners/multicultural, social science education, mathematics education, science education, instructional technology. Total annual research expenditures: $336,023. *Unit head:* Dr. Stephen Thornton, Chairperson, 813-974-3533, Fax: 813-974-3837, E-mail: thornton@usf.edu. *Application contact:* Dr. James White, Program Director, 813-974-1629, Fax: 813-974-3837, E-mail: jwhite@usf.edu.

The University of Tennessee, Graduate School, College of Education, Health and Human Sciences, Program in Education, Knoxville, TN 37996. Offers art education (MS); counseling education (PhD); cultural studies in education (PhD); curriculum (MS, Ed S); curriculum, educational research and evaluation (Ed D, PhD); early childhood education (PhD); early childhood special education (MS); education of deaf and hard of hearing (MS); educational administration and policy studies (Ed D, PhD); educational administration and supervision (Ed S); educational psychology (Ed D, PhD); elementary education (MS, Ed S); elementary teaching (MS); English education (MS, Ed S); exercise science (PhD); foreign language/ESL education (MS, Ed S); instructional technology (MS, Ed D, PhD, Ed S); literacy, language and ESL education (PhD); literacy, language education, and ESL education (Ed D); mathematics education (MS, Ed S); modified and comprehensive special education (MS); reading education (MS, Ed S); school counseling (Ed S); school psychology (PhD, Ed S); science education (MS, Ed S); secondary teaching (MS); social foundations (MS); social science education (MS, Ed S); socio-cultural foundations of sports and education (PhD); special education (Ed S); teacher education (Ed D, PhD). *Accreditation:* NCATE. Part-time and evening/weekend programs available. *Degree requirements:* For master's and Ed S, thesis optional; for doctorate, variable foreign language requirement, thesis/dissertation. *Entrance requirements:* For master's, minimum GPA of 2.7; for doctorate and Ed S, GRE General Test, minimum GPA of 2.7. Additional exam requirements/recommendations for international students: Required—TOEFL. Electronic applications accepted. *Expenses:* Tuition, state resident: full-time $6826; part-time $380 per semester hour. Tuition, nonresident: full-time $21,844; part-time $1147 per semester hour. Tuition and fees vary according to program.

The University of Texas at El Paso, Graduate School, College of Liberal Arts, Department of English, El Paso, TX 79968-0001. Offers bilingual professional writing (Certificate); English and American literature (MA); rhetoric and composition (PhD); rhetoric and writing studies (MA); teaching English (MAT). Part-time and evening/weekend programs available. *Degree requirements:* For master's, thesis optional. *Entrance requirements:* For master's, GRE General Test, minimum GPA of 3.0. Additional exam requirements/recommendations for international students: Required—TOEFL. Electronic applications accepted. *Faculty research:* Literature, creative writing, literary theory.

University of the Sacred Heart, Graduate Programs, Department of Education, San Juan, PR 00914-0383. Offers early childhood education (M Ed); information technology and multimedia (Certificate); instruction systems and education technology (M Ed), including English, information technology and multimedia, instructional design, mathematics, Spanish. Part-time and evening/weekend programs available. *Degree requirements:* For master's, thesis. *Entrance requirements:* For master's, EXADEP, minimum undergraduate GPA of 2.75, interview.

The University of Toledo, College of Graduate Studies, College of Education, Department of Curriculum and Instruction, Program in Education and English, Toledo, OH 43606-3390. Offers MAE.

University of Victoria, Faculty of Graduate Studies, Faculty of Education, Department of Curriculum and Instruction, Victoria, BC V8W 2Y2, Canada. Offers art education (M Ed, PhD); curriculum studies (M Ed, MA, PhD); early childhood education (M Ed, PhD); educational studies (PhD); language and literacy (M Ed, MA, PhD); mathematics (M Ed, MA, PhD); music education (M Ed, MA, PhD); science (M Ed, MA, PhD); social studies (M Ed, MA); social, cultural and foundational studies (MA, PhD); technology and environmental education (PhD). Part-time programs available. *Degree requirements:* For master's, thesis, project (M Ed); for doctorate, comprehensive exam, thesis/dissertation. *Entrance requirements:* For master's, minimum B average. Additional exam requirements/recommendations for international students: Required—TOEFL (minimum score 575 paper-based; 233 computer-based), IELTS (minimum score 7). Electronic applications accepted. *Faculty research:* Elementary and secondary English, language arts, curriculum theory and practice, educational media and technology, educational administration and leadership, history and philosophy of education.

University of Virginia, Curry School of Education, Department of Curriculum, Instruction, and Special Education, Program in Curriculum and Instruction, Charlottesville, VA 22903. Offers curriculum and instruction (M Ed, Ed S); elementary (M Ed, Ed D); English (M Ed, Ed D); foreign language (M Ed); mathematics (M Ed, Ed D); reading (M Ed, Ed D, Ed S); science (Ed D); social studies (M Ed). *Students:* 12 full-time (8 women), 30 part-time (24 women); includes 2 minority (1 Asian American or Pacific Islander, 1 Hispanic American), 1 international. Average age 36. 55 applicants, 69% accepted, 26 enrolled. In 2009, 247 master's, 14 doctorates, 10 other advanced degrees awarded. *Degree requirements:* For master's, comprehensive exam (for some programs); for doctorate, comprehensive exam, thesis/dissertation; for Ed S, comprehensive exam. *Entrance requirements:* For master's, doctorate, and Ed S, GRE General Test, 2 letters of recommendation. Additional exam requirements/recommendations for international students: Required—TOEFL (minimum score 600 paper-based; 250 computer-based; 90 iBT), IELTS (minimum score 7). *Application deadline:* Applications are processed on a rolling basis. Application fee: $60. Electronic applications accepted. *Financial support:* Fellowships with tuition reimbursements, research assistantships with tuition reimbursements, teaching assistantships with tuition reimbursements available. Financial award application deadline: 1/5; financial award applicants required to submit FAFSA.

University of Virginia, Curry School of Education, Program in Education, Charlottesville, VA 22903. Offers administration and supervision (PhD); applied developmental science (PhD); counselor education (PhD); curriculum and instruction (PhD); early childhood-developmental risk (MT); education evaluation (PhD); educational psychology (PhD); educational research (PhD); elementary (MT, PhD); English education (MT, PhD); foreign language education (MT); higher education (PhD); instructional technology (PhD); kinesiology (MT, PhD); math education (PhD); reading education (PhD); research statistics and evaluation (PhD); school psychology (PhD); science education (PhD); social studies education (MT, PhD); special education (PhD); world languages education (MT). *Students:* 336 full-time (239 women), 88 part-time (54 women); includes 43 minority (24 African Americans, 2 American Indian/Alaska Native, 11 Asian Americans or Pacific Islanders, 6 Hispanic Americans), 18 international. Average age 27. 199 applicants, 48% accepted, 55 enrolled. In 2009, 127 master's, 52 doctorates awarded. *Degree requirements:* For master's, comprehensive exam (for some programs), field project; for doctorate, comprehensive exam, thesis/dissertation. *Entrance requirements:* For doctorate, GRE General Test. Additional exam requirements/recommendations for international students: Required—TOEFL (minimum score 600 paper-based; 250 computer-based; 90 iBT), IELTS (minimum score 7). *Application deadline:* Applications are processed on a rolling basis. Application fee: $60. Electronic applications accepted. *Financial support:* Fellowships, research assistantships, teaching assistantships available. Financial award application deadline: 1/5; financial award applicants required to submit FAFSA.

University of Washington, Graduate School, College of Arts and Sciences, Department of English, Seattle, WA 98195. Offers creative writing (MFA); English as a second language (MAT); English literature and language (MA, MAT, PhD). Part-time programs available. Terminal master's awarded for partial completion of doctoral program. *Degree requirements:* For master's, one foreign language, thesis (for some programs); for doctorate, one foreign language, thesis/dissertation. *Entrance requirements:* For master's, GRE General Test, GRE Subject Test (MA and MAT in English), minimum GPA of 3.0; for doctorate, GRE General Test, GRE Subject Test. Additional exam requirements/recommendations for international students: Required—TOEFL. Electronic applications accepted. *Faculty research:* English and American literature, critical theory, creative writing, language theory.

University of Washington, Graduate School, College of Education, Seattle, WA 98195. Offers curriculum and instruction (M Ed, Ed D, PhD), including educational technology, general curriculum (Ed D, PhD), language, literacy, and culture, mathematics education, multicultural education, reading and language arts education (Ed D), science education, social studies education, teaching and curriculum (M Ed); educational leadership and policy studies (M Ed, Ed D, PhD), including administration (Ed D), educational policy, organization, and leadership (M Ed, PhD), higher education, leadership for learning (Ed D), social and cultural foundations of education (M Ed, PhD); educational psychology (M Ed, PhD), including educational psychology (PhD), human development and cognition (M Ed), learning sciences, measurement, statistics and research design (M Ed), school psychology (M Ed); instructional leadership (M Ed); intercollegiate athletic leadership (M Ed); special education (M Ed, Ed D, PhD), including early childhood special education (M Ed), emotional and behavioral disabilities (M Ed), learning disabilities (M Ed), low-incidence disabilities (M Ed), severe disabilities (M Ed), special education (Ed D, PhD); teacher education (MIT). *Accreditation:* APA. Part-time and evening/weekend programs available. *Degree requirements:* For master's, thesis optional; for doctorate, thesis/dissertation. *Entrance requirements:* For master's and doctorate, GRE General Test, minimum GPA of 3.0. Additional exam requirements/recommendations for international students: Required—TOEFL.

English Education

University of Washington (continued)

Electronic applications accepted. *Faculty research:* School restructuring/effective schools, special education interventions, literacy and writing, technology, school partnerships, teacher preparation.

The University of West Alabama, School of Graduate Studies, College of Liberal Arts, Department of English and Language Arts, Livingston, AL 35470. Offers language arts (MAT). *Accreditation:* NCATE.

University of West Georgia, Graduate School, College of Education, Department of Curriculum and Instruction, Carrollton, GA 30118. Offers art education (M Ed); art teacher education (Ed S); biology/secondary education (Ed S); business education (M Ed, Ed S); early childhood education (M Ed, Ed S); economics/secondary teacher education (Ed S); English teacher education (Ed S); French language teacher education (Ed S); history teacher education (Ed S); mathematics teacher education (Ed S); middle grades education (M Ed, Ed S); reading education (M Ed, Ed S); science teacher education (Ed S); secondary education (M Ed, Ed S); social science teacher education (Ed S); Spanish language teacher education (Ed S). Part-time and evening/weekend programs available. *Faculty:* 18 full-time (15 women), 7 part-time/adjunct (6 women). *Students:* 119 full-time (101 women), 358 part-time (280 women); includes 109 minority (97 African Americans, 3 American Indian/Alaska Native, 2 Asian Americans or Pacific Islanders, 7 Hispanic Americans). Average age 33. 193 applicants, 82% accepted, 34 enrolled. In 2009, 109 master's, 27 Ed Ss awarded. *Degree requirements:* For master's, comprehensive exam; for Ed S, research project. *Entrance requirements:* For master's, GRE General Test or MAT, minimum GPA of 2.7; for Ed S, GRE General Test, master's degree, minimum graduate GPA of 2.7. *Application deadline:* For fall admission, 7/17 for domestic students; for spring admission, 11/20 for domestic students. Applications are processed on a rolling basis. Application fee: $30. Electronic applications accepted. *Expenses:* Tuition, state resident: full-time $2952; part-time $164 per semester hour. Tuition, nonresident: full-time $11,808; part-time $656 per semester hour. Required fees: $42.90 per semester hour. $307 per semester. Tuition and fees vary according to course load. *Financial support:* In 2009–10, 5 research assistantships with full tuition reimbursements (averaging $3,000 per year) were awarded; career-related internships or fieldwork and scholarships/grants also available. Support available to part-time students. Financial award applicants required to submit FAFSA. *Unit head:* Dr. Donna Harkins, Chair, 678-839-6066, Fax: 678-839-6559, E-mail: dharkins@westga.edu. *Application contact:* Dr. Charles W. Clark, Dean, 678-839-6508, E-mail: cclark@westga.edu.

University of Wisconsin–Platteville, School of Graduate Studies, College of Liberal Arts and Education, School of Education, Platteville, WI 53818-3099. Offers adult education (MSE); elementary education (MSE); English education (MSE); middle school education (MSE); secondary education (MSE); vocational and technical education (MSE). *Accreditation:* NCATE. Part-time programs available. *Faculty:* 8 part-time/adjunct (3 women). *Students:* 16 full-time (12 women), 183 part-time (137 women); includes 35 minority (27 African Americans, 1 American Indian/Alaska Native, 1 Asian American or Pacific Islander, 6 Hispanic Americans), 63 international. 23 applicants, 100% accepted, 23 enrolled. In 2009, 85 master's awarded. *Degree requirements:* For master's, comprehensive exam, thesis or alternative. *Entrance requirements:* Additional exam requirements/recommendations for international students: Required—TOEFL (minimum score 500 paper-based; 173 computer-based; 61 iBT). *Application deadline:* For fall admission, 7/1 priority date for domestic students; for spring admission, 11/1 for domestic students. Applications are processed on a rolling basis. Application fee: $56. Electronic applications accepted. *Expenses:* Tuition, state resident: full-time $6706. Tuition, nonresident: full-time $16,772. *Financial support:* Research assistantships with partial tuition reimbursements, career-related internships or fieldwork, Federal Work-Study, institutionally sponsored loans, scholarships/grants, and unspecified assistantships available. Support available to part-time students. *Unit head:* Dr. Karen Stinson, Director, 608-342-1131, Fax: 608-342-1133. *Application contact:* Lisa Popp, School of Graduate Studies, 608-342-1322, Fax: 608-342-1389, E-mail: poppl@uwplatt.edu.

Vanderbilt University, Peabody College, Department of Teaching and Learning, Nashville, TN 37240-1001. Offers elementary education (M Ed); English language learners (M Ed); learning and instruction (M Ed); learning, diversity, and urban studies (M Ed); reading education (M Ed); secondary education (M Ed). *Accreditation:* NCATE. *Faculty:* 31 full-time (20 women), 23 part-time/adjunct (20 women). *Students:* 95 full-time (88 women), 21 part-time (6 women); includes 14 minority (6 African Americans, 4 Asian Americans or Pacific Islanders, 4 Hispanic Americans), 5 international. Average age 27. 150 applicants, 69% accepted, 59 enrolled. In 2009, 74 master's awarded. *Degree requirements:* For master's, comprehensive exam, thesis optional. *Entrance requirements:* For master's, GRE General Test, MAT. Additional exam requirements/recommendations for international students: Required—TOEFL (minimum score 550 paper-based; 213 computer-based). *Application deadline:* For fall admission, 12/31 priority date for domestic and international students; for spring admission, 11/1 priority date for domestic and international students. Applications are processed on a rolling basis. Application fee: $0. Electronic applications accepted. *Financial support:* In 2009–10, 104 students received support, including 27 research assistantships with full and partial tuition reimbursements available; fellowships with full and partial tuition reimbursements available, teaching assistantships with full and partial tuition reimbursements available, Federal Work-Study, institutionally sponsored loans, scholarships/grants, tuition waivers (partial), and unspecified assistantships also available. Support available to part-time students. Financial award application deadline: 2/1; financial award applicants required to submit FAFSA. *Faculty research:* Teaching and learning, development of mathematical and scientific knowledge, interventions to foster early literacy and numeracy, reading and writing in the digital age, teaching diverse learners. *Unit head:* Dr. David Dickinson, Acting Chair, 615-322-8100, Fax: 615-322-8999, E-mail: david.k.dickinson@vanderbilt.edu. *Application contact:* Angela Saylor, Educational Coordinator, 615-322-8092, Fax: 615-322-8999, E-mail: angela.saylor@vanderbilt.edu.

Virginia Polytechnic Institute and State University, Graduate School, College of Liberal Arts and Human Sciences, School of Education, Department of Teaching and Learning, Blacksburg, VA 24061. Offers career and technical education (MS Ed, Ed D, PhD, Ed S); curriculum and instruction (MA Ed, Ed D, PhD, Ed S); health and physical education (MS Ed); mathematics education (MA Ed, PhD); secondary English education (MA Ed). *Accreditation:* NCATE. Postbaccalaureate distance learning degree programs offered (no on-campus study). *Students:* 295 full-time (186 women), 374 part-time (272 women); includes 104 minority (1 African American, 39 American Indian/Alaska Native, 54 Asian Americans or Pacific Islanders, 10 Hispanic Americans), 23 international. Average age 34. 324 applicants, 85% accepted, 205 enrolled. In 2009, 235 master's, 34 doctorates, 1 other advanced degree awarded. *Entrance requirements:* For master's and doctorate, GRE, GMAT. Additional exam requirements/recommendations for international students: Required—TOEFL (minimum score 550 paper-based; 213 computer-based). *Application deadline:* For fall admission, 5/15 for international students; for spring admission, 10/15 for international students. Applications are processed on a rolling basis. Application fee: $65. Electronic applications accepted. *Expenses:* Tuition, area resident: Full-time $10,228; part-time $459 per credit hour. Tuition, nonresident: full-time $17,892; part-time $865 per credit hour. Required fees: $1966; $451 per semester. *Financial support:* Career-related internships or fieldwork, Federal Work-Study, scholarships/grants, and unspecified assistantships available. Financial award application deadline: 1/15. *Faculty research:* Instructional technology, teacher evaluation, school-change, literacy, teaching strategies. *Unit head:* Dr. Daisy L. Stewart, Dean, 540-231-8180, Fax: 540-231-3717, E-mail: daisys@vt.edu. *Application contact:* Dr. Daisy L. Stewart, Dean, 540-231-8180, Fax: 540-231-3717, E-mail: daisys@vt.edu.

Washington State University, Graduate School, College of Liberal Arts, Department of English, Pullman, WA 99164. Offers composition (MA); English (MA, PhD); teaching of English (MA). *Faculty:* 32. *Students:* 48 full-time (26 women), 5 part-time (4 women); includes 7 minority (4 African Americans, 3 American Indian/Alaska Native), 4 international. Average age 32. 105 applicants, 26% accepted, 10 enrolled. In 2009, 11 master's, 6 doctorates awarded. *Degree requirements:* For master's, one foreign language, comprehensive exam (for some programs), thesis (for some programs), oral exam; for doctorate, 2 foreign languages, comprehensive exam, thesis/dissertation, oral exam, written exam. *Entrance requirements:* For master's and doctorate, GRE General Test, GRE Subject Test, official transcripts; writing sample (approximately 10 pages); three letters of recommendation; statement of purpose (approximately 500 words); undergraduate major in English or other appropriate discipline. Additional exam requirements/recommendations for international students: Required—TOEFL, IELTS. *Application deadline:* For fall admission, 1/10 priority date for domestic students, 1/10 for international students. Applications are processed on a rolling basis. Application fee: $50. *Financial support:* In 2009–10, 48 students received support, including 1 fellowship (averaging $2,000 per year), 2 research assistantships with full and partial tuition reimbursements available (averaging $13,917 per year), 44 teaching assistantships with full and partial tuition reimbursements available (averaging $13,056 per year); career-related internships or fieldwork, Federal Work-Study, institutionally sponsored loans, scholarships/grants, health care benefits, and tuition waivers (partial) also available. Financial award application deadline: 2/10; financial award applicants required to submit FAFSA. *Faculty research:* Nationalism and gender in the American West, slavery and exploitation in nineteenth century Britain, photography and the color line, D. H. Lawrence and Mexico, social movement cultures and the arts. Total annual research expenditures: $5,000. *Unit head:* Dr. William Hamlin, Director, 509-335-7398, Fax: 509-335-2582, E-mail: whamlin@wsu.edu. *Application contact:* Graduate School Admissions, 800-GRADWSU, Fax: 509-335-1949, E-mail: gradsch@wsu.edu.

Wayne State College, School of Education and Counseling, Department of Educational Foundations and Leadership, Program in Curriculum and Instruction, Wayne, NE 68787. Offers alternative education (MSE); business and information technology education (MSE); communication arts education (MSE); early childhood education (MSE); elementary education (MSE); English as a second language (MSE); English education (MSE); family and consumer sciences education (MSE); industrial technology and vocational education (MSE); learning communities (MSE); mathematics education (MSE); music education (MSE); science education (MSE); social science education (MSE). *Accreditation:* NCATE. Part-time and evening/weekend programs available. *Degree requirements:* For master's, comprehensive exam, thesis optional. *Entrance requirements:* For master's, GRE General Test. Additional exam requirements/recommendations for international students: Required—TOEFL (minimum score 550 paper-based; 213 computer-based).

Wayne State University, College of Education, Division of Teacher Education, Detroit, MI 48202. Offers adult and continuing education (M Ed); art education (M Ed); bilingual/bicultural education (M Ed, MAT); business education (M Ed, MAT); career and technical education (M Ed, Ed D, PhD, Ed S); curriculum and instruction (Ed D, PhD, Ed S); distributive education (M Ed, MAT); early childhood education (M Ed); elementary education (M Ed, MAT, Ed D, PhD, Ed S); elementary education curriculum and instruction (M Ed); English education (M Ed); English education-secondary (M Ed, Ed S); foreign language education (M Ed); general education (Ed D, Ed S); health occupations education (M Ed); industrial education (M Ed); mathematics education (M Ed, Ed S); pre-school and parent education (M Ed); reading (M Ed, Ed D, Ed S); reading, languages and literature (Ed D); school music-vocal (M Ed); science education (M Ed, MAT, Ed S); secondary education (MAT); secondary school reading (M Ed); social studies education (M Ed, Ed S), including education-secondary (M Ed); special education (M Ed, Ed D, PhD, Ed S); teacher education (MAT, Ed D, PhD). *Degree requirements:* For doctorate, thesis/dissertation. *Entrance requirements:* For master's, Michigan Basic Skills Test (MA in teaching), minimum GPA of 2.6; for doctorate, minimum undergraduate GPA of 3.0, graduate 3.5; interview, curriculum vitae; references. Additional exam requirements/recommendations for international students: Required—TOEFL (minimum score 550 paper-based; 213 computer-based), TWE (minimum score 6). Electronic applications accepted. *Faculty research:* Reading and writing literacy and literature.

Western Connecticut State University, Division of Graduate Studies, School of Professional Studies, Department of Education and Educational Psychology, English Education Option, Danbury, CT 06810-6885. Offers MS. Part-time programs available. *Students:* 1 (woman) part-time. Average age 24. In 2009, 2 master's awarded. *Degree requirements:* For master's, comprehensive exam (for some programs), thesis or comprehensive exam, completion of program in 6 years. *Entrance requirements:* For master's, minimum GPA of 2.8, teaching certificate. Additional exam requirements/recommendations for international students: Recommended—TOEFL (minimum score 550 paper-based; 213 computer-based; 79 iBT), IELTS (minimum score 6). *Application deadline:* For fall admission, 8/5 priority date for domestic students; for spring admission, 1/5 priority date for domestic students. Applications are processed on a rolling basis. Application fee: $50. *Expenses:* Tuition, state resident: full-time $5012; part-time $278 per credit hour. Tuition, nonresident: full-time $13,962; part-time $284 per credit hour. Required fees: $3886; $139 per credit hour. Full-time tuition and fees vary according to course load and program. Part-time tuition and fees vary according to course level, degree level and program. *Financial support:* Applicants required to submit FAFSA. *Unit head:* Dr. Theresa Canada, Chairperson, Department of Education and Educational Psychology, 203-837-8509, Fax: 203-837-8413, E-mail: canadat@wcsu.edu. *Application contact:* Chris Shankle, Associate Director of Graduate Studies, 203-837-9005, Fax: 203-837-8326, E-mail: shanklec@wcsu.edu.

Western Governors University, Teachers College, Salt Lake City, UT 84107. Offers English language learning (K-12) (MA); learning and technology (M Ed, MA); management and innovation (M Ed); mathematics education (5-12) (MA); mathematics education (5-9) (MA); mathematics education (K-6) (MA); measurement and evaluation (M Ed); science (5-12) (MA), including biology, geology; science education (5-9) (MA); teaching (MAT); technology for principals (Post-Graduate Certificate). *Accreditation:* NCATE. Part-time and evening/weekend programs available. Postbaccalaureate distance learning degree programs offered (no on-campus study). *Degree requirements:* For master's, comprehensive exam. *Entrance requirements:* Additional exam requirements/recommendations for international students: Required—TOEFL (minimum score 450 paper-based). Electronic applications accepted. *Expenses:* Contact institution.

Western Kentucky University, Graduate Studies, Potter College of Arts and Letters, Department of English, Bowling Green, KY 42101. Offers education (MA); English (MA Ed); literature (MA), including American literature, British literature, literary theory, women writers, world literature; teaching English as a second language (MA); writing (MA). Part-time and evening/weekend programs available. *Degree requirements:* For master's, comprehensive exam, thesis optional, final exam. *Entrance requirements:* For master's, GRE General Test, minimum GPA of 2.75. Additional exam requirements/recommendations for international students: Required—TOEFL (minimum score 555 paper-based; 213 computer-based; 79 iBT). *Expenses:* Tuition, state resident: full-time $4160; part-time $416 per credit hour. Tuition, nonresident: full-time $9550; part-time $506 per credit hour. Tuition and fees vary according to campus/location and reciprocity agreements. *Faculty research:* Improving writing, linking teacher knowledge and performance, Victorian women writers, Kentucky women writers, Kentucky poets.

Western Michigan University, Graduate College, College of Arts and Sciences, Department of English, Kalamazoo, MI 49008. Offers creative writing (MFA, PhD); English (MA, PhD); English education (MA, PhD). *Faculty:* 39 full-time (18 women). *Students:* 82 full-time (60 women), 22 part-time (12 women); includes 9 minority (2 African Americans, 1 American Indian/Alaska Native, 6 Hispanic Americans), 4 international. 68 applicants, 76% accepted, 18 enrolled. In 2009, 22 master's, 5 doctorates awarded. *Degree requirements:* For master's, oral exams; for doctorate, one foreign language, thesis/dissertation, oral exam, written exams. *Entrance requirements:* For master's and doctorate, GRE General Test, GRE Subject Test. *Application deadline:* For fall admission, 2/1 priority date for domestic students. Applications are processed on a rolling basis. Application fee: $25. *Financial support:* Fellowships, research assistantships, teaching assistantships, Federal Work-Study available. Financial award application deadline: 2/15; financial award applicants required to submit FAFSA. *Unit head:* Richard Utz, Chairperson, 269-387-2571. *Application contact:* Admissions and Orientation, 269-387-2000, Fax: 269-387-2096.

Western New England College, School of Arts and Sciences, Program in English for Teachers, Springfield, MA 01119. Offers MAET. Part-time and evening/weekend programs available. *Students:* 31 part-time (27 women). In 2009, 7 master's awarded. *Entrance requirements:* For master's, recommendations, personal statement, resume. *Application deadline:* Applications are processed on a rolling basis. Application fee: $30. *Expenses:* Tuition: Part-time $552 per credit hour. Part-time tuition and fees vary according to program. *Financial support:* Available to part-time students. Application deadline: 4/1. *Unit head:* Dr. Saeed Ghahramani, Dean, 413-782-1218, Fax: 413-796-2118, E-mail: sghahram@wnec.edu. *Application contact:* Matt Fox, Director of Recruiting and Marketing for Adult Learners, 413-782-1249, Fax: 413-782-1779, E-mail: ce@wnec.edu.

Widener University, School of Human Service Professions, Center for Education, Chester, PA 19013-5792. Offers adult education (M Ed); counseling in higher education (M Ed); counselor education (M Ed); early childhood education (M Ed); educational foundations (M Ed); educational leadership (M Ed); educational psychology (M Ed); elementary education (M Ed); English and language arts (M Ed); health education (M Ed); higher education leadership (Ed D); home and school visitor (M Ed); human sexuality (M Ed); mathematics education (M Ed); middle school education (M Ed); principalship (M Ed); reading and language arts (Ed D); reading education (M Ed); school administration (Ed D); science education (M Ed); social studies education (M Ed); special education (M Ed); technology education (M Ed). *Accreditation:* NCATE. Part-time and evening/weekend programs available. *Faculty:* 34 full-time (22 women), 37 part-time/ adjunct (14 women). *Students:* 203 full-time (154 women), 415 part-time (298 women); includes 50 minority (34 African Americans, 1 American Indian/Alaska Native, 5 Asian Americans or Pacific Islanders, 10 Hispanic Americans), 3 international. Average age 39. 139 applicants, 88% accepted. In 2009, 168 master's, 31 doctorates awarded. Terminal master's awarded for partial completion of doctoral program. *Degree requirements:* For doctorate, thesis/dissertation. *Entrance requirements:* For master's, minimum GPA of 2.5; for doctorate, GRE or MAT, minimum GPA of 2.0 (undergraduate), 3.5 (graduate). *Application deadline:* Applications are processed on a rolling basis. Application fee: $25 ($300 for international students). Electronic applications accepted. *Expenses:* Contact institution. *Financial support:* Career-related internships or fieldwork, tuition waivers (full and partial), and unspecified assistantships available. Support available to part-time students. Financial award application deadline: 5/1. *Faculty research:* Reading and cognition, adult education, technology education, educational leadership, special education. *Unit head:* Dr. Michael W. LeDoux, Associate Dean, 610-499-4294, Fax: 610-499-4623, E-mail: mwledoux@widener.edu. *Application contact:* Dr. Roberta D. Nolan, Director of Graduate Admissions, 610-499-4125, E-mail: rdnolan@widener.edu.

Wilkes University, College of Graduate and Professional Studies, School of Education, Wilkes-Barre, PA 18766-0002. Offers classroom technology (MS Ed); educational computing (MS Ed); educational development and strategies (MS Ed); educational leadership (MS Ed); educational technology (Ed D); elementary education (MS Ed); higher education administration (Ed D); instructional technology (MS Ed); K-12 administration (Ed D); online teaching (MS Ed); school business leadership (MS Ed); secondary education (MS Ed), including biology, chemistry, English, history; special education (MS Ed). Part-time and evening/weekend programs available. Postbaccalaureate distance learning degree programs offered (minimal on-campus study). *Students:* 89 full-time (60 women), 2,849 part-time (2,058 women); includes 52 minority (10 African Americans, 2 American Indian/Alaska Native, 13 Asian Americans or Pacific Islanders, 27 Hispanic Americans), 6 international. Average age 33. In 2009, 947 master's awarded. *Entrance requirements:* Additional exam requirements/recommendations for international students: Required—TOEFL (minimum score 500 paper-based; 173 computer-based; 79 iBT). *Application deadline:* Applications are processed on a rolling basis. Application fee: $45. *Expenses:* Contact institution. *Financial support:* Federal Work-Study and unspecified assistantships available. Financial award application deadline: 3/1; financial award applicants required to submit FAFSA. *Unit head:* Dr. Michael Speziale, Dean, 570-408-4679, Fax: 570-408-4905, E-mail: michael.speziale@wilkes.edu. *Application contact:* Kathleen Houlihan, Director of Graduate Studies, 570-408-3235, Fax: 570-408-7846, E-mail: kathleen.houlihan@wilkes.edu.

William Carey University, School of Education, Hattiesburg, MS 39401-5499. Offers art education (M Ed); art of teaching (M Ed); elementary education (M Ed, Ed S); English education (M Ed); gifted education (M Ed); history and social science (M Ed); mild/moderate disabilities (M Ed); secondary education (M Ed). Part-time programs available. *Degree requirements:* For master's, comprehensive exam. *Entrance requirements:* For master's, GRE, MAT, minimum GPA of 2.5, Class A teacher's license. Additional exam requirements/recommendations for international students: Required—TOEFL (minimum score 550 paper-based; 213 computer-based).

Worcester State College, Graduate Studies, Program in English, Worcester, MA 01602-2597. Offers M Ed. Part-time programs available. *Faculty:* 2 full-time (1 woman). *Students:* 3 part-time (2 women). Average age 29. 3 applicants, 33% accepted, 0 enrolled. *Degree requirements:* For master's, one foreign language, comprehensive exam (for some programs), thesis optional. *Entrance requirements:* For master's, GRE General Test or MAT, 18 undergraduate credits in English, excluding composition. Additional exam requirements/recommendations for international students: Required—TOEFL (minimum score 550 paper-based; 213 computer-based; 79 iBT). *Application deadline:* Applications are processed on a rolling basis. Application fee: $30. *Expenses:* Tuition, area resident: Part-time $150 per credit. Tuition, state resident: part-time $150 per credit. Tuition, nonresident: part-time $150 per credit. Required fees: $85. *Financial support:* Career-related internships or fieldwork, scholarships/grants, and unspecified assistantships available. Financial award application deadline: 3/1; financial award applicants required to submit FAFSA. *Unit head:* Dr. Ruth Haber, Coordinator, 508-929-8706, Fax: 508-929-8174, E-mail: rhaber@worcester.edu. *Application contact:* Nicole Brown, Assistant Dean of Graduate and Continuing Education, 508-929-8787, Fax: 508-929-8100, E-mail: nbrown@worcester.edu.

Environmental Education

Alaska Pacific University, Graduate Programs, Environmental Science Department, Program in Outdoor and Environmental Education, Anchorage, AK 99508-4672. Offers MSOEE. Part-time programs available. *Degree requirements:* For master's, thesis. *Entrance requirements:* For master's, MAT or GRE, minimum GPA of 3.0. Additional exam requirements/recommendations for international students: Required—TOEFL (minimum score 550 paper-based; 79 computer-based).

Antioch University New England, Graduate School, Department of Environmental Studies, Program in Environmental Education, Keene, NH 03431-3552. Offers MS. *Degree requirements:* For master's, practicum. *Entrance requirements:* For master's, previous undergraduate course work in biology, chemistry, mathematics (environmental biology); resume; 3 letters of recommendation. Additional exam requirements/recommendations for international students: Required—TOEFL (minimum score 550 paper-based; 213 computer-based). Electronic applications accepted. *Expenses:* Contact institution. *Faculty research:* Sustainability, natural resources inventory.

Arcadia University, Graduate Studies, Department of Education, Glenside, PA 19038-3295. Offers art education (M Ed, MA Ed); biology education (MA Ed); chemistry education (MA Ed); child development (CAS); computer education (M Ed, CAS); computer education 7–12 (MA Ed); early childhood education (M Ed, CAS), including individualized (M Ed), master teacher (M Ed), research in child development (M Ed); educational leadership (M Ed, CAS); educational psychology (CAS); elementary education (M Ed, CAS); English education (MA Ed); environmental education (MA Ed, CAS); history education (MA Ed); language arts (M Ed, CAS); mathematics education (M Ed, MA Ed, CAS); music education (MA Ed); psychology (MA Ed); pupil personnel services (CAS); reading (M Ed, CAS); school library science (M Ed); science education (M Ed, CAS); secondary education (M Ed, CAS); special education (M Ed, Ed D, CAS); theater arts (MA Ed); written communication (MA Ed). *Accreditation:* NASAD. Part-time and evening/weekend programs available. Postbaccalaureate distance learning degree programs offered (minimal on-campus study). *Faculty:* 12 full-time (8 women), 38 part-time/adjunct (26 women). *Students:* 89 full-time (74 women), 622 part-time (487 women); includes 112 minority (94 African Americans, 9 Asian Americans or Pacific Islanders, 9 Hispanic Americans), 2 international. Average age 32. In 2009, 257 master's, 4 doctorates awarded. *Application deadline:* Applications are processed on a rolling basis. Application fee: $40. Electronic applications accepted. *Expenses:* Tuition: Full-time $30,450; part-time $620 per credit hour. Required fees: $165. Tuition and fees vary according to program. *Financial support:* Career-related internships or fieldwork, tuition waivers (partial), and unspecified assistantships available. *Unit head:* Dr. Steven P. Gulkus. *Application contact:* 215-572-2925, Fax: 215-572-2126, E-mail: grad@arcadia.edu.

Brooklyn College of the City University of New York, Division of Graduate Studies, School of Education, Program in Childhood Education, Brooklyn, NY 11210-2889. Offers bilingual education (MS Ed); liberal arts (MS Ed); mathematics (MS Ed); science/environmental education (MS Ed). Part-time and evening/weekend programs available. *Students:* 14 full-time (13 women), 245 part-time (209 women); includes 129 minority (60 African Americans, 2 American Indian/ Alaska Native, 20 Asian Americans or Pacific Islanders, 47 Hispanic Americans), 6 international. Average age 30. 114 applicants, 85% accepted, 65 enrolled. In 2009, 118 master's awarded. *Entrance requirements:* For master's, LAST, interview, previous course work in education, writing sample, resume, 2 letters of recommendation. Additional exam requirements/ recommendations for international students: Required—TOEFL (minimum score 500 paper-based; 173 computer-based; 61 iBT). *Application deadline:* For fall admission, 3/1 priority date for domestic students, 2/1 priority date for international students; for spring admission, 11/1 priority date for domestic students, 10/1 priority date for international students. Applications are processed on a rolling basis. Application fee: $125. Electronic applications accepted. *Expenses:* Tuition, state resident: full-time $7360; part-time $310 per credit hour. Tuition, nonresident: full-time $13,800; part-time $575 per credit hour. Required fees: $140.10 per semester. *Financial support:* Career-related internships or fieldwork, Federal Work-Study, institutionally sponsored loans, and scholarships/grants available. Support available to part-time students. Financial award application deadline: 5/1; financial award applicants required to submit FAFSA. *Faculty research:* Emotional intelligence, multiculturalism, arts immersion, the Holocaust. *Unit head:* Dr. Wayne Reed, Program Head, 718-951-5214, E-mail: wreed@brooklyn.cuny.edu. *Application contact:* Hernan Sierra, Graduate Admissions Coordinator, 718-951-4536, Fax: 718-951-4506, E-mail: grads@brooklyn.cuny.edu.

California State University, San Bernardino, Graduate Studies, College of Education, Program in Environmental Education, San Bernardino, CA 92407-2397. Offers MA. *Accreditation:* NCATE. *Faculty:* 1 full-time (0 women). *Students:* 1 (woman) full-time, 1 part-time (0 women). Average age 45. 2 applicants, 0% accepted, 0 enrolled. In 2009, 8 master's awarded. *Application deadline:* For fall admission, 8/31 priority date for domestic students. Application fee: $55. *Unit head:* Dr. Herbert Brunkhorst, Chair, 909-537-5613, Fax: 909-537-7522, E-mail: hkbrunkh@csusb.edu. *Application contact:* Olivia Rosas, Director of Admissions, 909-537-7577, Fax: 909-537-7034, E-mail: orosas@csusb.edu.

Chatham University, Program in Education, Pittsburgh, PA 15232-2826. Offers early childhood education (MAT); elementary education (MAT); English—secondary (MAT); environmental education (K-12) (MAT); secondary art (MAT); secondary biology education (MAT); secondary chemistry education (MAT); secondary English education (MAT); secondary math education (MAT); secondary physics education (MAT); secondary social studies education (MAT); special education (MAT). *Students:* 52 full-time (41 women), 20 part-time (16 women). Average age 30. 39 applicants, 79% accepted, 26 enrolled. In 2009, 37 master's awarded. *Degree requirements:* For master's, thesis, teaching experience. *Entrance requirements:* For master's, PRAXIS I, minimum GPA of 3.0, sample of written work, recommendation letters. Additional exam requirements/recommendations for international students: Required—TOEFL (minimum score 600 paper-based; 250 computer-based; 100 iBT), IELTS (minimum score 6.5), TWE. *Application deadline:* For fall admission, 5/1 priority date for domestic and international students; for spring admission, 10/15 priority date for domestic and international students. Applications are processed on a rolling basis. Application fee: $45. Electronic applications accepted. *Financial support:* Career-related internships or fieldwork available. Financial award applicants required to submit FAFSA. *Faculty research:* Gifted education, environmental education, technology in education, writing as learning, class size and achievement. *Unit head:* Dr. Barbara Biglan, Interim Director, 412-365-1170, E-mail: biglan@chatham.edu. *Application contact:* Dory Perry, Associate Director of Graduate Admissions, 412-365-2758, Fax: 412-365-1609, E-mail: gradadmissions@chatham.edu.

Concordia University Wisconsin, Graduate Programs, Department of Education, Mequon, WI 53097-2402. Offers art education (MS Ed); curriculum and instruction (MS Ed); early childhood (MS Ed); educational administration (MS Ed); environmental education (MS Ed); family studies (MS Ed); reading (MS Ed); school counseling (MS Ed); special education (MS Ed). Part-time and evening/weekend programs available. Postbaccalaureate distance learning degree programs offered (minimal on-campus study). *Degree requirements:* For master's, comprehensive exam, thesis or alternative. *Entrance requirements:* For master's, minimum GPA of 3.0, teaching license. Additional exam requirements/recommendations for international students: Required—TOEFL. *Faculty research:* Motivation, developmental learning, learning styles.

Florida Atlantic University, College of Education, Department of Teaching and Learning, Boca Raton, FL 33431-0991. Offers curriculum and instruction (M Ed); elementary education (M Ed); environmental education (M Ed); reading education (M Ed); social foundations of education (M Ed). *Accreditation:* NCATE. Part-time and evening/weekend programs available. *Faculty:* 35 full-time (29 women), 92 part-time/adjunct (61 women). *Students:* 56 full-time (50 women), 134 part-time (128 women); includes 36 minority (15 African Americans, 4 Asian Americans or Pacific Islanders, 17 Hispanic Americans), 2 international. Average age 32. 162 applicants, 74% accepted, 66 enrolled. In 2009, 52 master's awarded. *Entrance requirements:* For master's, GRE General Test, minimum GPA of 3.0 in last 2 years of undergraduate course work. Additional exam requirements/recommendations for international students: Required—TOEFL. *Application deadline:* For fall admission, 7/1 for domestic students, 2/15 for international students; for spring admission, 11/1 for domestic students, 7/15 for international students. Applications are processed on a rolling basis. Application fee: $30. *Expenses:* Tuition, state resident: full-time $7055; part-time $293.94 per credit hour. Tuition, nonresident: full-time $22,096; part-time $920.66 per credit hour. *Financial support:* Fellowships with partial tuition reimbursements, research assistantships with partial tuition reimbursements, teaching assistantships with partial tuition reimbursements, career-related internships or fieldwork, scholarships/grants, and unspecified assistantships available. *Faculty research:* Technology, teaching English to speakers of other languages, math teaching, electronic portfolio assessment, global perspectives through social studies. *Unit head:* Dr. Barbara Ridener, Chairperson, 561-297-3588. *Application contact:* Dr. Barbara Ridener, Chairperson, 561-297-3588.

Environmental Education

Florida Institute of Technology, Graduate Programs, College of Science, Department of Science and Mathematics Education, Melbourne, FL 32901-6975. Offers computer education (MS); elementary science education (M Ed); environmental education (MS); informal science education (M Ed); mathematics education (MS, Ed D, PhD, Ed S); science education (MS, Ed D, PhD, Ed S); teaching (MAT). Part-time and evening/weekend programs available. *Faculty:* 4 full-time (1 woman), 3 part-time/adjunct (2 women). *Students:* 15 full-time (9 women), 18 part-time (12 women); includes 5 minority (2 African Americans, 3 Hispanic Americans), 5 international. Average age 36. 42 applicants, 52% accepted, 7 enrolled. In 2009, 3 master's, 1 doctorate, 1 other advanced degree awarded. Terminal master's awarded for partial completion of doctoral program. *Degree requirements:* For master's, comprehensive exam (for some programs), thesis (for some programs), oral final exam; for doctorate, comprehensive exam, thesis/dissertation, oral defense of dissertation; for Ed S, comprehensive exam. *Entrance requirements:* For master's, minimum GPA of 3.0, resume, 3 letters of recommendation (elementary science education); for doctorate, minimum GPA of 3.2, resume, 3 letters of recommendation, statement of objectives, 3 years teaching experience (recommended); for Ed S, minimum GPA of 3.0, resume, 3 letters of recommendation, statement of objectives. Additional exam requirements/recommendations for international students: Required—TOEFL (minimum score 550 paper-based; 213 computer-based; 79 iBT). *Application deadline:* For fall admission, 4/1 for international students; for spring admission, 9/30 for international students. Applications are processed on a rolling basis. Application fee: $50. Electronic applications accepted. *Expenses:* Tuition: Part-time $1015 per credit. Tuition and fees vary according to campus/location and program. *Financial support:* In 2009–10, 3 students received support, including 3 teaching assistantships with full and partial tuition reimbursements available (averaging $6,212 per year); research assistantships with full and partial tuition reimbursements available, career-related internships or fieldwork, institutionally sponsored loans, tuition waivers (partial), unspecified assistantships, and tuition remissions also available. Support available to part-time students. Financial award application deadline: 3/1; financial award applicants required to submit FAFSA. *Faculty research:* Measurement and evaluation, computers in education, educational technology. Total annual research expenditures: $352,726. *Unit head:* Dr. David E. Cook, Department Head, 321-674-8126, Fax: 321-674-7598, E-mail: dcook@fit.edu. *Application contact:* Thomas M. Shea, Director of Graduate Admissions, 321-674-7577, Fax: 321-723-9468, E-mail: tshea@fit.edu.

Gannon University, School of Graduate Studies, College of Engineering and Business, School of Engineering and Computer Science, Program in Natural and Environmental Sciences, Erie, PA 16541-0001. Offers M Ed. Part-time and evening/weekend programs available. *Students:* 1 (woman) part-time. Average age 42. 1 applicant, 100% accepted, 0 enrolled. *Degree requirements:* For master's, research paper. *Entrance requirements:* Additional exam requirements/recommendations for international students: Required—TOEFL (minimum score 79 iBT). *Application deadline:* Applications are processed on a rolling basis. Application fee: $25. Electronic applications accepted. *Expenses:* Tuition: Full-time $13,590; part-time $755 per credit. Required fees: $524; $17 per credit. Tuition and fees vary according to course load, degree level, campus/location and program. *Financial support:* Career-related internships or fieldwork and scholarships/grants available. Financial award application deadline: 7/1; financial award applicants required to submit FAFSA. *Unit head:* Dr. Harry Diz, Chair, 814-871-7633, E-mail: diz001@gannon.edu. *Application contact:* Kara Morgan, Assistant Director of Graduate Admissions, 814-871-5831, Fax: 814-871-5827, E-mail: graduate@gannon.edu.

Goshen College, Merry Lea Environmental Learning Center, Goshen, IN 46526-4794. Offers MA. *Accreditation:* NCATE. *Faculty:* 1 full-time (0 women), 5 part-time/adjunct (1 woman). *Students:* 8 full-time (7 women); includes 1 African American, 1 international. 12 applicants, 75% accepted, 8 enrolled. In 2009, 3 master's awarded. *Entrance requirements:* Additional exam requirements/recommendations for international students: Required—TOEFL (minimum score 213 paper-based; 79 computer-based; 60 iBT). Application fee: $50. *Financial support:* In 2009–10, 8 students received support. Application deadline: 9/10. *Unit head:* Dr. Luke Gascho, Executive Director, 260-799-5869, E-mail: lukeag@goshen.edu. *Application contact:* Dr. David Ostergren, Director of Graduate Studies, 260-799-5869, E-mail: daveo@goshen.edu.

Hamline University, School of Education, St. Paul, MN 55104-1284. Offers education (MA Ed, Ed D); English as a second language (MAESL); literacy education (MALED); natural science and environmental education (MA Ed); teaching (MAT). *Accreditation:* NCATE (one or more programs are accredited). Part-time and evening/weekend programs available. *Faculty:* 27 full-time (18 women), 128 part-time/adjunct (100 women). *Students:* 324 full-time (242 women), 1,049 part-time (780 women); includes 116 minority (36 African Americans, 4 American Indian/Alaska Native, 42 Asian Americans or Pacific Islanders, 34 Hispanic Americans), 25 international. Average age 33. 501 applicants, 79% accepted, 311 enrolled. In 2009, 196 master's, 9 doctorates awarded. *Degree requirements:* For master's, thesis; for doctorate, comprehensive exam, thesis/dissertation. *Entrance requirements:* For doctorate, personal statement, master's degree, 3 years experience, letters of recommendation, writing sample, interview. Additional exam requirements/recommendations for international students: Required—TOEFL (minimum score 550 paper-based; 213 computer-based; 79 iBT), TWE (minimum score 5). *Application deadline:* Applications are processed on a rolling basis. Application fee: $0. Electronic applications accepted. *Expenses:* Tuition: Full-time $6816; part-time $426 per credit. Required fees: $6 per credit. One-time fee: $205. Tuition and fees vary according to degree level, campus/location and program. *Financial support:* In 2009–10, 8 students received support. Federal Work-Study and scholarships/grants available. Support available to part-time students. Financial award applicants required to submit FAFSA. *Faculty research:* Adult basic education, service learning, teacher dispositions, diversity, technology. *Unit head:* Dr. Sheila Wright, Dean, 651-523-2600, Fax: 651-523-2489, E-mail: swright04@hamline.edu. *Application contact:* Rae A. Lenway, Director, Graduate Recruitment and Admission, 651-523-2900, Fax: 651-523-3058, E-mail: rlenway@hamline.edu.

Lesley University, Graduate School of Arts and Social Sciences, Cambridge, MA 02138-2790. Offers clinical mental health counseling (MA), including expressive therapies counseling, holistic counseling, school and community counseling; counseling psychology (MA, CAGS), including professional counseling (MA), school counseling (MA); creative arts in learning (CAGS); creative writing (MFA); ecological teaching and learning (MS); environmental education (MS); expressive therapies (MA, PhD, CAGS), including art (MA), dance (MA), expressive therapies, music (MA); independent studies (CAGS); independent study (MA); intercultural relations (MA, CAGS); interdisciplinary studies (MA), including individualized studies, integrative holistic health, women's studies; urban environmental leadership (MA); visual arts (MFA). Part-time and evening/weekend programs available. Postbaccalaureate distance learning degree programs offered (minimal on-campus study). *Degree requirements:* For master's, internship, practicum, thesis (expressive therapies); for doctorate, thesis/dissertation, arts apprenticeship, field placement; for CAGS, thesis, internship (counseling psychology, expressive therapies). *Entrance requirements:* For master's, MAT (counseling psychology), interview, writing samples, art portfolio; for doctorate, GRE or MAT; for CAGS, interview, master's degree. Additional exam requirements/recommendations for international students: Required—TOEFL (minimum score 550 paper-based; 213 computer-based; 80 iBT). Electronic applications accepted. *Faculty research:* Psychotherapy and culture; psychotherapy and psychological trauma; women's issues in art, teaching and psychotherapy; community based art, psycho-spiritual inquiry.

Maryville University of Saint Louis, School of Education, St. Louis, MO 63141-7299. Offers art education (MA Ed); early childhood education (MA Ed); educational leadership (Ed D); educational leadership: principal certification (MA Ed); elementary education (MA Ed); elementary education/English (MA Ed); elementary education/psychology (MA Ed); environmental education (MA Ed); gifted education (MA Ed); literacy specialist (MA Ed); middle grades education (MA Ed); secondary teaching and inquiry (MA Ed); teacher as leader (MA Ed). *Accreditation:* NASAD; NCATE. Part-time and evening/weekend programs available. *Students:* 25 full-time (18 women), 198 part-time (145 women); includes 33 minority (27 African Americans, 2 American Indian/Alaska Native, 1 Asian American or Pacific Islander, 3 Hispanic Americans). Average age 36. In 2009, 61 master's, 45 doctorates awarded. *Degree requirements:* For master's, thesis, project. *Entrance requirements:* For master's and doctorate, minimum GPA of 3.0, 3 professional recommendations. Additional exam requirements/recommendations for international students: Required—TOEFL (minimum score 550 paper-based). *Application deadline:* Applications are processed on a rolling basis. Application fee: $40 ($60 for international students). Electronic applications accepted. *Expenses:* Tuition: Full-time $20,384; part-time $627.50 per credit hour. Required fees: $100 per semester. *Financial support:* Career-related internships or fieldwork, Federal Work-Study, tuition waivers (partial), and professional educator discounts available. Financial award application deadline: 3/1; financial award applicants required to submit FAFSA. *Faculty research:* Collaboration with public schools, pre-service program development, mathematics, diversity, literacy. *Unit head:* Dr. Sam Hausfather, Dean, 314-529-9466, Fax: 314-529-9921, E-mail: shausfather@maryville.edu. *Application contact:* Holly Stanwich, Graduate Admissions Coordinator, 314-529-9542, Fax: 314-529-9921, E-mail: teachered@maryville.edu.

New York University, Steinhardt School of Culture, Education, and Human Development, Department of Teaching and Learning, Program in Environmental Conservation Education, New York, NY 10012-1019. Offers MA. *Accreditation:* Teacher Education Accreditation Council. Part-time programs available. *Students:* 17 full-time (13 women), 18 part-time (14 women); includes 5 minority (1 African American, 4 Hispanic Americans), 3 international. Average age 30. 44 applicants, 84% accepted, 21 enrolled. In 2009, 5 master's awarded. *Degree requirements:* For master's, thesis (for some programs). *Entrance requirements:* Additional exam requirements/recommendations for international students: Required—TOEFL. *Application deadline:* For fall admission, 12/15 priority date for domestic and international students; for spring admission, 11/1 for domestic and international students. Applications are processed on a rolling basis. Application fee: $75. Electronic applications accepted. *Expenses:* Tuition: Full-time $30,528; part-time $1272 per credit. Required fees: $2177. *Financial support:* Career-related internships or fieldwork, Federal Work-Study, institutionally sponsored loans, and tuition waivers (partial) available. Support available to part-time students. Financial award application deadline: 2/1; financial award applicants required to submit FAFSA. *Faculty research:* Environmental ethics, values and policy, philosophy and geography. *Unit head:* Dr. Mary Leou, Acting Director, 212-998-5474, Fax: 212-995-4832. *Application contact:* 212-998-5030, Fax: 212-995-4328, E-mail: steinhardt.gradadmissions@nyu.edu.

Nova Southeastern University, Fischler School of Education and Human Services, Graduate Teacher Education Program, Fort Lauderdale, FL 33314-7796. Offers athletic administration (MS); brain research (MS, Ed S); charter school education/leadership (MS); cognitive and behavioral disabilities (MS); computer science education (Ed S); computer science education (K-12) (MS); curriculum and teaching (Ed S); curriculum, instruction and technology (MS); curriculum, instruction, management and administration (Ed S); early childhood education (MS); early literacy and reading (Ed S); early literacy education (MS); education technology (MS); educational leadership (administration K–12) (MS, Ed S); educational media (Ed S); educational media (K-12) (MS); elementary education (MS, Ed S), including ESOL endorsement (MS); English education (MS, Ed S); environmental education (MS); exceptional student education (MS), including ESOL endorsement; gifted education (MS, Ed S); interdisciplinary arts education (MS); management and administration of educational programs (MS); mathematics (MS); mathematics education (Ed S); multicultural early intervention (MS); pre-kindergarten/primary (MS); preschool education (MS); reading (MS); reading and TESOL (MS); reading education (Ed S); science (MS); science education (Ed S); secondary education (MS); social studies (MS, Ed S); Spanish language (MS); special education and reading (MS); teaching and learning (MA, MS), including curriculum and instruction (MA), elementary mathematics (MA), elementary reading (MA), K-12 technology integration (MA); teaching English to speakers of other languages (MS, Ed S); technology management and administration (Ed S); urban studies education (MS). Part-time and evening/weekend programs available. Postbaccalaureate distance learning degree programs offered (minimal on-campus study). *Faculty:* 72 full-time (43 women), 385 part-time/adjunct (252 women). *Students:* 196 full-time (175 women), 1,304 part-time (1,128 women); includes 594 minority (471 African Americans, 5 American Indian/Alaska Native, 18 Asian Americans or Pacific Islanders, 100 Hispanic Americans). Average age 37. 2,610 applicants, 72% accepted, 1352 enrolled. In 2009, 836 other advanced degrees awarded. *Degree requirements:* For master's and Ed S, thesis, practicum, internship. *Entrance requirements:* For master's, MAT, GRE, CLAST, CBEST, PRAXIS I, General Knowledge Test, minimum GPA of 2.5; for Ed S, MAT or GRE, master's degree, teaching certificate, minimum GPA of 3.0. Additional exam requirements/recommendations for international students: Required—TSE (recommended, minimum score 50); Recommended—TOEFL (minimum score 550 paper-based; 213 computer-based; 80 iBT), IELTS (minimum score 6). *Application deadline:* For fall admission, 9/25 priority date for domestic and international students; for winter admission, 2/23 priority date for domestic and international students; for spring admission, 4/25 priority date for domestic and international students. Applications are processed on a rolling basis. Application fee: $50. Electronic applications accepted. *Financial support:* Federal Work-Study available. Support available to part-time students. Financial award application deadline: 4/15; financial award applicants required to submit FAFSA. *Faculty research:* School effectiveness, critical thinking, leadership skills acquisition, child education, multicultural education. *Unit head:* Dr. Ronald Kern, Dean of Academic Affairs, 800-986-3223 Ext. 7809, Fax: 954-262-3606, E-mail: rk429@nsu.nova.edu. *Application contact:* Dr. Jennifer Quinones Nottingham, Dean of Student Affairs, 800-986-3223 Ext. 1559.

Prescott College, Graduate Programs, Program in Education, Prescott, AZ 86301. Offers early childhood education (MA); early childhood special education (MA); education (MA); elementary education (MA); environmental education leadership and administration (MA); equine-assisted experiential learning (MA); school guidance counseling (MA); secondary education (MA); special education, learning disability (MA); special education, mental retardation (MA); special education, serious emotional disability (MA); student-directed independent study (MA); sustainability education (PhD). Part-time programs available. Postbaccalaureate distance learning degree programs offered (minimal on-campus study). *Faculty:* 3 full-time (1 woman), 79 part-time/adjunct (41 women). *Students:* 75 full-time (44 women), 46 part-time (36 women); includes 18 minority (3 African Americans, 3 American Indian/Alaska Native, 4 Asian Americans or Pacific Islanders, 8 Hispanic Americans), 2 international. Average age 39. 66 applicants, 67% accepted, 31 enrolled. In 2009, 22 master's, 4 doctorates awarded. *Degree requirements:* For master's, thesis, fieldwork or internship, practicum; for doctorate, thesis/dissertation. *Entrance requirements:* For master's, 2 letters of recommendation, resume; for doctorate, 3 letters of recommendation, resume, official transcripts, personal statement, program proposal. Additional exam requirements/recommendations for international students: Required—TOEFL (minimum score 500 paper-based; 173 computer-based). *Application deadline:* For fall admission, 4/15 priority date for domestic and international students; for spring admission, 9/15 priority date for domestic and international students. Applications are processed on a rolling basis. Application fee: $40. Electronic applications accepted. *Expenses:* Tuition: Full-time $14,712; part-time $613 per credit. Required fees: $50 per term. One-time fee: $150. Tuition and fees vary according to course load and degree level. *Financial support:* Career-related internships or fieldwork and Federal Work-Study available. Financial award applicants required to submit FAFSA. *Unit head:* Noel Caniglia, Chair, 928-358-3201, Fax: 928-776-5151, E-mail: ncaniglia@prescott.edu. *Application contact:* Kerstin Alicki, Admissions Counselor, 877-412-8705, Fax: 928-277-4695, E-mail: admissions@prescott.edu.

Royal Roads University, Graduate Studies, Environment and Sustainability Program, Victoria, BC V9B 5Y2, Canada. Offers environment and management (M Sc, MA); environmental education and communication (MA, G Dip, Graduate Certificate); MA/MS. Postbaccalaureate distance learning degree programs offered (minimal on-campus study). *Degree requirements:* For master's, thesis. *Entrance requirements:* For master's, 5-7 years of related work experience. Electronic applications accepted. *Faculty research:* Sustainable development, atmospheric processes, sustainable communities, chemical fate and transport of persistent organic pollutants, educational technology.

Saint Vincent College, Program in Education, Latrobe, PA 15650-2690. Offers curriculum and instruction (MS); environmental education (MS); library media management (MS); school

administration (MS); special education (MS). Part-time and evening/weekend programs available. *Degree requirements:* For master's, comprehensive exam. *Entrance requirements:* For master's, GRE (if undergraduate GPA less than 3.0). Additional exam requirements/recommendations for international students: Required—TOEFL (minimum score 550 paper-based; 213 computer-based). *Faculty research:* Assessment and instructional technology.

Slippery Rock University of Pennsylvania, Graduate Studies (Recruitment), College of Health, Environment, and Science, Department of Parks, Recreation, and Environmental Education, Slippery Rock, PA 16057-1383. Offers environmental education (M Ed); resource management (MS). Part-time and evening/weekend programs available. *Degree requirements:* For master's, comprehensive exam (for some programs), thesis (for some programs). *Entrance requirements:* For master's, GRE General Test, MAT, minimum GPA of 2.75. Additional exam requirements/recommendations for international students: Required—TOEFL (minimum score 550 paper-based; 213 computer-based). *Application deadline:* For fall admission, 3/1 priority date for domestic students, 5/1 priority date for international students; for spring admission, 11/1 priority date for domestic students, 9/1 priority date for international students. Applications are processed on a rolling basis. Application fee: $25 ($30 for international students). Electronic applications accepted. *Expenses:* Tuition, state resident: full-time $6666; part-time $370 per credit. Tuition, nonresident: full-time $10,666; part-time $593 per credit. Required fees: $2184; $182 per credit. *Financial support:* Career-related internships or fieldwork, Federal Work-Study, scholarships/grants, and unspecified assistantships available. Support available to part-time students. Financial award application deadline: 5/1; financial award applicants required to submit FAFSA. *Unit head:* Dr. Daniel Dziubek, Graduate Coordinator, 724-738-2958, Fax: 724-738-2938, E-mail: daniel.dziubek@sru.edu. *Application contact:* Angela Piverotto, Interim Director of Graduate Studies, 724-738-2051, Fax: 724-738-2146, E-mail: graduate.admissions@sru.edu.

Southern Connecticut State University, School of Graduate Studies, School of Arts and Sciences, Department of Science Education and Environmental Studies, New Haven, CT 06515-1355. Offers environmental education (MS); science education (MS, Diploma). *Accreditation:* NCATE. Part-time and evening/weekend programs available. *Faculty:* 2 full-time, 1 part-time/adjunct. *Students:* 6 full-time (3 women), 19 part-time (12 women); includes 1 minority (African American). 37 applicants, 54% accepted, 13 enrolled. *Degree requirements:* For master's, thesis or alternative. *Entrance requirements:* For master's, interview; for Diploma, master's degree. *Application deadline:* For fall admission, 7/15 priority date for domestic students. Applications are processed on a rolling basis. Application fee: $50. Electronic applications accepted. Tuition and fees vary according to program. *Financial support:* Application deadline: 4/15. *Unit head:* Dr. Susan Cusato, Chairman, 203-392-6610, Fax: 203-392-6614, E-mail: hagemans1@southernct.edu. *Application contact:* Dr. Susan Cusato, Graduate Coordinator, 203-392-6610, Fax: 203-392-6614, E-mail: cusatos1@southernct.edu.

Southern Oregon University, Graduate Studies, Program in Environmental Education, Ashland, OR 97520. Offers MS. Part-time programs available. *Degree requirements:* For master's, thesis (for some programs), comprehensive exam (MA). *Entrance requirements:* For master's, GRE General Test, minimum GPA of 3.0. *Faculty research:* Ferroelectric, ecology environmental science, biotechnology, material science.

Universidad Metropolitana, Graduate Programs in Education, Program in Environmental Education, San Juan, PR 00928-1150. Offers M Ed.

Universidad Metropolitana, School of Environmental Affairs, Program in Environmental Education, San Juan, PR 00928-1150. Offers MA. Part-time programs available. *Degree requirements:* For master's, thesis or alternative. *Entrance requirements:* For master's, EXADEP, interview. Electronic applications accepted.

Université du Québec à Montréal, Graduate Programs, Program in Education, Montréal, QC H3C 3P8, Canada. Offers education (M Ed, MA, PhD); education of the environmental sciences (Diploma). Part-time programs available. *Degree requirements:* For master's, thesis (for some programs); for doctorate, thesis/dissertation. *Entrance requirements:* For master's and Diploma, appropriate bachelor's degree or equivalent, proficiency in French; for doctorate, appropriate master's degree or equivalent, proficiency in French.

University of Minnesota, Twin Cities Campus, Graduate School, College of Education and Human Development, Department of Curriculum and Instruction, Minneapolis, MN 55455-0213. Offers art education (M Ed, MA, PhD); children's literature (M Ed, MA, PhD); curriculum and instruction (MA, PhD); early childhood education (M Ed, PhD); elementary education (M Ed, MA, PhD); English education (MA, PhD); environmental education (M Ed); family education (M Ed, MA, Ed D, PhD); instructional systems and technology (M Ed, MA, PhD); language arts (MA, PhD); language immersion education (Certificate); literacy education (MA); mathematics education (MA, PhD); reading education (MA, PhD); science education (MA, PhD); second languages and cultures education (MA, PhD); social studies education (MA, PhD); teaching (M Ed), including Chinese, earth science, elementary special education, English, English as a second language, French, German, Hebrew, Japanese, life sciences, mathematics, middle school science, science, second languages and cultures, social studies, Spanish; technology enhanced learning (Certificate); writing education (M Ed, MA, PhD). *Faculty:* 34 full-time (21 women). *Students:* 436 full-time (307 women), 375 part-time (280 women); includes 80 minority (30 African Americans, 6 American Indian/Alaska Native, 33 Asian Americans or Pacific Islanders, 11 Hispanic Americans), 40 international. Average age 32. 660 applicants, 64% accepted, 379 enrolled. In 2009, 552 master's, 14 doctorates, 7 other advanced degrees awarded. *Financial support:* In 2009–10, 5 fellowships (averaging $27,000 per year), 47 research assistantships with full tuition reimbursements (averaging $25,682 per year), 60 teaching assistantships with full tuition reimbursements (averaging $29,889 per year) were awarded. *Faculty research:* Teaching and learning; quality of education; influence of cultural, linguistic, social, political, technological and economic factors on teaching, learning and educational research; relationship between educational practice and a democratic and just society. Total annual research expenditures: $1.8 million. *Unit head:* Dr. Ruth Thomas, Chair, 612-624-4772, Fax: 612-624-8277, E-mail: thoma006@umn.edu. *Application contact:* Dr. Mary Trettin, Associate Dean, 612-625-6501, Fax: 612-626-1580, E-mail: mtrettin@umn.edu.

University of New Hampshire, Graduate School, Interdisciplinary Programs, Program in Environmental Education, Durham, NH 03824. Offers MA. Program offered in summer only. Part-time programs available. *Faculty:* 32 full-time. *Students:* 6 full-time (5 women), 7 part-time (6 women). Average age 32. In 2009, 10 master's awarded. *Entrance requirements:* Additional exam requirements/recommendations for international students: Required—TOEFL (minimum score 550 paper-based; 213 computer-based; 80 iBT). *Application deadline:* For fall admission, 6/1 for domestic students, 4/1 for international students; for spring admission, 12/1 for domestic students. Applications are processed on a rolling basis. Application fee: $65. Electronic applications accepted. *Expenses:* Tuition, state resident: full-time $10,380; part-time $577 per credit hour. Tuition, nonresident: full-time $24,350; part-time $1002 per credit hour. Required fees: $1550; $387.50 per semester. Tuition and fees vary according to course load and program. *Financial support:* In 2009–10, 1 student received support; fellowships, research assistantships, teaching assistantships available. Financial award application deadline: 2/15. *Unit head:* Dr. Todd Demitchell, Chairperson, 603-862-5043, E-mail: education.department@unh.edu. *Application contact:* Lisa Canfield, Administrative Assistant, 603-862-2310, E-mail: education.department@unh.edu.

The University of North Carolina Wilmington, College of Arts and Sciences, Department of Environmental Studies, Wilmington, NC 28403-3297. Offers coastal management (MA); environmental education and interpretation (MA); environmental management (MA); individualized study (MA). Part-time programs available. *Degree requirements:* For master's, comprehensive exam, thesis or alternative, final project, practicum. *Entrance requirements:* For master's, GRE, 3 letters of recommendation. Additional exam requirements/recommendations for international students: Required—TOEFL (minimum score 550 paper-based; 217 computer-based; 79 iBT), IELTS (minimum score 6.5). Electronic applications accepted. *Faculty research:* Coastal management, environmental management, environmental education, environmental law, natural resource management.

University of South Africa, College of Human Sciences, Pretoria, South Africa. Offers adult education (M Ed); African languages (MA, PhD); African politics (MA, PhD); Afrikaans (MA, PhD); ancient history (MA, PhD); ancient Near Eastern studies (MA, PhD); anthropology (MA, PhD); applied linguistics (MA); Arabic (MA, PhD); archaeology (MA); art history (MA); Biblical archaeology (MA); Biblical studies (M Th, D Th, PhD); Christian spirituality (M Th, D Th); church history (M Th, D Th); classical studies (MA, PhD); clinical psychology (MA); communication (MA, PhD); comparative education (M Ed, Ed D); consulting psychology (D Admin, D Com, PhD); curriculum studies (M Ed, Ed D); development studies (M Admin, MA, D Admin, PhD); didactics (M Ed, Ed D); education (M Tech); education management (M Ed, Ed D); educational psychology (M Ed); English (MA); environmental education (M Ed); French (MA, PhD); German (MA, PhD); Greek (MA); guidance and counseling (M Ed); health studies (MA, PhD), including health sciences education (MA), health services management (MA), medical and surgical nursing science (critical care general) (MA), midwifery and neonatal nursing science (MA), trauma and emergency care (MA); history (MA, PhD); history of education (Ed D); inclusive education (M Ed, Ed D); information and communications technology policy and regulation (MA); information science (MA, MIS, PhD); international politics (MA, PhD); Islamic studies (MA, PhD); Italian (MA, PhD); Judaica (MA, PhD); linguistics (MA, PhD); mathematical education (M Ed); mathematics education (MA); missiology (M Th, D Th); modern Hebrew (MA, PhD); musicology (MA, MMus, D Mus, PhD); natural science education (M Ed); New Testament (M Th, D Th); Old Testament (D Th); pastoral therapy (M Th, D Th); philosophy (MA); philosophy of education (M Ed, Ed D); politics (MA, PhD); Portuguese (MA, PhD); practical theology (M Th, D Th); psychology (MA, MS, PhD); psychology of education (M Ed, Ed D); public health (MA); religious studies (MA, D Th, PhD); Romance languages (MA); Russian (MA, PhD); Semitic languages (MA, PhD); social behavior studies in HIV/AIDS (MA); social science (mental health) (MA); social science in development studies (MA); social science in psychology (MA); social science in social work (MA); social science in sociology (MA); social work (MSW, DSW, PhD); socio-education (M Ed, Ed D); sociolinguistics (MA); sociology (MA, PhD); Spanish (MA, PhD); systematic theology (M Th, D Th); TESOL (teaching English to speakers of other languages) (MA); theological ethics (M Th, D Th); theory of literature (MA, PhD); urban ministries (D Th); urban ministry (M Th).

University of Victoria, Faculty of Graduate Studies, Faculty of Education, Department of Curriculum and Instruction, Victoria, BC V8W 2Y2, Canada. Offers art education (M Ed, PhD); curriculum studies (M Ed, MA, PhD); early childhood education (M Ed, PhD); educational studies (PhD); language and literacy (M Ed, MA, PhD); mathematics (M Ed, MA, PhD); music education (M Ed, MA, PhD); science (M Ed, MA, PhD); social studies (M Ed, MA); social, cultural and foundational studies (MA, PhD); technology and environmental education (PhD). Part-time programs available. *Degree requirements:* For master's, thesis, project (M Ed); for doctorate, comprehensive exam, thesis/dissertation. *Entrance requirements:* For master's, minimum B average. Additional exam requirements/recommendations for international students: Required—TOEFL (minimum score 575 paper-based; 233 computer-based), IELTS (minimum score 7). Electronic applications accepted. *Faculty research:* Elementary and secondary English, language arts, curriculum theory and practice, educational media and technology, educational administration and leadership, history and philosophy of education.

Western Washington University, Graduate School, Huxley College of the Environment, Department of Environmental Studies, Program in Environmental Education, Bellingham, WA 98225-5996. Offers M Ed. Part-time programs available. *Degree requirements:* For master's, comprehensive exam, thesis optional. *Entrance requirements:* For master's, GRE or MAT, minimum GPA of 3.0 in last 60 semester hours. Additional exam requirements/recommendations for international students: Required—TOEFL (minimum score 567 paper-based; 227 computer-based). Electronic applications accepted. *Faculty research:* Role of wilderness in national park history; history of the conservation movement and sense of place in environmental education; environmental care and responsibility; conservation psychology and environmental education.

West Virginia University, Davis College of Agriculture, Forestry and Consumer Sciences, Division of Resource Management and Sustainable Development, Program in Agricultural and Extension Education, Morgantown, WV 26506. Offers agricultural and extension education (MS, PhD); teaching vocational-agriculture (MS). *Accreditation:* NCATE. Part-time programs available. *Degree requirements:* For master's, thesis. *Entrance requirements:* For master's, GRE General Test, minimum GPA of 2.75. Additional exam requirements/recommendations for international students: Required—TOEFL. *Faculty research:* Program development in vocational agriculture, agricultural extension, supervised experience programs, leadership development.

Foreign Languages Education

The American University in Cairo, Graduate Studies and Research, School of Humanities and Social Sciences, Arabic Language Institute, Cairo, Egypt. Offers teaching Arabic as a foreign language (MA). *Entrance requirements:* Additional exam requirements/recommendations for international students: Required—English entrance exam and/or TOEFL.

Andrews University, School of Graduate Studies, College of Arts and Sciences, Department of International Language Studies, Berrien Springs, MI 49104. Offers MAT. *Application deadline:* Applications are processed on a rolling basis. Application fee: $40. *Unit head:* Dr. Pedro A. Navia, Chairman, 269-471-3180. *Application contact:* Carolyn Hurst, Supervisor of Graduate Admission, 800-253-2874, Fax: 269-471-3228, E-mail: graduate@andrews.edu.

Andrews University, School of Graduate Studies, School of Education, Department of Teaching, Learning, and Curriculum, Berrien Springs, MI 49104. Offers curriculum and instruction (MA, Ed D, PhD, Ed S); elementary education (MAT); reading (MA); secondary education (MAT), including biology, education, English, English as a second language, French, history, physics; special education/learning disabilities (MS); teacher education (MAT). *Students:* 12 full-time (8 women), 30 part-time (19 women); includes 17 minority (14 African Americans, 1 Asian American or Pacific Islander, 2 Hispanic Americans), 10 international. Average age 43. 28 applicants, 54% accepted, 6 enrolled. In 2009, 11 master's, 4 doctorates, 1 other advanced degree awarded. *Entrance requirements:* For master's, GRE Subject Test. Additional exam requirements/recommendations for international students: Required—TOEFL (minimum score 550 paper-based). *Application deadline:* For fall admission, 8/15 for domestic students. Applications are processed on a rolling basis. Application fee: $40. *Unit head:* Dr. Lee C. Davidson, Chair, 269-471-6364. *Application contact:* Carolyn Hurst, Supervisor of Graduate Admission, 800-253-2874, Fax: 269-471-6321, E-mail: graduate@andrews.edu.

Appalachian State University, Cratis D. Williams Graduate School, Department of Foreign Languages and Literatures, Boone, NC 28608. Offers romance languages (MA), including

Foreign Languages Education

Appalachian State University (continued)
Spanish or French teaching. Part-time programs available. Postbaccalaureate distance learning degree programs offered (no on-campus study). *Faculty:* 15 full-time (8 women). *Students:* 3 full-time (1 woman), 16 part-time (13 women); includes 4 minority (1 African American, 3 Hispanic Americans). 13 applicants, 92% accepted, 7 enrolled. In 2009, 8 master's awarded. *Degree requirements:* For master's, one foreign language, comprehensive exam, thesis optional. *Entrance requirements:* For master's, GRE General Test, 3 letters of recommendation. Additional exam requirements/recommendations for international students: Required—TOEFL (minimum score 570 paper-based; 230 computer-based; 79 iBT), or IELTS (minimum score 6.5). *Application deadline:* For fall admission, 7/1 for domestic students, 2/1 for international students; for spring admission, 11/1 for domestic students, 7/1 for international students. Applications are processed on a rolling basis. Application fee: $50. Electronic applications accepted. *Expenses:* Tuition, state resident: full-time $2960. Tuition, nonresident: full-time $14,051. Required fees: $2320. *Financial support:* In 2009–10, 2 research assistantships (averaging $7,000 per year) were awarded; fellowships, teaching assistantships, career-related internships or fieldwork and unspecified assistantships also available. Financial award application deadline: 4/1; financial award applicants required to submit FAFSA. *Faculty research:* French and Spanish literature, Latin American culture, teaching foreign languages. Total annual research expenditures: $35,000. *Unit head:* Dr. Richard Carp, Chairperson, 828-262-3096, Fax: 828-262-3095, E-mail: carprm@appstate.edu. *Application contact:* Dr. Beverly Moser, Graduate Coordinator, 828-262-2929, E-mail: moserba@appstate.edu.

Auburn University, Graduate School, College of Education, Department of Curriculum and Teaching, Auburn University, AL 36849. Offers business education (M Ed, MS, PhD); early childhood education (M Ed, MS, PhD, Ed S); elementary education (M Ed, MS, PhD, Ed S); foreign languages (M Ed, MS); music education (M Ed, MS, PhD, Ed S); postsecondary education (PhD); reading education (PhD, Ed S); secondary education (M Ed, MS, PhD, Ed S), including English language arts, mathematics, science, social studies. *Accreditation:* NASM (one or more programs are accredited); NCATE. Part-time programs available. *Faculty:* 28 full-time (21 women), 8 part-time/adjunct (5 women). *Students:* 76 full-time (55 women), 186 part-time (139 women); includes 43 minority (29 African Americans, 1 American Indian/Alaska Native, 4 Asian Americans or Pacific Islanders, 9 Hispanic Americans), 4 international. Average age 33. 248 applicants, 65% accepted, 110 enrolled. In 2009, 102 master's, 12 doctorates, 6 other advanced degrees awarded. *Degree requirements:* For master's, thesis (for some programs); for doctorate, thesis/dissertation; for Ed S, field project. *Entrance requirements:* For master's, doctorate, and Ed S, GRE General Test. *Application deadline:* For fall admission, 7/7 for domestic students; for spring admission, 11/24 for domestic students. Applications are processed on a rolling basis. Application fee: $50 ($60 for international students). Electronic applications accepted. *Expenses:* Tuition, state resident: full-time $6240. Tuition, nonresident: full-time $18,720. International tuition: $18,938 full-time. Required fees: $492. Tuition and fees vary according to course load, program and reciprocity agreements. *Financial support:* Fellowships, teaching assistantships, career-related internships or fieldwork and Federal Work-Study available. Support available to part-time students. Financial award application deadline: 3/15; financial award applicants required to submit FAFSA. *Faculty research:* Emerging literacy, reading attitudes, music for at-risk youth, portfolio assessment. *Unit head:* Dr. Nancy H. Barry, Head, 334-844-4434. *Application contact:* Dr. George Flowers, Dean of the Graduate School, 334-844-2125.

Bennington College, Graduate Programs, MA in Teaching a Second Language Program, Bennington, VT 05201. Offers education (MATSL); foreign language education (MATSL); French (MATSL); Spanish (MATSL). Part-time programs available. *Faculty:* 1 full-time (0 women), 3 part-time/adjunct (2 women). *Students:* 16 part-time (14 women); includes 3 minority (1 African American, 2 Hispanic Americans). Average age 37. 16 applicants, 63% accepted, 9 enrolled. In 2009, 6 master's awarded. *Degree requirements:* For master's, one foreign language, 2 major projects and presentations. *Entrance requirements:* For master's, Oral Proficiency Interview (OPI). Additional exam requirements/recommendations for international students: Required—TOEFL (minimum score 577 paper-based; 233 computer-based; 91 iBT). *Application deadline:* For spring admission, 4/1 priority date for domestic and international students. Applications are processed on a rolling basis. Application fee: $60. *Expenses:* Contact institution. *Financial support:* In 2009–10, 1 student received support. Scholarships/grants available. Financial award application deadline: 4/1; financial award applicants required to submit FAFSA. *Faculty research:* Acquisition, evaluation, assessment, conceptual teaching and learning content-driven communication, applied linguistics. *Unit head:* Carol Meyer, Director, 802-440-4375, E-mail: cmeyer@bennington.edu. *Application contact:* Nancy Pearlman, Assistant Director, 802-440-4710, E-mail: matsl@bennington.edu.

Bennington College, Graduate Programs, MA in Teaching Program, Bennington, VT 05201. Offers art education (MAT); early childhood (MAT); elementary education (MAT); English education (MAT); foreign language education (MAT); k-12 education (MAT); mathematics education (MAT); music education (MAT); science education (MAT); secondary education (MAT); social studies education (MAT); theater arts (MAT). *Faculty:* 5 part-time/adjunct (3 women). *Students:* 8 full-time (5 women), 1 part-time (0 women). Average age 28. 11 applicants, 27% accepted, 1 enrolled. In 2009, 4 master's awarded. *Degree requirements:* For master's, comprehensive exam, 1 year teaching practicum, professional portfolio. *Entrance requirements:* For master's, interview. *Application deadline:* For fall admission, 3/1 for domestic students. Application fee: $60. *Expenses:* Contact institution. *Financial support:* In 2009–10, 6 students received support, including 4 fellowships (averaging $10,475 per year); scholarships/grants and unspecified assistantships also available. Financial award application deadline: 4/1; financial award applicants required to submit FAFSA. *Unit head:* Carol Meyer, Director of Programs in Teacher Education, 802-440-4375, E-mail: cmeyer@bennington.edu. *Application contact:* Nancy Pearlman, Assistant Director of Programs in Teacher Education, 802-440-4710, Fax: 802-440-4383, E-mail: npearlman@bennington.edu.

Boston College, Lynch Graduate School of Education, Department of Teacher Education/Special Education and Curriculum and Instruction, Program in Secondary Education, Chestnut Hill, MA 02467-3800. Offers biology (MST); chemistry (MST); English (MAT); French (MAT); geology (MST); history (MAT); Latin and classical humanities (MAT); mathematics (MST); physics (MST); secondary teaching (M Ed), including biology, chemistry, English, French, geology, history, Latin and classical humanities, mathematics, physics, Spanish; Spanish (MAT). *Accreditation:* Teacher Education Accreditation Council. Part-time and evening/weekend programs available. *Students:* 14 full-time (10 women), 68 part-time (37 women); includes 17 minority (9 African Americans, 3 Asian Americans or Pacific Islanders, 5 Hispanic Americans), 1 international. 252 applicants, 59% accepted, 47 enrolled. In 2009, 39 master's awarded. *Degree requirements:* For master's, comprehensive exam. *Entrance requirements:* For master's, GRE General Test or MAT. Additional exam requirements/recommendations for international students: Required—TOEFL (minimum score 550 paper-based; 213 computer-based; 81 iBT). *Application deadline:* For fall admission, 1/1 priority date for domestic students. Application fee: $60. Electronic applications accepted. *Financial support:* Fellowships with full and partial tuition reimbursements, research assistantships with full and partial tuition reimbursements, teaching assistantships with full and partial tuition reimbursements, career-related internships or fieldwork, Federal Work-Study, institutionally sponsored loans, scholarships/grants, traineeships, health care benefits, tuition waivers (full and partial), and unspecified assistantships available. Support available to part-time students. Financial award applicants required to submit FAFSA. *Faculty research:* School reform; urban science education; teacher research; critical literacy; poverty and achievement. *Unit head:* Dr. Maria E. Brisk, Chairperson, 617-552-4216, Fax: 617-552-0812, E-mail: brisk@bc.edu. *Application contact:* Adam Poluzzi, Director, Graduate Admission and Financial Aid, 617-552-4214, Fax: 617-552-0398, E-mail: poluzzi@bc.edu.

Boston University, School of Education, Department of Literacy and Language, Counseling and Development, Program in Modern Foreign Language Education, Boston, MA 02215. Offers Ed M, MAT. *Degree requirements:* For master's, thesis or alternative. *Entrance requirements:* For master's, GRE General Test or MAT. Additional exam requirements/recommendations for international students: Required—TOEFL. Electronic applications accepted. *Expenses:* Tuition: Full-time $37,910; part-time $1184 per credit hour. Required fees: $386; $40 per semester. Part-time tuition and fees vary according to class time, course level, degree level and program.

Bowling Green State University, Graduate College, College of Arts and Sciences, Department of German, Russian, and East Asian Languages, Bowling Green, OH 43403. Offers German (MA, MAT); MA/MA. Part-time programs available. *Degree requirements:* For master's, one foreign language, thesis or alternative. *Entrance requirements:* For master's, GRE General Test. Additional exam requirements/recommendations for international students: Required—TOEFL. Electronic applications accepted.

Bowling Green State University, Graduate College, College of Arts and Sciences, Department of Romance and Classical Studies, Program in French, Bowling Green, OH 43403. Offers French (MA); French education (MAT). Part-time programs available. *Degree requirements:* For master's, one foreign language, thesis or alternative. *Entrance requirements:* For master's, GRE General Test. Additional exam requirements/recommendations for international students: Required—TOEFL. Electronic applications accepted. *Faculty research:* Francophone literature, French cinema, business French, nineteenth and twentieth century literature.

Bowling Green State University, Graduate College, College of Arts and Sciences, Department of Romance and Classical Studies, Program in Spanish, Bowling Green, OH 43403. Offers Spanish (MA); Spanish education (MAT). Part-time programs available. *Degree requirements:* For master's, one foreign language, thesis or alternative. *Entrance requirements:* For master's, GRE General Test. Additional exam requirements/recommendations for international students: Required—TOEFL. Electronic applications accepted. *Faculty research:* U.S. Latino literature and culture, Latin American film and popular culture, applied linguistics, Spanish popular culture.

Brigham Young University, Graduate Studies, College of Humanities, Center for Language Studies, Provo, UT 84602-1001. Offers language acquisition and teaching (MA). *Faculty:* 21 full-time (3 women). *Students:* 13 full-time (8 women), 5 part-time (4 women), 3 international. Average age 29. 16 applicants, 69% accepted, 9 enrolled. In 2009, 6 master's awarded. *Degree requirements:* For master's, 2 foreign languages, thesis. *Entrance requirements:* For master's, GRE General Test (minimum 50th percentile recommended), interview, strong background in language of specialization, writing sample, minimum GPA of 3.5 (recommended), three letters of recommendation. Additional exam requirements/recommendations for international students: Required—TOEFL (minimum score 237 computer-based; 85 iBT). *Application deadline:* For fall admission, 2/1 for domestic and international students. Application fee: $50. Electronic applications accepted. *Expenses:* Tuition: Full-time $5580; part-time $301 per credit hour. Tuition and fees vary according to student's religious affiliation. *Financial support:* In 2009–10, 14 students received support, including 29 fellowships with partial tuition reimbursements available (averaging $1,877 per year); career-related internships or fieldwork, scholarships/grants, traineeships, tuition waivers (partial), and unspecified assistantships also available. Support available to part-time students. Financial award application deadline: 2/1. *Faculty research:* Second language vocabulary, applied linguistics, computer-assisted learning and instructing, language comprehension, testing sociolinguists. Total annual research expenditures: $2 million. *Unit head:* Dr. Ray T. Clifford, Director, 801-422-3263, Fax: 801-422-9741, E-mail: rayc@byu.edu. *Application contact:* Agnes Y. Welch, Program Manager, 801-422-5199, Fax: 801-422-9741, E-mail: agnes_welch@byu.edu.

Brigham Young University, Graduate Studies, College of Humanities, Department of Spanish and Portuguese, Provo, UT 84602. Offers hispanic literature (MA); Portuguese linguistics (MA); Portuguese literature (MA); Spanish linguistics (MA); Spanish teaching (MA). Part-time programs available. *Faculty:* 32 full-time (5 women). *Students:* 18 full-time (7 women), 21 part-time (10 women); includes 5 minority (all Hispanic Americans), 9 international. Average age 30. 25 applicants, 56% accepted, 14 enrolled. In 2009, 17 master's awarded. *Degree requirements:* For master's, one foreign language, comprehensive exam, thesis, 1 semester of teaching. *Entrance requirements:* For master's, minimum GPA of 3.5 in Spanish or Portuguese, 3.3 overall. Additional exam requirements/recommendations for international students: Required—TOEFL (minimum score 580 paper-based; 237 computer-based). *Application deadline:* For fall admission, 2/1 for domestic and international students. Application fee: $50. Electronic applications accepted. *Expenses:* Tuition: Full-time $5580; part-time $301 per credit hour. Tuition and fees vary according to student's religious affiliation. *Financial support:* In 2009–10, 39 students received support, including 39 teaching assistantships with partial tuition reimbursements available (averaging $8,787 per year); institutionally sponsored loans, scholarships/grants, tuition waivers (partial), and unspecified assistantships also available. Support available to part-time students. Financial award application deadline: 7/1. *Faculty research:* Mexican prose; Latin American theater, literature, phonetics, and phonology; pedagogy; classical Portuguese literature; Peninsular prose and theater. *Unit head:* Dr. Alvin F. Sherman, Chair, 801-422-3107, Fax: 801-422-0628, E-mail: alvin_sherman@byu.edu. *Application contact:* Arwen T. Wyatt, Graduate Secretary, 801-422-2196, Fax: 801-422-0628, E-mail: arwen_wyatt@byu.edu.

Brooklyn College of the City University of New York, Division of Graduate Studies, School of Education, Program in Adolescence Education and Special Subjects, Brooklyn, NY 11210-2889. Offers adolescence science education (MAT); art teacher (MA); biology teacher (MA); chemistry teacher (MA); earth science teacher (MAT); English teacher (MA); French teacher (MA); health and nutrition sciences: health teacher (MS Ed); mathematics teacher (MA); music education (CAS); music teacher (MA); physical education teacher (MS Ed); physics teacher (MA); social studies teacher (MA); Spanish teacher (MA). Part-time and evening/weekend programs available. *Students:* 23 full-time (15 women), 449 part-time (256 women); includes 147 minority (96 African Americans, 1 American Indian/Alaska Native, 18 Asian Americans or Pacific Islanders, 32 Hispanic Americans), 12 international. Average age 30. 251 applicants, 80% accepted, 141 enrolled. In 2009, 163 master's, 2 other advanced degrees awarded. *Degree requirements:* For master's, comprehensive exam (for some programs), thesis (for some programs). *Entrance requirements:* For master's, LAST, previous course work in education, resume, 2 letters of recommendation, essay. Additional exam requirements/recommendations for international students: Required—TOEFL (minimum score 500 paper-based; 173 computer-based; 61 iBT). *Application deadline:* For fall admission, 7/15 for domestic students, 7/1 for international students; for spring admission, 11/15 for domestic students, 10/1 for international students. Applications are processed on a rolling basis. Application fee: $125. Electronic applications accepted. *Expenses:* Tuition, state resident: full-time $7360; part-time $310 per credit hour. Tuition, nonresident: full-time $13,800; part-time $575 per credit hour. Required fees: $140.10 per semester. *Financial support:* Career-related internships or fieldwork, Federal Work-Study, institutionally sponsored loans, and scholarships/grants available. Support available to part-time students. Financial award application deadline: 5/1; financial award applicants required to submit FAFSA. *Faculty research:* Interdisciplinary education, semiotics, discourse analysis, autobiography, teacher identity. *Unit head:* Prof. Stephen Phillips, Program Head, 718-951-5214, E-mail: phillips@brooklyn.cuny.edu. *Application contact:* Hernan Sierra, Graduate Admissions Coordinator, 718-951-4536, Fax: 718-951-4506, E-mail: grads@brooklyn.cuny.edu.

California State University, Chico, Graduate School, Program in Teaching International Languages, Chico, CA 95929-0722. Offers MA. Part-time programs available. *Students:* 21 full-time (18 women), 10 part-time (9 women); includes 7 minority (1 African American, 1 Asian American or Pacific Islander, 5 Hispanic Americans), 7 international. Average age 35. 23 applicants, 91% accepted, 11 enrolled. In 2009, 8 master's awarded. *Degree requirements:* For master's, comprehensive exam (for some programs), thesis or alternative. *Entrance requirements:* For master's, 3 letters of recommendation. Additional exam requirements/recommendations for international students: Required—TOEFL (minimum score 550 paper-based; 213 computer-based; 80 iBT), IELTS (minimum score 6.5). *Application deadline:* For fall admission, 3/1 priority date for domestic students, 3/1 for international students; for spring admission, 9/15 priority date for domestic students, 9/15 for international students. Applications are processed on a rolling basis. Application fee: $55. Electronic applications accepted.

Unit head: Dr. Hilda I. Hernandez. *Application contact:* School of Graduate, International, and Interdisciplinary Studies, 530-898-6880, Fax: 530-898-6889, E-mail: grin@csuchico.edu.

California State University, Sacramento, Graduate Studies, College of Arts and Letters, Department of Foreign Languages, Sacramento, CA 95819. Offers MA. Part-time programs available. *Degree requirements:* For master's, one foreign language, thesis or alternative, writing proficiency exam. *Entrance requirements:* For master's, interview, minimum GPA of 2.5 during previous 2 years of course work. Additional exam requirements/recommendations for international students: Required—TOEFL. Electronic applications accepted.

Caribbean University, Graduate School, Bayamón, PR 00960-0493. Offers administration and supervision (MA Ed); criminal justice (MA); curriculum and instruction (MA Ed), including elementary education, English education, history education, mathematics education, primary education, science education, Spanish education; education (PhD); gerontology (MSN); human resources (MBA); museology, archiving and art history (MA Ed); neonatal pediatrics (MSN); physical education (MA Ed); special education (MA Ed). *Entrance requirements:* For master's, interview, minimum GPA of 2.5.

Central Connecticut State University, School of Graduate Studies, School of Arts and Sciences, Department of Modern Languages, Program in Modern Language, New Britain, CT 06050-4010. Offers French (MA, Certificate); German (Certificate); Italian (Certificate); modern language (MA); Spanish language and Hispanic culture (MA). Part-time and evening/weekend programs available. *Students:* 2 full-time (1 woman), 40 part-time (35 women); includes 14 minority (all Hispanic Americans). Average age 38. 16 applicants, 69% accepted, 9 enrolled. In 2009, 9 master's awarded. *Degree requirements:* For master's, one foreign language, comprehensive exam, thesis or alternative; for Certificate, qualifying exam. *Entrance requirements:* For master's, minimum undergraduate GPA of 2.7, 24 credits of undergraduate courses in either Italian or Spanish. Additional exam requirements/recommendations for international students: Required—TOEFL. *Application deadline:* For fall admission, 7/1 for domestic students; for spring admission, 12/1 for domestic students. Applications are processed on a rolling basis. Application fee: $50. Electronic applications accepted. *Expenses:* Tuition, area resident: Full-time $4662; part-time $440 per credit. Tuition, state resident: full-time $6994; part-time $440 per credit. Tuition, nonresident: full-time $12,988; part-time $440 per credit. Required fees: $3606. One-time fee: $62 part-time. *Faculty research:* Twentieth century French theater, seventeenth century French literature, French Middle Ages.

Christopher Newport University, Graduate Studies, Department of Teacher Preparation, Newport News, VA 23606-2998. Offers art (PK-12) (MAT); biology (6-12) (MAT); computer science (6-12) (MAT); elementary (PK-6) (MAT); English (6-12) (MAT); French (PK-12) (MAT); history and social science (6-12) (MAT); mathematics (6-12) (MAT); music (PK-12) (MAT), including choral, instrumental; physics (6-12) (MAT); Spanish (PK-12) (MAT). Part-time and evening/weekend programs available. *Faculty:* 24 full-time (13 women), 4 part-time/adjunct (2 women). *Students:* 76 full-time (66 women), 12 part-time (10 women); includes 3 minority (2 African Americans, 1 Hispanic American). Average age 24. 3 applicants, 100% accepted, 2 enrolled. In 2009, 58 master's awarded. *Degree requirements:* For master's, comprehensive exam, thesis or alternative. *Entrance requirements:* For master's, PRAXIS I, minimum GPA of 3.0. Additional exam requirements/recommendations for international students: Required—TOEFL (minimum score 580 paper-based; 237 computer-based; 92 iBT). *Application deadline:* For fall admission, 8/15 for domestic students, 4/1 for international students; for spring admission, 10/15 for domestic students, 10/1 for international students. Applications are processed on a rolling basis. Application fee: $45. Electronic applications accepted. *Expenses:* Tuition, area resident: Part-time $384 per credit hour. Tuition, state resident: part-time $384 per credit hour. Tuition, nonresident: part-time $701 per credit hour. *Financial support:* In 2009–10, 3 research assistantships with full and partial tuition reimbursements (averaging $2,000 per year) were awarded; career-related internships or fieldwork, Federal Work-Study, and unspecified assistantships also available. Support available to part-time students. Financial award application deadline: 3/1; financial award applicants required to submit FAFSA. *Faculty research:* Early literacy development, instructional innovations, professional teaching standards, multicultural issues, aesthetic education. *Unit head:* Dr. Marsha Sprague, Director, 757-594-7388, Fax: 757-594-7803, E-mail: msprague@cnu.edu. *Application contact:* Lyn Sawyer, Associate Director, Graduate Admissions, 757-594-7544, Fax: 757-594-7649, E-mail: gradstdy@cnu.edu.

Cleveland State University, College of Graduate Studies, College of Education and Human Services, Department of Teacher Education, Cleveland, OH 44115. Offers art education (M Ed); early childhood education (M Ed); foreign language education (M Ed); mathematics and science education (M Ed); middle childhood education (M Ed); special education (M Ed), including mild/moderate disabilities, moderate/intensive disabilities; teaching English to speakers of other languages (M Ed). Part-time and evening/weekend programs available. *Degree requirements:* For master's, comprehensive exam (for some programs), thesis or alternative. *Entrance requirements:* For master's, GRE General Test or MAT, minimum GPA of 2.75. Additional exam requirements/recommendations for international students: Required—TOEFL (minimum score 525 paper-based; 197 computer-based), IELTS (minimum score 6). *Faculty research:* Early literacy, professional development in reading, reading recovery, dual language, induction programs.

The College at Brockport, State University of New York, School of Education and Human Services, Department of Education and Human Development, Brockport, NY 14420-2997. Offers adolescence education (MS Ed), including adolescence biology education, adolescence chemistry education, adolescence earth science education, adolescence English education, adolescence mathematics education, adolescence physics education, adolescence social studies education; alternate adolescence inclusive education (MS Ed), including alternate adolescence English inclusive education, alternate adolescence mathematics inclusive education, alternate adolescence science inclusive education, alternate adolescence social studies inclusive education; bilingual education (MS Ed, AGC), including bilingual education, Spanish (AGC); childhood curriculum specialist (MS Ed); childhood literacy (MS Ed). *Accreditation:* NCATE. *Students:* 49 full-time (29 women), 245 part-time (182 women); includes 12 minority (4 African Americans, 3 Asian Americans or Pacific Islanders, 5 Hispanic Americans). 109 applicants, 54% accepted, 53 enrolled. In 2009, 92 master's awarded. *Degree requirements:* For master's, thesis or alternative. *Entrance requirements:* For master's, minimum GPA of 3.0, letters of recommendation, interview (for some programs). Additional exam requirements/recommendations for international students: Required—TOEFL (minimum score 550 paper-based; 213 computer-based; 79 iBT). *Application deadline:* For fall admission, 2/15 priority date for domestic and international students; for spring admission, 9/15 priority date for domestic and international students. Application fee: $80. Electronic applications accepted. *Expenses:* Tuition, state resident: full-time $8370; part-time $349 per credit. Tuition, nonresident: full-time $13,250; part-time $522 per credit. *Financial support:* In 2009–10, 1 teaching assistantship with full tuition reimbursement (averaging $6,000 per year) was awarded; Federal Work-Study, scholarships/grants, and unspecified assistantships also available. Support available to part-time students. Financial award application deadline: 3/15; financial award applicants required to submit FAFSA. *Faculty research:* Educational assessment, literacy education, inclusive education, teacher preparation, qualitative methodology. *Unit head:* Dr. Sue Novinger, Chairperson, 585-395-2205, Fax: 585-395-2172, E-mail: snovinge@brockport.edu. *Application contact:* Dr. Sue Novinger, Chairperson, 585-395-2205, Fax: 585-395-2172, E-mail: snovinge@brockport.edu.

College of Charleston, Graduate School, School of Education, Health, and Human Performance, Program in Languages, Charleston, SC 29424-0001. Offers M Ed. Part-time programs available. *Faculty:* 2 full-time (1 woman). *Students:* 5 full-time (4 women), 26 part-time (23 women); includes 8 minority (5 African Americans, 3 Hispanic Americans), 1 international. Average age 35. 9 applicants, 67% accepted, 4 enrolled. In 2009, 8 master's awarded. *Degree requirements:* For master's, comprehensive exam or portfolio. *Entrance requirements:* For master's, minimum GPA of 2.5. Additional exam requirements/recommendations for international students: Required—TOEFL. *Application deadline:* For fall admission, 4/1 for domestic students; for spring admission, 11/1 for domestic students.

Application fee: $45. Electronic applications accepted. *Financial support:* In 2009–10, 9 research assistantships were awarded; fellowships, scholarships/grants and unspecified assistantships also available. Financial award applicants required to submit FAFSA. *Unit head:* Dr. Robyn Holman, Director, 843-953-5459. *Application contact:* Susan Hallatt, Director of Graduate Admissions, 843-953-5614, Fax: 843-953-1434, E-mail: hallatts@cofc.edu.

The College of William and Mary, School of Education, Program in Curriculum and Instruction, Williamsburg, VA 23187-8795. Offers elementary education (MA Ed); gifted education (MA Ed); math specialist (MA Ed); reading education (MA Ed); secondary education (MA Ed), including English education, mathematics education, modern foreign languages education, science education, social studies education; special education (MA Ed), including general curriculum, resource collaborating teaching. *Accreditation:* NCATE. Part-time programs available. *Faculty:* 18 full-time (12 women), 17 part-time/adjunct (15 women). *Students:* 54 full-time (45 women), 12 part-time (all women); includes 3 minority (2 African Americans, 1 Asian American or Pacific Islander), 2 international. Average age 27. 120 applicants, 75% accepted. In 2009, 70 master's awarded. *Degree requirements:* For master's, project. *Entrance requirements:* For master's, GRE or MAT, minimum GPA of 2.5. Additional exam requirements/recommendations for international students: Required—TOEFL. *Application deadline:* For fall admission, 1/15 for domestic and international students; for spring admission, 10/1 for domestic and international students. Application fee: $45. Electronic applications accepted. *Expenses:* Tuition, state resident: full-time $6400; part-time $315 per credit hour. Tuition, nonresident: full-time $19,720; part-time $840 per credit hour. Required fees: $4114. *Financial support:* In 2009–10, 30 students received support, including 10 research assistantships with full and partial tuition reimbursements (averaging $5,500 per year); career-related internships or fieldwork, Federal Work-Study, institutionally sponsored loans, scholarships/grants, and unspecified assistantships also available. Financial award application deadline: 1/15; financial award applicants required to submit FAFSA. *Faculty research:* National Council of Teachers of Mathematics Standards, counseling, self-concept and self-esteem, special education, curriculum development. *Unit head:* Dr. C. Denise Johnson, Area Coordinator, 757-221-1528, E-mail: cdjohn@wm.edu. *Application contact:* Dorothy Smith Osborne, Director of Admissions, 757-221-2317, Fax: 757-221-2293, E-mail: dsosbo@wm.edu.

The Colorado College, Department of Education, Program in Secondary Education, Colorado Springs, CO 80903-3294. Offers art teaching (K-12) (MAT); English teaching (MAT); foreign language teaching (MAT); mathematics teaching (MAT); music teaching (MAT); science teaching (MAT); social studies teaching (MAT). *Faculty:* 3 full-time (2 women), 8 part-time/adjunct (6 women). *Students:* 15 full-time (5 women); includes 2 minority (1 American Indian/Alaska Native, 1 Asian American or Pacific Islander). Average age 27. 26 applicants, 81% accepted, 15 enrolled. In 2009, 17 master's awarded. *Degree requirements:* For master's, thesis, internship. *Entrance requirements:* For master's, PRAXIS II or PLACE Exam. *Application deadline:* For fall admission, 12/1 priority date for domestic students, 12/1 for international students. Applications are processed on a rolling basis. Application fee: $50. *Expenses:* Tuition: Part-time $2545 per credit. *Financial support:* In 2009–10, 15 students received support, including 7 teaching assistantships (averaging $16,000 per year); career-related internships or fieldwork, institutionally sponsored loans, health care benefits, and tuition waivers (partial) also available. Financial award application deadline: 2/15; financial award applicants required to submit FAFSA. *Unit head:* Mike Taber, Director, 719-389-6026, Fax: 719-389-6473, E-mail: mike.taber@coloradocollege.edu. *Application contact:* Debra Yazulla Mortenson, Education Services Manager, 719-389-6472, Fax: 719-389-6473, E-mail: debra.mortenson@coloradocollege.edu.

Colorado State University, Graduate School, College of Liberal Arts, Department of Foreign Languages and Literatures, Fort Collins, CO 80523-1774. Offers MA. TESL degrees offered jointly with Department of English. Part-time programs available. *Faculty:* 14 full-time (6 women), 1 (woman) part-time/adjunct. *Students:* 20 full-time (17 women), 6 part-time (4 women); includes 3 minority (all Hispanic Americans), 1 international. Average age 29. 17 applicants, 53% accepted, 6 enrolled. In 2009, 5 master's awarded. *Degree requirements:* For master's, one foreign language, comprehensive exam (for some programs), thesis or paper, competitive exams. *Entrance requirements:* For master's, minimum GPA of 3.0; undergraduate major/proficiency in foreign languages. Additional exam requirements/recommendations for international students: Required—TOEFL (minimum score 550 paper-based). *Application deadline:* For fall admission, 2/15 priority date for domestic students; for spring admission, 7/15 priority date for domestic students. Applications are processed on a rolling basis. Application fee: $50. Electronic applications accepted. *Expenses:* Tuition, state resident: full-time $6434; part-time $359.10 per credit. Tuition, nonresident: full-time $18,116; part-time $1006.45 per credit. Required fees: $1496; $83 per credit. *Financial support:* In 2009–10, 12 students received support, including 12 teaching assistantships with full tuition reimbursements available (averaging $11,245 per year); fellowships, career-related internships or fieldwork, scholarships/grants, and unspecified assistantships also available. Financial award application deadline: 3/1; financial award applicants required to submit FAFSA. *Faculty research:* French, German, and Hispanic literatures and cultures; video-assisted language learning; computer-assisted language learners; foreign language teaching methodologies; linguistics. Total annual research expenditures: $75,073. *Unit head:* Dr. Paola Malpezzi-Price, Chair, 970-491-3838, Fax: 970-491-2822, E-mail: paola.malpezzi_price@colostate.edu. *Application contact:* Dr. Maria del Mar Lopez-Cabrales, Graduate Coordinator, 970-491-5957, Fax: 970-491-2822, E-mail: maria.lopez-cabrales@colostate.edu.

Colorado State University–Pueblo, College of Education, Engineering and Professional Studies, Education Program, Pueblo, CO 81001-4901. Offers art education (M Ed); foreign language education (M Ed); health and physical education (M Ed); instructional technology (M Ed); linguistically diverse education (M Ed); music education (M Ed); special education (M Ed). *Accreditation:* Teacher Education Accreditation Council. Part-time programs available. *Degree requirements:* For master's, portfolio. *Entrance requirements:* For master's, 3 recommendations, teaching license. Additional exam requirements/recommendations for international students: Required—TOEFL (minimum score 500 paper-based; 173 computer-based). Electronic applications accepted. *Faculty research:* Portfolio assessment, math education, science education.

Concordia College, Program in Education, Moorhead, MN 56562. Offers world language instruction (M Ed). *Degree requirements:* For master's, thesis/seminar. *Entrance requirements:* For master's, 2 professional references, 1 personal reference.

Cornell University, Graduate School, Graduate Fields of Arts and Sciences, Field of Linguistics, Ithaca, NY 14853-0001. Offers applied linguistics (MA, PhD); East Asian linguistics (MA, PhD); English linguistics (MA, PhD); general linguistics (MA, PhD); Germanic linguistics (MA, PhD); Indo-European linguistics (MA, PhD); phonetics (MA, PhD); phonological theory (MA, PhD); Romance linguistics (MA, PhD); second language acquisition (MA, PhD); semantics (MA, PhD); Slavic linguistics (MA, PhD); sociolinguistics (MA, PhD); South Asian linguistics (MA, PhD); Southeast Asian linguistics (MA, PhD); syntactic theory (MA, PhD). *Faculty:* 21 full-time (10 women). *Students:* 31 full-time (17 women), 14 international. Average age 30. 95 applicants, 12% accepted, 5 enrolled. In 2009, 5 master's, 6 doctorates awarded. Terminal master's awarded for partial completion of doctoral program. *Degree requirements:* For master's, one foreign language, thesis; for doctorate, one foreign language, comprehensive exam, thesis/dissertation. *Entrance requirements:* For master's and doctorate, GRE General Test, 2 letters of recommendation. Additional exam requirements/recommendations for international students: Required—TOEFL (minimum score 600 paper-based; 250 computer-based; 77 iBT). *Application deadline:* For fall admission, 1/15 for domestic students. Application fee: $70. Electronic applications accepted. *Expenses:* Tuition: Full-time $29,500. Required fees: $70. Full-time tuition and fees vary according to degree level, program and student level. *Financial support:* In 2009–10, 3 fellowships with full tuition reimbursements, 1 teaching assistantship with full tuition reimbursement were awarded; research assistantships with full tuition reimbursements, institutionally sponsored loans, scholarships/grants, health care benefits, tuition waivers (full and partial), and unspecified assistantships also available. Financial award applicants required to submit FAFSA. *Faculty research:* Phonology and phonetics; syntax and semantics; historical linguistics; philosophy of language; language acquisition. *Unit head:* Director of Graduate

Foreign Languages Education

Cornell University *(continued)*
Studies, 607-255-1105. *Application contact:* Graduate Field Assistant, 607-255-1105, E-mail: lingfield@cornell.edu.

Delaware State University, Graduate Programs, Department of English and Foreign Languages, Dover, DE 19901-2277. Offers French (MA); Spanish (MA). *Entrance requirements:* Additional exam requirements/recommendations for international students: Required—TOEFL (minimum score 550 paper-based). Electronic applications accepted.

Drew University, Caspersen School of Graduate Studies, Program in Education, Madison, NJ 07940-1493. Offers biology (MAT); chemistry (MAT); English (MAT); French (MAT); Italian (MAT); math (MAT); physics (MAT); social studies (MAT); Spanish (MAT); theatre arts (MAT). Part-time programs available. *Students:* 21 full-time (10 women), 6 part-time (2 women); includes 1 minority (Hispanic American). Average age 24. 40 applicants, 90% accepted, 27 enrolled. In 2009, 13 master's awarded. *Entrance requirements:* For master's, transcripts, personal statement, recommendations. Additional exam requirements/recommendations for international students: Required—TOEFL, TWE. *Application deadline:* For fall admission, 2/1 priority date for domestic students. Applications are processed on a rolling basis. Application fee: $35. *Expenses:* Contact institution. *Financial support:* In 2009–10, 22 students received support. Federal Work-Study, scholarships/grants, and tuition waivers (partial) available. Support available to part-time students. Financial award application deadline: 2/15; financial award applicants required to submit FAFSA. *Unit head:* Dr. Ross Danis. *Application contact:* Carla J. Burns, Director of Graduate Admissions, 973-408-3110, Fax: 973-408-3242, E-mail: gradm@drew.edu.

Duquesne University, School of Education, Department of Instruction and Leadership, Program in Secondary Education, Pittsburgh, PA 15282-0001. Offers secondary education (MS Ed), including biology, chemistry, English, Latin, math, physics, social studies, Spanish. Part-time and evening/weekend programs available. *Faculty:* 4 full-time (3 women), 1 part-time/adjunct (0 women). *Students:* 56 full-time (34 women), 8 part-time (3 women); includes 6 minority (3 African Americans, 2 Asian Americans or Pacific Islanders, 1 Hispanic American), 2 international. Average age 29. 69 applicants, 70% accepted, 27 enrolled. In 2009, 36 master's awarded. *Degree requirements:* For master's, thesis optional. *Entrance requirements:* For master's, MAT, minimum GPA of 3.0. Additional exam requirements/recommendations for international students: Required—TOEFL (minimum score 550 paper-based; 80 computer-based). *Application deadline:* For fall admission, 8/1 for domestic students; for spring admission, 12/1 for domestic students. Applications are processed on a rolling basis. Application fee: $0. Electronic applications accepted. *Expenses:* Tuition: Part-time $851 per credit. Required fees: $81 per credit. *Financial support:* Research assistantships, Federal Work-Study available. Support available to part-time students. *Unit head:* Dr. Melissa Boston, Assistant Professor, 412-396-6109, E-mail: bostonm@duq.edu. *Application contact:* Michael Dolinger, Director of Student and Academic Services, 412-396-6647, Fax: 412-396-5585, E-mail: dolingerm@duq.edu.

Eastern Washington University, Graduate Studies, College of Arts and Letters, Department of Modern Languages and Literatures, Cheney, WA 99004-2431. Offers French education (M Ed). *Accreditation:* NCATE. *Degree requirements:* For master's, comprehensive exam. *Entrance requirements:* For master's, minimum GPA of 3.0. *Expenses:* Tuition, state resident: full-time $7476; part-time $249 per quarter hour. Tuition, nonresident: full-time $18,030; part-time $601 per quarter hour. Required fees: $3.50 per quarter hour. $142 per quarter.

Elms College, Division of Education, Chicopee, MA 01013-2839. Offers early childhood education (MAT); education (M Ed, CAGS); elementary education (MAT); English as a second language (MAT); reading (MAT); secondary education (MAT), including biology education, English education, Spanish education; special education (MAT). Part-time and evening/weekend programs available. *Faculty:* 12 full-time (8 women), 4 part-time/adjunct (2 women). *Students:* 17 full-time (14 women), 153 part-time (136 women); includes 5 minority (1 American Indian/Alaska Native, 4 Hispanic Americans). Average age 36. 43 applicants, 88% accepted, 37 enrolled. In 2009, 23 master's, 8 other advanced degrees awarded. *Degree requirements:* For master's, thesis (for some programs). *Entrance requirements:* For master's, Massachusetts Educators Certification Test, minimum GPA of 3.0; for CAGS, master's degree in education. Additional exam requirements/recommendations for international students: Required—TOEFL. *Application deadline:* For fall admission, 7/1 priority date for domestic students; for spring admission, 11/1 priority date for domestic students. Applications are processed on a rolling basis. Application fee: $30. *Financial support:* In 2009–10, 2 teaching assistantships with partial tuition reimbursements were awarded; tuition waivers (partial) also available. Support available to part-time students. Financial award applicants required to submit FAFSA. *Unit head:* Dr. Mary Janeczek, Director, 413-594-2761, Fax: 413-592-4871, E-mail: janeczeke@elms.edu. *Application contact:* Dana Malone, Associate Director for Graduate Studies and Continuing Education, 413-265-2445, Fax: 413-265-2459, E-mail: maloned@elms.edu.

Florida International University, College of Education, Department of Curriculum and Instruction, Program in Foreign Language Education—Teaching English to Speakers of Other Languages (TESOL), Miami, FL 33199. Offers foreign language education (Certificate); teaching English (MS). Part-time and evening/weekend programs available. *Entrance requirements:* For master's, GRE General Test, minimum GPA of 3.0. Additional exam requirements/recommendations for international students: Required—TOEFL (minimum score 550 paper-based; 213 computer-based; 80 iBT), IELTS (minimum score 6.3). Electronic applications accepted. *Expenses:* Tuition, state resident: full-time $8008; part-time $4004 per year. Tuition, nonresident: full-time $20,104; part-time $10,052 per year. Required fees: $298; $149 per term. *Faculty research:* Methodology, applied languages.

Florida International University, College of Education, Department of Curriculum and Instruction, Program in French Education—Initial Teacher Preparation, Miami, FL 33199. Offers MAT. Part-time and evening/weekend programs available. *Entrance requirements:* For master's, GRE General Test (minimum score 1000), minimum GPA of 3.0. Additional exam requirements/recommendations for international students: Required—TOEFL (minimum score 550 paper-based; 213 computer-based; 80 iBT), IELTS (minimum score 6.3). Electronic applications accepted. *Expenses:* Tuition, state resident: full-time $8008; part-time $4004 per year. Tuition, nonresident: full-time $20,104; part-time $10,052 per year. Required fees: $298; $149 per term.

Florida International University, College of Education, Department of Curriculum and Instruction, Program in Modern Language Education/Bilingual Education, Miami, FL 33199. Offers MS, Ed D. *Accreditation:* NCATE. Part-time and evening/weekend programs available. *Entrance requirements:* Additional exam requirements/recommendations for international students: Required—TOEFL. *Expenses:* Tuition, state resident: full-time $8008; part-time $4004 per year. Tuition, nonresident: full-time $20,104; part-time $10,052 per year. Required fees: $298; $149 per term. *Faculty research:* Language and business, teaching English to speakers of other languages (TESOL).

Florida International University, College of Education, Department of Curriculum and Instruction, Program in Spanish Education—Initial Teacher Preparation, Miami, FL 33199. Offers MAT. Part-time and evening/weekend programs available. *Entrance requirements:* For master's, GRE General Test (minimum score 1000), minimum GPA of 3.0. Additional exam requirements/recommendations for international students: Required—TOEFL (minimum score 550 paper-based; 213 computer-based; 80 iBT), IELTS (minimum score 6.3). Electronic applications accepted. *Expenses:* Tuition, state resident: full-time $8008; part-time $4004 per year. Tuition, nonresident: full-time $20,104; part-time $10,052 per year. Required fees: $298; $149 per term.

Framingham State University, Division of Graduate and Continuing Education, Program in Spanish, Framingham, MA 01701-9101. Offers M Ed.

George Mason University, College of Humanities and Social Sciences, Department of Modern and Classical Languages, Fairfax, VA 22030. Offers foreign languages (MA). *Faculty:* 30 full-time (21 women), 43 part-time/adjunct (35 women). *Students:* 7 full-time (4 women), 35 part-time (25 women); includes 11 minority (1 African American, 1 Asian American or Pacific Islander, 9 Hispanic Americans), 1 international. Average age 33. 24 applicants, 71% accepted, 13 enrolled. In 2009, 7 master's awarded. *Degree requirements:* For master's, comprehensive exam, thesis optional. *Entrance requirements:* Additional exam requirements/recommendations for international students: Required—TOEFL. Application fee: $75. Electronic applications accepted. *Expenses:* Tuition, state resident: full-time $7568; part-time $315.33 per credit hour. Tuition, nonresident: full-time $21,704; part-time $904.33 per credit hour. Required fees: $2184; $91 per credit hour. *Financial support:* In 2009–10, 1 student received support, including 1 teaching assistantship with full and partial tuition reimbursement available (averaging $10,080 per year); Federal Work-Study, scholarships/grants, unspecified assistantships, and health care benefits (full-time research or teaching assistantship recipients) also available. Support available to part-time students. Financial award application deadline: 3/1; financial award applicants required to submit FAFSA. *Faculty research:* French Renaissance studies, early Modern (sixteenth-eighteenth centuries) literary and cultural studies, history, literature and philosophy, women's studies. Total annual research expenditures: $41,661. *Unit head:* Julie Christensen, Chairperson, 703-993-1230, E-mail: jchriste@gmu.edu. *Application contact:* Antonio Carreno-Rodriguez, Information Contact, 703-993-4227, E-mail: acarreno@gmu.edu.

Georgia Southern University, Jack N. Averitt College of Graduate Studies, College of Education, Department of Teaching and Learning, Program in Spanish Education, Statesboro, GA 30460. Offers MAT. *Accreditation:* NCATE. Part-time and evening/weekend programs available. *Students:* 4 full-time (2 women), 3 part-time (2 women); includes 1 minority (Hispanic American). Average age 28. 1 applicant, 100% accepted, 1 enrolled. In 2009, 1 master's awarded. *Degree requirements:* For master's, portfolio, transition point assessments, exit assessment. *Entrance requirements:* For master's, GRE General Test or MAT; GACE Basic Skills and Content Assessments, minimum cumulative GPA of 2.5. Additional exam requirements/recommendations for international students: Required—TOEFL (minimum score 550 paper-based; 213 computer-based; 80 iBT). *Application deadline:* For fall admission, 3/1 for domestic students, 3/1 priority date for international students; for spring admission, 10/1 priority date for domestic students, 10/1 for international students. Applications are processed on a rolling basis. Application fee: $50. Electronic applications accepted. *Expenses:* Tuition, state resident: full-time $5040; part-time $210 per credit hour. Tuition, nonresident: full-time $20,136; part-time $839 per credit hour. Required fees: $1644. *Financial support:* In 2009–10, 5 students received support, including research assistantships with partial tuition reimbursements available (averaging $7,200 per year), teaching assistantships with partial tuition reimbursements available (averaging $7,200 per year); Federal Work-Study, scholarships/grants, tuition waivers (partial), and unspecified assistantships also available. Support available to part-time students. Financial award application deadline: 4/15; financial award applicants required to submit FAFSA. *Unit head:* Dr. Ronnie Sheppard, Department Chair, 912-478-5203, Fax: 912-478-0026, E-mail: sheppard@georgiasouthern.edu. *Application contact:* Dr. Charles Ziglar, Coordinator for Graduate Student Recruitment, 912-478-5635, Fax: 912-478-0740, E-mail: gradadmissions@georgiasouthern.edu.

Georgia Southern University, Jack N. Averitt College of Graduate Studies, College of Liberal Arts and Social Sciences, Department of Foreign Languages, Statesboro, GA 30460. Offers Spanish (MA). Part-time and evening/weekend programs available. *Students:* 6 full-time (3 women), 8 part-time (7 women); includes 1 minority (African American), 1 international. Average age 28. 8 applicants, 100% accepted, 6 enrolled. In 2009, 5 master's awarded. *Degree requirements:* For master's, one foreign language, thesis optional. *Entrance requirements:* For master's, GRE, minimum GPA of 3.0, letters of reference. Additional exam requirements/recommendations for international students: Required—TOEFL (minimum score 550 paper-based; 213 computer-based; 80 iBT). *Application deadline:* For fall admission, 3/1 priority date for domestic and international students; for spring admission, 10/1 priority date for domestic students, 10/1 for international students. Applications are processed on a rolling basis. Application fee: $50. Electronic applications accepted. *Expenses:* Tuition, state resident: full-time $5040; part-time $210 per credit hour. Tuition, nonresident: full-time $20,136; part-time $839 per credit hour. Required fees: $1644. *Financial support:* In 2009–10, 10 students received support, including research assistantships with partial tuition reimbursements available (averaging $7,200 per year), teaching assistantships with partial tuition reimbursements available (averaging $7,200 per year); career-related internships or fieldwork, Federal Work-Study, scholarships/grants, tuition waivers (partial), and unspecified assistantships also available. Support available to part-time students. Financial award application deadline: 4/15; financial award applicants required to submit FAFSA. *Unit head:* Dr. Eric Kartchner, Chair, 912-478-5281, Fax: 912-478-0652, E-mail: forlangs@georgiasouthern.edu. *Application contact:* Dr. Charles Ziglar, Coordinator for Graduate Student Recruitment, 912-478-5635, Fax: 912-478-0740, E-mail: gradadmissions@georgiasouthern.edu.

Harding University, College of Education, Searcy, AR 72149-0001. Offers advanced studies in teaching and learning (M Ed); art (MSE); behavioral science (MSE); counseling (MS, Ed S); early childhood special education (M Ed, MSE); education (MSE); educational leadership (M Ed, Ed S); elementary education (M Ed); English (MSE); family and consumer science (MSE); French (MSE); history/social science (MSE); kinesiology (MSE); math (MSE); physical science (MSE); reading (M Ed); secondary education (M Ed); Spanish (MSE); special education licensure (M Ed); teaching (MAT); teaching English as a second language (M Ed). *Accreditation:* NCATE. Part-time and evening/weekend programs available. *Faculty:* 11 full-time (4 women), 49 part-time/adjunct (26 women). *Students:* 104 full-time (85 women), 392 part-time (282 women); includes 77 minority (67 African Americans, 5 American Indian/Alaska Native, 1 Asian American or Pacific Islander, 4 Hispanic Americans), 5 international. Average age 36. 153 applicants, 92% accepted, 131 enrolled. In 2009, 153 master's, 6 other advanced degrees awarded. *Degree requirements:* For master's, comprehensive exam (for some programs), thesis optional, portfolio(s); for Ed S, comprehensive exam, portfolio, specialist project. *Entrance requirements:* For master's, GRE, MAT, PRAXIS; for Ed S, MAT or GRE. Additional exam requirements/recommendations for international students: Required—TOEFL (minimum score 550 paper-based; 79 iBT). *Application deadline:* For fall admission, 8/1 for domestic and international students; for spring admission, 1/1 for domestic and international students. Applications are processed on a rolling basis. Application fee: $35. *Expenses:* Tuition: Full-time $9720; part-time $540 per credit hour. Required fees: $22 per credit hour. Tuition and fees vary according to course load and program. *Financial support:* In 2009–10, 30 students received support. Unspecified assistantships available. *Faculty research:* Reading, comprehension, school violence, educational technology, behavior, college choice, differentiated instruction, brain-based teaching. *Unit head:* Dr. Clara Carroll, Chair, 501-279-4501, Fax: 501-279-4083, E-mail: ccarroll@harding.edu. *Application contact:* Information Contact, 501-279-4315, E-mail: gradstudiesedu@harding.edu.

Hofstra University, College of Liberal Arts and Sciences, Department of Romance Languages and Literatures, Hempstead, NY 11549. Offers Spanish (MA). Part-time and evening/weekend programs available. *Faculty:* 4 full-time (2 women), 1 (woman) part-time/adjunct. *Students:* 2 full-time (both women), 4 part-time (all women); includes 3 minority (all Hispanic Americans). Average age 31. 3 applicants, 100% accepted, 1 enrolled. In 2009, 3 master's awarded. *Degree requirements:* For master's, one foreign language, thesis. *Entrance requirements:* Additional exam requirements/recommendations for international students: Required—TOEFL (minimum score 550 paper-based; 213 computer-based; 80 iBT). *Application deadline:* Applications are processed on a rolling basis. Application fee: $60. Electronic applications accepted. *Expenses:* Tuition: Full-time $16,200; part-time $900 per credit hour. Required fees: $970; $145 per term. Tuition and fees vary according to program. *Financial support:* In 2009–10, 13 fellowships with full and partial tuition reimbursements (averaging $2,667 per year) were awarded; research assistantships with full and partial tuition reimbursements, career-related internships or fieldwork, Federal Work-Study, institutionally sponsored loans, scholarships/grants, and tuition waivers (full and partial) also available. Support available to part-time students. Financial award applicants required to submit FAFSA. *Faculty research:* Contemporary Spanish and Spanish American cultural studies; Spanish linguistics and history of the Spanish language; Latin American poetry; colonial Latin America, postcolonial studies, and decolonization theories, Spanish theater. *Unit head:* Dr. Benita Sampedro, Chairperson, 516-463-4521, Fax:

516-463-2310, E-mail: benita.sampedro@hofstra.edu. *Application contact:* Carol Drummer, Dean of Graduate Admissions, 516-463-4876, Fax: 516-463-4664, E-mail: gradstudent@hofstra.edu.

Hofstra University, School of Education, Health, and Human Services, Department of Curriculum and Teaching, Program in Foreign Language Education, Hempstead, NY 11549. Offers foreign language and TESOL (MS Ed); foreign language education (MA, MS Ed), including French, German, Russian, Spanish. Part-time and evening/weekend programs available. *Students:* 4 full-time (all women), 3 part-time (1 woman); includes 2 minority (both Hispanic Americans). Average age 29. 9 applicants, 67% accepted, 3 enrolled. In 2009, 2 master's awarded. *Degree requirements:* For master's, one foreign language. *Entrance requirements:* For master's, 2 letters of recommendation, teacher certification (MA). Additional exam requirements/recommendations for international students: Required—TOEFL (minimum score 550 paper-based; 213 computer-based; 80 iBT). *Application deadline:* Applications are processed on a rolling basis. Application fee: $60. Electronic applications accepted. *Expenses:* Tuition: Full-time $16,200; part-time $900 per credit hour. Required fees: $970; $145 per term. Tuition and fees vary according to program. *Financial support:* In 2009–10, 6 students received support, including 2 fellowships with full and partial tuition reimbursements available (averaging $2,878 per year); research assistantships with full and partial tuition reimbursements available, Federal Work-Study, institutionally sponsored loans, scholarships/grants, tuition waivers (full and partial), and unspecified assistantships also available. Support available to part-time students. Financial award applicants required to submit FAFSA. *Faculty research:* First language acquisition and second language learning; theory and practice in language teaching; technology and language teaching and learning; language and colonialism. *Unit head:* Dr. Mustapha Masrour, Program Director, 516-463-6033, Fax: 516-463-6266, E-mail: lalmzm@hofstra.edu. *Application contact:* Carol Drummer, Dean of Graduate Admissions, 516-463-4876, Fax: 516-463-4664, E-mail: gradstudent@hofstra.edu.

Hunter College of the City University of New York, Graduate School, School of Arts and Sciences, Department of Romance Languages, Program in French, New York, NY 10021-5085. Offers French (MA); French education (MA). Part-time and evening/weekend programs available. *Faculty:* 3 full-time (1 woman). *Students:* 4 part-time (1 woman). Average age 32. 8 applicants, 50% accepted, 1 enrolled. In 2009, 2 master's awarded. *Degree requirements:* For master's, 2 foreign languages, comprehensive exam, thesis optional. *Entrance requirements:* For master's, GRE General Test, GRE Subject Test, ability to read, speak, and write French; interview. Additional exam requirements/recommendations for international students: Required—TOEFL. *Application deadline:* For fall admission, 4/1 for domestic students, 2/1 for international students; for spring admission, 11/1 for domestic students, 9/1 for international students. Application fee: $125. *Expenses:* Tuition, state resident: full-time $7360; part-time $310 per credit. Required fees: $250 per semester. *Financial support:* Fellowships, Federal Work-Study, scholarships/grants, and tuition waivers (partial) available. Support available to part-time students. Financial award application deadline: 4/15. *Faculty research:* Contemporary French theater, Villiers-dell Isle-Adam, Voltaire, medieval folklore, fin-de-siécle. *Unit head:* Prof. Marlene Barloum, Graduate Advisor, 212-650-3511, E-mail: mbarloum@hunter.cuny.edu. *Application contact:* William Zlata, Director for Graduate Admissions, 212-772-4482, Fax: 212-650-3336, E-mail: admissions@hunter.cuny.edu.

Hunter College of the City University of New York, Graduate School, School of Arts and Sciences, Department of Romance Languages, Program in Italian, New York, NY 10021-5085. Offers Italian (MA); Italian education (MA). *Faculty:* 2 full-time (both women). *Students:* 6 part-time (4 women); includes 1 minority (Hispanic American). Average age 31. 7 applicants, 86% accepted, 4 enrolled. In 2009, 2 master's awarded. *Degree requirements:* For master's, 2 foreign languages, comprehensive exam, thesis optional. *Entrance requirements:* For master's, GRE General Test, GRE Subject Test, ability to read, speak, and write Italian; interview. Additional exam requirements/recommendations for international students: Required—TOEFL. *Application deadline:* For fall admission, 4/1 for domestic students, 2/1 for international students; for spring admission, 11/1 for domestic students, 9/1 for international students. Application fee: $125. *Expenses:* Tuition, state resident: full-time $7360; part-time $310 per credit. Required fees: $250 per semester. *Financial support:* Federal Work-Study, scholarships/grants, and tuition waivers (partial) available. Support available to part-time students. Financial award application deadline: 4/15. *Faculty research:* Dante, Middle Ages, Renaissance, contemporary Italian novel and poetry, late Renaissance and baroque. *Unit head:* Dr. Paolo Fasoli, Graduate Co-Adviser, 212-772-5129, Fax: 212-772-5094, E-mail: pfasoli@hunter.cuny.edu. *Application contact:* William Zlata, Director for Graduate Admissions, 212-772-4482, Fax: 212-650-3336, E-mail: admissions@hunter.cuny.edu.

Hunter College of the City University of New York, Graduate School, School of Arts and Sciences, Department of Romance Languages, Program in Spanish, New York, NY 10021-5085. Offers Spanish (MA); Spanish education (MA). Part-time and evening/weekend programs available. *Faculty:* 4 full-time (3 women). *Students:* 1 (woman) full-time, 12 part-time (11 women); includes 9 minority (all Hispanic Americans). Average age 35. 12 applicants, 100% accepted, 7 enrolled. In 2009, 6 master's awarded. *Degree requirements:* For master's, 2 foreign languages, comprehensive exam, thesis optional. *Entrance requirements:* For master's, GRE General Test, GRE Subject Test, ability to read, speak, and write Spanish; interview. Additional exam requirements/recommendations for international students: Required—TOEFL. *Application deadline:* For fall admission, 4/1 for domestic students, 2/1 for international students; for spring admission, 11/1 for domestic students, 9/1 for international students. Application fee: $125. *Expenses:* Tuition, state resident: full-time $7360; part-time $310 per credit. Required fees: $250 per semester. *Financial support:* Federal Work-Study and tuition waivers (partial) available. Support available to part-time students. Financial award application deadline: 4/15. *Faculty research:* Galician studies, contemporary Spanish poetry, Lope de Vega, comparative Hispanic literatures, contemporary Hispanic poetry. *Unit head:* Dr. James O. Pellier, Graduate Advisor, 212-772-5625, E-mail: jpellice@hunter.cuny.edu. *Application contact:* William Zlata, Director for Graduate Admissions, 212-772-4482, Fax: 212-650-3336, E-mail: admissions@hunter.cuny.edu.

Hunter College of the City University of New York, Graduate School, School of Education, Programs in Secondary Education, Concentration in French Education, New York, NY 10021-5085. Offers MA. *Accreditation:* NCATE. *Faculty:* 4 full-time (all women), 4 part-time/adjunct (3 women). *Students:* 6 part-time (5 women); includes 1 minority (African American). Average age 31. 4 applicants, 75% accepted, 3 enrolled. In 2009, 2 master's awarded. *Degree requirements:* For master's, thesis, professional teaching portfolio, New York State Teacher Certification Exam. *Entrance requirements:* For master's, 24 credits in French; minimum GPA of 3.0 in French, 2.8 overall; 2 letters of reference; interview. Additional exam requirements/recommendations for international students: Required—TOEFL, TWE. *Application deadline:* For fall admission, 4/1 for domestic students, 2/1 for international students; for spring admission, 11/1 for domestic students, 9/1 for international students. Applications are processed on a rolling basis. Application fee: $125. *Expenses:* Tuition, state resident: full-time $7360; part-time $310 per credit. Required fees: $250 per semester. *Financial support:* Federal Work-Study and tuition waivers (partial) available. Support available to part-time students. *Unit head:* Dr. Jenny M. Castillo, Graduate Advisor, 212-772-4614, E-mail: jmcastil@hunter.cuny.edu. *Application contact:* William Zlata, Director for Graduate Admissions, 212-772-4482, Fax: 212-650-3336, E-mail: admissions@hunter.cuny.edu.

Hunter College of the City University of New York, Graduate School, School of Education, Programs in Secondary Education, Concentration in Italian Education, New York, NY 10021-5085. Offers MA. *Accreditation:* NCATE. *Students:* 1 (woman) full-time, 4 part-time (3 women). Average age 28. 5 applicants, 40% accepted, 2 enrolled. In 2009, 2 master's awarded. *Degree requirements:* For master's, thesis, professional teaching portfolio, New York State Teacher Certification Exam, research project. *Entrance requirements:* For master's, minimum GPA of 3.0 in Italian, 2.8 overall; 24 credits of course work in Italian; 2 letters of reference; interview. Additional exam requirements/recommendations for international students: Required—TOEFL, TWE. *Application deadline:* For fall admission, 4/1 for domestic students, 2/1 for international students; for spring admission, 11/1 for domestic students, 9/1 for international students. Applications are processed on a rolling basis. Application fee: $125. *Expenses:* Tuition, state resident: full-time $7360; part-time $310 per credit. Required fees: $250 per semester. *Financial support:* Federal Work-Study and tuition waivers (partial) available. Support available to part-time students. *Unit head:* Dr. Paolo Fasoli, Chair, 212-772-5129, Fax: 212-772-5094, E-mail: pfasoli@hunter.cuny.edu. *Application contact:* William Zlata, Director for Graduate Admissions, 212-772-4482, Fax: 212-650-3336, E-mail: admissions@hunter.cuny.edu.

Hunter College of the City University of New York, Graduate School, School of Education, Programs in Secondary Education, Concentration in Spanish Education, New York, NY 10021-5085. Offers MA. *Accreditation:* NCATE. *Students:* 1 (woman) full-time, 39 part-time (28 women); includes 22 minority (1 African American, 21 Hispanic Americans). Average age 29. 10 applicants, 30% accepted, 2 enrolled. In 2009, 16 master's awarded. *Degree requirements:* For master's, thesis, professional teaching portfolio, New York State Teacher Certification Exam. *Entrance requirements:* For master's, minimum GPA of 3.0 in Spanish, 2.8 overall; 24 credits of course work in Spanish; 2 letters of reference; interview. Additional exam requirements/recommendations for international students: Required—TOEFL, TWE. *Application deadline:* For fall admission, 4/1 for domestic students, 2/1 for international students; for spring admission, 11/1 for domestic students, 9/1 for international students. Applications are processed on a rolling basis. Application fee: $125. *Expenses:* Tuition, state resident: full-time $7360; part-time $310 per credit. Required fees: $250 per semester. *Financial support:* Federal Work-Study and tuition waivers (partial) available. Support available to part-time students. *Unit head:* Dr. Magdalena Perkowska, Romance Language Advisor (Spanish), 212-772-5132, E-mail: mperkowsk@hunter.cuny.edu. *Application contact:* William Zlata, Director for Graduate Admissions, 212-772-4482, Fax: 212-650-3336, E-mail: admissions@hunter.cuny.edu.

Indiana University Bloomington, University Graduate School, College of Arts and Sciences, Department of French and Italian, Bloomington, IN 47405-7000. Offers French (MA, PhD), including French instruction (MA), French linguistics, French literature; Italian (MA, PhD). Part-time programs available. *Faculty:* 19 full-time (7 women). *Students:* 69 full-time (42 women), 5 part-time (4 women); includes 3 minority (1 American Indian/Alaska Native, 1 Asian American or Pacific Islander, 1 Hispanic American), 28 international. Average age 30. 48 applicants, 63% accepted, 15 enrolled. In 2009, 12 master's, 2 doctorates awarded. Terminal master's awarded for partial completion of doctoral program. *Degree requirements:* For master's, one foreign language, comprehensive exam, thesis optional; for doctorate, 2 foreign languages, comprehensive exam, thesis/dissertation. *Entrance requirements:* For master's and doctorate, GRE General Test. Additional exam requirements/recommendations for international students: Required—TOEFL (minimum score 550 paper-based; 213 computer-based; 79 iBT). *Application deadline:* For fall admission, 1/15 priority date for domestic students, 12/1 priority date for international students; for spring admission, 9/1 priority date for domestic and international students. Application fee: $55 ($65 for international students). Electronic applications accepted. *Financial support:* In 2009–10, 4 fellowships with partial tuition reimbursements (averaging $15,000 per year), 5 research assistantships with partial tuition reimbursements (averaging $13,025 per year), 39 teaching assistantships with partial tuition reimbursements (averaging $13,025 per year) were awarded. Financial award application deadline: 1/15. *Faculty research:* All periods of French and Italian literature and various areas of French linguistics, including the novel and political theory, literature and fine arts, literary theory, postcolonialism, French-Creole studies, French literature of Africa and its Diaspora, humanism, medieval folklore and mythology, humor in medieval and Renaissance literature, cinema Old Occitan and Old French, emigration, second language acquisition, syntax, sociolinguistics, phonology, lexicography. *Unit head:* Prof. Emanuel Mickel, Interim Chairman, 812-855-5458, Fax: 812-855-8877, E-mail: fritchr@indiana.edu. *Application contact:* Jocelyn Karlan, Secretary, 812-855-1088, Fax: 812-855-8877, E-mail: fritgs@indiana.edu.

Indiana University Bloomington, University Graduate School, College of Arts and Sciences, Department of Germanic Studies, Bloomington, IN 47405-7000. Offers German philology and linguistics (PhD); German studies (MA, PhD), including German (MA), German literature and culture (MA), German literature and linguistics (MA); medieval German studies (PhD); teaching German (MAT). *Faculty:* 13 full-time (4 women), 6 part-time/adjunct (2 women). *Students:* 34 full-time (19 women), 2 part-time (1 woman); includes 2 minority (1 African American, 1 Hispanic American), 9 international. Average age 30. 34 applicants, 41% accepted, 8 enrolled. In 2009, 3 master's, 2 doctorates awarded. Terminal master's awarded for partial completion of doctoral program. *Degree requirements:* For master's, one foreign language, project; for doctorate, one foreign language, comprehensive exam, thesis/dissertation. *Entrance requirements:* For master's, GRE General Test, BA in German or equivalent; for doctorate, GRE General Test, MA in German or equivalent. Additional exam requirements/recommendations for international students: Required—TOEFL. *Application deadline:* For fall admission, 1/15 priority date for domestic students, 12/15 for international students; for spring admission, 9/1 priority date for domestic students, 9/1 for international students. Applications are processed on a rolling basis. Application fee: $55 ($65 for international students). *Financial support:* In 2009–10, 8 fellowships with full and partial tuition reimbursements (averaging $20,000 per year), 1 research assistantship (averaging $13,025 per year), 20 teaching assistantships with full tuition reimbursements (averaging $13,025 per year) were awarded; Federal Work-Study, institutionally sponsored loans, scholarships/grants, and unspecified assistantships also available. Support available to part-time students. Financial award application deadline: 1/15; financial award applicants required to submit FAFSA. *Faculty research:* German and other European literature: medieval to modern/postmodern, German and culture studies, Germanic philology, literary theory, literature and the other arts. *Unit head:* William Rasch, Department Chairman, 812-855-7947, Fax: 812-855-8292, E-mail: wrasch@indiana.edu. *Application contact:* Michelle Dunbar, Graduate Secretary, 812-855-7947, E-mail: midunbar@indiana.edu.

Indiana University Bloomington, University Graduate School, College of Arts and Sciences, Department of Spanish and Portuguese, Bloomington, IN 47405-7000. Offers Hispanic linguistics (MA, PhD); Hispanic literature (MA); Luso-Brazilian literature (MA); Luso-Brazilian studies (PhD); Spanish literatures (PhD); teaching Spanish (MAT). *Faculty:* 18 full-time (10 women). *Students:* 84 full-time (47 women), 2 part-time (0 women); includes 17 minority (1 Asian American or Pacific Islander, 16 Hispanic Americans), 18 international. Average age 30. 55 applicants, 62% accepted, 15 enrolled. In 2009, 10 master's, 4 doctorates awarded. *Degree requirements:* For master's, one foreign language; for doctorate, 3 foreign languages, thesis/dissertation. *Entrance requirements:* For master's, GRE General Test, GRE Subject Test, bachelor's degree in Portuguese or Spanish, minimum GPA of 3.25; for doctorate, GRE General Test, GRE Subject Test, master's degree in Portuguese or Spanish, minimum GPA of 3.25. Additional exam requirements/recommendations for international students: Required—TOEFL. *Application deadline:* For fall admission, 1/15 priority date for domestic students, 12/15 for international students; for spring admission, 9/1 for domestic and international students. Application fee: $55 ($65 for international students). *Financial support:* In 2009–10, 1 fellowship with full tuition reimbursement (averaging $15,000 per year), 72 teaching assistantships with full tuition reimbursements (averaging $14,790 per year) were awarded; research assistantships, Federal Work-Study also available. Financial award application deadline: 1/15. *Faculty research:* Spanish-American literature, Spanish peninsular literature, Luso-Brazilian studies, Catalan studies. *Unit head:* Josep Miguel Sobrer, Chair, 812-855-8498. *Application contact:* Steven Wagschal, Student Contact, 812-855-9194, E-mail: swagscha@indiana.edu.

Indiana University–Purdue University Indianapolis, School of Education, Indianapolis, IN 46202-2896. Offers computer education (Certificate); curriculum and instruction (MS); early childhood (MS); educational leadership (MS, Certificate); English as a second language (Certificate); higher education and student affairs (MS); kindergarten (Certificate); language education (MS); reading (Certificate); school counseling (MS); special education (MS, Certificate). Part-time and evening/weekend programs available. *Faculty:* 41 full-time, 80 part-time/adjunct. *Students:* 72 full-time (60 women), 427 part-time (325 women); includes 57 minority (42 African Americans, 1 American Indian/Alaska Native, 4 Asian Americans or Pacific Islanders, 10 Hispanic Americans), 5 international. Average age 32. 181 applicants, 78% accepted, 112 enrolled. In 2009, 162 master's awarded. *Degree requirements:* For master's, thesis optional. *Entrance requirements:* For master's, GRE General Test, minimum GPA of 3.0. Additional

Foreign Languages Education

Indiana University–Purdue University Indianapolis (continued)
exam requirements/recommendations for international students: Required—TOEFL. *Application deadline:* For fall admission, 5/1 priority date for domestic students; for spring admission, 11/1 for domestic students. Application fee: $55 ($65 for international students). *Financial support:* In 2009–10, 2 fellowships (averaging $780 per year), 18 teaching assistantships (averaging $9,756 per year) were awarded; research assistantships with partial tuition reimbursements, Federal Work-Study, institutionally sponsored loans, scholarships/grants, and tuition waivers (partial) also available. Support available to part-time students. *Faculty research:* Teachers in the process of change, learning cycles, children's concepts of science. Total annual research expenditures: $614,458. *Unit head:* Dr. Chris Leland, Interim Executive Associate Dean, 317-274-6801, Fax: 317-274-6864. *Application contact:* Sarah Brandenburg, Graduate Advisor, 317-274-6801, Fax: 317-274-6864, E-mail: edugrad@iupui.edu.

Inter American University of Puerto Rico, Arecibo Campus, Programs in Education, Arecibo, PR 00614-4050. Offers administration and educational supervision (MA Ed); counseling and guidance (MA Ed); curriculum and teaching (MA Ed), including biology education, English as a second language, history education, math education, Spanish; elementary education (MA Ed). *Degree requirements:* For master's, comprehensive exam, thesis optional. *Entrance requirements:* For master's, GRE, EXADEP, bachelor's degree in education or teaching license (administration and supervision) or courses in education and psychology (counseling and guidance), minimum GPA of 2.5 in last 60 credits.

Iona College, School of Arts and Science, Program in Education, New Rochelle, NY 10801-1890. Offers biology education (MS Ed, MST); educational leadership (MS Ed); English education (MS Ed, MST); literacy education (MS Ed); mathematics education (MS Ed, MST); social studies education (MS Ed, MST); Spanish education (MS Ed, MST); teaching in childhood education (MST). *Accreditation:* NCATE. Part-time and evening/weekend programs available. *Faculty:* 24 full-time (13 women), 16 part-time/adjunct (10 women). *Students:* 41 full-time (35 women), 118 part-time (87 women); includes 15 minority (5 African Americans, 1 Asian American or Pacific Islander, 9 Hispanic Americans). Average age 28. 91 applicants, 67% accepted, 41 enrolled. In 2009, 61 master's awarded. *Degree requirements:* For master's, thesis or alternative. *Entrance requirements:* For master's, minimum GPA of 2.5 (MST), New York teaching certificate (MS Ed). Additional exam requirements/recommendations for international students: Required—TOEFL (minimum score 550 paper-based; 213 computer-based). *Application deadline:* Applications are processed on a rolling basis. Application fee: $50. Electronic applications accepted. *Expenses:* Tuition: Part-time $830 per credit. *Financial support:* Unspecified assistantships available. Support available to part-time students. Financial award application deadline: 4/15; financial award applicants required to submit FAFSA. *Faculty research:* Reading/writing, educational technology, administration, early literacy assessment, literacy development. *Unit head:* Dr. Catherine O'Callaghan, Chair, 914-633-2210, Fax: 914-633-2608, E-mail: cocallaghan@iona.edu. *Application contact:* Veronica Jarek-Prinz, Director of Graduate Admissions, 914-633-2420, Fax: 914-633-2277, E-mail: vjarekprinz@iona.edu.

Iona College, School of Arts and Science, Program in Foreign Languages, New Rochelle, NY 10801-1890. Offers Italian (MA); Spanish (MA). Part-time and evening/weekend programs available. *Faculty:* 4 full-time (2 women), 1 part-time/adjunct (0 women). *Students:* 14 part-time (13 women); includes 1 minority (Hispanic American). Average age 35. 4 applicants, 75% accepted, 2 enrolled. In 2009, 10 master's awarded. *Degree requirements:* For master's, thesis or alternative. *Entrance requirements:* For master's, minimum GPA of 3.0. Additional exam requirements/recommendations for international students: Required—TOEFL (minimum score 550 paper-based; 213 computer-based). *Application deadline:* Applications are processed on a rolling basis. Application fee: $50. Electronic applications accepted. *Expenses:* Tuition: Part-time $830 per credit. *Financial support:* Unspecified assistantships available. Support available to part-time students. Financial award application deadline: 4/15; financial award applicants required to submit FAFSA. *Faculty research:* Contemporary Spanish literature, linguistics, language acquisition, female Hispanic literature, Latina authors. *Unit head:* Dr. Victoria E. Ketz, Chair, 914-637-2738, E-mail: vketz@iona.edu. *Application contact:* Veronica Jarek-Prinz, Director of Graduate Admissions, 914-633-2420, Fax: 914-633-2277, E-mail: vjarekprinz@iona.edu.

Ithaca College, Division of Graduate and Professional Studies, School of Humanities and Sciences, Program in Adolescent Education, Ithaca, NY 14850. Offers biology 7-12 (MAT); chemistry 7-12 (MAT); English 7-12 (MAT); French 7-12 (MAT); math 7-12 (MAT); physics 7-12 (MAT); social studies 7-12 (MAT); Spanish (MAT). Part-time programs available. *Faculty:* 18 full-time (7 women). *Students:* 15 full-time (10 women), 2 part-time (1 woman); includes 1 minority (African American). Average age 26. 31 applicants, 68% accepted, 16 enrolled. In 2009, 31 master's awarded. *Degree requirements:* For master's, thesis or alternative, student teaching. *Entrance requirements:* For master's, minimum GPA of 3.0. Additional exam requirements/recommendations for international students: Required—TOEFL (minimum score 550 paper-based; 213 computer-based; 80 iBT). *Application deadline:* For fall admission, 5/15 for domestic and international students; for spring admission, 12/1 for domestic and international students. Applications are processed on a rolling basis. Application fee: $40. Electronic applications accepted. *Expenses:* Contact institution. *Financial support:* In 2009–10, 15 students received support, including 10 teaching assistantships (averaging $6,474 per year); career-related internships or fieldwork, Federal Work-Study, scholarships/grants, and unspecified assistantships also available. Support available to part-time students. Financial award applicants required to submit CSS PROFILE or FAFSA. *Faculty research:* Bilingual education, socio-linguistic perspective on literacy. *Unit head:* Dr. Linda Hanrahan, Chairperson, 607-274-3527, Fax: 607-274-1263, E-mail: gps@ithaca.edu. *Application contact:* Rob Gearhart, Dean, Graduate and Professional Studies, 607-274-3527, Fax: 607-274-1263, E-mail: gps@ithaca.edu.

The Johns Hopkins University, School of Education, Department of Teacher Preparation, Baltimore, MD 21218. Offers education (MS), including educational studies; elementary education (MAT); English for speakers of other languages (MAT); K-8 mathematics lead-teacher (Certificate); K-8 science lead-teacher (Certificate); secondary education (MAT), including biology, chemistry, earth/space/environmental science, English, French, mathematics, physics, social studies, Spanish. Part-time and evening/weekend programs available. *Faculty:* 13 full-time (11 women), 35 part-time/adjunct (21 women). *Students:* 162 full-time (119 women), 347 part-time (256 women); includes 138 minority (80 African Americans, 3 American Indian/Alaska Native, 38 Asian Americans or Pacific Islanders, 17 Hispanic Americans), 3 international. Average age 27. 89 applicants, 37% accepted, 24 enrolled. In 2009, 177 master's awarded. *Degree requirements:* For master's, portfolio, PRAXIS II, internship. *Entrance requirements:* For master's, PRAXIS I, SAT, ACT, or GRE (MAT), minimum undergraduate GPA of 3.0, interview, 1 letter of recommendation, curriculum vitae/resume; for Certificate, bachelor's degree, minimum undergraduate GPA of 3.0, essay/statement of goals, interview. Additional exam requirements/recommendations for international students: Required—TOEFL (minimum score 600 paper-based; 250 computer-based; 100 iBT). *Application deadline:* For fall admission, 5/1 for international students; for spring admission, 10/15 for international students. Applications are processed on a rolling basis. Application fee: $80. Electronic applications accepted. *Financial support:* Scholarships/grants available. Support available to part-time students. Financial award application deadline: 6/1; financial award applicants required to submit FAFSA. *Faculty research:* Teacher retention; STEM education reform; alternative certification programs; school-university partnerships; urban education; action research/data-informed instruction; family engagement. *Unit head:* Dr. Francis Masci, Chair, 410-516-9774, Fax: 410-516-9770, E-mail: matjhu@jhu.edu. *Application contact:* Jennifer Shaffer, Director of Admissions, 410-516-9797, Fax: 410-516-9799, E-mail: educationinfo@jhu.edu.

Kean University, College of Education, Program in Instruction and Curriculum, Union, NJ 07083. Offers bilingual/bicultural education (MA); classroom instruction (MA); earth science (MA); mathematics/science/computer education (MA); teaching (MA); teaching English as a second language (MA); world languages (Spanish) (MA). *Accreditation:* NCATE. Part-time and evening/weekend programs available. *Faculty:* 16 full-time (7 women). *Students:* 45 full-time (34 women), 131 part-time (104 women); includes 60 minority (11 African Americans, 6 Asian

Americans or Pacific Islanders, 43 Hispanic Americans), 6 international. Average age 33. 64 applicants, 94% accepted, 46 enrolled. In 2009, 58 master's awarded. *Entrance requirements:* For master's, GRE General Test or MAT, PRAXIS, minimum GPA of 3.0, 2 letters of recommendation, interview, teacher certification (for some programs). *Application deadline:* For fall admission, 5/1 for domestic students; for spring admission, 11/1 for domestic students. Application fee: $60 ($150 for international students). Electronic applications accepted. *Expenses:* Tuition, state resident: full-time $10,440; part-time $435 per credit. Tuition, nonresident: full-time $14,160; part-time $590 per credit. Required fees: $2642; $110 per credit. Part-time tuition and fees vary according to course load and degree level. *Financial support:* In 2009–10, 1 research assistantship with full tuition reimbursement (averaging $3,263 per year) was awarded; unspecified assistantships also available. *Unit head:* Dr. Thomas Walsh, Program Coordinator, 908-737-4296, E-mail: twalsh@kean.edu. *Application contact:* Ann-Marie Kay, Assistant Director of Graduate Admissions, 908-737-5922, Fax: 908-737-5965, E-mail: akay@kean.edu.

Kent State University, College of Arts and Sciences, Department of Modern and Classical Language Studies, Kent, OH 44242-0001. Offers French literature (MA); French, Spanish, German and Latin pedagogy (MA); German literature (MA); Spanish literature (MA); translation (MA), including French, German, Japanese, Russian, Spanish; translation studies (PhD). Part-time and evening/weekend programs available. *Degree requirements:* For master's, one foreign language, comprehensive exam (for some programs), thesis (for some programs); for doctorate, comprehensive exam, thesis/dissertation (for some programs). *Entrance requirements:* For master's, minimum GPA of 3.0, writing sample, audio tape or CD; for doctorate, 3 recommendations. Additional exam requirements/recommendations for international students: Required—TOEFL (minimum score 197 computer-based). Electronic applications accepted. *Faculty research:* Literature, pedagogy, applied linguistics, translation studies.

Long Island University, C.W. Post Campus, College of Liberal Arts and Sciences, Department of Foreign Languages, Brookville, NY 11548-1300. Offers Spanish (MA); Spanish education (MS). Part-time programs available. *Degree requirements:* For master's, 2 foreign languages, comprehensive exam, thesis or alternative. *Entrance requirements:* For master's, 24 credits of undergraduate course work in Spanish. Electronic applications accepted. *Faculty research:* Making of a superhero, dialogue in the 19th century novel, nicknames, Menendez Pidal and Spanish School of Philology, women writers of Latin America.

Long Island University, C.W. Post Campus, School of Education, Department of Curriculum and Instruction, Brookville, NY 11548-1300. Offers adolescence education (MS); adolescence education: biology (MS); adolescence education: earth science (MS); adolescence education: English (MS); adolescence education: mathematics (MS); adolescence education: social studies (MS); adolescence education: Spanish (MS); art education (MS); bilingual education (MS); childhood education (MS); early childhood education (MS); middle childhood education (MS); music education (MS); teaching English to speakers of other languages (MS). Part-time and evening/weekend programs available. *Degree requirements:* For master's, comprehensive exam or thesis, student teaching. *Entrance requirements:* For master's, minimum GPA of 2.75 in major, 2.5 overall. Electronic applications accepted. *Faculty research:* Ethics and education, teaching strategies.

Louisiana Tech University, Graduate School, College of Education, Department of Curriculum, Instruction and Leadership, Ruston, LA 71272. Offers curriculum and instruction (MS, Ed D); educational leadership (Ed D); secondary education (M Ed), including business education, English education, foreign language education, health and physical education, mathematics education, science education, social studies education, speech education. *Accreditation:* NCATE. Part-time programs available. *Degree requirements:* For doctorate, thesis/dissertation. *Entrance requirements:* For master's and doctorate, GRE General Test.

Manhattanville College, Graduate Programs, School of Education, Program in Middle Childhood/Adolescence Education (Grades 5-12), Purchase, NY 10577-2132. Offers biology (MAT); biology and special education (MPS); chemistry (MAT); chemistry and special education (MPS); English (MAT); English and special education (MPS); literacy (MPS), including reading and writing, writing; literacy and special education (MPS); math (MAT); math and special education (MPS); second language (MAT), including French, Italian, Latin, Spanish; social studies (MAT); social studies and special education (MPS); special education (MPS). Part-time and evening/weekend programs available. *Students:* 52 full-time (39 women), 106 part-time (71 women); includes 8 African Americans, 3 Asian Americans or Pacific Islanders, 4 Hispanic Americans, 1 international. In 2009, 82 master's awarded. *Degree requirements:* For master's, comprehensive exam or research project, field experience. *Entrance requirements:* For master's, minimum undergraduate GPA of 3.0, 2 letters of recommendation. Additional exam requirements/recommendations for international students: Required—TOEFL. *Application deadline:* Applications are processed on a rolling basis. Application fee: $70. Electronic applications accepted. *Financial support:* Career-related internships or fieldwork, Federal Work-Study, institutionally sponsored loans, and unspecified assistantships available. Support available to part-time students. Financial award application deadline: 3/1; financial award applicants required to submit FAFSA. *Unit head:* Dr. Shelley Wepner, Dean, 914-323-5192, Fax: 914-694-2386, E-mail: wepners@mville.edu. *Application contact:* Jeanine Pardey-Levine, Director of Admissions, 914-323-3208, Fax: 914-694-1732, E-mail: edschool@mville.edu.

Marquette University, Graduate School, College of Arts and Sciences, Department of Foreign Languages and Literatures, Milwaukee, WI 53201-1881. Offers Spanish (MA, MAT). Part-time programs available. *Faculty:* 33 full-time (21 women), 7 part-time/adjunct (5 women). *Students:* 7 full-time (4 women), 4 part-time (all women); includes 3 minority (all Hispanic Americans), 2 international. Average age 29. 10 applicants, 80% accepted, 5 enrolled. In 2009, 6 master's awarded. *Degree requirements:* For master's, one foreign language, comprehensive exam or thesis. *Entrance requirements:* Additional exam requirements/recommendations for international students: Required—TOEFL. Application fee: $40. *Financial support:* In 2009–10, 5 research assistantships were awarded; teaching assistantships, Federal Work-Study, institutionally sponsored loans, scholarships/grants, and tuition waivers (full and partial) also available. Support available to part-time students. Financial award application deadline: 2/15. *Faculty research:* Magic realism, African-Hispanic literature, women studies, Hispanic linguistics. *Unit head:* Dr. Belen Castaneda, Chair, 414-288-7063, Fax: 414-288-1578. *Application contact:* Dr. Armando Gonzales-Percz, Director of Graduate Studies, 414-288-7268, Fax: 414-288-1578.

McGill University, Faculty of Graduate and Postdoctoral Studies, Faculty of Education, Department of Integrated Studies in Education, Montréal, QC H3A 2T5, Canada. Offers culture and values in education (MA, PhD); curriculum studies (MA); educational leadership (MA, Certificate); educational studies (PhD); integrated studies in education (M Ed); second language education (MA, PhD).

Michigan State University, The Graduate School, College of Arts and Letters, Program in Second Language Studies, East Lansing, MI 48824. Offers PhD. *Accreditation:* Teacher Education Accreditation Council. *Students:* 29 full-time (20 women), 2 part-time (1 woman); includes 1 minority (African American), 21 international. Average age 32. 63 applicants, 10% accepted. In 2009, 2 doctorates awarded. *Entrance requirements:* Additional exam requirements/recommendations for international students: Required—TOEFL, Michigan State University ELT (minimum score 85), Michigan Michigan English Language Assessment Battery (minimum score 83). Electronic applications accepted. *Expenses:* Tuition, state resident: part-time $478.25 per credit hour. Tuition, nonresident: part-time $966.50 per credit hour. Part-time tuition and fees vary according to program. *Financial support:* In 2009–10, 14 research assistantships with tuition reimbursements (averaging $6,104 per year), 15 teaching assistantships with tuition reimbursements (averaging $6,114 per year) were awarded. *Unit head:* Dr. Susan Mary Gass, Director, 517-432-1812, Fax: 517-353-9637, E-mail: gass@msu.edu. *Application contact:* Joan Reid, Graduate Secretary, 517-432-1812, Fax: 517-353-9637, E-mail: sls@msu.edu.

Middle Tennessee State University, College of Graduate Studies, College of Liberal Arts, Department of Foreign Languages and Literatures, Murfreesboro, TN 37132. Offers English as a second language (M Ed); foreign language (MAT). Part-time and evening/weekend programs available. Postbaccalaureate distance learning degree programs offered. *Faculty:* 14 full-time

(8 women). *Students:* 5 full-time (3 women), 11 part-time (8 women); includes 3 minority (1 African American, 1 Asian American or Pacific Islander, 1 Hispanic American). Average age 30. 15 applicants, 87% accepted, 13 enrolled. In 2009, 6 master's awarded. *Degree requirements:* For master's, one foreign language, comprehensive exam. *Entrance requirements:* For master's, GRE. Additional exam requirements/recommendations for international students: Required—TOEFL (minimum score 525 paper-based; 195 computer-based; 71 iBT) or IELTS (minimum score 6). *Application deadline:* For fall admission, 6/1 for domestic and international students. Applications are processed on a rolling basis. Application fee: $25 ($30 for international students). Electronic applications accepted. *Expenses:* Tuition, state resident: full-time $4404. Tuition, nonresident: full-time $10,956. *Financial support:* In 2009–10, 15 students received support. Career-related internships or fieldwork and institutionally sponsored loans available. Support available to part-time students. Financial award application deadline: 5/1; financial award applicants required to submit FAFSA. *Faculty research:* Literature and linguistics, French literature, interactive material design, Holocaust literature, foreign language pedagogy. *Unit head:* Dr. Joan McRae, Chair, 615-898-2981, Fax: 615-898-5826, E-mail: jmcrae@mtsu.edu. *Application contact:* Dr. Michael Allen, Dean and Vice Provost for Research, 615-898-2840, Fax: 615-904-8020, E-mail: mallen@mtsu.edu.

Mills College, Graduate Studies, School of Education, Oakland, CA 94613-1000. Offers child life in hospitals (MA); early childhood education (MA); education (MA), including art education, curriculum and instruction, elementary education, English education, foreign language education, mathematics education, science education, secondary education, social studies education, teaching; educational leadership (MA, Ed D); infant mental health (MA). Part-time and evening/weekend programs available. *Faculty:* 11 full-time (9 women), 16 part-time/adjunct (14 women). *Students:* 138 full-time (119 women), 55 part-time (48 women); includes 71 minority (34 African Americans, 19 Asian Americans or Pacific Islanders, 18 Hispanic Americans), 3 international. Average age 34. 210 applicants, 82% accepted, 93 enrolled. In 2009, 54 master's, 15 doctorates awarded. Terminal master's awarded for partial completion of doctoral program. *Degree requirements:* For master's, comprehensive exam. *Entrance requirements:* For doctorate, GRE General Test. Additional exam requirements/recommendations for international students: Required—TOEFL. *Application deadline:* For fall admission, 2/1 for domestic and international students; for spring admission, 11/1 for domestic and international students. Applications are processed on a rolling basis. Application fee: $50. Electronic applications accepted. *Expenses:* Tuition: Full-time $26,326; part-time $6584 per course. Required fees: $896. One-time fee: $896 part-time. Tuition and fees vary according to program. *Financial support:* In 2009–10, 188 students received support, including 186 fellowships (averaging $6,499 per year), 28 teaching assistantships with partial tuition reimbursements available (averaging $3,187 per year); career-related internships or fieldwork and scholarships/grants also available. Support available to part-time students. Financial award application deadline: 2/1; financial award applicants required to submit FAFSA. *Faculty research:* Child development, gender and education, public policy, cross-cultural development, development of literacy. Total annual research expenditures: $1.2 million. *Unit head:* Joseph Kahne, Chairperson, 510-430-3190, Fax: 510-430-3314, E-mail: grad-studies@mills.edu. *Application contact:* Jessica King, Graduate Admission Specialist, 510-430-3305, Fax: 510-430-2159, E-mail: grad-studies@mills.edu.

Mississippi State University, College of Arts and Sciences, Department of Foreign Languages, Mississippi State, MS 39762. Offers foreign language (MA), including French, German, Spanish. Part-time programs available. *Faculty:* 8 full-time (3 women). *Students:* 9 full-time (7 women), 2 part-time (1 woman); includes 1 minority (Hispanic American), 3 international. Average age 31. 5 applicants, 100% accepted, 3 enrolled. In 2009, 5 master's awarded. *Degree requirements:* For master's, one foreign language, comprehensive exam (for some programs), thesis optional, comprehensive oral or written exam. *Entrance requirements:* For master's, minimum GPA of 2.75 on last two years of undergraduate courses. Additional exam requirements/recommendations for international students: Required—TOEFL (minimum score 525 paper-based). *Application deadline:* For fall admission, 7/1 for domestic students, 5/1 for international students; for spring admission, 11/1 for domestic students, 9/1 for international students. Applications are processed on a rolling basis. Application fee: $40. Electronic applications accepted. *Expenses:* Tuition, state resident: full-time $2575.50; part-time $286.25 per credit hour. Tuition, nonresident: full-time $6510; part-time $723.50 per credit hour. Tuition and fees vary according to course load. *Financial support:* In 2009–10, 7 teaching assistantships with full tuition reimbursements (averaging $8,766 per year) were awarded; Federal Work-Study, institutionally sponsored loans, and unspecified assistantships also available. Financial award application deadline: 4/1; financial award applicants required to submit FAFSA. *Faculty research:* French, German, Spanish literature from medieval era to present; gender and cultural studies in French; Spanish American literature; foreign language methodology; linguistics. *Unit head:* Dr. Jack Jordan, Professor/Head, 662-325-3480, Fax: 662-325-8209, E-mail: jordan@ra.msstate.edu. *Application contact:* Dr. Edward T. Potter, Assistant Professor/Graduate Coordinator, 662-325-2399, Fax: 662-325-8209, E-mail: ep75@.msstate.edu.

Missouri State University, Graduate College, College of Arts and Letters, Department of Modern and Classical Languages, Springfield, MO 65897. Offers secondary education (MS Ed), including Spanish. Part-time programs available. *Faculty:* 4 full-time (1 woman). *Students:* 1 (woman) full-time, 3 part-time (2 women); includes 1 minority (Hispanic American). Average age 37. In 2009, 1 master's awarded. *Entrance requirements:* For master's, grades 9-12 teaching certification. Additional exam requirements/recommendations for international students: Required—TOEFL (minimum score 550 paper-based; 213 computer-based; 79 iBT), IELTS (minimum score 6). *Application deadline:* For fall admission, 7/20 priority date for domestic students, 5/1 for international students; for spring admission, 12/20 priority date for domestic students, 9/1 for international students. Applications are processed on a rolling basis. Application fee: $35 ($50 for international students). Electronic applications accepted. *Expenses:* Tuition, state resident: full-time $3852; part-time $214 per credit hour. Tuition, nonresident: full-time $7524; part-time $418 per credit hour. Required fees: $696; $172 per semester. Tuition and fees vary according to course level, course load, degree level and program. *Financial support:* Federal Work-Study, scholarships/grants, and unspecified assistantships available. Financial award applicants required to submit FAFSA. *Unit head:* Dr. Madeleine Kernen, Head, 417-836-7626, E-mail: mcl@missouristate.edu. *Application contact:* Eric Eckert, Coordinator of Admissions and Recruitment, 417-836-5331, Fax: 417-836-6888, E-mail: ericeckert@missouristate.edu.

Monterey Institute of International Studies, Graduate School of Translation, Interpretation and Language Education, Program in Teaching Foreign Language, Monterey, CA 93940-2691. Offers MATFL. *Students:* 10 full-time (9 women), 28 part-time (15 women); includes 6 minority (2 African Americans, 4 Asian Americans or Pacific Islanders), 9 international. Average age 40. In 2009, 12 master's awarded. *Degree requirements:* For master's, one foreign language, portfolio, oral defense. *Entrance requirements:* For master's, minimum GPA of 3.0, proficiency in foreign language. Additional exam requirements/recommendations for international students: Required—TOEFL (minimum score 600 paper-based; 250 computer-based; 100 iBT). *Application deadline:* For fall admission, 3/15 priority date for domestic and international students; for spring admission, 10/1 priority date for domestic and international students. Applications are processed on a rolling basis. Application fee: $50. Electronic applications accepted. *Expenses:* Tuition: Full-time $31,000; part-time $1500 per credit. Required fees: $56. *Financial support:* Application deadline: 3/15. *Application contact:* 831-647-4123, Fax: 831-647-6405, E-mail: admit@miis.edu.

See Close-Up on page 1119.

Morehead State University, Graduate Programs, College of Education, Department of Middle Grades and Secondary Education, Morehead, KY 40351. Offers business and marketing education (MAT); English/language arts 5-9 (MAT); French (MAT); health P-12 (MAT); mathematics 5-9 (MAT); physical education P-12 (MAT); science 5-9 (MAT); secondary biology (MAT); secondary chemistry (MAT); secondary earth science (MAT); secondary English (MAT); secondary math (MAT); secondary physics (MAT); secondary social studies (MAT); social studies 5-9 (MAT); Spanish (MAT). Part-time and evening/weekend programs available. *Students:* 54 full-time (31 women), 233 part-time (142 women); includes 11 minority (5 African Americans, 1 American Indian/Alaska Native, 1 Asian American or Pacific Islander, 4 Hispanic Americans). Average age 32. 206 applicants, 71% accepted, 79 enrolled. In 2009, 101 master's awarded. *Degree requirements:* For master's, portfolio. *Entrance requirements:* For master's, GRE or PRAXIS II content exam, minimum overall undergraduate GPA of 2.5. Additional exam requirements/recommendations for international students: Required—TOEFL (minimum score 500 paper-based; 173 computer-based). *Application deadline:* For fall admission, 8/1 priority date for domestic and international students; for spring admission, 12/1 priority date for domestic and international students. Applications are processed on a rolling basis. Application fee: $30. Electronic applications accepted. *Expenses:* Tuition, state resident: full-time $6318; part-time $351 per credit hour. Tuition, nonresident: full-time $15,804; part-time $878 per credit hour. *Financial support:* In 2009–10, 1 research assistantship (averaging $10,000 per year) was awarded; career-related internships or fieldwork, Federal Work-Study, and unspecified assistantships also available. Financial award application deadline: 3/15; financial award applicants required to submit FAFSA. *Unit head:* Dr. Cathy Gunn, Dean, 606-783-2040, Fax: 606-783-5029, E-mail: c.gunn@moreheadstate.edu. *Application contact:* Michelle Barber, Graduate Recruitment and Retention Assistant Director, 606-783-5127, Fax: 606-783-5061, E-mail: m.barber@moreheadstate.edu.

New York University, NYU in Paris, Paris, NY 10012-1019, France. Offers teaching French as a foreign language (MA). *Students:* 7 full-time (6 women), 2 part-time (both women); includes 1 Asian American or Pacific Islander, 1 Hispanic American. Average age 29. 13 applicants, 85% accepted, 7 enrolled. In 2009, 20 master's awarded. Application fee: $90. *Expenses:* Tuition: Full-time $30,528; part-time $1272 per credit. Required fees: $2177. *Unit head:* Henriette Goldwyn, Acting Director, 212-998-7625, Fax: 212-995-4667, E-mail: nyuparis@nyu.edu. *Application contact:* Henriette Goldwyn, Acting Director, 212-998-7625, Fax: 212-995-4667, E-mail: nyuparis@nyu.edu.

New York University, Steinhardt School of Culture, Education, and Human Development, Department of Teaching and Learning, Program in Multilingual/Multicultural Studies, New York, NY 10012-1019. Offers bilingual education (MA, PhD, Advanced Certificate); foreign language education (MA, Advanced Certificate); foreign language education/TESOL (MA); teaching English to speakers of other languages (MA, PhD, Advanced Certificate); teaching French as a foreign language (MA). *Accreditation:* Teacher Education Accreditation Council. Part-time and evening/weekend programs available. *Students:* 138 full-time (121 women), 97 part-time (78 women); includes 49 minority (4 African Americans, 25 Asian Americans or Pacific Islanders, 20 Hispanic Americans), 79 international. Average age 28. 330 applicants, 75% accepted, 88 enrolled. In 2009, 120 master's, 5 doctorates, 13 other advanced degrees awarded. *Degree requirements:* For master's, thesis (for some programs); for doctorate, thesis/dissertation. *Entrance requirements:* For doctorate, GRE General Test, interview; for Advanced Certificate, master's degree. Additional exam requirements/recommendations for international students: Required—TOEFL. *Application deadline:* For fall admission, 12/15 priority date for domestic and international students; for spring admission, 11/1 for domestic and international students. Applications are processed on a rolling basis. Application fee: $75. Electronic applications accepted. *Expenses:* Tuition: Full-time $30,528; part-time $1272 per credit. Required fees: $2177. *Financial support:* Fellowships with full and partial tuition reimbursements, career-related internships or fieldwork, Federal Work-Study, institutionally sponsored loans, scholarships/grants, and tuition waivers (partial) available. Support available to part-time students. Financial award application deadline: 2/1; financial award applicants required to submit FAFSA. *Faculty research:* Second language acquisition, cross-cultural communication, technology-enhanced language learning, language variation, action learning. *Unit head:* Dr. Miriam Eisenstein Ebsworth, Director, 212-998-5460, Fax: 212-995-4049. *Application contact:* 212-998-5030, Fax: 212-995-4328, E-mail: steinhardt.gradadmissions@nyu.edu.

Northern Arizona University, Graduate College, College of Arts and Letters, Department of Modern Languages, Flagstaff, AZ 86011. Offers Spanish teaching (MAT); Spanish teaching/Spanish education (MAT). *Faculty:* 23 full-time (16 women). *Students:* 12 full-time (7 women), 1 (woman) part-time; includes 4 minority (all Hispanic Americans), 2 international. Average age 30. 5 applicants, 100% accepted, 4 enrolled. *Degree requirements:* For master's, thesis optional. *Entrance requirements:* For master's, BA in Spanish or other foreign language, or minimum GPA of 3.0. Additional exam requirements/recommendations for international students: Required—TOEFL (minimum score 550 paper-based; 213 computer-based; 80 iBT), IELTS (minimum score 7), or a bachelor's degree from an English-speaking university and demonstrated proficiency. *Application deadline:* For fall admission, 4/21 priority date for domestic students, 9/21 priority date for international students; for spring admission, 10/21 priority date for domestic students. Applications are processed on a rolling basis. Application fee: $65. Electronic applications accepted. *Financial support:* Teaching assistantships, tuition waivers (full and partial) available. Financial award application deadline: 3/30. *Unit head:* Joseph Collentine, Chair, 928-523-5334, Fax: 928-523-0963, E-mail: j.collentine@nau.edu. *Application contact:* Cecilia Ojeda, Coordinator, 928-523-5988, Fax: 928-523-0963, E-mail: cecilia.ojeda@nau.edu.

Occidental College, Graduate Studies, Department of Education, Program in Secondary Education, Los Angeles, CA 90041-3314. Offers English and comparative literary studies (MAT); history (MAT); life science (MAT); mathematics (MAT); physical science (MAT); social science (MAT); Spanish (MAT). Part-time programs available. *Degree requirements:* For master's, comprehensive exam, graduate synthesis paper. *Entrance requirements:* For master's, GRE General Test, minimum GPA of 3.0. Additional exam requirements/recommendations for international students: Required—TOEFL (minimum score 625 paper-based; 263 computer-based). *Expenses:* Contact institution.

Portland State University, Graduate Studies, College of Liberal Arts and Sciences, Department of Foreign Languages and Literatures, Portland, OR 97207-0751. Offers foreign literature and language (MA); French (MA); German (MA); Japanese (MA); Spanish (MA). Part-time programs available. *Degree requirements:* For master's, one foreign language, thesis (for some programs). *Entrance requirements:* Additional exam requirements/recommendations for international students: Required—TOEFL (minimum score 550 paper-based; 213 computer-based). *Faculty research:* Foreign language pedagogy, applied and social linguistics, literary history and criticism.

Purdue University, Graduate School, College of Liberal Arts, Department of Foreign Languages and Literatures, West Lafayette, IN 47907. Offers French (MA, MAT, PhD), including French (MA, PhD), French education (MAT); German (MA, MAT, PhD), including German (MA, PhD), German education (MAT); Spanish (MA, MAT, PhD), including Spanish (MA, PhD), Spanish education (MAT). Terminal master's awarded for partial completion of doctoral program. *Degree requirements:* For master's, one foreign language; for doctorate, 2 foreign languages, thesis/dissertation. *Entrance requirements:* For master's, GRE, sample recording of English and language of study; for doctorate, GRE, writing sample, sample recording of English and language of study. Additional exam requirements/recommendations for international students: Required—TOEFL. Electronic applications accepted. *Faculty research:* Linguistics, semiotics, literary criticism, pedagogy.

Purdue University, Graduate School, School of Education, Department of Curriculum and Instruction, West Lafayette, IN 47907. Offers agricultural and extension education (PhD, Ed S); agriculture and extension education (MS, MS Ed); art education (PhD); consumer and family sciences and extension education (MS Ed, PhD, Ed S); curriculum studies (MS Ed, PhD, Ed S); educational technology (MS Ed, PhD, Ed S); elementary education (MS Ed); foreign language education (MS Ed, PhD, Ed S); industrial technology (PhD, Ed S); language arts (MS Ed, PhD, Ed S); literacy (MS Ed, PhD, Ed S); mathematics/science education (MS, MS Ed, PhD, Ed S); social studies (MS Ed, PhD); social studies education (Ed S); vocational/industrial education (MS Ed, PhD, Ed S); vocational/technical education (MS Ed, PhD, Ed S). *Accreditation:* NCATE. Part-time and evening/weekend programs available. *Degree requirements:* For master's, thesis optional; for doctorate, thesis/dissertation, oral and written exams; for Ed S, oral presentation, project. *Entrance requirements:* For master's, GRE General Test, minimum B average; for doctorate, GRE General Test; for Ed S, GRE, minimum B average. Additional exam requirements/recommendations for international students: Required—TOEFL.

Foreign Languages Education

Purdue University (continued)

Electronic applications accepted. *Faculty research:* Literacy acquisition and development, teacher beliefs and knowledge, recruitment and retention of underrepresented students, economic education, literacy discourse.

Queens College of the City University of New York, Division of Graduate Studies, Division of Education, Department of Secondary Education, Flushing, NY 11367-1597. Offers art (MS Ed); biology (MS Ed, AC); chemistry (MS Ed, AC); earth sciences (MS Ed, AC); English (MS Ed, AC); French (MS Ed, AC); Italian (MS Ed, AC); mathematics (MS Ed, AC); music (MS Ed, AC); physics (MS Ed, AC); social studies (MS Ed, AC); Spanish (MS Ed, AC). Part-time and evening/weekend programs available. *Faculty:* 22 full-time (14 women). *Students:* 86 full-time (47 women), 1,118 part-time (736 women). 591 applicants, 60% accepted, 250 enrolled. In 2009, 187 master's awarded. *Degree requirements:* For master's, research project; for AC, thesis optional. *Entrance requirements:* For master's, minimum GPA of 3.0. Additional exam requirements/recommendations for international students: Required—TOEFL. *Application deadline:* For fall admission, 4/1 for domestic students; for spring admission, 11/1 for domestic students. Applications are processed on a rolling basis. Application fee: $125. *Expenses:* Tuition, state resident: full-time $7360; part-time $310 per credit. Tuition, nonresident: part-time $575 per credit. One-time fee: $195 full-time; $145.25 part-time. *Financial support:* Career-related internships or fieldwork, Federal Work-Study, institutionally sponsored loans, and tuition waivers (partial) available. Support available to part-time students. Financial award application deadline: 4/1; financial award applicants required to submit FAFSA. *Unit head:* Dr. Eleanor Armour-Thomas, Chairperson, 718-997-5150, E-mail: armourthomas@yahoo.com. *Application contact:* Mario Caruso, Director of Graduate Admissions, 718-997-5200, Fax: 718-997-5193, E-mail: graduate_admissions@qc.edu.

Quinnipiac University, Division of Education, Program in Secondary Education, Hamden, CT 06518-1940. Offers biology (MAT); English (MAT); history/social studies (MAT); mathematics (MAT); Spanish (MAT). *Accreditation:* NCATE. *Faculty:* 10 full-time (7 women), 5 part-time/adjunct (3 women). *Students:* 80 full-time (56 women), 2 part-time (1 woman); includes 6 minority (2 African Americans, 2 Asian Americans or Pacific Islanders, 2 Hispanic Americans). 77 applicants, 95% accepted, 66 enrolled. In 2009, 33 master's awarded. *Entrance requirements:* For master's, PRAXIS I, minimum GPA of 2.67, interview. Additional exam requirements/recommendations for international students: Required—TOEFL (minimum score 575 paper-based; 233 computer-based; 90 iBT), IELTS (minimum score 6.5). *Application deadline:* For fall admission, 3/31 priority date for domestic students. Applications are processed on a rolling basis. Application fee: $45. Electronic applications accepted. *Expenses:* Tuition: Full-time $16,030; part-time $770 per credit. Required fees: $630; $35 per credit. *Financial support:* Career-related internships or fieldwork, scholarships/grants, and tuition waivers (partial) available. Financial award application deadline: 4/15; financial award applicants required to submit FAFSA. *Faculty research:* Multicultural and urban education, role of technology in education, challenges of teaching diverse learners, socio-cultural nature of learning. *Unit head:* Dr. Bernadine Krawczyk, Assistant Dean, Division of Education, 203-582-3510, Fax: 203-582-3473, E-mail: bernadine.krawczyk@quinnipiac.edu. *Application contact:* Jennifer Boutin, Associate Director of Graduate Admissions, 800-462-1944, Fax: 203-582-3443, E-mail: jennifer.boutin@quinnipiac.edu.

Rhode Island College, School of Graduate Studies, Feinstein School of Education and Human Development, Department of Educational Studies, Providence, RI 02908-1991. Offers English (MAT); French (MAT); history (MAT); math (MAT); secondary education (MAT); Spanish (MAT); teaching English as a second language (M Ed); technology education (M Ed). *Accreditation:* NCATE. Part-time and evening/weekend programs available. *Faculty:* 10 full-time (5 women), 6 part-time/adjunct (5 women). *Students:* 8 full-time (all women), 56 part-time (40 women); includes 2 minority (both Hispanic Americans). Average age 35. In 2009, 28 master's awarded. *Degree requirements:* For master's, capstone or comprehensive assessment. *Entrance requirements:* For master's, GRE or MAT (for most programs), minimum undergraduate GPA of 3.0; baccalaureate degree in English, French, history, math or Spanish; evaluation of content area knowledge; 3 letters of recommendation; interview. Additional exam requirements/recommendations for international students: Recommended—TOEFL (minimum score 550 paper-based; 213 computer-based; 79 iBT). *Application deadline:* For fall admission, 3/15 for domestic students; for spring admission, 11/1 for domestic students. Applications are processed on a rolling basis. Application fee: $50. *Expenses:* Tuition, state resident: full-time $7440; part-time $310 per credit hour. Tuition, nonresident: full-time $14,784; part-time $616 per credit hour. Required fees: $552; $20 per credit. $70 per term. *Financial support:* Teaching assistantships with full tuition reimbursements, career-related internships or fieldwork, Federal Work-Study, scholarships/grants, health care benefits, and unspecified assistantships available. Support available to part-time students. Financial award application deadline: 5/15; financial award applicants required to submit FAFSA. *Faculty research:* School administration, school/college articulation. *Unit head:* Dr. Ellen Bigler, Chair, 401-456-8170. *Application contact:* Graduate Studies, 401-456-8700.

Rider University, Department of Graduate Education, Leadership and Counseling, Teacher Certification Program, Lawrenceville, NJ 08648-3001. Offers business education (Certificate); elementary education (Certificate); English as a second language (Certificate); English education (Certificate); mathematics education (Certificate); preschool to grade 3 (Certificate); science education (Certificate); social studies education (Certificate); world languages (Certificate), including French, German, Spanish. Part-time programs available. *Degree requirements:* For Certificate, internship, professional portfolio. *Entrance requirements:* For degree, PRAXIS, resume. Additional exam requirements/recommendations for international students: Required—TOEFL (minimum score 550 paper-based; 213 computer-based). Electronic applications accepted. *Faculty research:* Conceptual foundations for optimal development of creativity; creative theory, cognitive processes in mathematics learning, teacher collaboration.

Rivier College, School of Graduate Studies, Department of Modern Languages, Nashua, NH 03060. Offers Spanish (MAT). Part-time and evening/weekend programs available. *Application deadline:* Applications are processed on a rolling basis. Application fee: $25. *Expenses:* Tuition: Part-time $447 per credit. *Financial support:* Available to part-time students. Application deadline: 2/1. *Unit head:* Dr. Barry Jackson, Department Coordinator, 603-897-8204, E-mail: bjackson@rivier.edu. *Application contact:* Mathew Kittredge, Director of Graduate Admissions, 603-897-8229, Fax: 603-897-8810, E-mail: mkittredge@rivier.edu.

Rowan University, Graduate School, College of Education, Department of Teacher Education, Program in Foreign Language Education, Glassboro, NJ 08028-1701. Offers MST. Part-time and evening/weekend programs available. *Students:* 1 (woman) part-time. Average age 55. *Entrance requirements:* For master's, GRE General Test, minimum GPA of 2.8, 1year of teaching experience. Additional exam requirements/recommendations for international students: Required—TOEFL. *Application deadline:* Applications are processed on a rolling basis. Application fee: $50. Electronic applications accepted. *Expenses:* Tuition, state resident: full-time $10,624; part-time $590 per semester hour. Tuition, nonresident: full-time $10,624; part-time $590 per semester hour. Required fees: $2320; $125 per semester hour. *Financial support:* Career-related internships or fieldwork and unspecified assistantships available. Support available to part-time students. *Unit head:* Dr. Mira Lalovic-Hand, Interim Associate Provost/Director of Graduate School, 856-256-5120 Ext. 3812, E-mail: lalovic-hand@rowan.edu. *Application contact:* Karen Haynes, Graduate Coordinator, 856-256-4052, Fax: 856-256-4436, E-mail: haynes@rowan.edu.

Rutgers, The State University of New Jersey, New Brunswick, Graduate School-New Brunswick, Program in French, Piscataway, NJ 08854-8097. Offers French (MA, PhD); French studies (MAT). Part-time and evening/weekend programs available. Terminal master's awarded for partial completion of doctoral program. *Degree requirements:* For master's, one foreign language, written and oral exams (MA); for doctorate, 3 foreign languages, thesis/dissertation, qualifying exam. *Entrance requirements:* For master's and doctorate, GRE General Test. *Faculty research:* Literatures in French, literary history and theory, rhetoric and poetics.

Rutgers, The State University of New Jersey, New Brunswick, Graduate School-New Brunswick, Program in Italian, Piscataway, NJ 08854-8097. Offers Italian (MA, PhD); Italian literature and literary criticism (MA); language, literature and culture (MAT). Part-time and evening/weekend programs available. Terminal master's awarded for partial completion of doctoral program. *Degree requirements:* For master's, one foreign language, comprehensive exam (for some programs), thesis optional; for doctorate, 2 foreign languages, thesis/dissertation, qualifying exam. *Entrance requirements:* For master's and doctorate, GRE General Test. Additional exam requirements/recommendations for international students: Required—TOEFL. *Faculty research:* Literature.

Rutgers, The State University of New Jersey, New Brunswick, Graduate School-New Brunswick, Program in Spanish, Piscataway, NJ 08854-8097. Offers bilingualism and second language acquisition (MA, PhD); Spanish (MA, MAT, PhD); Spanish literature (MA, PhD); translation (MA). Part-time programs available. *Degree requirements:* For master's, comprehensive exam (for some programs), thesis (for some programs); for doctorate, 2 foreign languages, comprehensive exam, thesis/dissertation. *Entrance requirements:* For master's and doctorate, GRE General Test. Additional exam requirements/recommendations for international students: Required—TOEFL. Electronic applications accepted. *Faculty research:* Hispanic literature, Luso-Brazilian literature, Spanish linguistics, Spanish translation.

Rutgers, The State University of New Jersey, New Brunswick, Graduate School of Education, Department of Learning and Teaching, Program in Language Education, Piscataway, NJ 08854-8097. Offers English as a second language education (Ed M); language education (Ed M, Ed D). Part-time programs available. Terminal master's awarded for partial completion of doctoral program. *Degree requirements:* For master's, comprehensive exam; for doctorate, thesis/dissertation, concept paper, qualifying exam. *Entrance requirements:* For master's, GRE General Test, minimum GPA of 3.0; for doctorate, GRE General Test, minimum GPA of 3.5. Additional exam requirements/recommendations for international students: Required—TOEFL. Electronic applications accepted. *Faculty research:* Linguistics, sociolinguistics, cross-cultural/international communication.

St. John Fisher College, Ralph C. Wilson Jr. School of Education, Program in Adolescence Education/Special Education, Rochester, NY 14618-3597. Offers adolescence English (MS Ed); adolescence French (MS Ed); adolescence social studies (MS Ed); adolescence Spanish (MS Ed). Part-time and evening/weekend programs available. *Faculty:* 3 full-time (1 woman), 1 (woman) part-time/adjunct. *Students:* 39 full-time (18 women), 5 part-time (2 women); includes 7 minority (1 African American, 2 American Indian/Alaska Native, 1 Asian American or Pacific Islander, 3 Hispanic Americans). Average age 28. 39 applicants, 90% accepted, 20 enrolled. In 2009, 17 master's awarded. *Degree requirements:* For master's, field experiences, student teaching, LAST. *Entrance requirements:* For master's, 2 letters of recommendation, personal statement, current resume. Additional exam requirements/recommendations for international students: Required—TOEFL (minimum score 575 paper-based; 233 computer-based; 80 iBT). *Application deadline:* Applications are processed on a rolling basis. Application fee: $30. Electronic applications accepted. *Expenses:* Tuition: Part-time $680 per credit hour. Required fees: $25 per semester. Tuition and fees vary according to degree level and program. *Financial support:* In 2009–10, 40 students received support. Federal Work-Study and scholarships/grants available. Financial award applicants required to submit FAFSA. *Faculty research:* Arts and humanities, urban schools, constructivist learning, at risk students, mentoring. *Unit head:* Dr. Russell Coward, Program Director, 585-385-8114, E-mail: rcoward@sjfc.edu. *Application contact:* Jose Perales, Director of Graduate Admissions, 585-385-8067, E-mail: jperales@sjfc.edu.

Shippensburg University of Pennsylvania, School of Graduate Studies, College of Education and Human Services, Department of Teacher Education, Shippensburg, PA 17257-2299. Offers curriculum and instruction (M Ed), including biology, early childhood education, elementary education, English, foreign languages, geography/earth science, history, mathematics, middle school education; reading (M Ed). *Accreditation:* NCATE. Part-time and evening/weekend programs available. *Degree requirements:* For master's, comprehensive exam (for some programs), thesis optional, practicum or internship (for some programs). *Entrance requirements:* For master's, MAT (if GPA less than 2.75), interview, 3 letters of recommendation, writing sample of teaching background and future goals. Additional exam requirements/recommendations for international students: Required—TOEFL (minimum score 560 paper-based; 220 computer-based); Recommended—IELTS (minimum score 6). Electronic applications accepted.

SIT Graduate Institute, Graduate Programs, Programs in Language Teacher Education, Brattleboro, VT 05302-0676. Offers English for speakers of other languages (MAT); French (MAT); Spanish (MAT). *Degree requirements:* For master's, one foreign language, thesis, teaching practice. *Entrance requirements:* For master's, 4 letters of reference. Additional exam requirements/recommendations for international students: Required—TOEFL.

Smith College, Graduate and Special Programs, Department of Education and Child Study, Program in Secondary Education, Northampton, MA 01063. Offers biological sciences education (MAT); chemistry education (MAT); English education (MAT); French education (MAT); geology education (MAT); government education (MAT); history education (MAT); mathematics education (MAT); physics education (MAT); Spanish education (MAT). Part-time programs available. *Faculty:* 6 full-time (4 women), 3 part-time/adjunct (2 women). *Students:* 7 full-time (4 women), 1 part-time (0 women). Average age 25. 14 applicants, 100% accepted, 8 enrolled. In 2009, 9 master's awarded. *Entrance requirements:* Additional exam requirements/recommendations for international students: Required—TOEFL (minimum score 590 paper-based; 243 computer-based; 97 iBT). *Application deadline:* For fall admission, 4/1 for domestic students, 1/15 priority date for international students; for spring admission, 12/1 for domestic students. Application fee: $60. *Financial support:* In 2009–10, 6 students received support. Career-related internships or fieldwork, institutionally sponsored loans, and scholarships/grants available. Support available to part-time students. Financial award application deadline: 1/15; financial award applicants required to submit CSS PROFILE or FAFSA. *Unit head:* Rosetta Cohen, Graduate Student Advisor, 413-585-3266, E-mail: rcohen@smith.edu. *Application contact:* Ruth Morgan, Administrative Assistant, 413-585-3050, Fax: 413-585-3054, E-mail: gradstdy@smith.edu.

Smith College, Graduate and Special Programs, Department of Spanish and Portuguese, Northampton, MA 01063. Offers Spanish (MAT). Part-time programs available. *Faculty:* 9 full-time (6 women). *Entrance requirements:* Additional exam requirements/recommendations for international students: Required—TOEFL (minimum score 590 paper-based; 243 computer-based; 97 iBT). *Application deadline:* For fall admission, 4/1 for domestic students, 1/15 for international students; for spring admission, 12/1 for domestic students. Application fee: $60. *Financial support:* Career-related internships or fieldwork, institutionally sponsored loans, and scholarships/grants available. Support available to part-time students. Financial award application deadline: 1/15. *Unit head:* Michelle Joffroy, Chair, 413-585-3452, E-mail: mjoffroy@smith.edu. *Application contact:* Ruth Morgan, Administrative Assistant, 413-585-3050, Fax: 413-585-3054, E-mail: gradstdy@smith.edu.

Soka University of America, Graduate School, Aliso Viejo, CA 92656. Offers teaching Japanese as a foreign language (Certificate). Evening/weekend programs available. *Entrance requirements:* For degree, bachelor's degree with minimum GPA of 3.0, proficiency in Japanese. Additional exam requirements/recommendations for international students: Required—TOEFL (minimum score 600 paper-based; 100 iBT).

Southern Illinois University Edwardsville, Graduate Studies and Research, School of Education, Department of Curriculum and Instruction, Program in Secondary Education, Edwardsville, IL 62026-0001. Offers art (MS Ed); biology (MS Ed); chemistry (MS Ed); earth and space sciences (MS Ed); English/language arts (MS Ed); foreign languages (MS Ed); history (MS Ed); mathematics (MS Ed); physics (MS Ed). *Accreditation:* NCATE. Part-time and evening/weekend programs available. *Students:* 24 part-time (19 women); includes 2 minority (1 African American, 1 Hispanic American). Average age 26. 13 applicants, 31% accepted. In

2009, 5 master's awarded. *Degree requirements:* For master's, thesis or alternative, final exam/paper. *Entrance requirements:* Additional exam requirements/recommendations for international students: Required—TOEFL (minimum score 550 paper-based; 213 computer-based; 79 iBT), IELTS (minimum score 6.5). *Application deadline:* For fall admission, 7/23 for domestic students, 6/1 for international students; for spring admission, 12/11 for domestic students, 10/1 for international students. Applications are processed on a rolling basis. Application fee: $30. Electronic applications accepted. *Expenses:* Tuition, state resident: part-time $1252.50 per semester. Tuition, nonresident: part-time $3131.25 per semester. Required fees: $586.85 per semester. Tuition and fees vary according to course load. *Financial support:* Fellowships, research assistantships, teaching assistantships, career-related internships or fieldwork, Federal Work-Study, institutionally sponsored loans, scholarships/grants, traineeships, and unspecified assistantships available. Support available to part-time students. Financial award application deadline: 3/1; financial award applicants required to submit FAFSA. *Unit head:* Dr. Kathy Bushrow, Director, 618-650-3082, E-mail: kbushro@siue.edu. *Application contact:* Dr. Kathy Bushrow, Director, 618-650-3082, E-mail: kbushro@siue.edu.

Southern Oregon University, Graduate Studies, College of Arts and Sciences, Department of Foreign Languages and Literatures, Ashland, OR 97520. Offers Spanish language teaching (MA).

Stanford University, School of Education, Teacher Education Program, Stanford, CA 94305-9991. Offers English education (MA); languages education (MA); mathematics education (MA); science education (MA); social studies education (MA). *Degree requirements:* For master's, thesis. *Entrance requirements:* For master's, GRE General Test. Electronic applications accepted. *Expenses:* Tuition: Full-time $37,380; part-time $2760 per quarter. Required fees: $501.

State University of New York at Binghamton, Graduate School, School of Education, Program in Adolescence Education, Binghamton, NY 13902-6000. Offers biology education (MAT, MS Ed, MST); earth science education (MAT, MS Ed, MST); English education (MAT, MS Ed, MST); French education (MAT, MST); mathematical sciences education (MAT, MS Ed, MST); physics (MAT, MS Ed, MST); social studies (MAT, MS Ed, MST); Spanish education (MAT, MST). *Accreditation:* Teacher Education Accreditation Council. Part-time and evening/weekend programs available. *Students:* 93 full-time (37 women), 21 part-time (8 women); includes 6 minority (2 Asian Americans or Pacific Islanders, 4 Hispanic Americans), 1 international. Average age 27. 69 applicants, 81% accepted, 46 enrolled. In 2009, 53 master's awarded. *Entrance requirements:* For master's, GRE General Test. Additional exam requirements/recommendations for international students: Required—TOEFL (minimum score 550 paper-based; 213 computer-based; 80 iBT). *Application deadline:* For fall admission, 2/1 priority date for domestic and international students; for spring admission, 10/15 priority date for domestic and international students. Applications are processed on a rolling basis. Application fee: $60. Electronic applications accepted. *Financial support:* Fellowships with partial tuition reimbursements, research assistantships with full and partial tuition reimbursements, teaching assistantships with full tuition reimbursements, career-related internships or fieldwork, Federal Work-Study, institutionally sponsored loans, scholarships/grants, health care benefits, tuition waivers (full), and unspecified assistantships available. Financial award application deadline: 2/15; financial award applicants required to submit FAFSA. *Unit head:* Dr. S. G. Grant, Dean of School of Education, 607-777-7329, E-mail: sggrant@binghamton.edu. *Application contact:* Victoria Williams, Recruiting and Admissions Coordinator, 607-777-2151, Fax: 607-777-2501, E-mail: vwilliam@binghamton.edu.

State University of New York at Plattsburgh, Division of Education, Health, and Human Services, Program in Teacher Education: Adolescence MST, Plattsburgh, NY 12901-2681. Offers adolescence education (MST); biology 7-12 (MST); chemistry 7-12 (MST); earth science 7-12 (MST); English 7-12 (MST); French 7-12 (MST); mathematics 7-12 (MST); physics 7-12 (MST); social studies 7-12 (MST); Spanish 7-12 (MST). *Accreditation:* Teacher Education Accreditation Council. Part-time and evening/weekend programs available. *Faculty:* 4 full-time (3 women), 2 part-time/adjunct (0 women). *Students:* 83 full-time (49 women), 5 part-time (3 women); includes 9 minority (2 African Americans, 1 American Indian/Alaska Native, 1 Asian American or Pacific Islander, 5 Hispanic Americans), 2 international. Average age 27. 72 applicants, 71% accepted, 44 enrolled. In 2009, 57 master's awarded. *Degree requirements:* For master's, portfolio. *Entrance requirements:* For master's, minimum GPA of 2.75. Additional exam requirements/recommendations for international students: Required—TOEFL (minimum score 550 paper-based; 213 computer-based; 79 iBT). *Application deadline:* For fall admission, 2/15 priority date for domestic students. Applications are processed on a rolling basis. Application fee: $75. *Expenses:* Tuition, state resident: full-time $8370; part-time $349 per credit hour. Tuition, nonresident: full-time $13,250; part-time $552 per credit hour. Required fees: $1130. *Financial support:* Application deadline: 4/15. *Unit head:* Dr. Robert Ackland, Coordinator, 518-564-5131, E-mail: acklanrt@plattsburgh.edu. *Application contact:* Marguerite Adelman, Assistant Director, Graduate Admissions, 518-564-4723, Fax: 518-564-4722, E-mail: adelmaml@plattsburgh.edu.

State University of New York College at Cortland, Graduate Studies, School of Arts and Sciences, Programs in Adolescence Education, Cortland, NY 13045. Offers biology (MAT, MS Ed); chemistry (MAT, MS Ed); earth science (MAT, MS Ed); English (MS Ed); French (MS Ed); mathematics (MAT, MS Ed); physics (MAT, MS Ed); social studies (MS Ed); Spanish (MS Ed). *Accreditation:* NCATE. Part-time and evening/weekend programs available. *Degree requirements:* For master's, one foreign language, comprehensive exam (for some programs), thesis (for some programs). *Entrance requirements:* For master's, GRE General Test.

Stony Brook University, State University of New York, School of Professional Development, Stony Brook, NY 11794. Offers biology-grade 7-12 (MAT); chemistry-grade 7-12 (MAT); coaching (Graduate Certificate); computer integrated engineering (Graduate Certificate); earth science-grade 7-12 (MAT); educational computing (Graduate Certificate); educational leadership (Advanced Certificate); English-grade 7-12 (MAT); environmental management (Graduate Certificate); environmental/occupational health and safety (Graduate Certificate); French-grade 7-12 (MAT); German-grade 7-12 (MAT); human resource management (Graduate Certificate); information systems management (Graduate Certificate); Italian-grade 7-12 (MAT); liberal studies (MA); mathematics-grade 7-12 (MAT); operation research (Graduate Certificate); physics-grade 7-12 (MAT); school administration and supervision (Graduate Certificate); school building leadership (Graduate Certificate); school district administration (Graduate Certificate); school district business leadership (Advanced Certificate); school district leadership (Graduate Certificate); social science and the professions (MPS), including environmental waste management, human resource management; social studies-grade 7-12 (MAT); Spanish-grade 7-12 (MAT); waste management (Graduate Certificate). Part-time and evening/weekend programs available. Postbaccalaureate distance learning degree programs offered. *Faculty:* 5 full-time (3 women), 131 part-time/adjunct (53 women). *Students:* 317 full-time (187 women), 1,200 part-time (773 women); includes 187 minority (77 African Americans, 2 American Indian/Alaska Native, 22 Asian Americans or Pacific Islanders, 86 Hispanic Americans), 11 international. Average age 28. In 2009, 597 master's, 234 other advanced degrees awarded. *Degree requirements:* For master's, one foreign language, thesis or alternative. *Application deadline:* Applications are processed on a rolling basis. Application fee: $62. *Expenses:* Tuition, state resident: full-time $8370; part-time $349 per credit. Tuition, nonresident: full-time $13,250; part-time $552 per credit. Required fees: $933. *Financial support:* Fellowships, research assistantships, teaching assistantships, career-related internships or fieldwork available. Support available to part-time students. *Unit head:* Dr. Paul J. Edelson, Dean, 631-632-7052, Fax: 631-632-9046, E-mail: paul.edelson@stonybrook.edu. *Application contact:* Dr. Paul J. Edelson, Dean, 631-632-7052, Fax: 631-632-9046, E-mail: paul.edelson@stonybrook.edu.

Teachers College, Columbia University, Graduate Faculty of Education, Department of Arts and Humanities, Program in Teaching of Spanish, New York, NY 10027-6696. Offers Ed M, MA, Ed D, Ed DCT, PhD. *Accreditation:* NCATE. Part-time programs available. *Students:* 2 part-time (both women); both minorities (both Hispanic Americans). Average age 50. Terminal master's awarded for partial completion of doctoral program. *Degree requirements:* For doctorate,

thesis/dissertation. *Application deadline:* For fall admission, 5/15 for domestic students; for spring admission, 12/1 for domestic students. Application fee: $75. *Financial support:* Career-related internships or fieldwork, Federal Work-Study, institutionally sponsored loans, and tuition waivers (full and partial) available. Support available to part-time students. Financial award application deadline: 2/1. *Faculty research:* Content of teacher training, curriculum, applied linguistics in the teaching of Spanish, distance learning, poetry in Spanish. *Unit head:* Graeme Sullivan, Chair, 212-678-3799. *Application contact:* Mark E. Stearns, Associate Director of Admission, 212-678-3710, Fax: 212-678-4171.

Temple University, Graduate School, College of Education, Department of Curriculum, Instruction, and Technology in Education, Philadelphia, PA 19122-6096. Offers applied behavioral analysis (MS Ed); career and technical education (MS Ed); early childhood education and elementary education (MS Ed); English education (MS Ed); language arts education (Ed D); math/science education (Ed D); mathematics education (MS Ed); science education (MS Ed); second and foreign language education (MS Ed); special education (MS Ed); teaching English as a second language (MS Ed). Part-time and evening/weekend programs available. Terminal master's awarded for partial completion of doctoral program. *Degree requirements:* For master's, thesis or alternative; for doctorate, thesis/dissertation. *Entrance requirements:* For master's and doctorate, GRE General Test or MAT, minimum GPA of 3.0. Additional exam requirements/recommendations for international students: Required—TOEFL (minimum score 550 paper-based; 213 computer-based; 79 iBT). Electronic applications accepted. *Faculty research:* School improvement, problem solving, literacy, language development.

Texas A&M International University, Office of Graduate Studies and Research, College of Arts and Sciences, Department of Language and Literature, Laredo, TX 78041-1900. Offers English (MA); Hispanic studies (PhD); Spanish (MA). *Faculty:* 6 full-time (3 women). *Students:* 4 full-time (3 women), 49 part-time (33 women); includes 46 minority (all Hispanic Americans), 1 international. Average age 34. 26 applicants. In 2009, 3 master's awarded. *Entrance requirements:* For master's, GRE General Test. Additional exam requirements/recommendations for international students: Required—TOEFL (minimum score 550 paper-based; 213 computer-based). *Application deadline:* For fall admission, 4/30 priority date for domestic students; for spring admission, 11/30 for domestic students. Applications are processed on a rolling basis. Application fee: $25. *Financial support:* In 2009–10, 12 students received support, including 1 fellowship, 1 research assistantship, 6 teaching assistantships. Financial award application deadline: 11/1. *Unit head:* Dr. Manuel Broncano, Chair, 956-326-2470, E-mail: manuel.broncano@tamiu.edu. *Application contact:* Rosie Espinoza-Dickinson, Director of Admissions, 956-326-2200, Fax: 956-326-2199, E-mail: enroll@tamiu.edu.

Texas A&M University–Kingsville, College of Graduate Studies, College of Arts and Sciences, Department of Language and Literature, Kingsville, TX 78363. Offers English (MA, MS); Spanish (MA). Part-time and evening/weekend programs available. *Degree requirements:* For master's, comprehensive exam, thesis or alternative. *Entrance requirements:* For master's, GRE General Test, minimum GPA of 3.0. Additional exam requirements/recommendations for international students: Required—TOEFL. *Faculty research:* Linguistics, culture, Spanish American literature, Spanish peninsular literature, American literature.

Union Graduate College, School of Education, Schenectady, NY 12308-3107. Offers biology (MAT, MS); chemistry (MAT); Chinese (MAT); earth science (MAT); English (MAT); French (MAT); general science (MAT); German (MAT); Greek (MAT); languages (MAT); Latin (MAT); mathematics (MAT); mathematics and technology (MS); mentoring and teacher leadership (AC); middle childhood extension (AC); national board certificate and teacher leadership (AC); physical science (MS); physics (MAT); social studies (MAT); Spanish (MAT). *Accreditation:* Teacher Education Accreditation Council. *Faculty:* 3 full-time (1 woman), 39 part-time/adjunct (19 women). *Students:* 46 full-time (27 women), 45 part-time (39 women); includes 5 minority (1 Asian American or Pacific Islander, 4 Hispanic Americans), 2 international. Average age 33. 66 applicants, 73% accepted, 39 enrolled. In 2009, 44 master's awarded. *Degree requirements:* For master's, thesis or project. *Entrance requirements:* For master's, minimum GPA of 3.0, letters of recommendation. Additional exam requirements/recommendations for international students: Required—TOEFL (minimum score 550 paper-based; 213 computer-based). *Application deadline:* Applications are processed on a rolling basis. Application fee: $60. Electronic applications accepted. *Expenses:* Contact institution. *Financial support:* In 2009–10, 12 research assistantships with tuition reimbursements (averaging $3,000 per year) were awarded; Federal Work-Study, scholarships/grants, health care benefits, and tuition waivers (partial) also available. Support available to part-time students. Financial award applicants required to submit FAFSA. *Faculty research:* Transformative learning, science education, National Board Certification, teacher leadership, teacher quality. *Unit head:* Dr. Patrick Allen, Dean, 518-631-9870, Fax: 518-631-9901. *Application contact:* Christine Angley, Assistant, 518-631-9871, Fax: 518-631-9903, E-mail: angleyc@uniongraduatecollege.edu.

Universidad del Este, Graduate School, Carolina, PR 00984. Offers accounting (MBA); adult education (M Ed); agribusiness (MBA); bilingual education (M Ed); criminal justice and criminology (MA); early education (M Ed); elementary education (M Ed); human resources (MBA); information security management (MBA); information technology and Web business development (MBA); management (MBA); public policy (MPA); social work (MA), including clinical social work; special education (M Ed); strategic leadership (MBA); teaching English (M Ed); teaching Spanish (M Ed).

University at Buffalo, the State University of New York, Graduate School, Graduate School of Education, Department of Learning and Instruction, Buffalo, NY 14260. Offers biology education (Ed M, Certificate); chemistry education (Ed M, Certificate); childhood education (Ed M); childhood education with bilingual extension (Ed M); early childhood education (Ed M); earth science education (Ed M, Certificate); elementary education (Ed D, PhD); English education (Ed M, PhD, Certificate); English for speakers of other languages (Ed M); foreign and second language education (PhD); French education (Ed M, Certificate); general education (Ed M); German education (Ed M, Certificate); gifted education (online) (Certificate); Latin education (Ed M, Certificate); literary specialist (Ed M); mathematics education (Ed M, PhD, Certificate); music education (Ed M, Certificate); physics education (Ed M, Certificate); reading education (PhD); science and the public (online) (Ed M); science education (PhD); social studies education (Ed M, Certificate); Spanish education (Ed M, Certificate); special education (PhD); teaching and leading for diversity (Certificate); teaching English to speakers of other languages (Ed M). Part-time and evening/weekend programs available. Postbaccalaureate distance learning degree programs offered (no on-campus study). *Faculty:* 34 full-time (24 women), 50 part-time/adjunct (39 women). *Students:* 332 full-time (245 women), 365 part-time (272 women); includes 50 minority (18 African Americans, 4 American Indian/Alaska Native, 10 Asian Americans or Pacific Islanders, 18 Hispanic Americans), 55 international. Average age 30. 627 applicants, 78% accepted, 286 enrolled. In 2009, 255 master's, 16 doctorates, 51 other advanced degrees awarded. *Degree requirements:* For master's, comprehensive exam; for doctorate, thesis/dissertation, research analysis exam, research experience component. *Entrance requirements:* For doctorate, GRE General Test or MAT, interview, writing sample, letters of recommendation. Additional exam requirements/recommendations for international students: Required—TOEFL (minimum score 600 paper-based; 250 computer-based; 96 iBT). *Application deadline:* For fall admission, 2/1 priority date for domestic and international students; for spring admission, 11/15 priority date for domestic students, 10/1 for international students. Applications are processed on a rolling basis. Application fee: $50. Electronic applications accepted. *Financial support:* In 2009–10, 23 fellowships with full tuition reimbursements (averaging $9,000 per year), 42 research assistantships with full tuition reimbursements (averaging $10,000 per year) were awarded; teaching assistantships with full tuition reimbursements, career-related internships or fieldwork, Federal Work-Study, institutionally sponsored loans, scholarships/grants, tuition waivers (partial), and unspecified assistantships also available. Financial award application deadline: 2/28; financial award applicants required to submit FAFSA. *Faculty research:* Science assessment, foreign language teaching and learning, early learning, new literacies, gender and education. Total annual research expenditures: $1.8 million. *Unit head:* Dr. Suzanne Miller, Chair, 716-645-2455, Fax: 716-645-3161, E-mail: smiller@buffalo.edu.

Foreign Languages Education

University at Buffalo, the State University of New York (continued)
Application contact: Cathy Dimino, Admissions Assistant, 716-645-2110, Fax: 716-645-7937, E-mail: cadimino@buffalo.edu.

University of Arkansas at Little Rock, Graduate School, College of Arts, Humanities, and Social Science, Department of International and Second Language Studies, Little Rock, AR 72204-1099. Offers second languages (MA).

University of Calgary, Faculty of Graduate Studies, Faculty of Education, Graduate Division of Educational Research, Calgary, AB T2N 1N4, Canada. Offers community rehabilitation and disability studies (M Ed, M Sc, Ed D, PhD, Graduate Certificate, Graduate Diploma); curriculum, teaching and learning (M Ed, M Sc, MA, Ed D, PhD, Graduate Certificate, Graduate Diploma); educational contexts (M Ed, MA, Ed D, PhD, Graduate Certificate, Graduate Diploma); educational leadership (M Ed, MA, Ed D, PhD, Graduate Certificate, Graduate Diploma); educational technology (M Ed, M Sc, MA, Ed D, PhD, Graduate Certificate, Graduate Diploma); gifted education (M Sc, MA, Ed D, PhD, Graduate Certificate, Graduate Diploma); higher education administration (Ed D); interpretive studies in education (M Ed, M Sc, MA, Ed D, PhD, Graduate Certificate, Graduate Diploma); second language teaching (M Ed, Ed D, PhD, Graduate Certificate, Graduate Diploma); teaching English as a second language (M Ed, M Sc, MA, Ed D, PhD, Graduate Certificate, Graduate Diploma); workplace and adult learning (M Ed, MA, Ed D, PhD, Graduate Certificate, Graduate Diploma). Ed D in both higher education administration and educational leadership offered via distance delivery. Part-time and evening/weekend programs available. Postbaccalaureate distance learning degree programs offered (minimal on-campus study). *Degree requirements:* For master's, thesis (for some programs); for doctorate, thesis/dissertation, candidacy exam. *Entrance requirements:* For master's, minimum GPA of 3.0, 3 letters of reference; for doctorate, minimum GPA of 3.5, 3 letters of reference; for other advanced degree, minimum GPA of 3.0. Additional exam requirements/recommendations for international students: Required—TOEFL, IELTS. Electronic applications accepted. *Faculty research:* Curriculum, leadership, technology, contexts, gifted, second language teaching, work place and adult learning.

University of California, Irvine, Office of Graduate Studies, School of Humanities, Department of Spanish and Portuguese, Irvine, CA 92697. Offers Spanish (MA, MAT, PhD). *Students:* 39 full-time (19 women), 3 part-time (2 women); includes 29 minority (1 Asian American or Pacific Islander, 28 Hispanic Americans). Average age 32. 57 applicants, 30% accepted, 8 enrolled. In 2009, 2 master's, 7 doctorates awarded. *Degree requirements:* For doctorate, thesis/dissertation. *Entrance requirements:* For master's and doctorate, GRE General Test, minimum GPA of 3.0. Additional exam requirements/recommendations for international students: Required—TOEFL (minimum score 550 paper-based; 213 computer-based). *Application deadline:* For fall admission, 1/2 priority date for domestic students, 1/2 for international students. Applications are processed on a rolling basis. Application fee: $70 ($90 for international students). Electronic applications accepted. *Financial support:* Fellowships, teaching assistantships, institutionally sponsored loans, traineeships, health care benefits, and unspecified assistantships available. Financial award application deadline: 3/1; financial award applicants required to submit FAFSA. *Faculty research:* Latin American literature, Spanish literature, Spanish linguistics in Creole studies, Hispanic literature in the U.S., Luso-Brazilian literature. *Unit head:* Ana Paula Ferreira, Chair, 949-824-7265, Fax: 949-824-2803, E-mail: apferrei@uci.edu. *Application contact:* Linda T. Le, Graduate Coordinator, 949-824-8793, Fax: 949-824-2803, E-mail: ttle@uci.edu.

University of Central Arkansas, Graduate School, College of Liberal Arts, Department of Foreign Languages, Conway, AR 72035-0001. Offers MA. Part-time programs available. *Faculty:* 4 full-time (2 women). *Students:* 6 full-time (5 women), 6 part-time (4 women); includes 5 minority (1 African American, 4 Hispanic Americans). Average age 31. 5 applicants, 100% accepted, 5 enrolled. In 2009, 3 master's awarded. *Degree requirements:* For master's, one foreign language, comprehensive exam, thesis optional. *Entrance requirements:* For master's, GRE General Test, minimum GPA of 2.7. Additional exam requirements/recommendations for international students: Required—TOEFL (minimum score 550 paper-based; 213 computer-based). *Application deadline:* For fall admission, 3/1 priority date for domestic and international students; for spring admission, 10/1 priority date for domestic and international students. Application fee: $25 ($50 for international students). *Expenses:* Tuition, state resident: full-time $5136; part-time $214 per credit hour. Required fees: $379.50; $127 per term. Tuition and fees vary according to course level, course load and campus/location. *Financial support:* In 2009–10, 2 teaching assistantships with partial tuition reimbursements (averaging $10,000 per year) were awarded. Financial award application deadline: 2/15; financial award applicants required to submit FAFSA. *Unit head:* Dr. Phillip Bailey, Chair, 501-450-5645, Fax: 501-450-5185, E-mail: phillipb@mail.uca.edu. *Application contact:* Brenda Herring, Admissions Assistant, 501-450-5065, Fax: 501-450-5678, E-mail: bherring@uca.edu.

University of Connecticut, Graduate School, Neag School of Education, Department of Curriculum and Instruction, Program in World Languages Education, Storrs, CT 06269. Offers MA, PhD, Post-Master's Certificate. *Accreditation:* NCATE. *Faculty:* 15 full-time (10 women). *Students:* 10 full-time (all women), 1 (woman) part-time; includes 4 minority (1 African American, 3 Hispanic Americans). Average age 27. 12 applicants, 42% accepted, 4 enrolled. In 2009, 5 master's awarded. Terminal master's awarded for partial completion of doctoral program. *Degree requirements:* For master's, comprehensive exam, thesis or alternative; for doctorate, thesis/dissertation. *Entrance requirements:* For doctorate, GRE General Test. Additional exam requirements/recommendations for international students: Required—TOEFL (minimum score 550 paper-based; 213 computer-based). *Application deadline:* For fall admission, 2/1 priority date for domestic and international students; for spring admission, 11/1 for domestic students, 10/1 for international students. Applications are processed on a rolling basis. Application fee: $55. Electronic applications accepted. *Expenses:* Tuition, state resident: full-time $4725; part-time $525 per credit. Tuition, nonresident: full-time $12,267; part-time $1363 per credit. Required fees: $346 per semester. Tuition and fees vary according to course load. *Financial support:* Research assistantships with full tuition reimbursements, teaching assistantships with full tuition reimbursements, Federal Work-Study, scholarships/grants, health care benefits, and unspecified assistantships available. Financial award application deadline: 2/1; financial award applicants required to submit FAFSA. *Unit head:* Mary Anne Doyle, Head, 860-486-2433, Fax: 860-486-0280, E-mail: mary.dolye@uconn.edu. *Application contact:* Lisa Rasicot, Graduate Coordinator, 860-486-3065, Fax: 860-486-0210, E-mail: l.rasicot@uconn.edu.

University of Delaware, College of Arts and Sciences, Department of Foreign Languages and Literatures, Newark, DE 19716. Offers foreign languages and literatures (MA), including French, German, Spanish; foreign languages pedagogy (MA), including French, German, Spanish. *Degree requirements:* For master's, one foreign language, comprehensive exam, thesis optional. *Entrance requirements:* For master's, GRE General Test, letters of recommendation, writing sample. Additional exam requirements/recommendations for international students: Required—TOEFL. Electronic applications accepted. *Faculty research:* Medieval to Modern French and Spanish literature, Twentieth Century German, French, Spanish literature by women, computer-assisted instruction.

University of Georgia, Graduate School, College of Education, Department of Language and Literacy Education, Athens, GA 30602. Offers English education (M Ed, Ed S); language and literacy education (PhD); reading education (M Ed, Ed D, Ed S); teaching additional languages (M Ed, Ed S). *Accreditation:* NCATE. *Faculty:* 18 full-time (12 women). *Students:* 85 full-time (64 women), 112 part-time (98 women); includes 24 minority (12 African Americans, 3 Asian Americans or Pacific Islanders, 9 Hispanic Americans), 19 international. 110 applicants, 47% accepted, 47 enrolled. In 2009, 45 master's, 8 doctorates, 15 other advanced degrees awarded. *Degree requirements:* For doctorate, variable foreign language requirement. *Entrance requirements:* For master's and Ed S, GRE General Test or MAT; for doctorate, GRE General Test. Additional exam requirements/recommendations for international students: Required—TOEFL (minimum score 550 paper-based; 213 computer-based). *Application deadline:* For fall admission, 7/1 priority date for domestic students; for spring admission, 11/15 for domestic students. Application fee: $50. Electronic applications accepted. *Expenses:* Tuition, state resident: full-time $6000; part-time $250 per credit hour. Tuition, nonresident: full-time $20,904; part-time $871 per credit hour. Required fees: $730 per semester. *Faculty research:* Comprehension, critical literacy, literacy and technology, vocabulary instruction, content area reading. *Unit head:* Dr. Mark A. Faust, Head, 706-542-4515, Fax: 706-542-4509, E-mail: mfaust@uga.edu. *Application contact:* Dr. Elizabeth St. Pierre, Graduate Coordinator, 706-542-4526, E-mail: stpierre@uga.edu.

University of Hawaii at Hilo, Program in Hawaiian and Indigenous Language and Cultural Revitalization, Hilo, HI 96720-4091. Offers PhD.

University of Hawaii at Hilo, Program in Hawaiian Language and Literature, Hilo, HI 96720-4091. Offers MA.

University of Hawaii at Manoa, Graduate Division, College of Language, Linguistics and Literature, Department of Second Language Studies, Honolulu, HI 96822. Offers English as a second language (MA, Graduate Certificate); second language acquisition (PhD). Part-time programs available. *Faculty:* 23 full-time (9 women), 3 part-time/adjunct (2 women). *Students:* 83 full-time (53 women), 20 part-time (12 women); includes 20 minority (1 African American, 19 Asian Americans or Pacific Islanders), 62 international. Average age 31. 129 applicants, 45% accepted, 31 enrolled. In 2009, 28 master's, 2 doctorates, 1 other advanced degree awarded. *Degree requirements:* For master's, 2 foreign languages, thesis optional; for doctorate, 2 foreign languages, comprehensive exam, thesis/dissertation. *Entrance requirements:* For master's, GRE General Test, minimum GPA of 3.0; for doctorate, GRE General Test, MA, scholarly publications. Additional exam requirements/recommendations for international students: Required—TOEFL (minimum score 600 paper-based; 250 computer-based; 100 iBT), IELTS (minimum score 7). *Application deadline:* For fall admission, 1/15 for domestic and international students; for spring admission, 9/1 for domestic and international students. Applications are processed on a rolling basis. Application fee: $60. *Expenses:* Tuition, state resident: full-time $8900; part-time $372 per credit. Tuition, nonresident: full-time $21,400; part-time $898 per credit. Required fees: $207 per semester. *Financial support:* In 2009–10, 24 fellowships (averaging $3,677 per year), 9 research assistantships (averaging $16,850 per year), 26 teaching assistantships (averaging $13,795 per year) were awarded; career-related internships or fieldwork, Federal Work-Study, institutionally sponsored loans, scholarships/grants, and tuition waivers (full and partial) also available. Financial award application deadline: 2/1; financial award applicants required to submit FAFSA. *Faculty research:* Second language use, second language analysis, second language pedagogy and testing, second language learning, qualitative and quantitative research methods for second languages. Total annual research expenditures: $360,000. *Application contact:* Thomas Hudson, Graduate Chair, 808-956-2799, Fax: 808-956-2802, E-mail: tdh@hawaii.edu.

University of Hawaii at Manoa, Graduate Division, School of Hawaiian Knowledge, Program in Hawaiian, Honolulu, HI 96822. Offers MA. Part-time programs available. *Faculty:* 5 full-time (3 women), 3 part-time/adjunct (2 women). *Students:* 13 full-time (8 women), 12 part-time (4 women); includes 19 minority (all Asian Americans or Pacific Islanders). Average age 30. 12 applicants, 42% accepted, 5 enrolled. In 2009, 2 master's awarded. *Degree requirements:* For master's, thesis optional. *Entrance requirements:* Additional exam requirements/recommendations for international students: Required—TOEFL (minimum score 500 paper-based; 173 computer-based; 61 iBT), IELTS (minimum score 5). *Application deadline:* For fall admission, 3/1 for domestic and international students. Application fee: $60. *Expenses:* Tuition, state resident: full-time $8900; part-time $372 per credit. Tuition, nonresident: full-time $21,400; part-time $898 per credit. Required fees: $207 per semester. *Financial support:* In 2009–10, 1 student received support, including 5 fellowships (averaging $2,416 per year), 1 research assistantship (averaging $15,558 per year), 3 teaching assistantships (averaging $14,382 per year). *Application contact:* Sam Warner, Graduate Chair, 808-956-6480, Fax: 808-956-3560, E-mail: noeau@hawaii.edu.

University of Hawaii at Manoa, Graduate Division, School of Hawaiian Knowledge, Program in Hawaiian Studies, Honolulu, HI 96822. Offers MA. Part-time programs available. *Faculty:* 4 full-time (2 women), 4 part-time/adjunct (3 women). *Students:* 20 full-time (15 women), 8 part-time (5 women); includes 25 minority (all Asian Americans or Pacific Islanders). Average age 33. 12 applicants, 42% accepted, 5 enrolled. In 2009, 3 master's awarded. *Degree requirements:* For master's, thesis optional. *Entrance requirements:* Additional exam requirements/recommendations for international students: Required—TOEFL (minimum score 500 paper-based; 173 computer-based; 61 iBT), IELTS (minimum score 5). *Application deadline:* For fall admission, 2/1 for domestic and international students. Application fee: $60. *Expenses:* Tuition, state resident: full-time $8900; part-time $372 per credit. Tuition, nonresident: full-time $21,400; part-time $898 per credit. Required fees: $207 per semester. *Financial support:* In 2009–10, 6 fellowships (averaging $2,360 per year), 2 research assistantships (averaging $16,836 per year), 9 teaching assistantships (averaging $14,382 per year) were awarded. Total annual research expenditures: $3 million. *Application contact:* Ivy Andrade, Associate Director, 808-973-0989, Fax: 808-956-5699, E-mail: andrade@hawaii.edu.

University of Illinois at Urbana–Champaign, Graduate College, College of Liberal Arts and Sciences, School of Literatures, Cultures and Linguistics, Department of Spanish, Italian and Portuguese, Champaign, IL 61820. Offers Italian (MA, PhD); Portuguese (MA, PhD); Spanish (MA, PhD). *Faculty:* 18 full-time (11 women). *Students:* 46 full-time (35 women), 10 part-time (7 women); includes 15 minority (1 Asian American or Pacific Islander, 14 Hispanic Americans), 28 international. 46 applicants, 41% accepted, 12 enrolled. In 2009, 7 master's, 11 doctorates awarded. *Entrance requirements:* For master's, GRE General Test, minimum GPA of 3.0; writing sample; for doctorate, GRE, minimum GPA of 3.0; writing sample. Additional exam requirements/recommendations for international students: Required—TOEFL (minimum score 88 iBT). *Application deadline:* Applications are processed on a rolling basis. Application fee: $60 ($75 for international students). Electronic applications accepted. *Financial support:* In 2009–10, 10 fellowships, 3 research assistantships, 51 teaching assistantships were awarded; tuition waivers (full and partial) also available. *Unit head:* Diane Musumeci, Head, 217-333-3390, Fax: 217-244-8430, E-mail: musumeci@illinois.edu. *Application contact:* Lynn Stanke, Office Support Specialist, 217-333-6269, Fax: 217-244-3050, E-mail: stanke@illinois.edu.

University of Illinois at Urbana–Champaign, Graduate College, College of Liberal Arts and Sciences, School of Literatures, Cultures and Linguistics, Department of the Classics, Champaign, IL 61820. Offers classical philology (PhD); classics (MA); teaching of Latin (MA). *Faculty:* 8 full-time (4 women), 1 part-time/adjunct (0 women). *Students:* 9 full-time (4 women), 7 part-time (5 women); includes 4 minority (2 Asian Americans or Pacific Islanders, 2 Hispanic Americans), 1 international. 22 applicants, 32% accepted, 2 enrolled. In 2009, 3 master's, 1 doctorate awarded. *Entrance requirements:* For master's, GRE, minimum GPA of 3.0; for doctorate, GRE, writing sample; minimum GPA of 3.0. Additional exam requirements/recommendations for international students: Required—TOEFL (minimum score 79 iBT). *Application deadline:* Applications are processed on a rolling basis. Application fee: $60 ($75 for international students). Electronic applications accepted. *Financial support:* In 2009–10, 5 fellowships, 15 teaching assistantships were awarded; research assistantships, tuition waivers (full and partial) also available. *Faculty research:* Greek and Latin language, papyrology, epigraphy, classical archaeology. *Unit head:* David Sansone, Head, 217-333-7573, Fax: 217-244-8430, E-mail: dsansone@illinois.edu. *Application contact:* Lynn Stanke, Office Support Specialist, 217-333-6269, Fax: 217-244-3050, E-mail: stanke@illinois.edu.

University of Indianapolis, Graduate Programs, School of Education, Indianapolis, IN 46227-3697. Offers art education (MAT); biology (MAT); chemistry (MAT); curriculum and instruction (MA); earth sciences (MAT); education (MA, MAT); educational leadership (MA); elementary education (MA); English (MAT); French (MAT); math (MAT); physical education (MAT); physics (MAT); secondary education (MA), including art education, education, English education, social studies education; social studies (MAT); Spanish (MAT). *Accreditation:* NCATE. Part-time and evening/weekend programs available. *Faculty:* 4 full-time (3 women), 3 part-time/adjunct (2 women). *Students:* 52 full-time (28 women), 110 part-time (67 women); includes 3 minority (all African Americans), 2 international. Average age 33. *Entrance requirements:* For master's, GRE Subject Test, PRAXIS I, minimum GPA of 2.5, 3 letters of recommendation, interview,

writing exercise. Additional exam requirements/recommendations for international students: Required—TOEFL (minimum score 550 paper-based; 213 computer-based). *Application deadline:* Applications are processed on a rolling basis. Application fee: $50. *Financial support:* Federal Work-Study available. Financial award application deadline: 5/1; financial award applicants required to submit FAFSA. *Faculty research:* Assessment of teacher education, perceptions of prospective teachers by parents. *Unit head:* Dr. Kathy Moran, Dean, 317-788-3285, Fax: 317-788-3300, E-mail: kmoran@uindy.edu. *Application contact:* Chemain Slater, 317-788-2051, E-mail: slaterc@uindy.edu.

The University of Iowa, Graduate College, College of Education, Department of Teaching and Learning, Program in Secondary Education, Iowa City, IA 52242-1316. Offers art education (PhD); curriculum and supervision (PhD); curriculum supervision (MA); developmental reading (MA); English education (MA, MAT); foreign language education (MA, MAT); foreign language/ESL education (PhD); language, literature and culture (PhD); math education (PhD); mathematics education (MA); social studies (MA, PhD). *Degree requirements:* For master's, thesis optional, exam; for doctorate, comprehensive exam, thesis/dissertation. *Entrance requirements:* For master's and doctorate, GRE General Test, minimum GPA of 3.0. Additional exam requirements/recommendations for international students: Required—TOEFL (minimum score 550 paper-based; 213 computer-based; 81 iBT). Electronic applications accepted.

The University of Iowa, Graduate College, Program in Second Language Acquisition, Iowa City, IA 52242-1316. Offers PhD. *Degree requirements:* For doctorate, comprehensive exam, thesis/dissertation. *Entrance requirements:* For doctorate, GRE General Test, minimum GPA of 3.0. Additional exam requirements/recommendations for international students: Required—TOEFL (minimum score 600 paper-based; 250 computer-based; 100 iBT). Electronic applications accepted.

University of Kentucky, Graduate School, College of Arts and Sciences and College of Education, Program in Teaching World Languages, Lexington, KY 40506-0032. Offers MA. *Entrance requirements:* For master's, GRE General Test, minimum undergraduate GPA of 2.75. Additional exam requirements/recommendations for international students: Required—TOEFL (minimum score 550 paper-based; 213 computer-based). Electronic applications accepted.

University of Maine, Graduate School, College of Liberal Arts and Sciences, Department of Modern Languages and Classics, Orono, ME 04469. Offers French (MA, MAT). Part-time programs available. *Faculty:* 9 full-time (6 women), 7 part-time/adjunct (5 women). *Students:* 5 full-time (3 women), 2 part-time (1 woman); includes 1 minority (African American). Average age 31. 6 applicants, 83% accepted, 4 enrolled. In 2009, 9 master's awarded. *Degree requirements:* For master's, one foreign language, thesis (for some programs). *Entrance requirements:* For master's, GRE General Test. Additional exam requirements/recommendations for international students: Required—TOEFL. *Application deadline:* For fall admission, 2/1 priority date for domestic students. Applications are processed on a rolling basis. Application fee: $60. Electronic applications accepted. *Financial support:* In 2009–10, 3 teaching assistantships with tuition reimbursements (averaging $12,790 per year) were awarded; Federal Work-Study, tuition waivers (full and partial), and instructorships also available. Financial award application deadline: 3/1. *Faculty research:* Narratology, poetics, Quebec literature, theater, women's studies. *Unit head:* Dr. Jane Smith, Chair, 207-581-2079, Fax: 207-581-1832. *Application contact:* Scott G. Delcourt, Associate Dean of the Graduate School, 207-581-3291, Fax: 207-581-3232, E-mail: graduate@maine.edu.

University of Maryland, Baltimore County, Graduate School, College of Arts, Humanities and Social Sciences, Department of Education, Program in Teaching, Baltimore, MD 21250. Offers early childhood education (MAT); elementary education (MAT); secondary education (MAT), including art, biology, chemistry, dance, earth/space science, English, foreign language, mathematics, music, physics, theatre; secondary science (MAT), including social studies. Part-time and evening/weekend programs available. *Faculty:* 24 full-time (18 women), 25 part-time/adjunct (19 women). *Students:* 52 full-time (41 women), 64 part-time (55 women); includes 20 minority (5 African Americans, 1 American Indian/Alaska Native, 10 Asian Americans or Pacific Islanders, 4 Hispanic Americans), 3 international. Average age 31. 88 applicants, 57% accepted, 39 enrolled. In 2009, 106 master's awarded. *Degree requirements:* For master's, comprehensive exam (for some programs), thesis (for some programs). *Entrance requirements:* For master's, PRAXIS I and II, minimum GPA of 3.0. Additional exam requirements/recommendations for international students: Required—TOEFL. *Application deadline:* For fall admission, 6/1 for domestic students; for spring admission, 11/1 for domestic students. Applications are processed on a rolling basis. Application fee: $50. Electronic applications accepted. *Financial support:* In 2009–10, 6 students received support, including research assistantships with full tuition reimbursements available (averaging $12,000 per year); career-related internships or fieldwork, Federal Work-Study, scholarships/grants, tuition waivers, and unspecified assistantships also available. Financial award application deadline: 3/1. *Faculty research:* STEM teacher education, culturally sensitive pedagogy, ESOL/bilingual education, early childhood education, language, literacy and culture. *Unit head:* Dr. Susan M. Blunck, Director, 410-455-2869, Fax: 410-455-3986, E-mail: blunck@umbc.edu. *Application contact:* Dr. Susan M. Blunck, Director, 410-455-2869, Fax: 410-455-3986, E-mail: blunck@umbc.edu.

University of Maryland, College Park, Academic Affairs, College of Arts and Humanities, School of Languages, Literature, and Cultures, Program in Second Language Acquisition and Application, College Park, MD 20742. Offers French (MA); German (MA); Japanese (MA); Russian (MA); second language instruction (PhD); second language learning (PhD); second language measurement and assessment (PhD); second language use (PhD); Spanish (MA). *Students:* 12 full-time (10 women), 5 part-time (3 women); includes 2 minority (both Asian Americans or Pacific Islanders), 5 international. 47 applicants, 15% accepted, 3 enrolled. In 2009, 7 master's awarded. *Entrance requirements:* For master's, BA or BS in related field, demonstrated language competency, 3 letters of reference. *Application deadline:* For fall admission, 1/15 for domestic and international students; for spring admission, 6/1 for domestic and international students. Applications are processed on a rolling basis. Application fee: $60. Electronic applications accepted. *Expenses:* Tuition, area resident: Part-time $471 per credit hour. Tuition, state resident: part-time $471 per credit hour. Tuition, nonresident: part-time $1016 per credit hour. Required fees: $337.04 per term. *Financial support:* In 2009–10, 2 fellowships with full and partial tuition reimbursements (averaging $13,928 per year), 4 research assistantships (averaging $21,457 per year), 6 teaching assistantships (averaging $20,933 per year) were awarded. *Faculty research:* Second language acquisition, pedagogical perspectives, technological applications, language use in professional contexts. *Unit head:* Carol Mossman, Director, School of Languages, Literatures, and Cultures, 301-405-4025, E-mail: cmossman@umd.edu. *Application contact:* Dean of Graduate School, 301-405-0376, Fax: 301-314-9305.

University of Massachusetts Amherst, Graduate School, College of Humanities and Fine Arts, Department of Languages, Literatures, and Cultures, Program in French and Francophone Studies, Amherst, MA 01003. Offers French (MA, MAT). Part-time programs available. *Faculty:* 7 full-time (4 women). *Students:* 7 full-time (5 women), 3 part-time (1 woman), 1 international. Average age 34. 10 applicants, 80% accepted, 2 enrolled. In 2009, 4 master's awarded. *Degree requirements:* For master's, thesis or alternative. *Entrance requirements:* For master's, GRE General Test. Additional exam requirements/recommendations for international students: Required—TOEFL (minimum score 550 paper-based; 213 computer-based; 80 iBT), IELTS (minimum score 6.5). *Application deadline:* For fall admission, 2/1 for domestic and international students; for spring admission, 10/1 for domestic and international students. Applications are processed on a rolling basis. Application fee: $50 ($65 for international students). Electronic applications accepted. *Expenses:* Tuition, state resident: full-time $2640; part-time $110 per credit. Tuition, nonresident: full-time $9936; part-time $414 per credit. Tuition and fees vary according to course load. *Financial support:* In 2009–10, 17 teaching assistantships with full tuition reimbursements (averaging $12,253 per year) were awarded; fellowships, research assistantships, career-related internships or fieldwork, Federal Work-Study, scholarships/grants, traineeships, health care benefits, tuition waivers (full), and unspecified assistantships

also available. Support available to part-time students. Financial award application deadline: 2/1. *Unit head:* Dr. Luke P. Bouvier, Graduate Program Director, 413-545-2314, Fax: 412-545-4778. *Application contact:* Jean M. Ames, Supervisor of Admissions, 413-545-0722, Fax: 413-577-0100, E-mail: gradadm@grad.umass.edu.

University of Massachusetts Boston, Office of Graduate Studies, College of Liberal Arts, Program in Applied Linguistics, Boston, MA 02125-3393. Offers bilingual education (MA); English as a second language (MA); foreign language pedagogy (MA). Part-time and evening/weekend programs available. *Degree requirements:* For master's, one foreign language, comprehensive exam. *Entrance requirements:* For master's, minimum GPA of 2.75. *Faculty research:* Multicultural theory and curriculum development, foreign language pedagogy, language and culture, applied psycholinguistics, bilingual education.

University of Michigan, Horace H. Rackham School of Graduate Studies, College of Literature, Science, and the Arts, Department of Classical Studies, Ann Arbor, MI 48109. Offers classical studies (PhD); teaching Latin (MAT). *Faculty:* 21 full-time (8 women), 10 part-time/adjunct (6 women). *Students:* 26 full-time (17 women); includes 3 minority (2 Asian Americans or Pacific Islanders, 1 Hispanic American), 1 international. Average age 27. 98 applicants, 4% accepted, 3 enrolled. In 2009, 3 master's, 7 doctorates awarded. Terminal master's awarded for partial completion of doctoral program. *Degree requirements:* For master's, one foreign language, comprehensive exam; for doctorate, 4 foreign languages, thesis/dissertation, oral defense of dissertation, preliminary exams. *Entrance requirements:* For master's, GRE General Test; for doctorate, GRE General Test, minimum of 3 years of college-level Latin and 2 years of college-level Greek. Additional exam requirements/recommendations for international students: Required—TOEFL (minimum score 560 paper-based; 220 computer-based). *Application deadline:* For fall admission, 1/5 for domestic and international students. Application fee: $60 ($75 for international students). Electronic applications accepted. *Expenses:* Tuition, state resident: full-time $17,286; part-time $1099 per credit hour. Tuition, nonresident: full-time $34,944; part-time $2080 per credit hour. Required fees: $95 per semester. Tuition and fees vary according to course load, degree level and program. *Financial support:* In 2009–10, 26 students received support, including 3 fellowships with full tuition reimbursements available (averaging $18,000 per year), 15 teaching assistantships with full tuition reimbursements available (averaging $16,694 per year); career-related internships or fieldwork, Federal Work-Study, institutionally sponsored loans, scholarships/grants, traineeships, health care benefits, and unspecified assistantships also available. Financial award application deadline: 3/15. *Faculty research:* Greek and Latin literature, ancient history, papyrology, archaeology. *Unit head:* Prof. Ruth Scodel, Chair, 734-764-0360, Fax: 734-763-4959, E-mail: classics@umich.edu. *Application contact:* Michelle M. Biggs, Graduate Coordinator, 734-647-2330, Fax: 734-763-4959, E-mail: mbiggs@umich.edu.

University of Minnesota, Twin Cities Campus, Graduate School, College of Education and Human Development, Department of Curriculum and Instruction, Program in Teaching, Minneapolis, MN 55455-0213. Offers Chinese (M Ed); earth science (M Ed); elementary special education (M Ed); English (M Ed); English as a second language (M Ed); French (M Ed); German (M Ed); Hebrew (M Ed); Japanese (M Ed); life sciences (M Ed); mathematics (M Ed); middle school science (M Ed); science (M Ed); second languages and cultures (M Ed); social studies (M Ed); Spanish (M Ed). *Students:* 263 full-time (186 women), 117 part-time (83 women); includes 32 minority (10 African Americans, 2 American Indian/Alaska Native, 17 Asian Americans or Pacific Islanders, 3 Hispanic Americans), 4 international. Average age 27. 363 applicants, 74% accepted, 259 enrolled. In 2009, 497 master's awarded. *Unit head:* Dr. Ruth Thomas, Chair, 612-624-4772, Fax: 612-624-8277, E-mail: thoma006@umn.edu. *Application contact:* Dr. Mary Trettin, Associate Dean, 612-625-6501, Fax: 612-626-1580, E-mail: mtrettin@umn.edu.

University of Missouri, Graduate School, College of Arts and Sciences, Department of Romance Languages and Literature, Columbia, MO 65211. Offers French (MA, PhD); literature (MA); Spanish (MA, PhD); teaching (MA). *Faculty:* 21 full-time (13 women), 19 part-time/adjunct (15 women). *Students:* 16 full-time (12 women), 26 part-time (16 women); includes 11 minority (2 African Americans, 2 Asian Americans or Pacific Islanders, 7 Hispanic Americans), 9 international. Average age 35. 28 applicants, 71% accepted, 14 enrolled. In 2009, 2 master's awarded. Terminal master's awarded for partial completion of doctoral program. *Degree requirements:* For master's, one foreign language; for doctorate, 4 foreign languages, comprehensive exam, thesis/dissertation. *Entrance requirements:* For master's, GRE General Test, minimum GPA of 3.0 in field of major; bachelor's degree; for doctorate, GRE General Test, minimum GPA of 3.0 in field of major; master's degree. Additional exam requirements/recommendations for international students: Required—TOEFL (minimum score 500 paper-based; 173 computer-based; 61 iBT). *Application deadline:* For fall admission, 2/15 priority date for domestic students; for winter admission, 10/15 for domestic students. Applications are processed on a rolling basis. Application fee: $45 ($60 for international students). Electronic applications accepted. *Financial support:* In 2009–10, 37 teaching assistantships with full tuition reimbursements were awarded; research assistantships, institutionally sponsored loans, health care benefits, and unspecified assistantships also available. *Unit head:* Dr. Flore Zephir, Department Chair, E-mail: zephirf@missouri.edu. *Application contact:* Mary Harriss, Administrative Assistant, 573-882-5039, E-mail: harrisma@missouri.edu.

University of Missouri, Graduate School, College of Education, Department of Learning, Teaching and Curriculum, Columbia, MO 65211. Offers agricultural education (M Ed, PhD, Ed S); art education (M Ed, PhD, Ed S); business and office education (M Ed, PhD, Ed S); early childhood education (M Ed, PhD, Ed S); elementary education (M Ed, PhD, Ed S); English education (M Ed, PhD, Ed S); foreign language education (M Ed, PhD, Ed S); health education and promotion (M Ed, PhD); learning and instruction (M Ed); marketing education (M Ed, PhD, Ed S); mathematics education (M Ed, PhD, Ed S); music education (M Ed, PhD, Ed S); reading education (M Ed, PhD, Ed S); science education (M Ed, PhD, Ed S); social studies education (M Ed, PhD, Ed S); vocational education (M Ed, PhD, Ed S). Part-time programs available. Terminal master's awarded for partial completion of doctoral program. *Degree requirements:* For doctorate, thesis/dissertation. *Entrance requirements:* For master's and Ed S, GRE General Test or MAT, minimum GPA of 3.0; for doctorate, GRE General Test, minimum GPA of 3.0. Additional exam requirements/recommendations for international students: Required—TOEFL (minimum score 600 paper-based; 250 computer-based; 100 iBT). Electronic applications accepted.

University of Nebraska at Kearney, College of Graduate Study, College of Fine Arts and Humanities, Department of Modern Languages, Kearney, NE 68849-0001. Offers French (MA Ed); German (MA Ed); Spanish (MA Ed). *Accreditation:* NCATE. Part-time and evening/weekend programs available. *Degree requirements:* For master's, thesis optional. *Entrance requirements:* For master's, GRE General Test. Electronic applications accepted. *Faculty research:* Translation theory, Spanish linguistics; Heidegger, Rilke and Nietzsche; symotolistic poetry.

University of Nebraska at Omaha, Graduate Studies, College of Arts and Sciences, Program in Language Teaching, Omaha, NE 68182. Offers MA. Part-time and evening/weekend programs available. *Faculty:* 11 full-time (9 women). *Students:* 4 full-time (3 women), 18 part-time (15 women); includes 6 minority (2 Asian Americans or Pacific Islanders, 4 Hispanic Americans). Average age 40. 13 applicants, 46% accepted, 4 enrolled. In 2009, 5 master's awarded. *Degree requirements:* For master's, comprehensive exam, thesis (for some programs). *Entrance requirements:* For master's, letters of recommendation, oral and written language sample. Additional exam requirements/recommendations for international students: Required—TOEFL (minimum score 600 paper-based; 250 computer-based; 100 iBT). *Application deadline:* For fall admission, 7/1 priority date for domestic students; for spring admission, 11/15 priority date for domestic students. Application fee: $45. *Financial support:* In 2009–10, 8 students received support. Tuition waivers (partial) available. Financial award application deadline: 3/1; financial award applicants required to submit FAFSA. *Unit head:* Dr. Carolyn Gascoigne, Chairperson, 402-554-4841. *Application contact:* Dr. Melanie Bloom, Information Contact, 402-554-4841.

Foreign Languages Education

University of Nevada, Reno, Graduate School, College of Liberal Arts, Department of Foreign Languages and Literatures, Reno, NV 89557. Offers French (MA); German (MA); Spanish (MA). *Degree requirements:* For master's, one foreign language, thesis optional. *Entrance requirements:* For master's, GRE General Test, minimum GPA of 2.75. Additional exam requirements/recommendations for international students: Required—TOEFL (minimum score 500 paper-based; 173 computer-based; 61 iBT), IELTS (minimum score 6). *Faculty research:* Thirteenth century mysticism, contemporary Spanish and Latin American poetry and theater, French interrelation between narration and photography, exile literature and Holocaust.

The University of North Carolina at Chapel Hill, Graduate School, School of Education, Program in Secondary Education, Chapel Hill, NC 27599. Offers English (Grades 9-12) (MAT); English as a second language (MAT); French (Grades K-12) (MAT); German (Grades K-12) (MAT); Japanese (Grades K-12) (MAT); Latin (Grades 9-12) (MAT); mathematics (Grades 9-12) (MAT); music (Grades K-12) (MAT); science (Grades 9-12) (MAT); social studies (Grades 9-12) (MAT); Spanish (Grades K-12) (MAT). *Accreditation:* NCATE. *Students:* 53 full-time (35 women), 1 part-time (0 women); includes 8 minority (4 African Americans, 2 Asian Americans or Pacific Islanders, 2 Hispanic Americans), 3 international. Average age 25. 137 applicants, 77% accepted, 54 enrolled. In 2009, 39 master's awarded. *Degree requirements:* For master's, comprehensive exam. *Entrance requirements:* For master's, GRE General Test, minimum GPA of 3.0 during last 2 years of undergraduate course work. Additional exam requirements/recommendations for international students: Required—TOEFL (minimum score 550 paper-based; 79 computer-based). *Application deadline:* For fall admission, 12/15 priority date for domestic and international students. Applications are processed on a rolling basis. Application fee: $77. Electronic applications accepted. *Financial support:* Federal Work-Study available. Support available to part-time students. Financial award application deadline: 3/1; financial award applicants required to submit FAFSA. *Unit head:* Dr. James Trier, Coordinator, 919-843-4627, Fax: 919-962-1533. *Application contact:* Amy Butler, Student Services Assistant, 919-966-1346, Fax: 919-962-1533, E-mail: abutler@email.unc.edu.

The University of North Carolina at Charlotte, Graduate School, College of Education, Program in Teacher Education, Charlotte, NC 28223-0001. Offers art education (K-12) (MAT); dance education (K-12) (MAT); elementary education (K-6) (MAT); English as a second language (K-12) (MAT); foreign language education (K-12) (MAT); general teacher education (MAT); middle grades education (6-9) (MAT); music education (K-12) (MAT); secondary education (9-12) (MAT); special education (K-12) (MAT); theatre education (K-12) (MAT). *Faculty:* 108 full-time (64 women), 16 part-time/adjunct (12 women). *Students:* 29 full-time (20 women), 229 part-time (189 women); includes 32 minority (22 African Americans, 2 American Indian/Alaska Native, 3 Asian Americans or Pacific Islanders, 5 Hispanic Americans). Average age 32. 108 applicants, 92% accepted, 85 enrolled. In 2009, 59 master's awarded. *Entrance requirements:* For master's, GRE or MAT. Additional exam requirements/recommendations for international students: Required—TOEFL (minimum score 557 paper-based; 220 computer-based; 83 iBT). *Application deadline:* For fall admission, 7/1 for domestic students, 5/1 for international students; for spring admission, 11/1 for domestic students, 10/1 for international students. Applications are processed on a rolling basis. Application fee: $55. Electronic applications accepted. *Financial support:* In 2009–10, 5 students received support, including 1 research assistantship (averaging $18,000 per year), 3 teaching assistantships (averaging $12,183 per year); career-related internships or fieldwork, Federal Work-Study, institutionally sponsored loans, scholarships/grants, and administrative assistantship also available. Support available to part-time students. Financial award application deadline: 4/1; financial award applicants required to submit FAFSA. Total annual research expenditures: $5.1 million. *Unit head:* Dr. Kimberly J. Hartman, Coordinator, 704-687-8883, Fax: 704-687-6430, E-mail: khartman@uncc.edu. *Application contact:* Kathy B. Giddings, Director of Graduate Admissions, 704-687-5503, Fax: 704-687-3279, E-mail: gradadmn@uncc.edu.

The University of North Carolina at Greensboro, Graduate School, School of Education, Department of Curriculum and Instruction, Greensboro, NC 27412-5001. Offers college teaching and adult learning (Certificate); curriculum and instruction (M Ed), including chemistry education, elementary education, English as a second language, French education, instructional technology, mathematics education, middle grades education, reading education, science education, social studies education, Spanish education; curriculum and teaching (PhD), including higher education, teacher education and development; English as a second language (Certificate); higher education (M Ed); supervision (M Ed). *Accreditation:* NCATE. Part-time programs available. *Degree requirements:* For doctorate, thesis/dissertation. *Entrance requirements:* For master's and doctorate, GRE General Test. Additional exam requirements/recommendations for international students: Required—TOEFL. Electronic applications accepted. *Faculty research:* Community college literacy program, middle school mathematics/computer mathematics.

University of Northern Colorado, Graduate School, College of Humanities and Social Sciences, School of Modern Languages and Cultural Studies, Program in Foreign Languages, Greeley, CO 80639. Offers Spanish/teaching (MA). Part-time programs available. *Faculty:* 12 full-time (6 women). *Students:* 1 part-time (0 women), all international. Average age 50. 1 applicant, 100% accepted, 0 enrolled. In 2009, 4 master's awarded. *Degree requirements:* For master's, comprehensive exam, thesis or alternative. *Entrance requirements:* For master's, minimum undergraduate GPA of 3.0, BA in Spanish, 1 year of secondary teaching. *Application deadline:* Applications are processed on a rolling basis. Application fee: $50 ($60 for international students). Electronic applications accepted. *Expenses:* Tuition, state resident: full-time $5770; part-time $320.55 per credit hour. Tuition, nonresident: full-time $13,847; part-time $769.27 per credit hour. Required fees: $948.78; $52.72 per credit. *Financial support:* In 2009–10, 1 teaching assistantship (averaging $11,969 per year) was awarded; fellowships, research assistantships, unspecified assistantships also available. Financial award application deadline: 3/1; financial award applicants required to submit FAFSA. *Unit head:* Dr. Joy Landeira, Program Coordinator, 970-351-2221, Fax: 970-351-1571. *Application contact:* Linda Sisson, Graduate Student Admission Coordinator, 970-351-1807, Fax: 970-351-2371, E-mail: linda.sisson@unco.edu.

University of Pittsburgh, School of Education, Department of Instruction and Learning, Program in Secondary Education, Pittsburgh, PA 15260. Offers English/communications education (M Ed, MAT); foreign languages education (M Ed, MAT); mathematics education (M Ed, MAT, Ed D); science education (M Ed, MAT, MS, Ed D); social studies education (M Ed, MAT). Part-time and evening/weekend programs available. *Students:* 170 full-time (107 women), 70 part-time (54 women); includes 19 minority (11 African Americans, 6 Asian Americans or Pacific Islanders, 2 Hispanic Americans), 10 international. Average age 29. 220 applicants, 72% accepted, 128 enrolled. In 2009, 108 master's, 5 doctorates awarded. *Degree requirements:* For master's, thesis; for doctorate, thesis/dissertation. *Entrance requirements:* For master's, PRAXIS I; for doctorate, GRE General Test. Additional exam requirements/recommendations for international students: Required—TOEFL. *Application deadline:* For fall admission, 2/1 priority date for domestic students; for spring admission, 11/15 priority date for domestic students. Applications are processed on a rolling basis. Application fee: $50. Electronic applications accepted. *Expenses:* Tuition, state resident: full-time $16,402; part-time $665 per credit. Tuition, nonresident: full-time $28,694; part-time $1175 per credit. Required fees: $690; $175 per term. Tuition and fees vary according to program. *Financial support:* Fellowships, teaching assistantships, career-related internships or fieldwork, Federal Work-Study, tuition waivers (partial), and unspecified assistantships available. Support available to part-time students. Financial award application deadline: 3/15; financial award applicants required to submit FAFSA. *Unit head:* Dr. Richard Donato, Chairman, 412-624-7248, Fax: 412-648-7081, E-mail: donato@pitt.edu. *Application contact:* Joan M. Cutone, Director, School of Education Student Service Center, 412-648-2230, Fax: 412-648-1899, E-mail: soeinfo@pitt.edu.

University of Puerto Rico, Río Piedras, College of Education, Program in Curriculum and Teaching, San Juan, PR 00931-3300. Offers biology education (M Ed); chemistry education (M Ed); curriculum and teaching (Ed D); history education (M Ed); mathematics education (M Ed); physics education (M Ed); Spanish education (M Ed). Part-time programs available. *Degree requirements:* For master's, thesis; for doctorate, thesis/dissertation, internship. *Entrance requirements:* For master's, PAEG or GRE, minimum GPA of 3.0, letter of recommendation; for doctorate, GRE or PAEG, master's degree, minimum GPA of 3.0, letter of recommendation (2), interview. *Faculty research:* Curriculum, math teaching.

University of South Carolina, The Graduate School, College of Arts and Sciences, Department of Languages, Literatures, and Cultures, Columbia, SC 29208. Offers comparative literature (MA, PhD); foreign languages (MAT), including French, German, Spanish; French (MA); German (MA); Spanish (MA). MAT offered in cooperation with the College of Education. Part-time programs available. *Degree requirements:* For master's, one foreign language, comprehensive exam, thesis optional; for doctorate, 2 foreign languages, comprehensive exam, thesis/dissertation. *Entrance requirements:* For master's and doctorate, GRE General Test, writing sample. Additional exam requirements/recommendations for international students: Required—TOEFL (minimum score 230 computer-based; 75 iBT). Electronic applications accepted. *Faculty research:* Modern literature, linguistics, literature and culture, medieval literature, literary theory.

University of South Carolina, The Graduate School, College of Education, Department of Instruction and Teacher Education, Program in Secondary Education, Columbia, SC 29208. Offers art education (IMA, MAT); business education (IMA, MAT); English (MAT); foreign language (MAT); health education (MAT); mathematics (MAT); science (IMA, MAT); secondary (Ed D); secondary education (MT, PhD); social studies (MAT); theatre and speech (MAT). IMA and MT offered jointly with the subject areas. *Accreditation:* NCATE. *Degree requirements:* For master's, comprehensive exam, thesis (for some programs), foreign language (MA); for doctorate, one foreign language, comprehensive exam, thesis/dissertation. *Entrance requirements:* For master's, GRE General Test or MAT, teaching certificate (IMA, M Ed), interview; for doctorate, GRE General Test or MAT, interview. *Faculty research:* Middle school programs, professional development, school collaboration.

University of Southern Mississippi, Graduate School, College of Arts and Letters, Department of Foreign Languages and Literatures, Hattiesburg, MS 39406-0001. Offers French (MATL); Spanish (MATL); teaching English to speakers of other languages (TESOL) (MATL). *Faculty:* 9 full-time (5 women). *Students:* 10 full-time (7 women), 43 part-time (37 women); includes 6 minority (1 African American, 1 Asian American or Pacific Islander, 4 Hispanic Americans), 5 international. Average age 33. 29 applicants, 59% accepted, 14 enrolled. In 2009, 24 master's awarded. *Degree requirements:* For master's, comprehensive exam. *Entrance requirements:* For master's, GRE General Test, minimum GPA of 3.0 in field of study, 2.75 in last 2 years. Additional exam requirements/recommendations for international students: Required—TOEFL. *Application deadline:* For fall admission, 3/1 for domestic and international students. Applications are processed on a rolling basis. Application fee: $35. *Expenses:* Tuition, state resident: full-time $5096; part-time $284 per hour. Tuition, nonresident: full-time $13,052; part-time $726 per hour. Required fees: $402. Tuition and fees vary according to course level and course load. *Financial support:* In 2009–10, 8 teaching assistantships with full tuition reimbursements (averaging $8,350 per year) were awarded; research assistantships, Federal Work-Study, scholarships/grants, and unspecified assistantships also available. Financial award application deadline: 3/15; financial award applicants required to submit FAFSA. *Unit head:* Dr. Leah Fonder-Solano, Chair, 601-266-4964, Fax: 601-266-4853. *Application contact:* Dr. Joanne Burnett, 601-266-4964.

University of South Florida, Graduate School, College of Education–Main Campus, Department of Secondary Education, Tampa, FL 33620-9951. Offers English education (M Ed, MA, MAT, PhD); foreign language education/ESOL (M Ed, MA, MAT); instructional technology (M Ed, PhD, Ed S); mathematics education (M Ed, MA, MAT, PhD, Ed S); science education (M Ed, MA, MAT, PhD); second language acquisition/instructional technology (PhD); secondary education (M Ed, PhD); secondary education/TESOL (M Ed); social science education (M Ed, MA, MAT); teaching and learning in the content area (PhD). *Accreditation:* NCATE. Part-time and evening/weekend programs available. *Faculty:* 28 full-time (17 women), 3 part-time/adjunct (1 woman). *Students:* 144 full-time (97 women), 322 part-time (212 women); includes 100 minority (32 African Americans, 4 American Indian/Alaska Native, 17 Asian Americans or Pacific Islanders, 47 Hispanic Americans), 25 international. Average age 30. 230 applicants, 67% accepted, 122 enrolled. In 2009, 122 master's, 14 doctorates, 1 other advanced degree awarded. *Degree requirements:* For master's, variable foreign language requirement, comprehensive exam; for doctorate, variable foreign language requirement, comprehensive exam, thesis/dissertation. *Entrance requirements:* For master's, GRE General Test or General Knowledge Test, minimum GPA of 3.0; for doctorate, GRE General Test, minimum GPA of 3.5; for Ed S, GRE General Test. Additional exam requirements/recommendations for international students: Required—TOEFL (minimum score 550 paper-based; 213 computer-based; 79 iBT). *Application deadline:* For fall admission, 2/15 for domestic students, 1/2 for international students; for spring admission, 10/15 for domestic students, 6/1 for international students. Application fee: $30. Electronic applications accepted. *Financial support:* In 2009–10, 7 students received support, including 1 research assistantship with full tuition reimbursement available (averaging $10,000 per year), 55 teaching assistantships with full and partial tuition reimbursements available (averaging $7,900 per year); scholarships/grants and unspecified assistantships also available. Financial award application deadline: 4/15; financial award applicants required to submit FAFSA. *Faculty research:* English language learners/multicultural, social science education, mathematics education, science education, instructional technology. Total annual research expenditures: $336,023. *Unit head:* Dr. Stephen Thornton, Chairperson, 813-974-3533, Fax: 813-974-3837, E-mail: thornton@usf.edu. *Application contact:* Dr. James White, Program Director, 813-974-1629, Fax: 813-974-3837, E-mail: jwhite@usf.edu.

The University of Tennessee, Graduate School, College of Education, Health and Human Sciences, Program in Education, Knoxville, TN 37996. Offers art education (MS); counseling education (PhD); cultural studies in education (PhD); curriculum (MS, Ed S); curriculum, educational research and evaluation (Ed D, PhD); early childhood education (PhD); early childhood special education (MS); education of deaf and hard of hearing (MS); educational administration and policy studies (Ed D, PhD); educational administration and supervision (Ed S); educational psychology (Ed D, PhD); elementary education (MS, Ed S); elementary teaching (MS); English education (MS, Ed S); exercise science (PhD); foreign language/ESL education (MS, Ed S); instructional technology (MS, Ed D, PhD, Ed S); literacy, language and ESL education (PhD); literacy, language education, and ESL education (Ed D); mathematics education (MS, Ed S); modified and comprehensive special education (MS); reading education (MS, Ed S); school counseling (Ed S); school psychology (PhD, Ed S); science education (MS, Ed S); secondary teaching (MS); social foundations (MS); social science education (MS, Ed S); socio-cultural foundations of sports and education (PhD); special education (Ed S); teacher education (Ed D, PhD). *Accreditation:* NCATE. Part-time and evening/weekend programs available. *Degree requirements:* For master's and Ed S, thesis optional; for doctorate, variable foreign language requirement, thesis/dissertation. *Entrance requirements:* For master's, minimum GPA of 2.7; for doctorate and Ed S, GRE General Test, minimum GPA of 2.7. Additional exam requirements/recommendations for international students: Required—TOEFL. Electronic applications accepted. *Expenses:* Tuition, state resident: full-time $6826; part-time $380 per semester hour. Tuition, nonresident: full-time $21,844; part-time $1147 per semester hour. Tuition and fees vary according to program.

The University of Texas at Austin, Graduate School, College of Education, Program in Foreign Language Education, Austin, TX 78712-1111. Offers MA, PhD. Part-time programs available. *Degree requirements:* For master's, one foreign language, thesis; for doctorate, one foreign language, thesis/dissertation. *Entrance requirements:* For master's and doctorate, GRE General Test. Electronic applications accepted. *Faculty research:* Individual differences in language learning, culture, portfolio, assessment, biliteracy.

University of the Sacred Heart, Graduate Programs, Department of Education, San Juan, PR 00914-0383. Offers early childhood education (M Ed); information technology and multimedia (Certificate); instruction systems and education technology (M Ed), including English, information technology and multimedia, instructional design, mathematics, Spanish. Part-time and evening/weekend programs available. *Degree requirements:* For master's, thesis. *Entrance requirements:* For master's, EXADEP, minimum undergraduate GPA of 2.75, interview.

The University of Toledo, College of Graduate Studies, College of Education, Department of Curriculum and Instruction, Program in Education and French, Toledo, OH 43606-3390. Offers MAE.

The University of Toledo, College of Graduate Studies, College of Education, Department of Curriculum and Instruction, Program in Education and German, Toledo, OH 43606-3390. Offers MAE.

The University of Toledo, College of Graduate Studies, College of Education, Department of Curriculum and Instruction, Program in Education and Spanish, Toledo, OH 43606-3390. Offers MAE.

University of Utah, Graduate School, College of Humanities, Department of Languages and Literature, Salt Lake City, UT 84112-1107. Offers comparative literary and cultural studies (MA, PhD); French (MA, MALP); German (MA, MALP, PhD); Spanish (MA, MALP, PhD); world languages with secondary teaching licensure (MA). *Faculty:* 35 full-time (22 women), 1 part-time/adjunct (0 women). *Students:* 30 full-time (20 women), 10 part-time (9 women); includes 8 minority (1 American Indian/Alaska Native, 2 Asian Americans or Pacific Islanders, 5 Hispanic Americans), 6 international. Average age 35. 47 applicants, 40% accepted, 18 enrolled. In 2009, 7 master's, 3 doctorates awarded. Terminal master's awarded for partial completion of doctoral program. *Degree requirements:* For master's, 2 foreign languages, comprehensive exam, thesis, standard proficiency in 2 languages other than English; for doctorate, 3 foreign languages, comprehensive exam, thesis/dissertation, standard proficiency in 2 languages other than English and language of study, advanced proficiency in 1 language other than English and language of study. *Entrance requirements:* For master's, bachelor's degree or strong undergraduate record in target languages, minimum GPA of 3.0; for doctorate, GRE, MA, advanced proficiency in a target language. Additional exam requirements/recommendations for international students: Required—TOEFL (minimum score 500 paper-based; 173 computer-based). *Application deadline:* For fall admission, 1/15 priority date for domestic students, 12/15 priority date for international students. Application fee: $55 ($65 for international students). *Expenses:* Tuition, state resident: full-time $4004; part-time $1674 per semester. Tuition, nonresident: full-time $14,134; part-time $5915 per semester. Required fees: $324 per semester. Tuition and fees vary according to course load, degree level and program. *Financial support:* In 2009–10, 21 students received support, including 21 teaching assistantships with full tuition reimbursements available (averaging $11,000 per year); health care benefits also available. Financial award application deadline: 2/1; financial award applicants required to submit FAFSA. *Faculty research:* Literary theory, linguistics, cultural studies, comparative studies. Total annual research expenditures: $22,986. *Unit head:* Dr. Christine A. Jones, Director of Graduate Studies, 801-585-3002, Fax: 801-581-7581, E-mail: cjones@hum.utah.edu. *Application contact:* Virginia Ellinwood, Academic Advisor, 801-585-9437, Fax: 801-581-7581, E-mail: v.ellinwood@mail.hum.utah.edu.

University of Vermont, Graduate College, College of Arts and Sciences, Department of Classics, Burlington, VT 05405. Offers Greek (MA); Greek and Latin (MAT); Latin (MA). *Students:* 6 (3 women); includes 1 minority (Hispanic American). 11 applicants, 64% accepted, 4 enrolled. In 2009, 1 master's awarded. *Degree requirements:* For master's, one foreign language, thesis. *Entrance requirements:* For master's, GRE General Test. Additional exam requirements/recommendations for international students: Required—TOEFL (minimum score 550 paper-based; 213 computer-based; 80 iBT). *Application deadline:* For fall admission, 4/1 priority date for domestic students. Applications are processed on a rolling basis. Application fee: $40. Electronic applications accepted. *Expenses:* Tuition, state resident: part-time $508 per credit hour. Tuition, nonresident: part-time $1281 per credit hour. *Financial support:* Fellowships, teaching assistantships available. Financial award application deadline: 3/1. *Faculty research:* Early Greek literature. *Unit head:* Dr. Mark Usher, Chair, 802-656-3210. *Application contact:* Jacques Bailly, Coordinator, 802-656-3210.

University of Victoria, Faculty of Graduate Studies, Faculty of Humanities, Department of French, Victoria, BC V8W 2Y2, Canada. Offers literature (MA); teaching emphasis (MA). Part-time and evening/weekend programs available. *Degree requirements:* For master's, 2 foreign languages, thesis optional. *Entrance requirements:* For master's, BA in French. Additional exam requirements/recommendations for international students: Required—TOEFL (minimum score 575 paper-based; 233 computer-based), IELTS (minimum score 7). Electronic applications accepted. *Faculty research:* French-Canadian literature, stylistics, comparative literature, Francophone literature.

University of Virginia, Curry School of Education, Department of Curriculum, Instruction, and Special Education, Program in Curriculum and Instruction, Charlottesville, VA 22903. Offers curriculum and instruction (M Ed, Ed S); elementary (M Ed, Ed D); English (M Ed, Ed D); foreign language (M Ed); mathematics (M Ed, Ed D); reading (M Ed, Ed D, Ed S); science (Ed D); social studies (M Ed). *Students:* 12 full-time (8 women), 30 part-time (24 women); includes 2 minority (1 Asian American or Pacific Islander, 1 Hispanic American), 1 international. Average age 36. 55 applicants, 69% accepted, 26 enrolled. In 2009, 247 master's, 14 doctorates, 10 other advanced degrees awarded. *Degree requirements:* For master's, comprehensive exam (for some programs); for doctorate, comprehensive exam, thesis/dissertation; for Ed S, comprehensive exam. *Entrance requirements:* For master's, doctorate, and Ed S, GRE General Test, 2 letters of recommendation. Additional exam requirements/recommendations for international students: Required—TOEFL (minimum score 600 paper-based; 250 computer-based; 90 iBT), IELTS (minimum score 7). *Application deadline:* Applications are processed on a rolling basis. Application fee: $60. Electronic applications accepted. *Financial support:* Fellowships with tuition reimbursements, research assistantships with tuition reimbursements, teaching assistantships with tuition reimbursements available. Financial award application deadline: 1/5; financial award applicants required to submit FAFSA.

University of Virginia, Curry School of Education, Program in Education, Charlottesville, VA 22903. Offers administration and supervision (PhD); applied developmental science (PhD); counselor education (PhD); curriculum and instruction (PhD); early childhood-developmental risk (MT); education evaluation (PhD); educational psychology (PhD); educational research (PhD); elementary (MT, PhD); English education (MT, PhD); foreign language education (MT); higher education (PhD); instructional technology (PhD); kinesiology (MT, PhD); math education (PhD); reading education (PhD); research statistics and evaluation (PhD); school psychology (PhD); science education (PhD); social studies education (MT, PhD); special education (PhD); world languages education (MT). *Students:* 336 full-time (239 women), 88 part-time (54 women); includes 43 minority (24 African Americans, 2 American Indian/Alaska Native, 11 Asian Americans or Pacific Islanders, 6 Hispanic Americans), 18 international. Average age 27. 199 applicants, 48% accepted, 55 enrolled. In 2009, 127 master's, 52 doctorates awarded. *Degree requirements:* For master's, comprehensive exam (for some programs), field project; for doctorate, comprehensive exam, thesis/dissertation. *Entrance requirements:* For doctorate, GRE General Test. Additional exam requirements/recommendations for international students: Required—TOEFL (minimum score 600 paper-based; 250 computer-based; 90 iBT), IELTS (minimum score 7). *Application deadline:* Applications are processed on a rolling basis. Application fee: $60. Electronic applications accepted. *Financial support:* Fellowships, research assistantships, teaching assistantships available. Financial award application deadline: 1/5; financial award applicants required to submit FAFSA.

University of West Georgia, Graduate School, College of Arts and Sciences, Department of Foreign Languages and Literatures, Carrollton, GA 30118. Offers teaching foreign languages (MAT). *Expenses:* Tuition, state resident: full-time $2952; part-time $164 per semester hour. Tuition, nonresident: full-time $11,808; part-time $656 per semester hour. Required fees: $42.90 per semester hour. $307 per semester. Tuition and fees vary according to course load.

University of West Georgia, Graduate School, College of Education, Department of Curriculum and Instruction, Carrollton, GA 30118. Offers art education (M Ed); art teacher education (Ed S); biology/secondary education (Ed S); business education (M Ed, Ed S); early childhood education (M Ed, Ed S); economics/secondary teacher education (Ed S); English teacher education (Ed S); French language teacher education (Ed S); history teacher education (Ed S); mathematics teacher education (Ed S); middle grades education (M Ed, Ed S); reading education (M Ed, Ed S); science teacher education (Ed S); secondary education (M Ed, Ed S); social science teacher education (Ed S); Spanish language teacher education (Ed S). Part-time and evening/weekend programs available. *Faculty:* 18 full-time (15 women), 7 part-time/adjunct (6 women). *Students:* 119 full-time (101 women), 358 part-time (280 women); includes 109 minority (97 African Americans, 3 American Indian/Alaska Native, 2 Asian Americans or Pacific Islanders, 7 Hispanic Americans). Average age 33. 193 applicants, 82% accepted, 34 enrolled. In 2009, 109 master's, 27 Ed Ss awarded. *Degree requirements:* For master's, comprehensive exam; for Ed S, research project. *Entrance requirements:* For master's, GRE General Test or MAT, minimum GPA of 2.7; for Ed S, GRE General Test, master's degree, minimum graduate GPA of 2.7. *Application deadline:* For fall admission, 7/17 for domestic students; for spring admission, 11/20 for domestic students. Applications are processed on a rolling basis. Application fee: $30. Electronic applications accepted. *Expenses:* Tuition, state resident: full-time $2952; part-time $164 per semester hour. Tuition, nonresident: full-time $11,808; part-time $656 per semester hour. Required fees: $42.90 per semester hour. $307 per semester. Tuition and fees vary according to course load. *Financial support:* In 2009–10, 5 research assistantships with full tuition reimbursements (averaging $3,000 per year) were awarded; career-related internships or fieldwork and scholarships/grants also available. Support available to part-time students. Financial award applicants required to submit FAFSA. *Unit head:* Dr. Donna Harkins, Chair, 678-839-6066, Fax: 678-839-6559, E-mail: dharkins@westga.edu. *Application contact:* Dr. Charles W. Clark, Dean, 678-839-6508, E-mail: cclark@westga.edu.

University of Wisconsin–Madison, Graduate School, School of Education, Department of Curriculum and Instruction, Madison, WI 53706-1380. Offers art education (MA); curriculum and instruction (MS, PhD); education and mathematics (MA); French education (MA); German education (MA); music education (MS); science education (MS); Spanish education (MA). *Accreditation:* NASM (one or more programs are accredited). *Degree requirements:* For doctorate, thesis/dissertation. Application fee: $56. *Expenses:* Tuition, state resident: part-time $594 per credit. Tuition, nonresident: part-time $1504 per credit. Required fees: $65 per credit. Tuition and fees vary according to course load, program and reciprocity agreements. *Financial support:* Project assistantships available. *Unit head:* Dr. Gloria Ladson-Billings, Chair, 608-262-4000. *Application contact:* Dr. Gloria Ladson-Billings, Chair, 608-262-4000.

Vanderbilt University, Graduate School, Department of French and Italian, Nashville, TN 37240-1001. Offers French (MA, MAT, PhD). *Faculty:* 21 full-time (15 women). *Students:* 10 full-time (5 women); includes 1 minority (Hispanic American), 2 international. Average age 29. 41 applicants, 17% accepted, 2 enrolled.Terminal master's awarded for partial completion of doctoral program. *Degree requirements:* For master's, one foreign language, comprehensive exam; for doctorate, 2 foreign languages, comprehensive exam, thesis/dissertation, final and qualifying exams. *Entrance requirements:* For master's and doctorate, GRE General Test. Additional exam requirements/recommendations for international students: Required—TOEFL (minimum score 570 paper-based; 230 computer-based; 88 iBT). *Application deadline:* For fall admission, 1/15 for domestic and international students. Application fee: $0. Electronic applications accepted. *Financial support:* Fellowships with full and partial tuition reimbursements, teaching assistantships with full and partial tuition reimbursements, career-related internships or fieldwork, Federal Work-Study, institutionally sponsored loans, scholarships/grants, and health care benefits available. Financial award application deadline: 1/15; financial award applicants required to submit CSS PROFILE or FAFSA. *Faculty research:* Baudelaire, Rabelais, voyage literature, postcolonial literature, medieval epic. *Unit head:* Lynn Ramey, Chair, 615-322-6900, Fax: 615-343-6909, E-mail: lynn.ramey@vanderbilt.edu. *Application contact:* Robert Barsky, Director of Graduate Studies, 615-322-6900, Fax: 615-343-6909, E-mail: robert.barsky@vanderbilt.edu.

Vanderbilt University, Graduate School, Department of Germanic and Slavic Languages, Nashville, TN 37240-1001. Offers German (MA, MAT, PhD). *Faculty:* 11 full-time (5 women). *Students:* 20 full-time (13 women); includes 3 minority (1 African American, 1 Asian American or Pacific Islander, 1 Hispanic American), 7 international. Average age 32. 22 applicants, 32% accepted, 5 enrolled. In 2009, 2 master's, 1 doctorate awarded. Terminal master's awarded for partial completion of doctoral program. *Degree requirements:* For master's, one foreign language, comprehensive exam; for doctorate, 2 foreign languages, comprehensive exam, thesis/dissertation, qualifying and final exams. *Entrance requirements:* For master's and doctorate, GRE General Test, sample of written work. Additional exam requirements/recommendations for international students: Required—TOEFL (minimum score 570 paper-based; 230 computer-based; 88 iBT). *Application deadline:* For fall admission, 1/15 for domestic and international students. Application fee: $0. Electronic applications accepted. *Financial support:* Fellowships with full and partial tuition reimbursements, teaching assistantships with full and partial tuition reimbursements, career-related internships or fieldwork, Federal Work-Study, institutionally sponsored loans, scholarships/grants, and health care benefits available. Financial award application deadline: 1/15; financial award applicants required to submit CSS PROFILE or FAFSA. *Faculty research:* 1750 to present, Middle Ages, Baroque, language pedagogy, linguistics. *Unit head:* Barbara Hahn, Acting Chair, 615-322-2611, Fax: 615-343-7258, E-mail: barbara.hahn@vanderbilt.edu. *Application contact:* Meike Werner, Director of Graduate Studies, 615-322-2611, Fax: 615-343-7258, E-mail: meike.werner@vanderbilt.edu.

Vanderbilt University, Graduate School, Department of Spanish and Portuguese, Nashville, TN 37240-1001. Offers Portuguese (MA); Spanish (MA, MAT, PhD); Spanish and Portuguese (PhD). *Faculty:* 14 full-time (6 women). *Students:* 30 full-time (16 women), 1 part-time (0 women); includes 3 minority (1 African American, 1 American Indian/Alaska Native, 1 Hispanic American), 13 international. Average age 31. 66 applicants, 12% accepted, 7 enrolled. In 2009, 4 doctorates awarded. *Degree requirements:* For master's, one foreign language, thesis; for doctorate, 2 foreign languages, thesis/dissertation, final and qualifying exams. *Entrance requirements:* For master's, GRE General Test; for doctorate, GRE General Test, writing sample in Spanish. Additional exam requirements/recommendations for international students: Required—TOEFL (minimum score 570 paper-based; 230 computer-based; 88 iBT). *Application deadline:* For fall admission, 1/15 for domestic and international students. Application fee: $0. Electronic applications accepted. *Financial support:* Fellowships with full and partial tuition reimbursements, teaching assistantships with full tuition reimbursements, Federal Work-Study, institutionally sponsored loans, and health care benefits available. Financial award application deadline: 1/15; financial award applicants required to submit CSS PROFILE or FAFSA. *Faculty research:* Spanish, Portuguese, and Latin American literatures; foreign language pedagogy; Renaissance and Baroque poetry; nineteenth century Spanish novel. *Unit head:* Cathy L. Jrade, Chair, 615-322-6930, Fax: 615-343-7260, E-mail: cathy.l.jrade@vanderbilt.edu. *Application contact:* Christina Karageorgou-Bastea, Director of Graduate Studies, 615-322-6930, Fax: 615-343-7260, E-mail: christina.karageorgou@vanderbilt.edu.

Virginia Polytechnic Institute and State University, Graduate School, College of Liberal Arts and Human Sciences, Department of Foreign Languages and Literatures, Blacksburg, VA 24061. Offers MA. *Faculty:* 35 full-time (22 women). *Students:* 7 full-time (6 women); includes 1 minority (American Indian/Alaska Native). Average age 24. 8 applicants, 63% accepted, 3 enrolled. *Entrance requirements:* For master's, GRE, GMAT. Additional exam requirements/recommendations for international students: Required—TOEFL (minimum score 550 paper-based; 213 computer-based). *Application deadline:* For fall admission, 5/15 for international students; for spring admission, 10/15 for international students. Applications are processed on a rolling basis. Application fee: $65. Electronic applications accepted. *Expenses:* Tuition, area resident: Full-time $10,228; part-time $459 per credit hour. Tuition, nonresident: full-time $17,892; part-time $865 per credit hour. Required fees: $1966; $451 per semester. *Financial support:* In 2009–10, 4 teaching assistantships with full tuition reimbursements (averaging $9,279 per year) were awarded; career-related internships or fieldwork, Federal Work-Study, scholarships/grants, and unspecified assistantships also available. Financial award application deadline: 1/15. Total annual research expenditures: $258,207. *Unit head:* Dr. Richard L. Shryock, Head, 540-231-5361, Fax: 540-231-4812, E-mail: shryock@vt.edu. *Application contact:* Janell Watson, Student Contact, 540-231-9009, Fax: 540-231-4812, E-mail: rjwatson@vt.edu.

Washington State University, Graduate School, College of Liberal Arts, Department of Foreign Languages and Cultures, Pullman, WA 99164. Offers foreign languages with emphasis

Foreign Languages Education

Washington State University (continued)

in Spanish (MA). *Faculty:* 7. *Students:* 11 full-time (7 women); includes 4 minority (all Hispanic Americans), 2 international. Average age 28. 21 applicants, 48% accepted, 4 enrolled. In 2009, 3 master's awarded. *Degree requirements:* For master's, comprehensive exam (for some programs), thesis (for some programs), 4 written exams, oral exam, paper. *Entrance requirements:* For master's, three current letters of recommendation; all original transcripts including an official English translation; two writing samples; letter of application stating qualifications and personal goals; brief (3-5 minute) tape recordings of two informal dialogues between applicant and native speaker. Additional exam requirements/recommendations for international students: Required—TOEFL (minimum score 550 paper-based). *Application deadline:* For fall admission, 1/1 priority date for domestic and international students; for spring admission, 7/1 priority date for domestic students, 7/1 for international students. Application fee: $50. Electronic applications accepted. *Financial support:* In 2009–10, fellowships (averaging $2,200 per year), teaching assistantships with full and partial tuition reimbursements (averaging $13,056 per year) were awarded; career-related internships or fieldwork, Federal Work-Study, institutionally sponsored loans, scholarships/grants, and health care benefits also available. Financial award application deadline: 2/15; financial award applicants required to submit FAFSA. *Faculty research:* Spanish and Latin American literature, film, and culture; pedagogy; computer-aided instruction. Total annual research expenditures: $98,000. *Unit head:* Dr. Eloy Gonzalez, Chair, 509-335-2756, Fax: 509-335-3708, E-mail: eloygonz@wsunix.wsu.edu. *Application contact:* Graduate School Admissions, 800-GRADWSU, Fax: 509-335-1949, E-mail: gradsch@wsu.edu.

Wayne State University, College of Education, Division of Teacher Education, Detroit, MI 48202. Offers adult and continuing education (M Ed); art education (M Ed); bilingual/bicultural education (M Ed, MAT); business education (M Ed, MAT); career and technical education (M Ed, Ed D, PhD, Ed S); curriculum and instruction (Ed D, PhD, Ed S); distributive education (M Ed, MAT); early childhood education (M Ed); elementary education (M Ed, MAT, Ed D, PhD, Ed S); elementary education curriculum and instruction (M Ed); English education (M Ed); English education-secondary (M Ed, Ed S); foreign language education (M Ed); general education (Ed D, Ed S); health occupations education (M Ed); industrial education (M Ed); mathematics education (M Ed, Ed S); pre-school and parent education (M Ed); reading (M Ed, Ed D, Ed S); reading, languages and literature (Ed D); school music-vocal (M Ed); science education (M Ed, MAT, Ed S); secondary education (MAT); secondary school reading (M Ed); social studies education (M Ed, Ed S), including education-secondary (M Ed); special education (M Ed, Ed D, PhD, Ed S); teacher education (MAT, Ed D, PhD). *Degree requirements:* For doctorate, thesis/dissertation. *Entrance requirements:* For master's, Michigan Basic Skills Test (MA in teaching), minimum GPA of 2.6; for doctorate, minimum undergraduate GPA of 3.0, graduate 3.5; interview, curriculum vitae; references. Additional exam requirements/recommendations for international students: Required—TOEFL (minimum score 550 paper-based; 213 computer-based), TWE (minimum score 6). Electronic applications accepted. *Faculty research:* Reading and writing literacy and literature.

Wayne State University, College of Liberal Arts and Sciences, Department of Classical and Modern Languages, Literatures, and Cultures, Program in German and Slavic Studies, Detroit, MI 48202. Offers German (MA); language learning (MA); modern languages (PhD); Russian (MA). *Degree requirements:* For master's, one foreign language, thesis or alternative; for doctorate, 2 foreign languages, thesis/dissertation. *Entrance requirements:* For master's and doctorate, minimum GPA of 3.0. Additional exam requirements/recommendations for international students: Required—TOEFL (minimum score 550 paper-based; 213 computer-

based); Recommended—TWE (minimum score 6). Electronic applications accepted. *Faculty research:* Exile and Holocaust, minority literature, gender studies, fairytale studies, sociolinguistics.

Wayne State University, College of Liberal Arts and Sciences, Department of Classical and Modern Languages, Literatures, and Cultures, Program in Near Eastern and Asian Studies, Detroit, MI 48202. Offers language learning (MA); Near Eastern studies (MA). *Degree requirements:* For master's, one foreign language. *Entrance requirements:* For master's, GRE General Test. Additional exam requirements/recommendations for international students: Required—TOEFL (minimum score 550 paper-based; 213 computer-based); Recommended—TWE (minimum score 6). Electronic applications accepted. *Faculty research:* Modern Middle East history, Arabic language and culture studies, Chinese linguistics, Islamic studies, Judaic studies.

West Chester University of Pennsylvania, Office of Graduate Studies, College of Arts and Sciences, Department of Languages and Cultures, West Chester, PA 19383. Offers French (M Ed, MA, Teaching Certificate); German (M Ed, Teaching Certificate); Latin (M Ed, Teaching Certificate); Spanish (M Ed, MA, Teaching Certificate). Part-time and evening/weekend programs available. *Students:* 4 full-time (all women), 27 part-time (21 women); includes 6 minority (2 African Americans, 1 Asian American or Pacific Islander, 3 Hispanic Americans). Average age 33. 16 applicants, 94% accepted, 9 enrolled. In 2009, 7 master's awarded. *Degree requirements:* For master's, one foreign language, comprehensive exam, thesis optional. *Entrance requirements:* For master's, GRE or MAT, placement test. Additional exam requirements/recommendations for international students: Required—TOEFL (minimum score 550 paper-based; 213 computer-based; 80 iBT). *Application deadline:* For fall admission, 4/15 priority date for domestic students, 3/15 for international students; for spring admission, 10/15 for domestic students, 9/1 for international students. Applications are processed on a rolling basis. Application fee: $35. Electronic applications accepted. *Expenses:* Tuition, state resident: full-time $6666; part-time $370 per credit. Tuition, nonresident: full-time $10,666; part-time $593 per credit. Required fees: $122.56 per credit. *Financial support:* In 2009–10, 1 research assistantship with full and partial tuition reimbursement (averaging $5,000 per year) was awarded; unspecified assistantships also available. Support available to part-time students. Financial award application deadline: 2/15; financial award applicants required to submit FAFSA. *Faculty research:* Implementation of world languages curriculum framework. *Unit head:* Dr. Jerry Williams, Chair, 610-436-2700, Fax: 610-436-3048, E-mail: jwilliams2@wcupa.edu. *Application contact:* Dr. Rebecca Pauly, Graduate Coordinator, 610-436-2382, E-mail: rpauly@wcupa.edu.

Worcester State College, Graduate Studies, Program in Spanish, Worcester, MA 01602-2597. Offers M Ed. Part-time programs available. *Faculty:* 3 full-time (2 women). *Students:* 11 part-time (9 women); includes 1 minority (Hispanic American). Average age 32. 9 applicants, 100% accepted, 0 enrolled. In 2009, 1 master's awarded. *Degree requirements:* For master's, comprehensive exam (for some programs), thesis optional. *Entrance requirements:* Additional exam requirements/recommendations for international students: Required—TOEFL (minimum score 550 paper-based; 213 computer-based; 79 iBT). *Application deadline:* Applications are processed on a rolling basis. Application fee: $30. *Expenses:* Tuition, area resident: Part-time $150 per credit. Tuition, state resident: part-time $150 per credit. Tuition, nonresident: part-time $150 per credit. Required fees: $85. *Financial support:* Career-related internships or fieldwork, scholarships/grants, and unspecified assistantships available. Financial award application deadline: 3/1; financial award applicants required to submit FAFSA. *Unit head:* Dr. Juan Orbe, Head, 508-929-8704, Fax: 508-929-8174, E-mail: jorbe@worcester.edu. *Application contact:* Nicole Brown, Assistant Dean of Graduate and Continuing Education, 508-929-8787, Fax: 508-929-8100, E-mail: nbrown@worcester.edu.

Health Education

Adelphi University, School of Education, Program in Health Studies, Garden City, NY 11530-0701. Offers community health education (MA, Certificate); school health education (MA). Part-time and evening/weekend programs available. *Students:* 7 full-time (4 women), 73 part-time (41 women); includes 2 minority (1 Asian American or Pacific Islander, 1 Hispanic American). Average age 27. In 2009, 27 master's awarded. *Degree requirements:* For master's, internship. *Entrance requirements:* For master's, 3 letters of recommendation, resume, minimum cumulative GPA of 2.75. Additional exam requirements/recommendations for international students: Required—TOEFL (minimum score 550 paper-based; 213 computer-based; 80 iBT). *Application deadline:* For fall admission, 4/1 for international students; for spring admission, 11/1 for international students. Applications are processed on a rolling basis. Application fee: $50. Electronic applications accepted. *Expenses:* Tuition: Full-time $28,340; part-time $830 per credit. Required fees: $600; $250 per credit. Full-time tuition and fees vary according to course load and program. *Financial support:* Fellowships, research assistantships with partial tuition reimbursements, teaching assistantships, career-related internships or fieldwork, Federal Work-Study, institutionally sponsored loans, and tuition waivers (full) available. Support available to part-time students. Financial award application deadline: 2/15; financial award applicants required to submit FAFSA. *Faculty research:* Alcohol abuse, tobacco cessation, drug abuse, healthy family lives, healthy personal living. *Unit head:* Dr. Stanley Snegroff, Director, 516-877-4283, E-mail: snegroff@adelphi.edu. *Application contact:* Christine Murphy, Director of Admissions, 516-877-3050, Fax: 516-877-3039, E-mail: graduateadmissions@adelphi.edu.

Alabama State University, School of Graduate Studies, College of Education, Department of Health, Physical Education, and Recreation, Montgomery, AL 36101-0271. Offers health education (M Ed); physical education (M Ed). Part-time programs available. *Degree requirements:* For master's, comprehensive exam. *Entrance requirements:* For master's, GRE General Test, MAT, graduate writing competency test. Additional exam requirements/recommendations for international students: Required—TOEFL (minimum score 500 paper-based; 173 computer-based). *Faculty research:* Risk factors for heart disease in the college-age population, cardiovascular reactivity for the Cold Pressor Test.

Albany State University, College of Education, Program in Health and Physical Education, Albany, GA 31705-2717. Offers M Ed. *Accreditation:* NCATE. Part-time programs available. *Students:* 5 full-time (2 women), 17 part-time (6 women); includes 19 minority (all African Americans). Average age 32. 4 applicants, 100% accepted, 3 enrolled. In 2009, 1 master's awarded. *Degree requirements:* For master's, comprehensive exam, thesis optional. *Entrance requirements:* For master's, GRE General Test, MAT or NTE (GACE II). Additional exam requirements/recommendations for international students: Required—TOEFL. *Application deadline:* For fall admission, 11/16 for domestic students, 9/16 for international students; for spring admission, 4/19 for domestic students, 2/19 for international students. Applications are processed on a rolling basis. Application fee: $20. Electronic applications accepted. *Expenses:* Tuition, state resident: full-time $2970; part-time $162 per credit hour. Tuition, nonresident: full-time $12,168; part-time $676 per credit hour. Required fees: $962; $75 per credit hour. *Financial support:* Application deadline: 6/30. *Faculty research:* Neuromuscular function, nutrition, health, recreation, and physical education. *Unit head:* Dr. Richard H. Williams, Chair, 229-430-4762, Fax: 229-430-3020, E-mail: richard.williams@asurams.edu. *Application contact:* Dr. Rani George, Interim Graduate Admissions Officer, 229-430-4862, Fax: 229-430-6398, E-mail: nicole.lane@asurams.edu.

Alcorn State University, School of Graduate Studies, School of Psychology and Education, Alcorn State, MS 39096-7500. Offers agricultural education (MS Ed); elementary education (MS Ed, Ed S); guidance and counseling (MS Ed); industrial education (MS Ed); secondary

education (MS Ed), including health and physical education; special education (MS Ed). *Accreditation:* NCATE. *Degree requirements:* For master's, thesis optional.

Allen College, Program in Nursing, Waterloo, IA 50703. Offers acute care nurse practitioner (MSN); adult nurse practitioner (MSN); adult psychiatric-mental health nurse practitioner (MSN); family nurse practitioner (MSN); gerontological nurse practitioner (MSN); health education (MSN); leadership in health care delivery (MSN). *Accreditation:* AACN; NLN. Part-time programs available. *Faculty:* 2 full-time (both women), 8 part-time/adjunct (all women). *Students:* 37 full-time (35 women), 103 part-time (99 women); includes 1 minority (Asian American or Pacific Islander). Average age 38. *Degree requirements:* For master's, thesis optional. *Entrance requirements:* For master's, minimum GPA of 3.0. Additional exam requirements/recommendations for international students: Required—TOEFL (minimum score 550 paper-based). *Application deadline:* For fall admission, 7/15 priority date for domestic students; for spring admission, 12/1 priority date for domestic students. Applications are processed on a rolling basis. Application fee: $50. Electronic applications accepted. *Expenses:* Tuition: Full-time $12,550; part-time $651 per credit hour. Required fees: $826; $65 per credit hour. One-time fee: $425. Tuition and fees vary according to course load. *Financial support:* Teaching assistantships, institutionally sponsored loans, scholarships/grants, and traineeships available. Support available to part-time students. Financial award application deadline: 8/15; financial award applicants required to submit FAFSA. *Faculty research:* Pain and aged, congestive heart failure. *Unit head:* Nancy Kramer, Dean, School of Nursing, 319-226-2040, Fax: 319-226-2070, E-mail: kramerna@ihs.org. *Application contact:* Michelle Koehn, Admissions Counselor, 319-226-2002, Fax: 319-226-2051, E-mail: koehnml@ihs.org.

American University, College of Arts and Sciences, School of Education, Teaching, and Health, Washington, DC 20016-8030. Offers curriculum and instruction (M Ed, Certificate); early childhood education (MAT, Certificate); elementary education (MAT); English for speakers of other languages (MAT, Certificate); health promotion management (MS); international training and development (MAT); international training and education (MA); nutrition education (Certificate); secondary teaching (MAT, Certificate); special education (MA), including special education: learning disabilities; MAT/MA. *Accreditation:* NCATE. Part-time and evening/weekend programs available. *Faculty:* 15 full-time (9 women), 68 part-time/adjunct (45 women). *Students:* 74 full-time (56 women), 392 part-time (293 women); includes 110 minority (71 African Americans, 9 American Indian/Alaska Native, 11 Asian Americans or Pacific Islanders, 19 Hispanic Americans), 3 international. Average age 27. 354 applicants, 87% accepted, 218 enrolled. In 2009, 196 master's awarded. *Degree requirements:* For master's, comprehensive exam, thesis or alternative, PRAXIS II. *Entrance requirements:* For master's, GRE General Test, minimum GPA of 3.0; for Certificate, bachelor's degree. Additional exam requirements/recommendations for international students: Required—TOEFL. *Application deadline:* For fall admission, 2/1 priority date for domestic students; for spring admission, 10/1 priority date for domestic students. Applications are processed on a rolling basis. Application fee: $80. *Expenses:* Tuition: Full-time $22,266; part-time $1237 per credit hour. Required fees: $430. Tuition and fees vary according to program. *Financial support:* Fellowships, research assistantships with full and partial tuition reimbursements, teaching assistantships with full and partial tuition reimbursements, career-related internships or fieldwork, Federal Work-Study, and institutionally sponsored loans available. Support available to part-time students. Financial award application deadline: 2/1; financial award applicants required to submit FAFSA. *Faculty research:* Gender equity, socioeconomic technology, learning disabilities, gifted and talented education. *Unit head:* Dr. Sarah Irvine-Belson, Dean, 202-885-3714, Fax: 202-885-1187, E-mail: educate@american.edu. *Application contact:* Kathleen Clowery, Director, Graduate Admissions, 202-885-3621, Fax: 202-885-1505.

American University of Beirut, Graduate Programs, Faculty of Health Sciences, Beirut, Lebanon. Offers environmental sciences (MSES), including environmental health; epidemiology (MS); epidemiology and biostatistics (MPH); health behavior and education (MPH); population health (MS); public health (MPH). Part-time programs available. *Degree requirements:* For master's, one foreign language, comprehensive exam, thesis (for some programs). *Entrance requirements:* For master's, 2 letters of recommendation. Additional exam requirements/recommendations for international students: Required—TOEFL (minimum score 573 paper-based; 230 computer-based; 98 iBT), IELTS (minimum score 7.5). Electronic applications accepted. *Faculty research:* Urban health, childbirth, tobacco control, HIV/AIDS surveillance, health finance and policies.

Arcadia University, Graduate Studies, Department of Medical Science and Community Health, Program in Allied Health, Glenside, PA 19038-3295. Offers MPH, MSHE, MSPH. Part-time and evening/weekend programs available. *Faculty:* 1 (woman) full-time, 9 part-time/adjunct (5 women). *Students:* 54 full-time (40 women), 10 part-time (4 women); includes 3 minority (all African Americans), 6 international. Average age 27. In 2009, 14 master's awarded. *Entrance requirements:* For master's, GMAT or GRE (MHA). *Application deadline:* Applications are processed on a rolling basis. Application fee: $50. *Expenses:* Tuition: Full-time $30,450; part-time $620 per credit hour. Required fees: $165. Tuition and fees vary according to program. *Financial support:* Tuition waivers (partial) and unspecified assistantships available. *Unit head:* Dr. Andrea Crivelli-Kovach, Director. *Application contact:* 215-572-2910, Fax: 215-572-4049, E-mail: admiss@arcadia.edu.

Arkansas State University—Jonesboro, Graduate School, College of Nursing and Health Professions, Department of Physical Therapy, Jonesboro, State University, AR 72467. Offers aging studies (Certificate); health sciences (MS); health sciences education (Certificate); physical therapy (DPT). *Accreditation:* APTA. Part-time programs available. *Faculty:* 8 full-time (4 women), 1 (woman) part-time/adjunct. *Students:* 49 full-time (31 women), 26 part-time (19 women); includes 12 minority (all African Americans), 5 international. Average age 28. 53 applicants, 70% accepted, 32 enrolled. In 2009, 22 master's awarded. *Degree requirements:* For master's, comprehensive exam; for doctorate, comprehensive exam, thesis/dissertation. *Entrance requirements:* For master's, GRE General Test, Allied Health Profession Admissions Test, writing exam, appropriate bachelor's degree, letters of reference, resume, writing sample; for doctorate, GRE, Allied Health Professions Admissions Test, appropriate bachelor's or master's degree, letters of reference, resume, official transcript, volunteer experience, criminal background check, immunization records. Additional exam requirements/recommendations for international students: Required—TOEFL (minimum score 550 paper-based; 213 computer-based; 79 iBT), IELTS (minimum score 6). *Application deadline:* For fall admission, 3/1 for domestic and international students. Applications are processed on a rolling basis. Application fee: $50. Electronic applications accepted. *Expenses:* Contact institution. *Financial support:* In 2009–10, 7 students received support; fellowships, career-related internships or fieldwork, scholarships/grants, and unspecified assistantships available. Financial award application deadline: 7/1; financial award applicants required to submit FAFSA. *Unit head:* Dr. Patricia King, Chair, 870-972-3591, Fax: 870-972-3652, E-mail: pking@astate.edu. *Application contact:* Dr. Andrew Sustich, Dean of the Graduate School, 870-972-3029, Fax: 870-972-3857, E-mail: sustich@astate.edu.

A.T. Still University of Health Sciences, School of Health Management, Kirksville, MO 63501. Offers geriatric healthcare (MGH); health administration (MHA); health education (MH Ed, DH Ed); public health (MPH). Part-time and evening/weekend programs available. Postbaccalaureate distance learning degree programs offered (minimal on-campus study). *Faculty:* 12 full-time (6 women), 31 part-time/adjunct (12 women). *Students:* 84 full-time (59 women), 503 part-time (340 women); includes 179 minority (103 African Americans, 11 American Indian/Alaska Native, 37 Asian Americans or Pacific Islanders, 28 Hispanic Americans). Average age 32. 179 applicants, 100% accepted, 98 enrolled. In 2009, 98 master's, 22 doctorates awarded. *Degree requirements:* For master's, thesis (for some programs), integrated terminal project; for doctorate, thesis/dissertation. *Entrance requirements:* For master's, minimum GPA of 2.5, bachelor's degree or equivalent from U.S. institution; for doctorate, minimum GPA of 2.5, master's or terminal degree, employment. Additional exam requirements/recommendations for international students: Required—TOEFL (minimum score 550 paper-based; 213 computer-based; 80 iBT). *Application deadline:* For fall admission, 8/7 for domestic and international students; for winter admission, 10/23 for domestic and international students; for spring admission, 2/5 for domestic and international students. Applications are processed on a rolling basis. Application fee: $60. Electronic applications accepted. *Expenses:* Contact institution. *Financial support:* In 2009–10, 408 students received support. Application deadline: 5/1. *Unit head:* Dr. Kimberly O'Reilly, Interim Dean, 660-626-2820, Fax: 660-626-2826, E-mail: koreilley@atsu.edu. *Application contact:* Sarah Spencer, Director of Recruitment, 660-626-2820 Ext. 2669, Fax: 660-626-2826, E-mail: sbartlett@atsu.edu.

Auburn University, Graduate School, College of Education, Department of Kinesiology, Auburn University, AL 36849. Offers exercise science (M Ed, MS, PhD); health promotion (M Ed, MS); kinesiology (PhD); physical education/teacher education (M Ed, MS, Ed D, Ed S). *Accreditation:* NCATE. Part-time programs available. *Faculty:* 16 full-time (7 women), 1 part-time/adjunct (0 women). *Students:* 70 full-time (46 women), 21 part-time (8 women); includes 10 minority (8 African Americans, 2 Asian Americans or Pacific Islanders), 10 international. Average age 26. 109 applicants, 68% accepted, 53 enrolled. In 2009, 26 master's, 7 doctorates awarded. *Degree requirements:* For master's, thesis (for some programs); for doctorate, thesis/dissertation; for Ed S, exam, field project. *Entrance requirements:* For master's, GRE General Test; for doctorate and Ed S, GRE General Test, interview, master's degree. *Application deadline:* For fall admission, 7/7 for domestic students; for spring admission, 11/24 for domestic students. Applications are processed on a rolling basis. Application fee: $50 ($60 for international students). Electronic applications accepted. *Expenses:* Tuition, state resident: full-time $6240. Tuition, nonresident: full-time $18,720. International tuition: $18,938 full-time. Required fees: $492. Tuition and fees vary according to course load, program and reciprocity agreements. *Financial support:* Research assistantships, teaching assistantships, Federal Work-Study available. Support available to part-time students. Financial award application deadline: 3/15; financial award applicants required to submit FAFSA. *Faculty research:* Biomechanics, exercise physiology, motor skill learning, school health, curriculum development. *Unit head:* Dr. Mary E. Rudisill, Head, 334-844-4483. *Application contact:* Dr. George Flowers, Dean of the Graduate School, 334-844-2125.

Augusta State University, Graduate Studies, College of Education, Program in Health and Physical Education, Augusta, GA 30904-2200. Offers M Ed. *Entrance requirements:* For master's, GRE, MAT, minimum GPA of 2.5.

Austin Peay State University, College of Graduate Studies, College of Behavioral and Health Sciences, Department of Health and Human Performance, Clarksville, TN 37044. Offers health leadership (MS). Part-time and evening/weekend programs available. Postbaccalaureate distance learning degree programs offered (no on-campus study). *Faculty:* 5 full-time (3 women). *Students:* 28 full-time (19 women), 45 part-time (35 women); includes 33 minority (28 African Americans, 1 Asian American or Pacific Islander, 4 Hispanic Americans). Average age 32. 72 applicants, 96% accepted, 39 enrolled. In 2009, 23 master's awarded. *Degree requirements:* For master's, comprehensive exam, thesis optional. *Entrance requirements:* For master's, GRE General Test, 3 letters of recommendation, minimum undergraduate GPA of 2.5. Additional exam requirements/recommendations for international students: Required—TOEFL (minimum score 500 paper-based; 173 computer-based). *Application deadline:* For fall admission, 7/27 priority date for domestic students; for spring admission, 12/17 priority date for domestic students. Applications are processed on a rolling basis. Application fee: $25. Electronic applications accepted. *Expenses:* Tuition, state resident: full-time $6160; part-time $608 per credit hour. Tuition, nonresident: full-time $17,080; part-time $854 per credit hour. Required fees: $1224; $61.20 per credit hour. *Financial support:* In 2009–10, 9 students received support, including 9 research assistantships with full tuition reimbursements available (averaging $5,184 per year); career-related internships or fieldwork, Federal Work-Study, institutionally sponsored loans, scholarships/grants, and unspecified assistantships also available. Support available to part-time students. Financial award application deadline: 3/1; financial award applicants required to submit FAFSA. *Faculty research:* Aging and physical activity. *Unit head:* Dr. Marcy Maurer, Interim Chair, 931-221-6105, Fax: 931-221-7040, E-mail: maurerm@apsu.edu. *Application contact:* Dr. Dixie Dennis, Dean, College of Graduate Studies, 931-221-7662, Fax: 931-221-7641, E-mail: dennisdi@apsu.edu.

Averett University, Master in Education Program, Danville, VA 24541-3692. Offers art education (M Ed); biology (M Ed); biology education (M Ed); chemistry (M Ed); chemistry education (M Ed); curriculum and instruction (M Ed); elementary education (M Ed); English (M Ed); English education (M Ed); health and physical education (M Ed); history and social studies education (M Ed); math (M Ed); mathematics education (M Ed); physical science (M Ed); reading specialization (M Ed); special education (learning disabilities specialization PK-12) (M Ed). Program also offered at Richmond, VA regional campus location. Part-time and evening/weekend programs available. *Faculty:* 4 full-time (3 women), 36 part-time/adjunct (22 women). *Students:* 182 full-time (160 women), 110 part-time (94 women); includes 113 minority (94 African Americans, 1 American Indian/Alaska Native, 7 Asian Americans or Pacific Islanders, 11 Hispanic Americans). Average age 37. 119 applicants, 99% accepted, 98 enrolled. In 2009, 92 master's awarded. *Degree requirements:* For master's, comprehensive exam, thesis optional. *Entrance requirements:* For master's, PRAXIS, GRE General Test, MAT or NTE, writing proficiency exam, 3 letters of recommendation, current teacher's licensure or eligibility for licensure, minimum undergraduate GPA of 3.0 in previous 2 years. Additional exam requirements/recommendations for international students: Required—TOEFL (minimum score 600 paper-based; 200 computer-based). *Application deadline:* Applications are processed on a rolling basis. *Expenses:* Contact institution. *Financial support:* Career-related internships or fieldwork, Federal Work-Study, and scholarships/grants available. Financial award application deadline: 4/1; financial award applicants required to submit FAFSA. *Faculty research:* Literary assessment-PreK-6, handwriting instruction and assessment-PreK-6, written language instruction and assessment-PreK-6 and special needs students learning styles, curriculum and instruction processes. *Unit head:* Dr. Lynn H. Wolf, Chair/Associate Professor/Director, 434-793-3995, Fax: 434-791-4392, E-mail: lynn.wolf@averett.edu. *Application contact:* Dr. Lynn H. Wolf, Chair/Associate Professor/Director, 434-793-3995, Fax: 434-791-4392, E-mail: lynn.wolf@averett.edu.

Ball State University, Graduate School, College of Sciences and Humanities, Department of Physiology and Health Science, Program in Health Education, Muncie, IN 47306-1099. Offers MA, MAE. *Accreditation:* NCATE.

Baylor University, Graduate School, School of Education, Department of Health, Human Performance and Recreation, Waco, TX 76798. Offers exercise, nutrition and preventive health (PhD); health, human performance and recreation (MS Ed). *Accreditation:* NCATE. Part-time programs available. *Faculty:* 13 full-time (5 women), 3 part-time/adjunct (1 woman). *Students:* 66 full-time (35 women), 42 part-time (21 women); includes 14 minority (7 African Americans, 3 Asian Americans or Pacific Islanders, 4 Hispanic Americans), 5 international. 30 applicants, 87% accepted. In 2009, 48 master's, 6 doctorates awarded. *Degree requirements:* For master's, thesis optional. *Entrance requirements:* For master's, GRE General Test. *Application deadline:* For fall admission, 4/1 priority date for domestic students; for spring admission, 10/1 for domestic students. Applications are processed on a rolling basis. Application fee: $25. Electronic applications accepted. *Financial support:* In 2009–10, 35 students received support, including 22 teaching assistantships; career-related internships or fieldwork, Federal Work-Study, institutionally sponsored loans, tuition waivers (partial), and recreation supplements also available. *Faculty research:* Behavior change theory, pedagogy, nutrition and enzyme therapy, exercise testing, health planning. *Unit head:* Dr. Glenn Miller, Graduate Program Director, 254-710-4001, Fax: 254-710-3527, E-mail: glenn_miller@baylor.edu. *Application contact:* Eva Berger-Rhodes, Administrative Assistant, 254-710-4945, Fax: 254-710-3870, E-mail: eva_rhodes@baylor.edu.

Benedictine University, Graduate Programs, Program in Public Health, Lisle, IL 60532-0900. Offers administration of health care institutions (MPH); dietetics (MPH); disaster management (MPH); health education (MPH); health information systems (MPH); MBA/MPH; MPH/MS. Part-time and evening/weekend programs available. Postbaccalaureate distance learning degree programs offered. *Faculty:* 2 full-time (0 women), 8 part-time/adjunct (3 women). *Students:* 132 full-time (92 women), 354 part-time (286 women); includes 171 minority (112 African Americans, 1 American Indian/Alaska Native, 35 Asian Americans or Pacific Islanders, 23 Hispanic Americans), 14 international. Average age 33. 247 applicants, 94% accepted, 180 enrolled. In 2009, 77 master's awarded. *Entrance requirements:* For master's, MAT, GRE, or GMAT. Additional exam requirements/recommendations for international students: Required—TOEFL (minimum score 550 paper-based; 213 computer-based). *Application deadline:* For fall admission, 9/1 for domestic students; for winter admission, 12/1 for domestic students; for spring admission, 2/15 for domestic students. Application fee: $40. *Expenses:* Tuition: Part-time $750 per credit hour. Tuition and fees vary according to campus/location and program. *Financial support:* Career-related internships or fieldwork and health care benefits available. Support available to part-time students. *Unit head:* Dr. Alan Gorr, Director, 630-829-6566, Fax: 630-960-1126, E-mail: agorr@ben.edu. *Application contact:* Kari Gibbons, Director, Admissions, 630-829-6200, Fax: 630-829-6584, E-mail: kgibbons@ben.edu.

Boston University, School of Education, Department of Curriculum and Teaching, Program in Health Education, Boston, MA 02215. Offers Ed M, CAGS. *Degree requirements:* For master's, thesis optional; for CAGS, comprehensive exam. *Entrance requirements:* For master's and CAGS, GRE General Test or MAT. Additional exam requirements/recommendations for international students: Required—TOEFL. Electronic applications accepted. *Expenses:* Tuition: Full-time $37,910; part-time $1184 per credit hour. Required fees: $386; $40 per semester. Part-time tuition and fees vary according to class time, course level, degree level and program. *Faculty research:* Substance abuse, therapeutic recreation, motor development and performance, stress management.

Brandeis University, The Heller School for Social Policy and Management, Program in Social Policy, Waltham, MA 02454-9110. Offers assets and inequalities (PhD); children, youth and families (PhD); health and behavioral health (PhD). *Degree requirements:* For doctorate, thesis/dissertation, qualifying paper, 2-year residency. *Entrance requirements:* For doctorate, GRE General Test.

Brigham Young University, Graduate Studies, College of Life Sciences, Department of Health Science, Provo, UT 84602. Offers MPH. *Faculty:* 12 full-time (2 women). *Students:* 23 full-time (15 women); includes 4 minority (1 African American, 2 Asian Americans or Pacific Islanders, 1 Hispanic American). Average age 26. 47 applicants, 34% accepted, 10 enrolled. In 2009, 11 master's awarded. *Degree requirements:* For master's, thesis, oral defense. *Entrance requirements:* For master's, GRE General Test, minimum GPA of 3.0 in last 60 hours. Additional exam requirements/recommendations for international students: Required—TOEFL (minimum score 580 paper-based; 237 computer-based; 85 iBT), IELTS (minimum score 7). *Application deadline:* For fall admission, 2/1 for domestic and international students. Application fee: $50. Electronic applications accepted. *Expenses:* Tuition: Full-time $5580; part-time $301 per credit hour. Tuition and fees vary according to student's religious affiliation. *Financial support:* In 2009–10, 23 students received support, including 23 fellowships with partial tuition reimbursements available (averaging $3,260 per year), 23 research assistantships with partial tuition reimbursements available (averaging $950 per year); teaching assistantships, career-related internships or fieldwork, scholarships/grants, and tuition waivers (partial) also available. Financial award application deadline: 3/1. *Faculty research:* Social marketing, health communication, cancer, epidemiology, tobacco prevention and control, maternal and child health. Total annual research expenditures: $3,915. *Unit head:* Dr. Michael Dean Barnes, Chair, 801-422-3327, Fax: 801-422-0273, E-mail: micahel_barnes@byu.edu. *Application contact:* Dr. Carl Hanson, Graduate Coordinator, 801-422-9103, Fax: 801-422-0273, E-mail: carl_hanson@byu.edu.

Brooklyn College of the City University of New York, Division of Graduate Studies, School of Education, Program in Adolescence Education and Special Subjects, Brooklyn, NY 11210-

Health Education

Brooklyn College of the City University of New York *(continued)*
2889. Offers adolescence science education (MAT); art teacher (MA); biology teacher (MA); chemistry teacher (MA); earth science teacher (MAT); English teacher (MA); French teacher (MA); health and nutrition sciences: health teacher (MS Ed); mathematics teacher (MA); music education (CAS); music teacher (MA); physical education teacher (MS Ed); physics teacher (MA); social studies teacher (MA); Spanish teacher (MA). Part-time and evening/weekend programs available. *Students:* 23 full-time (15 women), 449 part-time (256 women); includes 147 minority (96 African Americans, 1 American Indian/Alaska Native, 18 Asian Americans or Pacific Islanders, 32 Hispanic Americans), 12 international. Average age 30. 251 applicants, 80% accepted, 141 enrolled. In 2009, 163 master's, 2 other advanced degrees awarded. *Degree requirements:* For master's, comprehensive exam (for some programs), thesis (for some programs). *Entrance requirements:* For master's, LAST, previous course work in education, resume, 2 letters of recommendation, essay. Additional exam requirements/recommendations for international students: Required—TOEFL (minimum score 500 paper-based; 173 computer-based; 61 iBT). *Application deadline:* For fall admission, 7/15 for domestic students, 7/1 for international students; for spring admission, 11/15 for domestic students, 10/1 for international students. Applications are processed on a rolling basis. Application fee: $125. Electronic applications accepted. *Expenses:* Tuition, state resident: full-time $7360; part-time $310 per credit hour. Tuition, nonresident: full-time $13,800; part-time $575 per credit hour. Required fees: $140.10 per semester. *Financial support:* Career-related internships or fieldwork, Federal Work-Study, institutionally sponsored loans, and scholarships/grants available. Support available to part-time students. Financial award application deadline: 5/1; financial award applicants required to submit FAFSA. *Faculty research:* Interdisciplinary education, semiotics, discourse analysis, autobiography, teacher identity. *Unit head:* Prof. Stephen Phillips, Program Head, 718-951-5214, E-mail: phillips@brooklyn.cuny.edu. *Application contact:* Hernan Sierra, Graduate Admissions Coordinator, 718-951-4536, Fax: 718-951-4506, E-mail: grads@brooklyn.cuny.edu.

California State University, Dominguez Hills, College of Professional Studies, School of Health and Human Services, Division of Health Sciences, Carson, CA 90747-0001. Offers MS. Part-time programs available. *Students:* 3 full-time (2 women), 8 part-time (6 women); includes 7 minority (4 African Americans, 3 Hispanic Americans). Average age 43. 1 applicant, 0% accepted, 0 enrolled. In 2009, 14 master's awarded. *Degree requirements:* For master's, comprehensive exam. *Entrance requirements:* Additional exam requirements/recommendations for international students: Required—TOEFL, TWE. *Application deadline:* For fall admission, 8/15 priority date for domestic students. Applications are processed on a rolling basis. Electronic applications accepted. *Expenses:* Tuition, nonresident: full-time $6696; part-time $372 per unit. Required fees: $5946; $1752 per semester. *Faculty research:* International health, health promotion and disease prevention, public health. *Unit head:* Dr. Mitchell T. Maki, Dean, 310-243-2046, Fax: 310-217-6800, E-mail: mmaki@csudh.edu. *Application contact:* Dr. Gayle Ball-Parker, Director of Admissions, 310-243-3645, E-mail: gball@csudh.edu.

California State University, Long Beach, Graduate Studies, College of Health and Human Services, Department of Health Science, Long Beach, CA 90840. Offers MPH, MS, MSN/MPH. *Accreditation:* CEPH; NCATE. Part-time programs available. *Faculty:* 3 full-time (1 woman). *Students:* 32 full-time (21 women), 18 part-time (13 women); includes 25 minority (4 African Americans, 8 Asian Americans or Pacific Islanders, 13 Hispanic Americans), 5 international. Average age 30. *Degree requirements:* For master's, thesis optional. *Entrance requirements:* For master's, GRE, minimum GPA of 3.0 in last 60 units. *Application deadline:* For fall admission, 3/1 for domestic students. Applications are processed on a rolling basis. Application fee: $55. Electronic applications accepted. *Expenses:* Required fees: $1802 per semester. Part-time tuition and fees vary according to course load. *Financial support:* Federal Work-Study, institutionally sponsored loans, and scholarships/grants available. Financial award application deadline: 3/2. *Unit head:* Dr. Robert Friis, Chair, 562-985-1537, Fax: 562-985-2384, E-mail: rfriis@csulb.edu. *Application contact:* Dr. Mohammed Forouzesh, Director, Graduate Studies, 562-985-4014, Fax: 562-985-2384, E-mail: mforouze@csulb.edu.

California State University, Los Angeles, Graduate Studies, College of Health and Human Services, School of Nursing, Los Angeles, CA 90032-8530. Offers health science (MA); nursing (MS). *Accreditation:* AACN. Part-time and evening/weekend programs available. *Faculty:* 17 part-time/adjunct (15 women). *Students:* 92 full-time (76 women), 130 part-time (114 women); includes 133 minority (18 African Americans, 89 Asian Americans or Pacific Islanders, 26 Hispanic Americans), 8 international. Average age 37. 149 applicants, 79% accepted, 53 enrolled. In 2009, 51 master's awarded. *Degree requirements:* For master's, comprehensive exam, project or thesis. *Entrance requirements:* For master's, minimum GPA of 3.0 in nursing, course work in nursing and statistics. Additional exam requirements/recommendations for international students: Required—TOEFL (minimum score 500 paper-based; 173 computer-based). *Application deadline:* For fall admission, 5/1 for domestic and international students. Applications are processed on a rolling basis. Application fee: $55. *Financial support:* Federal Work-Study available. Support available to part-time students. Financial award application deadline: 3/1. *Faculty research:* Family stress, geripsychiatric nursing, self-care counseling, holistic nursing, adult health. *Unit head:* Dr. Cynthia Hughes, Director, 323-343-4700, Fax: 323-343-6454, E-mail: chughes2@calstatela.edu. *Application contact:* Dr. Cheryl L. Ney, Associate Vice President for Academic Affairs and Dean of Graduate Studies, 323-343-3820, Fax: 323-343-5653, E-mail: cney@cslanet.calstatela.edu.

California State University, San Bernardino, Graduate Studies, College of Natural Sciences, Program in Health Science, San Bernardino, CA 92407-2397. Offers health science (MS); public health (MPH). *Faculty:* 5 full-time (1 woman), 2 part-time/adjunct (1 woman). *Students:* 10 full-time (9 women), 17 part-time (15 women); includes 14 minority (5 African Americans, 1 Asian American or Pacific Islander, 8 Hispanic Americans), 1 international. Average age 35. 12 applicants, 92% accepted, 3 enrolled. In 2009, 1 master's awarded. *Unit head:* Dr. Cynthia Paxton, Assistant Dean, 909-537-5343, Fax: 909-537-7037, E-mail: cpaxton@csusb.edu. *Application contact:* Olivia Rosas, Director of Admissions, 909-537-7577, Fax: 909-537-7034, E-mail: orosas@csusb.edu.

Cambridge College, School of Education, Cambridge, MA 02138-5304. Offers autism specialist (M Ed); autism/behavior analyst (M Ed); behavior analyst (Post-Master's Certificate); behavioral management (M Ed); early childhood teacher (M Ed); education specialist in curriculum and instruction (CAGS); educational leadership (Ed D); elementary teacher (M Ed); English as a second language (M Ed, Certificate); general science (M Ed); health education, health promotion (Post-Master's Certificate); health/family and consumer sciences (M Ed); history (M Ed); individualized degree (M Ed); information technology literacy (M Ed); instructional technology (M Ed); interdisciplinary studies (M Ed); library teacher (M Ed); literacy education (M Ed); mathematics (M Ed); mathematics specialist (Certificate); middle school mathematics and science (M Ed); school administration (M Ed, CAGS); school guidance counselor (M Ed); school nurse education (M Ed); school social worker/school adjustment counselor (M Ed); special education administrator (CAGS); special education/moderate disabilities (M Ed); teaching skills and methodologies (M Ed). Part-time and evening/weekend programs available. Post-baccalaureate distance learning degree programs offered (minimal on-campus study). *Faculty:* 10 full-time (3 women), 283 part-time/adjunct (187 women). *Students:* 974 full-time (755 women), 1,071 part-time (835 women); includes 940 minority (762 African Americans, 4 American Indian/Alaska Native, 22 Asian Americans or Pacific Islanders, 152 Hispanic Americans), 28 international. Average age 39. In 2009, 866 master's, 4 doctorates, 209 CAGSs awarded. *Degree requirements:* For master's, thesis, internship/practicum (licensure program only); for doctorate, thesis/dissertation; for other advanced degree, thesis. *Entrance requirements:* For master's, interview, resume, documentation of licensure, 2 professional references; for doctorate, official transcripts, interview, resume, documentation of licensure (if any), written personal statement/essay, portfolio of scholarly and professional work, qualifying assessment, 2 professional references, health insurance, immunizations form; for other advanced degree, official transcripts, interview, resume, documentation of licensure (if any), written personal statement/essay, 2 professional references, health insurance, immunizations form. Additional exam requirements/recommendations for international students: Required—TOEFL (minimum score 550 paper-based; 213 computer-based; 79 iBT); Recommended—IELTS

(minimum score 6). *Application deadline:* Applications are processed on a rolling basis. Application fee: $30. Electronic applications accepted. *Expenses:* Contact institution. *Financial support:* In 2009–10, 1,373 students received support. Career-related internships or fieldwork, Federal Work-Study, and scholarships/grants available. Financial award applicants required to submit FAFSA. *Faculty research:* Adult education, accelerated learning, mathematics education, brain compatible learning, special education and law. *Unit head:* Dr. N. Alan Sheppard, Interim Associate Dean, 617-873-0619, E-mail: alan.sheppard@cambridgecollege.edu. *Application contact:* Stephen Lyons, Director of Enrollment, Graduate and N.I.T.E. Programs, 617-868-1000, Fax: 617-349-3561, E-mail: stephen.lyons@cambridgecollege.edu.

The Citadel, The Military College of South Carolina, Citadel Graduate College, Department of Health, Exercise, and Sport Science, Charleston, SC 29409. Offers health, exercise, and sport science (MS); physical education (MAT). *Accreditation:* NCATE. Part-time and evening/weekend programs available. *Faculty:* 6 full-time (3 women), 2 part-time/adjunct (0 women). *Students:* 12 full-time (9 women), 49 part-time (22 women); includes 8 minority (6 African Americans, 1 American Indian/Alaska Native, 1 Hispanic American), 2 international. Average age 26. In 2009, 9 master's awarded. *Degree requirements:* For master's, comprehensive exam, thesis optional. *Entrance requirements:* For master's, GRE (minimum score 900) or MAT (minimum score 396), minimum undergraduate GPA of 2.5, 3 letters of recommendation, resume detailing previous work experience (for MS only). Additional exam requirements/recommendations for international students: Required—TOEFL (minimum score 550 paper-based; 213 computer-based; 79 iBT). *Application deadline:* Applications are processed on a rolling basis. Application fee: $30. Electronic applications accepted. *Expenses:* Tuition, state resident: part-time $400 per credit hour. Tuition, nonresident: part-time $657 per credit hour. Required fees: $40 per term. *Financial support:* Career-related internships or fieldwork, health care benefits, and unspecified assistantships available. Support available to part-time students. Financial award application deadline: 7/1; financial award applicants required to submit FAFSA. *Faculty research:* Risk management in sport and physical activity programs, legal aspects of sport (gender equity/interscholastic athletics), comparison of dietary habits of Greek vs. American hs students, school-wide physical activity programs, exercise intervention among HIV-infected individuals, exercise and dietary intervention among breast cancer survivors, factors influencing motor skill in SC physical education programs, physical activity influences on inflammation and risk of recurrent colorectal neoplasia. *Unit head:* Dr. John S. Carter, Department Head, 843-953-7953, Fax: 843-953-6798, E-mail: john.carter@citadel.edu. *Application contact:* Dr. Steve A. Nida, Associate Provost, The Citadel Graduate College, 843-953-5089, Fax: 843-953-7630, E-mail: cgc@citadel.edu.

Cleveland State University, College of Graduate Studies, College of Education and Human Services, Department of Health, Physical Education, Recreation and Dance, Cleveland, OH 44115. Offers community health education (M Ed); exercise science (M Ed); human performance (M Ed); physical education pedagogy (M Ed); public health (MPH); school health education (M Ed); sport and exercise psychology (M Ed); sports management (M Ed). Part-time programs available. *Degree requirements:* For master's, comprehensive exam, thesis optional. *Entrance requirements:* For master's, GRE General Test or MAT (if undergraduate GPA less than 2.75), minimum undergraduate GPA of 2.75. Additional exam requirements/recommendations for international students: Required—TOEFL (minimum score 525 paper-based; 197 computer-based), IELTS (minimum score 6). Electronic applications accepted. *Faculty research:* Bone density, marketing fitness centers, motor development of disabled, online learning and survey research.

The College at Brockport, State University of New York, School of Health and Human Performance, Department of Health Science, Brockport, NY 14420-2997. Offers health education (MS Ed), including community health education, health education K-12. *Students:* 3 full-time (1 woman), 6 part-time (5 women). 8 applicants, 38% accepted, 3 enrolled. In 2009, 10 master's awarded. *Degree requirements:* For master's, thesis or alternative. *Entrance requirements:* For master's, GRE General Test, minimum GPA of 3.0, letters of recommendation. Additional exam requirements/recommendations for international students: Required—TOEFL (minimum score 550 paper-based; 213 computer-based; 79 iBT). *Application deadline:* For fall admission, 4/1 priority date for domestic and international students; for spring admission, 11/1 priority date for domestic and international students. Application fee: $80. Electronic applications accepted. *Expenses:* Tuition, state resident: full-time $8370; part-time $349 per credit. Tuition, nonresident: full-time $13,250; part-time $522 per credit. *Financial support:* In 2009–10, 1 teaching assistantship with full tuition reimbursement (averaging $6,000 per year) was awarded; Federal Work-Study, scholarships/grants, and unspecified assistantships also available. Support available to part-time students. Financial award application deadline: 3/15; financial award applicants required to submit FAFSA. *Faculty research:* Nutrition, substance use, HIV/AIDS, bioethics, worksite health. *Unit head:* Dr. Patti Follensbee, Chairperson, 585-395-5483, Fax: 585-395-5246, E-mail: pfallons@brockport.edu. *Application contact:* Dr. Patti Follansbee, Admissions Coordinator, 585-395-5483, Fax: 585-395-5246, E-mail: pfollans@brockport.edu.

The College of New Jersey, Graduate Division, School of Nursing, Health and Exercise Science, Department of Health and Exercise Science, Program in Health Education, Ewing, NJ 08628. Offers health (MAT); physical education (M Ed). *Accreditation:* NCATE. Part-time programs available. *Students:* 2 full-time (0 women), 4 part-time (all women); includes 1 minority (Hispanic American). 5 applicants, 60% accepted. In 2009, 4 master's awarded. *Degree requirements:* For master's, comprehensive exam. *Entrance requirements:* For master's, GRE, minimum GPA of 3.0 in field or 2.75 overall. Additional exam requirements/recommendations for international students: Required—TOEFL. *Application deadline:* For fall admission, 2/1 priority date for domestic students; for spring admission, 10/1 priority date for domestic students. Application fee: $70. Electronic applications accepted. *Expenses:* Tuition, state resident: part-time $573.70 per credit. Tuition, nonresident: part-time $887.75 per credit. Required fees: $140.85 per credit. One-time fee: $10 part-time. *Financial support:* Tuition waivers (partial) and unspecified assistantships available. Financial award application deadline: 5/1; financial award applicants required to submit FAFSA. *Unit head:* Dr. Aristomen Chilakos, Coordinator, 609-771-3160, Fax: 609-637-5153, E-mail: chilako@tcnj.edu. *Application contact:* Susan L. Hydro, Assistant Dean, Office of Graduate Studies, 609-771-2300, Fax: 609-637-5105, E-mail: graduate@tcnj.edu.

College of Saint Mary, Program in Health Professions Education, Omaha, NE 68106. Offers Ed D. Part-time programs available.

Colorado State University–Pueblo, College of Education, Engineering and Professional Studies, Education Program, Pueblo, CO 81001-4901. Offers art education (M Ed); foreign language education (M Ed); health and physical education (M Ed); instructional technology (M Ed); linguistically diverse education (M Ed); music education (M Ed); special education (M Ed). *Accreditation:* Teacher Education Accreditation Council. Part-time programs available. *Degree requirements:* For master's, portfolio. *Entrance requirements:* For master's, 3 recommendations, teaching license. Additional exam requirements/recommendations for international students: Required—TOEFL (minimum score 500 paper-based; 173 computer-based). Electronic applications accepted. *Faculty research:* Portfolio assessment, math education, science education.

Dalhousie University, Faculty of Health Professions, School of Health and Human Performance, Program in Health Promotion, Halifax, NS B3H 3J5, Canada. Offers MA. Part-time programs available. *Faculty:* 5 full-time (3 women), 1 part-time/adjunct (0 women). *Students:* 8 full-time (7 women), 1 (woman) part-time; includes 2 minority (both Asian Americans or Pacific Islanders). 8 applicants, 25% accepted. In 2009, 3 master's awarded. *Degree requirements:* For master's, thesis. *Entrance requirements:* Additional exam requirements/recommendations for international students: Required—TOEFL, IELTS, CANTEST, CAEL, or Michigan English Language Assessment Battery. *Application deadline:* For fall admission, 6/1 priority date for domestic and international students. Applications are processed on a rolling basis. Application fee: $70. Electronic applications accepted. *Financial support:* In 2009–10, 4 students received support; research assistantships, teaching assistantships, institutionally sponsored loans available. *Faculty research:* AIDS research, health knowledge of adolescents, evaluating health promotion,

program evaluation. *Unit head:* Dr. Carol Putnam, Graduate Coordinator, 902-494-1167, Fax: 902-494-5120, E-mail: hahp@dal.ca. *Application contact:* Tracy Powell, Graduate Administrative Secretary, 902-494-1154, Fax: 902-494-5120, E-mail: tracy.powell@dal.ca.

D'Youville College, Doctoral Programs, Buffalo, NY 14201-1084. Offers educational leadership (Ed D); health education (Ed D); health policy (Ed D). Part-time and evening/weekend programs available. *Degree requirements:* For doctorate, comprehensive exam, thesis/dissertation, fieldwork. *Entrance requirements:* For doctorate, MS/MA; professional experience. *Faculty research:* Educational assessment, assessment reform, culture and education, market-based reform, men's health, electronic records.

East Carolina University, Graduate School, College of Health and Human Performance, Department of Health Education and Promotion, Greenville, NC 27858-4353. Offers environmental health (MS); health education (MA, MA Ed). *Accreditation:* NCATE. *Degree requirements:* For master's, comprehensive exam, thesis optional. *Entrance requirements:* For master's, GRE General Test or MAT. Additional exam requirements/recommendations for international students: Required—TOEFL. *Faculty research:* Community health education, worksite health promotion, school health education, environmental health.

Eastern Kentucky University, The Graduate School, College of Education, Department of Curriculum and Instruction, Program in Secondary and Higher Education, Richmond, KY 40475-3102. Offers secondary education (MA Ed), including agricultural education, art education, biological sciences education, business education, English education, geography education, history education, home economics education, industrial education, mathematical sciences education, physical education, school health education. *Accreditation:* NCATE. Part-time programs available. *Entrance requirements:* For master's, GRE General Test, minimum GPA of 2.5.

Eastern Michigan University, Graduate School, College of Health and Human Services, School of Health Promotion and Human Performance, Program in Health Education, Ypsilanti, MI 48197. Offers MS. Part-time and evening/weekend programs available. *Students:* 2 full-time (1 woman), 18 part-time (17 women); includes 3 minority (all African Americans). Average age 32. In 2009, 4 master's awarded. *Degree requirements:* For master's, thesis or project. *Entrance requirements:* For master's, teaching credential. Additional exam requirements/recommendations for international students: Required—TOEFL. *Application deadline:* For fall admission, 8/1 for domestic students, 5/1 for international students; for winter admission, 12/1 for domestic students, 10/1 for international students; for spring admission, 4/15 for domestic students, 3/1 for international students. Application fee: $35. Tuition and fees vary according to course level. *Unit head:* Dr. Joan Cowdery, Program Coordinator, 734-487-7120 Ext. 2698, Fax: 734-487-2024, E-mail: jcowdery@emich.edu. *Application contact:* Dr. Joan Cowdery, Program Coordinator, 734-487-7120 Ext. 2698, Fax: 734-487-2024, E-mail: jcowdery@emich.edu.

Eastern University, Graduate Education Programs, Program in School Health Services, St. Davids, PA 19087-3696. Offers M Ed. *Entrance requirements:* For master's, minimum GPA of 2.5. Additional exam requirements/recommendations for international students: Required—TOEFL.

East Stroudsburg University of Pennsylvania, Graduate School, College of Health Sciences, Department of Exercise Science, East Stroudsburg, PA 18301-2999. Offers cardiac rehabilitation and exercise science (MS). Part-time and evening/weekend programs available. *Faculty:* 3 full-time (1 woman). *Students:* 38 full-time (18 women), 3 part-time (2 women); includes 1 minority (Hispanic American), 4 international. Average age 25. In 2009, 35 master's awarded. *Degree requirements:* For master's, comprehensive exam, thesis or alternative, computer literacy. *Entrance requirements:* Additional exam requirements/recommendations for international students: Required—TOEFL (minimum score 560 paper-based; 220 computer-based; 83 iBT). *Application deadline:* For fall admission, 7/31 priority date for domestic students, 5/1 priority date for international students; for spring admission, 11/30 for domestic students, 10/1 for international students. Applications are processed on a rolling basis. Application fee: $50. *Expenses:* Tuition, state resident: full-time $9942; part-time $387 per credit. Tuition, nonresident: full-time $14,240; part-time $619 per credit. *Financial support:* In 2009–10, 57 research assistantships with full and partial tuition reimbursements (averaging $1,749 per year) were awarded; Federal Work-Study and institutionally sponsored loans also available. Financial award application deadline: 3/1. *Unit head:* Dr. Shala Davis, Graduate Coordinator, 570-422-3302, Fax: 570-422-3616, E-mail: sdavis@po-box.esu.edu. *Application contact:* Kevin Quintero, Graduate Admissions Coordinator, 570-422-3890, Fax: 570-422-2711, E-mail: kquintero@po-box.esu.edu.

East Stroudsburg University of Pennsylvania, Graduate School, College of Health Sciences, Department of Health, East Stroudsburg, PA 18301-2999. Offers community health education (MPH); health education (MS). *Accreditation:* CEPH (one or more programs are accredited). Part-time and evening/weekend programs available. *Faculty:* 6 full-time (3 women). *Students:* 7 full-time (6 women), 9 part-time (8 women); includes 1 minority (Hispanic American). Average age 29. In 2009, 3 degrees awarded. *Degree requirements:* For master's, oral comprehensive exam. *Entrance requirements:* For master's, GRE General Test, minimum GPA of 3.0 in major, 2.8 overall; undergraduate prerequisites in anatomy and physiology; 3 verifiable letters of recommendation; professional resume. Additional exam requirements/recommendations for international students: Required—TOEFL (minimum score 560 paper-based; 220 computer-based; 83 iBT) or IELTS (minimum score 6). *Application deadline:* For fall admission, 7/31 priority date for domestic students, 5/1 priority date for international students; for spring admission, 11/30 for domestic students, 10/1 for international students. Applications are processed on a rolling basis. Application fee: $50. *Expenses:* Tuition, state resident: full-time $9942; part-time $387 per credit. Tuition, nonresident: full-time $14,240; part-time $619 per credit. *Financial support:* In 2009–10, 9 research assistantships with full and partial tuition reimbursements (averaging $2,363 per year) were awarded; Federal Work-Study and institutionally sponsored loans also available. Financial award application deadline: 3/1; financial award applicants required to submit FAFSA. *Faculty research:* HIV prevention, wellness, international health issues. *Unit head:* Dr. Kathleen Hillman, Graduate Coordinator, 570-422-3727, Fax: 570-422-3848, E-mail: khillman@po-box.esu.edu. *Application contact:* Kevin Quintero, Graduate Admissions Coordinator, 570-422-3890, Fax: 570-422-2711, E-mail: kquintero@po-box.esu.edu.

East Stroudsburg University of Pennsylvania, Graduate School, College of Health Sciences, Department of Physical Education, East Stroudsburg, PA 18301-2999. Offers health and physical education (M Ed). *Faculty:* 1 (woman) full-time. *Students:* 2 full-time (1 woman), 6 part-time (3 women); includes 1 minority (African American). Average age 35. In 2009, 11 master's awarded. *Degree requirements:* For master's, computer literacy, portfolio exhibition as exiting research project. *Entrance requirements:* For master's, teacher certification in physical education or health and physical education. Additional exam requirements/recommendations for international students: Required—TOEFL (minimum score 560 paper-based; 220 computer-based; 83 iBT), or IELTS. *Application deadline:* For fall admission, 7/31 for domestic students, 5/1 for international students; for spring admission, 11/30 for domestic students, 10/1 for international students. Applications are processed on a rolling basis. Application fee: $50. *Expenses:* Tuition, state resident: full-time $9942; part-time $387 per credit. Tuition, nonresident: full-time $14,240; part-time $619 per credit. *Financial support:* Federal Work-Study and unspecified assistantships available. Financial award application deadline: 3/1; financial award applicants required to submit FAFSA. *Unit head:* Dr. Caroline Kuchinski, Graduate Admissions Coordinator, 570-422-3293, Fax: 570-422-3824, E-mail: ckuchinski@po-box.esu.edu. *Application contact:* Kevin Quintero, Graduate Admissions Coordinator, 570-422-3890, Fax: 570-422-2711, E-mail: kquintero@po-box.esu.edu.

Emory University, Rollins School of Public Health, Department of Behavioral Sciences and Health Education, Atlanta, GA 30322-1100. Offers MPH. *Accreditation:* CEPH. Part-time programs available. *Degree requirements:* For master's, comprehensive exam (for some programs), thesis, practicum. *Entrance requirements:* For master's, GRE General Test. Additional

exam requirements/recommendations for international students: Required—TOEFL (minimum score 550 paper-based; 220 computer-based; 80 iBT). Electronic applications accepted.

Florida Agricultural and Mechanical University, Division of Graduate Studies, Research, and Continuing Education, College of Education, Department of Health, Physical Education, and Recreation, Tallahassee, FL 32307-3200. Offers M Ed, MS Ed. *Accreditation:* NCATE. Part-time and evening/weekend programs available. *Faculty:* 10 full-time (6 women). *Students:* 11 full-time (9 women), 3 part-time (2 women); all minorities (all African Americans). In 2009, 2 master's awarded. *Degree requirements:* For master's, thesis optional. *Entrance requirements:* For master's, GRE General Test, minimum GPA of 3.0. Additional exam requirements/recommendations for international students: Required—TOEFL. *Application deadline:* For fall admission, 5/18 for domestic students, 12/18 for international students; for spring admission, 11/12 for domestic students, 5/12 for international students. Application fee: $20. *Financial support:* Teaching assistantships, Federal Work-Study and institutionally sponsored loans available. *Faculty research:* Administration/curriculum, work behavior, psychology. *Unit head:* Dr. E. Newton Jackson, Chairperson, 850-599-3135. *Application contact:* Dr. Chanta M. Haywood, Dean of Graduate Studies, Research, and Continuing Education, 850-599-3315, Fax: 850-599-3727.

Florida State University, The Graduate School, College of Human Sciences, Department of Nutrition, Food, and Exercise Sciences, Tallahassee, FL 32306-1493. Offers exercise science (MS, PhD), including exercise physiology; nutrition and food sciences (MS, PhD), including clinical nutrition (MS), food science, human nutrition (PhD), nutrition and sport (MS), nutrition science (MS), nutrition, education and health promotion (MS). Part-time programs available. *Faculty:* 13 full-time (8 women). *Students:* 88 full-time (58 women), 21 part-time (14 women); includes 28 minority (10 African Americans, 5 Asian Americans or Pacific Islanders, 13 Hispanic Americans), 23 international. 128 applicants, 52% accepted, 35 enrolled. In 2009, 30 master's, 8 doctorates awarded. *Degree requirements:* For master's, comprehensive exam (for some programs), thesis optional; for doctorate, thesis/dissertation. *Entrance requirements:* For master's, GRE General Test, minimum upper-division GPA of 3.0; for doctorate, GRE General Test, minimum upper-division GPA of 3.0, MS. Additional exam requirements/recommendations for international students: Required—TOEFL (minimum score 570 paper-based; 80 iBT). *Application deadline:* For fall admission, 7/1 for domestic students, 3/1 for international students; for spring admission, 11/1 for domestic students, 5/1 for international students. Application fee: $30. Electronic applications accepted. *Expenses:* Tuition, state resident: full-time $7413. Tuition, nonresident: full-time $22,567. *Financial support:* In 2009–10, 42 students received support, including 5 fellowships with partial tuition reimbursements available (averaging $10,000 per year), 8 research assistantships with partial tuition reimbursements available (averaging $8,000 per year), 31 teaching assistantships with partial tuition reimbursements available (averaging $8,000 per year); career-related internships or fieldwork, Federal Work-Study, institutionally sponsored loans, scholarships/grants, and unspecified assistantships also available. Financial award application deadline: 1/15; financial award applicants required to submit FAFSA. *Faculty research:* Body composition, functional food, chronic disease and aging response; food safety, food allergy, and safety/quality detection methods; sports nutrition, energy and human performance. *Unit head:* Dr. Bahram H. Arjmandi, Margaret A. Sitton Professor and Chair, 850-645-1517, Fax: 850-645-5000, E-mail: barjmandi@fsu.edu. *Application contact:* Ursula M. Tate, Administrative Support Assistant, 850-644-4800, Fax: 850-645-5000, E-mail: utate@fsu.edu.

Fort Hays State University, Graduate School, College of Health and Life Sciences, Department of Health and Human Performance, Hays, KS 67601-4099. Offers MS. Part-time programs available. *Degree requirements:* For master's, comprehensive exam, thesis optional. *Entrance requirements:* For master's, GRE General Test or MAT. Additional exam requirements/recommendations for international students: Required—TOEFL (minimum score 550 paper-based; 213 computer-based). Electronic applications accepted. *Faculty research:* Isoproterenol hydrochloride and exercise, dehydrogenase and high-density lipoprotein levels in athletics, venous blood parameters to adipose fat.

Framingham State University, Division of Graduate and Continuing Education, Programs in Food and Nutrition, Program in Human Nutrition: Education and Media Technologies, Framingham, MA 01701-9101. Offers MS.

Georgia College & State University, Graduate School, College of Health Sciences, Department of Kinesiology, Milledgeville, GA 31061. Offers health promotion (M Ed); human performance (M Ed); kinesiology (MAT); outdoor education (M Ed). *Accreditation:* NCATE (one or more programs are accredited). Part-time and evening/weekend programs available. *Faculty:* 12 full-time (5 women). *Students:* 25 full-time (13 women), 7 part-time (5 women); includes 4 minority (2 African Americans, 2 Hispanic Americans), 3 international. Average age 26. 23 applicants, 87% accepted, 19 enrolled. In 2009, 7 master's awarded. *Degree requirements:* For master's, thesis optional. *Entrance requirements:* For master's, GRE General Test or MAT, minimum GPA of 2.75 in upper-level undergraduate courses, 2 letters of reference. Additional exam requirements/recommendations for international students: Recommended—TOEFL (minimum score 550 paper-based; 213 computer-based; 79 iBT). *Application deadline:* For fall admission, 7/15 priority date for domestic students; for spring admission, 11/15 for domestic students. Applications are processed on a rolling basis. Application fee: $40. Electronic applications accepted. *Expenses:* Tuition, area resident: Part-time $241 per credit hour. Tuition, state resident: full-time $4338. Tuition, nonresident: full-time $17,352; part-time $964 per credit hour. Required fees: $609 per semester. Tuition and fees vary according to course load and campus/location. *Financial support:* In 2009–10, 20 research assistantships with full tuition reimbursements were awarded; career-related internships or fieldwork and unspecified assistantships also available. Support available to part-time students. Financial award applicants required to submit FAFSA. *Unit head:* Dr. Jude Hirsch, Chair, 478-445-4072, Fax: 478-445-1790, E-mail: jude.hirsch@gcsu.edu. *Application contact:* Dr. Jude Hirsch, Chair, 478-445-4072, Fax: 478-445-1790, E-mail: jude.hirsch@gcsu.edu.

Georgia Southern University, Jack N. Averitt College of Graduate Studies, College of Education, Department of Teaching and Learning, Program in Health and Physical Education, Statesboro, GA 30460. Offers M Ed. *Accreditation:* NCATE. Part-time and evening/weekend programs available. In 2009, 4 master's awarded. *Degree requirements:* For master's, comprehensive exam. *Entrance requirements:* For master's, GRE General Test or MAT, minimum GPA of 2.5. Additional exam requirements/recommendations for international students: Required—TOEFL (minimum score 550 paper-based; 213 computer-based; 80 iBT). *Application deadline:* For fall admission, 3/1 priority date for domestic and international students; for spring admission, 10/1 priority date for domestic students, 10/1 for international students. Applications are processed on a rolling basis. Application fee: $50. Electronic applications accepted. *Expenses:* Tuition, state resident: full-time $5040; part-time $210 per credit hour. Tuition, nonresident: full-time $20,136; part-time $839 per credit hour. Required fees: $1644. *Financial support:* In 2009–10, research assistantships with partial tuition reimbursements (averaging $6,850 per year), teaching assistantships with partial tuition reimbursements (averaging $6,850 per year) were awarded; career-related internships or fieldwork, Federal Work-Study, and tuition waivers (partial) also available. Support available to part-time students. Financial award application deadline: 4/15; financial award applicants required to submit FAFSA. *Unit head:* Dr. Tony Pritchard, Coordinator, 912-478-1323, Fax: 912-478-0026, E-mail: tpritchard@georgiasouthern.edu. *Application contact:* 912-478-5384, Fax: 912-478-0740, E-mail: gradadmissions@georgiasouthern.edu.

Georgia Southern University, Jack N. Averitt College of Graduate Studies, Jiann-Ping Hsu College of Public Health, Program in Public Health, Statesboro, GA 30460. Offers biostatistics (MPH, Dr PH); community health behavior and education (Dr PH); community health education (MPH); environmental health sciences (MPH); epidemiology (MPH); health services policy management (MPH); public health leadership (Dr PH). Part-time programs available. *Students:* 75 full-time (47 women), 23 part-time (15 women); includes 39 minority (36 African Americans, 3 Asian Americans or Pacific Islanders), 24 international. Average age 30. 50 applicants, 80% accepted, 20 enrolled. In 2009, 20 master's awarded. *Degree requirements:* For master's,

Health Education

Georgia Southern University (continued)
thesis optional, practicum; for doctorate, comprehensive exam, thesis/dissertation, practicum. *Entrance requirements:* For master's, GRE General Test, minimum GPA of 2.75, resume, 3 letters of reference; for doctorate, GRE, GMAT, MCAT, LSAT, 3 letters of reference, statement of purpose, resume or curriculum vitae. Additional exam requirements/recommendations for international students: Required—TOEFL (minimum score 550 paper-based; 213 computer-based; 80 iBT). *Application deadline:* For fall admission, 3/1 priority date for domestic and international students; for spring admission, 10/1 priority date for domestic students, 10/1 for international students. Applications are processed on a rolling basis. Application fee: $50. Electronic applications accepted. *Expenses:* Contact institution. *Financial support:* In 2009–10, 83 students received support, including research assistantships with partial tuition reimbursements available (averaging $7,200 per year), teaching assistantships with partial tuition reimbursements available (averaging $7,200 per year); career-related internships or fieldwork, Federal Work-Study, scholarships/grants, tuition waivers (partial), and unspecified assistantships also available. Support available to part-time students. Financial award application deadline: 4/15; financial award applicants required to submit FAFSA. *Faculty research:* Biostatistics, community health, environmental health sciences, epidemiology, health policy and management, community health behavior and education, public health leadership. *Unit head:* Dr. Charles Hardy, Dean, 912-478-2674, Fax: 912-478-5811, E-mail: chardy@georgiasouthern.edu. *Application contact:* Dr. Charles Ziglar, Coordinator for Graduate Student Recruitment, 912-478-5635, Fax: 912-478-0740, E-mail: gradadmissions@georgiasouthern.edu.

Georgia Southwestern State University, Graduate Studies, School of Education, Americus, GA 31709-4693. Offers early childhood education (M Ed, Ed S); health and physical education (M Ed); middle grades education (M Ed, Ed S); reading (M Ed); secondary education (M Ed); special education (M Ed). *Accreditation:* NCATE. *Degree requirements:* For master's, comprehensive exam. *Entrance requirements:* For master's, GRE General Test or MAT, minimum GPA of 2.5; for Ed S, GRE General Test or MAT, minimum graduate GPA of 3.25, M Ed from accredited college or university, 3 years teaching experience. Electronic applications accepted.

Georgia State University, College of Education, Department of Kinesiology and Health, Program in Health and Physical Education, Atlanta, GA 30302-3083. Offers M Ed. Part-time and evening/weekend programs available. *Degree requirements:* For master's, comprehensive exam. *Entrance requirements:* For master's, GRE General Test, minimum GPA of 2.5. *Faculty research:* Exercise science, teacher behavior.

Harding University, College of Education, Searcy, AR 72149-0001. Offers advanced studies in teaching and learning (M Ed); art (MSE); behavioral science (MSE); counseling (MS, Ed S); early childhood special education (M Ed, MSE); education (MSE); educational leadership (M Ed, Ed S); elementary education (M Ed); English (MSE); family and consumer science (MSE); French (MSE); history/social science (MSE); kinesiology (MSE); math (MSE); physical science (MSE); reading (M Ed); secondary education (M Ed); Spanish (MSE); special education licensure (M Ed); teaching (MAT); teaching English as a second language (M Ed). *Accreditation:* NCATE. Part-time and evening/weekend programs available. *Faculty:* 11 full-time (4 women), 49 part-time/adjunct (26 women). *Students:* 104 full-time (85 women), 392 part-time (282 women); includes 77 minority (67 African Americans, 5 American Indian/Alaska Native, 1 Asian American or Pacific Islander, 4 Hispanic Americans), 5 international. Average age 36. 153 applicants, 92% accepted, 131 enrolled. In 2009, 153 master's, 6 other advanced degrees awarded. *Degree requirements:* For master's, comprehensive exam (for some programs), thesis optional, portfolio(s); for Ed S, comprehensive exam, portfolio, specialist project. *Entrance requirements:* For master's, GRE, MAT, PRAXIS; for Ed S, MAT or GRE. Additional exam requirements/recommendations for international students: Required—TOEFL (minimum score 550 paper-based; 79 iBT). *Application deadline:* For fall admission, 8/1 for domestic and international students; for spring admission, 1/1 for domestic and international students. Applications are processed on a rolling basis. Application fee: $35. *Expenses:* Tuition: Full-time $9720; part-time $540 per credit hour. Required fees: $22 per credit hour. Tuition and fees vary according to course load and program. *Financial support:* In 2009–10, 30 students received support. Unspecified assistantships available. *Faculty research:* Reading, comprehension, school violence, educational technology, behavior, college choice, differentiated instruction, brain-based teaching. *Unit head:* Dr. Clara Carroll, Chair, 501-279-4501, Fax: 501-279-4083, E-mail: ccarroll@harding.edu. *Application contact:* Information Contact, 501-279-4315, E-mail: gradstudiesedu@harding.edu.

Hofstra University, School of Education, Health, and Human Services, Department of Health Professions and Family Studies, Program in Health Education, Hempstead, NY 11549. Offers MS. Part-time and evening/weekend programs available. *Students:* 37 full-time (21 women), 48 part-time (25 women); includes 7 minority (5 African Americans, 1 Asian American or Pacific Islander, 1 Hispanic American). Average age 28. 31 applicants, 97% accepted, 21 enrolled. In 2009, 32 master's awarded. *Degree requirements:* For master's, one foreign language, capstone course. *Entrance requirements:* For master's, interview, 2 letters of recommendation. Additional exam requirements/recommendations for international students: Required—TOEFL (minimum score 550 paper-based; 213 computer-based; 80 iBT). *Application deadline:* Applications are processed on a rolling basis. Application fee: $60. Electronic applications accepted. *Expenses:* Tuition: Full-time $16,200; part-time $900 per credit hour. Required fees: $970; $145 per term. Tuition and fees vary according to program. *Financial support:* In 2009–10, 32 students received support, including 9 fellowships with full and partial tuition reimbursements available (averaging $2,319 per year), 1 research assistantship with full and partial tuition reimbursement available (averaging $18,325 per year); Federal Work-Study, institutionally sponsored loans, scholarships/grants, tuition waivers (full and partial), and unspecified assistantships also available. Support available to part-time students. Financial award applicants required to submit FAFSA. *Faculty research:* Skill development and health behavior; cultural competence and health education; culturally sensitive instruction; decreasing adolescent pregnancy; assessment in health education. *Unit head:* Prof. Andrew Herman, Program Director, 516-463-6673, Fax: 516-463-4810, E-mail: hprazh@hofstra.edu. *Application contact:* Carol Drummer, Dean of Graduate Admissions, 516-463-4876, Fax: 516-463-4664, E-mail: gradstudent@hofstra.edu.

Howard University, Graduate School, Department of Health, Human Performance and Leisure Studies, Washington, DC 20059-0002. Offers exercise physiology (MS); health education (MS); sports studies (MS), including sociology of sports, sports management; urban recreation (MS), including leisure studies. Part-time and evening/weekend programs available. *Degree requirements:* For master's, comprehensive exam, thesis. *Entrance requirements:* For master's, BS in human performance or related field. Electronic applications accepted. *Faculty research:* Health promotion, cardiovascular hypertension, physical activity, sport and human rights issues.

Idaho State University, Office of Graduate Studies, Kasiska College of Health Professions, Department of Health and Nutrition Sciences, Program in Health Education, Pocatello, ID 83209-8109. Offers MHE. Part-time programs available. *Faculty:* 2 full-time (1 woman). *Students:* 7 full-time (5 women), 10 part-time (9 women); includes 2 minority (both Hispanic Americans), 2 international. Average age 32. In 2009, 6 master's awarded. *Degree requirements:* For master's, comprehensive exam, thesis or project. *Entrance requirements:* For master's, GRE General Test, previous coursework in statistics, natural sciences, tests and measurements. Additional exam requirements/recommendations for international students: Required—TOEFL (minimum score 600 paper-based; 213 computer-based). *Application deadline:* For fall admission, 7/1 for domestic students, 6/1 for international students; for spring admission, 12/1 for domestic students, 11/1 for international students. Applications are processed on a rolling basis. Application fee: $55. Electronic applications accepted. *Expenses:* Tuition, state resident: full-time $3318; part-time $297 per credit hour. Tuition, nonresident: full-time $13,120; part-time $437 per credit hour. Required fees: $2530. Tuition and fees vary according to program. *Financial support:* In 2009–10, research assistantships with full and partial tuition reimbursements (averaging $10,841 per year); teaching assistantships with full and partial tuition reimbursements, career-related internships or fieldwork, Federal Work-Study, institutionally sponsored loans, scholarships/grants, traineeships, health care benefits, tuition waivers (full and partial), and unspecified

assistantships also available. Support available to part-time students. Financial award application deadline: 1/1; financial award applicants required to submit FAFSA. *Faculty research:* Health and wellness. *Unit head:* Dr. Willis McAleese, Chairman, 208-282-2729, Fax: 208-282-4000, E-mail: mcalwill@isu.edu. *Application contact:* Tami Carson, Graduate School Technical Records Specialist, 208-282-2150, Fax: 208-282-4847, E-mail: carstami@isu.edu.

Illinois State University, Graduate School, College of Applied Science and Technology, School of Kinesiology and Recreation, Normal, IL 61790-2200. Offers health education (MS); physical education (MS). *Degree requirements:* For master's, thesis or alternative. *Entrance requirements:* For master's, GRE General Test, minimum GPA of 2.6 in last 60 hours of course work. *Faculty research:* Influences on positive youth development through sport, country-wide health fitness project, graduate practicum in athletic training, perceived exertion and self-selected intensity during resistance exercise in younger and older.

Indiana State University, School of Graduate Studies, College of Nursing, Health and Human Services, Department of Health, Safety, and Environmental Health Sciences, Terre Haute, IN 47809. Offers community health promotion (MA, MS); health and safety education (MA, MS); occupational safety management (MA, MS). *Accreditation:* NCATE (one or more programs are accredited). *Degree requirements:* For master's, thesis or alternative. *Entrance requirements:* For master's, GRE General Test. Electronic applications accepted.

Indiana University Bloomington, School of Health, Physical Education and Recreation, Department of Applied Health Science, Bloomington, IN 47405-7000. Offers health behavior (PhD); health promotion (MS); human development/family studies (MS); nutrition science (MS); public health (MPH); safety management (MS); school and college health programs (MS). *Accreditation:* CEPH (one or more programs are accredited). *Faculty:* 24 full-time (12 women). *Students:* 131 full-time (92 women), 22 part-time (20 women); includes 35 minority (22 African Americans, 1 American Indian/Alaska Native, 5 Asian Americans or Pacific Islanders, 7 Hispanic Americans), 29 international. Average age 31. 118 applicants, 71% accepted, 52 enrolled. In 2009, 43 master's, 6 doctorates awarded. *Degree requirements:* For master's, thesis optional; for doctorate, thesis/dissertation. *Entrance requirements:* For master's, GRE (MS in nutrition science), 3 recommendations; for doctorate, GRE, 3 recommendations. Additional exam requirements/recommendations for international students: Required—TOEFL (minimum score 550 paper-based; 213 computer-based; 79 iBT). *Application deadline:* For fall admission, 4/30 priority date for domestic students, 12/1 priority date for international students; for spring admission, 11/15 priority date for domestic students, 9/1 priority date for international students. Application fee: $55 ($65 for international students). *Financial support:* In 2009–10, 80 students received support, including 12 fellowships (averaging $2,316 per year), 50 research assistantships with full and partial tuition reimbursements available (averaging $6,973 per year), 27 teaching assistantships with full and partial tuition reimbursements available (averaging $11,067 per year); career-related internships or fieldwork, Federal Work-Study, institutionally sponsored loans, scholarships/grants, tuition waivers (partial), and fee remissions also available. Financial award application deadline: 3/1. *Faculty research:* Cancer education, HIV/AIDS and drug education, public health, parent-child interactions, safety education. Total annual research expenditures: $2.8 million. *Unit head:* Dr. Mohammad R. Torabi, Chair, 812-855-4808, Fax: 812-855-3936, E-mail: torabi@indiana.edu. *Application contact:* Dr. Mohammad R. Torabi, Chair, 812-855-4808, Fax: 812-855-3936, E-mail: torabi@indiana.edu.

Indiana University of Pennsylvania, School of Graduate Studies and Research, College of Health and Human Services, Department of Health and Physical Education, Indiana, PA 15705-1087. Offers aquatics administration and facilities management (MS); exercise science (MS); sport management (MS); sport science (MS). Part-time programs available. *Faculty:* 8 full-time (4 women). *Students:* 55 full-time (24 women), 33 part-time (10 women); includes 8 minority (all African Americans), 14 international. Average age 25. 154 applicants, 48% accepted, 48 enrolled. In 2009, 54 master's awarded. *Degree requirements:* For master's, thesis optional. *Entrance requirements:* For master's, 2 letters of recommendation. Additional exam requirements/recommendations for international students: Required—TOEFL. *Application deadline:* For fall admission, 7/1 priority date for domestic students; for spring admission, 11/1 for domestic students. Applications are processed on a rolling basis. Application fee: $40. *Expenses:* Tuition, state resident: full-time $6666; part-time $370 per credit hour. Tuition, nonresident: full-time $10,666; part-time $593 per credit hour. Required fees: $813 per semester. *Financial support:* In 2009–10, 1 fellowship (averaging $500 per year), 16 research assistantships with full and partial tuition reimbursements (averaging $4,335 per year) were awarded. Financial award application deadline: 3/15; financial award applicants required to submit FAFSA. *Unit head:* Dr. Elaine Blair, Chairperson, 724-357-2770, E-mail: eblair@iup.edu. *Application contact:* Dr. Elaine Blair, Chairperson, 724-357-2770, E-mail: eblair@iup.edu.

Indiana University–Purdue University Indianapolis, Indiana University School of Medicine, Department of Public Health, Indianapolis, IN 46202-2896. Offers behavioral health science (MPH); epidemiology (MPH); health policy and management (MPH). *Students:* 62 full-time (47 women), 71 part-time (54 women); includes 37 minority (24 African Americans, 12 Asian Americans or Pacific Islanders, 1 Hispanic American), 15 international. Average age 31. 17 applicants, 65% accepted, 6 enrolled.Application fee: $55 ($65 for international students). *Expenses:* Contact institution. *Financial support:* In 2009–10, 1 teaching assistantship (averaging $14,058 per year) was awarded. *Unit head:* Dr. Carole Kacius, Director, 317-274-3126. *Application contact:* Robert M. Stump, Director of Admissions, 317-274-3772, E-mail: inmedadm@iupui.edu.

Indiana University–Purdue University Indianapolis, Indiana University School of Medicine, School of Health and Rehabilitation Sciences, Indianapolis, IN 46202-2896. Offers health sciences education (MS); nutrition and dietetics (MS); occupational therapy (MS); physical therapy (DPT). Part-time and evening/weekend programs available. *Faculty:* 8 full-time (5 women). *Students:* 206 full-time (161 women), 11 part-time (8 women); includes 16 minority (5 African Americans, 1 American Indian/Alaska Native, 8 Asian Americans or Pacific Islanders, 2 Hispanic Americans), 1 international. Average age 26. 23 applicants, 83% accepted, 18 enrolled. In 2009, 9 master's, 32 doctorates awarded. *Degree requirements:* For master's, thesis (for some programs). *Entrance requirements:* For master's, GRE General Test, minimum GPA of 3.0. Additional exam requirements/recommendations for international students: Required—TOEFL. *Application deadline:* For fall admission, 1/15 priority date for domestic students; for spring admission, 10/15 for domestic students. Application fee: $55 ($65 for international students). *Financial support:* In 2009–10, 10 fellowships (averaging $2,485 per year), 1 teaching assistantship (averaging $3,600 per year) were awarded; research assistantships, Federal Work-Study, institutionally sponsored loans, and scholarships/grants also available. Support available to part-time students. Financial award applicants required to submit FAFSA. *Unit head:* Dr. Mark S. Sothmann, Dean, 317-274-4702, E-mail: msothman@iupui.edu. *Application contact:* Dr. Mark S. Sothmann, Dean, 317-274-4702, E-mail: msothman@iupui.edu.

Inter American University of Puerto Rico, Metropolitan Campus, Graduate Programs, Program in Physical Education, San Juan, PR 00919-1293. Offers teaching of physical education (MA); training and sport performance (MA). *Degree requirements:* For master's, comprehensive exam. *Entrance requirements:* For master's, GRE or EXADEP, interview. Electronic applications accepted.

Ithaca College, Division of Graduate and Professional Studies, School of Health Sciences and Human Performance, Program in Health Education, Ithaca, NY 14850. Offers MS. Part-time programs available. *Faculty:* 8 full-time (6 women), 1 (woman) part-time/adjunct. *Students:* 13 full-time (12 women), 1 (woman) part-time; includes 1 minority (Hispanic American), 1 international. Average age 25. 15 applicants, 87% accepted, 11 enrolled. In 2009, 11 master's awarded. *Degree requirements:* For master's, comprehensive exam (for some programs), thesis optional. *Entrance requirements:* For master's, GRE General Test, minimum GPA of 3.0. Additional exam requirements/recommendations for international students: Required—TOEFL (minimum score 550 paper-based; 213 computer-based; 80 iBT). *Application deadline:* For fall admission, 3/1 priority date for domestic and international students; for spring admission, 12/1 for domestic and international students. Applications are processed on a rolling basis. Application

fee: $40. Electronic applications accepted. *Expenses:* Contact institution. *Financial support:* In 2009–10, 14 students received support, including 13 teaching assistantships (averaging $6,522 per year); career-related internships or fieldwork, Federal Work-Study, scholarships/grants, and unspecified assistantships also available. Support available to part-time students. Financial award application deadline: 3/1; financial award applicants required to submit CSS PROFILE or FAFSA. *Faculty research:* Needs assessment evaluation of health education programs, minority health (includes diversity), employee health assessment and program planning, youth at risk/families, multicultural/international health, program planning/health behaviors, sexuality education in the family and school setting, parent-teacher and student-teacher relationships, attitude/interest/motivation, teaching effectiveness, student learning/achievement. *Unit head:* Dr. Srijana Bajacharya, Chairperson, 607-274-3527, Fax: 607-274-1263, E-mail: gps@ithaca.edu. *Application contact:* Rob Gearhart, Dean, Graduate and Professional Studies, 607-274-3527, Fax: 607-274-1263, E-mail: gps@ithaca.edu.

Jackson State University, Graduate School, School of Education, Department of Health, Physical Education and Recreation, Jackson, MS 39217. Offers MS Ed. *Accreditation:* NCATE. Part-time and evening/weekend programs available. *Degree requirements:* For master's, comprehensive exam, thesis or alternative. *Entrance requirements:* For master's, GRE General Test. Additional exam requirements/recommendations for international students: Required—TOEFL.

Jacksonville State University, College of Graduate Studies and Continuing Education, College of Education and Professional Studies, Program in Health and Physical Education, Jacksonville, AL 36265-1602. Offers MS Ed. *Accreditation:* NCATE. Part-time and evening/weekend programs available. *Degree requirements:* For master's, comprehensive exam, thesis (for some programs). *Entrance requirements:* For master's, GRE General Test or MAT. Electronic applications accepted.

James Madison University, The Graduate School, College of Integrated Science and Technology, Department of Health Sciences, Program in Health Education, Harrisonburg, VA 22807. Offers MS, MS Ed. Part-time programs available. *Students:* 9 full-time (8 women), 11 part-time (10 women); includes 4 minority (2 African Americans, 1 Asian American or Pacific Islander, 1 Hispanic American). Average age 27. In 2009, 22 master's awarded. *Entrance requirements:* For master's, GRE General Test. Additional exam requirements/recommendations for international students: Required—TOEFL. *Application deadline:* For fall admission, 5/1 priority date for domestic students; for spring admission, 9/1 priority date for domestic students. Application fee: $55. *Expenses:* Tuition, area resident: Part-time $305 per credit hour. Tuition, state resident: part-time $305 per credit hour. Tuition, nonresident: part-time $890 per credit hour. *Financial support:* In 2009–10, 12 students received support; teaching assistantships with full tuition reimbursements available available. Financial award application deadline: 3/1. *Unit head:* Dr. Maria T. Wessel, Coordinator, 540-568-3955. *Application contact:* Lynette M. Bible, Director of Graduate Admissions, 540-568-6395, Fax: 540-568-7860, E-mail: biblelm@jmu.edu.

John F. Kennedy University, Graduate School of Holistic Studies, Department of Integral Studies, Program in Holistic Health Education, Pleasant Hill, CA 94523-4817. Offers MA. Part-time and evening/weekend programs available. *Degree requirements:* For master's, thesis or alternative. *Entrance requirements:* For master's, interview. Additional exam requirements/recommendations for international students: Required—TOEFL.

The Johns Hopkins University, Bloomberg School of Public Health, Department of Health, Behavior and Society, Baltimore, MD 21218-2699. Offers genetic counseling (Sc M); health education and health communication (MHS); social and behavioral sciences (Dr PH, PhD, Sc D); social factors in health (MHS). *Faculty:* 43 full-time (30 women), 59 part-time/adjunct (40 women). *Students:* 100 full-time (89 women), 4 part-time (3 women); includes 28 minority (13 African Americans, 12 Asian Americans or Pacific Islanders, 3 Hispanic Americans), 13 international. Average age 29. 227 applicants, 31% accepted, 26 enrolled. In 2009, 25 master's, 8 doctorates awarded. *Degree requirements:* For master's, comprehensive exam (for some programs), thesis (for some programs); for doctorate, comprehensive exam, thesis/dissertation. *Entrance requirements:* For master's, GRE, curriculum vitae, 3 letters of recommendation; for doctorate, GRE, transcripts, curriculum vitae, 3 recommendation letters. Additional exam requirements/recommendations for international students: Required—TOEFL (minimum score 600 paper-based; 250 computer-based; 100 iBT). *Application deadline:* For fall admission, 12/1 for domestic and international students. Applications are processed on a rolling basis. Application fee: $45. Electronic applications accepted. *Financial support:* In 2009–10, 96 students received support, including 17 fellowships with tuition reimbursements available (averaging $23,634 per year), 30 research assistantships (averaging $7,800 per year), 25 teaching assistantships (averaging $2,759 per year); career-related internships or fieldwork, Federal Work-Study, scholarships/grants, traineeships, health care benefits, unspecified assistantships, and stipends also available. Financial award application deadline: 3/15. *Faculty research:* Social determinants of health, and structural- and community-level inventions to improve health; communication and health education; behavioral and social aspects of genetic counseling. Total annual research expenditures: $6.3 million. *Unit head:* Georgean Smith, Administrator, 410-502-3715, Fax: 410-502-4333, E-mail: gcsmith@jhsph.edu. *Application contact:* Barbara W. Diehl, Senior Academic Program Coordinator, 410-502-4415, Fax: 410-502-4333, E-mail: bdiehl@jhsph.edu.

Kent State University, Graduate School of Education, Health, and Human Services, School of Health Sciences, Program in Health Education and Promotion, Kent, OH 44242-0001. Offers M Ed, MA, PhD. *Accreditation:* NCATE. *Faculty:* 6 full-time (5 women), 6 part-time/adjunct (5 women). *Students:* 15 full-time (all women), 30 part-time (24 women); includes 9 minority (8 African Americans, 1 Hispanic American). 17 applicants, 65% accepted. In 2009, 8 master's awarded. *Degree requirements:* For doctorate, comprehensive exam, thesis/dissertation. *Entrance requirements:* For doctorate, GRE General Test. Additional exam requirements/recommendations for international students: Required—TOEFL. *Application deadline:* Applications are processed on a rolling basis. Application fee: $30. Electronic applications accepted. *Financial support:* In 2009–10, 3 fellowships with full tuition reimbursements (averaging $11,055 per year), research assistantships with full tuition reimbursements (averaging $7,903 per year) were awarded; teaching assistantships with full tuition reimbursements, Federal Work-Study, scholarships/grants, and unspecified assistantships also available. Financial award application deadline: 4/1; financial award applicants required to submit FAFSA. *Faculty research:* Substance use/abuse, sexuality, community health assessment, epidemiology, HIV/AIDS. *Unit head:* Dr. Dianne Kerr, Coordinator, 330-672-0677, E-mail: dkerr@kent.edu. *Application contact:* Nancy Miller, Academic Program Coordinator, Office of Graduate Student Services, 330-672-2586, Fax: 330-672-9162, E-mail: ogs@kent.edu.

Lake Erie College of Osteopathic Medicine, Professional Programs, Erie, PA 16509-1025. Offers biomedical sciences (Postbaccalaureate Certificate); medical education (MS); osteopathic medicine (DO); pharmacy (Pharm D). *Accreditation:* ACPE; AOsA. *Degree requirements:* For first professional degree, comprehensive exam, National Osteopathic Medical Licensing Exam, Levels 1 and 2; for Postbaccalaureate Certificate, comprehensive exam, North American Pharmacist Licensure Examination (NAPLEX). *Entrance requirements:* For first professional degree, MCAT, minimum GPA of 3.2, letters of recommendation; for Postbaccalaureate Certificate, PCAT, letters of recommendation, minimum GPA of 3.5. Electronic applications accepted. *Faculty research:* Cardiac smooth and skeletal muscle mechanics, chemotherapeutics and vitamins, osteopathic manipulation.

Lehman College of the City University of New York, Division of Natural and Social Sciences, Department of Health Sciences, Program in Health Education and Promotion, Bronx, NY 10468-1589. Offers MA. *Accreditation:* NCATE. Part-time and evening/weekend programs available. *Degree requirements:* For master's, thesis or alternative. *Entrance requirements:* For master's, minimum GPA of 2.7.

Lehman College of the City University of New York, Division of Natural and Social Sciences, Department of Health Sciences, Program in Health N–12 Teacher, Bronx, NY 10468-1589. Offers MS Ed. *Accreditation:* NCATE. *Degree requirements:* For master's, thesis or alternative.

Loma Linda University, School of Public Health, Programs in Health Promotion and Education, Loma Linda, CA 92350. Offers MPH, Dr PH. *Accreditation:* CEPH (one or more programs are accredited). *Degree requirements:* For doctorate, thesis/dissertation. *Entrance requirements:* For doctorate, GRE General Test. Additional exam requirements/recommendations for international students: Required—Michigan English Language Assessment Battery or TOEFL.

Long Island University, Brooklyn Campus, School of Health Professions, Division of Sports Sciences, Brooklyn, NY 11201-8423. Offers adapted physical education (MS); athletic training and sports sciences (MS); exercise physiology (MS); health sciences (MS). Part-time and evening/weekend programs available. *Entrance requirements:* For master's, 2 letters of recommendation. Additional exam requirements/recommendations for international students: Required—TOEFL (minimum score 500 paper-based; 173 computer-based). Electronic applications accepted.

Louisiana Tech University, Graduate School, College of Education, Department of Curriculum, Instruction and Leadership, Ruston, LA 71272. Offers curriculum and instruction (MS, Ed D); educational leadership (Ed D); secondary education (M Ed), including business education, English education, foreign language education, health and physical education, mathematics education, science education, social studies education, speech education. *Accreditation:* NCATE. Part-time programs available. *Degree requirements:* For doctorate, thesis/dissertation. *Entrance requirements:* For master's and doctorate, GRE General Test.

Louisiana Tech University, Graduate School, College of Education, Department of Health and Exercise Sciences, Ruston, LA 71272. Offers MS. *Accreditation:* NCATE. Part-time programs available. *Degree requirements:* For master's, thesis or alternative. *Entrance requirements:* For master's, GRE General Test.

Marshall University, Academic Affairs Division, College of Information Technology and Engineering, Division of Applied Science and Technology, Program in Safety, Huntington, WV 25755. Offers MS. *Accreditation:* NCATE. *Faculty:* 2 full-time (1 woman). *Students:* 12 full-time (2 women), 29 part-time (4 women); includes 1 minority (Hispanic American), 1 international. Average age 37. In 2009, 8 master's awarded. *Degree requirements:* For master's, thesis optional, comprehensive assessment. Application fee: $40. *Unit head:* Dr. D. Allen Stern, 304-696-3069, E-mail: stern@marshall.edu. *Application contact:* Information Contact, 304-746-1900, Fax: 304-746-1902, E-mail: services@marshall.edu.

Marywood University, Academic Affairs, Reap College of Education and Human Development, Department of Human Development, Emphasis in Health Promotion, Scranton, PA 18509-1598. Offers PhD. *Students:* 3 full-time (all women), 21 part-time (14 women). Average age 43. *Entrance requirements:* Additional exam requirements/recommendations for international students: Required—TOEFL (minimum score 550 paper-based; 213 computer-based; 79 iBT). *Application deadline:* For fall admission, 1/30 for domestic and international students. Application fee: $35. Electronic applications accepted. *Expenses:* Contact institution. *Financial support:* Career-related internships or fieldwork, scholarships/grants, and unspecified assistantships available. Support available to part-time students. Financial award application deadline: 6/30; financial award applicants required to submit FAFSA. *Unit head:* Dr. Brook Cannon, Director, 570-348-6211 Ext. 2324, E-mail: cannon@marywood.edu. *Application contact:* Tammy Manka, Assistant Director of Graduate Admissions, 866-279-9663, E-mail: tmanka@marywood.edu.

Middle Tennessee State University, College of Graduate Studies, College of Education and Behavioral Science, Department of Health and Human Performance, Program in Health, Physical Education and Recreation, Murfreesboro, TN 37132. Offers MS. Part-time and evening/weekend programs available. Postbaccalaureate distance learning degree programs offered. *Students:* 9 full-time (6 women), 59 part-time (27 women); includes 22 minority (19 African Americans, 2 Asian Americans or Pacific Islanders, 1 Hispanic American). 54 applicants, 74% accepted, 40 enrolled. In 2009, 36 master's awarded. *Degree requirements:* For master's, comprehensive exam, thesis optional. *Entrance requirements:* For master's, GRE or MAT. Additional exam requirements/recommendations for international students: Required—TOEFL (minimum score 525 paper-based; 195 computer-based; 71 iBT) or IELTS (minimum score 6). *Application deadline:* For fall admission, 6/1 for domestic and international students. Applications are processed on a rolling basis. Application fee: $25 ($30 for international students). *Expenses:* Tuition, state resident: full-time $4404. Tuition, nonresident: full-time $10,956. *Financial support:* In 2009–10, 14 students received support. Career-related internships or fieldwork and institutionally sponsored loans available. Support available to part-time students. Financial award application deadline: 5/1. *Unit head:* Dr. Scott Colclough, Interim Chair, 615-898-5073, Fax: 615-898-5020, E-mail: scolclou@mtsu.edu. *Application contact:* Dr. Michael Allen, Dean and Vice Provost for Research, 615-898-2840, Fax: 615-904-8020, E-mail: mallen@mtsu.edu.

Midwestern University, Glendale Campus, College of Health Sciences, Arizona Campus, Program in Health Professions Education, Glendale, AZ 85308. Offers MHPE. Part-time programs available. *Faculty:* 9 full-time (3 women). *Students:* 2 part-time (both women). Average age 37. 2 applicants, 100% accepted, 2 enrolled. In 2009, 5 master's awarded. *Entrance requirements:* For master's, GRE. *Application deadline:* Applications are processed on a rolling basis. Application fee: $50. *Unit head:* Terri Anderson, Director, 623-572-3622. *Application contact:* James Walter, Director of Admissions, 888-247-9277, Fax: 623-572-3229, E-mail: admissaz@midwestern.edu.

Mills College, Graduate Studies, School of Education, Oakland, CA 94613-1000. Offers child life in hospitals (MA); early childhood education (MA); education (MA), including art education, curriculum and instruction, elementary education, English education, foreign language education, mathematics education, science education, secondary education, social studies education, teaching; educational leadership (MA, Ed D); infant mental health (MA). Part-time and evening/weekend programs available. *Faculty:* 11 full-time (9 women), 16 part-time/adjunct (14 women). *Students:* 138 full-time (119 women), 55 part-time (48 women); includes 71 minority (34 African Americans, 19 Asian Americans or Pacific Islanders, 18 Hispanic Americans), 3 international. Average age 34. 210 applicants, 82% accepted, 93 enrolled. In 2009, 54 master's, 15 doctorates awarded. Terminal master's awarded for partial completion of doctoral program. *Degree requirements:* For master's, comprehensive exam. *Entrance requirements:* For doctorate, GRE General Test. Additional exam requirements/recommendations for international students: Required—TOEFL. *Application deadline:* For fall admission, 2/1 for domestic and international students; for spring admission, 11/1 for domestic and international students. Applications are processed on a rolling basis. Application fee: $50. Electronic applications accepted. *Expenses:* Tuition: Full-time $26,326; part-time $6584 per course. Required fees: $896. One-time fee: $896 part-time. Tuition and fees vary according to program. *Financial support:* In 2009–10, 188 students received support, including 186 fellowships (averaging $6,499 per year), 28 teaching assistantships with partial tuition reimbursements available (averaging $3,187 per year); career-related internships or fieldwork and scholarships/grants also available. Support available to part-time students. Financial award application deadline: 2/1; financial award applicants required to submit FAFSA. *Faculty research:* Child development, gender and education, public policy, cross-cultural development, development of literacy. Total annual research expenditures: $1.2 million. *Unit head:* Joseph Kahne, Chairperson, 510-430-3190, Fax: 510-430-3314, E-mail: grad-studies@mills.edu. *Application contact:* Jessica King, Graduate Admission Specialist, 510-430-3305, Fax: 510-430-2159, E-mail: grad-studies@mills.edu.

Minnesota State University Mankato, College of Graduate Studies, College of Allied Health and Nursing, Department of Health Science, Mankato, MN 56001. Offers community health (MS); health science (MS, MT); school health (MS). Part-time programs available. *Students:* 14 full-time (9 women), 39 part-time (20 women). *Degree requirements:* For master's, comprehensive exam, thesis or alternative. *Entrance requirements:* For master's, minimum GPA of 3.0 during previous 2 years. Additional exam requirements/recommendations for international students: Required—TOEFL (minimum score 500 paper-based; 173 computer-based; 61 iBT). *Application deadline:* For fall admission, 7/1 for domestic students, 5/1 for

Health Education

Minnesota State University Mankato (continued)

international students; for spring admission, 11/1 for domestic students, 10/1 for international students. Applications are processed on a rolling basis. Application fee: $40. Electronic applications accepted. *Expenses:* Tuition, state resident: full-time $5364. Tuition, nonresident: full-time $8314. *Financial support:* Research assistantships with full tuition reimbursements, teaching assistantships with full tuition reimbursements, career-related internships or fieldwork and Federal Work-Study available. Support available to part-time students. Financial award application deadline: 3/15; financial award applicants required to submit FAFSA. *Faculty research:* Teaching methods, stress prophylaxis and management, effects of alcohol. *Unit head:* Dr. Dawn Larsen, Graduate Coordinator, 507-389-2113. *Application contact:* 507-389-2321, E-mail: grad@mnsu.edu.

Mississippi University for Women, Graduate School, Division of Health and Kinesiology, Columbus, MS 39701-9998. Offers health education (MS). *Degree requirements:* For master's, comprehensive exam.

Montana State University, College of Graduate Studies, College of Education, Health, and Human Development, Department of Health and Human Development, Bozeman, MT 59717. Offers health and human development (MS), including counseling, exercise and nutrition sciences, family and consumer sciences, family financial planning, health promotion and education. *Accreditation:* ACA. Part-time programs available. Postbaccalaureate distance learning degree programs offered (no on-campus study). *Faculty:* 27 full-time (18 women), 7 part-time/adjunct (6 women). *Students:* 54 full-time (47 women), 18 part-time (15 women); includes 1 minority (Hispanic American). Average age 30. 32 applicants, 34% accepted, 10 enrolled. In 2009, 26 master's awarded. *Degree requirements:* For master's, comprehensive exam. *Entrance requirements:* For master's, GRE General Test. Additional exam requirements/recommendations for international students: Required—TOEFL (minimum score 550 paper-based; 213 computer-based). *Application deadline:* For fall admission, 7/15 priority date for domestic students, 5/15 priority date for international students; for spring admission, 12/1 priority date for domestic students, 10/1 priority date for international students. Applications are processed on a rolling basis. Application fee: $30. Electronic applications accepted. *Expenses:* Tuition, state resident: full-time $5635; part-time $3492 per year. Tuition, nonresident: full-time $17,212; part-time $7865.10 per year. Required fees: $1441; $153.15 per credit. Tuition and fees vary according to course load and program. *Financial support:* In 2009–10, 24 students received support, including 7 research assistantships (averaging $1,000 per year), 17 teaching assistantships with full tuition reimbursements available (averaging $8,000 per year). Financial award application deadline: 3/1; financial award applicants required to submit FAFSA. *Faculty research:* Gait analysis, cancer prevention, obesity prevention, energy expenditure, decision making. Total annual research expenditures: $2.8 million. *Unit head:* Dr. Tim Dunnagan, Head, 404-994-3242, Fax: 404-994-2013, E-mail: dunnagan@montana.edu. *Application contact:* Dr. Carl Fox.

Montclair State University, The Graduate School, College of Education and Human Services, Department of Curriculum and Teaching, Montclair, NJ 07043-1624. Offers education (M Ed); educational technology (M Ed); learning disabled teacher consultant (Certificate); school library media specialist (Certificate); teaching (MAT, Certificate), including art (MAT), biological science (MAT), early childhood education (P-3) (MAT), earth science (MAT), elementary education (K-8) (MAT), English (MAT), French (MAT), health and physical education (MAT), health education (MAT), home economics (MAT), mathematics (MAT), music (MAT), physical education (MAT), physical science (MAT), social studies (MAT), Spanish (MAT), teacher of ESL (MAT), teacher of students with disabilities (MAT). Part-time and evening/weekend programs available. *Faculty:* 17 full-time (12 women), 29 part-time/adjunct (21 women). *Students:* 124 full-time (63 women), 174 part-time (126 women). Average age 31. 112 applicants, 69% accepted, 59 enrolled. In 2009, 179 master's, 2 other advanced degrees awarded. *Degree requirements:* For master's, comprehensive exam, field experience. *Entrance requirements:* For master's, GRE, 2 letters of recommendation. Additional exam requirements/recommendations for international students: Required—TOEFL (minimum score 83 computer-based), or IELTS. *Application deadline:* For fall admission, 2/15 for domestic and international students; for spring admission, 9/15 for domestic and international students. Applications are processed on a rolling basis. Application fee: $60. Electronic applications accepted. *Expenses:* Tuition, area resident: Part-time $486.74 per credit. Tuition, state resident: part-time $486.74 per credit. Tuition, nonresident: part-time $751.34 per credit. Tuition and fees vary according to degree level and program. *Financial support:* In 2009–10, 12 research assistantships with full tuition reimbursements (averaging $7,000 per year) were awarded; Federal Work-Study, scholarships/grants, and unspecified assistantships also available. Support available to part-time students. Financial award application deadline: 3/1; financial award applicants required to submit FAFSA. *Unit head:* Dr. David Schwarzer, Chairperson, 973-655-5187. *Application contact:* Amy Aiello, Director of Graduate Admissions and Operations, 973-655-5147, Fax: 973-655-7869, E-mail: graduate.school@montclair.edu.

Montclair State University, The Graduate School, College of Education and Human Services, Department of Exercise Science and Physical Education, Montclair, NJ 07043-1624. Offers health and physical education (Certificate); nutrition and exercise science (Certificate); physical education (MA, Certificate), including coaching and sports administration (MA), exercise science (MA), physical education (MA), teaching and supervision of physical education (MA). Part-time and evening/weekend programs available. *Faculty:* 15 full-time (9 women), 17 part-time/adjunct (10 women). *Students:* 8 full-time (3 women), 38 part-time (19 women). Average age 30. 34 applicants, 56% accepted, 13 enrolled. In 2009, 9 master's awarded. *Degree requirements:* For master's, comprehensive exam. *Entrance requirements:* For master's, GRE General Test, 2 letters of recommendation; for Certificate, 2 letters of recommendation (nutrition and exercise science concentration). Additional exam requirements/recommendations for international students: Required—TOEFL (minimum score 83 computer-based), or IELTS. *Application deadline:* For fall admission, 6/1 for international students; for spring admission, 10/1 for international students. Applications are processed on a rolling basis. Application fee: $60. Electronic applications accepted. *Expenses:* Tuition, area resident: Part-time $486.74 per credit. Tuition, state resident: part-time $486.74 per credit. Tuition, nonresident: part-time $751.34 per credit. Tuition and fees vary according to degree level and program. *Financial support:* In 2009–10, 5 research assistantships with full tuition reimbursements (averaging $7,000 per year) were awarded; Federal Work-Study, scholarships/grants, and unspecified assistantships also available. Support available to part-time students. Financial award application deadline: 3/1; financial award applicants required to submit FAFSA. *Unit head:* Dr. Susana Juniu, Chairperson, 973-655-7093. *Application contact:* Amy Aliello, Director of Graduate Admissions and Operations, 973-655-5147, Fax: 973-655-7869, E-mail: graduate.school@montclair.edu.

Montclair State University, The Graduate School, College of Education and Human Services, Department of Health and Nutrition Sciences, Montclair, NJ 07043-1624. Offers American Dietetic Association (Certificate); community health education (MPH); food safety instructor (Certificate); health education (MA); nutrition and exercise science (MS); nutrition and food science (MS). Part-time and evening/weekend programs available. *Faculty:* 15 full-time (10 women), 55 part-time/adjunct (40 women). *Students:* 38 full-time (32 women), 78 part-time (68 women). Average age 32. 53 applicants, 64% accepted, 23 enrolled. In 2009, 19 master's, 2 other advanced degrees awarded. *Degree requirements:* For master's, comprehensive exam, thesis optional. *Entrance requirements:* For master's, GRE, 2 letters of recommendation. Additional exam requirements/recommendations for international students: Required—TOEFL (minimum score 83 computer-based), or IELTS. *Application deadline:* For fall admission, 6/1 for international students; for spring admission, 10/1 for international students. Application fee: $60. *Expenses:* Tuition, area resident: Part-time $486.74 per credit. Tuition, state resident: part-time $486.74 per credit. Tuition, nonresident: part-time $751.34 per credit. Tuition and fees vary according to degree level and program. *Financial support:* In 2009–10, 8 research assistantships with full tuition reimbursements (averaging $7,000 per year) were awarded; Federal Work-Study, scholarships/grants, and unspecified assistantships also available. Support available to part-time students. Financial award application deadline: 3/1; financial award applicants required to submit FAFSA. *Faculty research:* Adolescent physical activity. *Unit head:* Dr. Eva Goldfarb, Chairperson, 973-655-4154. *Application contact:* Amy Aiello, Director of Graduate Admissions and Operations, 973-655-5147, Fax: 973-655-7869, E-mail: graduate.school@montclair.edu.

Morehead State University, Graduate Programs, College of Education, Department of Middle Grades and Secondary Education, Morehead, KY 40351. Offers business and marketing education (MAT); English/language arts 5-9 (MAT); French (MAT); health P-12 (MAT); mathematics 5-9 (MAT); physical education P-12 (MAT); science 5-9 (MAT); secondary biology (MAT); secondary chemistry (MAT); secondary earth science (MAT); secondary English (MAT); secondary math (MAT); secondary physics (MAT); secondary social studies (MAT); social studies 5-9 (MAT); Spanish (MAT). Part-time and evening/weekend programs available. *Students:* 54 full-time (31 women), 233 part-time (142 women); includes 11 minority (5 African Americans, 1 American Indian/Alaska Native, 1 Asian American or Pacific Islander, 4 Hispanic Americans). Average age 32. 206 applicants, 71% accepted, 79 enrolled. In 2009, 101 master's awarded. *Degree requirements:* For master's, portfolio. *Entrance requirements:* For master's, GRE or PRAXIS II content exam, minimum overall undergraduate GPA of 2.5. Additional exam requirements/recommendations for international students: Required—TOEFL (minimum score 500 paper-based; 173 computer-based). *Application deadline:* For fall admission, 8/1 priority date for domestic and international students; for spring admission, 12/1 priority date for domestic and international students. Applications are processed on a rolling basis. Application fee: $30. Electronic applications accepted. *Expenses:* Tuition, state resident: full-time $6318; part-time $351 per credit hour. Tuition, nonresident: full-time $15,804; part-time $878 per credit hour. *Financial support:* In 2009–10, 1 research assistantship (averaging $10,000 per year) was awarded; career-related internships or fieldwork, Federal Work-Study, and unspecified assistantships also available. Financial award application deadline: 3/15; financial award applicants required to submit FAFSA. *Unit head:* Dr. Cathy Gunn, Dean, 606-783-2040, Fax: 606-783-5029, E-mail: c.gunn@moreheadstate.edu. *Application contact:* Michelle Barber, Graduate Recruitment and Retention Assistant Director, 606-783-5127, Fax: 606-783-5061, E-mail: m.barber@moreheadstate.edu.

Morehead State University, Graduate Programs, College of Science and Technology, Department of Health, Wellness and Human Performance, Morehead, KY 40351. Offers health/physical education (MA). *Accreditation:* NCATE. Part-time and evening/weekend programs available. *Faculty:* 5 full-time (4 women). *Students:* 8 full-time (4 women), 6 part-time (4 women); includes 1 African American. Average age 28. 9 applicants, 78% accepted, 6 enrolled. In 2009, 3 master's awarded. *Degree requirements:* For master's, comprehensive exam, thesis, oral exam, written core exam. *Entrance requirements:* For master's, GRE General Test or MAT, minimum GPA of 2.5; undergraduate major/minor in health, physical education, or recreation. Additional exam requirements/recommendations for international students: Required—TOEFL (minimum score 500 paper-based; 173 computer-based). *Application deadline:* For fall admission, 8/1 priority date for domestic and international students; for spring admission, 12/1 priority date for domestic and international students. Applications are processed on a rolling basis. Application fee: $30. Electronic applications accepted. *Expenses:* Tuition, state resident: full-time $6318; part-time $351 per credit hour. Tuition, nonresident: full-time $15,804; part-time $878 per credit hour. *Financial support:* In 2009–10, 1 research assistantship (averaging $10,000 per year), 3 teaching assistantships (averaging $10,000 per year) were awarded; career-related internships or fieldwork, Federal Work-Study, and unspecified assistantships also available. Financial award application deadline: 3/15; financial award applicants required to submit FAFSA. *Faculty research:* Child growth and performance, instructional strategies, outdoor leadership qualities, exercise science, athletic training. *Unit head:* Dr. Lynne Fitzgerald, Chair, 606-783-2466, Fax: 606-783-5058, E-mail: l.fitzgerald@moreheadstate.edu. *Application contact:* Michelle Barber, Graduate Recruitment and Retention Assistant Director, 606-783-5127, Fax: 606-783-5061, E-mail: m.barber@moreheadstate.edu.

Morehouse School of Medicine, Master of Public Health Program, Atlanta, GA 30310-1495. Offers epidemiology (MPH); health administration, management and policy (MPH); health education/health promotion (MPH); international health (MPH). *Accreditation:* CEPH. Part-time programs available. *Faculty:* 4 full-time (1 woman), 36 part-time/adjunct (21 women). *Students:* 54 full-time (37 women), 3 part-time (2 women); includes 34 minority (33 African Americans, 1 American Indian/Alaska Native). Average age 28. 62 applicants, 48% accepted, 29 enrolled. In 2009, 13 master's awarded. *Degree requirements:* For master's, thesis, practicum, public health leadership seminar. *Entrance requirements:* For master's, GRE General Test, writing test, public health or human service experience. Additional exam requirements/recommendations for international students: Required—TOEFL (minimum score 550 paper-based; 200 computer-based). *Application deadline:* For fall admission, 3/1 for domestic and international students. Application fee: $50. Electronic applications accepted. *Expenses:* Contact institution. *Financial support:* In 2009–10, 32 students received support, including 6 research assistantships with partial tuition reimbursements available (averaging $10,000 per year); fellowships, teaching assistantships, career-related internships or fieldwork, Federal Work-Study, institutionally sponsored loans, scholarships/grants, and unspecified assistantships also available. Support available to part-time students. Financial award application deadline: 5/1; financial award applicants required to submit FAFSA. *Faculty research:* Women's and adolescent health, violence prevention, cancer epidemiology/disparities, substance abuse prevention. Total annual research expenditures: $640,176. *Unit head:* Dr. Patricia Rodney, Director/Assistant Dean for Public Health Education, 404-752-1944, Fax: 404-752-1051, E-mail: prodney@msm.edu. *Application contact:* Dr. Sterling Roaf, Director of Admissions, 404-752-1650, Fax: 404-752-1512, E-mail: mphadmissions@msm.edu.

Mount Mary College, Graduate Programs, Program in Dietetics, Milwaukee, WI 53222-4597. Offers administrative dietetics (MS); clinical dietetics (MS); nutrition education (MS). Part-time and evening/weekend programs available. *Faculty:* 1 (woman) full-time, 5 part-time/adjunct (4 women). *Students:* 13 full-time (all women), 20 part-time (all women), 1 international. Average age 28. 60 applicants, 22% accepted, 12 enrolled. In 2009, 1 master's awarded. *Degree requirements:* For master's, thesis. *Entrance requirements:* For master's, minimum GPA of 2.75, completion of ADA and DPD requirements. Additional exam requirements/recommendations for international students: Required—TOEFL (minimum score 500 paper-based; 173 computer-based). *Application deadline:* For fall admission, 2/15 priority date for domestic students. Application fee: $35 ($100 for international students). *Expenses:* Tuition: Part-time $595 per credit. Tuition and fees vary according to program. *Financial support:* In 2009–10, 1 student received support. Career-related internships or fieldwork and Federal Work-Study available. Support available to part-time students. Financial award application deadline: 5/1; financial award applicants required to submit FAFSA. *Unit head:* Lisa Stark, Director, 414-258-4810 Ext. 398, E-mail: starkl@mtmary.edu. *Application contact:* Lisa Stark, Director, 414-258-4810 Ext. 398, E-mail: starkl@mtmary.edu.

New Jersey City University, Graduate Studies and Continuing Education, College of Professional Studies, Department of Health Sciences, Jersey City, NJ 07305-1597. Offers community health education (MS); health administration (MS); school health education (MS). Part-time and evening/weekend programs available. *Faculty:* 3. *Students:* 8 full-time (6 women), 42 part-time (32 women); includes 18 minority (10 African Americans, 1 American Indian/Alaska Native, 3 Asian Americans or Pacific Islanders, 4 Hispanic Americans), 3 international. Average age 41. In 2009, 21 master's awarded. *Degree requirements:* For master's, thesis or alternative, internship. *Entrance requirements:* For master's, GRE General Test or MAT. Additional exam requirements/recommendations for international students: Required—TOEFL. *Application deadline:* For fall admission, 8/1 priority date for domestic students; for spring admission, 12/1 for domestic students. Applications are processed on a rolling basis. Application fee: $0. *Expenses:* Tuition, area resident: Part-time $456.75 per credit. Tuition, nonresident: part-time $842.55 per credit. Required fees: $65 per term. *Financial support:* Career-related internships or fieldwork and unspecified assistantships available. *Unit head:* Dr. Gail Gordon, Chairperson, 201-200-3431, E-mail: ggordon@njcu.edu. *Application contact:* Dr. Gail Gordon, Chairperson, 201-200-3431, E-mail: ggordon@njcu.edu.

New Mexico Highlands University, Graduate Studies, School of Education, Department of Exercise and Sport Sciences, Las Vegas, NM 87701. Offers human performance and sport

(MA); sports administration (MA); teacher education (MA). Part-time programs available. *Degree requirements:* For master's, comprehensive exam, thesis or alternative. *Entrance requirements:* For master's, minimum undergraduate GPA of 3.0. Additional exam requirements/recommendations for international students: Required—TOEFL (minimum score 540 paper-based; 207 computer-based). *Faculty research:* Child obesity and physical inactivity, body composition and fitness assessment, motor development, sport marketing, sport finance.

New Mexico State University, Graduate School, College of Health and Social Services, Department of Health Science, Las Cruces, NM 88003-8001. Offers community health education (MPH). Part-time programs available. Postbaccalaureate distance learning degree programs offered (minimal on-campus study). *Faculty:* 9 full-time (5 women), 1 (woman) part-time/adjunct. *Students:* 51 full-time (40 women), 38 part-time (28 women); includes 41 minority (6 African Americans, 13 American Indian/Alaska Native, 2 Asian Americans or Pacific Islanders, 20 Hispanic Americans), 11 international. Average age 34. 64 applicants, 81% accepted, 29 enrolled. In 2009, 18 master's awarded. *Degree requirements:* For master's, thesis optional. *Entrance requirements:* For master's, GRE, 6 hours in psychosocial course work, 4 hours in biology, 3 hours in statistics. Additional exam requirements/recommendations for international students: Required—TOEFL. *Application deadline:* For fall admission, 4/1 for domestic students. Application fee: $30 ($50 for international students). *Expenses:* Tuition, state resident: full-time $4080; part-time $223 per credit. Tuition, nonresident: full-time $14,256; part-time $647 per credit. Required fees: $1278; $639 per semester. *Financial support:* In 2009–10, 2 research assistantships (averaging $3,950 per year), 21 teaching assistantships (averaging $5,047 per year) were awarded; fellowships, career-related internships or fieldwork and health care benefits also available. Financial award application deadline: 4/1. *Faculty research:* Community health education, health issues of U.S.-Mexico border, health policy and management, victims of violence, environmental and occupational health issues. *Unit head:* Dr. Stephen Arnold, Interim Head, 575-646-4300, Fax: 575-646-4343, E-mail: sarnold@nmsu.edu. *Application contact:* Dr. Stephen Arnold, Interim Head, 575-646-4300, Fax: 575-646-4343, E-mail: sarnold@nmsu.edu.

New York Medical College, School of Health Sciences and Practice, Department of Epidemiology and Community Health, Program in Health Education, Valhalla, NY 10595-1691. Offers Graduate Certificate. *Faculty:* 2 full-time, 9 part-time/adjunct. *Students:* 10 full-time, 18 part-time. Average age 32. 28 applicants, 75% accepted, 18 enrolled. *Entrance requirements:* Additional exam requirements/recommendations for international students: Required—TOEFL (minimum score 637 paper-based; 110 iBT), IELTS (minimum score 7). *Application deadline:* For fall admission, 8/1 for domestic students; for spring admission, 12/1 for domestic students. Applications are processed on a rolling basis. Application fee: $50 ($100 for international students). Electronic applications accepted. *Expenses:* Tuition: Full-time $18,170; part-time $790 per credit. Required fees: $790 per credit. $20 per semester. One-time fee: $100. Tuition and fees vary according to class time, course level, course load, degree level, program, student level and student's religious affiliation. *Unit head:* Dr. Chia-Ching Chen, Director, 914-594-3379, E-mail: chiaching_chen@nymc.edu. *Application contact:* Pamela Suett, Director of Recruitment, 914-594-4510, Fax: 914-594-4292, E-mail: shsp_admissions@nymc.edu.

New York University, Steinhardt School of Culture, Education, and Human Development, Department of Nutrition, Food Studies, and Public Health, Program in Community Public Health, New York, NY 10012-1019. Offers community public health (MPH), including community health, international community health, public health nutrition; public health (PhD). *Accreditation:* CEPH. Part-time programs available. *Students:* 90 full-time (77 women), 45 part-time (41 women); includes 34 minority (11 African Americans, 17 Asian Americans or Pacific Islanders, 6 Hispanic Americans), 10 international. Average age 28. 257 applicants, 81% accepted, 52 enrolled. In 2009, 36 master's awarded. *Degree requirements:* For master's, thesis (for some programs). *Entrance requirements:* For master's, GRE General Test; for doctorate, GRE General Test, interview. Additional exam requirements/recommendations for international students: Required—TOEFL. *Application deadline:* For fall admission, 12/15 priority date for domestic and international students; for spring admission, 11/1 for domestic and international students. Applications are processed on a rolling basis. Application fee: $75. Electronic applications accepted. *Expenses:* Tuition: Full-time $30,528; part-time $1272 per credit. Required fees: $2177. *Financial support:* Fellowships with full and partial tuition reimbursements, career-related internships or fieldwork, Federal Work-Study, institutionally sponsored loans, scholarships/grants, and tuition waivers (partial) available. Support available to part-time students. Financial award application deadline: 2/1; financial award applicants required to submit FAFSA. *Faculty research:* Social epidemiology, primary health care, global health, immigrants and health, infectious disease prevention, HIV/AIDS. *Unit head:* Director, 212-998-5580, Fax: 212-995-4192. *Application contact:* 212-998-5030, Fax: 212-995-4328, E-mail: steinhardt.gradadmissions@nyu.edu.

North Carolina Agricultural and Technical State University, Graduate School, School of Education, Department of Human Performance and Leisure Studies, Greensboro, NC 27411. Offers physical education (MAT, MS). *Accreditation:* NCATE. Part-time and evening/weekend programs available. *Degree requirements:* For master's, comprehensive exam, thesis or alternative, qualifying exam. *Entrance requirements:* For master's, GRE General Test, minimum GPA of 3.0.

Northeastern State University, Graduate College, College of Education, Department of Health and Human Performance, Tahlequah, OK 74464-2399. Offers health and kinesiology (MS Ed). Part-time and evening/weekend programs available. *Entrance requirements:* For master's, MAT or GRE, minimum GPA of 2.5. Additional exam requirements/recommendations for international students: Required—TOEFL (minimum score 213 computer-based).

Northern State University, Division of Graduate Studies in Education, Program in Teaching and Learning, Aberdeen, SD 57401-7198. Offers educational studies (MS Ed); elementary classroom teaching (MS Ed); health, physical education, and coaching (MS Ed); language and literacy (MS Ed); secondary classroom teaching (MS Ed); special education (MS Ed). *Accreditation:* NCATE. Part-time and evening/weekend programs available. *Faculty:* 10 full-time (8 women). *Students:* 23 full-time (16 women), 35 part-time (17 women); includes 2 minority (1 American Indian/Alaska Native, 1 Asian American or Pacific Islander). Average age 32. In 2009, 26 master's awarded. *Degree requirements:* For master's, thesis optional. *Entrance requirements:* For master's, minimum GPA of 2.75. Additional exam requirements/recommendations for international students: Required—TOEFL (minimum score 550 paper-based; 213 computer-based; 76 iBT). *Application deadline:* For fall admission, 8/15 priority date for domestic students; for spring admission, 12/15 for domestic students. Applications are processed on a rolling basis. Application fee: $35. Electronic applications accepted. *Financial support:* In 2009–10, 18 teaching assistantships with partial tuition reimbursements (averaging $5,558 per year) were awarded; career-related internships or fieldwork, Federal Work-Study, institutionally sponsored loans, scholarships/grants, and unspecified assistantships also available. Support available to part-time students. Financial award application deadline: 3/1; financial award applicants required to submit FAFSA. *Application contact:* Tammy K. Griffith, Program Assistant, 605-626-2558, Fax: 605-626-7190, E-mail: griffith@northern.edu.

Northwestern State University of Louisiana, Graduate Studies and Research, Department of Health and Human Performance, Natchitoches, LA 71497. Offers MS. *Degree requirements:* For master's, comprehensive exam, thesis or alternative. *Entrance requirements:* For master's, GRE General Test, minimum undergraduate GPA of 2.5.

Northwest Missouri State University, Graduate School, College of Education and Human Services, Department of Health, Physical Education, Recreation and Dance, Maryville, MO 64468-6001. Offers applied health science (MS); health and physical education (MS Ed); recreation (MS). *Accreditation:* NCATE. Part-time programs available. *Faculty:* 10 full-time (5 women). *Students:* 38 full-time (10 women), 12 part-time (5 women); includes 3 minority (2 African Americans, 1 Hispanic American), 2 international. 35 applicants, 77% accepted, 20 enrolled. In 2009, 10 master's awarded. *Degree requirements:* For master's, comprehensive exam. *Entrance requirements:* For master's, GRE General Test, minimum undergraduate GPA of 2.75, teaching certificate, writing sample. Additional exam requirements/recommendations

for international students: Required—TOEFL (minimum score 550 paper-based; 213 computer-based). *Application deadline:* For fall admission, 7/1 for domestic and international students; for spring admission, 11/15 for domestic and international students. Applications are processed on a rolling basis. Application fee: $0 ($50 for international students). *Expenses:* Tuition, state resident: part-time $296.34 per credit hour. Tuition, nonresident: part-time $510.43 per credit hour. *Financial support:* In 2009–10, 27 teaching assistantships with full tuition reimbursements (averaging $6,000 per year) were awarded; unspecified assistantships also available. Financial award application deadline: 4/1; financial award applicants required to submit FAFSA. *Unit head:* Dr. Terry Robertson, Program Director, 660-562-1781. *Application contact:* Dr. Gregory Haddock, Dean of Graduate School, 660-562-1145, Fax: 660-562-1096, E-mail: gradsch@nwmissouri.edu.

Nova Southeastern University, Fischler School of Education and Human Services, Program in Education, Fort Lauderdale, FL 33314-7796. Offers educational leadership (Ed D); health care education (Ed D); higher education leadership (Ed D); human services administration (Ed D); instructional leadership (Ed D); instructional technology and distance education (Ed D); organizational leadership (Ed D); special education (Ed D); speech language pathology (Ed D). Part-time and evening/weekend programs available. Postbaccalaureate distance learning degree programs offered (minimal on-campus study). *Faculty:* 88 full-time (46 women), 132 part-time/adjunct (63 women). *Students:* 2,805 full-time (2,128 women), 1,411 part-time (1,081 women); includes 2,629 minority (2,034 African Americans, 19 American Indian/Alaska Native, 62 Asian Americans or Pacific Islanders, 514 Hispanic Americans), 30 international. Average age 41. 964 applicants, 69% accepted, 513 enrolled. In 2009, 445 doctorates awarded. *Degree requirements:* For doctorate, thesis/dissertation. *Entrance requirements:* For doctorate, MAT or GRE, master's degree, 2 letters of recommendation, work experience. Additional exam requirements/recommendations for international students: Required—TSE (recommended, minimum score 50); Recommended—TOEFL (minimum score 550 paper-based; 213 computer-based; 80 iBT), IELTS (minimum score 6). *Application deadline:* For fall admission, 8/20 priority date for domestic and international students; for winter admission, 12/19 priority date for domestic and international students; for spring admission, 4/26 priority date for domestic students, 4/25 priority date for international students. Applications are processed on a rolling basis. Application fee: $50. Electronic applications accepted. *Financial support:* In 2009–10, 2 fellowships with full tuition reimbursements (averaging $30,000 per year) were awarded; scholarships/grants and tuition waivers (full) also available. Support available to part-time students. Financial award application deadline: 4/15; financial award applicants required to submit FAFSA. *Unit head:* Dr. Ronald Kern, Dean of Academic Affairs, 800-986-3223 Ext. 7809, Fax: 954-262-3606, E-mail: rk429@nsu.nova.edu. *Application contact:* Dr. Jennifer Quinones Nottingham, Dean of Student Affairs, 800-986-3223 Ext. 1546.

Nova Southeastern University, Fischler School of Education and Human Services, Programs for Higher Education, Fort Lauderdale, FL 33314-7796. Offers adult education (Ed D); computing and information technology (Ed D); health care education (Ed D); higher education (Ed D); vocational, occupational and technical education (Ed D). Part-time and evening/weekend programs available. Postbaccalaureate distance learning degree programs offered (minimal on-campus study). *Faculty:* 6 full-time (3 women), 8 part-time/adjunct (2 women). *Students:* 113 full-time (81 women), 2 part-time (both women); includes 57 minority (51 African Americans, 6 Hispanic Americans). 4 applicants, 75% accepted, 3 enrolled. In 2009, 13 doctorates awarded. *Degree requirements:* For doctorate, thesis/dissertation, practicum. *Entrance requirements:* For doctorate, MAT or GRE, master's degree, work experience in field, minimum GPA of 3.0. Additional exam requirements/recommendations for international students: Required—TSE (recommended, minimum score 50); Recommended—TOEFL (minimum score 550 paper-based; 213 computer-based; 80 iBT), IELTS (minimum score 6). *Application deadline:* For fall admission, 8/11 priority date for domestic and international students; for winter admission, 12/28 priority date for domestic and international students; for spring admission, 4/22 priority date for domestic and international students. Applications are processed on a rolling basis. Application fee: $50. Electronic applications accepted. *Expenses:* Contact institution. *Financial support:* Career-related internships or fieldwork and tuition waivers (full) available. Financial award application deadline: 1/7. *Unit head:* Dr. Karen D. Bowser, Associate Dean of Doctoral Programs, 954-262-8677, Fax: 954-262-3606, E-mail: bowserk@nova.edu. *Application contact:* Dr. Jennifer Quinones Nottingham, Dean of Student Affairs, 800-986-3223 Ext. 8624, Fax: 954-262-3883, E-mail: jlquinon@nova.edu.

Nova Southeastern University, Fischler School of Education and Human Services, Programs in Human Services, Fort Lauderdale, FL 33314-7796. Offers child and youth studies (Ed D); child protection (MHS); education (MS), including human services; health professions education (MS); substance abuse counseling and education (MS). Part-time and evening/weekend programs available. *Students:* 1,867 full-time (1,442 women), 1,273 part-time (976 women); includes 1,866 minority (1,545 African Americans, 16 American Indian/Alaska Native, 48 Asian Americans or Pacific Islanders, 257 Hispanic Americans), 27 international. In 2009, 118 doctorates awarded. *Degree requirements:* For master's, thesis, practicum; for doctorate, thesis/dissertation, practicum. *Entrance requirements:* For master's, GRE or MAT, work experience in field, minimum GPA of 2.5; for doctorate, GRE or MAT, master's degree, minimum GPA of 3.0, work experience. Additional exam requirements/recommendations for international students: Recommended—TOEFL (minimum score 550 paper-based; 213 computer-based), IELTS (minimum score 6). *Application deadline:* Applications are processed on a rolling basis. Application fee: $50. Electronic applications accepted. *Expenses:* Contact institution. *Financial support:* Career-related internships or fieldwork and Federal Work-Study available. Support available to part-time students. Financial award application deadline: 4/15; financial award applicants required to submit FAFSA. *Unit head:* Dr. Elda Veloso, Associate Dean, 954-262-8538, Fax: 954-262-2917, E-mail: veloso@nova.edu. *Application contact:* Dr. Jennifer Quinones Nottingham, Dean of Student Affairs, 800-986-3223 Ext. 8500.

Oklahoma State University, College of Education, School of Applied Health and Educational Psychology, Stillwater, OK 74078. Offers applied behavioral studies (Ed D). *Accreditation:* APA (one or more programs are accredited). Part-time programs available. *Faculty:* 38 full-time (17 women), 15 part-time/adjunct (10 women). *Students:* 188 full-time (141 women), 179 part-time (122 women); includes 73 minority (27 African Americans, 26 American Indian/Alaska Native, 9 Asian Americans or Pacific Islanders, 11 Hispanic Americans), 13 international. Average age 33. 267 applicants, 30% accepted, 58 enrolled. In 2009, 65 master's, 50 doctorates awarded. *Degree requirements:* For master's, thesis (for some programs); for doctorate, comprehensive exam, thesis/dissertation. *Entrance requirements:* For master's and doctorate, GRE or GMAT. Additional exam requirements/recommendations for international students: Required—TOEFL (minimum score 550 paper-based; 79 iBT). *Application deadline:* For fall admission, 3/1 priority date for international students; for spring admission, 8/1 priority date for international students. Applications are processed on a rolling basis. Application fee: $40 ($75 for international students). Electronic applications accepted. *Expenses:* Tuition, state resident: full-time $3716; part-time $154.85 per credit hour. Tuition, nonresident: full-time $14,448; part-time $602 per credit hour. Required fees: $1772; $73.85 per credit hour. One-time fee: $50. Tuition and fees vary according to course load and campus/location. *Financial support:* In 2009–10, 31 research assistantships (averaging $6,378 per year), 67 teaching assistantships (averaging $8,252 per year) were awarded; career-related internships or fieldwork, Federal Work-Study, scholarships/grants, health care benefits, tuition waivers (partial), and unspecified assistantships also available. Support available to part-time students. Financial award application deadline: 3/1; financial award applicants required to submit FAFSA. *Unit head:* Dr. John Romans, Head, 405-744-6040, Fax: 405-744-6779. *Application contact:* Dr. Gordon Emslie, Dean, 405-744-6368, Fax: 405-744-0355, E-mail: grad-i@okstate.edu.

Plymouth State University, College of Graduate Studies, Graduate Studies in Education, Program in Health Education, Plymouth, NH 03264-1595. Offers M Ed. Part-time and evening/weekend programs available. *Degree requirements:* For master's, PRAXIS. *Entrance requirements:* For master's, MAT, minimum GPA of 3.0.

Portland State University, Graduate Studies, College of Urban and Public Affairs, School of Community Health, Portland, OR 97207-0751. Offers aging (Certificate); health education

Health Education

Portland State University (continued)

(MA, MS); health education and health promotion (MPH); health studies (MPA, MPH), including health administration. *Accreditation:* CEPH. Part-time programs available. *Degree requirements:* For master's, oral and written exams. *Entrance requirements:* For master's, GRE General Test, 3 letters of recommendation, minimum GPA of 3.0. Additional exam requirements/recommendations for international students: Required—TOEFL (minimum score 550 paper-based; 213 computer-based).

Prairie View A&M University, College of Education, Department of Health and Human Performance, Prairie View, TX 77446-0519. Offers health education (M Ed, MS); physical education (M Ed, MS). *Accreditation:* NCATE. Part-time and evening/weekend programs available. *Faculty:* 3 full-time (0 women). *Students:* 14 part-time (8 women); includes 10 African Americans, 1 Hispanic American. Average age 31. 36 applicants, 100% accepted. In 2009, 6 master's awarded. *Entrance requirements:* For master's, GRE General Test. Additional exam requirements/recommendations for international students: Required—TOEFL. *Application deadline:* For fall admission, 10/2 priority date for domestic students; for spring admission, 2/19 for domestic students. Applications are processed on a rolling basis. Application fee: $50. *Expenses:* Tuition, state resident: full-time $2200. Tuition, nonresident: full-time $5600. Required fees: $1720. Tuition and fees vary according to course load. *Financial support:* In 2009–10, 8 fellowships with tuition reimbursements (averaging $1,200 per year), 10 research assistantships with tuition reimbursements (averaging $15,000 per year) were awarded; teaching assistantships with tuition reimbursements, career-related internships or fieldwork, Federal Work-Study, and institutionally sponsored loans also available. Support available to part-time students. Financial award application deadline: 4/1. *Unit head:* Dr. Patricia Hoffman-Miller, Interim Department Head, 936-261-3530, Fax: 936-261-3617. *Application contact:* Dr. William H. Parker, Dean of Graduate School, 936-261-3500, Fax: 936-261-3529, E-mail: whparker@pvamu.edu.

Regis University, Rueckert-Hartman School for Health Professions, Denver, CO 80221-1099. Offers clinical leadership for physician assistants (MS); family nurse practitioner (MSN); health informatics (Postbaccalaureate Certificate); health services administration (MS); healthcare education (Certificate); leadership in healthcare systems (MSN); neonatal nurse practitioner (MSN); nursing (MSN); pharmacy (Pharm D); physical therapy (DPT, TDPT). *Entrance requirements:* Additional exam requirements/recommendations for international students: Required—TOEFL (minimum score 550 paper-based; 213 computer-based; 82 iBT). Electronic applications accepted. *Expenses:* Contact institution. *Faculty research:* Normal and pathological balance and gait research, normal/pathological upper limb motor control/biomechanics, exercise energy/metabolism research, optical treatment protocols for therapeutic modalities.

Rhode Island College, School of Graduate Studies, Feinstein School of Education and Human Development, Department of Health and Physical Education, Providence, RI 02908-1991. Offers health education (M Ed); physical education (CGS). *Accreditation:* NCATE. Part-time and evening/weekend programs available. *Faculty:* 3 full-time (2 women). *Students:* 15 part-time (13 women). Average age 39. In 2009, 9 master's awarded. *Degree requirements:* For master's, comprehensive assessment. *Entrance requirements:* For master's, GRE General Test or MAT, undergraduate transcripts; minimum undergraduate GPA of 3.0; copy of teaching certificate (when applicable); 3 letters of recommendation; for CGS, GRE or MAT (for most programs), undergraduate transcripts; minimum undergraduate GPA of 3.0; copy of teaching certificate (when applicable); 3 letters of recommendation. Additional exam requirements/recommendations for international students: Recommended—TOEFL (minimum score 550 paper-based; 213 computer-based; 79 iBT). *Application deadline:* For fall admission, 3/15 for domestic students; for spring admission, 11/1 for domestic students. Applications are processed on a rolling basis. Application fee: $50. *Expenses:* Tuition, state resident: full-time $7440; part-time $310 per credit hour. Tuition, nonresident: full-time $14,784; part-time $616 per credit hour. Required fees: $552; $20 per credit. $70 per term. *Financial support:* Teaching assistantships with full tuition reimbursements, Federal Work-Study, scholarships/grants, health care benefits, and unspecified assistantships available. Support available to part-time students. Financial award application deadline: 5/15; financial award applicants required to submit FAFSA. *Unit head:* Dr. Betty Rauhe, Chair, 401-456-8046. *Application contact:* Graduate Studies, 401-456-8700.

Rosalind Franklin University of Medicine and Science, College of Health Professions, Department of Nutrition, North Chicago, IL 60064-3095. Offers clinical nutrition (MS); nutrition education (MS). Part-time and evening/weekend programs available. Postbaccalaureate distance learning degree programs offered (no on-campus study). *Faculty:* 3 full-time (all women), 3 part-time/adjunct (2 women). *Students:* 46; includes 6 minority (2 African Americans, 3 Asian Americans or Pacific Islanders, 1 Hispanic American). Average age 36. 34 applicants, 76% accepted, 23 enrolled. *Degree requirements:* For master's, thesis optional, portfolio. *Entrance requirements:* For master's, minimum GPA of 2.75, registered dietitian (RD), professional certificate or license. Additional exam requirements/recommendations for international students: Required—TOEFL. *Application deadline:* For fall admission, 8/6 priority date for domestic students; for winter admission, 10/29 for domestic students; for spring admission, 2/5 for domestic students. Applications are processed on a rolling basis. Application fee: $50. *Expenses:* Contact institution. *Financial support:* Institutionally sponsored loans available. Support available to part-time students. Financial award application deadline: 6/9; financial award applicants required to submit FAFSA. *Faculty research:* Nutrition education, distance learning, computer-based graduate education, childhood obesity, nutrition medical education. *Unit head:* Dr. Lynn Janas, Chair, 847-578-3324, Fax: 847-578-8623, E-mail: lynn.janas@rosalindfranklin.edu. *Application contact:* Melissa Knox, Admissions Officer, 847-578-8772, Fax: 847-775-6559, E-mail: melissa.knox@rosalindfranklin.edu.

Sage Graduate School, Graduate School, School of Education, Program in Community Health Education, Troy, NY 12180-4115. Offers MS. Part-time and evening/weekend programs available. *Faculty:* 15 full-time (9 women), 19 part-time/adjunct (16 women). *Students:* 5 full-time (3 women), 22 part-time (12 women); includes 3 minority (1 Asian American or Pacific Islander, 2 Hispanic Americans). Average age 29. 21 applicants, 48% accepted, 8 enrolled. In 2009, 8 master's awarded. *Degree requirements:* For master's, thesis optional. *Entrance requirements:* For master's, minimum GPA of 2.75, resume, 2 letters of recommendation, interview, assessment of writing skills. Additional exam requirements/recommendations for international students: Required—TOEFL (minimum score 550 paper-based; 213 computer-based). *Application deadline:* Applications are processed on a rolling basis. Application fee: $40. *Expenses:* Tuition: Full-time $10,620; part-time $590 per credit hour. *Financial support:* Federal Work-Study, scholarships/grants, tuition waivers (partial), and unspecified assistantships available. Support available to part-time students. Financial award application deadline: 3/1; financial award applicants required to submit FAFSA. *Unit head:* Dr. Nancy A. DeKorp, Director, 518-244-2496, E-mail: dekorn@sage.edu. *Application contact:* Wendy D. Diefendorf, Director of Graduate and Adult Admission, 518-244-2443, Fax: 518-244-6880, E-mail: diefew@sage.edu.

Sage Graduate School, Graduate School, School of Education, Program in School Health Education, Troy, NY 12180-4115. Offers MS. *Accreditation:* NCATE. Part-time and evening/weekend programs available. *Faculty:* 15 full-time (9 women), 19 part-time/adjunct (16 women). *Students:* 11 full-time (7 women), 18 part-time (10 women); includes 2 minority (1 American Indian/Alaska Native, 1 Hispanic American). Average age 26. 21 applicants, 62% accepted, 10 enrolled. In 2009, 12 master's awarded. *Degree requirements:* For master's, thesis optional. *Entrance requirements:* For master's, minimum GPA of 2.75, resume, 2 letters of recommendation, interview, assessment of writing skills. Additional exam requirements/recommendations for international students: Required—TOEFL (minimum score 550 paper-based; 213 computer-based). *Application deadline:* Applications are processed on a rolling basis. Application fee: $40. *Expenses:* Tuition: Full-time $10,620; part-time $590 per credit hour. *Financial support:* Fellowships, research assistantships, Federal Work-Study, scholarships/grants, and unspecified assistantships available. Support available to part-time students. Financial award application deadline: 3/1; financial award applicants required to submit FAFSA. *Faculty research:* Policy development in health education and health care. *Unit head:* Dr. John J. Pelizza, Director, 518-244-2326, Fax: 518-244-2334, E-mail: peliz@sage.edu. *Application contact:* Wendy D. Diefendorf, Director of Graduate and Adult Admission, 518-244-2443, Fax: 518-244-6880, E-mail: diefew@sage.edu.

Saint Francis University, Department of Physician Assistant Sciences, Health Science Program, Loretto, PA 15940-0600. Offers MHS. Part-time and evening/weekend programs available. Postbaccalaureate distance learning degree programs offered (no on-campus study). *Faculty:* 1 (woman) full-time, 11 part-time/adjunct (4 women). *Students:* 42 part-time (29 women); includes 30 minority (25 African Americans, 3 Asian Americans or Pacific Islanders, 2 Hispanic Americans). 28 applicants, 100% accepted, 28 enrolled. *Entrance requirements:* For master's, 2 letters of reference, minimum QPA of 2.5. *Application deadline:* For fall admission, 8/1 for domestic students; for spring admission, 12/1 for domestic students. Applications are processed on a rolling basis. Application fee: $50. Electronic applications accepted. *Expenses:* Contact institution. *Financial support:* Available to part-time students. Applicants required to submit FAFSA. *Unit head:* Deborah E. Budash, Director, 814-472-3919, Fax: 814-472-3137, E-mail: dbudash@francis.edu. *Application contact:* Cheryl Strittmatter, Office Assistant, 814-472-3136, Fax: 814-472-3137, E-mail: cstrittmatter@francis.edu.

Saint Joseph's University, College of Arts and Sciences, Department of Health Services, Philadelphia, PA 19131-1395. Offers health administration (MS, Post-Master's Certificate); health care ethics (Post-Master's Certificate); health education (MS, Post-Master's Certificate); health informatics (Post-Master's Certificate); healthcare ethics (MS); nurse anesthesia (MS); school nurse certification (MS). Part-time and evening/weekend programs available. *Students:* 10 full-time (5 women), 180 part-time (135 women); includes 67 minority (50 African Americans, 11 Asian Americans or Pacific Islanders, 6 Hispanic Americans), 8 international. Average age 36. In 2009, 72 master's awarded. *Entrance requirements:* For master's, GRE (if GPA less than 2.75), 2 letters of recommendation, minimum GPA of 2.75, resume. Additional exam requirements/recommendations for international students: Required—TOEFL (minimum score 550 paper-based; 213 computer-based; 79 iBT). *Application deadline:* For fall admission, 7/15 priority date for domestic students, 4/15 for international students; for winter admission, 1/15 for international students; for spring admission, 11/15 priority date for domestic students, 10/15 for international students. Applications are processed on a rolling basis. Application fee: $35. Electronic applications accepted. *Expenses:* Tuition: Part-time $729 per credit hour. Tuition and fees vary according to degree level and program. *Financial support:* Career-related internships or fieldwork and unspecified assistantships available. Financial award applicants required to submit FAFSA. *Unit head:* Nakia Henderson, Director, 610-660-2952, E-mail: nakia.henderson@sju.edu. *Application contact:* Kate McConnell, Director, Graduate College of Arts and Sciences Admissions and Retention, 610-660-3184, Fax: 610-660-3230, E-mail: kate.mcconnell@sju.edu.

San Francisco State University, Division of Graduate Studies, College of Behavioral and Social Sciences, Human Sexuality Studies Program, San Francisco, CA 94132-1722. Offers MA.

San Jose State University, Graduate Studies and Research, College of Applied Sciences and Arts, Department of Health Science, San Jose, CA 95192-0001. Offers applied social gerontology (Certificate); community health education (MPH). *Accreditation:* CEPH (one or more programs are accredited). Postbaccalaureate distance learning degree programs offered. *Students:* 26 full-time (21 women), 51 part-time (45 women); includes 42 minority (6 African Americans, 1 American Indian/Alaska Native, 16 Asian Americans or Pacific Islanders, 19 Hispanic Americans), 3 international. Average age 33. 121 applicants, 24% accepted, 25 enrolled. In 2009, 11 master's awarded. *Entrance requirements:* For master's, GRE General Test. *Application deadline:* For fall admission, 6/29 for domestic students; for spring admission, 11/30 for domestic students. Applications are processed on a rolling basis. Application fee: $59. Electronic applications accepted. *Financial support:* Career-related internships or fieldwork, Federal Work-Study, and institutionally sponsored loans available. Support available to part-time students. Financial award applicants required to submit FAFSA. *Faculty research:* Behavioral science in occupational and health care settings, epidemiology in health care settings. *Unit head:* Dr. Kathleen Roe, Chair, 408-924-2976, Fax: 408-924-2979. *Application contact:* Dr. Kathleen Roe, Chair, 408-924-2976, Fax: 408-924-2979.

Simmons College, College of Arts and Sciences Graduate Studies, Department of Education, Program in Special Education, Boston, MA 02115. Offers applied behavior analysis (PhD); assistive technology (MS Ed, Ed S); behavioral education (MS Ed, Ed S); health professions education (PhD); language and literacy (MS Ed, Ed S); moderate disabilities (Ed S); moderate special needs (MS Ed); severe disabilities (Ed S); severe special needs (MS Ed); special education administration (MS Ed, PhD, Ed S). Part-time and evening/weekend programs available. *Students:* 45 full-time (40 women), 316 part-time (271 women); includes 19 minority (7 African Americans, 1 American Indian/Alaska Native, 7 Asian Americans or Pacific Islanders, 4 Hispanic Americans), 2 international. 95 applicants, 89% accepted, 65 enrolled. In 2009, 145 master's awarded. *Degree requirements:* For master's, student teaching. *Entrance requirements:* For doctorate, GRE, research proposal, interview, BCBA credential. Additional exam requirements/recommendations for international students: Required—TOEFL (minimum score 600 paper-based; 250 computer-based; 100 iBT). *Application deadline:* For fall admission, 8/1 priority date for domestic and international students; for winter admission, 12/15 priority date for domestic students; for spring admission, 12/15 priority date for domestic and international students. Applications are processed on a rolling basis. Application fee: $35. Electronic applications accepted. *Expenses:* Contact institution. *Financial support:* Application deadline: 3/1. *Faculty research:* Development and application of the IEP for teachers, assistive technology, language-based disabilities, applied behavior analysis, communication challenges between general and special education teachers. *Unit head:* Paul Abraham, Chair, Department of Education, 617-521-2575, E-mail: paul.abraham@simmons.edu. *Application contact:* Kristen Haack, Director, Graduate Studies Admission, 617-521-2917, Fax: 617-521-3058, E-mail: gsa@simmons.edu.

Simmons College, School of Health Sciences, Graduate Nursing Program, Boston, MA 02115. Offers health professions education (PhD, CAGS); nursing (MSN, DNP); nursing practice (PhD); primary health care nursing (MS, CAGS). *Accreditation:* AACN. Part-time programs available. Postbaccalaureate distance learning degree programs offered (minimal on-campus study). *Faculty:* 37 full-time (31 women), 42 part-time/adjunct (31 women). *Students:* 99 full-time (97 women), 116 part-time (107 women); includes 22 minority (5 African Americans, 11 Asian Americans or Pacific Islanders, 6 Hispanic Americans). Average age 38. 306 applicants, 52% accepted, 72 enrolled. In 2009, 29 master's, 2 doctorates, 2 other advanced degrees awarded. *Degree requirements:* For master's, research project; for doctorate, capstone project (for DNP only). *Entrance requirements:* For master's, courses in statistics and health assessment; for CAGS, previous coursework in microbiology, statistics, developmental psychology, organic and inorganic chemistry. Additional exam requirements/recommendations for international students: Required—TOEFL (minimum score 570 paper-based; 230 computer-based; 88 iBT). *Application deadline:* For fall admission, 6/1 for domestic and international students; for spring admission, 11/1 for domestic students. Application fee: $50. *Expenses:* Contact institution. *Financial support:* Scholarships/grants available. Financial award application deadline: 3/1; financial award applicants required to submit FAFSA. *Faculty research:* Environmental effects on DNA, nursing care of the developmentally disabled, ethical decision-making, depression and grief of the elderly, cultural impressions of dementia. *Unit head:* Dr. Judy A. Beal, Chairperson, 617-521-2139, Fax: 617-521-3045, E-mail: judy.beal@simmons.edu. *Application contact:* Carmen Fortin, Assistant Dean/Director of Admission, 617-521-2605, Fax: 617-521-3137, E-mail: shs@simmons.edu.

Simmons College, School of Health Sciences, Program in Health Professions Education, Boston, MA 02115. Offers PhD, CAGS. Part-time programs available. *Faculty:* 3 full-time (all women), 1 (woman) part-time/adjunct. *Students:* 24 part-time (all women); includes 2 minority (both African Americans), 1 international. 17 applicants, 88% accepted, 15 enrolled. In 2009, 2 doctorates, 2 other advanced degrees awarded. *Degree requirements:* For doctorate, thesis/dissertation; for CAGS, capstone project. *Application deadline:* For fall admission, 2/1 for

domestic and international students; for winter admission, 9/1 for domestic and international students; for spring admission, 12/1 for domestic and international students. Applications are processed on a rolling basis. Application fee: $50. Electronic applications accepted. *Expenses:* Tuition: Part-time $925 per credit hour. Part-time tuition and fees vary according to program. *Faculty research:* Evidence-based practice, pediatric nursing, racial/class conflict in the healthcare workplace, curricular innovation. *Unit head:* Dr. Gerald P. Koocher, Dean, 617-521-2605, Fax: 617-521-3137, E-mail: gerald.koocher@simmons.edu. *Application contact:* Carmen Fortin, Assistant Dean/Director of Admission, 617-521-2651, Fax: 617-521-3137, E-mail: shs@simmons.edu.

South Dakota State University, Graduate School, College of Education and Human Sciences, Department of Health, Physical Education and Recreation, Brookings, SD 57007. Offers MS. Part-time programs available. *Degree requirements:* For master's, thesis, oral and written exams. *Entrance requirements:* Additional exam requirements/recommendations for international students: Required—TOEFL (minimum score 550 paper-based; 213 computer-based; 71 iBT). *Faculty research:* Effective teaching behaviors in physical education, sports nutrition, muscle/bone interaction, hormonal response to exercise.

Southeastern Louisiana University, College of Nursing and Health Sciences, Department of Kinesiology and Health Studies, Hammond, LA 70402. Offers health and kinesiology (MA), including exercise science, health promotion and exercise science, health studies, kinesiology. *Accreditation:* NCATE. Part-time and evening/weekend programs available. *Faculty:* 9 full-time (3 women). *Students:* 34 full-time (22 women), 18 part-time (11 women); includes 14 minority (13 African Americans, 1 Hispanic American), 10 international. Average age 26. 20 applicants, 95% accepted, 14 enrolled. In 2009, 11 master's awarded. *Degree requirements:* For master's, comprehensive exam (for some programs), thesis optional. *Entrance requirements:* For master's, GRE General Test (minimum score 800), minimum undergraduate cumulative GPA of 2.5 or 2.75 during last 60 hours of coursework. Additional exam requirements/recommendations for international students: Required—TOEFL (minimum score 500 paper-based; 173 computer-based; 61 iBT). *Application deadline:* For fall admission, 7/15 priority date for domestic students, 6/1 priority date for international students; for spring admission, 12/1 priority date for domestic students, 10/1 priority date for international students. Applications are processed on a rolling basis. Application fee: $20 ($30 for international students). Electronic applications accepted. *Expenses:* Tuition, state resident: full-time $3086; part-time $225 per credit hour. Tuition, nonresident: part-time $529 per credit hour. Required fees: $1195. Tuition and fees vary according to course level and course load. *Financial support:* In 2009–10, 12 students received support, including 8 research assistantships (averaging $9,412 per year), 4 teaching assistantships (averaging $9,412 per year); Federal Work-Study, institutionally sponsored loans, and administrative assistantships also available. Support available to part-time students. Financial award application deadline: 5/1; financial award applicants required to submit FAFSA. *Faculty research:* Relationship of exercise on body hormones, sexuality knowledge–attitudes and behaviors, drug and tobacco use and abuse, relationship of health and spirituality, exercise adherence and motivation. *Unit head:* Dr. Edward Hebert, Department Head, 985-549-2129, Fax: 985-549-5119, E-mail: ehebert@selu.edu. *Application contact:* Sandra Meyers, Graduate Admissions Analyst, 985-549-5620, Fax: 985-549-5632, E-mail: admissions@selu.edu.

Southern Connecticut State University, School of Graduate Studies, School of Education, Department of Exercise Science, Program in School Health Education, New Haven, CT 06515-1355. Offers MS. *Accreditation:* NCATE. Part-time and evening/weekend programs available. *Students:* 9 full-time (7 women), 55 part-time (32 women); includes 2 minority (1 African American, 1 Hispanic American). 23 applicants, 83% accepted, 18 enrolled. In 2009, 33 master's awarded. *Entrance requirements:* For master's, interview. *Application deadline:* For fall admission, 7/15 priority date for domestic students. Applications are processed on a rolling basis. Application fee: $50. Electronic applications accepted. Tuition and fees vary according to program. *Financial support:* Application deadline: 4/15. *Unit head:* Dr. Doris Marino, Graduate Coordinator, 203-392-6922, Fax: 203-392-6911, E-mail: marinod1@southernct.edu. *Application contact:* Dr. Doris Marino, Graduate Coordinator, 203-392-6922, Fax: 203-392-6911, E-mail: marinod1@southernct.edu.

Southern Illinois University Carbondale, Graduate School, College of Education, Department of Health Education and Recreation, Program in Community Health Education, Carbondale, IL 62901-4701. Offers MPH.

Southern Illinois University Carbondale, Graduate School, College of Education, Department of Health Education and Recreation, Program in Health Education, Carbondale, IL 62901-4701. Offers MS Ed, PhD. *Accreditation:* NCATE. Part-time programs available. *Degree requirements:* For master's, thesis; for doctorate, thesis/dissertation. *Entrance requirements:* For master's, MAT, minimum GPA of 2.7; for doctorate, MAT, minimum GPA of 3.25. Additional exam requirements/recommendations for international students: Required—TOEFL. *Faculty research:* Sexuality education, research design, injury control, program evaluation.

Southern Illinois University Edwardsville, Graduate Studies and Research, School of Education, Department of Kinesiology and Health Education, Edwardsville, IL 62026-0001. Offers kinesiology (MS Ed). *Accreditation:* NCATE. Part-time and evening/weekend programs available. *Faculty:* 12 full-time (5 women). *Students:* 25 full-time (16 women), 50 part-time (21 women); includes 6 minority (5 African Americans, 1 Hispanic American), 4 international. Average age 26. 81 applicants, 60% accepted. In 2009, 30 master's awarded. *Degree requirements:* For master's, thesis (for some programs), final exam. *Entrance requirements:* Additional exam requirements/recommendations for international students: Required—TOEFL (minimum score 550 paper-based; 213 computer-based; 79 iBT), IELTS (minimum score 6.5). *Application deadline:* For fall admission, 7/23 for domestic students, 6/1 for international students; for spring admission, 12/11 for domestic students, 10/1 for international students. Applications are processed on a rolling basis. Application fee: $30. Electronic applications accepted. *Expenses:* Tuition, state resident: part-time $1252.50 per semester. Tuition, nonresident: part-time $3131.25 per semester. Required fees: $586.85 per semester. Tuition and fees vary according to course load. *Financial support:* In 2009–10, 17 teaching assistantships with full tuition reimbursements (averaging $8,064 per year) were awarded; fellowships, research assistantships with full tuition reimbursements, career-related internships or fieldwork, Federal Work-Study, institutionally sponsored loans, scholarships/grants, traineeships, and unspecified assistantships also available. Support available to part-time students. Financial award application deadline: 3/1; financial award applicants required to submit FAFSA. *Unit head:* Dr. Curt Lox, Director, 618-650-2938, E-mail: clox@siue.edu. *Application contact:* Dr. Curt Lox, Director, 618-650-2938, E-mail: clox@siue.edu.

Springfield College, Graduate Programs, Programs in Physical Education, Springfield, MA 01109-3797. Offers adapted physical education (M Ed, MPE, MS); advanced level coaching (M Ed, MPE, MS); athletic administration (M Ed, MPE, MS); general physical education (PhD, CAGS); health education licensure (MPE, MS); health education licensure program (M Ed); physical education licensure (MPE, MS); physical education licensure program (M Ed); teaching and administration (MS). Part-time programs available. *Degree requirements:* For master's, comprehensive exam, thesis (for some programs). *Entrance requirements:* For master's and doctorate, GRE General Test. Additional exam requirements/recommendations for international students: Required—TOEFL (minimum score 550 paper-based; 213 computer-based). Electronic applications accepted. *Expenses:* Tuition: Full-time $19,800; part-time $825 per credit hour. Required fees: $150.

State University of New York College at Cortland, Graduate Studies, School of Professional Studies, Department of Health Education, Cortland, NY 13045. Offers MS Ed, MST. *Accreditation:* NCATE. Part-time and evening/weekend programs available. *Entrance requirements:* Additional exam requirements/recommendations for international students: Required—TOEFL.

Suffolk University, College of Arts and Sciences, Program in Women's Health, Boston, MA 02108-2770. Offers MA. *Faculty:* 15 full-time (10 women). *Students:* 25 full-time (all women), 14 part-time (all women); includes 24 minority (14 African Americans, 10 Hispanic Americans). Average age 27. 128 applicants, 50% accepted, 24 enrolled. In 2009, 3 master's awarded. *Entrance requirements:* For master's, statement of professional goals, official transcripts, 2 letters of recommendation, resume. Additional exam requirements/recommendations for international students: Required—TOEFL (minimum score 550 paper-based; 213 computer-based; 80 iBT). *Application deadline:* For fall admission, 6/15 priority date for domestic students, 6/15 for international students; for spring admission, 11/1 priority date for domestic students, 11/1 for international students. Applications are processed on a rolling basis. Application fee: $50. Electronic applications accepted. *Expenses:* Contact institution. *Financial support:* In 2009–10, 38 students received support, including 36 fellowships (averaging $6,929 per year). Financial award applicants required to submit FAFSA. *Unit head:* Dr. Amy Agigian, Co-Director, 617-573-8487, Fax: 617-994-4278, E-mail: aagigian@suffolk.edu. *Application contact:* Judith Reynolds, Director of Graduate Admissions, 617-573-8302, Fax: 617-305-1733, E-mail: grad.admission@suffolk.edu.

Teachers College, Columbia University, Graduate Faculty of Education, Department of Health and Behavioral Studies, Program in Community Nutrition Education, New York, NY 10027-6696. Offers Ed M.

Teachers College, Columbia University, Graduate Faculty of Education, Department of Health and Behavioral Studies, Program in Health Education, New York, NY 10027-6696. Offers MA, MS, Ed D. *Accreditation:* NCATE. Part-time and evening/weekend programs available. *Faculty:* 6 full-time (3 women). *Students:* 21 full-time (19 women), 93 part-time (81 women); includes 48 minority (30 African Americans, 8 Asian Americans or Pacific Islanders, 10 Hispanic Americans), 7 international. Average age 38. 35 applicants, 66% accepted, 12 enrolled. In 2009, 22 master's, 6 doctorates awarded. Terminal master's awarded for partial completion of doctoral program. *Degree requirements:* For master's, thesis optional, integrative project; for doctorate, thesis/dissertation. *Entrance requirements:* For doctorate, GRE or MAT. *Application deadline:* For fall admission, 5/15 for domestic students; for spring admission, 12/1 for domestic students. Application fee: $65. *Financial support:* Fellowships, research assistantships available. Financial award application deadline: 2/1. *Unit head:* Dr. Chuck Basch, Chair, 212-678-3964, E-mail: ceb35@columbia.edu. *Application contact:* Peter Shon, Assistant Director of Admission, 212-678-3305, Fax: 212-678-4171, E-mail: shon@exchange.tc.columbia.edu.

Temple University, Health Sciences Center and Graduate School, College of Health Professions, Department of Public Health, Program in Community Health Education, Philadelphia, PA 19122-6096. Offers MPH. *Accreditation:* CEPH. Part-time programs available. *Entrance requirements:* For master's, GRE General Test. Additional exam requirements/recommendations for international students: Required—TOEFL (minimum score 550 paper-based; 213 computer-based; 79 iBT). Electronic applications accepted.

Temple University, Health Sciences Center and Graduate School, College of Health Professions, Department of Public Health, Program in School Health Education, Philadelphia, PA 19122-6096. Offers Ed M. Part-time and evening/weekend programs available. *Entrance requirements:* For master's, GRE or MAT. Additional exam requirements/recommendations for international students: Required—TOEFL (minimum score 550 paper-based; 213 computer-based; 79 iBT). Electronic applications accepted.

Tennessee Technological University, Graduate School, College of Education, Department of Exercise Science, Physical Education and Wellness, Cookeville, TN 38505. Offers MA. *Accreditation:* NCATE. Part-time programs available. *Faculty:* 7 full-time (0 women). *Students:* 14 full-time (8 women), 32 part-time (17 women); includes 5 minority (4 African Americans, 1 American Indian/Alaska Native). Average age 27. 27 applicants, 93% accepted, 20 enrolled. In 2009, 17 master's awarded. *Degree requirements:* For master's, comprehensive exam, thesis or alternative. *Entrance requirements:* For master's, MAT or GRE. Additional exam requirements/recommendations for international students: Required—TOEFL (minimum score 550 paper-based; 79 iBT), IELTS (minimum score 5.5). *Application deadline:* For fall admission, 8/1 for domestic students, 5/1 for international students; for spring admission, 12/1 for domestic students, 10/1 for international students. Application fee: $25 ($30 for international students). Electronic applications accepted. *Expenses:* Tuition, state resident: full-time $7034; part-time $368 per credit hour. *Financial support:* In 2009–10, fellowships (averaging $8,000 per year), 3 research assistantships (averaging $4,000 per year), 4 teaching assistantships (averaging $4,000 per year) were awarded; career-related internships or fieldwork also available. Financial award application deadline: 4/1. *Unit head:* Dr. Patricia Jordan, Interim Chairperson, 931-372-3467, Fax: 931-372-6319. *Application contact:* Shelia K. Kendrick, Coordinator of Graduate Studies, 931-372-3808, Fax: 931-372-3497, E-mail: skendrick@tntech.edu.

Texas A&M Health Science Center, Baylor College of Dentistry, Graduate Division, Program in Health Professions Education, College Station, TX 77840. Offers MS. Part-time programs available. *Degree requirements:* For master's, thesis. *Entrance requirements:* For master's, GRE General Test, DDS or DMD. Additional exam requirements/recommendations for international students: Required—TOEFL. *Faculty research:* Craniofacial biology, dermatoglyphics, alternative curricula, admissions criteria, competency-based program assessment.

Texas A&M University, College of Education and Human Development, Department of Health and Kinesiology, College Station, TX 77843. Offers health education (M Ed, MS, Ed D, PhD); kinesiology (M Ed, MS, Ed D, PhD), including kinesiology (MS, PhD), physical education (M Ed, Ed D). Part-time programs available. *Faculty:* 33. *Students:* 132 full-time (57 women), 25 part-time (15 women); includes 26 minority (9 African Americans, 1 American Indian/Alaska Native, 7 Asian Americans or Pacific Islanders, 9 Hispanic Americans), 32 international. Average age 23. In 2009, 42 master's, 10 doctorates awarded. *Degree requirements:* For master's, thesis (for some programs); for doctorate, comprehensive exam, thesis/dissertation. *Entrance requirements:* For master's and doctorate, GRE General Test. Additional exam requirements/recommendations for international students: Required—TOEFL. *Application deadline:* Applications are processed on a rolling basis. Application fee: $50 ($75 for international students). Electronic applications accepted. *Expenses:* Tuition, state resident: full-time $3991; part-time $221.74 per credit hour. Tuition, nonresident: full-time $9049; part-time $502.74 per credit hour. *Financial support:* Fellowships with partial tuition reimbursements, research assistantships, teaching assistantships, career-related internships or fieldwork and institutionally sponsored loans available. Financial award application deadline: 2/15; financial award applicants required to submit FAFSA. *Unit head:* Head, 979-845-3491, Fax: 979-847-8987, E-mail: info@hlkn.tamu.edu. *Application contact:* Information Contact, 979-458-2673, Fax: 979-847-8987, E-mail: info@hlkn.tamu.edu.

Texas A&M University–Commerce, Graduate School, College of Education and Human Services, Department of Health and Human Performance, Commerce, TX 75429-3011. Offers exercise physiology (MS); health and human performance (M Ed); health promotion (MS); health, kinesiology and sports studies (Ed D); motor performance (MS); sport studies (MS). Part-time programs available. *Degree requirements:* For master's, comprehensive exam, thesis (for some programs). *Entrance requirements:* For master's, GRE General Test. Electronic applications accepted. *Faculty research:* Teaching, physical fitness.

Texas A&M University–Kingsville, College of Graduate Studies, College of Education, Department of Health and Kinesiology, Kingsville, TX 78363. Offers MA, MS. Part-time programs available. *Degree requirements:* For master's, comprehensive exam, thesis or alternative. *Entrance requirements:* For master's, GRE General Test, minimum GPA of 3.0. *Faculty research:* Body composition, electromyography.

Texas Southern University, College of Education, Department of Health and Kinesiology, Houston, TX 77004-4584. Offers health education (MS); human performance (MS). Part-time and evening/weekend programs available. *Faculty:* 5 full-time (2 women). *Students:* 13 full-time (7 women), 17 part-time (12 women); includes 26 minority (25 African Americans, 1 Hispanic American), 2 international. Average age 32. 13 applicants, 92% accepted, 10 enrolled. In 2009, 8 master's awarded. *Degree requirements:* For master's, comprehensive exam, thesis optional. *Entrance requirements:* For master's, GRE General Test, minimum GPA of 2.5. Additional exam requirements/recommendations for international students: Required—TOEFL. *Application deadline:* For fall admission, 7/1 for domestic and international students; for spring

Health Education

Texas Southern University *(continued)*

admission, 11/1 for domestic and international students. Applications are processed on a rolling basis. Application fee: $50 ($75 for international students). Electronic applications accepted. *Expenses:* Tuition, state resident: full-time $1805; part-time $100 per credit hour. Tuition, nonresident: full-time $6470; part-time $343 per credit hour. Tuition and fees vary according to course level, course load and degree level. *Financial support:* In 2009–10, 3 teaching assistantships (averaging $4,041 per year) were awarded; scholarships/grants and unspecified assistantships also available. Support available to part-time students. Financial award application deadline: 5/1. *Unit head:* Dr. Marie Horton, Interim Chair, 713-313-7087, E-mail: horton_mr@tsu.edu. *Application contact:* Dr. Gregory Maddox, Interim Dean of the Graduate School, 713-313-7011 Ext. 4410, Fax: 713-639-1876, E-mail: maddox_gh@tsu.edu.

Texas State University–San Marcos, Graduate School, College of Education, Department of Health and Human Performance, Program in Health Education, San Marcos, TX 78666. Offers M Ed. Part-time and evening/weekend programs available. *Faculty:* 1 full-time (0 women). *Students:* 11 full-time (10 women), 12 part-time (10 women); includes 7 minority (3 African Americans, 1 Asian American or Pacific Islander, 3 Hispanic Americans), 1 international. Average age 27. 17 applicants, 100% accepted, 11 enrolled. In 2009, 7 master's awarded. *Degree requirements:* For master's, comprehensive exam, thesis optional. *Entrance requirements:* For master's, GRE General Test, minimum GPA of 2.75 in last 60 hours of course work, 18 hours of health education background courses. Additional exam requirements/recommendations for international students: Required—TOEFL (minimum score 550 paper-based; 213 computer-based). *Application deadline:* For fall admission, 6/15 priority date for domestic students; for spring admission, 10/15 priority date for domestic students. Applications are processed on a rolling basis. Application fee: $40 ($90 for international students). Electronic applications accepted. *Expenses:* Tuition, state resident: full-time $5784; part-time $241 per credit hour. Tuition, nonresident: full-time $13,224; part-time $551 per credit hour. Required fees: $1728; $48 per credit hour. $306. Tuition and fees vary according to course load. *Financial support:* In 2009–10, 18 students received support, including 1 research assistantship (averaging $5,859 per year), 3 teaching assistantships (averaging $5,076 per year); career-related internships or fieldwork, Federal Work-Study, and institutionally sponsored loans also available. Support available to part-time students. Financial award application deadline: 4/1; financial award applicants required to submit FAFSA. *Faculty research:* AIDS education, employee wellness, isometric strength evaluation. *Unit head:* Dr. Duane Knudson, Chair, 512-245-2561, Fax: 512-245-8678. *Application contact:* Dr. Steve Furney, Graduate Adviser, 512-245-2561, Fax: 512-245-8678, E-mail: sf02@txstate.edu.

Texas Woman's University, Graduate School, College of Health Sciences, Department of Health Studies, Denton, TX 76201. Offers MS, Ed D, PhD. Part-time and evening/weekend programs available. *Faculty:* 11 full-time (9 women), 3 part-time/adjunct (2 women). *Students:* 16 full-time (15 women), 65 part-time (58 women); includes 36 minority (26 African Americans, 2 American Indian/Alaska Native, 2 Asian Americans or Pacific Islanders, 6 Hispanic Americans), 2 international. Average age 38. 32 applicants, 75% accepted, 16 enrolled. In 2009, 5 master's, 12 doctorates awarded. *Degree requirements:* For master's, comprehensive exam, thesis or alternative; for doctorate, comprehensive exam, thesis/dissertation, qualifying exam. *Entrance requirements:* For master's, GRE General Test, 2 letters of recommendation, curriculum vitae; for doctorate, GRE General Test, minimum GPA of 3.5, 2 letters of recommendation, curriculum vitae, essay. Additional exam requirements/recommendations for international students: Required—TOEFL (minimum score 575 paper-based; 213 computer-based; 79 iBT). *Application deadline:* For fall admission, 4/1 for domestic students, 3/1 for international students; for spring admission, 10/1 for domestic students, 7/1 for international students. Applications are processed on a rolling basis. Application fee: $50. Electronic applications accepted. *Expenses:* Tuition, state resident: full-time $3564; part-time $198 per credit hour. Tuition, nonresident: full-time $8550; part-time $475 per credit hour. Required fees: $69.26 per credit hour. Tuition and fees vary according to course load. *Financial support:* In 2009–10, 14 students received support, including 3 research assistantships (averaging $11,862 per year), 1 teaching assistantship (averaging $11,862 per year); career-related internships or fieldwork, Federal Work-Study, institutionally sponsored loans, scholarships/grants, traineeships, health care benefits, tuition waivers (partial), and unspecified assistantships also available. Support available to part-time students. Financial award application deadline: 3/1; financial award applicants required to submit FAFSA. *Faculty research:* Worksite health, adolescent health, minority health, women's health, HIV/AIDS prevention. *Unit head:* Dr. Gay James, Chair, 940-898-2860, Fax: 940-898-2859, E-mail: healthstudiesinfo@twu.edu. *Application contact:* Samuel Wheeler, Assistant Director of Admissions, 940-898-3188, Fax: 940-898-3081, E-mail: wheelersr@twu.edu.

TUI University, College of Health Sciences, Program in Health Sciences, Cypress, CA 90630. Offers clinical research administration (MS, Certificate); emergency and disaster management (MS, Certificate); environmental health science (Certificate); health care administration (PhD); health care management (MS), including health informatics; health education (MS, Certificate); health informatics (Certificate); health sciences (PhD); international health (MS); international health: educator or researcher option (PhD); international health: practitioner option (PhD); law and expert witness studies (MS, Certificate); public health (MS); quality assurance (Certificate). Part-time and evening/weekend programs available. Postbaccalaureate distance learning degree programs offered (no on-campus study). *Degree requirements:* For doctorate, comprehensive exam, thesis/dissertation, defense of dissertation. *Entrance requirements:* For master's, minimum GPA of 2.5 (students with GPA 3.0 or greater may transfer up to 30% of graduate level credits); for doctorate, minimum GPA of 3.4, curriculum vitae, course work in research methods or statistics. Additional exam requirements/recommendations for international students: Required—TOEFL. Electronic applications accepted.

Tulane University, School of Public Health and Tropical Medicine, Department of Community Health Sciences, Program in Health Education and Communication, New Orleans, LA 70118-5669. Offers MPH. *Accreditation:* CEPH. *Degree requirements:* For master's, comprehensive exam. *Entrance requirements:* For master's, GRE General Test. Additional exam requirements/recommendations for international students: Required—TOEFL.

Union College, Graduate Programs, Department of Education, Barbourville, KY 40906-1499. Offers elementary education (MA); health and physical education (MA); middle grades (MA); music education (MA); principalship (MA); reading specialist (MA); secondary education (MA); special education (MA). *Degree requirements:* For master's, thesis optional. *Entrance requirements:* For master's, GRE General Test, NTE.

Union College, Graduate Programs, Department of Health and Physical Education, Barbourville, KY 40906-1499. Offers health (MA Ed). *Degree requirements:* For master's, thesis optional. *Entrance requirements:* For master's, GRE General Test, NTE.

The University of Alabama, Graduate School, College of Human Environmental Sciences, Department of Health Science, Tuscaloosa, AL 35487-0311. Offers health education and promotion (PhD); health studies (MA). Part-time programs available. Postbaccalaureate distance learning degree programs offered (no on-campus study). *Faculty:* 6 full-time (4 women), 1 part-time/adjunct (0 women). *Students:* 40 full-time (31 women), 77 part-time (48 women); includes 38 minority (29 African Americans, 3 American Indian/Alaska Native, 4 Asian Americans or Pacific Islanders, 2 Hispanic Americans), 2 international. Average age 34. 112 applicants, 54% accepted, 37 enrolled. In 2009, 58 master's, 3 doctorates awarded. *Median time to degree:* Of those who began their doctoral program in fall 2001, 100% received their degree in 8 years or less. *Degree requirements:* For master's, comprehensive exam, thesis optional; for doctorate, one foreign language, comprehensive exam, thesis/dissertation. *Entrance requirements:* For master's, minimum GPA of 3.0; for doctorate, GRE General Test, minimum GPA of 3.0, prerequisites in health education. Additional exam requirements/recommendations for international students: Required—TOEFL. *Application deadline:* For fall admission, 3/15 priority date for domestic students, 3/15 for international students. Applications are processed on a rolling basis. Application fee: $50 ($60 for international students). Electronic applications accepted. *Expenses:* Tuition, state resident: full-time $7000. Tuition, nonresident: full-time $19,200. *Financial support:* In 2009–10, 2 research assistantships with full tuition reimburse-

ments (averaging $10,500 per year), 6 teaching assistantships with full tuition reimbursements (averaging $10,500 per year) were awarded; career-related internships or fieldwork, Federal Work-Study, institutionally sponsored loans, health care benefits, and unspecified assistantships also available. Financial award application deadline: 4/14. *Faculty research:* Program planning, substance abuse prevention, obesity prevention, nutrition, physical activity, athletic training, osteoporosis, health behavior. Total annual research expenditures: $66,836. *Unit head:* Dr. Lori W. Turner, Department Head and Professor, 205-348-2956, Fax: 205-348-7568, E-mail: lwturner@ches.ua.edu. *Application contact:* Dr. Stuart Usdan, Associate Professor and Doctoral Program Coordinator, 205-348-8373, Fax: 205-348-7568, E-mail: susdan@ches.ua.edu.

The University of Alabama at Birmingham, College of Arts and Sciences, School of Education, Program in Health Education, Birmingham, AL 35294. Offers MA Ed. *Accreditation:* NCATE. *Degree requirements:* For master's, thesis optional. *Entrance requirements:* For master's, GRE General Test, MAT, or NTE, minimum GPA of 3.0. Electronic applications accepted.

The University of Alabama at Birmingham, College of Arts and Sciences, School of Education, Program in Health Education and Promotion, Birmingham, AL 35294. Offers PhD. *Accreditation:* NCATE. *Degree requirements:* For doctorate, thesis/dissertation. *Entrance requirements:* For doctorate, GRE General Test, MAT, minimum GPA of 3.25. Electronic applications accepted.

The University of Alabama at Birmingham, School of Public Health, Program in Health Education and Promotion, Birmingham, AL 35294. Offers PhD.

University of Arkansas, Graduate School, College of Education and Health Professions, Department of Health Science, Kinesiology, Recreation and Dance, Program in Health Science, Fayetteville, AR 72701-1201. Offers MS, PhD. *Accreditation:* NCATE. *Students:* 25 full-time (21 women), 12 part-time (11 women); includes 12 minority (11 African Americans, 1 American Indian/Alaska Native), 4 international. In 2009, 5 master's, 1 doctorate awarded. *Degree requirements:* For doctorate, thesis/dissertation. *Entrance requirements:* For doctorate, GRE General Test. Application fee: $40 ($50 for international students). *Expenses:* Tuition, state resident: full-time $7355; part-time $356.58 per hour. Tuition, nonresident: full-time $17,401; part-time $775.17 per hour. Required fees: $1203. *Financial support:* In 2009–10, 2 fellowships with tuition reimbursements, 3 research assistantships, 4 teaching assistantships were awarded; career-related internships or fieldwork and Federal Work-Study also available. Support available to part-time students. Financial award application deadline: 4/1; financial award applicants required to submit FAFSA. *Unit head:* Dr. Sharon Hunt, Department Chairperson, 479-575-2857, Fax: 479-575-5778, E-mail: sbhunt@uark.edu. *Application contact:* Dr. Dean Gorman, Coordinator of Graduate Studies, 479-575-2890, E-mail: dgorman@uark.edu.

University of Calgary, Faculty of Medicine and Faculty of Graduate Studies, Department of Medical Science, Calgary, AB T2N 1N4, Canada. Offers cancer biology (M Sc, PhD); immunology (M Sc, PhD); joint injury and arthritis research (M Sc, PhD); medical education (M Sc, PhD); medical science (M Sc, PhD); mountain medicine and high altitude physiology (M Sc). *Degree requirements:* For master's, thesis; for doctorate, thesis/dissertation, candidacy exam. *Entrance requirements:* For master's, minimum undergraduate GPA of 3.2; for doctorate, minimum graduate GPA of 3.2. Additional exam requirements/recommendations for international students: Required—TOEFL (minimum score 600 paper-based; 250 computer-based). Electronic applications accepted. *Faculty research:* Cancer biology, immunology, joint injury and arthritis, medical education, population genomics.

University of Central Arkansas, Graduate School, College of Health and Behavioral Sciences, Department of Health Sciences, Conway, AR 72035-0001. Offers health education (MS); health systems (MS). *Faculty:* 9 full-time (5 women), 1 part-time/adjunct (0 women). *Students:* 10 full-time (8 women), 17 part-time (12 women); includes 8 minority (7 African Americans, 1 Asian American or Pacific Islander). Average age 27. 14 applicants, 100% accepted, 11 enrolled. In 2009, 9 master's awarded. *Degree requirements:* For master's, comprehensive exam, thesis optional. *Entrance requirements:* For master's, GRE General Test, minimum GPA of 2.7. Additional exam requirements/recommendations for international students: Required—TOEFL (minimum score 550 paper-based; 213 computer-based). *Application deadline:* For fall admission, 3/1 priority date for domestic students; for spring admission, 10/1 for domestic students. Applications are processed on a rolling basis. Application fee: $25 ($50 for international students). *Expenses:* Tuition, state resident: full-time $5136; part-time $214 per credit hour. Required fees: $379.50; $127 per term. Tuition and fees vary according to course level, course load and campus/location. *Financial support:* In 2009–10, 4 research assistantships (averaging $5,700 per year) were awarded; Federal Work-Study, scholarships/grants, tuition waivers (partial), and unspecified assistantships also available. Financial award application deadline: 2/15; financial award applicants required to submit FAFSA. *Unit head:* Emogene Fox, Chairperson, 501-450-5508, Fax: 501-450-5515, E-mail: emogenef@uca.edu. *Application contact:* Patti Hornor, Administrative Assistant, 501-450-5063, Fax: 501-450-5678, E-mail: pattih@uca.edu.

University of Central Oklahoma, College of Graduate Studies and Research, College of Education, Department of Occupational and Technical Education, Program in Professional Health Occupations, Edmond, OK 73034-5209. Offers M Ed. *Accreditation:* NCATE. Part-time programs available. *Faculty:* 2 full-time (1 woman), 1 (woman) part-time/adjunct. *Students:* 2 full-time (both women), 13 part-time (11 women); includes 1 minority (American Indian/Alaska Native). Average age 44. 6 applicants, 100% accepted. In 2009, 4 master's awarded. *Entrance requirements:* For master's, GRE General Test. Additional exam requirements/recommendations for international students: Required—TOEFL (minimum score 550 paper-based; 213 computer-based). *Application deadline:* For fall admission, 7/1 for international students; for spring admission, 11/1 for international students. Applications are processed on a rolling basis. Application fee: $25. Electronic applications accepted. *Expenses:* Tuition, state resident: full-time $4128; part-time $172 per credit hour. Tuition, nonresident: full-time $10,373; part-time $432.20 per credit hour. Required fees: $433.20; $18.05 per credit hour. *Financial support:* Unspecified assistantships available. Financial award application deadline: 3/31; financial award applicants required to submit FAFSA. *Unit head:* Dr. Candy Sebet, Adviser, 405-974-5780, Fax: 405-974-3822, E-mail: kbarnes@aix1.uco.edu. *Application contact:* Dr. Richard Bernard, Dean, Graduate College, 405-974-3493, Fax: 405-974-3852, E-mail: gradcoll@uco.edu.

University of Cincinnati, Graduate School, College of Education, Criminal Justice, and Human Services, Division of Human Services, Program in Health Promotion/Education, Cincinnati, OH 45221. Offers community health (MS); health education (MS, PhD); health promotion and education (M Ed). *Accreditation:* NCATE. Part-time and evening/weekend programs available. *Degree requirements:* For master's, thesis or alternative. *Entrance requirements:* For master's and doctorate, GRE General Test. Additional exam requirements/recommendations for international students: Required—TOEFL (minimum score 580 paper-based; 237 computer-based), OEPT. Electronic applications accepted.

University of Colorado Denver, College of Liberal Arts and Sciences, Program in Health and Behavioral Sciences, Denver, CO 80217-3364. Offers PhD. Part-time and evening/weekend programs available. *Students:* 3 full-time (all women), 20 part-time (15 women); includes 3 minority (1 African American, 2 Hispanic Americans), 1 international. 20 applicants, 30% accepted, 4 enrolled. In 2009, 6 doctorates awarded. *Degree requirements:* For doctorate, comprehensive exam, thesis/dissertation. *Entrance requirements:* For doctorate, GRE. Additional exam requirements/recommendations for international students: Required—TOEFL (minimum score 525 paper-based; 193 computer-based). *Application deadline:* For fall admission, 2/15 for domestic students. Applications are processed on a rolling basis. Application fee: $50 ($75 for international students). *Financial support:* Fellowships with tuition reimbursements, research assistantships with partial tuition reimbursements, career-related internships or fieldwork and Federal Work-Study available. Financial award application deadline: 4/1; financial award applicants required to submit FAFSA. *Faculty research:* HIV/AIDS prevention, tobacco control, globalization and primary health care, social inequality and health, maternal and child health. *Unit head:* Richard Miech, Director, 303-556-8422, Fax: 303-556-5801, E-mail: richard.miech@

ucdenver.edu. *Application contact:* Abby Fitch, Program Assistant, 303-556-4300, Fax: 303-556-8501, E-mail: abby.fitch@ucdenver.edu.

University of Florida, Graduate School, College of Health and Human Performance, Department of Health Education and Behavior, Gainesville, FL 32611. Offers health behavior (PhD); health communication (Graduate Certificate); health education and behavior (MS). *Accreditation:* NCATE (one or more programs are accredited). Part-time programs available. Terminal master's awarded for partial completion of doctoral program. *Degree requirements:* For master's, thesis (for some programs); for doctorate, thesis/dissertation. *Entrance requirements:* For master's and doctorate, GRE General Test, minimum GPA of 3.0. Additional exam requirements/recommendations for international students: Required—TOEFL (minimum score 550 paper-based; 213 computer-based). Electronic applications accepted. *Faculty research:* Adolescent health, human sexuality and HIV/AIDS, substance use, nutrition.

University of Georgia, College of Public Health, Department of Health Promotion and Behavior, Athens, GA 30602. Offers MA, MPH, PhD. *Accreditation:* CEPH; NCATE (one or more programs are accredited). *Faculty:* 7 full-time (5 women). *Students:* 12 full-time (9 women), 7 part-time (6 women); includes 8 minority (4 African Americans, 2 Asian Americans or Pacific Islanders, 2 Hispanic Americans), 1 international. 31 applicants, 26% accepted, 7 enrolled. In 2009, 3 doctorates awarded. *Degree requirements:* For master's, thesis (MA); for doctorate, thesis/dissertation. *Entrance requirements:* For master's, GRE General Test or MAT; for doctorate, GRE General Test. *Application deadline:* For fall admission, 7/1 priority date for domestic students; for spring admission, 11/15 for domestic students. Application fee: $50. Electronic applications accepted. *Expenses:* Tuition, state resident: full-time $6000; part-time $250 per credit hour. Tuition, nonresident: full-time $20,904; part-time $871 per credit hour. Required fees: $730 per semester. *Financial support:* Fellowships, research assistantships, teaching assistantships, unspecified assistantships available. *Unit head:* Dr. Mark G. Wilson, Head, 706-542-4364, Fax: 706-542-4956, E-mail: mwilson@coe.uga.edu. *Application contact:* Dr. Marsha Davis, Graduate Coordinator, 706-542-4364, Fax: 706-542-4956, E-mail: davism@uga.edu.

University of Georgia, Graduate School, Biomedical and Health Sciences Institute, Athens, GA 30602. Offers neuroscience (PhD). *Entrance requirements:* For doctorate, GRE, official transcripts, 3 letters of recommendation, statement of interest. Additional exam requirements/recommendations for international students: Required—TOEFL. *Expenses:* Tuition, state resident: full-time $6000; part-time $250 per credit hour. Tuition, nonresident: full-time $20,904; part-time $871 per credit hour. Required fees: $730 per semester. *Financial support:* Unspecified assistantships available. Financial award application deadline: 12/31. *Unit head:* Dr. Gaylen Edwards, Chair, 706-542-5922, Fax: 706-542-5285, E-mail: gedwards@uga.edu. *Application contact:* Philip V. Holmes, Graduate Coordinator, 706-542-5922.

University of Houston, College of Education, Department of Health and Human Performance, Houston, TX 77204. Offers allied health education and administration (M Ed, Ed D); exercise science (MS); health education (M Ed); human nutrition (MS); human space exploration sciences (MS); kinesiology (PhD); physical education (M Ed). *Accreditation:* NCATE (one or more programs are accredited). Part-time and evening/weekend programs available. *Faculty:* 12 full-time (4 women), 4 part-time/adjunct (3 women). *Students:* 53 full-time (26 women), 39 part-time (25 women); includes 21 minority (12 African Americans, 6 Asian Americans or Pacific Islanders, 3 Hispanic Americans), 14 international. Average age 29. 78 applicants, 64% accepted, 26 enrolled. In 2009, 20 master's, 2 doctorates awarded. *Degree requirements:* For master's, comprehensive exam, thesis (for some programs); for doctorate, comprehensive exam, thesis/dissertation, qualifying exam, candidacy paper. *Entrance requirements:* For master's, GRE (minimum 35th percentile on each section), minimum cumulative GPA of 3.0; for doctorate, GRE (minimum 35th percentile on each section), minimum cumulative GPA of 3.3. Additional exam requirements/recommendations for international students: Required—TOEFL (minimum score 550 paper-based; 79 iBT). *Application deadline:* For fall admission, 5/1 for domestic students, 4/1 for international students; for spring admission, 10/1 for domestic and international students. Applications are processed on a rolling basis. Application fee: $45 ($75 for international students). Electronic applications accepted. *Expenses:* Tuition, state resident: full-time $7676; part-time $320 per credit hour. Tuition, nonresident: full-time $14,324; part-time $597 per credit hour. Required fees: $3034. *Financial support:* In 2009–10, 7 fellowships with full tuition reimbursements (averaging $9,500 per year), 8 research assistantships with full tuition reimbursements (averaging $9,850 per year), 12 teaching assistantships with full tuition reimbursements (averaging $9,850 per year) were awarded; career-related internships or fieldwork, Federal Work-Study, institutionally sponsored loans, scholarships/grants, health care benefits, and unspecified assistantships also available. Support available to part-time students. Financial award application deadline: 2/1. *Faculty research:* Biomechanics, exercise physiology, obesity, nutrition, space exploration science. *Unit head:* Dr. Charles Layne, Chairperson, 713-743-9868, Fax: 713-743-9860, E-mail: clayne2@uh.edu. *Application contact:* Todd Boutte, Graduate Admission Counselor, 713-743-0571, Fax: 713-743-0123, E-mail: tboutte@mail.coe.uh.edu.

University of Illinois at Chicago, College of Medicine and Graduate College, Graduate Programs in Medicine, Department of Medical Education, Chicago, IL 60607-7128. Offers MHPE. Part-time programs available. *Degree requirements:* For master's, thesis. *Entrance requirements:* For master's, GRE General Test. Additional exam requirements/recommendations for international students: Required—TOEFL. Electronic applications accepted.

The University of Kansas, Graduate Studies, School of Education, Department of Health, Sport, and Exercise Sciences, Lawrence, KS 66045. Offers health and physical education (MS Ed, Ed D, PhD). *Accreditation:* NCATE. Part-time and evening/weekend programs available. *Students:* 53 full-time (28 women), 21 part-time (9 women); includes 5 minority (2 American Indian/Alaska Native, 2 Asian Americans or Pacific Islanders, 1 Hispanic American), 4 international. Average age 26. 73 applicants, 56% accepted, 31 enrolled. In 2009, 40 master's, 3 doctorates awarded. *Degree requirements:* For master's, comprehensive exam, thesis (for some programs); for doctorate, variable foreign language requirement, comprehensive exam, thesis/dissertation. *Entrance requirements:* For master's, GRE General Test (minimum score 1000, 450 verbal, 450 quantitative, 4.0 analytical), minimum GPA of 3.0; for doctorate, GRE General Test (minimum score 1100: verbal 500, quantitative 500, analytical 5.0), minimum graduate GPA of 3.5, undergraduate 3.0. Additional exam requirements/recommendations for international students: Required—TOEFL (minimum score 570 paper-based; 230 computer-based). *Application deadline:* For fall admission, 3/15 priority date for domestic students; for spring admission, 10/15 priority date for domestic students. Applications are processed on a rolling basis. Application fee: $45 ($55 for international students). Electronic applications accepted. *Expenses:* Tuition, state resident: full-time $6492; part-time $270.50 per credit hour. Tuition, nonresident: full-time $15,510; part-time $646.25 per credit hour. Required fees: $847; $70.56 per credit hour. Tuition and fees vary according to course load and program. *Financial support:* Research assistantships with full and partial tuition reimbursements, teaching assistantships with full and partial tuition reimbursements available. Financial award application deadline: 4/1. *Faculty research:* Character education, health education, ACE genotype, obesity prevention, force and torque production. *Unit head:* Dr. Andy Fry, Chair, 785-864-0784, Fax: 785-864-3343, E-mail: acfry@ku.edu. *Application contact:* Dr. Keith D. Tennant, Graduate Coordinator, 785-864-4656, Fax: 785-864-3343, E-mail: ktennant@ku.edu.

The University of Kansas, University of Kansas Medical Center, School of Nursing, Kansas City, KS 66160. Offers clinical research management (PMC); family nurse practitioner (PMC); health care informatics (PMC); health professions educator (PMC); nurse midwife (PMC); nursing (MS, DNP, PhD); organizational leadership (PMC); psychiatric/mental health nurse practitioner (PMC); public health nursing (PMC). *Accreditation:* AACN; ACNM/DOA. Part-time programs available. Postbaccalaureate distance learning degree programs offered (minimal on-campus study). *Faculty:* 65. *Students:* 59 full-time (56 women), 309 part-time (285 women); includes 37 minority (17 African Americans, 4 American Indian/Alaska Native, 7 Asian Americans or Pacific Islanders, 9 Hispanic Americans), 10 international. Average age 38. 138 applicants, 59% accepted, 82 enrolled. In 2009, 78 master's, 3 doctorates awarded. Terminal master's

awarded for partial completion of doctoral program. *Degree requirements:* For master's, thesis optional, general oral exam; for doctorate, one foreign language, thesis/dissertation, comprehensive oral and written exam. *Entrance requirements:* For master's, bachelor's degree in nursing, minimum GPA of 3.0, RN license, 1 year of clinical experience; for doctorate, GRE General Test, master's degree in nursing, minimum GPA of 3.5. Additional exam requirements/recommendations for international students: Required—TOEFL. *Application deadline:* For fall admission, 4/1 for domestic students; for spring admission, 9/1 for domestic students. Application fee: $60. Electronic applications accepted. *Expenses:* Tuition, state resident: full-time $6492; part-time $270.50 per credit hour. Tuition, nonresident: full-time $15,510; part-time $646.25 per credit hour. Required fees: $847; $70.56 per credit hour. Tuition and fees vary according to course load and program. *Financial support:* In 2009–10, 93 students received support, including 7 research assistantships (averaging $24,000 per year), 23 teaching assistantships with full and partial tuition reimbursements available (averaging $24,000 per year); traineeships also available. Financial award application deadline: 2/14; financial award applicants required to submit FAFSA. *Faculty research:* Breastfeeding practices of teen mothers, national database of nursing quality indicators, caregiving of families of patients using technology in the home, self care talk intervention partnership between caregivers of stroke survivors and nurses, smoking cessation. Total annual research expenditures: $5 million. *Unit head:* Dr. Karen L. Miller, Dean, 913-588-1601, Fax: 913-588-1660, E-mail: kmiller@kumc.edu. *Application contact:* Dr. Rita K. Clifford, Associate Dean, Student Affairs, 913-588-1619, Fax: 913-588-1615, E-mail: rcliffor@kumc.edu.

University of Louisville, Graduate School, College of Education and Human Development, Department of Health and Sport Sciences, Louisville, KY 40292-0001. Offers community health education (M Ed); exercise physiology (MS); health and physical education (MAT); sport administration (MS). Part-time and evening/weekend programs available. *Faculty:* 17 full-time (8 women), 1 part-time/adjunct (0 women). *Students:* 73 full-time (28 women), 28 part-time (17 women); includes 13 minority (11 African Americans, 2 Asian Americans or Pacific Islanders), 8 international. Average age 26. 154 applicants, 67% accepted, 59 enrolled. In 2009, 42 master's awarded. *Entrance requirements:* For master's, GRE General Test. Additional exam requirements/recommendations for international students: Required—TOEFL (minimum score 560 paper-based; 210 computer-based; 83 iBT). Application fee: $50. Electronic applications accepted. *Financial support:* In 2009–10, 21 students received support; fellowships, research assistantships, teaching assistantships, career-related internships or fieldwork, Federal Work-Study, scholarships/grants, and unspecified assistantships available. Financial award application deadline: 6/1; financial award applicants required to submit FAFSA. *Faculty research:* Impact of sports and sport marketing on society, factors associated with school and community health, cardiac and pulmonary rehabilitation, impact of participation in activities on student retention and graduation, strength and conditioning. Total annual research expenditures: $58,888. *Unit head:* Dr. David W. Britt, Chair, 502-852-6645, Fax: 502-852-4534, E-mail: david.britt@louisville.edu. *Application contact:* Libby Leggett, Director, Graduate Admissions, 502-852-3101, Fax: 502-852-6536, E-mail: gradadm@louisville.edu.

University of Louisville, Graduate School, School of Nursing, Louisville, KY 40202. Offers adult nurse practitioner (MSN); family nurse practitioner (MSN); health professions education (MSN); neonatal nurse practitioner (MSN); nursing research (PhD); psychiatric mental health nurse practitioner (MSN). *Accreditation:* AACN. Part-time programs available. *Faculty:* 28 full-time (25 women), 4 part-time/adjunct (3 women). *Students:* 72 full-time (66 women), 57 part-time (52 women); includes 15 minority (11 African Americans, 3 Asian Americans or Pacific Islanders, 1 Hispanic American), 4 international. Average age 35. 45 applicants, 82% accepted, 31 enrolled. In 2009, 28 master's, 3 doctorates awarded. Terminal master's awarded for partial completion of doctoral program. *Degree requirements:* For master's, thesis optional; for doctorate, comprehensive exam, thesis/dissertation. *Entrance requirements:* For master's, GRE General Test, bachelor's degree in nursing, minimum GPA of 3.0, RN license; for doctorate, GRE General Test, BSN and MSN with recommended minimum GPA of 3.0. Additional exam requirements/recommendations for international students: Required—TOEFL. *Application deadline:* For fall admission, 4/1 priority date for domestic students, 4/1 for international students; for spring admission, 10/1 priority date for domestic students, 10/1 for international students. Applications are processed on a rolling basis. Application fee: $50. Electronic applications accepted. *Financial support:* In 2009–10, 45 students received support, including 2 fellowships with full tuition reimbursements available (averaging $20,000 per year), 5 research assistantships with full tuition reimbursements available (averaging $18,000 per year), 5 teaching assistantships with full tuition reimbursements available (averaging $18,000 per year); institutionally sponsored loans, scholarships/grants, traineeships, health care benefits, and unspecified assistantships also available. Support available to part-time students. Financial award application deadline: 4/15; financial award applicants required to submit FAFSA. *Faculty research:* Maternal-child/family stress after pregnancy loss, postpartum depression, access to healthcare (underserved populations), quality of life issues, physical activity (impact on chronic/acute conditions). Total annual research expenditures: $363,876. *Unit head:* Dr. Marcia J. Hern, Dean, 502-852-8300, Fax: 502-852-5044, E-mail: m.hern@gwise.louisville.edu. *Application contact:* Dr. Rosalie O'Dell Mainous, Associate Dean for Graduate Academic Affairs, 502-852-8387, Fax: 502-852-8783, E-mail: romain01@louisville.edu.

University of Maryland, Baltimore County, Graduate School, College of Arts, Humanities and Social Sciences, Department of Emergency Health Services, Baltimore, MD 21250. Offers administration, planning, and policy (MS); education (MS); emergency health services (MS); emergency management (Postbaccalaureate Certificate); preventive medicine and epidemiology (MS). Part-time and evening/weekend programs available. Postbaccalaureate distance learning degree programs offered (no on-campus study). *Faculty:* 4 full-time (0 women), 7 part-time/adjunct (1 woman). *Students:* 20 full-time (8 women), 21 part-time (10 women); includes 2 minority (both African Americans), 6 international. Average age 32. 13 applicants, 85% accepted, 10 enrolled. In 2009, 13 master's awarded. *Degree requirements:* For master's, comprehensive exam, thesis (for some programs). *Entrance requirements:* For master's, GRE General Test, minimum GPA of 3.0. Additional exam requirements/recommendations for international students: Required—TOEFL (minimum score 550 paper-based; 213 computer-based; 80 iBT). *Application deadline:* For fall admission, 7/1 for domestic students, 4/1 for international students. Applications are processed on a rolling basis. Application fee: $45. Electronic applications accepted. *Financial support:* In 2009–10, 2 students received support, including fellowships with tuition reimbursements available (averaging $70,000 per year), research assistantships with tuition reimbursements available (averaging $21,000 per year); career-related internships or fieldwork, Federal Work-Study, health care benefits, and unspecified assistantships also available. Financial award application deadline: 5/30; financial award applicants required to submit FAFSA. *Faculty research:* EMS management, disaster health services, emergency management. Total annual research expenditures: $50,000. *Unit head:* Dr. Bruce Walz, Chairman, 410-455-3223. *Application contact:* Dr. Rick Bissell, Program Director, 410-455-3776, Fax: 410-455-3045, E-mail: bissell@umbc.edu.

University of Maryland, College Park, Academic Affairs, School of Public Health, Department of Public and Community Health, College Park, MD 20742. Offers biostatistics (MPH); community health education (MPH); environmental health sciences (MPH); epidemiology (MPH); public/community health (PhD). *Accreditation:* CEPH. Part-time and evening/weekend programs available. *Faculty:* 26 full-time (16 women), 7 part-time/adjunct (6 women). *Students:* 56 full-time (47 women), 31 part-time (29 women); includes 25 minority (19 African Americans, 4 Asian Americans or Pacific Islanders, 2 Hispanic Americans), 12 international. 252 applicants, 25% accepted, 25 enrolled. In 2009, 14 master's, 4 doctorates awarded. *Degree requirements:* For master's, thesis optional; for doctorate, comprehensive exam, thesis/dissertation. *Entrance requirements:* For master's, GRE General Test, minimum GPA of 3.0, 3 letters of recommendation; for doctorate, GRE General Test, minimum GPA of 3.5, 3 letters of recommendation. Additional exam requirements/recommendations for international students: Required—TOEFL. *Application deadline:* For fall admission, 1/15 for domestic and international students; for spring admission, 6/1 for international students. Applications are processed on a rolling basis. Application fee: $60. Electronic applications accepted. *Expenses:* Tuition, area resident: Part-time $471 per credit hour. Tuition, state resident: part-time $471 per credit hour. Tuition, nonresident:

Health Education

University of Maryland, College Park *(continued)*
part-time $1016 per credit hour. Required fees: $337.04 per term. *Financial support:* In 2009–10, 14 research assistantships with tuition reimbursements (averaging $15,827 per year), 21 teaching assistantships with tuition reimbursements (averaging $16,363 per year) were awarded; fellowships, career-related internships or fieldwork, Federal Work-Study, and scholarships/grants also available. Support available to part-time students. Financial award applicants required to submit FAFSA. *Faculty research:* Controlling stress and tension, women's health, aging and public policy, adolescent health, long-term care. Total annual research expenditures: $3.2 million. *Unit head:* Dr. Elbert Glover, Chair, 301-405-2467, Fax: 301-314-9167, E-mail: eglover1@umd.edu. *Application contact:* Dean of Graduate School, 301-405-0358.

University of Massachusetts Amherst, Graduate School, School of Public Health and Health Sciences, Department of Public Health, Amherst, MA 01003. Offers biostatistics (MS, PhD); community health education (MS); environmental health sciences (MPH, MS); epidemiology (MPH, MS); health policy and management (MPH, MS); nutrition (PhD); public health practice (MPH). *Accreditation:* CEPH (one or more programs are accredited). Part-time and evening/weekend programs available. Postbaccalaureate distance learning degree programs offered (no on-campus study). *Faculty:* 38 full-time (23 women). *Students:* 96 full-time (71 women), 232 part-time (153 women); includes 41 minority (14 African Americans, 17 Asian Americans or Pacific Islanders, 10 Hispanic Americans), 65 international. Average age 36. 316 applicants, 61% accepted, 79 enrolled. In 2009, 91 master's, 5 doctorates awarded. Terminal master's awarded for partial completion of doctoral program. *Degree requirements:* For master's, thesis (for some programs); for doctorate, comprehensive exam, thesis/dissertation. *Entrance requirements:* For master's and doctorate, GRE General Test. Additional exam requirements/recommendations for international students: Required—TOEFL (minimum score 550 paper-based; 213 computer-based; 80 iBT), IELTS (minimum score 6.5). *Application deadline:* For fall admission, 2/1 for domestic and international students. Applications are processed on a rolling basis. Application fee: $40 ($65 for international students). Electronic applications accepted. *Expenses:* Tuition, state resident: full-time $2640; part-time $110 per credit. Tuition, nonresident: full-time $9936; part-time $414 per credit. Tuition and fees vary according to course load. *Financial support:* In 2009–10, 3 fellowships with full tuition reimbursements (averaging $2,791 per year), 32 research assistantships with full tuition reimbursements (averaging $9,196 per year), 24 teaching assistantships with full tuition reimbursements (averaging $5,789 per year) were awarded; career-related internships or fieldwork, Federal Work-Study, scholarships/grants, traineeships, health care benefits, tuition waivers (full), and unspecified assistantships also available. Support available to part-time students. Financial award application deadline: 2/1. *Unit head:* Dr. Paula Stamps, Graduate Program Director, 413-545-2861, Fax: 413-545-0964. *Application contact:* Jean M. Ames, Supervisor of Admissions, 413-545-0722, Fax: 413-577-0010, E-mail: gradadm@grad.umass.edu.

University of Medicine and Dentistry of New Jersey, School of Health Related Professions, Department of Interdisciplinary Studies, Program in Health Sciences, Newark, NJ 07107-1709. Offers cardiopulmonary sciences (PhD); clinical laboratory sciences (PhD); health sciences (MS); interdisciplinary studies (PhD); nutrition (PhD); physical therapy/movement science (PhD). *Degree requirements:* For doctorate, thesis/dissertation. *Entrance requirements:* For doctorate, interview, writing sample. Additional exam requirements/recommendations for international students: Required—TOEFL. Electronic applications accepted.

University of Michigan–Flint, School of Health Professions and Studies, Program in Health Education, Flint, MI 48502-1950. Offers MS. Part-time programs available. *Faculty:* 4 full-time (3 women), 2 part-time/adjunct (both women). *Students:* 24 full-time (10 women), 3 part-time (0 women); includes 6 minority (4 African Americans, 2 Hispanic Americans), 1 international. Average age 34. 16 applicants, 63% accepted, 6 enrolled. In 2009, 3 master's awarded. *Degree requirements:* For master's, thesis or alternative, internship or current employment as health educator. *Entrance requirements:* For master's, minimum GPA of 2.8; course work in anatomy, physiology, statistics, speech, and developmental psychology. Additional exam requirements/recommendations for international students: Required—TOEFL (minimum score 560 paper-based; 220 computer-based; 84 iBT), IELTS (minimum score 6.5). *Application deadline:* For fall admission, 8/1 priority date for domestic students, 5/1 priority date for international students; for winter admission, 11/15 priority date for domestic students, 9/1 priority date for international students; for spring admission, 3/15 priority date for domestic students, 1/1 priority date for international students. Applications are processed on a rolling basis. Application fee: $55. Electronic applications accepted. *Expenses:* Contact institution. *Financial support:* Career-related internships or fieldwork, Federal Work-Study, scholarships/grants, and unspecified assistantships available. Support available to part-time students. Financial award application deadline: 6/1; financial award applicants required to submit FAFSA. *Faculty research:* Minority health, health disparities, cultural competency, HIV/AIDS, women's health. *Unit head:* Dr. Suzanne M. Selig, Director, 810-762-3172, Fax: 810-762-3003, E-mail: sselig@umich.edu. *Application contact:* Bradley T. Maki, Director of Graduate Admissions, 810-762-3171, Fax: 810-766-6789, E-mail: bmaki@umflint.edu.

University of Missouri, Graduate School, College of Education, Department of Learning, Teaching and Curriculum, Columbia, MO 65211. Offers agricultural education (M Ed, PhD, Ed S); art education (M Ed, PhD, Ed S); business and office education (M Ed, PhD, Ed S); early childhood education (M Ed, PhD, Ed S); elementary education (M Ed, PhD, Ed S); English education (M Ed, PhD, Ed S); foreign language education (M Ed, PhD, Ed S); health education and promotion (M Ed, PhD); learning and instruction (M Ed); marketing education (M Ed, PhD, Ed S); mathematics education (M Ed, PhD, Ed S); music education (M Ed, PhD, Ed S); reading education (M Ed, PhD, Ed S); science education (M Ed, PhD, Ed S); social studies education (M Ed, PhD, Ed S); vocational education (M Ed, PhD, Ed S). Part-time programs available. Terminal master's awarded for partial completion of doctoral program. *Degree requirements:* For doctorate, thesis/dissertation. *Entrance requirements:* For master's and Ed S, GRE General Test or MAT, minimum GPA of 3.0; for doctorate, GRE General Test, minimum GPA of 3.0. Additional exam requirements/recommendations for international students: Required—TOEFL (minimum score 600 paper-based; 250 computer-based; 100 iBT). Electronic applications accepted.

The University of Montana, Graduate School, School of Education, Department of Health and Human Performance, Missoula, MT 59812-0002. Offers exercise science (MS); health and human performance (MS); health promotion (MS). Part-time programs available. *Entrance requirements:* For master's, GRE General Test. Additional exam requirements/recommendations for international students: Required—TOEFL. *Faculty research:* Exercise physiology, performance psychology, nutrition, pre-employment physical screening, program evaluation.

University of Nebraska at Omaha, Graduate Studies, College of Education, School of Health, Physical Education, and Recreation, Omaha, NE 68182. Offers MA, MS. Part-time and evening/weekend programs available. *Faculty:* 12 full-time (4 women). *Students:* 43 full-time (25 women), 38 part-time (23 women); includes 5 minority (4 African Americans, 1 Asian American or Pacific Islander), 12 international. Average age 29. 49 applicants, 53% accepted, 16 enrolled. In 2009, 30 master's awarded. *Degree requirements:* For master's, comprehensive exam, thesis (for some programs). *Entrance requirements:* For master's, minimum GPA of 3.0. Additional exam requirements/recommendations for international students: Required—TOEFL (minimum score 550 paper-based; 213 computer-based; 80 iBT). *Application deadline:* For fall admission, 7/1 priority date for domestic students; for spring admission, 12/1 priority date for domestic students. Applications are processed on a rolling basis. Application fee: $45. Electronic applications accepted. *Financial support:* In 2009–10, 48 students received support, including 8 research assistantships with tuition reimbursements available; fellowships, Federal Work-Study, institutionally sponsored loans, scholarships/grants, tuition waivers (full), and unspecified assistantships also available. Support available to part-time students. Financial award application deadline: 3/1; financial award applicants required to submit FAFSA. *Unit head:* Dr. Dan Blanke, Director, 402-554-2670. *Application contact:* Penny Harmoney, Director, Graduate Studies, 402-554-2341, Fax: 402-554-3143, E-mail: graduate@unomaha.edu.

University of Nebraska–Lincoln, Graduate College, College of Agricultural Sciences and Natural Resources, Department of Agricultural Leadership, Education and Communication, Lincoln, NE 68588. Offers distance education specialization (MS); leadership development (MS); leadership education (MS); nutrition outreach education specialization (MS); teaching and extension education specialization (MS). *Degree requirements:* For master's, thesis optional. *Entrance requirements:* For master's, resume. Additional exam requirements/recommendations for international students: Required—TOEFL (minimum score 550 paper-based; 213 computer-based). Electronic applications accepted. *Faculty research:* Teaching and instruction, extension education, leadership and human resource development, international agricultural education.

University of New Mexico, Graduate School, College of Education, Department of Health, Exercise and Sports Sciences, Program in Health Education, Albuquerque, NM 87131-2039. Offers MS. *Accreditation:* NCATE. Part-time programs available. *Students:* 18 full-time (16 women), 17 part-time (16 women); includes 21 minority (3 African Americans, 5 American Indian/Alaska Native, 1 Asian American or Pacific Islander, 12 Hispanic Americans), 3 international. Average age 33. 23 applicants, 70% accepted, 13 enrolled. In 2009, 10 master's awarded. *Degree requirements:* For master's, comprehensive exam, thesis optional. *Entrance requirements:* For master's, 3 letters of reference, resume, minimum cumulative GPA of 3.0 in last 2 years of bachelor's degree, letter of intent. Additional exam requirements/recommendations for international students: Required—TOEFL (minimum score 550 paper-based; 213 computer-based). *Application deadline:* For fall admission, 6/15 priority date for domestic students; for spring admission, 11/1 priority date for domestic students. Applications are processed on a rolling basis. Application fee: $50. Electronic applications accepted. *Expenses:* Tuition, state resident: full-time $2099; part-time $233.20 per credit hour. Tuition, nonresident: full-time $6650. Required fees: $25 per semester. Tuition and fees vary according to course load, program and reciprocity agreements. *Financial support:* In 2009–10, 13 students received support, including 2 teaching assistantships with full tuition reimbursements available (averaging $10,815 per year); career-related internships or fieldwork, institutionally sponsored loans, scholarships/grants, and health care benefits also available. Financial award application deadline: 3/1; financial award applicants required to submit FAFSA. *Faculty research:* Alcohol and families, health behaviors and sexuality, multicultural health behavior, health promotion policy, school/community-based prevention, health and aging. *Unit head:* Dr. Elias Duryea, Coordinator, 505-277-5151, Fax: 505-277-6227, E-mail: duryea@unm.edu. *Application contact:* Carol Catania, Graduate Coordinator, 505-277-5151, Fax: 505-277-6227, E-mail: catania@unm.edu.

The University of North Carolina at Chapel Hill, Graduate School, School of Public Health, Department of Health Behavior and Health Education, Chapel Hill, NC 27599. Offers MPH, PhD, MPH/MRP. *Accreditation:* CEPH (one or more programs are accredited). *Degree requirements:* For master's, comprehensive exam, thesis, major paper; for doctorate, comprehensive exam, thesis/dissertation. *Entrance requirements:* For master's, GRE General Test, minimum GPA of 3.0; for doctorate, GRE General Test, minimum GPA of 3.0, master's degree. Additional exam requirements/recommendations for international students: Required—TOEFL. Electronic applications accepted. *Faculty research:* Cancer prevention and control, aging health promotion and disease prevention, adolescent health, nutrition intervention.

University of Northern Colorado, Graduate School, College of Natural and Health Sciences, School of Human Sciences, Program in Public Health, Greeley, CO 80639. Offers public health education (MPH). *Faculty:* 1 (woman) full-time. *Students:* 5 full-time (all women), 11 part-time (9 women); includes 2 minority (1 African American, 1 Hispanic American), 1 international. Average age 26. 1 applicant, 100% accepted, 1 enrolled. In 2009, 7 master's awarded. *Degree requirements:* For master's, comprehensive exam, thesis or alternative. *Entrance requirements:* For master's, GRE General Test, 2 letters of recommendation. *Application deadline:* Applications are processed on a rolling basis. Application fee: $50 ($60 for international students). Electronic applications accepted. *Expenses:* Tuition, state resident: full-time $5770; part-time $320.55 per credit hour. Tuition, nonresident: full-time $13,847; part-time $769.27 per credit hour. Required fees: $948.78; $52.72 per credit. *Financial support:* Fellowships, research assistantships, teaching assistantships, unspecified assistantships available. Financial award application deadline: 3/1; financial award applicants required to submit FAFSA. *Unit head:* Dr. Deborah Givray, Program Coordinator, 970-351-2403. *Application contact:* Linda Sisson, Graduate Student Admission Coordinator, 970-351-1807, Fax: 970-351-2371, E-mail: linda.sisson@unco.edu.

University of Northern Iowa, Graduate College, College of Education, School of Health, Physical Education, and Leisure Services, Program in Health Education, Cedar Falls, IA 50614. Offers MA, Ed D. Part-time and evening/weekend programs available. *Students:* 11 full-time (9 women), 6 part-time (2 women); includes 3 minority (1 African American, 1 Asian American or Pacific Islander, 1 Hispanic American), 2 international. 17 applicants, 59% accepted, 7 enrolled. In 2009, 2 master's, 1 doctorate awarded. *Degree requirements:* For master's, comprehensive exam, thesis or alternative; for doctorate, thesis/dissertation. *Entrance requirements:* For master's, minimum GPA of 3.0; for doctorate, GRE, minimum GPA of 3.5. Additional exam requirements/recommendations for international students: Required—TOEFL (minimum score 500 paper-based; 180 computer-based; 61 iBT). *Application deadline:* For fall admission, 8/1 priority date for domestic students. Applications are processed on a rolling basis. Application fee: $30 ($50 for international students). Electronic applications accepted. *Financial support:* Career-related internships or fieldwork, Federal Work-Study, and tuition waivers (full and partial) available. Support available to part-time students. Financial award application deadline: 2/1. *Unit head:* Dr. Catherine Zeman, Coordinator, 319-273-7090, E-mail: catherine.zeman@uni.edu. *Application contact:* Laurie S. Russell, Record Analyst, 319-273-2623, Fax: 319-273-6792, E-mail: laurie.russell@uni.edu.

University of Oklahoma Health Sciences Center, Graduate College, College of Allied Health, Department of Allied Health Sciences, Oklahoma City, OK 73190. Offers PhD. *Faculty:* 1 (woman) full-time, 2 part-time/adjunct (1 woman). *Students:* 1 (woman) full-time. Average age 22. 1 applicant, 100% accepted, 1 enrolled. In 2009, 1 doctorate awarded. *Degree requirements:* For doctorate, one foreign language, comprehensive exam, thesis/dissertation optional. *Entrance requirements:* For doctorate, GRE General Test, 3 letters of recommendation, master's degree. Additional exam requirements/recommendations for international students: Required—TOEFL (minimum score 550 paper-based). *Application deadline:* For fall admission, 7/1 for domestic students; for spring admission, 12/1 for domestic students. Application fee: $50. *Expenses:* Tuition, state resident: full-time $3120; part-time $156 per credit hour. Tuition, nonresident: full-time $11,314; part-time $409.70 per credit hour. Required fees: $1471; $51.20 per credit hour. $223.25 per term. *Financial support:* In 2009–10, research assistantships (averaging $15,000 per year). *Unit head:* Dr. Jan Womack, Associate Dean, Academic and Student Affairs, 405-271-6588, Fax: 405-271-3120, E-mail: jan-womack@ouhsc.edu. *Application contact:* Dr. Carole Sullivan, Dean, 405-271-2288, Fax: 405-271-1190, E-mail: carole-sullivan@ouhsc.edu.

University of Phoenix–Phoenix Campus, School of Business, College of Natural Sciences, Phoenix, AZ 85040-1958. Offers education (MHA); gerontology (MHA); health administration (MHA); informatics (MHA). Evening/weekend programs available. *Students:* 18 full-time (17 women); includes 16 minority (1 African American, 12 American Indian/Alaska Native, 2 Asian Americans or Pacific Islanders, 1 Hispanic American), 2 international. Average age 41. In 2009, 1 master's awarded. *Degree requirements:* For master's, thesis (for some programs). *Entrance requirements:* For master's, 3 years of work experience, minimum undergraduate GPA of 3.0. Additional exam requirements/recommendations for international students: Required—TOEFL (minimum score 550 paper-based; 213 computer-based; 79 iBT). *Application deadline:* Applications are processed on a rolling basis. Application fee: $45. Electronic applications accepted. *Expenses:* Tuition: Full-time $10,272. Required fees: $760. *Financial support:* Institutionally sponsored loans and scholarships/grants available. Financial award applicants required to submit FAFSA. *Unit head:* Dr. Hinrich Eyers, Dean/Executive Director, 480-557-7278, Fax: 602-557-7428, E-mail: hinrich.eyers@phoenix.edu. *Application contact:* Campus College Chair, 866-766-0766, Fax: 480-557-2320.

University of Phoenix–Southern Colorado Campus, The Artemis School, College of Health and Human Services, Colorado Springs, CO 80919-2335. Offers administration of justice and

security (MS); community counseling (MSC); education (MHA); gerontology (MHA); health administration (MHA); health care management (MBA); marriage, family and child therapy (MSC); nursing (MSN); psychology (MS); MSN/MBA. Evening/weekend programs available. *Degree requirements:* For master's, thesis (for some programs). *Entrance requirements:* For master's, minimum undergraduate GPA of 2.5, 3 years of work experience, RN license. Additional exam requirements/recommendations for international students: Required—TOEFL (minimum score 550 paper-based; 213 computer-based; 79 iBT). Electronic applications accepted.

University of Pittsburgh, Graduate School of Public Health, Department of Infectious Diseases and Microbiology, Pittsburgh, PA 15260. Offers bioscience of infectious diseases (MPH); community and behavioral intervention of infectious diseases (MPH); infectious diseases and microbiology (MS, Dr PH, PhD); LGBT health and wellness (Certificate). Part-time programs available. *Faculty:* 20 full-time (7 women), 2 part-time/adjunct (1 woman). *Students:* 46 full-time (33 women), 8 part-time (6 women); includes 7 minority (2 African Americans, 4 Asian Americans or Pacific Islanders, 1 Hispanic American), 6 international. Average age 28. 176 applicants, 43% accepted, 18 enrolled. In 2009, 11 master's, 9 doctorates awarded. Terminal master's awarded for partial completion of doctoral program. *Degree requirements:* For master's, one foreign language, comprehensive exam (for some programs), thesis; for doctorate, one foreign language, comprehensive exam, thesis/dissertation. *Entrance requirements:* For master's and doctorate, GRE General Test, MCAT, or DAT. Additional exam requirements/recommendations for international students: Required—TOEFL (minimum score 550 paper-based; 213 computer-based; 80 iBT). *Application deadline:* For fall admission, 1/4 for domestic students. Applications are processed on a rolling basis. Application fee: $95. Electronic applications accepted. *Expenses:* Tuition, state resident: full-time $16,402; part-time $665 per credit. Tuition, nonresident: full-time $28,694; part-time $1175 per credit. Required fees: $690; $175 per term. Tuition and fees vary according to program. *Financial support:* In 2009–10, 16 students received support, including 16 research assistantships with full tuition reimbursements available (averaging $23,500 per year). Financial award applicants required to submit FAFSA. *Faculty research:* HIV, Epstein-Barr virus, virology, immunology, malaria. Total annual research expenditures: $13.6 million. *Unit head:* Dr. Charles R. Rinaldo, Chairman, 412-624-3928, Fax: 412-624-4953, E-mail: rinaldo@pitt.edu. *Application contact:* Dr. Jeremy Martinson, Assistant Professor, 412-624-5646, Fax: 412-383-8926, E-mail: jmartins@pitt.edu.

University of Pittsburgh, School of Medicine, Programs in Medical Education, Pittsburgh, PA 15260. Offers medical education (MS, Certificate). Part-time programs available. *Faculty:* 24 full-time (11 women). *Students:* 13 part-time (9 women); includes 2 minority (both Asian Americans or Pacific Islanders), 1 international. Average age 32. 2 applicants, 100% accepted, 2 enrolled. In 2009, 6 master's awarded. *Degree requirements:* For master's, thesis. *Entrance requirements:* For master's, MCAT, GRE, or GMAT. Additional exam requirements/recommendations for international students: Required—TOEFL (minimum score 600 paper-based; 250 computer-based; 100 iBT). *Application deadline:* For fall admission, 10/31 priority date for domestic and international students; for spring admission, 4/15 priority date for domestic and international students. Applications are processed on a rolling basis. Application fee: $0. Electronic applications accepted. *Expenses:* Tuition, state resident: full-time $16,402; part-time $665 per credit. Tuition, nonresident: full-time $28,694; part-time $1175 per credit. Required fees: $690; $175 per term. Tuition and fees vary according to program. *Financial support:* Tuition waivers (partial) available. *Faculty research:* Medical education. *Unit head:* Dr. Wishwa Kapoor, Program Director, 412-692-2686, Fax: 412-586-9672, E-mail: kapoorwn@upmc.edu. *Application contact:* Jessica L. Dornin, Program Coordinator, 412-692-2686, Fax: 412-586-9672, E-mail: dorninjl@upmc.edu.

University of Puerto Rico, Medical Sciences Campus, Graduate School of Public Health, Program in Public Health Education, San Juan, PR 00936-5067. Offers MPHE. Part-time and evening/weekend programs available. *Degree requirements:* For master's, thesis. *Entrance requirements:* For master's, GRE, previous course work in education, social sciences, algebra, and natural sciences.

University of Rhode Island, Graduate School, College of Human Science and Services, Department of Kinesiology, Kingston, RI 02881. Offers cultural studies of sport and physical culture (MS); exercise science (MS); physical education pedagogy (MS); psychosocial/behavioral aspects of physical activity (MS). *Accreditation:* NCATE. Part-time programs available. *Faculty:* 13 full-time (7 women). *Students:* 16 full-time (8 women), 2 part-time (1 woman), 1 international. In 2009, 6 master's awarded. *Degree requirements:* For master's, thesis optional. *Entrance requirements:* For master's, GRE, 2 letters of recommendation. Additional exam requirements/recommendations for international students: Required—TOEFL (minimum score 550 paper-based; 213 computer-based). *Application deadline:* For fall admission, 4/15 for domestic students, 2/1 for international students; for spring admission, 11/15 for domestic students, 7/15 for international students. Application fee: $65. Electronic applications accepted. *Expenses:* Tuition, state resident: full-time $8828; part-time $490 per credit hour. Tuition, nonresident: full-time $22,100; part-time $1228 per credit hour. Required fees: $1118; $57 per semester. Tuition and fees vary according to program. *Financial support:* In 2009–10, 4 teaching assistantships with full and partial tuition reimbursements (averaging $7,939 per year) were awarded. Financial award application deadline: 4/15; financial award applicants required to submit FAFSA. *Faculty research:* Strength training and older adults, interventions to promote a healthy lifestyle as well as analysis of the psychosocial outcomes of those interventions, effects of exercise and nutrition on skeletal muscle of aging healthy adults with CVD and other metabolic related diseases, physical activity and fitness of deaf children and youth. Total annual research expenditures: $92,479. *Unit head:* Dr. Deborah Riebe, Chair, 401-874-5444, Fax: 401-874-4215, E-mail: debriebe@uri.edu. *Application contact:* Dr. Lori Ciccomascolo, Director of Graduate Studies, 401-874-5454, Fax: 401-874-4215, E-mail: lecicco@uri.edu.

University of Rochester, School of Nursing, Rochester, NY 14642. Offers acute care nurse practitioner (MS); adult nurse practitioner (MS); adult psychiatric mental health nurse practitioner (MS); adult/geriatric nurse practitioner (MS); care of children and families/pediatric nurse practitioner (MS); care of children and families/pediatric nurse practitioner with pediatric behavioral health (MS); care of children and families/pediatric nurse practitioner/neonatal nurse practitioner (MS); child and adolescent psychiatric mental health nurse practitioner (MS); clinical nurse leader (MS); disaster response and emergency preparedness (MS); family nurse practitioner (MS); health care organization management and leadership (MS); health practice research (PhD); health promotion, education and technology (MS); nursing (Certificate). *Accreditation:* AACN; NLN (one or more programs are accredited). Part-time programs available. Postbaccalaureate distance learning degree programs offered (minimal on-campus study). *Faculty:* 26 full-time (24 women), 20 part-time/adjunct (15 women). *Students:* 50 full-time (45 women), 178 part-time (165 women); includes 33 minority (17 African Americans, 2 American Indian/Alaska Native, 10 Asian Americans or Pacific Islanders, 4 Hispanic Americans), 11 international. Average age 35. 56 applicants, 80% accepted, 35 enrolled. In 2009, 53 master's, 5 doctorates awarded. Terminal master's awarded for partial completion of doctoral program. *Degree requirements:* For master's, comprehensive exam or thesis; for doctorate, thesis/dissertation. *Entrance requirements:* For master's, BS in nursing, minimum GPA of 3.0, course work in statistics; for doctorate, GRE General Test, MS in nursing, minimum GPA of 3.5; for Certificate, MS in nursing. Additional exam requirements/recommendations for international students: Recommended—TOEFL (minimum score 560 paper-based; 230 computer-based; 88 iBT). *Application deadline:* For fall admission, 11/1 priority date for domestic and international students. Application fee: $50. *Financial support:* In 2009–10, 53 students received support, including 14 fellowships with full and partial tuition reimbursements available (averaging $17,497 per year); scholarships/grants, traineeships, health care benefits, tuition waivers (partial), and unspecified assistantships also available. Support available to part-time students. Financial award application deadline: 6/30. *Faculty research:* Clinical research in aging, managing asthma in children, interventions to improve outcomes in critically ill children and their mothers, nurse home visitation studies, medical device evaluation, critical care clinical studies, high risk behavior and prevention, palliative care, pregnancy-related weight gain. Total annual research

expenditures: $4.8 million. *Unit head:* Dr. Kathy P. Parker, Dean, 585-273-5639, Fax: 585-273-1268, E-mail: kathy_parker@urmc.rochester.edu. *Application contact:* Elaine Andolina, Director of Admissions, 585-275-2375, Fax: 585-756-8299, E-mail: elaine_andolina@urmc.rochester.edu.

University of South Africa, College of Human Sciences, Pretoria, South Africa. Offers adult education (M Ed); African languages (MA, PhD); African politics (MA, PhD); Afrikaans (MA, PhD); ancient history (MA, PhD); ancient Near Eastern studies (MA, PhD); anthropology (MA, PhD); applied linguistics (MA); Arabic (MA, PhD); archaeology (MA); art history (MA); Biblical archaeology (MA); Biblical studies (M Th, D Th, PhD); Christian spirituality (M Th, D Th); church history (M Th, D Th); classical studies (MA, PhD); clinical psychology (MA); communication (MA, PhD); comparative education (M Ed, Ed D); consulting psychology (D Admin, D Com, PhD); curriculum studies (M Ed, Ed D); development studies (M Admin, MA, D Admin, PhD); didactics (M Ed, Ed D); education (M Tech); education management (M Ed, Ed D); educational psychology (M Ed); English (MA); environmental education (M Ed); French (MA, PhD); German (MA, PhD); Greek (MA); guidance and counseling (M Ed); health studies (MA, PhD), including health sciences education (MA), health services management (MA), medical and surgical nursing science (critical care general) (MA), midwifery and neonatal nursing science (MA), trauma and emergency care (MA); history (MA, PhD); history of education (Ed D); inclusive education (M Ed, Ed D); information and communications technology policy and regulation (MA); information science (MA, MIS, PhD); international politics (MA, PhD); Islamic studies (MA, PhD); Italian (MA, PhD); Judaica (MA, PhD); linguistics (MA, PhD); mathematical education (M Ed); mathematics education (MA); missiology (M Th, D Th); modern Hebrew (MA, PhD); musicology (MA, MMus, D Mus, PhD); natural science education (M Ed); New Testament (M Th, D Th); Old Testament (D Th); pastoral therapy (M Th, D Th); philosophy (MA); philosophy of education (M Ed, Ed D); politics (MA, PhD); Portuguese (MA, PhD); practical theology (M Th, D Th); psychology (MA, MS, PhD); psychology of education (M Ed, Ed D); public health (MA); religious studies (MA, D Th, PhD); Romance languages (MA); Russian (MA, PhD); Semitic languages (MA, PhD); social behavior studies in HIV/AIDS (MA); social science (mental health) (MA); social science in development studies (MA); social science in psychology (MA); social science in social work (MA); social science in sociology (MA); social work (MSW, DSW, PhD); socio-education (M Ed, Ed D); sociolinguistics (MA); sociology (MA, PhD); Spanish (MA, PhD); systematic theology (M Th, D Th); TESOL (teaching English to speakers of other languages) (MA); theological ethics (M Th, D Th); theory of literature (MA, PhD); urban ministries (D Th); urban ministry (M Th).

University of South Alabama, Graduate School, College of Education, Department of Health, Physical Education and Leisure Services, Mobile, AL 36688-0002. Offers exercise science (MS); health education (M Ed); physical education (M Ed); therapeutic recreation (MS). *Accreditation:* NCATE (one or more programs are accredited). Part-time programs available. *Degree requirements:* For master's, comprehensive exam. *Entrance requirements:* For master's, GRE General Test or MAT. *Expenses:* Tuition, state resident: part-time $218 per contact hour. Required fees: $1102 per year.

University of South Carolina, The Graduate School, Arnold School of Public Health, Department of Health Promotion, Education, and Behavior, Columbia, SC 29208. Offers health education (MAT); health promotion, education, and behavior (MPH, MS, MSPH, Dr PH, PhD); school health education (Certificate); MSW/MPH. MAT offered in cooperation with the College of Education. *Accreditation:* CEPH (one or more programs are accredited); NCATE (one or more programs are accredited). Part-time programs available. *Degree requirements:* For master's, comprehensive exam, thesis or alternative, practicum (MPH), project (MS); for doctorate, comprehensive exam, thesis/dissertation. *Entrance requirements:* For master's and doctorate, GRE General Test. Additional exam requirements/recommendations for international students: Required—TOEFL (minimum score 570 paper-based; 230 computer-based; 75 iBT). Electronic applications accepted. *Faculty research:* Health disparities and inequalities in communities, global health and nutrition, cancer and HIV/AIDS prevention, health communication, policy and program design.

University of South Carolina, The Graduate School, College of Education, Department of Instruction and Teacher Education, Program in Secondary Education, Columbia, SC 29208. Offers art education (IMA, MAT); business education (IMA, MAT); English (MAT); foreign language (MAT); health education (MAT); mathematics (MAT); science (IMA, MAT); secondary (Ed D); secondary education (MT, PhD); social studies (MAT); theatre and speech (MAT). IMA and MT offered jointly with the subject areas. *Accreditation:* NCATE. *Degree requirements:* For master's, comprehensive exam, thesis (for some programs), foreign language (MA); for doctorate, one foreign language, comprehensive exam, thesis/dissertation. *Entrance requirements:* For master's, GRE General Test or MAT, teaching certificate (IMA, M Ed), interview; for doctorate, GRE General Test or MAT, interview. *Faculty research:* Middle school programs, professional development, school collaboration.

The University of South Dakota, Graduate School, School of Education, Division of Health, Physical Education and Recreation, Vermillion, SD 57069-2390. Offers MA. *Accreditation:* NCATE. Part-time programs available. *Degree requirements:* For master's, comprehensive exam, thesis or alternative. *Entrance requirements:* For master's, GRE General Test, MAT, minimum GPA of 2.7. Additional exam requirements/recommendations for international students: Required—TOEFL (minimum score 550 paper-based; 213 computer-based; 79 iBT). Electronic applications accepted.

University of Southern Mississippi, Graduate School, College of Health, Department of Community Health Sciences, Hattiesburg, MS 39406-0001. Offers epidemiology and biostatistics (MPH); health education (MPH); health policy/administration (MPH); occupational/environmental health (MPH); public health nutrition (MPH). *Accreditation:* CEPH. Part-time and evening/weekend programs available. *Faculty:* 8 full-time (4 women), 1 part-time/adjunct (0 women). *Students:* 92 full-time (59 women), 20 part-time (14 women); includes 40 minority (36 African Americans, 1 Asian American or Pacific Islander, 3 Hispanic Americans), 13 international. Average age 32. 90 applicants, 73% accepted, 47 enrolled. In 2009, 4 master's awarded. *Degree requirements:* For master's, comprehensive exam, thesis (for some programs). *Entrance requirements:* For master's, GRE General Test, minimum GPA of 2.75 in last 60 hours. Additional exam requirements/recommendations for international students: Required—TOEFL. *Application deadline:* For fall admission, 3/1 for domestic and international students. Applications are processed on a rolling basis. Application fee: $35. *Expenses:* Tuition, state resident: full-time $5096; part-time $284 per hour. Tuition, nonresident: full-time $13,052; part-time $726 per hour. Required fees: $402. Tuition and fees vary according to course level and course load. *Financial support:* In 2009–10, 5 research assistantships with full tuition reimbursements (averaging $7,000 per year), 1 teaching assistantship with full tuition reimbursement (averaging $8,263 per year) were awarded; career-related internships or fieldwork and Federal Work-Study also available. Financial award application deadline: 3/15; financial award applicants required to submit FAFSA. *Faculty research:* Rural health care delivery, school health, nutrition of pregnant teens, risk factor reduction, sexually transmitted diseases. *Unit head:* Dr. James McGuire, Chair, 601-266-5437, Fax: 601-266-5043. *Application contact:* Shonna Breland, Manager of Graduate Admissions, 601-266-6563, Fax: 601-266-5138.

The University of Tennessee, Graduate School, College of Education, Health and Human Sciences, Program in Health Promotion and Health Education, Knoxville, TN 37996. Offers MS. *Accreditation:* CEPH. Part-time programs available. *Degree requirements:* For master's, thesis optional. *Entrance requirements:* For master's, minimum GPA of 2.7. Additional exam requirements/recommendations for international students: Required—TOEFL. Electronic applications accepted. *Expenses:* Tuition, state resident: full-time $6826; part-time $380 per semester hour. Tuition, nonresident: full-time $21,844; part-time $1147 per semester hour. Tuition and fees vary according to program.

The University of Tennessee, Graduate School, College of Education, Health and Human Sciences, Program in Safety, Knoxville, TN 37996. Offers MS. *Accreditation:* NCATE. Part-time programs available. *Degree requirements:* For master's, thesis optional. *Entrance requirements:* For master's, minimum GPA of 2.7. Additional exam requirements/recommendations for international students: Required—TOEFL. Electronic applications accepted. *Expenses:* Tuition,

Health Education

The University of Tennessee (continued)
state resident: full-time $6826; part-time $380 per semester hour. Tuition, nonresident: full-time $21,844; part-time $1147 per semester hour. Tuition and fees vary according to program.

The University of Texas at Austin, Graduate School, College of Education, Department of Kinesiology and Health Education, Austin, TX 78712-1111. Offers behavioral health (PhD); exercise and sport psychology (M Ed, MA); health education (M Ed, MA, Ed D, PhD); kinesiology (M Ed, MA). Part-time programs available. Terminal master's awarded for partial completion of doctoral program. *Degree requirements:* For master's, thesis (for some programs); for doctorate, thesis/dissertation. *Entrance requirements:* For master's and doctorate, GRE General Test. Additional exam requirements/recommendations for international students: Required—TOEFL. Electronic applications accepted. *Faculty research:* Health promotion, human performance and exercise biochemistry, motor behavior and biomechanics, sport management, aging and pediatric development.

The University of Texas at El Paso, Graduate School, College of Health Sciences, Department of Health Promotion, El Paso, TX 79968-0001. Offers public health (MPH). Part-time and evening/weekend programs available. *Students:* 26 (21 women); includes 20 minority (all Hispanic Americans), 4 international. Average age 34. In 2009, 6 master's awarded. *Degree requirements:* For master's, thesis optional. *Entrance requirements:* For master's, GRE, minimum GPA of 3.0, resume, letters of recommendation. Additional exam requirements/recommendations for international students: Required—TOEFL; Recommended—IELTS. *Application deadline:* For fall admission, 8/1 priority date for domestic students, 3/1 for international students; for spring admission, 11/1 priority date for domestic students, 9/1 for international students. Applications are processed on a rolling basis. Application fee: $45 ($80 for international students). Electronic applications accepted. *Financial support:* In 2009–10, research assistantships (averaging $18,825 per year), teaching assistantships with partial tuition reimbursements (averaging $18,000 per year) were awarded; fellowships with partial tuition reimbursements, institutionally sponsored loans, scholarships/grants, health care benefits, tuition waivers (partial), and unspecified assistantships also available. Support available to part-time students. Financial award application deadline: 3/15; financial award applicants required to submit FAFSA. *Unit head:* Dr. Maria O. Duarte-Gardea, Chair, 915-747-8214 Ext. 7252, E-mail: moduarte@utep.edu. *Application contact:* Dr. Patricia D. Witherspoon, Dean of the Graduate School, 915-747-5491, Fax: 915-747-5788, E-mail: withersp@utep.edu.

The University of Texas at San Antonio, College of Education and Human Development, Department of Health and Kinesiology, San Antonio, TX 78249-0617. Offers health and kinesiology (MS); kinesiology and health promotion (MA Ed). Part-time programs available. *Faculty:* 12 full-time (5 women). *Students:* 22 full-time (9 women), 49 part-time (31 women); includes 40 minority (5 African Americans, 1 Asian American or Pacific Islander, 34 Hispanic Americans), 3 international. Average age 29. 43 applicants, 91% accepted, 22 enrolled. In 2009, 14 master's awarded. *Degree requirements:* For master's, comprehensive exam (for some programs), thesis (for some programs). *Entrance requirements:* For master's, GRE or GMAT, minimum GPA of 3.0. Additional exam requirements/recommendations for international students: Required—TOEFL (minimum score 500 paper-based; 173 computer-based; 61 iBT), IELTS (minimum score 5). *Application deadline:* For fall admission, 6/1 for domestic students, 4/1 for international students; for spring admission, 11/1 for domestic students, 9/1 for international students. Applications are processed on a rolling basis. Application fee: $45 ($80 for international students). Electronic applications accepted. *Expenses:* Tuition, state resident: full-time $3975; part-time $221 per contact hour. Tuition, nonresident: full-time $13,947; part-time $775 per contact hour. Required fees: $1853. *Financial support:* In 2009–10, 3 students received support, including 14 research assistantships (averaging $10,754 per year); scholarships/grants, tuition waivers, and unspecified assistantships also available. Support available to part-time students. *Faculty research:* Motor learning/control, biomechanics, and sports psychology; exercise and military physiology; physical education and coaching; health disparities and nutrition; community and school health. Total annual research expenditures: $458,272. *Unit head:* Dr. Wanxiang Yao, Chair, 210-458-5650, E-mail: wanxiang.yao@utsa.edu. *Application contact:* Dr. Dorothy A. Flannagan, Dean of the Graduate School, 210-458-4330, Fax: 210-458-4332, E-mail: dorothy.flannagan@utsa.edu.

The University of Texas at Tyler, College of Nursing and Health Sciences, Department of Health and Kinesiology, Tyler, TX 75799-0001. Offers health and kinesiology (M Ed, MA); health sciences (MS); kinesiology (MS). Part-time programs available. Postbaccalaureate distance learning degree programs offered. *Faculty:* 7 full-time (2 women). *Students:* 23 full-time (16 women), 36 part-time (24 women); includes 9 minority (8 African Americans, 1 Hispanic American). Average age 29. 44 applicants, 100% accepted, 27 enrolled. In 2009, 13 master's awarded. *Degree requirements:* For master's, comprehensive exam (for some programs), thesis (for some programs). *Entrance requirements:* Additional exam requirements/recommendations for international students: Required—TOEFL (minimum score 79 computer-based). *Application deadline:* For fall admission, 8/17 priority date for domestic students, 7/1 priority date for international students; for spring admission, 12/21 priority date for domestic students, 11/1 priority date for international students. Applications are processed on a rolling basis. Application fee: $25 ($50 for international students). Electronic applications accepted. *Expenses:* Tuition, state resident: part-time $665 per semester hour. Tuition, nonresident: part-time $942 per semester hour. Part-time tuition and fees vary according to degree level and program. *Financial support:* In 2009–10, 2 teaching assistantships (averaging $6,000 per year) were awarded; research assistantships, Federal Work-Study and scholarships/grants also available. Financial award application deadline: 7/1. *Faculty research:* Osteoporosis, muscle soreness, economy of locomotion, adoption of rehabilitation programs, effect of inactivity and aging on muscle blood vessels, territoriality. *Unit head:* Dr. Scott Marzilli, Chair/Professor, 903-566-7178, Fax: 903-566-7065, E-mail: smarzilli@uttyler.edu. *Application contact:* Dr. Scott Marzilli.

The University of Toledo, College of Graduate Studies, College of Education, Department of Curriculum and Instruction, Program in Health Education, Toledo, OH 43606-3390. Offers ME.

The University of Toledo, College of Graduate Studies, College of Health Science and Human Service, Division of Human Services, Department of Health Education, Toledo, OH 43606-3390. Offers PhD.

University of Utah, Graduate School, College of Health, Department of Health Promotion and Education, Salt Lake City, UT 84112. Offers M Phil, MS, Ed D, PhD. Part-time and evening/weekend programs available. *Faculty:* 5 full-time (2 women), 2 part-time/adjunct (1 woman). *Students:* 31 full-time (24 women), 14 part-time (11 women); includes 2 minority (1 Asian American or Pacific Islander, 1 Hispanic American), 6 international. Average age 35. 32 applicants, 69% accepted, 17 enrolled. In 2009, 7 master's, 10 doctorates awarded. Terminal master's awarded for partial completion of doctoral program. *Degree requirements:* For master's, comprehensive exam, thesis or alternative, field experience; for doctorate, comprehensive exam, thesis/dissertation, field experience. *Entrance requirements:* For master's, GRE (for thesis option), minimum GPA of 3.0; for doctorate, GRE General Test, minimum GPA of 3.2. Additional exam requirements/recommendations for international students: Required—TOEFL (minimum score 500 paper-based; 173 computer-based). *Application deadline:* For fall admission, 10/15 for domestic and international students; for spring admission, 2/15 for domestic and international students. Applications are processed on a rolling basis. Application fee: $55 ($65 for international students). *Expenses:* Tuition, state resident: full-time $4004; part-time $1674 per semester. Tuition, nonresident: full-time $14,134; part-time $5915 per semester. Required fees: $324 per semester. Tuition and fees vary according to course load, degree level and program. *Financial support:* In 2009–10, 13 students received support, including 3 research assistantships with full tuition reimbursements available (averaging $11,500 per year), 3 teaching assistantships with full tuition reimbursements available (averaging $11,500 per year); career-related internships or fieldwork, Federal Work-Study, institutionally sponsored loans, and scholarships/grants also available. Financial award application deadline: 2/15; financial award applicants required to submit FAFSA. *Faculty research:* Health behavior and counseling, health service administration, evaluation of health programs. Total annual research expenditures: $3,583. *Unit head:* Dr. Glenn E. Richardson, Department Chair, 801-581-8039, Fax: 801-585-3646, E-mail: glenn.richardson@health.utah.edu. *Application contact:* Dr. Glenn P. Trunnell, Director of Graduate Studies, 801-581-4462, Fax: 801-585-3646, E-mail: eric.trunnell@health.utah.edu.

University of Virginia, Curry School of Education, Department of Human Services, Program in Health and Physical Education, Charlottesville, VA 22903. Offers kinesiology (M Ed, Ed D). *Students:* 38 full-time (27 women), 6 part-time (3 women); includes 3 minority (2 African Americans, 1 Hispanic American). Average age 24. 13 applicants, 92% accepted, 8 enrolled. In 2009, 43 master's, 1 doctorate awarded. *Entrance requirements:* For master's and doctorate, GRE General Test, 2 letters of recommendation. Additional exam requirements/recommendations for international students: Required—TOEFL (minimum score 600 paper-based; 250 computer-based; 90 iBT), IELTS (minimum score 7). *Application deadline:* Applications are processed on a rolling basis. Application fee: $60. Electronic applications accepted. *Financial support:* Applicants required to submit FAFSA.

University of Waterloo, Graduate Studies, Faculty of Applied Health Sciences, Department of Health Studies and Gerontology, Waterloo, ON N2L 3G1, Canada. Offers health studies and gerontology (M Sc, PhD); public health (MPH). Part-time programs available. *Degree requirements:* For master's, thesis; for doctorate, comprehensive exam, thesis/dissertation. *Entrance requirements:* For master's, honors degree, minimum B average, resume, writing sample; for doctorate, GRE (recommended), master's degree, minimum B average, resumé, writing sample. Additional exam requirements/recommendations for international students: Required—TOEFL, TWE. Electronic applications accepted. *Faculty research:* Population health, health promotion and disease prevention, healthy aging, health policy, planning and evaluation, health information management and health informatics, aging, health and well-being, work and health.

University of West Florida, College of Professional Studies, Division of Health, Leisure, and Exercise Science, Community Health Education, Pensacola, FL 32514-5750. Offers aging studies (MS); promotion and worksite wellness (MS); psycho-social (MS). Part-time and evening/weekend programs available. *Faculty:* 2 full-time (1 woman), 1 (woman) part-time/adjunct. *Students:* 7 full-time (6 women), 7 part-time (all women); includes 4 minority (1 African American, 1 American Indian/Alaska Native, 1 Asian American or Pacific Islander, 1 Hispanic American), 1 international. Average age 34. 7 applicants, 86% accepted, 5 enrolled. In 2009, 13 master's awarded. *Degree requirements:* For master's, thesis or alternative. *Entrance requirements:* For master's, GRE General Test, minimum GPA of 3.0. Additional exam requirements/recommendations for international students: Required—TOEFL (minimum score 550 paper-based; 213 computer-based). *Application deadline:* For fall admission, 6/1 for domestic students, 5/15 for international students; for spring admission, 11/1 for domestic students, 10/1 for international students. Applications are processed on a rolling basis. Application fee: $30. *Expenses:* Tuition, state resident: full-time $4982; part-time $260 per credit hour. Tuition, nonresident: full-time $20,059; part-time $919 per credit hour. Required fees: $1247; $52 per credit hour. *Financial support:* Research assistantships, teaching assistantships, unspecified assistantships available. *Unit head:* Dr. John Todorovich, Chairperson, 850-473-7248, Fax: 850-474-2106. *Application contact:* Terry McCray, Assistant Director of Graduate Admissions, 850-473-7718, Fax: 850-473-7714, E-mail: gradadmissions@uwf.edu.

University of West Florida, College of Professional Studies, Division of Health, Leisure, and Exercise Science, Program in Health, Leisure, and Exercise Science, Pensacola, FL 32514-5750. Offers exercise science (MS); physical education (MS). Part-time and evening/weekend programs available. *Faculty:* 5 full-time (2 women), 2 part-time/adjunct (1 woman). *Students:* 20 full-time (9 women), 23 part-time (10 women); includes 6 minority (3 African Americans, 1 Asian American or Pacific Islander, 2 Hispanic Americans), 4 international. Average age 28. 30 applicants, 83% accepted, 11 enrolled. In 2009, 26 master's awarded. *Degree requirements:* For master's, thesis or alternative. *Entrance requirements:* For master's, GRE General Test, minimum GPA of 3.0. Additional exam requirements/recommendations for international students: Required—TOEFL (minimum score 550 paper-based; 213 computer-based). *Application deadline:* For fall admission, 6/1 for domestic students, 5/15 for international students; for spring admission, 11/1 for domestic students, 10/1 for international students. Applications are processed on a rolling basis. Application fee: $30. Electronic applications accepted. *Expenses:* Tuition, state resident: full-time $4982; part-time $260 per credit hour. Tuition, nonresident: full-time $20,059; part-time $919 per credit hour. Required fees: $1247; $52 per credit hour. *Financial support:* Career-related internships or fieldwork, Federal Work-Study, scholarships/grants, and tuition waivers (partial) available. Support available to part-time students. Financial award application deadline: 4/15; financial award applicants required to submit FAFSA. *Unit head:* Dr. John Todorovich, Chairperson, 850-473-7248, Fax: 850-474-2106. *Application contact:* Terry McCray, Assistant Director of Graduate Admissions, 850-473-7718, Fax: 850-473-7714, E-mail: gradadmissions@uwf.edu.

University of Wisconsin–La Crosse, Office of University Graduate Studies, College of Science and Health, Department of Health Education and Health Promotion, Program in Community Health Education, La Crosse, WI 54601-3742. Offers MPH, MS. *Accreditation:* CEPH. *Students:* 13 full-time (11 women), 19 part-time (18 women); includes 1 minority (Asian American or Pacific Islander), 5 international. Average age 30. 10 applicants, 80% accepted, 7 enrolled. In 2009, 18 master's awarded. *Degree requirements:* For master's, thesis. *Entrance requirements:* For master's, GRE General Test, GRE Subject Test (MPH), 3 letters of recommendation. Additional exam requirements/recommendations for international students: Required—TOEFL (minimum score 550 paper-based; 213 computer-based; 79 iBT). Application fee: $56. Electronic applications accepted. *Financial support:* Research assistantships available. *Unit head:* Dr. Gary Gilmore, Director, 608-785-8163, E-mail: gilmore.gary@uwlax.edu. *Application contact:* Kathryn Kiefer, Director of Admissions, 608-785-8939, E-mail: admissions@uwlax.edu.

University of Wisconsin–La Crosse, Office of University Graduate Studies, College of Science and Health, Department of Health Education and Health Promotion, Program in School Health Education, La Crosse, WI 54601-3742. Offers MS. *Students:* 1 (woman) full-time, 4 part-time (3 women). Average age 32. 4 applicants, 50% accepted, 0 enrolled. In 2009, 3 master's awarded. *Entrance requirements:* For master's, GRE General Test, minimum GPA of 2.85. Additional exam requirements/recommendations for international students: Required—TOEFL (minimum score 550 paper-based; 213 computer-based; 79 iBT). Application fee: $56. Electronic applications accepted. *Financial support:* Research assistantships available. *Unit head:* Dr. Tracy Caravella, Director, 608-785-6788, E-mail: caravell.trac@uwlax.edu. *Application contact:* Kathryn Kiefer, Director of Admissions, 608-785-8939, E-mail: admissions@uwlax.edu.

University of Wisconsin–Milwaukee, Graduate School, College of Nursing, Milwaukee, WI 53201-0413. Offers family nursing practitioner (Post Master's Certificate); health professional education (Certificate); nursing (MS, PhD); public health (Certificate). *Accreditation:* AACN. Part-time programs available. *Faculty:* 34 full-time (33 women). *Students:* 159 full-time (148 women), 118 part-time (100 women); includes 32 minority (15 African Americans, 1 American Indian/Alaska Native, 11 Asian Americans or Pacific Islanders, 5 Hispanic Americans), 6 international. Average age 40. 123 applicants, 54% accepted, 37 enrolled. In 2009, 53 master's, 13 doctorates awarded. *Degree requirements:* For master's, thesis; for doctorate, thesis/dissertation. *Entrance requirements:* For master's, GRE General Test or MAT, autobiographical sketch; for doctorate, GRE, minimum GPA of 3.2. Additional exam requirements/recommendations for international students: Required—TOEFL (minimum score 550 paper-based; 79 iBT), IELTS (minimum score 6.5). *Application deadline:* For fall admission, 1/1 priority date for domestic students; for spring admission, 9/1 for domestic students. Applications are processed on a rolling basis. Application fee: $45 ($75 for international students). *Expenses:* Tuition, state resident: full-time $8800. Tuition, nonresident: full-time $20,760. Tuition and fees vary according to program and reciprocity agreements. *Financial support:* In 2009–10, 8 teaching assistantships were awarded; career-related internships or fieldwork, Federal Work-Study, and unspecified assistantships also available. Support available to part-time students. Financial award application deadline: 4/15. Total annual research expenditures: $3.4

million. *Unit head:* Dr. Sally Lundeen, Dean, 414-229-4189, E-mail: slundeen@uwm.edu. *Application contact:* Ellen K. Murphy, Representative, 414-229-5468.

University of Wyoming, College of Health Sciences, Division of Kinesiology and Health, Laramie, WY 82070. Offers MS. *Accreditation:* NCATE. Part-time programs available. Postbaccalaureate distance learning degree programs offered (no on-campus study). *Degree requirements:* For master's, comprehensive exam (for some programs), thesis (for some programs). *Entrance requirements:* For master's, GRE General Test, minimum GPA of 3.0. Additional exam requirements/recommendations for international students: Required—TOEFL. Electronic applications accepted. *Faculty research:* Teacher effectiveness, effects of exercising on heart function, physiological responses of overtraining, psychological benefits of physical activity, health behavior.

Utah State University, School of Graduate Studies, College of Education and Human Services, Department of Health, Physical Education and Recreation, Logan, UT 84322. Offers M Ed, MS. Part-time and evening/weekend programs available. Postbaccalaureate distance learning degree programs offered (minimal on-campus study). *Degree requirements:* For master's, thesis (for some programs). *Entrance requirements:* For master's, GRE General Test or MAT, minimum GPA of 3.0. Additional exam requirements/recommendations for international students: Required—TOEFL. *Faculty research:* Sport psychology intervention, motor learning biomechanics, pedagogy, physiology.

Virginia Polytechnic Institute and State University, Graduate School, College of Liberal Arts and Human Sciences, School of Education, Department of Teaching and Learning, Blacksburg, VA 24061. Offers career and technical education (MS Ed, Ed D, PhD, Ed S); curriculum and instruction (MA Ed, Ed D, PhD, Ed S); health and physical education (MS Ed); mathematics education (MA Ed, PhD); secondary English education (MA Ed). *Accreditation:* NCATE. Postbaccalaureate distance learning degree programs offered (no on-campus study). *Students:* 295 full-time (186 women), 374 part-time (272 women); includes 104 minority (1 African American, 39 American Indian/Alaska Native, 54 Asian Americans or Pacific Islanders, 10 Hispanic Americans), 23 international. Average age 34. 324 applicants, 85% accepted, 205 enrolled. In 2009, 235 master's, 34 doctorates, 1 other advanced degree awarded. *Entrance requirements:* For master's and doctorate, GRE, GMAT. Additional exam requirements/recommendations for international students: Required—TOEFL (minimum score 550 paper-based; 213 computer-based). *Application deadline:* For fall admission, 5/15 for international students; for spring admission, 10/15 for international students. Applications are processed on a rolling basis. Application fee: $65. Electronic applications accepted. *Expenses:* Tuition, area resident: Full-time $10,228; part-time $459 per credit hour. Tuition, nonresident: full-time $17,892; part-time $865 per credit hour. Required fees: $1966; $451 per semester. *Financial support:* Career-related internships or fieldwork, Federal Work-Study, scholarships/grants, and unspecified assistantships available. Financial award application deadline: 1/15. *Faculty research:* Instructional technology, teacher evaluation, school change, literacy, teaching strategies. *Unit head:* Dr. Daisy L. Stewart, Dean, 540-231-8180, Fax: 540-231-3717, E-mail: daisys@vt.edu. *Application contact:* Dr. Daisy L. Stewart, Dean, 540-231-8180, Fax: 540-231-3717, E-mail: daisys@vt.edu.

Virginia State University, School of Graduate Studies, Research, and Outreach, School of Engineering, Science and Technology, Department of Psychology, Petersburg, VA 23806-0001. Offers behavioral and community health sciences (PhD); clinical health psychology (PhD); clinical psychology (MS); general psychology (MS). *Degree requirements:* For master's, one foreign language, thesis. *Entrance requirements:* For master's, GRE General Test.

Wayne State University, College of Education, Division of Kinesiology, Health and Sports Studies, Detroit, MI 48202. Offers health education (M Ed); kinesiology (M Ed); physical education (M Ed); recreation and park services (MA); sports administration (MA). *Degree requirements:* For master's, thesis (for some programs). *Entrance requirements:* Additional exam requirements/recommendations for international students: Required—TOEFL; Recommended—TWE (minimum score 6). Electronic applications accepted. *Faculty research:* Fitness in urban children, motor development of crack babies, effects of caffeine on metabolism/exercise, body composition of elite youth sports participants, systematic observation of teaching.

Wayne State University, College of Education, Division of Teacher Education, Detroit, MI 48202. Offers adult and continuing education (M Ed); art education (M Ed); bilingual/bicultural education (M Ed, MAT); business education (M Ed, MAT); career and technical education (M Ed, Ed D, PhD, Ed S); curriculum and instruction (Ed D, PhD, Ed S); distributive education (M Ed, MAT); early childhood education (M Ed); elementary education (M Ed, MAT, Ed D, PhD, Ed S); elementary education curriculum and instruction (M Ed); English education (M Ed); English education-secondary (M Ed, Ed S); foreign language education (M Ed); general education (Ed D, Ed S); health occupations education (M Ed); industrial education (M Ed); mathematics education (M Ed, Ed S); pre-school and parent education (M Ed); reading (M Ed, Ed D, Ed S); reading, languages and literature (Ed D); school music-vocal (M Ed); science education (M Ed, MAT, Ed S); secondary education (MAT); secondary school reading (M Ed); social studies education (M Ed, Ed S), including education-secondary (M Ed); special education (M Ed, Ed D, PhD, Ed S); teacher education (MAT, Ed D, PhD). *Degree requirements:* For doctorate, thesis/dissertation. *Entrance requirements:* For master's, Michigan Basic Skills Test (MA in teaching), minimum GPA of 2.6; for doctorate, minimum undergraduate GPA of 3.0, graduate 3.5; interview, curriculum vitae; references. Additional exam requirements/recommendations for international students: Required—TOEFL (minimum score 550 paper-based; 213 computer-based), TWE (minimum score 6). Electronic applications accepted. *Faculty research:* Reading and writing literacy and literature.

Wayne State University, School of Medicine, Graduate Programs in Medicine, Medical Research Program, Detroit, MI 48202. Offers MS. *Entrance requirements:* For master's, GRE or MCAT, minimum GPA of 3.0, MD. Additional exam requirements/recommendations for international students: Required—TOEFL (minimum score 550 paper-based; 213 computer-based); Recommended—TWE (minimum score 6). Electronic applications accepted.

West Chester University of Pennsylvania, Office of Graduate Studies, College of Health Sciences, Department of Health, West Chester, PA 19383. Offers emergency preparedness (Certificate); health care administration (Certificate); integrative health (Certificate); public health (MPH), including administration, community, environment, integrative, nutrition; school health (M Ed). *Accreditation:* CEPH. Part-time and evening/weekend programs available. *Students:* 15 full-time (9 women), 128 part-time (91 women); includes 41 minority (34 African Americans, 2 American Indian/Alaska Native, 5 Asian Americans or Pacific Islanders), 22 international. Average age 30. 83 applicants, 88% accepted, 41 enrolled. In 2009, 45 master's, 8 other advanced degrees awarded. *Degree requirements:* For master's, thesis (for some programs). *Entrance requirements:* For master's, one-page statement of career objectives, two letters of reference. Additional exam requirements/recommendations for international students: Required—TOEFL (minimum score 550 paper-based; 213 computer-based; 80 iBT). *Application deadline:* For fall admission, 4/15 priority date for domestic students, 3/15 for international students; for spring admission, 10/15 for domestic students, 9/1 for international students. Applications are processed on a rolling basis. Application fee: $35. Electronic applications accepted. *Expenses:* Tuition, state resident: full-time $6666; part-time $370 per credit. Tuition, nonresident: full-time $10,666; part-time $593 per credit. Required fees: $122.56 per credit. *Financial support:* In 2009–10, 11 research assistantships with full and partial tuition reimbursements (averaging $5,000 per year) were awarded; unspecified assistantships also available. Support available to part-time students. Financial award application deadline: 2/15; financial award applicants required to submit FAFSA. *Faculty research:* HIV/AIDS education, teacher preparation, water quality. *Unit head:* Dr. Roger Mustalish, Chair, 610-436-2931, E-mail: rmustalish@wcupa.edu. *Application contact:* Dr. Bethann Cinelli, Graduate Coordinator, 610-436-2267, E-mail: bcinelli@wcupa.edu.

West Chester University of Pennsylvania, Office of Graduate Studies, College of Health Sciences, Department of Kinesiology, West Chester, PA 19383. Offers adapted physical education (Certificate); health and physical education (MS, Teaching Certificate), including exercise physiology (MS); physical education (MS); sport and athletic administration (MSA). Part-time and evening/weekend programs available. *Students:* 2 full-time (1 woman), 37 part-time (15 women); includes 2 minority (both African Americans), 3 international. Average age 25. 39 applicants, 90% accepted, 11 enrolled. In 2009, 25 master's awarded. *Degree requirements:* For master's, thesis (for some programs), thesis or report (MS), 2 internships (MSA). *Entrance requirements:* For master's, GRE (MS); GMAT, GRE General Test, or MAT (MSA), minimum GPA of 3.0 with interview (MS) or letters of recommendation (MSA). Additional exam requirements/recommendations for international students: Required—TOEFL (minimum score 550 paper-based; 213 computer-based; 80 iBT). *Application deadline:* For fall admission, 4/15 priority date for domestic students, 3/15 for international students; for spring admission, 10/15 for domestic students, 9/1 for international students. Applications are processed on a rolling basis. Application fee: $35. Electronic applications accepted. *Expenses:* Tuition, state resident: full-time $6666; part-time $370 per credit. Tuition, nonresident: full-time $10,666; part-time $593 per credit. Required fees: $122.56 per credit. *Financial support:* In 2009–10, 11 research assistantships with full and partial tuition reimbursements (averaging $5,000 per year) were awarded; unspecified assistantships also available. Support available to part-time students. Financial award application deadline: 2/15; financial award applicants required to submit FAFSA. *Faculty research:* Weight lifting and type 1 diabetes mellitus, martial arts, sexual harassment in sports. *Unit head:* Dr. Frank Fry, Chair, 610-436-2832, E-mail: ffry@wcupa.edu. *Application contact:* Dr. Sheri Melton, Graduate Coordinator, 610-436-2260, E-mail: smelton@wcupa.edu.

Western Illinois University, School of Graduate Studies, College of Education and Human Services, Department of Health Sciences, Macomb, IL 61455-1390. Offers health education (MS); health services administration (Certificate). *Accreditation:* NCATE. Part-time programs available. *Students:* 18 full-time (7 women), 33 part-time (27 women); includes 1 minority (African American), 14 international. Average age 33. 33 applicants, 79% accepted. In 2009, 19 master's awarded. *Degree requirements:* For master's, comprehensive exam, thesis or alternative. *Entrance requirements:* Additional exam requirements/recommendations for international students: Required—TOEFL (minimum score 550 paper-based; 213 computer-based; 80 iBT). *Application deadline:* Applications are processed on a rolling basis. Application fee: $30. Electronic applications accepted. *Expenses:* Tuition, state resident: full-time $4486; part-time $249.21 per credit hour. Tuition, nonresident: full-time $8972; part-time $498.42 per credit hour. Required fees: $72.62 per credit hour. *Financial support:* In 2009–10, 10 students received support, including 10 research assistantships with full tuition reimbursements available (averaging $7,280 per year). Financial award applicants required to submit FAFSA. *Unit head:* Dr. R. Mark Kelley, Chairperson, 309-298-1076. *Application contact:* Evelyn Hoing, Assistant Director of Graduate Studies, 309-298-1806, Fax: 309-298-2345, E-mail: grad-office@wiu.edu.

Western Michigan University, Graduate College, College of Health and Human Services, Interdisciplinary Health Sciences Program, Kalamazoo, MI 49008. Offers PhD. *Unit head:* Dr. Nickola Wolf Nelson, Director, 269-387-3800. *Application contact:* Admissions and Orientation, 269-387-2000, Fax: 269-387-2355.

Western Oregon University, Graduate Programs, College of Education, Division of Teacher Education, Program in Secondary Education, Monmouth, OR 97361-1394. Offers bilingual education (MS Ed); health (MS Ed); humanities (MAT, MS Ed); initial licensure (MAT); mathematics (MAT, MS Ed); science (MAT, MS Ed); social science (MAT, MS Ed). *Accreditation:* NCATE. Part-time and evening/weekend programs available. *Degree requirements:* For master's, thesis optional, written exam. *Entrance requirements:* For master's, minimum GPA of 3.0, teaching license. Additional exam requirements/recommendations for international students: Required—TOEFL (minimum score 550 paper-based; 213 computer-based; 79 iBT), IELTS (minimum score 6.5). *Faculty research:* Literacy, science in primary grades, geography education, retention, teacher burnout.

Western University of Health Sciences, College of Allied Health Professions, Program in Health Sciences, Pomona, CA 91766-1854. Offers MS. Part-time and evening/weekend programs available. *Entrance requirements:* For master's, minimum undergraduate GPA of 2.5, graduate 3.0; letters of recommendation; interview. *Expenses:* Contact institution.

West Virginia University, School of Physical Education, Morgantown, WV 26506. Offers athletic coaching education (MS); athletic training (MS); physical education/teacher education (MS, PhD), including curriculum and instruction (PhD), motor behavior (PhD), physical education supervision (PhD); sport and exercise psychology (PhD); sport management (MS). *Degree requirements:* For doctorate, comprehensive exam, thesis/dissertation, oral exam. *Entrance requirements:* For master's, GRE or MAT, minimum GPA of 3.0; for doctorate, GRE General Test or MAT, minimum GPA of 3.5. Additional exam requirements/recommendations for international students: Required—TOEFL (minimum score 550 paper-based; 213 computer-based). Electronic applications accepted. *Faculty research:* Sport psychosociology, teacher education, exercise psychology, counseling.

Widener University, School of Human Service Professions, Center for Education, Chester, PA 19013-5792. Offers adult education (M Ed); counseling in higher education (M Ed); counselor education (M Ed); early childhood education (M Ed); educational foundations (M Ed); educational leadership (M Ed); educational psychology (M Ed); elementary education (M Ed); English and language arts (M Ed); health education (M Ed); higher education leadership (Ed D); home and school visitor (M Ed); human sexuality (M Ed); mathematics education (M Ed); middle school education (M Ed); principalship (M Ed); reading and language arts (Ed D); reading education (M Ed); school administration (Ed D); science education (M Ed); social studies education (M Ed); special education (M Ed); technology education (M Ed). *Accreditation:* NCATE. Part-time and evening/weekend programs available. *Faculty:* 34 full-time (22 women), 37 part-time/adjunct (14 women). *Students:* 203 full-time (154 women), 415 part-time (298 women); includes 50 minority (34 African Americans, 1 American Indian/Alaska Native, 5 Asian Americans or Pacific Islanders, 10 Hispanic Americans), 3 international. Average age 39. 139 applicants, 88% accepted. In 2009, 168 master's, 31 doctorates awarded. Terminal master's awarded for partial completion of doctoral program. *Degree requirements:* For doctorate, thesis/dissertation. *Entrance requirements:* For master's, minimum GPA of 2.5; for doctorate, GRE or MAT, minimum GPA of 2.0 (undergraduate), 3.5 (graduate). *Application deadline:* Applications are processed on a rolling basis. Application fee: $25 ($300 for international students). Electronic applications accepted. *Expenses:* Contact institution. *Financial support:* Career-related internships or fieldwork, tuition waivers (full and partial), and unspecified assistantships available. Support available to part-time students. Financial award application deadline: 5/1. *Faculty research:* Reading and cognition, adult education, technology education, educational leadership, special education. *Unit head:* Dr. Michael W. LeDoux, Associate Dean, 610-499-4294, Fax: 610-499-4623, E-mail: mwledoux@widener.edu. *Application contact:* Dr. Roberta D. Nolan, Director of Graduate Admissions, 610-499-4125, E-mail: rdnolan@widener.edu.

Worcester State College, Graduate Studies, Program in Health Education, Worcester, MA 01602-2597. Offers M Ed. Part-time programs available. *Students:* 2 full-time (1 woman), 12 part-time (all women); includes 1 minority (Hispanic American). Average age 36. 10 applicants, 80% accepted, 4 enrolled. In 2009, 8 master's awarded. *Degree requirements:* For master's, comprehensive exam (for some programs), thesis optional. *Entrance requirements:* For master's, GRE General Test or MAT. Additional exam requirements/recommendations for international students: Required—TOEFL (minimum score 550 paper-based; 213 computer-based; 79 iBT). *Application deadline:* Applications are processed on a rolling basis. Application fee: $30. *Expenses:* Tuition, area resident: Part-time $150 per credit. Tuition, state resident: part-time $150 per credit. Tuition, nonresident: part-time $150 per credit. Required fees: $85. *Financial support:* Career-related internships or fieldwork, scholarships/grants, and unspecified assistantships available. Financial award application deadline: 3/1; financial award applicants required to submit FAFSA. *Unit head:* Dr. Nancy Brewer, Coordinator, 508-929-8838, Fax: 508-929-8164, E-mail: nbrewer@worcester.edu. *Application contact:* Nicole Brown, Assistant Dean of Graduate and Continuing Education, 508-929-8787, Fax: 508-929-8100, E-mail: nbrown@worcester.edu.

Wright State University, School of Graduate Studies, College of Education and Human Services, Department of Health, Physical Education, and Recreation, Dayton, OH 45435. Offers M Ed, MA. *Accreditation:* NCATE. *Degree requirements:* For master's, comprehensive exam, thesis (for some programs). *Entrance requirements:* For master's, GRE General Test, MAT. Additional exam requirements/recommendations for international students: Required—TOEFL. *Faculty research:* Motor learning, motor development, exercise physiology, adapted physical education.

Wright State University, School of Medicine, Program in Public Health, Dayton, OH 45435. Offers health promotion and education (MPH); public health management (MPH); public health nursing (MPH). *Accreditation:* CEPH.

Home Economics Education

Appalachian State University, Cratis D. Williams Graduate School, Department of Family and Consumer Sciences, Boone, NC 28608. Offers child development (MA); family and consumer science (MA), including food and nutrition; family and consumer science education (MA). Part-time programs available. Postbaccalaureate distance learning degree programs offered (no on-campus study). *Faculty:* 12 full-time (10 women), 2 part-time/adjunct (1 woman). *Students:* 17 full-time (16 women), 15 part-time (all women); includes 2 minority (both African Americans), 1 international. 29 applicants, 83% accepted, 20 enrolled. In 2009, 6 master's awarded. *Degree requirements:* For master's, comprehensive exam, thesis optional. *Entrance requirements:* For master's, GRE General Test, 3 letters of recommendation. Additional exam requirements/recommendations for international students: Required—TOEFL (minimum score 550 paper-based; 230 computer-based; 79 iBT), IELTS (minimum score 6.5). *Application deadline:* For fall admission, 7/1 for domestic students, 2/1 for international students; for spring admission, 11/1 for domestic students, 7/1 for international students. Applications are processed on a rolling basis. Application fee: $50. Electronic applications accepted. *Expenses:* Tuition, state resident: full-time $2960. Tuition, nonresident: full-time $14,051. Required fees: $2320. *Financial support:* In 2009–10, 5 research assistantships (averaging $8,000 per year) were awarded; career-related internships or fieldwork, scholarships/grants, and unspecified assistantships also available. Financial award application deadline: 7/1; financial award applicants required to submit FAFSA. *Faculty research:* Food antioxidants, preschool curriculum, children with special needs, family child care, FCS curriculum content. *Unit head:* Dr. Sarah Jordan, Chairperson, 828-262-2661, E-mail: jordansr@appstate.edu. *Application contact:* Dr. Sandy Krause, Director of Graduate Admissions and Recruiting, 828-262-2130, E-mail: krausesl@appstate.edu.

Cambridge College, School of Education, Cambridge, MA 02138-5304. Offers autism specialist (M Ed); autism/behavior analyst (M Ed); behavior analyst (Post-Master's Certificate); behavioral management (M Ed); early childhood teacher (M Ed); education specialist in curriculum and instruction (CAGS); educational leadership (Ed D); elementary teacher (M Ed); English as a second language (M Ed, Certificate); general science (M Ed); health education, health promotion (Post-Master's Certificate); health/family and consumer sciences (M Ed); history (M Ed); individualized degree (M Ed); information technology literacy (M Ed); instructional technology (M Ed); interdisciplinary studies (M Ed); library teacher (M Ed); literacy education (M Ed); mathematics (M Ed); mathematics specialist (Certificate); middle school mathematics and science (M Ed); school administration (M Ed, CAGS); school guidance counselor (M Ed); school nurse education (M Ed); school social worker/school adjustment counselor (M Ed); special education administrator (CAGS); special education/moderate disabilities (M Ed); teaching skills and methodologies (M Ed). Part-time and evening/weekend programs available. Postbaccalaureate distance learning degree programs offered (minimal on-campus study). *Faculty:* 10 full-time (3 women), 283 part-time/adjunct (187 women). *Students:* 974 full-time (755 women), 1,071 part-time (835 women); includes 940 minority (762 African Americans, 4 American Indian/Alaska Native, 22 Asian Americans or Pacific Islanders, 152 Hispanic Americans), 28 international. Average age 39. In 2009, 866 master's, 4 doctorates, 209 CAGSs awarded. *Degree requirements:* For master's, thesis, internship/practicum (licensure program only); for doctorate, thesis/dissertation; for other advanced degree, thesis. *Entrance requirements:* For master's, interview, resume, documentation of licensure, 2 professional references; for doctorate, official transcripts, interview, resume, documentation of licensure (if any), written personal statement/essay, portfolio of scholarly and professional work, qualifying assessment, 2 professional references, health insurance, immunizations form; for other advanced degree, official transcripts, interview, resume, documentation of licensure (if any), written personal statement/essay, 2 professional references, health insurance, immunizations form. Additional exam requirements/recommendations for international students: Required—TOEFL (minimum score 550 paper-based; 213 computer-based; 79 iBT); Recommended—IELTS (minimum score 6). *Application deadline:* Applications are processed on a rolling basis. Application fee: $30. Electronic applications accepted. *Expenses:* Contact institution. *Financial support:* In 2009–10, 1,373 students received support. Career-related internships or fieldwork, Federal Work-Study, and scholarships/grants available. Financial award applicants required to submit FAFSA. *Faculty research:* Adult education, accelerated learning, mathematics education, brain compatible learning, special education and law. *Unit head:* Dr. N. Alan Sheppard, Interim Associate Dean, 617-873-0619, E-mail: alan.sheppard@cambridgecollege.edu. *Application contact:* Stephen Lyons, Director of Enrollment, Graduate and N.I.T.E. Programs, 617-868-1000, Fax: 617-349-3561, E-mail: stephen.lyons@cambridgecollege.edu.

Central Washington University, Graduate Studies and Research, College of Education and Professional Studies, Department of Family and Consumer Sciences, Ellensburg, WA 98926. Offers family and consumer sciences education (MS); family studies (MS). Part-time programs available. *Faculty:* 14 full-time (9 women). *Students:* 11 full-time (10 women), 22 part-time (21 women); includes 1 minority (Asian American or Pacific Islander), 1 international. 9 applicants, 78% accepted, 7 enrolled. In 2009, 4 master's awarded. *Degree requirements:* For master's, thesis or alternative. *Entrance requirements:* For master's, minimum GPA of 3.0. Additional exam requirements/recommendations for international students: Required—TOEFL (minimum score 550 paper-based; 213 computer-based; 79 iBT). *Application deadline:* For fall admission, 2/1 priority date for domestic students; for winter admission, 10/1 for domestic students; for spring admission, 1/1 for domestic students. Applications are processed on a rolling basis. Application fee: $50. Electronic applications accepted. *Expenses:* Tuition, state resident: full-time $7353; part-time $245 per credit. Tuition, nonresident: full-time $16,383; part-time $546 per credit. Required fees: $882. Tuition and fees vary according to degree level. *Financial support:* In 2009–10, 1 research assistantship with full and partial tuition reimbursement (averaging $9,145 per year) was awarded; Federal Work-Study, health care benefits, and unspecified assistantships also available. Financial award application deadline: 3/1; financial award applicants required to submit FAFSA. *Unit head:* Dr. Jan Bowers, Chair, 509-963-2766, E-mail: bowersj@cwu.edu. *Application contact:* Justine Eason, Admissions Program Coordinator, 509-963-3103, Fax: 509-963-1799, E-mail: masters@cwu.edu.

Eastern Kentucky University, The Graduate School, College of Education, Department of Curriculum and Instruction, Program in Secondary and Higher Education, Richmond, KY 40475-3102. Offers secondary education (MA Ed), including agricultural education, art education, biological sciences education, business education, English education, geography education, history education, home economics education, industrial education, mathematical sciences education, physical education, school health education. *Accreditation:* NCATE. Part-time programs available. *Entrance requirements:* For master's, GRE General Test, minimum GPA of 2.5.

Harding University, College of Education, Searcy, AR 72149-0001. Offers advanced studies in teaching and learning (M Ed); art (MSE); behavioral science (MSE); counseling (MS, Ed S); early childhood special education (M Ed, MSE); education (MSE); educational leadership (M Ed, Ed S); elementary education (M Ed); English (MSE); family and consumer science (MSE); French (MSE); history/social science (MSE); kinesiology (MSE); math (MSE); physical science (MSE); reading (M Ed); secondary education (M Ed); Spanish (MSE); special education licensure (M Ed); teaching (MAT); teaching English as a second language (M Ed). *Accreditation:* NCATE. Part-time and evening/weekend programs available. *Faculty:* 11 full-time (4 women), 49 part-time/adjunct (26 women). *Students:* 104 full-time (85 women), 392 part-time (282 women); includes 77 minority (67 African Americans, 5 American Indian/Alaska Native, 1 Asian American or Pacific Islander, 4 Hispanic Americans), 5 international. Average age 36. 153 applicants, 92% accepted, 131 enrolled. In 2009, 153 master's, 6 other advanced degrees awarded. *Degree requirements:* For master's, comprehensive exam (for some programs), thesis optional, portfolio(s); for Ed S, comprehensive exam, portfolio, specialist project. *Entrance requirements:* For master's, GRE, MAT, PRAXIS; for Ed S, MAT or GRE. Additional exam requirements/recommendations for international students: Required—TOEFL (minimum score 550 paper-based; 79 iBT). *Application deadline:* For fall admission, 8/1 for domestic and international students; for spring admission, 1/1 for domestic and international students. Applications are processed on a rolling basis. Application fee: $35. *Expenses:* Tuition: Full-time $9720; part-time $540 per credit hour. Required fees: $22 per credit hour. Tuition and fees vary according to course load and program. *Financial support:* In 2009–10, 30 students received support. Unspecified assistantships available. *Faculty research:* Reading, comprehension, school violence, educational technology, behavior, college choice, differentiated instruction, brain-based teaching. *Unit head:* Dr. Clara Carroll, Chair, 501-279-4501, Fax: 501-279-4083, E-mail: ccarroll@harding.edu. *Application contact:* Information Contact, 501-279-4315, E-mail: gradstudiesedu@harding.edu.

Indiana State University, School of Graduate Studies, College of Arts and Sciences, Department of Family and Consumer Sciences, Terre Haute, IN 47809. Offers dietetics (MS); family and consumer sciences education (MS); inter-area option (MS). *Accreditation:* ADtA. Part-time programs available. *Degree requirements:* For master's, thesis optional. Electronic applications accepted.

Iowa State University of Science and Technology, Graduate College, College of Human Sciences, Department of Apparel, Education Studies, and Hospitality Management, Program in Family and Consumer Sciences Education and Studies, Ames, IA 50011. Offers M Ed, MS, PhD. *Students:* 20 part-time (18 women); includes 3 minority (all African Americans), 3 international. In 2009, 3 master's, 7 doctorates awarded. *Degree requirements:* For master's, thesis (for some programs); for doctorate, thesis/dissertation. *Entrance requirements:* For master's and doctorate, GRE General Test. Additional exam requirements/recommendations for international students: Required—TOEFL (minimum score 550 paper-based; 213 computer-based; 80 iBT) or IELTS (minimum score 6.5). Application fee: $40 ($90 for international students). *Expenses:* Tuition, state resident: full-time $6716. Tuition, nonresident: full-time $8908. Tuition and fees vary according to course level, course load, program and student level. *Financial support:* Research assistantships with full and partial tuition reimbursements, teaching assistantships with full and partial tuition reimbursements, scholarships/grants available. *Unit head:* Dr. Robert Bosselman, Director of Graduate Education, 515-294-7474. *Application contact:* Dr. Robert Bosselman, Director of Graduate Education, 515-294-7474.

Louisiana State University and Agricultural and Mechanical College, Graduate School, College of Agriculture, School of Human Resource Education and Workforce Development, Baton Rouge, LA 70803. Offers agriculture and extension education and youth development (MS, PhD); career and technical education (MS, PhD); comprehensive vocational education (MS, PhD); extension and international education (MS, PhD); human resource and leadership development (MS, PhD); industrial education (MS); vocational agriculture education (MS, PhD); vocational business education (MS); vocational home economics education (MS). *Accreditation:* NCATE. Part-time programs available. *Faculty:* 11 full-time (5 women), 2 part-time/adjunct (both women). *Students:* 39 full-time (22 women), 75 part-time (51 women); includes 14 African Americans, 1 Asian American or Pacific Islander, 2 Hispanic Americans, 7 international. Average age 37. 40 applicants, 93% accepted, 18 enrolled. In 2009, 16 master's, 13 doctorates awarded. Terminal master's awarded for partial completion of doctoral program. *Degree requirements:* For master's, thesis (for some programs); for doctorate, thesis/dissertation. *Entrance requirements:* For master's and doctorate, GRE General Test, minimum GPA of 3.0. Additional exam requirements/recommendations for international students: Required—TOEFL (minimum score 550 paper-based; 213 computer-based; 79 iBT) or IELTS (minimum score 6.5). *Application deadline:* For fall admission, 1/25 priority date for domestic students, 5/15 for international students; for spring admission, 10/15 for international students. Applications are processed on a rolling basis. Application fee: $50 ($70 for international students). Electronic applications accepted. *Financial support:* In 2009–10, 63 students received support, including 3 fellowships with full and partial tuition reimbursements available (averaging $24,885 per year), 5 research assistantships with full and partial tuition reimbursements available (averaging $14,440 per year), 4 teaching assistantships with partial tuition reimbursements available (averaging $13,750 per year); career-related internships or fieldwork, Federal Work-Study, institutionally sponsored loans, health care benefits, tuition waivers (full and partial), and unspecified assistantships also available. Financial award application deadline: 3/1; financial award applicants required to submit FAFSA. *Faculty research:* Adult education, history and philosophy of vocational education, curriculum and instruction, career decision making. Total annual research expenditures: $21,538. *Unit head:* Dr. Michael F. Burnett, Director, 225-578-5748, Fax: 225-578-2526, E-mail: vocbur@lsu.edu. *Application contact:* Paula Beecher, Recruiting Coordinator, 225-578-2468, E-mail: pbeeche@lsu.edu.

Montana State University, College of Graduate Studies, College of Education, Health, and Human Development, Department of Health and Human Development, Bozeman, MT 59717. Offers health and human development (MS), including counseling, exercise and nutrition sciences, family and consumer sciences, family financial planning, health promotion and education. *Accreditation:* ACA. Part-time programs available. Postbaccalaureate distance learning degree programs offered (no on-campus study). *Faculty:* 27 full-time (18 women), 7 part-time/adjunct (6 women). *Students:* 54 full-time (47 women), 18 part-time (15 women); includes 1 minority (Hispanic American). Average age 30. 32 applicants, 34% accepted, 10 enrolled. In 2009, 26 master's awarded. *Degree requirements:* For master's, comprehensive exam. *Entrance requirements:* For master's, GRE General Test. Additional exam requirements/recommendations for international students: Required—TOEFL (minimum score 550 paper-based; 213 computer-based). *Application deadline:* For fall admission, 7/15 priority date for domestic students, 5/15 priority date for international students; for spring admission, 12/1 priority date for domestic students, 10/1 priority date for international students. Applications are processed on a rolling basis. Application fee: $30. Electronic applications accepted. *Expenses:* Tuition, state resident: full-time $5635; part-time $3492 per year. Tuition, nonresident: full-time $17,212; part-time $7865.10 per year. Required fees: $1441; $153.15 per credit. Tuition and fees vary according to course load and program. *Financial support:* In 2009–10, 24 students received support, including 7 research assistantships (averaging $1,000 per year), 17 teaching

assistantships with full tuition reimbursements available (averaging $8,000 per year). Financial award application deadline: 3/1; financial award applicants required to submit FAFSA. *Faculty research:* Gait analysis, cancer prevention, obesity prevention, energy expenditure, decision making. Total annual research expenditures: $2.8 million. *Unit head:* Dr. Tim Dunnagan, Head, 404-994-3242, Fax: 404-994-2013, E-mail: dunnagan@montana.edu. *Application contact:* Dr. Carl Fox.

Montclair State University, The Graduate School, College of Education and Human Services, Department of Curriculum and Teaching, Montclair, NJ 07043-1624. Offers education (M Ed); educational technology (M Ed); learning disabled teacher consultant (Certificate); school library media specialist (Certificate); teaching (MAT, Certificate), including art (MAT), biological science (MAT), early childhood education (P-3) (MAT), earth science (MAT), elementary education (K-8) (MAT), English (MAT), French (MAT), health and physical education (MAT), health education (MAT), home economics (MAT), mathematics (MAT), music (MAT), physical education (MAT), physical science (MAT), social studies (MAT), Spanish (MAT), teacher of ESL (MAT), teacher of students with disabilities (MAT). Part-time and evening/weekend programs available. *Faculty:* 17 full-time (12 women), 29 part-time/adjunct (21 women). *Students:* 124 full-time (63 women), 174 part-time (126 women). Average age 31. 112 applicants, 69% accepted, 59 enrolled. In 2009, 179 master's, 2 other advanced degrees awarded. *Degree requirements:* For master's, comprehensive exam, field experience. *Entrance requirements:* For master's, GRE, 2 letters of recommendation. Additional exam requirements/recommendations for international students: Required—TOEFL (minimum score 83 computer-based), or IELTS. *Application deadline:* For fall admission, 2/15 for domestic and international students; for spring admission, 9/15 for domestic and international students. Applications are processed on a rolling basis. Application fee: $60. Electronic applications accepted. *Expenses:* Tuition, area resident: Part-time $486.74 per credit. Tuition, state resident: part-time $486.74 per credit. Tuition, nonresident: part-time $751.34 per credit. Tuition and fees vary according to degree level and program. *Financial support:* In 2009–10, 12 research assistantships with full tuition reimbursements (averaging $7,000 per year) were awarded; Federal Work-Study, scholarships/grants, and unspecified assistantships also available. Support available to part-time students. Financial award application deadline: 3/1; financial award applicants required to submit FAFSA. *Unit head:* Dr. David Schwarzer, Chairperson, 973-655-5187. *Application contact:* Amy Aiello, Director of Graduate Admissions and Operations, 973-655-5147, Fax: 973-655-7869, E-mail: graduate.school@montclair.edu.

Northwestern State University of Louisiana, Graduate Studies and Research, College of Education, Programs in Education, Natchitoches, LA 71497. Offers business and distributive education (M Ed); counseling (M Ed); early childhood education (M Ed); education (M Ed); education leadership (M Ed); educational technology (M Ed); elementary teaching (M Ed); English education (M Ed); home economics education (M Ed); mathematics education (M Ed); reading (M Ed); science education (M Ed); secondary teaching (M Ed); social sciences education (M Ed). *Degree requirements:* For master's, comprehensive exam, thesis or alternative. *Entrance requirements:* For master's, GRE General Test, minimum undergraduate GPA of 2.5.

Purdue University, Graduate School, School of Education, Department of Curriculum and Instruction, West Lafayette, IN 47907. Offers agricultural and extension education (PhD, Ed S); agriculture and extension education (MS, MS Ed); art education (PhD); consumer and family sciences and extension education (MS Ed, PhD, Ed S); curriculum studies (MS Ed, PhD, Ed S); educational technology (MS Ed, PhD, Ed S); elementary education (MS Ed); foreign language education (MS Ed, PhD, Ed S); industrial technology (PhD, Ed S); language arts (MS Ed, PhD, Ed S); literacy (MS Ed, PhD, Ed S); mathematics/science education (MS, MS Ed, PhD, Ed S); social studies (MS Ed, PhD); social studies education (Ed S); vocational/industrial education (MS Ed, PhD, Ed S); vocational/technical education (MS Ed, PhD, Ed S). *Accreditation:* NCATE. Part-time and evening/weekend programs available. *Degree requirements:* For master's, thesis optional; for doctorate, thesis/dissertation, oral and written exams; for Ed S, oral presentation, project. *Entrance requirements:* For master's, GRE General Test, minimum B average; for doctorate, GRE General Test; for Ed S, GRE, minimum B average. Additional exam requirements/recommendations for international students: Required—TOEFL. Electronic applications accepted. *Faculty research:* Literacy acquisition and development, teacher beliefs and knowledge, recruitment and retention of underrepresented students, economic education, literacy discourse.

Queens College of the City University of New York, Division of Graduate Studies, Mathematics and Natural Sciences Division, Department of Family, Nutrition and Exercise Sciences, Flushing, NY 11367-1597. Offers home economics (MS Ed); physical education and exercise sciences (MS Ed). Part-time and evening/weekend programs available. *Faculty:* 12 full-time (7 women). *Students:* 13 full-time (all women), 68 part-time (44 women). 58 applicants, 78% accepted, 25 enrolled. In 2009, 9 master's awarded. *Degree requirements:* For master's, research project. *Entrance requirements:* For master's, minimum GPA of 3.0. Additional exam requirements/recommendations for international students: Required—TOEFL. *Application deadline:* For fall admission, 4/1 for domestic students; for spring admission, 11/1 for domestic students. Applications are processed on a rolling basis. Application fee: $125. *Expenses:* Tuition, state resident: full-time $7360; part-time $310 per credit. Tuition, nonresident: part-time $575 per credit. One-time fee: $195 full-time; $145.25 part-time. *Financial support:* Career-related internships or fieldwork, Federal Work-Study, institutionally sponsored loans, and tuition waivers (partial) available. Support available to part-time students. Financial award application deadline: 4/1; financial award applicants required to submit FAFSA. *Faculty research:* Exercise and environmental physiology, interdisciplinary approaches to school curricula using outdoor education, program development in cardiac rehabilitation and adult fitness, nutrition education. *Unit head:* Dr. Elizabeth Lowe, Chairperson, 718-997-4168. *Application contact:* Mario Caruso, Director of Graduate Admissions, 718-997-5200, Fax: 718-997-5193, E-mail: graduate_admissions@qc.edu.

South Carolina State University, School of Graduate Studies, Department of Education, Orangeburg, SC 29117-0001. Offers early childhood and special education (M Ed); early childhood education (MAT); elementary education (M Ed, MAT); engineering (MAT); general science (MAT); mathematics (MAT); secondary education (M Ed), including biology education, business education, counselor education, English education, home economics education, industrial education, mathematics education, science education, social studies education; special education (M Ed), including emotionally handicapped, learning disabilities, mentally handicapped. *Accreditation:* NCATE. Part-time and evening/weekend programs available. *Degree requirements:* For master's, thesis optional, departmental qualifying exam. *Entrance requirements:* For master's, GRE General Test, NTE, interview, teaching certificate. Electronic applications accepted. *Expenses:* Tuition, state resident: part-time $470 per credit hour. Tuition, nonresident: part-time $924 per credit hour. *Faculty research:* Critical thinking, child abuse, stress, test-taking skills, conflict resolution, mainstreaming.

State University of New York College at Oneonta, Graduate Education, Division of Education, Department of Secondary Education, Oneonta, NY 13820-4015. Offers adolescence education (MS Ed); family and consumer science education (MS Ed). *Accreditation:* NCATE. Part-time and evening/weekend programs available. *Entrance requirements:* For master's, GRE General

Test. *Application deadline:* For fall admission, 3/25 priority date for domestic students; for spring admission, 10/1 priority date for domestic students. Applications are processed on a rolling basis. Application fee: $50. *Expenses:* Tuition, state resident: part-time $349 per credit hour. Tuition, nonresident: full-time $12,870; part-time $552 per credit hour. Required fees: $1280; $15.85 per credit hour. *Unit head:* Dr. Dennis Banks, Chair, 607-436-3391, Fax: 607-436-2554, E-mail: banksdn@oneonta.edu. *Application contact:* Dr. Dennis Banks, Chair, 607-436-3391, Fax: 607-436-2554, E-mail: banksdn@oneonta.edu.

Texas Tech University, Graduate School, College of Human Sciences, Department of Applied and Professional Studies, Program in Family and Consumer Sciences Education, Lubbock, TX 79409. Offers MS, PhD. Part-time and evening/weekend programs available. *Students:* 5 full-time (all women), 17 part-time (14 women), 2 international. Average age 41. 30 applicants, 47% accepted, 1 enrolled. In 2009, 5 master's, 4 doctorates awarded. Terminal master's awarded for partial completion of doctoral program. *Degree requirements:* For master's, thesis or alternative; for doctorate, thesis/dissertation. *Entrance requirements:* For master's and doctorate, GRE General Test. Additional exam requirements/recommendations for international students: Required—TOEFL (minimum score 500 paper-based; 213 computer-based). *Application deadline:* For fall admission, 3/1 priority date for international students; for spring admission, 11/1 priority date for international students. Applications are processed on a rolling basis. Application fee: $50 ($75 for international students). Electronic applications accepted. *Expenses:* Tuition, state resident: full-time $5100; part-time $213 per credit hour. Tuition, nonresident: full-time $11,748; part-time $490 per credit hour. Required fees: $2298; $50 per credit hour. $555 per semester. *Financial support:* Research assistantships with partial tuition reimbursements, teaching assistantships with partial tuition reimbursements, career-related internships or fieldwork, Federal Work-Study, institutionally sponsored loans, and scholarships/grants available. Support available to part-time students. Financial award application deadline: 4/15; financial award applicants required to submit FAFSA. *Faculty research:* Work and family interaction, intergenerational initiatives, gender equity, curriculum, supervision. *Unit head:* Sue Couch, Director, 806-742-5050. *Application contact:* Sue Couch, Director, 806-742-5050.

The University of British Columbia, Faculty of Education, Department of Curriculum and Pedagogy, Vancouver, BC V6T 1Z4, Canada. Offers art education (M Ed, MA); business education (MA); curriculum studies (M Ed, MA, PhD); home economics education (M Ed, MA); math education (M Ed, MA); music education (M Ed, MA); physical education (M Ed, MA); science education (M Ed, MA); social studies education (M Ed, MA); technology studies education (M Ed, MA). Part-time programs available. *Degree requirements:* For master's, thesis (MA); for doctorate, comprehensive exam, thesis/dissertation. *Entrance requirements:* Additional exam requirements/recommendations for international students: Required—TOEFL (minimum score 580 paper-based; 237 computer-based; 92 iBT). Electronic applications accepted. *Expenses:* Contact institution. *Faculty research:* School subjects, teaching and learning.

University of Central Oklahoma, College of Graduate Studies and Research, College of Education, Department of Human Environmental Sciences, Edmond, OK 73034-5209. Offers family and child studies (MS); family and consumer science education (MS); interior design (MS); nutrition-food management (MS). Part-time programs available. *Faculty:* 5 full-time (4 women), 7 part-time/adjunct (4 women). *Students:* 51 full-time (49 women), 43 part-time (all women); includes 31 minority (20 African Americans, 7 American Indian/Alaska Native, 1 Asian American or Pacific Islander, 3 Hispanic Americans), 3 international. Average age 30. 21 applicants, 95% accepted. In 2009, 30 master's awarded. *Entrance requirements:* Additional exam requirements/recommendations for international students: Required—TOEFL (minimum score 550 paper-based; 213 computer-based). *Application deadline:* For fall admission, 7/1 for international students; for spring admission, 11/1 for international students. Applications are processed on a rolling basis. Application fee: $25. Electronic applications accepted. *Expenses:* Tuition, state resident: full-time $4128; part-time $172 per credit hour. Tuition, nonresident: full-time $10,373; part-time $432.20 per credit hour. Required fees: $433.20; $18.05 per credit hour. *Financial support:* Career-related internships or fieldwork and unspecified assistantships available. Financial award application deadline: 3/31; financial award applicants required to submit FAFSA. *Faculty research:* Dietetics and food science. *Unit head:* Dr. Kaye Sears, Chairperson, 405-974-5786. *Application contact:* Dr. Richard Bernard, Dean, Graduate College, 405-974-3493, Fax: 405-974-3852, E-mail: gradcoll@uco.edu.

University of Nebraska–Lincoln, Graduate College, College of Education and Human Sciences, Department of Child, Youth and Family Studies, Lincoln, NE 68588. Offers child development/early childhood education (MS, PhD); child, youth and family studies (MS); family and consumer sciences education (MS, PhD); family financial planning (MS); family science (MS, PhD); gerontology (PhD); human sciences (PhD), including child, youth and family studies, gerontology, medical family therapy; marriage and family therapy (MS); medical family therapy (PhD); youth development (MS). *Accreditation:* AAMFT/COAMFTE (one or more programs are accredited). Postbaccalaureate distance learning degree programs offered. *Degree requirements:* For master's, thesis optional. *Entrance requirements:* For master's, GRE. Additional exam requirements/recommendations for international students: Required—TOEFL (minimum score 550 paper-based; 213 computer-based). Electronic applications accepted. *Faculty research:* Marriage and family therapy, child development/early childhood education, family financial management.

Utah State University, School of Graduate Studies, College of Agriculture, Department of Agricultural Systems Technology and Education, Logan, UT 84322. Offers agricultural systems technology (MS), including agricultural extension education, agricultural mechanization, international agricultural extension, secondary and postsecondary agricultural education; family and consumer sciences education (MS). Part-time programs available. Postbaccalaureate distance learning degree programs offered (minimal on-campus study). *Degree requirements:* For master's, comprehensive exam (for some programs), thesis (for some programs). *Entrance requirements:* For master's, GRE General Test, MAT, BS in agricultural education, agricultural extension, or related agricultural or science discipline; minimum GPA of 3.0. Additional exam requirements/recommendations for international students: Required—TOEFL. *Faculty research:* Extension and adult education; structures and environment; low-input agriculture; farm safety, systems, and mechanizations.

Wayne State College, School of Education and Counseling, Department of Educational Foundations and Leadership, Program in Curriculum and Instruction, Wayne, NE 68787. Offers alternative education (MSE); business and information technology education (MSE); communication arts education (MSE); early childhood education (MSE); elementary education (MSE); English as a second language (MSE); English education (MSE); family and consumer sciences education (MSE); industrial technology and vocational education (MSE); learning communities (MSE); mathematics education (MSE); music education (MSE); science education (MSE); social science education (MSE). *Accreditation:* NCATE. Part-time and evening/weekend programs available. *Degree requirements:* For master's, comprehensive exam, thesis optional. *Entrance requirements:* For master's, GRE General Test. Additional exam requirements/recommendations for international students: Required—TOEFL (minimum score 550 paper-based; 213 computer-based).

Mathematics Education

Acadia University, Faculty of Professional Studies, School of Education, Program in Curriculum Studies, Wolfville, NS B4P 2R6, Canada. Offers cultural and media studies (M Ed); learning and technology (M Ed); science, math and technology (M Ed). Evening/weekend programs available. *Faculty:* 12 full-time (5 women). *Students:* 7 full-time (all women), 49 part-time (33 women). 61 applicants, 80% accepted. In 2009, 32 master's awarded. *Degree requirements:* For master's, thesis optional. *Entrance requirements:* For master's, B Ed or the equivalent, minimum B average in undergraduate course work, 2 years of teaching experience. Additional exam requirements/recommendations for international students: Required—TOEFL (minimum score 580 paper-based; 237 computer-based; 93 iBT), IELTS (minimum score 6.5). *Application deadline:* For fall admission, 3/15 priority date for domestic and international students. Applications are processed on a rolling basis. Application fee: $50. *Financial support:* Teaching assistantships available. Financial award application deadline: 3/15. *Faculty research:* Literacy development, postmodern philosophy and curriculum theory, historiography, philosophy of education, learning and technology. *Unit head:* Ann Vibert, Director, E-mail: ann.vibert@acadiau.ca. *Application contact:* Sheila Langille, Secretary, 902-585-1229, Fax: 902-585-1071, E-mail: sheila.langille@acadiau.ca.

Alabama State University, School of Graduate Studies, College of Arts and Sciences, Department of Mathematics and Computer Science, Montgomery, AL 36101-0271. Offers mathematics (M Ed, MS, Ed S). Part-time programs available. *Degree requirements:* For Ed S, thesis. *Entrance requirements:* For master's, GRE, GRE Subject Test, graduate writing competence test; for Ed S, GRE General Test, MAT, graduate writing competency test. Additional exam requirements/recommendations for international students: Required—TOEFL (minimum score 500 paper-based; 173 computer-based). *Faculty research:* Discrete mathematics, symbolic dynamics, mathematical social sciences.

Alabama State University, School of Graduate Studies, College of Education, Department of Curriculum and Instruction, Program in Secondary Education, Montgomery, AL 36101-0271. Offers biology education (M Ed, Ed S); English/language arts (M Ed); history education (M Ed, Ed S); mathematics education (M Ed); secondary education (Ed S); social studies (Ed S). Part-time programs available. *Degree requirements:* For master's, comprehensive exam; for Ed S, comprehensive exam, thesis. *Entrance requirements:* For master's, GRE General Test, MAT, graduate writing competency test; for Ed S, graduate writing competency test, GRE, MAT. Additional exam requirements/recommendations for international students: Required—TOEFL (minimum score 500 paper-based; 173 computer-based).

Albany State University, College of Sciences and Health Professions, Program in Mathematics Education, Albany, GA 31705-2717. Offers mathematics (M Ed). *Accreditation:* NCATE. *Students:* 1 full-time (0 women), 3 part-time (1 woman); includes 2 minority (both African Americans). Average age 30. 4 applicants, 100% accepted, 2 enrolled. In 2009, 1 master's awarded. *Degree requirements:* For master's, comprehensive exam. *Entrance requirements:* For master's, GRE General Test, MAT or GACE I, minimum overall GPA of 2.5, initial Georgia teaching certification for secondary mathematics. Additional exam requirements/recommendations for international students: Required—TOEFL. *Application deadline:* For fall admission, 11/16 for domestic students, 9/16 for international students; for spring admission, 4/19 for domestic students, 2/19 for international students. Applications are processed on a rolling basis. Application fee: $20. Electronic applications accepted. *Expenses:* Tuition, state resident: full-time $2970; part-time $162 per credit hour. Tuition, nonresident: full-time $12,168; part-time $676 per credit hour. Required fees: $962; $75 per credit hour. *Financial support:* Application deadline: 6/30. *Faculty research:* Information assurance, high performance computing, programming languages, statistical methods, applied mathematics. Total annual research expenditures: $250,000. *Unit head:* Dr. Seyed Roosta, Chair, 229-430-4886, Fax: 229-430-7895, E-mail: seyed.roosta@asurams.edu. *Application contact:* Nicole Lane, Interim Graduate Admissions Officer, 229-430-4862, Fax: 229-430-6398, E-mail: nicole.lane@asurams.edu.

Alfred University, Graduate School, Division of Education, Alfred, NY 14802-1205. Offers literacy teacher (MS Ed); numeracy (MS). *Accreditation:* Teacher Education Accreditation Council. Part-time programs available. *Entrance requirements:* For master's, LAST, Assessment of Teaching Skills (written), Content Specialty Test. Additional exam requirements/recommendations for international students: Required—TOEFL (minimum score 590 paper-based; 243 computer-based; 90 iBT), IELTS (minimum score 6.5). Electronic applications accepted. *Expenses:* Tuition: Full-time $33,296; part-time $708 per credit hour. Required fees: $880; $144 per year. Full-time tuition and fees vary according to program. *Faculty research:* Whole language, ethics in counseling and psychotherapy.

Appalachian State University, Cratis D. Williams Graduate School, Department of Curriculum and Instruction, Boone, NC 28608. Offers curriculum specialist (MA); educational media (MA); elementary education (MA); middle grades education (MA), including language arts, mathematics, science, social studies. *Accreditation:* NCATE. Part-time and evening/weekend programs available. Postbaccalaureate distance learning degree programs offered (no on-campus study). *Faculty:* 32 full-time (22 women), 9 part-time/adjunct (3 women). *Students:* 16 full-time (12 women), 168 part-time (140 women); includes 2 minority (both African Americans), 1 international. 97 applicants, 99% accepted, 77 enrolled. In 2009, 78 master's awarded. *Degree requirements:* For master's, comprehensive exam, thesis or alternative. *Entrance requirements:* For master's, GRE General Test or MAT, 3 letters of recommendation. Additional exam requirements/recommendations for international students: Required—TOEFL (minimum score 570 paper-based; 230 computer-based; 79 iBT), IELTS (minimum score 6.5). *Application deadline:* For fall admission, 7/1 for domestic students, 2/1 for international students; for spring admission, 11/1 for domestic students, 7/1 for international students. Applications are processed on a rolling basis. Application fee: $50. Electronic applications accepted. *Expenses:* Tuition, state resident: full-time $2960. Tuition, nonresident: full-time $14,051. Required fees: $2320. *Financial support:* In 2009–10, 8 teaching assistantships (averaging $8,000 per year) were awarded; fellowships, research assistantships, career-related internships or fieldwork, Federal Work-Study, scholarships/grants, and unspecified assistantships also available. Financial award application deadline: 4/1; financial award applicants required to submit FAFSA. *Faculty research:* Media literacy, elementary teaching, curriculum development, online learning environments. Total annual research expenditures: $690,000. *Unit head:* Dr. Michael Jacobson, Chairperson, 828-262-2224. *Application contact:* Sandy Krause, Director of Admissions and Recruiting, 828-262-2130, Fax: 828-262-2709, E-mail: krausesl@appstate.edu.

Appalachian State University, Cratis D. Williams Graduate School, Department of Mathematical Sciences, Boone, NC 28608. Offers mathematics (MA); mathematics education (MA). Part-time programs available. Postbaccalaureate distance learning degree programs offered (no on-campus study). *Faculty:* 27 full-time (10 women). *Students:* 7 full-time (4 women), 11 part-time (10 women). 7 applicants, 100% accepted, 5 enrolled. In 2009, 11 master's awarded. *Degree requirements:* For master's, comprehensive exam, thesis optional. *Entrance requirements:* For master's, GRE General Test, 3 letters of recommendation. Additional exam requirements/recommendations for international students: Required—TOEFL (minimum score 570 paper-based; 230 computer-based; 79 iBT), IELTS (minimum score 6.5). *Application deadline:* For fall admission, 7/1 for domestic students, 2/1 for international students; for spring admission, 11/1 for domestic students, 7/1 for international students. Applications are processed on a rolling basis. Application fee: $50. Electronic applications accepted. *Expenses:* Tuition, state resident: full-time $2960. Tuition, nonresident: full-time $14,051. Required fees: $2320. *Financial support:* In 2009–10, 14 teaching assistantships (averaging $9,500 per year) were awarded; fellowships, research assistantships, career-related internships or fieldwork, Federal Work-Study, scholarships/grants, and unspecified assistantships also available. Financial award application deadline: 4/1; financial award applicants required to submit FAFSA. *Faculty research:* Graph theory, differential equations, logic, geometry, complex analysis, topology, algebra, mathematics education. Total annual research expenditures: $482,500. *Unit head:* Dr. Mark Ginn, Chair, 828-262-3050, Fax: 828-265-8617, E-mail: ginnmc@appstate.edu. *Application contact:* Dr. Greg Rhoads, Graduate Director, 828-262-3050, E-mail: rhoadsgs@appstate.edu.

Arcadia University, Graduate Studies, Department of Education, Glenside, PA 19038-3295. Offers art education (M Ed, MA Ed); biology education (MA Ed); chemistry education (MA Ed); child development (CAS); computer education (M Ed, CAS); computer education 7–12 (MA Ed); early childhood education (M Ed, CAS), including individualized (M Ed), master teacher (M Ed), research in child development (M Ed); educational leadership (M Ed, CAS); educational psychology (CAS); elementary education (M Ed, CAS); English education (MA Ed); environmental education (MA Ed, CAS); history education (MA Ed); language arts (M Ed, CAS); mathematics education (M Ed, MA Ed, CAS); music education (MA Ed); psychology (MA Ed); pupil personnel services (CAS); reading (M Ed, CAS); school library science (M Ed); science education (M Ed, CAS); secondary education (M Ed, CAS); special education (M Ed, Ed D, CAS); theater arts (MA Ed); written communication (MA Ed). *Accreditation:* NASAD. Part-time and evening/weekend programs available. Postbaccalaureate distance learning degree programs offered (minimal on-campus study). *Faculty:* 12 full-time (8 women), 38 part-time/adjunct (26 women). *Students:* 89 full-time (74 women), 622 part-time (487 women); includes 112 minority (94 African Americans, 9 Asian Americans or Pacific Islanders, 9 Hispanic Americans), 2 international. Average age 32. In 2009, 257 master's, 4 doctorates awarded. *Application deadline:* Applications are processed on a rolling basis. Application fee: $40. Electronic applications accepted. *Expenses:* Tuition: Full-time $30,450; part-time $620 per credit hour. Required fees: $165. Tuition and fees vary according to program. *Financial support:* Career-related internships or fieldwork, tuition waivers (partial), and unspecified assistantships available. *Unit head:* Dr. Steven P. Gulkus. *Application contact:* 215-572-2925, Fax: 215-572-2126, E-mail: grad@arcadia.edu.

Arkansas State University—Jonesboro, Graduate School, College of Sciences and Mathematics, Department of Mathematics and Statistics, Jonesboro, State University, AR 72467. Offers mathematics (MS); mathematics education (MSE). Part-time programs available. *Faculty:* 7 full-time (2 women). *Students:* 9 full-time (4 women), 12 part-time (6 women), 2 international. Average age 31. 12 applicants, 100% accepted, 11 enrolled. In 2009, 5 master's awarded. *Degree requirements:* For master's, comprehensive exam, thesis or alternative. *Entrance requirements:* For master's, GRE General Test or MAT, appropriate bachelor's degree. Additional exam requirements/recommendations for international students: Required—TOEFL (minimum score 550 paper-based; 213 computer-based; 79 iBT), IELTS (minimum score 6). *Application deadline:* For fall admission, 7/1 for domestic and international students; for spring admission, 11/15 for domestic students, 11/13 for international students. Applications are processed on a rolling basis. Application fee: $30 ($40 for international students). Electronic applications accepted. *Expenses:* Tuition, state resident: full-time $3744; part-time $208 per credit hour. Tuition, nonresident: full-time $9540; part-time $530 per credit hour. Required fees: $896; $47 per credit hour. $25 per term. One-time fee: $50. Tuition and fees vary according to course load and program. *Financial support:* In 2009–10, 8 students received support; teaching assistantships, career-related internships or fieldwork, scholarships/grants, and unspecified assistantships available. Financial award application deadline: 7/1; financial award applicants required to submit FAFSA. *Unit head:* Dr. Debra Ingram, Chair, 870-972-3090, Fax: 870-972-3950, E-mail: dingram@astate.edu. *Application contact:* Dr. Andrew Sustich, Dean of the Graduate School, 870-972-3029, Fax: 870-972-3857, E-mail: sustich@astate.edu.

Armstrong Atlantic State University, School of Graduate Studies, Program in Education, Savannah, GA 31419-1997. Offers adult education (M Ed); curriculum and instruction (M Ed); early childhood education (M Ed); education (M Ed); elementary education (M Ed); middle grades education (M Ed); secondary education (M Ed), including business education, English education, mathematics education, science education, social science education; special education (M Ed), including behavioral disorders, learning disabilities, speech-language pathology. *Accreditation:* NCATE. Part-time and evening/weekend programs available. Postbaccalaureate distance learning degree programs offered (minimal on-campus study). *Degree requirements:* For master's, comprehensive exam, portfolio. *Entrance requirements:* For master's, GRE General Test or MAT, minimum GPA of 2.5, letters of recommendation. Additional exam requirements/recommendations for international students: Required—TOEFL (minimum score 523 paper-based; 193 computer-based). Electronic applications accepted.

Asbury University, School of Graduate and Professional Studies, Wilmore, KY 40390-1198. Offers biology: alternative certificate (MA Ed); chemistry: alternative certificate (MA Ed); English (MA Ed); English as a second language (MA Ed); ESL (MA Ed); French (MA Ed); Latin: alternative certificate (MA Ed); mathematics: alternative certificate (MA Ed); reading/writing endorsement (MA Ed); social studies (MA Ed); social work (MSW), including child and family services; Spanish (MA Ed); special education (MA Ed); special education: alternative certificate (MA Ed); teacher as leader endorsement (MA Ed). *Accreditation:* NCATE. Part-time programs available. *Faculty:* 8 full-time (7 women), 9 part-time/adjunct (4 women). *Students:* 108 part-time (87 women); includes 8 minority (4 African Americans, 2 Asian Americans or Pacific Islanders, 2 Hispanic Americans). Average age 36. 36 applicants, 86% accepted, 24 enrolled. In 2009, 20 master's awarded. *Degree requirements:* For master's, action research project, portfolio. *Entrance requirements:* For master's, PRAXIS/NTE, minimum GPA of 2.75, letters of recommendation. Additional exam requirements/recommendations for international students: Required—TOEFL (minimum score 550 paper-based). *Application deadline:* Applications are processed on a rolling basis. Application fee: $25. Electronic applications accepted. *Financial support:* Scholarships/grants and traineeships available. Financial award applicants required to submit FAFSA. *Unit head:* Dr. Bonnie J. Banker, Dean, School of Graduate and Professional Studies, 859-858-3511 Ext. 2221, Fax: 859-858-3921, E-mail: bonnie.banker@asbury.edu. *Application contact:* Lenore A. Sweigard, Graduate Program Assistant and Certification Specialist, 859-858-3511 Ext. 2502, Fax: 859-858-3921, E-mail: graded@asbury.edu.

Auburn University, Graduate School, College of Education, Department of Curriculum and Teaching, Auburn University, AL 36849. Offers business education (M Ed, MS, PhD); early childhood education (M Ed, MS, PhD, Ed S); elementary education (M Ed, MS, PhD, Ed S); foreign languages (M Ed, MS); music education (M Ed, MS, PhD, Ed S); postsecondary education (PhD); reading education (PhD, Ed S); secondary education (M Ed, MS, PhD, Ed S), including English language arts, mathematics, science, social studies. *Accreditation:* NASM (one or more programs are accredited); NCATE. Part-time programs available. *Faculty:* 28 full-time (21 women), 8 part-time/adjunct (5 women). *Students:* 76 full-time (55 women), 186 part-time (139 women); includes 43 minority (29 African Americans, 1 American Indian/Alaska Native, 4 Asian Americans or Pacific Islanders, 9 Hispanic Americans), 4 international. Average age 33. 248 applicants, 65% accepted, 110 enrolled. In 2009, 102 master's, 12 doctorates, 6 other advanced degrees awarded. *Degree requirements:* For master's, thesis (for some programs); for doctorate, thesis/dissertation; for Ed S, field project. *Entrance requirements:* For master's, doctorate, and Ed S, GRE General Test. *Application deadline:* For fall admission, 7/7 for domestic students; for spring admission, 11/24 for domestic students. Applications are processed on a rolling basis. Application fee: $50 ($60 for international students). Electronic applications accepted. *Expenses:* Tuition, state resident: full-time $6240. Tuition, nonresident: full-time $18,720. International tuition: $18,938 full-time. Required fees: $492. Tuition and fees vary according to course load, program and reciprocity agreements. *Financial support:* Fellowships, teaching assistantships, career-related internships or fieldwork and Federal Work-Study available. Support available to part-time students. Financial award application deadline: 3/15; financial award applicants required to submit FAFSA. *Faculty research:* Emerging literacy, reading attitudes, music for at-risk youth, portfolio assessment. *Unit head:* Dr. Nancy H. Barry, Head, 334-844-4434. *Application contact:* Dr. George Flowers, Dean of the Graduate School, 334-844-2125.

Averett University, Master in Education Program, Danville, VA 24541-3692. Offers art education (M Ed); biology (M Ed); biology education (M Ed); chemistry (M Ed); chemistry education (M Ed); curriculum and instruction (M Ed); elementary education (M Ed); English (M Ed);

English education (M Ed); health and physical education (M Ed); history and social studies education (M Ed); math (M Ed); mathematics education (M Ed); physical science (M Ed); reading specialization (M Ed); special education (learning disabilities specialization PK-12) (M Ed). Program also offered at Richmond, VA regional campus location. Part-time and evening/weekend programs available. *Faculty:* 4 full-time (3 women), 36 part-time/adjunct (22 women). *Students:* 182 full-time (160 women), 110 part-time (94 women); includes 113 minority (94 African Americans, 1 American Indian/Alaska Native, 7 Asian Americans or Pacific Islanders, 11 Hispanic Americans). Average age 37. 119 applicants, 99% accepted, 98 enrolled. In 2009, 92 master's awarded. *Degree requirements:* For master's, comprehensive exam, thesis optional. *Entrance requirements:* For master's, PRAXIS, GRE General Test, MAT or NTE, writing proficiency exam, 3 letters of recommendation, current teacher's licensure or eligibility for licensure, minimum undergraduate GPA of 3.0 in previous 2 years. Additional exam requirements/recommendations for international students: Required—TOEFL (minimum score 600 paper-based; 200 computer-based). *Application deadline:* Applications are processed on a rolling basis. *Expenses:* Contact institution. *Financial support:* Career-related internships or fieldwork, Federal Work-Study, and scholarships/grants available. Financial award application deadline: 4/1; financial award applicants required to submit FAFSA. *Faculty research:* Literary assessment-PreK-6, handwriting instruction and assessment-PreK-6, written language instruction and assessment-PreK-6 and special needs students learning styles, curriculum and instruction processes. *Unit head:* Dr. Lynn H. Wolf, Chair/Associate Professor/Director, 434-793-3995, Fax: 434-791-4392, E-mail: lynn.wolf@averett.edu. *Application contact:* Dr. Lynn H. Wolf, Chair/Associate Professor/Director, 434-793-3995, Fax: 434-791-4392, E-mail: lynn.wolf@averett.edu.

Ball State University, Graduate School, College of Sciences and Humanities, Department of Mathematical Sciences, Program in Mathematics, Muncie, IN 47306-1099. Offers mathematics (MA, MS); mathematics education (MAE).

Bank Street College of Education, Graduate School, Programs in Educational Leadership, New York, NY 10025. Offers early childhood leadership (MS Ed); educational leadership (MS Ed); leadership for educational change (Ed M, MS Ed); leadership in mathematics education (MS Ed); leadership in museum education (MS Ed); leadership in the arts: creative writing (MS Ed); leadership in the arts: visual arts (MS Ed). *Students:* 76 full-time (60 women), 121 part-time (95 women); includes 67 minority (34 African Americans, 1 American Indian/Alaska Native, 6 Asian Americans or Pacific Islanders, 26 Hispanic Americans), 2 international. Average age 36. 124 applicants, 86% accepted, 98 enrolled. In 2009, 79 master's awarded. *Degree requirements:* For master's, thesis. *Entrance requirements:* For master's, interview, minimum of 2 years experience as a classroom teacher. Additional exam requirements/recommendations for international students: Required—TOEFL (minimum score 600 paper-based; 250 computer-based; 100 iBT), IELTS (minimum score 7). *Application deadline:* For fall admission, 3/1 priority date for domestic students; for spring admission, 11/1 priority date for domestic students. Applications are processed on a rolling basis. Application fee: $65. *Expenses:* Tuition: Part-time $1120 per credit. *Financial support:* Career-related internships or fieldwork, Federal Work-Study, scholarships/grants, and unspecified assistantships available. Support available to part-time students. Financial award application deadline: 4/15; financial award applicants required to submit FAFSA. *Faculty research:* Leadership in small schools, mathematics in elementary schools, professional development in early childhood, leadership in arts education, leadership in special education. *Unit head:* Dr. Rima Shore, Chairperson, 212-875-4478, Fax: 212-875-8753, E-mail: rshore@bankstreet.edu. *Application contact:* Ann Morgan, Director of Graduate Admissions, 212-875-4403, Fax: 212-875-4678, E-mail: amorgan@bankstreet.edu.

Belmont University, College of Arts and Sciences, School of Education, Nashville, TN 37212-3757. Offers education (M Ed); elementary education (MAT), including early childhood education, elementary education, language arts education; English (MAT); history (MAT); mathematics (MAT); middle grade education (MAT); science (MAT); secondary education (MAT); special education (MAT); sports administration (MSA). *Accreditation:* NCATE. Part-time and evening/weekend programs available. *Degree requirements:* For master's, comprehensive exam, thesis, culminating portfolio. *Entrance requirements:* For master's, MAT or GRE and/or LSAT or GMAT, minimum GPA of 2.75. Additional exam requirements/recommendations for international students: Required—TOEFL. *Expenses:* Contact institution. *Faculty research:* Improving secondary literacy, Montessori, classroom management strategies, teacher residency programs, online professional development, mentoring, leadership, sociological issues in sport, faculty development, coaching.

Bemidji State University, School of Graduate Studies, College of Social and Natural Sciences, Field of Mathematics, Bemidji, MN 56601-2699. Offers MS. Part-time programs available. *Entrance requirements:* For master's, letters of recommendation. Additional exam requirements/recommendations for international students: Required—TOEFL. Electronic applications accepted. *Faculty research:* Numerical partial differential equations, statistics, biostatistics, industrial statistics and production, math and statistics education, coding theory, graph theory.

Bennington College, Graduate Programs, MA in Teaching Program, Bennington, VT 05201. Offers art education (MAT); early childhood (MAT); elementary education (MAT); English education (MAT); foreign language education (MAT); k-12 education (MAT); mathematics education (MAT); music education (MAT); science education (MAT); secondary education (MAT); social studies education (MAT); theater arts (MAT). *Faculty:* 5 part-time/adjunct (3 women). *Students:* 8 full-time (5 women), 1 part-time (0 women). Average age 28. 11 applicants, 27% accepted, 1 enrolled. In 2009, 4 master's awarded. *Degree requirements:* For master's, comprehensive exam, 1 year teaching practicum, professional portfolio. *Entrance requirements:* For master's, interview. *Application deadline:* For fall admission, 3/1 for domestic students. Application fee: $60. *Expenses:* Contact institution. *Financial support:* In 2009–10, 6 students received support, including 4 fellowships (averaging $10,475 per year); scholarships/grants and unspecified assistantships also available. Financial award application deadline: 4/1; financial award applicants required to submit FAFSA. *Unit head:* Carol Meyer, Director of Programs in Teacher Education, 802-440-4375, E-mail: cmeyer@bennington.edu. *Application contact:* Nancy Pearlman, Assistant Director of Programs in Teacher Education, 802-440-4710, Fax: 802-440-4383, E-mail: npearlman@bennington.edu.

Bob Jones University, Graduate Programs, Greenville, SC 29614. Offers accountancy (MS); Bible (MA); Bible translation (MA); Biblical studies (Certificate); broadcast management (MS); business administration (MBA); church history (MA, PhD); church ministries (MA); church music (MM); cinema and video production (MA); counseling (MS); curriculum and instruction (Ed D); divinity (M Div); dramatic production (MA); educational leadership (MS, Ed D, Ed S); elementary education (M Ed, MAT); English (M Ed, MA, MAT); fine arts (MA); graphic design (MA); history (M Ed, MA); illustration (MA); interpretative speech (MA); mathematics (M Ed, MAT); medical missions (Certificate); ministry (MM, D Min); multi-categorical special education (M Ed, MAT); music (M Ed); New Testament interpretation (PhD); Old Testament interpretation (PhD); orchestral instrument performance (MM); organ performance (MM); pastoral studies (MA); personnel services (MS, Ed S); piano pedagogy (MM); piano performance (MM); platform arts (MA); radio and television broadcasting (MS); rhetoric and public address (MA); secondary education (M Ed); studio art (MA); teaching Bible (MA); theology (MA, PhD); voice performance (MM); youth ministries (MA); M Div/MM.

Boston College, Lynch Graduate School of Education, Department of Teacher Education/Special Education and Curriculum and Instruction, Program in Secondary Education, Chestnut Hill, MA 02467-3800. Offers biology (MST); chemistry (MST); English (MAT); French (MAT); geology (MST); history (MAT); Latin and classical humanities (MAT); mathematics (MST); physics (MST); secondary teaching (M Ed), including biology, chemistry, English, French, geology, history, Latin and classical humanities, mathematics, physics, Spanish; Spanish (MAT). *Accreditation:* Teacher Education Accreditation Council. Part-time and evening/weekend programs available. *Students:* 14 full-time (10 women), 68 part-time (37 women); includes 17 minority (9 African Americans, 3 Asian Americans or Pacific Islanders, 5 Hispanic Americans), 1 international. 252 applicants, 59% accepted, 47 enrolled. In 2009, 39 master's awarded. *Degree requirements:* For master's, comprehensive exam. *Entrance requirements:* For master's, GRE General Test or MAT. Additional exam requirements/recommendations for international students: Required—TOEFL (minimum score 550 paper-based; 213 computer-based; 81 iBT). *Application deadline:* For fall admission, 1/1 priority date for domestic students. Application fee: $60. Electronic applications accepted. *Financial support:* Fellowships with full and partial tuition reimbursements, research assistantships with full and partial tuition reimbursements, teaching assistantships with full and partial tuition reimbursements, career-related internships or fieldwork, Federal Work-Study, institutionally sponsored loans, scholarships/grants, traineeships, health care benefits, tuition waivers (full and partial), and unspecified assistantships available. Support available to part-time students. Financial award applicants required to submit FAFSA. *Faculty research:* School reform; urban science education; teacher research; critical literacy; poverty and achievement. *Unit head:* Dr. Maria E. Brisk, Chairperson, 617-552-4216, Fax: 617-552-0812, E-mail: brisk@bc.edu. *Application contact:* Adam Poluzzi, Director, Graduate Admission and Financial Aid, 617-552-4214, Fax: 617-552-0398, E-mail: poluzzi@bc.edu.

Boston University, School of Education, Department of Curriculum and Teaching, Program in Mathematics Education, Boston, MA 02215. Offers Ed M, MAT, Ed D, CAGS. *Degree requirements:* For master's, thesis optional; for doctorate, comprehensive exam, thesis/dissertation; for CAGS, comprehensive exam. *Entrance requirements:* For master's, doctorate, and CAGS, GRE General Test or MAT. Additional exam requirements/recommendations for international students: Required—TOEFL. Electronic applications accepted. *Expenses:* Tuition: Full-time $37,910; part-time $1184 per credit hour. Required fees: $386; $40 per semester. Part-time tuition and fees vary according to class time, course level, degree level and program. *Faculty research:* Learning theory, impact of computers, problem solving.

Bowling Green State University, Graduate College, College of Arts and Sciences, Department of Mathematics and Statistics, Bowling Green, OH 43403. Offers applied statistics (MS); mathematics (MA, MAT, PhD); statistics (PhD). Part-time programs available. *Degree requirements:* For master's, thesis or alternative; for doctorate, comprehensive exam, thesis/dissertation. *Entrance requirements:* For master's and doctorate, GRE General Test. Additional exam requirements/recommendations for international students: Required—TOEFL. Electronic applications accepted. *Faculty research:* Statistics and probability, algebra, analysis.

Bridgewater State University, School of Graduate Studies, School of Arts and Sciences, Department of Mathematics and Computer Science, Bridgewater, MA 02325-0001. Offers computer science (MS); mathematics (MAT). Part-time and evening/weekend programs available. *Entrance requirements:* For master's, GRE General Test.

Brigham Young University, Graduate Studies, College of Physical and Mathematical Sciences, Department of Mathematics Education, Provo, UT 84602-1001. Offers MA. Part-time programs available. *Faculty:* 8 full-time (2 women). *Students:* 10 full-time (8 women), 6 part-time (4 women); includes 1 minority (African American). Average age 30. In 2009, 5 master's awarded. *Degree requirements:* For master's, comprehensive exam, project or thesis, written exam. *Entrance requirements:* For master's, GRE General Test, teaching certificate, bachelor's degree in math education or equivalent. Additional exam requirements/recommendations for international students: Required—TOEFL. *Application deadline:* For fall and spring admission, 3/1 priority date for domestic and international students. Application fee: $50. Electronic applications accepted. *Expenses:* Tuition: Full-time $5580; part-time $301 per credit hour. Tuition and fees vary according to student's religious affiliation. *Financial support:* In 2009–10, 14 students received support, including 8 research assistantships with full tuition reimbursements available (averaging $3,000 per year), 10 teaching assistantships with full tuition reimbursements available (averaging $12,000 per year); institutionally sponsored loans, scholarships/grants, and tuition waivers (partial) also available. Financial award application deadline: 3/1. *Faculty research:* Pre-service mathematics teacher education, teaching and learning with technology, mathematics learning and teaching, communication in mathematics classrooms, mathematical knowledge for teaching. *Unit head:* Steven R. Williams, Chair, 801-422-2887, Fax: 801-422-0511, E-mail: williams@mathed.byu.edu. *Application contact:* Kathy Lee Garrett, Administrative Assistant, 801-422-1840, Fax: 801-422-0511, E-mail: kathylee@mathed.byu.edu.

Brooklyn College of the City University of New York, Division of Graduate Studies, School of Education, Program in Adolescence Education and Special Subjects, Brooklyn, NY 11210-2889. Offers adolescence science education (MAT); art teacher (MA); biology teacher (MA); chemistry teacher (MA); earth science teacher (MAT); English teacher (MA); French teacher (MA); health and nutrition sciences: health teacher (MS Ed); mathematics teacher (MA); music education (CAS); music teacher (MA); physical education teacher (MS Ed); physics teacher (MA); social studies teacher (MA); Spanish teacher (MA). Part-time and evening/weekend programs available. *Students:* 23 full-time (15 women), 449 part-time (256 women); includes 147 minority (96 African Americans, 1 American Indian/Alaska Native, 18 Asian Americans or Pacific Islanders, 32 Hispanic Americans), 12 international. Average age 30. 251 applicants, 80% accepted, 141 enrolled. In 2009, 163 master's, 2 other advanced degrees awarded. *Degree requirements:* For master's, comprehensive exam (for some programs), thesis (for some programs). *Entrance requirements:* For master's, LAST, previous course work in education, resume, 2 letters of recommendation, essay. Additional exam requirements/recommendations for international students: Required—TOEFL (minimum score 500 paper-based; 173 computer-based; 61 iBT). *Application deadline:* For fall admission, 7/15 for domestic students, 7/1 for international students; for spring admission, 11/15 for domestic students, 10/1 for international students. Applications are processed on a rolling basis. Application fee: $125. Electronic applications accepted. *Expenses:* Tuition, state resident: full-time $7360; part-time $310 per credit hour. Tuition, nonresident: full-time $13,800; part-time $575 per credit hour. Required fees: $140.10 per semester. *Financial support:* Career-related internships or fieldwork, Federal Work-Study, institutionally sponsored loans, and scholarships/grants available. Support available to part-time students. Financial award application deadline: 5/1; financial award applicants required to submit FAFSA. *Faculty research:* Interdisciplinary education, semiotics, discourse analysis, autobiography, teacher identity. *Unit head:* Prof. Stephen Phillips, Program Head, 718-951-5214, E-mail: phillips@brooklyn.cuny.edu. *Application contact:* Hernan Sierra, Graduate Admissions Coordinator, 718-951-4536, Fax: 718-951-4506, E-mail: grads@brooklyn.cuny.edu.

Brooklyn College of the City University of New York, Division of Graduate Studies, School of Education, Program in Childhood Education, Brooklyn, NY 11210-2889. Offers bilingual education (MS Ed); liberal arts (MS Ed); mathematics (MS Ed); science/environmental education (MS Ed). Part-time and evening/weekend programs available. *Students:* 14 full-time (13 women), 245 part-time (209 women); includes 129 minority (60 African Americans, 2 American Indian/Alaska Native, 20 Asian Americans or Pacific Islanders, 47 Hispanic Americans), 6 international. Average age 30. 114 applicants, 85% accepted, 65 enrolled. In 2009, 118 master's awarded. *Entrance requirements:* For master's, LAST, interview, previous course work in education, writing sample, resume, 2 letters of recommendation. Additional exam requirements/recommendations for international students: Required—TOEFL (minimum score 500 paper-based; 173 computer-based; 61 iBT). *Application deadline:* For fall admission, 3/1 priority date for domestic students, 2/1 priority date for international students; for spring admission, 11/1 priority date for domestic students, 10/1 priority date for international students. Applications are processed on a rolling basis. Application fee: $125. Electronic applications accepted. *Expenses:* Tuition, state resident: full-time $7360; part-time $310 per credit hour. Tuition, nonresident: full-time $13,800; part-time $575 per credit hour. Required fees: $140.10 per semester. *Financial support:* Career-related internships or fieldwork, Federal Work-Study, institutionally sponsored loans, and scholarships/grants available. Support available to part-time students. Financial award application deadline: 5/1; financial award applicants required to submit FAFSA. *Faculty research:* Emotional intelligence, multiculturalism, arts immersion, the Holocaust. *Unit head:* Dr. Wayne Reed, Program Head, 718-951-5214, E-mail: wreed@brooklyn.cuny.edu. *Application contact:* Hernan Sierra, Graduate Admissions Coordinator, 718-951-4536, Fax: 718-951-4506, E-mail: grads@brooklyn.cuny.edu.

Brooklyn College of the City University of New York, Division of Graduate Studies, School of Education, Program in Middle Childhood Education (Math), Brooklyn, NY 11210-2889.

Mathematics Education

Brooklyn College of the City University of New York (continued)
Offers MS Ed. *Students:* 1 (woman) full-time, 97 part-time (53 women); includes 47 minority (25 African Americans, 14 Asian Americans or Pacific Islanders, 8 Hispanic Americans), 2 international. Average age 30. 31 applicants, 84% accepted, 17 enrolled. In 2009, 63 master's awarded. *Entrance requirements:* For master's, LAST, 2 letters of recommendation, essay, resume. Additional exam requirements/recommendations for international students: Required—TOEFL (minimum score 500 paper-based; 173 computer-based; 61 iBT). *Application deadline:* For fall admission, 7/15 priority date for domestic students, 6/1 priority date for international students; for spring admission, 11/15 priority date for domestic students, 10/1 priority date for international students. Applications are processed on a rolling basis. Electronic applications accepted. *Expenses:* Tuition, state resident: full-time $7360; part-time $310 per credit hour. Tuition, nonresident: full-time $13,800; part-time $575 per credit hour. Required fees: $140.10 per semester. *Financial support:* Federal Work-Study, institutionally sponsored loans, and scholarships/grants available. Support available to part-time students. Financial award application deadline: 5/1; financial award applicants required to submit FAFSA. *Unit head:* Prof. Mary Chiusano, Program Head, 718-951-5214, E-mail: mchiusano@brooklyn.cuny.edu. *Application contact:* Hernan Sierra, Graduate Admissions Coordinator, 718-951-4536, Fax: 718-951-4506, E-mail: grads@brooklyn.cuny.edu.

Buffalo State College, State University of New York, The Graduate School, Faculty of Natural and Social Sciences, Department of Mathematics, Buffalo, NY 14222-1095. Offers mathematics education (MS Ed). *Accreditation:* NCATE. Part-time and evening/weekend programs available. *Degree requirements:* For master's, thesis or alternative. *Entrance requirements:* For master's, 18 undergraduate hours in upper-level mathematics, minimum GPA of 2.5 in undergraduate math courses. Additional exam requirements/recommendations for international students: Required—TOEFL (minimum score 550 paper-based; 213 computer-based).

California State University, Bakersfield, Division of Graduate Studies, School of Natural Sciences and Mathematics, Program in Teaching Mathematics, Bakersfield, CA 93311. Offers MA. *Entrance requirements:* For master's, minimum GPA of 2.5 for last 90 quarter units.

California State University, Chico, Graduate School, College of Natural Sciences, Program in Math Education, Chico, CA 95929-0722. Offers MS. Part-time programs available. *Students:* 1 applicant, 0% accepted, 0 enrolled. *Entrance requirements:* For master's, teaching credential. Additional exam requirements/recommendations for international students: Required—TOEFL (minimum score 550 paper-based; 213 computer-based; 80 iBT), IELTS (minimum score 6.5). *Application deadline:* For fall admission, 3/1 priority date for domestic students, 3/1 for international students. Application fee: $55. *Unit head:* Dr. Julie Monet, Graduate Coordinator, 530-898-3460. *Application contact:* Dr. Julie Monet, Graduate Coordinator, 530-898-3460.

California State University, Dominguez Hills, College of Natural and Behavioral Sciences, Program in Teaching of Mathematics, Carson, CA 90747-0001. Offers MA. Part-time and evening/weekend programs available. *Faculty:* 2 full-time (0 women). *Students:* 25 part-time (14 women); includes 18 minority (3 African Americans, 4 Asian Americans or Pacific Islanders, 11 Hispanic Americans). Average age 39. 9 applicants, 56% accepted, 4 enrolled. In 2009, 5 master's awarded. *Degree requirements:* For master's, comprehensive exam, thesis. *Entrance requirements:* For master's, 2 years of teaching experience. Additional exam requirements/recommendations for international students: Required—TOEFL. *Application deadline:* For fall admission, 6/1 priority date for domestic students; for spring admission, 11/1 priority date for domestic students. Applications are processed on a rolling basis. Application fee: $55. Electronic applications accepted. *Expenses:* Tuition, nonresident: full-time $6696; part-time $372 per unit. Required fees: $5946; $1752 per semester. *Unit head:* Dr. John Wilkins, Chair, 310-243-3380, E-mail: jwilkins@csudh.edu. *Application contact:* Dr. John Wilkins, Associate Professor, 310-243-3380, E-mail: jwilkins@csudh.edu.

California State University, Fresno, Division of Graduate Studies, College of Science and Mathematics, Department of Mathematics, Fresno, CA 93740-8027. Offers mathematics (MA); teaching (MA). Part-time programs available. *Degree requirements:* For master's, thesis or alternative. *Entrance requirements:* For master's, GRE General Test. Additional exam requirements/recommendations for international students: Required—TOEFL. Electronic applications accepted. *Faculty research:* Diagnostic testing project.

California State University, Fullerton, Graduate Studies, College of Education, Department of Secondary Education, Fullerton, CA 92834-9480. Offers middle school mathematics (MS); secondary education (MS); teacher induction (MS). Part-time programs available. *Students:* 1 (woman) full-time, 41 part-time (33 women); includes 15 minority (1 African American, 1 American Indian/Alaska Native, 4 Asian Americans or Pacific Islanders, 9 Hispanic Americans). Average age 32. 32 applicants, 63% accepted, 17 enrolled. In 2009, 39 master's awarded. Application fee: $55. *Expenses:* Tuition, nonresident: full-time $11,160; part-time $373 per credit. Required fees: $1440 per term. Tuition and fees vary according to course load, degree level and program. *Financial support:* Career-related internships or fieldwork, Federal Work-Study, institutionally sponsored loans, and scholarships/grants available. Support available to part-time students. Financial award application deadline: 3/1; financial award applicants required to submit FAFSA. *Unit head:* Dr. Victoria Costa, Head, 657-278-7037. *Application contact:* Admissions/Applications, 657-278-2371.

California State University, Fullerton, Graduate Studies, College of Natural Science and Mathematics, Department of Mathematics, Fullerton, CA 92834-9480. Offers applied mathematics (MA); mathematics (MA); mathematics for secondary school teachers (MA). Part-time programs available. *Students:* 15 full-time (8 women), 58 part-time (31 women); includes 30 minority (25 Asian Americans or Pacific Islanders, 5 Hispanic Americans), 3 international. Average age 30. 62 applicants, 76% accepted, 31 enrolled. In 2009, 25 master's awarded. *Degree requirements:* For master's, comprehensive exam or project. *Entrance requirements:* For master's, minimum GPA of 2.5 in last 60 units of course work, major in mathematics or related field. Application fee: $55. *Expenses:* Tuition, nonresident: full-time $11,160; part-time $373 per credit. Required fees: $1440 per term. Tuition and fees vary according to course load, degree level and program. *Financial support:* Research assistantships, teaching assistantships, career-related internships or fieldwork, Federal Work-Study, institutionally sponsored loans, and scholarships/grants available. Support available to part-time students. Financial award application deadline: 3/1; financial award applicants required to submit FAFSA. *Unit head:* Dr. Paul Deland, Chair, 657-278-3631. *Application contact:* Admissions/Applications, 657-278-2371.

California State University, Long Beach, Graduate Studies, College of Natural Sciences and Mathematics, Department of Mathematics and Statistics, Long Beach, CA 90840. Offers mathematics (MS), including applied mathematics, applied statistics, mathematics education for secondary school teachers. Part-time programs available. *Faculty:* 11 full-time (5 women). *Students:* 73 full-time (30 women), 90 part-time (36 women); includes 75 minority (6 African Americans, 47 Asian Americans or Pacific Islanders, 22 Hispanic Americans), 15 international. Average age 30. 123 applicants, 69% accepted, 44 enrolled. *Degree requirements:* For master's, comprehensive exam or thesis. *Application deadline:* For fall admission, 7/1 for domestic students; for spring admission, 12/1 for domestic students. Applications are processed on a rolling basis. Application fee: $55. Electronic applications accepted. *Expenses:* Required fees: $1802 per semester. Part-time tuition and fees vary according to course load. *Financial support:* Teaching assistantships, Federal Work-Study, institutionally sponsored loans, scholarships/grants, and traineeships available. Financial award application deadline: 3/2. *Faculty research:* Algebra, functional analysis, partial differential equations, operator theory, numerical analysis. *Unit head:* Dr. Robert Mena, Chair, 562-985-4721, Fax: 562-985-8227, E-mail: rmena@csulb.edu. *Application contact:* Dr. Ngo Viet, Graduate Associate Chair, 562-985-4721, Fax: 562-985-8227, E-mail: viet@csulb.edu.

California State University, Northridge, Graduate Studies, College of Education, Department of Secondary Education, Northridge, CA 91330. Offers educational technology (MA); English education (MA); mathematics education (MA); secondary science education (MA); teaching and learning (MA). *Accreditation:* NCATE. Part-time programs available. *Faculty:* 13 full-time (7 women), 41 part-time/adjunct (20 women). *Students:* 10 full-time (6 women), 99 part-time (65 women); includes 40 minority (6 African Americans, 2 American Indian/Alaska Native, 13 Asian Americans or Pacific Islanders, 19 Hispanic Americans). Average age 34. 86 applicants, 60% accepted, 40 enrolled. *Degree requirements:* For master's, thesis optional. *Entrance requirements:* For master's, GRE General Test or minimum GPA of 3.0. Additional exam requirements/recommendations for international students: Required—TOEFL. *Application deadline:* For fall admission, 11/30 for domestic students. Application fee: $55. *Financial support:* Application deadline: 3/1. *Unit head:* Dr. Bonnie Ericson, Chair, 818-677-2580. *Application contact:* Dr. Michael Rivas, Graduate Advisor, 818-677-6792, E-mail: michael.rivas@csun.edu.

California State University, Northridge, Graduate Studies, College of Science and Mathematics, Department of Mathematics, Northridge, CA 91330. Offers applied mathematics (MS); mathematics (MS); mathematics for educational careers (MS). Part-time and evening/weekend programs available. *Faculty:* 34 full-time (9 women), 36 part-time/adjunct (17 women). *Students:* 19 full-time (11 women), 34 part-time (12 women); includes 1 African American, 4 Asian Americans or Pacific Islanders, 9 Hispanic Americans, 2 international. Average age 31. 86 applicants, 49% accepted, 27 enrolled. In 2009, 16 master's awarded. *Degree requirements:* For master's, thesis (for some programs). *Entrance requirements:* For master's, GRE (if cumulative undergraduate GPA less than 3.0). Additional exam requirements/recommendations for international students: Required—TOEFL. *Application deadline:* For fall admission, 4/15 priority date for domestic students. Application fee: $55. *Financial support:* Teaching assistantships, Federal Work-Study and institutionally sponsored loans available. Support available to part-time students. Financial award application deadline: 3/1. *Unit head:* Dr. Werner Horn, Graduate Coordinator, 818-677-7794, E-mail: werner.horn@csun.edu. *Application contact:* Dr. Werner Horn, Graduate Coordinator, 818-677-7794, E-mail: werner.horn@csun.edu.

California State University, San Bernardino, Graduate Studies, College of Natural Sciences, Department of Mathematics, San Bernardino, CA 92407-2397. Offers mathematics (MA); teaching mathematics (MAT). Part-time programs available. *Faculty:* 13 full-time (4 women). *Students:* 36 full-time (15 women), 42 part-time (18 women); includes 36 minority (5 African Americans, 10 Asian Americans or Pacific Islanders, 21 Hispanic Americans), 2 international. Average age 34. 44 applicants, 75% accepted, 23 enrolled. In 2009, 11 master's awarded. *Degree requirements:* For master's, advancement to candidacy. *Entrance requirements:* For master's, writing exam, minimum GPA of 3.0 in math courses. Application fee: $55. *Financial support:* Teaching assistantships available. *Faculty research:* Mathematics education, technology in education, algebra, combinatorics, real analysis. *Unit head:* Dr. Peter D. Williams, Chair, 909-537-5361, Fax: 909-537-7119, E-mail: pwilliam@csusb.edu. *Application contact:* Olivia Rosas, Director of Admissions, 909-537-7577, Fax: 909-537-7034, E-mail: orosas@csusb.edu.

Cambridge College, School of Education, Cambridge, MA 02138-5304. Offers autism specialist (M Ed); autism/behavior analyst (M Ed); behavior analyst (Post-Master's Certificate); behavioral management (M Ed); early childhood teacher (M Ed); education specialist in curriculum and instruction (CAGS); educational leadership (Ed D); elementary teacher (M Ed); English as a second language (M Ed, Certificate); general science (M Ed); health education, health promotion (Post-Master's Certificate); health/family and consumer sciences (M Ed); history (M Ed); individualized degree (M Ed); information technology literacy (M Ed); instructional technology (M Ed); interdisciplinary studies (M Ed); library teacher (M Ed); literacy education (M Ed); mathematics (M Ed); mathematics specialist (Certificate); middle school mathematics and science (M Ed); school administration (M Ed, CAGS); school guidance counselor (M Ed); school nurse education (M Ed); school social worker/school adjustment counselor (M Ed); special education administrator (CAGS); special education/moderate disabilities (M Ed); teaching skills and methodologies (M Ed). Part-time and evening/weekend programs available. Postbaccalaureate distance learning degree programs offered (minimal on-campus study). *Faculty:* 10 full-time (3 women), 283 part-time/adjunct (187 women). *Students:* 974 full-time (755 women), 1,071 part-time (835 women); includes 940 minority (762 African Americans, 4 American Indian/Alaska Native, 22 Asian Americans or Pacific Islanders, 152 Hispanic Americans), 28 international. Average age 39. In 2009, 866 master's, 4 doctorates, 209 CAGSs awarded. *Degree requirements:* For master's, thesis, internship/practicum (licensure program only); for doctorate, thesis/dissertation; for other advanced degree, thesis. *Entrance requirements:* For master's, interview, resume, documentation of licensure, 2 professional references; for doctorate, official transcripts, interview, resume, documentation of licensure (if any), written personal statement/essay, portfolio of scholarly and professional work, qualifying assessment, 2 professional references, health insurance, immunizations form; for other advanced degree, official transcripts, interview, resume, documentation of licensure (if any), written personal statement/essay, 2 professional references, health insurance, immunizations form. Additional exam requirements/recommendations for international students: Required—TOEFL (minimum score 550 paper-based; 213 computer-based; 79 iBT); Recommended—IELTS (minimum score 6). *Application deadline:* Applications are processed on a rolling basis. Application fee: $30. Electronic applications accepted. *Expenses:* Contact institution. *Financial support:* In 2009–10, 1,373 students received support. Career-related internships or fieldwork, Federal Work-Study, and scholarships/grants available. Financial award applicants required to submit FAFSA. *Faculty research:* Adult education, accelerated learning, mathematics education, brain compatible learning, special education and law. *Unit head:* Dr. N. Alan Sheppard, Interim Associate Dean, 617-873-0619, E-mail: alan.sheppard@cambridgecollege.edu. *Application contact:* Stephen Lyons, Director of Enrollment, Graduate and N.I.T.E. Programs, 617-868-1000, Fax: 617-349-3561, E-mail: stephen.lyons@cambridgecollege.edu.

Campbell University, Graduate and Professional Programs, School of Education, Buies Creek, NC 27506. Offers administration (MSA); community counseling (MA); elementary education (M Ed); English education (M Ed); interdisciplinary studies (M Ed); mathematics education (M Ed); middle grades education (M Ed); physical education (M Ed); school counseling (M Ed); secondary education (M Ed); social science education (M Ed). *Accreditation:* NCATE. Part-time and evening/weekend programs available. *Degree requirements:* For master's, comprehensive exam. *Entrance requirements:* For master's, GRE General Test, minimum GPA of 2.7. *Faculty research:* Spiritual values and wellness issues in counseling, stress and professional burnout among counselors, thinking strategies, leadership, adaptive technology.

Caribbean University, Graduate School, Bayamón, PR 00960-0493. Offers administration and supervision (MA Ed); criminal justice (MA); curriculum and instruction (MA Ed), including elementary education, English education, history education, mathematics education, primary education, science education, Spanish education; education (PhD); gerontology (MSN); human resources (MBA); museology, archiving and art history (MA Ed); neonatal pediatrics (MSN); physical education (MA Ed); special education (MA Ed). *Entrance requirements:* For master's, interview, minimum GPA of 2.5.

Central Michigan University, College of Graduate Studies, College of Science and Technology, Department of Mathematics, Mount Pleasant, MI 48859. Offers mathematics (MA, PhD), including teaching of college mathematics (PhD). Part-time programs available. *Degree requirements:* For master's, thesis or alternative; for doctorate, thesis/dissertation. *Entrance requirements:* For master's, minimum GPA of 2.7, 20 hours of course work in mathematics; for doctorate, GRE, minimum GPA of 3.0, 20 hours of course work in mathematics. Electronic applications accepted. *Faculty research:* Combinatorics, approximation theory, applied mathematics, statistics, functional analysis and operator theory.

Chatham University, Program in Education, Pittsburgh, PA 15232-2826. Offers early childhood education (MAT); elementary education (MAT); English—secondary (MAT); environmental education (K-12) (MAT); secondary art (MAT); secondary biology education (MAT); secondary chemistry education (MAT); secondary English education (MAT); secondary math education (MAT); secondary physics education (MAT); secondary social studies education (MAT); special education (MAT). *Students:* 52 full-time (41 women), 20 part-time (16 women). Average age 30. 39 applicants, 79% accepted, 26 enrolled. In 2009, 37 master's awarded. *Degree*

requirements: For master's, thesis, teaching experience. *Entrance requirements:* For master's, PRAXIS I, minimum GPA of 3.0, sample of written work, recommendation letters. Additional exam requirements/recommendations for international students: Required—TOEFL (minimum score 600 paper-based; 250 computer-based; 100 iBT), IELTS (minimum score 6.5), TWE. *Application deadline:* For fall admission, 5/1 priority date for domestic and international students; for spring admission, 10/15 priority date for domestic and international students. Applications are processed on a rolling basis. Application fee: $45. Electronic applications accepted. *Financial support:* Career-related internships or fieldwork available. Financial award applicants required to submit FAFSA. *Faculty research:* Gifted education, environmental education, technology in education, writing as learning, class size and achievement. *Unit head:* Dr. Barbara Biglan, Interim Director, 412-365-1170, E-mail: biglan@chatham.edu. *Application contact:* Dory Perry, Associate Director of Graduate Admissions, 412-365-2758, Fax: 412-365-1609, E-mail: gradadmissions@chatham.edu.

Christopher Newport University, Graduate Studies, Department of Teacher Preparation, Newport News, VA 23606-2998. Offers art (PK-12) (MAT); biology (6-12) (MAT); computer science (6-12) (MAT); elementary (PK-6) (MAT); English (6-12) (MAT); French (PK-12) (MAT); history and social science (6-12) (MAT); mathematics (6-12) (MAT); music (PK-12) (MAT), including choral, instrumental; physics (6-12) (MAT); Spanish (PK-12) (MAT). Part-time and evening/weekend programs available. *Faculty:* 24 full-time (13 women), 4 part-time/adjunct (2 women). *Students:* 76 full-time (66 women), 12 part-time (10 women); includes 3 minority (2 African Americans, 1 Hispanic American). Average age 24. 3 applicants, 100% accepted, 2 enrolled. In 2009, 58 master's awarded. *Degree requirements:* For master's, comprehensive exam, thesis or alternative. *Entrance requirements:* For master's, PRAXIS I, minimum GPA of 3.0. Additional exam requirements/recommendations for international students: Required—TOEFL (minimum score 580 paper-based; 237 computer-based; 92 iBT). *Application deadline:* For fall admission, 8/15 for domestic students, 4/1 for international students; for spring admission, 10/15 for domestic students, 10/1 for international students. Applications are processed on a rolling basis. Application fee: $45. Electronic applications accepted. *Expenses:* Tuition, area resident: Part-time $384 per credit hour. Tuition, state resident: part-time $384 per credit hour. Tuition, nonresident: part-time $701 per credit hour. *Financial support:* In 2009–10, 3 research assistantships with full and partial tuition reimbursements (averaging $2,000 per year) were awarded; career-related internships or fieldwork, Federal Work-Study, and unspecified assistantships also available. Support available to part-time students. Financial award application deadline: 3/1; financial award applicants required to submit FAFSA. *Faculty research:* Early literacy development, instructional innovations, professional teaching standards, multicultural issues, aesthetic education. *Unit head:* Dr. Marsha Sprague, Director, 757-594-7388, Fax: 757-594-7803, E-mail: msprague@cnu.edu. *Application contact:* Lyn Sawyer, Associate Director, Graduate Admissions, 757-594-7544, Fax: 757-594-7649, E-mail: gradstdy@cnu.edu.

The Citadel, The Military College of South Carolina, Citadel Graduate College, Department of Mathematics and Computer Science, Charleston, SC 29409. Offers computer and information science (MS); mathematics education (MAE). *Accreditation:* NCATE (one or more programs are accredited). Part-time and evening/weekend programs available. *Faculty:* 3 full-time (0 women), 1 part-time/adjunct (0 women). *Students:* 1 (woman) full-time, 18 part-time (8 women); includes 1 minority (Asian American or Pacific Islander). Average age 35. In 2009, 3 master's awarded. *Degree requirements:* For master's, comprehensive exam (for some programs), thesis (for some programs). *Entrance requirements:* For master's, GRE (minimum score 1000 for MS; minimum score 900 verbal and quantitative for MAT, raw score of 396), minimum undergraduate GPA of 3.0 (MS) or 2.5 (MAT); competency, demonstrated through coursework, approved work experience, or a program-administrated competency exam, in the areas of basic computer architecture, object-oriented programming, discrete mathematics, and data structures (MS); successful completion of 7 courses (MAT). Additional exam requirements/recommendations for international students: Required—TOEFL (minimum score 550 paper-based; 213 computer-based; 79 iBT). *Application deadline:* Applications are processed on a rolling basis. Application fee: $30. Electronic applications accepted. *Expenses:* Tuition, state resident: part-time $400 per credit hour. Tuition, nonresident: part-time $657 per credit hour. Required fees: $40 per term. *Financial support:* Health care benefits and unspecified assistantships available. Support available to part-time students. Financial award application deadline: 7/1; financial award applicants required to submit FAFSA. *Unit head:* Dr. John I. Moore, Department Head, 843-953-5048, Fax: 843-953-7391, E-mail: john.moore@citadel.edu. *Application contact:* Dr. George L. Rudolph, Computer and Information Science Program Director, 843-953-5032, Fax: 843-953-7391, E-mail: george.rudolph@citadel.edu.

The Citadel, The Military College of South Carolina, Citadel Graduate College, School of Education, Program in Secondary Education, Charleston, SC 29409. Offers biology (MAT); English language arts (MAT); mathematics (MAT); social studies (MAT). *Accreditation:* NCATE. Part-time and evening/weekend programs available. *Faculty:* 12 full-time (7 women), 8 part-time/adjunct (5 women). *Students:* 27 full-time (18 women), 62 part-time (37 women); includes 15 minority (11 African Americans, 2 Asian Americans or Pacific Islanders, 2 Hispanic Americans). Average age 29. In 2009, 22 master's awarded. *Degree requirements:* For master's, comprehensive exam, internship. *Entrance requirements:* For master's, GRE (minimum score 900) or MAT (minimum score 396), minimum undergraduate GPA of 2.5. Additional exam requirements/recommendations for international students: Required—TOEFL (minimum score 550 paper-based; 213 computer-based). *Application deadline:* Applications are processed on a rolling basis. Application fee: $30. Electronic applications accepted. *Expenses:* Tuition, state resident: part-time $400 per credit hour. Tuition, nonresident: part-time $657 per credit hour. Required fees: $40 per term. *Financial support:* Career-related internships or fieldwork, health care benefits, and unspecified assistantships available. Support available to part-time students. Financial award application deadline: 7/1; financial award applicants required to submit FAFSA. *Unit head:* Dr. Kathryn A. Richardson-Jones, Coordinator, 843-953-3163, Fax: 843-953-7258, E-mail: kathryn.jones@citadel.edu. *Application contact:* Dr. Steve A. Nida, Associate Provost, The Citadel Graduate College, 843-953-5089, Fax: 843-953-7630, E-mail: cgc@citadel.edu.

City College of the City University of New York, Graduate School, School of Education, Department of Secondary Education, New York, NY 10031-9198. Offers adolescent mathematics education (MA, AC); English education (MA); middle school mathematics education (MS); science education (MA); social studies education (AC). *Accreditation:* NCATE. *Entrance requirements:* For master's, Liberal Arts and Sciences Test (LAST), Content Specialty Test (CST). Additional exam requirements/recommendations for international students: Required—TOEFL. *Expenses:* Tuition, state resident: part-time $310 per credit. Tuition, nonresident: part-time $575 per credit. Tuition and fees vary according to course load and program.

Clayton State University, School of Graduate Studies, Program in Education, Morrow, GA 30260-0285. Offers English (MAT); mathematics (MAT). *Accreditation:* NCATE. *Students:* 6 full-time (3 women), 2 part-time (1 woman); includes 2 African Americans, 1 international. Average age 24. 16 applicants, 56% accepted, 7 enrolled. *Application deadline:* For fall admission, 7/15 for domestic students, 5/1 for international students; for spring admission, 4/15 for domestic students, 2/1 for international students. Application fee: $50. *Unit head:* Dr. Ruth Caillouet, Program Coordinator, Master of Arts in Teaching English, 678-466-4735, Fax: 678-466-4899, E-mail: ruthcaillouet@clayton.edu. *Application contact:* Melanie Nolan, Administrative Assistant, Master of Arts in Teaching English, 678-466-4735, Fax: 678-466-4899, E-mail: melanienolan@clayton.edu.

Clemson University, Graduate School, College of Health, Education, and Human Development, School of Education, Program in Secondary Education, Clemson, SC 29634. Offers English (M Ed); mathematics (M Ed); natural sciences (M Ed); social studies (M Ed). *Accreditation:* NCATE. *Students:* 5 full-time (3 women), 4 part-time (2 women); includes 2 minority (1 Asian American or Pacific Islander, 1 Hispanic American), 2 international. Average age 29. 11 applicants, 82% accepted, 4 enrolled. In 2009, 2 master's awarded. *Entrance requirements:* For master's, GRE General Test, teaching certificate. Additional exam requirements/recommendations for international students: Required—TOEFL. *Application deadline:* Applications are processed on a rolling basis. Application fee: $70 ($80 for international students). Electronic applications accepted. *Expenses:* Contact institution. *Financial support:* In 2009–10, 2 students received support. Career-related internships or fieldwork, institutionally sponsored loans, scholarships/grants, health care benefits, and unspecified assistantships available. Support available to part-time students. Financial award application deadline: 6/1; financial award applicants required to submit FAFSA. *Unit head:* Dr. Michael J. Padilla, Director/Associate Dean, 864-656-4444, Fax: 864-656-0311, E-mail: padilla@clemson.edu. *Application contact:* Dr. David Fleming, Graduate Coordinator, 864-656-1881, Fax: 864-656-0311, E-mail: dflemin@clemson.edu.

Cleveland State University, College of Graduate Studies, College of Education and Human Services, Department of Teacher Education, Cleveland, OH 44115. Offers art education (M Ed); early childhood education (M Ed); foreign language education (M Ed); mathematics and science education (M Ed); middle childhood education (M Ed); special education (M Ed), including mild/moderate disabilities, moderate/intensive disabilities; teaching English to speakers of other languages (M Ed). Part-time and evening/weekend programs available. *Degree requirements:* For master's, comprehensive exam (for some programs), thesis or alternative. *Entrance requirements:* For master's, GRE General Test or MAT, minimum GPA of 2.75. Additional exam requirements/recommendations for international students: Required—TOEFL (minimum score 525 paper-based; 197 computer-based), IELTS (minimum score 6). *Faculty research:* Early literacy, professional development in reading, reading recovery, dual language, induction programs.

The College at Brockport, State University of New York, School of Education and Human Services, Department of Education and Human Development, Program in Adolescence Education, Brockport, NY 14420-2997. Offers adolescence biology education (MS Ed); adolescence chemistry education (MS Ed); adolescence earth science education (MS Ed); adolescence English education (MS Ed); adolescence mathematics education (MS Ed); adolescence physics education (MS Ed); adolescence social studies education (MS Ed). *Accreditation:* NCATE. Part-time programs available. *Students:* 10 full-time (6 women), 98 part-time (60 women); includes 1 minority (African American). 15 applicants, 67% accepted, 8 enrolled. In 2009, 60 master's awarded. *Degree requirements:* For master's, thesis or alternative. *Entrance requirements:* For master's, minimum GPA of 3.0, letters of recommendation. Additional exam requirements/recommendations for international students: Required—TOEFL (minimum score 550 paper-based; 213 computer-based; 79 iBT). *Application deadline:* For fall admission, 2/15 priority date for domestic and international students; for spring admission, 9/15 priority date for domestic and international students. Application fee: $80. Electronic applications accepted. *Expenses:* Tuition, state resident: full-time $8370; part-time $349 per credit. Tuition, nonresident: full-time $13,250; part-time $522 per credit. *Financial support:* Federal Work-Study, scholarships/grants, and unspecified assistantships available. Support available to part-time students. Financial award application deadline: 3/15; financial award applicants required to submit FAFSA. *Unit head:* Dr. Sue Novinger, Chairperson, 585-395-2205, Fax: 585-395-2172, E-mail: snovinge@brockport.edu. *Application contact:* Coordinator of Certification and Graduate Advisement.

The College at Brockport, State University of New York, School of Education and Human Services, Department of Education and Human Development, Program in Alternate Adolescence Inclusive Education, Brockport, NY 14420-2997. Offers alternate adolescence English inclusive education (MS Ed); alternate adolescence mathematics inclusive education (MS Ed); alternate adolescence science inclusive education (MS Ed); alternate adolescence social studies inclusive education (MS Ed). *Students:* 25 full-time (8 women), 5 part-time (3 women). 26 applicants, 50% accepted, 11 enrolled. *Degree requirements:* For master's, thesis or alternative. *Entrance requirements:* For master's, minimum GPA of 3.0, letters of recommendation, statement of objectives, academic major (or equivalent) in program discipline. Additional exam requirements/recommendations for international students: Required—TOEFL (minimum score 550 paper-based; 213 computer-based; 79 iBT). *Application deadline:* For fall admission, 2/15 priority date for domestic and international students; for spring admission, 9/15 priority date for domestic and international students. Application fee: $80. Electronic applications accepted. *Expenses:* Tuition, state resident: full-time $8370; part-time $349 per credit. Tuition, nonresident: full-time $13,250; part-time $522 per credit. *Financial support:* Federal Work-Study, scholarships/grants, and unspecified assistantships available. Support available to part-time students. Financial award application deadline: 3/15; financial award applicants required to submit FAFSA. *Unit head:* Dr. Sue Novinger, Chairperson, 585-395-2205, E-mail: snovinge@brockport.edu. *Application contact:* Coordinator of Certification and Graduate Advisement.

College of Charleston, Graduate School, School of Education, Health, and Human Performance, Program in Science and Mathematics for Teachers, Charleston, SC 29424-0001. Offers M Ed. *Accreditation:* NCATE. *Faculty:* 5 full-time (4 women). *Students:* 5 full-time (3 women), 17 part-time (16 women); includes 3 minority (2 African Americans, 1 Hispanic American), 1 international. Average age 29. 10 applicants, 70% accepted, 7 enrolled. In 2009, 6 master's awarded. *Degree requirements:* For master's, capstone project. *Entrance requirements:* For master's, GRE or PRAXIS, 2 letters of recommendation, copy of teaching certificate. Additional exam requirements/recommendations for international students: Required—TOEFL. *Application deadline:* For fall admission, 4/1 for domestic students; for spring admission, 11/1 for domestic students. Application fee: $45. Electronic applications accepted. *Financial support:* In 2009–10, research assistantships (averaging $12,400 per year), teaching assistantships (averaging $13,300 per year) were awarded; scholarships/grants and unspecified assistantships also available. Financial award applicants required to submit FAFSA. *Unit head:* Dr. Gary Harrison, Director, 843-953-5734, E-mail: harrisong@cofc.edu. *Application contact:* Susan Hallatt, Director of Graduate Admissions, 843-953-5614, Fax: 843-953-1434, E-mail: hallatts@cofc.edu.

The College of William and Mary, School of Education, Program in Curriculum and Instruction, Williamsburg, VA 23187-8795. Offers elementary education (MA Ed); gifted education (MA Ed); math specialist (MA Ed); reading education (MA Ed); secondary education (MA Ed), including English education, mathematics education, modern foreign languages education, science education, social studies education; special education (MA Ed), including general curriculum, resource collaborating teaching. *Accreditation:* NCATE. Part-time programs available. *Faculty:* 18 full-time (12 women), 17 part-time/adjunct (15 women). *Students:* 54 full-time (45 women), 12 part-time (all women); includes 3 minority (2 African Americans, 1 Asian American or Pacific Islander), 2 international. Average age 27. 120 applicants, 75% accepted. In 2009, 70 master's awarded. *Degree requirements:* For master's, project. *Entrance requirements:* For master's, GRE or MAT, minimum GPA of 2.5. Additional exam requirements/recommendations for international students: Required—TOEFL. *Application deadline:* For fall admission, 1/15 for domestic and international students; for spring admission, 10/1 for domestic and international students. Application fee: $45. Electronic applications accepted. *Expenses:* Tuition, state resident: full-time $6400; part-time $315 per credit hour. Tuition, nonresident: full-time $19,720; part-time $840 per credit hour. Required fees: $4114. *Financial support:* In 2009–10, 30 students received support, including 10 research assistantships with full and partial tuition reimbursements available (averaging $5,500 per year); career-related internships or fieldwork, Federal Work-Study, institutionally sponsored loans, scholarships/grants, and unspecified assistantships also available. Financial award application deadline: 1/15; financial award applicants required to submit FAFSA. *Faculty research:* National Council of Teachers of Mathematics Standards, counseling, self-concept and self-esteem, special education, curriculum development. *Unit head:* Dr. C. Denise Johnson, Area Coordinator, 757-221-1528, E-mail: cdjohn@wm.edu. *Application contact:* Dorothy Smith Osborne, Director of Admissions, 757-221-2317, Fax: 757-221-2293, E-mail: dsosbo@wm.edu.

The Colorado College, Department of Education, Program in Secondary Education, Colorado Springs, CO 80903-3294. Offers art teaching (K-12) (MAT); English teaching (MAT); foreign language teaching (MAT); mathematics teaching (MAT); music teaching (MAT); science teaching (MAT); social studies teaching (MAT). *Faculty:* 3 full-time (2 women), 8 part-time/adjunct (6 women). *Students:* 15 full-time (5 women); includes 2 minority (1 American Indian/Alaska Native, 1 Asian American or Pacific Islander). Average age 27. 26 applicants, 81% accepted, 15 enrolled. In 2009, 17 master's awarded. *Degree requirements:* For master's, thesis, internship. *Entrance requirements:* For master's, PRAXIS II or PLACE Exam. *Application deadline:* For

Mathematics Education

The Colorado College (continued)
fall admission, 12/1 priority date for domestic students, 12/1 for international students. Applications are processed on a rolling basis. Application fee: $50. *Expenses:* Tuition: Part-time $2545 per credit. *Financial support:* In 2009–10, 15 students received support, including 7 teaching assistantships (averaging $16,000 per year); career-related internships or fieldwork, institutionally sponsored loans, health care benefits, and tuition waivers (partial) also available. Financial award application deadline: 2/15; financial award applicants required to submit FAFSA. *Unit head:* Mike Taber, Director, 719-389-6026, Fax: 719-389-6473, E-mail: mike.taber@coloradocollege.edu. *Application contact:* Debra Yazulla Mortenson, Education Services Manager, 719-389-6472, Fax: 719-389-6473, E-mail: debra.mortenson@coloradocollege.edu.

Columbus State University, Graduate Studies, College of Education and Health Professions, Department of Teacher Education, Columbus, GA 31907-5645. Offers accomplished teaching (M Ed); early childhood education (M Ed, Ed S); health administration (MPA); instructional technology (MS); middle grades education (M Ed, Ed S); physical education (M Ed); secondary education (M Ed, MAT, Ed S), including English/language arts (M Ed, Ed S), general science (M Ed), mathematics (M Ed), social science (M Ed); special education (M Ed), including behavior disorders, mental retardation. *Accreditation:* NCATE. Part-time and evening/weekend programs available. Postbaccalaureate distance learning degree programs offered (minimal on-campus study). *Faculty:* 18 full-time (15 women), 14 part-time/adjunct (10 women). *Students:* 146 full-time (113 women), 312 part-time (261 women); includes 142 minority (120 African Americans, 1 American Indian/Alaska Native, 8 Asian Americans or Pacific Islanders, 13 Hispanic Americans), 2 international. Average age 31. 248 applicants, 64% accepted, 114 enrolled. In 2009, 103 master's, 22 other advanced degrees awarded. *Degree requirements:* For master's, thesis, exit exam; for Ed S, thesis or alternative. *Entrance requirements:* For master's, GRE General Test, minimum GPA of 2.75; for Ed S, GRE General Test. Additional exam requirements/recommendations for international students: Required—TOEFL (minimum score 550 paper-based; 213 computer-based; 79 iBT). *Application deadline:* For fall admission, 5/1 priority date for domestic students, 5/1 for international students; for spring admission, 11/1 for domestic and international students. Applications are processed on a rolling basis. Application fee: $30. Electronic applications accepted. *Financial support:* In 2009–10, 305 students received support, including 36 research assistantships with partial tuition reimbursements available (averaging $3,000 per year); career-related internships or fieldwork, Federal Work-Study, institutionally sponsored loans, scholarships/grants, tuition waivers (partial), and unspecified assistantships also available. Support available to part-time students. Financial award application deadline: 5/1; financial award applicants required to submit FAFSA. *Unit head:* Dr. Deborah Gober, Acting Chair, 706-568-2255, Fax: 706-568-3134, E-mail: gober_deborah@colstate.edu. *Application contact:* Katie Thornton, Graduate Admissions Specialist, 706-568-2035, Fax: 706-568-2462, E-mail: thornton_katie@colstate.edu.

Concordia University, School of Graduate Studies, Faculty of Arts and Science, Department of Mathematics and Statistics, Montréal, QC H3G 1M8, Canada. Offers mathematics (M Sc, MA, PhD); teaching of mathematics (MTM). *Degree requirements:* For master's, thesis optional; for doctorate, comprehensive exam, thesis/dissertation. *Entrance requirements:* For master's, honors degree in mathematics or equivalent. *Faculty research:* Number theory, computational algebra, mathematical physics, differential geometry, dynamical systems and statistics.

Converse College, School of Education and Graduate Studies, Program in Secondary Education, Spartanburg, SC 29302-0006. Offers biology (MAT); chemistry (MAT); English (M Ed, MAT); mathematics (M Ed, MAT); natural sciences (M Ed); social sciences (M Ed, MAT). Part-time programs available. *Degree requirements:* For master's, capstone paper. *Entrance requirements:* For master's, NTE or PRAXIS II (M Ed), minimum GPA of 2.75, 2 recommendations. Electronic applications accepted.

Cornell University, Graduate School, Graduate Fields of Agriculture and Life Sciences, Field of Education, Ithaca, NY 14853-0001. Offers agricultural education (MAT); biology (7-12) (MAT); chemistry (7-12) (MAT); curriculum and instruction (MPS, MS, PhD); earth science (7-12) (MAT); extension and adult education (MPS, MS, PhD); mathematics (7-12) (MAT); physics (7-12) (MAT). *Faculty:* 26 full-time (9 women). *Students:* 65 full-time (50 women); includes 15 minority (4 African Americans, 7 Asian Americans or Pacific Islanders, 4 Hispanic Americans), 2 international. Average age 34. 96 applicants, 33% accepted, 21 enrolled. In 2009, 27 master's, 2 doctorates awarded. Terminal master's awarded for partial completion of doctoral program. *Degree requirements:* For master's, thesis (MS); for doctorate, comprehensive exam, thesis/dissertation. *Entrance requirements:* For master's and doctorate, GRE General Test, sample of written work (recommended), 2 letters of recommendation. Additional exam requirements/recommendations for international students: Required—TOEFL (minimum score 550 paper-based; 213 computer-based; 77 iBT). *Application deadline:* For fall admission, 2/15 for domestic students. Application fee: $70. Electronic applications accepted. *Expenses:* Tuition: Full-time $29,500. Required fees: $70. Full-time tuition and fees vary according to degree level, program and student level. *Financial support:* In 2009–10, 33 students received support, including 3 fellowships with full tuition reimbursements available, 5 teaching assistantships with full tuition reimbursements available; research assistantships with full tuition reimbursements available, institutionally sponsored loans, scholarships/grants, health care benefits, tuition waivers (full and partial), and unspecified assistantships also available. Financial award applicants required to submit FAFSA. *Faculty research:* Moral development and professional ethics; public issues education and community development; socio/political issues in public education; teacher education and curriculum in agricultural science, and mathematics; extension research. *Unit head:* Director of Graduate Studies, 607-255-4278, Fax: 607-255-7905. *Application contact:* Graduate Field Assistant, 607-255-4278, Fax: 607-255-7905, E-mail: rh22@cornell.edu.

Delaware State University, Graduate Programs, Department of Mathematics, Program in Mathematics Education, Dover, DE 19901-2277. Offers MS. *Entrance requirements:* Additional exam requirements/recommendations for international students: Required—TOEFL (minimum score 550 paper-based). Electronic applications accepted.

Delta State University, Graduate Programs, College of Arts and Sciences, Department of Mathematics, Cleveland, MS 38733-0001. Offers mathematics education (M Ed). Part-time programs available. *Degree requirements:* For master's, thesis or alternative. *Expenses:* Tuition, state resident: full-time $4450; part-time $247 per credit hour. Tuition, nonresident: full-time $11,520; part-time $640 per credit hour.

DePaul University, College of Liberal Arts and Sciences, Department of Mathematical Sciences, Chicago, IL 60614. Offers applied mathematics (MS), including actuarial science or statistics; applied statistics (MS, Certificate); mathematics education (MA). Part-time and evening/weekend programs available. *Faculty:* 23 full-time (6 women), 18 part-time/adjunct (5 women). *Students:* 117 full-time (64 women), 67 part-time (37 women); includes 47 minority (22 African Americans, 15 Asian Americans or Pacific Islanders, 10 Hispanic Americans), 13 international. Average age 30. 40 applicants, 100% accepted. In 2009, 30 master's awarded. *Degree requirements:* For master's, comprehensive exam. *Entrance requirements:* Additional exam requirements/recommendations for international students: Required—TOEFL. *Application deadline:* For fall admission, 7/30 for domestic students, 6/30 for international students; for winter admission, 11/30 for domestic students, 10/31 for international students; for spring admission, 2/15 for domestic students. Applications are processed on a rolling basis. Application fee: $25. *Expenses:* Tuition: Full-time $37,525; part-time $620 per credit hour. *Financial support:* In 2009–10, 12 students received support, including research assistantships with partial tuition reimbursements available (averaging $6,000 per year); teaching assistantships, tuition waivers (full) also available. Financial award application deadline: 4/30. *Faculty research:* Verbally prime algebras, enveloping algebras of Lie, superalgebras and related rings, harmonic analysis, estimation theory. *Unit head:* Dr. Ahmed I. Zayed, Chairperson, 773-325-7806, Fax: 773-325-7807, E-mail: azayed@depaul.edu. *Application contact:* Ann Spittle, Director of Graduate Admissions, 312-362-8300, Fax: 312-362-5749, E-mail: admitdpu@depaul.edu.

DeSales University, Graduate Division, Program in Education, Center Valley, PA 18034-9568. Offers elementary education (M Ed); instructional technology for K-12 (M Ed); interdisciplinary

(M Ed); mathematics (M Ed); special education (M Ed); TESOL/ESL (M Ed). Part-time and evening/weekend programs available. Postbaccalaureate distance learning degree programs offered (no on-campus study). *Students:* 218 part-time. *Degree requirements:* For master's, thesis project. *Entrance requirements:* For master's, teaching certificate. Additional exam requirements/recommendations for international students: Required—TOEFL. *Application deadline:* Applications are processed on a rolling basis. Application fee: $35. Electronic applications accepted. *Expenses:* Tuition: Full-time $17,500; part-time $665 per credit. Full-time tuition and fees vary according to program. Part-time tuition and fees vary according to course load. *Financial support:* Application deadline: 5/1. *Faculty research:* Effective teaching, computer interfacing in chemistry labs, computer applications to teaching, history of philosophy, aesthetics multidrug-resistant cancer. *Unit head:* Dr. Lujean Baab, Director, 610-282-1100 Ext. 1739, Fax: 610-282-3734, E-mail: lujean.baab@desales.edu. *Application contact:* Caryn Stopper, Director of Graduate Admissions, 610-282-1100 Ext. 1768, Fax: 610-282-0525, E-mail: caryn.stopper@desales.edu.

Drew University, Caspersen School of Graduate Studies, Program in Education, Madison, NJ 07940-1493. Offers biology (MAT); chemistry (MAT); English (MAT); French (MAT); Italian (MAT); math (MAT); physics (MAT); social studies (MAT); Spanish (MAT); theatre arts (MAT). Part-time programs available. *Students:* 21 full-time (10 women), 6 part-time (2 women); includes 1 minority (Hispanic American). Average age 24. 40 applicants, 90% accepted, 27 enrolled. In 2009, 13 master's awarded. *Entrance requirements:* For master's, transcripts, personal statement, recommendations. Additional exam requirements/recommendations for international students: Required—TOEFL, TWE. *Application deadline:* For fall admission, 2/1 priority date for domestic students. Applications are processed on a rolling basis. Application fee: $35. *Expenses:* Contact institution. *Financial support:* In 2009–10, 22 students received support. Federal Work-Study, scholarships/grants, and tuition waivers (partial) available. Support available to part-time students. Financial award application deadline: 2/15; financial award applicants required to submit FAFSA. *Unit head:* Dr. Ross Danis. *Application contact:* Carla J. Burns, Director of Graduate Admissions, 973-408-3110, Fax: 973-408-3242, E-mail: gradm@drew.edu.

Drury University, Graduate Programs in Education, Springfield, MO 65802. Offers elementary education (M Ed); gifted education (M Ed); human services (M Ed); instructional mathematics K-8 (M Ed); instructional technology (M Ed); middle school teaching (M Ed); secondary education (M Ed); special education (M Ed); special reading (M Ed). *Accreditation:* NCATE. Part-time and evening/weekend programs available. *Degree requirements:* For master's, thesis. *Entrance requirements:* For master's, GRE or MAT, minimum GPA of 2.75. Additional exam requirements/recommendations for international students: Required—TOEFL. Electronic applications accepted. *Faculty research:* Cultural enrichment, research skills, parental involvement relating to reading skills, reading strategies for mainstreaming children.

Duquesne University, School of Education, Department of Instruction and Leadership, Program in Secondary Education, Pittsburgh, PA 15282-0001. Offers secondary education (MS Ed), including biology, chemistry, English, Latin, math, physics, social studies, Spanish. Part-time and evening/weekend programs available. *Faculty:* 4 full-time (3 women), 1 part-time/adjunct (0 women). *Students:* 56 full-time (34 women), 8 part-time (3 women); includes 6 minority (3 African Americans, 2 Asian Americans or Pacific Islanders, 1 Hispanic American), 2 international. Average age 29. 69 applicants, 70% accepted, 27 enrolled. In 2009, 36 master's awarded. *Degree requirements:* For master's, thesis optional. *Entrance requirements:* For master's, MAT, minimum GPA of 3.0. Additional exam requirements/recommendations for international students: Required—TOEFL (minimum score 550 paper-based; 80 computer-based). *Application deadline:* For fall admission, 8/1 for domestic students; for spring admission, 12/1 for domestic students. Applications are processed on a rolling basis. Application fee: $0. Electronic applications accepted. *Expenses:* Tuition: Part-time $851 per credit. Required fees: $81 per credit. *Financial support:* Research assistantships, Federal Work-Study available. Support available to part-time students. *Unit head:* Dr. Melissa Boston, Assistant Professor, 412-396-6109, E-mail: bostonm@duq.edu. *Application contact:* Michael Dolinger, Director of Student and Academic Services, 412-396-6647, Fax: 412-396-5585, E-mail: dolingerm@duq.edu.

East Carolina University, Graduate School, College of Education, Department of Mathematics and Science Education, Greenville, NC 27858-4353. Offers mathematics (MA Ed); science education (MA, MA Ed). Part-time and evening/weekend programs available. *Degree requirements:* For master's, comprehensive exam, thesis optional. *Entrance requirements:* For master's, GRE General Test or MAT, interview, minimum GPA of 2.5, bachelor's degree in related field, teaching license (MA Ed). Additional exam requirements/recommendations for international students: Required—TOEFL.

Eastern Illinois University, Graduate School, College of Sciences, Department of Mathematics and Computer Science, Charleston, IL 61920-3099. Offers mathematics (MA); mathematics education (MA). *Faculty:* 30 full-time (6 women). In 2009, 9 master's awarded. *Entrance requirements:* For master's, GRE General Test. *Application deadline:* For fall admission, 3/31 priority date for domestic students. Applications are processed on a rolling basis. Application fee: $30. *Expenses:* Tuition, state resident: full-time $9434; part-time $239 per credit hour. Tuition, nonresident: full-time $23,774; part-time $717 per credit hour. Required fees: $802.63. *Financial support:* In 2009–10, research assistantships with tuition reimbursements (averaging $8,100 per year), 8 teaching assistantships with tuition reimbursements (averaging $8,100 per year) were awarded. *Unit head:* Dr. Peter Andrews, Chair, 217-581-6275, Fax: 217-581-6284, E-mail: pgandrews@eiu.edu. *Application contact:* Dr. Keith Wolcott, Coordinator, 217-581-6279, Fax: 217-581-6284, E-mail: kwolcott@eiu.edu.

Eastern Kentucky University, The Graduate School, College of Education, Department of Curriculum and Instruction, Program in Secondary and Higher Education, Richmond, KY 40475-3102. Offers secondary education (MA Ed), including agricultural education, art education, biological sciences education, business education, English education, geography education, history education, home economics education, industrial education, mathematical sciences education, physical education, school health education. *Accreditation:* NCATE. Part-time programs available. *Entrance requirements:* For master's, GRE General Test, minimum GPA of 2.5.

Eastern Michigan University, Graduate School, College of Arts and Sciences, Department of Mathematics, Ypsilanti, MI 48197. Offers applied statistics (MA); computer science (MA); mathematics (MA); mathematics education (MA). Part-time and evening/weekend programs available. Postbaccalaureate distance learning degree programs offered (minimal on-campus study). *Faculty:* 25 full-time (10 women). *Students:* 11 full-time (7 women), 39 part-time (17 women); includes 2 minority (1 African American, 1 Asian American or Pacific Islander), 11 international. Average age 35. 28 applicants, 75% accepted, 14 enrolled. In 2009, 15 master's awarded. *Degree requirements:* For master's, thesis optional. *Entrance requirements:* Additional exam requirements/recommendations for international students: Required—TOEFL. *Application deadline:* Applications are processed on a rolling basis. Application fee: $35. Tuition and fees vary according to course level. *Financial support:* Fellowships, research assistantships with full tuition reimbursements, teaching assistantships with full tuition reimbursements, career-related internships or fieldwork, Federal Work-Study, institutionally sponsored loans, scholarships/grants, tuition waivers (partial), and unspecified assistantships available. Support available to part-time students. Financial award applicants required to submit FAFSA. *Unit head:* Dr. Christopher Gardiner, Interim Department Head, 734-487-1444, Fax: 734-487-2489, E-mail: cgardiner@emich.edu. *Application contact:* Dr. Bingwu Wang, Graduate Coordinator, 734-487-5044, Fax: 734-487-2489, E-mail: bwang@emich.edu.

Eastern Washington University, Graduate Studies, College of Science, Health and Engineering, Department of Mathematics, Cheney, WA 99004-2431. Offers mathematics (MS); teaching mathematics (MA). *Accreditation:* NCATE. Part-time programs available. *Degree requirements:* For master's, comprehensive exam, thesis (for some programs). *Entrance requirements:* For master's, GRE General Test, departmental qualifying exam, minimum GPA of 3.0. *Expenses:* Tuition, state resident: full-time $7476; part-time $249 per quarter hour.

Tuition, nonresident: full-time $18,030; part-time $601 per quarter hour. Required fees: $3.50 per quarter hour. $142 per quarter.

The Evergreen State College, Graduate Programs, Program in Curriculum and Instruction, Olympia, WA 98505. Offers English as a second language (M Ed); mathematics (M Ed). *Faculty:* 2 full-time (both women). *Students:* 40 part-time (30 women); includes 5 minority (1 African American, 1 American Indian/Alaska Native, 2 Asian Americans or Pacific Islanders, 1 Hispanic American). Average age 42. 23 applicants, 100% accepted, 17 enrolled. *Degree requirements:* For master's, research paper and presentation, passing score on WEST-E (math or ELL). *Entrance requirements:* For master's, bachelor's degree with 4-quarter/3-semester credits in child/adolescent development, lifespan development or another human development course covering the cognitive, affective, and psychological components of individuals; minimum GPA of 3.0 in last 90 quarter/60 semester credits; 1 year classroom teaching experience (preferred). *Application deadline:* For fall admission, 3/29 priority date for domestic and international students. Applications are processed on a rolling basis. Application fee: $50. Electronic applications accepted. *Expenses:* Contact institution. *Financial support:* In 2009–10, 1 student received support, including 1 fellowship (averaging $2,250 per year); scholarships/grants and tuition waivers (partial) also available. Financial award application deadline: 3/15; financial award applicants required to submit FAFSA. *Faculty research:* Multicultural education, bilingual education, ELL, qualitative research methodologies, critical theory, education leadership policy, math and science education. *Unit head:* Sherry Walton, Director, 360-867-6856, Fax: 360-867-6575, E-mail: adairl@evergreen.edu. *Application contact:* Lynne Adair, Program Coordinator, 360-867-6639, Fax: 360-867-6575, E-mail: adairl@evergreen.edu.

Florida Agricultural and Mechanical University, Division of Graduate Studies, Research, and Continuing Education, College of Education, Program in Secondary Education and Foundation, Tallahassee, FL 32307-3200. Offers biology (M Ed); chemistry (MS Ed); English (MS Ed); history (MS Ed); math (MS Ed); physics (MS Ed). *Accreditation:* NCATE. *Faculty:* 10 full-time (5 women). In 2009, 28 master's awarded. *Degree requirements:* For master's, thesis (for some programs). *Entrance requirements:* For master's, GRE General Test, minimum GPA of 3.0. Additional exam requirements/recommendations for international students: Required—TOEFL. *Application deadline:* For fall admission, 5/18 for domestic students, 12/18 for international students; for spring admission, 11/12 for domestic students, 5/12 for international students. Application fee: $20. *Unit head:* Dr. Bernadette Kelley, Chairperson, 850-599-3123. *Application contact:* Dr. Chanta M. Haywood, Dean of Graduate Studies, Research, and Continuing Education, 850-599-3315, Fax: 850-599-3727.

Florida Institute of Technology, Graduate Programs, College of Science, Department of Science and Mathematics Education, Melbourne, FL 32901-6975. Offers computer education (MS); elementary science education (M Ed); environmental education (MS); informal science education (M Ed); mathematics education (MS, Ed D, PhD, Ed S); science education (MS, Ed D, PhD, Ed S); teaching (MAT). Part-time and evening/weekend programs available. *Faculty:* 4 full-time (1 woman), 3 part-time/adjunct (2 women). *Students:* 15 full-time (9 women), 18 part-time (12 women); includes 5 minority (2 African Americans, 3 Hispanic Americans), 5 international. Average age 36. 42 applicants, 52% accepted, 7 enrolled. In 2009, 3 master's, 1 doctorate, 1 other advanced degree awarded. Terminal master's awarded for partial completion of doctoral program. *Degree requirements:* For master's, comprehensive exam (for some programs), thesis (for some programs), oral final exam; for doctorate, comprehensive exam, thesis/dissertation, oral defense of dissertation; for Ed S, comprehensive exam. *Entrance requirements:* For master's, minimum GPA of 3.0, resume, 3 letters of recommendation (elementary science education); for doctorate, minimum GPA of 3.2, resume, 3 letters of recommendation, statement of objectives, 3 years teaching experience (recommended); for Ed S, minimum GPA of 3.0, resume, 3 letters of recommendation, statement of objectives. Additional exam requirements/recommendations for international students: Required—TOEFL (minimum score 550 paper-based; 213 computer-based; 79 iBT). *Application deadline:* For fall admission, 4/1 for international students; for spring admission, 9/30 for international students. Applications are processed on a rolling basis. Application fee: $50. Electronic applications accepted. *Expenses:* Tuition: Part-time $1015 per credit. Tuition and fees vary according to campus/location and program. *Financial support:* In 2009–10, 3 students received support, including 3 teaching assistantships with full and partial tuition reimbursements available (averaging $6,212 per year); research assistantships with full and partial tuition reimbursements available, career-related internships or fieldwork, institutionally sponsored loans, tuition waivers (partial), unspecified assistantships, and tuition remissions also available. Support available to part-time students. Financial award application deadline: 3/1; financial award applicants required to submit FAFSA. *Faculty research:* Measurement and evaluation, computers in education, educational technology. Total annual research expenditures: $352,726. *Unit head:* Dr. David E. Cook, Department Head, 321-674-8126, Fax: 321-674-7598, E-mail: dcook@fit.edu. *Application contact:* Thomas M. Shea, Director of Graduate Admissions, 321-674-7577, Fax: 321-723-9468, E-mail: tshea@fit.edu.

Florida International University, College of Education, Department of Curriculum and Instruction, Program in Mathematics Education, Miami, FL 33199. Offers MAT, MS, Ed D, PhD. *Accreditation:* NCATE. Part-time and evening/weekend programs available. *Entrance requirements:* Additional exam requirements/recommendations for international students: Required—TOEFL. *Expenses:* Tuition, state resident: full-time $8008; part-time $4004 per year. Tuition, nonresident: full-time $20,104; part-time $10,052 per year. Required fees: $298; $149 per term. *Faculty research:* Problem solving, heuristics, microcomputers.

Florida State University, The Graduate School, College of Education, School of Teacher Education, Program in Mathematics Education, Tallahassee, FL 32306. Offers MS, PhD, Ed S. Part-time programs available. Postbaccalaureate distance learning degree programs offered. *Faculty:* 4 full-time (3 women). *Students:* 17 full-time (9 women), 66 part-time (47 women); includes 21 minority (10 African Americans, 1 American Indian/Alaska Native, 9 Asian Americans or Pacific Islanders, 1 Hispanic American). 59 applicants, 51% accepted, 20 enrolled. In 2009, 20 master's, 5 doctorates, 1 other advanced degree awarded. *Degree requirements:* For master's and Ed S, comprehensive exam, thesis optional; for doctorate, comprehensive exam, thesis/dissertation. *Entrance requirements:* For master's, doctorate, and Ed S, GRE General Test, minimum GPA of 3.0. Additional exam requirements/recommendations for international students: Required—TOEFL (minimum score 550 paper-based; 213 computer-based; 80 iBT). *Application deadline:* For fall admission, 7/1 priority date for domestic students; for spring admission, 11/1 for domestic students. Applications are processed on a rolling basis. Application fee: $30. *Expenses:* Tuition, state resident: full-time $7413. Tuition, nonresident: full-time $22,567. *Financial support:* In 2009–10, 1 fellowship with full and partial tuition reimbursement, 2 research assistantships with full and partial tuition reimbursements, 3 teaching assistantships with full and partial tuition reimbursements were awarded; career-related internships or fieldwork and Federal Work-Study also available. Financial award applicants required to submit FAFSA. *Faculty research:* History of mathematics, students' ability to develop thinking skills in calculus, development of algebraic thinking, teacher preparation in secondary mathematics. *Unit head:* Dr. Elizabeth Jakubowski, Head, 850-644-6553, Fax: 850-644-1880, E-mail: ejakubowski@coe.fsu.edu. *Application contact:* Amy McKnight, Office Manager, 850-644-7810, Fax: 850-644-1880, E-mail: amcknight@coe.fsu.edu.

Framingham State University, Division of Graduate and Continuing Education, Program in Mathematics, Framingham, MA 01701-9101. Offers M Ed. *Entrance requirements:* For master's, GRE General Test, minimum GPA of 3.0.

Fresno Pacific University, Graduate Programs, School of Education, Fresno, CA 93702-4709. Offers administration (MA Ed), including administrative services; foundations, curriculum and teaching (MA Ed), including curriculum and teaching, school library and information technology; language, literacy, and culture (MA Ed), including bilingual/cross-cultural education, language development, multilingual contexts, reading; mathematics/science/computer education (MA Ed), including educational technology, integrated mathematics/science education, mathematics education; pupil personnel services (MA Ed), including school counseling, school psychology; special education (MA Ed), including mild/moderate, moderate/severe, physical

and health impairments. Part-time and evening/weekend programs available. *Degree requirements:* For master's, thesis (for some programs). *Entrance requirements:* For master's, interview; GMAT, GRE, MAT, or 6 units of course work with a faculty recommendation. Additional exam requirements/recommendations for international students: Required—TOEFL (minimum score 550 paper-based; 213 computer-based). Electronic applications accepted.

Fresno Pacific University, Graduate Programs, School of Education, Division of Mathematics/Science/Computer Education, Program in Integrated Mathematics/Science Education, Fresno, CA 93702-4709. Offers MA Ed. Part-time and evening/weekend programs available. *Degree requirements:* For master's, thesis or alternative. *Entrance requirements:* Additional exam requirements/recommendations for international students: Required—TOEFL (minimum score 550 paper-based; 213 computer-based).

Fresno Pacific University, Graduate Programs, School of Education, Division of Mathematics/Science/Computer Education, Program in Mathematics Education, Fresno, CA 93702-4709. Offers elementary and middle school mathematics (MA Ed); secondary school mathematics (MA Ed). Part-time and evening/weekend programs available. *Degree requirements:* For master's, thesis or alternative. *Entrance requirements:* Additional exam requirements/recommendations for international students: Required—TOEFL (minimum score 550 paper-based; 213 computer-based).

Georgia Southern University, Jack N. Averitt College of Graduate Studies, College of Education, Department of Teaching and Learning, Program in Mathematics Education, Statesboro, GA 30460. Offers M Ed, MAT. *Accreditation:* NCATE. Part-time and evening/weekend programs available. *Students:* 1 (woman) full-time. Average age 27. *Degree requirements:* For master's, portfolio, transition point assessments, exit assessment. *Entrance requirements:* For master's, GRE General Test or MAT; GACE Basic Skills and Content Assessments (MAT), minimum cumulative GPA of 2.5. Additional exam requirements/recommendations for international students: Required—TOEFL (minimum score 550 paper-based; 213 computer-based; 80 iBT). *Application deadline:* For fall admission, 3/1 priority date for domestic and international students; for spring admission, 10/1 priority date for domestic students, 10/1 for international students. Applications are processed on a rolling basis. Application fee: $50. Electronic applications accepted. *Expenses:* Tuition, state resident: full-time $5040; part-time $210 per credit hour. Tuition, nonresident: full-time $20,136; part-time $839 per credit hour. Required fees: $1644. *Financial support:* In 2009–10, 1 student received support, including research assistantships with partial tuition reimbursements available (averaging $7,200 per year), teaching assistantships with partial tuition reimbursements available (averaging $7,200 per year); Federal Work-Study, scholarships/grants, tuition waivers (partial), and unspecified assistantships also available. Support available to part-time students. Financial award application deadline: 4/15; financial award applicants required to submit FAFSA. *Faculty research:* Technology applications. *Unit head:* Dr. Ronnie Sheppard, Department Chair, 912-478-7203, Fax: 912-478-0026, E-mail: sheppard@georgiasouthern.edu. *Application contact:* Dr. charles Ziglar, Coordinator for Graduate Student Recruitment, 912-478-5635, Fax: 912-478-0740, E-mail: gradadmissions@georgiasouthern.edu.

Georgia State University, College of Education, Department of Middle-Secondary Education and Instructional Technology, Programs in Secondary Education, Atlanta, GA 30302-3083. Offers art education (Ed S); English education (M Ed, Ed S); mathematics education (M Ed, PhD, Ed S); music education (PhD); science education (M Ed, PhD, Ed S); social studies education (M Ed, PhD, Ed S). *Accreditation:* NASM (one or more programs are accredited); NCATE. Part-time and evening/weekend programs available. *Degree requirements:* For master's, comprehensive exam; for doctorate, comprehensive exam, thesis/dissertation; for Ed S, project/exam. *Entrance requirements:* For master's, GRE General Test, minimum GPA of 2.5; for doctorate, GRE General Test or MAT, minimum GPA of 3.3; for Ed S, GRE General Test or MAT, minimum graduate GPA of 3.25. *Faculty research:* Women and science, problem solving in mathematics, dialects, economic education.

Grambling State University, School of Graduate Studies and Research, College of Education, Department of Educational Leadership, Grambling, LA 71245. Offers curriculum and instruction (Ed D); developmental education (MS, Ed D), including curriculum and instruction: reading (Ed D), English (MS), guidance and counseling (MS), higher education administration (Ed D), instructional systems and technology (Ed D), mathematics (MS), reading (MS), science (MS), student development and personnel services (Ed D); educational leadership (MS, Ed D). Part-time and evening/weekend programs available. *Faculty:* 19 full-time (12 women). *Students:* 23 full-time (18 women), 84 part-time (62 women); includes 81 minority (80 African Americans, 1 Asian American or Pacific Islander), 5 international. Average age 39. 72 applicants, 75% accepted, 39 enrolled. In 2009, 5 master's, 9 doctorates awarded. *Degree requirements:* For master's, comprehensive exam, thesis (for some programs); for doctorate, comprehensive exam, thesis/dissertation. *Entrance requirements:* For master's, GRE, minimum GPA of 2.5 on last degree; for doctorate, GRE (minimum 1000, 500 on Verbal), master's degree, minimum GPA of 3.0 on last degree. Additional exam requirements/recommendations for international students: Required—TOEFL (minimum score 500 paper-based; 173 computer-based; 61 iBT). *Application deadline:* For fall admission, 7/1 for domestic and international students; for spring admission, 12/1 for domestic and international students. Applications are processed on a rolling basis. Application fee: $20 ($30 for international students). Electronic applications accepted. *Expenses:* Tuition, state resident: full-time $2610. Tuition, nonresident: full-time $2610. *Financial support:* In 2009–10, 5 research assistantships (averaging $10,948 per year) were awarded; health care benefits, tuition waivers (full), and unspecified assistantships also available. Financial award application deadline: 5/31; financial award applicants required to submit FAFSA. *Unit head:* Dr. Olatunde Ogunyemi, Director, 318-274-6105, Fax: 318-274-2799, E-mail: ogunyemio@gram.edu. *Application contact:* Laketha Richards, Administrative Assistant III, 318-274-6105, Fax: 318-274-6249, E-mail: richardsl@gram.edu.

Harding University, College of Education, Searcy, AR 72149-0001. Offers advanced studies in teaching and learning (M Ed); art (MSE); behavioral science (MSE); counseling (MS, Ed S); early childhood special education (M Ed, MSE); education (MSE); educational leadership (M Ed, Ed S); elementary education (M Ed); English (MSE); family and consumer science (MSE); French (MSE); history/social science (MSE); kinesiology (MSE); math (MSE); physical science (MSE); reading (M Ed); secondary education (M Ed); Spanish (MSE); special education licensure (M Ed); teaching (MAT); teaching English as a second language (M Ed). *Accreditation:* NCATE. Part-time and evening/weekend programs available. *Faculty:* 11 full-time (4 women), 49 part-time/adjunct (26 women). *Students:* 104 full-time (85 women), 392 part-time (282 women); includes 77 minority (67 African Americans, 5 American Indian/Alaska Native, 1 Asian American or Pacific Islander, 4 Hispanic Americans), 5 international. Average age 36. 153 applicants, 92% accepted, 131 enrolled. In 2009, 153 master's, 6 other advanced degrees awarded. *Degree requirements:* For master's, comprehensive exam (for some programs), thesis optional, portfolio(s); for Ed S, comprehensive exam, portfolio, specialist project. *Entrance requirements:* For master's, GRE, MAT, PRAXIS; for Ed S, MAT or GRE. Additional exam requirements/recommendations for international students: Required—TOEFL (minimum score 550 paper-based; 79 iBT). *Application deadline:* For fall admission, 8/1 for domestic and international students; for spring admission, 1/1 for domestic and international students. Applications are processed on a rolling basis. Application fee: $35. *Expenses:* Tuition: Full-time $9720; part-time $540 per credit hour. Required fees: $22 per credit hour. Tuition and fees vary according to course load and program. *Financial support:* In 2009–10, 30 students received support. Unspecified assistantships available. *Faculty research:* Reading, comprehension, school violence, educational technology, behavior, college choice, differentiated instruction, brain-based teaching. *Unit head:* Dr. Clara Carroll, Chair, 501-279-4501, Fax: 501-279-4083, E-mail: ccarroll@harding.edu. *Application contact:* Information Contact, 501-279-4315, E-mail: gradstudiesedu@harding.edu.

Harvard University, Extension School, Cambridge, MA 02138-3722. Offers applied sciences (CAS); biotechnology (ALM); educational technologies (ALM); educational technology (CET); English for graduate and professional studies (DGP); environmental management (ALM, CEM); information technology (ALM); journalism (ALM); liberal arts (ALM); management (ALM,

Mathematics Education

Harvard University (continued)
CM); mathematics for teaching (ALM); museum studies (ALM); premedical studies (Diploma); publication and communication (CPC). Part-time and evening/weekend programs available. *Degree requirements:* For master's, thesis. *Entrance requirements:* For master's, 3 completed graduate courses with grade of B or higher. Additional exam requirements/recommendations for international students: Required—TOEFL (minimum score 600 paper-based; 250 computer-based), TWE (minimum score 5). *Expenses:* Contact institution.

Harvard University, Graduate School of Education, Master's Programs in Education, Cambridge, MA 02138. Offers arts in education (Ed M); education policy and management (Ed M); higher education (Ed M); human development and psychology (Ed M); international education policy (Ed M); language and literacy (Ed M); learning and teaching (Ed M); mid-career mathematics and science (teaching certificate) (Ed M); mind brain and education (Ed M); risk and prevention (Ed M); school leadership (Ed M); special studies (Ed M); teaching and curriculum (teaching certificate) (Ed M); technology innovation and education (Ed M). Part-time programs available. *Faculty:* 70 full-time (33 women), 36 part-time/adjunct (20 women). *Students:* 598 full-time (448 women), 76 part-time (60 women); includes 132 minority (40 African Americans, 2 American Indian/Alaska Native, 58 Asian Americans or Pacific Islanders, 32 Hispanic Americans), 103 international. Average age 28. 1,574 applicants, 58% accepted, 640 enrolled. In 2009, 556 master's awarded. *Entrance requirements:* For master's, GRE General Test, 3 letters of recommendation. Additional exam requirements/recommendations for international students: Required—TOEFL (minimum score 600 paper-based; 250 computer-based; 100 iBT), TWE (minimum score 5). *Application deadline:* For fall admission, 1/4 for domestic and international students. Application fee: $85. Electronic applications accepted. *Expenses:* Contact institution. *Financial support:* In 2009–10, 424 students received support, including 25 fellowships with full and partial tuition reimbursements available (averaging $15,890 per year); career-related internships or fieldwork, Federal Work-Study, institutionally sponsored loans, scholarships/grants, health care benefits, tuition waivers (full and partial), and unspecified assistantships also available. Support available to part-time students. Financial award application deadline: 2/1; financial award applicants required to submit FAFSA. *Faculty research:* Learning and development, educational leadership and organizations, educational policy analysis. Total annual research expenditures: $18.1 million. *Unit head:* Jennifer L. Petrallia, Assistant Dean, 617-495-8445. *Application contact:* Information Contact, 617-495-3414, Fax: 617-496-3577, E-mail: gseadmissions@harvard.edu.

Hofstra University, School of Education, Health, and Human Services, Department of Curriculum and Teaching, Program in Elementary Education—Math, Science, and Technology, Hempstead, NY 11549. Offers MA. Part-time and evening/weekend programs available. *Students:* 3 full-time (all women), 12 part-time (all women); includes 1 minority (Hispanic American). Average age 25. 7 applicants, 100% accepted, 5 enrolled. In 2009, 10 master's awarded. *Degree requirements:* For master's, thesis. *Entrance requirements:* For master's, 2 letters of recommendation, interview, teaching certificate (MA), essay. Additional exam requirements/recommendations for international students: Required—TOEFL (minimum score 550 paper-based; 213 computer-based; 80 iBT). *Application deadline:* Applications are processed on a rolling basis. Application fee: $60. Electronic applications accepted. *Expenses:* Tuition: Full-time $16,200; part-time $900 per credit hour. Required fees: $970; $145 per term. Tuition and fees vary according to program. *Financial support:* In 2009–10, 8 students received support, including 3 fellowships with full and partial tuition reimbursements available (averaging $3,167 per year); research assistantships with full and partial tuition reimbursements available, Federal Work-Study, institutionally sponsored loans, scholarships/grants, tuition waivers (full and partial), and unspecified assistantships also available. Support available to part-time students. Financial award applicants required to submit FAFSA. *Faculty research:* Constructivism, interdisciplinary curriculum, design and technology education, science inquiry, problem-based learning. *Unit head:* Dr. Irene Plonczak, Program Director, 516-463-5768, Fax: 516-463-6196, E-mail: catizp@hofstra.edu. *Application contact:* Carol Drummer, Dean of Graduate Admissions, 516-463-4876, Fax: 516-463-4664, E-mail: gradstudent@hofstra.edu.

Hofstra University, School of Education, Health, and Human Services, Department of Curriculum and Teaching, Program in Learning and Teaching, Hempstead, NY 11549. Offers learning and teaching (Ed D), including applied linguistics, art education, arts and humanities, early childhood education, English education, human development, math education, math, science, and technology, multicultural education, physical education, science education, social studies education, special education. Part-time and evening/weekend programs available. *Students:* 5 full-time (all women), 21 part-time (17 women); includes 2 minority (1 African American, 1 Hispanic American), 1 international. Average age 38. 22 applicants, 68% accepted, 11 enrolled. *Degree requirements:* For doctorate, comprehensive exam, thesis/dissertation. *Entrance requirements:* For doctorate, GRE, 3 letters of recommendation, interview, 2 years full-time teaching experience. Additional exam requirements/recommendations for international students: Required—TOEFL (minimum score 550 paper-based; 213 computer-based; 80 iBT). *Application deadline:* Applications are processed on a rolling basis. Application fee: $60. Electronic applications accepted. *Expenses:* Tuition: Full-time $16,200; part-time $900 per credit hour. Required fees: $970; $145 per term. Tuition and fees vary according to program. *Financial support:* In 2009–10, 24 students received support, including 20 fellowships with full and partial tuition reimbursements available (averaging $4,906 per year); research assistantships with full and partial tuition reimbursements available, Federal Work-Study, institutionally sponsored loans, scholarships/grants, and tuition waivers (full and partial) also available. Support available to part-time students. Financial award applicants required to submit FAFSA. *Faculty research:* Critical thinking, professional development, teacher quality, quantitative research. *Unit head:* Dr. Bruce A. Torff, Director, 516-463-5803, Fax: 516-463-6196, E-mail: catajs@hofstra.edu. *Application contact:* Carol Drummer, Dean of Graduate Admissions, 516-463-4876, Fax: 516-463-4664, E-mail: gradstudent@hofstra.edu.

Hofstra University, School of Education, Health, and Human Services, Department of Curriculum and Teaching, Program in Mathematics Education, Hempstead, NY 11549. Offers MA, MS Ed. Part-time and evening/weekend programs available. *Students:* 22 full-time (15 women), 17 part-time (10 women); includes 7 minority (1 African American, 1 American Indian/Alaska Native, 1 Asian American or Pacific Islander, 4 Hispanic Americans). Average age 25. 30 applicants, 90% accepted, 15 enrolled. In 2009, 31 master's awarded. *Degree requirements:* For master's, one foreign language, thesis, student teaching. *Entrance requirements:* For master's, 2 letters of recommendation, teacher certification (MA). Additional exam requirements/recommendations for international students: Required—TOEFL (minimum score 550 paper-based; 213 computer-based; 80 iBT). *Application deadline:* Applications are processed on a rolling basis. Application fee: $60. Electronic applications accepted. *Expenses:* Tuition: Full-time $16,200; part-time $900 per credit hour. Required fees: $970; $145 per term. Tuition and fees vary according to program. *Financial support:* In 2009–10, 20 students received support, including 3 fellowships with full and partial tuition reimbursements available (averaging $2,416 per year); research assistantships with full and partial tuition reimbursements available, career-related internships or fieldwork, Federal Work-Study, institutionally sponsored loans, scholarships/grants, tuition waivers (full and partial), and unspecified assistantships also available. Support available to part-time students. Financial award applicants required to submit FAFSA. *Faculty research:* Integrating technology into the 7-12 math curriculum, multiple intelligences, constructive teaching methods, integrating math, science and technology into the K-7 curriculum. *Unit head:* Dr. Sharon Whitton, Director, 516-463-6456, Fax: 516-463-6196, E-mail: catszw@hofstra.edu. *Application contact:* Carol Drummer, Dean of Graduate Admissions, 516-463-4876, Fax: 516-463-4664, E-mail: gradstudent@hofstra.edu.

Hood College, Graduate School, Department of Education, Frederick, MD 21701-8575. Offers curriculum and instruction (MS), including early childhood education, elementary education, elementary school science and mathematics, secondary education, special education; educational leadership (MS, Certificate); reading specialization (MS). Part-time and evening/weekend programs available. *Faculty:* 4 full-time (all women), 39 part-time/adjunct (21 women). *Students:* 2 full-time (both women), 397 part-time (326 women); includes 41 minority (29 African Americans, 5 Asian Americans or Pacific Islanders, 7 Hispanic Americans). Average age 33. 100 applicants, 92% accepted, 84 enrolled. In 2009, 73 master's, 65 other advanced degrees awarded. *Degree requirements:* For master's, action research project, portfolio (reading). *Entrance requirements:* For master's, minimum GPA of 2.75, teaching certification. *Application deadline:* For fall admission, 7/15 for domestic and international students; for spring admission, 12/15 for domestic and international students. Applications are processed on a rolling basis. Application fee: $35. Electronic applications accepted. *Expenses:* Tuition: Full-time $6480; part-time $360 per credit. Required fees: $100; $50 per term. *Financial support:* Applicants required to submit FAFSA. *Faculty research:* Leadership, action research, brain research, learning styles. *Unit head:* Dr. John George, Chairperson, 301-696-3471, Fax: 301-696-3597, E-mail: george@hood.edu. *Application contact:* Dr. Allen P. Flora, Dean of Graduate School, 301-696-3811, Fax: 301-696-3597, E-mail: gofurther@hood.edu.

Hood College, Graduate School, Program in Secondary Mathematics Education, Frederick, MD 21701-8575. Offers mathematics education (MS), including high school, middle school; secondary mathematics education (Certificate). Part-time and evening/weekend programs available. *Faculty:* 1 full-time (0 women), 2 part-time/adjunct (0 women). *Students:* 32 part-time (24 women); includes 1 minority (African American). Average age 34. 8 applicants, 88% accepted, 7 enrolled. In 2009, 1 master's, 1 other advanced degree awarded. *Degree requirements:* For master's, capstone/research project. *Entrance requirements:* For master's, minimum GPA of 2.75. *Application deadline:* For fall admission, 7/15 for domestic and international students; for spring admission, 12/15 for domestic and international students. Applications are processed on a rolling basis. Application fee: $35. Electronic applications accepted. *Expenses:* Tuition: Full-time $6480; part-time $360 per credit. Required fees: $100; $50 per term. *Financial support:* Applicants required to submit FAFSA. *Unit head:* Dr. Betty Mayfield, Chairperson, 301-696-3763, E-mail: mayfield@hood.edu. *Application contact:* Dr. Allen P. Flora, Dean of Graduate School, 301-696-3811, Fax: 301-696-3597, E-mail: gofurther@hood.edu.

Hunter College of the City University of New York, Graduate School, School of Arts and Sciences, Department of Mathematics and Statistics, New York, NY 10021-5085. Offers applied mathematics (MA); mathematics for secondary education (MA); pure mathematics (MA). Part-time and evening/weekend programs available. *Faculty:* 7 full-time (1 woman). *Students:* 19 full-time (7 women), 56 part-time (26 women); includes 24 minority (3 African Americans, 18 Asian Americans or Pacific Islanders, 3 Hispanic Americans). Average age 31. 43 applicants, 77% accepted, 21 enrolled. In 2009, 35 master's awarded. *Degree requirements:* For master's, one foreign language, comprehensive exam, thesis (for some programs). *Entrance requirements:* For master's, GRE General Test, 24 credits in mathematics. Additional exam requirements/recommendations for international students: Required—TOEFL. *Application deadline:* For fall admission, 4/1 for domestic students, 2/1 for international students; for spring admission, 11/1 for domestic students, 9/1 for international students. Application fee: $125. *Expenses:* Tuition, state resident: full-time $7360; part-time $310 per credit. Required fees: $250 per semester. *Financial support:* Federal Work-Study, institutionally sponsored loans, scholarships/grants, and tuition waivers (partial) available. Support available to part-time students. *Faculty research:* Data analysis, dynamical systems, computer graphics, topology, statistical decision theory. *Unit head:* Ada Peluso, Chairperson, 212-772-5300, Fax: 212-772-4858, E-mail: peluso@math.hunter.cuny.edu. *Application contact:* William Zlata, Director for Graduate Admissions, 212-772-4482, Fax: 212-650-3336, E-mail: admissions@hunter.cuny.edu.

Hunter College of the City University of New York, Graduate School, School of Education, Programs in Secondary Education, Concentration in Mathematics Education, New York, NY 10021-5085. Offers MA. *Accreditation:* NCATE. *Faculty:* 7 full-time (1 woman). *Students:* 3 full-time (1 woman), 45 part-time (19 women); includes 9 minority (2 African Americans, 6 Asian Americans or Pacific Islanders, 1 Hispanic American). Average age 35. 41 applicants, 46% accepted, 12 enrolled. In 2009, 22 master's awarded. *Degree requirements:* For master's, thesis, professional teaching portfolio, New York State Teacher Certification Exam, research project. *Entrance requirements:* For master's, minimum GPA of 2.8 overall, 2.7 in mathematics courses; 24 credits of course work in mathematics. Additional exam requirements/recommendations for international students: Required—TOEFL, TWE. *Application deadline:* For fall admission, 4/1 for domestic students, 2/1 for international students; for spring admission, 11/1 for domestic students, 9/1 for international students. Applications are processed on a rolling basis. Application fee: $125. *Expenses:* Tuition, state resident: full-time $7360; part-time $310 per credit. Required fees: $250 per semester. *Financial support:* Federal Work-Study and tuition waivers (partial) available. Support available to part-time students. *Unit head:* Dr. Ptrick Burke, Program Coordinator, 212-396-6043, E-mail: patrick.burkei@hunter.cuny.edu. *Application contact:* William Zlata, Director for Graduate Admissions, 212-772-4482, Fax: 212-650-3336, E-mail: admissions@hunter.cuny.edu.

Idaho State University, Office of Graduate Studies, College of Arts and Sciences, Department of Mathematics, Pocatello, ID 83209-8085. Offers mathematics (MS, DA); mathematics for secondary teachers (MA). Part-time programs available. *Faculty:* 18 full-time (3 women), 1 part-time/adjunct (0 women). *Students:* 13 full-time (3 women), 8 part-time (3 women); includes 2 minority (1 American Indian/Alaska Native, 1 Hispanic American), 3 international. Average age 35. *Degree requirements:* For master's, comprehensive exam, thesis (for some programs), oral and written exams; for doctorate, comprehensive exam, thesis/dissertation, teaching internships. *Entrance requirements:* For master's, GRE General Test, GRE Subject Test, course work in modern algebra, differential equations, advanced calculus, introductory analysis; for doctorate, GRE General Test, GRE Subject Test, minimum graduate GPA of 3.5, MS in mathematics, teaching experience, 3 letters of recommendation. Additional exam requirements/recommendations for international students: Required—TOEFL (minimum score 550 paper-based; 213 computer-based; 80 iBT). *Application deadline:* For fall admission, 7/1 for domestic students, 6/1 for international students; for spring admission, 12/1 for domestic students, 11/1 for international students. Applications are processed on a rolling basis. Application fee: $55. Electronic applications accepted. *Expenses:* Tuition, state resident: full-time $3318; part-time $297 per credit hour. Tuition, nonresident: full-time $13,120; part-time $437 per credit hour. Required fees: $2530. Tuition and fees vary according to program. *Financial support:* In 2009–10, 13 teaching assistantships with full and partial tuition reimbursements (averaging $10,841 per year) were awarded; fellowships with full and partial tuition reimbursements, career-related internships or fieldwork, Federal Work-Study, institutionally sponsored loans, scholarships/grants, health care benefits, tuition waivers (full and partial), and unspecified assistantships also available. Support available to part-time students. Financial award application deadline: 1/1; financial award applicants required to submit FAFSA. *Faculty research:* Algebra, analysis geometry, statistics, applied mathematics. *Unit head:* Dr. Robert Fisher, Chairman, 208-282-3604, Fax: 208-282-2636, E-mail: fishrobe@isu.edu. *Application contact:* Tami Carson, Graduate School Technical Records Specialist, 208-282-2150, Fax: 208-282-4847, E-mail: carstami@isu.edu.

Illinois Institute of Technology, Graduate College, College of Science and Letters, Department of Mathematics and Science Education, Chicago, IL 60616-3793. Offers collegiate mathematics education (PhD); mathematics education (MME, MS, PhD); science education (MS, MSE, PhD). *Faculty:* 8 full-time (4 women), 2 part-time/adjunct (1 woman). *Students:* 33 full-time (18 women), 61 part-time (44 women); includes 23 minority (15 African Americans, 2 Asian Americans or Pacific Islanders, 6 Hispanic Americans), 2 international. Average age 37. 34 applicants, 62% accepted, 11 enrolled. In 2009, 15 master's, 2 doctorates awarded. *Degree requirements:* For master's, comprehensive exam (for some programs), thesis or alternative; for doctorate, comprehensive exam, thesis/dissertation. *Entrance requirements:* For master's, GRE General Test, minimum undergraduate GPA of 3.0; for doctorate, GRE General Test, minimum GPA of 3.0, 3 years of teaching experience. Additional exam requirements/recommendations for international students: Required—TOEFL (minimum score 523 paper-based; 70 iBT). *Application deadline:* For fall admission, 5/1 for domestic and international students; for spring admission, 10/15 for domestic and international students. Applications are processed on a rolling basis. Application fee: $50. Electronic applications accepted. *Expenses:* Tuition: Full-time $17,550; part-time $888 per credit hour. Required fees: $850; $7.50 per credit hour. One-time fee: $50 full-time. Full-time tuition and fees vary according to program.

Financial support: Career-related internships or fieldwork, Federal Work-Study, institutionally sponsored loans, scholarships/grants, health care benefits, tuition waivers (partial), and unspecified assistantships available. Support available to part-time students. Financial award applicants required to submit FAFSA. *Faculty research:* Nature of science, scientific inquiry, pedagogical content knowledge, classroom discourse, model eliciting activities. Total annual research expenditures: $87,994. *Unit head:* Dr. Norman G. Lederman, Chair, Professor, 312-567-3659, Fax: 312-567-3659, E-mail: ledermann@iit.edu. *Application contact:* Dr. Norman G. Lederman, Chair, Professor, 312-567-3659, Fax: 312-567-3659, E-mail: ledermann@iit.edu.

Illinois State University, Graduate School, College of Arts and Sciences, Department of Mathematics, Program in Mathematics Education, Normal, IL 61790-2200. Offers PhD. *Degree requirements:* For doctorate, variable foreign language requirement, comprehensive exam, thesis/dissertation, 2 terms of residency. *Entrance requirements:* For doctorate, GRE General Test.

Indiana State University, School of Graduate Studies, College of Arts and Sciences, Department of Mathematics and Computer Science, Terre Haute, IN 47809. Offers math teaching (MA, MS); mathematics and computer science (MA); mathematics and computer sciences (MS). Part-time programs available. *Degree requirements:* For master's, thesis or alternative. *Entrance requirements:* For master's, 24 semester hours of course work in undergraduate mathematics. Electronic applications accepted.

Indiana University Bloomington, School of Education, Department of Curriculum and Instruction, Bloomington, IN 47405-7000. Offers art education (MS, Ed D, PhD); curriculum studies (Ed D, PhD); elementary education (MS, Ed D, PhD, Ed S); mathematics education (MS, Ed D, PhD); science education (MS, Ed D, PhD); secondary education (MS, Ed D, PhD); social studies education (MS, PhD); special education (MS, Ed D, PhD, Ed S). *Accreditation:* NCATE. Part-time and evening/weekend programs available. *Students:* 208 full-time (155 women), 44 part-time (25 women); includes 28 minority (9 African Americans, 3 American Indian/Alaska Native, 9 Asian Americans or Pacific Islanders, 7 Hispanic Americans), 34 international. Average age 34. 100 applicants, 68% accepted, 39 enrolled. In 2009, 48 master's, 20 doctorates awarded. Terminal master's awarded for partial completion of doctoral program. *Degree requirements:* For doctorate, thesis/dissertation; for Ed S, comprehensive exam or project. *Entrance requirements:* For master's, doctorate, and Ed S, GRE General Test. *Application deadline:* For fall admission, 6/1 priority date for domestic students, 3/1 for international students; for winter admission, 11/1 priority date for domestic students; for spring admission, 9/1 for international students. Applications are processed on a rolling basis. Application fee: $55 ($65 for international students). Electronic applications accepted. *Financial support:* Fellowships with full and partial tuition reimbursements, research assistantships with full and partial tuition reimbursements, teaching assistantships with full and partial tuition reimbursements, career-related internships or fieldwork, Federal Work-Study, institutionally sponsored loans, and tuition waivers (partial) available. Support available to part-time students. *Unit head:* Cary Buzzelli, Chairperson, 812-856-8100. *Application contact:* Bobbie Partenheimer, Admissions Services Coordinator, 812-856-8127, Fax: 812-856-8333, E-mail: partenhe@indiana.edu.

Indiana University Bloomington, University Graduate School, College of Arts and Sciences, Department of Mathematics, Bloomington, IN 47405-7000. Offers applied mathematics–numerical analysis (MA, PhD); mathematics education (MAT); probability-statistics (MA, PhD); pure mathematics (MA). *Faculty:* 46 full-time (4 women). *Students:* 131 full-time (26 women); includes 10 minority (1 African American, 1 American Indian/Alaska Native, 7 Asian Americans or Pacific Islanders, 1 Hispanic American), 67 international. Average age 28. 211 applicants, 29% accepted, 26 enrolled. In 2009, 13 master's, 18 doctorates awarded. Terminal master's awarded for partial completion of doctoral program. *Degree requirements:* For doctorate, one foreign language, thesis/dissertation. *Entrance requirements:* For master's and doctorate, GRE General Test, GRE Subject Test. Additional exam requirements/recommendations for international students: Required—TOEFL. *Application deadline:* For fall admission, 1/15 priority date for domestic and international students. Applications are processed on a rolling basis. Application fee: $55 ($65 for international students). Electronic applications accepted. *Financial support:* In 2009–10, 9 fellowships with full tuition reimbursements (averaging $20,000 per year), 5 research assistantships with full tuition reimbursements (averaging $16,440 per year), 106 teaching assistantships with full tuition reimbursements (averaging $15,940 per year) were awarded; scholarships/grants, health care benefits, and unspecified assistantships also available. Financial award application deadline: 1/15. *Faculty research:* Topology, geometry, algebra. *Unit head:* James F. Davis, Chair, 812-855-2200. *Application contact:* Kate Bowman, Graduate Secretary, 812-855-2645, Fax: 812-855-0046, E-mail: gradmath@indiana.edu.

Indiana University of Pennsylvania, School of Graduate Studies and Research, College of Natural Sciences and Mathematics, Department of Mathematics, Program in Elementary and Middle School Mathematics Education, Indiana, PA 15705-1087. Offers M Ed. *Accreditation:* NCATE. *Faculty:* 3 full-time (1 woman). *Students:* 2 full-time (both women), 15 part-time (13 women). Average age 33. 10 applicants, 70% accepted, 5 enrolled. In 2009, 10 master's awarded. *Degree requirements:* For master's, comprehensive exam (for some programs), thesis optional. *Entrance requirements:* For master's, 2 letters of recommendation. Additional exam requirements/recommendations for international students: Required—TOEFL. *Application deadline:* For fall admission, 7/1 priority date for domestic students; for spring admission, 11/1 for domestic students. Applications are processed on a rolling basis. Application fee: $40. *Expenses:* Tuition, state resident: full-time $6666; part-time $370 per credit hour. Tuition, nonresident: full-time $10,666; part-time $593 per credit hour. Required fees: $813 per semester. *Financial support:* In 2009–10, 1 research assistantship with full and partial tuition reimbursement (averaging $5,440 per year) was awarded; Federal Work-Study also available. Support available to part-time students. Financial award application deadline: 3/15; financial award applicants required to submit FAFSA. *Unit head:* Dr. Larry Feldman, Graduate Coordinator, 724-357-4764, E-mail: lmfeldmn@iup.edu. *Application contact:* Dr. Jacqueline Gorman, Dean's Associate, 724-357-2609, E-mail: jgorman@iup.edu.

Indiana University of Pennsylvania, School of Graduate Studies and Research, College of Natural Sciences and Mathematics, Department of Mathematics, Program in Mathematics Education, Indiana, PA 15705-1087. Offers M Ed. *Accreditation:* NCATE. Part-time programs available. *Faculty:* 2 full-time (1 woman). *Students:* 1 full-time (0 women), 4 part-time (3 women); includes 1 minority (Asian American or Pacific Islander). Average age 31. 4 applicants, 25% accepted, 1 enrolled. In 2009, 2 master's awarded. *Degree requirements:* For master's, thesis optional. *Entrance requirements:* For master's, 2 letters of recommendation. Additional exam requirements/recommendations for international students: Required—TOEFL. *Application deadline:* For fall admission, 7/1 priority date for domestic students; for spring admission, 11/1 for domestic students. Applications are processed on a rolling basis. Application fee: $40. *Expenses:* Tuition, state resident: full-time $6666; part-time $370 per credit hour. Tuition, nonresident: full-time $10,666; part-time $593 per credit hour. Required fees: $813 per semester. *Financial support:* Research assistantships, career-related internships or fieldwork and Federal Work-Study available. Support available to part-time students. Financial award application deadline: 3/15; financial award applicants required to submit FAFSA. *Unit head:* Dr. Margaret Stempien, Graduate Coordinator, 724-357-3791, E-mail: margaret.stempien@iup.edu. *Application contact:* Dr. Jacqueline Gorman, Dean's Associate, 724-357-2609, E-mail: jgorman@iup.edu.

Indiana University–Purdue University Indianapolis, School of Science, Department of Mathematical Sciences, Program in Math Education, Indianapolis, IN 46202-2896. Offers MS. Application fee: $50 ($60 for international students). *Unit head:* Slawomir Klimek, Director of Graduate Programs, 317-274-6918, E-mail: grad-program@math.iupui.edu. *Application contact:* Slawomir Klimek, Director of Graduate Programs, 317-274-6918, E-mail: grad-program@math.iupui.edu.

Instituto Tecnológico y de Estudios Superiores de Monterrey, Campus Ciudad Obregón, Programs in Education, Program in Mathematics, Ciudad Obregón, Mexico. Offers ME.

Inter American University of Puerto Rico, Arecibo Campus, Programs in Education, Arecibo, PR 00614-4050. Offers administration and educational supervision (MA Ed); counseling and guidance (MA Ed); curriculum and teaching (MA Ed), including biology education, English as a second language, history education, math education, Spanish; elementary education (MA Ed). *Degree requirements:* For master's, comprehensive exam, thesis optional. *Entrance requirements:* For master's, GRE, EXADEP, bachelor's degree in education or teaching license (administration and supervision) or courses in education and psychology (counseling and guidance), minimum GPA of 2.5 in last 60 credits.

Inter American University of Puerto Rico, Metropolitan Campus, Graduate Programs, Program in Teaching of Math, San Juan, PR 00919-1293. Offers MA.

Inter American University of Puerto Rico, Ponce Campus, Graduate School, Mercedita, PR 00715-1602. Offers accounting (MBA); biology (M Ed); chemistry (M Ed); criminal justice (MA); elementary education (M Ed); English as a Second Language (M Ed); finance (MBA); history (M Ed); human resources (MBA); marketing (MBA); mathematics (M Ed); Spanish (M Ed). *Entrance requirements:* For master's, minimum GPA of 2.5.

Iona College, School of Arts and Science, Program in Education, New Rochelle, NY 10801-1890. Offers biology education (MS Ed, MST); educational leadership (MS Ed); English education (MS Ed, MST); literacy education (MS Ed); mathematics education (MS Ed, MST); social studies education (MS Ed, MST); Spanish education (MS Ed, MST); teaching in childhood education (MST). *Accreditation:* NCATE. Part-time and evening/weekend programs available. *Faculty:* 24 full-time (13 women), 16 part-time/adjunct (10 women). *Students:* 41 full-time (35 women), 118 part-time (87 women); includes 15 minority (5 African Americans, 1 Asian American or Pacific Islander, 9 Hispanic Americans). Average age 28. 91 applicants, 67% accepted, 41 enrolled. In 2009, 61 master's awarded. *Degree requirements:* For master's, thesis or alternative. *Entrance requirements:* For master's, minimum GPA of 2.5 (MST), New York teaching certificate (MS Ed). Additional exam requirements/recommendations for international students: Required—TOEFL (minimum score 550 paper-based; 213 computer-based). *Application deadline:* Applications are processed on a rolling basis. Application fee: $50. Electronic applications accepted. *Expenses:* Tuition: Part-time $830 per credit. *Financial support:* Unspecified assistantships available. Support available to part-time students. Financial award application deadline: 4/15; financial award applicants required to submit FAFSA. *Faculty research:* Reading/writing, educational technology, administration, early literacy assessment, literacy development. *Unit head:* Dr. Catherine O'Callaghan, Chair, 914-633-2210, Fax: 914-633-2608, E-mail: cocallaghan@iona.edu. *Application contact:* Veronica Jarek-Prinz, Director of Graduate Admissions, 914-633-2420, Fax: 914-633-2277, E-mail: vjarekprinz@iona.edu.

Iowa State University of Science and Technology, Graduate College, College of Liberal Arts and Sciences, Department of Mathematics, Ames, IA 50011. Offers applied mathematics (MS, PhD); mathematics (MS, PhD); school mathematics (MSM). *Faculty:* 44 full-time (5 women), 2 part-time/adjunct (1 woman). *Students:* 76 full-time (18 women), 10 part-time (2 women); includes 4 minority (1 African American, 2 Asian Americans or Pacific Islanders, 1 Hispanic American), 38 international. 133 applicants, 25% accepted, 24 enrolled. In 2009, 12 master's, 10 doctorates awarded. *Degree requirements:* For master's, thesis or alternative; for doctorate, thesis/dissertation. *Entrance requirements:* For master's and doctorate, GRE General Test. Additional exam requirements/recommendations for international students: Required—TOEFL (minimum score 550 paper-based; 79 iBT) or IELTS (minimum score 6.5). *Application deadline:* For fall admission, 2/1 priority date for domestic and international students; for spring admission, 10/1 priority date for domestic and international students. Application fee: $40 ($90 for international students). Electronic applications accepted. *Expenses:* Tuition, state resident: full-time $6716. Tuition, nonresident: full-time $8908. Tuition and fees vary according to course level, course load, program and student level. *Financial support:* In 2009–10, 15 research assistantships with full and partial tuition reimbursements (averaging $13,500 per year), 66 teaching assistantships with full and partial tuition reimbursements (averaging $16,400 per year) were awarded; fellowships, scholarships/grants, health care benefits, and unspecified assistantships also available. *Unit head:* Dr. Wolfgang Kliemann, Chair, 515-294-1752, Fax: 515-294-5454, E-mail: gradmath@iastate.edu. *Application contact:* Dr. Paul Sacks, Director of Graduate Education, 515-294-0393, E-mail: gradmath@iastate.edu.

Ithaca College, Division of Graduate and Professional Studies, School of Humanities and Sciences, Program in Adolescent Education, Ithaca, NY 14850. Offers biology 7-12 (MAT); chemistry 7-12 (MAT); English 7-12 (MAT); French 7-12 (MAT); math 7-12 (MAT); physics 7-12 (MAT); social studies 7-12 (MAT); Spanish (MAT). Part-time programs available. *Faculty:* 18 full-time (7 women). *Students:* 15 full-time (10 women), 2 part-time (1 woman); includes 1 minority (African American). Average age 26. 31 applicants, 68% accepted, 16 enrolled. In 2009, 31 master's awarded. *Degree requirements:* For master's, thesis or alternative, student teaching. *Entrance requirements:* For master's, minimum GPA of 3.0. Additional exam requirements/recommendations for international students: Required—TOEFL (minimum score 550 paper-based; 213 computer-based; 80 iBT). *Application deadline:* For fall admission, 5/15 for domestic and international students; for spring admission, 12/1 for domestic and international students. Applications are processed on a rolling basis. Application fee: $40. Electronic applications accepted. *Expenses:* Contact institution. *Financial support:* In 2009–10, 15 students received support, including 10 teaching assistantships (averaging $6,474 per year); career-related internships or fieldwork, Federal Work-Study, scholarships/grants, and unspecified assistantships also available. Support available to part-time students. Financial award applicants required to submit CSS PROFILE or FAFSA. *Faculty research:* Bilingual education, sociolinguistic perspective on literacy. *Unit head:* Dr. Linda Hanrahan, Chairperson, 607-274-3527, Fax: 607-274-1263, E-mail: gps@ithaca.edu. *Application contact:* Rob Gearhart, Dean, Graduate and Professional Studies, 607-274-3527, Fax: 607-274-1263, E-mail: gps@ithaca.edu.

Jackson State University, Graduate School, School of Science and Technology, Department of Mathematics, Jackson, MS 39217. Offers mathematics (MS); mathematics education (MST). Part-time and evening/weekend programs available. *Degree requirements:* For master's, comprehensive exam, thesis (for some programs). *Entrance requirements:* For master's, GRE General Test. Additional exam requirements/recommendations for international students: Required—TOEFL.

Jacksonville University, College of Arts and Sciences, School of Education, Program in Mathematics Education, Jacksonville, FL 32211. Offers MAT. Part-time and evening/weekend programs available. *Degree requirements:* For master's, comprehensive exam. *Entrance requirements:* For master's, GRE General Test. Additional exam requirements/recommendations for international students: Required—TOEFL.

The Johns Hopkins University, School of Education, Department of Teacher Preparation, Baltimore, MD 21218. Offers education (MS), including educational studies; elementary education (MAT); English for speakers of other languages (MAT); K-8 mathematics lead-teacher (Certificate); K-8 science lead-teacher (Certificate); secondary education (MAT), including biology, chemistry, earth/space/environmental science, English, French, mathematics, physics, social studies, Spanish. Part-time and evening/weekend programs available. *Faculty:* 13 full-time (11 women), 35 part-time/adjunct (21 women). *Students:* 162 full-time (119 women), 347 part-time (256 women); includes 138 minority (80 African Americans, 3 American Indian/Alaska Native, 38 Asian Americans or Pacific Islanders, 17 Hispanic Americans), 3 international. Average age 27. 89 applicants, 37% accepted, 24 enrolled. In 2009, 177 master's awarded. *Degree requirements:* For master's, portfolio, PRAXIS II, internship. *Entrance requirements:* For master's, PRAXIS I, SAT, ACT, or GRE (MAT), minimum undergraduate GPA of 3.0, interview, 1 letter of recommendation, curriculum vitae/resume; for Certificate, bachelor's degree, minimum undergraduate GPA of 3.0, essay/statement of goals, interview. Additional exam requirements/recommendations for international students: Required—TOEFL (minimum score 600 paper-based; 250 computer-based; 100 iBT). *Application deadline:* For fall admission, 5/1 for international students; for spring admission, 10/15 for international students. Applications are processed on a rolling basis. Application fee: $80. Electronic applications accepted. *Financial support:* Scholarships/grants available. Support available to part-time students. Financial award application deadline: 6/1; financial award applicants required to submit FAFSA.

Mathematics Education

The Johns Hopkins University (continued)
Faculty research: Teacher retention; STEM education reform; alternative certification programs; school-university partnerships; urban education; action research/data-informed instruction; family engagement. *Unit head:* Dr. Francis Masci, Chair, 410-516-9774, Fax: 410-516-9770, E-mail: matjhu@jhu.edu. *Application contact:* Jennifer Shaffer, Director of Admissions, 410-516-9797, Fax: 410-516-9799, E-mail: educationinfo@jhu.edu.

Kaplan University, Davenport Campus, School of Teacher Education, Davenport, IA 52807-2095. Offers education (M Ed); secondary education (M Ed); teaching and learning (MA); teaching literacy and language: grades 6-12 (MA); teaching literacy and language: grades K-6 (MA); teaching mathematics: grades 6-8 (MA); teaching mathematics: grades 9-12 (MA); teaching mathematics: grades K-5 (MA); teaching science: grades 6-12 (MA); teaching science: grades K-6 (MA); teaching students with special needs (MA); teaching with technology (MA). Part-time and evening/weekend programs available. Postbaccalaureate distance learning degree programs offered (no on-campus study). *Entrance requirements:* Additional exam requirements/recommendations for international students: Required—TOEFL (minimum score 550 paper-based; 218 computer-based; 80 iBT).

Kean University, College of Education, Program in Instruction and Curriculum, Union, NJ 07083. Offers bilingual/bicultural education (MA); classroom instruction (MA); earth science (MA); mathematics/science/computer education (MA); teaching (MA); teaching English as a second language (MA); world languages (Spanish) (MA). *Accreditation:* NCATE. Part-time and evening/weekend programs available. *Faculty:* 16 full-time (7 women). *Students:* 45 full-time (34 women), 131 part-time (104 women); includes 60 minority (11 African Americans, 6 Asian Americans or Pacific Islanders, 43 Hispanic Americans), 6 international. Average age 33. 64 applicants, 94% accepted, 46 enrolled. In 2009, 58 master's awarded. *Entrance requirements:* For master's, GRE General Test or MAT, PRAXIS, minimum GPA of 3.0, 2 letters of recommendation, interview, teacher certification (for some programs). *Application deadline:* For fall admission, 5/1 for domestic students; for spring admission, 11/1 for domestic students. Application fee: $60 ($150 for international students). Electronic applications accepted. *Expenses:* Tuition, state resident: full-time $10,440; part-time $435 per credit. Tuition, nonresident: full-time $14,160; part-time $590 per credit. Required fees: $2642; $110 per credit. Part-time tuition and fees vary according to course load and degree level. *Financial support:* In 2009–10, 1 research assistantship with full tuition reimbursement (averaging $3,263 per year) was awarded; unspecified assistantships also available. *Unit head:* Dr. Thomas Walsh, Program Coordinator, 908-737-4296, E-mail: twalsh@kean.edu. *Application contact:* Ann-Marie Kay, Assistant Director of Graduate Admissions, 908-737-5922, Fax: 908-737-5965, E-mail: akay@kean.edu.

Kean University, College of Natural, Applied and Health Sciences, Program in Mathematics Education, Union, NJ 07083. Offers computer applications (MA); supervision of math education (MA); teaching of math (MA). Part-time and evening/weekend programs available. *Faculty:* 13 full-time (4 women). *Students:* 5 full-time (4 women), 5 part-time (1 woman); includes 4 minority (2 Asian Americans or Pacific Islanders, 2 Hispanic Americans), 1 international. Average age 31. 5 applicants, 80% accepted, 4 enrolled. In 2009, 5 master's awarded. *Degree requirements:* For master's, comprehensive exam, thesis. *Entrance requirements:* For master's, GRE General Test, minimum GPA of 3.0, undergraduate major or strong minor in math, 2 letters of recommendation, interview. *Application deadline:* For fall admission, 5/1 for domestic students; for spring admission, 11/1 for domestic students. Application fee: $60 ($150 for international students). Electronic applications accepted. *Expenses:* Tuition, state resident: full-time $10,440; part-time $435 per credit. Tuition, nonresident: full-time $14,160; part-time $590 per credit. Required fees: $2642; $110 per credit. Part-time tuition and fees vary according to course load and degree level. *Financial support:* In 2009–10, 2 research assistantships with full tuition reimbursements (averaging $3,263 per year) were awarded; unspecified assistantships also available. *Unit head:* Dr. Revathi Narasimhan, Program Coordinator, 908-737-3700, E-mail: rnarasim@kean.edu. *Application contact:* Reenat Hasan, Pre-Admissions Coordinator, 908-737-5923, Fax: 908-737-5965, E-mail: rhasan@exchange.kean.edu.

Kennesaw State University, Leland and Clarice C. Bagwell College of Education, Program in Teaching, Kennesaw, GA 30144-5591. Offers secondary English or mathematics (MAT); teaching English to speakers of other languages (MAT). Program offered only in summer. Part-time and evening/weekend programs available. *Students:* 120 full-time (94 women), 16 part-time (9 women); includes 23 minority (12 African Americans, 4 Asian Americans or Pacific Islanders, 7 Hispanic Americans), 1 international. Average age 33. 28 applicants, 79% accepted, 19 enrolled. In 2009, 50 master's awarded. *Entrance requirements:* For master's, GRE, GACE I (state certificate exam), minimum GPA of 2.75, 2 recommendations, resume. Additional exam requirements/recommendations for international students: Required—TOEFL (minimum score 550 paper-based; 213 computer-based; 80 iBT), IELTS (minimum score 6). *Application deadline:* For fall admission, 6/1 for domestic and international students; for spring admission, 3/1 for domestic and international students. Application fee: $60. Electronic applications accepted. *Expenses:* Tuition, state resident: full-time $2341; part-time $196 per credit hour. Tuition, nonresident: full-time $9396; part-time $783 per credit hour. Required fees: $573 per semester. *Financial support:* In 2009–10, 2 research assistantships with tuition reimbursements (averaging $4,000 per year) were awarded; unspecified assistantships also available. Financial award application deadline: 6/15; financial award applicants required to submit FAFSA. *Unit head:* Dr. Lynn Stallings, Director, 770-420-4477, E-mail: lstalling@kennesaw.edu. *Application contact:* Alisha Bello, Administrative Coordinator, 770-423-6043, Fax: 770-420-4435, E-mail: abello1@kennesaw.edu.

Kutztown University of Pennsylvania, College of Education, Program in Secondary Education, Kutztown, PA 19530-0730. Offers biology (M Ed); curriculum and instruction (M Ed); English (M Ed); mathematics (M Ed); secondary education (Certificate); social studies (M Ed). *Accreditation:* NCATE. Part-time and evening/weekend programs available. *Faculty:* 7 full-time (4 women). *Students:* 90 full-time (45 women), 84 part-time (56 women); includes 8 minority (4 African Americans, 1 Asian American or Pacific Islander, 3 Hispanic Americans), 2 international. Average age 29. 129 applicants, 76% accepted, 31 enrolled. In 2009, 36 master's awarded. *Degree requirements:* For master's, comprehensive exam, thesis optional. *Entrance requirements:* For master's, GRE General Test. Additional exam requirements/recommendations for international students: Required—TOEFL. *Application deadline:* For fall admission, 8/15 priority date for domestic and international students; for spring admission, 12/15 priority date for domestic and international students. Applications are processed on a rolling basis. Application fee: $35. Electronic applications accepted. *Expenses:* Tuition, state resident: full-time $6666; part-time $370 per credit. Tuition, nonresident: full-time $10,666; part-time $593 per credit. Required fees: $62 per credit. $60 per semester. *Financial support:* Career-related internships or fieldwork, Federal Work-Study, scholarships/grants, and unspecified assistantships available. Financial award application deadline: 3/1; financial award applicants required to submit FAFSA. *Unit head:* Dr. Theresa Stahler, Chairperson, 610-683-4259, Fax: 610-683-1338, E-mail: stahler@kutztown.edu. *Application contact:* Kelly D. Burr, Associate Director, Graduate Admissions, 610-683-4200, Fax: 610-683-1393, E-mail: graduate@kutztown.edu.

Lehman College of the City University of New York, Division of Education, Department of Middle and High School Education, Program in Mathematics 7–12, Bronx, NY 10468-1589. Offers MS Ed. *Accreditation:* NCATE. Part-time and evening/weekend programs available. *Degree requirements:* For master's, comprehensive exam or thesis. *Entrance requirements:* For master's, 18 credits in mathematics, 12 credits in education. *Faculty research:* Mathematical problem solving, Piagetian cognitive theory.

Lewis University, College of Education, Program in Secondary Education, Romeoville, IL 60446. Offers biology (MA); chemistry (MA); English (MA); history (MA); math (MA); physics (MA); psychology and social science (MA). Part-time programs available. *Students:* 20 full-time (12 women), 24 part-time (16 women); includes 2 minority (1 African American, 1 Hispanic American). Average age 29. 39 applicants, 51% accepted, 18 enrolled. In 2009, 15 master's awarded. *Entrance requirements:* For master's, departmental qualifying exam, writing exam, minimum GPA of 2.75, 2 letters of recommendation, interview. Additional exam requirements/recommendations for international students: Required—TOEFL (minimum score 550 paper-based; 213 computer-based). *Application deadline:* For fall admission, 5/1 priority date for international students; for spring admission, 11/15 priority date for international students. Applications are processed on a rolling basis. Application fee: $40. Electronic applications accepted. *Expenses:* Tuition: Full-time $6480; part-time $720 per credit. One-time fee: $40. Tuition and fees vary according to course load, degree level and program. *Financial support:* Federal Work-Study, scholarships/grants, and unspecified assistantships available. Financial award application deadline: 5/1; financial award applicants required to submit FAFSA. *Unit head:* Dr. Dorene Huvaere, Program Director, 815-838-0500 Ext. 5885, E-mail: huvaersdo@lewisu.edu. *Application contact:* Fran Welsh, Secretary, 815-838-0500 Ext. 5880, E-mail: welshfr@lewisu.edu.

Lipscomb University, Program in Education, Nashville, TN 37204-3951. Offers English language learners (MAT); instructional leadership (M Ed); instructional technology (M Ed); learning and teaching (MALT); math specialty (M Ed); school administration and supervision (M Ed); special education instruction, K-12 (MASE). *Accreditation:* NCATE. Part-time and evening/weekend programs available. *Faculty:* 4 full-time (1 woman), 12 part-time/adjunct (8 women). *Students:* 140 full-time (103 women), 200 part-time (144 women); includes 32 minority (29 African Americans, 3 Hispanic Americans). Average age 31. 206 applicants, 75% accepted. In 2009, 131 master's awarded. *Entrance requirements:* For master's, MAT or GRE General Test, 2 reference letters. Additional exam requirements/recommendations for international students: Required—TOEFL (minimum score 570 paper-based; 230 computer-based). *Application deadline:* For fall admission, 8/29 priority date for domestic students; for spring admission, 1/16 priority date for domestic students. Applications are processed on a rolling basis. Application fee: $50. *Expenses:* Tuition: Full-time $16,002; part-time $889 per credit hour. Tuition and fees vary according to program. *Financial support:* In 2009–10, 67 students received support. Federal Work-Study, tuition waivers (full), and unspecified assistantships available. Support available to part-time students. Financial award applicants required to submit FAFSA. *Faculty research:* Facilitative learning styles, leadership, student assessment, interactive multimedia inclusion. *Unit head:* Dr. Deborah Boyd, Director of M Ed Program, 615-966-6263. *Application contact:* Kristin Green, Administrative Assistant, 615-966-7628 Ext. 6081, Fax: 615-966-7628, E-mail: kristin.green@lipscomb.edu.

Long Island University, Brooklyn Campus, School of Education, Department of Teaching and Learning, Program in Secondary Education, Brooklyn, NY 11201-8423. Offers mathematics education (MS Ed). Part-time and evening/weekend programs available. *Degree requirements:* For master's, thesis optional. *Entrance requirements:* For master's, 2 letters of recommendation. Additional exam requirements/recommendations for international students: Required—TOEFL (minimum score 500 paper-based; 173 computer-based). Electronic applications accepted.

Long Island University, C.W. Post Campus, College of Liberal Arts and Sciences, Department of Mathematics, Brookville, NY 11548-1300. Offers applied mathematics (MS); mathematics education (MS); mathematics for secondary school teachers (MS). Part-time and evening/weekend programs available. *Degree requirements:* For master's, thesis or alternative, oral presentation. *Entrance requirements:* Additional exam requirements/recommendations for international students: Required—TOEFL. Electronic applications accepted. *Faculty research:* Differential geometry, topological groups, general topology, number theory, analysis and statistics, numerical analysis.

Long Island University, C.W. Post Campus, School of Education, Department of Curriculum and Instruction, Brookville, NY 11548-1300. Offers adolescence education (MS); adolescence education: biology (MS); adolescence education: earth science (MS); adolescence education: English (MS); adolescence education: mathematics (MS); adolescence education: social studies (MS); adolescence education: Spanish (MS); art education (MS); bilingual education (MS); childhood education (MS); early childhood education (MS); middle childhood education (MS); music education (MS); teaching English to speakers of other languages (MS). Part-time and evening/weekend programs available. *Degree requirements:* For master's, comprehensive exam or thesis, student teaching. *Entrance requirements:* For master's, minimum GPA of 2.75 in major, 2.5 overall. Electronic applications accepted. *Faculty research:* Ethics and education, teaching strategies.

Louisiana Tech University, Graduate School, College of Education, Department of Curriculum, Instruction and Leadership, Ruston, LA 71272. Offers curriculum and instruction (MS, Ed D); educational leadership (Ed D); secondary education (M Ed), including business education, English education, foreign language education, health and physical education, mathematics education, science education, social studies education, speech education. *Accreditation:* NCATE. Part-time programs available. *Degree requirements:* For doctorate, thesis/dissertation. *Entrance requirements:* For master's and doctorate, GRE General Test.

Loyola Marymount University, College of Science and Engineering, Department of Mathematics, Program in Teaching in Mathematics, Los Angeles, CA 90045. Offers MAT. Part-time programs available. *Faculty:* 21 full-time (8 women), 1 part-time/adjunct (0 women). *Students:* 1 (woman) part-time. 1 applicant, 0% accepted, 0 enrolled. In 2009, 1 master's awarded. *Entrance requirements:* For master's, 1 letter of recommendation addressing student's mathematical background and teaching experience. Additional exam requirements/recommendations for international students: Required—TOEFL (minimum score 550 paper-based; 213 computer-based; 80 iBT). *Application deadline:* For fall admission, 6/15 for domestic students; for spring admission, 11/15 for domestic students. Application fee: $50. Electronic applications accepted. *Financial support:* In 2009–10, 1 student received support. Scholarships/grants and unspecified assistantships available. Financial award application deadline: 6/1; financial award applicants required to submit FAFSA. Total annual research expenditures: $152,007. *Unit head:* Dr. Edward Mosteig, Graduate Director, 310-338-2381, Fax: 310-338-3768, E-mail: emosteig@lmu.edu. *Application contact:* Chake H. Kouyoumjian, Associate Dean of Graduate Admissions, 310-338-2721, Fax: 310-338-6086, E-mail: ckouyoum@lmu.edu.

Loyola University Chicago, School of Education, Program in Initial Teacher Preparation, Chicago, IL 60660. Offers elementary education (M Ed); math education (M Ed); reading specialist (M Ed); school technology (M Ed); science education (M Ed); secondary education (M Ed); special education (M Ed). *Accreditation:* NCATE. *Faculty:* 12 full-time (9 women), 12 part-time/adjunct (6 women). *Students:* 154. Average age 28. 125 applicants, 69% accepted, 38 enrolled. In 2009, 89 master's awarded. *Degree requirements:* For master's, comprehensive exam. *Entrance requirements:* For master's, Illinois Basic Skills Test, 3 letters of recommendation, minimum GPA of 3.0, resume. Additional exam requirements/recommendations for international students: Required—TOEFL (minimum score 550 paper-based; 213 computer-based; 79 iBT). *Application deadline:* For fall admission, 7/1 priority date for domestic and international students; for spring admission, 11/1 priority date for domestic and international students. Applications are processed on a rolling basis. Application fee: $50. Electronic applications accepted. *Expenses:* Tuition: Full-time $14,220; part-time $790 per credit hour. Required fees: $60 per semester hour. Tuition and fees vary according to program. *Financial support:* In 2009–10, 1 research assistantship with full tuition reimbursement (averaging $8,500 per year), 1 teaching assistantship were awarded. Financial award application deadline: 2/15. *Faculty research:* Positive behavior support, school reform, school improvement. *Unit head:* Dr. Dorothy Giroux, Director, 312-915-7027, E-mail: dgiroux@luc.edu. *Application contact:* Marie Rosin-Dittmar, Information Contact, 312-915-6800, E-mail: schleduc@luc.edu.

Manhattanville College, Graduate Programs, School of Education, Program in Middle Childhood/Adolescence Education (Grades 5-12), Purchase, NY 10577-2132. Offers biology (MAT); biology and special education (MPS); chemistry (MAT); chemistry and special education (MPS); English (MAT); English and special education (MPS); literacy (MPS), including reading and writing, writing; literacy and special education (MPS); math (MAT); math and special education (MPS); second language (MAT), including French, Italian, Latin, Spanish; social studies (MAT); social studies and special education (MPS); special education (MPS). Part-time and evening/weekend programs available. *Students:* 52 full-time (39 women), 106 part-time (71 women); includes 8 African Americans, 3 Asian Americans or Pacific Islanders, 4 Hispanic Americans, 1 international. In 2009, 82 master's awarded. *Degree requirements:* For master's,

comprehensive exam or research project, field experience. *Entrance requirements:* For master's, minimum undergraduate GPA of 3.0, 2 letters of recommendation. Additional exam requirements/recommendations for international students: Required—TOEFL. *Application deadline:* Applications are processed on a rolling basis. Application fee: $70. Electronic applications accepted. *Financial support:* Career-related internships or fieldwork, Federal Work-Study, institutionally sponsored loans, and unspecified assistantships available. Support available to part-time students. Financial award application deadline: 3/1; financial award applicants required to submit FAFSA. *Unit head:* Dr. Shelley Wepner, Dean, 914-323-5192, Fax: 914-694-2386, E-mail: wepners@mville.edu. *Application contact:* Jeanine Pardey-Levine, Director of Admissions, 914-323-3208, Fax: 914-694-1732, E-mail: edschool@mville.edu.

Marquette University, Graduate School, College of Arts and Sciences, Department of Mathematics, Statistics, and Computer Science, Milwaukee, WI 53201-1881. Offers bioinformatics (MS); computational sciences (PhD); computers (MS); mathematics education (MS). Part-time programs available. *Faculty:* 28 full-time (12 women), 7 part-time/adjunct (2 women). *Students:* 20 full-time (4 women), 25 part-time (4 women); includes 2 minority (both Asian Americans or Pacific Islanders), 20 international. Average age 31. 68 applicants, 47% accepted, 15 enrolled. In 2009, 16 master's, 1 doctorate awarded. Terminal master's awarded for partial completion of doctoral program. *Degree requirements:* For master's, comprehensive exam, thesis or alternative; for doctorate, 2 foreign languages, comprehensive exam, thesis/dissertation. *Entrance requirements:* For doctorate, sample of scholarly writing. Additional exam requirements/recommendations for international students: Required—TOEFL. Application fee: $40. *Financial support:* In 2009–10, 2 research assistantships, 20 teaching assistantships were awarded; Federal Work-Study, institutionally sponsored loans, scholarships/grants, and tuition waivers (full and partial) also available. Support available to part-time students. Financial award application deadline: 2/15. *Faculty research:* Models of physiological systems, mathematical immunology, computational group theory, mathematical logic, computational science. *Unit head:* Dr. Peter Jones, Chair, 414-288-3263, Fax: 414-288-1578. *Application contact:* Dr. Gary Krenz, Director of Graduate Studies, 414-288-6345.

Miami University, Graduate School, College of Arts and Science, Department of Mathematics, Oxford, OH 45056. Offers MA, MAT, MS. *Students:* 23 full-time (12 women), 2 part-time (1 woman), 1 international. *Entrance requirements:* Additional exam requirements/recommendations for international students: Required—TOEFL. Application fee: $50. *Expenses:* Tuition, state resident: full-time $11,280. Tuition, nonresident: full-time $24,912. Required fees: $516. *Financial support:* Research assistantships, teaching assistantships, health care benefits and unspecified assistantships available. Financial award application deadline: 3/1; financial award applicants required to submit FAFSA. *Unit head:* Dr. Patrick Dowling, Department Chair, 513-529-5818, E-mail: dowlinpn@muohio.edu. *Application contact:* Dr. Doug Ward, Director of Graduate Studies, 513-529-3534, E-mail: wardde@muohio.edu.

Miami University, Graduate School, School of Education and Allied Professions, Department of Teacher Education, Oxford, OH 45056. Offers elementary education (M Ed, MAT); reading education (M Ed); secondary education (M Ed, MAT), including adolescent education (MAT), elementary mathematics education (M Ed), secondary education. Part-time programs available. *Students:* 48 full-time (31 women), 70 part-time (60 women); includes 6 minority (3 African Americans, 3 Hispanic Americans), 5 international. *Entrance requirements:* For master's, GRE (MAT), minimum undergraduate GPA of 3.0 during previous 2 years or 2.75 overall. Application fee: $50. *Expenses:* Tuition, state resident: full-time $11,280. Tuition, nonresident: full-time $24,912. Required fees: $516. *Financial support:* Fellowships with full tuition reimbursements, research assistantships, teaching assistantships, career-related internships or fieldwork, Federal Work-Study, scholarships/grants, health care benefits, tuition waivers (full), and unspecified assistantships available. Financial award application deadline: 3/1. *Unit head:* Dr. James Shiveley, Chair, 513-529-6443, Fax: 513-529-4931, E-mail: shiveljm@muohio.edu. *Application contact:* Dr. Iris Johnson, Assistant Chair and Graduate Coordinator, 513-529-6443, Fax: 513-529-4931, E-mail: johnsoid@muohio.edu.

Michigan State University, The Graduate School, College of Natural Science, Department of Mathematics, East Lansing, MI 48824. Offers applied mathematics (MS, PhD); industrial mathematics (MS); mathematics (MAT, MS, PhD). *Faculty:* 54 full-time (7 women), 1 part-time/adjunct (0 women). *Students:* 116 full-time (24 women), 3 part-time (0 women); includes 4 minority (1 African American, 1 American Indian/Alaska Native, 1 Asian American or Pacific Islander, 1 Hispanic American), 63 international. Average age 26. 135 applicants, 21% accepted. In 2009, 15 master's, 7 doctorates awarded. *Entrance requirements:* Additional exam requirements/recommendations for international students: Required—TOEFL. Electronic applications accepted. *Expenses:* Tuition, state resident: part-time $478.25 per credit hour. Tuition, nonresident: part-time $966.50 per credit hour. Part-time tuition and fees vary according to program. *Financial support:* In 2009–10, 13 research assistantships with tuition reimbursements (averaging $7,120 per year), 94 teaching assistantships with tuition reimbursements (averaging $6,975 per year) were awarded. Total annual research expenditures: $3.3 million. *Unit head:* Dr. Yang Wang, Chairperson, 517-355-9680, Fax: 517-432-1562, E-mail: ywang@math.msu.edu. *Application contact:* Barbara S. Miller, Graduate Secretary, 517-353-6338, Fax: 517-432-1562, E-mail: grad@math.msu.edu.

Michigan State University, The Graduate School, College of Natural Science and College of Education, Division of Science and Mathematics Education, East Lansing, MI 48824. Offers biological, physical and general science for teachers (MAT, MS), including biological science (MS), general science (MAT), physical science (MS); mathematics education (MS, PhD). *Students:* 23 full-time (13 women), 2 part-time (1 woman); includes 2 minority (1 African American, 1 Asian American or Pacific Islander), 6 international. Average age 33. In 2009, 5 master's, 1 doctorate awarded. *Expenses:* Tuition, state resident: part-time $478.25 per credit hour. Tuition, nonresident: part-time $966.50 per credit hour. Part-time tuition and fees vary according to program. *Financial support:* In 2009–10, 14 research assistantships with tuition reimbursements (averaging $6,849 per year), 16 teaching assistantships with tuition reimbursements (averaging $6,752 per year) were awarded. *Unit head:* Dr. George Leroi, Interim Director, 517-432-1490 Ext. 103, Fax: 517-432-9868, E-mail: geleroi@msu.edu. *Application contact:* Margaret Iding, Graduate Secretary, 517-355-1708 Ext. 105, Fax: 517-432-9868, E-mail: dsme@msu.edu.

Middle Tennessee State University, College of Graduate Studies, College of Basic and Applied Sciences, Department of Mathematical Sciences, Murfreesboro, TN 37132. Offers mathematics (MS, MST). Part-time and evening/weekend programs available. Postbaccalaureate distance learning degree programs offered. *Faculty:* 21 full-time (9 women). *Students:* 3 full-time (2 women), 38 part-time (22 women); includes 11 minority (5 African Americans, 6 Asian Americans or Pacific Islanders). Average age 27. 17 applicants, 82% accepted, 14 enrolled. In 2009, 12 master's awarded. *Degree requirements:* For master's, comprehensive exam. *Entrance requirements:* For master's, GRE General Test or MAT. Additional exam requirements/recommendations for international students: Required—TOEFL (minimum score 525 paper-based; 195 computer-based; 71 iBT) or IELTS (minimum score 6). *Application deadline:* For fall admission, 6/1 for domestic and international students. Applications are processed on a rolling basis. Application fee: $25 ($30 for international students). Electronic applications accepted. *Expenses:* Tuition, state resident: full-time $4404. Tuition, nonresident: full-time $10,956. *Financial support:* In 2009–10, 11 students received support. Institutionally sponsored loans available. Support available to part-time students. Financial award application deadline: 5/1; financial award applicants required to submit FAFSA. *Unit head:* Dr. Donald Nelson, Interim Chair, 615-898-2704, Fax: 615-898-5422, E-mail: dnelson@mtsu.edu. *Application contact:* Dr. Michael Allen, Dean and Vice Provost for Research, 615-898-2840, Fax: 615-904-8020, E-mail: mallen@mtsu.edu.

Millersville University of Pennsylvania, College of Graduate and Professional Studies, School of Science and Mathematics, Department of Mathematics, Millersville, PA 17551-0302. Offers M Ed. *Accreditation:* NCATE. Part-time and evening/weekend programs available. *Faculty:* 22 full-time (6 women), 5 part-time/adjunct (4 women). *Students:* 4 full-time (2 women), 11 part-time (6 women). Average age 30. 5 applicants, 100% accepted, 2 enrolled. In 2009, 6 master's awarded. *Degree requirements:* For master's, thesis optional. *Entrance requirements:* For master's, 3 letters of recommendation. Additional exam requirements/recommendations for international students: Required—TOEFL (minimum score 500 paper-based; 183 computer-based; 65 iBT) or IELTS (minimum score 6). *Application deadline:* For fall admission, 1/15 priority date for domestic and international students; for winter admission, 10/1 priority date for domestic and international students; for spring admission, 10/1 priority date for domestic and international students. Applications are processed on a rolling basis. Application fee: $40 ($50 for international students). Electronic applications accepted. *Expenses:* Tuition, state resident: full-time $6666; part-time $370 per credit. Tuition, nonresident: full-time $10,666; part-time $593 per credit. Required fees: $1578.50; $76.25 per credit. One-time fee: $60 part-time. Tuition and fees vary according to course load. *Financial support:* In 2009–10, 1 student received support, including 1 research assistantship with full tuition reimbursement available (averaging $5,000 per year); institutionally sponsored loans and unspecified assistantships also available. Support available to part-time students. Financial award application deadline: 3/15; financial award applicants required to submit FAFSA. *Unit head:* Dr. Janet A. White, Assistant Chair, 717-872-3957, Fax: 717-871-2320, E-mail: janet.white@millersville.edu. *Application contact:* Dr. Victor S. DeSantis, Dean of Graduate and Professional Studies, 717-872-3099, Fax: 717-872-3453, E-mail: victor.desantis@millersville.edu.

Mills College, Graduate Studies, School of Education, Oakland, CA 94613-1000. Offers child life in hospitals (MA); early childhood education (MA); education (MA), including art education, curriculum and instruction, elementary education, English education, foreign language education, mathematics education, science education, secondary education, social studies education, teaching; educational leadership (MA, Ed D); infant mental health (MA). Part-time and evening/weekend programs available. *Faculty:* 11 full-time (9 women), 16 part-time/adjunct (14 women). *Students:* 138 full-time (119 women), 55 part-time (48 women); includes 71 minority (34 African Americans, 19 Asian Americans or Pacific Islanders, 18 Hispanic Americans), 3 international. Average age 34. 210 applicants, 82% accepted, 93 enrolled. In 2009, 54 master's, 15 doctorates awarded. Terminal master's awarded for partial completion of doctoral program. *Degree requirements:* For master's, comprehensive exam. *Entrance requirements:* For doctorate, GRE General Test. Additional exam requirements/recommendations for international students: Required—TOEFL. *Application deadline:* For fall admission, 2/1 for domestic and international students; for spring admission, 11/1 for domestic and international students. Applications are processed on a rolling basis. Application fee: $50. Electronic applications accepted. *Expenses:* Tuition: Full-time $26,326; part-time $6584 per course. Required fees: $896. One-time fee: $896 part-time. Tuition and fees vary according to program. *Financial support:* In 2009–10, 188 students received support, including 186 fellowships (averaging $6,499 per year), 28 teaching assistantships with partial tuition reimbursements available (averaging $3,187 per year); career-related internships or fieldwork and scholarships/grants also available. Support available to part-time students. Financial award application deadline: 2/1; financial award applicants required to submit FAFSA. *Faculty research:* Child development, gender and education, public policy, cross-cultural development, development of literacy. Total annual research expenditures: $1.2 million. *Unit head:* Joseph Kahne, Chairperson, 510-430-3190, Fax: 510-430-3314, E-mail: grad-studies@mills.edu. *Application contact:* Jessica King, Graduate Admission Specialist, 510-430-3305, Fax: 510-430-2159, E-mail: grad-studies@mills.edu.

Minnesota State University Mankato, College of Graduate Studies, College of Science, Engineering and Technology, Department of Mathematics and Statistics, Mankato, MN 56001. Offers mathematics (MA, MAT, MS); mathematics education (MS); statistics (MS). *Students:* 8 full-time (3 women), 11 part-time (3 women). *Degree requirements:* For master's, one foreign language, comprehensive exam, thesis or alternative. *Entrance requirements:* For master's, GRE General Test (if GPA less than 2.75), minimum GPA of 2.75 during previous 2 years of course work. Additional exam requirements/recommendations for international students: Required—TOEFL. *Application deadline:* For fall admission, 7/1 priority date for domestic students; for spring admission, 11/1 for domestic students. Applications are processed on a rolling basis. Application fee: $40. Electronic applications accepted. *Expenses:* Tuition, state resident: full-time $5364. Tuition, nonresident: full-time $8314. *Financial support:* Fellowships with partial tuition reimbursements, research assistantships with full tuition reimbursements, teaching assistantships with full tuition reimbursements, Federal Work-Study, institutionally sponsored loans, and unspecified assistantships available. Support available to part-time students. Financial award application deadline: 3/15; financial award applicants required to submit FAFSA. *Unit head:* Dr. Ernest Boyd, Chairperson, 507-389-1453. *Application contact:* 507-389-2321, E-mail: grad@mnsu.edu.

Minot State University, Graduate School, Department of Mathematics and Computer Science, Minot, ND 58707-0002. Offers mathematics (MAT). *Degree requirements:* For master's, thesis or alternative. *Entrance requirements:* For master's, minimum GPA of 2.75, undergraduate major in mathematics, teaching certificate. Additional exam requirements/recommendations for international students: Required—TOEFL. *Expenses:* Tuition, state resident: full-time $5720; part-time $283 per credit hour. Tuition, nonresident: full-time $5720; part-time $283 per credit hour. Required fees: $1034; $1034 per year. Tuition and fees vary according to course load, degree level and program. *Faculty research:* Mathematics education.

Mississippi College, Graduate School, School of Education, Department of Teacher Education and Leadership, Clinton, MS 39058. Offers art (M Ed); biological science (M Ed); business education (M Ed); computer science (M Ed); dyslexia therapy (M Ed); educational leadership (M Ed, Ed D, Ed S); elementary education (M Ed, Ed S); English (M Ed); higher education administration (MS); mathematics (M Ed); secondary education (M Ed); social studies (history) (M Ed); teaching arts (M Ed). Part-time programs available. Postbaccalaureate distance learning degree programs offered (no on-campus study). *Faculty:* 11 full-time (7 women), 13 part-time/adjunct (7 women). *Students:* 33 full-time (22 women), 282 part-time (240 women); includes 148 minority (146 African Americans, 2 American Indian/Alaska Native), 1 international. Average age 34. In 2009, 147 master's awarded. *Degree requirements:* For master's, comprehensive exam, thesis optional. *Entrance requirements:* For master's, NTE. Additional exam requirements/recommendations for international students: Recommended—IELTS. *Application deadline:* For fall admission, 8/15 priority date for domestic students. Applications are processed on a rolling basis. Application fee: $30. Electronic applications accepted. *Expenses:* Tuition: Part-time $452 per credit hour. Required fees: $101 per semester. Tuition and fees vary according to degree level, campus/location, program and student level. *Financial support:* Teaching assistantships, career-related internships or fieldwork, Federal Work-Study, scholarships/grants, and unspecified assistantships available. Support available to part-time students. Financial award applicants required to submit FAFSA. *Unit head:* Dr. Tom Williams, Chair, 601-925-3844, E-mail: twilliams@mc.edu. *Application contact:* Elnora Lewis, Secretary, 601-925-3225, Fax: 601-925-3889, E-mail: lewis09@mc.edu.

Missouri University of Science and Technology, Graduate School, Department of Mathematics and Statistics, Rolla, MO 65409. Offers applied mathematics (MS); mathematics (MST, PhD), including mathematics (PhD), mathematics education (MST), statistics (PhD). Terminal master's awarded for partial completion of doctoral program. *Degree requirements:* For master's, thesis or alternative; for doctorate, one foreign language, thesis/dissertation. *Entrance requirements:* For master's and doctorate, GRE General Test, GRE Subject Test. Electronic applications accepted. *Faculty research:* Analysis, differential equations, topology, statistics.

Montana State University, College of Graduate Studies, College of Letters and Science, Department of Mathematical Sciences, Bozeman, MT 59717. Offers mathematics (MS, PhD), including mathematics education option (MS); statistics (MS, PhD). Part-time programs available. Postbaccalaureate distance learning degree programs offered (minimal on-campus study). *Faculty:* 35 full-time (11 women), 7 part-time/adjunct (3 women). *Students:* 17 full-time (6 women), 71 part-time (33 women); includes 3 minority (1 American Indian/Alaska Native, 1 Asian American or Pacific Islander, 1 Hispanic American), 6 international. Average age 31. 53 applicants, 36% accepted, 15 enrolled. In 2009, 18 master's, 3 doctorates awarded. *Degree requirements:* For master's, comprehensive exam, thesis (for some programs); for doctorate, comprehensive exam, thesis/dissertation. *Entrance requirements:* For master's and doctorate,

Mathematics Education

Montana State University *(continued)*
GRE General Test. Additional exam requirements/recommendations for international students: Required—TOEFL (minimum score 550 paper-based; 213 computer-based). *Application deadline:* For fall admission, 7/15 priority date for domestic students, 5/15 priority date for international students; for spring admission, 12/1 priority date for domestic students, 10/1 priority date for international students. Applications are processed on a rolling basis. Application fee: $30. Electronic applications accepted. *Expenses:* Tuition, state resident: full-time $5635; part-time $3492 per year. Tuition, nonresident: full-time $17,212; part-time $7865.10 per year. Required fees: $1441; $153.15 per credit. Tuition and fees vary according to course load and program. *Financial support:* In 2009–10, 58 students received support, including 4 research assistantships with tuition reimbursements available (averaging $15,650 per year), 54 teaching assistantships with tuition reimbursements available (averaging $15,450 per year); career-related internships or fieldwork, scholarships/grants, tuition waivers (full), and unspecified assistantships also available. Support available to part-time students. Financial award application deadline: 3/1; financial award applicants required to submit FAFSA. *Faculty research:* Applied mathematics, dynamical systems, statistics, mathematics education, mathematical and computational biology. Total annual research expenditures: $248,209. *Unit head:* Dr. Kenneth Bowers, Head, 406-994-3604, Fax: 406-994-1789, E-mail: bowers@math.montana.edu. *Application contact:* Dr. Carl A. Fox, Vice Provost for Graduate Education, 406-994-4145, Fax: 406-994-7433, E-mail: gradstudy@montana.edu.

Montclair State University, The Graduate School, College of Education and Human Services, Department of Curriculum and Teaching, Montclair, NJ 07043-1624. Offers education (M Ed); educational technology (M Ed); learning disabled teacher consultant (Certificate); school library media specialist (Certificate); teaching (MAT, Certificate), including art (MAT), biological science (MAT), early childhood education (P-3) (MAT), earth science (MAT), elementary education (K-8) (MAT), English (MAT), French (MAT), health and physical education (MAT), health education (MAT), home economics (MAT), mathematics (MAT), music (MAT), physical education (MAT), physical science (MAT), social studies (MAT), Spanish (MAT), teacher of ESL (MAT), teacher of students with disabilities (MAT). Part-time and evening/weekend programs available. *Faculty:* 17 full-time (12 women), 29 part-time/adjunct (21 women). *Students:* 124 full-time (63 women), 174 part-time (126 women). Average age 31. 112 applicants, 69% accepted, 59 enrolled. In 2009, 179 master's, 2 other advanced degrees awarded. *Degree requirements:* For master's, comprehensive exam, field experience. *Entrance requirements:* For master's, GRE, 2 letters of recommendation. Additional exam requirements/recommendations for international students: Required—TOEFL (minimum score 83 computer-based), or IELTS. *Application deadline:* For fall admission, 2/15 for domestic and international students; for spring admission, 9/15 for domestic and international students. Applications are processed on a rolling basis. Application fee: $60. Electronic applications accepted. *Expenses:* Tuition, area resident: Part-time $486.74 per credit. Tuition, state resident: part-time $486.74 per credit. Tuition, nonresident: part-time $751.34 per credit. Tuition and fees vary according to degree level and program. *Financial support:* In 2009–10, 12 research assistantships with full tuition reimbursements (averaging $7,000 per year) were awarded; Federal Work-Study, scholarships/grants, and unspecified assistantships also available. Support available to part-time students. Financial award application deadline: 3/1; financial award applicants required to submit FAFSA. *Unit head:* Dr. David Schwarzer, Chairperson, 973-655-5187. *Application contact:* Amy Aiello, Director of Graduate Admissions and Operations, 973-655-5147, Fax: 973-655-7869, E-mail: graduate.school@montclair.edu.

Montclair State University, The Graduate School, College of Science and Mathematics, Department of Mathematics, Montclair, NJ 07043-1624. Offers math pedagogy (Ed D); mathematics (MS), including computer science, mathematics education, pure and applied mathematics, statistics; physical science (Certificate); teaching middle grades math (MS, Certificate). Part-time and evening/weekend programs available. *Faculty:* 30 full-time (10 women), 39 part-time/adjunct (19 women). *Students:* 15 full-time (7 women), 101 part-time (75 women). Average age 32. 55 applicants, 76% accepted, 31 enrolled. In 2009, 32 master's, 2 doctorates, 9 other advanced degrees awarded. *Degree requirements:* For master's, comprehensive exam. *Entrance requirements:* For master's, GRE General Test, 2 letters of recommendation. Additional exam requirements/recommendations for international students: Required—TOEFL (minimum score 83 computer-based), or IELTS. *Application deadline:* For fall admission, 6/1 for international students; for spring admission, 10/1 for international students. Applications are processed on a rolling basis. Application fee: $60. *Expenses:* Tuition, area resident: Part-time $486.74 per credit. Tuition, state resident: part-time $486.74 per credit. Tuition, nonresident: part-time $751.34 per credit. Tuition and fees vary according to degree level and program. *Financial support:* In 2009–10, 9 research assistantships with full tuition reimbursements (averaging $7,000 per year), 1 teaching assistantship with full tuition reimbursement (averaging $15,000 per year) were awarded; Federal Work-Study, scholarships/grants, and unspecified assistantships also available. Support available to part-time students. Financial award application deadline: 3/1; financial award applicants required to submit FAFSA. *Faculty research:* Infectious disease. *Unit head:* Dr. Helen Roberts, Chairperson, 973-655-5132. *Application contact:* Amy Aiello, Director of Graduate Admissions and Operations, 973-655-5147, Fax: 973-655-7869, E-mail: graduate.school@montclair.edu.

Morehead State University, Graduate Programs, College of Education, Department of Middle Grades and Secondary Education, Morehead, KY 40351. Offers business and marketing education (MAT); English/language arts 5-9 (MAT); French (MAT); health P-12 (MAT); mathematics 5-9 (MAT); physical education P-12 (MAT); science 5-9 (MAT); secondary biology (MAT); secondary chemistry (MAT); secondary earth science (MAT); secondary English (MAT); secondary math (MAT); secondary physics (MAT); secondary social studies (MAT); social studies 5-9 (MAT); Spanish (MAT). Part-time and evening/weekend programs available. *Students:* 54 full-time (31 women), 233 part-time (142 women); includes 11 minority (5 African Americans, 1 American Indian/Alaska Native, 1 Asian American or Pacific Islander, 4 Hispanic Americans). Average age 32. 206 applicants, 71% accepted, 79 enrolled. In 2009, 101 master's awarded. *Degree requirements:* For master's, portfolio. *Entrance requirements:* For master's, GRE or PRAXIS II content exam, minimum overall undergraduate GPA of 2.5. Additional exam requirements/recommendations for international students: Required—TOEFL (minimum score 500 paper-based; 173 computer-based). *Application deadline:* For fall admission, 8/1 priority date for domestic and international students; for spring admission, 12/1 priority date for domestic and international students. Applications are processed on a rolling basis. Application fee: $30. Electronic applications accepted. *Expenses:* Tuition, state resident: full-time $6318; part-time $351 per credit hour. Tuition, nonresident: full-time $15,804; part-time $878 per credit hour. *Financial support:* In 2009–10, 1 research assistantship (averaging $10,000 per year) was awarded; career-related internships or fieldwork, Federal Work-Study, and unspecified assistantships also available. Financial award application deadline: 3/15; financial award applicants required to submit FAFSA. *Unit head:* Dr. Cathy Gunn, Dean, 606-783-2040, Fax: 606-783-5029, E-mail: c.gunn@moreheadstate.edu. *Application contact:* Michelle Barber, Graduate Recruitment and Retention Assistant Director, 606-783-5127, Fax: 606-783-5061, E-mail: m.barber@moreheadstate.edu.

Morgan State University, School of Graduate Studies, School of Education and Urban Studies, Department of Advanced Studies, Leadership and Policy, Program in Mathematics Education, Baltimore, MD 21251. Offers Ms, Ed D. *Degree requirements:* For doctorate, comprehensive exam, thesis/dissertation. *Entrance requirements:* For doctorate, GRE General Test or MAT. Additional exam requirements/recommendations for international students: Required—TOEFL (minimum score 550 paper-based; 213 computer-based).

National-Louis University, National College of Education, Program in Mathematics Education, Chicago, IL 60603. Offers M Ed, MS Ed, CAS. Part-time and evening/weekend programs available. *Degree requirements:* For master's, thesis (for some programs). *Entrance requirements:* For master's, MAT or GRE, minimum GPA of 3.0, teaching certificate; for CAS, master's degree, teaching certificate. *Expenses:* Tuition: Full-time $17,160; part-time $715 per semester hour. Tuition and fees vary according to course load, degree level, campus/location and program.

New Jersey City University, Graduate Studies and Continuing Education, William J. Maxwell College of Arts and Sciences, Department of Mathematics, Jersey City, NJ 07305-1597. Offers mathematics education (MA). Part-time and evening/weekend programs available. *Faculty:* 6. *Students:* 3 full-time (2 women), 22 part-time (12 women); includes 10 minority (4 African Americans, 1 Asian American or Pacific Islander, 5 Hispanic Americans), 1 international. In 2009, 12 master's awarded. *Degree requirements:* For master's, comprehensive exam, thesis optional. *Entrance requirements:* For master's, GRE General Test or MAT. Additional exam requirements/recommendations for international students: Required—TOEFL. *Application deadline:* For fall admission, 8/1 priority date for domestic students; for spring admission, 12/1 for domestic students. Applications are processed on a rolling basis. Application fee: $0. *Expenses:* Tuition, area resident: Part-time $456.75 per credit. Tuition, nonresident: part-time $842.55 per credit. Required fees: $65 per term. *Financial support:* Unspecified assistantships available. *Unit head:* Dr. Bimnet Teclezghi, Chairperson, 201-200-3202, E-mail: bteclezghi@njcu.edu. *Application contact:* Dr. Bimnet Teclezghi, Chairperson, 201-200-3202, E-mail: bteclezghi@njcu.edu.

New York University, Steinhardt School of Culture, Education, and Human Development, Department of Teaching and Learning, Program in Mathematics Education, New York, NY 10012-1019. Offers MA. *Accreditation:* Teacher Education Accreditation Council. Part-time and evening/weekend programs available. *Students:* 48 full-time (31 women), 12 part-time (10 women); includes 18 minority (4 African Americans, 11 Asian Americans or Pacific Islanders, 3 Hispanic Americans), 2 international. Average age 25. 48 applicants, 73% accepted, 14 enrolled. In 2009, 28 master's awarded. *Degree requirements:* For master's, thesis (for some programs). *Entrance requirements:* Additional exam requirements/recommendations for international students: Required—TOEFL. *Application deadline:* For fall admission, 12/15 priority date for domestic and international students; for spring admission, 11/1 for domestic and international students. Applications are processed on a rolling basis. Application fee: $75. Electronic applications accepted. *Expenses:* Tuition: Full-time $30,528; part-time $1272 per credit. Required fees: $2177. *Financial support:* Career-related internships or fieldwork, Federal Work-Study, institutionally sponsored loans, scholarships/grants, and tuition waivers (partial) available. Support available to part-time students. Financial award application deadline: 2/1; financial award applicants required to submit FAFSA. *Faculty research:* Race, gender and mathematics learning; developing mathematical concepts through activity; innovative secondary school mathematics materials. *Unit head:* Dr. Orit Zaslavsky, Director, 212-998-5460, Fax: 212-995-4049. *Application contact:* 212-998-5030, Fax: 212-995-4328, E-mail: steinhardt.gradadmissions@nyu.edu.

Nicholls State University, Graduate Studies, College of Arts and Sciences, Department of Mathematics and Computer Science, Thibodaux, LA 70310. Offers community/technical college mathematics (MS). Part-time and evening/weekend programs available. *Degree requirements:* For master's, comprehensive exam. *Entrance requirements:* For master's, GRE General Test. Electronic applications accepted. *Faculty research:* Operations research, statistics, numerical analysis, algebra, topology.

North Carolina Agricultural and Technical State University, Graduate School, College of Arts and Sciences, Department of Mathematics, Greensboro, NC 27411. Offers mathematics education (MS), including applied mathematics, mathematics, secondary education. *Accreditation:* NCATE. Part-time and evening/weekend programs available. *Degree requirements:* For master's, comprehensive exam, thesis or alternative, qualifying exam. *Entrance requirements:* For master's, GRE General Test, minimum GPA of 3.0.

North Carolina Central University, Division of Academic Affairs, College of Science and Technology, Department of Mathematics and Computer Science, Durham, NC 27707-3129. Offers applied mathematics (MS); mathematics education (MS); pure mathematics (MS). Part-time and evening/weekend programs available. *Degree requirements:* For master's, one foreign language, comprehensive exam, thesis. *Entrance requirements:* For master's, minimum GPA of 3.0 in major, 2.5 overall. Additional exam requirements/recommendations for international students: Required—TOEFL. *Faculty research:* Structure theorems for Lie algebra, Kleene monoids and semi-groups, theoretical computer science, mathematics education.

North Carolina State University, Graduate School, College of Education, Department of Mathematics, Science, and Technology Education, Program in Mathematics Education, Raleigh, NC 27695. Offers M Ed, MS, PhD. *Accreditation:* NCATE. Part-time programs available. *Degree requirements:* For master's, thesis (for some programs), oral exam; for doctorate, one foreign language, thesis/dissertation, oral and written exams. *Entrance requirements:* For master's, GRE General Test or MAT, minimum GPA of 3.0; for doctorate, GRE General Test, minimum GPA of 3.0, interview. Electronic applications accepted. *Faculty research:* Teacher education using technology, curriculum development, scientific visualization, problem solving.

North Dakota State University, College of Graduate and Interdisciplinary Studies, College of Human Development and Education, School of Education, Fargo, ND 58108. Offers agricultural education (M Ed, MS), including agricultural education, agricultural extension education (MS); counseling (M Ed, MS, PhD); curriculum and instruction (M Ed, MS), including pedagogy, physical education and athletic administration; education (PhD); educational leadership (M Ed, MS, Ed S); family and consumer sciences education (M Ed, MS); history education (M Ed, MS); institutional analysis (Ed D); mathematics education (M Ed, MS); music education (M Ed, MS); occupational and adult education (Ed D); science education (M Ed, MS). *Accreditation:* NCATE. Part-time and evening/weekend programs available. Postbaccalaureate distance learning degree programs offered (minimal on-campus study). *Faculty:* 25 full-time (9 women), 3 part-time/adjunct (1 woman). *Students:* 29 full-time (25 women), 207 part-time (132 women); includes 15 minority (4 African Americans, 6 American Indian/Alaska Native, 3 Asian Americans or Pacific Islanders, 2 Hispanic Americans), 4 international. 88 applicants, 67% accepted, 56 enrolled. In 2009, 44 master's, 5 doctorates awarded. *Degree requirements:* For master's, comprehensive exam; for doctorate, thesis/dissertation; for Ed S, thesis. *Entrance requirements:* For degree, GRE General Test, master's degree, minimum GPA of 3.25. Additional exam requirements/recommendations for international students: Required—TOEFL. *Application deadline:* Applications are processed on a rolling basis. Application fee: $45 ($60 for international students). *Financial support:* Research assistantships, teaching assistantships, career-related internships or fieldwork, Federal Work-Study, institutionally sponsored loans, and tuition waivers (full) available. Financial award application deadline: 4/15. *Unit head:* Dr. William Martin, Chair, 701-231-7202, Fax: 701-231-7416, E-mail: william.martin@ndsu.edu. *Application contact:* Dr. William Martin, Chair, 701-231-7202, Fax: 701-231-7416, E-mail: william.martin@ndsu.edu.

Northeastern Illinois University, Graduate College, College of Arts and Sciences, Department of Mathematics, Programs in Mathematics, Chicago, IL 60625-4699. Offers mathematics (MS); mathematics for elementary school teachers (MA). Part-time and evening/weekend programs available. *Degree requirements:* For master's, comprehensive exam, thesis optional, project. *Entrance requirements:* For master's, minimum GPA of 2.75, 6 undergraduate courses in mathematics. Additional exam requirements/recommendations for international students: Required—TOEFL (minimum score 550 paper-based; 213 computer-based; 80 iBT). Electronic applications accepted. *Faculty research:* Numerical analysis, mathematical biology, operations research, statistics, geometry and mathematics of finance.

Northeastern State University, Graduate College, College of Education, Program in Mathematics Education, Tahlequah, OK 74464-2399. Offers M Ed. *Entrance requirements:* For master's, GRE or MAT, minimum GPA of 2.5. Additional exam requirements/recommendations for international students: Required—TOEFL (minimum score 213 computer-based). Electronic applications accepted.

Northern Arizona University, Graduate College, College of Engineering, Forestry and Natural Sciences, Center for Science Teaching and Learning, Flagstaff, AZ 86011. Offers mathematics or science teaching (Certificate); science teaching and learning (M Ed, MAST). Part-time programs available. Postbaccalaureate distance learning degree programs offered (minimal on-campus study). *Faculty:* 2 full-time (both women). *Students:* 6 full-time (5 women), 7

part-time (6 women); includes 1 African American, 1 Hispanic American. In 2009, 6 master's awarded. *Entrance requirements:* Additional exam requirements/recommendations for international students: Required—TOEFL (minimum score 550 paper-based; 213 computer-based; 80 iBT), IELTS (minimum score 7), or a bachelor's degree from an English-speaking university and demonstrated proficiency. Application fee: $65. *Financial support:* Career-related internships or fieldwork available. Support available to part-time students. Financial award application deadline: 3/30; financial award applicants required to submit FAFSA. *Unit head:* Julie Gess-Newsome, Director, 928-523-9527, E-mail: julie.gess-newsome@nau.edu. *Application contact:* Dr. Sharon Cardenas, Faculty Coordinator, 928-523-7430.

Northern Arizona University, Graduate College, College of Engineering, Forestry and Natural Sciences, Department of Mathematics and Statistics, Flagstaff, AZ 86011. Offers mathematics (MAT, MS); statistics (MS, Certificate). Part-time programs available. *Faculty:* 32 full-time (10 women). *Students:* 21 full-time (9 women), 22 part-time (14 women); includes 5 minority (3 Asian Americans or Pacific Islanders, 2 Hispanic Americans), 3 international. Average age 28. 34 applicants, 62% accepted, 14 enrolled. In 2009, 9 master's awarded. *Degree requirements:* For master's, comprehensive exam, thesis optional. *Entrance requirements:* For master's, minimum GPA of 3.0. Additional exam requirements/recommendations for international students: Required—TOEFL (minimum score 550 paper-based; 213 computer-based; 80 iBT), IELTS (minimum score 7), or a bachelor's degree from an English-speaking university and demonstrated proficiency. *Application deadline:* For fall admission, 3/15 priority date for domestic students, 9/1 priority date for international students; for spring admission, 10/15 priority date for domestic students. Applications are processed on a rolling basis. Application fee: $65. Electronic applications accepted. *Financial support:* In 2009–10, 22 teaching assistantships with partial tuition reimbursements (averaging $14,213 per year) were awarded; career-related internships or fieldwork, Federal Work-Study, tuition waivers (full and partial), and unspecified assistantships also available. Support available to part-time students. Financial award application deadline: 3/30; financial award applicants required to submit FAFSA. *Faculty research:* Topology, statistics, groups, ring theory, number theory. *Unit head:* Dr. Janet M. McShane, Chair, 928-523-1252, Fax: 928-523-5847, E-mail: janet.mcshane@nau.edu. *Application contact:* Dr. Jeffrey Allen Hovermill, Chair, 928-523-6897, Fax: 928-523-5847, E-mail: jeff.hovermill@nau.edu.

North Georgia College & State University, Graduate Studies, Program in Teacher Education, Dahlonega, GA 30597. Offers early childhood education (M Ed); educational leadership (Ed S); middle grades education (M Ed); secondary education (M Ed), including art education, biology education, chemistry education, English education, history education, mathematics education, physical education, science education; special education (M Ed), including interrelated special education, learning disabilities. *Accreditation:* NCATE. Part-time and evening/weekend programs available. Postbaccalaureate distance learning degree programs offered (minimal on-campus study). *Degree requirements:* For master's, comprehensive exam, thesis optional. *Entrance requirements:* For master's, GRE General Test or MAT, minimum GPA of 2.75; for Ed S, GRE General Test or MAT, 3 years of teaching experience, master's degree, minimum graduate GPA of 3.25. Electronic applications accepted. *Faculty research:* Computers and teachers' attitudes, rural versus urban teacher attitudes, teacher leadership roles, minority recruitment in teaching force.

Northwestern State University of Louisiana, Graduate Studies and Research, College of Education, Programs in Education, Natchitoches, LA 71497. Offers business and distributive education (M Ed); counseling (M Ed); early childhood education (M Ed); education (M Ed); education leadership (M Ed); educational technology (M Ed); elementary teaching (M Ed); English education (M Ed); home economics education (M Ed); mathematics education (M Ed); reading (M Ed); science education (M Ed); secondary teaching (M Ed); social sciences education (M Ed). *Degree requirements:* For master's, comprehensive exam, thesis or alternative. *Entrance requirements:* For master's, GRE General Test, minimum undergraduate GPA of 2.5.

Northwest Missouri State University, Graduate School, College of Arts and Sciences, Department of Mathematics and Statistics, Maryville, MO 64468-6001. Offers teaching mathematics (MS Ed). Part-time programs available. *Faculty:* 8 full-time (3 women). *Students:* 3 full-time (0 women), 1 (woman) part-time. 3 applicants, 100% accepted, 1 enrolled. In 2009, 1 master's awarded. *Degree requirements:* For master's, comprehensive exam. *Entrance requirements:* For master's, GRE General Test, minimum undergraduate GPA of 2.5, writing sample. Additional exam requirements/recommendations for international students: Required—TOEFL (minimum score 550 paper-based; 213 computer-based). *Application deadline:* For fall admission, 7/1 for domestic and international students; for spring admission, 11/15 for domestic and international students. Applications are processed on a rolling basis. Application fee: $0 ($50 for international students). *Expenses:* Tuition, state resident: part-time $296.34 per credit hour. Tuition, nonresident: part-time $510.43 per credit hour. *Financial support:* In 2009–10, 3 teaching assistantships with full tuition reimbursements (averaging $6,000 per year) were awarded. Financial award application deadline: 4/1; financial award applicants required to submit FAFSA. *Unit head:* Dr. Dennis Malm, Chairperson, 660-562-1807. *Application contact:* Dr. Gregory Haddock, Dean of Graduate School, 660-562-1145, Fax: 660-562-1096, E-mail: gradsch@nwmissouri.edu.

Nova Southeastern University, Fischler School of Education and Human Services, Graduate Teacher Education Program, Fort Lauderdale, FL 33314-7796. Offers athletic administration (MS); brain research (MS, Ed S); charter school education/leadership (MS); cognitive and behavioral disabilities (MS); computer science education (Ed S); computer science education (K-12) (MS); curriculum and teaching (Ed S); curriculum, instruction and technology (MS); curriculum, instruction, management and administration (Ed S); early childhood education (MS); early literacy and reading (Ed S); early literacy education (MS); education technology (MS); educational leadership (administration K–12) (MS, Ed S); educational media (Ed S); educational media (K-12) (MS); elementary education (MS, Ed S), including ESOL endorsement (MS); English education (MS, Ed S); environmental education (MS); exceptional student education (MS), including ESOL endorsement; gifted education (MS, Ed S); interdisciplinary arts education (MS); management and administration of educational programs (MS); mathematics (MS); mathematics education (Ed S); multicultural early intervention (MS); pre-kindergarten/primary (MS); preschool education (MS); reading (MS); reading and TESOL (MS); reading education (Ed S); science (MS); science education (Ed S); secondary education (MS); social studies (MS, Ed S); Spanish language (MS); special education and reading (MS); teaching and learning (MA, MS), including curriculum and instruction (MA), elementary mathematics (MA), elementary reading (MA), K-12 technology integration (MA); teaching English to speakers of other languages (MS, Ed S); technology management and administration (Ed S); urban studies education (MS). Part-time and evening/weekend programs available. Postbaccalaureate distance learning degree programs offered (minimal on-campus study). *Faculty:* 72 full-time (43 women), 385 part-time/adjunct (252 women). *Students:* 196 full-time (175 women), 1,304 part-time (1,128 women); includes 594 minority (471 African Americans, 5 American Indian/Alaska Native, 18 Asian Americans or Pacific Islanders, 100 Hispanic Americans). Average age 37. 2,610 applicants, 72% accepted, 1352 enrolled. In 2009, 836 other advanced degrees awarded. *Degree requirements:* For master's and Ed S, thesis, practicum, internship. *Entrance requirements:* For master's, MAT, GRE, CLAST, CBEST, PRAXIS I, General Knowledge Test, minimum GPA of 2.5; for Ed S, MAT or GRE, master's degree, teaching certificate, minimum GPA of 3.0. Additional exam requirements/recommendations for international students: Required—TSE (recommended, minimum score 50); Recommended—TOEFL (minimum score 550 paper-based; 213 computer-based; 80 iBT), IELTS (minimum score 6). *Application deadline:* For fall admission, 9/25 priority date for domestic and international students; for winter admission, 2/23 priority date for domestic and international students; for spring admission, 4/25 priority date for domestic and international students. Applications are processed on a rolling basis. Application fee: $50. Electronic applications accepted. *Financial support:* Federal Work-Study available. Support available to part-time students. Financial award application deadline: 4/15; financial award applicants required to submit FAFSA. *Faculty research:* School effectiveness, critical thinking, leadership skills acquisition, child education, multicultural education. *Unit head:* Dr. Ronald Kern, Dean of Academic Affairs, 800-986-3223 Ext. 7809, Fax: 954-262-3606, E-mail: rk429@nsu.nova.edu. *Application contact:* Dr. Jennifer Quinones Nottingham, Dean of Student Affairs, 800-986-3223 Ext. 1559.

Oakland University, Graduate Study and Lifelong Learning, School of Education and Human Services, Department of Human Development and Child Studies, Program in Early Childhood Education, Rochester, MI 48309-4401. Offers early childhood education (M Ed, PhD, Certificate); early mathematics education (Certificate). *Accreditation:* Teacher Education Accreditation Council. *Degree requirements:* For doctorate, thesis/dissertation. *Entrance requirements:* For master's, minimum GPA of 3.0 for unconditional admission; for doctorate, GRE General Test, minimum GPA of 3.0 for unconditional admission. Additional exam requirements/recommendations for international students: Required—TOEFL (minimum score 550 paper-based; 213 computer-based).

Occidental College, Graduate Studies, Department of Education, Program in Secondary Education, Los Angeles, CA 90041-3314. Offers English and comparative literary studies (MAT); history (MAT); life science (MAT); mathematics (MAT); physical science (MAT); social science (MAT); Spanish (MAT). Part-time programs available. *Degree requirements:* For master's, comprehensive exam, graduate synthesis paper. *Entrance requirements:* For master's, GRE General Test, minimum GPA of 3.0. Additional exam requirements/recommendations for international students: Required—TOEFL (minimum score 625 paper-based; 263 computer-based). *Expenses:* Contact institution.

Ohio University, Graduate College, College of Education, Department of Teacher Education, Athens, OH 45701-2979. Offers adolescent to young adult education (M Ed); curriculum and instruction (M Ed, PhD); early childhood/special education (M Ed); intervention specialist/mild-moderate needs (M Ed); intervention specialist/moderate-intensive needs (M Ed); mathematics education (PhD); middle child education (M Ed); reading education (M Ed); social studies education (PhD). Part-time and evening/weekend programs available. *Faculty:* 21 full-time (13 women), 7 part-time/adjunct (all women). *Students:* 105 full-time (75 women), 183 part-time (161 women); includes 9 minority (5 African Americans, 3 American Indian/Alaska Native, 1 Asian American or Pacific Islander), 14 international. 190 applicants, 80% accepted, 72 enrolled. *Degree requirements:* For master's, thesis or alternative; for doctorate, comprehensive exam, thesis/dissertation. *Entrance requirements:* For master's, GRE General Test or MAT (if GPA is below 2.9); for doctorate, GRE General Test, minimum GPA of 3.4, work experience. Additional exam requirements/recommendations for international students: Required—TOEFL (minimum score 550 paper-based; 80 iBT) or IELTS Academic (minimum score 6.5). *Application deadline:* For fall admission, 5/1 priority date for domestic students, 4/1 priority date for international students; for winter admission, 11/1 priority date for domestic students, 10/1 priority date for international students; for spring admission, 2/15 priority date for domestic students, 1/1 priority date for international students. Applications are processed on a rolling basis. Application fee: $50 ($55 for international students). Electronic applications accepted. *Expenses:* Tuition, state resident: full-time $7839; part-time $323 per quarter hour. Tuition, nonresident: full-time $15,831; part-time $654 per quarter hour. Required fees: $2931. *Financial support:* Research assistantships with full tuition reimbursements, teaching assistantships with full tuition reimbursements, Federal Work-Study, institutionally sponsored loans, tuition waivers (partial), and unspecified assistantships available. Financial award application deadline: 3/1. *Faculty research:* Cognition literacy, character education, teacher's education reform, disabilities. Total annual research expenditures: $46,933. *Unit head:* Dr. John Henning, Chair, 740-597-1830, Fax: 740-593-0477, E-mail: henningj@ohio.edu. *Application contact:* Floyd J. Doney, Director of Student Affairs, 740-593-4400, Fax: 740-593-9310, E-mail: doney@ohio.edu.

Oklahoma State University, College of Arts and Sciences, Department of Mathematics, Stillwater, OK 74078. Offers applied mathematics (MS, PhD); mathematics education (MS, PhD); pure mathematics (MS, PhD). *Faculty:* 32 full-time (4 women), 10 part-time/adjunct (6 women). *Students:* 31 full-time (7 women), 23 international. Average age 32. 72 applicants, 19% accepted, 6 enrolled. In 2009, 6 master's, 4 doctorates awarded. *Degree requirements:* For master's, thesis, creative component, or report; for doctorate, comprehensive exam, thesis/dissertation. *Entrance requirements:* For master's and doctorate, GRE (recommended). Additional exam requirements/recommendations for international students: Required—TOEFL (minimum score 550 paper-based; 79 iBT). *Application deadline:* For fall admission, 3/1 for domestic and international students; for spring admission, 10/15 for domestic students, 10/15 priority date for international students. Applications are processed on a rolling basis. Application fee: $40 ($75 for international students). Electronic applications accepted. *Expenses:* Tuition, state resident: full-time $3716; part-time $154.85 per credit hour. Tuition, nonresident: full-time $14,448; part-time $602 per credit hour. Required fees: $1772; $73.85 per credit hour. One-time fee: $50. Tuition and fees vary according to course load and campus/location. *Financial support:* In 2009–10, 29 teaching assistantships (averaging $14,046 per year) were awarded; fellowships, health care benefits and tuition waivers (partial) also available. Financial award application deadline: 3/1; financial award applicants required to submit FAFSA. *Unit head:* Dr. Dale Alspach, Head, 405-744-5688, Fax: 405-744-8275. *Application contact:* Dr. Mark Payton, Dean, 405-744-6368, Fax: 405-744-0355, E-mail: grad-i@okstate.edu.

Oregon State University, Graduate School, College of Science, Department of Science and Mathematics Education, Program in Mathematics Education, Corvallis, OR 97331. Offers MA, MS, PhD. *Accreditation:* NCATE. *Degree requirements:* For master's, variable foreign language requirement; for doctorate, one foreign language, thesis/dissertation. *Entrance requirements:* For master's, minimum GPA of 3.0 in last 90 hours of course work; for doctorate, GRE or MAT, minimum GPA of 3.0 in last 90 hours of course work. Additional exam requirements/recommendations for international students: Required—TOEFL. *Application deadline:* For fall admission, 3/1 for domestic students. Applications are processed on a rolling basis. Application fee: $50. *Expenses:* Tuition, state resident: full-time $9774; part-time $362 per credit. Tuition, nonresident: full-time $15,849; part-time $587 per credit. Required fees: $1639. Full-time tuition and fees vary according to course load and program. *Financial support:* Teaching assistantships, Federal Work-Study and institutionally sponsored loans available. Support available to part-time students. Financial award application deadline: 2/1. *Faculty research:* Teacher action when focused on standards, teacher belief, integration of technology. *Unit head:* Program Coordinator, 541-737-9286, Fax: 541-737-1817. *Application contact:* Dr. Mary Ann Matzke, Head Advisor, 541-737-3880, Fax: 541-737-1009, E-mail: maryann.matzke@oregonstate.edu.

Our Lady of the Lake University of San Antonio, School of Professional Studies, Program in Curriculum and Instruction, San Antonio, TX 78207-4689. Offers bilingual (M Ed); early childhood education (M Ed); English as a second language (M Ed); integrated math teaching (M Ed); integrated science teaching (M Ed); master reading teacher (M Ed); master technology teacher (M Ed); reading specialist (M Ed). *Students:* 2 full-time (1 woman), 112 part-time (94 women); includes 64 minority (5 African Americans, 1 American Indian/Alaska Native, 1 Asian American or Pacific Islander, 57 Hispanic Americans). Average age 38. In 2009, 49 master's awarded. *Expenses:* Tuition: Full-time $12,330; part-time $685 per contact hour. Required fees: $139; $12 per contact hour. $57 per semester. Tuition and fees vary according to campus/location. *Unit head:* Dr. Cullen Grinnan, 210-434-6711 Ext. 8928, E-mail: ctgrinnan@lake.ollusa.edu. *Application contact:* Dr. Cullen Grinnan, 210-434-6711 Ext. 8928, E-mail: ctgrinnan@lake.ollusa.edu.

Our Lady of the Lake University of San Antonio, School of Professional Studies, Program in Intermediate Education, San Antonio, TX 78207-4689. Offers math/science education (M Ed); professional studies (M Ed). Part-time and evening/weekend programs available. *Students:* 3 full-time (1 woman), 14 part-time (11 women); includes 11 minority (3 African Americans, 8 Hispanic Americans). Average age 36. In 2009, 4 master's awarded. *Expenses:* Tuition: Full-time $12,330; part-time $685 per contact hour. Required fees: $139; $12 per contact hour. $57 per semester. Tuition and fees vary according to campus/location. *Unit head:* Dr. Cullen Grinnen, E-mail: ctgrinnan@lake.ollusa.edu. *Application contact:* Dr. Cullen Grinnen, E-mail: ctgrinnan@lake.ollusa.edu.

Plymouth State University, College of Graduate Studies, Graduate Studies in Education, Program in Mathematics Education, Plymouth, NH 03264-1595. Offers M Ed. Part-time and

Mathematics Education

Plymouth State University (continued)
evening/weekend programs available. *Degree requirements:* For master's, comprehensive exam, thesis optional. *Entrance requirements:* For master's, MAT, minimum GPA of 3.0.

Portland State University, Graduate Studies, College of Liberal Arts and Sciences, Department of Mathematics and Statistics, Portland, OR 97207-0751. Offers mathematical sciences (PhD); mathematics education (PhD); statistics (MS); MA/MS. *Degree requirements:* For master's, thesis or alternative, exams; for doctorate, 2 foreign languages, thesis/dissertation, exams. *Entrance requirements:* For master's, GRE General Test, GRE Subject Test, minimum GPA of 3.0 in upper-division course work or 2.75 overall; for doctorate, GRE General Test. Additional exam requirements/recommendations for international students: Required—TOEFL (minimum score 550 paper-based; 213 computer-based). *Faculty research:* Algebra, topology, statistical distribution theory, control theory, statistical robustness.

Providence College, Graduate Studies, Department of Mathematics, Providence, RI 02918. Offers teaching mathematics (MA). Part-time and evening/weekend programs available. *Faculty:* 4 full-time (1 woman). *Students:* 2 full-time (both women), 20 part-time (14 women); includes 1 minority (Hispanic American). Average age 32. 12 applicants, 100% accepted. In 2009, 13 master's awarded. *Entrance requirements:* Additional exam requirements/recommendations for international students: Required—TOEFL (minimum score 550 paper-based; 213 computer-based; 80 iBT). *Application deadline:* For fall admission, 8/1 priority date for domestic and international students; for spring admission, 12/1 priority date for domestic and international students. Applications are processed on a rolling basis. Application fee: $55. *Expenses:* Tuition: Full-time $9909; part-time $367 per credit. One-time fee: $200. Tuition and fees vary according to course load and program. *Financial support:* In 2009–10, 1 research assistantship with full tuition reimbursement (averaging $8,400 per year) was awarded; institutionally sponsored loans and unspecified assistantships also available. Support available to part-time students. Financial award application deadline: 8/1; financial award applicants required to submit FAFSA. *Unit head:* Dr. Linda M. Wilkens, Program Director, 401-865-1896, Fax: 401-865-1356, E-mail: lwilkens@providence.edu. *Application contact:* Carol A. Daniels, Coordinator of Graduate Faculty and Administrative Services, 401-865-2247, Fax: 401-865-1147, E-mail: daniels@providence.edu.

Purdue University, Graduate School, School of Education, Department of Curriculum and Instruction, West Lafayette, IN 47907. Offers agricultural and extension education (PhD, Ed S); agriculture and extension education (MS, MS Ed); art education (PhD); consumer and family sciences and extension education (MS Ed, PhD, Ed S); curriculum studies (MS Ed, PhD, Ed S); educational technology (MS Ed, PhD, Ed S); elementary education (MS Ed); foreign language education (MS Ed, PhD, Ed S); industrial technology (PhD, Ed S); language arts (MS Ed, PhD, Ed S); literacy (MS Ed, PhD, Ed S); mathematics/science education (MS, MS Ed, PhD, Ed S); social studies (MS Ed, PhD); social studies education (Ed S); vocational/industrial education (MS Ed, PhD, Ed S); vocational/technical education (MS Ed, PhD, Ed S). *Accreditation:* NCATE. Part-time and evening/weekend programs available. *Degree requirements:* For master's, thesis optional; for doctorate, thesis/dissertation, oral and written exams; for Ed S, oral presentation, project. *Entrance requirements:* For master's, GRE General Test, minimum B average; for doctorate, GRE General Test; for Ed S, GRE, minimum B average. Additional exam requirements/recommendations for international students: Required—TOEFL. Electronic applications accepted. *Faculty research:* Literacy acquisition and development, teacher beliefs and knowledge, recruitment and retention of underrepresented students, economic education, literacy discourse.

Purdue University Calumet, Graduate School, School of Engineering, Mathematics, and Science, Department of Mathematics, Computer Science, and Statistics, Hammond, IN 46323-2094. Offers mathematics (MAT, MS). Part-time programs available. *Entrance requirements:* Additional exam requirements/recommendations for international students: Required—TOEFL. *Faculty research:* Topology, analysis, algebra, mathematics education.

Queens College of the City University of New York, Division of Graduate Studies, Division of Education, Department of Secondary Education, Flushing, NY 11367-1597. Offers art (MS Ed); biology (MS Ed, AC); chemistry (MS Ed, AC); earth sciences (MS Ed, AC); English (MS Ed, AC); French (MS Ed, AC); Italian (MS Ed, AC); mathematics (MS Ed, AC); music (MS Ed, AC); physics (MS Ed, AC); social studies (MS Ed, AC); Spanish (MS Ed, AC). Part-time and evening/weekend programs available. *Faculty:* 22 full-time (14 women). *Students:* 86 full-time (47 women), 1,118 part-time (736 women). 591 applicants, 60% accepted, 250 enrolled. In 2009, 187 master's awarded. *Degree requirements:* For master's, research project; for AC, thesis optional. *Entrance requirements:* For master's, minimum GPA of 3.0. Additional exam requirements/recommendations for international students: Required—TOEFL. *Application deadline:* For fall admission, 4/1 for domestic students; for spring admission, 11/1 for domestic students. Applications are processed on a rolling basis. Application fee: $125. *Expenses:* Tuition, state resident: full-time $7360; part-time $310 per credit. Tuition, nonresident: part-time $575 per credit. One-time fee: $195 full-time; $145.25 part-time. *Financial support:* Career-related internships or fieldwork, Federal Work-Study, institutionally sponsored loans, and tuition waivers (partial) available. Support available to part-time students. Financial award application deadline: 4/1; financial award applicants required to submit FAFSA. *Unit head:* Dr. Eleanor Armour-Thomas, Chairperson, 718-997-5150, E-mail: armourthomas@yahoo.com. *Application contact:* Mario Caruso, Director of Graduate Admissions, 718-997-5200, Fax: 718-997-5193, E-mail: graduate_admissions@qc.edu.

Quinnipiac University, Division of Education, Program in Secondary Education, Hamden, CT 06518-1940. Offers biology (MAT); English (MAT); history/social studies (MAT); mathematics (MAT); Spanish (MAT). *Accreditation:* NCATE. *Faculty:* 10 full-time (7 women), 5 part-time/adjunct (3 women). *Students:* 80 full-time (56 women), 2 part-time (1 woman); includes 6 minority (2 African Americans, 2 Asian Americans or Pacific Islanders, 2 Hispanic Americans). 77 applicants, 95% accepted, 66 enrolled. In 2009, 33 master's awarded. *Entrance requirements:* For master's, PRAXIS I, minimum GPA of 2.67, interview. Additional exam requirements/recommendations for international students: Required—TOEFL (minimum score 575 paper-based; 233 computer-based; 90 iBT), IELTS (minimum score 6.5). *Application deadline:* For fall admission, 3/31 priority date for domestic students. Applications are processed on a rolling basis. Application fee: $45. Electronic applications accepted. *Expenses:* Tuition: Full-time $16,030; part-time $770 per credit. Required fees: $630; $35 per credit. *Financial support:* Career-related internships or fieldwork, scholarships/grants, and tuition waivers (partial) available. Financial award application deadline: 4/15; financial award applicants required to submit FAFSA. *Faculty research:* Multicultural and urban education, role of technology in education, challenges of teaching diverse learners, socio-cultural nature of learning. *Unit head:* Dr. Bernadine Krawczyk, Assistant Dean, Division of Education, 203-582-3510, Fax: 203-582-3473, E-mail: bernadine.krawczyk@quinnipiac.edu. *Application contact:* Jennifer Boutin, Associate Director of Graduate Admissions, 800-462-1944, Fax: 203-582-3443, E-mail: jennifer.boutin@quinnipiac.edu.

Regent University, Graduate School, School of Education, Virginia Beach, VA 23464-9800. Offers career switcher (M Ed); Christian school program (M Ed); cross-categorical special education (M Ed); education (M Ed, Ed D); education licensure (M Ed); educational leadership (M Ed); elementary education (M Ed); individualized degree plan (M Ed); leadership in character education (M Ed); master teacher (M Ed); mathematics education (M Ed); special education leadership (Ed S); student affairs (M Ed); TESOL (M Ed). *Accreditation:* Teacher Education Accreditation Council. Part-time and evening/weekend programs available. Postbaccalaureate distance learning degree programs offered (minimal on-campus study). *Faculty:* 26 full-time (13 women), 104 part-time/adjunct (78 women). *Students:* 141 full-time (116 women), 622 part-time (488 women); includes 218 minority (186 African Americans, 1 American Indian/Alaska Native, 10 Asian Americans or Pacific Islanders, 21 Hispanic Americans), 8 international. Average age 39. 509 applicants, 60% accepted, 176 enrolled. In 2009, 212 master's, 15 doctorates awarded. *Degree requirements:* For master's, thesis or alternative; for doctorate, comprehensive exam, thesis/dissertation. *Entrance requirements:* For master's, MAT, minimum undergraduate GPA of 2.75, writing sample, resume, recommendations, interview; for doctorate, GRE, writing sample, 3 years of relevant professional experience, master's-level paper, copies of published work, resume, transcripts, interview, recommendations. Additional exam requirements/recommendations for international students: Required—TOEFL (minimum score 577 paper-based; 233 computer-based). *Application deadline:* For fall admission, 4/1 priority date for domestic students; for spring admission, 10/15 priority date for domestic students. Applications are processed on a rolling basis. Application fee: $50. Electronic applications accepted. *Expenses:* Contact institution. *Financial support:* In 2009–10, 480 students received support; fellowships, career-related internships or fieldwork, scholarships/grants, tuition waivers (full and partial), and unspecified assistantships available. Support available to part-time students. Financial award application deadline: 4/1; financial award applicants required to submit FAFSA. *Faculty research:* Character development and discipline for children, education leadership development, diversity in schools, classroom management, technology in education settings. *Unit head:* Dr. Alan A. Arroyo, Dean, 757-352-4261, Fax: 757-352-4318, E-mail: alanarr@regent.edu. *Application contact:* Matthew Chadwick, Director of Admissions, 800-373-5504, Fax: 757-352-4381, E-mail: admissions@regent.edu.

Rhode Island College, School of Graduate Studies, Feinstein School of Education and Human Development, Department of Educational Studies, Providence, RI 02908-1991. Offers English (MAT); French (MAT); history (MAT); math (MAT); secondary education (MAT); Spanish (MAT); teaching English as a second language (M Ed); technology education (M Ed). *Accreditation:* NCATE. Part-time and evening/weekend programs available. *Faculty:* 10 full-time (5 women), 6 part-time/adjunct (5 women). *Students:* 8 full-time (all women), 56 part-time (40 women); includes 2 minority (both Hispanic Americans). Average age 35. In 2009, 28 master's awarded. *Degree requirements:* For master's, capstone or comprehensive assessment. *Entrance requirements:* For master's, GRE or MAT (for most programs), minimum undergraduate GPA of 3.0; baccalaureate degree in English, French, history, math or Spanish; evaluation of content area knowledge; 3 letters of recommendation; interview. Additional exam requirements/recommendations for international students: Recommended—TOEFL (minimum score 550 paper-based; 213 computer-based; 79 iBT). *Application deadline:* For fall admission, 3/15 for domestic students; for spring admission, 11/1 for domestic students. Applications are processed on a rolling basis. Application fee: $50. *Expenses:* Tuition, state resident: full-time $7440; part-time $310 per credit hour. Tuition, nonresident: full-time $14,784; part-time $616 per credit hour. Required fees: $552; $20 per credit. $70 per term. *Financial support:* Teaching assistantships with full tuition reimbursements, career-related internships or fieldwork, Federal Work-Study, scholarships/grants, health care benefits, and unspecified assistantships available. Support available to part-time students. Financial award application deadline: 5/15; financial award applicants required to submit FAFSA. *Faculty research:* School administration, school/college articulation. *Unit head:* Dr. Ellen Bigler, Chair, 401-456-8170. *Application contact:* Graduate Studies, 401-456-8700.

Rider University, Department of Graduate Education, Leadership and Counseling, Teacher Certification Program, Lawrenceville, NJ 08648-3001. Offers business education (Certificate); elementary education (Certificate); English as a second language (Certificate); English education (Certificate); mathematics education (Certificate); preschool to grade 3 (Certificate); science education (Certificate); social studies education (Certificate); world languages (Certificate), including French, German, Spanish. Part-time programs available. *Degree requirements:* For Certificate, internship, professional portfolio. *Entrance requirements:* For degree, PRAXIS, resume. Additional exam requirements/recommendations for international students: Required—TOEFL (minimum score 550 paper-based; 213 computer-based). Electronic applications accepted. *Faculty research:* Conceptual foundations for optimal development of creativity; creative theory, cognitive processes in mathematics learning, teacher collaboration.

Rollins College, Hamilton Holt School, Program in Education, Winter Park, FL 32789-4499. Offers elementary education (M Ed, MAT); secondary education (MAT), including English, mathematics, music. Part-time and evening/weekend programs available. *Faculty:* 5 full-time (3 women), 3 part-time/adjunct (2 women). *Students:* 14 full-time (11 women), 26 part-time (25 women); includes 7 minority (4 African Americans, 3 Hispanic Americans). Average age 31. 27 applicants, 100% accepted, 27 enrolled. In 2009, 10 master's awarded. *Degree requirements:* For master's, comprehensive exam. *Entrance requirements:* For master's, GRE or MAT, interview. Additional exam requirements/recommendations for international students: Required—TOEFL. *Application deadline:* For fall admission, 7/16 for domestic students; for winter admission, 12/3 for domestic students; for spring admission, 4/22 for domestic students. Applications are processed on a rolling basis. Application fee: $50. *Expenses:* Contact institution. *Financial support:* Teaching assistantships, scholarships/grants available. Support available to part-time students. *Unit head:* Dr. J. Scott Hewit, Director, 407-646-2300, E-mail: jhewit@rollins.edu. *Application contact:* Rebecca Cordray, Coordinator of Records and Registration, 407-646-1568, Fax: 407-975-6430, E-mail: rcordray@rollins.edu.

Rutgers, The State University of New Jersey, New Brunswick, Graduate School of Education, Department of Learning and Teaching, Program in Mathematics Education, Piscataway, NJ 08854-8097. Offers Ed M, Ed D. Part-time programs available. Terminal master's awarded for partial completion of doctoral program. *Degree requirements:* For master's, comprehensive exam (for some programs); for doctorate, thesis/dissertation, qualifying exam. *Entrance requirements:* For master's, GRE General Test, minimum GPA of 3.0; for doctorate, GRE General Test, minimum GPA of 3.5. Additional exam requirements/recommendations for international students: Required—TOEFL. Electronic applications accepted.

Rutgers, The State University of New Jersey, New Brunswick, Graduate School of Education, Doctoral Program in Education, Piscataway, NJ 08854-8097. Offers educational policy (PhD); educational psychology (PhD); literacy education (PhD); mathematics education (PhD). Part-time programs available. *Degree requirements:* For doctorate, thesis/dissertation, qualifying exam. *Entrance requirements:* For doctorate, GRE General Test, GRE Subject Test (mathematics education). Additional exam requirements/recommendations for international students: Required—TOEFL (minimum score 575 paper-based; 233 computer-based; 83 iBT). Electronic applications accepted. *Faculty research:* Literacy education, math education, educational psychology, educational policy.

Sage Graduate School, Graduate School, School of Education, Program in Teaching, Troy, NY 12180-4115. Offers art education (MAT); English (MAT); mathematics (MAT); social studies (MAT). Part-time and evening/weekend programs available. *Faculty:* 15 full-time (9 women), 19 part-time/adjunct (16 women). *Students:* 32 full-time (25 women), 39 part-time (27 women); includes 4 minority (all Asian Americans or Pacific Islanders). Average age 27. 47 applicants, 55% accepted, 19 enrolled. In 2009, 36 master's awarded. *Entrance requirements:* For master's, minimum undergraduate GPA of 2.75 overall, 3.0 in content area; current resume; 2 letters of recommendation; assessment of writing skills. Additional exam requirements/recommendations for international students: Required—TOEFL (minimum score 550 paper-based; 213 computer-based). *Application deadline:* For fall admission, 8/1 for domestic students. Applications are processed on a rolling basis. Application fee: $40. *Expenses:* Tuition: Full-time $10,620; part-time $590 per credit hour. *Financial support:* Fellowships, research assistantships, Federal Work-Study, scholarships/grants, and unspecified assistantships available. Support available to part-time students. Financial award application deadline: 3/1; financial award applicants required to submit FAFSA. *Unit head:* Kelly Jones, Director, 518-244-2433. *Application contact:* Wendy D. Diefendorf, Director of Graduate and Adult Admission, 518-244-2443, Fax: 518-244-6880, E-mail: diefew@sage.edu.

St. John Fisher College, School of Arts and Sciences, Mathematics/Science/Technology Education Program, Rochester, NY 14618-3597. Offers MS. Part-time and evening/weekend programs available. *Faculty:* 3 full-time (2 women), 3 part-time/adjunct (1 woman). *Students:* 18 full-time (8 women), 45 part-time (24 women); includes 4 minority (2 African Americans, 2 Asian Americans or Pacific Islanders). Average age 31. 33 applicants, 85% accepted, 15 enrolled. In 2009, 18 master's awarded. *Degree requirements:* For master's, thesis, capstone experience. *Entrance requirements:* For master's, 2 letters of recommendation, personal statement, current resume, interview, teaching certification. Additional exam requirements/recommendations for international students: Required—TOEFL (minimum score 575 paper-

based; 233 computer-based; 80 iBT). *Application deadline:* Applications are processed on a rolling basis. Application fee: $30. Electronic applications accepted. *Expenses:* Tuition: Part-time $680 per credit hour. Required fees: $25 per semester. Tuition and fees vary according to degree level and program. *Financial support:* In 2009–10, 40 students received support. Federal Work-Study and scholarships/grants available. Financial award applicants required to submit FAFSA. *Faculty research:* Mathematics education, science and technology education. *Unit head:* Dr. Diane Barrett, Graduate Director, 585-385-8366, E-mail: dbarrett@sjfc.edu. *Application contact:* Jose Perales, Interim Director of Graduate Admissions, 585-385-8067, E-mail: jperales@sjfc.edu.

Salem State College, School of Graduate Studies, Program in Middle School Education, Salem, MA 01970-5353. Offers humanities (M Ed); math/science (MAT). Part-time and evening/weekend programs available. *Students:* 29 part-time (19 women). Average age 36. 8 applicants, 88% accepted, 7 enrolled. In 2009, 15 master's awarded. *Entrance requirements:* For master's, GRE or MAT. Additional exam requirements/recommendations for international students: Required—TOEFL (minimum score 550 paper-based; 80 iBT), or IELTS (minimum score 5.5). *Application deadline:* For fall admission, 5/1 for domestic students; for spring admission, 10/1 for domestic students. Applications are processed on a rolling basis. Application fee: $50. *Expenses:* Tuition, state resident: full-time $2520; part-time $275 per credit hour. Tuition, nonresident: full-time $4140; part-time $365 per credit hour. Required fees: $2430. *Financial support:* In 2009–10, 2 students received support. Career-related internships or fieldwork, Federal Work-Study, scholarships/grants, and unspecified assistantships available. Support available to part-time students. Financial award application deadline: 5/1; financial award applicants required to submit FAFSA. *Unit head:* Steve Prodanas, Program Coordinator, 978-542-6310, Fax: 978-542-7215, E-mail: spondanas@salemstate.edu. *Application contact:* Dr. Lee A. Brossoit, Assistant Dean of Graduate Admissions, 978-542-6675, Fax: 978-542-7215, E-mail: lbrossoit@salemstate.edu.

Salem State College, School of Graduate Studies, Program in Middle School Math, Salem, MA 01970-5353. Offers MAT. Part-time and evening/weekend programs available. *Students:* 21 part-time (14 women); includes 1 minority (Hispanic American). Average age 32. 10 applicants, 100% accepted, 10 enrolled. In 2009, 11 master's awarded. *Entrance requirements:* For master's, GRE or MAT. Additional exam requirements/recommendations for international students: Required—TOEFL (minimum score 550 paper-based; 80 iBT), or IELTS (minimum score 5.5). *Application deadline:* For fall admission, 5/1 for domestic students; for spring admission, 10/1 for domestic students. Applications are processed on a rolling basis. Application fee: $50. *Expenses:* Tuition, state resident: full-time $2520; part-time $275 per credit hour. Tuition, nonresident: full-time $4140; part-time $365 per credit hour. Required fees: $2430. *Financial support:* In 2009–10, 1 student received support. Career-related internships or fieldwork, Federal Work-Study, scholarships/grants, and unspecified assistantships available. Support available to part-time students. Financial award application deadline: 5/1; financial award applicants required to submit FAFSA. *Unit head:* Jule Belock, Program Coordinator, 978-542-6321, Fax: 978-542-7215, E-mail: jbelock@salemstate.edu. *Application contact:* Dr. Lee A. Brossoit, Assistant Dean of Graduate Admissions, 978-542-6675, Fax: 978-542-7215, E-mail: lbrossoit@salemstate.edu.

Salisbury University, Graduate Division, Program in Mathematics Education, Salisbury, MD 21801-6837. Offers MSME. Part-time and evening/weekend programs available. *Faculty:* 5 full-time (1 woman). *Students:* 10 part-time (9 women). Average age 32. 7 applicants, 14% accepted, 0 enrolled. In 2009, 9 master's awarded. *Entrance requirements:* Additional exam requirements/recommendations for international students: Required—TOEFL (minimum score 550 paper-based; 213 computer-based). *Application deadline:* Applications are processed on a rolling basis. Application fee: $45. Electronic applications accepted. *Expenses:* Tuition, area resident: Part-time $278 per credit hour. Tuition, state resident: part-time $278 per credit hour. Tuition, nonresident: part-time $574 per credit hour. Required fees: $57 per credit hour. *Financial support:* Applicants required to submit FAFSA. *Unit head:* Dr. Jennifer Bergner, Coordinator, 410-543-5381, Fax: 410-548-5559, E-mail: jabergner@salisbury.edu. *Application contact:* Dr. Jennifer Bergner, Coordinator, 410-543-5381, Fax: 410-548-5559, E-mail: jabergner@salisbury.edu.

San Diego State University, Graduate and Research Affairs, College of Sciences, Department of Mathematics and Statistics, San Diego, CA 92182. Offers applied mathematics (MS); mathematics (MA); mathematics and science education (PhD); statistics (MS). Part-time programs available. *Degree requirements:* For doctorate, thesis/dissertation. *Entrance requirements:* For master's, GRE General Test; for doctorate, GRE, minimum GPA of 3.25 in last 30 undergraduate semester units, minimum graduate GPA of 3.5, MSE recommendation form, 3 letters of recommendation. Additional exam requirements/recommendations for international students: Required—TOEFL. Electronic applications accepted. *Faculty research:* Teacher education in mathematics.

San Francisco State University, Division of Graduate Studies, College of Education, Department of Elementary Education, Program in Mathematics Education, San Francisco, CA 94132-1722. Offers MA. *Accreditation:* NCATE.

San Jose State University, Graduate Studies and Research, College of Science, Department of Mathematics, San Jose, CA 95192-0001. Offers applied mathematics (MS); mathematics (MA, MS); mathematics education (MA); statistics (MA). Part-time and evening/weekend programs available. *Students:* 13 full-time (7 women), 22 part-time (8 women); includes 17 minority (1 African American, 12 Asian Americans or Pacific Islanders, 4 Hispanic Americans), 5 international. Average age 34. 50 applicants, 30% accepted, 10 enrolled. In 2009, 7 master's awarded. *Degree requirements:* For master's, comprehensive exam, thesis (for some programs). *Entrance requirements:* For master's, GRE Subject Test. *Application deadline:* For fall admission, 6/29 for domestic students; for spring admission, 11/30 for domestic students. Applications are processed on a rolling basis. Application fee: $59. Electronic applications accepted. *Financial support:* Teaching assistantships, career-related internships or fieldwork and Federal Work-Study available. Support available to part-time students. Financial award applicants required to submit FAFSA. *Faculty research:* Artificial intelligence, algorithms, numerical analysis, software database, number theory. *Unit head:* Dr. Bradley Jackson, Chair, 408-924-5100, Fax: 408-924-5080. *Application contact:* Prof. Richard Kubelka, Graduate Coordinator, 408-924-5132, E-mail: kubelka@math.sjsu.edu.

Shippensburg University of Pennsylvania, School of Graduate Studies, College of Education and Human Services, Department of Teacher Education, Shippensburg, PA 17257-2299. Offers curriculum and instruction (M Ed), including biology, early childhood education, elementary education, English, foreign languages, geography/earth science, history, mathematics, middle school education; reading (M Ed). *Accreditation:* NCATE. Part-time and evening/weekend programs available. *Degree requirements:* For master's, comprehensive exam (for some programs), thesis optional, practicum or internship (for some programs). *Entrance requirements:* For master's, MAT (if GPA less than 2.75), interview, 3 letters of recommendation, writing sample of teaching background and future goals. Additional exam requirements/recommendations for international students: Required—TOEFL (minimum score 560 paper-based; 220 computer-based); Recommended—IELTS (minimum score 6). Electronic applications accepted.

Siena Heights University, Graduate College, Program in Teacher Education, Adrian, MI 49221-1796. Offers early childhood education (MA), including Montessori education; elementary education (MA), including elementary education/reading; mathematics education (MA); middle school education (MA); secondary education (MA), including secondary education/reading. Part-time programs available. *Degree requirements:* For master's, thesis, presentation. *Entrance requirements:* For master's, minimum GPA of 3.0, interview. *Faculty research:* Teaching/learning styles, outcomes-based teaching, multiple intelligences, assessment.

Simon Fraser University, Graduate Studies, Faculty of Education, Program in Mathematics Education, Burnaby, BC V5A 1S6, Canada. Offers M Ed, M Sc, PhD. *Degree requirements:* For master's, comprehensive exam or thesis; for doctorate, comprehensive exam, thesis/dissertation.

Slippery Rock University of Pennsylvania, Graduate Studies (Recruitment), College of Education, Department of Secondary Education/Foundations of Education, Slippery Rock, PA 16057-1383. Offers secondary education in math/science (M Ed). *Accreditation:* NCATE. *Degree requirements:* For master's, comprehensive exam (for some programs), thesis (for some programs). *Entrance requirements:* For master's, GRE General Test, MAT, minimum GPA of 2.75 (3.0 for initial certification programs). Additional exam requirements/recommendations for international students: Required—TOEFL (minimum score 550 paper-based; 213 computer-based). *Application deadline:* For fall admission, 3/1 priority date for domestic students, 5/1 priority date for international students; for spring admission, 11/1 priority date for domestic students, 9/1 priority date for international students. Applications are processed on a rolling basis. Application fee: $25 ($30 for international students). Electronic applications accepted. *Expenses:* Tuition, state resident: full-time $6666; part-time $370 per credit. Tuition, nonresident: full-time $10,666; part-time $593 per credit. Required fees: $2184; $182 per credit. *Financial support:* Career-related internships or fieldwork, Federal Work-Study, scholarships/grants, and unspecified assistantships available. Support available to part-time students. Financial award application deadline: 5/1; financial award applicants required to submit FAFSA. *Unit head:* Dr. Jeffrey Lehman, Graduate Coordinator, 724-738-2311, Fax: 724-738-4987, E-mail: jeffrey.lehman@sru.edu. *Application contact:* Angela Piverotto, Interim Director of Graduate Studies, 724-738-2051, Fax: 724-738-2146, E-mail: graduate.admissions@sru.edu.

Smith College, Graduate and Special Programs, Department of Education and Child Study, Program in Secondary Education, Northampton, MA 01063. Offers biological sciences education (MAT); chemistry education (MAT); English education (MAT); French education (MAT); geology education (MAT); government education (MAT); history education (MAT); mathematics education (MAT); physics education (MAT); Spanish education (MAT). Part-time programs available. *Faculty:* 6 full-time (4 women), 3 part-time/adjunct (2 women). *Students:* 7 full-time (4 women), 1 part-time (0 women). Average age 25. 14 applicants, 100% accepted, 8 enrolled. In 2009, 9 master's awarded. *Entrance requirements:* Additional exam requirements/recommendations for international students: Required—TOEFL (minimum score 590 paper-based; 243 computer-based; 97 iBT). *Application deadline:* For fall admission, 4/1 for domestic students, 1/15 priority date for international students; for spring admission, 12/1 for domestic students. Application fee: $60. *Financial support:* In 2009–10, 6 students received support. Career-related internships or fieldwork, institutionally sponsored loans, and scholarships/grants available. Support available to part-time students. Financial award application deadline: 1/15; financial award applicants required to submit CSS PROFILE or FAFSA. *Unit head:* Rosetta Cohen, Graduate Student Advisor, 413-585-3266, E-mail: rcohen@smith.edu. *Application contact:* Ruth Morgan, Administrative Assistant, 413-585-3050, Fax: 413-585-3054, E-mail: gradstdy@smith.edu.

Smith College, Graduate and Special Programs, Department of Mathematics, Northampton, MA 01063. Offers MAT. Part-time programs available. *Faculty:* 12 full-time (5 women). *Students:* 1 applicant, 100% accepted, 0 enrolled. In 2009, 1 master's awarded. *Entrance requirements:* Additional exam requirements/recommendations for international students: Required—TOEFL (minimum score 590 paper-based; 243 computer-based; 97 iBT). *Application deadline:* For fall admission, 4/1 for domestic students, 1/5 for international students; for spring admission, 2/1 for domestic students. Application fee: $60. *Financial support:* Career-related internships or fieldwork, institutionally sponsored loans, and scholarships/grants available. Support available to part-time students. Financial award application deadline: 1/15. *Unit head:* Christophe Gole, Chair, 413-585-3875, E-mail: cgole@smith.edu. *Application contact:* Ruth Morgan, Administrative Assistant, 413-585-3050, Fax: 413-585-3054, E-mail: gradstdy@smith.edu.

South Carolina State University, School of Graduate Studies, Department of Education, Orangeburg, SC 29117-0001. Offers early childhood and special education (M Ed); early childhood education (MAT); elementary education (M Ed, MAT); engineering (MAT); general science (MAT); mathematics (MAT); secondary education (M Ed), including biology education, business education, counselor education, English education, home economics education, industrial education, mathematics education, science education, social studies education; special education (M Ed), including emotionally handicapped, learning disabilities, mentally handicapped. *Accreditation:* NCATE. Part-time and evening/weekend programs available. *Degree requirements:* For master's, thesis optional, departmental qualifying exam. *Entrance requirements:* For master's, GRE General Test, NTE, interview, teaching certificate. Electronic applications accepted. *Expenses:* Tuition, state resident: part-time $470 per credit hour. Tuition, nonresident: part-time $924 per credit hour. *Faculty research:* Critical thinking, child abuse, stress, test-taking skills, conflict resolution, mainstreaming.

Southeastern Oklahoma State University, School of Education, Durant, OK 74701-0609. Offers math specialist (M Ed); reading specialist (M Ed); school administration (M Ed); school counseling (M Ed). *Accreditation:* NCATE. Part-time and evening/weekend programs available. *Faculty:* 52 full-time (19 women), 1 (woman) part-time/adjunct. *Students:* 14 full-time (11 women), 73 part-time (58 women); includes 22 minority (4 African Americans, 17 American Indian/Alaska Native, 1 Hispanic American). Average age 32. 18 applicants, 100% accepted, 18 enrolled. *Degree requirements:* For master's, comprehensive exam, thesis optional, portfolio (M Ed). *Entrance requirements:* For master's, GRE General Test (MBS), minimum GPA of 3.0 in last 60 hours or 2.75 overall. Additional exam requirements/recommendations for international students: Required—TOEFL (minimum score 550 paper-based; 213 computer-based). *Application deadline:* For fall admission, 8/1 for domestic students, 6/1 for international students; for spring admission, 1/5 for domestic students, 11/1 for international students. Application fee: $20 ($55 for international students). Electronic applications accepted. *Financial support:* In 2009–10, 1 teaching assistantship with full tuition reimbursement (averaging $5,000 per year) was awarded; Federal Work-Study, institutionally sponsored loans, and tuition waivers (partial) also available. Support available to part-time students. Financial award application deadline: 6/15; financial award applicants required to submit FAFSA. *Unit head:* Dr. Melanie Price, Chair, 580-745-2602, Fax: 580-745-7474, E-mail: mprice@se.edu. *Application contact:* Carrie Williamson, Graduate Secretary, 580-745-2200, Fax: 580-745-7474, E-mail: cwilliamson@se.edu.

Southern Illinois University Edwardsville, Graduate Studies and Research, School of Education, Department of Curriculum and Instruction, Program in Secondary Education, Edwardsville, IL 62026-0001. Offers art (MS Ed); biology (MS Ed); chemistry (MS Ed); earth and space sciences (MS Ed); English/language arts (MS Ed); foreign languages (MS Ed); history (MS Ed); mathematics (MS Ed); physics (MS Ed). *Accreditation:* NCATE. Part-time and evening/weekend programs available. *Students:* 24 part-time (19 women); includes 2 minority (1 African American, 1 Hispanic American). Average age 26. 13 applicants, 31% accepted. In 2009, 5 master's awarded. *Degree requirements:* For master's, thesis or alternative, final exam/paper. *Entrance requirements:* Additional exam requirements/recommendations for international students: Required—TOEFL (minimum score 550 paper-based; 213 computer-based; 79 iBT), IELTS (minimum score 6.5). *Application deadline:* For fall admission, 7/23 for domestic students, 6/1 for international students; for spring admission, 12/11 for domestic students, 10/1 for international students. Applications are processed on a rolling basis. Application fee: $30. Electronic applications accepted. *Expenses:* Tuition, state resident: part-time $1252.50 per semester. Tuition, nonresident: part-time $3131.25 per semester. Required fees: $586.85 per semester. Tuition and fees vary according to course load. *Financial support:* Fellowships, research assistantships, teaching assistantships, career-related internships or fieldwork, Federal Work-Study, institutionally sponsored loans, scholarships/grants, traineeships, and unspecified assistantships available. Support available to part-time students. Financial award application deadline: 3/1; financial award applicants required to submit FAFSA. *Unit head:* Dr. Kathy Bushrow, Director, 618-650-3082, E-mail: kbushro@siue.edu. *Application contact:* Dr. Kathy Bushrow, Director, 618-650-3082, E-mail: kbushro@siue.edu.

Southern University and Agricultural and Mechanical College, Graduate School, Department of Science/Mathematics Education, Baton Rouge, LA 70813. Offers PhD. *Accreditation:* NCATE. *Degree requirements:* For doctorate, thesis/dissertation. *Entrance requirements:* For doctorate, GRE General Test. Additional exam requirements/recommendations for international students: Required—TOEFL (minimum score 525 paper-based; 193 computer-based). *Faculty research:*

Mathematics Education

Southern University and Agricultural and Mechanical College (continued)
Performance assessment in science/mathematics education, equity in science/mathematics education, technology and distance learning, science/mathematics concept formation, cognitive themes, problem solving in science/mathematics education.

Southwestern Oklahoma State University, College of Arts and Sciences, Department of Mathematics, Weatherford, OK 73096-3098. Offers M Ed. Part-time programs available. *Degree requirements:* For master's, exam. *Entrance requirements:* For master's, GRE General Test or minimum undergraduate GPA of 3.0. Additional exam requirements/recommendations for international students: Required—TOEFL.

Stanford University, School of Education, Program in Curriculum Studies and Teacher Education, Stanford, CA 94305-9991. Offers art education (MA, PhD); dance education (MA); English education (MA, PhD); general curriculum studies (MA, PhD); mathematics education (MA, PhD); science education (MA, PhD); social studies education (PhD); teacher education (MA, PhD). *Degree requirements:* For master's, thesis (for some programs); for doctorate, thesis/dissertation. *Entrance requirements:* For master's and doctorate, GRE General Test. Electronic applications accepted. *Expenses:* Tuition: Full-time $37,380; part-time $2760 per quarter. Required fees: $501.

Stanford University, School of Education, Teacher Education Program, Stanford, CA 94305-9991. Offers English education (MA); languages education (MA); mathematics education (MA); science education (MA); social studies education (MA). *Degree requirements:* For master's, thesis. *Entrance requirements:* For master's, GRE General Test. Electronic applications accepted. *Expenses:* Tuition: Full-time $37,380; part-time $2760 per quarter. Required fees: $501.

State University of New York at Binghamton, Graduate School, School of Education, Program in Adolescence Education, Binghamton, NY 13902-6000. Offers biology education (MAT, MS Ed, MST); earth science education (MAT, MS Ed, MST); English education (MAT, MS Ed, MST); French education (MAT, MST); mathematical sciences education (MAT, MS Ed, MST); physics (MAT, MS Ed, MST); social studies (MAT, MS Ed, MST); Spanish education (MAT, MST). *Accreditation:* Teacher Education Accreditation Council. Part-time and evening/weekend programs available. *Students:* 93 full-time (37 women), 21 part-time (8 women); includes 6 minority (2 Asian Americans or Pacific Islanders, 4 Hispanic Americans), 1 international. Average age 27. 69 applicants, 81% accepted, 46 enrolled. In 2009, 53 master's awarded. *Entrance requirements:* For master's, GRE General Test. Additional exam requirements/recommendations for international students: Required—TOEFL (minimum score 550 paper-based; 213 computer-based; 80 iBT). *Application deadline:* For fall admission, 2/1 priority date for domestic and international students; for spring admission, 10/15 priority date for domestic and international students. Applications are processed on a rolling basis. Application fee: $60. Electronic applications accepted. *Financial support:* Fellowships with partial tuition reimbursements, research assistantships with full and partial tuition reimbursements, teaching assistantships with full tuition reimbursements, career-related internships or fieldwork, Federal Work-Study, institutionally sponsored loans, scholarships/grants, health care benefits, tuition waivers (full), and unspecified assistantships available. Financial award application deadline: 2/15; financial award applicants required to submit FAFSA. *Unit head:* Dr. S. G. Grant, Dean of School of Education, 607-777-7329, E-mail: sggrant@binghamton.edu. *Application contact:* Victoria Williams, Recruiting and Admissions Coordinator, 607-777-2151, Fax: 607-777-2501, E-mail: vwilliam@binghamton.edu.

State University of New York at Plattsburgh, Division of Education, Health, and Human Services, Program in Teacher Education: Adolescence MST, Plattsburgh, NY 12901-2681. Offers adolescence education (MST); biology 7-12 (MST); chemistry 7-12 (MST); earth science 7-12 (MST); English 7-12 (MST); French 7-12 (MST); mathematics 7-12 (MST); physics 7-12 (MST); social studies 7-12 (MST); Spanish 7-12 (MST). *Accreditation:* Teacher Education Accreditation Council. Part-time and evening/weekend programs available. *Faculty:* 4 full-time (3 women), 2 part-time/adjunct (0 women). *Students:* 83 full-time (49 women), 5 part-time (3 women); includes 9 minority (2 African Americans, 1 American Indian/Alaska Native, 1 Asian American or Pacific Islander, 5 Hispanic Americans), 2 international. Average age 27. 72 applicants, 71% accepted, 44 enrolled. In 2009, 57 master's awarded. *Degree requirements:* For master's, portfolio. *Entrance requirements:* For master's, minimum GPA of 2.75. Additional exam requirements/recommendations for international students: Required—TOEFL (minimum score 550 paper-based; 213 computer-based; 79 iBT). *Application deadline:* For fall admission, 2/15 priority date for domestic students. Applications are processed on a rolling basis. Application fee: $75. *Expenses:* Tuition, state resident: full-time $8370; part-time $349 per credit hour. Tuition, nonresident: full-time $13,250; part-time $552 per credit hour. Required fees: $1130. *Financial support:* Application deadline: 4/15. *Unit head:* Dr. Robert Ackland, Coordinator, 518-564-5131, E-mail: acklanrt@plattsburgh.edu. *Application contact:* Marguerite Adelman, Assistant Director, Graduate Admissions, 518-564-4723, Fax: 518-564-4722, E-mail: adelmaml@plattsburgh.edu.

State University of New York College at Cortland, Graduate Studies, School of Arts and Sciences, Programs in Adolescence Education, Cortland, NY 13045. Offers biology (MAT, MS Ed); chemistry (MAT, MS Ed); earth science (MAT, MS Ed); English (MS Ed); French (MS Ed); mathematics (MAT, MS Ed); physics (MAT, MS Ed); social studies (MS Ed); Spanish (MS Ed). *Accreditation:* NCATE. Part-time and evening/weekend programs available. *Degree requirements:* For master's, one foreign language, comprehensive exam (for some programs), thesis (for some programs). *Entrance requirements:* For master's, GRE General Test.

State University of New York College at Potsdam, School of Education and Professional Studies, Program in Secondary Education, Potsdam, NY 13676. Offers English (MST); mathematics (with grades 5-6 extension) (MST); science (MST), including biology, chemistry, earth science, physics; Social Studies (with grades 5-6 extension) (MST). *Accreditation:* NCATE. *Faculty:* 9 full-time (3 women), 3 part-time/adjunct (2 women). *Students:* 49 full-time (27 women), 6 part-time (1 woman); includes 5 minority (3 African Americans, 2 American Indian/Alaska Native), 7 international. 13 applicants, 62% accepted, 8 enrolled. In 2009, 49 master's awarded. *Degree requirements:* For master's, thesis optional, culminating experience. *Entrance requirements:* For master's, minimum GPA of 2.75 in last 60 hours of course work (3.0 for English program). Additional exam requirements/recommendations for international students: Required—TOEFL (minimum score 550 paper-based; 213 computer-based; 80 iBT), IELTS (minimum score 6). *Application deadline:* For fall admission, 4/1 priority date for domestic and international students; for spring admission, 10/15 priority date for domestic and international students. Applications are processed on a rolling basis. Application fee: $50. *Expenses:* Tuition, state resident: full-time $8370; part-time $349 per credit hour. Tuition, nonresident: full-time $13,250; part-time $552 per credit hour. Required fees: $942; $38.70 per credit hour. *Financial support:* Fellowships, teaching assistantships, career-related internships or fieldwork, Federal Work-Study, scholarships/grants, and unspecified assistantships available. Support available to part-time students. Financial award application deadline: 3/1; financial award applicants required to submit FAFSA. *Unit head:* Dr. Peter Brouwer, Chairperson, 315-267-3018, Fax: 315-267-4802, E-mail: brouweps@potsdam.edu. *Application contact:* Peter Cutler, Graduate Admissions Counselor, 315-267-3154, Fax: 315-267-4802, E-mail: cutlerpj@potsdam.edu.

Stephen F. Austin State University, Graduate School, College of Sciences and Mathematics, Department of Mathematics and Statistics, Nacogdoches, TX 75962. Offers mathematics (MS); mathematics education (MS); statistics (MS). *Degree requirements:* For master's, comprehensive exam, thesis optional. *Entrance requirements:* For master's, GRE General Test, minimum GPA of 2.8 in last 60 hours, 2.5 overall. Additional exam requirements/recommendations for international students: Required—TOEFL. *Faculty research:* Kernel type estimators, fractal mappings, spline curve fitting, robust regression continua theory.

Stony Brook University, State University of New York, School of Professional Development, Stony Brook, NY 11794. Offers biology-grade 7-12 (MAT); chemistry-grade 7-12 (MAT); coaching (Graduate Certificate); computer integrated engineering (Graduate Certificate); earth science-grade 7-12 (MAT); educational computing (Graduate Certificate); educational leadership (Advanced Certificate); English-grade 7-12 (MAT); environmental management (Graduate Certificate); environmental/occupational health and safety (Graduate Certificate); French-grade 7-12 (MAT); German-grade 7-12 (MAT); human resource management (Graduate Certificate); information systems management (Graduate Certificate); Italian-grade 7-12 (MAT); liberal studies (MA); mathematics-grade 7-12 (MAT); operation research (Graduate Certificate); physics-grade 7-12 (MAT); school administration and supervision (Graduate Certificate); school building leadership (Graduate Certificate); school district administration (Graduate Certificate); school district business leadership (Advanced Certificate); school district leadership (Graduate Certificate); social science and the professions (MPS), including environmental waste management, human resource management; social studies-grade 7-12 (MAT); Spanish-grade 7-12 (MAT); waste management (Graduate Certificate). Part-time and evening/weekend programs available. Postbaccalaureate distance learning degree programs offered. *Faculty:* 5 full-time (3 women), 131 part-time/adjunct (53 women). *Students:* 317 full-time (187 women), 1,200 part-time (773 women); includes 187 minority (77 African Americans, 2 American Indian/Alaska Native, 22 Asian Americans or Pacific Islanders, 86 Hispanic Americans), 11 international. Average age 28. In 2009, 597 master's, 234 other advanced degrees awarded. *Degree requirements:* For master's, one foreign language, thesis or alternative. *Application deadline:* Applications are processed on a rolling basis. Application fee: $62. *Expenses:* Tuition, state resident: full-time $8370; part-time $349 per credit. Tuition, nonresident: full-time $13,250; part-time $552 per credit. Required fees: $933. *Financial support:* Fellowships, research assistantships, teaching assistantships, career-related internships or fieldwork available. Support available to part-time students. *Unit head:* Dr. Paul J. Edelson, Dean, 631-632-7052, Fax: 631-632-9046, E-mail: paul.edelson@stonybrook.edu. *Application contact:* Dr. Paul J. Edelson, Dean, 631-632-7052, Fax: 631-632-9046, E-mail: paul.edelson@stonybrook.edu.

Syracuse University, School of Education, Program in Mathematics Education, Syracuse, NY 13244. Offers mathematics education (PhD); mathematics education: preparation 7-12 (MS). Part-time programs available. *Students:* 10 full-time (6 women), 2 part-time (both women), 2 international. Average age 32. 12 applicants, 67% accepted, 4 enrolled. In 2009, 2 master's, 2 doctorates awarded. *Degree requirements:* For master's, thesis or alternative; for doctorate, thesis/dissertation. *Entrance requirements:* For master's, GRE (for assistantship applicants); for doctorate, GRE, MS. Additional exam requirements/recommendations for international students: Required—TOEFL (minimum score 100 iBT). *Application deadline:* For fall admission, 2/1 priority date for domestic and international students; for spring admission, 10/15 for domestic students, 10/15 priority date for international students. Applications are processed on a rolling basis. Application fee: $75. Electronic applications accepted. *Expenses:* Tuition: Full-time $26,808; part-time $1117 per credit. Required fees: $1024. *Financial support:* Fellowships with full tuition reimbursements, teaching assistantships with full tuition reimbursements available. Financial award application deadline: 1/1; financial award applicants required to submit FAFSA. *Unit head:* Dr. Joanna Masingila, Chair, 315-443-1483, E-mail: jomasing@syr.edu. *Application contact:* Liza Rochelson, Graduate Recruiter, School of Education, 315-443-2505, E-mail: e-gradrcrt@syr.edu.

Teachers College, Columbia University, Graduate Faculty of Education, Department of Math, Science and Technology, Program in Mathematics Education, New York, NY 10027-6696. Offers Ed M, MA, MS, Ed D, Ed DCT, PhD. *Accreditation:* NCATE. *Faculty:* 3 full-time (1 woman). *Students:* 72 full-time (48 women), 117 part-time (68 women); includes 55 minority (18 African Americans, 30 Asian Americans or Pacific Islanders, 7 Hispanic Americans), 24 international. Average age 32. 88 applicants, 78% accepted, 37 enrolled. In 2009, 58 master's, 6 doctorates awarded. *Degree requirements:* For doctorate, thesis/dissertation. *Entrance requirements:* For master's, undergraduate major or minor in mathematics; for doctorate, MA in mathematics or mathematics education. *Application deadline:* For fall admission, 5/15 for domestic students; for spring admission, 12/1 for domestic students. Application fee: $65. *Financial support:* Career-related internships or fieldwork, Federal Work-Study, institutionally sponsored loans, and tuition waivers (full and partial) available. Support available to part-time students. Financial award application deadline: 2/1. *Faculty research:* Problem solving, curriculum development, international education, history of mathematics. *Unit head:* Dr. O. Roger Anderson, Chair, 212-678-3405. *Application contact:* Deanna Ghozati, Assistant Director of Admission, 212-678-4018, Fax: 212-678-4171, E-mail: ghozati@tc.edu.

Temple University, Graduate School, College of Education, Department of Curriculum, Instruction, and Technology in Education, Philadelphia, PA 19122-6096. Offers applied behavioral analysis (MS Ed); career and technical education (MS Ed); early childhood education and elementary education (MS Ed); English education (MS Ed); language arts education (Ed D); math/science education (Ed D); mathematics education (MS Ed); science education (MS Ed); second and foreign language education (MS Ed); special education (MS Ed); teaching English as a second language (MS Ed). Part-time and evening/weekend programs available. Terminal master's awarded for partial completion of doctoral program. *Degree requirements:* For master's, thesis or alternative; for doctorate, thesis/dissertation. *Entrance requirements:* For master's and doctorate, GRE General Test or MAT, minimum GPA of 3.0. Additional exam requirements/recommendations for international students: Required—TOEFL (minimum score 550 paper-based; 213 computer-based; 79 iBT). Electronic applications accepted. *Faculty research:* School improvement, problem solving, literacy, language development.

Texas A&M University, College of Education and Human Development, Department of Teaching, Learning, and Culture, College Station, TX 77843. Offers curriculum and instruction (M Ed, MS, PhD); mathematics education (M Ed, MS, PhD); multicultural/urban/ESL/international education (M Ed, MS, PhD); reading/language arts (M Ed, MS, PhD); science education (M Ed, MS, PhD); social studies education (M Ed, MS, PhD). Part-time programs available. *Faculty:* 33. *Students:* 145 full-time (113 women), 270 part-time (214 women); includes 110 minority (60 African Americans, 4 American Indian/Alaska Native, 4 Asian Americans or Pacific Islanders, 42 Hispanic Americans), 47 international. Average age 36. In 2009, 114 master's, 17 doctorates awarded. *Degree requirements:* For master's, comprehensive exam, thesis (for some programs); for doctorate, comprehensive exam, thesis/dissertation. *Entrance requirements:* For master's, GRE General Test, minimum GPA of 3.0; for doctorate, GRE General Test, 3 years of teaching experience. Additional exam requirements/recommendations for international students: Required—TOEFL (minimum score 550 paper-based; 213 computer-based). *Application deadline:* For fall admission, 1/15 priority date for domestic and international students; for spring admission, 9/15 priority date for domestic and international students. Applications are processed on a rolling basis. Application fee: $50 ($75 for international students). Electronic applications accepted. *Expenses:* Tuition, state resident: full-time $3991; part-time $221.74 per credit hour. Tuition, nonresident: full-time $9049; part-time $502.74 per credit hour. *Financial support:* In 2009–10, fellowships with partial tuition reimbursements (averaging $3,000 per year), teaching assistantships with partial tuition reimbursements (averaging $7,200 per year) were awarded; research assistantships with partial tuition reimbursements, career-related internships or fieldwork, Federal Work-Study, institutionally sponsored loans, scholarships/grants, tuition waivers (partial), and unspecified assistantships also available. Support available to part-time students. Financial award application deadline: 4/1; financial award applicants required to submit FAFSA. *Unit head:* Dr. Dennie Smith, Head, 979-845-8384, Fax: 979-845-9663, E-mail: krsmith@tamu.edu. *Application contact:* Graduate Admissions Supervisor, 979-845-8382, Fax: 979-845-9663, E-mail: krsmith@tamu.edu.

Texas A&M University–Corpus Christi, Graduate Studies and Research, College of Science and Technology, Program in Mathematics, Corpus Christi, TX 78412-5503. Offers applied and computational mathematics (MS); curriculum content (MS). Part-time programs available. *Degree requirements:* For master's, thesis (for some programs). *Entrance requirements:* For master's, 2 letters of recommendation.

Texas State University–San Marcos, Graduate School, College of Science, Department of Mathematics, Doctoral Program in Mathematics Education, San Marcos, TX 78666. Offers PhD. *Faculty:* 13 full-time (2 women). *Students:* 19 full-time (10 women), 3 part-time (all women); includes 4 minority (1 African American, 2 Asian Americans or Pacific Islanders, 1 Hispanic American). Average age 36. 12 applicants, 75% accepted, 8 enrolled. *Degree*

requirements: For doctorate, comprehensive exam, thesis/dissertation. *Entrance requirements:* For doctorate, GRE General Test; GRE Subject Test in mathematics (minimum score of 75th percentile), bachelor's degree or higher in mathematics, mathematics education, or related field; minimum GPA of 3.0 in last 60 hours of undergraduate work. Additional exam requirements/recommendations for international students: Required—TOEFL (minimum score 550 paper-based; 213 computer-based). *Application deadline:* For fall admission, 6/15 priority date for domestic students, 6/1 priority date for international students; for spring admission, 10/15 priority date for domestic students, 9/1 priority date for international students. Application fee: $40 ($90 for international students). *Expenses:* Tuition, state resident: full-time $5784; part-time $241 per credit hour. Tuition, nonresident: full-time $13,224; part-time $551 per credit hour. Required fees: $1728; $48 per credit hour. $306. Tuition and fees vary according to course load. *Financial support:* In 2009–10, 12 students received support, including 4 research assistantships (averaging $9,389 per year), 15 teaching assistantships (averaging $12,719 per year). *Unit head:* Dr. Stanley Wayment, Graduate Advisor, 512-245-2551, E-mail: sw05@txstate.edu. *Application contact:* Dr. Nathaniel Dean, Graduate Adviser, 512-245-2497, E-mail: nd17@txstate.edu.

Texas State University–San Marcos, Graduate School, College of Science, Department of Mathematics, Program in Middle School Mathematics Teaching, San Marcos, TX 78666. Offers M Ed. Part-time programs available. *Students:* 22 part-time (16 women); includes 7 minority (1 African American, 1 American Indian/Alaska Native, 5 Hispanic Americans), 2 international. Average age 38. 3 applicants, 100% accepted, 2 enrolled. In 2009, 9 master's awarded. *Degree requirements:* For master's, comprehensive exam. *Entrance requirements:* For master's, GRE, minimum GPA of 2.75 in last 60 hours of undergraduate course work. Additional exam requirements/recommendations for international students: Required—TOEFL (minimum score 550 paper-based; 213 computer-based). *Application deadline:* For fall admission, 6/15 priority date for domestic students, 6/1 priority date for international students; for spring admission, 10/15 priority date for domestic students, 10/1 priority date for international students. Applications are processed on a rolling basis. Application fee: $40 ($90 for international students). Electronic applications accepted. *Expenses:* Tuition, state resident: full-time $5784; part-time $241 per credit hour. Tuition, nonresident: full-time $13,224; part-time $551 per credit hour. Required fees: $1728; $48 per credit hour. $306. Tuition and fees vary according to course load. *Financial support:* In 2009–10, 16 students received support; teaching assistantships, Federal Work-Study and institutionally sponsored loans available. Support available to part-time students. Financial award application deadline: 4/1; financial award applicants required to submit FAFSA. *Unit head:* Dr. Stanley Wayment, Graduate Advisor, 512-245-3555, Fax: 512-245-3425, E-mail: sw05@txstaate.edu. *Application contact:* Dr. Gregory Passty, Graduate Adviser, 512-245-3446, Fax: 512-245-3425, E-mail: passty@txstate.edu.

Texas State University–San Marcos, Graduate School, Interdisciplinary Studies Program in Elementary Mathematics, Science, and Technology, San Marcos, TX 78666. Offers MSIS. *Students:* 1 full-time (0 women), 4 part-time (3 women). Average age 32. 1 applicant, 100% accepted, 0 enrolled. In 2009, 1 master's awarded. *Degree requirements:* For master's, comprehensive exam, thesis optional. *Entrance requirements:* For master's, minimum GPA of 2.75 in the last 60 hours of undergraduate work. Additional exam requirements/recommendations for international students: Required—TOEFL (minimum score 550 paper-based; 213 computer-based). *Application deadline:* For fall admission, 6/15 priority date for domestic students, 6/1 priority date for international students; for spring admission, 10/15 priority date for domestic students, 10/1 priority date for international students. Applications are processed on a rolling basis. Application fee: $40 ($90 for international students). Electronic applications accepted. *Expenses:* Tuition, state resident: full-time $5784; part-time $241 per credit hour. Tuition, nonresident: full-time $13,224; part-time $551 per credit hour. Required fees: $1728; $48 per credit hour. $306. Tuition and fees vary according to course load. *Financial support:* In 2009–10, 3 students received support; research assistantships, teaching assistantships available. Financial award application deadline: 4/1; financial award applicants required to submit FAFSA. *Unit head:* Dr. Sandra Mody, Acting Dean, 512-245-3360, Fax: 512-245-8095, E-mail: sw04@txstate.edu. *Application contact:* Dr. J. Michael Willoughby, Dean of Graduate School, 512-245-2581, Fax: 512-245-8365, E-mail: gradcollege@txstate.edu.

Texas Woman's University, Graduate School, College of Arts and Sciences, Department of Mathematics and Computer Science, Denton, TX 76201. Offers mathematics (MA, MS); mathematics teaching (MS). Part-time and evening/weekend programs available. *Faculty:* 10 full-time (7 women), 3 part-time/adjunct (2 women). *Students:* 9 full-time (6 women), 20 part-time (17 women); includes 9 minority (1 African American, 4 Asian Americans or Pacific Islanders, 4 Hispanic Americans), 2 international. Average age 37. 19 applicants, 89% accepted, 8 enrolled. In 2009, 9 master's awarded. *Degree requirements:* For master's, comprehensive exam, thesis (for some programs). *Entrance requirements:* For master's, 2 letters of reference. Additional exam requirements/recommendations for international students: Required—TOEFL (minimum score 550 paper-based; 213 computer-based; 79 iBT). *Application deadline:* For fall admission, 7/1 priority date for domestic students, 3/1 for international students; for spring admission, 12/1 priority date for domestic students, 7/1 for international students. Applications are processed on a rolling basis. Application fee: $50. Electronic applications accepted. *Expenses:* Tuition, state resident: full-time $3564; part-time $198 per credit hour. Tuition, nonresident: full-time $8550; part-time $475 per credit hour. Required fees: $69.26 per credit hour. Tuition and fees vary according to course load. *Financial support:* In 2009–10, 4 students received support, including 7 research assistantships (averaging $10,440 per year), 3 teaching assistantships (averaging $10,440 per year); career-related internships or fieldwork, Federal Work-Study, institutionally sponsored loans, scholarships/grants, traineeships, health care benefits, and unspecified assistantships also available. Support available to part-time students. Financial award application deadline: 3/1; financial award applicants required to submit FAFSA. *Faculty research:* Biopharmaceutical statistics, dynamic systems and control theory, Bayesian inference, math and computer science curriculum innovation, computer modeling of physical phenomenon. *Unit head:* Dr. Don E. Edwards, Chair, 940-898-2166, Fax: 940-898-2179, E-mail: mathcs@twu.edu. *Application contact:* Samuel Wheeler, Assistant Director of Admissions, 940-898-3188, Fax: 940-898-3081, E-mail: wheelersr@twu.edu.

Towson University, College of Graduate Studies and Research, Program in Mathematics Education, Towson, MD 21252-0001. Offers MS. *Accreditation:* NCATE. *Entrance requirements:* For master's, current certification for teaching secondary school mathematics, minimum GPA of 3.0. Electronic applications accepted.

Troy University, Graduate School, College of Education, Program in Postsecondary Education, Troy, AL 36082. Offers adult education (M Ed); biology (M Ed); criminal justice (M Ed); english (M Ed); foundations of education (M Ed); general science (M Ed); higher education administration (M Ed); history (M Ed); instructional technology (M Ed); mathematics (M Ed); music industry (M Ed); physical fitness (M Ed); political science (M Ed); public administration (M Ed); social science (M Ed); teaching english (M Ed). Also offered through the University College. *Accreditation:* NCATE. Part-time and evening/weekend programs available. *Students:* 267 full-time (192 women), 381 part-time (293 women); includes 326 minority (309 African Americans, 4 American Indian/Alaska Native, 5 Asian Americans or Pacific Islanders, 8 Hispanic Americans). Average age 34. 343 applicants, 90% accepted. In 2009, 480 master's awarded. *Degree requirements:* For master's, comprehensive exam, thesis. *Entrance requirements:* For master's, MAT (minimum score 385), minimum GPA of 2.5. Additional exam requirements/recommendations for international students: Required—TOEFL (minimum score 523 paper-based; 193 computer-based; 70 iBT), IELTS, or ACT Compass ESL (minimum score 270 on Listening, Reading, and Grammar with no individual score below 85 and a minimum score of 8 out of 12 on writing test). *Application deadline:* Applications are processed on a rolling basis. Application fee: $50. Electronic applications accepted. *Financial support:* Available to part-time students. Applicants required to submit FAFSA. *Unit head:* Dr. Andrew Creamer, Chair, 334-670-3350, E-mail: drcreamer@troy.edu. *Application contact:* Brenda K. Campbell, Director of Graduate Admissions, 334-670-3178, Fax: 334-670-3733, E-mail: bcamp@troy.edu.

Troy University, Graduate School, College of Education, Program in Secondary Education, Troy, AL 36082. Offers 5th year biology (MS); 5th year computer science (MS); 5th year history (MS); 5th year language arts (MS); 5th year mathematics (MS); 5th year social science (MS); educationtraditional language arts (MS); traditional biology (MS); traditional computer science (MS); traditional history (MS); traditional mathematics (MS); traditional social science (MS). *Accreditation:* NCATE. Part-time and evening/weekend programs available. *Students:* 17 full-time (12 women), 25 part-time (23 women); includes 8 minority (all African Americans). Average age 27. 10 applicants, 90% accepted. In 2009, 29 master's awarded. *Degree requirements:* For master's, comprehensive exam, thesis. *Entrance requirements:* For master's, minimum GPA of 2.5. Additional exam requirements/recommendations for international students: Required—TOEFL (minimum score 523 paper-based; 193 computer-based; 70 iBT), IELTS (minimum score 6). *Application deadline:* Applications are processed on a rolling basis. Application fee: $50. Electronic applications accepted. *Financial support:* Career-related internships or fieldwork available. Support available to part-time students. Financial award applicants required to submit FAFSA. *Unit head:* Dr. Marian Parker, Coordinator, 334-670-5661, Fax: 334-670-3548, E-mail: mjparker@troy.edu. *Application contact:* Brenda K. Campbell, Director of Graduate Admissions, 334-670-3178, Fax: 334-670-3733, E-mail: bcamp@troy.edu.

Union Graduate College, School of Education, Schenectady, NY 12308-3107. Offers biology (MAT, MS); chemistry (MAT); Chinese (MAT); earth science (MAT); English (MAT); French (MAT); general science (MAT); German (MAT); Greek (MAT); languages (MAT); Latin (MAT); mathematics (MAT); mathematics and technology (MS); mentoring and teacher leadership (AC); middle childhood extension (AC); national board certificate and teacher leadership (AC); physical science (MS); physics (MAT); social studies (MAT); Spanish (MAT). *Accreditation:* Teacher Education Accreditation Council. *Faculty:* 3 full-time (1 woman), 39 part-time/adjunct (19 women). *Students:* 46 full-time (27 women), 45 part-time (39 women); includes 5 minority (1 Asian American or Pacific Islander, 4 Hispanic Americans), 2 international. Average age 33. 66 applicants, 73% accepted, 39 enrolled. In 2009, 44 master's awarded. *Degree requirements:* For master's, thesis or project. *Entrance requirements:* For master's, minimum GPA of 3.0, letters of recommendation. Additional exam requirements/recommendations for international students: Required—TOEFL (minimum score 550 paper-based; 213 computer-based). *Application deadline:* Applications are processed on a rolling basis. Application fee: $60. Electronic applications accepted. *Expenses:* Contact institution. *Financial support:* In 2009–10, 12 research assistantships with tuition reimbursements (averaging $3,000 per year) were awarded; Federal Work-Study, scholarships/grants, health care benefits, and tuition waivers (partial) also available. Support available to part-time students. Financial award applicants required to submit FAFSA. *Faculty research:* Transformative learning, science education, National Board Certification, teacher leadership, teacher quality. *Unit head:* Dr. Patrick Allen, Dean, 518-631-9870, Fax: 518-631-9901. *Application contact:* Christine Angley, Assistant, 518-631-9871, Fax: 518-631-9903, E-mail: angleyc@uniongraduatecollege.edu.

Union Institute & University, M Ed Program–Vermont Campus, Montpelier, VT 05602. Offers school administration (M Ed), including principalship; school counseling (M Ed); teaching (M Ed), including art, early childhood, elementary, English, math, middle schools, science, social studies, special education. *Faculty:* 3 full-time (1 woman), 23 part-time/adjunct (19 women). *Students:* 41 part-time (29 women). Average age 38. In 2009, 15 master's awarded. *Degree requirements:* For master's, thesis. *Entrance requirements:* For master's, 3 letters of reference. *Application deadline:* Applications are processed on a rolling basis. Application fee: $50. *Expenses:* Contact institution. *Financial support:* Federal Work-Study, scholarships/grants, and tuition waivers available. Financial award applicants required to submit FAFSA. *Unit head:* Dr. Arlene Sacks, Dean, Graduate Programs in Education, 305-653-6713 Ext. 2152, E-mail: arlene.sacks@myunion.edu. *Application contact:* Dr. Arlene Sacks, Dean, Graduate Programs in Education, 305-653-6713 Ext. 2152, E-mail: arlene.sacks@myunion.edu.

Universidad Autonoma de Guadalajara, Graduate Programs, Guadalajara, Mexico. Offers administrative law and justice (LL M); advertising and corporate communications (MA); architecture (M Arch); business (MBA); computational science (MCC); education (Ed M, Ed D); English-Spanish translation (MA); fiscal law (MA); integrated management of digital animation (MA); international business (MIB); international corporate law (LL M); internet technologies (MS); labor health (MS); manufacturing systems (MMS); philosophy (MA, PhD); power electronics (MS); quality systems (MQS); renewable energy (MS); social evaluation of projects (MBA); strategic market research (MBA); teaching mathematics (MA).

University at Albany, State University of New York, College of Arts and Sciences, Department of Mathematics and Statistics, Albany, NY 12222-0001. Offers mathematics (PhD); secondary teaching (MA); statistics (MA). *Degree requirements:* For doctorate, one foreign language, thesis/dissertation. *Entrance requirements:* For doctorate, GRE General Test. Additional exam requirements/recommendations for international students: Required—TOEFL (minimum score 550 paper-based; 213 computer-based). Electronic applications accepted.

University at Buffalo, the State University of New York, Graduate School, Graduate School of Education, Department of Learning and Instruction, Buffalo, NY 14260. Offers biology education (Ed M, Certificate); chemistry education (Ed M, Certificate); childhood education (Ed M); childhood education with bilingual extension (Ed M); early childhood education (Ed M); earth science education (Ed M, Certificate); elementary education (Ed D, PhD); English education (Ed M, PhD, Certificate); English for speakers of other languages (Ed M); foreign and second language education (PhD); French education (Ed M, Certificate); general education (Ed M); German education (Ed M, Certificate); gifted education (online) (Certificate); Latin education (Ed M, Certificate); literary specialist (Ed M); mathematics education (Ed M, PhD, Certificate); music education (Ed M, Certificate); physics education (Ed M, Certificate); reading education (PhD); science and the public (online) (Ed M); science education (PhD); social studies education (Ed M, Certificate); Spanish education (Ed M, Certificate); special education (PhD); teaching and leading for diversity (Certificate); teaching English to speakers of other languages (Ed M). Part-time and evening/weekend programs available. Postbaccalaureate distance learning degree programs offered (no on-campus study). *Faculty:* 34 full-time (24 women), 50 part-time/adjunct (39 women). *Students:* 332 full-time (245 women), 365 part-time (272 women); includes 50 minority (18 African Americans, 4 American Indian/Alaska Native, 10 Asian Americans or Pacific Islanders, 18 Hispanic Americans), 55 international. Average age 30. 627 applicants, 78% accepted, 286 enrolled. In 2009, 255 master's, 16 doctorates, 51 other advanced degrees awarded. *Degree requirements:* For master's, comprehensive exam; for doctorate, thesis/dissertation, research analysis exam, research experience component. *Entrance requirements:* For doctorate, GRE General Test or MAT, interview, writing sample, letters of recommendation. Additional exam requirements/recommendations for international students: Required—TOEFL (minimum score 600 paper-based; 250 computer-based; 96 iBT). *Application deadline:* For fall admission, 2/1 priority date for domestic and international students; for spring admission, 11/15 priority date for domestic students, 10/1 for international students. Applications are processed on a rolling basis. Application fee: $50. Electronic applications accepted. *Financial support:* In 2009–10, 23 fellowships with full tuition reimbursements (averaging $9,000 per year), 42 research assistantships with full tuition reimbursements (averaging $10,000 per year) were awarded; teaching assistantships with full tuition reimbursements, career-related internships or fieldwork, Federal Work-Study, institutionally sponsored loans, scholarships/grants, tuition waivers (partial), and unspecified assistantships also available. Financial award application deadline: 2/28; financial award applicants required to submit FAFSA. *Faculty research:* Science assessment, foreign language teaching and learning, early learning, new literacies, gender and education. Total annual research expenditures: $1.8 million. *Unit head:* Dr. Suzanne Miller, Chair, 716-645-2455, Fax: 716-645-3161, E-mail: smiller@buffalo.edu. *Application contact:* Cathy Dimino, Admissions Assistant, 716-645-2110, Fax: 716-645-7937, E-mail: cadimino@buffalo.edu.

University of Arkansas, Graduate School, J. William Fulbright College of Arts and Sciences, Department of Mathematical Sciences, Program in Secondary Mathematics, Fayetteville, AR 72701-1201. Offers MA. *Accreditation:* NCATE. *Degree requirements:* For master's, written exam. Application fee: $40 ($50 for international students). *Expenses:* Tuition, state resident: full-time $7355; part-time $356.58 per hour. Tuition, nonresident: full-time $17,401; part-time $775.17 per hour. Required fees: $1203. *Financial support:* Fellowships, research assistantships, teaching assistantships, career-related internships or fieldwork and Federal Work-Study

Mathematics Education

University of Arkansas (continued)
available. Support available to part-time students. Financial award application deadline: 4/1; financial award applicants required to submit FAFSA. *Unit head:* Dr. Chaim Goodman-Strauss, Chair, 479-575-3351, Fax: 479-575-8630, E-mail: strauss@uark.edu. *Application contact:* Dr. Mark Johnson, Graduate Coordinator, 479-575-3351, Fax: 479-575-8630, E-mail: markj@uark.edu.

The University of British Columbia, Faculty of Education, Department of Curriculum and Pedagogy, Vancouver, BC V6T 1Z4, Canada. Offers art education (M Ed, MA); business education (MA); curriculum studies (M Ed, MA, PhD); home economics education (M Ed, MA); math education (M Ed, MA); music education (M Ed, MA); physical education (M Ed, MA); science education (M Ed, MA); social studies education (M Ed, MA); technology studies education (M Ed, MA). Part-time programs available. *Degree requirements:* For master's, thesis (MA); for doctorate, comprehensive exam, thesis/dissertation. *Entrance requirements:* Additional exam requirements/recommendations for international students: Required—TOEFL (minimum score 580 paper-based; 237 computer-based; 92 iBT). Electronic applications accepted. *Expenses:* Contact institution. *Faculty research:* School subjects, teaching and learning.

University of California, Berkeley, Graduate Division, School of Education, Group in Science and Mathematics Education, Berkeley, CA 94720-1500. Offers PhD, MA/Credential. *Students:* 21 full-time (15 women). Average age 30. 15 applicants, 5 enrolled. In 2009, 2 doctorates awarded. *Application deadline:* For fall admission, 12/1 for domestic students. Application fee: $70 ($90 for international students). Electronic applications accepted. *Financial support:* Unspecified assistantships available. *Application contact:* Information Contact, 510-642-4207, Fax: 510-642-4808, E-mail: smeinfo@berkeley.edu.

University of California, Berkeley, Graduate Division, School of Education, Programs in Education, Berkeley, CA 94720-1500. Offers development in mathematics and science (MA); education in mathematics, science, and technology (MA, PhD); human development and education (MA, PhD); special education (PhD); MA/Credential; Ph D/Credential; PhD/MA. *Students:* 374 full-time (270 women). Average age 33. 674 applicants, 111 enrolled. In 2009, 120 master's, 25 doctorates awarded. Terminal master's awarded for partial completion of doctoral program. *Degree requirements:* For master's, exam or thesis; for doctorate, thesis/dissertation, oral qualifying exam. *Entrance requirements:* For master's and doctorate, GRE General Test, minimum GPA of 3.0 during last 2 years of undergraduate course work. *Application deadline:* For fall admission, 12/1 for domestic students. Application fee: $70 ($90 for international students). Electronic applications accepted. *Financial support:* Fellowships, research assistantships, teaching assistantships, unspecified assistantships available. *Faculty research:* Human development, social and moral educational psychology, developmental teacher preparation. *Unit head:* Prof. P. David Pearson, Dean, 510-642-3726, E-mail: gsedeansoffice@lists.berkeley.edu. *Application contact:* Admissions Office, 510-642-0841, Fax: 510-642-4808, E-mail: gse_info@uclink.berkeley.edu.

University of California, San Diego, Office of Graduate Studies, Program in Mathematics and Science Education, La Jolla, CA 92093. Offers PhD. *Entrance requirements:* For doctorate, GRE General Test. Electronic applications accepted.

University of California, Santa Cruz, Division of Graduate Studies, Division of Social Sciences, Department of Education, Santa Cruz, CA 95064. Offers education (MA); language and literacy studies (PhD); mathematics and science education (PhD); social context and policy studies of education (PhD). Terminal master's awarded for partial completion of doctoral program. *Degree requirements:* For master's, thesis; for doctorate, thesis/dissertation. *Faculty research:* Bilingual/multicultural education, special education, curriculum and instruction, child development.

University of Central Arkansas, Graduate School, College of Natural Sciences and Math, Department of Mathematics, Conway, AR 72035-0001. Offers applied mathematics (MS); math education (MA). Part-time programs available. *Faculty:* 16 full-time (4 women). *Students:* 17 full-time (10 women), 8 part-time (6 women); includes 2 minority (1 African American, 1 Asian American or Pacific Islander), 2 international. Average age 28. 8 applicants, 100% accepted, 4 enrolled. In 2009, 5 master's awarded. *Degree requirements:* For master's, comprehensive exam, thesis optional. *Entrance requirements:* For master's, GRE General Test, minimum GPA of 2.7. Additional exam requirements/recommendations for international students: Required—TOEFL (minimum score 550 paper-based; 213 computer-based). *Application deadline:* For fall admission, 3/1 priority date for domestic students; for spring admission, 10/1 priority date for domestic students. Applications are processed on a rolling basis. Application fee: $25 ($50 for international students). *Expenses:* Tuition, state resident: full-time $5136; part-time $214 per credit hour. Required fees: $379.50; $127 per term. Tuition and fees vary according to course level, course load and campus/location. *Financial support:* In 2009–10, 11 teaching assistantships with partial tuition reimbursements (averaging $8,500 per year) were awarded; Federal Work-Study, scholarships/grants, and unspecified assistantships also available. Financial award application deadline: 2/15; financial award applicants required to submit FAFSA. *Unit head:* Dr. Ramesh Garimella, Chair, 501-450-3147, Fax: 501-450-5662, E-mail: rameshg@uca.edu. *Application contact:* Brenda Herring, Admissions Assistant, 501-450-5065, Fax: 501-450-5678, E-mail: bherring@uca.edu.

University of Central Florida, College of Education, Department of Teaching and Learning Principles, Program in K-8 Mathematics and Science Education, Orlando, FL 32816. Offers M Ed, Certificate. *Accreditation:* NCATE. *Students:* 32 part-time (23 women); includes 4 minority (2 African Americans, 1 Asian American or Pacific Islander, 1 Hispanic American). Average age 35. 1 applicant, 100% accepted, 1 enrolled. In 2009, 5 master's awarded. Application fee: $30. *Expenses:* Tuition, state resident: part-time $306.31 per credit hour. Tuition, nonresident: part-time $1099.01 per credit hour. Part-time tuition and fees vary according to degree level and program. *Financial support:* Fellowships available.

University of Central Florida, College of Education, Department of Teaching and Learning Principles, Program in Mathematics Education, Orlando, FL 32816. Offers M Ed, MA. *Accreditation:* NCATE. Part-time and evening/weekend programs available. *Students:* 13 full-time (12 women), 35 part-time (27 women); includes 13 minority (5 African Americans, 1 American Indian/Alaska Native, 2 Asian Americans or Pacific Islanders, 5 Hispanic Americans), 1 international. Average age 34. 34 applicants, 74% accepted, 19 enrolled. In 2009, 23 master's awarded. *Entrance requirements:* For master's, GRE General Test. Additional exam requirements/recommendations for international students: Required—TOEFL. *Application deadline:* For fall admission, 7/15 for domestic students; for spring admission, 12/1 for domestic students. Application fee: $30. Electronic applications accepted. *Expenses:* Tuition, state resident: part-time $306.31 per credit hour. Tuition, nonresident: part-time $1099.01 per credit hour. Part-time tuition and fees vary according to degree level and program. *Financial support:* Fellowships with partial tuition reimbursements, research assistantships with partial tuition reimbursements, teaching assistantships with partial tuition reimbursements, career-related internships or fieldwork, Federal Work-Study, institutionally sponsored loans, tuition waivers (partial), and unspecified assistantships available. Financial award application deadline: 3/1; financial award applicants required to submit FAFSA.

University of Central Florida, College of Education, Education PhD Program, Orlando, FL 32816. Offers communication sciences and disorders (PhD); counselor education (PhD); elementary education (PhD); exceptional education (PhD); higher education (PhD); hospitality education (PhD); instructional technology (PhD); mathematics education (PhD); science education (PhD); social science education (PhD). *Students:* 99 full-time (70 women), 14 part-time (9 women); includes 28 minority (17 African Americans, 2 Asian Americans or Pacific Islanders, 9 Hispanic Americans), 20 international. In 2009, 15 doctorates awarded. Application fee: $30. Electronic applications accepted. *Expenses:* Tuition, state resident: part-time $306.31 per credit hour. Tuition, nonresident: part-time $1099.01 per credit hour. Part-time tuition and fees vary according to degree level and program. *Financial support:* In 2009–10, 40 fellowships with partial tuition reimbursements (averaging $9,200 per year), 61 research assistantships with partial tuition reimbursements (averaging $7,800 per year), 18 teaching assistantships with partial tuition reimbursements (averaging $6,500 per year) were awarded. *Unit head:* Dr. B. Grant Hayes, Associate Dean, 407-823-5391, E-mail: ghayes@mail.ucf.edu. *Application contact:* Dr. B. Grant Hayes, Associate Dean, 407-823-5391, E-mail: ghayes@mail.ucf.edu.

University of Central Oklahoma, College of Graduate Studies and Research, College of Mathematics and Science, Department of Mathematics and Statistics, Edmond, OK 73034-5209. Offers applied mathematical sciences (MS), including computer science, mathematics, mathematics/computer science teaching, statistics. Part-time programs available. *Faculty:* 6 full-time (2 women). *Students:* 14 full-time (3 women), 13 part-time (5 women); includes 2 minority (1 American Indian/Alaska Native, 1 Asian American or Pacific Islander), 10 international. Average age 31. 14 applicants, 100% accepted. In 2009, 9 master's awarded. *Degree requirements:* For master's, thesis. *Entrance requirements:* Additional exam requirements/recommendations for international students: Required—TOEFL (minimum score 550 paper-based; 213 computer-based). *Application deadline:* For fall admission, 7/1 for international students; for spring admission, 11/1 for international students. Applications are processed on a rolling basis. Application fee: $25. Electronic applications accepted. *Expenses:* Tuition, state resident: full-time $4128; part-time $172 per credit hour. Tuition, nonresident: full-time $10,373; part-time $432.20 per credit hour. Required fees: $433.20; $18.05 per credit hour. *Financial support:* Federal Work-Study and unspecified assistantships available. Financial award application deadline: 3/31; financial award applicants required to submit FAFSA. *Faculty research:* Curvature, FAA, math education. *Unit head:* Dr. Charlotte Simmons, Chairperson, 405-974-5294. *Application contact:* Dr. Richard Bernard, Adviser, 405-974-3493, Fax: 405-974-3824, E-mail: jyates@aix1.uco.edu.

University of Cincinnati, Graduate School, McMicken College of Arts and Sciences, Department of Mathematical Sciences, Cincinnati, OH 45221. Offers applied mathematics (MS, PhD); mathematics education (MAT); pure mathematics (MS, PhD); statistics (MS, PhD). Part-time programs available. Terminal master's awarded for partial completion of doctoral program. *Degree requirements:* For master's, comprehensive exam, thesis or alternative; for doctorate, one foreign language, comprehensive exam, thesis/dissertation. *Entrance requirements:* For master's, GRE, teacher certification (MAT); for doctorate, GRE. Additional exam requirements/recommendations for international students: Required—TOEFL. Electronic applications accepted. *Faculty research:* Algebra, analysis, differential equations, numerical analysis, statistics.

University of Connecticut, Graduate School, Neag School of Education, Department of Curriculum and Instruction, Program in Mathematics Education, Storrs, CT 06269. Offers MA, PhD, Post-Master's Certificate. *Accreditation:* NCATE. *Faculty:* 15 full-time (10 women). *Students:* 14 full-time (10 women), 6 part-time (4 women); includes 2 minority (1 African American, 1 Asian American or Pacific Islander), 1 international. Average age 29. 25 applicants, 24% accepted, 5 enrolled. In 2009, 13 master's, 2 other advanced degrees awarded. Terminal master's awarded for partial completion of doctoral program. *Degree requirements:* For master's, comprehensive exam; for doctorate, thesis/dissertation. *Entrance requirements:* For doctorate, GRE General Test. Additional exam requirements/recommendations for international students: Required—TOEFL (minimum score 550 paper-based; 213 computer-based). *Application deadline:* For fall admission, 2/1 priority date for domestic and international students; for spring admission, 11/1 for domestic students, 10/1 for international students. Applications are processed on a rolling basis. Application fee: $55. Electronic applications accepted. *Expenses:* Tuition, state resident: full-time $4725; part-time $525 per credit. Tuition, nonresident: full-time $12,267; part-time $1363 per credit. Required fees: $346 per semester. Tuition and fees vary according to course load. *Financial support:* In 2009–10, 1 research assistantship with full tuition reimbursement, 1 teaching assistantship with full tuition reimbursement were awarded; fellowships, Federal Work-Study, scholarships/grants, health care benefits, and unspecified assistantships also available. Financial award application deadline: 2/1; financial award applicants required to submit FAFSA. *Unit head:* Mary Anne Doyle, Head, 860-486-2433, Fax: 860-486-0280, E-mail: mary.dolye@uconn.edu. *Application contact:* Lisa Rasicot, Graduate Coordinator, 860-486-3065, Fax: 860-486-0210, E-mail: l.rasicot@uconn.edu.

University of Detroit Mercy, College of Engineering and Science, Department of Mathematics and Computer Science, Detroit, MI 48221. Offers computer science (MSCS), including computer systems applications, software engineering; computer science education (MATM); mathematics education (MATM). Evening/weekend programs available. *Entrance requirements:* For master's, minimum GPA of 3.0.

University of Florida, Graduate School, College of Education, School of Teaching and Learning, Gainesville, FL 32611. Offers bilingual/ESOL education (M Ed, MAE, Ed D, PhD, Ed S); curriculum and instruction (M Ed, MAE, Ed D, PhD, Ed S); early childhood education (Ed D, PhD, Ed S); elementary education (M Ed, MAE); English education (M Ed, MAE); mathematics education (M Ed, MAE); reading education (M Ed, MAE); science education (M Ed, MAE); social foundations (M Ed, MAE, Ed D, PhD); social studies education (M Ed, MAE). *Accreditation:* NCATE. *Degree requirements:* For master's, thesis optional; for doctorate, variable foreign language requirement, thesis/dissertation. *Entrance requirements:* For master's and doctorate, GRE General Test, minimum GPA of 3.0; for Ed S, GRE General Test. Additional exam requirements/recommendations for international students: Required—TOEFL (minimum score 550 paper-based; 213 computer-based). Electronic applications accepted. *Faculty research:* Teacher education, inclusive education, classroom processes, curriculum and technology.

University of Georgia, Graduate School, College of Education, Department of Mathematics and Science Education, Athens, GA 30602. Offers mathematics education (M Ed, Ed D, PhD, Ed S); science education (M Ed, Ed D, PhD, Ed S). *Faculty:* 16 full-time (7 women), 1 (woman) part-time/adjunct. *Students:* 125 full-time (83 women), 71 part-time (42 women); includes 34 minority (24 African Americans, 5 Asian Americans or Pacific Islanders, 5 Hispanic Americans), 20 international. 88 applicants. In 2009, 31 master's, 14 doctorates, 10 other advanced degrees awarded. *Application deadline:* For fall admission, 7/1 priority date for domestic students; for spring admission, 11/15 for domestic students. Application fee: $50. *Expenses:* Tuition, state resident: full-time $6000; part-time $250 per credit hour. Tuition, nonresident: full-time $20,904; part-time $871 per credit hour. Required fees: $730 per semester. *Unit head:* Dr. Denise S. Mewborn, Head, 706-542-4548, Fax: 706-542-4551, E-mail: dmewborn@uga.edu. *Application contact:* Dr. David Jackson, Graduate Coordinator, 706-542-4637, Fax: 706-542-4551, E-mail: djackson@uga.edu.

University of Houston, College of Education, Department of Curriculum and Instruction, Houston, TX 77204. Offers art education (M Ed); bilingual education (M Ed); curriculum and instruction (M Ed, Ed D); early childhood education (M Ed); elementary education (M Ed); gifted and talented education (M Ed); instructional technology (M Ed); mathematics education (M Ed); reading and language arts education (M Ed); science education (M Ed); second language education (M Ed); secondary education (M Ed); social studies education (M Ed); teaching (M Ed). *Accreditation:* NCATE. Part-time and evening/weekend programs available. *Faculty:* 20 full-time (9 women), 22 part-time/adjunct (17 women). *Students:* 113 full-time (81 women), 195 part-time (150 women); includes 107 minority (43 African Americans, 29 Asian Americans or Pacific Islanders, 35 Hispanic Americans), 29 international. Average age 35. 150 applicants, 77% accepted, 55 enrolled. In 2009, 75 master's, 31 doctorates awarded. *Degree requirements:* For master's, comprehensive exam, thesis optional; for doctorate, comprehensive exam, thesis/dissertation. *Entrance requirements:* For master's and doctorate, GRE, minimum cumulative undergraduate GPA of 2.6. Additional exam requirements/recommendations for international students: Required—TOEFL (minimum score 550 paper-based; 79 iBT). *Application deadline:* For fall admission, 3/1 for domestic and international students; for spring admission, 10/1 for domestic and international students. Application fee: $45 ($75 for international students). Electronic applications accepted. *Expenses:* Tuition, state resident: full-time $7676; part-time $320 per credit hour. Tuition, nonresident: full-time $14,324; part-time $597 per credit hour. Required fees: $3034. *Financial support:* In 2009–10, 4 fellowships with full tuition reimbursements (averaging $9,500 per year), 6 research assistantships with full tuition reimbursements (averaging $8,800 per year), 25 teaching assistantships with full tuition reimbursements

(averaging $8,800 per year) were awarded; career-related internships or fieldwork, Federal Work-Study, institutionally sponsored loans, scholarships/grants, health care benefits, and unspecified assistantships also available. Support available to part-time students. Financial award application deadline: 2/1. *Faculty research:* Teaching-learning process, instructional technology in schools, teacher education, classroom management, at-risk students. *Unit head:* Dr. Laveria Hutchison, Chairperson, 713-743-4958, Fax: 713-743-4990, E-mail: lhutchison@uh.edu. *Application contact:* Renee C. Rattelade, Executive Secretary, 713-743-4997, Fax: 713-743-4990, E-mail: rrattelade@mail.coe.uh.edu.

University of Illinois at Chicago, Graduate College, College of Liberal Arts and Sciences, Department of Mathematics, Statistics, and Computer Science, Program in Teaching of Mathematics, Chicago, IL 60607-7128. Offers elementary (MST); secondary (MST). Part-time programs available. *Degree requirements:* For master's, comprehensive exam. *Entrance requirements:* For master's, GRE General Test, minimum GPA of 2.75. Additional exam requirements/recommendations for international students: Required—TOEFL. Electronic applications accepted.

University of Illinois at Urbana–Champaign, Graduate College, College of Liberal Arts and Sciences, Department of Mathematics, Champaign, IL 61820. Offers applied mathematics (MS); applied mathematics: actuarial science (MS); mathematics (MA, MS, PhD); teaching of mathematics (MS). *Faculty:* 67 full-time (5 women), 3 part-time/adjunct (0 women). *Students:* 161 full-time (40 women), 25 part-time (8 women); includes 13 minority (1 African American, 10 Asian Americans or Pacific Islanders, 2 Hispanic Americans), 107 international. 361 applicants, 25% accepted, 37 enrolled. In 2009, 41 master's, 23 doctorates awarded. *Entrance requirements:* For master's, GRE General Test, GRE Subject Test (mathematics), minimum GPA of 3.0; for doctorate, GRE General Test, GRE Subject Test (math), minimum GPA of 3.0. Additional exam requirements/recommendations for international students: Required—TOEFL (minimum score 550 paper-based; 213 computer-based). *Application deadline:* Applications are processed on a rolling basis. Application fee: $60 ($75 for international students). Electronic applications accepted. *Financial support:* In 2009–10, 22 fellowships, 44 research assistantships, 148 teaching assistantships were awarded; tuition waivers (full and partial) also available. *Unit head:* Sheldon Katz, Chair, 217-265-6258, Fax: 217-333-9576, E-mail: katzs@illinois.edu. *Application contact:* Marci Blocher, Office Support Specialist, 217-333-3350, Fax: 217-333-9576, E-mail: mblocher@illinois.edu.

University of Indianapolis, Graduate Programs, School of Education, Indianapolis, IN 46227-3697. Offers art education (MAT); biology (MAT); chemistry (MAT); curriculum and instruction (MA); earth sciences (MAT); education (MA, MAT); educational leadership (MA); elementary education (MA); English (MAT); French (MAT); math (MAT); physical education (MAT); physics (MAT); secondary education (MA), including art education, education, English education, social studies education; social studies (MAT); Spanish (MAT). *Accreditation:* NCATE. Part-time and evening/weekend programs available. *Faculty:* 4 full-time (3 women), 3 part-time/adjunct (2 women). *Students:* 52 full-time (28 women), 110 part-time (67 women); includes 3 minority (all African Americans), 2 international. Average age 33. *Entrance requirements:* For master's, GRE Subject Test, PRAXIS I, minimum GPA of 2.5, 3 letters of recommendation, interview, writing exercise. Additional exam requirements/recommendations for international students: Required—TOEFL (minimum score 550 paper-based; 213 computer-based). *Application deadline:* Applications are processed on a rolling basis. Application fee: $50. *Financial support:* Federal Work-Study available. Financial award application deadline: 5/1; financial award applicants required to submit FAFSA. *Faculty research:* Assessment of teacher education, perceptions of prospective teachers by parents. *Unit head:* Dr. Kathy Moran, Dean, 317-788-3285, Fax: 317-788-3300, E-mail: kmoran@uindy.edu. *Application contact:* Chemain Slater, 317-788-2051, E-mail: slaterc@uindy.edu.

The University of Iowa, Graduate College, College of Education, Department of Teaching and Learning, Program in Secondary Education, Iowa City, IA 52242-1316. Offers art education (PhD); curriculum and supervision (PhD); curriculum supervision (MA); developmental reading (MA); English education (MA, MAT); foreign language education (MA, MAT); foreign language/ESL education (PhD); language, literature and culture (PhD); math education (PhD); mathematics education (MA); social studies (MA, PhD). *Degree requirements:* For master's, thesis optional, exam; for doctorate, comprehensive exam, thesis/dissertation. *Entrance requirements:* For master's and doctorate, GRE General Test, minimum GPA of 3.0. Additional exam requirements/recommendations for international students: Required—TOEFL (minimum score 550 paper-based; 213 computer-based; 81 iBT). Electronic applications accepted.

University of Maryland, Baltimore County, Graduate School, College of Arts, Humanities and Social Sciences, Department of Education, Program in Education, Baltimore, MD 21250. Offers mathematics education (MA); science education (MA); STEM education (MA). Part-time and evening/weekend programs available. *Faculty:* 24 full-time (18 women), 25 part-time/adjunct (19 women). *Students:* 2 full-time (1 woman), 147 part-time (120 women); includes 9 African Americans, 2 Asian Americans or Pacific Islanders. Average age 34. 34 applicants, 97% accepted, 26 enrolled. In 2009, 106 master's awarded. *Degree requirements:* For master's, comprehensive exam (for some programs), thesis (for some programs). *Entrance requirements:* For master's, PRAXIS I, minimum GPA of 3.0. Additional exam requirements/recommendations for international students: Required—TOEFL. *Application deadline:* For fall admission, 6/1 for domestic students; for spring admission, 11/1 for domestic students. Applications are processed on a rolling basis. Application fee: $50. Electronic applications accepted. *Financial support:* In 2009–10, 12 students received support, including research assistantships with full tuition reimbursements available (averaging $12,000 per year); career-related internships or fieldwork, Federal Work-Study, scholarships/grants, tuition waivers, and unspecified assistantships also available. Financial award application deadline: 3/1; financial award applicants required to submit FAFSA. *Unit head:* Dr. Susan M. Blunck, Director, 410-455-2869, Fax: 410-455-3986, E-mail: blunck@umbc.edu. *Application contact:* Dr. Susan M. Blunck, Director, 410-455-2869, Fax: 410-455-3986, E-mail: blunck@umbc.edu.

University of Maryland, Baltimore County, Graduate School, College of Arts, Humanities and Social Sciences, Department of Education, Program in Teaching, Baltimore, MD 21250. Offers early childhood education (MAT); elementary education (MAT); secondary education (MAT), including art, biology, chemistry, dance, earth/space science, English, foreign language, mathematics, music, physics, theatre; secondary science (MAT), including social studies. Part-time and evening/weekend programs available. *Faculty:* 24 full-time (18 women), 25 part-time/adjunct (19 women). *Students:* 52 full-time (41 women), 64 part-time (55 women); includes 20 minority (5 African Americans, 1 American Indian/Alaska Native, 10 Asian Americans or Pacific Islanders, 4 Hispanic Americans), 3 international. Average age 31. 88 applicants, 57% accepted, 39 enrolled. In 2009, 106 master's awarded. *Degree requirements:* For master's, comprehensive exam (for some programs), thesis (for some programs). *Entrance requirements:* For master's, PRAXIS I and II, minimum GPA of 3.0. Additional exam requirements/recommendations for international students: Required—TOEFL. *Application deadline:* For fall admission, 6/1 for domestic students; for spring admission, 11/1 for domestic students. Applications are processed on a rolling basis. Application fee: $50. Electronic applications accepted. *Financial support:* In 2009–10, 6 students received support, including research assistantships with full tuition reimbursements available (averaging $12,000 per year); career-related internships or fieldwork, Federal Work-Study, scholarships/grants, tuition waivers, and unspecified assistantships also available. Financial award application deadline: 3/1. *Faculty research:* STEM teacher education, culturally sensitive pedagogy, ESOL/bilingual education, early childhood education, language, literacy and culture. *Unit head:* Dr. Susan M. Blunck, Director, 410-455-2869, Fax: 410-455-3986, E-mail: blunck@umbc.edu. *Application contact:* Dr. Susan M. Blunck, Director, 410-455-2869, Fax: 410-455-3986, E-mail: blunck@umbc.edu.

University of Massachusetts Dartmouth, Graduate School, School of Education, Public Policy, and Civic Engagement, Department of Science, Technology, Engineering and Mathematics (STEM), North Dartmouth, MA 02747-2300. Offers math education (PhD). Part-time programs available. *Faculty:* 4 full-time (2 women). *Students:* 1 full-time (0 women), 2 part-time (both women). Average age 31. 6 applicants, 67% accepted, 3 enrolled. *Entrance requirements:*

Additional exam requirements/recommendations for international students: Required—TOEFL (minimum score 550 paper-based; 213 computer-based). *Application deadline:* For fall admission, 4/20 for domestic students, 2/20 for international students; for spring admission, 11/15 for domestic students. Applications are processed on a rolling basis. Application fee: $40 ($60 for international students). *Expenses:* Tuition, state resident: full-time $2071; part-time $86.29 per credit. Tuition, nonresident: full-time $8099; part-time $337.46 per credit. Required fees: $9446. Tuition and fees vary according to class time, course load and reciprocity agreements. *Financial support:* Application deadline: 3/1. *Faculty research:* Algebraic thinking in early grades; use of dynamic, interactive technologies and their impact on mathematical experience; classroom connectivity and impact on participation and motivation; development of proof and reasoning across grades; international political economy. *Unit head:* Maria Blanton, Department Head, 508-999-9171, E-mail: mblanton@umassd.edu. *Application contact:* Elan Turcotte-Shamski, Graduate Admissions Officer, 508-999-8604, Fax: 508-999-8183, E-mail: graduate@umassd.edu.

University of Massachusetts Lowell, Graduate School of Education, Lowell, MA 01854-2881. Offers administration, planning, and policy (CAGS); curriculum and instruction (M Ed, CAGS); educational administration (M Ed); language arts and literacy (Ed D); leadership in schooling (Ed D); math and science education (Ed D); reading and language (M Ed, CAGS). *Accreditation:* NCATE. Part-time and evening/weekend programs available. Postbaccalaureate distance learning degree programs offered (no on-campus study). Terminal master's awarded for partial completion of doctoral program. *Degree requirements:* For doctorate, thesis/dissertation. *Entrance requirements:* For master's, doctorate, and CAGS, GRE General Test. Additional exam requirements/recommendations for international students: Required—TOEFL. Electronic applications accepted.

University of Miami, Graduate School, School of Education, Department of Teaching and Learning, Program in Teaching and Learning, Coral Gables, FL 33124. Offers language and literacy learning in multilingual settings (PhD); mathematics and science education (PhD); special education (PhD). *Students:* 30 full-time (22 women); includes 11 minority (3 African Americans, 8 Hispanic Americans), 7 international. Average age 35. 21 applicants, 43% accepted, 7 enrolled. In 2009, 5 doctorates awarded. *Degree requirements:* For doctorate, thesis/dissertation, qualifying exam. *Entrance requirements:* For doctorate, GRE General Test. Additional exam requirements/recommendations for international students: Required—TOEFL (minimum score 550 paper-based; 80 iBT); Recommended—IELTS (minimum score 6.5). *Application deadline:* For fall admission, 2/15 for domestic students, 10/15 for international students. Application fee: $65. Electronic applications accepted. *Financial support:* In 2009–10, 25 students received support. Application deadline: 3/1. *Faculty research:* Teacher education, multicultural education, technology, second language acquisition, math and science education. *Unit head:* Dr. Batya Elbaum, Associate Department Chairperson, 305-284-4218, Fax: 305-284-4439, E-mail: elbaum@miami.edu. *Application contact:* Tinisha Hollinshead, Admission Coordinator, 305-284-2102, Fax: 305-284-6998, E-mail: tinisha@miami.edu.

University of Michigan, Horace H. Rackham School of Graduate Studies, School of Education, Programs in Educational Studies, Ann Arbor, MI 48109. Offers cross specialization (PhD); curriculum development (MA); early childhood education (MA, PhD); educational administration and policy (MA, PhD); educational foundations and policy (MA, PhD); English education (MA); English language learning in school settings (MA); learning technologies (MA, PhD); literacy, language, and culture (MA, PhD); mathematics education (MA, PhD); postsecondary science education (MS); research methods (MA); science education (MA, PhD); social studies education (MA); teaching and teacher education (PhD); MA/Certification; MBA/MA; PhD/MA. Terminal master's awarded for partial completion of doctoral program. *Degree requirements:* For master's, thesis (for some programs); for doctorate, comprehensive exam, thesis/dissertation. *Entrance requirements:* For master's and doctorate, GRE General Test. Additional exam requirements/recommendations for international students: Required—TOEFL (minimum score 600 paper-based; 250 computer-based). *Application deadline:* For fall admission, 12/1 priority date for domestic students, 12/1 for international students. Application fee: $60 ($75 for international students). Electronic applications accepted. *Expenses:* Tuition, state resident: full-time $17,286; part-time $1099 per credit hour. Tuition, nonresident: full-time $34,944; part-time $2080 per credit hour. Required fees: $95 per semester. Tuition and fees vary according to course load, degree level and program. *Financial support:* Applicants required to submit FAFSA. *Unit head:* Dr. Addison Stone, Chairperson, 734-763-7500, Fax: 734-615-1290, E-mail: addison@umich.edu. *Application contact:* Laura Mayers, Student Services Assistant, 734-764-7563, Fax: 734-763-1495, E-mail: ed.grad.admit@umich.edu.

University of Minnesota, Twin Cities Campus, Graduate School, College of Education and Human Development, Department of Curriculum and Instruction, Program in Teaching, Minneapolis, MN 55455-0213. Offers Chinese (M Ed); earth science (M Ed); elementary special education (M Ed); English (M Ed); English as a second language (M Ed); French (M Ed); German (M Ed); Hebrew (M Ed); Japanese (M Ed); life sciences (M Ed); mathematics (M Ed); middle school science (M Ed); science (M Ed); second languages and cultures (M Ed); social studies (M Ed); Spanish (M Ed). *Students:* 263 full-time (186 women), 117 part-time (83 women); includes 32 minority (10 African Americans, 2 American Indian/Alaska Native, 17 Asian Americans or Pacific Islanders, 3 Hispanic Americans), 4 international. Average age 27. 363 applicants, 74% accepted, 259 enrolled. In 2009, 497 master's awarded. *Unit head:* Dr. Ruth Thomas, Chair, 612-624-4772, Fax: 612-624-8277, E-mail: thoma006@umn.edu. *Application contact:* Dr. Mary Trettin, Associate Dean, 612-625-6501, Fax: 612-626-1580, E-mail: mtrettin@umn.edu.

University of Missouri, Graduate School, College of Arts and Sciences, Department of Mathematics, Columbia, MO 65211. Offers applied mathematics (MS); mathematics (MA, MST, PhD). *Faculty:* 47 full-time (9 women), 11 part-time/adjunct (6 women). *Students:* 59 full-time (6 women), 14 part-time (5 women); includes 2 minority (both Hispanic Americans), 25 international. Average age 27. 107 applicants, 23% accepted, 16 enrolled. In 2009, 8 master's, 4 doctorates awarded. *Degree requirements:* For doctorate, 2 foreign languages, comprehensive exam, thesis/dissertation. *Entrance requirements:* For master's and doctorate, GRE General Test, minimum GPA of 3.0; bachelor's degree from accredited institution. Additional exam requirements/recommendations for international students: Required—TOEFL (minimum score 500 paper-based; 173 computer-based; 61 iBT). *Application deadline:* For fall admission, 1/15 for domestic students. Applications are processed on a rolling basis. Application fee: $45 ($60 for international students). Electronic applications accepted. *Financial support:* In 2009–10, 7 fellowships with full tuition reimbursements, 4 research assistantships with full tuition reimbursements, 64 teaching assistantships with full tuition reimbursements were awarded; institutionally sponsored loans, health care benefits, and unspecified assistantships also available. Financial award applicants required to submit FAFSA. *Faculty research:* Algebraic geometry, analysis (real, complex, functional and harmonic), analytic functions, applied mathematics, financial mathematics and mathematics of insurance, commutative rings, scattering theory, differential equations (ordinary and partial), differential geometry, dynamical systems, general relativity, mathematical physics, number theory, probabilistic analysis and topology. *Unit head:* Dr. Glen Himmelberg, Department Chair, E-mail: himmelbergg@missouri.edu. *Application contact:* Dr. Jan Segert, Director of Graduate Studies, 573-882-4926, E-mail: segertj@missouri.edu.

University of Missouri, Graduate School, College of Education, Department of Learning, Teaching and Curriculum, Columbia, MO 65211. Offers agricultural education (M Ed, PhD, Ed S); art education (M Ed, PhD, Ed S); business and office education (M Ed, PhD, Ed S); early childhood education (M Ed, PhD, Ed S); elementary education (M Ed, PhD, Ed S); English education (M Ed, PhD, Ed S); foreign language education (M Ed, PhD, Ed S); health education and promotion (M Ed, PhD); learning and instruction (M Ed); marketing education (M Ed, PhD, Ed S); mathematics education (M Ed, PhD, Ed S); music education (M Ed, PhD, Ed S); reading education (M Ed, PhD, Ed S); science education (M Ed, PhD, Ed S); social studies education (M Ed, PhD, Ed S); vocational education (M Ed, PhD, Ed S). Part-time programs available. Terminal master's awarded for partial completion of doctoral program. *Degree requirements:* For doctorate, thesis/dissertation. *Entrance requirements:* For master's and Ed S, GRE General Test or MAT, minimum GPA of 3.0; for doctorate, GRE General Test,

Mathematics Education

University of Missouri (continued)
minimum GPA of 3.0. Additional exam requirements/recommendations for international students: Required—TOEFL (minimum score 600 paper-based; 250 computer-based; 100 iBT). Electronic applications accepted.

The University of Montana, Graduate School, College of Arts and Sciences, Department of Mathematical Sciences, Missoula, MT 59812-0002. Offers mathematics (MA, PhD), including college teaching (PhD), traditional mathematics research (PhD); mathematics education (MA). Part-time programs available. Terminal master's awarded for partial completion of doctoral program. *Degree requirements:* For doctorate, thesis/dissertation. *Entrance requirements:* For master's and doctorate, GRE General Test. Additional exam requirements/recommendations for international students: Required—TOEFL (minimum score 525 paper-based; 195 computer-based).

University of Nevada, Reno, Graduate School, College of Science, Department of Mathematics and Statistics, Reno, NV 89557. Offers mathematics (MS); teaching mathematics (MATM). *Degree requirements:* For master's, thesis optional. *Entrance requirements:* For master's, GRE General Test, minimum GPA of 2.75. Additional exam requirements/recommendations for international students: Required—TOEFL (minimum score 500 paper-based; 173 computer-based; 61 iBT), IELTS (minimum score 6). Electronic applications accepted. *Faculty research:* Operator algebra, nonlinear systems, differential equations.

University of New Hampshire, Graduate School, College of Engineering and Physical Sciences, Department of Mathematics and Statistics, Durham, NH 03824. Offers applied mathematics (MS); industrial statistics (Postbaccalaureate Certificate); mathematics (MS, MST, PhD); mathematics education (PhD); statistics (MS). *Faculty:* 21 full-time (5 women). *Students:* 34 full-time (21 women), 24 part-time (8 women); includes 4 minority (1 Asian American or Pacific Islander, 3 Hispanic Americans), 20 international. Average age 29. 76 applicants, 50% accepted, 17 enrolled. In 2009, 17 master's, 7 doctorates, 1 other advanced degree awarded. Terminal master's awarded for partial completion of doctoral program. *Degree requirements:* For doctorate, 2 foreign languages, thesis/dissertation. *Entrance requirements:* Additional exam requirements/recommendations for international students: Required—TOEFL (minimum score 550 paper-based; 213 computer-based; 80 iBT). *Application deadline:* For fall admission, 4/1 priority date for domestic students, 4/1 for international students; for spring admission, 12/1 for domestic students. Applications are processed on a rolling basis. Application fee: $65. Electronic applications accepted. *Expenses:* Tuition, state resident: full-time $10,380; part-time $577 per credit hour. Tuition, nonresident: full-time $24,350; part-time $1002 per credit hour. Required fees: $1550; $387.50 per semester. Tuition and fees vary according to course load and program. *Financial support:* In 2009–10, 35 students received support, including 2 fellowships, 1 research assistantship, 32 teaching assistantships; Federal Work-Study, scholarships/grants, and tuition waivers (full and partial) also available. Support available to part-time students. Financial award application deadline: 2/15. *Faculty research:* Operator theory, complex analysis, algebra, nonlinear dynamics, statistics. *Unit head:* Dr. Eric Grinberg, Chairperson, 603-862-5772. *Application contact:* Jan Jankowski, Administrative Assistant, 603-862-2320, E-mail: jan.jankowski@unh.edu.

The University of North Carolina at Chapel Hill, Graduate School, School of Education, Program in Secondary Education, Chapel Hill, NC 27599. Offers English (Grades 9-12) (MAT); English as a second language (MAT); French (Grades K-12) (MAT); German (Grades K-12) (MAT); Japanese (Grades K-12) (MAT); Latin (Grades 9-12) (MAT); mathematics (Grades 9-12) (MAT); music (Grades K-12) (MAT); science (Grades 9-12) (MAT); social studies (Grades 9-12) (MAT); Spanish (Grades K-12) (MAT). *Accreditation:* NCATE. *Students:* 53 full-time (35 women), 1 part-time (0 women); includes 8 minority (4 African Americans, 2 Asian Americans or Pacific Islanders, 2 Hispanic Americans), 3 international. Average age 25. 137 applicants, 77% accepted, 54 enrolled. In 2009, 39 master's awarded. *Degree requirements:* For master's, comprehensive exam. *Entrance requirements:* For master's, GRE General Test, minimum GPA of 3.0 during last 2 years of undergraduate course work. Additional exam requirements/recommendations for international students: Required—TOEFL (minimum score 550 paper-based; 79 computer-based). *Application deadline:* For fall admission, 12/15 priority date for domestic and international students. Applications are processed on a rolling basis. Application fee: $77. Electronic applications accepted. *Financial support:* Federal Work-Study available. Support available to part-time students. Financial award application deadline: 3/1; financial award applicants required to submit FAFSA. *Unit head:* Dr. James Trier, Coordinator, 919-843-4627, Fax: 919-962-1533. *Application contact:* Amy Butler, Student Services Assistant, 919-966-1346, Fax: 919-962-1533, E-mail: abutler@email.unc.edu.

The University of North Carolina at Charlotte, Graduate School, College of Arts and Sciences, Department of Mathematics and Statistics, Program in Mathematics Education, Charlotte, NC 28223-0001. Offers MA. *Faculty:* 1 full-time (0 women). *Students:* 1 full-time (0 women), 11 part-time (7 women); includes 1 minority (African American). Average age 27. 3 applicants, 67% accepted, 2 enrolled. In 2009, 6 master's awarded. *Degree requirements:* For master's, comprehensive exam. *Entrance requirements:* For master's, GRE General Test, minimum GPA of 2.75 overall. Additional exam requirements/recommendations for international students: Required—TOEFL (minimum score 557 paper-based; 220 computer-based; 83 iBT). *Application deadline:* For fall admission, 7/15 for domestic students, 5/1 for international students; for spring admission, 11/15 for domestic students, 10/1 for international students. Application fee: $55. *Financial support:* Career-related internships or fieldwork, Federal Work-Study, institutionally sponsored loans, scholarships/grants, and administrative assistantship available. Support available to part-time students. Financial award application deadline: 4/1; financial award applicants required to submit FAFSA. *Unit head:* Dr. Alan Dow, Chair, 704-687-4560, Fax: 704-687-0415, E-mail: adow@uncc.edu. *Application contact:* Kathy B. Giddings, Director of Graduate Admissions, 704-687-5503, Fax: 704-687-3279, E-mail: gradadm@uncc.edu.

The University of North Carolina at Greensboro, Graduate School, School of Education, Department of Curriculum and Instruction, Greensboro, NC 27412-5001. Offers college teaching and adult learning (Certificate); curriculum and instruction (M Ed), including chemistry education, elementary education, English as a second language, French education, instructional technology, mathematics education, middle grades education, reading education, science education, social studies education, Spanish education; curriculum and teaching (PhD), including higher education, teacher education and development; English as a second language (Certificate); higher education (M Ed); supervision (M Ed). *Accreditation:* NCATE. Part-time programs available. *Degree requirements:* For doctorate, thesis/dissertation. *Entrance requirements:* For master's and doctorate, GRE General Test. Additional exam requirements/recommendations for international students: Required—TOEFL. Electronic applications accepted. *Faculty research:* Community college literacy program, middle school mathematics/computer mathematics.

The University of North Carolina at Pembroke, Graduate Studies, Department of Mathematics and Computer Science, Program in Mathematics Education, Pembroke, NC 28372-1510. Offers MA, MAT. *Accreditation:* NCATE. Part-time and evening/weekend programs available. *Degree requirements:* For master's, comprehensive exam, thesis optional. *Entrance requirements:* For master's, GRE General Test or MAT, bachelor's degree in mathematics or mathematics education; minimum GPA of 3.0 in major, 2.5 overall. Additional exam requirements/recommendations for international students: Required—TOEFL.

University of Northern Colorado, Graduate School, College of Natural and Health Sciences, School of Mathematical Sciences, Greeley, CO 80639. Offers mathematical teaching (MA); mathematics (MA, PhD); mathematics education (PhD); mathematics: liberal arts (MA). Part-time programs available. *Faculty:* 14 full-time (4 women). *Students:* 15 full-time (9 women), 16 part-time (12 women); includes 2 minority (1 American Indian/Alaska Native, 1 Hispanic American), 3 international. Average age 34. 15 applicants, 100% accepted, 7 enrolled. In 2009, 4 master's, 2 doctorates awarded. *Degree requirements:* For master's, comprehensive exam, thesis or alternative; for doctorate, comprehensive exam, thesis/dissertation. *Entrance requirements:* For master's, GRE General Test (liberal arts), 3 letters of recommendation; for doctorate, GRE General Test, 3 letters of recommendation. *Application deadline:* Applications are processed on a rolling basis. Application fee: $50 ($60 for international students). Electronic applications accepted. *Expenses:* Tuition, state resident: full-time $5770; part-time $320.55 per credit hour. Tuition, nonresident: full-time $13,847; part-time $769.27 per credit hour. Required fees: $948.78; $52.72 per credit. *Financial support:* In 2009–10, 3 research assistantships (averaging $7,835 per year), 13 teaching assistantships (averaging $12,032 per year) were awarded; fellowships, unspecified assistantships also available. Financial award application deadline: 3/1; financial award applicants required to submit FAFSA. *Unit head:* Dr. Dean Allison, Director, 970-351-2820, Fax: 970-351-2155. *Application contact:* Linda Sisson, Graduate Student Admission Coordinator, 970-351-1807, Fax: 970-351-2371, E-mail: linda.sisson@unco.edu.

University of Northern Iowa, Graduate College, College of Natural Sciences, Department of Mathematics, Cedar Falls, IA 50614. Offers mathematics (MA); mathematics for middle grades (MA). Part-time programs available. *Students:* 16 full-time (9 women), 41 part-time (27 women); includes 3 minority (1 African American, 2 Hispanic Americans), 5 international. 23 applicants, 78% accepted, 8 enrolled. In 2009, 13 master's awarded. *Degree requirements:* For master's, comprehensive exam (for some programs), thesis or alternative. *Entrance requirements:* For master's, minimum GPA of 3.0. Additional exam requirements/recommendations for international students: Required—TOEFL (minimum score 600 paper-based; 250 computer-based; 100 iBT). *Application deadline:* For fall admission, 8/1 priority date for domestic students. Applications are processed on a rolling basis. Application fee: $30 ($50 for international students). Electronic applications accepted. *Financial support:* Career-related internships or fieldwork, Federal Work-Study, scholarships/grants, and tuition waivers (full and partial) available. Support available to part-time students. Financial award application deadline: 2/1. *Unit head:* Dr. Douglas Mupasiri, Interim Head, 319-273-2012, Fax: 319-273-2546, E-mail: douglas.mupasiri@uni.edu. *Application contact:* Laurie S. Russell, Record Analyst, 319-273-2623, Fax: 319-273-6792, E-mail: laurie.russell@uni.edu.

University of Oklahoma, Graduate College, College of Education, Department of Instructional Leadership and Academic Curriculum, Norman, OK 73072. Offers education (Certificate); instructional leadership and academic curriculum (M Ed, PhD), including bilingual education, early childhood education, elementary education, English education, math education, reading education, science education, secondary education, social studies education. *Accreditation:* NCATE. Part-time and evening/weekend programs available. *Faculty:* 18 full-time (11 women). *Students:* 44 full-time (36 women), 117 part-time (92 women); includes 35 minority (11 African Americans, 14 American Indian/Alaska Native, 5 Asian Americans or Pacific Islanders, 5 Hispanic Americans), 2 international. 50 applicants, 84% accepted, 32 enrolled. In 2009, 31 master's, 6 doctorates awarded. Terminal master's awarded for partial completion of doctoral program. *Degree requirements:* For doctorate, thesis/dissertation. *Entrance requirements:* For master's, 12 hours of course work in education; for doctorate, GRE General Test, master's degree, minimum graduate GPA of 3.0. Additional exam requirements/recommendations for international students: Required—TOEFL (minimum score 550 paper-based; 213 computer-based). *Application deadline:* For fall admission, 6/1 priority date for domestic students, 4/1 for international students; for spring admission, 11/1 for domestic students, 9/1 for international students. Applications are processed on a rolling basis. Application fee: $40 ($90 for international students). Electronic applications accepted. *Expenses:* Tuition, state resident: full-time $3744; part-time $156 per credit hour. Tuition, nonresident: full-time $13,577; part-time $565.70 per credit hour. Required fees: $2415; $90.10 per credit hour. *Financial support:* In 2009–10, 107 students received support, including 1 research assistantship with partial tuition reimbursement available (averaging $9,630 per year), 6 teaching assistantships with partial tuition reimbursements available (averaging $10,801 per year); scholarships/grants, health care benefits, and unspecified assistantships also available. Financial award applicants required to submit FAFSA. *Faculty research:* English education, mathematics education, reading, science education, social studies education. Total annual research expenditures: $752,908. *Unit head:* Lawrence Baines, Chair, 405-325-1498, Fax: 405-325-4061, E-mail: lbaines@ou.edu. *Application contact:* Lynn Crussel, Administrative Assistant for Graduate Studies, 405-325-4843, Fax: 405-325-4061, E-mail: lcrussel@ou.edu.

University of Phoenix, College of Natural Sciences, College of Education, Phoenix, AZ 85034-7209. Offers administration and supervision (MAEd); adult education and training (MAEd); curriculum and instruction (MAEd); curriculum and instruction-adult education (MAEd); curriculum and instruction-computer education (MAEd); curriculum and instruction-English and language arts education (MAEd); curriculum and instruction-English as a second language (MAEd); curriculum and instruction-mathematics education (MAEd); curriculum education (MAEd); early childhood (MAEd); elementary teacher education (MAEd); secondary teacher education (MAEd); special education (MAEd); teacher leadership (MAEd). *Accreditation:* Teacher Education Accreditation Council. Evening/weekend programs available. Postbaccalaureate distance learning degree programs offered (no on-campus study). *Faculty:* 47 full-time (34 women), 844 part-time/adjunct (636 women). *Students:* 13,657 full-time (10,698 women); includes 4,000 minority (3,063 African Americans, 74 American Indian/Alaska Native, 241 Asian Americans or Pacific Islanders, 622 Hispanic Americans), 307 international. Average age 36. In 2009, 17,246 master's awarded. *Degree requirements:* For master's, thesis (for some programs). *Entrance requirements:* For master's, 3 years of work experience, minimum GPA of 2.5. Additional exam requirements/recommendations for international students: Required—TOEFL (minimum score 550 paper-based; 213 computer-based; 79 iBT). *Application deadline:* Applications are processed on a rolling basis. Application fee: $45. Electronic applications accepted. *Expenses:* Tuition: Full-time $13,272. Required fees: $660. Full-time tuition and fees vary according to course level, degree level and program. *Financial support:* Institutionally sponsored loans and scholarships/grants available. Financial award applicants required to submit FAFSA. *Unit head:* Dr. Meredith Curley, Dean/Executive Director, 480-557-1217, Fax: 480-557-1588, E-mail: meredith.curley@phoenix.edu. *Application contact:* Chair, 602-387-7000, Fax: 602-387-6020.

University of Phoenix–Central Florida Campus, The Artemis School, College of Education, Maitland, FL 32751-7057. Offers administration and supervision (MA Ed); curriculum and instruction (MA Ed); curriculum and instruction-computer education (MA Ed); curriculum and instruction-mathematics education (MA Ed); early childhood education (MA Ed); elementary teacher education (MA Ed); secondary teacher education (MA Ed). Evening/weekend programs available. *Degree requirements:* For master's, thesis (for some programs). *Entrance requirements:* For master's, 3 years of work experience, minimum undergraduate GPA of 2.5. Additional exam requirements/recommendations for international students: Required—TOEFL (minimum score 550 paper-based; 213 computer-based; 79 iBT). Electronic applications accepted.

University of Phoenix–North Florida Campus, The Artemis School, College of Education, Jacksonville, FL 32216-0959. Offers administration and supervision (MA Ed); curriculum and instruction (MA Ed), including computer education, mathematics education; early childhood education (MA Ed); elementary teacher education (MA Ed); secondary teacher education (MA Ed). Evening/weekend programs available. *Degree requirements:* For master's, thesis (for some programs). *Entrance requirements:* For master's, 3 years of work experience, minimum undergraduate GPA of 2.5. Additional exam requirements/recommendations for international students: Required—TOEFL (minimum score 550 paper-based; 213 computer-based; 49 iBT). Electronic applications accepted.

University of Phoenix–Omaha Campus, College of Education, Omaha, NE 68154-5240. Offers administration and supervision (MA Ed); curriculum and instruction (MA Ed), including adult education, computer education, curriculum and instruction, English and language arts education, English as a second language, mathematics education; elementary teacher education (MA Ed); secondary teacher education (MA Ed); special education (MA Ed).

University of Phoenix–Southern California Campus, College of Education, Costa Mesa, CA 92626. Offers administration and supervision (MA Ed); adult education and training (MA Ed); curriculum and instruction (MA Ed), including computer education, curriculum and instruction,

English and language arts, English as a second language, mathematics education; early childhood education (MA Ed); special education (MA Ed); teacher leadership (MA Ed). Evening/weekend programs available. *Faculty:* 47 full-time (34 women), 844 part-time/adjunct (636 women). *Students:* 558 full-time (391 women); includes 222 minority (60 African Americans, 4 American Indian/Alaska Native, 26 Asian Americans or Pacific Islanders, 132 Hispanic Americans), 9 international. Average age 34. In 2009, 303 master's awarded. *Degree requirements:* For master's, thesis (for some programs). *Entrance requirements:* For master's, minimum undergraduate GPA of 2.5, 3 years work experience. Additional exam requirements/recommendations for international students: Required—TOEFL (minimum score 550 paper-based; 213 computer-based; 79 iBT). *Application deadline:* Applications are processed on a rolling basis. Application fee: $45. Electronic applications accepted. *Expenses:* Tuition: Full-time $15,120. Required fees: $660. *Financial support:* Institutionally sponsored loans and scholarships/grants available. Financial award applicants required to submit FAFSA. *Unit head:* Dr. Meredith Curley, Dean/Executive Director, 480-557-1217, Fax: 480-557-1588, E-mail: meredith.curley@phoenix.edu. *Application contact:* Campus College Chair, 714-378-1878, Fax: 714-378-5875.

University of Phoenix–South Florida Campus, The Artemis School, College of Education, Fort Lauderdale, FL 33309. Offers administration and supervision (MA Ed); curriculum and instruction (MA Ed), including computer education, curriculum and instruction, mathematics education; early childhood education (MA Ed); elementary teacher education (MA Ed); secondary teacher education (MA Ed). Evening/weekend programs available. *Degree requirements:* For master's, thesis (for some programs). *Entrance requirements:* For master's, 3 years of work experience, minimum undergraduate GPA of 2.5. Additional exam requirements/recommendations for international students: Required—TOEFL (minimum score 550 paper-based; 213 computer-based; 79 iBT). Electronic applications accepted.

University of Phoenix–Springfield Campus, College of Education, Springfield, MO 65804-7211. Offers administration and supervision (MA Ed); curriculum and instruction (MA Ed), including computer education, curriculum and instruction, English and language arts education, English as a second language, mathematics education; English and language arts education (MA Ed).

University of Phoenix–West Florida Campus, The Artemis School, College of Education, Temple Terrace, FL 33637. Offers administration and supervision (MA Ed); curriculum and instruction (MA Ed), including computer education, curriculum and instruction, mathematics education; curriculum and technology (MA Ed); early childhood education (MA Ed); elementary teacher education (MA Ed); secondary teacher education (MA Ed). Evening/weekend programs available. *Degree requirements:* For master's, thesis (for some programs). *Entrance requirements:* For master's, 3 years of work experience, minimum undergraduate GPA of 2.5. Additional exam requirements/recommendations for international students: Required—TOEFL (minimum score 550 paper-based; 213 computer-based; 79 iBT).

University of Pittsburgh, School of Education, Department of Instruction and Learning, Program in Secondary Education, Pittsburgh, PA 15260. Offers English/communications education (M Ed, MAT); foreign languages education (M Ed, MAT); mathematics education (M Ed, MAT, Ed D); science education (M Ed, MAT, MS, Ed D); social studies education (M Ed, MAT). Part-time and evening/weekend programs available. *Students:* 170 full-time (107 women), 70 part-time (54 women); includes 19 minority (11 African Americans, 6 Asian Americans or Pacific Islanders, 2 Hispanic Americans), 10 international. Average age 29. 220 applicants, 72% accepted, 128 enrolled. In 2009, 108 master's, 5 doctorates awarded. *Degree requirements:* For master's, thesis; for doctorate, thesis/dissertation. *Entrance requirements:* For master's, PRAXIS I; for doctorate, GRE General Test. Additional exam requirements/recommendations for international students: Required—TOEFL. *Application deadline:* For fall admission, 2/1 priority date for domestic students; for spring admission, 11/15 priority date for domestic students. Applications are processed on a rolling basis. Application fee: $50. Electronic applications accepted. *Expenses:* Tuition: state resident: full-time $16,402; part-time $665 per credit. Tuition, nonresident: full-time $28,694; part-time $1175 per credit. Required fees: $690; $175 per term. Tuition and fees vary according to program. *Financial support:* Fellowships, teaching assistantships, career-related internships or fieldwork, Federal Work-Study, tuition waivers (partial), and unspecified assistantships available. Support available to part-time students. Financial award application deadline: 3/15; financial award applicants required to submit FAFSA. *Unit head:* Dr. Richard Donato, Chairman, 412-624-7248, Fax: 412-648-7081, E-mail: donato@pitt.edu. *Application contact:* Joan M. Cutone, Director, School of Education Student Service Center, 412-648-2230, Fax: 412-648-1899, E-mail: soeinfo@pitt.edu.

University of Puerto Rico, Río Piedras, College of Education, Program in Curriculum and Teaching, San Juan, PR 00931-3300. Offers biology education (M Ed); chemistry education (M Ed); curriculum and teaching (Ed D); history education (M Ed); mathematics education (M Ed); physics education (M Ed); Spanish education (M Ed). Part-time programs available. *Degree requirements:* For master's, thesis; for doctorate, thesis/dissertation, internship. *Entrance requirements:* For master's, PAEG or GRE, minimum GPA of 3.0, letter of recommendation; for doctorate, GRE or PAEG, master's degree, minimum GPA of 3.0, letter of recommendation (2), interview. *Faculty research:* Curriculum, math teaching.

University of Rio Grande, Graduate School, Rio Grande, OH 45674. Offers classroom teaching (M Ed), including fine arts, learning disabilities, mathematics, reading education. *Accreditation:* NCATE. Part-time and evening/weekend programs available. *Degree requirements:* For master's, final research project, portfolio. *Entrance requirements:* For master's, minimum GPA of 2.7 in major, 2.5 overall. Additional exam requirements/recommendations for international students: Required—TOEFL. *Faculty research:* Interagency collaboration, reading and mathematics, learning styles, college access, literacy.

University of St. Francis, College of Education, Joliet, IL 60435-6169. Offers educational leadership (MS), including reading; elementary education certification (M Ed); reading (MS); secondary education certification (M Ed), including English education, math education, science education, social studies education; special education (M Ed); teaching and learning (MS), including character education, curriculum and instruction, differentiated instruction, technology. *Accreditation:* NCATE. Part-time and evening/weekend programs available. *Faculty:* 10 full-time (8 women), 26 part-time/adjunct (18 women). *Students:* 60 full-time (45 women), 349 part-time (283 women); includes 36 minority (10 African Americans, 2 Asian Americans or Pacific Islanders, 24 Hispanic Americans). Average age 33. 211 applicants, 65% accepted, 102 enrolled. In 2009, 174 master's awarded. *Entrance requirements:* For master's, Illinois Basic Skills Test (M Ed), teaching certificate (MS), minimum undergraduate GPA of 2.75, 2 letters of recommendation, computer competency. Additional exam requirements/recommendations for international students: Required—TOEFL (minimum score 550 paper-based; 213 computer-based). *Application deadline:* Applications are processed on a rolling basis. Application fee: $30. Electronic applications accepted. *Expenses:* Contact institution. *Financial support:* In 2009–10, 254 students received support. Federal Work-Study, scholarships/grants, tuition waivers (partial), and unspecified assistantships available. Support available to part-time students. Financial award applicants required to submit FAFSA. *Unit head:* Dr. John Gambro, Dean, 815-740-3332, Fax: 815-740-2264, E-mail: jgambro@stfrancis.edu. *Application contact:* Sandra Sloka, Director of Admissions for Graduate and Degree Completion Programs, 800-735-7500, Fax: 815-740-5032, E-mail: ssloka@stfrancis.edu.

University of San Diego, School of Leadership and Education Sciences, Department of Learning and Teaching, San Diego, CA 92110-2492. Offers curriculum and instruction (M Ed); mathematics, science and technology education (M Ed); special education (M Ed); special education with deaf and hard of hearing (M Ed); teaching (MAT); TESOL, literacy and culture (M Ed). Part-time and evening/weekend programs available. *Faculty:* 13 full-time (9 women), 24 part-time/adjunct (21 women). *Students:* 77 full-time (63 women), 92 part-time (74 women); includes 46 minority (13 African Americans, 12 Asian Americans or Pacific Islanders, 21 Hispanic Americans), 6 international. Average age 31. 142 applicants, 75% accepted, 59 enrolled. In 2009, 64 master's awarded. *Degree requirements:* For master's, thesis (for some programs). *Entrance requirements:* For master's, minimum GPA of 3.0. Additional exam

requirements/recommendations for international students: Required—TOEFL (minimum score 580 paper-based; 237 computer-based; 83 iBT), TWE. *Application deadline:* For fall admission, 7/15 for domestic and international students; for spring admission, 12/1 for domestic and international students. Applications are processed on a rolling basis. Application fee: $45. Electronic applications accepted. *Expenses:* Tuition: Full-time $21,042; part-time $1169 per unit. Required fees: $224. Full-time tuition and fees vary according to course load and degree level. *Financial support:* In 2009–10, 113 students received support. Career-related internships or fieldwork, Federal Work-Study, institutionally sponsored loans, and stipends available. Support available to part-time students. Financial award application deadline: 4/1; financial award applicants required to submit FAFSA. *Faculty research:* Action research methodology, cultural studies, instructional theories and practices, second language acquisition, school reform. *Unit head:* Dr. Judy Mantle, Director, 619-260-7879, Fax: 619-260-6835, E-mail: jmantle@sandiego.edu. *Application contact:* Dr. John Mosby, Associate Director of Graduate Admissions, 619-260-4524, Fax: 619-260-4158, E-mail: grads@sandiego.edu.

University of South Africa, College of Human Sciences, Pretoria, South Africa. Offers adult education (M Ed); African languages (MA, PhD); African politics (MA, PhD); Afrikaans (MA, PhD); ancient history (MA, PhD); ancient Near Eastern studies (MA, PhD); anthropology (MA, PhD); applied linguistics (MA); Arabic (MA, PhD); archaeology (MA); art history (MA); Biblical archaeology (MA); Biblical studies (M Th, D Th, PhD); Christian spirituality (M Th, D Th); church history (M Th, D Th); classical studies (MA, PhD); clinical psychology (MA); communication (MA, PhD); comparative education (M Ed, Ed D); consulting psychology (D Admin, D Com, PhD); curriculum studies (M Ed, Ed D); development studies (M Admin, MA, D Admin, PhD); didactics (M Ed, Ed D); education (M Tech); education management (M Ed, Ed D); educational psychology (M Ed); English (MA); environmental education (M Ed); French (MA, PhD); German (MA, PhD); Greek (MA); guidance and counseling (M Ed); health studies (MA, PhD), including health sciences education (MA), health services management (MA), medical and surgical nursing science (critical care general) (MA), midwifery and neonatal nursing science (MA), trauma and emergency care (MA); history (MA, PhD); history of education (Ed D); inclusive education (M Ed, Ed D); information and communications technology policy and regulation (MA); information science (MA, MIS, PhD); international politics (MA, PhD); Islamic studies (MA, PhD); Italian (MA, PhD); Judaica (MA, PhD); linguistics (MA, PhD); mathematical education (M Ed); mathematics education (MA); missiology (M Th, D Th); modern Hebrew (MA, PhD); musicology (MA, MMus, D Mus, PhD); natural science education (M Ed); New Testament (M Th, D Th); Old Testament (D Th); pastoral therapy (M Th, D Th); philosophy (MA); philosophy of education (M Ed, Ed D); politics (MA, PhD); Portuguese (MA, PhD); practical theology (M Th, D Th); psychology (MA, MS, PhD); psychology of education (M Ed, Ed D); public health (MA); religious studies (MA, D Th, PhD); Romance languages (MA); Russian (MA, PhD); Semitic languages (MA, PhD); social behavior studies in HIV/AIDS (MA); social science (mental health) (MA); social science in development studies (MA); social science in psychology (MA); social science in social work (MA); social science in sociology (MA); social work (MSW, DSW, PhD); socio-education (M Ed, Ed D); sociolinguistics (MA); sociology (MA, PhD); Spanish (MA, PhD); systematic theology (M Th, D Th); TESOL (teaching English to speakers of other languages) (MA); theological ethics (M Th, D Th); theory of literature (MA, PhD); urban ministries (D Th); urban ministry (M Th).

University of South Africa, Institute for Science and Technology Education, Pretoria, South Africa. Offers mathematics, science and technology education (M Sc, PhD).

University of South Carolina, The Graduate School, College of Arts and Sciences, Department of Mathematics, Columbia, SC 29208. Offers mathematics (MA, MS, PhD); mathematics education (M Math, MAT). MAT offered in cooperation with the College of Education. Part-time programs available. Terminal master's awarded for partial completion of doctoral program. *Degree requirements:* For master's, comprehensive exam, thesis (for some programs); for doctorate, one foreign language, comprehensive exam, thesis/dissertation, admission to candidacy exam, residency. *Entrance requirements:* For master's and doctorate, GRE General Test. Additional exam requirements/recommendations for international students: Required—TOEFL (minimum score 600 paper-based; 250 computer-based; 100 iBT). Electronic applications accepted. *Faculty research:* Computational mathematics, analysis (classical/modern), discrete mathematics, algebra, number theory.

University of South Carolina, The Graduate School, College of Education, Department of Instruction and Teacher Education, Program in Secondary Education, Columbia, SC 29208. Offers art education (IMA, MAT); business education (IMA, MAT); English (MAT); foreign language (MAT); health education (MAT); mathematics (MAT); science (IMA, MAT); secondary (Ed D); secondary education (MT, PhD); social studies (MAT); theatre and speech (MAT). IMA and MT offered jointly with the subject areas. *Accreditation:* NCATE. *Degree requirements:* For master's, comprehensive exam, thesis (for some programs), foreign language (MA); for doctorate, one foreign language, comprehensive exam, thesis/dissertation. *Entrance requirements:* For master's, GRE General Test or MAT, teaching certificate (IMA, M Ed), interview; for doctorate, GRE General Test or MAT, interview. *Faculty research:* Middle school programs, professional development, school collaboration.

University of Southern Mississippi, Graduate School, College of Science and Technology, Center for Science and Mathematics Education, Hattiesburg, MS 39406-0001. Offers MS, PhD. *Faculty:* 1 full-time (0 women), 1 (woman) part-time/adjunct. *Students:* 18 full-time (14 women), 23 part-time (20 women); includes 6 minority (3 African Americans, 3 Asian Americans or Pacific Islanders), 3 international. Average age 35. 11 applicants, 91% accepted, 8 enrolled. In 2009, 6 master's, 4 doctorates awarded. *Degree requirements:* For master's, comprehensive exam, thesis or alternative; for doctorate, comprehensive exam, thesis/dissertation. *Entrance requirements:* For master's, GRE General Test, minimum GPA of 2.75 in last 60 hours; for doctorate, GRE General Test, minimum GPA of 3.5. Additional exam requirements/recommendations for international students: Required—TOEFL. *Application deadline:* For fall admission, 3/15 priority date for domestic students, 3/15 for international students. Applications are processed on a rolling basis. Application fee: $35. *Expenses:* Tuition, state resident: full-time $5096; part-time $284 per hour. Tuition, nonresident: full-time $13,052; part-time $726 per hour. Required fees: $402. Tuition and fees vary according to course level and course load. *Financial support:* In 2009–10, 1 fellowship with full tuition reimbursement (averaging $21,000 per year), 1 research assistantship with full tuition reimbursement (averaging $14,500 per year), 8 teaching assistantships with full tuition reimbursements (averaging $8,362 per year) were awarded; Federal Work-Study also available. Financial award application deadline: 3/15; financial award applicants required to submit FAFSA. *Unit head:* Dr. Sherry Herron, Director, 601-266-4739, Fax: 601-266-4741. *Application contact:* Shonna Breland, Manager of Graduate Admissions, 601-266-6563, Fax: 601-266-5138.

University of South Florida, Graduate School, College of Education–Main Campus, Department of Secondary Education, Tampa, FL 33620-9951. Offers English education (M Ed, MA, MAT, PhD); foreign language education/ESOL (M Ed, MA, MAT); instructional technology (M Ed, PhD, Ed S); mathematics education (M Ed, MA, MAT, PhD, Ed S); science education (M Ed, MA, MAT, PhD); second language acquisition/instructional technology (PhD); secondary education (M Ed, PhD); secondary education/TESOL (M Ed); social science education (M Ed, MA, MAT); teaching and learning in the content area (PhD). *Accreditation:* NCATE. Part-time and evening/weekend programs available. *Faculty:* 28 full-time (17 women), 3 part-time/adjunct (1 woman). *Students:* 144 full-time (97 women), 322 part-time (212 women); includes 100 minority (32 African Americans, 4 American Indian/Alaska Native, 17 Asian Americans or Pacific Islanders, 47 Hispanic Americans), 25 international. Average age 30. 230 applicants, 67% accepted, 122 enrolled. In 2009, 122 master's, 14 doctorates, 1 other advanced degree awarded. *Degree requirements:* For master's, variable foreign language requirement, comprehensive exam; for doctorate, variable foreign language requirement, comprehensive exam, thesis/dissertation. *Entrance requirements:* For master's, GRE General Test or General Knowledge Test, minimum GPA of 3.0; for doctorate, GRE General Test, minimum GPA of 3.5; for Ed S, GRE General Test. Additional exam requirements/recommendations for international students: Required—TOEFL (minimum score 550 paper-based; 213 computer-based; 79 iBT). *Application deadline:* For fall admission, 2/15 for domestic students, 1/2 for international

Mathematics Education

University of South Florida (continued)
students; for spring admission, 10/15 for domestic students, 6/1 for international students. Application fee: $30. Electronic applications accepted. *Financial support:* In 2009–10, 7 students received support, including 1 research assistantship with full tuition reimbursement available (averaging $10,000 per year), 55 teaching assistantships with full and partial tuition reimbursements available (averaging $7,900 per year); scholarships/grants and unspecified assistantships also available. Financial award application deadline: 4/15; financial award applicants required to submit FAFSA. *Faculty research:* English language learners/multicultural, social science education, mathematics education, science education, instructional technology. Total annual research expenditures: $336,023. *Unit head:* Dr. Stephen Thornton, Chairperson, 813-974-3533, Fax: 813-974-3837, E-mail: thornton@usf.edu. *Application contact:* Dr. James White, Program Director, 813-974-1629, Fax: 813-974-3837, E-mail: jwhite@usf.edu.

The University of Tampa, Program in Teaching, Tampa, FL 33606-1490. Offers curriculum and instruction (M Ed); math education (MAT); science education (MAT); social science education (MAT). Part-time and evening/weekend programs available. *Faculty:* 9 full-time (6 women), 5 part-time/adjunct (4 women). *Students:* 1 full-time (0 women), 68 part-time (51 women); includes 11 minority (3 African Americans, 1 Asian American or Pacific Islander, 7 Hispanic Americans), 1 international. Average age 30. 119 applicants, 71% accepted, 69 enrolled. In 2009, 36 master's awarded. *Degree requirements:* For master's, comprehensive exam, thesis. *Entrance requirements:* For master's, General Knowledge Test, GRE General Test, SAE Subject Area Exam, bachelor's degree in education or professional teaching certificate. Additional exam requirements/recommendations for international students: Required—TOEFL (minimum score 577 paper-based; 230 computer-based; 90 iBT), IELTS (minimum score 7). *Application deadline:* For fall admission, 5/1 for domestic students. Application fee: $40. *Expenses:* Tuition: Part-time $488 per credit hour. *Financial support:* In 2009–10, 67 students received support. Applicants required to submit FAFSA. *Unit head:* Dr. Martha Harrison, Associate Professor of Education, 813-253-3333 Ext. 3373, E-mail: mharrison@ut.edu. *Application contact:* Karen Full, Director of Admissions for Graduate and Continuing Studies, 813-257-3642, E-mail: kfull@ut.edu.

The University of Tennessee, Graduate School, College of Education, Health and Human Sciences, Program in Education, Knoxville, TN 37996. Offers art education (MS); counseling education (PhD); cultural studies in education (PhD); curriculum (MS, Ed S); curriculum, educational research and evaluation (Ed D, PhD); early childhood education (PhD); early childhood special education (MS); education of deaf and hard of hearing (MS); educational administration and policy studies (Ed D, PhD); educational administration and supervision (Ed S); educational psychology (Ed D, PhD); elementary education (MS, Ed S); elementary teaching (MS); English education (MS, Ed S); exercise science (PhD); foreign language/ESL education (MS, Ed S); instructional technology (MS, Ed D, PhD, Ed S); literacy, language and ESL education (PhD); literacy, language education, and ESL education (Ed D); mathematics education (MS, Ed S); modified and comprehensive special education (MS); reading education (MS, Ed S); school counseling (Ed S); school psychology (PhD, Ed S); science education (MS, Ed S); secondary teaching (MS); social foundations (MS); social science education (MS, Ed S); socio-cultural foundations of sports and education (PhD); special education (Ed S); teacher education (Ed D, PhD). *Accreditation:* NCATE. Part-time and evening/weekend programs available. *Degree requirements:* For master's and Ed S, thesis optional; for doctorate, variable foreign language requirement, thesis/dissertation. *Entrance requirements:* For master's, minimum GPA of 2.7; for doctorate and Ed S, GRE General Test, minimum GPA of 2.7. Additional exam requirements/recommendations for international students: Required—TOEFL. Electronic applications accepted. *Expenses:* Tuition, state resident: full-time $6826; part-time $380 per semester hour. Tuition, nonresident: full-time $21,844; part-time $1147 per semester hour. Tuition and fees vary according to program.

The University of Texas at Austin, Graduate School, College of Education, Program in Science and Mathematics Education, Austin, TX 78712-1111. Offers M Ed, MA, PhD. *Entrance requirements:* For master's and doctorate, GRE General Test. Electronic applications accepted.

The University of Texas at Dallas, School of Natural Sciences and Mathematics, Programs in Science and Mathematics Education, Richardson, TX 75080. Offers mathematics education (MAT); science education (MAT). Part-time and evening/weekend programs available. Post-baccalaureate distance learning degree programs offered (minimal on-campus study). *Faculty:* 8 full-time (1 woman). *Students:* 13 full-time (9 women), 53 part-time (39 women); includes 15 minority (7 African Americans, 5 Asian Americans or Pacific Islanders, 3 Hispanic Americans), 3 international. Average age 37. 58 applicants, 60% accepted, 29 enrolled. In 2009, 25 master's awarded. *Degree requirements:* For master's, thesis optional. *Entrance requirements:* For master's, GRE General Test, minimum GPA of 3.0 in upper-level coursework in field. Additional exam requirements/recommendations for international students: Required—TOEFL (minimum score 550 paper-based; 213 computer-based). *Application deadline:* For fall admission, 7/15 for domestic students, 5/1 priority date for international students; for spring admission, 11/15 for domestic students, 9/1 priority date for international students. Applications are processed on a rolling basis. Application fee: $50 ($100 for international students). Electronic applications accepted. *Expenses:* Tuition, state resident: full-time $11,068; part-time $461 per credit hour. Tuition, nonresident: full-time $21,178; part-time $882 per credit hour. Tuition and fees vary according to course load. *Financial support:* In 2009–10, 2 students received support, including 1 research assistantship with full tuition reimbursement available (averaging $13,500 per year), 2 teaching assistantships with full tuition reimbursements available (averaging $13,500 per year); fellowships, career-related internships or fieldwork, Federal Work-Study, institutionally sponsored loans, scholarships/grants, and unspecified assistantships also available. Support available to part-time students. Financial award application deadline: 4/30; financial award applicants required to submit FAFSA. *Faculty research:* Techniques for training teachers, philosophic definitions of science held by working scientists, science teachers, science students. *Unit head:* Dr. Robert Hillborn, Department Head, 972-883-2496, Fax: 972-883-6796, E-mail: scimathed@utdallas.edu. *Application contact:* Information Contact, 972-883-2496, Fax: 972-883-6796, E-mail: scimathed@utdallas.edu.

The University of Texas at El Paso, Graduate School, College of Science, Department of Mathematical Sciences, El Paso, TX 79968-0001. Offers mathematical sciences (MS); mathematics (teaching) (MAT); statistics (MS). Part-time and evening/weekend programs available. *Students:* 61 (30 women); includes 39 minority (1 Asian American or Pacific Islander, 38 Hispanic Americans), 13 international. Average age 34. In 2009, 17 master's awarded. *Degree requirements:* For master's, thesis optional. *Entrance requirements:* For master's, minimum GPA of 3.0, letters of recommendation. Additional exam requirements/recommendations for international students: Required—TOEFL; Recommended—IELTS. *Application deadline:* For fall admission, 8/1 priority date for domestic students, 3/1 for international students; for spring admission, 11/1 priority date for domestic students, 9/1 for international students. Applications are processed on a rolling basis. Application fee: $45 ($80 for international students). Electronic applications accepted. *Financial support:* In 2009–10, research assistantships with partial tuition reimbursements (averaging $21,812 per year), teaching assistantships with partial tuition reimbursements (averaging $17,450 per year) were awarded; fellowships with tuition reimbursements, institutionally sponsored loans, scholarships/grants, health care benefits, tuition waivers (partial), and unspecified assistantships also available. Support available to part-time students. Financial award application deadline: 3/15; financial award applicants required to submit FAFSA. *Unit head:* Dr. Maria C. Mariani, Chair, 915-747-5761, Fax: 915-747-6502, E-mail: mcmariani@utep.edu. *Application contact:* Dr. Patricia D. Witherspoon, Dean of the Graduate School, 915-747-5491, Fax: 915-747-5788, E-mail: withersp@utep.edu.

The University of Texas–Pan American, College of Science and Engineering, Department of Mathematics, Edinburg, TX 78539. Offers mathematical science (MS); mathematics teaching (MS). Part-time and evening/weekend programs available. *Degree requirements:* For master's, comprehensive exam. *Entrance requirements:* For master's, GRE General Test, minimum GPA of 3.0. *Expenses:* Tuition, state resident: full-time $3630.60; part-time $201.70 per credit hour. Tuition, nonresident: full-time $8617; part-time $478.70 per credit hour. Required fees: $806.50. *Faculty research:* Boundary value problems in differential equations, training of public school teachers in methods of presenting mathematics, harmonic analysis, inverse problems, commulative algebra.

University of the District of Columbia, College of Arts and Sciences, Department of Mathematics, Washington, DC 20008-1175. Offers applied statistics (MS); teaching mathematics (MST). Part-time and evening/weekend programs available. *Students:* 1 part-time (0 women). Average age 30. 33 applicants, 30% accepted. In 2009, 2 master's awarded. *Degree requirements:* For master's, comprehensive exam. *Entrance requirements:* For master's, GRE General Test, writing proficiency exam. *Application deadline:* For fall admission, 6/15 priority date for domestic students; for spring admission, 11/1 for domestic students. Applications are processed on a rolling basis. Application fee: $75 ($100 for international students). *Expenses:* Tuition, state resident: full-time $7580. Tuition, nonresident: full-time $14,580. Required fees: $620. *Unit head:* Dr. Vernise Steadman, Chair, 202-274-5153. *Application contact:* Ann Marie Waterman, Associate Vice President of Admission, Recruitment and Financial Aid, 202-274-6069.

University of the Sacred Heart, Graduate Programs, Department of Education, San Juan, PR 00914-0383. Offers early childhood education (M Ed); information technology and multimedia (Certificate); instruction systems and education technology (M Ed), including English, information technology and multimedia, instructional design, mathematics, Spanish. Part-time and evening/weekend programs available. *Degree requirements:* For master's, thesis. *Entrance requirements:* For master's, EXADEP, minimum undergraduate GPA of 2.75, interview.

University of the Virgin Islands, Graduate Programs, Division of Science and Mathematics, Program in Mathematics, Saint Thomas, VI 00802-9990. Offers mathematics for secondary teachers (MA). *Degree requirements:* For master's, action research paper. *Entrance requirements:* For master's, GRE, minimum GPA of 2.5, BA or BS. Additional exam requirements/recommendations for international students: Required—TOEFL (minimum score 550 paper-based; 213 computer-based).

The University of Toledo, College of Graduate Studies, College of Education, Department of Curriculum and Instruction, Program in Education and Mathematics, Toledo, OH 43606-3390. Offers MAE, MES.

University of Tulsa, Graduate School, College of Arts and Sciences, School of Education, Program in Mathematics and Science Education, Tulsa, OK 74104-3189. Offers MSMSE. Part-time programs available. *Students:* 2 part-time (both women); includes 1 minority (African American). Average age 46. 4 applicants, 50% accepted, 1 enrolled. In 2009, 1 master's awarded. *Entrance requirements:* For master's, GRE General Test. Additional exam requirements/recommendations for international students: Required—TOEFL (minimum score 575 paper-based; 231 computer-based), IELTS (minimum score 6.5). *Application deadline:* Applications are processed on a rolling basis. Application fee: $40. Electronic applications accepted. *Expenses:* Tuition: Full-time $16,182; part-time $899 per credit hour. Required fees: $4 per credit hour. Tuition and fees vary according to course load. *Financial support:* Fellowships with full and partial tuition reimbursements, research assistantships, teaching assistantships with full and partial tuition reimbursements, Federal Work-Study, scholarships/grants, tuition waivers (full and partial), and unspecified assistantships available. Support available to part-time students. Financial award application deadline: 2/1; financial award applicants required to submit FAFSA. *Unit head:* Dr. David Brown, Advisor, 918-631-2719, Fax: 918-631-2133, E-mail: david-brown@utulsa.edu. *Application contact:* Dr. David Brown, Advisor, 918-631-2719, Fax: 918-631-2133, E-mail: david-brown@utulsa.edu.

University of Vermont, Graduate College, College of Engineering and Mathematics, Department of Mathematics and Statistics, Program in Mathematics, Burlington, VT 05405. Offers mathematics (MS, PhD); mathematics education (MST). *Students:* 24 (8 women), 1 international. 39 applicants, 41% accepted, 6 enrolled. In 2009, 6 master's, 1 doctorate awarded. *Degree requirements:* For doctorate, thesis/dissertation. *Entrance requirements:* For master's and doctorate, GRE General Test. Additional exam requirements/recommendations for international students: Required—TOEFL (minimum score 550 paper-based; 213 computer-based; 80 iBT). *Application deadline:* For fall admission, 4/1 priority date for domestic students. Applications are processed on a rolling basis. Application fee: $40. Electronic applications accepted. *Expenses:* Tuition, state resident: part-time $508 per credit hour. Tuition, nonresident: part-time $1281 per credit hour. *Financial support:* Fellowships, research assistantships, teaching assistantships available. Financial award application deadline: 3/1. *Unit head:* Dr. M. Wilson, Coordinator, 802-656-2940. *Application contact:* Dr. M. Wilson, Coordinator, 802-656-2940.

University of Victoria, Faculty of Graduate Studies, Faculty of Education, Department of Curriculum and Instruction, Victoria, BC V8W 2Y2, Canada. Offers art education (M Ed, PhD); curriculum studies (M Ed, MA, PhD); early childhood education (M Ed, PhD); educational studies (PhD); language and literacy (M Ed, MA, PhD); mathematics (M Ed, MA, PhD); music education (M Ed, MA, PhD); science (M Ed, MA, PhD); social studies (M Ed, MA); social, cultural and foundational studies (MA, PhD); technology and environmental education (PhD). Part-time programs available. *Degree requirements:* For master's, thesis, project (M Ed); for doctorate, comprehensive exam, thesis/dissertation. *Entrance requirements:* For master's, minimum B average. Additional exam requirements/recommendations for international students: Required—TOEFL (minimum score 575 paper-based; 233 computer-based), IELTS (minimum score 7). Electronic applications accepted. *Faculty research:* Elementary and secondary English, language arts, curriculum theory and practice, educational media and technology, educational administration and leadership, history and philosophy of education.

University of Virginia, Curry School of Education, Department of Curriculum, Instruction, and Special Education, Program in Curriculum and Instruction, Charlottesville, VA 22903. Offers curriculum and instruction (M Ed, Ed S); elementary (M Ed, Ed D); English (M Ed, Ed D); foreign language (M Ed); mathematics (M Ed, Ed D); reading (M Ed, Ed D, Ed S); science (Ed D); social studies (M Ed). *Students:* 12 full-time (8 women), 30 part-time (24 women); includes 2 minority (1 Asian American or Pacific Islander, 1 Hispanic American), 1 international. Average age 36. 55 applicants, 69% accepted, 26 enrolled. In 2009, 247 master's, 14 doctorates, 10 other advanced degrees awarded. *Degree requirements:* For master's, comprehensive exam (for some programs); for doctorate, comprehensive exam, thesis/dissertation; for Ed S, comprehensive exam. *Entrance requirements:* For master's, doctorate, and Ed S, GRE General Test, 2 letters of recommendation. Additional exam requirements/recommendations for international students: Required—TOEFL (minimum score 600 paper-based; 250 computer-based; 90 iBT), IELTS (minimum score 7). *Application deadline:* Applications are processed on a rolling basis. Application fee: $60. Electronic applications accepted. *Financial support:* Fellowships with tuition reimbursements, research assistantships with tuition reimbursements, teaching assistantships with tuition reimbursements available. Financial award application deadline: 1/5; financial award applicants required to submit FAFSA.

University of Virginia, Curry School of Education, Program in Education, Charlottesville, VA 22903. Offers administration and supervision (PhD); applied developmental science (PhD); counselor education (PhD); curriculum and instruction (PhD); early childhood-developmental risk (MT); education evaluation (PhD); educational psychology (PhD); educational research (PhD); elementary (MT, PhD); English education (MT, PhD); foreign language education (MT); higher education (PhD); instructional technology (PhD); kinesiology (MT, PhD); math education (PhD); reading education (PhD); research statistics and evaluation (PhD); school psychology (PhD); science education (PhD); social studies education (MT, PhD); special education (PhD); world languages education (MT). *Students:* 336 full-time (239 women), 88 part-time (54 women); includes 43 minority (24 African Americans, 2 American Indian/Alaska Native, 11 Asian Americans or Pacific Islanders, 6 Hispanic Americans), 18 international. Average age 27. 199 applicants, 48% accepted, 55 enrolled. In 2009, 127 master's, 52 doctorates awarded. *Degree requirements:* For master's, comprehensive exam (for some programs), field project; for doctorate, comprehensive exam, thesis/dissertation. *Entrance requirements:* For doctorate, GRE General Test. Additional exam requirements/recommendations for international students:

Required—TOEFL (minimum score 600 paper-based; 250 computer-based; 90 iBT), IELTS (minimum score 7). *Application deadline:* Applications are processed on a rolling basis. Application fee: $60. Electronic applications accepted. *Financial support:* Fellowships, research assistantships, teaching assistantships available. Financial award application deadline: 1/5; financial award applicants required to submit FAFSA.

University of Washington, Graduate School, College of Education, Seattle, WA 98195. Offers curriculum and instruction (M Ed, Ed D, PhD), including educational technology, general curriculum (Ed D, PhD), language, literacy, and culture, mathematics education, multicultural education, reading and language arts education (Ed D), science education, social studies education, teaching and curriculum (M Ed); educational leadership and policy studies (M Ed, Ed D, PhD), including administration (Ed D), educational policy, organization, and leadership (M Ed, PhD), higher education, leadership for learning (Ed D), social and cultural foundations of education (M Ed, PhD); educational psychology (M Ed, PhD), including educational psychology (PhD), human development and cognition (M Ed), learning sciences, measurement, statistics and research design (M Ed), school psychology (M Ed); instructional leadership (M Ed); intercollegiate athletic leadership (M Ed); special education (M Ed, Ed D, PhD), including early childhood special education (M Ed), emotional and behavioral disabilities (M Ed), learning disabilities (M Ed), low-incidence disabilities (M Ed), severe disabilities (M Ed), special education (Ed D, PhD); teacher education (MIT). *Accreditation:* APA. Part-time and evening/weekend programs available. *Degree requirements:* For master's, thesis optional; for doctorate, thesis/dissertation. *Entrance requirements:* For master's and doctorate, GRE General Test, minimum GPA of 3.0. Additional exam requirements/recommendations for international students: Required—TOEFL. Electronic applications accepted. *Faculty research:* School restructuring/effective schools, special education interventions, literacy and writing, technology, school partnerships, teacher preparation.

The University of West Alabama, School of Graduate Studies, College of Natural Sciences and Mathematics, Department of Mathematics, Livingston, AL 35470. Offers MAT. *Accreditation:* NCATE.

University of West Georgia, Graduate School, College of Arts and Sciences, Department of Mathematics, Carrollton, GA 30118. Offers mathematics (MSM); teaching and applied mathematics (MS). *Faculty:* 13 full-time (2 women). *Students:* 3 full-time (1 woman), 3 part-time (1 woman); includes 1 minority (African American), 1 international. Average age 25. 6 applicants, 50% accepted, 1 enrolled. *Application deadline:* For fall admission, 7/17 for domestic students; for spring admission, 11/20 for domestic students. Applications are processed on a rolling basis. Application fee: $30. Electronic applications accepted. *Expenses:* Tuition, state resident: full-time $2952; part-time $164 per semester hour. Tuition, nonresident: full-time $11,808; part-time $656 per semester hour. Required fees: $42.90 per semester hour. $307 per semester. Tuition and fees vary according to course load. *Unit head:* Dr. Bruce Landman, Chair, 678-839-6489, E-mail: landman@westga.edu. *Application contact:* Dr. Charles W. Clark, Dean, 678-839-6508, E-mail: cclark@westga.edu.

University of West Georgia, Graduate School, College of Education, Department of Curriculum and Instruction, Carrollton, GA 30118. Offers art education (M Ed); art teacher education (Ed S); biology/secondary education (Ed S); business education (M Ed, Ed S); early childhood education (M Ed, Ed S); economics/secondary teacher education (Ed S); English teacher education (Ed S); French language teacher education (Ed S); history teacher education (Ed S); mathematics teacher education (Ed S); middle grades education (M Ed, Ed S); reading education (M Ed, Ed S); science teacher education (Ed S); secondary education (M Ed, Ed S); social science teacher education (Ed S); Spanish language teacher education (Ed S). Part-time and evening/weekend programs available. *Faculty:* 18 full-time (15 women), 7 part-time/adjunct (6 women). *Students:* 119 full-time (101 women), 358 part-time (280 women); includes 109 minority (97 African Americans, 3 American Indian/Alaska Native, 2 Asian Americans or Pacific Islanders, 7 Hispanic Americans). Average age 33. 193 applicants, 82% accepted, 34 enrolled. In 2009, 109 master's, 27 Ed Ss awarded. *Degree requirements:* For master's, comprehensive exam; for Ed S, research project. *Entrance requirements:* For master's, GRE General Test or MAT, minimum GPA of 2.7; for Ed S, GRE General Test, master's degree, minimum graduate GPA of 2.7. *Application deadline:* For fall admission, 7/17 for domestic students; for spring admission, 11/20 for domestic students. Applications are processed on a rolling basis. Application fee: $30. Electronic applications accepted. *Expenses:* Tuition, state resident: full-time $2952; part-time $164 per semester hour. Tuition, nonresident: full-time $11,808; part-time $656 per semester hour. Required fees: $42.90 per semester hour. $307 per semester. Tuition and fees vary according to course load. *Financial support:* In 2009–10, 5 research assistantships with full tuition reimbursements (averaging $3,000 per year) were awarded; career-related internships or fieldwork and scholarships/grants also available. Support available to part-time students. Financial award applicants required to submit FAFSA. *Unit head:* Dr. Donna Harkins, Chair, 678-839-6066, Fax: 678-839-6559, E-mail: dharkins@westga.edu. *Application contact:* Dr. Charles W. Clark, Dean, 678-839-6508, E-mail: cclark@westga.edu.

University of Wisconsin–Madison, Graduate School, School of Education, Department of Curriculum and Instruction, Madison, WI 53706-1380. Offers art education (MA); curriculum and instruction (MS, PhD); education and mathematics (MA); French education (MA); German education (MA); music education (MS); science education (MS); Spanish education (MA). *Accreditation:* NASM (one or more programs are accredited). *Degree requirements:* For doctorate, thesis/dissertation. Application fee: $56. *Expenses:* Tuition, state resident: part-time $594 per credit. Tuition, nonresident: part-time $1504 per credit. Required fees: $65 per credit. Tuition and fees vary according to course load, program and reciprocity agreements. *Financial support:* Project assistantships available. *Unit head:* Dr. Gloria Ladson-Billings, Chair, 608-262-4000. *Application contact:* Dr. Gloria Ladson-Billings, Chair, 608-262-4000.

University of Wisconsin–Oshkosh, The Office of Graduate Studies, College of Letters and Science, Department of Mathematics, Oshkosh, WI 54901. Offers mathematics education (MS). Part-time programs available. *Degree requirements:* For master's, comprehensive exam, thesis optional. *Entrance requirements:* For master's, 30 undergraduate credits in mathematics. Additional exam requirements/recommendations for international students: Required—TOEFL (minimum score 550 paper-based; 213 computer-based; 79 iBT). Electronic applications accepted. *Faculty research:* Problem solving, number theory, discrete mathematics, statistics.

University of Wisconsin–River Falls, Outreach and Graduate Studies, College of Arts and Science, Program in Mathematics, River Falls, WI 54022. Offers mathematics education (MSE). *Accreditation:* NCATE. Part-time programs available. *Degree requirements:* For master's, thesis (for some programs). *Entrance requirements:* For master's, minimum GPA of 2.75. Additional exam requirements/recommendations for international students: Required—TOEFL (minimum score 500 paper-based; 65 iBT), IELTS (minimum score 5.5). Electronic applications accepted.

University of Wyoming, College of Arts and Sciences, Department of Mathematics, Laramie, WY 82071. Offers mathematics (MA, MAT, MS, MST, PhD); mathematics/computer science (PhD). Part-time programs available. Terminal master's awarded for partial completion of doctoral program. *Degree requirements:* For master's, comprehensive exam, thesis, qualifying exam; for doctorate, comprehensive exam, thesis/dissertation, preliminary exam. *Entrance requirements:* For master's and doctorate, GRE General Test, minimum GPA of 3.0. Additional exam requirements/recommendations for international students: Required—TOEFL (minimum score 540 paper-based; 76 iBT). *Faculty research:* Numerical analysis, classical analysis, mathematical modeling, algebraic combinations.

Ursuline College, School of Graduate Studies, Program in Education, Pepper Pike, OH 44124-4398. Offers art education (MA); early childhood education (MA); language arts education (MA); life science education (MA); math education (MA); middle school education (MA); social studies education (MA); special education (MA). *Accreditation:* NCATE. *Faculty:* 1 (woman) full-time, 10 part-time/adjunct (8 women). *Students:* 53 full-time (40 women), 3 part-time (all women); includes 8 minority (7 African Americans, 1 Hispanic American). Average age 34. In 2009, 11 master's awarded. *Degree requirements:* For master's, comprehensive exam. *Entrance requirements:* For master's, minimum undergraduate GPA of 3.0. Additional exam requirements/recommendations for international students: Required—TOEFL (minimum score 500 paper-based; 173 computer-based). *Application deadline:* For fall admission, 8/1 priority date for domestic students. Applications are processed on a rolling basis. Application fee: $25. *Expenses:* Contact institution. *Financial support:* Federal Work-Study available. Financial award application deadline: 3/1. *Unit head:* Karen Godenschwager Nelson, Director, 440-684-8338, Fax: 440-684-6088, E-mail: kgodenschwager@ursuline.edu. *Application contact:* Melanie Steele, Secretary, 440-646-8199, Fax: 440-684-6138, E-mail: gradsch@ursuline.edu.

Virginia Polytechnic Institute and State University, Graduate School, College of Engineering, Department of Engineering Education, Blacksburg, VA 24061. Offers PhD. *Faculty:* 15 full-time (8 women). *Students:* 13 full-time (5 women), 2 part-time (both women); includes 3 minority (1 American Indian/Alaska Native, 2 Asian Americans or Pacific Islanders). Average age 30. 6 applicants, 50% accepted, 2 enrolled. *Entrance requirements:* For doctorate, GRE, GMAT. Additional exam requirements/recommendations for international students: Required—TOEFL (minimum score 550 paper-based; 213 computer-based). *Application deadline:* For fall admission, 5/15 for international students; for spring admission, 10/15 for international students. Applications are processed on a rolling basis. Application fee: $65. Electronic applications accepted. *Expenses:* Tuition, area resident: Full-time $10,228; part-time $459 per credit hour. Tuition, nonresident: full-time $17,892; part-time $865 per credit hour. Required fees: $1966; $451 per semester. *Financial support:* In 2009–10, 2 fellowships with full tuition reimbursements (averaging $5,358 per year), 16 research assistantships with full tuition reimbursements (averaging $19,324 per year), 22 teaching assistantships with full tuition reimbursements (averaging $14,225 per year) were awarded; career-related internships or fieldwork, Federal Work-Study, scholarships/grants, and unspecified assistantships also available. Financial award application deadline: 1/15. Total annual research expenditures: $3.4 million. *Unit head:* Dr. O. Hayden Griffin, Head, 540-231-6555, Fax: 540-231-6903, E-mail: hayden.griffin@vt.edu. *Application contact:* Maura Borrego, Information Contact, 540-231-9536, Fax: 540-231-6903, E-mail: mborrego@vt.edu.

Virginia Polytechnic Institute and State University, Graduate School, College of Liberal Arts and Human Sciences, School of Education, Department of Teaching and Learning, Blacksburg, VA 24061. Offers career and technical education (MS Ed, Ed D, PhD, Ed S); curriculum and instruction (MA Ed, Ed D, PhD, Ed S); health and physical education (MS Ed); mathematics education (MA Ed, PhD); secondary English education (MA Ed). *Accreditation:* NCATE. Postbaccalaureate distance learning degree programs offered (no on-campus study). *Students:* 295 full-time (186 women), 374 part-time (272 women); includes 104 minority (1 African American, 39 American Indian/Alaska Native, 54 Asian Americans or Pacific Islanders, 10 Hispanic Americans), 23 international. Average age 34. 324 applicants, 85% accepted, 205 enrolled. In 2009, 235 master's, 34 doctorates, 1 other advanced degree awarded. *Entrance requirements:* For master's and doctorate, GRE, GMAT. Additional exam requirements/recommendations for international students: Required—TOEFL (minimum score 550 paper-based; 213 computer-based). *Application deadline:* For fall admission, 5/15 for international students; for spring admission, 10/15 for international students. Applications are processed on a rolling basis. Application fee: $65. Electronic applications accepted. *Expenses:* Tuition, area resident: Full-time $10,228; part-time $459 per credit hour. Tuition, nonresident: full-time $17,892; part-time $865 per credit hour. Required fees: $1966; $451 per semester. *Financial support:* Career-related internships or fieldwork, Federal Work-Study, scholarships/grants, and unspecified assistantships available. Financial award application deadline: 1/15. *Faculty research:* Instructional technology, teacher evaluation, school change, literacy, teaching strategies. *Unit head:* Dr. Daisy L. Stewart, Dean, 540-231-8180, Fax: 540-231-3717, E-mail: daisys@vt.edu. *Application contact:* Dr. Daisy L. Stewart, Dean, 540-231-8180, Fax: 540-231-3717, E-mail: daisys@vt.edu.

Virginia State University, School of Graduate Studies, Research, and Outreach, School of Engineering, Science and Technology, Department of Mathematics and Computer Science, Petersburg, VA 23806-0001. Offers computer science (MS); mathematics (MS); mathematics education (M Ed). *Degree requirements:* For master's, thesis (for some programs).

Walden University, Graduate Programs, Richard W. Riley College of Education and Leadership, Minneapolis, MN 55401. Offers administrator leadership for teaching and learning (Ed D, Ed S); curriculum, instruction, and professional development (Ed S); early childhood education (birth-grade 3) (MAT); education (MS, PhD), including adolescent literacy and technology (grades 6-12) (MS), adult education leadership (PhD), community college leadership (PhD), curriculum, instruction, and assessment, early childhood education (PhD), educational leadership (MS), educational technology (PhD), elementary reading and literacy (MS), elementary reading and mathematics (MS), emotional/behavioral disorders (K-12) (MS), general program, higher education (PhD), integrating technology in the classroom (MS), K-12 educational leadership (PhD), learning disabilities (K-12) (MS), literacy and learning in the content areas (MS), mathematics (grades 6-8) (MS), mathematics (grades K-5) (MS), middle level education (grades 5-8) (MS), professional development (MS), science (grades K-8) (MS), self-designed (PhD), special education (PhD), special education (non-licensure) (MS), teacher leadership (grades K-12) (MS); educational leadership and administration (principal preparation) (Ed S); educational technology (Ed S); higher education and adult learning (Ed D); instructional design (Postbaccalaureate Certificate); instructional design and technology (MS), including general program (MS, PhD), online learning, training and performance improvement; special education: emotional/behavioral disorders (K-12) (MAT); special education: learning disabilities (K-12) (MAT); teacher leadership (Ed D, Ed S). Part-time and evening/weekend programs available. Postbaccalaureate distance learning degree programs offered (minimal on-campus study). *Faculty:* 54 full-time, 835 part-time/adjunct. *Students:* 13,940 full-time (11,339 women), 1,940 part-time (1,637 women); includes 4,626 minority (3,795 African Americans, 111 American Indian/Alaska Native, 199 Asian Americans or Pacific Islanders, 521 Hispanic Americans), 124 international. Average age 38. In 2009, 4,688 master's, 190 doctorates awarded. *Degree requirements:* For doctorate, thesis/dissertation (for some programs), residency; for other advanced degree, residency (for some programs). *Entrance requirements:* For master's, bachelor's degree or equivalent in related field; minimum GPA of 2.5; official transcripts; goal statement; access to computer and Internet; for doctorate, master's degree or equivalent in related field; minimum GPA of 3.0; official transcripts; three years' related professional/academic experience (preferred); access to computer and Internet; for other advanced degree, master's degree or equivalent in related field; minimum GPA of 3.0; 3 years related professional/academic experience (preferred); access to computer and Internet (Ed S). Additional exam requirements/recommendations for international students: Required—TOEFL (minimum score 550 paper-based; 213 computer-based), IELTS (minimum score 6.5), or Michigan English Language Assessment Battery (minimum score 82). *Application deadline:* Applications are processed on a rolling basis. Application fee: $50. Electronic applications accepted. *Expenses:* Tuition: Full-time $13,665; part-time $560 per credit. Required fees: $1375. Tuition and fees vary according to course load, degree level and program. *Financial support:* In 2009–10, 2,418 students received support; fellowships, Federal Work-Study, scholarships/grants, unspecified assistantships, and family tuition reduction, active duty/veteran tuition reduction, group tuition reduction, interest-free payment plans available. Support available to part-time students. Financial award applicants required to submit FAFSA. *Unit head:* Dr. Kate Steffens, Dean, 800-925-3368. *Application contact:* Jennifer Hall, Director of Enrollment, 866-4-WALDEN, E-mail: info@waldenu.edu.

Washington State University, Graduate School, College of Education, Department of Teaching and Learning, Pullman, WA 99164. Offers curriculum and instruction (Ed D, PhD); diverse languages (M Ed, MA); elementary education (M Ed, MA, MIT); exercise science (MS); literacy education (M Ed, MA, PhD); math education (PhD); secondary education (M Ed, MA). *Accreditation:* NCATE. *Degree requirements:* For master's, comprehensive exam (for some programs), thesis (for some programs), oral or written exam; for doctorate, comprehensive exam, thesis/dissertation, oral, written exam. *Entrance requirements:* For master's and doctorate, GRE General Test, minimum GPA of 3.0, 3 letters of recommendation. Additional exam requirements/recommendations for international students: Required—TOEFL. *Faculty research:* Evolution of middle school education issues in special education, computer-assisted language learning.

Mathematics Education

Washington State University, Graduate School, College of Sciences, Department of Mathematics, Pullman, WA 99164. Offers applied mathematics (MS, PhD); mathematics teaching (MS, PhD). Part-time programs available. *Faculty:* 26. *Students:* 33 full-time (11 women), 5 part-time (3 women); includes 3 minority (1 African American, 2 Asian Americans or Pacific Islanders), 10 international. Average age 29. 84 applicants, 29% accepted, 9 enrolled. In 2009, 7 master's, 1 doctorate awarded. *Degree requirements:* For master's, comprehensive exam (for some programs), thesis (for some programs), oral exam, project; for doctorate, 2 foreign languages, comprehensive exam, thesis/dissertation, oral exam, written exam. *Entrance requirements:* For master's and doctorate, minimum GPA of 3.0, 3 letters of recommendation. Additional exam requirements/recommendations for international students: Required—TOEFL (minimum score 600 paper-based; 250 computer-based), IELTS. *Application deadline:* For fall admission, 1/10 for domestic and international students; for spring admission, 7/1 for domestic and international students. Applications are processed on a rolling basis. Application fee: $50. Electronic applications accepted. *Financial support:* In 2009–10, 33 students received support, including 2 fellowships with tuition reimbursements available (averaging $2,500 per year), 3 research assistantships with full and partial tuition reimbursements available (averaging $14,634 per year), 27 teaching assistantships with full and partial tuition reimbursements available (averaging $13,383 per year); career-related internships or fieldwork, Federal Work-Study, institutionally sponsored loans, health care benefits, and tuition waivers (partial) also available. Financial award application deadline: 2/15; financial award applicants required to submit FAFSA. *Faculty research:* Computational mathematics, operations research, modeling in the natural sciences, applied statistics. *Unit head:* Dr. K. A. Ariyawansa, Chair, 509-335-4918, Fax: 509-335-1188, E-mail: ari@wsu.edu. *Application contact:* Graduate School Admissions, 800-GRADWSU, Fax: 509-335-1949, E-mail: gradsch@wsu.edu.

Wayne State College, School of Education and Counseling, Department of Educational Foundations and Leadership, Program in Curriculum and Instruction, Wayne, NE 68787. Offers alternative education (MSE); business and information technology education (MSE); communication arts education (MSE); early childhood education (MSE); elementary education (MSE); English as a second language (MSE); English education (MSE); family and consumer sciences education (MSE); industrial technology and vocational education (MSE); learning communities (MSE); mathematics education (MSE); music education (MSE); science education (MSE); social science education (MSE). *Accreditation:* NCATE. Part-time and evening/weekend programs available. *Degree requirements:* For master's, comprehensive exam, thesis optional. *Entrance requirements:* For master's, GRE General Test. Additional exam requirements/recommendations for international students: Required—TOEFL (minimum score 550 paper-based; 213 computer-based).

Wayne State University, College of Education, Division of Teacher Education, Detroit, MI 48202. Offers adult and continuing education (M Ed); art education (M Ed); bilingual/bicultural education (M Ed, MAT); business education (M Ed, MAT); career and technical education (M Ed, Ed D, PhD, Ed S); curriculum and instruction (Ed D, PhD, Ed S); distributive education (M Ed, MAT); early childhood education (M Ed); elementary education (M Ed, MAT, Ed D, PhD, Ed S); elementary education curriculum and instruction (M Ed); English education (M Ed); English education-secondary (M Ed, Ed S); foreign language education (M Ed); general education (Ed D, Ed S); health occupations education (M Ed); industrial education (M Ed); mathematics education (M Ed, Ed S); pre-school and parent education (M Ed); reading (M Ed, Ed D, Ed S); reading, languages and literature (Ed D); school music-vocal (M Ed); science education (M Ed, MAT, Ed S); secondary education (MAT); secondary school reading (M Ed); social studies education (M Ed, Ed S), including education-secondary (M Ed); special education (M Ed, Ed D, PhD, Ed S); teacher education (MAT, Ed D, PhD). *Degree requirements:* For doctorate, thesis/dissertation. *Entrance requirements:* For master's, Michigan Basic Skills Test (MA in teaching), minimum GPA of 2.6; for doctorate, minimum undergraduate GPA of 3.0, graduate 3.5; interview, curriculum vitae; references. Additional exam requirements/recommendations for international students: Required—TOEFL (minimum score 550 paper-based; 213 computer-based), TWE (minimum score 6). Electronic applications accepted. *Faculty research:* Reading and writing literacy and literature.

Webster University, School of Education, Department of Multidisciplinary Studies, St. Louis, MO 63119-3194. Offers administrative leadership (Ed S); education leadership (Ed S); educational technology (MAT); mathematics (MAT); multidisciplinary studies (MAT); school systems, superintendency and leadership (Ed S); social science (MAT); special education (MAT). Part-time programs available. *Entrance requirements:* For master's, minimum GPA of 2.5. Additional exam requirements/recommendations for international students: Required—TOEFL. *Expenses:* Tuition: Part-time $565 per credit hour. Tuition and fees vary according to degree level, campus/location and program.

Western Connecticut State University, Division of Graduate Studies, School of Professional Studies, Department of Education and Educational Psychology, Mathematics Education Option, Danbury, CT 06810-6885. Offers MS. Part-time programs available. *Students:* 2 part-time (both women). Average age 26. 1 applicant, 0% accepted, 0 enrolled. In 2009, 2 master's awarded. *Degree requirements:* For master's, thesis or alternative, completion of program in 6 years. *Entrance requirements:* For master's, minimum GPA of 2.8, teaching certificate. Additional exam requirements/recommendations for international students: Recommended—TOEFL (minimum score 550 paper-based; 213 computer-based; 79 iBT), IELTS (minimum score 6). *Application deadline:* For fall admission, 8/5 priority date for domestic students; for spring admission, 1/5 priority date for domestic students. Applications are processed on a rolling basis. Application fee: $50. *Expenses:* Tuition, state resident: full-time $5012; part-time $278 per credit hour. Tuition, nonresident: full-time $13,962; part-time $284 per credit hour. Required fees: $3886; $139 per credit hour. Full-time tuition and fees vary according to course load and program. Part-time tuition and fees vary according to course level, degree level and program. *Financial support:* Application deadline: 5/1. *Unit head:* Dr. Theresa Canada, Chairperson, Department of Education and Educational Psychology, 203-837-8509, Fax: 203-837-8413, E-mail: canadat@wcsu.edu. *Application contact:* Chris Shankle, Associate Director of Graduate Studies, 203-837-9005, Fax: 203-837-8326, E-mail: shanklec@wcsu.edu.

Western Connecticut State University, Division of Graduate Studies, School of Professional Studies, Department of Education and Educational Psychology, Program in Secondary Education, Danbury, CT 06810-6885. Offers biology option (MAT); mathematics option (MAT). Part-time programs available. *Students:* 18 full-time (9 women), 1 part-time (0 women); includes 1 African American. Average age 34. 30 applicants, 73% accepted, 19 enrolled. *Entrance requirements:* For master's, PRAXIS I Pre_Professional Skills Tests, PRAXIS II subject assessment(s), minimum combined undergraduate GPA of 2.8 or score rated at 35th percentile or higher on MAT. Additional exam requirements/recommendations for international students: Recommended—TOEFL (minimum score 550 paper-based; 213 computer-based; 79 iBT), IELTS (minimum score 6). *Application deadline:* For fall admission, 8/5 priority date for domestic students; for spring admission, 1/5 priority date for domestic students. Application fee: $50. *Expenses:* Tuition, state resident: full-time $5012; part-time $278 per credit hour. Tuition, nonresident: full-time $13,962; part-time $284 per credit hour. Required fees: $3886; $139 per credit hour. Full-time tuition and fees vary according to course load and program. Part-time tuition and fees vary according to course level, degree level and program. *Financial support:* Application deadline: 5/1. *Unit head:* Dr. Theresa Canada, Chairperson, Department of Education and Educational Psychology. *Application contact:* Chris Shankle, Associate Director of Graduate Studies, 203-837-9005, Fax: 203-837-8326, E-mail: shanklec@wcsu.edu.

Western Governors University, Teachers College, Salt Lake City, UT 84107. Offers English language learning (K-12) (MA); learning and technology (M Ed, MA); management and innovation (M Ed); mathematics education (5-12) (MA); mathematics education (5-9) (MA); mathematics education (K-6) (MA); measurement and evaluation (M Ed); science (5-12) (MA), including biology, geology; science education (5-9) (MA); teaching (MAT); technology for principals (Post-Graduate Certificate). *Accreditation:* NCATE. Part-time and evening/weekend programs available. Postbaccalaureate distance learning degree programs offered (no on-campus study). *Degree requirements:* For master's, comprehensive exam. *Entrance requirements:* Additional exam requirements/recommendations for international students: Required—TOEFL (minimum score 450 paper-based). Electronic applications accepted. *Expenses:* Contact institution.

Western Michigan University, Graduate College, College of Arts and Sciences, Department of Mathematics, Programs in Mathematics, Kalamazoo, MI 49008. Offers mathematics (MA, PhD); mathematics education (MA, PhD). *Faculty:* 28 full-time (9 women). *Students:* 21 full-time (11 women), 18 part-time (11 women); includes 2 minority (1 American Indian/Alaska Native, 1 Hispanic American), 9 international. 25 applicants, 60% accepted, 11 enrolled. In 2009, 15 master's, 1 doctorate awarded. *Degree requirements:* For master's, oral exams; for doctorate, one foreign language, thesis/dissertation, oral exams, 3 comprehensive exams, internship. *Entrance requirements:* For doctorate, GRE General Test. *Application deadline:* For fall admission, 2/15 priority date for domestic students. Applications are processed on a rolling basis. Application fee: $25. *Financial support:* Fellowships, research assistantships, teaching assistantships, Federal Work-Study available. Financial award application deadline: 2/15; financial award applicants required to submit FAFSA. *Unit head:* Dr. Jay A. Wood, Professor, 269-387-4812. *Application contact:* Admissions and Orientation, 269-387-2000, Fax: 269-387-2355.

Western New England College, School of Arts and Sciences, Program in Mathematics for Teachers, Springfield, MA 01119. Offers MAMT. Part-time and evening/weekend programs available. *Students:* 29 part-time (14 women); includes 2 Asian Americans or Pacific Islanders, 2 Hispanic Americans. In 2009, 8 master's awarded. *Entrance requirements:* For master's, recommendations, resume, personal statement. *Application deadline:* Applications are processed on a rolling basis. Application fee: $30. *Expenses:* Tuition: Part-time $552 per credit hour. Part-time tuition and fees vary according to program. *Financial support:* Available to part-time students. Applicants required to submit FAFSA. *Unit head:* Dr. Dennis Luciano, Chair, 413-782-1275, E-mail: dluciano@wnec.edu. *Application contact:* Matt Fox, Director of Recruiting and Marketing for Adult Learners, 413-782-1249, Fax: 413-782-1779, E-mail: ce@wnec.edu.

Western Oregon University, Graduate Programs, College of Education, Division of Teacher Education, Program in Secondary Education, Monmouth, OR 97361-1394. Offers bilingual education (MS Ed); health (MS Ed); humanities (MAT, MS Ed); initial licensure (MAT); mathematics (MAT, MS Ed); science (MAT, MS Ed); social science (MAT, MS Ed). *Accreditation:* NCATE. Part-time and evening/weekend programs available. *Degree requirements:* For master's, thesis optional, written exam. *Entrance requirements:* For master's, minimum GPA of 3.0, teaching license. Additional exam requirements/recommendations for international students: Required—TOEFL (minimum score 550 paper-based; 213 computer-based; 79 iBT), IELTS (minimum score 6.5). *Faculty research:* Literacy, science in primary grades, geography education, retention, teacher burnout.

West Virginia University, Eberly College of Arts and Sciences, Department of Mathematics, Morgantown, WV 26506. Offers applied mathematics (MS, PhD); discrete mathematics (PhD); interdisciplinary mathematics (MS); mathematics for secondary education (MS); pure mathematics (MS). Part-time programs available. Terminal master's awarded for partial completion of doctoral program. *Degree requirements:* For master's, comprehensive exam (for some programs), thesis optional; for doctorate, one foreign language, comprehensive exam, thesis/dissertation. *Entrance requirements:* For master's, GRE Subject Test (recommended), minimum GPA of 2.5; for doctorate, GRE Subject Test (recommended), master's degree in mathematics. Additional exam requirements/recommendations for international students: Required—TOEFL (paper-based 550; computer-based 213) or IELTS (paper-based 6). *Faculty research:* Combinatorics and graph theory, differential equations, applied and computational mathematics.

Widener University, School of Human Service Professions, Center for Education, Chester, PA 19013-5792. Offers adult education (M Ed); counseling in higher education (M Ed); counselor education (M Ed); early childhood education (M Ed); educational foundations (M Ed); educational leadership (M Ed); educational psychology (M Ed); elementary education (M Ed); English and language arts (M Ed); health education (M Ed); higher education leadership (Ed D); home and school visitor (M Ed); human sexuality (M Ed); mathematics education (M Ed); middle school education (M Ed); principalship (M Ed); reading and language arts (Ed D); reading education (M Ed); school administration (Ed D); science education (M Ed); social studies education (M Ed); special education (M Ed); technology education (M Ed). *Accreditation:* NCATE. Part-time and evening/weekend programs available. *Faculty:* 34 full-time (22 women), 37 part-time/adjunct (14 women). *Students:* 203 full-time (154 women), 415 part-time (298 women); includes 50 minority (34 African Americans, 1 American Indian/Alaska Native, 5 Asian Americans or Pacific Islanders, 10 Hispanic Americans), 3 international. Average age 39. 139 applicants, 88% accepted. In 2009, 168 master's, 31 doctorates awarded. Terminal master's awarded for partial completion of doctoral program. *Degree requirements:* For doctorate, thesis/dissertation. *Entrance requirements:* For master's, minimum GPA of 2.5; for doctorate, GRE or MAT, minimum GPA of 2.0 (undergraduate), 3.5 (graduate). *Application deadline:* Applications are processed on a rolling basis. Application fee: $25 ($300 for international students). Electronic applications accepted. *Expenses:* Contact institution. *Financial support:* Career-related internships or fieldwork, tuition waivers (full and partial), and unspecified assistantships available. Support available to part-time students. Financial award application deadline: 5/1. *Faculty research:* Reading and cognition, adult education, technology education, educational leadership, special education. *Unit head:* Dr. Michael W. LeDoux, Associate Dean, 610-499-4294, Fax: 610-499-4623, E-mail: mwledoux@widener.edu. *Application contact:* Dr. Roberta D. Nolan, Director of Graduate Admissions, 610-499-4125, E-mail: rdnolan@widener.edu.

Wilkes University, College of Graduate and Professional Studies, College of Science and Engineering, Department of Mathematics and Computer Science, Wilkes-Barre, PA 18766-0002. Offers mathematics (MS, MS Ed). Part-time programs available. *Students:* 1 full-time (0 women), 1 part-time (0 women). Average age 33. In 2009, 2 master's awarded. *Degree requirements:* For master's, thesis or alternative. *Entrance requirements:* For master's, GRE General Test. Additional exam requirements/recommendations for international students: Required—TOEFL (minimum score 500 paper-based; 173 computer-based; 79 iBT). *Application deadline:* Applications are processed on a rolling basis. Application fee: $45. *Financial support:* Federal Work-Study and unspecified assistantships available. Financial award application deadline: 3/1; financial award applicants required to submit FAFSA. *Unit head:* Dr. John Harrison, Chair, 570-408-4845, Fax: 570-408-7883, E-mail: john.harrison@wilkes.edu. *Application contact:* Kathleen Houlihan, Director of Graduate Studies, 570-408-3235, Fax: 570-408-7846, E-mail: kathleen.houlihan@wilkes.edu.

Wright State University, School of Graduate Studies, College of Science and Mathematics, Interdisciplinary Program in Science and Mathematics, Dayton, OH 45435. Offers MST.

Youngstown State University, Graduate School, College of Science, Technology, Engineering and Mathematics, Department of Mathematics and Statistics, Youngstown, OH 44555-0001. Offers applied mathematics (MS); computer science (MS); secondary mathematics (MS); statistics (MS). Part-time programs available. *Degree requirements:* For master's, comprehensive exam, thesis optional. *Entrance requirements:* For master's, minimum GPA of 2.7 in computer science and mathematics. Additional exam requirements/recommendations for international students: Required—TOEFL. *Faculty research:* Regression analysis, numerical analysis, statistics, Markov chain, topology and fuzzy sets.

Museum Education

Bank Street College of Education, Graduate School, Program in Museum Education, New York, NY 10025. Offers museum education (MS Ed); museum education: elemetary education certification (MS Ed); museum education: middle school certification (MS Ed). *Students:* 25 full-time (24 women), 34 part-time (33 women); includes 6 minority (1 African American, 1 Asian American or Pacific Islander, 4 Hispanic Americans). Average age 29. 45 applicants, 87% accepted, 25 enrolled. In 2009, 25 master's awarded. *Degree requirements:* For master's, thesis. *Entrance requirements:* For master's, interview. Additional exam requirements/recommendations for international students: Required—TOEFL (minimum score 600 paper-based; 250 computer-based; 100 iBT), IELTS (minimum score 7). *Application deadline:* For fall admission, 3/1 priority date for domestic and international students; for spring admission, 11/1 priority date for domestic and international students. Applications are processed on a rolling basis. Application fee: $65. *Expenses:* Tuition: Part-time $1120 per credit. *Financial support:* Federal Work-Study and scholarships/grants available. Support available to part-time students. Financial award application deadline: 4/15; financial award applicants required to submit FAFSA. *Faculty research:* Equitable access and openness to diversity in museum settings, exhibition display and development, museum/school partnerships. *Unit head:* Nina Jensen, Director, 212-875-4491, Fax: 212-875-4753, E-mail: ninajensen@bankstreet.edu. *Application contact:* Director of Graduate Admissions.

Bank Street College of Education, Graduate School, Programs in Educational Leadership, New York, NY 10025. Offers early childhood leadership (MS Ed); educational leadership (MS Ed); leadership for educational change (Ed M, MS Ed); leadership in mathematics education (MS Ed); leadership in museum education (MS Ed); leadership in the arts: creative writing (MS Ed); leadership in the arts: visual arts (MS Ed). *Students:* 76 full-time (60 women), 121 part-time (95 women); includes 67 minority (34 African Americans, 1 American Indian/Alaska Native, 6 Asian Americans or Pacific Islanders, 26 Hispanic Americans), 2 international. Average age 36. 124 applicants, 86% accepted, 98 enrolled. In 2009, 79 master's awarded. *Degree requirements:* For master's, thesis. *Entrance requirements:* For master's, interview, minimum of 2 years experience as a classroom teacher. Additional exam requirements/recommendations for international students: Required—TOEFL (minimum score 600 paper-based; 250 computer-based; 100 iBT), IELTS (minimum score 7). *Application deadline:* For fall admission, 3/1 priority date for domestic students; for spring admission, 11/1 priority date for domestic students. Applications are processed on a rolling basis. Application fee: $65. *Expenses:* Tuition: Part-time $1120 per credit. *Financial support:* Career-related internships or fieldwork, Federal Work-Study, scholarships/grants, and unspecified assistantships available. Support available to part-time students. Financial award application deadline: 4/15; financial award applicants required to submit FAFSA. *Faculty research:* Leadership in small schools, mathematics in elementary schools, professional development in early childhood, leadership in arts education, leadership in special education. *Unit head:* Dr. Rima Shore, Chairperson, 212-875-4478, Fax: 212-875-8753, E-mail: rshore@bankstreet.edu. *Application contact:* Ann Morgan, Director of Graduate Admissions, 212-875-4403, Fax: 212-875-4678, E-mail: amorgan@bankstreet.edu.

The George Washington University, Graduate School of Education and Human Development, Department of Educational Leadership, Program in Museum Education, Washington, DC 20052. Offers MAT. *Students:* 15 full-time (13 women), 1 part-time (0 women); includes 4 minority (1 American Indian/Alaska Native, 1 Asian American or Pacific Islander, 2 Hispanic Americans). Average age 26. 31 applicants, 100% accepted, 14 enrolled. In 2009, 20 master's awarded. *Degree requirements:* For master's, comprehensive exam. *Entrance requirements:* For master's, GRE General Test or MAT, minimum GPA of 2.75. *Application deadline:* For fall admission, 1/15 priority date for domestic students; for spring admission, 10/1 for domestic students. Applications are processed on a rolling basis. Application fee: $60. *Financial support:* In 2009–10, 7 students received support; fellowships, career-related internships or fieldwork, Federal Work-Study, and tuition waivers available. Financial award application deadline: 1/15; financial award applicants required to submit FAFSA. *Unit head:* Dr. Carol B. Stapp, Director, 202-994-4960, E-mail: cstapp@gwu.edu. *Application contact:* Sarah Lang, Director of Graduate Admissions, 202-994-1447, Fax: 202-994-7207, E-mail: slang@gwu.edu.

Seton Hall University, College of Arts and Sciences, Department of Art, Music and Design, South Orange, NJ 07079-2697. Offers museum professions (MA), including exhibition development, museum education, museum management, museum registration. Part-time and evening/weekend programs available. *Faculty:* 5 full-time (4 women), 8 part-time/adjunct (5 women). *Students:* 40 full-time (36 women), 32 part-time (26 women); includes 7 minority (2 African Americans, 1 Asian American or Pacific Islander, 4 Hispanic Americans), 1 international. Average age 28. 54 applicants, 80% accepted, 20 enrolled. In 2009, 12 master's awarded. *Degree requirements:* For master's, thesis. *Entrance requirements:* For master's, GRE General Test, previous course work in art history. Additional exam requirements/recommendations for international students: Required—TOEFL. *Application deadline:* For fall admission, 7/1 priority date for domestic and international students; for spring admission, 11/1 priority date for domestic and international students. Applications are processed on a rolling basis. Application fee: $50. Electronic applications accepted. *Financial support:* Research assistantships, career-related internships or fieldwork, Federal Work-Study, and unspecified assistantships available. Financial award applicants required to submit FAFSA. *Faculty research:* History of museums, museum education, theory of museums, nineteenth century art, African-American art, Renaissance art history, museum registration, museum ethics. *Unit head:* Dr. Susan Leshnoff, Chair, 973-761-9459, Fax: 973-275-2368, E-mail: leshnosu@shu.edu. *Application contact:* Dr. Petra Chu, Director of Graduate Studies, 973-761-9460, Fax: 973-275-2368, E-mail: chupetra@shu.edu.

The University of the Arts, College of Art and Design, Department of Museum Studies, Philadelphia, PA 19102-4944. Offers museum communication (MA); museum education (MA); museum exhibition planning and design (MFA). *Accreditation:* NASAD. Part-time programs available. *Degree requirements:* For master's, thesis, internship. *Entrance requirements:* For master's, portfolio. Additional exam requirements/recommendations for international students: Required—TOEFL (minimum score 550 paper-based; 213 computer-based).

Music Education

Alabama Agricultural and Mechanical University, School of Graduate Studies, School of Education, Area in Music Education, Huntsville, AL 35811. Offers music (MS); music education (M Ed). *Accreditation:* NCATE. Part-time and evening/weekend programs available. *Degree requirements:* For master's, comprehensive exam. *Entrance requirements:* For master's, GRE General Test. Additional exam requirements/recommendations for international students: Required—TOEFL (minimum score 500 paper-based; 173 computer-based; 61 iBT). Electronic applications accepted. *Faculty research:* Jazz and black music, Alabama folk music.

Albany State University, College of Arts and Humanities, Program in Music Education, Albany, GA 31705-2717. Offers music (M Ed). *Accreditation:* NCATE. *Degree requirements:* For master's, comprehensive exam, teaching demonstration. *Entrance requirements:* For master's, placement examination in music theory and music history. *Expenses:* Tuition, state resident: full-time $2970; part-time $162 per credit hour. Tuition, nonresident: full-time $12,168; part-time $676 per credit hour. Required fees: $962; $75 per credit hour.

Appalachian State University, Cratis D. Williams Graduate School, School of Music, Boone, NC 28608. Offers music education (MM); music performance (MM); music therapy (MMT). *Accreditation:* NASM. Part-time programs available. *Faculty:* 29 full-time (11 women), 2 part-time/adjunct (both women). *Students:* 26 full-time (17 women), 7 part-time (5 women); includes 1 minority (African American), 1 international. 24 applicants, 92% accepted, 9 enrolled. In 2009, 7 master's awarded. *Degree requirements:* For master's, comprehensive exam, thesis or alternative. *Entrance requirements:* For master's, GRE General Test, 3 letters of reference, audition. Additional exam requirements/recommendations for international students: Required—TOEFL (minimum score 550 paper-based; 230 computer-based; 79 iBT), IELTS (minimum score 6.5). *Application deadline:* For fall admission, 7/1 for domestic students, 2/1 for international students; for spring admission, 11/1 for domestic students, 7/1 for international students. Applications are processed on a rolling basis. Application fee: $50. Electronic applications accepted. *Expenses:* Tuition, state resident: full-time $2960. Tuition, nonresident: full-time $14,051. Required fees: $2320. *Financial support:* In 2009–10, 16 research assistantships (averaging $8,000 per year) were awarded; fellowships, teaching assistantships, career-related internships or fieldwork, Federal Work-Study, scholarships/grants, tuition waivers (partial), and unspecified assistantships also available. Financial award application deadline: 4/1; financial award applicants required to submit FAFSA. *Faculty research:* Music of the Holocaust, Celtic folk music, early nineteenth century performance practice, hypermeter and phase rhythm, world music, music and psychoneuroimmunology. *Unit head:* Dr. William Pelto, Dean, 828-262-6446, E-mail: peltowl@appstate.edu. *Application contact:* Dr. Nancy Schneeloch-Bingham, Graduate Program Director, 828-262-6463, E-mail: schneelochna@appstate.edu.

Arcadia University, Graduate Studies, Department of Education, Glenside, PA 19038-3295. Offers art education (M Ed, MA Ed); biology education (MA Ed); chemistry education (MA Ed); child development (CAS); computer education (M Ed, CAS); computer education 7–12 (MA Ed); early childhood education (M Ed, CAS), including individualized (M Ed), master teacher (M Ed), research in child development (M Ed); educational leadership (M Ed, CAS); educational psychology (CAS); elementary education (M Ed, CAS); English education (MA Ed); environmental education (MA Ed, CAS); history education (MA Ed); language arts (M Ed, CAS); mathematics education (M Ed, MA Ed, CAS); music education (MA Ed); psychology (MA Ed); pupil personnel services (CAS); reading (M Ed, CAS); school library science (M Ed); science education (M Ed, CAS); secondary education (M Ed, CAS); special education (M Ed, Ed D, CAS); theater arts (MA Ed); written communication (MA Ed). *Accreditation:* NASAD. Part-time and evening/weekend programs available. Postbaccalaureate distance learning degree programs offered (minimal on-campus study). *Faculty:* 12 full-time (8 women), 38 part-time/adjunct (26 women). *Students:* 89 full-time (74 women), 622 part-time (487 women); includes 112 minority (94 African Americans, 9 Asian Americans or Pacific Islanders, 9 Hispanic Americans), 2 international. Average age 32. In 2009, 257 master's, 4 doctorates awarded. *Application deadline:* Applications are processed on a rolling basis. Application fee: $40. Electronic applications accepted. *Expenses:* Tuition: Full-time $30,450; part-time $620 per credit hour. Required fees: $165. Tuition and fees vary according to program. *Financial support:* Career-related internships or fieldwork, tuition waivers (partial), and unspecified assistantships available. *Unit head:* Dr. Steven P. Gulkus. *Application contact:* 215-572-2925, Fax: 215-572-2126, E-mail: grad@arcadia.edu.

Arizona State University, Graduate College, Herberger College of the Arts, School of Music, Tempe, AZ 85287. Offers composition (MM); music (MA, DMA); music education (MM); music therapy (MM); performance (MM). *Accreditation:* NASM. *Degree requirements:* For doctorate, thesis/dissertation. *Entrance requirements:* For master's, GRE or MAT; for doctorate, GRE.

Arkansas State University—Jonesboro, Graduate School, College of Fine Arts, Department of Music, Jonesboro, State University, AR 72467. Offers music education (MME, SCCT); performance (MM). *Accreditation:* NASM (one or more programs are accredited). Part-time programs available. *Faculty:* 14 full-time (3 women), 2 part-time/adjunct (both women). *Students:* 6 full-time (3 women), 3 part-time (1 woman); includes 1 minority (American Indian/Alaska Native). Average age 29. 3 applicants, 67% accepted, 2 enrolled. In 2009, 5 master's awarded. *Degree requirements:* For master's, 2 foreign languages, comprehensive exam, thesis or alternative; for SCCT, comprehensive exam. *Entrance requirements:* For master's, GRE General Test or MAT, university entrance exam, appropriate bachelor's degree, audition; for SCCT, GRE General Test or MAT, interview, master's degree, official transcript, immunization records. Additional exam requirements/recommendations for international students: Required—TOEFL (minimum score 550 paper-based; 213 computer-based; 79 iBT), IELTS (minimum score 6). *Application deadline:* For fall admission, 7/1 for domestic and international students; for spring admission, 11/15 for domestic students, 11/13 for international students. Applications are processed on a rolling basis. Application fee: $30 ($40 for international students). Electronic applications accepted. *Expenses:* Tuition, state resident: full-time $3744; part-time $208 per credit hour. Tuition, nonresident: full-time $9540; part-time $530 per credit hour. Required fees: $896; $47 per credit hour. $25 per term. One-time fee: $50. Tuition and fees vary according to course load and program. *Financial support:* In 2009–10, 5 students received support; teaching assistantships, career-related internships or fieldwork, scholarships/grants, and unspecified assistantships available. Financial award application deadline: 7/1; financial award applicants required to submit FAFSA. *Unit head:* Ken Hatch, Interim Chair, 870-972-2094, Fax: 870-972-3932, E-mail: khatch@astate.edu. *Application contact:* Dr. Andrew Sustich, Dean of the Graduate School, 870-972-3029, Fax: 870-972-3857, E-mail: sustich@astate.edu.

Auburn University, Graduate School, College of Education, Department of Curriculum and Teaching, Auburn University, AL 36849. Offers business education (M Ed, MS, PhD); early childhood education (M Ed, MS, PhD, Ed S); elementary education (M Ed, MS, PhD, Ed S); foreign languages (M Ed, MS); music education (M Ed, MS, PhD, Ed S); postsecondary education (PhD); reading education (PhD, Ed S); secondary education (M Ed, MS, PhD, Ed S), including English language arts, mathematics, science, social studies. *Accreditation:* NASM (one or more programs are accredited); NCATE. Part-time programs available. *Faculty:* 28 full-time (21 women), 8 part-time/adjunct (5 women). *Students:* 76 full-time (55 women), 186 part-time (139 women); includes 43 minority (29 African Americans, 1 American Indian/Alaska Native, 4 Asian Americans or Pacific Islanders, 9 Hispanic Americans), 4 international. Average age 33. 248 applicants, 65% accepted, 110 enrolled. In 2009, 102 master's, 12 doctorates, 6 other advanced degrees awarded. *Degree requirements:* For master's, thesis (for some programs); for doctorate, thesis/dissertation; for Ed S, field project. *Entrance requirements:* For master's, doctorate, and Ed S, GRE General Test. *Application deadline:* For fall admission, 7/7 for domestic students; for spring admission, 11/24 for domestic students. Applications are processed on a rolling basis. Application fee: $50 ($60 for international students). Electronic applications accepted. *Expenses:* Tuition, state resident: full-time $6240. Tuition, nonresident: full-time $18,720. International tuition: $18,938 full-time. Required fees: $492. Tuition and fees vary according to course load, program and reciprocity agreements. *Financial support:* Fellowships, teaching assistantships, career-related internships or fieldwork and Federal Work-Study available. Support available to part-time students. Financial award application deadline: 3/15; financial award applicants required to submit FAFSA. *Faculty research:* Emerging literacy, reading attitudes, music for at-risk youth, portfolio assessment.

Music Education

Auburn University (continued)

Unit head: Dr. Nancy H. Barry, Head, 334-844-4434. *Application contact:* Dr. George Flowers, Dean of the Graduate School, 334-844-2125.

Austin College, Program in Education, Sherman, TX 75090-4400. Offers art education (MA); elementary education (MA); middle school education (MA); music education (MA); physical education and coaching (MA); secondary education (MA); theatre education (MA). Part-time programs available. *Faculty:* 5 full-time (3 women), 1 (woman) part-time/adjunct. *Students:* 29 full-time (21 women); includes 3 minority (1 Asian American or Pacific Islander, 2 Hispanic Americans). Average age 23. In 2009, 23 master's awarded. *Degree requirements:* For master's, one foreign language, thesis or alternative. *Entrance requirements:* For master's, Texas Academic Skills Program Test. *Application deadline:* For fall admission, 5/1 priority date for domestic students; for spring admission, 1/15 priority date for domestic students. Applications are processed on a rolling basis. Application fee: $35. Electronic applications accepted. *Expenses:* Tuition: Full-time $31,575. Required fees: $160. *Financial support:* Career-related internships or fieldwork, Federal Work-Study, scholarships/grants, and unspecified assistantships available. Support available to part-time students. Financial award application deadline: 4/1; financial award applicants required to submit FAFSA. *Unit head:* Dr. Barbara Sylvester, Director of Teaching Program, 903-813-2327, Fax: 903-813-2326, E-mail: bsylvester@austincollege.edu. *Application contact:* Dr. Barbara Sylvester, Director of Teaching Program, 903-813-2327, Fax: 903-813-2326, E-mail: bsylvester@austincollege.edu.

Austin Peay State University, College of Graduate Studies, College of Arts and Letters, Department of Music, Clarksville, TN 37044. Offers music education (M Mu); music performance (M Mu). *Accreditation:* NASM. Part-time programs available. *Faculty:* 16 full-time (7 women), 2 part-time/adjunct (both women). *Students:* 21 full-time (9 women), 3 part-time (1 woman); includes 4 minority (2 African Americans, 1 Asian American or Pacific Islander, 1 Hispanic American), 1 international. Average age 29. 20 applicants, 100% accepted, 10 enrolled. In 2009, 7 master's awarded. *Degree requirements:* For master's, comprehensive exam, thesis optional. *Entrance requirements:* For master's, GRE General Test, diagnostic exams, audition, bachelor's degree, 3 letters of recommendation. Additional exam requirements/recommendations for international students: Required—TOEFL (minimum score 500 paper-based; 173 computer-based). *Application deadline:* For fall admission, 7/27 priority date for domestic students; for spring admission, 12/17 priority date for domestic students. Applications are processed on a rolling basis. Application fee: $25. Electronic applications accepted. *Expenses:* Tuition, state resident: full-time $6160; part-time $608 per credit hour. Tuition, nonresident: full-time $17,080; part-time $854 per credit hour. Required fees: $1224; $61.20 per credit hour. *Financial support:* In 2009–10, 11 students received support, including 11 research assistantships with full tuition reimbursements available (averaging $5,184 per year); career-related internships or fieldwork, Federal Work-Study, institutionally sponsored loans, scholarships/grants, and unspecified assistantships also available. Support available to part-time students. Financial award application deadline: 3/1; financial award applicants required to submit FAFSA. *Unit head:* Dr. Douglas Rose, Chair, 931-221-7808, Fax: 931-221-7529, E-mail: rosed@apsu.edu. *Application contact:* Dr. Dixie Dennis, Dean, College of Graduate Studies, 931-221-7662, Fax: 931-221-7641, E-mail: dennisdi@apsu.edu.

Azusa Pacific University, School of Music, Azusa, CA 91702-7000. Offers education (M Mus); performance (M Mus). *Accreditation:* NASM. Part-time and evening/weekend programs available. *Degree requirements:* For master's, recital. *Entrance requirements:* For master's, interview, audition. Additional exam requirements/recommendations for international students: Required—TOEFL (minimum score 550 paper-based). *Faculty research:* Tribal music of northeast India, rare Motown recordings in England.

Ball State University, Graduate School, College of Fine Arts, School of Music, Muncie, IN 47306-1099. Offers music education (MA, MM, DA). *Accreditation:* NASM; NCATE (one or more programs are accredited). *Degree requirements:* For doctorate, thesis/dissertation. *Entrance requirements:* For master's, audition; for doctorate, GRE General Test, audition, minimum graduate GPA of 3.2, writing sample.

Belmont University, College of Visual and Performing Arts, School of Music, Nashville, TN 37212-3757. Offers church music (MM); composition (MM); music education (MM); pedagogy (MM); performance (MM). *Accreditation:* NASM. Part-time programs available. *Degree requirements:* For master's, comprehensive exam, thesis (for some programs). *Entrance requirements:* For master's, placement exam, GRE or MAT, audition, interview, minimum GPA of 2.75. Additional exam requirements/recommendations for international students: Required—TOEFL (minimum score 500 paper-based; 173 computer-based). Electronic applications accepted.

Bennington College, Graduate Programs, MA in Teaching Program, Bennington, VT 05201. Offers art education (MAT); early childhood (MAT); elementary education (MAT); English education (MAT); foreign language education (MAT); k-12 education (MAT); mathematics education (MAT); music education (MAT); science education (MAT); secondary education (MAT); social studies education (MAT); theater arts (MAT). *Faculty:* 5 part-time/adjunct (3 women). *Students:* 8 full-time (5 women), 1 part-time (0 women). Average age 28. 11 applicants, 27% accepted, 1 enrolled. In 2009, 4 master's awarded. *Degree requirements:* For master's, comprehensive exam, 1 year teaching practicum, professional portfolio. *Entrance requirements:* For master's, interview. *Application deadline:* For fall admission, 3/1 for domestic students. Application fee: $60. *Expenses:* Contact institution. *Financial support:* In 2009–10, 6 students received support, including 4 fellowships (averaging $10,475 per year); scholarships/grants and unspecified assistantships also available. Financial award application deadline: 4/1; financial award applicants required to submit FAFSA. *Unit head:* Carol Meyer, Director of Programs in Teacher Education, 802-440-4375, E-mail: cmeyer@bennington.edu. *Application contact:* Nancy Pearlman, Assistant Director of Programs in Teacher Education, 802-440-4710, Fax: 802-440-4383, E-mail: npearlman@bennington.edu.

Bob Jones University, Graduate Programs, Greenville, SC 29614. Offers accountancy (MS); Bible (MA); Bible translation (MA); Biblical studies (Certificate); broadcast management (MS); business administration (MBA); church history (MA, PhD); church ministries (MA); church music (MM); cinema and video production (MA); counseling (MS); curriculum and instruction (Ed D); divinity (M Div); dramatic production (MA); educational leadership (MS, Ed D, Ed S); elementary education (M Ed, MAT); English (M Ed, MA, MAT); fine arts (MA); graphic design (MA); history (M Ed, MA); illustration (MA); interpretative speech (MA); mathematics (M Ed, MAT); medical missions (Certificate); ministry (MM, D Min); multi-categorical special education (M Ed, MAT); music (M Ed); New Testament interpretation (PhD); Old Testament interpretation (PhD); orchestral instrument performance (MM); organ performance (MM); pastoral studies (MA); personnel services (MS, Ed S); piano pedagogy (MM); piano performance (MM); platform arts (MA); radio and television broadcasting (MS); rhetoric and public address (MA); secondary education (M Ed); studio art (MA); teaching Bible (MA); theology (MA, PhD); voice performance (MM); youth ministries (MA); M Div/MM.

Boise State University, Graduate College, College of Arts and Sciences, Department of Music, Program in Music Education, Boise, ID 83725-0399. Offers MM. *Accreditation:* NASM; NCATE. Part-time programs available. *Degree requirements:* For master's, thesis optional. *Entrance requirements:* For master's, minimum GPA of 3.0, performance demonstration. Electronic applications accepted. *Expenses:* Tuition, state resident: full-time $3106; part-time $209 per credit. Tuition, nonresident: part-time $284 per credit.

Boise State University, Graduate College, College of Arts and Sciences, Department of Music, Program in Pedagogy, Boise, ID 83725-0399. Offers MM. *Accreditation:* NCATE. Part-time programs available. *Degree requirements:* For master's, thesis optional. *Entrance requirements:* For master's, minimum GPA of 3.0, performance demonstration. Electronic applications accepted. *Expenses:* Tuition, state resident: full-time $3106; part-time $209 per credit. Tuition, nonresident: part-time $284 per credit.

The Boston Conservatory, Graduate Division, Boston, MA 02215. Offers choral conducting (MM); composition (MM); music (MM, ADP, Certificate), including music, music education (MM); music performance (MM, ADP, Certificate); opera (MM, ADP, Certificate); theater (MM). *Accreditation:* NASM (one or more programs are accredited). Part-time programs available. *Degree requirements:* For master's, recital or performance; for other advanced degree, recital. *Entrance requirements:* For master's and other advanced degree, audition. Additional exam requirements/recommendations for international students: Required—TOEFL (minimum score 580 paper-based; 237 computer-based). Electronic applications accepted.

The Boston Conservatory, Graduate Division, Music Division, Department of Music Education, Boston, MA 02215. Offers MM. *Accreditation:* NASM. Part-time programs available. *Degree requirements:* For master's, comprehensive oral exam, thesis or recital. *Entrance requirements:* For master's, audition, interview. Additional exam requirements/recommendations for international students: Required—TOEFL (minimum score 580 paper-based; 237 computer-based). Electronic applications accepted.

Boston University, College of Fine Arts, School of Music, Program in Music Education, Boston, MA 02215. Offers MM, DMA. *Accreditation:* NASM. *Students:* 483 full-time (255 women), 197 part-time (103 women); includes 90 minority (44 African Americans, 7 American Indian/Alaska Native, 12 Asian Americans or Pacific Islanders, 27 Hispanic Americans), 28 international. Average age 37. 31 applicants, 74% accepted, 15 enrolled. In 2009, 35 master's, 1 doctorate awarded. *Degree requirements:* For master's, thesis; for doctorate, 2 foreign languages, thesis/dissertation. *Entrance requirements:* For doctorate, GRE or MAT. Additional exam requirements/recommendations for international students: Required—TOEFL (minimum score 100 iBT), only iBT accepted. *Application deadline:* For fall admission, 1/1 priority date for domestic and international students. Applications are processed on a rolling basis. Application fee: $70. *Expenses:* Tuition: Full-time $37,910; part-time $1184 per credit hour. Required fees: $386; $40 per semester. Part-time tuition and fees vary according to class time, course level, degree level and program. *Financial support:* Fellowships, teaching assistantships available. Financial award application deadline: 1/1. *Application contact:* Mark Krone, Manager, Graduate Admissions, 617-353-3350, E-mail: arts@bu.edu.

Boston University, Graduate School of Arts and Sciences, Department of Music, Boston, MA 02215. Offers composition (MA); music education (MA); music history/theory (PhD); musicology (MA, PhD). *Accreditation:* NASM. *Students:* 2 part-time (1 woman); includes 1 minority (Hispanic American). Average age 28. 19 applicants, 32% accepted, 2 enrolled. In 2009, 1 master's awarded. *Degree requirements:* For master's, 2 foreign languages, comprehensive exam, thesis; for doctorate, 2 foreign languages, comprehensive exam, thesis/dissertation. *Entrance requirements:* For master's and doctorate, GRE General Test, musical composition or research paper, 3 letters of recommendation. Additional exam requirements/recommendations for international students: Required—TOEFL (minimum score 550 paper-based; 213 computer-based). *Application deadline:* For fall admission, 3/15 for domestic and international students; for spring admission, 10/15 for domestic and international students. Application fee: $70. Electronic applications accepted. *Expenses:* Tuition: Full-time $37,910; part-time $1184 per credit hour. Required fees: $386; $40 per semester. Part-time tuition and fees vary according to class time, course level, degree level and program. *Financial support:* Federal Work-Study, scholarships/grants, and unspecified assistantships available. Support available to part-time students. Financial award application deadline: 1/15; financial award applicants required to submit FAFSA. *Unit head:* Jeremy Yudkin, Director, 617-353-3362, Fax: 617-353-7455, E-mail: yudkinj@bu.edu. *Application contact:* Jessica Smith, Administrative Coordinator, 617-353-6887, Fax: 617-353-7455, E-mail: smithj08@bu.edu.

Bowling Green State University, Graduate College, College of Musical Arts, Bowling Green, OH 43403. Offers composition (MM); contemporary music (DMA), including composition, performance; ethnomusicology (MM); music education (MM), including choral, comprehensive, instrumental; music history (MM); music theory (MM); performance (MM). *Accreditation:* NASM. Part-time programs available. *Degree requirements:* For master's, thesis or alternative, recitals; for doctorate, comprehensive exam, thesis/dissertation. *Entrance requirements:* For master's, GRE General Test, diagnostic placement exams in music history and theory, audition, interview. Additional exam requirements/recommendations for international students: Required—TOEFL. Electronic applications accepted. *Faculty research:* Ethnomusicology.

Brandon University, School of Music, Brandon, MB R7A 6A9, Canada. Offers composition (M Mus); music education (M Mus); performance and literature (M Mus), including piano, strings. Part-time programs available. *Faculty:* 8 full-time (4 women). *Students:* 8 full-time (4 women), 1 part-time (0 women), 2 international. Average age 25. 7 applicants, 100% accepted. In 2009, 2 master's awarded. *Degree requirements:* For master's, comprehensive exam (for some programs), thesis (for some programs). *Entrance requirements:* For master's, B Mus. Additional exam requirements/recommendations for international students: Required—TOEFL (minimum score 580 paper-based; 237 computer-based) or IELTS. *Application deadline:* For spring admission, 5/1 priority date for domestic students. Applications are processed on a rolling basis. Application fee: $60 ($125 for international students). Electronic applications accepted. *Financial support:* In 2009–10, 4 students received support, including 1 research assistantship, 3 teaching assistantships (averaging $3,250 per year). Financial award application deadline: 5/1. *Faculty research:* Composition, community music, evaluation and assessment, performance anxiety, performance injuries, philosophy of music, teacher education. *Unit head:* Dr. Michael Kim, Dean, 204-727-9633, Fax: 204-728-6839, E-mail: kimm@brandonu.ca. *Application contact:* Dr. Sheila Scott, Joint Chair, 204-727-7435, Fax: 204-728-6839.

Brigham Young University, Graduate Studies, College of Fine Arts and Communications, School of Music, Provo, UT 84602-1001. Offers composition (MM); conducting (MM); music education (MA, MM); musicology (MA); performance (MM). *Accreditation:* NASM. *Faculty:* 44 full-time (8 women). *Students:* 56 full-time (40 women), 9 part-time (4 women); includes 4 minority (all Asian Americans or Pacific Islanders). Average age 28. 54 applicants, 57% accepted, 27 enrolled. In 2009, 25 master's awarded. *Degree requirements:* For master's, comprehensive exam (for some programs), thesis (for some programs), recital, project or composition (for some programs). *Entrance requirements:* For master's, placement exam, minimum GPA of 3.0 in last 60 hours, BM. Additional exam requirements/recommendations for international students: Required—TOEFL (minimum score 580 paper-based; 237 computer-based; 85 iBT). *Application deadline:* For fall admission, 2/1 priority date for domestic students, 1/15 priority date for international students. Application fee: $50. Electronic applications accepted. *Expenses:* Tuition: Full-time $5580; part-time $301 per credit hour. Tuition and fees vary according to student's religious affiliation. *Financial support:* In 2009–10, 56 students received support, including 39 teaching assistantships (averaging $5,000 per year); research assistantships, career-related internships or fieldwork, institutionally sponsored loans, scholarships/grants, tuition waivers (partial), and unspecified assistantships also available. Support available to part-time students. Financial award application deadline: 2/1; financial award applicants required to submit FAFSA. *Faculty research:* Louis Armstrong, rock and roll, Balinese gamelan. *Unit head:* Prof. Kory L. Katseanes, Director, 801-422-6304, Fax: 801-422-0533, E-mail: kory_katseanes@byu.edu. *Application contact:* Dr. Thomas L. Durham, Graduate Coordinator, 801-422-3226, Fax: 801-422-0533, E-mail: thomas_durham@byu.edu.

Brooklyn College of the City University of New York, Division of Graduate Studies, Conservatory of Music, Brooklyn, NY 11210-2889. Offers composition (MM); music (DMA, PhD); music education (MA); musicology (MA); performance (MM); performance practice (MA). Part-time programs available. *Students:* 1 full-time (0 women), 78 part-time (44 women); includes 15 minority (4 African Americans, 2 Asian Americans or Pacific Islanders, 9 Hispanic Americans), 14 international. Average age 28. 76 applicants, 79% accepted, 37 enrolled. In 2009, 24 master's awarded. *Degree requirements:* For master's, one foreign language, comprehensive exam, thesis. *Entrance requirements:* For master's, placement exam, 36 credits in music, audition, completed composition, writing sample. Additional exam requirements/recommendations for international students: Required—TOEFL (minimum score 550 paper-based; 213 computer-based; 79 iBT). *Application deadline:* For fall admission, 3/1 priority date for domestic students, 2/1 priority date for international students; for spring admission, 11/1

priority date for domestic students, 10/1 priority date for international students. Applications are processed on a rolling basis. Application fee: $125. Electronic applications accepted. *Expenses:* Tuition, state resident: full-time $7360; part-time $310 per credit hour. Tuition, nonresident: full-time $13,800; part-time $575 per credit hour. Required fees: $140.10 per semester. *Financial support:* Career-related internships or fieldwork, Federal Work-Study, institutionally sponsored loans, and scholarships/grants available. Support available to part-time students. Financial award application deadline: 5/1; financial award applicants required to submit FAFSA. *Faculty research:* American music, computer music. *Unit head:* Dr. Bruce MacIntyre, Chairperson, 718-951-5286, E-mail: brucem@brooklyn.cuny.edu. *Application contact:* Hernan Sierra, Graduate Admissions Coordinator, 718-951-4536, Fax: 718-951-4506, E-mail: grads@brooklyn.cuny.edu.

Brooklyn College of the City University of New York, Division of Graduate Studies, School of Education, Program in Adolescence Education and Special Subjects, Brooklyn, NY 11210-2889. Offers adolescence science education (MAT); art teacher (MA); biology teacher (MA); chemistry teacher (MA); earth science teacher (MAT); English teacher (MA); French teacher (MA); health and nutrition sciences: health teacher (MS Ed); mathematics teacher (MA); music education (CAS); music teacher (MA); physical education teacher (MS Ed); physics teacher (MA); social studies teacher (MA); Spanish teacher (MA). Part-time and evening/weekend programs available. *Students:* 23 full-time (15 women), 449 part-time (256 women); includes 147 minority (96 African Americans, 1 American Indian/Alaska Native, 18 Asian Americans or Pacific Islanders, 32 Hispanic Americans), 12 international. Average age 30. 251 applicants, 80% accepted, 141 enrolled. In 2009, 163 master's, 2 other advanced degrees awarded. *Degree requirements:* For master's, comprehensive exam (for some programs), thesis (for some programs). *Entrance requirements:* For master's, LAST, previous course work in education, resume, 2 letters of recommendation, essay. Additional exam requirements/recommendations for international students: Required—TOEFL (minimum score 500 paper-based; 173 computer-based; 61 iBT). *Application deadline:* For fall admission, 7/15 for domestic students, 7/1 for international students; for spring admission, 11/15 for domestic students, 10/1 for international students. Applications are processed on a rolling basis. Application fee: $125. Electronic applications accepted. *Expenses:* Tuition, state resident: full-time $7360; part-time $310 per credit hour. Tuition, nonresident: full-time $13,800; part-time $575 per credit hour. Required fees: $140.10 per semester. *Financial support:* Career-related internships or fieldwork, Federal Work-Study, institutionally sponsored loans, and scholarships/grants available. Support available to part-time students. Financial award application deadline: 5/1; financial award applicants required to submit FAFSA. *Faculty research:* Interdisciplinary education, semiotics, discourse analysis, autobiography, teacher identity. *Unit head:* Prof. Stephen Phillips, Program Head, 718-951-5214, E-mail: phillips@brooklyn.cuny.edu. *Application contact:* Hernan Sierra, Graduate Admissions Coordinator, 718-951-4536, Fax: 718-951-4506, E-mail: grads@brooklyn.cuny.edu.

Butler University, Jordan College of Fine Arts, Department of Music, Indianapolis, IN 46208-3485. Offers composition (MM); conducting (MM); music (MM); music education (MM); music history (MM); organ (MM); performance (MM). *Accreditation:* NASM. Part-time and evening/weekend programs available. *Faculty:* 14 full-time (3 women), 10 part-time/adjunct (3 women). *Students:* 20 full-time (8 women), 20 part-time (6 women), 5 international. Average age 27. 40 applicants, 48% accepted, 8 enrolled. In 2009, 10 master's awarded. *Degree requirements:* For master's, thesis (for some programs). *Entrance requirements:* For master's, GRE General Test, GRE Subject Test, audition, interview. *Application deadline:* For fall admission, 8/15 priority date for domestic students. Applications are processed on a rolling basis. Application fee: $35. Electronic applications accepted. *Financial support:* In 2009–10, 15 teaching assistantships with full tuition reimbursements (averaging $2,500 per year) were awarded; fellowships, career-related internships or fieldwork, institutionally sponsored loans, and scholarships/grants also available. Support available to part-time students. Financial award application deadline: 7/15; financial award applicants required to submit FAFSA. *Unit head:* Dr. Daniel Bolin, Head, 317-940-9988, Fax: 317-940-9658, E-mail: dbolin@butler.edu. *Application contact:* Kathy Lang, Admission Representative, 317-940-9646, Fax: 317-940-9658, E-mail: klang@butler.edu.

California Baptist University, Program in Music, Riverside, CA 92504-3206. Offers conducting (MM); music education (MM); performance (MM). *Accreditation:* NASM. Part-time programs available. *Faculty:* 4 full-time (1 woman), 1 (woman) part-time/adjunct. *Students:* 15 full-time (10 women), 4 part-time (3 women); includes 2 minority (both African Americans), 10 international. 12 applicants, 42% accepted, 4 enrolled. In 2009, 6 master's awarded. *Degree requirements:* For master's, thesis or alternative. *Entrance requirements:* For master's, minimum undergraduate GPA of 2.75; bachelor's degree in music. Additional exam requirements/recommendations for international students: Required—TOEFL (minimum score 575 paper-based; 230 computer-based; 89 iBT). *Application deadline:* For fall admission, 8/1 priority date for domestic students, 7/1 for international students; for spring admission, 12/1 priority date for domestic students, 10/15 for international students. Applications are processed on a rolling basis. Application fee: $45. Electronic applications accepted. *Expenses:* Tuition: Full-time $8352; part-time $464 per semester hour. Required fees: $125 per semester. Tuition and fees vary according to course load, campus/location and program. *Financial support:* Federal Work-Study and scholarships/grants available. Support available to part-time students. Financial award applicants required to submit FAFSA. *Unit head:* Dr. Gary Bonner, Dean, School of Music, 951-343-4251, Fax: 951-343-4570, E-mail: gbonner@calbaptist.edu. *Application contact:* Gail Ronveaux, Dean of Graduate Enrollment, 951-343-5045, Fax: 951-343-5095, E-mail: graduateadmissions@calbaptist.edu.

California State University, Fresno, Division of Graduate Studies, College of Arts and Humanities, Department of Music, Fresno, CA 93740-8027. Offers music (MA); music education (MA); performance (MA). *Accreditation:* NASM. Part-time programs available. *Degree requirements:* For master's, thesis or alternative. *Entrance requirements:* For master's, GRE General Test, BA in music, minimum GPA of 3.0. Additional exam requirements/recommendations for international students: Required—TOEFL. Electronic applications accepted. *Faculty research:* Technology transfer, folk art.

California State University, Fullerton, Graduate Studies, College of the Arts, Department of Music, Fullerton, CA 92834-9480. Offers music education (MA); music history and literature (MA); performance (MM); piano pedagogy (MA); theory-composition (MM). *Accreditation:* NASM. Part-time programs available. *Students:* 19 full-time (11 women), 53 part-time (31 women); includes 21 minority (1 African American, 15 Asian Americans or Pacific Islanders, 5 Hispanic Americans), 10 international. Average age 29. 68 applicants, 37% accepted, 18 enrolled. In 2009, 17 master's awarded. *Degree requirements:* For master's, comprehensive exam, project or thesis. *Entrance requirements:* For master's, audition, major in music or related field, minimum GPA of 2.5 in last 60 units of course work. Application fee: $55. *Expenses:* Tuition, nonresident: full-time $11,160; part-time $373 per credit. Required fees: $1440 per term. Tuition and fees vary according to course load, degree level and program. *Financial support:* Career-related internships or fieldwork, Federal Work-Study, institutionally sponsored loans, and scholarships/grants available. Support available to part-time students. Financial award application deadline: 3/1; financial award applicants required to submit FAFSA. *Unit head:* Dr. Marc Dickey, Chair, 657-278-3511. *Application contact:* Admissions/Applications, 657-278-2371.

California State University, Los Angeles, Graduate Studies, College of Arts and Letters, Department of Music, Los Angeles, CA 90032-8530. Offers music composition (MM); music education (MA); musicology (MA); performance (MM). *Accreditation:* NASM. Part-time and evening/weekend programs available. *Faculty:* 13 full-time (3 women), 10 part-time/adjunct (4 women). *Students:* 32 full-time (12 women), 34 part-time (13 women); includes 25 minority (4 African Americans, 5 Asian Americans or Pacific Islanders, 16 Hispanic Americans), 8 international. Average age 37. 21 applicants, 100% accepted, 11 enrolled. In 2009, 28 master's awarded. *Degree requirements:* For master's, comprehensive exam, project or thesis. *Entrance requirements:* For master's, audition. Additional exam requirements/recommendations for international students: Required—TOEFL (minimum score 500 paper-based; 173 computer-based). *Application deadline:* For fall admission, 5/1 for domestic and international students. Applications are processed on a rolling basis. Application fee: $55. Electronic applications accepted. *Financial support:* Career-related internships or fieldwork and Federal Work-Study

available. Support available to part-time students. Financial award application deadline: 3/1. *Faculty research:* Gregorian semiology, Baroque opera. *Unit head:* Dr. George DeGraffenreid, Chair, 323-343-4060, Fax: 323-343-4063, E-mail: gdegraf@calstatela.edu. *Application contact:* Dr. Cheryl L. Ney, Associate Vice President for Academic Affairs and Dean of Graduate Studies, 323-343-3820, Fax: 323-343-5653, E-mail: cney@cslanet.calstatela.edu.

California State University, Northridge, Graduate Studies, College of Arts, Media, and Communication, Department of Music, Northridge, CA 91330. Offers composition (MM); conducting (MM); music education (MA); performance (MM). *Accreditation:* NASM. *Faculty:* 22 full-time (6 women), 47 part-time/adjunct (15 women). *Students:* 29 full-time (20 women), 32 part-time (19 women); includes 16 minority (3 African Americans, 4 Asian Americans or Pacific Islanders, 9 Hispanic Americans), 10 international. Average age 29. 92 applicants, 36% accepted, 22 enrolled. In 2009, 17 master's awarded. *Degree requirements:* For master's, thesis. *Entrance requirements:* For master's, audition, GRE General Test or minimum GPA of 3.0. Additional exam requirements/recommendations for international students: Required—TOEFL. *Application deadline:* For fall admission, 11/30 for domestic students. Application fee: $55. *Financial support:* Application deadline: 3/1. *Faculty research:* Touring program. *Unit head:* Dr. Elizabeth Sellers, Chair, 816-677-4752, E-mail: elizabeth.a.sellers@csun.edu. *Application contact:* Julia Heinen, Graduate Advisor, 818-677-3168, E-mail: julia.heinen@csun.edu.

Campbellsville University, School of Music, Campbellsville, KY 42718-2799. Offers church music (MM); music (MA); music education (MM). *Accreditation:* NASM. Part-time programs available. *Degree requirements:* For master's, thesis (for some programs), paper or recital. *Entrance requirements:* For master's, GRE General Test or PRAXIS, minimum GPA of 2.75. Additional exam requirements/recommendations for international students: Required—TOEFL (minimum score 550 paper-based). Electronic applications accepted. *Expenses:* Tuition: Full-time $6750; part-time $375 per credit hour.

Capital University, Conservatory of Music, Columbus, OH 43209-2394. Offers music education (MM), including instrumental emphasis, Kodály emphasis. Program offered only in summer. *Accreditation:* NASM. Part-time programs available. *Degree requirements:* For master's, comprehensive exam, thesis or alternative, chamber performance exam. *Entrance requirements:* For master's, music theory exam, minimum undergraduate GPA of 3.0. Additional exam requirements/recommendations for international students: Required—TOEFL (minimum score 550 paper-based; 213 computer-based; 80 iBT). Electronic applications accepted. *Expenses:* Contact institution. *Faculty research:* Folk song research, Kodály method, performance, composition.

Carnegie Mellon University, College of Fine Arts, School of Music, Pittsburgh, PA 15213-3891. Offers composition (MM); conducting (MM); instrumental performance (MM); music and technology (MS); music education (MM); vocal performance (MM). *Accreditation:* NASM. Part-time programs available. *Degree requirements:* For master's, comprehensive exam, recital. *Entrance requirements:* For master's, audition. *Faculty research:* Computer music, music history.

Case Western Reserve University, School of Graduate Studies, Department of Music, Program in Music Education, Cleveland, OH 44106. Offers MA, PhD. *Accreditation:* NASM; Teacher Education Accreditation Council. *Faculty:* 13 full-time (5 women). *Students:* 13 full-time (6 women), 4 part-time (0 women); includes 2 minority (1 Asian American or Pacific Islander, 1 Hispanic American). Average age 31. 13 applicants, 62% accepted, 7 enrolled. In 2009, 5 master's awarded. *Degree requirements:* For master's, thesis (for some programs); for doctorate, thesis/dissertation. *Entrance requirements:* For master's, GRE, audition/interview, writing sample, 1 year of teaching; for doctorate, GRE, audition/interview, writing sample. Additional exam requirements/recommendations for international students: Required—TOEFL (minimum score 550 paper-based; 213 computer-based; 79 iBT). *Application deadline:* For fall admission, 2/15 for domestic students. Application fee: $50. Electronic applications accepted. *Financial support:* Fellowships, teaching assistantships, career-related internships or fieldwork, tuition waivers (full), and unspecified assistantships available. Financial award application deadline: 2/15; financial award applicants required to submit FAFSA. *Faculty research:* Psychology of music, creative thinking, computer applications, educational psychology. *Unit head:* Mary E. Davis, Chair, 216-368-2400, Fax: 216-368-6557, E-mail: mary.e.davis@case.edu. *Application contact:* Laura Stauffer, Admissions, 216-368-2400, Fax: 216-368-6557, E-mail: laura.stauffer@case.edu.

The Catholic University of America, The Benjamin T. Rome School of Music, Washington, DC 20064. Offers chamber music (MM); composition (MM, DMA), including concert music (DMA), stage music (MM); music (Certificate); musicology (MA, PhD), including music history (MA), music theory (MA); orchestral conducting (MM); orchestral instruments (DMA); piano pedagogy (MM, DMA); piano performance (MM); sacred music (MMSM, DMA); vocal pedagogy (MM); vocal performance (MM). *Accreditation:* NASM. Part-time programs available. *Faculty:* 17 full-time (4 women), 23 part-time/adjunct (9 women). *Students:* 45 full-time (23 women), 91 part-time (60 women); includes 25 minority (6 African Americans, 11 Asian Americans or Pacific Islanders, 8 Hispanic Americans), 25 international. Average age 33. 121 applicants, 60% accepted, 38 enrolled. In 2009, 18 master's, 13 doctorates awarded. *Degree requirements:* For master's, comprehensive exam (for some programs), thesis (for some programs); for doctorate, comprehensive exam (for some programs), thesis/dissertation (for some programs), minimum GPA of 3.0. *Entrance requirements:* For master's, theory placement test, 2 letters of recommendation, minimum undergraduate B average, BA in music, demonstration of performance proficiency; for doctorate, school qualifying exam, statement of purpose, official copies of academic transcripts, 4 letters of recommendation, audition/interview. Additional exam requirements/recommendations for international students: Required—TOEFL (minimum score 580 paper-based; 237 computer-based). *Application deadline:* For fall admission, 8/1 priority date for domestic students, 7/15 for international students; for spring admission, 12/1 priority date for domestic students, 10/15 for international students. Applications are processed on a rolling basis. Application fee: $55. Electronic applications accepted. *Expenses:* Tuition: Full-time $31,740; part-time $1245 per credit hour. Required fees: $50; $25 per semester hour. One-time fee: $425. *Financial support:* Fellowships, research assistantships, teaching assistantships, Federal Work-Study, scholarships/grants, tuition waivers (full and partial), and unspecified assistantships available. Financial award application deadline: 2/1; financial award applicants required to submit FAFSA. *Faculty research:* Composition, sacred music, orchestral instruments, piano, voice, music history and theory. *Unit head:* Murry Sidlin, Dean, 202-319-5417, Fax: 202-319-6280, E-mail: cua-music@cua.edu. *Application contact:* Julie Schwing, Director of Graduate Admissions, 202-319-5057, Fax: 202-319-6533, E-mail: cua-admissions@cua.edu.

Central Connecticut State University, School of Graduate Studies, School of Arts and Sciences, Department of Music, New Britain, CT 06050-4010. Offers music education (MS, Certificate). *Accreditation:* NASM. Part-time and evening/weekend programs available. *Faculty:* 10 full-time (4 women), 31 part-time/adjunct (15 women). *Students:* 2 full-time (1 woman), 10 part-time (6 women). Average age 27. 19 applicants, 37% accepted, 2 enrolled. In 2009, 8 master's, 1 other advanced degree awarded. *Degree requirements:* For master's, comprehensive exam, thesis or alternative; for Certificate, qualifying exam. *Entrance requirements:* For master's, audition, minimum undergraduate GPA of 2.7. Additional exam requirements/recommendations for international students: Required—TOEFL. *Application deadline:* For fall admission, 7/10 for domestic students; for spring admission, 12/10 for domestic students. Applications are processed on a rolling basis. Application fee: $50. Electronic applications accepted. *Expenses:* Tuition, area resident: Full-time $4662; part-time $440 per credit. Tuition, state resident: full-time $6994; part-time $440 per credit. Tuition, nonresident: full-time $12,988; part-time $440 per credit. Required fees: $3606. One-time fee: $62 part-time. *Financial support:* Application deadline: 3/1. *Faculty research:* Applied music. *Unit head:* Dr. Charles Menoche, Chair, 860-832-2912. *Application contact:* Dr. Charles Menoche, Chair, 860-832-2912.

Central Michigan University, College of Graduate Studies, College of Communication and Fine Arts, School of Music, Program in Music Education, Mount Pleasant, MI 48859. Offers

Music Education

Central Michigan University (continued)
MM. *Accreditation:* NASM. Part-time programs available. *Degree requirements:* For master's, thesis or alternative. Electronic applications accepted.

Christopher Newport University, Graduate Studies, Department of Teacher Preparation, Newport News, VA 23606-2998. Offers art (PK-12) (MAT); biology (6-12) (MAT); computer science (6-12) (MAT); elementary (PK-6) (MAT); English (6-12) (MAT); French (PK-12) (MAT); history and social science (6-12) (MAT); mathematics (6-12) (MAT); music (PK-12) (MAT), including choral, instrumental; physics (6-12) (MAT); Spanish (PK-12) (MAT). Part-time and evening/weekend programs available. *Faculty:* 24 full-time (13 women), 4 part-time/adjunct (2 women). *Students:* 76 full-time (66 women), 12 part-time (10 women); includes 3 minority (2 African Americans, 1 Hispanic American). Average age 24. 3 applicants, 100% accepted, 2 enrolled. In 2009, 58 master's awarded. *Degree requirements:* For master's, comprehensive exam, thesis or alternative. *Entrance requirements:* For master's, PRAXIS I, minimum GPA of 3.0. Additional exam requirements/recommendations for international students: Required—TOEFL (minimum score 580 paper-based; 237 computer-based; 92 iBT). *Application deadline:* For fall admission, 8/15 for domestic students, 4/1 for international students; for spring admission, 10/15 for domestic students, 10/1 for international students. Applications are processed on a rolling basis. Application fee: $45. Electronic applications accepted. *Expenses:* Tuition, area resident: Part-time $384 per credit hour. Tuition, state resident: part-time $384 per credit hour. Tuition, nonresident: part-time $701 per credit hour. *Financial support:* In 2009–10, 3 research assistantships with full and partial tuition reimbursements (averaging $2,000 per year) were awarded; career-related internships or fieldwork, Federal Work-Study, and unspecified assistantships also available. Support available to part-time students. Financial award application deadline: 3/1; financial award applicants required to submit FAFSA. *Faculty research:* Early literacy development, instructional innovations, professional teaching standards, multicultural issues, aesthetic education. *Unit head:* Dr. Marsha Sprague, Director, 757-594-7388, Fax: 757-594-7803, E-mail: msprague@cnu.edu. *Application contact:* Lyn Sawyer, Associate Director, Graduate Admissions, 757-594-7544, Fax: 757-594-7649, E-mail: gradstdy@cnu.edu.

Cleveland State University, College of Graduate Studies, College of Liberal Arts and Social Sciences, Department of Music, Cleveland, OH 44115. Offers composition (MM); music education (MM); performance (MM). *Accreditation:* NASM. Part-time and evening/weekend programs available. *Degree requirements:* For master's, comprehensive exam, thesis or recital. *Entrance requirements:* For master's, departmental assessment in music history, minimum undergraduate GPA of 2.75. Additional exam requirements/recommendations for international students: Required—TOEFL (minimum score 525 paper-based; 197 computer-based). *Faculty research:* Ethnomusicology, classical-romantic music, new performance practices, electronic music, interdisciplinary studies.

College of Charleston, Graduate School, School of Education, Health, and Human Performance, Department of Foundations, Secondary, and Special Education, Program in Performing Arts Education, Charleston, SC 29424-0001. Offers MAT. *Accreditation:* NASM. *Faculty:* 31 full-time (26 women), 11 part-time/adjunct (10 women). *Students:* 5 full-time (3 women), 1 part-time (0 women); includes 1 minority (African American). Average age 26. 5 applicants, 60% accepted, 3 enrolled. In 2009, 1 master's awarded. *Entrance requirements:* For master's, GRE, minimum GPA of 2.5 overall, 3.0 in last 60 hours of undergraduate coursework; 2 letters of recommendation; audition/interview. Additional exam requirements/recommendations for international students: Required—TOEFL. *Application deadline:* For fall admission, 7/1 for domestic students; for spring admission, 11/1 for domestic students. Application fee: $45. Electronic applications accepted. *Financial support:* Scholarships/grants and unspecified assistantships available. *Unit head:* Dr. Bonnie McCarty, Director, 843-953-8048, E-mail: mccarty@cofc.edu. *Application contact:* Susan Hallatt, Director of Graduate Admissions, 843-953-5614, Fax: 843-953-1434, E-mail: hallatts@cofc.edu.

College of Mount St. Joseph, Graduate Education Program, Cincinnati, OH 45233-1670. Offers adolescent young adult education (MA); art (MA); inclusive early childhood education (MA); instructional leadership (MA); middle childhood education (MA); multi-age education (MA); multicultural special education (MA); music (MA); reading (MA). *Accreditation:* Teacher Education Accreditation Council. Part-time and evening/weekend programs available. *Faculty:* 15 full-time (11 women), 9 part-time/adjunct (6 women). *Students:* 93 full-time (75 women), 99 part-time (66 women); includes 19 minority (18 African Americans, 1 American Indian/Alaska Native). Average age 34. 116 applicants, 97% accepted, 94 enrolled. In 2009, 51 master's awarded. *Degree requirements:* For master's, research project, student teaching, clinical and field-based experiences. *Entrance requirements:* For master's, GRE, PRAXIS II in teaching content area (math or science), 2 letters of recommendation, interview, resume. Additional exam requirements/recommendations for international students: Required—TOEFL (minimum score 560 paper-based; 220 computer-based; 83 iBT). *Application deadline:* Applications are processed on a rolling basis. Application fee: $50. Electronic applications accepted. *Expenses:* Tuition: Part-time $500 per hour. Required fees: $200 per year. Tuition and fees vary according to degree level and program. *Financial support:* In 2009–10, 51 students received support. Scholarships/grants available. Financial award applicants required to submit FAFSA. *Faculty research:* Foreign and second language learning problems/reading disabilities/hyperlexia, multicultural/bilingual special education, alternative educator licensure, science education, pedagogical content knowledge. *Unit head:* Dr. Mary West, Chair of Graduate Education, 513-244-3263, Fax: 513-244-4867, E-mail: mary_west@mail.msj.edu. *Application contact:* Marilyn Hoskins, Assistant Director of Graduate Recruitment, 513-244-4723, Fax: 513-244-4629, E-mail: marilyn_hoskins@mail.msj.edu.

The College of Saint Rose, Graduate Studies, School of Arts and Humanities, Music Department, Program in Music Education, Albany, NY 12203-1419. Offers MS Ed, Certificate. *Accreditation:* NASM; NCATE. *Degree requirements:* For master's, thesis optional, final project. *Entrance requirements:* For master's, audition, minimum undergraduate GPA of 3.0; for Certificate, placement test if undergraduate degree is not in music, audition. Additional exam requirements/recommendations for international students: Required—TOEFL (minimum score 550 paper-based; 213 computer-based). Electronic applications accepted.

The Colorado College, Department of Education, Program in Secondary Education, Colorado Springs, CO 80903-3294. Offers art teaching (K-12) (MAT); English teaching (MAT); foreign language teaching (MAT); mathematics teaching (MAT); music teaching (MAT); science teaching (MAT); social studies teaching (MAT). *Faculty:* 3 full-time (2 women), 8 part-time/adjunct (6 women). *Students:* 15 full-time (5 women); includes 2 minority (1 American Indian/Alaska Native, 1 Asian American or Pacific Islander). Average age 27. 26 applicants, 81% accepted, 15 enrolled. In 2009, 17 master's awarded. *Degree requirements:* For master's, thesis, internship. *Entrance requirements:* For master's, PRAXIS II or PLACE Exam. *Application deadline:* For fall admission, 12/1 priority date for domestic students, 12/1 for international students. Applications are processed on a rolling basis. Application fee: $50. *Expenses:* Tuition: Part-time $2545 per credit. *Financial support:* In 2009–10, 15 students received support, including 7 teaching assistantships (averaging $16,000 per year); career-related internships or fieldwork, institutionally sponsored loans, health care benefits, and tuition waivers (partial) also available. Financial award application deadline: 2/15; financial award applicants required to submit FAFSA. *Unit head:* Mike Taber, Director, 719-389-6026, Fax: 719-389-6473, E-mail: mike.taber@coloradocollege.edu. *Application contact:* Debra Yazulla Mortenson, Education Services Manager, 719-389-6472, Fax: 719-389-6473, E-mail: debra.mortenson@coloradocollege.edu.

Colorado State University–Pueblo, College of Education, Engineering and Professional Studies, Education Program, Pueblo, CO 81001-4901. Offers art education (M Ed); foreign language education (M Ed); health and physical education (M Ed); instructional technology (M Ed); linguistically diverse education (M Ed); music education (M Ed); special education (M Ed). *Accreditation:* Teacher Education Accreditation Council. Part-time programs available. *Degree requirements:* For master's, portfolio. *Entrance requirements:* For master's, 3 recommendations, teaching license. Additional exam requirements/recommendations for international students: Required—TOEFL (minimum score 500 paper-based; 173 computer-based). Electronic applications accepted. *Faculty research:* Portfolio assessment, math education, science education.

Columbus State University, Graduate Studies, College of the Arts, Schwob School of Music, Columbus, GA 31907-5645. Offers artist diploma (Postbaccalaureate Certificate); music education (MM). *Accreditation:* NASM; NCATE (one or more programs are accredited). Part-time and evening/weekend programs available. *Faculty:* 16 full-time (10 women). *Students:* 16 full-time (8 women); includes 2 minority (1 African American, 1 Hispanic American), 3 international. Average age 26. 22 applicants, 50% accepted, 11 enrolled. In 2009, 5 master's awarded. *Degree requirements:* For master's, exit exam. *Entrance requirements:* For master's, GRE General Test, audition. Additional exam requirements/recommendations for international students: Required—TOEFL (minimum score 550 paper-based; 213 computer-based; 79 iBT). *Application deadline:* For fall admission, 5/1 priority date for domestic students, 5/1 for international students; for spring admission, 11/1 for domestic and international students. Applications are processed on a rolling basis. Application fee: $30. Electronic applications accepted. *Financial support:* In 2009–10, 13 students received support, including 15 research assistantships with partial tuition reimbursements available (averaging $3,000 per year); career-related internships or fieldwork, Federal Work-Study, institutionally sponsored loans, scholarships/grants, tuition waivers (full), and unspecified assistantships also available. Support available to part-time students. Financial award application deadline: 5/1; financial award applicants required to submit FAFSA. *Unit head:* Dr. Fred Cohen, Director, 706-649-7244, E-mail: cohen_alfred@colstate.edu. *Application contact:* Katie Thornton, Graduate Admissions Specialist, 706-568-2035, Fax: 706-568-2462, E-mail: thornton_katie@colstate.edu.

Conservatorio de Musica, Program in Music Education, San Juan, PR 00918-2199. Offers MM Ed. *Entrance requirements:* For master's, EXADEP, 3 letters of recommendation, audition, bachelor's degree in music education, interview, minimum GPA of 2.5, performance video, teaching video. Additional exam requirements/recommendations for international students: Required—TOEFL.

Converse College, Carroll McDaniel Petrie School of Music, Spartanburg, SC 29302-0006. Offers instrumental performance (M Mus); music education (M Mus); piano pedagogy (M Mus); vocal performance (M Mus). *Accreditation:* NASM. Part-time and evening/weekend programs available. *Degree requirements:* For master's, variable foreign language requirement, comprehensive exam, thesis (for some programs), recitals. *Entrance requirements:* For master's, NTE (music education), audition, 3 letters of recommendation. Additional exam requirements/recommendations for international students: Required—TOEFL. Electronic applications accepted. *Faculty research:* Chamber music, opera, performance, composition, recording.

DePaul University, School of Music, Chicago, IL 60614. Offers applied music (performance) (MM, Certificate); jazz studies (MM), including composition, performance; music composition (MM); music education (MM). *Accreditation:* NASM (one or more programs are accredited). Part-time and evening/weekend programs available. *Faculty:* 11 full-time (2 women), 50 part-time/adjunct (14 women). *Students:* 53 full-time (23 women), 65 part-time (38 women); includes 10 minority (1 African American, 3 Asian Americans or Pacific Islanders, 6 Hispanic Americans), 25 international. Average age 24. 312 applicants, 31% accepted, 50 enrolled. In 2009, 40 master's, 5 Certificates awarded. *Degree requirements:* For master's, comprehensive exam, terminal project, recital (for performers); for Certificate, recital. *Entrance requirements:* For master's, bachelor's degree in music or related field, minimum GPA of 3.0, auditions (performance), scores (composition); for Certificate, master's degree in performance or related field, auditions (for performance majors). Additional exam requirements/recommendations for international students: Required—TOEFL (minimum score 550 paper-based; 213 computer-based; 80 iBT). *Application deadline:* For fall admission, 1/15 priority date for domestic and international students. Applications are processed on a rolling basis. Application fee: $40. Electronic applications accepted. *Expenses:* Contact institution. *Financial support:* In 2009–10, 4 fellowships with partial tuition reimbursements were awarded; teaching assistantships, career-related internships or fieldwork, Federal Work-Study, scholarships/grants, and tuition waivers also available. Support available to part-time students. Financial award application deadline: 1/15. *Unit head:* Dr. Donald E. Casey, Dean, 773-325-7256, E-mail: dcasey@depaul.edu. *Application contact:* Ross Beacraft, Director of Admissions, 773-325-7444, Fax: 773-325-7429, E-mail: rbeacraf@depaul.edu.

Duquesne University, Mary Pappert School of Music, Pittsburgh, PA 15282-0001. Offers music composition (MM); music education (MM); music performance (MM, AD); music technology (MM); music theory (MM); sacred music (MM). *Accreditation:* NASM. Part-time programs available. *Faculty:* 28 full-time (10 women), 73 part-time/adjunct (19 women). *Students:* 77 full-time (40 women), 16 part-time (7 women); includes 9 minority (5 African Americans, 2 Asian Americans or Pacific Islanders, 2 Hispanic Americans), 20 international. Average age 23. 95 applicants, 80% accepted, 36 enrolled. In 2009, 15 master's, 5 ADs awarded. *Degree requirements:* For master's, comprehensive exam, thesis (for some programs), recital (music performance); for AD, recital. *Entrance requirements:* For master's, audition, minimum undergraduate QPA of 3.0 in music, portfolio of original compositions, theoretical papers, or music education experience; for AD, audition. Additional exam requirements/recommendations for international students: Required—TOEFL (minimum score 550 paper-based; 213 computer-based; 79 iBT). *Application deadline:* For fall admission, 7/1 priority date for domestic and international students; for spring admission, 12/1 priority date for domestic and international students. Applications are processed on a rolling basis. Application fee: $50. Electronic applications accepted. *Expenses:* Contact institution. *Financial support:* In 2009–10, 50 students received support, including 45 fellowships with full and partial tuition reimbursements available; career-related internships or fieldwork, Federal Work-Study, institutionally sponsored loans, and tuition waivers (full and partial) also available. Support available to part-time students. Financial award application deadline: 4/1. *Faculty research:* Performance; computer-assisted instruction in music at elementary and secondary levels; electronic music; contemporary music, theory, and analysis; development of online graduate music courses. Total annual research expenditures: $8,000. *Unit head:* Dr. Edward W. Kocher, Dean, 412-396-6082, Fax: 412-396-1524, E-mail: kocher@duq.edu. *Application contact:* Peggy Eiseman, Administrative Assistant of Admissions, 412-396-5064, Fax: 412-396-5479, E-mail: eiseman@duq.edu.

East Carolina University, Graduate School, College of Fine Arts and Communication, School of Music, Greenville, NC 27858-4353. Offers music education (MM); music therapy (MM); performance (MM); theory and composition (MM). *Accreditation:* NASM. Part-time programs available. *Degree requirements:* For master's, comprehensive exam, thesis optional. *Entrance requirements:* For master's, GRE General Test or MAT. Additional exam requirements/recommendations for international students: Required—TOEFL.

Eastern Kentucky University, The Graduate School, College of Education, Department of Curriculum and Instruction, Richmond, KY 40475-3102. Offers elementary education (MA Ed), including early elementary education, reading; library science (MA Ed); music education (MA Ed); secondary and higher education (MA Ed), including secondary education; teaching (MAT). *Accreditation:* NCATE. Part-time programs available. *Degree requirements:* For master's, portfolio is part of exam. *Entrance requirements:* For master's, GRE General Test, PRAXIS II (KY), minimum GPA of 2.5. *Faculty research:* Technology in education, reading instruction, e-portfolios, induction to teacher education, dispositions of teachers.

Eastern Michigan University, Graduate School, College of Arts and Sciences, Department of Music and Dance, Ypsilanti, MI 48197. Offers music composition (MM); music education (MM); music pedagogy (MM); music performance (MM). *Accreditation:* NASM. Part-time and evening/weekend programs available. Postbaccalaureate distance learning degree programs offered (minimal on-campus study). *Faculty:* 26 full-time (10 women). *Students:* 3 full-time (1 woman), 33 part-time (18 women); includes 5 minority (2 African Americans, 1 Asian American or Pacific Islander, 2 Hispanic Americans), 5 international. Average age 31. 25 applicants, 80% accepted, 8 enrolled. In 2009, 8 master's awarded. *Entrance requirements:* Additional exam requirements/recommendations for international students: Required—TOEFL. *Application deadline:* Applications are processed on a rolling basis. Application fee: $35. Tuition and fees vary according to course level. *Financial support:* Fellowships, research assistantships with full tuition reimburse-

ments, teaching assistantships with full tuition reimbursements, career-related internships or fieldwork, Federal Work-Study, institutionally sponsored loans, scholarships/grants, tuition waivers (partial), and unspecified assistantships available. Support available to part-time students. Financial award applicants required to submit FAFSA. *Unit head:* Dr. David Woike, Department Head, 734-487-4380, Fax: 734-487-6939, E-mail: dwoike@emich.edu. *Application contact:* Dr. David Pierce, Coordinator of Music Advising, 734-487-4380, Fax: 734-487-6939, E-mail: david.pierce@emich.edu.

Eastern Washington University, Graduate Studies, College of Arts and Letters, Department of Music, Cheney, WA 99004-2431. Offers composition (MA); instrumental/vocal performance (MA); music education (MA); music history and literature (MA). *Accreditation:* NASM. Part-time programs available. *Degree requirements:* For master's, comprehensive exam, thesis or alternative. *Entrance requirements:* For master's, GRE General Test, minimum GPA of 3.0. *Expenses:* Tuition, state resident: full-time $7476; part-time $249 per quarter hour. Tuition, nonresident: full-time $18,030; part-time $601 per quarter hour. Required fees: $3.50 per quarter hour. $142 per quarter.

Emporia State University, School of Graduate Studies, College of Liberal Arts and Sciences, Department of Music, Emporia, KS 66801-5087. Offers music education (MM), including instrumental, vocal; performance (MM). *Accreditation:* NASM. Part-time programs available. *Faculty:* 13 full-time (4 women), 4 part-time/adjunct (all women). *Students:* 5 full-time (3 women), 4 part-time (3 women); includes 1 minority (Asian American or Pacific Islander), 2 international. In 2009, 11 master's awarded. *Degree requirements:* For master's, comprehensive exam or thesis. *Entrance requirements:* For master's, music qualifying exam, appropriate undergraduate degree. Additional exam requirements/recommendations for international students: Required—TOEFL (minimum score 520 paper-based; 133 computer-based; 68 iBT). *Application deadline:* For fall admission, 8/15 priority date for domestic students. Applications are processed on a rolling basis. Application fee: $30 ($75 for international students). Electronic applications accepted. *Expenses:* Tuition, state resident: full-time $4154; part-time $173 per credit hour. Tuition, nonresident: full-time $12,864; part-time $536 per credit hour. Required fees: $948; $58 per credit hour. Tuition and fees vary according to campus/location. *Financial support:* In 2009–10, 1 research assistantship with full tuition reimbursement (averaging $7,059 per year), 4 teaching assistantships with full tuition reimbursements (averaging $7,059 per year) were awarded; Federal Work-Study, institutionally sponsored loans, health care benefits, and unspecified assistantships also available. Financial award application deadline: 3/15; financial award applicants required to submit FAFSA. *Unit head:* Dr. Allan D. Comstock, Interim Chair, 620-341-5431, E-mail: acomstoc@emporia.edu. *Application contact:* Dr. Andrew Houchins, Graduate Coordinator, 620-341-6089, E-mail: ahouchin@emporia.edu.

Five Towns College, Department of Music, Dix Hills, NY 11746-6055. Offers jazz/commercial music (MM); music (DMA); music education (MM). Part-time programs available. *Faculty:* 5 full-time (2 women), 11 part-time/adjunct (2 women). *Students:* 17 full-time (4 women), 38 part-time (9 women); includes 5 minority (2 African Americans, 3 Hispanic Americans), 15 international. Average age 28. *Degree requirements:* For master's, exams, major composition or capstone project, recital; for doctorate, comprehensive exam, thesis/dissertation, final oral exam. *Entrance requirements:* For master's, audition, bachelor's degree in music or music education, minimum GPA of 2.75, 36 hours of course work in performance; for doctorate, master's degree in music, minimum GPA of 3.0, 3 letters of recommendation. Additional exam requirements/recommendations for international students: Required—TOEFL (minimum score 550 paper-based; 213 computer-based; 80 iBT). *Application deadline:* Applications are processed on a rolling basis. Application fee: $50. *Expenses:* Tuition: Full-time $11,880; part-time $495 per credit. Required fees: $110 per semester. *Financial support:* Fellowships with tuition reimbursements, tuition waivers (partial) available. Financial award applicants required to submit FAFSA. *Faculty research:* Teaching methods, teaching strategies and techniques, analysis of modern music, jazz. *Unit head:* Dr. Jill Miller-Thorn, Dean of Graduate Studies, 631-656-2142, Fax: 631-656-2172, E-mail: jmillerthorn@ftc.edu. *Application contact:* Jerry Cohen, Dean of Enrollment, 631-656-2121, Fax: 631-656-2172, E-mail: jcohen@ftc.edu.

Florida International University, College of Architecture and the Arts, School of Music, Program in Music Education, Miami, FL 33199. Offers MS. *Accreditation:* NASM. Part-time and evening/weekend programs available. *Students:* 1 (woman) full-time, 7 part-time (2 women); includes 6 minority (1 African American, 5 Hispanic Americans). Average age 29. 1 applicant, 100% accepted, 1 enrolled. *Degree requirements:* For master's, thesis. *Entrance requirements:* For master's, GRE, 2 letters of recommendation; audition, interview and/or writing sample (for some areas). Additional exam requirements/recommendations for international students: Required—TOEFL (minimum score 550 paper-based; 80 iBT). *Application deadline:* For fall admission, 6/1 for domestic students, 4/1 for international students; for spring admission, 10/1 for domestic students, 9/1 for international students. Applications are processed on a rolling basis. Application fee: $30. Electronic applications accepted. *Expenses:* Tuition, state resident: full-time $8008; part-time $4004 per year. Tuition, nonresident: full-time $20,104; part-time $10,052 per year. Required fees: $298; $149 per term. *Financial support:* Institutionally sponsored loans and scholarships/grants available. Financial award application deadline: 3/1; financial award applicants required to submit FAFSA. *Faculty research:* Psychology of music teaching, classroom methodology, biofeedback. *Unit head:* Orlando Garcia, Chair, School of Music, 305-348-3357, Fax: 305-348-4073, E-mail: orlando.garcia@fiu.edu. *Application contact:* Prof. Joel Galand, Graduate Program Director, 305-348-2896, Fax: 305-348-4073, E-mail: joel.galand@fiu.edu.

Florida State University, The Graduate School, College of Music, Program in Music Education, Tallahassee, FL 32306. Offers MM Ed, PhD. *Accreditation:* NASM. *Faculty:* 25 full-time. *Students:* 61 full-time (22 women); includes 14 minority (10 African Americans, 1 Asian American or Pacific Islander, 3 Hispanic Americans). Average age 23. 60 applicants, 90% accepted, 37 enrolled. In 2009, 23 master's, 11 doctorates awarded. *Degree requirements:* For master's, comprehensive exam (for some programs), thesis optional, departmental qualifying exam; for doctorate, thesis/dissertation, departmental qualifying exam. *Entrance requirements:* For master's and doctorate, minimum GPA of 3.0 or GRE General Test. Additional exam requirements/recommendations for international students: Required—TOEFL (minimum score 650 paper-based; 213 computer-based). *Application deadline:* For fall admission, 7/1 for domestic students, 5/2 for international students; for spring admission, 11/3 for domestic students, 9/1 for international students. Applications are processed on a rolling basis. Application fee: $30. *Expenses:* Tuition, state resident: full-time $7413. Tuition, nonresident: full-time $22,567. *Financial support:* In 2009–10, 9 students received support, including 9 teaching assistantships with full tuition reimbursements available (averaging $3,000 per year); career-related internships or fieldwork, Federal Work-Study, and tuition waivers (partial) also available. Support available to part-time students. Financial award application deadline: 2/28; financial award applicants required to submit FAFSA. *Unit head:* Don Gibson, Dean, 850-644-4361, Fax: 850-644-2033. *Application contact:* Dr. Seth Beckman, Assistant Dean for Academic Affairs/Director of Graduate Studies, 850-644-5848, Fax: 850-644-2033, E-mail: sbeckman@admin.fsu.edu.

George Mason University, College of Visual and Performing Arts, Department of Music, Fairfax, VA 22030. Offers instrumental performance artist (Certificate); music (MM); music education (PhD); musical arts (DMA); piano performance artist (Certificate); vocal performance artist (Certificate). *Accreditation:* NASM. Part-time and evening/weekend programs available. *Faculty:* 23 full-time (9 women), 20 part-time/adjunct (11 women). *Students:* 21 full-time (11 women), 44 part-time (28 women); includes 11 minority (6 African Americans, 3 Asian Americans or Pacific Islanders, 2 Hispanic Americans), 1 international. Average age 30. 46 applicants, 57% accepted, 15 enrolled. In 2009, 25 master's awarded. *Degree requirements:* For master's, recital (for all except MM in music education), summer auditions, portfolios, compositions. *Entrance requirements:* For master's, 2 letters of recommendation. Additional exam requirements/recommendations for international students: Required—TOEFL. *Application deadline:* For fall admission, 4/1 priority date for domestic students; for spring admission, 11/1 priority date for domestic students. Applications are processed on a rolling basis. Application fee: $75. Electronic applications accepted. *Expenses:* Contact institution. *Financial support:* Fellowships with partial tuition reimbursements, research assistantships, teaching assistantships with partial tuition reimbursements, unspecified assistantships and health care benefits (full-time research or teaching assistantship recipients) available. Financial award application deadline: 3/1; financial award applicants required to submit FAFSA. *Faculty research:* Single or multiple instruments, music education, composition, conducting, pedagogy. Total annual research expenditures: $25,586. *Unit head:* Mark Camphouse, Interim Director, 703-993-3598, Fax: 703-993-1394, E-mail: mcamphou@gmu.edu. *Application contact:* Victoria Salmon, Graduate Studies, 703-993-4541, E-mail: vsalmon@gmu.edu.

Georgia College & State University, Graduate School, College of Arts and Sciences, Department of Music, Milledgeville, GA 31061. Offers MM Ed. *Accreditation:* NASM. *Faculty:* 11 full-time (6 women). *Students:* 2 full-time (1 woman), 4 part-time (2 women). Average age 26. In 2009, 2 master's awarded. *Degree requirements:* For master's, comprehensive exam, thesis optional. *Entrance requirements:* For master's, GACE II or GRE, bachelor's degree in music education, 3 letters of recommendation. Additional exam requirements/recommendations for international students: Recommended—TOEFL (minimum score 550 paper-based; 213 computer-based; 79 iBT). *Application deadline:* For fall admission, 7/1 for domestic students; for spring admission, 11/15 for domestic students. Application fee: $40. Electronic applications accepted. *Expenses:* Tuition, area resident: Part-time $241 per credit hour. Tuition, state resident: full-time $4338. Tuition, nonresident: full-time $17,352; part-time $964 per credit hour. Required fees: $609 per semester. Tuition and fees vary according to course load and campus/location. *Financial support:* In 2009–10, 1 research assistantship was awarded. Financial award applicants required to submit FAFSA. *Unit head:* Dr. Jennifer Flory, Graduate Coordinator for Music Education, 478-445-4839, Fax: 478-445-1633, E-mail: jennifer.flory@gcsu.edu. *Application contact:* Dr. Jennifer Flory, Graduate Coordinator for Music Education, 478-445-4839, Fax: 478-445-1633, E-mail: jennifer.flory@gcsu.edu.

Georgia State University, College of Education, Department of Middle-Secondary Education and Instructional Technology, Programs in Secondary Education, Atlanta, GA 30302-3083. Offers art education (Ed S); English education (M Ed, Ed S); mathematics education (M Ed, PhD, Ed S); music education (PhD); science education (M Ed, PhD, Ed S); social studies education (M Ed, PhD, Ed S). *Accreditation:* NASM (one or more programs are accredited); NCATE. Part-time and evening/weekend programs available. *Degree requirements:* For master's, comprehensive exam; for doctorate, comprehensive exam, thesis/dissertation; for Ed S, project/exam. *Entrance requirements:* For master's, GRE General Test, minimum GPA of 2.5; for doctorate, GRE General Test or MAT, minimum GPA of 3.3; for Ed S, GRE General Test or MAT, minimum graduate GPA of 3.25. *Faculty research:* Women and science, problem solving in mathematics, dialects, economic education.

Gordon College, Graduate Education, Wenham, MA 01984-1899. Offers education (M Ed, MAT); music education (MME). *Accreditation:* NASM. Part-time and evening/weekend programs available. *Entrance requirements:* For master's, GRE or MAT, references. Additional exam requirements/recommendations for international students: Required—TOEFL (minimum score 550 paper-based; 213 computer-based). *Faculty research:* Reading, early childhood development, ELL (English Language Learners).

Hampton University, Graduate College, Department of Education, Program in Teaching, Hampton, VA 23668. Offers early childhood education (MT); middle school education (MT); music education (MT); secondary education (MT); special education (MT). *Entrance requirements:* For master's, GRE General Test.

Hardin-Simmons University, Graduate School, School of Music and Fine Arts, Abilene, TX 79698-0001. Offers church music (MM); music education (MM); music performance (MM); theory-composition (MM). *Accreditation:* NASM. Part-time programs available. *Faculty:* 13 full-time (3 women), 1 (woman) part-time/adjunct. *Students:* 6 full-time (2 women), 10 part-time (6 women). Average age 28. 7 applicants, 100% accepted, 3 enrolled. In 2009, 5 master's awarded. *Degree requirements:* For master's, one foreign language, comprehensive exam, thesis (for some programs). *Entrance requirements:* For master's, minimum undergraduate GPA of 3.0 in major, 2.7 overall; performance; writing sample; demonstrated knowledge in chosen area. Additional exam requirements/recommendations for international students: Required—TOEFL (minimum score 550 paper-based; 213 computer-based; 75 iBT). *Application deadline:* For fall admission, 8/15 priority date for domestic students, 4/1 for international students; for spring admission, 1/5 priority date for domestic students, 9/1 for international students. Applications are processed on a rolling basis. Application fee: $50. *Expenses:* Tuition: Full-time $11,430; part-time $635 per credit hour. Required fees: $650; $110 per semester. Tuition and fees vary according to degree level. *Financial support:* In 2009–10, 13 students received support; fellowships, career-related internships or fieldwork and scholarships/grants available. Support available to part-time students. Financial award application deadline: 6/30; financial award applicants required to submit FAFSA. *Unit head:* Dr. Leigh Anne Hunsaker, Director, 325-670-1391, Fax: 325-670-5873, E-mail: hunsaker@hsutx.edu. *Application contact:* Dr. Gary Stanlake, Dean of Graduate Studies, 325-670-1298, Fax: 325-670-1564, E-mail: gradoff@hsutx.edu.

Hebrew College, Program in Jewish Studies, Newton Centre, MA 02459. Offers Jewish liturgical music (Certificate); Jewish music education (Certificate); Jewish studies (MA). Part-time and evening/weekend programs available. Postbaccalaureate distance learning degree programs offered (minimal on-campus study). *Degree requirements:* For master's, one foreign language. *Entrance requirements:* For master's, GRE, interview. Additional exam requirements/recommendations for international students: Required—TOEFL.

Heidelberg University, Program in Music Education, Tiffin, OH 44883-2462. Offers MME. Summer program only. Part-time programs available. *Faculty:* 4 full-time (0 women). *Students:* 9 part-time (all women). Average age 35. 11 applicants, 100% accepted, 9 enrolled. *Entrance requirements:* For master's, BS in music education, minimum GPA of 2.2. Additional exam requirements/recommendations for international students: Required—TOEFL. *Application deadline:* Applications are processed on a rolling basis. Application fee: $25. *Expenses:* Tuition: Part-time $415 per credit hour. *Financial support:* Applicants required to submit FAFSA. *Unit head:* Dr. John Owen, Program Director, 419-448-2085, E-mail: jowen@heidelberg.edu. *Application contact:* Melissa Nye, Administrative Assistant, Graduate Studies Office, 419-448-2288, Fax: 419-448-2072, E-mail: mnye@heidelberg.edu.

Hofstra University, School of Education, Health, and Human Services, Department of Curriculum and Teaching, Program in Music Education, Hempstead, NY 11549. Offers music education (MA, MS Ed); wind conducting (MA). Part-time programs available. *Students:* 16 full-time (8 women), 25 part-time (19 women); includes 10 minority (4 African Americans, 1 Asian American or Pacific Islander, 5 Hispanic Americans). Average age 26. 24 applicants, 100% accepted, 16 enrolled. In 2009, 19 master's awarded. *Degree requirements:* For master's, one foreign language, thesis (for some programs). *Entrance requirements:* For master's, 2 letters of recommendation, teacher certification (MA). Additional exam requirements/recommendations for international students: Required—TOEFL (minimum score 550 paper-based; 213 computer-based; 80 iBT). *Application deadline:* Applications are processed on a rolling basis. Application fee: $60. Electronic applications accepted. *Expenses:* Tuition: Full-time $16,200; part-time $900 per credit hour. Required fees: $970; $145 per term. Tuition and fees vary according to program. *Financial support:* In 2009–10, 14 students received support, including 5 fellowships with full and partial tuition reimbursements available (averaging $4,290 per year), 1 research assistantship with full and partial tuition reimbursement available (averaging $500 per year); Federal Work-Study, institutionally sponsored loans, scholarships/grants, tuition waivers (full and partial), and unspecified assistantships also available. Support available to part-time students. Financial award applicants required to submit FAFSA. *Faculty research:* Creative thinking, musical thinking, curriculum design, teaching preparation. *Unit head:* Dr. Nathalie G. Robinson, Program Director, 516-463-4514, Fax: 516-463-6393, E-mail: musngr@hofstra.edu. *Application contact:* Carol Drummer, Dean of Graduate Admissions, 516-463-4876, Fax: 516-463-4664, E-mail: gradstudent@hofstra.edu.

Holy Names University, Graduate Division, Department of Music, Oakland, CA 94619-1699. Offers Kodaly specialist certificate (Certificate); Kodaly summer certificate (Certificate); music

Music Education

Holy Names University (continued)
education with Kodaly emphasis (MM); piano pedagogy (MM); piano pedagogy with Suzuki emphasis (MM); vocal pedagogy (MM). *Degree requirements:* For master's, comprehensive exam, recital. *Entrance requirements:* For master's, audition, minimum undergraduate GPA of 2.6 overall, 3.0 in major. Additional exam requirements/recommendations for international students: Required—TOEFL (minimum score 550 paper-based; 213 computer-based; 80 iBT). *Faculty research:* Performance practice with special interest in baroque, Romantic, and twentieth-century instrumental and vocal music, choral pedagogy, Hungarian music education.

Howard University, Graduate School, Division of Fine Arts, Department of Music, Washington, DC 20059-0002. Offers applied music (MM); instrument (MM Ed); jazz studies (MM); organ (MM Ed); piano (MM Ed); voice (MM Ed). *Accreditation:* NASM. Part-time programs available. *Degree requirements:* For master's, comprehensive exam, thesis or alternative, departmental qualifying exam, recital. *Entrance requirements:* For master's, minimum GPA of 3.0, bachelor's degree in music or music education. Additional exam requirements/recommendations for international students: Required—TOEFL.

Hunter College of the City University of New York, Graduate School, School of Arts and Sciences, Department of Music, New York, NY 10021-5085. Offers music (MA); music education (MA). Part-time and evening/weekend programs available. *Faculty:* 12 full-time (3 women), 2 part-time/adjunct (1 woman). *Students:* 3 full-time (all women), 30 part-time (18 women); includes 9 minority (1 African American, 8 Asian Americans or Pacific Islanders). Average age 32. 33 applicants, 52% accepted, 12 enrolled. In 2009, 13 master's awarded. *Degree requirements:* For master's, one foreign language, thesis, composition, essay, or recital; proficiency exam. *Entrance requirements:* For master's, undergraduate major in music (minimum 24 credits) or equivalent, sample of work, research paper. Additional exam requirements/recommendations for international students: Required—TOEFL. *Application deadline:* For fall admission, 4/1 for domestic students, 2/1 for international students; for spring admission, 11/1 for domestic students, 9/1 for international students. Applications are processed on a rolling basis. Application fee: $125. *Expenses:* Tuition, state resident: full-time $7360; part-time $310 per credit. Required fees: $250 per semester. *Financial support:* In 2009–10, 4 fellowships (averaging $1,000 per year) were awarded; Federal Work-Study, tuition waivers (partial), and lesson stipends also available. Support available to part-time students. Financial award application deadline: 4/15. *Faculty research:* African and African-American music, Bach, Renaissance music, early romantic music, theory of tonal music. *Unit head:* Dr. Ruth DeFord, Department Chair, 212-772-5026, Fax: 212-772-5022, E-mail: ruth.deford@hunter.cuny.edu. *Application contact:* L. Pondie Burstein, Graduate Adviser, 212-772-5152, E-mail: huntermust@aol.com.

Hunter College of the City University of New York, Graduate School, School of Education, Program in Music Education, New York, NY 10021-5085. Offers MA. *Accreditation:* NCATE. *Faculty:* 12 full-time (3 women), 2 part-time/adjunct (1 woman). *Students:* 5 full-time (2 women), 25 part-time (13 women); includes 7 minority (5 Asian Americans or Pacific Islanders, 2 Hispanic Americans). Average age 32. 24 applicants, 58% accepted, 11 enrolled. In 2009, 14 master's awarded. *Degree requirements:* For master's, one foreign language, comprehensive exam, thesis, professional teaching portfolio, New York State Teacher Certification Exams. *Entrance requirements:* For master's, minimum GPA of 2.8, 2 letters of reference. Additional exam requirements/recommendations for international students: Required—TOEFL, TWE. *Application deadline:* For fall admission, 4/1 for domestic students, 2/1 for international students; for spring admission, 11/1 for domestic students, 9/1 for international students. Applications are processed on a rolling basis. Application fee: $125. *Expenses:* Tuition, state resident: full-time $7360; part-time $310 per credit. Required fees: $250 per semester. *Financial support:* Federal Work-Study and tuition waivers (partial) available. Support available to part-time students. *Unit head:* Dr. Poundie Burstein, Music Department Adviser, 212-772-5154, E-mail: huntermust@aol.com. *Application contact:* Carla Asher, Education Advisor, 212-772-4651, E-mail: carla.asher@hunter.cuny.edu.

Indiana University of Pennsylvania, School of Graduate Studies and Research, College of Fine Arts, Department of Music and Music Education, Program in Music, Indiana, PA 15705-1087. Offers music education (MA); music history and literature (MA); music theory and composition (MA); performance (MA). *Accreditation:* NASM. Part-time programs available. *Faculty:* 14 full-time (6 women). *Students:* 10 full-time (4 women), 5 part-time (3 women). Average age 29. 17 applicants, 41% accepted, 4 enrolled. In 2009, 4 master's awarded. *Degree requirements:* For master's, thesis optional. *Entrance requirements:* For master's, 2 letters of recommendation, audition. Additional exam requirements/recommendations for international students: Required—TOEFL. *Application deadline:* For fall admission, 7/1 priority date for domestic students; for spring admission, 11/1 for domestic students. Applications are processed on a rolling basis. Application fee: $40. *Expenses:* Tuition, state resident: full-time $6666; part-time $370 per credit hour. Tuition, nonresident: full-time $10,666; part-time $593 per credit hour. Required fees: $813 per semester. *Financial support:* In 2009–10, 5 research assistantships with full and partial tuition reimbursements (averaging $4,906 per year) were awarded; fellowships, Federal Work-Study also available. Support available to part-time students. Financial award application deadline: 3/15; financial award applicants required to submit FAFSA. *Unit head:* Dr. Stephanie Caulder, Head, 724-357-4408, E-mail: stephanie.caulder@iup.edu. *Application contact:* Dr. Stephanie Caulder, Head, 724-357-4408, E-mail: stephanie.caulder@iup.edu.

Inter American University of Puerto Rico, Metropolitan Campus, Graduate Programs, Program in Music Education, San Juan, PR 00919-1293. Offers MM.

Inter American University of Puerto Rico, San Germán Campus, Graduate Studies Center, Program in Music Education, San Germán, PR 00683-5008. Offers MA. Part-time and evening/weekend programs available.

Ithaca College, Division of Graduate and Professional Studies, School of Music, Program in Music and Music Education, Ithaca, NY 14850. Offers composition (MM); conducting (MM); music education (MM, MS); performance (MM); Suzuki pedagogy (MM). *Accreditation:* NASM. Part-time programs available. *Faculty:* 58 full-time (21 women), 2 part-time/adjunct (1 woman). *Students:* 42 full-time (17 women), 2 part-time (1 woman); includes 2 minority (1 African American, 1 Hispanic American), 1 international. Average age 24. 154 applicants, 45% accepted, 25 enrolled. In 2009, 29 master's awarded. *Degree requirements:* For master's, comprehensive exam, thesis (for some programs). *Entrance requirements:* For master's, audition, minimum GPA of 3.0. Additional exam requirements/recommendations for international students: Required—TOEFL (minimum score 550 paper-based; 213 computer-based; 80 iBT). *Application deadline:* For fall admission, 3/1 for domestic and international students; for spring admission, 12/1 for domestic and international students. Applications are processed on a rolling basis. Application fee: $40. Electronic applications accepted. *Expenses:* Tuition: Full-time $18,960; part-time $632 per credit hour. *Financial support:* In 2009–10, 42 students received support, including 38 teaching assistantships (averaging $8,459 per year); career-related internships or fieldwork, Federal Work-Study, scholarships/grants, and unspecified assistantships also available. Support available to part-time students. Financial award application deadline: 4/1; financial award applicants required to submit CSS PROFILE or FAFSA. *Faculty research:* Musical performance and performance studies; musical composition; music theory and analysis; music education, teaching and learning; musical direction and conducting. *Unit head:* Dr. Timothy Johnson, Chairperson, Graduate Studies in Music, 607-274-3527, Fax: 607-274-1263, E-mail: gps@ithaca.edu. *Application contact:* Rob Gearhart, Dean, Graduate and Professional Studies, 607-274-3527, Fax: 607-274-1263, E-mail: gps@ithaca.edu.

Jackson State University, Graduate School, School of Liberal Arts, Department of Music, Jackson, MS 39217. Offers music education (MM Ed). *Accreditation:* NASM. Part-time and evening/weekend programs available. *Degree requirements:* For master's, comprehensive exam, thesis or alternative. *Entrance requirements:* For master's, GRE General Test. Additional exam requirements/recommendations for international students: Required—TOEFL.

Jacksonville University, College of Arts and Sciences, School of Education, Program in Music Education, Jacksonville, FL 32211. Offers MAT. *Accreditation:* NASM. Part-time and evening/weekend programs available. *Degree requirements:* For master's, comprehensive exam. *Entrance requirements:* For master's, GRE General Test, minimum GPA of 3.0. Additional exam requirements/recommendations for international students: Required—TOEFL.

James Madison University, The Graduate School, College of Visual and Performing Arts, School of Music, Harrisonburg, VA 22807. Offers conducting (MM); music education (MM); musical arts (DMA); performance (MM); theory-composition (MM). *Accreditation:* NASM. Part-time programs available. *Faculty:* 32 full-time (10 women), 2 part-time/adjunct (both women). *Students:* 17 full-time (8 women), 5 part-time (3 women), 1 international. Average age 27. In 2009, 11 master's awarded. *Degree requirements:* For master's, comprehensive exam. *Entrance requirements:* For master's, GRE General Test, audition, undergraduate degree with major in music and minimum GPA of 3.0. Additional exam requirements/recommendations for international students: Required—TOEFL. *Application deadline:* For fall admission, 4/1 priority date for domestic students, 4/1 for international students; for spring admission, 4/1 priority date for domestic students, 4/1 for international students. Applications are processed on a rolling basis. Application fee: $55. Electronic applications accepted. *Expenses:* Tuition, area resident: Part-time $305 per credit hour. Tuition, state resident: part-time $305 per credit hour. Tuition, nonresident: part-time $890 per credit hour. *Financial support:* In 2009–10, 12 students received support, including 2 teaching assistantships with full tuition reimbursements available (averaging $8,664 per year); Federal Work-Study also available. Financial award application deadline: 3/1; financial award applicants required to submit FAFSA. *Unit head:* Dr. Jeffrey A. Showell, Academic Unit Head, 540-568-6197. *Application contact:* Dr. Mary Jane Speare, Graduate Coordinator, 540-568-6197.

Kansas State University, Graduate School, College of Arts and Sciences, Department of Music, Manhattan, KS 66506. Offers music education (MM); music education/band conducting (MM); music history and literature (MM); performance (MM); performance with pedagogy emphasis (MM); theory and composition (MM). *Accreditation:* NASM. Part-time programs available. *Faculty:* 23 full-time (8 women), 1 (woman) part-time/adjunct. *Students:* 12 applicants, 92% accepted. In 2009, 10 master's awarded. *Degree requirements:* For master's, thesis optional. *Entrance requirements:* For master's, GRE, audition (in person or recording), interview (music education). Additional exam requirements/recommendations for international students: Required—TOEFL (minimum score 600 paper-based). *Application deadline:* For fall admission, 2/1 priority date for domestic and international students; for spring admission, 8/1 priority date for domestic and international students. Applications are processed on a rolling basis. Application fee: $40 ($55 for international students). Electronic applications accepted. *Financial support:* In 2009–10, 12 teaching assistantships with full tuition reimbursements (averaging $7,500 per year) were awarded; institutionally sponsored loans, scholarships/grants, and tuition waivers (full and partial) also available. Support available to part-time students. Financial award application deadline: 3/1; financial award applicants required to submit FAFSA. *Faculty research:* Music since 1945, music by women composers, American music, opera, current performance practices. Total annual research expenditures: $12,026. *Unit head:* Dr. Gary Mortenson, Head, 785-532-3828, Fax: 785-532-7732, E-mail: garym@ksu.edu. *Application contact:* Fred Burrack, Director, 785-532-5764, Fax: 785-532-7732, E-mail: fburrack@ksu.edu.

Kent State University, College of the Arts, Hugh A. Glauser School of Music, Kent, OH 44242-0001. Offers composition (MA); conducting (MM); ethnomusicology (MA); music education (MM, PhD); musicology (MA); musicology-ethnomusicology (PhD); performance (MM); theory (MA); theory and composition (PhD). *Accreditation:* NASM. *Degree requirements:* For master's, variable foreign language requirement, comprehensive exam, 2 recitals, essay and recital, or thesis; for doctorate, variable foreign language requirement, comprehensive exam, thesis/dissertation. *Entrance requirements:* For master's, diagnostic exams in music history and theory, audition, minimum GPA of 2.75; for doctorate, diagnostic exams in music history and theory, master's thesis or scholarly paper, minimum GPA of 3.0. Additional exam requirements/recommendations for international students: Required—TOEFL. Electronic applications accepted. *Faculty research:* Music composition, performance, teaching and history.

Kutztown University of Pennsylvania, College of Visual and Performing Arts, Program in Music Education, Kutztown, PA 19530-0730. Offers Certificate. *Accreditation:* NASM. Part-time programs available. *Students:* 7 full-time (3 women), 5 part-time (0 women); includes 2 minority (1 African American, 1 Hispanic American). 7 applicants, 86% accepted, 4 enrolled. *Entrance requirements:* Additional exam requirements/recommendations for international students: Required—TOEFL. *Application deadline:* For fall admission, 8/15 priority date for domestic and international students; for spring admission, 12/15 priority date for domestic and international students. Applications are processed on a rolling basis. Application fee: $35. Electronic applications accepted. *Expenses:* Tuition, state resident: full-time $6666; part-time $370 per credit. Tuition, nonresident: full-time $10,666; part-time $593 per credit. Required fees: $62 per credit. $60 per semester. *Financial support:* Career-related internships or fieldwork, Federal Work-Study, scholarships/grants, and unspecified assistantships available. Financial award application deadline: 3/1; financial award applicants required to submit FAFSA. *Unit head:* Dr. Willis Rapp, Chairperson, 610-683-4551, Fax: 610-683-1506, E-mail: rapp@kutztown.edu. *Application contact:* Kelly D. Burr, Associate Director, Graduate Admissions, 610-683-4200, Fax: 610-683-1393, E-mail: graduate@kutztown.edu.

Lamar University, College of Graduate Studies, College of Fine Arts and Communication, Department of Music, Theatre, and Dance, Beaumont, TX 77710. Offers music education (MM Ed); music performance (MM); theatre (MS). *Accreditation:* NASM (one or more programs are accredited). *Faculty:* 8 full-time (2 women). *Students:* 5 full-time (3 women), 3 part-time (2 women); includes 1 minority (African American). Average age 29. 9 applicants, 44% accepted, 4 enrolled. In 2009, 3 master's awarded. *Degree requirements:* For master's, comprehensive exam, thesis optional. *Entrance requirements:* For master's, GRE General Test, theory placement exams, audition. Additional exam requirements/recommendations for international students: Required—TOEFL. *Application deadline:* For fall admission, 8/1 for domestic students; for spring admission, 12/1 for domestic students. Applications are processed on a rolling basis. Application fee: $25 ($50 for international students). *Financial support:* In 2009–10, 4 fellowships with tuition reimbursements (averaging $2,000 per year), 2 teaching assistantships were awarded; institutionally sponsored loans and tuition waivers (partial) also available. Support available to part-time students. Financial award application deadline: 4/1. *Faculty research:* Performance: ensembles and personal. *Unit head:* Dr. L. Randolph Babin, Chair, 409-880-8144, Fax: 409-880-8143, E-mail: babinlr@hal.lamar.edu. *Application contact:* Dr. Robert M. Culbertson, Adviser, 409-880-8073, Fax: 409-880-8143, E-mail: culbertsrm@hal.lamar.edu.

Lebanon Valley College, Graduate Studies and Continuing Education, Program in Music Education, Annville, PA 17003-1400. Offers MME. *Accreditation:* NASM. Part-time programs available. *Students:* 1 (woman) part-time. Average age 30. In 2009, 2 master's awarded. *Degree requirements:* For master's, thesis. *Entrance requirements:* For master's, minimum GPA of 3.0, teaching certificate. *Application deadline:* Applications are processed on a rolling basis. Application fee: $30. Electronic applications accepted. *Expenses:* Tuition: Full-time $32,740; part-time $410 per credit hour. Required fees: $610. *Financial support:* Application deadline: 5/1. *Unit head:* Dr. Marian T. Dura, Director, 717-867-6213. *Application contact:* Elaine D. Feather, Director of Graduate Studies and Continuing Education, 717-867-6213, Fax: 717-867-6018, E-mail: feather@lvc.edu.

Lee University, Program in Music, Cleveland, TN 37320-3450. Offers church music (MCM); music education (MM); music performance (MM). *Accreditation:* NASM. Part-time programs available. *Faculty:* 21 full-time (5 women), 14 part-time/adjunct (7 women). *Students:* 15 full-time (6 women), 20 part-time (8 women); includes 3 minority (all African Americans), 5 international. Average age 30. 9 applicants, 100% accepted, 8 enrolled. In 2009, 8 master's awarded. *Degree requirements:* For master's, variable foreign language requirement, comprehensive exam, thesis, internship. *Entrance requirements:* For master's, audition, resume, interview, minimum GPA of 2.75. Additional exam requirements/recommendations for international students: Required—TOEFL (minimum score 450 paper-based; 45 computer-based).

Application deadline: For fall admission, 4/1 for domestic students; for spring admission, 10/1 for domestic students. Applications are processed on a rolling basis. Application fee: $25. *Expenses:* Tuition: Full-time $11,100; part-time $463 per credit. Required fees: $305. *Financial support:* Teaching assistantships, career-related internships or fieldwork, Federal Work-Study, institutionally sponsored loans, and scholarships/grants available. Financial award application deadline: 3/1; financial award applicants required to submit FAFSA. *Unit head:* Dr. Jim W. Burns, Director, 423-614-8240, Fax: 423-614-8242, E-mail: gradmusic@leeuniversity.edu. *Application contact:* Vicki Glasscock, Graduate Admissions Director, 423-614-8059, E-mail: vglasscock@leeuniversity.edu.

Lehman College of the City University of New York, Division of Arts and Humanities, Department of Music, Bronx, NY 10468-1589. Offers MAT. *Accreditation:* NCATE. Part-time and evening/weekend programs available. *Entrance requirements:* For master's, audition. *Faculty research:* Music and music education.

Lehman College of the City University of New York, Division of Education, Department of Middle and High School Education, Program in Music Education, Bronx, NY 10468-1589. Offers MS Ed. Part-time and evening/weekend programs available.

Long Island University, C.W. Post Campus, School of Education, Department of Curriculum and Instruction, Brookville, NY 11548-1300. Offers adolescence education (MS); adolescence education: biology (MS); adolescence education: earth science (MS); adolescence education: English (MS); adolescence education: mathematics (MS); adolescence education: social studies (MS); adolescence education: Spanish (MS); art education (MS); bilingual education (MS); childhood education (MS); early childhood education (MS); middle childhood education (MS); music education (MS); teaching English to speakers of other languages (MS). Part-time and evening/weekend programs available. *Degree requirements:* For master's, comprehensive exam or thesis, student teaching. *Entrance requirements:* For master's, minimum GPA of 2.75 in major, 2.5 overall. Electronic applications accepted. *Faculty research:* Ethics and education, teaching strategies.

Long Island University, C.W. Post Campus, School of Education, Department of Music, Brookville, NY 11548-1300. Offers music education (MS).

Long Island University, C.W. Post Campus, School of Visual and Performing Arts, Department of Music, Brookville, NY 11548-1300. Offers music (MA); music education (MS). Part-time programs available. *Degree requirements:* For master's, thesis. *Entrance requirements:* For master's, GRE General Test (MA), GRE Subject Test in music, minimum undergraduate GPA of 3.0, 2 professional and/or academic letters of recommendation, current resume. Electronic applications accepted. *Faculty research:* Performance, composing, musicology, conducting, computer-based music technology.

Louisiana State University and Agricultural and Mechanical College, Graduate School, College of Music and Dramatic Arts, School of Music, Baton Rouge, LA 70803. Offers music (MM, DMA, PhD); music education (PhD). *Accreditation:* NASM. Part-time programs available. *Faculty:* 50 full-time (15 women), 1 (woman) part-time/adjunct. *Students:* 155 full-time (79 women), 44 part-time (23 women); includes 21 minority (10 African Americans, 4 Asian Americans or Pacific Islanders, 7 Hispanic Americans), 37 international. Average age 29. 171 applicants, 51% accepted, 55 enrolled. In 2009, 40 master's, 16 doctorates awarded. Terminal master's awarded for partial completion of doctoral program. *Degree requirements:* For doctorate, thesis/dissertation (for some programs). *Entrance requirements:* For master's, minimum GPA of 3.0, audition/interview; for doctorate, GRE General Test, minimum GPA of 3.0, audition/interview. Additional exam requirements/recommendations for international students: Required—TOEFL (minimum score 550 paper-based; 213 computer-based; 79 iBT) or IELTS (minimum score 6.5). *Application deadline:* For fall admission, 3/15 priority date for domestic students, 5/15 for international students; for spring admission, 10/15 for international students. Applications are processed on a rolling basis. Application fee: $50 ($70 for international students). Electronic applications accepted. *Financial support:* In 2009–10, 158 students received support, including 3 fellowships (averaging $31,007 per year), 2 research assistantships with full and partial tuition reimbursements available (averaging $15,250 per year), 84 teaching assistantships with full and partial tuition reimbursements available (averaging $10,673 per year); Federal Work-Study, institutionally sponsored loans, scholarships/grants, health care benefits, tuition waivers (full and partial), and unspecified assistantships also available. Support available to part-time students. Financial award applicants required to submit FAFSA. *Faculty research:* Music education, music literature, formal and harmonic analysis, pedagogy, performance. Total annual research expenditures: $65,241. *Unit head:* Dr. Jane Cassidy, Interim Dean, 225-578-3261, Fax: 225-578-2562. *Application contact:* Dr. Lori Bade, Director of Graduate Studies, 225-578-3261, Fax: 225-578-2562, E-mail: lbade1@lsu.edu.

Manhattanville College, Graduate Programs, School of Education, Program in Music Education, Purchase, NY 10577-2132. Offers MAT. Part-time and evening/weekend programs available. *Students:* 4 full-time (all women), 7 part-time (4 women). In 2009, 2 master's awarded. *Degree requirements:* For master's, comprehensive exam or research project, field experience. *Entrance requirements:* For master's, audition, minimum undergraduate GPA of 3.0, 2 letters of recommendation. Additional exam requirements/recommendations for international students: Required—TOEFL. *Application deadline:* Applications are processed on a rolling basis. Application fee: $70. Electronic applications accepted. *Financial support:* Career-related internships or fieldwork, Federal Work-Study, institutionally sponsored loans, and unspecified assistantships available. Support available to part-time students. Financial award application deadline: 3/1; financial award applicants required to submit FAFSA. *Unit head:* Dr. Shelley Wepner, Dean, 914-323-5192, Fax: 914-694-2386, E-mail: wepners@mville.edu. *Application contact:* Jeanine Pardey-Levine, Director of Admissions, 914-323-3208, Fax: 914-694-1732, E-mail: edschool@mville.edu.

Marywood University, Academic Affairs, Insalaco College of Creative and Performing Arts, Music, Theatre and Dance Department, Program in Music Education, Scranton, PA 18509-1598. Offers MA. *Accreditation:* NASM; NCATE. *Students:* 2 full-time (0 women), 5 part-time (4 women). Average age 30. In 2009, 3 master's awarded. *Entrance requirements:* Additional exam requirements/recommendations for international students: Required—TOEFL (minimum score 550 paper-based; 213 computer-based; 79 iBT). *Application deadline:* For fall admission, 4/1 priority date for domestic students, 3/31 priority date for international students; for spring admission, 11/1 priority date for domestic students, 8/31 priority date for international students. Applications are processed on a rolling basis. Application fee: $35. Electronic applications accepted. *Expenses:* Tuition: Part-time $715 per credit. Required fees: $270 per semester. Tuition and fees vary according to degree level, campus/location and program. *Financial support:* Career-related internships or fieldwork, scholarships/grants, and unspecified assistantships available. Support available to part-time students. Financial award application deadline: 6/30; financial award applicants required to submit FAFSA. *Application contact:* Tammy Manka, Assistant Director of Graduate Admissions, 866-279-9663, E-mail: tmanka@marywood.edu.

McGill University, Faculty of Graduate and Postdoctoral Studies, Schulich School of Music, Montréal, QC H3A 2T5, Canada. Offers composition (M Mus, D Mus, PhD); music education (MA, PhD); music technology (MA, PhD); musicology (MA, PhD); performance (M Mus); performance studies (D Mus); sound recording (M Mus, PhD); theory (MA, PhD).

McKendree University, Graduate Programs, Master of Arts in Education Program, Lebanon, IL 62254-1299. Offers certification (MA Ed); educational administration and leadership (MA Ed); educational studies (MA Ed); higher education administrative services (MA Ed); music education (MA Ed); special education (MA Ed); teacher leadership (MA Ed); transition to teaching (MA Ed). *Accreditation:* NCATE. Part-time and evening/weekend programs available. Postbaccalaureate distance learning degree programs offered (no on-campus study). *Faculty:* 18 full-time (7 women), 56 part-time/adjunct (34 women). *Students:* 107 full-time (83 women), 445 part-time (325 women); includes 41 minority (32 African Americans, 3 Asian Americans or Pacific Islanders, 6 Hispanic Americans). Average age 35. 225 applicants, 77% accepted, 129 enrolled. In 2009, 200 master's awarded. *Entrance requirements:* For master's, official transcripts from institutions attended, minimum GPA of 3.0, resume, references. Additional exam requirements/recommendations for international students: Required—TOEFL. *Application deadline:* Applications are processed on a rolling basis. Application fee: $0. Electronic applications accepted. *Expenses:* Tuition: Full-time $6300; part-time $350 per credit hour. One-time fee: $125. *Financial support:* In 2009–10, 1 student received support. Application deadline: 6/30. *Unit head:* Dr. Joseph J. Cipfl, Interim Chair of the School of Education, 618-537-6462, Fax: 618-537-6417, E-mail: jjcipfl@mckendree.edu. *Application contact:* Sabrina Storner, Director of Graduate Admission, 618-537-6477, Fax: 618-537-6410, E-mail: skstorner@mckendree.edu.

McNeese State University, Doré School of Graduate Studies, College of Liberal Arts, Department of Performing Arts, Program in Music Education, Lake Charles, LA 70609. Offers instrumental (MM Ed); vocal (MM Ed). *Accreditation:* NASM; NCATE. Evening/weekend programs available. *Faculty:* 8 full-time (2 women). *Students:* 1 full-time (0 women), 3 part-time (1 woman); includes 1 minority (African American). In 2009, 2 master's awarded. *Entrance requirements:* For master's, GRE, teaching certificate in music education. *Application deadline:* For fall admission, 5/15 priority date for domestic and international students; for spring admission, 10/15 priority date for domestic and international students. Applications are processed on a rolling basis. Application fee: $20 ($30 for international students). *Expenses:* Tuition, area resident: Full-time $2556. Tuition, state resident: full-time $2556. Required fees: $1031. Tuition and fees vary according to course load. *Financial support:* Teaching assistantships available. Financial award application deadline: 5/1. *Unit head:* Michele Martin, Head, 337-475-5028, Fax: 337-475-5063, E-mail: mmartin@mcneese.edu. *Application contact:* Dr. George F. Mead, Interim Dean of Dore' School of Graduate Studies, 337-475-5396, Fax: 337-475-5397, E-mail: admissions@mcneese.edu.

Miami University, Graduate School, School of Fine Arts, Department of Music, Oxford, OH 45056. Offers music education (MM); music performance (MM). *Accreditation:* NASM. *Students:* 21 full-time (8 women), 2 part-time (both women); includes 6 minority (3 African Americans, 1 Asian American or Pacific Islander, 2 Hispanic Americans), 1 international. *Entrance requirements:* For master's, audition, minimum undergraduate GPA of 3.0 during previous 2 years or overall. Application fee: $50. *Expenses:* Tuition, state resident: full-time $11,280. Tuition, nonresident: full-time $24,912. Required fees: $516. *Financial support:* Fellowships with full tuition reimbursements, research assistantships, teaching assistantships, Federal Work-Study, health care benefits, tuition waivers (full), and unspecified assistantships available. Financial award application deadline: 3/1. *Unit head:* Dr. Richard Green, Chair, 513-529-3014, Fax: 513-529-3027. *Application contact:* Chair, Graduate Studies, 513-529-3014, E-mail: music@muohio.edu.

Michigan State University, The Graduate School, College of Music, East Lansing, MI 48824. Offers collaborative piano (M Mus); jazz studies (M Mus); music (PhD); music composition (M Mus, DMA); music conducting (M Mus, DMA); music education (M Mus); music performance (M Mus, DMA); music theory (M Mus); music therapy (M Mus); musicology (MA); piano pedagogy (M Mus). *Accreditation:* NASM. *Faculty:* 57 full-time (14 women), 2 part-time/adjunct (0 women). *Students:* 234 full-time (120 women), 41 part-time (28 women); includes 30 minority (9 African Americans, 6 American Indian/Alaska Native, 10 Asian Americans or Pacific Islanders, 5 Hispanic Americans), 107 international. Average age 29. 378 applicants, 21% accepted. In 2009, 57 master's, 34 doctorates awarded. *Entrance requirements:* Additional exam requirements/recommendations for international students: Required—TOEFL. Electronic applications accepted. *Expenses:* Tuition, state resident: part-time $478.25 per credit hour. Tuition, nonresident: part-time $966.50 per credit hour. Part-time tuition and fees vary according to program. *Financial support:* In 2009–10, 15 research assistantships with tuition reimbursements (averaging $6,188 per year), 86 teaching assistantships with tuition reimbursements (averaging $6,110 per year) were awarded. *Unit head:* Prof. James B. Forger, Dean, 517-355-4583, Fax: 517-432-7081, E-mail: forger@msu.edu. *Application contact:* Anne Simon, Assistant to the Associate Dean for Graduate Studies and Research, 517-353-9122, Fax: 517-432-2880, E-mail: musgrad@msu.edu.

Minot State University, Graduate School, Division of Music, Minot, ND 58707-0002. Offers music education (MME). Program offered during summer only. *Accreditation:* NASM. *Degree requirements:* For master's, thesis or alternative. *Entrance requirements:* For master's, music exam, minimum GPA of 2.75. Additional exam requirements/recommendations for international students: Required—TOEFL. *Expenses:* Tuition, state resident: full-time $5720; part-time $283 per credit hour. Tuition, nonresident: full-time $5720; part-time $283 per credit hour. Required fees: $1034; $1034 per year. Tuition and fees vary according to course load, degree level and program. *Faculty research:* Music education.

Mississippi College, Graduate School, College of Arts and Sciences, School of Christian Studies and the Arts, Department of Music, Clinton, MS 39058. Offers applied music performance (MM); conducting (MM); music education (MM); music performance: organ (MM); vocal pedagogy (MM). *Accreditation:* NASM. Part-time and evening/weekend programs available. *Faculty:* 9 full-time (5 women), 5 part-time/adjunct (3 women). *Students:* 8 full-time (6 women), 7 part-time (5 women), 8 international. Average age 26. In 2009, 12 master's awarded. *Degree requirements:* For master's, comprehensive exam, recital. *Entrance requirements:* For master's, GRE, minimum GPA of 2.5. Additional exam requirements/recommendations for international students: Recommended—IELTS. *Application deadline:* For fall admission, 8/15 priority date for domestic and international students. Applications are processed on a rolling basis. Application fee: $30. Electronic applications accepted. *Expenses:* Tuition: Part-time $452 per credit hour. Required fees: $101 per semester. Tuition and fees vary according to degree level, campus/location, program and student level. *Financial support:* Teaching assistantships, Federal Work-Study, scholarships/grants, and unspecified assistantships available. Support available to part-time students. Financial award application deadline: 4/1; financial award applicants required to submit FAFSA. *Unit head:* Dr. James Meaders, Chair, 601-925-3441, Fax: 601-925-3945, E-mail: meaders@mc.edu. *Application contact:* Elnora Lewis, Secretary, 601-925-3225, Fax: 601-925-3889, E-mail: lewis09@mc.edu.

Missouri State University, Graduate College, College of Arts and Letters, Department of Music, Springfield, MO 65897. Offers music (MM), including conducting, music education, music pedagogy, music theory and composition, performance; secondary education (MS Ed), including music. *Accreditation:* NASM. Part-time programs available. *Faculty:* 24 full-time (9 women). *Students:* 13 full-time (9 women), 29 part-time (14 women); includes 1 minority (Asian American or Pacific Islander), 4 international. Average age 30. 14 applicants, 100% accepted, 8 enrolled. In 2009, 12 master's awarded. *Degree requirements:* For master's, comprehensive exam, thesis or alternative. *Entrance requirements:* For master's, GRE, interview/audition (MM), 9-12 teaching certification (MS Ed). Additional exam requirements/recommendations for international students: Required—TOEFL (minimum score 550 paper-based; 213 computer-based; 79 iBT). *Application deadline:* For fall admission, 7/20 for domestic students, 5/1 for international students; for spring admission, 12/20 for domestic students, 9/1 for international students. Applications are processed on a rolling basis. Application fee: $35 ($50 for international students). Electronic applications accepted. *Expenses:* Tuition, state resident: full-time $3852; part-time $214 per credit hour. Tuition, nonresident: full-time $7524; part-time $418 per credit hour. Required fees: $696; $172 per semester. Tuition and fees vary according to course level, course load, degree level and program. *Financial support:* In 2009–10, 10 teaching assistantships with full tuition reimbursements (averaging $7,340 per year) were awarded; Federal Work-Study, institutionally sponsored loans, scholarships/grants, tuition waivers (partial), and unspecified assistantships also available. Financial award application deadline: 3/31; financial award applicants required to submit FAFSA. *Faculty research:* Bulgarian violin literature, Ozarks fiddle music, carillon, nineteenth century piano. *Unit head:* Diane C. Strickland, Head, 417-836-4122, Fax: 417-836-7665, E-mail: music@missouristate.edu. *Application contact:* Eric Eckert, Coordinator of Graduate Admissions and Recruitment, 417-836-5331, Fax: 417-836-6888.

Montclair State University, The Graduate School, College of Education and Human Services, Department of Curriculum and Teaching, Montclair, NJ 07043-1624. Offers education (M Ed); educational technology (M Ed); learning disabled teacher consultant (Certificate); school library media specialist (Certificate); teaching (MAT, Certificate), including art (MAT), biological science

Music Education

Montclair State University (continued)

(MAT), early childhood education (P-3) (MAT), earth science (MAT), elementary education (K-8) (MAT), English (MAT), French (MAT), health and physical education (MAT), health education (MAT), home economics (MAT), mathematics (MAT), music (MAT), physical education (MAT), physical science (MAT), social studies (MAT), Spanish (MAT), teacher of ESL (MAT), teacher of students with disabilities (MAT). Part-time and evening/weekend programs available. *Faculty:* 17 full-time (12 women), 29 part-time/adjunct (21 women). *Students:* 124 full-time (63 women), 174 part-time (126 women). Average age 31. 112 applicants, 69% accepted, 59 enrolled. In 2009, 179 master's, 2 other advanced degrees awarded. *Degree requirements:* For master's, comprehensive exam, field experience. *Entrance requirements:* For master's, GRE, 2 letters of recommendation. Additional exam requirements/recommendations for international students: Required—TOEFL (minimum score 83 computer-based), or IELTS. *Application deadline:* For fall admission, 2/15 for domestic and international students; for spring admission, 9/15 for domestic and international students. Applications are processed on a rolling basis. Application fee: $60. Electronic applications accepted. *Expenses:* Tuition, area resident: Part-time $486.74 per credit. Tuition, state resident: part-time $486.74 per credit. Tuition, nonresident: part-time $751.34 per credit. Tuition and fees vary according to degree level and program. *Financial support:* In 2009–10, 12 research assistantships with full tuition reimbursements (averaging $7,000 per year) were awarded; Federal Work-Study, scholarships/grants, and unspecified assistantships also available. Support available to part-time students. Financial award application deadline: 3/1; financial award applicants required to submit FAFSA. *Unit head:* Dr. David Schwarzer, Chairperson, 973-655-5187. *Application contact:* Amy Aiello, Director of Graduate Admissions and Operations, 973-655-5147, Fax: 973-655-7869, E-mail: graduate.school@montclair.edu.

Montclair State University, The Graduate School, School of the Arts, Department of Music, Montclair, NJ 07043-1624. Offers music (AD); music education (MA); music therapy (MA); performance (MA, Certificate); theory/composition (MA). *Accreditation:* NASM. Part-time and evening/weekend programs available. *Faculty:* 19 full-time (7 women), 95 part-time/adjunct (41 women). *Students:* 21 full-time (11 women), 43 part-time (25 women). Average age 31. 44 applicants, 68% accepted, 21 enrolled. In 2009, 7 master's, 4 other advanced degrees awarded. *Degree requirements:* For master's, comprehensive exam, compositions, recitals, or thesis. *Entrance requirements:* For master's, GRE General Test, audition; teaching certificate (MA in music education). Additional exam requirements/recommendations for international students: Required—TOEFL (minimum score 83 computer-based), or IELTS. *Application deadline:* For fall admission, 6/1 for international students; for spring admission, 10/1 for international students. Applications are processed on a rolling basis. Application fee: $60. Electronic applications accepted. *Expenses:* Tuition, area resident: Part-time $486.74 per credit. Tuition, state resident: part-time $486.74 per credit. Tuition, nonresident: part-time $751.34 per credit. Tuition and fees vary according to degree level and program. *Financial support:* In 2009–10, 3 research assistantships with full tuition reimbursements (averaging $7,000 per year) were awarded; Federal Work-Study, scholarships/grants, and unspecified assistantships also available. Support available to part-time students. Financial award application deadline: 3/1; financial award applicants required to submit FAFSA. *Unit head:* Prof. Robert Aldridge, Chairperson, 973-655-7212. *Application contact:* Amy Aiello, Director of Graduate Admissions and Operations, 973-655-5147, Fax: 973-655-7869, E-mail: graduate.school@montclair.edu.

Morehead State University, Graduate Programs, Caudill College of Arts, Humanities and Social Sciences, Department of Music, Theatre and Dance, Morehead, KY 40351. Offers music education (MM); music performance (MM). *Accreditation:* NASM. Part-time and evening/weekend programs available. *Faculty:* 16 full-time (5 women). *Students:* 8 full-time (5 women), 12 part-time (5 women), 2 international. Average age 26. 13 applicants, 69% accepted, 7 enrolled. In 2009, 9 master's awarded. *Degree requirements:* For master's, comprehensive exam, oral and written exams. *Entrance requirements:* For master's, music entrance exam, BA in music with minimum GPA of 3.0, 2.5 overall; audition. Additional exam requirements/recommendations for international students: Required—TOEFL (minimum score 550 paper-based; 173 computer-based). *Application deadline:* For fall admission, 8/1 priority date for domestic and international students; for spring admission, 12/1 priority date for domestic and international students. Applications are processed on a rolling basis. Application fee: $30. Electronic applications accepted. *Expenses:* Tuition, state resident: full-time $6318; part-time $351 per credit hour. Tuition, nonresident: full-time $15,804; part-time $878 per credit hour. *Financial support:* In 2009–10, 9 research assistantships (averaging $10,000 per year) were awarded; career-related internships or fieldwork, Federal Work-Study, and unspecified assistantships also available. Financial award application deadline: 3/15; financial award applicants required to submit FAFSA. *Faculty research:* Musical instrument digital interface (MIDI) applications, tonal concepts of euphonium and baritone horn, digital synthesis, computer-assisted instruction in music, musical composition. *Unit head:* Dr. Curtis Hammond, Interim Department Chair, 606-783-2473, E-mail: l.hammon@moreheadstate.edu. *Application contact:* Michelle Barber, Graduate Recruitment and Retention Assistant Director, 606-783-5127, Fax: 606-783-5061, E-mail: m.barber@moreheadstate.edu.

Murray State University, College of Humanities and Fine Arts, Program in Music, Murray, KY 42071. Offers music education (MME). *Accreditation:* NASM. Part-time programs available. *Entrance requirements:* For master's, GRE General Test or MAT. Additional exam requirements/recommendations for international students: Required—TOEFL.

Nazareth College of Rochester, Graduate Studies, Department of Music, Program in Music Education, Rochester, NY 14618-3790. Offers MS Ed. *Accreditation:* NASM; Teacher Education Accreditation Council. Part-time and evening/weekend programs available. *Entrance requirements:* For master's, audition, minimum GPA of 3.0.

New Jersey City University, Graduate Studies and Continuing Education, William J. Maxwell College of Arts and Sciences, Department of Music, Dance and Theatre, Jersey City, NJ 07305-1597. Offers music education (MA); performance (MM). *Accreditation:* NASM. Part-time and evening/weekend programs available. *Faculty:* 5. *Students:* 9 full-time (4 women), 8 part-time (2 women); includes 2 minority (both Hispanic Americans), 2 international. Average age 33. In 2009, 2 master's awarded. *Degree requirements:* For master's, thesis optional, recital. *Entrance requirements:* For master's, GRE General Test or MAT. Additional exam requirements/recommendations for international students: Required—TOEFL. *Application deadline:* For fall admission, 8/1 priority date for domestic students; for spring admission, 12/1 for domestic students. Applications are processed on a rolling basis. Application fee: $0. *Expenses:* Tuition, area resident: Part-time $456.75 per credit. Tuition, nonresident: part-time $842.55 per credit. Required fees: $65 per term. *Financial support:* Unspecified assistantships available. *Unit head:* Dr. Edward Raditz, Chairperson, 201-200-3157, E-mail: eraditz@njcu.edu. *Application contact:* Dr. Edward Raditz, Chairperson, 201-200-3157, E-mail: eraditz@njcu.edu.

New Mexico State University, Graduate School, College of Arts and Sciences, Department of Music, Las Cruces, NM 88003-8001. Offers conducting (MM); music education (MM); performance (MM). *Accreditation:* NASM. Part-time programs available. *Faculty:* 10 full-time (4 women), 1 part-time/adjunct (0 women). *Students:* 12 full-time (4 women), 11 part-time (5 women); includes 6 minority (1 African American, 5 Hispanic Americans), 6 international. Average age 32. 19 applicants, 89% accepted, 12 enrolled. In 2009, 2 master's awarded. *Degree requirements:* For master's, comprehensive exam (for some programs), thesis (for some programs), recital. *Entrance requirements:* For master's, diagnostic exam, audition, bachelor's degree or equivalent from an accredited institution. Additional exam requirements/recommendations for international students: Required—TOEFL. *Application deadline:* For fall admission, 7/1 priority date for domestic students; for spring admission, 11/1 for domestic students. Applications are processed on a rolling basis. Application fee: $30 ($50 for international students). Electronic applications accepted. *Expenses:* Contact institution. *Financial support:* In 2009–10, 13 students received support, including 5 teaching assistantships (averaging $14,220 per year); fellowships, Federal Work-Study and health care benefits also available. Support available to part-time students. Financial award application deadline: 3/1. *Faculty research:* Music education, contemporary wind band literature, performance. *Unit head:* Dr. Ken Van Winkle, Head, 575-646-2421, Fax: 575-646-8199, E-mail: kvanwink@nmsu.edu. *Application contact:* Dr. Lisa Van Winkle, Assistant Professor, 575-646-2523, Fax: 575-646-2472, E-mail: lvanwink@nmsu.edu.

New York University, Steinhardt School of Culture, Education, and Human Development, Department of Music and Performing Arts Professions, Program in Music Education, New York, NY 10012-1019. Offers MA, Ed D, PhD, Advanced Certificate. *Accreditation:* Teacher Education Accreditation Council. Part-time programs available. *Students:* 31 full-time (24 women), 24 part-time (17 women); includes 10 minority (2 African Americans, 7 Asian Americans or Pacific Islanders, 1 Hispanic American), 15 international. Average age 29. 50 applicants, 78% accepted, 13 enrolled. In 2009, 14 master's, 2 doctorates, 4 other advanced degrees awarded. *Degree requirements:* For master's, thesis (for some programs); for doctorate, thesis/dissertation. *Entrance requirements:* For master's, audition; for doctorate, GRE General Test, interview; for Advanced Certificate, master's degree. Additional exam requirements/recommendations for international students: Required—TOEFL. *Application deadline:* For fall admission, 12/15 priority date for domestic and international students; for spring admission, 11/1 for domestic and international students. Applications are processed on a rolling basis. Application fee: $75. Electronic applications accepted. *Expenses:* Tuition: Full-time $30,528; part-time $1272 per credit. Required fees: $2177. *Financial support:* Fellowships with full and partial tuition reimbursements, career-related internships or fieldwork, Federal Work-Study, scholarships/grants, and tuition waivers (partial) available. Support available to part-time students. Financial award application deadline: 2/1; financial award applicants required to submit FAFSA. *Faculty research:* Music education philosophy; community music education; integrated curriculum; multiple intelligences; technology in arts education; cognition, emotion, and music. *Unit head:* Dr. David Elliott, Director, 212-998-5424, E-mail: david.elliott@nyu.edu. *Application contact:* 212-998-5030, Fax: 212-995-4328, E-mail: steinhardt.gradadmissions@nyu.edu.

New York University, Steinhardt School of Culture, Education, and Human Development, Department of Music and Performing Arts Professions, Program in Music Performance and Composition, New York, NY 10012-1019. Offers instrumental performance (MM), including jazz instrumental performance; music theory and composition (MM, PhD), including scoring for film and multimedia (MM); piano performance (MM), including collaborative performance, solo piano; vocal pedagogy (Advanced Certificate); vocal performance (MM), including classical voice, music theatre performance; MM/Advanced Certificate. Part-time programs available. *Students:* 205 full-time (81 women), 78 part-time (37 women); includes 33 minority (7 African Americans, 14 Asian Americans or Pacific Islanders, 12 Hispanic Americans), 90 international. Average age 28. 396 applicants, 58% accepted, 133 enrolled. In 2009, 97 master's, 4 doctorates awarded. *Degree requirements:* For master's, thesis (for some programs); for doctorate, thesis/dissertation. *Entrance requirements:* For master's, audition; for doctorate, GRE General Test, audition, interview. Additional exam requirements/recommendations for international students: Required—TOEFL. *Application deadline:* For fall admission, 12/15 priority date for domestic and international students; for spring admission, 11/1 for domestic and international students. Applications are processed on a rolling basis. Application fee: $75. Electronic applications accepted. *Expenses:* Tuition: Full-time $30,528; part-time $1272 per credit. Required fees: $2177. *Financial support:* Fellowships with full and partial tuition reimbursements, Federal Work-Study, scholarships/grants, and tuition waivers (partial) available. Support available to part-time students. Financial award application deadline: 2/1; financial award applicants required to submit FAFSA. *Faculty research:* Aesthetics, performance analysis, twentieth century music, music methodologies for arts criticism and analysis. *Application contact:* 212-998-5030, Fax: 212-995-4328, E-mail: steinhardt.gradadmissions@nyu.edu.

Norfolk State University, School of Graduate Studies, School of Liberal Arts, Department of Music, Norfolk, VA 23504. Offers music (MM); music education (MM); performance (MM); theory and composition (MM). *Accreditation:* NASM. Part-time programs available. *Degree requirements:* For master's, thesis or alternative. *Entrance requirements:* For master's, minimum GPA of 2.7, letters of recommendation. Additional exam requirements/recommendations for international students: Required—TOEFL.

North Dakota State University, College of Graduate and Interdisciplinary Studies, College of Human Development and Education, School of Education, Fargo, ND 58108. Offers agricultural education (M Ed, MS), including agricultural education, agricultural extension education (MS); counseling (M Ed, MS, PhD); curriculum and instruction (M Ed, MS), including pedagogy, physical education and athletic administration; education (PhD); educational leadership (M Ed, MS, Ed S); family and consumer sciences education (M Ed, MS); history education (M Ed, MS); institutional analysis (Ed D); mathematics education (M Ed, MS); music education (M Ed, MS); occupational and adult education (Ed D); science education (M Ed, MS). *Accreditation:* NCATE. Part-time and evening/weekend programs available. Postbaccalaureate distance learning degree programs offered (minimal on-campus study). *Faculty:* 25 full-time (9 women), 3 part-time/adjunct (1 woman). *Students:* 29 full-time (25 women), 207 part-time (132 women); includes 15 minority (4 African Americans, 6 American Indian/Alaska Native, 3 Asian Americans or Pacific Islanders, 2 Hispanic Americans), 4 international. 88 applicants, 67% accepted, 56 enrolled. In 2009, 44 master's, 5 doctorates awarded. *Degree requirements:* For master's, comprehensive exam; for doctorate, thesis/dissertation; for Ed S, thesis. *Entrance requirements:* For degree, GRE General Test, master's degree, minimum GPA of 3.25. Additional exam requirements/recommendations for international students: Required—TOEFL. *Application deadline:* Applications are processed on a rolling basis. Application fee: $45 ($60 for international students). *Financial support:* Research assistantships, teaching assistantships, career-related internships or fieldwork, Federal Work-Study, institutionally sponsored loans, and tuition waivers (full) available. Financial award application deadline: 4/15. *Unit head:* Dr. William Martin, Chair, 701-231-7202, Fax: 701-231-7416, E-mail: william.martin@ndsu.edu. *Application contact:* Dr. William Martin, Chair, 701-231-7202, Fax: 701-231-7416, E-mail: william.martin@ndsu.edu.

Northwestern University, Henry and Leigh Bienen School of Music, Department of Music Studies, Evanston, IL 60208. Offers music composition (DM); music education (MM, PhD); music theory (MM, PhD); musicology (MM, PhD). PhD admissions and degree offered through The Graduate School. *Accreditation:* NASM. *Faculty:* 20 full-time (5 women). *Students:* 34 full-time (20 women). 176 applicants, 20% accepted, 18 enrolled. In 2009, 28 master's, 7 doctorates awarded. *Degree requirements:* For doctorate, comprehensive exam, thesis/dissertation. *Entrance requirements:* For master's, portfolio or research papers; for doctorate, GRE General Test (PhD), portfolio, research papers. Additional exam requirements/recommendations for international students: Required—TOEFL (minimum score 600 paper-based; 250 computer-based; 100 iBT), TOEFL (minimum score 560 paper-based; 220 computer-based) or IELTS (minimum score 6). *Application deadline:* For fall admission, 12/15 for domestic and international students. Application fee: $55. *Financial support:* In 2009–10, 30 students received support, including 10 fellowships with full tuition reimbursements available (averaging $20,000 per year); research assistantships, teaching assistantships, Federal Work-Study, institutionally sponsored loans, scholarships/grants, tuition waivers (partial), and unspecified assistantships also available. Financial award application deadline: 5/1; financial award applicants required to submit FAFSA. *Faculty research:* Music cognition, cognitive learning, aesthetic education, computer music, technology in education. *Unit head:* Dr. Peter Webster, Chair, 847-491-1682, Fax: 847-491-5260, E-mail: pwebster@northwestern.edu. *Application contact:* Ryan O'Mealey, Associate Director, Admission and Financial Aid, 847-491-3141, Fax: 847-467-7440, E-mail: r-omealey@northwestern.edu.

Northwest Missouri State University, Graduate School, College of Arts and Sciences, Department of Music, Maryville, MO 64468-6001. Offers teaching music (MS Ed). *Accreditation:* NASM. Part-time programs available. *Faculty:* 4 full-time (0 women). *Students:* 3 full-time (2 women), 2 part-time (both women). 3 applicants, 100% accepted, 1 enrolled. In 2009, 3 master's awarded. *Degree requirements:* For master's, comprehensive exam. *Entrance requirements:* For master's, GRE General Test, minimum undergraduate GPA of 2.5, writing

sample. Additional exam requirements/recommendations for international students: Required—TOEFL (minimum score 550 paper-based; 213 computer-based). *Application deadline:* For fall admission, 7/1 for domestic and international students; for spring admission, 11/15 for domestic and international students. Applications are processed on a rolling basis. Application fee: $0 ($50 for international students). *Expenses:* Tuition, state resident: part-time $296.34 per credit hour. Tuition, nonresident: part-time $510.43 per credit hour. *Financial support:* In 2009–10, 1 research assistantship (averaging $6,000 per year), 3 teaching assistantships with full tuition reimbursements (averaging $6,000 per year) were awarded. Financial award application deadline: 4/1; financial award applicants required to submit FAFSA. *Unit head:* Dr. Ernest Woodruff, Chairperson, 660-562-1317. *Application contact:* Dr. Gregory Haddock, Dean of Graduate School, 660-562-1145, Fax: 660-562-1096, E-mail: gradsch@nwmissouri.edu.

Oakland University, Graduate Study and Lifelong Learning, College of Arts and Sciences, Department of Music, Rochester, MI 48309-4401. Offers music (MM); music education (PhD). *Accreditation:* NASM. *Entrance requirements:* For master's, minimum GPA of 3.0 for unconditional admission. Additional exam requirements/recommendations for international students: Required—TOEFL (minimum score 550 paper-based; 213 computer-based). Electronic applications accepted. *Expenses:* Contact institution.

Ohio University, Graduate College, College of Fine Arts, School of Music, Athens, OH 45701-2979. Offers accompanying (MM); composition (MM); conducting (MM); history/literature (MM); music education (MM); music therapy (MM); performance (MM, Certificate); performance/pedagogy (MM); theory (MM). *Accreditation:* NASM. Part-time and evening/weekend programs available. Postbaccalaureate distance learning degree programs offered (minimal on-campus study). *Faculty:* 35 full-time (10 women), 1 part-time/adjunct (0 women). *Students:* 42 full-time (19 women), 11 part-time (8 women); includes 5 minority (2 African Americans, 1 Asian American or Pacific Islander, 2 Hispanic Americans), 10 international. 85 applicants, 59% accepted, 22 enrolled. In 2009, 22 master's awarded. *Degree requirements:* For master's, comprehensive exam, thesis (for some programs), oral exam. *Entrance requirements:* For master's, audition, interview, portfolio, recordings (varies by program). Additional exam requirements/recommendations for international students: Required—TOEFL (minimum score 550 paper-based; 80 iBT) or IELTS Academic (minimum score 6.5). *Application deadline:* For fall admission, 1/1 priority date for domestic and international students. Application fee: $50 ($55 for international students). Electronic applications accepted. *Expenses:* Tuition, state resident: full-time $7839; part-time $323 per quarter hour. Tuition, nonresident: full-time $15,831; part-time $654 per quarter hour. Required fees: $2931. *Financial support:* In 2009–10, 35 teaching assistantships with full and partial tuition reimbursements (averaging $4,500 per year) were awarded; career-related internships or fieldwork, Federal Work-Study, institutionally sponsored loans, and tuition waivers (full and partial) also available. Financial award application deadline: 1/1. *Unit head:* Dr. W. Michael Parkinson, Director, 740-593-4244, Fax: 740-593-1429, E-mail: parkinsw@ohio.edu. *Application contact:* Dr. Richard Wetzel, Graduate Chair, 740-593-1652, Fax: 740-593-1429, E-mail: wetzel@ohio.edu.

Oklahoma State University, College of Arts and Sciences, Department of Music, Stillwater, OK 74078. Offers pedagogy and performance (MM). *Accreditation:* NASM. *Faculty:* 28 full-time (11 women), 6 part-time/adjunct (4 women). *Students:* 10 full-time (2 women), 3 part-time (1 woman). Average age 30. 22 applicants, 45% accepted, 5 enrolled. In 2009, 4 master's awarded. *Degree requirements:* For master's, final project, oral exam. *Entrance requirements:* For master's, GRE, audition. Additional exam requirements/recommendations for international students: Required—TOEFL (minimum score 550 paper-based; 79 iBT). *Application deadline:* For fall admission, 3/1 priority date for international students; for spring admission, 8/1 priority date for international students. Applications are processed on a rolling basis. Application fee: $40 ($75 for international students). Electronic applications accepted. *Expenses:* Tuition, state resident: full-time $3716; part-time $154.85 per credit hour. Tuition, nonresident: full-time $14,448; part-time $602 per credit hour. Required fees: $1772; $73.85 per credit hour. One-time fee: $50. Tuition and fees vary according to course load and campus/location. *Financial support:* In 2009–10, 11 teaching assistantships (averaging $8,041 per year) were awarded; career-related internships or fieldwork, Federal Work-Study, scholarships/grants, health care benefits, tuition waivers (partial), and unspecified assistantships also available. Support available to part-time students. Financial award application deadline: 3/1; financial award applicants required to submit FAFSA. *Faculty research:* Discovery and presentation of music literature of other countries, transportation of ancient music literature to modern notation. *Unit head:* Dr. Brant Adams, Head, 405-744-6133, Fax: 405-744-9324. *Application contact:* Dr. Gordon Emslie, Dean, 405-744-6368, Fax: 405-744-0355, E-mail: grad-i@okstate.edu.

Old Dominion University, College of Arts and Letters, Program in Music Education, Norfolk, VA 23529. Offers MME. *Accreditation:* NASM. Part-time and evening/weekend programs available. *Faculty:* 10 full-time (2 women), 4 part-time/adjunct (1 woman). *Students:* 4 full-time (3 women), 16 part-time (9 women); includes 3 minority (1 African American, 1 Asian American or Pacific Islander, 1 Hispanic American). Average age 35. 8 applicants, 88% accepted, 7 enrolled. In 2009, 9 master's awarded. *Degree requirements:* For master's, comprehensive exam, thesis (for some programs), recital. *Entrance requirements:* For master's, music theory exam, diagnostic examination, baccalaureate degree in music theory, history education, or applied music; audition. *Application deadline:* Applications are processed on a rolling basis. Application fee: $40. Electronic applications accepted. *Expenses:* Tuition, state resident: full-time $8112; part-time $338 per credit. Tuition, nonresident: full-time $20,256; part-time $844 per credit. Required fees: $119 per semester. One-time fee: $50. *Financial support:* In 2009–10, 1 teaching assistantship with partial tuition reimbursement (averaging $8,000 per year) was awarded; scholarships/grants and unspecified assistantships also available. *Faculty research:* Performance, composition, conducting, music education. *Unit head:* Dr. Nancy K. Klein, Graduate Program Director, 757-683-4061, E-mail: nklein@odu.edu. *Application contact:* Dr. Robert Wojtowicz, Associate Dean, 757-683-6077, Fax: 757-683-5746, E-mail: rwojtowi@odu.edu.

Oregon State University, Graduate School, College of Education, Program in Music Education, Corvallis, OR 97331. Offers MAT. *Students:* 6. In 2009, 2 master's awarded. *Degree requirements:* For master's, thesis optional. *Entrance requirements:* For master's, minimum GPA of 3.0 in last 90 hours of course work. Additional exam requirements/recommendations for international students: Required—TOEFL. *Application deadline:* For fall admission, 3/1 for domestic students. Applications are processed on a rolling basis. Application fee: $50. *Expenses:* Tuition, state resident: full-time $9774; part-time $362 per credit. Tuition, nonresident: full-time $15,849; part-time $587 per credit. Required fees: $1639. Full-time tuition and fees vary according to course load and program. *Financial support:* Teaching assistantships, career-related internships or fieldwork, Federal Work-Study, and institutionally sponsored loans available. Support available to part-time students. Financial award application deadline: 2/1. *Faculty research:* Teaching skills and methods, verbal and nonverbal classroom teaching techniques. *Unit head:* Dr. Kenneth J. Winograd, Chair, 541-737-5988, Fax: 541-737-2040, E-mail: winograk@oregonstate.edu. *Application contact:* Dr. Kenneth J. Winograd, Chair, 541-737-5988, Fax: 541-737-2040, E-mail: winograk@oregonstate.edu.

Pittsburg State University, Graduate School, College of Arts and Sciences, Department of Music, Pittsburg, KS 66762. Offers instrumental music education (MM); music history/music literature (MM); performance (MM), including orchestral performance, organ, piano, voice; theory and composition (MM); vocal music education (MM). *Accreditation:* NASM. *Degree requirements:* For master's, thesis or alternative. *Expenses:* Tuition, state resident: full-time $4212; part-time $176 per credit. Tuition, nonresident: full-time $11,530; part-time $480 per credit. Required fees: $940; $43 per credit. Tuition and fees vary according to course level, course load, degree level, campus/location, reciprocity agreements and student level.

Portland State University, Graduate Studies, School of Fine and Performing Arts, Department of Music, Portland, OR 97207-0751. Offers conducting (MMC); music education (MAT, MST); performance (MMP). *Accreditation:* NASM. Part-time programs available. *Degree requirements:* For master's, variable foreign language requirement, exit exam. *Entrance requirements:* For master's, GRE General Test, departmental exam, minimum GPA of 3.0 in upper-division course work or 2.75 overall. Additional exam requirements/recommendations for international students: Required—TOEFL (minimum score 550 paper-based; 213 computer-based). *Faculty research:* Composition, music analysis, music history, jazz.

Queens College of the City University of New York, Division of Graduate Studies, Division of Education, Department of Secondary Education, Flushing, NY 11367-1597. Offers art (MS Ed); biology (MS Ed, AC); chemistry (MS Ed, AC); earth sciences (MS Ed, AC); English (MS Ed, AC); French (MS Ed, AC); Italian (MS Ed, AC); mathematics (MS Ed, AC); music (MS Ed, AC); physics (MS Ed, AC); social studies (MS Ed, AC); Spanish (MS Ed, AC). Part-time and evening/weekend programs available. *Faculty:* 22 full-time (14 women). *Students:* 86 full-time (47 women), 1,118 part-time (736 women). 591 applicants, 60% accepted, 250 enrolled. In 2009, 187 master's awarded. *Degree requirements:* For master's, research project; for AC, thesis optional. *Entrance requirements:* For master's, minimum GPA of 3.0. Additional exam requirements/recommendations for international students: Required—TOEFL. *Application deadline:* For fall admission, 4/1 for domestic students; for spring admission, 11/1 for domestic students. Applications are processed on a rolling basis. Application fee: $125. *Expenses:* Tuition, state resident: full-time $7360; part-time $310 per credit. Tuition, nonresident: part-time $575 per credit. One-time fee: $195 full-time; $145.25 part-time. *Financial support:* Career-related internships or fieldwork, Federal Work-Study, institutionally sponsored loans, and tuition waivers (partial) available. Support available to part-time students. Financial award application deadline: 4/1; financial award applicants required to submit FAFSA. *Unit head:* Dr. Eleanor Armour-Thomas, Chairperson, 718-997-5150, E-mail: armourthomas@yahoo.com. *Application contact:* Mario Caruso, Director of Graduate Admissions, 718-997-5200, Fax: 718-997-5193, E-mail: graduate_admissions@qc.edu.

Radford University, College of Graduate and Professional Studies, College of Visual and Performing Arts, Department of Music, Radford, VA 24142. Offers music (MA); music education (MS); music therapy (MS). *Accreditation:* NASM. Part-time programs available. *Faculty:* 9 full-time (2 women), 3 part-time/adjunct (1 woman). *Students:* 12 full-time (8 women), 4 part-time (all women); includes 3 minority (all African Americans), 1 international. Average age 26. 8 applicants, 88% accepted, 4 enrolled. In 2009, 5 master's awarded. *Degree requirements:* For master's, comprehensive exam, thesis or alternative. *Entrance requirements:* For master's, GRE, major field test in music or PRAXIS II (content knowledge), written diagnostics exams in music, minimum GPA of 2.75; 3 letters of reference. Additional exam requirements/recommendations for international students: Required—TOEFL (minimum score 550 paper-based; 213 computer-based; 79 iBT). *Application deadline:* For fall admission, 12/1 for international students; for spring admission, 7/1 for international students. Applications are processed on a rolling basis. Application fee: $50. Electronic applications accepted. *Expenses:* Tuition, state resident: full-time $5086; part-time $211 per credit hour. Tuition, nonresident: full-time $12,608; part-time $525 per credit hour. Required fees: $2508; $105 per credit hour. *Financial support:* In 2009–10, 10 students received support, including 3 research assistantships with partial tuition reimbursements available (averaging $8,000 per year), 8 teaching assistantships with partial tuition reimbursements available (averaging $8,700 per year); career-related internships or fieldwork, Federal Work-Study, institutionally sponsored loans, scholarships/grants, and unspecified assistantships also available. Financial award application deadline: 3/1; financial award applicants required to submit FAFSA. *Unit head:* Dr. Allen F. Wojtera, Chair, 540-831-5177, Fax: 540-831-6133, E-mail: awojtera@radford.edu. *Application contact:* Graduate Admissions, 540-831-5431, Fax: 540-831-6061, E-mail: gradcollege@radford.edu.

Reinhardt University, Program in Music, Waleska, GA 30183-2981. Offers conducting (MM); music education (MM); piano pedagogy (MM). *Accreditation:* NASM. *Entrance requirements:* For master's, GRE, audition (for piano pedagogy and conducting), 2 letters of reference. Additional exam requirements/recommendations for international students: Required—TOEFL. *Application deadline:* For fall admission, 5/7 for domestic and international students. Applications are processed on a rolling basis. Application fee: $25. Electronic applications accepted. *Expenses:* Tuition: Full-time $16,500; part-time $325 per credit hour. One-time fee: $100. Tuition and fees vary according to course load and program. *Financial support:* Application deadline: 5/1. *Unit head:* Dr. Paula Thomas-Lee, Graduate Program Coordinator, 770-720-5658, E-mail: ptl@reinhardt.edu. *Application contact:* Ray Schumacher, Admissions Counselor, 770-993-6971, Fax: 770-475-0263, E-mail: res@reinhardt.edu.

Rhode Island College, School of Graduate Studies, Faculty of Arts and Sciences, Department of Music, Theatre, and Dance, Providence, RI 02908-1991. Offers music education (MAT, MM Ed); theatre (MFA). Part-time and evening/weekend programs available. *Faculty:* 8 full-time (2 women), 1 (woman) part-time/adjunct. *Students:* 4 full-time (1 woman), 4 part-time (3 women). Average age 33. In 2009, 6 master's awarded. *Degree requirements:* For master's, comprehensive exam, thesis, final project (MFA). *Entrance requirements:* For master's, GRE General Test or MAT, exams in music education, theory, history and literature, audition, 3 letters of recommendation, evidence of musicianship, interview. Additional exam requirements/recommendations for international students: Recommended—TOEFL (minimum score 550 paper-based; 213 computer-based; 79 iBT). *Application deadline:* For fall admission, 4/1 for domestic students; for spring admission, 11/1 for domestic students. Applications are processed on a rolling basis. Application fee: $50. *Expenses:* Tuition, state resident: full-time $7440; part-time $310 per credit hour. Tuition, nonresident: full-time $14,784; part-time $616 per credit hour. Required fees: $552; $20 per credit. $70 per term. *Financial support:* Teaching assistantships with full tuition reimbursements, Federal Work-Study, scholarships/grants, health care benefits, and unspecified assistantships available. Support available to part-time students. Financial award application deadline: 5/15; financial award applicants required to submit FAFSA. *Unit head:* Dr. James Taylor, Chair, 401-456-8639. *Application contact:* Graduate Studies, 401-456-8700.

Rollins College, Hamilton Holt School, Program in Education, Winter Park, FL 32789-4499. Offers elementary education (M Ed, MAT); secondary education (MAT), including English, mathematics, music. Part-time and evening/weekend programs available. *Faculty:* 5 full-time (3 women), 3 part-time/adjunct (2 women). *Students:* 14 full-time (11 women), 26 part-time (25 women); includes 7 minority (4 African Americans, 3 Hispanic Americans). Average age 31. 27 applicants, 100% accepted, 27 enrolled. In 2009, 10 master's awarded. *Degree requirements:* For master's, comprehensive exam. *Entrance requirements:* For master's, GRE or MAT, interview. Additional exam requirements/recommendations for international students: Required—TOEFL. *Application deadline:* For fall admission, 7/16 for domestic students; for winter admission, 12/3 for domestic students; for spring admission, 4/22 for domestic students. Applications are processed on a rolling basis. Application fee: $50. *Expenses:* Contact institution. *Financial support:* Teaching assistantships, scholarships/grants available. Support available to part-time students. *Unit head:* Dr. J. Scott Hewit, Director, 407-646-2300, E-mail: jhewit@rollins.edu. *Application contact:* Rebecca Cordray, Coordinator of Records and Registration, 407-646-1568, Fax: 407-975-6430, E-mail: rcordray@rollins.edu.

Roosevelt University, Graduate Division, Chicago College of Performing Arts, The Music Conservatory, Chicago, IL 60605. Offers music (MM); piano pedagogy (Diploma). *Accreditation:* NASM. Part-time and evening/weekend programs available.

Rutgers, The State University of New Jersey, New Brunswick, Mason Gross School of the Arts, Program in Music, Piscataway, NJ 08854-8097. Offers collaborative piano (MM, DMA); conducting: choral (MM, DMA); conducting: instrumental (MM, DMA); conducting: orchestral (MM, DMA); jazz studies (MM); music (DMA, AD); music education (MM, DMA); music performance (MM). *Accreditation:* NASM. *Degree requirements:* For doctorate, one foreign language. *Entrance requirements:* For doctorate, audition. Additional exam requirements/recommendations for international students: Required—TOEFL (minimum score 550 paper-based; 213 computer-based). Electronic applications accepted. *Faculty research:* Performance, twentieth century music, jazz.

St. Cloud State University, School of Graduate Studies, College of Fine Arts and Humanities, Department of Music, St. Cloud, MN 56301-4498. Offers conducting and literature (MM); music education (MM); piano pedagogy (MM). *Accreditation:* NASM. *Faculty:* 16 full-time (7 women), 1 part-time/adjunct (0 women). *Students:* 2 full-time (1 woman), 13 part-time (5

Music Education

St. Cloud State University (continued)

women); includes 1 minority (Asian American or Pacific Islander), 1 international. 4 applicants, 100% accepted. In 2009, 7 master's awarded. *Degree requirements:* For master's, comprehensive exam (for some programs), thesis or alternative. *Entrance requirements:* For master's, GRE General Test, minimum GPA of 2.75. Additional exam requirements/recommendations for international students: Required—Michigan English Language Assessment Battery; Recommended—TOEFL (minimum score 550 paper-based; 213 computer-based), IELTS (minimum score 6.5). *Application deadline:* For fall admission, 6/1 priority date for domestic students, 4/1 for international students; for spring admission, 10/1 priority date for domestic students, 8/1 for international students. Applications are processed on a rolling basis. Application fee: $35. Electronic applications accepted. *Financial support:* Federal Work-Study, scholarships/grants, and unspecified assistantships available. Financial award application deadline: 3/1. *Unit head:* Dr. Mark Springer, Chairperson, 320-308-3223, Fax: 320-308-2902. *Application contact:* Linda Lou Krueger, School of Graduate Studies, 320-308-2113, Fax: 320-308-5371, E-mail: lekrueger@stcloudstate.edu.

Samford University, School of the Arts, Birmingham, AL 35229. Offers church music (MM); music (MME), including instrumental, vocal choral; piano pedagogy (MM). *Accreditation:* NASM. Part-time programs available. *Faculty:* 7 full-time (3 women), 4 part-time/adjunct (1 woman). *Students:* 8 full-time (4 women), 4 part-time (2 women); includes 1 minority (African American), 1 international. Average age 27. 7 applicants, 71% accepted, 5 enrolled. In 2009, 9 master's awarded. *Degree requirements:* For master's, oral exams, comprehensive exam (MME). *Entrance requirements:* For master's, GRE General Test or MAT, institutional exam, minimum GPA of 3.0. Additional exam requirements/recommendations for international students: Required—TOEFL (minimum score 550 paper-based; 213 computer-based). *Application deadline:* For fall admission, 5/1 priority date for domestic students; for spring admission, 12/1 priority date for domestic students. Applications are processed on a rolling basis. Application fee: $35. *Expenses:* Tuition: Full-time $26,660; part-time $595 per credit hour. Required fees: $110 per semester. *Financial support:* In 2009–10, 11 students received support, including research assistantships (averaging $4,000 per year); Federal Work-Study, scholarships/grants, and tuition waivers (partial) also available. Financial award application deadline: 9/1. *Faculty research:* Hymnology, choral techniques, assessment of music learning at elementary and secondary levels, piano pedagogy, special education and inclusion, learning theories. *Unit head:* Dr. Joseph H. Hopkins, Dean, 205-726-2165, E-mail: jhhopkin@samford.edu. *Application contact:* Dr. Moya Nordlund, Director, Graduate Studies, 205-726-2651, Fax: 205-726-2165, E-mail: mlnordlu@samford.edu.

Sam Houston State University, College of Arts and Sciences, School of Music, Huntsville, TX 77341. Offers music (MM); music education (MM). *Accreditation:* NASM. Part-time programs available. *Faculty:* 14 full-time (3 women), 1 part-time/adjunct (0 women). *Students:* 11 full-time (6 women), 7 part-time (4 women); includes 2 minority (both Hispanic Americans), 4 international. Average age 31. 11 applicants, 91% accepted, 9 enrolled. In 2009, 13 master's awarded. *Degree requirements:* For master's, thesis (for some programs), departmental qualifying exam. *Entrance requirements:* For master's, GRE General Test. Additional exam requirements/recommendations for international students: Required—TOEFL (minimum score 550 paper-based; 213 computer-based; 79 iBT). *Application deadline:* For fall admission, 8/1 for domestic and international students; for spring admission, 12/1 for domestic and international students. Applications are processed on a rolling basis. Application fee: $20. *Expenses:* Tuition, state resident: full-time $3690; part-time $205 per credit hour. Tuition, nonresident: full-time $8676; part-time $482 per credit hour. Required fees: $1474. Tuition and fees vary according to course load and campus/location. *Financial support:* Teaching assistantships, Federal Work-Study and scholarships/grants available. Financial award application deadline: 5/31; financial award applicants required to submit FAFSA. *Unit head:* Dr. James Bankhead, Director, 936-294-3808, Fax: 936-294-3765, E-mail: bankhead@shsu.edu. *Application contact:* Scott Plugge, Advisor, 936-294-1393, E-mail: plugge@shsu.edu.

San Diego State University, Graduate and Research Affairs, College of Professional Studies and Fine Arts, School of Music and Dance, San Diego, CA 92182. Offers composition (acoustic and electronic) (MM); conducting (MM); ethnomusicology (MA); jazz studies (MM); musicology (MA); performance (MM); piano pedagogy (MA); theory (MA). *Degree requirements:* For master's, comprehensive exam (for some programs), thesis (for some programs). *Entrance requirements:* For master's, GRE General Test, bachelor's degree in related field, 2 letters of reference. Additional exam requirements/recommendations for international students: Required—TOEFL. Electronic applications accepted.

San Francisco State University, Division of Graduate Studies, College of Creative Arts, School of Music and Dance, San Francisco, CA 94132-1722. Offers chamber music (MM); classical performance (MM); composition (MA); conducting (MM); music education (MA); music history (MA). *Accreditation:* NASM.

Shenandoah University, Shenandoah Conservatory, Winchester, VA 22601-5195. Offers arts administration (MS); church music (MM, Certificate); composition (MM); conducting (MM); dance (MA, MS); music education (MME, DMA); music therapy (MMT, Certificate); pedagogy (MM, DMA); performance (MM, DMA, Artist Diploma); piano accompanying (MM). *Accreditation:* NASM. *Faculty:* 39 full-time (15 women), 17 part-time/adjunct (5 women). *Students:* 72 full-time (42 women), 134 part-time (83 women); includes 40 minority (14 African Americans, 22 Asian Americans or Pacific Islanders, 4 Hispanic Americans), 16 international. Average age 35. 115 applicants, 88% accepted, 70 enrolled. In 2009, 40 master's, 5 doctorates, 9 other advanced degrees awarded. *Degree requirements:* For master's, comprehensive exam (for some programs), thesis (for some programs), internship (MS), recital (MM), research teaching project or thesis (MME), project (MA); for doctorate, comprehensive exam, thesis/dissertation (for some programs), dissertation or teaching project, recital; for other advanced degree, research project, recital. *Entrance requirements:* For master's, audition, minimum GPA of 2.5, writing sample, resume; for doctorate, audition, minimum GPA of 3.25, 2 letters of recommendation, writing sample, resume; for other advanced degree, bachelor's or master's degree; minimum GPA of 2.5. Additional exam requirements/recommendations for international students: Required—TOEFL (minimum score 550 paper-based; 213 computer-based; 79 iBT), IELTS (minimum score 6.5). *Application deadline:* Applications are processed on a rolling basis. Application fee: $30. Electronic applications accepted. *Expenses:* Tuition: Full-time $11,925; part-time $695 per credit. Required fees: $400 per semester. *Financial support:* Application deadline: 3/15. *Unit head:* Dr. Laurence A. Kaptain, Dean, 540-665-4600, Fax: 540-665-5402, E-mail: lkaptain@su.edu. *Application contact:* David Anthony, Dean of Admissions, 540-665-4581, Fax: 540-665-4627, E-mail: admit@su.edu.

Silver Lake College, Division of Graduate Studies, Program in Music Education, Manitowoc, WI 54220-9319. Offers music education-Kodaly emphasis (MM). *Accreditation:* NASM. Part-time programs available. Postbaccalaureate distance learning degree programs offered (minimal on-campus study). *Faculty:* 2 full-time (both women), 3 part-time/adjunct (all women). *Students:* 7 part-time (all women). Average age 40. 5 applicants, 80% accepted, 0 enrolled. In 2009, 4 master's awarded. *Degree requirements:* For master's, comprehensive exam, thesis. *Entrance requirements:* For master's, music performance exam, exam in music history and theory and conducting, interview, minimum undergraduate GPA of 3.0, writing sample, three letters of recommendation, audition. Additional exam requirements/recommendations for international students: Required—TOEFL. *Application deadline:* For fall admission, 8/1 for domestic students; for spring admission, 12/1 for domestic students. Applications are processed on a rolling basis. Application fee: $50. Electronic applications accepted. *Expenses:* Tuition: Full-time $7380; part-time $410 per credit. Required fees: $10 per term. Part-time tuition and fees vary according to course load. *Financial support:* In 2009–10, 4 students received support. Career-related internships or fieldwork, Federal Work-Study, and scholarships/grants available. Support available to part-time students. Financial award applicants required to submit FAFSA. *Faculty research:* Effects of prenatal music on bonding and stimulation, music and the brain, early childhood music, effective use of Smart Music for choral and general music areas. *Unit head:* Sr. Lorna Zemke, Director, 920-686-6161, Fax: 920-684-7082, E-mail: lzemke@silver.sl.edu. *Application contact:* Jamie Grant, Associate Director of Admissions, 800-236-4752 Ext. 186, Fax: 920-686-6322, E-mail: jgrant@silver.sl.edu.

Southeast Missouri State University, School of Graduate Studies, Department of Music, Cape Girardeau, MO 63701-4799. Offers music education (MME). *Accreditation:* NASM; NCATE. Part-time programs available. *Degree requirements:* For master's, comprehensive exam (for some programs), thesis or alternative, project. *Entrance requirements:* For master's, departmental exam in music theory, BME or valid teaching certificate, audition, minimum undergraduate GPA of 3.0. Additional exam requirements/recommendations for international students: Required—TOEFL (minimum score 550 paper-based; 213 computer-based); Recommended—IELTS (minimum score 6). Electronic applications accepted. *Expenses:* Tuition, state resident: full-time $4266; part-time $237 per credit hour. Tuition, nonresident: full-time $7506; part-time $417 per credit hour. Required fees: $427; $427.

Southern Illinois University Carbondale, Graduate School, College of Liberal Arts, School of Music, Carbondale, IL 62901-4701. Offers composition and theory (MM); history and literature (MM); music education (MM); opera/music theater (MM); performance (MM); piano pedagogy (MM). *Accreditation:* NASM. Part-time programs available. *Degree requirements:* For master's, one foreign language, thesis or alternative. *Entrance requirements:* For master's, audition, minimum GPA of 2.7. Additional exam requirements/recommendations for international students: Required—TOEFL. *Faculty research:* Performance practices, historical research, operatic development.

Southern Illinois University Edwardsville, Graduate Studies and Research, College of Arts and Sciences, Department of Music, Program in Music, Edwardsville, IL 62026-0001. Offers music education (MM); music performance (MM). Part-time programs available. *Faculty:* 15 full-time (4 women). *Students:* 10 full-time (5 women), 24 part-time (15 women); includes 4 minority (1 African American, 2 Asian Americans or Pacific Islanders, 1 Hispanic American), 2 international. Average age 26. 18 applicants, 39% accepted. In 2009, 10 master's awarded. *Degree requirements:* For master's, one foreign language, thesis (for some programs), recital. *Entrance requirements:* Additional exam requirements/recommendations for international students: Required—TOEFL (minimum score 550 paper-based; 213 computer-based; 79 iBT), IELTS (minimum score 6.5). *Application deadline:* For fall admission, 7/23 for domestic students, 6/1 for international students; for spring admission, 12/11 for domestic students, 10/1 for international students. Applications are processed on a rolling basis. Application fee: $30. Electronic applications accepted. *Expenses:* Tuition, state resident: part-time $1252.50 per semester. Tuition, nonresident: part-time $3131.25 per semester. Required fees: $586.85 per semester. Tuition and fees vary according to course load. *Financial support:* In 2009–10, 13 teaching assistantships with full tuition reimbursements (averaging $8,064 per year) were awarded; career-related internships or fieldwork, Federal Work-Study, institutionally sponsored loans, scholarships/grants, and traineeships also available. Support available to part-time students. Financial award application deadline: 3/1; financial award applicants required to submit FAFSA. *Unit head:* Dr. Audrey Tallant, Chair, 618-650-3900, E-mail: atallan@siue.edu. *Application contact:* Dr. Darryl Coan, Director, 618-650-2012, E-mail: dcoan@siue.edu.

Southern Illinois University Edwardsville, Graduate Studies and Research, College of Arts and Sciences, Department of Music, Program in Piano Pedagogy, Edwardsville, IL 62026-0001. Offers Postbaccalaureate Certificate. Part-time programs available. *Students:* 3 part-time (2 women). Average age 26. 1 applicant, 100% accepted. *Entrance requirements:* Additional exam requirements/recommendations for international students: Required—TOEFL (minimum score 550 paper-based; 213 computer-based; 6 iBT), IELTS (minimum score 6.5). *Application deadline:* For fall admission, 7/23 for domestic students, 6/1 for international students; for spring admission, 12/11 for domestic students, 10/1 for international students. Applications are processed on a rolling basis. Application fee: $30. Electronic applications accepted. *Expenses:* Tuition, state resident: part-time $1252.50 per semester. Tuition, nonresident: part-time $3131.25 per semester. Required fees: $586.85 per semester. Tuition and fees vary according to course load. *Financial support:* Fellowships, research assistantships, teaching assistantships, career-related internships or fieldwork, Federal Work-Study, institutionally sponsored loans, scholarships/grants, traineeships, and unspecified assistantships available. Support available to part-time students. Financial award application deadline: 3/1; financial award applicants required to submit FAFSA. *Unit head:* Dr. Audrey Tallant, Chair, 618-650-3900, E-mail: atallan@siue.edu. *Application contact:* Dr. Linda Perry, Director, 618-650-3593, E-mail: lperry@siue.edu.

Southern Illinois University Edwardsville, Graduate Studies and Research, College of Arts and Sciences, Department of Music, Program in Vocal Pedagogy, Edwardsville, IL 62026-0001. Offers Postbaccalaureate Certificate. Part-time programs available. *Students:* 2 part-time (1 woman). Average age 26. 1 applicant, 100% accepted. *Entrance requirements:* Additional exam requirements/recommendations for international students: Required—TOEFL (minimum score 550 paper-based; 213 computer-based; 79 iBT), IELTS (minimum score 6.5). *Application deadline:* For fall admission, 7/23 for domestic students, 6/1 for international students; for spring admission, 12/11 for domestic students, 10/1 for international students. Applications are processed on a rolling basis. Application fee: $30. Electronic applications accepted. *Expenses:* Tuition, state resident: part-time $1252.50 per semester. Tuition, nonresident: part-time $3131.25 per semester. Required fees: $586.85 per semester. Tuition and fees vary according to course load. *Financial support:* Fellowships, research assistantships, teaching assistantships, career-related internships or fieldwork, Federal Work-Study, institutionally sponsored loans, scholarships/grants, traineeships, and unspecified assistantships available. Support available to part-time students. Financial award application deadline: 3/1; financial award applicants required to submit FAFSA. *Unit head:* Dr. Audrey Tallant, Chair, 618-650-3900, E-mail: atallan@siue.edu. *Application contact:* Dr. Emily Truckenbrod, Director, 618-650-5394, E-mail: etrucke@siue.edu.

Southern Methodist University, Meadows School of the Arts, Division of Music, Dallas, TX 75275. Offers conducting (MM); music composition (MM); music education (MM); music history (MM); music theory (MM); performance (MM); piano performance and pedagogy (MM); sacred music (MSM). *Accreditation:* NASM. Part-time programs available. *Faculty:* 34 full-time (12 women), 39 part-time/adjunct (16 women). *Students:* 18 full-time (7 women), 78 part-time (47 women); includes 18 minority (9 African Americans, 3 Asian Americans or Pacific Islanders, 6 Hispanic Americans), 14 international. Average age 27. 148 applicants, 54% accepted, 55 enrolled. In 2009, 44 master's, 13 Certificates awarded. *Degree requirements:* For master's, variable foreign language requirement, comprehensive exam, project, recital, or thesis. *Entrance requirements:* For master's, placement exams in music history and theory, audition; bachelor's degree in music or equivalent; minimum GPA of 3.0; research paper in history, theory, education. Additional exam requirements/recommendations for international students: Required—TOEFL (minimum score 550 paper-based; 213 computer-based; 80 iBT). *Application deadline:* For fall admission, 3/1 priority date for domestic and international students; for spring admission, 11/1 for domestic and international students. Applications are processed on a rolling basis. Application fee: $75. Electronic applications accepted. *Financial support:* In 2009–10, 77 students received support, including 70 teaching assistantships with full and partial tuition reimbursements available (averaging $4,000 per year); career-related internships or fieldwork, Federal Work-Study, scholarships/grants, tuition waivers (full and partial), and unspecified assistantships also available. Financial award application deadline: 3/1; financial award applicants required to submit FAFSA. *Faculty research:* Music perception and cognition, computer-based instruction, music medicine and therapy, theoretical and historical analysis–medieval to contemporary. *Unit head:* Dr. Sam Holland, Director, 214-768-1951, Fax: 214-768-4669, E-mail: sholland@smu.edu. *Application contact:* Joe S. Hoselton, Graduate Admissions and Records Coordinator, 214-768-3765, Fax: 214-768-3272, E-mail: hoselton@smu.edu.

Southwestern Oklahoma State University, College of Arts and Sciences, Department of Music, Weatherford, OK 73096-3098. Offers music education (MM); performance (MM). *Accreditation:* NASM. Part-time programs available. *Degree requirements:* For master's, comprehensive exam, recital (music performance). *Entrance requirements:* For master's, minimum GPA of 2.5. Additional exam requirements/recommendations for international students: Required—TOEFL.

State University of New York at Fredonia, Graduate Studies, School of Music, Program in Music Education, Fredonia, NY 14063-1136. Offers MM. *Accreditation:* NASM. Part-time and evening/weekend programs available. *Degree requirements:* For master's, thesis optional. *Expenses:* Tuition, state resident: full-time $8370; part-time $349 per credit. Tuition, nonresident: full-time $13,250; part-time $552 per credit. Required fees: $1289; $53.55 per credit.

State University of New York College at Potsdam, Crane School of Music, Potsdam, NY 13676. Offers music composition (MM); music education (MM); music performance (MM). Part-time programs available. *Faculty:* 25 full-time (9 women), 5 part-time/adjunct (1 woman). *Students:* 22 full-time (10 women), 3 part-time (2 women); includes 1 minority (Asian American or Pacific Islander), 2 international. 27 applicants, 67% accepted, 18 enrolled. In 2009, 23 master's awarded. *Degree requirements:* For master's, variable foreign language requirement, thesis. *Entrance requirements:* For master's, audition, minimum GPA of 3.0. Additional exam requirements/recommendations for international students: Required—TOEFL (minimum score 550 paper-based; 213 computer-based; 80 iBT), IELTS (minimum score 6). *Application deadline:* For fall admission, 3/1 for domestic and international students. Applications are processed on a rolling basis. Application fee: $50. *Expenses:* Tuition, state resident: full-time $8370; part-time $349 per credit hour. Tuition, nonresident: full-time $13,250; part-time $552 per credit hour. Required fees: $942; $38.70 per credit hour. *Financial support:* In 2009–10, 1 student received support; teaching assistantships with full tuition reimbursements available, career-related internships or fieldwork, Federal Work-Study, scholarships/grants, and unspecified assistantships available. Support available to part-time students. Financial award application deadline: 3/1; financial award applicants required to submit FAFSA. *Unit head:* Dr. Michael R. Sitton, Dean, 315-267-2415, Fax: 315-267-2413, E-mail: sittonmr@potsdam.edu. *Application contact:* Karen Miller, Secretary, 315-267-3418, Fax: 315-267-2413, E-mail: millerkl@potsdam.edu.

Syracuse University, School of Education, Program in Music Education, Syracuse, NY 13244. Offers music education/professional certification (M Mus, MS); music education: teacher preparation (MS). *Accreditation:* NASM. Part-time and evening/weekend programs available. *Students:* 16 full-time (12 women), 13 part-time (10 women); includes 3 minority (1 African American, 1 Asian American or Pacific Islander, 1 Hispanic American). Average age 27. 13 applicants, 69% accepted, 5 enrolled. In 2009, 8 master's awarded. *Degree requirements:* For master's, thesis or alternative. *Entrance requirements:* For master's, New York state teacher certification or eligibility. Additional exam requirements/recommendations for international students: Required—TOEFL (minimum score 100 iBT). *Application deadline:* For fall admission, 2/1 priority date for domestic and international students; for spring admission, 10/15 for domestic and international students. Applications are processed on a rolling basis. Application fee: $75. Electronic applications accepted. *Expenses:* Tuition: Full-time $26,808; part-time $1117 per credit. Required fees: $1024. *Financial support:* Fellowships with tuition reimbursements, teaching assistantships with tuition reimbursements, tuition waivers (partial) available. Financial award application deadline: 1/1. *Unit head:* Dr. John Coggiola, Program Coordinator, 315-443-5896, E-mail: jecoggio@syr.edu. *Application contact:* Liza Rochelson, Graduate Recruiter, School of Education, 315-443-2505, E-mail: e-gradrcrt@syr.edu.

Tarleton State University, College of Graduate Studies, College of Liberal and Fine Arts, Department of Fine Arts, Stephenville, TX 76402. Offers music education (MM). *Accreditation:* NASM. Part-time and evening/weekend programs available. *Degree requirements:* For master's, comprehensive exam, thesis optional. *Entrance requirements:* For master's, GRE, minimum GPA of 3.0. Additional exam requirements/recommendations for international students: Required—TOEFL (minimum score 550 paper-based; 213 computer-based; 80 iBT). Electronic applications accepted.

Teachers College, Columbia University, Graduate Faculty of Education, Department of Arts and Humanities, Program in Music and Music Education, New York, NY 10027-6696. Offers Ed M, MA, Ed D, Ed DCT. *Accreditation:* NCATE. Part-time programs available. *Students:* 44 full-time (29 women), 134 part-time (99 women); includes 43 minority (9 African Americans, 30 Asian Americans or Pacific Islanders, 4 Hispanic Americans), 19 international. Average age 33. 85 applicants, 76% accepted, 37 enrolled. In 2009, 55 master's, 11 doctorates awarded. Terminal master's awarded for partial completion of doctoral program. *Degree requirements:* For master's, thesis, project; for doctorate, variable foreign language requirement, thesis/dissertation. *Entrance requirements:* For master's and doctorate, diagnostic exam. *Application deadline:* For fall admission, 5/15 for domestic students. Application fee: $65. *Financial support:* Fellowships, research assistantships, teaching assistantships, career-related internships or fieldwork, Federal Work-Study, institutionally sponsored loans, and tuition waivers (full and partial) available. Support available to part-time students. Financial award application deadline: 2/1. *Faculty research:* Artistry, creativity, and proficiency in production and performance; educational theory and practice; piano pedagogy; research strategies in music pedagogy. *Unit head:* Graeme Sullivan, Chair, 212-678-3799. *Application contact:* Mark E. Stearns, Associate Director of Admission, 212-678-3710, Fax: 212-678-4171.

Temple University, Graduate School, Esther Boyer College of Music and Dance, Department of Keyboard Instruction, Philadelphia, PA 19122-6096. Offers MM, DMA. Part-time programs available. *Entrance requirements:* Additional exam requirements/recommendations for international students: Required—TOEFL. Electronic applications accepted.

Temple University, Graduate School, Esther Boyer College of Music and Dance, Department of Music Education and Therapy, Philadelphia, PA 19122-6096. Offers music education (MM, PhD); music therapy (MMT, PhD). *Accreditation:* NASM. Part-time and evening/weekend programs available. *Degree requirements:* For master's, thesis; for doctorate, thesis/dissertation. *Entrance requirements:* Additional exam requirements/recommendations for international students: Required—TOEFL. Electronic applications accepted. *Faculty research:* Music learning theory, guided imagery in music, computer learning theory.

Tennessee State University, The School of Graduate Studies and Research, College of Arts and Sciences, Department of Music, Nashville, TN 37209-1561. Offers music education (MS). *Accreditation:* NASM. *Degree requirements:* For master's, thesis optional. *Entrance requirements:* For master's, MAT. *Faculty research:* Applications of technology in music education; K-12 vocal, instrumental and general music pedagogy: historical research in American music education; classical guitar performance practice.

Texas A&M University–Commerce, Graduate School, College of Arts and Sciences, Department of Music, Commerce, TX 75429-3011. Offers music (MA, MS); music composition (MA, MM); music education (MA, MM, MS); music literature (MA); music performance (MA, MM); music theory (MA, MM). *Accreditation:* NASM. Part-time programs available. *Degree requirements:* For master's, comprehensive exam, thesis (for some programs). *Entrance requirements:* For master's, GRE General Test. Electronic applications accepted.

Texas A&M University–Kingsville, College of Graduate Studies, College of Arts and Sciences, Department of Music, Kingsville, TX 78363. Offers music education (MM). *Accreditation:* NASM. *Degree requirements:* For master's, comprehensive exam, thesis or alternative. *Entrance requirements:* For master's, GRE General Test, minimum GPA of 3.0. Additional exam requirements/recommendations for international students: Required—TOEFL.

Texas Christian University, College of Fine Arts, School of Music, Fort Worth, TX 76129-0002. Offers composition (DMA); conducting (M Mus, DMA); music education (MM Ed); musicology (M Mus); organ performance (M Mus); pedagogy (DMA); performance (DMA); piano (Artist Diploma); piano pedagogy (M Mus); piano performance (M Mus); string performance (M Mus); theory/composition (M Mus); vocal performance (M Mus); voice pedagogy (M Mus); wind and percussion performance (M Mus). *Accreditation:* NASM. *Degree requirements:* For master's, one foreign language, comprehensive exam, thesis (for some programs), thesis or recital; for doctorate, one foreign language, comprehensive exam, thesis/dissertation. *Entrance requirements:* For master's, GRE General Test (theory/composition, musicology), audition or composition/theory, letters of recommendation; for doctorate, GRE General Test, on site entrance exam, audition, interview. Additional exam requirements/recommendations for international students: Required—TOEFL iBT (minimum score 80; 100 for DMA). *Application deadline:* For fall admission, 1/15 for domestic and international students; for spring admission, 10/1 for domestic and international students. Application fee: $0. *Expenses:* Tuition: Full-time $17,640; part-time $980 per credit hour. Tuition and fees vary according to program. *Financial support:* Application deadline: 1/15. *Unit head:* Dr. Richard Gipson, Director, 817-257-7602. *Application contact:* Dr. Joseph Butler, Associate Dean, College of Fine Arts, E-mail: j.butler@tcu.edu.

Texas State University–San Marcos, Graduate School, College of Fine Arts and Communication, School of Music, Program in Music Education, San Marcos, TX 78666. Offers MM. *Accreditation:* NASM. Part-time programs available. *Faculty:* 7 full-time (1 woman), 2 part-time/adjunct (1 woman). *Students:* 2 full-time (0 women), 5 part-time (3 women); includes 2 minority (1 African American, 1 Hispanic American). Average age 33. 2 applicants, 50% accepted, 1 enrolled. In 2009, 7 master's awarded. *Degree requirements:* For master's, comprehensive exam. *Entrance requirements:* For master's, minimum GPA of 2.75 in last 60 hours of course work. Additional exam requirements/recommendations for international students: Required—TOEFL (minimum score 550 paper-based; 213 computer-based). *Application deadline:* For fall admission, 6/15 priority date for domestic students; for spring admission, 10/15 priority date for domestic students. Applications are processed on a rolling basis. Application fee: $40 ($90 for international students). Electronic applications accepted. *Expenses:* Tuition, state resident: full-time $5784; part-time $241 per credit hour. Tuition, nonresident: full-time $13,224; part-time $551 per credit hour. Required fees: $1728; $48 per credit hour. $306. Tuition and fees vary according to course load. *Financial support:* In 2009–10, 3 students received support, including 2 teaching assistantships (averaging $3,074 per year); career-related internships or fieldwork, Federal Work-Study, institutionally sponsored loans, and scholarships/grants also available. Support available to part-time students. Financial award application deadline: 4/1; financial award applicants required to submit FAFSA. *Unit head:* Dr. Kevin Mooney, Graduate Advisor, 512-245-2651, Fax: 512-245-8181, E-mail: km30@txstate.edu. *Application contact:* Dr. J. Michael Willoughby, Dean of Graduate School, 512-245-2581, Fax: 512-245-8365, E-mail: gradcollege@txstate.edu.

Texas Tech University, Graduate School, College of Visual and Performing Arts, School of Music, Lubbock, TX 79409. Offers composition (MM, DMA); conducting (DMA); fine arts-music (PhD); music education (MM Ed); music theory (MM); musicology (MM); pedagogy (MM); performance (MM, DMA); piano pedagogy (DMA). *Accreditation:* NASM. Part-time programs available. *Faculty:* 40 full-time (15 women), 1 part-time/adjunct (0 women). *Students:* 105 full-time (41 women), 28 part-time (15 women); includes 17 minority (5 African Americans, 12 Hispanic Americans), 27 international. Average age 30. 123 applicants, 60% accepted, 37 enrolled. In 2009, 19 master's, 20 doctorates awarded. *Degree requirements:* For master's, thesis or alternative; for doctorate, thesis/dissertation. *Entrance requirements:* For master's and doctorate, GRE General Test. Additional exam requirements/recommendations for international students: Required—TOEFL (minimum score 550 paper-based; 213 computer-based). *Application deadline:* For fall admission, 3/1 priority date for international students; for spring admission, 11/1 priority date for international students. Applications are processed on a rolling basis. Application fee: $50 ($75 for international students). Electronic applications accepted. *Expenses:* Tuition, state resident: full-time $5100; part-time $213 per credit hour. Tuition, nonresident: full-time $11,748; part-time $490 per credit hour. Required fees: $2298; $50 per credit hour. $555 per semester. *Financial support:* In 2009–10, 32 teaching assistantships with partial tuition reimbursements (averaging $8,206 per year) were awarded; research assistantships with partial tuition reimbursements, Federal Work-Study and institutionally sponsored loans also available. Support available to part-time students. Financial award application deadline: 4/15; financial award applicants required to submit FAFSA. *Faculty research:* Strategies for music pedagogy in grades K-12, performance practice of traditional music, role of the woman piano virtuoso, vernacular music center, voice health and culture. Total annual research expenditures: $9,083. *Unit head:* Prof. William Ballenger, Director, 806-742-2270, Fax: 806-742-2294, E-mail: william.ballenger@ttu.edu. *Application contact:* Carin Wanner, Admissions and Scholarship Coordinator, 806-742-2270 Ext. 225, Fax: 806-742-2294, E-mail: melissacarin.wanner@ttu.edu.

Towson University, College of Graduate Studies and Research, Program in Music Education, Towson, MD 21252-0001. Offers MS, Certificate. *Accreditation:* NASM; NCATE. Part-time and evening/weekend programs available. *Degree requirements:* For master's, thesis optional, exam. *Entrance requirements:* For master's, bachelor's degree in music education or certification as public school music teacher, minimum GPA of 3.0; for Certificate, bachelor's degree in music or certification as public school music teacher. Electronic applications accepted.

Troy University, Graduate School, College of Education, Program in Postsecondary Education, Troy, AL 36082. Offers adult education (M Ed); biology (M Ed); criminal justice (M Ed); english (M Ed); foundations of education (M Ed); general science (M Ed); higher education administration (M Ed); history (M Ed); instructional technology (M Ed); mathematics (M Ed); music industry (M Ed); physical fitness (M Ed); political science (M Ed); public administration (M Ed); social science (M Ed); teaching english (M Ed). Also offered through the University College. *Accreditation:* NCATE. Part-time and evening/weekend programs available. *Students:* 267 full-time (192 women), 381 part-time (293 women); includes 326 minority (309 African Americans, 4 American Indian/Alaska Native, 5 Asian Americans or Pacific Islanders, 8 Hispanic Americans). Average age 34. 343 applicants, 90% accepted. In 2009, 480 master's awarded. *Degree requirements:* For master's, comprehensive exam, thesis. *Entrance requirements:* For master's, MAT (minimum score 385), minimum GPA of 2.5. Additional exam requirements/recommendations for international students: Required—TOEFL (minimum score 523 paper-based; 193 computer-based; 70 iBT), IELTS, or ACT Compass ESL (minimum score 270 on Listening, Reading, and Grammar with no individual score below 85 and a minimum score of 8 out of 12 on writing test). *Application deadline:* Applications are processed on a rolling basis. Application fee: $50. Electronic applications accepted. *Financial support:* Available to part-time students. Applicants required to submit FAFSA. *Unit head:* Dr. Andrew Creamer, Chair, 334-670-3350, E-mail: drcreamer@troy.edu. *Application contact:* Brenda K. Campbell, Director of Graduate Admissions, 334-670-3178, Fax: 334-670-3733, E-mail: bcamp@troy.edu.

Troy University, Graduate School, College of Education, Program in Teacher Education-Multiple Levels, Troy, AL 36082. Offers alternative 5th year art education (MS); alternative 5th year instrumental (MS); alternative 5th year physical education (MS); alternative 5th year vocal/choral (MS); traditional art education (MS); traditional gifted education (MS); traditional instrumental (MS); traditional physical education (MS); traditional reading specialist (MS); traditional vocal/choral (MS). Part-time and evening/weekend programs available. *Students:* 5 full-time (3 women), 21 part-time (12 women); includes 11 minority (9 African Americans, 1 American Indian/Alaska Native, 1 Asian American or Pacific Islander). Average age 30. 2 applicants, 50% accepted. In 2009, 8 master's awarded. *Degree requirements:* For master's, comprehensive exam, thesis. *Entrance requirements:* For master's, minimum GPA of 2.5. Additional exam requirements/recommendations for international students: Required—TOEFL (minimum score 523 paper-based; 193 computer-based; 70 iBT), IELTS (minimum score 6). *Application deadline:* Applications are processed on a rolling basis. Application fee: $50. Electronic applications accepted. *Financial support:* Available to part-time students. Applicants required to submit FAFSA. *Unit head:* Dr. Marian Parker, Coordinator, 334-670-5661, Fax: 334-670-3548, E-mail: mjparker@troy.edu. *Application contact:* Brenda K. Campbell, Director of Graduate Admissions, 334-670-3178, Fax: 334-670-3733, E-mail: bcamp@troy.edu.

Union College, Graduate Programs, Department of Education, Barbourville, KY 40906-1499. Offers elementary education (MA); health and physical education (MA); middle grades (MA); music education (MA); principalship (MA); reading specialist (MA); secondary education (MA); special education (MA). *Degree requirements:* For master's, thesis optional. *Entrance requirements:* For master's, GRE General Test, NTE.

Université Laval, Faculty of Music, Programs in Music, Québec, QC G1K 7P4, Canada. Offers composition (M Mus); instrumental didactics (M Mus); interpretation (M Mus); music education (M Mus, PhD); musicology (M Mus, PhD). Terminal master's awarded for partial completion of doctoral program. *Degree requirements:* For master's, thesis (for some programs); for doctorate, comprehensive exam, thesis/dissertation. *Entrance requirements:* For master's,

Music Education

Université Laval (continued)

English exam, audition, knowledge of French; for doctorate, English exam, knowledge of French, third language. Electronic applications accepted.

University at Buffalo, the State University of New York, Graduate School, Graduate School of Education, Department of Learning and Instruction, Buffalo, NY 14260. Offers biology education (Ed M, Certificate); chemistry education (Ed M, Certificate); childhood education (Ed M); childhood education with bilingual extension (Ed M); early childhood education (Ed M); earth science education (Ed M, Certificate); elementary education (Ed D, PhD); English education (Ed M, PhD, Certificate); English for speakers of other languages (Ed M); foreign and second language education (PhD); French education (Ed M, Certificate); general education (Ed M); German education (Ed M, Certificate); gifted education (online) (Certificate); Latin education (Ed M, Certificate); literary specialist (Ed M); mathematics education (Ed M, PhD, Certificate); music education (Ed M, Certificate); physics education (Ed M, Certificate); reading education (PhD); science and the public (online) (Ed M); science education (PhD); social studies education (Ed M, Certificate); Spanish education (Ed M, Certificate); special education (PhD); teaching and leading for diversity (Certificate); teaching English to speakers of other languages (Ed M). Part-time and evening/weekend programs available. Postbaccalaureate distance learning degree programs offered (no on-campus study). *Faculty:* 34 full-time (24 women), 50 part-time/adjunct (39 women). *Students:* 332 full-time (245 women), 365 part-time (272 women); includes 50 minority (18 African Americans, 4 American Indian/Alaska Native, 10 Asian Americans or Pacific Islanders, 18 Hispanic Americans), 55 international. Average age 30. 627 applicants, 78% accepted, 286 enrolled. In 2009, 255 master's, 16 doctorates, 51 other advanced degrees awarded. *Degree requirements:* For master's, comprehensive exam; for doctorate, thesis/dissertation, research analysis exam, research experience component. *Entrance requirements:* For doctorate, GRE General Test or MAT, interview, writing sample, letters of recommendation. Additional exam requirements/recommendations for international students: Required—TOEFL (minimum score 600 paper-based; 250 computer-based; 96 iBT). *Application deadline:* For fall admission, 2/1 priority date for domestic and international students; for spring admission, 11/15 priority date for domestic students, 10/1 for international students. Applications are processed on a rolling basis. Application fee: $50. Electronic applications accepted. *Financial support:* In 2009–10, 23 fellowships with full tuition reimbursements (averaging $9,000 per year), 42 research assistantships with full tuition reimbursements (averaging $10,000 per year) were awarded; teaching assistantships with full tuition reimbursements, career-related internships or fieldwork, Federal Work-Study, institutionally sponsored loans, scholarships/grants, tuition waivers (partial), and unspecified assistantships also available. Financial award application deadline: 2/28; financial award applicants required to submit FAFSA. *Faculty research:* Science assessment, foreign language teaching and learning, early learning, new literacies, gender and education. Total annual research expenditures: $1.8 million. *Unit head:* Dr. Suzanne Miller, Chair, 716-645-2455, Fax: 716-645-3161, E-mail: smiller@buffalo.edu. *Application contact:* Cathy Dimino, Admissions Assistant, 716-645-2110, Fax: 716-645-7937, E-mail: cadimino@buffalo.edu.

The University of Akron, Graduate School, College of Creative and Professional Arts, School of Music, Program in Music Education, Akron, OH 44325. Offers MM. *Accreditation:* NCATE. *Students:* 11 full-time (9 women), 21 part-time (14 women); includes 1 minority (Asian American or Pacific Islander). Average age 32. 13 applicants, 92% accepted, 8 enrolled. In 2009, 8 master's awarded. *Degree requirements:* For master's, comprehensive exam, thesis optional. *Entrance requirements:* For master's, minimum GPA of 2.75, interview, audition, letters of recommendation. Additional exam requirements/recommendations for international students: Required—TOEFL (minimum score 550 paper-based; 213 computer-based; 79 iBT). *Application deadline:* Applications are processed on a rolling basis. Application fee: $30 ($40 for international students). Electronic applications accepted. *Expenses:* Tuition, state resident: full-time $6570; part-time $365 per credit hour. Tuition, nonresident: full-time $11,250; part-time $625 per credit hour. *Unit head:* Laurie Lafferty, Head, 330-972-5761, E-mail: laffert@uakron.edu. *Application contact:* Laurie Lafferty, Head, 330-972-5761, E-mail: laffert@uakron.edu.

The University of Alabama, Graduate School, College of Arts and Sciences, School of Music, Tuscaloosa, AL 35487. Offers arranging (MM); choral conducting (MM, DMA); composition (MM, DMA); music education (MA, PhD); music history (MM); performance (MM, DMA); theory (MM); wind conducting (MM, DMA). *Accreditation:* NASM. *Faculty:* 32 full-time (11 women). *Students:* 63 full-time (35 women), 26 part-time (11 women); includes 13 minority (5 African Americans, 5 Asian Americans or Pacific Islanders, 3 Hispanic Americans), 13 international. Average age 30. 66 applicants, 42% accepted, 22 enrolled. In 2009, 12 master's, 4 doctorates awarded. *Median time to degree:* Of those who began their doctoral program in fall 2001, 50% received their degree in 8 years or less. *Degree requirements:* For master's, comprehensive exam, thesis, oral and written exams, recital; for doctorate, comprehensive exam, thesis/dissertation, oral and written exams, recital. *Entrance requirements:* For master's and doctorate, audition. Additional exam requirements/recommendations for international students: Required—TOEFL, or IELTS. *Application deadline:* For fall admission, 2/1 priority date for domestic and international students; for winter admission, 2/1 for domestic students, 2/1 priority date for international students; for spring admission, 2/1 priority date for domestic and international students. Applications are processed on a rolling basis. Application fee: $50 ($60 for international students). Electronic applications accepted. *Expenses:* Tuition, state resident: full-time $7000. Tuition, nonresident: full-time $19,200. *Financial support:* In 2009–10, 22 students received support, including 1 fellowship with tuition reimbursement available (averaging $30,000 per year), 40 teaching assistantships with full and partial tuition reimbursements available (averaging $8,181 per year); Federal Work-Study, institutionally sponsored loans, and unspecified assistantships also available. Financial award application deadline: 7/14. *Faculty research:* Performance practice, musicology, theory, composition. *Unit head:* Charles G. Snead, Director, 205-348-7110, Fax: 205-348-1473, E-mail: ssnead@music.ua.edu. *Application contact:* Dr. Marvin Johnson, Director of Graduate Studies, 205-348-6604, Fax: 205-348-1473, E-mail: mjohnson@music.ua.edu.

The University of Alabama, Graduate School, College of Education, Department of Music Education, Tuscaloosa, AL 35487-0366. Offers choral music education (MA); instrumental music education (MA); music education (Ed D, PhD, Ed S). *Accreditation:* NASM. Part-time programs available. *Students:* 1 applicant, 0% accepted, 0 enrolled. In 2009, 1 degree awarded. *Median time to degree:* Of those who began their doctoral program in fall 2001, 100% received their degree in 8 years or less. *Degree requirements:* For master's, comprehensive exam, thesis optional; for doctorate, comprehensive exam, thesis/dissertation, oral exam (PhD). *Entrance requirements:* For master's, GRE or MAT, video of teaching, letters of recommendation; for doctorate, GRE or MAT, interview, writing sample, video of teaching, letters of recommendation; for Ed S, GRE or MAT. Additional exam requirements/recommendations for international students: Required—TOEFL (minimum score 550 paper-based; 213 computer-based). *Application deadline:* For fall admission, 7/1 priority date for domestic students; for spring admission, 11/1 priority date for domestic students. Applications are processed on a rolling basis. Application fee: $50 ($60 for international students). Electronic applications accepted. *Expenses:* Tuition, state resident: full-time $7000. Tuition, nonresident: full-time $19,200. *Financial support:* Research assistantships with full and partial tuition reimbursements, teaching assistantships with full and partial tuition reimbursements available. Financial award application deadline: 3/1. *Faculty research:* Elementary music, music for students with special needs, choral music. *Unit head:* Dr. Carol A. Prickett, Department Head and Professor, 205-348-1432, Fax: 205-348-1675, E-mail: cpricket@bama.ua.edu. *Application contact:* Cathie M. Daniels, Senior Office Associate, 205-348-6054, Fax: 205-348-1675, E-mail: cdaniels@bama.ua.edu.

University of Alaska Fairbanks, College of Liberal Arts, Department of Music, Fairbanks, AK 99775-5660. Offers conducting (MA); music education (MA); music history (MA); music theory/composition (MA); performance (MA). *Accreditation:* NASM. Part-time programs available. *Faculty:* 12 full-time (3 women), 6 part-time/adjunct (4 women). *Students:* 11 full-time (6 women), 4 part-time (2 women). Average age 36. 18 applicants, 67% accepted, 11 enrolled. In 2009, 5 master's awarded. *Degree requirements:* For master's, comprehensive exam, thesis or alternative, oral exam, oral defense. *Entrance requirements:* For master's, evaluative preliminary examination in music theory and history. Additional exam requirements/recommendations for international students: Required—TOEFL (minimum score 550 paper-based; 213 computer-based; 80 iBT). *Application deadline:* For fall admission, 6/1 for domestic students, 3/1 for international students; for spring admission, 10/15 for domestic students, 9/1 for international students. Applications are processed on a rolling basis. Application fee: $60. Electronic applications accepted. *Expenses:* Tuition, state resident: full-time $7584; part-time $316 per credit. Tuition, nonresident: full-time $15,504; part-time $646 per credit. Required fees: $23 per credit. $135 per semester. Tuition and fees vary according to course level, course load and reciprocity agreements. *Financial support:* In 2009–10, 4 teaching assistantships (averaging $12,472 per year) were awarded; fellowships, Federal Work-Study, scholarships/grants, health care benefits, and unspecified assistantships also available. Support available to part-time students. Financial award application deadline: 7/1; financial award applicants required to submit FAFSA. *Faculty research:* Symphony, opera, jazz, chamber and solo performance. *Unit head:* Dr. Eduard Zilberkant, Department Chair, 907-474-7555, Fax: 907-474-6420, E-mail: uaf.music@alaska.edu. *Application contact:* Dr. Eduard Zilberkant, Department Chair, 907-474-7555, Fax: 907-474-6420, E-mail: uaf.music@alaska.edu.

The University of Arizona, Graduate College, College of Fine Arts, School of Music, Tucson, AZ 85721. Offers composition (MM, A Mus D); conducting (MM, A Mus D); music education (MM, PhD); music theory (MM, PhD); musicology (MM); performance (MM, A Mus D). *Accreditation:* NASD (one or more programs are accredited); NASM (one or more programs are accredited). Part-time programs available. *Faculty:* 42. *Students:* 117 full-time (47 women), 100 part-time (47 women); includes 4 Hispanic Americans, 49 international. Average age 32. 162 applicants, 48% accepted, 50 enrolled. In 2009, 19 master's, 15 doctorates awarded. *Degree requirements:* For master's, thesis or alternative, orals; for doctorate, comprehensive exam, thesis/dissertation or alternative. *Entrance requirements:* For master's, 3 letters of recommendation; for doctorate, 3 letters of recommendation, statement of purpose. Additional exam requirements/recommendations for international students: Required—TOEFL (minimum score 550 paper-based; 213 computer-based; 79 iBT). *Application deadline:* For fall admission, 6/1 for domestic students, 12/1 for international students; for spring admission, 10/1 for domestic students, 6/1 for international students. Applications are processed on a rolling basis. Application fee: $75. Electronic applications accepted. *Expenses:* Tuition, state resident: full-time $9028. Tuition, nonresident: full-time $24,890. *Financial support:* In 2009–10, 51 teaching assistantships with full tuition reimbursements (averaging $12,473 per year) were awarded; career-related internships or fieldwork, institutionally sponsored loans, scholarships/grants, health care benefits, tuition waivers (full), and unspecified assistantships also available. Support available to part-time students. Financial award application deadline: 2/15; financial award applicants required to submit FAFSA. *Faculty research:* Music in general education, psychology of music learning, innovation in string music education, Zarzuela, Franz Liszt's work. Total annual research expenditures: $934. *Unit head:* Dr. Peter A. McAllister, Director, 520-621-7023, Fax: 520-621-1351, E-mail: pmcallis@email.arizona.edu. *Application contact:* Lyneen Elmore, 520-621-5929, Fax: 520-621-8118, E-mail: lyneen@u.arizona.edu.

The University of British Columbia, Faculty of Education, Department of Curriculum and Pedagogy, Vancouver, BC V6T 1Z4, Canada. Offers art education (M Ed, MA); business education (MA); curriculum studies (M Ed, MA, PhD); home economics education (M Ed, MA); math education (M Ed, MA); music education (M Ed, MA); physical education (M Ed, MA); science education (M Ed, MA); social studies education (M Ed, MA); technology studies education (M Ed, MA). Part-time programs available. *Degree requirements:* For master's, thesis (MA); for doctorate, comprehensive exam, thesis/dissertation. *Entrance requirements:* Additional exam requirements/recommendations for international students: Required—TOEFL (minimum score 580 paper-based; 237 computer-based; 92 iBT). Electronic applications accepted. *Expenses:* Contact institution. *Faculty research:* School subjects, teaching and learning.

University of Central Arkansas, Graduate School, College of Fine Arts and Communication, Department of Music, Conway, AR 72035-0001. Offers choral conducting (MM); instrumental conducting (MM); music education (MM); music theory (MM); performance (MM). *Accreditation:* NASM. Part-time programs available. *Faculty:* 12 full-time (4 women), 1 part-time/adjunct (0 women). *Students:* 15 full-time (7 women), 2 part-time (both women); includes 4 minority (3 African Americans, 1 Asian American or Pacific Islander), 2 international. Average age 27. 10 applicants, 100% accepted, 8 enrolled. In 2009, 8 master's awarded. *Degree requirements:* For master's, comprehensive exam, thesis optional. *Entrance requirements:* For master's, GRE General Test, minimum GPA of 2.7. Additional exam requirements/recommendations for international students: Required—TOEFL (minimum score 550 paper-based; 213 computer-based). *Application deadline:* For fall admission, 3/1 priority date for domestic students; for spring admission, 10/1 priority date for domestic students. Applications are processed on a rolling basis. Application fee: $25 ($50 for international students). *Expenses:* Tuition, state resident: full-time $5136; part-time $214 per credit hour. Required fees: $379.50; $127 per term. Tuition and fees vary according to course level, course load and campus/location. *Financial support:* Federal Work-Study, scholarships/grants, tuition waivers (partial), and unspecified assistantships available. Financial award application deadline: 2/15; financial award applicants required to submit FAFSA. *Unit head:* Jeffrey Jarvis, Unit Head, 501-450-3163. *Application contact:* Brenda Herring, Admissions Assistant, 501-450-5065, Fax: 501-450-5678, E-mail: bherring@uca.edu.

University of Central Oklahoma, College of Graduate Studies and Research, College of Fine Arts and Design, Department of Music, Edmond, OK 73034-5209. Offers music education (MM); performance (MM). *Accreditation:* NASM. Part-time programs available. *Faculty:* 17 full-time (6 women), 6 part-time/adjunct (0 women). *Students:* 18 full-time (6 women), 14 part-time (4 women); includes 10 minority (8 African Americans, 1 American Indian/Alaska Native, 1 Hispanic American), 3 international. Average age 28. 10 applicants, 100% accepted. In 2009, 17 master's awarded. *Entrance requirements:* Additional exam requirements/recommendations for international students: Required—TOEFL (minimum score 550 paper-based; 213 computer-based). *Application deadline:* For fall admission, 7/1 for international students; for spring admission, 11/1 for international students. Applications are processed on a rolling basis. Application fee: $25. Electronic applications accepted. *Expenses:* Tuition, state resident: full-time $4128; part-time $172 per credit hour. Tuition, nonresident: full-time $10,373; part-time $432.20 per credit hour. Required fees: $433.20; $18.05 per credit hour. *Financial support:* Federal Work-Study and unspecified assistantships available. Financial award application deadline: 3/31; financial award applicants required to submit FAFSA. *Faculty research:* Opera/orchestral composition, western/world music, ethnomusicology, literature for librettos. *Unit head:* Dr. Kent Kidwell, Chair, 405-974-5175. *Application contact:* Dr. Kent Kidwell, Chair, 405-974-5175.

University of Cincinnati, Graduate School, College-Conservatory of Music, Division of Music Education, Cincinnati, OH 45221. Offers MM. *Accreditation:* NASM; NCATE. *Degree requirements:* For master's, comprehensive exam, paper or thesis. *Entrance requirements:* For master's, GRE General Test, interview. Additional exam requirements/recommendations for international students: Required—TOEFL (minimum score 520 paper-based; 190 computer-based). Electronic applications accepted. *Faculty research:* Choral, orchestral, and wind conducting; Kodaly; Orff-Schulwerk; jazz studies; string education.

University of Colorado at Boulder, Graduate School, College of Music, Boulder, CO 80309. Offers composition (M Mus, D Mus A); conducting (M Mus); instrumental conducting and literature (D Mus A); literature and performance of choral music (D Mus A); music education (M Mus Ed, PhD); musicology (PhD); performance (M Mus, D Mus A); performance/pedagogy (M Mus, D Mus A); theory (M Mus). *Accreditation:* NASM. *Faculty:* 55 full-time (19 women). *Students:* 194 full-time (108 women), 56 part-time (30 women); includes 25 minority (3 African Americans, 1 American Indian/Alaska Native, 10 Asian Americans or Pacific Islanders, 11 Hispanic Americans), 28 international. Average age 30. 440 applicants, 32% accepted, 67 enrolled. In 2009, 53 master's, 25 doctorates awarded. Terminal master's awarded for partial completion of doctoral program. *Degree requirements:* For master's, variable foreign language

requirement, comprehensive exam, thesis or alternative, recital; for doctorate, variable foreign language requirement, thesis/dissertation. *Entrance requirements:* For master's, GRE General Test, GRE Subject Test (music literature), minimum undergraduate GPA of 2.75; for doctorate, GRE General Test, GRE Subject Test, audition, sample of research. *Application deadline:* For fall admission, 3/1 priority date for domestic students, 12/1 for international students. Applications are processed on a rolling basis. Application fee: $50 ($60 for international students). *Financial support:* In 2009–10, 88 fellowships (averaging $3,325 per year), 38 research assistantships (averaging $6,550 per year) were awarded; tuition waivers (full) also available. Financial award application deadline: 3/1. Total annual research expenditures: $22,375.

University of Connecticut, Graduate School, School of Fine Arts, Department of Music, Storrs, CT 06269. Offers conducting (M Mus, DMA); historical musicology (MA); music (Performer's Certificate); music education (M Mus, PhD); music theory (MA); music theory and history (PhD); performance (M Mus, DMA). *Accreditation:* NASM. *Faculty:* 19 full-time (5 women). *Students:* 38 full-time (19 women), 25 part-time (12 women); includes 5 minority (1 African American, 1 American Indian/Alaska Native, 1 Asian American or Pacific Islander, 2 Hispanic Americans), 9 international. Average age 32. 60 applicants, 33% accepted, 11 enrolled. In 2009, 13 master's, 6 doctorates, 4 other advanced degrees awarded. Terminal master's awarded for partial completion of doctoral program. *Degree requirements:* For master's, comprehensive exam; for doctorate, thesis/dissertation. *Entrance requirements:* For master's, GRE General Test, GRE Subject Test, audition; for doctorate, GRE Subject Test, MAT, audition. Additional exam requirements/recommendations for international students: Required—TOEFL (minimum score 550 paper-based; 213 computer-based). *Application deadline:* For fall admission, 2/1 priority date for domestic and international students; for spring admission, 11/1 for domestic students, 10/1 for international students. Application fee: $55. *Expenses:* Tuition, state resident: full-time $4725; part-time $525 per credit. Tuition, nonresident: full-time $12,267; part-time $1363 per credit. Required fees: $346 per semester. Tuition and fees vary according to course load. *Financial support:* In 2009–10, 9 research assistantships with full tuition reimbursements, 25 teaching assistantships with full tuition reimbursements were awarded; fellowships, Federal Work-Study, health care benefits, and unspecified assistantships also available. Financial award application deadline: 2/1; financial award applicants required to submit FAFSA. *Unit head:* Karla Fox, Head, 860-486-1361, E-mail: karla.fox@uconn.edu. *Application contact:* David Maker, Associate Head, 860-486-1617, E-mail: david.maker@uconn.edu.

University of Dayton, Graduate School, School of Education and Allied Professions, Department of Teacher Education, Dayton, OH 45469-1300. Offers adolescent/young adult (MS Ed); art education (MS Ed); early childhood education (MS Ed); inclusive early childhood (MS Ed); interdisciplinary education (MS Ed); intervention specialist education, mild/moderate (MS Ed); literacy (MS Ed); middle childhood (MS Ed); multi-age education (MS Ed); music education (MS Ed); teacher as leader (MS Ed); technology in education (MS Ed). Part-time and evening/weekend programs available. *Faculty:* 17 full-time (13 women), 27 part-time/adjunct (21 women). *Students:* 105 full-time (76 women), 152 part-time (131 women); includes 25 minority (21 African Americans, 1 Asian American or Pacific Islander, 3 Hispanic Americans), 8 international. Average age 33. 199 applicants, 58% accepted, 48 enrolled. In 2009, 139 master's awarded. *Degree requirements:* For master's, thesis, capstone research project. *Entrance requirements:* For master's, GRE General Test, minimum GPA of 2.75. Additional exam requirements/recommendations for international students: Required—TOEFL (minimum score 550 paper-based; 213 computer-based; 80 iBT). *Application deadline:* For fall admission, 3/15 priority date for domestic students, 3/1 priority date for international students; for winter admission, 7/1 priority date for international students; for spring admission, 1/1 priority date for international students. Applications are processed on a rolling basis. Application fee: $0 ($50 for international students). Electronic applications accepted. *Expenses:* Contact institution. *Financial support:* In 2009–10, 5 research assistantships with full and partial tuition reimbursements (averaging $8,000 per year) were awarded; career-related internships or fieldwork, institutionally sponsored loans, health care benefits, and unspecified assistantships also available. Financial award applicants required to submit FAFSA. *Faculty research:* Diversity, literacy, art representation by young children, preservice teacher preparation. *Unit head:* Dr. Katie A. Kinnucan-Welsch, Chair, 937-229-3346. *Application contact:* Graduate Admissions, 937-229-4411, Fax: 937-229-4729, E-mail: gradadmission@udayton.edu.

University of Delaware, College of Arts and Sciences, Department of Music, Newark, DE 19716. Offers composition (MM); music education (MM); performance (MM). *Accreditation:* NASM. Part-time programs available. *Entrance requirements:* For master's, audition. Additional exam requirements/recommendations for international students: Required—TOEFL. Electronic applications accepted. *Faculty research:* Teaching of music.

University of Denver, Division of Arts, Humanities and Social Sciences, Lamont School of Music, Denver, CO 80208. Offers composition (MA); conducting (MA); jazz and commercial music (Certificate); music (MM); music education (MA); music history and literature (MA); Orff-Schulwerk (MA); performance (MA); piano pedagogy (MA); Suzuki pedagogy (MA); Suzuki teaching (Certificate); theory (MA). *Accreditation:* NASM. Part-time programs available. *Faculty:* 27 full-time (9 women), 37 part-time/adjunct (16 women). *Students:* 19 full-time (8 women), 45 part-time (27 women); includes 5 minority (2 African Americans, 2 Asian Americans or Pacific Islanders, 1 Hispanic American), 6 international. Average age 28. 85 applicants, 69% accepted, 39 enrolled. In 2009, 20 master's, 2 other advanced degrees awarded. *Degree requirements:* For master's, thesis (for some programs), recital or project, 2 years language (performance, music history and literature). *Entrance requirements:* For master's, GRE General Test, music history and theory qualifying exams. Additional exam requirements/recommendations for international students: Required—TOEFL. *Application deadline:* Applications are processed on a rolling basis. Application fee: $50. Electronic applications accepted. *Expenses:* Tuition: Full-time $34,596; part-time $961 per quarter hour. Required fees: $4 per quarter hour. Tuition and fees vary according to course load, campus/location and program. *Financial support:* In 2009–10, 37 teaching assistantships with full and partial tuition reimbursements (averaging $4,500 per year) were awarded; career-related internships or fieldwork, Federal Work-Study, institutionally sponsored loans, and scholarships/grants also available. Support available to part-time students. Financial award application deadline: 4/15; financial award applicants required to submit FAFSA. *Unit head:* Joseph Docksey, Director, 303-871-6986. *Application contact:* Information Contact, 303-871-6400.

University of Florida, Graduate School, College of Fine Arts, School of Music, Gainesville, FL 32611. Offers choral conducting (MM, PhD); composition/theory (MM, PhD); ethnomusicology (PhD); instrumental conducting (MM, PhD); music (MM, PhD); music education (MM, PhD); music history and literature (MM); musicology (PhD); performance (MM); sacred music (MM). *Accreditation:* NASM. *Degree requirements:* For master's, variable foreign language requirement, thesis; for doctorate, thesis/dissertation. *Entrance requirements:* For master's and doctorate, audition, GRE General Test or minimum GPA of 3.0. Additional exam requirements/recommendations for international students: Required—TOEFL (minimum score 550 paper-based; 213 computer-based). Electronic applications accepted.

University of Georgia, Graduate School, College of Education, Program in Music Education, Athens, GA 30602. Offers MM Ed, Ed D, Ed S. *Accreditation:* NASM; NCATE. *Students:* 11 full-time (5 women), 27 part-time (16 women); includes 11 minority (8 African Americans, 3 Asian Americans or Pacific Islanders), 2 international. 34 applicants, 59% accepted, 11 enrolled. In 2009, 21 master's, 2 doctorates, 1 other advanced degree awarded. *Degree requirements:* For doctorate, thesis/dissertation. *Entrance requirements:* For master's, GRE General Test, MAT; for doctorate, GRE General Test; for Ed S, GRE General Test or MAT. *Application deadline:* For fall admission, 7/1 priority date for domestic students; for spring admission, 11/15 for domestic students. Application fee: $50. Electronic applications accepted. *Expenses:* Tuition, state resident: full-time $6000; part-time $250 per credit hour. Tuition, nonresident: full-time $20,904; part-time $871 per credit hour. Required fees: $730 per semester. *Financial support:* Fellowships, research assistantships, teaching assistantships, unspecified assistantships available. *Unit head:* Dr. Donald R. Lowe, Director, 706-542-2276, Fax: 706-542-2773, E-mail: dlowe@uga.edu. *Application contact:* Dr. Kenneth M. Fischer, Graduate Coordinator, 206-542-2743, E-mail: kfischer@uga.edu.

University of Hartford, The Hartt School, West Hartford, CT 06117-1599. Offers choral conducting (MM Ed); composition (MM, DMA, Artist Diploma, Diploma); conducting (MM, DMA, Artist Diploma, Diploma), including choral (MM, Diploma), instrumental (MM, Diploma); early childhood education (MM Ed); instrumental conducting (MM Ed); Kodály (MM Ed); music (CAGS); music education (DMA, PhD); music history (MM); music theory (MM); pedagogy (MM Ed); performance (MM, MM Ed, DMA, Artist Diploma, Diploma); research (MM Ed); technology (MM Ed). Part-time programs available. *Degree requirements:* For master's, variable foreign language requirement, thesis (for some programs), recital; for doctorate, variable foreign language requirement, thesis/dissertation (for some programs), recital; for other advanced degree, recital. *Entrance requirements:* For master's, audition, letters of recommendation; for doctorate, proficiency exam, audition, interview, research paper; for other advanced degree, audition. Additional exam requirements/recommendations for international students: Required—TOEFL. Electronic applications accepted. *Expenses:* Contact institution.

University of Illinois at Urbana–Champaign, Graduate College, College of Fine and Applied Arts, School of Music, Champaign, IL 61820. Offers music (M Mus, DMA, AD); music education (MME, Ed D, PhD); musicology (PhD). *Accreditation:* NASM. *Faculty:* 68 full-time (11 women), 6 part-time/adjunct (2 women). *Students:* 282 full-time (133 women), 94 part-time (59 women); includes 27 minority (7 African Americans, 1 American Indian/Alaska Native, 10 Asian Americans or Pacific Islanders, 9 Hispanic Americans), 136 international. 551 applicants, 39% accepted, 105 enrolled. In 2009, 69 master's, 50 doctorates awarded. *Entrance requirements:* For master's and doctorate, minimum GPA of 3.0. Additional exam requirements/recommendations for international students: Required—TOEFL (minimum score 590 paper-based; 243 computer-based). *Application deadline:* Applications are processed on a rolling basis. Application fee: $60 ($75 for international students). Electronic applications accepted. *Financial support:* In 2009–10, 29 fellowships, 9 research assistantships, 120 teaching assistantships were awarded; tuition waivers (full and partial) also available. *Unit head:* Karl Kramer, Director, 217-244-2676, Fax: 217-244-4585, E-mail: kramerk@illinois.edu. *Application contact:* Jennifer Phillips, Office Manager, 217-244-8385, Fax: 217-244-4585, E-mail: jhorn@illinois.edu.

The University of Kansas, Graduate Studies, School of Music, Program in Music Education, Lawrence, KS 66045. Offers MME, PhD. *Accreditation:* NASM. *Students:* 14 full-time (8 women), 13 part-time (9 women); includes 1 minority (Asian American or Pacific Islander). Average age 35. 15 applicants, 67% accepted, 10 enrolled. In 2009, 4 master's, 4 doctorates awarded. *Degree requirements:* For master's, comprehensive exam, thesis or alternative; for doctorate, comprehensive exam, thesis/dissertation. *Entrance requirements:* For master's, GRE, minimum GPA of 3.0, video, letters of reference; for doctorate, GRE, MEMT diagnostic exam, minimum graduate GPA of 3.5, video, reference letters, transcripts, writing sample, proof of professional experience. Additional exam requirements/recommendations for international students: Required—TOEFL (minimum score 570 paper-based; 230 computer-based; 92 iBT), or IELTS; Recommended—TWE. *Application deadline:* For fall admission, 2/15 priority date for domestic students, 2/15 for international students. Applications are processed on a rolling basis. Application fee: $45 ($55 for international students). Electronic applications accepted. *Expenses:* Tuition, state resident: full-time $6492; part-time $270.50 per credit hour. Tuition, nonresident: full-time $15,510; part-time $646.25 per credit hour. Required fees: $847; $70.56 per credit hour. Tuition and fees vary according to course load and program. *Financial support:* Fellowships with tuition reimbursements, research assistantships, teaching assistantships with full and partial tuition reimbursements, institutionally sponsored loans, scholarships/grants, and unspecified assistantships available. Financial award application deadline: 12/15; financial award applicants required to submit FAFSA. *Faculty research:* Psychology of music, performance, assessment, listener responses, functional music, philosophy of music education, choral pedagogy, choir acoustics, voice science, children's choirs, music in society. *Unit head:* Robert Walzel, Dean, 785-864-3436, Fax: 785-864-5387, E-mail: music@ku.edu. *Application contact:* Dr. James Daugherty, Director of Graduate Studies, 785-864-9637, Fax: 785-864-9640, E-mail: jdaugher@ku.edu.

University of Kentucky, Graduate School, College of Fine Arts, Program in Music, Lexington, KY 40506-0032. Offers music (PhD); music composition (MM); music education (MM); music performance (MM); music theory (MA); musical arts (DMA); musicology (MA). *Accreditation:* NASM. Part-time and evening/weekend programs available. *Degree requirements:* For master's, variable foreign language requirement, comprehensive exam, thesis (for some programs); for doctorate, variable foreign language requirement, comprehensive exam, thesis/dissertation. *Entrance requirements:* For master's, GRE General Test, minimum undergraduate GPA of 2.75; for doctorate, GRE General Test, minimum undergraduate GPA of 2.75, graduate 3.0. Additional exam requirements/recommendations for international students: Required—TOEFL (minimum score 550 paper-based; 213 computer-based). Electronic applications accepted. *Faculty research:* Musicology, music theory, jazz, music education, performance and conducting.

University of Louisiana at Lafayette, College of the Arts, School of Music, Lafayette, LA 70504. Offers conducting (MM); pedagogy (MM); vocal and instrumental performance (MM). *Accreditation:* NASM. *Degree requirements:* For master's, thesis or alternative. *Entrance requirements:* For master's, GRE General Test, minimum GPA of 2.75. Additional exam requirements/recommendations for international students: Required—TOEFL (minimum score 550 paper-based; 213 computer-based). Electronic applications accepted. *Faculty research:* Nineteenth century American music, trumpet pedagogy, fifteenth century Renaissance polyphony, Charles Ives.

University of Louisville, Graduate School, College of Education and Human Development, Department of Teaching and Learning, Louisville, KY 40292-0001. Offers art education (MAT); curriculum and instruction (PhD); early elementary education (MAT); instructional technology (M Ed); interdisciplinary early childhood education (MAT); middle school education (MAT); music education (MAT); reading education (M Ed); secondary education (MAT); special education (M Ed, MAT); teacher leadership (M Ed). Part-time and evening/weekend programs available. *Faculty:* 43 full-time (33 women), 43 part-time/adjunct (36 women). *Students:* 207 full-time (144 women), 410 part-time (306 women); includes 68 minority (43 African Americans, 2 American Indian/Alaska Native, 14 Asian Americans or Pacific Islanders, 9 Hispanic Americans), 5 international. Average age 33. 216 applicants, 68% accepted, 112 enrolled. In 2009, 269 master's, 6 doctorates awarded. *Degree requirements:* For doctorate, comprehensive exam, thesis/dissertation. *Entrance requirements:* For master's, GRE General Test, PRAXIS II (for some programs); for doctorate, GRE General Test. Additional exam requirements/recommendations for international students: Required—TOEFL (minimum score 560 paper-based; 210 computer-based; 83 iBT). Application fee: $50. Electronic applications accepted. *Financial support:* In 2009–10, 172 students received support; fellowships, research assistantships, teaching assistantships, career-related internships or fieldwork, Federal Work-Study, scholarships/grants, and unspecified assistantships available. Financial award application deadline: 6/1; financial award applicants required to submit FAFSA. *Faculty research:* Assessment of cognitive and language abilities in infants and preschool children; mathematics teachers' conceptions and beliefs, effect, and understanding of mathematics; incorporating nanoscience and nanotechnology into middle and high school science classrooms; urban teacher preparation through inquiry, action and advocacy; impacts of cognitive coaching on teacher practice and student achievement. Total annual research expenditures: $3.7 million. *Unit head:* Dr. Ann E. Larson, Acting Chair, 502-852-6431, Fax: 502-852-1497, E-mail: ann@louisville.edu. *Application contact:* Libby Leggett, Director, Graduate Admissions, 502-852-3101, Fax: 502-852-6536, E-mail: gradadm@louisville.edu.

University of Louisville, Graduate School, School of Music, Louisville, KY 40292-0001. Offers music composition (MM); music education (MME); music history and literature (MM); music theory (MM); performance (MM). *Accreditation:* NASM. Part-time and evening/weekend programs available. *Faculty:* 33 full-time (10 women), 38 part-time/adjunct (10 women). *Students:* 52 full-time (17 women), 9 part-time (6 women); includes 7 minority (4 African Americans, 3 Hispanic Americans), 9 international. Average age 28. 75 applicants, 56% accepted, 28 enrolled. In 2009, 25 master's awarded. *Degree requirements:* For master's, one foreign language, thesis (for some programs), recital (performance), paper (music education), major composition (composition). *Entrance requirements:* For master's, GRE General Test, music

Music Education

University of Louisville (continued)
history and theory exam, jazz exam, audition, portfolio. Additional exam requirements/recommendations for international students: Required—TOEFL (minimum score 550 paper-based; 213 computer-based; 79 iBT). *Application deadline:* For fall admission, 3/15 priority date for domestic and international students; for spring admission, 11/15 priority date for domestic and international students. Applications are processed on a rolling basis. Application fee: $50. *Financial support:* In 2009–10, 50 students received support, including 4 fellowships with full tuition reimbursements available (averaging $12,000 per year), 24 teaching assistantships with full tuition reimbursements available (averaging $12,000 per year); scholarships/grants, health care benefits, tuition waivers (full and partial), and unspecified assistantships also available. Financial award application deadline: 3/15; financial award applicants required to submit FAFSA. *Faculty research:* Performance, composition, music education, music therapy, music history. *Unit head:* Dr. Christopher Doane, Dean, 502-852-6907, Fax: 502-852-1874, E-mail: doane@louisville.edu. *Application contact:* Toni Robinson, Esq., Admissions Counselor, 502-852-1623, Fax: 502-852-0520, E-mail: toni.robinson@louisville.edu.

University of Maryland, Baltimore County, Graduate School, College of Arts, Humanities and Social Sciences, Department of Education, Program in Teaching, Baltimore, MD 21250. Offers early childhood education (MAT); elementary education (MAT); secondary education (MAT), including art, biology, chemistry, dance, earth/space science, English, foreign language, mathematics, music, physics, theatre; secondary science (MAT), including social studies. Part-time and evening/weekend programs available. *Faculty:* 24 full-time (18 women), 25 part-time/adjunct (19 women). *Students:* 52 full-time (41 women), 64 part-time (55 women); includes 20 minority (5 African Americans, 1 American Indian/Alaska Native, 10 Asian Americans or Pacific Islanders, 4 Hispanic Americans), 3 international. Average age 31. 88 applicants, 57% accepted, 39 enrolled. In 2009, 106 master's awarded. *Degree requirements:* For master's, comprehensive exam (for some programs), thesis (for some programs). *Entrance requirements:* For master's, PRAXIS I and II, minimum GPA of 3.0. Additional exam requirements/recommendations for international students: Required—TOEFL. *Application deadline:* For fall admission, 6/1 for domestic students; for spring admission, 11/1 for domestic students. Applications are processed on a rolling basis. Application fee: $50. Electronic applications accepted. *Financial support:* In 2009–10, 6 students received support, including research assistantships with full tuition reimbursements available (averaging $12,000 per year); career-related internships or fieldwork, Federal Work-Study, scholarships/grants, tuition waivers, and unspecified assistantships also available. Financial award application deadline: 3/1. *Faculty research:* STEM teacher education, culturally sensitive pedagogy, ESOL/bilingual education, early childhood education, language, literacy and culture. *Unit head:* Dr. Susan M. Blunck, Director, 410-455-2869, Fax: 410-455-3986, E-mail: blunck@umbc.edu. *Application contact:* Dr. Susan M. Blunck, Director, 410-455-2869, Fax: 410-455-3986, E-mail: blunck@umbc.edu.

University of Maryland, College Park, Academic Affairs, College of Arts and Humanities, School of Music, Program in Music, College Park, MD 20742. Offers M Ed, MA, MM, DMA, Ed D, PhD. *Students:* 172 full-time (110 women), 66 part-time (33 women); includes 43 minority (9 African Americans, 30 Asian Americans or Pacific Islanders, 4 Hispanic Americans), 41 international. 586 applicants, 19% accepted, 52 enrolled. In 2009, 38 master's, 29 doctorates awarded. *Entrance requirements:* Additional exam requirements/recommendations for international students: Required—TOEFL. *Application deadline:* For fall admission, 12/1 for domestic and international students. Application fee: $60. *Expenses:* Tuition, area resident: Part-time $471 per credit hour. Tuition, state resident: part-time $471 per credit hour. Tuition, nonresident: part-time $1016 per credit hour. Required fees: $337.04 per term. *Financial support:* In 2009–10, 1 fellowship with full tuition reimbursement (averaging $15,711 per year), 109 teaching assistantships (averaging $15,897 per year) were awarded. *Unit head:* Dr. Robert Gibson, Director, 301-405-5553, Fax: 301-314-9504, E-mail: rgibson@umd.edu. *Application contact:* Dean of Graduate School, 301-405-0358, Fax: 301-314-9305.

University of Massachusetts Lowell, College of Arts and Sciences, Department of Music, Lowell, MA 01854-2881. Offers music education (MM); sound recording technology (MM). *Accreditation:* NASM. Part-time programs available. *Degree requirements:* For master's, one foreign language, thesis. *Entrance requirements:* For master's, MAT, audition. Electronic applications accepted.

University of Memphis, Graduate School, College of Communication and Fine Arts, Rudi E. Scheidt School of Music, Memphis, TN 38152. Offers applied music (M Mu, DMA); composition (M Mu, DMA); conducting (M Mu, DMA); historical musicology (PhD); jazz and studio performance (M Mu); music education (M Mu, DMA); musicology (M Mu). *Accreditation:* NASM. Part-time programs available. *Faculty:* 36 full-time (7 women), 7 part-time/adjunct (4 women). *Students:* 84 full-time (34 women), 44 part-time (21 women); includes 24 minority (17 African Americans, 2 Asian Americans or Pacific Islanders, 5 Hispanic Americans), 24 international. Average age 32. 76 applicants, 87% accepted, 42 enrolled. In 2009, 13 master's, 10 doctorates awarded. Terminal master's awarded for partial completion of doctoral program. *Degree requirements:* For master's, comprehensive exam, thesis or alternative; for doctorate, one foreign language, comprehensive exam, thesis/dissertation, exam. *Entrance requirements:* For master's, GRE General Test or MAT, proficiency exam, audition; for doctorate, GRE General Test or MAT, proficiency exam, audition, master's degree. Additional exam requirements/recommendations for international students: Required—TOEFL. *Application deadline:* For fall admission, 8/1 for domestic students; for spring admission, 12/1 for domestic students. Applications are processed on a rolling basis. Application fee: $35 ($60 for international students). *Expenses:* Tuition, state resident: full-time $6246; part-time $347 per credit hour. Tuition, nonresident: full-time $15,894; part-time $883 per credit hour. Required fees: $1160. Full-time tuition and fees vary according to course load, degree level and program. *Financial support:* In 2009–10, 73 students received support; research assistantships with full and partial tuition reimbursements available, teaching assistantships with full and partial tuition reimbursements available, Federal Work-Study, scholarships/grants, and unspecified assistantships available. Financial award application deadline: 2/15; financial award applicants required to submit FAFSA. *Faculty research:* Spanish Renaissance, twentieth century music, Project OPTIMUS, composition, musical performance, regional music, performance, performance practice, composition. *Unit head:* Dr. Patricia J. Hoy, Director, 901-678-2541, Fax: 901-678-3096, E-mail: phoy@memphis.edu. *Application contact:* Dr. John Baur, Assistant Director for Graduate Admissions, 901-678-3362, Fax: 901-678-3096, E-mail: jbaur@memphis.edu.

University of Miami, Graduate School, Frost School of Music, Department of Music Education and Music Therapy, Coral Gables, FL 33124. Offers music education (MM, PhD, Spec M); music therapy (MM). *Accreditation:* NASM. *Degree requirements:* For master's, thesis; for doctorate, thesis/dissertation, 2 research tools; for Spec M, thesis, research project. *Entrance requirements:* For master's and doctorate, GRE General Test. Additional exam requirements/recommendations for international students: Required—TOEFL (minimum score 550 paper-based; 213 computer-based; 59 iBT). Electronic applications accepted. *Faculty research:* Motivation, quantitative research, early childhood, instrumental music, elementary music.

University of Michigan, Horace H. Rackham School of Graduate Studies, School of Music, Theatre, and Dance, Program in Music Education, Ann Arbor, MI 48109-2085. Offers MM, PhD, Spec M. *Accreditation:* NASM. *Faculty:* 4 full-time (3 women), 1 (woman) part-time/adjunct. *Students:* 5 full-time (2 women). Average age 35. *Degree requirements:* For doctorate, thesis/dissertation, oral and preliminary exams. *Entrance requirements:* For doctorate, MAT, writing sample, portfolio. Additional exam requirements/recommendations for international students: Required—TOEFL (minimum score 600 paper-based; 250 computer-based; 100 iBT). *Application deadline:* For fall admission, 12/1 for domestic and international students. Applications are processed on a rolling basis. Application fee: $60 ($75 for international students). Electronic applications accepted. *Expenses:* Tuition, state resident: full-time $17,286; part-time $1099 per credit hour. Tuition, nonresident: full-time $34,944; part-time $2080 per credit hour. Required fees: $95 per semester. Tuition and fees vary according to course load, degree level and program. *Financial support:* In 2009–10, 5 teaching assistantships with full and partial tuition reimbursements (averaging $38,208 per year) were awarded. Financial award application deadline: 2/1. *Unit head:* Steven M. Whiting, Associate Dean for Graduate Studies, 734-764-0590, Fax: 734-764-5097, E-mail: stevenmw@umich.edu. *Application contact:* Karen A. Frye, Administrative Assistant, 734-764-0590, Fax: 734-763-5097, E-mail: hoshi@umich.edu.

University of Minnesota, Duluth, Graduate School, School of Fine Arts, Department of Music, Duluth, MN 55812-2496. Offers music education (MM); performance (MM). *Accreditation:* NASM. Part-time programs available. *Degree requirements:* For master's, comprehensive exam, thesis (for some programs), recital (MM in performance). *Entrance requirements:* For master's, audition, minimum GPA of 3.0, sample of written work, interview, bachelor's degree in music, video of teaching. Additional exam requirements/recommendations for international students: Required—TOEFL (minimum score 550 paper-based; 213 computer-based). *Faculty research:* Band composition, music aesthetics, learning theory, value theory, music advocacy.

University of Missouri, Graduate School, College of Education, Department of Learning, Teaching and Curriculum, Columbia, MO 65211. Offers agricultural education (M Ed, PhD, Ed S); art education (M Ed, PhD, Ed S); business and office education (M Ed, PhD, Ed S); early childhood education (M Ed, PhD, Ed S); elementary education (M Ed, PhD, Ed S); English education (M Ed, PhD, Ed S); foreign language education (M Ed, PhD, Ed S); health education and promotion (M Ed, PhD); learning and instruction (M Ed); marketing education (M Ed, PhD, Ed S); mathematics education (M Ed, PhD, Ed S); music education (M Ed, PhD, Ed S); reading education (M Ed, PhD, Ed S); science education (M Ed, PhD, Ed S); social studies education (M Ed, PhD, Ed S); vocational education (M Ed, PhD, Ed S). Part-time programs available. Terminal master's awarded for partial completion of doctoral program. *Degree requirements:* For doctorate, thesis/dissertation. *Entrance requirements:* For master's and Ed S, GRE General Test or MAT, minimum GPA of 3.0; for doctorate, GRE General Test, minimum GPA of 3.0. Additional exam requirements/recommendations for international students: Required—TOEFL (minimum score 600 paper-based; 250 computer-based; 100 iBT). Electronic applications accepted.

University of Missouri–Kansas City, Conservatory of Music, Kansas City, MO 64110-2499. Offers composition (MM, DMA); conducting (MM, DMA); music (MA); music education (MME, PhD); music history and literature (MM); music theory (MM); performance (MM, DMA). PhD (interdisciplinary) offered through the School of Graduate Studies. *Accreditation:* NASM. Part-time programs available. *Faculty:* 58 full-time (24 women), 29 part-time/adjunct (13 women). *Students:* 143 full-time (65 women), 103 part-time (58 women); includes 12 minority (7 African Americans, 1 American Indian/Alaska Native, 2 Asian Americans or Pacific Islanders, 2 Hispanic Americans), 64 international. Average age 29. 267 applicants, 45% accepted, 59 enrolled. In 2009, 43 master's, 21 doctorates awarded. *Degree requirements:* For master's, variable foreign language requirement, comprehensive exam, thesis (for some programs); for doctorate, variable foreign language requirement, comprehensive exam, thesis/dissertation or alternative. *Entrance requirements:* For master's, minimum GPA of 3.0 in major, auditions (performance); for doctorate, minimum graduate GPA of 3.5, auditions (performance degrees), portfolio of compositions. Additional exam requirements/recommendations for international students: Required—TOEFL (minimum score 550 paper-based; 213 computer-based; 80 iBT). *Application deadline:* For fall admission, 1/15 priority date for domestic students, 1/15 for international students. Application fee: $45 ($50 for international students). *Expenses:* Tuition, state resident: full-time $5378; part-time $299 per credit hour. Tuition, nonresident: full-time $13,881; part-time $771 per credit hour. Required fees: $641; $71 per credit hour. Tuition and fees vary according to course load and program. *Financial support:* In 2009–10, 52 teaching assistantships with partial tuition reimbursements (averaging $8,772 per year) were awarded; career-related internships or fieldwork, Federal Work-Study, institutionally sponsored loans, scholarships/grants, tuition waivers (partial), and unspecified assistantships also available. Support available to part-time students. Financial award application deadline: 3/1; financial award applicants required to submit FAFSA. *Faculty research:* Electro-acoustic composition, affective music responses, American music theatre, Russian choral music, music therapy and Alzheimer's. Total annual research expenditures: $8,559. *Unit head:* Peter Witte, Dean, 816-235-2731, Fax: 816-235-5265, E-mail: wittep@umkc.edu. *Application contact:* James Elswick, Associate Director, 816-235-2932, Fax: 816-235-5264, E-mail: cadmissions@umkc.edu.

University of Missouri–St. Louis, College of Fine Arts and Communication, Program in Music Education, St. Louis, MO 63121. Offers MME. *Accreditation:* NASM. Part-time and evening/weekend programs available. *Faculty:* 17 full-time (4 women), 7 part-time/adjunct (4 women). *Students:* 20 full-time (13 women), 1 (woman) part-time; includes 3 minority (all African Americans). Average age 34. In 2009, 5 master's awarded. *Entrance requirements:* For master's, 3 letters of recommendation, BA in music education. Additional exam requirements/recommendations for international students: Required—TOEFL (minimum score 550 paper-based; 213 computer-based). *Application deadline:* For fall admission, 7/1 priority date for domestic and international students; for spring admission, 12/1 for domestic students, 12/1 priority date for international students. Applications are processed on a rolling basis. Application fee: $35 ($40 for international students). Electronic applications accepted. *Expenses:* Tuition, state resident: full-time $5377; part-time $297.70 per credit hour. Tuition, nonresident: full-time $13,882; part-time $771.20 per credit hour. Required fees: $220; $12.20 per credit hour. One-time fee: $12. Tuition and fees vary according to course level, campus/location and program. *Financial support:* In 2009–10, 1 teaching assistantship with full and partial tuition reimbursement (averaging $5,625 per year) was awarded. Financial award applicants required to submit FAFSA. *Faculty research:* Music technology, musicology, music education methods, history of music education, psychology of music. *Unit head:* Dr. Fred Willman, Director of Graduate Studies, 314-516-5980, Fax: 314-516-6593, E-mail: fred_willman@umsl.edu. *Application contact:* 314-516-5458, Fax: 314-516-6996, E-mail: gradadm@umsl.edu.

The University of Montana, Graduate School, School of Fine Arts, Department of Music, Missoula, MT 59812-0002. Offers music (MM), including composition/technology, music education, musical theater, performance. *Accreditation:* NASM. *Entrance requirements:* For master's, GRE General Test, GRE Subject Test, portfolio.

University of Nebraska at Kearney, College of Graduate Study, College of Fine Arts and Humanities, Department of Music, Kearney, NE 68849-0001. Offers music education (MA Ed). *Accreditation:* NASM; NCATE. Part-time and evening/weekend programs available. *Degree requirements:* For master's, thesis optional. *Entrance requirements:* For master's, interview/audition, portfolio, letters of recommendation. *Faculty research:* Contemporary American music, musical theatre, opera, woodwind performance and pedagogy.

University of Nebraska–Lincoln, Graduate College, College of Fine and Performing Arts, School of Music, Lincoln, NE 68588. Offers composition (MM, DMA); conducting (MM, DMA); music education (MM, PhD); music history (MM); music theory (MM); performance (MM, DMA); piano pedagogy (MM); woodwind specialties (MM). *Accreditation:* NASM. *Degree requirements:* For master's, thesis optional; for doctorate, comprehensive exam, thesis/dissertation. *Entrance requirements:* For master's and doctorate, audition. Additional exam requirements/recommendations for international students: Required—TOEFL. Electronic applications accepted. *Faculty research:* Mozart, Tchaikovsky, Josquin des Prez, practice of J.S. Bach's organ works, instructional strategies in music education.

University of New Hampshire, Graduate School, College of Liberal Arts, Department of Music, Durham, NH 03824. Offers music education (MA); music history (MA). *Accreditation:* NASM. *Faculty:* 17 full-time (3 women). *Students:* 7 full-time (1 woman), 5 part-time (3 women); includes 1 minority (Hispanic American), 1 international. Average age 28. 9 applicants, 100% accepted, 5 enrolled. In 2009, 5 master's awarded. *Degree requirements:* For master's, one foreign language. *Entrance requirements:* For master's, audition. Additional exam requirements/recommendations for international students: Required—TOEFL (minimum score 550 paper-based; 213 computer-based; 80 iBT). *Application deadline:* For fall admission, 4/1 priority date for domestic students, 4/1 for international students; for spring admission, 12/1 for domestic students. Applications are processed on a rolling basis. Application fee: $65. Electronic applications accepted. *Expenses:* Tuition, state resident: full-time $10,380; part-time $577 per credit hour. Tuition, nonresident: full-time $24,350; part-time $1002 per credit hour. Required

fees: $1550; $387.50 per semester. Tuition and fees vary according to course load and program. *Financial support:* In 2009–10, 5 students received support, including 4 teaching assistantships; fellowships, research assistantships, career-related internships or fieldwork, Federal Work-Study, scholarships/grants, and tuition waivers (full and partial) also available. Support available to part-time students. Financial award application deadline: 2/15. *Unit head:* Dr. Rob Stibler, Chairperson, 603-862-2418. *Application contact:* Alexis Zaricki, Administrative Assistant, 603-862-2418, E-mail: grad.music@unh.edu.

The University of North Carolina at Chapel Hill, Graduate School, School of Education, Program in Secondary Education, Chapel Hill, NC 27599. Offers English (Grades 9-12) (MAT); English as a second language (MAT); French (Grades K-12) (MAT); German (Grades K-12) (MAT); Japanese (Grades K-12) (MAT); Latin (Grades 9-12) (MAT); mathematics (Grades 9-12) (MAT); music (Grades K-12) (MAT); science (Grades 9-12) (MAT); social studies (Grades 9-12) (MAT); Spanish (Grades K-12) (MAT). *Accreditation:* NCATE. *Students:* 53 full-time (35 women), 1 part-time (0 women); includes 8 minority (4 African Americans, 2 Asian Americans or Pacific Islanders, 2 Hispanic Americans), 3 international. Average age 25. 137 applicants, 77% accepted, 54 enrolled. In 2009, 39 master's awarded. *Degree requirements:* For master's, comprehensive exam. *Entrance requirements:* For master's, GRE General Test, minimum GPA of 3.0 during last 2 years of undergraduate course work. Additional exam requirements/recommendations for international students: Required—TOEFL (minimum score 550 paper-based; 79 computer-based). *Application deadline:* For fall admission, 12/15 priority date for domestic and international students. Applications are processed on a rolling basis. Application fee: $77. Electronic applications accepted. *Financial support:* Federal Work-Study available. Support available to part-time students. Financial award application deadline: 3/1; financial award applicants required to submit FAFSA. *Unit head:* Dr. James Trier, Coordinator, 919-843-4627, Fax: 919-962-1533. *Application contact:* Amy Butler, Student Services Assistant, 919-966-1346, Fax: 919-962-1533, E-mail: abutler@email.unc.edu.

The University of North Carolina at Charlotte, Graduate School, College of Education, Program in Teacher Education, Charlotte, NC 28223-0001. Offers art education (K-12) (MAT); dance education (K-12) (MAT); elementary education (K-6) (MAT); English as a second language (K-12) (MAT); foreign language education (K-12) (MAT); general teacher education (MAT); middle grades education (6-9) (MAT); music education (K-12) (MAT); secondary education (9-12) (MAT); special education (K-12) (MAT); theatre education (K-12) (MAT). *Faculty:* 108 full-time (64 women), 16 part-time/adjunct (12 women). *Students:* 29 full-time (20 women), 229 part-time (189 women); includes 32 minority (22 African Americans, 2 American Indian/Alaska Native, 3 Asian Americans or Pacific Islanders, 5 Hispanic Americans). Average age 32. 108 applicants, 92% accepted, 85 enrolled. In 2009, 59 master's awarded. *Entrance requirements:* For master's, GRE or MAT. Additional exam requirements/recommendations for international students: Required—TOEFL (minimum score 557 paper-based; 220 computer-based; 83 iBT). *Application deadline:* For fall admission, 7/1 for domestic students, 5/1 for international students; for spring admission, 11/1 for domestic students, 10/1 for international students. Applications are processed on a rolling basis. Application fee: $55. Electronic applications accepted. *Financial support:* In 2009–10, 5 students received support, including 1 research assistantship (averaging $18,000 per year), 3 teaching assistantships (averaging $12,183 per year); career-related internships or fieldwork, Federal Work-Study, institutionally sponsored loans, scholarships/grants, and administrative assistantship also available. Support available to part-time students. Financial award application deadline: 4/1; financial award applicants required to submit FAFSA. Total annual research expenditures: $5.1 million. *Unit head:* Dr. Kimberly J. Hartman, Coordinator, 704-687-8883, Fax: 704-687-6430, E-mail: khartman@uncc.edu. *Application contact:* Kathy B. Giddings, Director of Graduate Admissions, 704-687-5503, Fax: 704-687-3279, E-mail: gradadmn@uncc.edu.

The University of North Carolina at Greensboro, Graduate School, School of Music, Greensboro, NC 27412-5001. Offers composition (MM); education (MM); music education (PhD); performance (MM, DMA). *Accreditation:* NASM. *Degree requirements:* For master's, variable foreign language requirement, thesis (for some programs), recital; for doctorate, comprehensive exam, thesis/dissertation, diagnostic exam, recital. *Entrance requirements:* For master's, GRE General Test, NTE, audition; for doctorate, GRE General Test, GRE Subject Test (music), audition. Additional exam requirements/recommendations for international students: Required—TOEFL. Electronic applications accepted.

The University of North Carolina at Pembroke, Graduate Studies, Program in Music Education, Pembroke, NC 28372-1510. Offers MA, MAT. *Accreditation:* NASM. *Entrance requirements:* For master's, GRE or MAT, minimum GPA of 3.0 in major, 2.5 overall; audition. Additional exam requirements/recommendations for international students: Required—TOEFL.

University of North Dakota, Graduate School, College of Arts and Sciences, Department of Music, Grand Forks, ND 58202. Offers music (M Mus); music education (M Mus, DMEd). *Accreditation:* NASM. Part-time programs available. *Degree requirements:* For master's, comprehensive exam, thesis or alternative. *Entrance requirements:* For master's, minimum GPA of 3.0. Additional exam requirements/recommendations for international students: Required—TOEFL (minimum score 550 paper-based; 213 computer-based; 79 iBT), IELTS (minimum score 6.5). Electronic applications accepted.

University of Northern Colorado, Graduate School, College of Performing and Visual Arts, School of Music, Greeley, CO 80639. Offers collaborative keyboard (MM); conducting (MM); instrumental performance (MM); jazz studies (MM); music conducting (DA); music education (MM, DA); music history and literature (MM, DA); music performance (DA); music theory and composition (MM, DA); vocal performance (MM). *Accreditation:* NASM; NCATE (one or more programs are accredited). Part-time programs available. *Faculty:* 30 full-time (8 women). *Students:* 76 full-time (28 women), 19 part-time (8 women); includes 3 minority (2 Asian Americans or Pacific Islanders, 1 Hispanic American), 14 international. Average age 29. 79 applicants, 82% accepted, 38 enrolled. In 2009, 22 master's, 2 doctorates awarded. *Degree requirements:* For master's, comprehensive exam, thesis or alternative; for doctorate, comprehensive exam, thesis/dissertation. *Entrance requirements:* For master's, audition; for doctorate, GRE General Test, audition, 3 letters of recommendation. *Application deadline:* Applications are processed on a rolling basis. Application fee: $50 ($60 for international students). Electronic applications accepted. *Expenses:* Tuition, state resident: full-time $5770; part-time $320.55 per credit hour. Tuition, nonresident: full-time $13,847; part-time $769.27 per credit hour. Required fees: $948.78; $52.72 per credit. *Financial support:* In 2009–10, 30 research assistantships (averaging $4,101 per year), 17 teaching assistantships (averaging $5,787 per year) were awarded; fellowships, unspecified assistantships also available. Financial award application deadline: 3/1; financial award applicants required to submit FAFSA. *Unit head:* David Caffey, Director, 970-351-2679. *Application contact:* Linda Sisson, Graduate Student Admission Coordinator, 970-351-1807, Fax: 970-351-2371, E-mail: linda.sisson@unco.edu.

University of Northern Iowa, Graduate College, College of Humanities and Fine Arts, School of Music, Program in Music Education, Cedar Falls, IA 50614. Offers jazz pedagogy (MM); music (MA); music education (MM); piano performance and pedagogy (MM). *Accreditation:* NASM. Part-time and evening/weekend programs available. *Students:* 2 full-time (both women), 14 part-time (11 women). 7 applicants, 57% accepted, 0 enrolled. In 2009, 7 master's awarded. *Degree requirements:* For master's, comprehensive exam, thesis or alternative. *Entrance requirements:* For master's, written diagnostic exam in theory, music history, expository writing skills, and in the area of claimed competency, portfolio, tape recordings of compositions, in person auditions, minimum GPA of 3.0. Additional exam requirements/recommendations for international students: Required—TOEFL (minimum score 500 paper-based; 180 computer-based; 61 iBT). *Application deadline:* For fall admission, 8/1 priority date for domestic students. Applications are processed on a rolling basis. Application fee: $30 ($50 for international students). Electronic applications accepted. *Financial support:* Career-related internships or fieldwork, Federal Work-Study, and tuition waivers (full and partial) available. Support available to part-time students. Financial award application deadline: 2/1. *Unit head:* Dr. Rebecca

Burkhardt, Coordinator, 319-273-4723, E-mail: rebecca.burkhardt@uni.edu. *Application contact:* Laurie S. Russell, Record Analyst, 319-273-2623, Fax: 319-273-6792, E-mail: laurie.russell@uni.edu.

University of North Texas, Robert B. Toulouse School of Graduate Studies, College of Music, Denton, TX 76203. Offers composition (MM, DMA); jazz studies (MM); music (MA); music education (MM, MME, PhD); music theory (MM, PhD); musicology (MM, PhD); performance (MM, DMA). *Accreditation:* NASM. In 2009, 82 master's awarded. Terminal master's awarded for partial completion of doctoral program. *Degree requirements:* For master's, one foreign language, comprehensive exam (for some programs), thesis (for some programs); for doctorate, one foreign language, comprehensive exam (for some programs), thesis/dissertation (for some programs). *Entrance requirements:* For master's and doctorate, audition, writing samples. Additional exam requirements/recommendations for international students: Required—proof of English language proficiency; Recommended—TOEFL (minimum score 550 paper-based; 213 computer-based). *Application deadline:* Applications are processed on a rolling basis. Application fee: $50 ($75 for international students). Electronic applications accepted. *Expenses:* Tuition, state resident: full-time $4298; part-time $239 per contact hour. Tuition, nonresident: full-time $9878; part-time $549 per contact hour. Required fees: $265 per contact hour. *Financial support:* Fellowships with partial tuition reimbursements, research assistantships, teaching assistantships with partial tuition reimbursements, career-related internships or fieldwork, Federal Work-Study, institutionally sponsored loans, and scholarships/grants available. Financial award application deadline: 4/1. *Faculty research:* Electro-acoustical music, intermedia, music and medicine, music performance. *Application contact:* Admissions and Scholarship Services, 940-367-7771, Fax: 940-565-2002.

University of Oklahoma, Graduate College, College of Fine Arts, School of Music, Norman, OK 73019-0390. Offers choral conducting (M Mus); conducting (M Mus Ed, DMA); general (M Mus Ed); instrumental (M Mus Ed); instrumental conducting (M Mus); music composition (M Mus, DMA); music education (M Mus Ed, PhD); music theory (M Mus); musicology (M Mus); organ (M Mus, DMA); piano (M Mus, DMA); voice (M Mus, DMA); wind/percussion/string (M Mus, DMA). *Accreditation:* NASM. *Faculty:* 53 full-time (16 women), 1 part-time/adjunct (0 women). *Students:* 102 full-time (60 women), 59 part-time (29 women); includes 15 minority (1 African American, 3 American Indian/Alaska Native, 9 Asian Americans or Pacific Islanders, 2 Hispanic Americans), 17 international. 88 applicants, 69% accepted, 44 enrolled. In 2009, 44 master's, 14 doctorates awarded. *Degree requirements:* For master's, variable foreign language requirement, thesis (for some programs), departmental qualifying exam, oral and preliminary exams; for doctorate, variable foreign language requirement, thesis/dissertation, departmental qualifying exam, general and oral exams. *Entrance requirements:* For master's, audition, BA in music, minimum GPA of 3.0; for doctorate, audition, minimum GPA of 3.0. Additional exam requirements/recommendations for international students: Required—TOEFL (minimum score 550 paper-based; 213 computer-based). *Application deadline:* For fall admission, 6/1 priority date for domestic students, 4/1 for international students; for spring admission, 11/1 for domestic students, 9/1 for international students. Applications are processed on a rolling basis. Application fee: $40 ($90 for international students). Electronic applications accepted. *Expenses:* Tuition, state resident: full-time $3744; part-time $156 per credit hour. Tuition, nonresident: full-time $13,577; part-time $565.70 per credit hour. Required fees: $2415; $90.10 per credit hour. *Financial support:* In 2009–10, 116 students received support, including 9 fellowships with full tuition reimbursements available (averaging $5,000 per year), 22 research assistantships with partial tuition reimbursements available (averaging $10,918 per year), 76 teaching assistantships with partial tuition reimbursements available (averaging $10,055 per year); unspecified assistantships also available. Financial award application deadline: 4/7; financial award applicants required to submit FAFSA. *Faculty research:* Piano pedagogy, vocal and instrumental performance, music education. Total annual research expenditures: $37,246. *Unit head:* Dr. Steven Curtis, Director, 405-325-2081, Fax: 405-325-7574, E-mail: scurtis@ou.edu. *Application contact:* Jan Russell, Office Assistant, 405-325-5393, Fax: 405-325-7574, E-mail: jrussell@ou.edu.

University of Oklahoma—Tulsa, Kodaly Certification Programs, Tulsa, OK 74135-2512. Offers Kodaly biography (Certificate); Kodaly concept (Certificate); Kodaly philosophy (Certificate).

University of Oregon, Graduate School, School of Music, Program in Music Education, Eugene, OR 97403. Offers M Mus, DMA, PhD. *Accreditation:* NASM. Part-time programs available. Terminal master's awarded for partial completion of doctoral program. *Degree requirements:* For master's, variable foreign language requirement, thesis (for some programs); for doctorate, one foreign language, comprehensive exam, thesis/dissertation. *Entrance requirements:* For master's, minimum GPA of 3.0, videotape or interview; for doctorate, GRE General Test, minimum GPA of 3.0, videotape or interview. Additional exam requirements/recommendations for international students: Required—TOEFL. *Faculty research:* Psalms of DeLasso, stress and muscular tension in stringed instrument performance, piano music of Stravinsky, learning aptitudes in elementary music.

University of Ottawa, Faculty of Graduate and Postdoctoral Studies, Faculty of Arts, Department of Music, Ottawa, ON K1N 6N5, Canada. Offers music (M Mus, MA); orchestral studies (Certificate); piano pedagogy research (Certificate). *Degree requirements:* For master's, thesis optional. *Entrance requirements:* For master's, honors degree or equivalent, minimum B+ average. Electronic applications accepted. *Faculty research:* Performance, theory, musicology.

University of Rhode Island, Graduate School, College of Arts and Sciences, Department of Music, Kingston, RI 02881. Offers music education (MM); music performance (MM). *Accreditation:* NASM. Part-time programs available. *Faculty:* 14 full-time (5 women). *Students:* 9 full-time (3 women), 5 part-time (1 woman); includes 1 minority (Asian American or Pacific Islander). In 2009, 5 master's awarded. *Entrance requirements:* For master's, 2 letters of recommendation, audition. Additional exam requirements/recommendations for international students: Required—TOEFL (minimum score 550 paper-based; 213 computer-based). *Application deadline:* For fall admission, 7/15 for domestic students, 2/1 for international students; for spring admission, 7/15 for international students. Application fee: $65. Electronic applications accepted. *Expenses:* Tuition, state resident: full-time $8828; part-time $490 per credit hour. Tuition, nonresident: full-time $22,100; part-time $1228 per credit hour. Required fees: $1118; $57 per semester. Tuition and fees vary according to program. *Financial support:* In 2009–10, 3 teaching assistantships with full and partial tuition reimbursements (averaging $6,368 per year) were awarded. Financial award application deadline: 3/15; financial award applicants required to submit FAFSA. *Unit head:* Dr. Ronald T. Lee, Chair, 401-874-2431, Fax: 401-874-2772, E-mail: rlee@uri.edu. *Application contact:* Dr. Eliane Aberdam, Co-Director of Graduate Studies, 401-874-2794, Fax: 401-874-2772, E-mail: eliane@uri.edu.

University of Rhode Island, Graduate School, College of Human Science and Services, School of Education, Kingston, RI 02881. Offers adult education (MA); education (PhD); elementary education (MA); music education (MM); reading education (MA); secondary education (MA); special education (MA); MS/PhD. *Accreditation:* NCATE. Part-time and evening/weekend programs available. *Faculty:* 19 full-time (12 women), 5 part-time/adjunct (1 woman). *Students:* 44 full-time (33 women), 128 part-time (101 women); includes 14 minority (8 African Americans, 2 American Indian/Alaska Native, 2 Asian Americans or Pacific Islanders, 2 Hispanic Americans), 3 international. In 2009, 44 master's, 7 doctorates awarded. *Degree requirements:* For master's, comprehensive exam (for some programs), thesis optional; for doctorate, comprehensive exam, thesis/dissertation. *Entrance requirements:* For master's, 2 letters of recommendation; interview (for special education applicants); for doctorate, GRE, 3 letters of recommendation, resume. Additional exam requirements/recommendations for international students: Required—TOEFL (minimum score 600 paper-based; 250 computer-based; 100 iBT). *Application deadline:* For fall admission, 1/31 for international students. Application fee: $65. Electronic applications accepted. *Expenses:* Tuition, state resident: full-time $8828; part-time $490 per credit hour. Tuition, nonresident: full-time $22,100; part-time $1228 per credit hour. Required fees: $1118; $57 per semester. Tuition and fees vary according to program. *Financial support:* In 2009–10, 5 research assistantships with full and partial tuition

Music Education

University of Rhode Island *(continued)*
reimbursements (averaging $11,518 per year), 3 teaching assistantships with full and partial tuition reimbursements (averaging $10,421 per year) were awarded; career-related internships or fieldwork also available. Financial award applicants required to submit FAFSA. Total annual research expenditures: $3.4 million. *Unit head:* Dr. David Byrd, Director, 401-874-5484, Fax: 401-874-5471, E-mail: dbyrd@uri.edu. *Application contact:* Dr. John Boulmetis, Coordinator of Graduate Studies, 401-874-4159, Fax: 401-874-7610, E-mail: johnb@uri.edu.

University of Rochester, Eastman School of Music, Rochester, NY 14627. Offers composition (MA, MM, DMA, PhD); conducting (MM, DMA); education (MA, PhD); jazz studies/contemporary media (MM); music education (MM, DMA); musicology (MA, PhD); pedagogy of music theory (MA); performance and literature (MM, DMA); piano accompanying and chamber music (MM, DMA); theory (MA, PhD). *Accreditation:* NASM. Part-time programs available. *Degree requirements:* For master's, thesis (for some programs); for doctorate, comprehensive exam (for some programs), thesis/dissertation (for some programs). *Entrance requirements:* For master's and doctorate, GRE. *Expenses:* Contact institution.

University of St. Thomas, Graduate Studies, College of Arts and Sciences, Program in Music Education, St. Paul, MN 55105-1096. Offers MA. *Accreditation:* NASM; NCATE. Part-time programs available. *Faculty:* 10 full-time (5 women), 20 part-time/adjunct (10 women). *Students:* 276 part-time (221 women); includes 10 minority (all African Americans). Average age 30. 15 applicants, 80% accepted, 12 enrolled. In 2009, 24 master's awarded. *Degree requirements:* For master's, comprehensive exam, thesis, 2 teaching videotape assessments. *Entrance requirements:* For master's, teaching videotape, performance assessment hearing, interview. Additional exam requirements/recommendations for international students: Required—TOEFL (minimum score 550 paper-based). *Application deadline:* For fall admission, 7/1 for domestic students; for winter admission, 12/1 for domestic students; for spring admission, 4/1 for domestic students. Applications are processed on a rolling basis. Application fee: $50. *Financial support:* In 2009–10, 14 students received support; fellowships, research assistantships, teaching assistantships, career-related internships or fieldwork, institutionally sponsored loans, scholarships/grants, and tuition waivers (partial) available. Financial award application deadline: 4/1. *Faculty research:* Kodaly, choral conducting, piano pedagogy. *Unit head:* Dr. Bruce P. Gleason, Director, 800-328-6819 Ext. 25729, Fax: 651-962-5886, E-mail: bpgleason@stthomas.edu. *Application contact:* Beverly H. Johnson, Program Coordinator, 800-328-6819 Ext. 25870, Fax: 651-962-5886, E-mail: bhjohnson@stthomas.edu.

University of South Carolina, The Graduate School, School of Music, Columbia, SC 29208. Offers composition (MM, DMA); conducting (MM, DMA); jazz studies (MM); music education (MM Ed, PhD); music history (MM); music performance (Certificate); music theory (MM); opera theater (MM); performance (MM, DMA); piano pedagogy (MM, DMA). *Accreditation:* NASM (one or more programs are accredited). Part-time programs available. *Degree requirements:* For master's, 5 foreign languages, comprehensive exam, thesis (for some programs); for doctorate, one foreign language, comprehensive exam, thesis/dissertation; for Certificate, recitals. *Entrance requirements:* For master's and doctorate, GRE General Test or MAT, music diagnostic exam. Additional exam requirements/recommendations for international students: Required—TOEFL (minimum score 570 paper-based; 230 computer-based). Electronic applications accepted. *Expenses:* Contact institution. *Faculty research:* Music skills in pre-school children, evaluation of school performing ensembles.

University of Southern California, Graduate School, Thornton School of Music, Los Angeles, CA 90089. Offers brass performance (MM, DMA, Graduate Certificate); choral and sacred music (MM, DMA); classical guitar (MM, DMA, Graduate Certificate); composition (MM, DMA); early music (MA, DMA); harp performance (MM, DMA, Graduate Certificate); historical musicology (PhD); jazz studies (MM, DMA, Graduate Certificate); keyboard collaborative arts (MM, Graduate Certificate); music education (MM, DMA); organ performance (MM, DMA, Graduate Certificate); percussion performance (MM, DMA, Graduate Certificate); piano performance (MM, DMA, Graduate Certificate); scoring for motion pictures and television (Graduate Certificate); strings performance (MM, DMA, Graduate Certificate); studio jazz guitar (MM, DMA, Graduate Certificate); teaching music (MA); vocal arts (classical voice) (opera) (MM, DMA, Graduate Certificate); woodwind performance (MM, DMA, Graduate Certificate). *Accreditation:* NASM. Part-time and evening/weekend programs available. *Faculty:* 74 full-time (14 women), 120 part-time/adjunct (29 women). *Students:* 354 full-time (155 women), 43 part-time (32 women); includes 72 minority (5 African Americans, 2 American Indian/Alaska Native, 47 Asian Americans or Pacific Islanders, 18 Hispanic Americans), 111 international. 784 applicants, 36% accepted, 145 enrolled. In 2009, 54 master's, 2 doctorates, 96 other advanced degrees awarded. Terminal master's awarded for partial completion of doctoral program. *Degree requirements:* For master's, variable foreign language requirement, comprehensive exam (for some programs); thesis (for some programs); for doctorate, variable foreign language requirement, comprehensive exam, thesis/dissertation (for some programs). *Entrance requirements:* For master's, GRE (for MA, MM in music education); for doctorate, GRE (for DMA). Additional exam requirements/recommendations for international students: Required—TOEFL (minimum score 560 paper-based; 220 computer-based; 83 iBT). *Application deadline:* For fall admission, 12/1 for domestic and international students; for spring admission, 10/1 for domestic and international students. Application fee: $85. Electronic applications accepted. *Expenses:* Contact institution. *Financial support:* In 2009–10, 65 teaching assistantships with full tuition reimbursements (averaging $9,600 per year) were awarded; tuition waivers also available. Financial award application deadline: 12/1; financial award applicants required to submit FAFSA. *Faculty research:* Early Modern musical improvisation and composition, maternal sound stimulation of the premature infant, physiological characteristics of jazz guitarists, the musical experience of the very young child, electronic music. *Unit head:* PJ Woolston, Dean, 213-740-2311, E-mail: woolston@thornton.usc.edu. *Application contact:* Ligaya J. Jones, Admission Coordinator, 213-740-8986, E-mail: ljones@thornton.usc.edu.

University of Southern Mississippi, Graduate School, College of Arts and Letters, School of Music, Hattiesburg, MS 39406-0001. Offers conducting (MM); history and literature (MM); music education (MME, PhD); performance (MM); performance and pedagogy (DMA); theory and composition (MM); woodwind performance (MM). *Accreditation:* NASM. *Faculty:* 33 full-time (10 women), 2 part-time/adjunct (0 women). *Students:* 72 full-time (24 women), 24 part-time (7 women); includes 7 minority (4 African Americans, 3 Hispanic Americans), 15 international. Average age 32. 71 applicants, 73% accepted, 35 enrolled. In 2009, 26 master's, 11 doctorates awarded. Terminal master's awarded for partial completion of doctoral program. *Degree requirements:* For master's, comprehensive exam, thesis (for some programs); for doctorate, comprehensive exam, thesis/dissertation. *Entrance requirements:* For master's, GRE General Test, minimum GPA of 2.75 in last 60 hours; for doctorate, GRE General Test, minimum GPA of 3.5. Additional exam requirements/recommendations for international students: Required—TOEFL. *Application deadline:* For fall admission, 3/1 priority date for domestic students; for spring admission, 12/13 for domestic students. Applications are processed on a rolling basis. Application fee: $35. *Expenses:* Tuition, state resident: full-time $5096; part-time $284 per hour. Tuition, nonresident: full-time $13,052; part-time $726 per hour. Required fees: $402. Tuition and fees vary according to course level and course load. *Financial support:* In 2009–10, 1 fellowship with full tuition reimbursement (averaging $12,000 per year), 51 teaching assistantships with full tuition reimbursements (averaging $6,000 per year) were awarded; research assistantships, Federal Work-Study, scholarships/grants, tuition waivers (partial), and unspecified assistantships also available. Financial award application deadline: 3/15; financial award applicants required to submit FAFSA. *Faculty research:* Music theory, composition. *Unit head:* Dr. Charles Elliott, Director, 601-266-5543, Fax: 601-266-6427, E-mail: celliott@usm.edu. *Application contact:* Graduate Coordinator, 601-266-5369, Fax: 601-266-6427.

University of South Florida, Graduate School, College of The Arts, School of Music, Tampa, FL 33620-9951. Offers chamber music (MM); composition (MM); conducting (MM); electro-acoustic music (MM); jazz studies (MM), including composition, performance; music education (MA, PhD); piano pedagogy (MM); theory (MM). *Accreditation:* NASM. Part-time and evening/weekend programs available. *Faculty:* 19 full-time (8 women), 10 part-time/adjunct (4 women). *Students:* 61 full-time (29 women), 28 part-time (14 women); includes 10 minority (2 African Americans, 3 Asian Americans or Pacific Islanders, 5 Hispanic Americans), 11 international. Average age 32. 81 applicants, 84% accepted, 36 enrolled. In 2009, 37 master's, 1 doctorate awarded. *Degree requirements:* For master's, comprehensive exam, thesis, 30-34 credit hours; for doctorate, comprehensive exam, thesis/dissertation. *Entrance requirements:* For master's, diagnostic exam in theory and history, audition, portfolio, minimum GPA of 3.0; for doctorate, GRE, writing samples, interview, teaching video. Additional exam requirements/recommendations for international students: Required—TOEFL (minimum score 550 paper-based; 213 computer-based). *Application deadline:* For fall admission, 2/15 priority date for domestic students, 3/15 for international students; for spring admission, 10/15 for domestic students, 6/1 for international students. Application fee: $30. *Financial support:* In 2009–10, teaching assistantships with tuition reimbursements (averaging $19,251 per year); unspecified assistantships also available. Financial award application deadline: 2/15. *Faculty research:* Education, conducting, performance, history, theory. *Unit head:* Wade Weast, Director, 813-974-2311, Fax: 813-974-8721, E-mail: wweast@usf.edu. *Application contact:* David Williams, Program Director, 813-974-2311, Fax: 813-974-8721, E-mail: davidw@usf.edu.

The University of Tennessee, Graduate School, College of Arts and Sciences, School of Music, Knoxville, TN 37996. Offers accompanying (MM); choral conducting (MM); composition (MM); instrumental conducting (MM); jazz (MM); music education (MM); music theory (MM); musicology (MM); performance (MM); piano pedagogy and literature (MM). *Accreditation:* NASM. Part-time programs available. *Degree requirements:* For master's, thesis (for some programs). *Entrance requirements:* For master's, audition, minimum GPA of 2.7. Additional exam requirements/recommendations for international students: Required—TOEFL. Electronic applications accepted. *Expenses:* Tuition, state resident: full-time $6826; part-time $380 per semester hour. Tuition, nonresident: full-time $21,844; part-time $1147 per semester hour. Tuition and fees vary according to program.

The University of Tennessee at Chattanooga, Graduate School, College of Arts and Sciences, Department of Music, Chattanooga, TN 37403. Offers music education (MM); performance (MM). *Accreditation:* NASM. Part-time programs available. *Faculty:* 7 full-time (1 woman). *Students:* 7 full-time (4 women), 10 part-time (6 women); includes 1 minority (African American), 2 international. Average age 32. 4 applicants, 100% accepted, 4 enrolled. In 2009, 6 master's awarded. *Degree requirements:* For master's, comprehensive exam, thesis or alternative, senior recital. *Entrance requirements:* For master's, GRE General Test or MAT, bachelor's degree in music, audition for placement. Additional exam requirements/recommendations for international students: Required—TOEFL (minimum score 550 paper-based; 213 computer-based; 79 iBT), IELTS (minimum score 6). *Application deadline:* For fall admission, 8/1 priority date for domestic students, 6/1 for international students; for spring admission, 12/1 priority date for domestic students, 10/1 for international students. Applications are processed on a rolling basis. Application fee: $35. Electronic applications accepted. *Expenses:* Tuition, state resident: full-time $5404; part-time $300 per credit hour. Tuition, nonresident: full-time $16,702; part-time $928 per credit hour. Required fees: $1150; $130 per credit hour. *Financial support:* In 2009–10, 5 research assistantships with full and partial tuition reimbursements (averaging $5,500 per year) were awarded; Federal Work-Study, scholarships/grants, and unspecified assistantships also available. *Faculty research:* Music education, conducting, opera, vocal instruction, orchestras. *Unit head:* Dr. Lee Harris, Department Head, 423-425-4601, Fax: 423-425-4603, E-mail: lee-harris@utc.edu. *Application contact:* Dr. Stephanie Bellar, Dean of Graduate Studies, 423-425-4666, Fax: 423-425-5223, E-mail: stephanie-bellar@utc.edu.

The University of Texas at Arlington, Graduate School, College of Liberal Arts, Department of Music, Arlington, TX 76019. Offers education (MM); performance (MM). *Accreditation:* NASM. Part-time and evening/weekend programs available. *Faculty:* 24 full-time (9 women). *Students:* 9 full-time (3 women), 25 part-time (14 women); includes 6 minority (2 African Americans, 4 Hispanic Americans), 9 international. 13 applicants, 100% accepted, 10 enrolled. In 2009, 6 master's awarded. *Degree requirements:* For master's, comprehensive exam, thesis optional. *Entrance requirements:* For master's, GRE, 3 letters of recommendation, minimum GPA of 3.0 in last 60 hours of course work. Additional exam requirements/recommendations for international students: Required—TOEFL (minimum score 550 paper-based; 213 computer-based). *Application deadline:* For fall admission, 6/1 for domestic students. Application fee: $35 ($50 for international students). *Financial support:* In 2009–10, 2 research assistantships (averaging $6,500 per year), 5 teaching assistantships with partial tuition reimbursements (averaging $6,500 per year) were awarded; scholarships/grants also available. *Unit head:* Dr. John Burton, Chair, 817-272-3471, Fax: 817-272-3434. *Application contact:* Assistant Chair/Graduate Advisor.

The University of Texas at El Paso, Graduate School, College of Liberal Arts, Department of Music, El Paso, TX 79968-0001. Offers music education (MM); music performance (MM). *Accreditation:* NASM. Part-time and evening/weekend programs available. *Students:* 23 (7 women); includes 13 minority (1 African American, 1 American Indian/Alaska Native, 11 Hispanic Americans), 4 international. Average age 34. In 2009, 8 master's awarded. *Degree requirements:* For master's, thesis optional. *Entrance requirements:* For master's, audition, interview, letters of recommendation. Additional exam requirements/recommendations for international students: Required—TOEFL; Recommended—IELTS. *Application deadline:* For fall admission, 8/1 priority date for domestic students, 3/1 for international students; for spring admission, 11/1 priority date for domestic students, 9/1 for international students. Applications are processed on a rolling basis. Application fee: $45 ($80 for international students). Electronic applications accepted. *Financial support:* In 2009–10, research assistantships (averaging $18,625 per year), teaching assistantships with partial tuition reimbursements (averaging $14,900 per year) were awarded; fellowships with partial tuition reimbursements, institutionally sponsored loans, scholarships/grants, health care benefits, tuition waivers (partial), and unspecified assistantships also available. Support available to part-time students. Financial award application deadline: 3/15; financial award applicants required to submit FAFSA. *Unit head:* Dr. Lowell Graham, Chair, 915-747-5606, Fax: 915-747-5023, E-mail: legraham@utep.edu. *Application contact:* Dr. Patricia D. Witherspoon, Dean of the Graduate School, 915-747-5491, Fax: 915-747-5788, E-mail: withersp@utep.edu.

The University of Texas–Pan American, College of Arts and Humanities, Department of Music, Edinburg, TX 78539. Offers ethnomusicology (M Mus); interdisciplinary studies (MAIS); music education (M Mus); performance (M Mus). Part-time programs available. *Degree requirements:* For master's, comprehensive exam, thesis optional, recital (performance). *Entrance requirements:* For master's, audition for performance area, bachelor's degree in music. *Expenses:* Tuition, state resident: full-time $3630.60; part-time $201.70 per credit hour. Tuition, nonresident: full-time $8617; part-time $478.70 per credit hour. Required fees: $806.50. *Faculty research:* Music history, instrumental pedagogy, vocal pedagogy, music education, ethnomusicology.

The University of the Arts, College of Performing Arts, School of Music, Division of Music Education, Philadelphia, PA 19102-4944. Offers MAT. *Accreditation:* NASM. Part-time programs available. *Degree requirements:* For master's, student teaching experience. *Entrance requirements:* For master's, audition. Additional exam requirements/recommendations for international students: Required—TOEFL (minimum score 550 paper-based; 213 computer-based).

University of the Pacific, Conservatory of Music, Program in Music Education, Stockton, CA 95211-0197. Offers MM. *Faculty:* 2 full-time (1 woman), 4 part-time/adjunct (2 women). *Students:* 4 part-time (2 women). Average age 24. 7 applicants, 100% accepted, 2 enrolled. In 2009, 3 master's awarded. *Entrance requirements:* For master's, 3 letters of recommendation. Additional exam requirements/recommendations for international students: Required—TOEFL (minimum score 475 paper-based; 150 computer-based). *Application deadline:* For fall admission, 3/1 priority date for domestic students; for spring admission, 10/1 priority date for domestic students. Applications are processed on a rolling basis. Application fee: $75. *Financial support:*

Application deadline: 3/1. *Unit head:* Dr. Ruth Brittin, Associate Professor, 209-946-2408, E-mail: rbrittin@pacific.edu. *Application contact:* Dr. Therese West, Chairperson, 209-946-3194.

The University of Toledo, College of Graduate Studies, College of Education, Department of Curriculum and Instruction, Program in Music Education, Toledo, OH 43606-3390. Offers MME.

University of Toronto, School of Graduate Studies, Humanities Division, Faculty of Music, Toronto, ON M5S 1A1, Canada. Offers composition (M Mus, DMA); music education (MA, PhD); musicology/theory (MA, PhD); performance (M Mus, DMA). Part-time programs available. *Degree requirements:* For master's, comprehensive exam (for some programs), oral examination (Mus M in composition), 1 foreign language (MA); for doctorate, thesis/dissertation (for some programs), recital of original works (Mus Doc), thesis (PhD). *Entrance requirements:* For master's, Bachelor of Music in area of specialization with minimum B average in final 2 years, original compositions (Mus M in composition); for doctorate, master's degree in area of specialization, minimum B+ average, at least 2 extended compositions (Mus Doc).

University of Victoria, Faculty of Graduate Studies, Faculty of Education, Department of Curriculum and Instruction, Victoria, BC V8W 2Y2, Canada. Offers art education (M Ed, PhD); curriculum studies (M Ed, MA, PhD); early childhood education (M Ed, PhD); educational studies (PhD); language and literacy (M Ed, MA, PhD); mathematics (M Ed, MA, PhD); music education (M Ed, MA, PhD); science (M Ed, MA, PhD); social studies (M Ed, MA); social, cultural and foundational studies (MA, PhD); technology and environmental education (PhD). Part-time programs available. *Degree requirements:* For master's, thesis, project (M Ed); for doctorate, comprehensive exam, thesis/dissertation. *Entrance requirements:* For master's, minimum B average. Additional exam requirements/recommendations for international students: Required—TOEFL (minimum score 575 paper-based; 233 computer-based), IELTS (minimum score 7). Electronic applications accepted. *Faculty research:* Elementary and secondary English, language arts, curriculum theory and practice, educational media and technology, educational administration and leadership, history and philosophy of education.

University of Washington, Graduate School, College of Arts and Sciences, School of Music, Concentration in Music Education, Seattle, WA 98195. Offers MA, PhD. *Accreditation:* NASM. *Degree requirements:* For doctorate, thesis/dissertation. *Entrance requirements:* For master's, GRE General Test, GRE Subject Test, minimum GPA of 3.0; for doctorate, GRE General Test, GRE Subject Test, minimum GPA of 3.0, sample of scholarly writing, videotape of teaching, 1 year of teaching experience. Additional exam requirements/recommendations for international students: Required—TOEFL. Electronic applications accepted. *Faculty research:* Multiethnic issues in music instruction, affective responses to music.

University of West Georgia, Graduate School, College of Arts and Sciences, Department of Music, Carrollton, GA 30118. Offers music education (M Mus); performance (M Mus). *Accreditation:* NASM. Part-time programs available. *Faculty:* 7 full-time (3 women), 3 part-time/adjunct (2 women). *Students:* 3 full-time (2 women), 11 part-time (7 women); includes 3 minority (all African Americans). Average age 32. 4 applicants, 75% accepted, 2 enrolled. In 2009, 3 master's awarded. *Degree requirements:* For master's, comprehensive exam, thesis optional, recital (MM in performance), departmental qualifying exam. *Entrance requirements:* For master's, qualifying exam, minimum GPA of 2.5, bachelor's degree in music education or teacher certification (music education), performance evaluation. *Application deadline:* For fall admission, 7/17 for domestic students; for spring admission, 11/20 for domestic students. Applications are processed on a rolling basis. Application fee: $30. Electronic applications accepted. *Expenses:* Tuition, state resident: full-time $2952; part-time $164 per semester hour. Tuition, nonresident: full-time $11,808; part-time $656 per semester hour. Required fees: $42.90 per semester hour. $307 per semester. Tuition and fees vary according to course load. *Financial support:* In 2009–10, 2 students received support, including 2 research assistantships with full tuition reimbursements available (averaging $6,000 per year); career-related internships or fieldwork, tuition waivers (full), and unspecified assistantships also available. Support available to part-time students. Financial award application deadline: 7/1; financial award applicants required to submit FAFSA. *Faculty research:* Ethnomusicology, instrumental music/music education, jazz performance, French music, Latin American music. *Unit head:* Dr. Kevin Hibbard, Chair, 678-839-6516, Fax: 678-839-6259, E-mail: khibbard@westga.edu. *Application contact:* Dr. Charles W. Clark, Dean, 678-839-6508, E-mail: cclark@westga.edu.

University of Wisconsin–Madison, Graduate School, College of Letters and Science, School of Music, Program in Music Education, Madison, WI 53706-1380. Offers curriculum and instruction (MS, PhD); music education (MM). *Accreditation:* NASM. *Degree requirements:* For doctorate, 2 foreign languages, thesis/dissertation. *Entrance requirements:* For doctorate, GRE General Test. *Expenses:* Tuition, state resident: part-time $594 per credit. Tuition, nonresident: part-time $1504 per credit. Required fees: $65 per credit. Tuition and fees vary according to course load, program and reciprocity agreements.

University of Wisconsin–Madison, Graduate School, School of Education, Department of Curriculum and Instruction, Madison, WI 53706-1380. Offers art education (MA); curriculum and instruction (MS, PhD); education and mathematics (MA); French education (MA); German education (MA); music education (MS); science education (MS); Spanish education (MA). *Accreditation:* NASM (one or more programs are accredited). *Degree requirements:* For doctorate, thesis/dissertation. Application fee: $56. *Expenses:* Tuition, state resident: part-time $594 per credit. Tuition, nonresident: part-time $1504 per credit. Required fees: $65 per credit. Tuition and fees vary according to course load, program and reciprocity agreements. *Financial support:* Project assistantships available. *Unit head:* Dr. Gloria Ladson-Billings, Chair, 608-262-4000. *Application contact:* Dr. Gloria Ladson-Billings, Chair, 608-262-4000.

University of Wisconsin–Milwaukee, Graduate School, Peck School of the Arts, Department of Music, Milwaukee, WI 53201-0413. Offers chamber music performance (Certificate); music composition (MM); music education (MM); music history and literature (MM); opera and vocal arts (Certificate); string pedagogy (MM); MLIS/MM. *Accreditation:* NASM. Part-time programs available. *Faculty:* 24 full-time (6 women). *Students:* 38 full-time (19 women), 28 part-time (14 women); includes 3 minority (2 Asian Americans or Pacific Islanders, 1 Hispanic American), 7 international. Average age 27. 54 applicants, 72% accepted, 22 enrolled. In 2009, 22 master's awarded. *Degree requirements:* For master's, variable foreign language requirement, comprehensive exam, thesis or alternative. *Entrance requirements:* For master's, GRE General Test, GRE Subject Test, audition, interview. Additional exam requirements/recommendations for international students: Required—TOEFL (minimum score 550 paper-based; 79 iBT), IELTS (minimum score 6.5). *Application deadline:* For fall admission, 1/1 priority date for domestic students; for spring admission, 9/1 for domestic students. Applications are processed on a rolling basis. Application fee: $45 ($75 for international students). *Expenses:* Contact institution. *Financial support:* In 2009–10, 9 teaching assistantships were awarded; career-related internships or fieldwork and unspecified assistantships also available. Support available to part-time students. Financial award application deadline: 4/15. *Unit head:* Timothy Noonan, Representative, 414-229-2286, Fax: 414-229-2776, E-mail: tpnoonan@uwm.edu. *Application contact:* General Information Contact, 414-229-4982, Fax: 414-229-6967, E-mail: gradschool@uwm.edu.

University of Wisconsin–Stevens Point, College of Fine Arts and Communication, Department of Music, Stevens Point, WI 54481-3897. Offers MM Ed. *Accreditation:* NASM. Part-time programs available. *Students:* 1 (woman) full-time, 1 (woman) part-time. *Degree requirements:* For master's, thesis or alternative. *Entrance requirements:* For master's, teaching certificate. *Application deadline:* For fall admission, 5/1 priority date for domestic students. Applications are processed on a rolling basis. Application fee: $45. *Expenses:* Tuition, state resident: full-time $7740; part-time $430 per credit hour. Tuition, nonresident: full-time $17,804; part-time $989 per credit hour. Tuition and fees vary according to course load and reciprocity agreements. *Financial support:* Career-related internships or fieldwork, Federal Work-Study, institutionally sponsored loans, and unspecified assistantships available. Support available to part-time students. Financial award application deadline: 5/1; financial award applicants required to submit FAFSA. *Faculty research:* Music education, music composition, music performance. *Unit head:* Dr. Patricia Holland, Chair, 715-346-3107, Fax: 715-346-3163, E-mail: pholland@uwsp.edu. *Application contact:* Dr. Patricia Holland, Chair, 715-346-3107, Fax: 715-346-3163, E-mail: pholland@uwsp.edu.

University of Wyoming, College of Arts and Sciences, Department of Music, Laramie, WY 82070. Offers music education (MME); performance (MM). *Accreditation:* NASM. *Degree requirements:* For master's, comprehensive exam, thesis or alternative. *Entrance requirements:* For master's, minimum GPA of 3.0. Additional exam requirements/recommendations for international students: Required—TOEFL (minimum score 540 paper-based; 207 computer-based). Electronic applications accepted.

VanderCook College of Music, Program in Music Education, Chicago, IL 60616-3731. Offers MM Ed. Offered during summer only. *Accreditation:* NASM. Part-time programs available. *Faculty:* 10 full-time (6 women), 60 part-time/adjunct (22 women). *Students:* 181 full-time (94 women), 59 part-time (38 women). Average age 31. *Degree requirements:* For master's, comprehensive exam, project. *Entrance requirements:* For master's, minimum of one year of teaching experience, or its equivalent, in music; official transcripts; 3 letters of recommendation. *Application deadline:* Applications are processed on a rolling basis. Application fee: $50. *Expenses:* Tuition: Full-time $5280; part-time $440 per semester hour. Required fees: $435 per term. *Financial support:* Teaching assistantships with partial tuition reimbursements, scholarships/grants and tuition waivers (partial) available. Financial award application deadline: 5/1. *Faculty research:* Pedagogy in elementary music. *Unit head:* Peter Berghoff, Graduate Dean's Assistant, 312-225-6288, Fax: 312-225-5211, E-mail: pberghoff@vandercook.edu. *Application contact:* Peter Berghoff, Graduate Dean's Assistant, 312-225-6288, Fax: 312-225-5211, E-mail: pberghoff@vandercook.edu.

Virginia Commonwealth University, Graduate School, School of the Arts, Department of Music, Richmond, VA 23284-9005. Offers education (MM). *Accreditation:* NASM. *Degree requirements:* For master's, departmental qualifying exam, recital. *Entrance requirements:* For master's, department examination, audition or tapes, portfolio. *Faculty research:* Composition, conducting, education, performance.

Washington State University, Graduate School, College of Liberal Arts, School of Music and Theatre Arts, Pullman, WA 99164. Offers composition (MA); jazz (MA); music (MA); music education (MA); performance (MA). *Accreditation:* NASM. *Faculty:* 38. *Students:* 17 full-time (10 women); includes 2 minority (1 African American, 1 Hispanic American), 3 international. Average age 30. 14 applicants, 64% accepted, 5 enrolled. In 2009, 7 master's awarded. *Degree requirements:* For master's, comprehensive exam (for some programs), thesis (for some programs), oral exam. *Entrance requirements:* For master's, audition, minimum GPA of 3.0, 3 letters of recommendation, composition portfolio and recording (composition), writing sample and written philosophy (music education), writing sample (music history), in-depth audition (performance). Additional exam requirements/recommendations for international students: Required—TOEFL, IELTS. *Application deadline:* For fall admission, 1/10 priority date for domestic students, 1/10 for international students; for spring admission, 7/1 for domestic and international students. Applications are processed on a rolling basis. Application fee: $50. Electronic applications accepted. *Financial support:* In 2009–10, 1 fellowship (averaging $3,500 per year), research assistantships (averaging $13,917 per year), 11 teaching assistantships with full and partial tuition reimbursements (averaging $13,056 per year) were awarded; career-related internships or fieldwork, Federal Work-Study, institutionally sponsored loans, and tuition waivers (partial) also available. Financial award application deadline: 2/15; financial award applicants required to submit FAFSA. Total annual research expenditures: $3,000. *Unit head:* Dr. Gerald Berthiaume, Director, 509-335-2509, Fax: 509-335-4245, E-mail: berthia@wsu.edu. *Application contact:* Graduate School Admissions, 800-GRADWSU, Fax: 509-335-1949, E-mail: gradsch@wsu.edu.

Wayne State College, School of Education and Counseling, Department of Educational Foundations and Leadership, Program in Curriculum and Instruction, Wayne, NE 68787. Offers alternative education (MSE); business and information technology education (MSE); communication arts education (MSE); early childhood education (MSE); elementary education (MSE); English as a second language (MSE); English education (MSE); family and consumer sciences education (MSE); industrial technology and vocational education (MSE); learning communities (MSE); mathematics education (MSE); music education (MSE); science education (MSE); social science education (MSE). *Accreditation:* NCATE. Part-time and evening/weekend programs available. *Degree requirements:* For master's, comprehensive exam, thesis optional. *Entrance requirements:* For master's, GRE General Test. Additional exam requirements/recommendations for international students: Required—TOEFL (minimum score 550 paper-based; 213 computer-based).

Wayne State University, College of Fine, Performing and Communication Arts, Department of Music, Detroit, MI 48202. Offers choral conducting (MM); composition (MM); music (MA, MM); music education (MM); orchestral studies (Certificate); performance (MM); theory (MM). *Accreditation:* NASM. *Degree requirements:* For master's, variable foreign language requirement. *Entrance requirements:* For master's, audition, interview. Additional exam requirements/recommendations for international students: Required—TOEFL (minimum score 550 paper-based; 213 computer-based); Recommended—TWE (minimum score 6). Electronic applications accepted. *Faculty research:* Teacher training, pedagogy, musicology, composition/theory, conducting/performance practice.

Webster University, Leigh Gerdine College of Fine Arts, Department of Music, St. Louis, MO 63119-3194. Offers church music (MM); composition (MM); conducting (MM); jazz studies (MM); music (MA); music education (MM); performance (MM); piano (MM). *Accreditation:* NASM. *Entrance requirements:* Additional exam requirements/recommendations for international students: Required—TOEFL. *Expenses:* Tuition: Part-time $565 per credit hour. Tuition and fees vary according to degree level, campus/location and program.

West Chester University of Pennsylvania, Office of Graduate Studies, College of Visual and Performing Arts, Department of Applied Music, West Chester, PA 19383. Offers accompanying (MM); performance (MM); piano pedagogy (MM, Certificate). Part-time and evening/weekend programs available. *Students:* 3 full-time (2 women), 29 part-time (15 women); includes 6 minority (3 African Americans, 2 Asian Americans or Pacific Islanders, 1 Hispanic American), 5 international. Average age 27. 23 applicants, 91% accepted, 15 enrolled. In 2009, 5 master's awarded. *Degree requirements:* For master's, comprehensive exam, thesis optional, recital. *Entrance requirements:* For master's and Certificate, GRE General Test, School of Music Graduate Admission Test (GAT), audition, interview. Additional exam requirements/recommendations for international students: Required—TOEFL (minimum score 550 paper-based; 213 computer-based; 80 iBT). *Application deadline:* For fall admission, 4/15 priority date for domestic students, 3/15 for international students; for spring admission, 10/15 for domestic students, 9/1 for international students. Applications are processed on a rolling basis. Application fee: $35. Electronic applications accepted. *Expenses:* Tuition, state resident: full-time $6666; part-time $370 per credit. Tuition, nonresident: full-time $10,666; part-time $593 per credit. Required fees: $122.56 per credit. *Financial support:* In 2009–10, 7 research assistantships with full and partial tuition reimbursements (averaging $5,000 per year) were awarded; unspecified assistantships also available. Support available to part-time students. Financial award application deadline: 2/15; financial award applicants required to submit FAFSA. *Unit head:* Dr. Chris Hanning, Interim Chair, 610-436-4178, E-mail: channing@wcupa.edu. *Application contact:* Dr. J. Bryan Burton, Graduate Coordinator, 610-436-2222, E-mail: jburton@wcupa.edu.

West Chester University of Pennsylvania, Office of Graduate Studies, College of Visual and Performing Arts, Department of Music Education, West Chester, PA 19383. Offers 21st Century music education (Certificate); Kodaly methodology (Certificate); music education (Teaching Certificate); music technology (Certificate); Orff-Schulwerk (Certificate); performance (MM), including performance; research (MM), including research; technology (MM), including technology. *Accreditation:* NASM; NCATE. Part-time and evening/weekend programs available.

Music Education

West Chester University of Pennsylvania (continued)

Students: 38 part-time (29 women); includes 1 minority (Asian American or Pacific Islander). Average age 28. 35 applicants, 91% accepted, 14 enrolled. In 2009, 19 master's, 5 Certificates awarded. *Degree requirements:* For master's, comprehensive exam, thesis optional, recital. *Entrance requirements:* For master's and other advanced degree, GRE General Test, School of Music Graduate Admission Test (GAT), audition, interview. Additional exam requirements/recommendations for international students: Required—TOEFL (minimum score 550 paper-based; 213 computer-based; 80 iBT). *Application deadline:* For fall admission, 4/15 priority date for domestic students, 3/15 for international students; for spring admission, 10/15 for domestic students, 9/1 for international students. Applications are processed on a rolling basis. Application fee: $35. Electronic applications accepted. *Expenses:* Tuition, state resident: full-time $6666; part-time $370 per credit. Tuition, nonresident: full-time $10,666; part-time $593 per credit. Required fees: $122.56 per credit. *Financial support:* In 2009–10, research assistantships with full and partial tuition reimbursements (averaging $5,000 per year) unspecified assistantships also available. Support available to part-time students. Financial award application deadline: 2/15; financial award applicants required to submit FAFSA. *Faculty research:* Developing music listening skills. *Unit head:* Dr. J. Bryan Burton, Chair and Graduate Coordinator, 610-436-2222, E-mail: jburton@wcupa.edu. *Application contact:* Dr. J. Bryan Burton, Chair and Graduate Coordinator, 610-436-2222, E-mail: jburton@wcupa.edu.

Western Carolina University, Graduate School, College of Fine and Performing Arts, Department of Educational Leadership and Foundations, Cullowhee, NC 28723. Offers comprehensive education: music (MA Ed, MAT). *Students:* 7 full-time (all women), 7 part-time (3 women). Average age 33. 10 applicants, 90% accepted, 8 enrolled.Application fee: $45. *Unit head:* Dr. Jacqueline Jacobs, Head, 828-227-7415, Fax: 828-227-7607, E-mail: jjacobs@email.wcu.edu. *Application contact:* Admissions Specialist for Fine and Performing Arts, 828-227-7398, Fax: 828-227-7480, E-mail: gradsch@email.wcu.edu.

Western Connecticut State University, Division of Graduate Studies, School of Visual and Performing Arts, Music Department, Danbury, CT 06810-6885. Offers music education (MS). *Accreditation:* NASM. Part-time programs available. *Faculty:* 1 (woman) full-time, 1 (woman) part-time/adjunct. *Students:* 17 part-time (14 women). Average age 31. 7 applicants, 71% accepted, 3 enrolled. In 2009, 13 master's awarded. *Degree requirements:* For master's, thesis or comprehensive exam, completion of program within 6 years. *Entrance requirements:* For master's, minimum GPA of 2.8, teaching certificate. Additional exam requirements/recommendations for international students: Recommended—TOEFL (minimum score 550 paper-based; 213 computer-based; 79 iBT), IELTS (minimum score 6). *Application deadline:* For fall admission, 8/5 priority date for domestic students; for spring admission, 1/5 for domestic students. Applications are processed on a rolling basis. Application fee: $50. *Expenses:* Tuition, state resident: full-time $5012; part-time $278 per credit hour. Tuition, nonresident: full-time $13,962; part-time $284 per credit hour. Required fees: $3886; $139 per credit hour. Full-time tuition and fees vary according to course load and program. Part-time tuition and fees vary according to course level, degree level and program. *Financial support:* Application deadline: 5/1. *Unit head:* Dr. Kevin Isaacs, Graduate Coordinator, 203-837-8355, Fax: 203-837-8630, E-mail: isaacsk@wcsu.edu. *Application contact:* Chris Shankle, Associate Director of Graduate Studies, 203-837-9005, Fax: 203-837-8326, E-mail: shanklec@wcsu.edu.

Western Kentucky University, Graduate Studies, Potter College of Arts and Letters, Department of Music, Bowling Green, KY 42101. Offers MA Ed. *Accreditation:* NASM; NCATE. Part-time and evening/weekend programs available. *Degree requirements:* For master's, comprehensive exam, written exam. *Entrance requirements:* For master's, GRE General Test, minimum GPA of 3.0. Additional exam requirements/recommendations for international students: Required—TOEFL (minimum score 555 paper-based; 213 computer-based; 79 iBT). *Expenses:* Tuition, state resident: full-time $4160; part-time $416 per credit hour. Tuition, nonresident: full-time $9550; part-time $506 per credit hour. Tuition and fees vary according to campus/location and reciprocity agreements. *Faculty research:* Music education, music technology, performance.

Western Michigan University, Graduate College, College of Fine Arts, School of Music, Kalamazoo, MI 49008. Offers composition (MM); conducting (MM); music (MA); music education (MM); music therapy (MM); performance (MM). *Accreditation:* NASM. *Faculty:* 40 full-time (9 women). *Students:* 59 full-time (29 women), 18 part-time (14 women); includes 4 minority (3 African Americans, 1 Asian American or Pacific Islander), 16 international. 78 applicants, 83% accepted, 28 enrolled. In 2009, 24 master's awarded. *Application deadline:* For fall admission, 2/15 priority date for domestic students. Applications are processed on a rolling basis. Application fee: $25. *Financial support:* Fellowships, research assistantships, teaching assistantships, Federal Work-Study available. Financial award application deadline: 2/15; financial award applicants required to submit FAFSA. *Unit head:* David Colson, Director, 269-387-4667. *Application contact:* Admissions and Orientation, 269-387-2000, Fax: 269-387-2355.

Westminster Choir College of Rider University, Graduate Programs in Music, Program in Music Education, Princeton, NJ 08540-3899. Offers MM, MME. *Accreditation:* NASM. *Entrance requirements:* For master's, audition, interview, repertoire list, 2 letters of reference, resume. Additional exam requirements/recommendations for international students: Required—TOEFL (minimum score 525 paper-based; 195 computer-based). Electronic applications accepted.

West Virginia University, College of Creative Arts, Division of Music, Morgantown, WV 26506. Offers music composition (MM, DMA); music education (MM, PhD); music history (MM); music performance (MM, DMA); music theory (MM). *Accreditation:* NASM. *Degree requirements:* For master's, comprehensive exam, thesis (for some programs), recitals; for doctorate, variable foreign language requirement, comprehensive exam, thesis/dissertation, recitals (DMA). *Entrance requirements:* For master's, GRE General Test (music history), minimum GPA of 3.0, audition; for doctorate, GRE General Test (music education), minimum GPA of 3.0, audition. Additional exam requirements/recommendations for international students: Required—TOEFL. *Faculty research:* Jazz history, seventeenth century French court music, nineteenth century composition theory.

Wichita State University, Graduate School, College of Fine Arts, School of Music, Wichita, KS 67260. Offers music (MM); music education (MME). *Accreditation:* NASM. Part-time programs available. *Expenses:* Tuition, state resident: full-time $4247; part-time $235.95 per credit hour. Tuition, nonresident: full-time $11,171; part-time $620.60 per credit hour. Required fees: $34; $3.60 per credit hour. $17 per term. Tuition and fees vary according to campus/location and program. *Unit head:* Prof. Russ Widener, Director, 316-978-6435, Fax: 316-978-3625, E-mail: russ.widener@wichita.edu. *Application contact:* Prof. Russ Widener, Director, 316-978-6435, Fax: 316-978-3625, E-mail: russ.widener@wichita.edu.

Winthrop University, College of Visual and Performing Arts, Department of Music, Rock Hill, SC 29733. Offers conducting (MM); music education (MME); performance (MM). *Accreditation:* NASM. Part-time programs available. *Degree requirements:* For master's, oral and written exams, recital (MM). *Entrance requirements:* For master's, GRE General Test, audition, minimum GPA of 3.0, 2 recitals. Electronic applications accepted.

Wright State University, School of Graduate Studies, College of Liberal Arts, Department of Music, Dayton, OH 45435. Offers music education (M Mus); performance (M Mus). *Accreditation:* NASM. Part-time programs available. *Degree requirements:* For master's, thesis or alternative, oral exam. *Entrance requirements:* For master's, theory placement test, BA in music. Additional exam requirements/recommendations for international students: Required—TOEFL. *Faculty research:* General music, current needs, role of teacher, expectations in music education.

Youngstown State University, Graduate School, College of Fine and Performing Arts, Dana School of Music, Youngstown, OH 44555-0001. Offers jazz studies (MM); music education (MM); music history and literature (MM); music theory and composition (MM); performance (MM). *Accreditation:* NASM. Part-time and evening/weekend programs available. *Degree requirements:* For master's, one foreign language, thesis optional, final qualifying exam. *Entrance requirements:* For master's, audition; GRE General Test or minimum GPA of 2.7. Additional exam requirements/recommendations for international students: Required—TOEFL. *Faculty research:* Teaching education, use of computers, conducting.

Reading Education

Adelphi University, School of Education, Program in Literacy, Garden City, NY 11530-0701. Offers birth-grade 12 (MS); birth-grade 6 (MS); grades 5-12 (MS). Part-time and evening/weekend programs available. *Students:* 6 full-time (all women), 71 part-time (67 women); includes 5 minority (4 African Americans, 1 Asian American or Pacific Islander). Average age 30. In 2009, 33 master's awarded. *Entrance requirements:* For master's, 2 letters of recommendation, resume, valid New York state teaching certification. Additional exam requirements/recommendations for international students: Required—TOEFL (minimum score 550 paper-based; 213 computer-based; 80 iBT). *Application deadline:* For fall admission, 4/1 priority date for domestic students, 4/1 for international students; for spring admission, 11/1 priority date for domestic students, 11/1 for international students. Applications are processed on a rolling basis. Application fee: $50. Electronic applications accepted. *Expenses:* Tuition: Full-time $28,340; part-time $830 per credit. Required fees: $600; $250 per credit. Full-time tuition and fees vary according to course load and program. *Financial support:* Fellowships, research assistantships with partial tuition reimbursements, teaching assistantships, career-related internships or fieldwork, Federal Work-Study, institutionally sponsored loans, and tuition waivers (full) available. Support available to part-time students. Financial award application deadline: 2/15; financial award applicants required to submit FAFSA. *Faculty research:* Assessment and intervention, literacy education and development, higher and teacher education, human and adult development, achieving styles and human motivation. *Unit head:* Dr. Lori Wolf, Director, 516-877-4104, E-mail: wolf@adelphi.edu. *Application contact:* Christine Murphy, Director of Admissions, 516-877-3050, Fax: 516-877-3039, E-mail: graduateadmissions@adelphi.edu.

Alfred University, Graduate School, Division of Education, Alfred, NY 14802-1205. Offers literacy teacher (MS Ed); numeracy (MS). *Accreditation:* Teacher Education Accreditation Council. Part-time programs available. *Entrance requirements:* For master's, LAST, Assessment of Teaching Skills (written), Content Specialty Test. Additional exam requirements/recommendations for international students: Required—TOEFL (minimum score 590 paper-based; 243 computer-based; 90 iBT), IELTS (minimum score 6.5). Electronic applications accepted. *Expenses:* Tuition: Full-time $33,296; part-time $708 per credit hour. Required fees: $880; $144 per year. Full-time tuition and fees vary according to program. *Faculty research:* Whole language, ethics in counseling and psychotherapy.

Alverno College, School of Education, Milwaukee, WI 53234-3922. Offers adaptive education (MA); administrative leadership (MA); adult education and organizational development (MA); adult educational and instructional design (MA); adult educational and instructional technology (MA); global connections in the humanities (MA); instructional leadership (MA); instructional technology for K-12 settings (MA); professional development (MA); reading education (MA); reading education with adaptive education (MA); science education (MA); teaching in alternative schools (MA). *Accreditation:* NCATE. Part-time and evening/weekend programs available. *Faculty:* 10 full-time (all women), 17 part-time/adjunct (15 women). *Students:* 65 full-time (59 women), 82 part-time (75 women); includes 31 minority (24 African Americans, 1 American Indian/Alaska Native, 1 Asian American or Pacific Islander, 5 Hispanic Americans), 2 international. Average age 38. 113 applicants, 64% accepted, 61 enrolled. In 2009, 56 master's awarded. *Degree requirements:* For master's, presentation/defense of proposal, conference presentation of inquiry projects. *Entrance requirements:* For master's, bachelor's degree in related field,

communication samples from work setting, 3 letters of recommendation. Additional exam requirements/recommendations for international students: Required—TOEFL. *Application deadline:* For fall admission, 7/15 priority date for domestic and international students; for spring admission, 12/15 priority date for domestic and international students. Applications are processed on a rolling basis. Application fee: $50. Electronic applications accepted. *Financial support:* In 2009–10, 92 students received support. Federal Work-Study available. Support available to part-time students. Financial award application deadline: 4/15; financial award applicants required to submit FAFSA. *Faculty research:* Student self-assessment, self-reflection, integration of curriculum, identifying needs of students in strategic situations and designing appropriate classroom strategies. *Unit head:* Dr. Mary Diez, Graduate Dean, 414-382-6214, Fax: 414-382-6332, E-mail: mary.diez@alverno.edu. *Application contact:* Angela Peterson-Adams, Graduate Recruiter, 414-382-6104, Fax: 414-382-6354, E-mail: angela.peterson-adams@alverno.edu.

American International College, School of Arts, Education and Sciences, Department of Education, Springfield, MA 01109-3189. Offers early childhood education (M Ed, CAGS); educational leadership and supervision (Ed D); elementary education (M Ed, CAGS); middle/secondary education (M Ed, CAGS); moderate disabilities (M Ed, CAGS); reading (M Ed, CAGS); school adjustment counseling (MA, CAGS); school administration (M Ed, CAGS); school guidance counseling (MA, CAGS); teaching (MA, MS); teaching and learning (Ed D). Part-time and evening/weekend programs available. Terminal master's awarded for partial completion of doctoral program. *Degree requirements:* For master's, comprehensive exam (for some programs), thesis (for some programs), practicum; for doctorate, comprehensive exam (for some programs), thesis/dissertation; for CAGS, practicum. *Entrance requirements:* For master's, minimum B- average in undergraduate course work; for doctorate, GRE General Test, interview. Additional exam requirements/recommendations for international students: Required—TOEFL. Electronic applications accepted. *Expenses:* Tuition: Full-time $12,510; part-time $695 per credit hour. Required fees: $35 per term.

Andrews University, School of Graduate Studies, School of Education, Department of Teaching, Learning, and Curriculum, Program in Reading, Berrien Springs, MI 49104. Offers MA. *Degree requirements:* For master's, thesis optional. *Entrance requirements:* For master's, GRE Subject Test. *Application deadline:* For fall admission, 8/15 for domestic students. Applications are processed on a rolling basis. Application fee: $40. *Financial support:* Fellowships, research assistantships, teaching assistantships, career-related internships or fieldwork, Federal Work-Study, institutionally sponsored loans, and tuition waivers (partial) available. Support available to part-time students. *Application contact:* Carolyn Hurst, Supervisor of Graduate Admission, 800-253-2874, Fax: 269-471-3228, E-mail: graduate@andrews.edu.

Angelo State University, College of Graduate Studies, College of Education, Department of Teacher Education, Program in Reading Specialist, San Angelo, TX 76909. Offers M Ed. Part-time and evening/weekend programs available. *Faculty:* 17 full-time (12 women). *Students:* 10 part-time (all women); includes 2 minority (both Hispanic Americans). Average age 41. 5 applicants, 100% accepted, 5 enrolled. In 2009, 5 master's awarded. *Degree requirements:* For master's, comprehensive exam. *Entrance requirements:* For master's, GRE General Test.

Additional exam requirements/recommendations for international students: Required—TOEFL or IELTS. *Application deadline:* For fall admission, 7/15 priority date for domestic students, 6/10 for international students; for spring admission, 12/1 priority date for domestic students, 11/1 for international students). Applications are processed on a rolling basis. Application fee: $40 ($50 for international students). Electronic applications accepted. *Expenses:* Tuition, state resident: full-time $3396; part-time $142 per credit hour. Tuition, nonresident: full-time $10,152; part-time $423 per credit hour. Required fees: $1786; $36.25 per credit hour. $494 per semester. Full-time tuition and fees vary according to course load, degree level and program. *Financial support:* In 2009–10, 3 students received support. Career-related internships or fieldwork, Federal Work-Study, scholarships/grants, tuition waivers (partial), and unspecified assistantships available. Support available to part-time students. Financial award application deadline: 3/1; financial award applicants required to submit FAFSA. *Unit head:* Dr. Ann Bullion-Mears, Graduate Advisor, 325-942-2052 Ext. 283, Fax: 325-942-2039, E-mail: ann.bullion-mears@angelo.edu. *Application contact:* Theresa Fortin, Graduate Admissions Assistant, 325-942-2169, Fax: 325-942-2194, E-mail: theresa.fortin@angelo.edu.

Appalachian State University, Cratis D. Williams Graduate School, Department of Language, Reading, and Exceptionalities, Boone, NC 28608. Offers reading education (MA); special education (MA); speech-language pathology (MA). *Accreditation:* ASHA. Part-time programs available. Postbaccalaureate distance learning degree programs offered (no on-campus study). *Faculty:* 37 full-time (25 women), 6 part-time/adjunct (all women). *Students:* 89 full-time (84 women), 202 part-time (192 women); includes 7 minority (3 African Americans, 1 Asian American or Pacific Islander, 3 Hispanic Americans). 291 applicants, 57% accepted, 105 enrolled. In 2009, 95 master's awarded. *Degree requirements:* For master's, comprehensive exam, thesis optional. *Entrance requirements:* For master's, GRE General Test or MAT, 3 letters of recommendation. Additional exam requirements/recommendations for international students: Required—TOEFL (minimum score 570 paper-based; 230 computer-based; 79 iBT), IELTS (minimum score 6.5). *Application deadline:* For fall admission, 7/1 for domestic students, 2/1 for international students; for spring admission, 11/1 for domestic students, 7/1 for international students. Applications are processed on a rolling basis. Application fee: $50. Electronic applications accepted. *Expenses:* Tuition, state resident: full-time $2960. Tuition, nonresident: full-time $14,051. Required fees: $2320. *Financial support:* In 2009–10, 21 research assistantships (averaging $8,000 per year) were awarded; Federal Work-Study, scholarships/grants, and unspecified assistantships also available. Financial award application deadline: 4/1; financial award applicants required to submit FAFSA. *Faculty research:* Speech pathology, special education, language arts, reading. Total annual research expenditures: $160,500. *Unit head:* Dr. Monica Lambert, Chairperson, 828-262-7173, Fax: 828-262-6767, E-mail: lambertma@appstate.edu. *Application contact:* Eveline Watts, Graduate Student Coordinator, 828-262-2182, E-mail: wattsem@appstate.edu.

Arcadia University, Graduate Studies, Department of Education, Glenside, PA 19038-3295. Offers art education (M Ed, MA Ed); biology education (MA Ed); chemistry education (MA Ed); child development (CAS); computer education (M Ed, CAS); computer education 7–12 (MA Ed); early childhood education (M Ed, CAS), including individualized (M Ed), master teacher (M Ed), research in child development (M Ed); educational leadership (M Ed, CAS); educational psychology (CAS); elementary education (M Ed, CAS); English education (MA Ed); environmental education (MA Ed, CAS); history education (MA Ed); language arts (M Ed, CAS); mathematics education (M Ed, MA Ed, CAS); music education (MA Ed); psychology (MA Ed); pupil personnel services (CAS); reading (M Ed, CAS); school library science (M Ed); science education (M Ed, CAS); secondary education (M Ed, CAS); special education (M Ed, Ed D, CAS); theater arts (MA Ed); written communication (MA Ed). *Accreditation:* NASAD. Part-time and evening/weekend programs available. Postbaccalaureate distance learning degree programs offered (minimal on-campus study). *Faculty:* 12 full-time (8 women), 38 part-time/adjunct (26 women). *Students:* 89 full-time (74 women), 622 part-time (487 women); includes 112 minority (94 African Americans, 9 Asian Americans or Pacific Islanders, 9 Hispanic Americans), 2 international. Average age 32. In 2009, 257 master's, 4 doctorates awarded. *Application deadline:* Applications are processed on a rolling basis. Application fee: $40. Electronic applications accepted. *Expenses:* Tuition: Full-time $30,450; part-time $620 per credit hour. Required fees: $165. Tuition and fees vary according to program. *Financial support:* Career-related internships or fieldwork, tuition waivers (partial), and unspecified assistantships available. *Unit head:* Dr. Steven P. Gulkus. *Application contact:* 215-572-2925, Fax: 215-572-2126, E-mail: grad@arcadia.edu.

Arkansas State University—Jonesboro, Graduate School, College of Education, Department of Teacher Education, Jonesboro, State University, AR 72467. Offers early childhood education (MSE); early childhood services (MS); middle level education (MSE); reading (MSE, SCCT). *Accreditation:* NCATE. Part-time programs available. *Faculty:* 5 full-time (4 women), 4 part-time/adjunct (3 women). *Students:* 10 full-time (all women), 87 part-time (84 women); includes 40 minority (39 African Americans, 1 American Indian/Alaska Native). Average age 35. 63 applicants, 79% accepted, 39 enrolled. In 2009, 31 master's awarded. *Degree requirements:* For master's, comprehensive exam, thesis or alternative; for SCCT, comprehensive exam. *Entrance requirements:* For master's, GRE General Test or MAT, appropriate bachelor's degree; for SCCT, GRE General Test or MAT, interview, master's degree, official transcript, immunization records. Additional exam requirements/recommendations for international students: Required—TOEFL (minimum score 550 paper-based; 213 computer-based; 79 iBT), IELTS (minimum score 6). *Application deadline:* For fall admission, 7/15 for domestic students, 7/1 for international students; for spring admission, 12/1 for domestic students, 11/13 for international students. Applications are processed on a rolling basis. Application fee: $30 ($40 for international students). Electronic applications accepted. *Expenses:* Tuition, state resident: full-time $3744; part-time $208 per credit hour. Tuition, nonresident: full-time $9540; part-time $530 per credit hour. Required fees: $896; $47 per credit hour. $25 per term. One-time fee: $50. Tuition and fees vary according to course load and program. *Financial support:* In 2009–10, 16 students received support; teaching assistantships, career-related internships or fieldwork, scholarships/grants, and unspecified assistantships available. Financial award application deadline: 7/1; financial award applicants required to submit FAFSA. *Unit head:* Dr. Dianne Lawler-Prince, Chair, 870-972-3059, Fax: 870-972-3344, E-mail: dprince@astate.edu. *Application contact:* Dr. Andrew Sustich, Dean of the Graduate School, 870-972-3029, Fax: 870-972-3857, E-mail: sustich@astate.edu.

Asbury University, School of Graduate and Professional Studies, Wilmore, KY 40390-1198. Offers biology: alternative certificate (MA Ed); chemistry: alternative certificate (MA Ed); English (MA Ed); English as a second language (MA Ed); ESL (MA Ed); French (MA Ed); Latin: alternative certificate (MA Ed); mathematics: alternative certificate (MA Ed); reading/writing endorsement (MA Ed); social studies (MA Ed); social work (MSW), including child and family services; Spanish (MA Ed); special education (MA Ed); special education: alternative certificate (MA Ed); teacher as leader endorsement (MA Ed). *Accreditation:* NCATE. Part-time programs available. *Faculty:* 8 full-time (7 women), 9 part-time/adjunct (4 women). *Students:* 108 part-time (87 women); includes 8 minority (4 African Americans, 2 Asian Americans or Pacific Islanders, 2 Hispanic Americans). Average age 36. 36 applicants, 86% accepted, 24 enrolled. In 2009, 20 master's awarded. *Degree requirements:* For master's, action research project, portfolio. *Entrance requirements:* For master's, PRAXIS/NTE, minimum GPA of 2.75, letters of recommendation. Additional exam requirements/recommendations for international students: Required—TOEFL (minimum score 550 paper-based). *Application deadline:* Applications are processed on a rolling basis. Application fee: $25. Electronic applications accepted. *Financial support:* Scholarships/grants and traineeships available. Financial award applicants required to submit FAFSA. *Unit head:* Dr. Bonnie J. Banker, Dean, School of Graduate and Professional Studies, 859-858-3511 Ext. 2221, Fax: 859-858-3921, E-mail: bonnie.banker@asbury.edu. *Application contact:* Lenore A. Sweigard, Graduate Program Assistant and Certification Specialist, 859-858-3511 Ext. 2502, Fax: 859-858-3921, E-mail: graded@asbury.edu.

Ashland University, Dwight Schar College of Education, Department of Curriculum and Instruction, Ashland, OH 44805-3702. Offers intervention specialist–mild/moderate (M Ed); intervention specialist–moderate/intensive (M Ed); literacy (M Ed); technology facilitator (M Ed). *Accreditation:* NCATE. Part-time and evening/weekend programs available. *Faculty:* 20 full-time (14 women), 83 part-time/adjunct (53 women). *Students:* 137 full-time (116 women), 309 part-time (278 women); includes 22 minority (16 African Americans, 2 American Indian/Alaska Native, 4 Hispanic Americans), 1 international. Average age 33. 160 applicants, 98% accepted, 152 enrolled. In 2009, 245 master's awarded. *Degree requirements:* For master's, thesis or alternative, internship, practicum, inquiry seminar. *Entrance requirements:* For master's, teaching certificate or license, bachelor's degree, minimum cumulative GPA of 2.75. Additional exam requirements/recommendations for international students: Required—TOEFL. *Application deadline:* For fall admission, 8/27 for domestic students; for spring admission, 1/14 for domestic students. Applications are processed on a rolling basis. Application fee: $30. Electronic applications accepted. *Financial support:* In 2009–10, 192 students received support. Institutionally sponsored loans and scholarships/grants available. Financial award application deadline: 4/15. *Faculty research:* Gender equity, postmodern children's and young adult literature, outdoor/experimental education, re-examining literature study in middle grades, morality and giftedness. *Unit head:* Dr. David J. Kommer, Chair, 419-289-5203, E-mail: dkommer@ashland.edu. *Application contact:* Dr. David J. Kommer, Chair, 419-289-5203, E-mail: dkommer@ashland.edu.

Auburn University, Graduate School, College of Education, Department of Curriculum and Teaching, Auburn University, AL 36849. Offers business education (M Ed, MS, PhD); early childhood education (M Ed, MS, PhD, Ed S); elementary education (M Ed, MS, PhD, Ed S); foreign languages (M Ed, MS); music education (M Ed, MS, PhD, Ed S); postsecondary education (PhD); reading education (PhD, Ed S); secondary education (M Ed, MS, PhD, Ed S), including English language arts, mathematics, science, social studies. *Accreditation:* NASM (one or more programs are accredited); NCATE. Part-time programs available. *Faculty:* 28 full-time (21 women), 8 part-time/adjunct (5 women). *Students:* 76 full-time (55 women), 186 part-time (139 women); includes 43 minority (29 African Americans, 1 American Indian/Alaska Native, 4 Asian Americans or Pacific Islanders, 9 Hispanic Americans), 4 international. Average age 33. 248 applicants, 65% accepted, 110 enrolled. In 2009, 102 master's, 12 doctorates, 6 other advanced degrees awarded. *Degree requirements:* For master's, thesis (for some programs); for doctorate, thesis/dissertation; for Ed S, field project. *Entrance requirements:* For master's, doctorate, and Ed S, GRE General Test. *Application deadline:* For fall admission, 7/7 for domestic students; for spring admission, 11/24 for domestic students. Applications are processed on a rolling basis. Application fee: $50 ($60 for international students). Electronic applications accepted. *Expenses:* Tuition, state resident: full-time $6240. Tuition, nonresident: full-time $18,720. International tuition: $18,938 full-time. Required fees: $492. Tuition and fees vary according to course load, program and reciprocity agreements. *Financial support:* Fellowships, teaching assistantships, career-related internships or fieldwork and Federal Work-Study available. Support available to part-time students. Financial award application deadline: 3/15; financial award applicants required to submit FAFSA. *Faculty research:* Emerging literacy, reading attitudes, music for at-risk youth, portfolio assessment. *Unit head:* Dr. Nancy H. Barry, Head, 334-844-4434. *Application contact:* Dr. George Flowers, Dean of the Graduate School, 334-844-2125.

Auburn University Montgomery, School of Education, Department of Early Childhood, Elementary, and Reading Education, Montgomery, AL 36124-4023. Offers early childhood education (M Ed, Ed S); elementary education (M Ed, Ed S); reading education (M Ed, Ed S). *Accreditation:* NCATE. Part-time and evening/weekend programs available. *Faculty:* 5 full-time (all women). *Students:* 56 full-time (54 women), 71 part-time (65 women); includes 45 minority (all African Americans). Average age 31. In 2009, 42 master's awarded. *Degree requirements:* For master's and Ed S, comprehensive exam. *Entrance requirements:* For master's, GRE General Test or MAT, certification, BS in teaching; for Ed S, GRE General Test or MAT, certification. *Application deadline:* Applications are processed on a rolling basis. Electronic applications accepted. *Expenses:* Tuition, state resident: full-time $2841; part-time $225 per credit hour. Tuition, nonresident: full-time $8241; part-time $675 per credit hour. Required fees: $282; $8 per hour. $45 per term. *Financial support:* In 2009–10, 1 teaching assistantship was awarded; career-related internships or fieldwork and scholarships/grants also available. Support available to part-time students. Financial award application deadline: 3/1; financial award applicants required to submit FAFSA. *Unit head:* Dr. Lynne Mills, Head, 334-244-3283, Fax: 334-244-3835, E-mail: lmills@mail.aum.edu. *Application contact:* Dr. Sam Flynt, Associate Graduate Coordinator, 334-244-3270, Fax: 334-244-3835, E-mail: sflynt@mail.aum.edu.

Aurora University, College of Education, Aurora, IL 60506-4892. Offers curriculum and instruction (Ed D); education (MAT); education and administration (Ed D); educational leadership (MEL); reading instruction (MA). *Accreditation:* NCATE. Part-time and evening/weekend programs available. *Degree requirements:* For doctorate, thesis/dissertation. *Entrance requirements:* For master's, 2 years of teaching experience, valid teaching certificate. Additional exam requirements/recommendations for international students: Required—TOEFL (minimum score 550 paper-based; 213 computer-based). Electronic applications accepted. *Expenses:* Contact institution.

Austin Peay State University, College of Graduate Studies, College of Education, Department of Teaching and Learning, Clarksville, TN 37044. Offers elementary education K-6 (MAT); reading (MA Ed); secondary education 7-12 (MAT); special education K-12 (MAT). Part-time and evening/weekend programs available. Postbaccalaureate distance learning degree programs offered. *Faculty:* 8 full-time (6 women), 3 part-time/adjunct (all women). *Students:* 91 full-time (74 women), 84 part-time (67 women); includes 14 minority (12 African Americans, 2 Asian Americans or Pacific Islanders), 1 international. Average age 32. 122 applicants, 94% accepted, 75 enrolled. In 2009, 61 master's awarded. *Degree requirements:* For master's, comprehensive exam, thesis optional. *Entrance requirements:* For master's, GRE General Test, 3 letters of recommendation, minimum undergraduate GPA of 2.75. Additional exam requirements/recommendations for international students: Required—TOEFL (minimum score 500 paper-based; 173 computer-based). *Application deadline:* For fall admission, 7/27 priority date for domestic students; for spring admission, 12/17 priority date for domestic students. Applications are processed on a rolling basis. Application fee: $25. Electronic applications accepted. *Expenses:* Tuition, state resident: full-time $6160; part-time $608 per credit hour. Tuition, nonresident: full-time $17,080; part-time $854 per credit hour. Required fees: $1224; $61.20 per credit hour. *Financial support:* Career-related internships or fieldwork, Federal Work-Study, institutionally sponsored loans, scholarships/grants, and unspecified assistantships available. Support available to part-time students. Financial award application deadline: 3/1; financial award applicants required to submit FAFSA. *Unit head:* Dr. Rebecca McMahan, Interim Chair, 931-221-7513, Fax: 931-221-1292, E-mail: mcmahanb@apsu.edu. *Application contact:* Dr. Dixie Dennis, Dean, College of Graduate Studies, 931-221-7662, Fax: 931-221-7641, E-mail: dennisdi@apsu.edu.

Averett University, Master in Education Program, Danville, VA 24541-3692. Offers art education (M Ed); biology (M Ed); biology education (M Ed); chemistry (M Ed); chemistry education (M Ed); curriculum and instruction (M Ed); elementary education (M Ed); English (M Ed); English education (M Ed); health and physical education (M Ed); history and social studies education (M Ed); math (M Ed); mathematics education (M Ed); physical science (M Ed); reading specialization (M Ed); special education (learning disabilities specialization PK-12) (M Ed). Program also offered at Richmond, VA regional campus location. Part-time and evening/weekend programs available. *Faculty:* 4 full-time (3 women), 36 part-time/adjunct (22 women). *Students:* 182 full-time (160 women), 110 part-time (94 women); includes 113 minority (94 African Americans, 1 American Indian/Alaska Native, 7 Asian Americans or Pacific Islanders, 11 Hispanic Americans). Average age 37. 119 applicants, 99% accepted, 98 enrolled. In 2009, 92 master's awarded. *Degree requirements:* For master's, comprehensive exam, thesis optional. *Entrance requirements:* For master's, PRAXIS, GRE General Test, MAT or NTE, writing proficiency exam, 3 letters of recommendation, current teacher's licensure or eligibility for licensure, minimum undergraduate GPA of 3.0 in previous 2 years. Additional exam requirements/recommendations for international students: Required—TOEFL (minimum score 600 paper-based; 200 computer-based). *Application deadline:* Applications are processed on a rolling basis. *Expenses:* Contact institution. *Financial support:* Career-related internships or fieldwork,

Reading Education

Averett University (continued)

Federal Work-Study, and scholarships/grants available. Financial award application deadline: 4/1; financial award applicants required to submit FAFSA. *Faculty research:* Literary assessment-PreK-6, handwriting instruction and assessment-PreK-6, written language instruction and assessment-PreK-6 and special needs students learning styles, curriculum and instruction processes. *Unit head:* Dr. Lynn H. Wolf, Chair/Associate Professor/Director, 434-793-3995, Fax: 434-791-4392, E-mail: lynn.wolf@averett.edu. *Application contact:* Dr. Lynn H. Wolf, Chair/Associate Professor/Director, 434-793-3995, Fax: 434-791-4392, E-mail: lynn.wolf@averett.edu.

Baldwin-Wallace College, Graduate Programs, Division of Education, Specialization in Literacy, Berea, OH 44017-2088. Offers MA Ed. *Accreditation:* NCATE. Part-time and evening/weekend programs available. *Students:* 24 full-time (20 women), 20 part-time (all women); includes 2 minority (both African Americans). Average age 31. 15 applicants, 80% accepted, 9 enrolled. In 2009, 38 master's awarded. *Degree requirements:* For master's, comprehensive exam. *Entrance requirements:* For master's, bachelor's degree in field, MAT or minimum GPA of 2.75. Additional exam requirements/recommendations for international students: Required—TOEFL (minimum score 523 paper-based; 193 computer-based; 70 iBT). *Application deadline:* For fall admission, 8/15 priority date for domestic students; for spring admission, 12/15 priority date for domestic students. Applications are processed on a rolling basis. Application fee: $25. Electronic applications accepted. *Expenses:* Tuition: Full-time $14,174; part-time $682 per credit. Tuition and fees vary according to program. *Financial support:* Career-related internships or fieldwork available. Support available to part-time students. Financial award application deadline: 5/1; financial award applicants required to submit FAFSA. *Faculty research:* Metacognition and the reading process, language acquisition, genres and the reader response theory, cultural responsiveness, content area literacy. *Unit head:* Karen Kaye, Chair, 440-826-2168, Fax: 440-826-3779, E-mail: kkaye@bw.edu. *Application contact:* Winifred W. Gerhardt, Director of Admission for the Evening and Weekend College, 440-826-2222, Fax: 440-826-3830, E-mail: admission@bw.edu.

Bank Street College of Education, Graduate School, Program in Reading and Literacy, New York, NY 10025. Offers advanced literacy specialization (Ed M); reading and literacy (MS Ed); teaching literacy (MS Ed); teaching literacy and childhood general education (MS Ed). *Students:* 29 full-time (all women), 50 part-time (45 women); includes 13 minority (6 African Americans, 4 Asian Americans or Pacific Islanders, 3 Hispanic Americans). Average age 31. 48 applicants, 81% accepted, 28 enrolled. In 2009, 50 master's awarded. *Degree requirements:* For master's, thesis. *Entrance requirements:* For master's, interview. Additional exam requirements/recommendations for international students: Required—TOEFL (minimum score 600 paper-based; 250 computer-based; 100 iBT), IELTS (minimum score 7). *Application deadline:* For fall admission, 3/1 priority date for domestic students; for spring admission, 11/1 priority date for domestic students. Applications are processed on a rolling basis. Application fee: $65. *Expenses:* Tuition: Part-time $1120 per credit. *Financial support:* Career-related internships or fieldwork, Federal Work-Study, scholarships/grants, and unspecified assistantships available. Support available to part-time students. Financial award application deadline: 4/15; financial award applicants required to submit FAFSA. *Faculty research:* Language development, children's literature, whole language, the reading and writing processes, reading difficulties in multi-cultural classrooms. *Unit head:* Dr. Susan Goetz-Haver, Director, 212-875-4692, Fax: 212-875-4753, E-mail: sgoetz-haver@bankstreet.edu. *Application contact:* Ann Morgan, Director of Graduate Admissions, 212-875-4403, Fax: 212-875-4678, E-mail: amorgan@bankstreet.edu.

Barry University, School of Education, Program in Curriculum and Instruction, Miami Shores, FL 33161-6695. Offers accomplished teacher (Ed S); culture, language and literacy (TESOL) (PhD); curriculum evaluation and research (PhD); early childhood (Ed S); early childhood education (PhD); elementary (Ed S); elementary education (PhD); ESOL (Ed S); gifted (Ed S); Montessori (Ed S); PKP/elementary (Ed S); reading (Ed S); reading, language and cognition (PhD). *Entrance requirements:* For doctorate, GRE, minimum GPA of 3.25.

Barry University, School of Education, Program in Reading, Miami Shores, FL 33161-6695. Offers MS, Ed S. Part-time and evening/weekend programs available. *Degree requirements:* For master's, comprehensive exam, practicum; for Ed S, practicum. *Entrance requirements:* For master's, GRE General Test or MAT, minimum GPA of 3.0, course work in children's literature; for Ed S, GRE General Test, minimum GPA of 3.0. Electronic applications accepted.

Bellarmine University, Annsley Frazier Thornton School of Education, Louisville, KY 40205-0671. Offers early elementary education (MA, MAT); instructional leadership and school administration/school principal (MA); learning and behavior disorders (MA); middle school education (MA, MAT); reading and writing endorsement (MA); secondary school education (MAT); Waldorf inspired curriculum (MA). *Accreditation:* NCATE. Part-time and evening/weekend programs available. *Faculty:* 16 full-time (11 women), 20 part-time/adjunct (13 women). *Students:* 67 full-time (47 women), 140 part-time (111 women); includes 14 minority (10 African Americans, 1 American Indian/Alaska Native, 3 Asian Americans or Pacific Islanders), 1 international. Average age 33. In 2009, 106 degrees awarded. *Degree requirements:* For master's, comprehensive exam, thesis (for some programs). *Entrance requirements:* For master's, GRE, baccalaureate degree from an accredited institution; minimum overall GPA of 2.75, 3.0 in major; letters of recommendation; valid Kentucky provisional or professional certificate. Additional exam requirements/recommendations for international students: Required—TOEFL (minimum score 550 paper-based; 213 computer-based; 80 iBT). *Application deadline:* Applications are processed on a rolling basis. Application fee: $25. *Expenses:* Contact institution. *Financial support:* Scholarships/grants available. Financial award applicants required to submit FAFSA. *Faculty research:* Literacy, service learning, dispositions, educational technology, special education. *Unit head:* Dr. Cindy Gnadinger, Dean, 502-452-8191, Fax: 502-452-8189, E-mail: cgnadinger@bellarmine.edu. *Application contact:* Theresa Klapheke, Administrative Director of Graduate Programs, 502-452-8271, Fax: 502-452-8002, E-mail: tklapheke@bellarmine.edu.

Benedictine University, Graduate Programs, Program in Education, Lisle, IL 60532-0900. Offers curriculum and instruction and collaborative teaching (M Ed); elementary education (MA Ed); leadership and administration (M Ed); reading and literacy (M Ed); secondary education (MA Ed); special education (MA Ed). Part-time and evening/weekend programs available. *Faculty:* 4 full-time (2 women), 52 part-time/adjunct (30 women). *Students:* 286 full-time (252 women), 443 part-time (349 women); includes 61 minority (22 African Americans, 11 Asian Americans or Pacific Islanders, 28 Hispanic Americans), 5 international. Average age 33. 341 applicants, 90% accepted, 264 enrolled. In 2009, 299 master's awarded. *Degree requirements:* For master's, comprehensive exam, thesis (for some programs). *Entrance requirements:* For master's, GRE or MAT. Additional exam requirements/recommendations for international students: Required—TOEFL (minimum score 550 paper-based; 213 computer-based). *Application deadline:* For fall admission, 9/1 for domestic students; for winter admission, 12/1 for domestic students; for spring admission, 2/15 for domestic students. Applications are processed on a rolling basis. Application fee: $40. Electronic applications accepted. *Expenses:* Contact institution. *Financial support:* Career-related internships or fieldwork and health care benefits available. Support available to part-time students. *Unit head:* Dr. Richard Campbell, Director, 630-829-6242, Fax: 630-960-1126, E-mail: rcampbell@ben.edu. *Application contact:* Kari Gibbons, Director, Admissions, 630-829-6200, Fax: 630-829-6584, E-mail: kgibbons@ben.edu.

Berry College, Graduate Programs, Graduate Programs in Education, Program in Middle-Grades Education and Reading, Mount Berry, GA 30149-0159. Offers M Ed. *Accreditation:* NCATE. Part-time programs available. *Faculty:* 13 part-time/adjunct (8 women). *Students:* 1 full-time (0 women), 35 part-time (27 women); includes 1 minority (African American). Average age 33. In 2009, 6 master's awarded. *Degree requirements:* For master's, thesis optional, oral exams. *Entrance requirements:* For master's, GRE General Test, MAT, or NTE, minimum GPA of 2.5. Additional exam requirements/recommendations for international students: Required—TOEFL (minimum score 550 paper-based; 213 computer-based). *Application deadline:* For fall admission, 5/1 for domestic and international students; for spring admission, 10/1 for domestic and international students. Applications are processed on a rolling basis. Application fee: $25 ($30 for international students). *Expenses:* Contact institution. *Financial support:* In 2009–10, 14 students received support, including 3 research assistantships with full tuition reimbursements available (averaging $3,399 per year); scholarships/grants, tuition waivers (partial), and unspecified assistantships also available. Support available to part-time students. Financial award application deadline: 4/1; financial award applicants required to submit FAFSA. *Faculty research:* Curriculum development, teacher training, pedagogy. *Unit head:* Dr. Jacqueline McDowell, 706-236-1717, Fax: 706-238-5827, E-mail: jmcdowell@berry.edu. *Application contact:* Brett Kennedy, Director of Admissions, 706-236-2215, Fax: 706-290-2178, E-mail: admissions@berry.edu.

Bethel University, Graduate School, Department of Education, St. Paul, MN 55112-6999. Offers education K-12 (MA), including autism spectrum disorders, coordinator of work-based learning, differentiation, international baccalaureate, literacy, special education; educational administration (Ed D), including director of special education, K-12 principal license, superintendent license; literacy (Certificate); literacy education (MA); special education (MA), including autism spectrum disorders; teaching (MA). *Accreditation:* Teacher Education Accreditation Council. Evening/weekend programs available. Postbaccalaureate distance learning degree programs offered (minimal on-campus study). *Faculty:* 17 full-time (11 women), 37 part-time/adjunct (17 women). *Students:* 182 full-time (119 women), 172 part-time (120 women); includes 18 minority (2 African Americans, 1 American Indian/Alaska Native, 6 Asian Americans or Pacific Islanders, 9 Hispanic Americans), 1 international. Average age 35. 236 applicants, 79% accepted, 173 enrolled. In 2009, 51 master's, 5 doctorates awarded. *Degree requirements:* For master's, thesis, practicum; for doctorate, comprehensive exam, thesis/dissertation, internship. *Entrance requirements:* For master's, baccalaureate degree, statement of purpose essay, interview, current teaching license (if applicable), minimum GPA of 3.0, teaching experience (if applicable), letters of reference; for doctorate, MAT or GRE, minimum GPA of 3.0, letters of reference, statement of purpose essay, pre-assessment of prior experience and preparation, current license (if applicable), master's degree, interview, work experience in education. Additional exam requirements/recommendations for international students: Required—TOEFL (minimum score 550 paper-based; 213 computer-based; 80 iBT). *Application deadline:* For fall admission, 8/1 priority date for domestic students; for winter admission, 12/5 priority date for domestic students; for spring admission, 5/1 priority date for domestic students. Applications are processed on a rolling basis. Application fee: $25. Electronic applications accepted. *Expenses:* Contact institution. *Financial support:* Applicants required to submit FAFSA. *Unit head:* Dr. Judi Landrum, Assistant Dean, 651-635-8000, Fax: 651-638-8004, E-mail: j-landrum@bethel.edu. *Application contact:* Michael Price, Director of Admissions, 651-635-8000, Fax: 651-635-8004, E-mail: m-price@bethel.edu.

Bloomsburg University of Pennsylvania, School of Graduate Studies, College of Professional Studies, School of Education, Department of Exceptionality Programs, Program in Reading, Bloomsburg, PA 17815-1301. Offers M Ed. *Accreditation:* NCATE. *Entrance requirements:* For master's, minimum QPA of 3.0, teaching certificate. Additional exam requirements/recommendations for international students: Required—TOEFL (minimum score 550 paper-based; 213 computer-based; 79 iBT). Electronic applications accepted. *Faculty research:* Diagnosis, remediation, parental involvement, language arts, child literacy.

Boise State University, Graduate College, College of Education, Programs in Teacher Education, Program in Reading, Boise, ID 83725-0399. Offers MA. *Accreditation:* NCATE. Part-time programs available. *Degree requirements:* For master's, thesis optional. *Entrance requirements:* For master's, minimum GPA of 3.0. Electronic applications accepted. *Expenses:* Tuition, state resident: full-time $3106; part-time $209 per credit. Tuition, nonresident: part-time $284 per credit.

Boston College, Lynch Graduate School of Education, Department of Teacher Education/Special Education and Curriculum and Instruction, Reading Specialist Program, Chestnut Hill, MA 02467-3800. Offers M Ed, CAES. *Accreditation:* Teacher Education Accreditation Council. Part-time and evening/weekend programs available. *Students:* 17 part-time (15 women); includes 5 minority (1 African American, 3 Asian Americans or Pacific Islanders, 1 Hispanic American). 31 applicants, 48% accepted, 7 enrolled. In 2009, 6 master's awarded. *Degree requirements:* For master's and CAES, comprehensive exam. *Entrance requirements:* For master's, GRE General Test or MAT, general licensure, one year of teaching experience; for CAES, GRE General Test or MAT. Additional exam requirements/recommendations for international students: Required—TOEFL (minimum score 550 paper-based; 213 computer-based; 81 iBT). *Application deadline:* For fall admission, 1/1 priority date for domestic students. Application fee: $60. Electronic applications accepted. *Financial support:* Fellowships with full and partial tuition reimbursements, research assistantships with full and partial tuition reimbursements, teaching assistantships with full and partial tuition reimbursements, career-related internships or fieldwork, Federal Work-Study, scholarships/grants, traineeships, health care benefits, tuition waivers (full and partial), and unspecified assistantships available. Support available to part-time students. Financial award applicants required to submit FAFSA. *Faculty research:* Creating literacy learning environments; critical literacy and literacy development. *Unit head:* Dr. Maria E. Brisk, Chairperson, 617-552-4216, Fax: 617-552-0812, E-mail: brisk@bc.edu. *Application contact:* Adam Poluzzi, Director, Graduate Admission and Financial Aid, 617-552-4214, Fax: 617-552-0398, E-mail: poluzzi@bc.edu.

Boston University, School of Education, Department of Literacy and Language, Counseling and Development, Program in Reading Education, Boston, MA 02215. Offers literacy and language (Ed D); reading education (Ed M, CAGS). *Degree requirements:* For doctorate, comprehensive exam, thesis/dissertation; for CAGS, comprehensive exam. *Entrance requirements:* For master's, doctorate, and CAGS, GRE General Test or MAT. Additional exam requirements/recommendations for international students: Required—TOEFL. Electronic applications accepted. *Expenses:* Tuition: Full-time $37,910; part-time $1184 per credit hour. Required fees: $386; $40 per semester. Part-time tuition and fees vary according to class time, course level, degree level and program. *Faculty research:* Reading diagnosis (disabilities), professional preparation.

Bowie State University, Graduate Programs, Program in Reading Education, Bowie, MD 20715-9465. Offers M Ed. *Accreditation:* NCATE. Part-time and evening/weekend programs available. *Degree requirements:* For master's, comprehensive exam, thesis optional, research paper. *Entrance requirements:* For master's, minimum GPA of 2.5, teaching certificate, teaching experience. *Faculty research:* Literacy education, multicultural education.

Bowling Green State University, Graduate College, College of Education and Human Development, School of Education and Intervention Services, Teaching and Learning Division, Program in Reading, Bowling Green, OH 43403. Offers M Ed, Ed S. *Accreditation:* NCATE. Part-time programs available. *Degree requirements:* For master's, thesis or alternative; for Ed S, practicum or field experience. *Entrance requirements:* For master's and Ed S, GRE General Test. Additional exam requirements/recommendations for international students: Required—TOEFL. Electronic applications accepted. *Faculty research:* Children's literature, attention deficit disorder (ADD)/reading correlation, content area reading, reading instruction, reading/writing connection.

Bridgewater State University, School of Graduate Studies, School of Education and Allied Science, Department of Elementary and Early Childhood Education, Program in Reading, Bridgewater, MA 02325-0001. Offers M Ed, CAGS. *Accreditation:* NCATE. Part-time and evening/weekend programs available. *Entrance requirements:* For master's, GRE General Test, 1 year of teaching experience.

Brigham Young University, Graduate Studies, David O. McKay School of Education, Department of Teacher Education, Provo, UT 84602. Offers literacy education (MA); stem (MA); teacher education (MA). *Accreditation:* NCATE. Part-time programs available. *Faculty:* 22 full-time (13 women). *Students:* 27 part-time (24 women). Average age 32. 21 applicants, 86% accepted, 17 enrolled. In 2009, 6 master's awarded. *Degree requirements:* For master's, thesis. *Entrance requirements:* For master's, GRE General Test, minimum 1 year of teaching experience, minimum GPA of 3.25 in last 60 hours of course work, valid teaching credential.

Additional exam requirements/recommendations for international students: Required—TOEFL (minimum score 500 paper-based). *Application deadline:* For fall admission, 2/1 priority date for domestic and international students; for spring admission, 3/15 for domestic students. Application fee: $50. Electronic applications accepted. *Expenses:* Tuition: Full-time $5580; part-time $301 per credit hour. Tuition and fees vary according to student's religious affiliation. *Financial support:* In 2009–10, 27 students received support, including 10 research assistantships (averaging $4,650 per year); teaching assistantships with partial tuition reimbursements available, scholarships/grants and tuition waivers (full and partial) also available. *Faculty research:* History pedagogy, early childhood and socio-emotional development, teacher socialization, problem solving in mathematics, technology in teacher education. *Unit head:* Dr. Janet Young, Graduate Coordinator, 801-422-4979, Fax: 801-422-0652, E-mail: janet_young@byu.edu. *Application contact:* Lori Bikhazi, Graduate Secretary, 801-422-4079, Fax: 801-422-0652, E-mail: ted201asec@byu.edu.

Bucknell University, Graduate Studies, College of Arts and Sciences, Department of Education, Specialization in Reading, Lewisburg, PA 17837. Offers MA, MS Ed. *Degree requirements:* For master's, thesis or alternative. *Entrance requirements:* For master's, GRE General Test, minimum GPA of 2.8. Additional exam requirements/recommendations for international students: Required—TOEFL.

Buffalo State College, State University of New York, The Graduate School, Faculty of Applied Science and Education, Department of Elementary Education and Reading, Programs in Literacy Specialist, Buffalo, NY 14222-1095. Offers literacy specialist (birth-grade 6) (MS Ed); literacy specialist (grades 5-12) (MPS). *Accreditation:* NCATE. Part-time and evening/weekend programs available. *Degree requirements:* For master's, project. *Entrance requirements:* For master's, minimum GPA of 3.0 in last 60 hours. Additional exam requirements/recommendations for international students: Required—TOEFL (minimum score 550 paper-based; 213 computer-based).

Butler University, College of Education, Indianapolis, IN 46208-3485. Offers administration (MS); elementary education (MS); reading (MS); school counseling (MS); secondary education (MS); special education (MS). *Accreditation:* ACA; NCATE. Part-time and evening/weekend programs available. *Faculty:* 9 full-time (7 women), 7 part-time/adjunct (6 women). *Students:* 18 full-time (11 women), 137 part-time (111 women); includes 17 minority (14 African Americans, 1 American Indian/Alaska Native, 2 Asian Americans or Pacific Islanders), 9 international. Average age 31. 57 applicants, 77% accepted, 24 enrolled. In 2009, 61 master's awarded. *Entrance requirements:* For master's, GRE General Test, MAT, interview. *Application deadline:* For fall admission, 8/15 priority date for domestic students. Applications are processed on a rolling basis. Application fee: $35. Electronic applications accepted. *Financial support:* Institutionally sponsored loans available. Support available to part-time students. Financial award application deadline: 7/15; financial award applicants required to submit FAFSA. *Faculty research:* Ethics in cybercounseling, history of sports for disabled, effect of fetal alcohol syndrome on perceptual learning, reading recovery's theoretical framework in teacher education. *Unit head:* Dr. Ena Shelley, Dean, 317-940-9752, Fax: 317-940-6481. *Application contact:* Karen Farrell, Department Secretary, 317-940-9220, E-mail: kfarrell@butler.edu.

California Baptist University, Program in Education, Riverside, CA 92504-3206. Offers cross-cultural language and academic development (MA); educational leadership (MS); educational leadership and faith-based instruction (MS); educational technology (MS); instructional computer applications (MS); reading (MS); school counseling (MS); school psychology (MS); special education (MS); special education in mild/moderate disabilities (MS); special education in moderate/severe disabilities (MS); teaching (MS); teaching and learning (MS Ed). Part-time programs available. *Faculty:* 16 full-time (9 women), 10 part-time/adjunct (all women). *Students:* 73 full-time (60 women), 368 part-time (298 women); includes 170 minority (34 African Americans, 4 American Indian/Alaska Native, 18 Asian Americans or Pacific Islanders, 114 Hispanic Americans). 266 applicants, 72% accepted, 169 enrolled. In 2009, 120 master's awarded. *Degree requirements:* For master's, comprehensive exam (for some programs), thesis optional. *Entrance requirements:* For master's, minimum undergraduate GPA of 2.75, 12 semester hours of pre-requisite course work in education. Additional exam requirements/recommendations for international students: Required—TOEFL (minimum score 575 paper-based; 230 computer-based; 89 iBT). *Application deadline:* For fall admission, 8/1 priority date for domestic students, 7/1 for international students; for spring admission, 12/1 priority date for domestic students, 10/15 priority date for international students. Applications are processed on a rolling basis. Application fee: $45. Electronic applications accepted. *Expenses:* Tuition: Full-time $8352; part-time $464 per semester hour. Required fees: $125 per semester. Tuition and fees vary according to course load, campus/location and program. *Financial support:* Career-related internships or fieldwork, Federal Work-Study, and scholarships/grants available. Support available to part-time students. Financial award applicants required to submit FAFSA. *Unit head:* Dr. Mary Crist, Dean, School of Education, 951-343-4313, Fax: 951-343-4516, E-mail: mcrist@calbaptist.edu. *Application contact:* Gail Ronveaux, Dean of Graduate Enrollment, 951-343-5045, Fax: 951-343-5095, E-mail: graduateadmissions@calbaptist.edu.

California Lutheran University, Graduate Studies, School of Education, Emphasis in Curriculum and Instruction, Thousand Oaks, CA 91360-2787. Offers reading education (MA). *Accreditation:* NCATE. Part-time and evening/weekend programs available. *Degree requirements:* For master's, thesis or comprehensive exam. *Entrance requirements:* For master's, GRE General Test, interview, minimum GPA of 3.0.

California State University, Bakersfield, Division of Graduate Studies, School of Education, Graduate Reading/Literacy Program, Bakersfield, CA 93311. Offers MA Ed, Certificate.

California State University, Chico, Graduate School, College of Communication and Education, Department of Professional Studies in Education, Option in Reading/Language Arts, Chico, CA 95929-0722. Offers MA. Part-time and evening/weekend programs available. *Students:* 5 part-time (all women). Average age 43. In 2009, 1 master's awarded. *Entrance requirements:* Additional exam requirements/recommendations for international students: Required—TOEFL (minimum score 550 paper-based; 213 computer-based; 80 iBT), IELTS (minimum score 6.5). *Application deadline:* For fall admission, 3/1 priority date for domestic students, 3/1 for international students; for spring admission, 9/15 priority date for domestic students, 9/15 for international students. Applications are processed on a rolling basis. Application fee: $55. Electronic applications accepted.

California State University, East Bay, Graduate Programs, College of Education and Allied Studies, Department of Teacher Education, Hayward, CA 94542-3000. Offers education (MS), including curriculum, early childhood education, educational technology leadership, reading instruction. *Faculty:* 18 full-time (10 women), 4 part-time/adjunct (3 women). *Students:* Average age 37. In 2009, 135 master's awarded. *Degree requirements:* For master's, project or thesis. *Entrance requirements:* For master's, minimum GPA of 3.0 in field, 2.5 overall; teaching experience. Additional exam requirements/recommendations for international students: Required—TOEFL (minimum score 550 paper-based; 213 computer-based). *Application deadline:* For fall admission, 6/30 for domestic and international students. Application fee: $55. Electronic applications accepted. *Financial support:* Career-related internships or fieldwork, Federal Work-Study, and institutionally sponsored loans available. Support available to part-time students. Financial award application deadline: 3/1; financial award applicants required to submit FAFSA. *Unit head:* Dr. Jeanette Bicais, Chair, 510-885-3027, E-mail: jeanette.bicais@csueastbay.edu. *Application contact:* Donna Wiley, Interim Associate Director, 510-885-2928, Fax: 510-885-4777, E-mail: donna.wiley@csueastbay.edu.

California State University, Fresno, Division of Graduate Studies, School of Education and Human Development, Department of Literacy and Early Education, Fresno, CA 93740-8027. Offers education (MA), including early childhood education, reading/language arts. *Accreditation:* NCATE. Part-time and evening/weekend programs available. *Degree requirements:* For master's, thesis or alternative. *Entrance requirements:* For master's, GRE General Test, MAT, minimum GPA of 2.75. Additional exam requirements/recommendations for international students:

Required—TOEFL. Electronic applications accepted. *Faculty research:* Reading recovery, monitoring/tutoring programs, character and academics, professional ethics, low-performing partnership schools.

California State University, Fullerton, Graduate Studies, College of Education, Department of Reading, Fullerton, CA 92834-9480. Offers MS. Part-time programs available. *Students:* 11 full-time (all women), 115 part-time (110 women); includes 52 minority (3 African Americans, 16 Asian Americans or Pacific Islanders, 33 Hispanic Americans), 1 international. Average age 35. 47 applicants, 87% accepted, 33 enrolled. In 2009, 64 master's awarded. Application fee: $55. *Expenses:* Tuition, nonresident: full-time $11,160; part-time $373 per credit. Required fees: $1440 per term. Tuition and fees vary according to course load, degree level and program. *Financial support:* Career-related internships or fieldwork, Federal Work-Study, institutionally sponsored loans, and scholarships/grants available. Support available to part-time students. Financial award application deadline: 3/1; financial award applicants required to submit FAFSA. *Unit head:* Dr. Ula Manzo, Chair, 657-278-3357. *Application contact:* Admissions/Applications, 657-278-2371.

California State University, Los Angeles, Graduate Studies, Charter College of Education, Division of Curriculum and Instruction, Los Angeles, CA 90032-8530. Offers elementary teaching (MA); reading (MA); secondary teaching (MA). Part-time and evening/weekend programs available. *Faculty:* 8 full-time (6 women), 7 part-time/adjunct (4 women). *Students:* 308 full-time (217 women), 297 part-time (211 women); includes 399 minority (22 African Americans, 98 Asian Americans or Pacific Islanders, 279 Hispanic Americans), 19 international. Average age 32. 53 applicants, 100% accepted, 30 enrolled. In 2009, 101 master's awarded. *Entrance requirements:* For master's, minimum GPA of 2.75 in last 90 units of course work, teaching certificate. Additional exam requirements/recommendations for international students: Required—TOEFL (minimum score 500 paper-based; 173 computer-based). *Application deadline:* For fall admission, 5/1 for domestic and international students. Applications are processed on a rolling basis. Application fee: $55. Electronic applications accepted. *Financial support:* Federal Work-Study available. Support available to part-time students. Financial award application deadline: 3/1. *Faculty research:* Media, language arts, mathematics, computers, drug-free schools. *Unit head:* Dr. Ramakrishan Menon, Chair, 323-343-4350, Fax: 323-343-5458, E-mail: rmenon@calstatela.edu. *Application contact:* Dr. Cheryl L. Ney, Associate Vice President for Academic Affairs and Dean of Graduate Studies, 323-343-3820 Ext. 3827, Fax: 323-343-5653, E-mail: cney@cslanet.calstatela.edu.

California State University, Northridge, Graduate Studies, College of Education, Department of Elementary Education, Northridge, CA 91330. Offers curriculum and instruction (MA); language and literacy (MA); multilingual/multicultural education (MA); teaching and learning (MA). *Accreditation:* NCATE. Part-time and evening/weekend programs available. *Faculty:* 18 full-time (14 women), 32 part-time/adjunct (24 women). *Students:* 29 full-time (all women), 61 part-time (57 women); includes 38 minority (1 African American, 10 Asian Americans or Pacific Islanders, 27 Hispanic Americans), 1 international. Average age 31. 64 applicants, 64% accepted, 28 enrolled. *Degree requirements:* For master's, comprehensive exam. *Entrance requirements:* For master's, GRE General Test or minimum GPA of 3.0. Additional exam requirements/recommendations for international students: Required—TOEFL. *Application deadline:* For fall admission, 11/30 for domestic students. Application fee: $55. *Financial support:* Federal Work-Study available. Financial award application deadline: 3/1. *Unit head:* Dr. David Kretschmer, Chair, 818-677-2621. *Application contact:* Joyce Burstein, Graduate Coordinator, 818-677-2621 Ext. 6850, E-mail: joyce.burstein@csun.edu.

California State University, Sacramento, Graduate Studies, College of Education, Department of Teacher Education, Sacramento, CA 95819. Offers curriculum and instruction (MA); early childhood education (MA); reading education (MA). Part-time programs available. *Degree requirements:* For master's, thesis or alternative, writing proficiency exam. *Entrance requirements:* Additional exam requirements/recommendations for international students: Required—TOEFL. Electronic applications accepted.

California State University, San Bernardino, Graduate Studies, College of Education, Program in Reading, San Bernardino, CA 92407-2397. Offers MA. *Accreditation:* NCATE. Part-time and evening/weekend programs available. *Faculty:* 2 full-time (both women), 3 part-time/adjunct (all women). *Students:* 45 full-time (40 women), 20 part-time (16 women); includes 19 minority (4 African Americans, 2 Asian Americans or Pacific Islanders, 13 Hispanic Americans). Average age 40. 31 applicants, 97% accepted, 17 enrolled. In 2009, 34 master's awarded. *Degree requirements:* For master's, comprehensive exam (for some programs), thesis or alternative. *Entrance requirements:* For master's, minimum GPA of 3.0 in education. *Application deadline:* For fall admission, 8/31 priority date for domestic students. Application fee: $55. *Financial support:* Career-related internships or fieldwork and Federal Work-Study available. Support available to part-time students. *Unit head:* Dr. Mary Jo Skillings, Chair, 909-537-5639, Fax: 909-537-5992, E-mail: maryjosk@csusb.edu. *Application contact:* Olivia Rosas, Director of Admissions, 909-537-7577, Fax: 909-537-7034, E-mail: orosas@csusb.edu.

California State University, Stanislaus, College of Education, Department of Teacher Education, Turlock, CA 95382. Offers curriculum and instruction (MA), including elementary education, multilingual education, reading, secondary education; education (MA); middle/junior high studies (Graduate Certificate). Part-time and evening/weekend programs available. *Degree requirements:* For master's, thesis. *Entrance requirements:* For master's, MAT or GRE, 3 letters of recommendation. Additional exam requirements/recommendations for international students: Required—TOEFL (minimum score 550 paper-based; 213 computer-based). Electronic applications accepted. *Faculty research:* Children's perspectives on historical events, method elementary schools dual language education, K-12 reading and CYRM programs.

California University of Pennsylvania, School of Graduate Studies and Research, School of Education, Department of Elementary Education, Program in Reading Specialist, California, PA 15419-1394. Offers M Ed. *Accreditation:* NCATE. Part-time and evening/weekend programs available. *Degree requirements:* For master's, comprehensive exam, thesis optional, practicum. *Entrance requirements:* For master's, MAT, PRAXIS, minimum GPA of 3.0, teaching certificate. Additional exam requirements/recommendations for international students: Required—TOEFL (minimum score 550 paper-based; 213 computer-based; 80 iBT). Electronic applications accepted. *Faculty research:* Online education in reading supervision, phonetics education, remedial reading, injury and reading remediation in brain patients.

Calvin College, Graduate Programs in Education, Grand Rapids, MI 49546-4388. Offers curriculum and instruction (M Ed); educational leadership (M Ed); learning disabilities (M Ed); literacy (M Ed). Part-time programs available. *Faculty:* 3 full-time (2 women), 4 part-time/adjunct (1 woman). *Students:* 7 full-time (6 women), 113 part-time (79 women); includes 9 minority (2 African Americans, 5 Asian Americans or Pacific Islanders, 2 Hispanic Americans). Average age 29. In 2009, 27 master's awarded. *Degree requirements:* For master's, thesis or seminar. *Entrance requirements:* For master's, teaching certificate. Additional exam requirements/recommendations for international students: Required—TOEFL (minimum score 550 paper-based; 213 computer-based). *Application deadline:* For fall admission, 8/1 priority date for domestic students, 6/1 priority date for international students; for spring admission, 1/1 priority date for domestic students, 2/1 priority date for international students. Applications are processed on a rolling basis. Application fee: $0. Electronic applications accepted. *Expenses:* Tuition: Full-time $10,080. *Financial support:* Federal Work-Study, scholarships/grants, and tuition waivers (full and partial) available. Support available to part-time students. Financial award application deadline: 4/3. *Faculty research:* Literacy, racialized gender and gendered identity, teacher learning, learning disabilities identification. *Unit head:* Dr. Debra Buursma, Graduate Program Director, 616-526-6231, Fax: 616-526-6505, E-mail: dbuursma@calvin.edu. *Application contact:* Cindi Hoekstra, Program Coordinator, 616-526-6158, Fax: 616-526-6505, E-mail: choekstr@calvin.edu.

Cambridge College, School of Education, Cambridge, MA 02138-5304. Offers autism specialist (M Ed); autism/behavior analyst (M Ed); behavior analyst (Post-Master's Certificate); behavioral management (M Ed); early childhood teacher (M Ed); education specialist in curriculum and

Reading Education

Cambridge College (continued)

instruction (CAGS); educational leadership (Ed D); elementary teacher (M Ed); English as a second language (M Ed, Certificate); general science (M Ed); health education, health promotion (Post-Master's Certificate); health/family and consumer sciences (M Ed); history (M Ed); individualized degree (M Ed); information technology literacy (M Ed); instructional technology (M Ed); interdisciplinary studies (M Ed); library teacher (M Ed); literacy education (M Ed); mathematics (M Ed); mathematics specialist (Certificate); middle school mathematics and science (M Ed); school administration (M Ed, CAGS); school guidance counselor (M Ed); school nurse education (M Ed); school social worker/school adjustment counselor (M Ed); special education administrator (CAGS); special education/moderate disabilities (M Ed); teaching skills and methodologies (M Ed). Part-time and evening/weekend programs available. Post-baccalaureate distance learning degree programs offered (minimal on-campus study). *Faculty:* 10 full-time (3 women), 283 part-time/adjunct (187 women). *Students:* 974 full-time (755 women), 1,071 part-time (835 women); includes 940 minority (762 African Americans, 4 American Indian/Alaska Native, 22 Asian Americans or Pacific Islanders, 152 Hispanic Americans), 28 international. Average age 39. In 2009, 866 master's, 4 doctorates, 209 CAGSs awarded. *Degree requirements:* For master's, thesis, internship/practicum (licensure program only); for doctorate, thesis/dissertation; for other advanced degree, thesis. *Entrance requirements:* For master's, interview, resume, documentation of licensure, 2 professional references; for doctorate, official transcripts, interview, resume, documentation of licensure (if any), written personal statement/essay, portfolio of scholarly and professional work, qualifying assessment, 2 professional references, health insurance, immunizations form; for other advanced degree, official transcripts, interview, resume, documentation of licensure (if any), written personal statement/essay, 2 professional references, health insurance, immunizations form. Additional exam requirements/recommendations for international students: Required—TOEFL (minimum score 550 paper-based; 213 computer-based; 79 iBT); Recommended—IELTS (minimum score 6). *Application deadline:* Applications are processed on a rolling basis. Application fee: $30. Electronic applications accepted. *Expenses:* Contact institution. *Financial support:* In 2009–10, 1,373 students received support. Career-related internships or fieldwork, Federal Work-Study, and scholarships/grants available. Financial award applicants required to submit FAFSA. *Faculty research:* Adult education, accelerated learning, mathematics education, brain compatible learning, special education and law. *Unit head:* Dr. N. Alan Sheppard, Interim Associate Dean, 617-873-0619, E-mail: alan.sheppard@cambridgecollege.edu. *Application contact:* Stephen Lyons, Director of Enrollment, Graduate and N.I.T.E. Programs, 617-868-1000, Fax: 617-349-3561, E-mail: stephen.lyons@cambridgecollege.edu.

Canisius College, Graduate Division, School of Education and Human Services, Department of Graduate Education, Buffalo, NY 14208-1098. Offers adolescence education (grades 7-12) (MS); childhood education (grades 1-6) (MS); college student personnel administration (MS); deaf education (MS); differentiated instruction (MS Ed); educational administration and supervision (MS); general education (MS Ed); initial teacher certification (elementary education) (MS); initial teacher certification (secondary education) (MS); literacy (MS Ed); special education (MS). *Accreditation:* NCATE. Part-time and evening/weekend programs available. *Faculty:* 22 full-time (14 women), 84 part-time/adjunct (54 women). *Students:* 409 full-time (288 women), 261 part-time (187 women); includes 29 minority (24 African Americans, 5 Hispanic Americans), 156 international. Average age 30. 518 applicants, 74% accepted, 240 enrolled. In 2009, 346 master's awarded. Application fee: $25. *Financial support:* Research assistantships with full tuition reimbursements, career-related internships or fieldwork, institutionally sponsored loans, scholarships/grants, health care benefits, tuition waivers (full and partial), and unspecified assistantships available. *Faculty research:* Autism, Asperger's disease, private higher education, reading strategies. *Unit head:* Rev. Paul Nochelski, Chair of Graduate Education and Leadership, 716-888-3297, Fax: 716-888-3299. *Application contact:* James D. Bagwell, Director of Graduate Recruitment and Admissions, 716-888-2544, Fax: 716-888-3290, E-mail: bagwellj@canisius.edu.

Capella University, School of Education, Minneapolis, MN 55402. Offers college teaching (Certificate); curriculum and instruction (MS, PhD); education (MS); enrollment management (MS); instructional design for online learning (MS, PhD); k-12 studies in education (MS, PhD); leadership for higher education (MS, PhD); leadership in education administration (Certificate); leadership in educational administration (MS, PhD); postsecondary and adult education (MS, PhD); professional studies in education (MS, PhD); reading and literacy (MS); training and performance improvement (MS, PhD). Part-time and evening/weekend programs available. Postbaccalaureate distance learning degree programs offered (minimal on-campus study). Terminal master's awarded for partial completion of doctoral program. *Degree requirements:* For master's, thesis optional, integrative project; for doctorate, comprehensive exam, thesis/dissertation. *Entrance requirements:* Additional exam requirements/recommendations for international students: Required—TOEFL (minimum score 550 paper-based; 213 computer-based), TWE (minimum score 4). Electronic applications accepted. *Faculty research:* Higher education administration, distance learning, adult education, training and curriculum design.

Cardinal Stritch University, College of Education, Department of Literacy, Milwaukee, WI 53217-3985. Offers literacy/English as a second language (MA); reading/language arts (MA); reading/learning disability (MA). *Accreditation:* NCATE. Part-time and evening/weekend programs available. *Degree requirements:* For master's, comprehensive exam, thesis, faculty recommendation, research project. *Entrance requirements:* For master's, letters of recommendation (2), minimum GPA of 2.75.

Carthage College, Division of Teacher Education, Kenosha, WI 53140. Offers classroom guidance and counseling (M Ed); creative arts (M Ed); gifted and talented children (M Ed); language arts (M Ed); modern language (M Ed); natural sciences (M Ed); reading (M Ed, Certificate); social sciences (M Ed); teacher leadership (M Ed). Part-time and evening/weekend programs available. *Degree requirements:* For master's, thesis optional. *Entrance requirements:* For master's, MAT, minimum B average, letters of reference.

Castleton State College, Division of Graduate Studies, Department of Education, Program in Language Arts and Reading, Castleton, VT 05735. Offers MA Ed, CAGS. Part-time and evening/weekend programs available. *Degree requirements:* For master's, thesis or alternative; for CAGS, publishable paper, written exams. *Entrance requirements:* For master's, GRE General Test, MAT, interview, minimum undergraduate GPA of 3.0; for CAGS, educational research, master's degree, minimum undergraduate GPA of 3.0. *Expenses:* Tuition, state resident: full-time $10,290; part-time $429 per credit. Tuition, nonresident: full-time $15,420; part-time $643 per credit. One-time fee: $200 full-time.

Central Connecticut State University, School of Graduate Studies, School of Education and Professional Studies, Department of Reading and Language Arts, New Britain, CT 06050-4010. Offers MS, Sixth Year Certificate. Part-time and evening/weekend programs available. *Faculty:* 8 full-time (6 women), 9 part-time/adjunct (5 women). *Students:* 2 full-time (both women), 138 part-time (131 women); includes 7 minority (5 African Americans, 2 Hispanic Americans), 1 international. Average age 36. 47 applicants, 43% accepted, 16 enrolled. In 2009, 34 master's, 13 other advanced degrees awarded. *Degree requirements:* For master's, comprehensive exam, thesis or alternative; for Sixth Year Certificate, qualifying exam. *Entrance requirements:* For master's, minimum undergraduate GPA of 2.7, teacher certification, interview; for Sixth Year Certificate, master's degree, essay, teacher certification, interview. Additional exam requirements/recommendations for international students: Required—TOEFL. *Application deadline:* For fall admission, 7/1 for domestic students; for spring admission, 12/1 for domestic students. Applications are processed on a rolling basis. Application fee: $50. Electronic applications accepted. *Expenses:* Tuition, area resident: Full-time $4662; part-time $440 per credit. Tuition, state resident: full-time $6994; part-time $440 per credit. Tuition, nonresident: full-time $12,988; part-time $440 per credit. Required fees: $3606. One-time fee: $62 part-time. *Financial support:* In 2009–10, 4 students received support. Career-related internships or fieldwork, Federal Work-Study, scholarships/grants, and unspecified assistantships available. Support available to part-time students. Financial award application deadline: 3/1; financial award applicants required to submit FAFSA. *Faculty research:* Developmental, clinical, and

administrative aspects of reading and language arts instruction. *Unit head:* Dr. Helen Abadiano, Chair, 860-832-2175. *Application contact:* Dr. Helen Abadiano, Chair, 860-832-2175.

Central Michigan University, Central Michigan University Off-Campus Programs, Program in Education, Mount Pleasant, MI 48859. Offers adult education (MA); community college (MA); education (MA); guidance and development (MA); instructional (MA); reading and literacy K-12 (MA). Part-time and evening/weekend programs available. *Entrance requirements:* For master's, minimum GPA of 2.7 in major. Additional exam requirements/recommendations for international students: Required—TOEFL. *Application deadline:* Applications are processed on a rolling basis. Application fee: $50. Electronic applications accepted. *Financial support:* Scholarships/grants available. Support available to part-time students. *Unit head:* Jennifer Cochran, Director, 989-774-2584, E-mail: jennifer.cochran@cmich.edu. *Application contact:* 877-268-4636, E-mail: cmuoffcampus@cmich.edu.

Central Michigan University, College of Graduate Studies, College of Education and Human Services, Department of Teacher Education and Professional Development, Mount Pleasant, MI 48859. Offers educational technology (MA); elementary education (MA), including classroom teaching, early childhood; middle level education (MA); reading and literacy K-12 (MA); secondary education (MA). Part-time and evening/weekend programs available. *Degree requirements:* For master's, thesis or alternative. Electronic applications accepted. *Faculty research:* Integrating literacy across the curriculum; science teaching and aesthetic learning in science; diversity education; educational technology; educational psychology and child development.

Central Washington University, Graduate Studies and Research, College of Education and Professional Studies, Department of Education, Program in Reading Education, Ellensburg, WA 98926. Offers M Ed. Part-time programs available. *Faculty:* 4 full-time (2 women). *Students:* 5 part-time (all women); includes 1 minority (American Indian/Alaska Native). 1 applicant, 0% accepted. In 2009, 11 master's awarded. *Degree requirements:* For master's, thesis or alternative. *Entrance requirements:* For master's, minimum GPA of 3.0. Additional exam requirements/recommendations for international students: Required—TOEFL (minimum score 550 paper-based; 213 computer-based; 79 iBT). *Application deadline:* For fall admission, 2/1 priority date for domestic students; for winter admission, 10/1 for domestic students; for spring admission, 1/1 for domestic students. Applications are processed on a rolling basis. Application fee: $50. *Expenses:* Tuition, state resident: full-time $7353; part-time $245 per credit. Tuition, nonresident: full-time $16,383; part-time $546 per credit. Required fees: $882. Tuition and fees vary according to degree level. *Financial support:* Research assistantships with full and partial tuition reimbursements, teaching assistantships with full and partial tuition reimbursements, Federal Work-Study, health care benefits, and unspecified assistantships available. Financial award application deadline: 3/1; financial award applicants required to submit FAFSA. *Unit head:* Dr. Carol Butterfield, Program Director, 509-963-1480, E-mail: butterfc@cwu.edu. *Application contact:* Justine Eason, Admissions Program Coordinator, 509-963-3103, Fax: 509-963-1799, E-mail: masters@cwu.edu.

Chapman University, Graduate Studies, College of Educational Studies, Concentration in Reading Education, Orange, CA 92866. Offers MA, Credential. Part-time and evening/weekend programs available. *Faculty:* 19 full-time (13 women), 20 part-time/adjunct (12 women). *Students:* 5 part-time (all women). Average age 38. 4 applicants, 100% accepted, 3 enrolled. *Degree requirements:* For master's, comprehensive exam, thesis optional. *Entrance requirements:* For master's, GRE General Test, MAT, or California Subject Examinations for Teachers, minimum undergraduate GPA of 2.5. Additional exam requirements/recommendations for international students: Required—TOEFL (minimum score 550 paper-based). *Application deadline:* Applications are processed on a rolling basis. Application fee: $55. Electronic applications accepted. *Expenses:* Contact institution. *Financial support:* Fellowships, Federal Work-Study and scholarships/grants available. Financial award application deadline: 6/30; financial award applicants required to submit FAFSA. *Unit head:* Dr. Sally Thomas, Coordinator, 714-997-6781, E-mail: sthomas@chapman.edu. *Application contact:* Rika Judd, Information Contact, 714-997-6786, Fax: 714-997-6713, E-mail: rjudd@chapman.edu.

Chapman University, Graduate Studies, College of Educational Studies, Program in Education, Orange, CA 92866. Offers curriculum and foundations (MA); educational leadership and administration (MA); reading and literacy (MA). Part-time and evening/weekend programs available. *Faculty:* 24 full-time (15 women), 25 part-time/adjunct (16 women). *Students:* 7 full-time (all women), 35 part-time (25 women); includes 20 minority (1 African American, 8 Asian Americans or Pacific Islanders, 11 Hispanic Americans). Average age 32. 18 applicants, 89% accepted, 9 enrolled. In 2009, 32 master's awarded. *Degree requirements:* For master's, comprehensive exam, thesis optional. *Entrance requirements:* For master's, GRE General Test, MAT, or California Subject Examinations for Teachers, minimum undergraduate GPA of 2.5. Additional exam requirements/recommendations for international students: Required—TOEFL (minimum score 550 paper-based). *Application deadline:* Applications are processed on a rolling basis. Application fee: $55. Electronic applications accepted. *Expenses:* Contact institution. *Financial support:* Fellowships, Federal Work-Study and scholarships/grants available. Financial award application deadline: 6/30; financial award applicants required to submit FAFSA. *Unit head:* Dr. Barbara Tye, Coordinator, 714-997-6781. *Application contact:* Rika Judd, Information Contact, 714-997-6786, Fax: 714-997-6713, E-mail: rjudd@chapman.edu.

Chicago State University, School of Graduate and Professional Studies, College of Education, Department of Reading, Elementary Education, Library Information and Media Studies, Program in Reading, Chicago, IL 60628. Offers teaching of reading (MS Ed). *Accreditation:* NCATE. *Entrance requirements:* For master's, minimum GPA of 2.75.

The Citadel, The Military College of South Carolina, Citadel Graduate College, School of Education, Program in Reading, Charleston, SC 29409. Offers literacy education (M Ed). *Accreditation:* NCATE. Part-time and evening/weekend programs available. *Faculty:* 12 full-time (7 women), 8 part-time/adjunct (5 women). *Students:* 1 (woman) full-time, 53 part-time (51 women); includes 5 minority (all African Americans). Average age 30. In 2009, 22 master's awarded. *Degree requirements:* For master's, comprehensive exam. *Entrance requirements:* For master's, GRE (minimum score 900) or MAT (minimum score 396), minimum undergraduate GPA of 2.5, valid teaching certificate. Additional exam requirements/recommendations for international students: Required—TOEFL (minimum score 550 paper-based; 213 computer-based; 79 iBT). *Application deadline:* Applications are processed on a rolling basis. Application fee: $30. Electronic applications accepted. *Expenses:* Tuition, state resident: part-time $400 per credit hour. Tuition, nonresident: part-time $657 per credit hour. Required fees: $40 per term. *Financial support:* Career-related internships or fieldwork, health care benefits, and unspecified assistantships available. Support available to part-time students. Financial award application deadline: 7/1; financial award applicants required to submit FAFSA. *Unit head:* Dr. Jennifer L. Altieri, Coordinator, 843-953-3162, Fax: 843-953-7258, E-mail: jennifer.altieri@citadel.edu. *Application contact:* Dr. Steve A. Nida, Associate Provost, The Citadel Graduate College, 843-953-5089, Fax: 843-953-7630, E-mail: cgc@citadel.edu.

City College of the City University of New York, Graduate School, College of Liberal Arts and Science, Division of the Humanities and Arts, Department of English, Program in Language and Literacy, New York, NY 10031-9198. Offers MA. *Accreditation:* NCATE. *Entrance requirements:* For master's, 2 writing samples. Additional exam requirements/recommendations for international students: Required—TOEFL (minimum score 600 paper-based; 100 iBT). Electronic applications accepted. *Expenses:* Tuition, state resident: part-time $310 per credit. Tuition, nonresident: part-time $575 per credit. Tuition and fees vary according to course load and program.

City University of Seattle, Graduate Division, Gordon Albright School of Education, Bellevue, WA 98005. Offers curriculum and instruction (M Ed); educational leadership (M Ed); educational leadership: administrator certification (Certificate); executive leadership: superintendent certification (Certificate); guidance and counseling (M Ed); leadership (M Ed); leadership and school counseling (M Ed); professional certification for teachers (Certificate); reading and literacy (M Ed); reading and literacy in education (M Ed); teacher certification (elementary K-8)

(MIT); teacher certification (special education K-12) (MIT); technology, curriculum, and instruction (M Ed). Part-time and evening/weekend programs available. Postbaccalaureate distance learning degree programs offered (no on-campus study). *Entrance requirements:* Additional exam requirements/recommendations for international students: Required—TOEFL (minimum score 540 paper-based; 207 computer-based); Recommended—IELTS. Electronic applications accepted. *Expenses:* Contact institution.

Clarion University of Pennsylvania, Office of Research and Graduate Studies, College of Education and Human Services, Department of Education, Program in Education, Clarion, PA 16214. Offers curriculum and instruction (M Ed); early childhood (M Ed); English (M Ed); history (M Ed); literacy (M Ed); science (M Ed); technology (M Ed). *Accreditation:* NCATE. Part-time programs available. *Degree requirements:* For master's, comprehensive exam, thesis or alternative. *Entrance requirements:* For master's, minimum QPA of 3.0, teacher certification. Additional exam requirements/recommendations for international students: Required—TOEFL (minimum score 550 paper-based; 213 computer-based; 80 iBT). Electronic applications accepted.

Clarion University of Pennsylvania, Office of Research and Graduate Studies, College of Education and Human Services, Department of Education, Program in Reading, Clarion, PA 16214. Offers M Ed. *Accreditation:* NCATE. Part-time programs available. *Degree requirements:* For master's, comprehensive exam, thesis or alternative, National Teacher Exam. *Entrance requirements:* For master's, minimum QPA of 3.0, teacher certification. Additional exam requirements/recommendations for international students: Required—TOEFL (minimum score 550 paper-based; 213 computer-based; 80 iBT). Electronic applications accepted.

Clarke College, Program in Education, Dubuque, IA 52001-3198. Offers early childhood/special education (MAE); educational administration: elementary and secondary (MAE); educational media: elementary and secondary (MAE); multi-categorical resource k-12 (MAE); multidisciplinary studies (MAE); reading: elementary (MAE); technology in education (MAE). Part-time and evening/weekend programs available. Postbaccalaureate distance learning degree programs offered (minimal on-campus study). *Faculty:* 5 full-time (all women). *Students:* 1 (woman) full-time, 45 part-time (40 women). Average age 31. 19 applicants, 74% accepted, 13 enrolled. In 2009, 11 master's awarded. *Degree requirements:* For master's, comprehensive exam, thesis optional. *Entrance requirements:* For master's, GRE General Test or MAT, minimum GPA of 2.75. *Application deadline:* Applications are processed on a rolling basis. Application fee: $25. Electronic applications accepted. *Expenses:* Tuition: Full-time $10,836; part-time $602 per credit hour. Required fees: $30 per credit hour. *Financial support:* Career-related internships or fieldwork available. Financial award applicants required to submit FAFSA. *Unit head:* Dr. Larry Bice, Chair, 319-588-6397, Fax: 319-584-8604. *Application contact:* Joan Coates, Information Contact, 563-588-6354, Fax: 563-588-6789, E-mail: graduate@clarke.edu.

Clemson University, Graduate School, College of Health, Education, and Human Development, School of Education, Program in Reading, Clemson, SC 29634. Offers M Ed. *Accreditation:* NCATE. *Students:* 4 full-time (3 women), 24 part-time (23 women). Average age 28. 22 applicants, 68% accepted, 15 enrolled. In 2009, 3 master's awarded. *Entrance requirements:* For master's, GRE General Test, teaching certificate. Additional exam requirements/recommendations for international students: Required—TOEFL. *Application deadline:* Applications are processed on a rolling basis. Application fee: $70 ($80 for international students). Electronic applications accepted. *Expenses:* Contact institution. *Financial support:* Career-related internships or fieldwork, institutionally sponsored loans, scholarships/grants, health care benefits, and unspecified assistantships available. Support available to part-time students. Financial award application deadline: 6/1; financial award applicants required to submit FAFSA. *Faculty research:* Literature, writing, reading recovery across the curriculum. *Unit head:* Dr. Michael J. Padilla, Director/Associate Dean, 864-656-4444, Fax: 864-656-0311, E-mail: padilla@clemson.edu. *Application contact:* Dr. David Fleming, Graduate Coordinator, 864-656-1881, Fax: 864-656-0311, E-mail: dflemin@clemson.edu.

The College at Brockport, State University of New York, School of Education and Human Services, Department of Education and Human Development, Program in Childhood Literacy, Brockport, NY 14420-2997. Offers MS Ed. *Accreditation:* NCATE. Part-time programs available. *Students:* 2 full-time (both women), 86 part-time (76 women); includes 2 minority (both African Americans). 52 applicants, 44% accepted, 21 enrolled. *Degree requirements:* For master's, thesis or alternative. *Entrance requirements:* For master's, minimum GPA of 3.0, letters of recommendation, interview. Additional exam requirements/recommendations for international students: Required—TOEFL (minimum score 550 paper-based; 213 computer-based; 79 iBT). *Application deadline:* For fall admission, 2/15 priority date for domestic and international students. Application fee: $80. Electronic applications accepted. *Expenses:* Tuition, state resident: full-time $8370; part-time $349 per credit. Tuition, nonresident: full-time $13,250; part-time $522 per credit. *Financial support:* Federal Work-Study and scholarships/grants available. Support available to part-time students. Financial award application deadline: 3/15; financial award applicants required to submit FAFSA. *Unit head:* Dr. Sue Novinger, Chairperson, 585-395-2205, Fax: 585-395-2172, E-mail: snovinge@brockport.edu. *Application contact:* Dr. Sue Novinger, Chairperson, 585-395-2205, Fax: 585-395-2172, E-mail: snovinge@brockport.edu.

College of Mount St. Joseph, Graduate Education Program, Cincinnati, OH 45233-1670. Offers adolescent young adult education (MA); art (MA); inclusive early childhood education (MA); instructional leadership (MA); middle childhood education (MA); multi-age education (MA); multicultural special education (MA); music (MA); reading (MA). *Accreditation:* Teacher Education Accreditation Council. Part-time and evening/weekend programs available. *Faculty:* 15 full-time (11 women), 9 part-time/adjunct (6 women). *Students:* 93 full-time (75 women), 99 part-time (66 women); includes 19 minority (18 African Americans, 1 American Indian/Alaska Native). Average age 34. 116 applicants, 97% accepted, 94 enrolled. In 2009, 51 master's awarded. *Degree requirements:* For master's, research project, student teaching, clinical and field-based experiences. *Entrance requirements:* For master's, GRE, PRAXIS II in teaching content area (math or science), 2 letters of recommendation, interview, resume. Additional exam requirements/recommendations for international students: Required—TOEFL (minimum score 560 paper-based; 220 computer-based; 83 iBT). *Application deadline:* Applications are processed on a rolling basis. Application fee: $50. Electronic applications accepted. *Expenses:* Tuition: Part-time $500 per hour. Required fees: $200 per year. Tuition and fees vary according to degree level and program. *Financial support:* In 2009–10, 51 students received support. Scholarships/grants available. Financial award applicants required to submit FAFSA. *Faculty research:* Foreign and second language learning problems/reading disabilities/hyperlexia, multicultural/bilingual special education, alternative educator licensure, science education, pedagogical content knowledge. *Unit head:* Dr. Mary West, Chair of Graduate Education, 513-244-3263, Fax: 513-244-4867, E-mail: mary_west@mail.msj.edu. *Application contact:* Marilyn Hoskins, Assistant Director of Graduate Recruitment, 513-244-4723, Fax: 513-244-4629, E-mail: marilyn_hoskins@mail.msj.edu.

The College of New Jersey, Graduate Division, School of Education, Department of Special Education, Language and Literacy, Program in Developmental Reading, Ewing, NJ 08628. Offers M Ed. *Accreditation:* NCATE. Part-time programs available. *Students:* 23 part-time (22 women). 20 applicants, 70% accepted. In 2009, 8 master's awarded. *Degree requirements:* For master's, comprehensive exam. *Entrance requirements:* For master's, GRE General Test, minimum GPA of 3.0 in field or 2.75 overall. Additional exam requirements/recommendations for international students: Required—TOEFL. *Application deadline:* For fall admission, 2/1 priority date for domestic students; for spring admission, 10/1 priority date for domestic students. Application fee: $70. Electronic applications accepted. *Expenses:* Tuition, state resident: part-time $573.70 per credit. Tuition, nonresident: part-time $887.75 per credit. Required fees: $140.85 per credit. One-time fee: $10 part-time. *Financial support:* Tuition waivers (partial) and unspecified assistantships available. Financial award application deadline: 5/1; financial award applicants required to submit FAFSA. *Unit head:* Dr. Kathryne Speaker, Graduate Coordinator, 609-771-2321. *Application contact:* Susan L. Hydro, Assistant Dean, Office of Graduate Studies, 609-771-2300, Fax: 609-637-5105, E-mail: graduate@tcnj.edu.

The College of New Jersey, Graduate Division, School of Education, Department of Special Education, Language and Literacy, Program in Reading Certification, Ewing, NJ 08628. Offers Certificate. Part-time programs available. *Students:* 1 (woman) full-time, 6 part-time (all women); includes 2 minority (both African Americans). 4 applicants, 50% accepted. In 2009, 2 Certificates awarded. *Entrance requirements:* Additional exam requirements/recommendations for international students: Required—TOEFL. *Application deadline:* For fall admission, 2/1 priority date for domestic students; for spring admission, 10/1 priority date for domestic students. Application fee: $70. Electronic applications accepted. *Expenses:* Tuition, state resident: part-time $573.70 per credit. Tuition, nonresident: part-time $887.75 per credit. Required fees: $140.85 per credit. One-time fee: $10 part-time. *Financial support:* Tuition waivers (partial) and unspecified assistantships available. Financial award application deadline: 5/1; financial award applicants required to submit FAFSA. *Unit head:* Dr. Kathryne Speaker, Graduate Coordinator, 609-771-2321. *Application contact:* Susan L. Hydro, Assistant Dean, Office of Graduate Studies, 609-771-2300, Fax: 609-637-5105, E-mail: graduate@tcnj.edu.

The College of New Rochelle, Graduate School, Division of Education, Program in Literacy Education, New Rochelle, NY 10805-2308. Offers MS Ed. Part-time and evening/weekend programs available. *Degree requirements:* For master's, practicum. *Entrance requirements:* For master's, interview, minimum GPA of 3.0 in field, 2.7 overall, early elementary teacher certification.

College of St. Joseph, Graduate Programs, Division of Education, Program in Reading, Rutland, VT 05701-3899. Offers M Ed. Part-time and evening/weekend programs available. *Degree requirements:* For master's, comprehensive exam. *Entrance requirements:* For master's, interview, current licensure in another area, 2 letters of reference. Electronic applications accepted. *Expenses:* Tuition: Full-time $13,500; part-time $350 per credit. Required fees: $45 per term. One-time fee: $445. Tuition and fees vary according to program.

The College of Saint Rose, Graduate Studies, School of Education, Department of Literacy and Special Education, Albany, NY 12203-1419. Offers literacy: birth-grade 6 (MS Ed); literacy: grades 5-12 (MS Ed); reading (Certificate), including literacy: birth—grade 6, literacy: grades 5-12; special education (MS Ed), including adolescent education, childhood education, special education advanced study. Part-time and evening/weekend programs available. *Entrance requirements:* For master's, minimum undergraduate GPA of 3.0. Additional exam requirements/recommendations for international students: Required—TOEFL (minimum score 550 paper-based; 213 computer-based). Electronic applications accepted.

The College of William and Mary, School of Education, Program in Curriculum and Instruction, Williamsburg, VA 23187-8795. Offers elementary education (MA Ed); gifted education (MA Ed); math specialist (MA Ed); reading education (MA Ed); secondary education (MA Ed), including English education, mathematics education, modern foreign languages education, science education, social studies education; special education (MA Ed), including general curriculum, resource collaborating teaching. *Accreditation:* NCATE. Part-time programs available. *Faculty:* 18 full-time (12 women), 17 part-time/adjunct (15 women). *Students:* 54 full-time (45 women), 12 part-time (all women); includes 3 minority (2 African Americans, 1 Asian American or Pacific Islander), 2 international. Average age 27. 120 applicants, 75% accepted. In 2009, 70 master's awarded. *Degree requirements:* For master's, project. *Entrance requirements:* For master's, GRE or MAT, minimum GPA of 2.5. Additional exam requirements/recommendations for international students: Required—TOEFL. *Application deadline:* For fall admission, 1/15 for domestic and international students; for spring admission, 10/1 for domestic and international students. Application fee: $45. Electronic applications accepted. *Expenses:* Tuition, state resident: full-time $6400; part-time $315 per credit hour. Tuition, nonresident: full-time $19,720; part-time $840 per credit hour. Required fees: $4114. *Financial support:* In 2009–10, 30 students received support, including 10 research assistantships with full and partial tuition reimbursements available (averaging $5,500 per year); career-related internships or fieldwork, Federal Work-Study, institutionally sponsored loans, scholarships/grants, and unspecified assistantships also available. Financial award application deadline: 1/15; financial award applicants required to submit FAFSA. *Faculty research:* National Council of Teachers of Mathematics Standards, counseling, self-concept and self-esteem, special education, curriculum development. *Unit head:* Dr. C. Denise Johnson, Area Coordinator, 757-221-1528, E-mail: cdjohn@wm.edu. *Application contact:* Dorothy Smith Osborne, Director of Admissions, 757-221-2317, Fax: 757-221-2293, E-mail: dsosbo@wm.edu.

Concordia University Chicago, College of Education, Program in Reading Education, River Forest, IL 60305-1499. Offers MA. Part-time and evening/weekend programs available. *Degree requirements:* For master's, comprehensive exam, thesis optional. *Entrance requirements:* For master's, minimum GPA of 2.9. Additional exam requirements/recommendations for international students: Required—TOEFL (minimum score 550 paper-based; 195 computer-based). Electronic applications accepted. *Faculty research:* Early literacy, classroom management and organization in reading, minority students and reading.

Concordia University, Nebraska, Graduate Programs in Education, Program in Reading Education, Seward, NE 68434-1599. Offers M Ed. *Accreditation:* NCATE. Part-time programs available. *Degree requirements:* For master's, thesis or alternative. *Entrance requirements:* For master's, GRE, MAT, or NTE, minimum GPA of 3.0, BS in education or equivalent.

Concordia University, St. Paul, College of Education, St. Paul, MN 55104-5494. Offers curriculum and instruction (MA Ed), including K-12 reading endorsement; differentiated instruction (MA Ed); early childhood education (MA Ed); educational leadership (MA Ed); family life education (MA); K-12 reading endorsement (Certificate); special education (Certificate); sports management (MA). *Accreditation:* NCATE. Evening/weekend programs available. Postbaccalaureate distance learning degree programs offered (minimal on-campus study). *Faculty:* 12 full-time (8 women), 59 part-time/adjunct (47 women). *Students:* 697 full-time (571 women), 13 part-time (12 women); includes 64 minority (31 African Americans, 1 American Indian/Alaska Native, 21 Asian Americans or Pacific Islanders, 11 Hispanic Americans), 1 international. Average age 34. In 2009, 402 master's, 29 other advanced degrees awarded. *Application deadline:* Applications are processed on a rolling basis. Application fee: $50. Electronic applications accepted. *Financial support:* Applicants required to submit FAFSA. *Unit head:* Dr. Donald Helmstetter, Dean, 651-641-8227, Fax: 651-641-8807, E-mail: helmstetter@csp.edu. *Application contact:* Kimberly Craig, Director of Graduate and Cohort Admission, 651-603-6223, Fax: 651-603-6320, E-mail: craig@csp.edu.

Concordia University Wisconsin, Graduate Programs, Department of Education, Program in Reading, Mequon, WI 53097-2402. Offers MS Ed. Part-time and evening/weekend programs available. Postbaccalaureate distance learning degree programs offered (minimal on-campus study). *Degree requirements:* For master's, comprehensive exam, thesis or alternative. *Entrance requirements:* For master's, minimum GPA of 3.0. Additional exam requirements/recommendations for international students: Required—TOEFL.

Concord University, Graduate Studies, Athens, WV 24712-1000. Offers behavioral science (M Ed); educational leadership and supervision (M Ed); geography (M Ed); health promotion (M Ed); reading specialist (M Ed); social studies (M Ed). Postbaccalaureate distance learning degree programs offered. *Entrance requirements:* For master's, GRE or MAT, baccalaureate degree with minimum GPA of 2.5 GPA from regionally accredited institution; teaching license; 2 letters of recommendation.

Coppin State University, Division of Graduate Studies, Division of Education, Baltimore, MD 21216-3698. Offers adult and general education (MS); curriculum and instruction (M Ed, MAT, MS), including curriculum and instruction (M Ed), reading education (MS), teaching (MAT); special education (M Ed). *Accreditation:* NCATE. Part-time and evening/weekend programs available. Postbaccalaureate distance learning degree programs offered. *Degree requirements:* For master's, comprehensive exam (for some programs), thesis (for some programs).

Coppin State University, Division of Graduate Studies, Division of Education, Department of Curriculum and Instruction, Program in Reading Education, Baltimore, MD 21216-3698. Offers MS. Part-time programs available. *Degree requirements:* For master's, 3 hours of capstone

Reading Education

Coppin State University (continued)
experience in urban literacy. *Entrance requirements:* For master's, MAT or GRE, resume, references, teacher certification, 3 years of teaching experience.

Curry College, Graduate Studies, Program in Education, Milton, MA 02186-9984. Offers educational administration (M Ed); educational diagnostic assessment (Certificate); educational therapy (Certificate); elementary education (M Ed); foundations (non-license) (M Ed); learning disabilities across the lifespan (Certificate); reading (M Ed, Certificate); special education (M Ed). Part-time and evening/weekend programs available. *Faculty:* 6 full-time (4 women), 12 part-time/adjunct (9 women). *Students:* 101 part-time (82 women). Average age 37. In 2009, 25 master's awarded. *Degree requirements:* For master's, project or thesis. *Entrance requirements:* For master's, MAT or GRE, interview, recommendations, resume, written statement. Additional exam requirements/recommendations for international students: Required—TOEFL (minimum score 550 paper-based; 213 computer-based; 80 iBT). *Application deadline:* For fall admission, 8/1 priority date for domestic students, 6/1 for international students; for winter admission, 10/1 for international students; for spring admission, 1/1 for domestic students, 1/28 for international students. Applications are processed on a rolling basis. Application fee: $50. *Expenses:* Contact institution. *Financial support:* Career-related internships or fieldwork and tuition waivers (partial) available. *Faculty research:* Classroom trauma, therapeutic writing, inclusionary practices. *Unit head:* Dr. Donald Gratz, Director and Associate Professor, 617-333-2243, E-mail: dgratz0703@curry.edu. *Application contact:* John Bresnahan, Director of Graduate Enrollment and Student Services, 617-333-2243, Fax: 617-979-3535, E-mail: jbresnah0104@curry.edu.

Dallas Baptist University, Dorothy M. Bush College of Education, Program in Reading and English as a Second Language, Dallas, TX 75211-9299. Offers English as a second language (M Ed); master reading teacher (M Ed); reading specialist (M Ed). Part-time and evening/weekend programs available. *Entrance requirements:* For master's, GRE General Test, minimum GPA of 3.0. Additional exam requirements/recommendations for international students: Required—TOEFL, IELTS. *Expenses:* Tuition: Full-time $10,674; part-time $593 per credit hour.

Delaware State University, Graduate Programs, College of Education, Program in Adult Literacy and Basic Education, Dover, DE 19901-2277. Offers MA. *Entrance requirements:* Additional exam requirements/recommendations for international students: Required—TOEFL (minimum score 550 paper-based). Electronic applications accepted.

DePaul University, School of Education, Chicago, IL 60106. Offers bilingual and bicultural education (M Ed, MA); curriculum studies (M Ed, MA, Ed D); educational leadership (M Ed, MA, Ed D), including administration and supervision (M Ed, MA), Catholic school leadership (M Ed, MA), physical education (M Ed, MA); human development and learning (MA); human services and counseling (M Ed, MA), including agencies, family concerns, and higher education, elementary schools, human services management, secondary schools; reading and learning disabilities (M Ed, MA); social culture studies in education and development (M Ed, MA), including curriculum studies/development; teaching and learning (early childhood, elementary and secondary) (M Ed), including elementary education (M Ed, MA), secondary education (M Ed, MA); teaching and learning (early childhood, elementary, and secondary) (MA), including elementary education (M Ed, MA), secondary education (M Ed, MA). *Accreditation:* NCATE. Part-time and evening/weekend programs available. *Faculty:* 61 full-time (40 women), 66 part-time/adjunct (41 women). *Students:* 799 full-time (779 women), 470 part-time (365 women); includes 319 minority (153 African Americans, 3 American Indian/Alaska Native, 48 Asian Americans or Pacific Islanders, 115 Hispanic Americans), 15 international. Average age 30. 635 applicants, 74% accepted, 318 enrolled. In 2009, 604 master's, 5 doctorates awarded. *Degree requirements:* For doctorate, thesis/dissertation. *Entrance requirements:* For master's, interview, minimum GPA of 2.75, 2 letters of recommendation; for doctorate, interview, master's degree, writing sample, 3 letters of recommendation. Additional exam requirements/recommendations for international students: Required—TOEFL (minimum score 550 paper-based; 213 computer-based; 80 iBT). *Application deadline:* Applications are processed on a rolling basis. Application fee: $40. Electronic applications accepted. *Expenses:* Tuition: Full-time $37,525; part-time $620 per credit hour. *Financial support:* In 2009–10, 14 research assistantships with tuition reimbursements (averaging $5,800 per year) were awarded; career-related internships or fieldwork also available. *Faculty research:* Reflective teaching, children at risk, loss, ethnicity, urban education. Total annual research expenditures: $1.6 million. *Unit head:* Dr. Marie Donovan, Dean, 773-325-7581, Fax: 773-325-7713, E-mail: mdonovan@depaul.edu. *Application contact:* Brandon Washington, Data Project Manager, 773-325-1152, Fax: 773-325-2270, E-mail: bwashin3@depaul.edu.

Dominican University, School of Education, River Forest, IL 60305-1099. Offers curriculum and instruction (MA Ed); early childhood education (MS); education (MAT); educational administration (MA); elementary (online) (MS); English as a second language (online) (MS); reading (online) (MS); special education (MS). Part-time and evening/weekend programs available. Postbaccalaureate distance learning degree programs offered. *Faculty:* 16 full-time (12 women), 59 part-time/adjunct (46 women). *Students:* 236 full-time (182 women), 622 part-time (509 women); includes 180 minority (54 African Americans, 3 American Indian/Alaska Native, 36 Asian Americans or Pacific Islanders, 87 Hispanic Americans), 2 international. Average age 32. In 2009, 199 master's awarded. *Entrance requirements:* For master's, Illinois certification test of basic skills. Additional exam requirements/recommendations for international students: Required—TOEFL (minimum score 550 paper-based; 213 computer-based; 79 iBT). *Application deadline:* Applications are processed on a rolling basis. Application fee: $25. *Expenses:* Contact institution. *Financial support:* Career-related internships or fieldwork, scholarships/grants, and tuition waivers (partial) available. Support available to part-time students. Financial award application deadline: 8/15; financial award applicants required to submit FAFSA. *Faculty research:* Governance of private education institutions, reading and language arts, inclusion, organizational planning, leadership and vision. *Unit head:* Dr. Colleen Reardon, Dean, 718-524-6643, Fax: 708-524-6665, E-mail: creardon@dom.edu. *Application contact:* Keven Hansen, Coordinator of Recruitment and Admissions, 708-524-6921, Fax: 708-524-6665, E-mail: educate@dom.edu.

Dowling College, Graduate Programs in Education, Oakdale, NY 11769-1999. Offers adolescence education (MS Ed), including educational administration; advanced certificate in gifted education (AC); childhood and early childhood education (MS Ed); childhood education (MS Ed); educational administration (AC, PD), including computers in education (PD), school administration and supervision (PD), school district administration (PD); educational technology specialist (AC); literacy (MS Ed); literacy/special education (MS Ed); secondary education (MS Ed); special education (MS Ed). *Accreditation:* NCATE. Part-time and evening/weekend programs available. Postbaccalaureate distance learning degree programs offered. *Faculty:* 32 full-time (18 women), 98 part-time/adjunct (59 women). *Students:* 563 full-time (393 women), 885 part-time (668 women); includes 133 minority (47 African Americans, 2 American Indian/Alaska Native, 10 Asian Americans or Pacific Islanders, 74 Hispanic Americans). Average age 32. 363 applicants, 89% accepted, 213 enrolled. In 2009, 459 master's, 85 ACs awarded. *Degree requirements:* For master's and other advanced degree, comprehensive exam. *Entrance requirements:* For master's, minimum GPA of 3.0; for other advanced degree, teaching certificate. Additional exam requirements/recommendations for international students: Required—TOEFL (minimum score 550 paper-based). *Application deadline:* For fall admission, 9/1 priority date for domestic students; for winter admission, 1/1 priority date for domestic students; for spring admission, 2/1 priority date for domestic students. Applications are processed on a rolling basis. Application fee: $50. Electronic applications accepted. *Expenses:* Tuition: Full-time $14,490; part-time $805 per credit. Required fees: $346 per term. *Financial support:* Career-related internships or fieldwork and Federal Work-Study available. Support available to part-time students. Financial award application deadline: 6/30; financial award applicants required to submit FAFSA. *Faculty research:* Natural readers, Korean styles and learning strategies, mothers of children with disabilities, computers in instruction, cultural background and organizational roadblocks to problem solving. *Unit head:* Dr. Clyde Payne, Dean of the School of Education, 631-244-3404, Fax: 631-589-6644, E-mail: paynec@dowling.edu. *Application contact:* Glenn M. Berman, Assistant Vice President for Enrollment Services/Dean of Admissions, 631-244-3357, Fax: 631-244-1059, E-mail: glenn.berman@dowling.edu.

Drury University, Graduate Programs in Education, Springfield, MO 65802. Offers elementary education (M Ed); gifted education (M Ed); human services (M Ed); instructional mathematics K-8 (M Ed); instructional technology (M Ed); middle school teaching (M Ed); secondary education (M Ed); special education (M Ed); special reading (M Ed). *Accreditation:* NCATE. Part-time and evening/weekend programs available. *Degree requirements:* For master's, thesis. *Entrance requirements:* For master's, GRE or MAT, minimum GPA of 2.75. Additional exam requirements/recommendations for international students: Required—TOEFL. Electronic applications accepted. *Faculty research:* Cultural enrichment, research skills, parental involvement relating to reading skills, reading strategies for mainstreaming children.

Duquesne University, School of Education, Department of Instruction and Leadership, Program in Reading and Language Arts, Pittsburgh, PA 15282-0001. Offers MS Ed. Part-time and evening/weekend programs available. *Faculty:* 3 full-time (2 women), 4 part-time/adjunct (2 women). *Students:* 22 full-time (20 women), 21 part-time (all women); includes 1 minority (African American). Average age 30. 13 applicants, 77% accepted, 9 enrolled. In 2009, 15 master's awarded. *Degree requirements:* For master's, thesis optional. *Entrance requirements:* For master's, MAT, minimum GPA of 3.0. Additional exam requirements/recommendations for international students: Required—TOEFL (minimum score 550 paper-based; 80 computer-based). *Application deadline:* For fall admission, 8/1 for domestic students; for spring admission, 12/1 for domestic students. Applications are processed on a rolling basis. Application fee: $0. Electronic applications accepted. *Expenses:* Tuition: Part-time $851 per credit. Required fees: $81 per credit. *Financial support:* Research assistantships, Federal Work-Study available. Support available to part-time students. *Unit head:* Dr. Rosemary T. Mautino, Director, 412-396-6089, Fax: 412-396-1759, E-mail: mautino@duq.edu. *Application contact:* Michael Dolinger, Director of Student and Academic Services, 412-396-6647, Fax: 412-396-5585, E-mail: dolingerm@duq.edu.

East Carolina University, Graduate School, College of Education, Department of Curriculum and Instruction, Greenville, NC 27858-4353. Offers behavior/emotional disabilities (MA Ed); elementary education (MA Ed); English education (MA Ed); learning disabilities (MA Ed); low incidence disabilities (MA Ed); mental retardation (MA Ed); middle grade education (MA Ed); reading education (MA Ed); social studies education (MA Ed). Part-time programs available. Postbaccalaureate distance learning degree programs offered. *Degree requirements:* For master's, comprehensive exam, thesis optional. *Entrance requirements:* For master's, GRE General Test or MAT, interview, bachelor's degree in related field, minimum GPA of 2.5, teaching license. Additional exam requirements/recommendations for international students: Required—TOEFL.

Eastern Connecticut State University, School of Education and Professional Studies/Graduate Division, Program in Reading and Language Arts, Willimantic, CT 06226-2295. Offers MS. *Accreditation:* NCATE. Part-time and evening/weekend programs available. *Degree requirements:* For master's, comprehensive exam or thesis. *Entrance requirements:* For master's, minimum GPA of 2.7, teaching certificate. Additional exam requirements/recommendations for international students: Required—TOEFL (minimum score 550 paper-based; 213 computer-based).

Eastern Michigan University, Graduate School, College of Education, Department of Teacher Education, Program in Reading, Ypsilanti, MI 48197. Offers MA. *Accreditation:* NCATE. Part-time and evening/weekend programs available. Postbaccalaureate distance learning degree programs offered (minimal on-campus study). *Students:* 1 (woman) full-time, 107 part-time (104 women); includes 15 minority (11 African Americans, 1 American Indian/Alaska Native, 1 Asian American or Pacific Islander, 2 Hispanic Americans). Average age 33. In 2009, 36 master's awarded. *Entrance requirements:* For master's, GRE. Additional exam requirements/recommendations for international students: Required—TOEFL. *Application deadline:* Applications are processed on a rolling basis. Application fee: $35. Tuition and fees vary according to course level. *Financial support:* Fellowships, research assistantships with full tuition reimbursements, teaching assistantships with full tuition reimbursements, career-related internships or fieldwork, Federal Work-Study, institutionally sponsored loans, scholarships/grants, tuition waivers (partial), and unspecified assistantships available. Support available to part-time students. Financial award applicants required to submit FAFSA. *Unit head:* Dr. Mary Rearick, Coordinator, 734-487-3260, Fax: 734-487-2101, E-mail: mrearick@emich.edu. *Application contact:* Dr. Mary Rearick, Coordinator, 734-487-3260, Fax: 734-487-2101, E-mail: mrearick@emich.edu.

Eastern Nazarene College, Adult and Graduate Studies, Division of Education, Quincy, MA 02170. Offers early childhood education (M Ed, Certificate); elementary education (M Ed, Certificate); English as a second language (M Ed, Certificate); instructional enrichment and development (M Ed, Certificate); middle school education (M Ed, Certificate); moderate special needs education (M Ed, Certificate); principal (Certificate); program development and supervision (M Ed, Certificate); secondary education (M Ed, Certificate); special education administrator (Certificate); supervisor (Certificate); teacher of reading (M Ed, Certificate). M Ed and Certificate also available through weekend program for administration, special needs, and reading only. Part-time and evening/weekend programs available. *Entrance requirements:* Additional exam requirements/recommendations for international students: Required—TOEFL (minimum score 550 paper-based).

Eastern Washington University, Graduate Studies, College of Education and Human Development, Department of Education, Program in Literacy, Cheney, WA 99004-2431. Offers M Ed. *Accreditation:* NCATE. *Degree requirements:* For master's, comprehensive exam. *Entrance requirements:* For master's, minimum GPA of 3.0. *Expenses:* Tuition, state resident: full-time $7476; part-time $249 per quarter hour. Tuition, nonresident: full-time $18,030; part-time $601 per quarter hour. Required fees: $3.50 per quarter hour. $142 per quarter.

East Stroudsburg University of Pennsylvania, Graduate School, College of Education, Department of Reading, East Stroudsburg, PA 18301-2999. Offers M Ed. Part-time and evening/weekend programs available. *Faculty:* 3 full-time (all women), 3 part-time/adjunct (all women). *Students:* 20 full-time (all women), 155 part-time (150 women); includes 9 minority (3 African Americans, 4 Asian Americans or Pacific Islanders, 2 Hispanic Americans), 1 international. Average age 32. In 2009, 53 master's awarded. *Degree requirements:* For master's, comprehensive exam, research paper, electronic program portfolio. *Entrance requirements:* For master's, PRAXIS/teacher certification, letter of recommendation, Pennsylvania Department of Education requirements. Additional exam requirements/recommendations for international students: Required—TOEFL (minimum score 560 paper-based; 220 computer-based; 83 iBT). *Application deadline:* For fall admission, 7/31 priority date for domestic students, 5/1 priority date for international students; for spring admission, 11/30 for domestic students, 10/1 for international students. Applications are processed on a rolling basis. Application fee: $50. *Expenses:* Tuition, state resident: full-time $9942; part-time $387 per credit. Tuition, nonresident: full-time $14,240; part-time $619 per credit. *Financial support:* In 2009–10, 17 research assistantships with full and partial tuition reimbursements (averaging $2,207 per year) were awarded; Federal Work-Study and institutionally sponsored loans also available. Financial award application deadline: 3/1; financial award applicants required to submit FAFSA. *Faculty research:* Portfolio assessment, reading assessment. *Unit head:* Dr. Stephanie Romano, Graduate Coordinator, 570-422-3415, Fax: 570-422-3920, E-mail: sromano@po-box.esu.edu. *Application contact:* Kevin Quintero, Graduate Admissions Coordinator, 570-422-3890, Fax: 570-422-2711, E-mail: kquintero@po-box.esu.edu.

East Tennessee State University, School of Graduate Studies, College of Education, Department of Curriculum and Instruction, Johnson City, TN 37614. Offers 7-12 (MAT); classroom technology (M Ed); educational communication (M Ed); educational media/educational technology (M Ed); elementary education (M Ed, MAT); K-12 (MAT); reading and storytelling (M Ed, MA); reading education (M Ed, MA); school library media (M Ed); secondary education (M Ed, MAT). *Accreditation:* NCATE. Part-time and evening/weekend programs available.

Degree requirements: For master's, thesis (for some programs). *Entrance requirements:* For master's, GRE, minimum GPA of 3.0. Additional exam requirements/recommendations for international students: Required—TOEFL (minimum score 550 paper-based; 213 computer-based). *Faculty research:* Critical thinking, curriculum development, cultural diversity, cognitive processes, effective teaching strategies.

Edinboro University of Pennsylvania, School of Graduate Studies and Research, School of Education, Department of Elementary, Middle and Secondary Education, Edinboro, PA 16444. Offers character education (Certificate); elementary education (M Ed), including character education, early childhood education, elementary education; reading (M Ed, Certificate), including reading (M Ed), reading specialist (Certificate). Part-time and evening/weekend programs available. *Faculty:* 10 full-time (6 women), 3 part-time/adjunct (2 women). *Students:* 106 full-time (63 women), 172 part-time (126 women); includes 7 minority (4 African Americans, 3 Hispanic Americans). Average age 31. In 2009, 153 master's, 7 Certificates awarded. *Degree requirements:* For master's, comprehensive exam, thesis or alternative, project; for Certificate, thesis or alternative, exam. *Entrance requirements:* For master's and Certificate, GRE or MAT, minimum QPA of 2.5. *Application deadline:* Applications are processed on a rolling basis. Application fee: $30. Electronic applications accepted. *Expenses:* Tuition, state resident: full-time $6666; part-time $370 per credit. Tuition, nonresident: full-time $10,666; part-time $593 per credit. Required fees: $2206.28. One-time fee: $204 part-time. *Financial support:* In 2009–10, 14 research assistantships with full and partial tuition reimbursements (averaging $4,050 per year) were awarded; career-related internships or fieldwork, Federal Work-Study, scholarships/grants, and unspecified assistantships also available. Support available to part-time students. Financial award application deadline: 2/15; financial award applicants required to submit FAFSA. *Unit head:* Dr. Maureen Walcavich, Program Head, Elementary Education, 814-732-2303, E-mail: mwalcavich@edinboro.edu.

Elms College, Division of Education, Chicopee, MA 01013-2839. Offers early childhood education (MAT); education (M Ed, CAGS); elementary education (MAT); English as a second language (MAT); reading (MAT); secondary education (MAT), including biology education, English education, Spanish education; special education (MAT). Part-time and evening/weekend programs available. *Faculty:* 12 full-time (8 women), 4 part-time/adjunct (2 women). *Students:* 17 full-time (14 women), 153 part-time (136 women); includes 5 minority (1 American Indian/Alaska Native, 4 Hispanic Americans). Average age 36. 43 applicants, 88% accepted, 37 enrolled. In 2009, 23 master's, 8 other advanced degrees awarded. *Degree requirements:* For master's, thesis (for some programs). *Entrance requirements:* For master's, Massachusetts Educators Certification Test, minimum GPA of 3.0; for CAGS, master's degree in education. Additional exam requirements/recommendations for international students: Required—TOEFL. *Application deadline:* For fall admission, 7/1 priority date for domestic students; for spring admission, 11/1 priority date for domestic students. Applications are processed on a rolling basis. Application fee: $30. *Financial support:* In 2009–10, 2 teaching assistantships with partial tuition reimbursements were awarded; tuition waivers (partial) also available. Support available to part-time students. Financial award applicants required to submit FAFSA. *Unit head:* Dr. Mary Janeczek, Director, 413-594-2761, Fax: 413-592-4871, E-mail: janeczeke@elms.edu. *Application contact:* Dana Malone, Associate Director for Graduate Studies and Continuing Education, 413-265-2445, Fax: 413-265-2459, E-mail: maloned@elms.edu.

Emory & Henry College, Graduate Programs, Emory, VA 24327-0947. Offers American history (MA Ed); organizational leadership (MOL); professional studies (M Ed); reading specialist (MA Ed). Part-time and evening/weekend programs available. *Entrance requirements:* For master's, GRE or PRAXIS I, recommendations, writing sample.

Emporia State University, School of Graduate Studies, The Teachers College, Department of Early Childhood/Elementary Teacher Education, Program in Master Teacher, Emporia, KS 66801-5087. Offers elementary subject matter (MS); English as a second language (MS); reading (MS); secondary subject matter (MS). *Accreditation:* NCATE. Part-time programs available. *Students:* 3 full-time (all women), 87 part-time (84 women); includes 6 minority (1 African American, 1 American Indian/Alaska Native, 2 Asian Americans or Pacific Islanders, 2 Hispanic Americans). 14 applicants, 100% accepted, 12 enrolled. In 2009, 40 master's awarded. *Degree requirements:* For master's, comprehensive exam or thesis, practicum. *Entrance requirements:* For master's, GRE General Test or MAT, graduate essay exam, appropriate bachelor's degree, letters of recommendation. Additional exam requirements/recommendations for international students: Required—TOEFL (minimum score 520 paper-based; 133 computer-based; 68 iBT). *Application deadline:* For fall admission, 8/15 priority date for domestic students. Applications are processed on a rolling basis. Application fee: $30 ($75 for international students). Electronic applications accepted. *Expenses:* Tuition, state resident: full-time $4154; part-time $173 per credit hour. Tuition, nonresident: full-time $12,864; part-time $536 per credit hour. Required fees: $948; $58 per credit hour. Tuition and fees vary according to campus/location. *Financial support:* Federal Work-Study, institutionally sponsored loans, health care benefits, and unspecified assistantships available. Financial award application deadline: 3/15; financial award applicants required to submit FAFSA. *Unit head:* Dr. Jean Morrow, Chair, 620-341-5766, E-mail: jmorrow@emporia.edu. *Application contact:* Mary Sewell, Admissions Coordinator, 800-950-GRAD, Fax: 620-341-5909, E-mail: msewell@emporia.edu.

Endicott College, Van Loan School of Graduate and Professional Studies, Program in Reading and Literacy, Beverly, MA 01915-2096. Offers initial and professional licensure (M Ed). Part-time and evening/weekend programs available. *Faculty:* 1 full-time (0 women), 7 part-time/adjunct (5 women). *Students:* 29 part-time (all women). Average age 34. 15 applicants, 100% accepted, 15 enrolled. In 2009, 2 master's awarded. *Degree requirements:* For master's, comprehensive exam, practicum. *Entrance requirements:* For master's, MAT or GRE, Massachusetts teaching certificate, letters of recommendation. Additional exam requirements/recommendations for international students: Required—TOEFL. *Application deadline:* Applications are processed on a rolling basis. Application fee: $50. *Expenses:* Contact institution. *Financial support:* Career-related internships or fieldwork, Federal Work-Study, and institutionally sponsored loans available. *Unit head:* Dr. John D. MacLean, Director of Licensure Programs, 978-232-2408, E-mail: jmaclean@endicott.edu. *Application contact:* Dr. John D. MacLean, Director of Licensure Programs, 978-232-2408, E-mail: jmaclean@endicott.edu.

Evangel University, Department of Education, Springfield, MO 65802. Offers educational leadership (M Ed); reading education (M Ed); secondary teaching (M Ed); teaching (MA). *Accreditation:* NCATE. Part-time and evening/weekend programs available. *Faculty:* 4 full-time (2 women), 5 part-time/adjunct (3 women). *Students:* 10 full-time (6 women), 40 part-time (31 women). Average age 33. 14 applicants, 86% accepted, 11 enrolled. In 2009, 23 master's awarded. *Degree requirements:* For master's, comprehensive exam, thesis optional. *Entrance requirements:* For master's, PRAXIS II (preferred) or GRE. Additional exam requirements/recommendations for international students: Required—TOEFL (minimum score 550 paper-based; 213 computer-based). *Application deadline:* For fall admission, 7/15 priority date for domestic students; for spring admission, 11/15 priority date for domestic students. Applications are processed on a rolling basis. Application fee: $25. *Financial support:* In 2009–10, 3 students received support. Career-related internships or fieldwork, institutionally sponsored loans, and scholarships/grants available. Support available to part-time students. Financial award application deadline: 3/1; financial award applicants required to submit FAFSA. *Unit head:* Dr. Colleen Hardy, Program Coordinator, 417-865-2815 Ext. 8553, E-mail: hardyc@evangel.edu. *Application contact:* Charity H. Fahlstrom, Admissions Representative, Graduate and Professional Studies, 417-865-2811 Ext. 7227, Fax: 417-865-9599.

Fairleigh Dickinson University, College at Florham, University College: Arts, Sciences, and Professional Studies, Peter Sammartino School of Education, Madison, NJ 07940-1099. Offers education for certified teachers (MA, Certificate); educational leadership (MA); instructional technology (Certificate); literacy/reading (Certificate); teaching (MAT). *Students:* 66 full-time (53 women), 49 part-time (25 women). Average age 27. 91 applicants, 87% accepted, 68 enrolled. In 2009, 74 master's awarded. *Application deadline:* Applications are processed on a rolling basis. Application fee: $40. *Application contact:* Susan Brooman, University Director, Graduate Admissions, 973-443-8905, Fax: 973-443-8088, E-mail: grad@fdu.edu.

Fairleigh Dickinson University, Metropolitan Campus, University College: Arts, Sciences, and Professional Studies, Peter Sammartino School of Education, Teaneck, NJ 07666-1914. Offers dyslexia specialist (Certificate); education for certified teachers (MA); educational leadership (MA); instructional technology (Certificate); learning disabilities (MA); literacy/reading (Certificate); multilingual education (MA); teacher of the handicapped (Certificate); teaching (MAT). *Accreditation:* Teacher Education Accreditation Council. Part-time programs available. *Students:* 61 full-time (56 women), 530 part-time (464 women), 10 international. Average age 36. 283 applicants, 93% accepted, 231 enrolled. In 2009, 152 master's awarded. *Degree requirements:* For master's, research project (MAT). *Application deadline:* Applications are processed on a rolling basis. Application fee: $40. *Unit head:* Dr. Vicki Cohen, Director, 201-692-2525, Fax: 201-692-2603, E-mail: vicki_cohen@fdu.edu. *Application contact:* Susan Brooman, University Director of Graduate Admissions, 201-692-2554, Fax: 201-692-2560, E-mail: globaleducation@fdu.edu.

Fairmont State University, Graduate Studies, Programs in Education, Fairmont, WV 26554. Offers education (MAT); leadership studies (M Ed); online learning (M Ed); professional studies (M Ed); reading (M Ed); special education (M Ed). *Accreditation:* NCATE.

Fayetteville State University, Graduate School, Program in Middle Grades, Secondary and Special Education, Fayetteville, NC 28301-4298. Offers biology (MA Ed); history (MA Ed); mathematics (MA Ed); middle grades (MA Ed); political science (MA Ed); reading (MA Ed); sociology (MA Ed); special education (MA Ed), including behavioral-emotional handicaps, mentally handicapped, specific training disability. *Accreditation:* NCATE. Part-time and evening/weekend programs available. *Faculty:* 15 full-time (10 women), 3 part-time/adjunct (2 women). *Students:* 16 full-time (12 women), 70 part-time (57 women); includes 55 minority (50 African Americans, 1 American Indian/Alaska Native, 1 Asian American or Pacific Islander, 3 Hispanic Americans). Average age 35. 14 applicants, 100% accepted, 14 enrolled. In 2009, 32 master's awarded. *Degree requirements:* For master's, comprehensive exam, internship. *Application deadline:* For fall admission, 4/15 for domestic students; for spring admission, 10/15 for domestic students. Applications are processed on a rolling basis. Application fee: $35. Electronic applications accepted. *Unit head:* Dr. Charletta Barringer-Brown, Interim Chair, 910-672-1182, E-mail: cbarringerbrown@uncfsu.edu. *Application contact:* Roxie Shabazz, Associate Vice-Chancellor for Enrollment Management, 910-672-1784, Fax: 910-672-2209, E-mail: rshabazz@uncfsu.edu.

Ferris State University, College of Education and Human Services, School of Education, Big Rapids, MI 49307. Offers administration (MSCTE); curriculum and instruction (M Ed), including administration, elementary education, experiential education, philanthropic education, reading, secondary education, special education, subject matter option; education technology (MSCTE); instructor (MSCTE); post-secondary administration (MSCTE); training and development (MSCTE). Part-time and evening/weekend programs available. Postbaccalaureate distance learning degree programs offered. *Faculty:* 12 full-time (8 women), 11 part-time/adjunct (5 women). *Students:* 19 full-time (13 women), 185 part-time (122 women); includes 24 minority (20 African Americans, 1 Asian American or Pacific Islander, 3 Hispanic Americans), 1 international. Average age 36. 37 applicants, 32% accepted, 11 enrolled. In 2009, 73 master's awarded. *Degree requirements:* For master's, thesis, research paper. *Entrance requirements:* For master's, 2 years of work experience for vocational setting, minimum GPA of 2.75. Additional exam requirements/recommendations for international students: Recommended—TOEFL (minimum score 500 paper-based; 173 computer-based; 61 iBT). *Application deadline:* For fall admission, 7/1 priority date for domestic students; for spring admission, 11/1 priority date for domestic students. Applications are processed on a rolling basis. Application fee: $30. *Financial support:* Career-related internships or fieldwork and scholarships/grants available. Support available to part-time students. Financial award applicants required to submit FAFSA. *Faculty research:* Suicide prevention, reading, women in education, special needs, administration. *Unit head:* Dr. Liza Ing, Director, 231-591-5362, Fax: 231-591-2041. *Application contact:* Kimisue Worrall, Secretary, 231-591-5361, Fax: 231-591-2043.

Florida Atlantic University, College of Education, Department of Teaching and Learning, Boca Raton, FL 33431-0991. Offers curriculum and instruction (M Ed); elementary education (M Ed); environmental education (M Ed); reading education (M Ed); social foundations of education (M Ed). *Accreditation:* NCATE. Part-time and evening/weekend programs available. *Faculty:* 35 full-time (29 women), 92 part-time/adjunct (61 women). *Students:* 56 full-time (50 women), 134 part-time (128 women); includes 36 minority (15 African Americans, 4 Asian Americans or Pacific Islanders, 17 Hispanic Americans), 2 international. Average age 32. 162 applicants, 74% accepted, 66 enrolled. In 2009, 52 master's awarded. *Entrance requirements:* For master's, GRE General Test, minimum GPA of 3.0 in last 2 years of undergraduate course work. Additional exam requirements/recommendations for international students: Required—TOEFL. *Application deadline:* For fall admission, 7/1 for domestic students, 2/15 for international students; for spring admission, 11/1 for domestic students, 7/15 for international students. Applications are processed on a rolling basis. Application fee: $30. *Expenses:* Tuition, state resident: full-time $7055; part-time $293.94 per credit hour. Tuition, nonresident: full-time $22,096; part-time $920.66 per credit hour. *Financial support:* Fellowships with partial tuition reimbursements, research assistantships with partial tuition reimbursements, teaching assistantships with partial tuition reimbursements, career-related internships or fieldwork, scholarships/grants, and unspecified assistantships available. *Faculty research:* Technology, teaching English to speakers of other languages, math teaching, electronic portfolio assessment, global perspectives through social studies. *Unit head:* Dr. Barbara Ridener, Chairperson, 561-297-3588. *Application contact:* Dr. Barbara Ridener, Chairperson, 561-297-3588.

Florida Gulf Coast University, College of Education, Program in Reading Education, Fort Myers, FL 33965-6565. Offers M Ed. Part-time and evening/weekend programs available. *Faculty:* 31 full-time (24 women), 39 part-time/adjunct (28 women). *Students:* 48 full-time (47 women), 15 part-time (all women); includes 11 minority (3 African Americans, 2 American Indian/Alaska Native, 6 Hispanic Americans). Average age 33. 34 applicants, 85% accepted, 28 enrolled. In 2009, 22 master's awarded. *Entrance requirements:* For master's, GRE General Test, MAT, minimum GPA of 3.0. Additional exam requirements/recommendations for international students: Required—TOEFL (minimum score 550 paper-based; 213 computer-based). *Application deadline:* For fall admission, 7/1 priority date for domestic students; for spring admission, 10/15 for domestic students. Applications are processed on a rolling basis. Application fee: $30. Electronic applications accepted. *Faculty research:* Struggling readers, reading and writing connection, involving families in reading. *Unit head:* Dr. Patricia Wachholz, Head, 239-590-7808, Fax: 239-590-7801, E-mail: pwachhol@fgcu.edu. *Application contact:* Edward Beckett, Adviser/Counselor, 239-590-7759, Fax: 239-590-7801, E-mail: ebeckett@fgcu.edu.

Florida International University, College of Education, Department of Curriculum and Instruction, Program in Reading Education, Miami, FL 33199. Offers MS, Ed D. *Accreditation:* NCATE. Part-time and evening/weekend programs available. *Degree requirements:* For master's, thesis optional. *Entrance requirements:* For master's, minimum GPA of 3.0, professional certification. Additional exam requirements/recommendations for international students: Required—TOEFL (minimum score 550 paper-based; 213 computer-based; 80 iBT), IELTS (minimum score 6.3). Electronic applications accepted. *Expenses:* Tuition, state resident: full-time $8008; part-time $4004 per year. Tuition, nonresident: full-time $20,104; part-time $10,052 per year. Required fees: $298; $149 per term. *Faculty research:* Understanding reading comprehension, improving reading instruction, racial issues in reading and learning.

Florida Memorial University, School of Education, Miami-Dade, FL 33054. Offers elementary education (MS); exceptional student education (MS); reading (MS). *Degree requirements:* For master's, comprehensive exam or thesis, field and clinical experiences, exit exam. *Entrance requirements:* For master's, GRE, CLAST, PRAXIS I, baccalaureate or graduate degree with minimum GPA of 3.0 in last 60 hours, 3 recommendations.

Florida State University, The Graduate School, College of Education, School of Teacher Education, Tallahassee, FL 32306. Offers early childhood education (MS, Ed D, PhD, Ed S); elementary education (MS, Ed D, PhD, Ed S); English education (MS, PhD, Ed S); mathematics

Reading Education

Florida State University (continued)
education (MS, PhD, Ed S); reading education/language arts (MS, Ed D, PhD, Ed S); science education (MS, PhD, Ed S); social science education (MS, PhD, Ed S); special education (MS, PhD, Ed S), including emotional disturbance/learning disabilities (MS), mental retardation (MS), rehabilitation counseling, special education (PhD, Ed S), visual disabilities (MS). Part-time programs available. *Faculty:* 24 full-time (19 women), 3 part-time/adjunct (all women). *Students:* 85 full-time (73 women), 205 part-time (189 women); includes 60 minority (36 African Americans, 2 American Indian/Alaska Native, 13 Asian Americans or Pacific Islanders, 9 Hispanic Americans). 189 applicants, 61% accepted, 71 enrolled. In 2009, 76 master's, 7 doctorates, 5 other advanced degrees awarded. *Degree requirements:* For master's and Ed S, comprehensive exam, thesis optional; for doctorate, comprehensive exam, thesis/dissertation, preliminary exam, prospectus defense. *Entrance requirements:* For master's, doctorate, and Ed S, GRE General Test, minimum GPA of 3.0. Additional exam requirements/recommendations for international students: Required—TOEFL (minimum score 550 paper-based; 213 computer-based; 80 iBT). *Application deadline:* For fall admission, 7/1 priority date for domestic students; for spring admission, 11/1 for domestic students. Applications are processed on a rolling basis. Application fee: $30. *Expenses:* Tuition, state resident: full-time $7413. Tuition, nonresident: full-time $22,567. *Financial support:* In 2009–10, 2 fellowships with full and partial tuition reimbursements, 4 research assistantships with full and partial tuition reimbursements, 12 teaching assistantships with full and partial tuition reimbursements were awarded; career-related internships or fieldwork, Federal Work-Study, scholarships/grants, and unspecified assistantships also available. Financial award applicants required to submit FAFSA. *Faculty research:* Teaching and learning practices and policies, twenty-first century literacies, impact of teacher education programs of student gains. *Unit head:* Dr. Walt Wager, Chair, 850-644-6553, Fax: 850-644-1880, E-mail: wwager@fsu.edu. *Application contact:* Timolin Lynette Bodison-Baker, Program Assistant, 850-644-5458, Fax: 850-644-7736, E-mail: bodison@coe.fsu.edu.

Fordham University, Graduate School of Education, Division of Curriculum and Teaching, New York, NY 10023. Offers adult education (MS, MSE); bilingual teacher education (MSE); curriculum and teaching (MSE); early childhood education (MSE); elementary education (MST); language, literacy, and learning (PhD); reading education (MSE, Adv C); secondary education (MAT, MSE); special education (MSE, Adv C); teaching English as a second language (MSE). *Accreditation:* NCATE. *Degree requirements:* For doctorate, thesis/dissertation; for Adv C, thesis. *Entrance requirements:* For doctorate, MAT, GRE General Test.

Framingham State University, Division of Graduate and Continuing Education, Program in Literacy and Language, Framingham, MA 01701-9101. Offers M Ed. Part-time and evening/weekend programs available. *Entrance requirements:* For master's, MAT.

Fresno Pacific University, Graduate Programs, School of Education, Fresno, CA 93702-4709. Offers administration (MA Ed), including administrative services; foundations, curriculum and teaching (MA Ed), including curriculum and teaching, school library and information technology; language, literacy, and culture (MA Ed), including bilingual/cross-cultural education, language development, multilingual contexts, reading; mathematics/science/computer education (MA Ed), including educational technology, integrated mathematics/science education, mathematics education; pupil personnel services (MA Ed), including school counseling, school psychology; special education (MA Ed), including mild/moderate, moderate/severe, physical and health impairments. Part-time and evening/weekend programs available. *Degree requirements:* For master's, thesis (for some programs). *Entrance requirements:* For master's, interview; GMAT, GRE, MAT, or 6 units of course work with a faculty recommendation. Additional exam requirements/recommendations for international students: Required—TOEFL (minimum score 550 paper-based; 213 computer-based). Electronic applications accepted.

Fresno Pacific University, Graduate Programs, School of Education, Division of Language, Literacy, and Culture, Program in Language Development, Fresno, CA 93702-4709. Offers MA Ed. Part-time and evening/weekend programs available. *Degree requirements:* For master's, thesis or alternative. *Entrance requirements:* Additional exam requirements/recommendations for international students: Required—TOEFL (minimum score 550 paper-based; 213 computer-based). Electronic applications accepted.

Fresno Pacific University, Graduate Programs, School of Education, Division of Language, Literacy, and Culture, Program in Literacy in Multilingual Contexts, Fresno, CA 93702-4709. Offers MA Ed. Part-time and evening/weekend programs available. *Degree requirements:* For master's, thesis or alternative. *Entrance requirements:* Additional exam requirements/recommendations for international students: Required—TOEFL (minimum score 550 paper-based; 213 computer-based). Electronic applications accepted.

Fresno Pacific University, Graduate Programs, School of Education, Division of Language, Literacy, and Culture, Program in Reading, Fresno, CA 93702-4709. Offers reading/English as a second language (MA Ed); reading/language arts (MA Ed). Part-time and evening/weekend programs available. *Degree requirements:* For master's, thesis or alternative. *Entrance requirements:* Additional exam requirements/recommendations for international students: Required—TOEFL (minimum score 550 paper-based; 213 computer-based). Electronic applications accepted.

Frostburg State University, Graduate School, College of Education, Department of Educational Professions, Program in Reading, Frostburg, MD 21532-1099. Offers M Ed. *Accreditation:* NCATE. *Faculty:* 5. *Students:* 13 full-time (all women), 58 part-time (56 women); includes 1 minority (Asian American or Pacific Islander), 1 international. Average age 30. 13 applicants, 85% accepted, 8 enrolled. In 2009, 21 master's awarded. *Degree requirements:* For master's, thesis or alternative, in-service. *Entrance requirements:* For master's, teaching certificate. Additional exam requirements/recommendations for international students: Required—TOEFL. *Application deadline:* For fall admission, 7/15 priority date for domestic students. Applications are processed on a rolling basis. Application fee: $30. Electronic applications accepted. *Expenses:* Tuition, state resident: full-time $5706; part-time $317 per credit hour. Tuition, nonresident: full-time $6948; part-time $386 per credit hour. Required fees: $1476; $82 per credit hour. $11 per term. One-time fee: $30 full-time. *Financial support:* In 2009–10, 1 research assistantship with full tuition reimbursement (averaging $5,000 per year) was awarded; career-related internships or fieldwork also available. Financial award application deadline: 4/1; financial award applicants required to submit FAFSA. *Unit head:* Dr. Roger Dow, Coordinator, 301-687-4431, E-mail: rdow@frostburg.edu. *Application contact:* Vickie Mazer, Director, Graduate Services, 301-687-7053, Fax: 301-687-4597, E-mail: vmmazer@frostburg.edu.

Furman University, Graduate Division, Department of Education, Greenville, SC 29613. Offers curriculum and instruction (MA); early childhood education (MA); English as a second language (MA); literacy (MA); school leadership (MA); special education (MA). *Accreditation:* NCATE. Part-time programs available. Postbaccalaureate distance learning degree programs offered (minimal on-campus study). *Faculty:* 14 full-time (8 women), 10 part-time/adjunct (6 women). *Students:* 114 part-time (93 women); includes 13 minority (10 African Americans, 3 Asian Americans or Pacific Islanders). Average age 29. 24 applicants, 100% accepted, 23 enrolled. In 2009, 71 master's awarded. *Degree requirements:* For master's, comprehensive exam (for some programs), thesis or alternative. *Entrance requirements:* For master's, PRAXIS II. *Application deadline:* For fall admission, 8/1 priority date for domestic students, 7/15 priority date for international students; for spring admission, 12/1 priority date for domestic and international students. Applications are processed on a rolling basis. Application fee: $50. *Financial support:* In 2009–10, 43 students received support; fellowships, scholarships/grants available. Financial award application deadline: 5/15; financial award applicants required to submit FAFSA. *Faculty research:* Literacy, pedagogy and practice, social justice, advanced leadership, achievement in high poverty schools. *Unit head:* Dr. Nelly Hecker, Head, 864-294-3385. *Application contact:* Helen Reynolds, Department Assistant, 864-294-2213, Fax: 864-294-3579, E-mail: helen.reynolds@furman.edu.

Gannon University, School of Graduate Studies, College of Humanities, Education, and Social Sciences, School of Education, Program in Reading, Erie, PA 16541-0001. Offers M Ed, Certificate. Part-time and evening/weekend programs available. *Students:* 3 full-time (2 women), 13 part-time (12 women). Average age 35. 16 applicants, 100% accepted, 7 enrolled. In 2009, 2 master's awarded. *Degree requirements:* For master's, comprehensive exam, thesis; for Certificate, comprehensive exam. *Entrance requirements:* For master's and Certificate, bachelor's degree, minimum QPA of 3.0, teacher certification. Additional exam requirements/recommendations for international students: Required—TOEFL (minimum score 79 iBT). *Application deadline:* Applications are processed on a rolling basis. Application fee: $25. Electronic applications accepted. *Expenses:* Contact institution. *Financial support:* Scholarships/grants available. Financial award application deadline: 7/1; financial award applicants required to submit FAFSA. *Unit head:* Dr. Kathleen Kingston, Director, 814-871-5626, E-mail: kingston002@gannon.edu. *Application contact:* Kara Morgan, Assistant Director of Graduate Admissions, 814-871-5831, Fax: 814-871-5827, E-mail: graduate@gannon.edu.

Geneva College, Program in Reading, Beaver Falls, PA 15010-3599. Offers M Ed. Part-time and evening/weekend programs available. *Faculty:* 4 full-time (all women). *Students:* 8 part-time (7 women). 2 applicants, 100% accepted, 2 enrolled. In 2009, 7 master's awarded. *Degree requirements:* For master's, 100 hours of field experience. *Entrance requirements:* For master's, 2 letters of recommendation, resume, copy of current certificate. Additional exam requirements/recommendations for international students: Required—TOEFL. *Application deadline:* Applications are processed on a rolling basis. Electronic applications accepted. *Expenses:* Tuition: Full-time $11,250; part-time $625 per credit. Tuition and fees vary according to program. *Financial support:* Scholarships/grants available. Financial award applicants required to submit FAFSA. *Unit head:* Dr. Adel Aiken, Program Director, 724-847-5002, E-mail: reading@geneva.edu. *Application contact:* Lori Hartge, Graduate Student Support Specialist, 724-846-6571, E-mail: reading@geneva.edu.

George Fox University, School of Education, Educational Foundations and Leadership Program, Newberg, OR 97132-2697. Offers continuing administrator license (Certificate); curriculum and instruction (M Ed); educational leadership (M Ed, Ed D); higher education (M Ed); initial administrator license (Certificate); library media (M Ed, Certificate); literacy (M Ed); reading (M Ed); secondary education (M Ed). *Accreditation:* NCATE. Part-time and evening/weekend programs available. Postbaccalaureate distance learning degree programs offered (minimal on-campus study). *Faculty:* 10 full-time (3 women), 7 part-time/adjunct (3 women). *Students:* 1 (woman) full-time, 151 part-time (101 women); includes 15 minority (1 African American, 4 American Indian/Alaska Native, 4 Asian Americans or Pacific Islanders, 6 Hispanic Americans), 1 international. Average age 40. 44 applicants, 75% accepted, 26 enrolled. In 2009, 44 master's, 27 doctorates, 82 Certificates awarded. *Degree requirements:* For master's, thesis (for some programs); for doctorate, comprehensive exam, thesis/dissertation, project. *Entrance requirements:* For master's, minimum undergraduate GPA of 3.0 during previous 2 years of course work, resume, 3 professional recommendations on university forms, copy of teaching license (if applicable); for doctorate, GRE or MAT, master's degree with minimum GPA of 3.25, 3 years of relevant professional experience, interview, personal essay, scholarly work, 3 professional recommendations on university forms along with 3 written letters of recommendation, official transcripts. Additional exam requirements/recommendations for international students: Required—TOEFL (minimum score 577 paper-based; 233 computer-based; 90 iBT). *Application deadline:* For fall admission, 7/15 for domestic and international students; for winter admission, 11/1 for domestic and international students; for spring admission, 4/1 for domestic and international students. Applications are processed on a rolling basis. Application fee: $40. Electronic applications accepted. *Expenses:* Contact institution. *Financial support:* Career-related internships or fieldwork available. Financial award applicants required to submit FAFSA. *Unit head:* Dr. Scott Headley, Chair, 503-554-2836, E-mail: sheadley@georgefox.edu. *Application contact:* Kristie DeHaven, Admissions Counselor, 800-631-0921, Fax: 503-554-3110, E-mail: edfl@georgefox.edu.

George Fox University, School of Education, Master of Arts in Teaching Program, Newberg, OR 97132-2697. Offers teaching (MAT); teaching plus ESOL (MAT); teaching plus ESOL/bilingual (MAT); teaching plus reading (MAT). MAT program is offered in Oregon and Idaho. Part-time and evening/weekend programs available. *Faculty:* 16 full-time (13 women), 22 part-time/adjunct (15 women). *Students:* 158 full-time (116 women), 70 part-time (49 women); includes 22 minority (1 African American, 2 American Indian/Alaska Native, 8 Asian Americans or Pacific Islanders, 11 Hispanic Americans), 1 international. Average age 32. 59 applicants, 75% accepted, 35 enrolled. In 2009, 195 master's awarded. *Entrance requirements:* For master's, CBEST or PRAXIS PPST, bachelor's degree from regionally-accredited college or university with minimum GPA of 3.0 in last two years of course work. Additional exam requirements/recommendations for international students: Required—TOEFL (minimum score 577 paper-based; 233 computer-based; 90 iBT). *Application deadline:* For fall admission, 6/1 for domestic and international students; for winter admission, 10/1 for domestic and international students; for spring admission, 2/1 for domestic and international students. Applications are processed on a rolling basis. Application fee: $40. Electronic applications accepted. *Expenses:* Contact institution. *Financial support:* In 2009–10, 20 students received support. Scholarships/grants available. Financial award application deadline: 2/1; financial award applicants required to submit FAFSA. *Unit head:* Kristin Dixon, Chair, 971-239-4934, E-mail: kdixon@georgefox.edu. *Application contact:* Beth Molzahn, Admissions Counselor, Oregon Master of Arts in Teaching Programs, 800-631-0921, Fax: 503-554-3110, E-mail: mat@georgefox.edu.

Georgetown College, Department of Education, Georgetown, KY 40324-1696. Offers reading and writing (MA Ed); special education (MA Ed); teaching (MA Ed). *Accreditation:* NCATE. Part-time programs available. *Degree requirements:* For master's, portfolio. *Entrance requirements:* For master's, teaching certificate, minimum GPA of 2.7 or GRE General Test.

Georgia Southern University, Jack N. Averitt College of Graduate Studies, College of Education, Department of Curriculum, Foundations, and Reading, Program in Reading Education, Statesboro, GA 30460. Offers M Ed. *Accreditation:* NCATE. Part-time and evening/weekend programs available. *Students:* 6 full-time (all women), 18 part-time (all women); includes 1 minority (African American). Average age 27. 3 applicants, 100% accepted, 2 enrolled. In 2009, 23 master's awarded. *Degree requirements:* For master's, comprehensive exam, transition point assessments. *Entrance requirements:* For master's, GRE General Test or MAT, minimum GPA of 2.5. Additional exam requirements/recommendations for international students: Required—TOEFL (minimum score 550 paper-based; 213 computer-based; 80 iBT). *Application deadline:* For fall admission, 3/1 priority date for domestic and international students; for spring admission, 10/1 priority date for domestic students, 10/1 for international students. Applications are processed on a rolling basis. Application fee: $50. Electronic applications accepted. *Expenses:* Tuition, state resident: full-time $5040; part-time $210 per credit hour. Tuition, nonresident: full-time $20,136; part-time $839 per credit hour. Required fees: $1644. *Financial support:* In 2009–10, 14 students received support, including research assistantships with partial tuition reimbursements available (averaging $7,200 per year), teaching assistantships with partial tuition reimbursements available (averaging $7,200 per year); career-related internships or fieldwork, Federal Work-Study, scholarships/grants, tuition waivers (partial), and unspecified assistantships also available. Support available to part-time students. Financial award application deadline: 4/15; financial award applicants required to submit FAFSA. *Faculty research:* Emerging literacy, content literacy, literature groups, phonics/whole language, qualitative research methods. *Unit head:* Dr. Michael Moore, Coordinator, 912-478-0211, Fax: 912-478-5382, E-mail: mmoore@georgiasouthern.edu. *Application contact:* Dr. Charles Ziglar, Coordinator for Graduate Student Recruitment, 912-478-5635, Fax: 912-478-0740, E-mail: gradadmissions@georgiasouthern.edu.

Georgia Southwestern State University, Graduate Studies, School of Education, Americus, GA 31709-4693. Offers early childhood education (M Ed, Ed S); health and physical education (M Ed); middle grades education (M Ed, Ed S); reading (M Ed); secondary education (M Ed); special education (M Ed). *Accreditation:* NCATE. *Degree requirements:* For master's, comprehensive exam. *Entrance requirements:* For master's, GRE General Test or MAT, minimum GPA of 2.5; for Ed S, GRE General Test or MAT, minimum graduate GPA of 3.25, M Ed from accredited college or university, 3 years teaching experience. Electronic applications accepted.

Georgia State University, College of Education, Department of Middle-Secondary Education and Instructional Technology, Program in Reading Instruction, Atlanta, GA 30302-3083. Offers reading, language and literacy (M Ed); reading, language, and literacy (PhD, Ed S); teaching English as a second language (M Ed). *Accreditation:* NCATE. Part-time and evening/weekend programs available. *Degree requirements:* For master's, comprehensive exam; for Ed S, project/exam. *Entrance requirements:* For master's, GRE General Test, minimum GPA of 2.5; for Ed S, GRE General Test or MAT, minimum graduate GPA of 3.25. *Faculty research:* Language development, attribution theory, linguistics.

Gonzaga University, School of Education, Program in Literacy, Spokane, WA 99258. Offers M Ed. *Students:* 4 part-time (all women). Average age 35. In 2009, 1 master's awarded. *Degree requirements:* For master's, comprehensive exam. *Entrance requirements:* For master's, GRE General Test or MAT, minimum B average in undergraduate course work. *Application deadline:* For fall admission, 3/1 for domestic students. Application fee: $40. Tuition and fees vary according to course level, course load, degree level, campus/location and program. *Financial support:* Application deadline: 3/1. *Unit head:* Dr. John Sunderland, Dean, 509-328-4220 Ext. 3503, Fax: 509-324-5812, E-mail: sunderland@gonzaga.edu. *Application contact:* Julie McCulloh, Dean of Admissions, 509-323-6592, Fax: 509-323-5780, E-mail: mcculloh@gu.gonzaga.edu.

Governors State University, College of Education, Program in Reading, University Park, IL 60466-0975. Offers MA. *Accreditation:* NCATE.

Grambling State University, School of Graduate Studies and Research, College of Education, Department of Educational Leadership, Grambling, LA 71245. Offers curriculum and instruction (Ed D); developmental education (MS, Ed D), including curriculum and instruction: reading (Ed D), English (MS), guidance and counseling (MS), higher education administration (Ed D), instructional systems and technology (Ed D), mathematics (MS), reading (MS), science (MS), student development and personnel services (Ed D); educational leadership (MS, Ed D). Part-time and evening/weekend programs available. *Faculty:* 19 full-time (12 women). *Students:* 23 full-time (18 women), 84 part-time (62 women); includes 81 minority (80 African Americans, 1 Asian American or Pacific Islander), 5 international. Average age 39. 72 applicants, 75% accepted, 39 enrolled. In 2009, 5 master's, 9 doctorates awarded. *Degree requirements:* For master's, comprehensive exam, thesis (for some programs); for doctorate, comprehensive exam, thesis/dissertation. *Entrance requirements:* For master's, GRE, minimum GPA of 2.5 on last degree; for doctorate, GRE (minimum 1000, 500 on Verbal), master's degree, minimum GPA of 3.0 on last degree. Additional exam requirements/recommendations for international students: Required—TOEFL (minimum score 500 paper-based; 173 computer-based; 61 iBT). *Application deadline:* For fall admission, 7/1 for domestic and international students; for spring admission, 12/1 for domestic and international students. Applications are processed on a rolling basis. Application fee: $20 ($30 for international students). Electronic applications accepted. *Expenses:* Tuition, state resident: full-time $2610. Tuition, nonresident: full-time $2610. *Financial support:* In 2009–10, 5 research assistantships (averaging $10,948 per year) were awarded; health care benefits, tuition waivers (full), and unspecified assistantships also available. Financial award application deadline: 5/31; financial award applicants required to submit FAFSA. *Unit head:* Dr. Olatunde Ogunyemi, Director, 318-274-6105, Fax: 318-274-2799, E-mail: ogunyemio@gram.edu. *Application contact:* Laketha Richards, Administrative Assistant III, 318-274-6105, Fax: 318-274-6249, E-mail: richardsl@gram.edu.

Grand Valley State University, College of Education, Program in Literacy Studies, Allendale, MI 49401-9403. Offers M Ed. *Expenses:* Tuition, state resident: part-time $471 per credit hour. Tuition, nonresident: part-time $646 per credit hour. Tuition and fees vary according to course level.

Grand Valley State University, College of Education, Program in Reading and Language Arts, Allendale, MI 49401-9403. Offers M Ed. *Accreditation:* NCATE. Part-time and evening/weekend programs available. *Faculty:* 5 full-time (4 women), 2 part-time/adjunct (both women). *Students:* 3 full-time (all women), 183 part-time (182 women); includes 6 minority (2 African Americans, 2 Asian Americans or Pacific Islanders, 2 Hispanic Americans). Average age 31. 29 applicants, 100% accepted, 21 enrolled. In 2009, 42 master's awarded. *Degree requirements:* For master's, thesis. *Entrance requirements:* For master's, GRE General Test or minimum GPA of 3.0. Additional exam requirements/recommendations for international students: Required—TOEFL. *Application deadline:* Applications are processed on a rolling basis. Application fee: $30. Electronic applications accepted. *Expenses:* Tuition, state resident: part-time $471 per credit hour. Tuition, nonresident: part-time $646 per credit hour. Tuition and fees vary according to course level. *Financial support:* In 2009–10, 16 students received support, including 15 fellowships (averaging $1,733 per year), 1 research assistantship with full and partial tuition reimbursement available (averaging $8,000 per year); career-related internships or fieldwork, Federal Work-Study, scholarships/grants, and unspecified assistantships also available. *Faculty research:* Culture of literacy, literacy acquisition, assessment, content area literacy, writing pedagogy. *Unit head:* Dr. Nancy Patterson, Director, 616-331-6226, E-mail: patterson@gvsu.edu. *Application contact:* Stephen Worst, 616-331-6831, Fax: 616-331-6217, E-mail: busmando@gvsu.edu.

Gwynedd-Mercy College, School of Education, Gwynedd Valley, PA 19437-0901. Offers educational administration (MS); master teacher (MS); reading (MS); school counseling (MS); special education (MS). Part-time and evening/weekend programs available. *Degree requirements:* For master's, thesis, internship, practicum. *Entrance requirements:* For master's, GRE or MAT; PRAXIS I Test, minimum GPA of 3.0. *Faculty research:* Learning and the brain, reading literacy, ethics and moral judgment, leadership, teaching and multicultural education.

Hamline University, School of Education, St. Paul, MN 55104-1284. Offers education (MA Ed, Ed D); English as a second language (MAESL); literacy education (MALED); natural science and environmental education (MA Ed); teaching (MAT). *Accreditation:* NCATE (one or more programs are accredited). Part-time and evening/weekend programs available. *Faculty:* 27 full-time (18 women), 128 part-time/adjunct (100 women). *Students:* 324 full-time (242 women), 1,049 part-time (780 women); includes 116 minority (36 African Americans, 4 American Indian/Alaska Native, 42 Asian Americans or Pacific Islanders, 34 Hispanic Americans), 25 international. Average age 33. 501 applicants, 79% accepted, 311 enrolled. In 2009, 196 master's, 9 doctorates awarded. *Degree requirements:* For master's, thesis; for doctorate, comprehensive exam, thesis/dissertation. *Entrance requirements:* For doctorate, personal statement, master's degree, 3 years experience, letters of recommendation, writing sample, interview. Additional exam requirements/recommendations for international students: Required—TOEFL (minimum score 550 paper-based; 213 computer-based; 79 iBT), TWE (minimum score 5). *Application deadline:* Applications are processed on a rolling basis. Application fee: $0. Electronic applications accepted. *Expenses:* Tuition: Full-time $6816; part-time $426 per credit. Required fees: $6 per credit. One-time fee: $205. Tuition and fees vary according to degree level, campus/location and program. *Financial support:* In 2009–10, 8 students received support. Federal Work-Study and scholarships/grants available. Support available to part-time students. Financial award applicants required to submit FAFSA. *Faculty research:* Adult basic education, service learning, teacher dispositions, diversity, technology. *Unit head:* Dr. Sheila Wright, Dean, 651-523-2600, Fax: 651-523-2489, E-mail: swright04@hamline.edu. *Application contact:* Rae A. Lenway, Director, Graduate Recruitment and Admission, 651-523-2900, Fax: 651-523-3058, E-mail: rlenway@hamline.edu.

Hannibal-LaGrange College, Program in Education, Hannibal, MO 63401-1999. Offers literacy (MS Ed); teaching and learning (MS Ed). Part-time and evening/weekend programs available. *Entrance requirements:* For master's, copy of current teaching certificate.

Harding University, College of Education, Searcy, AR 72149-0001. Offers advanced studies in teaching and learning (M Ed); art (MSE); behavioral science (MSE); counseling (MS, Ed S); early childhood special education (M Ed, MSE); education (MSE); educational leadership (M Ed, Ed S); elementary education (M Ed); English (MSE); family and consumer science (MSE); French (MSE); history/social science (MSE); kinesiology (MSE); math (MSE); physical science (MSE); reading (M Ed); secondary education (M Ed); Spanish (MSE); special education licensure (M Ed); teaching (MAT); teaching English as a second language (M Ed). *Accreditation:* NCATE. Part-time and evening/weekend programs available. *Faculty:* 11 full-time (4 women), 49 part-time/adjunct (26 women). *Students:* 104 full-time (85 women), 392 part-time (282 women); includes 77 minority (67 African Americans, 5 American Indian/Alaska Native, 1 Asian American or Pacific Islander, 4 Hispanic Americans), 5 international. Average age 36. 153 applicants, 92% accepted, 131 enrolled. In 2009, 153 master's, 6 other advanced degrees awarded. *Degree requirements:* For master's, comprehensive exam (for some programs), thesis optional, portfolio(s); for Ed S, comprehensive exam, portfolio, specialist project. *Entrance requirements:* For master's, GRE, MAT, PRAXIS; for Ed S, MAT or GRE. Additional exam requirements/recommendations for international students: Required—TOEFL (minimum score 550 paper-based; 79 iBT). *Application deadline:* For fall admission, 8/1 for domestic and international students; for spring admission, 1/1 for domestic and international students. Applications are processed on a rolling basis. Application fee: $35. *Expenses:* Tuition: Full-time $9720; part-time $540 per credit hour. Required fees: $22 per credit hour. Tuition and fees vary according to course load and program. *Financial support:* In 2009–10, 30 students received support. Unspecified assistantships available. *Faculty research:* Reading, comprehension, school violence, educational technology, behavior, college choice, differentiated instruction, brain-based teaching. *Unit head:* Dr. Clara Carroll, Chair, 501-279-4501, Fax: 501-279-4083, E-mail: ccarroll@harding.edu. *Application contact:* Information Contact, 501-279-4315, E-mail: gradstudiesedu@harding.edu.

Hardin-Simmons University, Graduate School, Irvin School of Education, Department of Educational Studies, Program in Reading Specialist Education, Abilene, TX 79698-0001. Offers M Ed. Part-time programs available. *Faculty:* 3 full-time (all women), 1 part-time/adjunct (0 women). *Students:* 6 part-time (all women); includes 1 minority (Hispanic American). Average age 25. 3 applicants, 100% accepted, 1 enrolled. In 2009, 5 master's awarded. *Degree requirements:* For master's, comprehensive exam. *Entrance requirements:* For master's, minimum undergraduate GPA of 3.0 in major, 2.7 overall. Additional exam requirements/recommendations for international students: Required—TOEFL (minimum score 550 paper-based; 213 computer-based; 75 iBT). *Application deadline:* For fall admission, 8/15 priority date for domestic students, 4/1 for international students; for spring admission, 1/5 priority date for domestic students, 9/1 for international students. Applications are processed on a rolling basis. Application fee: $50. *Expenses:* Tuition: Full-time $11,430; part-time $635 per credit hour. Required fees: $650; $110 per semester. Tuition and fees vary according to degree level. *Financial support:* In 2009–10, 3 students received support, including 1 fellowship (averaging $2,400 per year); scholarships/grants also available. Support available to part-time students. Financial award application deadline: 6/30; financial award applicants required to submit FAFSA. *Faculty research:* Social networking as a gatekeeper, reflective process of teachers, growth of reflective practice in pre-service teachers, multicultural children's literature. *Unit head:* Dr. Mary Christopher, Director, 325-670-1510, E-mail: mchris@hsutx.edu. *Application contact:* Dr. Gary Stanlake, Dean of Graduate Studies, 325-670-1298, Fax: 325-670-1564, E-mail: gradoff@hsutx.edu.

Harvard University, Graduate School of Education, Master's Programs in Education, Cambridge, MA 02138. Offers arts in education (Ed M); education policy and management (Ed M); higher education (Ed M); human development and psychology (Ed M); international education policy (Ed M); language and literacy (Ed M); learning and teaching (Ed M); mid-career mathematics and science (teaching certificate) (Ed M); mind brain and education (Ed M); risk and prevention (Ed M); school leadership (Ed M); special studies (Ed M); teaching and curriculum (teaching certificate) (Ed M); technology innovation and education (Ed M). Part-time programs available. *Faculty:* 70 full-time (33 women), 36 part-time/adjunct (20 women). *Students:* 598 full-time (448 women), 76 part-time (60 women); includes 132 minority (40 African Americans, 2 American Indian/Alaska Native, 58 Asian Americans or Pacific Islanders, 32 Hispanic Americans), 103 international. Average age 28. 1,574 applicants, 58% accepted, 640 enrolled. In 2009, 556 master's awarded. *Entrance requirements:* For master's, GRE General Test, 3 letters of recommendation. Additional exam requirements/recommendations for international students: Required—TOEFL (minimum score 600 paper-based; 250 computer-based; 100 iBT), TWE (minimum score 5). *Application deadline:* For fall admission, 1/4 for domestic and international students. Application fee: $85. Electronic applications accepted. *Expenses:* Contact institution. *Financial support:* In 2009–10, 424 students received support, including 25 fellowships with full and partial tuition reimbursements available (averaging $15,890 per year); career-related internships or fieldwork, Federal Work-Study, institutionally sponsored loans, scholarships/grants, health care benefits, tuition waivers (full and partial), and unspecified assistantships also available. Support available to part-time students. Financial award application deadline: 2/1; financial award applicants required to submit FAFSA. *Faculty research:* Learning and development, educational leadership and organizations, educational policy analysis. Total annual research expenditures: $18.1 million. *Unit head:* Jennifer L. Petrallia, Assistant Dean, 617-495-8445. *Application contact:* Information Contact, 617-495-3414, Fax: 617-496-3577, E-mail: gseadmissions@harvard.edu.

Henderson State University, Graduate Studies, School of Education, Department of Advanced Instructional Studies, Arkadelphia, AR 71999-0001. Offers early childhood (P-4) (MSE); education (MAT); middle school (MSE); reading (MSE); special education (MSE). *Accreditation:* NCATE. Part-time programs available. *Faculty:* 7 full-time (4 women), 2 part-time/adjunct (both women). *Students:* 7 full-time (all women), 131 part-time (119 women); includes 16 minority (11 African Americans, 1 Asian American or Pacific Islander, 4 Hispanic Americans). Average age 33. 25 applicants, 100% accepted, 25 enrolled. In 2009, 53 master's awarded. *Entrance requirements:* For master's, GRE General Test or MAT, minimum GPA of 2.7, teacher certification. Additional exam requirements/recommendations for international students: Required—TOEFL (minimum score 550 paper-based; 213 computer-based); Recommended—IELTS (minimum score 6). *Application deadline:* For fall admission, 8/1 priority date for domestic students, 6/30 priority date for international students; for spring admission, 1/1 priority date for domestic students, 11/30 priority date for international students. Application fee: $25 ($75 for international students). Electronic applications accepted. *Expenses:* Tuition, state resident: full-time $3798; part-time $211 per credit hour. Tuition, nonresident: full-time $7596; part-time $422 per credit hour. Required fees: $903. *Financial support:* Research assistantships, teaching assistantships with tuition reimbursements available. *Unit head:* Dr. Gary Smithey, Chairperson, 870-230-5361, Fax: 870-230-5455, E-mail: smitheg@hsu.edu. *Application contact:* Dr. Marck L. Beggs, Graduate Dean, 870-230-5126, Fax: 870-230-5479, E-mail: beggsm@hsu.edu.

Heritage University, Graduate Programs in Education, Program in Professional Studies, Toppenish, WA 98948-9599. Offers bilingual education/ESL (M Ed); biology (M Ed); English and literature (M Ed); reading/literacy (M Ed); special education (M Ed). Part-time and evening/weekend programs available. *Degree requirements:* For master's, comprehensive exam (for some programs), thesis (for some programs).

Hofstra University, School of Education, Health, and Human Services, Department of Counseling, Research, Special Education and Rehabilitation, Program in Special Education, Hempstead, NY 11549. Offers early childhood special education (MS Ed, Advanced Certificate); gifted education (Advanced Certificate); inclusive early childhood special education (MS Ed); inclusive elementary special education (MS Ed); inclusive secondary special education (MS Ed); literacy studies and special education (MS Ed); special education (MA, MS Ed, PD); special education assessment and diagnosis (Advanced Certificate); teaching students with severe or multiple disabilities (Advanced Certificate). Part-time and evening/weekend programs available. *Students:* 113 full-time (96 women), 105 part-time (95 women); includes 39 minority (18 African Americans, 1 American Indian/Alaska Native, 3 Asian Americans or Pacific Islanders, 17 Hispanic Americans). Average age 29. 134 applicants, 71% accepted, 74 enrolled. In 2009, 88 master's, 7 other advanced degrees awarded. *Degree requirements:* For master's, comprehensive exam (for some programs), thesis (for some programs), seminars, student teaching. *Entrance requirements:* For master's, interview, 3 letters of reference, initial/professional certification; for other advanced degree, interview, 3 letters of recommendation, resume, master's degree, certification. Additional exam requirements/recommendations for international students: Required—TOEFL (minimum score 550 paper-based; 213 computer-

Reading Education

Hofstra University (continued)

based; 80 iBT). *Application deadline:* Applications are processed on a rolling basis. Application fee: $60. Electronic applications accepted. *Expenses:* Tuition: Full-time $16,200; part-time $900 per credit hour. Required fees: $970; $145 per term. Tuition and fees vary according to program. *Financial support:* In 2009–10, 78 students received support, including 10 fellowships with full and partial tuition reimbursements available (averaging $2,541 per year), 4 research assistantships with full and partial tuition reimbursements available (averaging $7,210 per year); Federal Work-Study, institutionally sponsored loans, scholarships/grants, tuition waivers (full and partial), and unspecified assistantships also available. Support available to part-time students. Financial award applicants required to submit FAFSA. *Faculty research:* Inclusive schooling, autism spectrum disorders related services, cultural competency and culturally responsive instruction, co-teaching student teaching, universal design for learning. *Unit head:* Dr. George Guiliani, Director, 516-463-5143, Fax: 516-463-6184, E-mail: cprgag@hofstra.edu. *Application contact:* Carol Drummer, Dean of Graduate Admissions, 516-463-4876, Fax: 516-463-4664, E-mail: gradstudent@hofstra.edu.

Hofstra University, School of Education, Health, and Human Services, Department of Literacy Studies, Hempstead, NY 11549. Offers literacy studies (MA, MS Ed, Ed D, PhD, CAS, PD), including advanced literacy studies (birth-6) (PD), advanced literacy studies (grades 5-12) (PD), literacy studies (Ed D, PhD), literacy studies (birth-grade 6) (MS Ed, CAS), literacy studies (grades 5-12) (MS Ed, CAS), teaching of writing (birth-grade 6) (MA), teaching of writing (grades 5-12) (MA). Part-time and evening/weekend programs available. *Faculty:* 8 full-time (7 women), 9 part-time/adjunct (8 women). *Students:* 35 full-time (33 women), 126 part-time (121 women); includes 20 minority (8 African Americans, 3 Asian Americans or Pacific Islanders, 9 Hispanic Americans), 2 international. Average age 31. 85 applicants, 73% accepted, 52 enrolled. In 2009, 58 master's, 2 doctorates, 4 other advanced degrees awarded. *Degree requirements:* For master's, comprehensive exam, portfolio; for doctorate, one foreign language, comprehensive exam, thesis/dissertation, qualifying hearing. *Entrance requirements:* For master's, interview, teaching certificate, 2 letters of recommendation; for doctorate, GRE or MAT, interview, resume, essay, master's degree, 3 letters of recommendation, writing sample; for other advanced degree, 2 letters of recommendation, interview, teaching certificate, essay, master's degree. Additional exam requirements/recommendations for international students: Required—TOEFL (minimum score 550 paper-based; 213 computer-based; 80 iBT). *Application deadline:* Applications are processed on a rolling basis. Application fee: $60. Electronic applications accepted. *Expenses:* Tuition: Full-time $16,200; part-time $900 per credit hour. Required fees: $970; $145 per term. Tuition and fees vary according to program. *Financial support:* In 2009–10, 79 students received support, including 41 fellowships with full and partial tuition reimbursements available (averaging $3,273 per year); research assistantships with full and partial tuition reimbursements available, career-related internships or fieldwork, Federal Work-Study, institutionally sponsored loans, scholarships/grants, tuition waivers (full and partial), and unspecified assistantships also available. Support available to part-time students. Financial award applicants required to submit FAFSA. *Faculty research:* Miscue analysis; literature for children and adolescents; eye movement/miscue analysis; digital literacy. Total annual research expenditures: $20,000. *Unit head:* Dr. Debra Goodman, Chairperson, 516-463-5563, Fax: 516-463-5949, E-mail: readzg@hofstra.edu. *Application contact:* Carol Drummer, Dean of Graduate Admissions, 516-463-4876, Fax: 516-463-4664, E-mail: gradstudent@hofstra.edu.

Holy Family University, Graduate School, School of Education, Philadelphia, PA 19114. Offers education (M Ed); education leadership (M Ed); elementary education (M Ed); reading specialist (M Ed); secondary education (M Ed); special education (M Ed). Part-time and evening/weekend programs available. *Faculty:* 14 full-time (10 women), 42 part-time/adjunct (23 women). *Students:* 63 full-time (48 women), 608 part-time (487 women); includes 45 minority (23 African Americans, 7 Asian Americans or Pacific Islanders, 15 Hispanic Americans), 1 international. Average age 31. 202 applicants, 86% accepted, 146 enrolled. In 2009, 248 master's awarded. *Degree requirements:* For master's, thesis optional. *Entrance requirements:* For master's, GRE or MAT, interview. *Application deadline:* For fall admission, 7/1 priority date for domestic students; for winter admission, 11/1 priority date for domestic students. Applications are processed on a rolling basis. Application fee: $25. *Expenses:* Tuition: Part-time $600 per credit. Required fees: $58 per semester. *Financial support:* Research assistantships, Federal Work-Study available. Support available to part-time students. Financial award application deadline: 2/15; financial award applicants required to submit FAFSA. *Faculty research:* Cognition, developmental issues, sociological issues in education. *Unit head:* Dr. Leonard Soroka, Dean, 267-341-3565, Fax: 215-824-2438, E-mail: lsoroka@holyfamily.edu. *Application contact:* Gidget Marie Montelibano, Graduate Admissions Counselor, 267-341-3558, Fax: 215-637-1478, E-mail: gmontelibano@holyfamily.edu.

Hood College, Graduate School, Department of Education, Frederick, MD 21701-8575. Offers curriculum and instruction (MS), including early childhood education, elementary education, elementary school science and mathematics, secondary education, special education; educational leadership (MS, Certificate); reading specialization (MS). Part-time and evening/weekend programs available. *Faculty:* 4 full-time (all women), 39 part-time/adjunct (21 women). *Students:* 2 full-time (both women), 397 part-time (326 women); includes 41 minority (29 African Americans, 5 Asian Americans or Pacific Islanders, 7 Hispanic Americans). Average age 33. 100 applicants, 92% accepted, 84 enrolled. In 2009, 73 master's, 65 other advanced degrees awarded. *Degree requirements:* For master's, action research project, portfolio (reading). *Entrance requirements:* For master's, minimum GPA of 2.75, teaching certification. *Application deadline:* For fall admission, 7/15 for domestic and international students; for spring admission, 12/15 for domestic and international students. Applications are processed on a rolling basis. Application fee: $35. Electronic applications accepted. *Expenses:* Tuition: Full-time $6480; part-time $360 per credit. Required fees: $100; $50 per term. *Financial support:* Applicants required to submit FAFSA. *Faculty research:* Leadership, action research, brain research, learning styles. *Unit head:* Dr. John George, Chairperson, 301-696-3471, Fax: 301-696-3597, E-mail: george@hood.edu. *Application contact:* Dr. Allen P. Flora, Dean of Graduate School, 301-696-3811, Fax: 301-696-3597, E-mail: gofurther@hood.edu.

Houston Baptist University, College of Education and Behavioral Sciences, Programs in Education, Houston, TX 77074-3298. Offers bilingual education (M Ed); counselor education (M Ed); curriculum and instruction (M Ed); educational administration (M Ed); educational diagnostician (M Ed); reading education (M Ed). Part-time programs available. *Entrance requirements:* For master's, GRE General Test or MAT. Additional exam requirements/recommendations for international students: Required—TOEFL (minimum score 550 paper-based; 213 computer-based).

Howard University, School of Education, Department of Curriculum and Instruction, Program in Reading, Washington, DC 20059-0002. Offers M Ed, MA, MAT, CAGS. MA offered through the Graduate School of Arts and Sciences. *Accreditation:* NCATE. Part-time programs available. *Faculty:* 1 full-time (0 women). *Students:* 1 (woman) part-time; minority (African American). Average age 50. 1 applicant, 100% accepted, 1 enrolled. In 2009, 1 master's awarded. *Degree requirements:* For master's, comprehensive exam, thesis (for some programs), expository writing exam, internships, practicum; for CAGS, thesis or alternative. *Entrance requirements:* For master's, GRE General Test (MA), minimum GPA of 2.7. *Application deadline:* For fall admission, 2/15 priority date for domestic students; for spring admission, 11/1 for domestic students. Applications are processed on a rolling basis. Application fee: $45. Electronic applications accepted. *Financial support:* In 2009–10, fellowships with full and partial tuition reimbursements (averaging $15,000 per year), research assistantships with full and partial tuition reimbursements (averaging $13,000 per year) were awarded; career-related internships or fieldwork, Federal Work-Study, institutionally sponsored loans, scholarships/grants, and unspecified assistantships also available. Financial award application deadline: 2/15. *Faculty research:* Recruiting teachers, multicultural literature, early reading, teacher-made materials. *Unit head:* Dr. Kenneth Anderson, Assistant Professor/Coordinator, 202-806-6703, Fax: 202-806-5297, E-mail: kenanderson@howard.edu. *Application contact:* June L. Harris, Administrative Assistant, Department of Curriculum and Instruction, 202-806-7343, Fax: 202-806-5297, E-mail: jlharris@howard.edu.

Hunter College of the City University of New York, Graduate School, School of Education, Department of Curriculum and Teaching, New York, NY 10021-5085. Offers bilingual education (MS); corrective reading (K-12) (MS Ed); early childhood education (MS); educational supervision and administration (AC); elementary education (MS); literacy education (MS); teaching English as a second language (MA). *Faculty:* 30 full-time (22 women), 122 part-time/adjunct (95 women). *Students:* 170 full-time (157 women), 1,035 part-time (889 women); includes 268 minority (74 African Americans, 5 American Indian/Alaska Native, 71 Asian Americans or Pacific Islanders, 118 Hispanic Americans). Average age 31. 1,339 applicants, 43% accepted, 410 enrolled. In 2009, 365 master's, 90 other advanced degrees awarded. *Degree requirements:* For master's, thesis; for AC, portfolio review. *Entrance requirements:* For degree, minimum B average in graduate course work, teaching certificate, minimum 3 years of full-time teaching experience, interview, 2 letters of support. Additional exam requirements/recommendations for international students: Required—TOEFL, TWE. *Application deadline:* For fall admission, 4/1 for domestic students; for spring admission, 11/1 for domestic students. Applications are processed on a rolling basis. Application fee: $125. *Expenses:* Tuition, state resident: full-time $7360; part-time $310 per credit. Required fees: $250 per semester. *Financial support:* Federal Work-Study, scholarships/grants, and tuition waivers (partial) available. Support available to part-time students. *Faculty research:* Teacher opportunity corps-mentor program for first-year teachers, adult literacy, student literacy corporation. *Unit head:* Dr. Anne M. Ediger, Head, 212-777-4686, E-mail: anne.ediger@hunter.cuny.edu. *Application contact:* Milena Solo, Director for Graduate Admissions, 212-772-4482, Fax: 212-650-3336, E-mail: milena.solo@hunter.cuny.edu.

Idaho State University, Office of Graduate Studies, College of Education, Department of Educational Foundations, Pocatello, ID 83209-8059. Offers child and family studies (M Ed); curriculum leadership (M Ed); education (M Ed); educational administration (M Ed); educational foundations (5th Year Certificate); elementary education (M Ed), including K-12 education, literacy, secondary education. Part-time programs available. *Faculty:* 13 full-time (8 women). *Students:* 15 full-time (9 women), 100 part-time (64 women); includes 2 minority (1 African American, 1 Hispanic American), 3 international. Average age 39. In 2009, 25 master's awarded. *Degree requirements:* For master's, comprehensive exam, thesis optional, oral exam, written exam; for 5th Year Certificate, comprehensive exam, thesis (for some programs), oral exam, written exam. *Entrance requirements:* For master's, GRE General Test or MAT, minimum undergraduate GPA of 3.0; for 5th Year Certificate, GRE General Test, minimum undergraduate GPA of 3.0, master's degree. Additional exam requirements/recommendations for international students: Required—TOEFL (minimum score 550 paper-based; 213 computer-based; 80 iBT). *Application deadline:* For fall admission, 7/1 for domestic students, 6/1 for international students; for spring admission, 12/1 for domestic students, 11/1 for international students. Applications are processed on a rolling basis. Application fee: $55. Electronic applications accepted. *Expenses:* Tuition, state resident: full-time $3318; part-time $297 per credit hour. Tuition, nonresident: full-time $13,120; part-time $437 per credit hour. Required fees: $2530. Tuition and fees vary according to program. *Financial support:* Research assistantships with full and partial tuition reimbursements, teaching assistantships with full and partial tuition reimbursements, career-related internships or fieldwork, Federal Work-Study, institutionally sponsored loans, scholarships/grants, traineeships, health care benefits, tuition waivers (full and partial), and unspecified assistantships available. Support available to part-time students. Financial award application deadline: 1/1; financial award applicants required to submit FAFSA. *Faculty research:* Child and families studies; business education; special education; math, science, and technology education. *Unit head:* Dr. Beverly Ray, Chair, 208-282-4516, Fax: 208-282-3791, E-mail: raybeve@isu.edu. *Application contact:* Dr. Peter Denner, Assistant Dean, 208-282-3807, Fax: 208-282-4697, E-mail: dennpete@isu.edu.

Illinois State University, Graduate School, College of Education, Department of Curriculum and Instruction, Program in Reading, Normal, IL 61790-2200. Offers MS Ed. *Accreditation:* NCATE. *Degree requirements:* For master's, practicum. *Entrance requirements:* For master's, GRE General Test, minimum GPA of 3.0 in last 60 hours of course work, course work in reading.

Indiana University Bloomington, School of Education, Department of Literacy, Culture, and Language Education, Bloomington, IN 47405-7000. Offers MS, Ed D, PhD, Ed S. *Accreditation:* NCATE. Part-time and evening/weekend programs available. Postbaccalaureate distance learning degree programs offered (no on-campus study). *Faculty:* 15 full-time (9 women), 26 part-time/adjunct (21 women). *Students:* 142 full-time (104 women), 57 part-time (47 women); includes 23 minority (4 African Americans, 1 American Indian/Alaska Native, 10 Asian Americans or Pacific Islanders, 8 Hispanic Americans), 75 international. Average age 35. 67 applicants, 84% accepted, 27 enrolled. In 2009, 53 master's, 5 doctorates awarded. Terminal master's awarded for partial completion of doctoral program. *Degree requirements:* For doctorate, thesis/dissertation, internship; for Ed S, comprehensive exam or project. *Entrance requirements:* For master's, GRE General Test or minimum GPA of 3.0; for doctorate, GRE General Test, minimum graduate GPA of 3.5; for Ed S, GRE General Test. Additional exam requirements/recommendations for international students: Required—TOEFL. *Application deadline:* For fall admission, 6/1 for domestic students, 3/1 for international students; for spring admission, 9/1 for international students. Applications are processed on a rolling basis. Application fee: $55 ($65 for international students). *Financial support:* Fellowships with tuition reimbursements, research assistantships with partial tuition reimbursements, teaching assistantships with partial tuition reimbursements, career-related internships or fieldwork, Federal Work-Study, institutionally sponsored loans, and tuition waivers (full and partial) available. Support available to part-time students. *Faculty research:* Discourse analysis, sociolinguistics, critical literacy, cultural studies. *Unit head:* MaryBeth Hines, Chair, 812-856-8270, Fax: 812-856-8287. *Application contact:* Office Manager, 812-856-8270.

Indiana University of Pennsylvania, School of Graduate Studies and Research, College of Education and Educational Technology, Department of Professional Studies in Education, Program in Literacy, Indiana, PA 15705-1087. Offers literacy (M Ed); reading (M Ed). *Accreditation:* NCATE. Part-time programs available. *Faculty:* 1 (woman) full-time. *Students:* 8 full-time (7 women), 38 part-time (37 women), 1 international. Average age 27. 28 applicants, 82% accepted, 21 enrolled. In 2009, 23 master's awarded. *Degree requirements:* For master's, thesis optional. *Entrance requirements:* For master's, 2 letters of recommendation. Additional exam requirements/recommendations for international students: Required—TOEFL. *Application deadline:* For fall admission, 7/1 priority date for domestic students; for spring admission, 11/1 for domestic students. Applications are processed on a rolling basis. Application fee: $40. *Expenses:* Tuition, state resident: full-time $6666; part-time $370 per credit hour. Tuition, nonresident: full-time $10,666; part-time $593 per credit hour. Required fees: $813 per semester. *Financial support:* In 2009–10, 6 research assistantships with full and partial tuition reimbursements (averaging $5,440 per year) were awarded; career-related internships or fieldwork and Federal Work-Study also available. Support available to part-time students. Financial award application deadline: 3/15; financial award applicants required to submit FAFSA. *Unit head:* Dr. Anne Creany, Graduate Coordinator, 724-357-2409. *Application contact:* Dr. Anne Creany, Graduate Coordinator, 724-357-2409.

Indiana University–Purdue University Indianapolis, School of Education, Indianapolis, IN 46202-2896. Offers computer education (Certificate); curriculum and instruction (MS); early childhood (MS); educational leadership (MS, Certificate); English as a second language (Certificate); higher education and student affairs (MS); kindergarten (Certificate); language education (MS); reading (Certificate); school counseling (MS); special education (MS, Certificate). Part-time and evening/weekend programs available. *Faculty:* 41 full-time, 80 part-time/adjunct. *Students:* 72 full-time (60 women), 427 part-time (325 women); includes 57 minority (42 African Americans, 1 American Indian/Alaska Native, 4 Asian Americans or Pacific Islanders, 10 Hispanic Americans), 5 international. Average age 32. 181 applicants, 78% accepted, 112 enrolled. In 2009, 162 master's awarded. *Degree requirements:* For master's, thesis optional. *Entrance requirements:* For master's, GRE General Test, minimum GPA of 3.0. Additional

exam requirements/recommendations for international students: Required—TOEFL. *Application deadline:* For fall admission, 5/1 priority date for domestic students; for spring admission, 11/1 for domestic students. Application fee: $55 ($65 for international students). *Financial support:* In 2009–10, 2 fellowships (averaging $780 per year), 18 teaching assistantships (averaging $9,756 per year) were awarded; research assistantships with partial tuition reimbursements, Federal Work-Study, institutionally sponsored loans, scholarships/grants, and tuition waivers (partial) also available. Support available to part-time students. *Faculty research:* Teachers in the process of change, learning cycles, children's concepts of science. Total annual research expenditures: $614,458. *Unit head:* Dr. Chris Leland, Interim Executive Associate Dean, 317-274-6801, Fax: 317-274-6864. *Application contact:* Sarah Brandenburg, Graduate Advisor, 317-274-6801, Fax: 317-274-6864, E-mail: edugrad@iupui.edu.

Iona College, School of Arts and Science, Program in Education, New Rochelle, NY 10801-1890. Offers biology education (MS Ed, MST); educational leadership (MS Ed); English education (MS Ed, MST); literacy education (MS Ed); mathematics education (MS Ed, MST); social studies education (MS Ed, MST); Spanish education (MS Ed, MST); teaching in childhood education (MST). *Accreditation:* NCATE. Part-time and evening/weekend programs available. *Faculty:* 24 full-time (13 women), 16 part-time/adjunct (10 women). *Students:* 41 full-time (35 women), 118 part-time (87 women); includes 15 minority (5 African Americans, 1 Asian American or Pacific Islander, 9 Hispanic Americans). Average age 28. 91 applicants, 67% accepted, 41 enrolled. In 2009, 61 master's awarded. *Degree requirements:* For master's, thesis or alternative. *Entrance requirements:* For master's, minimum GPA of 2.5 (MST), New York teaching certificate (MS Ed). Additional exam requirements/recommendations for international students: Required—TOEFL (minimum score 550 paper-based; 213 computer-based). *Application deadline:* Applications are processed on a rolling basis. Application fee: $50. Electronic applications accepted. *Expenses:* Tuition: Part-time $830 per credit. *Financial support:* Unspecified assistantships available. Support available to part-time students. Financial award application deadline: 4/15; financial award applicants required to submit FAFSA. *Faculty research:* Reading/writing, educational technology, administration, early literacy assessment, literacy development. *Unit head:* Dr. Catherine O'Callaghan, Chair, 914-633-2210, Fax: 914-633-2608, E-mail: cocallaghan@iona.edu. *Application contact:* Veronica Jarek-Prinz, Director of Graduate Admissions, 914-633-2420, Fax: 914-633-2277, E-mail: vjarekprinz@iona.edu.

Jacksonville State University, College of Graduate Studies and Continuing Education, College of Education and Professional Studies, Program in Reading Specialist, Jacksonville, AL 36265-1602. Offers MS Ed. Part-time and evening/weekend programs available. *Degree requirements:* For master's, comprehensive exam, thesis (for some programs). Electronic applications accepted.

Jacksonville University, College of Arts and Sciences, School of Education, Program in Reading Education, Jacksonville, FL 32211. Offers MAT. Part-time and evening/weekend programs available. *Degree requirements:* For master's, comprehensive exam. *Entrance requirements:* For master's, GRE General Test, minimum GPA of 3.0. Additional exam requirements/recommendations for international students: Required—TOEFL.

James Madison University, The Graduate School, College of Education, Early, Elementary, and Reading Education Department, Program in Reading Education, Harrisonburg, VA 22807. Offers M Ed. *Accreditation:* NCATE. Part-time programs available. *Students:* Average age 27. *Entrance requirements:* For master's, GRE General Test. Additional exam requirements/recommendations for international students: Required—TOEFL. *Application deadline:* For fall admission, 5/1 priority date for domestic students; for spring admission, 9/1 priority date for domestic students. Applications are processed on a rolling basis. Application fee: $55. Electronic applications accepted. *Expenses:* Tuition, area resident: Part-time $305 per credit hour. Tuition, state resident: part-time $305 per credit hour. Tuition, nonresident: part-time $890 per credit hour. *Financial support:* Federal Work-Study and unspecified assistantships available. Financial award application deadline: 3/1; financial award applicants required to submit FAFSA. *Unit head:* Dr. Martha Ross, Academic Unit Head, 540-568-6255. *Application contact:* Lynette M. Bible, Director of Graduate Admissions, 540-568-6395, Fax: 540-568-7860, E-mail: biblelm@jmu.edu.

The Johns Hopkins University, School of Education, Department of Teacher Development and Leadership, Baltimore, MD 21218-2699. Offers adolescent literacy education (Certificate); data-based decision making and organizational improvement (Certificate); education (MS), including reading, school administration and supervision, technology for educators; educational leadership for independent schools (Certificate); effective teaching of reading (Certificate); emergent literacy education (Certificate); English as a second language instruction (Certificate); gifted education (Certificate); leadership for school, family, and community collaboration (Certificate); leadership in technology integration (Certificate); school administration and supervision (Certificate); teacher development and leadership (Ed D); teacher leadership (Certificate); technology for educators (MS). Part-time and evening/weekend programs available. Postbaccalaureate distance learning degree programs offered (minimal on-campus study). *Faculty:* 8 full-time (2 women), 53 part-time/adjunct (36 women). *Students:* 17 full-time (16 women), 462 part-time (358 women); includes 117 minority (77 African Americans, 25 Asian Americans or Pacific Islanders, 15 Hispanic Americans), 11 international. Average age 33. 217 applicants, 62% accepted, 107 enrolled. In 2009, 85 master's, 2 doctorates, 181 other advanced degrees awarded. *Degree requirements:* For master's and Certificate, portfolio; for doctorate, comprehensive exam (for some programs), thesis/dissertation, portfolio or comprehensive exam. *Entrance requirements:* For master's and Certificate, bachelor's degree; minimum undergraduate GPA of 3.0; essay/statement of goals; for doctorate, GRE, essay/statement of goals; three letters of recommendation; curriculum vitae/resume; K-12 professional experience; interview; writing assessment. Additional exam requirements/recommendations for international students: Required—TOEFL (minimum score 600 paper-based; 250 computer-based; 100 iBT). *Application deadline:* For fall admission, 5/1 for international students; for spring admission, 10/15 for international students. Applications are processed on a rolling basis. Application fee: $80. Electronic applications accepted. *Financial support:* In 2009–10, 5 research assistantships, 1 teaching assistantship were awarded; scholarships/grants also available. Support available to part-time students. Financial award application deadline: 6/1; financial award applicants required to submit FAFSA. *Faculty research:* Application of psychoanalytic concepts to teaching, schools, and education reform; adolescent literacies; use of emerging technologies for teaching, learning, and school leadership; quantitative analyses of the social contexts of education; school, family, and community collaboration; program evaluation methodologies. *Unit head:* Dr. Edward Pajak, Chair, 410-516-9755, Fax: 410-516-9770, E-mail: mbuckingham@jhu.edu. *Application contact:* Jennifer Shaffer, Director of Admissions, 410-516-9797, Fax: 410-516-9799, E-mail: educationinfo@jhu.edu.

Johnson State College, Graduate Program in Education, Program in Literacy, Johnson, VT 05656. Offers MA Ed. *Degree requirements:* For master's, comprehensive exam, thesis or alternative. *Entrance requirements:* For master's, interview. Additional exam requirements/recommendations for international students: Required—TOEFL. *Expenses:* Tuition, area resident: Part-time $416 per credit. Tuition, state resident: part-time $416 per credit. Tuition, nonresident: part-time $899 per credit.

Judson University, Graduate Programs, Elgin, IL 60123-1498. Offers architecture (M Arch); literacy (M Ed); organizational leadership (MA); teaching (M Ed). Part-time and evening/weekend programs available. Postbaccalaureate distance learning degree programs offered (no on-campus study). *Degree requirements:* For master's, comprehensive exam (for some programs), thesis. *Entrance requirements:* For master's, interviews.

Kaplan University, Davenport Campus, School of Teacher Education, Davenport, IA 52807-2095. Offers education (M Ed); secondary education (M Ed); teaching and learning (MA); teaching literacy and language: grades 6-12 (MA); teaching literacy and language: grades K-6 (MA); teaching mathematics: grades 6-8 (MA); teaching mathematics: grades 9-12 (MA); teaching mathematics: grades K-5 (MA); teaching science: grades 6-12 (MA); teaching science: grades K-6 (MA); teaching students with special needs (MA); teaching with technology (MA). Part-time and evening/weekend programs available. Postbaccalaureate distance learning degree programs offered (no on-campus study). *Entrance requirements:* Additional exam requirements/recommendations for international students: Required—TOEFL (minimum score 550 paper-based; 218 computer-based; 80 iBT).

Kean University, College of Education, Program in Reading Specialization, Union, NJ 07083. Offers adult literacy (MA); basic skills (MA); reading specialization (MA). *Faculty:* 15 full-time (13 women). *Students:* 3 full-time (all women), 69 part-time (63 women); includes 8 minority (3 African Americans, 4 Asian Americans or Pacific Islanders, 1 Hispanic American). Average age 32. 22 applicants, 100% accepted, 19 enrolled. In 2009, 28 master's awarded. *Degree requirements:* For master's, thesis, practicum, clinical, research seminar. *Entrance requirements:* For master's, GRE General Test or MAT, minimum GPA of 3.0, 2 letters of recommendation, interview, teaching certification. *Application deadline:* For fall admission, 5/1 for domestic students; for spring admission, 11/1 for domestic students. Application fee: $60 ($150 for international students). Electronic applications accepted. *Expenses:* Tuition, state resident: full-time $10,440; part-time $435 per credit. Tuition, nonresident: full-time $14,160; part-time $590 per credit. Required fees: $2642; $110 per credit. Part-time tuition and fees vary according to course load and degree level. *Financial support:* In 2009–10, research assistantships with full tuition reimbursements (averaging $3,263 per year); unspecified assistantships also available. *Unit head:* Dr. Joan M. Kastner, Program Coordinator, 908-737-3942, E-mail: jkastner@kean.edu. *Application contact:* Reenat Hasan, Pre-Admission Coordinator, 908-737-5923, Fax: 908-737-5965, E-mail: rhasan@exchange.kean.edu.

Kent State University, Graduate School of Education, Health, and Human Services, School of Teaching, Learning and Curriculum Studies, Program in Reading Specialization, Kent, OH 44242-0001. Offers M Ed, MA. *Accreditation:* NCATE. Part-time and evening/weekend programs available. *Faculty:* 12 full-time (9 women), 4 part-time/adjunct (all women). *Students:* 1 full-time (0 women), 108 part-time (104 women); includes 4 minority (2 African Americans, 1 Asian American or Pacific Islander, 1 Hispanic American), 2 international. 60 applicants, 95% accepted. In 2009, 59 master's awarded. *Degree requirements:* For master's, thesis (for some programs). *Entrance requirements:* Additional exam requirements/recommendations for international students: Required—TOEFL. *Application deadline:* Applications are processed on a rolling basis. Application fee: $30 ($60 for international students). Electronic applications accepted. *Financial support:* In 2009–10, 1 research assistantship with full tuition reimbursement (averaging $9,000 per year) was awarded; Federal Work-Study, scholarships/grants, and unspecified assistantships also available. Financial award application deadline: 4/1; financial award applicants required to submit FAFSA. *Faculty research:* Adolescent literacy, adult and family literacy, school change in literacy education, struggling readers. *Unit head:* Dr. Nancy Padak, Coordinator, 330-672-0648, E-mail: npadak@kent.edu. *Application contact:* Nancy Miller, Academic Program Coordinator, Office of Graduate Student Services, 330-672-2576, Fax: 330-672-9162, E-mail: ogs@kent.edu.

King's College, Program in Reading, Wilkes-Barre, PA 18711-0801. Offers M Ed. *Accreditation:* NCATE. Part-time and evening/weekend programs available. *Degree requirements:* For master's, thesis. *Entrance requirements:* Additional exam requirements/recommendations for international students: Required—TOEFL (minimum score 600 paper-based; 250 computer-based).

Kutztown University of Pennsylvania, College of Education, Program in Reading, Kutztown, PA 19530-0730. Offers M Ed. *Accreditation:* NCATE. Part-time and evening/weekend programs available. *Students:* 3 full-time (2 women), 118 part-time (112 women); includes 4 minority (1 African American, 1 American Indian/Alaska Native, 1 Asian American or Pacific Islander, 1 Hispanic American), 1 international. Average age 28. 48 applicants, 79% accepted, 13 enrolled. In 2009, 31 master's awarded. *Degree requirements:* For master's, comprehensive project. *Entrance requirements:* For master's, GRE General Test. Additional exam requirements/recommendations for international students: Required—TOEFL. *Application deadline:* For fall admission, 8/15 priority date for domestic and international students; for spring admission, 12/15 priority date for domestic and international students. Applications are processed on a rolling basis. Application fee: $35. Electronic applications accepted. *Expenses:* Tuition, state resident: full-time $6666; part-time $370 per credit. Tuition, nonresident: full-time $10,666; part-time $593 per credit. Required fees: $62 per credit. $60 per semester. *Financial support:* Career-related internships or fieldwork, Federal Work-Study, scholarships/grants, and unspecified assistantships available. Financial award application deadline: 3/1; financial award applicants required to submit FAFSA. *Unit head:* Dr. Elsa Geskus, Chairperson, 610-683-4262, Fax: 610-683-1327, E-mail: geskus@kutztown.edu. *Application contact:* Kelly D. Burr, Associate Director, Graduate Admissions, 610-683-4200, Fax: 610-683-1393, E-mail: graduate@kutztown.edu.

Lake Erie College, Division of Education, Painesville, OH 44077-3389. Offers curriculum and instruction (MS Ed); education (MS Ed); educational leadership (MS Ed); reading (MS Ed). Part-time and evening/weekend programs available. *Degree requirements:* For master's, comprehensive exam (for some programs), thesis optional, applied research project. *Entrance requirements:* For master's, GRE General Test or minimum GPA of 3.0. Additional exam requirements/recommendations for international students: Required—TOEFL (minimum score 590 paper-based). Electronic applications accepted. *Expenses:* Contact institution. *Faculty research:* Cooperative learning, portfolio assessment, education systems abroad, Web-based instruction.

Lehman College of the City University of New York, Division of Education, Department of Specialized Services in Education, Program in Reading Teacher, Bronx, NY 10468-1589. Offers MS Ed. *Accreditation:* NCATE. Evening/weekend programs available. *Entrance requirements:* For master's, interview, minimum GPA of 2.7. *Faculty research:* Emergent literacy, language-based classrooms, primary and secondary social contexts of language and literacy, innovative in-service education models, adult literacy.

Lesley University, School of Education, Cambridge, MA 02138-2790. Offers curriculum and instruction (M Ed, CAGS); early childhood education (M Ed); educational studies (PhD); elementary education (M Ed); individually designed (M Ed); middle school education (M Ed); moderate special needs (M Ed); reading (M Ed, CAGS); science in education (M Ed); severe special needs (M Ed); special needs (CAGS); technology in education (M Ed, CAGS). *Accreditation:* Teacher Education Accreditation Council. Part-time and evening/weekend programs available. Postbaccalaureate distance learning degree programs offered (no on-campus study). *Degree requirements:* For master's, practicum; for doctorate, thesis/dissertation. *Entrance requirements:* For doctorate, GRE General Test or MAT, interview, master's degree, resume; for CAGS, interview, master's degree. Additional exam requirements/recommendations for international students: Required—TOEFL (minimum score 550 paper-based; 213 computer-based; 80 iBT). Electronic applications accepted. *Faculty research:* Assessment in literacy, mathematics and science; autism spectrum disorders; instructional technology and online learning; multicultural education and ELL.

Lewis University, College of Education, Programs in Reading and Literacy, Romeoville, IL 60446. Offers M Ed, MA. Part-time and evening/weekend programs available. In 2009, 13 master's awarded. *Entrance requirements:* For master's, departmental qualifying exam, writing exam, minimum GPA of 2.75, 2 letters of recommendation, interview. Additional exam requirements/recommendations for international students: Required—TOEFL (minimum score 550 paper-based; 213 computer-based). *Application deadline:* For fall admission, 5/1 priority date for international students; for spring admission, 11/15 priority date for international students. Application fee: $40. *Expenses:* Tuition: Full-time $6480; part-time $720 per credit. One-time fee: $40. Tuition and fees vary according to course load, degree level and program. *Financial support:* Scholarships/grants and unspecified assistantships available. Support available to part-time students. Financial award application deadline: 5/1; financial award applicants required to submit FAFSA. *Unit head:* Dr. Deborah Augsburger, Program Director, 815-838-0500 Ext. 5883, E-mail: augsbude@lewisu.edu. *Application contact:* Maggi Pfrommer, Information Contact, 815-838-0500 Ext. 5650.

Reading Education

Liberty University, School of Education, Lynchburg, VA 24502. Offers administration and supervision (M Ed); curriculum and instruction (M Ed); early childhood education (M Ed); education specialist (Ed S); educational leadership (Ed D); elementary education (M Ed); gifted education (M Ed); reading specialist (M Ed); school counseling (M Ed); secondary education (M Ed); special education (M Ed). *Accreditation:* NCATE. Part-time programs available. Postbaccalaureate distance learning degree programs offered (minimal on-campus study). *Degree requirements:* For doctorate, comprehensive exam, thesis/dissertation. *Entrance requirements:* For master's, GRE General Test or MAT (aken in or before 1999), 2 letters of recommendation, minimum undergraduate GPA of 3.0, curriculum vitae; for doctorate, GRE General Test or MAT (if taken before 1999), minimum master's GPA of 3.0, 3 years of teacher experience; for Ed S, GRE General Test or MAT (if taken before 1999), minimum master's GPA of 3.0, 3 years of teaching experience. Additional exam requirements/recommendations for international students: Required—TOEFL (minimum score 600 paper-based; 250 computer-based). Electronic applications accepted. *Expenses:* Contact institution. *Faculty research:* Self-determination, character education, bibliotherapy, learning styles, distance education.

Lincoln University, Graduate Center, Lincoln University, PA 19352. Offers administration (MSA), including finance, human resources management; early childhood education (M Ed); elementary education (M Ed); human services (M Hum Svcs); reading (MSR). Evening/weekend programs available. *Degree requirements:* For master's, thesis. *Entrance requirements:* For master's, 5 years of work experience in human services. *Faculty research:* Gerontology/minority aging, computers in composition instruction.

Long Island University at Riverhead, Education Division, Program in Literacy Education, Riverhead, NY 11901. Offers MS Ed. *Accreditation:* Teacher Education Accreditation Council. Part-time programs available. *Faculty:* 4 full-time, 6 part-time/adjunct. *Students:* 2 full-time (both women), 31 part-time (30 women); includes 1 African American. Average age 30. In 2009, 12 master's awarded. *Degree requirements:* For master's, comprehensive exam. *Entrance requirements:* For master's, minimum undergraduate GPA of 2.75, NYSTC-New York State Provisional or Initial Teacher Certification. Additional exam requirements/recommendations for international students: Required—TOEFL (minimum score 550 paper-based; 250 computer-based). *Application deadline:* Applications are processed on a rolling basis. Electronic applications accepted. *Financial support:* Scholarships/grants and unspecified assistantships available. Support available to part-time students. Financial award applicants required to submit FAFSA. *Unit head:* Dr. Erica Pecorale, Head, 631-287-8010, Fax: 631-287-8253, E-mail: erica.pecorale@liu.edu. *Application contact:* Andrea Borra, Admissions Counselor, 631-287-8010, Fax: 631-287-8253, E-mail: andrea.borra@liu.edu.

Long Island University, Brentwood Campus, School of Education, Brentwood, NY 11717. Offers childhood education (MS); early childhood education (MS); literacy (MS); mental health counseling (MS); school counseling (MS); special education (MS). Part-time and evening/weekend programs available.

Long Island University, Brooklyn Campus, School of Education, Department of Teaching and Learning, Program in Reading, Brooklyn, NY 11201-8423. Offers MS Ed. Part-time and evening/weekend programs available. *Degree requirements:* For master's, thesis optional. *Entrance requirements:* For master's, 2 letters of recommendation. Additional exam requirements/recommendations for international students: Required—TOEFL (minimum score 500 paper-based; 173 computer-based). Electronic applications accepted.

Long Island University, C.W. Post Campus, School of Education, Department of Special Education and Literacy, Brookville, NY 11548-1300. Offers childhood education/literacy (MS); childhood education/special education (MS); literacy (MS Ed); special education (MS Ed). *Accreditation:* Teacher Education Accreditation Council. Part-time and evening/weekend programs available. *Degree requirements:* For master's, research project, comprehensive exam or thesis. *Entrance requirements:* For master's, interview; minimum GPA of 2.75 in major, 2.5 overall. Electronic applications accepted. *Faculty research:* Autism, mainstreaming, robotics and microcomputers in special education, transition from school to work.

Long Island University, Rockland Graduate Campus, Graduate School, Programs in Special Education and Literacy, Orangeburg, NY 10962. Offers childhood/literacy (MS); childhood/special education (MS); literacy (MS Ed); special education (MS Ed); special education autism (MS Ed). Part-time programs available. *Faculty:* 1 (woman) full-time, 10 part-time/adjunct (6 women). *Students:* 30 full-time (25 women), 130 part-time (114 women). In 2009, 81 master's awarded. *Application deadline:* Applications are processed on a rolling basis. Application fee: $30. *Expenses:* Tuition: Part-time $930 per credit. Required fees: $200 per semester. *Financial support:* Applicants required to submit FAFSA. *Unit head:* Prof. Elaine B. Geller, Program Director, 845-359-7200 Ext. 5407, Fax: 845-359-7248, E-mail: elaineb.geller@liu.edu. *Application contact:* Peter S. Reiner, Director of Admissions and Marketing, 845-359-7200, Fax: 845-359-7248, E-mail: peter.reiner@liu.edu.

Long Island University, Westchester Graduate Campus, Programs in Education-Teaching, Program in Literacy Education, Purchase, NY 10577. Offers MS Ed, Advanced Certificate. Part-time and evening/weekend programs available.

Longwood University, Office of Graduate Studies, College of Education and Human Services, Farmville, VA 23909. Offers communication sciences and disorders (MS); community and college counseling (MS); curriculum and instruction specialist-elementary (MS), including mild disabilities, modern languages; curriculum and instruction specialist-secondary (MS), including English, mild disabilities, modern languages; educational leadership (MS); guidance and counseling (MS); literacy and culture (MS); school library media (MS). *Accreditation:* NCATE. Part-time and evening/weekend programs available. *Degree requirements:* For master's, comprehensive exam, thesis optional. *Entrance requirements:* For master's, GRE (communication sciences and disorders), minimum GPA of 2.75. Additional exam requirements/recommendations for international students: Required—TOEFL (minimum score 550 paper-based; 213 computer-based).

Loyola Marymount University, School of Education, Department of Elementary and Secondary Education, Program in Child/Adolescent Literacy, Los Angeles, CA 90045. Offers MA. Part-time and evening/weekend programs available. Postbaccalaureate distance learning degree programs offered (no on-campus study). *Faculty:* 6 full-time (5 women), 11 part-time/adjunct (6 women). *Students:* 21 full-time (all women), 15 part-time (14 women); includes 21 minority (1 African American, 3 Asian Americans or Pacific Islanders, 17 Hispanic Americans). Average age 26. 27 applicants, 78% accepted, 17 enrolled. In 2009, 30 master's awarded. *Degree requirements:* For master's, comprehensive exam. *Entrance requirements:* For master's, CBEST, teaching credentials. Additional exam requirements/recommendations for international students: Required—TOEFL (minimum score 600 paper-based; 250 computer-based; 100 iBT). *Application deadline:* For fall admission, 6/15 for domestic students; for spring admission, 11/15 for domestic students. Application fee: $50. Electronic applications accepted. *Financial support:* In 2009–10, 25 students received support, including 1 research assistantship (averaging $1,440 per year); scholarships/grants and unspecified assistantships also available. Support available to part-time students. Financial award application deadline: 6/15; financial award applicants required to submit FAFSA. *Unit head:* Dr. Irene Oliver, Chair, 310-338-7302, E-mail: ioliver@lmu.edu. *Application contact:* Chake H. Kouyoumjian, Director, Graduate Admissions, 310-338-2721, Fax: 310-338-6086, E-mail: ckouyoum@lmu.edu.

Loyola Marymount University, School of Education, Department of Elementary and Secondary Education, Program in Literacy Education, Los Angeles, CA 90045. Offers MA. Part-time and evening/weekend programs available. *Faculty:* 6 full-time (5 women), 11 part-time/adjunct (6 women). *Students:* 3 full-time (2 women), 1 (woman) part-time; all minorities (2 Asian Americans or Pacific Islanders, 2 Hispanic Americans). Average age 30. 3 applicants, 67% accepted, 2 enrolled. In 2009, 3 master's awarded. *Degree requirements:* For master's, comprehensive exam. *Entrance requirements:* For master's, CBEST. Additional exam requirements/recommendations for international students: Required—TOEFL (minimum score 600 paper-based; 250 computer-based; 100 iBT). *Application deadline:* For fall admission, 6/15 for domestic students; for spring admission, 11/15 for domestic students. Application fee: $50. Electronic applications accepted. *Financial support:* In 2009–10, 3 students received support. Scholarships/grants and unspecified assistantships available. Support available to part-time students. Financial award application deadline: 6/15; financial award applicants required to submit FAFSA. *Unit head:* Dr. Irene Oliver, Chair, 310-338-7302, E-mail: ioliver@lmu.edu. *Application contact:* Chake H. Kouyoumjian, Director, Graduate Admissions, 310-338-2721, Fax: 310-338-6086, E-mail: ckouyoum@lmu.edu.

Loyola Marymount University, School of Education, Department of Elementary and Secondary Education, Program in Literacy/Language Arts, Los Angeles, CA 90045. Offers MA. Part-time and evening/weekend programs available. *Faculty:* 6 full-time (5 women), 11 part-time/adjunct (6 women). *Students:* 24 full-time (23 women), 4 part-time (all women); includes 13 minority (2 African Americans, 3 Asian Americans or Pacific Islanders, 8 Hispanic Americans). Average age 28. 6 applicants, 67% accepted, 4 enrolled. In 2009, 10 master's awarded. *Degree requirements:* For master's, comprehensive exam. *Entrance requirements:* For master's, CBEST, CSET, 3 letters of recommendation. Additional exam requirements/recommendations for international students: Required—TOEFL (minimum score 600 paper-based; 250 computer-based; 100 iBT). *Application deadline:* For fall admission, 6/15 for domestic students; for spring admission, 11/15 for domestic students. Application fee: $50. Electronic applications accepted. *Financial support:* In 2009–10, 13 students received support. Scholarships/grants and unspecified assistantships available. Support available to part-time students. Financial award application deadline: 6/15; financial award applicants required to submit FAFSA. *Unit head:* Dr. Irene Oliver, Chair, 310-338-7302, E-mail: ioliver@lmu.edu. *Application contact:* Chake H. Kouyoumjian, Director, Graduate Admissions, 310-338-2721, Fax: 310-338-6086, E-mail: ckouyoum@lmu.edu.

Loyola University Chicago, School of Education, Program in Initial Teacher Preparation, Chicago, IL 60660. Offers elementary education (M Ed); math education (M Ed); reading specialist (M Ed); school technology (M Ed); science education (M Ed); secondary education (M Ed); special education (M Ed). *Accreditation:* NCATE. *Faculty:* 12 full-time (9 women), 12 part-time/adjunct (6 women). *Students:* 154. Average age 28. 125 applicants, 69% accepted, 38 enrolled. In 2009, 89 master's awarded. *Degree requirements:* For master's, comprehensive exam. *Entrance requirements:* For master's, Illinois Basic Skills Test, 3 letters of recommendation, minimum GPA of 3.0, resume. Additional exam requirements/recommendations for international students: Required—TOEFL (minimum score 550 paper-based; 213 computer-based; 79 iBT). *Application deadline:* For fall admission, 7/1 priority date for domestic and international students; for spring admission, 11/1 priority date for domestic and international students. Applications are processed on a rolling basis. Application fee: $50. Electronic applications accepted. *Expenses:* Tuition: Full-time $14,220; part-time $790 per credit hour. Required fees: $60 per semester hour. Tuition and fees vary according to program. *Financial support:* In 2009–10, 1 research assistantship with full tuition reimbursement (averaging $8,500 per year), 1 teaching assistantship were awarded. Financial award application deadline: 2/15. *Faculty research:* Positive behavior support, school reform, school improvement. *Unit head:* Dr. Dorothy Giroux, Director, 312-915-7027, E-mail: dgiroux@luc.edu. *Application contact:* Marie Rosin-Dittmar, Information Contact, 312-915-6800, E-mail: schleduc@luc.edu.

Loyola University Maryland, Graduate Programs, College of Arts and Sciences, Department of Education, Program in Reading, Baltimore, MD 21210-2699. Offers M Ed, CAS. *Accreditation:* NCATE. Part-time and evening/weekend programs available. *Entrance requirements:* For master's and CAS, GRE General Test, GRE Subject Test (recommended). Additional exam requirements/recommendations for international students: Required—TOEFL (minimum score 550 paper-based; 213 computer-based).

Lynchburg College, Graduate Studies, School of Education and Human Development, Lynchburg, VA 24501-3199. Offers community counseling (M Ed); counselor education (M Ed), including community counseling; curriculum and instruction (M Ed); educational leadership (M Ed); English education (M Ed); reading (M Ed); school counseling (M Ed); science education (M Ed); special education (M Ed), including autism spectrum disorder, early childhood special education, mental retardation, teaching children with learning disabilities, teaching the emotionally disturbed. Part-time and evening/weekend programs available. *Degree requirements:* For master's, comprehensive exam. *Entrance requirements:* For master's, GRE, minimum undergraduate GPA of 3.0. Additional exam requirements/recommendations for international students: Required—TOEFL. *Expenses:* Tuition: Full-time $7020; part-time $390 per credit hour.

Lyndon State College, Graduate Programs in Education, Department of Education, Lyndonville, VT 05851-0919. Offers curriculum and instruction (M Ed); reading specialist (M Ed); special education (M Ed); teaching and counseling (M Ed). Part-time and evening/weekend programs available. *Degree requirements:* For master's, exam or major field project. *Entrance requirements:* Additional exam requirements/recommendations for international students: Recommended—TOEFL (minimum score 500 paper-based; 173 computer-based).

Madonna University, Programs in Education, Livonia, MI 48150-1173. Offers Catholic school leadership (MSA); educational leadership (MSA); learning disabilities (MAT); literacy education (MAT); teaching and learning (MAT). *Accreditation:* NCATE. Part-time and evening/weekend programs available. *Degree requirements:* For master's, thesis or alternative. Electronic applications accepted.

Malone University, Graduate Program in Education, Canton, OH 44709. Offers curriculum and instruction (MA); curriculum, instruction, and professional development (MA); instructional technology (MA); intervention specialist (MA); reading (MA). Part-time and evening/weekend programs available. *Faculty:* 7 full-time (4 women), 7 part-time/adjunct (5 women). *Students:* 2 full-time (1 woman), 64 part-time (55 women); includes 1 minority (African American). Average age 34. In 2009, 27 master's awarded. *Degree requirements:* For master's, research project. *Entrance requirements:* For master's, minimum GPA of 3.0, teaching license. Additional exam requirements/recommendations for international students: Required—TOEFL (minimum score 550 paper-based; 213 computer-based; 79 iBT). *Application deadline:* Applications are processed on a rolling basis. Application fee: $25. *Expenses:* Tuition: Part-time $450 per semester hour. *Financial support:* Tuition waivers (partial) available. Support available to part-time students. Financial award application deadline: 6/30. *Faculty research:* The Bible as children's literature, special needs students and literacy development, middle level education, school/university partnerships and professional development, child/adolescent literature and popular culture. *Unit head:* Dr. Alice E. Christie, Director, 330-478-8541, Fax: 330-471-8563, E-mail: achristie@malone.edu. *Application contact:* David L. Kleffman, Assistant Director of Enrollment, 330-471-8447, Fax: 330-471-8343, E-mail: dkleffman@malone.edu.

Manhattanville College, Graduate Programs, School of Education, Program in Early Childhood Education, Purchase, NY 10577-2132. Offers childhood and early childhood education (MAT); early childhood education (birth-grade 2) (MAT); literacy (birth-grade 6) (MPS), including reading, writing; literacy (birth-grade 6) and special education (grades 1-6) (MPS); special education (birth-grade 2) (MPS); special education (birth-grade 6) (MPS). Part-time and evening/weekend programs available. *Students:* 43 full-time (42 women), 62 part-time (59 women); includes 1 African American, 1 Asian American or Pacific Islander, 7 Hispanic Americans. In 2009, 5 master's awarded. *Degree requirements:* For master's, comprehensive exam or research project, field experience. *Entrance requirements:* For master's, minimum undergraduate GPA of 3.0, 2 letters of recommendation. Additional exam requirements/recommendations for international students: Required—TOEFL. *Application deadline:* Applications are processed on a rolling basis. Application fee: $70. Electronic applications accepted. *Financial support:* Career-related internships or fieldwork and institutionally sponsored loans available. Support available to part-time students. *Unit head:* Dr. Shelley Wepner, Dean, 914-323-5192, Fax: 914-694-2386, E-mail: wepners@mville.edu. *Application contact:* Jeanine Pardey-Levine, Director of Admissions, 914-323-3208, Fax: 914-694-1732, E-mail: edschool@mville.edu.

Manhattanville College, Graduate Programs, School of Education, Program in Middle Childhood/Adolescence Education (Grades 5-12), Purchase, NY 10577-2132. Offers biology (MAT); biology and special education (MPS); chemistry (MAT); chemistry and special education

(MPS); English (MAT); English and special education (MPS); literacy (MPS), including reading and writing, writing; literacy and special education (MPS); math (MAT); math and special education (MPS); second language (MAT), including French, Italian, Latin, Spanish; social studies (MAT); social studies and special education (MPS); special education (MPS). Part-time and evening/weekend programs available. *Students:* 52 full-time (39 women), 106 part-time (71 women); includes 8 African Americans, 3 Asian Americans or Pacific Islanders, 4 Hispanic Americans, 1 international. In 2009, 82 master's awarded. *Degree requirements:* For master's, comprehensive exam or research project, field experience. *Entrance requirements:* For master's, minimum undergraduate GPA of 3.0, 2 letters of recommendation. Additional exam requirements/recommendations for international students: Required—TOEFL. *Application deadline:* Applications are processed on a rolling basis. Application fee: $70. Electronic applications accepted. *Financial support:* Career-related internships or fieldwork, Federal Work-Study, institutionally sponsored loans, and unspecified assistantships available. Support available to part-time students. Financial award application deadline: 3/1; financial award applicants required to submit FAFSA. *Unit head:* Dr. Shelley Wepner, Dean, 914-323-5192, Fax: 914-694-2386, E-mail: wepners@mville.edu. *Application contact:* Jeanine Pardey-Levine, Director of Admissions, 914-323-3208, Fax: 914-694-1732, E-mail: edschool@mville.edu.

Marshall University, Academic Affairs Division, Graduate School of Education and Professional Development, Program in Reading Education, Huntington, WV 25755. Offers MA, Ed S. *Accreditation:* NCATE. Part-time and evening/weekend programs available. *Faculty:* 3 full-time (1 woman), 22 part-time/adjunct (18 women). *Students:* 18 full-time (16 women), 129 part-time (124 women); includes 2 minority (1 African American, 1 American Indian/Alaska Native). Average age 35. In 2009, 39 master's awarded. *Degree requirements:* For master's, thesis optional, comprehensive or oral assessment, final project; for Ed S, thesis optional, research project. *Entrance requirements:* For master's, GRE General Test or MAT; for Ed S, master's degree in reading, minimum GPA of 3.0. Application fee: $40. *Financial support:* Federal Work-Study, tuition waivers (full and partial), and unspecified assistantships available. Support available to part-time students. Financial award applicants required to submit FAFSA. *Unit head:* Dr. Barbara O'Byrne, Program Director, 304-746-1986, E-mail: bobyrne@marshall.edu. *Application contact:* Information Contact, 304-746-1900, Fax: 304-746-1902, E-mail: services@marshall.edu.

Marygrove College, Graduate Division, Program in Reading and Literacy, Detroit, MI 48221-2599. Offers M Ed. Part-time and evening/weekend programs available. *Degree requirements:* For master's, practicum, research project. *Entrance requirements:* For master's, MAT, interview, minimum undergraduate GPA of 3.0, teaching certificate.

Maryville University of Saint Louis, School of Education, St. Louis, MO 63141-7299. Offers art education (MA Ed); early childhood education (MA Ed); educational leadership (Ed D); educational leadership: principal certification (MA Ed); elementary education (MA Ed); elementary education/English (MA Ed); elementary education/psychology (MA Ed); environmental education (MA Ed); gifted education (MA Ed); literacy specialist (MA Ed); middle grades education (MA Ed); secondary teaching and inquiry (MA Ed); teacher as leader (MA Ed). *Accreditation:* NASAD; NCATE. Part-time and evening/weekend programs available. *Students:* 25 full-time (18 women), 198 part-time (145 women); includes 33 minority (27 African Americans, 2 American Indian/Alaska Native, 1 Asian American or Pacific Islander, 3 Hispanic Americans). Average age 36. In 2009, 61 master's, 45 doctorates awarded. *Degree requirements:* For master's, thesis, project. *Entrance requirements:* For master's and doctorate, minimum GPA of 3.0, 3 professional recommendations. Additional exam requirements/recommendations for international students: Required—TOEFL (minimum score 550 paper-based). *Application deadline:* Applications are processed on a rolling basis. Application fee: $40 ($60 for international students). Electronic applications accepted. *Expenses:* Tuition: Full-time $20,384; part-time $627.50 per credit hour. Required fees: $100 per semester. *Financial support:* Career-related internships or fieldwork, Federal Work-Study, tuition waivers (partial), and professional educator discounts available. Financial award application deadline: 3/1; financial award applicants required to submit FAFSA. *Faculty research:* Collaboration with public schools, pre-service program development, mathematics, diversity, literacy. *Unit head:* Dr. Sam Hausfather, Dean, 314-529-9466, Fax: 314-529-9921, E-mail: shausfather@maryville.edu. *Application contact:* Holly Stanwich, Graduate Admissions Coordinator, 314-529-9542, Fax: 314-529-9921, E-mail: teachered@maryville.edu.

Marywood University, Academic Affairs, Reap College of Education and Human Development, Department of Education, Program in Reading Education, Scranton, PA 18509-1598. Offers MS. *Accreditation:* NCATE. *Students:* 22 part-time (21 women). Average age 32. 4 applicants, 100% accepted. In 2009, 12 master's awarded. *Entrance requirements:* Additional exam requirements/recommendations for international students: Required—TOEFL (minimum score 550 paper-based; 213 computer-based; 79 iBT). *Application deadline:* For fall admission, 4/1 priority date for domestic students, 3/31 priority date for international students; for spring admission, 11/1 priority date for domestic students, 8/31 priority date for international students. Applications are processed on a rolling basis. Application fee: $30. Electronic applications accepted. *Expenses:* Tuition: Part-time $715 per credit. Required fees: $270 per semester. Tuition and fees vary according to degree level, campus/location and program. *Financial support:* Career-related internships or fieldwork, scholarships/grants, and unspecified assistantships available. Support available to part-time students. Financial award application deadline: 6/30; financial award applicants required to submit FAFSA. *Faculty research:* Design of school reading programs, whole language. *Application contact:* Tammy Manka, Assistant Director of Graduate Admissions, 866-279-9663, E-mail: tmanka@marywood.edu.

Massachusetts College of Liberal Arts, Program in Education, North Adams, MA 01247-4100. Offers curriculum (M Ed); educational administration (M Ed); reading (M Ed); special education (M Ed). Part-time and evening/weekend programs available. *Degree requirements:* For master's, thesis. *Entrance requirements:* For master's, writing sample. *Faculty research:* Anxiety, methodology, mainstreaming.

McDaniel College, Graduate and Professional Studies, Program in Reading Education, Westminster, MD 21157-4390. Offers MS. *Accreditation:* NCATE. Part-time and evening/weekend programs available. *Degree requirements:* For master's, comprehensive exam, thesis optional. *Entrance requirements:* For master's, GRE General Test, MAT, or NTE/PRAXIS I, letters of reference (3). Additional exam requirements/recommendations for international students: Required—TOEFL (minimum score 213 computer-based). *Expenses:* Tuition: Part-time $325 per credit hour.

Medaille College, Program in Education, Buffalo, NY 14214-2695. Offers adolescent education (MS Ed); curriculum and instruction (MS Ed); education preparation (MS Ed); literacy (MS Ed); special education (MS). *Accreditation:* Teacher Education Accreditation Council. Part-time and evening/weekend programs available. *Faculty:* 22 full-time (16 women), 47 part-time/adjunct (36 women). *Students:* 721 full-time (596 women), 2 part-time (both women); includes 34 minority (16 African Americans, 1 American Indian/Alaska Native, 14 Asian Americans or Pacific Islanders, 3 Hispanic Americans). Average age 26. 621 applicants, 46% accepted, 288 enrolled. In 2009, 608 master's awarded. *Degree requirements:* For master's, thesis or alternative. *Entrance requirements:* For master's, minimum undergraduate GPA of 2.7. Additional exam requirements/recommendations for international students: Required—TOEFL (minimum score 550 paper-based; 213 computer-based). *Application deadline:* For fall admission, 8/15 priority date for domestic students; for spring admission, 1/15 priority date for domestic students. Applications are processed on a rolling basis. Application fee: $35. Electronic applications accepted. *Financial support:* In 2009–10, 501 students received support. Federal Work-Study available. Financial award applicants required to submit FAFSA. *Faculty research:* Curriculum planning, truancy, tracking minority students, curriculum design, mentoring students. *Unit head:* Dr. Robert DiSibio, Director of Graduate Programs, 716-932-2548, Fax: 716-631-1380, E-mail: rdisibio@medaille.edu. *Application contact:* Jacqueline Matheny, Executive Director of Marketing and Enrollment, 716-932-2541, Fax: 716-632-1811, E-mail: jmatheny@medaille.edu.

Mercer University, Graduate Studies, Cecil B. Day Campus, Tift College of Education (Atlanta), Macon, GA 31207-0003. Offers curriculum and instruction (PhD); early childhood education (M Ed, MAT); educational leadership (PhD, Ed S); middle grades education (M Ed, MAT); reading education (M Ed); secondary education (M Ed, MAT); teacher leadership (Ed S). *Accreditation:* NCATE. Part-time and evening/weekend programs available. *Faculty:* 27 full-time (14 women), 6 part-time/adjunct (3 women). *Students:* 302 full-time (251 women), 543 part-time (430 women); includes 334 minority (311 African Americans, 1 American Indian/Alaska Native, 21 Asian Americans or Pacific Islanders, 1 Hispanic American), 7 international. Average age 34. In 2009, 195 master's, 20 doctorates awarded. *Degree requirements:* For master's and Ed S, research project; for doctorate, thesis/dissertation. *Entrance requirements:* For master's, GRE or MAT, minimum undergraduate GPA of 2.75; for doctorate, GRE; for Ed S, GRE or MAT, minimum GPA of 3.25, 3 years of teaching experience. Additional exam requirements/recommendations for international students: Required—TOEFL. *Application deadline:* For fall admission, 8/1 for domestic and international students; for spring admission, 12/1 for domestic and international students. Applications are processed on a rolling basis. Application fee: $25. *Expenses:* Contact institution. *Financial support:* Federal Work-Study available. Support available to part-time students. Financial award application deadline: 5/1. *Faculty research:* Educational computing, content area reading, concept learning, importance of play for young children, multicultural literature. *Unit head:* Dr. Carl R. Martray, Dean, 478-301-5397, Fax: 478-301-2280, E-mail: martray_cr@mercer.edu. *Application contact:* Dr. Allison Gilmore, Associate Dean for Graduate Teacher Education, 678-547-6330, Fax: 678-547-6055, E-mail: gilmore_a@mercer.edu.

Mercy College, School of Education, Program in Teaching Literacy, Birth-6, Dobbs Ferry, NY 10522. Offers MS. Part-time and evening/weekend programs available. *Students:* 34 full-time (32 women), 82 part-time (73 women); includes 28 minority (7 African Americans, 1 American Indian/Alaska Native, 2 Asian Americans or Pacific Islanders, 18 Hispanic Americans). Average age 31. 35 applicants, 71% accepted, 17 enrolled. In 2009, 103 master's awarded. *Entrance requirements:* For master's, resume, interview by faculty advisor and/or program director. Additional exam requirements/recommendations for international students: Required—TOEFL (minimum score 600 paper-based; 250 computer-based; 100 iBT). *Application deadline:* For fall admission, 8/1 for international students. Applications are processed on a rolling basis. Application fee: $40. Electronic applications accepted. *Expenses:* Tuition: Full-time $13,158; part-time $731 per credit. Required fees: $500. Tuition and fees vary according to degree level and program. *Financial support:* In 2009–10, 2 students received support. Career-related internships or fieldwork, Federal Work-Study, scholarships/grants, and unspecified assistantships available. Support available to part-time students. Financial award applicants required to submit FAFSA. *Faculty research:* Linguistics, literacy. *Unit head:* Dr. Andrew Peiser, Chairperson, 914-674-7489, Fax: 914-674-7352, E-mail: apeiser@mercy.edu. *Application contact:* Mary Ellen Hoffman, Director, Graduate Education Programs, 914-674-7334, E-mail: mhoffman@mercy.edu.

Mercy College, School of Education, Program in Teaching Literacy/Birth-Grade 12, Dobbs Ferry, NY 10522-1189. Offers MS. Part-time and evening/weekend programs available. *Students:* 2 full-time (both women), 16 part-time (13 women); includes 2 minority (1 African American, 1 Hispanic American). Average age 33. 8 applicants, 100% accepted, 6 enrolled. *Entrance requirements:* Additional exam requirements/recommendations for international students: Required—TOEFL (minimum score 600 paper-based; 250 computer-based; 100 iBT). *Application deadline:* For fall admission, 8/1 for international students. Applications are processed on a rolling basis. Application fee: $40. Electronic applications accepted. *Expenses:* Tuition: Full-time $13,158; part-time $731 per credit. Required fees: $500. Tuition and fees vary according to degree level and program. *Faculty research:* Linguistics, literacy. *Unit head:* Dr. Andrew Peiser, Chairperson, 914-674-7489, Fax: 914-674-7352, E-mail: apeiser@mercy.edu. *Application contact:* Mary Ellen Hoffman, Director, Graduate Education Programs, 914-674-7334, E-mail: mhoffman@mercy.edu.

Mercy College, School of Education, Program in Teaching Literacy/Grades 5-12, Dobbs Ferry, NY 10522-1189. Offers MS. Part-time and evening/weekend programs available. *Students:* 1 (woman) full-time, 19 part-time (14 women); includes 3 minority (1 American Indian/Alaska Native, 2 Hispanic Americans). Average age 30. 9 applicants, 67% accepted, 4 enrolled. In 2009, 13 master's awarded. *Entrance requirements:* Additional exam requirements/recommendations for international students: Required—TOEFL (minimum score 600 paper-based; 250 computer-based; 100 iBT). *Application deadline:* For fall admission, 8/1 for international students. Applications are processed on a rolling basis. Application fee: $40. Electronic applications accepted. *Expenses:* Tuition: Full-time $13,158; part-time $731 per credit. Required fees: $500. Tuition and fees vary according to degree level and program. *Faculty research:* Linguistics, literacy. *Unit head:* Dr. Andrew Peiser, Chairperson, 914-674-7489, Fax: 914-674-7352, E-mail: aperiser@mercy.edu. *Application contact:* Mary Ellen Hoffman, Director, Graduate Education Programs, 914-674-7334, E-mail: mhoffman@mercy.edu.

MGH Institute of Health Professions, Graduate Programs, School of Health and Rehabilitation Sciences, Department of Communication Sciences and Disorders, Boston, MA 02129. Offers reading (Certificate); speech-language pathology (MS). *Accreditation:* ASHA (one or more programs are accredited). Part-time programs available. *Faculty:* 12 full-time (9 women), 3 part-time/adjunct (all women). *Students:* 101 full-time (98 women), 21 part-time (20 women); includes 12 minority (2 African Americans, 6 Asian Americans or Pacific Islanders, 4 Hispanic Americans). Average age 29. 295 applicants, 48% accepted, 68 enrolled. In 2009, 41 master's, 11 other advanced degrees awarded. *Degree requirements:* For master's, thesis or alternative, research proposal. *Entrance requirements:* For master's, GRE General Test. Additional exam requirements/recommendations for international students: Required—TOEFL (minimum score 550 paper-based; 213 computer-based; 80 iBT). *Application deadline:* For fall admission, 1/28 for domestic and international students. Application fee: $50. Electronic applications accepted. *Expenses:* Tuition: Part-time $943 per credit. Required fees: $943 per credit. Tuition and fees vary according to course load. *Financial support:* In 2009–10, 84 students received support; research assistantships, teaching assistantships, career-related internships or fieldwork, scholarships/grants, tuition waivers (full and partial), and unspecified assistantships available. Support available to part-time students. Financial award application deadline: 3/1; financial award applicants required to submit FAFSA. *Faculty research:* Children's language disorders, reading, speech disorders, voice disorders, augmentative communication, autism. *Unit head:* Dr. Gregory L. Lof, Department Chair, 617-724-6313, E-mail: glot@mghihp.edu. *Application contact:* Maureen Rika Judd, Manager of Admissions, 617-726-6069, Fax: 617-726-8010, E-mail: admissions@mghihp.edu.

Miami University, Graduate School, School of Education and Allied Professions, Department of Teacher Education, Oxford, OH 45056. Offers elementary education (M Ed, MAT); reading education (M Ed); secondary education (M Ed, MAT), including adolescent education (MAT), elementary mathematics education (M Ed), secondary education. Part-time programs available. *Students:* 48 full-time (31 women), 70 part-time (60 women); includes 6 minority (3 African Americans, 3 Hispanic Americans), 5 international. *Entrance requirements:* For master's, GRE (MAT), minimum undergraduate GPA of 3.0 during previous 2 years or 2.75 overall. Application fee: $50. *Expenses:* Tuition, state resident: full-time $11,280. Tuition, nonresident: full-time $24,912. Required fees: $516. *Financial support:* Fellowships with full tuition reimbursements, research assistantships, teaching assistantships, career-related internships or fieldwork, Federal Work-Study, scholarships/grants, health care benefits, tuition waivers (full), and unspecified assistantships available. Financial award application deadline: 3/1. *Unit head:* Dr. James Shiveley, Chair, 513-529-6443, Fax: 513-529-4931, E-mail: shiveljm@muohio.edu. *Application contact:* Dr. Iris Johnson, Assistant Chair and Graduate Coordinator, 513-529-6443, Fax: 513-529-4931, E-mail: johnsoid@muohio.edu.

Michigan State University, The Graduate School, College of Education, Program in Literacy Instruction, East Lansing, MI 48824. Offers MA. *Accreditation:* Teacher Education Accreditation Council. Part-time programs available. *Students:* 29 part-time (27 women); includes 2 minority (both African Americans). Average age 29. 18 applicants, 78% accepted. In 2009, 23 master's awarded. *Degree requirements:* For master's, comprehensive exam (for some programs), final

Reading Education

Michigan State University (continued)
exam or portfolio. *Entrance requirements:* Additional exam requirements/recommendations for international students: Required—TOEFL, Michigan State University ELT (minimum score 85), Michigan Michigan English Language Assessment Battery (minimum score 83). Electronic applications accepted. *Expenses:* Tuition, state resident: part-time $478.25 per credit hour. Tuition, nonresident: part-time $966.50 per credit hour. Part-time tuition and fees vary according to program. *Unit head:* Dr. Douglas Hartman, Literacy Coordinator, 517-432-9603, Fax: 517-432-5092, E-mail: dhartman@msu.edu. *Application contact:* Linda Brandau, Program Secretary, 517-432-7705, Fax: 517-432-5092, E-mail: malit@msu.edu.

Middle Tennessee State University, College of Graduate Studies, College of Education and Behavioral Science, Department of Elementary and Special Education, Major in Reading, Murfreesboro, TN 37132. Offers M Ed. *Accreditation:* NCATE. Part-time and evening/weekend programs available. Postbaccalaureate distance learning degree programs offered. *Students:* 1 (woman) full-time, 18 part-time (all women). 11 applicants, 100% accepted, 11 enrolled. In 2009, 8 master's awarded. *Degree requirements:* For master's, comprehensive exam. *Entrance requirements:* For master's, GRE, MAT or PRAXIS. Additional exam requirements/recommendations for international students: Required—TOEFL (minimum score 525 paper-based; 195 computer-based; 71 iBT) or IELTS (minimum score 6). *Application deadline:* For fall admission, 6/1 for domestic and international students. Applications are processed on a rolling basis. Application fee: $25 ($30 for international students). Electronic applications accepted. *Expenses:* Tuition, state resident: full-time $4404. Tuition, nonresident: full-time $10,956. *Financial support:* Application deadline: 5/1. *Unit head:* Dr. Connie Jones, Chair, 615-898-2680, Fax: 615-898-5309, E-mail: cojones@mtsu.edu. *Application contact:* Dr. Michael Allen, Dean and Vice Provost for Research, 615-898-2840, Fax: 615-904-8020, E-mail: mallen@mtsu.edu.

Middle Tennessee State University, College of Graduate Studies, College of Education and Behavioral Science, PhD in Literacy Studies Program, Murfreesboro, TN 37132. Offers PhD. Part-time and evening/weekend programs available. Postbaccalaureate distance learning degree programs offered. *Faculty:* 1 full-time (0 women), 2 part-time/adjunct (both women). *Students:* 1 (woman) full-time, 9 part-time (8 women). Average age 33. 10 applicants, 60% accepted, 6 enrolled. *Degree requirements:* For doctorate, comprehensive exam, thesis/dissertation. *Entrance requirements:* For doctorate, GRE. Additional exam requirements/recommendations for international students: Required—TOEFL (minimum score 525 paper-based; 195 computer-based; 71 iBT) or IELTS (minimum score 6). *Application deadline:* For fall admission, 6/1 for domestic and international students. Applications are processed on a rolling basis. Application fee: $25 ($30 for international students). *Expenses:* Tuition, state resident: full-time $4404. Tuition, nonresident: full-time $10,956. *Financial support:* In 2009–10, 3 students received support. Institutionally sponsored loans available. Support available to part-time students. Financial award application deadline: 5/1. *Unit head:* Dr. Diane Sawyer, Chair, 615-898-5642. *Application contact:* Dr. Michael Allen, Dean and Vice Provost for Research, 615-898-2840, Fax: 615-904-8020, E-mail: mallen@mtsu.edu.

Midwestern State University, Graduate Studies, College of Education, Program in Reading Education, Wichita Falls, TX 76308. Offers M Ed. Part-time and evening/weekend programs available. *Degree requirements:* For master's, comprehensive exam. *Entrance requirements:* For master's, GRE General Test, MAT or GMAT. Additional exam requirements/recommendations for international students: Required—TOEFL (minimum score 550 paper-based; 213 computer-based). Electronic applications accepted. *Expenses:* Tuition, state resident: full-time $1620; part-time $90 per credit hour. Tuition, nonresident: full-time $2160; part-time $120 per credit hour. International tuition: $7506 full-time. Required fees: $3068.80; $145.60 per credit hour. $179 per semester.

Millersville University of Pennsylvania, College of Graduate and Professional Studies, School of Education, Department of Elementary and Early Childhood Education, Program in Language and Literacy Education, Millersville, PA 17551-0302. Offers M Ed. *Accreditation:* NCATE. Part-time and evening/weekend programs available. *Faculty:* 18 full-time (14 women), 15 part-time/adjunct (7 women). *Students:* 89 part-time (86 women); includes 1 minority (Asian American or Pacific Islander). Average age 30. 11 applicants, 100% accepted, 9 enrolled. In 2009, 28 master's awarded. *Degree requirements:* For master's, thesis optional. *Entrance requirements:* For master's, GRE or MAT, 3 letters of recommendation, copy of teaching certificate. Additional exam requirements/recommendations for international students: Required—TOEFL (minimum score 500 paper-based; 183 computer-based; 65 iBT) or IELTS (minimum score 6). *Application deadline:* For fall admission, 1/15 priority date for domestic and international students; for winter admission, 10/1 priority date for domestic and international students; for spring admission, 10/1 priority date for domestic and international students. Applications are processed on a rolling basis. Application fee: $40 ($50 for international students). Electronic applications accepted. *Expenses:* Tuition, state resident: full-time $6666; part-time $370 per credit. Tuition, nonresident: full-time $10,666; part-time $593 per credit. Required fees: $1578.50; $76.25 per credit. One-time fee: $60 part-time. Tuition and fees vary according to course load. *Financial support:* In 2009–10, 3 students received support, including 3 research assistantships with full tuition reimbursements available (averaging $5,000 per year); institutionally sponsored loans and unspecified assistantships also available. Support available to part-time students. Financial award application deadline: 3/15; financial award applicants required to submit FAFSA. *Faculty research:* Integration of technology and literacy, ethnographic teacher research, literacy coaching, content area literacy, emergent/early literacy. *Unit head:* Dr. Mary Ann C. Gray-Schlegel, Coordinator, 717-872-3397, Fax: 717-871-5462, E-mail: maryann.gray-schlegel@millersville.edu. *Application contact:* Dr. Victor S. DeSantis, Dean of Graduate and Professional Studies, 717-872-3099, Fax: 717-872-3453, E-mail: victor.desantis@millersville.edu.

Minnesota State University Moorhead, Graduate Studies, College of Education and Human Services, Program in Reading, Moorhead, MN 56563-0002. Offers MS. *Accreditation:* NCATE. Part-time and evening/weekend programs available. *Degree requirements:* For master's, comprehensive exam, final oral exam, project or thesis. *Entrance requirements:* For master's, MAT, minimum GPA of 2.75, 2 years of teaching experience. Additional exam requirements/recommendations for international students: Required—TOEFL (minimum score 550 paper-based; 213 computer-based). Electronic applications accepted.

Missouri State University, Graduate College, College of Education, Department of Reading, Foundations, and Technology, Program in Reading Education, Springfield, MO 65897. Offers reading (MS Ed). Part-time programs available. *Students:* 8 full-time (7 women), 51 part-time (50 women). Average age 34. 16 applicants, 100% accepted, 11 enrolled. In 2009, 16 master's awarded. *Degree requirements:* For master's, comprehensive exam, thesis or alternative. *Entrance requirements:* For master's, GRE or minimum GPA of 3.0, teaching certificate. Additional exam requirements/recommendations for international students: Required—TOEFL (minimum score 550 paper-based; 213 computer-based; 79 iBT). *Application deadline:* For fall admission, 7/20 priority date for domestic students, 5/1 for international students; for spring admission, 12/20 for domestic students, 9/1 for international students. Applications are processed on a rolling basis. Application fee: $35 ($50 for international students). Electronic applications accepted. *Expenses:* Tuition, state resident: full-time $3852; part-time $214 per credit hour. Tuition, nonresident: full-time $7524; part-time $418 per credit hour. Required fees: $696; $172 per semester. Tuition and fees vary according to course level, course load, degree level and program. *Financial support:* Federal Work-Study, institutionally sponsored loans, scholarships/grants, and unspecified assistantships available. Financial award application deadline: 3/31; financial award applicants required to submit FAFSA. *Unit head:* Dr. Deanne Camp, Graduate Program Director, 417-836-6983, E-mail: deannecamp@missouristate.edu. *Application contact:* Eric Eckert, Coordinator of Graduate Admissions and Recruitment, 417-836-5331, Fax: 417-836-6200, E-mail: ericeckert@missouristate.edu.

Monmouth University, Graduate School, School of Education, West Long Branch, NJ 07764-1898. Offers education (M Ed); initial certification (MAT), including elementary level, K-12, secondary level; learning disabilities-teacher consultant (Certificate); principal (MS Ed); principal/school administrator (MS Ed); reading specialist (MS Ed, Certificate); school counseling (MS Ed); special education (MS Ed), including autism, learning disabilities teacher consultant, teacher of students with disabilities, teaching in inclusive settings; supervisor (Certificate); teacher of the handicapped (Certificate); teaching english to speakers of other languages (TESOL) (Certificate). *Accreditation:* NCATE. Part-time and evening/weekend programs available. *Faculty:* 20 full-time (13 women), 32 part-time/adjunct (22 women). *Students:* 182 full-time (146 women), 353 part-time (286 women); includes 40 minority (15 African Americans, 3 American Indian/Alaska Native, 5 Asian Americans or Pacific Islanders, 17 Hispanic Americans), 1 international. Average age 29. 361 applicants, 96% accepted, 176 enrolled. In 2009, 178 master's awarded. *Entrance requirements:* For master's, minimum GPA of 3.0 in major, 2.75 overall; 2 letters of recommendation (for some programs). Additional exam requirements/recommendations for international students: Required—TOEFL (minimum score 550 paper-based; 213 computer-based; 79 iBT), IELTS (minimum score 5), Michigan English Language Assessment Battery (minimum score 77), Cambridge A, B, C. *Application deadline:* For fall admission, 7/15 priority date for domestic students, 7/1 for international students; for spring admission, 11/15 priority date for domestic students, 11/1 for international students. Applications are processed on a rolling basis. Application fee: $50. Electronic applications accepted. *Expenses:* Tuition: Part-time $773 per credit. Required fees: $157 per semester. *Financial support:* In 2009–10, 326 students received support, including 211 fellowships (averaging $1,824 per year), 23 research assistantships (averaging $7,943 per year); career-related internships or fieldwork, scholarships/grants, and unspecified assistantships also available. Support available to part-time students. Financial award applicants required to submit FAFSA. *Faculty research:* Multicultural literacy, science and mathematics teaching strategies, teacher as reflective practitioner, children with disabilities, varied contexts of learning. *Unit head:* Dr. Terri Rothman, Associate Dean, 732-571-7507, Fax: 732-263-5277, E-mail: trothman@monmouth.edu. *Application contact:* Kevin Roane, Director, Office of Graduate Admission, 732-571-3452, Fax: 732-263-5123, E-mail: gradadm@monmouth.edu.

Montana State University Billings, College of Education, Department of Special Education, Counseling, Reading and Early Childhood, Option in Reading, Billings, MT 59101-0298. Offers M Ed. *Accreditation:* NCATE. Part-time programs available. *Degree requirements:* For master's, thesis or professional paper and/or field experience. *Entrance requirements:* For master's, GRE General Test or MAT, minimum GPA of 3.0 (undergraduate), 3.25 (graduate).

Montclair State University, The Graduate School, College of Education and Human Services, Department of Early Childhood, Elementary and Literacy Education, Montclair, NJ 07043-1624. Offers early childhood education and teaching students with disabilities (MAT); early childhood special education (M Ed, Certificate); early childhood/elementary education (M Ed); elementary education with disabilities (MAT); elementary school teacher (Certificate); learning disabilities (Certificate); reading (MA, Certificate); reading specialist (Certificate). Part-time and evening/weekend programs available. *Faculty:* 17 full-time (15 women), 68 part-time/adjunct (52 women). *Students:* 124 full-time (105 women), 274 part-time (257 women). Average age 31. 139 applicants, 65% accepted, 75 enrolled. In 2009, 85 master's awarded. *Degree requirements:* For master's, comprehensive exam, clinical experience, portfolio. *Entrance requirements:* For master's, GRE, 2 letters of recommendation. Additional exam requirements/recommendations for international students: Required—TOEFL (minimum score 83 computer-based), or IELTS. *Application deadline:* For fall admission, 6/1 for international students; for spring admission, 10/1 for international students. Applications are processed on a rolling basis. Application fee: $60. Electronic applications accepted. *Expenses:* Tuition, area resident: Part-time $486.74 per credit. Tuition, state resident: part-time $486.74 per credit. Tuition, nonresident: part-time $751.34 per credit. Tuition and fees vary according to degree level and program. *Financial support:* In 2009–10, 12 research assistantships with full tuition reimbursements (averaging $7,000 per year) were awarded; Federal Work-Study, scholarships/grants, and unspecified assistantships also available. Support available to part-time students. Financial award application deadline: 3/1; financial award applicants required to submit FAFSA. *Unit head:* Dr. Tina Jacobowitz, Chairperson, 973-655-7191. *Application contact:* Amy Aiello, Director of Graduate Admissions and Operations, 973-655-5147, Fax: 973-655-7869, E-mail: graduate.school@montclair.edu.

Morehead State University, Graduate Programs, College of Education, Department of Curriculum and Instruction, Morehead, KY 40351. Offers curriculum and instruction (Ed S); elementary education (MA Ed), including elementary education, international education, middle school education, reading; secondary education (MA Ed); special education (MA Ed); teaching (MAT). Part-time and evening/weekend programs available. *Faculty:* 25 full-time (17 women), 2 part-time/adjunct (1 woman). *Students:* 25 full-time (22 women), 165 part-time (139 women); includes 4 minority (1 African American, 2 American Indian/Alaska Native, 1 Hispanic American). Average age 33. 148 applicants, 68% accepted, 48 enrolled. In 2009, 178 master's awarded. *Degree requirements:* For master's, comprehensive exam, thesis optional; for Ed S, thesis, oral exam. *Entrance requirements:* For master's, GRE General Test, minimum GPA of 2.75, teaching certificate; for Ed S, GRE General Test, interview, master's degree, minimum GPA of 3.5, work experience. Additional exam requirements/recommendations for international students: Required—TOEFL (minimum score 500 paper-based; 173 computer-based). *Application deadline:* For fall admission, 8/1 priority date for domestic and international students; for spring admission, 12/1 priority date for domestic and international students. Applications are processed on a rolling basis. Application fee: $30. Electronic applications accepted. *Expenses:* Tuition, state resident: full-time $6318; part-time $351 per credit hour. Tuition, nonresident: full-time $15,804; part-time $878 per credit hour. *Financial support:* In 2009–10, 2 teaching assistantships (averaging $6,000 per year) were awarded; career-related internships or fieldwork, Federal Work-Study, and unspecified assistantships also available. Financial award application deadline: 3/15; financial award applicants required to submit FAFSA. *Faculty research:* Communicative competence of learning-disabled students, teaching social studies in elementary schools, ungraded primary school organization, study skills. *Unit head:* Dr. James Knoll, Chair, 606-783-2598, Fax: 606-783-5044, E-mail: j.knoll@moreheadstate.edu. *Application contact:* Michelle Barber, Graduate Recruitment and Retention Assistant Director, 606-783-5127, Fax: 606-783-5061, E-mail: m.barber@moreheadstate.edu.

Morehead State University, Graduate Programs, College of Education, Department of Foundational and Graduate Studies in Education, Morehead, KY 40351. Offers adult and higher education (MA, Ed S); certified professional counselor (Ed S); counseling P-12 (MA); curriculum and instruction (Ed S); educational technology (MA Ed); instructional leadership (Ed S); school administration (MA); school counseling (Ed S); teacher leader business and marketing- content (MA Ed); teacher leader business and marketing- technology (MA Ed); teacher leader educational technology (MA Ed); teacher leader English (MA Ed); teacher leader gifted educ (MA Ed); teacher leader IECE—non-certification (MA Ed); teacher leader IECE certification (MA Ed); teacher leader interdisciplanary educaction P-5 (MA Ed); teacher leader middle grades 5-9 (MA Ed); teacher leader reading/writing—non-certification (MA Ed); teacher leader reading/writing certification (MA Ed); teacher leader school communication—non-certification (MA Ed); teacher leader school communication certification (MA Ed); teacher leader social studies (MA Ed); teacher leader special education (MA Ed). *Accreditation:* NCATE. Part-time and evening/weekend programs available. *Faculty:* 20 full-time (10 women), 7 part-time/adjunct (3 women). *Students:* 26 full-time (18 women), 371 part-time (295 women); includes 11 minority (9 African Americans, 1 American Indian/Alaska Native, 1 Hispanic American). Average age 35. 201 applicants, 73% accepted, 73 enrolled. In 2009, 105 master's, 5 other advanced degrees awarded. *Degree requirements:* For master's, thesis optional, oral and/or written comprehensive exams; for Ed S, thesis, oral exam. *Entrance requirements:* For master's, GRE General Test, minimum overall undergraduate GPA of 2.5; for Ed S, GRE General Test, interview, master's degree, minimum GPA of 3.5, work experience. Additional exam requirements/recommendations for international students: Required—TOEFL (minimum score 500 paper-based; 173 computer-based). *Application deadline:* For fall admission, 8/1 priority date for domestic and international students; for spring admission, 12/1 priority date for domestic and international students. Applications are processed on a rolling basis. Application fee: $30. Electronic applications accepted. *Expenses:* Tuition, state resident: full-time $6318; part-time $351 per credit hour. Tuition, nonresident: full-time $15,804; part-time $878 per credit

hour. *Financial support:* In 2009–10, 2 research assistantships (averaging $10,000 per year) were awarded; career-related internships or fieldwork, Federal Work-Study, and unspecified assistantships also available. Financial award application deadline: 3/15; financial award applicants required to submit FAFSA. *Faculty research:* Character education, school accountability, computer applications for school administrators. *Unit head:* Dr. Cathy Gunn, Dean and Professor, 606-783-2040, Fax: 606-783-5029, E-mail: c.gunn@moreheadstate.edu. *Application contact:* Michelle Barber, Graduate Recruitment and Retention Assistant Director, 606-783-5127, Fax: 606-783-5061, E-mail: m.barber@moreheadstate.edu.

Mount Mercy College, Program in Education, Cedar Rapids, IA 52402-4797. Offers reading (MA Ed); special education (MA Ed). *Entrance requirements:* For master's, minimum cumulative GPA of 3.0, 2 letters of recommendation, resume, valid teaching license. Additional exam requirements/recommendations for international students: Required—TOEFL (minimum score 570 paper-based; 88 iBT). Electronic applications accepted.

Mount Saint Mary College, Division of Education, Newburgh, NY 12550-3494. Offers adolescence and special education (MS Ed); adolescence education (MS Ed); childhood and special education (MS Ed); childhood education (MS Ed); literacy (5-12) (Advanced Certificate); literacy (birth-6) (Advanced Certificate); literacy and special education (MS Ed); literacy/childhood (MS Ed); middle school (5-6) (MS Ed); middle school (7-9) (MS Ed); special education (1-6) (MS Ed); special education (7-12) (MS Ed). *Accreditation:* NCATE. Part-time and evening/weekend programs available. *Faculty:* 15 full-time (13 women), 16 part-time/adjunct (10 women). *Students:* 76 full-time (63 women), 226 part-time (188 women); includes 27 minority (7 African Americans, 3 Asian Americans or Pacific Islanders, 17 Hispanic Americans). Average age 30. 141 applicants, 56% accepted, 44 enrolled. In 2009, 142 master's awarded. *Application deadline:* Applications are processed on a rolling basis. Application fee: $45. *Expenses:* Tuition: Full-time $13,356; part-time $742 per credit. Required fees: $50 per semester. *Financial support:* In 2009–10, 106 students received support. Unspecified assistantships available. Financial award application deadline: 4/15; financial award applicants required to submit FAFSA. *Faculty research:* Learning and teaching styles, computers in special education, language development. *Unit head:* Dr. Theresa Lewis, Coordinator, 845-569-3149, Fax: 845-569-3535, E-mail: tlewis@msmc.edu. *Application contact:* Dr. Theresa Lewis, Coordinator, 845-569-3149, Fax: 845-569-3535, E-mail: tlewis@msmc.edu.

Mount Saint Vincent University, Graduate Programs, Faculty of Education, Program in Literacy Education, Halifax, NS B3M 2J6, Canada. Offers M Ed, MA Ed, MA-R. Part-time and evening/weekend programs available. Postbaccalaureate distance learning degree programs offered (no on-campus study). *Degree requirements:* For master's, thesis (for some programs). *Entrance requirements:* For master's, minimum B average, 1 year of teaching experience, bachelor's degree in related field. Electronic applications accepted. *Faculty research:* Writing processes and instruction, assessment and evaluation of literacy education, critical literacy, early literacy development, gender and literacy.

Murray State University, College of Education, Department of Early Childhood and Elementary Education, Programs in Elementary Education/Reading and Writing, Murray, KY 42071. Offers elementary education (MA Ed, Ed S); reading and writing (MA Ed). *Accreditation:* NCATE. Part-time programs available. *Degree requirements:* For master's, comprehensive exam, thesis optional; for Ed S, comprehensive exam. *Entrance requirements:* For master's, minimum GPA of 2.5 for conditional admittance, 3.0 for unconditional; for Ed S, GRE General Test or MAT. Additional exam requirements/recommendations for international students: Required—TOEFL.

National-Louis University, National College of Education, Doctoral Programs in Education, Program in Reading and Language, Chicago, IL 60603. Offers Ed D. Part-time and evening/weekend programs available. *Degree requirements:* For doctorate, comprehensive exam, thesis/dissertation, internship. *Entrance requirements:* For doctorate, GRE General Test, minimum GPA of 3.25, interview, resume, writing sample. *Expenses:* Tuition: Full-time $17,160; part-time $715 per semester hour. Tuition and fees vary according to course load, degree level, campus/location and program.

National-Louis University, National College of Education, Programs in Reading and Language, Chicago, IL 60603. Offers language and literacy (M Ed, MS Ed, CAS); reading recovery (CAS); reading specialist (M Ed, MS Ed, CAS). Part-time and evening/weekend programs available. *Degree requirements:* For master's, thesis (for some programs). *Entrance requirements:* For master's, MAT or GRE, minimum GPA of 3.0, teaching certificate; for CAS, master's degree, teaching certificate. *Expenses:* Tuition: Full-time $17,160; part-time $715 per semester hour. Tuition and fees vary according to course load, degree level, campus/location and program.

Nazareth College of Rochester, Graduate Studies, Department of Education, Program in Literacy Education, Rochester, NY 14618-3790. Offers MS Ed. *Accreditation:* Teacher Education Accreditation Council. Part-time and evening/weekend programs available. *Entrance requirements:* For master's, minimum GPA of 3.0.

New Jersey City University, Graduate Studies and Continuing Education, Debra Cannon Partridge Wolfe College of Education, Department of Literacy Education, Jersey City, NJ 07305-1597. Offers elementary school reading (MA); reading specialist (MA); secondary school reading (MA). Part-time and evening/weekend programs available. *Faculty:* 6. *Students:* 4 full-time (3 women), 58 part-time (54 women); includes 17 minority (6 African Americans, 1 Asian American or Pacific Islander, 10 Hispanic Americans), 1 international. Average age 31. In 2009, 20 master's awarded. *Degree requirements:* For master's, comprehensive exam. *Entrance requirements:* For master's, GRE General Test or MAT. Additional exam requirements/recommendations for international students: Required—TOEFL. *Application deadline:* For fall admission, 8/1 priority date for domestic students; for spring admission, 12/1 for domestic students. Applications are processed on a rolling basis. Application fee: $0. *Expenses:* Tuition, area resident: Part-time $456.75 per credit. Tuition, nonresident: part-time $842.55 per credit. Required fees: $65 per term. *Financial support:* Research assistantships, unspecified assistantships available. *Faculty research:* Reading clinic. *Unit head:* Dr. Debra Woo, Chairperson, 201-200-3521, E-mail: dwoo@njcu.edu. *Application contact:* Dr. Debra Woo, Chairperson, 201-200-3521, E-mail: dwoo@njcu.edu.

New York University, Steinhardt School of Culture, Education, and Human Development, Department of Teaching and Learning, Program in Literacy Education, New York, NY 10012-1019. Offers literacy education (MA), including literacy education: birth-grade 6, literacy education: grades 5-12. *Accreditation:* Teacher Education Accreditation Council. Part-time programs available. *Students:* 11 full-time (10 women), 18 part-time (17 women); includes 4 minority (1 African American, 1 Asian American or Pacific Islander, 2 Hispanic Americans), 1 international. Average age 25. 50 applicants, 88% accepted, 16 enrolled. In 2009, 22 master's awarded. *Degree requirements:* For master's, thesis (for some programs). *Entrance requirements:* For master's, teacher certification. Additional exam requirements/recommendations for international students: Required—TOEFL. *Application deadline:* For fall admission, 12/15 priority date for domestic and international students. Applications are processed on a rolling basis. Application fee: $75. Electronic applications accepted. *Expenses:* Tuition: Full-time $30,528; part-time $1272 per credit. Required fees: $2177. *Financial support:* Career-related internships or fieldwork, Federal Work-Study, institutionally sponsored loans, scholarships/grants, and tuition waivers (partial) available. Support available to part-time students. Financial award application deadline: 2/1; financial award applicants required to submit FAFSA. *Faculty research:* Early literacy intervention and development, psycho and sociolinguistics, multicultural education, literacy assessment and instruction. *Unit head:* Dr. Kay Stahl, Director, 212-998-5402, Fax: 212-995-4049, E-mail: kay.stahl@nyu.edu. *Application contact:* Office of Graduate Admissions, 212-998-5030, Fax: 212-995-4328, E-mail: steinhardt.gradadmissions@nyu.edu.

Niagara University, Graduate Division of Education, Concentration in Literacy Instruction, Niagara Falls, Niagara University, NY 14109. Offers MS Ed.

North Carolina Agricultural and Technical State University, Graduate School, School of Education, Department of Curriculum and Instruction, Program in Reading, Greensboro, NC 27411. Offers MA Ed. *Accreditation:* NCATE. Part-time and evening/weekend programs available. *Degree requirements:* For master's, comprehensive exam, thesis or alternative, qualifying exam. *Entrance requirements:* For master's, GRE General Test, minimum GPA of 3.0.

Northeastern Illinois University, Graduate College, College of Education, School of Teacher Education, Program in Reading, Chicago, IL 60625-4699. Offers MA. Part-time and evening/weekend programs available. *Degree requirements:* For master's, comprehensive exam, thesis optional. *Entrance requirements:* For master's, ISBE, previous course work in psychology or tests and measurements, minimum GPA of 2.75. Additional exam requirements/recommendations for international students: Required—TOEFL (minimum score 550 paper-based; 213 computer-based; 80 iBT). Electronic applications accepted. *Faculty research:* Early literacy, reading disabilities, cognitive processes, multicultural and linguistic diversity, use of literature in the classroom.

Northeastern State University, Graduate College, College of Education, Department of Curriculum and Instruction, Program in Reading, Tahlequah, OK 74464-2399. Offers M Ed. Part-time and evening/weekend programs available. *Degree requirements:* For master's, thesis. *Entrance requirements:* For master's, MAT or GRE, minimum GPA of 2.5. Additional exam requirements/recommendations for international students: Required—TOEFL (minimum score 213 computer-based). Electronic applications accepted.

Northern Illinois University, Graduate School, College of Education, Department of Literacy Education, De Kalb, IL 60115-2854. Offers curriculum and instruction (Ed D), including reading; literacy education (MS Ed). Part-time and evening/weekend programs available. *Faculty:* 12 full-time (10 women), 1 part-time/adjunct (0 women). *Students:* 5 full-time (4 women), 198 part-time (183 women); includes 31 minority (3 African Americans, 2 American Indian/Alaska Native, 4 Asian Americans or Pacific Islanders, 22 Hispanic Americans), 1 international. Average age 35. 37 applicants, 68% accepted, 21 enrolled. In 2009, 61 master's, 21 doctorates awarded. *Degree requirements:* For master's, comprehensive exam, thesis optional; for doctorate, thesis/dissertation, candidacy exam, dissertation defense. *Entrance requirements:* For master's, GRE General Test or MAT, minimum undergraduate GPA of 2.75; for doctorate, GRE General Test, minimum GPA of 2.75 (undergraduate), 3.2 (graduate). Additional exam requirements/recommendations for international students: Required—TOEFL (minimum score 550 paper-based; 213 computer-based). *Application deadline:* For fall admission, 3/1 priority date for domestic students, 5/1 for international students; for spring admission, 11/1 for domestic students, 10/1 for international students. Applications are processed on a rolling basis. Application fee: $30. Electronic applications accepted. *Expenses:* Tuition, state resident: full-time $6576; part-time $274 per credit hour. Tuition, nonresident: full-time $13,152; part-time $548 per credit hour. Required fees: $1813; $75.53 per credit hour. Part-time tuition and fees vary according to course load. *Financial support:* In 2009–10, 19 teaching assistantships with full tuition reimbursements were awarded; fellowships with full tuition reimbursements, research assistantships with full tuition reimbursements, career-related internships or fieldwork, Federal Work-Study, scholarships/grants, tuition waivers (full), and staff assistantships also available. Support available to part-time students. Financial award applicants required to submit FAFSA. *Faculty research:* Early reading development, literacy for bilingual students, family literacy, expository writing, fluency. *Unit head:* Dr. Norm Stahl, Chair, 815-753-9032, E-mail: stahl@niu.edu. *Application contact:* Graduate School Office, 815-753-0395, E-mail: gradsch@niu.edu.

Northern Michigan University, College of Graduate Studies, College of Professional Studies, School of Education, Programs in Reading Education, Marquette, MI 49855-5301. Offers literacy leadership (Ed S); reading (MA Ed); reading specialist (MA Ed). Postbaccalaureate distance learning degree programs offered.

Northern State University, Division of Graduate Studies in Education, Program in Teaching and Learning, Aberdeen, SD 57401-7198. Offers educational studies (MS Ed); elementary classroom teaching (MS Ed); health, physical education, and coaching (MS Ed); language and literacy (MS Ed); secondary classroom teaching (MS Ed); special education (MS Ed). *Accreditation:* NCATE. Part-time and evening/weekend programs available. *Faculty:* 10 full-time (8 women). *Students:* 23 full-time (16 women), 35 part-time (17 women); includes 2 minority (1 American Indian/Alaska Native, 1 Asian American or Pacific Islander). Average age 32. In 2009, 26 master's awarded. *Degree requirements:* For master's, thesis optional. *Entrance requirements:* For master's, minimum GPA of 2.75. Additional exam requirements/recommendations for international students: Required—TOEFL (minimum score 550 paper-based; 213 computer-based; 76 iBT). *Application deadline:* For fall admission, 8/15 priority date for domestic students; for spring admission, 12/15 for domestic students. Applications are processed on a rolling basis. Application fee: $35. Electronic applications accepted. *Financial support:* In 2009–10, 18 teaching assistantships with partial tuition reimbursements (averaging $5,558 per year) were awarded; career-related internships or fieldwork, Federal Work-Study, institutionally sponsored loans, scholarships/grants, and unspecified assistantships also available. Support available to part-time students. Financial award application deadline: 3/1; financial award applicants required to submit FAFSA. *Application contact:* Tammy K. Griffith, Program Assistant, 605-626-2558, Fax: 605-626-7190, E-mail: griffith@northern.edu.

Northwestern Oklahoma State University, School of Professional Studies, Reading Specialist Program, Alva, OK 73717-2799. Offers M Ed. *Accreditation:* NCATE. Part-time programs available. *Faculty:* 10 full-time (7 women). *Students:* 12 part-time (all women). 6 applicants, 67% accepted. In 2009, 3 master's awarded. *Degree requirements:* For master's, thesis optional, portfolio. *Entrance requirements:* For master's, GRE General Test or MAT, minimum GPA of 2.75. *Application deadline:* Applications are processed on a rolling basis. Application fee: $15. *Financial support:* Application deadline: 5/1. *Unit head:* Dr. Martie Young, Coordinator, 580-213-3195. *Application contact:* Leah Haines, Coordinator of Graduate Studies, 580-327-8410, E-mail: ldhaines@nwosu.edu.

Northwestern State University of Louisiana, Graduate Studies and Research, College of Education, Programs in Education, Natchitoches, LA 71497. Offers business and distributive education (M Ed); counseling (M Ed); early childhood education (M Ed); education (M Ed); education leadership (M Ed); educational technology (M Ed); elementary teaching (M Ed); English education (M Ed); home economics education (M Ed); mathematics education (M Ed); reading (M Ed); science education (M Ed); secondary teaching (M Ed); social sciences education (M Ed). *Degree requirements:* For master's, comprehensive exam, thesis or alternative. *Entrance requirements:* For master's, GRE General Test, minimum undergraduate GPA of 2.5.

Northwestern State University of Louisiana, Graduate Studies and Research, College of Education, Programs in Educational Leadership and Instruction, Natchitoches, LA 71497. Offers counseling (Ed S); educational leadership (Ed S); educational technology (Ed S); elementary teaching (Ed S); reading (Ed S); secondary teaching (Ed S); special education (Ed S). *Entrance requirements:* For degree, GRE General Test.

Northwest Missouri State University, Graduate School, College of Education and Human Services, Department of Curriculum and Instruction, Program in Reading, Maryville, MO 64468-6001. Offers MS Ed. *Accreditation:* NCATE. Part-time programs available. *Faculty:* 12 full-time (all women). *Students:* 8 full-time (all women), 35 part-time (all women); includes 2 minority (1 African American, 1 Hispanic American). 15 applicants, 93% accepted, 11 enrolled. In 2009, 16 master's awarded. *Degree requirements:* For master's, comprehensive exam. *Entrance requirements:* For master's, GRE General Test, minimum undergraduate GPA of 2.75, teaching certificate, writing sample. Additional exam requirements/recommendations for international students: Required—TOEFL (minimum score 550 paper-based; 213 computer-based). *Application deadline:* For fall admission, 7/1 for domestic and international students; for spring admission, 11/15 for domestic and international students. Applications are processed on a rolling basis. Application fee: $0 ($50 for international students). *Expenses:* Tuition, state resident: part-time $296.34 per credit hour. Tuition, nonresident: part-time $510.43 per credit hour. *Financial support:* Application deadline: 3/1. *Unit head:* Dr. Margaret Drew, Director, 660-562-1668, E-mail: mdrew@mail.nwmissouri.edu. *Application contact:* Dr. Gregory Haddock, Dean of Graduate School, 660-562-1145, Fax: 660-562-1096, E-mail: gradsch@nwmissouri.edu.

Reading Education

Northwest Nazarene University, Graduate Studies, Program in Teacher Education, Nampa, ID 83686-5897. Offers curriculum and instruction (M Ed); educational leadership (M Ed); exceptional child (M Ed); reading education (M Ed); school counseling (M Ed). *Accreditation:* ACA; NCATE. Part-time programs available. *Degree requirements:* For master's, comprehensive exam (for some programs), action research project. *Entrance requirements:* For master's, minimum undergraduate GPA of 2.8 overall or 3.0 during final 30 semester credits. *Faculty research:* Action research, cooperative learning, accountability, institutional accreditation.

Notre Dame College, Graduate Studies, South Euclid, OH 44121-4293. Offers accounting (Certificate); creative critical thinking (M Ed); financial services management (Certificate); information systems (Certificate); learning disabilities (M Ed); management (Certificate); paralegal (Certificate); pastoral ministry (Certificate); reading (M Ed); teacher education (Certificate). Part-time and evening/weekend programs available. *Degree requirements:* For master's, thesis. *Entrance requirements:* For master's, GRE General Test, MAT, minimum GPA of 2.75, valid teaching certificate. *Faculty research:* Cognitive psychology, teaching critical thinking in the classroom.

Notre Dame de Namur University, Division of Academic Affairs, School of Education and Leadership, Program in Reading, Belmont, CA 94002-1908. Offers MA, Certificate. Part-time programs available. In 2009, 4 master's, 8 other advanced degrees awarded. *Entrance requirements:* Additional exam requirements/recommendations for international students: Required—TOEFL (minimum score 550 paper-based; 213 computer-based; 79 iBT). *Expenses:* Tuition: Part-time $720 per credit. Required fees: $35 per semester hour. *Financial support:* Career-related internships or fieldwork available. Support available to part-time students. Financial award applicants required to submit FAFSA. *Unit head:* Dr. Shadrack Msengi, Director, 650-508-4154, E-mail: smsengi@ndnu.edu. *Application contact:* Candace Hallmark, Director of Graduate Admissions, 650-508-3592, Fax: 650-508-3426, E-mail: grad.admit@ndnu.edu.

Nova Southeastern University, Fischler School of Education and Human Services, Graduate Teacher Education Program, Fort Lauderdale, FL 33314-7796. Offers athletic administration (MS); brain research (MS, Ed S); charter school education/leadership (MS); cognitive and behavioral disabilities (MS); computer science education (Ed S); computer science education (K-12) (MS); curriculum and teaching (Ed S); curriculum, instruction and technology (MS); curriculum, instruction, management and administration (Ed S); early childhood education (MS); early literacy and reading (Ed S); early literacy education (MS); education technology (MS); educational leadership (administration K–12) (MS, Ed S); educational media (Ed S); educational media (K-12) (MS); elementary education (MS, Ed S), including ESOL endorsement (MS); English education (MS, Ed S); environmental education (MS); exceptional student education (MS), including ESOL endorsement; gifted education (MS, Ed S); interdisciplinary arts education (MS); management and administration of educational programs (MS); mathematics (MS); mathematics education (Ed S); multicultural early intervention (MS); pre-kindergarten/primary (MS); preschool education (MS); reading (MS); reading and TESOL (MS); reading education (Ed S); science (MS); science education (Ed S); secondary education (MS); social studies (MS, Ed S); Spanish language (MS); special education and reading (MS); teaching and learning (MA, MS), including curriculum and instruction (MA), elementary mathematics (MA), elementary reading (MA), K-12 technology integration (MA); teaching English to speakers of other languages (MS, Ed S); technology management and administration (Ed S); urban studies education (MS). Part-time and evening/weekend programs available. Postbaccalaureate distance learning degree programs offered (minimal on-campus study). *Faculty:* 72 full-time (43 women), 385 part-time/adjunct (252 women). *Students:* 196 full-time (175 women), 1,304 part-time (1,128 women); includes 594 minority (471 African Americans, 5 American Indian/Alaska Native, 18 Asian Americans or Pacific Islanders, 100 Hispanic Americans). Average age 37. 2,610 applicants, 72% accepted, 1352 enrolled. In 2009, 836 other advanced degrees awarded. *Degree requirements:* For master's and Ed S, thesis, practicum, internship. *Entrance requirements:* For master's, MAT, GRE, CLAST, CBEST, PRAXIS I, General Knowledge Test, minimum GPA of 2.5; for Ed S, MAT or GRE, master's degree, teaching certificate, minimum GPA of 3.0. Additional exam requirements/recommendations for international students: Required—TSE (recommended, minimum score 50); Recommended—TOEFL (minimum score 550 paper-based; 213 computer-based; 80 iBT), IELTS (minimum score 6). *Application deadline:* For fall admission, 9/25 priority date for domestic and international students; for winter admission, 2/23 priority date for domestic and international students; for spring admission, 4/25 priority date for domestic and international students. Applications are processed on a rolling basis. Application fee: $50. Electronic applications accepted. *Financial support:* Federal Work-Study available. Support available to part-time students. Financial award application deadline: 4/15; financial award applicants required to submit FAFSA. *Faculty research:* School effectiveness, critical thinking, leadership skills acquisition, child education, multicultural education. *Unit head:* Dr. Ronald Kern, Dean of Academic Affairs, 800-986-3223 Ext. 7809, Fax: 954-262-3606, E-mail: rk429@nsu.nova.edu. *Application contact:* Dr. Jennifer Quinones Nottingham, Dean of Student Affairs, 800-986-3223 Ext. 1559.

Oakland University, Graduate Study and Lifelong Learning, School of Education and Human Services, Program in Reading and Language Arts, Rochester, MI 48309-4401. Offers reading (Certificate); reading and language arts (MAT); reading education (PhD); reading, language arts and literature (Certificate). *Accreditation:* Teacher Education Accreditation Council. *Degree requirements:* For doctorate, thesis/dissertation. *Entrance requirements:* For master's, minimum GPA of 3.0 for unconditional admission; for doctorate, MAT, minimum GPA of 3.0 for unconditional admission. Electronic applications accepted.

Ohio University, Graduate College, College of Education, Department of Teacher Education, Athens, OH 45701-2979. Offers adolescent to young adult education (M Ed); curriculum and instruction (M Ed, PhD); early childhood/special education (M Ed); intervention specialist/mild-moderate needs (M Ed); intervention specialist/moderate-intensive needs (M Ed); mathematics education (PhD); middle child education (M Ed); reading education (M Ed); social studies education (PhD). Part-time and evening/weekend programs available. *Faculty:* 21 full-time (13 women), 7 part-time/adjunct (all women). *Students:* 105 full-time (75 women), 183 part-time (161 women); includes 9 minority (5 African Americans, 3 American Indian/Alaska Native, 1 Asian American or Pacific Islander), 14 international. 190 applicants, 80% accepted, 72 enrolled. *Degree requirements:* For master's, thesis or alternative; for doctorate, comprehensive exam, thesis/dissertation. *Entrance requirements:* For master's, GRE General Test or MAT (if GPA is below 2.9); for doctorate, GRE General Test, minimum GPA of 3.4, work experience. Additional exam requirements/recommendations for international students: Required—TOEFL (minimum score 550 paper-based; 80 iBT) or IELTS Academic (minimum score 6.5). *Application deadline:* For fall admission, 5/1 priority date for domestic students, 4/1 priority date for international students; for winter admission, 11/1 priority date for domestic students, 10/1 priority date for international students; for spring admission, 2/15 priority date for domestic students, 1/1 priority date for international students. Applications are processed on a rolling basis. Application fee: $50 ($55 for international students). Electronic applications accepted. *Expenses:* Tuition, state resident: full-time $7839; part-time $323 per quarter hour. Tuition, nonresident: full-time $15,831; part-time $654 per quarter hour. Required fees: $2931. *Financial support:* Research assistantships with full tuition reimbursements, teaching assistantships with full tuition reimbursements, Federal Work-Study, institutionally sponsored loans, tuition waivers (partial), and unspecified assistantships available. Financial award application deadline: 3/1. *Faculty research:* Cognition literacy, character education, teacher's education reform, disabilities. Total annual research expenditures: $46,933. *Unit head:* Dr. John Henning, Chair, 740-597-1830, Fax: 740-593-0477, E-mail: henningj@ohio.edu. *Application contact:* Floyd J. Doney, Director of Student Affairs, 740-593-4400, Fax: 740-593-9310, E-mail: doney@ohio.edu.

Old Dominion University, Darden College of Education, Program in Literacy Leadership, Norfolk, VA 23529. Offers PhD. Part-time and evening/weekend programs available. *Faculty:* 6 full-time (all women). *Students:* 1 (woman) full-time, 10 part-time (all women); includes 2 minority (1 African American, 1 Asian American or Pacific Islander). Average age 47. 2 applicants, 100% accepted, 2 enrolled. *Degree requirements:* For doctorate, comprehensive exam, thesis/dissertation. *Entrance requirements:* For doctorate, GRE, minimum GPA of 3.0, MS in reading or related degree, letters of recommendatoin. Additional exam requirements/recommendations for international students: Required—TOEFL (minimum score 600 paper-based; 250 computer-based). *Application deadline:* For fall admission, 3/15 for domestic and international students; for spring admission, 11/15 for domestic and international students. Applications are processed on a rolling basis. Application fee: $50. Electronic applications accepted. *Expenses:* Tuition, state resident: full-time $8112; part-time $338 per credit. Tuition, nonresident: full-time $20,256; part-time $844 per credit. Required fees: $119 per semester. One-time fee: $50. *Financial support:* In 2009–10, 1 teaching assistantship with full tuition reimbursement was awarded; career-related internships or fieldwork, scholarships/grants, and unspecified assistantships also available. *Faculty research:* Literacy for students with special needs, children's Reading First instruction, reading in the content area. Total annual research expenditures: $600,000. *Unit head:* Dr. Charlene Fleener, Graduate Program Director, 757-683-4387, E-mail: cfleener@odu.edu. *Application contact:* Dr. Charlene Fleener, Graduate Program Director, 757-683-4387, E-mail: cfleener@odu.edu.

Old Dominion University, Darden College of Education, Program in Reading Education, Norfolk, VA 23529. Offers MS Ed. *Accreditation:* NCATE. Part-time and evening/weekend programs available. Postbaccalaureate distance learning degree programs offered (no on-campus study). *Faculty:* 6 full-time (all women), 26 part-time/adjunct (25 women). *Students:* 2 full-time (both women), 61 part-time (55 women); includes 19 minority (16 African Americans, 2 American Indian/Alaska Native, 1 Asian American or Pacific Islander). Average age 37. 17 applicants, 76% accepted, 13 enrolled. In 2009, 23 master's awarded. *Degree requirements:* For master's, comprehensive exam, thesis optional. *Entrance requirements:* For master's, GRE General Test or MAT, minimum GPA of 3.0 in major, 2.8 overall; teaching certificate. Additional exam requirements/recommendations for international students: Required—TOEFL. *Application deadline:* For fall admission, 6/1 for domestic students, 4/15 for international students; for spring admission, 11/1 for domestic students, 10/1 for international students. Applications are processed on a rolling basis. Application fee: $50. Electronic applications accepted. *Expenses:* Tuition, state resident: full-time $8112; part-time $338 per credit. Tuition, nonresident: full-time $20,256; part-time $844 per credit. Required fees: $119 per semester. One-time fee: $50. *Financial support:* In 2009–10, 7 students received support, including 1 research assistantship with partial tuition reimbursement available (averaging $9,000 per year); career-related internships or fieldwork, Federal Work-Study, institutionally sponsored loans, scholarships/grants, and unspecified assistantships also available. Support available to part-time students. Financial award application deadline: 2/15; financial award applicants required to submit FAFSA. *Faculty research:* Metacognition and reading, strategies for improving comprehension in reading science, reading in content areas, vocabulary instruction for adolescents, literacy with special needs children, Reading First instruction, reading in the content area, vocabulary, diversity and literacy. Total annual research expenditures: $150,000. *Unit head:* Dr. Charlene Fleener, Graduate Program Director, 757-683-4387, Fax: 757-683-3284, E-mail: cfleener@odu.edu. *Application contact:* Alice McAdory, Director of Admissions, 757-683-3685, Fax: 757-683-3255, E-mail: gradadmit@odu.edu.

Olivet Nazarene University, Graduate School, Division of Education, Program in Reading Specialist, Bourbonnais, IL 60914. Offers MAE.

Oregon State University, Graduate School, College of Education, Program in Language Arts Education, Corvallis, OR 97331. Offers MAT. *Accreditation:* NCATE. Part-time programs available. In 2009, 1 master's awarded. *Degree requirements:* For master's, thesis (for some programs). *Entrance requirements:* For master's, California Basic Educational Skills Test, NTE, minimum GPA of 3.0 in last 90 hours of course work. Additional exam requirements/recommendations for international students: Required—TOEFL. *Application deadline:* For fall admission, 3/1 for domestic students. Applications are processed on a rolling basis. Application fee: $50. *Expenses:* Tuition, state resident: full-time $9774; part-time $362 per credit. Tuition, nonresident: full-time $15,849; part-time $587 per credit. Required fees: $1639. Full-time tuition and fees vary according to course load and program. *Financial support:* Research assistantships, teaching assistantships, career-related internships or fieldwork, Federal Work-Study, and institutionally sponsored loans available. Support available to part-time students. Financial award application deadline: 2/1. *Unit head:* Dr. Kenneth J. Winograd, Chair, 541-737-5988, Fax: 541-737-2040, E-mail: winograk@oregonstate.edu. *Application contact:* Dr. Kenneth J. Winograd, Chair, 541-737-5988, Fax: 541-737-2040, E-mail: winograk@oregonstate.edu.

Our Lady of the Lake University of San Antonio, School of Professional Studies, Program in Curriculum and Instruction, San Antonio, TX 78207-4689. Offers bilingual (M Ed); early childhood education (M Ed); English as a second language (M Ed); integrated math teaching (M Ed); integrated science teaching (M Ed); master reading teacher (M Ed); master technology teacher (M Ed); reading specialist (M Ed). *Students:* 2 full-time (1 woman), 112 part-time (94 women); includes 64 minority (5 African Americans, 1 American Indian/Alaska Native, 1 Asian American or Pacific Islander, 57 Hispanic Americans). Average age 38. In 2009, 49 master's awarded. *Expenses:* Tuition: Full-time $12,330; part-time $685 per contact hour. Required fees: $139; $12 per contact hour. $57 per semester. Tuition and fees vary according to campus/location. *Unit head:* Dr. Cullen Grinnan, 210-434-6711 Ext. 8928, E-mail: ctgrinnan@lake.ollusa.edu. *Application contact:* Dr. Cullen Grinnan, 210-434-6711 Ext. 8928, E-mail: ctgrinnan@lake.ollusa.edu.

Pace University, School of Education, New York, NY 10038. Offers administration and supervision (MS Ed); adolescent education (MST); childhood education (MST); curriculum and instruction (MS); education (MST); literacy (MSE); school business management (Certificate); teaching students with disabilities (MSE); teaching visual arts (MST). *Accreditation:* NCATE. Part-time and evening/weekend programs available. *Students:* 235 full-time (177 women), 766 part-time (515 women); includes 158 minority (58 African Americans, 1 American Indian/Alaska Native, 37 Asian Americans or Pacific Islanders, 62 Hispanic Americans), 7 international. Average age 30. 332 applicants, 83% accepted, 165 enrolled. In 2009, 669 master's, 34 other advanced degrees awarded. *Degree requirements:* For master's, internship. *Entrance requirements:* For master's, interview, teaching certificate. Additional exam requirements/recommendations for international students: Required—TOEFL. *Application deadline:* For fall admission, 7/31 priority date for domestic students; for spring admission, 11/30 for domestic students. Applications are processed on a rolling basis. Application fee: $70. Electronic applications accepted. *Expenses:* Contact institution. *Financial support:* Research assistantships, career-related internships or fieldwork and Federal Work-Study available. Support available to part-time students. Financial award applicants required to submit FAFSA. *Unit head:* Dr. Harriet Feldman, Interim Dean, 212-346-1512. *Application contact:* Susan Ford-Goldschein, Director of Admissions, 212-346-1652, Fax: 212-346-1585, E-mail: gradnyc@pace.edu.

Pittsburg State University, Graduate School, College of Education, Department of Curriculum and Instruction, Pittsburg, KS 66762. Offers classroom reading teacher (MS); early childhood education (MS); elementary education (MS); reading (MS); reading specialist (MS); secondary education (MS); teaching (MAT). *Accreditation:* NCATE. *Degree requirements:* For master's, thesis or alternative. *Entrance requirements:* For master's, GRE or MAT. *Expenses:* Tuition, state resident: full-time $4212; part-time $176 per credit. Tuition, nonresident: full-time $11,530; part-time $480 per credit. Required fees: $940; $43 per credit. Tuition and fees vary according to course level, course load, degree level, campus/location, reciprocity agreements and student level.

Plymouth State University, College of Graduate Studies, Graduate Studies in Education, Program in Reading and Writing Specialist, Plymouth, NH 03264-1595. Offers M Ed. Part-time and evening/weekend programs available. *Degree requirements:* For master's, PRAXIS. *Entrance requirements:* For master's, GRE General Test or MAT, minimum GPA of 3.0.

Portland State University, Graduate Studies, School of Education, Department of Curriculum and Instruction, Portland, OR 97207-0751. Offers early childhood education (MA, MS); education (M Ed, MA, MS); educational leadership: curriculum and instruction (Ed D); educational media/school librarianship (MA, MS); elementary education (M Ed, MAT, MST); reading (MA, MS); secondary education (M Ed, MAT, MST). *Accreditation:* NCATE. Part-time programs available.

Degree requirements: For master's, comprehensive exam, thesis or alternative; for doctorate, thesis/dissertation. *Entrance requirements:* For master's, California Basic Educational Skills Test, minimum GPA of 3.0 in upper-division course work or 2.75 overall. Additional exam requirements/recommendations for international students: Required—TOEFL (minimum score 550 paper-based; 213 computer-based). *Faculty research:* Early literacy, characteristics of successful teachers of at-risk students, participation of women/minorities in technology courses, selection of cooperating teachers.

Providence College, Graduate Studies, Department of Education, Program in Literacy, Providence, RI 02918. Offers M Ed. Part-time and evening/weekend programs available. *Faculty:* 4 full-time (3 women), 39 part-time/adjunct (22 women). *Students:* 10 full-time (all women), 29 part-time (27 women). Average age 31. 9 applicants, 100% accepted. In 2009, 16 master's awarded. *Degree requirements:* For master's, comprehensive exam. *Entrance requirements:* For master's, GRE General Test. Additional exam requirements/recommendations for international students: Required—TOEFL (minimum score 550 paper-based; 213 computer-based; 80 iBT). *Application deadline:* For fall admission, 8/1 priority date for domestic and international students; for spring admission, 12/1 priority date for domestic and international students. Applications are processed on a rolling basis. Application fee: $55. *Expenses:* Tuition: Full-time $9909; part-time $367 per credit. One-time fee: $200. Tuition and fees vary according to course load and program. *Financial support:* In 2009–10, 1 research assistantship with full tuition reimbursement (averaging $8,400 per year) was awarded; career-related internships or fieldwork, institutionally sponsored loans, and unspecified assistantships also available. Support available to part-time students. Financial award application deadline: 8/1; financial award applicants required to submit FAFSA. *Unit head:* E. Sharon Capobianco, Director, 401-865-1987, Fax: 401-865-1147, E-mail: escapobi@providence.edu. *Application contact:* Carol A. Daniels, Coordinator of Graduate Faculty and Administrative Services, 401-865-2247, Fax: 401-865-1147, E-mail: daniels@providence.edu.

Purdue University, Graduate School, School of Education, Department of Curriculum and Instruction, West Lafayette, IN 47907. Offers agricultural and extension education (PhD, Ed S); agriculture and extension education (MS, MS Ed); art education (PhD); consumer and family sciences and extension education (MS Ed, PhD, Ed S); curriculum studies (MS Ed, PhD, Ed S); educational technology (MS Ed, PhD, Ed S); elementary education (MS Ed); foreign language education (MS Ed, PhD, Ed S); industrial technology (PhD, Ed S); language arts (MS Ed, PhD, Ed S); literacy (MS Ed, PhD, Ed S); mathematics/science education (MS, MS Ed, PhD, Ed S); social studies (MS Ed, PhD); social studies education (Ed S); vocational/industrial education (MS Ed, PhD, Ed S); vocational/technical education (MS Ed, PhD, Ed S). *Accreditation:* NCATE. Part-time and evening/weekend programs available. *Degree requirements:* For master's, thesis optional; for doctorate, thesis/dissertation, oral and written exams; for Ed S, oral presentation, project. *Entrance requirements:* For master's, GRE General Test, minimum B average; for doctorate, GRE General Test; for Ed S, GRE, minimum B average. Additional exam requirements/recommendations for international students: Required—TOEFL. Electronic applications accepted. *Faculty research:* Literacy acquisition and development, teacher beliefs and knowledge, recruitment and retention of underrepresented students, economic education, literacy discourse.

Queens College of the City University of New York, Division of Graduate Studies, Division of Education, Department of Elementary and Early Childhood Education, Program in Literacy, Flushing, NY 11367-1597. Offers MS Ed. Part-time programs available. *Faculty:* 8 full-time (6 women). *Students:* 142 part-time (137 women). 74 applicants, 92% accepted, 54 enrolled. In 2009, 140 master's awarded. *Degree requirements:* For master's, research project. *Entrance requirements:* For master's, minimum GPA of 3.0. Additional exam requirements/recommendations for international students: Required—TOEFL. *Application deadline:* For fall admission, 4/1 for domestic students; for spring admission, 11/1 for domestic students. Applications are processed on a rolling basis. Application fee: $125. *Expenses:* Tuition, state resident: full-time $7360; part-time $310 per credit. Tuition, nonresident: part-time $575 per credit. One-time fee: $195 full-time; $145.25 part-time. *Financial support:* Career-related internships or fieldwork, Federal Work-Study, institutionally sponsored loans, and tuition waivers (partial) available. Support available to part-time students. Financial award application deadline: 4/1; financial award applicants required to submit FAFSA. *Unit head:* Dr. Marcia Braghban, Coordinator, 718-997-5339. *Application contact:* Mario Caruso, Director of Graduate Admissions, 718-997-5200, Fax: 718-997-5193, E-mail: graduate_admissions@qc.edu.

Queens University of Charlotte, Wayland H. Cato, Jr. School of Education, Charlotte, NC 28274-0002. Offers education in literacy (M Ed); elementary education (MAT); school administration (MSA). *Accreditation:* NCATE. Part-time and evening/weekend programs available. *Degree requirements:* For master's, comprehensive exam. *Entrance requirements:* For master's, GRE General Test. *Expenses:* Contact institution.

Quincy University, Program in Education, Quincy, IL 62301-2699. Offers curriculum and instruction (MS Ed); leadership (MRS); reading education (MS Ed); school administration (MS Ed); special education (MS Ed); teaching certification (MS Ed). Part-time programs available. Postbaccalaureate distance learning degree programs offered. *Faculty:* 3 full-time (2 women), 19 part-time/adjunct (16 women). *Students:* 328 full-time (222 women), 88 part-time (57 women); includes 60 African Americans, 9 Asian Americans or Pacific Islanders, 69 Hispanic Americans. In 2009, 10 master's awarded. *Degree requirements:* For master's, thesis. *Entrance requirements:* For master's, MAT or GRE. Additional exam requirements/recommendations for international students: Required—TOEFL. *Application deadline:* Applications are processed on a rolling basis. Application fee: $25. Electronic applications accepted. *Expenses:* Tuition: Full-time $8400; part-time $350 per credit hour. Required fees: $360; $15 per credit hour. Tuition and fees vary according to course load, campus/location and program. *Financial support:* Available to part-time students. Applicants required to submit FAFSA. *Unit head:* Dot Nelson, Director, 217-228-5432 Ext. 3111, E-mail: nelsodo@quincy.edu. *Application contact:* Jennifer O'Donnell, Coordinator of Adult Studies, 217-228-5404, Fax: 217-228-5479, E-mail: admissions@quincy.edu.

Radford University, College of Graduate and Professional Studies, College of Education and Human Development, School of Teacher Education and Leadership, Program in Literacy Education, Radford, VA 24142. Offers MS. *Accreditation:* NCATE. Part-time and evening/weekend programs available. *Faculty:* 4 full-time (3 women), 1 (woman) part-time/adjunct. *Students:* 16 part-time (all women); includes 1 minority (Hispanic American). Average age 36. 28 applicants, 100% accepted. In 2009, 27 master's awarded. *Degree requirements:* For master's, comprehensive exam. *Entrance requirements:* For master's, GRE or MAT, minimum GPA of 2.75; copy of teaching license; 2 letters of reference. Additional exam requirements/recommendations for international students: Required—TOEFL (minimum score 550 paper-based; 213 computer-based; 79 iBT). *Application deadline:* For fall admission, 12/1 for international students; for spring admission, 7/1 for international students. Applications are processed on a rolling basis. Application fee: $50. Electronic applications accepted. *Expenses:* Tuition, state resident: full-time $5086; part-time $211 per credit hour. Tuition, nonresident: full-time $12,608; part-time $525 per credit hour. Required fees: $2508; $105 per credit hour. *Financial support:* Career-related internships or fieldwork, Federal Work-Study, institutionally sponsored loans, scholarships/grants, and unspecified assistantships available. Financial award application deadline: 3/1; financial award applicants required to submit FAFSA. *Unit head:* Dr. Donald B. Langrehr, Coordinator, 540-831-6580, Fax: 540-831-5059, E-mail: dlangreh@radford.edu. *Application contact:* Graduate Admissions, 540-831-5431, Fax: 540-831-6061, E-mail: gradcollege@radford.edu.

Regis College, Department of Education, Weston, MA 02493. Offers elementary teacher (MAT); reading (MAT); special education (MAT). Part-time and evening/weekend programs available. *Faculty:* 2 full-time (both women), 5 part-time/adjunct (all women). *Students:* 2 full-time (both women), 49 part-time (42 women); includes 1 minority (Asian American or Pacific Islander). Average age 36. 8 applicants, 88% accepted, 4 enrolled. In 2009, 11 master's awarded. *Degree requirements:* For master's, thesis. *Entrance requirements:* For master's, GRE or MAT. Additional exam requirements/recommendations for international students: Required—TOEFL. *Application deadline:* Applications are processed on a rolling basis. Application fee: $50. Electronic applications accepted. *Expenses:* Tuition: Full-time $29,000; part-time $800 per credit. Tuition and fees vary according to course load, degree level and program. *Financial support:* In 2009–10, 1 student received support, including 1 fellowship with full tuition reimbursement available (averaging $11,970 per year); Federal Work-Study and scholarships/grants also available. Financial award applicants required to submit FAFSA. *Faculty research:* Reflective teaching, gender-based education, integrated teaching. *Unit head:* Dr. Leona McCaughey-Oreszak, Program Director, 781-768-7421, Fax: 781-768-7159, E-mail: leona.mccaughey-oreszak@regiscollege.edu. *Application contact:* Christine Petherick, Administrative Coordinator, Graduate Admission, 866-438-7344, Fax: 781-768-7071, E-mail: christine.petherick@regiscollege.edu.

Regis University, College for Professional Studies, Program in Teacher Education, Denver, CO 80221-1099. Offers adult learning, training, and development (M Ed); curriculum, instruction, and assessment (M Ed); early childhood (M Ed); educational technology (Certificate); elementary (M Ed); ESL (M Ed); fine arts (M Ed), including arts, music; instructional technology (M Ed); professional leadership (M Ed); reading (M Ed); secondary (M Ed); self-designed (M Ed); space studies (M Ed); special education (M Ed); teacher licensure (M Ed). Program also offered in Henderson and Las Vegas (Summerlin), NV. *Accreditation:* Teacher Education Accreditation Council. Part-time and evening/weekend programs available. Postbaccalaureate distance learning degree programs offered (no on-campus study). *Degree requirements:* For master's, thesis. *Entrance requirements:* For master's, resume, minimum GPA of 2.75, criminal background check. Additional exam requirements/recommendations for international students: Required—TOEFL (minimum score 213 computer-based), TWE (minimum score 5). Electronic applications accepted. *Faculty research:* Issues of equity in the middle school classroom, professional learning communities, school reform, socialinguistic and discursive obstacles to student integration, inclusive language arts curriculum.

Rhode Island College, School of Graduate Studies, Feinstein School of Education and Human Development, Department of Elementary Education, Providence, RI 02908-1991. Offers early childhood education (M Ed); elementary education (M Ed, MAT); reading (M Ed). *Accreditation:* NCATE. Part-time and evening/weekend programs available. *Faculty:* 10 full-time (6 women), 7 part-time/adjunct (5 women). *Students:* 15 full-time (12 women), 40 part-time (all women); includes 1 minority (Asian American or Pacific Islander), 1 international. Average age 32. In 2009, 47 master's awarded. *Degree requirements:* For master's, comprehensive exam (for some programs), comprehensive assessment. *Entrance requirements:* For master's, GRE General Test or MAT, PRAXIS II (elementary content knowledge), undergraduate transcripts; minimum undergraduate GPA of 3.0; copy of teaching certificate (when applicable); 3 letters of recommendation. Additional exam requirements/recommendations for international students: Recommended—TOEFL (minimum score 550 paper-based; 213 computer-based; 79 iBT). *Application deadline:* For fall admission, 3/15 for domestic students; for spring admission, 11/1 for domestic students. Applications are processed on a rolling basis. Application fee: $50. *Expenses:* Tuition, state resident: full-time $7440; part-time $310 per credit hour. Tuition, nonresident: full-time $14,784; part-time $616 per credit hour. Required fees: $552; $20 per credit. $70 per term. *Financial support:* Teaching assistantships with full tuition reimbursements, Federal Work-Study, scholarships/grants, and health care benefits available. Support available to part-time students. Financial award application deadline: 5/15; financial award applicants required to submit FAFSA. *Unit head:* Dr. Patricia Cordeiro, Chair, 401-456-8016. *Application contact:* Graduate Studies, 401-456-8700.

Rider University, Department of Graduate Education, Leadership and Counseling, Program in Reading/Language Arts, Lawrenceville, NJ 08648-3001. Offers reading specialist (Certificate); reading/language arts (MA). *Accreditation:* NCATE. Part-time and evening/weekend programs available. *Degree requirements:* For master's, comprehensive exam, research project. *Entrance requirements:* For master's, interview, resume. Additional exam requirements/recommendations for international students: Required—TOEFL (minimum score 550 paper-based; 213 computer-based). Electronic applications accepted. *Faculty research:* Ethnography in the reading/language arts process.

Rivier College, School of Graduate Studies, Department of Education, Nashua, NH 03060. Offers curriculum and instruction (M Ed); early childhood education (M Ed); educational administration (M Ed); educational studies (M Ed); elementary education (M Ed); elementary education and general special education (M Ed); emotional and behavioral disorders (M Ed); general social education (M Ed); leadership and learning (Ed D, CAGS); learning disabilities (M Ed); learning disabilities and reading (M Ed); mental health counseling (MA); reading (M Ed); school counseling (M Ed). Part-time and evening/weekend programs available. *Faculty:* 13 full-time (9 women), 38 part-time/adjunct (25 women). *Students:* 87 full-time (78 women), 293 part-time (246 women); includes 10 minority (3 African Americans, 4 Asian Americans or Pacific Islanders, 3 Hispanic Americans). Average age 38. 182 applicants, 82% accepted, 72 enrolled. In 2009, 110 master's, 18 other advanced degrees awarded. *Degree requirements:* For master's, comprehensive exam (for some programs), internships. *Entrance requirements:* For master's, GRE General Test or MAT. *Application deadline:* Applications are processed on a rolling basis. Application fee: $25. *Expenses:* Tuition: Part-time $447 per credit. *Financial support:* Available to part-time students. Application deadline: 2/1. *Unit head:* Dr. Patricia Howson, Chairman, 603-897-8562, E-mail: phowson@rivier.edu. *Application contact:* Mathew Kittredge, Director of Graduate Admissions, 603-897-8129, Fax: 603-897-8810, E-mail: mkittredge@rivier.edu.

Roberts Wesleyan College, Division of Teacher Education, Rochester, NY 14624-1997. Offers adolescence education (M Ed); childhood and special education (M Ed); literacy education (M Ed); urban education (M Ed). Part-time and evening/weekend programs available. *Degree requirements:* For master's, thesis.

Rockford College, Graduate Studies, Department of Education, Program in Reading, Rockford, IL 61108-2393. Offers MAT. Part-time and evening/weekend programs available. *Degree requirements:* For master's, thesis optional. *Entrance requirements:* For master's, GRE General Test, 3 letters of recommendation. Additional exam requirements/recommendations for international students: Required—TOEFL (minimum score 550 paper-based; 213 computer-based; 79 iBT). Electronic applications accepted.

Roger Williams University, School of Education, Program in Literacy Education, Bristol, RI 02809. Offers literacy (MA). Part-time and evening/weekend programs available. *Degree requirements:* For master's, state-mandated exams. *Entrance requirements:* For master's, interview, teacher's certification, 2 recommendation letters, curriculum vitae/resume. Additional exam requirements/recommendations for international students: Recommended—IELTS. Electronic applications accepted. *Expenses:* Contact institution. *Faculty research:* Assessment of reading difficulties, action research in reading, comprehension and writing, student mediation techniques.

Roosevelt University, Graduate Division, College of Education, Program in Language and Literacy, Chicago, IL 60605. Offers reading teacher education (MA).

Rowan University, Graduate School, College of Education, Department of Reading Education, Glassboro, NJ 08028-1701. Offers MA. *Accreditation:* NCATE. Part-time and evening/weekend programs available. *Faculty:* 2 part-time/adjunct (both women). *Students:* 33 part-time (32 women); includes 2 minority (both African Americans). Average age 33. 5 applicants, 80% accepted, 4 enrolled. In 2009, 20 master's awarded. *Degree requirements:* For master's, comprehensive exam, thesis. *Entrance requirements:* For master's, GRE General Test, GRE Subject Test, interview, minimum GPA of 2.8. Additional exam requirements/recommendations for international students: Required—TOEFL. *Application deadline:* Applications are processed on a rolling basis. Application fee: $50. Electronic applications accepted. *Expenses:* Tuition, state resident: full-time $10,624; part-time $590 per semester hour. Tuition, nonresident: full-time $10,624; part-time $590 per semester hour. Required fees: $2320; $125 per semester hour. *Financial support:* Career-related internships or fieldwork, Federal Work-Study, scholarships/grants, and unspecified assistantships available. Support available to part-time

Reading Education

Rowan University (continued)

students. *Unit head:* Dr. Mira Lalovic-Hand, Interim Associate Provost/Director of Graduate School, 856-256-5120, E-mail: lalovic-hand@rowan.edu. *Application contact:* Karen Haynes, Graduate Coordinator, 856-256-4052, Fax: 856-256-4436, E-mail: haynes@rowan.edu.

Rutgers, The State University of New Jersey, New Brunswick, Graduate School of Education, Department of Learning and Teaching, Program in Literacy Education, Piscataway, NJ 08854-8097. Offers Ed M, Ed D. Part-time programs available. Terminal master's awarded for partial completion of doctoral program. *Degree requirements:* For master's, comprehensive exam; for doctorate, thesis/dissertation, qualifying exam. *Entrance requirements:* For master's, GRE General Test, minimum undergraduate GPA of 3.0; for doctorate, GRE General Test, 2 years of teaching experience, certification, minimum graduate GPA of 3.5. Additional exam requirements/recommendations for international students: Required—TOEFL. Electronic applications accepted. *Faculty research:* Early childhood literacy development, discourse analysis-adult literacy.

Rutgers, The State University of New Jersey, New Brunswick, Graduate School of Education, Department of Learning and Teaching, Program in Reading Education, Piscataway, NJ 08854-8097. Offers Ed M. Part-time programs available. *Degree requirements:* For master's, comprehensive exam or paper. *Entrance requirements:* For master's, GRE General Test. Electronic applications accepted.

Rutgers, The State University of New Jersey, New Brunswick, Graduate School of Education, Doctoral Program in Education, Piscataway, NJ 08854-8097. Offers educational policy (PhD); educational psychology (PhD); literacy education (PhD); mathematics education (PhD). Part-time programs available. *Degree requirements:* For doctorate, thesis/dissertation, qualifying exam. *Entrance requirements:* For doctorate, GRE General Test, GRE Subject Test (mathematics education). Additional exam requirements/recommendations for international students: Required—TOEFL (minimum score 575 paper-based; 233 computer-based; 83 iBT). Electronic applications accepted. *Faculty research:* Literacy education, math education, educational psychology, educational policy.

Sacred Heart University, Graduate Programs, College of Education and Health Professions, Isabelle Farrington School of Education, Fairfield, CT 06825-1000. Offers administration (CAS); educational technology (MAT); elementary education (MAT); reading (CAS); secondary education (MAT); teaching (CAS). Part-time and evening/weekend programs available. Postbaccalaureate distance learning degree programs offered (minimal on-campus study). *Faculty:* 23 full-time (10 women). *Students:* 377 full-time (291 women), 691 part-time (495 women); includes 63 minority (31 African Americans, 2 American Indian/Alaska Native, 8 Asian Americans or Pacific Islanders, 22 Hispanic Americans), 2 international. Average age 34. 429 applicants, 90% accepted, 338 enrolled. In 2009, 409 master's, 66 other advanced degrees awarded. *Degree requirements:* For master's, thesis or alternative. *Entrance requirements:* For master's, PRAXIS (teacher certification/MAT); for CAS, PRAXIS I. Additional exam requirements/recommendations for international students: Required—TOEFL (minimum score 550 paper-based; 213 computer-based). *Application deadline:* Applications are processed on a rolling basis. Application fee: $50 ($100 for international students). Electronic applications accepted. *Expenses:* Contact institution. *Financial support:* Teaching assistantships with partial tuition reimbursements, career-related internships or fieldwork, institutionally sponsored loans, traineeships, tuition waivers (partial), and unspecified assistantships available. Support available to part-time students. Financial award applicants required to submit FAFSA. *Faculty research:* Reading education, learning theory, teacher preparation, education of underachievers. *Unit head:* Dr. Edward Malin, Director, 203-371-7800, Fax: 203-365-7513. *Application contact:* Kathy Dilks, Assistant Dean of Graduate Admissions, 203-365-7619, Fax: 203-365-4732, E-mail: gradstudies@sacredheart.edu.

Sage Graduate School, Graduate School, School of Education, Program in Childhood Education/Literacy, Troy, NY 12180-4115. Offers MS. Part-time and evening/weekend programs available. *Faculty:* 15 full-time (9 women), 19 part-time/adjunct (16 women). *Students:* 5 full-time (all women), 18 part-time (16 women). Average age 27. 12 applicants, 50% accepted, 4 enrolled. In 2009, 5 master's awarded. *Degree requirements:* For master's, thesis optional. *Entrance requirements:* For master's, minimum GPA of 2.75, resume, 2 letters of recommendation, interview, assessment of writing skills. Additional exam requirements/recommendations for international students: Required—TOEFL (minimum score 550 paper-based; 213 computer-based). *Application deadline:* Applications are processed on a rolling basis. Application fee: $40. *Expenses:* Tuition: Full-time $10,620; part-time $590 per credit hour. *Financial support:* Fellowships, research assistantships, Federal Work-Study, scholarships/grants, and unspecified assistantships available. Support available to part-time students. Financial award application deadline: 3/1. *Unit head:* Ellen Adams, Assistant Professor, Education Department, 518-244-2054, E-mail: adamse@sage.edu. *Application contact:* Wendy D. Diefendorf, Director of Graduate and Adult Admission, 518-244-2443, Fax: 518-244-6880, E-mail: diefew@sage.edu.

Sage Graduate School, Graduate School, School of Education, Program in Literacy, Troy, NY 12180-4115. Offers MS Ed. *Accreditation:* NCATE. Part-time and evening/weekend programs available. *Faculty:* 15 full-time (9 women), 19 part-time/adjunct (16 women). *Students:* 5 full-time (all women), 34 part-time (32 women). Average age 25. 23 applicants, 83% accepted, 13 enrolled. In 2009, 32 master's awarded. *Entrance requirements:* For master's, minimum GPA of 2.75, resume, 2 letters of recommendation. Additional exam requirements/recommendations for international students: Required—TOEFL (minimum score 550 paper-based; 213 computer-based). *Application deadline:* Applications are processed on a rolling basis. Application fee: $40. *Expenses:* Tuition: Full-time $10,620; part-time $590 per credit hour. *Financial support:* Fellowships, research assistantships, Federal Work-Study, scholarships/grants, and unspecified assistantships available. Support available to part-time students. Financial award application deadline: 3/1; financial award applicants required to submit FAFSA. *Faculty research:* Literacy development in at-risk children. *Unit head:* Peter McDermott, Director, 518-244-2493, Fax: 518-244-2334, E-mail: mcderp@sage.edu. *Application contact:* Wendy D. Diefendorf, Director of Graduate and Adult Admission, 518-244-2443, Fax: 518-244-6880, E-mail: diefew@sage.edu.

Sage Graduate School, Graduate School, School of Education, Program in Literacy/Childhood Special Education, Troy, NY 12180-4115. Offers MS Ed. *Accreditation:* NCATE. Part-time and evening/weekend programs available. *Faculty:* 15 full-time (9 women), 19 part-time/adjunct (16 women). *Students:* 3 full-time (all women), 13 part-time (12 women); includes 1 minority (Hispanic American). Average age 27. 8 applicants. In 2009, 6 master's awarded. *Entrance requirements:* For master's, minimum GPA of 2.75, resume, 2 letters of recommendation, interview with advisor, assessment of writing skills. Additional exam requirements/recommendations for international students: Required—TOEFL (minimum score 550 paper-based; 213 computer-based). *Application deadline:* Applications are processed on a rolling basis. Application fee: $40. *Expenses:* Tuition: Full-time $10,620; part-time $590 per credit hour. *Financial support:* Fellowships, research assistantships, Federal Work-Study, scholarships/grants, and unspecified assistantships available. Support available to part-time students. Financial award application deadline: 3/1; financial award applicants required to submit FAFSA. *Faculty research:* Commonalities in the roles of reading specialists and resource/consultant teachers. *Unit head:* Michelle Reilly, Director, 518-244-4539, Fax: 518-244-2334, E-mail: reillm@sage.edu. *Application contact:* Wendy D. Diefendorf, Director of Graduate and Adult Admission, 518-244-2443, Fax: 518-244-6880, E-mail: diefew@sage.edu.

Saginaw Valley State University, College of Education, Program in Reading Education, University Center, MI 48710. Offers MAT. *Accreditation:* NCATE. Part-time and evening/weekend programs available. *Students:* 151 part-time (144 women); includes 6 minority (3 African Americans, 3 Hispanic Americans), 1 international. Average age 33. 21 applicants, 100% accepted, 17 enrolled. In 2009, 32 master's awarded. *Degree requirements:* For master's, capstone course, practicum. *Entrance requirements:* For master's, minimum GPA of 3.0, teaching certificate. Additional exam requirements/recommendations for international students: Required—TOEFL (minimum score 525 paper-based; 197 computer-based; 71 iBT). *Application deadline:* Applications are processed on a rolling basis. Application fee: $25. Electronic applications accepted. *Financial support:* Federal Work-Study and scholarships/grants available. Support available to part-time students. Financial award applicants required to submit FAFSA. *Faculty research:* Pre-service, middle school, secondary teacher, literacy education. *Unit head:* Dr. Steve P. Barbus, Dean, 989-964-6067, Fax: 989-790-4385, E-mail: barbus@svsu.edu. *Application contact:* Dr. Steve P. Barbus, Dean, 989-964-6067, Fax: 989-790-4385, E-mail: barbus@svsu.edu.

St. Bonaventure University, School of Graduate Studies, School of Education, Literacy Programs, St. Bonaventure, NY 14778-2284. Offers adolescent literacy 5-12 (MS Ed); childhood literacy B-6 (MS Ed). *Accreditation:* NCATE. Part-time and evening/weekend programs available. *Faculty:* 2 full-time (1 woman), 1 (woman) part-time/adjunct. *Students:* 37 full-time (33 women), 33 part-time (31 women); includes 1 minority (Hispanic American). Average age 27. 37 applicants, 86% accepted, 26 enrolled. In 2009, 45 master's awarded. *Degree requirements:* For master's, comprehensive exam, thesis optional. *Entrance requirements:* For master's, interview, writing sample, minimum undergraduate GPA of 3.0. Additional exam requirements/recommendations for international students: Required—TOEFL. *Application deadline:* For fall admission, 8/1 for domestic students; for spring admission, 11/1 priority date for domestic students. Applications are processed on a rolling basis. Application fee: $30. Electronic applications accepted. *Expenses:* Tuition: Full-time $11,700; part-time $650 per credit. *Financial support:* In 2009–10, 9 research assistantships with full and partial tuition reimbursements were awarded; scholarships/grants also available. Support available to part-time students. Financial award application deadline: 4/15; financial award applicants required to submit FAFSA. *Faculty research:* Children's literary tastes, reading diagnosis. *Unit head:* Dr. Joseph Zimmer, Director, 716-375-2388. *Application contact:* Bruce Campbell, 716-375-2429, E-mail: gradsch@sbu.edu.

Saint Francis University, Graduate Education Program, Loretto, PA 15940-0600. Offers education (M Ed); leadership (M Ed); reading (M Ed). Part-time and evening/weekend programs available. *Faculty:* 29 part-time/adjunct (7 women). *Students:* 150 part-time (100 women); includes 3 minority (2 African Americans, 1 Hispanic American). Average age 30. 20 applicants, 100% accepted, 20 enrolled. In 2009, 50 master's awarded. *Degree requirements:* For master's, comprehensive exam, thesis optional. *Entrance requirements:* For master's, GRE or MAT (if undergraduate GPA less than 2.8), minimum undergraduate QPA of 2.5. *Application deadline:* Applications are processed on a rolling basis. Application fee: $30. *Expenses:* Contact institution. *Financial support:* Applicants required to submit FAFSA. *Unit head:* Dr. Janette D. Kelly, Director, Graduate Education, 814-472-3068, Fax: 814-472-3864, E-mail: jkelly@francis.edu. *Application contact:* Sherri L. Toth, Coordinator, 814-472-3058, Fax: 814-472-3864, E-mail: stoth@francis.edu.

St. John Fisher College, Ralph C. Wilson Jr. School of Education, Program in Literacy Education, Rochester, NY 14618-3597. Offers literacy birth to grade 6 (MS); literacy grades 5 to 12 (MS). Part-time and evening/weekend programs available. *Faculty:* 4 full-time (all women), 7 part-time/adjunct (all women). *Students:* 10 full-time (9 women), 77 part-time (all women); includes 6 minority (4 African Americans, 2 Hispanic Americans). Average age 27. 71 applicants, 83% accepted, 30 enrolled. In 2009, 69 master's awarded. *Degree requirements:* For master's, capstone project, practicum. *Entrance requirements:* For master's, teacher certification, 2 letters of recommendation, personal statement, current resume. Additional exam requirements/recommendations for international students: Required—TOEFL (minimum score 575 paper-based; 233 computer-based; 80 iBT). *Application deadline:* Applications are processed on a rolling basis. Application fee: $30. Electronic applications accepted. *Expenses:* Tuition: Part-time $680 per credit hour. Required fees: $25 per semester. Tuition and fees vary according to degree level and program. *Financial support:* In 2009–10, 57 students received support. Federal Work-Study and scholarships/grants available. Financial award applicants required to submit FAFSA. *Faculty research:* Adolescent use of new literacies (instant messaging), referral practices, at risk early literacy, new literacies (Internet, technology), equity in education. *Unit head:* Dr. Kathleen Broikou, Program Director, 585-385-8112, E-mail: kbroikou@sjfc.edu. *Application contact:* Jose Perales, Interim Director of Graduate Admissions, 585-385-8067, E-mail: jperales@sjfc.edu.

St. John's University, The School of Education, Department of Human Services and Counseling, Literacy Program, Queens, NY 11439. Offers teaching literacy 5-12 (MS Ed); teaching literacy B-12 (MS Ed); teaching literacy B-6 (MS Ed). Part-time and evening/weekend programs available. *Students:* 20 full-time (all women), 67 part-time (64 women); includes 6 minority (1 African American, 5 Hispanic Americans). Average age 28. 56 applicants, 79% accepted, 30 enrolled. In 2009, 38 master's awarded. *Degree requirements:* For master's, comprehensive exam. *Entrance requirements:* For master's, minimum GPA of 3.0. Additional exam requirements/recommendations for international students: Required—TOEFL (minimum score 500 paper-based; 173 computer-based; 61 iBT), IELTS (minimum score 5.5). *Application deadline:* For fall admission, 4/1 priority date for domestic students, 6/1 priority date for international students; for spring admission, 11/1 priority date for domestic and international students. Applications are processed on a rolling basis. Application fee: $70. Electronic applications accepted. *Expenses:* Tuition: Full-time $16,290; part-time $905 per credit. Required fees: $300; $150 per semester. Tuition and fees vary according to program. *Financial support:* Research assistantships, career-related internships or fieldwork and scholarships/grants available. Support available to part-time students. Financial award application deadline: 3/1; financial award applicants required to submit FAFSA. *Faculty research:* Higher order reading comprehension development and instruction, children's literature theory and children's reading interests, critical comprehension development, early writing development at the primary level, self-efficacy with textbook formats, out of school time program effects for at-risk students, teacher training effects for low performing parochial school students. *Unit head:* Dr. Francine Guastello, Acting Chair, 718-990-1475, E-mail: guastelf@stjohns.edu. *Application contact:* Dr. Kelly K. Ronayne, Associate Dean of Graduate Admissions, 718-990-2303, Fax: 718-990-2343, E-mail: graded@stjohns.edu.

St. Joseph's College, Long Island Campus, Program in Literacy and Cognition, Patchogue, NY 11772-2399. Offers MA.

St. Joseph's College, New York, Graduate Programs, Program in Education, Field of Literacy and Cognition, Brooklyn, NY 11205-3688. Offers MA.

Saint Joseph's University, College of Arts and Sciences, Department of Education, Philadelphia, PA 19131-1395. Offers educational leadership (Ed D); elementary education (MS); instructional technology (MS); organizational development and leadership (MS); professional education (MS); reading specialist (MS); secondary education (MS); special education (MS). Part-time and evening/weekend programs available. *Students:* 5 full-time (3 women), 750 part-time (561 women); includes 100 minority (76 African Americans, 1 American Indian/Alaska Native, 11 Asian Americans or Pacific Islanders, 12 Hispanic Americans), 3 international. Average age 33. In 2009, 210 master's, 14 doctorates awarded. *Entrance requirements:* For master's, 2 letters of recommendation, minimum GPA of 3.0, application, official transcripts, personal statement; for doctorate, GRE, master's degree from accredited institution, minimum graduate GPA of 3.5, computer competence, commitment to participate in cohort, interview with program director. Additional exam requirements/recommendations for international students: Required—TOEFL (minimum score 550 paper-based; 213 computer-based; 79 iBT). *Application deadline:* For fall admission, 7/15 priority date for domestic students, 4/15 for international students; for winter admission, 11/15 for domestic students, 1/15 for international students; for spring admission, 11/15 priority date for domestic students, 10/15 for international students. Applications are processed on a rolling basis. Application fee: $35. Electronic applications accepted. *Expenses:* Contact institution. *Financial support:* Unspecified assistantships available. Financial award applicants required to submit FAFSA. *Faculty research:* Early childhood course design, public education professional development. Total annual research expenditures: $91,900. *Unit head:* Dr. Teri Sosa, Director of Graduate Education, 610-660-3162, E-mail: tsosa@sju.edu. *Application contact:* Kate McConnell, Director, Graduate College of Arts and

Sciences Admissions and Retention, 610-660-3184, Fax: 610-660-3230, E-mail: kate.mcconnell@sju.edu.

Saint Leo University, Graduate Studies in Education, Saint Leo, FL 33574-6665. Offers educational leadership (M Ed, Ed S); exceptional student education (M Ed); higher education leadership (Ed S); instructional design (MS); instructional leadership (M Ed); reading (M Ed). Part-time and evening/weekend programs available. Postbaccalaureate distance learning degree programs offered (minimal on-campus study). *Faculty:* 13 full-time (10 women), 12 part-time/adjunct (9 women). *Students:* 432 full-time (355 women), 35 part-time (24 women); includes 56 minority (40 African Americans, 2 American Indian/Alaska Native, 2 Asian Americans or Pacific Islanders, 12 Hispanic Americans), 1 international. Average age 37. In 2009, 131 master's awarded. *Degree requirements:* For master's, comprehensive exam, appropriate State of Florida Certification Tests. *Entrance requirements:* For master's, GRE (minimum score of 1000) or MAT (minimum score of 410) if undergraduate GPA for last 60 hours of coursework was below 3.0 (for M Ed), bachelor's degree from regionally-accredited college or university with minimum GPA of 3.0 for last 60 hours of coursework, 2 recommendations, resume, statement of professional goals, copy of valid teaching certificate (for M Ed); for Ed S, GRE (minimum score 1000) or MAT (minimum score 410) if undergraduate GPA for last 60 hours of coursework less than 3.0, bachelor's degree from regionally-accredited college or university with minimum GPA of 3.0 for last 60 hours of coursework, 2 recommendations, resume, valid teaching certificate. Additional exam requirements/recommendations for international students: Required—TOEFL (minimum score 550 paper-based; 213 computer-based; 80 iBT). *Application deadline:* For fall admission, 7/1 priority date for domestic students; for spring admission, 11/12 priority date for domestic students. Applications are processed on a rolling basis. Application fee: $75. Electronic applications accepted. *Expenses:* Tuition: Part-time $1767 per course. Required fees: $115 per course. *Financial support:* Career-related internships or fieldwork, Federal Work-Study, and health care benefits available. Financial award application deadline: 3/1; financial award applicants required to submit FAFSA. *Faculty research:* The role of the school leader in data analysis of student achievement, teacher recruitment, and teacher effectiveness. *Unit head:* Dr. John Smith, Director, 352-588-8309, Fax: 352-588-8861, E-mail: med@saintleo.edu. *Application contact:* Jared Welling, Director, Graduate/Weekend and Evening Admission, 800-707-8846, Fax: 352-588-7873, E-mail: grad.admissions@saintleo.edu.

Saint Martin's University, Graduate Programs, College of Education, Lacey, WA 98503. Offers administration (M Ed); English as a second language (M Ed); guidance and counseling (M Ed); reading (M Ed); special education (M Ed); teaching (MIT); technology in education (M Ed). *Accreditation:* Teacher Education Accreditation Council. Part-time and evening/weekend programs available. *Faculty:* 13 full-time (9 women), 11 part-time/adjunct (7 women). *Students:* 61 full-time (42 women), 23 part-time (17 women); includes 7 minority (2 African Americans, 1 American Indian/Alaska Native, 3 Asian Americans or Pacific Islanders, 1 Hispanic American), 1 international. Average age 35. 26 applicants, 92% accepted, 22 enrolled. In 2009, 12 master's awarded. *Degree requirements:* For master's, comprehensive exam (for some programs), thesis or alternative, project or comprehensives. *Entrance requirements:* For master's, GRE General Test or MAT, resume. Additional exam requirements/recommendations for international students: Required—TOEFL (minimum score 560 paper-based; 220 computer-based; 83 iBT). *Application deadline:* For fall admission, 6/1 priority date for domestic and international students; for spring admission, 10/1 priority date for domestic and international students. Applications are processed on a rolling basis. Application fee: $35. *Expenses:* Tuition: Full-time $12,440; part-time $827 per credit hour. *Financial support:* In 2009–10, 62 students received support. Career-related internships or fieldwork, Federal Work-Study, institutionally sponsored loans, and unspecified assistantships available. Support available to part-time students. Financial award application deadline: 3/1; financial award applicants required to submit FAFSA. *Faculty research:* Reader's theatre and reader/writer workshops, curriculum and assessment integration, gender and equity, classroom evaluations, organizational leadership. *Unit head:* Dr. Joyce Westgard, Director, 360-438-4509, Fax: 360-438-4486, E-mail: westgard@stmartin.edu. *Application contact:* Ryan M. Smith, Administrative Assistant, 360-438-4333, Fax: 360-438-4486, E-mail: ryan.smith@stmartin.edu.

Saint Mary's College of California, Kalmanovitz School of Education, Program in Reading Leadership, Moraga, CA 94556. Offers MA. Part-time and evening/weekend programs available. *Faculty:* 1 (woman) full-time. *Students:* 10 part-time (all women); includes 1 minority (Hispanic American). Average age 38. In 2009, 5 master's awarded. *Degree requirements:* For master's, thesis or alternative. *Entrance requirements:* For master's, interview, minimum GPA of 3.0. *Application deadline:* Applications are processed on a rolling basis. Application fee: $50. *Expenses:* Tuition: Full-time $35,087; part-time $956 per credit hour. One-time fee: $50 full-time. Part-time tuition and fees vary according to course level, course load, degree level, campus/location and program. *Financial support:* Career-related internships or fieldwork available. Support available to part-time students. Financial award application deadline: 2/15. *Unit head:* Dr. Mary Kay Moskal, Director, 925-631-4726, Fax: 925-376-8379, E-mail: mmoskal@stmarys-ca.edu. *Application contact:* Jane Joyce, Coordinator, Recruitment and Admissions, 925-631-4700, Fax: 925-376-8379, E-mail: soereq@stmarys-ca.edu.

St. Mary's University, Graduate School, Department of Teacher Education, Program in Reading, San Antonio, TX 78228-8507. Offers MA. Part-time programs available. Postbaccalaureate distance learning degree programs offered (no on-campus study). *Degree requirements:* For master's, comprehensive exam. *Entrance requirements:* For master's, GRE. Additional exam requirements/recommendations for international students: Required—TOEFL (minimum score 550 paper-based; 213 computer-based; 80 iBT). Electronic applications accepted. *Expenses:* Tuition: Full-time $8004. Required fees: $536. One-time fee: $5 full-time. Full-time tuition and fees vary according to program.

Saint Mary's University of Minnesota, Schools of Graduate and Professional Programs, Graduate School of Education, Literacy Education Program, Winona, MN 55987-1399. Offers K-12 reading teacher (Certificate); literacy education (MA). *Unit head:* Dr. Jane Anderson, Director, 507-457-6621, E-mail: janders1@smumn.edu. *Application contact:* Jami Spitzer, Director of Admissions for Graduate and Professional Programs, 507-457-7500, E-mail: jspitzer@smumn.edu.

Saint Michael's College, Graduate Programs, Program in Education, Colchester, VT 05439. Offers administration (M Ed, CAGS); arts in education (CAGS); curriculum and instruction (M Ed, CAGS); information technology (CAGS); reading (M Ed); special education (M Ed, CAGS); technology (M Ed). Part-time and evening/weekend programs available. *Degree requirements:* For master's, thesis. *Entrance requirements:* For master's, minimum GPA of 3.0. Electronic applications accepted. *Faculty research:* Integrative curriculum, moral and spiritual dimensions of education, learning styles, multiple intelligences, integrating technology into the curriculum.

Saint Peter's College, Graduate Programs in Education, Program in Special Education, Jersey City, NJ 07306-5997. Offers special education (MA), including applied behavior analysis, literacy. *Degree requirements:* For master's, comprehensive exam. *Entrance requirements:* Additional exam requirements/recommendations for international students: Required—TOEFL. *Application deadline:* Applications are processed on a rolling basis. Electronic applications accepted. *Expenses:* Tuition: Part-time $971 per credit. *Financial support:* Career-related internships or fieldwork, Federal Work-Study, and institutionally sponsored loans available. *Unit head:* Dr. Anthony Sciarrillo, Chairperson, 201-761-6473, Fax: 201-435-5270. *Application contact:* Dr. Anthony Sciarrillo, Chairperson, 201-761-6473, Fax: 201-435-5270.

Saint Peter's College, Graduate Programs in Education, Reading Specialist Program, Jersey City, NJ 07306-5997. Offers reading (MA). *Accreditation:* Teacher Education Accreditation Council. Part-time and evening/weekend programs available. *Faculty:* 1. *Degree requirements:* For master's, comprehensive exam. *Entrance requirements:* For master's, GRE or MAT. Additional exam requirements/recommendations for international students: Required—TOEFL. *Application deadline:* Applications are processed on a rolling basis. Electronic applications accepted. *Expenses:* Tuition: Part-time $971 per credit. *Financial support:* Career-related internships or fieldwork, Federal Work-Study, and institutionally sponsored loans available. *Unit head:* Dr. Anthony Sciarrillo, Chairperson, 201-761-6473, Fax: 201-435-5270. *Application contact:* Dr. Anthony Sciarrillo, Chairperson, 201-761-6473, Fax: 201-435-5270.

St. Thomas Aquinas College, Division of Teacher Education, Sparkill, NY 10976. Offers adolescence education (MST); childhood and special education (MST); childhood education (MST); educational leadership (MS Ed); reading (MS Ed, PMC); special education (MS Ed, PMC); teaching (MS Ed), including elementary education, middle school education, secondary education. *Accreditation:* NCATE. Part-time and evening/weekend programs available. *Degree requirements:* For master's, comprehensive exam, comprehensive professional portfolio; for PMC, action research project. *Entrance requirements:* For master's, New York State Qualifying Exam, GRE General Test or minimum GPA of 3.0, teaching certificate; for PMC, GRE General Test or minimum GPA of 3.0. Electronic applications accepted. *Faculty research:* Computer applications in education, adolescent special education students, literacy development, inclusive practices for special education students.

St. Thomas University, School of Leadership Studies, Institute for Education, Miami Gardens, FL 33054-6459. Offers earth/space science (Certificate); educational administration (MS, Certificate); educational leadership (Ed D); elementary education (MS); ESOL (Certificate); gifted education (Certificate); instructional technology (MS, Certificate); professional/studies (Certificate); reading (MS, Certificate); special education (MS). Part-time and evening/weekend programs available. *Degree requirements:* For master's, comprehensive exam; for doctorate, comprehensive exam, thesis/dissertation. *Entrance requirements:* For master's, interview, minimum GPA of 3.0 or GRE; for doctorate, GRE or MAT. Additional exam requirements/recommendations for international students: Required—TOEFL (minimum score 550 paper-based; 213 computer-based; 79 iBT). Electronic applications accepted.

Saint Xavier University, Graduate Studies, School of Education, Chicago, IL 60655-3105. Offers counseling (MA); counselor education (MA); curriculum and instruction (MA); early childhood education (MA); education (CAS); educational administration (MA); elementary education (MA); field-based education (MA); general educational studies (MA); individualized program (MA); learning disabilities (MA); reading (MA); secondary education (MA). *Accreditation:* NCATE. Part-time and evening/weekend programs available. *Degree requirements:* For master's, thesis or project. *Entrance requirements:* For master's, minimum GPA of 3.0. *Expenses:* Contact institution.

Salem College, Department of Education, Winston-Salem, NC 27101. Offers early education and leadership (MAT); elementary education (MAT); English as a second language (MAT); language and literacy (M Ed); middle school education (MAT); secondary education (MAT); special education (MAT). *Accreditation:* NCATE. Part-time and evening/weekend programs available. *Degree requirements:* For master's, comprehensive exam, practicum (MAT), project (M Ed), oral and written comprehensive exams. *Entrance requirements:* For master's, GRE, minimum GPA of 2.5. *Faculty research:* Content area reading strategies, literacy development, brain compatible instruction.

Salem State College, School of Graduate Studies, Program in Reading, Salem, MA 01970-5353. Offers M Ed. *Accreditation:* NCATE. Part-time and evening/weekend programs available. *Students:* 1 (woman) full-time, 57 part-time (55 women); includes 1 minority (African American). Average age 35. 1 applicant, 100% accepted, 1 enrolled. In 2009, 47 master's awarded. *Entrance requirements:* For master's, GRE or MAT. Additional exam requirements/recommendations for international students: Required—TOEFL (minimum score 550 paper-based; 80 iBT), or IELTS (minimum score 5.5). *Application deadline:* For fall admission, 5/1 for domestic students; for spring admission, 10/1 for domestic students. Applications are processed on a rolling basis. Application fee: $50. *Expenses:* Tuition, state resident: full-time $2520; part-time $275 per credit hour. Tuition, nonresident: full-time $4140; part-time $365 per credit hour. Required fees: $2430. *Financial support:* In 2009–10, 5 students received support. Career-related internships or fieldwork, Federal Work-Study, scholarships/grants, and unspecified assistantships available. Support available to part-time students. Financial award application deadline: 5/1; financial award applicants required to submit FAFSA. *Unit head:* Francesca Pomerantz, Coordinator, 978-542-6310, Fax: 978-542-7023, E-mail: fpomerantz@salemstate.edu. *Application contact:* Dr. Lee Brossoit, Assistant Dean of Graduate Admissions, 978-542-6675, Fax: 978-542-7215, E-mail: lbrossoit@salemstate.edu.

Salisbury University, Graduate Division, Department of Education, Salisbury, MD 21801-6837. Offers educational leadership (M Ed); general (M Ed); reading specialist (M Ed); teaching (MAT). *Accreditation:* NCATE. Part-time and evening/weekend programs available. *Faculty:* 23 full-time (14 women), 9 part-time/adjunct (8 women). *Students:* 33 full-time (18 women), 129 part-time (100 women); includes 14 minority (12 African Americans, 1 Asian American or Pacific Islander, 1 Hispanic American), 1 international. Average age 31. 71 applicants, 54% accepted, 12 enrolled. In 2009, 70 master's awarded. *Degree requirements:* For master's, comprehensive exam (for some programs). *Entrance requirements:* For master's, minimum GPA of 2.75. Additional exam requirements/recommendations for international students: Required—TOEFL (minimum score 550 paper-based; 213 computer-based). *Application deadline:* For fall admission, 3/3 for domestic students; for spring admission, 10/1 for domestic students. Applications are processed on a rolling basis. Application fee: $45. Electronic applications accepted. *Expenses:* Tuition, area resident: Part-time $278 per credit hour. Tuition, state resident: part-time $278 per credit hour. Tuition, nonresident: part-time $574 per credit hour. Required fees: $57 per credit hour. *Financial support:* In 2009–10, 30 students received support. Career-related internships or fieldwork and scholarships/grants available. Support available to part-time students. Financial award applicants required to submit FAFSA. *Unit head:* Dr. Laura Marasco, Program Coordinator, 410-546-6012, E-mail: llmarasco@salisbury.edu. *Application contact:* Tina Melczarek, Administrative Assistant I, 410-543-6281, Fax: 410-548-2593, E-mail: tmmelczarek@salisbury.edu.

Sam Houston State University, College of Education and Applied Science, Department of Language, Literacy, and Special Populations, Huntsville, TX 77341. Offers reading (M Ed, MA, Ed D); special education (M Ed, MA). Part-time and evening/weekend programs available. *Faculty:* 15 full-time (12 women), 1 (woman) part-time/adjunct. *Students:* 2 full-time (both women), 135 part-time (129 women); includes 32 minority (15 African Americans, 1 Asian American or Pacific Islander, 16 Hispanic Americans), 3 international. Average age 36. 55 applicants, 98% accepted, 37 enrolled. In 2009, 24 master's, 1 doctorate awarded. *Entrance requirements:* For master's, GRE General Test, minimum GPA of 2.5. Additional exam requirements/recommendations for international students: Required—TOEFL (minimum score 550 paper-based; 213 computer-based; 79 iBT). *Application deadline:* For fall admission, 8/1 for domestic students; for spring admission, 12/1 for domestic students. Application fee: $20. *Expenses:* Tuition, state resident: full-time $3690; part-time $205 per credit hour. Tuition, nonresident: full-time $8676; part-time $482 per credit hour. Required fees: $1474. Tuition and fees vary according to course load and campus/location. *Financial support:* Teaching assistantships available. Financial award application deadline: 5/31; financial award applicants required to submit FAFSA. *Unit head:* Dr. Sharon Lynch, Chair, 936-294-1122, Fax: 936-294-1131, E-mail: edu_sal@shsu.edu. *Application contact:* Molly Doughtie, Advisor, 936-294-1105, E-mail: edu_mxd@shsu.edu.

San Diego State University, Graduate and Research Affairs, College of Education, School of Teacher Education, Program in Reading Education, San Diego, CA 92182. Offers MA. *Accreditation:* NCATE. Part-time programs available. *Entrance requirements:* For master's, GRE General Test, letters of reference. Additional exam requirements/recommendations for international students: Required—TOEFL. Electronic applications accepted. *Faculty research:* Literacy, writing, reading/writing connection, class size reduction in reading, book clubs, evaluation instruments in reading/language arts.

San Francisco State University, Division of Graduate Studies, College of Education, Department of Elementary Education, Program in Language and Literacy Education, San Francisco, CA 94132-1722. Offers MA.

Reading Education

San Francisco State University, Division of Graduate Studies, College of Humanities, Department of English Language and Literature, San Francisco, CA 94132-1722. Offers composition (MA, Certificate); linguistics (MA); literature (MA); teaching composition (Certificate); teaching English to speakers of other languages (MA); teaching post-secondary reading (Certificate). Part-time programs available.

San Jose State University, Graduate Studies and Research, Connie L. Lurie College of Education, Department of Elementary Education, San Jose, CA 95192-0001. Offers curriculum and instruction (MA); reading (Certificate). *Accreditation:* NCATE. *Students:* 318 full-time (270 women), 163 part-time (140 women); includes 166 minority (5 African Americans, 97 Asian Americans or Pacific Islanders, 64 Hispanic Americans), 7 international. Average age 32. 257 applicants, 87% accepted, 189 enrolled. In 2009, 40 master's awarded. *Degree requirements:* For master's, thesis or alternative. *Application deadline:* For fall admission, 6/29 for domestic students; for spring admission, 11/30 for domestic students. Applications are processed on a rolling basis. Application fee: $59. Electronic applications accepted. *Financial support:* Career-related internships or fieldwork available. Financial award applicants required to submit FAFSA. *Unit head:* Dr. Andrea Whittaker, Chair, 408-924-3751, Fax: 408-924-3775. *Application contact:* Dr. Andrea Whittaker, Chair, 408-924-3751, Fax: 408-924-3775.

Santa Clara University, School of Education and Counseling Psychology, Department of Education, Program in Interdisciplinary Education, Santa Clara, CA 95053. Offers interdisciplinary education (MA), including Catholic education, curriculum and instruction, reading, STEEM, teaching and learning. Part-time and evening/weekend programs available. *Students:* 6 full-time (all women), 73 part-time (60 women); includes 18 minority (1 African American, 1 American Indian/Alaska Native, 9 Asian Americans or Pacific Islanders, 7 Hispanic Americans), 1 international. Average age 34. 35 applicants. In 2009, 36 master's awarded. *Degree requirements:* For master's, comprehensive exam. *Entrance requirements:* For master's, GRE or MAT, minimum GPA of 3.0. Additional exam requirements/recommendations for international students: Required—TOEFL. *Application deadline:* Applications are processed on a rolling basis. *Expenses:* Contact institution. *Financial support:* Fellowships, Federal Work-Study, institutionally sponsored loans, and scholarships/grants available. Support available to part-time students. Financial award application deadline: 5/15; financial award applicants required to submit FAFSA. *Unit head:* Dr. Sara Garcia, Director, 408-554-4507. *Application contact:* Dr. Sara Garcia, Director, 408-554-4507.

Seattle Pacific University, M Ed in Curriculum and Instruction Program, Seattle, WA 98119-1997. Offers reading/language arts education (M Ed). *Accreditation:* NCATE. Part-time and evening/weekend programs available. *Faculty:* 3 full-time (all women), 9 part-time/adjunct (6 women). *Students:* 7 full-time (6 women), 86 part-time (70 women); includes 4 minority (1 Asian American or Pacific Islander, 3 Hispanic Americans), 1 international. Average age 33. 35 applicants, 74% accepted, 26 enrolled. In 2009, 11 master's awarded. *Degree requirements:* For master's, comprehensive exam. *Entrance requirements:* For master's, GRE General Test or MAT, minimum GPA of 3.0. Additional exam requirements/recommendations for international students: Required—TOEFL (minimum score 550 paper-based). *Application deadline:* For fall admission, 7/1 priority date for domestic students, 7/1 for international students; for spring admission, 3/1 priority date for domestic students, 3/1 for international students. Applications are processed on a rolling basis. Application fee: $50. Electronic applications accepted. *Expenses:* Contact institution. *Financial support:* In 2009–10, 61 students received support. Applicants required to submit FAFSA. *Faculty research:* Educational technology, classroom environments, character education. *Unit head:* Dr. Andrew Lumpe, Chair, 206-281-2369. *Application contact:* The Grad Center, 206-281-2091.

Seattle Pacific University, M Ed in Literacy Program, Seattle, WA 98119-1997. Offers M Ed. Part-time programs available. *Faculty:* 2 full-time (1 woman), 1 (woman) part-time/adjunct. *Students:* 1 (woman) full-time, 16 part-time (15 women). Average age 33. 8 applicants, 88% accepted, 7 enrolled. In 2009, 1 master's awarded. *Degree requirements:* For master's, comprehensive exam. *Entrance requirements:* For master's, MAT or GRE (unless minimum undergraduate GPA of 3.4 or master's degree from accredited university). *Application deadline:* Applications are processed on a rolling basis. Application fee: $50. Electronic applications accepted. *Expenses:* Tuition: Part-time $485 per credit. Part-time tuition and fees vary according to course level, degree level and program. *Financial support:* In 2009–10, 8 students received support. Scholarships/grants available. Financial award applicants required to submit FAFSA. *Unit head:* Dr. William Nagy, Co-Chair, 206-281-2253, E-mail: wnagy@spu.edu. *Application contact:* The Grad Center, 206-281-2091.

Seattle University, College of Education, Program in Literacy, Seattle, WA 98122-1090. Offers M Ed, Post-Master's Certificate. *Entrance requirements:* For master's, GRE, MAT or minimum GPA of 3.0, 1 year of K-12 work experience; for Post-Master's Certificate, GRE, MAT or minimum GPA of 3.0, master's degree, WA state teaching certification. Additional exam requirements/recommendations for international students: Required—TOEFL.

Shenandoah University, School of Education and Human Development, Winchester, VA 22601-5195. Offers administrative leadership (D Ed); advanced professional teaching English to speakers of other languages (Certificate); education (MSE); elementary education (Certificate); middle school education (Certificate); organizational leadership (MS); professional studies (Certificate); professional studies (for initial teacher licensure) (Certificate); professional studies (for special education teacher licensure) (Certificate); professional studies (for VA licensure reading specialists) (Certificate); professional studies (for VA licensure) (Certificate); professional teaching English to speakers of other languages (Certificate); public management (Certificate); school reform (Certificate); secondary education (Certificate). *Accreditation:* Teacher Education Accreditation Council. Part-time and evening/weekend programs available. Postbaccalaureate distance learning degree programs offered (minimal on-campus study). *Faculty:* 13 full-time (7 women), 27 part-time/adjunct (20 women). *Students:* 11 full-time (8 women), 382 part-time (276 women); includes 35 minority (17 African Americans, 1 American Indian/Alaska Native, 6 Asian Americans or Pacific Islanders, 11 Hispanic Americans), 4 international. Average age 39. 272 applicants, 95% accepted, 218 enrolled. In 2009, 103 master's, 2 doctorates awarded. *Degree requirements:* For master's, comprehensive exam (for some programs), thesis (for some programs), internship; for doctorate, comprehensive exam, thesis/dissertation; for Certificate, full time teaching in area for 1 year. *Entrance requirements:* For master's, minimum GPA of 3.0 or satisfactory GRE, 3 letters of recommendation, valid teaching license, essay; for doctorate, minimum graduate GPA of 3.5, 3 years of teaching experience, 3 letters of recommendation, writing samples; for Certificate, minimum undergraduate GPA of 3.0, essay, 3 letters of recommendation. Additional exam requirements/recommendations for international students: Required—TOEFL (minimum score 550 paper-based; 213 computer-based; 79 iBT), IELTS (minimum score 6.5). *Application deadline:* For fall admission, 7/1 for domestic and international students; for spring admission, 10/15 for domestic and international students. Application fee: $30. Electronic applications accepted. *Expenses:* Tuition: Full-time $11,925; part-time $695 per credit. Required fees: $400 per semester. *Financial support:* Application deadline: 3/15. *Unit head:* Dr. Steven E. Humphries, Dean, 540-535-3574, E-mail: shumphri@su.edu. *Application contact:* David Anthony, Dean of Admissions, 540-665-4581, Fax: 540-665-4627, E-mail: admit@su.edu.

Shippensburg University of Pennsylvania, School of Graduate Studies, College of Education and Human Services, Department of Teacher Education, Shippensburg, PA 17257-2299. Offers curriculum and instruction (M Ed), including biology, early childhood education, elementary education, English, foreign languages, geography/earth science, history, mathematics, middle school education; reading (M Ed). *Accreditation:* NCATE. Part-time and evening/weekend programs available. *Degree requirements:* For master's, comprehensive exam (for some programs), thesis optional, practicum or internship (for some programs). *Entrance requirements:* For master's, MAT (if GPA less than 2.75), interview, 3 letters of recommendation, writing sample of teaching background and future goals. Additional exam requirements/recommendations for international students: Required—TOEFL (minimum score 560 paper-based; 220 computer-based); Recommended—IELTS (minimum score 6). Electronic applications accepted.

Siena Heights University, Graduate College, Program in Teacher Education, Concentration in Elementary Education, Adrian, MI 49221-1796. Offers elementary education/reading (MA). Part-time programs available. *Degree requirements:* For master's, thesis, presentation. *Entrance requirements:* For master's, interview, minimum GPA of 3.0.

Siena Heights University, Graduate College, Program in Teacher Education, Concentration in Secondary Education, Adrian, MI 49221-1796. Offers secondary education/reading (MA). Part-time programs available. *Degree requirements:* For master's, thesis, presentation. *Entrance requirements:* For master's, minimum GPA of 3.0, interview.

Slippery Rock University of Pennsylvania, Graduate Studies (Recruitment), College of Education, Department of Elementary Education and Early Childhood, Slippery Rock, PA 16057-1383. Offers reading (M Ed). *Accreditation:* NCATE. Part-time and evening/weekend programs available. *Degree requirements:* For master's, comprehensive exam (for some programs), thesis (for some programs), reflective presentation. *Entrance requirements:* For master's, GRE General Test, MAT, minimum GPA of 2.75 (3.0 for initial certification programs). Additional exam requirements/recommendations for international students: Required—TOEFL (minimum score 550 paper-based; 213 computer-based). *Application deadline:* For fall admission, 3/1 priority date for domestic students, 5/1 priority date for international students; for spring admission, 11/1 priority date for domestic students, 9/1 priority date for international students. Applications are processed on a rolling basis. Application fee: $25 ($30 for international students). Electronic applications accepted. *Expenses:* Tuition, state resident: full-time $6666; part-time $370 per credit. Tuition, nonresident: full-time $10,666; part-time $593 per credit. Required fees: $2184; $182 per credit. *Financial support:* Career-related internships or fieldwork, Federal Work-Study, scholarships/grants, and unspecified assistantships available. Support available to part-time students. Financial award application deadline: 5/1; financial award applicants required to submit FAFSA. *Unit head:* Dr. Suzanne Rose, Graduate Coordinator, 724-738-2863, Fax: 724-738-4987, E-mail: suzanne.rose@sru.edu. *Application contact:* Angela Piverotto, Interim Director of Graduate Studies, 724-738-2051, Fax: 724-738-2146, E-mail: graduate.admissions@sru.edu.

Sojourner-Douglass College, Graduate Program, Baltimore, MD 21205-1814. Offers human services (MASS); public administration (MASS); urban education (reading) (MASS). Part-time and evening/weekend programs available. *Degree requirements:* For master's, comprehensive exam, written proposal oral defense. *Entrance requirements:* For master's, Graduate Examination.

Southeastern Louisiana University, College of Arts, Humanities and Social Sciences, Department of English, Hammond, LA 70402. Offers creative writing (MA); language and literacy (MA); professional writing (MA). Part-time and evening/weekend programs available. *Faculty:* 15 full-time (7 women), 1 (woman) part-time/adjunct. *Students:* 27 full-time (15 women), 22 part-time (15 women); includes 4 minority (3 African Americans, 1 Asian American or Pacific Islander). Average age 29. 16 applicants, 94% accepted, 11 enrolled. In 2009, 12 master's awarded. *Degree requirements:* For master's, one foreign language, comprehensive exam, thesis optional. *Entrance requirements:* For master's, GRE General Test (850 or better), 24 undergraduate credit hours in English, minimum GPA of 2.5. Additional exam requirements/recommendations for international students: Required—TOEFL (minimum score 500 paper-based; 173 computer-based; 61 iBT). *Application deadline:* For fall admission, 7/15 priority date for domestic students, 6/1 priority date for international students; for spring admission, 12/1 priority date for domestic students, 10/1 priority date for international students. Applications are processed on a rolling basis. Application fee: $20 ($30 for international students). Electronic applications accepted. *Expenses:* Tuition, state resident: full-time $3086; part-time $225 per credit hour. Tuition, nonresident: part-time $529 per credit hour. Required fees: $1195. Tuition and fees vary according to course level and course load. *Financial support:* In 2009–10, 11 students received support, including 1 fellowship (averaging $13,050 per year), 9 research assistantships (averaging $8,078 per year), 1 teaching assistantship (averaging $6,700 per year); career-related internships or fieldwork, Federal Work-Study, institutionally sponsored loans, scholarships/grants, and administrative assistantships also available. Support available to part-time students. Financial award application deadline: 5/1; financial award applicants required to submit FAFSA. *Faculty research:* Composition/rhetoric, professional and technical writing, film and performance studies, literary criticism, creative writing. Total annual research expenditures: $34,307. *Unit head:* Dr. David Hanson, Department Head, 985-549-2100, Fax: 985-549-5021, E-mail: dhanson@selu.edu. *Application contact:* Sandra Meyers, Graduate Admissions Analyst, 985-549-5620, Fax: 985-549-5632, E-mail: admissions@selu.edu.

Southeastern Oklahoma State University, School of Education, Durant, OK 74701-0609. Offers math specialist (M Ed); reading specialist (M Ed); school administration (M Ed); school counseling (M Ed). *Accreditation:* NCATE. Part-time and evening/weekend programs available. *Faculty:* 52 full-time (19 women), 1 (woman) part-time/adjunct. *Students:* 14 full-time (11 women), 73 part-time (58 women); includes 22 minority (4 African Americans, 17 American Indian/Alaska Native, 1 Hispanic American). Average age 32. 18 applicants, 100% accepted, 18 enrolled. *Degree requirements:* For master's, comprehensive exam, thesis optional, portfolio (M Ed). *Entrance requirements:* For master's, GRE General Test (MBS), minimum GPA of 3.0 in last 60 hours or 2.75 overall. Additional exam requirements/recommendations for international students: Required—TOEFL (minimum score 550 paper-based; 213 computer-based). *Application deadline:* For fall admission, 8/1 for domestic students, 6/1 for international students; for spring admission, 1/5 for domestic students, 11/1 for international students. Application fee: $20 ($55 for international students). Electronic applications accepted. *Financial support:* In 2009–10, 1 teaching assistantship with full tuition reimbursement (averaging $5,000 per year) was awarded; Federal Work-Study, institutionally sponsored loans, and tuition waivers (partial) also available. Support available to part-time students. Financial award application deadline: 6/15; financial award applicants required to submit FAFSA. *Unit head:* Dr. Melanie Price, Chair, 580-745-2602, Fax: 580-745-7474, E-mail: mprice@se.edu. *Application contact:* Carrie Williamson, Graduate Secretary, 580-745-2200, Fax: 580-745-7474, E-mail: cwilliamson@se.edu.

Southern Adventist University, School of Education and Psychology, Collegedale, TN 37315-0370. Offers clinical mental health counseling (MS); inclusive education (MS Ed); instructional leadership (MS Ed); literacy education (MS Ed); outdoor teacher education (MS Ed); school counseling (MS). *Accreditation:* NCATE. Part-time and evening/weekend programs available. *Faculty:* 4 full-time (2 women), 8 part-time/adjunct (5 women). *Students:* 33 full-time (15 women), 17 part-time (13 women); includes 16 minority (7 African Americans, 9 Hispanic Americans). Average age 30. In 2009, 23 master's awarded. *Degree requirements:* For master's, comprehensive exam (for some programs), thesis optional, position paper (MS), portfolio (MS Ed in outdoor teacher education). *Entrance requirements:* For master's, interview (MS); 9 semester hours of upper division course work in psychology or related field, including 1 course in psychology research or statistics; 9 semester hours of education (MS Ed). Additional exam requirements/recommendations for international students: Required—TOEFL (minimum score 600 paper-based; 250 computer-based; 100 iBT). *Application deadline:* For fall admission, 7/1 priority date for domestic students, 6/1 priority date for international students; for winter admission, 11/1 priority date for domestic students, 10/1 priority date for international students; for spring admission, 4/1 priority date for domestic students, 3/1 priority date for international students. Applications are processed on a rolling basis. Application fee: $25. Electronic applications accepted. *Expenses:* Tuition: Full-time $13,149; part-time $487 per credit hour. *Financial support:* In 2009–10, 7 students received support, including 1 research assistantship with full tuition reimbursement available (averaging $15,000 per year), 5 teaching assistantships with full tuition reimbursements available (averaging $15,000 per year); career-related internships or fieldwork, scholarships/grants, tuition waivers (partial), and unspecified assistantships also available. Support available to part-time students. Financial award application deadline: 4/1; financial award applicants required to submit FAFSA. *Unit head:* Dr. Wesley Taylor, Dean, 423-236-2444, Fax: 423-236-1765, E-mail: jwtv@southern.edu. *Application contact:* Mikhaile Spence, Information Contact, 423-236-2496, Fax: 423-236-1765, E-mail: maspence@southern.edu.

Southern Arkansas University–Magnolia, Graduate Programs, Magnolia, AR 71753. Offers agriculture (MS); business administration (MBA); computer and information sciences (MS); counseling (MS); education (M Ed), including counseling and development, curriculum and instruction emphasis, educational administration and supervision, elementary education, middle level emphasis, reading emphasis, secondary education, TESOL emphasis; kinesiology (MS); library media and information specialist (M Ed); mental health and clinical counseling (MS); public administration (EMPA); school counseling (M Ed); teaching (MAT). *Accreditation:* NCATE. Part-time and evening/weekend programs available. *Faculty:* 43 full-time (24 women), 12 part-time/adjunct (7 women). *Students:* 116 full-time (78 women), 333 part-time (255 women); includes 105 minority (98 African Americans, 3 American Indian/Alaska Native, 3 Asian Americans or Pacific Islanders, 1 Hispanic American), 11 international. Average age 33. In 2009, 88 master's awarded. *Degree requirements:* For master's, comprehensive exam, thesis optional. *Entrance requirements:* For master's, GRE, MAT or GMAT, minimum GPA of 2.75. *Application deadline:* For fall admission, 8/15 for domestic students; for winter admission, 1/8 for domestic students; for spring admission, 1/8 for domestic students. Applications are processed on a rolling basis. Application fee: $0. *Expenses:* Tuition, state resident: full-time $3798; part-time $211 per hour. Tuition, nonresident: full-time $5580; part-time $310 per hour. Required fees: $584. *Financial support:* Career-related internships or fieldwork, Federal Work-Study, scholarships/grants, tuition waivers (full), and unspecified assistantships available. Financial award applicants required to submit FAFSA. *Faculty research:* Alternative certification for teachers, supervision of instruction, instructional leadership, counseling. *Unit head:* Dr. Kim Bloss, Dean, Graduate Studies, 870-235-4150, Fax: 870-235-5227, E-mail: kkbloss@saumag.edu. *Application contact:* Dr. Kim Bloss, Dean, Graduate Studies, 870-235-4150, Fax: 870-235-5227, E-mail: kkbloss@saumag.edu.

Southern Connecticut State University, School of Graduate Studies, School of Education, Program in Reading, New Haven, CT 06515-1355. Offers MS, Diploma. Part-time and evening/weekend programs available. *Students:* 5 full-time (all women), 193 part-time (189 women); includes 2 minority (1 Asian American or Pacific Islander, 1 Hispanic American). 67 applicants, 66% accepted, 29 enrolled. In 2009, 37 master's, 16 other advanced degrees awarded. *Degree requirements:* For master's, thesis or alternative. *Entrance requirements:* For master's, interview, teaching certificate; for Diploma, master's degree. *Application deadline:* For fall admission, 7/15 priority date for domestic students. Applications are processed on a rolling basis. Application fee: $50. Electronic applications accepted. Tuition and fees vary according to program. *Financial support:* Application deadline: 4/15. *Unit head:* Dr. Deborah Newton, Chairperson, 203-392-5941, Fax: 203-392-5927, E-mail: newtond2@southernct.edu. *Application contact:* Dr. Nancy Boyles, Graduate Coordinator, 203-392-5946, E-mail: boylesn1@southernct.edu.

Southern Illinois University Edwardsville, Graduate Studies and Research, School of Education, Department of Curriculum and Instruction, Program in Literacy Education, Edwardsville, IL 62026-0001. Offers MS Ed. Part-time programs available. *Students:* 38 part-time (all women); includes 1 minority (African American). Average age 26. 13 applicants, 92% accepted. In 2009, 11 master's awarded. *Degree requirements:* For master's, comprehensive exam, research paper. *Entrance requirements:* Additional exam requirements/recommendations for international students: Required—TOEFL (minimum score 550 paper-based; 213 computer-based; 79 iBT), IELTS (minimum score 6.5). *Application deadline:* For fall admission, 7/23 for domestic students, 6/1 for international students; for spring admission, 12/11 for domestic students, 10/1 for international students. Applications are processed on a rolling basis. Application fee: $30. Electronic applications accepted. *Expenses:* Tuition, state resident: part-time $1252.50 per semester. Tuition, nonresident: part-time $3131.25 per semester. Required fees: $586.85 per semester. Tuition and fees vary according to course load. *Financial support:* In 2009–10, 1 teaching assistantship (averaging $8,064 per year) was awarded; fellowships, research assistantships, career-related internships or fieldwork, Federal Work-Study, institutionally sponsored loans, scholarships/grants, traineeships, and unspecified assistantships also available. Support available to part-time students. Financial award application deadline: 3/1; financial award applicants required to submit FAFSA. *Unit head:* Dr. Stephanie McAndrews, Director, 618-650-3426, E-mail: smcandr@siue.edu. *Application contact:* Dr. Stephanie McAndrews, Director, 618-650-3426, E-mail: smcandr@siue.edu.

Southern Illinois University Edwardsville, Graduate Studies and Research, School of Education, Department of Curriculum and Instruction, Program in Literacy Specialist, Edwardsville, IL 62026-0001. Offers Post-Master's Certificate. Part-time programs available. *Students:* 9 part-time (all women). Average age 26. 5 applicants, 80% accepted. In 2009, 2 Post-Master's Certificates awarded. *Entrance requirements:* Additional exam requirements/recommendations for international students: Required—TOEFL (minimum score 550 paper-based; 213 computer-based; 79 iBT), IELTS (minimum score 6.5). *Application deadline:* For fall admission, 7/23 for domestic students, 6/1 for international students; for spring admission, 12/11 for domestic students, 10/1 for international students. Applications are processed on a rolling basis. Application fee: $30. Electronic applications accepted. *Expenses:* Tuition, state resident: part-time $1252.50 per semester. Tuition, nonresident: part-time $3131.25 per semester. Required fees: $586.85 per semester. Tuition and fees vary according to course load. *Financial support:* Fellowships with full tuition reimbursements, research assistantships with full tuition reimbursements, teaching assistantships with full tuition reimbursements, career-related internships or fieldwork, Federal Work-Study, institutionally sponsored loans, scholarships/grants, traineeships, and unspecified assistantships available. Support available to part-time students. Financial award application deadline: 3/1; financial award applicants required to submit FAFSA. *Unit head:* Dr. Stephanie McAndrews, Director, 618-650-3426, E-mail: smcandr@siue.edu. *Application contact:* Dr. Stephanie McAndrews, Director, 618-650-3426, E-mail: smcandr@siue.edu.

Southern Oregon University, Graduate Studies, School of Education, Ashland, OR 97520. Offers elementary education (MA Ed, MS Ed), including classroom teacher, early childhood, handicapped learner, reading, supervision; secondary education (MA Ed, MS Ed), including classroom teacher, handicapped learner, reading, supervision; teaching (MAT). *Degree requirements:* For master's, thesis optional. *Entrance requirements:* For master's, GRE General Test, minimum GPA of 3.0. Electronic applications accepted.

Southwestern Adventist University, Education Department, Graduate Program, Keene, TX 76059. Offers curriculum and instruction with reading emphasis (M Ed); educational leadership (M Ed). Part-time and evening/weekend programs available. *Degree requirements:* For master's, thesis or alternative, professional paper. *Entrance requirements:* For master's, GRE General Test.

State University of New York at Binghamton, Graduate School, School of Education, Program in Literacy Education, Binghamton, NY 13902-6000. Offers MS Ed. *Accreditation:* Teacher Education Accreditation Council. Part-time and evening/weekend programs available. *Students:* 12 full-time (11 women), 32 part-time (29 women); includes 1 minority (Hispanic American). Average age 27. 19 applicants, 84% accepted, 13 enrolled. In 2009, 27 master's awarded. *Entrance requirements:* For master's, GRE General Test. Additional exam requirements/recommendations for international students: Required—TOEFL (minimum score 550 paper-based; 213 computer-based; 80 iBT). *Application deadline:* For fall admission, 2/1 priority date for domestic and international students; for spring admission, 10/15 priority date for domestic and international students. Applications are processed on a rolling basis. Application fee: $60. Electronic applications accepted. *Financial support:* Fellowships, research assistantships, career-related internships or fieldwork, Federal Work-Study, institutionally sponsored loans, scholarships/grants, health care benefits, tuition waivers, and unspecified assistantships available. Financial award application deadline: 2/15; financial award applicants required to submit FAFSA. *Unit head:* Dr. S. G. Grant, Dean of School of Education, 607-777-7329, E-mail: sggrant@binghamton.edu. *Application contact:* Victoria Williams, Recruiting and Admissions Coordinator, 607-777-2151, Fax: 607-777-2501, E-mail: vwilliam@binghamton.edu.

State University of New York at Fredonia, Graduate Studies, College of Education, Program in Literacy, Fredonia, NY 14063-1136. Offers MS Ed. *Accreditation:* NCATE. Part-time and

evening/weekend programs available. *Degree requirements:* For master's, thesis optional. *Expenses:* Tuition, state resident: full-time $8370; part-time $349 per credit. Tuition, nonresident: full-time $13,250; part-time $552 per credit. Required fees: $1289; $53.55 per credit.

State University of New York at New Paltz, Graduate School, School of Education, Department of Educational Studies, Program in Special Education, New Paltz, NY 12561. Offers adolescence (7-12) (MS Ed); adolescence special education and literacy education (MS Ed); childhood (1-6) (MS Ed); childhood special education and literacy education (MS Ed); early childhood (B-2) (MS Ed). *Accreditation:* NCATE. Part-time and evening/weekend programs available. *Faculty:* 5 full-time (3 women), 7 part-time/adjunct (all women). *Students:* 33 full-time (30 women), 73 part-time (58 women); includes 4 minority (1 African American, 1 American Indian/Alaska Native, 1 Asian American or Pacific Islander, 1 Hispanic American). Average age 31. 53 applicants, 45% accepted, 19 enrolled. In 2009, 48 master's awarded. *Degree requirements:* For master's, portfolio. *Entrance requirements:* For master's, minimum GPA of 3.0 (3.2 for special education and literacy programs), NYS teaching certificate. Additional exam requirements/recommendations for international students: Required—TOEFL (minimum score 550 paper-based; 213 computer-based; 80 iBT), IELTS (minimum score 6.5). *Application deadline:* For fall admission, 3/15 priority date for domestic students, 3/15 for international students; for spring admission, 11/1 for domestic and international students. Application fee: $50. Electronic applications accepted. *Financial support:* In 2009–10, 1 student received support, including 1 fellowship (averaging $9,000 per year); career-related internships or fieldwork, Federal Work-Study, and institutionally sponsored loans also available. Financial award application deadline: 8/1; financial award applicants required to submit FAFSA. *Faculty research:* Grouping formats. *Unit head:* Dr. Spencer Salend, Coordinator, 845-257-2831, E-mail: salends@newpaltz.edu. *Application contact:* Dr. Catherine Whittaker, Coordinator, 845-257-2831, E-mail: whittakc@newpaltz.edu.

State University of New York at New Paltz, Graduate School, School of Education, Department of Elementary Education, New Paltz, NY 12561. Offers childhood education (MS Ed); childhood education (1-6) (MST); literacy education (5-12) (MS Ed); literacy education (B-6) (MS Ed); literacy education and adolescence special education (MS Ed); literacy education and childhood education and childhood special education (MS Ed). *Accreditation:* NCATE. Part-time and evening/weekend programs available. *Faculty:* 7 full-time (all women), 7 part-time/adjunct (5 women). *Students:* 61 full-time (54 women), 139 part-time (126 women); includes 8 minority (1 African American, 2 American Indian/Alaska Native, 2 Asian Americans or Pacific Islanders, 3 Hispanic Americans). Average age 30. 122 applicants, 63% accepted, 63 enrolled. In 2009, 81 master's awarded. *Degree requirements:* For master's, comprehensive exam (for some programs), portfolio. *Entrance requirements:* For master's, GRE and MAT (MST), minimum GPA of 3.0 (3.2 for literacy and special education), NYS teaching certificate (MS Ed). Additional exam requirements/recommendations for international students: Required—TOEFL (minimum score 550 paper-based; 213 computer-based; 80 iBT), IELTS (minimum score 6.5). *Application deadline:* For fall admission, 4/1 for domestic and international students; for spring admission, 11/15 for domestic and international students. Application fee: $50. Electronic applications accepted. *Financial support:* Federal Work-Study and institutionally sponsored loans available. Financial award application deadline: 8/1; financial award applicants required to submit FAFSA. *Faculty research:* Multi-sensory teaching methods, volunteer tutoring programs for struggling readers, school readiness and transition, math/science/technology, university-school partnerships. *Unit head:* Dr. Aaron Isabelle, Chair, 845-257-2860, E-mail: isabella@newpaltz.edu. *Application contact:* Caroline Murphy, Graduate Admissions Advisor, 845-257-3285, Fax: 845-257-3284, E-mail: gradschool@newpaltz.edu.

State University of New York at Oswego, Graduate Studies, School of Education, Department of Curriculum and Instruction, Oswego, NY 13126. Offers art education (MAT); elementary education (MS Ed); literacy education (MS Ed); secondary education (MS Ed); special education (MS Ed). Part-time and evening/weekend programs available. *Degree requirements:* For master's, comprehensive exam (for some programs), thesis optional. *Entrance requirements:* For master's, GRE General Test, minimum GPA of 2.7, provisional teaching certificate. Additional exam requirements/recommendations for international students: Required—TOEFL (minimum score 560 paper-based; 220 computer-based). *Faculty research:* Classroom applications for microcomputers; classroom questioning, wait-time, and achievement; values clarification and academic achievement.

State University of New York at Plattsburgh, Division of Education, Health, and Human Services, Program in Teacher Education: Literacy Education, Plattsburgh, NY 12901-2681. Offers birth-grade 6 (MS Ed); grades 5-12 (MS Ed). *Accreditation:* Teacher Education Accreditation Council. Part-time and evening/weekend programs available. *Faculty:* 5 full-time (4 women), 8 part-time/adjunct (7 women). *Students:* 7 full-time (6 women), 15 part-time (13 women); includes 1 minority (American Indian/Alaska Native). Average age 27. 12 applicants, 67% accepted, 6 enrolled. In 2009, 23 master's awarded. *Degree requirements:* For master's, comprehensive exam, thesis, portfolio. *Entrance requirements:* For master's, minimum GPA of 2.75. Additional exam requirements/recommendations for international students: Required—TOEFL (minimum score 550 paper-based; 213 computer-based; 79 iBT). *Application deadline:* For fall admission, 2/15 priority date for domestic students; for spring admission, 10/15 priority date for domestic students. Applications are processed on a rolling basis. Application fee: $75. *Expenses:* Tuition, state resident: full-time $8370; part-time $349 per credit hour. Tuition, nonresident: full-time $13,250; part-time $552 per credit hour. Required fees: $1130. *Financial support:* Federal Work-Study available. Support available to part-time students. Financial award application deadline: 4/15; financial award applicants required to submit FAFSA. *Faculty research:* Reading pedagogy, early childhood literacy, children's literature, integrated language arts. *Unit head:* Dr. Heidi Schnackenberg, Coordinator, 518-564-5143, E-mail: schnachl@plattsburgh.edu. *Application contact:* Marguerite Adelman, Assistant Director, Graduate Admissions, 518-564-4723, Fax: 518-564-4722, E-mail: adelmaml@plattsburgh.edu.

State University of New York College at Cortland, Graduate Studies, School of Education, Program in Literacy, Cortland, NY 13045. Offers MS Ed. *Accreditation:* NCATE. Part-time and evening/weekend programs available. *Degree requirements:* For master's, one foreign language, comprehensive exam, thesis (for some programs). *Entrance requirements:* Additional exam requirements/recommendations for international students: Required—TOEFL.

State University of New York College at Geneseo, Graduate Studies, School of Education, Program in Reading, Geneseo, NY 14454-1401. Offers MS Ed. Part-time and evening/weekend programs available. *Faculty:* 6 full-time (3 women). *Students:* 17 full-time (16 women), 52 part-time (46 women); includes 2 minority (1 African American, 1 Asian American or Pacific Islander). Average age 26. 46 applicants, 100% accepted, 36 enrolled. In 2009, 36 master's awarded. *Degree requirements:* For master's, reading clinics, action research project. *Application deadline:* For fall admission, 3/1 priority date for domestic students; for spring admission, 10/1 for domestic students. Application fee: $50. *Expenses:* Tuition, state resident: full-time $8370; part-time $349 per credit hour. Tuition, nonresident: full-time $13,250; part-time $552 per credit hour. Required fees: $700.52; $29 per credit hour. *Financial support:* In 2009–10, 3 students received support. Scholarships/grants, health care benefits, tuition waivers (full), and unspecified assistantships available. Support available to part-time students. Financial award application deadline: 4/1; financial award applicants required to submit FAFSA. *Unit head:* Dr. Osman Alawiye, Dean/Chairperson, 585-245-5560, Fax: 585-245-5220, E-mail: alawiyeo@geneseo.edu. *Application contact:* Dr. Susan Salmon, Assistant to the Dean/Graduate Liaison, 585-245-5560, Fax: 585-245-5220, E-mail: salmon@geneseo.edu.

State University of New York College at Oneonta, Graduate Education, Division of Education, Department of Elementary Education and Reading, Oneonta, NY 13820-4015. Offers childhood education (MS Ed); literacy education (MS Ed). *Accreditation:* NCATE. Part-time and evening/weekend programs available. *Entrance requirements:* For master's, GRE General Test. *Application deadline:* For fall admission, 3/25 priority date for domestic students; for spring admission, 10/1 priority date for domestic students. Applications are processed on a rolling basis. Application fee: $50. *Expenses:* Tuition, state resident: part-time $349 per credit hour. Tuition, nonresident: full-time $12,870; part-time $552 per credit hour. Required fees: $1280;

Reading Education

State University of New York College at Oneonta (continued)
$15.85 per credit hour. *Unit head:* Dr. Constance Feldt-Golden, Chair, 607-436-3176, Fax: 607-436-2554, E-mail: feldtcc@oneonta.edu. *Application contact:* Dr. Constance Feldt-Golden, Chair, 607-436-3176, Fax: 607-436-2554, E-mail: feldtcc@oneonta.edu.

State University of New York College at Potsdam, School of Education and Professional Studies, Program in Literacy, Potsdam, NY 13676. Offers literacy educator (MS Ed); literacy specialist (MS Ed), including birth-grade 6, grades 5-12. *Accreditation:* NCATE. Part-time programs available. Postbaccalaureate distance learning degree programs offered (minimal on-campus study). *Faculty:* 5 full-time (3 women), 9 part-time/adjunct (all women). *Students:* 52 full-time (49 women), 51 part-time (43 women); includes 1 minority (American Indian/Alaska Native), 1 international. 27 applicants, 100% accepted, 26 enrolled. In 2009, 79 master's awarded. *Degree requirements:* For master's, thesis optional, culminating experience. *Entrance requirements:* For master's, minimum GPA of 2.75 in last 60 hours of course work. Additional exam requirements/recommendations for international students: Required—TOEFL (minimum score 550 paper-based; 213 computer-based; 80 iBT), IELTS (minimum score 6). *Application deadline:* For fall admission, 4/1 priority date for domestic and international students; for spring admission, 10/15 priority date for domestic and international students. Applications are processed on a rolling basis. Application fee: $50. *Expenses:* Tuition, state resident: full-time $8370; part-time $349 per credit hour. Tuition, nonresident: full-time $13,250; part-time $552 per credit hour. Required fees: $942; $38.70 per credit hour. *Financial support:* In 2009–10, 2 students received support; fellowships, teaching assistantships with full tuition reimbursements available, career-related internships or fieldwork, Federal Work-Study, scholarships/grants, and unspecified assistantships available. Support available to part-time students. Financial award application deadline: 3/1; financial award applicants required to submit FAFSA. *Unit head:* Dr. Lynn Hall, Chairperson, 315-267-2540, Fax: 315-267-4802, E-mail: hallla@potsdam.edu. *Application contact:* Peter Cutler, Graduate Admissions Counselor, 315-267-3154, Fax: 315-267-4802, E-mail: cutlerpj@potsdam.edu.

Stetson University, College of Arts and Sciences, Division of Education, Department of Teacher Education, Program in Reading Education, DeLand, FL 32723. Offers M Ed. *Students:* 35 part-time (34 women); includes 12 minority (5 African Americans, 1 American Indian/Alaska Native, 6 Hispanic Americans). Average age 31. In 2009, 17 master's awarded. Tuition and fees vary according to course load, campus/location and program. *Unit head:* Dr. Gail Choice, Coordinator, 386-822-7075. *Application contact:* Diana Belian, Office of Graduate Studies, 386-822-7075, Fax: 386-822-7388, E-mail: dbelian@stetson.edu.

Sul Ross State University, Rio Grande College of Sul Ross State University, Alpine, TX 79832. Offers business administration (MBA); teacher education (M Ed), including bilingual education, counseling, educational diagnostics, elementary education, general education, reading, school administration, secondary education. Part-time and evening/weekend programs available. *Degree requirements:* For master's, thesis optional. *Entrance requirements:* For master's, GMAT or GRE General Test, minimum GPA of 2.5 in last 60 hours of undergraduate work. *Faculty research:* Drug and substance abuse counseling, U.S.-Mexico border economic development.

Sul Ross State University, School of Professional Studies, Department of Teacher Education, Program in Reading Specialist, Alpine, TX 79832. Offers M Ed. Part-time and evening/weekend programs available. *Degree requirements:* For master's, thesis optional. *Entrance requirements:* For master's, GMAT or GRE General Test, minimum GPA of 2.5 in last 60 hours of undergraduate work.

Syracuse University, School of Education, Program in Literacy Education: Birth-Grade 6, Syracuse, NY 13244. Offers MS. Part-time programs available. *Students:* 7 full-time (all women), 4 part-time (all women). Average age 24. 12 applicants, 100% accepted, 4 enrolled. In 2009, 15 master's awarded. *Degree requirements:* For master's, thesis or alternative. *Entrance requirements:* For master's, New York state teacher certification. Additional exam requirements/recommendations for international students: Required—TOEFL (minimum score 100 iBT). *Application deadline:* For fall admission, 2/1 priority date for domestic and international students; for spring admission, 10/15 for domestic students, 10/15 priority date for international students. Applications are processed on a rolling basis. Application fee: $75. Electronic applications accepted. *Expenses:* Tuition: Full-time $26,808; part-time $1117 per credit. Required fees: $1024. *Financial support:* Fellowships with tuition reimbursements, teaching assistantships with tuition reimbursements available. Financial award application deadline: 1/1; financial award applicants required to submit FAFSA. *Faculty research:* Literacy, knowledge modeling, assessment, teaching of literature, writing. *Unit head:* Dr. Rachel Brown, Program Coordinator, 315-443-5672, E-mail: rfbrown@syr.edu. *Application contact:* Liza Rochelson, Graduate Recruiter, School of Education, 315-443-2505, E-mail: e-gradrcrt@syr.edu.

Syracuse University, School of Education, Program in Literacy Education: Grades 5-12, Syracuse, NY 13244. Offers MS. Part-time programs available. *Students:* 7 full-time (5 women), 7 part-time (6 women); includes 4 minority (2 African Americans, 2 Hispanic Americans). Average age 29. 8 applicants, 100% accepted, 5 enrolled. In 2009, 5 master's awarded. *Entrance requirements:* For master's, New York state teacher certification or eligibility. Additional exam requirements/recommendations for international students: Required—TOEFL (minimum score 100 iBT). *Application deadline:* For fall admission, 2/1 priority date for domestic and international students. Application fee: $75. Electronic applications accepted. *Expenses:* Tuition: Full-time $26,808; part-time $1117 per credit. Required fees: $1024. *Financial support:* Fellowships with tuition reimbursements, teaching assistantships with tuition reimbursements, tuition waivers (partial) available. Financial award application deadline: 1/1. *Unit head:* Dr. Rachel Brown, Program Coordinator, 315-443-5183, E-mail: rfbrown@syr.edu. *Application contact:* Liza Rochelson, Graduate Recruiter, School of Education, 315-443-2505, E-mail: e-gradrcrt@syr.edu.

Syracuse University, School of Education, Program in Reading Education, Syracuse, NY 13244. Offers PhD. Part-time programs available. *Students:* 6 full-time (5 women), 8 part-time (7 women). Average age 38. 3 applicants, 0% accepted, 0 enrolled. *Degree requirements:* For doctorate, thesis/dissertation. *Entrance requirements:* For doctorate, GRE. Additional exam requirements/recommendations for international students: Required—TOEFL (minimum score 100 iBT). *Application deadline:* For fall admission, 2/1 priority date for domestic and international students; for spring admission, 10/15 priority date for domestic and international students. Applications are processed on a rolling basis. Application fee: $75. Electronic applications accepted. *Expenses:* Tuition: Full-time $26,808; part-time $1117 per credit. Required fees: $1024. *Financial support:* Fellowships with tuition reimbursements, research assistantships with tuition reimbursements, teaching assistantships with tuition reimbursements available. Financial award application deadline: 1/1. *Unit head:* Dr. Kathleen Hinchman, Graduate Chair, 315-443-4757, E-mail: kahinchm@syr.edu. *Application contact:* Liza Rochelson, Graduate Recruiter, School of Education, 315-443-2505, E-mail: e-gradrcrt@syr.edu.

Teachers College, Columbia University, Graduate Faculty of Education, Department of Curriculum and Teaching, Program in Literacy Specialist, New York, NY 10027-6696. Offers MA. *Students:* 24 full-time (all women), 52 part-time (50 women); includes 7 minority (1 African American, 5 Asian Americans or Pacific Islanders, 1 Hispanic American), 1 international. Average age 27. 34 applicants, 79% accepted, 10 enrolled. In 2009, 48 master's awarded. Application fee: $65. *Unit head:* Marjorie Siegel, Chair, 212-678-3765. *Application contact:* Peter Shon, Assistant Director of Admission, 212-678-3305, Fax: 212-678-4171, E-mail: shon@exchange.tc.columbia.edu.

Teachers College, Columbia University, Graduate Faculty of Education, Department of Health and Behavioral Studies, Program in Reading Specialist, New York, NY 10027-6696. Offers MA. *Faculty:* 2 full-time (both women), 6 part-time/adjunct. *Students:* 10 full-time (all women), 35 part-time (all women); includes 6 minority (2 African Americans, 4 Hispanic Americans). Average age 31. 29 applicants, 62% accepted, 12 enrolled. In 2009, 21 master's awarded. *Application deadline:* For fall admission, 5/15 for domestic students. Application fee: $65. *Financial support:* Application deadline: 2/1. *Unit head:* Dr. Chuck Basch, Chair, 212-678-3964, E-mail: ceb35@columbia.edu. *Application contact:* Peter Shon, Assistant Director of Admission, 212-678-3305, Fax: 212-678-4171, E-mail: shon@exchange.tc.columbia.edu.

Temple University, Graduate School, College of Education, Department of Curriculum, Instruction, and Technology in Education, Philadelphia, PA 19122-6096. Offers applied behavioral analysis (MS Ed); career and technical education (MS Ed); early childhood education and elementary education (MS Ed); English education (MS Ed); language arts education (Ed D); math/science education (Ed D); mathematics education (MS Ed); science education (MS Ed); second and foreign language education (MS Ed); special education (MS Ed); teaching English as a second language (MS Ed). Part-time and evening/weekend programs available. Terminal master's awarded for partial completion of doctoral program. *Degree requirements:* For master's, thesis or alternative; for doctorate, thesis/dissertation. *Entrance requirements:* For master's and doctorate, GRE General Test or MAT, minimum GPA of 3.0. Additional exam requirements/recommendations for international students: Required—TOEFL (minimum score 550 paper-based; 213 computer-based; 79 iBT). Electronic applications accepted. *Faculty research:* School improvement, problem solving, literacy, language development.

Tennessee Technological University, Graduate School, College of Education, Department of Curriculum and Instruction, Program in Exceptional Learning, Cookeville, TN 38505. Offers applied behavior and learning (PhD); literacy (PhD); program planning and evaluation (PhD). *Students:* 11 full-time (10 women), 14 part-time (11 women); includes 3 minority (2 African Americans, 1 Asian American or Pacific Islander). 22 applicants, 18% accepted, 4 enrolled. In 2009, 4 doctorates awarded. *Degree requirements:* For doctorate, comprehensive exam, thesis/dissertation. *Entrance requirements:* For doctorate, GRE, minimum GPA of 3.0. Additional exam requirements/recommendations for international students: Required—TOEFL (minimum score 550 paper-based; 79 iBT), IELTS (minimum score 5.5). *Application deadline:* For fall admission, 8/1 for domestic students, 5/1 for international students; for spring admission, 12/1 for domestic students, 10/1 for international students. Application fee: $25 ($30 for international students). Electronic applications accepted. *Expenses:* Tuition, state resident: full-time $7034; part-time $368 per credit hour. *Financial support:* In 2009–10, 4 fellowships (averaging $8,000 per year), 10 research assistantships (averaging $12,000 per year), 1 teaching assistantship (averaging $12,000 per year) were awarded. Financial award application deadline: 4/1. *Unit head:* Dr. John J. Wheeler, Director, Doctoral Studies, 931-372-3078, Fax: 931-372-3517. *Application contact:* Shelia K. Kendrick, Coordinator of Graduate Studies, 931-372-3808, Fax: 931-372-3497, E-mail: skendrick@Tntech.edu.

Tennessee Technological University, Graduate School, College of Education, Department of Curriculum and Instruction, Program in Reading, Cookeville, TN 38505. Offers MA, Ed S. *Accreditation:* NCATE. Part-time and evening/weekend programs available. *Faculty:* 2 full-time (both women). *Students:* 16 full-time (all women), 34 part-time (all women); includes 1 minority (Hispanic American). Average age 27. 10 applicants, 80% accepted, 6 enrolled. In 2009, 15 master's, 11 other advanced degrees awarded. *Degree requirements:* For master's and Ed S, comprehensive exam, thesis or alternative. *Entrance requirements:* For master's and Ed S, MAT or GRE. Additional exam requirements/recommendations for international students: Required—TOEFL (minimum score 550 paper-based; 79 iBT), IELTS (minimum score 5.5). *Application deadline:* For fall admission, 8/1 for domestic students, 5/1 for international students; for spring admission, 12/1 for domestic students, 10/1 for international students. Application fee: $25 ($30 for international students). Electronic applications accepted. *Expenses:* Tuition, state resident: full-time $7034; part-time $368 per credit hour. *Financial support:* In 2009–10, fellowships (averaging $8,000 per year), 4 teaching assistantships (averaging $4,000 per year) were awarded; research assistantships, career-related internships or fieldwork also available. Financial award application deadline: 4/1. *Unit head:* Dr. Matthew R. Smith, Chairperson, 931-372-3181, Fax: 931-372-6270. *Application contact:* Shelia K. Kendrick, Coordinator of Graduate Studies, 931-372-3808, Fax: 931-372-3497, E-mail: skendrick@tntech.edu.

Texas A&M International University, Office of Graduate Studies and Research, College of Education, Department of Curriculum and Instruction, Laredo, TX 78041-1900. Offers bilingual education (PhD); curriculum and instruction (MS, PhD); early childhood education (PhD); reading (MS). *Faculty:* 4 full-time (3 women). *Students:* 7 full-time (3 women), 120 part-time (105 women); includes 117 minority (all Hispanic Americans), 2 international. Average age 36. 50 applicants, 64% accepted, 29 enrolled. In 2009, 34 master's awarded. *Application deadline:* For fall admission, 4/30 priority date for domestic students; for spring admission, 11/30 for domestic students. *Unit head:* Dr. Cathy Guerra, Interim Chair, 956-326-2438, E-mail: cgsakta@tamiu.edu. *Application contact:* Rosie Dickinson, Director of Admissions, 956-326-2200.

Texas A&M University, College of Education and Human Development, Department of Teaching, Learning, and Culture, College Station, TX 77843. Offers curriculum and instruction (M Ed, MS, PhD); mathematics education (M Ed, MS, PhD); multicultural/urban/ESL/international education (M Ed, MS, PhD); reading/language arts (M Ed, MS, PhD); science education (M Ed, MS, PhD); social studies education (M Ed, MS, PhD). Part-time programs available. *Faculty:* 33. *Students:* 145 full-time (113 women), 270 part-time (214 women); includes 110 minority (60 African Americans, 4 American Indian/Alaska Native, 4 Asian Americans or Pacific Islanders, 42 Hispanic Americans), 47 international. Average age 36. In 2009, 114 master's, 17 doctorates awarded. *Degree requirements:* For master's, comprehensive exam, thesis (for some programs); for doctorate, comprehensive exam, thesis/dissertation. *Entrance requirements:* For master's, GRE General Test, minimum GPA of 3.0; for doctorate, GRE General Test, 3 years of teaching experience. Additional exam requirements/recommendations for international students: Required—TOEFL (minimum score 550 paper-based; 213 computer-based). *Application deadline:* For fall admission, 1/15 priority date for domestic and international students; for spring admission, 9/15 priority date for domestic and international students. Applications are processed on a rolling basis. Application fee: $50 ($75 for international students). Electronic applications accepted. *Expenses:* Tuition, state resident: full-time $3991; part-time $221.74 per credit hour. Tuition, nonresident: full-time $9049; part-time $502.74 per credit hour. *Financial support:* In 2009–10, fellowships with partial tuition reimbursements (averaging $3,000 per year), teaching assistantships with partial tuition reimbursements (averaging $7,200 per year) were awarded; research assistantships with partial tuition reimbursements, career-related internships or fieldwork, Federal Work-Study, institutionally sponsored loans, scholarships/grants, tuition waivers (partial), and unspecified assistantships also available. Support available to part-time students. Financial award application deadline: 4/1; financial award applicants required to submit FAFSA. *Unit head:* Dr. Dennie Smith, Head, 979-845-8384, Fax: 979-845-9663, E-mail: krsmith@tamu.edu. *Application contact:* Graduate Admissions Supervisor, 979-845-8382, Fax: 979-845-9663, E-mail: krsmith@tamu.edu.

Texas A&M University–Commerce, Graduate School, College of Education and Human Services, Department of Curriculum and Instruction, Commerce, TX 75429-3011. Offers bilingual/ESL education (M Ed, MS); early childhood education (M Ed, MS); elementary education (M Ed, MS); reading (M Ed, MS); secondary education (M Ed, MS); supervision, curriculum and instruction: elementary education (Ed D). Part-time programs available. Terminal master's awarded for partial completion of doctoral program. *Degree requirements:* For master's, comprehensive exam, thesis (for some programs); for doctorate, 2 foreign languages, thesis/dissertation, departmental qualifying exam. *Entrance requirements:* For master's and doctorate, GRE General Test. Electronic applications accepted. *Faculty research:* Literacy and learning, early childhood, preservice teacher education, technology.

Texas A&M University–Corpus Christi, Graduate Studies and Research, College of Education, Corpus Christi, TX 78412-5503. Offers counseling (MS, PhD), including counseling (MS), counselor education (PhD); curriculum and instruction (MS, Ed D); early childhood education (MS); educational administration (MS); educational leadership (Ed D); educational technology (MS); elementary education (MS); kinesiology (MS); reading (MS); secondary education (MS); special education (MS). Part-time and evening/weekend programs available. *Degree requirements:* For master's, comprehensive exam, thesis (for some programs); for doctorate, comprehensive exam, thesis/dissertation. *Entrance requirements:* For master's, GRE General

Test. Additional exam requirements/recommendations for international students: Required—TOEFL. Electronic applications accepted.

Texas A&M University–Kingsville, College of Graduate Studies, College of Education, Department of Education, Program in Reading Specialization, Kingsville, TX 78363. Offers MS. Part-time and evening/weekend programs available. *Degree requirements:* For master's, comprehensive exam, mini-thesis. *Entrance requirements:* For master's, GRE General Test, MAT, minimum GPA of 3.0. *Faculty research:* Reading programs for preparing the handicapped, reading methods in elementary education, literature-based reading instruction.

Texas State University–San Marcos, Graduate School, College of Education, Department of Curriculum and Instruction, Program in Reading Education, San Marcos, TX 78666. Offers M Ed. Part-time and evening/weekend programs available. *Faculty:* 5 full-time (4 women), 1 (woman) part-time/adjunct. *Students:* 2 full-time (both women), 32 part-time (all women); includes 8 minority (2 African Americans, 1 American Indian/Alaska Native, 5 Hispanic Americans). Average age 36. 4 applicants, 100% accepted, 4 enrolled. In 2009, 3 master's awarded. *Degree requirements:* For master's, comprehensive exam, thesis optional. *Entrance requirements:* For master's, minimum GPA of 2.75 in last 60 hours of course work, teaching experience. Additional exam requirements/recommendations for international students: Required—TOEFL (minimum score 550 paper-based; 213 computer-based). *Application deadline:* For fall admission, 6/15 priority date for domestic students; for spring admission, 10/15 priority date for domestic students. Applications are processed on a rolling basis. Application fee: $40 ($90 for international students). Electronic applications accepted. *Expenses:* Tuition, state resident: full-time $5784; part-time $241 per credit hour. Tuition, nonresident: full-time $13,224; part-time $551 per credit hour. Required fees: $1728; $48 per credit hour. $306. Tuition and fees vary according to course load. *Financial support:* In 2009–10, 16 students received support; research assistantships, teaching assistantships, career-related internships or fieldwork, Federal Work-Study, and institutionally sponsored loans available. Support available to part-time students. Financial award application deadline: 4/1; financial award applicants required to submit FAFSA. *Faculty research:* Reading comprehension, computer-assisted instruction. *Unit head:* Dr. Gwynne Ash, Graduate Advisor, 512-245-2157, Fax: 512-245-8365, E-mail: ga13@txstate.edu. *Application contact:* Dr. J. Michael Willoughby, Dean of Graduate School, 512-245-2581, Fax: 512-245-8365, E-mail: gradcollege@txstate.edu.

Texas Tech University, Graduate School, College of Education, Division of Curriculum and Instruction, Lubbock, TX 79409. Offers bilingual education (M Ed); curriculum and instruction (M Ed, PhD); elementary education (M Ed); language and literacy education (M Ed); secondary education (M Ed). *Accreditation:* NCATE. Part-time programs available. *Students:* 72 full-time (54 women), 109 part-time (85 women); includes 50 minority (11 African Americans, 1 American Indian/Alaska Native, 4 Asian Americans or Pacific Islanders, 34 Hispanic Americans), 11 international. Average age 35. 228 applicants, 54% accepted, 56 enrolled. In 2009, 59 master's, 5 doctorates awarded. *Degree requirements:* For master's, thesis or alternative; for doctorate, thesis/dissertation. *Entrance requirements:* For master's and doctorate, GRE General Test. Additional exam requirements/recommendations for international students: Required—TOEFL (minimum score 550 paper-based; 213 computer-based). *Application deadline:* For fall admission, 3/1 priority date for international students; for spring admission, 11/1 priority date for international students. Applications are processed on a rolling basis. Application fee: $50 ($75 for international students). Electronic applications accepted. *Expenses:* Tuition, state resident: full-time $5100; part-time $213 per credit hour. Tuition, nonresident: full-time $11,748; part-time $490 per credit hour. Required fees: $2298; $50 per credit hour. $555 per semester. *Financial support:* Research assistantships with partial tuition reimbursements, teaching assistantships with partial tuition reimbursements, career-related internships or fieldwork, Federal Work-Study, and institutionally sponsored loans available. Support available to part-time students. Financial award application deadline: 4/15; financial award applicants required to submit FAFSA. *Faculty research:* Multicultural foundations of education, teacher education, instruction and pedagogy in subject areas, curriculum theory, language and literary. *Unit head:* Dr. Walter Smith, Chair, 806-742-1988 Ext. 437, Fax: 806-742-2179, E-mail: walter.smith@ttu.edu. *Application contact:* Dr. Walter Smith, Chair, 806-742-1988 Ext. 437, Fax: 806-742-2179, E-mail: walter.smith@ttu.edu.

Texas Woman's University, Graduate School, College of Professional Education, Department of Reading, Denton, TX 76201. Offers reading education (M Ed, MA, MS, Ed D, PhD). Part-time and evening/weekend programs available. *Students:* 3 full-time (all women), 61 part-time (60 women); includes 25 minority (8 African Americans, 1 American Indian/Alaska Native, 2 Asian Americans or Pacific Islanders, 14 Hispanic Americans). Average age 42. 25 applicants, 84% accepted, 10 enrolled. In 2009, 14 master's, 2 doctorates awarded. Terminal master's awarded for partial completion of doctoral program. *Degree requirements:* For master's, thesis; for doctorate, comprehensive exam, thesis/dissertation. *Entrance requirements:* For master's, GRE General Test (minimum score 350 verbal, 350 quantitative); for doctorate, GRE General Test (Verbal 500, Quantitative 500), graduate degree, minimum GPA of 3.5, on-site writing sample, interview, 3 letters of reference, resume, 1-2 page statement of professional experience and goals in pursuing a doctoral degree, teaching experience (preferred). Additional exam requirements/recommendations for international students: Required—TOEFL (minimum score 550 paper-based; 213 computer-based; 79 iBT). *Application deadline:* For fall admission, 7/1 priority date for domestic students, 3/1 for international students; for spring admission, 12/1 priority date for domestic students, 7/1 for international students. Applications are processed on a rolling basis. Application fee: $50. Electronic applications accepted. *Expenses:* Tuition, state resident: full-time $3564; part-time $198 per credit hour. Tuition, nonresident: full-time $8550; part-time $475 per credit hour. Required fees: $69.26 per credit hour. Tuition and fees vary according to course load. *Financial support:* In 2009–10, 12 students received support, including 3 research assistantships (averaging $10,440 per year); career-related internships or fieldwork, Federal Work-Study, institutionally sponsored loans, scholarships/grants, traineeships, health care benefits, and unspecified assistantships also available. Support available to part-time students. Financial award application deadline: 3/1; financial award applicants required to submit FAFSA. *Faculty research:* Teacher change, home/school partnerships, literacy-middle grades, early literacy, language acquisition. *Unit head:* Dr. Margaret Compton, Chair, 940-898-2227, Fax: 940-898-2224, E-mail: reading@twu.edu. *Application contact:* Samuel Wheeler, Assistant Director of Admissions, 940-898-3188, Fax: 940-898-3081, E-mail: wheelersr@twu.edu.

Towson University, College of Graduate Studies and Research, Program in Reading, Towson, MD 21252-0001. Offers reading (M Ed); reading education (CAS). *Accreditation:* NCATE. Part-time and evening/weekend programs available. Postbaccalaureate distance learning degree programs offered (minimal on-campus study). *Degree requirements:* For master's, exam. *Entrance requirements:* For master's, minimum GPA of 3.0; for CAS, letters of reference, portfolio, master's degree in reading or related field. Electronic applications accepted. *Faculty research:* Teacher training, early literacy, adolescent literacy, reading clinics, family literacy.

Trevecca Nazarene University, Graduate Division, School of Education, Major in Reading PreK-12, Nashville, TN 37210-2877. Offers M Ed. *Accreditation:* NCATE. Part-time and evening/weekend programs available. *Students:* 19 full-time (18 women), 1 (woman) part-time; includes 3 minority (all African Americans). In 2009, 9 master's awarded. *Degree requirements:* For master's, exit assessment. *Entrance requirements:* For master's, GRE General Test, MAT, minimum GPA of 2.7, 2 reference forms. Additional exam requirements/recommendations for international students: Required—TOEFL (minimum score 550 paper-based; 213 computer-based). *Application deadline:* Applications are processed on a rolling basis. Application fee: $25. *Expenses:* Contact institution. *Financial support:* Applicants required to submit FAFSA. *Unit head:* Dr. Esther Swink, Dean, School of Education/Director of Graduate Education Program, 615-248-1201, Fax: 615-248-1597, E-mail: admissions_ged@trevecca.edu. *Application contact:* Admissions Office, 615-248-1201, Fax: 615-248-1597, E-mail: admissions_ged@trevecca.edu.

Trinity (Washington) University, School of Education, Washington, DC 20017-1094. Offers counseling (MA); early childhood education (MAT); educating for change (M Ed); educational administration (MSA); elementary education (MAT); school counseling (MA); secondary education (MAT), including English, social studies; special education (MAT); teaching English as a second language (MAT); teaching English to speakers of other languages (M Ed); the teaching of reading (M Ed). *Accreditation:* NCATE. Part-time and evening/weekend programs available. *Degree requirements:* For master's, thesis (for some programs), capstone project(s). *Entrance requirements:* For master's, PRAXIS I, minimum GPA of 2.8. Additional exam requirements/recommendations for international students: Required—TOEFL (minimum score 550 paper-based; 213 computer-based). *Faculty research:* Technology, literacy, special education, organizations, inclusion models.

Troy University, Graduate School, College of Education, Program in Secondary Education, Troy, AL 36082. Offers 5th year biology (MS); 5th year computer science (MS); 5th year history (MS); 5th year language arts (MS); 5th year mathematics (MS); 5th year social science (MS); educationtraditional language arts (MS); traditional biology (MS); traditional computer science (MS); traditional history (MS); traditional mathematics (MS); traditional social science (MS). *Accreditation:* NCATE. Part-time and evening/weekend programs available. *Students:* 17 full-time (12 women), 25 part-time (23 women); includes 8 minority (all African Americans). Average age 27. 10 applicants, 90% accepted. In 2009, 29 master's awarded. *Degree requirements:* For master's, comprehensive exam, thesis. *Entrance requirements:* For master's, minimum GPA of 2.5. Additional exam requirements/recommendations for international students: Required—TOEFL (minimum score 523 paper-based; 193 computer-based; 70 iBT), IELTS (minimum score 6). *Application deadline:* Applications are processed on a rolling basis. Application fee: $50. Electronic applications accepted. *Financial support:* Career-related internships or fieldwork available. Support available to part-time students. Financial award applicants required to submit FAFSA. *Unit head:* Dr. Marian Parker, Coordinator, 334-670-5661, Fax: 334-670-3548, E-mail: mjparker@troy.edu. *Application contact:* Brenda K. Campbell, Director of Graduate Admissions, 334-670-3178, Fax: 334-670-3733, E-mail: bcamp@troy.edu.

TUI University, College of Education, Program in Education, Cypress, CA 90630. Offers adult education (MA Ed); aviation education (MA Ed); children's literacy development (MA Ed); e-learning (MA Ed); early childhood education (MA Ed); enrollment management (MA Ed); higher education (MA Ed); teaching and instruction (MA Ed); training and development (MA Ed). Part-time and evening/weekend programs available. Postbaccalaureate distance learning degree programs offered (no on-campus study). *Degree requirements:* For master's, capstone project with integrative paper. *Entrance requirements:* For master's, minimum GPA of 2.5 (students with GPA 3.0 or greater may transfer up to 30% of graduate level credits). Additional exam requirements/recommendations for international students: Required—TOEFL (minimum score 525 paper-based). Electronic applications accepted.

Union College, Graduate Programs, Department of Education, Barbourville, KY 40906-1499. Offers elementary education (MA); health and physical education (MA); middle grades (MA); music education (MA); principalship (MA); reading specialist (MA); secondary education (MA); special education (MA). *Degree requirements:* For master's, thesis optional. *Entrance requirements:* For master's, GRE General Test, NTE.

Union Institute & University, Education Programs—Florida Center, North Miami Beach, FL 33162. Offers educational leadership (M Ed, Ed S); exceptional student education (M Ed, Ed S); guidance and counseling (M Ed, Ed S); reading (M Ed, Ed S). *Faculty:* 3 full-time (1 woman), 23 part-time/adjunct (19 women). *Students:* 32 full-time (21 women); includes 23 minority (21 African Americans, 2 Hispanic Americans). Average age 37. In 2009, 8 master's, 3 Ed Ss awarded. *Degree requirements:* For master's, thesis or alternative, portfolio. *Entrance requirements:* For master's, letters of recommendation. *Application deadline:* Applications are processed on a rolling basis. Application fee: $50. *Expenses:* Contact institution. *Financial support:* Federal Work-Study, scholarships/grants, and tuition waivers (partial) available. Financial award applicants required to submit FAFSA. *Unit head:* Dr. Arlene Sacks, Dean, 305-653-6713 Ext. 2152, E-mail: arlene.sacks@myunion.edu. *Application contact:* Josefina Rosario, Admissions Counselor, 305-653-6713 Ext. 2172, E-mail: admissions@tui.edu.

University at Albany, State University of New York, School of Education, Department of Reading, Albany, NY 12222-0001. Offers MS, Ed D, CAS. Evening/weekend programs available. *Degree requirements:* For doctorate, one foreign language, thesis/dissertation. *Entrance requirements:* For doctorate, GRE General Test. Additional exam requirements/recommendations for international students: Required—TOEFL (minimum score 550 paper-based; 213 computer-based). Electronic applications accepted.

University at Buffalo, the State University of New York, Graduate School, Graduate School of Education, Department of Learning and Instruction, Buffalo, NY 14260. Offers biology education (Ed M, Certificate); chemistry education (Ed M, Certificate); childhood education (Ed M); childhood education with bilingual extension (Ed M); early childhood education (Ed M); earth science education (Ed M, Certificate); elementary education (Ed D, PhD); English education (Ed M, PhD, Certificate); English for speakers of other languages (Ed M); foreign and second language education (PhD); French education (Ed M, Certificate); general education (Ed M); German education (Ed M, Certificate); gifted education (online) (Certificate); Latin education (Ed M, Certificate); literary specialist (Ed M); mathematics education (Ed M, PhD, Certificate); music education (Ed M, Certificate); physics education (Ed M, Certificate); reading education (PhD); science and the public (online) (Ed M); science education (PhD); social studies education (Ed M, Certificate); Spanish education (Ed M, Certificate); special education (PhD); teaching and leading for diversity (Certificate); teaching English to speakers of other languages (Ed M). Part-time and evening/weekend programs available. Postbaccalaureate distance learning degree programs offered (no on-campus study). *Faculty:* 34 full-time (24 women), 50 part-time/adjunct (39 women). *Students:* 332 full-time (245 women), 365 part-time (272 women); includes 50 minority (18 African Americans, 4 American Indian/Alaska Native, 10 Asian Americans or Pacific Islanders, 18 Hispanic Americans), 55 international. Average age 30. 627 applicants, 78% accepted, 286 enrolled. In 2009, 255 master's, 16 doctorates, 51 other advanced degrees awarded. *Degree requirements:* For master's, comprehensive exam; for doctorate, thesis/dissertation, research analysis exam, research experience component. *Entrance requirements:* For doctorate, GRE General Test or MAT, interview, writing sample, letters of recommendation. Additional exam requirements/recommendations for international students: Required—TOEFL (minimum score 600 paper-based; 250 computer-based; 96 iBT). *Application deadline:* For fall admission, 2/1 priority date for domestic and international students; for spring admission, 11/15 priority date for domestic students, 10/1 for international students. Applications are processed on a rolling basis. Application fee: $50. Electronic applications accepted. *Financial support:* In 2009–10, 23 fellowships with full tuition reimbursements (averaging $9,000 per year), 42 research assistantships with full tuition reimbursements (averaging $10,000 per year) were awarded; teaching assistantships with full tuition reimbursements, career-related internships or fieldwork, Federal Work-Study, institutionally sponsored loans, scholarships/grants, tuition waivers (partial), and unspecified assistantships also available. Financial award application deadline: 2/28; financial award applicants required to submit FAFSA. *Faculty research:* Science assessment, foreign language teaching and learning, early learning, new literacies, gender and education. Total annual research expenditures: $1.8 million. *Unit head:* Dr. Suzanne Miller, Chair, 716-645-2455, Fax: 716-645-3161, E-mail: smiller@buffalo.edu. *Application contact:* Cathy Dimino, Admissions Assistant, 716-645-2110, Fax: 716-645-7937, E-mail: cadimino@buffalo.edu.

University of Alaska Fairbanks, School of Education, Program in Education, Fairbanks, AK 99775. Offers curriculum and instruction (M Ed); education (M Ed); elementary education (M Ed); language and literacy (M Ed); reading (M Ed); secondary education (M Ed). *Faculty:* 23 full-time (15 women), 10 part-time/adjunct (9 women). *Students:* 35 full-time (26 women), 58 part-time (43 women); includes 25 minority (2 African Americans, 17 American Indian/Alaska Native, 4 Asian Americans or Pacific Islanders, 2 Hispanic Americans), 1 international. Average age 36. 94 applicants, 64% accepted, 42 enrolled. In 2009, 19 master's, 18 other advanced degrees awarded. *Degree requirements:* For master's, comprehensive exam, thesis, oral defense. *Entrance requirements:* Additional exam requirements/recommendations for international students: Required—TOEFL (minimum score 550 paper-based; 213 computer-

Reading Education

University of Alaska Fairbanks (continued)
based; 80 iBT). *Application deadline:* For fall admission, 5/1 for domestic students, 3/1 for international students; for spring admission, 10/15 for domestic students, 8/1 for international students. Applications are processed on a rolling basis. Application fee: $60. Electronic applications accepted. *Expenses:* Tuition, state resident: full-time $7584; part-time $316 per credit. Tuition, nonresident: full-time $15,504; part-time $646 per credit. Required fees: $23 per credit. $135 per semester. Tuition and fees vary according to course level, course load and reciprocity agreements. *Financial support:* In 2009–10, 1 teaching assistantship (averaging $11,955 per year) was awarded; fellowships, career-related internships or fieldwork, Federal Work-Study, scholarships/grants, health care benefits, and unspecified assistantships also available. Support available to part-time students. Financial award application deadline: 6/1; financial award applicants required to submit FAFSA. *Unit head:* Dr. Eric C. Madsen, Dean, 907-474-7341, Fax: 907-474-5451, E-mail: fysoed@uaf.edu. *Application contact:* Dr. Eric C. Madsen, Dean, 907-474-7341, Fax: 907-474-5451, E-mail: fysoed@uaf.edu.

The University of Arizona, Graduate College, College of Education, Department of Teaching, Learning and Sociocultural Studies, Tucson, AZ 85721. Offers bilingual education (M Ed); bilingual/multicultural education (MA); language, reading and culture (MA, Ed D, PhD, Ed S). Part-time programs available. *Faculty:* 11. *Students:* 40 full-time (34 women), 103 part-time (80 women); includes 37 minority (3 African Americans, 11 American Indian/Alaska Native, 3 Asian Americans or Pacific Islanders, 20 Hispanic Americans), 25 international. Average age 39. 63 applicants, 71% accepted, 30 enrolled. In 2009, 17 master's, 10 doctorates awarded. Terminal master's awarded for partial completion of doctoral program. *Degree requirements:* For master's, thesis optional, thesis (MA); for doctorate, comprehensive exam, thesis/dissertation; for Ed S, thesis optional. *Entrance requirements:* For master's, 2 letters of recommendation, resume; for doctorate, GRE or MAT, 2 letters of recommendation, resume; for Ed S, GRE, MAT. Additional exam requirements/recommendations for international students: Required—TOEFL (minimum score 550 paper-based; 213 computer-based; 79 iBT). *Application deadline:* For fall admission, 2/1 for domestic and international students. Application fee: $65. Electronic applications accepted. *Expenses:* Tuition, state resident: full-time $9028. Tuition, nonresident: full-time $24,890. *Financial support:* In 2009–10, 3 research assistantships with full tuition reimbursements (averaging $12,123 per year), 12 teaching assistantships with full tuition reimbursements (averaging $12,437 per year) were awarded; career-related internships or fieldwork, scholarships/grants, health care benefits, tuition waivers (full and partial), and unspecified assistantships also available. Financial award application deadline: 3/7; financial award applicants required to submit FAFSA. *Faculty research:* Reading, Native American education, language policy, children's literature, bilingual/bicultural literacy. Total annual research expenditures: $686,878. *Unit head:* Dr. Norma E. Gonzalez, Department Head, 520-621-1311, Fax: 520-621-1853, E-mail: ngonzale@email.arizona.edu. *Application contact:* Information Contact, 520-621-1311, Fax: 520-621-1853, E-mail: lrcinfo@email.arizona.edu.

University of Arkansas at Little Rock, Graduate School, College of Education, Department of Teacher Education, Program in Reading Education, Little Rock, AR 72204-1099. Offers literacy coach (Graduate Certificate); reading (M Ed, Ed S).

University of Bridgeport, School of Education and Human Resources, Division of Education, Program in Secondary Education, Bridgeport, CT 06604. Offers computer specialist (Diploma); international education (Diploma); reading specialist (MS, Diploma); secondary education (MS, Diploma). Part-time and evening/weekend programs available. *Degree requirements:* For master's, final exam, final project, or thesis; for Diploma, thesis or alternative, final project. *Entrance requirements:* For master's, minimum undergraduate QPA of 2.67; for Diploma, minimum graduate QPA of 3.0. Additional exam requirements/recommendations for international students: Recommended—TOEFL (minimum score 550 paper-based; 213 computer-based; 80 iBT), IELTS (minimum score 6.5). Electronic applications accepted. *Faculty research:* Self-concept, internship assessment, stress and situational development, follow-up of graduation, trend analysis.

The University of British Columbia, Faculty of Education, Program in Language and Literacy Education, Vancouver, BC V6T 1Z1, Canada. Offers library education (M Ed); literacy education (M Ed, MA, PhD); modern language education (M Ed, MA, PhD); teaching English as a second language (M Ed, MA, PhD). Part-time and evening/weekend programs available. *Degree requirements:* For master's, thesis (MA); for doctorate, thesis/dissertation. *Entrance requirements:* For master's and doctorate, minimum B+ average in last 2 years with minimum 2 courses at A standing. Additional exam requirements/recommendations for international students: Required—TOEFL (minimum score 580 paper-based; 237 computer-based; 92 iBT), TWE (minimum score 5). Electronic applications accepted. *Faculty research:* Language and literacy development, second language acquisition, Asia Pacific language curriculum, children's literature, whole language instruction.

University of California, Riverside, Graduate Division, Graduate School of Education, Riverside, CA 92521-0102. Offers autism (M Ed); curriculum and instruction (MA, PhD); diversity and equity (M Ed); educational leadership and policy (MA, PhD); educational psychology (MA, PhD); general education (M Ed); higher education administration and policy (M Ed, PhD); leadership (M Ed); reading (M Ed); school psychology (PhD); special education (M Ed, MA, PhD). *Faculty:* 23 full-time (12 women), 12 part-time/adjunct (8 women). *Students:* 230 full-time (183 women), 6 part-time (3 women); includes 75 minority (12 African Americans, 1 American Indian/Alaska Native, 21 Asian Americans or Pacific Islanders, 41 Hispanic Americans), 6 international. Average age 32. 288 applicants, 60% accepted, 118 enrolled. In 2009, 68 master's, 13 doctorates awarded. Terminal master's awarded for partial completion of doctoral program. *Degree requirements:* For master's, comprehensive exam (for some programs), comprehensive exams or thesis (MA), case study or analytical report (M Ed); for doctorate, thesis/dissertation, written and oral qualifying exams, college teaching practicum. *Entrance requirements:* For master's, GRE General Test, GRE Subject Test, CBEST, CSET, minimum GPA of 3.2; for doctorate, GRE General Test, GRE Subject Test, master's degree (desirable), minimum GPA of 3.2. Additional exam requirements/recommendations for international students: Required—TOEFL (minimum score 550 paper-based; 213 computer-based; 80 iBT). *Application deadline:* For fall admission, 9/1 for domestic students, 4/1 for international students; for winter admission, 12/1 for domestic students, 9/1 for international students; for spring admission, 3/1 for domestic students, 10/1 for international students. Applications are processed on a rolling basis. Application fee: $70 ($85 for international students). Electronic applications accepted. *Financial support:* In 2009–10, 55 students received support, including 13 fellowships with full and partial tuition reimbursements available (averaging $26,809 per year), 21 research assistantships with full and partial tuition reimbursements available (averaging $14,238 per year), 1 teaching assistantship with full and partial tuition reimbursement available (averaging $16,638 per year); career-related internships or fieldwork, Federal Work-Study, institutionally sponsored loans, scholarships/grants, and unspecified assistantships also available. Financial award application deadline: 1/5; financial award applicants required to submit FAFSA. *Faculty research:* Responsiveness to intervention, faculty core, response to intervention of English language learners, advanced modeling techniques, study on social capital, trust, and motivation. Total annual research expenditures: $5.6 million. *Unit head:* Dr. Steven T. Bossert, Dean, 951-827-5802, Fax: 951-827-3942, E-mail: steven.bossert@ucr.edu. *Application contact:* Dr. John Wills, Graduate Advisor for Admission, 951-827-6362, Fax: 951-827-3942, E-mail: edgrad@ucr.edu.

University of California, Santa Cruz, Division of Graduate Studies, Division of Social Sciences, Department of Education, Santa Cruz, CA 95064. Offers education (MA); language and literacy studies (PhD); mathematics and science education (PhD); social context and policy studies of education (PhD). Terminal master's awarded for partial completion of doctoral program. *Degree requirements:* For master's, thesis; for doctorate, thesis/dissertation. *Faculty research:* Bilingual/multicultural education, special education, curriculum and instruction, child development.

University of Central Arkansas, Graduate School, College of Education, Department of Early Childhood and Special Education, Program in Reading Education, Conway, AR 72035-0001. Offers MSE. *Accreditation:* NCATE. Part-time programs available. *Faculty:* 2 full-time (1 woman). *Students:* 3 full-time (all women), 29 part-time (all women); includes 2 minority (both African Americans), 1 international. Average age 29. 9 applicants, 100% accepted, 7 enrolled. In 2009, 33 master's awarded. *Degree requirements:* For master's, comprehensive exam, thesis optional. *Entrance requirements:* For master's, GRE General Test, minimum GPA of 2.7. Additional exam requirements/recommendations for international students: Required—TOEFL (minimum score 550 paper-based; 213 computer-based). *Application deadline:* For fall admission, 3/1 priority date for domestic and international students; for spring admission, 10/1 priority date for domestic and international students. Applications are processed on a rolling basis. Application fee: $25 ($50 for international students). *Expenses:* Tuition, state resident: full-time $5136; part-time $214 per credit hour. Required fees: $379.50; $127 per term. Tuition and fees vary according to course level, course load and campus/location. *Financial support:* Federal Work-Study, scholarships/grants, tuition waivers (partial), and unspecified assistantships available. Support available to part-time students. Financial award application deadline: 2/15; financial award applicants required to submit FAFSA. *Unit head:* Mary Mosley, Coordinator, 501-450-5461, Fax: 501-450-5358, E-mail: marym@uca.edu. *Application contact:* Brenda Herring, Admissions Assistant, 501-450-5065, Fax: 501-450-5678, E-mail: bherring@uca.edu.

University of Central Florida, College of Education, Department of Teaching and Learning Principles, Program in Reading Education, Orlando, FL 32816. Offers M Ed, Certificate. *Accreditation:* NCATE. Part-time and evening/weekend programs available. *Students:* 14 full-time (all women), 50 part-time (48 women); includes 12 minority (3 African Americans, 1 American Indian/Alaska Native, 8 Hispanic Americans). In 2009, 30 master's, 53 Certificates awarded. *Degree requirements:* For master's, thesis or alternative. *Entrance requirements:* For master's, GRE General Test. Additional exam requirements/recommendations for international students: Required—TOEFL. *Application deadline:* For fall admission, 7/15 for domestic students; for spring admission, 12/1 for domestic students. Application fee: $30. Electronic applications accepted. *Expenses:* Tuition, state resident: part-time $306.31 per credit hour. Tuition, nonresident: part-time $1099.01 per credit hour. Part-time tuition and fees vary according to degree level and program. *Financial support:* In 2009–10, 2 research assistantships with partial tuition reimbursements (averaging $9,000 per year) were awarded; fellowships with partial tuition reimbursements, teaching assistantships with partial tuition reimbursements, career-related internships or fieldwork, Federal Work-Study, institutionally sponsored loans, tuition waivers (full), and unspecified assistantships also available. Financial award application deadline: 3/1; financial award applicants required to submit FAFSA. *Unit head:* Dr. Karri Williams, Coordinator, 321-433-7920, E-mail: kjwilliams@mail.ucf.edu. *Application contact:* Dr. Karri Williams, Coordinator, 321-433-7920, E-mail: kjwilliams@mail.ucf.edu.

University of Central Missouri, The Graduate School, College of Education, Warrensburg, MO 64093. Offers career and technical education administration (MS); career and technical education industry training (MS); career and technical education leadership/teaching (MS); college student personnel administration (MS); counseling (MS); curriculum and instruction (Ed S); educational leadership (Ed D); educational technology (MS); elementary education/educational foundations and literacy (MSE); elementary school administration (MSE); elementary school principalship (Ed S); human services/learning resources (Ed S); human services/professional counseling (Ed S); human services/special education (Ed S); human services/technology and occupational education (Ed S); K-12 education/educational foundations and literacy (MSE); K-12 special education (MSE); library science and information services (MS); literacy education (MSE); secondary education/educational foundations & literacy (MSE); secondary school administration (MSE); secondary school principalship (Ed S); superintendency (Ed S); teaching (MAT). Part-time programs available. Postbaccalaureate distance learning degree programs offered. *Faculty:* 42. *Students:* 123 full-time (82 women), 721 part-time (552 women); includes 58 minority (38 African Americans, 3 American Indian/Alaska Native, 6 Asian Americans or Pacific Islanders, 11 Hispanic Americans), 6 international. Average age 34. 229 applicants, 88% accepted, 190 enrolled. In 2009, 212 master's, 47 other advanced degrees awarded. *Entrance requirements:* Additional exam requirements/recommendations for international students: Required—TOEFL (minimum score 550 paper-based; 79 computer-based). *Application deadline:* For fall admission, 6/1 priority date for domestic students, 5/1 for international students; for spring admission, 10/1 priority date for domestic students, 10/1 for international students. Applications are processed on a rolling basis. Application fee: $30 ($75 for international students). Electronic applications accepted. *Expenses:* Tuition, area resident: Part-time $245.80 per credit hour. Tuition, nonresident: part-time $491.60 per credit hour. Required fees: $24.20 per credit hour. Full-time tuition and fees vary according to course load, degree level, campus/location and reciprocity agreements. *Financial support:* Research assistantships with full and partial tuition reimbursements, teaching assistantships with full and partial tuition reimbursements, career-related internships or fieldwork, Federal Work-Study, scholarships/grants, and administrative and laboratory assistantships available. Support available to part-time students. Financial award application deadline: 3/1; financial award applicants required to submit FAFSA. *Unit head:* Dr. Michael Wright, Dean, 660-543-4272, Fax: 660-543-8753, E-mail: mwright@ucmo.edu. *Application contact:* Laurie Delap, Admissions Coordinator, 660-543-4621, Fax: 660-543-4778, E-mail: gradinfo@ucmo.edu.

University of Central Oklahoma, College of Graduate Studies and Research, College of Education, Department of Special Services, Program in Reading, Edmond, OK 73034-5209. Offers M Ed. *Accreditation:* NCATE. Part-time programs available. *Faculty:* 2 full-time (both women), 1 part-time/adjunct (0 women). *Students:* 4 full-time (all women), 33 part-time (all women); includes 3 minority (1 African American, 2 American Indian/Alaska Native). Average age 34. 15 applicants, 100% accepted. In 2009, 8 master's awarded. *Entrance requirements:* For master's, GRE General Test. Additional exam requirements/recommendations for international students: Required—TOEFL (minimum score 550 paper-based; 213 computer-based). *Application deadline:* For fall admission, 7/1 for international students; for spring admission, 11/1 for international students. Applications are processed on a rolling basis. Application fee: $25. Electronic applications accepted. *Expenses:* Tuition, state resident: full-time $4128; part-time $172 per credit hour. Tuition, nonresident: full-time $10,373; part-time $432.20 per credit hour. Required fees: $433.20; $18.05 per credit hour. *Financial support:* Unspecified assistantships available. Financial award application deadline: 3/31; financial award applicants required to submit FAFSA. *Unit head:* Dr. Barbara Green, Director, 405-974-5283, Fax: 405-974-3822, E-mail: mmonfort@aix1.uco.edu. *Application contact:* Dr. Richard Bernard, Dean, Graduate College, 405-974-3493, Fax: 405-974-3852, E-mail: gradcoll@uco.edu.

University of Cincinnati, Graduate School, College of Education, Criminal Justice, and Human Services, Division of Teacher Education, Program in Reading/Literacy, Cincinnati, OH 45221. Offers M Ed, Ed D. *Accreditation:* NCATE. Part-time programs available. *Degree requirements:* For master's, thesis or alternative; for doctorate, thesis/dissertation. *Entrance requirements:* For master's, GRE General Test. Additional exam requirements/recommendations for international students: Required—TOEFL (minimum score 550 paper-based; 213 computer-based), TWE (minimum score 4.5), OEPT. Electronic applications accepted.

University of Connecticut, Graduate School, Neag School of Education, Department of Curriculum and Instruction, Program in Reading Education, Storrs, CT 06269. Offers MA, PhD, Post-Master's Certificate. *Accreditation:* NCATE. *Faculty:* 15 full-time (10 women). *Students:* 6 full-time (all women), 17 part-time (16 women). Average age 38. 5 applicants, 40% accepted, 0 enrolled. In 2009, 1 master's, 5 other advanced degrees awarded. Terminal master's awarded for partial completion of doctoral program. *Degree requirements:* For master's, comprehensive exam, thesis or alternative; for doctorate, thesis/dissertation. *Entrance requirements:* For doctorate, GRE General Test. Additional exam requirements/recommendations for international students: Required—TOEFL (minimum score 550 paper-based; 213 computer-based). *Application deadline:* For fall admission, 2/1 priority date for domestic and international students; for spring admission, 11/1 for domestic students, 10/1 for international students. Applications are processed on a rolling basis. Application fee: $55. Electronic applications accepted. *Expenses:* Tuition, state resident: full-time $4725; part-time $525 per credit. Tuition, nonresident: full-time $12,267; part-time $1363 per credit. Required fees: $346 per semester. Tuition and fees vary according to course load. *Financial support:* In 2009–10, 3 research

assistantships with full tuition reimbursements, 1 teaching assistantship with full tuition reimbursement were awarded; fellowships, Federal Work-Study, scholarships/grants, health care benefits, and unspecified assistantships also available. Financial award application deadline: 2/1; financial award applicants required to submit FAFSA. *Unit head:* Mary Anne Doyle, Head, 860-486-2433, Fax: 860-486-0280, E-mail: mary.dolye@uconn.edu. *Application contact:* Lisa Rasicot, Graduate Coordinator, 860-486-3065, Fax: 860-486-0210, E-mail: l.rasicot@uconn.edu.

University of Dayton, Graduate School, School of Education and Allied Professions, Department of Teacher Education, Dayton, OH 45469-1300. Offers adolescent/young adult (MS Ed); art education (MS Ed); early childhood education (MS Ed); inclusive early childhood (MS Ed); interdisciplinary education (MS Ed); intervention specialist education, mild/moderate (MS Ed); literacy (MS Ed); middle childhood (MS Ed); multi-age education (MS Ed); music education (MS Ed); teacher as leader (MS Ed); technology in education (MS Ed). Part-time and evening/weekend programs available. *Faculty:* 17 full-time (13 women), 27 part-time/adjunct (21 women). *Students:* 105 full-time (76 women), 152 part-time (131 women); includes 25 minority (21 African Americans, 1 Asian American or Pacific Islander, 3 Hispanic Americans), 8 international. Average age 33. 199 applicants, 58% accepted, 48 enrolled. In 2009, 139 master's awarded. *Degree requirements:* For master's, thesis, capstone research project. *Entrance requirements:* For master's, GRE General Test, minimum GPA of 2.75. Additional exam requirements/recommendations for international students: Required—TOEFL (minimum score 550 paper-based; 213 computer-based; 80 iBT). *Application deadline:* For fall admission, 3/15 priority date for domestic students, 3/1 priority date for international students; for winter admission, 7/1 priority date for international students; for spring admission, 1/1 priority date for international students. Applications are processed on a rolling basis. Application fee: $0 ($50 for international students). Electronic applications accepted. *Expenses:* Contact institution. *Financial support:* In 2009–10, 5 research assistantships with full and partial tuition reimbursements (averaging $8,000 per year) were awarded; career-related internships or fieldwork, institutionally sponsored loans, health care benefits, and unspecified assistantships also available. Financial award applicants required to submit FAFSA. *Faculty research:* Diversity, literacy, art representation by young children, preservice teacher preparation. *Unit head:* Dr. Katie A. Kinnucan-Welsch, Chair, 937-229-3346. *Application contact:* Graduate Admissions, 937-229-4411, Fax: 937-229-4729, E-mail: gradadmission@udayton.edu.

University of Florida, Graduate School, College of Education, School of Teaching and Learning, Gainesville, FL 32611. Offers bilingual/ESOL education (M Ed, MAE, Ed D, PhD, Ed S); curriculum and instruction (M Ed, MAE, Ed D, PhD, Ed S); early childhood education (Ed D, PhD, Ed S); elementary education (M Ed, MAE); English education (M Ed, MAE); mathematics education (M Ed, MAE); reading education (M Ed, MAE); science education (M Ed, MAE); social foundations (M Ed, MAE, Ed D, PhD); social studies education (M Ed, MAE). *Accreditation:* NCATE. *Degree requirements:* For master's, thesis optional; for doctorate, variable foreign language requirement, thesis/dissertation. *Entrance requirements:* For master's and doctorate, GRE General Test, minimum GPA of 3.0; for Ed S, GRE General Test. Additional exam requirements/recommendations for international students: Required—TOEFL (minimum score 550 paper-based; 213 computer-based). Electronic applications accepted. *Faculty research:* Teacher education, inclusive education, classroom processes, curriculum and technology.

University of Georgia, Graduate School, College of Education, Department of Language and Literacy Education, Athens, GA 30602. Offers English education (M Ed, Ed S); language and literacy education (PhD); reading education (M Ed, Ed D, Ed S); teaching additional languages (M Ed, Ed S). *Accreditation:* NCATE. *Faculty:* 18 full-time (12 women). *Students:* 85 full-time (64 women), 112 part-time (98 women); includes 24 minority (12 African Americans, 3 Asian Americans or Pacific Islanders, 9 Hispanic Americans), 19 international. 110 applicants, 47% accepted, 47 enrolled. In 2009, 45 master's, 8 doctorates, 15 other advanced degrees awarded. *Degree requirements:* For doctorate, variable foreign language requirement. *Entrance requirements:* For master's and Ed S, GRE General Test or MAT; for doctorate, GRE General Test. Additional exam requirements/recommendations for international students: Required—TOEFL (minimum score 550 paper-based; 213 computer-based). *Application deadline:* For fall admission, 7/1 priority date for domestic students; for spring admission, 11/15 for domestic students. Application fee: $50. Electronic applications accepted. *Expenses:* Tuition, state resident: full-time $6000; part-time $250 per credit hour. Tuition, nonresident: full-time $20,904; part-time $871 per credit hour. Required fees: $730 per semester. *Faculty research:* Comprehension, critical literacy, literacy and technology, vocabulary instruction, content area reading. *Unit head:* Dr. Mark A. Faust, Head, 706-542-4515, Fax: 706-542-4509, E-mail: mfaust@uga.edu. *Application contact:* Dr. Elizabeth St. Pierre, Graduate Coordinator, 706-542-4526, E-mail: stpierre@uga.edu.

University of Guam, Office of Graduate Studies, School of Education, Program in Language and Literacy, Mangilao, GU 96923. Offers M Ed. Part-time programs available. *Degree requirements:* For master's, comprehensive oral and written exams, special project or thesis. *Entrance requirements:* For master's, GRE General Test. Additional exam requirements/recommendations for international students: Required—TOEFL.

University of Houston, College of Education, Department of Curriculum and Instruction, Houston, TX 77204. Offers art education (M Ed); bilingual education (M Ed); curriculum and instruction (M Ed, Ed D); early childhood education (M Ed); elementary education (M Ed); gifted and talented education (M Ed); instructional technology (M Ed); mathematics education (M Ed); reading and language arts education (M Ed); science education (M Ed); second language education (M Ed); secondary education (M Ed); social studies education (M Ed); teaching (M Ed). *Accreditation:* NCATE. Part-time and evening/weekend programs available. *Faculty:* 20 full-time (9 women), 22 part-time/adjunct (17 women). *Students:* 113 full-time (81 women), 195 part-time (150 women); includes 107 minority (43 African Americans, 29 Asian Americans or Pacific Islanders, 35 Hispanic Americans), 29 international. Average age 35. 150 applicants, 77% accepted, 55 enrolled. In 2009, 75 master's, 31 doctorates awarded. *Degree requirements:* For master's, comprehensive exam, thesis optional; for doctorate, comprehensive exam, thesis/dissertation. *Entrance requirements:* For master's and doctorate, GRE, minimum cumulative undergraduate GPA of 2.6. Additional exam requirements/recommendations for international students: Required—TOEFL (minimum score 550 paper-based; 79 iBT). *Application deadline:* For fall admission, 3/1 for domestic and international students; for spring admission, 10/1 for domestic and international students. Application fee: $45 ($75 for international students). Electronic applications accepted. *Expenses:* Tuition, state resident: full-time $7676; part-time $320 per credit hour. Tuition, nonresident: full-time $14,324; part-time $597 per credit hour. Required fees: $3034. *Financial support:* In 2009–10, 4 fellowships with full tuition reimbursements (averaging $9,500 per year), 6 research assistantships with full tuition reimbursements (averaging $8,800 per year), 25 teaching assistantships with full tuition reimbursements (averaging $8,800 per year) were awarded; career-related internships or fieldwork, Federal Work-Study, institutionally sponsored loans, scholarships/grants, health care benefits, and unspecified assistantships also available. Support available to part-time students. Financial award application deadline: 2/1. *Faculty research:* Teaching-learning process, instructional technology in schools, teacher education, classroom management, at-risk students. *Unit head:* Dr. Laveria Hutchison, Chairperson, 713-743-4958, Fax: 713-743-4990, E-mail: lhutchison@uh.edu. *Application contact:* Renee C. Rattelade, Executive Secretary, 713-743-4997, Fax: 713-743-4990, E-mail: rrattelade@mail.coe.uh.edu.

University of Houston–Clear Lake, School of Education, Program in Curriculum and Instruction, Houston, TX 77058-1098. Offers curriculum and instruction (MS); early childhood education (MS); reading (MS); school library and information science (MS). Part-time and evening/weekend programs available. *Degree requirements:* For master's, thesis (for some programs). *Entrance requirements:* For master's, GRE or minimum GPA of 3.0 in last 60 hours. Additional exam requirements/recommendations for international students: Required—TOEFL (minimum score 550 paper-based; 213 computer-based). Electronic applications accepted.

University of Illinois at Chicago, Graduate College, College of Education, Department of Curriculum and Instruction, Chicago, IL 60607-7128. Offers curriculum studies (PhD); educational studies (M Ed); elementary education (M Ed); literacy, language and culture (M Ed, PhD); secondary education (M Ed). Part-time and evening/weekend programs available. *Degree requirements:* For doctorate, thesis/dissertation. *Entrance requirements:* For master's, minimum GPA of 2.75; for doctorate, GRE General Test, minimum GPA of 2.75. Additional exam requirements/recommendations for international students: Required—TOEFL. Electronic applications accepted. *Faculty research:* Curriculum theory, curriculum development, research on teaching, curriculum and context, reading/literacy.

University of La Verne, College of Education and Organizational Leadership, Program in Reading, La Verne, CA 91750-4443. Offers reading (M Ed, Certificate); reading and language arts specialist (Credential). *Faculty:* 19 full-time (14 women), 35 part-time/adjunct (27 women). *Students:* 2 full-time (both women), 43 part-time (41 women); includes 24 minority (1 African American, 2 Asian Americans or Pacific Islanders, 21 Hispanic Americans). Average age 38. In 2009, 9 master's awarded. *Degree requirements:* For master's, thesis optional. *Entrance requirements:* For master's, MAT, California Basic Educational Skills Test, minimum GPA of 3.0, basic teaching credential, interview, 3 letters of reference. *Application deadline:* Applications are processed on a rolling basis. Application fee: $50. *Expenses:* Contact institution. *Financial support:* Institutionally sponsored loans, scholarships/grants, and unspecified assistantships available. Financial award application deadline: 3/2; financial award applicants required to submit FAFSA. *Unit head:* Dr. Janice Pilgreen, Chairperson, 909-593-3511 Ext. 4624, E-mail: jpilgreen@laverne.edu. *Application contact:* Christy Ranells, Program and Admission Specialist, 909-593-3511 Ext. 4644, Fax: 909-392-2761, E-mail: cranells@laverne.edu.

University of Louisiana at Monroe, Graduate School, College of Education and Human Development, Department of Curriculum and Instruction, Program in Curriculum and Instruction, Monroe, LA 71209-0001. Offers curriculum and instruction (Ed D); elementary education (1-5) (M Ed); reading education (K-12) (M Ed); SPED-academically gifted education (K-12) (M Ed); SPED-early intervention education (birth-3) (M Ed); SPED-educational diagnostics education (PreK-12) (M Ed). *Accreditation:* NCATE. *Faculty:* 17 full-time (all women), 2 part-time/adjunct (both women). *Students:* 15 full-time (13 women), 125 part-time (118 women); includes 38 minority (36 African Americans, 1 Asian American or Pacific Islander, 1 Hispanic American). Average age 37. In 2009, 11 master's, 4 doctorates awarded. *Degree requirements:* For master's, comprehensive exam (for some programs), thesis; for doctorate, thesis/dissertation, internships. *Entrance requirements:* For master's, GRE General Test; for doctorate, GRE General Test, minimum undergraduate GPA of 2.75, graduate 3.25. Additional exam requirements/recommendations for international students: Required—TOEFL (minimum score 500 paper-based; 173 computer-based; 61 iBT). *Application deadline:* For fall admission, 8/24 priority date for domestic students, 7/1 for international students; for winter admission, 12/14 priority date for domestic students; for spring admission, 1/19 for domestic students, 11/1 for international students. Applications are processed on a rolling basis. Application fee: $20 ($30 for international students). Electronic applications accepted. *Expenses:* Tuition, state resident: part-time $159 per credit hour. Tuition, nonresident: part-time $159 per credit hour. Required fees: $1300 per year. Tuition and fees vary according to course load. *Financial support:* In 2009–10, 8 teaching assistantships with full tuition reimbursements (averaging $2,969 per year) were awarded; career-related internships or fieldwork, Federal Work-Study, and unspecified assistantships also available. Financial award application deadline: 4/1; financial award applicants required to submit FAFSA. *Unit head:* Dr. Dorothy Schween, Coordinator, 318-342-1269, Fax: 318-342-3131, E-mail: schween@ulm.edu. *Application contact:* Whitney Sutherland, Administrative Assistant to the Department Head, 318-342-1266, Fax: 318-342-3131, E-mail: sutherland@ulm.edu.

University of Louisville, Graduate School, College of Education and Human Development, Department of Teaching and Learning, Louisville, KY 40292-0001. Offers art education (MAT); curriculum and instruction (PhD); early elementary education (MAT); instructional technology (M Ed); interdisciplinary early childhood education (MAT); middle school education (MAT); music education (MAT); reading education (M Ed); secondary education (MAT); special education (M Ed, MAT); teacher leadership (M Ed). Part-time and evening/weekend programs available. *Faculty:* 43 full-time (33 women), 43 part-time/adjunct (36 women). *Students:* 207 full-time (144 women), 410 part-time (306 women); includes 68 minority (43 African Americans, 2 American Indian/Alaska Native, 14 Asian Americans or Pacific Islanders, 9 Hispanic Americans), 5 international. Average age 33. 216 applicants, 68% accepted, 112 enrolled. In 2009, 269 master's, 6 doctorates awarded. *Degree requirements:* For doctorate, comprehensive exam, thesis/dissertation. *Entrance requirements:* For master's, GRE General Test, PRAXIS II (for some programs); for doctorate, GRE General Test. Additional exam requirements/recommendations for international students: Required—TOEFL (minimum score 560 paper-based; 210 computer-based; 83 iBT). Application fee: $50. Electronic applications accepted. *Financial support:* In 2009–10, 172 students received support; fellowships, research assistantships, teaching assistantships, career-related internships or fieldwork, Federal Work-Study, scholarships/grants, and unspecified assistantships available. Financial award application deadline: 6/1; financial award applicants required to submit FAFSA. *Faculty research:* Assessment of cognitive and language abilities in infants and preschool children; mathematics teachers' conceptions and beliefs, effect, and understanding of mathematics; incorporating nanoscience and nanotechnology into middle and high school science classrooms; urban teacher preparation through inquiry, action and advocacy; impacts of cognitive coaching on teacher practice and student achievement. Total annual research expenditures: $3.7 million. *Unit head:* Dr. Ann E. Larson, Acting Chair, 502-852-6431, Fax: 502-852-1497, E-mail: ann@louisville.edu. *Application contact:* Libby Leggett, Director, Graduate Admissions, 502-852-3101, Fax: 502-852-6536, E-mail: gradadm@louisville.edu.

University of Maine, Graduate School, College of Education and Human Development, Program in Literacy Education, Orono, ME 04469. Offers M Ed, MA, MS, Ed D, CAS. *Accreditation:* NCATE. Part-time and evening/weekend programs available. *Students:* 26 full-time (24 women), 88 part-time (82 women); includes 3 minority (2 Asian Americans or Pacific Islanders, 1 Hispanic American), 1 international. Average age 42. 21 applicants, 62% accepted, 12 enrolled. In 2009, 10 master's, 1 other advanced degree awarded. *Degree requirements:* For master's, thesis or alternative; for doctorate, thesis/dissertation. *Entrance requirements:* For master's, MAT; for doctorate, GRE General Test, MA, M Ed, or MS; for CAS, MAT, MA, M Ed, or MS. Additional exam requirements/recommendations for international students: Required—TOEFL. *Application deadline:* For fall admission, 2/1 priority date for domestic students. Applications are processed on a rolling basis. Application fee: $65. Electronic applications accepted. *Financial support:* Career-related internships or fieldwork, Federal Work-Study, institutionally sponsored loans, tuition waivers (full and partial), and unspecified assistantships available. Support available to part-time students. Financial award application deadline: 3/1. *Unit head:* Dr. Janet Spector, Coordinator, 207-581-2444, Fax: 207-581-2423. *Application contact:* Scott G. Delcourt, Associate Dean of the Graduate School, 207-581-3291, Fax: 207-581-3232, E-mail: graduate@maine.edu.

University of Maine at Farmington, Program in Education, Farmington, ME 04938-1990. Offers administration (MS Ed); educational technology (MS Ed); studies in literature and literacy (MS Ed). *Accreditation:* NCATE. *Entrance requirements:* For master's, teaching certificate, 2 years' teaching experience.

University of Mary, Program in Education, Bismarck, ND 58504-9652. Offers college teaching (M Ed); curriculum, instruction and assessment (M Ed); early childhood education (M Ed); early childhood special education (M Ed); elementary education administration (M Ed); emotional disorders (M Ed); learning disabilities (M Ed); reading (M Ed); secondary education administration (M Ed); special education (M Ed); special education strategist (M Ed). Part-time programs available. *Degree requirements:* For master's, portfolio or thesis. *Entrance requirements:* For master's, interview, letters of reference. Additional exam requirements/recommendations for international students: Required—TOEFL (minimum score 550 paper-based). *Expenses:* Tuition: Full-time $10,062; part-time $430 per credit. Tuition and fees vary according to course load, degree level, program and student level. *Faculty research:* Innovative pedagogy in higher education, technology in education, content standards, children of poverty, children with diverse learning needs.

Reading Education

University of Mary Hardin-Baylor, Graduate Studies in Education, Belton, TX 76513. Offers educational administration (M Ed, Ed D); educational psychology (M Ed); exercise and sport science (M Ed); general studies (M Ed); reading education (M Ed). Part-time and evening/weekend programs available. *Degree requirements:* For master's, comprehensive exam; for doctorate, thesis/dissertation. *Entrance requirements:* For master's, GRE General Test, minimum GPA of 2.75, Texas teaching certificate. Electronic applications accepted.

University of Maryland, Baltimore County, Graduate School, College of Arts, Humanities and Social Sciences, Department of Education, Baltimore, MD 21250. Offers computer/web-based instruction (Postbaccalaureate Certificate); distance education (Postbaccalaureate Certificate); education (MA), including mathematics education, science education, STEM education; elementary/middle science education (Postbaccalaureate Certificate); instructional systems development: training systems (MA, Graduate Certificate), including distance education (Graduate Certificate), e-learning in instructional design (Graduate Certificate), instructional systems development, instructional technology (Graduate Certificate); language, literacy, culture (PhD); math education (Postbaccalaureate Certificate); STEM education (Postbaccalaureate Certificate); teaching (MAT), including early childhood education, elementary education, secondary education; teaching English to speakers of other languages (MA, Postbaccalaureate Certificate). *Accreditation:* NCATE. Part-time and evening/weekend programs available. Postbaccalaureate distance learning degree programs offered (no on-campus study). *Faculty:* 24 full-time (18 women), 25 part-time/adjunct (19 women). *Students:* 90 full-time (79 women), 320 part-time (264 women); includes 64 minority (36 African Americans, 2 American Indian/Alaska Native, 16 Asian Americans or Pacific Islanders, 10 Hispanic Americans), 21 international. Average age 34. 209 applicants, 63% accepted, 98 enrolled. In 2009, 106 master's, 3 doctorates awarded. *Degree requirements:* For master's, comprehensive exam (for some programs), thesis (for some programs); for doctorate, comprehensive exam, thesis/dissertation. *Entrance requirements:* For master's, GRE General Test, GRE Subject Test (MA), PRAXIS I (MAT), minimum GPA of 3.0. Additional exam requirements/recommendations for international students: Required—TOEFL. *Application deadline:* For fall admission, 6/1 for domestic students; for spring admission, 11/1 for domestic students. Applications are processed on a rolling basis. Application fee: $50. Electronic applications accepted. *Financial support:* In 2009–10, 12 students received support, including research assistantships with full tuition reimbursements available (averaging $12,000 per year); fellowships, teaching assistantships, career-related internships or fieldwork, Federal Work-Study, scholarships/grants, tuition waivers (partial), and unspecified assistantships also available. Financial award application deadline: 3/1. *Faculty research:* Teacher leadership; STEM education; ESOL/bilingual education; early childhood education; language, literacy and culture. Total annual research expenditures: $1.3 million. *Unit head:* Dr. Eugene Schaffer, Department Chair, 410-455-2465, Fax: 410-455-3986, E-mail: schaffer@umbc.edu. *Application contact:* Dr. Susan M. Blunck, Director, 410-455-2869, Fax: 410-455-3986, E-mail: blunck@umbc.edu.

University of Maryland, College Park, Academic Affairs, College of Education, Department of Curriculum and Instruction, College Park, MD 20742. Offers reading (M Ed, MA, PhD, CAGS); secondary education (M Ed, MA, Ed D, PhD, CAGS); teaching English to speakers of other languages (M Ed). *Accreditation:* NCATE. Part-time and evening/weekend programs available. Postbaccalaureate distance learning degree programs offered (no on-campus study). *Faculty:* 57 full-time (36 women), 35 part-time/adjunct (30 women). *Students:* 280 full-time (216 women), 181 part-time (150 women); includes 117 minority (60 African Americans, 2 American Indian/Alaska Native, 33 Asian Americans or Pacific Islanders, 22 Hispanic Americans), 51 international. 300 applicants, 40% accepted, 85 enrolled. In 2009, 143 master's, 20 doctorates awarded. *Degree requirements:* For master's, comprehensive exam, seminar paper; for doctorate, comprehensive exam, thesis/dissertation, published paper, oral exam. *Entrance requirements:* For master's, GRE General Test or MAT, minimum GPA of 3.0, 3 letters of recommendation; for doctorate, GRE General Test or MAT, minimum undergraduate GPA of 3.0, graduate 3.5; 3 letters of recommendation. *Application deadline:* For fall admission, 1/20 priority date for domestic students, 1/20 for international students; for spring admission, 9/1 priority date for domestic students, 6/1 for international students. Applications are processed on a rolling basis. Application fee: $60. Electronic applications accepted. *Expenses:* Tuition, area resident: Part-time $471 per credit hour. Tuition, state resident: part-time $471 per credit hour. Tuition, nonresident: part-time $1016 per credit hour. Required fees: $337.04 per term. *Financial support:* In 2009–10, 19 research assistantships with tuition reimbursements (averaging $18,124 per year), 76 teaching assistantships with tuition reimbursements (averaging $17,105 per year) were awarded; fellowships, Federal Work-Study and scholarships/grants also available. Support available to part-time students. Financial award applicants required to submit FAFSA. *Faculty research:* Teacher preparation, curriculum study, inservice education. Total annual research expenditures: $3.9 million. *Unit head:* Dr. Linda M. Valli, Interim Chair, 301-405-3117, E-mail: lrv@umd.edu. *Application contact:* Dean of Graduate School, 301-405-0358.

University of Massachusetts Amherst, Graduate School, School of Education, Program in Education, Amherst, MA 01003. Offers bilingual, English as a second language, and multicultural education (M Ed, CAGS); child study and early education (M Ed); children, families and schools (Ed D, CAGS); early childhood and elementary teacher education (M Ed); education policy and leadership (CAGS); educational administration (M Ed, CAGS); educational policy and leadership (Ed D); higher education (M Ed, CAGS); international education (M Ed); language, literacy and culture (Ed D); learning, media and technology (M Ed, CAGS); mathematics, science, and learning technologies (Ed D); policy studies (M Ed); policy studies in education (CAGS); reading and writing (M Ed); research and evaluation methods (Ed D); school counselor education (M Ed, CAGS); school psychology (CAGS); science education (CAGS); secondary teacher education (M Ed); social justice education (M Ed, Ed D, CAGS); special education (M Ed, Ed D, CAGS). *Accreditation:* NCATE. Part-time programs available. Postbaccalaureate distance learning degree programs offered (minimal on-campus study). *Faculty:* 74 full-time (41 women). *Students:* 377 full-time (268 women), 347 part-time (232 women); includes 115 minority (59 African Americans, 2 American Indian/Alaska Native, 16 Asian Americans or Pacific Islanders, 38 Hispanic Americans), 108 international. Average age 35. 708 applicants, 68% accepted, 266 enrolled. In 2009, 183 master's, 17 doctorates awarded. Terminal master's awarded for partial completion of doctoral program. *Degree requirements:* For master's, thesis or alternative; for doctorate, comprehensive exam, thesis/dissertation. *Entrance requirements:* Additional exam requirements/recommendations for international students: Required—TOEFL (minimum score 550 paper-based; 213 computer-based; 80 iBT), IELTS (minimum score 6.5). *Application deadline:* For fall admission, 1/15 for domestic and international students. Applications are processed on a rolling basis. Application fee: $50 ($65 for international students). Electronic applications accepted. *Expenses:* Tuition, state resident: full-time $2640; part-time $110 per credit. Tuition, nonresident: full-time $9936; part-time $414 per credit. Tuition and fees vary according to course load. *Financial support:* In 2009–10, 1 fellowship with full tuition reimbursement (averaging $8,036 per year), 92 research assistantships with full tuition reimbursements (averaging $8,555 per year), 83 teaching assistantships with full tuition reimbursements (averaging $4,661 per year) were awarded; career-related internships or fieldwork, Federal Work-Study, scholarships/grants, traineeships, health care benefits, tuition waivers (full), and unspecified assistantships also available. Support available to part-time students. Financial award application deadline: 1/15. *Unit head:* Dr. Linda L. Griffin, Graduate Program Director, 413-545-6984, Fax: 413-545-2873. *Application contact:* Jean M. Ames, Supervisor of Admissions, 413-545-0722, Fax: 413-577-0010, E-mail: gradadm@grad.umass.edu.

University of Massachusetts Lowell, Graduate School of Education, Lowell, MA 01854-2881. Offers administration, planning, and policy (CAGS); curriculum and instruction (M Ed, CAGS); educational administration (M Ed); language arts and literacy (Ed D); leadership in schooling (Ed D); math and science education (Ed D); reading and language (M Ed, CAGS). *Accreditation:* NCATE. Part-time and evening/weekend programs available. Postbaccalaureate distance learning degree programs offered (no on-campus study). Terminal master's awarded for partial completion of doctoral program. *Degree requirements:* For doctorate, thesis/dissertation. *Entrance requirements:* For master's, doctorate, and CAGS, GRE General Test. Additional exam requirements/recommendations for international students: Required—TOEFL. Electronic applications accepted.

University of Memphis, Graduate School, College of Education, Department of Instruction and Curriculum Leadership, Memphis, TN 38152. Offers early childhood education (MAT, MS, Ed D); elementary education (MAT); instruction and curriculum (MS, Ed D); instruction design and technology (MS, Ed D); middle grades education (MAT); reading (MS, Ed D); secondary education (MAT); special education (MAT, MS, Ed D). *Accreditation:* NCATE (one or more programs are accredited). Part-time programs available. *Faculty:* 40 full-time (28 women), 20 part-time/adjunct (15 women). *Students:* 119 full-time (90 women), 631 part-time (505 women); includes 348 minority (331 African Americans, 2 American Indian/Alaska Native, 4 Asian Americans or Pacific Islanders, 11 Hispanic Americans), 7 international. Average age 34. 202 applicants, 77% accepted, 29 enrolled. In 2009, 137 master's, 10 doctorates awarded. Terminal master's awarded for partial completion of doctoral program. *Degree requirements:* For master's, comprehensive exam, thesis or alternative; for doctorate, comprehensive exam, thesis/dissertation. *Entrance requirements:* For master's, GRE General Test, minimum GPA of 2.5; for doctorate, GRE General Test, GRE Subject Test, 2 years of teaching experience. *Application deadline:* For fall admission, 8/1 for domestic students; for spring admission, 12/1 for domestic students. Applications are processed on a rolling basis. Application fee: $35 ($60 for international students). Electronic applications accepted. *Expenses:* Tuition, state resident: full-time $6246; part-time $347 per credit hour. Tuition, nonresident: full-time $15,894; part-time $883 per credit hour. Required fees: $1160. Full-time tuition and fees vary according to course load, degree level and program. *Financial support:* In 2009–10, 635 students received support; research assistantships with full tuition reimbursements available, teaching assistantships with full tuition reimbursements available, career-related internships or fieldwork, Federal Work-Study, institutionally sponsored loans, scholarships/grants, traineeships, and unspecified assistantships available. Support available to part-time students. Financial award application deadline: 2/15; financial award applicants required to submit FAFSA. *Faculty research:* Effective urban teachers, preparation and retention of urban teachers, technology utilization in schools, field-based teacher preparation programs, effective use of online instruction. *Unit head:* Dr. Sandra Cooley-Nichols, Interim Chair, 901-678-2365. *Application contact:* Dr. Sally Blake, Director of Graduate Studies, 901-678-4861.

University of Miami, Graduate School, School of Education, Department of Teaching and Learning, Program in Teaching and Learning, Coral Gables, FL 33124. Offers language and literacy learning in multilingual settings (PhD); mathematics and science education (PhD); special education (PhD). *Students:* 30 full-time (22 women); includes 11 minority (3 African Americans, 8 Hispanic Americans), 7 international. Average age 35. 21 applicants, 43% accepted, 7 enrolled. In 2009, 5 doctorates awarded. *Degree requirements:* For doctorate, thesis/dissertation, qualifying exam. *Entrance requirements:* For doctorate, GRE General Test. Additional exam requirements/recommendations for international students: Required—TOEFL (minimum score 550 paper-based; 80 iBT); Recommended—IELTS (minimum score 6.5). *Application deadline:* For fall admission, 2/15 for domestic students, 10/15 for international students. Application fee: $65. Electronic applications accepted. *Financial support:* In 2009–10, 25 students received support. Application deadline: 3/1. *Faculty research:* Teacher education, multicultural education, technology, second language acquisition, math and science education. *Unit head:* Dr. Batya Elbaum, Associate Department Chairperson, 305-284-4218, Fax: 305-284-4439, E-mail: elbaum@miami.edu. *Application contact:* Tinisha Hollinshead, Admission Coordinator, 305-284-2102, Fax: 305-284-6998, E-mail: tinisha@miami.edu.

University of Michigan, Horace H. Rackham School of Graduate Studies, School of Education, Programs in Educational Studies, Ann Arbor, MI 48109. Offers cross specialization (PhD); curriculum development (MA); early childhood education (MA, PhD); educational administration and policy (MA, PhD); educational foundations and policy (MA, PhD); English education (MA); English language learning in school settings (MA); learning technologies (MA, PhD); literacy, language, and culture (MA, PhD); mathematics education (MA, PhD); postsecondary science education (MS); research methods (MA); science education (MA, PhD); social studies education (MA); teaching and teacher education (PhD); MA/Certification; MBA/MA; PhD/MA. Terminal master's awarded for partial completion of doctoral program. *Degree requirements:* For master's, thesis (for some programs); for doctorate, comprehensive exam, thesis/dissertation. *Entrance requirements:* For master's and doctorate, GRE General Test. Additional exam requirements/recommendations for international students: Required—TOEFL (minimum score 600 paper-based; 250 computer-based). *Application deadline:* For fall admission, 12/1 priority date for domestic students, 12/1 for international students. Application fee: $60 ($75 for international students). Electronic applications accepted. *Expenses:* Tuition, state resident: full-time $17,286; part-time $1099 per credit hour. Tuition, nonresident: full-time $34,944; part-time $2080 per credit hour. Required fees: $95 per semester. Tuition and fees vary according to course load, degree level and program. *Financial support:* Applicants required to submit FAFSA. *Unit head:* Dr. Addison Stone, Chairperson, 734-763-7500, Fax: 734-615-1290, E-mail: addison@umich.edu. *Application contact:* Laura Mayers, Student Services Assistant, 734-764-7563, Fax: 734-763-1495, E-mail: ed.grad.admit@umich.edu.

University of Michigan–Flint, School of Education and Human Services, Department of Education, Flint, MI 48502-1950. Offers education (MA); elementary education with teaching certification (MA); literacy (K-12) (MA); special education (MA); technology in education (MA). Part-time programs available. *Faculty:* 14 full-time (12 women), 8 part-time/adjunct (4 women). *Students:* 27 full-time (24 women), 215 part-time (186 women); includes 22 minority (20 African Americans, 2 American Indian/Alaska Native). Average age 35. 63 applicants, 86% accepted, 43 enrolled. In 2009, 91 master's awarded. *Entrance requirements:* For master's, BS with minimum GPA of 3.0. Additional exam requirements/recommendations for international students: Required—TOEFL (minimum score 560 paper-based; 220 computer-based; 84 iBT), IELTS (minimum score 6.5). *Application deadline:* For fall admission, 8/1 priority date for domestic students, 5/1 priority date for international students; for winter admission, 11/15 priority date for domestic students, 9/15 priority date for international students; for spring admission, 3/15 priority date for domestic students, 1/15 priority date for international students. Application fee: $55. *Expenses:* Contact institution. *Financial support:* Federal Work-Study, scholarships/grants, and unspecified assistantships available. Support available to part-time students. Financial award application deadline: 6/1; financial award applicants required to submit FAFSA. *Unit head:* Dr. Beverly Schumer, Director, 810-424-5215, E-mail: bschumer@umflint.edu. *Application contact:* Beulah Alexander, Executive Secretary, 810-766-6879, Fax: 810-766-6891, E-mail: beulaha@umflint.edu.

University of Minnesota, Twin Cities Campus, Graduate School, College of Education and Human Development, Department of Curriculum and Instruction, Minneapolis, MN 55455-0213. Offers art education (M Ed, MA, PhD); children's literature (M Ed, MA, PhD); curriculum and instruction (MA, PhD); early childhood education (M Ed, PhD); elementary education (M Ed, MA, PhD); English education (MA, PhD); environmental education (M Ed); family education (M Ed, MA, Ed D, PhD); instructional systems and technology (M Ed, MA, PhD); language arts (MA, PhD); language immersion education (Certificate); literacy education (MA); mathematics education (MA, PhD); reading education (MA, PhD); science education (MA, PhD); second languages and cultures education (MA, PhD); social studies education (MA, PhD); teaching (M Ed), including Chinese, earth science, elementary special education, English, English as a second language, French, German, Hebrew, Japanese, life sciences, mathematics, middle school science, science, second languages and cultures, social studies, Spanish; technology enhanced learning (Certificate); writing education (M Ed, MA, PhD). *Faculty:* 34 full-time (21 women). *Students:* 436 full-time (307 women), 375 part-time (280 women); includes 80 minority (30 African Americans, 6 American Indian/Alaska Native, 33 Asian Americans or Pacific Islanders, 11 Hispanic Americans), 40 international. Average age 32. 660 applicants, 64% accepted, 379 enrolled. In 2009, 552 master's, 14 doctorates, 7 other advanced degrees awarded. *Financial support:* In 2009–10, 5 fellowships (averaging $27,000 per year), 47 research assistantships with full tuition reimbursements (averaging $25,682 per year), 60 teaching assistantships with full tuition reimbursements (averaging $29,889 per year) were awarded. *Faculty research:* Teaching and learning; quality of education; influence of cultural,

linguistic, social, political, technological and economic factors on teaching, learning and educational research; relationship between educational practice and a democratic and just society. Total annual research expenditures: $1.8 million. *Unit head:* Dr. Ruth Thomas, Chair, 612-624-4772, Fax: 612-624-8277, E-mail: thoma006@umn.edu. *Application contact:* Dr. Mary Trettin, Associate Dean, 612-626-6501, Fax: 612-626-1580, E-mail: mtrettin@umn.edu.

University of Missouri, Graduate School, College of Education, Department of Learning, Teaching and Curriculum, Columbia, MO 65211. Offers agricultural education (M Ed, PhD, Ed S); art education (M Ed, PhD, Ed S); business and office education (M Ed, PhD, Ed S); early childhood education (M Ed, PhD, Ed S); elementary education (M Ed, PhD, Ed S); English education (M Ed, PhD, Ed S); foreign language education (M Ed, PhD, Ed S); health education and promotion (M Ed, PhD); learning and instruction (M Ed); marketing education (M Ed, PhD, Ed S); mathematics education (M Ed, PhD, Ed S); music education (M Ed, PhD, Ed S); reading education (M Ed, PhD, Ed S); science education (M Ed, PhD, Ed S); social studies education (M Ed, PhD, Ed S); vocational education (M Ed, PhD, Ed S). Part-time programs available. Terminal master's awarded for partial completion of doctoral program. *Degree requirements:* For doctorate, thesis/dissertation. *Entrance requirements:* For master's and Ed S, GRE General Test or MAT, minimum GPA of 3.0; for doctorate, GRE General Test, minimum GPA of 3.0. Additional exam requirements/recommendations for international students: Required—TOEFL (minimum score 600 paper-based; 250 computer-based; 100 iBT). Electronic applications accepted.

University of Missouri–Kansas City, School of Education, Kansas City, MO 64110-2499. Offers administration (Ed D); counseling and guidance (MA, Ed S); counseling psychology (PhD); curriculum and instruction (MA, Ed S); education (PhD); educational administration (Ed S); reading education (MA, Ed S); special education (MA). PhD with concentration in education (interdisciplinary) is offered through the School of Graduate Studies. *Accreditation:* NCATE. Part-time and evening/weekend programs available. *Faculty:* 62 full-time (52 women), 45 part-time/adjunct (34 women). *Students:* 207 full-time (154 women), 401 part-time (290 women); includes 142 minority (107 African Americans, 14 Asian Americans or Pacific Islanders, 21 Hispanic Americans), 18 international. Average age 34. 294 applicants, 61% accepted, 150 enrolled. In 2009, 184 master's, 9 doctorates, 49 other advanced degrees awarded. *Degree requirements:* For doctorate, thesis/dissertation, internship, practicum. *Entrance requirements:* For master's, GRE, minimum GPA of 2.75, 2 letters of reference, written statement of purpose; for doctorate, GRE, minimum GPA of 3.0; for Ed S, minimum GPA of 3.0. Additional exam requirements/recommendations for international students: Required—TOEFL (minimum score 550 paper-based; 213 computer-based; 80 iBT). *Application deadline:* For fall admission, 4/1 priority date for domestic and international students; for spring admission, 11/1 priority date for domestic and international students. Applications are processed on a rolling basis. Application fee: $45 ($50 for international students). *Expenses:* Tuition, state resident: full-time $5378; part-time $299 per credit hour. Tuition, nonresident: full-time $13,881; part-time $771 per credit hour. Required fees: $641; $71 per credit hour. Tuition and fees vary according to course load and program. *Financial support:* In 2009–10, 19 research assistantships with partial tuition reimbursements (averaging $9,821 per year) were awarded; career-related internships or fieldwork, Federal Work-Study, institutionally sponsored loans, and tuition waivers (full and partial) also available. Support available to part-time students. Financial award application deadline: 3/1; financial award applicants required to submit FAFSA. *Faculty research:* Urban education, inquiry-based field study, theories of counseling and psychotherapy, school literacy, educational technology. Total annual research expenditures: $2.9 million. *Unit head:* Dr. Wanda Blanchett, Dean, 816-235-2234, Fax: 816-235-5270, E-mail: education@umkc.edu. *Application contact:* Erica Hernandez-Scott, Student Recruiter, 816-235-1295, Fax: 816-235-5270, E-mail: hernandeze@umkc.edu.

University of Missouri–St. Louis, College of Education, Division of Teaching and Learning, St. Louis, MO 63121. Offers elementary education (M Ed), including early childhood, general, reading; secondary education (M Ed), including curriculum and instruction, general, middle level education, reading, teaching English to speakers of other languages (TESOL); secondary school teaching (Certificate); special education (M Ed), including behavioral disorders, early childhood special education, general, learning disabilities, mental retardation; teaching English to speakers of other languages (Certificate). Part-time and evening/weekend programs available. *Faculty:* 36 full-time (23 women), 51 part-time/adjunct (42 women). *Students:* 123 full-time (77 women), 569 part-time (435 women); includes 137 minority (110 African Americans, 4 American Indian/Alaska Native, 10 Asian Americans or Pacific Islanders, 13 Hispanic Americans), 11 international. Average age 32. In 2009, 1,852 master's awarded. *Degree requirements:* For master's, comprehensive exam. *Entrance requirements:* Additional exam requirements/recommendations for international students: Recommended—TOEFL (minimum score 550 paper-based; 213 computer-based). *Application deadline:* For fall admission, 7/1 priority date for domestic and international students; for spring admission, 12/1 priority date for domestic and international students. Application fee: $35 ($40 for international students). Electronic applications accepted. *Expenses:* Tuition, state resident: full-time $5377; part-time $297.70 per credit hour. Tuition, nonresident: full-time $13,882; part-time $771.20 per credit hour. Required fees: $220; $12.20 per credit hour. One-time fee: $12. Tuition and fees vary according to course level, campus/location and program. *Financial support:* In 2009–10, 5 research assistantships (averaging $10,339 per year), 2 teaching assistantships (averaging $6,800 per year) were awarded. Financial award application deadline: 4/1; financial award applicants required to submit FAFSA. *Unit head:* Dr. Joseph Polman, Chair, 314-516-5791. *Application contact:* 314-516-5458, Fax: 314-516-6996, E-mail: gadadm@umsl.edu.

University of Nebraska at Kearney, College of Graduate Study, College of Education, Department of Teacher Education, Kearney, NE 68849-0001. Offers curriculum and instruction (MS Ed); instructional technology (MS Ed); reading education (MA Ed); special education (MA Ed). Part-time and evening/weekend programs available. *Degree requirements:* For master's, comprehensive exam, thesis optional. *Entrance requirements:* For master's, portfolio or GRE. Additional exam requirements/recommendations for international students: Required—TOEFL (minimum score 550 paper-based; 213 computer-based). Electronic applications accepted.

University of Nebraska at Omaha, Graduate Studies, College of Education, Department of Teacher Education, Program in Reading Education, Omaha, NE 68182. Offers MS. *Accreditation:* NCATE. Part-time and evening/weekend programs available. *Faculty:* 4 full-time (3 women). *Students:* 2 full-time (both women), 65 part-time (all women); includes 2 minority (1 African American, 1 Hispanic American). Average age 33. 7 applicants, 86% accepted, 6 enrolled. In 2009, 23 master's awarded. *Degree requirements:* For master's, comprehensive exam, thesis (for some programs). *Entrance requirements:* For master's, minimum GPA of 3.0. Additional exam requirements/recommendations for international students: Required—TOEFL (minimum score 550 paper-based; 213 computer-based; 80 iBT). *Application deadline:* For fall admission, 7/1 priority date for domestic students; for spring admission, 12/1 priority date for domestic students. Applications are processed on a rolling basis. Application fee: $45. Electronic applications accepted. *Financial support:* In 2009–10, 15 students received support; fellowships, teaching assistantships with tuition reimbursements available, Federal Work-Study, institutionally sponsored loans, scholarships/grants, tuition waivers (full), and unspecified assistantships available. Support available to part-time students. Financial award application deadline: 3/1. *Application contact:* Dr. Wilma Kuhlman, Student Contact, 402-554-2212.

University of Nevada, Reno, Graduate School, College of Education, Department of Educational Specialties, Program in Literacy Studies, Reno, NV 89557. Offers M Ed, MA, Ed D, PhD. Terminal master's awarded for partial completion of doctoral program. *Degree requirements:* For master's, thesis optional; for doctorate, thesis/dissertation. *Entrance requirements:* For master's, minimum GPA of 2.75; for doctorate, GRE General Test, minimum GPA of 3.0. Additional exam requirements/recommendations for international students: Required—TOEFL (minimum score 500 paper-based; 173 computer-based; 61 iBT), IELTS (minimum score 6). Electronic applications accepted. *Faculty research:* Cognitive language process, literacy.

University of New England, College of Arts and Sciences, Program in Education, Biddeford, ME 04005-9526. Offers curriculm and instruction strategy (MS Ed); educational leadership (MS Ed); general studies (MS Ed); literacy (MS Ed); teaching methodologies (MS Ed). Part-time programs available. Postbaccalaureate distance learning degree programs offered (minimal on-campus study). *Faculty:* 2 full-time (1 woman), 25 part-time/adjunct (15 women). *Students:* 473 full-time (362 women), 177 part-time (133 women); includes 29 African Americans, 12 Asian Americans or Pacific Islanders, 16 Hispanic Americans. In 2009, 319 master's awarded. *Degree requirements:* For master's, collaborative action research project, integrative seminar portfolio. *Entrance requirements:* For master's, teaching certificate, 2 years of teaching experience. Additional exam requirements/recommendations for international students: Required—TOEFL. *Application deadline:* For fall admission, 9/15 for domestic students; for spring admission, 1/15 for domestic students. Applications are processed on a rolling basis. Application fee: $40. Electronic applications accepted. *Expenses:* Contact institution. *Financial support:* Application deadline: 5/1. *Faculty research:* Distance learning, effective teaching, transition planning, adult learning. *Unit head:* Dr. Doug Lynch, Chair of Education Department, 207-283-0171 Ext. 2888, E-mail: dlynch@une.edu. *Application contact:* Stacy Gato, Assistant Director of Graduate Admissions, 207-221-4225, Fax: 207-221-4898, E-mail: gradadmissions@une.edu.

University of New Hampshire, Graduate School, College of Liberal Arts, Department of Education, Program in Reading, Durham, NH 03824. Offers M Ed. Part-time programs available. *Faculty:* 32 full-time. *Students:* 2 full-time (both women), 12 part-time (all women). Average age 38. 6 applicants, 33% accepted, 2 enrolled. In 2009, 11 master's awarded. *Degree requirements:* For master's, thesis or alternative. *Entrance requirements:* For master's, GRE General Test. Additional exam requirements/recommendations for international students: Required—TOEFL (minimum score 550 paper-based; 213 computer-based; 80 iBT). *Application deadline:* For fall admission, 4/1 for domestic and international students. Applications are processed on a rolling basis. Application fee: $65. Electronic applications accepted. *Expenses:* Tuition, state resident: full-time $10,380; part-time $577 per credit hour. Tuition, nonresident: full-time $24,350; part-time $1002 per credit hour. Required fees: $1550; $387.50 per semester. Tuition and fees vary according to course load and program. *Financial support:* In 2009–10, 1 student received support, including 1 teaching assistantship; fellowships, research assistantships, career-related internships or fieldwork, Federal Work-Study, scholarships/grants, and tuition waivers (full and partial) also available. Support available to part-time students. Financial award application deadline: 2/15. *Faculty research:* Reading foundations; clinical components; consultant, supervisory, and research skills. *Unit head:* Dr. John Carney, Coordinator, 603-862-2373, E-mail: education.department@unh.edu. *Application contact:* Dr. John Carney, Coordinator, 603-862-2373, E-mail: education.department@unh.edu.

The University of North Carolina at Chapel Hill, Graduate School, School of Education, Program in Education, Chapel Hill, NC 27599. Offers culture, curriculum and change (MA, PhD); early childhood, intervention and literacy (MA, PhD); educational psychology, measurement and evaluation (MA, PhD). *Accreditation:* NCATE. *Degree requirements:* For master's, thesis; for doctorate, comprehensive exam, thesis/dissertation. *Entrance requirements:* For master's, GRE General Test, minimum GPA of 3.0 during last 2 years of undergraduates course work; for doctorate, GRE General Test, minimum GPA of 3.0 during last 2 years of undergraduate course work. Additional exam requirements/recommendations for international students: Required—TOEFL (minimum score 550 paper-based; 213 computer-based). Electronic applications accepted.

The University of North Carolina at Charlotte, Graduate School, College of Education, Department of Reading and Elementary Education, Charlotte, NC 28223-0001. Offers elementary education (M Ed); reading, language and literacy (M Ed). Part-time and evening/weekend programs available. Postbaccalaureate distance learning degree programs offered (no on-campus study). *Faculty:* 23 full-time (13 women), 3 part-time/adjunct (2 women). *Students:* 4 full-time (all women), 64 part-time (all women); includes 4 minority (3 African Americans, 1 Hispanic American). Average age 30. 17 applicants, 94% accepted, 12 enrolled. In 2009, 18 master's awarded. *Entrance requirements:* For master's, GRE or MAT. Additional exam requirements/recommendations for international students: Required—TOEFL (minimum score 557 paper-based; 220 computer-based; 83 iBT). *Application deadline:* For fall admission, 7/1 for domestic students, 5/1 for international students; for spring admission, 11/1 for domestic students, 10/1 for international students. Applications are processed on a rolling basis. Application fee: $55. Electronic applications accepted. *Financial support:* In 2009–10, 2 students received support, including 2 teaching assistantships (averaging $24,000 per year); fellowships, research assistantships, career-related internships or fieldwork, Federal Work-Study, institutionally sponsored loans, scholarships/grants, and unspecified assistantships also available. Support available to part-time students. Financial award application deadline: 4/1; financial award applicants required to submit FAFSA. *Unit head:* Dr. Robert J. Rickelman, Chair, 704-687-8890, Fax: 704-687-3749, E-mail: rjrickel@uncc.edu. *Application contact:* Kathy B. Giddings, Director of Graduate Admissions, 704-687-5503, Fax: 704-687-3279, E-mail: gradadm@uncc.edu.

The University of North Carolina at Greensboro, Graduate School, School of Education, Department of Curriculum and Instruction, Greensboro, NC 27412-5001. Offers college teaching and adult learning (Certificate); curriculum and instruction (M Ed), including chemistry education, elementary education, English as a second language, French education, instructional technology, mathematics education, middle grades education, reading education, science education, social studies education, Spanish education; curriculum and teaching (PhD), including higher education, teacher education and development; English as a second language (Certificate); higher education (M Ed); supervision (M Ed). *Accreditation:* NCATE. Part-time programs available. *Degree requirements:* For doctorate, thesis/dissertation. *Entrance requirements:* For master's and doctorate, GRE General Test. Additional exam requirements/recommendations for international students: Required—TOEFL. Electronic applications accepted. *Faculty research:* Community college literacy program, middle school mathematics/computer mathematics.

The University of North Carolina at Pembroke, Graduate Studies, School of Education, Program in Reading Education, Pembroke, NC 28372-1510. Offers MA Ed. *Accreditation:* NCATE. Part-time and evening/weekend programs available. *Degree requirements:* For master's, comprehensive exam, thesis optional. *Entrance requirements:* For master's, GRE General Test or MAT, minimum GPA of 3.0 in major, 2.5 overall; teaching license. Additional exam requirements/recommendations for international students: Required—TOEFL.

The University of North Carolina Wilmington, School of Education, Department of Elementary, Middle Level and Literacy Education, Program in Language and Literacy Education, Wilmington, NC 28403-3297. Offers M Ed. *Accreditation:* NCATE. Part-time and evening/weekend programs available. *Degree requirements:* For master's, comprehensive exam. *Entrance requirements:* For master's, GRE General Test, MAT, minimum B average in upper-division undergraduate course work.

University of North Dakota, Graduate School, College of Education and Human Development, Program in Reading Education, Grand Forks, ND 58202. Offers M Ed, MS. *Accreditation:* NCATE. Part-time programs available. Postbaccalaureate distance learning degree programs offered (minimal on-campus study). *Degree requirements:* For master's, comprehensive exam, thesis or alternative. *Entrance requirements:* For master's, minimum GPA of 3.0. Additional exam requirements/recommendations for international students: Required—TOEFL (minimum score 550 paper-based; 213 computer-based; 79 iBT), IELTS (minimum score 6.5). Electronic applications accepted. *Faculty research:* Whole language, multicultural education, child-focused learning, experiential science, cooperative learning.

University of Northern Colorado, Graduate School, College of Education and Behavioral Sciences, School of Teacher Education, Program in Reading, Greeley, CO 80639. Offers MA. *Accreditation:* NCATE. Part-time and evening/weekend programs available. Postbaccalaureate distance learning degree programs offered (no on-campus study). *Faculty:* 2 full-time (1 woman). *Students:* 1 (woman) full-time, 13 part-time (12 women); includes 1 minority (Hispanic American). Average age 35. 4 applicants, 75% accepted, 1 enrolled. In 2009, 37 master's

Reading Education

University of Northern Colorado (continued)

awarded. *Degree requirements:* For master's, comprehensive exam, thesis or alternative. *Entrance requirements:* For master's, GRE General Test (if undergraduate GPA less than 3.0), resume, letters of reference. *Application deadline:* Applications are processed on a rolling basis. Application fee: $50 ($60 for international students). Electronic applications accepted. *Expenses:* Tuition, state resident: full-time $5770; part-time $320.55 per credit hour. Tuition, nonresident: full-time $13,847; part-time $769.27 per credit hour. Required fees: $948.78; $52.72 per credit. *Financial support:* Fellowships, research assistantships, teaching assistantships, unspecified assistantships available. Financial award application deadline: 3/1; financial award applicants required to submit FAFSA. *Unit head:* Dr. Michael Opitz, Program Coordinator, 970-351-1605. *Application contact:* Linda Sisson, Graduate Student Admission Coordinator, 970-351-1807, Fax: 970-351-2371, E-mail: linda.sisson@unco.edu.

University of Northern Iowa, Graduate College, College of Education, Department of Curriculum and Instruction, Program in Reading, Cedar Falls, IA 50614. Offers elementary reading and language arts (MAE); reading education (MAE); secondary reading (MAE). Part-time and evening/weekend programs available. *Students:* 1 full-time (0 women), 18 part-time (all women); includes 3 minority (2 African Americans, 1 Hispanic American). 3 applicants, 33% accepted, 1 enrolled. In 2009, 14 master's awarded. *Degree requirements:* For master's, comprehensive exam, thesis or alternative. *Entrance requirements:* For master's, writing exam, minimum GPA of 3.0, two recommendations from professional educators. Additional exam requirements/recommendations for international students: Required—TOEFL (minimum score 500 paper-based; 180 computer-based; 61 iBT). *Application deadline:* For fall admission, 8/1 priority date for domestic students. Applications are processed on a rolling basis. Application fee: $30 ($50 for international students). Electronic applications accepted. *Financial support:* Career-related internships or fieldwork, Federal Work-Study, and tuition waivers (full and partial) available. Support available to part-time students. Financial award application deadline: 2/1. *Unit head:* Dr. Deborah Tidwell, Coordinator, 319-273-2070, Fax: 319-273-5886, E-mail: deborah.tidwell@uni.edu. *Application contact:* Laurie S. Russell, Record Analyst, 319-273-2623, Fax: 319-273-6792, E-mail: laurie.russell@uni.edu.

University of North Florida, College of Education and Human Services, Department of Childhood Education, Jacksonville, FL 32224. Offers literacy K-12 (M Ed); professional education—elementary ed (M Ed); TESOL K-12 (M Ed). *Accreditation:* NCATE. Part-time and evening/weekend programs available. *Faculty:* 11 full-time (8 women). *Students:* 11 full-time (all women), 22 part-time (21 women); includes 7 minority (4 African Americans, 1 Asian American or Pacific Islander, 2 Hispanic Americans). Average age 30. 17 applicants, 35% accepted, 3 enrolled. In 2009, 23 master's awarded. *Entrance requirements:* For master's, GRE General Test, minimum GPA of 3.0 in last 60 hours, 3 letters of recommendation, interview. Additional exam requirements/recommendations for international students: Required—TOEFL (minimum score 500 paper-based; 173 computer-based). *Application deadline:* For fall admission, 7/1 priority date for domestic students, 5/1 for international students; for spring admission, 11/1 priority date for domestic students, 10/1 for international students. Applications are processed on a rolling basis. Application fee: $30. Electronic applications accepted. *Expenses:* Tuition, state resident: full-time $6649.20; part-time $277.05 per credit hour. Tuition, nonresident: full-time $22,970; part-time $957.08 per credit hour. Required fees: $985; $41.03 per credit hour. *Financial support:* In 2009–10, 12 students received support. Federal Work-Study and tuition waivers (partial) available. Support available to part-time students. Financial award application deadline: 4/1; financial award applicants required to submit FAFSA. *Faculty research:* The social context of and processes in learning, inter-disciplinary instruction, cross-cultural conflict resolution, the Vygotskian perspective on literacy diagnosis and instruction, performance poetry and teaching the language arts through drama. Total annual research expenditures: $256,831. *Unit head:* Dr. Ronghua Ouyang, Chair, 904-620-2611, Fax: 904-620-1025, E-mail: ronghua.ouyang@unf.edu. *Application contact:* Dr. John Kemppainen, Director, Office of Student Services, 904-620-2530, Fax: 904-620-1135, E-mail: jkemppai@unf.edu.

University of North Texas, Robert B. Toulouse School of Graduate Studies, College of Education, Department of Teacher Education and Administration, Program in Reading Education, Denton, TX 76203. Offers M Ed, MS, Ed D, PhD. *Accreditation:* NCATE. Part-time and evening/weekend programs available. *Degree requirements:* For master's, portfolio development and presentation; for doctorate, comprehensive exam, thesis/dissertation. *Entrance requirements:* For master's, GRE General Test, goals statement, writing sample, curriculum vitae/resume; for doctorate, GRE General Test, curriculum vitae/resume, writing sample, 3 letters of recommendation, screening interview. Additional exam requirements/recommendations for international students: Required—proof of English language proficiency required for non-native English speakers; Recommended—TOEFL (minimum score 550 paper-based; 213 computer-based; 79 iBT). *Application deadline:* Applications are processed on a rolling basis. Application fee: $50 ($75 for international students). Electronic applications accepted. *Expenses:* Tuition, state resident: full-time $4298; part-time $239 per contact hour. Tuition, nonresident: full-time $9878; part-time $549 per contact hour. Required fees: $265 per contact hour. *Financial support:* Fellowships, research assistantships, teaching assistantships, career-related internships or fieldwork, Federal Work-Study, and institutionally sponsored loans available. Financial award application deadline: 4/15; financial award applicants required to submit FAFSA. *Faculty research:* Writing instruction for adolescent ELL, literacy development in Thailand, language acquisition literacy development in emergent readers, current children's/adolescent literature relating to global issues, policy issues in bilingual/ESL education.

University of Oklahoma, Graduate College, College of Education, Department of Instructional Leadership and Academic Curriculum, Norman, OK 73072. Offers education (Certificate); instructional leadership and academic curriculum (M Ed, PhD), including bilingual education, early childhood education, elementary education, English education, math education, reading education, science education, secondary education, social studies education. *Accreditation:* NCATE. Part-time and evening/weekend programs available. *Faculty:* 18 full-time (11 women). *Students:* 44 full-time (36 women), 117 part-time (92 women); includes 35 minority (11 African Americans, 14 American Indian/Alaska Native, 5 Asian Americans or Pacific Islanders, 5 Hispanic Americans), 2 international. 50 applicants, 84% accepted, 32 enrolled. In 2009, 31 master's, 6 doctorates awarded. Terminal master's awarded for partial completion of doctoral program. *Degree requirements:* For doctorate, thesis/dissertation. *Entrance requirements:* For master's, 12 hours of course work in education; for doctorate, GRE General Test, master's degree, minimum graduate GPA of 3.0. Additional exam requirements/recommendations for international students: Required—TOEFL (minimum score 550 paper-based; 213 computer-based). *Application deadline:* For fall admission, 6/1 priority date for domestic students, 4/1 for international students; for spring admission, 11/1 for domestic students, 9/1 for international students. Applications are processed on a rolling basis. Application fee: $40 ($90 for international students). Electronic applications accepted. *Expenses:* Tuition, state resident: full-time $3744; part-time $156 per credit hour. Tuition, nonresident: full-time $13,577; part-time $565.70 per credit hour. Required fees: $2415; $90.10 per credit hour. *Financial support:* In 2009–10, 107 students received support, including 1 research assistantship with partial tuition reimbursement available (averaging $9,630 per year), 6 teaching assistantships with partial tuition reimbursements available (averaging $10,801 per year); scholarships/grants, health care benefits, and unspecified assistantships also available. Financial award applicants required to submit FAFSA. *Faculty research:* English education, mathematics education, reading, science education, social studies education. Total annual research expenditures: $752,908. *Unit head:* Lawrence Baines, Chair, 405-325-1498, Fax: 405-325-4061, E-mail: lbaines@ou.edu. *Application contact:* Lynn Crussel, Administrative Assistant for Graduate Studies, 405-325-4843, Fax: 405-325-4061, E-mail: lcrussel@ou.edu.

University of Oklahoma Health Sciences Center, Graduate College, College of Allied Health, Department of Communication Sciences and Disorders, Oklahoma City, OK 73190. Offers audiology (MS, Au D, PhD); communication sciences and disorders (Certificate), including reading, speech-language pathology; education of the deaf (MS); speech-language pathology (MS, PhD). *Accreditation:* ASHA (one or more programs are accredited). Part-time programs available. *Faculty:* 13 full-time (10 women), 2 part-time/adjunct (1 woman). *Students:* 67 full-time (66 women), 4 part-time (3 women); includes 10 minority (8 American Indian/Alaska Native, 1 Asian American or Pacific Islander, 1 Hispanic American). Average age 25. 92 applicants, 49% accepted, 25 enrolled. In 2009, 24 master's, 7 doctorates awarded. Terminal master's awarded for partial completion of doctoral program. *Degree requirements:* For master's, comprehensive exam, thesis optional; for doctorate, one foreign language, comprehensive exam, thesis/dissertation. *Entrance requirements:* For master's and doctorate, GRE General Test, 3 letters of recommendation. Additional exam requirements/recommendations for international students: Required—TOEFL (minimum score 550 paper-based). *Application deadline:* For fall admission, 2/1 for domestic students. Applications are processed on a rolling basis. Application fee: $50. *Expenses:* Tuition, state resident: full-time $3120; part-time $156 per credit hour. Tuition, nonresident: full-time $11,314; part-time $409.70 per credit hour. Required fees: $1471; $51.20 per credit hour. $223.25 per term. *Financial support:* In 2009–10, 8 research assistantships (averaging $16,000 per year) were awarded; fellowships, career-related internships or fieldwork, Federal Work-Study, institutionally sponsored loans, and traineeships also available. Support available to part-time students. *Faculty research:* Event-related potentials, cleft palate, fluency disorders, language disorders, hearing and speech science. *Unit head:* Dr. Stephen Painton, Chair, 405-271-4214, E-mail: stephen-painton@ouhsc.edu. *Application contact:* Dr. Sarah Christman, Graduate Liaison, 405-271-4214, Fax: 405-271-1153, E-mail: sarah-christman@ouhsc.edu.

University of Pennsylvania, Graduate School of Education, Division of Language in Education, Program in Reading, Writing, and Literacy, Philadelphia, PA 19104. Offers MS Ed, Ed D, PhD. Part-time programs available. *Students:* 87 full-time (77 women), 43 part-time (41 women); includes 31 minority (14 African Americans, 14 Asian Americans or Pacific Islanders, 3 Hispanic Americans), 4 international. 104 applicants, 71% accepted, 46 enrolled. In 2009, 33 master's, 3 doctorates awarded. *Degree requirements:* For master's, comprehensive exam; for doctorate, one foreign language, thesis/dissertation, preliminary exam. *Entrance requirements:* For master's and doctorate, GRE General Test or MAT. Additional exam requirements/recommendations for international students: Required—TOEFL. *Application deadline:* For fall admission, 12/15 priority date for domestic students. Applications are processed on a rolling basis. Application fee: $70. Electronic applications accepted. *Expenses:* Contact institution. *Financial support:* Fellowships, institutionally sponsored loans, scholarships/grants, traineeships, health care benefits, and unspecified assistantships available. *Faculty research:* Reading and writing relationships, classroom teachers as researchers, comprehension processes.

University of Pittsburgh, School of Education, Department of Instruction and Learning, Program in Reading Education, Pittsburgh, PA 15260. Offers M Ed, Ed D, PhD. *Students:* 8 full-time (all women), 68 part-time (65 women); includes 7 minority (6 African Americans, 1 Hispanic American), 2 international. Average age 31. 68 applicants, 81% accepted, 51 enrolled. In 2009, 27 master's, 4 doctorates awarded. *Degree requirements:* For master's, thesis; for doctorate, thesis/dissertation. *Entrance requirements:* For master's, PRAXIS I; for doctorate, GRE General Test. Additional exam requirements/recommendations for international students: Required—TOEFL. *Application deadline:* For fall admission, 2/15 for domestic students. Application fee: $50. *Expenses:* Tuition, state resident: full-time $16,402; part-time $665 per credit. Tuition, nonresident: full-time $28,694; part-time $1175 per credit. Required fees: $690; $175 per term. Tuition and fees vary according to program. *Financial support:* Application deadline: 3/15. *Unit head:* Dr. Richard Donato, Chairman, 412-624-7248, Fax: 412-648-7081, E-mail: donato@pitt.edu. *Application contact:* Dr. Marjie Schermer, Graduate Enrollment Manager, 412-648-2230, Fax: 412-648-1899, E-mail: soeinfo@pitt.edu.

University of Rhode Island, Graduate School, College of Human Science and Services, School of Education, Kingston, RI 02881. Offers adult education (MA); education (PhD); elementary education (MA); music education (MM); reading education (MA); secondary education (MA); special education (MA); MS/PhD. *Accreditation:* NCATE. Part-time and evening/weekend programs available. *Faculty:* 19 full-time (12 women), 5 part-time/adjunct (1 woman). *Students:* 44 full-time (33 women), 128 part-time (101 women); includes 14 minority (8 African Americans, 2 American Indian/Alaska Native, 2 Asian Americans or Pacific Islanders, 2 Hispanic Americans), 3 international. In 2009, 44 master's, 7 doctorates awarded. *Degree requirements:* For master's, comprehensive exam (for some programs), thesis optional; for doctorate, comprehensive exam, thesis/dissertation. *Entrance requirements:* For master's, 2 letters of recommendation; interview (for special education applicants); for doctorate, GRE, 3 letters of recommendation, resume. Additional exam requirements/recommendations for international students: Required—TOEFL (minimum score 600 paper-based; 250 computer-based; 100 iBT). *Application deadline:* For fall admission, 1/31 for international students. Application fee: $65. Electronic applications accepted. *Expenses:* Tuition, state resident: full-time $8828; part-time $490 per credit hour. Tuition, nonresident: full-time $22,100; part-time $1228 per credit hour. Required fees: $1118; $57 per semester. Tuition and fees vary according to program. *Financial support:* In 2009–10, 5 research assistantships with full and partial tuition reimbursements (averaging $11,518 per year), 3 teaching assistantships with full and partial tuition reimbursements (averaging $10,421 per year) were awarded; career-related internships or fieldwork also available. Financial award applicants required to submit FAFSA. Total annual research expenditures: $3.4 million. *Unit head:* Dr. David Byrd, Director, 401-874-5484, Fax: 401-874-5471, E-mail: dbyrd@uri.edu. *Application contact:* Dr. John Boulmetis, Coordinator of Graduate Studies, 401-874-4159, Fax: 401-874-7610, E-mail: johnb@uri.edu.

University of Rio Grande, Graduate School, Rio Grande, OH 45674. Offers classroom teaching (M Ed), including fine arts, learning disabilities, mathematics, reading education. *Accreditation:* NCATE. Part-time and evening/weekend programs available. *Degree requirements:* For master's, final research project, portfolio. *Entrance requirements:* For master's, minimum GPA of 2.7 in major, 2.5 overall. Additional exam requirements/recommendations for international students: Required—TOEFL. *Faculty research:* Interagency collaboration, reading and mathematics, learning styles, college access, literacy.

University of St. Francis, College of Education, Joliet, IL 60435-6169. Offers educational leadership (MS), including reading; elementary education certification (M Ed); reading (MS); secondary education certification (M Ed), including English education, math education, science education, social studies education; special education (M Ed); teaching and learning (MS), including character education, curriculum and instruction, differentiated instruction, technology. *Accreditation:* NCATE. Part-time and evening/weekend programs available. *Faculty:* 10 full-time (8 women), 26 part-time/adjunct (18 women). *Students:* 60 full-time (45 women), 349 part-time (283 women); includes 36 minority (10 African Americans, 2 Asian Americans or Pacific Islanders, 24 Hispanic Americans). Average age 33. 211 applicants, 65% accepted, 102 enrolled. In 2009, 174 master's awarded. *Entrance requirements:* For master's, Illinois Basic Skills Test (M Ed), teaching certificate (MS), minimum undergraduate GPA of 2.75, 2 letters of recommendation, computer competency. Additional exam requirements/recommendations for international students: Required—TOEFL (minimum score 550 paper-based; 213 computer-based). *Application deadline:* Applications are processed on a rolling basis. Application fee: $30. Electronic applications accepted. *Expenses:* Contact institution. *Financial support:* In 2009–10, 254 students received support. Federal Work-Study, scholarships/grants, tuition waivers (partial), and unspecified assistantships available. Support available to part-time students. Financial award applicants required to submit FAFSA. *Unit head:* Dr. John Gambro, Dean, 815-740-3332, Fax: 815-740-2264, E-mail: jgambro@stfrancis.edu. *Application contact:* Sandra Sloka, Director of Admissions for Graduate and Degree Completion Programs, 800-735-7500, Fax: 815-740-5032, E-mail: ssloka@stfrancis.edu.

University of St. Thomas, Graduate Studies, School of Education, Department of Teacher Education, St. Paul, MN 55105-1096. Offers curriculum and instruction (MA), including elementary, individualized, K-12, secondary; elementary (MAT); multicultural education (Certificate); reading (MA, Certificate), including elementary (MA), K-12 (MA). *Accreditation:* NCATE. Part-time and evening/weekend programs available. *Faculty:* 10 full-time (7 women), 25 part-time/adjunct (16 women). *Students:* 31 full-time (25 women), 260 part-time (195 women); includes 19 minority (6 African Americans, 7 Asian Americans or Pacific Islanders, 6 Hispanic Americans), 3 international. Average age 34. 325 applicants, 72% accepted, 225 enrolled. In 2009, 135 master's, 17 other advanced degrees awarded. *Entrance requirements:*

For master's, minimum GPA of 3.0 or MAT. Additional exam requirements/recommendations for international students: Required—TOEFL (minimum score 550 paper-based; 210 computer-based; 80 iBT). *Application deadline:* For fall admission, 6/1 for domestic students; for spring admission, 11/1 for domestic students. Applications are processed on a rolling basis. Application fee: $50. *Financial support:* Fellowships, research assistantships, institutionally sponsored loans and scholarships/grants available. Support available to part-time students. Financial award applicants required to submit FAFSA. *Unit head:* Dr. Douglas F. Warring, Department Chair, 651-962-4877, Fax: 651-962-4169, E-mail: dfwarring@stthomas.edu. *Application contact:* Kathy J. Neary, Department Assistant, 651-962-4420, Fax: 651-962-4169, E-mail: kjneary@stthomas.edu.

University of San Diego, School of Leadership and Education Sciences, Department of Learning and Teaching, San Diego, CA 92110-2492. Offers curriculum and instruction (M Ed); mathematics, science and technology education (M Ed); special education (M Ed); special education with deaf and hard of hearing (M Ed); teaching (MAT); TESOL, literacy and culture (M Ed). Part-time and evening/weekend programs available. *Faculty:* 13 full-time (9 women), 24 part-time/adjunct (21 women). *Students:* 77 full-time (63 women), 92 part-time (74 women); includes 46 minority (13 African Americans, 12 Asian Americans or Pacific Islanders, 21 Hispanic Americans), 6 international. Average age 31. 142 applicants, 75% accepted, 59 enrolled. In 2009, 64 master's awarded. *Degree requirements:* For master's, thesis (for some programs). *Entrance requirements:* For master's, minimum GPA of 3.0. Additional exam requirements/recommendations for international students: Required—TOEFL (minimum score 580 paper-based; 237 computer-based; 83 iBT), TWE. *Application deadline:* For fall admission, 7/15 for domestic and international students; for spring admission, 12/1 for domestic and international students. Applications are processed on a rolling basis. Application fee: $45. Electronic applications accepted. *Expenses:* Tuition: Full-time $21,042; part-time $1169 per unit. Required fees: $224. Full-time tuition and fees vary according to course load and degree level. *Financial support:* In 2009–10, 113 students received support. Career-related internships or fieldwork, Federal Work-Study, institutionally sponsored loans, and stipends available. Support available to part-time students. Financial award application deadline: 4/1; financial award applicants required to submit FAFSA. *Faculty research:* Action research methodology, cultural studies, instructional theories and practices, second language acquisition, school reform. *Unit head:* Dr. Judy Mantle, Director, 619-260-7879, Fax: 619-260-6835, E-mail: jmantle@sandiego.edu. *Application contact:* Dr. John Mosby, Associate Director of Graduate Admissions, 619-260-4524, Fax: 619-260-4158, E-mail: grads@sandiego.edu.

University of San Francisco, School of Education, Department of Learning and Instruction, San Francisco, CA 94117-1080. Offers digital media and learning (MA); learning and instruction (MA, Ed D); teaching (MA); teaching reading (MA). *Faculty:* 10 full-time (6 women), 1 part-time/adjunct (0 women). *Students:* 89 full-time (64 women), 40 part-time (27 women); includes 36 minority (9 African Americans, 4 American Indian/Alaska Native, 13 Asian Americans or Pacific Islanders, 10 Hispanic Americans), 1 international. Average age 40. 88 applicants, 72% accepted, 42 enrolled. In 2009, 17 master's, 9 doctorates awarded. *Degree requirements:* For doctorate, thesis/dissertation. *Application fee:* $55 ($65 for international students). *Expenses:* Tuition: Full-time $19,710; part-time $1095 per unit. Part-time tuition and fees vary according to degree level, campus/location and program. *Financial support:* In 2009–10, 77 students received support; fellowships, research assistantships, teaching assistantships available. Financial award application deadline: 3/2; financial award applicants required to submit FAFSA. *Unit head:* Dr. Robert Burns, Chair, 415-422-6289. *Application contact:* Beth Teague, Associate Director of Graduate Outreach, 415-422-5467, E-mail: schoolofeducation@usfca.edu.

The University of Scranton, College of Graduate and Continuing Education, Department of Education, Program in Reading Education, Scranton, PA 18510. Offers MS. *Accreditation:* NCATE. Part-time and evening/weekend programs available. *Students:* 7 full-time (all women), 4 part-time (all women). Average age 26. 4 applicants, 100% accepted. In 2009, 7 master's awarded. *Degree requirements:* For master's, comprehensive exam, thesis (for some programs), capstone experience. *Entrance requirements:* For master's, minimum GPA of 2.75. Additional exam requirements/recommendations for international students: Required—TOEFL (minimum score 500 paper-based; 173 computer-based), IELTS (minimum score 5.5). *Application deadline:* Applications are processed on a rolling basis. Application fee: $0. *Financial support:* Fellowships, teaching assistantships, career-related internships or fieldwork, Federal Work-Study, and unspecified assistantships available. Support available to part-time students. Financial award application deadline: 3/1. *Unit head:* Dr. Art Chambers, Director, 570-941-4668, Fax: 570-941-5515, E-mail: chambersa2@scranton.edu. *Application contact:* Joseph M. Roback, Director of Admissions, 570-941-4385, Fax: 570-941-5928, E-mail: robackj2@scranton.edu.

University of Sioux Falls, Fredrikson School of Education, Sioux Falls, SD 57105-1699. Offers leadership (M Ed); reading (M Ed); superintendent (Ed S); teaching (M Ed); technology (M Ed). Summer admission only. *Accreditation:* NCATE. Part-time and evening/weekend programs available. *Degree requirements:* For master's, comprehensive exam (for some programs), research application project; for Ed S, comprehensive exam, portfolio. *Entrance requirements:* For master's, minimum GPA of 3.0, 1 year of teaching experience; for Ed S, minimum 3 years of teaching experience, minimum cumulative GPA of 3.5, 1 year of administrative experience. Additional exam requirements/recommendations for international students: Required—TOEFL. *Faculty research:* Reading, literacy, leadership.

University of South Alabama, Graduate School, College of Education, Department of Leadership and Teacher Education, Mobile, AL 36688-0002. Offers early childhood education (M Ed); educational administration (Ed S); educational leadership (M Ed); elementary education (M Ed); reading education (M Ed); science education (M Ed); secondary education (M Ed); special education (M Ed, Ed S). *Accreditation:* NCATE. Part-time programs available. *Degree requirements:* For master's, comprehensive exam. *Entrance requirements:* For master's, GRE General Test or MAT, minimum GPA of 3.0. *Expenses:* Tuition, state resident: part-time $218 per contact hour. Required fees: $1102 per year.

University of South Carolina, The Graduate School, College of Education, Department of Instruction and Teacher Education, Program in Language and Literacy, Columbia, SC 29208. Offers M Ed, PhD. *Accreditation:* NCATE. *Degree requirements:* For master's, comprehensive exam; for doctorate, one foreign language, comprehensive exam, thesis/dissertation. *Entrance requirements:* For master's, GRE General Test, Miller Analogies Test, teaching certificate, resume, letters of reference, letter of intent; for doctorate, GRE General Test, Miller Analogies Test, resumé, letters of reference, letter of intent, interview. *Faculty research:* Remedial and compensatory education, metacognition and learning, literacy, learning, teacher change.

University of Southern Maine, College of Education and Human Development, Program in Literacy Education, Portland, ME 04104-9300. Offers applied literacy (MS Ed); early language and literacy (Certificate); English as a second language (MS Ed, CAS); literacy education (MS Ed, CAS, Certificate). *Accreditation:* Teacher Education Accreditation Council. Part-time and evening/weekend programs available. *Faculty:* 2 full-time (both women), 6 part-time/adjunct (4 women). *Students:* 9 full-time (8 women), 41 part-time (37 women); includes 1 minority (Hispanic American). 19 applicants, 89% accepted, 14 enrolled. In 2009, 33 master's, 8 CASs awarded. *Degree requirements:* For master's, comprehensive exam, thesis or alternative; for other advanced degree, thesis or alternative. *Entrance requirements:* For master's, teacher certification; for other advanced degree, master's degree. Additional exam requirements/recommendations for international students: Required—TOEFL (minimum score 550 paper-based; 213 computer-based; 79 iBT). *Application deadline:* For fall admission, 5/1 priority date for domestic students; for spring admission, 10/15 priority date for domestic students. Applications are processed on a rolling basis. Application fee: $50. Electronic applications accepted. *Financial support:* In 2009–10, 3 students received support, including research assistantships with tuition reimbursements available (averaging $4,500 per year); career-related internships or fieldwork, Federal Work-Study, institutionally sponsored loans, scholarships/grants, and unspecified assistantships also available. Support available to part-time students. Financial award application deadline: 3/1; financial award applicants required to submit FAFSA. *Unit head:* Dr. James Curry, Chair, Professional Education Department, 207-780-5400, Fax: 207-

780-8277, E-mail: jcurry@usm.maine.edu. *Application contact:* Mary Sloan, Director of Graduate Admissions, 207-780-4386, Fax: 207-780-4969, E-mail: msloan@usm.maine.edu.

University of Southern Mississippi, Graduate School, College of Education and Psychology, Department of Curriculum, Instruction, and Special Education, Hattiesburg, MS 39406-0001. Offers alternative secondary teacher education (MAT); early childhood education (M Ed, Ed S); education of the gifted (M Ed, Ed D, PhD, Ed S); elementary education (M Ed, Ed D, PhD, Ed S); reading (M Ed, MS, Ed S); secondary education (M Ed, MS, Ed D, PhD, Ed S); special education (M Ed, Ed D, PhD, Ed S). *Faculty:* 23 full-time (17 women), 3 part-time/adjunct (2 women). *Students:* 31 full-time (26 women), 77 part-time (68 women); includes 18 minority (15 African Americans, 3 Hispanic Americans). Average age 37. 50 applicants, 52% accepted, 19 enrolled. In 2009, 43 master's, 3 doctorates, 2 other advanced degrees awarded. *Degree requirements:* For master's, comprehensive exam, thesis (for some programs); for doctorate, comprehensive exam, thesis/dissertation; for Ed S, comprehensive exam, thesis. *Entrance requirements:* For master's, GRE General Test, MAT, minimum GPA of 3.0; for doctorate, GRE General Test, minimum GPA of 3.5; for Ed S, GRE General Test, MAT, minimum GPA of 3.25. Additional exam requirements/recommendations for international students: Required—TOEFL. *Application deadline:* For fall admission, 3/1 priority date for domestic students, 3/1 for international students. Applications are processed on a rolling basis. Application fee: $35. *Expenses:* Tuition, state resident: full-time $5096; part-time $284 per hour. Tuition, nonresident: full-time $13,052; part-time $726 per hour. Required fees: $402. Tuition and fees vary according to course level and course load. *Financial support:* In 2009–10, 9 research assistantships with tuition reimbursements (averaging $18,316 per year), 2 teaching assistantships with full tuition reimbursements (averaging $8,500 per year) were awarded; Federal Work-Study, institutionally sponsored loans, and tuition waivers (partial) also available. Financial award application deadline: 3/15; financial award applicants required to submit FAFSA. *Faculty research:* Mathematical problem solving, integrative curriculum, writing process, teacher education models. Total annual research expenditures: $100,000. *Unit head:* Dr. David Daves, Chair, 601-266-4547, Fax: 601-266-4175. *Application contact:* Rachea Cawthorn, Administrative Assistant, 601-266-6987, Fax: 601-266-4548.

University of South Florida, Graduate School, College of Education–Main Campus, Department of Childhood Education, Tampa, FL 33620-9951. Offers early childhood education (M Ed, MA, PhD); elementary education (MA, MAT); reading/language arts (MA, PhD, Ed S). *Accreditation:* NCATE. Part-time and evening/weekend programs available. *Faculty:* 24 full-time (21 women), 2 part-time/adjunct (both women). *Students:* 92 full-time (84 women), 165 part-time (157 women); includes 62 minority (36 African Americans, 1 American Indian/Alaska Native, 6 Asian Americans or Pacific Islanders, 19 Hispanic Americans), 9 international. Average age 30. 192 applicants, 76% accepted, 113 enrolled. In 2009, 94 master's, 11 doctorates awarded. *Degree requirements:* For master's, comprehensive exam; for doctorate, comprehensive exam, thesis/dissertation. *Entrance requirements:* For master's, GRE (if GPA less than 3.0), minimum GPA of 3.0 in last 60 hours of course work; for doctorate, GRE General Test, minimum GPA of 3.0 undergraduate, 3.5 graduate; interview; for Ed S, GRE General Test, interview. Additional exam requirements/recommendations for international students: Required—TOEFL (minimum score 550 paper-based; 213 computer-based). *Application deadline:* For fall admission, 2/15 for domestic students, 1/2 for international students; for winter admission, 2/15 for domestic students, 1/2 for international students; for spring admission, 10/15 for domestic students, 6/1 for international students. Application fee: $30. Electronic applications accepted. *Financial support:* In 2009–10, 7 teaching assistantships with full tuition reimbursements (averaging $10,300 per year) were awarded; institutionally sponsored loans, scholarships/grants, and unspecified assistantships also available. Financial award applicants required to submit FAFSA. *Faculty research:* Evaluating interventions for struggling users, prevention and intervention services for young children at risk for behavioral and mental health challenges, preservice teacher education and young adolescent middle school experience, art and inquiry-based approaches to teaching and learning, study of children's writing development. Total annual research expenditures: $381,048. *Unit head:* Dr. Diane Yendol-Hoppey, Chairperson, 813-974-3460, Fax: 813-974-0938. *Application contact:* Dr. Diane Yendol-Hoppey, Chairperson, 813-974-3460, Fax: 813-974-0938.

The University of Tennessee, Graduate School, College of Education, Health and Human Sciences, Program in Education, Knoxville, TN 37996. Offers art education (MS); counseling education (PhD); cultural studies in education (PhD); curriculum (MS, Ed S); curriculum, educational research and evaluation (Ed D, PhD); early childhood education (PhD); early childhood special education (MS); education of deaf and hard of hearing (MS); educational administration and policy studies (Ed D, PhD); educational administration and supervision (Ed S); educational psychology (Ed D, PhD); elementary education (MS, Ed S); elementary teaching (MS); English education (MS, Ed S); exercise science (PhD); foreign language/ESL education (MS, Ed S); instructional technology (MS, Ed D, PhD, Ed S); literacy, language and ESL education (PhD); literacy, language education, and ESL education (Ed D); mathematics education (MS, Ed S); modified and comprehensive special education (MS); reading education (MS, Ed S); school counseling (Ed S); school psychology (PhD, Ed S); science education (MS, Ed S); secondary teaching (MS); social foundations (MS); social science education (MS, Ed S); socio-cultural foundations of sports and education (PhD); special education (Ed S); teacher education (Ed D, PhD). *Accreditation:* NCATE. Part-time and evening/weekend programs available. *Degree requirements:* For master's and Ed S, thesis optional; for doctorate, variable foreign language requirement, thesis/dissertation. *Entrance requirements:* For master's, minimum GPA of 2.7; for doctorate and Ed S, GRE General Test, minimum GPA of 2.7. Additional exam requirements/recommendations for international students: Required—TOEFL. Electronic applications accepted. *Expenses:* Tuition, state resident: full-time $6826; part-time $380 per semester hour. Tuition, nonresident: full-time $21,844; part-time $1147 per semester hour. Tuition and fees vary according to program.

The University of Texas at Brownsville, Graduate Studies, School of Education, Brownsville, TX 78520-4991. Offers bilingual education (M Ed); counseling and guidance (M Ed); curriculum and instruction (M Ed); early childhood education (M Ed); educational administration (M Ed); educational technology (M Ed); English as a second language (M Ed); reading specialist (M Ed); special education/educational diagnostician (M Ed). Part-time and evening/weekend programs available. Postbaccalaureate distance learning degree programs offered (minimal on-campus study). *Degree requirements:* For master's, thesis optional. *Entrance requirements:* For master's, GRE General Test. Additional exam requirements/recommendations for international students: Required—TOEFL.

The University of Texas at El Paso, Graduate School, College of Education, Department of Teacher Education, El Paso, TX 79968-0001. Offers education (MA); instruction (M Ed); reading education (M Ed); teaching, learning, and culture (PhD). Part-time and evening/weekend programs available. *Degree requirements:* For master's, thesis optional. *Entrance requirements:* For master's, GRE General Test, minimum graduate GPA of 3.0. Additional exam requirements/recommendations for international students: Required—TOEFL. Electronic applications accepted.

The University of Texas at San Antonio, College of Education and Human Development, Department of Interdisciplinary Learning and Teaching, San Antonio, TX 78249-0617. Offers curriculum and instruction (MA); early childhood education (MA); instructional technology (MA); reading (MA); special education (MA). Part-time and evening/weekend programs available. *Faculty:* 28 full-time (24 women), 1 part-time/adjunct (0 women). *Students:* 103 full-time (83 women), 317 part-time (253 women); includes 227 minority (36 African Americans, 11 Asian Americans or Pacific Islanders, 180 Hispanic Americans), 17 international. Average age 33. 212 applicants, 90% accepted, 140 enrolled. In 2009, 74 master's awarded. *Degree requirements:* For master's, comprehensive exam (for some programs), thesis (for some programs). *Entrance requirements:* For master's, GRE General Test, minimum GPA of 3.0. Additional exam requirements/recommendations for international students: Required—TOEFL (minimum score 500 paper-based; 173 computer-based; 61 iBT), IELTS (minimum score 5). *Application deadline:* For fall admission, 7/1 for domestic students, 4/1 for international students; for spring admission, 11/1 for domestic students, 9/1 for international students. Applications

Reading Education

The University of Texas at San Antonio (continued)

are processed on a rolling basis. Application fee: $45 ($80 for international students). Electronic applications accepted. *Expenses:* Tuition, state resident: full-time $3975; part-time $221 per contact hour. Tuition, nonresident: full-time $13,947; part-time $775 per contact hour. Required fees: $1853. *Financial support:* In 2009–10, 76 students received support, including 25 research assistantships (averaging $11,599 per year), 4 teaching assistantships (averaging $8,800 per year); scholarships/grants, tuition waivers, and unspecified assistantships also available. Support available to part-time students. *Faculty research:* Adult education; early childhood education; literacy; special education; science, technology, engineering and math fields. Total annual research expenditures: $57,097. *Unit head:* Dr. Belinda B. Flores, Chair, 210-458-5969, Fax: 210-458-7281, E-mail: belinda.flores@utsa.edu. *Application contact:* Mari Cortez, Graduate Advisor, 210-458-4414, E-mail: mari.cortez@utsa.edu.

The University of Texas at Tyler, College of Education and Psychology, School of Education, Tyler, TX 75799-0001. Offers early childhood education (M Ed, MA); reading (M Ed, MA); special education (M Ed, MA). Part-time and evening/weekend programs available. *Faculty:* 18 full-time (8 women). *Students:* 4 full-time (3 women), 30 part-time (all women); includes 4 minority (3 African Americans, 1 Hispanic American), 2 international. Average age 37. 13 applicants, 100% accepted, 6 enrolled. In 2009, 14 master's awarded. *Degree requirements:* For master's, comprehensive exam, thesis (for some programs), research project. *Entrance requirements:* For master's, GRE General Test. Additional exam requirements/recommendations for international students: Required—TOEFL (minimum score 79 computer-based). *Application deadline:* For fall admission, 8/17 priority date for domestic students, 7/1 priority date for international students; for spring admission, 12/21 priority date for domestic students, 11/1 priority date for international students. Applications are processed on a rolling basis. Application fee: $25 ($50 for international students). Electronic applications accepted. *Expenses:* Tuition, state resident: part-time $665 per semester hour. Tuition, nonresident: part-time $942 per semester hour. Part-time tuition and fees vary according to degree level and program. *Financial support:* In 2009–10, 2 research assistantships (averaging $12,000 per year) were awarded; scholarships/grants also available. Financial award application deadline: 7/1. *Faculty research:* Improving quality in childcare settings, play and creativity, teacher interactions, effects of modeling on early childhood teachers, biofeedback, literacy instruction. *Unit head:* Dr. Kathy L. Morrison, Interim Director, 903-566-7016, Fax: 903-565-5560, E-mail: kmorrison@uttyler.edu. *Application contact:* Dr. Kathy Morrison, Program Director for Curriculum and Instruction and Early Childhood, 903-566-7016, Fax: 903-565-5560, E-mail: kmorrison@uttyler.edu.

The University of Texas of the Permian Basin, Office of Graduate Studies, School of Education, Program in Reading, Odessa, TX 79762-0001. Offers MA. *Degree requirements:* For master's, comprehensive exam (for some programs), thesis (for some programs). *Entrance requirements:* For master's, GRE General Test. Additional exam requirements/recommendations for international students: Required—TOEFL (minimum score 550 paper-based; 213 computer-based).

The University of Texas–Pan American, College of Education, Department of Curriculum and Instruction: Elementary and Secondary, Edinburg, TX 78539. Offers bilingual education (M Ed); early childhood education (M Ed); elementary education (M Ed); reading (M Ed); secondary education (M Ed). Part-time programs available. *Degree requirements:* For master's, comprehensive exam, thesis optional. *Entrance requirements:* For master's, GRE. Additional exam requirements/recommendations for international students: Required—TOEFL, IELTS. *Expenses:* Tuition, state resident: full-time $3630.60; part-time $201.70 per credit hour. Tuition, nonresident: full-time $8617; part-time $478.70 per credit hour. Required fees: $806.50. *Faculty research:* Dual language instruction, literacy and technology, teacher education in diverse populations, mathematics and science education.

University of the Cumberlands, Graduate Programs in Education, Reading and Writing Specialist Program, Williamsburg, KY 40769-1372. Offers MA Ed. Evening/weekend programs available. *Degree requirements:* For master's, comprehensive exam. *Entrance requirements:* For master's, GRE or NTE, Kentucky teaching certificate.

University of the Incarnate Word, School of Graduate Studies and Research, Dreeben School of Education, Programs in Education, San Antonio, TX 78209-6397. Offers adult education (M Ed, MA); cross-cultural education (M Ed, MA); early childhood literacy (M Ed, MA); general education (M Ed, MA); Higher Education (PhD); instructional technology (M Ed, MA); international education and entrepreneurship (PhD); kinesiology (M Ed, MA); literacy (M Ed, MA); organizational leadership (PhD); organizational learning and learning (M Ed, MA); reading (M Ed, MA); special education (M Ed, MA); teacher leadership (M Ed, MA). Part-time and evening/weekend programs available. *Students:* 20 full-time (11 women), 201 part-time (122 women); includes 113 minority (29 African Americans, 2 American Indian/Alaska Native, 2 Asian Americans or Pacific Islanders, 80 Hispanic Americans), 30 international. Average age 41. In 2009, 26 master's, 19 doctorates awarded. *Degree requirements:* For master's, capstone; for doctorate, thesis/dissertation, qualifying exam. *Entrance requirements:* For master's, baccalaureate degree; minimum foundation GPA of 2.5; interview; for doctorate, master's degree; interview; supervised writing sample. Additional exam requirements/recommendations for international students: Required—TOEFL (minimum score 560 paper-based; 220 computer-based; 83 iBT). *Application deadline:* Applications are processed on a rolling basis. Application fee: $20. Electronic applications accepted. *Expenses:* Tuition: Full-time $12,150; part-time $675 per credit hour. Required fees: $83 per credit hour. *Financial support:* Federal Work-Study and scholarships/grants available. Financial award applicants required to submit FAFSA. *Unit head:* Dr. Denise Staudt, Dean, Dreeben School of Education, 210-829-2762, E-mail: staudt@uiwtx.edu. *Application contact:* Andrea Cyterski-Acosta, Dean of Enrollment, 210-829-6005, Fax: 210-829-3921, E-mail: admis@uiwtx.edu.

University of the Southwest, Graduate Programs, Hobbs, NM 88240-9129. Offers business administration (MBA); curriculum and instruction (MSE); curriculum and instruction: bilingual (MSE); curriculum and instruction: reading (MSE); curriculum and instruction: TESOL (MSE); early childhood education (MSE); educational diagnostician (MSE); mental health counseling (MSE); school business administration (MSE); school counseling (MSE); special education (MSE). Part-time and evening/weekend programs available. Postbaccalaureate distance learning degree programs offered (no on-campus study). *Faculty:* 10 full-time (6 women), 10 part-time/adjunct (4 women). *Students:* 112 full-time (93 women), 99 part-time (72 women). Average age 35. 94 applicants, 47% accepted, 39 enrolled. In 2009, 32 master's awarded. *Degree requirements:* For master's, comprehensive exam. *Application deadline:* For fall admission, 3/1 priority date for domestic students; for spring admission, 10/1 for domestic students. Applications are processed on a rolling basis. Application fee: $25. Electronic applications accepted. *Expenses:* Tuition: Part-time $512 per hour. Tuition and fees vary according to course load. *Financial support:* In 2009–10, 196 students received support; research assistantships with partial tuition reimbursements available, Federal Work-Study, scholarships/grants, and tuition waivers (partial) available. Support available to part-time students. Financial award application deadline: 4/1; financial award applicants required to submit FAFSA. *Unit head:* Dr. Mary Harris, Dean of Education, 575-392-6561 Ext. 1056, Fax: 575-392-6006, E-mail: mharris@usw.edu. *Application contact:* Ryanne Evans, Assistant Registrar, 575-392-6561 Ext. 1031, Fax: 575-392-6006, E-mail: revans@usw.edu.

University of Utah, Graduate School, College of Education, Department of Educational Psychology, Salt Lake City, UT 84112. Offers counseling psychology (PhD); educational psychology (MA); instructional design and educational technology (M Ed); learning and cognition (MS, PhD); professional counseling (MS); professional psychology (M Ed); reading and literacy (M Ed, PhD); school counseling (M Ed, MS); school psychology (MS, PhD); statistics (M Stat). *Accreditation:* APA (one or more programs are accredited). Evening/weekend programs available. Postbaccalaureate distance learning degree programs offered (minimal on-campus study). *Faculty:* 21 full-time (11 women), 8 part-time/adjunct (5 women). *Students:* 92 full-time (67 women), 74 part-time (43 women); includes 16 minority (4 Asian Americans or Pacific Islanders, 12 Hispanic Americans), 2 international. Average age 33. 177 applicants, 34% accepted, 50 enrolled. In 2009, 44 master's, 9 doctorates awarded. *Degree requirements:* For master's, variable foreign language requirement, comprehensive exam, thesis (for some programs); for doctorate, variable foreign language requirement, thesis/dissertation, oral exam. *Entrance requirements:* For master's and doctorate, GRE General Test, minimum GPA of 3.0. Additional exam requirements/recommendations for international students: Required—TOEFL (minimum score 500 paper-based; 173 computer-based). *Application deadline:* For fall admission, 4/1 for domestic and international students; for spring admission, 11/1 for domestic and international students. Application fee: $55 ($65 for international students). *Expenses:* Tuition, state resident: full-time $4004; part-time $1674 per semester. Tuition, nonresident: full-time $14,134; part-time $5915 per semester. Required fees: $324 per semester. Tuition and fees vary according to course load, degree level and program. *Financial support:* In 2009–10, 55 students received support, including 20 fellowships with full tuition reimbursements available (averaging $11,000 per year), 5 research assistantships with full tuition reimbursements available (averaging $11,000 per year), 32 teaching assistantships with full and partial tuition reimbursements available (averaging $11,000 per year); career-related internships or fieldwork, Federal Work-Study, institutionally sponsored loans, scholarships/grants, and unspecified assistantships also available. Financial award application deadline: 2/1; financial award applicants required to submit FAFSA. *Faculty research:* Autism, computer technology and instruction, cognitive behavior, aging, group counseling. Total annual research expenditures: $151,911. *Unit head:* Dr. Elaine Clark, Chair, 801-581-7148, Fax: 801-581-5566, E-mail: clark@ed.utah.edu. *Application contact:* Jenna Atkinson, Academic Program Specialist, 801-581-7148, Fax: 801-581-5566, E-mail: jenna.atkinson@utah.edu.

University of Vermont, Graduate College, College of Education and Social Services, Department of Education, Program in Reading and Language Arts, Burlington, VT 05405. Offers M Ed. *Accreditation:* NCATE. *Students:* 3 (all women). 3 applicants, 33% accepted, 1 enrolled. In 2009, 4 master's awarded. *Degree requirements:* For master's, thesis or alternative. *Entrance requirements:* Additional exam requirements/recommendations for international students: Required—TOEFL (minimum score 550 paper-based; 213 computer-based; 80 iBT). *Application deadline:* For fall admission, 8/1 priority date for domestic students. Applications are processed on a rolling basis. Application fee: $40. Electronic applications accepted. *Expenses:* Tuition, state resident: part-time $508 per credit hour. Tuition, nonresident: part-time $1281 per credit hour. *Financial support:* Teaching assistantships, career-related internships or fieldwork available. Financial award application deadline: 3/1. *Unit head:* Dr. James Mosenthal, Coordinator, 802-656-3356. *Application contact:* Dr. James Mosenthal, Coordinator, 802-656-3356.

University of Victoria, Faculty of Graduate Studies, Faculty of Education, Department of Curriculum and Instruction, Victoria, BC V8W 2Y2, Canada. Offers art education (M Ed, PhD); curriculum studies (M Ed, MA, PhD); early childhood education (M Ed, PhD); educational studies (PhD); language and literacy (M Ed, MA, PhD); mathematics (M Ed, MA, PhD); music education (M Ed, MA, PhD); science (M Ed, MA, PhD); social studies (M Ed, MA); social, cultural and foundational studies (MA, PhD); technology and environmental education (PhD). Part-time programs available. *Degree requirements:* For master's, thesis, project (M Ed); for doctorate, comprehensive exam, thesis/dissertation. *Entrance requirements:* For master's, minimum B average. Additional exam requirements/recommendations for international students: Required—TOEFL (minimum score 575 paper-based; 233 computer-based), IELTS (minimum score 7). Electronic applications accepted. *Faculty research:* Elementary and secondary English, language arts, curriculum theory and practice, educational media and technology, educational administration and leadership, history and philosophy of education.

University of Virginia, Curry School of Education, Department of Curriculum, Instruction, and Special Education, Program in Curriculum and Instruction, Charlottesville, VA 22903. Offers curriculum and instruction (M Ed, Ed S); elementary (M Ed, Ed D); English (M Ed, Ed D); foreign language (M Ed); mathematics (M Ed, Ed D); reading (M Ed, Ed D, Ed S); science (Ed D); social studies (M Ed). *Students:* 12 full-time (8 women), 30 part-time (24 women); includes 2 minority (1 Asian American or Pacific Islander, 1 Hispanic American), 1 international. Average age 36. 55 applicants, 69% accepted, 26 enrolled. In 2009, 247 master's, 14 doctorates, 10 other advanced degrees awarded. *Degree requirements:* For master's, comprehensive exam (for some programs); for doctorate, comprehensive exam, thesis/dissertation; for Ed S, comprehensive exam. *Entrance requirements:* For master's, doctorate, and Ed S, GRE General Test, 2 letters of recommendation. Additional exam requirements/recommendations for international students: Required—TOEFL (minimum score 600 paper-based; 250 computer-based; 90 iBT), IELTS (minimum score 7). *Application deadline:* Applications are processed on a rolling basis. Application fee: $60. Electronic applications accepted. *Financial support:* Fellowships with tuition reimbursements, research assistantships with tuition reimbursements, teaching assistantships with tuition reimbursements available. Financial award application deadline: 1/5; financial award applicants required to submit FAFSA.

University of Virginia, Curry School of Education, Program in Education, Charlottesville, VA 22903. Offers administration and supervision (PhD); applied developmental science (PhD); counselor education (PhD); curriculum and instruction (PhD); early childhood-developmental risk (MT); education evaluation (PhD); educational psychology (PhD); educational research (PhD); elementary (MT, PhD); English education (MT, PhD); foreign language education (MT); higher education (PhD); instructional technology (PhD); kinesiology (MT, PhD); math education (PhD); reading education (PhD); research statistics and evaluation (PhD); school psychology (PhD); science education (PhD); social studies education (MT, PhD); special education (PhD); world languages education (MT). *Students:* 336 full-time (239 women), 88 part-time (54 women); includes 43 minority (24 African Americans, 2 American Indian/Alaska Native, 11 Asian Americans or Pacific Islanders, 6 Hispanic Americans), 18 international. Average age 27. 199 applicants, 48% accepted, 55 enrolled. In 2009, 127 master's, 52 doctorates awarded. *Degree requirements:* For master's, comprehensive exam (for some programs), field project; for doctorate, comprehensive exam, thesis/dissertation. *Entrance requirements:* For doctorate, GRE General Test. Additional exam requirements/recommendations for international students: Required—TOEFL (minimum score 600 paper-based; 250 computer-based; 90 iBT), IELTS (minimum score 7). *Application deadline:* Applications are processed on a rolling basis. Application fee: $60. Electronic applications accepted. *Financial support:* Fellowships, research assistantships, teaching assistantships available. Financial award application deadline: 1/5; financial award applicants required to submit FAFSA.

University of Washington, Graduate School, College of Education, Seattle, WA 98195. Offers curriculum and instruction (M Ed, Ed D, PhD), including educational technology, general curriculum (Ed D, PhD), language, literacy, and culture, mathematics education, multicultural education, reading and language arts education (Ed D), science education, social studies education, teaching and curriculum (M Ed); educational leadership and policy studies (M Ed, Ed D, PhD), including administration (Ed D), educational policy, organization, and leadership (M Ed, PhD), higher education, leadership for learning (Ed D), social and cultural foundations of education (M Ed, PhD); educational psychology (M Ed, PhD), including educational psychology (PhD), human development and cognition (M Ed), learning sciences, measurement, statistics and research design (M Ed), school psychology (M Ed); instructional leadership (M Ed); intercollegiate athletic leadership (M Ed); special education (M Ed, Ed D, PhD), including early childhood special education (M Ed), emotional and behavioral disabilities (M Ed), learning disabilities (M Ed), low-incidence disabilities (M Ed), severe disabilities (M Ed), special education (Ed D, PhD); teacher education (MIT). *Accreditation:* APA. Part-time and evening/weekend programs available. *Degree requirements:* For master's, thesis optional; for doctorate, thesis/dissertation. *Entrance requirements:* For master's and doctorate, GRE General Test, minimum GPA of 3.0. Additional exam requirements/recommendations for international students: Required—TOEFL. Electronic applications accepted. *Faculty research:* School restructuring/effective schools, special education interventions, literacy and writing, technology, school partnerships, teacher preparation.

University of West Florida, College of Professional Studies, School of Education, Program in Reading Education, Pensacola, FL 32514-5750. Offers M Ed. Part-time and evening/weekend programs available. *Students:* 5 full-time (all women), 35 part-time (34 women); includes 1 minority (Hispanic American). Average age 38. 7 applicants, 86% accepted, 6 enrolled. In

2009, 9 master's awarded. *Degree requirements:* For master's, portfolio, teacher certification exams (general knowledge, professional, reading subject area). *Entrance requirements:* For master's, GRE (minimum score 450 verbal) or MAT (minimum score 396) if bachelor's GPA less than 3.0, state teaching certification; letter of intent; two professional references. Additional exam requirements/recommendations for international students: Required—TOEFL (minimum score 550 paper-based; 213 computer-based). *Application deadline:* For fall admission, 6/1 for domestic students, 5/15 for international students; for spring admission, 11/1 for domestic students, 10/1 for international students. Applications are processed on a rolling basis. Application fee: $30. *Expenses:* Tuition, state resident: full-time $4982; part-time $260 per credit hour. Tuition, nonresident: full-time $20,059; part-time $919 per credit hour. Required fees: $1247; $52 per credit hour. *Financial support:* Fellowships, teaching assistantships, career-related internships or fieldwork, Federal Work-Study, scholarships/grants, and unspecified assistantships available. Financial award application deadline: 4/15; financial award applicants required to submit FAFSA. *Unit head:* Dr. David Stout, Chairperson, 850-474-2284, Fax: 850-474-2844. *Application contact:* Terry McCray, Assistant Director of Graduate Admissions, 850-473-7718, Fax: 850-473-7714, E-mail: gradadmissions@uwf.edu.

University of West Georgia, Graduate School, College of Education, Department of Curriculum and Instruction, Carrollton, GA 30118. Offers art education (M Ed); art teacher education (Ed S); biology/secondary education (Ed S); business education (M Ed, Ed S); early childhood education (M Ed, Ed S); economics/secondary teacher education (Ed S); English teacher education (Ed S); French language teacher education (Ed S); history teacher education (Ed S); mathematics teacher education (Ed S); middle grades education (M Ed, Ed S); reading education (M Ed, Ed S); science teacher education (Ed S); secondary education (M Ed, Ed S); social science teacher education (Ed S); Spanish language teacher education (Ed S). Part-time and evening/weekend programs available. *Faculty:* 18 full-time (15 women), 7 part-time/adjunct (6 women). *Students:* 119 full-time (101 women), 358 part-time (280 women); includes 109 minority (97 African Americans, 3 American Indian/Alaska Native, 2 Asian Americans or Pacific Islanders, 7 Hispanic Americans). Average age 33. 193 applicants, 82% accepted, 34 enrolled. In 2009, 109 master's, 27 Ed Ss awarded. *Degree requirements:* For master's, comprehensive exam; for Ed S, research project. *Entrance requirements:* For master's, GRE General Test or MAT, minimum GPA of 2.7; for Ed S, GRE General Test, master's degree, minimum graduate GPA of 2.7. *Application deadline:* For fall admission, 7/17 for domestic students; for spring admission, 11/20 for domestic students. Applications are processed on a rolling basis. Application fee: $30. Electronic applications accepted. *Expenses:* Tuition, state resident: full-time $2952; part-time $164 per semester hour. Tuition, nonresident: full-time $11,808; part-time $656 per semester hour. Required fees: $42.90 per semester hour. $307 per semester. Tuition and fees vary according to course load. *Financial support:* In 2009–10, 5 research assistantships with full tuition reimbursements (averaging $3,000 per year) were awarded; career-related internships or fieldwork and scholarships/grants also available. Support available to part-time students. Financial award applicants required to submit FAFSA. *Unit head:* Dr. Donna Harkins, Chair, 678-839-6066, Fax: 678-839-6559, E-mail: dharkins@westga.edu. *Application contact:* Dr. Charles W. Clark, Dean, 678-839-6508, E-mail: cclark@westga.edu.

University of Wisconsin–Eau Claire, College of Education and Human Sciences, Program in Reading, Eau Claire, WI 54702-4004. Offers MST. Part-time programs available. *Faculty:* 13 full-time (8 women). *Students:* 9 part-time (8 women); includes 1 minority (American Indian/Alaska Native). Average age 34. 2 applicants, 50% accepted, 0 enrolled. In 2009, 10 master's awarded. *Degree requirements:* For master's, portfolio with an oral examination. *Entrance requirements:* For master's, certification to teach. Additional exam requirements/recommendations for international students: Required—TOEFL (minimum score 550 paper-based; 213 computer-based; 79 iBT). *Application deadline:* For fall admission, 7/1 priority date for domestic students, 6/1 priority date for international students; for spring admission, 12/1 priority date for domestic students, 11/1 priority date for international students. Applications are processed on a rolling basis. Application fee: $56. Electronic applications accepted. *Expenses:* Tuition, state resident: full-time $6705.90; part-time $372.55 per credit. Tuition, nonresident: full-time $16,771; part-time $931.74 per credit. Required fees: $925.50; $51.19 per credit. One-time fee: $56. *Financial support:* In 2009–10, 3 students received support. Federal Work-Study and unspecified assistantships available. Financial award application deadline: 3/1; financial award applicants required to submit FAFSA. *Unit head:* Dr. Dwight Watson, Chair, 715-836-2013, Fax: 715-836-4868, E-mail: watsondc@uwec.edu. *Application contact:* Kristina Anderson, Director of Admissions, 715-836-5415, Fax: 715-836-2409, E-mail: admissions@uwec.edu.

University of Wisconsin–Milwaukee, Graduate School, School of Education, Department of Curriculum and Instruction, Milwaukee, WI 53201-0413. Offers curriculum planning and instruction improvement (MS); early childhood education (MS); elementary education (MS); junior high/middle school education (MS); reading education (MS); secondary education (MS); teaching in an urban setting (MS). Part-time programs available. *Faculty:* 22 full-time (17 women). *Students:* 23 full-time (14 women), 64 part-time (58 women); includes 8 minority (4 African Americans, 1 American Indian/Alaska Native, 3 Hispanic Americans), 1 international. Average age 31. 46 applicants, 57% accepted, 12 enrolled. In 2009, 28 master's awarded. *Degree requirements:* For master's, thesis or alternative. *Entrance requirements:* Additional exam requirements/recommendations for international students: Required—TOEFL (minimum score 550 paper-based; 79 iBT), IELTS (minimum score 6.5). *Application deadline:* For fall admission, 1/1 priority date for domestic students; for spring admission, 9/1 for domestic students. Applications are processed on a rolling basis. Application fee: $45 ($75 for international students). *Expenses:* Tuition, state resident: full-time $8800. Tuition, nonresident: full-time $20,760. Tuition and fees vary according to program and reciprocity agreements. *Financial support:* Career-related internships or fieldwork and unspecified assistantships available. Support available to part-time students. Financial award application deadline: 4/15. Total annual research expenditures: $65,946. *Unit head:* Hope Longwell-Grice, Chair, 414-229-4884, Fax: 414-229-5571, E-mail: hope@uwm.edu. *Application contact:* General Information Contact, 414-229-4982, Fax: 414-229-6967, E-mail: gradschool@uwm.edu.

University of Wisconsin–Oshkosh, The Office of Graduate Studies, College of Education and Human Services, Department of Reading Education, Oshkosh, WI 54901. Offers MSE. Part-time programs available. *Degree requirements:* For master's, thesis or alternative, reflective journey course. *Entrance requirements:* For master's, interview, teaching certificate, undergraduate degree in teacher education, letters of recommendation. Additional exam requirements/recommendations for international students: Required—TOEFL (minimum score 550 paper-based; 213 computer-based; 79 iBT). Electronic applications accepted. *Faculty research:* Writing and reading, assessment, learner-centered instruction, multicultural literature, family literacy.

University of Wisconsin–River Falls, Outreach and Graduate Studies, College of Education and Professional Studies, Department of Teacher Education, River Falls, WI 54022. Offers elementary education (MSE); professional development shared inquiry communities (MSE); reading (MSE). Part-time programs available. *Degree requirements:* For master's, comprehensive exam, thesis or alternative. *Entrance requirements:* For master's, minimum GPA of 2.75. Additional exam requirements/recommendations for international students: Required—TOEFL (minimum score 500 paper-based; 65 iBT), IELTS (minimum score 5.5). Electronic applications accepted.

University of Wisconsin–Stevens Point, College of Professional Studies, School of Education, Program in Education—General/Reading, Stevens Point, WI 54481-3897. Offers MSE. Part-time programs available. *Students:* 2 full-time (1 woman), 35 part-time (21 women); includes 1 Asian American or Pacific Islander. Average age 25. *Degree requirements:* For master's, comprehensive exam, thesis or alternative. *Entrance requirements:* For master's, minimum undergraduate GPA of 3.0, teacher certification, 2 years teaching experience, letters of recommendation. Additional exam requirements/recommendations for international students: Required—TOEFL (minimum score 523 paper-based; 193 computer-based). *Application deadline:* For fall admission, 5/1 priority date for domestic students. Applications are processed on a rolling basis. Application fee: $45. *Expenses:* Tuition, state resident: full-time $7740; part-time $430 per credit hour. Tuition, nonresident: full-time $17,804; part-time $989 per credit hour. Tuition and fees vary according to course load and reciprocity agreements. *Financial support:* In 2009–10, 4 research assistantships with partial tuition reimbursements (averaging $9,807 per year) were awarded; Federal Work-Study and unspecified assistantships also available. Support available to part-time students. Financial award application deadline: 5/1; financial award applicants required to submit FAFSA. *Faculty research:* Reading strategies in the content areas, gifted education, curriculum and instruction, standards-based education. *Application contact:* Dr. Patricia Caro, Director, 715-346-4403, Fax: 715-346-4846, E-mail: pcaro@uwsp.edu.

University of Wisconsin–Superior, Graduate Division, Department of Teacher Education, Program in Teaching Reading, Superior, WI 54880-4500. Offers MSE. Part-time and evening/weekend programs available. *Faculty:* 2 full-time (both women). *Students:* 12 full-time (8 women), 27 part-time (24 women); includes 1 minority (American Indian/Alaska Native). 4 applicants, 100% accepted. In 2009, 3 master's awarded. *Degree requirements:* For master's, comprehensive exam, thesis or alternative, research project. *Entrance requirements:* For master's, minimum GPA of 2.75, teaching certificate. *Application deadline:* For fall admission, 4/1 priority date for domestic students; for spring admission, 10/15 priority date for domestic students. Applications are processed on a rolling basis. Application fee: $45. *Financial support:* Federal Work-Study and tuition waivers (partial) available. Support available to part-time students. Financial award application deadline: 4/15; financial award applicants required to submit FAFSA. *Unit head:* Dr. Peggy Marciniec, Coordinator, 715-394-8585, E-mail: pmarcini@uwsuper.edu. *Application contact:* Sandy Wallgren, Program Assistant/Status Examiner, 715-394-8295, Fax: 715-394-8040, E-mail: gradstudy@uwsuper.edu.

University of Wisconsin–Whitewater, School of Graduate Studies, College of Education, Program in Reading, Whitewater, WI 53190-1790. Offers MS Ed. Part-time and evening/weekend programs available. Postbaccalaureate distance learning degree programs offered (no on-campus study). *Entrance requirements:* Additional exam requirements/recommendations for international students: Required—TOEFL (minimum score 550 paper-based; 213 computer-based).

Ursuline College, School of Graduate Studies, Program in Education, Pepper Pike, OH 44124-4398. Offers art education (MA); early childhood education (MA); language arts education (MA); life science education (MA); math education (MA); middle school education (MA); social studies education (MA); special education (MA). *Accreditation:* NCATE. *Faculty:* 1 (woman) full-time, 10 part-time/adjunct (8 women). *Students:* 53 full-time (40 women), 3 part-time (all women); includes 8 minority (7 African Americans, 1 Hispanic American). Average age 34. In 2009, 11 master's awarded. *Degree requirements:* For master's, comprehensive exam. *Entrance requirements:* For master's, minimum undergraduate GPA of 3.0. Additional exam requirements/recommendations for international students: Required—TOEFL (minimum score 500 paper-based; 173 computer-based). *Application deadline:* For fall admission, 8/1 priority date for domestic students. Applications are processed on a rolling basis. Application fee: $25. *Expenses:* Contact institution. *Financial support:* Federal Work-Study available. Financial award application deadline: 3/1. *Unit head:* Karen Godenschwager Nelson, Director, 440-684-8338, Fax: 440-684-6088, E-mail: kgodenschwager@ursuline.edu. *Application contact:* Melanie Steele, Secretary, 440-646-8199, Fax: 440-684-6138, E-mail: gradsch@ursuline.edu.

Valdosta State University, Graduate School, Department of Early Childhood and Reading Education, Valdosta, GA 31698. Offers early childhood education (M Ed, Ed S); reading education (M Ed). *Accreditation:* NCATE. Part-time and evening/weekend programs available. *Degree requirements:* For master's, comprehensive written and/or oral exams; for Ed S, thesis. *Entrance requirements:* For master's and Ed S, GRE General Test or MAT. Additional exam requirements/recommendations for international students: Required—TOEFL (minimum score 523 paper-based; 193 computer-based). Electronic applications accepted.

Vanderbilt University, Peabody College, Department of Teaching and Learning, Nashville, TN 37240-1001. Offers elementary education (M Ed); English language learners (M Ed); learning and instruction (M Ed); learning, diversity, and urban studies (M Ed); reading education (M Ed); secondary education (M Ed). *Accreditation:* NCATE. *Faculty:* 31 full-time (20 women), 23 part-time/adjunct (20 women). *Students:* 95 full-time (88 women), 21 part-time (6 women); includes 14 minority (6 African Americans, 4 Asian Americans or Pacific Islanders, 4 Hispanic Americans), 5 international. Average age 27. 150 applicants, 69% accepted, 59 enrolled. In 2009, 74 master's awarded. *Degree requirements:* For master's, comprehensive exam, thesis optional. *Entrance requirements:* For master's, GRE General Test, MAT. Additional exam requirements/recommendations for international students: Required—TOEFL (minimum score 550 paper-based; 213 computer-based). *Application deadline:* For fall admission, 12/31 priority date for domestic and international students; for spring admission, 11/1 priority date for domestic and international students. Applications are processed on a rolling basis. Application fee: $0. Electronic applications accepted. *Financial support:* In 2009–10, 104 students received support, including 27 research assistantships with full and partial tuition reimbursements available; fellowships with full and partial tuition reimbursements available, teaching assistantships with full and partial tuition reimbursements available, Federal Work-Study, institutionally sponsored loans, scholarships/grants, tuition waivers (partial), and unspecified assistantships also available. Support available to part-time students. Financial award application deadline: 2/1; financial award applicants required to submit FAFSA. *Faculty research:* Teaching and learning, development of mathematical and scientific knowledge, interventions to foster early literacy and numeracy, reading and writing in the digital age, teaching diverse learners. *Unit head:* Dr. David Dickinson, Acting Chair, 615-322-8100, Fax: 615-322-8999, E-mail: david.k.dickinson@vanderbilt.edu. *Application contact:* Angela Saylor, Educational Coordinator, 615-322-8092, Fax: 615-322-8999, E-mail: angela.saylor@vanderbilt.edu.

Virginia Commonwealth University, Graduate School, School of Education, Program in Adult and Organizational Learning, Richmond, VA 23284-9005. Offers adult literacy (M Ed); adults with disabilities (M Ed); human resource development (M Ed). *Accreditation:* NCATE. Part-time programs available. *Entrance requirements:* For master's, GRE General Test or MAT. *Faculty research:* Adult development and learning, program planning and evaluation.

Virginia Commonwealth University, Graduate School, School of Education, Program in Reading, Richmond, VA 23284-9005. Offers M Ed. *Accreditation:* NCATE. *Degree requirements:* For master's, comprehensive exam. *Entrance requirements:* For master's, GRE General Test or MAT.

Wagner College, Division of Graduate Studies, Department of Education, Program in Literacy (B-6), Staten Island, NY 10301-4495. Offers MS Ed. Part-time programs available. *Degree requirements:* For master's, thesis. *Entrance requirements:* For master's, minimum GPA of 2.75. Additional exam requirements/recommendations for international students: Required—TOEFL (minimum score 550 paper-based; 217 computer-based). *Expenses:* Tuition: Full-time $15,570; part-time $865 per credit. Required fees: $2.

Walden University, Graduate Programs, Richard W. Riley College of Education and Leadership, Minneapolis, MN 55401. Offers administrator leadership for teaching and learning (Ed D, Ed S); curriculum, instruction, and professional development (Ed S); early childhood education (birth-grade 3) (MAT); education (MS, PhD), including adolescent literacy and technology (grades 6-12) (MS), adult education leadership (PhD), community college leadership (PhD), curriculum, instruction, and assessment, early childhood education (PhD), educational leadership (MS), educational technology (PhD), elementary reading and literacy (MS), elementary reading and mathematics (MS), emotional/behavioral disorders (K-12) (MS), general program, higher education (PhD), integrating technology in the classroom (MS), K-12 educational leadership (PhD), learning disabilities (K-12) (MS), literacy and learning in the content areas (MS), mathematics (grades 6-8) (MS), mathematics (grades K-5) (MS), middle level education (grades 5-8) (MS), professional development (MS), science (grades K-8) (MS), self-designed (PhD), special education (PhD), special education (non-licensure) (MS), teacher leadership (grades K-12) (MS); educational leadership and administration (principal preparation) (Ed S); educational technology (Ed S); higher education and adult learning (Ed D); instructional design

Reading Education

Walden University (continued)
(Postbaccalaureate Certificate); instructional design and technology (MS), including general program (MS, PhD), online learning, training and performance improvement; special education: emotional/behavioral disorders (K-12) (MAT); special education: learning disabilities (K-12) (MAT); teacher leadership (Ed D, Ed S). Part-time and evening/weekend programs available. Postbaccalaureate distance learning degree programs offered (minimal on-campus study). *Faculty:* 54 full-time, 835 part-time/adjunct. *Students:* 13,940 full-time (11,339 women), 1,940 part-time (1,637 women); includes 4,626 minority (3,795 African Americans, 111 American Indian/Alaska Native, 199 Asian Americans or Pacific Islanders, 521 Hispanic Americans), 124 international. Average age 38. In 2009, 4,688 master's, 190 doctorates awarded. *Degree requirements:* For doctorate, thesis/dissertation (for some programs), residency; for other advanced degree, residency (for some programs). *Entrance requirements:* For master's, bachelor's degree or equivalent in related field; minimum GPA of 2.5; official transcripts; goal statement; access to computer and Internet; for doctorate, master's degree or equivalent in related field; minimum GPA of 3.0; official transcripts; three years' related professional/academic experience (preferred); access to computer and Internet; for other advanced degree, master's degree or equivalent in related field; minimum GPA of 3.0; 3 years related professional/academic experience (preferred); access to computer and Internet (Ed S). Additional exam requirements/recommendations for international students: Required—TOEFL (minimum score 550 paper-based; 213 computer-based), IELTS (minimum score 6.5), or Michigan English Language Assessment Battery (minimum score 82). *Application deadline:* Applications are processed on a rolling basis. Application fee: $50. Electronic applications accepted. *Expenses:* Tuition: Full-time $13,665; part-time $560 per credit. Required fees: $1375. Tuition and fees vary according to course load, degree level and program. *Financial support:* In 2009–10, 2,418 students received support; fellowships, Federal Work-Study, scholarships/grants, unspecified assistantships, and family tuition reduction, active duty/veteran tuition reduction, group tuition reduction, interest-free payment plans available. Support available to part-time students. Financial award applicants required to submit FAFSA. *Unit head:* Dr. Kate Steffens, Dean, 800-925-3368. *Application contact:* Jennifer Hall, Director of Enrollment, 866-4-WALDEN, E-mail: info@waldenu.edu.

Walla Walla University, Graduate School, School of Education and Psychology, College Place, WA 99324-1198. Offers counseling psychology (MA); curriculum and instruction (M Ed, MA, MAT); educational leadership (M Ed, MA, MAT); literacy instruction (M Ed, MA, MAT); students at risk (M Ed, MA, MAT); teaching (MAT). Part-time programs available. *Faculty:* 7 full-time (3 women), 1 part-time/adjunct (0 women). *Students:* 32 full-time (14 women), 9 part-time (7 women); includes 5 minority (1 African American, 1 American Indian/Alaska Native, 2 Asian Americans or Pacific Islanders, 1 Hispanic American). Average age 30. 41 applicants, 80% accepted, 21 enrolled. In 2009, 29 master's awarded. *Entrance requirements:* For master's, GRE General Test, minimum GPA of 2.75. Additional exam requirements/recommendations for international students: Required—TOEFL (minimum score 550 paper-based; 213 computer-based; 79 iBT). *Application deadline:* For fall admission, 4/1 priority date for domestic students. Applications are processed on a rolling basis. Application fee: $50. Electronic applications accepted. *Expenses:* Tuition: Full-time $19,929. *Financial support:* In 2009–10, 29 students received support; research assistantships, teaching assistantships, Federal Work-Study and tuition waivers (partial) available. Support available to part-time students. Financial award application deadline: 4/1; financial award applicants required to submit FAFSA. *Faculty research:* Admissions/retention, instructional psychology, moral development, teaching of reading. *Unit head:* Dr. Julian Melgosa, Dean, 509-527-2272, Fax: 509-527-2248, E-mail: julian.melgosa@wallawalla.edu. *Application contact:* Dr. Joe G. Galusha, Dean of Graduate Studies, 509-527-2421, Fax: 509-527-2237, E-mail: joe.galusha@wallawalla.edu.

Washburn University, College of Arts and Sciences, Department of Education, Program in Reading, Topeka, KS 66621. Offers M Ed. *Accreditation:* NCATE. Part-time programs available. *Degree requirements:* For master's, portfolio. *Entrance requirements:* For master's, GRE General Test, MAT, minimum GPA of 3.0 during previous 2 years.

Washington State University, Graduate School, College of Education, Department of Teaching and Learning, Pullman, WA 99164. Offers curriculum and instruction (Ed D, PhD); diverse languages (M Ed, MA); elementary education (M Ed, MA, MIT); exercise science (MS); literacy education (M Ed, MA, PhD); math education (PhD); secondary education (M Ed, MA). *Accreditation:* NCATE. *Degree requirements:* For master's, comprehensive exam (for some programs), thesis (for some programs), oral or written exam; for doctorate, comprehensive exam, thesis/dissertation, oral, written exam. *Entrance requirements:* For master's and doctorate, GRE General Test, minimum GPA of 3.0, 3 letters of recommendation. Additional exam requirements/recommendations for international students: Required—TOEFL. *Faculty research:* Evolution of middle school education issues in special education, computer-assisted language learning.

Washington State University Tri-Cities, Graduate Programs, Program in Education, Richland, WA 99354. Offers counseling (Ed M); educational leadership (Ed M, Ed D); literacy (Ed M); secondary certification (Ed M); teaching (MIT). Part-time programs available. *Faculty:* 24. *Students:* 11 full-time (8 women), 97 part-time (80 women); includes 17 minority (1 African American, 3 Asian Americans or Pacific Islanders, 13 Hispanic Americans). Average age 36. In 2009, 39 master's awarded. *Degree requirements:* For master's, comprehensive exam, thesis or alternative; for doctorate, comprehensive exam, thesis/dissertation. *Entrance requirements:* For master's, GRE, minimum GPA of 3.0, Working with Youth form, Character and Fitness form, 3 letters of recommendation. Additional exam requirements/recommendations for international students: Required—TOEFL. *Application deadline:* For fall admission, 1/10 priority date for domestic students, 1/10 for international students; for spring admission, 7/1 priority date for domestic students, 7/1 for international students. Applications are processed on a rolling basis. Application fee: $50. Electronic applications accepted. *Expenses:* Tuition, state resident: part-time $423 per credit. Tuition, nonresident: part-time $1032 per credit. *Financial support:* In 2009–10, 59 students received support, including research assistantships (averaging $14,634 per year), teaching assistantships (averaging $13,383 per year); Federal Work-Study, scholarships/grants, and unspecified assistantships also available. Financial award application deadline: 2/15. *Faculty research:* Multicultural counseling, socio-cultural influences in schools, diverse learners, teacher education, K-12 educational leadership. *Unit head:* Dr. Elizabeth Nagel, Director, 509-372-7398, E-mail: elizabeth_nagel@tricity.wsu.edu. *Application contact:* Helen Berry, Academic Coordinator, 800-GRADWSU, Fax: 509-372-3796, E-mail: hberry@tricity.wsu.edu.

Wayne State University, College of Education, Division of Teacher Education, Detroit, MI 48202. Offers adult and continuing education (M Ed); art education (M Ed); bilingual/bicultural education (M Ed, MAT); business education (M Ed, MAT); career and technical education (M Ed, Ed D, PhD, Ed S); curriculum and instruction (Ed D, PhD, Ed S); distributive education (M Ed, MAT); early childhood education (M Ed); elementary education (M Ed, MAT, Ed D, PhD, Ed S); elementary education curriculum and instruction (M Ed); English education (M Ed); English education-secondary (M Ed, Ed S); foreign language education (M Ed); general education (Ed D, Ed S); health occupations education (M Ed); industrial education (M Ed); mathematics education (M Ed, Ed S); pre-school and parent education (M Ed); reading (M Ed, Ed D, Ed S); reading, languages and literature (Ed D); school music-vocal (M Ed); science education (M Ed, MAT, Ed S); secondary education (MAT); secondary school reading (M Ed); social studies education (M Ed, Ed S), including education-secondary (M Ed); special education (M Ed, Ed D, PhD, Ed S); teacher education (MAT, Ed D, PhD). *Degree requirements:* For doctorate, thesis/dissertation. *Entrance requirements:* For master's, Michigan Basic Skills Test (MA in teaching), minimum GPA of 2.6; for doctorate, minimum undergraduate GPA of 3.0, graduate 3.5; interview, curriculum vitae; references. Additional exam requirements/recommendations for international students: Required—TOEFL (minimum score 550 paper-based; 213 computer-based), TWE (minimum score 6). Electronic applications accepted. *Faculty research:* Reading and writing literacy and literature.

West Chester University of Pennsylvania, Office of Graduate Studies, College of Education, Department of Literacy, West Chester, PA 19383. Offers literacy (Certificate); literacy coaching (Certificate); reading (M Ed, Teaching Certificate). Part-time and evening/weekend programs available. *Students:* 180 part-time (177 women); includes 5 minority (2 African Americans, 1 Asian American or Pacific Islander, 2 Hispanic Americans). Average age 28. 47 applicants, 100% accepted, 29 enrolled. In 2009, 54 master's, 1 Certificate awarded. *Degree requirements:* For master's, comprehensive exam. *Entrance requirements:* For master's, GRE or MAT (if GPA is below 3.0), minimum GPA of 3.0, teaching certificate, three letters of reference. Additional exam requirements/recommendations for international students: Required—TOEFL (minimum score 550 paper-based; 213 computer-based; 80 iBT). *Application deadline:* For fall admission, 4/15 priority date for domestic students, 3/15 for international students; for spring admission, 10/15 priority date for domestic students, 9/1 for international students. Applications are processed on a rolling basis. Application fee: $35. Electronic applications accepted. *Expenses:* Tuition, state resident: full-time $6666; part-time $370 per credit. Tuition, nonresident: full-time $10,666; part-time $593 per credit. Required fees: $122.56 per credit. *Financial support:* In 2009–10, 1 research assistantship with full and partial tuition reimbursement (averaging $5,000 per year) was awarded; unspecified assistantships also available. Support available to part-time students. Financial award application deadline: 2/15; financial award applicants required to submit FAFSA. *Faculty research:* Teaching and mentoring pre-service teachers to teach reading in urban settings. *Unit head:* Dr. Sunita Mayor, Chair, 610-436-2282, E-mail: smayor@wcupa.edu. *Application contact:* Dr. Robert Szabo, Graduate Coordinator, 610-436-3318, E-mail: rszabo@wcupa.edu.

Western Connecticut State University, Division of Graduate Studies, School of Professional Studies, Department of Education and Educational Psychology, Reading Option, Danbury, CT 06810-6885. Offers MS. Part-time programs available. *Students:* 2 full-time (both women), 35 part-time (32 women); includes 1 minority (Hispanic American). Average age 28. 18 applicants, 78% accepted, 14 enrolled. In 2009, 13 master's awarded. *Degree requirements:* For master's, thesis or research project, completion of program in 6 years. *Entrance requirements:* For master's, minimum GPA of 2.8, teaching certificate in elementary education. Additional exam requirements/recommendations for international students: Recommended—TOEFL (minimum score 550 paper-based; 213 computer-based; 79 iBT), IELTS (minimum score 6). *Application deadline:* For fall admission, 8/5 priority date for domestic students; for spring admission, 1/5 priority date for domestic students. Applications are processed on a rolling basis. Application fee: $50. *Expenses:* Tuition, state resident: full-time $5012; part-time $278 per credit hour. Tuition, nonresident: full-time $13,962; part-time $284 per credit hour. Required fees: $3886; $139 per credit hour. Full-time tuition and fees vary according to course load and program. Part-time tuition and fees vary according to course level, degree level and program. *Financial support:* In 2009–10, 1 student received support. Scholarships/grants available. Financial award application deadline: 5/1; financial award applicants required to submit FAFSA. *Unit head:* Dr. Theresa Canada, Chairperson, Department of Education and Educational Psychology, 203-837-8509, Fax: 203-837-8413, E-mail: canadat@wcsu.edu. *Application contact:* Chris Shankle, Associate Director of Graduate Studies, 203-837-9005, Fax: 203-837-8326, E-mail: shanklec@wcsu.edu.

Western Illinois University, School of Graduate Studies, College of Education and Human Services, Department of Curriculum and Instruction, Program in Reading, Macomb, IL 61455-1390. Offers MS Ed. *Accreditation:* NCATE. Part-time programs available. *Students:* 1 (woman) full-time, 151 part-time (146 women); includes 7 minority (3 African Americans, 1 Asian American or Pacific Islander, 3 Hispanic Americans). Average age 34. 16 applicants, 94% accepted. In 2009, 30 master's awarded. *Degree requirements:* For master's, thesis or alternative. *Entrance requirements:* For master's, teacher certification. Additional exam requirements/recommendations for international students: Required—TOEFL (minimum score 550 paper-based; 213 computer-based; 80 iBT). *Application deadline:* Applications are processed on a rolling basis. Application fee: $30. Electronic applications accepted. *Expenses:* Tuition, state resident: full-time $4486; part-time $249.21 per credit hour. Tuition, nonresident: full-time $8972; part-time $498.42 per credit hour. Required fees: $72.62 per credit hour. *Financial support:* Research assistantships with full tuition reimbursements available. Financial award applicants required to submit FAFSA. *Unit head:* Dr. Cindy Dooley, Department Chair, 309-298-1961. *Application contact:* Evelyn Hoing, Assistant Director of Graduate Studies, 309-298-1806, Fax: 309-298-2345, E-mail: grad-office@wiu.edu.

Western Kentucky University, Graduate Studies, College of Education and Behavioral Sciences, Department of Special Instructional Programs, Bowling Green, KY 42101. Offers exceptional child education (MAE); interdisciplinary early child education (MAE); library media education (MS); literacy (MAE). Part-time and evening/weekend programs available. Postbaccalaureate distance learning degree programs offered (minimal on-campus study). *Degree requirements:* For master's, comprehensive exam. *Entrance requirements:* For master's, GRE General Test. Additional exam requirements/recommendations for international students: Required—TOEFL (minimum score 555 paper-based; 213 computer-based; 79 iBT). *Expenses:* Tuition, state resident: full-time $4160; part-time $416 per credit hour. Tuition, nonresident: full-time $9550; part-time $506 per credit hour. Tuition and fees vary according to campus/location and reciprocity agreements. *Faculty research:* Teacher preparation in moderate/severe disabilities.

Western Michigan University, Graduate College, College of Education, Department of Special Education and Literacy Studies, Kalamazoo, MI 49008. Offers literacy studies (MA); special education (MA, Ed D); teaching children with visual impairments (MA). *Unit head:* Dan Morgan, Chair, 269-387-2968. *Application contact:* Admissions and Orientation, 269-387-2000, Fax: 269-387-2355.

Western New Mexico University, Graduate Division, School of Education, Silver City, NM 88062-0680. Offers bilingual education (MAT); counseling (MA); educational leadership (MA); elementary education (MAT); reading (MAT); school psychology (MA); secondary education (MAT); special education (MAT); TESOL (teaching English to speakers of other languages) (MAT). *Accreditation:* NCATE. *Degree requirements:* For master's, comprehensive exam. *Entrance requirements:* For master's, GRE General Test, GRE Subject Test, minimum GPA of 3.2 in last 64 hours of undergraduate study. Additional exam requirements/recommendations for international students: Required—TOEFL (minimum score 550 paper-based; 213 computer-based). Electronic applications accepted.

Westfield State College, Division of Graduate and Continuing Education, Department of Education, Program in Reading, Westfield, MA 01086. Offers M Ed. *Accreditation:* NCATE. Part-time and evening/weekend programs available. *Degree requirements:* For master's, comprehensive exam, practicum. *Entrance requirements:* For master's, GRE General Test or MAT, minimum undergraduate GPA of 2.7.

Westminster College, Programs in Education, Program in Reading, New Wilmington, PA 16172-0001. Offers M Ed, Certificate. Part-time and evening/weekend programs available. *Degree requirements:* For master's, comprehensive exam, portfolio. *Entrance requirements:* For master's, minimum GPA of 3.0.

West Texas A&M University, College of Education and Social Sciences, Division of Education, Program in Reading, Canyon, TX 79016-0001. Offers M Ed. Part-time and evening/weekend programs available. *Degree requirements:* For master's, comprehensive exam. *Entrance requirements:* For master's, GRE General Test, interview with master's committee chairperson, state certification as a reading specialist with 3 years of teaching experience. Electronic applications accepted. *Faculty research:* Multicultural child and adolescent literature, bilingual, dual language, monolingual classrooms.

West Virginia University, College of Human Resources and Education, Department of Curriculum and Instruction-Literacy, Program in Reading, Morgantown, WV 26506. Offers MA. *Accreditation:* NCATE. Part-time programs available. *Degree requirements:* For master's, thesis optional, content exams. *Entrance requirements:* For master's, minimum GPA of 2.75. Additional exam requirements/recommendations for international students: Required—TOEFL.

Electronic applications accepted. *Faculty research:* Teacher education, current practices, protocol research, metacognitive studies.

Wheelock College, Graduate Programs, Division of Education, Boston, MA 02215-4176. Offers early childhood education (MS); education leadership (MS); elementary education (MS); language, literacy, and reading (MS); teaching students with moderate disabilities (MS). *Accreditation:* NCATE. Postbaccalaureate distance learning degree programs offered (minimal on-campus study). *Degree requirements:* For master's, comprehensive exam. *Entrance requirements:* Additional exam requirements/recommendations for international students: Required—TOEFL. Electronic applications accepted. *Faculty research:* Symbolic learning, emergent literacy, diversity inclusion, beginning reading language and culture, math education.

Widener University, School of Human Service Professions, Center for Education, Chester, PA 19013-5792. Offers adult education (M Ed); counseling in higher education (M Ed); counselor education (M Ed); early childhood education (M Ed); educational foundations (M Ed); educational leadership (M Ed); educational psychology (M Ed); elementary education (M Ed); English and language arts (M Ed); health education (M Ed); higher education leadership (Ed D); home and school visitor (M Ed); human sexuality (M Ed); mathematics education (M Ed); middle school education (M Ed); principalship (M Ed); reading and language arts (Ed D); reading education (M Ed); school administration (Ed D); science education (M Ed); social studies education (M Ed); special education (M Ed); technology education (M Ed). *Accreditation:* NCATE. Part-time and evening/weekend programs available. *Faculty:* 34 full-time (22 women), 37 part-time/adjunct (14 women). *Students:* 203 full-time (154 women), 415 part-time (298 women); includes 50 minority (34 African Americans, 1 American Indian/Alaska Native, 5 Asian Americans or Pacific Islanders, 10 Hispanic Americans), 3 international. Average age 39. 139 applicants, 88% accepted. In 2009, 168 master's, 31 doctorates awarded. Terminal master's awarded for partial completion of doctoral program. *Degree requirements:* For doctorate, thesis/dissertation. *Entrance requirements:* For master's, minimum GPA of 2.5; for doctorate, GRE or MAT, minimum GPA of 2.0 (undergraduate), 3.5 (graduate). *Application deadline:* Applications are processed on a rolling basis. Application fee: $25 ($300 for international students). Electronic applications accepted. *Expenses:* Contact institution. *Financial support:* Career-related internships or fieldwork, tuition waivers (full and partial), and unspecified assistantships available. Support available to part-time students. Financial award application deadline: 5/1. *Faculty research:* Reading and cognition, adult education, technology education, educational leadership, special education. *Unit head:* Dr. Michael W. LeDoux, Associate Dean, 610-499-4294, Fax: 610-499-4623, E-mail: mwledoux@widener.edu. *Application contact:* Dr. Roberta D. Nolan, Director of Graduate Admissions, 610-499-4125, E-mail: rdnolan@widener.edu.

William Paterson University of New Jersey, College of Education, Wayne, NJ 07470-8420. Offers curriculum and learning (M Ed); educational leadership (M Ed); reading (M Ed); special education and counseling services (M Ed), including counseling services, special education; teaching (MAT). *Accreditation:* NCATE. Part-time and evening/weekend programs available. *Students:* 119 full-time (100 women), 662 part-time (550 women); includes 111 minority (25 African Americans, 1 American Indian/Alaska Native, 9 Asian Americans or Pacific Islanders, 76 Hispanic Americans), 2 international. *Degree requirements:* For master's, comprehensive exam. *Entrance requirements:* For master's, GRE General Test, MAT, minimum GPA of 2.75, teaching certificate. *Application deadline:* Applications are processed on a rolling basis. Application fee: $50. Electronic applications accepted. *Financial support:* Research assistantships with full tuition reimbursements, career-related internships or fieldwork, Federal Work-Study, and unspecified assistantships available. Support available to part-time students. Financial award application deadline: 4/1; financial award applicants required to submit FAFSA. *Faculty research:* Urban community service. *Unit head:* Dr. Candace Burns, Dean, 973-720-2137, Fax: 973-720-2955, E-mail: burnsc@wpunj.edu. *Application contact:* Liana Fornarotto, Assistant Director, Graduate Admissions, 973-720-3578, Fax: 973-720-2035, E-mail: fornarottol@wpunj.edu.

Wilmington College, Department of Education, Wilmington, OH 45177. Offers reading (M Ed); special education (M Ed). Part-time programs available. *Degree requirements:* For master's, comprehensive exam. *Entrance requirements:* For master's, GRE or MAT, minimum GPA of 3.0, 2 letters of recommendation. Additional exam requirements/recommendations for international students: Required—TOEFL. *Faculty research:* Reading instruction, special education practices, conflict resolution in the schools, models of higher education for teachers.

Wilmington University, College of Education, New Castle, DE 19720-6491. Offers applied education technology (M Ed); career and technical education (M Ed); elementary and secondary school counseling (M Ed); elementary special education (M Ed); elementary studies (M Ed); instruction: gifted and talented (M Ed); instruction: teaching and learning (M Ed); literacy (M Ed); reading (M Ed); school leadership (M Ed); secondary teaching (MAT). *Accreditation:* NCATE. Part-time and evening/weekend programs available. *Entrance requirements:* For master's, 2 letters of recommendation, interview. Additional exam requirements/recommendations for international students: Required—TOEFL (minimum score 500 paper-based; 173 computer-based). Electronic applications accepted.

Winthrop University, College of Education, Program in Reading Education, Rock Hill, SC 29733. Offers M Ed. *Accreditation:* NCATE. Part-time programs available. *Entrance requirements:* For master's, PRAXIS, South Carolina Class III Teaching Certificate, 1 year of teaching experience. Electronic applications accepted.

Worcester State College, Graduate Studies, Department of Education, Program in Reading, Worcester, MA 01602-2597. Offers M Ed, CAGS. Part-time and evening/weekend programs available. *Faculty:* 9 full-time (7 women), 19 part-time/adjunct (7 women). *Students:* 1 (woman) full-time, 13 part-time (all women); includes 1 minority (African American). Average age 36. 15 applicants, 60% accepted, 2 enrolled. In 2009, 5 master's, 10 CAGSs awarded. *Degree requirements:* For master's, comprehensive exam (for some programs), thesis optional. *Entrance requirements:* For master's, GRE General Test or MAT, teaching certificate. Additional exam requirements/recommendations for international students: Required—TOEFL (minimum score 550 paper-based; 213 computer-based; 79 iBT). *Application deadline:* Applications are processed on a rolling basis. Application fee: $30. *Expenses:* Tuition, area resident: Part-time $150 per credit. Tuition, state resident: part-time $150 per credit. Tuition, nonresident: part-time $150 per credit. Required fees: $85. *Financial support:* Career-related internships or fieldwork, scholarships/grants, and unspecified assistantships available. Financial award application deadline: 3/1; financial award applicants required to submit FAFSA. *Unit head:* Dr. Margaret Pray-Bouchard, Coordinator, 508-929-8840, Fax: 508-929-8164, E-mail: mbouchard@worcester.edu. *Application contact:* Nicole Brown, Assistant Dean of Graduate and Continuing Education, 508-929-8787, Fax: 508-929-8100, E-mail: nbrown@worcester.edu.

Xavier University, College of Social Sciences, Health and Education, School of Education, Department of Childhood Education and Literacy, Program in Reading, Cincinnati, OH 45207. Offers M Ed. Part-time and evening/weekend programs available. Postbaccalaureate distance learning degree programs offered (minimal on-campus study). *Faculty:* 3 full-time (2 women), 6 part-time/adjunct (5 women). *Students:* 5 full-time (all women), 50 part-time (49 women); includes 4 minority (3 African Americans, 1 Hispanic American). Average age 33. 8 applicants, 100% accepted, 2 enrolled. In 2009, 51 master's awarded. *Degree requirements:* For master's, comprehensive exam. *Entrance requirements:* For master's, GRE or MAT. Additional exam requirements/recommendations for international students: Required—TOEFL. *Application deadline:* Applications are processed on a rolling basis. Application fee: $35. Electronic applications accepted. *Expenses:* Tuition: Part-time $697 per credit hour. One-time fee: $35 part-time. *Financial support:* In 2009–10, 49 students received support. Tuition waivers (partial) and unspecified assistantships available. Financial award applicants required to submit FAFSA. *Faculty research:* Multicultural literacy/fluency, content area literacy, early literacy development, writing/creative and across curriculum, assessment of reading abilities, multicultural literature for children and young adults. *Unit head:* Dr. Leslie Prosak-Beres, Director, 513-745-3652, Fax: 513-745-1052, E-mail: prosak-b@xavier.edu. *Application contact:* Roger Bosse, Director of Graduate Studies, 513-745-3357, Fax: 513-745-1048, E-mail: bosse@xavier.edu.

Youngstown State University, Graduate School, Beeghly College of Education, Department of Teacher Education, Youngstown, OH 44555-0001. Offers adolescent/young adult education (MS Ed); content area concentration (MS Ed); early childhood education (MS Ed); educational technology (MS Ed); literacy (MS Ed); middle childhood education (MS Ed); special education (MS Ed), including gifted and talented education, special education. *Accreditation:* NCATE. Part-time and evening/weekend programs available. *Degree requirements:* For master's, comprehensive exam. *Entrance requirements:* For master's, GRE, MAT, or teaching certificate; minimum GPA of 2.7. Additional exam requirements/recommendations for international students: Required—TOEFL. *Faculty research:* Multicultural literacy, hands-on mathematics teaching, integrated instruction, reading comprehension, emergent curriculum.

Religious Education

Andover Newton Theological School, Graduate and Professional Programs, Newton Centre, MA 02459-2243. Offers divinity (M Div); general (MA); psychology and religion (MA); religious education (MA); research (MA); sacred theology (STM); theology (D Min); theology and the arts (MA). *Accreditation:* ACIPE; ATS. Part-time programs available. *Degree requirements:* For master's, comprehensive exam (for some programs), thesis (for some programs); for doctorate, comprehensive exam, thesis/dissertation. *Entrance requirements:* For doctorate, M Div or equivalent. Additional exam requirements/recommendations for international students: Required—TOEFL (minimum score 550 paper-based; 213 computer-based). Electronic applications accepted.

Andrews University, School of Graduate Studies, Seventh-day Adventist Theological Seminary, Program in Religious Education, Berrien Springs, MI 49104. Offers MA, Ed D, PhD, Ed S. Part-time programs available. *Students:* 9 full-time (8 women), 11 part-time (9 women); includes 7 minority (3 African Americans, 4 Hispanic Americans), 8 international. Average age 33. 20 applicants, 55% accepted, 7 enrolled. In 2009, 5 master's, 2 doctorates awarded. Terminal master's awarded for partial completion of doctoral program. *Degree requirements:* For doctorate, thesis/dissertation. *Entrance requirements:* For master's, GRE Subject Test. Additional exam requirements/recommendations for international students: Required—TOEFL (minimum score 550 paper-based). *Application deadline:* For fall admission, 8/31 for domestic students. Applications are processed on a rolling basis. Application fee: $40. *Financial support:* Fellowships, research assistantships, teaching assistantships, career-related internships or fieldwork available. Financial award application deadline: 6/1. *Faculty research:* Marriage and family, spiritual gifts and temperament. *Unit head:* Coordinator, 269-471-8618. *Application contact:* Carolyn Hurst, Supervisor of Graduate Admission, 800-253-2874, Fax: 269-471-6321, E-mail: graduate@andrews.edu.

Asbury Theological Seminary, Graduate and Professional Programs, Wilmore, KY 40390-1199. Offers MA, MAC, MACE, MACL, MAPC, MAYM, Th M, D Miss, PhD, Certificate. *Accreditation:* ATS. Part-time programs available. Postbaccalaureate distance learning degree programs offered (minimal on-campus study). *Faculty:* 64 full-time (11 women), 74 part-time/adjunct (14 women). *Students:* 760 full-time (226 women), 768 part-time (279 women); includes 155 minority (85 African Americans, 13 American Indian/Alaska Native, 25 Asian Americans or Pacific Islanders, 32 Hispanic Americans), 141 international. Average age 25. 765 applicants, 75% accepted, 364 enrolled. In 2009, 95 master's, 15 doctorates, 38 other advanced degrees awarded. Terminal master's awarded for partial completion of doctoral program. *Degree requirements:* For master's, thesis (for some programs); for doctorate, thesis/dissertation, qualifying exam. *Entrance requirements:* For master's, minimum GPA of 2.75; for doctorate, minimum GPA of 3.0. Additional exam requirements/recommendations for international students: Required—TOEFL, IELTS. *Application deadline:* Applications are processed on a rolling basis. Application fee: $50. Electronic applications accepted. *Financial support:* In 2009–10, 1,317 students received support. Career-related internships or fieldwork, Federal Work-Study, institutionally sponsored loans, and scholarships/grants available. Support available to part-time students. Financial award applicants required to submit FAFSA. *Unit head:* Dr. Leslie A. Andrews, Provost, 859-858-2206, Fax: 859-858-2025, E-mail: leslie.andrews@asburyseminary.edu. *Application contact:* Kevin Bush, Vice President of Enrollment Management, 859-858-2211, Fax: 859-858-2287, E-mail: admissions.office@asburyseminary.edu.

Azusa Pacific University, Haggard School of Theology, Program in Christian Education in Youth Ministry, Azusa, CA 91702-7000. Offers Christian education (MA). *Accreditation:* NCATE.

Baptist Bible College of Pennsylvania, Baptist Bible Seminary, Clarks Summit, PA 18411-1297. Offers biblical studies (PhD); church planting (M Div); global missions (M Div); military chaplaincy (M Div); ministry (M Min, D Min); pastor of church education (M Div); pastor of outreach (M Div); pastoral counseling (M Div); pastoral leadership (M Div); theology (M Div, Th M); youth pastor (M Div). Part-time and evening/weekend programs available. Postbaccalaureate distance learning degree programs offered (minimal on-campus study). Terminal master's awarded for partial completion of doctoral program. *Degree requirements:* For master's, 2 foreign languages, thesis; for doctorate, 2 foreign languages, comprehensive exam (for some programs), thesis/dissertation, oral exam; for M Div, 2 foreign languages, thesis/dissertation, oral exam. *Entrance requirements:* For doctorate, Greek and Hebrew entrance exams (PhD). Electronic applications accepted.

Baptist Bible College of Pennsylvania, Graduate School, Clarks Summit, PA 18411-1297. Offers Bible (MA); biblical ministries (MS); Christian school education (MS); counseling (MS). Part-time and evening/weekend programs available. Postbaccalaureate distance learning degree programs offered (no on-campus study). *Faculty:* 2 full-time (0 women), 1 part-time/adjunct (0 women). *Students:* 12 full-time (7 women), 61 part-time (40 women); includes 3 minority (all African Americans), 1 international. Average age 31. In 2009, 13 master's awarded. *Entrance requirements:* Additional exam requirements/recommendations for international students: Required—TOEFL (minimum score 500 paper-based; 173 computer-based). *Application deadline:* Applications are processed on a rolling basis. Application fee: $30. *Financial support:* In 2009–10, 43 students received support. Institutionally sponsored loans and scholarships/grants available. Financial award application deadline: 8/20; financial award applicants required to submit FAFSA. *Unit head:* Dr. James Lytle, Provost, 570-586-2400 Ext. 9222, Fax: 570-586-1753. *Application contact:* Drew Whipple, Assistant Director of Enrollment, 570-585-9370, Fax: 570-585-9299, E-mail: gradadmissions@bbc.edu.

Baptist Theological Seminary at Richmond, Graduate and Professional Programs, Richmond, VA 23227. Offers biblical interpretation (M Div); Christian education (M Div); theology (D Min); youth and student ministries (M Div); M Div/MS; M Div/MSW. *Accreditation:* ATS. Part-time programs available. Postbaccalaureate distance learning degree programs offered (minimal on-campus study). *Faculty:* 8 full-time (2 women), 9 part-time/adjunct (3 women). *Students:* 59 full-time (33 women), 30 part-time (17 women); includes 9 minority (all African Americans), 3

Religious Education

Baptist Theological Seminary at Richmond (continued)

international. Average age 46. In 2009, 29 first professional degrees, 6 doctorates awarded. *Degree requirements:* For doctorate, one foreign language, comprehensive exam, thesis/dissertation, field study, independent study; for M Div, one foreign language, comprehensive exam (for some programs), thesis/dissertation optional, mission immersion experience, internship. *Entrance requirements:* For doctorate, MAT, M Div, 3 years of full-time ministry experience. Additional exam requirements/recommendations for international students: Required—TOEFL (minimum score 550 paper-based; 213 computer-based). *Application deadline:* For fall admission, 8/1 priority date for domestic students, 5/1 priority date for international students; for winter admission, 12/1 priority date for domestic students, 9/1 priority date for international students; for spring admission, 1/1 priority date for domestic students, 10/1 priority date for international students. Applications are processed on a rolling basis. Application fee: $35. *Financial support:* In 2009–10, 16 teaching assistantships (averaging $1,650 per year) were awarded; scholarships/grants and tuition waivers (partial) also available. Financial award application deadline: 2/1. *Faculty research:* New Testament studies, Old Testament studies, pastoral care, church history, theology. *Unit head:* Dr. Ronald W. Crawford, President, 804-204-1201, Fax: 804-355-8182, E-mail: rcrawford@btsr.edu. *Application contact:* Tiffany Kellogg Pittman, Director of Admissions, 804-204-1208, Fax: 804-355-8182, E-mail: admissions@btsr.edu.

Bethel Seminary, Graduate and Professional Programs, St. Paul, MN 55112-6998. Offers applied ministry (MA); biblical studies (MATS, Certificate); children's and family ministry (MACFM); Christian education (MACE); Christian thought (M Div, MACT); church leadership (D Min); community ministry leadership (MA, Certificate); congregation and family care (D Min); global and contextual studies (MA, MATS); historical studies (MATS); lay ministry (Certificate); marriage and family studies (M Div, MATS); marriage and family therapy (MAMFT, Certificate); ministry leadership (Certificate); pastoral care and counseling (MATS); pastoral ministries (M Div); spiritual formation (Certificate); theological studies (MATS, Certificate); transformational leadership (MATL, Certificate); youth ministries (MACE). *Accreditation:* ACIPE; ATS (one or more programs are accredited). Part-time and evening/weekend programs available. Post-baccalaureate distance learning degree programs offered (minimal on-campus study). *Faculty:* 26 full-time (3 women), 76 part-time/adjunct (30 women). *Students:* 725 full-time (269 women), 300 part-time (104 women); includes 204 minority (115 African Americans, 1 American Indian/Alaska Native, 65 Asian Americans or Pacific Islanders, 23 Hispanic Americans), 13 international. Average age 37. 516 applicants, 78% accepted, 261 enrolled. In 2009, 50 first professional degrees, 100 master's, 6 doctorates awarded. *Degree requirements:* For master's, variable foreign language requirement, thesis (for some programs); for doctorate, thesis/dissertation; for M Div, one foreign language. *Entrance requirements:* For M Div and master's, letters of reference, transcripts, personal statement; for doctorate, M Div, letters of reference, organizational support. Additional exam requirements/recommendations for international students: Required—TOEFL (minimum score 550 paper-based; 213 computer-based; 87 iBT). *Application deadline:* For fall admission, 8/1 priority date for domestic students, 3/1 for international students; for winter admission, 12/1 priority date for domestic students; for spring admission, 3/1 priority date for domestic students. Applications are processed on a rolling basis. Application fee: $20. Electronic applications accepted. *Financial support:* In 2009–10, 847 students received support, including 18 teaching assistantships; career-related internships or fieldwork, Federal Work-Study, scholarships/grants, and tuition waivers (full) also available. Financial award application deadline: 7/15; financial award applicants required to submit FAFSA. *Faculty research:* Nature of theology, ethics, Biblical commentaries, nature of God, science and theology. *Unit head:* Dr. David Ridder, Vice President and Dean, 651-638-6553. *Application contact:* Joseph V. Dworak, Director of Admissions, 651-638-6288, Fax: 651-638-6002, E-mail: j-dworak@bethel.edu.

Biola University, Talbot School of Theology, La Mirada, CA 90639-0001. Offers Bible exposition (MA); biblical and theological studies (MA); Christian education (MACE); Christian ministry and leadership (MA); divinity (M Div); education (PhD); ministry (MA Min); New Testament (MA); Old Testament (MA); philosophy of religion and ethics (MA); spiritual formation (MA); spiritual formation and soul care (MA); theology (MA, Th M, D Min). *Accreditation:* ATS. Part-time and evening/weekend programs available. *Degree requirements:* For master's, variable foreign language requirement, thesis or alternative; for doctorate, variable foreign language requirement, thesis/dissertation; for M Div, thesis/dissertation or alternative. *Entrance requirements:* For M Div, minimum GPA of 2.6; for master's, minimum undergraduate GPA of 3.0; for doctorate, minimum GPA of 3.25. Additional exam requirements/recommendations for international students: Required—TOEFL (minimum score 550 paper-based; 213 computer-based). *Faculty research:* Moral development; biological, medical, and social ethics; ancient Near Eastern historical philosophy.

Boston College, Graduate School of Arts and Sciences, School of Theology and Ministry, Chestnut Hill, MA 02467-3800. Offers church leadership (MA); divinity (M Div); pastoral ministry (MA), including Hispanic ministry, liturgy and worship, pastoral care and counseling, spirituality; religious education (MA, PhD); sacred theology (STD, STL); social justice/social ministry (MA); spiritual direction (MA); theological studies (MTS); theology (Th M, PhD); youth ministry (MA); MA/MA; MS/MA; MSW/MA. *Accreditation:* Teacher Education Accreditation Council. Part-time programs available. *Degree requirements:* For doctorate, one foreign language, thesis/dissertation. *Entrance requirements:* For doctorate, GRE. Additional exam requirements/recommendations for international students: Required—TOEFL (minimum score 550 paper-based; 213 computer-based). Electronic applications accepted. *Faculty research:* Philosophy and practice of religious education, pastoral psychology, liturgical and spiritual theology, spiritual formation for the practice of ministry.

Boston College, Lynch Graduate School of Education, Department of Teacher Education/Special Education and Curriculum and Instruction, Religious Education Specialization, Chestnut Hill, MA 02467-3800. Offers M Ed, CAES. *Accreditation:* Teacher Education Accreditation Council. Part-time and evening/weekend programs available. *Students:* 1 (woman) full-time, 23 part-time (17 women); includes 3 minority (1 Asian American or Pacific Islander, 2 Hispanic Americans), 5 international. In 2009, 3 master's awarded. *Degree requirements:* For master's and CAES, comprehensive exam. *Entrance requirements:* For master's, GRE General Test or MAT. Additional exam requirements/recommendations for international students: Required—TOEFL. Application fee: $60. Electronic applications accepted. *Financial support:* Fellowships with full and partial tuition reimbursements, research assistantships with full and partial tuition reimbursements, teaching assistantships with full and partial tuition reimbursements, career-related internships or fieldwork, Federal Work-Study, scholarships/grants, traineeships, health care benefits, tuition waivers (full and partial), and unspecified assistantships available. Support available to part-time students. Financial award applicants required to submit FAFSA. *Faculty research:* Curriculum development, inter-religious dialogue, ethical and value issues and pedagogy. *Unit head:* Dr. Maria E. Brisk, Chairperson, 617-552-4216, Fax: 617-552-0812, E-mail: brisk@bc.edu. *Application contact:* Adam Poluzzi, Director, Graduate Admission and Financial Aid, 617-552-4214, Fax: 617-552-0398, E-mail: poluzzi@bc.edu.

Brandeis University, Graduate School of Arts and Sciences, Teaching Program, Waltham, MA 02454-9110. Offers elementary education (public) (MAT); Jewish day school (MAT); secondary education (English, history, biology, Bible) (MAT). *Faculty:* 4 full-time (3 women), 12 part-time/adjunct (9 women). *Students:* 24 full-time (20 women), 1 part-time (0 women), 2 international. Average age 27. 61 applicants, 70% accepted, 24 enrolled. In 2009, 31 master's awarded. *Entrance requirements:* For master's, GRE General Test, 3 letters of recommendation, resume. Additional exam requirements/recommendations for international students: Required—TOEFL (minimum score 600 paper-based; 250 computer-based; 100 iBT); Recommended—IELTS (minimum score 7). *Application deadline:* For fall admission, 1/15 priority date for domestic and international students. Applications are processed on a rolling basis. Application fee: $75. Electronic applications accepted. *Expenses:* Contact institution. *Financial support:* Scholarships/grants and tuition waivers (partial) available. Financial award applicants required to submit FAFSA. *Faculty research:* Teacher education, induction, philosophy, education, democracy education, social justice. *Unit head:* Prof. Dirck Roosevelt, Director, MAT Program, 781-736-2020, Fax: 781-736-5020, E-mail: drooseve@brandeis.edu. *Application contact:* Manuel Tuan, Department Administrator, 781-736-2633, Fax: 781-736-5020, E-mail: tuan@brandeis.edu.

Brigham Young University, Graduate Studies, College of Religious Education, Provo, UT 84602-1001. Offers MA. *Faculty:* 69 full-time (4 women). *Students:* 8 full-time (1 woman), 5 part-time (0 women). Average age 32. In 2009, 2 master's awarded. *Degree requirements:* For master's, thesis. *Entrance requirements:* For master's, GRE, minimum GPA of 3.0 in last 60 hours, letter of recommendation. *Application deadline:* For fall admission, 12/1 for international students; for winter admission, 12/1 for domestic students. Application fee: $50. *Expenses:* Tuition: Full-time $5580; part-time $301 per credit hour. Tuition and fees vary according to student's religious affiliation. *Financial support:* Scholarships/grants available. *Unit head:* Dr. Terry B. Ball, Dean, 801-422-2736, Fax: 801-422-0616, E-mail: terry_ball@byu.edu. *Application contact:* Dr. Clyde J. Williams, Professor of Ancient Scripture, 801-422-2124, Fax: 801-422-0616.

Calvin Theological Seminary, Graduate and Professional Programs, Grand Rapids, MI 49546-4387. Offers Bible and theology (MA); divinity (M Div), including ancient near eastern languages and literature, contextual ministry, evangelism and teaching, history of Christianity, new church development, New Testament, Old Testament, pastoral care and leadership, preaching and worship, theological studies, youth and family ministries; educational ministry (MA); historical theology (PhD); missions and evangelism (MA); pastoral care (MA); philosophical and moral theology (PhD); systematic theology (PhD); theological studies (MTS); theology (Th M); worship (MA); youth and family ministries (MA). *Accreditation:* ACIPE; ATS. Part-time programs available. *Faculty:* 28 full-time (2 women), 20 part-time/adjunct (7 women). *Students:* 203 full-time (39 women), 48 part-time (19 women); includes 28 minority (10 African Americans, 13 Asian Americans or Pacific Islanders, 5 Hispanic Americans), 69 international. Average age 31. 152 applicants, 89% accepted, 98 enrolled. In 2009, 45 first professional degrees, 42 master's, 6 doctorates awarded. *Degree requirements:* For master's, thesis (for some programs); for doctorate, 4 foreign languages, comprehensive exam, thesis/dissertation; for M Div, 2 foreign languages. *Entrance requirements:* For doctorate, GRE General Test, Hebrew, Greek, and a modern foreign language. Additional exam requirements/recommendations for international students: Required—TOEFL (minimum score 550 paper-based; 213 computer-based), TWE (minimum score 4). *Application deadline:* For fall admission, 3/1 priority date for domestic and international students. Applications are processed on a rolling basis. Application fee: $25. Electronic applications accepted. *Expenses:* Tuition: Full-time $11,814; part-time $358 per semester hour. Tuition and fees vary according to degree level. *Financial support:* In 2009–10, 187 students received support, including 4 fellowships with full tuition reimbursements available (averaging $8,405 per year), 4 teaching assistantships with full tuition reimbursements available (averaging $5,760 per year); career-related internships or fieldwork, institutionally sponsored loans, scholarships/grants, and tuition waivers (full) also available. Support available to part-time students. Financial award application deadline: 3/1; financial award applicants required to submit FAFSA. *Faculty research:* Recent Trinity theory, Christian anthropology, Proverbs, reformed confessions, Paul's view of law. *Unit head:* Dr. Cornelius Plantinga, Head, 616-957-6024, Fax: 616-957-6536, E-mail: sempres@calvinseminary.edu. *Application contact:* Rev. Gregory Janke, Director of Admissions, 616-957-7035, Fax: 616-957-6101, E-mail: gjanke@calvinseminary.edu.

Campbell University, Graduate and Professional Programs, Divinity School, Buies Creek, NC 27506. Offers Christian education (MA); divinity (M Div); ministry (D Min); M Div/MA; M Div/MBA. *Accreditation:* ATS. *Degree requirements:* For doctorate, final project. *Entrance requirements:* For master's, minimum GPA of 2.5; for doctorate, MAT, M Div, minimum graduate GPA of 3.0. Additional exam requirements/recommendations for international students: Required—TOEFL (minimum score 580 paper-based; 237 computer-based). *Expenses:* Contact institution. *Faculty research:* New Testament, theology, spiritual formation, Old Testament, Christian leadership.

Canadian Southern Baptist Seminary, Graduate Programs, Cochrane, AB T4C 2G1, Canada. Offers Christian education (MACE); ministry (M Div). *Accreditation:* ATS. Part-time programs available. *Faculty:* 8 full-time (0 women), 3 part-time/adjunct (1 woman). *Students:* 17 full-time (3 women), 25 part-time (4 women); includes 9 minority (1 African American, 5 Asian Americans or Pacific Islanders, 3 Hispanic Americans), 12 international. *Entrance requirements:* Additional exam requirements/recommendations for international students: Required—TOEFL (minimum score 560 paper-based; 220 computer-based), IELTS (minimum score 6.5). *Application deadline:* For fall admission, 7/1 priority date for domestic and international students; for winter admission, 11/15 priority date for domestic and international students. Applications are processed on a rolling basis. Application fee: $50. Tuition and fees charges are reported in Canadian dollars. *Expenses:* Tuition: Full-time $5280 Canadian dollars; part-time $220 Canadian dollars per credit hour. Required fees: $480 Canadian dollars; $20 Canadian dollars per credit hour. *Unit head:* Steve Booth, Academic Dean, 403-932-6622. *Application contact:* Kathleen McNaughton, Registrar, 403-932-6622 Ext. 221, E-mail: kathleen.mcnaughton@csbs.ca.

The Catholic University of America, School of Theology and Religious Studies, Washington, DC 20064. Offers Biblical studies (STB, MA, PhD, STL); Catholic educational leadership (MA); church history (PhD); Hispanic pastoral leadership (Certificate); Hispanic/Latino ministry (M Div); historical theology (STB, STD); history of religions (Hinduism/Islam) (MA, PhD); liturgical studies/sacramental theology (MA, PhD, STD, STL); moral theology/ethics (STB, MA, PhD, STD, STL); pastoral studies (M Div, Certificate); religion and culture (PhD); religious education/catechetics (MA, MRE, PhD); spirituality (STB, PhD, STD, STL); systematic and historical theology (MA, PhD, STD, STL). *Accreditation:* ATS (one or more programs are accredited). Part-time programs available. *Faculty:* 40 full-time (6 women), 10 part-time/adjunct (2 women). *Students:* 169 full-time (26 women), 225 part-time (57 women); includes 33 minority (10 African Americans, 1 American Indian/Alaska Native, 9 Asian Americans or Pacific Islanders, 13 Hispanic Americans), 73 international. Average age 36. 226 applicants, 72% accepted, 75 enrolled. In 2009, 9 first professional degrees, 14 master's, 26 doctorates awarded. *Degree requirements:* For master's, variable foreign language requirement, comprehensive exam, thesis (for some programs); for doctorate, variable foreign language requirement, comprehensive exam, thesis/dissertation; for first professional degree, comprehensive exam. *Entrance requirements:* For first professional degree and master's, GRE General Test, statement of purpose, official copies of academic transcripts, three letters of recommendation; for doctorate, GRE General Test, 3 letters of recommendation. Additional exam requirements/recommendations for international students: Required—TOEFL (minimum score 580 paper-based; 237 computer-based). *Application deadline:* For fall admission, 8/1 priority date for domestic students, 7/15 for international students; for spring admission, 12/1 priority date for domestic students, 10/15 for international students. Applications are processed on a rolling basis. Application fee: $55. Electronic applications accepted. *Expenses:* Tuition: Full-time $31,740; part-time $1245 per credit hour. Required fees: $50; $25 per semester hour. One-time fee: $425. *Financial support:* Fellowships, research assistantships, teaching assistantships, Federal Work-Study, scholarships/grants, tuition waivers (full and partial), and unspecified assistantships available. Financial award application deadline: 2/1; financial award applicants required to submit FAFSA. *Faculty research:* Historical and systematic theology, religious education and catechetics, moral theology and ethics, Biblical studies, liturgical studies and sacramental theology. Total annual research expenditures: $66,740. *Unit head:* Msgr. Kevin W. Irwin, Dean, 202-319-5683, Fax: 202-319-4967, E-mail: irwin@cua.edu. *Application contact:* Julie Schwing, Director of Graduate Admissions, 202-319-5057, Fax: 202-319-6533, E-mail: cua-admissions@cua.edu.

Claremont School of Theology, Graduate and Professional Programs, Program in Religion, Claremont, CA 91711-3199. Offers practical theology (PhD), including religious education, spiritual care and counseling; religion (PhD), including Hebrew Bible, New Testament and Christian origins, process studies, religion, ethics, and society; religion and theology (MA); religious education (MARE). *Accreditation:* ACIPE; ATS. Terminal master's awarded for partial completion of doctoral program. *Degree requirements:* For master's, thesis; for doctorate, 2 foreign languages, thesis/dissertation. *Entrance requirements:* For doctorate, GRE General Test. Additional exam requirements/recommendations for international students: Required—TOEFL (minimum score 250 computer-based). Electronic applications accepted.

College of Mount St. Joseph, Graduate Program in Religious Studies, Cincinnati, OH 45233-1670. Offers religious education (Certificate); spiritual and pastoral care (MA, Certificate); spiritual direction (Certificate). Part-time and evening/weekend programs available. *Faculty:* 4 full-time (2 women). *Students:* 25 part-time (20 women); includes 1 minority (African American). Average age 49. 5 applicants, 100% accepted, 3 enrolled. In 2009, 9 master's awarded. *Degree requirements:* For master's, comprehensive exam, integrating project. *Entrance requirements:* For master's, 3 letters of recommendation, interview, minimum GPA of 3.0. Additional exam requirements/recommendations for international students: Required—TOEFL (minimum score 560 paper-based; 220 computer-based; 83 iBT). *Application deadline:* Applications are processed on a rolling basis. Application fee: $50. Electronic applications accepted. *Expenses:* Tuition: Part-time $500 per hour. Required fees: $200 per year. Tuition and fees vary according to degree level and program. *Financial support:* In 2009–10, 20 students received support. Scholarships/grants available. Financial award applicants required to submit FAFSA. *Faculty research:* Contextual/cultural/systematic theology, historical/spiritual theology, business/economics ethics, social justice, Biblical/cultural/pastoral theology. *Unit head:* Dr. John Trokan, Chair of Religious/Pastoral Studies, 513-244-4272, Fax: 513-244-4222, E-mail: john_trokan@mail.msj.edu. *Application contact:* Marilyn Hoskins, Assistant Director of Graduate Recruitment, 513-244-4723, Fax: 513-244-4629, E-mail: marilyn_hoskins@mail.msj.edu.

Columbia International University, Columbia Biblical Seminary and School of Missions, Columbia, SC 29230-3122. Offers academic ministries (M Div); bible exposition (M Div, MABE); biblical studies (Certificate); counseling ministries (Certificate); divinity (M Div); educational ministries (M Div, MAEM, Certificate); intercultural studies (M Div, MAIS, Certificate); leadership (D Min); leadership for evangelism/mobilization (MALM); member care (D Min); ministry (Certificate); missions (D Min); pastoral counseling and spiritual formation (M Div, MAPS); preaching (D Min); theology (MA). *Accreditation:* ATS (one or more programs are accredited). Part-time and evening/weekend programs available. *Degree requirements:* For master's, integrative seminar; for doctorate, comprehensive exam, thesis/dissertation; for M Div, internship. *Entrance requirements:* For master's, minimum GPA of 2.7; for doctorate, 3 years of ministerial experience, M Div. Additional exam requirements/recommendations for international students: Required—TOEFL. Electronic applications accepted.

Columbia International University, Columbia Graduate School, Columbia, SC 29230-3122. Offers Bible teaching (MABT); Christian higher education leadership (Ed D); Christian school educational leadership (Ed D); counseling (MACN); curriculum and instruction (M Ed), including Christian school guidance, English as a second language, learning disabilities, school technology; early childhood and elementary education (MAT); educational administration (M Ed); teaching English as a foreign language (Certificate); teaching English as a foreign language and intercultural studies (MATF). Part-time and evening/weekend programs available. *Degree requirements:* For master's, internships, professional project. *Entrance requirements:* For master's, Minnesota Multiphasic Personality Inventory, MAT, minimum GPA of 2.7. Additional exam requirements/recommendations for international students: Required—TOEFL. Electronic applications accepted.

Concordia University Chicago, College of Education, Program in Christian Education, River Forest, IL 60305-1499. Offers MA. *Entrance requirements:* Additional exam requirements/recommendations for international students: Required—TOEFL (minimum score 550 paper-based; 195 computer-based). Electronic applications accepted.

Concordia University, Nebraska, Graduate Programs in Education, Program in Parish Education, Seward, NE 68434-1599. Offers MPE. *Accreditation:* NCATE. Part-time and evening/weekend programs available. *Degree requirements:* For master's, thesis or alternative. *Entrance requirements:* For master's, GRE, MAT, or NTE, minimum GPA of 3.0, BS in education or equivalent.

Concordia University, St. Paul, College of Vocation and Ministry, St. Paul, MN 55104-5494. Offers Christian education (Certificate); Christian outreach (MA); christian outreach (Certificate). Evening/weekend programs available. Postbaccalaureate distance learning degree programs offered (minimal on-campus study). *Faculty:* 4 full-time (0 women), 2 part-time/adjunct (1 woman). *Students:* 14 full-time (8 women), 4 part-time (2 women); includes 1 minority (Asian American or Pacific Islander). Average age 38. In 2009, 5 master's, 10 other advanced degrees awarded. *Application deadline:* Applications are processed on a rolling basis. Application fee: $50. Electronic applications accepted. *Financial support:* Applicants required to submit FAFSA. *Unit head:* Dr. David Lumpp, Dean, 651-641-8217, E-mail: lumpp@csp.edu. *Application contact:* Kimberly Craig, Director of Graduate and Cohort Admission, 651-603-6223, Fax: 651-603-6320, E-mail: craig@csp.edu.

Dallas Baptist University, Gary Cook School of Leadership, Program in Christian Education, Dallas, TX 75211-9299. Offers adult ministry (MA); business ministry (MA); childhood ministry (MA); collegiate ministry (MA); communication ministry (MA); counseling ministry (MA); education ministry (MA); general ministry (MA); missions ministry (MA); student ministry (MA); worship ministry (MA). Part-time and evening/weekend programs available. *Entrance requirements:* For master's, minimum GPA of 3.0. Additional exam requirements/recommendations for international students: Required—TOEFL. Electronic applications accepted. *Expenses:* Tuition: Full-time $10,674; part-time $593 per credit hour.

Dallas Baptist University, Gary Cook School of Leadership, Program in Christian Education and Business Administration, Dallas, TX 75211-9299. Offers MA, MBA. Part-time and evening/weekend programs available. *Entrance requirements:* For master's, GMAT, minimum GPA of 3.0. Additional exam requirements/recommendations for international students: Required—TOEFL, IELTS. *Expenses:* Tuition: Full-time $10,674; part-time $593 per credit hour.

Dallas Baptist University, Gary Cook School of Leadership, Program in Christian Education: Childhood Ministry, Dallas, TX 75211-9299. Offers MA. Part-time and evening/weekend programs available. *Entrance requirements:* For master's, minimum GPA of 3.0. Additional exam requirements/recommendations for international students: Required—TOEFL, IELTS. *Expenses:* Tuition: Full-time $10,674; part-time $593 per credit hour.

Dallas Baptist University, Gary Cook School of Leadership, Program in Christian Education: Student Ministry, Dallas, TX 75211-9299. Offers MA. Part-time and evening/weekend programs available. *Entrance requirements:* For master's, minimum GPA of 3.0. Additional exam requirements/recommendations for international students: Required—TOEFL, IELTS. *Expenses:* Tuition: Full-time $10,674; part-time $593 per credit hour.

Dallas Baptist University, Gary Cook School of Leadership, Program in Global Leadership, Dallas, TX 75211-9299. Offers business communication (MA); Christian education/missions (MA); ESL (MA); general studies (MA); global studies (MA); international business (MA); missions (MA); worship/missions (MA). Part-time and evening/weekend programs available. *Entrance requirements:* For master's, minimum GPA of 3.0. Additional exam requirements/recommendations for international students: Required—TOEFL, IELTS. *Expenses:* Tuition: Full-time $10,674; part-time $593 per credit hour.

Dallas Theological Seminary, Graduate Programs, Dallas, TX 75204-6499. Offers academic ministries (Th M); Bible translation (Th M); biblical and theological studies (CGS); biblical counseling (MA, Th M); biblical exegesis and linguistics (MA); biblical exposition (PhD); biblical studies (MA); Christian education (MA, D Min); cross-cultural ministries (MA, Th M); educational leadership (Th M); evangelism and discipleship (Th M); interdisciplinary studies (Th M); media and communication (MA); media arts in ministry (Th M); ministry (D Min); New Testament studies (Th M, PhD); Old Testament studies (PhD); parachurch ministries (Th M); pastoral ministries (Th M); sacred theology (STM); theological studies (PhD); women's ministry (Th M). *Accreditation:* ATS (one or more programs are accredited). Part-time and evening/weekend programs available. *Degree requirements:* For master's, variable foreign language requirement, thesis (for some programs); for doctorate, 2 foreign languages, thesis/dissertation. *Entrance requirements:* Additional exam requirements/recommendations for international students: Required—TOEFL, TWE. Electronic applications accepted.

Emmanuel School of Religion, Graduate and Professional Programs, Johnson City, TN 37601-9438. Offers Christian care and counseling (M Div); Christian doctrine (MAR); Christian education (M Div); church history (MAR); ministry (D Min); New Testament (MAR); Old Testament (MAR); urban ministry (M Div); world missions (M Div). *Accreditation:* ACIPE; ATS. Part-time programs available. *Faculty:* 10 full-time (2 women), 5 part-time/adjunct (0 women). *Students:* 108 full-time (27 women), 48 part-time (13 women). Average age 32. *Degree requirements:* For master's, 2 foreign languages, thesis; for M Div, 2 foreign languages, thesis/dissertation or alternative. *Entrance requirements:* For doctorate, GRE General Test, Minnesota Multiphasic Personality Inventory, M Div or equivalent. *Application deadline:* For fall admission, 8/1 priority date for domestic students. Applications are processed on a rolling basis. Application fee: $25. *Expenses:* Tuition: Full-time $7800; part-time $325 per credit hour. Required fees: $137.50 per semester. One-time fee: $240. Tuition and fees vary according to course load. *Financial support:* Teaching assistantships with partial tuition reimbursements, career-related internships or fieldwork, institutionally sponsored loans, scholarships/grants, and tuition waivers (partial) available. Support available to part-time students. Financial award application deadline: 4/1; financial award applicants required to submit FAFSA. *Faculty research:* Theology of Old Testament prophets, spiritual formation for Christian leaders, history of African churches and religions, social world of early Christianity, lay pastoral counseling. Total annual research expenditures: $12,000. *Unit head:* Dr. Rollin A. Ramsaran, Dean and Professor of New Testament, 423-461-1524, Fax: 423-926-6198, E-mail: ramsaranr@esr.edu. *Application contact:* Shelley Gasser, Administrative Assistant for Admissions, 423-461-1535, Fax: 423-926-6198, E-mail: gassers@esr.edu.

Felician College, Program in Religious Education, Lodi, NJ 07644-2117. Offers MA, Certificate. *Accreditation:* Teacher Education Accreditation Council. Part-time and evening/weekend programs available. Postbaccalaureate distance learning degree programs offered (no on-campus study). *Students:* 52 part-time (34 women); includes 1 African American, 2 Asian Americans or Pacific Islanders, 3 Hispanic Americans. Average age 48. 24 applicants, 79% accepted, 18 enrolled. *Degree requirements:* For master's, thesis. *Entrance requirements:* For master's, minimum GPA of 3.0, 1 letter of recommendation. Additional exam requirements/recommendations for international students: Recommended—TOEFL (minimum score 550 paper-based; 213 computer-based). *Application deadline:* Applications are processed on a rolling basis. Application fee: $40. *Financial support:* Scholarships/grants and tuition waivers (partial) available. *Faculty research:* Spirituality, race and ethnicity in religious settings. *Unit head:* Dr. Dolores M. Henchy, Director, 201-559-6053, Fax: 973-472-8936, E-mail: henchyd@felician.edu. *Application contact:* Dr. Wendy Lin-Cook, Director of Adult and Graduate Admission, 201-559-6077, Fax: 201-559-6138, E-mail: adultandgraduate@felician.edu.

Fordham University, Graduate School of Religion and Religious Education, New York, NY 10458. Offers pastoral counseling and spiritual care (MA); pastoral ministry/spirituality/pastoral counseling (D Min); religion and religious education (MA); religious education (MS, PhD, PD); spiritual direction (Certificate). Part-time programs available. Terminal master's awarded for partial completion of doctoral program. *Degree requirements:* For master's, research paper; for doctorate, comprehensive exam, thesis/dissertation. *Entrance requirements:* For doctorate, MAT. Electronic applications accepted. *Expenses:* Contact institution. *Faculty research:* Spirituality and spiritual direction, pastoral care and counseling, adult family and community, growth and young adult.

Gardner-Webb University, School of Divinity, Boiling Springs, NC 28017. Offers biblical studies (M Div); Christian education and formation (M Div); ministry (D Min); missiology (M Div); pastoral care and counseling (M Div); pastoral studies (M Div); M Div/MA; M Div/MBA. *Accreditation:* ACIPE; ATS. Part-time programs available. *Degree requirements:* For M Div, 2 foreign languages. *Entrance requirements:* For M Div, minimum GPA of 2.0; for doctorate, minimum GPA of 2.75. *Application deadline:* For fall admission, 8/1 priority date for domestic students; for spring admission, 12/15 priority date for domestic students. Applications are processed on a rolling basis. Application fee: $25. *Expenses:* Contact institution. *Financial support:* Fellowships, institutionally sponsored loans and unspecified assistantships available. Support available to part-time students. Financial award application deadline: 5/15. *Faculty research:* Jewish Christian dialogue, Islam. *Unit head:* Dr. Robert W. Canoy, Dean, 704-406-4400, Fax: 704-406-3935, E-mail: rcanoy@gardner-webb.edu. *Application contact:* Jeremy Fern, Director of Admissions, 704-406-3205, Fax: 704-406-3935, E-mail: jfern@gardner-webb.edu.

Garrett-Evangelical Theological Seminary, Graduate and Professional Programs, Evanston, IL 60201-3298. Offers Bible and culture (PhD); Christian education (MA); Christian education and congregational studies (PhD); contemporary theology and culture (PhD); divinity (M Div); ethics, church, and society (MA); liturgical studies (PhD); ministry (D Min); music ministry (MA); pastoral care and counseling (MA); pastoral theology, personality, and culture (PhD); spiritual formation and evangelism (MA); theological studies (MTS); M Div/MSW. *Accreditation:* ACIPE; ATS (one or more programs are accredited). Part-time programs available. *Degree requirements:* For master's, thesis (for some programs); for doctorate, thesis/dissertation. *Entrance requirements:* For doctorate, GRE (PhD). Additional exam requirements/recommendations for international students: Required—TOEFL (minimum score 560 paper-based; 230 computer-based). Electronic applications accepted.

Georgian Court University, School of Arts and Humanities, Lakewood, NJ 08701-2697. Offers Catholic school leadership (Certificate); parish business management (Certificate); pastoral administration (Certificate); pastoral ministry (Certificate); religious education (Certificate); theology (MA, Certificate). Part-time and evening/weekend programs available. *Faculty:* 3 full-time (2 women), 1 (woman) part-time/adjunct. *Students:* 57 part-time (39 women); includes 8 minority (3 African Americans, 1 Asian American or Pacific Islander, 4 Hispanic Americans). Average age 52. 20 applicants, 100% accepted, 14 enrolled. In 2009, 6 master's awarded. *Degree requirements:* For master's, thesis (for some programs). *Entrance requirements:* For master's, 3 letters of recommendation. Additional exam requirements/recommendations for international students: Required—TOEFL (minimum score 550 paper-based; 213 computer-based). *Application deadline:* For fall admission, 8/1 priority date for domestic students, 4/1 for international students; for spring admission, 1/1 priority date for domestic students, 7/1 for international students. Applications are processed on a rolling basis. Application fee: $40. Electronic applications accepted. *Expenses:* Tuition: Full-time $12,510; part-time $695 per credit. Required fees: $416 per year. Tuition and fees vary according to campus/location. *Financial support:* Scholarships/grants, health care benefits, and unspecified assistantships available. Financial award application deadline: 4/15; financial award applicants required to submit FAFSA. *Unit head:* Dr. Linda James, Dean, 732-987-2617, Fax: 732-987-2007. *Application contact:* Eugene Soltys, Director of Graduate Admissions, 732-987-2770, Fax: 732-987-2084, E-mail: graduateadmissions@georgian.edu.

Global University, Graduate School of Theology, Springfield, MO 65804. Offers biblical studies (MA); divinity (M Div); ministerial studies (MA), including education, leadership, missions, New Testament, Old Testament. Part-time and evening/weekend programs available. Postbaccalaureate distance learning degree programs offered (no on-campus study). *Degree requirements:* For master's, thesis (for some programs). *Entrance requirements:* For M Div, minimum undergraduate GPA of 3.0; for master's, minimum undergraduate GPA of 3.0, 15 undergraduate credit hours of course work in Bible or theology. Electronic applications accepted. *Faculty research:* Higher education, cross-cultural missions.

Grand Rapids Theological Seminary of Cornerstone University, Graduate Programs, Grand Rapids, MI 49525-5897. Offers biblical counseling (MA); Biblical counseling (M Div); chaplaincy (M Div); Christian education (M Div, MA); intercultural studies (M Div, MA); New Testament (MA, Th M); Old Testament (MA, Th M); pastoral studies (M Div); systematic theology (MA); theology (Th M). *Accreditation:* ATS. Part-time programs available. Postbaccalaureate distance learning degree programs offered (minimal on-campus study). *Entrance requirements:* Additional exam requirements/recommendations for international students: Required—TOEFL (minimum score 577 paper-based; 233 computer-based; 90 iBT). Electronic applications accepted.

Religious Education

Gratz College, Graduate Programs, Program in Jewish Education, Melrose Park, PA 19027. Offers MA, Ed D, Certificate, MA/MA. Part-time and evening/weekend programs available. Postbaccalaureate distance learning degree programs offered. *Degree requirements:* For master's, one foreign language, internship. *Entrance requirements:* For master's, interview.

Hebrew College, Shoolman Graduate School of Education, Newton Centre, MA 02459. Offers early childhood Jewish education (Certificate); Jewish day school education (Certificate); Jewish education (MJ Ed); Jewish family education (Certificate); Jewish special education (Certificate); Jewish youth education, informal education and camping (Certificate). Part-time and evening/weekend programs available. Postbaccalaureate distance learning degree programs offered. *Degree requirements:* For master's, one foreign language. *Entrance requirements:* For master's, GRE, interview. Additional exam requirements/recommendations for international students: Required—TOEFL.

Hebrew Union College–Jewish Institute of Religion, Rhea Hirsch School of Education, Los Angeles, CA 90007-3796. Offers day school teaching: California state teaching credential (Certificate); Jewish education (MAJE, PhD); MAJCS/MAJE. Terminal master's awarded for partial completion of doctoral program. *Degree requirements:* For master's, one foreign language, thesis or alternative, Hebrew; for doctorate, one foreign language, thesis/dissertation, Hebrew. *Entrance requirements:* For master's, GRE General Test, Hebrew, interview, minimum undergraduate GPA of 3.0; for doctorate, GRE General Test, interview, knowledge of Hebrew, minimum GPA of 3.0. Additional exam requirements/recommendations for international students: Required—TOEFL (minimum score 550 paper-based). Electronic applications accepted.

Hebrew Union College–Jewish Institute of Religion, School of Education, New York, NY 10012-1186. Offers MARE. Part-time programs available. *Degree requirements:* For master's, one foreign language, thesis. *Entrance requirements:* For master's, GRE, minimum 2 years of college-level Hebrew.

Inter American University of Puerto Rico, Metropolitan Campus, Graduate Programs, Program in Christian Education, San Juan, PR 00919-1293. Offers PhD.

The Jewish Theological Seminary, William Davidson Graduate School of Jewish Education, New York, NY 10027-4649. Offers MA, Ed D. Offered in conjunction with Rabbinical School; H. L. Miller Cantorial School and College of Jewish Music; Teacher's College, Columbia University; and Union Theological Seminary. Part-time programs available. Postbaccalaureate distance learning degree programs offered (minimal on-campus study). *Degree requirements:* For master's, one foreign language, thesis optional; for doctorate, one foreign language, comprehensive exam, thesis/dissertation. *Entrance requirements:* For master's, GRE or MAT, 3 letters of recommendation; for doctorate, GRE or MAT, writing sample, 3 letters of recommendation. *Expenses:* Tuition: Full-time $21,200; part-time $1000 per credit. Required fees: $400 per semester. Tuition and fees vary according to degree level.

See Close-Up on page 1355.

Jewish University of America, Graduate School, Program in Jewish Education, Skokie, IL 60077-3248. Offers MJ Ed, DJ Ed. *Degree requirements:* For master's, thesis optional; for doctorate, one foreign language, thesis/dissertation. *Entrance requirements:* For master's and doctorate, interview.

Lancaster Theological Seminary, Graduate and Professional Programs, Lancaster, PA 17603-2812. Offers biblical studies (MAR); Christian education (MAR); Christianity and the arts (MAR); church history (MAR); congregational life (MAR); lay leadership (Certificate); theological studies (M Div); theology (D Min); theology and ethics (MAR). *Accreditation:* ACIPE; ATS. *Faculty:* 11 full-time (4 women), 13 part-time/adjunct (9 women). *Students:* 91 full-time (48 women), 42 part-time (33 women). *Degree requirements:* For doctorate, thesis/dissertation; for M Div, one foreign language. *Application deadline:* For fall admission, 4/1 priority date for domestic students, 1/1 for international students; for spring admission, 11/15 priority date for domestic students. Applications are processed on a rolling basis. Application fee: $50. *Expenses:* Tuition: Full-time $12,600; part-time $490 per credit. Required fees: $125 per semester. One-time fee: $3000. Tuition and fees vary according to program and student level. *Financial support:* Career-related internships or fieldwork, scholarships/grants, and tuition waivers (partial) available. Financial award application deadline: 4/15; financial award applicants required to submit FAFSA. *Unit head:* Dr. Edwin D. Aponte, Vice President of Academic Affairs and Dean of the Seminary, 717-290-8754, Fax: 717-393-0423, E-mail: eaponte@lancasterseminary.edu. *Application contact:* Virginia Whitaker-Brooks, Assistant Director of Recruitment and Admissions, 717-290-8741, Fax: 717-393-0423.

La Sierra University, School of Religion, Riverside, CA 92515. Offers pastoral ministry (M Div); religion (MA); religious education (MA); religious studies (MA). *Accreditation:* ATS. Part-time programs available. *Degree requirements:* For master's, one foreign language, thesis or alternative. *Entrance requirements:* For master's, GRE General Test, minimum GPA of 3.0.

Laura and Alvin Siegal College of Judaic Studies, Graduate Programs, Program in Religious Education, Beachwood, OH 44122-7116. Offers Jewish education (MAJS); Judaic studies (MAJS). Part-time and evening/weekend programs available. Postbaccalaureate distance learning degree programs offered (minimal on-campus study). *Degree requirements:* For master's, one foreign language, thesis. *Entrance requirements:* For master's, interview.

Lincoln Christian Seminary, Graduate and Professional Programs, Lincoln, IL 62656-2167. Offers Bible and theology (MA); Christian ministries (MA); counseling (MA); divinity (M Div); leadership ministry (D Min); religious education (MRE). *Accreditation:* ACIPE; ATS. Part-time programs available. *Degree requirements:* For master's, 2 foreign languages, thesis; for doctorate, thesis/dissertation; for M Div, 2 foreign languages. *Entrance requirements:* For M Div and master's, minimum GPA of 2.5; for doctorate, M Div or equivalent. Additional exam requirements/recommendations for international students: Required—TOEFL (minimum score 550 paper-based; 213 computer-based). Electronic applications accepted.

Loyola Marymount University, School of Education, Department of Educational Support Services, Program in Catholic Inclusive Education, Los Angeles, CA 90045. Offers MA. Part-time programs available. *Faculty:* 9 full-time (6 women), 22 part-time/adjunct (19 women). *Students:* 6 full-time (all women), 12 part-time (all women); includes 8 minority (1 African American, 1 Asian American or Pacific Islander, 6 Hispanic Americans). Average age 40. 2 applicants, 100% accepted, 1 enrolled. In 2009, 15 master's awarded. *Degree requirements:* For master's, comprehensive exam. *Entrance requirements:* For master's, CBEST, CSET, full-time employment in Archdiocese of Los Angeles, 2 letters of recommendation. Additional exam requirements/recommendations for international students: Required—TOEFL (minimum score 600 paper-based; 250 computer-based; 100 iBT). *Application deadline:* For fall admission, 5/15 for domestic students; for spring admission, 11/15 for domestic students. Application fee: $50. Electronic applications accepted. *Financial support:* In 2009–10, 18 students received support. Scholarships/grants and unspecified assistantships available. Support available to part-time students. Financial award application deadline: 5/15; financial award applicants required to submit FAFSA. Total annual research expenditures: $5,992. *Unit head:* Dr. Tom Batsis, Chair, 310-338-7303, E-mail: tbatsis@lmu.edu. *Application contact:* Chake H. Kouyoumjian, Associate Dean of Graduate Studies, 310-338-2721, Fax: 310-338-6086, E-mail: ckouyoum@lmu.edu.

Loyola University Chicago, Institute of Pastoral Studies, Program in Religious Education, Chicago, IL 60660. Offers MA, Certificate. *Students:* 7 full-time (5 women), 4 part-time (all women); includes 2 minority (1 African American, 1 Hispanic American). Average age 41. 3 applicants, 67% accepted, 2 enrolled. In 2009, 4 master's awarded. *Application deadline:* Applications are processed on a rolling basis. Application fee: $50. *Expenses:* Tuition: Full-time $14,220; part-time $790 per credit hour. Required fees: $60 per semester hour. Tuition and fees vary according to program. *Financial support:* Application deadline: 3/1. *Unit head:* Eileen Daily, Program Director, 312-915-7477, E-mail: edaily@luc.edu. *Application contact:* Randy Gibbons, Administrative Assistant, 312-915-7450, Fax: 312-915-7410, E-mail: rgibbon@luc.edu.

Luther Rice University, Graduate Programs, Lithonia, GA 30038-2454. Offers Bible/theology (M Div); Christian education (M Div); Christian studies (MA); church ministry (D Min); counseling (M Div); discipleship counseling (MA); ministry (M Div, MA); missions/evangelism (M Div). Part-time programs available. Postbaccalaureate distance learning degree programs offered (no on-campus study). *Degree requirements:* For doctorate, thesis/dissertation. *Entrance requirements:* Additional exam requirements/recommendations for international students: Required—TOEFL (minimum score 500 paper-based; 173 computer-based).

Maple Springs Baptist Bible College and Seminary, Graduate and Professional Programs, Capitol Heights, MD 20743. Offers biblical studies (MA, Certificate); Christian counseling (MA); church administration (MA); divinity (M Div); ministry (D Min); religious education (MRE).

Michigan Theological Seminary, Graduate Programs, Plymouth, MI 48170. Offers Bible (Graduate Certificate); Christian education (MA); counseling psychology (MA); divinity (M Div); theological studies (MA). *Accreditation:* ATS. Part-time and evening/weekend programs available. *Degree requirements:* For master's, one foreign language, thesis; for M Div, 2 foreign languages. *Faculty research:* Judaism, cults, world religions.

Midwestern Baptist Theological Seminary, Graduate and Professional Programs, Kansas City, MO 64118-4697. Offers Biblical archaeology (MA); Biblical languages (MA); Christian education (M Div, MACE); Christian foundations—lay ministry (Graduate Certificate); collegiate ministries (M Div); counseling (MA); educational ministry (D Ed Min); international church planting (M Div); ministry (M Div, D Min); North American church planting (M Div); sacred music (MCM); urban ministry (M Div); worship leadership (M Div); youth ministry (M Div). *Accreditation:* ATS. Part-time programs available. Postbaccalaureate distance learning degree programs offered (minimal on-campus study). *Degree requirements:* For doctorate, thesis/dissertation; for M Div, 2 foreign languages. *Entrance requirements:* For doctorate, MAT. Electronic applications accepted. *Faculty research:* Ministerial studies, Biblical and theological studies, missions, counseling.

Nazarene Theological Seminary, Graduate and Professional Programs, Kansas City, MO 64131-1263. Offers Christian education (MA); intercultural studies (MA); theological studies (MA); theology (M Div, D Min). *Accreditation:* ACIPE; ATS. Part-time programs available. *Faculty:* 19 full-time (3 women), 12 part-time/adjunct (2 women). *Students:* 136 full-time (32 women), 118 part-time (32 women); includes 21 minority (5 African Americans, 1 American Indian/Alaska Native, 7 Asian Americans or Pacific Islanders, 8 Hispanic Americans), 14 international. Average age 31. 129 applicants, 77% accepted, 71 enrolled. In 2009, 40 first professional degrees, 22 master's, 2 doctorates awarded. *Degree requirements:* For master's, comprehensive exam (for some programs), thesis (for some programs); for doctorate, thesis/dissertation. *Entrance requirements:* Additional exam requirements/recommendations for international students: Required—TOEFL. *Application deadline:* For fall admission, 3/1 priority date for domestic and international students; for spring admission, 10/1 priority date for domestic and international students. Applications are processed on a rolling basis. Application fee: $25 ($200 for international students). Electronic applications accepted. *Financial support:* In 2009–10, 235 students received support, including 15 teaching assistantships (averaging $1,400 per year); institutionally sponsored loans and scholarships/grants also available. Support available to part-time students. Financial award application deadline: 3/1; financial award applicants required to submit FAFSA. *Unit head:* Dr. Roger L. Hahn, Dean of the Faculty, 816-268-5412, Fax: 816-268-5500, E-mail: rlhahn@nts.edu. *Application contact:* Jay A. Sandbloom, Director of Admissions, 816-268-5451, Fax: 816-268-5500, E-mail: jasandbloom@nts.edu.

Newman Theological College, Religious Education Program, Edmonton, AB T6V 1H3, Canada. Offers Catholic school administration (CCSA); religious education (MRE, GDRE). Part-time programs available. Postbaccalaureate distance learning degree programs offered (no on-campus study). *Degree requirements:* For master's, thesis or alternative. *Entrance requirements:* For master's, 2 years of successful teaching experience, graduate diploma in religious education; for other advanced degree, bachelor's degree in education, teaching certificate. Additional exam requirements/recommendations for international students: Required—TOEFL (minimum score 560 paper-based; 220 computer-based). Tuition and fees charges are reported in Canadian dollars. *Expenses:* Tuition: Full-time $5150 Canadian dollars; part-time $515 Canadian dollars per course. Required fees: $40 Canadian dollars per semester. Tuition and fees vary according to course level, course load, campus/location and program.

New Orleans Baptist Theological Seminary, Graduate and Professional Programs, Division of Christian Education Ministries, New Orleans, LA 70126-4858. Offers Christian education (M Div, MACE, D Min, DEM, PhD). Evening/weekend programs available. *Degree requirements:* For doctorate, thesis/dissertation; for M Div, project report. *Entrance requirements:* For doctorate, GRE General Test.

The Nigerian Baptist Theological Seminary, Graduate Studies, Ogbomoso, Nigeria. Offers church music (M Div, M Th, Diploma); divinity (M Div); ministry (D Min); religious education (M Div, M Th, PhD); theological studies (MATS); theology (M Th, PhD). Part-time programs available. *Degree requirements:* For master's, thesis, 2 Nigerian languages; for M Div, thesis/dissertation (for some programs), 2 biblical languages; for Diploma, thesis or alternative.

Oral Roberts University, School of Theology and Missions, Tulsa, OK 74171. Offers biblical literature (MA), including advanced languages, Judaic-Christian studies; Christian counseling (MA), including marriage and family therapy; divinity (M Div); missions (MA); practical theology (MA); theological/historical studies (MA); theology (D Min). *Accreditation:* ATS; NASM. Part-time programs available. Postbaccalaureate distance learning degree programs offered (minimal on-campus study). *Faculty:* 17 full-time (2 women). *Students:* 371 full-time (156 women), 110 part-time (65 women); includes 177 minority (127 African Americans, 5 American Indian/Alaska Native, 20 Asian Americans or Pacific Islanders, 25 Hispanic Americans), 82 international. Average age 36. 159 applicants, 95% accepted, 124 enrolled. In 2009, 38 first professional degrees, 52 master's, 10 doctorates awarded. *Degree requirements:* For master's, thesis (for some programs), practicum/internship; for doctorate, thesis/dissertation, applied research project; for M Div, one foreign language, field experience. *Entrance requirements:* For M Div and master's, GRE General Test or MAT, minimum GPA of 2.5; for doctorate, M Div, minimum GPA of 3.0, 3 years of full-time ministry experience. Additional exam requirements/recommendations for international students: Required—TOEFL (minimum score 550 paper-based; 213 computer-based; 79 iBT). *Application deadline:* For fall admission, 7/1 priority date for domestic and international students; for spring admission, 12/1 priority date for domestic students, 10/1 priority date for international students. Applications are processed on a rolling basis. Application fee: $35. Electronic applications accepted. *Financial support:* In 2009–10, teaching assistantships (averaging $3,600 per year); scholarships/grants and employment assistantships also available. Financial award application deadline: 6/1; financial award applicants required to submit FAFSA. *Unit head:* Dr. Thomson K. Mathew, Dean, 918-495-7016, Fax: 918-495-6259, E-mail: tmathew@oru.edu. *Application contact:* Debra E. Watkins, Graduate Theology Representative, 918-495-6618, Fax: 918-495-6725, E-mail: dwatkins@oru.edu.

Pfeiffer University, School of Religion and Christian Education, Misenheimer, NC 28109-0960. Offers MACE. Part-time and evening/weekend programs available. *Entrance requirements:* For master's, minimum GPA of 2.75.

Phillips Theological Seminary, Programs in Theology, Tulsa, OK 74116. Offers administration of church agencies (M Div); campus ministry (M Div); church-related social work (M Div); college and seminary teaching (M Div); global mission work (M Div); institutional chaplaincy (M Div); ministerial vocations in Christian education (M Div); ministry (D Min), including parish ministry, pastoral counseling, practices of ministry; ministry and culture (MAMC), including Christian education, congregational leadership, history and practice of Christian spirituality, theology, ethics, and culture; ministry of music (M Div); pastoral care and counseling (M Div); pastoral ministry (M Div); theological studies (MTS). *Accreditation:* ATS. Part-time programs available. Postbaccalaureate distance learning degree programs offered (minimal on-campus study). *Degree requirements:* For master's, thesis (for some programs); for doctorate, thesis/dissertation. *Entrance requirements:* For master's, minimum GPA of 2.5; for doctorate, M Div,

minimum GPA of 3.0. *Faculty research:* Biblical studies, historical studies, theology and culture, practical theology, theology and film.

Pontifical Catholic University of Puerto Rico, College of Education, Program in Religious Education, Ponce, PR 00717-0777. Offers MRE.

Providence College and Theological Seminary, Theological Seminary, Otterburne, MB R0A 1G0, Canada. Offers children's ministry (Certificate); Christian studies (MA, Certificate); counseling (MA); cross-cultural discipleship (Certificate); divinity (M Div); educational studies (MA), including counseling psychology, educational ministries, student development, teaching English to speakers of other languages, training teachers of English to speakers of other languages; global studies (MA); lay counseling (Diploma); ministry (D Min); teaching English to speakers of other languages (Certificate); theological studies (MA); training teacher of English to speakers of other languages (Certificate); youth ministry (Certificate). *Accreditation:* ATS. Part-time programs available. *Degree requirements:* For master's, variable foreign language requirement, thesis (for some programs); for doctorate, thesis/dissertation; for M Div, 2 foreign languages, comprehensive exam, thesis/dissertation (for some programs). *Entrance requirements:* Additional exam requirements/recommendations for international students: Recommended—TOEFL (minimum score 550 paper-based; 213 computer-based). *Faculty research:* Studies in Isaiah, theology of sin.

Reformed Theological Seminary–Jackson Campus, Graduate and Professional Programs, Jackson, MS 39209-3099. Offers Bible, theology, and missions (Certificate); biblical studies (MA); Christian education (M Div, MA); counseling (M Div); divinity (M Div, Diploma); marriage and family therapy (MA); ministry (D Min); missions (M Div, MA, D Min); New Testament (Th M); Old Testament (Th M); theological studies (MA); theology (Th M); M Div/MA. *Accreditation:* AAMFT/COAMFTE (one or more programs are accredited); ATS (one or more programs are accredited). *Degree requirements:* For master's, thesis (for some programs), fieldwork; for doctorate, 2 foreign languages, thesis/dissertation; for M Div, 2 foreign languages, thesis/dissertation (for some programs). *Entrance requirements:* For M Div and master's, minimum GPA of 2.6; for doctorate, minimum GPA of 3.0. Additional exam requirements/recommendations for international students: Required—TOEFL.

Regent University, Graduate School, School of Education, Virginia Beach, VA 23464-9800. Offers career switcher (M Ed); Christian school program (M Ed); cross-categorical special education (M Ed); education (M Ed, Ed D); education licensure (M Ed); educational leadership (M Ed); elementary education (M Ed); individualized degree plan (M Ed); leadership in character education (M Ed); master teacher (M Ed); mathematics education (M Ed); special education leadership (Ed S); student affairs (M Ed); TESOL (M Ed). *Accreditation:* Teacher Education Accreditation Council. Part-time and evening/weekend programs available. Postbaccalaureate distance learning degree programs offered (minimal on-campus study). *Faculty:* 26 full-time (13 women), 104 part-time/adjunct (78 women). *Students:* 141 full-time (116 women), 622 part-time (488 women); includes 218 minority (186 African Americans, 1 American Indian/Alaska Native, 10 Asian Americans or Pacific Islanders, 21 Hispanic Americans), 8 international. Average age 39. 509 applicants, 60% accepted, 176 enrolled. In 2009, 212 master's, 15 doctorates awarded. *Degree requirements:* For master's, thesis or alternative; for doctorate, comprehensive exam, thesis/dissertation. *Entrance requirements:* For master's, MAT, minimum undergraduate GPA of 2.75, writing sample, resume, recommendations, interview; for doctorate, GRE, writing sample, 3 years of relevant professional experience, master's-level paper, copies of published work, resume, transcripts, interview, recommendations. Additional exam requirements/recommendations for international students: Required—TOEFL (minimum score 577 paper-based; 233 computer-based). *Application deadline:* For fall admission, 4/1 priority date for domestic students; for spring admission, 10/15 priority date for domestic students. Applications are processed on a rolling basis. Application fee: $50. Electronic applications accepted. *Expenses:* Contact institution. *Financial support:* In 2009–10, 480 students received support; fellowships, career-related internships or fieldwork, scholarships/grants, tuition waivers (full and partial), and unspecified assistantships available. Support available to part-time students. Financial award application deadline: 4/1; financial award applicants required to submit FAFSA. *Faculty research:* Character development and discipline for children, education leadership development, diversity in schools, classroom management, technology in education settings. *Unit head:* Dr. Alan A. Arroyo, Dean, 757-352-4261, Fax: 757-352-4318, E-mail: alanarr@regent.edu. *Application contact:* Matthew Chadwick, Director of Admissions, 800-373-5504, Fax: 757-352-4381, E-mail: admissions@regent.edu.

Rochester College, Center for Missional Leadership, Rochester Hills, MI 48307-2764. Offers MRE.

St. Augustine's Seminary of Toronto, Graduate and Professional Programs, Scarborough, ON M1M 1M3, Canada. Offers divinity (M Div); lay ministry (Diploma); religious education (MRE); theological studies (MTS, Diploma). *Accreditation:* ATS. Part-time and evening/weekend programs available. *Degree requirements:* For M Div, comprehensive exam (for some programs), thesis/dissertation optional, field education. *Entrance requirements:* Course work in philosophy. Additional exam requirements/recommendations for international students: Required—TOEFL (minimum score 580 paper-based; 237 computer-based), TWE (minimum score 5).

Saint Mary's University of Minnesota, Schools of Graduate and Professional Programs, Graduate School of Education, Institute for LaSallian Studies, Winona, MN 55987-1399. Offers LaSallian leadership (MA); LaSallian studies (MA). *Unit head:* Dr. Roxanne Eubank, Director, 612-728-5217, E-mail: reubank@smumn.edu. *Application contact:* Yasin Alsaidi, Director of Admissions for Graduate and Professional Programs, 612-728-5207, Fax: 612-728-5121, E-mail: yalsaidi@smumn.edu.

St. Petersburg Theological Seminary, Graduate Programs, St. Petersburg, FL 33708. Offers Biblical studies (MA); counseling (MA); divinity (M Div); education (MA); Judaic studies (MA); ministry (MA, D Min); religious teacher (MA). Part-time and evening/weekend programs available. Postbaccalaureate distance learning degree programs offered (minimal on-campus study). *Degree requirements:* For master's, thesis; for doctorate, thesis/dissertation. *Entrance requirements:* For M Div, Bachelor degree; for doctorate, Master degree. Electronic applications accepted.

Saints Cyril and Methodius Seminary, Graduate and Professional Programs, Orchard Lake, MI 48324. Offers pastoral ministry (MAPM); religious education (MARE); theology (M Div, MA). *Accreditation:* ATS. Part-time programs available.

St. Vladimir's Orthodox Theological Seminary, Graduate School of Theology, Crestwood, NY 10707-1699. Offers general theological studies (MA); liturgical music (MA); religious education (MA); theology (M Div, M Th, D Min); M Div/MA. MA in general theological studies, M Div offered jointly with St. Nersess Seminary. *Accreditation:* ATS. Part-time programs available. *Degree requirements:* For master's, one foreign language, thesis, fieldwork; for doctorate, thesis/dissertation, fieldwork; for M Div, one foreign language, thesis/dissertation, fieldwork. *Entrance requirements:* For doctorate, M Div, minimum GPA of 3.0. Additional exam requirements/recommendations for international students: Required—TOEFL (minimum score 250 computer-based).

Shasta Bible College, Program in Biblical Counseling, Redding, CA 96002. Offers biblical counseling and Christian family life education (MA). Part-time programs available. *Degree requirements:* For master's, comprehensive exam (for some programs), thesis or alternative. *Entrance requirements:* For master's, minimum GPA of 2.5. Additional exam requirements/recommendations for international students: Required—TOEFL (minimum score 550 paper-based; 213 computer-based).

Southeastern Baptist Theological Seminary, Graduate and Professional Programs, Wake Forest, NC 27588-1889. Offers advanced biblical studies (M Div); Christian education (M Div, MACE); Christian ethics (PhD); Christian ministry (M Div); Christian planting (M Div); church music (MACM); counseling (MACO); evangelism (PhD); language (M Div); ministry (D Min); New Testament (PhD); Old Testament (PhD); philosophy (PhD); theology (Th M, PhD); women's studies (M Div). *Accreditation:* ACIPE; ATS (one or more programs are accredited). *Degree requirements:* For master's, thesis (for some programs), oral exam; for doctorate, thesis/dissertation, fieldwork; for M Div, supervised ministry. *Entrance requirements:* For master's, Cooperative English Test, minimum GPA of 2.0, M Div or equivalent (Th M); for doctorate, GRE General Test or MAT, Cooperative English Test, M Div or equivalent, 3 years of professional experience.

Southern Adventist University, School of Religion, Collegedale, TN 37315-0370. Offers Biblical and theological studies (MA); church leadership and management (M Min); church ministry and homiletics (M Min); evangelism and world mission (M Min); religious studies (MA). Part-time programs available. *Faculty:* 5 full-time (0 women). *Students:* 1 (woman) full-time, 1 part-time (0 women); includes 1 minority (African American). Average age 36. 2 applicants, 100% accepted, 2 enrolled. In 2009, 6 master's awarded. *Degree requirements:* For master's, comprehensive exam, thesis (for some programs). *Entrance requirements:* For master's, GRE. Additional exam requirements/recommendations for international students: Required—TOEFL (minimum score 600 paper-based; 250 computer-based). *Application deadline:* For spring admission, 5/1 priority date for domestic students, 4/30 for international students. Applications are processed on a rolling basis. Application fee: $25. *Expenses:* Tuition: Full-time $13,149; part-time $487 per credit hour. *Financial support:* Tuition waivers (full) available. Support available to part-time students. Financial award application deadline: 4/1; financial award applicants required to submit FAFSA. *Faculty research:* Biblical archaeology. *Unit head:* Dr. Greg A. King, Dean, 423-236-2975, Fax: 423-236-1976, E-mail: gking@southern.edu. *Application contact:* Susan L. Brown, Administrative Assistant, 423-236-2977, Fax: 423-236-1977, E-mail: sbrown@southern.edu.

Southern Baptist Theological Seminary, School of Leadership and Church Ministry, Louisville, KY 40280-0004. Offers advanced youth ministry (M Div); Christian education (M Div, MACE); leadership (Ed D); leadership and church ministry (PhD); ministry (D Ed Min); women's leadership (M Div); youth ministry (M Div, MAYM). Part-time programs available. Postbaccalaureate distance learning degree programs offered (minimal on-campus study). *Degree requirements:* For doctorate, thesis/dissertation; for M Div, 2 foreign languages. *Entrance requirements:* For doctorate, GRE General Test, interview, M Div or MACE. Additional exam requirements/recommendations for international students: Required—TWE. *Faculty research:* Gerontology, creative teaching methods, faith development in children, faith development in youth, transformational learning.

Southern Evangelical Seminary, Graduate School of Ministry and Missions, Matthews, NC 28105. Offers apologetics (Certificate); Christian education (MA); church ministry (MA, Certificate); divinity (Certificate), including apologetics (M Div, Certificate); Islamic studies (Certificate); theology (M Div), including apologetics (M Div, Certificate), Biblical studies; youth ministry (MA). Part-time and evening/weekend programs available. Postbaccalaureate distance learning degree programs offered. *Degree requirements:* For master's, thesis (for some programs); for M Div, one foreign language. *Entrance requirements:* Additional exam requirements/recommendations for international students: Required—TOEFL (minimum score 600 paper-based; 250 computer-based).

Southwestern Assemblies of God University, Thomas F. Harrison School of Graduate Studies, Program in Education, Waxahachie, TX 75165-5735. Offers Christian school administration (MS); curriculum development (MS); early education administration (M Ed); middle and secondary education (M Ed). *Degree requirements:* For master's, comprehensive written and oral exams. *Entrance requirements:* For master's, GRE General Test, minimum GPA of 2.5. Electronic applications accepted.

Southwestern Baptist Theological Seminary, School of Educational Ministries, Fort Worth, TX 76122-0000. Offers MA Comm, MACC, MACCM, MACE, MACSE, MAMFC, DEM, PhD, SPEM. Part-time and evening/weekend programs available. Terminal master's awarded for partial completion of doctoral program. *Degree requirements:* For master's, thesis; for doctorate, thesis/dissertation, statistics comprehensive exam. *Entrance requirements:* For doctorate, GRE or MAT, MACE or equivalent, minimum GPA of 3.0; for SPEM, 3 years of ministry experience after master's degree, MACE or equivalent. Additional exam requirements/recommendations for international students: Required—TOEFL, TWE. Electronic applications accepted.

Spertus Institute of Jewish Studies, Graduate Programs, Program in Jewish Education, Chicago, IL 60605-1901. Offers MAJ Ed. Part-time and evening/weekend programs available. *Degree requirements:* For master's, one foreign language, thesis. *Entrance requirements:* For master's, bachelor of arts in Jewish studies.

Teachers College, Columbia University, Graduate Faculty of Education, Department of Arts and Humanities, Program in Religion and Education, New York, NY 10027-6696. Offers Ed M, MA, Ed D. *Accreditation:* NCATE. *Students:* 3 part-time (2 women); includes 1 minority (Asian American or Pacific Islander), 1 international. Average age 48. In 2009, 1 doctorate awarded. *Degree requirements:* For doctorate, thesis/dissertation. *Application deadline:* For fall admission, 5/15 for domestic students; for spring admission, 12/1 for domestic students. Application fee: $65. *Financial support:* Career-related internships or fieldwork, Federal Work-Study, institutionally sponsored loans, and tuition waivers (full and partial) available. Support available to part-time students. Financial award application deadline: 2/1. *Faculty research:* Epistemology; science and education; Waldorf education; epistemological, cultural, and spiritual foundations of education. *Unit head:* Graeme Sullivan, Chair, 212-678-3799. *Application contact:* Mark E. Stearns, Associate Director of Admission, 212-678-3710, Fax: 212-678-4171.

Temple Baptist Seminary, Program in Theology, Chattanooga, TN 37404-3530. Offers biblical languages (M Div); Biblical studies (MABS); Christian education (MACE); English Bible û language tools (M Div); theology (MM, D Min). Part-time and evening/weekend programs available. Postbaccalaureate distance learning degree programs offered (minimal on-campus study). *Degree requirements:* For doctorate, thesis/dissertation; for M Div, proficiency in Greek and Hebrew. *Entrance requirements:* For doctorate, minimum GPA of 3.0, M Div.

Towson University, College of Graduate Studies and Research, Baltimore Hebrew Institute, Towson, MD 21252. Offers Jewish communal service (MAJCS); Jewish education (MAJE); Jewish studies (MAJS).

Trinity Baptist College, Graduate Programs, Jacksonville, FL 32221. Offers Bible (M Ed); Christian school administration (M Ed); classroom practices (M Ed); ministry (M Min); special education (M Ed). Postbaccalaureate distance learning degree programs offered. *Entrance requirements:* For master's, GRE (M Ed), 2 letters of recommendation; minimum GPA of 2.5 (M Min) or 3.0 (M Ed); computer proficiency.

Trinity International University, Trinity Evangelical Divinity School, Deerfield, IL 60015-1284. Offers Biblical and Near Eastern archaeology and languages (MA); Christian studies (MA, Certificate); Christian thought (MA); church history (MA, Th M); congregational ministry: pastor-teacher (M Div); congregational ministry: team ministry (M Div); counseling ministries (MA); counseling psychology (MA); cross-cultural ministry (M Div); educational studies (PhD); evangelism (MA); history of Christianity in America (MA); intercultural studies (MA, PhD); leadership and ministry management (D Min); military chaplaincy (D Min); ministry (MA); mission and evangelism (Th M); missions and evangelism (D Min); New Testament (MA, Th M); Old Testament (Th M); Old Testament and Semitic languages (MA); pastoral care (M Div); pastoral care and counseling (D Min); pastoral counseling and psychology (Th M); pastoral theology (Th M); philosophy of religion (MA); preaching (D Min); religion (MA); research ministry (M Div); systematic theology (Th M); theological studies (PhD); urban ministry (MA). *Accreditation:* ATS (one or more programs are accredited). Part-time programs available. Postbaccalaureate distance learning degree programs offered (minimal on-campus study). *Degree requirements:* For master's, comprehensive exam, thesis, fieldwork; for doctorate, comprehensive exam (for some programs), thesis/dissertation; for M Div, 2 foreign languages, fieldwork; for Certificate, comprehensive exam, integrative papers. *Entrance requirements:* For M Div, GRE, MAT; for master's, GRE, MAT, minimum cumulative undergraduate GPA of 3.0;

Religious Education

Trinity International University (continued)
for doctorate, GRE, minimum cumulative graduate GPA of 3.2; for Certificate, GRE, MAT, minimum undergraduate GPA of 2.5. Additional exam requirements/recommendations for international students: Required—TOEFL (minimum score 580 paper-based; 237 computer-based), TWE (minimum score 4). Electronic applications accepted.

Trinity Lutheran Seminary, Graduate and Professional Programs, Columbus, OH 43209-2334. Offers Christian education (MA); church music (MA); divinity (M Div); sacred theology (STM); theological studies (MTS); youth and family ministry (MA); MSN/MTS; MTS/JD. *Accreditation:* ACIPE; ATS. Part-time programs available. *Faculty:* 15 full-time (7 women), 10 part-time/adjunct (3 women). *Students:* 99 full-time (38 women), 44 part-time (18 women); includes 21 minority (15 African Americans, 4 Asian Americans or Pacific Islanders, 2 Hispanic Americans), 4 international. Average age 35. 71 applicants, 77% accepted, 49 enrolled. In 2009, 29 first professional degrees, 9 master's awarded. *Degree requirements:* For master's, comprehensive exam (for some programs), thesis (for some programs); for M Div, 2 foreign languages, internship. *Entrance requirements:* For master's, M Div or equivalent (STM). Additional exam requirements/recommendations for international students: Required—TOEFL (minimum score 500 paper-based; 173 computer-based; 61 iBT). *Application deadline:* For fall admission, 7/15 priority date for domestic and international students. Applications are processed on a rolling basis. Application fee: $25. *Expenses:* Tuition: Full-time $11,400; part-time $380 per semester hour. Required fees: $115 per semester. One-time fee: $150 full-time. *Financial support:* In 2009–10, 102 students received support. Career-related internships or fieldwork, Federal Work-Study, institutionally sponsored loans, and scholarships/grants available. Support available to part-time students. Financial award application deadline: 5/1; financial award applicants required to submit FAFSA. *Unit head:* Dr. James M. Childs, Interim Academic Dean, 614-235-4136, Fax: 614-384-4635, E-mail: jchilds@trinitylutheranseminary.edu. *Application contact:* Rev. Sheri L. Ayers, Director of Admissions, 614-235-4136 Ext. 4614, Fax: 866-610-8572, E-mail: sayers@trinitylutheranseminary.edu.

Union Theological Seminary and Presbyterian School of Christian Education, School of Christian Education, Richmond, VA 23227-4597. Offers MA, MATS, M Div/MA, M Div/MSW, MSW/MA. Part-time and evening/weekend programs available. Postbaccalaureate distance learning degree programs offered (minimal on-campus study). *Degree requirements:* For master's, oral and written exams. *Entrance requirements:* Additional exam requirements/recommendations for international students: Required—TOEFL (minimum score 550 paper-based; 213 computer-based), TWE (minimum score 4).

University of St. Michael's College, Faculty of Theology, Toronto, ON M5S 1J4, Canada. Offers Catholic leadership (MA); eastern Christian studies (Diploma); religious education (Diploma); theological studies (Diploma); theology (M Div, MA, MRE, MTS, D Min, PhD, Th D); theology and Jewish studies (MA). *Accreditation:* ATS (one or more programs are accredited). Part-time programs available. *Faculty:* 9 full-time (2 women), 23 part-time/adjunct (6 women). *Students:* 106 full-time (35 women), 98 part-time (59 women); includes 35 minority (13 African Americans, 21 Asian Americans or Pacific Islanders, 1 Hispanic American), 24 international. Average age 40. 72 applicants, 75% accepted, 44 enrolled. In 2009, 29 first professional degrees, 7 master's, 2 doctorates, 3 other advanced degrees awarded. *Degree requirements:* For master's, thesis (for some programs), 1 foreign language (MA), 2 foreign languages (Th M); for doctorate, 3 foreign languages, comprehensive exam, thesis/dissertation; for M Div, thesis/dissertation optional; for other advanced degree, thesis optional. *Entrance requirements:* For M Div and other advanced degree, minimum GPA of 2.7; for master's, M Div or BA, course work in an ancient or modern language, minimum GPA of 3.3; for doctorate, MA in theology, Th M, or M Div with thesis, minimum GPA of 3.7. Additional exam requirements/recommendations for international students: Required—TOEFL (minimum score 600 paper-based; 250 computer-based). *Application deadline:* For fall admission, 1/15 for domestic and international students. Applications are processed on a rolling basis. Application fee: $25 Canadian dollars. Electronic applications accepted. *Expenses:* Contact institution. *Financial support:* In 2009–10, 45 students received support, including fellowships with partial tuition reimbursements available (averaging $2,500 per year), research assistantships with partial tuition reimbursements available (averaging $2,400 per year), 4 teaching assistantships with partial tuition reimbursements available (averaging $2,400 per year); scholarships/grants, tuition waivers (partial), and bursaries also available. Financial award application deadline: 2/1. *Faculty research:* Patristics, eastern Christianity, ecology and theology, ecumenism, Jewish Christian studies. *Unit head:* Fr. Dr. Mario O. D'Souza, Dean, 416-926-7265, Fax: 416-926-7294, E-mail: mario.dsouza@utoronto.ca. *Application contact:* Allen Croxall, Student Recruitment and Advancement Officer, 416-926-1300 Ext. 3281, Fax: 416-926-7294, E-mail: allen.croxall@utoronto.ca.

University of St. Thomas, Graduate Studies, Saint Paul Seminary School of Divinity, Program in Theology/Pastoral Studies, St. Paul, MN 55105-1096. Offers religious education (MARE); theology (MA). *Accreditation:* ATS. Part-time and evening/weekend programs available. *Degree requirements:* For master's, one foreign language, comprehensive exam, thesis or alternative. *Entrance requirements:* For master's, GRE, interview, 3 letters of recommendation. Additional exam requirements/recommendations for international students: Required—TOEFL (minimum score 550 paper-based; 213 computer-based). Electronic applications accepted. *Expenses:* Contact institution. *Faculty research:* Theological education.

University of San Francisco, School of Education, Catholic Educational Leadership Program, San Francisco, CA 94117-1080. Offers Catholic school leadership (MA, Ed D); Catholic school teaching (MA). *Faculty:* 1 (woman) full-time, 3 part-time/adjunct (2 women). *Students:* 12 full-time (3 women), 21 part-time (8 women); includes 1 minority (Hispanic American), 2 international. Average age 42. 20 applicants, 65% accepted, 4 enrolled. In 2009, 13 master's, 2 doctorates awarded. *Degree requirements:* For doctorate, thesis/dissertation. Application fee: $55 ($65 for international students). *Expenses:* Tuition: Full-time $19,710; part-time $1095 per unit. Part-time tuition and fees vary according to degree level, campus/location and program. *Financial support:* In 2009–10, 6 students received support; fellowships, research assistantships, teaching assistantships available. Financial award application deadline: 3/2; financial award applicants required to submit FAFSA. *Unit head:* Br. Ray Vercruysse, Chair, 415-422-6226. *Application contact:* Beth Teague, Associate Director of Graduate Outreach, 415-422-5467, E-mail: schoolofeducation@usfca.edu.

Wesley Biblical Seminary, Graduate Programs, Jackson, MS 39206. Offers apologetics (MA); Biblical studies (MA); Christian studies (MA); evangelism (M Div); family life ministry (M Div); honors research (M Div); missions (M Div); pastoral ministry (M Div); teaching (M Div); theological studies (MA). *Accreditation:* ATS. Part-time programs available. *Faculty:* 11 full-time (2 women), 5 part-time/adjunct (0 women). *Students:* 43 full-time (5 women), 89 part-time (33 women). *Degree requirements:* For master's, thesis. *Entrance requirements:* Additional exam requirements/recommendations for international students: Required—TOEFL. *Application deadline:* For fall admission, 7/1 priority date for domestic students; for spring admission, 12/1 priority date for domestic students. Applications are processed on a rolling basis. Application fee: $40. Electronic applications accepted. *Expenses:* Tuition: Full-time $8000; part-time $320 per credit hour. Required fees: $310; $160 per semester. Tuition and fees vary according to course load, campus/location and program. *Financial support:* Scholarships/grants available. Support available to part-time students. *Faculty research:* Patristics, missiology, culture, hermeneutics. *Unit head:* Dr. Ray R. Easley, Vice President for Academic Affairs, 601-366-8880 Ext. 112, Fax: 601-366-8832. *Application contact:* Laura McMillan, Assistant to the Vice President for Business and Student Development, 601-366-8880 Ext. 110, Fax: 601-366-8832, E-mail: admissions@wbs.edu.

Wheaton College, Graduate School, Department of Christian Formation and Ministry, Wheaton, IL 60187-5593. Offers MA. Part-time programs available. *Degree requirements:* For master's, thesis or alternative. *Entrance requirements:* For master's, GRE General Test or MAT. Electronic applications accepted.

Xavier University, College of Arts and Sciences, Department of Theology, Cincinnati, OH 45207. Offers theology (MA), including religious education, social and pastoral ministry, theology. Part-time programs available. *Faculty:* 7 full-time (2 women). *Students:* 5 full-time (2 women), 23 part-time (10 women); includes 1 minority (Hispanic American). Average age 33. 11 applicants, 100% accepted, 11 enrolled. In 2009, 5 master's awarded. *Degree requirements:* For master's, thesis optional, final paper and defense. *Entrance requirements:* For master's, MAT or GRE, letters of recommendation. Additional exam requirements/recommendations for international students: Required—TOEFL (minimum score 550 paper-based; 213 computer-based). *Application deadline:* Applications are processed on a rolling basis. Application fee: $35. Electronic applications accepted. *Expenses:* Tuition: Part-time $697 per credit hour. One-time fee: $35 part-time. *Financial support:* In 2009–10, 26 students received support. Scholarships/grants and unspecified assistantships available. Financial award applicants required to submit FAFSA. *Faculty research:* Scripture, ethics, constructive theology, historical theology. *Unit head:* Dr. Sarah Melcher, Chair, 513-745-2043, Fax: 513-745-3215, E-mail: melcher@xavier.edu. *Application contact:* Dr. Sarah Melcher, Chair, 513-745-2043, Fax: 513-745-3215, E-mail: melcher@xavier.edu.

Yeshiva University, Azrieli Graduate School of Jewish Education and Administration, New York, NY 10033-4391. Offers MS, Ed D, Specialist. Part-time and evening/weekend programs available. *Faculty:* 3 full-time (0 women), 11 part-time/adjunct (5 women). *Students:* 67 full-time (30 women), 136 part-time (52 women); includes 1 African American. Average age 25. 47 applicants, 83% accepted. In 2009, 46 master's, 4 doctorates, 2 other advanced degrees awarded. Terminal master's awarded for partial completion of doctoral program. *Degree requirements:* For master's, one foreign language, student teaching experience, comprehensive exam or thesis; for doctorate, one foreign language, comprehensive exam, thesis/dissertation, certifying exams, internship; for Specialist, one foreign language, comprehensive exam, certifying exams, internship. *Entrance requirements:* For master's, GRE General Test, BA in Jewish studies or equivalent; for doctorate and Specialist, GRE General Test, master's degree in Jewish education, 2 years of teaching experience. *Application deadline:* Applications are processed on a rolling basis. Application fee: $35. *Expenses:* Contact institution. *Financial support:* In 2009–10, 149 students received support, including 39 fellowships with full and partial tuition reimbursements available (averaging $2,500 per year); institutionally sponsored loans, scholarships/grants, and tuition waivers (partial) also available. Support available to part-time students. Financial award application deadline: 4/1. *Faculty research:* Social patterns of American and Israeli Jewish population, special education, adult education, technology in education, return to religious values. *Unit head:* Dr. Yitzchak S. Handel, Associate Dean, 212-340-7705, Fax: 212-340-7787. *Application contact:* Michael Kranzler, Associate Director of Admissions, 212-960-5277, Fax: 212-960-0086.

Science Education

Acadia University, Faculty of Professional Studies, School of Education, Program in Curriculum Studies, Wolfville, NS B4P 2R6, Canada. Offers cultural and media studies (M Ed); learning and technology (M Ed); science, math and technology (M Ed). Evening/weekend programs available. *Faculty:* 12 full-time (5 women). *Students:* 7 full-time (all women), 49 part-time (33 women). 61 applicants, 80% accepted. In 2009, 32 master's awarded. *Degree requirements:* For master's, thesis optional. *Entrance requirements:* For master's, B Ed or the equivalent, minimum B average in undergraduate course work, 2 years of teaching experience. Additional exam requirements/recommendations for international students: Required—TOEFL (minimum score 580 paper-based; 237 computer-based; 93 iBT), IELTS (minimum score 6.5). *Application deadline:* For fall admission, 3/15 priority date for domestic and international students. Applications are processed on a rolling basis. Application fee: $50. *Financial support:* Teaching assistantships available. Financial award application deadline: 3/15. *Faculty research:* Literacy development, postmodern philosophy and curriculum theory, historiography, philosophy of education, learning and technology. *Unit head:* Ann Vibert, Director, E-mail: ann.vibert@acadiau.ca. *Application contact:* Sheila Langille, Secretary, 902-585-1229, Fax: 902-585-1071, E-mail: sheila.langille@acadiau.ca.

Alabama State University, School of Graduate Studies, College of Education, Department of Curriculum and Instruction, Program in Secondary Education, Montgomery, AL 36101-0271. Offers biology education (M Ed, Ed S); English/language arts (M Ed); history education (M Ed, Ed S); mathematics education (M Ed); secondary education (Ed S); social studies (Ed S). Part-time programs available. *Degree requirements:* For master's, comprehensive exam; for Ed S, comprehensive exam, thesis. *Entrance requirements:* For master's, GRE General Test, MAT, graduate writing competency test; for Ed S, graduate writing competency test, GRE, MAT. Additional exam requirements/recommendations for international students: Required—TOEFL (minimum score 500 paper-based; 173 computer-based).

Albany State University, College of Natural Sciences, Program in Science Education, Albany, GA 31705-2717. Offers M Ed. *Accreditation:* NCATE. *Students:* 4 part-time (all women); includes 2 minority (both African Americans). Average age 32. 3 applicants, 100% accepted, 2 enrolled. In 2009, 1 master's awarded. *Degree requirements:* For master's, comprehensive exam. *Entrance requirements:* For master's, GRE General Test, MAT or NTE. Additional exam requirements/recommendations for international students: Required—TOEFL. *Application deadline:* For fall admission, 11/16 for domestic students, 9/16 for international students; for spring admission, 4/19 for domestic students, 2/19 for international students. Applications are processed on a rolling basis. Application fee: $20. Electronic applications accepted. *Expenses:* Tuition, state resident: full-time $2970; part-time $162 per credit hour. Tuition, nonresident: full-time $12,168; part-time $676 per credit hour. Required fees: $962; $75 per credit hour. *Financial support:* Application deadline: 6/30. *Unit head:* Dr. Louise Wrensford, Dean, 229-430-4823, Fax: 229-430-4765, E-mail: joyce.johnson@asurams.edu. *Application contact:* Nicole Lane, Interim Graduate Admissions Officer, 229-430-4862, Fax: 229-430-6398, E-mail: nicole.lane@asurams.edu.

Alverno College, School of Education, Milwaukee, WI 53234-3922. Offers adaptive education (MA); administrative leadership (MA); adult education and organizational development (MA); adult educational and instructional design (MA); adult educational and instructional technology (MA); global connections in the humanities (MA); instructional leadership (MA); instructional technology for K-12 settings (MA); professional development (MA); reading education (MA); reading education with adaptive education (MA); science education (MA); teaching in alternative schools (MA). *Accreditation:* NCATE. Part-time and evening/weekend programs available. *Faculty:* 10 full-time (all women), 17 part-time/adjunct (15 women). *Students:* 65 full-time (59 women), 82 part-time (75 women); includes 31 minority (24 African Americans, 1 American Indian/Alaska Native, 1 Asian American or Pacific Islander, 5 Hispanic Americans), 2 international. Average age 38. 113 applicants, 64% accepted, 61 enrolled. In 2009, 56 master's awarded. *Degree requirements:* For master's, presentation/defense of proposal, conference presentation

of inquiry projects. *Entrance requirements:* For master's, bachelor's degree in related field, communication samples from work setting, 3 letters of recommendation. Additional exam requirements/recommendations for international students: Required—TOEFL. *Application deadline:* For fall admission, 7/15 priority date for domestic and international students; for spring admission, 12/15 priority date for domestic and international students. Applications are processed on a rolling basis. Application fee: $50. Electronic applications accepted. *Financial support:* In 2009–10, 92 students received support. Federal Work-Study available. Support available to part-time students. Financial award application deadline: 4/15; financial award applicants required to submit FAFSA. *Faculty research:* Student self-assessment, self-reflection, integration of curriculum, identifying needs of students in strategic situations and designing appropriate classroom strategies. *Unit head:* Dr. Mary Diez, Graduate Dean, 414-382-6214, Fax: 414-382-6332, E-mail: mary.diez@alverno.edu. *Application contact:* Angela Peterson-Adams, Graduate Recruiter, 414-382-6104, Fax: 414-382-6354, E-mail: angela.peterson-adams@alverno.edu.

American University of Puerto Rico, Program in Education, Bayamón, PR 00960-2037. Offers art history (M Ed); elementary education (4-6) (M Ed); elementary education (k-3) (M Ed); general science education (M Ed); physical education (k-12) (M Ed); special education at secondary level (transition) (M Ed). *Faculty:* 1 full-time (0 women), 22 part-time/adjunct (6 women). *Students:* 121 full-time (98 women), 64 part-time (50 women); includes all Hispanic Americans. Average age 30. 250 applicants, 80% accepted, 185 enrolled. *Entrance requirements:* For master's, EXADEP or GRE or MAT, 2 letters of recommendation, minimum GPA of 2.5. *Application deadline:* For fall admission, 8/4 for domestic students; for winter admission, 10/18 for domestic students; for spring admission, 3/22 for domestic students. Applications are processed on a rolling basis. Application fee: $50. *Application contact:* Information Contact, E-mail: oficnaadmisiones@aupr.edu.

Andrews University, School of Graduate Studies, College of Arts and Sciences, Department of Biology, Berrien Springs, MI 49104. Offers MAT, MS. *Faculty:* 7 full-time (0 women). *Students:* 3 full-time (2 women), 1 (woman) part-time, 1 international. Average age 24. 8 applicants, 50% accepted, 2 enrolled. In 2009, 4 master's awarded. *Degree requirements:* For master's, comprehensive exam, thesis. *Entrance requirements:* For master's, GRE Subject Test. Additional exam requirements/recommendations for international students: Required—TOEFL (minimum score 550 paper-based). *Application deadline:* Applications are processed on a rolling basis. Application fee: $40. *Financial support:* Fellowships, research assistantships, teaching assistantships, career-related internships or fieldwork, Federal Work-Study, and institutionally sponsored loans available. Financial award application deadline: 3/15. *Unit head:* Dr. David A. Steen, Chairman, 269-471-3243. *Application contact:* Carolyn Hurst, Supervisor of Graduate Admission, 800-253-2874, Fax: 269-471-6321, E-mail: graduate@andrews.edu.

Andrews University, School of Graduate Studies, School of Education, Department of Teaching, Learning, and Curriculum, Berrien Springs, MI 49104. Offers curriculum and instruction (MA, Ed D, PhD, Ed S); elementary education (MAT); reading (MA); secondary education (MAT), including biology, education, English, English as a second language, French, history, physics; special education/learning disabilities (MS); teacher education (MAT). *Students:* 12 full-time (8 women), 30 part-time (19 women); includes 17 minority (14 African Americans, 1 Asian American or Pacific Islander, 2 Hispanic Americans), 10 international. Average age 43. 28 applicants, 54% accepted, 6 enrolled. In 2009, 11 master's, 4 doctorates, 1 other advanced degree awarded. *Entrance requirements:* For master's, GRE Subject Test. Additional exam requirements/recommendations for international students: Required—TOEFL (minimum score 550 paper-based). *Application deadline:* For fall admission, 8/15 for domestic students. Applications are processed on a rolling basis. Application fee: $40. *Unit head:* Dr. Lee C. Davidson, Chair, 269-471-6364. *Application contact:* Carolyn Hurst, Supervisor of Graduate Admission, 800-253-2874, Fax: 269-471-6321, E-mail: graduate@andrews.edu.

Antioch University New England, Graduate School, Department of Environmental Studies, Science Teacher Certification Program, Keene, NH 03431-3552. Offers MS. *Degree requirements:* For master's, practicum, seminar, student teaching.

Appalachian State University, Cratis D. Williams Graduate School, Department of Curriculum and Instruction, Boone, NC 28608. Offers curriculum specialist (MA); educational media (MA); elementary education (MA); middle grades education (MA), including language arts, mathematics, science, social studies. *Accreditation:* NCATE. Part-time and evening/weekend programs available. Postbaccalaureate distance learning degree programs offered (no on-campus study). *Faculty:* 32 full-time (22 women), 9 part-time/adjunct (3 women). *Students:* 16 full-time (12 women), 168 part-time (140 women); includes 2 minority (both African Americans), 1 international. 97 applicants, 99% accepted, 77 enrolled. In 2009, 78 master's awarded. *Degree requirements:* For master's, comprehensive exam, thesis or alternative. *Entrance requirements:* For master's, GRE General Test or MAT, 3 letters of recommendation. Additional exam requirements/recommendations for international students: Required—TOEFL (minimum score 570 paper-based; 230 computer-based; 79 iBT), IELTS (minimum score 6.5). *Application deadline:* For fall admission, 7/1 for domestic students, 2/1 for international students; for spring admission, 11/1 for domestic students, 7/1 for international students. Applications are processed on a rolling basis. Application fee: $50. Electronic applications accepted. *Expenses:* Tuition, state resident: full-time $2960. Tuition, nonresident: full-time $14,051. Required fees: $2320. *Financial support:* In 2009–10, 8 teaching assistantships (averaging $8,000 per year) were awarded; fellowships, research assistantships, career-related internships or fieldwork, Federal Work-Study, scholarships/grants, and unspecified assistantships also available. Financial award application deadline: 4/1; financial award applicants required to submit FAFSA. *Faculty research:* Media literacy, elementary teaching, curriculum development, online learning environments. Total annual research expenditures: $690,000. *Unit head:* Dr. Michael Jacobson, Chairperson, 828-262-2224. *Application contact:* Sandy Krause, Director of Admissions and Recruiting, 828-262-2130, Fax: 828-262-2709, E-mail: krausesl@appstate.edu.

Arcadia University, Graduate Studies, Department of Education, Glenside, PA 19038-3295. Offers art education (M Ed, MA Ed); biology education (MA Ed); chemistry education (MA Ed); child development (CAS); computer education (M Ed, CAS); computer education 7–12 (MA Ed); early childhood education (M Ed, CAS), including individualized (M Ed), master teacher (M Ed), research in child development (M Ed); educational leadership (M Ed, CAS); educational psychology (CAS); elementary education (M Ed, CAS); English education (MA Ed); environmental education (MA Ed, CAS); history education (MA Ed); language arts (M Ed, CAS); mathematics education (M Ed, MA Ed, CAS); music education (MA Ed); psychology (MA Ed); pupil personnel services (CAS); reading (M Ed, CAS); school library science (M Ed); science education (M Ed, CAS); secondary education (M Ed, CAS); special education (M Ed, Ed D, CAS); theater arts (MA Ed); written communication (MA Ed). *Accreditation:* NASAD. Part-time and evening/weekend programs available. Postbaccalaureate distance learning degree programs offered (minimal on-campus study). *Faculty:* 12 full-time (8 women), 38 part-time/adjunct (26 women). *Students:* 89 full-time (74 women), 622 part-time (487 women); includes 112 minority (94 African Americans, 9 Asian Americans or Pacific Islanders, 9 Hispanic Americans), 2 international. Average age 32. In 2009, 257 master's, 4 doctorates awarded. *Application deadline:* Applications are processed on a rolling basis. Application fee: $40. Electronic applications accepted. *Expenses:* Tuition: Full-time $30,450; part-time $620 per credit hour. Required fees: $165. Tuition and fees vary according to program. *Financial support:* Career-related internships or fieldwork, tuition waivers (partial), and unspecified assistantships available. *Unit head:* Dr. Steven P. Gulkus. *Application contact:* 215-572-2925, Fax: 215-572-2126, E-mail: grad@arcadia.edu.

Arkansas State University—Jonesboro, Graduate School, College of Sciences and Mathematics, Department of Biological Sciences, Jonesboro, State University, AR 72467. Offers biological sciences (MA); biology (MS); biology education (MSE, SCCT). Part-time programs available. *Faculty:* 14 full-time (4 women), 1 part-time/adjunct (0 women). *Students:* 22 full-time (7 women), 14 part-time (4 women); includes 1 minority (American Indian/Alaska Native), 12 international. Average age 27. 24 applicants, 75% accepted, 12 enrolled. In 2009, 5 master's awarded. *Degree requirements:* For master's, comprehensive exam, thesis (for some programs); for SCCT, comprehensive exam. *Entrance requirements:* For master's, GRE General Test, appropriate bachelor's degree, letters of reference, interview; for SCCT, GRE General Test or MAT, interview, master's degree, letters of reference, official transcript, personal statement, immunization records. Additional exam requirements/recommendations for international students: Required—TOEFL (minimum score 550 paper-based; 213 computer-based; 79 iBT), IELTS (minimum score 6). *Application deadline:* For fall admission, 7/1 for domestic and international students; for spring admission, 11/15 for domestic students, 11/13 for international students. Applications are processed on a rolling basis. Application fee: $30 ($40 for international students). Electronic applications accepted. *Expenses:* Tuition, state resident: full-time $3744; part-time $208 per credit hour. Tuition, nonresident: full-time $9540; part-time $530 per credit hour. Required fees: $896; $47 per credit hour. $25 per term. One-time fee: $50. Tuition and fees vary according to course load and program. *Financial support:* In 2009–10, 19 students received support; research assistantships, career-related internships or fieldwork, scholarships/grants, and unspecified assistantships available. Financial award application deadline: 7/1; financial award applicants required to submit FAFSA. *Unit head:* Dr. Stanley Trauth, Interim Chair, 870-972-3082, Fax: 870-972-2638, E-mail: strauth@astate.edu. *Application contact:* Dr. Andrew Sustich, Dean of the Graduate School, 870-972-3029, Fax: 870-972-3857, E-mail: sustich@astate.edu.

Arkansas State University—Jonesboro, Graduate School, College of Sciences and Mathematics, Department of Chemistry and Physics, Jonesboro, State University, AR 72467. Offers chemistry (MS); chemistry education (MSE, SCCT). Part-time programs available. *Faculty:* 8 full-time (3 women), 2 part-time/adjunct (1 woman). *Students:* 6 full-time (4 women), 8 part-time (4 women), 11 international. Average age 24. 11 applicants, 55% accepted, 3 enrolled. In 2009, 3 master's awarded. *Degree requirements:* For master's, comprehensive exam, thesis or alternative; for SCCT, comprehensive exam. *Entrance requirements:* For master's, GRE General Test or MAT, appropriate bachelor's degree; for SCCT, GRE General Test or MAT, interview, master's degree, official transcript, immunization records. Additional exam requirements/recommendations for international students: Required—TOEFL (minimum score 550 paper-based; 213 computer-based; 79 iBT), IELTS (minimum score 6). *Application deadline:* For fall admission, 7/1 for domestic and international students; for spring admission, 11/15 for domestic students, 11/13 for international students. Applications are processed on a rolling basis. Application fee: $30 ($40 for international students). Electronic applications accepted. *Expenses:* Tuition, state resident: full-time $3744; part-time $208 per credit hour. Tuition, nonresident: full-time $9540; part-time $530 per credit hour. Required fees: $896; $47 per credit hour. $25 per term. One-time fee: $50. Tuition and fees vary according to course load and program. *Financial support:* In 2009–10, 7 students received support; teaching assistantships, career-related internships or fieldwork, scholarships/grants, and unspecified assistantships available. Financial award application deadline: 7/1; financial award applicants required to submit FAFSA. *Unit head:* Dr. John Pratte, Chair, 870-972-3086, Fax: 870-972-3089, E-mail: jpratte@astate.edu. *Application contact:* Dr. Andrew Sustich, Dean of the Graduate School, 870-972-3029, Fax: 870-972-3857, E-mail: sustich@astate.edu.

Armstrong Atlantic State University, School of Graduate Studies, Program in Education, Savannah, GA 31419-1997. Offers adult education (M Ed); curriculum and instruction (M Ed); early childhood education (M Ed); education (M Ed); elementary education (M Ed); middle grades education (M Ed); secondary education (M Ed), including business education, English education, mathematics education, science education, social science education; special education (M Ed), including behavioral disorders, learning disabilities, speech-language pathology. *Accreditation:* NCATE. Part-time and evening/weekend programs available. Postbaccalaureate distance learning degree programs offered (minimal on-campus study). *Degree requirements:* For master's, comprehensive exam, portfolio. *Entrance requirements:* For master's, GRE General Test or MAT, minimum GPA of 2.5, letters of recommendation. Additional exam requirements/recommendations for international students: Required—TOEFL (minimum score 523 paper-based; 193 computer-based). Electronic applications accepted.

Asbury University, School of Graduate and Professional Studies, Wilmore, KY 40390-1198. Offers biology: alternative certificate (MA Ed); chemistry: alternative certificate (MA Ed); English (MA Ed); English as a second language (MA Ed); ESL (MA Ed); French (MA Ed); Latin: alternative certificate (MA Ed); mathematics: alternative certificate (MA Ed); reading/writing endorsement (MA Ed); social studies (MA Ed); social work (MSW), including child and family services; Spanish (MA Ed); special education (MA Ed); special education: alternative certificate (MA Ed); teacher as leader endorsement (MA Ed). *Accreditation:* NCATE. Part-time programs available. *Faculty:* 8 full-time (7 women), 9 part-time/adjunct (4 women). *Students:* 108 part-time (87 women); includes 8 minority (4 African Americans, 2 Asian Americans or Pacific Islanders, 2 Hispanic Americans). Average age 36. 36 applicants, 86% accepted, 24 enrolled. In 2009, 20 master's awarded. *Degree requirements:* For master's, action research project, portfolio. *Entrance requirements:* For master's, PRAXIS/NTE, minimum GPA of 2.75, letters of recommendation. Additional exam requirements/recommendations for international students: Required—TOEFL (minimum score 550 paper-based). *Application deadline:* Applications are processed on a rolling basis. Application fee: $25. Electronic applications accepted. *Financial support:* Scholarships/grants and traineeships available. Financial award applicants required to submit FAFSA. *Unit head:* Dr. Bonnie J. Banker, Dean, School of Graduate and Professional Studies, 859-858-3511 Ext. 2221, Fax: 859-858-3921, E-mail: bonnie.banker@asbury.edu. *Application contact:* Lenore A. Sweigard, Graduate Program Assistant and Certification Specialist, 859-858-3511 Ext. 2502, Fax: 859-858-3921, E-mail: graded@asbury.edu.

Auburn University, Graduate School, College of Education, Department of Curriculum and Teaching, Auburn University, AL 36849. Offers business education (M Ed, MS, PhD); early childhood education (M Ed, MS, PhD, Ed S); elementary education (M Ed, MS, PhD, Ed S); foreign languages (M Ed, MS); music education (M Ed, MS, PhD, Ed S); postsecondary education (PhD); reading education (PhD, Ed S); secondary education (M Ed, MS, PhD, Ed S), including English language arts, mathematics, science, social studies. *Accreditation:* NASM (one or more programs are accredited); NCATE. Part-time programs available. *Faculty:* 28 full-time (21 women), 8 part-time/adjunct (5 women). *Students:* 76 full-time (55 women), 186 part-time (139 women); includes 43 minority (29 African Americans, 1 American Indian/Alaska Native, 4 Asian Americans or Pacific Islanders, 9 Hispanic Americans), 4 international. Average age 33. 248 applicants, 65% accepted, 110 enrolled. In 2009, 102 master's, 12 doctorates, 6 other advanced degrees awarded. *Degree requirements:* For master's, thesis (for some programs); for doctorate, thesis/dissertation; for Ed S, field project. *Entrance requirements:* For master's, doctorate, and Ed S, GRE General Test. *Application deadline:* For fall admission, 7/7 for domestic students; for spring admission, 11/24 for domestic students. Applications are processed on a rolling basis. Application fee: $50 ($60 for international students). Electronic applications accepted. *Expenses:* Tuition, state resident: full-time $6240. Tuition, nonresident: full-time $18,720. International tuition: $18,938 full-time. Required fees: $492. Tuition and fees vary according to course load, program and reciprocity agreements. *Financial support:* Fellowships, teaching assistantships, career-related internships or fieldwork and Federal Work-Study available. Support available to part-time students. Financial award application deadline: 3/15; financial award applicants required to submit FAFSA. *Faculty research:* Emerging literacy, reading attitudes, music for at-risk youth, portfolio assessment. *Unit head:* Dr. Nancy H. Barry, Head, 334-844-4434. *Application contact:* Dr. George Flowers, Dean of the Graduate School, 334-844-2125.

Averett University, Master in Education Program, Danville, VA 24541-3692. Offers art education (M Ed); biology (M Ed); biology education (M Ed); chemistry (M Ed); chemistry education (M Ed); curriculum and instruction (M Ed); elementary education (M Ed); English (M Ed); English education (M Ed); health and physical education (M Ed); history and social studies education (M Ed); math (M Ed); mathematics education (M Ed); physical science (M Ed); reading specialization (M Ed); special education (learning disabilities specialization PK-12) (M Ed). Program also offered at Richmond, VA regional campus location. Part-time and evening/weekend programs available. *Faculty:* 4 full-time (3 women), 36 part-time/adjunct (22

Science Education

Averett University (continued)

women). *Students:* 182 full-time (160 women), 110 part-time (94 women); includes 113 minority (94 African Americans, 1 American Indian/Alaska Native, 7 Asian Americans or Pacific Islanders, 11 Hispanic Americans). Average age 37. 119 applicants, 99% accepted, 98 enrolled. In 2009, 92 master's awarded. *Degree requirements:* For master's, comprehensive exam, thesis optional. *Entrance requirements:* For master's, PRAXIS, GRE General Test, MAT or NTE, writing proficiency exam, 3 letters of recommendation, current teacher's licensure or eligibility for licensure, minimum undergraduate GPA of 3.0 in previous 2 years. Additional exam requirements/recommendations for international students: Required—TOEFL (minimum score 600 paper-based; 200 computer-based). *Application deadline:* Applications are processed on a rolling basis. *Expenses:* Contact institution. *Financial support:* Career-related internships or fieldwork, Federal Work-Study, and scholarships/grants available. Financial award application deadline: 4/1; financial award applicants required to submit FAFSA. *Faculty research:* Literary assessment-PreK-6, handwriting instruction and assessment-PreK-6, written language instruction and assessment-PreK-6 and special needs students learning styles, curriculum and instruction processes. *Unit head:* Dr. Lynn H. Wolf, Chair/Associate Professor/Director, 434-793-3995, Fax: 434-791-4392, E-mail: lynn.wolf@averett.edu. *Application contact:* Dr. Lynn H. Wolf, Chair/Associate Professor/Director, 434-793-3995, Fax: 434-791-4392, E-mail: lynn.wolf@averett.edu.

Ball State University, Graduate School, College of Sciences and Humanities, Department of Biology, Muncie, IN 47306-1099. Offers biology (MA, MAE, MS); biology education (Ed D). *Degree requirements:* For doctorate, thesis/dissertation. *Entrance requirements:* For master's, GRE General Test; for doctorate, GRE General Test, minimum graduate GPA of 3.2. *Faculty research:* Aquatics and fisheries, tumors, water and air pollution, developmental biology and genetics.

Belmont University, College of Arts and Sciences, School of Education, Nashville, TN 37212-3757. Offers education (M Ed); elementary education (MAT), including early childhood education, elementary education, language arts education; English (MAT); history (MAT); mathematics (MAT); middle grade education (MAT); science (MAT); secondary education (MAT); special education (MAT); sports administration (MSA). *Accreditation:* NCATE. Part-time and evening/weekend programs available. *Degree requirements:* For master's, comprehensive exam, thesis, culminating portfolio. *Entrance requirements:* For master's, MAT or GRE and/or LSAT or GMAT, minimum GPA of 2.75. Additional exam requirements/recommendations for international students: Required—TOEFL. *Expenses:* Contact institution. *Faculty research:* Improving secondary literacy, Montessori, classroom management strategies, teacher residency programs, online professional development, mentoring, leadership, sociological issues in sport, faculty development, coaching.

Bemidji State University, School of Graduate Studies, College of Social and Natural Sciences, Field of Science, Bemidji, MN 56601-2699. Offers MS. Part-time programs available. *Entrance requirements:* For master's, letters of recommendation. Additional exam requirements/recommendations for international students: Required—TOEFL. Electronic applications accepted. *Faculty research:* Science education, physical engineering.

Benedictine University, Graduate Programs, Program in Science Content and Process, Lisle, IL 60532-0900. Offers MSSCP. *Students:* 5 part-time (3 women). 12 applicants, 83% accepted, 8 enrolled. In 2009, 9 master's awarded. *Application deadline:* For fall admission, 9/1 for domestic students; for winter admission, 12/1 for domestic students; for spring admission, 2/15 for domestic students. Application fee: $40. *Expenses:* Tuition: Part-time $750 per credit hour. Tuition and fees vary according to campus/location and program. *Unit head:* Dr. John Mickus, Director, 630-829-6539. *Application contact:* Kari Gibbons, Director, Admissions, 630-829-6200, Fax: 630-829-6584, E-mail: kgibbons@ben.edu.

Bennington College, Graduate Programs, MA in Teaching Program, Bennington, VT 05201. Offers art education (MAT); early childhood (MAT); elementary education (MAT); English education (MAT); foreign language education (MAT); k-12 education (MAT); mathematics education (MAT); music education (MAT); science education (MAT); secondary education (MAT); social studies education (MAT); theater arts (MAT). *Faculty:* 5 part-time/adjunct (3 women). *Students:* 8 full-time (5 women), 1 part-time (0 women). Average age 28. 11 applicants, 27% accepted, 1 enrolled. In 2009, 4 master's awarded. *Degree requirements:* For master's, comprehensive exam, 1 year teaching practicum, professional portfolio. *Entrance requirements:* For master's, interview. *Application deadline:* For fall admission, 3/1 for domestic students. Application fee: $60. *Expenses:* Contact institution. *Financial support:* In 2009–10, 6 students received support, including 4 fellowships (averaging $10,475 per year); scholarships/grants and unspecified assistantships also available. Financial award application deadline: 4/1; financial award applicants required to submit FAFSA. *Unit head:* Carol Meyer, Director of Programs in Teacher Education, 802-440-4375, E-mail: cmeyer@bennington.edu. *Application contact:* Nancy Pearlman, Assistant Director of Programs in Teacher Education, 802-440-4710, Fax: 802-440-4383, E-mail: npearlman@bennington.edu.

Bethel University, Program in Education, McKenzie, TN 38201. Offers administration and supervision (MA Ed); biology education K8-12 (MAT); elementary education (MAT); English education K8-12 (MAT); history education K8-12 (MAT); physical education K8-12 (MAT); special education K8-12 (MAT). Part-time and evening/weekend programs available. *Degree requirements:* For master's, thesis (for some programs). *Entrance requirements:* For master's, GRE General Test or MAT, minimum undergraduate GPA of 2.5.

Bloomsburg University of Pennsylvania, School of Graduate Studies, College of Science and Technology, Department of Biological and Allied Health Sciences, Program in Biology Education, Bloomsburg, PA 17815-1301. Offers M Ed. *Accreditation:* NCATE. *Degree requirements:* For master's, thesis or alternative. *Entrance requirements:* For master's, teaching certificate, minimum QPA of 3.0. Additional exam requirements/recommendations for international students: Required—TOEFL (minimum score 550 paper-based; 213 computer-based; 79 iBT). Electronic applications accepted.

Boise State University, Graduate College, College of Arts and Sciences, Department of Geosciences, Boise, ID 83725-0399. Offers earth science (MS); geology (MS, PhD); geophysics (MS, PhD). Part-time programs available. *Degree requirements:* For master's, thesis. *Entrance requirements:* For master's, GRE General Test, BS in related field, minimum GPA of 3.0; for doctorate, GRE General Test. Electronic applications accepted. *Expenses:* Tuition, state resident: full-time $3106; part-time $209 per credit. Tuition, nonresident: part-time $284 per credit. *Faculty research:* Seismology, geothermal aquifers, sedimentation, tectonics, seismo-acoustic propagation.

Boston College, Graduate School of Arts and Sciences, Department of Chemistry, Chestnut Hill, MA 02467-3800. Offers biochemistry (PhD); inorganic chemistry (PhD); organic chemistry (PhD); physical chemistry (PhD); science education (MST). Part-time programs available. *Students:* 110 full-time (49 women); includes 8 minority (6 Asian Americans or Pacific Islanders, 2 Hispanic Americans), 49 international. 216 applicants, 34% accepted, 22 enrolled. In 2009, 3 master's, 20 doctorates awarded. *Degree requirements:* For doctorate, thesis/dissertation, qualifying exam. *Entrance requirements:* For doctorate, GRE General Test, GRE Subject Test. Additional exam requirements/recommendations for international students: Required—TOEFL (minimum score 600 paper-based; 250 computer-based; 100 iBT). *Application deadline:* For fall admission, 1/2 for domestic and international students. Application fee: $70. Electronic applications accepted. *Financial support:* In 2009–10, fellowships with full tuition reimbursements (averaging $25,000 per year), research assistantships with full tuition reimbursements (averaging $25,000 per year), teaching assistantships with full tuition reimbursements (averaging $25,000 per year) were awarded; Federal Work-Study also available. Support available to part-time students. Financial award application deadline: 3/1; financial award applicants required to submit FAFSA. *Unit head:* Dr. Amir Hoveyda, Chairperson, 617-552-1735, E-mail: amir.hoveyda@bc.edu. *Application contact:* Dr. Marc Snapper, Graduate Program Director, 617-552-8096, Fax: 617-552-0833, E-mail: marc.snapper@bc.edu.

Boston College, Lynch Graduate School of Education, Department of Teacher Education/Special Education and Curriculum and Instruction, Program in Secondary Education, Chestnut Hill, MA 02467-3800. Offers biology (MST); chemistry (MST); English (MAT); French (MAT); geology (MST); history (MAT); Latin and classical humanities (MAT); mathematics (MST); physics (MST); secondary teaching (M Ed), including biology, chemistry, English, French, geology, history, Latin and classical humanities, mathematics, physics, Spanish; Spanish (MAT). *Accreditation:* Teacher Education Accreditation Council. Part-time and evening/weekend programs available. *Students:* 14 full-time (10 women), 68 part-time (37 women); includes 17 minority (9 African Americans, 3 Asian Americans or Pacific Islanders, 5 Hispanic Americans), 1 international. 252 applicants, 59% accepted, 47 enrolled. In 2009, 39 master's awarded. *Degree requirements:* For master's, comprehensive exam. *Entrance requirements:* For master's, GRE General Test or MAT. Additional exam requirements/recommendations for international students: Required—TOEFL (minimum score 550 paper-based; 213 computer-based; 81 iBT). *Application deadline:* For fall admission, 1/1 priority date for domestic students. Application fee: $60. Electronic applications accepted. *Financial support:* Fellowships with full and partial tuition reimbursements, research assistantships with full and partial tuition reimbursements, teaching assistantships with full and partial tuition reimbursements, career-related internships or fieldwork, Federal Work-Study, institutionally sponsored loans, scholarships/grants, traineeships, health care benefits, tuition waivers (full and partial), and unspecified assistantships available. Support available to part-time students. Financial award applicants required to submit FAFSA. *Faculty research:* School reform; urban science education; teacher research; critical literacy; poverty and achievement. *Unit head:* Dr. Maria E. Brisk, Chairperson, 617-552-4216, Fax: 617-552-0812, E-mail: brisk@bc.edu. *Application contact:* Adam Poluzzi, Director, Graduate Admission and Financial Aid, 617-552-4214, Fax: 617-552-0398, E-mail: poluzzi@bc.edu.

Boston University, School of Education, Department of Curriculum and Teaching, Program in Science Education, Boston, MA 02215. Offers Ed M, MAT, Ed D, CAGS. *Degree requirements:* For master's, thesis optional; for doctorate, comprehensive exam, thesis/dissertation; for CAGS, comprehensive exam. *Entrance requirements:* For master's, doctorate, and CAGS, GRE General Test or MAT. Additional exam requirements/recommendations for international students: Required—TOEFL. Electronic applications accepted. *Expenses:* Tuition: Full-time $37,910; part-time $1184 per credit hour. Required fees: $386; $40 per semester. Part-time tuition and fees vary according to class time, course level, degree level and program. *Faculty research:* Teacher training, leadership.

Bowling Green State University, Graduate College, College of Arts and Sciences, Department of Physics and Astronomy, Bowling Green, OH 43403. Offers geophysics (MS); physics (MAT, MS). *Degree requirements:* For master's, thesis or alternative. *Entrance requirements:* For master's, GRE General Test. Additional exam requirements/recommendations for international students: Required—TOEFL. Electronic applications accepted. *Faculty research:* Computational physics, solid-state physics, materials science, theoretical physics.

Bridgewater State University, School of Graduate Studies, School of Arts and Sciences, Department of Biological Sciences, Bridgewater, MA 02325-0001. Offers MAT. Part-time and evening/weekend programs available. *Entrance requirements:* For master's, GRE General Test.

Bridgewater State University, School of Graduate Studies, School of Arts and Sciences, Department of Physics, Bridgewater, MA 02325-0001. Offers MAT. *Accreditation:* NCATE. Part-time and evening/weekend programs available. *Entrance requirements:* For master's, GRE General Test.

Bridgewater State University, School of Graduate Studies, School of Arts and Sciences, Program in Physical Sciences, Bridgewater, MA 02325-0001. Offers MAT. *Accreditation:* NCATE. Part-time and evening/weekend programs available. *Entrance requirements:* For master's, GRE General Test.

Brigham Young University, Graduate Studies, College of Life Sciences, Department of Biology, Provo, UT 84602. Offers biological science education (MS); biology (MS, PhD). *Faculty:* 22 full-time (2 women). *Students:* 35 full-time (13 women), 3 part-time (0 women); includes 9 minority (4 Asian Americans or Pacific Islanders, 5 Hispanic Americans). Average age 30. 15 applicants, 67% accepted, 9 enrolled. In 2009, 7 master's awarded. *Degree requirements:* For master's, comprehensive exam, thesis, prospectus, defense of research, defense of thesis; for doctorate, comprehensive exam, thesis/dissertation, prospectus, defense of research, defense of dissertation. *Entrance requirements:* For master's and doctorate, GRE General Test, minimum GPA of 3.0 for last 60 credit hours of course work. Additional exam requirements/recommendations for international students: Required—TOEFL (minimum score 580 paper-based; 85 iBT). *Application deadline:* For fall admission, 1/31 for domestic and international students. Application fee: $50. Electronic applications accepted. *Expenses:* Tuition: Full-time $5580; part-time $301 per credit hour. Tuition and fees vary according to student's religious affiliation. *Financial support:* In 2009–10, 2 students received support, including 2 fellowships with full and partial tuition reimbursements available (averaging $2,607 per year); research assistantships with full and partial tuition reimbursements available, teaching assistantships with full and partial tuition reimbursements available, career-related internships or fieldwork, institutionally sponsored loans, scholarships/grants, health care benefits, tuition waivers (full and partial), and unspecified assistantships also available. Financial award application deadline: 2/1; financial award applicants required to submit FAFSA. *Faculty research:* Systematics, bioinformatics, ecology, evolution. Total annual research expenditures: $1.4 million. *Unit head:* Dr. Keith A. Crandall, Chair, 801-422-3495, Fax: 801-422-0090, E-mail: keith_crandall@byu.edu. *Application contact:* Hilary H. Oldroyd, Graduate Secretary, 801-422-2010, Fax: 801-422-0090, E-mail: hilary_oldroyd@byu.edu.

Brooklyn College of the City University of New York, Division of Graduate Studies, School of Education, Program in Adolescence Education and Special Subjects, Brooklyn, NY 11210-2889. Offers adolescence science education (MAT); art teacher (MA); biology teacher (MA); chemistry teacher (MA); earth science teacher (MAT); English teacher (MA); French teacher (MA); health and nutrition sciences: health teacher (MS Ed); mathematics teacher (MA); music education (CAS); music teacher (MA); physical education teacher (MS Ed); physics teacher (MA); social studies teacher (MA); Spanish teacher (MA). Part-time and evening/weekend programs available. *Students:* 23 full-time (15 women), 449 part-time (256 women); includes 147 minority (96 African Americans, 1 American Indian/Alaska Native, 18 Asian Americans or Pacific Islanders, 32 Hispanic Americans), 12 international. Average age 30. 251 applicants, 80% accepted, 141 enrolled. In 2009, 163 master's, 2 other advanced degrees awarded. *Degree requirements:* For master's, comprehensive exam (for some programs), thesis (for some programs). *Entrance requirements:* For master's, LAST, previous course work in education, resume, 2 letters of recommendation, essay. Additional exam requirements/recommendations for international students: Required—TOEFL (minimum score 500 paper-based; 173 computer-based; 61 iBT). *Application deadline:* For fall admission, 7/15 for domestic students, 7/1 for international students; for spring admission, 11/15 for domestic students, 10/1 for international students. Applications are processed on a rolling basis. Application fee: $125. Electronic applications accepted. *Expenses:* Tuition, state resident: full-time $7360; part-time $310 per credit hour. Tuition, nonresident: full-time $13,800; part-time $575 per credit hour. Required fees: $140.10 per semester. *Financial support:* Career-related internships or fieldwork, Federal Work-Study, institutionally sponsored loans, and scholarships/grants available. Support available to part-time students. Financial award application deadline: 5/1; financial award applicants required to submit FAFSA. *Faculty research:* Interdisciplinary education, semiotics, discourse analysis, autobiography, teacher identity. *Unit head:* Prof. Stephen Phillips, Program Head, 718-951-5214, E-mail: phillips@brooklyn.cuny.edu. *Application contact:* Hernan Sierra, Graduate Admissions Coordinator, 718-951-4536, Fax: 718-951-4506, E-mail: grads@brooklyn.cuny.edu.

Brooklyn College of the City University of New York, Division of Graduate Studies, School of Education, Program in Childhood Education, Brooklyn, NY 11210-2889. Offers bilingual education (MS Ed); liberal arts (MS Ed); mathematics (MS Ed); science/environmental education (MS Ed). Part-time and evening/weekend programs available. *Students:* 14 full-time (13 women),

245 part-time (209 women); includes 129 minority (60 African Americans, 2 American Indian/Alaska Native, 20 Asian Americans or Pacific Islanders, 47 Hispanic Americans), 6 international. Average age 30. 114 applicants, 85% accepted, 65 enrolled. In 2009, 118 master's awarded. *Entrance requirements:* For master's, LAST, interview, previous course work in education, writing sample, resume, 2 letters of recommendation. Additional exam requirements/recommendations for international students: Required—TOEFL (minimum score 500 paper-based; 173 computer-based; 61 iBT). *Application deadline:* For fall admission, 3/1 priority date for domestic students, 2/1 priority date for international students; for spring admission, 11/1 priority date for domestic students, 10/1 priority date for international students. Applications are processed on a rolling basis. Application fee: $125. Electronic applications accepted. *Expenses:* Tuition, state resident: full-time $7360; part-time $310 per credit hour. Tuition, nonresident: full-time $13,800; part-time $575 per credit hour. Required fees: $140.10 per semester. *Financial support:* Career-related internships or fieldwork, Federal Work-Study, institutionally sponsored loans, and scholarships/grants available. Support available to part-time students. Financial award application deadline: 5/1; financial award applicants required to submit FAFSA. *Faculty research:* Emotional intelligence, multiculturalism, arts immersion, the Holocaust. *Unit head:* Dr. Wayne Reed, Program Head, 718-951-5214, E-mail: wreed@brooklyn.cuny.edu. *Application contact:* Hernan Sierra, Graduate Admissions Coordinator, 718-951-4536, Fax: 718-951-4506, E-mail: grads@brooklyn.cuny.edu.

Brooklyn College of the City University of New York, Division of Graduate Studies, School of Education, Program in Middle Childhood Education (Science), Brooklyn, NY 11210-2889. Offers biology (MA); chemistry (MA); earth science (MA); general science (MA); physics (MA). Part-time and evening/weekend programs available. *Students:* 2 full-time (both women), 80 part-time (55 women); includes 34 minority (22 African Americans, 3 Asian Americans or Pacific Islanders, 9 Hispanic Americans), 4 international. Average age 31. 43 applicants, 98% accepted, 31 enrolled. In 2009, 29 master's awarded. *Entrance requirements:* For master's, LAST, interview, previous course work in education and mathematics, resume, 2 letters of recommendation, essay. Additional exam requirements/recommendations for international students: Required—TOEFL (minimum score 500 paper-based; 173 computer-based; 61 iBT). *Application deadline:* For fall admission, 7/15 priority date for domestic students, 6/1 priority date for international students; for spring admission, 11/15 priority date for domestic students, 10/1 priority date for international students. Applications are processed on a rolling basis. Application fee: $125. Electronic applications accepted. *Expenses:* Tuition, state resident: full-time $7360; part-time $310 per credit hour. Tuition, nonresident: full-time $13,800; part-time $575 per credit hour. Required fees: $140.10 per semester. *Financial support:* Federal Work-Study, institutionally sponsored loans, and scholarships/grants available. Support available to part-time students. Financial award application deadline: 5/1; financial award applicants required to submit FAFSA. *Faculty research:* Geometric thinking, mastery of basic facts, problem-solving strategies, history of mathematics. *Unit head:* Dr. Jennifer Adams, Program Head, 718-951-5214, E-mail: jadams@brooklyn.cuny.edu. *Application contact:* Hernan Sierra, Graduate Admissions Coordinator, 718-951-4536, Fax: 718-951-4506, E-mail: grads@brooklyn.cuny.edu.

Brown University, Graduate School, Department of Education, Program in Teaching, Providence, RI 02912. Offers biology (MAT); elementary education (MAT); English (MAT); history/social studies (MAT). *Faculty:* 4 full-time (3 women), 6 part-time/adjunct (all women). *Students:* 27 full-time (21 women); includes 3 minority (2 African Americans, 1 Asian American or Pacific Islander). Average age 26. 94 applicants, 62% accepted, 27 enrolled. In 2009, 21 master's awarded. *Degree requirements:* For master's, student teaching, portfolio. *Entrance requirements:* For master's, GRE General Test, transcript, personal statement, letters of recommendation, interview, writing sample (English applicants only). Additional exam requirements/recommendations for international students: Required—TOEFL (minimum score 577 paper-based; 90 computer-based). *Application deadline:* For winter admission, 1/15 for domestic students. Application fee: $75. Electronic applications accepted. *Financial support:* In 2009–10, 23 students received support, including 4 fellowships; Federal Work-Study, institutionally sponsored loans, scholarships/grants, tuition waivers (partial), and proctorships also available. Financial award application deadline: 2/1; financial award applicants required to submit FAFSA. *Faculty research:* Literacy, biodiversity, English language learners, diversity, special education. *Unit head:* Laura Snyder, Director of Graduate Study for the MAT. *Application contact:* Carin Algava, Assistant Director, 401-863-3364, Fax: 401-863-1276, E-mail: carin_algava@brown.edu.

Buffalo State College, State University of New York, The Graduate School, Faculty of Natural and Social Sciences, Department of Biology, Buffalo, NY 14222-1095. Offers biology (MA); secondary education (MS Ed), including biology. Evening/weekend programs available. *Degree requirements:* For master's, thesis (for some programs), project. *Entrance requirements:* For master's, minimum GPA of 2.75. Additional exam requirements/recommendations for international students: Required—TOEFL (minimum score 550 paper-based; 213 computer-based).

Buffalo State College, State University of New York, The Graduate School, Faculty of Natural and Social Sciences, Department of Chemistry, Buffalo, NY 14222-1095. Offers chemistry (MA); secondary education (MS Ed), including chemistry. Part-time and evening/weekend programs available. *Degree requirements:* For master's, thesis (for some programs), project. *Entrance requirements:* For master's, minimum GPA of 2.6, New York teaching certificate (MS Ed). Additional exam requirements/recommendations for international students: Required—TOEFL (minimum score 550 paper-based; 213 computer-based).

Buffalo State College, State University of New York, The Graduate School, Faculty of Natural and Social Sciences, Department of Earth Science and Science Education, Buffalo, NY 14222-1095. Offers secondary education (MS Ed), including geoscience, science. *Accreditation:* NCATE. Part-time and evening/weekend programs available. *Degree requirements:* For master's, thesis or alternative, project. *Entrance requirements:* For master's, 36 undergraduate hours in mathematics and science. Additional exam requirements/recommendations for international students: Required—TOEFL (minimum score 550 paper-based; 213 computer-based).

Buffalo State College, State University of New York, The Graduate School, Faculty of Natural and Social Sciences, Department of Physics, Buffalo, NY 14222-1095. Offers secondary education physics (MS Ed). *Degree requirements:* For master's, project. *Entrance requirements:* For master's, minimum GPA of 2.5, New York State teaching certification. Additional exam requirements/recommendations for international students: Required—TOEFL (minimum score 550 paper-based; 213 computer-based).

California State University, Chico, Graduate School, Interdisciplinary Programs, Chico, CA 95929-0722. Offers interdisciplinary studies (MA, MS); science teaching (MS); simulation science (MS). Part-time programs available. *Students:* 21 full-time (18 women), 10 part-time (9 women); includes 7 minority (1 African American, 1 Asian American or Pacific Islander, 5 Hispanic Americans), 7 international. Average age 35. 23 applicants, 91% accepted, 11 enrolled. In 2009, 8 master's awarded. *Degree requirements:* For master's, thesis or alternative, oral exam. *Entrance requirements:* For master's, GRE General Test or MAT, 3 letters of recommendation. Additional exam requirements/recommendations for international students: Required—TOEFL (minimum score 550 paper-based; 213 computer-based; 80 iBT), IELTS (minimum score 6.5). *Application deadline:* For fall admission, 3/1 priority date for domestic students, 3/1 for international students; for spring admission, 9/15 priority date for domestic students, 9/15 for international students. Applications are processed on a rolling basis. Application fee: $55. *Financial support:* Fellowships, Federal Work-Study available. Support available to part-time students. *Unit head:* Dr. Sara Trechter, Graduate Coordinator, 530-898-5447. *Application contact:* School of Graduate, International, and Interdisciplinary Studies, 530-898-6880, Fax: 530-898-6889, E-mail: grin@csuchico.edu.

California State University, Fullerton, Graduate Studies, College of Natural Science and Mathematics, Program in Science Education, Fullerton, CA 92834-9480. Offers teaching science (MAT). Part-time programs available. *Students:* 11 part-time (8 women); includes 6 minority (2 Asian Americans or Pacific Islanders, 4 Hispanic Americans). Average age 36. 4 applicants, 75% accepted, 2 enrolled. In 2009, 2 master's awarded. *Degree requirements:* For master's, project or thesis. *Entrance requirements:* For master's, diagnostic exam, minimum GPA of 2.5 in last 60 units of course work, teaching credential, bachelor's degree in science. Application fee: $55. *Expenses:* Tuition, nonresident: full-time $11,160; part-time $373 per credit. Required fees: $1440 per term. Tuition and fees vary according to course load, degree level and program. *Financial support:* Teaching assistantships, career-related internships or fieldwork, Federal Work-Study, institutionally sponsored loans, and scholarships/grants available. Support available to part-time students. Financial award application deadline: 3/1; financial award applicants required to submit FAFSA. *Faculty research:* Earth and space science education. *Unit head:* Dr. Victoria Costa, Director, 657-278-2307. *Application contact:* Admissions/Applications, 657-278-2731.

California State University, Long Beach, Graduate Studies, College of Natural Sciences and Mathematics, Department of Science Education, Long Beach, CA 90840. Offers MS. *Faculty:* 7 full-time (3 women). *Students:* 3 full-time (all women), 30 part-time (26 women); includes 6 minority (1 African American, 2 Asian Americans or Pacific Islanders, 3 Hispanic Americans). Average age 33. *Expenses:* Required fees: $1802 per semester. Part-time tuition and fees vary according to course load. *Unit head:* Laura Henriques, Chair, 562-985-4801, E-mail: lhenriqu@csulb.edu. *Application contact:* Dr. Henry Fung, Associate Dean for Curriculum and Instruction, 562-985-7898, Fax: 562-985-2315, E-mail: hcfung@csulb.edu.

California State University, Northridge, Graduate Studies, College of Education, Department of Secondary Education, Northridge, CA 91330. Offers educational technology (MA); English education (MA); mathematics education (MA); secondary science education (MA); teaching and learning (MA). *Accreditation:* NCATE. Part-time programs available. *Faculty:* 13 full-time (7 women), 41 part-time/adjunct (20 women). *Students:* 10 full-time (6 women), 99 part-time (65 women); includes 40 minority (6 African Americans, 2 American Indian/Alaska Native, 13 Asian Americans or Pacific Islanders, 19 Hispanic Americans). Average age 34. 86 applicants, 60% accepted, 40 enrolled. *Degree requirements:* For master's, thesis optional. *Entrance requirements:* For master's, GRE General Test or minimum GPA of 3.0. Additional exam requirements/recommendations for international students: Required—TOEFL. *Application deadline:* For fall admission, 11/30 for domestic students. Application fee: $55. *Financial support:* Application deadline: 3/1. *Unit head:* Dr. Bonnie Ericson, Chair, 818-677-2580. *Application contact:* Dr. Michael Rivas, Graduate Advisor, 818-677-6792, E-mail: michael.rivas@csun.edu.

California State University, San Bernardino, Graduate Studies, College of Education, Program in Teaching of Science, San Bernardino, CA 92407-2397. Offers MA. *Accreditation:* NCATE. *Faculty:* 2 full-time (0 women). *Students:* 7 full-time (4 women), 5 part-time (4 women); includes 4 minority (1 African American, 2 Asian Americans or Pacific Islanders, 1 Hispanic American). Average age 41. 15 applicants, 80% accepted, 3 enrolled. In 2009, 1 master's awarded. *Entrance requirements:* For master's, minimum GPA of 3.0. Application fee: $55. *Unit head:* Dr. Herbert Brunkhorst, Coordinator, 909-537-5613, Fax: 909-537-7119, E-mail: hkbrunkh@csusb.edu. *Application contact:* Olivia Rosas, Director of Admissions, 909-537-7577, Fax: 909-537-7034, E-mail: orosas@csusb.edu.

Cambridge College, School of Education, Cambridge, MA 02138-5304. Offers autism specialist (M Ed); autism/behavior analyst (M Ed); behavior analyst (Post-Master's Certificate); behavioral management (M Ed); early childhood teacher (M Ed); education specialist in curriculum and instruction (CAGS); educational leadership (Ed D); elementary teacher (M Ed); English as a second language (M Ed, Certificate); general science (M Ed); health education, health promotion (Post-Master's Certificate); health/family and consumer sciences (M Ed); history (M Ed); individualized degree (M Ed); information technology literacy (M Ed); instructional technology (M Ed); interdisciplinary studies (M Ed); library teacher (M Ed); literacy education (M Ed); mathematics (M Ed); mathematics specialist (Certificate); middle school mathematics and science (M Ed); school administration (M Ed, CAGS); school guidance counselor (M Ed); school nurse education (M Ed); school social worker/school adjustment counselor (M Ed); special education administrator (CAGS); special education/moderate disabilities (M Ed); teaching skills and methodologies (M Ed). Part-time and evening/weekend programs available. Post-baccalaureate distance learning degree programs offered (minimal on-campus study). *Faculty:* 10 full-time (3 women), 283 part-time/adjunct (187 women). *Students:* 974 full-time (755 women), 1,071 part-time (835 women); includes 940 minority (762 African Americans, 4 American Indian/Alaska Native, 22 Asian Americans or Pacific Islanders, 152 Hispanic Americans), 28 international. Average age 39. In 2009, 866 master's, 4 doctorates, 209 CAGSs awarded. *Degree requirements:* For master's, thesis, internship/practicum (licensure program only); for doctorate, thesis/dissertation; for other advanced degree, thesis. *Entrance requirements:* For master's, interview, resume, documentation of licensure, 2 professional references; for doctorate, official transcripts, interview, resume, documentation of licensure (if any), written personal statement/essay, portfolio of scholarly and professional work, qualifying assessment, 2 professional references, health insurance, immunizations form; for other advanced degree, official transcripts, interview, resume, documentation of licensure (if any), written personal statement/essay, 2 professional references, health insurance, immunizations form. Additional exam requirements/recommendations for international students: Required—TOEFL (minimum score 550 paper-based; 213 computer-based; 79 iBT); Recommended—IELTS (minimum score 6). *Application deadline:* Applications are processed on a rolling basis. Application fee: $30. Electronic applications accepted. *Expenses:* Contact institution. *Financial support:* In 2009–10, 1,373 students received support. Career-related internships or fieldwork, Federal Work-Study, and scholarships/grants available. Financial award applicants required to submit FAFSA. *Faculty research:* Adult education, accelerated learning, mathematics education, brain compatible learning, special education and law. *Unit head:* Dr. N. Alan Sheppard, Interim Associate Dean, 617-873-0619, E-mail: alan.sheppard@cambridgecollege.edu. *Application contact:* Stephen Lyons, Director of Enrollment, Graduate and N.I.T.E. Programs, 617-868-1000, Fax: 617-349-3561, E-mail: stephen.lyons@cambridgecollege.edu.

Caribbean University, Graduate School, Bayamón, PR 00960-0493. Offers administration and supervision (MA Ed); criminal justice (MA); curriculum and instruction (MA Ed), including elementary education, English education, history education, mathematics education, primary education, science education, Spanish education; education (PhD); gerontology (MSN); human resources (MBA); museology, archiving and art history (MA Ed); neonatal pediatrics (MSN); physical education (MA Ed); special education (MA Ed). *Entrance requirements:* For master's, interview, minimum GPA of 2.5.

Carthage College, Division of Teacher Education, Kenosha, WI 53140. Offers classroom guidance and counseling (M Ed); creative arts (M Ed); gifted and talented children (M Ed); language arts (M Ed); modern language (M Ed); natural sciences (M Ed); reading (M Ed, Certificate); social sciences (M Ed); teacher leadership (M Ed). Part-time and evening/weekend programs available. *Degree requirements:* For master's, thesis optional. *Entrance requirements:* For master's, MAT, minimum B average, letters of reference.

Central Connecticut State University, School of Graduate Studies, School of Arts and Sciences, Department of Biology, New Britain, CT 06050-4010. Offers biological sciences (MA, MS), including anesthesia (MS), ecology and environmental sciences (MA), general biology (MA), health sciences specialization (MS), professional education program (MS); biology (Certificate). Part-time and evening/weekend programs available. *Faculty:* 13 full-time (4 women), 7 part-time/adjunct (4 women). *Students:* 99 full-time (58 women), 32 part-time (25 women); includes 29 minority (11 African Americans, 12 Asian Americans or Pacific Islanders, 6 Hispanic Americans), 1 international. Average age 32. 36 applicants, 28% accepted, 7 enrolled. In 2009, 37 master's, 5 other advanced degrees awarded. *Degree requirements:* For master's, comprehensive exam, thesis or alternative; for Certificate, qualifying exam. *Entrance requirements:* For master's, minimum undergraduate GPA of 2.7. Additional exam requirements/recommendations for international students: Required—TOEFL. *Application deadline:* For fall admission, 7/1 for domestic students; for spring admission, 12/1 for domestic students. Applications are processed on a rolling basis. Application fee: $50. Electronic applications accepted. *Expenses:* Tuition, area resident: Full-time $4662; part-time $440 per credit. Tuition, state

Science Education

Central Connecticut State University (continued)
resident: full-time $6994; part-time $440 per credit. Tuition, nonresident: full-time $12,988; part-time $440 per credit. Required fees: $3606. One-time fee: $62 part-time. *Financial support:* In 2009–10, 20 students received support, including 3 research assistantships; career-related internships or fieldwork, Federal Work-Study, scholarships/grants, and unspecified assistantships also available. Support available to part-time students. Financial award application deadline: 3/1; financial award applicants required to submit FAFSA. *Faculty research:* Environmental science, anesthesia, health sciences, zoology, animal behavior. *Unit head:* Dr. Jeremiah Jarrett, Chair, 860-832-2645. *Application contact:* Dr. Jeremiah Jarrett, Chair, 860-832-2645.

Central Connecticut State University, School of Graduate Studies, School of Arts and Sciences, Department of Physics and Earth Science, New Britain, CT 06050-4010. Offers natural sciences (MS); science education (Certificate). Part-time and evening/weekend programs available. *Faculty:* 12 full-time (4 women), 15 part-time/adjunct (4 women). *Students:* 22 part-time (11 women); includes 2 minority (1 African American, 1 Asian American or Pacific Islander). Average age 37. 14 applicants, 79% accepted, 7 enrolled. In 2009, 10 master's, 1 other advanced degree awarded. *Degree requirements:* For master's, comprehensive exam, thesis or alternative; for Certificate, qualifying exam. *Entrance requirements:* For master's, minimum undergraduate GPA of 2.7. Additional exam requirements/recommendations for international students: Required—TOEFL. *Application deadline:* For fall admission, 7/1 for domestic students; for spring admission, 12/1 for domestic students. Applications are processed on a rolling basis. Application fee: $50. Electronic applications accepted. *Expenses:* Tuition, area resident: Full-time $4662; part-time $440 per credit. Tuition, state resident: full-time $6994; part-time $440 per credit. Tuition, nonresident: full-time $12,988; part-time $440 per credit. Required fees: $3606. One-time fee: $62 part-time. *Financial support:* In 2009–10, 1 student received support. Career-related internships or fieldwork, Federal Work-Study, scholarships/grants, and unspecified assistantships available. Support available to part-time students. Financial award application deadline: 3/1; financial award applicants required to submit FAFSA. *Faculty research:* Elementary/secondary science education, particle and solid states, weather patterns, planetary studies. *Unit head:* Dr. Ali Antar, Chair, 860-832-2930. *Application contact:* Dr. Ali Antar, Chair, 860-832-2930.

Central Michigan University, College of Graduate Studies, College of Science and Technology, Department of Chemistry, Mount Pleasant, MI 48859. Offers chemistry (MS); teaching chemistry (MA), including teaching college chemistry, teaching high school chemistry. Part-time programs available. *Degree requirements:* For master's, comprehensive exam, thesis or alternative. *Entrance requirements:* For master's, GRE. Electronic applications accepted. *Faculty research:* Analytical and organic-inorganic chemistry, biochemistry, catalysis, dendrimer and polymer studies, nanotechnology.

Chatham University, Program in Education, Pittsburgh, PA 15232-2826. Offers early childhood education (MAT); elementary education (MAT); English—secondary (MAT); environmental education (K-12) (MAT); secondary art (MAT); secondary biology education (MAT); secondary chemistry education (MAT); secondary English education (MAT); secondary math education (MAT); secondary physics education (MAT); secondary social studies education (MAT); special education (MAT). *Students:* 52 full-time (41 women), 20 part-time (16 women). Average age 30. 39 applicants, 79% accepted, 26 enrolled. In 2009, 37 master's awarded. *Degree requirements:* For master's, thesis, teaching experience. *Entrance requirements:* For master's, PRAXIS I, minimum GPA of 3.0, sample of written work, recommendation letters. Additional exam requirements/recommendations for international students: Required—TOEFL (minimum score 600 paper-based; 250 computer-based; 100 iBT), IELTS (minimum score 6.5), TWE. *Application deadline:* For fall admission, 5/1 priority date for domestic and international students; for spring admission, 10/15 priority date for domestic and international students. Applications are processed on a rolling basis. Application fee: $45. Electronic applications accepted. *Financial support:* Career-related internships or fieldwork available. Financial award applicants required to submit FAFSA. *Faculty research:* Gifted education, environmental education, technology in education, writing as learning, class size and achievement. *Unit head:* Dr. Barbara Biglan, Interim Director, 412-365-1170, E-mail: biglan@chatham.edu. *Application contact:* Dory Perry, Associate Director of Graduate Admissions, 412-365-2758, Fax: 412-365-1609, E-mail: gradadmissions@chatham.edu.

Christopher Newport University, Graduate Studies, Department of Teacher Preparation, Newport News, VA 23606-2998. Offers art (PK-12) (MAT); biology (6-12) (MAT); computer science (6-12) (MAT); elementary (PK-6) (MAT); English (6-12) (MAT); French (PK-12) (MAT); history and social science (6-12) (MAT); mathematics (6-12) (MAT); music (PK-12) (MAT), including choral, instrumental; physics (6-12) (MAT); Spanish (PK-12) (MAT). Part-time and evening/weekend programs available. *Faculty:* 24 full-time (13 women), 4 part-time/adjunct (2 women). *Students:* 76 full-time (66 women), 12 part-time (10 women); includes 3 minority (2 African Americans, 1 Hispanic American). Average age 24. 3 applicants, 100% accepted, 2 enrolled. In 2009, 58 master's awarded. *Degree requirements:* For master's, comprehensive exam, thesis or alternative. *Entrance requirements:* For master's, PRAXIS I, minimum GPA of 3.0. Additional exam requirements/recommendations for international students: Required—TOEFL (minimum score 580 paper-based; 237 computer-based; 92 iBT). *Application deadline:* For fall admission, 8/15 for domestic students, 4/1 for international students; for spring admission, 10/15 for domestic students, 10/1 for international students. Applications are processed on a rolling basis. Application fee: $45. Electronic applications accepted. *Expenses:* Tuition, area resident: Part-time $384 per credit hour. Tuition, state resident: part-time $384 per credit hour. Tuition, nonresident: part-time $701 per credit hour. *Financial support:* In 2009–10, 3 research assistantships with full and partial tuition reimbursements (averaging $2,000 per year) were awarded; career-related internships or fieldwork, Federal Work-Study, and unspecified assistantships also available. Support available to part-time students. Financial award application deadline: 3/1; financial award applicants required to submit FAFSA. *Faculty research:* Early literacy development, instructional innovations, professional teaching standards, multicultural issues, aesthetic education. *Unit head:* Dr. Marsha Sprague, Director, 757-594-7388, Fax: 757-594-7803, E-mail: msprague@cnu.edu. *Application contact:* Lyn Sawyer, Associate Director, Graduate Admissions, 757-594-7544, Fax: 757-594-7649, E-mail: gradstdy@cnu.edu.

The Citadel, The Military College of South Carolina, Citadel Graduate College, School of Education, Program in Secondary Education, Charleston, SC 29409. Offers biology (MAT); English language arts (MAT); mathematics (MAT); social studies (MAT). *Accreditation:* NCATE. Part-time and evening/weekend programs available. *Faculty:* 12 full-time (7 women), 8 part-time/adjunct (5 women). *Students:* 27 full-time (18 women), 62 part-time (37 women); includes 15 minority (11 African Americans, 2 Asian Americans or Pacific Islanders, 2 Hispanic Americans). Average age 29. In 2009, 22 master's awarded. *Degree requirements:* For master's, comprehensive exam, internship. *Entrance requirements:* For master's, GRE (minimum score 900) or MAT (minimum score 396), minimum undergraduate GPA of 2.5. Additional exam requirements/recommendations for international students: Required—TOEFL (minimum score 550 paper-based; 213 computer-based). *Application deadline:* Applications are processed on a rolling basis. Application fee: $30. Electronic applications accepted. *Expenses:* Tuition, state resident: part-time $400 per credit hour. Tuition, nonresident: part-time $657 per credit hour. Required fees: $40 per term. *Financial support:* Career-related internships or fieldwork, health care benefits, and unspecified assistantships available. Support available to part-time students. Financial award application deadline: 7/1; financial award applicants required to submit FAFSA. *Unit head:* Dr. Kathryn A. Richardson-Jones, Coordinator, 843-953-3163, Fax: 843-953-7258, E-mail: kathryn.jones@citadel.edu. *Application contact:* Dr. Steve A. Nida, Associate Provost, The Citadel Graduate College, 843-953-5089, Fax: 843-953-7630, E-mail: cgc@citadel.edu.

City College of the City University of New York, Graduate School, School of Education, Department of Secondary Education, Program in Science Education, New York, NY 10031-9198. Offers MA. *Accreditation:* NCATE. *Entrance requirements:* For master's, Liberal Arts and Sciences Test (LAST), Content Specialty Test (CST). Additional exam requirements/recommendations for international students: Required—TOEFL. *Expenses:* Tuition, state resident: part-time $310 per credit. Tuition, nonresident: part-time $575 per credit. Tuition and fees vary according to course load and program.

Clarion University of Pennsylvania, Office of Research and Graduate Studies, College of Education and Human Services, Department of Education, Program in Education, Clarion, PA 16214. Offers curriculum and instruction (M Ed); early childhood (M Ed); English (M Ed); history (M Ed); literacy (M Ed); science (M Ed); technology (M Ed). *Accreditation:* NCATE. Part-time programs available. *Degree requirements:* For master's, comprehensive exam, thesis or alternative. *Entrance requirements:* For master's, minimum QPA of 3.0, teacher certification. Additional exam requirements/recommendations for international students: Required—TOEFL (minimum score 550 paper-based; 213 computer-based; 80 iBT). Electronic applications accepted.

Clarion University of Pennsylvania, Office of Research and Graduate Studies, College of Education and Human Services, Department of Education, Program in Science Education, Clarion, PA 16214. Offers M Ed. *Degree requirements:* For master's, comprehensive exam, thesis or alternative. *Entrance requirements:* For master's, minimum QPA of 3.0. Additional exam requirements/recommendations for international students: Required—TOEFL (minimum score 550 paper-based; 213 computer-based; 80 iBT). Electronic applications accepted.

Clemson University, Graduate School, College of Health, Education, and Human Development, School of Education, Program in Secondary Education, Clemson, SC 29634. Offers English (M Ed); mathematics (M Ed); natural sciences (M Ed); social studies (M Ed). *Accreditation:* NCATE. *Students:* 5 full-time (3 women), 4 part-time (2 women); includes 2 minority (1 Asian American or Pacific Islander, 1 Hispanic American), 2 international. Average age 29. 11 applicants, 82% accepted, 4 enrolled. In 2009, 2 master's awarded. *Entrance requirements:* For master's, GRE General Test, teaching certificate. Additional exam requirements/recommendations for international students: Required—TOEFL. *Application deadline:* Applications are processed on a rolling basis. Application fee: $70 ($80 for international students). Electronic applications accepted. *Expenses:* Contact institution. *Financial support:* In 2009–10, 2 students received support. Career-related internships or fieldwork, institutionally sponsored loans, scholarships/grants, health care benefits, and unspecified assistantships available. Support available to part-time students. Financial award application deadline: 6/1; financial award applicants required to submit FAFSA. *Unit head:* Dr. Michael J. Padilla, Director/Associate Dean, 864-656-4444, Fax: 864-656-0311, E-mail: padilla@clemson.edu. *Application contact:* Dr. David Fleming, Graduate Coordinator, 864-656-1881, Fax: 864-656-0311, E-mail: dflemin@clemson.edu.

Cleveland State University, College of Graduate Studies, College of Education and Human Services, Department of Teacher Education, Cleveland, OH 44115. Offers art education (M Ed); early childhood education (M Ed); foreign language education (M Ed); mathematics and science education (M Ed); middle childhood education (M Ed); special education (M Ed), including mild/moderate disabilities, moderate/intensive disabilities; teaching English to speakers of other languages (M Ed). Part-time and evening/weekend programs available. *Degree requirements:* For master's, comprehensive exam (for some programs), thesis or alternative. *Entrance requirements:* For master's, GRE General Test or MAT, minimum GPA of 2.75. Additional exam requirements/recommendations for international students: Required—TOEFL (minimum score 525 paper-based; 197 computer-based), IELTS (minimum score 6). *Faculty research:* Early literacy, professional development in reading, reading recovery, dual language, induction programs.

The College at Brockport, State University of New York, School of Education and Human Services, Department of Education and Human Development, Program in Adolescence Education, Brockport, NY 14420-2997. Offers adolescence biology education (MS Ed); adolescence chemistry education (MS Ed); adolescence earth science education (MS Ed); adolescence English education (MS Ed); adolescence mathematics education (MS Ed); adolescence physics education (MS Ed); adolescence social studies education (MS Ed). *Accreditation:* NCATE. Part-time programs available. *Students:* 10 full-time (6 women), 98 part-time (60 women); includes 1 minority (African American). 15 applicants, 67% accepted, 8 enrolled. In 2009, 60 master's awarded. *Degree requirements:* For master's, thesis or alternative. *Entrance requirements:* For master's, minimum GPA of 3.0, letters of recommendation. Additional exam requirements/recommendations for international students: Required—TOEFL (minimum score 550 paper-based; 213 computer-based; 79 iBT). *Application deadline:* For fall admission, 2/15 priority date for domestic and international students; for spring admission, 9/15 priority date for domestic and international students. Application fee: $80. Electronic applications accepted. *Expenses:* Tuition, state resident: full-time $8370; part-time $349 per credit. Tuition, nonresident: full-time $13,250; part-time $522 per credit. *Financial support:* Federal Work-Study, scholarships/grants, and unspecified assistantships available. Support available to part-time students. Financial award application deadline: 3/15; financial award applicants required to submit FAFSA. *Unit head:* Dr. Sue Novinger, Chairperson, 585-395-2205, Fax: 585-395-2172, E-mail: snovinge@brockport.edu. *Application contact:* Coördinator of Certification and Graduate Advisement.

The College at Brockport, State University of New York, School of Education and Human Services, Department of Education and Human Development, Program in Alternate Adolescence Inclusive Education, Brockport, NY 14420-2997. Offers alternate adolescence English inclusive education (MS Ed); alternate adolescence mathematics inclusive education (MS Ed); alternate adolescence science inclusive education (MS Ed); alternate adolescence social studies inclusive education (MS Ed). *Students:* 25 full-time (8 women), 5 part-time (3 women). 26 applicants, 50% accepted, 11 enrolled. *Degree requirements:* For master's, thesis or alternative. *Entrance requirements:* For master's, minimum GPA of 3.0, letters of recommendation, statement of objectives, academic major (or equivalent) in program discipline. Additional exam requirements/recommendations for international students: Required—TOEFL (minimum score 550 paper-based; 213 computer-based; 79 iBT). *Application deadline:* For fall admission, 2/15 priority date for domestic and international students; for spring admission, 9/15 priority date for domestic and international students. Application fee: $80. Electronic applications accepted. *Expenses:* Tuition, state resident: full-time $8370; part-time $349 per credit. Tuition, nonresident: full-time $13,250; part-time $522 per credit. *Financial support:* Federal Work-Study, scholarships/grants, and unspecified assistantships available. Support available to part-time students. Financial award application deadline: 3/15; financial award applicants required to submit FAFSA. *Unit head:* Dr. Sue Novinger, Chairperson, 585-395-2205, E-mail: snovinge@brockport.edu. *Application contact:* Coordinator of Certification and Graduate Advisement.

College of Charleston, Graduate School, School of Education, Health, and Human Performance, Program in Science and Mathematics for Teachers, Charleston, SC 29424-0001. Offers M Ed. *Accreditation:* NCATE. *Faculty:* 5 full-time (4 women). *Students:* 5 full-time (3 women), 17 part-time (16 women); includes 3 minority (2 African Americans, 1 Hispanic American), 1 international. Average age 29. 10 applicants, 70% accepted, 7 enrolled. In 2009, 6 master's awarded. *Degree requirements:* For master's, capstone project. *Entrance requirements:* For master's, GRE or PRAXIS, 2 letters of recommendation, copy of teaching certificate. Additional exam requirements/recommendations for international students: Required—TOEFL. *Application deadline:* For fall admission, 4/1 for domestic students; for spring admission, 11/1 for domestic students. Application fee: $45. Electronic applications accepted. *Financial support:* In 2009–10, research assistantships (averaging $12,400 per year), teaching assistantships (averaging $13,300 per year) were awarded; scholarships/grants and unspecified assistantships also available. Financial award applicants required to submit FAFSA. *Unit head:* Dr. Gary Harrison, Director, 843-953-5734, E-mail: harrisong@cofc.edu. *Application contact:* Susan Hallatt, Director of Graduate Admissions, 843-953-5614, Fax: 843-953-1434, E-mail: hallatts@cofc.edu.

College of the Humanities and Sciences, Harrison Middleton University, Graduate Program, Tempe, AZ 85282. Offers education (MA, Ed D); humanities (MA); imaginative literature (MA); interdisciplinary studies (DA); jurisprudence (MA); natural science (MA); philosophy and religion (MA); social science (MA). Part-time and evening/weekend programs available. Postbaccalaureate distance learning degree programs offered (no on-campus study). *Faculty:* 17

full-time (7 women), 14 part-time/adjunct (6 women). *Students:* 49 full-time (18 women). In 2009, 4 master's awarded. *Application deadline:* Applications are processed on a rolling basis. Application fee: $50. Electronic applications accepted. *Application contact:* Deborah Deacon, Dean of Graduate Studies, 877-248-6724, Fax: 800-762-1622, E-mail: ddeacon@chumsci.edu.

The College of William and Mary, School of Education, Program in Curriculum and Instruction, Williamsburg, VA 23187-8795. Offers elementary education (MA Ed); gifted education (MA Ed); math specialist (MA Ed); reading education (MA Ed); secondary education (MA Ed), including English education, mathematics education, modern foreign languages education, science education, social studies education; special education (MA Ed), including general curriculum, resource collaborating teaching. *Accreditation:* NCATE. Part-time programs available. *Faculty:* 18 full-time (12 women), 17 part-time/adjunct (15 women). *Students:* 54 full-time (45 women), 12 part-time (all women); includes 3 minority (2 African Americans, 1 Asian American or Pacific Islander), 2 international. Average age 27. 120 applicants, 75% accepted. In 2009, 70 master's awarded. *Degree requirements:* For master's, project. *Entrance requirements:* For master's, GRE or MAT, minimum GPA of 2.5. Additional exam requirements/recommendations for international students: Required—TOEFL. *Application deadline:* For fall admission, 1/15 for domestic and international students; for spring admission, 10/1 for domestic and international students. Application fee: $45. Electronic applications accepted. *Expenses:* Tuition, state resident: full-time $6400; part-time $315 per credit hour. Tuition, nonresident: full-time $19,720; part-time $840 per credit hour. Required fees: $4114. *Financial support:* In 2009–10, 30 students received support, including 10 research assistantships with full and partial tuition reimbursements available (averaging $5,500 per year); career-related internships or fieldwork, Federal Work-Study, institutionally sponsored loans, scholarships/grants, and unspecified assistantships also available. Financial award application deadline: 1/15; financial award applicants required to submit FAFSA. *Faculty research:* National Council of Teachers of Mathematics Standards, counseling, self-concept and self-esteem, special education, curriculum development. *Unit head:* Dr. C. Denise Johnson, Area Coordinator, 757-221-1528, E-mail: cdjohn@wm.edu. *Application contact:* Dorothy Smith Osborne, Director of Admissions, 757-221-2317, Fax: 757-221-2293, E-mail: dsosbo@wm.edu.

The Colorado College, Department of Education, Program in Secondary Education, Colorado Springs, CO 80903-3294. Offers art teaching (K-12) (MAT); English teaching (MAT); foreign language teaching (MAT); mathematics teaching (MAT); music teaching (MAT); science teaching (MAT); social studies teaching (MAT). *Faculty:* 3 full-time (2 women), 8 part-time/adjunct (6 women). *Students:* 15 full-time (5 women); includes 2 minority (1 American Indian/Alaska Native, 1 Asian American or Pacific Islander). Average age 27. 26 applicants, 81% accepted, 15 enrolled. In 2009, 17 master's awarded. *Degree requirements:* For master's, thesis, internship. *Entrance requirements:* For master's, PRAXIS II or PLACE Exam. *Application deadline:* For fall admission, 12/1 priority date for domestic students, 12/1 for international students. Applications are processed on a rolling basis. Application fee: $50. *Expenses:* Tuition: Part-time $2545 per credit. *Financial support:* In 2009–10, 15 students received support, including 7 teaching assistantships (averaging $16,000 per year); career-related internships or fieldwork, institutionally sponsored loans, health care benefits, and tuition waivers (partial) also available. Financial award application deadline: 2/15; financial award applicants required to submit FAFSA. *Unit head:* Mike Taber, Director, 719-389-6026, Fax: 719-389-6473, E-mail: mike.taber@coloradocollege.edu. *Application contact:* Debra Yazulla Mortenson, Education Services Manager, 719-389-6472, Fax: 719-389-6473, E-mail: debra.mortenson@coloradocollege.edu.

Columbia University, College of Dental Medicine and Graduate School of Arts and Sciences, Programs in Dental Specialties, New York, NY 10027. Offers advanced education in general dentistry (Certificate); biomedical informatics (MA, PhD); endodontics (Certificate); orthodontics (MS, Certificate); periodontics (MS, Certificate); prosthodontics (MS, Certificate); science education (MA). *Degree requirements:* For master's, thesis, presentation of seminar. *Entrance requirements:* For master's, GRE General Test, DDS or equivalent. *Expenses:* Contact institution. *Faculty research:* Analysis of growth/form, pulpal microcirculation, implants, microbiology of oral environment, calcified tissues.

Columbus State University, Graduate Studies, College of Education and Health Professions, Department of Teacher Education, Columbus, GA 31907-5645. Offers accomplished teaching (M Ed); early childhood education (M Ed, Ed S); health administration (MPA); instructional technology (MS); middle grades education (M Ed, Ed S); physical education (M Ed); secondary education (M Ed, MAT, Ed S), including English/language arts (M Ed, Ed S), general science (M Ed), mathematics (M Ed), social science (M Ed); special education (M Ed), including behavior disorders, mental retardation. *Accreditation:* NCATE. Part-time and evening/weekend programs available. Postbaccalaureate distance learning degree programs offered (minimal on-campus study). *Faculty:* 18 full-time (15 women), 14 part-time/adjunct (10 women). *Students:* 146 full-time (113 women), 312 part-time (261 women); includes 142 minority (120 African Americans, 1 American Indian/Alaska Native, 8 Asian Americans or Pacific Islanders, 13 Hispanic Americans), 2 international. Average age 31. 248 applicants, 64% accepted, 114 enrolled. In 2009, 103 master's, 22 other advanced degrees awarded. *Degree requirements:* For master's, thesis, exit exam; for Ed S, thesis or alternative. *Entrance requirements:* For master's, GRE General Test, minimum GPA of 2.75; for Ed S, GRE General Test. Additional exam requirements/recommendations for international students: Required—TOEFL (minimum score 550 paper-based; 213 computer-based; 79 iBT). *Application deadline:* For fall admission, 5/1 priority date for domestic students, 5/1 for international students; for spring admission, 11/1 for domestic and international students. Applications are processed on a rolling basis. Application fee: $30. Electronic applications accepted. *Financial support:* In 2009–10, 305 students received support, including 36 research assistantships with partial tuition reimbursements available (averaging $3,000 per year); career-related internships or fieldwork, Federal Work-Study, institutionally sponsored loans, scholarships/grants, tuition waivers (partial), and unspecified assistantships also available. Support available to part-time students. Financial award application deadline: 5/1; financial award applicants required to submit FAFSA. *Unit head:* Dr. Deborah Gober, Acting Chair, 706-568-2255, Fax: 706-568-3134, E-mail: gober_deborah@colstate.edu. *Application contact:* Katie Thornton, Graduate Admissions Specialist, 706-568-2035, Fax: 706-568-2462, E-mail: thornton_katie@colstate.edu.

Converse College, School of Education and Graduate Studies, Program in Secondary Education, Spartanburg, SC 29302-0006. Offers biology (MAT); chemistry (MAT); English (M Ed, MAT); mathematics (M Ed, MAT); natural sciences (M Ed); social sciences (M Ed, MAT). Part-time programs available. *Degree requirements:* For master's, capstone paper. *Entrance requirements:* For master's, NTE or PRAXIS II (M Ed), minimum GPA of 2.75, 2 recommendations. Electronic applications accepted.

Cornell University, Graduate School, Graduate Fields of Agriculture and Life Sciences, Field of Education, Ithaca, NY 14853-0001. Offers agricultural education (MAT); biology (7-12) (MAT); chemistry (7-12) (MAT); curriculum and instruction (MPS, MS, PhD); earth science (7-12) (MAT); extension, and adult education (MPS, MS, PhD); mathematics (7-12) (MAT); physics (7-12) (MAT). *Faculty:* 26 full-time (9 women). *Students:* 65 full-time (50 women); includes 15 minority (4 African Americans, 7 Asian Americans or Pacific Islanders, 4 Hispanic Americans), 2 international. Average age 34. 96 applicants, 33% accepted, 21 enrolled. In 2009, 27 master's, 2 doctorates awarded. Terminal master's awarded for partial completion of doctoral program. *Degree requirements:* For master's, thesis (MS); for doctorate, comprehensive exam, thesis/dissertation. *Entrance requirements:* For master's and doctorate, GRE General Test, sample of written work (recommended), 2 letters of recommendation. Additional exam requirements/recommendations for international students: Required—TOEFL (minimum score 550 paper-based; 213 computer-based; 77 iBT). *Application deadline:* For fall admission, 2/15 for domestic students. Application fee: $70. Electronic applications accepted. *Expenses:* Tuition: Full-time $29,500. Required fees: $70. Full-time tuition and fees vary according to degree level, program and student level. *Financial support:* In 2009–10, 33 students received support, including 3 fellowships with full tuition reimbursements available, 5 teaching assistantships with full tuition reimbursements available; research assistantships with full tuition reimbursements available, institutionally sponsored loans, scholarships/grants, health care benefits, tuition waivers (full and partial), and unspecified assistantships also available. Financial award applicants required to submit FAFSA. *Faculty research:* Moral development and professional ethics; public issues education and community development; socio/political issues in public education; teacher education and curriculum in agricultural science, and mathematics; extension research. *Unit head:* Director of Graduate Studies, 607-255-4278, Fax: 607-255-7905. *Application contact:* Graduate Field Assistant, 607-255-4278, Fax: 607-255-7905, E-mail: rh22@cornell.edu.

Delaware State University, Graduate Programs, College of Education, Program in Science Education, Dover, DE 19901-2277. Offers MA. Part-time and evening/weekend programs available. *Degree requirements:* For master's, comprehensive exam, thesis optional. *Entrance requirements:* For master's, GRE General Test, minimum GPA of 3.0 in major, 2.75 overall. Electronic applications accepted. *Faculty research:* Science reform in schools, inquiry science.

Delaware State University, Graduate Programs, Department of Biology, Program in Biology Education, Dover, DE 19901-2277. Offers MS. *Entrance requirements:* Additional exam requirements/recommendations for international students: Required—TOEFL (minimum score 550 paper-based).

Delaware State University, Graduate Programs, Department of Physics, Dover, DE 19901-2277. Offers applied optics (MS); optics (PhD); physics (MS); physics teaching (MS). Part-time and evening/weekend programs available. *Entrance requirements:* For master's, minimum GPA of 3.0 in major, 2.75 overall. Additional exam requirements/recommendations for international students: Required—TOEFL. Electronic applications accepted. *Faculty research:* Thermal properties of solids, nuclear physics, radiation damage in solids.

Delta State University, Graduate Programs, College of Arts and Sciences, Division of Biological and Physical Sciences, Cleveland, MS 38733-0001. Offers biological science (MSNS); physical science (MSNS). Part-time programs available. *Degree requirements:* For master's, research project or thesis. *Entrance requirements:* For master's, GRE General Test. *Expenses:* Tuition, state resident: full-time $4450; part-time $247 per credit hour. Tuition, nonresident: full-time $11,520; part-time $640 per credit hour.

Drew University, Caspersen School of Graduate Studies, Program in Education, Madison, NJ 07940-1493. Offers biology (MAT); chemistry (MAT); English (MAT); French (MAT); Italian (MAT); math (MAT); physics (MAT); social studies (MAT); Spanish (MAT); theatre arts (MAT). Part-time programs available. *Students:* 21 full-time (10 women), 6 part-time (2 women); includes 1 minority (Hispanic American). Average age 24. 40 applicants, 90% accepted, 27 enrolled. In 2009, 13 master's awarded. *Entrance requirements:* For master's, transcripts, personal statement, recommendations. Additional exam requirements/recommendations for international students: Required—TOEFL, TWE. *Application deadline:* For fall admission, 2/1 priority date for domestic students. Applications are processed on a rolling basis. Application fee: $35. *Expenses:* Contact institution. *Financial support:* In 2009–10, 22 students received support. Federal Work-Study, scholarships/grants, and tuition waivers (partial) available. Support available to part-time students. Financial award application deadline: 2/15; financial award applicants required to submit FAFSA. *Unit head:* Dr. Ross Danis. *Application contact:* Carla J. Burns, Director of Graduate Admissions, 973-408-3110, Fax: 973-408-3242, E-mail: gradm@drew.edu.

Duquesne University, School of Education, Department of Instruction and Leadership, Program in Secondary Education, Pittsburgh, PA 15282-0001. Offers secondary education (MS Ed), including biology, chemistry, English, Latin, math, physics, social studies, Spanish. Part-time and evening/weekend programs available. *Faculty:* 4 full-time (3 women), 1 part-time/adjunct (0 women). *Students:* 56 full-time (34 women), 8 part-time (3 women); includes 6 minority (3 African Americans, 2 Asian Americans or Pacific Islanders, 1 Hispanic American), 2 international. Average age 29. 69 applicants, 70% accepted, 27 enrolled. In 2009, 36 master's awarded. *Degree requirements:* For master's, thesis optional. *Entrance requirements:* For master's, MAT, minimum GPA of 3.0. Additional exam requirements/recommendations for international students: Required—TOEFL (minimum score 550 paper-based; 80 computer-based). *Application deadline:* For fall admission, 8/1 for domestic students; for spring admission, 12/1 for domestic students. Applications are processed on a rolling basis. Application fee: $0. Electronic applications accepted. *Expenses:* Tuition: Part-time $851 per credit. Required fees: $81 per credit. *Financial support:* Research assistantships, Federal Work-Study available. Support available to part-time students. *Unit head:* Dr. Melissa Boston, Assistant Professor, 412-396-6109, E-mail: bostonm@duq.edu. *Application contact:* Michael Dolinger, Director of Student and Academic Services, 412-396-6647, Fax: 412-396-5585, E-mail: dolingerm@duq.edu.

East Carolina University, Graduate School, College of Education, Department of Mathematics and Science Education, Greenville, NC 27858-4353. Offers mathematics (MA Ed); science education (MA, MA Ed). Part-time and evening/weekend programs available. *Degree requirements:* For master's, comprehensive exam, thesis optional. *Entrance requirements:* For master's, GRE General Test or MAT, interview, minimum GPA of 2.5, bachelor's degree in related field, teaching license (MA Ed). Additional exam requirements/recommendations for international students: Required—TOEFL.

Eastern Connecticut State University, School of Education and Professional Studies/Graduate Division, Program in Science Education, Willimantic, CT 06226-2295. Offers MS. *Accreditation:* NCATE. Part-time and evening/weekend programs available. *Degree requirements:* For master's, comprehensive exam or thesis. *Entrance requirements:* For master's, minimum GPA of 2.7, teaching certificate. Additional exam requirements/recommendations for international students: Required—TOEFL (minimum score 550 paper-based; 213 computer-based).

Eastern Kentucky University, The Graduate School, College of Education, Department of Curriculum and Instruction, Program in Secondary and Higher Education, Richmond, KY 40475-3102. Offers secondary education (MA Ed), including agricultural education, art education, biological sciences education, business education, English education, geography education, history education, home economics education, industrial education, mathematical sciences education, physical education, school health education. *Accreditation:* NCATE. Part-time programs available. *Entrance requirements:* For master's, GRE General Test, minimum GPA of 2.5.

Eastern Michigan University, Graduate School, College of Arts and Sciences, Department of Biology, Ypsilanti, MI 48197. Offers cell and molecular biology (MS); community college biology teaching (MS); ecology and organismal biology (MS); general biology (MS); water resources (MS). Part-time and evening/weekend programs available. Postbaccalaureate distance learning degree programs offered (minimal on-campus study). *Faculty:* 20 full-time (5 women). *Students:* 10 full-time (8 women), 35 part-time (21 women); includes 3 minority (2 African Americans, 1 Asian American or Pacific Islander), 7 international. Average age 28. 57 applicants, 63% accepted, 20 enrolled. In 2009, 17 master's awarded. *Entrance requirements:* For master's, GRE General Test, GRE Subject Test. Additional exam requirements/recommendations for international students: Required—TOEFL. *Application deadline:* Applications are processed on a rolling basis. Application fee: $35. Tuition and fees vary according to course level. *Financial support:* In 2009–10, 22 teaching assistantships with full tuition reimbursements (averaging $8,660 per year) were awarded; fellowships, research assistantships with full tuition reimbursements, career-related internships or fieldwork, Federal Work-Study, institutionally sponsored loans, scholarships/grants, tuition waivers (partial), and unspecified assistantships also available. Support available to part-time students. Financial award applicants required to submit FAFSA. *Unit head:* Dr. Marianne Laporte, Department Head, 734-487-4242, Fax: 734-487-9235, E-mail: mlaporte@emich.edu. *Application contact:* Dr. Marianne Laporte, Department Head, 734-487-4242, Fax: 734-487-9235, E-mail: mlaporte@emich.edu.

Eastern Michigan University, Graduate School, College of Arts and Sciences, Department of Geography and Geology, Program in Earth Science Education, Ypsilanti, MI 48197. Offers MS. *Students:* 2 full-time (both women), 9 part-time (4 women). Average age 35. In 2009, 1 master's awarded. Application fee: $35. Tuition and fees vary according to course level. *Application contact:* Dr. Sandra Rutherford, Program Advisor, 734-487-8588, Fax: 734-487-6979, E-mail: srutherf@emich.edu.

Science Education

Eastern Michigan University, Graduate School, College of Arts and Sciences, Department of Physics and Astronomy, Ypsilanti, MI 48197. Offers general science (MS); physics (MS); physics education (MS). Part-time and evening/weekend programs available. Postbaccalaureate distance learning degree programs offered (minimal on-campus study). *Faculty:* 10 full-time (4 women). *Students:* 2 full-time (0 women), 14 part-time (7 women); includes 3 minority (2 African Americans, 1 Asian American or Pacific Islander), 1 international. Average age 29. 16 applicants, 88% accepted, 8 enrolled. In 2009, 6 master's awarded. *Entrance requirements:* Additional exam requirements/recommendations for international students: Required—TOEFL. *Application deadline:* Applications are processed on a rolling basis. Application fee: $35. Tuition and fees vary according to course level. *Financial support:* In 2009–10, 8 teaching assistantships with full tuition reimbursements (averaging $8,562 per year) were awarded; fellowships, research assistantships with full tuition reimbursements, career-related internships or fieldwork, Federal Work-Study, institutionally sponsored loans, scholarships/grants, tuition waivers, and unspecified assistantships also available. Support available to part-time students. Financial award applicants required to submit FAFSA. *Unit head:* James Carroll, Interim Department Head, 734-487-4144, Fax: 734-487-0989, E-mail: jcarroll@emich.edu. *Application contact:* Graduate Admissions, 734-487-3400, Fax: 734-487-6559, E-mail: graduate. admissions@emich.edu.

East Stroudsburg University of Pennsylvania, Graduate School, College of Arts and Sciences, Department of Biology, East Stroudsburg, PA 18301-2999. Offers M Ed, MS. Part-time and evening/weekend programs available. *Faculty:* 11 full-time (4 women). *Students:* 24 full-time (13 women), 28 part-time (14 women); includes 4 minority (2 African Americans, 2 Asian Americans or Pacific Islanders). Average age 29. In 2009, 25 master's awarded. *Degree requirements:* For master's, comprehensive exam, thesis or alternative. *Entrance requirements:* For master's, GRE, resume, undergraduate major in life science (or equivalent), completion of organic chemistry (minimum two semesters), 3 letters of recommendation, letter of intent. Additional exam requirements/recommendations for international students: Required—TOEFL (minimum score 560 paper-based; 220 computer-based; 83 iBT), or IELTS. *Application deadline:* For fall admission, 7/31 for domestic students, 5/1 priority date for international students; for spring admission, 11/30 for domestic students, 10/1 for international students. Applications are processed on a rolling basis. Application fee: $50. *Expenses:* Tuition, state resident: full-time $9942; part-time $387 per credit. Tuition, nonresident: full-time $14,240; part-time $619 per credit. *Financial support:* In 2009–10, 31 research assistantships with full and partial tuition reimbursements (averaging $1,654 per year) were awarded; Federal Work-Study and institutionally sponsored loans also available. Financial award application deadline: 3/1; financial award applicants required to submit FAFSA. *Unit head:* Dr. Jane Huffman, Graduate Coordinator, 570-422-3725, Fax: 570-422-3724, E-mail: jhuffman@po-box.esu.edu. *Application contact:* Kevin Quintero, Associate Provost for Enrollment Management, 570-422-3890, Fax: 570-422-3711, E-mail: kquintero@po-box.esu.edu.

Elms College, Division of Education, Chicopee, MA 01013-2839. Offers early childhood education (MAT); education (M Ed, CAGS); elementary education (MAT); English as a second language (MAT); reading (MAT); secondary education (MAT), including biology education, English education, Spanish education; special education (MAT). Part-time and evening/weekend programs available. *Faculty:* 12 full-time (8 women), 4 part-time/adjunct (2 women). *Students:* 17 full-time (14 women), 153 part-time (136 women); includes 5 minority (1 American Indian/Alaska Native, 4 Hispanic Americans). Average age 36. 43 applicants, 88% accepted, 37 enrolled. In 2009, 23 master's, 8 other advanced degrees awarded. *Degree requirements:* For master's, thesis (for some programs). *Entrance requirements:* For master's, Massachusetts Educators Certification Test, minimum GPA of 3.0; for CAGS, master's degree in education. Additional exam requirements/recommendations for international students: Required—TOEFL. *Application deadline:* For fall admission, 7/1 priority date for domestic students; for spring admission, 11/1 priority date for domestic students. Applications are processed on a rolling basis. Application fee: $30. *Financial support:* In 2009–10, 2 teaching assistantships with partial tuition reimbursements were awarded; tuition waivers (partial) also available. Support available to part-time students. Financial award applicants required to submit FAFSA. *Unit head:* Dr. Mary Janeczek, Director, 413-594-2761, Fax: 413-592-4871, E-mail: janeczeke@elms.edu. *Application contact:* Dana Malone, Associate Director for Graduate Studies and Continuing Education, 413-265-2445, Fax: 413-265-2459, E-mail: maloned@elms.edu.

Fairleigh Dickinson University, Metropolitan Campus, University College: Arts, Sciences, and Professional Studies, School of Natural Sciences, Program in Science, Teaneck, NJ 07666-1914. Offers MA. *Accreditation:* Teacher Education Accreditation Council. *Students:* 15 full-time (11 women), 25 part-time (18 women), 13 international. Average age 30. 24 applicants, 63% accepted, 10 enrolled. In 2009, 18 master's awarded. *Application deadline:* Applications are processed on a rolling basis. Application fee: $40. *Application contact:* Susan Brooman, University Director of Graduate Admissions, 201-692-2554, Fax: 201-692-2560, E-mail: globaleducation@fdu.edu.

Fitchburg State University, Division of Graduate and Continuing Education, Program in Science Education, Fitchburg, MA 01420-2697. Offers M Ed. *Accreditation:* NCATE. Part-time and evening/weekend programs available. *Students:* 1 full-time (0 women), 6 part-time (4 women). Average age 33. 1 applicant, 100% accepted, 1 enrolled. In 2009, 2 master's awarded. *Entrance requirements:* For master's, GRE General Test, teaching certificate, appropriate bachelor's degree, letters of recommendation, resume. Additional exam requirements/recommendations for international students: Required—TOEFL (minimum score 550 paper-based; 213 computer-based; 79 iBT). *Application deadline:* Applications are processed on a rolling basis. Application fee: $25 ($50 for international students). *Expenses:* Tuition, area resident: Part-time $150 per credit. Tuition, state resident: part-time $150 per credit. Tuition, nonresident: part-time $150 per credit. Required fees: $120 per credit. *Financial support:* In 2009–10, research assistantships with partial tuition reimbursements (averaging $5,500 per year); Federal Work-Study, scholarships/grants, and unspecified assistantships also available. Support available to part-time students. Financial award application deadline: 3/1; financial award applicants required to submit FAFSA. *Unit head:* Dr. Christopher Cratsley, Chair, 978-665-3617, Fax: 978-665-3658, E-mail: gce@fsc.edu. *Application contact:* Director of Admissions, 978-665-3144, Fax: 978-665-4540, E-mail: admissions@fsc.edu.

Fitchburg State University, Division of Graduate and Continuing Education, Programs in Biology and Teaching Biology (Secondary Level), Fitchburg, MA 01420-2697. Offers MA, MAT, Certificate. *Accreditation:* NCATE. Part-time and evening/weekend programs available. *Students:* 1 full-time (0 women), 4 part-time (all women). Average age 36. 3 applicants, 100% accepted, 1 enrolled. In 2009, 5 master's awarded. *Entrance requirements:* For master's, GRE General Test, letters of recommendation, resume. Additional exam requirements/recommendations for international students: Required—TOEFL (minimum score 550 paper-based; 213 computer-based; 79 iBT). *Application deadline:* Applications are processed on a rolling basis. Application fee: $25 ($50 for international students). *Expenses:* Tuition, area resident: Part-time $150 per credit. Tuition, state resident: part-time $150 per credit. Tuition, nonresident: part-time $150 per credit. Required fees: $120 per credit. *Financial support:* In 2009–10, research assistantships with partial tuition reimbursements (averaging $5,500 per year); Federal Work-Study, scholarships/grants, and unspecified assistantships also available. Support available to part-time students. Financial award application deadline: 3/1; financial award applicants required to submit FAFSA. *Unit head:* Dr. Christopher Cratsley, Chair, 978-665-3617, Fax: 978-665-3658, E-mail: gce@fsc.edu. *Application contact:* Director of Admissions, 978-665-3144, Fax: 978-665-4540, E-mail: admissions@fsc.edu.

Florida Agricultural and Mechanical University, Division of Graduate Studies, Research, and Continuing Education, College of Education, Program in Secondary Education and Foundation, Tallahassee, FL 32307-3200. Offers biology (M Ed); chemistry (MS Ed); English (MS Ed); history (MS Ed); math (MS Ed); physics (MS Ed). *Accreditation:* NCATE. *Faculty:* 10 full-time (5 women). In 2009, 28 master's awarded. *Degree requirements:* For master's, thesis (for some programs). *Entrance requirements:* For master's, GRE General Test, minimum GPA of 3.0. Additional exam requirements/recommendations for international students: Required—TOEFL. *Application deadline:* For fall admission, 5/18 for domestic students, 12/18 for international students; for spring admission, 11/12 for domestic students, 5/12 for international students. Application fee: $20. *Unit head:* Dr. Bernadette Kelley, Chairperson, 850-599-3123. *Application contact:* Dr. Chanta M. Haywood, Dean of Graduate Studies, Research, and Continuing Education, 850-599-3315, Fax: 850-599-3727.

Florida Institute of Technology, Graduate Programs, College of Science, Department of Science and Mathematics Education, Melbourne, FL 32901-6975. Offers computer education (MS); elementary science education (M Ed); environmental education (MS); informal science education (M Ed); mathematics education (MS, Ed D, PhD, Ed S); science education (MS, Ed D, PhD, Ed S); teaching (MAT). Part-time and evening/weekend programs available. *Faculty:* 4 full-time (1 woman), 3 part-time/adjunct (2 women). *Students:* 15 full-time (9 women), 18 part-time (12 women); includes 5 minority (2 African Americans, 3 Hispanic Americans), 5 international. Average age 36. 42 applicants, 52% accepted, 7 enrolled. In 2009, 3 master's, 1 doctorate, 1 other advanced degree awarded. Terminal master's awarded for partial completion of doctoral program. *Degree requirements:* For master's, comprehensive exam (for some programs), thesis (for some programs), oral final exam; for doctorate, comprehensive exam, thesis/dissertation, oral defense of dissertation; for Ed S, comprehensive exam. *Entrance requirements:* For master's, minimum GPA of 3.0, resume, 3 letters of recommendation (elementary science education); for doctorate, minimum GPA of 3.2, resume, 3 letters of recommendation, statement of objectives, 3 years teaching experience (recommended); for Ed S, minimum GPA of 3.0, resume, 3 letters of recommendation, statement of objectives. Additional exam requirements/recommendations for international students: Required—TOEFL (minimum score 550 paper-based; 213 computer-based; 79 iBT). *Application deadline:* For fall admission, 4/1 for international students; for spring admission, 9/30 for international students. Applications are processed on a rolling basis. Application fee: $50. Electronic applications accepted. *Expenses:* Tuition: Part-time $1015 per credit. Tuition and fees vary according to campus/location and program. *Financial support:* In 2009–10, 3 students received support, including 3 teaching assistantships with full and partial tuition reimbursements available (averaging $6,212 per year); research assistantships with full and partial tuition reimbursements available, career-related internships or fieldwork, institutionally sponsored loans, tuition waivers (partial), unspecified assistantships, and tuition remissions also available. Support available to part-time students. Financial award application deadline: 3/1; financial award applicants required to submit FAFSA. *Faculty research:* Measurement and evaluation, computers in education, educational technology. Total annual research expenditures: $352,726. *Unit head:* Dr. David E. Cook, Department Head, 321-674-8126, Fax: 321-674-7598, E-mail: dcook@fit.edu. *Application contact:* Thomas M. Shea, Director of Graduate Admissions, 321-674-7577, Fax: 321-723-9468, E-mail: tshea@fit.edu.

Florida International University, College of Education, Department of Curriculum and Instruction, Program in Science Education, Miami, FL 33199. Offers MAT, MS, Ed D, PhD. *Accreditation:* NCATE. Part-time and evening/weekend programs available. *Entrance requirements:* Additional exam requirements/recommendations for international students: Required—TOEFL. *Expenses:* Tuition, state resident: full-time $8008; part-time $4004 per year. Tuition, nonresident: full-time $20,104; part-time $10,052 per year. Required fees: $298; $149 per term. *Faculty research:* Science processes, attitudes, bilingual science education, computers in science education.

Florida State University, The Graduate School, College of Education, School of Teacher Education, Program in Science Education, Tallahassee, FL 32306. Offers MS, PhD, Ed S. Part-time programs available. Postbaccalaureate distance learning degree programs offered. *Faculty:* 3 full-time (2 women), 1 part-time/adjunct (0 women). *Students:* 6 full-time (4 women), 35 part-time (22 women); includes 11 minority (5 African Americans, 2 Asian Americans or Pacific Islanders, 4 Hispanic Americans). 24 applicants, 46% accepted, 7 enrolled. In 2009, 4 master's, 2 doctorates awarded. *Degree requirements:* For master's and Ed S, comprehensive exam, thesis optional; for doctorate, comprehensive exam, thesis/dissertation. *Entrance requirements:* For master's, doctorate, and Ed S, GRE General Test, minimum GPA of 3.0. Additional exam requirements/recommendations for international students: Required—TOEFL (minimum score 550 paper-based; 213 computer-based; 80 iBT). *Application deadline:* For fall admission, 6/1 priority date for domestic and international students; for spring admission, 10/1 priority date for domestic and international students. Applications are processed on a rolling basis. Application fee: $30. *Expenses:* Tuition, state resident: full-time $7413. Tuition, nonresident: full-time $22,567. *Financial support:* Fellowships with full and partial tuition reimbursements, research assistantships with full and partial tuition reimbursements, teaching assistantships with full and partial tuition reimbursements, career-related internships or fieldwork and Federal Work-Study available. Financial award applicants required to submit FAFSA. *Unit head:* Dr. Sherry Southerland, Head, 850-644-6553, Fax: 850-644-1880, E-mail: southerl@coe.fsu.edu. *Application contact:* Amy McKnight, Office Manager, 850-644-7810, Fax: 850-644-1880, E-mail: amcknight@coe.fsu.edu.

Fresno Pacific University, Graduate Programs, School of Education, Fresno, CA 93702-4709. Offers administration (MA Ed), including administrative services; foundations, curriculum and teaching (MA Ed), including curriculum and teaching, school library and information technology; language, literacy, and culture (MA Ed), including bilingual/cross-cultural education, language development, multilingual contexts, reading; mathematics/science/computer education (MA Ed), including educational technology, integrated mathematics/science education, mathematics education; pupil personnel services (MA Ed), including school counseling, school psychology; special education (MA Ed), including mild/moderate, moderate/severe, physical and health impairments. Part-time and evening/weekend programs available. *Degree requirements:* For master's, thesis (for some programs). *Entrance requirements:* For master's, interview; GMAT, GRE, MAT, or 6 units of course work with a faculty recommendation. Additional exam requirements/recommendations for international students: Required—TOEFL (minimum score 550 paper-based; 213 computer-based). Electronic applications accepted.

Fresno Pacific University, Graduate Programs, School of Education, Division of Mathematics/Science/Computer Education, Program in Integrated Mathematics/Science Education, Fresno, CA 93702-4709. Offers MA Ed. Part-time and evening/weekend programs available. *Degree requirements:* For master's, thesis or alternative. *Entrance requirements:* Additional exam requirements/recommendations for international students: Required—TOEFL (minimum score 550 paper-based; 213 computer-based).

Gannon University, School of Graduate Studies, College of Engineering and Business, School of Engineering and Computer Science, Program in Natural and Environmental Sciences, Erie, PA 16541-0001. Offers M Ed. Part-time and evening/weekend programs available. *Students:* 1 (woman) part-time. Average age 42. 1 applicant, 100% accepted, 0 enrolled. *Degree requirements:* For master's, research paper. *Entrance requirements:* Additional exam requirements/recommendations for international students: Required—TOEFL (minimum score 79 iBT). *Application deadline:* Applications are processed on a rolling basis. Application fee: $25. Electronic applications accepted. *Expenses:* Tuition: Full-time $13,590; part-time $755 per credit. Required fees: $524; $17 per credit. Tuition and fees vary according to course load, degree level, campus/location and program. *Financial support:* Career-related internships or fieldwork and scholarships/grants available. Financial award application deadline: 7/1; financial award applicants required to submit FAFSA. *Unit head:* Dr. Harry Diz, Chair, 814-871-7633, E-mail: diz001@gannon.edu. *Application contact:* Kara Morgan, Assistant Director of Graduate Admissions, 814-871-5831, Fax: 814-871-5827, E-mail: graduate@gannon.edu.

Georgia Southern University, Jack N. Averitt College of Graduate Studies, College of Education, Department of Teaching and Learning, Program in Science Education, Statesboro, GA 30460. Offers M Ed, MAT. *Accreditation:* NCATE. Part-time and evening/weekend programs available. *Students:* 7 full-time (5 women), 2 part-time (1 woman); includes 1 minority (Hispanic American). Average age 27. 4 applicants, 100% accepted, 3 enrolled. In 2009, 4 master's awarded. *Degree requirements:* For master's, portfolio, transition point assessments, exit assessment. *Entrance requirements:* For master's, GRE General Test or MAT; GACE Basic Skills and Content Assessments (MAT), minimum GPA of 2.5. Additional exam requirements/recommendations for international students: Required—TOEFL (minimum score 550 paper-

based; 213 computer-based; 80 iBT). *Application deadline:* For fall admission, 3/1 priority date for domestic and international students; for spring admission, 10/1 priority date for domestic students, 10/1 for international students. Applications are processed on a rolling basis. Application fee: $50. Electronic applications accepted. *Expenses:* Tuition, state resident: full-time $5040; part-time $210 per credit hour. Tuition, nonresident: full-time $20,136; part-time $839 per credit hour. Required fees: $1644. *Financial support:* In 2009–10, 9 students received support, including research assistantships with partial tuition reimbursements available (averaging $7,200 per year); teaching assistantships with partial tuition reimbursements available (averaging $7,200 per year); Federal Work-Study, scholarships/grants, tuition waivers (partial), and unspecified assistantships also available. Support available to part-time students. Financial award application deadline: 4/15; financial award applicants required to submit FAFSA. *Faculty research:* Gender. *Unit head:* Dr. Ronnie Sheppard, Department Chair, 912-478-5203, Fax: 912-478-0026, E-mail: sheppard@georgiasouthern.edu. *Application contact:* Dr. Charles Ziglar, Coordinator for Graduate Student Recruitment, 912-478-5635, Fax: 912-478-0740, E-mail: gradadmissions@georgiasouthern.edu.

Georgia State University, College of Education, Department of Middle-Secondary Education and Instructional Technology, Programs in Secondary Education, Atlanta, GA 30302-3083. Offers art education (Ed S); English education (M Ed, Ed S); mathematics education (M Ed, PhD, Ed S); music education (PhD); science education (M Ed, PhD, Ed S); social studies education (M Ed, PhD, Ed S). *Accreditation:* NASM (one or more programs are accredited); NCATE. Part-time and evening/weekend programs available. *Degree requirements:* For master's, comprehensive exam; for doctorate, comprehensive exam, thesis/dissertation; for Ed S, project/exam. *Entrance requirements:* For master's, GRE General Test, minimum GPA of 2.5; for doctorate, GRE General Test or MAT, minimum GPA of 3.3; for Ed S, GRE General Test or MAT, minimum graduate GPA of 3.25. *Faculty research:* Women and science, problem solving in mathematics, dialects, economic education.

Grambling State University, School of Graduate Studies and Research, College of Education, Department of Educational Leadership, Grambling, LA 71245. Offers curriculum and instruction (Ed D); developmental education (MS, Ed D), including curriculum and instruction: reading (Ed D), English (MS), guidance and counseling (MS), higher education administration (Ed D), instructional systems and technology (Ed D), mathematics (MS), reading (MS), science (MS), student development and personnel services (Ed D); educational leadership (MS, Ed D). Part-time and evening/weekend programs available. *Faculty:* 19 full-time (12 women). *Students:* 23 full-time (18 women), 84 part-time (62 women); includes 81 minority (80 African Americans, 1 Asian American or Pacific Islander), 5 international. Average age 39. 72 applicants, 75% accepted, 39 enrolled. In 2009, 5 master's, 9 doctorates awarded. *Degree requirements:* For master's, comprehensive exam, thesis (for some programs); for doctorate, comprehensive exam, thesis/dissertation. *Entrance requirements:* For master's, GRE, minimum GPA of 2.5 on last degree; for doctorate, GRE (minimum 1000, 500 on Verbal), master's degree, minimum GPA of 3.0 on last degree. Additional exam requirements/recommendations for international students: Required—TOEFL (minimum score 500 paper-based; 173 computer-based; 61 iBT). *Application deadline:* For fall admission, 7/1 for domestic and international students; for spring admission, 12/1 for domestic and international students. Applications are processed on a rolling basis. Application fee: $20 ($30 for international students). Electronic applications accepted. *Expenses:* Tuition, state resident: full-time $2610. Tuition, nonresident: full-time $2610. *Financial support:* In 2009–10, 5 research assistantships (averaging $10,948 per year) were awarded; health care benefits, tuition waivers (full), and unspecified assistantships also available. Financial award application deadline: 5/31; financial award applicants required to submit FAFSA. *Unit head:* Dr. Olatunde Ogunyemi, Director, 318-274-6105, Fax: 318-274-2799, E-mail: ogunyemio@gram.edu. *Application contact:* Laketha Richards, Administrative Assistant III, 318-274-6105, Fax: 318-274-6249, E-mail: richardsl@gram.edu.

Hamline University, School of Education, St. Paul, MN 55104-1284. Offers education (MA Ed, Ed D); English as a second language (MAESL); literacy education (MALED); natural science and environmental education (MA Ed); teaching (MAT). *Accreditation:* NCATE (one or more programs are accredited). Part-time and evening/weekend programs available. *Faculty:* 27 full-time (18 women), 128 part-time/adjunct (100 women). *Students:* 324 full-time (242 women), 1,049 part-time (780 women); includes 116 minority (36 African Americans, 4 American Indian/Alaska Native, 42 Asian Americans or Pacific Islanders, 34 Hispanic Americans), 25 international. Average age 33. 501 applicants, 79% accepted, 311 enrolled. In 2009, 196 master's, 9 doctorates awarded. *Degree requirements:* For master's, thesis; for doctorate, comprehensive exam, thesis/dissertation. *Entrance requirements:* For doctorate, personal statement, master's degree, 3 years experience, letters of recommendation, writing sample, interview. Additional exam requirements/recommendations for international students: Required—TOEFL (minimum score 550 paper-based; 213 computer-based; 79 iBT), TWE (minimum score 5). *Application deadline:* Applications are processed on a rolling basis. Application fee: $0. Electronic applications accepted. *Expenses:* Tuition: Full-time $6816; part-time $426 per credit. Required fees: $6 per credit. One-time fee: $205. Tuition and fees vary according to degree level, campus/location and program. *Financial support:* In 2009–10, 8 students received support. Federal Work-Study and scholarships/grants available. Support available to part-time students. Financial award applicants required to submit FAFSA. *Faculty research:* Adult basic education, service learning, teacher dispositions, diversity, technology. *Unit head:* Dr. Sheila Wright, Dean, 651-523-2600, Fax: 651-523-2489, E-mail: swright04@hamline.edu. *Application contact:* Rae A. Lenway, Director, Graduate Recruitment and Admission, 651-523-2900, Fax: 651-523-3058, E-mail: rlenway@hamline.edu.

Harding University, College of Education, Searcy, AR 72149-0001. Offers advanced studies in teaching and learning (M Ed); art (MSE); behavioral science (MSE); counseling (MS, Ed S); early childhood special education (M Ed, MSE); education (MSE); educational leadership (M Ed, Ed S); elementary education (M Ed); English (MSE); family and consumer science (MSE); French (MSE); history/social science (MSE); kinesiology (MSE); math (MSE); physical science (MSE); reading (M Ed); secondary education (M Ed); Spanish (MSE); special education licensure (M Ed); teaching (MAT); teaching English as a second language (M Ed). *Accreditation:* NCATE. Part-time and evening/weekend programs available. *Faculty:* 11 full-time (4 women), 49 part-time/adjunct (26 women). *Students:* 104 full-time (85 women), 392 part-time (282 women); includes 77 minority (67 African Americans, 5 American Indian/Alaska Native, 1 Asian American or Pacific Islander, 4 Hispanic Americans), 5 international. Average age 36. 153 applicants, 92% accepted, 131 enrolled. In 2009, 153 master's, 6 other advanced degrees awarded. *Degree requirements:* For master's, comprehensive exam (for some programs), thesis optional, portfolio(s); for Ed S, comprehensive exam, portfolio, specialist project. *Entrance requirements:* For master's, GRE, MAT, PRAXIS; for Ed S, MAT or GRE. Additional exam requirements/recommendations for international students: Required—TOEFL (minimum score 550 paper-based; 79 iBT). *Application deadline:* For fall admission, 8/1 for domestic and international students; for spring admission, 1/1 for domestic and international students. Applications are processed on a rolling basis. Application fee: $35. *Expenses:* Tuition: Full-time $9720; part-time $540 per credit hour. Required fees: $22 per credit hour. Tuition and fees vary according to course load and program. *Financial support:* In 2009–10, 30 students received support. Unspecified assistantships available. *Faculty research:* Reading, comprehension, school violence, educational technology, behavior, college choice, differentiated instruction, brain-based teaching. *Unit head:* Dr. Clara Carroll, Chair, 501-279-4501, Fax: 501-279-4083, E-mail: ccarroll@harding.edu. *Application contact:* Information Contact, 501-279-4315, E-mail: gradstudiesedu@harding.edu.

Hardin-Simmons University, Graduate School, Holland School of Sciences and Mathematics, Abilene, TX 79698-0001. Offers MS, DPT. Part-time programs available. *Faculty:* 4 full-time (0 women). *Students:* 6 full-time (1 woman), 1 (woman) part-time; includes 1 minority (Hispanic American). Average age 29. 6 applicants, 83% accepted, 5 enrolled. In 2009, 2 master's awarded. *Degree requirements:* For master's, comprehensive exam, thesis or alternative, internship; for doctorate, comprehensive exam, thesis/dissertation or alternative. *Entrance requirements:* For master's, minimum undergraduate GPA of 3.0 in major, 2.7 overall; 2 semesters of course work each in biology, chemistry and geology; interview; writing sample;

occupational experience; for doctorate, letters of recommendation, interview, writing sample. Additional exam requirements/recommendations for international students: Required—TOEFL (minimum score 550 paper-based; 213 computer-based; 75 iBT). *Application deadline:* For fall admission, 8/15 priority date for domestic students, 4/1 for international students; for spring admission, 1/5 priority date for domestic students, 9/1 for international students. Applications are processed on a rolling basis. Application fee: $50. *Expenses:* Tuition: Full-time $11,430; part-time $635 per credit hour. Required fees: $650; $110 per semester. Tuition and fees vary according to degree level. *Financial support:* Fellowships, career-related internships or fieldwork and scholarships/grants available. Support available to part-time students. Financial award application deadline: 6/30; financial award applicants required to submit FAFSA. *Unit head:* Dr. Christopher McNair, Dean, 325-670-1401, Fax: 325-670-1385, E-mail: cmcnair@hsutx.edu. *Application contact:* Dr. Gary Stanlake, Dean of Graduate Studies, 325-670-1298, Fax: 325-670-1564, E-mail: gradoff@hsutx.edu.

Harvard University, Graduate School of Education, Master's Programs in Education, Cambridge, MA 02138. Offers arts in education (Ed M); education policy and management (Ed M); higher education (Ed M); human development and psychology (Ed M); international education policy (Ed M); language and literacy (Ed M); learning and teaching (Ed M); mid-career mathematics and science (teaching certificate) (Ed M); mind brain and education (Ed M); risk and prevention (Ed M); school leadership (Ed M); special studies (Ed M); teaching and curriculum (teaching certificate) (Ed M); technology innovation and education (Ed M). Part-time programs available. *Faculty:* 70 full-time (33 women), 36 part-time/adjunct (20 women). *Students:* 598 full-time (448 women), 76 part-time (60 women); includes 132 minority (40 African Americans, 2 American Indian/Alaska Native, 58 Asian Americans or Pacific Islanders, 32 Hispanic Americans), 103 international. Average age 28. 1,574 applicants, 58% accepted, 640 enrolled. In 2009, 556 master's awarded. *Entrance requirements:* For master's, GRE General Test, 3 letters of recommendation. Additional exam requirements/recommendations for international students: Required—TOEFL (minimum score 600 paper-based; 250 computer-based; 100 iBT), TWE (minimum score 5). *Application deadline:* For fall admission, 1/4 fpr domestic and international students. Application fee: $85. Electronic applications accepted. *Expenses:* Contact institution. *Financial support:* In 2009–10, 424 students received support, including 25 fellowships with full and partial tuition reimbursements available (averaging $15,890 per year); career-related internships or fieldwork, Federal Work-Study, institutionally sponsored loans, scholarships/grants, health care benefits, tuition waivers (full and partial), and unspecified assistantships also available. Support available to part-time students. Financial award application deadline: 2/1; financial award applicants required to submit FAFSA. *Faculty research:* Learning and development, educational leadership and organizations, educational policy analysis. Total annual research expenditures: $18.1 million. *Unit head:* Jennifer L. Petrallia, Assistant Dean, 617-495-8445. *Application contact:* Information Contact, 617-495-3414, Fax: 617-496-3577, E-mail: gseadmissions@harvard.edu.

Heritage University, Graduate Programs in Education, Toppenish, WA 98948-9599. Offers counseling (M Ed); educational administration (M Ed); professional studies (M Ed), including bilingual education/ESL, biology, English and literature, reading/literacy, special education; teaching (MIT). Part-time and evening/weekend programs available. *Degree requirements:* For master's, comprehensive exam, thesis (for some programs). *Entrance requirements:* For master's, interview, letters of recommendation, teaching certificate. Additional exam requirements/recommendations for international students: Recommended—TOEFL (minimum score 550 paper-based; 213 computer-based).

Hofstra University, School of Education, Health, and Human Services, Department of Curriculum and Teaching, Program in Elementary Education—Math, Science, and Technology, Hempstead, NY 11549. Offers MA. Part-time and evening/weekend programs available. *Students:* 3 full-time (all women), 12 part-time (all women); includes 1 minority (Hispanic American). Average age 25. 7 applicants, 100% accepted, 5 enrolled. In 2009, 10 master's awarded. *Degree requirements:* For master's, thesis. *Entrance requirements:* For master's, 2 letters of recommendation, interview, teaching certificate (MA), essay. Additional exam requirements/recommendations for international students: Required—TOEFL (minimum score 550 paper-based; 213 computer-based; 80 iBT). *Application deadline:* Applications are processed on a rolling basis. Application fee: $60. Electronic applications accepted. *Expenses:* Tuition: Full-time $16,200; part-time $900 per credit hour. Required fees: $970; $145 per term. Tuition and fees vary according to program. *Financial support:* In 2009–10, 8 students received support, including 3 fellowships with full and partial tuition reimbursements available (averaging $3,167 per year); research assistantships with full and partial tuition reimbursements available, Federal Work-Study, institutionally sponsored loans, scholarships/grants, tuition waivers (full and partial), and unspecified assistantships also available. Support available to part-time students. Financial award applicants required to submit FAFSA. *Faculty research:* Constructivism, interdisciplinary curriculum, design and technology education, science inquiry, problem-based learning. *Unit head:* Dr. Irene Plonczak, Program Director, 516-463-5768, Fax: 516-463-6196, E-mail: catizp@hofstra.edu. *Application contact:* Carol Drummer, Dean of Graduate Admissions, 516-463-4876, Fax: 516-463-4664, E-mail: gradstudent@hofstra.edu.

Hofstra University, School of Education, Health, and Human Services, Department of Curriculum and Teaching, Program in Learning and Teaching, Hempstead, NY 11549. Offers learning and teaching (Ed D), including applied linguistics, art education, arts and humanities, early childhood education, English education, human development, math education, math, science, and technology, multicultural education, physical education, science education, social studies education, special education. Part-time and evening/weekend programs available. *Students:* 5 full-time (all women), 21 part-time (17 women); includes 2 minority (1 African American, 1 Hispanic American), 1 international. Average age 38. 22 applicants, 68% accepted, 11 enrolled. *Degree requirements:* For doctorate, comprehensive exam, thesis/dissertation. *Entrance requirements:* For doctorate, GRE, 3 letters of recommendation, interview, 2 years full-time teaching experience. Additional exam requirements/recommendations for international students: Required—TOEFL (minimum score 550 paper-based; 213 computer-based; 80 iBT). *Application deadline:* Applications are processed on a rolling basis. Application fee: $60. Electronic applications accepted. *Expenses:* Tuition: Full-time $16,200; part-time $900 per credit hour. Required fees: $970; $145 per term. Tuition and fees vary according to program. *Financial support:* In 2009–10, 24 students received support, including 20 fellowships with full and partial tuition reimbursements available (averaging $4,906 per year); research assistantships with full and partial tuition reimbursements available, Federal Work-Study, institutionally sponsored loans, scholarships/grants, and tuition waivers (full and partial) also available. Support available to part-time students. Financial award applicants required to submit FAFSA. *Faculty research:* Critical thinking, professional development, teacher quality, quantitative research. *Unit head:* Dr. Bruce A. Torff, Director, 516-463-5803, Fax: 516-463-6196, E-mail: catajs@hofstra.edu. *Application contact:* Carol Drummer, Dean of Graduate Admissions, 516-463-4876, Fax: 516-463-4664, E-mail: gradstudent@hofstra.edu.

Hofstra University, School of Education, Health, and Human Services, Department of Curriculum and Teaching, Program in Science Education, Hempstead, NY 11549. Offers science education (MA, MS Ed), including biology, chemistry, earth science, geology, physics. Part-time programs available. *Students:* 16 full-time (11 women), 10 part-time (7 women); includes 4 minority (1 African American, 2 Asian Americans or Pacific Islanders, 1 Hispanic American). Average age 27. 13 applicants, 92% accepted, 5 enrolled. In 2009, 19 master's awarded. *Degree requirements:* For master's, one foreign language, comprehensive exam (for some programs), thesis optional, electronic portfolio. *Entrance requirements:* For master's, 2 letters of recommendation, teacher certification (MA). Additional exam requirements/recommendations for international students: Required—TOEFL (minimum score 550 paper-based; 213 computer-based; 80 iBT). *Application deadline:* Applications are processed on a rolling basis. Application fee: $60. Electronic applications accepted. *Expenses:* Tuition: Full-time $16,200; part-time $900 per credit hour. Required fees: $970; $145 per term. Tuition and fees vary according to program. *Financial support:* In 2009–10, 14 students received support, including 4 fellowships with full and partial tuition reimbursements available (averaging $3,533 per year); research assistantships with full and partial tuition reimbursements available, Federal Work-Study,

Science Education

Hofstra University (continued)

institutionally sponsored loans, scholarships/grants, tuition waivers (full and partial), and unspecified assistantships also available. Support available to part-time students. Financial award applicants required to submit FAFSA. *Faculty research:* Cognitive science, inclusive science education, science, technology and twenty-first century skills, environmental education. *Unit head:* Dr. Jacqueline G. Brooks, Director, 516-463-5777, Fax: 516-463-6196, E-mail: catjgb@hofstra.edu. *Application contact:* Carol Drummer, Dean of Graduate Admissions, 516-463-4876, Fax: 516-463-4664, E-mail: gradstudent@hofstra.edu.

Hood College, Graduate School, Department of Education, Frederick, MD 21701-8575. Offers curriculum and instruction (MS), including early childhood education, elementary education, elementary school science and mathematics, secondary education, special education; educational leadership (MS, Certificate); reading specialization (MS). Part-time and evening/weekend programs available. *Faculty:* 4 full-time (all women), 39 part-time/adjunct (21 women). *Students:* 2 full-time (both women), 397 part-time (326 women); includes 41 minority (29 African Americans, 5 Asian Americans or Pacific Islanders, 7 Hispanic Americans). Average age 33. 100 applicants, 92% accepted, 84 enrolled. In 2009, 73 master's, 65 other advanced degrees awarded. *Degree requirements:* For master's, action research project, portfolio (reading). *Entrance requirements:* For master's, minimum GPA of 2.75, teaching certification. *Application deadline:* For fall admission, 7/15 for domestic and international students; for spring admission, 12/15 for domestic and international students. Applications are processed on a rolling basis. Application fee: $35. Electronic applications accepted. *Expenses:* Tuition: Full-time $6480; part-time $360 per credit. Required fees: $100; $50 per term. *Financial support:* Applicants required to submit FAFSA. *Faculty research:* Leadership, action research, brain research, learning styles. *Unit head:* Dr. John George, Chairperson, 301-696-3471, Fax: 301-696-3597, E-mail: george@hood.edu. *Application contact:* Dr. Allen P. Flora, Dean of Graduate School, 301-696-3811, Fax: 301-696-3597, E-mail: gofurther@hood.edu.

Hunter College of the City University of New York, Graduate School, School of Arts and Sciences, Department of Geography, New York, NY 10021-5085. Offers analytical geography (MA); earth system science (MA); environmental and social issues (MA); geographic information science (Certificate); geographic information systems (MA); teaching earth science (MA). Part-time and evening/weekend programs available. *Faculty:* 12 full-time (5 women), 4 part-time/adjunct (0 women). *Students:* 17 full-time (16 women), 20 part-time (19 women); includes 9 minority (1 African American, 1 American Indian/Alaska Native, 4 Asian Americans or Pacific Islanders, 3 Hispanic Americans). Average age 31. 13 applicants, 92% accepted, 9 enrolled. In 2009, 10 master's, 3 other advanced degrees awarded. *Degree requirements:* For master's, comprehensive exam or thesis. *Entrance requirements:* For master's, GRE General Test, minimum B average in major, B- overall; 18 credits of course work in geography; 2 letters of recommendation; for Certificate, minimum B average in major, B- overall. Additional exam requirements/recommendations for international students: Required—TOEFL. *Application deadline:* For fall admission, 4/1 for domestic students; for spring admission, 11/1 for domestic students. Applications are processed on a rolling basis. Application fee: $125. *Expenses:* Tuition, state resident: full-time $7360; part-time $310 per credit. Required fees: $250 per semester. *Financial support:* In 2009–10, 1 fellowship (averaging $3,000 per year), 2 research assistantships (averaging $10,000 per year), 10 teaching assistantships (averaging $6,000 per year) were awarded; career-related internships or fieldwork, Federal Work-Study, institutionally sponsored loans, and unspecified assistantships also available. Financial award application deadline: 3/1. *Faculty research:* Urban geography, economic geography, geographic information science, demographic methods, climate change. *Unit head:* Prof. William Solecki, Chair, 212-772-4536, Fax: 212-772-5268, E-mail: wsolecki@hunter.cuny.edu. *Application contact:* Prof. Marianna Pavlovskaya, Graduate Adviser, 212-772-5320, Fax: 212-772-5268, E-mail: mpavlov@geo.hunter.cuny.edu.

Hunter College of the City University of New York, Graduate School, School of Education, Programs in Secondary Education, Concentration in Biology Education, New York, NY 10021-5085. Offers MA. *Accreditation:* NCATE. *Faculty:* 17 full-time (8 women), 16 part-time/adjunct (13 women). *Students:* 2 full-time (both women), 16 part-time (12 women); includes 3 minority (2 African Americans, 1 Asian American or Pacific Islander). Average age 33. 18 applicants, 28% accepted, 1 enrolled. In 2009, 6 master's awarded. *Degree requirements:* For master's, thesis, professional teaching portfolio, New York State Teacher Certification Exams, research project. *Entrance requirements:* For master's, minimum GPA of 2.8, 2 letters of reference, 21 credits of course work in biology. Additional exam requirements/recommendations for international students: Required—TOEFL, TWE. *Application deadline:* For fall admission, 4/1 for domestic students, 2/1 for international students; for spring admission, 11/1 for domestic students, 9/1 for international students. Application fee: $125. *Expenses:* Tuition, state resident: full-time $7360; part-time $310 per credit. Required fees: $250 per semester. *Financial support:* Federal Work-Study and tuition waivers (partial) available. Support available to part-time students. *Unit head:* Dr. Steve Demeo, Program Advisor, 212-772-4776, E-mail: sdemeo@hunter.cuny.edu. *Application contact:* William Zlata, Director for Graduate Admissions, 212-772-4482, Fax: 212-650-3336, E-mail: admissions@hunter.cuny.edu.

Hunter College of the City University of New York, Graduate School, School of Education, Programs in Secondary Education, Concentration in Chemistry Education, New York, NY 10021-5085. Offers MA. *Accreditation:* NCATE. *Faculty:* 4 full-time (3 women), 15 part-time/adjunct (12 women). *Students:* 2 full-time (both women), 5 part-time (3 women); includes 2 minority (both Asian Americans or Pacific Islanders). Average age 27. 5 applicants, 60% accepted, 2 enrolled. In 2009, 5 master's awarded. *Degree requirements:* For master's, thesis, professional teaching portfolio, New York State Teacher Certification Exam. *Entrance requirements:* For master's, minimum GPA of 2.8, 2 letters of reference, minimum of 29 credits in science and mathematics. *Application deadline:* For fall admission, 4/1 for domestic students, 2/1 for international students; for spring admission, 11/1 for domestic students, 9/1 for international students. Application fee: $125. *Expenses:* Tuition, state resident: full-time $7360; part-time $310 per credit. Required fees: $250 per semester. *Financial support:* Federal Work-Study and tuition waivers (partial) available. Support available to part-time students. *Unit head:* Dr. Stephen DeMeo, Education Advisor, 212-772-4776, E-mail: sdemeo@patsy.hunter.cuny.edu. *Application contact:* Pamela Mills, Chemistry Department Advisor, 212-772-5331, E-mail: pam.mills@hunter.cuny.edu.

ICR Graduate School, Graduate Programs, Santee, CA 92071. Offers astro/geophysics (MS); biology (MS); geology (MS); science education (MS). Part-time programs available. *Degree requirements:* For master's, comprehensive exam (for some programs), thesis (for some programs). *Entrance requirements:* For master's, minimum undergraduate GPA of 3.0, bachelor's degree in science or science education. *Faculty research:* Age of the earth, limits of variation, catastrophe, optimum methods for teaching.

Illinois Institute of Technology, Graduate College, College of Science and Letters, Department of Computer Science, Chicago, IL 60616-3793. Offers computer science (MCS, MS, PhD); teaching (MST); telecommunications and software engineering (MTSE); MS/M Ch E. Part-time and evening/weekend programs available. Postbaccalaureate distance learning degree programs offered (no on-campus study). *Faculty:* 26 full-time (5 women), 3 part-time/adjunct (0 women). *Students:* 227 full-time (60 women), 167 part-time (37 women); includes 15 minority (5 African Americans, 6 Asian Americans or Pacific Islanders, 4 Hispanic Americans), 334 international. Average age 27. 1,016 applicants, 59% accepted, 111 enrolled. In 2009, 151 master's, 8 doctorates awarded. Terminal master's awarded for partial completion of doctoral program. *Degree requirements:* For master's, thesis (for some programs); for doctorate, comprehensive exam, thesis/dissertation. *Entrance requirements:* For master's and doctorate, GRE General Test, minimum undergraduate GPA of 3.0. Additional exam requirements/recommendations for international students: Required—TOEFL (minimum score 523 paper-based; 70 iBT). *Application deadline:* For fall admission, 5/1 for domestic and international students; for spring admission, 10/15 for domestic and international students. Applications are processed on a rolling basis. Application fee: $50. Electronic applications accepted. *Expenses:* Tuition: Full-time $17,550; part-time $888 per credit hour. Required fees: $850; $7.50 per credit hour. One-time fee: $50 full-time. Full-time tuition and fees vary according to program. *Financial support:* In 2009–10, 2 fellowships with full and partial tuition reimbursements (averaging $7,500 per year), 17 research assistantships with full and partial tuition reimbursements (averaging $6,000 per year), 23 teaching assistantships with full and partial tuition reimbursements (averaging $6,000 per year) were awarded; career-related internships or fieldwork, Federal Work-Study, institutionally sponsored loans, scholarships/grants, traineeships, health care benefits, tuition waivers (partial), and unspecified assistantships also available. Support available to part-time students. Financial award applicants required to submit FAFSA. *Faculty research:* Information retrieval, parallel and distributed computing, networking, algorithms, natural language processing. *Unit head:* Dr. Xian-He Sun, Chair & Professor of Computer Science, 312-567-5260, Fax: 312-567-5067, E-mail: sun@cs.iit.edu. *Application contact:* Dr. Xian-He Sun, Chair & Professor of Computer Science, 312-567-5260, Fax: 312-567-5067, E-mail: sun@cs.iit.edu.

Illinois Institute of Technology, Graduate College, College of Science and Letters, Department of Mathematics and Science Education, Chicago, IL 60616-3793. Offers collegiate mathematics education (PhD); mathematics education (MME, MS, PhD); science education (MS, MSE, PhD). *Faculty:* 8 full-time (4 women), 2 part-time/adjunct (1 woman). *Students:* 33 full-time (18 women), 61 part-time (44 women); includes 23 minority (15 African Americans, 2 Asian Americans or Pacific Islanders, 6 Hispanic Americans), 2 international. Average age 37. 34 applicants, 62% accepted, 11 enrolled. In 2009, 15 master's, 2 doctorates awarded. *Degree requirements:* For master's, comprehensive exam (for some programs), thesis or alternative; for doctorate, comprehensive exam, thesis/dissertation. *Entrance requirements:* For master's, GRE General Test, minimum undergraduate GPA of 3.0; for doctorate, GRE General Test, minimum GPA of 3.0, 3 years of teaching experience. Additional exam requirements/recommendations for international students: Required—TOEFL (minimum score 523 paper-based; 70 iBT). *Application deadline:* For fall admission, 5/1 for domestic and international students; for spring admission, 10/15 for domestic and international students. Applications are processed on a rolling basis. Application fee: $50. Electronic applications accepted. *Expenses:* Tuition: Full-time $17,550; part-time $888 per credit hour. Required fees: $850; $7.50 per credit hour. One-time fee: $50 full-time. Full-time tuition and fees vary according to program. *Financial support:* Career-related internships or fieldwork, Federal Work-Study, institutionally sponsored loans, scholarships/grants, health care benefits, tuition waivers (partial), and unspecified assistantships available. Support available to part-time students. Financial award applicants required to submit FAFSA. *Faculty research:* Nature of science, scientific inquiry, pedagogical content knowledge, classroom discourse, model eliciting activities. Total annual research expenditures: $87,994. *Unit head:* Dr. Norman G. Lederman, Chair, Professor, 312-567-3659, Fax: 312-567-3659, E-mail: ledermann@iit.edu. *Application contact:* Dr. Norman G. Lederman, Chair, Professor, 312-567-3659, Fax: 312-567-3659, E-mail: ledermann@iit.edu.

Indiana State University, School of Graduate Studies, College of Arts and Sciences, Department of Biology, Terre Haute, IN 47809. Offers ecology (PhD); life sciences (MS); microbiology (PhD); physiology (PhD); science education (MS). *Degree requirements:* For master's, thesis (for some programs); for doctorate, comprehensive exam, thesis/dissertation. *Entrance requirements:* For master's and doctorate, GRE General Test. Electronic applications accepted.

Indiana State University, School of Graduate Studies, College of Arts and Sciences, Department of Science Education, Terre Haute, IN 47809. Offers MS. *Accreditation:* NCATE. *Degree requirements:* For master's, thesis optional. Electronic applications accepted.

Indiana Tech, Program in Science, Fort Wayne, IN 46803-1297. Offers MSE. Part-time and evening/weekend programs available. *Students:* 10 full-time (3 women), 1 part-time (0 women), 3 international. Average age 38. *Entrance requirements:* For master's, undergraduate transcript from accredited university with minimum GPA of 2.5, 3 letters of recommendation. *Application deadline:* Applications are processed on a rolling basis. Application fee: $25. Electronic applications accepted. *Expenses:* Tuition: Full-time $5160; part-time $430 per credit hour. Tuition and fees vary according to degree level and program. *Financial support:* Applicants required to submit FAFSA. *Unit head:* Dave Aschliman, Dean of Engineering, 260-422-5561 Ext. 2102, E-mail: daaschliman@indianatech.edu. *Application contact:* Steve Herendeen, Associate Vice President of College of Professional Studies Admissions, 260-422-5561 Ext. 2121, E-mail: saherendeen@indianatech.edu.

Indiana University Bloomington, School of Education, Department of Curriculum and Instruction, Bloomington, IN 47405-7000. Offers art education (MS, Ed D, PhD); curriculum studies (Ed D, PhD); elementary education (MS, Ed D, PhD, Ed S); mathematics education (MS, Ed D, PhD); science education (MS, Ed D, PhD); secondary education (MS, Ed D, PhD); social studies education (MS, PhD); special education (MS, Ed D, PhD, Ed S). *Accreditation:* NCATE. Part-time and evening/weekend programs available. *Students:* 208 full-time (155 women), 44 part-time (25 women); includes 28 minority (9 African Americans, 3 American Indian/Alaska Native, 9 Asian Americans or Pacific Islanders, 7 Hispanic Americans), 34 international. Average age 34. 100 applicants, 68% accepted, 39 enrolled. In 2009, 48 master's, 20 doctorates awarded. Terminal master's awarded for partial completion of doctoral program. *Degree requirements:* For doctorate, thesis/dissertation; for Ed S, comprehensive exam or project. *Entrance requirements:* For master's, doctorate, and Ed S, GRE General Test. *Application deadline:* For fall admission, 6/1 priority date for domestic students, 3/1 for international students; for winter admission, 11/1 priority date for domestic students; for spring admission, 9/1 for international students. Applications are processed on a rolling basis. Application fee: $55 ($65 for international students). Electronic applications accepted. *Financial support:* Fellowships with full and partial tuition reimbursements, research assistantships with full and partial tuition reimbursements, teaching assistantships with full and partial tuition reimbursements, career-related internships or fieldwork, Federal Work-Study, institutionally sponsored loans, and tuition waivers (partial) available. Support available to part-time students. *Unit head:* Cary Buzzelli, Chairperson, 812-856-8100. *Application contact:* Bobbie Partenheimer, Admissions Services Coordinator, 812-856-8127, Fax: 812-856-8333, E-mail: partenhe@indiana.edu.

Indiana University Bloomington, University Graduate School, College of Arts and Sciences, Department of Biology, Bloomington, IN 47405. Offers biology teaching (MAT); biotechnology (MA); evolution, ecology, and behavior (MA, PhD); genetics (PhD); microbiology (MA, PhD); molecular, cellular, and developmental biology (PhD); plant sciences (MA, PhD); zoology (MA, PhD). *Faculty:* 58 full-time (15 women), 21 part-time/adjunct (6 women). *Students:* 165 full-time (95 women); includes 14 minority (6 African Americans, 1 American Indian/Alaska Native, 7 Asian Americans or Pacific Islanders), 56 international. Average age 27. 312 applicants, 19% accepted, 24 enrolled. In 2009, 4 master's, 22 doctorates awarded. Terminal master's awarded for partial completion of doctoral program. *Degree requirements:* For master's, thesis, oral defense; for doctorate, thesis/dissertation, oral defense. *Entrance requirements:* For master's and doctorate, GRE General Test. Additional exam requirements/recommendations for international students: Required—TOEFL (minimum score 100 iBT). *Application deadline:* For fall admission, 1/5 priority date for domestic students, 12/1 priority date for international students. Application fee: $55 ($65 for international students). Electronic applications accepted. *Financial support:* In 2009–10, 165 students received support, including 62 fellowships with tuition reimbursements available (averaging $19,484 per year), 27 research assistantships with tuition reimbursements available (averaging $22,605 per year), 76 teaching assistantships with tuition reimbursements available (averaging $20,528 per year); scholarships/grants, traineeships, health care benefits, and unspecified assistantships also available. Financial award application deadline: 1/5. *Faculty research:* Evolution, ecology and behavior; microbiology; molecular biology and genetics; plant biology. *Unit head:* Dr. Roger Innes, Chair, 812-855-2219, Fax: 812-855-6082, E-mail: rinnes@indiana.edu. *Application contact:* Tracey D. Stohr, Graduate Student Recruitment Coordinator, 812-856-6303, Fax: 812-855-6082, E-mail: gradbio@indiana.edu.

Indiana University Bloomington, University Graduate School, College of Arts and Sciences, Department of Chemistry, Bloomington, IN 47405-7000. Offers analytical chemistry (PhD); biological chemistry (PhD); chemistry (MAT); inorganic chemistry (PhD); physical chemistry

(PhD). *Faculty:* 39 full-time (3 women). *Students:* 190 full-time (67 women), 1 (woman) part-time; includes 13 minority (4 African Americans, 1 American Indian/Alaska Native, 5 Asian Americans or Pacific Islanders, 3 Hispanic Americans), 66 international. Average age 26. 207 applicants, 60% accepted, 49 enrolled. In 2009, 10 master's, 20 doctorates awarded. Terminal master's awarded for partial completion of doctoral program. *Degree requirements:* For master's, thesis; for doctorate, thesis/dissertation. *Entrance requirements:* For master's and doctorate, GRE General Test, GRE Subject Test. Additional exam requirements/recommendations for international students: Required—TOEFL. *Application deadline:* For fall admission, 1/15 priority date for domestic students, 12/15 for international students; for spring admission, 9/1 priority date for domestic students, 9/1 for international students. Applications are processed on a rolling basis. Application fee: $55 ($65 for international students). *Financial support:* Fellowships with full tuition reimbursements, research assistantships with full tuition reimbursements, teaching assistantships with full tuition reimbursements, Federal Work-Study and institutionally sponsored loans available. *Faculty research:* Synthesis of complex natural products, organic reaction mechanisms, organic electrochemistry, transitive-metal chemistry, solid-state and surface chemistry. Total annual research expenditures: $7.7 million. *Unit head:* Jim Reilly, Chairperson, 812-855-6239, E-mail: chemchair@indiana.edu. *Application contact:* Martin Jarrold, Director of Graduate Admissions, 812-855-2069, E-mail: mfj@indiana.edu.

Instituto Tecnológico y de Estudios Superiores de Monterrey, Campus Monterrey, Graduate and Research Division, Program in Natural and Social Sciences, Monterrey, Mexico. Offers biotechnology (MS); chemistry (MS, PhD); communications (MS); education (MA). Part-time programs available. *Degree requirements:* For master's, one foreign language, thesis; for doctorate, one foreign language, thesis/dissertation. *Entrance requirements:* For master's, EXADEP; for doctorate, EXADEP, master's degree in related field. Additional exam requirements/recommendations for international students: Required—TOEFL. *Faculty research:* Cultural industries, mineral substances, bioremediation, food processing, CQ in industrial chemical processing.

Inter American University of Puerto Rico, Arecibo Campus, Programs in Education, Arecibo, PR 00614-4050. Offers administration and educational supervision (MA Ed); counseling and guidance (MA Ed); curriculum and teaching (MA Ed), including biology education, English as a second language, history education, math education, Spanish; elementary education (MA Ed). *Degree requirements:* For master's, comprehensive exam, thesis optional. *Entrance requirements:* For master's, GRE, EXADEP, bachelor's degree in education or teaching license (administration and supervision) or courses in education and psychology (counseling and guidance), minimum GPA of 2.5 in last 60 credits.

Inter American University of Puerto Rico, Metropolitan Campus, Graduate Programs, Program in Teaching of Science, San Juan, PR 00919-1293. Offers MA. *Degree requirements:* For master's, comprehensive exam. *Entrance requirements:* For master's, GRE or EXADEP, interview. Electronic applications accepted.

Inter American University of Puerto Rico, Ponce Campus, Graduate School, Mercedita, PR 00715-1602. Offers accounting (MBA); biology (M Ed); chemistry (M Ed); criminal justice (MA); elementary education (M Ed); English as a Second Language (M Ed); finance (MBA); history (M Ed); human resources (MBA); marketing (MBA); mathematics (M Ed); Spanish (M Ed). *Entrance requirements:* For master's, minimum GPA of 2.5.

Inter American University of Puerto Rico, San Germán Campus, Graduate Studies Center, Program in Science Education, San Germán, PR 00683-5008. Offers MA. Part-time and evening/weekend programs available. *Degree requirements:* For master's, comprehensive exam. *Entrance requirements:* For master's, GRE General Test or EXADEP, minimum GPA of 3.0.

Iona College, School of Arts and Science, Program in Education, New Rochelle, NY 10801-1890. Offers biology education (MS Ed, MST); educational leadership (MS Ed); English education (MS Ed, MST); literacy education (MS Ed); mathematics education (MS Ed, MST); social studies education (MS Ed, MST); Spanish education (MS Ed, MST); teaching in childhood education (MST). *Accreditation:* NCATE. Part-time and evening/weekend programs available. *Faculty:* 24 full-time (13 women), 16 part-time/adjunct (10 women). *Students:* 41 full-time (35 women), 118 part-time (87 women); includes 15 minority (5 African Americans, 1 Asian American or Pacific Islander, 9 Hispanic Americans). Average age 28. 91 applicants, 67% accepted, 41 enrolled. In 2009, 61 master's awarded. *Degree requirements:* For master's, thesis or alternative. *Entrance requirements:* For master's, minimum GPA of 2.5 (MST), New York teaching certificate (MS Ed). Additional exam requirements/recommendations for international students: Required—TOEFL (minimum score 550 paper-based; 213 computer-based). *Application deadline:* Applications are processed on a rolling basis. Application fee: $50. Electronic applications accepted. *Expenses:* Tuition: Part-time $830 per credit. *Financial support:* Unspecified assistantships available. Support available to part-time students. Financial award application deadline: 4/15; financial award applicants required to submit FAFSA. *Faculty research:* Reading/writing, educational technology, administration, early literacy assessment, literacy development. *Unit head:* Dr. Catherine O'Callaghan, Chair, 914-633-2210, Fax: 914-633-2608, E-mail: cocallaghan@iona.edu. *Application contact:* Veronica Jarek-Prinz, Director of Graduate Admissions, 914-633-2420, Fax: 914-633-2277, E-mail: vjarekprinz@iona.edu.

Ithaca College, Division of Graduate and Professional Studies, School of Humanities and Sciences, Program in Adolescent Education, Ithaca, NY 14850. Offers biology 7-12 (MAT); chemistry 7-12 (MAT); English 7-12 (MAT); French 7-12 (MAT); math 7-12 (MAT); physics 7-12 (MAT); social studies 7-12 (MAT); Spanish (MAT). Part-time programs available. *Faculty:* 18 full-time (7 women). *Students:* 15 full-time (10 women), 2 part-time (1 woman); includes 1 minority (African American). Average age 26. 31 applicants, 68% accepted, 16 enrolled. In 2009, 31 master's awarded. *Degree requirements:* For master's, thesis or alternative, student teaching. *Entrance requirements:* For master's, minimum GPA of 3.0. Additional exam requirements/recommendations for international students: Required—TOEFL (minimum score 550 paper-based; 213 computer-based; 80 iBT). *Application deadline:* For fall admission, 5/15 for domestic and international students; for spring admission, 12/1 for domestic and international students. Applications are processed on a rolling basis. Application fee: $40. Electronic applications accepted. *Expenses:* Contact institution. *Financial support:* In 2009–10, 15 students received support, including 10 teaching assistantships (averaging $6,474 per year); career-related internships or fieldwork, Federal Work-Study, scholarships/grants, and unspecified assistantships also available. Support available to part-time students. Financial award applicants required to submit CSS PROFILE or FAFSA. *Faculty research:* Bilingual education, socio-linguistic perspective on literacy. *Unit head:* Dr. Linda Hanrahan, Chairperson, 607-274-3527, Fax: 607-274-1263, E-mail: gps@ithaca.edu. *Application contact:* Rob Gearhart, Dean, Graduate and Professional Studies, 607-274-3527, Fax: 607-274-1263, E-mail: gps@ithaca.edu.

Jackson State University, Graduate School, School of Science and Technology, Department of Biology, Jackson, MS 39217. Offers biology education (MST); environmental science (MS, PhD). Part-time and evening/weekend programs available. *Degree requirements:* For master's, comprehensive exam, thesis (alternative accepted for MST); for doctorate, comprehensive exam, thesis/dissertation. *Entrance requirements:* For master's, GRE General Test; for doctorate, MAT. Additional exam requirements/recommendations for international students: Required—TOEFL. *Faculty research:* Comparative studies on the carbohydrate composition of marine macroalgae, host-parasite relationship between the spruce budworm and entomepathogen fungus.

Jackson State University, Graduate School, School of Science and Technology, Department of Physics, Atmospheric Sciences, and General Science, Jackson, MS 39217. Offers science education (MST). Part-time and evening/weekend programs available. *Degree requirements:* For master's, comprehensive exam. *Entrance requirements:* For master's, GRE General Test. Additional exam requirements/recommendations for international students: Required—TOEFL.

John Carroll University, Graduate School, Program in Integrated Science, University Heights, OH 44118-4581. Offers MA. Part-time programs available. *Degree requirements:* For master's, thesis optional. *Entrance requirements:* For master's, minimum GPA of 2.5, teachers license. Electronic applications accepted.

The Johns Hopkins University, School of Education, Department of Interdisciplinary Studies in Education, Baltimore, MD 21218. Offers earth/space science (Certificate); education (MS), including educational studies; mind, brain, and teaching (Certificate); teaching the adult learner (Certificate); urban education (Certificate). Part-time and evening/weekend programs available. Postbaccalaureate distance learning degree programs offered (minimal on-campus study). *Faculty:* 2 full-time (1 woman), 6 part-time/adjunct (5 women). *Students:* 8 full-time (7 women), 171 part-time (150 women); includes 44 minority (29 African Americans, 1 American Indian/Alaska Native, 11 Asian Americans or Pacific Islanders, 3 Hispanic Americans), 7 international. Average age 34. 77 applicants, 68% accepted, 39 enrolled. In 2009, 69 master's, 17 other advanced degrees awarded. *Degree requirements:* For master's, capstone course. *Entrance requirements:* For master's and Certificate, minimum undergraduate GPA of 3.0. Additional exam requirements/recommendations for international students: Required—TOEFL (minimum score 600 paper-based; 250 computer-based; 100 iBT). *Application deadline:* For fall admission, 5/1 for international students; for spring admission, 10/15 for international students. Applications are processed on a rolling basis. Application fee: $80. Electronic applications accepted. *Financial support:* Scholarships/grants available. Support available to part-time students. Financial award application deadline: 6/1; financial award applicants required to submit FAFSA. *Faculty research:* Neuro-education; urban school reform; leadership development; teacher leadership; charter schools; techniques for teaching reading to adolescents with delayed reading skills; school culture. *Unit head:* Dr. Mariale Hardiman, Assistant Dean and Chair, 410-516-8225, Fax: 410-516-3939, E-mail: mclean@jhu.edu. *Application contact:* Jennifer Shaffer, Director of Admissions, 410-516-9797, Fax: 410-516-9799, E-mail: educationinfo@jhu.edu.

The Johns Hopkins University, School of Education, Department of Teacher Preparation, Baltimore, MD 21218. Offers education (MS), including educational studies; elementary education (MAT); English for speakers of other languages (MAT); K-8 mathematics lead-teacher (Certificate); K-8 science lead-teacher (Certificate); secondary education (MAT), including biology, chemistry, earth/space/environmental science, English, French, mathematics, physics, social studies, Spanish. Part-time and evening/weekend programs available. *Faculty:* 13 full-time (11 women), 35 part-time/adjunct (21 women). *Students:* 162 full-time (119 women), 347 part-time (256 women); includes 138 minority (80 African Americans, 3 American Indian/Alaska Native, 38 Asian Americans or Pacific Islanders, 17 Hispanic Americans), 3 international. Average age 27. 89 applicants, 37% accepted, 24 enrolled. In 2009, 177 master's awarded. *Degree requirements:* For master's, portfolio, PRAXIS II, internship. *Entrance requirements:* For master's, PRAXIS I, SAT, ACT, or GRE (MAT), minimum undergraduate GPA of 3.0, interview, 1 letter of recommendation, curriculum vitae/resume; for Certificate, bachelor's degree, minimum undergraduate GPA of 3.0, essay/statement of goals, interview. Additional exam requirements/recommendations for international students: Required—TOEFL (minimum score 600 paper-based; 250 computer-based; 100 iBT). *Application deadline:* For fall admission, 5/1 for international students; for spring admission, 10/15 for international students. Applications are processed on a rolling basis. Application fee: $80. Electronic applications accepted. *Financial support:* Scholarships/grants available. Support available to part-time students. Financial award application deadline: 6/1; financial award applicants required to submit FAFSA. *Faculty research:* Teacher retention; STEM education reform; alternative certification programs; school-university partnerships; urban education; action research/data-informed instruction; family engagement. *Unit head:* Dr. Francis Masci, Chair, 410-516-9774, Fax: 410-516-9770, E-mail: matjhu@jhu.edu. *Application contact:* Jennifer Shaffer, Director of Admissions, 410-516-9797, Fax: 410-516-9799, E-mail: educationinfo@jhu.edu.

Johnson State College, Graduate Program in Education, Program in Science Education, Johnson, VT 05656. Offers MA Ed. *Expenses:* Tuition, area resident: Part-time $416 per credit. Tuition, state resident: part-time $416 per credit. Tuition, nonresident: part-time $899 per credit.

Kaplan University, Davenport Campus, School of Teacher Education, Davenport, IA 52807-2095. Offers education (M Ed); secondary education (M Ed); teaching and learning (MA); teaching literacy and language: grades 6-12 (MA); teaching literacy and language: grades K-6 (MA); teaching mathematics: grades 6-8 (MA); teaching mathematics: grades 9-12 (MA); teaching mathematics: grades K-5 (MA); teaching science: grades 6-12 (MA); teaching science: grades K-6 (MA); teaching students with special needs (MA); teaching with technology (MA). Part-time and evening/weekend programs available. Postbaccalaureate distance learning degree programs offered (no on-campus study). *Entrance requirements:* Additional exam requirements/recommendations for international students: Required—TOEFL (minimum score 550 paper-based; 218 computer-based; 80 iBT).

Kean University, College of Education, Program in Instruction and Curriculum, Union, NJ 07083. Offers bilingual/bicultural education (MA); classroom instruction (MA); earth science (MA); mathematics/science/computer education (MA); teaching (MA); teaching English as a second language (MA); world languages (Spanish) (MA). *Accreditation:* NCATE. Part-time and evening/weekend programs available. *Faculty:* 16 full-time (7 women). *Students:* 45 full-time (34 women), 131 part-time (104 women); includes 60 minority (11 African Americans, 6 Asian Americans or Pacific Islanders, 43 Hispanic Americans), 6 international. Average age 33. 64 applicants, 94% accepted, 46 enrolled. In 2009, 58 master's awarded. *Entrance requirements:* For master's, GRE General Test or MAT, PRAXIS, minimum GPA of 3.0, 2 letters of recommendation, interview, teacher certification (for some programs). *Application deadline:* For fall admission, 5/1 for domestic students; for spring admission, 11/1 for domestic students. Application fee: $60 ($150 for international students). Electronic applications accepted. *Expenses:* Tuition, state resident: full-time $10,440; part-time $435 per credit. Tuition, nonresident: full-time $14,160; part-time $590 per credit. Required fees: $2642; $110 per credit. Part-time tuition and fees vary according to course load and degree level. *Financial support:* In 2009–10, 1 research assistantship with full tuition reimbursement (averaging $3,263 per year) was awarded; unspecified assistantships also available. *Unit head:* Dr. Thomas Walsh, Program Coordinator, 908-737-4296, E-mail: twalsh@kean.edu. *Application contact:* Ann-Marie Kay, Assistant Director of Graduate Admissions, 908-737-5922, Fax: 908-737-5965, E-mail: akay@kean.edu.

Kutztown University of Pennsylvania, College of Education, Program in Secondary Education, Kutztown, PA 19530-0730. Offers biology (M Ed); curriculum and instruction (M Ed); English (M Ed); mathematics (M Ed); secondary education (Certificate); social studies (M Ed). *Accreditation:* NCATE. Part-time and evening/weekend programs available. *Faculty:* 7 full-time (4 women). *Students:* 90 full-time (45 women), 84 part-time (56 women); includes 8 minority (4 African Americans, 1 Asian American or Pacific Islander, 3 Hispanic Americans), 2 international. Average age 29. 129 applicants, 76% accepted, 31 enrolled. In 2009, 36 master's awarded. *Degree requirements:* For master's, comprehensive exam, thesis optional. *Entrance requirements:* For master's, GRE General Test. Additional exam requirements/recommendations for international students: Required—TOEFL. *Application deadline:* For fall admission, 8/15 priority date for domestic and international students; for spring admission, 12/15 priority date for domestic and international students. Applications are processed on a rolling basis. Application fee: $35. Electronic applications accepted. *Expenses:* Tuition, state resident: full-time $6666; part-time $370 per credit. Tuition, nonresident: full-time $10,666; part-time $593 per credit. Required fees: $62 per credit. $60 per semester. *Financial support:* Career-related internships or fieldwork, Federal Work-Study, scholarships/grants, and unspecified assistantships available. Financial award application deadline: 3/1; financial award applicants required to submit FAFSA. *Unit head:* Dr. Theresa Stahler, Chairperson, 610-683-4259, Fax: 610-683-1338, E-mail: stahler@kutztown.edu. *Application contact:* Kelly D. Burr, Associate Director, Graduate Admissions, 610-683-4200, Fax: 610-683-1393, E-mail: graduate@kutztown.edu.

Laurentian University, School of Graduate Studies and Research, Programme in Science Communication, Sudbury, ON P3E 2C6, Canada. Offers G Dip.

Lawrence Technological University, College of Arts and Sciences, Southfield, MI 48075-1058. Offers computer science (MS); educational technology (MET); science education (MSE);

Science Education

Lawrence Technological University (continued)
technical communication (MS). Part-time and evening/weekend programs available. *Faculty:* 14 full-time (6 women), 14 part-time/adjunct (4 women). *Students:* 6 full-time (3 women), 80 part-time (49 women); includes 19 minority (14 African Americans, 5 Asian Americans or Pacific Islanders), 12 international. Average age 35. 87 applicants, 57% accepted, 20 enrolled. In 2009, 34 master's awarded. *Degree requirements:* For master's, thesis (for some programs). *Entrance requirements:* For master's, GRE. Additional exam requirements/recommendations for international students: Required—TOEFL (minimum score 550 paper-based; 213 computer-based; 79 iBT). *Application deadline:* For fall admission, 8/1 priority date for domestic students, 6/1 for international students; for winter admission, 12/1 priority date for domestic students, 10/1 for international students; for spring admission, 5/1 priority date for domestic students, 3/1 for international students. Applications are processed on a rolling basis. Application fee: $50. Electronic applications accepted. *Expenses:* Tuition: Full-time $11,320; part-time $798 per credit hour. *Financial support:* Federal Work-Study available. Financial award application deadline: 4/1; financial award applicants required to submit FAFSA. *Unit head:* Dr. Hsiao-Ping Moore, Dean, 248-204-3500, Fax: 248-204-3518, E-mail: scidean@ltu.edu. *Application contact:* Jane Rohrback, Director of Admissions, 248-204-3160, Fax: 248-204-3188, E-mail: admissions@ltu.edu.

Lebanon Valley College, Graduate Studies and Continuing Education, Program in Science Education, Annville, PA 17003-1400. Offers MSE. Part-time and evening/weekend programs available. *Faculty:* 6 part-time/adjunct (4 women). *Students:* 44 part-time (33 women). Average age 36. In 2009, 15 master's awarded. *Degree requirements:* For master's, thesis. *Entrance requirements:* For master's, minimum GPA of 3.0, teacher certification. *Application deadline:* Applications are processed on a rolling basis. Application fee: $30. *Expenses:* Tuition: Full-time $32,740; part-time $410 per credit hour. Required fees: $610. *Financial support:* Application deadline: 5/1. *Unit head:* Patricia Woods, Coordinator, 717-867-6190, Fax: 717-867-6018. *Application contact:* Elaine D. Feather, Director of Graduate Studies and Continuing Education, 717-867-6213, Fax: 717-867-6018, E-mail: feather@lvc.edu.

Lehman College of the City University of New York, Division of Education, Department of Middle and High School Education, Program in Science Education, Bronx, NY 10468-1589. Offers MS Ed. *Accreditation:* NCATE.

Lesley University, School of Education, Cambridge, MA 02138-2790. Offers curriculum and instruction (M Ed, CAGS); early childhood education (M Ed); educational studies (PhD); elementary education (M Ed); individually designed (M Ed); middle school education (M Ed); moderate special needs (M Ed); reading (M Ed, CAGS); science in education (M Ed); severe special needs (M Ed); special needs (CAGS); technology in education (M Ed, CAGS). *Accreditation:* Teacher Education Accreditation Council. Part-time and evening/weekend programs available. Postbaccalaureate distance learning degree programs offered (no on-campus study). *Degree requirements:* For master's, practicum; for doctorate, thesis/dissertation. *Entrance requirements:* For doctorate, GRE General Test or MAT, interview, master's degree, resume; for CAGS, interview, master's degree. Additional exam requirements/recommendations for international students: Required—TOEFL (minimum score 550 paper-based; 213 computer-based; 80 iBT). Electronic applications accepted. *Faculty research:* Assessment in literacy, mathematics and science; autism spectrum disorders; instructional technology and online learning; multicultural education and ELL.

Lewis University, College of Education, Program in Secondary Education, Romeoville, IL 60446. Offers biology (MA); chemistry (MA); English (MA); history (MA); math (MA); physics (MA); psychology and social science (MA). Part-time programs available. *Students:* 20 full-time (12 women), 24 part-time (16 women); includes 2 minority (1 African American, 1 Hispanic American). Average age 29. 39 applicants, 51% accepted, 18 enrolled. In 2009, 15 master's awarded. *Entrance requirements:* For master's, departmental qualifying exam, writing exam, minimum GPA of 2.75, 2 letters of recommendation, interview. Additional exam requirements/recommendations for international students: Required—TOEFL (minimum score 550 paper-based; 213 computer-based). *Application deadline:* For fall admission, 5/1 priority date for international students; for spring admission, 11/15 priority date for international students. Applications are processed on a rolling basis. Application fee: $40. Electronic applications accepted. *Expenses:* Tuition: Full-time $6480; part-time $720 per credit. One-time fee: $40. Tuition and fees vary according to course load, degree level and program. *Financial support:* Federal Work-Study, scholarships/grants, and unspecified assistantships available. Financial award application deadline: 5/1; financial award applicants required to submit FAFSA. *Unit head:* Dr. Dorene Huvaere, Program Director, 815-838-0500 Ext. 5885, E-mail: huvaersdo@lewisu.edu. *Application contact:* Fran Welsh, Secretary, 815-838-0500 Ext. 5880, E-mail: welshfr@lewisu.edu.

Long Island University, C.W. Post Campus, College of Liberal Arts and Sciences, Department of Biology, Brookville, NY 11548-1300. Offers biology (MS); biology education (MS). Part-time and evening/weekend programs available. *Degree requirements:* For master's, thesis optional. *Entrance requirements:* For master's, GRE General Test, minimum GPA of 2.75 in major. Electronic applications accepted. *Faculty research:* Immunology, molecular biology, systematics, behavioral ecology, microbiology.

Long Island University, C.W. Post Campus, College of Liberal Arts and Sciences, Department of Earth and Environmental Science, Brookville, NY 11548-1300. Offers earth science (MS); earth science education (MS); environmental studies (MS).

Long Island University, C.W. Post Campus, School of Education, Department of Curriculum and Instruction, Brookville, NY 11548-1300. Offers adolescence education (MS); adolescence education: biology (MS); adolescence education: earth science (MS); adolescence education: English (MS); adolescence education: mathematics (MS); adolescence education: social studies (MS); adolescence education: Spanish (MS); art education (MS); bilingual education (MS); childhood education (MS); early childhood education (MS); middle childhood education (MS); music education (MS); teaching English to speakers of other languages (MS). Part-time and evening/weekend programs available. *Degree requirements:* For master's, comprehensive exam or thesis, student teaching. *Entrance requirements:* For master's, minimum GPA of 2.75 in major, 2.5 overall. Electronic applications accepted. *Faculty research:* Ethics and education, teaching strategies.

Louisiana Tech University, Graduate School, College of Education, Department of Curriculum, Instruction and Leadership, Ruston, LA 71272. Offers curriculum and instruction (MS, Ed D); educational leadership (Ed D); secondary education (M Ed), including business education, English education, foreign language education, health and physical education, mathematics education, science education, social studies education, speech education. *Accreditation:* NCATE. Part-time programs available. *Degree requirements:* For doctorate, thesis/dissertation. *Entrance requirements:* For master's and doctorate, GRE General Test.

Loyola University Chicago, School of Education, Program in Initial Teacher Preparation, Chicago, IL 60660. Offers elementary education (M Ed); math education (M Ed); reading specialist (M Ed); school technology (M Ed); science education (M Ed); secondary education (M Ed); special education (M Ed). *Accreditation:* NCATE. *Faculty:* 12 full-time (9 women), 12 part-time/adjunct (6 women). *Students:* 154. Average age 28. 125 applicants, 69% accepted, 38 enrolled. In 2009, 89 master's awarded. *Degree requirements:* For master's, comprehensive exam. *Entrance requirements:* For master's, Illinois Basic Skills Test, 3 letters of recommendation, minimum GPA of 3.0, resume. Additional exam requirements/recommendations for international students: Required—TOEFL (minimum score 550 paper-based; 213 computer-based; 79 iBT). *Application deadline:* For fall admission, 7/1 priority date for domestic and international students; for spring admission, 11/1 priority date for domestic and international students. Applications are processed on a rolling basis. Application fee: $50. Electronic applications accepted. *Expenses:* Tuition: Full-time $14,220; part-time $790 per credit hour. Required fees: $60 per semester hour. Tuition and fees vary according to program. *Financial support:* In 2009–10, 1 research assistantship with full tuition reimbursement (averaging $8,500 per year), 1 teaching assistantship were awarded. Financial award application deadline: 2/15. *Faculty research:* Positive behavior support, school reform, school improvement. *Unit head:* Dr. Dorothy Giroux, Director, 312-915-7027, E-mail: dgiroux@luc.edu. *Application contact:* Marie Rosin-Dittmar, Information Contact, 312-915-6800, E-mail: schleduc@luc.edu.

Lynchburg College, Graduate Studies, School of Education and Human Development, Lynchburg, VA 24501-3199. Offers community counseling (M Ed); counselor education (M Ed), including community counseling; curriculum and instruction (M Ed); educational leadership (M Ed); English education (M Ed); reading (M Ed); school counseling (M Ed); science education (M Ed); special education (M Ed), including autism spectrum disorder, early childhood special education, mental retardation, teaching children with learning disabilities, teaching the emotionally disturbed. Part-time and evening/weekend programs available. *Degree requirements:* For master's, comprehensive exam. *Entrance requirements:* For master's, GRE, minimum undergraduate GPA of 3.0. Additional exam requirements/recommendations for international students: Required—TOEFL. *Expenses:* Tuition: Full-time $7020; part-time $390 per credit hour.

Lyndon State College, Graduate Programs in Education, Department of Natural Sciences, Lyndonville, VT 05851-0919. Offers science education (MST). Part-time programs available. *Degree requirements:* For master's, exam or major field project. *Entrance requirements:* Additional exam requirements/recommendations for international students: Recommended—TOEFL (minimum score 500 paper-based; 173 computer-based). *Faculty research:* Fern genetics, comparative butterfly research.

Manhattanville College, Graduate Programs, School of Education, Program in Middle Childhood/Adolescence Education (Grades 5-12), Purchase, NY 10577-2132. Offers biology (MAT); biology and special education (MPS); chemistry (MAT); chemistry and special education (MPS); English (MAT); English and special education (MPS); literacy (MPS), including reading and writing, writing; literacy and special education (MPS); math (MAT); math and special education (MPS); second language (MAT), including French, Italian, Latin, Spanish; social studies (MAT); social studies and special education (MPS); special education (MPS). Part-time and evening/weekend programs available. *Students:* 52 full-time (39 women), 106 part-time (71 women); includes 8 African Americans, 3 Asian Americans or Pacific Islanders, 4 Hispanic Americans, 1 international. In 2009, 82 master's awarded. *Degree requirements:* For master's, comprehensive exam or research project, field experience. *Entrance requirements:* For master's, minimum undergraduate GPA of 3.0, 2 letters of recommendation. Additional exam requirements/recommendations for international students: Required—TOEFL. *Application deadline:* Applications are processed on a rolling basis. Application fee: $70. Electronic applications accepted. *Financial support:* Career-related internships or fieldwork, Federal Work-Study, institutionally sponsored loans, and unspecified assistantships available. Support available to part-time students. Financial award application deadline: 3/1; financial award applicants required to submit FAFSA. *Unit head:* Dr. Shelley Wepner, Dean, 914-323-5192, Fax: 914-694-2386, E-mail: wepners@mville.edu. *Application contact:* Jeanine Pardey-Levine, Director of Admissions, 914-323-3208, Fax: 914-694-1732, E-mail: edschool@mville.edu.

McNeese State University, Doré School of Graduate Studies, College of Science, Department of Chemistry, Program in Environmental and Chemical Sciences, Lake Charles, LA 70609. Offers chemistry (MS); chemistry/environmental science education (MS). Evening/weekend programs available. *Faculty:* 6 full-time (1 woman). *Students:* 14 full-time (5 women), 4 part-time (3 women); includes 2 minority (both African Americans), 10 international. In 2009, 6 master's awarded. *Degree requirements:* For master's, comprehensive exam, thesis or alternative. *Entrance requirements:* For master's, GRE. *Application deadline:* For fall admission, 5/15 priority date for domestic and international students; for spring admission, 10/15 priority date for domestic and international students. Applications are processed on a rolling basis. Application fee: $20 ($30 for international students). *Expenses:* Tuition, area resident: Full-time $2556. Tuition, state resident: full-time $2556. Required fees: $1031. Tuition and fees vary according to course load. *Financial support:* Application deadline: 5/1. *Unit head:* Dr. Bruce C. Wyman, Coordinator, 337-475-5669, Fax: 337-475-5677, E-mail: wyman@mcneese.edu. *Application contact:* Dr. Bruce C. Wyman, Coordinator, 337-475-5669, Fax: 337-475-5677, E-mail: wyman@mcneese.edu.

Michigan State University, The Graduate School, College of Natural Science and College of Education, Division of Science and Mathematics Education, East Lansing, MI 48824. Offers biological, physical and general science for teachers (MAT, MS), including biological science (MS), general science (MAT), physical science (MS); mathematics education (MS, PhD). *Students:* 23 full-time (13 women), 2 part-time (1 woman); includes 2 minority (1 African American, 1 Asian American or Pacific Islander), 6 international. Average age 33. In 2009, 5 master's, 1 doctorate awarded. *Expenses:* Tuition, state resident: part-time $478.25 per credit hour. Tuition, nonresident: part-time $966.50 per credit hour. Part-time tuition and fees vary according to program. *Financial support:* In 2009–10, 14 research assistantships with tuition reimbursements (averaging $6,849 per year), 16 teaching assistantships with tuition reimbursements (averaging $6,752 per year) were awarded. *Unit head:* Dr. George Leroi, Interim Director, 517-432-1490 Ext. 103, Fax: 517-432-9868, E-mail: geleroi@msu.edu. *Application contact:* Margaret Iding, Graduate Secretary, 517-355-1708 Ext. 105, Fax: 517-432-9868, E-mail: dsme@msu.edu.

Michigan Technological University, Graduate School, College of Sciences and Arts, Division of Teacher Education, Program in Applied Science Education, Houghton, MI 49931. Offers MS. Part-time programs available. *Degree requirements:* For master's, internship, project, final paper, defense. *Entrance requirements:* For master's, teaching certification (science or math preferred), 1 year of teaching experience. Additional exam requirements/recommendations for international students: Required—TOEFL. Electronic applications accepted.

Middle Tennessee State University, College of Graduate Studies, College of Basic and Applied Sciences, Department of Aerospace, Program in Aerospace Education, Murfreesboro, TN 37132. Offers M Ed. Part-time and evening/weekend programs available. Postbaccalaureate distance learning degree programs offered. *Students:* 7 applicants, 57% accepted. *Degree requirements:* For master's, one foreign language, comprehensive exam. *Entrance requirements:* For master's, GRE or MAT. Additional exam requirements/recommendations for international students: Required—TOEFL (minimum score 525 paper-based; 195 computer-based; 71 iBT) or IELTS (minimum score 6). *Application deadline:* For fall admission, 6/1 for domestic and international students. Applications are processed on a rolling basis. Application fee: $25 ($30 for international students). *Expenses:* Tuition, state resident: full-time $4404. Tuition, nonresident: full-time $10,956. *Financial support:* Institutionally sponsored loans available. Support available to part-time students. Financial award application deadline: 5/1. *Unit head:* Dr. Wayne Dornan, Chair, 615-898-2788, E-mail: wdornan@mtsu.edu. *Application contact:* Dr. Wayne Dornan, Chair, 615-898-2788, E-mail: wdornan@mtsu.edu.

Mills College, Graduate Studies, School of Education, Oakland, CA 94613-1000. Offers child life in hospitals (MA); early childhood education (MA); education (MA), including art education, curriculum and instruction, elementary education, English education, foreign language education, mathematics education, science education, secondary education, social studies education, teaching; educational leadership (MA, Ed D); infant mental health (MA). Part-time and evening/weekend programs available. *Faculty:* 11 full-time (9 women), 16 part-time/adjunct (14 women). *Students:* 138 full-time (119 women), 55 part-time (48 women); includes 71 minority (34 African Americans, 19 Asian Americans or Pacific Islanders, 18 Hispanic Americans), 3 international. Average age 34. 210 applicants, 82% accepted, 93 enrolled. In 2009, 54 master's, 15 doctorates awarded. Terminal master's awarded for partial completion of doctoral program. *Degree requirements:* For master's, comprehensive exam. *Entrance requirements:* For doctorate, GRE General Test. Additional exam requirements/recommendations for international students: Required—TOEFL. *Application deadline:* For fall admission, 2/1 for domestic and international students; for spring admission, 11/1 for domestic and international students. Applications are processed on a rolling basis. Application fee: $50. Electronic applications accepted. *Expenses:* Tuition: Full-time $26,326; part-time $6584 per course. Required fees: $896. One-time fee: $896 part-time. Tuition and fees vary according to program. *Financial support:* In 2009–10, 188 students received support, including 186 fellowships (averaging $6,499 per year), 28

teaching assistantships with partial tuition reimbursements available (averaging $3,187 per year); career-related internships or fieldwork and scholarships/grants also available. Support available to part-time students. Financial award application deadline: 2/1; financial award applicants required to submit FAFSA. *Faculty research:* Child development, gender and education, public policy, cross-cultural development, development of literacy. Total annual research expenditures: $1.2 million. *Unit head:* Joseph Kahne, Chairperson, 510-430-3190, Fax: 510-430-3314, E-mail: grad-studies@mills.edu. *Application contact:* Jessica King, Graduate Admission Specialist, 510-430-3305, Fax: 510-430-2159, E-mail: grad-studies@mills.edu.

Minnesota State University Mankato, College of Graduate Studies, College of Science, Engineering and Technology, Department of Biological Sciences, Mankato, MN 56001. Offers biology (MS); biology education (MS); environmental sciences (MS). Part-time programs available. *Students:* 9 full-time (2 women), 40 part-time (17 women). *Degree requirements:* For master's, one foreign language, comprehensive exam, thesis or alternative. *Entrance requirements:* For master's, minimum GPA of 3.0 during previous 2 years of course work. Additional exam requirements/recommendations for international students: Required—TOEFL. *Application deadline:* For fall admission, 7/1 priority date for domestic students; for spring admission, 11/1 for domestic students. Applications are processed on a rolling basis. Application fee: $40. Electronic applications accepted. *Expenses:* Tuition, state resident: full-time $5364. Tuition, nonresident: full-time $8314. *Financial support:* Fellowships, research assistantships with full tuition reimbursements, teaching assistantships with full tuition reimbursements, career-related internships or fieldwork, Federal Work-Study, institutionally sponsored loans, and unspecified assistantships available. Support available to part-time students. Financial award application deadline: 3/15; financial award applicants required to submit FAFSA. *Faculty research:* Limnology, enzyme analysis, membrane engineering, converters. *Unit head:* Dr. Penny Knoblich, Chairperson, 507-389-5736. *Application contact:* 507-389-2321, E-mail: grad@mnsu.edu.

Minot State University, Graduate School, Program in Biological and Agricultural Sciences, Minot, ND 58707-0002. Offers science (MAT). *Degree requirements:* For master's, thesis. *Entrance requirements:* For master's, minimum GPA of 3.0 or GRE General Test, secondary teaching certificate. Additional exam requirements/recommendations for international students: Required—TOEFL. *Expenses:* Tuition, state resident: full-time $5720; part-time $283 per credit hour. Tuition, nonresident: full-time $5720; part-time $283 per credit hour. Required fees: $1034; $1034 per year. Tuition and fees vary according to course load, degree level and program.

Mississippi College, Graduate School, School of Education, Department of Teacher Education and Leadership, Clinton, MS 39058. Offers art (M Ed); biological science (M Ed); business education (M Ed); computer science (M Ed); dyslexia therapy (M Ed); educational leadership (M Ed, Ed D, Ed S); elementary education (M Ed, Ed S); English (M Ed); higher education administration (MS); mathematics (M Ed); secondary education (M Ed); social studies (history) (M Ed); teaching arts (M Ed). Part-time programs available. Postbaccalaureate distance learning degree programs offered (no on-campus study). *Faculty:* 11 full-time (7 women), 13 part-time/adjunct (7 women). *Students:* 33 full-time (22 women), 282 part-time (240 women); includes 148 minority (146 African Americans, 2 American Indian/Alaska Native), 1 international. Average age 34. In 2009, 147 master's awarded. *Degree requirements:* For master's, comprehensive exam, thesis optional. *Entrance requirements:* For master's, NTE. Additional exam requirements/recommendations for international students: Recommended—IELTS. *Application deadline:* For fall admission, 8/15 priority date for domestic students. Applications are processed on a rolling basis. Application fee: $30. Electronic applications accepted. *Expenses:* Tuition: Part-time $452 per credit hour. Required fees: $101 per semester. Tuition and fees vary according to degree level, campus/location, program and student level. *Financial support:* Teaching assistantships, career-related internships or fieldwork, Federal Work-Study, scholarships/grants, and unspecified assistantships available. Support available to part-time students. Financial award applicants required to submit FAFSA. *Unit head:* Dr. Tom Williams, Chair, 601-925-3844, E-mail: twilliams@mc.edu. *Application contact:* Elnora Lewis, Secretary, 601-925-3225, Fax: 601-925-3889, E-mail: lewis09@mc.edu.

Missouri State University, Graduate College, College of Natural and Applied Sciences, Department of Physics, Astronomy, and Materials Science, Springfield, MO 65897. Offers materials science (MS); physics, astronomy, and materials science (MNAS); secondary education (MS Ed), including physics. Part-time programs available. *Faculty:* 13 full-time (0 women). *Students:* 6 full-time (2 women), 7 part-time (1 woman), 3 international. Average age 31. 12 applicants, 58% accepted, 6 enrolled. In 2009, 12 master's awarded. *Degree requirements:* For master's, comprehensive exam, thesis. *Entrance requirements:* For master's, GRE (MS, MNAS), minimum undergraduate GPA of 3.0 (MS and MNAS), 9-12 teaching certification (MS Ed). Additional exam requirements/recommendations for international students: Required—TOEFL (minimum score 550 paper-based; 213 computer-based; 79 iBT). *Application deadline:* For fall admission, 7/20 priority date for domestic students, 5/1 for international students; for spring admission, 12/20 priority date for domestic students, 9/1 for international students. Applications are processed on a rolling basis. Application fee: $35 ($50 for international students). Electronic applications accepted. *Expenses:* Tuition, state resident: full-time $3852; part-time $214 per credit hour. Tuition, nonresident: full-time $7524; part-time $418 per credit hour. Required fees: $696; $172 per semester. Tuition and fees vary according to course level, course load, degree level and program. *Financial support:* In 2009–10, 8 teaching assistantships with full tuition reimbursements (averaging $8,834 per year) were awarded; research assistantships with full tuition reimbursements, Federal Work-Study, institutionally sponsored loans, scholarships/grants, and unspecified assistantships also available. Financial award application deadline: 3/31; financial award applicants required to submit FAFSA. *Faculty research:* Nanocomposites, ferroelectricity, infrared focal plane array sensors, biosensors, pulsating stars. *Unit head:* Dr. Robert Patterson, Head, 417-836-5131, Fax: 417-836-6226, E-mail: physics@missouristate.edu. *Application contact:* Eric Eckert, Coordinator of Admissions and Recruitment, 417-836-5331, Fax: 417-836-6200, E-mail: ericeckertn@missouristate.edu.

Montclair State University, The Graduate School, College of Education and Human Services, Department of Curriculum and Teaching, Montclair, NJ 07043-1624. Offers education (M Ed); educational technology (M Ed); learning disabled teacher consultant (Certificate); school library media specialist (Certificate); teaching (MAT, Certificate), including art (MAT), biological science (MAT), early childhood education (P-3) (MAT), earth science (MAT), elementary education (K-8) (MAT), English (MAT), French (MAT), health and physical education (MAT), health education (MAT), home economics (MAT), mathematics (MAT), music (MAT), physical education (MAT), physical science (MAT), social studies (MAT), Spanish (MAT), teacher of ESL (MAT), teacher of students with disabilities (MAT). Part-time and evening/weekend programs available. *Faculty:* 17 full-time (12 women), 29 part-time/adjunct (21 women). *Students:* 124 full-time (63 women), 174 part-time (126 women). Average age 31. 112 applicants, 69% accepted, 59 enrolled. In 2009, 179 master's, 2 other advanced degrees awarded. *Degree requirements:* For master's, comprehensive exam, field experience. *Entrance requirements:* For master's, GRE, 2 letters of recommendation. Additional exam requirements/recommendations for international students: Required—TOEFL (minimum score 83 computer-based), or IELTS. *Application deadline:* For fall admission, 2/15 for domestic and international students; for spring admission, 9/15 for domestic and international students. Applications are processed on a rolling basis. Application fee: $60. Electronic applications accepted. *Expenses:* Tuition, area resident: Part-time $486.74 per credit. Tuition, state resident: part-time $486.74 per credit. Tuition, nonresident: part-time $751.34 per credit. Tuition and fees vary according to degree level and program. *Financial support:* In 2009–10, 12 research assistantships with full tuition reimbursements (averaging $7,000 per year) were awarded; Federal Work-Study, scholarships/grants, and unspecified assistantships also available. Support available to part-time students. Financial award application deadline: 3/1; financial award applicants required to submit FAFSA. *Unit head:* Dr. David Schwarzer, Chairperson, 973-655-5187. *Application contact:* Amy Aiello, Director of Graduate Admissions and Operations, 973-655-5147, Fax: 973-655-7869, E-mail: graduate.school@montclair.edu.

Montclair State University, The Graduate School, College of Science and Mathematics, Department of Biology and Molecular Biology, Montclair, NJ 07043-1624. Offers biology (MS), including biology science education, molecular biology; molecular biology (Certificate). Part-time and evening/weekend programs available. *Faculty:* 21 full-time (8 women), 27 part-time/adjunct (13 women). *Students:* 35 full-time (23 women), 57 part-time (44 women). Average age 28. 53 applicants, 64% accepted, 23 enrolled. In 2009, 26 master's, 2 other advanced degrees awarded. *Degree requirements:* For master's, comprehensive exam, thesis or alternative. *Entrance requirements:* For master's, GRE General Test, 24 credits of course work in undergraduate biology, 2 letters of recommendation, teaching certificate (biology sciences education concentration). Additional exam requirements/recommendations for international students: Required—TOEFL (minimum score 83 computer-based), or IELTS. *Application deadline:* For fall admission, 6/1 for international students; for spring admission, 10/1 for international students. Applications are processed on a rolling basis. Application fee: $60. Electronic applications accepted. *Expenses:* Tuition, area resident: Part-time $486.74 per credit. Tuition, state resident: part-time $486.74 per credit. Tuition, nonresident: part-time $751.34 per credit. Tuition and fees vary according to degree level and program. *Financial support:* In 2009–10, 13 research assistantships with full tuition reimbursements (averaging $7,000 per year) were awarded; Federal Work-Study, scholarships/grants, and unspecified assistantships also available. Support available to part-time students. Financial award application deadline: 3/1; financial award applicants required to submit FAFSA. *Faculty research:* Cells, algae blooms, scallops, New Jersey bays, Barnegat Bay. *Unit head:* Dr. Quinn Vega, Chairperson, 973-655-7178. *Application contact:* Amy Aiello, Director of Graduate Admissions and Operations, 973-655-5147, Fax: 973-655-7869, E-mail: graduate.school@montclair.edu.

Montclair State University, The Graduate School, College of Science and Mathematics, Department of Earth and Environmental Studies, Montclair, NJ 07043-1624. Offers earth science (Certificate); environmental management (MA, D Env M); environmental studies (MS), including environmental education, environmental health, environmental management, environmental science; geographic information science (Certificate); geoscience (MS, Certificate), including geoscience (MS), water resource management (Certificate). Part-time and evening/weekend programs available. *Faculty:* 16 full-time (2 women), 13 part-time/adjunct (4 women). *Students:* 36 full-time (17 women), 60 part-time (26 women). Average age 34. 42 applicants, 60% accepted, 17 enrolled. In 2009, 11 degrees awarded. *Degree requirements:* For master's, comprehensive exam, thesis or alternative; for doctorate, thesis/dissertation. *Entrance requirements:* For master's, GRE General Test, 2 letters of recommendation; for doctorate, GRE General Test, 3 letters of recommendation. Additional exam requirements/recommendations for international students: Required—TOEFL (minimum score 83 computer-based), or IELTS. *Application deadline:* For fall admission, 6/1 for international students; for spring admission, 10/1 for international students. Applications are processed on a rolling basis. Application fee: $60. Electronic applications accepted. *Expenses:* Tuition, area resident: Part-time $486.74 per credit. Tuition, state resident: part-time $486.74 per credit. Tuition, nonresident: part-time $751.34 per credit. Tuition and fees vary according to degree level and program. *Financial support:* In 2009–10, 3 fellowships (averaging $15,000 per year), 12 research assistantships with full tuition reimbursements (averaging $8,500 per year), 11 teaching assistantships with full tuition reimbursements (averaging $15,000 per year) were awarded; Federal Work-Study, scholarships/grants, and unspecified assistantships also available. Support available to part-time students. Financial award application deadline: 3/1; financial award applicants required to submit FAFSA. *Faculty research:* Antarctica, carbon pools, contaminated sediments, wetlands. *Unit head:* Dr. Duke Ophori, Chairperson, 973-655-7558. *Application contact:* Amy Aiello, Director of Graduate Admissions and Operations, 973-655-5147, Fax: 973-655-7869, E-mail: graduate.school@montclair.edu.

Montclair State University, The Graduate School, College of Science and Mathematics, Department of Mathematics, Montclair, NJ 07043-1624. Offers math pedagogy (Ed D); mathematics (MS), including computer science, mathematics education, pure and applied mathematics, statistics; physical science (Certificate); teaching middle grades math (MS, Certificate). Part-time and evening/weekend programs available. *Faculty:* 30 full-time (10 women), 39 part-time/adjunct (19 women). *Students:* 15 full-time (7 women), 101 part-time (75 women). Average age 32. 55 applicants, 76% accepted, 31 enrolled. In 2009, 32 master's, 2 doctorates, 9 other advanced degrees awarded. *Degree requirements:* For master's, comprehensive exam. *Entrance requirements:* For master's, GRE General Test, 2 letters of recommendation. Additional exam requirements/recommendations for international students: Required—TOEFL (minimum score 83 computer-based), or IELTS. *Application deadline:* For fall admission, 6/1 for international students; for spring admission, 10/1 for international students. Applications are processed on a rolling basis. Application fee: $60. *Expenses:* Tuition, area resident: Part-time $486.74 per credit. Tuition, state resident: part-time $486.74 per credit. Tuition, nonresident: part-time $751.34 per credit. Tuition and fees vary according to degree level and program. *Financial support:* In 2009–10, 9 research assistantships with full tuition reimbursements (averaging $7,000 per year), 1 teaching assistantship with full tuition reimbursement (averaging $15,000 per year) were awarded; Federal Work-Study, scholarships/grants, and unspecified assistantships also available. Support available to part-time students. Financial award application deadline: 3/1; financial award applicants required to submit FAFSA. *Faculty research:* Infectious disease. *Unit head:* Dr. Helen Roberts, Chairperson, 973-655-5132. *Application contact:* Amy Aiello, Director of Graduate Admissions and Operations, 973-655-5147, Fax: 973-655-7869, E-mail: graduate.school@montclair.edu.

Morehead State University, Graduate Programs, College of Education, Department of Middle Grades and Secondary Education, Morehead, KY 40351. Offers business and marketing education (MAT); English/language arts 5-9 (MAT); French (MAT); health P-12 (MAT); mathematics 5-9 (MAT); physical education P-12 (MAT); science 5-9 (MAT); secondary biology (MAT); secondary chemistry (MAT); secondary earth science (MAT); secondary English (MAT); secondary math (MAT); secondary physics (MAT); secondary social studies (MAT); social studies 5-9 (MAT); Spanish (MAT). Part-time and evening/weekend programs available. *Students:* 54 full-time (31 women), 233 part-time (142 women); includes 11 minority (5 African Americans, 1 American Indian/Alaska Native, 1 Asian American or Pacific Islander, 4 Hispanic Americans). Average age 32. 206 applicants, 71% accepted, 79 enrolled. In 2009, 101 master's awarded. *Degree requirements:* For master's, portfolio. *Entrance requirements:* For master's, GRE or PRAXIS II content exam, minimum overall undergraduate GPA of 2.5. Additional exam requirements/recommendations for international students: Required—TOEFL (minimum score 500 paper-based; 173 computer-based). *Application deadline:* For fall admission, 8/1 priority date for domestic and international students; for spring admission, 12/1 priority date for domestic and international students. Applications are processed on a rolling basis. Application fee: $30. Electronic applications accepted. *Expenses:* Tuition, state resident: full-time $6318; part-time $351 per credit hour. Tuition, nonresident: full-time $15,804; part-time $878 per credit hour. *Financial support:* In 2009–10, 1 research assistantship (averaging $10,000 per year) was awarded; career-related internships or fieldwork, Federal Work-Study, and unspecified assistantships also available. Financial award application deadline: 3/15; financial award applicants required to submit FAFSA. *Unit head:* Dr. Cathy Gunn, Dean, 606-783-2040, Fax: 606-783-5029, E-mail: c.gunn@moreheadstate.edu. *Application contact:* Michelle Barber, Graduate Recruitment and Retention Assistant Director, 606-783-5127, Fax: 606-783-5061, E-mail: m.barber@moreheadstate.edu.

Morgan State University, School of Graduate Studies, School of Education and Urban Studies, Department of Advanced Studies, Leadership and Policy, Program in Science Education, Baltimore, MD 21251. Offers MS, Ed D. *Entrance requirements:* Additional exam requirements/recommendations for international students: Required—TOEFL (minimum score 550 paper-based; 213 computer-based).

National-Louis University, National College of Education, Program in Science Education, Chicago, IL 60603. Offers M Ed, MS Ed, CAS. Part-time and evening/weekend programs available. *Degree requirements:* For master's, thesis (for some programs). *Entrance requirements:* For master's, MAT or GRE, minimum GPA of 3.0, teaching certificate; for CAS, master's degree, teaching certificate. *Expenses:* Tuition: Full-time $17,160; part-time $715 per

Science Education

National-Louis University (continued)
semester hour. Tuition and fees vary according to course load, degree level, campus/location and program.

New Mexico Institute of Mining and Technology, Graduate Studies, Program in Science Teaching, Socorro, NM 87801. Offers MST. *Degree requirements:* For master's, thesis optional. *Entrance requirements:* For master's, GRE General Test. Additional exam requirements/recommendations for international students: Required—TOEFL (minimum score 540 paper-based; 207 computer-based). Electronic applications accepted. *Faculty research:* Teaching secondary school science and/or mathematics.

New York University, Steinhardt School of Culture, Education, and Human Development, Department of Teaching and Learning, Program in Science Education, New York, NY 10012-1019. Offers biology grades 7-12 (MA); chemistry grades 7-12 (MA); physics grades 7-12 (MA). Part-time and evening/weekend programs available. *Students:* 17 full-time (11 women), 12 part-time (9 women); includes 11 minority (1 African American, 1 American Indian/Alaska Native, 4 Asian Americans or Pacific Islanders, 5 Hispanic Americans), 2 international. Average age 29. 38 applicants, 84% accepted, 16 enrolled. In 2009, 23 master's awarded. *Degree requirements:* For master's, thesis (for some programs). *Entrance requirements:* Additional exam requirements/recommendations for international students: Required—TOEFL. *Application deadline:* For fall admission, 12/15 priority date for domestic and international students; for spring admission, 11/1 for domestic and international students. Applications are processed on a rolling basis. Application fee: $50. Electronic applications accepted. *Expenses:* Tuition: Full-time $30,528; part-time $1272 per credit. Required fees: $2177. *Financial support:* Career-related internships or fieldwork, Federal Work-Study, institutionally sponsored loans, scholarships/grants, and tuition waivers (partial) available. Support available to part-time students. Financial award application deadline: 2/1; financial award applicants required to submit FAFSA. *Faculty research:* Science curriculum development, gender and ethnicity, technology use, history and philosophy of school science, science in urban schools. *Unit head:* Dr. Pamela Fraser-Abder, Director, 212-998-5460, Fax: 212-995-4049. *Application contact:* 212-998-5030, Fax: 212-995-4328, E-mail: steinhardt.gradadmissions@nyu.edu.

North Carolina Agricultural and Technical State University, Graduate School, College of Arts and Sciences, Department of Biology, Greensboro, NC 27411. Offers biology (MS); biology education (MAT). Part-time and evening/weekend programs available. *Degree requirements:* For master's, comprehensive exam, thesis (for some programs), qualifying exam. *Entrance requirements:* For master's, GRE General Test, minimum GPA of 2.6. *Faculty research:* Physical ecology, cytochemistry, botany, parasitology, microbiology.

North Carolina State University, Graduate School, College of Education, Department of Mathematics, Science, and Technology Education, Program in Science Education, Raleigh, NC 27695. Offers M Ed, MS, PhD. *Accreditation:* NCATE. Part-time programs available. *Degree requirements:* For master's, thesis (for some programs), oral exam; for doctorate, one foreign language, thesis/dissertation, oral and written exams. *Entrance requirements:* For master's, GRE General Test or MAT, minimum GPA of 3.0; for doctorate, GRE General Test, minimum GPA of 3.0, interview. Electronic applications accepted. *Faculty research:* Teacher development, sociocultural issues in learning, student science misconceptions, technical applications to science teaching.

North Dakota State University, College of Graduate and Interdisciplinary Studies, College of Human Development and Education, School of Education, Fargo, ND 58108. Offers agricultural education (M Ed, MS), including agricultural education, agricultural extension education (MS); counseling (M Ed, MS, PhD); curriculum and instruction (M Ed, MS), including pedagogy, physical education and athletic administration; education (PhD); educational leadership (M Ed, MS, Ed S); family and consumer sciences education (M Ed, MS); history education (M Ed, MS); institutional analysis (Ed D); mathematics education (M Ed, MS); music education (M Ed, MS); occupational and adult education (Ed D); science education (M Ed, MS). *Accreditation:* NCATE. Part-time and evening/weekend programs available. Postbaccalaureate distance learning degree programs offered (minimal on-campus study). *Faculty:* 25 full-time (9 women), 3 part-time/adjunct (1 woman). *Students:* 29 full-time (25 women), 207 part-time (132 women); includes 15 minority (4 African Americans, 6 American Indian/Alaska Native, 3 Asian Americans or Pacific Islanders, 2 Hispanic Americans), 4 international. 88 applicants, 67% accepted, 56 enrolled. In 2009, 44 master's, 5 doctorates awarded. *Degree requirements:* For master's, comprehensive exam; for doctorate, thesis/dissertation; for Ed S, thesis. *Entrance requirements:* For degree, GRE General Test, master's degree, minimum GPA of 3.25. Additional exam requirements/recommendations for international students: Required—TOEFL. *Application deadline:* Applications are processed on a rolling basis. Application fee: $45 ($60 for international students). *Financial support:* Research assistantships, teaching assistantships, career-related internships or fieldwork, Federal Work-Study, institutionally sponsored loans, and tuition waivers (full) available. Financial award application deadline: 4/15. *Unit head:* Dr. William Martin, Chair, 701-231-7202, Fax: 701-231-7416, E-mail: william.martin@ndsu.edu. *Application contact:* Dr. William Martin, Chair, 701-231-7202, Fax: 701-231-7416, E-mail: william.martin@ndsu.edu.

Northeastern State University, Graduate College, College of Science and Health Professions, Program in Science Education, Tahlequah, OK 74464-2399. Offers M Ed. Part-time and evening/weekend programs available. *Entrance requirements:* For master's, MAT or GRE, minimum GPA of 2.5.

Northern Arizona University, Graduate College, College of Engineering, Forestry and Natural Sciences, Center for Science Teaching and Learning, Flagstaff, AZ 86011. Offers mathematics or science teaching (Certificate); science teaching and learning (M Ed, MAST). Part-time programs available. Postbaccalaureate distance learning degree programs offered (minimal on-campus study). *Faculty:* 2 full-time (both women). *Students:* 6 full-time (5 women), 7 part-time (6 women); includes 1 African American, 1 Hispanic American. In 2009, 6 master's awarded. *Entrance requirements:* Additional exam requirements/recommendations for international students: Required—TOEFL (minimum score 550 paper-based; 213 computer-based; 80 iBT), IELTS (minimum score 7), or a bachelor's degree from an English-speaking university and demonstrated proficiency. Application fee: $65. *Financial support:* Career-related internships or fieldwork available. Support available to part-time students. Financial award application deadline: 3/30; financial award applicants required to submit FAFSA. *Unit head:* Julie Gess-Newsome, Director, 928-523-9527, E-mail: julie.gess-newsome@nau.edu. *Application contact:* Dr. Sharon Cardenas, Faculty Coordinator, 928-523-7430.

Northern Arizona University, Graduate College, College of Engineering, Forestry and Natural Sciences, Department of Physics and Astronomy, Flagstaff, AZ 86011. Offers applied physics (MS); science education (MAT). Part-time programs available. *Faculty:* 13 full-time (2 women). *Students:* 13 full-time (5 women), 4 part-time (2 women); includes 2 minority (1 American Indian/Alaska Native, 1 Asian American or Pacific Islander), 1 international. Average age 37. 14 applicants, 71% accepted, 7 enrolled. In 2009, 7 master's awarded. *Degree requirements:* For master's, thesis optional. *Entrance requirements:* For master's, GRE. Additional exam requirements/recommendations for international students: Required—TOEFL (minimum score 550 paper-based; 213 computer-based; 80 iBT), IELTS (minimum score 7), or a bachelor's degree from an English-speaking university and demonstrated proficiency. *Application deadline:* For fall admission, 3/15 priority date for domestic students, 9/1 for international students; for spring admission, 10/15 priority date for domestic students. Applications are processed on a rolling basis. Application fee: $65. Electronic applications accepted. *Financial support:* In 2009–10, 1 research assistantship with partial tuition reimbursement (averaging $12,390 per year), 9 teaching assistantships with partial tuition reimbursements (averaging $12,390 per year) were awarded; career-related internships or fieldwork, Federal Work-Study, health care benefits, tuition waivers (full and partial), and unspecified assistantships also available. Support available to part-time students. Financial award application deadline: 3/30; financial award applicants required to submit FAFSA. *Unit head:* Dr. Nadine Barlow, Chair, 928-523-5452, Fax: 928-523-1371, E-mail: nadine.barlow@nau.edu. *Application contact:* Dr. Gary Bowman, Graduate Coordinator, 928-523-1114, Fax: 928-523-1371, E-mail: gary.bowman@nau.edu.

Northern Michigan University, College of Graduate Studies, College of Professional Studies, School of Education, Program in Science Education, Marquette, MI 49855-5301. Offers MS. Postbaccalaureate distance learning degree programs offered.

North Georgia College & State University, Graduate Studies, Program in Teacher Education, Dahlonega, GA 30597. Offers early childhood education (M Ed); educational leadership (Ed S); middle grades education (M Ed); secondary education (M Ed), including art education, biology education, chemistry education, English education, history education, mathematics education, physical education, science education; special education (M Ed), including interrelated special education, learning disabilities. *Accreditation:* NCATE. Part-time and evening/weekend programs available. Postbaccalaureate distance learning degree programs offered (minimal on-campus study). *Degree requirements:* For master's, comprehensive exam, thesis optional. *Entrance requirements:* For master's, GRE General Test or MAT, minimum GPA of 2.75; for Ed S, GRE General Test or MAT, 3 years of teaching experience, master's degree, minimum graduate GPA of 3.25. Electronic applications accepted. *Faculty research:* Computers and teachers' attitudes, rural versus urban teacher attitudes, teacher leadership roles, minority recruitment in teaching force.

Northwestern State University of Louisiana, Graduate Studies and Research, College of Education, Programs in Education, Natchitoches, LA 71497. Offers business and distributive education (M Ed); counseling (M Ed); early childhood education (M Ed); education (M Ed); education leadership (M Ed); educational technology (M Ed); elementary teaching (M Ed); English education (M Ed); home economics education (M Ed); mathematics education (M Ed); reading (M Ed); science education (M Ed); secondary teaching (M Ed); social sciences education (M Ed). *Degree requirements:* For master's, comprehensive exam, thesis or alternative. *Entrance requirements:* For master's, GRE General Test, minimum undergraduate GPA of 2.5.

Northwest Missouri State University, Graduate School, College of Arts and Sciences, Program in Teaching: Science, Maryville, MO 64468-6001. Offers MS Ed. *Accreditation:* NCATE. Part-time programs available. *Faculty:* 10 full-time (2 women). *Students:* 1 (woman) full-time. 2 applicants, 0% accepted, 0 enrolled. In 2009, 6 master's awarded. *Degree requirements:* For master's, comprehensive exam, thesis optional. *Entrance requirements:* For master's, GRE General Test, minimum GPA of 2.75 in major, 2.5 overall; teaching certificate; writing sample. Additional exam requirements/recommendations for international students: Required—TOEFL (minimum score 550 paper-based; 213 computer-based). *Application deadline:* For fall admission, 7/1 for domestic and international students; for spring admission, 11/15 for domestic and international students. Applications are processed on a rolling basis. Application fee: $0 ($50 for international students). *Expenses:* Tuition, state resident: part-time $296.34 per credit hour. Tuition, nonresident: part-time $510.43 per credit hour. *Financial support:* In 2009–10, 2 research assistantships with full tuition reimbursements (averaging $6,000 per year) were awarded; teaching assistantships. Financial award application deadline: 4/1; financial award applicants required to submit FAFSA. *Unit head:* Dr. Rafia Islam, Chairperson, 660-562-1210. *Application contact:* Dr. Gregory Haddock, Dean of Graduate School, 660-562-1145, Fax: 660-562-1096, E-mail: gradsch@nwmissouri.edu.

Norwich University, School of Graduate and Continuing Studies, Program in Military History, Northfield, VT 05663. Offers race and gender in military history (MA); U. S. military history (MA). Evening/weekend programs available. *Faculty:* 33 part-time/adjunct (2 women). *Students:* 531 full-time (85 women); includes 30 minority (3 African Americans, 6 American Indian/Alaska Native, 6 Asian Americans or Pacific Islanders, 15 Hispanic Americans). Average age 42. 736 applicants, 80% accepted, 531 enrolled. In 2009, 503 master's awarded. *Entrance requirements:* For master's, minimum undergraduate GPA of 2.75. Additional exam requirements/recommendations for international students: Required—TOEFL (minimum score 550 paper-based; 212 computer-based; 83 iBT). *Application deadline:* For fall admission, 8/10 for domestic and international students; for winter admission, 11/7 for domestic and international students; for spring admission, 2/6 for domestic and international students. Application fee: $50. Electronic applications accepted. Full-time tuition and fees vary according to course level and course load. *Financial support:* Scholarships/grants available. Financial award applicants required to submit FAFSA. *Unit head:* Dr. James Erhman, Program Director, 802-485-2567, Fax: 802-485-2533. *Application contact:* Lars Nielsen, Administrative Director, 802-485-2853, Fax: 802-485-2533, E-mail: lnielsen@norwich.edu.

Nova Southeastern University, Fischler School of Education and Human Services, Graduate Teacher Education Program, Fort Lauderdale, FL 33314-7796. Offers athletic administration (MS); brain research (MS, Ed S); charter school education/leadership (MS); cognitive and behavioral disabilities (MS); computer science education (Ed S); computer science education (K-12) (MS); curriculum and teaching (Ed S); curriculum, instruction and technology (MS); curriculum, instruction, management and administration (Ed S); early childhood education (MS); early literacy and reading (Ed S); early literacy education (MS); education technology (MS); educational leadership (administration K–12) (MS, Ed S); educational media (Ed S); educational media (K-12) (MS); elementary education (MS, Ed S), including ESOL endorsement (MS); English education (MS, Ed S); environmental education (MS); exceptional student education (MS), including ESOL endorsement; gifted education (MS, Ed S); interdisciplinary arts education (MS); management and administration of educational programs (MS); mathematics (MS); mathematics education (Ed S); multicultural early intervention (MS); pre-kindergarten/primary (MS); preschool education (MS); reading (MS); reading and TESOL (MS); reading education (Ed S); science (MS); science education (Ed S); secondary education (MS); social studies (MS, Ed S); Spanish language (MS); special education and reading (MS); teaching and learning (MA, MS), including curriculum and instruction (MA), elementary mathematics (MA), elementary reading (MA), K-12 technology integration (MA); teaching English to speakers of other languages (MS, Ed S); technology management and administration (Ed S); urban studies education (MS). Part-time and evening/weekend programs available. Postbaccalaureate distance learning degree programs offered (minimal on-campus study). *Faculty:* 72 full-time (43 women), 385 part-time/adjunct (252 women). *Students:* 196 full-time (175 women), 1,304 part-time (1,128 women); includes 594 minority (471 African Americans, 5 American Indian/Alaska Native, 18 Asian Americans or Pacific Islanders, 100 Hispanic Americans). Average age 37. 2,610 applicants, 72% accepted, 1352 enrolled. In 2009, 836 other advanced degrees awarded. *Degree requirements:* For master's and Ed S, thesis, practicum, internship. *Entrance requirements:* For master's, MAT, GRE, CLAST, CBEST, PRAXIS I, General Knowledge Test, minimum GPA of 2.5; for Ed S, MAT or GRE, master's degree, teaching certificate, minimum GPA of 3.0. Additional exam requirements/recommendations for international students: Required—TSE (recommended, minimum score 50); Recommended—TOEFL (minimum score 550 paper-based; 213 computer-based; 80 iBT), IELTS (minimum score 6). *Application deadline:* For fall admission, 9/25 priority date for domestic and international students; for winter admission, 2/23 priority date for domestic and international students; for spring admission, 4/25 priority date for domestic and international students. Applications are processed on a rolling basis. Application fee: $50. Electronic applications accepted. *Financial support:* Federal Work-Study available. Support available to part-time students. Financial award application deadline: 4/15; financial award applicants required to submit FAFSA. *Faculty research:* School effectiveness, critical thinking, leadership skills acquisition, child education, multicultural education. *Unit head:* Dr. Ronald Kern, Dean of Academic Affairs, 800-986-3223 Ext. 7809, Fax: 954-262-3606, E-mail: rk429@nsu.nova.edu. *Application contact:* Dr. Jennifer Quinones Nottingham, Dean of Student Affairs, 800-986-3223 Ext. 1559.

Occidental College, Graduate Studies, Department of Education, Program in Secondary Education, Los Angeles, CA 90041-3314. Offers English and comparative literary studies (MAT); history (MAT); life science (MAT); mathematics (MAT); physical science (MAT); social science (MAT); Spanish (MAT). Part-time programs available. *Degree requirements:* For master's, comprehensive exam, graduate synthesis paper. *Entrance requirements:* For master's, GRE General Test, minimum GPA of 3.0. Additional exam requirements/recommendations for

international students: Required—TOEFL (minimum score 625 paper-based; 263 computer-based). *Expenses:* Contact institution.

Ohio University, Graduate College, College of Arts and Sciences, Department of Geological Sciences, Athens, OH 45701-2979. Offers environmental geochemistry (MS); environmental geology (MS); environmental/hydrology (MS); geology (MS); geology education (MS); geomorphology/surficial processes (MS); geophysics (MS); hydrogeology (MS); sedimentology (MS); structure/tectonics (MS). Part-time programs available. *Faculty:* 10 full-time (4 women), 4 part-time/adjunct (1 woman). *Students:* 18 full-time (13 women), 1 part-time (0 women), 9 international. 15 applicants, 67% accepted, 6 enrolled. In 2009, 5 master's awarded. *Degree requirements:* For master's, thesis. *Entrance requirements:* Additional exam requirements/recommendations for international students: Required—TOEFL (minimum score 550 paper-based; 80 iBT) or IELTS Academic (minimum score 6.5). *Application deadline:* For fall admission, 2/1 priority date for domestic and international students. Application fee: $50 ($55 for international students). Electronic applications accepted. *Expenses:* Tuition, state resident: full-time $7839; part-time $323 per quarter hour. Tuition, nonresident: full-time $15,831; part-time $654 per quarter hour. Required fees: $2931. *Financial support:* Research assistantships with full tuition reimbursements, teaching assistantships with full tuition reimbursements, Federal Work-Study, institutionally sponsored loans, scholarships/grants, tuition waivers (partial), and unspecified assistantships available. Financial award application deadline: 2/1. *Faculty research:* Geoscience education, tectonics, fluvial geomorphology, invertebrate paleontology, mine/hydrology. Total annual research expenditures: $649,020. *Unit head:* Dr. Gregory Nadon, Chair, 740-593-4212, Fax: 740-593-0486, E-mail: nadon@ohio.edu. *Application contact:* Dr. Douglas Green, Graduate Chair, 740-593-1843, Fax: 740-593-0486, E-mail: green@ohio.edu.

Old Dominion University, Darden College of Education, Programs in Secondary Education, Norfolk, VA 23529. Offers biology (MS Ed); chemistry (MS Ed); English (MS Ed); instructional technology (MS Ed); library science (MS Ed); secondary education (MS Ed). *Accreditation:* NCATE. Part-time and evening/weekend programs available. Postbaccalaureate distance learning degree programs offered (minimal on-campus study). *Faculty:* 20 full-time (16 women). *Students:* 74 full-time (54 women), 137 part-time (92 women); includes 41 minority (22 African Americans, 1 American Indian/Alaska Native, 11 Asian Americans or Pacific Islanders, 7 Hispanic Americans). Average age 33. 67 applicants, 79% accepted, 53 enrolled. In 2009, 131 master's awarded. *Degree requirements:* For master's, comprehensive exam, thesis. *Entrance requirements:* For master's, GRE General Test or MAT, PRAXIS I (for licensure), minimum GPA of 2.8, teaching certificate. Additional exam requirements/recommendations for international students: Required—TOEFL. *Application deadline:* For fall admission, 6/1 for domestic and international students; for winter admission, 11/1 for domestic and international students; for spring admission, 3/1 for domestic and international students. Applications are processed on a rolling basis. Application fee: $50. Electronic applications accepted. *Expenses:* Tuition, state resident: full-time $8112; part-time $338 per credit. Tuition, nonresident: full-time $20,256; part-time $844 per credit. Required fees: $119 per semester. One-time fee: $50. *Financial support:* In 2009–10, 56 students received support, including fellowships (averaging $15,000 per year), 2 research assistantships with tuition reimbursements available (averaging $9,000 per year), 3 teaching assistantships with tuition reimbursements available (averaging $12,500 per year); career-related internships or fieldwork, Federal Work-Study, institutionally sponsored loans, scholarships/grants, and tuition waivers (partial) also available. Support available to part-time students. Financial award application deadline: 2/15; financial award applicants required to submit FAFSA. *Faculty research:* Use of technology, writing project for teachers, geography teaching, reading. *Unit head:* Dr. Robert Lucking, Graduate Program Director, 757-683-5545, Fax: 757-683-5862, E-mail: rlucking@odu.edu. *Application contact:* Dr. Robert Lucking, Graduate Program Director, 757-683-5545, Fax: 757-683-5862, E-mail: rlucking@odu.edu.

Oregon State University, Graduate School, College of Science, Department of Science and Mathematics Education, Program in Biology Education, Corvallis, OR 97331. Offers MS. *Accreditation:* NCATE. *Entrance requirements:* For master's, minimum GPA of 3.0 in last 90 hours. Additional exam requirements/recommendations for international students: Required—TOEFL. *Application deadline:* For fall admission, 1/15 for domestic students. Application fee: $50. *Expenses:* Tuition, state resident: full-time $9774; part-time $362 per credit. Tuition, nonresident: full-time $15,849; part-time $587 per credit. Required fees: $1639. Full-time tuition and fees vary according to course load and program. *Unit head:* Program Coordinator, 541-737-9286, Fax: 541-737-1817. *Application contact:* Dr. Mary Ann Matzke, Head Advisor, 541-737-3880, Fax: 541-737-1009, E-mail: maryann.matzke@oregonstate.edu.

Oregon State University, Graduate School, College of Science, Department of Science and Mathematics Education, Program in Chemistry Education, Corvallis, OR 97331. Offers MS. *Accreditation:* NCATE. *Entrance requirements:* For master's, minimum GPA of 3.0 in last 90 hours of course work. Additional exam requirements/recommendations for international students: Required—TOEFL. *Application deadline:* For fall admission, 1/15 for domestic students. Application fee: $50. *Expenses:* Tuition, state resident: full-time $9774; part-time $362 per credit. Tuition, nonresident: full-time $15,849; part-time $587 per credit. Required fees: $1639. Full-time tuition and fees vary according to course load and program. *Unit head:* Program Coordinator, 541-737-9286, Fax: 541-737-1817. *Application contact:* Dr. Mary Ann Matzke, Head Advisor, 541-737-3880, Fax: 541-737-1009, E-mail: maryann.matzke@oregonstate.edu.

Oregon State University, Graduate School, College of Science, Department of Science and Mathematics Education, Program in Integrated Science Education, Corvallis, OR 97331. Offers MS. *Accreditation:* NCATE. In 2009, 30 master's awarded. *Entrance requirements:* For master's, minimum GPA of 3.0 in last 90 hours. Additional exam requirements/recommendations for international students: Required—TOEFL. *Application deadline:* For fall admission, 3/1 for domestic students. Application fee: $50. *Expenses:* Tuition, state resident: full-time $9774; part-time $362 per credit. Tuition, nonresident: full-time $15,849; part-time $587 per credit. Required fees: $1639. Full-time tuition and fees vary according to course load and program. *Financial support:* Application deadline: 2/1. *Unit head:* Program Coordinator, 541-737-9286, Fax: 541-737-1817. *Application contact:* Dr. Mary Ann Matzke, Head Advisor, 541-737-3880, Fax: 541-737-1009, E-mail: maryann.matzke@oregonstate.edu.

Oregon State University, Graduate School, College of Science, Department of Science and Mathematics Education, Program in Physics Education, Corvallis, OR 97331. Offers MS. *Accreditation:* NCATE. Part-time programs available. *Degree requirements:* For master's, thesis (for some programs). *Entrance requirements:* For master's, minimum GPA of 3.0 in last 90 hours of course work. Additional exam requirements/recommendations for international students: Required—TOEFL. *Application deadline:* For fall admission, 1/15 for domestic students. Application fee: $50. *Expenses:* Tuition, state resident: full-time $9774; part-time $362 per credit. Tuition, nonresident: full-time $15,849; part-time $587 per credit. Required fees: $1639. Full-time tuition and fees vary according to course load and program. *Financial support:* Application deadline: 2/1. *Unit head:* Program Coordinator, 541-737-9286, Fax: 541-737-1817. *Application contact:* Dr. Mary Ann Matzke, Head Advisor, 541-737-3880, Fax: 541-737-1009, E-mail: maryann.matzke@oregonstate.edu.

Oregon State University, Graduate School, College of Science, Department of Science and Mathematics Education, Program in Science Education, Corvallis, OR 97331. Offers MA, MS, PhD. *Accreditation:* NCATE. *Degree requirements:* For doctorate, thesis/dissertation. *Entrance requirements:* For master's, minimum GPA of 3.0 in last 90 hours; for doctorate, GRE or MAT, minimum GPA of 3.0 in last 90 hours. Additional exam requirements/recommendations for international students: Required—TOEFL. *Application deadline:* For fall admission, 3/1 for domestic students. Application fee: $50. *Expenses:* Tuition, state resident: full-time $9774; part-time $362 per credit. Tuition, nonresident: full-time $15,849; part-time $587 per credit. Required fees: $1639. Full-time tuition and fees vary according to course load and program. *Financial support:* Teaching assistantships, Federal Work-Study and institutionally sponsored loans available. Support available to part-time students. Financial award application deadline: 2/1. *Faculty research:* Teacher thought processes, pedagogical content knowledge and teacher preparation. *Unit head:* Dr. Lawrence B. Flick, Chair, 541-737-3664, Fax: 541-737-1817, E-mail: flickl@science.oregonstate.edu. *Application contact:* Dr. Mary Ann Matzke, Head Advisor, 541-737-3880, Fax: 541-737-1009, E-mail: maryann.matzke@oregonstate.edu.

Our Lady of the Lake University of San Antonio, School of Professional Studies, Program in Curriculum and Instruction, San Antonio, TX 78207-4689. Offers bilingual (M Ed); early childhood education (M Ed); English as a second language (M Ed); integrated math teaching (M Ed); integrated science teaching (M Ed); master reading teacher (M Ed); master technology teacher (M Ed); reading specialist (M Ed). *Students:* 2 full-time (1 woman), 112 part-time (94 women); includes 64 minority (5 African Americans, 1 American Indian/Alaska Native, 1 Asian American or Pacific Islander, 57 Hispanic Americans). Average age 38. In 2009, 49 master's awarded. *Expenses:* Tuition: Full-time $12,330; part-time $685 per contact hour. Required fees: $139; $12 per contact hour. $57 per semester. Tuition and fees vary according to campus/location. *Unit head:* Dr. Cullen Grinnan, 210-434-6711 Ext. 8928, E-mail: ctgrinnan@lake.ollusa.edu. *Application contact:* Dr. Cullen Grinnan, 210-434-6711 Ext. 8928, E-mail: ctgrinnan@lake.ollusa.edu.

Our Lady of the Lake University of San Antonio, School of Professional Studies, Program in Intermediate Education, San Antonio, TX 78207-4689. Offers math/science education (M Ed); professional studies (M Ed). Part-time and evening/weekend programs available. *Students:* 3 full-time (1 woman), 14 part-time (11 women); includes 11 minority (3 African Americans, 8 Hispanic Americans). Average age 36. In 2009, 4 master's awarded. *Expenses:* Tuition: Full-time $12,330; part-time $685 per contact hour. Required fees: $139; $12 per contact hour. $57 per semester. Tuition and fees vary according to campus/location. *Unit head:* Dr. Cullen Grinnen, E-mail: ctgrinnan@lake.ollusa.edu. *Application contact:* Dr. Cullen Grinnen, E-mail: ctgrinnan@lake.ollusa.edu.

Plymouth State University, College of Graduate Studies, Graduate Studies in Education, Program in Science, Plymouth, NH 03264-1595. Offers applied meteorology (MS); environmental science and policy (MS); science education (MS).

Portland State University, Graduate Studies, College of Liberal Arts and Sciences, Department of Geology, Portland, OR 97207-0751. Offers environmental sciences and resources (PhD); geology (MA, MS); science/geology (MAT, MST). Part-time programs available. *Degree requirements:* For master's, comprehensive exam, thesis, field comprehensive; for doctorate, thesis/dissertation, 2 years of residency. *Entrance requirements:* For master's, GRE General Test, GRE Subject Test, BA/BS in geology, minimum GPA of 3.0 in upper-division course work or 2.75 overall. Additional exam requirements/recommendations for international students: Required—TOEFL (minimum score 550 paper-based; 213 computer-based). *Faculty research:* Sediment transport, volcanic environmental geology, coastal and fluvial processes.

Portland State University, Graduate Studies, College of Liberal Arts and Sciences, Interdisciplinary Program in Environmental Sciences and Management, Portland, OR 97207-0751. Offers environmental management (MEM); environmental sciences/biology (PhD); environmental sciences/chemistry (PhD); environmental sciences/civil engineering (PhD); environmental sciences/geography (PhD); environmental sciences/geology (PhD); environmental sciences/physics (PhD); environmental studies (MS); science/environmental science (MST). Part-time programs available. *Degree requirements:* For master's, thesis or alternative; for doctorate, variable foreign language requirement, comprehensive exam, thesis/dissertation, oral and qualifying exams. *Entrance requirements:* For master's, GRE General Test, 3 letters of recommendation; for doctorate, minimum GPA of 3.0 in upper-division course work or 2.75 overall. Additional exam requirements/recommendations for international students: Required—TOEFL (minimum score 550 paper-based; 213 computer-based). *Faculty research:* Environmental aspects of biology, chemistry, civil engineering, geology, physics.

Portland State University, Graduate Studies, College of Liberal Arts and Sciences, Interdisciplinary Programs in General Science, General Social Science, and General Arts and Letters, Portland, OR 97207-0751. Offers general arts and letters education (MAT, MST); general science education (MAT, MST); general social science education (MAT, MST). Part-time and evening/weekend programs available. *Degree requirements:* For master's, variable foreign language requirement, written exam. *Entrance requirements:* For master's, minimum GPA of 3.0 in upper-division course work or 2.75 overall. Additional exam requirements/recommendations for international students: Required—TOEFL (minimum score 550 paper-based; 213 computer-based).

Purdue University, Graduate School, College of Science, Department of Chemistry, West Lafayette, IN 47907. Offers analytical chemistry (MS, PhD); biochemistry (MS, PhD); chemical education (MS, PhD); inorganic chemistry (MS, PhD); organic chemistry (MS, PhD); physical chemistry (MS, PhD). Terminal master's awarded for partial completion of doctoral program. *Degree requirements:* For master's, thesis; for doctorate, thesis/dissertation. *Entrance requirements:* Additional exam requirements/recommendations for international students: Required—TOEFL. Electronic applications accepted.

Purdue University, Graduate School, School of Education, Department of Curriculum and Instruction, West Lafayette, IN 47907. Offers agricultural and extension education (PhD, Ed S); agriculture and extension education (MS, MS Ed); art education (PhD); consumer and family sciences and extension education (MS Ed, PhD, Ed S); curriculum studies (MS Ed, PhD, Ed S); educational technology (MS Ed, PhD, Ed S); elementary education (MS Ed); foreign language education (MS Ed, PhD, Ed S); industrial technology (PhD, Ed S); language arts (MS Ed, PhD, Ed S); literacy (MS Ed, PhD, Ed S); mathematics/science education (MS, MS Ed, PhD, Ed S); social studies (MS Ed, PhD); social studies education (Ed S); vocational/industrial education (MS Ed, PhD, Ed S); vocational/technical education (MS Ed, PhD, Ed S). *Accreditation:* NCATE. Part-time and evening/weekend programs available. *Degree requirements:* For master's, thesis optional; for doctorate, thesis/dissertation, oral and written exams; for Ed S, oral presentation, project. *Entrance requirements:* For master's, GRE General Test, minimum B average; for doctorate, GRE General Test; for Ed S, GRE, minimum B average. Additional exam requirements/recommendations for international students: Required—TOEFL. Electronic applications accepted. *Faculty research:* Literacy acquisition and development, teacher beliefs and knowledge, recruitment and retention of underrepresented students, economic education, literacy discourse.

Purdue University Calumet, Graduate School, School of Engineering, Mathematics, and Science, Department of Biological Sciences, Hammond, IN 46323-2094. Offers biology (MS); biology teaching (MS); biotechnology (MS). *Entrance requirements:* For master's, GRE. Additional exam requirements/recommendations for international students: Required—TOEFL. Electronic applications accepted. *Faculty research:* Cell biology, molecular biology, genetics, microbiology, neurophysiology.

Queens College of the City University of New York, Division of Graduate Studies, Division of Education, Department of Secondary Education, Flushing, NY 11367-1597. Offers art (MS Ed); biology (MS Ed, AC); chemistry (MS Ed, AC); earth sciences (MS Ed, AC); English (MS Ed, AC); French (MS Ed, AC); Italian (MS Ed, AC); mathematics (MS Ed, AC); music (MS Ed, AC); physics (MS Ed, AC); social studies (MS Ed, AC); Spanish (MS Ed, AC). Part-time and evening/weekend programs available. *Faculty:* 22 full-time (14 women). *Students:* 86 full-time (47 women), 1,118 part-time (736 women). 591 applicants, 60% accepted, 250 enrolled. In 2009, 187 master's awarded. *Degree requirements:* For master's, research project; for AC, thesis optional. *Entrance requirements:* For master's, minimum GPA of 3.0. Additional exam requirements/recommendations for international students: Required—TOEFL. *Application deadline:* For fall admission, 4/1 for domestic students; for spring admission, 11/1 for domestic students. Applications are processed on a rolling basis. Application fee: $125. *Expenses:* Tuition, state resident: full-time $7360; part-time $310 per credit. Tuition, nonresident: part-time $575 per credit. One-time fee: $195 full-time; $145.25 part-time. *Financial support:* Career-related internships or fieldwork, Federal Work-Study, institutionally sponsored loans, and tuition waivers (partial) available. Support available to part-time students. Financial award application deadline: 4/1; financial award applicants required to submit FAFSA. *Unit head:* Dr. Eleanor Armour-Thomas, Chairperson, 718-997-5150, E-mail: armourthomas@yahoo.com.

Science Education

Queens College of the City University of New York (continued)
Application contact: Mario Caruso, Director of Graduate Admissions, 718-997-5200, Fax: 718-997-5193, E-mail: graduate_admissions@qc.edu.

Quinnipiac University, Division of Education, Program in Secondary Education, Hamden, CT 06518-1940. Offers biology (MAT); English (MAT); history/social studies (MAT); mathematics (MAT); Spanish (MAT). *Accreditation:* NCATE. *Faculty:* 10 full-time (7 women), 5 part-time/adjunct (3 women). *Students:* 80 full-time (56 women), 2 part-time (1 woman); includes 6 minority (2 African Americans, 2 Asian Americans or Pacific Islanders, 2 Hispanic Americans). 77 applicants, 95% accepted, 66 enrolled. In 2009, 33 master's awarded. *Entrance requirements:* For master's, PRAXIS I, minimum GPA of 2.67, interview. Additional exam requirements/recommendations for international students: Required—TOEFL (minimum score 575 paper-based; 233 computer-based; 90 iBT), IELTS (minimum score 6.5). *Application deadline:* For fall admission, 3/31 priority date for domestic students. Applications are processed on a rolling basis. Application fee: $45. Electronic applications accepted. *Expenses:* Tuition: Full-time $16,030; part-time $770 per credit. Required fees: $630; $35 per credit. *Financial support:* Career-related internships or fieldwork, scholarships/grants, and tuition waivers (partial) available. Financial award application deadline: 4/15; financial award applicants required to submit FAFSA. *Faculty research:* Multicultural and urban education, role of technology in education, challenges of teaching diverse learners, socio-cultural nature of learning. *Unit head:* Dr. Bernadine Krawczyk, Assistant Dean, Division of Education, 203-582-3510, Fax: 203-582-3473, E-mail: bernadine.krawczyk@quinnipiac.edu. *Application contact:* Jennifer Boutin, Associate Director of Graduate Admissions, 800-462-1944, Fax: 203-582-3443, E-mail: jennifer.boutin@quinnipiac.edu.

Regis University, College for Professional Studies, Program in Teacher Education, Denver, CO 80221-1099. Offers adult learning, training, and development (M Ed); curriculum, instruction, and assessment (M Ed); early childhood (M Ed); educational technology (Certificate); elementary (M Ed); ESL (M Ed); fine arts (M Ed), including arts, music; instructional technology (M Ed); professional leadership (M Ed); reading (M Ed); secondary (M Ed); self-designed (M Ed); space studies (M Ed); special education (M Ed); teacher licensure (M Ed). Program also offered in Henderson and Las Vegas (Summerlin), NV. *Accreditation:* Teacher Education Accreditation Council. Part-time and evening/weekend programs available. Postbaccalaureate distance learning degree programs offered (no on-campus study). *Degree requirements:* For master's, thesis. *Entrance requirements:* For master's, resume, minimum GPA of 2.75, criminal background check. Additional exam requirements/recommendations for international students: Required—TOEFL (minimum score 213 computer-based), TWE (minimum score 5). Electronic applications accepted. *Faculty research:* Issues of equity in the middle school classroom, professional learning communities, school reform, socialinguistic and discursive obstacles to student integration, inclusive language arts curriculum.

Rice University, Graduate Programs, Wiess School of Natural Sciences, Department of Physics and Astronomy, Houston, TX 77251-1892. Offers nanoscale physics (MS); physics and astronomy (PhD); science teaching (MST). Part-time programs available. *Faculty:* 39 full-time (4 women), 9 part-time/adjunct (1 woman). *Students:* 124 full-time (19 women), 12 part-time (7 women); includes 8 minority (5 Asian Americans or Pacific Islanders, 3 Hispanic Americans), 70 international. Average age 28. 192 applicants, 26% accepted, 22 enrolled. In 2009, 16 master's, 21 doctorates awarded. *Degree requirements:* For master's, thesis (for some programs); for doctorate, thesis/dissertation, minimum B average. *Entrance requirements:* For master's, GRE General Test; for doctorate, GRE General Test, GRE Subject Test. Additional exam requirements/recommendations for international students: Required—TOEFL (minimum score 600 paper-based; 250 computer-based; 90 iBT). *Application deadline:* For fall admission, 2/1 priority date for domestic and international students. Application fee: $70. Electronic applications accepted. *Financial support:* In 2009–10, 124 students received support, including 22 fellowships with full tuition reimbursements available (averaging $25,700 per year), 102 research assistantships with full tuition reimbursements available (averaging $25,700 per year). Financial award application deadline: 2/1. *Faculty research:* Optical physics; ultra cold atoms; membrane electr-statics, peptides, proteins and lipids; solar astrophysics; stellar activity; magnetic fields; young stars. *Unit head:* Rose Berridge, Department Administrator, 713-348-4938, Fax: 713-348-4510, E-mail: physics@rice.edu. *Application contact:* Bridgitt G. Ayers, Graduate Program Coordinator, 713-348-6348, Fax: 713-348-4150, E-mail: physgrad@rice.edu.

Rider University, Department of Graduate Education, Leadership and Counseling, Teacher Certification Program, Lawrenceville, NJ 08648-3001. Offers business education (Certificate); elementary education (Certificate); English as a second language (Certificate); English education (Certificate); mathematics education (Certificate); preschool to grade 3 (Certificate); science education (Certificate); social studies education (Certificate); world languages (Certificate), including French, German, Spanish. Part-time programs available. *Degree requirements:* For Certificate, internship, professional portfolio. *Entrance requirements:* For degree, PRAXIS, resume. Additional exam requirements/recommendations for international students: Required—TOEFL (minimum score 550 paper-based; 213 computer-based). Electronic applications accepted. *Faculty research:* Conceptual foundations for optimal development of creativity; creative theory, cognitive processes in mathematics learning, teacher collaboration.

Rutgers, The State University of New Jersey, New Brunswick, Graduate School of Education, Department of Learning and Teaching, Program in Science Education, Piscataway, NJ 08854-8097. Offers Ed M, Ed D. Part-time programs available. Terminal master's awarded for partial completion of doctoral program. *Degree requirements:* For master's, comprehensive exam (for some programs); for doctorate, thesis/dissertation, qualifying exam. *Entrance requirements:* For master's, GRE General Test, minimum GPA of 3.0; for doctorate, GRE General Test, minimum GPA of 3.5. Additional exam requirements/recommendations for international students: Required—TOEFL. Electronic applications accepted.

Saginaw Valley State University, College of Education, Program in Natural Science Teaching, University Center, MI 48710. Offers elementary (MAT); middle school (MAT); secondary school (MAT). *Accreditation:* NCATE. Part-time and evening/weekend programs available. *Students:* 20 part-time (16 women); includes 2 minority (1 African American, 1 Hispanic American), 1 international. Average age 35. 5 applicants, 100% accepted, 3 enrolled. In 2009, 14 master's awarded. *Degree requirements:* For master's, capstone course. *Entrance requirements:* For master's, minimum GPA of 3.0, teaching certificate. Additional exam requirements/recommendations for international students: Required—TOEFL (minimum score 525 paper-based; 197 computer-based; 71 iBT). *Application deadline:* Applications are processed on a rolling basis. Application fee: $25. Electronic applications accepted. *Financial support:* Federal Work-Study and scholarships/grants available. Support available to part-time students. Financial award applicants required to submit FAFSA. *Unit head:* Dr. Steve P. Barbus, Dean, 989-964-6067, Fax: 989-790-4385, E-mail: barbus@svsu.edu. *Application contact:* Dr. Steve P. Barbus, Dean, 989-964-6067, Fax: 989-790-4385, E-mail: barbus@svsu.edu.

St. John Fisher College, School of Arts and Sciences, Mathematics/Science/Technology Education Program, Rochester, NY 14618-3597. Offers MS. Part-time and evening/weekend programs available. *Faculty:* 3 full-time (2 women), 3 part-time/adjunct (1 woman). *Students:* 18 full-time (8 women), 45 part-time (24 women); includes 4 minority (2 African Americans, 2 Asian Americans or Pacific Islanders). Average age 31. 33 applicants, 85% accepted, 15 enrolled. In 2009, 18 master's awarded. *Degree requirements:* For master's, thesis, capstone experience. *Entrance requirements:* For master's, 2 letters of recommendation, personal statement, current resume, interview, teaching certification. Additional exam requirements/recommendations for international students: Required—TOEFL (minimum score 575 paper-based; 233 computer-based; 80 iBT). *Application deadline:* Applications are processed on a rolling basis. Application fee: $30. Electronic applications accepted. *Expenses:* Tuition: Part-time $680 per credit hour. Required fees: $25 per semester. Tuition and fees vary according to degree level and program. *Financial support:* In 2009–10, 40 students received support. Federal Work-Study and scholarships/grants available. Financial award applicants required to submit FAFSA. *Faculty research:* Mathematics education, science and technology education. *Unit head:* Dr. Diane Barrett, Graduate Director, 585-385-8366, E-mail: dbarrett@sjfc.edu. *Application contact:* Jose Perales, Interim Director of Graduate Admissions, 585-385-8067, E-mail: jperales@sjfc.edu.

Salem State College, School of Graduate Studies, Program in Biology, Salem, MA 01970-5353. Offers MAT. Part-time and evening/weekend programs available. *Students:* 3 part-time (0 women). Average age 35. 1 applicant, 0% accepted, 0 enrolled. In 2009, 3 master's awarded. *Entrance requirements:* For master's, GRE or MAT. Additional exam requirements/recommendations for international students: Required—TOEFL (minimum score 550 paper-based; 80 iBT), or IELTS (minimum score 5.5). *Application deadline:* For fall admission, 5/1 for domestic students; for spring admission, 10/1 for domestic students. Applications are processed on a rolling basis. Application fee: $50. *Expenses:* Tuition, state resident: full-time $2520; part-time $275 per credit hour. Tuition, nonresident: full-time $4140; part-time $365 per credit hour. Required fees: $2430. *Financial support:* Career-related internships or fieldwork, Federal Work-Study, scholarships/grants, and unspecified assistantships available. Support available to part-time students. Financial award application deadline: 5/1; financial award applicants required to submit FAFSA. *Unit head:* Dr. Mark R. Fregeau, Professor, 978-542-6321, E-mail: mfregeau@salemstate.edu. *Application contact:* Dr. Lee A. Brossoit, Assistant Dean of Graduate Admissions, 978-542-6673, Fax: 978-542-7215, E-mail: lbrossoit@salemstate.edu.

Salem State College, School of Graduate Studies, Program in Chemistry, Salem, MA 01970-5353. Offers MAT. Part-time and evening/weekend programs available. *Students:* 4 part-time (3 women). Average age 37. In 2009, 1 master's awarded. *Entrance requirements:* For master's, GRE or MAT. Additional exam requirements/recommendations for international students: Required—TOEFL (minimum score 550 paper-based; 80 iBT), or IELTS (minimum score 5.5). *Application deadline:* For fall admission, 5/1 for domestic students; for spring admission, 10/1 for domestic students. Applications are processed on a rolling basis. Application fee: $50. *Expenses:* Tuition, state resident: full-time $2520; part-time $275 per credit hour. Tuition, nonresident: full-time $4140; part-time $365 per credit hour. Required fees: $2430. *Financial support:* In 2009–10, 1 student received support. Career-related internships or fieldwork, Federal Work-Study, scholarships/grants, and unspecified assistantships available. Support available to part-time students. Financial award application deadline: 5/1; financial award applicants required to submit FAFSA. *Unit head:* Christine MacTaylor, Associate Professor, 978-542-6321, E-mail: cmactaylor@salemstate.edu. *Application contact:* Dr. Lee A. Brossoit, Assistant Dean of Graduate Admissions, 978-542-6673, Fax: 978-542-7215, E-mail: lbrossoit@salemstate.edu.

Salem State College, School of Graduate Studies, Program in Middle School General Science, Salem, MA 01970-5353. Offers MAT. Part-time and evening/weekend programs available. *Students:* 3 part-time (2 women). Average age 35. In 2009, 2 master's awarded. *Entrance requirements:* For master's, GRE or MAT. Additional exam requirements/recommendations for international students: Required—TOEFL (minimum score 550 paper-based; 80 iBT), or IELTS (minimum score 5.5). *Application deadline:* For fall admission, 5/1 for domestic students; for spring admission, 10/1 for domestic students. Applications are processed on a rolling basis. Application fee: $50. *Expenses:* Tuition, state resident: full-time $2520; part-time $275 per credit hour. Tuition, nonresident: full-time $4140; part-time $365 per credit hour. Required fees: $2430. *Financial support:* In 2009–10, 2 students received support. Career-related internships or fieldwork, Federal Work-Study, scholarships/grants, and unspecified assistantships available. Support available to part-time students. Financial award application deadline: 5/1; financial award applicants required to submit FAFSA. *Unit head:* Lindley Hanson, Program Coordinator, 978-542-6321, Fax: 978-542-7215, E-mail: lhanson@salemstate.edu. *Application contact:* Dr. Lee A. Brossoit, Assistant Dean of Graduate Admissions, 978-542-6675, Fax: 978-542-7215, E-mail: lbrossoit@salemstate.edu.

San Diego State University, Graduate and Research Affairs, College of Sciences, Department of Mathematics and Statistics, San Diego, CA 92182. Offers applied mathematics (MS); mathematics (MA); mathematics and science education (PhD); statistics (MS). Part-time programs available. *Degree requirements:* For doctorate, thesis/dissertation. *Entrance requirements:* For master's, GRE General Test; for doctorate, GRE, minimum GPA of 3.25 in last 30 undergraduate semester units, minimum graduate GPA of 3.5, MSE recommendation form, 3 letters of recommendation. Additional exam requirements/recommendations for international students: Required—TOEFL. Electronic applications accepted. *Faculty research:* Teacher education in mathematics.

San Jose State University, Graduate Studies and Research, College of Science, Program in Science Education, San Jose, CA 95192-0001. Offers natural science (MA). *Degree requirements:* For master's, project or thesis. *Unit head:* Dr. Ellen Metzger, Director, 408-924-5048, Fax: 408-924-5180. *Application contact:* Dr. Ellen Metzger, Director, 408-924-5048, Fax: 408-924-5180.

Shippensburg University of Pennsylvania, School of Graduate Studies, College of Education and Human Services, Department of Teacher Education, Shippensburg, PA 17257-2299. Offers curriculum and instruction (M Ed), including biology, early childhood education, elementary education, English, foreign languages, geography/earth science, history, mathematics, middle school education; reading (M Ed). *Accreditation:* NCATE. Part-time and evening/weekend programs available. *Degree requirements:* For master's, comprehensive exam (for some programs), thesis optional, practicum or internship (for some programs). *Entrance requirements:* For master's, MAT (if GPA less than 2.75), interview, 3 letters of recommendation, writing sample of teaching background and future goals. Additional exam requirements/recommendations for international students: Required—TOEFL (minimum score 560 paper-based; 220 computer-based); Recommended—IELTS (minimum score 6). Electronic applications accepted.

Slippery Rock University of Pennsylvania, Graduate Studies (Recruitment), College of Education, Department of Secondary Education/Foundations of Education, Slippery Rock, PA 16057-1383. Offers secondary education in math/science (M Ed). *Accreditation:* NCATE. *Degree requirements:* For master's, comprehensive exam (for some programs), thesis (for some programs). *Entrance requirements:* For master's, GRE General Test, MAT, minimum GPA of 2.75 (3.0 for initial certification programs). Additional exam requirements/recommendations for international students: Required—TOEFL (minimum score 550 paper-based; 213 computer-based). *Application deadline:* For fall admission, 3/1 priority date for domestic students, 5/1 priority date for international students; for spring admission, 11/1 priority date for domestic students, 9/1 priority date for international students. Applications are processed on a rolling basis. Application fee: $25 ($30 for international students). Electronic applications accepted. *Expenses:* Tuition, state resident: full-time $6666; part-time $370 per credit. Tuition, nonresident: full-time $10,666; part-time $593 per credit. Required fees: $2184; $182 per credit. *Financial support:* Career-related internships or fieldwork, Federal Work-Study, scholarships/grants, and unspecified assistantships available. Support available to part-time students. Financial award application deadline: 5/1; financial award applicants required to submit FAFSA. *Unit head:* Dr. Jeffrey Lehman, Graduate Coordinator, 724-738-2311, Fax: 724-738-4987, E-mail: jeffrey.lehman@sru.edu. *Application contact:* Angela Piverotto, Interim Director of Graduate Studies, 724-738-2051, Fax: 724-738-2146, E-mail: graduate.admissions@sru.edu.

Smith College, Graduate and Special Programs, Department of Education and Child Study, Program in Secondary Education, Northampton, MA 01063. Offers biological sciences education (MAT); chemistry education (MAT); English education (MAT); French education (MAT); geology education (MAT); government education (MAT); history education (MAT); mathematics education (MAT); physics education (MAT); Spanish education (MAT). Part-time programs available. *Faculty:* 6 full-time (4 women), 3 part-time/adjunct (2 women). *Students:* 7 full-time (4 women), 1 part-time (0 women). Average age 25. 14 applicants, 100% accepted, 8 enrolled. In 2009, 9 master's awarded. *Entrance requirements:* Additional exam requirements/recommendations for international students: Required—TOEFL (minimum score 590 paper-based; 243 computer-based; 97 iBT). *Application deadline:* For fall admission, 4/1 for domestic students, 1/15 priority date for international students; for spring admission, 12/1 for domestic students. Application fee: $60. *Financial support:* In 2009–10, 6 students received support. Career-

related internships or fieldwork, institutionally sponsored loans, and scholarships/grants available. Support available to part-time students. Financial award application deadline: 1/15; financial award applicants required to submit CSS PROFILE or FAFSA. *Unit head:* Rosetta Cohen, Graduate Student Advisor, 413-585-3266, E-mail: rcohen@smith.edu. *Application contact:* Ruth Morgan, Administrative Assistant, 413-585-3050, Fax: 413-585-3054, E-mail: gradstdy@smith.edu.

South Carolina State University, School of Graduate Studies, Department of Education, Orangeburg, SC 29117-0001. Offers early childhood and special education (M Ed); early childhood education (MAT); elementary education (M Ed, MAT); engineering (MAT); general science (MAT); mathematics (MAT); secondary education (M Ed), including biology education, business education, counselor education, English education, home economics education, industrial education, mathematics education, science education, social studies education; special education (M Ed), including emotionally handicapped, learning disabilities, mentally handicapped. *Accreditation:* NCATE. Part-time and evening/weekend programs available. *Degree requirements:* For master's, thesis optional, departmental qualifying exam. *Entrance requirements:* For master's, GRE General Test, NTE, interview, teaching certificate. Electronic applications accepted. *Expenses:* Tuition, state resident: part-time $470 per credit hour. Tuition, nonresident: part-time $924 per credit hour. *Faculty research:* Critical thinking, child abuse, stress, test-taking skills, conflict resolution, mainstreaming.

Southeast Missouri State University, School of Graduate Studies, Godwin Center for Science and Mathematics Education, Cape Girardeau, MO 63701-4799. Offers science education (MNS). Part-time programs available. Postbaccalaureate distance learning degree programs offered (minimal on-campus study). *Degree requirements:* For master's, comprehensive exam, thesis optional, graduate paper reporting action research project. *Entrance requirements:* For master's, PRAXIS II or GRE, minimum undergraduate GPA of 2.75, valid teaching certificate. Additional exam requirements/recommendations for international students: Required—TOEFL (minimum score 550 paper-based; 213 computer-based); Recommended—IELTS (minimum score 6). Electronic applications accepted. *Expenses:* Tuition, state resident: full-time $4266; part-time $237 per credit hour. Tuition, nonresident: full-time $7506; part-time $417 per credit hour. Required fees: $427; $427. *Faculty research:* Teacher development in science with NASA equipment and materials; investigative case-based learning (PBL) with computer simulations, tools, models; inquiry science in forensic chemistry; pre-K-G science education emphasizing constuctivist, engaged learning.

Southern Connecticut State University, School of Graduate Studies, School of Arts and Sciences, Department of Science Education and Environmental Studies, New Haven, CT 06515-1355. Offers environmental education (MS); science education (MS, Diploma). *Accreditation:* NCATE. Part-time and evening/weekend programs available. *Faculty:* 2 full-time, 1 part-time/adjunct. *Students:* 6 full-time (3 women), 19 part-time (12 women); includes 1 minority (African American). 37 applicants, 54% accepted, 13 enrolled. *Degree requirements:* For master's, thesis or alternative. *Entrance requirements:* For master's, interview; for Diploma, master's degree. *Application deadline:* For fall admission, 7/15 priority date for domestic students. Applications are processed on a rolling basis. Application fee: $50. Electronic applications accepted. Tuition and fees vary according to program. *Financial support:* Application deadline: 4/15. *Unit head:* Dr. Susan Cusato, Chairman, 203-392-6610, Fax: 203-392-6614, E-mail: hagemans1@southernct.edu. *Application contact:* Dr. Susan Cusato, Graduate Coordinator, 203-392-6610, Fax: 203-392-6614, E-mail: cusatos1@southernct.edu.

Southern Illinois University Edwardsville, Graduate Studies and Research, School of Education, Department of Curriculum and Instruction, Program in Secondary Education, Edwardsville, IL 62026-0001. Offers art (MS Ed); biology (MS Ed); chemistry (MS Ed); earth and space sciences (MS Ed); English/language arts (MS Ed); foreign languages (MS Ed); history (MS Ed); mathematics (MS Ed); physics (MS Ed). *Accreditation:* NCATE. Part-time and evening/weekend programs available. *Students:* 24 part-time (19 women); includes 2 minority (1 African American, 1 Hispanic American). Average age 26. 13 applicants, 31% accepted. In 2009, 5 master's awarded. *Degree requirements:* For master's, thesis or alternative, final exam/paper. *Entrance requirements:* Additional exam requirements/recommendations for international students: Required—TOEFL (minimum score 550 paper-based; 213 computer-based; 79 iBT), IELTS (minimum score 6.5). *Application deadline:* For fall admission, 7/23 for domestic students, 6/1 for international students; for spring admission, 12/11 for domestic students, 10/1 for international students. Applications are processed on a rolling basis. Application fee: $30. Electronic applications accepted. *Expenses:* Tuition, state resident: part-time $1252.50 per semester. Tuition, nonresident: part-time $3131.25 per semester. Required fees: $586.85 per semester. Tuition and fees vary according to course load. *Financial support:* Fellowships, research assistantships, teaching assistantships, career-related internships or fieldwork, Federal Work-Study, institutionally sponsored loans, scholarships/grants, traineeships, and unspecified assistantships available. Support available to part-time students. Financial award application deadline: 3/1; financial award applicants required to submit FAFSA. *Unit head:* Dr. Kathy Bushrow, Director, 618-650-3082, E-mail: kbushro@siue.edu. *Application contact:* Dr. Kathy Bushrow, Director, 618-650-3082, E-mail: kbushro@siue.edu.

Southern University and Agricultural and Mechanical College, Graduate School, Department of Science/Mathematics Education, Baton Rouge, LA 70813. Offers PhD. *Accreditation:* NCATE. *Degree requirements:* For doctorate, thesis/dissertation. *Entrance requirements:* For doctorate, GRE General Test. Additional exam requirements/recommendations for international students: Required—TOEFL (minimum score 525 paper-based; 193 computer-based). *Faculty research:* Performance assessment in science/mathematics education, equity in science/mathematics education, technology and distance learning, science/mathematics concept formation, cognitive themes, problem solving in science/mathematics education.

Southwestern Oklahoma State University, College of Arts and Sciences, Specialization in Natural Sciences, Weatherford, OK 73096-3098. Offers M Ed. Part-time programs available. *Degree requirements:* For master's, exam. *Entrance requirements:* For master's, GRE General Test or minimum undergraduate GPA of 3.0. Additional exam requirements/recommendations for international students: Required—TOEFL.

Stanford University, School of Education, Program in Curriculum Studies and Teacher Education, Stanford, CA 94305-9991. Offers art education (MA, PhD); dance education (MA); English education (MA, PhD); general curriculum studies (MA, PhD); mathematics education (MA, PhD); science education (MA, PhD); social studies education (PhD); teacher education (MA, PhD). *Degree requirements:* For master's, thesis (for some programs); for doctorate, thesis/dissertation. *Entrance requirements:* For master's and doctorate, GRE General Test. Electronic applications accepted. *Expenses:* Tuition: Full-time $37,380; part-time $2760 per quarter. Required fees: $501.

Stanford University, School of Education, Teacher Education Program, Stanford, CA 94305-9991. Offers English education (MA); languages education (MA); mathematics education (MA); science education (MA); social studies education (MA). *Degree requirements:* For master's, thesis. *Entrance requirements:* For master's, GRE General Test. Electronic applications accepted. *Expenses:* Tuition: Full-time $37,380; part-time $2760 per quarter. Required fees: $501.

State University of New York at Binghamton, Graduate School, School of Education, Program in Adolescence Education, Binghamton, NY 13902-6000. Offers biology education (MAT, MS Ed, MST); earth science education (MAT, MS Ed, MST); English education (MAT, MS Ed, MST); French education (MAT, MST); mathematical sciences education (MAT, MS Ed, MST); physics (MAT, MS Ed, MST); social studies (MAT, MS Ed, MST); Spanish education (MAT, MST). *Accreditation:* Teacher Education Accreditation Council. Part-time and evening/weekend programs available. *Students:* 93 full-time (37 women), 21 part-time (8 women); includes 6 minority (2 Asian Americans or Pacific Islanders, 4 Hispanic Americans), 1 international. Average age 27. 69 applicants, 81% accepted, 46 enrolled. In 2009, 53 master's awarded. *Entrance requirements:* For master's, GRE General Test. Additional exam requirements/recommendations for international students: Required—TOEFL (minimum score 550 paper-based; 213 computer-based; 80 iBT). *Application deadline:* For fall admission, 2/1 priority date for domestic and international students; for spring admission, 10/15 priority date for domestic and international students. Applications are processed on a rolling basis. Application fee: $60. Electronic applications accepted. *Financial support:* Fellowships with partial tuition reimbursements, research assistantships with full and partial tuition reimbursements, teaching assistantships with full tuition reimbursements, career-related internships or fieldwork, Federal Work-Study, institutionally sponsored loans, scholarships/grants, health care benefits, tuition waivers (full), and unspecified assistantships available. Financial award application deadline: 2/15; financial award applicants required to submit FAFSA. *Unit head:* Dr. S. G. Grant, Dean of School of Education, 607-777-7329, E-mail: sggrant@binghamton.edu. *Application contact:* Victoria Williams, Recruiting and Admissions Coordinator, 607-777-2151, Fax: 607-777-2501, E-mail: vwilliam@binghamton.edu.

State University of New York at Fredonia, Graduate Studies, Department of Chemistry and Biochemistry, Fredonia, NY 14063-1136. Offers chemistry (MS); curriculum and instruction science education (MS Ed). Part-time and evening/weekend programs available. *Degree requirements:* For master's, thesis optional. *Expenses:* Tuition, state resident: full-time $8370; part-time $349 per credit. Tuition, nonresident: full-time $13,250; part-time $552 per credit. Required fees: $1289; $53.55 per credit.

State University of New York at New Paltz, Graduate School, School of Education, Department of Secondary Education, New Paltz, NY 12561. Offers adolescence education: biology (MAT, MS Ed); adolescence education: english (MAT); adolescence education: English (MS Ed); adolescence education: social studies (MAT, MS Ed); English as a second language (MS Ed); second language education (MS Ed). *Accreditation:* NCATE. Part-time and evening/weekend programs available. *Faculty:* 9 full-time (5 women), 4 part-time/adjunct (3 women). *Students:* 86 full-time (51 women), 102 part-time (74 women); includes 22 minority (4 African Americans, 1 American Indian/Alaska Native, 3 Asian Americans or Pacific Islanders, 14 Hispanic Americans), 2 international. Average age 30. 122 applicants, 54% accepted, 53 enrolled. In 2009, 81 master's awarded. *Degree requirements:* For master's, comprehensive exam (for some programs), portfolio. *Entrance requirements:* For master's, minimum GPA of 3.0, NYS teaching certificate (MS Ed). Additional exam requirements/recommendations for international students: Required—TOEFL (minimum score 550 paper-based; 213 computer-based; 80 iBT), IELTS (minimum score 6.5). *Application deadline:* For fall admission, 3/1 priority date for domestic students, 3/1 for international students; for spring admission, 10/1 priority date for domestic students, 10/1 for international students. Application fee: $50. Electronic applications accepted. *Financial support:* In 2009–10, 4 students received support, including 3 fellowships (averaging $9,000 per year); Federal Work-Study, institutionally sponsored loans, and tuition waivers (full) also available. Financial award application deadline: 8/1; financial award applicants required to submit FAFSA. *Unit head:* Dr. Devon Duhaney, Chair, 845-257-2850, E-mail: duhaneyd@newpaltz.edu. *Application contact:* Caroline Murphy, Graduate Admissions Advisor, 845-257-3285, Fax: 845-257-3284, E-mail: gradschool@newpaltz.edu.

State University of New York at Plattsburgh, Division of Education, Health, and Human Services, Program in Teacher Education: Adolescence MST, Plattsburgh, NY 12901-2681. Offers adolescence education (MST); biology 7-12 (MST); chemistry 7-12 (MST); earth science 7-12 (MST); English 7-12 (MST); French 7-12 (MST); mathematics 7-12 (MST); physics 7-12 (MST); social studies 7-12 (MST); Spanish 7-12 (MST). *Accreditation:* Teacher Education Accreditation Council. Part-time and evening/weekend programs available. *Faculty:* 4 full-time (3 women), 2 part-time/adjunct (0 women). *Students:* 83 full-time (49 women), 5 part-time (3 women); includes 9 minority (2 African Americans, 1 American Indian/Alaska Native, 1 Asian American or Pacific Islander, 5 Hispanic Americans), 2 international. Average age 27. 72 applicants, 71% accepted, 44 enrolled. In 2009, 57 master's awarded. *Degree requirements:* For master's, portfolio. *Entrance requirements:* For master's, minimum GPA of 2.75. Additional exam requirements/recommendations for international students: Required—TOEFL (minimum score 550 paper-based; 213 computer-based; 79 iBT). *Application deadline:* For fall admission, 2/15 priority date for domestic students. Applications are processed on a rolling basis. Application fee: $75. *Expenses:* Tuition, state resident: full-time $8370; part-time $349 per credit hour. Tuition, nonresident: full-time $13,250; part-time $552 per credit hour. Required fees: $1130. *Financial support:* Application deadline: 4/15. *Unit head:* Dr. Robert Ackland, Coordinator, 518-564-5131, E-mail: acklanrt@plattsburgh.edu. *Application contact:* Marguerite Adelman, Assistant Director, Graduate Admissions, 518-564-4723, Fax: 518-564-4722, E-mail: adelmaml@plattsburgh.edu.

State University of New York at Plattsburgh, Faculty of Arts and Science, Program in Natural Science, Plattsburgh, NY 12901-2681. Offers MS. *Accreditation:* Teacher Education Accreditation Council. Part-time programs available. *Faculty:* 20 full-time (8 women), 1 (woman) part-time/adjunct. *Students:* 3 full-time (2 women), 3 part-time (0 women). Average age 30. 10 applicants, 80% accepted, 4 enrolled. *Degree requirements:* For master's, comprehensive exam, thesis, project. *Entrance requirements:* For master's, GRE General Test (minimum score of 1200), bachelor's degree in science discipline, minimum GPA of 3.0. Additional exam requirements/recommendations for international students: Required—TOEFL (minimum score 550 paper-based; 213 computer-based; 79 iBT). *Application deadline:* For fall admission, 2/15 priority date for domestic students; for spring admission, 10/15 priority date for domestic students. Applications are processed on a rolling basis. Application fee: $75. *Expenses:* Tuition, state resident: full-time $8370; part-time $349 per credit hour. Tuition, nonresident: full-time $13,250; part-time $552 per credit hour. Required fees: $1130. *Financial support:* Federal Work-Study available. Support available to part-time students. Financial award application deadline: 4/15; financial award applicants required to submit FAFSA. *Unit head:* Dr. Timothy B. Mihuc, Program Coordinator, 518-564-3039, Fax: 518-564-3036, E-mail: timothy.mihuc@plattsburgh.edu. *Application contact:* Marguerite Adelman, Assistant Director, Graduate Admissions, 518-564-4723, Fax: 518-564-4722, E-mail: adelmaml@plattsburgh.edu.

State University of New York College at Cortland, Graduate Studies, School of Arts and Sciences, Programs in Adolescence Education, Cortland, NY 13045. Offers biology (MAT, MS Ed); chemistry (MAT, MS Ed); earth science (MAT, MS Ed); English (MS Ed); French (MS Ed); mathematics (MAT, MS Ed); physics (MAT, MS Ed); social studies (MS Ed); Spanish (MS Ed). *Accreditation:* NCATE. Part-time and evening/weekend programs available. *Degree requirements:* For master's, one foreign language, comprehensive exam (for some programs), thesis (for some programs). *Entrance requirements:* For master's, GRE General Test.

State University of New York College at Potsdam, School of Education and Professional Studies, Program in Secondary Education, Potsdam, NY 13676. Offers English (MST); mathematics (with grades 5-6 extension) (MST); science (MST), including biology, chemistry, earth science, physics; Social Studies (with grades 5-6 extension) (MST). *Accreditation:* NCATE. *Faculty:* 9 full-time (3 women), 3 part-time/adjunct (2 women). *Students:* 49 full-time (27 women), 6 part-time (1 woman); includes 5 minority (3 African Americans, 2 American Indian/Alaska Native), 7 international. 13 applicants, 62% accepted, 8 enrolled. In 2009, 49 master's awarded. *Degree requirements:* For master's, thesis optional, culminating experience. *Entrance requirements:* For master's, minimum GPA of 2.75 in last 60 hours of course work (3.0 for English program). Additional exam requirements/recommendations for international students: Required—TOEFL (minimum score 550 paper-based; 213 computer-based; 80 iBT), IELTS (minimum score 6). *Application deadline:* For fall admission, 4/1 priority date for domestic and international students; for spring admission, 10/15 priority date for domestic and international students. Applications are processed on a rolling basis. Application fee: $50. *Expenses:* Tuition, state resident: full-time $8370; part-time $349 per credit hour. Tuition, nonresident: full-time $13,250; part-time $552 per credit hour. Required fees: $942; $38.70 per credit hour. *Financial support:* Fellowships, teaching assistantships, career-related internships or fieldwork, Federal Work-Study, scholarships/grants, and unspecified assistantships available. Support available to part-time students. Financial award application deadline: 3/1; financial award applicants required to submit FAFSA. *Unit head:* Dr. Peter Brouwer, Chairperson, 315-267-3018, Fax: 315-267-4802, E-mail: brouweps@potsdam.edu. *Application contact:* Peter Cutler, Graduate Admissions Counselor, 315-267-3154, Fax: 315-267-4802, E-mail: cutlerpj@potsdam.edu.

Science Education

Stony Brook University, State University of New York, Graduate School, College of Arts and Sciences, Department of Physics and Astronomy, Program in Physics, Stony Brook, NY 11794. Offers modern research instrumentation (MS); physics (MA, PhD); physics education (MAT). *Students:* 183 full-time (34 women), 2 part-time (0 women); includes 12 minority (1 African American, 3 Asian Americans or Pacific Islanders, 8 Hispanic Americans), 100 international. *Degree requirements:* For doctorate, one foreign language, thesis/dissertation. *Entrance requirements:* For master's and doctorate, GRE General Test. Additional exam requirements/recommendations for international students: Required—TOEFL. *Application deadline:* For fall admission, 1/15 for domestic students. Application fee: $60. *Expenses:* Tuition, state resident: full-time $8370; part-time $349 per credit. Tuition, nonresident: full-time $13,250; part-time $552 per credit. Required fees: $933. *Financial support:* Fellowships, research assistantships, teaching assistantships available. Financial award application deadline: 2/1. *Unit head:* Dr. Peter M. Koch, Chair, 631-632-8100, Fax: 631-632-8176, E-mail: peter.koch@stonybrook.edu. *Application contact:* Dr. Lazlo W. Mihaly, Director, 631-632-8279, Fax: 631-632-8176, E-mail: lazlo.mihaly@stonybrook.edu.

Stony Brook University, State University of New York, Graduate School, College of Arts and Sciences, Program in Science Education, Stony Brook, NY 11794. Offers PhD. *Degree requirements:* For doctorate, comprehensive exam, thesis/dissertation. *Entrance requirements:* For doctorate, GRE. Additional exam requirements/recommendations for international students: Required—TOEFL (minimum score 550 paper-based; 213 computer-based; 90 iBT), IELTS (minimum score 6.5). *Application deadline:* For fall admission, 1/15 for domestic students; for spring admission, 10/1 for domestic students. *Expenses:* Tuition, state resident: full-time $8370; part-time $349 per credit. Tuition, nonresident: full-time $13,250; part-time $552 per credit. Required fees: $933. *Unit head:* Dr. Keith Sheppard, Director, E-mail: keith.sheppard@stonybrook.edu. *Application contact:* Dr. Kent Marks, Assistant Dean, Admissions and Records, 631-632-4723, Fax: 631-632-7243, E-mail: kmarks@notes.cc.sunysb.edu.

Stony Brook University, State University of New York, School of Professional Development, Stony Brook, NY 11794. Offers biology-grade 7-12 (MAT); chemistry-grade 7-12 (MAT); coaching (Graduate Certificate); computer integrated engineering (Graduate Certificate); earth science-grade 7-12 (MAT); educational computing (Graduate Certificate); educational leadership (Advanced Certificate); English-grade 7-12 (MAT); environmental management (Graduate Certificate); environmental/occupational health and safety (Graduate Certificate); French-grade 7-12 (MAT); German-grade 7-12 (MAT); human resource management (Graduate Certificate); information systems management (Graduate Certificate); Italian-grade 7-12 (MAT); liberal studies (MA); mathematics-grade 7-12 (MAT); operation research (Graduate Certificate); physics-grade 7-12 (MAT); school administration and supervision (Graduate Certificate); school building leadership (Graduate Certificate); school district administration (Graduate Certificate); school district business leadership (Advanced Certificate); school district leadership (Graduate Certificate); social science and the professions (MPS), including environmental waste management, human resource management; social studies-grade 7-12 (MAT); Spanish-grade 7-12 (MAT); waste management (Graduate Certificate). Part-time and evening/weekend programs available. Postbaccalaureate distance learning degree programs offered. *Faculty:* 5 full-time (3 women), 131 part-time/adjunct (53 women). *Students:* 317 full-time (187 women), 1,200 part-time (773 women); includes 187 minority (77 African Americans, 2 American Indian/Alaska Native, 22 Asian Americans or Pacific Islanders, 86 Hispanic Americans), 11 international. Average age 28. In 2009, 597 master's, 234 other advanced degrees awarded. *Degree requirements:* For master's, one foreign language, thesis or alternative. *Application deadline:* Applications are processed on a rolling basis. Application fee: $62. *Expenses:* Tuition, state resident: full-time $8370; part-time $349 per credit. Tuition, nonresident: full-time $13,250; part-time $552 per credit. Required fees: $933. *Financial support:* Fellowships, research assistantships, teaching assistantships, career-related internships or fieldwork available. Support available to part-time students. *Unit head:* Dr. Paul J. Edelson, Dean, 631-632-7052, Fax: 631-632-9046, E-mail: paul.edelson@stonybrook.edu. *Application contact:* Dr. Paul J. Edelson, Dean, 631-632-7052, Fax: 631-632-9046, E-mail: paul.edelson@stonybrook.edu.

Syracuse University, College of Arts and Sciences, Program in College Science Teaching, Syracuse, NY 13244. Offers PhD. Part-time programs available. *Students:* 4 full-time (3 women), 5 part-time (2 women); includes 1 minority (Asian American or Pacific Islander). Average age 39. *Entrance requirements:* For doctorate, GRE General Test, GRE Subject Test. Additional exam requirements/recommendations for international students: Required—TOEFL (minimum score 100 iBT). *Application deadline:* Applications are processed on a rolling basis. Application fee: $75. Electronic applications accepted. *Expenses:* Tuition: Full-time $26,808; part-time $1117 per credit. Required fees: $1024. *Financial support:* Fellowships with full tuition reimbursements, teaching assistantships with full and partial tuition reimbursements available. Financial award application deadline: 1/1; financial award applicants required to submit FAFSA. *Unit head:* Dr. John Tillotson, Director of Graduate Studies, 315-443-9137, E-mail: jwtillot@syr.edu. *Application contact:* Cynthia Daley, Information Contact, 315-443-2586.

Syracuse University, School of Education, Emphasis in Biology Education, Syracuse, NY 13244. Offers MS. Part-time programs available. *Students:* 17 full-time (10 women), 1 (woman) part-time; includes 1 minority (Asian American or Pacific Islander), 1 international. Average age 27. 15 applicants, 80% accepted, 8 enrolled. In 2009, 3 master's awarded. *Entrance requirements:* Additional exam requirements/recommendations for international students: Required—TOEFL (minimum score 100 iBT). *Application deadline:* For fall admission, 2/1 priority date for domestic and international students. Applications are processed on a rolling basis. Application fee: $75. Electronic applications accepted. *Expenses:* Tuition: Full-time $26,808; part-time $1117 per credit. Required fees: $1024. *Financial support:* Fellowships with full and partial tuition reimbursements, teaching assistantships, scholarships/grants and tuition waivers (full and partial) available. Financial award application deadline: 1/1; financial award applicants required to submit FAFSA. *Unit head:* Dr. John Tillotson, Program Director, 315-443-9137, E-mail: jwtillot@syr.edu. *Application contact:* Liza Rochelson, Graduate Recruiter, School of Education, 315-443-2505, E-mail: e-gradrcrt@syr.edu.

Syracuse University, School of Education, Emphasis in Chemistry Education, Syracuse, NY 13244. Offers MS. Part-time programs available. *Students:* 1 (woman) full-time. Average age 48. 2 applicants, 100% accepted, 1 enrolled. In 2009, 1 master's awarded. *Entrance requirements:* Additional exam requirements/recommendations for international students: Required—TOEFL (minimum score 100 iBT). *Application deadline:* For fall admission, 2/1 priority date for domestic and international students. Applications are processed on a rolling basis. Application fee: $75. Electronic applications accepted. *Expenses:* Tuition: Full-time $26,808; part-time $1117 per credit. Required fees: $1024. *Financial support:* Fellowships with full and partial tuition reimbursements, teaching assistantships with full and partial tuition reimbursements, scholarships/grants and tuition waivers (partial) available. Financial award application deadline: 1/1; financial award applicants required to submit FAFSA. *Unit head:* Dr. John Tillotson, Program Director, 315-443-9137, E-mail: jwtillot@syr.edu. *Application contact:* Liza Rochelson, Graduate Recruiter, School of Education, 315-443-2505, E-mail: e-gradrcrt@syr.edu.

Syracuse University, School of Education, Emphasis in Earth Science Education, Syracuse, NY 13244. Offers MS. Part-time programs available. *Students:* 3 applicants, 67% accepted, 0 enrolled. *Entrance requirements:* Additional exam requirements/recommendations for international students: Required—TOEFL (minimum score 100 iBT). *Application deadline:* For fall admission, 2/1 priority date for domestic and international students. Applications are processed on a rolling basis. Electronic applications accepted. *Expenses:* Tuition: Full-time $26,808; part-time $1117 per credit. Required fees: $1024. *Financial support:* Fellowships with full and partial tuition reimbursements, teaching assistantships with full and partial tuition reimbursements, scholarships/grants and tuition waivers (full and partial) available. Financial award application deadline: 1/1; financial award applicants required to submit FAFSA. *Unit head:* Dr. John Tillotson, Program Director, 315-443-9137, E-mail: jwtillot@syr.edu. *Application contact:* Liza Rochelson, Graduate Recruiter, School of Education, 315-443-2505, E-mail: e-gradrcrt@syr.edu.

Syracuse University, School of Education, Emphasis in Physics Education, Syracuse, NY 13244. Offers MS. *Students:* 1 (woman) full-time. Average age 22. 1 applicant, 100% accepted, 1 enrolled. In 2009, 2 master's awarded. *Entrance requirements:* Additional exam requirements/recommendations for international students: Required—TOEFL (minimum score 100 iBT). *Application deadline:* For fall admission, 2/1 priority date for domestic and international students. Applications are processed on a rolling basis. Application fee: $75. Electronic applications accepted. *Expenses:* Tuition: Full-time $26,808; part-time $1117 per credit. Required fees: $1024. *Financial support:* Fellowships with full and partial tuition reimbursements, teaching assistantships with full and partial tuition reimbursements, scholarships/grants and tuition waivers (full and partial) available. Financial award application deadline: 1/1; financial award applicants required to submit FAFSA. *Unit head:* Dr. John Tillotson, Program Director, 315-443-9137, E-mail: jwtillot@syr.edu. *Application contact:* Liza Rochelson, Graduate Recruiter, School of Education, 315-443-2505, E-mail: e-gradrcrt@syr.edu.

Syracuse University, School of Education, Program in Science Education, Syracuse, NY 13244. Offers PhD. Part-time programs available. *Students:* 12 full-time (6 women), 8 part-time (6 women); includes 1 minority (Asian American or Pacific Islander), 1 international. Average age 33. 5 applicants, 80% accepted, 3 enrolled. In 2009, 9 doctorates awarded. *Degree requirements:* For doctorate, thesis/dissertation. *Entrance requirements:* For doctorate, GRE. Additional exam requirements/recommendations for international students: Required—TOEFL (minimum score 100 iBT). *Application deadline:* For fall admission, 2/1 priority date for domestic and international students; for spring admission, 10/15 priority date for domestic and international students. Applications are processed on a rolling basis. Application fee: $75. Electronic applications accepted. *Expenses:* Tuition: Full-time $26,808; part-time $1117 per credit. Required fees: $1024. *Financial support:* Fellowships with tuition reimbursements, research assistantships with tuition reimbursements, teaching assistantships with tuition reimbursements available. Financial award application deadline: 1/1. *Unit head:* Dr. John Tillotson, Coordinator, 315-443-9137, E-mail: jwtillot@syr.edu. *Application contact:* Liza Rochelson, Graduate Recruiter, School of Education, 315-443-2505, E-mail: e-gradrcrt@syr.edu.

Teachers College, Columbia University, Graduate Faculty of Education, Department of Math, Science and Technology, Program in Science Education, New York, NY 10027-6696. Offers Ed D, PhD.

Teachers College, Columbia University, Graduate Faculty of Education, Department of Math, Science and Technology, Program in Supervision in Science Education, New York, NY 10027-6696. Offers MA.

Teachers College, Columbia University, Graduate Faculty of Education, Department of Math, Science and Technology, Programs in Science Education, New York, NY 10027-6696. Offers Ed M, MA, MS, Ed D, Ed DCT, PhD. *Accreditation:* NCATE. Part-time and evening/weekend programs available. *Students:* 26 full-time (19 women), 57 part-time (41 women); includes 13 minority (5 African Americans, 7 Asian Americans or Pacific Islanders, 1 Hispanic American), 5 international. Average age 33. 55 applicants, 60% accepted, 9 enrolled. In 2009, 32 master's, 13 doctorates awarded. Terminal master's awarded for partial completion of doctoral program. *Degree requirements:* For master's, culminating paper; for doctorate, thesis/dissertation. *Entrance requirements:* For master's and doctorate, 24 credits in science. *Application deadline:* For fall admission, 5/15 for domestic students; for spring admission, 12/1 for domestic students. Application fee: $65. *Financial support:* Fellowships, career-related internships or fieldwork, Federal Work-Study, institutionally sponsored loans, and tuition waivers (full and partial) available. Support available to part-time students. Financial award application deadline: 2/1. *Faculty research:* Cell biology and physiological ecology of protozoa, teaching and learning of pre-college and college sciences, homelessness. Total annual research expenditures: $100,000. *Unit head:* Dr. O. Roger Anderson, Chair, 212-678-3405. *Application contact:* Deanna Ghozati, Assistant Director of Admission, 212-678-4018, Fax: 212-678-4171, E-mail: ghozati@tc.edu.

Temple University, Graduate School, College of Education, Department of Curriculum, Instruction, and Technology in Education, Philadelphia, PA 19122-6096. Offers applied behavioral analysis (MS Ed); career and technical education (MS Ed); early childhood education and elementary education (MS Ed); English education (MS Ed); language arts education (Ed D); math/science education (Ed D); mathematics education (MS Ed); science education (MS Ed); second and foreign language education (MS Ed); special education (MS Ed); teaching English as a second language (MS Ed). Part-time and evening/weekend programs available. Terminal master's awarded for partial completion of doctoral program. *Degree requirements:* For master's, thesis or alternative; for doctorate, thesis/dissertation. *Entrance requirements:* For master's and doctorate, GRE General Test or MAT, minimum GPA of 3.0. Additional exam requirements/recommendations for international students: Required—TOEFL (minimum score 550 paper-based; 213 computer-based; 79 iBT). Electronic applications accepted. *Faculty research:* School improvement, problem solving, literacy, language development.

Texas A&M University, College of Education and Human Development, Department of Teaching, Learning, and Culture, College Station, TX 77843. Offers curriculum and instruction (M Ed, MS, PhD); mathematics education (M Ed, MS, PhD); multicultural/urban/ESL/international education (M Ed, MS, PhD); reading/language arts (M Ed, MS, PhD); science education (M Ed, MS, PhD); social studies education (M Ed, MS, PhD). Part-time programs available. *Faculty:* 33. *Students:* 145 full-time (113 women), 270 part-time (214 women); includes 110 minority (60 African Americans, 4 American Indian/Alaska Native, 4 Asian Americans or Pacific Islanders, 42 Hispanic Americans), 47 international. Average age 36. In 2009, 114 master's, 17 doctorates awarded. *Degree requirements:* For master's, comprehensive exam, thesis (for some programs); for doctorate, comprehensive exam, thesis/dissertation. *Entrance requirements:* For master's, GRE General Test, minimum GPA of 3.0; for doctorate, GRE General Test, 3 years of teaching experience. Additional exam requirements/recommendations for international students: Required—TOEFL (minimum score 550 paper-based; 213 computer-based). *Application deadline:* For fall admission, 1/15 priority date for domestic and international students; for spring admission, 9/15 priority date for domestic and international students. Applications are processed on a rolling basis. Application fee: $50 ($75 for international students). Electronic applications accepted. *Expenses:* Tuition, state resident: full-time $3991; part-time $221.74 per credit hour. Tuition, nonresident: full-time $9049; part-time $502.74 per credit hour. *Financial support:* In 2009–10, fellowships with partial tuition reimbursements (averaging $3,000 per year), teaching assistantships with partial tuition reimbursements (averaging $7,200 per year) were awarded; research assistantships with partial tuition reimbursements, career-related internships or fieldwork, Federal Work-Study, institutionally sponsored loans, scholarships/grants, tuition waivers (partial), and unspecified assistantships also available. Support available to part-time students. Financial award application deadline: 4/1; financial award applicants required to submit FAFSA. *Unit head:* Dr. Dennie Smith, Head, 979-845-8384, Fax: 979-845-9663, E-mail: krsmith@tamu.edu. *Application contact:* Graduate Admissions Supervisor, 979-845-8382, Fax: 979-845-9663, E-mail: krsmith@tamu.edu.

Texas Christian University, College of Education, Program in Educational Studies: Science Education, Fort Worth, TX 76129-0002. Offers PhD. Part-time and evening/weekend programs available. *Entrance requirements:* For doctorate, GRE or MAT. Additional exam requirements/recommendations for international students: Required—TOEFL (minimum score 550 paper-based; 213 computer-based; 80 iBT). *Application deadline:* For fall admission, 2/1 for domestic and international students. Application fee: $50. *Expenses:* Tuition: Full-time $17,640; part-time $980 per credit hour. Tuition and fees vary according to program. *Financial support:* Teaching assistantships with full tuition reimbursements, career-related internships or fieldwork and unspecified assistantships available. Financial award application deadline: 3/15; financial award applicants required to submit FAFSA. *Unit head:* Dr. Kay B. Stevens, Associate Dean, 817-257-7661, E-mail: k.stevens2@tcu.edu. *Application contact:* Robyn P. Shepheard, Academic Program Specialist, 817-257-7661, E-mail: r.shepheard@tcu.edu.

Texas Christian University, College of Education, Program in Science Education, Fort Worth, TX 76129-0002. Offers M Ed. Part-time and evening/weekend programs available. *Degree requirements:* For master's, thesis optional. *Entrance requirements:* Additional exam

requirements/recommendations for international students: Required—TOEFL (minimum score 550 paper-based; 213 computer-based; 80 iBT). *Application deadline:* For fall admission, 7/15 for domestic and international students; for spring admission, 11/15 for domestic and international students. Applications are processed on a rolling basis. Application fee: $50. *Expenses:* Tuition: Full-time $17,640; part-time $980 per credit hour. Tuition and fees vary according to program. *Financial support:* Teaching assistantships with full tuition reimbursements, career-related internships or fieldwork and unspecified assistantships available. Financial award application deadline: 3/15; financial award applicants required to submit FAFSA. *Unit head:* Dr. Kay B. Stevens, Associate Dean, 817-257-7661, E-mail: k.stevens2@tcu.edu. *Application contact:* Robyn P. Shepheard, Academic Program Specialist, 817-257-7651, E-mail: r.shepheard@tcu.edu.

Texas State University–San Marcos, Graduate School, Interdisciplinary Studies Program in Elementary Mathematics, Science, and Technology, San Marcos, TX 78666. Offers MSIS. *Students:* 1 full-time (0 women), 4 part-time (3 women). Average age 32. 1 applicant, 100% accepted, 0 enrolled. In 2009, 1 master's awarded. *Degree requirements:* For master's, comprehensive exam, thesis optional. *Entrance requirements:* For master's, minimum GPA of 2.75 in the last 60 hours of undergraduate work. Additional exam requirements/recommendations for international students: Required—TOEFL (minimum score 550 paper-based; 213 computer-based). *Application deadline:* For fall admission, 6/15 priority date for domestic students, 6/1 priority date for international students; for spring admission, 10/15 priority date for domestic students, 10/1 priority date for international students. Applications are processed on a rolling basis. Application fee: $40 ($90 for international students). Electronic applications accepted. *Expenses:* Tuition, state resident: full-time $5784; part-time $241 per credit hour. Tuition, nonresident: full-time $13,224; part-time $551 per credit hour. Required fees: $1728; $48 per credit hour. $306. Tuition and fees vary according to course load. *Financial support:* In 2009–10, 3 students received support; research assistantships, teaching assistantships available. Financial award application deadline: 4/1; financial award applicants required to submit FAFSA. *Unit head:* Dr. Sandra Mody, Acting Dean, 512-245-3360, Fax: 512-245-8095, E-mail: sw04@txstate.edu. *Application contact:* Dr. J. Michael Willoughby, Dean of Graduate School, 512-245-2581, Fax: 512-245-8365, E-mail: gradcollege@txstate.edu.

Texas Woman's University, Graduate School, College of Arts and Sciences, Department of Biology, Denton, TX 76201. Offers biology (MS); biology teaching (MS); molecular biology (PhD). Part-time programs available. *Faculty:* 12 full-time (8 women), 1 (woman) part-time/adjunct. *Students:* 25 full-time (17 women), 16 part-time (9 women); includes 6 minority (4 African Americans, 2 Hispanic Americans), 29 international. Average age 28. 29 applicants, 79% accepted, 12 enrolled. In 2009, 2 master's, 4 doctorates awarded. Terminal master's awarded for partial completion of doctoral program. *Degree requirements:* For master's, comprehensive exam, thesis (for some programs); for doctorate, comprehensive exam, thesis/dissertation, residency. *Entrance requirements:* For master's, GRE General Test (minimum score 425 verbal, 425 quantitative), 3 letters of reference; for doctorate, GRE General Test (minimum score: Verbal 425, Quantitative 425), 3 letters of reference, letter of interest. Additional exam requirements/recommendations for international students: Required—TOEFL (minimum score 550 paper-based; 213 computer-based; 79 iBT). *Application deadline:* For fall admission, 7/1 priority date for domestic students, 3/1 for international students; for spring admission, 12/1 priority date for domestic students, 7/1 for international students. Applications are processed on a rolling basis. Application fee: $50. Electronic applications accepted. *Expenses:* Tuition, state resident: full-time $3564; part-time $198 per credit hour. Tuition, nonresident: full-time $8550; part-time $475 per credit hour. Required fees: $69.26 per credit hour. Tuition and fees vary according to course load. *Financial support:* In 2009–10, 5 students received support, including 47 research assistantships (averaging $11,862 per year); career-related internships or fieldwork, Federal Work-Study, institutionally sponsored loans, scholarships/grants, traineeships, health care benefits, and unspecified assistantships also available. Support available to part-time students. Financial award application deadline: 3/1; financial award applicants required to submit FAFSA. *Faculty research:* Interacerebral effects of 8-OH-DPAT, rna purification, mechanisms in pathogenesis of gatroduodenal disorders, HHS MBRS program. *Unit head:* Dr. Sarah McIntire, Chair, 940-898-2351, Fax: 940-898-2382, E-mail: biology@twu.edu. *Application contact:* Samuel Wheeler, Assistant Director of Admissions, 940-898-3188, Fax: 940-898-3081, E-mail: wheelersr@twu.edu.

Texas Woman's University, Graduate School, College of Arts and Sciences, Department of Chemistry and Physics, Denton, TX 76201. Offers chemistry (MS); chemistry teaching (MS); science teaching (MS). Part-time programs available. *Faculty:* 6 full-time (1 woman), 1 part-time/adjunct (0 women). *Students:* 6 full-time (all women), 2 part-time (both women), 2 international. Average age 28. 6 applicants, 67% accepted, 3 enrolled. In 2009, 3 master's awarded. *Degree requirements:* For master's, comprehensive exam, thesis. *Entrance requirements:* For master's, GRE General Test (minimum score 400 verbal, 550 quantitative), bachelor's degree in chemistry or equivalent, 2 reference contacts. Additional exam requirements/recommendations for international students: Required—TOEFL (minimum score 550 paper-based; 213 computer-based; 79 iBT). *Application deadline:* For fall admission, 7/1 priority date for domestic students, 3/1 for international students; for spring admission, 12/1 priority date for domestic students, 7/1 for international students. Applications are processed on a rolling basis. Application fee: $50. Electronic applications accepted. *Expenses:* Tuition, state resident: full-time $3564; part-time $198 per credit hour. Tuition, nonresident: full-time $8550; part-time $475 per credit hour. Required fees: $69.26 per credit hour. Tuition and fees vary according to course load. *Financial support:* In 2009–10, 4 students received support, including 3 research assistantships (averaging $10,440 per year), 2 teaching assistantships (averaging $10,440 per year); career-related internships or fieldwork, Federal Work-Study, institutionally sponsored loans, scholarships/grants, traineeships, health care benefits, and unspecified assistantships also available. Support available to part-time students. Financial award application deadline: 3/1; financial award applicants required to submit FAFSA. *Faculty research:* Glutathione synthetase, MRI-acquisition of a circular dichroism spectropolarimeter, construction and analysis of aqueous enzyme phase diagrams, development of metallopolymers, basic chemical research. *Unit head:* Dr. Richard Sheardy, Chair, 940-898-2550, Fax: 940-898-2548, E-mail: rsheardy@mail.twu.edu. *Application contact:* Samuel Wheeler, Assistant Director of Admissions, 940-898-3188, Fax: 940-898-3081, E-mail: wheelersr@twu.edu.

Towson University, College of Graduate Studies and Research, Program in Science Education, Towson, MD 21252-0001. Offers MS. *Entrance requirements:* For master's, secondary school teacher certification BA in science or 24 credits in related course work, minimum GPA of 3.0.

Troy University, Graduate School, College of Education, Program in Postsecondary Education, Troy, AL 36082. Offers adult education (M Ed); biology (M Ed); criminal justice (M Ed); english (M Ed); foundations of education (M Ed); general science (M Ed); higher education administration (M Ed); history (M Ed); instructional technology (M Ed); mathematics (M Ed); music industry (M Ed); physical fitness (M Ed); political science (M Ed); public administration (M Ed); social science (M Ed); teaching english (M Ed). Also offered through the University College. *Accreditation:* NCATE. Part-time and evening/weekend programs available. *Students:* 267 full-time (192 women), 381 part-time (293 women); includes 326 minority (309 African Americans, 4 American Indian/Alaska Native, 5 Asian Americans or Pacific Islanders, 8 Hispanic Americans). Average age 34. 343 applicants, 90% accepted. In 2009, 480 master's awarded. *Degree requirements:* For master's, comprehensive exam, thesis. *Entrance requirements:* For master's, MAT (minimum score 385), minimum GPA of 2.5. Additional exam requirements/recommendations for international students: Required—TOEFL (minimum score 523 paper-based; 193 computer-based; 70 iBT), IELTS, or ACT Compass ESL (minimum score 270 on Listening, Reading, and Grammar with no individual score below 85 and a minimum score of 8 out of 12 on writing test). *Application deadline:* Applications are processed on a rolling basis. Application fee: $50. Electronic applications accepted. *Financial support:* Available to part-time students. Applicants required to submit FAFSA. *Unit head:* Dr. Andrew Creamer, Chair, 334-670-3350, E-mail: drcreamer@troy.edu. *Application contact:* Brenda K. Campbell, Director of Graduate Admissions, 334-670-3178, Fax: 334-670-3733, E-mail: bcamp@troy.edu.

Troy University, Graduate School, College of Education, Program in Secondary Education, Troy, AL 36082. Offers 5th year biology (MS); 5th year computer science (MS); 5th year history

(MS); 5th year language arts (MS); 5th year mathematics (MS); 5th year social science (MS); educationtraditional language arts (MS); traditional biology (MS); traditional computer science (MS); traditional history (MS); traditional mathematics (MS); traditional social science (MS). *Accreditation:* NCATE. Part-time and evening/weekend programs available. *Students:* 17 full-time (12 women), 25 part-time (23 women); includes 8 minority (all African Americans). Average age 27. 10 applicants, 90% accepted. In 2009, 29 master's awarded. *Degree requirements:* For master's, comprehensive exam, thesis. *Entrance requirements:* For master's, minimum GPA of 2.5. Additional exam requirements/recommendations for international students: Required—TOEFL (minimum score 523 paper-based; 193 computer-based; 70 iBT), IELTS (minimum score 6). *Application deadline:* Applications are processed on a rolling basis. Application fee: $50. Electronic applications accepted. *Financial support:* Career-related internships or fieldwork available. Support available to part-time students. Financial award applicants required to submit FAFSA. *Unit head:* Dr. Marian Parker, Coordinator, 334-670-5661, Fax: 334-670-3548, E-mail: mjparker@troy.edu. *Application contact:* Brenda K. Campbell, Director of Graduate Admissions, 334-670-3178, Fax: 334-670-3733, E-mail: bcamp@troy.edu.

Union Graduate College, School of Education, Schenectady, NY 12308-3107. Offers biology (MAT, MS); chemistry (MAT); Chinese (MAT); earth science (MAT); English (MAT); French (MAT); general science (MAT); German (MAT); Greek (MAT); languages (MAT); Latin (MAT); mathematics (MAT); mathematics and technology (MS); mentoring and teacher leadership (AC); middle childhood extension (AC); national board certificate and teacher leadership (AC); physical science (MS); physics (MAT); social studies (MAT); Spanish (MAT). *Accreditation:* Teacher Education Accreditation Council. *Faculty:* 3 full-time (1 woman), 39 part-time/adjunct (19 women). *Students:* 46 full-time (27 women), 45 part-time (39 women); includes 5 minority (1 Asian American or Pacific Islander, 4 Hispanic Americans), 2 international. Average age 33. 66 applicants, 73% accepted, 39 enrolled. In 2009, 44 master's awarded. *Degree requirements:* For master's, thesis or project. *Entrance requirements:* For master's, minimum GPA of 3.0, letters of recommendation. Additional exam requirements/recommendations for international students: Required—TOEFL (minimum score 550 paper-based; 213 computer-based). *Application deadline:* Applications are processed on a rolling basis. Application fee: $60. Electronic applications accepted. *Expenses:* Contact institution. *Financial support:* In 2009–10, 12 research assistantships with tuition reimbursements (averaging $3,000 per year) were awarded; Federal Work-Study, scholarships/grants, health care benefits, and tuition waivers (partial) also available. Support available to part-time students. Financial award applicants required to submit FAFSA. *Faculty research:* Transformative learning, science education, National Board Certification, teacher leadership, teacher quality. *Unit head:* Dr. Patrick Allen, Dean, 518-631-9870, Fax: 518-631-9901. *Application contact:* Christine Angley, Assistant, 518-631-9871, Fax: 518-631-9903, E-mail: angleyc@uniongraduatecollege.edu.

Union Institute & University, M Ed Program–Vermont Campus, Montpelier, VT 05602. Offers school administration (M Ed), including principalship; school counseling (M Ed); teaching (M Ed), including art, early childhood, elementary, English, math, middle schools, science, social studies, special education. *Faculty:* 3 full-time (1 woman), 23 part-time/adjunct (19 women). *Students:* 41 part-time (29 women). Average age 38. In 2009, 15 master's awarded. *Degree requirements:* For master's, thesis. *Entrance requirements:* For master's, 3 letters of reference. *Application deadline:* Applications are processed on a rolling basis. Application fee: $50. *Expenses:* Contact institution. *Financial support:* Federal Work-Study, scholarships/grants, and tuition waivers available. Financial award applicants required to submit FAFSA. *Unit head:* Dr. Arlene Sacks, Dean, Graduate Programs in Education, 305-653-6713 Ext. 2152, E-mail: arlene.sacks@myunion.edu. *Application contact:* Dr. Arlene Sacks, Dean, Graduate Programs in Education, 305-653-6713 Ext. 2152, E-mail: arlene.sacks@myunion.edu.

University at Albany, State University of New York, College of Arts and Sciences, Department of Mathematics and Statistics, Albany, NY 12222-0001. Offers mathematics (PhD); secondary teaching (MA); statistics (MA). *Degree requirements:* For doctorate, one foreign language, thesis/dissertation. *Entrance requirements:* For doctorate, GRE General Test. Additional exam requirements/recommendations for international students: Required—TOEFL (minimum score 550 paper-based; 213 computer-based). Electronic applications accepted.

University at Buffalo, the State University of New York, Graduate School, Graduate School of Education, Department of Learning and Instruction, Buffalo, NY 14260. Offers biology education (Ed M, Certificate); chemistry education (Ed M, Certificate); childhood education (Ed M); childhood education with bilingual extension (Ed M); early childhood education (Ed M); earth science education (Ed M, Certificate); elementary education (Ed D, PhD); English education (Ed M, PhD, Certificate); English for speakers of other languages (Ed M); foreign and second language education (PhD); French education (Ed M, Certificate); general education (Ed M); German education (Ed M, Certificate); gifted education (online) (Certificate); Latin education (Ed M, Certificate); literary specialist (Ed M); mathematics education (Ed M, PhD, Certificate); music education (Ed M, Certificate); physics education (Ed M, Certificate); reading education (PhD); science and the public (online) (Ed M); science education (PhD); social studies education (Ed M, Certificate); Spanish education (Ed M, Certificate); special education (PhD); teaching and leading for diversity (Certificate); teaching English to speakers of other languages (Ed M). Part-time and evening/weekend programs available. Postbaccalaureate distance learning degree programs offered (no on-campus study). *Faculty:* 34 full-time (24 women), 50 part-time/adjunct (39 women). *Students:* 332 full-time (245 women), 365 part-time (272 women); includes 50 minority (18 African Americans, 4 American Indian/Alaska Native, 10 Asian Americans or Pacific Islanders, 18 Hispanic Americans), 55 international. Average age 30. 627 applicants, 78% accepted, 286 enrolled. In 2009, 255 master's, 16 doctorates, 51 other advanced degrees awarded. *Degree requirements:* For master's, comprehensive exam; for doctorate, thesis/dissertation, research analysis exam, research experience component. *Entrance requirements:* For doctorate, GRE General Test or MAT, interview, writing sample, letters of recommendation. Additional exam requirements/recommendations for international students: Required—TOEFL (minimum score 600 paper-based; 250 computer-based; 96 iBT). *Application deadline:* For fall admission, 2/1 priority date for domestic and international students; for spring admission, 11/15 priority date for domestic students, 10/1 for international students. Applications are processed on a rolling basis. Application fee: $50. Electronic applications accepted. *Financial support:* In 2009–10, 23 fellowships with full tuition reimbursements (averaging $9,000 per year), 42 research assistantships with full tuition reimbursements (averaging $10,000 per year) were awarded; teaching assistantships with full tuition reimbursements, career-related internships or fieldwork, Federal Work-Study, institutionally sponsored loans, scholarships/grants, tuition waivers (partial), and unspecified assistantships also available. Financial award application deadline: 2/28; financial award applicants required to submit FAFSA. *Faculty research:* Science assessment, foreign language teaching and learning, early learning, new literacies, gender and education. Total annual research expenditures: $1.8 million. *Unit head:* Dr. Suzanne Miller, Chair, 716-645-2455, Fax: 716-645-3161, E-mail: smiller@buffalo.edu. *Application contact:* Cathy Dimino, Admissions Assistant, 716-645-2110, Fax: 716-645-7937, E-mail: cadimino@buffalo.edu.

University of Arkansas at Pine Bluff, Program in Education, Pine Bluff, AR 71601-2799. Offers elementary education (M Ed); secondary education (M Ed), including general science, physical education, social studies. *Accreditation:* NCATE. Part-time and evening/weekend programs available. *Degree requirements:* For master's, comprehensive exam. *Entrance requirements:* For master's, GRE, minimum GPA of 2.75, NTE or Standard Arkansas Teaching Certificate. *Faculty research:* Teacher certification, accreditation, assessment, standards, portfolio development, rehabilitation, technology.

The University of British Columbia, Faculty of Education, Department of Curriculum and Pedagogy, Vancouver, BC V6T 1Z4, Canada. Offers art education (M Ed, MA); business education (MA); curriculum studies (M Ed, MA, PhD); home economics education (M Ed, MA); math education (M Ed, MA); music education (M Ed, MA); physical education (M Ed, MA); science education (M Ed, MA); social studies education (M Ed, MA); technology studies education (M Ed, MA). Part-time programs available. *Degree requirements:* For master's, thesis (MA); for doctorate, comprehensive exam, thesis/dissertation. *Entrance requirements:* Additional exam requirements/recommendations for international students: Required—TOEFL

Science Education

The University of British Columbia (continued)
(minimum score 580 paper-based; 237 computer-based; 92 iBT). Electronic applications accepted. *Expenses:* Contact institution. *Faculty research:* School subjects, teaching and learning.

University of California, Berkeley, Graduate Division, School of Education, Group in Science and Mathematics Education, Berkeley, CA 94720-1500. Offers PhD, MA/Credential. *Students:* 21 full-time (15 women). Average age 30. 15 applicants, 5 enrolled. In 2009, 2 doctorates awarded. *Application deadline:* For fall admission, 12/1 for domestic students. Application fee: $70 ($90 for international students). Electronic applications accepted. *Financial support:* Unspecified assistantships available. *Application contact:* Information Contact, 510-642-4207, Fax: 510-642-4808, E-mail: smeinfo@berkeley.edu.

University of California, Berkeley, Graduate Division, School of Education, Programs in Education, Berkeley, CA 94720-1500. Offers development in mathematics and science (MA); education in mathematics, science, and technology (MA, PhD); human development and education (MA, PhD); special education (PhD); MA/Credential; Ph D/Credential; PhD/MA. *Students:* 374 full-time (270 women). Average age 33. 674 applicants, 111 enrolled. In 2009, 120 master's, 25 doctorates awarded. Terminal master's awarded for partial completion of doctoral program. *Degree requirements:* For master's, exam or thesis; for doctorate, thesis/dissertation, oral qualifying exam. *Entrance requirements:* For master's and doctorate, GRE General Test, minimum GPA of 3.0 during last 2 years of undergraduate course work. *Application deadline:* For fall admission, 12/1 for domestic students. Application fee: $70 ($90 for international students). Electronic applications accepted. *Financial support:* Fellowships, research assistantships, teaching assistantships, unspecified assistantships available. *Faculty research:* Human development, social and moral educational psychology, developmental teacher preparation. *Unit head:* Prof. P. David Pearson, Dean, 510-642-3726, E-mail: gsedeansoffice@lists.berkeley.edu. *Application contact:* Admissions Office, 510-642-0841, Fax: 510-642-4808, E-mail: gse_info@uclink.berkeley.edu.

University of California, Los Angeles, Graduate Division, College of Letters and Science, Department of Physics and Astronomy, Program in Physics, Los Angeles, CA 90095. Offers physics (MS, PhD); physics education (MAT). MAT admits only applicants whose objective is PhD. *Students:* 143 full-time (19 women); includes 19 minority (3 African Americans, 14 Asian Americans or Pacific Islanders, 2 Hispanic Americans), 30 international. Average age 26. 287 applicants, 20% accepted, 23 enrolled. In 2009, 15 master's, 30 doctorates awarded. Terminal master's awarded for partial completion of doctoral program. *Degree requirements:* For master's, comprehensive exam; for doctorate, thesis/dissertation, oral and written qualifying exams. *Entrance requirements:* For master's, GRE General Test, GRE Subject Test (physics), minimum GPA of 3.0, BS in related field; for doctorate, GRE General Test, GRE Subject Test (physics), minimum undergraduate GPA of 3.0, BS in related field. *Application deadline:* For fall admission, 12/15 for domestic and international students. Application fee: $70 ($90 for international students). Electronic applications accepted. *Financial support:* In 2009–10, 94 fellowships with full and partial tuition reimbursements, 103 research assistantships with full and partial tuition reimbursements, 94 teaching assistantships with full and partial tuition reimbursements were awarded; Federal Work-Study, institutionally sponsored loans, scholarships/grants, health care benefits, tuition waivers (full and partial), and unspecified assistantships also available. Financial award application deadline: 3/1; financial award applicants required to submit FAFSA. *Unit head:* Dr. Ferdinand Coroniti, Chair, 310-825-3440. *Application contact:* Carol Finn, Graduate Counselor, 310-825-2307, E-mail: apply@physics.ucla.edu.

University of California, San Diego, Office of Graduate Studies, Program in Mathematics and Science Education, La Jolla, CA 92093. Offers PhD. *Entrance requirements:* For doctorate, GRE General Test. Electronic applications accepted.

University of California, Santa Cruz, Division of Graduate Studies, Division of Social Sciences, Department of Education, Santa Cruz, CA 95064. Offers education (MA); language and literacy studies (PhD); mathematics and science education (PhD); social context and policy studies of education (PhD). Terminal master's awarded for partial completion of doctoral program. *Degree requirements:* For master's, thesis; for doctorate, thesis/dissertation. *Faculty research:* Bilingual/multicultural education, special education, curriculum and instruction, child development.

University of Central Florida, College of Education, Department of Teaching and Learning Principles, Program in K-8 Mathematics and Science Education, Orlando, FL 32816. Offers M Ed, Certificate. *Accreditation:* NCATE. *Students:* 32 part-time (23 women); includes 4 minority (2 African Americans, 1 Asian American or Pacific Islander, 1 Hispanic American). Average age 35. 1 applicant, 100% accepted, 1 enrolled. In 2009, 5 master's awarded. Application fee: $30. *Expenses:* Tuition, state resident: part-time $306.31 per credit hour. Tuition, nonresident: part-time $1099.01 per credit hour. Part-time tuition and fees vary according to degree level and program. *Financial support:* Fellowships available.

University of Central Florida, College of Education, Department of Teaching and Learning Principles, Program in Science Education, Orlando, FL 32816. Offers biology (MA); chemistry (MA); middle school science (MA); physics (MA); science education (M Ed). *Accreditation:* NCATE. Part-time and evening/weekend programs available. *Students:* 11 full-time (6 women), 19 part-time (15 women); includes 6 minority (all Hispanic Americans). Average age 34. 12 applicants, 92% accepted, 10 enrolled. In 2009, 13 master's awarded. *Entrance requirements:* For master's, GRE General Test. Additional exam requirements/recommendations for international students: Required—TOEFL. *Application deadline:* For fall admission, 7/15 for domestic students; for spring admission, 12/1 for domestic students. Application fee: $30. Electronic applications accepted. *Expenses:* Tuition, state resident: part-time $306.31 per credit hour. Tuition, nonresident: part-time $1099.01 per credit hour. Part-time tuition and fees vary according to degree level and program. *Financial support:* Career-related internships or fieldwork, Federal Work-Study, institutionally sponsored loans, tuition waivers (partial), and unspecified assistantships available. Financial award application deadline: 3/1; financial award applicants required to submit FAFSA.

University of Central Florida, College of Education, Education PhD Program, Orlando, FL 32816. Offers communication sciences and disorders (PhD); counselor education (PhD); elementary education (PhD); exceptional education (PhD); higher education (PhD); hospitality education (PhD); instructional technology (PhD); mathematics education (PhD); science education (PhD); social science education (PhD). *Students:* 99 full-time (70 women), 14 part-time (9 women); includes 28 minority (17 African Americans, 2 Asian Americans or Pacific Islanders, 9 Hispanic Americans), 20 international. In 2009, 15 doctorates awarded. Application fee: $30. Electronic applications accepted. *Expenses:* Tuition, state resident: part-time $306.31 per credit hour. Tuition, nonresident: part-time $1099.01 per credit hour. Part-time tuition and fees vary according to degree level and program. *Financial support:* In 2009–10, 40 fellowships with partial tuition reimbursements (averaging $9,200 per year), 61 research assistantships with partial tuition reimbursements (averaging $7,800 per year), 18 teaching assistantships with partial tuition reimbursements (averaging $6,500 per year) were awarded. *Unit head:* Dr. B. Grant Hayes, Associate Dean, 407-823-5391, E-mail: ghayes@mail.ucf.edu. *Application contact:* Dr. B. Grant Hayes, Associate Dean, 407-823-5391, E-mail: ghayes@mail.ucf.edu.

University of Chicago, Division of Social Sciences, Committee on Conceptual and Historical Studies of Science, Chicago, IL 60637-1513. Offers PhD. *Students:* 7. *Degree requirements:* For doctorate, thesis/dissertation. *Entrance requirements:* For doctorate, GRE General Test, GRE Subject Test. Additional exam requirements/recommendations for international students: Required—TOEFL, IELTS (minimum score 7). *Application deadline:* For fall admission, 12/10 for domestic and international students. Application fee: $55. Electronic applications accepted. *Financial support:* Fellowships, teaching assistantships, Federal Work-Study, institutionally sponsored loans, scholarships/grants, traineeships, health care benefits, and unspecified assistantships available. Financial award application deadline: 12/28; financial award applicants required to submit FAFSA. *Unit head:* Prof. Adrian Johns, Chair, 773-702-8261. *Application contact:* Office of the Dean of Students, 773-702-8415, E-mail: admissions@ssd.uchicago.edu.

University of Cincinnati, Graduate School, College of Education, Criminal Justice, and Human Services, Division of Teacher Education, Cincinnati, OH 45221. Offers curriculum and instruction (M Ed, Ed D); deaf studies (Certificate); early childhood education (M Ed); middle childhood education (M Ed); postsecondary literacy instruction (Certificate); reading/literacy (M Ed, Ed D); secondary education (M Ed); special education (M Ed, Ed D); teaching English as a second language (M Ed, Ed D, Certificate); teaching science (MS). Part-time programs available. *Degree requirements:* For doctorate, thesis/dissertation. *Entrance requirements:* For master's, GRE General Test. Electronic applications accepted.

University of Connecticut, Graduate School, Neag School of Education, Department of Curriculum and Instruction, Program in Science Education, Storrs, CT 06269. Offers MA, PhD. *Accreditation:* NCATE. *Faculty:* 15 full-time (10 women). *Students:* 23 full-time (18 women), 1 (woman) part-time; includes 1 minority (African American). Average age 26. 37 applicants, 14% accepted, 5 enrolled. In 2009, 23 master's, 1 doctorate awarded. Terminal master's awarded for partial completion of doctoral program. *Degree requirements:* For master's, comprehensive exam, thesis or alternative; for doctorate, thesis/dissertation. *Entrance requirements:* For doctorate, GRE General Test. Additional exam requirements/recommendations for international students: Required—TOEFL (minimum score 550 paper-based; 213 computer-based). *Application deadline:* For fall admission, 2/1 priority date for domestic and international students; for spring admission, 11/1 for domestic students, 10/1 for international students. Applications are processed on a rolling basis. Application fee: $55. Electronic applications accepted. *Expenses:* Tuition, state resident: full-time $4725; part-time $525 per credit. Tuition, nonresident: full-time $12,267; part-time $1363 per credit. Required fees: $346 per semester. Tuition and fees vary according to course load. *Financial support:* In 2009–10, 1 research assistantship with full tuition reimbursement, 1 teaching assistantship with full tuition reimbursement were awarded; fellowships, Federal Work-Study, scholarships/grants, health care benefits, and unspecified assistantships also available. Financial award application deadline: 2/1; financial award applicants required to submit FAFSA. *Unit head:* Mary Anne Doyle, Head, 860-486-2433, Fax: 860-486-0280, E-mail: mary.dolye@uconn.edu. *Application contact:* Lisa Rasicot, Graduate Coordinator, 860-486-3065, Fax: 860-486-0210, E-mail: l.rasicot@uconn.edu.

University of Florida, Graduate School, College of Education, School of Teaching and Learning, Gainesville, FL 32611. Offers bilingual/ESOL education (M Ed, MAE, Ed D, PhD, Ed S); curriculum and instruction (M Ed, MAE, Ed D, PhD, Ed S); early childhood education (Ed D, PhD, Ed S); elementary education (M Ed, MAE); English education (M Ed, MAE); mathematics education (M Ed, MAE); reading education (M Ed, MAE); science education (M Ed, MAE); social foundations (M Ed, MAE, Ed D, PhD); social studies education (M Ed, MAE). *Accreditation:* NCATE. *Degree requirements:* For master's, thesis optional; for doctorate, variable foreign language requirement, thesis/dissertation. *Entrance requirements:* For master's and doctorate, GRE General Test, minimum GPA of 3.0; for Ed S, GRE General Test. Additional exam requirements/recommendations for international students: Required—TOEFL (minimum score 550 paper-based; 213 computer-based). Electronic applications accepted. *Faculty research:* Teacher education, inclusive education, classroom processes, curriculum and technology.

University of Florida, Graduate School, College of Liberal Arts and Sciences, Department of Geological Sciences, Gainesville, FL 32611. Offers geology (MS, MST, PhD). Terminal master's awarded for partial completion of doctoral program. *Degree requirements:* For master's, thesis (for some programs); for doctorate, one foreign language, thesis/dissertation. *Entrance requirements:* For master's and doctorate, GRE General Test, GRE Subject Test, minimum GPA of 3.0. Additional exam requirements/recommendations for international students: Required—TOEFL (minimum score 550 paper-based; 213 computer-based). Electronic applications accepted. *Faculty research:* Paleoclimatology, tectonophysics, petrochemistry, marine geology, geochemistry, hydrology.

University of Georgia, Graduate School, College of Education, Department of Mathematics and Science Education, Athens, GA 30602. Offers mathematics education (M Ed, Ed D, PhD, Ed S); science education (M Ed, Ed D, PhD, Ed S). *Faculty:* 16 full-time (7 women), 1 (woman) part-time/adjunct. *Students:* 125 full-time (83 women), 71 part-time (42 women); includes 34 minority (24 African Americans, 5 Asian Americans or Pacific Islanders, 5 Hispanic Americans), 20 international. 88 applicants. In 2009, 31 master's, 14 doctorates, 10 other advanced degrees awarded. *Application deadline:* For fall admission, 7/1 priority date for domestic students; for spring admission, 11/15 for domestic students. Application fee: $50. *Expenses:* Tuition, state resident: full-time $6000; part-time $250 per credit hour. Tuition, nonresident: full-time $20,904; part-time $871 per credit hour. Required fees: $730 per semester. *Unit head:* Dr. Denise S. Mewborn, Head, 706-542-4548, Fax: 706-542-4551, E-mail: dmewborn@uga.edu. *Application contact:* Dr. David Jackson, Graduate Coordinator, 706-542-4637, Fax: 706-542-4551, E-mail: djackson@uga.edu.

University of Houston, College of Education, Department of Curriculum and Instruction, Houston, TX 77204. Offers art education (M Ed); bilingual education (M Ed); curriculum and instruction (M Ed, Ed D); early childhood education (M Ed); elementary education (M Ed); gifted and talented education (M Ed); instructional technology (M Ed); mathematics education (M Ed); reading and language arts education (M Ed); science education (M Ed); second language education (M Ed); secondary education (M Ed); social studies education (M Ed); teaching (M Ed). *Accreditation:* NCATE. Part-time and evening/weekend programs available. *Faculty:* 20 full-time (9 women), 22 part-time/adjunct (17 women). *Students:* 113 full-time (81 women), 195 part-time (150 women); includes 107 minority (43 African Americans, 29 Asian Americans or Pacific Islanders, 35 Hispanic Americans), 29 international. Average age 35. 150 applicants, 77% accepted, 55 enrolled. In 2009, 75 master's, 31 doctorates awarded. *Degree requirements:* For master's, comprehensive exam, thesis optional; for doctorate, comprehensive exam, thesis/dissertation. *Entrance requirements:* For master's and doctorate, GRE, minimum cumulative undergraduate GPA of 2.6. Additional exam requirements/recommendations for international students: Required—TOEFL (minimum score 550 paper-based; 79 iBT). *Application deadline:* For fall admission, 3/1 for domestic and international students; for spring admission, 10/1 for domestic and international students. Application fee: $45 ($75 for international students). Electronic applications accepted. *Expenses:* Tuition, state resident: full-time $7676; part-time $320 per credit hour. Tuition, nonresident: full-time $14,324; part-time $597 per credit hour. Required fees: $3034. *Financial support:* In 2009–10, 4 fellowships with full tuition reimbursements (averaging $9,500 per year), 6 research assistantships with full tuition reimbursements (averaging $8,800 per year), 25 teaching assistantships with full tuition reimbursements (averaging $8,800 per year) were awarded; career-related internships or fieldwork, Federal Work-Study, institutionally sponsored loans, scholarships/grants, health care benefits, and unspecified assistantships also available. Support available to part-time students. Financial award application deadline: 2/1. *Faculty research:* Teaching-learning process, instructional technology in schools, teacher education, classroom management, at-risk students. *Unit head:* Dr. Laveria Hutchison, Chairperson, 713-743-4958, Fax: 713-743-4990, E-mail: lhutchison@uh.edu. *Application contact:* Renee C. Rattelade, Executive Secretary, 713-743-4997, Fax: 713-743-4990, E-mail: rrattelade@mail.coe.uh.edu.

University of Illinois at Urbana–Champaign, Graduate College, College of Engineering, Department of Physics, Champaign, IL 61820. Offers physics (MS, PhD); teaching of physics (MS). *Faculty:* 56 full-time (6 women), 1 part-time/adjunct (0 women). *Students:* 195 full-time (25 women), 80 part-time (12 women); includes 21 minority (2 African Americans, 15 Asian Americans or Pacific Islanders, 4 Hispanic Americans), 136 international. 582 applicants, 5% accepted, 27 enrolled. In 2009, 16 master's, 33 doctorates awarded. *Entrance requirements:* For master's, GRE, minimum GPA of 3.0; for doctorate, GRE, minimum GPA of 3.5. Additional exam requirements/recommendations for international students: Required—TOEFL (minimum score 550 paper-based; 213 computer-based; 79 iBT), or IELTS (minimum score 6.5). *Application deadline:* Applications are processed on a rolling basis. Application fee: $60 ($75 for international students). Electronic applications accepted. *Financial support:* In 2009–10, 18 fellowships, 185 research assistantships, 133 teaching assistantships were awarded; tuition waivers (full and partial) also available. *Unit head:* Dale J. VanHarlingen, Head, 217-333-3760, Fax:

217-244-4293, E-mail: dvh@illinois.edu. *Application contact:* Melodee Jo Schweighart, Office Manager, 217-333-3645, Fax: 217-244-5073, E-mail: mschweig@illinois.edu.

University of Illinois at Urbana–Champaign, Graduate College, College of Liberal Arts and Sciences, School of Chemical Sciences, Department of Chemistry, Champaign, IL 61820. Offers astrochemistry (PhD); chemical physics (PhD); chemistry (MA, MS, PhD); teaching of chemistry (MS); MS/JD; MS/MBA. *Faculty:* 34 full-time (6 women). *Students:* 308 full-time (91 women), 4 part-time (1 woman); includes 34 minority (6 African Americans, 3 American Indian/Alaska Native, 18 Asian Americans or Pacific Islanders, 7 Hispanic Americans), 69 international. 502 applicants, 13% accepted, 63 enrolled. In 2009, 14 master's, 51 doctorates awarded. *Entrance requirements:* For master's and doctorate, GRE General Test, GRE Subject Test, minimum GPA of 3.0. Additional exam requirements/recommendations for international students: Required—TOEFL (minimum score 580 paper-based; 237 computer-based). *Application deadline:* Applications are processed on a rolling basis. Application fee: $60 ($75 for international students). Electronic applications accepted. *Financial support:* In 2009–10, 108 fellowships, 186 research assistantships, 164 teaching assistantships were awarded; tuition waivers (full and partial) also available. *Unit head:* Steven C. Zimmerman, Head, 217-333-6655, Fax: 217-244-5943, E-mail: sczimmer@illinois.edu. *Application contact:* Dorothy Ann Gordon, Assistant to the Head, 217-244-0618, Fax: 217-244-5943, E-mail: dorothyh@illinois.edu.

University of Illinois at Urbana–Champaign, Graduate College, College of Liberal Arts and Sciences, School of Earth, Society and Environment, Department of Geology, Champaign, IL 61820. Offers geology (MS, PhD); teaching of earth sciences (MS). *Faculty:* 14 full-time (4 women). *Students:* 30 full-time (16 women), 2 part-time (1 woman); includes 2 minority (both Asian Americans or Pacific Islanders), 11 international. 53 applicants, 36% accepted, 8 enrolled. In 2009, 8 master's, 4 doctorates awarded. Terminal master's awarded for partial completion of doctoral program. *Entrance requirements:* For master's and doctorate, GRE General Test, minimum GPA of 3.0. Additional exam requirements/recommendations for international students: Required—TOEFL. *Application deadline:* Applications are processed on a rolling basis. Application fee: $60 ($75 for international students). Electronic applications accepted. *Financial support:* In 2009–10, 3 fellowships, 16 research assistantships, 16 teaching assistantships were awarded; Federal Work-Study and tuition waivers (full and partial) also available. *Faculty research:* Hydrogeology, structure/tectonics, mineral science. *Unit head:* Wang-Ping Chen, Head, 217-333-2744, Fax: 217-244-4996, E-mail: wpchen@illinois.edu. *Application contact:* Marilyn K. Whalen, Office Administrator, 217-333-3542, Fax: 217-244-4996, E-mail: mkt@illinois.edu.

University of Indianapolis, Graduate Programs, School of Education, Indianapolis, IN 46227-3697. Offers art education (MAT); biology (MAT); chemistry (MAT); curriculum and instruction (MA); earth sciences (MAT); education (MA, MAT); educational leadership (MA); elementary education (MA); English (MAT); French (MAT); math (MAT); physical education (MAT); physics (MAT); secondary education (MA), including art education, education, English education, social studies education; social studies (MAT); Spanish (MAT). *Accreditation:* NCATE. Part-time and evening/weekend programs available. *Faculty:* 4 full-time (3 women), 3 part-time/adjunct (2 women). *Students:* 52 full-time (28 women), 110 part-time (67 women); includes 3 minority (all African Americans), 2 international. Average age 33. *Entrance requirements:* For master's, GRE Subject Test, PRAXIS I, minimum GPA of 2.5, 3 letters of recommendation, interview, writing exercise. Additional exam requirements/recommendations for international students: Required—TOEFL (minimum score 550 paper-based; 213 computer-based). *Application deadline:* Applications are processed on a rolling basis. Application fee: $50. *Financial support:* Federal Work-Study available. Financial award application deadline: 5/1; financial award applicants required to submit FAFSA. *Faculty research:* Assessment of teacher education, perceptions of prospective teachers by parents. *Unit head:* Dr. Kathy Moran, Dean, 317-788-3285, Fax: 317-788-3300, E-mail: kmoran@uindy.edu. *Application contact:* Chemain Slater, 317-788-2051, E-mail: slaterc@uindy.edu.

The University of Iowa, Graduate College, College of Liberal Arts and Sciences, Program in Science Education, Iowa City, IA 52242-1316. Offers MS, PhD. *Degree requirements:* For master's, thesis, exam; for doctorate, comprehensive exam, thesis/dissertation. *Entrance requirements:* For master's and doctorate, GRE General Test, minimum GPA of 3.0. Additional exam requirements/recommendations for international students: Required—TOEFL (minimum score 550 paper-based; 213 computer-based; 81 iBT). Electronic applications accepted.

University of Maine, Graduate School, College of Education and Human Development, Program in Science Education, Orono, ME 04469. Offers M Ed, MS, CAS. *Accreditation:* NCATE. Part-time and evening/weekend programs available. *Students:* 3 full-time (all women), 3 part-time (1 woman). Average age 34. In 2009, 6 master's awarded. *Degree requirements:* For master's, thesis or alternative. *Entrance requirements:* For master's, MAT; for CAS, MA, M Ed, or MS. Additional exam requirements/recommendations for international students: Required—TOEFL. *Application deadline:* For fall admission, 2/1 priority date for domestic students. Applications are processed on a rolling basis. Application fee: $65. Electronic applications accepted. *Financial support:* Federal Work-Study, institutionally sponsored loans, and tuition waivers (full and partial) available. Financial award application deadline: 3/1. *Unit head:* Dr. Janet Spector, Coordinator, 207-581-2444, Fax: 207-581-2423. *Application contact:* Scott G. Delcourt, Associate Dean of the Graduate School, 207-581-3291, Fax: 207-581-3232, E-mail: graduate@maine.edu.

University of Maryland, Baltimore County, Graduate School, College of Arts, Humanities and Social Sciences, Department of Education, Program in Education, Baltimore, MD 21250. Offers mathematics education (MA); science education (MA); STEM education (MA). Part-time and evening/weekend programs available. *Faculty:* 24 full-time (18 women), 25 part-time/adjunct (19 women). *Students:* 2 full-time (1 woman), 147 part-time (120 women); includes 9 African Americans, 2 Asian Americans or Pacific Islanders. Average age 34. 34 applicants, 97% accepted, 26 enrolled. In 2009, 106 master's awarded. *Degree requirements:* For master's, comprehensive exam (for some programs), thesis (for some programs). *Entrance requirements:* For master's, PRAXIS I, minimum GPA of 3.0. Additional exam requirements/recommendations for international students: Required—TOEFL. *Application deadline:* For fall admission, 6/1 for domestic students; for spring admission, 11/1 for domestic students. Applications are processed on a rolling basis. Application fee: $50. Electronic applications accepted. *Financial support:* In 2009–10, 12 students received support, including research assistantships with full tuition reimbursements available (averaging $12,000 per year); career-related internships or fieldwork, Federal Work-Study, scholarships/grants, tuition waivers, and unspecified assistantships also available. Financial award application deadline: 3/1; financial award applicants required to submit FAFSA. *Unit head:* Dr. Susan M. Blunck, Director, 410-455-2869, Fax: 410-455-3986, E-mail: blunck@umbc.edu. *Application contact:* Dr. Susan M. Blunck, Director, 410-455-2869, Fax: 410-455-3986, E-mail: blunck@umbc.edu.

University of Maryland, Baltimore County, Graduate School, College of Arts, Humanities and Social Sciences, Department of Education, Program in Teaching, Baltimore, MD 21250. Offers early childhood education (MAT); elementary education (MAT); secondary education (MAT), including art, biology, chemistry, dance, earth/space science, English, foreign language, mathematics, music, physics, theatre; secondary science (MAT), including social studies. Part-time and evening/weekend programs available. *Faculty:* 24 full-time (18 women), 25 part-time/adjunct (19 women). *Students:* 52 full-time (41 women), 64 part-time (55 women); includes 20 minority (5 African Americans, 1 American Indian/Alaska Native, 10 Asian Americans or Pacific Islanders, 4 Hispanic Americans), 3 international. Average age 31. 88 applicants, 57% accepted, 39 enrolled. In 2009, 106 master's awarded. *Degree requirements:* For master's, comprehensive exam (for some programs), thesis (for some programs). *Entrance requirements:* For master's, PRAXIS I and II, minimum GPA of 3.0. Additional exam requirements/recommendations for international students: Required—TOEFL. *Application deadline:* For fall admission, 6/1 for domestic students; for spring admission, 11/1 for domestic students. Applications are processed on a rolling basis. Application fee: $50. Electronic applications accepted. *Financial support:* In 2009–10, 6 students received support, including research assistantships

with full tuition reimbursements available (averaging $12,000 per year); career-related internships or fieldwork, Federal Work-Study, scholarships/grants, tuition waivers, and unspecified assistantships also available. Financial award application deadline: 3/1. *Faculty research:* STEM teacher education, culturally sensitive pedagogy, ESOL/bilingual education, early childhood education, language, literacy and culture. *Unit head:* Dr. Susan M. Blunck, Director, 410-455-2869, Fax: 410-455-3986, E-mail: blunck@umbc.edu. *Application contact:* Dr. Susan M. Blunck, Director, 410-455-2869, Fax: 410-455-3986, E-mail: blunck@umbc.edu.

University of Massachusetts Amherst, Graduate School, School of Education, Program in Education, Amherst, MA 01003. Offers bilingual, English as a second language, and multicultural education (M Ed, CAGS); child study and early education (M Ed); children, families and schools (Ed D, CAGS); early childhood and elementary teacher education (M Ed); education policy and leadership (CAGS); educational administration (M Ed, CAGS); educational policy and leadership (Ed D); higher education (M Ed, CAGS); international education (M Ed); language, literacy and culture (Ed D); learning, media and technology (M Ed, CAGS); mathematics, science, and learning technologies (Ed D); policy studies (M Ed); policy studies in education (CAGS); reading and writing (M Ed); research and evaluation methods (Ed D); school counselor education (M Ed, CAGS); school psychology (CAGS); science education (CAGS); secondary teacher education (M Ed); social justice education (M Ed, Ed D, CAGS); special education (M Ed, Ed D, CAGS). *Accreditation:* NCATE. Part-time programs available. Postbaccalaureate distance learning degree programs offered (minimal on-campus study). *Faculty:* 74 full-time (41 women). *Students:* 377 full-time (268 women), 347 part-time (232 women); includes 115 minority (59 African Americans, 2 American Indian/Alaska Native, 16 Asian Americans or Pacific Islanders, 38 Hispanic Americans), 108 international. Average age 35. 708 applicants, 68% accepted, 266 enrolled. In 2009, 183 master's, 17 doctorates awarded. Terminal master's awarded for partial completion of doctoral program. *Degree requirements:* For master's, thesis or alternative; for doctorate, comprehensive exam, thesis/dissertation. *Entrance requirements:* Additional exam requirements/recommendations for international students: Required—TOEFL (minimum score 550 paper-based; 213 computer-based; 80 iBT), IELTS (minimum score 6.5). *Application deadline:* For fall admission, 1/15 for domestic and international students. Applications are processed on a rolling basis. Application fee: $50 ($65 for international students). Electronic applications accepted. *Expenses:* Tuition, state resident: full-time $2640; part-time $110 per credit. Tuition, nonresident: full-time $9936; part-time $414 per credit. Tuition and fees vary according to course load. *Financial support:* In 2009–10, 1 fellowship with full tuition reimbursement (averaging $8,036 per year), 92 research assistantships with full tuition reimbursements (averaging $8,555 per year), 83 teaching assistantships with full tuition reimbursements (averaging $4,661 per year) were awarded; career-related internships or fieldwork, Federal Work-Study, scholarships/grants, traineeships, health care benefits, tuition waivers (full), and unspecified assistantships also available. Support available to part-time students. Financial award application deadline: 1/15. *Unit head:* Dr. Linda L. Griffin, Graduate Program Director, 413-545-6984, Fax: 413-545-2873. *Application contact:* Jean M. Ames, Supervisor of Admissions, 413-545-0722, Fax: 413-577-0010, E-mail: gradadm@grad.umass.edu.

University of Massachusetts Lowell, Graduate School of Education, Lowell, MA 01854-2881. Offers administration, planning, and policy (CAGS); curriculum and instruction (M Ed, CAGS); educational administration (M Ed); language arts and literacy (Ed D); leadership in schooling (Ed D); math and science education (Ed D); reading and language (M Ed, CAGS). *Accreditation:* NCATE. Part-time and evening/weekend programs available. Postbaccalaureate distance learning degree programs offered (no on-campus study). Terminal master's awarded for partial completion of doctoral program. *Degree requirements:* For doctorate, thesis/dissertation. *Entrance requirements:* For master's, doctorate, and CAGS, GRE General Test. Additional exam requirements/recommendations for international students: Required—TOEFL. Electronic applications accepted.

University of Miami, Graduate School, School of Education, Department of Teaching and Learning, Program in Teaching and Learning, Coral Gables, FL 33124. Offers language and literacy learning in multilingual settings (PhD); mathematics and science education (PhD); special education (PhD). *Students:* 30 full-time (22 women); includes 11 minority (3 African Americans, 8 Hispanic Americans), 7 international. Average age 35. 21 applicants, 43% accepted, 7 enrolled. In 2009, 5 doctorates awarded. *Degree requirements:* For doctorate, thesis/dissertation, qualifying exam. *Entrance requirements:* For doctorate, GRE General Test. Additional exam requirements/recommendations for international students: Required—TOEFL (minimum score 550 paper-based; 80 iBT); Recommended—IELTS (minimum score 6.5). *Application deadline:* For fall admission, 2/15 for domestic students, 10/15 for international students. Application fee: $65. Electronic applications accepted. *Financial support:* In 2009–10, 25 students received support. Application deadline: 3/1. *Faculty research:* Teacher education, multicultural education, technology, second language acquisition, math and science education. *Unit head:* Dr. Batya Elbaum, Associate Department Chairperson, 305-284-4218, Fax: 305-284-4439, E-mail: elbaum@miami.edu. *Application contact:* Tinisha Hollinshead, Admission Coordinator, 305-284-2102, Fax: 305-284-6998, E-mail: tinisha@miami.edu.

University of Michigan, Horace H. Rackham School of Graduate Studies, School of Education, Programs in Educational Studies, Ann Arbor, MI 48109. Offers cross specialization (PhD); curriculum development (MA); early childhood education (MA, PhD); educational administration and policy (MA, PhD); educational foundations and policy (MA, PhD); English education (MA); English language learning in school settings (MA); learning technologies (MA, PhD); literacy, language, and culture (MA, PhD); mathematics education (MA, PhD); postsecondary science education (MS); research methods (MA); science education (MA, PhD); social studies education (MA); teaching and teacher education (PhD); MA/Certification; MBA/MA; PhD/MA. Terminal master's awarded for partial completion of doctoral program. *Degree requirements:* For master's, thesis (for some programs); for doctorate, comprehensive exam, thesis/dissertation. *Entrance requirements:* For master's and doctorate, GRE General Test. Additional exam requirements/recommendations for international students: Required—TOEFL (minimum score 600 paper-based; 250 computer-based). *Application deadline:* For fall admission, 12/1 priority date for domestic students, 12/1 for international students. Application fee: $60 ($75 for international students). Electronic applications accepted. *Expenses:* Tuition, state resident: full-time $17,286; part-time $1099 per credit hour. Tuition, nonresident: full-time $34,944; part-time $2080 per credit hour. Required fees: $95 per semester. Tuition and fees vary according to course load, degree level and program. *Financial support:* Applicants required to submit FAFSA. *Unit head:* Dr. Addison Stone, Chairperson, 734-763-7500, Fax: 734-615-1290, E-mail: addison@umich.edu. *Application contact:* Laura Mayers, Student Services Assistant, 734-764-7563, Fax: 734-763-1495, E-mail: ed.grad.admit@umich.edu.

University of Michigan–Dearborn, School of Education, Program in Science Education, Dearborn, MI 48126. Offers MS. Part-time and evening/weekend programs available. Postbaccalaureate distance learning degree programs offered (minimal on-campus study). *Faculty:* 11 full-time (7 women), 1 part-time/adjunct (0 women). *Students:* 20 part-time (16 women). Average age 35. 3 applicants, 100% accepted, 3 enrolled. In 2009, 10 master's awarded. *Entrance requirements:* For master's, Michigan Test for Teacher Certification, minimum GPA of 3.0, 2 letters of recommendation from supervisors or university faculty. Additional exam requirements/recommendations for international students: Required—TOEFL (minimum score 560 paper-based; 220 computer-based; 84 iBT), TWE. *Application deadline:* For fall admission, 9/5 priority date for domestic students, 9/5 for international students; for winter admission, 12/22 for domestic and international students; for spring admission, 5/5 for domestic and international students. Applications are processed on a rolling basis. Application fee: $30. Electronic applications accepted. *Expenses:* Tuition, state resident: part-time $504.10 per credit hour. Tuition, nonresident: part-time $957.90 per credit hour. *Financial support:* Available to part-time students. Applicants required to submit FAFSA. *Faculty research:* Inquiry pedagogy. *Unit head:* Dr. Susan A. Everett, Program Coordinator, 313-593-5133, Fax: 313-593-4748, E-mail: everetts@umd.umich.edu. *Application contact:* Elizabeth M. Morden, Graduate Secretary, 313-583-6333, Fax: 313-593-4748, E-mail: emorden@umd.umich.edu.

University of Minnesota, Twin Cities Campus, Graduate School, College of Education and Human Development, Department of Curriculum and Instruction, Program in Teaching, Min-

Science Education

University of Minnesota, Twin Cities Campus (continued)
neapolis, MN 55455-0213. Offers Chinese (M Ed); earth science (M Ed); elementary special education (M Ed); English (M Ed); English as a second language (M Ed); French (M Ed); German (M Ed); Hebrew (M Ed); Japanese (M Ed); life sciences (M Ed); mathematics (M Ed); middle school science (M Ed); science (M Ed); second languages and cultures (M Ed); social studies (M Ed); Spanish (M Ed). *Students:* 263 full-time (186 women), 117 part-time (83 women); includes 32 minority (10 African Americans, 2 American Indian/Alaska Native, 17 Asian Americans or Pacific Islanders, 3 Hispanic Americans), 4 international. Average age 27. 363 applicants, 74% accepted, 259 enrolled. In 2009, 497 master's awarded. *Unit head:* Dr. Ruth Thomas, Chair, 612-624-4772, Fax: 612-624-8277, E-mail: thoma006@umn.edu. *Application contact:* Dr. Mary Trettin, Associate Dean, 612-625-6501, Fax: 612-626-1580, E-mail: mtrettin@umn.edu.

University of Missouri, Graduate School, College of Education, Department of Learning, Teaching and Curriculum, Columbia, MO 65211. Offers agricultural education (M Ed, PhD, Ed S); art education (M Ed, PhD, Ed S); business and office education (M Ed, PhD, Ed S); early childhood education (M Ed, PhD, Ed S); elementary education (M Ed, PhD, Ed S); English education (M Ed, PhD, Ed S); foreign language education (M Ed, PhD, Ed S); health education and promotion (M Ed, PhD); learning and instruction (M Ed); marketing education (M Ed, PhD, Ed S); mathematics education (M Ed, PhD, Ed S); music education (M Ed, PhD, Ed S); reading education (M Ed, PhD, Ed S); science education (M Ed, PhD, Ed S); social studies education (M Ed, PhD, Ed S); vocational education (M Ed, PhD, Ed S). Part-time programs available. Terminal master's awarded for partial completion of doctoral program. *Degree requirements:* For doctorate, thesis/dissertation. *Entrance requirements:* For master's and Ed S, GRE General Test or MAT, minimum GPA of 3.0; for doctorate, GRE General Test, minimum GPA of 3.0. Additional exam requirements/recommendations for international students: Required—TOEFL (minimum score 600 paper-based; 250 computer-based; 100 iBT). Electronic applications accepted.

University of Nebraska at Kearney, College of Graduate Study, College of Natural and Social Sciences, Department of Biology, Kearney, NE 68849-0001. Offers biology (MS); science education (MS Ed). Part-time and evening/weekend programs available. *Degree requirements:* For master's, thesis optional. *Entrance requirements:* For master's, GRE General Test. Additional exam requirements/recommendations for international students: Required—TOEFL (minimum score 550 paper-based; 213 computer-based). Electronic applications accepted. *Faculty research:* Pollution injury, molecular biology-viral gene expression, prairie range condition modeling, evolution of symbiotic nitrogen fixation.

University of New Hampshire, Graduate School, College of Engineering and Physical Sciences, Department of Chemistry, Durham, NH 03824. Offers chemistry (MS, MST, PhD); chemistry education (PhD). *Faculty:* 28 full-time (17 women). *Students:* 35 full-time (13 women), 18 part-time (7 women); includes 2 minority (1 African American, 1 Hispanic American), 15 international. Average age 31. 55 applicants, 45% accepted, 12 enrolled. In 2009, 7 master's, 3 doctorates awarded. Terminal master's awarded for partial completion of doctoral program. *Degree requirements:* For master's, thesis; for doctorate, one foreign language, thesis/dissertation. *Entrance requirements:* Additional exam requirements/recommendations for international students: Required—TOEFL (minimum score 550 paper-based; 213 computer-based; 80 iBT). *Application deadline:* For fall admission, 4/1 priority date for domestic students, 4/1 for international students; for spring admission, 12/1 for domestic students. Applications are processed on a rolling basis. Application fee: $65. *Expenses:* Tuition, state resident: full-time $10,380; part-time $577 per credit hour. Tuition, nonresident: full-time $24,350; part-time $1002 per credit hour. Required fees: $1550; $387.50 per semester. Tuition and fees vary according to course load and program. *Financial support:* In 2009–10, 44 students received support, including 1 fellowship, 6 research assistantships, 36 teaching assistantships; Federal Work-Study, scholarships/grants, and tuition waivers (full and partial) also available. Support available to part-time students. Financial award application deadline: 2/15. *Faculty research:* Analytical, physical, organic, and inorganic chemistry. *Unit head:* Dr. Chris Bauer, Chairperson, 603-862-1550. *Application contact:* Cindi Rohwer, Coordinator, 603-862-1550, E-mail: chem.dept@unh.edu.

The University of North Carolina at Chapel Hill, Graduate School, School of Education, Program in Secondary Education, Chapel Hill, NC 27599. Offers English (Grades 9-12) (MAT); English as a second language (MAT); French (Grades K-12) (MAT); German (Grades K-12) (MAT); Japanese (Grades K-12) (MAT); Latin (Grades 9-12) (MAT); mathematics (Grades 9-12) (MAT); music (Grades K-12) (MAT); science (Grades 9-12) (MAT); social studies (Grades 9-12) (MAT); Spanish (Grades K-12) (MAT). *Accreditation:* NCATE. *Students:* 53 full-time (35 women), 1 part-time (0 women); includes 8 minority (4 African Americans, 2 Asian Americans or Pacific Islanders, 2 Hispanic Americans), 3 international. Average age 25. 137 applicants, 77% accepted, 54 enrolled. In 2009, 39 master's awarded. *Degree requirements:* For master's, comprehensive exam. *Entrance requirements:* For master's, GRE General Test, minimum GPA of 3.0 during last 2 years of undergraduate course work. Additional exam requirements/recommendations for international students: Required—TOEFL (minimum score 550 paper-based; 79 computer-based). *Application deadline:* For fall admission, 12/15 priority date for domestic and international students. Applications are processed on a rolling basis. Application fee: $77. Electronic applications accepted. *Financial support:* Federal Work-Study available. Support available to part-time students. Financial award application deadline: 3/1; financial award applicants required to submit FAFSA. *Unit head:* Dr. James Trier, Coordinator, 919-843-4627, Fax: 919-962-1533. *Application contact:* Amy Butler, Student Services Assistant, 919-966-1346, Fax: 919-962-1533, E-mail: abutler@email.unc.edu.

The University of North Carolina at Greensboro, Graduate School, School of Education, Department of Curriculum and Instruction, Greensboro, NC 27412-5001. Offers college teaching and adult learning (Certificate); curriculum and instruction (M Ed), including chemistry education, elementary education, English as a second language, French education, instructional technology, mathematics education, middle grades education, reading education, science education, social studies education, Spanish education; curriculum and teaching (PhD), including higher education, teacher education and development; English as a second language (Certificate); higher education (M Ed); supervision (M Ed). *Accreditation:* NCATE. Part-time programs available. *Degree requirements:* For doctorate, thesis/dissertation. *Entrance requirements:* For master's and doctorate, GRE General Test. Additional exam requirements/recommendations for international students: Required—TOEFL. Electronic applications accepted. *Faculty research:* Community college literacy program, middle school mathematics/computer mathematics.

The University of North Carolina at Pembroke, Graduate Studies, Department of Biology, Pembroke, NC 28372-1510. Offers science education (MA). Part-time and evening/weekend programs available. *Degree requirements:* For master's, thesis. *Entrance requirements:* For master's, GRE or MAT, minimum GPA of 3.0 in major or 2.5 overall.

University of Northern Colorado, Graduate School, College of Natural and Health Sciences, School of Biological Sciences, Program in Biological Education, Greeley, CO 80639. Offers PhD. Part-time programs available. *Faculty:* 14 full-time (5 women). *Students:* 12 full-time (4 women); includes 1 minority (Asian American or Pacific Islander). Average age 32. 6 applicants, 50% accepted, 1 enrolled. *Degree requirements:* For doctorate, comprehensive exam, thesis/dissertation. *Entrance requirements:* For doctorate, GRE General Test, 3 letters of recommendation. *Application deadline:* Applications are processed on a rolling basis. Application fee: $50 ($60 for international students). Electronic applications accepted. *Expenses:* Tuition, state resident: full-time $5770; part-time $320.55 per credit hour. Tuition, nonresident: full-time $13,847; part-time $769.27 per credit hour. Required fees: $948.78; $52.72 per credit. *Financial support:* Teaching assistantships available. Financial award application deadline: 3/1; financial award applicants required to submit FAFSA. *Unit head:* Dr. Susan Keenan, Program Coordinator, 970-351-2921, Fax: 970-951-2335. *Application contact:* Linda Sisson, Graduate Student Admission Coordinator, 970-351-1807, Fax: 970-351-2371, E-mail: linda.sisson@unco.edu.

University of Northern Colorado, Graduate School, College of Natural and Health Sciences, School of Chemistry, Earth Sciences and Physics, Program in Chemistry, Greeley, CO 80639. Offers chemistry education (PhD); chemistry: education (MS); chemistry: research (MS). Part-time programs available. *Faculty:* 9 full-time (3 women). *Students:* 12 full-time (5 women), 3 part-time (2 women), 1 international. Average age 31. 15 applicants, 53% accepted, 4 enrolled. In 2009, 2 master's, 3 doctorates awarded. *Degree requirements:* For master's, comprehensive exam, thesis or alternative; for doctorate, comprehensive exam, thesis/dissertation. *Entrance requirements:* For master's, 3 letters of reference; for doctorate, GRE General Test, 3 letters of reference. *Application deadline:* Applications are processed on a rolling basis. Application fee: $50 ($60 for international students). Electronic applications accepted. *Expenses:* Tuition, state resident: full-time $5770; part-time $320.55 per credit hour. Tuition, nonresident: full-time $13,847; part-time $769.27 per credit hour. Required fees: $948.78; $52.72 per credit. *Financial support:* In 2009–10, 6 research assistantships (averaging $4,950 per year), 4 teaching assistantships (averaging $11,019 per year) were awarded; fellowships, unspecified assistantships also available. Financial award application deadline: 3/1; financial award applicants required to submit FAFSA. *Unit head:* Dr. Richard Hyslop, Program Coordinator, 970-351-2559. *Application contact:* Linda Sisson, Graduate Student Admission Coordinator, 970-351-1807, Fax: 970-351-2371, E-mail: linda.sisson@unco.edu.

University of Northern Iowa, Graduate College, College of Natural Sciences, Program in Science Education, Cedar Falls, IA 50614. Offers MA. *Students:* 3 full-time (all women), 14 part-time (10 women). 7 applicants, 71% accepted, 5 enrolled. In 2009, 6 master's awarded. *Degree requirements:* For master's, comprehensive exam (for some programs), thesis or alternative. *Entrance requirements:* For master's, minimum GPA of 3.0. Additional exam requirements/recommendations for international students: Required—TOEFL (minimum score 500 paper-based; 180 computer-based; 61 iBT). *Application deadline:* For fall admission, 8/1 priority date for domestic students. Applications are processed on a rolling basis. Application fee: $30 ($50 for international students). Electronic applications accepted. *Financial support:* Application deadline: 2/1. *Unit head:* Dr. Cherin A. Lee, Director, 319-273-2499, Fax: 319-273-3051, E-mail: cherin.lee@uni.edu. *Application contact:* Laurie S. Russell, Record Analyst, 319-273-2623, Fax: 319-273-6792, E-mail: laurie.russell@uni.edu.

University of North Texas Health Science Center at Fort Worth, Graduate School of Biomedical Sciences, Fort Worth, TX 76107-2699. Offers anatomy and cell biology (MS, PhD); biochemistry and molecular biology (MS, PhD); biomedical sciences (MS, PhD); biotechnology (MS); forensic genetics (MS); integrative physiology (MS, PhD); medical science (MS); microbiology and immunology (MS, PhD); pharmacology (MS, PhD); science education (MS); DO/MS; DO/PhD. Terminal master's awarded for partial completion of doctoral program. *Degree requirements:* For master's, thesis; for doctorate, thesis/dissertation. *Entrance requirements:* For master's and doctorate, GRE General Test. Additional exam requirements/recommendations for international students: Required—TOEFL. *Expenses:* Contact institution. *Faculty research:* Alzheimer's disease, aging, eye diseases, cancer, cardiovascular disease.

University of Oklahoma, Graduate College, College of Education, Department of Instructional Leadership and Academic Curriculum, Norman, OK 73072. Offers education (Certificate); instructional leadership and academic curriculum (M Ed, PhD), including bilingual education, early childhood education, elementary education, English education, math education, reading education, science education, secondary education, social studies education. *Accreditation:* NCATE. Part-time and evening/weekend programs available. *Faculty:* 18 full-time (11 women). *Students:* 44 full-time (36 women), 117 part-time (92 women); includes 35 minority (11 African Americans, 14 American Indian/Alaska Native, 5 Asian Americans or Pacific Islanders, 5 Hispanic Americans), 2 international. 50 applicants, 84% accepted, 32 enrolled. In 2009, 31 master's, 6 doctorates awarded. Terminal master's awarded for partial completion of doctoral program. *Degree requirements:* For doctorate, thesis/dissertation. *Entrance requirements:* For master's, 12 hours of course work in education; for doctorate, GRE General Test, master's degree, minimum graduate GPA of 3.0. Additional exam requirements/recommendations for international students: Required—TOEFL (minimum score 550 paper-based; 213 computer-based). *Application deadline:* For fall admission, 6/1 priority date for domestic students, 4/1 for international students; for spring admission, 11/1 for domestic students, 9/1 for international students. Applications are processed on a rolling basis. Application fee: $40 ($90 for international students). Electronic applications accepted. *Expenses:* Tuition, state resident: full-time $3744; part-time $156 per credit hour. Tuition, nonresident: full-time $13,577; part-time $565.70 per credit hour. Required fees: $2415; $90.10 per credit hour. *Financial support:* In 2009–10, 107 students received support, including 1 research assistantship with partial tuition reimbursement available (averaging $9,630 per year), 6 teaching assistantships with partial tuition reimbursements available (averaging $10,801 per year); scholarships/grants, health care benefits, and unspecified assistantships also available. Financial award applicants required to submit FAFSA. *Faculty research:* English education, mathematics education, reading, science education, social studies education. Total annual research expenditures: $752,908. *Unit head:* Lawrence Baines, Chair, 405-325-1498, Fax: 405-325-4061, E-mail: lbaines@ou.edu. *Application contact:* Lynn Crussel, Administrative Assistant for Graduate Studies, 405-325-4843, Fax: 405-325-4061, E-mail: lcrussel@ou.edu.

University of Pittsburgh, School of Education, Department of Instruction and Learning, Program in Secondary Education, Pittsburgh, PA 15260. Offers English/communications education (M Ed, MAT); foreign languages education (M Ed, MAT); mathematics education (M Ed, MAT, Ed D); science education (M Ed, MAT, MS, Ed D); social studies education (M Ed, MAT). Part-time and evening/weekend programs available. *Students:* 170 full-time (107 women), 70 part-time (54 women); includes 19 minority (11 African Americans, 6 Asian Americans or Pacific Islanders, 2 Hispanic Americans), 10 international. Average age 29. 220 applicants, 72% accepted, 128 enrolled. In 2009, 108 master's, 5 doctorates awarded. *Degree requirements:* For master's, thesis; for doctorate, thesis/dissertation. *Entrance requirements:* For master's, PRAXIS I; for doctorate, GRE General Test. Additional exam requirements/recommendations for international students: Required—TOEFL. *Application deadline:* For fall admission, 2/1 priority date for domestic students; for spring admission, 11/15 priority date for domestic students. Applications are processed on a rolling basis. Application fee: $50. Electronic applications accepted. *Expenses:* Tuition, state resident: full-time $16,402; part-time $665 per credit. Tuition, nonresident: full-time $28,694; part-time $1175 per credit. Required fees: $690; $175 per term. Tuition and fees vary according to program. *Financial support:* Fellowships, teaching assistantships, career-related internships or fieldwork, Federal Work-Study, tuition waivers (partial), and unspecified assistantships available. Support available to part-time students. Financial award application deadline: 3/15; financial award applicants required to submit FAFSA. *Unit head:* Dr. Richard Donato, Chairman, 412-624-7248, Fax: 412-648-7081, E-mail: donato@pitt.edu. *Application contact:* Joan M. Cutone, Director, School of Education Student Service Center, 412-648-2230, Fax: 412-648-1899, E-mail: soeinfo@pitt.edu.

University of Puerto Rico, Río Piedras, College of Education, Program in Curriculum and Teaching, San Juan, PR 00931-3300. Offers biology education (M Ed); chemistry education (M Ed); curriculum and teaching (Ed D); history education (M Ed); mathematics education (M Ed); physics education (M Ed); Spanish education (M Ed). Part-time programs available. *Degree requirements:* For master's, thesis; for doctorate, thesis/dissertation, internship. *Entrance requirements:* For master's, PAEG or GRE, minimum GPA of 3.0, letter of recommendation; for doctorate, GRE or PAEG, master's degree, minimum GPA of 3.0, letter of recommendation (2), interview. *Faculty research:* Curriculum, math teaching.

University of St. Francis, College of Education, Joliet, IL 60435-6169. Offers educational leadership (MS), including reading; elementary education certification (M Ed); reading (MS); secondary education certification (M Ed), including English education, math education, science education, social studies education; special education (M Ed); teaching and learning (MS), including character education, curriculum and instruction, differentiated instruction, technology. *Accreditation:* NCATE. Part-time and evening/weekend programs available. *Faculty:* 10 full-time (8 women), 26 part-time/adjunct (18 women). *Students:* 60 full-time (45 women), 349 part-time (283 women); includes 36 minority (10 African Americans, 2 Asian Americans or Pacific Islanders, 24 Hispanic Americans). Average age 33. 211 applicants, 65% accepted, 102

enrolled. In 2009, 174 master's awarded. *Entrance requirements:* For master's, Illinois Basic Skills Test (M Ed), teaching certificate (MS), minimum undergraduate GPA of 2.75, 2 letters of recommendation, computer competency. Additional exam requirements/recommendations for international students: Required—TOEFL (minimum score 550 paper-based; 213 computer-based). *Application deadline:* Applications are processed on a rolling basis. Application fee: $30. Electronic applications accepted. *Expenses:* Contact institution. *Financial support:* In 2009–10, 254 students received support. Federal Work-Study, scholarships/grants, tuition waivers (partial), and unspecified assistantships available. Support available to part-time students. Financial award applicants required to submit FAFSA. *Unit head:* Dr. John Gambro, Dean, 815-740-3332, Fax: 815-740-2264, E-mail: jgambro@stfrancis.edu. *Application contact:* Sandra Sloka, Director of Admissions for Graduate and Degree Completion Programs, 800-735-7500, Fax: 815-740-5032, E-mail: ssloka@stfrancis.edu.

University of San Diego, School of Leadership and Education Sciences, Department of Learning and Teaching, San Diego, CA 92110-2492. Offers curriculum and instruction (M Ed); mathematics, science and technology education (M Ed); special education (M Ed); special education with deaf and hard of hearing (M Ed); teaching (MAT); TESOL, literacy and culture (M Ed). Part-time and evening/weekend programs available. *Faculty:* 13 full-time (9 women), 24 part-time/adjunct (21 women). *Students:* 77 full-time (63 women), 92 part-time (74 women); includes 46 minority (13 African Americans, 12 Asian Americans or Pacific Islanders, 21 Hispanic Americans), 6 international. Average age 31. 142 applicants, 75% accepted, 59 enrolled. In 2009, 64 master's awarded. *Degree requirements:* For master's, thesis (for some programs). *Entrance requirements:* For master's, minimum GPA of 3.0. Additional exam requirements/recommendations for international students: Required—TOEFL (minimum score 580 paper-based; 237 computer-based; 83 iBT), TWE. *Application deadline:* For fall admission, 7/15 for domestic and international students; for spring admission, 12/1 for domestic and international students. Applications are processed on a rolling basis. Application fee: $45. Electronic applications accepted. *Expenses:* Tuition: Full-time $21,042; part-time $1169 per unit. Required fees: $224. Full-time tuition and fees vary according to course load and degree level. *Financial support:* In 2009–10, 113 students received support. Career-related internships or fieldwork, Federal Work-Study, institutionally sponsored loans, and stipends available. Support available to part-time students. Financial award application deadline: 4/1; financial award applicants required to submit FAFSA. *Faculty research:* Action research methodology, cultural studies, instructional theories and practices, second language acquisition, school reform. *Unit head:* Dr. Judy Mantle, Director, 619-260-7879, Fax: 619-260-6835, E-mail: jmantle@sandiego.edu. *Application contact:* Dr. John Mosby, Associate Director of Graduate Admissions, 619-260-4524, Fax: 619-260-4158, E-mail: grads@sandiego.edu.

University of South Africa, College of Human Sciences, Pretoria, South Africa. Offers adult education (M Ed); African languages (MA, PhD); African politics (MA, PhD); Afrikaans (MA, PhD); ancient history (MA, PhD); ancient Near Eastern studies (MA, PhD); anthropology (MA, PhD); applied linguistics (MA); Arabic (MA, PhD); archaeology (MA); art history (MA); Biblical archaeology (MA); Biblical studies (M Th, D Th, PhD); Christian spirituality (M Th, D Th); church history (M Th, D Th); classical studies (MA, PhD); clinical psychology (MA); communication (MA, PhD); comparative education (M Ed, Ed D); consulting psychology (D Admin, D Com, PhD); curriculum studies (M Ed, Ed D); development studies (M Admin, MA, D Admin, PhD); didactics (M Ed, Ed D); education (M Tech); education management (M Ed, Ed D); educational psychology (M Ed); English (MA); environmental education (M Ed); French (MA, PhD); German (MA, PhD); Greek (MA); guidance and counseling (M Ed); health studies (MA, PhD), including health sciences education (MA), health services management (MA), medical and surgical nursing science (critical care general) (MA), midwifery and neonatal nursing science (MA), trauma and emergency care (MA); history (MA, PhD); history of education (Ed D); inclusive education (M Ed, Ed D); information and communications technology policy and regulation (MA); information science (MA, MIS, PhD); international politics (MA, PhD); Islamic studies (MA, PhD); Italian (MA, PhD); Judaica (MA, PhD); linguistics (MA, PhD); mathematical education (M Ed); mathematics education (MA); missiology (M Th, D Th); modern Hebrew (MA, PhD); musicology (MA, MMus, D Mus, PhD); natural science education (M Ed); New Testament (M Th, D Th); Old Testament (D Th); pastoral therapy (M Th, D Th); philosophy (MA); philosophy of education (M Ed, Ed D); politics (MA, PhD); Portuguese (MA, PhD); practical theology (M Th, D Th); psychology (MA, MS, PhD); psychology of education (M Ed, Ed D); public health (MA); religious studies (MA, D Th, PhD); Romance languages (MA); Russian (MA, PhD); Semitic languages (MA, PhD); social behavior studies in HIV/AIDS (MA); social science (mental health) (MA); social science in development studies (MA); social science in psychology (MA); social science in social work (MA); social science in sociology (MA); social work (MSW, DSW, PhD); socio-education (M Ed, Ed D); sociolinguistics (MA); sociology (MA, PhD); Spanish (MA, PhD); systematic theology (M Th, D Th); TESOL (teaching English to speakers of other languages) (MA); theological ethics (M Th, D Th); theory of literature (MA, PhD); urban ministries (D Th); urban ministry (M Th).

University of South Africa, Institute for Science and Technology Education, Pretoria, South Africa. Offers mathematics, science and technology education (M Sc, PhD).

University of South Alabama, Graduate School, College of Education, Department of Leadership and Teacher Education, Mobile, AL 36688-0002. Offers early childhood education (M Ed); educational administration (Ed S); educational leadership (M Ed); elementary education (M Ed); reading education (M Ed); science education (M Ed); secondary education (M Ed); special education (M Ed, Ed S). *Accreditation:* NCATE. Part-time programs available. *Degree requirements:* For master's, comprehensive exam. *Entrance requirements:* For master's, GRE General Test or MAT, minimum GPA of 3.0. *Expenses:* Tuition, state resident: part-time $218 per contact hour. Required fees: $1102 per year.

University of South Carolina, The Graduate School, College of Arts and Sciences, Department of Biological Sciences, Columbia, SC 29208. Offers biology (MS, PhD); biology education (IMA, MAT); ecology, evolution and organismal biology (MS, PhD); molecular, cellular, and developmental biology (MS, PhD). IMA and MAT offered in cooperation with the College of Education. Terminal master's awarded for partial completion of doctoral program. *Degree requirements:* For master's, one foreign language, thesis (for some programs); for doctorate, one foreign language, thesis/dissertation. *Entrance requirements:* For master's and doctorate, GRE General Test, minimum GPA of 3.0 in science. Electronic applications accepted. *Faculty research:* Marine ecology, population and evolutionary biology, molecular biology and genetics, development.

University of South Carolina, The Graduate School, College of Arts and Sciences, Department of Geography, Columbia, SC 29208. Offers geography (MA, MS, PhD); geography education (IMA). IMA and MAT offered in cooperation with the College of Education. Part-time programs available. *Degree requirements:* For master's, comprehensive exam, thesis (for some programs); for doctorate, comprehensive exam, thesis/dissertation. *Entrance requirements:* For master's, GRE General Test; for doctorate, GRE General Test, master's degree. Electronic applications accepted. *Faculty research:* Geographic information processing; economic, cultural, physical, and environmental geography.

University of South Carolina, The Graduate School, College of Education, Department of Instruction and Teacher Education, Program in Secondary Education, Columbia, SC 29208. Offers art education (IMA, MAT); business education (IMA, MAT); English (MAT); foreign language (MAT); health education (MAT); mathematics (MAT); science (IMA, MAT); secondary (Ed D); secondary education (MT, PhD); social studies (MAT); theatre and speech (MAT). IMA and MT offered jointly with the subject areas. *Accreditation:* NCATE. *Degree requirements:* For master's, comprehensive exam, thesis (for some programs), foreign language (MA); for doctorate, one foreign language, comprehensive exam, thesis/dissertation. *Entrance requirements:* For master's, GRE General Test or MAT, teaching certificate (IMA, M Ed), interview; for doctorate, GRE General Test or MAT, interview. *Faculty research:* Middle school programs, professional development, school collaboration.

University of Southern Mississippi, Graduate School, College of Science and Technology, Center for Science and Mathematics Education, Hattiesburg, MS 39406-0001. Offers MS, PhD. *Faculty:* 1 full-time (0 women), 1 (woman) part-time/adjunct. *Students:* 18 full-time (14 women), 23 part-time (20 women); includes 6 minority (3 African Americans, 3 Asian Americans or Pacific Islanders), 3 international. Average age 35. 11 applicants, 91% accepted, 8 enrolled. In 2009, 6 master's, 4 doctorates awarded. *Degree requirements:* For master's, comprehensive exam, thesis or alternative; for doctorate, comprehensive exam, thesis/dissertation. *Entrance requirements:* For master's, GRE General Test, minimum GPA of 2.75 in last 60 hours; for doctorate, GRE General Test, minimum GPA of 3.5. Additional exam requirements/recommendations for international students: Required—TOEFL. *Application deadline:* For fall admission, 3/15 priority date for domestic students, 3/15 for international students. Applications are processed on a rolling basis. Application fee: $35. *Expenses:* Tuition, state resident: full-time $5096; part-time $284 per hour. Tuition, nonresident: full-time $13,052; part-time $726 per hour. Required fees: $402. Tuition and fees vary according to course level and course load. *Financial support:* In 2009–10, 1 fellowship with full tuition reimbursement (averaging $21,000 per year), 1 research assistantship with full tuition reimbursement (averaging $14,500 per year), 8 teaching assistantships with full tuition reimbursements (averaging $8,362 per year) were awarded; Federal Work-Study also available. Financial award application deadline: 3/15; financial award applicants required to submit FAFSA. *Unit head:* Dr. Sherry Herron, Director, 601-266-4739, Fax: 601-266-4741. *Application contact:* Shonna Breland, Manager of Graduate Admissions, 601-266-6563, Fax: 601-266-5138.

University of South Florida, Graduate School, College of Education–Main Campus, Department of Secondary Education, Tampa, FL 33620-9951. Offers English education (M Ed, MA, MAT, PhD); foreign language education/ESOL (M Ed, MA, MAT); instructional technology (M Ed, PhD, Ed S); mathematics education (M Ed, MA, MAT, PhD, Ed S); science education (M Ed, MA, MAT, PhD); second language acquisition/instructional technology (PhD); secondary education (M Ed, PhD); secondary education/TESOL (M Ed, MA); social science education (M Ed, MA, MAT); teaching and learning in the content area (PhD). *Accreditation:* NCATE. Part-time and evening/weekend programs available. *Faculty:* 28 full-time (17 women), 3 part-time/adjunct (1 woman). *Students:* 144 full-time (97 women), 322 part-time (212 women); includes 100 minority (32 African Americans, 4 American Indian/Alaska Native, 17 Asian Americans or Pacific Islanders, 47 Hispanic Americans), 25 international. Average age 30. 230 applicants, 67% accepted, 122 enrolled. In 2009, 122 master's, 14 doctorates, 1 other advanced degree awarded. *Degree requirements:* For master's, variable foreign language requirement, comprehensive exam; for doctorate, variable foreign language requirement, comprehensive exam, thesis/dissertation. *Entrance requirements:* For master's, GRE General Test or General Knowledge Test, minimum GPA of 3.0; for doctorate, GRE General Test, minimum GPA of 3.5; for Ed S, GRE General Test. Additional exam requirements/recommendations for international students: Required—TOEFL (minimum score 550 paper-based; 213 computer-based; 79 iBT). *Application deadline:* For fall admission, 2/15 for domestic students, 1/2 for international students; for spring admission, 10/15 for domestic students, 6/1 for international students. Application fee: $30. Electronic applications accepted. *Financial support:* In 2009–10, 7 students received support, including 1 research assistantship with full tuition reimbursement available (averaging $10,000 per year), 55 teaching assistantships with full and partial tuition reimbursements available (averaging $7,900 per year); scholarships/grants and unspecified assistantships also available. Financial award application deadline: 4/15; financial award applicants required to submit FAFSA. *Faculty research:* English language learners/multicultural, social science education, mathematics education, science education, instructional technology. Total annual research expenditures: $336,023. *Unit head:* Dr. Stephen Thornton, Chairperson, 813-974-3533, Fax: 813-974-3837, E-mail: thornton@usf.edu. *Application contact:* Dr. James White, Program Director, 813-974-1629, Fax: 813-974-3837, E-mail: jwhite@usf.edu.

The University of Tampa, Program in Teaching, Tampa, FL 33606-1490. Offers curriculum and instruction (M Ed); math education (MAT); science education (MAT); social science education (MAT). Part-time and evening/weekend programs available. *Faculty:* 9 full-time (6 women), 5 part-time/adjunct (4 women). *Students:* 1 full-time (0 women), 68 part-time (51 women); includes 11 minority (3 African Americans, 1 Asian American or Pacific Islander, 7 Hispanic Americans), 1 international. Average age 30. 119 applicants, 71% accepted, 69 enrolled. In 2009, 36 master's awarded. *Degree requirements:* For master's, comprehensive exam, thesis. *Entrance requirements:* For master's, General Knowledge Test, GRE General Test, SAE Subject Area Exam, bachelor's degree in education or professional teaching certificate. Additional exam requirements/recommendations for international students: Required—TOEFL (minimum score 577 paper-based; 230 computer-based; 90 iBT), IELTS (minimum score 7). *Application deadline:* For fall admission, 5/1 for domestic students. Application fee: $40. *Expenses:* Tuition: Part-time $488 per credit hour. *Financial support:* In 2009–10, 67 students received support. Applicants required to submit FAFSA. *Unit head:* Dr. Martha Harrison, Associate Professor of Education, 813-253-3333 Ext. 3373, E-mail: mharrison@ut.edu. *Application contact:* Karen Full, Director of Admissions for Graduate and Continuing Studies, 813-257-3642, E-mail: kfull@ut.edu.

The University of Tennessee, Graduate School, College of Education, Health and Human Sciences, Program in Education, Knoxville, TN 37996. Offers art education (MS); counseling education (PhD); cultural studies in education (PhD); curriculum (MS, Ed S); curriculum, educational research and evaluation (Ed D, PhD); early childhood education (PhD); early childhood special education (MS); education of deaf and hard of hearing (MS); educational administration and policy studies (Ed D, PhD); educational administration and supervision (Ed S); educational psychology (Ed D, PhD); elementary education (MS, Ed S); elementary teaching (MS); English education (MS, Ed S); exercise science (PhD); foreign language/ESL education (MS, Ed S); instructional technology (MS, Ed D, PhD, Ed S); literacy, language and ESL education (PhD); literacy, language education, and ESL education (Ed D); mathematics education (MS, Ed S); modified and comprehensive special education (MS); reading education (MS, Ed S); school counseling (Ed S); school psychology (PhD, Ed S); science education (MS, Ed S); secondary teaching (MS); social foundations (MS); social science education (MS, Ed S); socio-cultural foundations of sports and education (PhD); special education (Ed S); teacher education (Ed D, PhD). *Accreditation:* NCATE. Part-time and evening/weekend programs available. *Degree requirements:* For master's and Ed S, thesis optional; for doctorate, variable foreign language requirement, thesis/dissertation. *Entrance requirements:* For master's, minimum GPA of 2.7; for doctorate and Ed S, GRE General Test, minimum GPA of 2.7. Additional exam requirements/recommendations for international students: Required—TOEFL. Electronic applications accepted. *Expenses:* Tuition, state resident: full-time $6826; part-time $380 per semester hour. Tuition, nonresident: full-time $21,844; part-time $1147 per semester hour. Tuition and fees vary according to program.

The University of Texas at Austin, Graduate School, College of Education, Program in Science and Mathematics Education, Austin, TX 78712-1111. Offers M Ed, MA, PhD. *Entrance requirements:* For master's and doctorate, GRE General Test. Electronic applications accepted.

The University of Texas at Dallas, School of Natural Sciences and Mathematics, Programs in Science and Mathematics Education, Richardson, TX 75080. Offers mathematics education (MAT); science education (MAT). Part-time and evening/weekend programs available. Post-baccalaureate distance learning degree programs offered (minimal on-campus study). *Faculty:* 8 full-time (1 woman). *Students:* 13 full-time (9 women), 53 part-time (39 women); includes 15 minority (7 African Americans, 5 Asian Americans or Pacific Islanders, 3 Hispanic Americans), 3 international. Average age 37. 58 applicants, 60% accepted, 29 enrolled. In 2009, 25 master's awarded. *Degree requirements:* For master's, thesis optional. *Entrance requirements:* For master's, GRE General Test, minimum GPA of 3.0 in upper-level coursework in field. Additional exam requirements/recommendations for international students: Required—TOEFL (minimum score 550 paper-based; 213 computer-based). *Application deadline:* For fall admission, 7/15 for domestic students, 5/1 priority date for international students; for spring admission, 11/15 for domestic students, 9/1 priority date for international students. Applications are processed on a rolling basis. Application fee: $50 ($100 for international students). Electronic applications accepted. *Expenses:* Tuition, state resident: full-time $11,068; part-time $461 per credit hour. Tuition, nonresident: full-time $21,178; part-time $882 per credit hour. Tuition and fees vary according to course load. *Financial support:* In 2009–10, 2 students received

Science Education

The University of Texas at Dallas (continued)

support, including 1 research assistantship with full tuition reimbursement available (averaging $13,500 per year), 2 teaching assistantships with full tuition reimbursements available (averaging $13,500 per year); fellowships, career-related internships or fieldwork, Federal Work-Study, institutionally sponsored loans, scholarships/grants, and unspecified assistantships also available. Support available to part-time students. Financial award application deadline: 4/30; financial award applicants required to submit FAFSA. *Faculty research:* Techniques for training teachers, philosophic definitions of science held by working scientists, science teachers, science students. *Unit head:* Dr. Robert Hillborn, Department Head, 972-883-2496, Fax: 972-883-6796, E-mail: scimathed@utdallas.edu. *Application contact:* Information Contact, 972-883-2496, Fax: 972-883-6796, E-mail: scimathed@utdallas.edu.

The University of Texas at El Paso, Graduate School, College of Science, Teaching Science Program, El Paso, TX 79968-0001. Offers MAT. Part-time and evening/weekend programs available. *Students:* 25 (15 women); includes 19 minority (2 African Americans, 17 Hispanic Americans), 1 international. *Degree requirements:* For master's, thesis optional. *Entrance requirements:* For master's, minimum GPA of 3.0. Additional exam requirements/recommendations for international students: Required—TOEFL; Recommended—IELTS. *Application deadline:* For fall admission, 8/1 for domestic students, 3/1 for international students; for spring admission, 11/1 for domestic students, 9/1 for international students. Applications are processed on a rolling basis. Application fee: $45 ($80 for international students). Electronic applications accepted. *Financial support:* Fellowships with tuition reimbursements, research assistantships with tuition reimbursements, teaching assistantships with tuition reimbursements, institutionally sponsored loans, scholarships/grants, health care benefits, tuition waivers (partial), and unspecified assistantships available. Support available to part-time students. Financial award application deadline: 3/15; financial award applicants required to submit FAFSA. *Unit head:* Dr. Laura Serpa, Coordinator, 915-747-6085, Fax: 915-747-6807, E-mail: lfserpa@utep.edu. *Application contact:* Dr. Patricia D. Witherspoon, Dean of the Graduate School, 915-747-5491, Fax: 915-747-5788, E-mail: withersp@utep.edu.

University of the Incarnate Word, School of Graduate Studies and Research, School of Mathematics, Science, and Engineering, Program in Mathematics, San Antonio, TX 78209-6397. Offers mathematics teaching (MA); research statistics (MS). Part-time and evening/weekend programs available. *Students:* 1 full-time (0 women), 1 (woman) part-time; includes 1 minority (Hispanic American). Average age 49. In 2009, 2 master's awarded. *Degree requirements:* For master's, capstone or prerequisite knowledge (for research statistics). *Entrance requirements:* For master's, GRE (minimum score 800 verbal and quantitative), 18 hours of undergraduate mathematics with minimum GPA of 3.0; letter of recommendation by a professional in the field, writing sample, teaching experience at the precollege level. Additional exam requirements/recommendations for international students: Required—TOEFL (minimum score 560 paper-based; 220 computer-based; 83 iBT). *Application deadline:* Applications are processed on a rolling basis. Application fee: $20. Electronic applications accepted. *Expenses:* Tuition: Full-time $12,150; part-time $675 per credit hour. Required fees: $83 per credit hour. *Financial support:* Federal Work-Study and scholarships/grants available. Financial award applicants required to submit FAFSA. *Unit head:* Dr. Zhanbo Yang, Graduate Programs Coordinator, 210-283-5008, Fax: 210-829-3153, E-mail: yang@uiwtx.edu. *Application contact:* Andrea Cyterski-Acosta, Dean of Enrollment, 210-829-6005, Fax: 210-829-3921, E-mail: admis@uiwtx.edu.

The University of Toledo, College of Graduate Studies, College of Education, Department of Curriculum and Instruction, Program in Education and Biology, Toledo, OH 43606-3390. Offers MES.

The University of Toledo, College of Graduate Studies, College of Education, Department of Curriculum and Instruction, Program in Education and Chemistry, Toledo, OH 43606-3390. Offers MES.

The University of Toledo, College of Graduate Studies, College of Education, Department of Curriculum and Instruction, Program in Education and Geology, Toledo, OH 43606-3390. Offers MES.

The University of Toledo, College of Graduate Studies, College of Education, Department of Curriculum and Instruction, Program in Education and Physics, Toledo, OH 43606-3390. Offers MES.

University of Tulsa, Graduate School, College of Arts and Sciences, School of Education, Program in Mathematics and Science Education, Tulsa, OK 74104-3189. Offers MSMSE. Part-time programs available. *Students:* 2 part-time (both women); includes 1 minority (African American). Average age 46. 4 applicants, 50% accepted, 1 enrolled. In 2009, 1 master's awarded. *Entrance requirements:* For master's, GRE General Test. Additional exam requirements/recommendations for international students: Required—TOEFL (minimum score 575 paper-based; 231 computer-based), IELTS (minimum score 6.5). *Application deadline:* Applications are processed on a rolling basis. Application fee: $40. Electronic applications accepted. *Expenses:* Tuition: Full-time $16,182; part-time $899 per credit hour. Required fees: $4 per credit hour. Tuition and fees vary according to course load. *Financial support:* Fellowships with full and partial tuition reimbursements, research assistantships, teaching assistantships with full and partial tuition reimbursements, Federal Work-Study, scholarships/grants, tuition waivers (full and partial), and unspecified assistantships available. Support available to part-time students. Financial award application deadline: 2/1; financial award applicants required to submit FAFSA. *Unit head:* Dr. David Brown, Advisor, 918-631-2719, Fax: 918-631-2133, E-mail: david-brown@utulsa.edu. *Application contact:* Dr. David Brown, Advisor, 918-631-2719, Fax: 918-631-2133, E-mail: david-brown@utulsa.edu.

University of Utah, Graduate School, College of Science, Department of Chemistry, Salt Lake City, UT 84112-0850. Offers chemical physics (PhD); chemistry (M Phil, MA, MS, PhD); science teacher education (MS). Part-time programs available. Postbaccalaureate distance learning degree programs offered. *Faculty:* 30 full-time (4 women), 4 part-time/adjunct (1 woman). *Students:* 145 full-time (47 women), 27 part-time (12 women); includes 10 minority (1 African American, 5 Asian Americans or Pacific Islanders, 4 Hispanic Americans), 68 international. Average age 28. 352 applicants, 24% accepted, 31 enrolled. In 2009, 9 master's, 29 doctorates awarded. Terminal master's awarded for partial completion of doctoral program. *Degree requirements:* For master's, thesis optional, 20 hours course work, 10 hours research; for doctorate, thesis/dissertation, 18 hours course work, 14 hours research. *Entrance requirements:* For master's and doctorate, GRE General Test, minimum GPA of 3.0. Additional exam requirements/recommendations for international students: Required—TOEFL (minimum score 620 paper-based; 260 computer-based; 105 iBT). *Application deadline:* For fall admission, 4/1 for domestic and international students; for spring admission, 11/1 for domestic and international students. Application fee: $55 ($65 for international students). Electronic applications accepted. *Expenses:* Tuition, state resident: full-time $4004; part-time $1674 per semester. Tuition, nonresident: full-time $14,134; part-time $5915 per semester. Required fees: $324 per semester. Tuition and fees vary according to course load, degree level and program. *Financial support:* In 2009–10, 1 fellowship with tuition reimbursement (averaging $22,000 per year), 116 research assistantships with tuition reimbursements (averaging $22,500 per year), 50 teaching assistantships with tuition reimbursements (averaging $22,000 per year) were awarded; scholarships/grants and tuition waivers (full) also available. Financial award application deadline: 4/1; financial award applicants required to submit FAFSA. *Faculty research:* Biological, theoretical, inorganic, organic, and physical-analytical chemistry. Total annual research expenditures: $14.2 million. *Unit head:* Dr. Henry S. White, Chair, 801-585-6256, Fax: 801-581-8433, E-mail: chair@chemistry.utah.edu. *Application contact:* Jo Hoovey, Graduate Coordinator, 801-581-4393, Fax: 801-581-5408, E-mail: jhoovey@chem.utah.edu.

University of Utah, Graduate School, College of Science, Department of Physics and Astronomy, Salt Lake City, UT 84112. Offers chemical physics (PhD); medical physics (MS, PhD); physics (MA, MS, PhD); physics teaching (PhD). Part-time programs available. *Faculty:* 32 full-time (1 woman), 2 part-time/adjunct (0 women). *Students:* 76 full-time (16 women), 25 part-time (6 women); includes 3 minority (1 Asian American or Pacific Islander, 2 Hispanic Americans), 48 international. Average age 30. 135 applicants, 25% accepted, 17 enrolled. In 2009, 5 master's, 14 doctorates awarded. Terminal master's awarded for partial completion of doctoral program. *Degree requirements:* For master's, comprehensive exam (for some programs), thesis or alternative, teaching experience, departmental exam; for doctorate, comprehensive exam, thesis/dissertation, departmental qualifying exam. *Entrance requirements:* For master's and doctorate, GRE General Test, GRE Subject Test, minimum GPA of 3.0. Additional exam requirements/recommendations for international students: Required—TOEFL (minimum score 500 paper-based; 173 computer-based; 69 iBT). *Application deadline:* For fall admission, 2/1 priority date for domestic students, 2/1 for international students. Applications are processed on a rolling basis. Application fee: $55 ($65 for international students). Electronic applications accepted. *Expenses:* Tuition, state resident: full-time $4004; part-time $1674 per semester. Tuition, nonresident: full-time $14,134; part-time $5915 per semester. Required fees: $324 per semester. Tuition and fees vary according to course load, degree level and program. *Financial support:* In 2009–10, 3 fellowships with full tuition reimbursements (averaging $19,000 per year), 27 research assistantships with full and partial tuition reimbursements (averaging $19,420 per year), 45 teaching assistantships with full and partial tuition reimbursements (averaging $14,626 per year) were awarded; Federal Work-Study, institutionally sponsored loans, and scholarships/grants also available. Financial award application deadline: 2/15; financial award applicants required to submit FAFSA. *Faculty research:* High-energy, cosmic-ray, astrophysics, medical physics, condensed matter, relativity applied physics. Total annual research expenditures: $4.7 million. *Unit head:* Dr. David Kieda, Chair, 801-581-6901, Fax: 801-581-4801, E-mail: kieda@physics.utah.edu. *Application contact:* Jackie Hadley, Graduate Secretary, 801-581-6861, Fax: 801-581-4801, E-mail: jackie@physics.utah.edu.

University of Vermont, Graduate College, College of Arts and Sciences, Department of Biology, Burlington, VT 05405. Offers biology (MS, PhD); biology education (MST). *Faculty:* 17. *Students:* 34 (18 women); includes 3 minority (1 African American, 2 Hispanic Americans), 13 international. 43 applicants, 23% accepted, 4 enrolled. In 2009, 3 doctorates awarded. *Degree requirements:* For master's, thesis; for doctorate, thesis/dissertation. *Entrance requirements:* For master's and doctorate, GRE General Test. Additional exam requirements/recommendations for international students: Required—TOEFL (minimum score 550 paper-based; 213 computer-based; 80 iBT). *Application deadline:* For fall admission, 1/15 priority date for domestic students. Applications are processed on a rolling basis. Application fee: $40. Electronic applications accepted. *Expenses:* Tuition, state resident: part-time $508 per credit hour. Tuition, nonresident: part-time $1281 per credit hour. *Financial support:* Fellowships, research assistantships, teaching assistantships available. Financial award application deadline: 3/1. *Unit head:* Dr. Jim Vigoreaux, Chairperson, 802-656-2922. *Application contact:* Dr. Judith Van Houten, Coordinator, 802-656-2922.

University of Victoria, Faculty of Graduate Studies, Faculty of Education, Department of Curriculum and Instruction, Victoria, BC V8W 2Y2, Canada. Offers art education (M Ed, PhD); curriculum studies (M Ed, MA, PhD); early childhood education (M Ed, PhD); educational studies (PhD); language and literacy (M Ed, MA, PhD); mathematics (M Ed, MA, PhD); music education (M Ed, MA, PhD); science (M Ed, MA, PhD); social studies (M Ed, MA); social, cultural and foundational studies (MA, PhD); technology and environmental education (PhD). Part-time programs available. *Degree requirements:* For master's, thesis, project (M Ed); for doctorate, comprehensive exam, thesis/dissertation. *Entrance requirements:* For master's, minimum B average. Additional exam requirements/recommendations for international students: Required—TOEFL (minimum score 575 paper-based; 233 computer-based), IELTS (minimum score 7). Electronic applications accepted. *Faculty research:* Elementary and secondary English, language arts, curriculum theory and practice, educational media and technology, educational administration and leadership, history and philosophy of education.

University of Virginia, College and Graduate School of Arts and Sciences, Department of Physics, Charlottesville, VA 22903. Offers physics (MA, MS, PhD); physics education (MA). *Faculty:* 38 full-time (4 women). *Students:* 96 full-time (24 women), 1 part-time (0 women); includes 1 minority (Asian American or Pacific Islander), 59 international. Average age 26. 201 applicants, 33% accepted, 24 enrolled. In 2009, 15 master's, 9 doctorates awarded. *Degree requirements:* For master's, thesis (for some programs); for doctorate, comprehensive exam, thesis/dissertation. *Entrance requirements:* For master's and doctorate, GRE General Test, GRE Subject Test, 2 or more letters of recommendation. Additional exam requirements/recommendations for international students: Required—TOEFL (minimum score 600 paper-based; 250 computer-based; 90 iBT), IELTS. *Application deadline:* For fall admission, 1/7 for domestic and international students. Applications are processed on a rolling basis. Application fee: $60. Electronic applications accepted. *Financial support:* Fellowships, research assistantships, teaching assistantships available. Financial award applicants required to submit FAFSA. *Unit head:* Dinko Pocanic, Chair, 434-924-3781, Fax: 434-924-4576, E-mail: phys-chair@physics.virginia.edu. *Application contact:* Charles Sackett, Associate Chair for Graduate Studies, 434-924-3781, Fax: 434-924-4576, E-mail: grad-info-request@physics.virginia.edu.

University of Virginia, Curry School of Education, Department of Curriculum, Instruction, and Special Education, Program in Curriculum and Instruction, Charlottesville, VA 22903. Offers curriculum and instruction (M Ed, Ed S); elementary (M Ed, Ed D); English (M Ed, Ed D); foreign language (M Ed); mathematics (M Ed, Ed D); reading (M Ed, Ed D, Ed S); science (Ed D); social studies (M Ed). *Students:* 12 full-time (8 women), 30 part-time (24 women); includes 2 minority (1 Asian American or Pacific Islander, 1 Hispanic American), 1 international. Average age 36. 55 applicants, 69% accepted, 26 enrolled. In 2009, 247 master's, 14 doctorates, 10 other advanced degrees awarded. *Degree requirements:* For master's, comprehensive exam (for some programs); for doctorate, comprehensive exam, thesis/dissertation; for Ed S, comprehensive exam. *Entrance requirements:* For master's, doctorate, and Ed S, GRE General Test, 2 letters of recommendation. Additional exam requirements/recommendations for international students: Required—TOEFL (minimum score 600 paper-based; 250 computer-based; 90 iBT), IELTS (minimum score 7). *Application deadline:* Applications are processed on a rolling basis. Application fee: $60. Electronic applications accepted. *Financial support:* Fellowships with tuition reimbursements, research assistantships with tuition reimbursements, teaching assistantships with tuition reimbursements available. Financial award application deadline: 1/5; financial award applicants required to submit FAFSA.

University of Virginia, Curry School of Education, Program in Education, Charlottesville, VA 22903. Offers administration and supervision (PhD); applied developmental science (PhD); counselor education (PhD); curriculum and instruction (PhD); early childhood-developmental risk (MT); education evaluation (PhD); educational psychology (PhD); educational research (PhD); elementary (MT, PhD); English education (MT, PhD); foreign language education (MT); higher education (PhD); instructional technology (PhD); kinesiology (MT, PhD); math education (PhD); reading education (PhD); research statistics and evaluation (PhD); school psychology (PhD); science education (PhD); social studies education (MT, PhD); special education (PhD); world languages education (MT). *Students:* 336 full-time (239 women), 88 part-time (54 women); includes 43 minority (24 African Americans, 2 American Indian/Alaska Native, 11 Asian Americans or Pacific Islanders, 6 Hispanic Americans), 18 international. Average age 27. 199 applicants, 48% accepted, 55 enrolled. In 2009, 127 master's, 52 doctorates awarded. *Degree requirements:* For master's, comprehensive exam (for some programs), field project; for doctorate, comprehensive exam, thesis/dissertation. *Entrance requirements:* For doctorate, GRE General Test. Additional exam requirements/recommendations for international students: Required—TOEFL (minimum score 600 paper-based; 250 computer-based; 90 iBT), IELTS (minimum score 7). *Application deadline:* Applications are processed on a rolling basis. Application fee: $60. Electronic applications accepted. *Financial support:* Fellowships, research assistantships, teaching assistantships available. Financial award application deadline: 1/5; financial award applicants required to submit FAFSA.

University of Washington, Graduate School, College of Education, Seattle, WA 98195. Offers curriculum and instruction (M Ed, Ed D, PhD), including educational technology, general curriculum (Ed D, PhD), language, literacy, and culture, mathematics education, multicultural education, reading and language arts education (Ed D), science education, social studies

education, teaching and curriculum (M Ed); educational leadership and policy studies (M Ed, Ed D, PhD), including administration (Ed D), educational policy, organization, and leadership (M Ed, PhD), higher education, leadership for learning (Ed D), social and cultural foundations of education (M Ed, PhD); educational psychology (M Ed, PhD), including educational psychology (PhD), human development and cognition (M Ed), learning sciences, measurement, statistics and research design (M Ed), school psychology (M Ed); instructional leadership (M Ed); intercollegiate athletic leadership (M Ed); special education (M Ed, Ed D, PhD), including early childhood special education (M Ed), emotional and behavioral disabilities (M Ed), learning disabilities (M Ed), low-incidence disabilities (M Ed), severe disabilities (M Ed), special education (Ed D, PhD); teacher education (MIT). *Accreditation:* APA. Part-time and evening/weekend programs available. *Degree requirements:* For master's, thesis optional; for doctorate, thesis/dissertation. *Entrance requirements:* For master's and doctorate, GRE General Test, minimum GPA of 3.0. Additional exam requirements/recommendations for international students: Required—TOEFL. Electronic applications accepted. *Faculty research:* School restructuring/effective schools, special education interventions, literacy and writing, technology, school partnerships, teacher preparation.

University of Washington, Graduate School, Interdisciplinary Program in Biology for Teachers, Seattle, WA 98195. Offers MS. Part-time programs available. *Degree requirements:* For master's, research project and oral exam. *Entrance requirements:* For master's, GRE General Test, minimum GPA of 3.0, teaching certificate or professional teaching experience. Electronic applications accepted.

University of Washington, Tacoma, Graduate Programs, Program in Education, Tacoma, WA 98402-3100. Offers educational administrator (M Ed); K-8 teacher education (M Ed); professional certification (M Ed); secondary science (M Ed); special education (M Ed). Part-time and evening/weekend programs available. *Faculty:* 13 full-time (8 women), 9 part-time/adjunct (8 women). *Students:* 85 full-time (66 women), 118 part-time (99 women); includes 24 minority (4 African Americans, 9 Asian Americans or Pacific Islanders, 11 Hispanic Americans). Average age 33. 36 applicants, 75% accepted, 23 enrolled. In 2009, 68 master's awarded. *Entrance requirements:* For master's, official sealed transcript from every college/university attended, personal goal statement, letters of recommendation, copy of valid teaching certificate. *Application deadline:* For fall admission, 8/1 for domestic students; for winter admission, 11/1 priority date for domestic students; for spring admission, 2/1 priority date for domestic students. Applications are processed on a rolling basis. Application fee: $65. Electronic applications accepted. *Expenses:* Tuition, state resident: full-time $10,660; part-time $484 per credit. Tuition, nonresident: full-time $24,000; part-time $1119 per credit. Required fees: $150 per term. Tuition and fees vary according to course load and program. *Faculty research:* Global learning communities for English/Chinese languages, evaluation of mathematics and reading intervention programs, response to intervention, school wide behavioral and emotional support, mathematics education and culturally responsive mathematics education. *Unit head:* Dr. Karen Landenburger, Chancellor, 253-692-4430, Fax: 253-692-5612, E-mail: uwted@u.washington.edu. *Application contact:* Dr. Carla Van Rossum, Recruiter/Advisor, 253-692-4430, Fax: 253-692-5612, E-mail: uwted@u.washington.edu.

The University of West Alabama, School of Graduate Studies, College of Natural Sciences and Mathematics, Department of Biological Sciences, Livingston, AL 35470. Offers MAT. *Accreditation:* NCATE.

University of West Florida, College of Arts and Sciences: Sciences, School of Allied Health and Life Sciences, Department of Biology, Program in Biology Education, Pensacola, FL 32514-5750. Offers MST. Part-time programs available. *Students:* 1 part-time (0 women); includes Hispanic American. Average age 42. In 2009, 2 master's awarded. *Entrance requirements:* For master's, GRE General Test, bachelor's degree in biological science. Additional exam requirements/recommendations for international students: Required—TOEFL (minimum score 550 paper-based; 213 computer-based). *Application deadline:* For fall admission, 6/1 for domestic students, 5/15 for international students; for spring admission, 11/1 for domestic students, 10/1 for international students. Applications are processed on a rolling basis. *Expenses:* Tuition, state resident: full-time $4982; part-time $260 per credit hour. Tuition, nonresident: full-time $20,059; part-time $919 per credit hour. Required fees: $1247; $52 per credit hour. *Unit head:* Dr. George L. Stewart, Chairperson, 850-474-2748. *Application contact:* Terry McCray, Assistant Director of Graduate Admissions, 850-473-7718, Fax: 850-473-7714, E-mail: gradadmissions@uwf.edu.

University of West Georgia, Graduate School, College of Education, Department of Curriculum and Instruction, Carrollton, GA 30118. Offers art education (M Ed); art teacher education (Ed S); biology/secondary education (Ed S); business education (M Ed, Ed S); early childhood education (M Ed, Ed S); economics/secondary teacher education (Ed S); English teacher education (Ed S); French language teacher education (Ed S); history teacher education (Ed S); mathematics teacher education (Ed S); middle grades education (M Ed, Ed S); reading education (M Ed, Ed S); science teacher education (Ed S); secondary education (M Ed, Ed S); social science teacher education (Ed S); Spanish language teacher education (Ed S). Part-time and evening/weekend programs available. *Faculty:* 18 full-time (15 women), 7 part-time/adjunct (6 women). *Students:* 119 full-time (101 women), 358 part-time (280 women); includes 109 minority (97 African Americans, 3 American Indian/Alaska Native, 2 Asian Americans or Pacific Islanders, 7 Hispanic Americans). Average age 33. 193 applicants, 82% accepted, 34 enrolled. In 2009, 109 master's, 27 Ed Ss awarded. *Degree requirements:* For master's, comprehensive exam; for Ed S, research project. *Entrance requirements:* For master's, GRE General Test or MAT, minimum GPA of 2.7; for Ed S, GRE General Test, master's degree, minimum graduate GPA of 2.7. *Application deadline:* For fall admission, 7/17 for domestic students; for spring admission, 11/20 for domestic students. Applications are processed on a rolling basis. Application fee: $30. Electronic applications accepted. *Expenses:* Tuition, state resident: full-time $2952; part-time $164 per semester hour. Tuition, nonresident: full-time $11,808; part-time $656 per semester hour. Required fees: $42.90 per semester hour. $307 per semester. Tuition and fees vary according to course load. *Financial support:* In 2009–10, 5 research assistantships with full tuition reimbursements (averaging $3,000 per year) were awarded; career-related internships or fieldwork and scholarships/grants also available. Support available to part-time students. Financial award applicants required to submit FAFSA. *Unit head:* Dr. Donna Harkins, Chair, 678-839-6066, Fax: 678-839-6559, E-mail: dharkins@westga.edu. *Application contact:* Dr. Charles W. Clark, Dean, 678-839-6508, E-mail: cclark@westga.edu.

University of Wisconsin–Madison, Graduate School, School of Education, Department of Curriculum and Instruction, Madison, WI 53706-1380. Offers art education (MA); curriculum and instruction (MS, PhD); education and mathematics (MA); French education (MA); German education (MA); music education (MS); science education (MS); Spanish education (MA). *Accreditation:* NASM (one or more programs are accredited). *Degree requirements:* For doctorate, thesis/dissertation. Application fee: $56. *Expenses:* Tuition, state resident: part-time $594 per credit. Tuition, nonresident: part-time $1504 per credit. Required fees: $65 per credit. Tuition and fees vary according to course load, program and reciprocity agreements. *Financial support:* Project assistantships available. *Unit head:* Dr. Gloria Ladson-Billings, Chair, 608-262-4000. *Application contact:* Dr. Gloria Ladson-Billings, Chair, 608-262-4000.

University of Wisconsin–River Falls, Outreach and Graduate Studies, College of Arts and Science, Program in Science, River Falls, WI 54022. Offers science education (MSE). Part-time programs available. *Degree requirements:* For master's, comprehensive exam, thesis or alternative. *Entrance requirements:* For master's, minimum GPA of 2.75. Additional exam requirements/recommendations for international students: Required—TOEFL (minimum score 500 paper-based; 65 iBT), IELTS (minimum score 5.5). Electronic applications accepted.

University of Wisconsin–Stevens Point, College of Letters and Science, Department of Biology, Stevens Point, WI 54481-3897. Offers MST. *Students:* 1 (woman) part-time. *Degree requirements:* For master's, thesis or alternative. *Entrance requirements:* For master's, minimum overall undergraduate GPA of 2.75, bachelor's degree in biology with minimum GPA of 3.0, teacher's license. *Application deadline:* For fall admission, 5/1 priority date for domestic students. Applications are processed on a rolling basis. Application fee: $45. *Expenses:* Tuition, state resident: full-time $7740; part-time $430 per credit hour. Tuition, nonresident: full-time $17,804; part-time $989 per credit hour. Tuition and fees vary according to course load and reciprocity agreements. *Financial support:* Federal Work-Study available. Financial award application deadline: 5/1; financial award applicants required to submit FAFSA. *Unit head:* Dr. Chris Yahnke, Chair, 715-346-2455. *Application contact:* Dr. Eric Wild, Coordinator, 715-346-2159, Fax: 715-346-3624, E-mail: ewild@uwsp.edu.

University of Wyoming, College of Education, Science and Mathematics Teaching Center, Laramie, WY 82070. Offers MS, MST. *Degree requirements:* For master's, thesis. *Entrance requirements:* For master's, GRE General Test, minimum GPA of 3.0, writing sample, 3 letters of recommendation. Electronic applications accepted.

Ursuline College, School of Graduate Studies, Program in Education, Pepper Pike, OH 44124-4398. Offers art education (MA); early childhood education (MA); language arts education (MA); life science education (MA); math education (MA); middle school education (MA); social studies education (MA); special education (MA). *Accreditation:* NCATE. *Faculty:* 1 (woman) full-time, 10 part-time/adjunct (8 women). *Students:* 53 full-time (40 women), 3 part-time (all women); includes 8 minority (7 African Americans, 1 Hispanic American). Average age 34. In 2009, 11 master's awarded. *Degree requirements:* For master's, comprehensive exam. *Entrance requirements:* For master's, minimum undergraduate GPA of 3.0. Additional exam requirements/recommendations for international students: Required—TOEFL (minimum score 500 paper-based; 173 computer-based). *Application deadline:* For fall admission, 8/1 priority date for domestic students. Applications are processed on a rolling basis. Application fee: $25. *Expenses:* Contact institution. *Financial support:* Federal Work-Study available. Financial award application deadline: 3/1. *Unit head:* Karen Godenschwager Nelson, Director, 440-684-8338, Fax: 440-684-6088, E-mail: kgodenschwager@ursuline.edu. *Application contact:* Melanie Steele, Secretary, 440-646-8199, Fax: 440-684-6138, E-mail: gradsch@ursuline.edu.

Vanderbilt University, Graduate School, Department of Physics and Astronomy, Nashville, TN 37240-1001. Offers astronomy (MS); physics (MA, MAT, MS, PhD). *Faculty:* 52 full-time (5 women). *Students:* 66 full-time (16 women), 2 part-time (1 woman); includes 11 minority (5 African Americans, 2 Asian Americans or Pacific Islanders, 4 Hispanic Americans), 16 international. Average age 29. 167 applicants, 21% accepted, 13 enrolled. In 2009, 10 master's, 6 doctorates awarded. *Degree requirements:* For master's, thesis; for doctorate, comprehensive exam, thesis/dissertation, final and qualifying exams. *Entrance requirements:* For master's, GRE General Test; for doctorate, GRE General Test, GRE Subject Test. Additional exam requirements/recommendations for international students: Required—TOEFL (minimum score 570 paper-based; 230 computer-based; 88 iBT). *Application deadline:* For fall admission, 1/15 for domestic and international students. Application fee: $0. Electronic applications accepted. *Financial support:* Fellowships with full and partial tuition reimbursements, research assistantships with full tuition reimbursements, teaching assistantships with full tuition reimbursements, career-related internships or fieldwork, Federal Work-Study, and institutionally sponsored loans available. Financial award application deadline: 1/15; financial award applicants required to submit CSS PROFILE or FAFSA. *Faculty research:* Experimental and theoretical physics, free electron laser, living-state physics, heavy-ion physics, nuclear structure. *Unit head:* Robert J. Scherrer, Chair, 615-322-2828, Fax: 615-343-7263, E-mail: robert.scherrer@vanderbilt.edu. *Application contact:* Richard Haglund, Director of Graduate Studies, 615-322-2828, Fax: 615-343-7263, E-mail: physastro-grad@vanderbilt.edu.

Walden University, Graduate Programs, Richard W. Riley College of Education and Leadership, Minneapolis, MN 55401. Offers administrator leadership for teaching and learning (Ed D, Ed S); curriculum, instruction, and professional development (Ed S); early childhood education (birth-grade 3) (MAT); education (MS, PhD), including adolescent literacy and technology (grades 6-12) (MS), adult education leadership (PhD), community college leadership (PhD), curriculum, instruction, and assessment, early childhood education (PhD), educational leadership (MS), educational technology (PhD), elementary reading and literacy (MS), elementary reading and mathematics (MS), emotional/behavioral disorders (K-12) (MS), general program, higher education (PhD), integrating technology in the classroom (MS), K-12 educational leadership (PhD), learning disabilities (K-12) (MS), literacy and learning in the content areas (MS), mathematics (grades 6-8) (MS), mathematics (grades K-5) (MS), middle level education (grades 5-8) (MS), professional development (MS), science (grades K-8) (MS), self-designed (PhD), special education (PhD), special education (non-licensure) (MS), teacher leadership (grades K-12) (MS); educational leadership and administration (principal preparation) (Ed S); educational technology (Ed S); higher education and adult learning (Ed D); instructional design (Postbaccalaureate Certificate); instructional design and technology (MS), including general program (MS, PhD), online learning, training and performance improvement; special education: emotional/behavioral disorders (K-12) (MAT); special education: learning disabilities (K-12) (MAT); teacher leadership (Ed D, Ed S). Part-time and evening/weekend programs available. Postbaccalaureate distance learning degree programs offered (minimal on-campus study). *Faculty:* 54 full-time, 835 part-time/adjunct. *Students:* 13,940 full-time (11,339 women), 1,940 part-time (1,637 women); includes 4,626 minority (3,795 African Americans, 111 American Indian/Alaska Native, 199 Asian Americans or Pacific Islanders, 521 Hispanic Americans), 124 international. Average age 38. In 2009, 4,688 master's, 190 doctorates awarded. *Degree requirements:* For doctorate, thesis/dissertation (for some programs), residency; for other advanced degree, residency (for some programs). *Entrance requirements:* For master's, bachelor's degree or equivalent in related field; minimum GPA of 2.5; official transcripts; goal statement; access to computer and Internet; for doctorate, master's degree or equivalent in related field; minimum GPA of 3.0; official transcripts; three years' related professional/academic experience (preferred); access to computer and Internet; for other advanced degree, master's degree or equivalent in related field; minimum GPA of 3.0; 3 years related professional/academic experience (preferred); access to computer and Internet (Ed S). Additional exam requirements/recommendations for international students: Required—TOEFL (minimum score 550 paper-based; 213 computer-based), IELTS (minimum score 6.5), or Michigan English Language Assessment Battery (minimum score 82). *Application deadline:* Applications are processed on a rolling basis. Application fee: $50. Electronic applications accepted. *Expenses:* Tuition: Full-time $13,665; part-time $560 per credit. Required fees: $1375. Tuition and fees vary according to course load, degree level and program. *Financial support:* In 2009–10, 2,418 students received support; fellowships, Federal Work-Study, scholarships/grants, unspecified assistantships, and family tuition reduction, active duty/veteran tuition reduction, group tuition reduction, interest-free payment plans available. Support available to part-time students. Financial award applicants required to submit FAFSA. *Unit head:* Dr. Kate Steffens, Dean, 800-925-3368. *Application contact:* Jennifer Hall, Director of Enrollment, 866-4-WALDEN, E-mail: info@waldenu.edu.

Wayne State College, School of Education and Counseling, Department of Educational Foundations and Leadership, Program in Curriculum and Instruction, Wayne, NE 68787. Offers alternative education (MSE); business and information technology education (MSE); communication arts education (MSE); early childhood education (MSE); elementary education (MSE); English as a second language (MSE); English education (MSE); family and consumer sciences education (MSE); industrial technology and vocational education (MSE); learning communities (MSE); mathematics education (MSE); music education (MSE); science education (MSE); social science education (MSE). *Accreditation:* NCATE. Part-time and evening/weekend programs available. *Degree requirements:* For master's, comprehensive exam, thesis optional. *Entrance requirements:* For master's, GRE General Test. Additional exam requirements/recommendations for international students: Required—TOEFL (minimum score 550 paper-based; 213 computer-based).

Wayne State University, College of Education, Division of Teacher Education, Detroit, MI 48202. Offers adult and continuing education (M Ed); art education (M Ed); bilingual/bicultural education (M Ed, MAT); business education (M Ed, MAT); career and technical education (M Ed, Ed D, PhD, Ed S); curriculum and instruction (Ed D, PhD, Ed S); distributive education (M Ed, MAT); early childhood education (M Ed); elementary education (M Ed, MAT, Ed D, PhD, Ed S); elementary education curriculum and instruction (M Ed); English education (M Ed); English education-secondary (M Ed, Ed S); foreign language education (M Ed); general

Science Education

Wayne State University (continued)
education (Ed D, Ed S); health occupations education (M Ed); industrial education (M Ed); mathematics education (M Ed, Ed S); pre-school and parent education (M Ed); reading (M Ed, Ed D, Ed S); reading, languages and literature (Ed D); school music-vocal (M Ed); science education (M Ed, MAT, Ed S); secondary education (MAT); secondary school reading (M Ed); social studies education (M Ed, Ed S), including education-secondary (M Ed); special education (M Ed, Ed D, PhD, Ed S); teacher education (MAT, Ed D, PhD). *Degree requirements:* For doctorate, thesis/dissertation. *Entrance requirements:* For master's, Michigan Basic Skills Test (MA in teaching), minimum GPA of 2.6; for doctorate, minimum undergraduate GPA of 3.0, graduate 3.5; interview, curriculum vitae; references. Additional exam requirements/recommendations for international students: Required—TOEFL (minimum score 550 paper-based; 213 computer-based), TWE (minimum score 6). Electronic applications accepted. *Faculty research:* Reading and writing literacy and literature.

West Chester University of Pennsylvania, Office of Graduate Studies, College of Arts and Sciences, Department of Biology, West Chester, PA 19383. Offers biology (MS, Teaching Certificate); biology—thesis (MS); biology–natural science (MS). Part-time and evening/weekend programs available. *Students:* 6 full-time (4 women), 30 part-time (17 women); includes 4 minority (1 African American, 2 Asian Americans or Pacific Islanders, 1 Hispanic American). Average age 29. 38 applicants, 92% accepted, 16 enrolled. In 2009, 9 master's awarded. *Degree requirements:* For master's, comprehensive exam, thesis (for some programs). *Entrance requirements:* For master's, 3 letters of reference. Additional exam requirements/recommendations for international students: Required—TOEFL (minimum score 550 paper-based; 213 computer-based; 80 iBT). *Application deadline:* For fall admission, 4/15 priority date for domestic students, 3/15 for international students; for spring admission, 10/15 for domestic students, 9/1 for international students. Applications are processed on a rolling basis. Application fee: $35. Electronic applications accepted. *Expenses:* Tuition, state resident: full-time $6666; part-time $370 per credit. Tuition, nonresident: full-time $10,666; part-time $593 per credit. Required fees: $122.56 per credit. *Financial support:* In 2009–10, 8 research assistantships with full and partial tuition reimbursements (averaging $5,000 per year) were awarded; unspecified assistantships also available. Support available to part-time students. Financial award application deadline: 2/15; financial award applicants required to submit FAFSA. *Faculty research:* Cell physiology of insect ovarian follicles, field inventory of reptiles and amphibians. *Unit head:* Dr. Jack Waber, Chair, 610-436-2319, E-mail: jwaber@wcupa.edu. *Application contact:* Dr. Judith Greenamyer, Graduate Coordinator, 610-436-1023, E-mail: jgreenamyer@wcupa.edu.

West Chester University of Pennsylvania, Office of Graduate Studies, College of Arts and Sciences, Department of Physics, West Chester, PA 19383. Offers Teaching Certificate. Part-time and evening/weekend programs available. *Students:* 1 full-time (0 women). Average age 26. 1 applicant, 100% accepted, 1 enrolled. *Entrance requirements:* For degree, GMAT, GRE General Test, or MAT . Additional exam requirements/recommendations for international students: Required—TOEFL (minimum score 550 paper-based; 213 computer-based; 80 iBT). *Application deadline:* For fall admission, 4/15 for domestic students, 3/5 for international students; for spring admission, 10/15 for domestic students, 9/1 for international students. Applications are processed on a rolling basis. Application fee: $35. Electronic applications accepted. *Expenses:* Tuition, state resident: full-time $6666; part-time $370 per credit. Tuition, nonresident: full-time $10,666; part-time $593 per credit. Required fees: $122.56 per credit. *Financial support:* In 2009–10, research assistantships with full and partial tuition reimbursements (averaging $5,000 per year); unspecified assistantships also available. Support available to part-time students. Financial award application deadline: 2/15; financial award applicants required to submit FAFSA. *Unit head:* Dr. Anthony J. Nicastro, Chairperson and Graduate Coordinator, 610-436-2497. *Application contact:* Office of Graduate Studies, 610-436-2943, Fax: 610-436-2763, E-mail: gradstudy@wcupa.edu.

Western Connecticut State University, Division of Graduate Studies, School of Professional Studies, Department of Education and Educational Psychology, Program in Secondary Education, Danbury, CT 06810-6885. Offers biology option (MAT); mathematics option (MAT). Part-time programs available. *Students:* 18 full-time (9 women), 1 part-time (0 women); includes 1 African American. Average age 34. 30 applicants, 73% accepted, 19 enrolled. *Entrance requirements:* For master's, PRAXIS I Pre_Professional Skills Tests, PRAXIS II subject assessment(s), minimum combined undergraduate GPA of 2.8 or score rated at 35th percentile or higher on MAT. Additional exam requirements/recommendations for international students: Recommended—TOEFL (minimum score 550 paper-based; 213 computer-based; 79 iBT), IELTS (minimum score 6). *Application deadline:* For fall admission, 8/5 priority date for domestic students; for spring admission, 1/5 priority date for domestic students. Application fee: $50. *Expenses:* Tuition, state resident: full-time $5012; part-time $278 per credit hour. Tuition, nonresident: full-time $13,962; part-time $284 per credit hour. Required fees: $3886; $139 per credit hour. Full-time tuition and fees vary according to course load and program. Part-time tuition and fees vary according to course level, degree level and program. *Financial support:* Application deadline: 5/1. *Unit head:* Dr. Theresa Canada, Chairperson, Department of Education and Educational Psychology. *Application contact:* Chris Shankle, Associate Director of Graduate Studies, 203-837-9005, Fax: 203-837-8326, E-mail: shanklec@wcsu.edu.

Western Governors University, Teachers College, Salt Lake City, UT 84107. Offers English language learning (K-12) (MA); learning and technology (M Ed, MA); management and innovation (M Ed); mathematics education (5-12) (MA); mathematics education (5-9) (MA); mathematics education (K-6) (MA); measurement and evaluation (M Ed); science (5-12) (MA), including biology, geology; science education (5-9) (MA); teaching (MAT); technology for principals (Post-Graduate Certificate). *Accreditation:* NCATE. Part-time and evening/weekend programs available. Postbaccalaureate distance learning degree programs offered (no on-campus study). *Degree requirements:* For master's, comprehensive exam. *Entrance requirements:* Additional exam requirements/recommendations for international students: Required—TOEFL (minimum score 450 paper-based). Electronic applications accepted. *Expenses:* Contact institution.

Western Kentucky University, Graduate Studies, Ogden College of Science and Engineering, Department of Biology, Bowling Green, KY 42101. Offers biology (MA Ed, MS). *Degree requirements:* For master's, comprehensive exam, thesis optional, research tool. *Entrance requirements:* For master's, GRE General Test, minimum GPA of 2.75. Additional exam requirements/recommendations for international students: Required—TOEFL (minimum score 555 paper-based; 213 computer-based; 79 iBT). *Expenses:* Tuition, state resident: full-time $4160; part-time $416 per credit hour. Tuition, nonresident: full-time $9550; part-time $506 per credit hour. Tuition and fees vary according to campus/location and reciprocity agreements. *Faculty research:* Phytoremediation, culturing of salt water organisms, PCR-based standards, biological monitoring (water) bioremediation, genetic diversity.

Western Kentucky University, Graduate Studies, Ogden College of Science and Engineering, Department of Chemistry, Bowling Green, KY 42101. Offers chemistry (MA Ed, MS). *Degree requirements:* For master's, comprehensive exam, thesis. *Entrance requirements:* For master's, GRE General Test, minimum GPA of 2.75. Additional exam requirements/recommendations for international students: Required—TOEFL (minimum score 555 paper-based; 213 computer-based). *Expenses:* Tuition, state resident: full-time $4160; part-time $416 per credit hour. Tuition, nonresident: full-time $9550; part-time $506 per credit hour. Tuition and fees vary according to campus/location and reciprocity agreements. *Faculty research:* Catatonic surfactants, directed orthometalation reactions, thermal stability and degradation mechanisms, co-firing refused derived fuels, laser fluorescence.

Western Michigan University, Graduate College, College of Arts and Sciences, Mallinson Institute for Science Education, Kalamazoo, MI 49008-5444. Offers MA, PhD. *Faculty:* 8 full-time (4 women), 2 part-time/adjunct (1 woman). *Students:* 86; includes 1 minority (American Indian/Alaska Native), 7 international. Average age 30. 12 applicants, 42% accepted, 4 enrolled. In 2009, 2 doctorates awarded. *Degree requirements:* For doctorate, thesis/dissertation, oral and written exams. *Entrance requirements:* For master's, undergraduate degree in a science or science education, teacher certification (or appropriate education courses); for doctorate, GRE General Test, master's degree in a science or science education. *Application deadline:* For fall admission, 2/15 for domestic students. Applications are processed on a rolling basis. Electronic applications accepted. *Financial support:* Application deadline: 2/15. *Faculty research:* History and philosophy of science, curriculum and instruction, science content learning, college science teaching and learning, social and cultural factors in science education. *Unit head:* Dr. William W. Cobern, Director, 269-387-5407, Fax: 269-387-4998, E-mail: bill.cobern@wmich.edu. *Application contact:* Admissions and Orientation, 269-387-2000, Fax: 269-387-2096.

See Close-Up on page 1359.

Western Oregon University, Graduate Programs, College of Education, Division of Teacher Education, Program in Secondary Education, Monmouth, OR 97361-1394. Offers bilingual education (MS Ed); health (MS Ed); humanities (MAT, MS Ed); initial licensure (MAT); mathematics (MAT, MS Ed); science (MAT, MS Ed); social science (MAT, MS Ed). *Accreditation:* NCATE. Part-time and evening/weekend programs available. *Degree requirements:* For master's, thesis optional, written exam. *Entrance requirements:* For master's, minimum GPA of 3.0, teaching license. Additional exam requirements/recommendations for international students: Required—TOEFL (minimum score 550 paper-based; 213 computer-based; 79 iBT), IELTS (minimum score 6.5). *Faculty research:* Literacy, science in primary grades, geography education, retention, teacher burnout.

Western Washington University, Graduate School, College of Sciences and Technology, Program in Natural Science/Science Education, Bellingham, WA 98225-5996. Offers M Ed. Electronic applications accepted. *Faculty research:* Science education reform.

Widener University, School of Human Service Professions, Center for Education, Chester, PA 19013-5792. Offers adult education (M Ed); counseling in higher education (M Ed); counselor education (M Ed); early childhood education (M Ed); educational foundations (M Ed); educational leadership (M Ed); educational psychology (M Ed); elementary education (M Ed); English and language arts (M Ed); health education (M Ed); higher education leadership (Ed D); home and school visitor (M Ed); human sexuality (M Ed); mathematics education (M Ed); middle school education (M Ed); principalship (M Ed); reading and language arts (Ed D); reading education (M Ed); school administration (Ed D); science education (M Ed); social studies education (M Ed); special education (M Ed); technology education (M Ed). *Accreditation:* NCATE. Part-time and evening/weekend programs available. *Faculty:* 34 full-time (22 women), 37 part-time/adjunct (14 women). *Students:* 203 full-time (154 women), 415 part-time (298 women); includes 50 minority (34 African Americans, 1 American Indian/Alaska Native, 5 Asian Americans or Pacific Islanders, 10 Hispanic Americans), 3 international. Average age 39. 139 applicants, 88% accepted. In 2009, 168 master's, 31 doctorates awarded. Terminal master's awarded for partial completion of doctoral program. *Degree requirements:* For doctorate, thesis/dissertation. *Entrance requirements:* For master's, minimum GPA of 2.5; for doctorate, GRE or MAT, minimum GPA of 2.0 (undergraduate), 3.5 (graduate). *Application deadline:* Applications are processed on a rolling basis. Application fee: $25 ($300 for international students). Electronic applications accepted. *Expenses:* Contact institution. *Financial support:* Career-related internships or fieldwork, tuition waivers (full and partial), and unspecified assistantships available. Support available to part-time students. Financial award application deadline: 5/1. *Faculty research:* Reading and cognition, adult education, technology education, educational leadership, special education. *Unit head:* Dr. Michael W. LeDoux, Associate Dean, 610-499-4294, Fax: 610-499-4623, E-mail: mwledoux@widener.edu. *Application contact:* Dr. Roberta D. Nolan, Director of Graduate Admissions, 610-499-4125, E-mail: rdnolan@widener.edu.

Wilkes University, College of Graduate and Professional Studies, School of Education, Wilkes-Barre, PA 18766-0002. Offers classroom technology (MS Ed); educational computing (MS Ed); educational development and strategies (MS Ed); educational leadership (MS Ed); educational technology (Ed D); elementary education (MS Ed); higher education administration (Ed D); instructional technology (MS Ed); K-12 administration (Ed D); online teaching (MS Ed); school business leadership (MS Ed); secondary education (MS Ed), including biology, chemistry, English, history; special education (MS Ed). Part-time and evening/weekend programs available. Postbaccalaureate distance learning degree programs offered (minimal on-campus study). *Students:* 89 full-time (60 women), 2,849 part-time (2,058 women); includes 52 minority (10 African Americans, 2 American Indian/Alaska Native, 13 Asian Americans or Pacific Islanders, 27 Hispanic Americans), 6 international. Average age 33. In 2009, 947 master's awarded. *Entrance requirements:* Additional exam requirements/recommendations for international students: Required—TOEFL (minimum score 500 paper-based; 173 computer-based; 79 iBT). *Application deadline:* Applications are processed on a rolling basis. Application fee: $45. *Expenses:* Contact institution. *Financial support:* Federal Work-Study and unspecified assistantships available. Financial award application deadline: 3/1; financial award applicants required to submit FAFSA. *Unit head:* Dr. Michael Speziale, Dean, 570-408-4679, Fax: 570-408-4905, E-mail: michael.speziale@wilkes.edu. *Application contact:* Kathleen Houlihan, Director of Graduate Studies, 570-408-3235, Fax: 570-408-7846, E-mail: kathleen.houlihan@wilkes.edu.

Wright State University, School of Graduate Studies, College of Science and Mathematics, Department of Earth and Environmental Sciences, Program in Earth Science Education, Dayton, OH 45435. Offers MST. *Entrance requirements:* For master's, GRE General Test. Additional exam requirements/recommendations for international students: Required—TOEFL. *Faculty research:* Pedagogy.

Wright State University, School of Graduate Studies, College of Science and Mathematics, Department of Physics, Program in Physics Education, Dayton, OH 45435. Offers MST. Part-time and evening/weekend programs available. *Entrance requirements:* Additional exam requirements/recommendations for international students: Required—TOEFL. *Faculty research:* Pedagogy.

Wright State University, School of Graduate Studies, College of Science and Mathematics, Interdisciplinary Program in Science and Mathematics, Dayton, OH 45435. Offers MST.

Youngstown State University, Graduate School, College of Science, Technology, Engineering and Mathematics, Department of Chemistry, Youngstown, OH 44555-0001. Offers analytical chemistry (MS); biochemistry (MS); chemistry education (MS); inorganic chemistry (MS); organic chemistry (MS); physical chemistry (MS). Part-time programs available. *Degree requirements:* For master's, thesis. *Entrance requirements:* For master's, bachelor's degree in chemistry, minimum GPA of 2.7. Additional exam requirements/recommendations for international students: Required—TOEFL. *Faculty research:* Analysis of antioxidants, chromatography, defects and disorder in crystalline oxides, hydrogen bonding, novel organic and organometallic materials.

Social Sciences Education

Acadia University, Faculty of Professional Studies, School of Education, Program in Curriculum Studies, Wolfville, NS B4P 2R6, Canada. Offers cultural and media studies (M Ed); learning and technology (M Ed); science, math and technology (M Ed). Evening/weekend programs available. *Faculty:* 12 full-time (5 women). *Students:* 7 full-time (all women), 49 part-time (33 women). 61 applicants, 80% accepted. In 2009, 32 master's awarded. *Degree requirements:* For master's, thesis optional. *Entrance requirements:* For master's, B Ed or the equivalent, minimum B average in undergraduate course work, 2 years of teaching experience. Additional exam requirements/recommendations for international students: Required—TOEFL (minimum score 580 paper-based; 237 computer-based; 93 iBT), IELTS (minimum score 6.5). *Application deadline:* For fall admission, 3/15 priority date for domestic and international students. Applications are processed on a rolling basis. Application fee: $50. *Financial support:* Teaching assistantships available. Financial award application deadline: 3/15. *Faculty research:* Literacy development, postmodern philosophy and curriculum theory, historiography, philosophy of education, learning and technology. *Unit head:* Ann Vibert, Director, E-mail: ann.vibert@acadiau.ca. *Application contact:* Sheila Langille, Secretary, 902-585-1229, Fax: 902-585-1071, E-mail: sheila.langille@acadiau.ca.

Alabama State University, School of Graduate Studies, College of Education, Department of Curriculum and Instruction, Program in Secondary Education, Montgomery, AL 36101-0271. Offers biology education (M Ed, Ed S); English/language arts (M Ed); history education (M Ed, Ed S); mathematics education (M Ed); secondary education (Ed S); social studies (Ed S). Part-time programs available. *Degree requirements:* For master's, comprehensive exam; for Ed S, comprehensive exam, thesis. *Entrance requirements:* For master's, GRE General Test, MAT, graduate writing competency test; for Ed S, graduate writing competency test, GRE, MAT. Additional exam requirements/recommendations for international students: Required—TOEFL (minimum score 500 paper-based; 173 computer-based).

Andrews University, School of Graduate Studies, College of Arts and Sciences, Department of History, Berrien Springs, MI 49104. Offers MA, MAT. Part-time programs available. *Faculty:* 5 full-time (3 women). *Degree requirements:* For master's, variable foreign language requirement, thesis optional. *Entrance requirements:* For master's, GRE Subject Test. *Application deadline:* Applications are processed on a rolling basis. Application fee: $40. *Financial support:* Fellowships, Federal Work-Study, institutionally sponsored loans, and unspecified assistantships available. Financial award application deadline: 6/1. *Faculty research:* American intellectual history, Civil War, American church history, modern German history. *Unit head:* Dr. Gary G. Land, Chairman, 269-471-3292. *Application contact:* Carolyn Hurst, Supervisor of Graduate Admission, 800-253-2874, Fax: 269-471-3228, E-mail: graduate@andrews.edu.

Andrews University, School of Graduate Studies, School of Education, Department of Teaching, Learning, and Curriculum, Berrien Springs, MI 49104. Offers curriculum and instruction (MA, Ed D, PhD, Ed S); elementary education (MAT); reading (MA); secondary education (MAT), including biology, education, English, English as a second language, French, history, physics; special education/learning disabilities (MS); teacher education (MAT). *Students:* 12 full-time (8 women), 30 part-time (19 women); includes 17 minority (14 African Americans, 1 Asian American or Pacific Islander, 2 Hispanic Americans), 10 international. Average age 43. 28 applicants, 54% accepted, 6 enrolled. In 2009, 11 master's, 4 doctorates, 1 other advanced degree awarded. *Entrance requirements:* For master's, GRE Subject Test. Additional exam requirements/recommendations for international students: Required—TOEFL (minimum score 550 paper-based). *Application deadline:* For fall admission, 8/15 for domestic students. Applications are processed on a rolling basis. Application fee: $40. *Unit head:* Dr. Lee C. Davidson, Chair, 269-471-6364. *Application contact:* Carolyn Hurst, Supervisor of Graduate Admission, 800-253-2874, Fax: 269-471-6321, E-mail: graduate@andrews.edu.

Appalachian State University, Cratis D. Williams Graduate School, Department of Curriculum and Instruction, Boone, NC 28608. Offers curriculum specialist (MA); educational media (MA); elementary education (MA); middle grades education (MA), including language arts, mathematics, science, social studies. *Accreditation:* NCATE. Part-time and evening/weekend programs available. Postbaccalaureate distance learning degree programs offered (no on-campus study). *Faculty:* 32 full-time (22 women), 9 part-time/adjunct (3 women). *Students:* 16 full-time (12 women), 168 part-time (140 women); includes 2 minority (both African Americans), 1 international. 97 applicants, 99% accepted, 77 enrolled. In 2009, 78 master's awarded. *Degree requirements:* For master's, comprehensive exam, thesis or alternative. *Entrance requirements:* For master's, GRE General Test or MAT, 3 letters of recommendation. Additional exam requirements/recommendations for international students: Required—TOEFL (minimum score 570 paper-based; 230 computer-based; 79 iBT), IELTS (minimum score 6.5). *Application deadline:* For fall admission, 7/1 for domestic students, 2/1 for international students; for spring admission, 11/1 for domestic students, 7/1 for international students. Applications are processed on a rolling basis. Application fee: $50. Electronic applications accepted. *Expenses:* Tuition, state resident: full-time $2960. Tuition, nonresident: full-time $14,051. Required fees: $2320. *Financial support:* In 2009–10, 8 teaching assistantships (averaging $8,000 per year) were awarded; fellowships, research assistantships, career-related internships or fieldwork, Federal Work-Study, scholarships/grants, and unspecified assistantships also available. Financial award application deadline: 4/1; financial award applicants required to submit FAFSA. *Faculty research:* Media literacy, elementary teaching, curriculum development, online learning environments. Total annual research expenditures: $690,000. *Unit head:* Dr. Michael Jacobson, Chairperson, 828-262-2224. *Application contact:* Sandy Krause, Director of Admissions and Recruiting, 828-262-2130, Fax: 828-262-2709, E-mail: krausesl@appstate.edu.

Appalachian State University, Cratis D. Williams Graduate School, Department of History, Boone, NC 28608. Offers history (MA); history education (MA); public history (MA). Part-time programs available. Postbaccalaureate distance learning degree programs offered (no on-campus study). *Faculty:* 26 full-time (8 women), 3 part-time/adjunct (1 woman). *Students:* 29 full-time (13 women), 15 part-time (3 women); includes 1 minority (African American). 33 applicants, 76% accepted, 16 enrolled. In 2009, 15 master's awarded. *Degree requirements:* For master's, one foreign language, comprehensive exam, thesis (for some programs). *Entrance requirements:* For master's, GRE General Test, 3 letters of recommendation. Additional exam requirements/recommendations for international students: Required—TOEFL (minimum score 570 paper-based; 230 computer-based; 79 iBT), IELTS (minimum score 6.5). *Application deadline:* For fall admission, 7/1 for domestic students, 2/1 for international students; for spring admission, 11/1 for domestic students, 7/1 for international students. Applications are processed on a rolling basis. Application fee: $50. Electronic applications accepted. *Expenses:* Tuition, state resident: full-time $2960. Tuition, nonresident: full-time $14,051. Required fees: $2320. *Financial support:* In 2009–10, 4 research assistantships (averaging $10,000 per year), 7 teaching assistantships (averaging $8,000 per year) were awarded; fellowships, career-related internships or fieldwork, Federal Work-Study, scholarships/grants, and unspecified assistantships also available. Financial award application deadline: 4/1; financial award applicants required to submit FAFSA. *Faculty research:* Women's history, social/cultural history, U.S. history, Latin America, medieval studies. Total annual research expenditures: $126,000. *Unit head:* Dr. Lucinda Beier, Chairperson, 828-262-2282, E-mail: beierlm@appstate.edu. *Application contact:* Dr. Lisa Holliday, Graduate Program Director, 828-262-6014, E-mail: hollidaylr@appstate.edu.

Arcadia University, Graduate Studies, Department of Education, Glenside, PA 19038-3295. Offers art education (M Ed, MA Ed); biology education (MA Ed); chemistry education (MA Ed); child development (CAS); computer education (M Ed, CAS); computer education 7–12 (MA Ed); early childhood education (M Ed, CAS), including individualized (M Ed), master teacher (M Ed), research in child development (M Ed); educational leadership (M Ed, CAS); educational psychology (CAS); elementary education (M Ed, CAS); English education (MA Ed); environmental education (MA Ed, CAS); history education (MA Ed); language arts (M Ed, CAS); mathematics education (M Ed, MA Ed, CAS); music education (MA Ed); psychology (MA Ed); pupil personnel services (CAS); reading (M Ed, CAS); school library science (M Ed); science education (M Ed, CAS); secondary education (M Ed, CAS); special education (M Ed, Ed D, CAS); theater arts (MA Ed); written communication (MA Ed). *Accreditation:* NASAD. Part-time and evening/weekend programs available. Postbaccalaureate distance learning degree programs offered (minimal on-campus study). *Faculty:* 12 full-time (8 women), 38 part-time/adjunct (26 women). *Students:* 89 full-time (74 women), 622 part-time (487 women); includes 112 minority (94 African Americans, 9 Asian Americans or Pacific Islanders, 9 Hispanic Americans), 2 international. Average age 32. In 2009, 257 master's, 4 doctorates awarded. *Application deadline:* Applications are processed on a rolling basis. Application fee: $40. Electronic applications accepted. *Expenses:* Tuition: Full-time $30,450; part-time $620 per credit hour. Required fees: $165. Tuition and fees vary according to program. *Financial support:* Career-related internships or fieldwork, tuition waivers (partial), and unspecified assistantships available. *Unit head:* Dr. Steven P. Gulkus. *Application contact:* 215-572-2925, Fax: 215-572-2126, E-mail: grad@arcadia.edu.

Arkansas State University—Jonesboro, Graduate School, College of Humanities and Social Sciences, Department of Criminology, Sociology, and Geography, Jonesboro, State University, AR 72467. Offers criminal justice (MA, Certificate); sociology (MA); sociology education (SCCT). Part-time programs available. *Faculty:* 7 full-time (4 women). *Students:* 9 full-time (7 women), 32 part-time (23 women); includes 15 minority (all African Americans). Average age 33. 29 applicants, 59% accepted, 12 enrolled. In 2009, 7 master's awarded. *Degree requirements:* For master's, one foreign language, comprehensive exam, thesis or alternative; for other advanced degree, comprehensive exam. *Entrance requirements:* For master's, GRE General Test or MAT, appropriate bachelor's degree, letters of recommendation; for other advanced degree, GRE General Test or MAT, interview, master's degree, official transcript, immunization records. Additional exam requirements/recommendations for international students: Required—TOEFL (minimum score 550 paper-based; 213 computer-based; 79 iBT), IELTS (minimum score 6). *Application deadline:* For fall admission, 7/1 for domestic and international students; for spring admission, 11/15 for domestic students, 11/13 for international students. Applications are processed on a rolling basis. Application fee: $30 ($40 for international students). Electronic applications accepted. *Expenses:* Tuition, state resident: full-time $3744; part-time $208 per credit hour. Tuition, nonresident: full-time $9540; part-time $530 per credit hour. Required fees: $896; $47 per credit hour. $25 per term. One-time fee: $50. Tuition and fees vary according to course load and program. *Financial support:* In 2009–10, 8 students received support. Career-related internships or fieldwork, scholarships/grants, and unspecified assistantships available. Financial award application deadline: 7/1; financial award applicants required to submit FAFSA. *Unit head:* Dr. Anthony Troy Adams, Chair, 870-972-3705, Fax: 870-972-3694, E-mail: aadams@astate.edu. *Application contact:* Dr. Andrew Sustich, Dean of the Graduate School, 870-972-3029, Fax: 870-972-3857, E-mail: sustich@astate.edu.

Arkansas State University—Jonesboro, Graduate School, College of Humanities and Social Sciences, Department of History, Jonesboro, State University, AR 72467. Offers history (MA); history education (MSE, SCCT); social science education (MSE). Part-time programs available. *Faculty:* 14 full-time (7 women), 2 part-time/adjunct (both women). *Students:* 13 full-time (7 women), 30 part-time (16 women); includes 5 minority (4 African Americans, 1 Hispanic American). Average age 33. 30 applicants, 90% accepted, 21 enrolled. In 2009, 14 master's, 3 other advanced degrees awarded. *Degree requirements:* For master's, comprehensive exam, thesis or alternative; for SCCT, comprehensive exam. *Entrance requirements:* For master's, GRE General Test or MAT, GMAT, appropriate bachelor's degree, letters of reference, official transcript, valid teaching certificate (for MSE), immunization records; for SCCT, GRE General Test or MAT, interview, master's degree, letters of reference, official transcript, immunization records. Additional exam requirements/recommendations for international students: Required—TOEFL (minimum score 550 paper-based; 213 computer-based; 79 iBT), IELTS (minimum score 6). *Application deadline:* For fall admission, 7/1 for domestic and international students; for spring admission, 11/15 for domestic students, 11/13 for international students. Applications are processed on a rolling basis. Application fee: $30 ($40 for international students). Electronic applications accepted. *Expenses:* Tuition, state resident: full-time $3744; part-time $208 per credit hour. Tuition, nonresident: full-time $9540; part-time $530 per credit hour. Required fees: $896; $47 per credit hour. $25 per term. One-time fee: $50. Tuition and fees vary according to course load and program. *Financial support:* In 2009–10, 10 students received support. Career-related internships or fieldwork, scholarships/grants, and unspecified assistantships available. Financial award application deadline: 7/1; financial award applicants required to submit FAFSA. *Unit head:* Dr. Gina Hogue, Chair, 870-972-3046, Fax: 870-972-2880, E-mail: ghogue@astate.edu. *Application contact:* Dr. Andrew Sustich, Dean of the Graduate School, 870-972-3029, Fax: 870-972-3857, E-mail: sustich@astate.edu.

Arkansas State University—Jonesboro, Graduate School, College of Humanities and Social Sciences, Department of Political Science, Jonesboro, State University, AR 72467. Offers political science (MA); political science education (SCCT); public administration (MPA). *Accreditation:* NASPAA (one or more programs are accredited). Part-time programs available. *Faculty:* 8 full-time (3 women), 1 (woman) part-time/adjunct. *Students:* 24 full-time (8 women), 21 part-time (11 women); includes 12 minority (11 African Americans, 1 American Indian/Alaska Native), 7 international. Average age 32. 27 applicants, 89% accepted, 21 enrolled. In 2009, 17 master's awarded. *Degree requirements:* For master's, comprehensive exam, thesis or alternative; for SCCT, comprehensive exam. *Entrance requirements:* For master's, GRE General Test or MAT, GMAT, appropriate bachelor's degree, letters of recommendation; for SCCT, GRE General Test or MAT, GMAT, interview, master's degree, official transcript, letters of recommendation, immunization records. Additional exam requirements/recommendations for international students: Required—TOEFL (minimum score 550 paper-based; 213 computer-based; 79 iBT), IELTS (minimum score 6). *Application deadline:* For fall admission, 7/1 for domestic and international students; for spring admission, 11/15 for domestic students, 11/13 for international students. Applications are processed on a rolling basis. Application fee: $30 ($40 for international students). Electronic applications accepted. *Expenses:* Tuition, state resident: full-time $3744; part-time $208 per credit hour. Tuition, nonresident: full-time $9540; part-time $530 per credit hour. Required fees: $896; $47 per credit hour. $25 per term. One-time fee: $50. Tuition and fees vary according to course load and program. *Financial support:* In 2009–10, 11 students received support; teaching assistantships, career-related internships or fieldwork, scholarships/grants, and unspecified assistantships available. Financial award application deadline: 7/1; financial award applicants required to submit FAFSA. *Unit head:* Dr. Richard Wang, Chair, 870-972-3048, Fax: 870-972-2720, E-mail: rwang@astate.edu. *Application contact:* Dr. Andrew Sustich, Dean of the Graduate School, 870-972-3029, Fax: 870-972-3857, E-mail: sustich@astate.edu.

Armstrong Atlantic State University, School of Graduate Studies, Program in Education, Savannah, GA 31419-1997. Offers adult education (M Ed); curriculum and instruction (M Ed); early childhood education (M Ed); education (M Ed); elementary education (M Ed); middle grades education (M Ed); secondary education (M Ed), including business education, English education, mathematics education, science education, social science education; special education (M Ed), including behavioral disorders, learning disabilities, speech-language pathology. *Accreditation:* NCATE. Part-time and evening/weekend programs available. Postbaccalaureate distance learning degree programs offered (minimal on-campus study). *Degree requirements:* For master's, comprehensive exam, portfolio. *Entrance requirements:* For master's, GRE General Test or MAT, minimum GPA of 2.5, letters of recommendation. Additional exam requirements/recommendations for international students: Required—TOEFL (minimum score 523 paper-based; 193 computer-based). Electronic applications accepted.

Asbury University, School of Graduate and Professional Studies, Wilmore, KY 40390-1198. Offers biology: alternative certificate (MA Ed); chemistry: alternative certificate (MA Ed); English (MA Ed); English as a second language (MA Ed); ESL (MA Ed); French (MA Ed); Latin: alternative certificate (MA Ed); mathematics: alternative certificate (MA Ed); reading/writing

Social Sciences Education

Asbury University (continued)
endorsement (MA Ed); social studies (MA Ed); social work (MSW), including child and family services; Spanish (MA Ed); special education (MA Ed); special education: alternative certificate (MA Ed); teacher as leader endorsement (MA Ed). *Accreditation:* NCATE. Part-time programs available. *Faculty:* 8 full-time (7 women), 9 part-time/adjunct (4 women). *Students:* 108 part-time (87 women); includes 8 minority (4 African Americans, 2 Asian Americans or Pacific Islanders, 2 Hispanic Americans). Average age 36. 36 applicants, 86% accepted, 24 enrolled. In 2009, 20 master's awarded. *Degree requirements:* For master's, action research project, portfolio. *Entrance requirements:* For master's, PRAXIS/NTE, minimum GPA of 2.75, letters of recommendation. Additional exam requirements/recommendations for international students: Required—TOEFL (minimum score 550 paper-based). *Application deadline:* Applications are processed on a rolling basis. Application fee: $25. Electronic applications accepted. *Financial support:* Scholarships/grants and traineeships available. Financial award applicants required to submit FAFSA. *Unit head:* Dr. Bonnie J. Banker, Dean, School of Graduate and Professional Studies, 859-858-3511 Ext. 2221, Fax: 859-858-3921, E-mail: bonnie.banker@asbury.edu. *Application contact:* Lenore A. Sweigard, Graduate Program Assistant and Certification Specialist, 859-858-3511 Ext. 2502, Fax: 859-858-3921, E-mail: graded@asbury.edu.

Auburn University, Graduate School, College of Education, Department of Curriculum and Teaching, Auburn University, AL 36849. Offers business education (M Ed, MS, PhD); early childhood education (M Ed, MS, PhD, Ed S); elementary education (M Ed, MS, PhD, Ed S); foreign languages (M Ed, MS); music education (M Ed, MS, PhD, Ed S); postsecondary education (PhD); reading education (PhD, Ed S); secondary education (M Ed, MS, PhD, Ed S), including English language arts, mathematics, science, social studies. *Accreditation:* NASM (one or more programs are accredited); NCATE. Part-time programs available. *Faculty:* 28 full-time (21 women), 8 part-time/adjunct (5 women). *Students:* 76 full-time (55 women), 186 part-time (139 women); includes 43 minority (29 African Americans, 1 American Indian/Alaska Native, 4 Asian Americans or Pacific Islanders, 9 Hispanic Americans), 4 international. Average age 33. 248 applicants, 65% accepted, 110 enrolled. In 2009, 102 master's, 12 doctorates, 6 other advanced degrees awarded. *Degree requirements:* For master's, thesis (for some programs); for doctorate, thesis/dissertation; for Ed S, field project. *Entrance requirements:* For master's, doctorate, and Ed S, GRE General Test. *Application deadline:* For fall admission, 7/7 for domestic students; for spring admission, 11/24 for domestic students. Applications are processed on a rolling basis. Application fee: $50 ($60 for international students). Electronic applications accepted. *Expenses:* Tuition, state resident: full-time $6240. Tuition, nonresident: full-time $18,720. International tuition: $18,938 full-time. Required fees: $492. Tuition and fees vary according to course load, program and reciprocity agreements. *Financial support:* Fellowships, teaching assistantships, career-related internships or fieldwork and Federal Work-Study available. Support available to part-time students. Financial award application deadline: 3/15; financial award applicants required to submit FAFSA. *Faculty research:* Emerging literacy, reading attitudes, music for at-risk youth, portfolio assessment. *Unit head:* Dr. Nancy H. Barry, Head, 334-844-4434. *Application contact:* Dr. George Flowers, Dean of the Graduate School, 334-844-2125.

Averett University, Master in Education Program, Danville, VA 24541-3692. Offers art education (M Ed); biology (M Ed); biology education (M Ed); chemistry (M Ed); chemistry education (M Ed); curriculum and instruction (M Ed); elementary education (M Ed); English (M Ed); English education (M Ed); health and physical education (M Ed); history and social studies education (M Ed); math (M Ed); mathematics education (M Ed); physical science (M Ed); reading specialization (M Ed); special education (learning disabilities specialization PK-12) (M Ed). Program also offered at Richmond, VA regional campus location. Part-time and evening/weekend programs available. *Faculty:* 4 full-time (3 women), 36 part-time/adjunct (22 women). *Students:* 182 full-time (160 women), 110 part-time (94 women); includes 113 minority (94 African Americans, 1 American Indian/Alaska Native, 7 Asian Americans or Pacific Islanders, 11 Hispanic Americans). Average age 37. 119 applicants, 99% accepted, 98 enrolled. In 2009, 92 master's awarded. *Degree requirements:* For master's, comprehensive exam, thesis optional. *Entrance requirements:* For master's, PRAXIS, GRE General Test, MAT or NTE, writing proficiency exam, 3 letters of recommendation, current teacher's licensure or eligibility for licensure, minimum undergraduate GPA of 3.0 in previous 2 years. Additional exam requirements/recommendations for international students: Required—TOEFL (minimum score 600 paper-based; 200 computer-based). *Application deadline:* Applications are processed on a rolling basis. *Expenses:* Contact institution. *Financial support:* Career-related internships or fieldwork, Federal Work-Study, and scholarships/grants available. Financial award application deadline: 4/1; financial award applicants required to submit FAFSA. *Faculty research:* Literary assessment-PreK-6, handwriting instruction and assessment-PreK-6, written language instruction and assessment-PreK-6 and special needs students learning styles, curriculum and instruction processes. *Unit head:* Dr. Lynn H. Wolf, Chair/Associate Professor/Director, 434-793-3995, Fax: 434-791-4392, E-mail: lynn.wolf@averett.edu. *Application contact:* Dr. Lynn H. Wolf, Chair/Associate Professor/Director, 434-793-3995, Fax: 434-791-4392, E-mail: lynn.wolf@averett.edu.

Belmont University, College of Arts and Sciences, School of Education, Nashville, TN 37212-3757. Offers education (M Ed); elementary education (MAT), including early childhood education, elementary education, language arts education; English (MAT); history (MAT); mathematics (MAT); middle grade education (MAT); science (MAT); secondary education (MAT); special education (MAT); sports administration (MSA). *Accreditation:* NCATE. Part-time and evening/weekend programs available. *Degree requirements:* For master's, comprehensive exam, thesis, culminating portfolio. *Entrance requirements:* For master's, MAT or GRE and/or LSAT or GMAT, minimum GPA of 2.75. Additional exam requirements/recommendations for international students: Required—TOEFL. *Expenses:* Contact institution. *Faculty research:* Improving secondary literacy, Montessori, classroom management strategies, teacher residency programs, online professional development, mentoring, leadership, sociological issues in sport, faculty development, coaching.

Bennington College, Graduate Programs, MA in Teaching Program, Bennington, VT 05201. Offers art education (MAT); early childhood (MAT); elementary education (MAT); English education (MAT); foreign language education (MAT); k-12 education (MAT); mathematics education (MAT); music education (MAT); science education (MAT); secondary education (MAT); social studies education (MAT); theater arts (MAT). *Faculty:* 5 part-time/adjunct (3 women). *Students:* 8 full-time (5 women), 1 part-time (0 women). Average age 28. 11 applicants, 27% accepted, 1 enrolled. In 2009, 4 master's awarded. *Degree requirements:* For master's, comprehensive exam, 1 year teaching practicum, professional portfolio. *Entrance requirements:* For master's, interview. *Application deadline:* For fall admission, 3/1 for domestic students. Application fee: $60. *Expenses:* Contact institution. *Financial support:* In 2009–10, 6 students received support, including 4 fellowships (averaging $10,475 per year); scholarships/grants and unspecified assistantships also available. Financial award application deadline: 4/1; financial award applicants required to submit FAFSA. *Unit head:* Carol Meyer, Director of Programs in Teacher Education, 802-440-4375, E-mail: cmeyer@bennington.edu. *Application contact:* Nancy Pearlman, Assistant Director of Programs in Teacher Education, 802-440-4710, Fax: 802-440-4383, E-mail: npearlman@bennington.edu.

Bethel University, Program in Education, McKenzie, TN 38201. Offers administration and supervision (MA Ed); biology education K8-12 (MAT); elementary education (MAT); English education K8-12 (MAT); history education K8-12 (MAT); physical education K8-12 (MAT); special education K8-12 (MAT). Part-time and evening/weekend programs available. *Degree requirements:* For master's, thesis (for some programs). *Entrance requirements:* For master's, GRE General Test or MAT, minimum undergraduate GPA of 2.5.

Bob Jones University, Graduate Programs, Greenville, SC 29614. Offers accountancy (MS); Bible (MA); Bible translation (MA); Biblical studies (Certificate); broadcast management (MS); business administration (MBA); church history (MA, PhD); church ministries (MA); church music (MM); cinema and video production (MA); counseling (MS); curriculum and instruction (Ed D); divinity (M Div); dramatic production (MA); educational leadership (MS, Ed D, Ed S); elementary education (M Ed, MAT); English (M Ed, MA, MAT); fine arts (MA); graphic design (MA); history (M Ed, MA); illustration (MA); interpretative speech (MA); mathematics (M Ed, MAT); medical missions (Certificate); ministry (MM, D Min); multi-categorical special education (M Ed, MAT); music (M Ed); New Testament interpretation (PhD); Old Testament interpretation (PhD); orchestral instrument performance (MM); organ performance (MM); pastoral studies (MA); personnel services (MS, Ed S); piano pedagogy (MM); piano performance (MM); platform arts (MA); radio and television broadcasting (MS); rhetoric and public address (MA); secondary education (M Ed); studio art (MA); teaching Bible (MA); theology (MA, PhD); voice performance (MM); youth ministries (MA); M Div/MM.

Boston College, Lynch Graduate School of Education, Department of Teacher Education/Special Education and Curriculum and Instruction, Program in Secondary Education, Chestnut Hill, MA 02467-3800. Offers biology (MST); chemistry (MST); English (MAT); French (MAT); geology (MST); history (MAT); Latin and classical humanities (MAT); mathematics (MST); physics (MST); secondary teaching (M Ed), including biology, chemistry, English, French, geology, history, Latin and classical humanities, mathematics, physics, Spanish; Spanish (MAT). *Accreditation:* Teacher Education Accreditation Council. Part-time and evening/weekend programs available. *Students:* 14 full-time (10 women), 68 part-time (37 women); includes 17 minority (9 African Americans, 3 Asian Americans or Pacific Islanders, 5 Hispanic Americans), 1 international. 252 applicants, 59% accepted, 47 enrolled. In 2009, 39 master's awarded. *Degree requirements:* For master's, comprehensive exam. *Entrance requirements:* For master's, GRE General Test or MAT. Additional exam requirements/recommendations for international students: Required—TOEFL (minimum score 550 paper-based; 213 computer-based; 81 iBT). *Application deadline:* For fall admission, 1/1 priority date for domestic students. Application fee: $60. Electronic applications accepted. *Financial support:* Fellowships with full and partial tuition reimbursements, research assistantships with full and partial tuition reimbursements, teaching assistantships with full and partial tuition reimbursements, career-related internships or fieldwork, Federal Work-Study, institutionally sponsored loans, scholarships/grants, traineeships, health care benefits, tuition waivers (full and partial), and unspecified assistantships available. Support available to part-time students. Financial award applicants required to submit FAFSA. *Faculty research:* School reform; urban science education; teacher research; critical literacy; poverty and achievement. *Unit head:* Dr. Maria E. Brisk, Chairperson, 617-552-4216, Fax: 617-552-0812, E-mail: brisk@bc.edu. *Application contact:* Adam Poluzzi, Director, Graduate Admission and Financial Aid, 617-552-4214, Fax: 617-552-0398, E-mail: poluzzi@bc.edu.

Boston University, School of Education, Department of Curriculum and Teaching, Program in Social Studies Education, Boston, MA 02215. Offers Ed M, MAT, Ed D, CAGS. *Degree requirements:* For master's, thesis optional; for doctorate, comprehensive exam, thesis/dissertation; for CAGS, comprehensive exam. *Entrance requirements:* For master's, doctorate, and CAGS, GRE General Test or MAT. Additional exam requirements/recommendations for international students: Required—TOEFL. Electronic applications accepted. *Expenses:* Tuition: Full-time $37,910; part-time $1184 per credit hour. Required fees: $386; $40 per semester. Part-time tuition and fees vary according to class time, course level, degree level and program. *Faculty research:* Law-focused and intercultural education.

Bridgewater State University, School of Graduate Studies, School of Arts and Sciences, Department of History, Bridgewater, MA 02325-0001. Offers MAT. Part-time and evening/weekend programs available. *Entrance requirements:* For master's, GRE General Test.

Brooklyn College of the City University of New York, Division of Graduate Studies, School of Education, Program in Adolescence Education and Special Subjects, Brooklyn, NY 11210-2889. Offers adolescence science education (MAT); art teacher (MA); biology teacher (MA); chemistry teacher (MA); earth science teacher (MAT); English teacher (MA); French teacher (MA); health and nutrition sciences: health teacher (MS Ed); mathematics teacher (MA); music education (CAS); music teacher (MA); physical education teacher (MS Ed); physics teacher (MA); social studies teacher (MA); Spanish teacher (MA). Part-time and evening/weekend programs available. *Students:* 23 full-time (15 women), 449 part-time (256 women); includes 147 minority (96 African Americans, 1 American Indian/Alaska Native, 18 Asian Americans or Pacific Islanders, 32 Hispanic Americans), 12 international. Average age 30. 251 applicants, 80% accepted, 141 enrolled. In 2009, 163 master's, 2 other advanced degrees awarded. *Degree requirements:* For master's, comprehensive exam (for some programs), thesis (for some programs). *Entrance requirements:* For master's, LAST, previous course work in education, resume, 2 letters of recommendation, essay. Additional exam requirements/recommendations for international students: Required—TOEFL (minimum score 500 paper-based; 173 computer-based; 61 iBT). *Application deadline:* For fall admission, 7/15 for domestic students, 7/1 for international students; for spring admission, 11/15 for domestic students, 10/1 for international students. Applications are processed on a rolling basis. Application fee: $125. Electronic applications accepted. *Expenses:* Tuition, state resident: full-time $7360; part-time $310 per credit hour. Tuition, nonresident: full-time $13,800; part-time $575 per credit hour. Required fees: $140.10 per semester. *Financial support:* Career-related internships or fieldwork, Federal Work-Study, institutionally sponsored loans, and scholarships/grants available. Support available to part-time students. Financial award application deadline: 5/1; financial award applicants required to submit FAFSA. *Faculty research:* Interdisciplinary education, semiotics, discourse analysis, autobiography, teacher identity. *Unit head:* Prof. Stephen Phillips, Program Head, 718-951-5214, E-mail: phillips@brooklyn.cuny.edu. *Application contact:* Hernan Sierra, Graduate Admissions Coordinator, 718-951-4536, Fax: 718-951-4506, E-mail: grads@brooklyn.cuny.edu.

Brown University, Graduate School, Department of Education, Program in Teaching, Providence, RI 02912. Offers biology (MAT); elementary education (MAT); English (MAT); history/social studies (MAT). *Faculty:* 4 full-time (3 women), 6 part-time/adjunct (all women). *Students:* 27 full-time (21 women); includes 3 minority (2 African Americans, 1 Asian American or Pacific Islander). Average age 26. 94 applicants, 62% accepted, 27 enrolled. In 2009, 21 master's awarded. *Degree requirements:* For master's, student teaching, portfolio. *Entrance requirements:* For master's, GRE General Test, transcript, personal statement, letters of recommendation, interview, writing sample (English applicants only). Additional exam requirements/recommendations for international students: Required—TOEFL (minimum score 577 paper-based; 90 computer-based). *Application deadline:* For winter admission, 1/15 for domestic students. Application fee: $75. Electronic applications accepted. *Financial support:* In 2009–10, 23 students received support, including 4 fellowships; Federal Work-Study, institutionally sponsored loans, scholarships/grants, tuition waivers (partial), and proctorships also available. Financial award application deadline: 2/1; financial award applicants required to submit FAFSA. *Faculty research:* Literacy, biodiversity, English language learners, diversity, special education. *Unit head:* Laura Snyder, Director of Graduate Study for the MAT. *Application contact:* Carin Algava, Assistant Director, 401-863-3364, Fax: 401-863-1276, E-mail: carin_algava@brown.edu.

Buffalo State College, State University of New York, The Graduate School, Faculty of Natural and Social Sciences, Department of History and Social Studies, Buffalo, NY 14222-1095. Offers history (MA); secondary education (MS Ed), including social studies. Part-time and evening/weekend programs available. *Degree requirements:* For master's, one foreign language, thesis (for some programs), project (MS Ed). *Entrance requirements:* For master's, minimum GPA of 2.75, 30 hours in history (MA), 36 hours in history or social sciences (MS Ed). Additional exam requirements/recommendations for international students: Required—TOEFL (minimum score 550 paper-based; 213 computer-based).

California State University, Chico, Graduate School, College of Behavioral and Social Sciences, Social Science Program, Chico, CA 95929-0722. Offers social science (MA); social science education (MA). *Students:* 8 full-time (6 women), 12 part-time (8 women); includes 4 minority (1 Asian American or Pacific Islander, 3 Hispanic Americans), 1 international. Average age 34. 16 applicants, 88% accepted, 7 enrolled. In 2009, 4 master's awarded. *Degree requirements:* For master's, thesis or alternative. *Entrance requirements:* For master's, GRE General Test or MAT. Additional exam requirements/recommendations for international students: Required—TOEFL (minimum score 550 paper-based; 213 computer-based; 80 iBT), IELTS

(minimum score 6.5). *Application deadline:* For fall admission, 3/1 priority date for domestic students, 3/1 for international students; for spring admission, 9/15 priority date for domestic students, 9/15 for international students. Applications are processed on a rolling basis. Application fee: $55. Electronic applications accepted. *Financial support:* Fellowships, teaching assistantships available. *Unit head:* Dr. Gwen Sheldon, Graduate Coordinator, 530-895-5204. *Application contact:* School of Graduate, International, and Interdisciplinary Studies, 530-898-6880, Fax: 530-898-6889, E-mail: grin@csuchico.edu.

California State University, Fresno, Division of Graduate Studies, College of Social Sciences, Department of History, Fresno, CA 93740-8027. Offers history-teaching option (MA); history-traditional track (MA). Part-time and evening/weekend programs available. *Degree requirements:* For master's, thesis or alternative. *Entrance requirements:* For master's, GRE General Test, minimum GPA of 3.0. Additional exam requirements/recommendations for international students: Required—TOEFL. Electronic applications accepted. *Faculty research:* International education, classical art history, improving teacher quality.

California State University, San Bernardino, Graduate Studies, College of Education, San Bernardino, CA 92407-2397. Offers bilingual/cross-cultural education (MA); curriculum and instruction (MA); educational administration (MA); educational leadership and curriculum (Ed D); educational psychology and counseling (MA, MS), including correctional and alternative education (MA), counseling and guidance (MS), rehabilitation counseling (MA); elementary education (MA); English as a second language (MA); environmental education (MA); general education (MA); history and English for secondary teachers (MA); instructional technology (MA); reading (MA); secondary education (MA); special education and rehabilitation counseling (MA), including rehabilitation counseling, special education; teaching of science (MA); vocational and career education (MA). *Accreditation:* NCATE. Part-time and evening/weekend programs available. *Faculty:* 35 full-time (15 women), 24 part-time/adjunct (15 women). *Students:* 921 full-time (710 women), 716 part-time (490 women); includes 751 minority (137 African Americans, 12 American Indian/Alaska Native, 73 Asian Americans or Pacific Islanders, 529 Hispanic Americans), 18 international. Average age 36. 493 applicants, 86% accepted, 243 enrolled. In 2009, 370 master's awarded. *Degree requirements:* For master's, comprehensive exam (for some programs), thesis (for some programs), advancement to candidacy. *Entrance requirements:* For master's, minimum GPA of 3.0 in education. *Application deadline:* For fall admission, 8/31 priority date for domestic students. Application fee: $55. *Financial support:* Career-related internships or fieldwork and Federal Work-Study available. Support available to part-time students. *Faculty research:* Multicultural education, brain-based learning, science education, social studies/global education. *Unit head:* Dr. Patricia Arlin, Dean, 909-537-5600, Fax: 909-537-7011, E-mail: parlin@csusb.edu. *Application contact:* Olivia Rosas, Director of Admissions, 909-537-7577, Fax: 909-537-7034, E-mail: orosas@csusb.edu.

Cambridge College, School of Education, Cambridge, MA 02138-5304. Offers autism specialist (M Ed); autism/behavior analyst (M Ed); behavior analyst (Post-Master's Certificate); behavioral management (M Ed); early childhood teacher (M Ed); education specialist in curriculum and instruction (CAGS); educational leadership (Ed D); elementary teacher (M Ed); English as a second language (M Ed, Certificate); general science (M Ed); health education, health promotion (Post-Master's Certificate); health/family and consumer sciences (M Ed); history (M Ed); individualized degree (M Ed); information technology literacy (M Ed); instructional technology (M Ed); interdisciplinary studies (M Ed); library teacher (M Ed); literacy education (M Ed); mathematics (M Ed); mathematics specialist (Certificate); middle school mathematics and science (M Ed); school administration (M Ed, CAGS); school guidance counselor (M Ed); school nurse education (M Ed); school social worker/school adjustment counselor (M Ed); special education administrator (CAGS); special education/moderate disabilities (M Ed); teaching skills and methodologies (M Ed). Part-time and evening/weekend programs available. Postbaccalaureate distance learning degree programs offered (minimal on-campus study). *Faculty:* 10 full-time (3 women), 283 part-time/adjunct (187 women). *Students:* 974 full-time (755 women), 1,071 part-time (835 women); includes 940 minority (762 African Americans, 4 American Indian/Alaska Native, 22 Asian Americans or Pacific Islanders, 152 Hispanic Americans), 28 international. Average age 39. In 2009, 866 master's, 4 doctorates, 209 CAGSs awarded. *Degree requirements:* For master's, thesis, internship/practicum (licensure program only); for doctorate, thesis/dissertation; for other advanced degree, thesis. *Entrance requirements:* For master's, interview, resume, documentation of licensure, 2 professional references; for doctorate, official transcripts, interview, resume, documentation of licensure (if any), written personal statement/essay, portfolio of scholarly and professional work, qualifying assessment, 2 professional references, health insurance, immunizations form; for other advanced degree, official transcripts, interview, resume, documentation of licensure (if any), written personal statement/essay, 2 professional references, health insurance, immunizations form. Additional exam requirements/recommendations for international students: Required—TOEFL (minimum score 550 paper-based; 213 computer-based; 79 iBT); Recommended—IELTS (minimum score 6). *Application deadline:* Applications are processed on a rolling basis. Application fee: $30. Electronic applications accepted. *Expenses:* Contact institution. *Financial support:* In 2009–10, 1,373 students received support. Career-related internships or fieldwork, Federal Work-Study, and scholarships/grants available. Financial award applicants required to submit FAFSA. *Faculty research:* Adult education, accelerated learning, mathematics education, brain compatible learning, special education and law. *Unit head:* Dr. N. Alan Sheppard, Interim Associate Dean, 617-873-0619, E-mail: alan.sheppard@cambridgecollege.edu. *Application contact:* Stephen Lyons, Director of Enrollment, Graduate and N.I.T.E. Programs, 617-868-1000, Fax: 617-349-3561, E-mail: stephen.lyons@cambridgecollege.edu.

Campbell University, Graduate and Professional Programs, School of Education, Buies Creek, NC 27506. Offers administration (MSA); community counseling (MA); elementary education (M Ed); English education (M Ed); interdisciplinary studies (M Ed); mathematics education (M Ed); middle grades education (M Ed); physical education (M Ed); school counseling (M Ed); secondary education (M Ed); social science education (M Ed). *Accreditation:* NCATE. Part-time and evening/weekend programs available. *Degree requirements:* For master's, comprehensive exam. *Entrance requirements:* For master's, GRE General Test, minimum GPA of 2.7. *Faculty research:* Spiritual values and wellness issues in counseling, stress and professional burnout among counselors, thinking strategies, leadership, adaptive technology.

Caribbean University, Graduate School, Bayamón, PR 00960-0493. Offers administration and supervision (MA Ed); criminal justice (MA); curriculum and instruction (MA Ed), including elementary education, English education, history education, mathematics education, primary education, science education, Spanish education; education (PhD); gerontology (MSN); human resources (MBA); museology, archiving and art history (MA Ed); neonatal pediatrics (MSN); physical education (MA Ed); special education (MA Ed). *Entrance requirements:* For master's, interview, minimum GPA of 2.5.

Carthage College, Division of Teacher Education, Kenosha, WI 53140. Offers classroom guidance and counseling (M Ed); creative arts (M Ed); gifted and talented children (M Ed); language arts (M Ed); modern language (M Ed); natural sciences (M Ed); reading (M Ed, Certificate); social sciences (M Ed); teacher leadership (M Ed). Part-time and evening/weekend programs available. *Degree requirements:* For master's, thesis optional. *Entrance requirements:* For master's, MAT, minimum B average, letters of reference.

Chadron State College, School of Professional and Graduate Studies, Department of Education, Chadron, NE 69337. Offers business (MA Ed); community counseling (MA Ed); educational administration (MS Ed, Sp Ed); elementary education (MS Ed); history (MA Ed); language and literature (MA Ed); secondary administration (MS Ed); secondary education (MS Ed). *Accreditation:* NCATE. Part-time and evening/weekend programs available. Postbaccalaureate distance learning degree programs offered. *Degree requirements:* For master's, thesis optional. *Entrance requirements:* For master's, GRE General Test, GRE Writing Test, minimum GPA of 2.75 or 12 graduate hours at CSC with minimum GPA of 3.25. Additional exam requirements/recommendations for international students: Required—TOEFL. Electronic applications accepted. *Faculty research:* Rural education, technology, mental health.

Chaminade University of Honolulu, Graduate Services, Program in Education, Honolulu, HI 96816-1578. Offers social science via peace education (M Ed). Part-time and evening/weekend programs available. Postbaccalaureate distance learning degree programs offered (minimal on-campus study). *Degree requirements:* For master's, thesis or alternative. *Entrance requirements:* For master's, minimum GPA of 2.75, 3 letters of recommendation. Additional exam requirements/recommendations for international students: Required—TOEFL (minimum score 550 paper-based). *Faculty research:* Peace and curriculum education.

Chatham University, Program in Education, Pittsburgh, PA 15232-2826. Offers early childhood education (MAT); elementary education (MAT); English—secondary (MAT); environmental education (K-12) (MAT); secondary art (MAT); secondary biology education (MAT); secondary chemistry education (MAT); secondary English education (MAT); secondary math education (MAT); secondary physics education (MAT); secondary social studies education (MAT); special education (MAT). *Students:* 52 full-time (41 women), 20 part-time (16 women). Average age 30. 39 applicants, 79% accepted, 26 enrolled. In 2009, 37 master's awarded. *Degree requirements:* For master's, thesis, teaching experience. *Entrance requirements:* For master's, PRAXIS I, minimum GPA of 3.0, sample of written work, recommendation letters. Additional exam requirements/recommendations for international students: Required—TOEFL (minimum score 600 paper-based; 250 computer-based; 100 iBT), IELTS (minimum score 6.5), TWE. *Application deadline:* For fall admission, 5/1 priority date for domestic and international students; for spring admission, 10/15 priority date for domestic and international students. Applications are processed on a rolling basis. Application fee: $45. Electronic applications accepted. *Financial support:* Career-related internships or fieldwork available. Financial award applicants required to submit FAFSA. *Faculty research:* Gifted education, environmental education, technology in education, writing as learning, class size and achievement. *Unit head:* Dr. Barbara Biglan, Interim Director, 412-365-1170, E-mail: biglan@chatham.edu. *Application contact:* Dory Perry, Associate Director of Graduate Admissions, 412-365-2758, Fax: 412-365-1609, E-mail: gradadmissions@chatham.edu.

Christopher Newport University, Graduate Studies, Department of Teacher Preparation, Newport News, VA 23606-2998. Offers art (PK-12) (MAT); biology (6-12) (MAT); computer science (6-12) (MAT); elementary (PK-6) (MAT); English (6-12) (MAT); French (PK-12) (MAT); history and social science (6-12) (MAT); mathematics (6-12) (MAT); music (PK-12) (MAT), including choral, instrumental; physics (6-12) (MAT); Spanish (PK-12) (MAT). Part-time and evening/weekend programs available. *Faculty:* 24 full-time (13 women), 4 part-time/adjunct (2 women). *Students:* 76 full-time (66 women), 12 part-time (10 women); includes 3 minority (2 African Americans, 1 Hispanic American). Average age 24. 3 applicants, 100% accepted, 2 enrolled. In 2009, 58 master's awarded. *Degree requirements:* For master's, comprehensive exam, thesis or alternative. *Entrance requirements:* For master's, PRAXIS I, minimum GPA of 3.0. Additional exam requirements/recommendations for international students: Required—TOEFL (minimum score 580 paper-based; 237 computer-based; 92 iBT). *Application deadline:* For fall admission, 8/15 for domestic students, 4/1 for international students; for spring admission, 10/15 for domestic students, 10/1 for international students. Applications are processed on a rolling basis. Application fee: $45. Electronic applications accepted. *Expenses:* Tuition, area resident: Part-time $384 per credit hour. Tuition, state resident: part-time $384 per credit hour. Tuition, nonresident: part-time $701 per credit hour. *Financial support:* In 2009–10, 3 research assistantships with full and partial tuition reimbursements (averaging $2,000 per year) were awarded; career-related internships or fieldwork, Federal Work-Study, and unspecified assistantships also available. Support available to part-time students. Financial award application deadline: 3/1; financial award applicants required to submit FAFSA. *Faculty research:* Early literacy development, instructional innovations, professional teaching standards, multicultural issues, aesthetic education. *Unit head:* Dr. Marsha Sprague, Director, 757-594-7388, Fax: 757-594-7803, E-mail: msprague@cnu.edu. *Application contact:* Lyn Sawyer, Associate Director, Graduate Admissions, 757-594-7544, Fax: 757-594-7649, E-mail: gradstdy@cnu.edu.

The Citadel, The Military College of South Carolina, Citadel Graduate College, School of Education, Program in Secondary Education, Charleston, SC 29409. Offers biology (MAT); English language arts (MAT); mathematics (MAT); social studies (MAT). *Accreditation:* NCATE. Part-time and evening/weekend programs available. *Faculty:* 12 full-time (7 women), 8 part-time/adjunct (5 women). *Students:* 27 full-time (18 women), 62 part-time (37 women); includes 15 minority (11 African Americans, 2 Asian Americans or Pacific Islanders, 2 Hispanic Americans). Average age 29. In 2009, 22 master's awarded. *Degree requirements:* For master's, comprehensive exam, internship. *Entrance requirements:* For master's, GRE (minimum score 900) or MAT (minimum score 396), minimum undergraduate GPA of 2.5. Additional exam requirements/recommendations for international students: Required—TOEFL (minimum score 550 paper-based; 213 computer-based). *Application deadline:* Applications are processed on a rolling basis. Application fee: $30. Electronic applications accepted. *Expenses:* Tuition, state resident: part-time $400 per credit hour. Tuition, nonresident: part-time $657 per credit hour. Required fees: $40 per term. *Financial support:* Career-related internships or fieldwork, health care benefits, and unspecified assistantships available. Support available to part-time students. Financial award application deadline: 7/1; financial award applicants required to submit FAFSA. *Unit head:* Dr. Kathryn A. Richardson-Jones, Coordinator, 843-953-3163, Fax: 843-953-7258, E-mail: kathryn.jones@citadel.edu. *Application contact:* Dr. Steve A. Nida, Associate Provost, The Citadel Graduate College, 843-953-5089, Fax: 843-953-7630, E-mail: cgc@citadel.edu.

City College of the City University of New York, Graduate School, School of Education, Department of Secondary Education, New York, NY 10031-9198. Offers adolescent mathematics education (MA, AC); English education (MA); middle school mathematics education (MS); science education (MA); social studies education (AC). *Accreditation:* NCATE. *Entrance requirements:* For master's, Liberal Arts and Sciences Test (LAST), Content Specialty Test (CST). Additional exam requirements/recommendations for international students: Required—TOEFL. *Expenses:* Tuition, state resident: part-time $310 per credit. Tuition, nonresident: part-time $575 per credit. Tuition and fees vary according to course load and program.

Clarion University of Pennsylvania, Office of Research and Graduate Studies, College of Education and Human Services, Department of Education, Program in Education, Clarion, PA 16214. Offers curriculum and instruction (M Ed); early childhood (M Ed); English (M Ed); history (M Ed); literacy (M Ed); science (M Ed); technology (M Ed). *Accreditation:* NCATE. Part-time programs available. *Degree requirements:* For master's, comprehensive exam, thesis or alternative. *Entrance requirements:* For master's, minimum QPA of 3.0, teacher certification. Additional exam requirements/recommendations for international students: Required—TOEFL (minimum score 550 paper-based; 213 computer-based; 80 iBT). Electronic applications accepted.

Clemson University, Graduate School, College of Health, Education, and Human Development, School of Education, Program in Secondary Education, Clemson, SC 29634. Offers English (M Ed); mathematics (M Ed); natural sciences (M Ed); social studies (M Ed). *Accreditation:* NCATE. *Students:* 5 full-time (3 women), 4 part-time (2 women); includes 2 minority (1 Asian American or Pacific Islander, 1 Hispanic American), 2 international. Average age 29. 11 applicants, 82% accepted, 4 enrolled. In 2009, 2 master's awarded. *Entrance requirements:* For master's, GRE General Test, teaching certificate. Additional exam requirements/recommendations for international students: Required—TOEFL. *Application deadline:* Applications are processed on a rolling basis. Application fee: $70 ($80 for international students). Electronic applications accepted. *Expenses:* Contact institution. *Financial support:* In 2009–10, 2 students received support. Career-related internships or fieldwork, institutionally sponsored loans, scholarships/grants, health care benefits, and unspecified assistantships available. Support available to part-time students. Financial award application deadline: 6/1; financial award applicants required to submit FAFSA. *Unit head:* Dr. Michael J. Padilla, Director/Associate Dean, 864-656-4444, Fax: 864-656-0311, E-mail: padilla@clemson.edu. *Application contact:* Dr. David Fleming, Graduate Coordinator, 864-656-1881, Fax: 864-656-0311, E-mail: dflemin@clemson.edu.

The College at Brockport, State University of New York, School of Education and Human Services, Department of Education and Human Development, Program in Adolescence

Social Sciences Education

The College at Brockport, State University of New York (continued)
Education, Brockport, NY 14420-2997. Offers adolescence biology education (MS Ed); adolescence chemistry education (MS Ed); adolescence earth science education (MS Ed); adolescence English education (MS Ed); adolescence mathematics education (MS Ed); adolescence physics education (MS Ed); adolescence social studies education (MS Ed). *Accreditation:* NCATE. Part-time programs available. *Students:* 10 full-time (6 women), 98 part-time (60 women); includes 1 minority (African American). 15 applicants, 67% accepted, 8 enrolled. In 2009, 60 master's awarded. *Degree requirements:* For master's, thesis or alternative. *Entrance requirements:* For master's, minimum GPA of 3.0, letters of recommendation. Additional exam requirements/recommendations for international students: Required—TOEFL (minimum score 550 paper-based; 213 computer-based; 79 iBT). *Application deadline:* For fall admission, 2/15 priority date for domestic and international students; for spring admission, 9/15 priority date for domestic and international students. Application fee: $80. Electronic applications accepted. *Expenses:* Tuition, state resident: full-time $8370; part-time $349 per credit. Tuition, nonresident: full-time $13,250; part-time $522 per credit. *Financial support:* Federal Work-Study, scholarships/grants, and unspecified assistantships available. Support available to part-time students. Financial award application deadline: 3/15; financial award applicants required to submit FAFSA. *Unit head:* Dr. Sue Novinger, Chairperson, 585-395-2205, Fax: 585-395-2172, E-mail: snovinge@brockport.edu. *Application contact:* Coordinator of Certification and Graduate Advisement.

The College at Brockport, State University of New York, School of Education and Human Services, Department of Education and Human Development, Program in Alternate Adolescence Inclusive Education, Brockport, NY 14420-2997. Offers alternate adolescence English inclusive education (MS Ed); alternate adolescence mathematics inclusive education (MS Ed); alternate adolescence science inclusive education (MS Ed); alternate adolescence social studies inclusive education (MS Ed). *Students:* 25 full-time (8 women), 5 part-time (3 women). 26 applicants, 50% accepted, 11 enrolled. *Degree requirements:* For master's, thesis or alternative. *Entrance requirements:* For master's, minimum GPA of 3.0, letters of recommendation, statement of objectives, academic major (or equivalent) in program discipline. Additional exam requirements/ recommendations for international students: Required—TOEFL (minimum score 550 paper-based; 213 computer-based; 79 iBT). *Application deadline:* For fall admission, 2/15 priority date for domestic and international students; for spring admission, 9/15 priority date for domestic and international students. Application fee: $80. Electronic applications accepted. *Expenses:* Tuition, state resident: full-time $8370; part-time $349 per credit. Tuition, nonresident: full-time $13,250; part-time $522 per credit. *Financial support:* Federal Work-Study, scholarships/ grants, and unspecified assistantships available. Support available to part-time students. Financial award application deadline: 3/15; financial award applicants required to submit FAFSA. *Unit head:* Dr. Sue Novinger, Chairperson, 585-395-2205, E-mail: snovinge@brockport.edu. *Application contact:* Coordinator of Certification and Graduate Advisement.

College of St. Joseph, Graduate Programs, Division of Education, Program in Secondary Education, Rutland, VT 05701-3899. Offers English (M Ed); social studies (M Ed). Part-time and evening/weekend programs available. *Entrance requirements:* For master's, PRAXIS I, 2 letters of recommendation, minimum GPA of 3.0, interview. Electronic applications accepted. *Expenses:* Tuition: Full-time $13,500; part-time $350 per credit. Required fees: $45 per term. One-time fee: $445. Tuition and fees vary according to program.

The College of William and Mary, School of Education, Program in Curriculum and Instruction, Williamsburg, VA 23187-8795. Offers elementary education (MA Ed); gifted education (MA Ed); math specialist (MA Ed); reading education (MA Ed); secondary education (MA Ed), including English education, mathematics education, modern foreign languages education, science education, social studies education; special education (MA Ed), including general curriculum, resource collaborating teaching. *Accreditation:* NCATE. Part-time programs available. *Faculty:* 18 full-time (12 women), 17 part-time/adjunct (15 women). *Students:* 54 full-time (45 women), 12 part-time (all women); includes 3 minority (2 African Americans, 1 Asian American or Pacific Islander), 2 international. Average age 27. 120 applicants, 75% accepted. In 2009, 70 master's awarded. *Degree requirements:* For master's, project. *Entrance requirements:* For master's, GRE or MAT, minimum GPA of 2.5. Additional exam requirements/recommendations for international students: Required—TOEFL. *Application deadline:* For fall admission, 1/15 for domestic and international students; for spring admission, 10/1 for domestic and international students. Application fee: $45. Electronic applications accepted. *Expenses:* Tuition, state resident: full-time $6400; part-time $315 per credit hour. Tuition, nonresident: full-time $19,720; part-time $840 per credit hour. Required fees: $4114. *Financial support:* In 2009–10, 30 students received support, including 10 research assistantships with full and partial tuition reimbursements available (averaging $5,500 per year); career-related internships or fieldwork, Federal Work-Study, institutionally sponsored loans, scholarships/grants, and unspecified assistantships also available. Financial award application deadline: 1/15; financial award applicants required to submit FAFSA. *Faculty research:* National Council of Teachers of Mathematics Standards, counseling, self-concept and self-esteem, special education, curriculum development. *Unit head:* Dr. C. Denise Johnson, Area Coordinator, 757-221-1528, E-mail: cdjohn@wm.edu. *Application contact:* Dorothy Smith Osborne, Director of Admissions, 757-221-2317, Fax: 757-221-2293, E-mail: dsosbo@wm.edu.

The Colorado College, Department of Education, Program in Secondary Education, Colorado Springs, CO 80903-3294. Offers art teaching (K-12) (MAT); English teaching (MAT); foreign language teaching (MAT); mathematics teaching (MAT); music teaching (MAT); science teaching (MAT); social studies teaching (MAT). *Faculty:* 3 full-time (2 women), 8 part-time/adjunct (6 women). *Students:* 15 full-time (5 women); includes 2 minority (1 American Indian/Alaska Native, 1 Asian American or Pacific Islander). Average age 27. 26 applicants, 81% accepted, 15 enrolled. In 2009, 17 master's awarded. *Degree requirements:* For master's, thesis, internship. *Entrance requirements:* For master's, PRAXIS II or PLACE Exam. *Application deadline:* For fall admission, 12/1 priority date for domestic students, 12/1 for international students. Applications are processed on a rolling basis. Application fee: $50. *Expenses:* Tuition: Part-time $2545 per credit. *Financial support:* In 2009–10, 15 students received support, including 7 teaching assistantships (averaging $16,000 per year); career-related internships or fieldwork, institutionally sponsored loans, health care benefits, and tuition waivers (partial) also available. Financial award application deadline: 2/15; financial award applicants required to submit FAFSA. *Unit head:* Mike Taber, Director, 719-389-6026, Fax: 719-389-6473, E-mail: mike. taber@coloradocollege.edu. *Application contact:* Debra Yazulla Mortenson, Education Services Manager, 719-389-6472, Fax: 719-389-6473, E-mail: debra.mortenson@coloradocollege.edu.

Columbus State University, Graduate Studies, College of Education and Health Professions, Department of Teacher Education, Columbus, GA 31907-5645. Offers accomplished teaching (M Ed); early childhood education (M Ed, Ed S); health administration (MPA); instructional technology (MS); middle grades education (M Ed, Ed S); physical education (M Ed); secondary education (M Ed, MAT, Ed S), including English/language arts (M Ed, Ed S), general science (M Ed), mathematics (M Ed), social science (M Ed); special education (M Ed), including behavior disorders, mental retardation. *Accreditation:* NCATE. Part-time and evening/weekend programs available. Postbaccalaureate distance learning degree programs offered (minimal on-campus study). *Faculty:* 18 full-time (15 women), 14 part-time/adjunct (10 women). *Students:* 146 full-time (113 women), 312 part-time (261 women); includes 142 minority (120 African Americans, 1 American Indian/Alaska Native, 8 Asian Americans or Pacific Islanders, 13 Hispanic Americans), 2 international. Average age 31. 248 applicants, 64% accepted, 114 enrolled. In 2009, 103 master's, 22 other advanced degrees awarded. *Degree requirements:* For master's, thesis, exit exam; for Ed S, thesis or alternative. *Entrance requirements:* For master's, GRE General Test, minimum GPA of 2.75; for Ed S, GRE General Test. Additional exam requirements/ recommendations for international students: Required—TOEFL (minimum score 550 paper-based; 213 computer-based; 79 iBT). *Application deadline:* For fall admission, 5/1 priority date for domestic students, 5/1 for international students; for spring admission, 11/1 for domestic and international students. Applications are processed on a rolling basis. Application fee: $30. Electronic applications accepted. *Financial support:* In 2009–10, 305 students received support, including 36 research assistantships with partial tuition reimbursements available (averaging

$3,000 per year); career-related internships or fieldwork, Federal Work-Study, institutionally sponsored loans, scholarships/grants, tuition waivers (partial), and unspecified assistantships also available. Support available to part-time students. Financial award application deadline: 5/1; financial award applicants required to submit FAFSA. *Unit head:* Dr. Deborah Gober, Acting Chair, 706-568-2255, Fax: 706-568-3134, E-mail: gober_deborah@colstate.edu. *Application contact:* Katie Thornton, Graduate Admissions Specialist, 706-568-2035, Fax: 706-568-2462, E-mail: thornton_katie@colstate.edu.

Concord University, Graduate Studies, Athens, WV 24712-1000. Offers behavioral science (M Ed); educational leadership and supervision (M Ed); geography (M Ed); health promotion (M Ed); reading specialist (M Ed); social studies (M Ed). Postbaccalaureate distance learning degree programs offered. *Entrance requirements:* For master's, GRE or MAT, baccalaureate degree with minimum GPA of 2.5 GPA from regionally accredited institution; teaching license; 2 letters of recommendation.

Converse College, School of Education and Graduate Studies, Program in Secondary Education, Spartanburg, SC 29302-0006. Offers biology (MAT); chemistry (MAT); English (M Ed, MAT); mathematics (M Ed, MAT); natural sciences (M Ed); social sciences (M Ed, MAT). Part-time programs available. *Degree requirements:* For master's, capstone paper. *Entrance requirements:* For master's, NTE or PRAXIS II (M Ed), minimum GPA of 2.75, 2 recommendations. Electronic applications accepted.

Delta State University, Graduate Programs, College of Arts and Sciences, Department of History, Cleveland, MS 38733-0001. Offers history education (M Ed). Part-time programs available. *Degree requirements:* For master's, thesis or alternative. *Entrance requirements:* For master's, GRE General Test or MAT. *Expenses:* Tuition, state resident: full-time $4450; part-time $247 per credit hour. Tuition, nonresident: full-time $11,520; part-time $640 per credit hour.

Delta State University, Graduate Programs, College of Arts and Sciences, Division of Social Sciences, Program in Social Science Secondary Education, Cleveland, MS 38733-0001. Offers M Ed. Part-time programs available. *Degree requirements:* For master's, thesis or alternative. *Expenses:* Tuition, state resident: full-time $4450; part-time $247 per credit hour. Tuition, nonresident: full-time $11,520; part-time $640 per credit hour.

Drew University, Caspersen School of Graduate Studies, Program in Education, Madison, NJ 07940-1493. Offers biology (MAT); chemistry (MAT); English (MAT); French (MAT); Italian (MAT); math (MAT); physics (MAT); social studies (MAT); Spanish (MAT); theatre arts (MAT). Part-time programs available. *Students:* 21 full-time (10 women), 6 part-time (2 women); includes 1 minority (Hispanic American). Average age 24. 40 applicants, 90% accepted, 27 enrolled. In 2009, 13 master's awarded. *Entrance requirements:* For master's, transcripts, personal statement, recommendations. Additional exam requirements/recommendations for international students: Required—TOEFL, TWE. *Application deadline:* For fall admission, 2/1 priority date for domestic students. Applications are processed on a rolling basis. Application fee: $35. *Expenses:* Contact institution. *Financial support:* In 2009–10, 22 students received support. Federal Work-Study, scholarships/grants, and tuition waivers (partial) available. Support available to part-time students. Financial award application deadline: 2/15; financial award applicants required to submit FAFSA. *Unit head:* Dr. Ross Danis. *Application contact:* Carla J. Burns, Director of Graduate Admissions, 973-408-3110, Fax: 973-408-3242, E-mail: gradm@drew.edu.

Duquesne University, School of Education, Department of Instruction and Leadership, Program in Secondary Education, Pittsburgh, PA 15282-0001. Offers secondary education (MS Ed), including biology, chemistry, English, Latin, math, physics, social studies, Spanish. Part-time and evening/weekend programs available. *Faculty:* 4 full-time (3 women), 1 part-time/adjunct (0 women). *Students:* 56 full-time (34 women), 8 part-time (3 women); includes 6 minority (3 African Americans, 2 Asian Americans or Pacific Islanders, 1 Hispanic American), 2 international. Average age 29. 69 applicants, 70% accepted, 27 enrolled. In 2009, 36 master's awarded. *Degree requirements:* For master's, thesis optional. *Entrance requirements:* For master's, MAT, minimum GPA of 3.0. Additional exam requirements/recommendations for international students: Required—TOEFL (minimum score 550 paper-based; 80 computer-based). *Application deadline:* For fall admission, 8/1 for domestic students; for spring admission, 12/1 for domestic students. Applications are processed on a rolling basis. Application fee: $0. Electronic applications accepted. *Expenses:* Tuition: Part-time $851 per credit. Required fees: $81 per credit. *Financial support:* Research assistantships, Federal Work-Study available. Support available to part-time students. *Unit head:* Dr. Melissa Boston, Assistant Professor, 412-396-6109, E-mail: bostonm@duq.edu. *Application contact:* Michael Dolinger, Director of Student and Academic Services, 412-396-6647, Fax: 412-396-5585, E-mail: dolingerm@duq.edu.

East Carolina University, Graduate School, College of Education, Department of Curriculum and Instruction, Greenville, NC 27858-4353. Offers behavior/emotional disabilities (MA Ed); elementary education (MA Ed); English education (MA Ed); learning disabilities (MA Ed); low incidence disabilities (MA Ed); mental retardation (MA Ed); middle grade education (MA Ed); reading education (MA Ed); social studies education (MA Ed). Part-time programs available. Postbaccalaureate distance learning degree programs offered. *Degree requirements:* For master's, comprehensive exam, thesis optional. *Entrance requirements:* For master's, GRE General Test or MAT, interview, bachelor's degree in related field, minimum GPA of 2.5, teaching license. Additional exam requirements/recommendations for international students: Required—TOEFL.

Eastern Kentucky University, The Graduate School, College of Education, Department of Curriculum and Instruction, Program in Secondary and Higher Education, Richmond, KY 40475-3102. Offers secondary education (MA Ed), including agricultural education, art education, biological sciences education, business education, English education, geography education, history education, home economics education, industrial education, mathematical sciences education, physical education, school health education. *Accreditation:* NCATE. Part-time programs available. *Entrance requirements:* For master's, GRE General Test, minimum GPA of 2.5.

East Stroudsburg University of Pennsylvania, Graduate School, College of Arts and Sciences, Department of History, East Stroudsburg, PA 18301-2999. Offers M Ed, MA. Part-time and evening/weekend programs available. *Faculty:* 5 full-time (1 woman). *Students:* 9 full-time (3 women), 20 part-time (8 women); includes 2 minority (1 African American, 1 Asian American or Pacific Islander). Average age 31. In 2009, 6 master's awarded. *Degree requirements:* For master's, comprehensive exam, thesis, thesis defense. *Entrance requirements:* For master's, Commonwealth of Pennsylvania Department of Education Certification Requirements (M Ed). Additional exam requirements/recommendations for international students: Required—TOEFL (minimum score 560 paper-based; 220 computer-based; 83 iBT). *Application deadline:* For fall admission, 7/31 priority date for domestic students, 5/1 priority date for international students; for spring admission, 11/30 for domestic students, 10/1 for international students. Applications are processed on a rolling basis. Application fee: $50. *Expenses:* Tuition, state resident: full-time $9942; part-time $387 per credit. Tuition, nonresident: full-time $14,240; part-time $619 per credit. *Financial support:* In 2009–10, 17 research assistantships with full and partial tuition reimbursements (averaging $1,643 per year) were awarded; Federal Work-Study and institutionally sponsored loans also available. Financial award application deadline: 3/1; financial award applicants required to submit FAFSA. *Unit head:* Dr. Lawrence Squeri, Graduate Coordinator, 570-422-3284, Fax: 570-422-3506, E-mail: lsqueri@po-box.esu.edu. *Application contact:* Kevin Quintero, Graduate Admissions Coordinator, 570-422-3890, Fax: 570-422-2711, E-mail: kquintero@po-box.esu.edu.

East Stroudsburg University of Pennsylvania, Graduate School, College of Arts and Sciences, Department of Political Science, East Stroudsburg, PA 18301-2999. Offers M Ed, MA. Part-time and evening/weekend programs available. *Faculty:* 8 full-time (3 women). *Students:* 24 full-time (16 women), 30 part-time (18 women); includes 10 minority (8 African Americans, 2 Hispanic Americans), 1 international. Average age 32. In 2009, 20 master's awarded. *Degree requirements:* For master's, variable foreign language requirement, comprehensive

exam, thesis or alternative. *Entrance requirements:* Additional exam requirements/recommendations for international students: Required—TOEFL (minimum score 560 paper-based; 220 computer-based; 83 iBT). *Application deadline:* For fall admission, 7/31 priority date for domestic students, 5/1 priority date for international students; for spring admission, 11/30 for domestic students, 10/1 for international students. Applications are processed on a rolling basis. Application fee: $50. *Expenses:* Tuition, state resident: full-time $9942; part-time $387 per credit. Tuition, nonresident: full-time $14,240; part-time $619 per credit. *Financial support:* In 2009–10, 17 research assistantships with full and partial tuition reimbursements (averaging $1,618 per year) were awarded; Federal Work-Study and institutionally sponsored loans also available. Financial award application deadline: 3/1; financial award applicants required to submit FAFSA. *Unit head:* Dr. Patricia Crotty, Graduate Coordinator, 570-422-3271, Fax: 570-422-3506, E-mail: pcrotty@po-box.esu.edu. *Application contact:* Kevin Quintero, Graduate Admissions Coordinator, 570-422-3890, Fax: 570-422-2711, E-mail: kquintero@po-box.esu.edu.

Emporia State University, School of Graduate Studies, College of Liberal Arts and Sciences, Department of Social Sciences, Program in Social Sciences, Emporia, KS 66801-5087. Offers American history (MAT); anthropology (MAT); economics (MAT); geography (MAT); political science (MAT); social studies education (MAT); sociology (MAT); world history (MAT). *Accreditation:* NCATE. Part-time programs available. *Students:* 2 full-time (0 women), 8 part-time (4 women); includes 1 minority (Asian American or Pacific Islander). 4 applicants, 75% accepted, 3 enrolled. In 2009, 2 master's awarded. *Degree requirements:* For master's, comprehensive exam or thesis. *Entrance requirements:* For master's, appropriate bachelor's degree, teacher certification. Additional exam requirements/recommendations for international students: Required—TOEFL (minimum score 520 paper-based; 133 computer-based; 68 iBT). *Application deadline:* For fall admission, 8/15 priority date for domestic students. Applications are processed on a rolling basis. Application fee: $30 ($75 for international students). Electronic applications accepted. *Expenses:* Tuition, state resident: full-time $4154; part-time $173 per credit hour. Tuition, nonresident: full-time $12,864; part-time $536 per credit hour. Required fees: $948; $58 per credit hour. Tuition and fees vary according to campus/location. *Financial support:* Federal Work-Study, institutionally sponsored loans, health care benefits, and unspecified assistantships available. Financial award application deadline: 3/15; financial award applicants required to submit FAFSA. *Application contact:* Dr. Christopher Lovett, Associate Professor, 620-341-5577, E-mail: clovett@emporia.edu.

Fayetteville State University, Graduate School, Program in Middle Grades, Secondary and Special Education, Fayetteville, NC 28301-4298. Offers biology (MA Ed); history (MA Ed); mathematics (MA Ed); middle grades (MA Ed); political science (MA Ed); reading (MA Ed); sociology (MA Ed); special education (MA Ed), including behavioral-emotional handicaps, mentally handicapped, specific training disability. *Accreditation:* NCATE. Part-time and evening/weekend programs available. *Faculty:* 15 full-time (10 women), 3 part-time/adjunct (2 women). *Students:* 16 full-time (12 women), 70 part-time (57 women); includes 55 minority (50 African Americans, 1 American Indian/Alaska Native, 1 Asian American or Pacific Islander, 3 Hispanic Americans). Average age 35. 14 applicants, 100% accepted, 14 enrolled. In 2009, 32 master's awarded. *Degree requirements:* For master's, comprehensive exam, internship. *Application deadline:* For fall admission, 4/15 for domestic students; for spring admission, 10/15 for domestic students. Applications are processed on a rolling basis. Application fee: $35. Electronic applications accepted. *Unit head:* Dr. Charletta Barringer-Brown, Interim Chair, 910-672-1182, E-mail: cbarringerbrown@uncfsu.edu. *Application contact:* Roxie Shabazz, Associate Vice-Chancellor for Enrollment Management, 910-672-1784, Fax: 910-672-2209, E-mail: rshabazz@uncfsu.edu.

Fitchburg State University, Division of Graduate and Continuing Education, Programs in History and Teaching History (Secondary Level), Fitchburg, MA 01420-2697. Offers MA, MAT, Certificate. *Accreditation:* NCATE. Part-time and evening/weekend programs available. *Students:* 2 full-time (1 woman), 26 part-time (15 women). Average age 32. 12 applicants, 100% accepted, 8 enrolled. In 2009, 8 master's awarded. *Entrance requirements:* For master's, GRE General Test or MAT, appropriate bachelor's degree, letters of recommendation, resume. Additional exam requirements/recommendations for international students: Required—TOEFL (minimum score 550 paper-based; 213 computer-based; 79 iBT). *Application deadline:* Applications are processed on a rolling basis. Application fee: $25 ($50 for international students). *Expenses:* Tuition, area resident: Part-time $150 per credit. Tuition, state resident: part-time $150 per credit. Tuition, nonresident: part-time $150 per credit. Required fees: $120 per credit. *Financial support:* In 2009–10, research assistantships with partial tuition reimbursements (averaging $5,500 per year); Federal Work-Study, scholarships/grants, and unspecified assistantships also available. Support available to part-time students. Financial award application deadline: 3/1; financial award applicants required to submit FAFSA. *Unit head:* Dr. Laura Baker, Chair, 978-665-3379, Fax: 978-665-3658, E-mail: gce@fsc.edu. *Application contact:* Director of Admissions, 978-665-3144, Fax: 978-665-4540, E-mail: admissions@fsc.edu.

Florida Agricultural and Mechanical University, Division of Graduate Studies, Research, and Continuing Education, College of Education, Program in Secondary Education and Foundation, Tallahassee, FL 32307-3200. Offers biology (M Ed); chemistry (MS Ed); English (MS Ed); history (MS Ed); math (MS Ed); physics (MS Ed). *Accreditation:* NCATE. *Faculty:* 10 full-time (5 women). In 2009, 28 master's awarded. *Degree requirements:* For master's, thesis (for some programs). *Entrance requirements:* For master's, GRE General Test, minimum GPA of 3.0. Additional exam requirements/recommendations for international students: Required—TOEFL. *Application deadline:* For fall admission, 5/18 for domestic students, 12/18 for international students; for spring admission, 11/12 for domestic students, 5/12 for international students. Application fee: $20. *Unit head:* Dr. Bernadette Kelley, Chairperson, 850-599-3123. *Application contact:* Dr. Chanta M. Haywood, Dean of Graduate Studies, Research, and Continuing Education, 850-599-3315, Fax: 850-599-3727.

Florida International University, College of Education, Department of Curriculum and Instruction, Program in Social Studies Education, Miami, FL 33199. Offers MAT, MS, Ed D. *Accreditation:* NCATE. Part-time and evening/weekend programs available. *Entrance requirements:* Additional exam requirements/recommendations for international students: Required—TOEFL. *Expenses:* Tuition, state resident: full-time $8008; part-time $4004 per year. Tuition, nonresident: full-time $20,104; part-time $10,052 per year. Required fees: $298; $149 per term. *Faculty research:* Pedagogical knowledge base for teaching social studies, global education.

Florida State University, The Graduate School, College of Education, School of Teacher Education, Program in Social Science Education, Tallahassee, FL 32306. Offers MS. Part-time programs available. *Faculty:* 3 full-time (2 women), 1 part-time/adjunct (0 women). *Students:* 9 full-time (4 women), 16 part-time (3 women); includes 4 minority (2 African Americans, 2 Hispanic Americans). 7 applicants, 43% accepted, 1 enrolled. In 2009, 3 master's awarded. *Degree requirements:* For master's, comprehensive exam, thesis optional. *Entrance requirements:* For master's, GRE General Test, minimum GPA of 3.0. Additional exam requirements/recommendations for international students: Required—TOEFL (minimum score 550 paper-based; 213 computer-based; 80 iBT). *Application deadline:* For fall admission, 6/1 priority date for domestic students, 6/1 for international students; for spring admission, 10/1 for domestic and international students. Applications are processed on a rolling basis. Application fee: $30. *Expenses:* Tuition, state resident: full-time $7413. Tuition, nonresident: full-time $22,567. *Financial support:* Fellowships with full and partial tuition reimbursements, research assistantships with full and partial tuition reimbursements, teaching assistantships with full and partial tuition reimbursements, career-related internships or fieldwork and Federal Work-Study available. Financial award applicants required to submit FAFSA. *Faculty research:* Globalization, desegregation and civil rights in the Deep South. *Unit head:* Dr. Helge Swanson, Head, 850-644-6553, Fax: 850-644-1880, E-mail: swanson@coe.fsu.edu. *Application contact:* Amy McKnight, Office Manager, 850-644-7810, Fax: 850-644-1880, E-mail: amcknight@coe.fsu.edu.

Framingham State University, Division of Graduate and Continuing Education, Program in History, Framingham, MA 01701-9101. Offers M Ed.

Georgia Southern University, Jack N. Averitt College of Graduate Studies, College of Education, Department of Teaching and Learning, Program in Social Science Education, Statesboro, GA 30460. Offers M Ed, MAT. *Accreditation:* NCATE. Part-time and evening/weekend programs available. *Students:* 13 full-time (7 women), 2 part-time (0 women); includes 2 minority (1 African American, 1 Hispanic American). Average age 26. 5 applicants, 100% accepted, 5 enrolled. In 2009, 6 master's awarded. *Degree requirements:* For master's, portfolio, transition point assessments, exit assessment. *Entrance requirements:* For master's, GRE General Test or MAT; GACE Basic Skills and Content Assessments (MAT), minimum cumulative GPA of 2.5. Additional exam requirements/recommendations for international students: Required—TOEFL (minimum score 550 paper-based; 213 computer-based; 80 iBT). *Application deadline:* For fall admission, 3/1 priority date for domestic and international students; for spring admission, 10/1 priority date for domestic students, 10/1 for international students. Applications are processed on a rolling basis. Application fee: $50. Electronic applications accepted. *Expenses:* Tuition, state resident: full-time $5040; part-time $210 per credit hour. Tuition, nonresident: full-time $20,136; part-time $839 per credit hour. Required fees: $1644. *Financial support:* In 2009–10, 12 students received support, including 1 research assistantship with partial tuition reimbursement available (averaging $7,200 per year), teaching assistantships with partial tuition reimbursements available (averaging $7,200 per year); Federal Work-Study, scholarships/grants, tuition waivers (partial), and unspecified assistantships also available. Support available to part-time students. Financial award application deadline: 4/15; financial award applicants required to submit FAFSA. *Faculty research:* Environmental issues. *Unit head:* Dr. Ronnie Sheppard, Department Chair, 912-478-5203, Fax: 912-478-0026, E-mail: sheppard@georgiasouthern.edu. *Application contact:* Dr. Charles Ziglar, Coordinator for Graduate Student Recruitment, 912-478-5635, Fax: 912-478-0740, E-mail: gradadmissions@georgiasouthern.edu.

Georgia State University, College of Education, Department of Middle-Secondary Education and Instructional Technology, Programs in Secondary Education, Atlanta, GA 30302-3083. Offers art education (Ed S); English education (M Ed, Ed S); mathematics education (M Ed, PhD, Ed S); music education (PhD); science education (M Ed, PhD, Ed S); social studies education (M Ed, PhD, Ed S). *Accreditation:* NASM (one or more programs are accredited); NCATE. Part-time and evening/weekend programs available. *Degree requirements:* For master's, comprehensive exam; for doctorate, comprehensive exam, thesis/dissertation; for Ed S, project/exam. *Entrance requirements:* For master's, GRE General Test, minimum GPA of 2.5; for doctorate, GRE General Test or MAT, minimum GPA of 3.3; for Ed S, GRE General Test or MAT, minimum graduate GPA of 3.25. *Faculty research:* Women and science, problem solving in mathematics, dialects, economic education.

Grambling State University, School of Graduate Studies and Research, College of Arts and Sciences, Program in Social Sciences, Grambling, LA 71245. Offers MAT. Part-time programs available. *Faculty:* 6 full-time (3 women). *Students:* 31 full-time (24 women), 11 part-time (9 women); includes 40 minority (all African Americans), 1 international. Average age 32. 16 applicants, 88% accepted, 12 enrolled. In 2009, 7 master's awarded. *Degree requirements:* For master's, comprehensive exam (for some programs), thesis optional. *Entrance requirements:* For master's, GRE, minimum GPA of 3.0 on last degree. Additional exam requirements/recommendations for international students: Required—TOEFL (minimum score 500 paper-based; 173 computer-based; 61 iBT). *Application deadline:* For fall admission, 7/1 for domestic and international students; for spring admission, 12/1 for domestic and international students. Applications are processed on a rolling basis. Application fee: $20 ($30 for international students). Electronic applications accepted. *Expenses:* Tuition, state resident: full-time $2610. Tuition, nonresident: full-time $2610. *Financial support:* In 2009–10, 2 research assistantships (averaging $6,500 per year) were awarded; traineeships, health care benefits, tuition waivers (full), and unspecified assistantships also available. Financial award application deadline: 5/31; financial award applicants required to submit FAFSA. *Unit head:* Dr. Ronnie L. Davis, Director, 318-274-2235, E-mail: davisr@gram.edu. *Application contact:* Katina Crowe, Special Assistant to Associate Vice President/Dean, 318-274-2158, Fax: 318-274-7373, E-mail: croweks@gram.edu.

Harding University, College of Education, Searcy, AR 72149-0001. Offers advanced studies in teaching and learning (M Ed); art (MSE); behavioral science (MSE); counseling (MS, Ed S); early childhood special education (M Ed, MSE); education (MSE); educational leadership (M Ed, Ed S); elementary education (M Ed); English (MSE); family and consumer science (MSE); French (MSE); history/social science (MSE); kinesiology (MSE); math (MSE); physical science (MSE); reading (M Ed); secondary education (M Ed); Spanish (MSE); special education licensure (M Ed); teaching (MAT); teaching English as a second language (M Ed). *Accreditation:* NCATE. Part-time and evening/weekend programs available. *Faculty:* 11 full-time (4 women), 49 part-time/adjunct (26 women). *Students:* 104 full-time (85 women), 392 part-time (282 women); includes 77 minority (67 African Americans, 5 American Indian/Alaska Native, 1 Asian American or Pacific Islander, 4 Hispanic Americans), 5 international. Average age 36. 153 applicants, 92% accepted, 131 enrolled. In 2009, 153 master's, 6 other advanced degrees awarded. *Degree requirements:* For master's, comprehensive exam (for some programs), thesis optional, portfolio(s); for Ed S, comprehensive exam, portfolio, specialist project. *Entrance requirements:* For master's, GRE, MAT, PRAXIS; for Ed S, MAT or GRE. Additional exam requirements/recommendations for international students: Required—TOEFL (minimum score 550 paper-based; 79 iBT). *Application deadline:* For fall admission, 8/1 for domestic and international students; for spring admission, 1/1 for domestic and international students. Applications are processed on a rolling basis. Application fee: $35. *Expenses:* Tuition: Full-time $9720; part-time $540 per credit hour. Required fees: $22 per credit hour. Tuition and fees vary according to course load and program. *Financial support:* In 2009–10, 30 students received support. Unspecified assistantships available. *Faculty research:* Reading, comprehension, school violence, educational technology, behavior, college choice, differentiated instruction, brain-based teaching. *Unit head:* Dr. Clara Carroll, Chair, 501-279-4501, Fax: 501-279-4083, E-mail: ccarroll@harding.edu. *Application contact:* Information Contact, 501-279-4315, E-mail: gradstudiesedu@harding.edu.

Hofstra University, School of Education, Health, and Human Services, Department of Curriculum and Teaching, Program in Learning and Teaching, Hempstead, NY 11549. Offers learning and teaching (Ed D), including applied linguistics, art education, arts and humanities, early childhood education, English education, human development, math education, math, science, and technology, multicultural education, physical education, science education, social studies education, special education. Part-time and evening/weekend programs available. *Students:* 5 full-time (all women), 21 part-time (17 women); includes 2 minority (1 African American, 1 Hispanic American), 1 international. Average age 38. 22 applicants, 68% accepted, 11 enrolled. *Degree requirements:* For doctorate, comprehensive exam, thesis/dissertation. *Entrance requirements:* For doctorate, GRE, 3 letters of recommendation, interview, 2 years full-time teaching experience. Additional exam requirements/recommendations for international students: Required—TOEFL (minimum score 550 paper-based; 213 computer-based; 80 iBT). *Application deadline:* Applications are processed on a rolling basis. Application fee: $60. Electronic applications accepted. *Expenses:* Tuition: Full-time $16,200; part-time $900 per credit hour. Required fees: $970; $145 per term. Tuition and fees vary according to program. *Financial support:* In 2009–10, 24 students received support, including 20 fellowships with full and partial tuition reimbursements available (averaging $4,906 per year); research assistantships with full and partial tuition reimbursements available, Federal Work-Study, institutionally sponsored loans, scholarships/grants, and tuition waivers (full and partial) also available. Support available to part-time students. Financial award applicants required to submit FAFSA. *Faculty research:* Critical thinking, professional development, teacher quality, quantitative research. *Unit head:* Dr. Bruce A. Torff, Director, 516-463-5803, Fax: 516-463-6196, E-mail: catajs@hofstra.edu. *Application contact:* Carol Drummer, Dean of Graduate Admissions, 516-463-4876, Fax: 516-463-4664, E-mail: gradstudent@hofstra.edu.

Hofstra University, School of Education, Health, and Human Services, Department of Curriculum and Teaching, Program in Social Studies Education, Hempstead, NY 11549. Offers MA, MS Ed, Advanced Certificate. Part-time programs available. *Students:* 38 full-time (18

Social Sciences Education

Hofstra University (continued)
women), 14 part-time (7 women); includes 11 minority (6 African Americans, 1 Asian American or Pacific Islander, 4 Hispanic Americans), 1 international. Average age 26. 56 applicants, 89% accepted, 26 enrolled. In 2009, 28 master's awarded. *Degree requirements:* For master's, one foreign language, exit project. *Entrance requirements:* For master's, 2 letters of recommendation, teacher certification (MA). Additional exam requirements/recommendations for international students: Required—TOEFL (minimum score 550 paper-based; 213 computer-based; 80 iBT). *Application deadline:* Applications are processed on a rolling basis. Application fee: $60. Electronic applications accepted. *Expenses:* Tuition: Full-time $16,200; part-time $900 per credit hour. Required fees: $970; $145 per term. Tuition and fees vary according to program. *Financial support:* In 2009–10, 47 students received support, including 2 fellowships with full and partial tuition reimbursements available (averaging $3,781 per year), 1 research assistantship with full and partial tuition reimbursement available (averaging $18,950 per year); Federal Work-Study, institutionally sponsored loans, scholarships/grants, and tuition waivers (full and partial) also available. Support available to part-time students. Financial award applicants required to submit FAFSA. *Faculty research:* Urban education, multicultural education, assessment and instruction, teaching for understanding, curriculum development. *Unit head:* Dr. Alan J. Singer, Director, 516-463-5853, Fax: 516-463-6196, E-mail: catajs@hofstra.edu. *Application contact:* Carol Drummer, Dean of Graduate Admissions, 516-463-4876, Fax: 516-463-4664, E-mail: gradstudent@hofstra.edu.

Hunter College of the City University of New York, Graduate School, School of Education, Programs in Secondary Education, Concentration in Social Studies Education, New York, NY 10021-5085. Offers MA. *Accreditation:* NCATE. *Faculty:* 5 full-time (1 woman), 3 part-time/adjunct (2 women). *Students:* 10 full-time (6 women), 41 part-time (19 women); includes 5 minority (all Hispanic Americans). Average age 29. 79 applicants, 43% accepted, 13 enrolled. In 2009, 13 master's awarded. *Degree requirements:* For master's, thesis, professional teaching portfolio, New York State Teacher Certification Exam, research project. *Entrance requirements:* For master's, minimum GPA of 3.0 in history, 2.8 overall; 2 letters of reference; minimum of 30 credits in social studies areas. Additional exam requirements/recommendations for international students: Required—TOEFL, TWE. *Application deadline:* For fall admission, 4/1 for domestic students, 2/1 for international students; for spring admission, 11/1 for domestic students, 9/1 for international students. Applications are processed on a rolling basis. Application fee: $125. *Expenses:* Tuition, state resident: full-time $7360; part-time $310 per credit. Required fees: $250 per semester. *Financial support:* Federal Work-Study and tuition waivers (partial) available. Support available to part-time students. *Unit head:* Dr. Barbara Welter, Graduate Advisor, 212-772-5487, E-mail: bwelter@shiva.hunter.cuny.edu. *Application contact:* William Zlata, Director for Graduate Admissions, 212-772-4482, Fax: 212-650-3336, E-mail: admissions@hunter.cuny.edu.

Indiana University Bloomington, School of Education, Department of Curriculum and Instruction, Bloomington, IN 47405-7000. Offers art education (MS, Ed D, PhD); curriculum studies (Ed D, PhD); elementary education (MS, Ed D, PhD, Ed S); mathematics education (MS, Ed D, PhD); science education (MS, Ed D, PhD); secondary education (MS, Ed D, PhD); social studies education (MS, PhD); special education (MS, Ed D, PhD, Ed S). *Accreditation:* NCATE. Part-time and evening/weekend programs available. *Students:* 208 full-time (155 women), 44 part-time (25 women); includes 28 minority (9 African Americans, 3 American Indian/Alaska Native, 9 Asian Americans or Pacific Islanders, 7 Hispanic Americans), 34 international. Average age 34. 100 applicants, 68% accepted, 39 enrolled. In 2009, 48 master's, 20 doctorates awarded. Terminal master's awarded for partial completion of doctoral program. *Degree requirements:* For doctorate, thesis/dissertation; for Ed S, comprehensive exam or project. *Entrance requirements:* For master's, doctorate, and Ed S, GRE General Test. *Application deadline:* For fall admission, 6/1 priority date for domestic students, 3/1 for international students; for winter admission, 11/1 priority date for domestic students; for spring admission, 9/1 for international students. Applications are processed on a rolling basis. Application fee: $55 ($65 for international students). Electronic applications accepted. *Financial support:* Fellowships with full and partial tuition reimbursements, research assistantships with full and partial tuition reimbursements, teaching assistantships with full and partial tuition reimbursements, career-related internships or fieldwork, Federal Work-Study, institutionally sponsored loans, and tuition waivers (partial) available. Support available to part-time students. *Unit head:* Cary Buzzelli, Chairperson, 812-856-8100. *Application contact:* Bobbie Partenheimer, Admissions Services Coordinator, 812-856-8127, Fax: 812-856-8333, E-mail: partenhe@indiana.edu.

Instituto Tecnologico de Santo Domingo, Graduate School, Santo Domingo, Dominican Republic. Offers applied linguistics (MA); construction administration (M Mgmt); corporate finance (M Mgmt); education (M Ed); engineering (M Eng), including data telecommunications, industrial engineering, logistics and supply chain, maintenance engineering, sanitary and environmental engineering, structural engineering; environmental science (M En S), including environmental education, environmental management, marine and coastal ecosystems, natural resources management; family therapy (MA); food science and technology (MS); human development (MA); human resources administration (M Mgmt); international business (M Mgmt); labor risks (M Mgmt); management (M Mgmt); marketing (M Mgmt); mathematics (MS); organizational development (M Mgmt); planning and taxation (M Mgmt); psychology (MA); social science (M Ed); upper management (M Mgmt). *Entrance requirements:* For master's, birth certificate, minimum GPA of 2.0.

Inter American University of Puerto Rico, Arecibo Campus, Programs in Education, Arecibo, PR 00614-4050. Offers administration and educational supervision (MA Ed); counseling and guidance (MA Ed); curriculum and teaching (MA Ed), including biology education, English as a second language, history education, math education, Spanish; elementary education (MA Ed). *Degree requirements:* For master's, comprehensive exam, thesis optional. *Entrance requirements:* For master's, GRE, EXADEP, bachelor's degree in education or teaching license (administration and supervision) or courses in education and psychology (counseling and guidance), minimum GPA of 2.5 in last 60 credits.

Inter American University of Puerto Rico, Ponce Campus, Graduate School, Mercedita, PR 00715-1602. Offers accounting (MBA); biology (M Ed); chemistry (M Ed); criminal justice (MA); elementary education (M Ed); English as a Second Language (M Ed); finance (MBA); history (M Ed); human resources (MBA); marketing (MBA); mathematics (M Ed); Spanish (M Ed). *Entrance requirements:* For master's, minimum GPA of 2.5.

Iona College, School of Arts and Science, Program in Education, New Rochelle, NY 10801-1890. Offers biology education (MS Ed, MST); educational leadership (MS Ed); English education (MS Ed, MST); literacy education (MS Ed); mathematics education (MS Ed, MST); social studies education (MS Ed, MST); Spanish education (MS Ed, MST); teaching in childhood education (MST). *Accreditation:* NCATE. Part-time and evening/weekend programs available. *Faculty:* 24 full-time (13 women), 16 part-time/adjunct (10 women). *Students:* 41 full-time (35 women), 118 part-time (87 women); includes 15 minority (5 African Americans, 1 Asian American or Pacific Islander, 9 Hispanic Americans). Average age 28. 91 applicants, 67% accepted, 41 enrolled. In 2009, 61 master's awarded. *Degree requirements:* For master's, thesis or alternative. *Entrance requirements:* For master's, minimum GPA of 2.5 (MST), New York teaching certificate (MS Ed). Additional exam requirements/recommendations for international students: Required—TOEFL (minimum score 550 paper-based; 213 computer-based). *Application deadline:* Applications are processed on a rolling basis. Application fee: $50. Electronic applications accepted. *Expenses:* Tuition: Part-time $830 per credit. *Financial support:* Unspecified assistantships available. Support available to part-time students. Financial award application deadline: 4/15; financial award applicants required to submit FAFSA. *Faculty research:* Reading/writing, educational technology, administration, early literacy assessment, literacy development. *Unit head:* Dr. Catherine O'Callaghan, Chair, 914-633-2210, Fax: 914-633-2608, E-mail: cocallaghan@iona.edu. *Application contact:* Veronica Jarek-Prinz, Director of Graduate Admissions, 914-633-2420, Fax: 914-633-2277, E-mail: vjarekprinz@iona.edu.

Ithaca College, Division of Graduate and Professional Studies, School of Humanities and Sciences, Program in Adolescent Education, Ithaca, NY 14850. Offers biology 7-12 (MAT); chemistry 7-12 (MAT); English 7-12 (MAT); French 7-12 (MAT); math 7-12 (MAT); physics 7-12 (MAT); social studies 7-12 (MAT); Spanish (MAT). Part-time programs available. *Faculty:* 18 full-time (7 women). *Students:* 15 full-time (10 women), 2 part-time (1 woman); includes 1 minority (African American). Average age 26. 31 applicants, 68% accepted, 16 enrolled. In 2009, 31 master's awarded. *Degree requirements:* For master's, thesis or alternative, student teaching. *Entrance requirements:* For master's, minimum GPA of 3.0. Additional exam requirements/recommendations for international students: Required—TOEFL (minimum score 550 paper-based; 213 computer-based; 80 iBT). *Application deadline:* For fall admission, 5/15 for domestic and international students; for spring admission, 12/1 for domestic and international students. Applications are processed on a rolling basis. Application fee: $40. Electronic applications accepted. *Expenses:* Contact institution. *Financial support:* In 2009–10, 15 students received support, including 10 teaching assistantships (averaging $6,474 per year); career-related internships or fieldwork, Federal Work-Study, scholarships/grants, and unspecified assistantships also available. Support available to part-time students. Financial award applicants required to submit CSS PROFILE or FAFSA. *Faculty research:* Bilingual education, sociolinguistic perspective on literacy. *Unit head:* Dr. Linda Hanrahan, Chairperson, 607-274-3527, Fax: 607-274-1263, E-mail: gps@ithaca.edu. *Application contact:* Rob Gearhart, Dean, Graduate and Professional Studies, 607-274-3527, Fax: 607-274-1263, E-mail: gps@ithaca.edu.

The Johns Hopkins University, School of Education, Department of Teacher Preparation, Baltimore, MD 21218. Offers education (MS), including educational studies; elementary education (MAT); English for speakers of other languages (MAT); K-8 mathematics lead-teacher (Certificate); K-8 science lead-teacher (Certificate); secondary education (MAT), including biology, chemistry, earth/space/environmental science, English, French, mathematics, physics, social studies, Spanish. Part-time and evening/weekend programs available. *Faculty:* 13 full-time (11 women), 35 part-time/adjunct (21 women). *Students:* 162 full-time (119 women), 347 part-time (256 women); includes 138 minority (80 African Americans, 3 American Indian/Alaska Native, 38 Asian Americans or Pacific Islanders, 17 Hispanic Americans), 3 international. Average age 27. 89 applicants, 37% accepted, 24 enrolled. In 2009, 177 master's awarded. *Degree requirements:* For master's, portfolio, PRAXIS II, internship. *Entrance requirements:* For master's, PRAXIS I, SAT, ACT, or GRE (MAT), minimum undergraduate GPA of 3.0, interview, 1 letter of recommendation, curriculum vitae/resume; for Certificate, bachelor's degree, minimum undergraduate GPA of 3.0, essay/statement of goals, interview. Additional exam requirements/recommendations for international students: Required—TOEFL (minimum score 600 paper-based; 250 computer-based; 100 iBT). *Application deadline:* For fall admission, 5/1 for international students; for spring admission, 10/15 for international students. Applications are processed on a rolling basis. Application fee: $80. Electronic applications accepted. *Financial support:* Scholarships/grants available. Support available to part-time students. Financial award application deadline: 6/1; financial award applicants required to submit FAFSA. *Faculty research:* Teacher retention; STEM education reform; alternative certification programs; school-university partnerships; urban education; action research/data-informed instruction; family engagement. *Unit head:* Dr. Francis Masci, Chair, 410-516-9774, Fax: 410-516-9770, E-mail: matjhu@jhu.edu. *Application contact:* Jennifer Shaffer, Director of Admissions, 410-516-9797, Fax: 410-516-9799, E-mail: educationinfo@jhu.edu.

Kutztown University of Pennsylvania, College of Education, Program in Secondary Education, Kutztown, PA 19530-0730. Offers biology (M Ed); curriculum and instruction (M Ed); English (M Ed); mathematics (M Ed); secondary education (Certificate); social studies (M Ed). *Accreditation:* NCATE. Part-time and evening/weekend programs available. *Faculty:* 7 full-time (4 women). *Students:* 90 full-time (45 women), 84 part-time (56 women); includes 8 minority (4 African Americans, 1 Asian American or Pacific Islander, 3 Hispanic Americans), 2 international. Average age 29. 129 applicants, 76% accepted, 31 enrolled. In 2009, 36 master's awarded. *Degree requirements:* For master's, comprehensive exam, thesis optional. *Entrance requirements:* For master's, GRE General Test. Additional exam requirements/recommendations for international students: Required—TOEFL. *Application deadline:* For fall admission, 8/15 priority date for domestic and international students; for spring admission, 12/15 priority date for domestic and international students. Applications are processed on a rolling basis. Application fee: $35. Electronic applications accepted. *Expenses:* Tuition, state resident: full-time $6666; part-time $370 per credit. Tuition, nonresident: full-time $10,666; part-time $593 per credit. Required fees: $62 per credit. $60 per semester. *Financial support:* Career-related internships or fieldwork, Federal Work-Study, scholarships/grants, and unspecified assistantships available. Financial award application deadline: 3/1; financial award applicants required to submit FAFSA. *Unit head:* Dr. Theresa Stahler, Chairperson, 610-683-4259, Fax: 610-683-1338, E-mail: stahler@kutztown.edu. *Application contact:* Kelly D. Burr, Associate Director, Graduate Admissions, 610-683-4200, Fax: 610-683-1393, E-mail: graduate@kutztown.edu.

Lehman College of the City University of New York, Division of Education, Department of Middle and High School Education, Program in Social Studies 7–12, Bronx, NY 10468-1589. Offers MA. *Accreditation:* NCATE. *Entrance requirements:* For master's, minimum GPA of 3.0 in social sciences, 2.7 overall.

Le Moyne College, Department of Education, Syracuse, NY 13214. Offers adolescent education (MS Ed, MST); adolescent education/special education (MS Ed, MST); adolescent English (grades 7-12) (MST); adolescent history (grades 7-12) (MST); childhood education (MS Ed); childhood education/special education (MS Ed); elementary education (MS Ed); general professional education (MS Ed); inclusive childhood education (MST); middle child specialist/special education (MS Ed); middle childhood specialist (MS Ed); school building leadership (MS Ed, CAS); school district business leader (MS Ed, CAS); school district leadership (MS Ed, CAS); secondary education (MS Ed); special education (MS Ed). *Accreditation:* Teacher Education Accreditation Council. Part-time and evening/weekend programs available. *Faculty:* 15 full-time (8 women), 61 part-time/adjunct (33 women). *Students:* 40 full-time (30 women), 260 part-time (180 women); includes 25 minority (11 African Americans, 3 American Indian/Alaska Native, 3 Asian Americans or Pacific Islanders, 8 Hispanic Americans). Average age 31. 168 applicants, 89% accepted, 140 enrolled. In 2009, 180 master's awarded. *Degree requirements:* For master's, thesis. *Entrance requirements:* For master's, GRE General Test, 2 letters of recommendation. Additional exam requirements/recommendations for international students: Required—TOEFL (minimum score 550 paper-based; 213 computer-based; 79 iBT). *Application deadline:* For fall admission, 4/1 priority date for domestic and international students; for spring admission, 10/1 priority date for domestic and international students. Applications are processed on a rolling basis. Application fee: $50. *Expenses:* Contact institution. *Financial support:* In 2009–10, 28 students received support. Career-related internships or fieldwork and health care benefits available. Support available to part-time students. Financial award applicants required to submit FAFSA. *Faculty research:* Recruitment/retention strategies, minority teachers, special education, multiculturalism, literacy, technology, video games learning, autism, school district organization. *Unit head:* Dr. Norbert J. Henry, Interim Chair/Director, 315-445-4376, Fax: 315-445-4744, E-mail: henry@lemoyne.edu. *Application contact:* Kristen P. Trapasso, Director of Graduate Admission, 315-445-4265, Fax: 315-445-6027, E-mail: trapaskp@lemoyne.edu.

Lewis University, College of Education, Program in Secondary Education, Romeoville, IL 60446. Offers biology (MA); chemistry (MA); English (MA); history (MA); math (MA); physics (MA); psychology and social science (MA). Part-time programs available. *Students:* 20 full-time (12 women), 24 part-time (16 women); includes 2 minority (1 African American, 1 Hispanic American). Average age 29. 39 applicants, 51% accepted, 18 enrolled. In 2009, 15 master's awarded. *Entrance requirements:* For master's, departmental qualifying exam, writing exam, minimum GPA of 2.75, 2 letters of recommendation, interview. Additional exam requirements/recommendations for international students: Required—TOEFL (minimum score 550 paper-based; 213 computer-based). *Application deadline:* For fall admission, 5/1 priority date for international students; for spring admission, 11/15 priority date for international students. Applications are processed on a rolling basis. Application fee: $40. Electronic applications accepted. *Expenses:* Tuition: Full-time $6480; part-time $720 per credit. One-time fee: $40.

Tuition and fees vary according to course load, degree level and program. *Financial support:* Federal Work-Study, scholarships/grants, and unspecified assistantships available. Financial award application deadline: 5/1; financial award applicants required to submit FAFSA. *Unit head:* Dr. Dorene Huvaere, Program Director, 815-838-0500 Ext. 5885, E-mail: huvaersdo@lewisu.edu. *Application contact:* Fran Welsh, Secretary, 815-838-0500 Ext. 5880, E-mail: welshfr@lewisu.edu.

Louisiana Tech University, Graduate School, College of Education, Department of Curriculum, Instruction and Leadership, Ruston, LA 71272. Offers curriculum and instruction (MS, Ed D); educational leadership (Ed D); secondary education (M Ed), including business education, English education, foreign language education, health and physical education, mathematics education, science education, social studies education, speech education. *Accreditation:* NCATE. Part-time programs available. *Degree requirements:* For doctorate, thesis/dissertation. *Entrance requirements:* For master's and doctorate, GRE General Test.

Manhattanville College, Graduate Programs, School of Education, Program in Middle Childhood/Adolescence Education (Grades 5-12), Purchase, NY 10577-2132. Offers biology (MAT); biology and special education (MPS); chemistry (MAT); chemistry and special education (MPS); English (MAT); English and special education (MPS); literacy (MPS), including reading and writing, writing; literacy and special education (MPS); math (MAT); math and special education (MPS); second language (MAT), including French, Italian, Latin, Spanish; social studies (MAT); social studies and special education (MPS); special education (MPS). Part-time and evening/weekend programs available. *Students:* 52 full-time (39 women), 106 part-time (71 women); includes 8 African Americans, 3 Asian Americans or Pacific Islanders, 4 Hispanic Americans, 1 international. In 2009, 82 master's awarded. *Degree requirements:* For master's, comprehensive exam or research project, field experience. *Entrance requirements:* For master's, minimum undergraduate GPA of 3.0, 2 letters of recommendation. Additional exam requirements/recommendations for international students: Required—TOEFL. *Application deadline:* Applications are processed on a rolling basis. Application fee: $70. Electronic applications accepted. *Financial support:* Career-related internships or fieldwork, Federal Work-Study, institutionally sponsored loans, and unspecified assistantships available. Support available to part-time students. Financial award application deadline: 3/1; financial award applicants required to submit FAFSA. *Unit head:* Dr. Shelley Wepner, Dean, 914-323-5192, Fax: 914-694-2386, E-mail: wepners@mville.edu. *Application contact:* Jeanine Pardey-Levine, Director of Admissions, 914-323-3208, Fax: 914-694-1732, E-mail: edschool@mville.edu.

Michigan State University, The Graduate School, College of Social Science, Department of History, East Lansing, MI 48824. Offers history (MA, PhD); history-secondary school teaching (MA). *Faculty:* 48 full-time (20 women). *Students:* 71 full-time (37 women), 6 part-time (3 women); includes 15 minority (5 African Americans, 2 American Indian/Alaska Native, 1 Asian American or Pacific Islander, 7 Hispanic Americans), 11 international. Average age 30. 53 applicants, 28% accepted. In 2009, 1 master's, 14 doctorates awarded. *Entrance requirements:* Additional exam requirements/recommendations for international students: Required—TOEFL. Electronic applications accepted. *Expenses:* Tuition, state resident: part-time $478.25 per credit hour. Tuition, nonresident: part-time $966.50 per credit hour. Part-time tuition and fees vary according to program. *Financial support:* In 2009–10, 4 research assistantships with tuition reimbursements (averaging $6,061 per year), 39 teaching assistantships with tuition reimbursements (averaging $6,001 per year) were awarded. Total annual research expenditures: $130,678. *Unit head:* Dr. Keely D. Stauter-Halstead, Acting Chairperson, 517-355-7500, Fax: 517-353-5599, E-mail: stauterh@msu.edu. *Application contact:* Kelli Kolasa, Graduate Secretary, 517-355-7500, Fax: 517-353-5599, E-mail: kolasa@msu.edu.

Mills College, Graduate Studies, School of Education, Oakland, CA 94613-1000. Offers child life in hospitals (MA); early childhood education (MA); education (MA), including art education, curriculum and instruction, elementary education, English education, foreign language education, mathematics education, science education, secondary education, social studies education, teaching; educational leadership (MA, Ed D); infant mental health (MA). Part-time and evening/weekend programs available. *Faculty:* 11 full-time (9 women), 16 part-time/adjunct (14 women). *Students:* 138 full-time (119 women), 55 part-time (48 women); includes 71 minority (34 African Americans, 19 Asian Americans or Pacific Islanders, 18 Hispanic Americans), 3 international. Average age 34. 210 applicants, 82% accepted, 93 enrolled. In 2009, 54 master's, 15 doctorates awarded. Terminal master's awarded for partial completion of doctoral program. *Degree requirements:* For master's, comprehensive exam. *Entrance requirements:* For doctorate, GRE General Test. Additional exam requirements/recommendations for international students: Required—TOEFL. *Application deadline:* For fall admission, 2/1 for domestic and international students; for spring admission, 11/1 for domestic and international students. Applications are processed on a rolling basis. Application fee: $50. Electronic applications accepted. *Expenses:* Tuition: Full-time $26,326; part-time $6584 per course. Required fees: $896. One-time fee: $896 part-time. Tuition and fees vary according to program. *Financial support:* In 2009–10, 188 students received support, including 186 fellowships (averaging $6,499 per year), 28 teaching assistantships with partial tuition reimbursements available (averaging $3,187 per year); career-related internships or fieldwork and scholarships/grants also available. Support available to part-time students. Financial award application deadline: 2/1; financial award applicants required to submit FAFSA. *Faculty research:* Child development, gender and education, public policy, cross-cultural development, development of literacy. Total annual research expenditures: $1.2 million. *Unit head:* Joseph Kahne, Chairperson, 510-430-3190, Fax: 510-430-3314, E-mail: grad-studies@mills.edu. *Application contact:* Jessica King, Graduate Admission Specialist, 510-430-3305, Fax: 510-430-2159, E-mail: grad-studies@mills.edu.

Minnesota State University Mankato, College of Graduate Studies, College of Social and Behavioral Sciences, Department of History, Mankato, MN 56001. Offers history (MA, MS); social studies (MAT). *Students:* 4 full-time (3 women), 9 part-time (1 woman). *Degree requirements:* For master's, one foreign language, comprehensive exam, thesis or alternative. *Entrance requirements:* For master's, minimum GPA of 3.0 during previous 2 years. Additional exam requirements/recommendations for international students: Required—TOEFL. *Application deadline:* For fall admission, 7/1 priority date for domestic students; for spring admission, 11/1 for domestic students. Applications are processed on a rolling basis. Application fee: $40. Electronic applications accepted. *Expenses:* Tuition, state resident: full-time $5364. Tuition, nonresident: full-time $8314. *Financial support:* Research assistantships, teaching assistantships with full tuition reimbursements, career-related internships or fieldwork, Federal Work-Study, institutionally sponsored loans, and unspecified assistantships available. Support available to part-time students. Financial award application deadline: 3/15. *Faculty research:* Charivaris, Lindbergh in the U. S., Dutch trade to South America in the seventeenth and eighteenth centuries. *Unit head:* Dr. Kathleen Gorman, Graduate Coordinator, 507-389-2720. *Application contact:* 507-389-2321, E-mail: grad@mnsu.edu.

Mississippi College, Graduate School, School of Education, Department of Teacher Education and Leadership, Clinton, MS 39058. Offers art (M Ed); biological science (M Ed); business education (M Ed); computer science (M Ed); dyslexia therapy (M Ed); educational leadership (M Ed, Ed D, Ed S); elementary education (M Ed, Ed S); English (M Ed); higher education administration (MS); mathematics (M Ed); secondary education (M Ed); social studies (history) (M Ed); teaching arts (M Ed). Part-time programs available. Postbaccalaureate distance learning degree programs offered (no on-campus study). *Faculty:* 11 full-time (7 women), 13 part-time/adjunct (7 women). *Students:* 33 full-time (22 women), 282 part-time (240 women); includes 148 minority (146 African Americans, 2 American Indian/Alaska Native), 1 international. Average age 34. In 2009, 147 master's awarded. *Degree requirements:* For master's, comprehensive exam, thesis optional. *Entrance requirements:* For master's, NTE. Additional exam requirements/recommendations for international students: Recommended—IELTS. *Application deadline:* For fall admission, 8/15 priority date for domestic students. Applications are processed on a rolling basis. Application fee: $30. Electronic applications accepted. *Expenses:* Tuition: Part-time $452 per credit hour. Required fees: $101 per semester. Tuition and fees vary according to degree level, campus/location, program and student level. *Financial support:* Teaching assistantships, career-related internships or fieldwork, Federal Work-Study, scholarships/grants, and unspecified assistantships available. Support available to part-time students. Financial award applicants required to submit FAFSA. *Unit head:* Dr. Tom Williams, Chair, 601-925-3844, E-mail: twilliams@mc.edu. *Application contact:* Elnora Lewis, Secretary, 601-925-3225, Fax: 601-925-3889, E-mail: lewis09@mc.edu.

Missouri State University, Graduate College, College of Humanities and Public Affairs, Department of History, Springfield, MO 65897. Offers history (MA); secondary education (MS Ed), including history, social science. Part-time programs available. *Faculty:* 17 full-time (4 women). *Students:* 18 full-time (7 women), 46 part-time (17 women). Average age 33. 19 applicants, 84% accepted, 15 enrolled. In 2009, 6 master's awarded. *Degree requirements:* For master's, comprehensive exam, thesis or alternative. *Entrance requirements:* For master's, minimum GPA of 2.75, 24 hours of undergraduate course work in history (MA), 9-12 teaching certification (MS Ed). Additional exam requirements/recommendations for international students: Required—TOEFL (minimum score 550 paper-based; 213 computer-based; 79 iBT). *Application deadline:* For fall admission, 7/20 priority date for domestic students, 5/1 for international students; for spring admission, 12/20 priority date for domestic students, 9/1 for international students. Applications are processed on a rolling basis. Application fee: $35 ($50 for international students). Electronic applications accepted. *Expenses:* Tuition, state resident: full-time $3852; part-time $214 per credit hour. Tuition, nonresident: full-time $7524; part-time $418 per credit hour. Required fees: $696; $172 per semester. Tuition and fees vary according to course level, course load, degree level and program. *Financial support:* In 2009–10, 5 teaching assistantships with full tuition reimbursements (averaging $7,340 per year) were awarded; Federal Work-Study, scholarships/grants, and unspecified assistantships also available. Support available to part-time students. Financial award application deadline: 3/31; financial award applicants required to submit FAFSA. *Faculty research:* U.S. history, Native American history, Latin American history, women's history, ancient Near East. *Unit head:* Thomas S. Dicke, Head, 417-836-5511, Fax: 417-836-5523, E-mail: history@missouristate.edu. *Application contact:* Eric Eckert, Coordinator of Admissions and Recruitment, 417-836-5331, Fax: 417-836-6200, E-mail: ericeckert@missouristate.edu.

Montclair State University, The Graduate School, College of Humanities and Social Sciences, Department of History, Montclair, NJ 07043-1624. Offers social sciences (MA), including history; social studies (Certificate). Part-time and evening/weekend programs available. *Faculty:* 16 full-time (6 women), 24 part-time/adjunct (6 women). *Students:* 1 full-time (0 women), 18 part-time (7 women). Average age 32. 12 applicants, 33% accepted, 2 enrolled. In 2009, 4 master's awarded. *Degree requirements:* For master's, comprehensive exam. *Entrance requirements:* For master's, GRE General Test, 2 letters of recommendation. Additional exam requirements/recommendations for international students: Required—TOEFL (minimum score 83 computer-based), or IELTS. *Application deadline:* For fall admission, 6/1 for international students; for spring admission, 11/1 for international students. Applications are processed on a rolling basis. Application fee: $60. Electronic applications accepted. *Expenses:* Tuition, area resident: Part-time $486.74 per credit. Tuition, state resident: part-time $486.74 per credit. Tuition, nonresident: part-time $751.34 per credit. Tuition and fees vary according to degree level and program. *Financial support:* In 2009–10, 5 research assistantships with full tuition reimbursements (averaging $7,000 per year) were awarded; Federal Work-Study, scholarships/grants, and unspecified assistantships also available. Support available to part-time students. Financial award application deadline: 3/1. *Unit head:* Dr. Michael Whelan, Chairperson, 973-655-7848. *Application contact:* Amy Aiello, Director of Admissions and Operations, 973-655-5147, Fax: 973-655-7869, E-mail: graduate.school@montclair.edu.

Morehead State University, Graduate Programs, College of Education, Department of Foundational and Graduate Studies in Education, Morehead, KY 40351. Offers adult and higher education (MA, Ed S); certified professional counselor (Ed S); counseling P-12 (MA); curriculum and instruction (Ed S); educational technology (MA Ed); instructional leadership (Ed S); school administration (MA); school counseling (Ed S); teacher leader business and marketing- content (MA Ed); teacher leader business and marketing- technology (MA Ed); teacher leader educational technology (MA Ed); teacher leader English (MA Ed); teacher leader gifted educ (MA Ed); teacher leader IECE—non-certification (MA Ed); teacher leader IECE certification (MA Ed); teacher leader interdisciplanary education P-5 (MA Ed); teacher leader middle grades 5-9 (MA Ed); teacher leader reading/writing—non-certification (MA Ed); teacher leader reading/writing certification (MA Ed); teacher leader school communication—non-certification (MA Ed); teacher leader school communication certification (MA Ed); teacher leader social studies (MA Ed); teacher leader special education (MA Ed). *Accreditation:* NCATE. Part-time and evening/weekend programs available. *Faculty:* 20 full-time (10 women), 7 part-time/adjunct (3 women). *Students:* 26 full-time (18 women), 371 part-time (295 women); includes 11 minority (9 African Americans, 1 American Indian/Alaska Native, 1 Hispanic American). Average age 35. 201 applicants, 73% accepted, 73 enrolled. In 2009, 105 master's, 5 other advanced degrees awarded. *Degree requirements:* For master's, thesis optional, oral and/or written comprehensive exams; for Ed S, thesis, oral exam. *Entrance requirements:* For master's, GRE General Test, minimum overall undergraduate GPA of 2.5; for Ed S, GRE General Test, interview, master's degree, minimum GPA of 3.5, work experience. Additional exam requirements/recommendations for international students: Required—TOEFL (minimum score 500 paper-based; 173 computer-based). *Application deadline:* For fall admission, 8/1 priority date for domestic and international students; for spring admission, 12/1 priority date for domestic and international students. Applications are processed on a rolling basis. Application fee: $30. Electronic applications accepted. *Expenses:* Tuition, state resident: full-time $6318; part-time $351 per credit hour. Tuition, nonresident: full-time $15,804; part-time $878 per credit hour. *Financial support:* In 2009–10, 2 research assistantships (averaging $10,000 per year) were awarded; career-related internships or fieldwork, Federal Work-Study, and unspecified assistantships also available. Financial award application deadline: 3/15; financial award applicants required to submit FAFSA. *Faculty research:* Character education, school accountability, computer applications for school administrators. *Unit head:* Dr. Cathy Gunn, Dean and Professor, 606-783-2040, Fax: 606-783-5029, E-mail: c.gunn@moreheadstate.edu. *Application contact:* Michelle Barber, Graduate Recruitment and Retention Assistant Director, 606-783-5127, Fax: 606-783-5061, E-mail: m.barber@moreheadstate.edu.

Morehead State University, Graduate Programs, College of Education, Department of Middle Grades and Secondary Education, Morehead, KY 40351. Offers business and marketing education (MAT); English/language arts 5-9 (MAT); French (MAT); health P-12 (MAT); mathematics 5-9 (MAT); physical education P-12 (MAT); science 5-9 (MAT); secondary biology (MAT); secondary chemistry (MAT); secondary earth science (MAT); secondary English (MAT); secondary math (MAT); secondary physics (MAT); secondary social studies (MAT); social studies 5-9 (MAT); Spanish (MAT). Part-time and evening/weekend programs available. *Students:* 54 full-time (31 women), 233 part-time (142 women); includes 11 minority (5 African Americans, 1 American Indian/Alaska Native, 1 Asian American or Pacific Islander, 4 Hispanic Americans). Average age 32. 206 applicants, 71% accepted, 79 enrolled. In 2009, 101 master's awarded. *Degree requirements:* For master's, portfolio. *Entrance requirements:* For master's, GRE or PRAXIS II content exam, minimum overall undergraduate GPA of 2.5. Additional exam requirements/recommendations for international students: Required—TOEFL (minimum score 500 paper-based; 173 computer-based). *Application deadline:* For fall admission, 8/1 priority date for domestic and international students; for spring admission, 12/1 priority date for domestic and international students. Applications are processed on a rolling basis. Application fee: $30. Electronic applications accepted. *Expenses:* Tuition, state resident: full-time $6318; part-time $351 per credit hour. Tuition, nonresident: full-time $15,804; part-time $878 per credit hour. *Financial support:* In 2009–10, 1 research assistantship (averaging $10,000 per year) was awarded; career-related internships or fieldwork, Federal Work-Study, and unspecified assistantships also available. Financial award application deadline: 3/15; financial award applicants required to submit FAFSA. *Unit head:* Dr. Cathy Gunn, Dean, 606-783-2040, Fax: 606-783-5029, E-mail: c.gunn@moreheadstate.edu. *Application contact:* Michelle Barber, Graduate Recruitment and Retention Assistant Director, 606-783-5127, Fax: 606-783-5061, E-mail: m.barber@moreheadstate.edu.

New York University, Steinhardt School of Culture, Education, and Human Development, Department of Music and Performing Arts Professions, Program in Educational Theatre, New

Social Sciences Education

New York University (continued)
York, NY 10012-1019. Offers dual degree: educational theatre and social studies (MA); educational theatre (Ed D, PhD, Advanced Certificate); educational theatre for colleges and communities (MA); educational theatre with English 7-12 (MA); teaching educational theatre, all grades (MA). Part-time programs available. *Students:* 78 full-time (64 women), 65 part-time (43 women); includes 24 minority (10 African Americans, 1 American Indian/Alaska Native, 4 Asian Americans or Pacific Islanders, 9 Hispanic Americans), 7 international. Average age 30. 104 applicants, 84% accepted, 58 enrolled. In 2009, 74 master's, 2 doctorates awarded. *Degree requirements:* For master's, thesis (for some programs); for doctorate, thesis/dissertation. *Entrance requirements:* For master's, audition; for doctorate, GRE General Test, interview; for Advanced Certificate, master's degree. Additional exam requirements/recommendations for international students: Required—TOEFL. *Application deadline:* For fall admission, 12/15 priority date for domestic and international students; for spring admission, 11/1 for domestic and international students. Applications are processed on a rolling basis. Application fee: $75. Electronic applications accepted. *Expenses:* Tuition: Full-time $30,528; part-time $1272 per credit. Required fees: $2177. *Financial support:* Teaching assistantships with partial tuition reimbursements, career-related internships or fieldwork, Federal Work-Study, institutionally sponsored loans, and scholarships/grants available. Support available to part-time students. Financial award application deadline: 2/1; financial award applicants required to submit FAFSA. *Faculty research:* Theatre for young audiences, drama in education, applied theatre, arts education assessment, reflective praxis. *Unit head:* Dr. Philip Taylor, Director, 212-998-5424, Fax: 212-995-4043. *Application contact:* 212-998-5030, Fax: 212-995-4328, E-mail: steinhardt.gradadmissions@nyu.edu.

New York University, Steinhardt School of Culture, Education, and Human Development, Department of Teaching and Learning, Program in Social Studies Education, New York, NY 10012-1019. Offers MA. *Accreditation:* Teacher Education Accreditation Council. Part-time and evening/weekend programs available. *Students:* 18 full-time (13 women), 9 part-time (5 women); includes 6 minority (1 American Indian/Alaska Native, 1 Asian American or Pacific Islander, 4 Hispanic Americans). Average age 27. 43 applicants, 81% accepted, 8 enrolled. In 2009, 26 master's awarded. *Degree requirements:* For master's, thesis (for some programs). *Entrance requirements:* Additional exam requirements/recommendations for international students: Required—TOEFL. *Application deadline:* For fall admission, 12/15 priority date for domestic and international students; for spring admission, 11/1 for domestic and international students. Applications are processed on a rolling basis. Application fee: $75. Electronic applications accepted. *Expenses:* Tuition: Full-time $30,528; part-time $1272 per credit. Required fees: $2177. *Financial support:* Career-related internships or fieldwork, Federal Work-Study, institutionally sponsored loans, scholarships/grants, and tuition waivers (partial) available. Support available to part-time students. Financial award application deadline: 2/1; financial award applicants required to submit FAFSA. *Faculty research:* Social studies education reform, ethnography and oral history, civic education, labor history and social studies curriculum, material culture. *Application contact:* 212-998-5030, Fax: 212-995-4328, E-mail: steinhardt.gradadmissions@nyu.edu.

North Carolina Agricultural and Technical State University, Graduate School, College of Arts and Sciences, Department of History and Social Science Education, Greensboro, NC 27411. Offers history education (MAT, MS); social studies education (MS). *Accreditation:* NCATE (one or more programs are accredited). *Degree requirements:* For master's, comprehensive exam, qualifying exam. *Entrance requirements:* For master's, GRE General Test.

North Carolina State University, Graduate School, College of Education, Department of Curriculum and Instruction, Program in Social Studies Education, Raleigh, NC 27695. Offers M Ed. *Entrance requirements:* For master's, GRE or MAT, 3 letters of reference, interview, minimum GPA of 3.0.

North Dakota State University, College of Graduate and Interdisciplinary Studies, College of Human Development and Education, School of Education, Fargo, ND 58108. Offers agricultural education (M Ed, MS), including agricultural education, agricultural extension education (MS); counseling (M Ed, MS, PhD); curriculum and instruction (M Ed, MS), including pedagogy, physical education and athletic administration; education (PhD); educational leadership (M Ed, MS, Ed S); family and consumer sciences education (M Ed, MS); history education (M Ed, MS); institutional analysis (Ed D); mathematics education (M Ed, MS); music education (M Ed, MS); occupational and adult education (Ed D); science education (M Ed, MS). *Accreditation:* NCATE. Part-time and evening/weekend programs available. Postbaccalaureate distance learning degree programs offered (minimal on-campus study). *Faculty:* 25 full-time (9 women), 3 part-time/adjunct (1 woman). *Students:* 29 full-time (25 women), 207 part-time (132 women); includes 15 minority (4 African Americans, 6 American Indian/Alaska Native, 3 Asian Americans or Pacific Islanders, 2 Hispanic Americans), 4 international. 88 applicants, 67% accepted, 56 enrolled. In 2009, 44 master's, 5 doctorates awarded. *Degree requirements:* For master's, comprehensive exam; for doctorate, thesis/dissertation; for Ed S, thesis. *Entrance requirements:* For degree, GRE General Test, master's degree, minimum GPA of 3.25. Additional exam requirements/recommendations for international students: Required—TOEFL. *Application deadline:* Applications are processed on a rolling basis. Application fee: $45 ($60 for international students). *Financial support:* Research assistantships, teaching assistantships, career-related internships or fieldwork, Federal Work-Study, institutionally sponsored loans, and tuition waivers (full) available. Financial award application deadline: 4/15. *Unit head:* Dr. William Martin, Chair, 701-231-7202, Fax: 701-231-7416, E-mail: william.martin@ndsu.edu. *Application contact:* Dr. William Martin, Chair, 701-231-7202, Fax: 701-231-7416, E-mail: william.martin@ndsu.edu.

North Georgia College & State University, Graduate Studies, Program in Teacher Education, Dahlonega, GA 30597. Offers early childhood education (M Ed); educational leadership (Ed S); middle grades education (M Ed); secondary education (M Ed), including art education, biology education, chemistry education, English education, history education, mathematics education, physical education, science education; special education (M Ed), including interrelated special education, learning disabilities. *Accreditation:* NCATE. Part-time and evening/weekend programs available. Postbaccalaureate distance learning degree programs offered (minimal on-campus study). *Degree requirements:* For master's, comprehensive exam, thesis optional. *Entrance requirements:* For master's, GRE General Test or MAT, minimum GPA of 2.75; for Ed S, GRE General Test or MAT, 3 years of teaching experience, master's degree, minimum graduate GPA of 3.25. Electronic applications accepted. *Faculty research:* Computers and teachers' attitudes, rural versus urban teacher attitudes, teacher leadership roles, minority recruitment in teaching force.

Northwestern State University of Louisiana, Graduate Studies and Research, College of Education, Programs in Education, Natchitoches, LA 71497. Offers business and distributive education (M Ed); counseling (M Ed); early childhood education (M Ed); education (M Ed); education leadership (M Ed); educational technology (M Ed); elementary teaching (M Ed); English education (M Ed); home economics education (M Ed); mathematics education (M Ed); reading (M Ed); science education (M Ed); secondary teaching (M Ed); social sciences education (M Ed). *Degree requirements:* For master's, comprehensive exam, thesis or alternative. *Entrance requirements:* For master's, GRE General Test, minimum undergraduate GPA of 2.5.

Northwest Missouri State University, Graduate School, College of Arts and Sciences, Department of History, Humanities, and Political Science, Maryville, MO 64468-6001. Offers history (MA); teaching history (MS Ed). Part-time programs available. *Faculty:* 6 full-time (2 women). *Students:* 9 full-time (7 women), 4 part-time (0 women). 8 applicants, 88% accepted, 3 enrolled. In 2009, 4 master's awarded. *Degree requirements:* For master's, comprehensive exam, thesis. *Entrance requirements:* For master's, GRE General Test, undergraduate major/minor in social studies/humanities, minimum undergraduate GPA of 2.5, writing sample. Additional exam requirements/recommendations for international students: Required—TOEFL (minimum score 550 paper-based; 213 computer-based). *Application deadline:* For fall admission, 7/1 for domestic and international students; for spring admission, 11/15 for domestic and international students. Applications are processed on a rolling basis. Application fee: $0 ($50 for international students). *Expenses:* Tuition, state resident: part-time $296.34 per credit hour. Tuition, nonresident: part-time $510.43 per credit hour. *Financial support:* In 2009–10, 2 research assistantships with full tuition reimbursements (averaging $6,000 per year) were awarded. Financial award application deadline: 4/1; financial award applicants required to submit FAFSA. *Unit head:* Dr. Richard Frucht, Chairperson, 660-562-1614. *Application contact:* Dr. Gregory Haddock, Dean of Graduate School, 660-562-1145, Fax: 660-562-1096, E-mail: gradsch@nwmissouri.edu.

Nova Southeastern University, Fischler School of Education and Human Services, Graduate Teacher Education Program, Fort Lauderdale, FL 33314-7796. Offers athletic administration (MS); brain research (MS, Ed S); charter school education/leadership (MS); cognitive and behavioral disabilities (MS); computer science education (Ed S); computer science education (K-12) (MS); curriculum and teaching (Ed S); curriculum, instruction and technology (MS); curriculum, instruction, management and administration (Ed S); early childhood education (MS); early literacy and reading (Ed S); early literacy education (MS); education technology (MS); educational leadership (administration K–12) (MS, Ed S); educational media (Ed S); educational media (K-12) (MS); elementary education (MS, Ed S), including ESOL endorsement (MS); English education (MS, Ed S); environmental education (MS); exceptional student education (MS), including ESOL endorsement; gifted education (MS, Ed S); interdisciplinary arts education (MS); management and administration of educational programs (MS); mathematics (MS); mathematics education (Ed S); multicultural early intervention (MS); pre-kindergarten/primary (MS); preschool education (MS); reading (MS); reading and TESOL (MS); reading education (Ed S); science (MS); science education (Ed S); secondary education (MS); social studies (MS, Ed S); Spanish language (MS); special education and reading (MS); teaching and learning (MA, MS), including curriculum and instruction (MA), elementary mathematics (MA), elementary reading (MA), K-12 technology integration (MA); teaching English to speakers of other languages (MS, Ed S); technology management and administration (Ed S); urban studies education (MS). Part-time and evening/weekend programs available. Postbaccalaureate distance learning degree programs offered (minimal on-campus study). *Faculty:* 72 full-time (43 women), 385 part-time/adjunct (252 women). *Students:* 196 full-time (175 women), 1,304 part-time (1,128 women); includes 594 minority (471 African Americans, 5 American Indian/Alaska Native, 18 Asian Americans or Pacific Islanders, 100 Hispanic Americans). Average age 37. 2,610 applicants, 72% accepted, 1352 enrolled. In 2009, 836 other advanced degrees awarded. *Degree requirements:* For master's and Ed S, thesis, practicum, internship. *Entrance requirements:* For master's, MAT, GRE, CLAST, CBEST, PRAXIS I, General Knowledge Test, minimum GPA of 2.5; for Ed S, MAT or GRE, master's degree, teaching certificate, minimum GPA of 3.0. Additional exam requirements/recommendations for international students: Required—TSE (recommended, minimum score 50); Recommended—TOEFL (minimum score 550 paper-based; 213 computer-based; 80 iBT), IELTS (minimum score 6). *Application deadline:* For fall admission, 9/25 priority date for domestic and international students; for winter admission, 2/23 priority date for domestic and international students; for spring admission, 4/25 priority date for domestic and international students. Applications are processed on a rolling basis. Application fee: $50. Electronic applications accepted. *Financial support:* Federal Work-Study available. Support available to part-time students. Financial award application deadline: 4/15; financial award applicants required to submit FAFSA. *Faculty research:* School effectiveness, critical thinking, leadership skills acquisition, child education, multicultural education. *Unit head:* Dr. Ronald Kern, Dean of Academic Affairs, 800-986-3223 Ext. 7809, Fax: 954-262-3606, E-mail: rk429@nsu.nova.edu. *Application contact:* Dr. Jennifer Quinones Nottingham, Dean of Student Affairs, 800-986-3223 Ext. 1559.

Occidental College, Graduate Studies, Department of Education, Program in Secondary Education, Los Angeles, CA 90041-3314. Offers English and comparative literary studies (MAT); history (MAT); life science (MAT); mathematics (MAT); physical science (MAT); social science (MAT); Spanish (MAT). Part-time programs available. *Degree requirements:* For master's, comprehensive exam, graduate synthesis paper. *Entrance requirements:* For master's, GRE General Test, minimum GPA of 3.0. Additional exam requirements/recommendations for international students: Required—TOEFL (minimum score 625 paper-based; 263 computer-based). *Expenses:* Contact institution.

Ohio University, Graduate College, College of Education, Department of Teacher Education, Athens, OH 45701-2979. Offers adolescent to young adult education (M Ed); curriculum and instruction (M Ed, PhD); early childhood/special education (M Ed); intervention specialist/mild-moderate needs (M Ed); intervention specialist/moderate-intensive needs (M Ed); mathematics education (PhD); middle child education (M Ed); reading education (M Ed, PhD); social studies education (PhD). Part-time and evening/weekend programs available. *Faculty:* 21 full-time (13 women), 7 part-time/adjunct (all women). *Students:* 105 full-time (75 women), 183 part-time (161 women); includes 9 minority (5 African Americans, 3 American Indian/Alaska Native, 1 Asian American or Pacific Islander), 14 international. 190 applicants, 80% accepted, 72 enrolled. *Degree requirements:* For master's, thesis or alternative; for doctorate, comprehensive exam, thesis/dissertation. *Entrance requirements:* For master's, GRE General Test or MAT (if GPA is below 2.9); for doctorate, GRE General Test, minimum GPA of 3.4, work experience. Additional exam requirements/recommendations for international students: Required—TOEFL (minimum score 550 paper-based; 80 iBT) or IELTS Academic (minimum score 6.5). *Application deadline:* For fall admission, 5/1 priority date for domestic students, 4/1 priority date for international students; for winter admission, 11/1 priority date for domestic students, 10/1 priority date for international students; for spring admission, 2/15 priority date for domestic students, 1/1 priority date for international students. Applications are processed on a rolling basis. Application fee: $50 ($55 for international students). Electronic applications accepted. *Expenses:* Tuition, state resident: full-time $7839; part-time $323 per quarter hour. Tuition, nonresident: full-time $15,831; part-time $654 per quarter hour. Required fees: $2931. *Financial support:* Research assistantships with full tuition reimbursements, teaching assistantships with full tuition reimbursements, Federal Work-Study, institutionally sponsored loans, tuition waivers (partial), and unspecified assistantships available. Financial award application deadline: 3/1. *Faculty research:* Cognition literacy, character education, teacher's education reform, disabilities. Total annual research expenditures: $46,933. *Unit head:* Dr. John Henning, Chair, 740-597-1830, Fax: 740-593-0477, E-mail: henningj@ohio.edu. *Application contact:* Floyd J. Doney, Director of Student Affairs, 740-593-4400, Fax: 740-593-9310, E-mail: doney@ohio.edu.

Portland State University, Graduate Studies, College of Liberal Arts and Sciences, Interdisciplinary Programs in General Science, General Social Science, and General Arts and Letters, Portland, OR 97207-0751. Offers general arts and letters education (MAT, MST); general science education (MAT, MST); general social science education (MAT, MST). Part-time and evening/weekend programs available. *Degree requirements:* For master's, variable foreign language requirement, written exam. *Entrance requirements:* For master's, minimum GPA of 3.0 in upper-division course work or 2.75 overall. Additional exam requirements/recommendations for international students: Required—TOEFL (minimum score 550 paper-based; 213 computer-based).

Purdue University, Graduate School, School of Education, Department of Curriculum and Instruction, West Lafayette, IN 47907. Offers agricultural and extension education (PhD, Ed S); agriculture and extension education (MS, MS Ed); art education (PhD); consumer and family sciences and extension education (MS Ed, PhD, Ed S); curriculum studies (MS Ed, PhD, Ed S); educational technology (MS Ed, PhD, Ed S); elementary education (MS Ed); foreign language education (MS Ed, PhD, Ed S); industrial technology (PhD, Ed S); language arts (MS Ed, PhD, Ed S); literacy (MS Ed, PhD, Ed S); mathematics/science education (MS, MS Ed, PhD, Ed S); social studies (MS Ed, PhD); social studies education (Ed S); vocational/industrial education (MS Ed, PhD, Ed S); vocational/technical education (MS Ed, PhD, Ed S). *Accreditation:* NCATE. Part-time and evening/weekend programs available. *Degree requirements:* For master's, thesis optional; for doctorate, thesis/dissertation, oral and written exams; for Ed S, oral presentation, project. *Entrance requirements:* For master's, GRE General Test, minimum B average; for doctorate, GRE General Test; for Ed S, GRE, minimum B average.

Additional exam requirements/recommendations for international students: Required—TOEFL. Electronic applications accepted. *Faculty research:* Literacy acquisition and development, teacher beliefs and knowledge, recruitment and retention of underrepresented students, economic education, literacy discourse.

Queens College of the City University of New York, Division of Graduate Studies, Division of Education, Department of Secondary Education, Flushing, NY 11367-1597. Offers art (MS Ed); biology (MS Ed, AC); chemistry (MS Ed, AC); earth sciences (MS Ed, AC); English (MS Ed, AC); French (MS Ed, AC); Italian (MS Ed, AC); mathematics (MS Ed, AC); music (MS Ed, AC); physics (MS Ed, AC); social studies (MS Ed, AC); Spanish (MS Ed, AC). Part-time and evening/weekend programs available. *Faculty:* 22 full-time (14 women). *Students:* 86 full-time (47 women), 1,118 part-time (736 women). 591 applicants, 60% accepted, 250 enrolled. In 2009, 187 master's awarded. *Degree requirements:* For master's, research project; for AC, thesis optional. *Entrance requirements:* For master's, minimum GPA of 3.0. Additional exam requirements/recommendations for international students: Required—TOEFL. *Application deadline:* For fall admission, 4/1 for domestic students; for spring admission, 11/1 for domestic students. Applications are processed on a rolling basis. Application fee: $125. *Expenses:* Tuition, state resident: full-time $7360; part-time $310 per credit. Tuition, nonresident: part-time $575 per credit. One-time fee: $195 full-time; $145.25 part-time. *Financial support:* Career-related internships or fieldwork, Federal Work-Study, institutionally sponsored loans, and tuition waivers (partial) available. Support available to part-time students. Financial award application deadline: 4/1; financial award applicants required to submit FAFSA. *Unit head:* Dr. Eleanor Armour-Thomas, Chairperson, 718-997-5150, E-mail: armourthomas@yahoo.com. *Application contact:* Mario Caruso, Director of Graduate Admissions, 718-997-5200, Fax: 718-997-5193, E-mail: graduate_admissions@qc.edu.

Quinnipiac University, Division of Education, Program in Secondary Education, Hamden, CT 06518-1940. Offers biology (MAT); English (MAT); history/social studies (MAT); mathematics (MAT); Spanish (MAT). *Accreditation:* NCATE. *Faculty:* 10 full-time (7 women), 5 part-time/adjunct (3 women). *Students:* 80 full-time (56 women), 2 part-time (1 woman); includes 6 minority (2 African Americans, 2 Asian Americans or Pacific Islanders, 2 Hispanic Americans). 77 applicants, 95% accepted, 66 enrolled. In 2009, 33 master's awarded. *Entrance requirements:* For master's, PRAXIS I, minimum GPA of 2.67, interview. Additional exam requirements/recommendations for international students: Required—TOEFL (minimum score 575 paper-based; 233 computer-based; 90 iBT), IELTS (minimum score 6.5). *Application deadline:* For fall admission, 3/31 priority date for domestic students. Applications are processed on a rolling basis. Application fee: $45. Electronic applications accepted. *Expenses:* Tuition: Full-time $16,030; part-time $770 per credit. Required fees: $630; $35 per credit. *Financial support:* Career-related internships or fieldwork, scholarships/grants, and tuition waivers (partial) available. Financial award application deadline: 4/15; financial award applicants required to submit FAFSA. *Faculty research:* Multicultural and urban education, role of technology in education, challenges of teaching diverse learners, socio-cultural nature of learning. *Unit head:* Dr. Bernadine Krawczyk, Assistant Dean, Division of Education, 203-582-3510, Fax: 203-582-3473, E-mail: bernadine.krawczyk@quinnipiac.edu. *Application contact:* Jennifer Boutin, Associate Director of Graduate Admissions, 800-462-1944, Fax: 203-582-3443, E-mail: jennifer.boutin@quinnipiac.edu.

Rhode Island College, School of Graduate Studies, Feinstein School of Education and Human Development, Department of Educational Studies, Providence, RI 02908-1991. Offers English (MAT); French (MAT); history (MAT); math (MAT); secondary education (MAT); Spanish (MAT); teaching English as a second language (M Ed); technology education (M Ed). *Accreditation:* NCATE. Part-time and evening/weekend programs available. *Faculty:* 10 full-time (5 women), 6 part-time/adjunct (5 women). *Students:* 8 full-time (all women), 56 part-time (40 women); includes 2 minority (both Hispanic Americans). Average age 35. In 2009, 28 master's awarded. *Degree requirements:* For master's, capstone or comprehensive assessment. *Entrance requirements:* For master's, GRE or MAT (for most programs), minimum undergraduate GPA of 3.0; baccalaureate degree in English, French, history, math or Spanish; evaluation of content area knowledge; 3 letters of recommendation; interview. Additional exam requirements/recommendations for international students: Recommended—TOEFL (minimum score 550 paper-based; 213 computer-based; 79 iBT). *Application deadline:* For fall admission, 3/15 for domestic students; for spring admission, 11/1 for domestic students. Applications are processed on a rolling basis. Application fee: $50. *Expenses:* Tuition, state resident: full-time $7440; part-time $310 per credit hour. Tuition, nonresident: full-time $14,784; part-time $616 per credit hour. Required fees: $552; $20 per credit. $70 per term. *Financial support:* Teaching assistantships with full tuition reimbursements, career-related internships or fieldwork, Federal Work-Study, scholarships/grants, health care benefits, and unspecified assistantships available. Support available to part-time students. Financial award application deadline: 5/15; financial award applicants required to submit FAFSA. *Faculty research:* School administration, school/college articulation. *Unit head:* Dr. Ellen Bigler, Chair, 401-456-8170. *Application contact:* Graduate Studies, 401-456-8700.

Rider University, Department of Graduate Education, Leadership and Counseling, Teacher Certification Program, Lawrenceville, NJ 08648-3001. Offers business education (Certificate); elementary education (Certificate); English as a second language (Certificate); English education (Certificate); mathematics education (Certificate); preschool to grade 3 (Certificate); science education (Certificate); social studies education (Certificate); world languages (Certificate), including French, German, Spanish. Part-time programs available. *Degree requirements:* For Certificate, internship, professional portfolio. *Entrance requirements:* For degree, PRAXIS, resume. Additional exam requirements/recommendations for international students: Required—TOEFL (minimum score 550 paper-based; 213 computer-based). Electronic applications accepted. *Faculty research:* Conceptual foundations for optimal development of creativity; creative theory, cognitive processes in mathematics learning, teacher collaboration.

Rivier College, School of Graduate Studies, Department of History, Law and Government, Nashua, NH 03060. Offers social studies education (MAT). *Faculty:* 3 full-time (1 woman), 3 part-time/adjunct (1 woman). *Students:* 7 full-time (5 women), 13 part-time (7 women). Average age 36. In 2009, 5 master's awarded. Application fee: $25. *Expenses:* Tuition: Part-time $447 per credit. *Unit head:* Martin Menke, Chairperson, 603-897-8603. *Application contact:* Mathew Kittredge, Director of Graduate Admissions, 603-897-8129, Fax: 603-897-8810, E-mail: mkittredge@rivier.edu.

Rutgers, The State University of New Jersey, New Brunswick, Graduate School of Education, Department of Educational Theory, Policy and Administration, Program in Social Studies Education, Piscataway, NJ 08854-8097. Offers Ed M, Ed D. Part-time and evening/weekend programs available. Terminal master's awarded for partial completion of doctoral program. *Degree requirements:* For master's, comprehensive exam; for doctorate, thesis/dissertation, qualifying exam. *Entrance requirements:* For master's and doctorate, GRE General Test. Additional exam requirements/recommendations for international students: Required—TOEFL. Electronic applications accepted. *Faculty research:* Academic freedom, equal educational opportunity, social studies curricula.

Sage Graduate School, Graduate School, School of Education, Program in Teaching, Troy, NY 12180-4115. Offers art education (MAT); English (MAT); mathematics (MAT); social studies (MAT). Part-time and evening/weekend programs available. *Faculty:* 15 full-time (9 women), 19 part-time/adjunct (16 women). *Students:* 32 full-time (25 women), 39 part-time (27 women); includes 4 minority (all Asian Americans or Pacific Islanders). Average age 27. 47 applicants, 55% accepted, 19 enrolled. In 2009, 36 master's awarded. *Entrance requirements:* For master's, minimum undergraduate GPA of 2.75 overall, 3.0 in content area; current resume; 2 letters of recommendation; assessment of writing skills. Additional exam requirements/recommendations for international students: Required—TOEFL (minimum score 550 paper-based; 213 computer-based). *Application deadline:* For fall admission, 8/1 for domestic students. Applications are processed on a rolling basis. Application fee: $40. *Expenses:* Tuition: Full-time $10,620; part-time $590 per credit hour. *Financial support:* Fellowships, research assistantships, Federal Work-Study, scholarships/grants, and unspecified assistantships available. Support available to part-time students. Financial award application deadline: 3/1; financial award applicants required to submit FAFSA. *Unit head:* Kelly Jones, Director, 518-244-2433. *Application contact:* Wendy D. Diefendorf, Director of Graduate and Adult Admission, 518-244-2443, Fax: 518-244-6880, E-mail: diefew@sage.edu.

St. John Fisher College, Ralph C. Wilson Jr. School of Education, Program in Adolescence Education/Special Education, Rochester, NY 14618-3597. Offers adolescence English (MS Ed); adolescence French (MS Ed); adolescence social studies (MS Ed); adolescence Spanish (MS Ed). Part-time and evening/weekend programs available. *Faculty:* 3 full-time (1 woman), 1 (woman) part-time/adjunct. *Students:* 39 full-time (18 women), 5 part-time (2 women); includes 7 minority (1 African American, 2 American Indian/Alaska Native, 1 Asian American or Pacific Islander, 3 Hispanic Americans). Average age 28. 39 applicants, 90% accepted, 20 enrolled. In 2009, 17 master's awarded. *Degree requirements:* For master's, field experiences, student teaching, LAST. *Entrance requirements:* For master's, 2 letters of recommendation, personal statement, current resume. Additional exam requirements/recommendations for international students: Required—TOEFL (minimum score 575 paper-based; 233 computer-based; 80 iBT). *Application deadline:* Applications are processed on a rolling basis. Application fee: $30. Electronic applications accepted. *Expenses:* Tuition: Part-time $680 per credit hour. Required fees: $25 per semester. Tuition and fees vary according to degree level and program. *Financial support:* In 2009–10, 40 students received support. Federal Work-Study and scholarships/grants available. Financial award applicants required to submit FAFSA. *Faculty research:* Arts and humanities, urban schools, constructivist learning, at risk students, mentoring. *Unit head:* Dr. Russell Coward, Program Director, 585-385-8114, E-mail: rcoward@sjfc.edu. *Application contact:* Jose Perales, Director of Graduate Admissions, 585-385-8067, E-mail: jperales@sjfc.edu.

Smith College, Graduate and Special Programs, Department of Education and Child Study, Program in Secondary Education, Northampton, MA 01063. Offers biological sciences education (MAT); chemistry education (MAT); English education (MAT); French education (MAT); geology education (MAT); government education (MAT); history education (MAT); mathematics education (MAT); physics education (MAT); Spanish education (MAT). Part-time programs available. *Faculty:* 6 full-time (4 women), 3 part-time/adjunct (2 women). *Students:* 7 full-time (4 women), 1 part-time (0 women). Average age 25. 14 applicants, 100% accepted, 8 enrolled. In 2009, 9 master's awarded. *Entrance requirements:* Additional exam requirements/recommendations for international students: Required—TOEFL (minimum score 590 paper-based; 243 computer-based; 97 iBT). *Application deadline:* For fall admission, 4/1 for domestic students, 1/15 priority date for international students; for spring admission, 12/1 for domestic students. Application fee: $60. *Financial support:* In 2009–10, 6 students received support. Career-related internships or fieldwork, institutionally sponsored loans, and scholarships/grants available. Support available to part-time students. Financial award application deadline: 1/15; financial award applicants required to submit CSS PROFILE or FAFSA. *Unit head:* Rosetta Cohen, Graduate Student Advisor, 413-585-3266, E-mail: rcohen@smith.edu. *Application contact:* Ruth Morgan, Administrative Assistant, 413-585-3050, Fax: 413-585-3054, E-mail: gradstdy@smith.edu.

South Carolina State University, School of Graduate Studies, Department of Education, Orangeburg, SC 29117-0001. Offers early childhood and special education (M Ed); early childhood education (MAT); elementary education (M Ed, MAT); engineering (MAT); general science (MAT); mathematics (MAT); secondary education (M Ed), including biology education, business education, counselor education, English education, home economics education, industrial education, mathematics education, science education, social studies education; special education (M Ed), including emotionally handicapped, learning disabilities, mentally handicapped. *Accreditation:* NCATE. Part-time and evening/weekend programs available. *Degree requirements:* For master's, thesis optional, departmental qualifying exam. *Entrance requirements:* For master's, GRE General Test, NTE, interview, teaching certificate. Electronic applications accepted. *Expenses:* Tuition, state resident: part-time $470 per credit hour. Tuition, nonresident: part-time $924 per credit hour. *Faculty research:* Critical thinking, child abuse, stress, test-taking skills, conflict resolution, mainstreaming.

Southern Illinois University Edwardsville, Graduate Studies and Research, School of Education, Department of Curriculum and Instruction, Program in Secondary Education, Edwardsville, IL 62026-0001. Offers art (MS Ed); biology (MS Ed); chemistry (MS Ed); earth and space sciences (MS Ed); English/language arts (MS Ed); foreign languages (MS Ed); history (MS Ed); mathematics (MS Ed); physics (MS Ed). *Accreditation:* NCATE. Part-time and evening/weekend programs available. *Students:* 24 part-time (19 women); includes 2 minority (1 African American, 1 Hispanic American). Average age 26. 13 applicants, 31% accepted. In 2009, 5 master's awarded. *Degree requirements:* For master's, thesis or alternative, final exam/paper. *Entrance requirements:* Additional exam requirements/recommendations for international students: Required—TOEFL (minimum score 550 paper-based; 213 computer-based; 79 iBT), IELTS (minimum score 6.5). *Application deadline:* For fall admission, 7/23 for domestic students, 6/1 for international students; for spring admission, 12/11 for domestic students, 10/1 for international students. Applications are processed on a rolling basis. Application fee: $30. Electronic applications accepted. *Expenses:* Tuition, state resident: part-time $1252.50 per semester. Tuition, nonresident: part-time $3131.25 per semester. Required fees: $586.85 per semester. Tuition and fees vary according to course load. *Financial support:* Fellowships, research assistantships, teaching assistantships, career-related internships or fieldwork, Federal Work-Study, institutionally sponsored loans, scholarships/grants, traineeships, and unspecified assistantships available. Support available to part-time students. Financial award application deadline: 3/1; financial award applicants required to submit FAFSA. *Unit head:* Dr. Kathy Bushrow, Director, 618-650-3082, E-mail: kbushro@siue.edu. *Application contact:* Dr. Kathy Bushrow, Director, 618-650-3082, E-mail: kbushro@siue.edu.

Southwestern Oklahoma State University, College of Arts and Sciences, Department of Social Sciences, Weatherford, OK 73096-3098. Offers M Ed. *Degree requirements:* For master's, exam. *Entrance requirements:* For master's, GRE General Test or minimum undergraduate GPA of 3.0. Additional exam requirements/recommendations for international students: Required—TOEFL.

Spring Hill College, Graduate Programs, Program in Liberal Arts, Mobile, AL 36608-1791. Offers fine arts (MLA); history and social science (MLA); leadership and ethics (MLA); literature (MLA). Part-time and evening/weekend programs available. *Faculty:* 11 full-time (4 women), 3 part-time/adjunct (2 women). *Students:* 1 (woman) full-time, 33 part-time (16 women); includes 6 minority (5 African Americans, 1 Hispanic American), 2 international. Average age 35. 27 applicants, 41% accepted, 6 enrolled. In 2009, 6 master's awarded. *Degree requirements:* For master's, capstone course, completion of program within 6 years of initial admittance. *Entrance requirements:* For master's, bachelor's degree with minimum undergraduate GPA of 3.0 or graduate/professional degree. Additional exam requirements/recommendations for international students: Required—TOEFL (minimum score 550 paper-based; 213 computer-based; 80 iBT), IELTS (minimum score 6.5). *Application deadline:* For fall admission, 8/1 priority date for domestic and international students; for spring admission, 12/1 priority date for domestic and international students. Applications are processed on a rolling basis. Application fee: $25 ($35 for international students). Electronic applications accepted. *Expenses:* Contact institution. *Financial support:* In 2009–10, 30 students received support. Career-related internships or fieldwork, institutionally sponsored loans, and scholarships/grants available. Support available to part-time students. Financial award applicants required to submit FAFSA. *Unit head:* Dr. Alexander R. Landi, Director, 251-380-3056, Fax: 251-460-2115, E-mail: landi@shc.edu. *Application contact:* Donna B. Tarasavage, Director of Marketing and Recruiting, Graduate and Continuing Studies, 251-380-3067, Fax: 251-460-2190, E-mail: dtarasavage@shc.edu.

Stanford University, School of Education, Program in Curriculum Studies and Teacher Education, Stanford, CA 94305-9991. Offers art education (MA, PhD); dance education (MA); English education (MA, PhD); general curriculum studies (MA, PhD); mathematics education (MA, PhD); science education (MA, PhD); social studies education (PhD); teacher education (MA, PhD). *Degree requirements:* For master's, thesis (for some programs); for doctorate,

Social Sciences Education

Stanford University (continued)
thesis/dissertation. *Entrance requirements:* For master's and doctorate, GRE General Test. Electronic applications accepted. *Expenses:* Tuition: Full-time $37,380; part-time $2760 per quarter. Required fees: $501.

Stanford University, School of Education, Teacher Education Program, Stanford, CA 94305-9991. Offers English education (MA); languages education (MA); mathematics education (MA); science education (MA); social studies education (MA). *Degree requirements:* For master's, thesis. *Entrance requirements:* For master's, GRE General Test. Electronic applications accepted. *Expenses:* Tuition: Full-time $37,380; part-time $2760 per quarter. Required fees: $501.

State University of New York at Binghamton, Graduate School, School of Education, Program in Adolescence Education, Binghamton, NY 13902-6000. Offers biology education (MAT, MS Ed, MST); earth science education (MAT, MS Ed, MST); English education (MAT, MS Ed, MST); French education (MAT, MST); mathematical sciences education (MAT, MS Ed, MST); physics (MAT, MS Ed, MST); social studies (MAT, MS Ed, MST); Spanish education (MAT, MST). *Accreditation:* Teacher Education Accreditation Council. Part-time and evening/weekend programs available. *Students:* 93 full-time (37 women), 21 part-time (8 women); includes 6 minority (2 Asian Americans or Pacific Islanders, 4 Hispanic Americans), 1 international. Average age 27. 69 applicants, 81% accepted, 46 enrolled. In 2009, 53 master's awarded. *Entrance requirements:* For master's, GRE General Test. Additional exam requirements/recommendations for international students: Required—TOEFL (minimum score 550 paper-based; 213 computer-based; 80 iBT). *Application deadline:* For fall admission, 2/1 priority date for domestic and international students; for spring admission, 10/15 priority date for domestic and international students. Applications are processed on a rolling basis. Application fee: $60. Electronic applications accepted. *Financial support:* Fellowships with partial tuition reimbursements, research assistantships with full and partial tuition reimbursements, teaching assistantships with full tuition reimbursements, career-related internships or fieldwork, Federal Work-Study, institutionally sponsored loans, scholarships/grants, health care benefits, tuition waivers (full), and unspecified assistantships available. Financial award application deadline: 2/15; financial award applicants required to submit FAFSA. *Unit head:* Dr. S. G. Grant, Dean of School of Education, 607-777-7329, E-mail: sggrant@binghamton.edu. *Application contact:* Victoria Williams, Recruiting and Admissions Coordinator, 607-777-2151, Fax: 607-777-2501, E-mail: vwilliam@binghamton.edu.

State University of New York at New Paltz, Graduate School, School of Education, Department of Secondary Education, New Paltz, NY 12561. Offers adolescence education: biology (MAT, MS Ed); adolescence education: english (MAT); adolescence education: English (MS Ed); adolescence education: social studies (MAT, MS Ed); English as a second language (MS Ed); second language education (MS Ed). *Accreditation:* NCATE. Part-time and evening/weekend programs available. *Faculty:* 9 full-time (5 women), 4 part-time/adjunct (3 women). *Students:* 86 full-time (51 women), 102 part-time (74 women); includes 22 minority (4 African Americans, 1 American Indian/Alaska Native, 3 Asian Americans or Pacific Islanders, 14 Hispanic Americans), 2 international. Average age 30. 122 applicants, 54% accepted, 53 enrolled. In 2009, 81 master's awarded. *Degree requirements:* For master's, comprehensive exam (for some programs), portfolio. *Entrance requirements:* For master's, minimum GPA of 3.0, NYS teaching certificate (MS Ed). Additional exam requirements/recommendations for international students: Required—TOEFL (minimum score 550 paper-based; 213 computer-based; 80 iBT), IELTS (minimum score 6.5). *Application deadline:* For fall admission, 3/1 priority date for domestic students, 3/1 for international students; for spring admission, 10/1 priority date for domestic students, 10/1 for international students. Application fee: $50. Electronic applications accepted. *Financial support:* In 2009–10, 4 students received support, including 3 fellowships (averaging $9,000 per year); Federal Work-Study, institutionally sponsored loans, and tuition waivers (full) also available. Financial award application deadline: 8/1; financial award applicants required to submit FAFSA. *Unit head:* Dr. Devon Duhaney, Chair, 845-257-2850, E-mail: duhaneyd@newpaltz.edu. *Application contact:* Caroline Murphy, Graduate Admissions Advisor, 845-257-3285, Fax: 845-257-3284, E-mail: gradschool@newpaltz.edu.

State University of New York at Plattsburgh, Division of Education, Health, and Human Services, Program in Teacher Education: Adolescence MST, Plattsburgh, NY 12901-2681. Offers adolescence education (MST); biology 7-12 (MST); chemistry 7-12 (MST); earth science 7-12 (MST); English 7-12 (MST); French 7-12 (MST); mathematics 7-12 (MST); physics 7-12 (MST); social studies 7-12 (MST); Spanish 7-12 (MST). *Accreditation:* Teacher Education Accreditation Council. Part-time and evening/weekend programs available. *Faculty:* 4 full-time (3 women), 2 part-time/adjunct (0 women). *Students:* 83 full-time (49 women), 5 part-time (3 women); includes 9 minority (2 African Americans, 1 American Indian/Alaska Native, 1 Asian American or Pacific Islander, 5 Hispanic Americans), 2 international. Average age 27. 72 applicants, 71% accepted, 44 enrolled. In 2009, 57 master's awarded. *Degree requirements:* For master's, portfolio. *Entrance requirements:* For master's, minimum GPA of 2.75. Additional exam requirements/recommendations for international students: Required—TOEFL (minimum score 550 paper-based; 213 computer-based; 79 iBT). *Application deadline:* For fall admission, 2/15 priority date for domestic students. Applications are processed on a rolling basis. Application fee: $75. *Expenses:* Tuition, state resident: full-time $8370; part-time $349 per credit hour. Tuition, nonresident: full-time $13,250; part-time $552 per credit hour. Required fees: $1130. *Financial support:* Application deadline: 4/15. *Unit head:* Dr. Robert Ackland, Coordinator, 518-564-5131, E-mail: acklanrt@plattsburgh.edu. *Application contact:* Marguerite Adelman, Assistant Director, Graduate Admissions, 518-564-4723, Fax: 518-564-4722, E-mail: adelmaml@plattsburgh.edu.

State University of New York College at Cortland, Graduate Studies, School of Arts and Sciences, Programs in Adolescence Education, Cortland, NY 13045. Offers biology (MAT, MS Ed); chemistry (MAT, MS Ed); earth science (MAT, MS Ed); English (MS Ed); French (MS Ed); mathematics (MAT, MS Ed); physics (MAT, MS Ed); social studies (MS Ed); Spanish (MS Ed). *Accreditation:* NCATE. Part-time and evening/weekend programs available. *Degree requirements:* For master's, one foreign language, comprehensive exam (for some programs), thesis (for some programs). *Entrance requirements:* For master's, GRE General Test.

State University of New York College at Potsdam, School of Education and Professional Studies, Program in Secondary Education, Potsdam, NY 13676. Offers English (MST); mathematics (with grades 5-6 extension) (MST); science (MST), including biology, chemistry, earth science, physics; Social Studies (with grades 5-6 extension) (MST). *Accreditation:* NCATE. *Faculty:* 9 full-time (3 women), 3 part-time/adjunct (2 women). *Students:* 49 full-time (27 women), 6 part-time (1 woman); includes 5 minority (3 African Americans, 2 American Indian/Alaska Native), 7 international. 13 applicants, 62% accepted, 8 enrolled. In 2009, 49 master's awarded. *Degree requirements:* For master's, thesis optional, culminating experience. *Entrance requirements:* For master's, minimum GPA of 2.75 in last 60 hours of course work (3.0 for English program). Additional exam requirements/recommendations for international students: Required—TOEFL (minimum score 550 paper-based; 213 computer-based; 80 iBT), IELTS (minimum score 6). *Application deadline:* For fall admission, 4/1 priority date for domestic and international students; for spring admission, 10/15 priority date for domestic and international students. Applications are processed on a rolling basis. Application fee: $50. *Expenses:* Tuition, state resident: full-time $8370; part-time $349 per credit hour. Tuition, nonresident: full-time $13,250; part-time $552 per credit hour. Required fees: $942; $38.70 per credit hour. *Financial support:* Fellowships, teaching assistantships, career-related internships or fieldwork, Federal Work-Study, scholarships/grants, and unspecified assistantships available. Support available to part-time students. Financial award application deadline: 3/1; financial award applicants required to submit FAFSA. *Unit head:* Dr. Peter Brouwer, Chairperson, 315-267-3018, Fax: 315-267-4802, E-mail: brouweps@potsdam.edu. *Application contact:* Peter Cutler, Graduate Admissions Counselor, 315-267-3154, Fax: 315-267-4802, E-mail: cutlerpj@potsdam.edu.

Stony Brook University, State University of New York, School of Professional Development, Stony Brook, NY 11794. Offers biology-grade 7-12 (MAT); chemistry-grade 7-12 (MAT); coaching (Graduate Certificate); computer integrated engineering (Graduate Certificate); earth science-grade 7-12 (MAT); educational computing (Graduate Certificate); educational leadership (Advanced Certificate); English-grade 7-12 (MAT); environmental management (Graduate Certificate); environmental/occupational health and safety (Graduate Certificate); French-grade 7-12 (MAT); German-grade 7-12 (MAT); human resource management (Graduate Certificate); information systems management (Graduate Certificate); Italian-grade 7-12 (MAT); liberal studies (MA); mathematics-grade 7-12 (MAT); operation research (Graduate Certificate); physics-grade 7-12 (MAT); school administration and supervision (Graduate Certificate); school building leadership (Graduate Certificate); school district administration (Graduate Certificate); school district business leadership (Advanced Certificate); school district leadership (Graduate Certificate); social science and the professions (MPS), including environmental waste management, human resource management; social studies-grade 7-12 (MAT); Spanish-grade 7-12 (MAT); waste management (Graduate Certificate). Part-time and evening/weekend programs available. Postbaccalaureate distance learning degree programs offered. *Faculty:* 5 full-time (3 women), 131 part-time/adjunct (53 women). *Students:* 317 full-time (187 women), 1,200 part-time (773 women); includes 187 minority (77 African Americans, 2 American Indian/Alaska Native, 22 Asian Americans or Pacific Islanders, 86 Hispanic Americans), 11 international. Average age 28. In 2009, 597 master's, 234 other advanced degrees awarded. *Degree requirements:* For master's, one foreign language, thesis or alternative. *Application deadline:* Applications are processed on a rolling basis. Application fee: $62. *Expenses:* Tuition, state resident: full-time $8370; part-time $349 per credit. Tuition, nonresident: full-time $13,250; part-time $552 per credit. Required fees: $933. *Financial support:* Fellowships, research assistantships, teaching assistantships, career-related internships or fieldwork available. Support available to part-time students. *Unit head:* Dr. Paul J. Edelson, Dean, 631-632-7052, Fax: 631-632-9046, E-mail: paul.edelson@stonybrook.edu. *Application contact:* Dr. Paul J. Edelson, Dean, 631-632-7052, Fax: 631-632-9046, E-mail: paul.edelson@stonybrook.edu.

Syracuse University, School of Education, Program in Social Studies Education: Preparation 7-12, Syracuse, NY 13244. Offers MS. Part-time and evening/weekend programs available. *Students:* 13 full-time (7 women); includes 2 minority (1 African American, 1 Asian American or Pacific Islander). Average age 24. 9 applicants, 67% accepted, 4 enrolled. In 2009, 4 master's awarded. *Degree requirements:* For master's, thesis or alternative. *Entrance requirements:* Additional exam requirements/recommendations for international students: Required—TOEFL (minimum score 100 iBT). *Application deadline:* For fall admission, 2/1 priority date for domestic and international students; for spring admission, 10/15 priority date for domestic and international students. Applications are processed on a rolling basis. Application fee: $75. Electronic applications accepted. *Expenses:* Tuition: Full-time $26,808; part-time $1117 per credit. Required fees: $1024. *Financial support:* Fellowships with tuition reimbursements, teaching assistantships with tuition reimbursements, tuition waivers (partial) available. Financial award application deadline: 1/1; financial award applicants required to submit FAFSA. *Unit head:* Dr. Jeffery Mangram, Program Coordinator, 315-443-9077, E-mail: jamangra@syr.edu. *Application contact:* Liza Rochelson, Graduate Recruiter, School of Education, 315-443-2505, E-mail: e-gradrcrt@syr.edu.

Teachers College, Columbia University, Graduate Faculty of Education, Department of Arts and Humanities, Program in Social Studies Education, New York, NY 10027-6696. Offers Ed M, MA, Ed D, PhD. *Accreditation:* NCATE. Part-time and evening/weekend programs available. *Faculty:* 4 full-time (3 women). *Students:* 46 full-time (27 women), 57 part-time (29 women); includes 14 minority (7 African Americans, 4 Asian Americans or Pacific Islanders, 3 Hispanic Americans), 3 international. Average age 30. 109 applicants, 67% accepted, 34 enrolled. In 2009, 61 master's, 2 doctorates awarded. Terminal master's awarded for partial completion of doctoral program. *Degree requirements:* For doctorate, thesis/dissertation. *Application deadline:* For fall admission, 5/15 for domestic students. Application fee: $65. *Financial support:* Fellowships, research assistantships, teaching assistantships, career-related internships or fieldwork, Federal Work-Study, institutionally sponsored loans, and tuition waivers (full and partial) available. Support available to part-time students. Financial award application deadline: 2/1. *Faculty research:* History of social studies education, social studies curriculum and teaching, women's history, gender and diversity issues in the classroom. *Unit head:* Graeme Sullivan, Chair, 212-678-3799. *Application contact:* Mark E. Stearns, Associate Director of Admission, 212-678-3710, Fax: 212-678-4171.

Texas A&M University–Commerce, Graduate School, College of Arts and Sciences, Department of History, Commerce, TX 75429-3011. Offers history (MA, MS); social sciences (M Ed, MS). Part-time programs available. *Degree requirements:* For master's, comprehensive exam, thesis (for some programs). *Entrance requirements:* For master's, GRE General Test. Electronic applications accepted. *Faculty research:* American foreign policy, colonial America, Texas politics, Medieval England.

Texas State University–San Marcos, Graduate School, College of Liberal Arts, Department of Geography, Program in Environmental Geography, Geography Education, and Geography Information Science, San Marcos, TX 78666. Offers environmental geography (PhD); geography education (PhD); information science (PhD). Part-time programs available. *Students:* 46 full-time (22 women), 25 part-time (12 women); includes 16 minority (3 African Americans, 7 Asian Americans or Pacific Islanders, 6 Hispanic Americans), 3 international. Average age 39. 23 applicants, 83% accepted, 8 enrolled. In 2009, 6 doctorates awarded. *Degree requirements:* For doctorate, thesis/dissertation. *Entrance requirements:* For doctorate, GRE General Test, minimum GPA of 3.5, master's degree in geography, demonstrated scholarly research. Additional exam requirements/recommendations for international students: Required—TOEFL (minimum score 550 paper-based; 213 computer-based). *Application deadline:* For fall admission, 6/15 priority date for domestic students, 6/1 for international students; for spring admission, 10/15 priority date for domestic students, 10/1 for international students. Applications are processed on a rolling basis. Application fee: $40 ($90 for international students). Electronic applications accepted. *Expenses:* Tuition, state resident: full-time $5784; part-time $241 per credit hour. Tuition, nonresident: full-time $13,224; part-time $551 per credit hour. Required fees: $1728; $48 per credit hour. $306. Tuition and fees vary according to course load. *Financial support:* In 2009–10, 60 students received support, including 17 research assistantships (averaging $10,552 per year), 26 teaching assistantships (averaging $9,874 per year); career-related internships or fieldwork, Federal Work-Study, and institutionally sponsored loans also available. Support available to part-time students. Financial award application deadline: 4/1; financial award applicants required to submit FAFSA. *Unit head:* Dr. David Butler, Graduate Adviser, 512-245-2170, Fax: 512-245-8353, E-mail: db25@txstate.edu. *Application contact:* Dr. J. Michael Willoughby, Dean of Graduate School, 512-245-2581, Fax: 512-245-8365, E-mail: gradcollege@txstate.edu.

Trinity (Washington) University, School of Education, Washington, DC 20017-1094. Offers counseling (MA); early childhood education (MAT); educating for change (M Ed); educational administration (MSA); elementary education (MAT); school counseling (MA); secondary education (MAT), including English, social studies; special education (MAT); teaching English as a second language (MAT); teaching English to speakers of other languages (M Ed); the teaching of reading (M Ed). *Accreditation:* NCATE. Part-time and evening/weekend programs available. *Degree requirements:* For master's, thesis (for some programs), capstone project(s). *Entrance requirements:* For master's, PRAXIS I, minimum GPA of 2.8. Additional exam requirements/recommendations for international students: Required—TOEFL (minimum score 550 paper-based; 213 computer-based). *Faculty research:* Technology, literacy, special education, organizations, inclusion models.

Troy University, Graduate School, College of Education, Program in Postsecondary Education, Troy, AL 36082. Offers adult education (M Ed); biology (M Ed); criminal justice (M Ed); english (M Ed); foundations of education (M Ed); general science (M Ed); higher education administration (M Ed); history (M Ed); instructional technology (M Ed); mathematics (M Ed); music industry (M Ed); physical fitness (M Ed); political science (M Ed); public administration (M Ed); social science (M Ed); teaching english (M Ed). Also offered through the University College. *Accreditation:* NCATE. Part-time and evening/weekend programs available. *Students:* 267 full-time (192 women), 381 part-time (293 women); includes 326 minority (309 African Americans,

4 American Indian/Alaska Native, 5 Asian Americans or Pacific Islanders, 8 Hispanic Americans). Average age 34. 343 applicants, 90% accepted. In 2009, 480 master's awarded. *Degree requirements:* For master's, comprehensive exam, thesis. *Entrance requirements:* For master's, MAT (minimum score 385), minimum GPA of 2.5. Additional exam requirements/recommendations for international students: Required—TOEFL (minimum score 523 paper-based; 193 computer-based; 70 iBT), IELTS, or ACT Compass ESL (minimum score 270 on Listening, Reading, and Grammar with no individual score below 85 and a minimum score of 8 out of 12 on writing test). *Application deadline:* Applications are processed on a rolling basis. Application fee: $50. Electronic applications accepted. *Financial support:* Available to part-time students. Applicants required to submit FAFSA. *Unit head:* Dr. Andrew Creamer, Chair, 334-670-3350, E-mail: drcreamer@troy.edu. *Application contact:* Brenda K. Campbell, Director of Graduate Admissions, 334-670-3178, Fax: 334-670-3733, E-mail: bcamp@troy.edu.

Troy University, Graduate School, College of Education, Program in Secondary Education, Troy, AL 36082. Offers 5th year biology (MS); 5th year computer science (MS); 5th year history (MS); 5th year language arts (MS); 5th year mathematics (MS); 5th year social science (MS); educationtraditional language arts (MS); traditional biology (MS); traditional computer science (MS); traditional history (MS); traditional mathematics (MS); traditional social science (MS). *Accreditation:* NCATE. Part-time and evening/weekend programs available. *Students:* 17 full-time (12 women), 25 part-time (23 women); includes 8 minority (all African Americans). Average age 27. 10 applicants, 90% accepted. In 2009, 29 master's awarded. *Degree requirements:* For master's, comprehensive exam, thesis. *Entrance requirements:* For master's, minimum GPA of 2.5. Additional exam requirements/recommendations for international students: Required—TOEFL (minimum score 523 paper-based; 193 computer-based; 70 iBT), IELTS (minimum score 6). *Application deadline:* Applications are processed on a rolling basis. Application fee: $50. Electronic applications accepted. *Financial support:* Career-related internships or fieldwork available. Support available to part-time students. Financial award applicants required to submit FAFSA. *Unit head:* Dr. Marian Parker, Coordinator, 334-670-5661, Fax: 334-670-3548, E-mail: mjparker@troy.edu. *Application contact:* Brenda K. Campbell, Director of Graduate Admissions, 334-670-3178, Fax: 334-670-3733, E-mail: bcamp@troy.edu.

Union Graduate College, School of Education, Schenectady, NY 12308-3107. Offers biology (MAT, MS); chemistry (MAT); Chinese (MAT); earth science (MAT); English (MAT); French (MAT); general science (MAT); German (MAT); Greek (MAT); languages (MAT); Latin (MAT); mathematics (MAT); mathematics and technology (MS); mentoring and teacher leadership (AC); middle childhood extension (AC); national board certificate and teacher leadership (AC); physical science (MS); physics (MAT); social studies (MAT); Spanish (MAT). *Accreditation:* Teacher Education Accreditation Council. *Faculty:* 3 full-time (1 woman), 39 part-time/adjunct (19 women). *Students:* 46 full-time (27 women), 45 part-time (39 women); includes 5 minority (1 Asian American or Pacific Islander, 4 Hispanic Americans), 2 international. Average age 33. 66 applicants, 73% accepted, 39 enrolled. In 2009, 44 master's awarded. *Degree requirements:* For master's, thesis or project. *Entrance requirements:* For master's, minimum GPA of 3.0, letters of recommendation. Additional exam requirements/recommendations for international students: Required—TOEFL (minimum score 550 paper-based; 213 computer-based). *Application deadline:* Applications are processed on a rolling basis. Application fee: $60. Electronic applications accepted. *Expenses:* Contact institution. *Financial support:* In 2009–10, 12 research assistantships with tuition reimbursements (averaging $3,000 per year) were awarded; Federal Work-Study, scholarships/grants, health care benefits, and tuition waivers (partial) also available. Support available to part-time students. Financial award applicants required to submit FAFSA. *Faculty research:* Transformative learning, science education, National Board Certification, teacher leadership, teacher quality. *Unit head:* Dr. Patrick Allen, Dean, 518-631-9870, Fax: 518-631-9901. *Application contact:* Christine Angley, Assistant, 518-631-9871, Fax: 518-631-9903, E-mail: angleyc@uniongraduatecollege.edu.

Union Institute & University, M Ed Program–Vermont Campus, Montpelier, VT 05602. Offers school administration (M Ed), including principalship; school counseling (M Ed); teaching (M Ed), including art, early childhood, elementary, English, math, middle schools, science, social studies, special education. *Faculty:* 3 full-time (1 woman), 23 part-time/adjunct (19 women). *Students:* 41 part-time (29 women). Average age 38. In 2009, 15 master's awarded. *Degree requirements:* For master's, thesis. *Entrance requirements:* For master's, 3 letters of reference. *Application deadline:* Applications are processed on a rolling basis. Application fee: $50. *Expenses:* Contact institution. *Financial support:* Federal Work-Study, scholarships/grants, and tuition waivers available. Financial award applicants required to submit FAFSA. *Unit head:* Dr. Arlene Sacks, Dean, Graduate Programs in Education, 305-653-6713 Ext. 2152, E-mail: arlene.sacks@myunion.edu. *Application contact:* Dr. Arlene Sacks, Dean, Graduate Programs in Education, 305-653-6713 Ext. 2152, E-mail: arlene.sacks@myunion.edu.

University at Buffalo, the State University of New York, Graduate School, Graduate School of Education, Department of Learning and Instruction, Buffalo, NY 14260. Offers biology education (Ed M, Certificate); chemistry education (Ed M, Certificate); childhood education (Ed M); childhood education with bilingual extension (Ed M); early childhood education (Ed M); earth science education (Ed M, Certificate); elementary education (Ed D, PhD); English education (Ed M, PhD, Certificate); English for speakers of other languages (Ed M); foreign and second language education (PhD); French education (Ed M, Certificate); general education (Ed M); German education (Ed M, Certificate); gifted education (online) (Certificate); Latin education (Ed M, Certificate); literary specialist (Ed M); mathematics education (Ed M, PhD, Certificate); music education (Ed M, Certificate); physics education (Ed M, Certificate); reading education (PhD); science and the public (online) (Ed M); science education (PhD); social studies education (Ed M, Certificate); Spanish education (Ed M, Certificate); special education (PhD); teaching and leading for diversity (Certificate); teaching English to speakers of other languages (Ed M). Part-time and evening/weekend programs available. Postbaccalaureate distance learning degree programs offered (no on-campus study). *Faculty:* 34 full-time (24 women), 50 part-time/adjunct (39 women). *Students:* 332 full-time (245 women), 365 part-time (272 women); includes 50 minority (18 African Americans, 4 American Indian/Alaska Native, 10 Asian Americans or Pacific Islanders, 18 Hispanic Americans), 55 international. Average age 30. 627 applicants, 78% accepted, 286 enrolled. In 2009, 255 master's, 16 doctorates, 51 other advanced degrees awarded. *Degree requirements:* For master's, comprehensive exam; for doctorate, thesis/dissertation, research analysis exam, research experience component. *Entrance requirements:* For doctorate, GRE General Test or MAT, interview, writing sample, letters of recommendation. Additional exam requirements/recommendations for international students: Required—TOEFL (minimum score 600 paper-based; 250 computer-based; 96 iBT). *Application deadline:* For fall admission, 2/1 priority date for domestic and international students; for spring admission, 11/15 priority date for domestic students, 10/1 for international students. Applications are processed on a rolling basis. Application fee: $50. Electronic applications accepted. *Financial support:* In 2009–10, 23 fellowships with full tuition reimbursements (averaging $9,000 per year), 42 research assistantships with full tuition reimbursements (averaging $10,000 per year) were awarded; teaching assistantships with full tuition reimbursements, career-related internships or fieldwork, Federal Work-Study, institutionally sponsored loans, scholarships/grants, tuition waivers (partial), and unspecified assistantships also available. Financial award application deadline: 2/28; financial award applicants required to submit FAFSA. *Faculty research:* Science assessment, foreign language teaching and learning, early learning, new literacies, gender and education. Total annual research expenditures: $1.8 million. *Unit head:* Dr. Suzanne Miller, Chair, 716-645-2455, Fax: 716-645-3161, E-mail: smiller@buffalo.edu. *Application contact:* Cathy Dimino, Admissions Assistant, 716-645-2110, Fax: 716-645-7937, E-mail: cadimino@buffalo.edu.

University of Arkansas at Pine Bluff, Program in Education, Pine Bluff, AR 71601-2799. Offers elementary education (M Ed); secondary education (M Ed), including general science, physical education, social studies. *Accreditation:* NCATE. Part-time and evening/weekend programs available. *Degree requirements:* For master's, comprehensive exam. *Entrance requirements:* For master's, GRE, minimum GPA of 2.75, NTE or Standard Arkansas Teaching Certificate. *Faculty research:* Teacher certification, accreditation, assessment, standards, portfolio development, rehabilitation, technology.

The University of British Columbia, Faculty of Education, Department of Curriculum and Pedagogy, Vancouver, BC V6T 1Z4, Canada. Offers art education (M Ed, MA); business education (MA); curriculum studies (M Ed, MA, PhD); home economics education (M Ed, MA); math education (M Ed, MA); music education (M Ed, MA); physical education (M Ed, MA); science education (M Ed, MA); social studies education (M Ed, MA); technology studies education (M Ed, MA). Part-time programs available. *Degree requirements:* For master's, thesis (MA); for doctorate, comprehensive exam, thesis/dissertation. *Entrance requirements:* Additional exam requirements/recommendations for international students: Required—TOEFL (minimum score 580 paper-based; 237 computer-based; 92 iBT). Electronic applications accepted. *Expenses:* Contact institution. *Faculty research:* School subjects, teaching and learning.

University of California, Santa Cruz, Division of Graduate Studies, Division of Social Sciences, Program in Social Documentation, Santa Cruz, CA 95064. Offers MA. *Entrance requirements:* For master's, resume or curriculum vitae, sample of documentary production work. Electronic applications accepted.

University of Central Florida, College of Education, Department of Teaching and Learning Principles, Program in Social Science Education, Orlando, FL 32816. Offers M Ed, MA. *Accreditation:* NCATE. Part-time and evening/weekend programs available. *Students:* 29 full-time (17 women), 31 part-time (18 women); includes 11 minority (5 African Americans, 1 Asian American or Pacific Islander, 5 Hispanic Americans). Average age 29. 43 applicants, 95% accepted, 27 enrolled. In 2009, 12 master's awarded. *Entrance requirements:* For master's, GRE General Test. Additional exam requirements/recommendations for international students: Required—TOEFL. *Application deadline:* For fall admission, 7/15 for domestic students; for spring admission, 12/1 for domestic students. Application fee: $30. Electronic applications accepted. *Expenses:* Tuition, state resident: part-time $306.31 per credit hour. Tuition, nonresident: part-time $1099.01 per credit hour. Part-time tuition and fees vary according to degree level and program. *Financial support:* Career-related internships or fieldwork, Federal Work-Study, institutionally sponsored loans, tuition waivers (partial), and unspecified assistantships available. Financial award application deadline: 3/1; financial award applicants required to submit FAFSA.

University of Central Florida, College of Education, Education PhD Program, Orlando, FL 32816. Offers communication sciences and disorders (PhD); counselor education (PhD); elementary education (PhD); exceptional education (PhD); higher education (PhD); hospitality education (PhD); instructional technology (PhD); mathematics education (PhD); science education (PhD); social science education (PhD). *Students:* 99 full-time (70 women), 14 part-time (9 women); includes 28 minority (17 African Americans, 2 Asian Americans or Pacific Islanders, 9 Hispanic Americans), 20 international. In 2009, 15 doctorates awarded. Application fee: $30. Electronic applications accepted. *Expenses:* Tuition, state resident: part-time $306.31 per credit hour. Tuition, nonresident: part-time $1099.01 per credit hour. Part-time tuition and fees vary according to degree level and program. *Financial support:* In 2009–10, 40 fellowships with partial tuition reimbursements (averaging $9,200 per year), 61 research assistantships with partial tuition reimbursements (averaging $7,800 per year), 18 teaching assistantships with partial tuition reimbursements (averaging $6,500 per year) were awarded. *Unit head:* Dr. B. Grant Hayes, Associate Dean, 407-823-5391, E-mail: ghayes@mail.ucf.edu. *Application contact:* Dr. B. Grant Hayes, Associate Dean, 407-823-5391, E-mail: ghayes@mail.ucf.edu.

University of Cincinnati, Graduate School, College of Education, Criminal Justice, and Human Services, Division of Teacher Education, Cincinnati, OH 45221. Offers curriculum and instruction (M Ed, Ed D); deaf studies (Certificate); early childhood education (M Ed); middle childhood education (M Ed); postsecondary literacy instruction (Certificate); reading/literacy (M Ed, Ed D); secondary education (M Ed); special education (M Ed, Ed D); teaching English as a second language (M Ed, Ed D, Certificate); teaching science (MS). Part-time programs available. *Degree requirements:* For doctorate, thesis/dissertation. *Entrance requirements:* For master's, GRE General Test. Electronic applications accepted.

University of Connecticut, Graduate School, Neag School of Education, Department of Curriculum and Instruction, Program in History and Social Sciences Education, Storrs, CT 06269. Offers MA, PhD, Post-Master's Certificate. *Accreditation:* NCATE. *Faculty:* 15 full-time (10 women). *Students:* 37 full-time (16 women), 3 part-time (all women); includes 2 minority (1 Asian American or Pacific Islander, 1 Hispanic American), 1 international. Average age 25. 49 applicants, 0% accepted, 0 enrolled. In 2009, 24 master's, 1 doctorate awarded. Terminal master's awarded for partial completion of doctoral program. *Degree requirements:* For master's, comprehensive exam, thesis or alternative; for doctorate, thesis/dissertation. *Entrance requirements:* For doctorate, GRE General Test. Additional exam requirements/recommendations for international students: Required—TOEFL (minimum score 550 paper-based; 213 computer-based). *Application deadline:* For fall admission, 2/1 priority date for domestic and international students; for spring admission, 11/1 for domestic students, 10/1 for international students. Applications are processed on a rolling basis. Application fee: $55. Electronic applications accepted. *Expenses:* Tuition, state resident: full-time $4725; part-time $525 per credit. Tuition, nonresident: full-time $12,267; part-time $1363 per credit. Required fees: $346 per semester. Tuition and fees vary according to course load. *Financial support:* In 2009–10, 1 research assistantship with full tuition reimbursement, 1 teaching assistantship with full tuition reimbursement were awarded; fellowships, Federal Work-Study, scholarships/grants, health care benefits, and unspecified assistantships also available. Financial award application deadline: 2/1; financial award applicants required to submit FAFSA. *Unit head:* Mary Anne Doyle, Head, 860-486-2433, Fax: 860-486-0280, E-mail: mary.dolye@uconn.edu. *Application contact:* Lisa Rasicot, Graduate Coordinator, 860-486-3065, Fax: 860-486-0210, E-mail: l.rasicot@uconn.edu.

University of Florida, Graduate School, College of Education, School of Teaching and Learning, Gainesville, FL 32611. Offers bilingual/ESOL education (M Ed, MAE, Ed D, PhD, Ed S); curriculum and instruction (M Ed, MAE, Ed D, PhD, Ed S); early childhood education (Ed D, PhD, Ed S); elementary education (M Ed, MAE); English education (M Ed, MAE); mathematics education (M Ed, MAE); reading education (M Ed, MAE); science education (M Ed, MAE); social foundations (M Ed, MAE, Ed D, PhD); social studies education (M Ed, MAE). *Accreditation:* NCATE. *Degree requirements:* For master's, thesis optional; for doctorate, variable foreign language requirement, thesis/dissertation. *Entrance requirements:* For master's and doctorate, GRE General Test, minimum GPA of 3.0; for Ed S, GRE General Test. Additional exam requirements/recommendations for international students: Required—TOEFL (minimum score 550 paper-based; 213 computer-based). Electronic applications accepted. *Faculty research:* Teacher education, inclusive education, classroom processes, curriculum and technology.

University of Florida, Graduate School, College of Liberal Arts and Sciences, Department of Political Science, Gainesville, FL 32611. Offers international development policy and administration (MA, Certificate); international relations (MA, MAT); political campaigning (MA, Certificate); political science (MA, MAT, PhD); public affairs (MA, Certificate); JD/MA. Part-time programs available. Terminal master's awarded for partial completion of doctoral program. *Degree requirements:* For master's, variable foreign language requirement, thesis or alternative; for doctorate, variable foreign language requirement, thesis/dissertation. *Entrance requirements:* For master's and doctorate, GRE General Test, minimum GPA of 3.0. Additional exam requirements/recommendations for international students: Required—TOEFL (minimum score 550 paper-based; 213 computer-based). Electronic applications accepted. *Faculty research:* U.S. political development, religion and politics, environmental politics and policy, developing societies, international relations.

University of Georgia, Graduate School, College of Education, Department of Elementary and Social Studies Education, Athens, GA 30602. Offers early childhood education (M Ed, MAT, PhD, Ed S), including child and family development (MAT); elementary education (PhD); middle school education (M Ed, PhD, Ed S); social studies education (M Ed, Ed D, PhD, Ed S). *Faculty:* 14 full-time (9 women). *Students:* 114 full-time (94 women), 130 part-time (112 women); includes 37 minority (20 African Americans, 1 American Indian/Alaska Native, 11 Asian Americans or Pacific Islanders, 5 Hispanic Americans), 9 international. 168 applicants,

Social Sciences Education

University of Georgia (continued)

57% accepted, 48 enrolled. In 2009, 75 master's, 9 doctorates, 12 other advanced degrees awarded. *Entrance requirements:* For master's and Ed S, GRE General Test or MAT; for doctorate, GRE General Test. *Application deadline:* For fall admission, 7/1 priority date for domestic students; for spring admission, 11/15 for domestic students. Application fee: $50. Electronic applications accepted. *Expenses:* Tuition, state resident: full-time $6000; part-time $250 per credit hour. Tuition, nonresident: full-time $20,904; part-time $871 per credit hour. Required fees: $730 per semester. *Financial support:* Fellowships, research assistantships, teaching assistantships, unspecified assistantships available. *Unit head:* Dr. Ronald L. VanSickle, Interim Head, 706-542-7265, Fax: 706-542-6506, E-mail: rvansick@uga.edu. *Application contact:* Dr. Ronald E. Butchart, Graduate Coordinator, 706-542-6490, Fax: 706-542-8996, E-mail: essegrad@uga.edu.

University of Houston, College of Education, Department of Curriculum and Instruction, Houston, TX 77204. Offers art education (M Ed); bilingual education (M Ed); curriculum and instruction (M Ed, Ed D); early childhood education (M Ed); elementary education (M Ed); gifted and talented education (M Ed); instructional technology (M Ed); mathematics education (M Ed); reading and language arts education (M Ed); science education (M Ed); second language education (M Ed); secondary education (M Ed); social studies education (M Ed); teaching (M Ed). *Accreditation:* NCATE. Part-time and evening/weekend programs available. *Faculty:* 20 full-time (9 women), 22 part-time/adjunct (17 women). *Students:* 113 full-time (81 women), 195 part-time (150 women); includes 107 minority (43 African Americans, 29 Asian Americans or Pacific Islanders, 35 Hispanic Americans), 29 international. Average age 35. 150 applicants, 77% accepted, 55 enrolled. In 2009, 75 master's, 31 doctorates awarded. *Degree requirements:* For master's, comprehensive exam, thesis optional; for doctorate, comprehensive exam, thesis/dissertation. *Entrance requirements:* For master's and doctorate, GRE, minimum cumulative undergraduate GPA of 2.6. Additional exam requirements/recommendations for international students: Required—TOEFL (minimum score 550 paper-based; 79 iBT). *Application deadline:* For fall admission, 3/1 for domestic and international students; for spring admission, 10/1 for domestic and international students. Application fee: $45 ($75 for international students). Electronic applications accepted. *Expenses:* Tuition, state resident: full-time $7676; part-time $320 per credit hour. Tuition, nonresident: full-time $14,324; part-time $597 per credit hour. Required fees: $3034. *Financial support:* In 2009–10, 4 fellowships with full tuition reimbursements (averaging $9,500 per year), 6 research assistantships with full tuition reimbursements (averaging $8,800 per year), 25 teaching assistantships with full tuition reimbursements (averaging $8,800 per year) were awarded; career-related internships or fieldwork, Federal Work-Study, institutionally sponsored loans, scholarships/grants, health care benefits, and unspecified assistantships also available. Support available to part-time students. Financial award application deadline: 2/1. *Faculty research:* Teaching-learning process, instructional technology in schools, teacher education, classroom management, at-risk students. *Unit head:* Dr. Laveria Hutchison, Chairperson, 713-743-4958, Fax: 713-743-4990, E-mail: lhutchison@uh.edu. *Application contact:* Renee C. Rattelade, Executive Secretary, 713-743-4997, Fax: 713-743-4990, E-mail: rrattelade@mail.coe.uh.edu.

University of Indianapolis, Graduate Programs, School of Education, Indianapolis, IN 46227-3697. Offers art education (MAT); biology (MAT); chemistry (MAT); curriculum and instruction (MA); earth sciences (MAT); education (MA, MAT); educational leadership (MA); elementary education (MA); English (MAT); French (MAT); math (MAT); physical education (MAT); physics (MAT); secondary education (MA), including art education, education, English education, social studies education; social studies (MAT); Spanish (MAT). *Accreditation:* NCATE. Part-time and evening/weekend programs available. *Faculty:* 4 full-time (3 women), 3 part-time/adjunct (2 women). *Students:* 52 full-time (28 women), 110 part-time (67 women); includes 3 minority (all African Americans), 2 international. Average age 33. *Entrance requirements:* For master's, GRE Subject Test, PRAXIS I, minimum GPA of 2.5, 3 letters of recommendation, interview, writing exercise. Additional exam requirements/recommendations for international students: Required—TOEFL (minimum score 550 paper-based; 213 computer-based). *Application deadline:* Applications are processed on a rolling basis. Application fee: $50. *Financial support:* Federal Work-Study available. Financial award application deadline: 5/1; financial award applicants required to submit FAFSA. *Faculty research:* Assessment of teacher education, perceptions of prospective teachers by parents. *Unit head:* Dr. Kathy Moran, Dean, 317-788-3285, Fax: 317-788-3300, E-mail: kmoran@uindy.edu. *Application contact:* Chemain Slater, 317-788-2051, E-mail: slaterc@uindy.edu.

The University of Iowa, Graduate College, College of Education, Department of Teaching and Learning, Program in Secondary Education, Iowa City, IA 52242-1316. Offers art education (PhD); curriculum and supervision (PhD); curriculum supervision (MA); developmental reading (MA); English education (MA, MAT); foreign language education (MA, MAT); foreign language/ESL education (PhD); language, literature and culture (PhD); math education (PhD); mathematics education (MA); social studies (MA, PhD). *Degree requirements:* For master's, thesis optional, exam; for doctorate, comprehensive exam, thesis/dissertation. *Entrance requirements:* For master's and doctorate, GRE General Test, minimum GPA of 3.0. Additional exam requirements/recommendations for international students: Required—TOEFL (minimum score 550 paper-based; 213 computer-based; 81 iBT). Electronic applications accepted.

University of Maine, Graduate School, College of Education and Human Development, Program in Social Studies Education, Orono, ME 04469. Offers M Ed, MA, MS, CAS. *Accreditation:* NCATE. Part-time and evening/weekend programs available. *Students:* 1 (woman) full-time, 1 part-time (0 women); includes 1 minority (American Indian/Alaska Native). Average age 28. 4 applicants, 0% accepted, 0 enrolled. In 2009, 1 master's, 1 other advanced degree awarded. *Degree requirements:* For master's, thesis or alternative. *Entrance requirements:* For master's, MAT; for CAS, MA, M Ed, or MS. Additional exam requirements/recommendations for international students: Required—TOEFL. *Application deadline:* For fall admission, 2/1 priority date for domestic students. Applications are processed on a rolling basis. Application fee: $65. Electronic applications accepted. *Financial support:* Tuition waivers (full and partial) available. Financial award application deadline: 3/1. *Unit head:* Dr. Janet Spector, Coordinator, 207-581-2444, Fax: 207-581-2423. *Application contact:* Scott G. Delcourt, Associate Dean of the Graduate School, 207-581-3291, Fax: 207-581-3232, E-mail: graduate@maine.edu.

University of Maryland, Baltimore County, Graduate School, College of Arts, Humanities and Social Sciences, Department of Education, Program in Teaching, Baltimore, MD 21250. Offers early childhood education (MAT); elementary education (MAT); secondary education (MAT), including art, biology, chemistry, dance, earth/space science, English, foreign language, mathematics, music, physics, theatre; secondary science (MAT), including social studies. Part-time and evening/weekend programs available. *Faculty:* 24 full-time (18 women), 25 part-time/adjunct (19 women). *Students:* 52 full-time (41 women), 64 part-time (55 women); includes 20 minority (5 African Americans, 1 American Indian/Alaska Native, 10 Asian Americans or Pacific Islanders, 4 Hispanic Americans), 3 international. Average age 31. 88 applicants, 57% accepted, 39 enrolled. In 2009, 106 master's awarded. *Degree requirements:* For master's, comprehensive exam (for some programs), thesis (for some programs). *Entrance requirements:* For master's, PRAXIS I and II, minimum GPA of 3.0. Additional exam requirements/recommendations for international students: Required—TOEFL. *Application deadline:* For fall admission, 6/1 for domestic students; for spring admission, 11/1 for domestic students. Applications are processed on a rolling basis. Application fee: $50. Electronic applications accepted. *Financial support:* In 2009–10, 6 students received support, including research assistantships with full tuition reimbursements available (averaging $12,000 per year); career-related internships or fieldwork, Federal Work-Study, scholarships/grants, tuition waivers, and unspecified assistantships also available. Financial award application deadline: 3/1. *Faculty research:* STEM teacher education, culturally sensitive pedagogy, ESOL/bilingual education, early childhood education, language, literacy and culture. *Unit head:* Dr. Susan M. Blunck, Director, 410-455-2869, Fax: 410-455-3986, E-mail: blunck@umbc.edu. *Application contact:* Dr. Susan M. Blunck, Director, 410-455-2869, Fax: 410-455-3986, E-mail: blunck@umbc.edu.

University of Michigan, Horace H. Rackham School of Graduate Studies, School of Education, Programs in Educational Studies, Ann Arbor, MI 48109. Offers cross specialization (PhD); curriculum development (MA); early childhood education (MA, PhD); educational administration and policy (MA, PhD); educational foundations and policy (MA, PhD); English education (MA); English language learning in school settings (MA); learning technologies (MA, PhD); literacy, language, and culture (MA, PhD); mathematics education (MA, PhD); postsecondary science education (MS); research methods (MA); science education (MA, PhD); social studies education (MA); teaching and teacher education (PhD); MA/Certification; MBA/MA; PhD/MA. Terminal master's awarded for partial completion of doctoral program. *Degree requirements:* For master's, thesis (for some programs); for doctorate, comprehensive exam, thesis/dissertation. *Entrance requirements:* For master's and doctorate, GRE General Test. Additional exam requirements/recommendations for international students: Required—TOEFL (minimum score 600 paper-based; 250 computer-based). *Application deadline:* For fall admission, 12/1 priority date for domestic students, 12/1 for international students. Application fee: $60 ($75 for international students). Electronic applications accepted. *Expenses:* Tuition, state resident: full-time $17,286; part-time $1099 per credit hour. Tuition, nonresident: full-time $34,944; part-time $2080 per credit hour. Required fees: $95 per semester. Tuition and fees vary according to course load, degree level and program. *Financial support:* Applicants required to submit FAFSA. *Unit head:* Dr. Addison Stone, Chairperson, 734-763-7500, Fax: 734-615-1290, E-mail: addison@umich.edu. *Application contact:* Laura Mayers, Student Services Assistant, 734-764-7563, Fax: 734-763-1495, E-mail: ed.grad.admit@umich.edu.

University of Minnesota, Twin Cities Campus, Graduate School, College of Education and Human Development, Department of Curriculum and Instruction, Program in Teaching, Minneapolis, MN 55455-0213. Offers Chinese (M Ed); earth science (M Ed); elementary special education (M Ed); English (M Ed); English as a second language (M Ed); French (M Ed); German (M Ed); Hebrew (M Ed); Japanese (M Ed); life sciences (M Ed); mathematics (M Ed); middle school science (M Ed); science (M Ed); second languages and cultures (M Ed); social studies (M Ed); Spanish (M Ed). *Students:* 263 full-time (186 women), 117 part-time (83 women); includes 32 minority (10 African Americans, 2 American Indian/Alaska Native, 17 Asian Americans or Pacific Islanders, 3 Hispanic Americans), 4 international. Average age 27. 363 applicants, 74% accepted, 259 enrolled. In 2009, 497 master's awarded. *Unit head:* Dr. Ruth Thomas, Chair, 612-624-4772, Fax: 612-624-8277, E-mail: thoma006@umn.edu. *Application contact:* Dr. Mary Trettin, Associate Dean, 612-625-6501, Fax: 612-626-1580, E-mail: mtrettin@umn.edu.

University of Missouri, Graduate School, College of Education, Department of Learning, Teaching and Curriculum, Columbia, MO 65211. Offers agricultural education (M Ed, PhD, Ed S); art education (M Ed, PhD, Ed S); business and office education (M Ed, PhD, Ed S); early childhood education (M Ed, PhD, Ed S); elementary education (M Ed, PhD, Ed S); English education (M Ed, PhD, Ed S); foreign language education (M Ed, PhD, Ed S); health education and promotion (M Ed, PhD); learning and instruction (M Ed); marketing education (M Ed, PhD, Ed S); mathematics education (M Ed, PhD, Ed S); music education (M Ed, PhD, Ed S); reading education (M Ed, PhD, Ed S); science education (M Ed, PhD, Ed S); social studies education (M Ed, PhD, Ed S); vocational education (M Ed, PhD, Ed S). Part-time programs available. Terminal master's awarded for partial completion of doctoral program. *Degree requirements:* For doctorate, thesis/dissertation. *Entrance requirements:* For master's and Ed S, GRE General Test or MAT, minimum GPA of 3.0; for doctorate, GRE General Test, minimum GPA of 3.0. Additional exam requirements/recommendations for international students: Required—TOEFL (minimum score 600 paper-based; 250 computer-based; 100 iBT). Electronic applications accepted.

The University of North Carolina at Chapel Hill, Graduate School, School of Education, Program in Secondary Education, Chapel Hill, NC 27599. Offers English (Grades 9-12) (MAT); English as a second language (MAT); French (Grades K-12) (MAT); German (Grades K-12) (MAT); Japanese (Grades K-12) (MAT); Latin (Grades 9-12) (MAT); mathematics (Grades 9-12) (MAT); music (Grades K-12) (MAT); science (Grades 9-12) (MAT); social studies (Grades 9-12) (MAT); Spanish (Grades K-12) (MAT). *Accreditation:* NCATE. *Students:* 53 full-time (35 women), 1 part-time (0 women); includes 8 minority (4 African Americans, 2 Asian Americans or Pacific Islanders, 2 Hispanic Americans), 3 international. Average age 25. 137 applicants, 77% accepted, 54 enrolled. In 2009, 39 master's awarded. *Degree requirements:* For master's, comprehensive exam. *Entrance requirements:* For master's, GRE General Test, minimum GPA of 3.0 during last 2 years of undergraduate course work. Additional exam requirements/recommendations for international students: Required—TOEFL (minimum score 550 paper-based; 79 computer-based). *Application deadline:* For fall admission, 12/15 priority date for domestic and international students. Applications are processed on a rolling basis. Application fee: $77. Electronic applications accepted. *Financial support:* Federal Work-Study available. Support available to part-time students. Financial award application deadline: 3/1; financial award applicants required to submit FAFSA. *Unit head:* Dr. James Trier, Coordinator, 919-843-4627, Fax: 919-962-1533. *Application contact:* Amy Butler, Student Services Assistant, 919-966-1346, Fax: 919-962-1533, E-mail: abutler@email.unc.edu.

The University of North Carolina at Greensboro, Graduate School, School of Education, Department of Curriculum and Instruction, Greensboro, NC 27412-5001. Offers college teaching and adult learning (Certificate); curriculum and instruction (M Ed), including chemistry education, elementary education, English as a second language, French education, instructional technology, mathematics education, middle grades education, reading education, science education, social studies education, Spanish education; curriculum and teaching (PhD), including higher education, teacher education and development; English as a second language (Certificate); higher education (M Ed); supervision (M Ed). *Accreditation:* NCATE. Part-time programs available. *Degree requirements:* For doctorate, thesis/dissertation. *Entrance requirements:* For master's and doctorate, GRE General Test. Additional exam requirements/recommendations for international students: Required—TOEFL. Electronic applications accepted. *Faculty research:* Community college literacy program, middle school mathematics/computer mathematics.

The University of North Carolina at Pembroke, Graduate Studies, Department of History, Program in Social Studies Education, Pembroke, NC 28372-1510. Offers MA, MAT. Part-time and evening/weekend programs available. *Degree requirements:* For master's, thesis optional. *Entrance requirements:* For master's, GRE or MAT, minimum GPA of 3.0 in major, 2.5 overall. Additional exam requirements/recommendations for international students: Required—TOEFL.

University of Oklahoma, Graduate College, College of Education, Department of Instructional Leadership and Academic Curriculum, Norman, OK 73072. Offers education (Certificate); instructional leadership and academic curriculum (M Ed, PhD), including bilingual education, early childhood education, elementary education, English education, math education, reading education, science education, secondary education, social studies education. *Accreditation:* NCATE. Part-time and evening/weekend programs available. *Faculty:* 18 full-time (11 women). *Students:* 44 full-time (36 women), 117 part-time (92 women); includes 35 minority (11 African Americans, 14 American Indian/Alaska Native, 5 Asian Americans or Pacific Islanders, 5 Hispanic Americans), 2 international. 50 applicants, 84% accepted, 32 enrolled. In 2009, 31 master's, 6 doctorates awarded. Terminal master's awarded for partial completion of doctoral program. *Degree requirements:* For doctorate, thesis/dissertation. *Entrance requirements:* For master's, 12 hours of course work in education; for doctorate, GRE General Test, master's degree, minimum graduate GPA of 3.0. Additional exam requirements/recommendations for international students: Required—TOEFL (minimum score 550 paper-based; 213 computer-based). *Application deadline:* For fall admission, 6/1 priority date for domestic students, 4/1 for international students; for spring admission, 11/1 for domestic students, 9/1 for international students. Applications are processed on a rolling basis. Application fee: $40 ($90 for international students). Electronic applications accepted. *Expenses:* Tuition, state resident: full-time $3744; part-time $156 per credit hour. Tuition, nonresident: full-time $13,577; part-time $565.70 per credit hour. Required fees: $2415; $90.10 per credit hour. *Financial support:* In 2009–10, 107 students received support, including 1 research assistantship with partial tuition reimbursement available (averaging $9,630 per year), 6 teaching assistantships with partial tuition reimbursements available (averaging $10,801 per year); scholarships/grants, health care benefits, and unspecified assistantships also available. Financial award applicants required to submit FAFSA. *Faculty research:* English education, mathematics education, reading, science

education, social studies education. Total annual research expenditures: $752,908. *Unit head:* Lawrence Baines, Chair, 405-325-1498, Fax: 405-325-4061, E-mail: lbaines@ou.edu. *Application contact:* Lynn Crussel, Administrative Assistant for Graduate Studies, 405-325-4843, Fax: 405-325-4061, E-mail: lcrussel@ou.edu.

University of Pittsburgh, School of Education, Department of Instruction and Learning, Program in Secondary Education, Pittsburgh, PA 15260. Offers English/communications education (M Ed, MAT); foreign languages education (M Ed, MAT); mathematics education (M Ed, MAT, Ed D); science education (M Ed, MAT, MS, Ed D); social studies education (M Ed, MAT). Part-time and evening/weekend programs available. *Students:* 170 full-time (107 women), 70 part-time (54 women); includes 19 minority (11 African Americans, 6 Asian Americans or Pacific Islanders, 2 Hispanic Americans), 10 international. Average age 29. 220 applicants, 72% accepted, 128 enrolled. In 2009, 108 master's, 5 doctorates awarded. *Degree requirements:* For master's, thesis; for doctorate, thesis/dissertation. *Entrance requirements:* For master's, PRAXIS I; for doctorate, GRE General Test. Additional exam requirements/recommendations for international students: Required—TOEFL. *Application deadline:* For fall admission, 2/1 priority date for domestic students; for spring admission, 11/15 priority date for domestic students. Applications are processed on a rolling basis. Application fee: $50. Electronic applications accepted. *Expenses:* Tuition, state resident: full-time $16,402; part-time $665 per credit. Tuition, nonresident: full-time $28,694; part-time $1175 per credit. Required fees: $690; $175 per term. Tuition and fees vary according to program. *Financial support:* Fellowships, teaching assistantships, career-related internships or fieldwork, Federal Work-Study, tuition waivers (partial), and unspecified assistantships available. Support available to part-time students. Financial award application deadline: 3/15; financial award applicants required to submit FAFSA. *Unit head:* Dr. Richard Donato, Chairman, 412-624-7248, Fax: 412-648-7081, E-mail: donato@pitt.edu. *Application contact:* Joan M. Cutone, Director, School of Education Student Service Center, 412-648-2230, Fax: 412-648-1899, E-mail: soeinfo@pitt.edu.

University of Puerto Rico, Río Piedras, College of Education, Program in Curriculum and Teaching, San Juan, PR 00931-3300. Offers biology education (M Ed); chemistry education (M Ed); curriculum and teaching (Ed D); history education (M Ed); mathematics education (M Ed); physics education (M Ed); Spanish education (M Ed). Part-time programs available. *Degree requirements:* For master's, thesis; for doctorate, thesis/dissertation, internship. *Entrance requirements:* For master's, PAEG or GRE, minimum GPA of 3.0, letter of recommendation; for doctorate, GRE or PAEG, master's degree, minimum GPA of 3.0, letter of recommendation (2), interview. *Faculty research:* Curriculum, math teaching.

University of St. Francis, College of Education, Joliet, IL 60435-6169. Offers educational leadership (MS), including reading; elementary education certification (M Ed); reading (MS); secondary education certification (M Ed), including English education, math education, science education, social studies education; special education (M Ed); teaching and learning (MS), including character education, curriculum and instruction, differentiated instruction, technology. *Accreditation:* NCATE. Part-time and evening/weekend programs available. *Faculty:* 10 full-time (8 women), 26 part-time/adjunct (18 women). *Students:* 60 full-time (45 women), 349 part-time (283 women); includes 36 minority (10 African Americans, 2 Asian Americans or Pacific Islanders, 24 Hispanic Americans). Average age 33. 211 applicants, 65% accepted, 102 enrolled. In 2009, 174 master's awarded. *Entrance requirements:* For master's, Illinois Basic Skills Test (M Ed), teaching certificate (MS), minimum undergraduate GPA of 2.75, 2 letters of recommendation, computer competency. Additional exam requirements/recommendations for international students: Required—TOEFL (minimum score 550 paper-based; 213 computer-based). *Application deadline:* Applications are processed on a rolling basis. Application fee: $30. Electronic applications accepted. *Expenses:* Contact institution. *Financial support:* In 2009–10, 254 students received support. Federal Work-Study, scholarships/grants, tuition waivers (partial), and unspecified assistantships available. Support available to part-time students. Financial award applicants required to submit FAFSA. *Unit head:* Dr. John Gambro, Dean, 815-740-3332, Fax: 815-740-2264, E-mail: jgambro@stfrancis.edu. *Application contact:* Sandra Sloka, Director of Admissions for Graduate and Degree Completion Programs, 800-735-7500, Fax: 815-740-5032, E-mail: ssloka@stfrancis.edu.

University of South Carolina, The Graduate School, College of Education, Department of Instruction and Teacher Education, Program in Secondary Education, Columbia, SC 29208. Offers art education (IMA, MAT); business education (IMA, MAT); English (MAT); foreign language (MAT); health education (MAT); mathematics (MAT); science (IMA, MAT); secondary (Ed D); secondary education (MT, PhD); social studies (MAT); theatre and speech (MAT). IMA and MT offered jointly with the subject areas. *Accreditation:* NCATE. *Degree requirements:* For master's, comprehensive exam, thesis (for some programs), foreign language (MA); for doctorate, one foreign language, comprehensive exam, thesis/dissertation. *Entrance requirements:* For master's, GRE General Test or MAT, teaching certificate (IMA, M Ed), interview; for doctorate, GRE General Test or MAT, interview. *Faculty research:* Middle school programs, professional development, school collaboration.

University of Southern Mississippi, Graduate School, College of Education and Psychology, Department of Curriculum, Instruction, and Special Education, Hattiesburg, MS 39406-0001. Offers alternative secondary teacher education (MAT); early childhood education (M Ed, Ed S); education of the gifted (M Ed, Ed D, PhD, Ed S); elementary education (M Ed, Ed D, PhD, Ed S); reading (M Ed, MS, Ed S); secondary education (M Ed, MS, Ed D, PhD, Ed S); special education (M Ed, Ed D, PhD, Ed S). *Faculty:* 23 full-time (17 women), 3 part-time/adjunct (2 women). *Students:* 31 full-time (26 women), 77 part-time (68 women); includes 18 minority (15 African Americans, 3 Hispanic Americans). Average age 37. 50 applicants, 52% accepted, 19 enrolled. In 2009, 43 master's, 3 doctorates, 2 other advanced degrees awarded. *Degree requirements:* For master's, comprehensive exam, thesis (for some programs); for doctorate, comprehensive exam, thesis/dissertation; for Ed S, comprehensive exam, thesis. *Entrance requirements:* For master's, GRE General Test, MAT, minimum GPA of 3.0; for doctorate, GRE General Test, minimum GPA of 3.5; for Ed S, GRE General Test, MAT, minimum GPA of 3.25. Additional exam requirements/recommendations for international students: Required—TOEFL. *Application deadline:* For fall admission, 3/1 priority date for domestic students, 3/1 for international students. Applications are processed on a rolling basis. Application fee: $35. *Expenses:* Tuition, state resident: full-time $5096; part-time $284 per hour. Tuition, nonresident: full-time $13,052; part-time $726 per hour. Required fees: $402. Tuition and fees vary according to course level and course load. *Financial support:* In 2009–10, 9 research assistantships with tuition reimbursements (averaging $18,316 per year), 2 teaching assistantships with full tuition reimbursements (averaging $8,500 per year) were awarded; Federal Work-Study, institutionally sponsored loans, and tuition waivers (partial) also available. Financial award application deadline: 3/15; financial award applicants required to submit FAFSA. *Faculty research:* Mathematical problem solving, integrative curriculum, writing process, teacher education models. Total annual research expenditures: $100,000. *Unit head:* Dr. David Daves, Chair, 601-266-4547, Fax: 601-266-4175. *Application contact:* Rachea Cawthorn, Administrative Assistant, 601-266-6987, Fax: 601-266-4548.

University of South Florida, Graduate School, College of Education–Main Campus, Department of Secondary Education, Tampa, FL 33620-9951. Offers English education (M Ed, MA, MAT, PhD); foreign language education/ESOL (M Ed, MA, MAT); instructional technology (M Ed, PhD, Ed S); mathematics education (M Ed, MA, MAT, PhD, Ed S); science education (M Ed, MA, MAT, PhD); second language acquisition/instructional technology (PhD); secondary education (M Ed, PhD); secondary education/TESOL (M Ed); social science education (M Ed, MA, MAT); teaching and learning in the content area (PhD). *Accreditation:* NCATE. Part-time and evening/weekend programs available. *Faculty:* 28 full-time (17 women), 3 part-time/adjunct (1 woman). *Students:* 144 full-time (97 women), 322 part-time (212 women); includes 100 minority (32 African Americans, 4 American Indian/Alaska Native, 17 Asian Americans or Pacific Islanders, 47 Hispanic Americans), 25 international. Average age 30. 230 applicants, 67% accepted, 122 enrolled. In 2009, 122 master's, 14 doctorates, 1 other advanced degree awarded. *Degree requirements:* For master's, variable foreign language requirement, comprehensive exam; for doctorate, variable foreign language requirement, comprehensive exam, thesis/dissertation. *Entrance requirements:* For master's, GRE General Test or General

Knowledge Test, minimum GPA of 3.0; for doctorate, GRE General Test, minimum GPA of 3.5; for Ed S, GRE General Test. Additional exam requirements/recommendations for international students: Required—TOEFL (minimum score 550 paper-based; 213 computer-based; 79 iBT). *Application deadline:* For fall admission, 2/15 for domestic students, 1/2 for international students; for spring admission, 10/15 for domestic students, 6/1 for international students. Application fee: $30. Electronic applications accepted. *Financial support:* In 2009–10, 7 students received support, including 1 research assistantship with full tuition reimbursement available (averaging $10,000 per year), 55 teaching assistantships with full and partial tuition reimbursements available (averaging $7,900 per year); scholarships/grants and unspecified assistantships also available. Financial award application deadline: 4/15; financial award applicants required to submit FAFSA. *Faculty research:* English language learners/multicultural, social science education, mathematics education, science education, instructional technology. Total annual research expenditures: $336,023. *Unit head:* Dr. Stephen Thornton, Chairperson, 813-974-3533, Fax: 813-974-3837, E-mail: thornton@usf.edu. *Application contact:* Dr. James White, Program Director, 813-974-1629, Fax: 813-974-3837, E-mail: jwhite@usf.edu.

The University of Tampa, Program in Teaching, Tampa, FL 33606-1490. Offers curriculum and instruction (M Ed); math education (MAT); science education (MAT); social science education (MAT). Part-time and evening/weekend programs available. *Faculty:* 9 full-time (6 women), 5 part-time/adjunct (4 women). *Students:* 1 full-time (0 women), 68 part-time (51 women); includes 11 minority (3 African Americans, 1 Asian American or Pacific Islander, 7 Hispanic Americans), 1 international. Average age 30. 119 applicants, 71% accepted, 69 enrolled. In 2009, 36 master's awarded. *Degree requirements:* For master's, comprehensive exam, thesis. *Entrance requirements:* For master's, General Knowledge Test, GRE General Test, SAE Subject Area Exam, bachelor's degree in education or professional teaching certificate. Additional exam requirements/recommendations for international students: Required—TOEFL (minimum score 577 paper-based; 230 computer-based; 90 iBT), IELTS (minimum score 7). *Application deadline:* For fall admission, 5/1 for domestic students. Application fee: $40. *Expenses:* Tuition: Part-time $488 per credit hour. *Financial support:* In 2009–10, 67 students received support. Applicants required to submit FAFSA. *Unit head:* Dr. Martha Harrison, Associate Professor of Education, 813-253-3333 Ext. 3373, E-mail: mharrison@ut.edu. *Application contact:* Karen Full, Director of Admissions for Graduate and Continuing Studies, 813-257-3642, E-mail: kfull@ut.edu.

The University of Tennessee, Graduate School, College of Education, Health and Human Sciences, Program in Education, Knoxville, TN 37996. Offers art education (MS); counseling education (PhD); cultural studies in education (PhD); curriculum (MS, Ed S); curriculum, educational research and evaluation (Ed D, PhD); early childhood education (PhD); early childhood special education (MS); education of deaf and hard of hearing (MS); educational administration and policy studies (Ed D, PhD); educational administration and supervision (Ed S); educational psychology (Ed D, PhD); elementary education (MS, Ed S); elementary teaching (MS); English education (MS, Ed S); exercise science (PhD); foreign language/ESL education (MS, Ed S); instructional technology (MS, Ed D, PhD, Ed S); literacy, language and ESL education (PhD); literacy, language education, and ESL education (Ed D); mathematics education (MS, Ed S); modified and comprehensive special education (MS); reading education (MS, Ed S); school counseling (Ed S); school psychology (PhD, Ed S); science education (MS, Ed S); secondary teaching (MS); social foundations (MS); social science education (MS, Ed S); socio-cultural foundations of sports and education (PhD); special education (Ed S); teacher education (Ed D, PhD). *Accreditation:* NCATE. Part-time and evening/weekend programs available. *Degree requirements:* For master's and Ed S, thesis optional; for doctorate, variable foreign language requirement, thesis/dissertation. *Entrance requirements:* For master's, minimum GPA of 2.7; for doctorate and Ed S, GRE General Test, minimum GPA of 2.7. Additional exam requirements/recommendations for international students: Required—TOEFL. Electronic applications accepted. *Expenses:* Tuition, state resident: full-time $6826; part-time $380 per semester hour. Tuition, nonresident: full-time $21,844; part-time $1147 per semester hour. Tuition and fees vary according to program.

The University of Toledo, College of Graduate Studies, College of Education, Department of Curriculum and Instruction, Program in Education and History, Toledo, OH 43606-3390. Offers MAE.

The University of Toledo, College of Graduate Studies, College of Education, Department of Curriculum and Instruction, Program in Education and Political Science, Toledo, OH 43606-3390. Offers MAE.

The University of Toledo, College of Graduate Studies, College of Education, Department of Curriculum and Instruction, Program in Education and Sociology, Toledo, OH 43606-3390. Offers MAE.

University of Victoria, Faculty of Graduate Studies, Faculty of Education, Department of Curriculum and Instruction, Victoria, BC V8W 2Y2, Canada. Offers art education (M Ed, PhD); curriculum studies (M Ed, MA, PhD); early childhood education (M Ed, PhD); educational studies (PhD); language and literacy (M Ed, MA, PhD); mathematics (M Ed, MA, PhD); music education (M Ed, MA, PhD); science (M Ed, MA, PhD); social studies (M Ed, MA); social, cultural and foundational studies (MA, PhD); technology and environmental education (PhD). Part-time programs available. *Degree requirements:* For master's, thesis, project (M Ed); for doctorate, comprehensive exam, thesis/dissertation. *Entrance requirements:* For master's, minimum B average. Additional exam requirements/recommendations for international students: Required—TOEFL (minimum score 575 paper-based; 233 computer-based), IELTS (minimum score 7). Electronic applications accepted. *Faculty research:* Elementary and secondary English, language arts, curriculum theory and practice, educational media and technology, educational administration and leadership, history and philosophy of education.

University of Virginia, Curry School of Education, Department of Curriculum, Instruction, and Special Education, Program in Curriculum and Instruction, Charlottesville, VA 22903. Offers curriculum and instruction (M Ed, Ed S); elementary (M Ed, Ed D); English (M Ed, Ed D); foreign language (M Ed); mathematics (M Ed, Ed D); reading (M Ed, Ed D, Ed S); science (Ed D); social studies (M Ed). *Students:* 12 full-time (8 women), 30 part-time (24 women); includes 2 minority (1 Asian American or Pacific Islander, 1 Hispanic American), 1 international. Average age 36. 55 applicants, 69% accepted, 26 enrolled. In 2009, 247 master's, 14 doctorates, 10 other advanced degrees awarded. *Degree requirements:* For master's, comprehensive exam (for some programs); for doctorate, comprehensive exam, thesis/dissertation; for Ed S, comprehensive exam. *Entrance requirements:* For master's, doctorate, and Ed S, GRE General Test, 2 letters of recommendation. Additional exam requirements/recommendations for international students: Required—TOEFL (minimum score 600 paper-based; 250 computer-based; 90 iBT), IELTS (minimum score 7). *Application deadline:* Applications are processed on a rolling basis. Application fee: $60. Electronic applications accepted. *Financial support:* Fellowships with tuition reimbursements, research assistantships with tuition reimbursements, teaching assistantships with tuition reimbursements available. Financial award application deadline: 1/5; financial award applicants required to submit FAFSA.

University of Virginia, Curry School of Education, Program in Education, Charlottesville, VA 22903. Offers administration and supervision (PhD); applied developmental science (PhD); counselor education (PhD); curriculum and instruction (PhD); early childhood-developmental risk (MT); education evaluation (PhD); educational psychology (PhD); educational research (PhD); elementary (MT, PhD); English education (MT, PhD); foreign language education (MT); higher education (PhD); instructional technology (PhD); kinesiology (MT, PhD); math education (PhD); reading education (PhD); research statistics and evaluation (PhD); school psychology (PhD); science education (PhD); social studies education (MT, PhD); special education (PhD); world languages education (MT). *Students:* 336 full-time (239 women), 88 part-time (54 women); includes 43 minority (24 African Americans, 2 American Indian/Alaska Native, 11 Asian Americans or Pacific Islanders, 6 Hispanic Americans), 18 international. Average age 27. 199 applicants, 48% accepted, 55 enrolled. In 2009, 127 master's, 52 doctorates awarded. *Degree requirements:* For master's, comprehensive exam (for some programs), field project; for doctorate, comprehensive exam, thesis/dissertation. *Entrance requirements:* For doctorate,

Social Sciences Education

University of Virginia (continued)
GRE General Test. Additional exam requirements/recommendations for international students: Required—TOEFL (minimum score 600 paper-based; 250 computer-based; 90 iBT), IELTS (minimum score 7). *Application deadline:* Applications are processed on a rolling basis. Application fee: $60. Electronic applications accepted. *Financial support:* Fellowships, research assistantships, teaching assistantships available. Financial award application deadline: 1/5; financial award applicants required to submit FAFSA.

University of Washington, Graduate School, College of Education, Seattle, WA 98195. Offers curriculum and instruction (M Ed, Ed D, PhD), including educational technology, general curriculum (Ed D, PhD), language, literacy, and culture, mathematics education, multicultural education, reading and language arts education (Ed D), science education, social studies education, teaching and curriculum (M Ed); educational leadership and policy studies (M Ed, Ed D, PhD), including administration (Ed D), educational policy, organization, and leadership (M Ed, PhD), higher education, leadership for learning (Ed D), social and cultural foundations of education (M Ed, PhD); educational psychology (M Ed, PhD), including educational psychology (PhD), human development and cognition (M Ed), learning sciences, measurement, statistics and research design (M Ed), school psychology (M Ed); instructional leadership (M Ed); intercollegiate athletic leadership (M Ed); special education (M Ed, Ed D, PhD), including early childhood special education (M Ed), emotional and behavioral disabilities (M Ed), learning disabilities (M Ed), low-incidence disabilities (M Ed), severe disabilities (M Ed), special education (Ed D, PhD); teacher education (MIT). *Accreditation:* APA. Part-time and evening/weekend programs available. *Degree requirements:* For master's, thesis optional; for doctorate, thesis/dissertation. *Entrance requirements:* For master's and doctorate, GRE General Test, minimum GPA of 3.0. Additional exam requirements/recommendations for international students: Required—TOEFL. Electronic applications accepted. *Faculty research:* School restructuring/effective schools, special education interventions, literacy and writing, technology, school partnerships, teacher preparation.

The University of West Alabama, School of Graduate Studies, College of Liberal Arts, Department of History and Social Sciences, Livingston, AL 35470. Offers history (MAT); social science (MAT). *Accreditation:* NCATE.

University of West Georgia, Graduate School, College of Education, Department of Curriculum and Instruction, Carrollton, GA 30118. Offers art education (M Ed); art teacher education (Ed S); biology/secondary education (Ed S); business education (M Ed, Ed S); early childhood education (M Ed, Ed S); economics/secondary teacher education (Ed S); English teacher education (Ed S); French language teacher education (Ed S); history teacher education (Ed S); mathematics teacher education (Ed S); middle grades education (M Ed, Ed S); reading education (M Ed, Ed S); science teacher education (Ed S); secondary education (M Ed, Ed S); social science teacher education (Ed S); Spanish language teacher education (Ed S). Part-time and evening/weekend programs available. *Faculty:* 18 full-time (15 women), 7 part-time/adjunct (6 women). *Students:* 119 full-time (101 women), 358 part-time (280 women); includes 109 minority (97 African Americans, 3 American Indian/Alaska Native, 2 Asian Americans or Pacific Islanders, 7 Hispanic Americans). Average age 33. 193 applicants, 82% accepted, 34 enrolled. In 2009, 109 master's, 27 Ed Ss awarded. *Degree requirements:* For master's, comprehensive exam; for Ed S, research project. *Entrance requirements:* For master's, GRE General Test or MAT, minimum GPA of 2.7; for Ed S, GRE General Test, master's degree, minimum graduate GPA of 2.7. *Application deadline:* For fall admission, 7/17 for domestic students; for spring admission, 11/20 for domestic students. Applications are processed on a rolling basis. Application fee: $30. Electronic applications accepted. *Expenses:* Tuition, state resident: full-time $2952; part-time $164 per semester hour. Tuition, nonresident: full-time $11,808; part-time $656 per semester hour. Required fees: $42.90 per semester hour. $307 per semester. Tuition and fees vary according to course load. *Financial support:* In 2009–10, 5 research assistantships with full tuition reimbursements (averaging $3,000 per year) were awarded; career-related internships or fieldwork and scholarships/grants also available. Support available to part-time students. Financial award applicants required to submit FAFSA. *Unit head:* Dr. Donna Harkins, Chair, 678-839-6066, Fax: 678-839-6559, E-mail: dharkins@westga.edu. *Application contact:* Dr. Charles W. Clark, Dean, 678-839-6508, E-mail: cclark@westga.edu.

University of Wisconsin–River Falls, Outreach and Graduate Studies, College of Arts and Science, Department of History and Philosophy, River Falls, WI 54022. Offers social science education (MSE). Part-time programs available. *Degree requirements:* For master's, thesis (for some programs). *Entrance requirements:* For master's, minimum GPA of 2.75. Additional exam requirements/recommendations for international students: Required—TOEFL (minimum score 500 paper-based; 65 iBT), IELTS (minimum score 5.5). Electronic applications accepted. *Faculty research:* WW II, Hitler, modern China, women's history, immigration history.

Ursuline College, School of Graduate Studies, Program in Education, Pepper Pike, OH 44124-4398. Offers art education (MA); early childhood education (MA); language arts education (MA); life science education (MA); math education (MA); middle school education (MA); social studies education (MA); special education (MA). *Accreditation:* NCATE. *Faculty:* 1 (woman) full-time, 10 part-time/adjunct (8 women). *Students:* 53 full-time (40 women), 3 part-time (all women); includes 8 minority (7 African Americans, 1 Hispanic American). Average age 34. In 2009, 11 master's awarded. *Degree requirements:* For master's, comprehensive exam. *Entrance requirements:* For master's, minimum undergraduate GPA of 3.0. Additional exam requirements/recommendations for international students: Required—TOEFL (minimum score 500 paper-based; 173 computer-based). *Application deadline:* For fall admission, 8/1 priority date for domestic students. Applications are processed on a rolling basis. Application fee: $25. *Expenses:* Contact institution. *Financial support:* Federal Work-Study available. Financial award application deadline: 3/1. *Unit head:* Karen Godenschwager Nelson, Director, 440-684-8338, Fax: 440-684-6088, E-mail: kgodenschwager@ursuline.edu. *Application contact:* Melanie Steele, Secretary, 440-646-8199, Fax: 440-684-6138, E-mail: gradsch@ursuline.edu.

Virginia Commonwealth University, Graduate School, School of Education, Program in Teaching and Learning, Richmond, VA 23284-9005. Offers early education (MT); middle education (MT); secondary education (MT, Certificate); special education (MT). *Accreditation:* NCATE. Part-time programs available. *Entrance requirements:* For master's, GRE General Test or MAT.

Wayne State College, School of Education and Counseling, Department of Educational Foundations and Leadership, Program in Curriculum and Instruction, Wayne, NE 68787. Offers alternative education (MSE); business and information technology education (MSE); communication arts education (MSE); early childhood education (MSE); elementary education (MSE); English as a second language (MSE); English education (MSE); family and consumer sciences education (MSE); industrial technology and vocational education (MSE); learning communities (MSE); mathematics education (MSE); music education (MSE); science education (MSE); social science education (MSE). *Accreditation:* NCATE. Part-time and evening/weekend programs available. *Degree requirements:* For master's, comprehensive exam, thesis optional. *Entrance requirements:* For master's, GRE General Test. Additional exam requirements/recommendations for international students: Required—TOEFL (minimum score 550 paper-based; 213 computer-based).

Wayne State University, College of Education, Division of Teacher Education, Detroit, MI 48202. Offers adult and continuing education (M Ed); art education (M Ed); bilingual/bicultural education (M Ed, MAT); business education (M Ed, MAT); career and technical education (M Ed, Ed D, PhD, Ed S); curriculum and instruction (Ed D, PhD, Ed S); distributive education (M Ed, MAT); early childhood education (M Ed); elementary education (M Ed, MAT, Ed D, PhD, Ed S); elementary education curriculum and instruction (M Ed); English education (M Ed); English education-secondary (M Ed, Ed S); foreign language education (M Ed); general education (Ed D, Ed S); health occupations education (M Ed); industrial education (M Ed); mathematics education (M Ed, Ed S); pre-school and parent education (M Ed); reading (M Ed, Ed D, Ed S); reading, languages and literature (Ed D); school music-vocal (M Ed); science education (M Ed, MAT, Ed S); secondary education (MAT); secondary school reading (M Ed); social studies education (M Ed, Ed S), including education-secondary (M Ed); special education (M Ed, Ed D, PhD, Ed S); teacher education (MAT, Ed D, PhD). *Degree requirements:* For doctorate, thesis/dissertation. *Entrance requirements:* For master's, Michigan Basic Skills Test (MA in teaching), minimum GPA of 2.6; for doctorate, minimum undergraduate GPA of 3.0, graduate 3.5; interview, curriculum vitae; references. Additional exam requirements/recommendations for international students: Required—TOEFL (minimum score 550 paper-based; 213 computer-based), TWE (minimum score 6). Electronic applications accepted. *Faculty research:* Reading and writing literacy and literature.

Wayne State University, College of Education, Division of Theoretical and Behavioral Foundations, Detroit, MI 48202. Offers counseling (M Ed, MA, Ed D, PhD, Ed S); education evaluation and research (M Ed, Ed D, PhD); educational psychology (M Ed, Ed D, PhD, Ed S); educational sociology (M Ed, Ed D, PhD, Ed S); history and philosophy of education (M Ed, Ed D, PhD); rehabilitation counseling and community inclusion (MA, Ed S); school and community psychology (MA, Ed S); school clinical psychology (Ed S). *Accreditation:* ACA (one or more programs are accredited); CORE (one or more programs are accredited). Evening/weekend programs available. *Degree requirements:* For doctorate, thesis/dissertation. *Entrance requirements:* For master's, GRE; for doctorate, GRE, interview, minimum GPA of 3.0, curriculum vitae, references. Additional exam requirements/recommendations for international students: Required—TOEFL (minimum score 550 paper-based; 213 computer-based), TWE (minimum score 6). Electronic applications accepted. *Faculty research:* Adolescents at risk, supervision of counseling.

Webster University, School of Education, Department of Multidisciplinary Studies, St. Louis, MO 63119-3194. Offers administrative leadership (Ed S); education leadership (Ed S); educational technology (MAT); mathematics (MAT); multidisciplinary studies (MAT); school systems, superintendency and leadership (Ed S); social science (MAT); special education (MAT). Part-time programs available. *Entrance requirements:* For master's, minimum GPA of 2.5. Additional exam requirements/recommendations for international students: Required—TOEFL. *Expenses:* Tuition: Part-time $565 per credit hour. Tuition and fees vary according to degree level, campus/location and program.

West Chester University of Pennsylvania, Office of Graduate Studies, College of Arts and Sciences, Department of History, West Chester, PA 19383. Offers history (M Ed, MA); holocaust and genocide studies (MA, Certificate); social studies/history (Teaching Certificate). Part-time and evening/weekend programs available. *Students:* 58 part-time (30 women); includes 3 minority (1 African American, 2 Asian Americans or Pacific Islanders). Average age 28. 38 applicants, 95% accepted, 24 enrolled. In 2009, 14 master's awarded. *Degree requirements:* For master's, thesis optional. *Entrance requirements:* For master's, GMAT, statement of professional goals, writing sample, minimum GPA of 3.0 in history, three letters of recommendation . Additional exam requirements/recommendations for international students: Required—TOEFL (minimum score 550 paper-based; 213 computer-based; 80 iBT). *Application deadline:* For fall admission, 4/15 priority date for domestic students, 3/15 for international students; for spring admission, 10/15 for domestic students, 9/1 for international students. Applications are processed on a rolling basis. Application fee: $35. Electronic applications accepted. *Expenses:* Tuition, state resident: full-time $6666; part-time $370 per credit. Tuition, nonresident: full-time $10,666; part-time $593 per credit. Required fees: $122.56 per credit. *Financial support:* In 2009–10, 5 research assistantships with full and partial tuition reimbursements (averaging $5,000 per year) were awarded; unspecified assistantships also available. Support available to part-time students. Financial award application deadline: 2/15; financial award applicants required to submit FAFSA. *Faculty research:* Oral histories, siege of Leningrad. *Unit head:* Dr. Wayne Hanley, Chair, 610-436-2201, E-mail: whanley@wcupa.edu. *Application contact:* Dr. Jonathan Friedman, Director of the Holocaust/Genocide Education Center and Graduate Coordinator of Holocaust and Genocide Studies, 610-436-2972, E-mail: jfriedmans@wcupa.edu.

Western Oregon University, Graduate Programs, College of Education, Division of Teacher Education, Program in Secondary Education, Monmouth, OR 97361-1394. Offers bilingual education (MS Ed); health (MS Ed); humanities (MAT, MS Ed); initial licensure (MAT); mathematics (MAT, MS Ed); science (MAT, MS Ed); social science (MAT, MS Ed). *Accreditation:* NCATE. Part-time and evening/weekend programs available. *Degree requirements:* For master's, thesis optional, written exam. *Entrance requirements:* For master's, minimum GPA of 3.0, teaching license. Additional exam requirements/recommendations for international students: Required—TOEFL (minimum score 550 paper-based; 213 computer-based; 79 iBT), IELTS (minimum score 6.5). *Faculty research:* Literacy, science in primary grades, geography education, retention, teacher burnout.

Widener University, School of Human Service Professions, Center for Education, Chester, PA 19013-5792. Offers adult education (M Ed); counseling in higher education (M Ed); counselor education (M Ed); early childhood education (M Ed); educational foundations (M Ed); educational leadership (M Ed); educational psychology (M Ed); elementary education (M Ed); English and language arts (M Ed); health education (M Ed); higher education leadership (Ed D); home and school visitor (M Ed); human sexuality (M Ed); mathematics education (M Ed); middle school education (M Ed); principalship (M Ed); reading and language arts (Ed D); reading education (M Ed); school administration (Ed D); science education (M Ed); social studies education (M Ed); special education (M Ed); technology education (M Ed). *Accreditation:* NCATE. Part-time and evening/weekend programs available. *Faculty:* 34 full-time (22 women), 37 part-time/adjunct (14 women). *Students:* 203 full-time (154 women), 415 part-time (298 women); includes 50 minority (34 African Americans, 1 American Indian/Alaska Native, 5 Asian Americans or Pacific Islanders, 10 Hispanic Americans), 3 international. Average age 39. 139 applicants, 88% accepted. In 2009, 168 master's, 31 doctorates awarded. Terminal master's awarded for partial completion of doctoral program. *Degree requirements:* For doctorate, thesis/dissertation. *Entrance requirements:* For master's, minimum GPA of 2.5; for doctorate, GRE or MAT, minimum GPA of 2.0 (undergraduate), 3.5 (graduate). *Application deadline:* Applications are processed on a rolling basis. Application fee: $25 ($300 for international students). Electronic applications accepted. *Expenses:* Contact institution. *Financial support:* Career-related internships or fieldwork, tuition waivers (full and partial), and unspecified assistantships available. Support available to part-time students. Financial award application deadline: 5/1. *Faculty research:* Reading and cognition, adult education, technology education, educational leadership, special education. *Unit head:* Dr. Michael W. LeDoux, Associate Dean, 610-499-4294, Fax: 610-499-4623, E-mail: mwledoux@widener.edu. *Application contact:* Dr. Roberta D. Nolan, Director of Graduate Admissions, 610-499-4125, E-mail: rdnolan@widener.edu.

Wilkes University, College of Graduate and Professional Studies, School of Education, Wilkes-Barre, PA 18766-0002. Offers classroom technology (MS Ed); educational computing (MS Ed); educational development and strategies (MS Ed); educational leadership (MS Ed); educational technology (Ed D); elementary education (MS Ed); higher education administration (Ed D); instructional technology (MS Ed); K-12 administration (Ed D); online teaching (MS Ed); school business leadership (MS Ed); secondary education (MS Ed), including biology, chemistry, English, history; special education (MS Ed). Part-time and evening/weekend programs available. Postbaccalaureate distance learning degree programs offered (minimal on-campus study). *Students:* 89 full-time (60 women), 2,849 part-time (2,058 women); includes 52 minority (10 African Americans, 2 American Indian/Alaska Native, 13 Asian Americans or Pacific Islanders, 27 Hispanic Americans), 6 international. Average age 33. In 2009, 947 master's awarded. *Entrance requirements:* Additional exam requirements/recommendations for international students: Required—TOEFL (minimum score 500 paper-based; 173 computer-based; 79 iBT). *Application deadline:* Applications are processed on a rolling basis. Application fee: $45. *Expenses:* Contact institution. *Financial support:* Federal Work-Study and unspecified assistantships available. Financial award application deadline: 3/1; financial award applicants required to submit FAFSA. *Unit head:* Dr. Michael Speziale, Dean, 570-408-4679, Fax: 570-408-4905, E-mail: michael.speziale@wilkes.edu. *Application contact:* Kathleen Houlihan, Director of Graduate Studies, 570-408-3235, Fax: 570-408-7846, E-mail: kathleen.houlihan@wilkes.edu.

William Carey University, School of Education, Hattiesburg, MS 39401-5499. Offers art education (M Ed); art of teaching (M Ed); elementary education (M Ed, Ed S); English education (M Ed); gifted education (M Ed); history and social science (M Ed); mild/moderate disabilities

(M Ed); secondary education (M Ed). Part-time programs available. *Degree requirements:* For master's, comprehensive exam. *Entrance requirements:* For master's, GRE, MAT, minimum GPA of 2.5, Class A teacher's license. Additional exam requirements/recommendations for international students: Required—TOEFL (minimum score 550 paper-based; 213 computer-based).

Worcester State College, Graduate Studies, Program in History, Worcester, MA 01602-2597. Offers M Ed. Part-time programs available. *Faculty:* 3 full-time (1 woman), 2 part-time/adjunct (0 women). *Students:* 16 part-time (5 women); includes 1 minority (Asian American or Pacific Islander). Average age 36. 11 applicants, 45% accepted, 3 enrolled. In 2009, 9 master's awarded. *Degree requirements:* For master's, comprehensive exam (for some programs), thesis optional. *Entrance requirements:* For master's, GRE General Test or MAT, 18 undergraduate credits in history, including U. S. history and Western civilizations. Additional exam requirements/recommendations for international students: Required—TOEFL (minimum score 550 paper-based; 213 computer-based; 79 iBT). *Application deadline:* Applications are processed on a rolling basis. Application fee: $30. *Expenses:* Tuition, area resident: Part-time $150 per credit. Tuition, state resident: part-time $150 per credit. Tuition, nonresident: part-time $150 per credit. Required fees: $85. *Financial support:* In 2009–10, 1 student received support, including 1 research assistantship with full tuition reimbursement available (averaging $4,800 per year); career-related internships or fieldwork, scholarships/grants, and unspecified assistantships also available. Financial award application deadline: 3/1; financial award applicants required to submit FAFSA. *Faculty research:* Labor history, Middle East politics, American-Russian relations, American–East Asian relations. *Unit head:* Dr. Charlotte Haller, Coordinator, 508-929-8046, Fax: 508-929-8155, E-mail: challer1@worcester.edu. *Application contact:* Nicole Brown, Assistant Dean of Graduate and Continuing Education, 508-929-8787, Fax: 508-929-8100, E-mail: nbrown@worcester.edu.

Vocational and Technical Education

Alabama Agricultural and Mechanical University, School of Graduate Studies, School of Engineering and Technology, Department of Industrial Technology, Huntsville, AL 35811. Offers M Ed, MS. *Accreditation:* NCATE. Part-time and evening/weekend programs available. *Degree requirements:* For master's, comprehensive exam, thesis optional. *Entrance requirements:* For master's, GRE General Test. Additional exam requirements/recommendations for international students: Required—TOEFL (minimum score 500 paper-based; 173 computer-based; 61 iBT). Electronic applications accepted. *Faculty research:* Ionized gases, hypersonic flow, phenomenology, robotic systems development.

Alcorn State University, School of Graduate Studies, Department of Advanced Technologies, Alcorn State, MS 39096-7500. Offers workforce education leadership (MS).

Alcorn State University, School of Graduate Studies, School of Psychology and Education, Alcorn State, MS 39096-7500. Offers agricultural education (MS Ed); elementary education (MS Ed, Ed S); guidance and counseling (MS Ed); industrial education (MS Ed); secondary education (MS Ed), including health and physical education; special education (MS Ed). *Accreditation:* NCATE. *Degree requirements:* For master's, thesis optional.

Appalachian State University, Cratis D. Williams Graduate School, Department of Technology, Boone, NC 28608. Offers appropriate technology (MA); technology education (MA). Part-time programs available. *Faculty:* 16 full-time (4 women), 3 part-time/adjunct (1 woman). *Students:* 30 full-time (6 women), 6 part-time (2 women); includes 2 minority (1 African American, 1 Hispanic American). 26 applicants, 92% accepted, 19 enrolled. In 2009, 20 master's awarded. *Degree requirements:* For master's, comprehensive exam, thesis optional. *Entrance requirements:* For master's, GRE General Test, 3 letters of recommendation. Additional exam requirements/recommendations for international students: Required—TOEFL (minimum score 550 paper-based; 230 computer-based; 79 iBT), IELTS (minimum score 6.5). *Application deadline:* For fall admission, 7/1 for domestic students, 2/1 for international students; for spring admission, 11/1 for domestic students, 7/1 for international students. Applications are processed on a rolling basis. Application fee: $50. Electronic applications accepted. *Expenses:* Tuition, state resident: full-time $2960. Tuition, nonresident: full-time $14,051. Required fees: $2320. *Financial support:* In 2009–10, 14 research assistantships (averaging $9,000 per year) were awarded; fellowships, teaching assistantships, career-related internships or fieldwork, Federal Work-Study, institutionally sponsored loans, scholarships/grants, and unspecified assistantships also available. Financial award application deadline: 4/1; financial award applicants required to submit FAFSA. *Faculty research:* Wind power, biofuels, green construction, solar energy production. Total annual research expenditures: $450,000. *Unit head:* Dr. Jeff Tiller, Chair, 828-262-6351, E-mail: tillerjs@appstate.edu. *Application contact:* Dr. Marie Hoepfl, Graduate Program Director, 828-262-6351, E-mail: hoepflmc@appstate.edu.

Ball State University, Graduate School, College of Applied Science and Technology, Department of Industry and Technology, Muncie, IN 47306-1099. Offers MA, MAE. *Accreditation:* NCATE (one or more programs are accredited).

Bemidji State University, School of Graduate Studies, College of Professional Studies, Field of Industrial Technology, Bemidji, MN 56601-2699. Offers technical education (MS). Part-time programs available. *Degree requirements:* For master's, thesis. *Entrance requirements:* For master's, letters of recommendation. Additional exam requirements/recommendations for international students: Required—TOEFL. Electronic applications accepted.

Bemidji State University, School of Graduate Studies, College of Professional Studies, Field of Technology/Career Technical Education, Bemidji, MN 56601-2699. Offers MS. Part-time programs available. *Entrance requirements:* For master's, letters of recommendation. Electronic applications accepted.

Bowling Green State University, Graduate College, College of Technology, Program in Career and Technology Education, Bowling Green, OH 43403. Offers career and technology education (M Ed), including technology. Part-time programs available. *Degree requirements:* For master's, thesis or alternative. *Entrance requirements:* For master's, GRE General Test. Additional exam requirements/recommendations for international students: Required—TOEFL. Electronic applications accepted. *Faculty research:* Curriculum in technology education.

Buffalo State College, State University of New York, The Graduate School, Faculty of Applied Science and Education, Department of Educational Foundations, Program in Career and Technical Education, Buffalo, NY 14222-1095. Offers MS Ed. *Accreditation:* NCATE. Part-time and evening/weekend programs available. *Degree requirements:* For master's, thesis or project. *Entrance requirements:* For master's, minimum GPA of 2.5 in last 60 hours, New York teaching certificate. Additional exam requirements/recommendations for international students: Required—TOEFL (minimum score 550 paper-based; 213 computer-based).

Buffalo State College, State University of New York, The Graduate School, Faculty of Applied Science and Education, Department of Technology, Program in Technology Education, Buffalo, NY 14222-1095. Offers MS Ed. *Accreditation:* NCATE. *Degree requirements:* For master's, thesis or project. *Entrance requirements:* For master's, minimum GPA of 2.5 in last 60 hours, New York teaching certificate. Additional exam requirements/recommendations for international students: Required—TOEFL (minimum score 550 paper-based; 213 computer-based).

California Baptist University, Program in Education, Riverside, CA 92504-3206. Offers cross-cultural language and academic development (MA); educational leadership (MS); educational leadership and faith-based instruction (MS); educational technology (MS); instructional computer applications (MS); reading (MS); school counseling (MS); school psychology (MS); special education (MS); special education in mild/moderate disabilities (MS); special education in moderate/severe disabilities (MS); teaching (MS); teaching and learning (MS Ed). Part-time programs available. *Faculty:* 16 full-time (9 women), 10 part-time/adjunct (all women). *Students:* 73 full-time (60 women), 368 part-time (298 women); includes 170 minority (34 African Americans, 4 American Indian/Alaska Native, 18 Asian Americans or Pacific Islanders, 114 Hispanic Americans). 266 applicants, 72% accepted, 169 enrolled. In 2009, 120 master's awarded. *Degree requirements:* For master's, comprehensive exam (for some programs), thesis optional. *Entrance requirements:* For master's, minimum undergraduate GPA of 2.75, 12 semester hours of pre-requisite course work in education. Additional exam requirements/recommendations for international students: Required—TOEFL (minimum score 575 paper-based; 230 computer-based; 89 iBT). *Application deadline:* For fall admission, 8/1 priority date for domestic students, 7/1 for international students; for spring admission, 12/1 priority date for domestic students, 10/15 priority date for international students. Applications are processed on a rolling basis. Application fee: $45. Electronic applications accepted. *Expenses:* Tuition: Full-time $8352; part-time $464 per semester hour. Required fees: $125 per semester. Tuition and fees vary according to course load, campus/location and program. *Financial support:* Career-related internships or fieldwork, Federal Work-Study, and scholarships/grants available. Support available to part-time students. Financial award applicants required to submit FAFSA. *Unit head:* Dr. Mary Crist, Dean, School of Education, 951-343-4313, Fax: 951-343-4516, E-mail: mcrist@calbaptist.edu. *Application contact:* Gail Ronveaux, Dean of Graduate Enrollment, 951-343-5045, Fax: 951-343-5095, E-mail: graduateadmissions@calbaptist.edu.

California State University, Sacramento, Graduate Studies, College of Education, Department of Special Education, Rehabilitation, and School Psychology, Sacramento, CA 95819. Offers school psychology (MS); special education (MA); vocational rehabilitation (MS). *Accreditation:* CORE. Part-time programs available. *Degree requirements:* For master's, thesis or alternative, writing proficiency exam. *Entrance requirements:* For master's, minimum GPA of 2.5. Additional exam requirements/recommendations for international students: Required—TOEFL. Electronic applications accepted.

California State University, San Bernardino, Graduate Studies, College of Education, Program in Vocational and Career Education, San Bernardino, CA 92407-2397. Offers MA. *Accreditation:* NCATE. Part-time and evening/weekend programs available. *Faculty:* 1 full-time (0 women). *Students:* 19 full-time (12 women), 7 part-time (4 women); includes 11 minority (1 African American, 2 Asian Americans or Pacific Islanders, 8 Hispanic Americans). Average age 48. 13 applicants, 69% accepted, 6 enrolled. In 2009, 20 master's awarded. *Degree requirements:* For master's, thesis. *Entrance requirements:* For master's, minimum GPA of 3.0 in education, vocational teaching credential. *Application deadline:* For fall admission, 8/31 priority date for domestic students. Application fee: $55. *Financial support:* Career-related internships or fieldwork and Federal Work-Study available. Support available to part-time students. *Unit head:* Dr. Herbert Brunkhorst, Coordinator, Designated Subjects, 909-537-5613. *Application contact:* Olivia Rosas, Director of Admissions, 909-537-7577, Fax: 909-537-7034, E-mail: orosas@csusb.edu.

California University of Pennsylvania, School of Graduate Studies and Research, School of Education, Department of Technology Education, California, PA 15419-1394. Offers M Ed. *Accreditation:* NCATE. Part-time and evening/weekend programs available. *Degree requirements:* For master's, comprehensive exam, thesis optional. *Entrance requirements:* For master's, MAT, minimum GPA of 3.0, teaching experience in industrial arts. Additional exam requirements/recommendations for international students: Required—TOEFL (minimum score 550 paper-based; 213 computer-based; 80 iBT). Electronic applications accepted. *Faculty research:* Curriculum, trends in technology, standards-based assessment.

Central Connecticut State University, School of Graduate Studies, School of Technology, Department of Technology Engineering Education, New Britain, CT 06050-4010. Offers MS, Certificate. Part-time and evening/weekend programs available. *Faculty:* 5 full-time (1 woman), 2 part-time/adjunct (0 women). *Students:* 6 full-time (0 women), 26 part-time (0 women); includes 2 minority (1 American Indian/Alaska Native, 1 Hispanic American). Average age 38. 17 applicants, 76% accepted, 7 enrolled. In 2009, 3 master's, 3 other advanced degrees awarded. *Degree requirements:* For master's, comprehensive exam, thesis or alternative; for Certificate, qualifying exam. *Entrance requirements:* For master's, minimum undergraduate GPA of 2.7. Additional exam requirements/recommendations for international students: Required—TOEFL. *Application deadline:* For fall admission, 7/1 for domestic students; for spring admission, 12/1 for domestic students. Applications are processed on a rolling basis. Application fee: $50. Electronic applications accepted. *Expenses:* Tuition, area resident: Full-time $4662; part-time $440 per credit. Tuition, state resident: full-time $6994; part-time $440 per credit. Tuition, nonresident: full-time $12,988; part-time $440 per credit. Required fees: $3606. One-time fee: $62 part-time. *Financial support:* In 2009–10, 1 student received support. Career-related internships or fieldwork, Federal Work-Study, scholarships/grants, and unspecified assistantships available. Support available to part-time students. Financial award application deadline: 3/1; financial award applicants required to submit FAFSA. *Faculty research:* Instruction, curriculum development, administration, occupational training. *Unit head:* Dr. James DeLaura, Chair, 860-832-1850. *Application contact:* Dr. James DeLaura, Chair, 860-832-1850.

Chicago State University, School of Graduate and Professional Studies, College of Education, Department of Technology and Education, Chicago, IL 60628. Offers secondary education (MAT); technology and education (MS Ed). Postbaccalaureate distance learning degree programs offered. *Degree requirements:* For master's, thesis optional. *Entrance requirements:* For master's, minimum GPA of 2.75.

Clarion University of Pennsylvania, Office of Research and Graduate Studies, College of Education and Human Services, Department of Education, Program in Education, Clarion, PA 16214. Offers curriculum and instruction (M Ed); early childhood (M Ed); English (M Ed); history (M Ed); literacy (M Ed); science (M Ed); technology (M Ed). *Accreditation:* NCATE. Part-time programs available. *Degree requirements:* For master's, comprehensive exam, thesis or alternative. *Entrance requirements:* For master's, minimum QPA of 3.0, teacher certification. Additional exam requirements/recommendations for international students: Required—TOEFL (minimum score 550 paper-based; 213 computer-based; 80 iBT). Electronic applications accepted.

Colorado State University, Graduate School, College of Applied Human Sciences, School of Education, Fort Collins, CO 80523-1588. Offers adult education and training (M Ed); community college leadership (PhD); counseling and career development (M Ed); education and human resource studies (M Ed, PhD); educational leadership (M Ed, PhD); interdisciplinary studies (PhD); organizational performance and change (M Ed, PhD); student affairs in higher education (MS). *Accreditation:* ACA; Teacher Education Accreditation Council. Part-time and evening/weekend programs available. *Faculty:* 21 full-time (10 women). *Students:* 195 full-time (132 women), 469 part-time (292 women); includes 114 minority (31 African Americans, 12 American Indian/Alaska Native, 22 Asian Americans or Pacific Islanders, 49 Hispanic Americans),

Vocational and Technical Education

Colorado State University (continued)

24 international. Average age 38. 451 applicants, 41% accepted, 141 enrolled. In 2009, 175 master's, 54 doctorates awarded. *Degree requirements:* For master's, comprehensive exam (for some programs), thesis optional; for doctorate, comprehensive exam, thesis/dissertation, minimum of 60 credits. *Entrance requirements:* For master's, GRE, minimum undergraduate GPA of 3.0, 3 letters of recommendation, curriculum vitae/resume; for doctorate, minimum GPA of 3.0, 3 letters of recommendation, curriculum vitae. Additional exam requirements/recommendations for international students: Required—TOEFL (minimum score 550 paper-based; 213 computer-based). *Application deadline:* For fall admission, 3/15 for domestic and international students; for spring admission, 11/1 for domestic students, 10/1 for international students. Applications are processed on a rolling basis. Application fee: $50. Electronic applications accepted. *Expenses:* Tuition, state resident: full-time $6434; part-time $359.10 per credit. Tuition, nonresident: full-time $18,116; part-time $1006.45 per credit. Required fees: $1496; $83 per credit. *Financial support:* In 2009–10, 8 students received support, including 3 research assistantships with full tuition reimbursements available (averaging $13,790 per year), 5 teaching assistantships with full tuition reimbursements available (averaging $10,253 per year); fellowships, Federal Work-Study, scholarships/grants, and unspecified assistantships also available. Financial award applicants required to submit FAFSA. *Faculty research:* Innovative instruction, diverse learners, transition, scientifically-based evaluation methods, leadership and organizational development. Total annual research expenditures: $655,700. *Unit head:* Dr. Carole Makela, Interim Director, 970-491-6317, Fax: 970-491-1317, E-mail: carole.makela@colostate.edu. *Application contact:* Dr. Sharon Anderson, Director of Graduate Programs, 970-491-6861, Fax: 970-491-1317, E-mail: sharon.anderson@colostate.edu.

East Carolina University, Graduate School, College of Education, Department of Business, Career, and Technical Education, Greenville, NC 27858-4353. Offers information technologies (MS); vocation education (MA Ed). *Accreditation:* NCATE. Part-time and evening/weekend programs available. Postbaccalaureate distance learning degree programs offered (no on-campus study). *Degree requirements:* For master's, comprehensive exam, thesis optional. *Entrance requirements:* For master's, GRE or MAT, minimum GPA of 2.5, bachelor's degree in related field, teaching license (MA Ed). Additional exam requirements/recommendations for international students: Required—TOEFL.

Eastern Kentucky University, The Graduate School, College of Business and Technology, Department of Technology, Program in Industrial Education, Richmond, KY 40475-3102. Offers occupational training and development (MS); technical administration (MS); technology education (MS). *Accreditation:* NCATE. Part-time programs available. *Entrance requirements:* For master's, GRE General Test, minimum GPA of 2.5.

Eastern Kentucky University, The Graduate School, College of Education, Department of Curriculum and Instruction, Program in Secondary and Higher Education, Richmond, KY 40475-3102. Offers secondary education (MA Ed), including agricultural education, art education, biological sciences education, business education, English education, geography education, history education, home economics education, industrial education, mathematical sciences education, physical education, school health education. *Accreditation:* NCATE. Part-time programs available. *Entrance requirements:* For master's, GRE General Test, minimum GPA of 2.5.

Eastern Michigan University, Graduate School, College of Technology, School of Technology Studies, Program in Career, Technical and Workforce Education, Ypsilanti, MI 48197. Offers MS. Part-time and evening/weekend programs available. Postbaccalaureate distance learning degree programs offered (minimal on-campus study). *Students:* 3 part-time (2 women). Average age 44. In 2009, 1 master's awarded. *Entrance requirements:* Additional exam requirements/recommendations for international students: Required—TOEFL. *Application deadline:* Applications are processed on a rolling basis. Application fee: $35. Tuition and fees vary according to course level. *Financial support:* Fellowships, research assistantships with full tuition reimbursements, teaching assistantships with full tuition reimbursements, career-related internships or fieldwork, Federal Work-Study, institutionally sponsored loans, scholarships/grants, tuition waivers (partial), and unspecified assistantships available. Support available to part-time students. Financial award applicants required to submit FAFSA. *Unit head:* Dr. Ronald Fulkert, Program Coordinator, 734-487-1161, Fax: 734-487-7690, E-mail: rfulkert@emich.edu. *Application contact:* Dr. Ronald Fulkert, Program Coordinator, 734-487-1161, Fax: 734-487-7690, E-mail: rfulkert@emich.edu.

East Tennessee State University, School of Graduate Studies, College of Business and Technology, Department of Technology and Geomatics, Johnson City, TN 37614. Offers digital media (MS); engineering technology (MS); industrial arts/technology education (MS). Part-time programs available. *Degree requirements:* For master's, thesis or alternative, final oral exam. *Entrance requirements:* For master's, bachelor's degree in technical or related area, minimum GPA of 3.0. Additional exam requirements/recommendations for international students: Required—TOEFL (minimum score 550 paper-based; 213 computer-based). *Faculty research:* Computer-integrated manufacturing, technology education, CAD/CAM, organizational change.

Fitchburg State University, Division of Graduate and Continuing Education, Program in Occupational Education, Fitchburg, MA 01420-2697. Offers M Ed. *Accreditation:* NCATE. Part-time and evening/weekend programs available. *Students:* 17 part-time (11 women). Average age 46. 6 applicants, 100% accepted, 5 enrolled. In 2009, 4 master's awarded. *Entrance requirements:* For master's, GRE General Test or MAT, teaching certificate, letters of recommendation, resume. Additional exam requirements/recommendations for international students: Required—TOEFL (minimum score 550 paper-based; 213 computer-based; 79 iBT). *Application deadline:* Applications are processed on a rolling basis. Application fee: $25 ($50 for international students). *Expenses:* Tuition, area resident: Part-time $150 per credit. Tuition, state resident: part-time $150 per credit. Tuition, nonresident: part-time $150 per credit. Required fees: $120 per credit. *Financial support:* In 2009–10, research assistantships with partial tuition reimbursements (averaging $5,500 per year); Federal Work-Study, scholarships/grants, and unspecified assistantships also available. Support available to part-time students. Financial award application deadline: 3/1; financial award applicants required to submit FAFSA. *Unit head:* Dr. James Alicata, Chair, 978-665-3047, Fax: 978-665-3658, E-mail: gce@fsc.edu. *Application contact:* Director of Admissions, 978-665-3144, Fax: 978-665-4540, E-mail: admissions@fsc.edu.

Fitchburg State University, Division of Graduate and Continuing Education, Program in Technology Education, Fitchburg, MA 01420-2697. Offers M Ed. *Accreditation:* NCATE. Part-time and evening/weekend programs available. *Students:* 1 full-time (0 women), 5 part-time (1 woman). Average age 46. 1 applicant, 100% accepted, 1 enrolled. In 2009, 8 master's awarded. *Entrance requirements:* For master's, GRE General Test or MAT, teaching certificate, letters of recommendation, resume. Additional exam requirements/recommendations for international students: Required—TOEFL (minimum score 550 paper-based; 213 computer-based; 79 iBT). *Application deadline:* Applications are processed on a rolling basis. Application fee: $25 ($50 for international students). *Expenses:* Tuition, area resident: Part-time $150 per credit. Tuition, state resident: part-time $150 per credit. Tuition, nonresident: part-time $150 per credit. Required fees: $120 per credit. *Financial support:* In 2009–10, research assistantships with partial tuition reimbursements (averaging $5,500 per year); Federal Work-Study, scholarships/grants, and unspecified assistantships also available. Support available to part-time students. Financial award application deadline: 3/1; financial award applicants required to submit FAFSA. *Unit head:* Wayne Whitfield, Chair, 978-665-4807, Fax: 978-665-3658, E-mail: gce@fsc.edu. *Application contact:* Director of Admissions, 978-665-3144, Fax: 978-665-4540, E-mail: admissions@fsc.edu.

Florida Agricultural and Mechanical University, Division of Graduate Studies, Research, and Continuing Education, College of Education, Department of Vocational Education, Tallahassee, FL 32307-3200. Offers business education (MBE); industrial education (M Ed, MS Ed). *Accreditation:* NCATE. *Faculty:* 2 full-time (both women). *Students:* 7 full-time (6 women); all minorities (all African Americans). *Degree requirements:* For master's, thesis (for some programs). *Entrance requirements:* For master's, GRE General Test, minimum GPA of 3.0. Additional exam requirements/recommendations for international students: Required—TOEFL. *Application deadline:* For fall admission, 5/18 for domestic students, 12/18 for international students; for spring admission, 11/12 for domestic students, 5/12 for international students. Application fee: $20. *Unit head:* Dr. Mary Young, Chairperson, 850-599-3061. *Application contact:* Dr. Chanta M. Haywood, Dean of Graduate Studies, Research, and Continuing Education, 850-599-3315, Fax: 850-599-3727.

Georgia Southern University, Jack N. Averitt College of Graduate Studies, College of Education, Department of Teaching and Learning, Program in Technology Education, Statesboro, GA 30460. Offers M Ed. Part-time and evening/weekend programs available. In 2009, 1 master's awarded. *Degree requirements:* For master's, exit assessment. *Entrance requirements:* For master's, GRE General Test or MAT, minimum GPA of 2.5. Additional exam requirements/recommendations for international students: Required—TOEFL (minimum score 550 paper-based; 213 computer-based; 80 iBT). *Application deadline:* For fall admission, 3/1 priority date for domestic and international students; for spring admission, 10/1 priority date for domestic and international students. Applications are processed on a rolling basis. Application fee: $50. Electronic applications accepted. *Expenses:* Tuition, state resident: full-time $5040; part-time $210 per credit hour. Tuition, nonresident: full-time $20,136; part-time $839 per credit hour. Required fees: $1644. *Financial support:* In 2009–10, research assistantships with partial tuition reimbursements (averaging $6,850 per year), teaching assistantships with partial tuition reimbursements (averaging $6,850 per year) were awarded; Federal Work-Study, scholarships/grants, tuition waivers (partial), and unspecified assistantships also available. Support available to part-time students. Financial award application deadline: 4/15; financial award applicants required to submit FAFSA. *Unit head:* Dr. Michelle Reidel, Coordinator, 912-478-5806, E-mail: mreidel@georgiasouthern.edu. *Application contact:* 912-478-5384, Fax: 912-478-0740, E-mail: gradadmissions@georgiasouthern.edu.

Idaho State University, Office of Graduate Studies, College of Technology, Department of Human Resource Training and Development, Pocatello, ID 83209-8380. Offers MTD. Part-time and evening/weekend programs available. *Faculty:* 2 full-time (1 woman). *Students:* 14 full-time (6 women), 50 part-time (24 women); includes 4 minority (2 American Indian/Alaska Native, 2 Hispanic Americans), 1 international. Average age 42. 2 applicants, 100% accepted, 1 enrolled. In 2009, 22 master's awarded. *Degree requirements:* For master's, comprehensive exam, thesis optional, statistical procedures. *Entrance requirements:* For master's, GRE or MAT, minimum GPA of 3.0 in upper-division courses. Additional exam requirements/recommendations for international students: Required—TOEFL (minimum score 550 paper-based; 213 computer-based; 80 iBT). *Application deadline:* For fall admission, 7/1 for domestic students, 6/1 for international students; for spring admission, 12/1 for domestic students, 11/1 for international students. Applications are processed on a rolling basis. Application fee: $55. Electronic applications accepted. *Expenses:* Tuition, state resident: full-time $3318; part-time $297 per credit hour. Tuition, nonresident: full-time $13,120; part-time $437 per credit hour. Required fees: $2530. Tuition and fees vary according to program. *Financial support:* Teaching assistantships with full and partial tuition reimbursements, career-related internships or fieldwork, Federal Work-Study, institutionally sponsored loans, scholarships/grants, health care benefits, tuition waivers (full and partial), and unspecified assistantships available. Support available to part-time students. Financial award application deadline: 1/1; financial award applicants required to submit FAFSA. *Faculty research:* Learning styles, instructional methodology, leadership administration. *Unit head:* Dr. Robert Croker, Chair, 208-282-2884, Fax: 208-282-4496, E-mail: crocobe@isu.edu. *Application contact:* Debra K. Ronneburg, Director of Admissions and Student Services, 208-282-2622, Fax: 208-282-5195, E-mail: ctech@isu.edu.

Indiana State University, School of Graduate Studies, College of Technology, Department of Industrial Technology Education, Terre Haute, IN 47809. Offers career and technical education (MS); human resource development (MS); technology education (MS); MA/MS. *Accreditation:* NCATE (one or more programs are accredited). *Entrance requirements:* For master's, bachelor's degree in industrial technology or related field. Additional exam requirements/recommendations for international students: Required—TOEFL. Electronic applications accepted.

Inter American University of Puerto Rico, Metropolitan Campus, Graduate Programs, Program in Occupational Education, San Juan, PR 00919-1293. Offers MA. *Degree requirements:* For master's, comprehensive exam. *Entrance requirements:* For master's, GRE or EXADEP, interview. Electronic applications accepted.

Iowa State University of Science and Technology, Graduate College, College of Agriculture, Program in Industrial Agriculture and Technology, Ames, IA 50011. Offers MS, PhD. *Faculty:* 27 full-time (1 woman), 3 part-time/adjunct (0 women). *Students:* 14 full-time (4 women), 15 part-time (3 women); includes 2 minority (1 African American, 1 American Indian/Alaska Native), 7 international. 7 applicants, 57% accepted, 4 enrolled. In 2009, 1 master's, 3 doctorates awarded. *Degree requirements:* For master's, thesis or alternative; for doctorate, thesis/dissertation. *Entrance requirements:* For master's and doctorate, GRE General Test. Additional exam requirements/recommendations for international students: Required—TOEFL (minimum score 550 paper-based; 79 iBT) or IELTS (minimum score 6.5). *Application deadline:* For fall admission, 2/1 priority date for domestic and international students; for spring admission, 7/1 for domestic and international students. Application fee: $40 ($90 for international students). Electronic applications accepted. *Expenses:* Tuition, state resident: full-time $6716. Tuition, nonresident: full-time $8908. Tuition and fees vary according to course level, course load, program and student level. *Financial support:* In 2009–10, 9 research assistantships with full and partial tuition reimbursements (averaging $14,580 per year) were awarded; fellowships, teaching assistantships with full and partial tuition reimbursements, scholarships/grants, health care benefits, and unspecified assistantships also available. *Faculty research:* Industrial technology, technology education, training and development, technical education. *Unit head:* Dr. Ramesh Kanwar, Chair, 515-294-1434. *Application contact:* Dr. Steven Freeman, Director of Graduate Education, 515-294-9541, E-mail: sfreeman@iastate.edu.

Jackson State University, Graduate School, School of Science and Technology, Department of Technology and Industrial Arts, Jackson, MS 39217. Offers hazardous materials management (MS); industrial arts education (MS Ed). Part-time and evening/weekend programs available. *Degree requirements:* For master's, comprehensive exam, thesis or alternative. *Entrance requirements:* For master's, GRE General Test. Additional exam requirements/recommendations for international students: Required—TOEFL.

James Madison University, The Graduate School, College of Education, Adult Education Department, Program in Adult Education/Human Resource Development, Harrisonburg, VA 22807. Offers MS Ed. *Accreditation:* NCATE. Part-time and evening/weekend programs available. *Students:* 19 full-time (14 women), 14 part-time (12 women); includes 11 minority (10 African Americans, 1 Hispanic American), 1 international. Average age 27. In 2009, 8 master's awarded. *Entrance requirements:* For master's, GRE General Test. Additional exam requirements/recommendations for international students: Required—TOEFL. *Application deadline:* For fall admission, 5/1 priority date for domestic students; for spring admission, 9/1 priority date for domestic students. Applications are processed on a rolling basis. Application fee: $55. Electronic applications accepted. *Expenses:* Tuition, area resident: Part-time $305 per credit hour. Tuition, state resident: part-time $305 per credit hour. Tuition, nonresident: part-time $890 per credit hour. *Financial support:* In 2009–10, 9 students received support. Application deadline: 3/1. *Unit head:* Dr. Diane Foucar-Szocki, Academic Unit Head, 540-568-6794. *Application contact:* Lynette M. Bible, Director of Graduate Admissions, 540-568-6395, Fax: 540-568-7860, E-mail: biblelm@jmu.edu.

Kansas State University, Graduate School, College of Education, Department of Educational Leadership, Manhattan, KS 66506. Offers adult and continuing education (Ed D); adult, occupational and continuing education (MS); educational administration and leadership (MS, Ed D). *Accreditation:* NCATE. *Faculty:* 10 full-time (5 women), 3 part-time/adjunct (1 woman). *Students:* 41 full-time (27 women), 169 part-time (72 women); includes 19 minority (12 African Americans, 1 American Indian/Alaska Native, 3 Asian Americans or Pacific Islanders, 3 Hispanic Americans), 1 international. Average age 41. 46 applicants, 96% accepted, 39 enrolled. In

2009, 79 master's, 9 doctorates awarded. *Degree requirements:* For master's, thesis or alternative, final written exam; for doctorate, comprehensive exam, thesis/dissertation, preliminary exam, residency. *Entrance requirements:* For master's, GRE General Test, MAT, minimum undergraduate GPA of 3.0; for doctorate, GRE General Test, MAT, minimum GPA of 3.0. Additional exam requirements/recommendations for international students: Required—TOEFL. *Application deadline:* For fall admission, 2/1 priority date for domestic and international students; for spring admission, 8/1 priority date for domestic and international students. Applications are processed on a rolling basis. Application fee: $40 ($55 for international students). Electronic applications accepted. *Financial support:* Career-related internships or fieldwork, institutionally sponsored loans, and scholarships/grants available. Support available to part-time students. Financial award application deadline: 3/1; financial award applicants required to submit FAFSA. *Faculty research:* Educational law, finance, technology ethics, application, and leadership in education; distance learning/education; program evaluation. Total annual research expenditures: $71,091. *Unit head:* David C. Thompson, Head, 785-532-5535, Fax: 785-532-7304, E-mail: thomsond@ksu.edu. *Application contact:* Gail Shroyer, Director, 785-532-6737, Fax: 785-532-7304, E-mail: gshroyer@ksu.edu.

Kent State University, Graduate School of Education, Health, and Human Services, School of Teaching, Learning and Curriculum Studies, Program in Career Technical Teacher Education, Kent, OH 44242-0001. Offers M Ed, MA, Ed S. Part-time and evening/weekend programs available. *Faculty:* 3 full-time (1 woman), 4 part-time/adjunct (1 woman). *Students:* 3 full-time (all women), 32 part-time (23 women); includes 5 minority (all African Americans). 7 applicants, 86% accepted. In 2009, 10 master's awarded. *Degree requirements:* For master's, thesis (for some programs). *Entrance requirements:* Additional exam requirements/recommendations for international students: Required—TOEFL. *Application deadline:* Applications are processed on a rolling basis. Application fee: $30 ($60 for international students). Electronic applications accepted. *Financial support:* In 2009–10, research assistantships with full tuition reimbursements (averaging $9,000 per year); Federal Work-Study, scholarships/grants, and unspecified assistantships also available. Financial award application deadline: 4/1; financial award applicants required to submit FAFSA. *Faculty research:* Workforce education/development, adult education, training and organizational change. *Unit head:* Dr. Patrick O'Connor, Coordinator, 330-672-0689, E-mail: poconnor@kent.edu. *Application contact:* Nancy Miller, Academic Program Coordinator, Office of Graduate Student Services, 330-672-2576, Fax: 330-672-9162, E-mail: ogs@kent.edu.

Louisiana State University and Agricultural and Mechanical College, Graduate School, College of Agriculture, School of Human Resource Education and Workforce Development, Baton Rouge, LA 70803. Offers agriculture and extension education and youth development (MS, PhD); career and technical education (MS, PhD); comprehensive vocational education (MS, PhD); extension and international education (MS, PhD); human resource and leadership development (MS, PhD); industrial education (MS); vocational agriculture education (MS, PhD); vocational business education (MS); vocational home economics education (MS). *Accreditation:* NCATE. Part-time programs available. *Faculty:* 11 full-time (5 women), 2 part-time/adjunct (both women). *Students:* 39 full-time (22 women), 75 part-time (51 women); includes 14 African Americans, 1 Asian American or Pacific Islander, 2 Hispanic Americans, 7 international. Average age 37. 40 applicants, 93% accepted, 18 enrolled. In 2009, 16 master's, 13 doctorates awarded. Terminal master's awarded for partial completion of doctoral program. *Degree requirements:* For master's, thesis (for some programs); for doctorate, thesis/dissertation. *Entrance requirements:* For master's and doctorate, GRE General Test, minimum GPA of 3.0. Additional exam requirements/recommendations for international students: Required—TOEFL (minimum score 550 paper-based; 213 computer-based; 79 iBT) or IELTS (minimum score 6.5). *Application deadline:* For fall admission, 1/25 priority date for domestic students, 5/15 for international students; for spring admission, 10/15 for international students. Applications are processed on a rolling basis. Application fee: $50 ($70 for international students). Electronic applications accepted. *Financial support:* In 2009–10, 63 students received support, including 3 fellowships with full and partial tuition reimbursements available (averaging $24,885 per year), 5 research assistantships with full and partial tuition reimbursements available (averaging $14,440 per year), 4 teaching assistantships with partial tuition reimbursements available (averaging $13,750 per year); career-related internships or fieldwork, Federal Work-Study, institutionally sponsored loans, health care benefits, tuition waivers (full and partial), and unspecified assistantships also available. Financial award application deadline: 3/1; financial award applicants required to submit FAFSA. *Faculty research:* Adult education, history and philosophy of vocational education, curriculum and instruction, career decision making. Total annual research expenditures: $21,538. *Unit head:* Dr. Michael F. Burnett, Director, 225-578-5748, Fax: 225-578-2526, E-mail: vocbur@lsu.edu. *Application contact:* Paula Beecher, Recruiting Coordinator, 225-578-2468, E-mail: pbeeche@lsu.edu.

Marshall University, Academic Affairs Division, College of Education and Human Services, Division of Human Development and Allied Technology, Program in Adult and Technical Education, Huntington, WV 25755. Offers MS. *Accreditation:* NCATE. Evening/weekend programs available. *Faculty:* 7 full-time (4 women), 15 part-time/adjunct (8 women). *Students:* 88 full-time (57 women), 93 part-time (65 women); includes 22 minority (18 African Americans, 2 Asian Americans or Pacific Islanders, 2 Hispanic Americans), 40 international. Average age 35. In 2009, 71 master's awarded. *Degree requirements:* For master's, thesis optional, comprehensive assessment. Application fee: $40. *Unit head:* Dr. Lee Olson, Program Coordinator, 304-696-6757, E-mail: olsonl@marshall.edu. *Application contact:* Graduate Admission.

Middle Tennessee State University, College of Graduate Studies, College of Basic and Applied Sciences, Department of Engineering Technology and Industrial Studies, Murfreesboro, TN 37132. Offers engineering technology (MS). Part-time and evening/weekend programs available. Postbaccalaureate distance learning degree programs offered. *Faculty:* 11 full-time (3 women). *Students:* 1 (woman) full-time, 21 part-time (2 women); includes 6 minority (1 African American, 5 Asian Americans or Pacific Islanders). Average age 32. 30 applicants, 47% accepted, 14 enrolled. In 2009, 6 master's awarded. *Degree requirements:* For master's, one foreign language, comprehensive exam. *Entrance requirements:* For master's, GRE. Additional exam requirements/recommendations for international students: Required—TOEFL (minimum score 525 paper-based; 195 computer-based; 71 iBT) or IELTS (minimum score 6). *Application deadline:* For fall admission, 6/1 for domestic and international students. Applications are processed on a rolling basis. Application fee: $25 ($30 for international students). Electronic applications accepted. *Expenses:* Tuition, state resident: full-time $4404. Tuition, nonresident: full-time $10,956. *Financial support:* In 2009–10, 9 students received support. Institutionally sponsored loans available. Support available to part-time students. Financial award application deadline: 5/1; financial award applicants required to submit FAFSA. *Faculty research:* Concrete pavement technology and management, high temperature gas properties, metal forming, modeling and simulation, robotics work cell design. *Unit head:* Dr. Walter W. Boles, Chair, 615-898-5009, Fax: 615-898-5697. *Application contact:* Dr. Michael Allen, Dean and Vice Provost for Research, 615-898-2840, Fax: 615-904-8020, E-mail: mallen@mtsu.edu.

Millersville University of Pennsylvania, College of Graduate and Professional Studies, School of Education, Department of Industry and Technology, Millersville, PA 17551-0302. Offers technology education (M Ed). *Accreditation:* NCATE. Part-time and evening/weekend programs available. *Faculty:* 18 full-time (2 women), 4 part-time/adjunct (0 women). *Students:* 2 full-time (0 women), 7 part-time (0 women). Average age 29. 1 applicant, 100% accepted, 1 enrolled. *Degree requirements:* For master's, thesis optional. *Entrance requirements:* For master's, GRE or MAT, 3 letters of recommendation. Additional exam requirements/recommendations for international students: Required—TOEFL (minimum score 500 paper-based; 183 computer-based; 65 iBT) or IELTS (minimum score 6). *Application deadline:* For fall admission, 1/15 priority date for domestic and international students; for winter admission, 10/1 priority date for domestic and international students; for spring admission, 10/1 priority date for domestic and international students. Applications are processed on a rolling basis. Application fee: $40 ($50 for international students). Electronic applications accepted. *Expenses:* Tuition, state resident: full-time $6666; part-time $370 per credit. Tuition, nonresident: full-time $10,666; part-time $593 per credit. Required fees: $1578.50; $76.25 per credit. One-time fee: $60 part-time. Tuition and fees vary according to course load. *Financial support:* In 2009–10, 2 students received support, including 2 research assistantships with full tuition reimbursements available (averaging $5,200 per year); institutionally sponsored loans and unspecified assistantships also available. Support available to part-time students. Financial award application deadline: 3/15; financial award applicants required to submit FAFSA. *Faculty research:* Recruitment and retention of women into STEM fields, design-based learning, recruitment and retention of under-represented students into STEM fields, remote-controlled vehicles for IED detection, satellite communication systems. Total annual research expenditures: $47,000. *Unit head:* Dr. Barry G. David, Chair, 717-872-3327, Fax: 717-872-3318, E-mail: barry.david@millersville.edu. *Application contact:* Dr. Victor S. DeSantis, Dean of Graduate and Professional Studies, 717-872-3099, Fax: 717-872-3453, E-mail: victor.desantis@millersville.edu.

Mississippi State University, College of Education, Department of Instructional Systems and Workforce Development, Mississippi State, MS 39762. Offers education (Ed D, Ed S), including technology; instructional systems and workforce development (PhD); instructional technology (MSIT); technology (MS). *Faculty:* 10 full-time (7 women). *Students:* 29 full-time (14 women), 115 part-time (97 women); includes 69 minority (all African Americans), 5 international. Average age 36. 35 applicants, 74% accepted, 19 enrolled. In 2009, 30 master's, 11 doctorates, 1 other advanced degree awarded. *Degree requirements:* For master's, comprehensive exam, thesis optional, comprehensive oral or written exam; for doctorate, comprehensive exam, thesis/dissertation, comprehensive oral and written exam; for Ed S, comprehensive exam, thesis, comprehensive written exam. *Entrance requirements:* For master's, GRE, minimum GPA of 2.75 in junior and senior courses; for doctorate and Ed S, GRE. Additional exam requirements/recommendations for international students: Required—TOEFL (minimum score 550 paper-based; 213 computer-based; 79 iBT); Recommended—IELTS (minimum score 6.5). *Application deadline:* For fall admission, 7/1 for domestic students, 5/1 for international students; for spring admission, 11/1 for domestic students, 9/1 for international students. Applications are processed on a rolling basis. Application fee: $40. Electronic applications accepted. *Expenses:* Tuition, state resident: full-time $2575.50; part-time $286.25 per credit hour. Tuition, nonresident: full-time $6510; part-time $723.50 per credit hour. Tuition and fees vary according to course load. *Financial support:* In 2009–10, 5 teaching assistantships with full tuition reimbursements (averaging $10,078 per year) were awarded; Federal Work-Study, institutionally sponsored loans, and unspecified assistantships also available. Financial award application deadline: 4/1; financial award applicants required to submit FAFSA. *Faculty research:* Computer technology, nontraditional students, interactive video, instructional technology, educational leadership. *Unit head:* Dr. Linda Cornelius, Professor and Interim Head, 662-325-2281, Fax: 662-325-7599, E-mail: lcornelius@colled.msstate.edu. *Application contact:* Interim Associate Vice President for Academic Affairs/Interim Dean of Graduate Studies.

Morehead State University, Graduate Programs, College of Science and Technology, Department of Industrial and Engineering Technology, Morehead, KY 40351. Offers career and technical education (MS); engineering technology (MS). Part-time and evening/weekend programs available. *Faculty:* 6 full-time (2 women). *Students:* 11 full-time (2 women), 14 part-time (5 women); includes 1 minority (African American), 3 international. Average age 33. 17 applicants, 41% accepted, 6 enrolled. In 2009, 18 master's awarded. *Degree requirements:* For master's, completion and defense of thesis or written and oral comprehensive exit exams. *Entrance requirements:* For master's, GRE, minimum undergraduate GPA of 3.0 in major. Additional exam requirements/recommendations for international students: Required—TOEFL (minimum score 500 paper-based; 173 computer-based). *Application deadline:* For fall admission, 8/1 priority date for domestic and international students; for spring admission, 12/1 priority date for domestic and international students. Applications are processed on a rolling basis. Application fee: $30. Electronic applications accepted. *Expenses:* Tuition, state resident: full-time $6318; part-time $351 per credit hour. Tuition, nonresident: full-time $15,804; part-time $878 per credit hour. *Financial support:* In 2009–10, 1 research assistantship (averaging $10,000 per year), 3 teaching assistantships (averaging $10,000 per year) were awarded; unspecified assistantships also available. Financial award application deadline: 3/15; financial award applicants required to submit FAFSA. *Unit head:* Dr. Ahmad Zargari, Chair and Professor, 606-783-2425, Fax: 606-783-5030, E-mail: a.zargar@moreheadstate.edu. *Application contact:* Michelle Barber, Graduate Recruitment and Retention Assistant Director, 606-783-5127, Fax: 606-783-5061, E-mail: b.cowsert@moreheadstate.edu.

Murray State University, College of Education, Department of Adolescent, Career and Special Education, Program in Industrial and Technical Education, Murray, KY 42071. Offers MS. *Accreditation:* NCATE. Part-time programs available. *Degree requirements:* For master's, thesis (for some programs), portfolio. *Entrance requirements:* For master's, GRE General Test. Additional exam requirements/recommendations for international students: Required—TOEFL.

North Carolina Agricultural and Technical State University, Graduate School, School of Technology, Department of Graphic Communication Systems and Technological Studies, Greensboro, NC 27411. Offers industrial arts education (MS); technology education (MS); technology management (PhD); vocational-industrial education (MS); workforce development director (MS). *Accreditation:* NCATE (one or more programs are accredited). Part-time and evening/weekend programs available. *Degree requirements:* For master's, comprehensive exam, thesis or alternative, qualifying exam. *Entrance requirements:* For master's, GRE General Test, minimum GPA of 3.0.

North Dakota State University, College of Graduate and Interdisciplinary Studies, College of Human Development and Education, School of Education, Fargo, ND 58108. Offers agricultural education (M Ed, MS), including agricultural education, agricultural extension education (MS); counseling (M Ed, MS, PhD); curriculum and instruction (M Ed, MS), including pedagogy, physical education and athletic administration; education (PhD); educational leadership (M Ed, MS, Ed S); family and consumer sciences education (M Ed, MS); history education (M Ed, MS); institutional analysis (Ed D); mathematics education (M Ed, MS); music education (M Ed, MS); occupational and adult education (Ed D); science education (M Ed, MS). *Accreditation:* NCATE. Part-time and evening/weekend programs available. Postbaccalaureate distance learning degree programs offered (minimal on-campus study). *Faculty:* 25 full-time (9 women), 3 part-time/adjunct (1 woman). *Students:* 29 full-time (25 women), 207 part-time (132 women); includes 15 minority (4 African Americans, 6 American Indian/Alaska Native, 3 Asian Americans or Pacific Islanders, 2 Hispanic Americans), 4 international. 88 applicants, 67% accepted, 56 enrolled. In 2009, 44 master's, 5 doctorates awarded. *Degree requirements:* For master's, comprehensive exam; for doctorate, thesis/dissertation; for Ed S, thesis. *Entrance requirements:* For degree, GRE General Test, master's degree, minimum GPA of 3.25. Additional exam requirements/recommendations for international students: Required—TOEFL. *Application deadline:* Applications are processed on a rolling basis. Application fee: $45 ($60 for international students). *Financial support:* Research assistantships, teaching assistantships, career-related internships or fieldwork, Federal Work-Study, institutionally sponsored loans, and tuition waivers (full) available. Financial award application deadline: 4/15. *Unit head:* Dr. William Martin, Chair, 701-231-7202, Fax: 701-231-7416, E-mail: william.martin@ndsu.edu. *Application contact:* Dr. William Martin, Chair, 701-231-7202, Fax: 701-231-7416, E-mail: william.martin@ndsu.edu.

Northern Arizona University, Graduate College, College of Education, Department of Educational Specialties, Flagstaff, AZ 86011. Offers autism spectrum disorders (Certificate); bilingual/multicultural education (M Ed), including bilingual education, ESL education; career and technical education (M Ed, Certificate); curriculum and instruction (Ed D); early childhood special education (M Ed); early intervention (Certificate); educational technology (M Ed, Certificate); special education (M Ed). *Faculty:* 29 full-time (16 women). *Students:* 153 full-time (118 women), 360 part-time (291 women); includes 152 minority (12 African Americans, 43 American Indian/Alaska Native, 5 Asian Americans or Pacific Islanders, 92 Hispanic Americans), 9 international. Average age 30. 215 applicants, 87% accepted, 133 enrolled. In 2009, 200 master's, 8 doctorates awarded. *Degree requirements:* For master's, comprehensive exam (for some programs), thesis (for some programs). *Entrance requirements:* For master's, minimum GPA of 3.0. Additional exam requirements/recommendations for international students:

Vocational and Technical Education

Northern Arizona University (continued)

Required—TOEFL (minimum score 550 paper-based; 213 computer-based; 80 iBT), IELTS (minimum score 7), or a bachelor's degree from an English-speaking university and demonstrated proficiency. *Application deadline:* For fall admission, 2/1 for domestic students, 8/1 for international students; for spring admission, 12/1 for domestic students. Applications are processed on a rolling basis. Application fee: $65. Electronic applications accepted. *Financial support:* In 2009–10, 2 research assistantships with partial tuition reimbursements (averaging $10,000 per year), 8 teaching assistantships with partial tuition reimbursements (averaging $10,000 per year) were awarded. Financial award application deadline: 3/30. *Unit head:* Dr. Lawrence Gallagher, Chair, 928-523-5083, E-mail: lawrence.gallagher@nau.edu. *Application contact:* Dr. Lawrence Gallagher, Chair, 928-523-5083, E-mail: lawrence.gallagher@nau.edu.

Nova Southeastern University, Fischler School of Education and Human Services, Programs for Higher Education, Fort Lauderdale, FL 33314-7796. Offers adult education (Ed D); computing and information technology (Ed D); health care education (Ed D); higher education (Ed D); vocational, occupational and technical education (Ed D). Part-time and evening/weekend programs available. Postbaccalaureate distance learning degree programs offered (minimal on-campus study). *Faculty:* 6 full-time (3 women), 8 part-time/adjunct (2 women). *Students:* 113 full-time (81 women), 2 part-time (both women); includes 57 minority (51 African Americans, 6 Hispanic Americans). 4 applicants, 75% accepted, 3 enrolled. In 2009, 13 doctorates awarded. *Degree requirements:* For doctorate, thesis/dissertation, practicum. *Entrance requirements:* For doctorate, MAT or GRE, master's degree, work experience in field, minimum GPA of 3.0. Additional exam requirements/recommendations for international students: Required—TSE (recommended, minimum score 50); Recommended—TOEFL (minimum score 550 paper-based; 213 computer-based; 80 iBT), IELTS (minimum score 6). *Application deadline:* For fall admission, 8/11 priority date for domestic and international students; for winter admission, 12/28 priority date for domestic and international students; for spring admission, 4/22 priority date for domestic and international students. Applications are processed on a rolling basis. Application fee: $50. Electronic applications accepted. *Expenses:* Contact institution. *Financial support:* Career-related internships or fieldwork and tuition waivers (full) available. Financial award application deadline: 1/7. *Unit head:* Dr. Karen D. Bowser, Associate Dean of Doctoral Programs, 954-262-8677, Fax: 954-262-3606, E-mail: bowserk@nova.edu. *Application contact:* Dr. Jennifer Quinones Nottingham, Dean of Student Affairs, 800-986-3223 Ext. 8624, Fax: 954-262-3883, E-mail: jlquinon@nova.edu.

Old Dominion University, Darden College of Education, Programs in Occupational and Technical Studies, Norfolk, VA 23529. Offers business and industry training (MS); career and technical education (MS, PhD); community college teaching (MS); human resources training (PhD); technology education (PhD). *Accreditation:* NCATE (one or more programs are accredited). Part-time and evening/weekend programs available. Postbaccalaureate distance learning degree programs offered (minimal on-campus study). *Faculty:* 6 full-time (1 woman), 8 part-time/adjunct (3 women). *Students:* 17 full-time (12 women), 67 part-time (39 women); includes 21 minority (17 African Americans, 1 Asian American or Pacific Islander, 3 Hispanic Americans), 2 international. Average age 41. 44 applicants, 95% accepted, 37 enrolled. In 2009, 18 master's, 7 doctorates awarded. *Degree requirements:* For master's, comprehensive exam, thesis optional, writing exam, candidacy exam; for doctorate, comprehensive exam, thesis/dissertation, writing exam, candidacy exam. *Entrance requirements:* For master's, GRE General Test or MAT, minimum GPA of 2.8, 2 letters of reference; for doctorate, GRE, minimum GPA of 3.0, 3 letters of reference. Additional exam requirements/recommendations for international students: Required—TOEFL. *Application deadline:* For fall admission, 6/1 priority date for domestic students, 6/1 for international students; for winter admission, 11/1 priority date for domestic students, 11/1 for international students; for spring admission, 3/1 priority date for domestic students, 3/1 for international students. Applications are processed on a rolling basis. Application fee: $40. Electronic applications accepted. *Expenses:* Tuition, state resident: full-time $8112; part-time $338 per credit. Tuition, nonresident: full-time $20,256; part-time $844 per credit. Required fees: $119 per semester. One-time fee: $50. *Financial support:* In 2009–10, 19 students received support, including 1 fellowship with full tuition reimbursement available (averaging $15,000 per year), 2 research assistantships with partial tuition reimbursements available (averaging $9,000 per year), 4 teaching assistantships with partial tuition reimbursements available (averaging $15,000 per year); career-related internships or fieldwork, scholarships/grants, tuition waivers (partial), and unspecified assistantships also available. Support available to part-time students. Financial award application deadline: 2/15; financial award applicants required to submit FAFSA. *Faculty research:* Training and development, marketing, technology, special populations, support of academic subjects. Total annual research expenditures: $799,773. *Unit head:* Dr. John M. Ritz, Graduate Program Director, 757-683-4305, Fax: 757-683-5227, E-mail: jritz@odu.edu. *Application contact:* Dr. John M. Ritz, Graduate Program Director, 757-683-4305, Fax: 757-683-5227, E-mail: jritz@odu.edu.

Our Lady of the Lake University of San Antonio, School of Professional Studies, Program in Curriculum and Instruction, San Antonio, TX 78207-4689. Offers bilingual (M Ed); early childhood education (M Ed); English as a second language (M Ed); integrated math teaching (M Ed); integrated science teaching (M Ed); master reading teacher (M Ed); master technology teacher (M Ed); reading specialist (M Ed). *Students:* 2 full-time (1 woman), 112 part-time (94 women); includes 64 minority (5 African Americans, 1 American Indian/Alaska Native, 1 Asian American or Pacific Islander, 57 Hispanic Americans). Average age 38. In 2009, 49 master's awarded. *Expenses:* Tuition: Full-time $12,330; part-time $685 per contact hour. Required fees: $139; $12 per contact hour. $57 per semester. Tuition and fees vary according to campus/location. *Unit head:* Dr. Cullen Grinnan, 210-434-6711 Ext. 8928, E-mail: ctgrinnan@lake.ollusa.edu. *Application contact:* Dr. Cullen Grinnan, 210-434-6711 Ext. 8928, E-mail: ctgrinnan@lake.ollusa.edu.

Penn State University Park, Graduate School, College of Education, Department of Learning and Performance Systems, State College, University Park, PA 16802-1503. Offers M Ed, MS, D Ed, PhD.

Pittsburg State University, Graduate School, College of Technology, Department of Technology Studies, Pittsburg, KS 66762. Offers technical teacher education (MS); technology education (MS). *Degree requirements:* For master's, thesis or alternative. *Expenses:* Tuition, state resident: full-time $4212; part-time $176 per credit. Tuition, nonresident: full-time $11,530; part-time $480 per credit. Required fees: $940; $43 per credit. Tuition and fees vary according to course level, course load, degree level, campus/location, reciprocity agreements and student level.

Pittsburg State University, Graduate School, College of Technology, Departments of Graphics and Imaging Technologies and Technology Management, Pittsburg, KS 66762. Offers human resource development (MS); industrial education (Ed S); technology (MS), including printing management. *Degree requirements:* For master's, thesis or alternative. *Expenses:* Tuition, state resident: full-time $4212; part-time $176 per credit. Tuition, nonresident: full-time $11,530; part-time $480 per credit. Required fees: $940; $43 per credit. Tuition and fees vary according to course level, course load, degree level, campus/location, reciprocity agreements and student level.

Purdue University, Graduate School, College of Technology, Graduate Program in Industrial Technology, West Lafayette, IN 47907. Offers MS. Part-time programs available. Postbaccalaureate distance learning degree programs offered (minimal on-campus study). *Degree requirements:* For master's, oral exam. *Entrance requirements:* For master's, GRE General Test, minimum GPA of 3.0. Additional exam requirements/recommendations for international students: Required—TOEFL. Electronic applications accepted.

Purdue University, Graduate School, School of Education, Department of Curriculum and Instruction, West Lafayette, IN 47907. Offers agricultural and extension education (PhD, Ed S); agriculture and extension education (MS, MS Ed); art education (PhD); consumer and family sciences and extension education (MS Ed, PhD, Ed S); curriculum studies (MS Ed, PhD, Ed S); educational technology (MS Ed, PhD, Ed S); elementary education (MS Ed); foreign language education (MS Ed, PhD, Ed S); industrial technology (PhD, Ed S); language arts (MS Ed, PhD, Ed S); literacy (MS Ed, PhD, Ed S); mathematics/science education (MS, MS Ed, PhD, Ed S); social studies (MS Ed, PhD); social studies education (Ed S); vocational/industrial education (MS Ed, PhD, Ed S); vocational/technical education (MS Ed, PhD, Ed S). *Accreditation:* NCATE. Part-time and evening/weekend programs available. *Degree requirements:* For master's, thesis optional; for doctorate, thesis/dissertation, oral and written exams; for Ed S, oral presentation, project. *Entrance requirements:* For master's, GRE General Test, minimum B average; for doctorate, GRE General Test; for Ed S, GRE, minimum B average. Additional exam requirements/recommendations for international students: Required—TOEFL. Electronic applications accepted. *Faculty research:* Literacy acquisition and development, teacher beliefs and knowledge, recruitment and retention of underrepresented students, economic education, literacy discourse.

Rhode Island College, School of Graduate Studies, Feinstein School of Education and Human Development, Department of Educational Studies, Providence, RI 02908-1991. Offers English (MAT); French (MAT); history (MAT); math (MAT); secondary education (MAT); Spanish (MAT); teaching English as a second language (M Ed); technology education (M Ed). *Accreditation:* NCATE. Part-time and evening/weekend programs available. *Faculty:* 10 full-time (5 women), 6 part-time/adjunct (5 women). *Students:* 8 full-time (all women), 56 part-time (40 women); includes 2 minority (both Hispanic Americans). Average age 35. In 2009, 28 master's awarded. *Degree requirements:* For master's, capstone or comprehensive assessment. *Entrance requirements:* For master's, GRE or MAT (for most programs), minimum undergraduate GPA of 3.0; baccalaureate degree in English, French, history, math or Spanish; evaluation of content area knowledge; 3 letters of recommendation; interview. Additional exam requirements/recommendations for international students: Recommended—TOEFL (minimum score 550 paper-based; 213 computer-based; 79 iBT). *Application deadline:* For fall admission, 3/15 for domestic students; for spring admission, 11/1 for domestic students. Applications are processed on a rolling basis. Application fee: $50. *Expenses:* Tuition, state resident: full-time $7440; part-time $310 per credit hour. Tuition, nonresident: full-time $14,784; part-time $616 per credit hour. Required fees: $552; $20 per credit. $70 per term. *Financial support:* Teaching assistantships with full tuition reimbursements, career-related internships or fieldwork, Federal Work-Study, scholarships/grants, health care benefits, and unspecified assistantships available. Support available to part-time students. Financial award application deadline: 5/15; financial award applicants required to submit FAFSA. *Faculty research:* School administration, school/college articulation. *Unit head:* Dr. Ellen Bigler, Chair, 401-456-8170. *Application contact:* Graduate Studies, 401-456-8700.

Saint Martin's University, Graduate Programs, College of Education, Lacey, WA 98503. Offers administration (M Ed); English as a second language (M Ed); guidance and counseling (M Ed); reading (M Ed); special education (M Ed); teaching (MIT); technology in education (M Ed). *Accreditation:* Teacher Education Accreditation Council. Part-time and evening/weekend programs available. *Faculty:* 13 full-time (9 women), 11 part-time/adjunct (7 women). *Students:* 61 full-time (42 women), 23 part-time (17 women); includes 7 minority (2 African Americans, 1 American Indian/Alaska Native, 3 Asian Americans or Pacific Islanders, 1 Hispanic American), 1 international. Average age 35. 26 applicants, 92% accepted, 22 enrolled. In 2009, 12 master's awarded. *Degree requirements:* For master's, comprehensive exam (for some programs), thesis or alternative, project or comprehensives. *Entrance requirements:* For master's, GRE General Test or MAT, resume. Additional exam requirements/recommendations for international students: Required—TOEFL (minimum score 560 paper-based; 220 computer-based; 83 iBT). *Application deadline:* For fall admission, 6/1 priority date for domestic and international students; for spring admission, 10/1 priority date for domestic and international students. Applications are processed on a rolling basis. Application fee: $35. *Expenses:* Tuition: Full-time $12,440; part-time $827 per credit hour. *Financial support:* In 2009–10, 62 students received support. Career-related internships or fieldwork, Federal Work-Study, institutionally sponsored loans, and unspecified assistantships available. Support available to part-time students. Financial award application deadline: 3/1; financial award applicants required to submit FAFSA. *Faculty research:* Reader's theatre and reader/writer workshops, curriculum and assessment integration, gender and equity, classroom evaluations, organizational leadership. *Unit head:* Dr. Joyce Westgard, Director, 360-438-4509, Fax: 360-438-4486, E-mail: westgard@stmartin.edu. *Application contact:* Ryan M. Smith, Administrative Assistant, 360-438-4333, Fax: 360-438-4486, E-mail: ryan.smith@stmartin.edu.

South Carolina State University, School of Graduate Studies, Department of Education, Orangeburg, SC 29117-0001. Offers early childhood and special education (M Ed); early childhood education (MAT); elementary education (M Ed, MAT); engineering (MAT); general science (MAT); mathematics (MAT); secondary education (M Ed), including biology education, business education, counselor education, English education, home economics education, industrial education, mathematics education, science education, social studies education; special education (M Ed), including emotionally handicapped, learning disabilities, mentally handicapped. *Accreditation:* NCATE. Part-time and evening/weekend programs available. *Degree requirements:* For master's, thesis optional, departmental qualifying exam. *Entrance requirements:* For master's, GRE General Test, NTE, interview, teaching certificate. Electronic applications accepted. *Expenses:* Tuition, state resident: part-time $470 per credit hour. Tuition, nonresident: part-time $924 per credit hour. *Faculty research:* Critical thinking, child abuse, stress, test-taking skills, conflict resolution, mainstreaming.

Southern Illinois University Carbondale, Graduate School, College of Education, Department of Workforce Education and Development, Carbondale, IL 62901-4701. Offers MS Ed, PhD. *Accreditation:* NCATE. Part-time programs available. *Degree requirements:* For master's, thesis; for doctorate, thesis/dissertation. *Entrance requirements:* For master's, minimum GPA of 2.7; for doctorate, GRE General Test, minimum GPA of 3.25. Additional exam requirements/recommendations for international students: Required—TOEFL. *Faculty research:* Career education, technical training, curriculum development, competency-based instruction, impact of technology on workplace and workforce.

Southern New Hampshire University, School of Education, Manchester, NH 03106-1045. Offers business education (MS); child development (M Ed); computer technology education (Certificate); curriculum and instruction (M Ed); education (M Ed, CAS); elementary education (M Ed); general special education (Certificate); school business administrator (Certificate); secondary education (M Ed); training and development (Certificate). Part-time and evening/weekend programs available. Postbaccalaureate distance learning degree programs offered (no on-campus study). *Degree requirements:* For master's, comprehensive exam (for some programs), thesis or alternative. *Entrance requirements:* For master's, PRAXIS I, minimum GPA of 2.75. Additional exam requirements/recommendations for international students: Required—TOEFL (minimum score 550 paper-based; 213 computer-based). Electronic applications accepted. *Expenses:* Contact institution.

State University of New York at Oswego, Graduate Studies, School of Education, Department of Technology, Oswego, NY 13126. Offers MS Ed. *Accreditation:* NCATE. Part-time programs available. *Degree requirements:* For master's, thesis optional, departmental exam. *Entrance requirements:* For master's, provisional teaching certificate in technology education. Additional exam requirements/recommendations for international students: Required—TOEFL (minimum score 560 paper-based; 220 computer-based). *Faculty research:* Curriculum development, microcomputer applications.

State University of New York at Oswego, Graduate Studies, School of Education, Department of Vocational Teacher Preparation, Oswego, NY 13126. Offers agriculture (MS Ed); business and marketing (MS Ed); family and consumer sciences (MS Ed); health careers (MS Ed); technical education (MS Ed); trade education (MS Ed). *Accreditation:* NCATE. Part-time and evening/weekend programs available. *Degree requirements:* For master's, thesis or alternative. *Entrance requirements:* Additional exam requirements/recommendations for international students: Required—TOEFL (minimum score 560 paper-based; 220 computer-based).

Temple University, Graduate School, College of Education, Department of Curriculum, Instruction, and Technology in Education, Philadelphia, PA 19122-6096. Offers applied behavioral

analysis (MS Ed); career and technical education (MS Ed); early childhood education and elementary education (MS Ed); English education (MS Ed); language arts education (Ed D); math/science education (Ed D); mathematics education (MS Ed); science education (MS Ed); second and foreign language education (MS Ed); special education (MS Ed); teaching English as a second language (MS Ed). Part-time and evening/weekend programs available. Terminal master's awarded for partial completion of doctoral program. *Degree requirements:* For master's, thesis or alternative; for doctorate, thesis/dissertation. *Entrance requirements:* For master's and doctorate, GRE General Test or MAT, minimum GPA of 3.0. Additional exam requirements/recommendations for international students: Required—TOEFL (minimum score 550 paper-based; 213 computer-based; 79 iBT). Electronic applications accepted. *Faculty research:* School improvement, problem solving, literacy, language development.

Texas State University–San Marcos, Graduate School, College of Applied Arts, Program in Management of Technical Education, San Marcos, TX 78666. Offers M Ed. Part-time and evening/weekend programs available. *Faculty:* 1 full-time (0 women), 1 part-time/adjunct (0 women). *Students:* 2 full-time (1 woman), 21 part-time (13 women); includes 10 minority (2 African Americans, 1 Asian American or Pacific Islander, 7 Hispanic Americans). Average age 42. 12 applicants, 100% accepted, 7 enrolled. In 2009, 11 master's awarded. *Degree requirements:* For master's, comprehensive exam. *Entrance requirements:* For master's, minimum GPA of 2.75 in last 60 hours of course work. Additional exam requirements/recommendations for international students: Required—TOEFL (minimum score 550 paper-based; 213 computer-based). *Application deadline:* For fall admission, 6/15 for domestic students; for spring admission, 10/15 for domestic students. Applications are processed on a rolling basis. Application fee: $40 ($90 for international students). Electronic applications accepted. *Expenses:* Tuition, state resident: full-time $5784; part-time $241 per credit hour. Tuition, nonresident: full-time $13,224; part-time $551 per credit hour. Required fees: $1728; $48 per credit hour. $306. Tuition and fees vary according to course load. *Financial support:* In 2009–10, 13 students received support, including 1 teaching assistantship (averaging $5,076 per year); research assistantships, career-related internships or fieldwork, Federal Work-Study, and institutionally sponsored loans also available. Support available to part-time students. Financial award application deadline: 4/1; financial award applicants required to submit FAFSA. *Unit head:* Dr. Stephen Springer, Director, 512-245-2115, E-mail: ss01@txstate.edu. *Application contact:* Dr. J. Michael Willoughby, Dean of Graduate School, 512-245-2581, Fax: 512-245-8365, E-mail: gradcollege@txstate.edu.

Texas State University–San Marcos, Graduate School, Interdisciplinary Studies Program in Occupational Education, San Marcos, TX 78666. Offers MAIS, MSIS. *Faculty:* 4 full-time (0 women), 1 (woman) part-time/adjunct. *Students:* 8 full-time (4 women), 51 part-time (26 women); includes 28 minority (9 African Americans, 19 Hispanic Americans), 1 international. Average age 41. 23 applicants, 100% accepted, 12 enrolled. In 2009, 8 master's awarded. *Degree requirements:* For master's, comprehensive exam, thesis optional. *Entrance requirements:* For master's, minimum GPA of 2.75 for undergraduate work, statement of personal goals. Additional exam requirements/recommendations for international students: Required—TOEFL (minimum score 550 paper-based; 213 computer-based). *Application deadline:* For fall admission, 6/15 priority date for domestic students, 6/1 priority date for international students; for spring admission, 10/15 priority date for domestic students, 10/1 priority date for international students. Applications are processed on a rolling basis. Application fee: $40 ($90 for international students). *Expenses:* Tuition, state resident: full-time $5784; part-time $241 per credit hour. Tuition, nonresident: full-time $13,224; part-time $551 per credit hour. Required fees: $1728; $48 per credit hour. $306. Tuition and fees vary according to course load. *Financial support:* In 2009–10, 37 students received support, including 2 teaching assistantships (averaging $5,076 per year). Financial award application deadline: 4/1; financial award applicants required to submit FAFSA. *Unit head:* Dr. Stephen Springer, Director, 512-245-2115, E-mail: ss01@txstate.edu. *Application contact:* Dr. J. Michael Willoughby, Dean of Graduate School, 512-245-2581, Fax: 512-245-8365, E-mail: gradcollege@txstate.edu.

Trevecca Nazarene University, Graduate Division, School of Education, Major in Instructional Technology, Nashville, TN 37210-2877. Offers M Ed. *Accreditation:* NCATE. Part-time and evening/weekend programs available. *Students:* 10 full-time (5 women); includes 4 minority (2 African Americans, 2 Hispanic Americans). *Degree requirements:* For master's, exit assessment. *Entrance requirements:* For master's, GRE General Test, MAT, minimum GPA of 2.7, 2 reference forms. Additional exam requirements/recommendations for international students: Required—TOEFL (minimum score 550 paper-based; 213 computer-based). *Application deadline:* Applications are processed on a rolling basis. Application fee: $25. *Expenses:* Contact institution. *Financial support:* Applicants required to submit FAFSA. *Unit head:* Dr. Esther Swink, Dean, School of Education/Director of Graduate Education Program, 615-248-1201, Fax: 615-248-1597, E-mail: admissions_ged@trevecca.edu. *Application contact:* Admissions Office, 615-248-1201, Fax: 615-248-1597, E-mail: admissions_ged@trevecca.edu.

The University of Akron, Graduate School, College of Education, Department of Educational Foundations and Leadership, Program in Technical Education, Akron, OH 44325. Offers MS. *Accreditation:* NCATE. *Students:* 12 full-time (8 women), 145 part-time (109 women); includes 13 minority (8 African Americans, 3 Asian Americans or Pacific Islanders, 2 Hispanic Americans), 3 international. Average age 41. 12 applicants, 92% accepted, 6 enrolled. In 2009, 11 master's awarded. *Degree requirements:* For master's, comprehensive exam, cumulative portfolio. *Entrance requirements:* For master's, minimum GPA of 2.75. Additional exam requirements/recommendations for international students: Required—TOEFL (minimum score 550 paper-based; 213 computer-based; 79 iBT). *Application deadline:* Applications are processed on a rolling basis. Application fee: $30 ($40 for international students). Electronic applications accepted. *Expenses:* Tuition, state resident: full-time $6570; part-time $365 per credit hour. Tuition, nonresident: full-time $11,250; part-time $625 per credit hour. *Financial support:* Fellowships, research assistantships, teaching assistantships available. *Unit head:* Dr. Qetler Jensrud, Head, 330-972-6403. *Application contact:* Dr. Qetler Jensrud, Head, 330-972-6403.

University of Arkansas, Graduate School, College of Education and Health Professions, Department of Rehabilitation, Human Resources and Communication Disorders, Program in Workforce Development Education, Fayetteville, AR 72701-1201. Offers M Ed, Ed D. Part-time and evening/weekend programs available. Postbaccalaureate distance learning degree programs offered. *Students:* 21 full-time (15 women), 155 part-time (113 women); includes 44 minority (41 African Americans, 1 American Indian/Alaska Native, 2 Hispanic Americans), 3 international. In 2009, 41 master's, 7 doctorates awarded. *Expenses:* Tuition, state resident: full-time $7355; part-time $356.58 per hour. Tuition, nonresident: full-time $17,401; part-time $775.17 per hour. Required fees: $1203. *Financial support:* In 2009–10, 2 research assistantships were awarded; fellowships, teaching assistantships, career-related internships or fieldwork and Federal Work-Study also available. Support available to part-time students. Financial award application deadline: 4/1; financial award applicants required to submit FAFSA. *Unit head:* Dr. Fran Hagstrom, Department Chairperson, 479-575-4758, Fax: 479-575-2492, E-mail: fhagstr@uark.edu. *Application contact:* Dr. Brent Williams, Graduate Coordinator, 479-575-4758, E-mail: btwilli@uark.edu.

The University of British Columbia, Faculty of Education, Department of Curriculum and Pedagogy, Vancouver, BC V6T 1Z4, Canada. Offers art education (M Ed, MA); business education (MA); curriculum studies (M Ed, MA, PhD); home economics education (M Ed, MA); math education (M Ed, MA); music education (M Ed, MA); physical education (M Ed, MA); science education (M Ed, MA); social studies education (M Ed, MA); technology studies education (M Ed, MA). Part-time programs available. *Degree requirements:* For master's, thesis (MA); for doctorate, comprehensive exam, thesis/dissertation. *Entrance requirements:* Additional exam requirements/recommendations for international students: Required—TOEFL (minimum score 580 paper-based; 237 computer-based; 92 iBT). Electronic applications accepted. *Expenses:* Contact institution. *Faculty research:* School subjects, teaching and learning.

University of Calgary, Faculty of Graduate Studies, Faculty of Education, Graduate Division of Educational Research, Calgary, AB T2N 1N4, Canada. Offers community rehabilitation and disability studies (M Ed, M Sc, Ed D, PhD, Graduate Certificate, Graduate Diploma); curriculum, teaching and learning (M Ed, M Sc, MA, Ed D, PhD, Graduate Certificate, Graduate Diploma); educational contexts (M Ed, MA, Ed D, PhD, Graduate Certificate, Graduate Diploma); educational leadership (M Ed, MA, Ed D, PhD, Graduate Certificate, Graduate Diploma); educational technology (M Ed, M Sc, MA, Ed D, PhD, Graduate Certificate, Graduate Diploma); gifted education (M Sc, MA, Ed D, PhD, Graduate Certificate, Graduate Diploma); higher education administration (Ed D); interpretive studies in education (M Ed, M Sc, MA, Ed D, PhD, Graduate Certificate, Graduate Diploma); second language teaching (M Ed, Ed D, PhD, Graduate Certificate, Graduate Diploma); teaching English as a second language (M Ed, M Sc, MA, Ed D, PhD, Graduate Certificate, Graduate Diploma); workplace and adult learning (M Ed, MA, Ed D, PhD, Graduate Certificate, Graduate Diploma). Ed D in both higher education administration and educational leadership offered via distance delivery. Part-time and evening/weekend programs available. Postbaccalaureate distance learning degree programs offered (minimal on-campus study). *Degree requirements:* For master's, thesis (for some programs); for doctorate, thesis/dissertation, candidacy exam. *Entrance requirements:* For master's, minimum GPA of 3.0, 3 letters of reference; for doctorate, minimum GPA of 3.5, 3 letters of reference; for other advanced degree, minimum GPA of 3.0. Additional exam requirements/recommendations for international students: Required—TOEFL, IELTS. Electronic applications accepted. *Faculty research:* Curriculum, leadership, technology, contexts, gifted, second language teaching, work place and adult learning.

University of Central Florida, College of Education, Department of Teaching and Learning Principles, Program in Career and Technical Education, Orlando, FL 32816. Offers MA. *Accreditation:* NCATE. Part-time and evening/weekend programs available. *Students:* 6 full-time (5 women), 33 part-time (26 women); includes 12 minority (8 African Americans, 4 Hispanic Americans). Average age 40. 15 applicants, 93% accepted, 7 enrolled. In 2009, 8 master's awarded. *Entrance requirements:* For master's, GRE General Test. Additional exam requirements/recommendations for international students: Required—TOEFL. *Application deadline:* For fall admission, 7/15 for domestic students; for spring admission, 12/1 for domestic students. Electronic applications accepted. *Expenses:* Tuition, state resident: part-time $306.31 per credit hour. Tuition, nonresident: part-time $1099.01 per credit hour. Part-time tuition and fees vary according to degree level and program. *Financial support:* Fellowships with partial tuition reimbursements, research assistantships with partial tuition reimbursements, teaching assistantships with partial tuition reimbursements, career-related internships or fieldwork, Federal Work-Study, institutionally sponsored loans, tuition waivers (partial), and unspecified assistantships available. Financial award application deadline: 3/1; financial award applicants required to submit FAFSA.

University of Central Missouri, The Graduate School, College of Education, Warrensburg, MO 64093. Offers career and technical education administration (MS); career and technical education industry training (MS); career and technical education leadership/teaching (MS); college student personnel administration (MS); counseling (MS); curriculum and instruction (Ed S); educational leadership (Ed D); educational technology (MS); elementary education/educational foundations and literacy (MSE); elementary school administration (MSE); elementary school principalship (Ed S); human services/learning resources (Ed S); human services/professional counseling (Ed S); human services/special education (Ed S); human services/technology and occupational education (Ed S); K-12 education/educational foundations and literacy (MSE); K-12 special education (MSE); library science and information services (MS); literacy education (MSE); secondary education/educational foundations & literacy (MSE); secondary school administration (MSE); secondary school principalship (Ed S); superintendency (Ed S); teaching (MAT). Part-time programs available. Postbaccalaureate distance learning degree programs offered. *Faculty:* 42. *Students:* 123 full-time (82 women), 721 part-time (552 women); includes 58 minority (38 African Americans, 3 American Indian/Alaska Native, 6 Asian Americans or Pacific Islanders, 11 Hispanic Americans), 6 international. Average age 34. 229 applicants, 88% accepted, 190 enrolled. In 2009, 212 master's, 47 other advanced degrees awarded. *Entrance requirements:* Additional exam requirements/recommendations for international students: Required—TOEFL (minimum score 550 paper-based; 79 computer-based). *Application deadline:* For fall admission, 6/1 priority date for domestic students, 5/1 for international students; for spring admission, 10/1 priority date for domestic students, 10/1 for international students. Applications are processed on a rolling basis. Application fee: $30 ($75 for international students). Electronic applications accepted. *Expenses:* Tuition, area resident: Part-time $245.80 per credit hour. Tuition, nonresident: part-time $491.60 per credit hour. Required fees: $24.20 per credit hour. Full-time tuition and fees vary according to course load, degree level, campus/location and reciprocity agreements. *Financial support:* Research assistantships with full and partial tuition reimbursements, teaching assistantships with full and partial tuition reimbursements, career-related internships or fieldwork, Federal Work-Study, scholarships/grants, and administrative and laboratory assistantships available. Support available to part-time students. Financial award application deadline: 3/1; financial award applicants required to submit FAFSA. *Unit head:* Dr. Michael Wright, Dean, 660-543-4272, Fax: 660-543-8753, E-mail: mwright@ucmo.edu. *Application contact:* Laurie Delap, Admissions Coordinator, 660-543-4621, Fax: 660-543-4778, E-mail: gradinfo@ucmo.edu.

University of Georgia, Graduate School, College of Education, Department of Workforce Education, Leadership and Social Foundations, Athens, GA 30602. Offers educational leadership (Ed D); human resources and organization design (M Ed); occupational studies (MAT, Ed D, PhD, Ed S); social foundations of education (PhD). *Accreditation:* NCATE. *Faculty:* 19 full-time (8 women). *Students:* 33 full-time (20 women), 127 part-time (81 women); includes 24 minority (19 African Americans, 2 American Indian/Alaska Native, 1 Asian American or Pacific Islander, 2 Hispanic Americans), 6 international. 140 applicants, 71% accepted, 46 enrolled. In 2009, 18 master's, 11 doctorates, 9 other advanced degrees awarded. *Entrance requirements:* For master's, GRE General Test, MAT; for doctorate, GRE General Test; for Ed S, GRE General Test or MAT. *Application deadline:* For fall admission, 7/1 priority date for domestic students; for spring admission, 11/15 for domestic students. Application fee: $50. Electronic applications accepted. *Expenses:* Tuition, state resident: full-time $6000; part-time $250 per credit hour. Tuition, nonresident: full-time $20,904; part-time $871 per credit hour. Required fees: $730 per semester. *Financial support:* Fellowships, research assistantships, teaching assistantships, unspecified assistantships available. *Unit head:* Dr. Roger B. Hill, Interim Head, 706-542-4100, Fax: 706-542-4054, E-mail: rbhill@uga.edu. *Application contact:* Dr. Myra N. Womble, Graduate Coordinator, 706-542-4091, Fax: 706-542-4054, E-mail: mwomble@uga.edu.

University of Idaho, College of Graduate Studies, College of Education, Department of Adult, Career, and Technology Education, Program in Professional-Technical and Technology Education, Moscow, ID 83844-2282. Offers M Ed, Ed Sp PTE. *Accreditation:* NCATE. *Students:* 8 full-time, 16 part-time. In 2009, 15 master's, 1 other advanced degree awarded. *Entrance requirements:* For master's, minimum GPA of 2.8. *Application deadline:* For fall admission, 8/1 for domestic students; for spring admission, 12/15 for domestic students. Application fee: $55 ($60 for international students). *Expenses:* Tuition, state resident: full-time $6120. Tuition, nonresident: full-time $17,712. *Financial support:* Application deadline: 2/15. *Unit head:* Dr. Charles W. Gagel, Head, 208-885-6492. *Application contact:* Dr. Charles W. Gagel, Head, 208-885-6492.

University of Illinois at Urbana–Champaign, Graduate College, College of Education, Department of Human Resource Education, Champaign, IL 61820. Offers Ed M, MS, Ed D, PhD, CAS, MBA/M Ed. Part-time and evening/weekend programs available. Postbaccalaureate distance learning degree programs offered (no on-campus study). *Faculty:* 6 full-time (1 woman). *Students:* 48 full-time (21 women), 118 part-time (81 women); includes 30 minority (19 African Americans, 6 Asian Americans or Pacific Islanders, 5 Hispanic Americans), 38 international. 104 applicants, 63% accepted, 29 enrolled. In 2009, 87 master's, 9 doctorates, 3 other advanced degrees awarded. *Entrance requirements:* For master's, minimum GPA of 3.0; for doctorate, GRE, minimum GPA of 3.0. Additional exam requirements/recommendations for international students: Required—TOEFL (minimum score 96 iBT). *Application deadline:* Applications are processed on a rolling basis. Application fee: $60 ($75 for international students). Electronic applications accepted. *Financial support:* In 2009–10, 3 fellowships, 8 research

Vocational and Technical Education

University of Illinois at Urbana–Champaign (continued)
assistantships, 11 teaching assistantships were awarded; tuition waivers (full and partial) also available. *Unit head:* Steven R. Aragon, Interim Head, 217-333-0807, Fax: 217-244-5632, E-mail: aragon@illinois.edu. *Application contact:* Laura Ketchum, Secretary, 217-333-0807, Fax: 217-244-5632, E-mail: lirle@illinois.edu.

University of Kentucky, Graduate School, College of Agriculture, Program in Career, Technology and Leadership Education, Lexington, KY 40506-0032. Offers MS. *Accreditation:* NCATE. Terminal master's awarded for partial completion of doctoral program. *Degree requirements:* For master's, comprehensive exam, thesis optional. *Entrance requirements:* For master's, GRE General Test, minimum undergraduate GPA of 2.75. Additional exam requirements/recommendations for international students: Required—TOEFL (minimum score 550 paper-based; 213 computer-based). Electronic applications accepted.

University of Maryland Eastern Shore, Graduate Programs, Department of Technology, Princess Anne, MD 21853-1299. Offers career and technology education (M Ed). Part-time and evening/weekend programs available. *Degree requirements:* For master's, comprehensive exam, seminar paper. *Entrance requirements:* For master's, PRAXIS, writing sample. Additional exam requirements/recommendations for international students: Required—TOEFL (minimum score 213 computer-based; 80 iBT). Electronic applications accepted. *Faculty research:* Doppler Radar study.

University of Minnesota, Twin Cities Campus, Graduate School, College of Education and Human Development, Department of Organizational Leadership, Policy and Development, Minneapolis, MN 55455-0213. Offers adult education (M Ed, MA, Ed D, PhD, Certificate); agricultural, food and environmental education (M Ed, MA, Ed D, PhD); business and industry education (M Ed, MA, Ed D, PhD); business education (M Ed); comparative and international development education (MA, PhD); disability policy and services (Certificate); educational administration (MA, Ed D, PhD); evaluation studies (MA, PhD); higher education (MA, PhD); human resource development (M Ed, MA, Ed D, PhD, Certificate); marketing education (M Ed); postsecondary administration (Ed D); program evaluation (Certificate); school-to-work (Certificate); staff development (Certificate); teacher leadership (M Ed); technical education (Certificate); technology education (M Ed, MA); work and human resource education (M Ed, MA, Ed D, PhD); youth development leadership (M Ed). *Faculty:* 24 full-time (11 women). *Students:* 334 full-time (220 women), 479 part-time (307 women); includes 120 minority (60 African Americans, 9 American Indian/Alaska Native, 30 Asian Americans or Pacific Islanders, 21 Hispanic Americans), 92 international. Average age 38. 452 applicants, 79% accepted, 261 enrolled. In 2009, 109 master's, 55 doctorates, 134 other advanced degrees awarded. *Financial support:* In 2009–10, 4 fellowships (averaging $32,881 per year), 34 research assistantships with full tuition reimbursements (averaging $24,977 per year), 16 teaching assistantships with full tuition reimbursements (averaging $26,078 per year) were awarded. *Faculty research:* Organization effects of schools, postsecondary institutions and business entities on leadership; program evaluation in shaping organizational reforms; international human resource development and change; effects of gender and race/ethnicity on learning and leadership; effects of initiatives to develop intercultural sensitivity and global awareness; the development of theory and pedagogy in pre-K through graduate school and in work contexts (including adult education and literacy). Total annual research expenditures: $757,278. *Unit head:* Dr. Darwin Hendel, Chair, 612-625-0129, Fax: 612-624-3377, E-mail: hende001@umn.edu. *Application contact:* Dr. Mary Trettin, Associate Dean, 612-625-6501, Fax: 612-626-1580, E-mail: mtrettin@umn.edu.

University of Missouri, Graduate School, College of Education, Department of Learning, Teaching and Curriculum, Columbia, MO 65211. Offers agricultural education (M Ed, PhD, Ed S); art education (M Ed, PhD, Ed S); business and office education (M Ed, PhD, Ed S); early childhood education (M Ed, PhD, Ed S); elementary education (M Ed, PhD, Ed S); English education (M Ed, PhD, Ed S); foreign language education (M Ed, PhD, Ed S); health education and promotion (M Ed, PhD); learning and instruction (M Ed); marketing education (M Ed, PhD, Ed S); mathematics education (M Ed, PhD, Ed S); music education (M Ed, PhD, Ed S); reading education (M Ed, PhD, Ed S); science education (M Ed, PhD, Ed S); social studies education (M Ed, PhD, Ed S); vocational education (M Ed, PhD, Ed S). Part-time programs available. Terminal master's awarded for partial completion of doctoral program. *Degree requirements:* For doctorate, thesis/dissertation. *Entrance requirements:* For master's and Ed S, GRE General Test or MAT, minimum GPA of 3.0; for doctorate, GRE General Test, minimum GPA of 3.0. Additional exam requirements/recommendations for international students: Required—TOEFL (minimum score 600 paper-based; 250 computer-based; 100 iBT). Electronic applications accepted.

University of Nebraska–Lincoln, Graduate College, College of Education and Human Sciences, Department of Teaching, Learning and Teacher Education, Lincoln, NE 68588. Offers adult and continuing education (MA); educational studies (Ed D, PhD), including special education (Ed D); teaching, learning and teacher education (M Ed, MA, MST, Ed D, PhD); vocational and adult education (M Ed, MA). *Accreditation:* NCATE. *Degree requirements:* For master's, thesis optional. *Entrance requirements:* Additional exam requirements/recommendations for international students: Required—TOEFL (minimum score 550 paper-based; 213 computer-based). Electronic applications accepted. *Faculty research:* Teacher education, instructional leadership, literacy education, technology, improvement of school curriculum.

University of Northern Iowa, Graduate College, College of Natural Sciences, Department of Industrial Technology, Cedar Falls, IA 50614. Offers MA, PSM, DIT. *Students:* 16 full-time (3 women), 19 part-time (3 women), 13 international. 41 applicants, 51% accepted, 16 enrolled. In 2009, 1 master's, 1 doctorate awarded. *Degree requirements:* For master's, comprehensive exam, thesis or alternative; for doctorate, thesis/dissertation. *Entrance requirements:* For master's, GRE, minimum GPA of 3.0, 3 professional references; for doctorate, GRE, minimum GPA of 3.5. Additional exam requirements/recommendations for international students: Required—TOEFL (minimum score 600 paper-based; 250 computer-based; 100 iBT). *Application deadline:* For fall admission, 8/1 priority date for domestic students. Applications are processed on a rolling basis. Application fee: $30 ($50 for international students). Electronic applications accepted. *Financial support:* Teaching assistantships, career-related internships or fieldwork, Federal Work-Study, scholarships/grants, and tuition waivers (full and partial) available. Support available to part-time students. Financial award application deadline: 2/1. *Unit head:* Dr. Barton Bergquist, Acting Head, 319-273-2563, Fax: 319-273-5818, E-mail: bart.bergquist@uni.edu. *Application contact:* Laurie S. Russell, Record Analyst, 319-273-2623, Fax: 319-273-6792, E-mail: laurie.russell@uni.edu.

University of North Texas, College of Information, Department of Learning Technologies, Program in Applied Technology, Training and Development, Denton, TX 76203. Offers M Ed, MS, Ed D, PhD. *Accreditation:* NCATE. *Degree requirements:* For doctorate, one foreign language, thesis/dissertation, internship. *Entrance requirements:* For master's, GRE General Test; for doctorate, GRE General Test, admissions exam. Additional exam requirements/recommendations for international students: Required—proof of English language proficiency required for non-native English speakers; Recommended—TOEFL (minimum score 550 paper-based; 213 computer-based; 79 iBT). Application fee: $50 ($75 for international students). *Expenses:* Tuition, state resident: full-time $4298; part-time $239 per contact hour. Tuition, nonresident: full-time $9878; part-time $549 per contact hour. Required fees: $265 per contact hour. *Financial support:* Fellowships, research assistantships, teaching assistantships, career-related internships or fieldwork, Federal Work-Study, and institutionally sponsored loans available. Financial award application deadline: 4/1; financial award applicants required to submit FAFSA. *Application contact:* Associate Dean, 940-565-2383, Fax: 940-565-2141.

University of North Texas, College of Information, Department of Library and Information Sciences, Denton, TX 76203-5017. Offers information science (MS, PhD); learning technologies (M Ed, Ed D), including applied technology, training and development (M Ed), computer education and cognitive systems, educational computing; library science (MS). *Accreditation:* ALA (one or more programs are accredited). Part-time and evening/weekend programs available. *Degree requirements:* For master's, comprehensive exam; for doctorate, comprehensive exam, thesis/dissertation. *Entrance requirements:* For master's, GRE General Test, MAT; for doctorate, GRE General Test. Additional exam requirements/recommendations for international students: Required—proof of English language proficiency required for non-native English speakers; Recommended—TOEFL (minimum score 550 paper-based; 213 computer-based; 79 iBT). *Application deadline:* Applications are processed on a rolling basis. Application fee: $50 ($75 for international students). Electronic applications accepted. *Expenses:* Tuition, state resident: full-time $4298; part-time $239 per contact hour. Tuition, nonresident: full-time $9878; part-time $549 per contact hour. Required fees: $265 per contact hour. *Financial support:* Fellowships, research assistantships, teaching assistantships, career-related internships or fieldwork, Federal Work-Study, institutionally sponsored loans, scholarships/grants, health care benefits, and library assistantships available. Financial award application deadline: 4/1; financial award applicants required to submit FAFSA. *Faculty research:* Information resources and services, information management and retrieval, computer-based information systems, human information behavior. *Application contact:* Graduate Academic Counselor, 940-369-2873, Fax: 940-565-3101.

University of South Africa, Institute for Science and Technology Education, Pretoria, South Africa. Offers mathematics, science and technology education (M Sc, PhD).

University of Southern Mississippi, Graduate School, College of Education and Psychology, Department of Technology Education, Hattiesburg, MS 39406-0001. Offers business technology education (MS); instructional technology (MS); technical occupational education (MS). Part-time programs available. *Faculty:* 6 full-time (3 women). *Students:* 11 full-time (5 women), 11 part-time (9 women); includes 4 minority (all African Americans), 2 international. Average age 37. 20 applicants, 65% accepted, 9 enrolled. In 2009, 8 master's awarded. *Degree requirements:* For master's, comprehensive exam, thesis (for some programs). *Entrance requirements:* For master's, GRE General Test, MAT, minimum GPA of 2.75 in last 60 hours. Additional exam requirements/recommendations for international students: Required—TOEFL. *Application deadline:* For fall admission, 3/1 priority date for domestic students, 3/1 for international students. Applications are processed on a rolling basis. Application fee: $35. *Expenses:* Tuition, state resident: full-time $5096; part-time $284 per hour. Tuition, nonresident: full-time $13,052; part-time $726 per hour. Required fees: $402. Tuition and fees vary according to course level and course load. *Financial support:* In 2009–10, 2 research assistantships with full tuition reimbursements (averaging $9,000 per year), 1 teaching assistantship with full tuition reimbursement (averaging $10,000 per year) were awarded; Federal Work-Study also available. Financial award application deadline: 3/15; financial award applicants required to submit FAFSA. *Faculty research:* Occupational competency, professional development for vocational-technical. Total annual research expenditures: $166,068. *Unit head:* Dr. Edward C. Mann, Chair, 601-266-4446, Fax: 601-266-5957, E-mail: edward.mann@usm.edu. *Application contact:* Shonna Breland, Manager of Graduate Admissions, 601-266-6563, Fax: 601-266-5138.

University of South Florida, Graduate School, College of Education–Main Campus, Department of Adult, Career and Higher Education, Tampa, FL 33620-9951. Offers adult education (MA, Ed D, PhD, Ed S); career and technical education (MA); career and workforce education (PhD); higher education/community college teaching (MA, Ed D, PhD); vocational education (Ed S). Part-time programs available. *Faculty:* 9 full-time (3 women), 4 part-time/adjunct (3 women). *Students:* 52 full-time (34 women), 211 part-time (149 women); includes 71 minority (41 African Americans, 1 American Indian/Alaska Native, 5 Asian Americans or Pacific Islanders, 24 Hispanic Americans), 6 international. Average age 30. 94 applicants, 69% accepted, 58 enrolled. In 2009, 31 master's, 11 doctorates awarded. *Degree requirements:* For master's, comprehensive exam; for doctorate, comprehensive exam, thesis/dissertation; for Ed S, comprehensive exam, thesis. *Entrance requirements:* For master's, minimum GPA of 3.0 in last 60 hours of course work; for doctorate and Ed S, GRE General Test, GRE Writing Test. Additional exam requirements/recommendations for international students: Required—TOEFL (minimum score 500 paper-based; 213 computer-based; 91 iBT). *Application deadline:* For fall admission, 2/15 for domestic students, 1/2 for international students; for spring admission, 10/15 for domestic students, 6/1 for international students. Applications are processed on a rolling basis. Application fee: $30. Electronic applications accepted. *Financial support:* Career-related internships or fieldwork, scholarships/grants, and unspecified assistantships available. Financial award applicants required to submit FAFSA. *Faculty research:* Community college leadership; integration of academic, career and technical education; competency-based education; continuing education administration; adult learning and development. Total annual research expenditures: $9,807. *Unit head:* Dr. Ann Cranston-Gingras, Chairperson, 813-974-6036, Fax: 813-974-3366, E-mail: cranston@usf.edu. *Application contact:* Dr. William Young, Program Director, 813-974-1861, Fax: 813-974-3366, E-mail: williamyoung@usf.edu.

The University of Texas at Tyler, College of Business and Technology, School of Human Resource Development and Technology, Tyler, TX 75799-0001. Offers human resource development (MS, PhD); industrial management (MS). Part-time and evening/weekend programs available. Postbaccalaureate distance learning degree programs offered (no on-campus study). *Faculty:* 5 full-time (1 woman). *Students:* 28 full-time (14 women), 51 part-time (29 women); includes 24 minority (14 African Americans, 10 Hispanic Americans), 3 international. Average age 35. 34 applicants, 97% accepted, 23 enrolled. In 2009, 31 master's awarded. *Degree requirements:* For master's, comprehensive exam. *Entrance requirements:* For master's, GRE General Test or MAT. Additional exam requirements/recommendations for international students: Required—TOEFL (minimum score 79 computer-based). *Application deadline:* For fall admission, 8/17 priority date for domestic students, 5/30 for international students; for spring admission, 12/21 priority date for domestic students, 10/30 for international students. Application fee: $25 ($50 for international students). Electronic applications accepted. *Expenses:* Tuition, state resident: part-time $665 per semester hour. Tuition, nonresident: part-time $942 per semester hour. Part-time tuition and fees vary according to degree level and program. *Financial support:* Career-related internships or fieldwork, institutionally sponsored loans, scholarships/grants, and health care benefits available. Support available to part-time students. Financial award application deadline: 7/1. *Faculty research:* Human resource development. *Unit head:* Dr. Paul B. Roberts, Interim Chair, 903-566-7334, Fax: 903-565-5650, E-mail: proberts@uttyler.edu. *Application contact:* Dr. Greg Wang, Director of Graduate Studies, 903-565-5910, Fax: 903-565-5650, E-mail: gwang@uttyler.edu.

The University of Toledo, College of Graduate Studies, College of Education, Department of Curriculum and Instruction, Program in Career and Technical Education, Toledo, OH 43606-3390. Offers Ed S.

The University of Toledo, College of Graduate Studies, College of Education, Department of Educational Foundations and Leadership, Program in Career and Technical Training, Toledo, OH 43606-3390. Offers ME.

University of Victoria, Faculty of Graduate Studies, Faculty of Education, Department of Curriculum and Instruction, Victoria, BC V8W 2Y2, Canada. Offers art education (M Ed, PhD); curriculum studies (M Ed, MA, PhD); early childhood education (M Ed, PhD); educational studies (PhD); language and literacy (M Ed, MA, PhD); mathematics (M Ed, MA, PhD); music education (M Ed, MA, PhD); science (M Ed, MA, PhD); social studies (M Ed, MA); social, cultural and foundational studies (MA, PhD); technology and environmental education (PhD). Part-time programs available. *Degree requirements:* For master's, thesis, project (M Ed); for doctorate, comprehensive exam, thesis/dissertation. *Entrance requirements:* For master's, minimum B average. Additional exam requirements/recommendations for international students: Required—TOEFL (minimum score 575 paper-based; 233 computer-based), IELTS (minimum score 7). Electronic applications accepted. *Faculty research:* Elementary and secondary English, language arts, curriculum theory and practice, educational media and technology, educational administration and leadership, history and philosophy of education.

University of West Florida, College of Professional Studies, Department of Engineering and Computer Technology, Program in Career and Technical Education, Pensacola, FL 32514-

5750. Offers M Ed. *Students:* 2 part-time (both women); both minorities (1 African American, 1 Hispanic American). Average age 40. In 2009, 4 master's awarded. *Expenses:* Tuition, state resident: full-time $4982; part-time $260 per credit hour. Tuition, nonresident: full-time $20,059; part-time $919 per credit hour. Required fees: $1247; $52 per credit hour. *Unit head:* Dr. Karen Rasmussen. *Application contact:* Terry McCray, Assistant Director of Graduate Admissions, 850-473-7718, Fax: 850-473-7714, E-mail: gradadmissions@uwf.edu.

University of Wisconsin–Platteville, School of Graduate Studies, College of Liberal Arts and Education, School of Education, Platteville, WI 53818-3099. Offers adult education (MSE); elementary education (MSE); English education (MSE); middle school education (MSE); secondary education (MSE); vocational and technical education (MSE). *Accreditation:* NCATE. Part-time programs available. *Faculty:* 8 part-time/adjunct (3 women). *Students:* 16 full-time (12 women), 183 part-time (137 women); includes 35 minority (27 African Americans, 1 American Indian/Alaska Native, 1 Asian American or Pacific Islander, 6 Hispanic Americans), 63 international. 23 applicants, 100% accepted, 23 enrolled. In 2009, 85 master's awarded. *Degree requirements:* For master's, comprehensive exam, thesis or alternative. *Entrance requirements:* Additional exam requirements/recommendations for international students: Required—TOEFL (minimum score 500 paper-based; 173 computer-based; 61 iBT). *Application deadline:* For fall admission, 7/1 priority date for domestic students; for spring admission, 11/1 for domestic students. Applications are processed on a rolling basis. Application fee: $56. Electronic applications accepted. *Expenses:* Tuition, state resident: full-time $6706. Tuition, nonresident: full-time $16,772. *Financial support:* Research assistantships with partial tuition reimbursements, career-related internships or fieldwork, Federal Work-Study, institutionally sponsored loans, scholarships/grants, and unspecified assistantships available. Support available to part-time students. *Unit head:* Dr. Karen Stinson, Director, 608-342-1131, Fax: 608-342-1133. *Application contact:* Lisa Popp, School of Graduate Studies, 608-342-1322, Fax: 608-342-1389, E-mail: poppl@uwplatt.edu.

University of Wisconsin–Stout, Graduate School, School of Education, Program in Career and Technical Education, Menomonie, WI 54751. Offers MS, Ed S. Part-time programs available. *Degree requirements:* For master's and Ed S, thesis. *Entrance requirements:* For master's, minimum GPA of 2.75; for Ed S, minimum GPA of 3.25. Additional exam requirements/recommendations for international students: Required—TOEFL (minimum score 500 paper-based; 173 computer-based; 61 iBT). Electronic applications accepted. *Faculty research:* Needs assessment, task analysis, instructional development, learning technologies.

University of Wisconsin–Stout, Graduate School, School of Education, Program in Industrial/Technology Education, Menomonie, WI 54751. Offers MS. Part-time programs available. *Degree requirements:* For master's, thesis. *Entrance requirements:* For master's, minimum GPA of 2.75. Additional exam requirements/recommendations for international students: Required—TOEFL (minimum score 500 paper-based; 173 computer-based; 61 iBT). Electronic applications accepted. *Faculty research:* Gender equity, instructional design, cognitive processes, socio-cultural impacts.

Utah State University, School of Graduate Studies, College of Engineering, Department of Engineering and Technology Education, Logan, UT 84322. Offers industrial technology (MS). Part-time and evening/weekend programs available. *Degree requirements:* For master's, thesis optional. *Entrance requirements:* For master's, GRE General Test, MAT, minimum GPA of 3.0 in last 30 hours of course work. Additional exam requirements/recommendations for international students: Required—TOEFL. *Faculty research:* Computer-aided design drafting, technology and the public school, materials, electronics, aviation.

Valley City State University, School of Education and Graduate Studies, Valley City, ND 58072. Offers English language learners (ELL) (M Ed); library and information technologies (M Ed); teaching and technology (M Ed); technology education (M Ed). *Accreditation:* NCATE. Part-time and evening/weekend programs available. Postbaccalaureate distance learning degree programs offered (no on-campus study). *Faculty:* 19 full-time (13 women), 4 part-time/adjunct (3 women). *Students:* 7 full-time (4 women), 115 part-time (73 women); includes 4 minority (1 African American, 1 American Indian/Alaska Native, 1 Asian American or Pacific Islander, 1 Hispanic American). Average age 36. 33 applicants, 97% accepted, 22 enrolled. In 2009, 22 master's awarded. *Degree requirements:* For master's, action research report, comprehensive portfolio. *Entrance requirements:* For master's, GRE, MAT, PRAXIS II or National Teaching Board for Professional Standards (if GPAless than 3.0). Additional exam requirements/recommendations for international students: Required—TOEFL (minimum score 525 paper-based; 193 computer-based). *Application deadline:* For fall admission, 5/24 priority date for domestic and international students; for winter admission, 12/11 priority date for domestic and international students; for spring admission, 4/24 priority date for domestic and international students. Applications are processed on a rolling basis. Application fee: $35. Electronic applications accepted. *Expenses:* Tuition, state resident: full-time $4266; part-time $237.40 per credit hour. Tuition, nonresident: full-time $4266; part-time $237.40 per credit hour. Required fees: $237.40 per credit hour. One-time fee: $35. *Financial support:* In 2009–10, 30 students received support. Applicants required to submit FAFSA. *Faculty research:* Academically at-risk students in higher education, communication pedagogy and technology, gender communication, computer mediated communication, creativity in music. Total annual research expenditures: $26,000. *Unit head:* Dr. Gary Thompson, Dean, 701-845-7197, E-mail: gary.thompson@vcsu.edu. *Application contact:* Misty Lindgren, 701-845-7303, Fax: 701-845-7305, E-mail: misty.lindgren@vcsu.edu.

Virginia Polytechnic Institute and State University, Graduate School, College of Liberal Arts and Human Sciences, School of Education, Department of Teaching and Learning, Program in Career and Technical Education, Blacksburg, VA 24061. Offers MS Ed, Ed D, PhD, Ed S. *Expenses:* Tuition, area resident: Full-time $10,228; part-time $459 per credit hour. Tuition, nonresident: full-time $17,892; part-time $865 per credit hour. Required fees: $1966; $451 per semester.

Virginia Polytechnic Institute and State University, VT Online, Blacksburg, VA 24061. Offers aerospace engineering (MS); business information systems (Graduate Certificate); career and technical education (MS); computer engineering (M Eng, MS); decision support systems (Graduate Certificate); eLearning leadership (MA); electrical engineering (M Eng, MS); engineering administration (MEA); environmental politics and policy (Graduate Certificate); foundations of political analysis (Graduate Certificate); health product risk management (Graduate Certificate); information policy and society (Graduate Certificate); information security (Graduate Certificate); instructional technology (MA); liberal arts (Graduate Certificate); life sciences: health product risk management (MS); natural resources (MNR, Graduate Certificate); networking (Graduate Certificate); nonprofit and nongovernmental organization management (Graduate Certificate); ocean engineering (MS); political science (MA); security studies (Graduate Certificate); software development (Graduate Certificate). *Expenses:* Tuition, area resident: Full-time $10,228; part-time $459 per credit hour. Tuition, nonresident: full-time $17,892; part-time $865 per credit hour. Required fees: $1966; $451 per semester.

Virginia State University, School of Graduate Studies, Research, and Outreach, School of Liberal Arts and Education, Department of Graduate Professional Education Programs, Program in Career and Technical Studies, Petersburg, VA 23806-0001. Offers M Ed, MS, CAGS. *Degree requirements:* For master's, thesis (for some programs).

Wayne State College, School of Education and Counseling, Department of Educational Foundations and Leadership, Program in Curriculum and Instruction, Wayne, NE 68787. Offers alternative education (MSE); business and information technology education (MSE); communication arts education (MSE); early childhood education (MSE); elementary education (MSE); English as a second language (MSE); English education (MSE); family and consumer sciences education (MSE); industrial technology and vocational education (MSE); learning communities (MSE); mathematics education (MSE); music education (MSE); science education (MSE); social science education (MSE). *Accreditation:* NCATE. Part-time and evening/weekend programs available. *Degree requirements:* For master's, comprehensive exam, thesis optional. *Entrance requirements:* For master's, GRE General Test. Additional exam requirements/recommendations for international students: Required—TOEFL (minimum score 550 paper-based; 213 computer-based).

Wayne State University, College of Education, Division of Teacher Education, Detroit, MI 48202. Offers adult and continuing education (M Ed); art education (M Ed); bilingual/bicultural education (M Ed, MAT); business education (M Ed, MAT); career and technical education (M Ed, Ed D, PhD, Ed S); curriculum and instruction (Ed D, PhD, Ed S); distributive education (M Ed, MAT); early childhood education (M Ed); elementary education (M Ed, MAT, Ed D, PhD, Ed S); elementary education curriculum and instruction (M Ed); English education (M Ed); English education-secondary (M Ed, Ed S); foreign language education (M Ed); general education (Ed D, Ed S); health occupations education (M Ed); industrial education (M Ed); mathematics education (M Ed, Ed S); pre-school and parent education (M Ed); reading (M Ed, Ed D, Ed S); reading, languages and literature (Ed D); school music-vocal (M Ed); science education (M Ed, MAT, Ed S); secondary education (MAT); secondary school reading (M Ed); social studies education (M Ed, Ed S), including education-secondary (M Ed); special education (M Ed, Ed D, PhD, Ed S); teacher education (MAT, Ed D, PhD). *Degree requirements:* For doctorate, thesis/dissertation. *Entrance requirements:* For master's, Michigan Basic Skills Test (MA in teaching), minimum GPA of 2.6; for doctorate, minimum undergraduate GPA of 3.0, graduate 3.5; interview, curriculum vitae; references. Additional exam requirements/recommendations for international students: Required—TOEFL (minimum score 550 paper-based; 213 computer-based), TWE (minimum score 6). Electronic applications accepted. *Faculty research:* Reading and writing literacy and literature.

Western Michigan University, Graduate College, College of Education, Department of Family and Consumer Sciences, Program in Career and Technical Education, Kalamazoo, MI 49008. Offers MA. *Accreditation:* NCATE. *Faculty:* 18 full-time (15 women). *Students:* 10 full-time (7 women), 32 part-time (18 women); includes 3 minority (2 African Americans, 1 American Indian/Alaska Native), 1 international. 15 applicants, 100% accepted, 9 enrolled. In 2009, 20 master's awarded. *Application deadline:* For fall admission, 2/15 priority date for domestic students. Applications are processed on a rolling basis. Application fee: $25. *Financial support:* Application deadline: 2/15. *Unit head:* Dr. Linda Dannison, Chair, 269-387-3704. *Application contact:* Admissions and Orientation, 269-387-2000, Fax: 269-387-2355.

Westfield State College, Division of Graduate and Continuing Education, Department of Education, Program in Occupational Education, Westfield, MA 01086. Offers M Ed, CAGS. *Accreditation:* NCATE. Part-time and evening/weekend programs available. *Degree requirements:* For master's, comprehensive exam. *Entrance requirements:* For master's, GRE General Test or MAT, minimum undergraduate GPA of 2.7.

Wilmington University, College of Education, New Castle, DE 19720-6491. Offers applied education technology (M Ed); career and technical education (M Ed); elementary and secondary school counseling (M Ed); elementary special education (M Ed); elementary studies (M Ed); instruction: gifted and talented (M Ed); instruction: teaching and learning (M Ed); literacy (M Ed); reading (M Ed); school leadership (M Ed); secondary teaching (MAT). *Accreditation:* NCATE. Part-time and evening/weekend programs available. *Entrance requirements:* For master's, 2 letters of recommendation, interview. Additional exam requirements/recommendations for international students: Required—TOEFL (minimum score 500 paper-based; 173 computer-based). Electronic applications accepted.

Wright State University, School of Graduate Studies, College of Education and Human Services, Department of Educational Leadership, Programs in Educational Leadership, Dayton, OH 45435. Offers curriculum and instruction: teacher leader (MA); educational administrative specialist: teacher leader (M Ed); educational administrative specialist: vocational education administration (M Ed, MA); student affairs in higher education-administration (M Ed, MA). *Accreditation:* NCATE. *Degree requirements:* For master's, thesis (for some programs). *Entrance requirements:* For master's, GRE General Test, MAT. Additional exam requirements/recommendations for international students: Required—TOEFL.

Wright State University, School of Graduate Studies, College of Education and Human Services, Department of Teacher Education, Programs in Workforce Education, Dayton, OH 45435. Offers career, technology and vocational education (M Ed, MA); computer/technology education (M Ed, MA); library/media (M Ed, MA); vocational education (M Ed, MA). *Accreditation:* NCATE. *Degree requirements:* For master's, thesis (for some programs). *Entrance requirements:* For master's, GRE General Test, MAT. Additional exam requirements/recommendations for international students: Required—TOEFL.

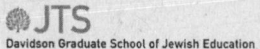

THE JEWISH THEOLOGICAL SEMINARY

William Davidson Graduate School of Jewish Education

Programs of Study	The William Davidson Graduate School of Jewish Education of the Jewish Theological Seminary (JTS) offers master of arts (M.A.) and doctoral (Ed.D.) programs in Jewish education.
	Through its master's program, the Davidson School prepares students to become educators in Jewish educational settings, both formal (day school and synagogue school) and informal (youth groups, camps, Jewish community centers, and adult education programs). The doctoral program prepares students for work in administration, supervision, curriculum design, and research and scholarship in Jewish education. In addition to the full-time doctoral program, part-time doctoral studies can be structured to fit the needs of students. In the fall of 2009, the Davidson School launched a new executive doctorate program that allows students to pursue doctoral course work through a combination of distance learning opportunities and intensive two-day seminars.
	The Davidson School has plans to launch three new programs in September 2011. The first is an M.A. in Jewish early childhood education, which will offer two distinct early childhood tracks: an M.A. in teaching and an M.A. in leadership. Many of the courses in this program will be offered in collaboration with the Bank Street College of Education. The second is a program in experiential education, which will offer an M.A. and a certificate in experiential education for educators interested in pursuing a career in summer camps, museums, and Jewish Community Centers (JCCs). The third is a certificate in teaching Israel. The new program will allow distinguished Davidson School students the opportunity to spend a full academic semester studying in Israel.
	Through a consortium academia agreement, Davidson School students can enroll in courses at Teachers College, Columbia University, and Union Theological Seminary. The Davidson School is open to men and women without regard to age, race, religion, sexual orientation, or national origin.
	Prospective students are strongly encouraged to utilize the resources found on the Davidson School's admissions page at http://www.jtsa.edu/davidsonadmissions. Applicants will find program descriptions, sample M.A. and Ed.D. curricula, information on alumni, and more.
Research Facilities	The Library of the Jewish Theological Seminary houses the most complete collection of Judaica in the Western Hemisphere. With more than 400,000 volumes on open shelves, it is ideally suited for the research needs of graduate students. The library's special collections, with more than 78,000 items, afford ample opportunity for original scholarship. All matriculated Davidson School students also benefit from the resources of neighboring Teachers College.
Financial Aid	Thanks to the generosity of the Jim Joseph Foundation, the M.A. program at the Davidson School offers a significant number of full-tuition fellowships for exceptional students. When prospective students submit their applications for admission, they are automatically considered for the M.A. tuition fellowship. There is no additional fellowship application. Fellowships—including both tuition aid and a significant living stipend—are available for full-time doctoral students.
	In addition, the Davidson School has an exciting philanthropic partnership with the Wexner Foundation (http://www.wexnerfoundation.org). The partnership's goal is to create an annual cohort of ten Davidson Scholars as part of the prestigious Wexner Graduate Fellowship. Wexner graduate fellows are awarded $20,000 each year for a two-year term with the possibility of renewal for a third year. The purpose of the fellowship is to build a cohesive community of fellows while enhancing the leadership skills of each individual. Fellows receive leadership training, peer support, professional mentoring, and networking across career choices and denominational affiliations, both during school and throughout their lives. Fellowships are granted for full-time study that begins in the fall. Applications are available on the Wexner Foundation Web site and are typically due in February. See http://www.wexnerfoundation.org for more information.
Cost of Study	For the 2010–11 academic year, tuition is $27,900 for full-time Ed.D. study and $22,300 for full-time M.A. study. Part-time students are charged $1050 per credit. In addition to tuition, a fee of $520 per semester is charged.
Living and Housing Costs	Residence halls (150 units) are available to single students at a cost of approximately $10,490 per academic year. Apartments of various costs are available to single or married students with families. For more information, students should contact the Office of Residence Life at 212-678-8035 or reslife@jtsa.edu.
Student Group	As of December 2009, 91 students were enrolled in the Davidson School. There were 27 students enrolled in the full-time doctoral program and 7 students enrolled in the executive doctoral program. There were 57 M.A. students enrolled solely in Davidson, while 21 M.A. students were in dual-degree JTS programs with the Rabbinical School, H. L. Miller Cantorial and College of Jewish Music, or the Graduate School. In addition, 5 students were enrolled in the distance learning M.A. program.
Location	JTS is located on the vibrant Upper West Side of New York City. Its proximity to Columbia University, Union Theological Seminary, and the Manhattan School of Music puts the Davidson School in the heart of a dynamic academic community. Students are encouraged to explore the wealth of cultural activities that New York City offers—from music and dance at Lincoln Center to theater on and off Broadway, from art at the Metropolitan and Whitney museums to the galleries in SoHo, Chelsea, and Williamsburg.
The Seminary	The Jewish Theological Seminary of America is a preeminent institution of Jewish higher education that integrates rigorous academic scholarship and teaching with a commitment to strengthening Jewish tradition, Jewish lives, and Jewish communities.
	JTS articulates a vision of Judaism that is learned and passionate, pluralist and authentic, traditional and egalitarian; one that is thoroughly grounded in Jewish texts, history, and practices, and fully engaged with the societies and cultures of the present. Its vision joins faith with inquiry; the covenant of Jewish ancestors with the creative insights of today; intense involvement in the society and state of Israel with devotion to the flowering of Judaism throughout the world; service to the Jewish community, as well as to all of the communities of which Jews are a part: society, their country, and the world.
	JTS serves North American Jewry by educating intellectual and spiritual leaders for Conservative Judaism and the vital religious center, training rabbis, cantors, scholars, educators, communal professionals, and lay activists who are inspired by the JTS vision of the Torah and dedicated to assisting in its realization.
Applying	Applications for admission to degree programs should be made as early as possible. M.A. applicants are encouraged to complete the application process by May 1 for consideration for fall admission, and by November 15 for spring admission. Ed.D. applications are due on January 2 for fall admission. Applications are received and reviewed throughout the year on a rolling basis. A $65 application fee, official college transcripts, three letters of recommendation (two academic references), and GRE scores are required. Doctoral applicants must also submit two academic writing samples.
Correspondence and Information	William Davidson Graduate School of Jewish Education The Jewish Theological Seminary 3080 Broadway New York, New York 10027-4649 Phone: 212-678-8022 E-mail: edschool@jtsa.edu Web site: http://www.jtsa.edu

The Jewish Theological Seminary

THE FACULTY

Arnold M. Eisen, Chancellor.
Michael B. Greenbaum, Vice Chancellor and Chief Operating Officer.
Marc Wolf, Vice Chancellor and Chief Development Officer.
Alan Cooper, Provost.
Stephen Garfinkel, Associate Provost.
Barry Holtz, Dean of the William Davidson Graduate School of Jewish Education.
Ofra Backenroth, Associate Dean of the William Davidson Graduate School of Jewish Education.

Department of Jewish Education

Full-time Faculty:
Ofra Backenroth, Adjunct Assistant Professor.
Aryeh Davidson, Assistant Professor.
Shira Epstein, Assistant Professor (on leave, fall 2010).
Barry Holtz, Professor.
Jeff Kress, Associate Professor and Senior Researcher.
Michelle Lynn-Sachs, Assistant Professor.

Adjunct Faculty:
Mary C. Boys
Amy Wallk Katz
Alvan Kaunfer
Cheryl Magen
Alvin Mars
Deborah Miller
Alex Sinclair

Rabbi In Residence:
Jonathan Lipnick

Prospective students are encouraged to visit http://www.jtsa.edu/davidsonfaculty to learn more about the Davidson School faculty and their accomplishments and contributions to the field of Jewish and general education.

VILLANOVA UNIVERSITY

Graduate Program in Counseling and Human Relations

Program of Study

In the Graduate Program in Counseling and Human Relations (CHR) a student can choose one of the following three course concentrations: elementary school counseling, secondary school counseling, or clinical mental health. Prerequisites for school counseling are 6 credits of mathematics and 6 credits of English at the undergraduate level. The elementary and secondary school counseling concentrations lead to approval for certification by the Pennsylvania Department of Education, and the clinical mental health concentration can lead to licensure as a professional counselor with the Bureau of Social Workers, Marriage and Family Therapists, and Professional Counselors. All students take the core program, including electives relating to the area of concentration, and the comprehensive examination, an integral part of the program. They must also demonstrate proficiency in counseling skills during a two-semester internship. A total of 48 credits are required for the degree.

Students have up to six years to complete the program, which begins when they take their first course—transfer or otherwise. Students must take CHR 8605 Laboratory in Counseling Skills and CHR 8655 Laboratory in Group Dynamics within the first 12 hours of graduate work. A thesis is not required but may be done in lieu of a comprehensive exam upon completing required course work.

Research Facilities

The Falvey Memorial Library at Villanova University houses about 600,000 volumes and 3,000 periodicals. An interlibrary loan system operates with the efficiency of e-mail. The library is located in the middle of the campus and includes numerous public-use computer stations that are equipped with sophisticated search engines and data retrieval mechanisms.

Financial Aid

Financial assistance is available, for those who qualify, through a variety of methods. A limited number of full-time graduate assistantships and part-time lab technician positions are available through the department. These positions include tuition remission of either 12 or 6 credits, in addition to a stipend for the full-time positions. Through a local bank, Villanova University has negotiated a student-loan package for which all students may apply. Several scholarships based on academic merit and other factors are available for students. Some provide full tuition. To help with the cost of tuition, Villanova may suggest a number of payment options, including credit card, deferred payment option, and employer tuition reimbursement (if available). Students should contact the Financial Assistance Office at 610-519-6456 for more information.

Students become eligible for financial assistance when they are enrolled for 9 or more credit hours per semester.

Cost of Study

Fees and expenses for graduate students in 2010–11 are $50 for the application fee, $650 per credit for tuition, and $60 per semester for general University fees. Additional tuition and fee information is available by calling the Bursar's Office at 610-519-4258.

Living and Housing Costs

A variety of affordable housing possibilities are available near the Villanova University campus. Housing costs vary in accordance with the option chosen. Room and board for a single graduate student may average about $8000 for a twelve-month period. Villanova University does not provide on-campus housing for graduate students.

Student Group

Students in the graduate CHR program combine a variety of academic backgrounds, professional interests, and personal aims. There are usually about 160 students matriculated in the program, with about one third full-time. The qualities most often mentioned and appreciated among the students are a collegial atmosphere, a high level of intellectual intensity, and practical experience.

Student Outcomes

The Graduate Program in Counseling and Human Relations prepares students to be counselors in school and community mental health agency settings. The school counseling track leads to certification as a school counselor through the Pennsylvania Department of Education, while the clinical mental health track leads to a license in professional counseling through the Bureau of Social Workers, Marriage and Family Therapists, and Professional Counselors. The counseling program is widely recognized both locally and nationally for preparing counselors who know not only what it means to be a counselor but also how to be a professional counselor. Graduates of the program have been readily accepted into many other graduate programs nationwide (e.g., at the Universities of Massachusetts, Connecticut, Colorado, Michigan, and Delaware) and have gone on to distinguish themselves in many counseling programs.

Location

Villanova University is situated on the historic Main Line, in a safe, western suburb of Philadelphia. Villanova is located on Lancaster Avenue (Route 30), 2 minutes from the Blue Route (Route 476) and 5 minutes from the Pennsylvania Turnpike, the Schuylkill Expressway, and Route 202. With ample parking and mass transit stops right on campus grounds, students can travel easily to and from the campus by car, bus, or train.

The University

Villanova University is an institution that is rich in history and Catholic tradition. From its modest beginnings on the country estate of a Revolutionary War officer, the University has seen significant growth in its student population as well as in its position as a leading coeducational institution of higher learning.

Applying

All students interested in graduate studies in counseling and human relations that lead to certification as a school counselor or licensure as a professional counselor must choose the appropriate track prior to admission. Applications for admission are required to include two complete undergraduate transcripts; three letters of recommendation from people who know the candidate personally, professionally, and/or academically; a completed departmental Work Experience and Goals worksheet; and test scores from either the Graduate Record Examinations or the Miller Analogies Test.

Applicants should submit the following materials: three letters of recommendation, work experience and goals form, a current resume, application for admission, the nonrefundable application fee, all official postsecondary transcripts, and the GRE or MAT scores; all should be sent to Graduate Studies in the College of Liberal Arts and Sciences, Villanova University, 800 Lancaster Avenue, Villanova, Pennsylvania 19085-1699. Application forms are available online or from the Office of Graduate Studies. The CHR manual is posted on the University's Web site; it is recommended that students download and print this document. The manual provides a wealth of information about the program and includes many of the forms required during the program.

The deadline for receipt of applications for the fall semester is May 1. Applications for financial aid are due by February 1.

Correspondence and Information

Department of Education and Human Services
Villanova University
800 Lancaster Avenue
Villanova, Pennsylvania 19085

Phone: 610-519-4620
Fax: 610-519-4623
E-mail: eduhs@villanova.edu
Web site: http://education.villanova.edu

Villanova University

THE FACULTY

Krista Malott, Assistant Professor; Ph.D., Northern Colorado, 2005.
Rayna D. Markin, Assistant Professor; Ph.D., Maryland, College Park, 2007.
Michael Mason, Assistant Professor; Ph.D., Oregon State, 1992.
Joan Q. Monnig, Assistant Professor; Ed.D., Massachusetts, 1973.
Robert J. Murray, O.S.A., Assistant Professor and Program Director; Ph.D., Temple, 1995.
Christopher D. Schmidt, Assistant Professor; William and Mary, Ph.D., 2007.

WESTERN MICHIGAN UNIVERSITY

The Mallinson Institute for Science Education

Programs of Study

Science education is an interdisciplinary discipline that is devoted to the study and improvement of how people teach and learn science. As an academic discipline, it lies at the intersection between science, education, psychology, and the history, philosophy, and sociology of science. The George G. Mallinson Institute for Science Education is proud to offer one of the largest faculties of science education specialists in the country, including biology, chemistry, earth science, and physics educators. One indication of its growing prominence among science education programs is that its faculty members were ranked third in terms of faculty productivity (papers written and cited, grants) among all science education Ph.D.-granting programs in the *Chronicle for Higher Education*'s *Almanac for Higher Education 2007–08*. The ranking was the result of an extensive survey of academic programs all across the country conducted by the *Chronicle of Higher Education* in association with Academic Analysis, a higher-education consulting firm.

The Ph.D. in science education is designed for those with a science or science education background who wish to pursue careers as college science teachers, science education researchers, curriculum specialists, or professionals in science education–related agencies. The program has three tracks: college science teaching, college science teaching with a discipline-specific research focus, and curriculum and instruction (K–12). Each track provides an understanding of the history of science education and a background in the diverse approaches to educational research. Doctoral candidates are required to complete 72 credit hours, including 15 hours in science education core courses, 24 hours in science core courses, 12 hours in research tools and techniques courses, 6 hours in electives, and 15 hours in a dissertation.

In addition, Western Michigan University (WMU) offers a concurrent-enrollment program in science education, in which students complete a master's degree program in a particular science (biology, chemistry, earth science (physical geography or geology), environmental science, or physics) and then a doctoral degree in one of the three tracks listed above.

The Master of Arts in science education is designed for secondary school science teachers who wish to expand their teaching skills as well as for students who are beginning work toward a Ph.D. in science education. Elementary school teachers with a strong science background may qualify for admission. In order to earn the degree, students must complete 30 credit hours, including 9 hours in science education core courses, 15 hours in science core courses, and 6 hours in electives, a thesis, or an independent research project.

Research Facilities

The Dwight B. Waldo Library forms the nerve center of the entire University community. It contains more than 4.3 million print and electronic items, including more than 2.1 million titles, 9,700 journal subscriptions, and 25,000 tapes and CDs. In addition, the library has a full depository for Michigan state documents and a selective depository for United States government documents. The science reference section contains reference and research sources in biology, chemistry, geology, mathematics, physics, and all areas of medicine and engineering. The science reference desk is also the service point for all current periodicals, newspapers, and the associated microfilm editions of periodicals and newspapers.

Financial Aid

The Institute offers a limited number of graduate assistantships and doctoral associateships each year for full-time graduate students. These positions typically include a stipend, tuition costs, conference costs, and research costs. Students who receive these awards typically teach a section of one of the introductory science courses for prospective teachers, including courses in life, physical, and earth science. Interested students should apply by February 15. Other teaching and research assistantships are available from the University. Students may also borrow under the Federal PLUS or Perkins Loan programs or other student loan programs.

Cost of Study

Information about tuition and fees can be found at http://www.wmich.edu/registrar/tuition.

Living and Housing Costs

Information about the cost of on-campus room and board can be found at http://www.wmich.edu/housing. Students living off campus typically pay $400 to $800 per month for a one-bedroom apartment or $500 to $1000 per month for a two bedroom.

Student Group

Students in the program are required to hold undergraduate or graduate degrees in science or science education or have teaching certification. Many of them are also science teachers at the elementary, secondary, or university level. Graduates of the program find employment in science education programs as teachers, curriculum specialists, or researchers.

Location

Kalamazoo, the fifth-largest city in Michigan, is located midway between Chicago and Detroit, a 2½-hour drive from each. Kalamazoo hosts a number of festivals throughout the year as well as theater, music, and ballet performances. Kalamazoo is just 40 minutes from Lake Michigan beaches and only 3 to 4 hours from Michigan's ski country, which is considered the best skiing in the central U.S.

The University

Western Michigan University is a nationally recognized student-centered research university. With an enrollment of more than 26,000, it is one of the fifty largest universities in the nation. Students may choose from more than 250 degree programs and participate in nearly 300 registered student organizations. *U.S. News & World Report* ranks WMU as one of the nation's top 100 public universities.

Applying

Prospective students are required to submit an online application for admission (with a $40 fee) through the Office of Admissions and Orientation (http://www.wmich.edu/admissions/graduate). Applicants should note that the Office of Admissions and Orientation has its own admissions requirements. The Mallinson Institute for Science Education also requires students to submit the following materials directly to the Institute: official transcripts of all previous college work, official GRE scores, a two-page essay describing the student's reasons for entering the program, and three letters of recommendation. For additional information, students should visit http://www.wmich.edu/science.

Correspondence and Information

Mallinson Institute for Science Education
3225 Wood Hall
Western Michigan University
Kalamazoo, Michigan 49008-5444
Phone: 269-387-5398
Fax: 269-387-4998
E-mail: sci-ed@wmich.edu
Web site: http://www.wmich.edu/science/

Western Michigan University

THE FACULTY AND THEIR RESEARCH

William W. Cobern, Professor of Biological Sciences and Science Education and Director of the Mallinson Institute for Science Education; Ph.D., Colorado at Boulder. The role of culture in the teaching and learning of science, the experimental study of science teaching effectiveness, the improvement of biology education.

Marcia Fetters, Associate Professor of Science Education; Ph.D., Michigan State. The needs of individuals marginalized from the science education community, science in informal settings, use of toys to teach science concepts.

Charles Henderson, Assistant Professor of Physics; Ph.D., Minnesota. Educational change, science teachers' beliefs about teaching and learning, student-centered instructional strategies in physics.

Mark Jenness, Senior Researcher and Director of Science and Mathematics Program Improvement; Ed.D., Western Michigan. Evaluation and technical assistance in the areas of science, mathematics, and environmental education.

Heather Petcovic, Assistant Professor of Geological Sciences; Ph.D., Oregon State. A combined approach to understanding how dikes fed lava flows of the Columbia River flood basalts, role of field experience in geoscience education, alternative conceptions in earth sciences, role of informal education programs in promoting scientific literacy in the general public.

David W. Rudge, Associate Professor of Biological Sciences; Ph.D., Pittsburgh. How the history and philosophy of science can be used to inform the teaching of science, H. B. D. Kettlewell's famous experiments on industrial melanism.

David Schuster, Associate Professor of Physics; Ph.D., Witwatersrand (South Africa). Cognition, assessment, teaching and learning in science, educational design, curriculum development, epistemology and inquiry.

Reneé Schwartz, Assistant Professor of Biological Sciences; Ph.D., Oregon State. Developments in learning and teaching of nature of science and scientific inquiry, effective means to utilize authentic scientific experiences to enhance learners' epistemological views of science, scientific inquiry within science classrooms and authentic settings.

Brandy Skjold, Laboratory Instructional Specialist; M.S., Northern Michigan. Biology education, ecological effects of climate change on microorganisms, the role of language in college science teaching and in research laboratories.

Joseph P. Stoltman, Professor of Geography and Science Education; Ph.D., Georgia. Teaching and learning of geography, global change education, spatial analysis of educational reform in Michigan.

ACADEMIC AND PROFESSIONAL PROGRAMS IN THE HEALTH-RELATED PROFESSIONS

Section 27
Allied Health

This section contains a directory of institutions offering graduate work in allied health, followed by in-depth entries submitted by institutions that chose to prepare detailed program descriptions. Additional information about programs listed in the directory but not augmented by an in-depth entry may be obtained by writing directly to the dean of a graduate school or chair of a department at the address given in the directory.

For programs offering related work, see also in this book *Administration, Instruction, and Theory (Educational Psychology); Dentistry and Dental Sciences; Health Services; Public Health; Special Focus (Education of the Multiply Handicapped); Social Work;* and *Subject Areas (Counselor Education).* In the other guides in this series:

Graduate Programs in the Humanities, Arts & Social Sciences
See *Art and Art History (Art Therapy), Family and Consumer Sciences (Gerontology), Performing Arts (Therapies),* and *Psychology and Counseling*

Graduate Programs in the Biological Sciences
See *Anatomy, Biophysics, Microbiological Sciences, Pathology and Pathobiology,* and *Physiology*

Graduate Programs in the Physical Sciences, Mathematics, Agricultural Sciences, the Environment & Natural Resources
See *Physics (Acoustics)*

Graduate Programs in Engineering & Applied Sciences
See *Agricultural Engineering and Bioengineering (Bioengineering), Biomedical Engineering and Biotechnology,* and *Energy and Power Engineering (Nuclear Engineering)*

CONTENTS

Allied Health—General

Alabama State University, School of Graduate Studies, College of Health Sciences, Montgomery, AL 36101-0271. Offers DPT. *Entrance requirements:* Additional exam requirements/recommendations for international students: Required—TOEFL (minimum score 500 paper-based; 173 computer-based).

American College of Healthcare Sciences, Graduate Programs, Portland, OR 97239-3719. Offers complementary alternative medicine (MS). Postbaccalaureate distance learning degree programs offered. *Degree requirements:* For master's, capstone project. *Entrance requirements:* For master's, interview, letters of recommendation, essay. *Application deadline:* For fall admission, 11/15 for domestic students. Application fee: $0. *Expenses:* Tuition: Part-time $370 per semester hour. *Application contact:* Tracey Miller, Dean of Admissions, 800-487-8839, Fax: 503-244-0727, E-mail: admissions@achs.edu.

Andrews University, School of Graduate Studies, College of Arts and Sciences, Department of Clinical and Laboratory Sciences, Berrien Springs, MI 49104. Offers MSMT. *Accreditation:* APTA. *Faculty:* 4 full-time (2 women). *Students:* 1 (woman) part-time; minority (African American). Average age 29. 1 applicant, 0% accepted, 0 enrolled. *Entrance requirements:* For master's, GRE. Additional exam requirements/recommendations for international students: Required—TOEFL (minimum score 550 paper-based). *Application deadline:* Applications are processed on a rolling basis. Application fee: $40. *Unit head:* Dr. Marcia A. Kilsby, Chair, 269-471-3336. *Application contact:* Carolyn Hurst, Supervisor of Graduate Admission, 800-253-2874, Fax: 269-471-6321, E-mail: graduate@andrews.edu.

Athabasca University, Centre for Nursing and Health Studies, Athabasca, AB T9S 3A3, Canada. Offers advanced nursing practice (MN, Advanced Diploma); generalist (MN); health studies-leadership (MHS). Part-time programs available. Postbaccalaureate distance learning degree programs offered. *Faculty:* 11 full-time (all women), 1 (woman) part-time/adjunct. *Students:* 542 part-time. Average age 38. 428 applicants, 51 enrolled. In 2009, 181 master's, 6 other advanced degrees awarded. *Degree requirements:* For master's, comprehensive exam (for some programs). *Entrance requirements:* For master's, bachelor's degree in health-related field, 2 years professional health service experience (MHS), bachelor's degree in nursing, 2 years nursing experience (MN), minimum GPA of 3.0 in final 30 credits; for Advanced Diploma, RN license, 2 years health care experience. *Application deadline:* For fall admission, 3/1 for domestic and international students. Application fee: $80. Electronic applications accepted. *Expenses:* Contact institution. *Unit head:* Dr. Donna Romyn, Dean, 800-788-9041 Ext. 6794, Fax: 780-675-6468, E-mail: dromyn@athabascau.ca. *Application contact:* Donna Dunn Hart, Academic Student Advisor—Graduate Programs, 800-788-9041 Ext. 6300, Fax: 780-675-6468, E-mail: donnad@athabascau.ca.

A.T. Still University of Health Sciences, Arizona School of Health Sciences, Mesa, AZ 85206. Offers advanced occupational therapy (MS); advanced physician assistant (MS); athletic training (MS); audiology (Au D); health sciences (DHSc); human movement (MS); occupational therapy (MS); physical therapy (MS, DPT); physician assistant (MS); transitional audiology (Au D); transitional physical therapy (DPT). *Accreditation:* AOTA (one or more programs are accredited); ASHA. Postbaccalaureate distance learning degree programs offered (no on-campus study). *Faculty:* 53 full-time (30 women), 205 part-time/adjunct (117 women). *Students:* 491 full-time (353 women), 1,251 part-time (874 women); includes 319 minority (70 African Americans, 11 American Indian/Alaska Native, 176 Asian Americans or Pacific Islanders, 62 Hispanic Americans), 3 international. Average age 31. 2,697 applicants, 22% accepted, 420 enrolled. In 2009, 225 master's, 523 doctorates awarded. *Degree requirements:* For master's, thesis (for some programs); for doctorate, thesis/dissertation (for some programs). *Entrance requirements:* For master's, GRE General Test; for doctorate, GRE, Evaluation of Practicing Audiologists Capabilities (Au D), Physical Therapy Evaluation Tool (DPT), current state licensure, master's degree or equivalent (Au D), minimum GPA of 2.7. Additional exam requirements/recommendations for international students: Recommended—TOEFL (minimum score 550 paper-based; 213 computer-based; 80 iBT). *Application deadline:* For fall admission, 2/1 priority date for domestic and international students. Applications are processed on a rolling basis. Application fee: $60. *Expenses:* Contact institution. *Financial support:* In 2009–10, 651 students received support. Federal Work-Study and scholarships/grants available. Financial award application deadline: 5/1; financial award applicants required to submit FAFSA. *Faculty research:* Adolescent health-related quality of life, clinical outcomes following sport related injury, pediatric concussion, shoulder stability and neuromuscular control, sport conditioning, exercise and sport psychology, geriatric exercise and wellness. Total annual research expenditures: $61,527. *Unit head:* Dr. Randy Danielsen, Dean, 480-219-6000, Fax: 480-219-6110, E-mail: rdanielsen@atsu.edu. *Application contact:* Donna Sparks, Associate Director for Admissions, 660-626-2237, Fax: 660-626-2969, E-mail: admissions@atsu.edu.

Baylor University, Graduate School, Military Programs, Waco, TX 76798. Offers MHA, MPT, MS, D Sc, D Sc PA, DPT. *Accreditation:* APTA (one or more programs are accredited). *Students:* 166 full-time (66 women); includes 27 minority (9 African Americans, 1 American Indian/Alaska Native, 9 Asian Americans or Pacific Islanders, 8 Hispanic Americans). In 2009, 49 master's, 63 doctorates awarded. *Entrance requirements:* For master's, GRE General Test. *Application deadline:* Applications are processed on a rolling basis. Application fee: $25. *Expenses:* Contact institution. *Unit head:* Col. Darwin L. Fretwell, Dean, 210-221-8715, Fax: 210-221-7306. *Application contact:* Suzanne Keener, Administrative Assistant, 254-710-3588, Fax: 254-710-3870.

Belmont University, College of Health Sciences, Nashville, TN 37212-3757. Offers Pharm D, MSN, MSOT, DPT, OTD. Part-time programs available. Postbaccalaureate distance learning degree programs offered (minimal on-campus study). *Degree requirements:* For master's, thesis; for doctorate, thesis/dissertation. *Entrance requirements:* For master's, GRE, BSN, minimum GPA of 3.0; for doctorate, 1 year experience as a licensed healthcare professional. Additional exam requirements/recommendations for international students: Required—TOEFL (minimum score 550 paper-based; 213 computer-based). Electronic applications accepted. *Expenses:* Contact institution.

Bennington College, Graduate Programs, Postbaccalaureate Premedical Program, Bennington, VT 05201. Offers allied and health sciences (Certificate). *Faculty:* 8 full-time (3 women), 2 part-time/adjunct (1 woman). *Students:* 10 full-time (5 women); includes 1 minority (Asian American or Pacific Islander). Average age 29. 64 applicants, 41% accepted. In 2009, 7 Certificates awarded. *Application deadline:* For fall admission, 2/15 priority date for domestic students. Applications are processed on a rolling basis. Application fee: $60. *Expenses:* Contact institution. *Financial support:* Scholarships/grants available. Financial award application deadline: 4/1; financial award applicants required to submit FAFSA. *Faculty research:* Cellular functions of Hsp90; foundations of quantum mechanics; history and philosophy of physics; cytosolic quality control; forest ecology; plate tectonics of rift systems; amphibian evolutionary physiology; photochemistry of gold complexes. *Unit head:* Dr. Janet Foley, Chief Health Professions Adviser, 802-440-4463, Fax: 802-440-4461, E-mail: jfoley@bennington.edu. *Application contact:* Ferrilyn Sourdiffe, Postbaccalaureate Admissions Counselor, 802-440-4885, Fax: 802-440-4320, E-mail: fsourdiffe@bennington.edu.

Boston University, College of Health and Rehabilitation Sciences—Sargent College, Boston, MA 02215. Offers MS, MSOT, D Sc, DPT, OTD, PhD, CAGS. *Accreditation:* APTA (one or more programs are accredited). Postbaccalaureate distance learning degree programs offered (minimal on-campus study). *Faculty:* 54 full-time (42 women), 44 part-time/adjunct (28 women). *Students:* 371 full-time (332 women), 81 part-time (72 women); includes 57 minority (2 African Americans, 39 Asian Americans or Pacific Islanders, 16 Hispanic Americans), 24 international. Average age 27. 763 applicants, 42% accepted, 110 enrolled. In 2009, 140 master's, 141 doctorates awarded. Terminal master's awarded for partial completion of doctoral program. *Degree requirements:* For master's, comprehensive exam (for some programs), thesis optional; for doctorate, variable foreign language requirement, comprehensive exam (for some programs), thesis/dissertation (for some programs). *Entrance requirements:* For master's, doctorate, and

CAGS, GRE General Test. Additional exam requirements/recommendations for international students: Required—TOEFL (minimum score 550 paper-based; 84 computer-based). *Application deadline:* For fall admission, 2/1 priority date for domestic students. Applications are processed on a rolling basis. Application fee: $70. Electronic applications accepted. *Expenses:* Tuition: Full-time $37,910; part-time $1184 per credit hour. Required fees: $386; $40 per semester. Part-time tuition and fees vary according to class time, course level, degree level and program. *Financial support:* In 2009–10, 300 students received support, including 119 fellowships with full and partial tuition reimbursements available (averaging $15,000 per year), 9 research assistantships with partial tuition reimbursements available (averaging $18,000 per year), 15 teaching assistantships with partial tuition reimbursements available (averaging $6,000 per year); career-related internships or fieldwork, Federal Work-Study, institutionally sponsored loans, scholarships/grants, and health care benefits also available. Support available to part-time students. Financial award application deadline: 4/15; financial award applicants required to submit FAFSA. *Faculty research:* Outcome measurement, gerontology, neuroanatomy, aphasia, autism. Total annual research expenditures: $9 million. *Unit head:* Dr. Gloria S. Waters, Dean, 617-353-2704, Fax: 617-353-7500, E-mail: gwaters@bu.edu. *Application contact:* Sharon Sankey, Director, Student Services, 617-353-2713, Fax: 617-353-7500, E-mail: ssankey@bu.edu.

Brock University, Faculty of Graduate Studies, Faculty of Applied Health Sciences, St. Catharines, ON L2S 3A1, Canada. Offers M Sc, MA, PhD. *Degree requirements:* For master's, thesis. *Entrance requirements:* For master's, honors degree, BA and/or B Sc. Additional exam requirements/recommendations for international students: Required—TOEFL (minimum score 550 paper-based; 213 computer-based; 80 iBT), IELTS (minimum score 6.5), TWE (minimum score 4). Electronic applications accepted. *Faculty research:* Health and physical activity, aging and health, health advocacy, exercise psychology, community development.

Cleveland State University, College of Graduate Studies, College of Science, Department of Health Sciences, Program in Health Sciences, Cleveland, OH 44115. Offers health sciences (MS); online health sciences (MS). Part-time and evening/weekend programs available. Postbaccalaureate distance learning degree programs offered (no on-campus study). *Degree requirements:* For master's, thesis. *Faculty research:* Assisted technologies, biomechanics, clinical administration, cultural health, gerontology.

Creighton University, School of Pharmacy and Health Professions, Omaha, NE 68178-0001. Offers Pharm D, MS, DPT, OTD, Pharm D/MS. *Accreditation:* ACPE (one or more programs are accredited). Postbaccalaureate distance learning degree programs offered (minimal on-campus study). *Entrance requirements:* PCAT. Electronic applications accepted. *Expenses:* Contact institution. *Faculty research:* Patient safety in health services research, health information technology and health services research, interdisciplinary educational research in the health professions, outcomes research in the health professions, cross-cultural care in the health professions .

Dominican College, Division of Allied Health, Orangeburg, NY 10962-1210. Offers MBA, MS, DPT. Part-time and evening/weekend programs available. Postbaccalaureate distance learning degree programs offered (minimal on-campus study). *Faculty:* 15 full-time (11 women), 30 part-time/adjunct (20 women). *Students:* 149 full-time (115 women), 188 part-time (127 women); includes 111 minority (25 African Americans, 1 American Indian/Alaska Native, 64 Asian Americans or Pacific Islanders, 21 Hispanic Americans), 3 international. Average age 40. In 2009, 50 master's, 38 doctorates awarded. *Unit head:* Dr. Sandra Countee, Division Director, 845-848-6039, Fax: 845-398-4893, E-mail: sandra.countee@dc.edu. *Application contact:* Joyce Elbe, Director of Admissions, 845-848-7896 Ext. 15, Fax: 845-365-3150, E-mail: admissions@dc.edu.

Drexel University, College of Nursing and Health Professions, Philadelphia, PA 19104-2875. Offers MA, MFT, MHS, MS, MSN, DPT, PhD, Certificate, PMC, PPDPT. *Accreditation:* NLN. Part-time and evening/weekend programs available. Terminal master's awarded for partial completion of doctoral program. *Degree requirements:* For master's, comprehensive exam, thesis (for some programs); for doctorate, thesis/dissertation, qualifying exam. *Entrance requirements:* For doctorate, GRE General Test. Electronic applications accepted.

Duquesne University, John G. Rangos, Sr. School of Health Sciences, Pittsburgh, PA 15282-0001. Offers health management systems (MHMS); occupational therapy (MS); physical therapy (DPT); physician assistant studies (MPAS); rehabilitation science (MS, PhD); speech-language pathology (MS); MBA/MHMS. *Accreditation:* AOTA (one or more programs are accredited); APTA (one or more programs are accredited); ASHA. *Faculty:* 35 full-time (23 women), 17 part-time/adjunct (10 women). *Students:* 309 full-time (258 women), 11 part-time (7 women); includes 11 minority (5 African Americans, 5 Asian Americans or Pacific Islanders, 1 Hispanic American), 6 international. Average age 23. 454 applicants, 20% accepted, 20 enrolled. In 2009, 92 master's, 23 doctorates awarded. *Degree requirements:* For doctorate, thesis/dissertation. *Entrance requirements:* For master's, GRE General Test (speech-language pathology), 3 letters of recommendation; minimum GPA of 2.75 (health management systems, occupational therapy), minimum GPA of 3.0 (speech-language pathology); for doctorate, GRE General Test (for physical therapy), 3 letters of recommendation, minimum GPA of 3.0, personal interview. Additional exam requirements/recommendations for international students: Required—TOEFL (minimum score 550 paper-based; 233 computer-based; 90 iBT). *Application deadline:* Applications are processed on a rolling basis. Electronic applications accepted. *Expenses:* Contact institution. *Financial support:* Federal Work-Study available. *Faculty research:* Neuronal processing, electrical stimulation on peripheral neuropathy, CNS stimulatory and inhibitory signals, behavioral genetic methodologies to development disorders of speech, neurogenic communication disorders. Total annual research expenditures: $338,404. *Unit head:* Dr. Gregory H. Frazer, Dean, 412-396-5303, Fax: 412-396-5554, E-mail: frazer@duq.edu. *Application contact:* Christopher R. Hilf, Recruiter/Academic Advisor, 412-396-5653, Fax: 412-396-5554, E-mail: hilfc@duq.edu.

East Carolina University, Graduate School, School of Allied Health Sciences, Greenville, NC 27858-4353. Offers MPT, MS, MSOT, DPT, PhD. Part-time and evening/weekend programs available. Postbaccalaureate distance learning degree programs offered (no on-campus study). *Degree requirements:* For master's, comprehensive exam. *Entrance requirements:* For master's, GRE General Test. Additional exam requirements/recommendations for international students: Required—TOEFL. *Faculty research:* Hearing, stuttering, therapeutic activities, ACL injury.

Eastern Kentucky University, The Graduate School, College of Health Sciences, Richmond, KY 40475-3102. Offers MPH, MS, MSN. Part-time programs available. *Entrance requirements:* For master's, GRE General Test, minimum GPA of 2.75.

East Tennessee State University, School of Graduate Studies, College of Public and Allied Health, Johnson City, TN 37614. Offers MPH, MS, MSEH, Au D, DPT, Certificate. Part-time and evening/weekend programs available. *Entrance requirements:* For master's and doctorate, GRE. Additional exam requirements/recommendations for international students: Required—TOEFL (minimum score 550 paper-based; 213 computer-based).

Emory University, School of Medicine, Programs in Allied Health Professions, Atlanta, GA 30322-1100. Offers anesthesiology (MM Sc); anesthesiology/patient monitoring systems (MM Sc); ophthalmic technology (MM Sc); physical therapy (DPT); physician assistant (MM Sc). Postbaccalaureate distance learning degree programs offered. *Faculty:* 29 full-time (19 women), 18 part-time/adjunct (8 women). *Students:* 381 full-time (273 women), 3 part-time (2 women); includes 80 minority (43 African Americans, 2 American Indian/Alaska Native, 20 Asian Americans or Pacific Islanders, 15 Hispanic Americans), 5 international. Average age 27. 1,299 applicants, 16% accepted, 149 enrolled. In 2009, 99 master's, 41 doctorates awarded. *Entrance requirements:* For master's, GRE or MCAT; for doctorate, GRE. *Application deadline:* Applications are processed on a rolling basis. Electronic applications accepted. *Expenses:* Contact institution. *Financial support:* In 2009–10, 275 students received support. Institutionally sponsored

loans and scholarships/grants available. Financial award application deadline: 3/1; financial award applicants required to submit FAFSA. *Unit head:* Dr. J. Alan Otsuki, Assistant Dean, Office of Medical Education and Student Affairs, 404-727-5655, Fax: 404-727-0045, E-mail: jotsuki@emory.edu. *Application contact:* Marvell Nesmith, Associate Director of Registration and Student Affairs, 404-712-9921, Fax: 404-727-0045, E-mail: marvell.nesmith@emory.edu.

Ferris State University, College of Allied Health Sciences, Big Rapids, MI 49307. Offers MS. Part-time programs available. Postbaccalaureate distance learning degree programs offered (no on-campus study). *Faculty:* 1 (woman) full-time, 69 part-time/adjunct (63 women). *Students:* 1 (woman) full-time, 64 part-time (58 women). Average age 42. 30 applicants, 53% accepted, 11 enrolled. In 2009, 9 master's awarded. *Degree requirements:* For master's, comprehensive exam. *Entrance requirements:* For master's, BS in nursing, minimum GPA of 3.0, writing sample, 3 professional references. Additional exam requirements/recommendations for international students: Required—TOEFL (minimum score 500 paper-based; 173 computer-based; 61 iBT). *Application deadline:* For fall admission, 7/15 priority date for domestic students. Application fee: $30. *Financial support:* In 2009–10, 4 students received support. Career-related internships or fieldwork and scholarships/grants available. Financial award applicants required to submit FAFSA. *Unit head:* Dr. Julie Coon, Director of School of Nursing, 231-591-2267, Fax: 231-591-2325, E-mail: coonj@ferris.edu. *Application contact:* Debby Buck, Off Campus Student Support, 231-591-2094, Fax: 231-591-3788, E-mail: buckd@ferris.edu.

Florida Agricultural and Mechanical University, Division of Graduate Studies, Research, and Continuing Education, School of Allied Health Sciences, Tallahassee, FL 32307-3200. Offers health administration (MS); physical therapy (MPT). *Faculty:* 19 full-time (5 women). *Students:* 133 full-time (100 women), 13 part-time (10 women); includes 134 minority (133 African Americans, 1 Asian American or Pacific Islander), 3 international. In 2009, 27 master's awarded. *Degree requirements:* For master's, thesis (for some programs). *Entrance requirements:* For master's, GRE General Test or GMAT, minimum GPA of 3.0. Additional exam requirements/recommendations for international students: Required—TOEFL (minimum score 550 paper-based). *Application deadline:* For fall admission, 5/18 for domestic students, 12/18 for international students; for spring admission, 11/12 for domestic students, 5/12 for international students. Application fee: $30. *Unit head:* Dr. Cynthia Hughes-Harris, Dean, 850-599-3818, Fax: 850-561-2502. *Application contact:* Dr. Chanta M. Haywood, Dean of Graduate Studies, Research, and Continuing Education, 850-599-3315, Fax: 850-599-3727.

Florida Gulf Coast University, College of Health Professions, Fort Myers, FL 33965-6565. Offers MS, MSN, DPT. *Accreditation:* AOTA. Part-time and evening/weekend programs available. Postbaccalaureate distance learning degree programs offered (minimal on-campus study). *Faculty:* 42 full-time (33 women), 30 part-time/adjunct (20 women). *Students:* 149 full-time (113 women), 76 part-time (61 women); includes 40 minority (18 African Americans, 2 American Indian/Alaska Native, 10 Asian Americans or Pacific Islanders, 10 Hispanic Americans), 1 international. Average age 31. 188 applicants, 44% accepted, 64 enrolled. In 2009, 36 master's awarded. *Degree requirements:* For master's, thesis or alternative. *Entrance requirements:* For master's, GRE General Test or MAT, minimum GPA of 3.0. Additional exam requirements/recommendations for international students: Required—TOEFL (minimum score 550 paper-based; 213 computer-based). *Application deadline:* Applications are processed on a rolling basis. Application fee: $30. Electronic applications accepted. *Financial support:* Career-related internships or fieldwork, Federal Work-Study, and institutionally sponsored loans available. *Faculty research:* Gerontology, health care policy, health administration, community-based services. Total annual research expenditures: $181,623. *Unit head:* Dr. Denise Heinemann, Dean, 239-590-7511, Fax: 239-590-7474. *Application contact:* Lynn O'Hare, Administrative Assistant, 239-590-7451, Fax: 239-590-7474, E-mail: lohare@fgcu.edu.

Georgia Southern University, Jack N. Averitt College of Graduate Studies, College of Health and Human Sciences, Statesboro, GA 30460. Offers MS, MSN, DNP, Certificate. Part-time and evening/weekend programs available. Postbaccalaureate distance learning degree programs offered (no on-campus study). *Faculty:* 63 full-time (40 women). *Students:* 109 full-time (56 women), 132 part-time (89 women); includes 40 minority (31 African Americans, 1 American Indian/Alaska Native, 3 Asian Americans or Pacific Islanders, 5 Hispanic Americans), 5 international. Average age 31. 138 applicants, 76% accepted, 78 enrolled. In 2009, 53 master's awarded. *Degree requirements:* For master's, comprehensive exam (for some programs), thesis (for some programs), exams; for doctorate, comprehensive exam, practicum. *Entrance requirements:* For master's, GRE General Test, MAT or GMAT; for doctorate, GRE or MAT. Additional exam requirements/recommendations for international students: Required—TOEFL (minimum score 550 paper-based; 213 computer-based; 80 iBT). *Application deadline:* For fall admission, 3/1 priority date for domestic students, 3/1 for international students; for spring admission, 10/1 priority date for domestic students, 10/1 for international students. Applications are processed on a rolling basis. Application fee: $50. Electronic applications accepted. *Expenses:* Tuition, state resident: full-time $5040; part-time $210 per credit hour. Tuition, nonresident: full-time $20,136; part-time $839 per credit hour. Required fees: $1644. *Financial support:* In 2009–10, 226 students received support, including 57 research assistantships with partial tuition reimbursements available (averaging $7,200 per year), teaching assistantships with partial tuition reimbursements available (averaging $7,200 per year); career-related internships or fieldwork, Federal Work-Study, scholarships/grants, traineeships, tuition waivers (partial), and unspecified assistantships also available. Support available to part-time students. Financial award application deadline: 4/15; financial award applicants required to submit FAFSA. *Unit head:* Dr. June Alberto, Dean, 912-478-5322, Fax: 912-478-5349, E-mail: jalberto@georgiasouthern.edu. *Application contact:* Dr. Charles Ziglar, Coordinator for Graduate Student Recruitment, 912-478-5635, Fax: 912-478-0740, E-mail: gradadmissions@georgiasouthern.edu.

Georgia State University, College of Health and Human Sciences, Atlanta, GA 30302-3083. Offers MPH, MS, MSW, DPT, PhD, Certificate. *Accreditation:* CSWE. Part-time and evening/weekend programs available. *Degree requirements:* For master's, thesis (for some programs); for doctorate, comprehensive exam, thesis/dissertation. *Entrance requirements:* For master's, GRE (some programs accept MAT, GMAT); for doctorate, GRE General Test, RN license, interview. Additional exam requirements/recommendations for international students: Required—TOEFL (minimum score 550 paper-based; 213 computer-based). Electronic applications accepted. *Faculty research:* Public health issues, obesity, life-cycle health, substance abuse prevention, women's health.

Georgia State University, College of Health and Human Sciences, School of Health Professions, Division of Respiratory Therapy, Atlanta, GA 30302-3083. Offers MS. Part-time programs available. *Degree requirements:* For master's, project-P. *Entrance requirements:* For master's, GRE. *Faculty research:* Aerosol drug delivery, tuberculosis education, respiratory therapy pharmacology.

Grand Valley State University, College of Health Professions, Allendale, MI 49401-9403. Offers MPAS, MS, DPT. *Faculty:* 27 full-time (14 women), 7 part-time/adjunct (5 women). *Students:* 261 full-time (208 women), 1 (woman) part-time; includes 10 minority (1 African American, 1 American Indian/Alaska Native, 5 Asian Americans or Pacific Islanders, 3 Hispanic Americans), 1 international. Average age 25. 220 applicants, 29% accepted, 64 enrolled. In 2009, 45 master's, 42 doctorates awarded. *Entrance requirements:* For master's, volunteer work, interview, minimum GPA of 3.0, writing sample; for doctorate, GRE, 50 hours of volunteer work, interview, minimum GPA of 3.0 in last 60 hours and in prerequisites, writing sample. Additional exam requirements/recommendations for international students: Required—TOEFL (minimum score 610 paper-based; 253 computer-based). *Application deadline:* For winter admission, 1/15 priority date for domestic and international students. Applications are processed on a rolling basis. Electronic applications accepted. *Expenses:* Tuition, state resident: part-time $471 per credit hour. Tuition, nonresident: part-time $646 per credit hour. Tuition and fees vary according to course level. *Financial support:* In 2009–10, 54 students received support, including 25 fellowships (averaging $3,660 per year), 40 research assistantships with partial tuition reimbursements available (averaging $4,136 per year); career-related internships or fieldwork, Federal Work-Study, institutionally sponsored loans, and scholarships/grants also available. Financial award application deadline: 2/15. *Faculty research:* Skeletal muscle structure, blood platelets, thrombospondin activity, FES exercise for quadriplegics, balance. *Unit head:* Dr. Roy Olsson, Dean, 616-331-3356, Fax: 616-331-3350. *Application contact:* Darlene Zwart, Student Services Coordinator, 616-331-3958, E-mail: zwartda@gvsu.edu.

Idaho State University, Office of Graduate Studies, Kasiska College of Health Professions, Pocatello, ID 83209-8090. Offers M Coun, MHE, MOT, MPAS, MPH, MS, Au D, DPT, PhD, Certificate, Ed S, Post-Doctoral Certificate, Post-Master's Certificate, Postbaccalaureate Certificate. *Accreditation:* APTA (one or more programs are accredited). Part-time programs available. *Faculty:* 34 full-time (21 women), 1 part-time/adjunct (0 women). *Students:* 485 full-time (318 women), 196 part-time (156 women); includes 57 minority (5 African Americans, 3 American Indian/Alaska Native, 23 Asian Americans or Pacific Islanders, 26 Hispanic Americans), 14 international. Average age 32. 323 applicants, 36% accepted, 68 enrolled. In 2009, 131 master's, 34 doctorates, 3 other advanced degrees awarded. *Degree requirements:* For master's, comprehensive exam, thesis (for some programs), 8-week externship; for doctorate, comprehensive exam, thesis/dissertation, clinical rotation (for some programs); for other advanced degree, comprehensive exam, thesis, case study, oral exam. *Entrance requirements:* For master's, GRE General Test or MAT, minimum GPA of 3.0, 3 letters of recommendation; for doctorate, GRE General Test or MAT, minimum GPA of 3.0, counseling license, professional research, interview, work experience, 3 letters of recommendation; for other advanced degree, GRE General Test or MAT, master's degree in similar field of study, 3 letters of recommendation, 2 years of work experience. Additional exam requirements/recommendations for international students: Required—TOEFL (minimum score 600 paper-based; 250 computer-based; 80 iBT). *Application deadline:* For fall admission, 7/1 for domestic students, 6/1 for international students; for spring admission, 12/1 for domestic students, 11/1 for international students. Applications are processed on a rolling basis. Application fee: $55. Electronic applications accepted. *Expenses:* Contact institution. *Financial support:* In 2009–10, 1 research assistantship with full and partial tuition reimbursement (averaging $9,401 per year), 26 teaching assistantships with full and partial tuition reimbursements (averaging $10,841 per year) were awarded; career-related internships or fieldwork, Federal Work-Study, institutionally sponsored loans, scholarships/grants, traineeships, health care benefits, tuition waivers (full and partial), and unspecified assistantships also available. Support available to part-time students. Financial award application deadline: 1/1; financial award applicants required to submit FAFSA. *Faculty research:* Mental health, information technology, dental health, nursing. *Unit head:* Dr. Stephen Feit, Dean, 208-282-3992, Fax: 208-282-4000, E-mail: feitstep@isu.edu. *Application contact:* Tami Carson, Graduate School Technical Records Specialist, 208-282-2150, Fax: 208-282-4847, E-mail: carstami@isu.edu.

Ithaca College, Division of Graduate and Professional Studies, School of Health Sciences and Human Performance, Ithaca, NY 14850. Offers MS, DPT. Part-time programs available. *Faculty:* 53 full-time (32 women), 6 part-time/adjunct (5 women). *Students:* 291 full-time (219 women), 14 part-time (10 women); includes 19 minority (2 African Americans, 1 American Indian/Alaska Native, 6 Asian Americans or Pacific Islanders, 10 Hispanic Americans), 14 international. Average age 23. In 2009, 141 master's, 58 doctorates awarded. Terminal master's awarded for partial completion of doctoral program. *Degree requirements:* For master's, comprehensive exam (for some programs), thesis optional; for doctorate, thesis/dissertation optional. *Entrance requirements:* Additional exam requirements/recommendations for international students: Required—TOEFL (minimum score 550 paper-based; 213 computer-based; 80 iBT). Application fee: $40. *Expenses:* Contact institution. *Financial support:* In 2009–10, 264 students received support, including 66 teaching assistantships (averaging $9,271 per year); career-related internships or fieldwork, Federal Work-Study, scholarships/grants, and unspecified assistantships also available. Support available to part-time students. Financial award applicants required to submit CSS PROFILE or FAFSA. *Unit head:* Dr. Steven Siconolfi, Dean, 607-274-3237, Fax: 607-274-1263, E-mail: gps@ithaca.edu. *Application contact:* Rob Gearhart, Dean, Graduate and Professional Studies, 607-274-3527, Fax: 607-274-1263, E-mail: gps@ithaca.edu.

Loma Linda University, School of Allied Health Professions, Loma Linda, CA 92350. Offers MHIS, MOT, MPT, MS, D Sc, DPT, DPTSc, OTD. *Accreditation:* AOTA; APTA. *Entrance requirements:* For master's, minimum GPA of 2.0; for doctorate, minimum 2.0 GPA, associate degree in physical therapy. Additional exam requirements/recommendations for international students: Required—TOEFL (minimum score 550 paper-based; 213 computer-based). Electronic applications accepted.

Long Island University, C.W. Post Campus, School of Health Professions and Nursing, Brookville, NY 11548-1300. Offers MS, Certificate. Part-time and evening/weekend programs available. Postbaccalaureate distance learning degree programs offered. *Degree requirements:* For master's, thesis. Electronic applications accepted. *Faculty research:* PCR techniques, breast CA-mammography compliance, smoking patterns.

Louisiana State University Health Sciences Center, School of Allied Health Professions, Program in Health Science, New Orleans, LA 70112-2223. Offers clinical concepts (MHS); education (MHS); management administration (MHS). Part-time and evening/weekend programs available. *Degree requirements:* For master's, comprehensive exam, thesis optional, research project. *Entrance requirements:* For master's, GRE General Test, minimum GPA of 2.5. *Faculty research:* Healthcare management, stroke, ambulation, neurological gait, early intervention.

Marymount University, School of Health Professions, Arlington, VA 22207-4299. Offers MS, MSN, DNP, DPT, Certificate. Part-time and evening/weekend programs available. *Faculty:* 13 full-time (11 women), 3 part-time/adjunct (2 women). *Students:* 116 full-time (92 women), 84 part-time (74 women); includes 71 minority (46 African Americans, 16 Asian Americans or Pacific Islanders, 9 Hispanic Americans), 9 international. Average age 31. 422 applicants, 44% accepted, 74 enrolled. In 2009, 32 master's, 127 doctorates awarded. *Entrance requirements:* For master's, GRE, MAT, 2 letters of recommendation, interview, resume; for doctorate, GRE, 2 letters of recommendation, resume; for Certificate, interview. Additional exam requirements/recommendations for international students: Required—TOEFL (minimum score 600 paper-based; 250 computer-based; 96 iBT), IELTS (minimum score 6.5). *Application deadline:* For fall admission, 7/1 for international students; for spring admission, 10/15 for international students. Applications are processed on a rolling basis. Application fee: $40. Electronic applications accepted. *Expenses:* Tuition: Full-time $13,050; part-time $725 per credit hour. Required fees: $135; $7.50 per credit hour. *Financial support:* In 2009–10, 21 students received support; research assistantships with full and partial tuition reimbursements available, career-related internships or fieldwork, Federal Work-Study, scholarships/grants, and unspecified assistantships also available. Support available to part-time students. Financial award applicants required to submit FAFSA. *Unit head:* Dr. Tess Cappello, Dean, 703-284-1580, Fax: 703-284-3819, E-mail: tess.cappello@marymount.edu. *Application contact:* Francesca Reed, Director, Graduate Admissions, 703-284-5901, Fax: 703-527-3815, E-mail: grad.admissions@marymount.edu.

Maryville University of Saint Louis, School of Health Professions, St. Louis, MO 63141-7299. Offers MARC, MMT, MOT, MSN, DNP, DPT, CAGS. *Accreditation:* CORE. Part-time and evening/weekend programs available. *Students:* 81 full-time (65 women), 131 part-time (117 women); includes 25 minority (13 African Americans, 7 Asian Americans or Pacific Islanders, 5 Hispanic Americans), 2 international. Average age 33. In 2009, 95 master's awarded. *Entrance requirements:* Additional exam requirements/recommendations for international students: Required—TOEFL. *Application deadline:* Applications are processed on a rolling basis. Application fee: $40 ($60 for international students). Electronic applications accepted. *Expenses:* Tuition: Full-time $20,384; part-time $627.50 per credit hour. Required fees: $100 per semester. *Financial support:* Career-related internships or fieldwork, Federal Work-Study, and campus employment available. Financial award application deadline: 3/1; financial award applicants required to submit FAFSA. *Faculty research:* Disability work transition, assessment, reducing work-related musculoskeletal injuries, women's health–AIDS. *Unit head:* Dr. Charles Gulas, Dean, 314-529-9625, Fax: 314-529-9495, E-mail: hlthprofessions@maryville.edu. *Application contact:* Dr. Charles Gulas, Dean, 314-529-9625, Fax: 314-529-9495, E-mail: hlthprofessions@maryville.edu.

Allied Health—General

Medical College of Georgia, School of Graduate Studies, Program in Allied Health Sciences, Augusta, GA 30912. Offers MS. Part-time programs available. Postbaccalaureate distance learning degree programs offered (no on-campus study). *Degree requirements:* For master's, thesis. *Entrance requirements:* For master's, GRE General Test. Additional exam requirements/recommendations for international students: Required—TOEFL (minimum score 550 paper-based; 213 computer-based; 79 iBT). Electronic applications accepted. Full-time tuition and fees vary according to campus/location, program and student level. *Faculty research:* Patient-and family-centered care, public health informatics, vascular health promotion through physical activity, improving air quality for school children, and movement therapies for Parkinson's Disease.

Medical University of South Carolina, College of Health Professions, Charleston, SC 29425. Offers MHA, MRA, MS, DHA, DPT, PhD. *Accreditation:* CAHME (one or more programs are accredited). Part-time programs available. *Faculty:* 39 full-time (17 women), 6 part-time/adjunct (4 women). *Students:* 623 full-time (488 women), 41 part-time (29 women); includes 83 minority (46 African Americans, 3 American Indian/Alaska Native, 14 Asian Americans or Pacific Islanders, 20 Hispanic Americans), 1 international. Average age 28. 1,158 applicants, 33% accepted, 292 enrolled. In 2009, 209 master's, 70 doctorates awarded. *Degree requirements:* For doctorate, comprehensive exam, thesis/dissertation. *Entrance requirements:* For master's, GRE. Additional exam requirements/recommendations for international students: Required—TOEFL (minimum score 600 paper-based; 250 computer-based). Application fee: $85. Electronic applications accepted. *Expenses:* Contact institution. *Financial support:* In 2009–10, 20 students received support. Career-related internships or fieldwork, Federal Work-Study, scholarships/grants, and tuition waivers (partial) available. Support available to part-time students. Financial award application deadline: 3/10; financial award applicants required to submit FAFSA. *Faculty research:* Spinal cord injury, geriatrics, health economics, health psychology, behavioral medicine. Total annual research expenditures: $2.7 million. *Unit head:* Dr. Mark S. Sothmann, Dean, 843-792-3328, Fax: 843-792-3322, E-mail: sothmann@musc.edu. *Application contact:* Lauren Smith, Recruitment and Student Affairs Coordinator, 843-792-8476, Fax: 843-792-0253, E-mail: smilau@musc.edu.

Mercy College, School of Health and Natural Sciences, Dobbs Ferry, NY 10522-1189. Offers communication disorders (MS); nursing (MS), including nursing administration (MS, Certificate), nursing education (MS, Certificate); nursing education (Certificate), including nursing administration (MS, Certificate), nursing education (MS, Certificate); occupational therapy (MS); physical therapy (MS, DPT); physician assistant (MS), including physician assistant studies. Part-time and evening/weekend programs available. Postbaccalaureate distance learning degree programs offered (minimal on-campus study). *Faculty:* 20 full-time (17 women), 17 part-time/adjunct (5 women). *Students:* 360 full-time (287 women), 189 part-time (168 women); includes 212 minority (95 African Americans, 1 American Indian/Alaska Native, 56 Asian Americans or Pacific Islanders, 60 Hispanic Americans), 22 international. Average age 34. 687 applicants, 26% accepted, 149 enrolled. In 2009, 130 master's, 16 doctorates, 3 other advanced degrees awarded. *Entrance requirements:* For master's, interview, resume, essay, letters of recommendation; for doctorate, 2 references, typewritten essay, work experience, minimum GPA of 3.0. Additional exam requirements/recommendations for international students: Required—TOEFL (minimum score 600 paper-based; 250 computer-based; 100 iBT). *Application deadline:* For fall admission, 8/1 for international students. Applications are processed on a rolling basis. Application fee: $65. Electronic applications accepted. *Expenses:* Tuition: Full-time $13,158; part-time $731 per credit. Required fees: $500. Tuition and fees vary according to degree level and program. *Financial support:* In 2009–10, 1 student received support. Career-related internships or fieldwork, Federal Work-Study, scholarships/grants, and unspecified assistantships available. Financial award applicants required to submit FAFSA. *Unit head:* Dr. Pat Chute, Dean, 914-674-7746, E-mail: pchute@mercy.edu. *Application contact:* Dr. Pat Chute, Dean, 914-674-7746, E-mail: pchute@mercy.edu.

MGH Institute of Health Professions, Graduate Programs, Boston, MA 02129-4557. Offers MS, MSN, DNP, DPT, Certificate. Part-time and evening/weekend programs available. Postbaccalaureate distance learning degree programs offered (no on-campus study). *Faculty:* 62 full-time (52 women), 22 part-time/adjunct (21 women). *Students:* 552 full-time (462 women), 278 part-time (227 women); includes 106 minority (30 African Americans, 2 American Indian/Alaska Native, 60 Asian Americans or Pacific Islanders, 14 Hispanic Americans). Average age 31. 1,676 applicants, 48% accepted, 418 enrolled. In 2009, 119 master's, 115 doctorates, 37 other advanced degrees awarded. *Degree requirements:* For master's, thesis optional; for doctorate, thesis/dissertation optional. *Entrance requirements:* For master's, GRE General Test. Additional exam requirements/recommendations for international students: Required—TOEFL (minimum score 550 paper-based; 213 computer-based; 80 iBT). *Application deadline:* For fall admission, 1/1 priority date for domestic students, 3/1 for international students; for winter admission, 11/1 priority date for domestic students, 7/1 for international students; for spring admission, 3/1 priority date for domestic students, 11/1 for international students. Application fee: $50. Electronic applications accepted. *Expenses:* Tuition: Part-time $943 per credit. Required fees: $943 per credit. Tuition and fees vary according to course load. *Financial support:* In 2009–10, 543 students received support, including 56 research assistantships; teaching assistantships, career-related internships or fieldwork, scholarships/grants, traineeships, tuition waivers (partial), and unspecified assistantships also available. Support available to part-time students. Financial award application deadline: 3/1; financial award applicants required to submit FAFSA. *Faculty research:* Long-term care, pain mechanisms, communication disorders, patient self-care, disability in the elderly. *Unit head:* Dr. Janis P. Bellack, President, 617-726-8002, Fax: 617-726-3716, E-mail: jbellack@mghihp.edu. *Application contact:* Maureen Rika Judd, Manager of Admissions, 617-726-6069, Fax: 617-726-8010, E-mail: admissions@mghihp.edu.

Midwestern University, Downers Grove Campus, College of Health Sciences, Illinois Campus, Downers Grove, IL 60515-1235. Offers MA, MBS, MMS, MOT, DPT, Psy D. *Accreditation:* AOTA (one or more programs are accredited). *Faculty:* 37 full-time (28 women). *Students:* 539 full-time (435 women), 16 part-time (8 women); includes 60 minority (10 African Americans, 33 Asian Americans or Pacific Islanders, 17 Hispanic Americans), 4 international. Average age 25. 1,425 applicants, 33% accepted, 221 enrolled. In 2009, 96 master's, 28 doctorates awarded. *Entrance requirements:* For master's, GRE General Test. *Application deadline:* Applications are processed on a rolling basis. Application fee: $50. *Expenses:* Contact institution. *Financial support:* In 2009–10, 229 students received support. Federal Work-Study, institutionally sponsored loans, and scholarships/grants available. Financial award applicants required to submit FAFSA. *Unit head:* Dr. Jacquelyn J. Smith, Dean, 630-515-6388. *Application contact:* Michael Laken, Director of Admissions, 630-515-6171, Fax: 630-971-6086, E-mail: admissil@midwestern.edu.

Midwestern University, Glendale Campus, College of Health Sciences, Arizona Campus, Glendale, AZ 85308. Offers DPM, MA, MBS, MCVS, MHPE, MMS, MOT, MS, Psy D, Certificate. Part-time programs available. *Faculty:* 44 full-time (21 women), 4 part-time/adjunct (3 women). *Students:* 538 full-time (329 women), 11 part-time (8 women); includes 98 minority (20 African Americans, 4 American Indian/Alaska Native, 48 Asian Americans or Pacific Islanders, 26 Hispanic Americans). Average age 27. 1,349 applicants, 31% accepted, 230 enrolled. In 2009, 107 master's awarded. *Entrance requirements:* MCAT, DAT, GRE or PCAT, 2 professional letters of recommendation. *Application deadline:* For fall admission, 6/4 for domestic students. Applications are processed on a rolling basis. Application fee: $50. *Expenses:* Contact institution. *Financial support:* Federal Work-Study available. *Unit head:* Dr. Jacquelyn Smith, Dean, 623-572-3601, Fax: 623-572-3601. *Application contact:* James Walter, Director of Admissions, 888-247-9277, Fax: 623-572-3229, E-mail: admissaz@midwestern.edu.

Minnesota State University Mankato, College of Graduate Studies, College of Allied Health and Nursing, Mankato, MN 56001. Offers MA, MS, MSN, MT, DNP, SP. Part-time programs available. *Students:* 124 full-time (92 women), 209 part-time (138 women). *Degree requirements:* For master's, comprehensive exam; for SP, thesis. *Entrance requirements:* For master's, GRE (for some programs), minimum GPA of 3.0 during previous 2 years; for SP, GRE General Test, minimum GPA of 3.0. *Application deadline:* Applications are processed on a rolling basis.

Application fee: $40. Electronic applications accepted. *Expenses:* Tuition, state resident: full-time $5364. Tuition, nonresident: full-time $8314. *Financial support:* Research assistantships with full tuition reimbursements, teaching assistantships with full tuition reimbursements, career-related internships or fieldwork, Federal Work-Study, institutionally sponsored loans, and unspecified assistantships available. Support available to part-time students. Financial award application deadline: 3/15; financial award applicants required to submit FAFSA. *Unit head:* Dr. Kaye Herth, Dean, 507-389-6315. *Application contact:* 507-389-2321, E-mail: grad@mnsu.edu.

Misericordia University, College of Health Sciences, Dallas, PA 18612-1098. Offers MSN, MSOT, MSPT, MSSLP, DPT, OTD. Part-time and evening/weekend programs available. *Faculty:* 19 full-time (14 women), 15 part-time/adjunct (11 women). *Students:* 89 full-time (76 women), 126 part-time (108 women); includes 1 minority (Hispanic American). Average age 29. In 2009, 91 master's, 11 doctorates awarded. *Entrance requirements:* For master's, GRE General Test or MAT, references. Additional exam requirements/recommendations for international students: Required—TOEFL. *Application deadline:* Applications are processed on a rolling basis. Application fee: $25. Electronic applications accepted. *Financial support:* In 2009–10, 125 students received support; teaching assistantships, career-related internships or fieldwork, Federal Work-Study, scholarships/grants, traineeships, and tuition waivers (partial) available. Support available to part-time students. Financial award application deadline: 6/30; financial award applicants required to submit FAFSA. *Unit head:* Dr. Jean A. Dyer, Dean, 570-674-8152, E-mail: jdyer@misericordia.edu. *Application contact:* Larree Brown, Coordinator of Part-Time Undergraduate and Graduate Programs, 570-674-6451, Fax: 570-674-6232, E-mail: lbrown@misericordia.edu.

Moravian College, Moravian College Comenius Center, Business and Management Programs, Bethlehem, PA 18018-6650. Offers general management (MBA); health care management (MBA); leadership (MSHRM); learning and performance management (MSHRM); supply chain management (MBA). Part-time and evening/weekend programs available. *Faculty:* 6 full-time (2 women), 10 part-time/adjunct (3 women). *Students:* 59 part-time (30 women). Average age 29. 27 applicants, 74% accepted, 10 enrolled. In 2009, 20 master's awarded. *Entrance requirements:* For master's, GMAT. Additional exam requirements/recommendations for international students: Required—TOEFL (minimum score 550 paper-based; 260 computer-based; 90 iBT). *Application deadline:* Applications are processed on a rolling basis. Application fee: $40. *Expenses:* Contact institution. *Financial support:* In 2009–10, 1 fellowship with full tuition reimbursement was awarded. *Faculty research:* Leadership, change management, human resources. *Unit head:* Dr. William A. Kleintop, Associate Dean for Business and Management Programs, 610-507-1400, Fax: 610-861-1400, E-mail: comenius@moravian.edu. *Application contact:* Linda J. Doyle, Information Contact, 610-861-1400, Fax: 610-861-1466, E-mail: mba@moravian.edu.

Mountain State University, Graduate Studies, Program in Health Science, Beckley, WV 25802-9003. Offers MHS. Part-time and evening/weekend programs available. Postbaccalaureate distance learning degree programs offered (no on-campus study). *Faculty:* 5 full-time (2 women), 9 part-time/adjunct (3 women). *Students:* 16 full-time (9 women); includes 2 minority (both African Americans), 5 international. Average age 32. 22 applicants, 64% accepted, 13 enrolled. In 2009, 5 master's awarded. *Degree requirements:* For master's, thesis or alternative. *Entrance requirements:* Additional exam requirements/recommendations for international students: Required—TOEFL (minimum score 550 paper-based; 213 computer-based); Recommended—IELTS (minimum score 6.5). *Application deadline:* For fall admission, 5/31 priority date for domestic and international students. Applications are processed on a rolling basis. Application fee: $25 ($50 for international students). Electronic applications accepted. *Expenses:* Tuition: Full-time $6450. Tuition and fees vary according to program. *Financial support:* Federal Work-Study, scholarships/grants, and unspecified assistantships available. Support available to part-time students. Financial award applicants required to submit FAFSA. *Unit head:* Dr. William White, Interim Dean, School of Graduate Studies/Dean, School of Leadership and Professional Development, 304-929-1658, Fax: 304-929-1637, E-mail: wwhite@mountainstate.edu. *Application contact:* Anita Diaz, Enrollment Coordinator of Graduate Studies, 304-461-3213, Fax: 304-929-1637, E-mail: adiaz@mountainstate.edu.

New Jersey City University, Graduate Studies and Continuing Education, College of Professional Studies, Department of Health Sciences, Jersey City, NJ 07305-1597. Offers community health education (MS); health administration (MS); school health education (MS). Part-time and evening/weekend programs available. *Faculty:* 3. *Students:* 8 full-time (6 women), 42 part-time (32 women); includes 18 minority (10 African Americans, 1 American Indian/Alaska Native, 3 Asian Americans or Pacific Islanders, 4 Hispanic Americans), 3 international. Average age 41. In 2009, 21 master's awarded. *Degree requirements:* For master's, thesis or alternative, internship. *Entrance requirements:* For master's, GRE General Test or MAT. Additional exam requirements/recommendations for international students: Required—TOEFL. *Application deadline:* For fall admission, 8/1 priority date for domestic students; for spring admission, 12/1 for domestic students. Applications are processed on a rolling basis. Application fee: $0. *Expenses:* Tuition, area resident: Part-time $456.75 per credit. Tuition, nonresident: part-time $842.55 per credit. Required fees: $65 per term. *Financial support:* Career-related internships or fieldwork and unspecified assistantships available. *Unit head:* Dr. Gail Gordon, Chairperson, 201-200-3431, E-mail: ggordon@njcu.edu. *Application contact:* Dr. Gail Gordon, Chairperson, 201-200-3431, E-mail: ggordon@njcu.edu.

Northeastern University, Bouvé College of Health Sciences Graduate School, Boston, MA 02115-5096. Offers Pharm D, MPH, MS, MS Ed, PSM, Au D, DPT, PhD, CAGS, CAS, MS/MBA. *Accreditation:* ACPE (one or more programs are accredited). Part-time and evening/weekend programs available. *Students:* 904 full-time (705 women), 160 part-time (136 women). 1,844 applicants, 35% accepted. In 2009, 338 master's, 71 doctorates, 31 other advanced degrees awarded. *Degree requirements:* For doctorate, thesis/dissertation, qualifying exam; for other advanced degree, comprehensive exam. *Entrance requirements:* For Pharm D, prior admission to undergraduate pharmacy program; for master's and other advanced degree, GRE General Test or MAT; for doctorate, GRE General Test. Additional exam requirements/recommendations for international students: Required—TOEFL. Application fee: $50. Electronic applications accepted. *Financial support:* Fellowships, research assistantships with full tuition reimbursements, teaching assistantships with full tuition reimbursements, career-related internships or fieldwork, Federal Work-Study, institutionally sponsored loans, scholarships/grants, traineeships, tuition waivers (full and partial), and administrative assistantships available. Support available to part-time students. Financial award application deadline: 3/1; financial award applicants required to submit FAFSA. *Faculty research:* Counseling, physical therapy, biomedical sciences, cardiopulmonary sciences, nursing. *Unit head:* Suzanne B. Greenberg, Director, 617-373-3195, E-mail: s.greenberg@neu.edu. *Application contact:* Margaret Schnabel, Director of Graduate Admissions, 617-373-2708, E-mail: bouvegrad@neu.edu.

Northern Arizona University, Graduate College, College of Health and Human Services, Flagstaff, AZ 86011. Offers M Ad, MPH, MS, MSN, DPT, Certificate, PPDPT. *Accreditation:* APTA (one or more programs are accredited). Part-time programs available. *Faculty:* 85 full-time (69 women). *Students:* 261 full-time (180 women), 73 part-time (48 women); includes 37 minority (3 African Americans, 10 American Indian/Alaska Native, 9 Asian Americans or Pacific Islanders, 15 Hispanic Americans), 6 international. Average age 31. 192 applicants, 63% accepted. In 2009, 56 master's, 41 doctorates awarded. Application fee: $65. *Financial support:* In 2009–10, 4 research assistantships, 5 teaching assistantships were awarded; fellowships, career-related internships or fieldwork, traineeships, tuition waivers (full and partial), and unspecified assistantships also available. *Unit head:* Leslie Schulz, Executive Dean, 928-523-4331. *Application contact:* Leslie Schulz, Executive Dean, 928-523-4331.

Nova Southeastern University, Health Professions Division, College of Allied Health and Nursing, Fort Lauderdale, FL 33314-7796. Offers MH Sc, MMS, MOT, MSN, Au D, DHSc, DPT, OTD, PhD, TDPT. Postbaccalaureate distance learning degree programs offered (minimal on-campus study). *Faculty:* 43 full-time (25 women), 8 part-time/adjunct (4 women). *Students:* 790 full-time (559 women), 489 part-time (341 women); includes 381 minority (138 African

Americans, 5 American Indian/Alaska Native, 92 Asian Americans or Pacific Islanders, 146 Hispanic Americans), 13 international. In 2009, 196 master's, 158 doctorates awarded. *Degree requirements:* For master's, thesis; for doctorate, comprehensive exam, thesis/dissertation. *Entrance requirements:* For master's and doctorate, GRE General Test. *Application deadline:* Applications are processed on a rolling basis. Application fee: $50. *Expenses:* Contact institution. *Financial support:* Teaching assistantships, institutionally sponsored loans and unspecified assistantships available. *Unit head:* Dr. Richard Davis, Dean, 954-262-1203, E-mail: redavis@nova.edu. *Application contact:* Marla Frolinger, Admissions Counselor, 954-262-1100, E-mail: marlaf@nova.edu.

Oakland University, Graduate Study and Lifelong Learning, School of Health Sciences, Rochester, MI 48309-4401. Offers MS, MSPT, DPT, Dr Sc PT, Certificate. *Accreditation:* APTA (one or more programs are accredited). *Entrance requirements:* For master's, minimum GPA of 3.0 for unconditional admission; for doctorate, GRE General Test. Additional exam requirements/recommendations for international students: Required—TOEFL (minimum score 550 paper-based; 213 computer-based). Electronic applications accepted. *Expenses:* Contact institution. *Faculty research:* Community emergency response team preparedness; appropriateness, comprehensiveness, sensitivity, and practicality of outcome measures; assessing effectiveness of innovative intervention program for spinal cord injuries.

The Ohio State University, College of Medicine, School of Allied Medical Professions, Columbus, OH 43210. Offers allied medicine (MS); circulation technology (MS); occupational therapy (MOT); physical therapy (MPT). *Accreditation:* AOTA; APTA. Part-time programs available. *Degree requirements:* For master's, thesis or alternative. *Entrance requirements:* Additional exam requirements/recommendations for international students: Required—TOEFL (paper-based 550; computer-based 213) or Michigan English Language Assessment Battery (82). Electronic applications accepted. *Expenses:* Tuition, state resident: full-time $10,683. Tuition, nonresident: full-time $25,923. Tuition and fees vary according to course load and program. *Faculty research:* Geriatrics, quality assurance, nutrition, interdisciplinary health care.

Old Dominion University, College of Health Sciences, Norfolk, VA 23529. Offers MPH, MS, MSN, DNP, DPT, PhD. Part-time and evening/weekend programs available. Postbaccalaureate distance learning degree programs offered (minimal on-campus study). *Faculty:* 42 full-time (31 women), 17 part-time/adjunct (14 women). *Students:* 315 full-time (264 women), 188 part-time (168 women); includes 122 minority (74 African Americans, 3 American Indian/Alaska Native, 32 Asian Americans or Pacific Islanders, 13 Hispanic Americans), 9 international. Average age 34. 688 applicants, 48% accepted, 258 enrolled. In 2009, 107 master's, 41 doctorates awarded. *Degree requirements:* For doctorate, comprehensive exam. *Entrance requirements:* Additional exam requirements/recommendations for international students: Required—TOEFL. *Application deadline:* Applications are processed on a rolling basis. Application fee: $40. Electronic applications accepted. *Expenses:* Tuition, state resident: full-time $8112; part-time $338 per credit. Tuition, nonresident: full-time $20,256; part-time $844 per credit. Required fees: $119 per semester. One-time fee: $50. *Financial support:* In 2009–10, 210 students received support, including 6 fellowships with full tuition reimbursements available (averaging $15,000 per year), 9 research assistantships with tuition reimbursements available (averaging $10,000 per year), 9 teaching assistantships with tuition reimbursements available (averaging $10,000 per year); career-related internships or fieldwork, institutionally sponsored loans, scholarships/grants, traineeships, tuition waivers (partial), and unspecified assistantships also available. Support available to part-time students. Financial award application deadline: 2/15; financial award applicants required to submit FAFSA. *Faculty research:* Health promotion and wellness, health care ethics, health policy, health services, cultural competency. Total annual research expenditures: $1.6 million. *Unit head:* Dr. Andrew Balas, Dean, 757-683-4960, Fax: 757-683-3674, E-mail: abalas@odu.edu. *Application contact:* Dr. Andrew Balas, Dean, 757-683-4960, Fax: 757-683-3674, E-mail: abalas@odu.edu.

Quinnipiac University, School of Health Sciences, Hamden, CT 06518-1940. Offers MHS, MHS, MOT, MPT, MS, MSN, DPT, Post Master's Certificate. *Accreditation:* AOTA. *Faculty:* 46 full-time (31 women), 56 part-time/adjunct (17 women). *Students:* 505 full-time (386 women), 147 part-time (121 women); includes 74 minority (21 African Americans, 28 Asian Americans or Pacific Islanders, 25 Hispanic Americans), 22 international. 1,126 applicants, 23% accepted, 216 enrolled. In 2009, 176 master's, 19 doctorates awarded. *Entrance requirements:* Additional exam requirements/recommendations for international students: Required—TOEFL (minimum score 575 paper-based; 233 computer-based; 90 iBT), IELTS (minimum score 6.5). *Application deadline:* For fall admission, 4/30 priority date for international students; for spring admission, 9/15 priority date for international students. Applications are processed on a rolling basis. Application fee: $45. Electronic applications accepted. *Expenses:* Tuition: Full-time $16,030; part-time $770 per credit. Required fees: $630; $35 per credit. *Financial support:* Career-related internships or fieldwork, traineeships, tuition waivers (partial), and unspecified assistantships available. Support available to part-time students. Financial award application deadline: 4/15; financial award applicants required to submit FAFSA. *Unit head:* Dr. Edward O'Connor, Dean, 203-582-8710, Fax: 203-582-8706. *Application contact:* Kristin Parent, Assistant Director of Graduate Health Sciences Admissions, 800-462-1944, Fax: 203-582-3443, E-mail: kristin.parent@quinnipiac.edu.

Regis University, Rueckert-Hartman School for Health Professions, Denver, CO 80221-1099. Offers clinical leadership for physician assistants (MS); family nurse practitioner (MSN); health informatics (Postbaccalaureate Certificate); health services administration (MS); healthcare education (Certificate); leadership in healthcare systems (MSN); neonatal nurse practitioner (MSN); nursing (MSN); pharmacy (Pharm D); physical therapy (DPT, TDPT). *Entrance requirements:* Additional exam requirements/recommendations for international students: Required—TOEFL (minimum score 550 paper-based; 213 computer-based; 82 iBT). Electronic applications accepted. *Expenses:* Contact institution. *Faculty research:* Normal and pathological balance and gait research, normal/pathological upper limb motor control/biomechanics, exercise energy/metabolism research, optical treatment protocols for therapeutic modalities.

Rosalind Franklin University of Medicine and Science, College of Health Professions, North Chicago, IL 60064-3095. Offers MS, D Sc, DPT, PhD, TDPT, Certificate. Part-time programs available. Postbaccalaureate distance learning degree programs offered (minimal on-campus study). *Faculty:* 39 full-time (26 women), 48 part-time/adjunct (22 women). *Students:* 38 full-time (26 women), 48 part-time (22 women). Terminal master's awarded for partial completion of doctoral program. *Application deadline:* Applications are processed on a rolling basis. Application fee: $50. *Financial support:* Fellowships, research assistantships, teaching assistantships, career-related internships or fieldwork, Federal Work-Study, institutionally sponsored loans, scholarships/grants, and tuition waivers (partial) available. Support available to part-time students. Financial award applicants required to submit FAFSA. *Unit head:* Dr. Wendy Rheault, Dean, 847-578-8805, E-mail: wendy.rheault@rosalindfranklin.edu. *Application contact:* Melissa Knox, Admissions Officer, 847-578-8772, Fax: 847-775-6559, E-mail: melissa.knox@rosalindfranklin.edu.

Saint Louis University, Graduate School, Doisy College of Health Sciences, St. Louis, MO 63103-2097. Offers MAT, MMS, MOT, MS, MSN, MSN-R, DNP, DPT, PhD, Certificate. Part-time programs available. *Degree requirements:* For master's, comprehensive exam. *Entrance requirements:* Additional exam requirements/recommendations for international students: Required—TOEFL (minimum score 525 paper-based; 194 computer-based).

Seton Hall University, School of Health and Medical Sciences, Department of Graduate Programs in Health Sciences, South Orange, NJ 07079-2697. Offers MS, PhD. Part-time and evening/weekend programs available. Terminal master's awarded for partial completion of doctoral program. *Degree requirements:* For master's, research project; for doctorate, comprehensive exam (for some programs), thesis/dissertation, candidacy exam, practicum, research projects. *Entrance requirements:* For master's, interview, minimum GPA of 3.0, letters of recommendation; for doctorate, GRE (preferred), interview, minimum GPA of 3.0, letters of recommendation. Additional exam requirements/recommendations for international students: Required—TOEFL. Electronic applications accepted. *Faculty research:* Movement science, motor learning, dual tasks, clinical decision making, online education, teaching strategies.

Shenandoah University, School of Health Professions, Winchester, VA 22601-5195. Offers MS, MSN, DNP, DPT, Certificate. Part-time programs available. Postbaccalaureate distance learning degree programs offered. *Faculty:* 30 full-time (25 women), 22 part-time/adjunct (18 women). *Students:* 310 full-time (247 women), 213 part-time (181 women); includes 45 minority (13 African Americans, 1 American Indian/Alaska Native, 17 Asian Americans or Pacific Islanders, 14 Hispanic Americans), 7 international. Average age 33. 1,160 applicants, 29% accepted, 236 enrolled. In 2009, 61 master's, 84 doctorates, 6 other advanced degrees awarded. *Entrance requirements:* For master's and doctorate, GRE. Additional exam requirements/recommendations for international students: Required—TOEFL (minimum score 550 paper-based; 213 computer-based; 79 iBT), IELTS (minimum score 6.5). *Application deadline:* Applications are processed on a rolling basis. Application fee: $30. Electronic applications accepted. *Expenses:* Tuition: Full-time $11,925; part-time $695 per credit. Required fees: $400 per semester. *Financial support:* Application deadline: 3/15. *Application contact:* Information Contact, 540-665-5500, Fax: 540-665-5519.

South Carolina State University, School of Graduate Studies, Department of Health Sciences, Orangeburg, SC 29117-0001. Offers speech/language pathology (MA). *Accreditation:* ASHA. Part-time and evening/weekend programs available. *Degree requirements:* For master's, thesis optional, departmental qualifying exam. *Entrance requirements:* For master's, GRE or NTE, minimum GPA of 3.0. Electronic applications accepted. *Expenses:* Tuition, state resident: part-time $470 per credit hour. Tuition, nonresident: part-time $924 per credit hour.

Southwestern Oklahoma State University, College of Professional and Graduate Studies, School of Behavioral Sciences and Education, Specialization in Health Sciences and Microbiology, Weatherford, OK 73096-3098. Offers M Ed.

Temple University, Health Sciences Center and Graduate School, College of Health Professions, Philadelphia, PA 19122-6096. Offers Ed M, MA, MOT, MPH, MS, MSN, DPT, PhD. *Accreditation:* APTA (one or more programs are accredited). Part-time and evening/weekend programs available. Postbaccalaureate distance learning degree programs offered (minimal on-campus study). *Degree requirements:* For doctorate, thesis/dissertation. *Faculty research:* Balance dysfunction, repetitive stress injury, neurobehavioral disorders, bilingual speech-language therapy, smoking cessation.

Tennessee State University, The School of Graduate Studies and Research, College of Health Sciences, Nashville, TN 37209-1561. Offers MPT, MS, DPT. *Accreditation:* ASHA (one or more programs are accredited). Part-time and evening/weekend programs available. *Entrance requirements:* For master's, GRE General Test, MAT, minimum GPA of 3.5. Electronic applications accepted. *Faculty research:* Community problems of the elderly, language disorders in children, aphasia, sickle cell disturbances, regional and foreign dialects.

Texas Christian University, Harris College of Nursing and Health Sciences, Fort Worth, TX 76129-0002. Offers MS, MSN, MSNA, DNP. Part-time programs available. Postbaccalaureate distance learning degree programs offered (minimal on-campus study). *Degree requirements:* For master's, professional project. *Entrance requirements:* For master's, GRE General Test. *Application deadline:* For fall admission, 2/1 for domestic students. Application fee: $0. *Expenses:* Tuition: Full-time $17,640; part-time $980 per credit hour. Tuition and fees vary according to program. *Financial support:* Application deadline: 2/1. *Unit head:* Dr. Paulette Burns, Dean, 817-257-6742, Fax: 817-257-6751. *Application contact:* Sybil J. White, Assistant to the Dean of Graduate Studies, 817-257-6750, Fax: 817-257-6751, E-mail: s.white@tcu.edu.

Texas State University–San Marcos, Graduate School, College of Health Professions, San Marcos, TX 78666. Offers MA, MHA, MS, MSCD, DPT. Part-time and evening/weekend programs available. *Faculty:* 27 full-time (11 women), 6 part-time/adjunct (5 women). *Students:* 167 full-time (117 women), 54 part-time (39 women); includes 71 minority (11 African Americans, 2 American Indian/Alaska Native, 10 Asian Americans or Pacific Islanders, 48 Hispanic Americans), 5 international. Average age 27. 238 applicants, 32% accepted, 63 enrolled. In 2009, 102 master's awarded. *Degree requirements:* For master's, comprehensive exam. *Entrance requirements:* For master's, GRE General Test (for some programs); for doctorate, GRE (minimum score of 1000 Verbal and Quantitative), bachelor's degree in physical therapy. Additional exam requirements/recommendations for international students: Required—TOEFL (minimum score 550 paper-based; 213 computer-based). *Application deadline:* For fall admission, 6/15 for domestic students, 6/1 for international students; for spring admission, 10/15 priority date for domestic students, 10/1 for international students. Applications are processed on a rolling basis. Application fee: $40 ($90 for international students). Electronic applications accepted. *Expenses:* Tuition, state resident: full-time $5784; part-time $241 per credit hour. Tuition, nonresident: full-time $13,224; part-time $551 per credit hour. Required fees: $1728; $48 per credit hour. $306. Tuition and fees vary according to course load. *Financial support:* In 2009–10, 195 students received support, including 7 research assistantships (averaging $2,304 per year), 23 teaching assistantships (averaging $2,625 per year); fellowships, career-related internships or fieldwork, Federal Work-Study, institutionally sponsored loans, scholarships/grants, and stipends also available. Support available to part-time students. Financial award application deadline: 4/1; financial award applicants required to submit FAFSA. *Faculty research:* Project La Costa, MRSA in Texas county jail, thoracic manipulation, medical ID theft, care gap analysis. Total annual research expenditures: $126,457. *Unit head:* Dr. Ruth Welborn, Dean, 512-245-3300, Fax: 512-245-3791, E-mail: mw01@txstate.edu. *Application contact:* Dr. J. Michael Willoughby, Dean of Graduate School, 512-245-2581, Fax: 512-245-8365, E-mail: gradcollege@txstate.edu.

Texas Tech University Health Sciences Center, School of Allied Health Sciences, Lubbock, TX 79430. Offers MAT, MOT, MPAS, MPT, MRC, MS, Au D, DPT, PhD, Sc D. *Accreditation:* APTA (one or more programs are accredited). *Faculty:* 75 full-time (38 women). *Students:* 738 full-time (528 women), 103 part-time (56 women); includes 221 minority (55 African Americans, 7 American Indian/Alaska Native, 39 Asian Americans or Pacific Islanders, 120 Hispanic Americans), 3 international. Average age 29. 1,636 applicants, 27% accepted, 443 enrolled. In 2009, 172 master's, 82 doctorates awarded. *Entrance requirements:* Additional exam requirements/recommendations for international students: Required—TOEFL, IELTS. Application fee: $35. Electronic applications accepted. *Financial support:* Fellowships, research assistantships, teaching assistantships, career-related internships or fieldwork, institutionally sponsored loans, scholarships/grants, and tuition waivers (full) available. Financial award application deadline: 9/1; financial award applicants required to submit FAFSA. *Unit head:* Lindsay R. Johnson, Assistant Dean for Admissions and Student Affairs, 806-743-3220, Fax: 806-743-2994, E-mail: lindsay.johnson@ttuhsc.edu. *Application contact:* Jeri Moravcik, Assistant Director of Admissions and Student Affairs, 806-743-3220, Fax: 806-743-2994, E-mail: jeri.moravcik@ttuhsc.edu.

Texas Woman's University, Graduate School, College of Health Sciences, Denton, TX 76201. Offers MA, MHA, MOT, MS, DPT, Ed D, PhD. Part-time and evening/weekend programs available. Postbaccalaureate distance learning degree programs offered. *Faculty:* 107 full-time (80 women), 14 part-time/adjunct (12 women). *Students:* 932 full-time (816 women), 541 part-time (449 women); includes 446 minority (140 African Americans, 10 American Indian/Alaska Native, 117 Asian Americans or Pacific Islanders, 179 Hispanic Americans), 95 international. Average age 33. 1,188 applicants, 88% accepted, 328 enrolled. In 2009, 292 master's, 46 doctorates awarded. Terminal master's awarded for partial completion of doctoral program. *Degree requirements:* For doctorate, thesis/dissertation, qualifying exam. *Entrance requirements:* For master's and doctorate, minimum GPA of 3.0. Additional exam requirements/recommendations for international students: Required—TOEFL (minimum score 550 paper-based; 213 computer-based; 79 iBT). *Application deadline:* For fall admission, 7/1 priority date for domestic students, 3/1 for international students; for spring admission, 12/1 priority date for domestic students, 7/1 for international students. Applications are processed on a rolling basis. Application fee: $50. Electronic applications accepted. *Expenses:* Tuition, state resident:

Allied Health—General

Texas Woman's University (continued)
full-time $3564; part-time $198 per credit hour. Tuition, nonresident: full-time $8550; part-time $475 per credit hour. Required fees: $69.26 per credit hour. Tuition and fees vary according to course load. *Financial support:* In 2009–10, 503 students received support, including 51 research assistantships (averaging $10,484 per year), 15 teaching assistantships (averaging $10,820 per year); career-related internships or fieldwork, Federal Work-Study, institutionally sponsored loans, scholarships/grants, traineeships, health care benefits, and unspecified assistantships also available. Support available to part-time students. Financial award application deadline: 3/1; financial award applicants required to submit FAFSA. *Unit head:* Dr. Jimmy Ishee, Dean, 940-898-2852, Fax: 940-898-2853, E-mail: jishee@twu.edu. *Application contact:* Samuel Wheeler, Assistant Director of Admissions, 940-898-3188, Fax: 940-898-3081, E-mail: wheelersr@twu.edu.

Towson University, College of Graduate Studies and Research, Program in Health Science, Towson, MD 21252-0001. Offers MS. Part-time and evening/weekend programs available. *Degree requirements:* For master's, thesis optional. *Entrance requirements:* For master's, previous course work in health sciences, minimum GPA of 2.75. Electronic applications accepted. *Faculty research:* Issues of the aging, drug and alcohol use prevention, health education, health policy, adolescent/student health.

University at Buffalo, the State University of New York, Graduate School, School of Public Health and Health Professions, Buffalo, NY 14260. Offers MA, MPH, MS, DPT, PhD, Certificate. Part-time programs available. *Faculty:* 64 full-time (30 women), 43 part-time/adjunct (26 women). *Students:* 393 full-time (242 women), 71 part-time (53 women); includes 75 minority (24 African Americans, 2 American Indian/Alaska Native, 38 Asian Americans or Pacific Islanders, 11 Hispanic Americans), 83 international. Average age 30. 539 applicants, 52% accepted, 132 enrolled. In 2009, 87 master's, 42 doctorates, 1 other advanced degree awarded. Terminal master's awarded for partial completion of doctoral program. *Degree requirements:* For master's, comprehensive exam (for some programs), thesis (for some programs); for doctorate, comprehensive exam, thesis/dissertation. *Entrance requirements:* For master's and doctorate, GRE General Test. Additional exam requirements/recommendations for international students: Required—TOEFL (minimum score 250 computer-based; 79 iBT). *Application deadline:* For fall admission, 2/1 for domestic and international students. Application fee: $50. Electronic applications accepted. *Financial support:* In 2009–10, 29 students received support, including 12 fellowships with full tuition reimbursements available (averaging $2,500 per year), 2 research assistantships with full tuition reimbursements available (averaging $15,000 per year), 15 teaching assistantships with full tuition reimbursements available (averaging $8,500 per year); career-related internships or fieldwork, Federal Work-Study, institutionally sponsored loans, scholarships/grants, tuition waivers (full and partial), and unspecified assistantships also available. Financial award application deadline: 3/15; financial award applicants required to submit FAFSA. *Faculty research:* Public health, epidemiology, rehabilitation, assistive technology, exercise and nutrition science. Total annual research expenditures: $8.7 million. *Unit head:* Dr. Lynn Kozlowski, Dean, 716-829-6951, Fax: 716-829-6040, E-mail: lk22@buffalo.edu. *Application contact:* Diane Gayles, Associate Director, Student Advisement and Recruitment Services, 716-829-6769, Fax: 716-829-2034, E-mail: sphhp-mph@buffalo.edu.

The University of Alabama at Birmingham, School of Health Professions, Birmingham, AL 35294. Offers MNA, MS, MSHA, MSHI, MSPAS, D Sc, DPT, PhD. *Accreditation:* AANA/CANAEP (one or more programs are accredited); APTA (one or more programs are accredited); CAHME (one or more programs are accredited). Part-time programs available. *Degree requirements:* For doctorate, thesis/dissertation. Electronic applications accepted. *Expenses:* Contact institution.

University of Arkansas at Little Rock, Graduate School, College of Professional Studies, Department of Health Sciences, Little Rock, AR 72204-1099. Offers MS. Part-time and evening/weekend programs available. *Degree requirements:* For master's, directed study or residency. *Entrance requirements:* For master's, GMAT or GRE General Test, interview, minimum GPA of 2.75.

University of Connecticut, Graduate School, College of Agriculture and Natural Resources, Department of Allied Health Sciences, Storrs, CT 06269. Offers MS. *Accreditation:* APTA. *Faculty:* 13 full-time (7 women). *Students:* 18 full-time (16 women), 3 part-time (all women); includes 3 minority (1 African American, 1 Asian American or Pacific Islander, 1 Hispanic American), 3 international. Average age 25. 18 applicants, 11% accepted, 1 enrolled. In 2009, 5 master's awarded. *Degree requirements:* For master's, comprehensive exam. *Entrance requirements:* For master's, GRE General Test. Additional exam requirements/recommendations for international students: Required—TOEFL (minimum score 550 paper-based; 213 computer-based). *Application deadline:* For fall admission, 2/1 priority date for domestic and international students; for spring admission, 11/1 for domestic students, 10/1 for international students. Applications are processed on a rolling basis. Application fee: $55. Electronic applications accepted. *Expenses:* Tuition, state resident: full-time $4725; part-time $525 per credit. Tuition, nonresident: full-time $12,267; part-time $1363 per credit. Required fees: $346 per semester. Tuition and fees vary according to course load. *Financial support:* In 2009–10, 16 research assistantships with full tuition reimbursements, 2 teaching assistantships with full tuition reimbursements were awarded; fellowships, Federal Work-Study, scholarships/grants, health care benefits, and unspecified assistantships also available. Financial award application deadline: 2/1; financial award applicants required to submit FAFSA. *Unit head:* Lawrence Silbart, Head, 860-486-0028, Fax: 860-486-5375, E-mail: lawrence.silbart@uconn.edu. *Application contact:* Pouran D. Faghri, Chairperson, 860-486-0018, Fax: 860-486-5375, E-mail: pouran.faghri@uconn.edu.

University of Detroit Mercy, College of Health Professions, Detroit, MI 48221. Offers MHSA, MS, MSN, Certificate. *Entrance requirements:* For master's, GRE General Test, minimum GPA of 3.0. *Faculty research:* Research design, respiratory physiology, AIDS prevention, adolescent health, community, low income health education.

University of Florida, Graduate School, College of Public Health and Health Professions, Gainesville, FL 32611. Offers MHA, MHS, MOT, MPH, Au D, DPT, PhD. *Accreditation:* CAHME (one or more programs are accredited). Part-time programs available. *Degree requirements:* For doctorate, thesis/dissertation. *Entrance requirements:* For master's, GRE General Test; for doctorate, GRE General Test, minimum GPA of 3.0. Additional exam requirements/recommendations for international students: Required—TOEFL (minimum score 550 paper-based; 213 computer-based). Electronic applications accepted.

University of Illinois at Chicago, Graduate College, College of Applied Health Sciences, Chicago, IL 60607-7128. Offers MS, DPT, OTD, PhD. *Accreditation:* AOTA. Part-time programs available. *Degree requirements:* For doctorate, thesis/dissertation. *Entrance requirements:* For master's, GRE General Test, minimum GPA of 2.75. Additional exam requirements/recommendations for international students: Required—TOEFL. Electronic applications accepted. *Faculty research:* Care of the elderly, nutritional status for various diseases, immunohematology, computer-aided graphics.

The University of Kansas, University of Kansas Medical Center, School of Allied Health, Lawrence, KS 66045. Offers MA, MOT, MS, Au D, DPT, OTD, PhD, Certificate. Part-time programs available. Postbaccalaureate distance learning degree programs offered (minimal on-campus study). *Faculty:* 98 full-time, 67 part-time/adjunct. *Students:* 275 full-time (218 women), 119 part-time (87 women); includes 31 minority (11 African Americans, 5 American Indian/Alaska Native, 13 Asian Americans or Pacific Islanders, 2 Hispanic Americans), 55 international. Average age 28. 390 applicants, 41% accepted, 132 enrolled. In 2009, 69 master's, 59 doctorates awarded. *Entrance requirements:* Additional exam requirements/recommendations for international students: Required—TOEFL. Application fee: $60. Electronic applications accepted. *Expenses:* Tuition, state resident: full-time $6492; part-time $270.50 per credit hour. Tuition, nonresident: full-time $15,510; part-time $646.25 per credit hour. Required fees: $847; $70.56 per credit hour. Tuition and fees vary according to course load and program. *Financial support:* In 2009–10, 1 fellowship, 9 teaching assistantships with full tuition reimbursements (averaging $20,124 per year) were awarded; health care benefits and unspecified assistantships also available. Financial award applicants required to submit FAFSA. *Faculty research:* Diabetes, obesity, DHA in brain development, mapping the inner ear. Total annual research expenditures: $2.3 million. *Unit head:* Dr. Karen L. Miller, Dean, 913-588-5235, Fax: 913-588-5254, E-mail: kmiller@kumc.edu. *Application contact:* Moffett Ferguson, Student Affairs Coordinator, 913-588-5275, Fax: 913-588-5254, E-mail: mfergus1@kumc.edu.

University of Kentucky, Graduate School, College of Health Sciences, Lexington, KY 40506-0032. Offers MS, MSCD, MSHP, MSPAS, MSPT, MSRMP, DS, PhD. Part-time programs available. *Degree requirements:* For master's, comprehensive exam, thesis (for some programs). *Entrance requirements:* For master's, GRE General Test, minimum undergraduate GPA of 2.75; for doctorate, GRE General Test, minimum undergraduate GPA of 3.0. Additional exam requirements/recommendations for international students: Required—TOEFL (minimum score 550 paper-based; 213 computer-based). Electronic applications accepted.

University of Massachusetts Lowell, School of Health and Environment, Lowell, MA 01854-2881. Offers MS, DPT, PhD, Sc D, Certificate, Graduate Certificate. *Accreditation:* APTA (one or more programs are accredited). Part-time programs available. *Degree requirements:* For master's, thesis optional; for doctorate, thesis/dissertation. *Entrance requirements:* For master's and doctorate, GRE General Test.

University of Medicine and Dentistry of New Jersey, School of Health Related Professions, Newark, NJ 07107-3001. Offers MPT, MS, DCN, DPT, PhD, Certificate, DMD/MS, MD/MS. *Accreditation:* APTA (one or more programs are accredited); NAACLS. Part-time programs available. *Degree requirements:* For master's, thesis (for some programs). *Entrance requirements:* For master's, GRE. Additional exam requirements/recommendations for international students: Required—TOEFL. Electronic applications accepted. *Expenses:* Contact institution. *Faculty research:* Clinical outcomes.

University of Mississippi Medical Center, School of Health Related Professions, Jackson, MS 39216-4505. Offers MOT, MPT. *Accreditation:* AOTA; NAACLS. Part-time programs available.

University of Nebraska Medical Center, School of Allied Health Professions, Omaha, NE 68198. Offers MPAS, MPS, DPT, Certificate. *Accreditation:* APTA (one or more programs are accredited).

University of Nevada, Las Vegas, Graduate College, School of Allied Health Sciences, Las Vegas, NV 89154-3018. Offers MS, DPT. Part-time programs available. *Faculty:* 29 full-time (10 women), 3 part-time/adjunct (2 women). *Students:* 114 full-time (60 women), 34 part-time (10 women); includes 9 minority (6 Asian Americans or Pacific Islanders, 3 Hispanic Americans), 7 international. Average age 29. 62 applicants, 84% accepted, 21 enrolled. In 2009, 13 master's, 30 doctorates awarded. *Degree requirements:* For master's, thesis optional. *Entrance requirements:* Additional exam requirements/recommendations for international students: Required—TOEFL (minimum score 550 paper-based; 213 computer-based; 80 iBT), IELTS (minimum score 7). *Application deadline:* For fall admission, 8/1 for domestic students, 5/1 for international students; for spring admission, 12/1 for domestic students, 10/1 for international students. Applications are processed on a rolling basis. Application fee: $60 ($95 for international students). Electronic applications accepted. *Financial support:* In 2009–10, 34 students received support, including 31 research assistantships with partial tuition reimbursements available (averaging $10,986 per year), 3 teaching assistantships with partial tuition reimbursements available (averaging $10,000 per year); institutionally sponsored loans, scholarships/grants, health care benefits, and unspecified assistantships also available. Financial award application deadline: 3/1. *Faculty research:* Childhood obesity; human performance; injury prevention, assessment and rehabilitation techniques; diagnostic imaging and therapeutics; nuclear waste management and nuclear forensics. Total annual research expenditures: $3.5 million. *Unit head:* Dr. Carolyn Yucha, Interim Dean, 702-895-3906, Fax: 702-895-5050, E-mail: carolyn.yucha@unlv.edu. *Application contact:* Graduate College Admissions Evaluator, 702-895-3320, Fax: 702-895-4180, E-mail: gradcollege@unlv.edu.

The University of North Carolina at Chapel Hill, School of Medicine and Graduate School, Graduate Programs in Medicine, Department of Allied Health Sciences, Chapel Hill, NC 27599. Offers human movement science (PhD); occupational science (MS, PhD), including occupational science; physical therapy (DPT), including physical therapy—off campus, physical therapy—on campus; rehabilitation counseling and psychology (MS); speech and hearing sciences (MS, Au D, PhD), including audiology (Au D), speech and hearing sciences (MS, PhD). *Accreditation:* APTA (one or more programs are accredited). Postbaccalaureate distance learning degree programs offered. *Faculty:* 133 full-time (100 women), 52 part-time/adjunct (39 women). *Students:* 297 full-time (250 women), 31 part-time (29 women); includes 51 minority (28 African Americans, 17 Asian Americans or Pacific Islanders, 6 Hispanic Americans). Average age 30. 643 applicants, 26% accepted, 124 enrolled. In 2009, 53 master's, 8 doctorates awarded. *Entrance requirements:* For master's, GRE General Test; for doctorate, GRE General Test, minimum GPA of 3.0. Additional exam requirements/recommendations for international students: Required—TOEFL (minimum score 550 paper-based; 79 computer-based), TWE. *Application deadline:* For fall admission, 1/1 for domestic and international students. Application fee: $75. Electronic applications accepted. *Financial support:* In 2009–10, 20 research assistantships with partial tuition reimbursements (averaging $3,424 per year), 5 teaching assistantships (averaging $7,000 per year) were awarded; fellowships with partial tuition reimbursements, career-related internships or fieldwork, Federal Work-Study, institutionally sponsored loans, traineeships, and unspecified assistantships also available. Financial award applicants required to submit FAFSA. Total annual research expenditures: $3.8 million. *Unit head:* Dr. Lee K. McLean, Chairman, 919-966-9040, Fax: 919-966-8384. *Application contact:* Seletha L. Shaw, Student Services Manager, 919-966-2343, Fax: 919-966-8384, E-mail: slshaw@med.unc.edu.

University of North Florida, Brooks College of Health, Jacksonville, FL 32224. Offers MHA, MPH, MS, MSH, MSN, DNP, DPT, Certificate. Part-time and evening/weekend programs available. *Faculty:* 66 full-time (46 women). *Students:* 294 full-time (217 women), 149 part-time (119 women); includes 83 minority (38 African Americans, 2 American Indian/Alaska Native, 23 Asian Americans or Pacific Islanders, 20 Hispanic Americans), 10 international. Average age 32. 573 applicants, 23% accepted, 56 enrolled. In 2009, 106 master's, 28 doctorates awarded. *Entrance requirements:* For master's, GRE General Test, minimum GPA of 3.0 in last 60 hours. Additional exam requirements/recommendations for international students: Required—TOEFL (minimum score 500 paper-based; 173 computer-based). *Application deadline:* For fall admission, 7/1 priority date for domestic students, 5/1 for international students; for spring admission, 11/1 priority date for domestic students, 10/1 for international students. Applications are processed on a rolling basis. Application fee: $30. Electronic applications accepted. *Expenses:* Contact institution. *Financial support:* In 2009–10, 113 students received support, including 1 teaching assistantship (averaging $1,004 per year); research assistantships, career-related internships or fieldwork, Federal Work-Study, scholarships/grants, and tuition waivers (partial) also available. Support available to part-time students. Financial award application deadline: 4/1; financial award applicants required to submit FAFSA. *Faculty research:* Adolescent substance abuse, detection of bacterial agents, spirituality and health, non-vitamin and non-mineral supplements, analyzing ticks and their ability to transfer diseases to humans. Total annual research expenditures: $1.3 million. *Unit head:* Dr. Pamela Chally, Dean, 904-620-2810, Fax: 904-620-1030, E-mail: pchally@unf.edu. *Application contact:* Heather Kenney, Director of Advising, 904-620-2810, Fax: 904-620-1030, E-mail: heather.kenney@unf.edu.

University of Oklahoma Health Sciences Center, College of Medicine, Program in Physician Associate, Oklahoma City, OK 73190. Offers MHS. *Faculty:* 10 full-time (8 women). *Students:* 198 full-time (148 women); includes 22 minority (3 African Americans, 11 American Indian/Alaska Native, 7 Asian Americans or Pacific Islanders, 1 Hispanic American). Average age 27. 213 applicants, 29% accepted, 50 enrolled. In 2009, 51 master's awarded. *Expenses:* Tuition, state resident: full-time $3120; part-time $156 per credit hour. Tuition, nonresident: full-time $11,314; part-time $409.70 per credit hour. Required fees: $1471; $51.20 per credit hour. $223.25 per term. *Unit head:* Dr. Daniel McNeill, Program Director, 405-271-2058. *Application*

contact: Dr. James J. Tomasek, Dean of the Graduate College, 405-271-2085, Fax: 405-271-1155, E-mail: james-tomasek@ouhsc.edu.

University of Oklahoma Health Sciences Center, Graduate College, College of Allied Health, Oklahoma City, OK 73190. Offers MOT, MPT, MS, Au D, PhD, Certificate. *Accreditation:* AOTA; APTA. Part-time programs available. *Faculty:* 38 full-time (28 women), 5 part-time/adjunct (3 women). *Students:* 335 full-time (288 women), 71 part-time (65 women); includes 65 minority (5 African Americans, 36 American Indian/Alaska Native, 15 Asian Americans or Pacific Islanders, 9 Hispanic Americans), 1 international. Average age 26. 437 applicants, 46% accepted, 145 enrolled. In 2009, 125 master's, 8 doctorates, 26 other advanced degrees awarded. Terminal master's awarded for partial completion of doctoral program. *Degree requirements:* For master's, comprehensive exam, thesis optional; for doctorate, one foreign language, comprehensive exam, thesis/dissertation. *Entrance requirements:* For master's and doctorate, GRE General Test, 3 letters of recommendation. Additional exam requirements/recommendations for international students: Required—TOEFL. *Application deadline:* For fall admission, 7/1 priority date for domestic students; for winter admission, 5/1 for domestic students; for spring admission, 12/1 for domestic students. Application fee: $50. *Expenses:* Tuition, state resident: full-time $3120; part-time $156 per credit hour. Tuition, nonresident: full-time $11,314; part-time $409.70 per credit hour. Required fees: $1471; $51.20 per credit hour. $223.25 per term. *Financial support:* Fellowships, career-related internships or fieldwork, Federal Work-Study, institutionally sponsored loans, and traineeships available. Support available to part-time students. *Unit head:* Dr. Carole Sullivan, Dean, 405-271-2288, Fax: 405-271-1190, E-mail: carole-sullivan@ouhsc.edu. *Application contact:* Dr. Jan Womack, Associate Dean, Academic and Student Affairs, 405-271-6588, Fax: 405-271-3120, E-mail: jan-womack@ouhsc.edu.

University of Phoenix–Charlotte Campus, The Artemis School, College of Health and Human Services, Charlotte, NC 28273-3409. Offers health care management (MBA). Evening/weekend programs available. *Degree requirements:* For master's, thesis (for some programs). *Entrance requirements:* For master's, minimum undergraduate GPA of 2.5, 3 years work experience. Additional exam requirements/recommendations for international students: Required—TOEFL (minimum score 550 paper-based; 213 computer-based; 79 iBT). Electronic applications accepted.

University of Phoenix–Las Vegas Campus, The Artemis School, College of Health and Human Services, Las Vegas, NV 89128. Offers administration of justice and security (MS); health administration (MHA); health care management (MBA); marriage, family, and child therapy (MSC); mental health counseling (MSC); nursing (MSN); nursing/health care education (MSN); psychology (MS); MSN/MBA; MSN/MHA. Postbaccalaureate distance learning degree programs offered. *Entrance requirements:* For master's, minimum undergraduate GPA of 2.5, 3 years of work experience. Additional exam requirements/recommendations for international students: Required—TOEFL (minimum score 550 paper-based; 213 computer-based; 79 iBT). Electronic applications accepted.

University of Puerto Rico, Medical Sciences Campus, School of Health Professions, San Juan, PR 00936-5067. Offers MS, Au D, Certificate. *Degree requirements:* For master's, one foreign language, thesis (for some programs). *Entrance requirements:* For master's, GRE or EXADEP, interview; for doctorate, EXADEP; for Certificate, Allied Health Professions Admissions Test, minimum GPA of 2.5, interview. Electronic applications accepted. *Faculty research:* Infantile autism, aphasia, language problems, toxicology, immunohematology, medical record documentation and quality.

University of St. Francis, College of Nursing and Allied Health, Joliet, IL 60435-6169. Offers nursing (MSN), including adult health clinical nurse specialist, adult nurse practitioner, family nurse practitioner; nursing practice (DNP). *Accreditation:* AACN. Part-time and evening/weekend programs available. Postbaccalaureate distance learning degree programs offered. *Faculty:* 10 full-time (all women), 11 part-time/adjunct (10 women). *Students:* 13 full-time (10 women), 164 part-time (153 women); includes 41 minority (22 African Americans, 1 American Indian/Alaska Native, 6 Asian Americans or Pacific Islanders, 12 Hispanic Americans). Average age 40. 161 applicants, 43% accepted, 56 enrolled. In 2009, 10 master's awarded. *Entrance requirements:* For master's, GRE General Test (MS), minimum GPA of 2.75, 2 years of work experience in clinical nursing, CPR certification, computer competency, 3 letters of recommendation, interview, RN license, current licensure, immunizations, liability insurance, resume, work history (MSN); for doctorate, master's degree in nursing with minimum GPA of 3.0, national certification as nurse practitioner or clinical nurse specialist, current RN licensure, interview, computer competency, CPR certification, immunizations, medical history, physical form, drug screen, criminal background check, liability insurance, letter of recommendation, resume. Additional exam requirements/recommendations for international students: Required—TOEFL (minimum score 550 paper-based; 213 computer-based). *Application deadline:* Applications are processed on a rolling basis. Application fee: $30. Electronic applications accepted. *Expenses:* Contact institution. *Financial support:* In 2009–10, 135 students received support. Scholarships/grants, traineeships, and tuition waivers (partial) available. Support available to part-time students. Financial award applicants required to submit FAFSA. *Unit head:* Dr. Maria Connolly, Dean, 815-740-3840, Fax: 815-740-4243, E-mail: mconnolly@stfrancis.edu. *Application contact:* Sandra Sloka, Director of Admissions for Graduate and Degree Completion Programs, 800-735-7500, Fax: 815-740-5032, E-mail: ssloka@stfrancis.edu.

University of Saint Francis, Graduate School, Department of Allied Health, Fort Wayne, IN 46808-3994. Offers physician assistant studies (MS). *Accreditation:* ARC-PA. *Entrance requirements:* For master's, GRE or MCAT, previous courses in biology, chemistry, and psychology, previous direct patient care.

University of South Alabama, Graduate School, College of Allied Health Professions, Mobile, AL 36688-0002. Offers MHS, MS, Au D, DPT, PhD. *Degree requirements:* For master's, thesis optional, externship; for doctorate, thesis/dissertation, clinical internship. *Entrance requirements:* For master's, GRE General Test. *Expenses:* Tuition, state resident: part-time $218 per contact hour. Required fees: $1102 per year.

The University of South Dakota, School of Medicine and Health Sciences and Graduate School, Graduate Programs in Health Sciences, Vermillion, SD 57069-2390. Offers occupational therapy (MS); physical therapy (DPT); physician assistant studies (MS). Part-time programs available. *Entrance requirements:* For master's, GRE General Test, GRE Subject Test. *Faculty research:* Occupational therapy, physical therapy, vision, pediatrics, geriatrics.

The University of Tennessee Health Science Center, College of Allied Health Sciences, Memphis, TN 38163-0002. Offers MCP, MDH, MHIIM, MOT, MSCLS, MSPT, DPT, ScDPT, TDPT. *Accreditation:* AOTA; APTA. Part-time and evening/weekend programs available. Postbaccalaureate distance learning degree programs offered (minimal on-campus study). Terminal master's awarded for partial completion of doctoral program. *Degree requirements:* For master's, comprehensive exam, thesis; for doctorate, comprehensive exam, residency. *Entrance requirements:* For master's, GRE (MOT, MSCLS), minimum GPA of 3.0, 3 letters of reference, state license (MDH), national accreditation (MSCLS), GRE if GPA is less than 3.0 (MCP); for doctorate, GRE. Additional exam requirements/recommendations for international students: Required—TOEFL (minimum score 550 paper-based; 213 computer-based; 80 iBT). Electronic applications accepted. *Expenses:* Contact institution. *Faculty research:* Gait deviation, muscular dystrophy and strength, hemophilia and exercise, pediatric neurology, self-efficacy.

The University of Texas at El Paso, Graduate School, College of Health Sciences, Program in Interdisciplinary Health Sciences, El Paso, TX 79968-0001. Offers PhD. *Students:* 32 (24 women); includes 20 minority (3 African Americans, 1 American Indian/Alaska Native, 2 Asian Americans or Pacific Islanders, 14 Hispanic Americans), 7 international. In 2009, 2 doctorates awarded. *Degree requirements:* For doctorate, thesis/dissertation. *Entrance requirements:* For doctorate, GRE, letters of reference, relevant personal/professional experience, master's degree in health. Additional exam requirements/recommendations for international students: Required—TOEFL; Recommended—IELTS. *Application deadline:* For fall admission, 8/1 for domestic students, 3/1 for international students; for spring admission, 11/1 for domestic students, 9/1 for international students. Applications are processed on a rolling basis. Application fee: $45 ($80 for international students). Electronic applications accepted. *Financial support:* Fellowships with partial tuition reimbursements, research assistantships with partial tuition reimbursements, teaching assistantships with partial tuition reimbursements, institutionally sponsored loans, scholarships/grants, health care benefits, tuition waivers (partial), and unspecified assistantships available. Support available to part-time students. Financial award application deadline: 3/15; financial award applicants required to submit FAFSA. *Unit head:* Dr. Gloria McKee Lopez, Director, 915-747-7234, Fax: 915-747-7207, E-mail: gmckee@utep.edu. *Application contact:* Dr. Patricia D. Witherspoon, Dean of the Graduate School, 915-747-5491, Fax: 915-747-5788, E-mail: withersp@utep.edu.

The University of Texas Medical Branch, School of Health Professions, Galveston, TX 77555. Offers MOT, MPAS, MPT, DPT. *Students:* 423 full-time (356 women), 22 part-time (19 women); includes 139 minority (26 African Americans, 3 American Indian/Alaska Native, 47 Asian Americans or Pacific Islanders, 63 Hispanic Americans), 2 international. Average age 26. In 2009, 109 master's, 21 doctorates awarded. *Degree requirements:* For master's, thesis or alternative; for doctorate, thesis/dissertation or alternative. *Entrance requirements:* For master's, GRE, experience in field, minimum GPA of 3.0; for doctorate, GRE, documentation of 40 hours experience. Additional exam requirements/recommendations for international students: Required—TOEFL (minimum score 550 paper-based; 212 computer-based). *Application deadline:* For fall admission, 11/1 for domestic students. Applications are processed on a rolling basis. Application fee: $30. Electronic applications accepted. *Financial support:* Career-related internships or fieldwork, Federal Work-Study, institutionally sponsored loans, and scholarships/grants available. Financial award applicants required to submit FAFSA. *Unit head:* Dr. Elizabeth J. Protas, Dean, 409-772-3001, Fax: 409-747-1623, E-mail: ejprotas@utmb.edu. *Application contact:* Dr. Henry Cavazos, Associate Dean for Academic and Student Affairs, 409-772-3004, E-mail: hcavazos@utmb.edu.

University of Vermont, Graduate College, College of Nursing and Health Sciences, Burlington, VT 05405. Offers MS, DPT. Part-time programs available. *Students:* 181 (148 women); includes 18 minority (4 African Americans, 3 American Indian/Alaska Native, 9 Asian Americans or Pacific Islanders, 2 Hispanic Americans), 2 international. 270 applicants, 44% accepted, 11 enrolled. In 2009, 4 master's, 8 doctorates awarded. *Degree requirements:* For master's, thesis. *Entrance requirements:* For master's, GRE General Test. Additional exam requirements/recommendations for international students: Required—TOEFL (minimum score 550 paper-based; 213 computer-based; 80 iBT). *Application deadline:* For fall admission, 4/1 priority date for domestic students. Applications are processed on a rolling basis. Application fee: $40. Electronic applications accepted. *Expenses:* Tuition, state resident: part-time $508 per credit hour. Tuition, nonresident: part-time $1281 per credit hour. *Financial support:* Fellowships, research assistantships, teaching assistantships, Federal Work-Study available. Financial award application deadline: 3/1. *Unit head:* Dr. Patricia Prelock, Dean, 802-656-3830. *Application contact:* Dr. Patricia Prelock, Dean, 802-656-3830.

University of Wisconsin–Milwaukee, Graduate School, College of Health Sciences, Milwaukee, WI 53211. Offers MS, DPT, PhD, Certificate. Part-time programs available. *Faculty:* 44 full-time (24 women). *Students:* 186 full-time (143 women), 33 part-time (24 women); includes 7 minority (3 African Americans, 1 American Indian/Alaska Native, 2 Asian Americans or Pacific Islanders, 1 Hispanic American), 16 international. Average age 27. 226 applicants, 35% accepted, 36 enrolled. In 2009, 73 master's, 2 doctorates awarded. *Degree requirements:* For master's, thesis; for doctorate, comprehensive exam, thesis/dissertation. *Entrance requirements:* For doctorate, GRE General Test, master's degree. Additional exam requirements/recommendations for international students: Required—TOEFL (minimum score 600 paper-based; 250 computer-based), IELTS (minimum score 6.5). *Application deadline:* For fall admission, 1/1 priority date for domestic students; for spring admission, 9/1 for domestic students. Applications are processed on a rolling basis. Application fee: $45 ($75 for international students). *Expenses:* Contact institution. *Financial support:* In 2009–10, 9 research assistantships, 15 teaching assistantships were awarded; career-related internships or fieldwork, Federal Work-Study, and unspecified assistantships also available. Support available to part-time students. Financial award application deadline: 4/15. Total annual research expenditures: $3 million. *Unit head:* Chukuka S. Enwemeka, Dean, 414-229-4712, E-mail: enwemeka@uwm.edu. *Application contact:* Roger O. Smith, General Information Contact, 414-229-6697, Fax: 414-229-6697, E-mail: smithro@uwm.edu.

Virginia Commonwealth University, Graduate School, School of Allied Health Professions, Department of Health Administration, Doctoral Program in Health Related Sciences, Richmond, VA 23284-9005. Offers clinical laboratory sciences (PhD); gerontology (PhD); health administration (PhD); nurse anesthesia (PhD); occupational therapy (PhD); physical therapy (PhD); radiation sciences (PhD); rehabilitation leadership (PhD).

Washington University in St. Louis, School of Medicine, Graduate Programs in Medicine, St. Louis, MO 63130-4899. Offers occupational therapy (MSOT, OTD); physical therapy (DPT, PhD, PPDPT), including movement science (PhD), physical therapy (DPT, PPDPT). *Students:* 561. *Degree requirements:* For doctorate, thesis/dissertation. *Expenses:* Contact institution. *Financial support:* Fellowships, research assistantships, career-related internships or fieldwork, Federal Work-Study, and institutionally sponsored loans available. Support available to part-time students. Financial award applicants required to submit FAFSA. *Unit head:* Dr. Larry Shapiro, Dean, 314-362-6827. *Application contact:* Dr. W. Edwin Dodson, Associate Dean, 314-362-6848, Fax: 314-362-4658, E-mail: wumscoa@msnotes.wustl.edu.

Western University of Health Sciences, College of Allied Health Professions, Pomona, CA 91766-1854. Offers MS, DPT. *Accreditation:* APTA (one or more programs are accredited). *Entrance requirements:* For master's, minimum undergraduate GPA of 2.5, graduate 3.0; for doctorate, GRE General Test, minimum GPA of 2.8, letters of recommendation, interview. *Expenses:* Contact institution.

Wichita State University, Graduate School, College of Health Professions, Wichita, KS 67260. Offers communication sciences and disorders (MA, Au D, PhD); nursing (MSN, DNP), including clinical nurse specialist (MSN), nurse midwifery (MSN), nurse practitioner (MSN), nursing and healthcare systems administration (MSN), nursing practice (DNP); physical therapy (DPT); physician assistant (MPA); MSN/MBA. *Accreditation:* APTA (one or more programs are accredited). Part-time programs available. *Expenses:* Tuition, state resident: full-time $4247; part-time $235.95 per credit hour. Tuition, nonresident: full-time $11,171; part-time $620.60 per credit hour. Required fees: $34; $3.60 per credit hour. $17 per term. Tuition and fees vary according to campus/location and program. *Unit head:* Dr. Peter A. Cohen, Dean, 316-978-3600, Fax: 316-978-3025, E-mail: peter.cohen@wichita.edu. *Application contact:* Dr. Peter A. Cohen, Dean, 316-978-3600, Fax: 316-978-3025, E-mail: peter.cohen@wichita.edu.

Anesthesiologist Assistant Studies

Case Western Reserve University, School of Medicine and School of Graduate Studies, Graduate Programs in Medicine, Department of Anesthesiology, Cleveland, OH 44106. Offers MS. *Accreditation:* AANA/CANAEP. *Degree requirements:* For master's, thesis. *Entrance requirements:* For master's, MCAT. Additional exam requirements/recommendations for international students: Required—TOEFL. Electronic applications accepted. *Faculty research:* Metabolism of bioamines, cerebral metabolism, cardiovascular hemodynamics, genetics.

Emory University, School of Medicine, Programs in Allied Health Professions, Department of Anesthesiology, Atlanta, GA 30322-1100. Offers MM Sc. *Faculty:* 10 part-time/adjunct (3 women). *Students:* 79 full-time (38 women); includes 16 minority (7 African Americans, 1 American Indian/Alaska Native, 6 Asian Americans or Pacific Islanders, 2 Hispanic Americans). Average age 29. 232 applicants, 18% accepted, 38 enrolled. In 2009, 45 master's awarded. *Entrance requirements:* For master's, GRE General Test or MCAT. Additional exam requirements/recommendations for international students: Required—TOEFL (minimum score 613 paper-based; 257 computer-based). *Application deadline:* For fall admission, 1/1 for domestic and international students. Applications are processed on a rolling basis. Application fee: $60. Electronic applications accepted. *Expenses:* Contact institution. *Financial support:* In 2009–10, 69 students received support. Institutionally sponsored loans and scholarships/grants available. Financial award application deadline: 3/1; financial award applicants required to submit FAFSA. *Unit head:* Dr. Richard G. Brouillard, Director of Academic Affairs, 404-727-5910, Fax: 404-727-3021. *Application contact:* Jerri J. Elder, Admissions Services Coordinator, 404-727-7125, Fax: 404-727-3021.

South University, Graduate Programs, College of Health Professions, Program in Anesthesiologist Assistant, Savannah, GA 31406. Offers MM Sc.

See Close-Up on page 1431.

Université Laval, Faculty of Medicine, Post-Professional Programs in Medical Studies, Québec, QC G1K 7P4, Canada. Offers anatomy–pathology (DESS); anesthesiology (DESS); cardiology (DESS); care of older people (Diploma); clinical research (DESS); community health (DESS); dermatology (DESS); diagnostic radiology (DESS); emergency medicine (Diploma); family medicine (DESS); general surgery (DESS); geriatrics (DESS); hematology (DESS); internal medicine (DESS); maternal and fetal medicine (Diploma); medical biochemistry (DESS); medical microbiology and infectious diseases (DESS); medical oncology (DESS); nephrology (DESS); neurology (DESS); neurosurgery (DESS); obstetrics and gynecology (DESS); ophthalmology (DESS); orthopedic surgery (DESS); oto-rhino-laryngology (DESS); palliative medicine (Diploma); pediatrics (DESS); plastic surgery (DESS); psychiatry (DESS); pulmonary medicine (DESS); radiology–oncology (DESS); thoracic surgery (DESS); urology (DESS). *Degree requirements:* For other advanced degree, comprehensive exam. *Entrance requirements:* For degree, knowledge of French. Electronic applications accepted.

University of Guelph, Ontario Veterinary College and Graduate Program Services, Graduate Programs in Veterinary Sciences, Department of Clinical Studies, Guelph, ON N1G 2W1, Canada. Offers anesthesiology (M Sc, DV Sc); cardiology (DV Sc, Diploma); clinical studies (Diploma); dermatology (M Sc); diagnostic imaging (M Sc, DV Sc); emergency/critical care (M Sc, DV Sc, Diploma); medicine (M Sc, DV Sc); neurology (M Sc, DV Sc); ophthalmology (M Sc, DV Sc); surgery (M Sc, DV Sc). *Degree requirements:* For master's, thesis; for doctorate, comprehensive exam, thesis/dissertation. *Entrance requirements:* Additional exam requirements/recommendations for international students: Required—TOEFL (minimum score 550 paper-based; 213 computer-based), IELTS (minimum score 6.5). Electronic applications accepted. *Faculty research:* Orthopedics, respirology, oncology, exercise physiology, cardiology.

Clinical Laboratory Sciences/Medical Technology

Austin Peay State University, College of Graduate Studies, College of Science and Mathematics, Department of Biology, Clarksville, TN 37044. Offers clinical laboratory science (MS); radiologic science (MS). Part-time programs available. *Faculty:* 6 full-time (1 woman). *Students:* 5 full-time (all women), 18 part-time (11 women); includes 6 minority (1 African American, 5 Hispanic Americans), 1 international. Average age 29. 19 applicants, 100% accepted, 9 enrolled. In 2009, 4 master's awarded. *Degree requirements:* For master's, comprehensive exam, thesis optional. *Entrance requirements:* For master's, GRE General Test, 3 letters of recommendation, minimum undergraduate GPA of 2.5. Additional exam requirements/recommendations for international students: Required—TOEFL (minimum score 500 paper-based; 173 computer-based). *Application deadline:* For fall admission, 7/27 priority date for domestic students; for spring admission, 12/17 priority date for domestic students. Applications are processed on a rolling basis. Application fee: $25. Electronic applications accepted. *Expenses:* Tuition, state resident: full-time $6160; part-time $608 per credit hour. Tuition, nonresident: full-time $17,080; part-time $854 per credit hour. Required fees: $1224; $61.20 per credit hour. *Financial support:* In 2009–10, 10 students received support, including 10 research assistantships with full tuition reimbursements available (averaging $5,184 per year); career-related internships or fieldwork, Federal Work-Study, institutionally sponsored loans, scholarships/grants, and unspecified assistantships also available. Support available to part-time students. Financial award application deadline: 3/1. *Faculty research:* Non-paint source pollution, amphibian biomonitoring, aquatic toxicology, biological indicators of water quality, taxonomy. *Unit head:* Dr. Don Dailey, Chair, 931-221-7781, Fax: 931-221-6323, E-mail: daileyd@apsu.edu. *Application contact:* Dr. Dixie Dennis Pinder, Dean, College of Graduate Studies, 931-221-7662, Fax: 931-221-7641, E-mail: dennisdi@apsu.edu.

Baylor College of Medicine, Graduate School of Biomedical Sciences, Program in Clinical Scientist Training, Houston, TX 77030-3498. Offers MS, PhD. *Faculty:* 55 full-time (17 women). *Students:* 36 full-time (22 women); includes 15 minority (1 African American, 10 Asian Americans or Pacific Islanders, 4 Hispanic Americans), 6 international. Average age 34. In 2009, 3 master's, 2 doctorates awarded. Terminal master's awarded for partial completion of doctoral program. *Degree requirements:* For master's, thesis; for doctorate, thesis/dissertation, public defense. *Application deadline:* For fall admission, 1/1 priority date for domestic students. Application fee: $0. Electronic applications accepted. *Financial support:* Fellowships with full tuition reimbursements, research assistantships with full tuition reimbursements, career-related internships or fieldwork, Federal Work-Study, institutionally sponsored loans, health care benefits, and students receive a scholarship unless there are grant funds available to pay tuition available. *Unit head:* Dr. Morey Haymond, Director, 713-798-6776, Fax: 713-798-7119, E-mail: mhaymond@bcm.edu. *Application contact:* Dr. Olga Watkins, Graduate Program Administrator/Co-Director, 713-798-7132, Fax: 713-798-7119, E-mail: owatkins@bcm.edu.

The Catholic University of America, School of Arts and Sciences, Department of Biology, Washington, DC 20064. Offers cell and microbial biology (MS, PhD), including cell biology, microbiology; clinical laboratory science (MS, PhD); MSLS/MS. Part-time programs available. *Faculty:* 7 full-time (4 women), 2 part-time/adjunct (both women). *Students:* 3 full-time (2 women), 23 part-time (15 women); includes 8 minority (2 African Americans, 3 Asian Americans or Pacific Islanders, 3 Hispanic Americans), 8 international. Average age 29. 30 applicants, 47% accepted, 3 enrolled. In 2009, 3 doctorates awarded. *Degree requirements:* For master's, comprehensive exam, thesis or alternative; for doctorate, comprehensive exam, thesis/dissertation. *Entrance requirements:* For master's and doctorate, GRE General Test, GRE Subject Test, statement of purpose, official copies of academic transcripts, three letters of recommendation. Additional exam requirements/recommendations for international students: Required—TOEFL (minimum score 580 paper-based; 237 computer-based). *Application deadline:* For fall admission, 8/1 priority date for domestic students, 7/15 for international students; for spring admission, 12/1 priority date for domestic students, 10/15 for international students. Applications are processed on a rolling basis. Application fee: $55. Electronic applications accepted. *Expenses:* Tuition: Full-time $31,740; part-time $1245 per credit hour. Required fees: $50; $25 per semester hour. One-time fee: $425. *Financial support:* Fellowships, research assistantships, teaching assistantships, Federal Work-Study, scholarships/grants, tuition waivers (full and partial), and unspecified assistantships available. Financial award application deadline: 2/1; financial award applicants required to submit FAFSA. *Faculty research:* Cell and microbiology, microbial pathogenesis, molecular biology of cell proliferation, cellular effects of electromagnetic radiation, biotechnology. Total annual research expenditures: $853,913. *Unit head:* Dr. Venigalla Rao, Chair, 202-319-5271, Fax: 202-319-5721, E-mail: rao@cua.edu. *Application contact:* Julie Schwing, Director of Graduate Admissions, 202-319-5057, Fax: 202-319-6533, E-mail: cua-admissions@cua.edu.

The Catholic University of America, School of Engineering, Department of Biomedical Engineering, Washington, DC 20064. Offers bioinstrumentation (MBE, MSE, D Engr); biomechanics (MBE, D Engr, PhD); biosignal processing and medical imaging (MBE, MSE, PhD); home care technologies (MBE, MSE, D Engr); rehabilitation engineering (MBE, MSE, D Engr); telemedicine (MBE, MSE, D Engr). Part-time programs available. *Faculty:* 6 full-time (1 woman), 1 part-time/adjunct (0 women). *Students:* 13 full-time (6 women), 10 part-time (4 women); includes 6 minority (3 African Americans, 3 Hispanic Americans), 6 international. Average age 29. 30 applicants, 63% accepted, 12 enrolled. In 2009, 15 master's awarded. *Degree requirements:* For master's, thesis or alternative; for doctorate, comprehensive exam, thesis/dissertation, oral exams. *Entrance requirements:* For master's, GRE (minimum score: 1250), minimum GPA of 3.0, statement of purpose, official copies of academic transcripts, three letters of recommendation; for doctorate, GRE (minimum score 1300), minimum GPA of 3.5, 3 letters of recommendation. Additional exam requirements/recommendations for international students: Required—TOEFL (minimum score 580 paper-based; 237 computer-based). *Application deadline:* For fall admission, 8/1 priority date for domestic students, 7/15 for international students; for spring admission, 12/1 priority date for domestic students, 10/15 for international students. Applications are processed on a rolling basis. Application fee: $55. Electronic applications accepted. *Expenses:* Contact institution. *Financial support:* Fellowships, research assistantships, teaching assistantships, Federal Work-Study, scholarships/grants, tuition waivers (full and partial), and unspecified assistantships available. Financial award application deadline: 2/1; financial award applicants required to submit FAFSA. *Faculty research:* Cardiopulmonary biomechanics, robotics and human motor control, cell and tissue engineering, biomechanics, rehabilitation engineering. Total annual research expenditures: $780,403. *Unit head:* Dr. Binh Q. Tran, Chair, 202-319-5181, Fax: 202-319-4287, E-mail: tran@cua.edu. *Application contact:* Julie Schwing, Director of Graduate Admissions, 202-319-5057, Fax: 202-319-6533, E-mail: cua-admissions@cua.edu.

Duke University, School of Medicine, Clinical Leadership Program, Durham, NC 27701. Offers MHS. *Faculty:* 4 full-time (2 women), 1 part-time/adjunct (0 women). *Students:* 4 part-time (2 women); includes 3 minority (all Asian Americans or Pacific Islanders). 1 applicant, 100% accepted. *Degree requirements:* For master's, project. *Entrance requirements:* For master's, GRE. *Application deadline:* For fall admission, 6/30 priority date for domestic students. Applications are processed on a rolling basis. Application fee: $100. *Financial support:* Fellowships, research assistantships, teaching assistantships available. Financial award application deadline: 5/1; financial award applicants required to submit FAFSA. *Unit head:* Anh N. Tran, Assistant Professor, 919-681-5744, Fax: 919-613-6899, E-mail: anh.tran@duke.edu. *Application contact:* Jennifer Barnett, Administrative Assistant, 919-681-5744, Fax: 919-681-3371, E-mail: jennifer.barnett@duke.edu.

Emory University, School of Medicine, Programs in Allied Health Professions, Atlanta, GA 30322-1100. Offers anesthesiology (MM Sc); anesthesiology/patient monitoring systems (MM Sc); ophthalmic technology (MM Sc); physical therapy (DPT); physician assistant (MM Sc). Postbaccalaureate distance learning degree programs offered. *Faculty:* 29 full-time (19 women), 18 part-time/adjunct (8 women). *Students:* 381 full-time (273 women), 3 part-time (2 women); includes 80 minority (43 African Americans, 2 American Indian/Alaska Native, 20 Asian Americans or Pacific Islanders, 15 Hispanic Americans), 5 international. Average age 27. 1,299 applicants, 16% accepted, 149 enrolled. In 2009, 99 master's, 41 doctorates awarded. *Entrance requirements:* For master's, GRE or MCAT; for doctorate, GRE. *Application deadline:* Applications are processed on a rolling basis. Electronic applications accepted. *Expenses:* Contact institution. *Financial support:* In 2009–10, 275 students received support. Institutionally sponsored loans and scholarships/grants available. Financial award application deadline: 3/1; financial award applicants required to submit FAFSA. *Unit head:* Dr. J. Alan Otsuki, Assistant Dean, Office of Medical Education and Student Affairs, 404-727-5655, Fax: 404-727-0045, E-mail: jotsuki@emory.edu. *Application contact:* Marvell Nesmith, Associate Director of Registration and Student Affairs, 404-712-9921, Fax: 404-727-0045, E-mail: marvell.nesmith@emory.edu.

Fairleigh Dickinson University, Metropolitan Campus, University College: Arts, Sciences, and Professional Studies, Henry P. Becton School of Nursing and Allied Health, Program in Medical Technology, Teaneck, NJ 07666-1914. Offers MS. *Students:* 2 applicants, 0% accepted. *Application deadline:* Applications are processed on a rolling basis. Application fee: $40. *Application contact:* Susan Brooman, University Director of Graduate Admissions, 201-692-2554, Fax: 201-692-2560, E-mail: globaleducation@fdu.edu.

Inter American University of Puerto Rico, Metropolitan Campus, Graduate Programs, Program in Medical Technology, San Juan, PR 00919-1293. Offers administration of clinical laboratories (MS); molecular microbiology (MS). *Accreditation:* NAACLS. Part-time programs available. *Degree requirements:* For master's, comprehensive exam. *Entrance requirements:* For master's, BS in medical technology, minimum GPA of 2.5. Electronic applications accepted.

Long Island University, C.W. Post Campus, School of Health Professions and Nursing, Department of Biomedical Sciences, Brookville, NY 11548-1300. Offers cardiovascular perfusion (MS); clinical laboratory management (MS); medical biology (MS), including hematology, immunology, medical biology, medical chemistry, medical microbiology. Part-time and evening/weekend programs available. Postbaccalaureate distance learning degree programs offered. *Degree requirements:* For master's, thesis. *Entrance requirements:* For master's, minimum GPA of 2.75 in major. Electronic applications accepted.

Medical College of Wisconsin, Graduate School of Biomedical Sciences, Program in Health Care Technologies Management, Milwaukee, WI 53226-0509. Offers MS. *Entrance requirements:* Additional exam requirements/recommendations for international students: Required—TOEFL.

Medical College of Wisconsin, Graduate School of Biomedical Sciences, Program in Translational Science, Milwaukee, WI 53226-0509. Offers clinical translational science (MS); translational science (PhD).

Michigan State University, The Graduate School, College of Natural Science, Biomedical Laboratory Diagnostics Program, East Lansing, MI 48824. Offers biomedical laboratory operations (MS); clinical laboratory sciences (MS). *Accreditation:* NAACLS. *Faculty:* 4 full-time (1 woman). *Students:* 4 full-time (all women), 23 part-time (14 women); includes 3 minority (all Hispanic Americans), 2 international. Average age 39. 21 applicants, 29% accepted. In 2009, 6 master's awarded. *Entrance requirements:* Additional exam requirements/recommendations for international students: Required—TOEFL. Electronic applications accepted. *Expenses:* Tuition, state resident: part-time $478.25 per credit hour. Tuition, nonresident: part-time $966.50 per credit hour. Part-time tuition and fees vary according to program. *Financial support:* In 2009–10, 2 research assistantships with tuition reimbursements (averaging $6,061 per year), 2 teaching assistantships with tuition reimbursements (averaging $5,919 per year) were awarded. Total annual research expenditures: $6,624. *Unit head:* Dr. John Gerlach, Director, 517-432-3467, Fax: 517-432-2006, E-mail: gerlach@cns.msu.edu. *Application contact:* Mark Bitman, Application Contact, 517-353-9225, Fax: 517-432-2006, E-mail: bld@msu.edu.

Milwaukee School of Engineering, Department of Electrical Engineering and Computer Science, Program in Perfusion, Milwaukee, WI 53202-3109. Offers MS. Part-time and evening/weekend programs available. *Faculty:* 1 full-time (0 women), 4 part-time/adjunct (1 woman). *Students:* 10 full-time (2 women); includes 2 minority (both Asian Americans or Pacific Islanders). Average age 33. 31 applicants, 32% accepted, 7 enrolled. In 2009, 1 master's awarded. *Degree requirements:* For master's, comprehensive exam, thesis. *Entrance requirements:* For master's, GRE General Test or GMAT, BS in appropriate discipline, undergraduate work in human physiology or anatomy, 3 letters of recommendation, interview, observation of 2 perfusion cases. Additional exam requirements/recommendations for international students: Required—TOEFL (minimum score 79 iBT). *Application deadline:* Applications are processed on a rolling basis. Application fee: $30. Electronic applications accepted. *Expenses:* Tuition: Part-time $603 per credit. *Financial support:* In 2009–10, 8 students received support. Career-related internships or fieldwork available. Support available to part-time students. Financial award applicants required to submit FAFSA. *Faculty research:* Heart medicine. *Unit head:* Dr. Ronald Gerrits, Director, 414-277-7561, Fax: 414-277-7494, E-mail: gerrits@msoe.edu. *Application contact:* David E. Tietyen, Graduate Admissions Director, 800-332-6763, Fax: 414-277-7475, E-mail: wp@msoe.edu.

Pontifical Catholic University of Puerto Rico, College of Sciences, Department of Medical Technology, Ponce, PR 00717-0777. Offers Certificate. *Entrance requirements:* For degree, letters of recommendation, interview, minimum GPA of 2.75.

Quinnipiac University, School of Health Sciences, Program for Pathologists' Assistant, Hamden, CT 06518-1940. Offers MHS. *Accreditation:* NAACLS. *Faculty:* 2 full-time (0 women), 3 part-time/adjunct (1 woman). *Students:* 37 full-time (31 women); includes 5 minority (1 African American, 3 Asian Americans or Pacific Islanders, 1 Hispanic American), 5 international. Average age 27. 109 applicants, 19% accepted, 18 enrolled. In 2009, 18 master's awarded. *Degree requirements:* For master's, residency. *Entrance requirements:* For master's, interview, coursework in biological and health sciences, minimum GPA of 2.8. Additional exam requirements/recommendations for international students: Required—TOEFL (minimum score 575 paper-based; 233 computer-based; 90 iBT), IELTS (minimum score 6.5). *Application deadline:* For fall admission, 12/15 for domestic students. Applications are processed on a rolling basis. Application fee: $45. Electronic applications accepted. *Expenses:* Tuition: Full-time $16,030; part-time $770 per credit. Required fees: $630; $35 per credit. *Financial support:* Career-related internships or fieldwork, tuition waivers (partial), and unspecified assistantships available. Financial award application deadline: 4/15; financial award applicants required to submit FAFSA. *Unit head:* Dr. Kenneth Kaloustian, Director, 203-582-8676, Fax: 203-582-3443, E-mail: ken.kaloustian@quinnipiac.edu. *Application contact:* Kristin Parent, Assistant Director of Graduate Health Sciences Admissions, 800-462-1944, Fax: 203-582-3443, E-mail: kristin.parent@quinnipiac.edu.

Quinnipiac University, School of Health Sciences, Program in Medical Laboratory Sciences, Hamden, CT 06518-1940. Offers biomedical sciences (MHS); laboratory management (MHS); microbiology (MHS). *Accreditation:* NAACLS. Part-time programs available. *Faculty:* 9 full-time (5 women), 12 part-time/adjunct (3 women). *Students:* 30 full-time (16 women), 22 part-time (13 women); includes 7 minority (3 African Americans, 1 Asian American or Pacific Islander, 3 Hispanic Americans), 13 international. Average age 28. 44 applicants, 86% accepted, 29 enrolled. In 2009, 15 master's awarded. *Degree requirements:* For master's, comprehensive exam, thesis optional. *Entrance requirements:* For master's, minimum GPA of 2.75; bachelor's degree in biological, medical, or health sciences. Additional exam requirements/recommendations for international students: Required—TOEFL (minimum score 575 paper-based; 233 computer-based; 90 iBT), IELTS (minimum score 6.5). *Application deadline:* For fall admission, 7/30 priority date for domestic students, 4/30 priority date for international students; for spring admission, 12/15 priority date for domestic students, 9/15 priority date for international students. Applications are processed on a rolling basis. Application fee: $45. Electronic applications accepted. *Expenses:* Tuition: Full-time $16,030; part-time $770 per credit. Required fees: $630; $35 per credit. *Financial support:* Federal Work-Study, tuition waivers (partial), and unspecified assistantships available. Support available to part-time students. Financial award application deadline: 4/15; financial award applicants required to submit FAFSA. *Faculty research:* Microbial physiology, fermentation technology. *Unit head:* Dr. Kenneth Kaloustian, Director, 203-582-8676, Fax: 203-582-3443, E-mail: ken.kaloustian@quinnipiac.edu. *Application contact:* Kristin Parent, Assistant Director of Graduate Health Sciences Admissions, 800-462-1944, Fax: 203-582-3443, E-mail: kristin.parent@quinnipiac.edu.

Rochester Institute of Technology, Graduate Enrollment Services, College of Science, Department of Medical Sciences, Program in Clinical Chemistry, Rochester, NY 14623-5603. Offers MS. Part-time programs available. *Students:* 4 full-time (1 woman), 4 part-time (0 women); includes 1 Asian American or Pacific Islander, 6 international. Average age 31. 14 applicants, 43% accepted, 4 enrolled. *Degree requirements:* For master's, thesis. *Entrance requirements:* For master's, GRE General Test (recommended), minimum GPA of 3.0. Additional exam requirements/recommendations for international students: Required—TOEFL (minimum score 575 paper-based; 233 computer-based; 90 iBT), or IELTS (minimum score 6.5). *Application deadline:* For fall admission, 2/15 priority date for domestic and international students; for winter admission, 11/1 for domestic students; for spring admission, 2/1 for domestic students. Applications are processed on a rolling basis. Application fee: $50. Electronic applications accepted. *Expenses:* Tuition: Full-time $31,533; part-time $876 per credit hour. Required fees: $210. *Financial support:* In 2009–10, 4 students received support; research assistantships with partial tuition reimbursements available, career-related internships or fieldwork, scholarships/grants, and unspecified assistantships available. Support available to part-time students. Financial award applicants required to submit FAFSA. *Unit head:* James Aumer, Program Director, 585-475-2526, Fax: 585-475-5809, E-mail: jcascl@rit.edu. *Application contact:* Diane Ellison, Assistant Vice President, Graduate Enrollment Services, 585-475-2229, Fax: 585-475-7164, E-mail: gradinfo@rit.edu.

Rush University, College of Health Sciences, Department of Clinical Laboratory Sciences, Chicago, IL 60612-3832. Offers clinical laboratory management (MS); clinical laboratory science (MS). *Accreditation:* NAACLS. Part-time programs available. *Degree requirements:* For master's, comprehensive exam, graduate project. *Entrance requirements:* For master's, 16 semester hours of chemistry, 12 semester hours of biology, 3 semester hours of mathematics, interview. Additional exam requirements/recommendations for international students: Required—TOEFL. Electronic applications accepted. *Faculty research:* Hematopoietic disorders, molecular techniques, biochemistry, microbial susceptibility, immunology.

San Francisco State University, Division of Graduate Studies, College of Science and Engineering, Department of Biology, San Francisco, CA 94132-1722. Offers biomedical laboratory science (MS); cell and molecular biology (MS); conservation biology (MS); ecology and systematic biology (MS); marine biology (MS); marine science (MS); microbiology (MS); physiology and behavioral biology (MS).

State University of New York Upstate Medical University, Program in Medical Technology, Syracuse, NY 13210-2334. Offers MS. *Accreditation:* NAACLS. *Faculty:* 6 full-time (4 women). *Students:* 10 full-time (6 women), 1 (woman) part-time; includes 9 minority (7 African Americans, 2 Hispanic Americans). Average age 31. 16 applicants, 81% accepted, 6 enrolled. In 2009, 7 master's awarded. *Degree requirements:* For master's, thesis. *Entrance requirements:* For master's, GRE General Test, GRE Subject Test, 2 years of medical technology experience. *Application deadline:* For fall admission, 4/1 priority date for domestic students. Applications are processed on a rolling basis. Application fee: $40. *Financial support:* In 2009–10, 10 students received support. Federal Work-Study available. Support available to part-time students. Financial award application deadline: 3/1; financial award applicants required to submit FAFSA. *Unit head:* Susan S. Graham, Department Chair, 315-464-4608, E-mail: cls@upstate.edu. *Application contact:* Donna Vavonese, Associate Director of Admissions, 315-464-4570, Fax: 315-464-8867, E-mail: vavonesd@upstate.edu.

Thomas Jefferson University, Jefferson College of Health Professions, Program in Bioscience Technologies, Philadelphia, PA 19107. Offers MS. *Accreditation:* NAACLS. Part-time and evening/weekend programs available. *Entrance requirements:* For master's, GRE General Test or MAT. Additional exam requirements/recommendations for international students: Required—TOEFL (minimum score 213 computer-based). Electronic applications accepted. *Expenses:* Tuition: Full-time $26,858; part-time $879 per credit. Required fees: $525. *Faculty research:* Molecular biology of BCR-ABL in chronic myeloid leukemia, diagnostic cytogenetics, ATP binding cassette (ABC), gene family, education outcome studies.

Universidad de las Américas–Puebla, Division of Graduate Studies, School of Sciences, Program in Clinical Analysis (Biomedicine), Puebla, Mexico. Offers MS. Part-time and evening/weekend programs available. *Degree requirements:* For master's, one foreign language, thesis. *Faculty research:* Clinical techniques, clinical research.

Université de Montréal, Faculty of Medicine, Program in Specialized Studies, Montréal, QC H3C 3J7, Canada. Offers anesthesia (DES); diagnostic radiology (DES); family medicine (DES); gastroenterology (DES); geriatry (DES); intensive care (DES); medical biochemistry (DES); medical genetics (DES); medicine (DES); microbiology and infectious diseases (DES); nuclear medicine (DES); obstetrics and gynecology (DES); ophthalmology (DES); pediatrics (DES); pneumology (DES); psychiatry (DES); radiology-oncology (DES); rheumatology (DES); surgery (DES). *Faculty:* 154 full-time (40 women), 333 part-time/adjunct (100 women). *Students:* 930 full-time (580 women), 7 part-time (all women). 74 applicants, 77% accepted, 29 enrolled. *Application deadline:* For fall admission, 2/1 priority date for domestic students; for winter admission, 11/1 priority date for domestic students; for spring admission, 2/1 priority date for domestic students. Application fee: $100. Electronic applications accepted. *Unit head:* Lorraine Locas, Assistant to the Vice Dean of Graduate Studies, 514-343-6269, Fax: 514-343-5751, E-mail: lorraine.locas@umontreal.ca. *Application contact:* Dr. Andre Ferron, Vice Dean Graduate Studies, 514-343-6111 Ext. 0933, Fax: 514-343-5751, E-mail: andre.ferron@umontreal.ca.

Université de Sherbrooke, Faculty of Medicine and Health Sciences, Graduate Programs in Medicine, Program in Clinical Sciences, Sherbrooke, QC J1H 5N4, Canada. Offers M Sc, PhD. Part-time programs available. Terminal master's awarded for partial completion of doctoral program. *Degree requirements:* For master's, thesis; for doctorate, thesis/dissertation. Electronic applications accepted. *Faculty research:* Population health, health services, ethics, clinical research.

University at Buffalo, the State University of New York, Graduate School, School of Medicine and Biomedical Sciences, Graduate Programs in Medicine and Biomedical Sciences, Department of Biotechnical and Clinical Laboratory Sciences, Buffalo, NY 14260. Offers biotechnology (MS). *Accreditation:* NAACLS. Part-time programs available. *Faculty:* 9 full-time (6 women), 5 part-time/adjunct (3 women). *Students:* 27 full-time (11 women), 1 (woman) part-time, 24 international. Average age 24. 115 applicants, 63% accepted, 10 enrolled. In 2009, 12 master's awarded. *Degree requirements:* For master's, thesis. *Entrance requirements:* For master's, GRE General Test, background in biology, chemistry or related field. Additional exam requirements/recommendations for international students: Required—TOEFL (minimum score 233 computer-based; 79 iBT). *Application deadline:* For fall admission, 3/1 priority date for domestic students, 2/1 for international students. Applications are processed on a rolling basis. Application fee: $50. Electronic applications accepted. *Financial support:* In 2009–10, 15 students received support, including research assistantships with full and partial tuition reimbursements available (averaging $10,000 per year), 15 teaching assistantships with full tuition reimbursements available (averaging $9,000 per year); Federal Work-Study and unspecified assistantships also available. Financial award application deadline: 3/1. *Faculty research:* Endocrine-immune interaction, tumor immunology, molecular biology, oxidative stress, cell differentiation. Total annual research expenditures: $1.1 million. *Unit head:* Dr. Paul Kostyniak, Chair, 716-829-3630 Ext. 107, Fax: 716-829-3601. *Application contact:* Dr. Stephen T. Koury, Director of Graduate Studies, 716-829-3630 Ext. 111, Fax: 716-829-3601, E-mail: stvkoury@buffalo.edu.

University of Alberta, Faculty of Medicine and Dentistry and Faculty of Graduate Studies and Research, Graduate Programs in Medicine, Department of Laboratory Medicine and Pathology, Edmonton, AB T6G 2E1, Canada. Offers medical sciences (M Sc, PhD). Part-time programs available. *Faculty:* 8 full-time. *Students:* 8 full-time (4 women), 3 part-time (all women). 25 applicants, 20% accepted. In 2009, 1 master's, 2 doctorates awarded. Terminal master's awarded for partial completion of doctoral program. *Degree requirements:* For master's, thesis; for doctorate, thesis/dissertation, candidacy exam. *Entrance requirements:* For master's and doctorate, 3 letters of recommendation, minimum GPA of 3.0. Additional exam requirements/recommendations for international students: Required—TOEFL. *Application deadline:* For fall admission, 5/15 for international students; for winter admission, 9/15 for international students; for spring admission, 1/15 for international students. Applications are processed on a rolling basis. Application fee: $0. Tuition and fee charges are reported in Canadian dollars. *Expenses:* Tuition, area resident: Full-time $4626 Canadian dollars; part-time $99.72 Canadian dollars per unit. International tuition: $8216 Canadian dollars full-time. Required fees: $3590 Canadian dollars; $99.72 Canadian dollars per unit. $215 Canadian dollars per term. *Financial support:* In 2009–10, 3 fellowships with full tuition reimbursements (averaging $16,000 per year), 6 research assistantships (averaging $12,000 per year), 1 teaching assistantship (averaging $8,000 per year) were awarded; scholarships/grants and unspecified assistantships also available. *Faculty research:* Transplantation, renal pathology, molecular mechanisms of diseases, cryobiology, immunodiagnostics, informatics/cyber medicine, neuroimmunology, microbiology. Total annual research expenditures: $550,000. *Unit head:* Br. John J. O'Connnor. *Application contact:* Dr. Gregory J. Tyrrell, Graduate Coordinator, 780-407-8949, Fax: 780-407-3964, E-mail: g.tyrrell@provlab.ab.ca.

University of Colorado Denver, School of Medicine, Program in Clinical Science, Denver, CO 80217-3364. Offers MS, PhD. *Students:* 32 full-time (17 women), 12 part-time (9 women); includes 6 minority (2 American Indian/Alaska Native, 3 Asian Americans or Pacific Islanders, 1 Hispanic American), 1 international. In 2009, 1 doctorate awarded. *Degree requirements:* For doctorate, comprehensive exam, thesis/dissertation. *Entrance requirements:* For master's and doctorate, GRE General Test or MCAT, minimum GPA of 3.0. Additional exam requirements/recommendations for international students: Required—TOEFL (minimum score 550 paper-based; 213 computer-based). *Application deadline:* For fall admission, 1/31 for domestic students. Application fee: $50. *Financial support:* Fellowships, research assistantships, teaching assistantships, Federal Work-Study and institutionally sponsored loans available. Support available to part-time students. Financial award application deadline: 3/15; financial award applicants required to submit FAFSA. *Unit head:* Dr. Lisa Cicutto, Program Director, 303-398-

Clinical Laboratory Sciences/Medical Technology

University of Colorado Denver (continued)
1538, E-mail: cicuttol@njc.org. *Application contact:* Lori Stepp, Administrator, 303-398-1657, Fax: 303-270-2249, E-mail: steppl@njc.org.

University of Kentucky, Graduate School, College of Health Sciences, Program in Clinical Sciences, Lexington, KY 40506-0032. Offers MS, DS. *Accreditation:* NAACLS. *Degree requirements:* For master's, comprehensive exam; for doctorate, comprehensive exam, thesis/dissertation. *Entrance requirements:* For master's, GRE General Test, minimum undergraduate GPA of 2.75; for doctorate, GRE General Test, minimum undergraduate GPA of 3.0. Additional exam requirements/recommendations for international students: Required—TOEFL (minimum score 550 paper-based; 213 computer-based). Electronic applications accepted.

University of Maryland, Baltimore, Graduate School, Department of Medical and Research Technology, Baltimore, MD 21201. Offers MS. *Accreditation:* NAACLS. Part-time programs available. *Students:* 6 full-time (3 women), 9 part-time (7 women); includes 8 minority (6 African Americans, 2 Hispanic Americans), 4 international. Average age 31. 10 applicants, 70% accepted, 4 enrolled. In 2009, 3 master's awarded. *Degree requirements:* For master's, thesis or management project. *Entrance requirements:* For master's, GRE General Test, minimum GPA of 3.0. Additional exam requirements/recommendations for international students: Required—TOEFL (minimum score 550 paper-based; 213 computer-based; 80 iBT), or IELTS (minimum score 7). *Application deadline:* For fall admission, 5/1 priority date for domestic students, 1/15 for international students; for spring admission, 11/30 priority date for domestic students. Application fee: $50. Electronic applications accepted. *Expenses:* Tuition, state resident: full-time $7290; part-time $405 per credit hour. Tuition, nonresident: full-time $12,780; part-time $710 per credit hour. Required fees: $774; $10 per credit hour. $297 per semester. Tuition and fees vary according to course load, degree level and program. *Financial support:* Fellowships, research assistantships available. Financial award application deadline: 3/1; financial award applicants required to submit FAFSA. *Faculty research:* Clinical microbiology, immunology, immunohematology, hematology, clinical chemistry, molecular biology. *Unit head:* Dr. Sanford Stass, Chair, 410-328-1237. *Application contact:* Dr. Kimberly Walker, Graduate Director, 410-706-2627, Fax: 410-706-5229, E-mail: kwalker@som.umaryland.edu.

University of Massachusetts Lowell, School of Health and Environment, Department of Clinical Laboratory and Nutritional Sciences, Lowell, MA 01854-2881. Offers clinical laboratory sciences (MS); clinical pathology (Graduate Certificate); nutritional sciences (Graduate Certificate); public health laboratory sciences (Graduate Certificate). *Accreditation:* NAACLS. Part-time programs available. Postbaccalaureate distance learning degree programs offered. *Degree requirements:* For master's, thesis optional. *Entrance requirements:* For master's, GRE General Test, minimum GPA of 3.0, letters of recommendation. *Faculty research:* Cardiovascular disease, lipoprotein metabolism, micronutrient evaluation, alcohol metabolism, mycobacterial drug resistance.

University of Medicine and Dentistry of New Jersey, School of Health Related Professions, Department of Interdisciplinary Studies, Program in Health Sciences, Newark, NJ 07107-1709. Offers cardiopulmonary sciences (PhD); clinical laboratory sciences (PhD); health sciences (MS); interdisciplinary studies (PhD); nutrition (PhD); physical therapy/movement science (PhD). *Degree requirements:* For doctorate, thesis/dissertation. *Entrance requirements:* For doctorate, interview, writing sample. Additional exam requirements/recommendations for international students: Required—TOEFL. Electronic applications accepted.

University of Mississippi Medical Center, School of Graduate Studies in the Health Sciences, Program in Clinical Health Sciences, Jackson, MS 39216-4505. Offers MS, PhD. Part-time programs available. Terminal master's awarded for partial completion of doctoral program. *Degree requirements:* For master's, thesis; for doctorate, thesis/dissertation. *Entrance requirements:* For master's and doctorate, GRE, 1 year of clinical experience. Additional exam requirements/recommendations for international students: Required—TOEFL. *Faculty research:* Clinical outcomes assessment via qualitative measures; health information systems; experimental laboratory evaluation of materials, drugs, hormones, and techniques used in clinical practice.

University of Nebraska Medical Center, School of Allied Health Professions, Program in Clinical Perfusion Education, Omaha, NE 68198-4144. Offers distance education perfusion education (MPS); perfusion science (MPS). *Accreditation:* NAACLS. Postbaccalaureate distance learning degree programs offered. *Degree requirements:* For master's, comprehensive exam, thesis. *Entrance requirements:* For master's, GRE. Electronic applications accepted. *Faculty research:* Platelet gel, hemoconcentrators.

University of Nebraska Medical Center, School of Allied Health Professions, Program in Cytotechnology, Omaha, NE 68198. Offers Certificate. *Accreditation:* NAACLS. Postbaccalaureate distance learning degree programs offered (minimal on-campus study). Electronic applications accepted. *Faculty research:* HPV vaccine.

University of New Mexico, School of Medicine, Program in Clinical Laboratory Science, Albuquerque, NM 87131-2039. Offers MS. *Expenses:* Tuition, state resident: full-time $2099; part-time $233.20 per credit hour. Tuition, nonresident: full-time $6650. Required fees: $25 per semester. Tuition and fees vary according to course load, program and reciprocity agreements.

University of North Dakota, School of Medicine and Health Sciences and Graduate School, Graduate Programs in Medicine, Department of Clinical Laboratory Science, Grand Forks, ND 58202. Offers MS. *Accreditation:* NAACLS. Postbaccalaureate distance learning degree programs offered (minimal on-campus study). *Degree requirements:* For master's, comprehensive exam, thesis or alternative. *Entrance requirements:* For master's, minimum GPA of 3.0. Additional exam requirements/recommendations for international students: Required—TOEFL (minimum score 550 paper-based; 213 computer-based; 79 iBT), IELTS (minimum score 5.5). Electronic applications accepted.

University of Pittsburgh, School of Medicine, Programs in Clinical Research, Program in Clinical and Translational Science, Pittsburgh, PA 15260. Offers PhD. Part-time programs available. *Faculty:* 48 full-time (18 women). *Students:* 5 part-time (1 woman); includes 1 minority (Hispanic American), 1 international. Average age 35. 4 applicants, 50% accepted, 2 enrolled. *Degree requirements:* For doctorate, comprehensive exam, thesis/dissertation. *Entrance requirements:* For doctorate, MCAT, GRE or GMAT. Additional exam requirements/recommendations for international students: Required—TOEFL (minimum score 600 paper-based; 250 computer-based; 100 iBT). *Application deadline:* For spring admission, 4/15 priority date for domestic and international students. Application fee: $0. Electronic applications accepted. *Expenses:* Tuition, state resident: full-time $16,402; part-time $665 per credit. Tuition, nonresident: full-time $28,694; part-time $1175 per credit. Required fees: $690; $175 per term. Tuition and fees vary according to program. *Faculty research:* Research design and methodology, healthcare outcomes and process assessment, organ and tissue donation and transplantation, measuring and improving function in patients with chronic kidney disease. *Unit head:* Dr. Wishwa Kapoor, Program Director, 412-586-9670, Fax: 412-586-9672, E-mail: kapoorwn@upmc.edu. *Application contact:* Benjamin M. Huffman, Program Coordinator, 412-586-9670, Fax: 412-586-9672, E-mail: huffmanbm@upmc.edu.

University of Puerto Rico, Medical Sciences Campus, School of Health Professions, Program in Clinical Laboratory Science, San Juan, PR 00936-5067. Offers MS. *Accreditation:* NAACLS. Part-time and evening/weekend programs available. *Degree requirements:* For master's, one foreign language, thesis or alternative. *Entrance requirements:* For master's, EXADEP or GRE General Test, minimum GPA of 2.75, bachelor's degree in medical technology, 1 year lab experience, interview. *Faculty research:* Toxicology, virology, biochemistry, immunohematology, nervous system regeneration.

University of Puerto Rico, Medical Sciences Campus, School of Health Professions, Program in Cytotechnology, San Juan, PR 00936-5067. Offers Certificate. *Degree requirements:* For Certificate, one foreign language, research project. *Entrance requirements:* For degree, minimum GPA of 2.5, interview.

University of Puerto Rico, Medical Sciences Campus, School of Health Professions, Program in Medical Technology, San Juan, PR 00936-5067. Offers Certificate. Part-time programs available. *Degree requirements:* For Certificate, one foreign language, clinical practice. *Entrance requirements:* For degree, bachelor's degree in science, minimum GPA of 2.5.

University of Rhode Island, Graduate School, College of the Environment and Life Sciences, Department of Cell and Molecular Biology, Kingston, RI 02881. Offers biochemistry (MS, PhD); clinical laboratory sciences (MS), including biotechnology, clinical laboratory science, cytopathology; microbiology (MS, PhD); molecular genetics (MS, PhD). Part-time programs available. *Faculty:* 12 full-time (4 women). *Students:* 29 full-time (17 women), 43 part-time (31 women); includes 13 minority (5 African Americans, 4 Asian Americans or Pacific Islanders, 4 Hispanic Americans), 3 international. In 2009, 5 master's, 2 doctorates awarded. *Degree requirements:* For master's, comprehensive exam (for some programs); for doctorate, comprehensive exam. *Entrance requirements:* For master's and doctorate, GRE, 2 letters of recommendation. Additional exam requirements/recommendations for international students: Required—TOEFL (minimum score 550 paper-based; 213 computer-based). *Application deadline:* For fall admission, 7/15 for domestic students, 2/1 for international students; for spring admission, 11/15 for domestic students, 7/15 for international students. Application fee: $65. Electronic applications accepted. *Expenses:* Tuition, state resident: full-time $8828; part-time $490 per credit hour. Tuition, nonresident: full-time $22,100; part-time $1228 per credit hour. Required fees: $1118; $57 per semester. Tuition and fees vary according to program. *Financial support:* In 2009–10, 2 research assistantships with full and partial tuition reimbursements (averaging $10,535 per year), 10 teaching assistantships with full and partial tuition reimbursements (averaging $13,449 per year) were awarded. Financial award application deadline: 7/15; financial award applicants required to submit FAFSA. *Faculty research:* Genomics and Sequencing Center: an interdisciplinary genomics research and undergraduate and graduate student training program which provides researchers access to cutting-edge technologies in the field of genomics. Total annual research expenditures: $1.2 million. *Unit head:* Dr. Jay Sperry, Chairperson, 401-874-2201, Fax: 401-874-2202, E-mail: jsperry@mail.uri.edu. *Application contact:* Dr. Jay Sperry, Chairperson, 401-874-2201, Fax: 401-874-2202, E-mail: jsperry@mail.uri.edu.

University of Southern Mississippi, Graduate School, College of Health, Department of Medical Technology, Hattiesburg, MS 39406-0001. Offers MS. *Accreditation:* NAACLS. Part-time programs available. *Faculty:* 5 full-time (all women). *Students:* 7 full-time (all women), 3 part-time (2 women); includes 4 minority (3 African Americans, 1 Hispanic American), 1 international. Average age 28. 3 applicants, 67% accepted, 2 enrolled. *Degree requirements:* For master's, comprehensive exam, thesis (for some programs). *Entrance requirements:* For master's, GRE General Test, minimum GPA of 2.75. Additional exam requirements/recommendations for international students: Required—TOEFL. *Application deadline:* For fall admission, 3/1 priority date for domestic students, 3/1 for international students. Application fee: $35. Electronic applications accepted. *Expenses:* Tuition, state resident: full-time $5096; part-time $284 per hour. Tuition, nonresident: full-time $13,052; part-time $726 per hour. Required fees: $402. Tuition and fees vary according to course level and course load. *Financial support:* In 2009–10, 3 teaching assistantships with full tuition reimbursements (averaging $6,000 per year) were awarded; research assistantships, Federal Work-Study also available. Financial award application deadline: 3/15; financial award applicants required to submit FAFSA. *Faculty research:* Clinical chemistry, clinical microbiology, hematology, clinical management and education, immunohematology. *Unit head:* Dr. Jane Hudson, Chair, 601-266-4908. *Application contact:* Shonna Breland, Manager of Graduate Admissions, 601-266-6563, Fax: 601-266-5138.

The University of Texas Health Science Center at San Antonio, School of Allied Health Sciences, San Antonio, TX 78229-3900. Offers clinical laboratory sciences (MS); deaf education and hearing science (MED); dental hygiene (MS); occupational therapy (MOT); physical therapy (MPT); physician assistant studies (MS). *Accreditation:* AOTA; APTA; ARC-PA. *Expenses:* Tuition, state resident: full-time $2832; part-time $118 per credit hour. Tuition, nonresident: full-time $10,896; part-time $454 per credit hour. Required fees: $884 per semester. One-time fee: $70.

The University of Texas Medical Branch, Graduate School of Biomedical Sciences, Program in Clinical Science, Galveston, TX 77555. Offers MS, PhD. *Unit head:* Dr. Karl E. Anderson, Director, 409-772-4661, Fax: 409-772-8097, E-mail: kanderso@utmb.edu. *Application contact:* Marie Carr, Application Contact, 409-772-1484, Fax: 409-772-8097, E-mail: mcarr@utmb.edu.

University of Utah, School of Medicine and Graduate School, Graduate Programs in Medicine, Department of Pathology, Program in Laboratory Medicine and Biomedical Science, Salt Lake City, UT 84112-1107. Offers MS. Part-time programs available. *Degree requirements:* For master's, comprehensive exam, thesis, thesis research. *Entrance requirements:* For master's, minimum GPA of 3.0 during last 2 years of undergraduate course work, BS in medical laboratory science or related field. Additional exam requirements/recommendations for international students: Required—TOEFL (minimum score 550 paper-based). *Expenses:* Tuition, state resident: full-time $4004; part-time $1674 per semester. Tuition, nonresident: full-time $14,134; part-time $5915 per semester. Required fees: $324 per semester. Tuition and fees vary according to course load, degree level and program. *Faculty research:* Clinical chemistry, hematology, diagnostic microbiology, immunohematology, cell biology, immunology.

University of Vermont, College of Medicine and Graduate College, Graduate Programs in Medicine, Program in Clinical and Translational Science, Burlington, VT 05405. Offers MS, PhD. *Students:* 7 (4 women). 9 applicants, 56% accepted, 2 enrolled. *Entrance requirements:* For master's and doctorate, GRE. Additional exam requirements/recommendations for international students: Recommended—TOEFL (minimum score 550 paper-based; 213 computer-based; 80 iBT). *Application deadline:* For fall admission, 4/1 for domestic students. Applications are processed on a rolling basis. Application fee: $40. Electronic applications accepted. *Expenses:* Tuition, state resident: part-time $508 per credit hour. Tuition, nonresident: part-time $1281 per credit hour. *Financial support:* Teaching assistantships available. *Unit head:* Dr. Alan Rubin, Director, 802-847-8268, E-mail: alan.rubin@uvm.edu. *Application contact:* Dr. Alan Rubin, Director, 802-847-8268, E-mail: alan.rubin@uvm.edu.

University of Washington, Graduate School, School of Medicine and Graduate School, Graduate Programs in Medicine, Department of Laboratory Medicine, Seattle, WA 98195. Offers MS. *Accreditation:* NAACLS. Part-time programs available. *Degree requirements:* For master's, thesis. *Entrance requirements:* For master's, GRE General Test, medical technology certification or specialist in an area of laboratory medicine.

University of Wisconsin–Milwaukee, Graduate School, College of Health Sciences, Program in Clinical Laboratory Science, Milwaukee, WI 53211. Offers MS. *Accreditation:* NAACLS. Part-time programs available. *Faculty:* 7 full-time (3 women). *Students:* 9 full-time (8 women), 3 part-time (2 women); includes 4 minority (1 African American, 1 American Indian/Alaska Native, 1 Asian American or Pacific Islander, 1 Hispanic American), 2 international. Average age 28. 21 applicants, 52% accepted, 3 enrolled. *Degree requirements:* For master's, thesis. *Entrance requirements:* For master's, GRE General Test. Additional exam requirements/recommendations for international students: Required—TOEFL (minimum score 550 paper-based; 79 iBT), IELTS (minimum score 6.5). *Application deadline:* For fall admission, 1/1 priority date for domestic students; for spring admission, 9/1 for domestic students. Applications are processed on a rolling basis. Application fee: $45 ($75 for international students). *Expenses:* Tuition, state resident: full-time $8800. Tuition, nonresident: full-time $20,760. Tuition and fees vary according to program and reciprocity agreements. *Financial support:* In 2009–10, 1 research assistantship, 5 teaching assistantships were awarded; fellowships, career-related internships or fieldwork and unspecified assistantships also available. Support available to part-time students. Financial award application deadline: 4/15. Total annual research expenditures: $170,547. *Unit head:* Jeri-Anne Lyons, Representative, 414-229-3812, E-mail: jlyons@uwm.edu. *Application contact:* Jeri-Anne Lyons, Representative, 414-229-3812, E-mail: jlyons@uwm.edu.

Virginia Commonwealth University, Graduate School, School of Allied Health Professions, Department of Clinical Laboratory Sciences, Richmond, VA 23284-9005. Offers MS. *Accreditation:* NAACLS. *Degree requirements:* For master's, one foreign language, thesis. *Entrance requirements:* For master's, GRE General Test, current medical technologist certification. *Faculty research:* Educational outcomes assessment, virtual instrumentation development, cost-effective treatment of bacteremia using third generation cephalosporins.

Virginia Commonwealth University, Graduate School, School of Allied Health Professions, Department of Health Administration, Doctoral Program in Health Related Sciences, Richmond, VA 23284-9005. Offers clinical laboratory sciences (PhD); gerontology (PhD); health administration (PhD); nurse anesthesia (PhD); occupational therapy (PhD); physical therapy (PhD); radiation sciences (PhD); rehabilitation leadership (PhD).

Wayne State University, Eugene Applebaum College of Pharmacy and Health Sciences, Department of Fundamental and Applied Sciences, Program in Clinical Laboratory Sciences, Detroit, MI 48202. Offers clinical laboratory science (MS); medical technology (Certificate). *Accreditation:* NAACLS. *Degree requirements:* For master's, thesis optional. *Entrance requirements:* Additional exam requirements/recommendations for international students: Required—TOEFL (minimum score 550 paper-based; 213 computer-based); Recommended—TWE (minimum score 6). Electronic applications accepted. *Faculty research:* Clinical microbiology, molecular diagnostics, development and evaluation of molecular assays for the diagnosis of infectious diseases.

Clinical Research

Case Western Reserve University, School of Medicine, Clinical Research Scholars Program, Cleveland, OH 44106. Offers MS.

Duke University, School of Medicine, Clinical Research Program, Durham, NC 27708-0586. Offers MHS. Part-time programs available. *Faculty:* 21 part-time/adjunct (3 women). *Students:* 13 full-time (6 women), 121 part-time (71 women); includes 47 minority (9 African Americans, 1 American Indian/Alaska Native, 36 Asian Americans or Pacific Islanders, 1 Hispanic American). 78 applicants, 97% accepted, 72 enrolled. In 2009, 32 master's awarded. *Degree requirements:* For master's, research project. *Entrance requirements:* For master's, GRE. *Application deadline:* For fall admission, 5/15 for domestic students. *Expenses:* Contact institution. *Financial support:* In 2009–10, 2 students received support; fellowships, research assistantships, teaching assistantships, scholarships/grants available. Financial award application deadline: 5/1; financial award applicants required to submit FAFSA. *Unit head:* Dr. Eugene Oddone, Director, 919-681-4560, Fax: 919-681-4569, E-mail: oddon001@mc.duke.edu. *Application contact:* Gail Ladd, Program Coordinator, 919-681-4560, Fax: 919-681-4569, E-mail: ladd0002@mc.duke.edu.

Eastern Michigan University, Graduate School, College of Health and Human Services, School of Health Sciences, Program in Clinical Research Administration, Ypsilanti, MI 48197. Offers MS, Graduate Certificate. Part-time and evening/weekend programs available. Post-baccalaureate distance learning degree programs offered (minimal on-campus study). *Students:* 21 full-time (15 women), 67 part-time (45 women); includes 16 minority (9 African Americans, 6 Asian Americans or Pacific Islanders, 1 Hispanic American), 42 international. Average age 31. In 2009, 7 master's, 8 other advanced degrees awarded. *Entrance requirements:* Additional exam requirements/recommendations for international students: Required—TOEFL. *Application deadline:* Applications are processed on a rolling basis. Application fee: $35. Tuition and fees vary according to course level. *Financial support:* Fellowships, research assistantships with full tuition reimbursements, teaching assistantships with full tuition reimbursements, career-related internships or fieldwork, Federal Work-Study, institutionally sponsored loans, scholarships/grants, tuition waivers (partial), and unspecified assistantships available. Support available to part-time students. Financial award applicants required to submit FAFSA. *Unit head:* Dr. Stephen Sonstein, Program Coordinator, 734-487-1238, Fax: 734-487-4095, E-mail: stephen.sonstein@emich.edu. *Application contact:* Dr. Stephen Sonstein, Program Coordinator, 734-487-1238, Fax: 734-487-4095, E-mail: stephen.sonstein@emich.edu.

Emory University, Graduate School of Arts and Sciences, Program in Clinical Research, Atlanta, GA 30322-1100. Offers MS. Part-time programs available. *Degree requirements:* For master's, thesis.

The Johns Hopkins University, Bloomberg School of Public Health, Graduate Training Program in Clinical Investigation, Baltimore, MD 21287. Offers MHS, Sc M, PhD. *Faculty:* 18 full-time (5 women). *Students:* 16 full-time (8 women), 30 part-time (17 women); includes 12 minority (2 African Americans, 10 Asian Americans or Pacific Islanders), 3 international. Average age 36. 24 applicants, 71% accepted, 14 enrolled. In 2009, 10 master's, 11 doctorates awarded. *Degree requirements:* For master's, comprehensive exam, thesis; for doctorate, comprehensive exam, thesis/dissertation. *Entrance requirements:* For master's, GRE or MCAT; United States Medical Licensing Exam, 2 letters of recommendation, curriculum vitae, transcripts, statement of purpose; for doctorate, GRE or MCAT; United States Medical Licensing Exam, 2 letters of recommendation, curriculum vitae. Additional exam requirements/recommendations for international students: Required—TOEFL (minimum score 600 paper-based; 250 computer-based). *Application deadline:* For spring admission, 3/1 for domestic and international students. Applications are processed on a rolling basis. Application fee: $45. Electronic applications accepted. *Financial support:* In 2009–10, 46 students received support, including 51 fellowships with partial tuition reimbursements available (averaging $27,480 per year); institutionally sponsored loans, scholarships/grants, and stipends also available. Support available to part-time students. Financial award application deadline: 3/15; financial award applicants required to submit FAFSA. *Faculty research:* Ethical issues, biomedical writing, grant writing, epidemiology, biostatistics. *Unit head:* Dr. N. Franklin Adkinson, Director, 410-550-2051, Fax: 410-550-2055, E-mail: fadkinso@jhmi.edu. *Application contact:* Cristina A. DeNardo, Academic Program Manager, 410-502-9734, Fax: 410-502-6966, E-mail: gtpci@jhsph.edu.

Medical College of Georgia, School of Graduate Studies, Program in Clinical and Translational Science, Augusta, GA 30912. Offers MCTS, CCTS. Full-time tuition and fees vary according to campus/location, program and student level.

Medical University of South Carolina, College of Graduate Studies, Program in Clinical Research, Charleston, SC 29425. Offers MS. *Faculty:* 10 full-time (2 women). *Students:* 10 full-time (3 women), 16 part-time (10 women); includes 1 African American, 2 Asian Americans or Pacific Islanders, 3 international. Average age 33. 16 applicants, 94% accepted, 12 enrolled. In 2009, 22 master's awarded. *Entrance requirements:* Additional exam requirements/recommendations for international students: Required—TOEFL (minimum score 600 paper-based; 250 computer-based; 100 iBT). *Application deadline:* For fall admission, 5/21 priority date for domestic and international students. Applications are processed on a rolling basis. Application fee: $85. Electronic applications accepted. *Financial support:* Federal Work-Study and scholarships/grants available. Support available to part-time students. Financial award application deadline: 3/10; financial award applicants required to submit FAFSA. *Unit head:* Dr. Thomas C. Hulsey, Director, 843-792-9907, Fax: 843-792-0227, E-mail: hulseytc@musc.edu. *Application contact:* Erica B. Brown, Program Coordinator, 843-792-8449, Fax: 843-792-0227, E-mail: blendere@musc.edu.

Memorial University of Newfoundland, Faculty of Medicine and School of Graduate Studies, Graduate Programs in Medicine, Division of Applied Health Services Research, St. John's, NL A1C 5S7, Canada. Offers M Sc.

Morehouse School of Medicine, Master of Science in Clinical Research Program, Atlanta, GA 30310-1495. Offers MS. Part-time programs available. *Faculty:* 15 full-time (3 women), 10 part-time/adjunct (2 women). *Students:* 11 full-time (10 women); all minorities (9 African Americans, 2 Asian Americans or Pacific Islanders). Average age 32. 5 applicants, 60% accepted, 3 enrolled. In 2009, 3 master's awarded. *Degree requirements:* For master's, thesis. *Application deadline:* For fall admission, 4/6 for domestic students, 4/6 priority date for international students. Application fee: $0. Electronic applications accepted. *Expenses:* Tuition: Full-time $29,484; part-time $446 per credit hour. Required fees: $7230. Tuition and fees vary according to class time, course level, course load, degree level, program, reciprocity agreements and student level. *Financial support:* Applicants required to submit FAFSA. *Unit head:* Dr. Elizabeth Ofili, Director, 404-752-1192, E-mail: ofilie@msm.edu. *Application contact:* Dr. Sterling Roaf, Director of Admissions, 404-752-1650, Fax: 404-752-1512, E-mail: sroaf@msm.edu.

Mount Sinai School of Medicine of New York University, Graduate School of Biological Sciences, New York, NY 10029-6504. Offers bioethics (MS); biological sciences (PhD); clinical research (MS); community medicine (MPH); genetic counseling (MS); neurosciences (PhD); MD/PhD. Terminal master's awarded for partial completion of doctoral program. *Degree requirements:* For master's, thesis; for doctorate, comprehensive exam, thesis/dissertation. *Entrance requirements:* For master's, GRE General Test; for doctorate, GRE General Test, GRE Subject Test, 3 years of college pre-med course work. Additional exam requirements/recommendations for international students: Required—TOEFL. Electronic applications accepted. *Faculty research:* Cancer, genetics and genomics, immunology, neuroscience, developmental and stem cell biology, translational research.

New York University, College of Dentistry, Program in Clinical Research, New York, NY 10010. Offers MS. *Students:* 21 full-time (12 women), 4 part-time (all women); includes 19 minority (1 African American, 16 Asian Americans or Pacific Islanders, 2 Hispanic Americans). Average age 31. 13 applicants, 100% accepted, 11 enrolled. In 2009, 12 master's awarded. *Entrance requirements:* For master's, GRE. Additional exam requirements/recommendations for international students: Required—TOEFL (minimum score 570 paper-based; 230 computer-based; 88 iBT). *Application deadline:* For fall admission, 2/28 priority date for domestic and international students. Application fee: $100. Electronic applications accepted. *Expenses:* Tuition: Full-time $30,528; part-time $1272 per credit. Required fees: $2177. *Financial support:* Application deadline: 3/1. *Unit head:* Dr. Ralph V. Katz, Chair, 212-998-9550, Fax: 212-995-4436, E-mail: ralph.katz@nyu.edu. *Application contact:* Dr. Anthony M. Palatta, Assistant Dean for Student Affairs and Admissions, 212-998-9918, Fax: 212-995-4240, E-mail: ap16@nyu.edu.

New York University, School of Medicine, New York, NY 10012-1019. Offers biomedical sciences (PhD), including biomedical imaging, cellular and molecular biology, computational biology, developmental genetics, medical and molecular parasitology, microbiology, molecular oncobiology and immunology, neuroscience and physiology, pathobiology, pharmacology, structural biology; clinical investigation (MS); medicine (MD); MD/MA; MD/MPA; MD/MS; MD/PhD. *Accreditation:* LCME/AMA (one or more programs are accredited). *Faculty:* 1,493 full-time (558 women), 327 part-time/adjunct (122 women). *Students:* 747 full-time (360 women); includes 275 minority (23 African Americans, 5 American Indian/Alaska Native, 199 Asian Americans or Pacific Islanders, 48 Hispanic Americans), 2 international. Average age 24. 7,568 applicants, 7% accepted, 213 enrolled. In 2009, 164 first professional degrees, 13 master's, 50 doctorates awarded. *Degree requirements:* For master's, comprehensive exam, thesis; for doctorate, comprehensive exam, thesis/dissertation. *Entrance requirements:* MCAT. Additional exam requirements/recommendations for international students: Required—TOEFL. *Application deadline:* For fall admission, 10/15 for domestic students; for winter admission, 12/18 for domestic students, 12/15 for international students. Application fee: $100. *Expenses:* Contact institution. *Financial support:* In 2009–10, 524 students received support, including 29 fellowships with full tuition reimbursements available (averaging $31,000 per year), 47 research assistantships with full tuition reimbursements available (averaging $31,000 per year); teaching assistantships, Federal Work-Study, institutionally sponsored loans, and health care benefits also available. Financial award application deadline: 3/1; financial award applicants required to submit FAFSA. *Faculty research:* AIDS, cancer, neuroscience, molecular biology, neuroscience, cell biology and molecular genetics, structural biology, microbial pathogenesis and host defense, pharmacology, molecular oncology and immunology. Total annual research expenditures: $201.1 million. *Unit head:* Dr. Robert Grossman, Dean, 212-263-3269, Fax: 212-263- 1828. *Application contact:* Dr. Nancy Genieser, Associate Dean, Admissions, 212-263-5290, Fax: 212-263-0720, E-mail: nancy.genieser@nyumc.org.

Northwestern University, The Graduate School, Program in Clinical Investigation, Evanston, IL 60208. Offers MSCI, Certificate. Part-time and evening/weekend programs available. *Faculty research:* Wide range of epidemiologic, clinical and bench research across all medical school departments.

Northwestern University, Northwestern University Feinberg School of Medicine, Department of Clinical Investigation, Evanston, IL 60208. Offers MSCI. Part-time and evening/weekend programs available. *Entrance requirements:* For master's, GRE or MCAT, doctoral degree in healthcare-related field. Additional exam requirements/recommendations for international students: Required—TOEFL. Electronic applications accepted. *Faculty research:* Clinical research.

Northwestern University, School of Continuing Studies, Program in Clinical Research and Regulatory Administration, Evanston, IL 60208. Offers MS.

Palmer College of Chiropractic, Division of Graduate Studies, Davenport, IA 52803-5287. Offers clinical research (MS). *Faculty:* 133 full-time (40 women). *Students:* 8 full-time (3 women), 4 part-time (1 woman). *Degree requirements:* For master's, comprehensive exam, thesis. *Entrance requirements:* For master's, GRE General Test, minimum GPA of 2.5. Additional exam requirements/recommendations for international students: Required—TOEFL. *Application deadline:* For fall admission, 9/1 for domestic students; for spring admission, 5/28 for domestic students. Applications are processed on a rolling basis. Application fee: $50. Electronic applications accepted. *Expenses:* Contact institution. *Financial support:* In 2009–10, 5 students received support, including teaching assistantships with full and partial tuition reimbursements available (averaging $6,269 per year); research assistantships, Federal Work-Study, institutionally sponsored loans, tuition waivers (full), and stipends also available. Support available to part-time students. Financial award application deadline: 4/1; financial award applicants required to submit FAFSA. *Unit head:* Dr. Jean Murray, Administrator, 563-884-5672, Fax: 563-884-5505. *Application contact:* Dr. Brian McMaster, Assistant Dean, 563-884-5163, Fax: 563-884-5226, E-mail: brian.mcmaster@plamer.edu.

Thomas Jefferson University, Jefferson College of Graduate Studies, Program in Clinical Research, Public Health, and Research Management, Philadelphia, PA 19107. Offers Certificate. *Students:* 17 part-time (14 women); includes 8 minority (4 African Americans, 4 Asian Americans or Pacific Islanders), 2 international. 17 applicants, 94% accepted, 13 enrolled. In 2009, 5

Clinical Research

Thomas Jefferson University (continued)

Certificates awarded. *Entrance requirements:* For degree, GRE General Test (recommended). Additional exam requirements/recommendations for international students: Required—TOEFL (minimum score 250 computer-based; 100 iBT), or IELTS. *Application deadline:* For fall admission, 8/1 priority date for domestic students, 3/1 priority date for international students; for winter admission, 12/1 priority date for domestic students, 6/1 priority date for international students; for spring admission, 4/1 priority date for domestic students. Applications are processed on a rolling basis. Application fee: $50. Electronic applications accepted. *Expenses:* Tuition: Full-time $26,858; part-time $879 per credit. Required fees: $525. *Financial support:* Federal Work-Study and institutionally sponsored loans available. Support available to part-time students. Financial award applicants required to submit FAFSA. *Faculty research:* Pharmacoeconomics, epidemiology, clinical research, performance improvement, statistics. *Unit head:* Dr. Dennis M. Gross, Associate Dean, 215-503-0156, Fax: 215-503-3433, E-mail: dennis.gross@jefferson.edu. *Application contact:* Eleanor M. Gorman, Assistant Coordinator, Graduate Center Programs, 215-503-5799, Fax: 215-503-3433, E-mail: eleanor.gorman@jefferson.edu.

Tufts University, Sackler School of Graduate Biomedical Sciences, Division of Clinical Care Research, Medford, MA 02155. Offers MS, PhD. *Faculty:* 37 full-time (11 women). *Students:* 23 full-time (15 women), 1 part-time (0 women); includes 5 minority (1 African American, 4 Asian Americans or Pacific Islanders), 10 international. Average age 33. 32 applicants, 41% accepted, 13 enrolled. In 2009, 7 master's awarded. Terminal master's awarded for partial completion of doctoral program. *Degree requirements:* For master's, thesis; for doctorate, thesis/dissertation. *Entrance requirements:* For master's and doctorate, MD or PhD, strong clinical research background. Additional exam requirements/recommendations for international students: Required—TOEFL. *Application deadline:* For fall admission, 12/15 for domestic and international students. Applications are processed on a rolling basis. Application fee: $70. Electronic applications accepted. *Expenses:* Tuition: Full-time $38,096; part-time $3962 per credit. Required fees: $686; $40 per year. Tuition and fees vary according to course level, course load, degree level, program and student level. *Financial support:* In 2009–10, 27 fellowships with full tuition reimbursements were awarded. Financial award application deadline: 12/15. *Faculty research:* Clinical study design, mathematical modeling, meta analysis, epidemiologic research, coronary heart disease. *Unit head:* Dr. Harry P. Selker, Program Director, 617-636-5009, Fax: 617-636-8023, E-mail: hselker@lifespan.org. *Application contact:* Kellie Johnston, Associate Director of Admissions, 617-636-6767, Fax: 617-636-0375, E-mail: sackler-school@tufts.edu.

TUI University, College of Health Sciences, Program in Health Sciences, Cypress, CA 90630. Offers clinical research administration (MS, Certificate); emergency and disaster management (MS, Certificate); environmental health science (Certificate); health care administration (PhD); health care management (MS), including health informatics; health education (MS, Certificate); health informatics (Certificate); health sciences (PhD); international health (MS); international health: educator or researcher option (PhD); international health: practitioner option (PhD); law and expert witness studies (MS, Certificate); public health (MS); quality assurance (Certificate). Part-time and evening/weekend programs available. Postbaccalaureate distance learning degree programs offered (no on-campus study). *Degree requirements:* For doctorate, comprehensive exam, thesis/dissertation, defense of dissertation. *Entrance requirements:* For master's, minimum GPA of 2.5 (students with GPA 3.0 or greater may transfer up to 30% of graduate level credits); for doctorate, minimum GPA of 3.4, curriculum vitae, course work in research methods or statistics. Additional exam requirements/recommendations for international students: Required—TOEFL. Electronic applications accepted.

University of California, Berkeley, UC Berkeley Extension, Certificate Programs in Sciences, Biotechnology and Mathematics, Berkeley, CA 94720-1500. Offers clinical research conduct and management (Certificate). Postbaccalaureate distance learning degree programs offered. *Unit head:* Diana Wu, Dean, 510-642-4181. *Application contact:* Sciences, Biotechnology, and Mathematics, 510-643-0598, E-mail: science@unex.berkeley.edu.

University of California, Davis, Graduate Studies, Graduate Group in Clinical Research, Davis, CA 95616. Offers MAS. *Degree requirements:* For master's, comprehensive exam. *Entrance requirements:* Additional exam requirements/recommendations for international students: Required—TOEFL (minimum score 550 paper-based; 213 computer-based).

University of California, Los Angeles, David Geffen School of Medicine and Graduate Division, Graduate Programs in Medicine, Department of Biomathematics, Program in Clinical Research, Los Angeles, CA 90095. Offers MS.

University of California, San Diego, School of Medicine, Program in Clinical Research, La Jolla, CA 92093. Offers MAS.

University of Connecticut, Graduate School, University of Connecticut Health Center, Field of Clinical and Translational Research, Storrs, CT 06269. Offers MS. *Students:* 2 full-time (1 woman), 8 part-time (4 women); includes 5 minority (1 African American, 4 Asian Americans or Pacific Islanders). Average age 39. 6 applicants, 83% accepted, 1 enrolled. *Degree requirements:* For master's, comprehensive exam. *Entrance requirements:* Additional exam requirements/recommendations for international students: Required—TOEFL (minimum score 550 paper-based; 213 computer-based). *Application deadline:* For fall admission, 2/1 priority date for domestic and international students; for spring admission, 11/1 for domestic students, 10/1 for international students. Applications are processed on a rolling basis. Electronic applications accepted. *Expenses:* Tuition, state resident: full-time $4725; part-time $525 per credit. Tuition, nonresident: full-time $12,267; part-time $1363 per credit. Required fees: $346 per semester. Tuition and fees vary according to course load. *Financial support:* Teaching assistantships with full tuition reimbursements, Federal Work-Study, scholarships/grants, health care benefits, and unspecified assistantships available. Financial award application deadline: 2/1; financial award applicants required to submit FAFSA. *Unit head:* Lawrence Klobutcher, Associate Dean, 860-679-2816, Fax: 860-679-3408, E-mail: klobutcher@nso2.uchc.edu. *Application contact:* Lisa Godin, Administrative Coordinator, 860-679-4145, E-mail: godin@nso.echc.edu.

University of Connecticut Health Center, Graduate School, Program in Clinical and Translational Research, Farmington, CT 06030. Offers MS. Part-time programs available. *Faculty:* 40 part-time/adjunct (12 women). *Students:* 2 full-time (1 woman), 8 part-time (4 women); includes 5 minority (1 African American, 4 Asian Americans or Pacific Islanders). 13 applicants, 54% accepted, 6 enrolled. In 2009, 2 master's awarded. *Entrance requirements:* For master's, GRE. Additional exam requirements/recommendations for international students: Required—TOEFL (minimum score 600 paper-based; 250 computer-based). *Application deadline:* For fall admission, 3/31 for domestic students. Applications are processed on a rolling basis. Application fee: $55. *Unit head:* Dr. Anne Kenny. *Application contact:* Lisa Godin, Administrative Program Coordinator, 860-679-4145, Fax: 860-679-1454, E-mail: godin@nso.uchc.edu.

University of Florida, College of Medicine, Program in Clinical Investigation, Gainesville, FL 32611. Offers clinical investigation (MS); epidemiology (MS); public health (MPH). Part-time programs available. *Entrance requirements:* For master's, GRE, MD, PhD, DMD/DDS or Pharm D.

The University of Iowa, Graduate College, College of Public Health, Department of Epidemiology, Iowa City, IA 52242-1316. Offers clinical investigation (MS); epidemiology (MS, PhD). *Degree requirements:* For master's, thesis optional, exam; for doctorate, comprehensive exam, thesis/dissertation. *Entrance requirements:* For master's and doctorate, GRE General Test, minimum GPA of 3.0. Additional exam requirements/recommendations for international students: Required—TOEFL (minimum score 600 paper-based; 250 computer-based; 100 iBT). Electronic applications accepted.

The University of Kansas, University of Kansas Medical Center, School of Medicine, Department of Preventive Medicine, Kansas City, KS 66160. Offers clinical research (MS); public health (MPH); MD/MPH. Part-time programs available. *Faculty:* 31 full-time, 9 part-time/adjunct. *Students:* 37 full-time (32 women), 55 part-time (36 women); includes 22 minority (8 African Americans, 3 American Indian/Alaska Native, 4 Asian Americans or Pacific Islanders, 7 Hispanic Americans), 15 international. Average age 32. 57 applicants, 56% accepted, 24 enrolled. In 2009, 32 master's awarded. *Degree requirements:* For master's, thesis. *Entrance requirements:* For master's, GRE, MCAT, LSAT, GMAT or other equivalent graduate professional exam, minimum GPA of 3.0. Additional exam requirements/recommendations for international students: Required—TOEFL. *Application deadline:* For fall admission, 3/31 for domestic and international students. Applications are processed on a rolling basis. Application fee: $35. *Expenses:* Tuition, state resident: full-time $6492; part-time $270.50 per credit hour. Tuition, nonresident: full-time $15,510; part-time $646.25 per credit hour. Required fees: $847; $70.56 per credit hour. Tuition and fees vary according to course load and program. *Financial support:* In 2009–10, 25 research assistantships (averaging $6,400 per year) were awarded; career-related internships or fieldwork, Federal Work-Study, scholarships/grants, and unspecified assistantships also available. Financial award application deadline: 3/30; financial award applicants required to submit FAFSA. *Faculty research:* Cancer screening and prevention, smoking cessation, obesity and physical activity, health services/outcomes research. Total annual research expenditures: $6.6 million. *Unit head:* Dr. Edward F. Ellerbeck, Chairman, 913-588-2774, Fax: 913-588-2780, E-mail: eellerbe@kumc.edu. *Application contact:* Tanya Honderick, Assistant Director, KU-MPH, 913-588-2720, Fax: 913-588-8505, E-mail: mwoirhaye@kumc.edu.

University of Louisville, Graduate School, School of Public Health and Information Sciences, Louisville, KY 40292-0001. Offers bioinformatics and biostatistics (MS, PhD), including biostatistics (MPH, MS, PhD), decision science (MS); clinical investigation sciences (Certificate); population health and epidemiology (MS, PhD), including epidemiology (MPH, MS, PhD), public health sciences (PhD); public health (MPH), including biostatistics (MPH, MS, PhD), environmental and occupational health, epidemiology (MPH, MS, PhD), health management (MPH, PhD), health promotion and behavior; public health sciences (PhD), including environmental health, epidemiology (MPH, MS, PhD), health management (MPH, PhD), health promotion. Part-time and evening/weekend programs available. *Faculty:* 39 full-time (13 women), 1 part-time/adjunct (0 women). *Students:* 92 full-time (52 women), 72 part-time (47 women); includes 36 minority (15 African Americans, 19 Asian Americans or Pacific Islanders, 2 Hispanic Americans), 21 international. Average age 33. 194 applicants, 47% accepted, 65 enrolled. In 2009, 35 master's, 4 doctorates awarded. *Degree requirements:* For master's, thesis; for doctorate, thesis/dissertation. *Entrance requirements:* For master's, GRE General Test, GMAT, DAT, MCAT, minimum of 2 letters of recommendation; for doctorate, GRE General Test, minimum of 2 letters of recommendation. Additional exam requirements/recommendations for international students: Required—TOEFL (minimum score 600 paper-based; 250 computer-based; 100 iBT). *Application deadline:* For fall admission, 2/1 for domestic and international students. Applications are processed on a rolling basis. Application fee: $50. Electronic applications accepted. *Financial support:* In 2009–10, 30 students received support, including 11 research assistantships with full tuition reimbursements available (averaging $20,000 per year); unspecified assistantships also available. Financial award application deadline: 5/1; financial award applicants required to submit FAFSA. *Faculty research:* Clinical research training, cancer and environmental exposure, health effects of air pollution, occupational injuries and illness, network science applications in health. Total annual research expenditures: $3.2 million. *Unit head:* Dr. Pete Walton, Associate Dean for Academic Affairs, 502-852-4493, Fax: 502-852-3291, E-mail: pete.walton@gwise.louisville.edu. *Application contact:* Vicki Lewis, Administrative Assistant, 502-852-1798, Fax: 502-852-3294, E-mail: vicki.lewis@louisville.edu.

University of Maryland, Baltimore, School of Medicine, Department of Epidemiology and Preventive Medicine, Baltimore, MD 21201. Offers biostatistics (MS); clinical research (MS); epidemiology (PhD); epidemiology and preventive medicine (MPH, MS); gerontology (PhD); human genetics and genomic (MS, PhD); molecular epidemiology (PhD); toxicology (MS, PhD); JD/MS; MD/PhD; MS/PhD. *Accreditation:* CEPH. Part-time programs available. *Students:* 64 full-time (42 women), 60 part-time (40 women); includes 40 minority (17 African Americans, 19 Asian Americans or Pacific Islanders, 4 Hispanic Americans), 16 international. Average age 31. 207 applicants, 48% accepted, 50 enrolled. In 2009, 24 master's, 9 doctorates awarded. *Entrance requirements:* For master's and doctorate, GRE General Test, minimum GPA of 3.0. Additional exam requirements/recommendations for international students: Required—TOEFL; Recommended—IELTS. *Application deadline:* For fall admission, 1/15 for domestic and international students. Application fee: $50. Electronic applications accepted. *Expenses:* Tuition, state resident: full-time $7290; part-time $405 per credit hour. Tuition, nonresident: full-time $12,780; part-time $710 per credit hour. Required fees: $774; $10 per credit hour. $297 per semester. Tuition and fees vary according to course load, degree level and program. *Financial support:* In 2009–10, research assistantships with partial tuition reimbursements (averaging $25,000 per year); fellowships also available. Financial award application deadline: 3/1. *Unit head:* Dr. Patricia Langenberg, Program Director, 410-706-3251, Fax: 410-706-8013. *Application contact:* Rachael Holmes, Academic Coordinator, 410-706-8492, Fax: 410-706-4225, E-mail: rholmes@epi.umaryland.edu.

University of Massachusetts Worcester, Graduate School of Biomedical Sciences, Program in Clinical and Population Health Research, Worcester, MA 01655-0115. Offers PhD. *Degree requirements:* For doctorate, comprehensive exam, thesis/dissertation. *Entrance requirements:* For doctorate, GRE General Test, master's degree in public health, clinical research, or in one of the social, psychological, physical, or biological sciences, with adequate introductory course work in biostatistics and epidemiology; 3 letters of recommendation. Additional exam requirements/recommendations for international students: Required—TOEFL (minimum score 600 paper-based; 250 computer-based; 100 iBT). Electronic applications accepted.

University of Massachusetts Worcester, Graduate School of Biomedical Sciences, Program in Clinical Investigation, Worcester, MA 01655-0115. Offers MS.

University of Michigan, School of Public Health, Program in Clinical Research Design and Statistical Analysis, Ann Arbor, MI 48109. Offers MS. Offered through the Horace H. Rackham School of Graduate Studies. Program admits applicants in odd-numbered calendar years only. Evening/weekend programs available. *Faculty:* 11 full-time (4 women), 1 part-time/adjunct (0 women). *Students:* 36 full-time (14 women); includes 8 minority (1 African American, 7 Asian Americans or Pacific Islanders), 4 international. Average age 33. 44 applicants, 84% accepted, 30 enrolled. In 2009, 36 master's awarded. *Degree requirements:* For master's, comprehensive exam. *Entrance requirements:* For master's, GRE General Test or MCAT. Additional exam requirements/recommendations for international students: Recommended—TOEFL (minimum score 560 paper-based; 220 computer-based; 84 iBT). *Application deadline:* For fall admission, 3/1 priority date for international students. Applications are processed on a rolling basis. Application fee: $60 ($75 for international students). Electronic applications accepted. *Expenses:* Contact institution. *Financial support:* Institutionally sponsored loans and scholarships/grants available. Financial award application deadline: 3/15; financial award applicants required to submit FAFSA. *Faculty research:* Survival analysis, missing data, Bayesian inference, health economics, quality of life. Total annual research expenditures: $14.4 million. *Unit head:* Dr. Trivellore Raghunathan, Director, 734-615-9832, E-mail: teraghu@umich.edu. *Application contact:* Fatma Nedjari, Information Contact, 734-615-9812, Fax: 734-763-2215, E-mail: sph.bio.inquiries@umich.edu.

University of Minnesota, Twin Cities Campus, School of Public Health, Major in Clinical Research, Minneapolis, MN 55455-0213. Offers MS. Part-time programs available. *Degree requirements:* For master's, thesis. *Entrance requirements:* For master's, advanced health professional degree. Additional exam requirements/recommendations for international students: Required—TOEFL. Electronic applications accepted. *Faculty research:* Osteoporosis prevention; heart disease prevention; role of inflammatory dental disease in the genesis of atherosclerosis; interventional research into AIDS and cancer.

University of Pittsburgh, School of Medicine, Programs in Clinical Research, Pittsburgh, PA 15260. Offers clinical and translational science (PhD); clinical research (MS, Certificate). Part-time programs available. *Faculty:* 48 full-time (18 women). *Students:* 47 part-time (21 women); includes 9 minority (2 African Americans, 1 American Indian/Alaska Native, 6 Asian

Americans or Pacific Islanders), 18 international. Average age 32. 11 applicants, 82% accepted, 9 enrolled. In 2009, 19 master's, 16 other advanced degrees awarded. *Degree requirements:* For master's, thesis. *Entrance requirements:* For master's, MCAT, GRE, or GMAT. Additional exam requirements/recommendations for international students: Required—TOEFL (minimum score 600 paper-based; 250 computer-based; 100 iBT). *Application deadline:* For fall admission, 10/31 priority date for domestic and international students; for spring admission, 4/15 priority date for domestic and international students. Applications are processed on a rolling basis. Application fee: $0. Electronic applications accepted. *Expenses:* Tuition, state resident: full-time $16,402; part-time $665 per credit. Tuition, nonresident: full-time $28,694; part-time $1175 per credit. Required fees: $690; $175 per term. Tuition and fees vary according to program. *Financial support:* Tuition waivers (partial) available. *Faculty research:* Quality of life, mood disorders in children, pediatric palliative care, female pelvic medicines, antibiotic use and racial variations medication use. *Unit head:* Dr. Wishwa Kapoor, Program Director, 412-692-2686, Fax: 412-586-9672, E-mail: kapoorwn@upmc.edu. *Application contact:* Jessica L. Dornin, Program Coordinator, 412-692-2686, Fax: 412-586-9672, E-mail: dorninjl@upmc.edu.

University of Puerto Rico, Medical Sciences Campus, School of Health Professions, Program in Clinical Research, San Juan, PR 00936-5067. Offers MS, Graduate Certificate.

University of Southern California, Graduate School, School of Pharmacy, Regulatory Science Programs, Los Angeles, CA 90089. Offers clinical research design and management (Graduate Certificate); food safety (Graduate Certificate); patient and product safety (Graduate Certificate); preclinical drug development (Graduate Certificate); regulatory and clinical affairs (Graduate Certificate); regulatory science (MS, DRSc). Part-time and evening/weekend programs available. Postbaccalaureate distance learning degree programs offered (minimal on-campus study). *Faculty:* 6 full-time (2 women), 7 part-time/adjunct (5 women). *Students:* 23 full-time (11 women), 80 part-time (52 women); includes 38 minority (7 African Americans, 1 American Indian/Alaska Native, 25 Asian Americans or Pacific Islanders, 5 Hispanic Americans), 19 international. 57 applicants, 54% accepted, 31 enrolled. In 2009, 32 master's, 28 other advanced degrees awarded. Terminal master's awarded for partial completion of doctoral program. *Degree requirements:* For master's, thesis optional; for doctorate, comprehensive exam, thesis/dissertation. *Entrance requirements:* For master's, GRE. Additional exam requirements/recommendations for international students: Required—TOEFL (minimum score 250 computer-based; 100 iBT). *Application deadline:* For fall admission, 6/15 priority date for domestic and international students; for winter admission, 2/15 priority date for domestic and international students; for spring admission, 10/15 priority date for domestic and international students. Application fee: $85. Electronic applications accepted. *Expenses:* Tuition: Full-time $25,980; part-time $1315 per unit. Required fees: $554. One-time fee: $35 full-time. Full-time tuition and fees vary according to degree level and program. *Unit head:* Dr. Frances J. R. Richmond, Director, 323-442-3531, Fax: 323-442-2333, E-mail: fjr@hsc.usc.edu. *Application contact:* Dr. Kathy Rolle, Program Manager, 323-442-3102, Fax: 323-442-2333, E-mail: regsci@usc.edu.

University of Virginia, School of Medicine, Department of Public Health Sciences, Program in Clinical Research, Charlottesville, VA 22903. Offers clinical investigation and patient-oriented research (MS); informatics in medicine (MS). Part-time programs available. *Students:* 4 full-time (2 women), 14 part-time (7 women); includes 4 minority (3 Asian Americans or Pacific Islanders, 1 Hispanic American). Average age 35. 4 applicants, 100% accepted, 3 enrolled. In 2009, 13 master's awarded. *Degree requirements:* For master's, thesis (for some programs). *Entrance requirements:* For master's, 2 letters of recommendation. Additional exam requirements/recommendations for international students: Required—TOEFL (minimum score 600 paper-based; 250 computer-based; 90 iBT). *Application deadline:* For fall admission, 3/1 priority date for domestic and international students. Application fee: $60. Electronic applications accepted. *Financial support:* Career-related internships or fieldwork available. Financial award applicants required to submit FAFSA. *Unit head:* Dr. William A. Knaus, Chair, 434-924-8430, Fax: 434-924-8437. *Application contact:* Tracey L. Brookman, Academic Programs Administrator, 434-924-8430, Fax: 434-924-8437, E-mail: ms-hes@virginia.edu.

University of Washington, Graduate School, School of Public Health, Department of Biostatistics, Seattle, WA 98195. Offers biostatistics (MPH, MS, PhD); clinical research (MS); including biostatistics; statistical genetics (PhD). Part-time programs available. *Faculty:* 41 full-time (15 women), 8 part-time/adjunct (1 woman). *Students:* 80 full-time (47 women), 5 part-time (2 women); includes 8 minority (7 Asian Americans or Pacific Islanders, 1 Hispanic American), 31 international. Average age 30. 187 applicants, 20% accepted, 21 enrolled. In 2009, 4 master's, 8 doctorates awarded. Terminal master's awarded for partial completion of doctoral program. *Degree requirements:* For master's, comprehensive exam, thesis, computer proficiency, consulting, departmental qualifying exams; for doctorate, comprehensive exam, thesis/dissertation, computer proficiency, consulting, departmental qualifying exams. *Entrance requirements:* For master's and doctorate, GRE General Test, 2 years of course work in advanced calculus, 1 course each in linear algebra and mathematical probability, 30 credits in math/statistics, minimum GPA of 3.0. Additional exam requirements/recommendations for international students: Required—TOEFL. *Application deadline:* For fall admission, 1/5 for domestic students. Application fee: $50. Electronic applications accepted. *Financial support:* In 2009–10, 79 students received support, including 75 research assistantships with full and partial tuition reimbursements available (averaging $22,000 per year), 10 teaching assistantships with full and partial tuition reimbursements available (averaging $22,000 per year); traineeships, health care benefits, and tuition waivers (partial) also available. *Faculty research:* Statistical methods for survival data analysis, clinical trials, epidemiological case control and cohort studies, statistical genetics. *Unit head:* Dr. Bruce Weir, Department Chair, 206-543-1044. *Application contact:* Alex Mackenzie, Counseling Services Coordinator, 206-543-1044, Fax: 206-543-3286, E-mail: alexam@u.washington.edu.

University of Washington, Graduate School, School of Public Health, Department of Epidemiology, Seattle, WA 98195. Offers clinical research (MS); epidemiology (MPH, MS, PhD); global health (MPH); maternal/child health (MPH); nutritional sciences (MPH, MS, PhD); public health genetics (MPH, MS, PhD), including genetic epidemiology (MS); public health genetics (MPH, PhD). *Accreditation:* CEPH (one or more programs are accredited). Part-time programs available. *Faculty:* 66 full-time (40 women), 46 part-time/adjunct (20 women). *Students:* 145 full-time (101 women), 43 part-time (26 women); includes 33 minority (6 African Americans, 1 American Indian/Alaska Native, 18 Asian Americans or Pacific Islanders, 8 Hispanic Americans), 20 international. Average age 32. 236 applicants, 48% accepted, 60 enrolled. In 2009, 44 master's, 16 doctorates awarded. Terminal master's awarded for partial completion of doctoral program. *Degree requirements:* For master's, thesis; for doctorate, comprehensive exam, thesis/dissertation, preliminary exam, original data collection. *Entrance requirements:* For master's, GRE General Test (except applicants with U.S. doctorate); for doctorate, GRE General Test. Additional exam requirements/recommendations for international students: Required—TOEFL (minimum score 580 paper-based; 237 computer-based; 92 iBT) or IELTS (minimum score 7). *Application deadline:* For fall admission, 12/1 for domestic students, 11/1 for international students. Application fee: $50. Electronic applications accepted. *Expenses:* Contact institution. *Financial support:* In 2009–10, 90 fellowships with full tuition reimbursements (averaging $20,976 per year), 43 research assistantships with full tuition reimbursements (averaging $19,668 per year), 12 teaching assistantships with full tuition reimbursements (averaging $16,398 per year) were awarded; career-related internships or fieldwork, Federal Work-Study, institutionally sponsored loans, scholarships/grants, traineeships, health care benefits, unspecified assistantships, and tuition waiver also available. Financial award application deadline: 2/15; financial award applicants required to submit FAFSA. *Faculty research:* Chronic diseases, sexually transmitted diseases, injury, materials and child health, molecular and genetic epidemiology. *Unit head:* Dr. Scott Davis, Chair, 206-543-1065, Fax: 206-543-1065, E-mail: sdavis@fhcrc.org. *Application contact:* Kate O'Brien, Student Services Manager, 206-543-1065, Fax: 206-543-8525, E-mail: apply@u.washington.edu.

University of Washington, Graduate School, School of Public Health, Department of Health Services, Seattle, WA 98195. Offers bioinformatics (PhD); cancer prevention and control (PhD); clinical research (MS); community oriented public health practice (MPH); economics or finance (PhD); evaluation sciences (PhD); executive program (MHA); health behavior and health promotion (PhD); health care and population health research (MPH); health policy analysis and process (PhD); health policy and analysis and process (MPH); health services (MS, PhD); health services administration (EMHA, MHA); in residence program (MHA); occupational health (PhD); population health and social determinants (PhD); social and behavioral sciences (MPH); sociology and demography (PhD); JD/MHA; MHA/MBA; MHA/MD; MHA/MPA; MPH/JD; MPH/MD; MPH/MN; MPH/MPA; MPH/MSD; MPH/MSW; MPH/PhD. Part-time and evening/weekend programs available. Postbaccalaureate distance learning degree programs offered (minimal on-campus study). *Faculty:* 52 full-time (24 women), 60 part-time/adjunct (28 women). *Students:* 104 full-time (83 women), 100 part-time (76 women); includes 21 minority (6 African Americans, 1 American Indian/Alaska Native, 11 Asian Americans or Pacific Islanders, 3 Hispanic Americans), 6 international. Average age 34. 375 applicants, 17% accepted, 24 enrolled. In 2009, 33 master's awarded. Terminal master's awarded for partial completion of doctoral program. *Degree requirements:* For master's, thesis (for some programs), practicum (MPH); for doctorate, comprehensive exam, thesis/dissertation. *Entrance requirements:* For master's and doctorate, GRE General Test, minimum GPA of 3.0. Additional exam requirements/recommendations for international students: Required—TOEFL. *Application deadline:* For fall admission, 1/15 for domestic students, 11/1 for international students. Application fee: 50 Albanian leks. Electronic applications accepted. *Financial support:* In 2009–10, 64 students received support, including 10 fellowships with full and partial tuition reimbursements available (averaging $21,000 per year), 10 research assistantships with full and partial tuition reimbursements available (averaging $18,000 per year), 3 teaching assistantships with full and partial tuition reimbursements available (averaging $18,000 per year); career-related internships or fieldwork, Federal Work-Study, institutionally sponsored loans, and traineeships also available. Financial award application deadline: 2/28; financial award applicants required to submit FAFSA. *Faculty research:* Health promotion and disease prevention, maternal and child health, health services research design, program evaluation, health policy. Total annual research expenditures: $10.5 million. *Unit head:* Dr. Larry Kessler, Chair, 206-543-616-2930. *Application contact:* Kitty A. Andert, Program Manager, 206-616-2926, Fax: 206-543-3964, E-mail: kitander@u.washington.edu.

University of Wisconsin–Madison, School of Medicine and Public Health and Graduate School, Graduate Programs in Medicine, Department of Population Health Sciences, Madison, WI 53726. Offers clinical research (MS, PhD); epidemiology (MS, PhD); health services research (MS, PhD); population health sciences (MPH); social and behavioral health sciences (MS, PhD); DPT/MPH; DVM/MPH; MD/MPH; MPA/MPH; MS/MPH; Pharm D/MPH. *Accreditation:* CEPH. Part-time programs available. *Faculty:* 104 full-time (54 women), 2 part-time/adjunct (0 women). *Students:* 105 full-time (76 women), 38 part-time (31 women); includes 19 minority (8 African Americans, 8 Asian Americans or Pacific Islanders, 3 Hispanic Americans), 15 international. Average age 30. 126 applicants, 75% accepted, 58 enrolled. In 2009, 13 master's, 8 doctorates awarded. Terminal master's awarded for partial completion of doctoral program. *Degree requirements:* For master's, thesis, defense; for doctorate, comprehensive exam, thesis/dissertation, qualifying exam, preliminary exam, dissertation defense. *Entrance requirements:* For master's and doctorate, GRE (separate guidelines for those with doctoral degrees), minimum GPA of 3.0, quantitative preparation (calculus, statistics, or other) with minimum B average. Additional exam requirements/recommendations for international students: Required—TOEFL (minimum score 600 paper-based; 250 computer-based; 100 iBT). *Application deadline:* For fall admission, 1/15 for domestic and international students. Application fee: $56. Electronic applications accepted. *Expenses:* Tuition, state resident: part-time $594 per credit. Tuition, nonresident: part-time $1504 per credit. Required fees: $65 per credit. Tuition and fees vary according to course load, program and reciprocity agreements. *Financial support:* In 2009–10, 73 students received support, including 16 fellowships with full tuition reimbursements available (averaging $21,000 per year), 38 research assistantships with full tuition reimbursements available (averaging $17,300 per year), 7 teaching assistantships with full tuition reimbursements available (averaging $17,300 per year); scholarships/grants, traineeships, health care benefits, and unspecified assistantships also available. Support available to part-time students. *Faculty research:* Epidemiology (cancer, environmental, aging, infectious disease and genetic), determinants of population health, health services research, social and behavioral health sciences, biostatistics. Total annual research expenditures: $11.4 million. *Unit head:* Dr. F. Javier Nieto, Chair, 608-265-5242, Fax: 608-263-2820, E-mail: fjnieto@wisc.edu. *Application contact:* Kelly Haslam, Graduate Program Coordinator, 608-265-8108, Fax: 608-263-2820, E-mail: haslam@wisc.edu.

Vanderbilt University, School of Medicine, Clinical Investigation Program, Nashville, TN 37240-1001. Offers MS. *Entrance requirements:* Additional exam requirements/recommendations for international students: Required—TOEFL.

Walden University, Graduate Programs, School of Health Sciences, Minneapolis, MN 55401. Offers clinical research administration (MS); health informatics (MS); health services (PhD), including community health promotion and education, general program, health management and policy; healthcare administration (MHA); public health (MPH, PhD), including community health promotion and education (PhD), epidemiology (PhD). Part-time and evening/weekend programs available. Postbaccalaureate distance learning degree programs offered (minimal on-campus study). *Faculty:* 14 full-time, 136 part-time/adjunct. *Students:* 2,121 full-time (1,670 women), 724 part-time (568 women); includes 1,370 minority (1,149 African Americans, 20 American Indian/Alaska Native, 95 Asian Americans or Pacific Islanders, 106 Hispanic Americans), 134 international. Average age 40. In 2009, 232 master's, 24 doctorates awarded. *Degree requirements:* For doctorate, thesis/dissertation, residency. *Entrance requirements:* For master's, bachelor's degree or equivalent in related field, minimum GPA of 2.5; for doctorate, master's degree or equivalent in related field; minimum GPA of 3.0; official transcripts; three years of related professional/academic experience (preferred); access to computer and Internet. Additional exam requirements/recommendations for international students: Required—TOEFL (minimum score 550 paper-based; 213 computer-based), IELTS (minimum score 6.5), or Michigan English Language Assessment Battery (minimum score 82). *Application deadline:* Applications are processed on a rolling basis. Application fee: $50. Electronic applications accepted. *Expenses:* Tuition: Full-time $13,665; part-time $560 per credit. Required fees: $1375. Tuition and fees vary according to course load, degree level and program. *Financial support:* In 2009–10, 152 students received support; fellowships, Federal Work-Study, scholarships/grants, unspecified assistantships, and family tuition reduction, active duty/veteran tuition reduction, group tuition reduction, interest-free payment plans available. Support available to part-time students. Financial award applicants required to submit FAFSA. *Unit head:* Dr. Jorg Westermann, Interim Associate Dean, 800-925-3368. *Application contact:* Jennifer Hall, Director of Enrollment, 866-4-WALDEN, E-mail: info@waldenu.edu.

Washington University in St. Louis, School of Medicine, Program in Clinical Investigation, St. Louis, MO 63130-4899. Offers MS. Part-time programs available. *Students:* 35. *Application deadline:* For fall admission, 3/1 for domestic students. Application fee: $0. *Unit head:* Dr. Bradley Evanoff, Division Chief—General Medical Sciences, 314-454-8638, Fax: 314-454-5113, E-mail: bevanoff@wustl.edu. *Application contact:* Rachel Driskell, Curriculum Coordinator, 314-362-8719, Fax: 314-454-8279, E-mail: rdriskel@dom.wustl.edu.

Communication Disorders

Abilene Christian University, Graduate School, College of Education and Human Services, Department of Communication Sciences and Disorders, Abilene, TX 79699-9100. Offers MS. *Accreditation:* ASHA. *Faculty:* 8 part-time/adjunct (7 women). *Students:* 24 full-time (22 women); includes 4 minority (2 African Americans, 1 Asian American or Pacific Islander, 1 Hispanic American). 56 applicants, 23% accepted, 11 enrolled. In 2009, 10 master's awarded. *Degree requirements:* For master's, one foreign language, comprehensive exam. *Entrance requirements:* For master's, GRE General Test. *Application deadline:* For fall admission, 4/1 priority date for domestic students; for spring admission, 11/1 for domestic students. Applications are processed on a rolling basis. Application fee: $40. Electronic applications accepted. *Expenses:* Tuition: Full-time $11,520; part-time $640 per hour. Required fees: $1090; $53.50 per hour. $10 per term. Tuition and fees vary according to program. *Financial support:* In 2009–10, 22 students received support. Application deadline: 4/1. *Unit head:* Dr. Terry Baggs, Graduate Adviser, 325-674-4819, Fax: 325-674-2552, E-mail: terry.baggs@acu.edu. *Application contact:* William Horn, Graduate Admissions Counselor, 325-674-2656, Fax: 325-674-6717, E-mail: gradinfo@acu.edu.

Adelphi University, School of Education, Program in Communication Sciences and Disorders, Garden City, NY 11530-0701. Offers audiology (MS, DA); speech-language pathology (MS, DA). *Accreditation:* ASHA. Part-time programs available. *Students:* 192 full-time (189 women), 59 part-time (55 women); includes 19 minority (5 African Americans, 6 Asian Americans or Pacific Islanders, 8 Hispanic Americans), 1 international. Average age 26. In 2009, 81 master's, 1 doctorate awarded. *Degree requirements:* For master's, comprehensive exam, clinical practice; for doctorate, one foreign language, comprehensive exam, thesis/dissertation. *Entrance requirements:* For master's, GRE General Test and writing exam, 3 letters of recommendation, interview, resume, 19 credits of prerequisite course work or communications disorders training; for doctorate, GRE General Test, 3 letters of recommendation, interview. Additional exam requirements/recommendations for international students: Required—TOEFL (minimum score 550 paper-based; 213 computer-based; 80 iBT). *Application deadline:* For fall admission, 3/1 priority date for domestic students, 3/1 for international students; for spring admission, 10/1 priority date for domestic students, 10/1 for international students. Applications are processed on a rolling basis. Application fee: $50. Electronic applications accepted. *Expenses:* Tuition: Full-time $28,340; part-time $830 per credit. Required fees: $600; $250 per credit. Full-time tuition and fees vary according to course load and program. *Financial support:* Fellowships, research assistantships with partial tuition reimbursements, teaching assistantships, career-related internships or fieldwork, Federal Work-Study, institutionally sponsored loans, tuition waivers (full), and unspecified assistantships available. Support available to part-time students. Financial award application deadline: 2/15; financial award applicants required to submit FAFSA. *Faculty research:* Pediatric audiology, child speech perception with hearing loss, auditory deprivation, fluency, cultural diversity. *Unit head:* Dr. Robert Goldfarb, Chairperson, 516-877-4785, E-mail: goldfarb2@adelphi.edu. *Application contact:* Christine Murphy, Director of Admissions, 516-877-3050, Fax: 516-877-3039, E-mail: graduateadmissions@adelphi.edu.

Alabama Agricultural and Mechanical University, School of Graduate Studies, School of Education, Department of Counseling and Special Education, Area in Communicative Disorders, Huntsville, AL 35811. Offers M Ed, MS. *Accreditation:* ASHA. Part-time programs available. *Degree requirements:* For master's, comprehensive exam. *Entrance requirements:* For master's, GRE General Test, minimum GPA of 2.5. Additional exam requirements/recommendations for international students: Required—TOEFL (minimum score 500 paper-based; 173 computer-based; 61 iBT). Electronic applications accepted. *Faculty research:* Alternative methods of teaching speech and language to handicapped individuals.

Appalachian State University, Cratis D. Williams Graduate School, Department of Language, Reading, and Exceptionalities, Boone, NC 28608. Offers reading education (MA); special education (MA); speech-language pathology (MA). *Accreditation:* ASHA. Part-time programs available. Postbaccalaureate distance learning degree programs offered (no on-campus study). *Faculty:* 37 full-time (25 women), 6 part-time/adjunct (all women). *Students:* 89 full-time (84 women), 202 part-time (192 women); includes 7 minority (3 African Americans, 1 Asian American or Pacific Islander, 3 Hispanic Americans). 291 applicants, 57% accepted, 105 enrolled. In 2009, 95 master's awarded. *Degree requirements:* For master's, comprehensive exam, thesis optional. *Entrance requirements:* For master's, GRE General Test or MAT, 3 letters of recommendation. Additional exam requirements/recommendations for international students: Required—TOEFL (minimum score 570 paper-based; 230 computer-based; 79 iBT), IELTS (minimum score 6.5). *Application deadline:* For fall admission, 7/1 for domestic students, 2/1 for international students; for spring admission, 11/1 for domestic students, 7/1 for international students. Applications are processed on a rolling basis. Application fee: $50. Electronic applications accepted. *Expenses:* Tuition, state resident: full-time $2960. Tuition, nonresident: full-time $14,051. Required fees: $2320. *Financial support:* In 2009–10, 21 research assistantships (averaging $8,000 per year) were awarded; Federal Work-Study, scholarships/grants, and unspecified assistantships also available. Financial award application deadline: 4/1; financial award applicants required to submit FAFSA. *Faculty research:* Speech pathology, special education, language arts, reading. Total annual research expenditures: $160,500. *Unit head:* Dr. Monica Lambert, Chairperson, 828-262-7173, Fax: 828-262-6767, E-mail: lambertma@appstate.edu. *Application contact:* Eveline Watts, Graduate Student Coordinator, 828-262-2182, E-mail: wattsem@appstate.edu.

Arizona State University, Graduate College, College of Liberal Arts and Sciences, Division of Natural Sciences, Department of Speech and Hearing Science, Tempe, AZ 85287. Offers audiology (Au D); communication disorders (MS); speech and hearing science (PhD). *Accreditation:* ASHA (one or more programs are accredited). *Degree requirements:* For master's, thesis or alternative, oral and written exams. *Entrance requirements:* For master's, GRE.

Arkansas State University—Jonesboro, Graduate School, College of Nursing and Health Professions, Department of Communication Disorders, Jonesboro, State University, AR 72467. Offers MCD. *Accreditation:* ASHA. Part-time programs available. *Faculty:* 4 full-time (3 women), 2 part-time/adjunct (1 woman). *Students:* 35 full-time (all women), 2 part-time (both women); includes 3 minority (2 African Americans, 1 Hispanic American), 1 international. Average age 25. 25 applicants, 92% accepted, 23 enrolled. In 2009, 18 master's awarded. *Degree requirements:* For master's, comprehensive exam, thesis or alternative. *Entrance requirements:* For master's, GRE General Test, appropriate bachelor's degree, letters of recommendation. Additional exam requirements/recommendations for international students: Required—TOEFL (minimum score 550 paper-based; 213 computer-based; 79 iBT), IELTS (minimum score 6). *Application deadline:* For fall admission, 2/15 for domestic and international students. Applications are processed on a rolling basis. Application fee: $30 ($40 for international students). Electronic applications accepted. *Expenses:* Contact institution. *Financial support:* In 2009–10, 9 students received support. Career-related internships or fieldwork, scholarships/grants, and unspecified assistantships available. Financial award application deadline: 7/1; financial award applicants required to submit FAFSA. *Unit head:* Dr. Richard Neeley, Director, 870-972-3301, Fax: 870-972-3788, E-mail: rneeley@astate.edu. *Application contact:* Dr. Andrew Sustich, Dean of the Graduate School, 870-972-3029, Fax: 870-972-3857, E-mail: sustich@astate.edu.

Armstrong Atlantic State University, School of Graduate Studies, Program in Education, Savannah, GA 31419-1997. Offers adult education (M Ed); curriculum and instruction (M Ed); early childhood education (M Ed); education (M Ed); elementary education (M Ed); middle grades education (M Ed); secondary education (M Ed), including business education, English education, mathematics education, science education, social science education; special education (M Ed), including behavioral disorders, learning disabilities, speech-language pathology. *Accreditation:* NCATE. Part-time and evening/weekend programs available. Postbaccalaureate distance learning degree programs offered (minimal on-campus study). *Degree requirements:* For master's, comprehensive exam, portfolio. *Entrance requirements:* For master's, GRE General Test or MAT, minimum GPA of 2.5, letters of recommendation. Additional exam requirements/recommendations for international students: Required—TOEFL (minimum score 523 paper-based; 193 computer-based). Electronic applications accepted.

A.T. Still University of Health Sciences, Arizona School of Health Sciences, Mesa, AZ 85206. Offers advanced occupational therapy (MS); advanced physician assistant (MS); athletic training (MS); audiology (Au D); health sciences (DHSc); human movement (MS); occupational therapy (MS); physical therapy (MS, DPT); physician assistant (MS); transitional audiology (Au D); transitional physical therapy (DPT). *Accreditation:* AOTA (one or more programs are accredited); ASHA. Postbaccalaureate distance learning degree programs offered (no on-campus study). *Faculty:* 53 full-time (30 women), 205 part-time/adjunct (117 women). *Students:* 491 full-time (353 women), 1,251 part-time (874 women); includes 319 minority (70 African Americans, 11 American Indian/Alaska Native, 176 Asian Americans or Pacific Islanders, 62 Hispanic Americans), 3 international. Average age 31. 2,697 applicants, 22% accepted, 420 enrolled. In 2009, 225 master's, 523 doctorates awarded. *Degree requirements:* For master's, thesis (for some programs); for doctorate, thesis/dissertation (for some programs). *Entrance requirements:* For master's, GRE General Test; for doctorate, GRE, Evaluation of Practicing Audiologists Capabilities (Au D), Physical Therapy Evaluation Tool (DPT), current state licensure, master's degree or equivalent (Au D), minimum GPA of 2.7. Additional exam requirements/recommendations for international students: Recommended—TOEFL (minimum score 550 paper-based; 213 computer-based; 80 iBT). *Application deadline:* For fall admission, 2/1 priority date for domestic and international students. Applications are processed on a rolling basis. Application fee: $60. *Expenses:* Contact institution. *Financial support:* In 2009–10, 651 students received support. Federal Work-Study and scholarships/grants available. Financial award application deadline: 5/1; financial award applicants required to submit FAFSA. *Faculty research:* Adolescent health-related quality of life, clinical outcomes following sport related injury, pediatric concussion, shoulder stability and neuromuscular control, sport conditioning, exercise and sport psychology, geriatric exercise and wellness. Total annual research expenditures: $61,527. *Unit head:* Dr. Randy Danielsen, Dean, 480-219-6000, Fax: 480-219-6110, E-mail: rdanielsen@atsu.edu. *Application contact:* Donna Sparks, Associate Director for Admissions, 660-626-2237, Fax: 660-626-2969, E-mail: admissions@atsu.edu.

Auburn University, Graduate School, College of Liberal Arts, Department of Communication Disorders, Auburn University, AL 36849. Offers audiology (MCD, MS, Au D); speech pathology (MCD, MS). *Accreditation:* ASHA (one or more programs are accredited). Part-time programs available. *Faculty:* 15 full-time (11 women), 3 part-time/adjunct (all women). *Students:* 71 full-time (67 women), 9 part-time (all women); includes 7 minority (4 African Americans, 2 Asian Americans or Pacific Islanders, 1 Hispanic American). Average age 24. 152 applicants, 29% accepted, 32 enrolled. In 2009, 19 master's awarded. *Degree requirements:* For master's, comprehensive exam (MCD), thesis (MS). *Entrance requirements:* For master's, GRE General Test. *Application deadline:* For fall admission, 7/7 for domestic students; for spring admission, 11/24 for domestic students. Applications are processed on a rolling basis. Application fee: $50 ($60 for international students). Electronic applications accepted. *Expenses:* Tuition, state resident: full-time $6240. Tuition, nonresident: full-time $18,720. International tuition: $18,938 full-time. Required fees: $492. Tuition and fees vary according to course load, program and reciprocity agreements. *Financial support:* Research assistantships, teaching assistantships, Federal Work-Study available. Support available to part-time students. Financial award application deadline: 3/15; financial award applicants required to submit FAFSA. *Unit head:* Dr. Lawrence F. Molt, Chair, 334-844-9600. *Application contact:* Dr. George Flowers, Dean of the Graduate School, 334-844-2125.

Ball State University, Graduate School, College of Sciences and Humanities, Department of Speech Pathology and Audiology, Muncie, IN 47306-1099. Offers MA, Au D. *Accreditation:* ASHA. *Entrance requirements:* For master's, GRE General Test; for doctorate, GRE General Test, interview. *Faculty research:* Adult neurological disorders, stuttering, tinnitus masking, brain stem responses.

Barry University, School of Education, Program in Education for Teachers of Students with Hearing Impairments, Miami Shores, FL 33161-6695. Offers MS.

Baylor University, Graduate School, College of Arts and Sciences, Department of Communication Sciences and Disorders, Waco, TX 76798. Offers MA, MSCSD. *Accreditation:* ASHA (one or more programs are accredited). *Faculty:* 9 full-time (6 women), 1 (woman) part-time/adjunct. *Students:* 48 full-time (46 women); includes 8 minority (3 African Americans, 5 Hispanic Americans). In 2009, 30 master's awarded. *Entrance requirements:* For master's, GRE General Test. *Application deadline:* Applications are processed on a rolling basis. Application fee: $25. *Expenses:* Contact institution. *Financial support:* In 2009–10, 25 students received support, including 20 fellowships; Federal Work-Study, institutionally sponsored loans, and tuition waivers (partial) also available. Financial award application deadline: 5/1. *Faculty research:* Nasality, language impairment, stuttering, Spanish speech perception. *Unit head:* Dr. David Garrett, Program Director, 254-710-2567, Fax: 254-710-2590. *Application contact:* Kathryn Williams, Administrative Assistant, 254-710-3588, Fax: 254-710-3870, E-mail: kathryn_williams@baylor.edu.

Bloomsburg University of Pennsylvania, School of Graduate Studies, College of Professional Studies, School of Education, Department of Exceptionality Programs, Program in Education of the Deaf/Hard of Hearing, Bloomsburg, PA 17815-1301. Offers MS. *Entrance requirements:* For master's, PRAXIS, minimum QPA of 3.0. Additional exam requirements/recommendations for international students: Required—TOEFL (minimum score 550 paper-based; 213 computer-based; 79 iBT). Electronic applications accepted. *Faculty research:* Teaching sign language and speech reading through videodisc technology, oral communication skills, sign language.

Bloomsburg University of Pennsylvania, School of Graduate Studies, College of Professional Studies, School of Health Sciences, Department of Audiology and Speech Pathology, Program in Audiology, Bloomsburg, PA 17815-1301. Offers Au D. *Accreditation:* ASHA. *Entrance requirements:* For doctorate, GRE, 3 letters of recommendation. Additional exam requirements/recommendations for international students: Required—TOEFL. Electronic applications accepted. *Faculty research:* Electrophysiological, industrial, and clinical audiology; hearing aid education; pediatric audiology; auditory processing.

Bloomsburg University of Pennsylvania, School of Graduate Studies, College of Professional Studies, School of Health Sciences, Department of Audiology and Speech Pathology, Program in Speech Pathology, Bloomsburg, PA 17815-1301. Offers MS. *Accreditation:* ASHA. *Entrance requirements:* For master's, GRE General Test, minimum QPA of 3.0, 3 letters of recommendation. Additional exam requirements/recommendations for international students: Required—TOEFL (minimum score 550 paper-based; 213 computer-based; 79 iBT). Electronic applications accepted. *Faculty research:* Language disorders in children, augmentative communication, neurogenic disorders of speech and language, stuttering, speech science.

Boston University, College of Health and Rehabilitation Sciences—Sargent College, Department of Speech, Language and Hearing Sciences, Boston, MA 02215. Offers audiology (PhD); speech-language pathology (MS, PhD, CAGS). *Accreditation:* ASHA. *Faculty:* 12 full-time (10 women), 12 part-time/adjunct (5 women). *Students:* 63 full-time (62 women), 1 (woman) part-time; includes 7 minority (6 Asian Americans or Pacific Islanders, 1 Hispanic American). Average age 26. 307 applicants, 45% accepted, 31 enrolled. In 2009, 28 master's awarded. *Degree requirements:* For master's, comprehensive exam, thesis optional; for doctorate, one foreign language, comprehensive exam, thesis/dissertation. *Entrance requirements:* For master's, doctorate, and CAGS, GRE General Test. Additional exam requirements/recommendations for international students: Required—TOEFL (minimum score 550 paper-based; 84 computer-based). *Application deadline:* For fall admission, 1/15 priority date for domestic students; for spring admission, 10/1 for domestic students. Applications are processed on a rolling basis. Application fee: $70. Electronic applications accepted. *Expenses:* Tuition: Full-time $37,910;

part-time $1184 per credit hour. Required fees: $386; $40 per semester. Part-time tuition and fees vary according to class time, course level, degree level and program. *Financial support:* In 2009–10, 54 students received support, including 8 fellowships with partial tuition reimbursements available (averaging $15,000 per year), 2 research assistantships with full tuition reimbursements available (averaging $18,000 per year), 11 teaching assistantships with partial tuition reimbursements available (averaging $2,400 per year); career-related internships or fieldwork, Federal Work-Study, institutionally sponsored loans, scholarships/grants, and tuition waivers (partial) also available. Financial award application deadline: 4/15; financial award applicants required to submit FAFSA. *Faculty research:* Child language, fluency, autism, speech science, perception of complex sounds. *Unit head:* Dr. Melanie Matthies, Chair, 617-353-3188, E-mail: matthies@bu.edu. *Application contact:* Sharon Sankey, Director, Student Services, 617-353-2713, Fax: 617-353-7500, E-mail: ssankey@bu.edu.

Bowling Green State University, Graduate College, College of Education and Human Development, School of Education and Intervention Services, Intervention Services Division, Program in Special Education, Bowling Green, OH 43403. Offers assistive technology (M Ed); early childhood intervention (M Ed); gifted education (M Ed); hearing impaired intervention (M Ed); mild/moderate intervention (M Ed); moderate/intensive intervention (M Ed). *Accreditation:* NCATE. Part-time programs available. *Degree requirements:* For master's, thesis or alternative. *Entrance requirements:* For master's, GRE General Test. Additional exam requirements/recommendations for international students: Required—TOEFL. Electronic applications accepted. *Faculty research:* Reading and special populations, deafness, early childhood, gifted and talented, behavior disorders.

Bowling Green State University, Graduate College, College of Health and Human Services, Department of Communication Disorders, Bowling Green, OH 43403. Offers communication disorders (PhD); speech-language pathology (MS). *Accreditation:* ASHA (one or more programs are accredited). *Degree requirements:* For master's, thesis or alternative; for doctorate, comprehensive exam, thesis/dissertation, foreign language or research tool. *Entrance requirements:* For master's, GRE General Test, minimum GPA of 3.0; for doctorate, GRE General Test, minimum GPA of 3.2. Additional exam requirements/recommendations for international students: Required—TOEFL. Electronic applications accepted. *Faculty research:* Rehabilitation and mental disorders, forensic rehabilitation, rehabilitation and substance abuse, private rehabilitation and disability management, adjustment to disability.

Brigham Young University, Graduate Studies, David O. McKay School of Education, Department of Communication Disorders, Provo, UT 84602-1001. Offers MS. *Accreditation:* ASHA. *Faculty:* 10 full-time (4 women), 4 part-time/adjunct (3 women). *Students:* 12 full-time (10 women), 20 part-time (all women); includes 1 minority (Asian American or Pacific Islander). Average age 27. 44 applicants, 41% accepted, 9 enrolled. In 2009, 25 master's awarded. *Degree requirements:* For master's, comprehensive exam, thesis, exit interview. *Entrance requirements:* For master's, GRE General Test, 3 letters of recommendation. Additional exam requirements/recommendations for international students: Required—TOEFL (minimum score 580 paper-based; 237 computer-based; 85 iBT). *Application deadline:* For fall admission, 2/1 for domestic and international students. Application fee: $50. Electronic applications accepted. *Expenses:* Tuition: Full-time $5580; part-time $301 per credit hour. Tuition and fees vary according to student's religious affiliation. *Financial support:* In 2009–10, 16 research assistantships (averaging $1,701 per year), 17 teaching assistantships (averaging $2,786 per year) were awarded; fellowships, institutionally sponsored loans, scholarships/grants, and tuition waivers (partial) also available. *Faculty research:* Foreign language speech audiometry materials; language sample analysis, language measurement; speech motor control physiology; acrodynamic and kenematic analysis of speech production; social skills and outcomes of children with language impairment. *Unit head:* Dr. Christopher Dromey, Chair, 801-422-6461, Fax: 801-422-0197, E-mail: christopher_dromey@byu.edu. *Application contact:* Sandy Alger, Department Secretary, 801-422-5117, Fax: 801-422-0197, E-mail: sandy_alger@byu.edu.

Brooklyn College of the City University of New York, Division of Graduate Studies, Department of Speech Communication Arts and Sciences, Brooklyn, NY 11210-2889. Offers audiology (Au D); speech (MA), including public communication; speech and hearing sciences (PhD); speech pathology (MS). *Accreditation:* ASHA (one or more programs are accredited). Part-time programs available. *Students:* 31 full-time (all women), 51 part-time (50 women); includes 14 minority (6 African Americans, 2 Asian Americans or Pacific Islanders, 6 Hispanic Americans), 1 international. Average age 26. 313 applicants, 23% accepted, 31 enrolled. In 2009, 42 master's awarded. Terminal master's awarded for partial completion of doctoral program. *Degree requirements:* For master's, comprehensive exam, NTE. *Entrance requirements:* For master's, GRE, minimum GPA of 3.0, interview, essay. Additional exam requirements/recommendations for international students: Required—TOEFL (minimum score 500 paper-based; 173 computer-based; 61 iBT). *Application deadline:* For fall admission, 2/1 priority date for domestic and international students. Applications are processed on a rolling basis. Electronic applications accepted. *Expenses:* Tuition, state resident: full-time $7360; part-time $310 per credit hour. Tuition, nonresident: full-time $13,800; part-time $575 per credit hour. Required fees: $140.10 per semester. *Financial support:* Career-related internships or fieldwork, Federal Work-Study, institutionally sponsored loans, scholarships/grants, and traineeships available. Support available to part-time students. Financial award application deadline: 5/1; financial award applicants required to submit FAFSA. *Faculty research:* Language and learning disorders, aphasia, auditory disorders, public and business communication, voice and fluency disorders. *Unit head:* Dr. Michele Emmer, Chairperson, 718-951-5225, Fax: 718-951-4167, E-mail: memmer@brooklyn.cuny.edu. *Application contact:* Hernan Sierra, Graduate Admissions Coordinator, 718-951-4536, Fax: 718-951-4506, E-mail: grads@brooklyn.cuny.edu.

Buffalo State College, State University of New York, The Graduate School, Faculty of Applied Science and Education, Department of Speech-Language Pathology, Buffalo, NY 14222-1095. Offers MS Ed. *Accreditation:* ASHA. Part-time and evening/weekend programs available. *Degree requirements:* For master's, thesis or alternative, project. *Entrance requirements:* For master's, minimum GPA of 3.0 in last 60 hours, 22 hours in communication disorders. Additional exam requirements/recommendations for international students: Required—TOEFL (minimum score 550 paper-based; 213 computer-based).

California State University, Chico, Graduate School, College of Communication and Education, Department of Communication Arts and Sciences, Program in Communication Science and Disorders, Chico, CA 95929-0722. Offers MA. *Accreditation:* ASHA. *Students:* 35 full-time (32 women), 6 part-time (all women); includes 10 minority (3 Asian Americans or Pacific Islanders, 7 Hispanic Americans). Average age 27. 94 applicants, 22% accepted, 19 enrolled. In 2009, 21 master's awarded. *Degree requirements:* For master's, thesis or alternative. *Entrance requirements:* For master's, GRE General Test, 3 letters of recommendation, resume. Additional exam requirements/recommendations for international students: Required—TOEFL (minimum score 550 paper-based; 213 computer-based; 80 iBT), IELTS (minimum score 6.5). *Application deadline:* For fall admission, 3/1 for domestic and international students. Application fee: $55. Electronic applications accepted. *Financial support:* Teaching assistantships, career-related internships or fieldwork available. *Unit head:* Dr. Patrick McCaffrey, Graduate Coordinator, 530-898-6394. *Application contact:* Dr. Ruth Guzley, Graduate Coordinator, 530-898-5751.

California State University, East Bay, Graduate Programs, College of Letters, Arts, and Social Sciences, Department of Communicative Sciences and Disorders, Hayward, CA 94542-3000. Offers speech pathology and audiology (MS). *Accreditation:* ASHA. Part-time programs available. *Faculty:* 5 full-time (4 women). *Students:* 89 full-time (83 women), 44 part-time (14 women); includes 23 minority (3 African Americans, 16 Asian Americans or Pacific Islanders, 4 Hispanic Americans), 3 international. Average age 31. 254 applicants, 15% accepted, 30 enrolled. In 2009, 35 master's awarded. *Degree requirements:* For master's, comprehensive exam, internship or thesis. *Entrance requirements:* For master's, minimum GPA of 3.0 in last 2 years of course work. Additional exam requirements/recommendations for international students: Required—TOEFL (minimum score 550 paper-based; 213 computer-based). *Application deadline:* For fall admission, 2/15 for domestic and international students. Application fee: $55. Electronic applications accepted. *Financial support:* Fellowships, teaching assistantships, career-related internships or fieldwork, Federal Work-Study, institutionally sponsored loans, and scholarships/grants available. Support available to part-time students. Financial award application deadline: 3/1. *Unit head:* Prof. Robert Peppard, Graduate Coordinator, 510-885-4310, Fax: 510-885-2186, E-mail: robert.peppard@csueastbay.edu. *Application contact:* Donna Wiley, Interim Associate Director, 510-885-2928, Fax: 510-885-4777, E-mail: donna.wiley@csueastbay.edu.

California State University, Fresno, Division of Graduate Studies, College of Health and Human Services, Department of Communicative Disorders, Fresno, CA 93740-8027. Offers communicative disorders (MA), including deaf education, speech/language pathology. *Accreditation:* ASHA. Part-time programs available. *Degree requirements:* For master's, thesis or alternative. *Entrance requirements:* For master's, GRE General Test, minimum GPA of 3.0. Additional exam requirements/recommendations for international students: Required—TOEFL. Electronic applications accepted. *Faculty research:* Disabilities education, technology, writing skills at multiple levels, stuttering treatment.

California State University, Fullerton, Graduate Studies, College of Communications, Department of Human Communications, Fullerton, CA 92834-9480. Offers communicative disorders (MA); speech communication (MA). *Accreditation:* ASHA. Part-time programs available. *Students:* 79 full-time (69 women), 42 part-time (31 women); includes 44 minority (8 African Americans, 14 Asian Americans or Pacific Islanders, 22 Hispanic Americans), 6 international. Average age 31. 266 applicants, 14% accepted, 29 enrolled. In 2009, 47 master's awarded. *Degree requirements:* For master's, comprehensive exam, thesis or alternative. *Entrance requirements:* For master's, minimum GPA of 3.0 in major. Application fee: $55. *Expenses:* Tuition, nonresident: full-time $11,160; part-time $373 per credit. Required fees: $1440 per term. Tuition and fees vary according to course load, degree level and program. *Financial support:* Teaching assistantships, career-related internships or fieldwork, Federal Work-Study, institutionally sponsored loans, and scholarships/grants available. Support available to part-time students. Financial award application deadline: 3/1; financial award applicants required to submit FAFSA. *Faculty research:* Speech therapy. *Unit head:* Dr. John Reinard, Chair, 657-278-3617. *Application contact:* Dr. John Reinard, Chair, 657-278-3617.

California State University, Fullerton, Graduate Studies, College of Humanities and Social Sciences, Program in Linguistics, Fullerton, CA 92834-9480. Offers analysis of specific language structures (MA); anthropological linguistics (MA); applied linguistics (MA); communication and semantics (MA); disorders of communication (MA); experimental phonetics (MA). Part-time programs available. *Students:* 20 full-time (10 women), 8 part-time (5 women); includes 5 minority (1 Asian American or Pacific Islander, 4 Hispanic Americans), 11 international. Average age 31. 21 applicants, 71% accepted, 8 enrolled. In 2009, 3 master's awarded. *Degree requirements:* For master's, one foreign language, thesis or alternative, project. *Entrance requirements:* For master's, minimum GPA of 3.0, undergraduate major in linguistics or related field. Application fee: $55. *Expenses:* Tuition, nonresident: full-time $11,160; part-time $373 per credit. Required fees: $1440 per term. Tuition and fees vary according to course load, degree level and program. *Financial support:* Career-related internships or fieldwork, Federal Work-Study, institutionally sponsored loans, and scholarships/grants available. Support available to part-time students. Financial award application deadline: 3/1; financial award applicants required to submit FAFSA. *Unit head:* Dr. Franz Muller-Gotama, Adviser, 657-278-2441. *Application contact:* Admissions/Applications, 657-278-2371.

California State University, Long Beach, Graduate Studies, College of Health and Human Services, Department of Communicative Disorders, Long Beach, CA 90840. Offers MA. *Accreditation:* ASHA. Part-time programs available. *Faculty:* 16 full-time (15 women), 4 part-time/adjunct (all women). *Students:* 68 full-time (63 women), 40 part-time (all women); includes 41 minority (3 African Americans, 19 Asian Americans or Pacific Islanders, 19 Hispanic Americans), 2 international. Average age 29. 286 applicants, 15% accepted, 36 enrolled. *Degree requirements:* For master's, comprehensive exam or thesis. *Entrance requirements:* For master's, GRE, minimum GPA of 3.0 in last 60 units. *Application deadline:* For fall admission, 2/1 for domestic students. Applications are processed on a rolling basis. Application fee: $55. Electronic applications accepted. *Expenses:* Required fees: $1802 per semester. Part-time tuition and fees vary according to course load. *Financial support:* Federal Work-Study, institutionally sponsored loans, and scholarships/grants available. Financial award application deadline: 3/2. *Unit head:* Dr. Carolyn Conway Madding, Chair, 562-985-5283, Fax: 562-985-4584, E-mail: madding@csulb.edu. *Application contact:* Dr. Jennifer Ostergren, Graduate Advisor, 562-985-8843, Fax: 562-985-4584, E-mail: ostergren@msn.com.

California State University, Los Angeles, Graduate Studies, College of Health and Human Services, Department of Communication Disorders, Los Angeles, CA 90032-8530. Offers speech and hearing (MA); speech-language pathology (MA). *Accreditation:* ASHA. Part-time and evening/weekend programs available. *Faculty:* 3 full-time (2 women), 2 part-time/adjunct (1 woman). *Students:* 60 full-time (56 women), 32 part-time (28 women); includes 49 minority (5 African Americans, 18 Asian Americans or Pacific Islanders, 26 Hispanic Americans), 4 international. Average age 30. 133 applicants, 98% accepted, 13 enrolled. In 2009, 13 master's awarded. *Degree requirements:* For master's, comprehensive exam. *Entrance requirements:* For master's, undergraduate major in communication disorders or related area, minimum GPA of 2.75 in last 90 units. Additional exam requirements/recommendations for international students: Required—TOEFL (minimum score 500 paper-based; 173 computer-based). *Application deadline:* For fall admission, 5/1 for domestic and international students. Applications are processed on a rolling basis. Application fee: $55. *Financial support:* Career-related internships or fieldwork and Federal Work-Study available. Support available to part-time students. Financial award application deadline: 3/1. *Faculty research:* Language disabilities, minority child language learning. *Unit head:* Dr. Edward Klein, Chair, 323-343-4690, Fax: 323-343-4698, E-mail: eklein@cslanet.calstatela.edu. *Application contact:* Dr. Cheryl L. Ney, Associate Vice President for Academic Affairs and Dean of Graduate Studies, 323-343-3820, Fax: 323-343-5653, E-mail: ncey@cslanet.calstatela.edu.

California State University, Northridge, Graduate Studies, College of Health and Human Development, Department of Communication Disorders and Sciences, Northridge, CA 91330. Offers audiology (MS); speech language pathology (MS). *Accreditation:* ASHA. *Faculty:* 8 full-time (5 women), 16 part-time/adjunct (15 women). *Students:* 105 full-time (101 women), 49 part-time (45 women); includes 2 African Americans, 14 Asian Americans or Pacific Islanders, 13 Hispanic Americans, 4 international. Average age 30. 296 applicants, 10% accepted, 26 enrolled. In 2009, 74 master's awarded. *Degree requirements:* For master's, PRAXIS. *Entrance requirements:* For master's, GRE or minimum GPA of 3.5. Additional exam requirements/recommendations for international students: Required—TOEFL. *Application deadline:* For fall admission, 11/30 for domestic students. Application fee: $55. *Financial support:* Application deadline: 3/1. *Faculty research:* Infant stimulation, early intervention program. *Unit head:* Dr. J. Stephen Sinclair, Chair, 818-677-2852. *Application contact:* Dr. J. Stephen Sinclair, Chair, 818-677-2852.

California State University, Sacramento, Graduate Studies, College of Health and Human Services, Department of Speech Pathology and Audiology, Sacramento, CA 95819. Offers audiology (MS); speech pathology (MS). *Accreditation:* ASHA. *Degree requirements:* For master's, thesis, writing proficiency exam. *Entrance requirements:* For master's, GRE General Test, appropriate bachelor's degree, minimum GPA of 3.0 in last 2 years of course work. Additional exam requirements/recommendations for international students: Required—TOEFL. Electronic applications accepted.

California University of Pennsylvania, School of Graduate Studies and Research, School of Education, Department of Communication Disorders, California, PA 15419-1394. Offers MS. *Accreditation:* ASHA. Part-time and evening/weekend programs available. *Degree requirements:* For master's, comprehensive exam, thesis optional. *Entrance requirements:* For master's, GRE General Test, minimum GPA of 3.0, references. Additional exam requirements/recommendations for international students: Required—TOEFL (minimum score 550 paper-based; 213 computer-based; 80 iBT). Electronic applications accepted. *Faculty research:* Normative voice database, communication disorders and health.

Communication Disorders

Canisius College, Graduate Division, School of Education and Human Services, Department of Graduate Education, Buffalo, NY 14208-1098. Offers adolescence education (grades 7-12) (MS); childhood education (grades 1-6) (MS); college student personnel administration (MS); deaf education (MS); differentiated instruction (MS Ed); educational administration and supervision (MS); general education (MS Ed); initial teacher certification (elementary education) (MS); initial teacher certification (secondary education) (MS); literacy (MS Ed); special education (MS). *Accreditation:* NCATE. Part-time and evening/weekend programs available. *Faculty:* 22 full-time (14 women), 84 part-time/adjunct (54 women). *Students:* 409 full-time (288 women), 261 part-time (187 women); includes 29 minority (24 African Americans, 5 Hispanic Americans), 156 international. Average age 30. 518 applicants, 74% accepted, 240 enrolled. In 2009, 346 master's awarded. Application fee: $25. *Financial support:* Research assistantships with full tuition reimbursements, career-related internships or fieldwork, institutionally sponsored loans, scholarships/grants, health care benefits, tuition waivers (full and partial), and unspecified assistantships available. *Faculty research:* Autism, Asperger's disease, private higher education, reading strategies. *Unit head:* Rev. Paul Nochelski, Chair of Graduate Education and Leadership, 716-888-3297, Fax: 716-888-3299. *Application contact:* James D. Bagwell, Director of Graduate Recruitment and Admissions, 716-888-2544, Fax: 716-888-3290, E-mail: bagwellj@canisius.edu.

Carlos Albizu University, Graduate Programs, San Juan, PR 00901. Offers clinical psychology (MS, PhD, Psy D); general psychology (PhD); industrial/organizational psychology (MS, PhD); speech and language pathology (MS). *Accreditation:* APA (one or more programs are accredited). Part-time and evening/weekend programs available. Terminal master's awarded for partial completion of doctoral program. *Degree requirements:* For master's, one foreign language, comprehensive exam, thesis; for doctorate, one foreign language, comprehensive exam, thesis/dissertation, written qualifying exams. *Entrance requirements:* For master's, GRE General Test or EXADEP, interview; minimum GPA of 3.0 (industrial/organizational psychology), 3.25 (speech and language pathology); for doctorate, GRE General Test or EXADEP, interview; minimum GPA of 3.0 (industrial/organizational psychology), 3.25 (PhD and Psy D in clinical psychology). *Faculty research:* Psychotherapeutic techniques for Hispanics, psychology of the aged, school dropouts, stress, violence.

Case Western Reserve University, School of Graduate Studies, Department of Communication Sciences, Cleveland, OH 44106. Offers speech-language pathology (MA, PhD). *Accreditation:* ASHA (one or more programs are accredited). Part-time programs available. *Faculty:* 5 full-time (all women), 4 part-time/adjunct (2 women). *Students:* 11 full-time (all women), 6 part-time (5 women); includes 1 minority (Hispanic American), 1 international. Average age 24. 58 applicants, 29% accepted, 6 enrolled. In 2009, 6 master's awarded. Terminal master's awarded for partial completion of doctoral program. *Degree requirements:* For master's, comprehensive exam, thesis optional; for doctorate, thesis/dissertation. *Entrance requirements:* For master's and doctorate, GRE General Test. Additional exam requirements/recommendations for international students: Required—TOEFL (minimum score 550 paper-based; 213 computer-based; 79 iBT). *Application deadline:* For fall admission, 2/15 for domestic students. Applications are processed on a rolling basis. Application fee: $50. Electronic applications accepted. *Financial support:* Research assistantships, tuition waivers (partial) and unspecified assistantships available. Financial award application deadline: 2/15; financial award applicants required to submit FAFSA. *Faculty research:* Traumatic brain injury, phonological disorders, child language disorders, communication problems in the aged and Alzheimer's patients, cleft palate, voice disorders. *Unit head:* Stephen E. Haynesworth, Interim Chair, 216-368-2470, Fax: 216-368-6078, E-mail: stephen.haynesworth@case.edu. *Application contact:* Patricia Maar, Assistant, 216-368-2470, Fax: 216-368-6078, E-mail: cosgrad@case.edu.

Central Michigan University, College of Graduate Studies, The Herbert H. and Grace A. Dow College of Health Professions, Department of Communications Disorders, Doctor of Audiology Program, Mount Pleasant, MI 48859. Offers Au D. *Accreditation:* ASHA. *Degree requirements:* For doctorate, comprehensive exam, thesis/dissertation or alternative. *Entrance requirements:* For doctorate, GRE, interview. Electronic applications accepted. *Faculty research:* Auditory electrophysiology, auditory process disorders, neuroanatomy, pediatric audiology, rehabilitative audiology.

Central Michigan University, College of Graduate Studies, The Herbert H. and Grace A. Dow College of Health Professions, Department of Communications Disorders, Program in Speech-Language Pathology, Mount Pleasant, MI 48859. Offers MA. *Accreditation:* ASHA. *Degree requirements:* For master's, thesis or alternative. Electronic applications accepted. *Expenses:* Contact institution. *Faculty research:* Traumatic brain injury, neuro-linguistics, multidisciplinary and transdisciplinary therapy, speech audiometry, phonological disorders.

Chapman University, Graduate Studies, College of Educational Studies, Program in Communication Sciences and Disorders, Orange, CA 92866. Offers MS. *Faculty:* 24 full-time (15 women), 25 part-time/adjunct (16 women). *Students:* 28 full-time (25 women); includes 6 minority (3 Asian Americans or Pacific Islanders, 3 Hispanic Americans). Average age 26. 87 applicants, 43% accepted. *Entrance requirements:* For master's, GRE, 3 letters of recommendation. *Application deadline:* For fall admission, 2/27 for domestic students. Application fee: $55. Tuition and fees vary according to course load, degree level and program. *Financial support:* Fellowships, institutionally sponsored loans and scholarships/grants available. *Unit head:* Dr. Judy Montgomery, Director, 714-628-7263, E-mail: montgome@chapman.edu. *Application contact:* Rika Judd, Graduate Admission Counselor, 714-997-6786, Fax: 714-997-6713, E-mail: rjudd@chapman.edu.

Clarion University of Pennsylvania, Office of Research and Graduate Studies, College of Education and Human Services, Department of Speech Language Pathology, Clarion, PA 16214. Offers MS. *Accreditation:* ASHA. Part-time programs available. *Degree requirements:* For master's, thesis or alternative. *Entrance requirements:* For master's, minimum QPA of 3.0. Additional exam requirements/recommendations for international students: Required—TOEFL (minimum score 573 paper-based; 230 computer-based; 89 iBT). Electronic applications accepted.

Cleveland State University, College of Graduate Studies, College of Science, Department of Health Sciences, Program in Speech Pathology and Audiology, Cleveland, OH 44115. Offers MA. *Accreditation:* ASHA. *Degree requirements:* For master's, comprehensive exam, thesis optional. *Entrance requirements:* For master's, GRE. Additional exam requirements/recommendations for international students: Required—TOEFL. Electronic applications accepted. *Faculty research:* Child language and literacy development, cultural diversity, variant dialects, voice disorders, neurogenic communication disorders.

The College of Saint Rose, Graduate Studies, School of Education, Department of Communication Disorders, Albany, NY 12203-1419. Offers MS Ed. *Accreditation:* ASHA. Part-time and evening/weekend programs available. *Degree requirements:* For master's, comprehensive exam or thesis. *Entrance requirements:* For master's, minimum undergraduate GPA of 3.0, on-campus interview, 32 undergraduate credits if undergraduate degree is not in communication disorders. Additional exam requirements/recommendations for international students: Required—TOEFL (minimum score 550 paper-based; 213 computer-based). Electronic applications accepted.

Dalhousie University, Faculty of Health Professions, School of Human Communication Disorders, Halifax, NS B3H 1R2, Canada. Offers audiology (M Sc); speech-language pathology (M Sc). *Faculty:* 8 full-time (6 women), 8 part-time/adjunct (4 women). *Students:* 92 full-time (87 women); includes 7 minority (4 Asian Americans or Pacific Islanders, 3 Hispanic Americans). Average age 25. 190 applicants, 17% accepted. In 2009, 27 master's awarded. *Degree requirements:* For master's, thesis or alternative. *Entrance requirements:* Additional exam requirements/recommendations for international students: Required—TOEFL, IELTS, CANTEST, CAEL, or Michigan English Language Assessment Battery. *Application deadline:* For fall admission, 1/15 priority date for domestic and international students. Applications are processed on a rolling basis. Application fee: $70. Electronic applications accepted. *Expenses:* Contact institution. *Financial support:* In 2009–10, 16 students received support, including 14 research

assistantships (averaging $1,500 per year), 2 teaching assistantships (averaging $500 per year); career-related internships or fieldwork and bursaries also available. *Faculty research:* Audiology, hearing aids, speech and voice disorders, language development and disorders, treatment efficacy. *Unit head:* Dr. Joy Armson, Graduate Coordinator, 902-494-7052, Fax: 902-494-5151, E-mail: hcdwww@dal.ca. *Application contact:* Joanne Fenerty, Administrative Assistant, 902-494-5161, Fax: 902-494-5151, E-mail: jfenerty@dal.ca.

Duquesne University, John G. Rangos, Sr. School of Health Sciences, Pittsburgh, PA 15282-0001. Offers health management systems (MHMS); occupational therapy (MS); physical therapy (DPT); physician assistant studies (MPAS); rehabilitation science (MS, PhD); speech-language pathology (MS); MBA/MHMS. *Accreditation:* AOTA (one or more programs are accredited); APTA (one or more programs are accredited); ASHA. *Faculty:* 35 full-time (23 women), 17 part-time/adjunct (10 women). *Students:* 309 full-time (258 women), 11 part-time (7 women); includes 11 minority (5 African Americans, 5 Asian Americans or Pacific Islanders, 1 Hispanic American), 6 international. Average age 23. 454 applicants, 20% accepted, 20 enrolled. In 2009, 92 master's, 23 doctorates awarded. *Degree requirements:* For doctorate, thesis/dissertation. *Entrance requirements:* For master's, GRE General Test (speech-language pathology), 3 letters of recommendation; minimum GPA of 2.75 (health management systems, occupational therapy), minimum GPA of 3.0 (speech-language pathology); for doctorate, GRE General Test (for physical therapy), 3 letters of recommendation, minimum GPA of 3.0, personal interview. Additional exam requirements/recommendations for international students: Required—TOEFL (minimum score 550 paper-based; 233 computer-based; 90 iBT). *Application deadline:* Applications are processed on a rolling basis. Electronic applications accepted. *Expenses:* Contact institution. *Financial support:* Federal Work-Study available. *Faculty research:* Neuronal processing, electrical stimulation on peripheral neuropathy, CNS stimulatory and inhibitory signals, behavioral genetic methodologies to development disorders of speech, neurogenic communication disorders. Total annual research expenditures: $338,404. *Unit head:* Dr. Gregory H. Frazer, Dean, 412-396-5303, Fax: 412-396-5554, E-mail: frazer@duq.edu. *Application contact:* Christopher R. Hilf, Recruiter/Academic Advisor, 412-396-5653, Fax: 412-396-5554, E-mail: hilfc@duq.edu.

East Carolina University, Graduate School, School of Allied Health Sciences, Department of Communication Sciences and Disorders, Greenville, NC 27858-4353. Offers communication sciences and disorders (PhD); speech, language and auditory pathology (MS). *Accreditation:* ASHA (one or more programs are accredited). Postbaccalaureate distance learning degree programs offered (no on-campus study). *Degree requirements:* For master's, comprehensive exam, thesis or alternative; for doctorate, comprehensive exam, thesis/dissertation. *Entrance requirements:* For master's and doctorate, GRE General Test. Additional exam requirements/recommendations for international students: Required—TOEFL. *Faculty research:* Hearing, language disorders, stuttering, reading disorder.

Eastern Illinois University, Graduate School, College of Sciences, Department of Communication Disorders and Sciences, Charleston, IL 61920-3099. Offers MS. *Accreditation:* ASHA. *Faculty:* 10 full-time (6 women). In 2009, 23 master's awarded. *Degree requirements:* For master's, comprehensive exam. *Application deadline:* For fall admission, 3/31 priority date for domestic students. Applications are processed on a rolling basis. Application fee: $30. *Expenses:* Tuition, state resident: full-time $9434; part-time $239 per credit hour. Tuition, nonresident: full-time $23,774; part-time $717 per credit hour. Required fees: $802.63. *Financial support:* In 2009–10, 4 research assistantships with tuition reimbursements (averaging $8,100 per year), 5 teaching assistantships with tuition reimbursements (averaging $8,100 per year) were awarded. *Unit head:* Dr. Gail Richard, Chairperson, 217-581-2016, Fax: 217-581-2722, E-mail: gjrichard@eiu.edu. *Application contact:* Dr. Tina Veale, Coordinator, 217-581-2712, Fax: 217-581-7105, E-mail: tkveale@eiu.edu.

Eastern Kentucky University, The Graduate School, College of Education, Department of Special Education, Program in Communication Disorders, Richmond, KY 40475-3102. Offers MA Ed. *Accreditation:* ASHA. *Degree requirements:* For master's, comprehensive exam, thesis optional, 375 clinical clock hours. *Entrance requirements:* For master's, GRE General Test, minimum GPA of 3.0. *Faculty research:* Distance learning, fluency, phonemic awareness, technology, autism.

Eastern Michigan University, Graduate School, College of Education, Department of Special Education, Program in Hearing Impairment, Ypsilanti, MI 48197. Offers MA. *Students:* 2 full-time (both women). Average age 30.Application fee: $35. Tuition and fees vary according to course level. *Unit head:* Linda Polter, Coordinator, 734-487-3300, Fax: 734-487-2473, E-mail: linda.polter@emich.edu. *Application contact:* Linda Polter, Coordinator, 734-487-3300, Fax: 734-487-2473, E-mail: linda.polter@emich.edu.

Eastern Michigan University, Graduate School, College of Education, Department of Special Education, Program in Speech and Language Pathology, Ypsilanti, MI 48197. Offers MA. *Accreditation:* ASHA. Part-time and evening/weekend programs available. Postbaccalaureate distance learning degree programs offered (minimal on-campus study). *Students:* 49 full-time (47 women), 25 part-time (21 women); includes 4 minority (all African Americans). Average age 27. In 2009, 39 master's awarded. *Entrance requirements:* For master's, GRE General Test. Additional exam requirements/recommendations for international students: Required—TOEFL. *Application deadline:* Applications are processed on a rolling basis. Application fee: $35. Tuition and fees vary according to course level. *Financial support:* Fellowships, research assistantships with full tuition reimbursements, teaching assistantships with full tuition reimbursements, career-related internships or fieldwork, Federal Work-Study, institutionally sponsored loans, scholarships/grants, tuition waivers (partial), and unspecified assistantships available. Support available to part-time students. Financial award applicants required to submit FAFSA. *Unit head:* Dr. Lizbeth Stevens, Coordinator, 734-487-3300, Fax: 734-487-2473, E-mail: lizbeth.stevens@emich.edu. *Application contact:* Dr. Sarah Ginsberg, Advisor, 734-487-3300, Fax: 734-487-2473, E-mail: sarah.ginsberg@emich.edu.

Eastern New Mexico University, Graduate School, College of Liberal Arts and Sciences, Department of Health and Human Services, Portales, NM 88130. Offers speech pathology and audiology (MS). *Accreditation:* ASHA. Part-time programs available. Postbaccalaureate distance learning degree programs offered (minimal on-campus study). *Faculty:* 4 full-time (3 women). *Students:* 11 full-time (10 women), 41 part-time (39 women); includes 22 minority (1 African American, 2 American Indian/Alaska Native, 1 Asian American or Pacific Islander, 18 Hispanic Americans). Average age 29. 33 applicants, 58% accepted, 19 enrolled. In 2009, 11 master's awarded. *Degree requirements:* For master's, comprehensive exam, thesis optional, professional portfolio. *Entrance requirements:* For master's, GRE, minimum GPA of 3.0, 3 letters of recommendation. Additional exam requirements/recommendations for international students: Required—TOEFL (minimum score 550 paper-based; 213 computer-based; 79 iBT), IELTS (minimum score 6). *Application deadline:* For fall admission, 3/1 priority date for domestic and international students; for spring admission, 10/15 priority date for domestic and international students. Applications are processed on a rolling basis. Application fee: $10. Electronic applications accepted. *Expenses:* Tuition, state resident: full-time $2922; part-time $121.75 per credit hour. Tuition, nonresident: full-time $8454; part-time $352.25 per credit hour. Required fees: $1038; $43.25 per credit hour. *Financial support:* In 2009–10, 6 research assistantships with full tuition reimbursements (averaging $4,250 per year) were awarded; fellowships, teaching assistantships, unspecified assistantships also available. Support available to part-time students. Financial award applicants required to submit FAFSA. *Unit head:* Dr. Adrienne Bratcher, Graduate Coordinator, 575-562-2159, E-mail: adrienne.bratcher@enmu.edu. *Application contact:* Dean, Graduate School.

Eastern Washington University, Graduate Studies, College of Science, Health and Engineering, Department of Communication Disorders, Cheney, WA 99004-2431. Offers MS. *Accreditation:* ASHA. *Degree requirements:* For master's, comprehensive exam, thesis or alternative. *Entrance requirements:* For master's, GRE General Test, minimum GPA of 3.0. *Expenses:* Tuition, state resident: full-time $7476; part-time $249 per quarter hour. Tuition, nonresident: full-time $18,030; part-time $601 per quarter hour. Required fees: $3.50 per quarter hour. $142 per quarter.

East Stroudsburg University of Pennsylvania, Graduate School, College of Health Sciences, Department of Speech Pathology and Audiology, East Stroudsburg, PA 18301-2999. Offers MS. *Accreditation:* ASHA. Part-time and evening/weekend programs available. *Faculty:* 7 full-time (6 women). *Students:* 51 full-time (50 women), 7 part-time (all women); includes 4 minority (1 African American, 3 Asian Americans or Pacific Islanders). Average age 27. In 2009, 18 master's awarded. *Degree requirements:* For master's, comprehensive exam, portfolio. *Entrance requirements:* For master's, GRE General Test, minimum undergraduate QPA of 3.0 overall and in major, 3 letters of recommendation. Additional exam requirements/recommendations for international students: Required—TOEFL (minimum score 560 paper-based; 220 computer-based; 83 iBT). *Application deadline:* For fall admission, 2/1 priority date for domestic and international students; for spring admission, 2/1 for domestic and international students. Applications are processed on a rolling basis. Application fee: $50. *Expenses:* Tuition, state resident: full-time $9942; part-time $387 per credit. Tuition, nonresident: full-time $14,240; part-time $619 per credit. *Financial support:* In 2009–10, 33 research assistantships with full and partial tuition reimbursements (averaging $1,578 per year) were awarded; Federal Work-Study and institutionally sponsored loans also available. Financial award application deadline: 3/1; financial award applicants required to submit FAFSA. *Faculty research:* Computer-assisted classroom instruction. *Unit head:* Dr. Robert Acakerman, Graduate Coordinator, 570-422-3247, Fax: 570-422-3506, E-mail: rackerman@po-box.esu.edu. *Application contact:* Kevin Quintero, Graduate Admissions Coordinator, 570-422-3890, Fax: 570-422-2711, E-mail: kquintero@po-box.esu.edu.

East Tennessee State University, School of Graduate Studies, College of Public and Allied Health, Department of Communicative Disorders, Johnson City, TN 37614. Offers audiology (MS, Au D); communicative disorders (MS); special education audiology pre-K-12 (MS); special education speech pathology pre-K-12 (MS); speech pathology (MS). *Accreditation:* ASHA (one or more programs are accredited). Part-time and evening/weekend programs available. *Degree requirements:* For master's, comprehensive exam, thesis or alternative. *Entrance requirements:* For master's, GRE General Test, minimum GPA of 3.0; for doctorate, GRE. Additional exam requirements/recommendations for international students: Required—TOEFL (minimum score 550 paper-based; 213 computer-based). *Faculty research:* Treatment efficacy, hearing aid trials, language development of cleft palate children, phonological processes, neurogenic disorders.

Edinboro University of Pennsylvania, School of Graduate Studies and Research, School of Liberal Arts, Department of Speech, Language and Hearing, Edinboro, PA 16444. Offers speech language pathology (MA). *Accreditation:* ASHA. Part-time and evening/weekend programs available. *Faculty:* 4 full-time (2 women), 4 part-time/adjunct (3 women). *Students:* 44 full-time (40 women), 1 (woman) part-time. Average age 26. In 2009, 20 master's awarded. *Degree requirements:* For master's, thesis or alternative, competency exam. *Entrance requirements:* For master's, GRE or MAT, minimum QPA of 2.5. *Application deadline:* Applications are processed on a rolling basis. Application fee: $30. Electronic applications accepted. *Expenses:* Tuition, state resident: full-time $6666; part-time $370 per credit. Tuition, nonresident: full-time $10,666; part-time $593 per credit. Required fees: $2206.28. One-time fee: $204 part-time. *Financial support:* In 2009–10, 12 research assistantships with full and partial tuition reimbursements (averaging $4,050 per year) were awarded; career-related internships or fieldwork, Federal Work-Study, scholarships/grants, and unspecified assistantships also available. Support available to part-time students. Financial award application deadline: 2/15; financial award applicants required to submit FAFSA. *Unit head:* Dr. Charlotte Molrine, Coordinator, 814-732-2432, Fax: 814-732-2629, E-mail: cmolrine@edinboro.edu. *Application contact:* Dr. Charlotte Molrine, Coordinator, 814-732-2432, Fax: 814-732-2629, E-mail: cmolrine@edinboro.edu.

Elms College, Division of Communication Sciences and Disorders, Chicopee, MA 01013-2839. Offers autism spectrum disorders (MS, CAGS); autism spectrum disorders with practicum (MS, CAGS); communication sciences and disorders (CAGS). Part-time programs available. *Faculty:* 5 part-time/adjunct (4 women). *Students:* 1 full-time (0 women), 13 part-time (12 women); includes 2 minority (1 African American, 1 Hispanic American). Average age 35. 22 applicants, 100% accepted. In 2009, 3 other advanced degrees awarded. *Entrance requirements:* For degree, minimum GPA of 3.0. Additional exam requirements/recommendations for international students: Required—TOEFL. *Application deadline:* For fall admission, 7/1 priority date for domestic students; for spring admission, 11/1 priority date for domestic students. Applications are processed on a rolling basis. Application fee: $30. *Financial support:* Applicants required to submit FAFSA. *Unit head:* Dr. Kathryn James, Chair, 413-265-2253, E-mail: jamesk@elms.edu. *Application contact:* Donna Harvey, Assistant Director for Graduate Studies and Continuing Education, 413-265-2445, Fax: 413-265-2459, E-mail: harveyd@elms.edu.

Emerson College, Graduate Studies, School of Communication, Department of Communication Sciences and Disorders, Program in Communication Disorders, Boston, MA 02116-4624. Offers MS. *Accreditation:* ASHA. *Faculty:* 15 full-time (7 women), 8 part-time/adjunct (6 women). *Students:* 90 full-time (87 women), 1 (woman) part-time; includes 10 minority (2 African Americans, 5 Asian Americans or Pacific Islanders, 3 Hispanic Americans), 1 international. Average age 26. 490 applicants, 26% accepted, 45 enrolled. In 2009, 49 master's awarded. *Degree requirements:* For master's, comprehensive exam, thesis or alternative. *Entrance requirements:* For master's, GRE General Test. Additional exam requirements/recommendations for international students: Required—TOEFL (minimum score 550 paper-based; 213 computer-based; 80 iBT), IELTS (minimum score 6.5). *Application deadline:* For fall admission, 2/15 priority date for domestic and international students. Applications are processed on a rolling basis. Application fee: $60 ($75 for international students). Electronic applications accepted. *Expenses:* Tuition: Full-time $22,056; part-time $919 per credit. Required fees: $120. One-time fee: $170 full-time. *Financial support:* In 2009–10, 54 students received support, including 5 fellowships with partial tuition reimbursements available (averaging $14,000 per year), 14 research assistantships with partial tuition reimbursements available (averaging $12,000 per year); Federal Work-Study, scholarships/grants, and unspecified assistantships also available. Financial award application deadline: 2/15; financial award applicants required to submit FAFSA. *Unit head:* Dr. Cynthia Bartlett, Graduate Program Director, 617-824-8730, E-mail: cynthia_bartlett@emerson.edu. *Application contact:* Office of Graduate Admission, 617-824-8610, Fax: 617-824-8614, E-mail: gradapp@emerson.edu.

Florida Atlantic University, College of Education, Department of Communication Sciences and Disorders, Boca Raton, FL 33431-0991. Offers speech-language pathology (MS). *Accreditation:* ASHA. *Faculty:* 6 full-time (4 women), 8 part-time/adjunct (5 women). *Students:* 47 full-time (all women), 12 part-time (all women); includes 11 minority (2 Asian Americans or Pacific Islanders, 9 Hispanic Americans), 1 international. Average age 28. 106 applicants, 53% accepted, 10 enrolled. In 2009, 11 master's awarded. *Degree requirements:* For master's, thesis optional. *Entrance requirements:* For master's, GRE General Test, minimum undergraduate GPA of 3.0 in last 60 hours of course work or minimum graduate GPA of 3.5. *Application deadline:* For fall admission, 2/1 for domestic and international students. Application fee: $30. *Expenses:* Tuition, state resident: full-time $7055; part-time $293.94 per credit hour. Tuition, nonresident: full-time $22,096; part-time $920.66 per credit hour. *Financial support:* Career-related internships or fieldwork available. *Faculty research:* Fluency disorders, auditory processing, child language, adult language and cognition, multicultural speech and language issues. *Unit head:* Dr. Deena Louise Wener, Chair, 561-297-2258, Fax: 561-297-2268, E-mail: wener@fau.edu. *Application contact:* Dr. Eliah Watlington, Associate Dean, 561-296-8520, Fax: 261-297-2991, E-mail: ewatling@fau.edu.

Florida International University, College of Nursing and Health Sciences, Department of Communication Sciences and Disorders, Miami, FL 33199. Offers speech-language pathology (MS). *Accreditation:* ASHA. Part-time and evening/weekend programs available. *Faculty:* 4 full-time (3 women). *Students:* 65 full-time (64 women), 6 part-time (5 women); includes 53 minority (6 African Americans, 47 Hispanic Americans). Average age 32. 144 applicants, 24% accepted, 35 enrolled. In 2009, 31 master's awarded. *Degree requirements:* For master's, thesis optional. *Entrance requirements:* For master's, minimum undergraduate GPA of 3.0 in upper-level coursework; letter of intent; 2 letters of recommendation. Additional exam requirements/recommendations for international students: Required—TOEFL (minimum score 550 paper-based; 80 iBT). *Application deadline:* For fall admission, 2/1 for domestic and international students. Application fee: $30. Electronic applications accepted. *Expenses:* Tuition, state resident: full-time $8008; part-time $4004 per year. Tuition, nonresident: full-time $20,104; part-time $10,052 per year. Required fees: $298; $149 per term. *Financial support:* Institutionally sponsored loans, scholarships/grants, and unspecified assistantships available. Financial award application deadline: 3/1; financial award applicants required to submit FAFSA. *Unit head:* Dr. Eliane Ramos, Chair, 305-348-2710, Fax: 305-348-2740, E-mail: eliane.ramos@fiu.edu. *Application contact:* Nanett Rojas, Assistant Director of Graduate Admissions, 305-348-7442, Fax: 305-348-7441, E-mail: gradadm@fiu.edu.

Florida State University, The Graduate School, College of Communication and Information, School of Communication Science and Disorders, Tallahassee, FL 32306-1200. Offers communication sciences and disorders (Adv M, MS, PhD). *Accreditation:* ASHA (one or more programs are accredited). Part-time programs available. Postbaccalaureate distance learning degree programs offered (minimal on-campus study). *Faculty:* 15 full-time (12 women), 10 part-time/adjunct (all women). *Students:* 89 full-time (83 women), 61 part-time (all women); includes 30 minority (20 African Americans, 2 Asian Americans or Pacific Islanders, 8 Hispanic Americans), 2 international. Average age 25. 150 applicants, 64% accepted, 61 enrolled. In 2009, 36 master's, 7 doctorates awarded. *Degree requirements:* For master's, thesis optional; for doctorate, thesis/dissertation. *Entrance requirements:* For master's, GRE General Test, minimum GPA of 3.0; for doctorate, GRE General Test, minimum GPA of 3.0 (undergraduate), 3.5 (graduate). Additional exam requirements/recommendations for international students: Required—TOEFL (minimum score 550 paper-based; 213 computer-based; 80 iBT). *Application deadline:* For fall admission, 1/15 for domestic and international students. Application fee: $30. Electronic applications accepted. *Expenses:* Tuition, state resident: full-time $7413. Tuition, nonresident: full-time $22,567. *Financial support:* In 2009–10, 49 students received support, including 1 fellowship with full tuition reimbursement available (averaging $16,500 per year), 21 research assistantships with full and partial tuition reimbursements available (averaging $12,750 per year), 16 teaching assistantships with full and partial tuition reimbursements available (averaging $8,100 per year); career-related internships or fieldwork, Federal Work-Study, institutionally sponsored loans, scholarships/grants, tuition waivers (partial), and unspecified assistantships also available. Financial award application deadline: 1/1; financial award applicants required to submit FAFSA. *Faculty research:* Autism, neurogenic disorders, early intervention, child language disorders, literacy development and disorders, augmentative communication, dialectal influences on language development, speech development. Total annual research expenditures: $2.3 million. *Unit head:* Dr. Kenn Apel, School Director, 850-645-6566, Fax: 850-645-8994, E-mail: kenn.apel@cci.fsu.edu. *Application contact:* Erica A. Lee, Academic Coordinator, 850-644-2253, Fax: 850-644-8994, E-mail: erica.lee@cci.fsu.edu.

Fontbonne University, Graduate Programs, Department of Communication Disorders and Deaf Education, Studies in Early Intervention in Deaf Education, St. Louis, MO 63105-3098. Offers MA. *Faculty:* 5 full-time (4 women), 4 part-time/adjunct (all women). *Students:* 9 full-time (all women), 2 part-time (both women), 2 international. Average age 28. In 2009, 8 master's awarded. *Entrance requirements:* For master's, minimum GPA of 3.0. *Application deadline:* For fall admission, 2/1 for domestic students. Application fee: $25. *Expenses:* Tuition: Part-time $562 per credit hour. *Financial support:* Application deadline: 4/1. *Unit head:* Dr. Gale Rice, Chair, 314-889-1407, Fax: 314-719-8016, E-mail: grice@fontbonne.edu. *Application contact:* Dr. Susan Lenihan, Director, 314-889-1461, Fax: 314-719-8016, E-mail: slenihan@fontbonne.edu.

Fontbonne University, Graduate Programs, Department of Communication Disorders and Deaf Education, Studies in Speech-Language Pathology, St. Louis, MO 63105-3098. Offers MS. *Faculty:* 6 full-time (5 women), 3 part-time/adjunct (all women). *Students:* 29 full-time (27 women), 28 part-time (all women), 1 international. Average age 28. In 2009, 25 master's awarded. *Entrance requirements:* For master's, minimum GPA of 3.0. *Application deadline:* For fall admission, 2/1 for domestic students. Application fee: $25. *Expenses:* Tuition: Part-time $562 per credit hour. *Financial support:* Application deadline: 4/1. *Unit head:* Dr. Gale Rice, Chair, 314-889-1407, Fax: 314-719-8016, E-mail: grice@fontbonne.edu. *Application contact:* Dr. Lynne Shields, Director, 314-889-1464, Fax: 314-719-8016, E-mail: lshields@fontbonne.edu.

Fort Hays State University, Graduate School, College of Health and Life Sciences, Department of Communication Disorders, Hays, KS 67601-4099. Offers speech-language pathology (MS). *Accreditation:* ASHA. Part-time programs available. *Degree requirements:* For master's, comprehensive exam, thesis optional. *Entrance requirements:* For master's, GRE General Test. Additional exam requirements/recommendations for international students: Required—TOEFL (minimum score 550 paper-based; 213 computer-based). Electronic applications accepted. *Faculty research:* Aural rehabilitation, phonological and articulation skills, middle ear diseases, output capability of stereo cassette units, language development.

Gallaudet University, The Graduate School, Department of Administration and Supervision, Washington, DC 20002-3625. Offers administration (MS); administration and supervision (PhD); change leadership on deaf education (Ed S); leadership (Certificate); management (Certificate); special education administration (PhD). *Degree requirements:* For master's, thesis optional; for doctorate, 2 foreign languages, thesis/dissertation; for other advanced degree, 2 foreign languages, thesis (for some programs). *Entrance requirements:* For master's, GRE General Test or MAT; for doctorate, GRE General Test or MAT, interview. Electronic applications accepted.

Gallaudet University, The Graduate School, Department of Hearing, Speech, and Language Sciences, Washington, DC 20002-3625. Offers MA, MS, Au D, Au D/PhD. *Accreditation:* ASHA. Part-time programs available. *Degree requirements:* For master's, thesis optional; for doctorate, thesis/dissertation. *Entrance requirements:* For master's, GRE General Test or MAT; for doctorate, GRE General Test or MAT, interview. Electronic applications accepted. *Faculty research:* Aural rehabilitation, speech production, sign language linguistics, sign language interpretation.

Gallaudet University, The Graduate School, Department of Interpretation, Washington, DC 20002-3625. Offers MA.

The George Washington University, Columbian College of Arts and Sciences, Department of Speech and Hearing Sciences, Washington, DC 20052. Offers speech-language pathology (MA). *Accreditation:* ASHA. *Faculty:* 9 full-time (6 women), 10 part-time/adjunct (all women). *Students:* 42 full-time (41 women), 24 part-time (23 women); includes 9 minority (3 African Americans, 2 Asian Americans or Pacific Islanders, 4 Hispanic Americans). Average age 24. 217 applicants, 47% accepted, 37 enrolled. In 2009, 22 master's awarded. *Degree requirements:* For master's, comprehensive exam, thesis or alternative. *Entrance requirements:* For master's, GRE General Test, interview, minimum GPA of 3.0. Additional exam requirements/recommendations for international students: Required—TOEFL (minimum score 550 paper-based; 213 computer-based; 80 iBT). *Application deadline:* For fall admission, 2/1 priority date for domestic students, 1/15 priority date for international students. Applications are processed on a rolling basis. Application fee: $60. Electronic applications accepted. *Financial support:* In 2009–10, 16 students received support; fellowships with tuition reimbursements available, teaching assistantships with tuition reimbursements available, career-related internships or fieldwork, Federal Work-Study, and tuition waivers available. Financial award application deadline: 1/15. *Unit head:* Geralyn M. Schulz, Chair, 202-994-6130, E-mail: schulz@gwu.edu. *Application contact:* Information Contact, 202-994-7362, Fax: 202-994-2589, E-mail: gwusphr@gwu.edu.

Georgia State University, College of Education, Department of Educational Psychology and Special Education, Program in Communication Disorders, Atlanta, GA 30302-3083. Offers M Ed. *Accreditation:* ASHA; NCATE. *Degree requirements:* For master's, portfolio. *Entrance requirements:* For master's, GRE General Test, minimum GPA of 2.5, 2 letters of recommendation. *Faculty research:* Language development, adult language disorders, voice disorders.

Communication Disorders

Governors State University, College of Health Professions, Program in Communication Disorders, University Park, IL 60466-0975. Offers MHS. *Accreditation:* ASHA. Part-time and evening/weekend programs available. *Degree requirements:* For master's, comprehensive exam, thesis or alternative, practicum. *Entrance requirements:* For master's, minimum GPA of 3.3. *Faculty research:* Speech perception of hearing-impaired, effects of binaural listening, communication assessment of infants, voice characteristics of head-neck cancer patients.

Graduate School and University Center of the City University of New York, Graduate Studies, Program in Audiology, New York, NY 10016-4039. Offers Au D. *Students:* 42 full-time (39 women), 6 part-time (5 women); includes 3 minority (1 African American, 1 Asian American or Pacific Islander, 1 Hispanic American), 1 international. Average age 28. 63 applicants, 30% accepted, 14 enrolled. In 2009, 7 doctorates awarded. *Entrance requirements:* For doctorate, GRE General Test. Additional exam requirements/recommendations for international students: Required—TOEFL. *Application deadline:* For fall admission, 2/1 for domestic students. Application fee: $125. Electronic applications accepted. *Financial support:* In 2009–10, 14 students received support. *Unit head:* Dr. Barbara Weinstein, Executive Officer, 212-817-7980, E-mail: bweinstein@gc.cuny.edu. *Application contact:* Les Gribben, Director of Admissions, 212-817-7470, Fax: 212-817-1624, E-mail: lgribben@gc.cuny.edu.

Graduate School and University Center of the City University of New York, Graduate Studies, Program in Speech and Hearing Sciences, New York, NY 10016-4039. Offers PhD. *Faculty:* 19 full-time (3 women). *Students:* 60 full-time (50 women), 3 part-time (all women); includes 11 minority (3 African Americans, 1 Asian American or Pacific Islander, 7 Hispanic Americans), 15 international. Average age 37. 23 applicants, 52% accepted, 6 enrolled. In 2009, 3 doctorates awarded. *Degree requirements:* For doctorate, one foreign language, thesis/dissertation. *Entrance requirements:* For doctorate, GRE General Test. Additional exam requirements/recommendations for international students: Required—TOEFL. *Application deadline:* For fall admission, 2/1 priority date for domestic students; for spring admission, 11/15 for domestic students. Application fee: $125. Electronic applications accepted. *Financial support:* In 2009–10, 29 students received support, including 35 fellowships, 1 teaching assistantship; research assistantships, career-related internships or fieldwork, Federal Work-Study, institutionally sponsored loans, and tuition waivers (full and partial) also available. Financial award application deadline: 2/1; financial award applicants required to submit FAFSA. *Unit head:* Dr. Martin Gitterman, Executive Officer, 212-817-8802, Fax: 212-817-1537. *Application contact:* Les Gribben, Director of Admissions, 212-817-7470, Fax: 212-817-1624, E-mail: lgribben@gc.cuny.edu.

Hampton University, Graduate College, Program in Communicative Sciences and Disorders, Hampton, VA 23668. Offers MA. *Accreditation:* ASHA. Part-time and evening/weekend programs available. *Entrance requirements:* For master's, GRE General Test. *Faculty research:* Language development, language pathology.

Harding University, College of Communication, Searcy, AR 72149-0001. Offers speech-language pathology (MS). *Faculty:* 7 part-time/adjunct (5 women). *Students:* 26 full-time (all women); includes 4 minority (3 African Americans, 1 American Indian/Alaska Native). Average age 26. 32 applicants, 91% accepted, 13 enrolled. *Degree requirements:* For master's, 400 clinical hours. *Entrance requirements:* For master's, GRE (minimum 900). *Application deadline:* For fall admission, 3/1 for domestic students. Application fee: $25. *Expenses:* Tuition: Full-time $9720; part-time $540 per credit hour. Required fees: $22 per credit hour. Tuition and fees vary according to course load and program. *Financial support:* In 2009–10, 7 students received support. Unspecified assistantships available. Financial award applicants required to submit FAFSA. *Unit head:* Dr. Rebecca O. Weaver, Chair, Department of Communication Sciences and Disorders/Graduate Program Director, 501-279-4640, Fax: 501-279-4325, E-mail: bweaver@harding.edu. *Application contact:* Martha Vendetti, Secretary, 501-279-4648, E-mail: mvendett@harding.edu.

Harvard University, Harvard Medical School and Graduate School of Arts and Sciences, Division of Health Sciences and Technology, Speech and Hearing Bioscience and Technology Program, Cambridge, MA 02138. Offers PhD, Sc D. Degrees are offered jointly with Massachusetts Institute of Technology. *Faculty:* 66 full-time (18 women). *Students:* 42 full-time (17 women); includes 13 minority (1 American Indian/Alaska Native, 11 Asian Americans or Pacific Islanders, 1 Hispanic American), 5 international. Average age 29. 28 applicants, 18% accepted, 3 enrolled. In 2009, 9 doctorates awarded. *Degree requirements:* For doctorate, thesis/dissertation. *Entrance requirements:* For doctorate, bachelor's degree in engineering or science, previous coursework in differential equations. Additional exam requirements/recommendations for international students: Required—TOEFL. *Application deadline:* For fall admission, 12/15 for domestic and international students. Application fee: $70. Electronic applications accepted. *Expenses:* Contact institution. *Financial support:* In 2009–10, 42 students received support, including 48 fellowships with full and partial tuition reimbursements available (averaging $27,156 per year), 19 research assistantships with full and partial tuition reimbursements available (averaging $44,556 per year), 5 teaching assistantships with full and partial tuition reimbursements available (averaging $10,060 per year); career-related internships or fieldwork, scholarships/grants, traineeships, health care benefits, and unspecified assistantships also available. Financial award application deadline: 12/15. *Faculty research:* Neuroscience audition, physiology, hearing science psychoacoustics, speech communications. *Unit head:* Dr. Louis D. Braida, Director, 617-253-2575, E-mail: braida@mit.edu. *Application contact:* Dr. Christopher Shera, Co-Chair, Admissions Committee, 617-573-4235, Fax: 617-720-4408, E-mail: shera@mit.edu.

Hofstra University, College of Liberal Arts and Sciences, Department of Speech Language-Hearing Sciences, Hempstead, NY 11549. Offers audiology (Au D); speech-language pathology (MA). *Accreditation:* ASHA (one or more programs are accredited). *Faculty:* 13 full-time (9 women), 5 part-time/adjunct (4 women). *Students:* 82 full-time (79 women), 7 part-time (6 women); includes 4 minority (1 African American, 1 Asian American or Pacific Islander, 2 Hispanic Americans). Average age 24. 284 applicants, 41% accepted, 39 enrolled. In 2009, 33 master's awarded. *Degree requirements:* For master's, comprehensive exam, thesis optional; for doctorate, comprehensive exam, thesis/dissertation. *Entrance requirements:* For master's, GRE, 3 letters of recommendation; for doctorate, GRE or master's degree, 3 letters of recommendation, essay. Additional exam requirements/recommendations for international students: Required—TOEFL (minimum score 550 paper-based; 213 computer-based; 80 iBT). *Application deadline:* For fall admission, 1/15 for domestic and international students. Application fee: $60. Electronic applications accepted. *Expenses:* Tuition: Full-time $16,200; part-time $900 per credit hour. Required fees: $970; $145 per term. Tuition and fees vary according to program. *Financial support:* In 2009–10, 35 students received support, including 25 fellowships with full and partial tuition reimbursements available (averaging $3,460 per year); research assistantships with full and partial tuition reimbursements available, Federal Work-Study, institutionally sponsored loans, scholarships/grants, tuition waivers (full and partial), and unspecified assistantships also available. Support available to part-time students. Financial award applicants required to submit FAFSA. *Faculty research:* Efficacy of storytelling strategies in aphasia, language and literacy development in internationally adopted children, aerodynamic aspects of speech in people who stutter, second language acquisition and first language attrition, acoustic aspects of normal and disordered speech production. *Unit head:* Dr. Carole T. Ferrand, Graduate Program Director, 516-463-5511, Fax: 516-463-5260, E-mail: sphctf@hofstra.edu. *Application contact:* Carol Drummer, Dean of Graduate Admissions, 516-463-4876, Fax: 516-463-4664, E-mail: gradstudent@hofstra.edu.

Howard University, School of Communications, Department of Communication Sciences and Disorders, Washington, DC 20059-0002. Offers communication sciences (PhD); speech pathology (MS). Offered through the Graduate School of Arts and Sciences. *Accreditation:* ASHA (one or more programs are accredited). Part-time programs available. *Degree requirements:* For master's, comprehensive exam, thesis or alternative; for doctorate, one foreign language, comprehensive exam, thesis/dissertation. *Entrance requirements:* For master's, GRE General Test, minimum GPA of 3.2; for doctorate, GRE General Test, minimum GPA of 3.5. Additional exam requirements/recommendations for international students: Required—

TOEFL. Electronic applications accepted. *Faculty research:* Multiculturalism, augmentative communication, adult neurological disorders, child language disorders.

Hunter College of the City University of New York, Graduate School, Schools of the Health Professions, School of Health Sciences, Communication Sciences Program, New York, NY 10021-5085. Offers audiology (MS); speech language pathology (MS); teacher of speech and hearing handicapped (MS). *Accreditation:* ASHA. Part-time programs available. *Degree requirements:* For master's, comprehensive exam (for some programs), NTE, research project. *Entrance requirements:* For master's, GRE, letters of reference. Additional exam requirements/recommendations for international students: Required—TOEFL. *Expenses:* Tuition, state resident: full-time $7360; part-time $310 per credit. Required fees: $250 per semester. *Faculty research:* Aging and communication disorders, fluency, speech science, diagnostic audiology, amplification.

Idaho State University, Office of Graduate Studies, Kasiska College of Health Professions, Department of Communication Sciences and Disorders and Education of the Deaf, Pocatello, ID 83209-8116. Offers audiology (MS, Au D); communication sciences and disorders (Postbaccalaureate Certificate); communication sciences and disorders and education of the deaf (Certificate); deaf education (MS); speech language pathology (MS). *Accreditation:* ASHA (one or more programs are accredited). Part-time programs available. *Faculty:* 5 full-time (1 woman). *Students:* 89 full-time (78 women), 32 part-time (27 women); includes 6 minority (1 African American, 1 American Indian/Alaska Native, 4 Asian Americans or Pacific Islanders), 3 international. Average age 30. In 2009, 26 master's, 4 doctorates awarded. *Degree requirements:* For master's, thesis optional, written and oral comprehensive exams; for doctorate, comprehensive exam, thesis/dissertation optional, externship, 1 year full time clinical practicum, 3rd year spent in Boise. *Entrance requirements:* For master's, GRE General Test, minimum GPA of 3.0, 3 letters of recommendation; for doctorate, GRE General Test (at least 2 scores minimum 40th percentile), minimum GPA of 3.0, 3 letters of recommendation, bachelor's degree. Additional exam requirements/recommendations for international students: Required—TOEFL (minimum score 600 paper-based; 250 computer-based; 80 iBT). *Application deadline:* For fall admission, 7/1 for domestic students, 6/1 for international students; for spring admission, 12/1 for domestic students, 11/1 for international students. Applications are processed on a rolling basis. Application fee: $55. Electronic applications accepted. *Expenses:* Tuition, state resident: full-time $3318; part-time $297 per credit hour. Tuition, nonresident: full-time $13,120; part-time $437 per credit hour. Required fees: $2530. Tuition and fees vary according to program. *Financial support:* In 2009–10, 8 teaching assistantships with full and partial tuition reimbursements (averaging $10,841 per year) were awarded; career-related internships or fieldwork, Federal Work-Study, institutionally sponsored loans, scholarships/grants, health care benefits, tuition waivers (full and partial), and unspecified assistantships also available. Support available to part-time students. Financial award application deadline: 1/1; financial award applicants required to submit FAFSA. *Faculty research:* Neurogenic disorders, central auditory processing disorders, vestibular disorders, cochlear implants, language disorders, professional burnout, swallowing disorders. *Unit head:* Dr. Kathleen Kangas, Interim Chairman, 208-282-4196, Fax: 208-282-4571, E-mail: kangkath@isu.edu. *Application contact:* Tami Carson, Graduate School Technical Records Specialist, 208-282-2150, Fax: 208-282-4847, E-mail: carstami@isu.edu.

Illinois State University, Graduate School, College of Arts and Sciences, Department of Communication Sciences and Disorders, Normal, IL 61790-2200. Offers MA, MS. *Accreditation:* ASHA. *Degree requirements:* For master's, thesis or alternative, 1 term of residency, 2 practica. *Entrance requirements:* For master's, GRE General Test, minimum GPA of 3.0 in last 60 hours.

Indiana University Bloomington, University Graduate School, College of Arts and Sciences, Department of Speech and Hearing Sciences, Clinical Program in Audiology, Bloomington, IN 47405-7000. Offers Au D. *Students:* 28 full-time (26 women), 1 (woman) part-time; includes 2 minority (1 African American, 1 Asian American or Pacific Islander), 2 international. Average age 26. 53 applicants, 64% accepted, 7 enrolled. In 2009, 8 doctorates awarded. Application fee: $55 ($65 for international students). *Unit head:* Karen Forrest, Chairperson, 812-855-2602, E-mail: kforrest@indiana.edu. *Application contact:* Jennifer J. Lentz, Graduate Advisor, 812-855-8945, E-mail: jjlentz@indiana.edu.

Indiana University Bloomington, University Graduate School, College of Arts and Sciences, Department of Speech and Hearing Sciences, Program in Speech and Hearing Sciences, Bloomington, IN 47405-7000. Offers auditory sciences (PhD); language sciences (PhD); speech and voice sciences (PhD); speech-language pathology (MA). *Students:* 78 full-time (76 women), 5 part-time (all women); includes 7 minority (1 African American, 1 Asian American or Pacific Islander, 5 Hispanic Americans), 6 international. Average age 25. 218 applicants, 39% accepted, 37 enrolled. In 2009, 29 master's, 1 doctorate awarded. Application fee: $55 ($65 for international students). *Unit head:* Karen Forrest, Chairperson, 812-855-2602, E-mail: kforrest@indiana.edu. *Application contact:* Kimberly Elkins, Graduate Secretary, 812-855-4202, E-mail: kelkins@indiana.edu.

Indiana University of Pennsylvania, School of Graduate Studies and Research, College of Education and Educational Technology, Department of Special Education and Clinical Services, Program in Speech-Language Pathology, Indiana, PA 15705-1087. Offers MS. *Accreditation:* ASHA. *Faculty:* 1 (woman) full-time. *Students:* 42 full-time (41 women). Average age 23. 114 applicants, 18% accepted, 20 enrolled. In 2009, 21 master's awarded. *Degree requirements:* For master's, comprehensive exam, thesis optional. *Entrance requirements:* For master's, 2 letters of recommendation. Additional exam requirements/recommendations for international students: Required—TOEFL. *Application deadline:* For fall admission, 7/1 priority date for domestic students; for spring admission, 11/1 for domestic students. Applications are processed on a rolling basis. Application fee: $40. *Expenses:* Tuition, state resident: full-time $6666; part-time $370 per credit hour. Tuition, nonresident: full-time $10,666; part-time $593 per credit hour. Required fees: $813 per semester. *Financial support:* In 2009–10, 12 research assistantships with full and partial tuition reimbursements (averaging $2,947 per year) were awarded; career-related internships or fieldwork and Federal Work-Study also available. Support available to part-time students. Financial award application deadline: 3/15; financial award applicants required to submit FAFSA. *Unit head:* Dr. Shari Robertson, Graduate Coordinator, 724-357-2454, E-mail: shari.robertson@iup.edu. *Application contact:* Dr. Edward Nardi, Interim Associate Dean, 724-357-2480, Fax: 724-357-5595, E-mail: ewnardi@iup.edu.

Indiana University–Purdue University Fort Wayne, College of Arts and Sciences, Department of Communication Sciences and Disorders, Fort Wayne, IN 46805-1499. Offers speech and language pathology (MA). *Expenses:* Tuition, state resident: full-time $4595; part-time $255 per credit. Tuition, nonresident: full-time $10,963; part-time $609 per credit. Required fees: $528; $29.35 per credit. Tuition and fees vary according to course load. *Unit head:* Dr. Lucille Hess, Chair and Associate Professor, 260-481-6411, Fax: 260-481-6985. *Application contact:* Dr. Lucille Hess, Chair and Associate Professor, 260-481-6411, Fax: 260-481-6985.

Ithaca College, Division of Graduate and Professional Studies, School of Health Sciences and Human Performance, Program in Speech-Language Pathology and Audiology, Ithaca, NY 14850. Offers speech pathology (MS); teacher of students with speech and language disabilities (MS). *Accreditation:* ASHA. *Faculty:* 9 full-time (6 women). *Students:* 52 full-time (50 women), 2 part-time (both women); includes 1 minority (Hispanic American), 5 international. Average age 25. 158 applicants, 26% accepted, 23 enrolled. In 2009, 21 master's awarded. *Degree requirements:* For master's, comprehensive exam (for some programs), thesis optional. *Entrance requirements:* For master's, GRE General Test, minimum GPA of 3.0. Additional exam requirements/recommendations for international students: Required—TOEFL (minimum score 550 paper-based; 213 computer-based; 80 iBT). *Application deadline:* For fall admission, 2/1 priority date for domestic and international students; for spring admission, 12/1 for domestic and international students. Applications are processed on a rolling basis. Application fee: $40. Electronic applications accepted. *Expenses:* Tuition: Full-time $18,960; part-time $632 per credit hour. *Financial support:* In 2009–10, 48 students received support, including 17 teaching assistantships (averaging $10,625 per year); career-related internships or fieldwork, Federal

Work-Study, scholarships/grants, and unspecified assistantships also available. Support available to part-time students. Financial award application deadline: 2/1; financial award applicants required to submit CSS PROFILE or FAFSA. *Faculty research:* Learning enhancement in higher education, augmentative/alternative communication, cultural and linguistic variables in communication, language and literacy acquisition. *Unit head:* Dr. Richard Schissel, Graduate Chair, 607-274-3527, Fax: 607-274-1263, E-mail: gps@ithaca.edu. *Application contact:* Rob Gearhart, Dean, Graduate and Professional Studies, 607-274-3527, Fax: 607-274-1263, E-mail: gps@ithaca.edu.

Jackson State University, Graduate School, College of Public Service, Department of Communicative Disorders, Jackson, MS 39217. Offers MS. *Accreditation:* ASHA. *Degree requirements:* For master's, comprehensive exam. *Entrance requirements:* For master's, GRE General Test. Additional exam requirements/recommendations for international students: Required—TOEFL.

James Madison University, The Graduate School, College of Integrated Science and Technology, Department of Communication Sciences and Disorders, Program in Audiology, Harrisonburg, VA 22807. Offers Au D. *Accreditation:* ASHA. Part-time programs available. *Students:* 22 full-time (20 women), 1 (woman) part-time; includes 1 minority (African American). Average age 27. In 2009, 7 doctorates awarded. *Entrance requirements:* For doctorate, 3 letters of recommendation, interview. Additional exam requirements/recommendations for international students: Required—TOEFL. *Application deadline:* For fall admission, 2/1 for domestic students. Applications are processed on a rolling basis. Application fee: $55. Electronic applications accepted. *Expenses:* Tuition, area resident: Part-time $305 per credit hour. Tuition, state resident: part-time $305 per credit hour. Tuition, nonresident: part-time $890 per credit hour. *Financial support:* In 2009–10, 21 students received support. Application deadline: 3/1. *Application contact:* Dr. Charles Runyan, Graduate Coordinator, 540-568-6440.

James Madison University, The Graduate School, College of Integrated Science and Technology, Department of Communication Sciences and Disorders, Program in Speech-Language Pathology, Harrisonburg, VA 22807. Offers audiology (PhD); clinical audiology (PhD); speech-language pathology (MS, PhD). *Accreditation:* ASHA. Part-time programs available. *Students:* 68 full-time (65 women), 17 part-time (15 women); includes 4 minority (1 African American, 3 Asian Americans or Pacific Islanders). Average age 27. In 2009, 27 master's, 1 doctorate awarded. *Degree requirements:* For master's, thesis. *Entrance requirements:* For master's, GRE General Test, 2 letters of recommendation; for doctorate, GRE, 3 letters of recommendation, interview. Additional exam requirements/recommendations for international students: Required—TOEFL. *Application deadline:* For fall admission, 5/1 priority date for domestic students. Applications are processed on a rolling basis. Application fee: $55. Electronic applications accepted. *Expenses:* Tuition, area resident: Part-time $305 per credit hour. Tuition, state resident: part-time $305 per credit hour. Tuition, nonresident: part-time $890 per credit hour. *Financial support:* In 2009–10, 27 students received support, including 2 teaching assistantships with full tuition reimbursements available (averaging $8,664 per year); Federal Work-Study also available. Financial award application deadline: 3/1; financial award applicants required to submit FAFSA. *Unit head:* Dr. Vicki A. Reed, Academic Unit Head, 540-568-6440. *Application contact:* Dr. Charles Runyan, Graduate Coordinator, 540-568-6440.

Kansas State University, Graduate School, College of Human Ecology, School of Family Studies and Human Services, Manhattan, KS 66506. Offers communication sciences and disorders (MS); early childhood education (MS); family studies (MS); life span human development (MS); marriage and family therapy (MS). *Accreditation:* AAMFT/COAMFTE; ASHA. Part-time programs available. *Faculty:* 25 full-time (15 women), 3 part-time/adjunct (2 women). *Students:* 76 full-time (67 women), 101 part-time (61 women); includes 17 minority (7 African Americans, 1 American Indian/Alaska Native, 2 Asian Americans or Pacific Islanders, 7 Hispanic Americans), 1 international. Average age 32. 117 applicants, 68% accepted, 47 enrolled. In 2009, 63 master's awarded. *Degree requirements:* For master's, thesis or alternative, oral exam, residency. *Entrance requirements:* For master's, GRE, minimum GPA of 3.0 in last 2 years of undergraduate study. Additional exam requirements/recommendations for international students: Required—TOEFL (minimum score 600 paper-based; 250 computer-based). *Application deadline:* For fall admission, 2/1 priority date for domestic and international students; for spring admission, 8/1 priority date for domestic and international students. Applications are processed on a rolling basis. Application fee: $40 ($55 for international students). Electronic applications accepted. *Financial support:* In 2009–10, 26 research assistantships (averaging $10,867 per year), 17 teaching assistantships with full and partial tuition reimbursements (averaging $11,635 per year) were awarded; Federal Work-Study, institutionally sponsored loans, scholarships/grants, and unspecified assistantships also available. Support available to part-time students. Financial award application deadline: 3/1; financial award applicants required to submit FAFSA. *Faculty research:* Health and security of military families, personal and family risk assessment and evaluation, disorders of communication and swallowing, families and health. Total annual research expenditures: $10.1 million. *Unit head:* Dr. Maurice McDonald, Head, 785-532-1472, E-mail: morey@ksu.edu. *Application contact:* Connie Fechter, Administrative Specialist, 785-532-1473, Fax: 785-532-5505, E-mail: fechter@ksu.edu.

Kean University, College of Education, Program in Speech Language Pathology, Union, NJ 07083. Offers MA. *Accreditation:* ASHA. Part-time and evening/weekend programs available. *Faculty:* 7 full-time (5 women). *Students:* 89 full-time (85 women), 46 part-time (42 women); includes 30 minority (7 African Americans, 6 Asian Americans or Pacific Islanders, 17 Hispanic Americans). Average age 29. 254 applicants, 44% accepted, 48 enrolled. In 2009, 33 master's awarded. *Degree requirements:* For master's, comprehensive exam, thesis, practicum, clinical, PRAXIS. *Entrance requirements:* For master's, GRE General Test, minimum GPA of 3.2, 3 letters of recommendation, interview. *Application deadline:* For fall admission, 2/1 for domestic students. Application fee: $60 ($150 for international students). Electronic applications accepted. *Expenses:* Tuition, state resident: full-time $10,440; part-time $435 per credit. Tuition, nonresident: full-time $14,160; part-time $590 per credit. Required fees: $2642; $110 per credit. Part-time tuition and fees vary according to course load and degree level. *Financial support:* In 2009–10, 14 research assistantships with full tuition reimbursements (averaging $3,263 per year) were awarded; unspecified assistantships also available. *Unit head:* Dr. Barbara D. Glazewski, Program Coordinator, 908-737-5800, E-mail: bglazews@kean.edu. *Application contact:* Reenat Hasan, Pre-Admissions Coordinator, 908-737-5923, Fax: 908-737-5965, E-mail: rhasan@exchange.kean.edu.

Kent State University, Graduate School of Education, Health, and Human Services, School of Health Sciences, Program in Audiology, Kent, OH 44242-0001. Offers Au D, PhD. *Faculty:* 3 full-time (1 woman), 3 part-time/adjunct (all women). *Students:* 41 full-time (38 women); includes 8 minority (2 African Americans, 4 Asian Americans or Pacific Islanders, 2 Hispanic Americans). 42 applicants, 52% accepted. In 2009, 1 doctorate awarded. *Entrance requirements:* For doctorate, GRE. Application fee: $30. *Financial support:* In 2009–10, 3 fellowships (averaging $11,330 per year), research assistantships (averaging $5,665 per year) were awarded; Federal Work-Study, scholarships/grants, and unspecified assistantships also available. *Unit head:* John Hawks, Coordinator, 330-672-0251, Fax: 330-672-2643, E-mail: jhawks@kent.edu. *Application contact:* Nancy Miller, Academic Program Coordinator, 330-672-2576, Fax: 330-672-9162, E-mail: ogs@kent.edu.

Kent State University, Graduate School of Education, Health, and Human Services, School of Health Sciences, Program in Speech Language Pathology, Kent, OH 44242-0001. Offers MA, PhD. *Accreditation:* ASHA. *Faculty:* 11 full-time (10 women), 5 part-time/adjunct (4 women). *Students:* 78 full-time (all women), 5 part-time (all women); includes 3 minority (2 African Americans, 1 Asian American or Pacific Islander). 224 applicants, 25% accepted. In 2009, 36 master's, 3 doctorates awarded. Application fee: $30. *Financial support:* In 2009–10, fellowships (averaging $11,330 per year), 20 research assistantships (averaging $5,665 per year) were awarded; Federal Work-Study, institutionally sponsored loans, and unspecified assistantships also available. *Unit head:* John Hawks, Coordinator, 330-672-0251, E-mail: jhawks@

kent.edu. *Application contact:* Nancy Miller, Academic Program Coordinator, Office of Graduate Student Services, 330-672-2576, Fax: 330-672-9162, E-mail: ogs@kent.edu.

Lamar University, College of Graduate Studies, College of Fine Arts and Communication, Department of Speech and Hearing Science, Beaumont, TX 77710. Offers audiology (MS, Au D); speech language pathology (MS). *Faculty:* 9 full-time (6 women). *Students:* 60 full-time (55 women), 1 (woman) part-time; includes 19 minority (8 African Americans, 1 American Indian/Alaska Native, 3 Asian Americans or Pacific Islanders, 7 Hispanic Americans), 2 international. Average age 26. 114 applicants, 27% accepted, 26 enrolled. In 2009, 10 master's, 24 doctorates awarded. *Degree requirements:* For master's, thesis optional; for doctorate, thesis/dissertation. *Entrance requirements:* For master's, GRE General Test, performance IQ score of 115 (for deaf students), minimum GPA of 2.5; for doctorate, GRE General Test, performance IQ score of 115 (for deaf students). Additional exam requirements/recommendations for international students: Required—TOEFL. *Application deadline:* For fall admission, 8/1 priority date for domestic students; for spring admission, 12/1 for domestic students. Applications are processed on a rolling basis. Application fee: $25 ($50 for international students). *Financial support:* Fellowships with tuition reimbursements, teaching assistantships, institutionally sponsored loans available. Support available to part-time students. Financial award application deadline: 4/1. *Unit head:* Dr. Russ A. Schultz, Dean, 409-880-8137, Fax: 409-880-2286, E-mail: russ.schultz@lamar.edu. *Application contact:* Debbie Piper, Coordinator of Graduate Admissions, 409-880-8356, Fax: 409-880-8414, E-mail: gradmissions@hal.lamar.edu.

La Salle University, School of Nursing and Health Sciences, Program in Speech-Language-Hearing Science, Philadelphia, PA 19141-1199. Offers MS. *Accreditation:* ASHA.

Lehman College of the City University of New York, Division of Arts and Humanities, Department of Speech–Language–Hearing Sciences, Bronx, NY 10468-1589. Offers speech-language pathology and audiology (MA). *Accreditation:* ASHA. Part-time and evening/weekend programs available. *Degree requirements:* For master's, thesis or alternative.

Lewis & Clark College, Graduate School of Education and Counseling, Department of Teacher Education, Program in Special Education, Portland, OR 97219-7899. Offers M Ed. *Accreditation:* NCATE. Part-time and evening/weekend programs available. *Faculty:* 1 (woman) full-time, 2 part-time/adjunct (both women). *Students:* 14 part-time (12 women). Average age 41. 14 applicants, 100% accepted, 9 enrolled. In 2009, 4 master's awarded. *Entrance requirements:* For master's, minimum GPA of 2.75. Additional exam requirements/recommendations for international students: Required—TOEFL (minimum score 575 paper-based; 233 computer-based). *Application deadline:* Applications are processed on a rolling basis. Application fee: $50. Electronic applications accepted. *Expenses:* Tuition: Part-time $713 per semester hour. Tuition and fees vary according to course level and campus/location. *Financial support:* In 2009–10, 14 students received support. Career-related internships or fieldwork, Federal Work-Study, institutionally sponsored loans, scholarships/grants, health care benefits, and tuition waivers (partial) available. Support available to part-time students. Financial award application deadline: 3/1; financial award applicants required to submit FAFSA. *Unit head:* Christine Moore, Program Coordinator, 503-768-6128, E-mail: cmoore@lclark.edu. *Application contact:* Becky Haas, Director of Admissions, 503-768-6200, Fax: 503-768-6205, E-mail: gseadmit@lclark.edu.

Loma Linda University, School of Allied Health Professions, Department of Speech-Language Pathology and Audiology, Loma Linda, CA 92350. Offers MS. *Accreditation:* ASHA. Part-time programs available. *Degree requirements:* For master's, thesis or alternative. *Entrance requirements:* For master's, GRE General Test. Additional exam requirements/recommendations for international students: Required—TOEFL (minimum score 550 paper-based; 213 computer-based). Electronic applications accepted.

Long Island University, Brooklyn Campus, Richard L. Conolly College of Liberal Arts and Sciences, Department of Communication Sciences and Disorders, Brooklyn, NY 11201-8423. Offers speech-language pathology (MS). *Accreditation:* ASHA. *Entrance requirements:* For master's, 2 letters of recommendation. Additional exam requirements/recommendations for international students: Required—TOEFL (minimum score 500 paper-based; 173 computer-based). Electronic applications accepted.

Long Island University, C.W. Post Campus, School of Education, Department of Communication Sciences and Disorders, Brookville, NY 11548-1300. Offers speech language pathology (MA). *Accreditation:* ASHA. Part-time and evening/weekend programs available. *Degree requirements:* For master's, comprehensive exam or thesis. *Entrance requirements:* For master's, minimum GPA of 3.0, bachelor's degree in communication sciences and disorders. Electronic applications accepted. *Faculty research:* Aural rehabilitation, spouses' perceptions of speech therapy with their ephasic partners, establish norms associated with swallowing.

Longwood University, Office of Graduate Studies, College of Education and Human Services, Program in Communication Sciences and Disorders, Farmville, VA 23909. Offers MS. *Accreditation:* ASHA.

Louisiana State University and Agricultural and Mechanical College, Graduate School, College of Arts and Sciences, Department of Communication Sciences and Disorders, Baton Rouge, LA 70803. Offers MA, PhD. *Accreditation:* ASHA (one or more programs are accredited). *Faculty:* 14 full-time (12 women). *Students:* 48 full-time (all women), 8 part-time (7 women); includes 5 minority (all African Americans), 3 international. Average age 27. 74 applicants, 49% accepted, 21 enrolled. In 2009, 20 master's, 2 doctorates awarded. *Degree requirements:* For doctorate, thesis/dissertation. *Entrance requirements:* For master's and doctorate, GRE General Test, minimum GPA of 3.0. Additional exam requirements/recommendations for international students: Required—TOEFL (minimum score 550 paper-based; 213 computer-based; 79 iBT) or IELTS (minimum score 6.5). *Application deadline:* For fall admission, 1/25 priority date for domestic students, 5/15 for international students; for spring admission, 10/15 for international students. Application fee: $25. Electronic applications accepted. *Financial support:* In 2009–10, 34 students received support, including 3 fellowships with full tuition reimbursements available (averaging $29,375 per year), 8 research assistantships with partial tuition reimbursements available (averaging $10,912 per year), 9 teaching assistantships with partial tuition reimbursements available (averaging $12,516 per year); Federal Work-Study, institutionally sponsored loans, health care benefits, and unspecified assistantships also available. Financial award application deadline: 4/1; financial award applicants required to submit FAFSA. *Faculty research:* Language development, language intervention, aphasia, language of the deaf. Total annual research expenditures: $47,585. *Unit head:* Dr. Paul R. Hoffman, Chair, 225-578-2545, Fax: 225-578-2995, E-mail: cdhoff@lsu.edu. *Application contact:* Dr. Hugh Buckingham, Graduate Adviser, 225-578-6682, Fax: 225-578-6447, E-mail: hbuck@lsu.edu.

Louisiana State University Health Sciences Center, School of Allied Health Professions, Program in Communication Disorders, New Orleans, LA 70112-2223. Offers audiology (Au D); speech pathology (MCD). *Accreditation:* ASHA (one or more programs are accredited). *Degree requirements:* For master's, comprehensive exam or thesis. *Entrance requirements:* For master's, GRE General Test, minimum undergraduate GPA of 3.0, 3 letters recommendation; for doctorate, GRE general test, 3 letters recommendation. *Faculty research:* Hearing aids, clinical audiology, swallowing respiration, language acquisition, speech science.

Louisiana Tech University, Graduate School, College of Liberal Arts, Department of Speech, Ruston, LA 71272. Offers speech (MA); speech pathology and audiology (MA). *Accreditation:* ASHA. *Degree requirements:* For master's, thesis or alternative. *Entrance requirements:* For master's, GRE General Test.

Loyola University Maryland, Graduate Programs, College of Arts and Sciences, Department of Speech-Language Pathology and Audiology, Baltimore, MD 21210-2699. Offers MS, CAS. *Accreditation:* ASHA (one or more programs are accredited). Evening/weekend programs available. *Entrance requirements:* For master's and CAS, GRE General Test, GRE Subject Test (recommended). Additional exam requirements/recommendations for international students: Required—TOEFL (minimum score 550 paper-based; 213 computer-based).

Communication Disorders

Marquette University, Graduate School, College of Health Sciences, Department of Speech Pathology and Audiology, Milwaukee, WI 53201-1881. Offers speech-language pathology (MS). *Accreditation:* ASHA. *Faculty:* 13 full-time (9 women), 4 part-time/adjunct (all women). *Students:* 49 full-time (48 women), 2 part-time (both women); includes 22 minority (5 African Americans, 1 American Indian/Alaska Native, 7 Asian Americans or Pacific Islanders, 9 Hispanic Americans), 3 international. Average age 24. 159 applicants, 41% accepted, 27 enrolled. In 2009, 26 master's awarded. *Degree requirements:* For master's, comprehensive exam. *Entrance requirements:* For master's, GRE General Test. Additional exam requirements/recommendations for international students: Required—TOEFL. Application fee: $40. *Financial support:* Research assistantships, teaching assistantships, career-related internships or fieldwork, Federal Work-Study, institutionally sponsored loans, and tuition waivers (full and partial) available. Support available to part-time students. Financial award application deadline: 2/15. *Faculty research:* Language processing in the brain, vocal aging, early language development, birth-to-three intervention, computer applications. *Unit head:* Dr. Kim Halula, Chair, 414-288-9658, Fax: 414-288-3980. *Application contact:* Erin Fox, Assistant Director for Recruitment, 414-288-5319, Fax: 414-288-1902, E-mail: erin.fox@marquette.edu.

Marshall University, Academic Affairs Division, College of Health Professions, Department of Communication Disorders, Huntington, WV 25755. Offers MA. *Accreditation:* ASHA. *Faculty:* 11 full-time (all women), 2 part-time/adjunct (both women). *Students:* 40 full-time (all women), 4 part-time (all women); includes 2 minority (1 African American, 1 Hispanic American), 1 international. Average age 25. In 2009, 17 master's awarded. *Degree requirements:* For master's, thesis optional. *Entrance requirements:* For master's, GRE General Test. Application fee: $40. *Financial support:* Fellowships available. *Unit head:* Kathryn Chezik, Chairperson, 304-696-2979, E-mail: chezik@marshall.edu. *Application contact:* Information Contact, 304-746-1900, Fax: 304-746-1902, E-mail: services@marshall.edu.

Marywood University, Academic Affairs, Reap College of Education and Human Development, Department of Communication Sciences and Disorders, Program in Speech-Language Pathology, Scranton, PA 18509-1598. Offers MS. *Students:* 19 full-time (18 women), 11 part-time (10 women); includes 2 minority (1 American Indian/Alaska Native, 1 Asian American or Pacific Islander). Average age 24. In 2009, 18 master's awarded. *Entrance requirements:* Additional exam requirements/recommendations for international students: Required—TOEFL (minimum score 550 paper-based; 213 computer-based; 79 iBT). *Application deadline:* For fall admission, 2/16 priority date for domestic and international students. Application fee: $35. Electronic applications accepted. *Expenses:* Tuition: Part-time $715 per credit. Required fees: $270 per semester. Tuition and fees vary according to degree level, campus/location and program. *Financial support:* Career-related internships or fieldwork, scholarships/grants, and unspecified assistantships available. Support available to part-time students. Financial award application deadline: 6/30; financial award applicants required to submit FAFSA. *Unit head:* Dr. Mona Griffer, Chairperson, 570-348-6211 Ext. 2363. *Application contact:* Tammy Manka, 866-279-9663, E-mail: tmanka@marywood.edu.

Massachusetts Institute of Technology, Harvard-MIT Division of Health Sciences and Technology, Speech and Hearing Bioscience and Technology Program, Cambridge, MA 02139-4307. Offers PhD, Sc D. *Faculty:* 66 full-time (18 women). *Students:* 42 full-time (17 women); includes 13 minority (1 American Indian/Alaska Native, 11 Asian Americans or Pacific Islanders, 1 Hispanic American), 5 international. Average age 29. 28 applicants, 18% accepted, 3 enrolled. In 2009, 9 doctorates awarded. *Degree requirements:* For doctorate, thesis/dissertation. *Entrance requirements:* For doctorate, BS in engineering or science, previous course work in differential equations. Additional exam requirements/recommendations for international students: Required—TOEFL. *Application deadline:* For fall admission, 12/15 for domestic and international students. Application fee: $70. Electronic applications accepted. *Expenses:* Contact institution. *Financial support:* In 2009–10, 42 students received support, including 48 fellowships with full and partial tuition reimbursements available (averaging $27,156 per year), 19 research assistantships with full and partial tuition reimbursements available (averaging $44,556 per year), 5 teaching assistantships with full and partial tuition reimbursements available (averaging $10,060 per year); career-related internships or fieldwork, scholarships/grants, traineeships, health care benefits, and unspecified assistantships also available. Financial award application deadline: 12/15. *Faculty research:* Neuroscience, auditory physiology, hearing science, psychoacoustics, speech communications. *Unit head:* Dr. Louis D. Braida, Director, 617-253-2575, Fax: 617-258-7354, E-mail: braida@cbgrle.mit.edu. *Application contact:* Dr. Christopher Shera, Co-Chair, Admissions Committee, 617-573-4235, Fax: 617-720-4408, E-mail: shera@mit.edu.

McGill University, Faculty of Graduate and Postdoctoral Studies, Faculty of Medicine, School of Communication Sciences and Disorders, Montréal, QC H3A 2T5, Canada. Offers communication science and disorders (M Sc); communication sciences and disorders (PhD); speech-language pathology (M Sc A). *Accreditation:* ASHA.

Mercy College, School of Health and Natural Sciences, Program in Communication Disorders, Dobbs Ferry, NY 10522-1189. Offers MS. *Accreditation:* ASHA. Part-time and evening/weekend programs available. *Students:* 86 full-time (84 women), 22 part-time (all women); includes 29 minority (7 African Americans, 4 Asian Americans or Pacific Islanders, 18 Hispanic Americans). Average age 28. 236 applicants, 25% accepted, 44 enrolled. In 2009, 41 master's awarded. *Entrance requirements:* For master's, interview, resume, 2 letters of recommendation. Additional exam requirements/recommendations for international students: Required—TOEFL (minimum score 600 paper-based; 250 computer-based; 100 iBT). *Application deadline:* For fall admission, 2/15 for domestic students. Application fee: $65. *Expenses:* Contact institution. *Financial support:* In 2009–10, 2 students received support. Career-related internships or fieldwork, Federal Work-Study, scholarships/grants, and unspecified assistantships available. Support available to part-time students. Financial award applicants required to submit FAFSA. *Faculty research:* Phonology, articulation, hearing deficits, fluency, attention. *Unit head:* Dr. Helen Buhler, Director, 914-674-7743, E-mail: hbuhler@mercy.edu. *Application contact:* Dr. Helen Buhler, Director, 914-674-7743, E-mail: hbuhler@mercy.edu.

MGH Institute of Health Professions, Graduate Programs, School of Health and Rehabilitation Sciences, Department of Communication Sciences and Disorders, Boston, MA 02129. Offers reading (Certificate); speech-language pathology (MS). *Accreditation:* ASHA (one or more programs are accredited). Part-time programs available. *Faculty:* 12 full-time (9 women), 3 part-time/adjunct (all women). *Students:* 101 full-time (98 women), 21 part-time (20 women); includes 12 minority (2 African Americans, 6 Asian Americans or Pacific Islanders, 4 Hispanic Americans). Average age 29. 295 applicants, 48% accepted, 68 enrolled. In 2009, 41 master's, 11 other advanced degrees awarded. *Degree requirements:* For master's, thesis or alternative, research proposal. *Entrance requirements:* For master's, GRE General Test. Additional exam requirements/recommendations for international students: Required—TOEFL (minimum score 550 paper-based; 213 computer-based; 80 iBT). *Application deadline:* For fall admission, 1/28 for domestic and international students. Application fee: $50. Electronic applications accepted. *Expenses:* Tuition: Part-time $943 per credit. Required fees: $943 per credit. Tuition and fees vary according to course load. *Financial support:* In 2009–10, 84 students received support; research assistantships, teaching assistantships, career-related internships or fieldwork, scholarships/grants, tuition waivers (full and partial), and unspecified assistantships available. Support available to part-time students. Financial award application deadline: 3/1; financial award applicants required to submit FAFSA. *Faculty research:* Children's language disorders, reading, speech disorders, voice disorders, augmentative communication, autism. *Unit head:* Dr. Gregory L. Lof, Department Chair, 617-724-6313, E-mail: glot@mghihp.edu. *Application contact:* Maureen Rika Judd, Manager of Admissions, 617-726-6069, Fax: 617-726-8010, E-mail: admissions@mghihp.edu.

Miami University, Graduate School, College of Arts and Science, Department of Speech Pathology and Audiology, Oxford, OH 45056. Offers MA, MS. *Accreditation:* ASHA. Part-time programs available. *Students:* 35 full-time (34 women), 3 part-time (all women); includes 1 minority (Asian American or Pacific Islander). *Entrance requirements:* For master's, GRE, minimum undergraduate GPA of 3.0 during previous 2 years or 2.75 overall. Additional exam requirements/recommendations for international students: Required—TOEFL. Application fee: $50. *Expenses:* Tuition, state resident: full-time $11,280. Tuition, nonresident: full-time $24,912. Required fees: $516. *Financial support:* Fellowships with full tuition reimbursements, research assistantships, teaching assistantships, career-related internships or fieldwork, Federal Work-Study, health care benefits, and unspecified assistantships available. Financial award application deadline: 3/1; financial award applicants required to submit FAFSA. *Unit head:* Dr. Kathleen Hutchinson, Chair, 513-529-2500, E-mail: spa@muohio.edu. *Application contact:* Dr. Laura J. Kelly, Graduate Program Coordinator, 513-529-2500, E-mail: spa@muohio.edu.

Michigan State University, The Graduate School, College of Communication Arts and Sciences, Department of Communicative Sciences and Disorders, East Lansing, MI 48824. Offers MA, PhD. *Accreditation:* ASHA (one or more programs are accredited). *Faculty:* 10 full-time (2 women). *Students:* 62 full-time (57 women); includes 3 minority (1 African American, 2 Hispanic Americans), 1 international. Average age 26. 210 applicants, 17% accepted. In 2009, 21 master's awarded. *Entrance requirements:* Additional exam requirements/recommendations for international students: Required—TOEFL. Electronic applications accepted. *Expenses:* Tuition, state resident: part-time $478.25 per credit hour. Tuition, nonresident: part-time $966.50 per credit hour. Part-time tuition and fees vary according to program. *Financial support:* Scholarships/grants available. Total annual research expenditures: $69,860. *Unit head:* Dr. Frank Boster, Acting Chairperson, 517-355-0120, Fax: 517-353-3176. *Application contact:* Heather Brown, Graduate Program Secretary, 517-353-8641, Fax: 516-353-3176, E-mail: comdis@msu.edu.

Minnesota State University Mankato, College of Graduate Studies, College of Allied Health and Nursing, Program in Communication Disorders, Mankato, MN 56001. Offers MS. *Accreditation:* ASHA. Part-time programs available. *Students:* 34 full-time (all women), 4 part-time (all women). *Degree requirements:* For master's, comprehensive exam, thesis or alternative. *Entrance requirements:* For master's, GRE General Test, minimum GPA of 3.0 during previous 2 years, references, writing sample. Additional exam requirements/recommendations for international students: Required—TOEFL. *Application deadline:* For fall admission, 2/1 priority date for domestic students. Applications are processed on a rolling basis. Application fee: $40. *Expenses:* Tuition, state resident: full-time $5364. Tuition, nonresident: full-time $8314. *Financial support:* Research assistantships with full tuition reimbursements, teaching assistantships with full tuition reimbursements, career-related internships or fieldwork, Federal Work-Study, and institutionally sponsored loans available. Support available to part-time students. Financial award application deadline: 3/15; financial award applicants required to submit FAFSA. *Faculty research:* Internet/technology issues related to speech-language pathology. *Unit head:* Dr. Bruce Poburka, Graduate Coordinator, 507-389-5843. *Application contact:* 507-389-2321, E-mail: grad@mnsu.edu.

Minnesota State University Moorhead, Graduate Studies, College of Education and Human Services, Program in Speech-Language Pathology, Moorhead, MN 56563-0002. Offers MS. *Accreditation:* ASHA. *Degree requirements:* For master's, comprehensive exam, final oral exam, project or thesis. *Entrance requirements:* For master's, GRE General Test, minimum GPA of 2.75, undergraduate major in speech/language/hearing sciences, 3 letters of recommendation. Additional exam requirements/recommendations for international students: Required—TOEFL (minimum score 550 paper-based; 213 computer-based). Electronic applications accepted.

Minot State University, Graduate School, Department of Communication Disorders, Minot, ND 58707-0002. Offers audiology (MS); speech-language pathology (MS). *Accreditation:* ASHA. *Degree requirements:* For master's, comprehensive exam (for some programs), thesis (for some programs). *Entrance requirements:* For master's, GRE General Test, minimum GPA of 3.0. Additional exam requirements/recommendations for international students: Required—TOEFL. *Expenses:* Tuition, state resident: full-time $5720; part-time $283 per credit hour. Tuition, nonresident: full-time $5720; part-time $283 per credit hour. Required fees: $1034; $1034 per year. Tuition and fees vary according to course load, degree level and program. *Faculty research:* Auditory evoked potentials, pathologies of auditory system, newborn hearing screening, cleft palate research, intervention, the diagnostic process, early language, the pedagogy of clinical teaching, phonology, geriatric communication problems, dysphagia, and brain functioning after injury.

Misericordia University, College of Health Sciences, Department of Speech-Language Pathology, Dallas, PA 18612-1098. Offers MSSLP. *Accreditation:* ASHA. *Faculty:* 4 full-time (2 women), 3 part-time/adjunct (2 women). *Students:* 23 full-time (all women). Average age 23. In 2009, 24 master's awarded. *Application deadline:* For fall admission, 2/1 priority date for domestic students. Application fee: $25. *Financial support:* In 2009–10, 22 students received support. Scholarships/grants available. Support available to part-time students. Financial award application deadline: 6/30; financial award applicants required to submit FAFSA. *Unit head:* Dr. Glen Tellis, Chair, 570-674-6471, E-mail: gtellis@misericordia.edu. *Application contact:* Dr. Glen Tellis, Chair, 570-674-6471, E-mail: gtellis@misericordia.edu.

Mississippi University for Women, Graduate School, College of Nursing and Speech-Language Pathology, Columbus, MS 39701-9998. Offers nursing (MSN, PMC); speech/language pathology (MS). *Accreditation:* AACN. Part-time programs available. *Degree requirements:* For master's, comprehensive exam, thesis. *Entrance requirements:* For master's, GRE General Test, bachelor's degree in nursing, previous course work in statistics, proficiency in English.

Missouri State University, Graduate College, College of Health and Human Services, Department of Communication Sciences and Disorders, Springfield, MO 65897. Offers audiology (Au D); communication sciences and disorders (MS), including education of deaf/hard of hearing, speech-language pathology. *Accreditation:* ASHA (one or more programs are accredited). *Faculty:* 18 full-time (12 women). *Students:* 100 full-time (89 women), 3 part-time (all women); includes 1 minority (Hispanic American), 4 international. Average age 26. 72 applicants, 69% accepted, 25 enrolled. In 2009, 31 master's, 5 doctorates awarded. *Degree requirements:* For master's, comprehensive exam, thesis or alternative; for doctorate, comprehensive exam, thesis/dissertation or alternative, clinical externship. *Entrance requirements:* For master's and doctorate, GRE, minimum GPA of 3.0. Additional exam requirements/recommendations for international students: Required—TOEFL (minimum score 550 paper-based; 213 computer-based; 79 iBT). *Application deadline:* For fall admission, 2/1 for domestic and international students. Application fee: $35 ($50 for international students). Electronic applications accepted. *Expenses:* Tuition, state resident: full-time $3852; part-time $214 per credit hour. Tuition, nonresident: full-time $7524; part-time $418 per credit hour. Required fees: $696; $172 per semester. Tuition and fees vary according to course level, course load, degree level and program. *Financial support:* Career-related internships or fieldwork, Federal Work-Study, scholarships/grants, and unspecified assistantships available. Support available to part-time students. Financial award application deadline: 3/31; financial award applicants required to submit FAFSA. *Faculty research:* Dysphagia, phonological intervention, elderly adult aural rehabilitation, vestibular disorders. *Unit head:* Dr. Neil DiSarno, Head, 417-836-5368, Fax: 417-836-4242, E-mail: neildisarno@missouristate.edu. *Application contact:* Eric Eckert, Coordinator of Admissions and Recruitment, 417-836-5331, Fax: 417-836-6200, E-mail: ericeckert@missouristate.edu.

Montclair State University, The Graduate School, College of Humanities and Social Sciences, Department of Communication Sciences and Disorders, Montclair, NJ 07043-1624. Offers audiology (Au D, Sc D); speech/language pathology (MA). *Accreditation:* ASHA (one or more programs are accredited). Part-time and evening/weekend programs available. *Faculty:* 8 full-time (7 women), 8 part-time/adjunct (6 women). *Students:* 95 full-time (88 women), 28 part-time (26 women). Average age 28. 298 applicants, 22% accepted, 40 enrolled. In 2009, 31 master's awarded. *Degree requirements:* For master's, thesis (for some programs), comprehensive exam or fieldwork/project. *Entrance requirements:* For master's, GRE General Test, 2 letters of recommendation; for doctorate, GRE, 3 letters of recommendation. Additional exam requirements/recommendations for international students: Required—TOEFL (minimum score 83 computer-based), or IELTS. *Application deadline:* For fall admission, 3/1 for domestic

and international students. Applications are processed on a rolling basis. Application fee: $60. Electronic applications accepted. *Expenses:* Tuition, area resident: Part-time $486.74 per credit. Tuition, state resident: part-time $486.74 per credit. Tuition, nonresident: part-time $751.34 per credit. Tuition and fees vary according to degree level and program. *Financial support:* In 2009–10, 8 research assistantships with tuition reimbursements (averaging $7,000 per year), 6 teaching assistantships (averaging $15,000 per year) were awarded; Federal Work-Study, scholarships/grants, and unspecified assistantships also available. Support available to part-time students. Financial award application deadline: 3/1; financial award applicants required to submit FAFSA. *Unit head:* Dr. Janet Koehnke, Chairperson, 973-655-3305. *Application contact:* Amy Aiello, Director of Graduate Admissions and Operations, 973-655-5147, Fax: 973-655-7869, E-mail: graduate.school@montclair.edu.

Murray State University, College of Health Sciences and Human Services, Department of Wellness and Therapeutic Sciences, Program in Speech-Language Pathology, Murray, KY 42071. Offers MS. *Accreditation:* ASHA. Part-time programs available. *Degree requirements:* For master's, comprehensive exam, thesis optional. *Entrance requirements:* For master's, GRE General Test or MAT, minimum GPA of 3.0. Additional exam requirements/recommendations for international students: Required—TOEFL.

National University, Academic Affairs, School of Education, Department of Special Education, La Jolla, CA 92037-1011. Offers deaf and hard-of-hearing education (MS); juvenile justice special education (MS); special education (MS). Part-time and evening/weekend programs available. Postbaccalaureate distance learning degree programs offered (no on-campus study). *Degree requirements:* For master's, thesis (for some programs). *Entrance requirements:* For master's, interview, minimum GPA of 2.5. Additional exam requirements/recommendations for international students: Required—TOEFL (minimum score 550 paper-based; 213 computer-based; 79 iBT), IELTS (minimum score 6). *Application deadline:* Applications are processed on a rolling basis. Application fee: $60 ($65 for international students). Electronic applications accepted. *Expenses:* Tuition: Part-time $338 per quarter hour. *Financial support:* Career-related internships or fieldwork, institutionally sponsored loans, scholarships/grants, and tuition waivers (partial) available. Support available to part-time students. Financial award application deadline: 6/30; financial award applicants required to submit FAFSA. *Unit head:* Dr. Britt Ferguson, Department Chair, 858-642-8346, Fax: 858-642-8729, E-mail: mferguson@nu.edu. *Application contact:* Dr. Britt Ferguson, Department Chair, 858-642-8346, Fax: 858-642-8729, E-mail: mferguson@nu.edu.

Nazareth College of Rochester, Graduate Studies, Department of Speech-Language Pathology, Communication Sciences and Disorders Program, Rochester, NY 14618-3790. Offers MS. *Accreditation:* ASHA. Part-time programs available. Postbaccalaureate distance learning degree programs offered. *Degree requirements:* For master's, comprehensive exam. *Entrance requirements:* For master's, GRE General Test, minimum GPA of 3.0.

New Mexico State University, Graduate School, College of Education, Department of Special Education and Communication Disorders, Las Cruces, NM 88003-8001. Offers bilingual/multicultural special education (Ed D, PhD); communication disorders (MA); special education (MA, Ed D, PhD). *Accreditation:* ASHA (one or more programs are accredited); NCATE. Part-time and evening/weekend programs available. Postbaccalaureate distance learning degree programs offered. *Faculty:* 16 full-time (13 women), 3 part-time/adjunct (all women). *Students:* 59 full-time (56 women), 61 part-time (47 women); includes 54 minority (5 American Indian/Alaska Native, 2 Asian Americans or Pacific Islanders, 47 Hispanic Americans). Average age 34. 93 applicants, 77% accepted, 48 enrolled. In 2009, 21 master's, 1 doctorate awarded. *Degree requirements:* For master's, comprehensive exam, thesis optional; for doctorate, comprehensive exam, thesis/dissertation. *Entrance requirements:* For master's, GRE General Test or MAT. Additional exam requirements/recommendations for international students: Required—TOEFL. *Application deadline:* For fall admission, 2/1 priority date for domestic students. Applications are processed on a rolling basis. Application fee: $30 ($50 for international students). Electronic applications accepted. *Expenses:* Tuition, state resident: full-time $4080; part-time $223 per credit. Tuition, nonresident: full-time $14,256; part-time $647 per credit. Required fees: $1278; $639 per semester. *Financial support:* In 2009–10, 28 students received support, including 2 research assistantships (averaging $10,715 per year), 12 teaching assistantships (averaging $4,617 per year); fellowships, career-related internships or fieldwork, Federal Work-Study, and health care benefits also available. Support available to part-time students. Financial award application deadline: 3/1; financial award applicants required to submit FAFSA. *Faculty research:* Multicultural special education, multicultural communication disorders, mild disability, multicultural assessment, deaf education, early childhood, bilingual special education. *Unit head:* Dr. Eric Joseph Lopez, Interim Department Head, 575-646-2402, Fax: 575-646-7712, E-mail: leric@nmsu.edu. *Application contact:* Coordinator.

New York Medical College, School of Health Sciences and Practice, Department of Speech-Language Pathology, Valhalla, NY 10595-1691. Offers MS. *Accreditation:* ASHA. *Faculty:* 5 full-time, 15 part-time/adjunct. *Students:* 75 full-time. Average age 27. 70 applicants, 43% accepted, 25 enrolled. In 2009, 25 master's awarded. *Degree requirements:* For master's, comprehensive exam. *Entrance requirements:* For master's, GRE, minimum GPA of 3.4. Additional exam requirements/recommendations for international students: Required—TOEFL (minimum score 637 paper-based; 250 computer-based; 117 iBT), IELTS (minimum score 7). *Application deadline:* For fall admission, 3/15 priority date for domestic students, 3/30 for international students. Applications are processed on a rolling basis. Application fee: $75 ($100 for international students). Electronic applications accepted. *Expenses:* Tuition: Full-time $18,170; part-time $790 per credit. Required fees: $790 per credit. $20 per semester. One-time fee: $100. Tuition and fees vary according to class time, course level, course load, degree level, program, student level and student's religious affiliation. *Financial support:* Applicants required to submit FAFSA. *Unit head:* Dr. Ben C. Watson, Chair, 914-594-4239, Fax: 914-594-4853, E-mail: slp_sph@nymc.edu. *Application contact:* Pamela Suett, Director of Recruitment, 914-594-4510, Fax: 914-594-4292, E-mail: shsp_admissions@nymc.edu.

New York University, Steinhardt School of Culture, Education, and Human Development, Department of Communication Sciences and Disorders, New York, NY 10003-6860. Offers MS, PhD. *Accreditation:* ASHA. Part-time programs available. *Faculty:* 10 full-time (7 women), 26 part-time/adjunct (22 women). *Students:* 170 full-time (166 women), 41 part-time (all women); includes 29 minority (7 African Americans, 12 Asian Americans or Pacific Islanders, 10 Hispanic Americans), 10 international. Average age 24. 512 applicants, 53% accepted, 69 enrolled. In 2009, 55 master's, 1 doctorate awarded. *Degree requirements:* For master's, thesis (for some programs); for doctorate, thesis/dissertation. *Entrance requirements:* For doctorate, GRE General Test, interview. Additional exam requirements/recommendations for international students: Required—TOEFL. *Application deadline:* For fall admission, 12/15 priority date for domestic and international students. Applications are processed on a rolling basis. Application fee: $75. Electronic applications accepted. *Expenses:* Tuition: Full-time $30,528; part-time $1272 per credit. Required fees: $2177. *Financial support:* Fellowships with full and partial tuition reimbursements, research assistantships with full and partial tuition reimbursements, career-related internships or fieldwork, Federal Work-Study, institutionally sponsored loans, scholarships/grants, tuition waivers (partial), and unspecified assistantships available. Support available to part-time students. Financial award application deadline: 2/1; financial award applicants required to submit FAFSA. *Faculty research:* Evidence-based practice, phonological acquisition, dysphagia, child language acquisition and disorders, neuromotor disorders. *Unit head:* Dr. Celia Stewart, Chairperson, 212-998-5230, Fax: 212-995-4356. *Application contact:* 212-998-5030, Fax: 212-995-4328, E-mail: steinhardt.gradadmissions@nyu.edu.

North Carolina Central University, Division of Academic Affairs, School of Education, Department of Communication Disorders, Durham, NC 27707-3129. Offers M Ed. *Accreditation:* ASHA. Part-time and evening/weekend programs available. *Degree requirements:* For master's, comprehensive exam, thesis or alternative. *Entrance requirements:* For master's, GRE, minimum GPA of 3.0 in major, 2.5 overall. Additional exam requirements/recommendations for international students: Required—TOEFL. *Faculty research:* Vocational programs for special needs learners.

Northeastern State University, Graduate College, College of Science and Health Professions, Department of Speech-Language Pathology, Tahlequah, OK 74464-2399. Offers MS. *Accreditation:* ASHA. Part-time and evening/weekend programs available. *Degree requirements:* For master's, thesis, capstone experience. *Entrance requirements:* For master's, GRE, minimum GPA of 2.75. Additional exam requirements/recommendations for international students: Required—TOEFL (minimum score 213 computer-based). Electronic applications accepted.

Northeastern University, Bouvé College of Health Sciences Graduate School, Department of Speech-Language Pathology, Boston, MA 02115-5096. Offers audiology (Au D); speech-language pathology (MS). *Accreditation:* ASHA. *Faculty:* 12 full-time (8 women), 6 part-time/adjunct (5 women). *Students:* 65 full-time (all women), 1 (woman) part-time; includes 3 Asian Americans or Pacific Islanders, 3 Hispanic Americans, 2 international. 359 applicants, 35% accepted, 32 enrolled. In 2009, 37 master's awarded. *Degree requirements:* For master's, comprehensive exam, thesis optional. *Entrance requirements:* For master's, GRE General Test or MAT. Additional exam requirements/recommendations for international students: Required—TOEFL (minimum score 100 iBT). *Application deadline:* For fall admission, 2/15 for domestic students. Applications are processed on a rolling basis. Application fee: $50. Electronic applications accepted. *Financial support:* Research assistantships with full tuition reimbursements, teaching assistantships with full tuition reimbursements, career-related internships or fieldwork, Federal Work-Study, scholarships/grants, tuition waivers (partial), and unspecified assistantships available. Support available to part-time students. Financial award application deadline: 3/1; financial award applicants required to submit FAFSA. *Faculty research:* Psychoacoustics, applied and theoretical aspects of aphasia, developmentally delayed children, hearing impairments. *Unit head:* Dr. Therese O'Neil-Pirozzi, Director, 617-373-5750, Fax: 617-373-8756, E-mail: t.oneil-pirozzi@neu.edu. *Application contact:* Margaret Schnabel, Director of Graduate Admissions, 617-373-2708, E-mail: bouvegrad@neu.edu.

Northern Arizona University, Graduate College, College of Health and Human Services, Department of Communication Sciences and Disorders, Flagstaff, AZ 86011. Offers clinical speech pathology (MS). *Accreditation:* ASHA. Part-time programs available. *Faculty:* 17 full-time (10 women). *Students:* 58 full-time (54 women), 27 part-time (25 women); includes 9 minority (1 African American, 1 American Indian/Alaska Native, 2 Asian Americans or Pacific Islanders, 5 Hispanic Americans), 1 international. Average age 28. 122 applicants, 25% accepted, 24 enrolled. In 2009, 44 master's awarded. *Entrance requirements:* For master's, GRE General Test, minimum GPA of 3.0. Additional exam requirements/recommendations for international students: Required—TOEFL (minimum score 550 paper-based; 213 computer-based; 80 iBT), IELTS (minimum score 7). *Application deadline:* For fall admission, 1/31 priority date for domestic students, 9/15 for international students. Application fee: $65. Electronic applications accepted. *Financial support:* In 2009–10, 2 teaching assistantships with partial tuition reimbursements were awarded; career-related internships or fieldwork also available. Financial award application deadline: 3/31. *Faculty research:* Meta-analysis of language, laryngeal speech, aphasia. *Unit head:* Mary Towle Harmon, Chair, 928-523-4315, E-mail: mary.harmon@nau.edu. *Application contact:* Mary Towle Harmon, Chair, 928-523-4315, E-mail: mary.harmon@nau.edu.

Northern Illinois University, Graduate School, College of Health and Human Sciences, School of Allied Health and Communicative Disorders, Program in Communicative Disorders, De Kalb, IL 60115-2854. Offers MA, Au D. *Accreditation:* ASHA (one or more programs are accredited); CORE. *Faculty:* 9 full-time (6 women), 2 part-time/adjunct (1 woman). *Students:* 93 full-time (91 women), 2 part-time (1 woman); includes 18 minority (3 African Americans, 5 Asian Americans or Pacific Islanders, 10 Hispanic Americans), 3 international. Average age 26. 270 applicants, 33% accepted, 37 enrolled. In 2009, 35 master's, 5 doctorates awarded. *Degree requirements:* For master's, comprehensive exam, thesis optional, practicum; for doctorate, practicum, research project. *Entrance requirements:* For master's, GRE General Test, minimum undergraduate GPA of 3.0; for doctorate, GRE General Test, minimum undergraduate GPA of 3.2. Additional exam requirements/recommendations for international students: Required—TOEFL (minimum score 550 paper-based; 213 computer-based). *Application deadline:* For fall admission, 2/1 priority date for domestic students, 5/1 for international students; for spring admission, 9/1 priority date for domestic students, 10/1 for international students. Applications are processed on a rolling basis. Application fee: $30. Electronic applications accepted. *Expenses:* Tuition, state resident: full-time $6576; part-time $274 per credit hour. Tuition, nonresident: full-time $13,152; part-time $548 per credit hour. Required fees: $1813; $75.53 per credit hour. Part-time tuition and fees vary according to course load. *Financial support:* In 2009–10, 40 research assistantships with full tuition reimbursements were awarded; fellowships with full tuition reimbursements, teaching assistantships with full tuition reimbursements, career-related internships or fieldwork, Federal Work-Study, scholarships/grants, tuition waivers (full), and unspecified assistantships also available. Support available to part-time students. Financial award applicants required to submit FAFSA. *Faculty research:* Impact of disability employment, deaf education, American Sign Language, autism, bilingualism. *Unit head:* Dr. Sue Ouellette, Chair, 815-753-1484, Fax: 815-753-9123, E-mail: souellette@niu.edu. *Application contact:* Graduate School Office, 815-753-0395, E-mail: gradsch@niu.edu.

Northwestern University, The Graduate School, School of Communication, The Roxelyn and Richard Pepper Department of Communication Sciences and Disorders, Program in Audiology and Hearing Sciences, Evanston, IL 60208. Offers MA, PhD. Admissions and degrees offered through The Graduate School. *Accreditation:* ASHA. Terminal master's awarded for partial completion of doctoral program. *Degree requirements:* For master's, thesis optional, seminar paper; for doctorate, pre-dissertation research project, qualifying exam. *Entrance requirements:* For master's and doctorate, GRE General Test, letters of recommendation. Additional exam requirements/recommendations for international students: Required—TOEFL. *Faculty research:* Auditory physiology, psychoacoustics, auditory evoked potentials, amplification, audiologic assessment and rehabilitation, speech perception, hearing loss and aging.

See Close-Up on page 1427.

Northwestern University, The Graduate School, School of Communication, The Roxelyn and Richard Pepper Department of Communication Sciences and Disorders, Program in Speech and Language Pathology, Evanston, IL 60208. Offers MA, PhD. Admissions and degrees offered through The Graduate School. *Accreditation:* ASHA. Part-time programs available. Terminal master's awarded for partial completion of doctoral program. *Degree requirements:* For master's, thesis optional; for doctorate, 2 pre-dissertation research projects. *Entrance requirements:* For master's and doctorate, GRE General Test, letters of recommendation. Additional exam requirements/recommendations for international students: Required—TOEFL. *Faculty research:* Voice science, language development, acquired neurogenic speech and language, swallowing physiology, acoustics of speech.

See Close-Up on page 1427.

Northwestern University, The Graduate School, School of Communication, The Roxelyn and Richard Pepper Department of Communication Sciences and Disorders, Program in Speech and Language Pathology and Learning Disabilities, Evanston, IL 60208. Offers MA. Admissions and degree offered through The Graduate School. *Accreditation:* ASHA. *Degree requirements:* For master's, thesis optional, seminar paper. *Entrance requirements:* For master's, GRE General Test, letters of recommendation. Additional exam requirements/recommendations for international students: Required—TOEFL. *Faculty research:* Language and cognitive development, phonological and reading development.

See Close-Up on page 1427.

Nova Southeastern University, Fischler School of Education and Human Services, Program in Education, Fort Lauderdale, FL 33314-7796. Offers educational leadership (Ed D); health care education (Ed D); higher education leadership (Ed D); human services administration (Ed D); instructional leadership (Ed D); instructional technology and distance education (Ed D); organizational leadership (Ed D); special education (Ed D); speech language pathology (Ed D). Part-time and evening/weekend programs available. Postbaccalaureate distance learning degree programs offered (minimal on-campus study). *Faculty:* 88 full-time (46 women), 132 part-time/

Communication Disorders

Nova Southeastern University (continued)

adjunct (63 women). *Students:* 2,805 full-time (2,128 women), 1,411 part-time (1,081 women); includes 2,629 minority (2,034 African Americans, 19 American Indian/Alaska Native, 62 Asian Americans or Pacific Islanders, 514 Hispanic Americans), 30 international. Average age 41. 964 applicants, 69% accepted, 513 enrolled. In 2009, 445 doctorates awarded. *Degree requirements:* For doctorate, thesis/dissertation. *Entrance requirements:* For doctorate, MAT or GRE, master's degree, 2 letters of recommendation, work experience. Additional exam requirements/recommendations for international students: Required—TSE (recommended, minimum score 50); Recommended—TOEFL (minimum score 550 paper-based; 213 computer-based; 80 iBT), IELTS (minimum score 6). *Application deadline:* For fall admission, 8/20 priority date for domestic and international students; for winter admission, 12/19 priority date for domestic and international students; for spring admission, 4/26 priority date for domestic students, 4/25 priority date for international students. Applications are processed on a rolling basis. Application fee: $50. Electronic applications accepted. *Financial support:* In 2009–10, 2 fellowships with full tuition reimbursements (averaging $30,000 per year) were awarded; scholarships/grants and tuition waivers (full) also available. Support available to part-time students. Financial award application deadline: 4/15; financial award applicants required to submit FAFSA. *Unit head:* Dr. Ronald Kern, Dean of Academic Affairs, 800-986-3223 Ext. 7809, Fax: 954-262-3606, E-mail: rk429@nsu.nova.edu. *Application contact:* Dr. Jennifer Quinones Nottingham, Dean of Student Affairs, 800-986-3223 Ext. 1546.

Nova Southeastern University, Fischler School of Education and Human Services, Programs in Communication Sciences and Disorders, Fort Lauderdale, FL 33314-7796. Offers speech-language pathology (MS, SLPD). *Accreditation:* ASHA. Part-time and evening/weekend programs available. Postbaccalaureate distance learning degree programs offered (minimal on-campus study). *Faculty:* 25 full-time (22 women), 46 part-time/adjunct (39 women). *Students:* 213 full-time (207 women), 527 part-time (514 women); includes 187 minority (83 African Americans, 4 American Indian/Alaska Native, 18 Asian Americans or Pacific Islanders, 82 Hispanic Americans), 5 international. Average age 30. 469 applicants, 34% accepted, 109 enrolled. In 2009, 108 master's, 8 doctorates awarded. *Degree requirements:* For master's, practicum; for doctorate, thesis/dissertation, practicum. *Entrance requirements:* For master's, interview, minimum GPA of 3.0, 2 letters of recommendation, background check; for doctorate, GRE or MAT, minimum GPA of 3.2, curriculum vitae, interview, 3 letters of recommendation. Additional exam requirements/recommendations for international students: Required—TSE (recommended, minimum score 50); Recommended—TOEFL (minimum score 550 paper-based; 213 computer-based; 80 iBT), IELTS (minimum score 6). *Application deadline:* For fall admission, 5/15 priority date for domestic students, 4/14 priority date for international students; for winter admission, 12/19 priority date for domestic students, 12/19 for international students; for spring admission, 4/15 priority date for domestic and international students. Applications are processed on a rolling basis. Application fee: $50. Electronic applications accepted. *Expenses:* Contact institution. *Financial support:* Research assistantships, career-related internships or fieldwork, Federal Work-Study, scholarships/grants, tuition waivers (full), and unspecified assistantships available. Support available to part-time students. Financial award application deadline: 4/15. *Unit head:* Dr. Wren Newman, Associate Dean for Speech Programs, 954-262-3606, Fax: 954-262-3940, E-mail: newmanw@nova.edu. *Application contact:* Dr. Jennifer Quinones Nottingham, Dean of Student Affairs, 800-986-3223 Ext. 1559.

Nova Southeastern University, Health Professions Division, College of Allied Health and Nursing, Audiology Department, Fort Lauderdale, FL 33314-7796. Offers Au D. *Accreditation:* ASHA. *Faculty:* 7 full-time (5 women), 4 part-time/adjunct (1 woman). *Students:* 41 full-time (34 women), 29 part-time (21 women); includes 22 minority (5 African Americans, 9 Asian Americans or Pacific Islanders, 8 Hispanic Americans), 6 international. 75 applicants, 27% accepted, 16 enrolled. In 2009, 10 doctorates awarded. *Degree requirements:* For doctorate, didactic and clinical competencies. *Entrance requirements:* For doctorate, letters of recommendation. Additional exam requirements/recommendations for international students: Required—TOEFL (minimum score 600 paper-based). *Application deadline:* For winter admission, 3/1 priority date for domestic students. Applications are processed on a rolling basis. Application fee: $50. *Financial support:* In 2009–10, 6 teaching assistantships (averaging $8,400 per year) were awarded. *Faculty research:* Amplification, ethics, professionalism, auditory processing, tinnitus. *Unit head:* Dr. Erica Friedland, Interim Chair, 954-262-7765, Fax: 954-262-1181. *Application contact:* Marla Frolinger, Admissions Counselor, 954-262-1100, E-mail: marlaf@nova.edu.

The Ohio State University, Graduate School, College of Social and Behavioral Sciences, School of Social and Behavioral Science, Department of Speech and Hearing Science, Program in Audiology, Columbus, OH 43210. Offers Au D. *Students:* 28 full-time (27 women), 6 part-time (5 women); includes 3 minority (1 African American, 1 American Indian/Alaska Native, 1 Asian American or Pacific Islander). Average age 24. In 2009, 7 doctorates awarded. *Application deadline:* Applications are processed on a rolling basis. Application fee: $40 ($50 for international students). Electronic applications accepted. *Expenses:* Tuition, state resident: full-time $10,683. Tuition, nonresident: full-time $25,923. Tuition and fees vary according to course load and program.

The Ohio State University, Graduate School, College of Social and Behavioral Sciences, School of Social and Behavioral Science, Department of Speech and Hearing Science, Program in Speech-Language Pathology, Columbus, OH 43210. Offers MA, PhD. Electronic applications accepted. *Expenses:* Tuition, state resident: full-time $10,683. Tuition, nonresident: full-time $25,923. Tuition and fees vary according to course load and program.

Ohio University, Graduate College, College of Health and Human Services, School of Hearing, Speech and Language Sciences, Athens, OH 45701-2979. Offers audiology (Au D); hearing, speech and language sciences (PhD); speech language pathology (MA). *Accreditation:* ASHA (one or more programs are accredited). *Faculty:* 20 full-time (12 women), 10 part-time/adjunct (5 women). *Students:* 71 full-time (64 women), 18 part-time (16 women); includes 2 minority (both Hispanic Americans), 12 international. 234 applicants, 15% accepted, 31 enrolled. In 2009, 20 master's, 5 doctorates awarded. *Degree requirements:* For doctorate, comprehensive exam (for some programs), thesis/dissertation (for some programs). *Entrance requirements:* For master's, GRE, resume; for doctorate, GRE. Additional exam requirements/recommendations for international students: Required—TOEFL (minimum score 550 paper-based; 80 iBT) or IELTS Academic (minimum score 6.5). *Application deadline:* For fall admission, 2/1 for domestic and international students. Applications are processed on a rolling basis. Application fee: $50 ($55 for international students). Electronic applications accepted. *Expenses:* Contact institution. *Financial support:* Fellowships with full tuition reimbursements, research assistantships with full tuition reimbursements, teaching assistantships with full tuition reimbursements, career-related internships or fieldwork, Federal Work-Study, institutionally sponsored loans, scholarships/grants, tuition waivers (partial), and unspecified assistantships available. Financial award application deadline: 2/1. *Faculty research:* Neurogenic communication disorders, speech perception and production, hearing science, swallowing, language disorders. Total annual research expenditures: $350,000. *Unit head:* Dr. M. Brooke Hallowell, Director, 740-593-1407, Fax: 740-593-1356, E-mail: hallowel@ohio.edu. *Application contact:* Teresa M. Tyson-Drummer, Administrative Associate, 740-593-1407, Fax: 740-593-0287, E-mail: tyson-dr@ohio.edu.

Oklahoma State University, College of Arts and Sciences, Department of Communications Sciences and Disorders, Stillwater, OK 74078. Offers MS. *Accreditation:* ASHA. *Faculty:* 10 full-time (7 women), 6 part-time/adjunct (5 women). *Students:* 31 full-time (all women), 1 (woman) part-time; includes 4 minority (all American Indian/Alaska Native). Average age 25. 50 applicants, 52% accepted, 16 enrolled. In 2009, 23 master's awarded. *Degree requirements:* For master's, thesis or creative research project, clinical practicum experience. *Entrance requirements:* For master's, GRE, minimum GPA of 3.0 in undergraduate major. Additional exam requirements/recommendations for international students: Required—TOEFL (minimum score 550 paper-based; 79 iBT). *Application deadline:* For fall admission, 3/1 priority date for international students; for spring admission, 8/1 priority date for international students. Applications are processed on a rolling basis. Application fee: $40 ($75 for international students). Electronic applications accepted. *Expenses:* Tuition, state resident: full-time $3716; part-time $154.85 per credit hour. Tuition, nonresident: full-time $14,448; part-time $602 per credit hour. Required fees: $1772; $73.85 per credit hour. One-time fee: $50. Tuition and fees vary according to course load and campus/location. *Financial support:* In 2009–10, 11 teaching assistantships (averaging $5,514 per year) were awarded; career-related internships or fieldwork, Federal Work-Study, scholarships/grants, health care benefits, tuition waivers (partial), and unspecified assistantships also available. Support available to part-time students. Financial award application deadline: 3/1; financial award applicants required to submit FAFSA. *Faculty research:* Speech communications. *Unit head:* Dr. Bruce Crauder, Interim Head, 405-744-8938, Fax: 405-744-8070. *Application contact:* Dr. Gordon Emslie, Dean, 405-744-6368, Fax: 405-744-0355, E-mail: grad-i@okstate.edu.

Old Dominion University, Darden College of Education, Program in Speech-Language Pathology, Norfolk, VA 23529. Offers MS Ed. *Accreditation:* ASHA. *Faculty:* 9 full-time (6 women), 5 part-time/adjunct (all women). *Students:* 47 full-time (45 women), 4 part-time (all women); includes 3 minority (1 African American, 1 American Indian/Alaska Native, 1 Hispanic American). Average age 23. 112 applicants, 21% accepted, 24 enrolled. In 2009, 18 master's awarded. *Degree requirements:* For master's, comprehensive exam, thesis, written exams, practica. *Entrance requirements:* For master's, GRE General Test, minimum GPA of 3.0 in major, 2.8 overall. *Application deadline:* For fall admission, 3/14 for domestic students; for spring admission, 11/1 for domestic students. Applications are processed on a rolling basis. Application fee: $40. Electronic applications accepted. *Expenses:* Tuition, state resident: full-time $8112; part-time $338 per credit. Tuition, nonresident: full-time $20,256; part-time $844 per credit. Required fees: $119 per semester. One-time fee: $50. *Financial support:* In 2009–10, 14 students received support, including 10 fellowships (averaging $5,000 per year), 1 teaching assistantship with tuition reimbursement available (averaging $6,000 per year); career-related internships or fieldwork, scholarships/grants, and tuition waivers (partial) also available. Financial award application deadline: 2/15; financial award applicants required to submit CSS PROFILE or FAFSA. *Faculty research:* Childhood language disorders, phonological disorders, stuttering, social dialects, aphasia. Total annual research expenditures: $255,000. *Unit head:* Dr. Nicholas G. Bountress, Graduate Program Director, 757-683-4117, Fax: 757-683-5593, E-mail: nbountre@odu.edu. *Application contact:* Dr. Nicholas G. Bountress, Graduate Program Director, 757-683-4117, Fax: 757-683-5593, E-mail: nbountre@odu.edu.

Our Lady of the Lake University of San Antonio, School of Professional Studies, Program in Communication and Learning Disorders, San Antonio, TX 78207-4689. Offers MA. *Accreditation:* ASHA. Part-time and evening/weekend programs available. *Students:* 45 full-time (44 women), 6 part-time (all women); includes 35 minority (1 African American, 1 Asian American or Pacific Islander, 33 Hispanic Americans), 1 international. Average age 28. In 2009, 18 master's awarded. *Degree requirements:* For master's, thesis optional, comprehensive clinical practicum. *Entrance requirements:* For master's, GRE General Test or MAT, interview. Additional exam requirements/recommendations for international students: Required—TOEFL. *Application deadline:* For fall admission, 2/1 for domestic and international students. Application fee: $25 ($50 for international students). Electronic applications accepted. *Expenses:* Tuition: Full-time $12,330; part-time $685 per contact hour. Required fees: $139; $12 per contact hour. $57 per semester. Tuition and fees vary according to campus/location. *Financial support:* Research assistantships, teaching assistantships, career-related internships or fieldwork available. Support available to part-time students. Financial award application deadline: 3/15. *Faculty research:* Multicultural issues, neurogenic disorders, neural networks, equivalence learning. *Unit head:* Dr. Mary Ann Acevedo, Head, 210-434-6711 Ext. 2410, E-mail: acevm@lake.ollusa.edu. *Application contact:* 210-434-6711 Ext. 2314, Fax: 210-431-4036, E-mail: gradadm@lake.ollusa.edu.

Penn State University Park, Graduate School, College of Health and Human Development, Department of Communication Sciences and Disorders, State College, University Park, PA 16802-1503. Offers MS, PhD. *Accreditation:* ASHA (one or more programs are accredited).

Portland State University, Graduate Studies, College of Liberal Arts and Sciences, Department of Speech and Hearing Sciences, Portland, OR 97207-0751. Offers speech-language pathology (MA, MS). *Accreditation:* ASHA (one or more programs are accredited). *Degree requirements:* For master's, variable foreign language requirement, thesis or alternative, oral exam. *Entrance requirements:* For master's, GRE General Test, minimum GPA of 3.0 in upper-division course work or 2.75 overall, BA/BS in speech and hearing sciences. Additional exam requirements/recommendations for international students: Required—TOEFL (minimum score 550 paper-based; 213 computer-based). *Faculty research:* Adolescents with clefts, spectral analysis of stuttering, communication in late talkers, speech intelligibility, brainstem response in fitting hearing aids.

Purdue University, Graduate School, College of Liberal Arts, Department of Speech, Language, and Hearing Sciences, West Lafayette, IN 47907. Offers audiology (MS, Au D, PhD); linguistics (MS, PhD); speech and hearing science (MS, PhD); speech-language pathology (MS, PhD). *Accreditation:* ASHA. *Degree requirements:* For master's, thesis optional; for doctorate, thesis/dissertation. *Entrance requirements:* For master's and doctorate, GRE. Additional exam requirements/recommendations for international students: Required—TOEFL. Electronic applications accepted. *Faculty research:* Psychoacoustics, speech perception, speech physiology, stuttering, child language.

Queens College of the City University of New York, Division of Graduate Studies, Arts and Humanities Division, Department of Linguistics and Communication Disorders, Program in Speech Pathology, Flushing, NY 11367-1597. Offers MA. *Accreditation:* ASHA. *Faculty:* 9 full-time (6 women). *Students:* 32 full-time (31 women). 274 applicants, 7% accepted, 16 enrolled. In 2009, 17 master's awarded. *Degree requirements:* For master's, thesis optional, clinical internships. *Entrance requirements:* For master's, GRE General Test, minimum GPA of 3.0. Additional exam requirements/recommendations for international students: Required—TOEFL. *Application deadline:* For fall admission, 2/1 for domestic students. Applications are processed on a rolling basis. Application fee: $125. *Expenses:* Tuition, state resident: full-time $7360; part-time $310 per credit. Tuition, nonresident: part-time $575 per credit. One-time fee: $195 full-time; $145.25 part-time. *Financial support:* Career-related internships or fieldwork, Federal Work-Study, institutionally sponsored loans, and tuition waivers (partial) available. Support available to part-time students. Financial award application deadline: 4/1; financial award applicants required to submit FAFSA. *Unit head:* Dr. Sima Gerber, Graduate Adviser, 718-520-2934, E-mail: sima_gerber@qc.edu. *Application contact:* Mario Caruso, Director of Graduate Admissions, 718-997-5200, Fax: 718-997-5193, E-mail: graduate_admissions@qc.edu.

Radford University, College of Graduate and Professional Studies, Waldron College of Health and Human Services, Department of Communication Sciences and Disorders, Radford, VA 24142. Offers speech-language pathology (MS). *Accreditation:* ASHA (one or more programs are accredited). Part-time programs available. *Faculty:* 4 full-time (all women), 6 part-time/adjunct (2 women). *Students:* 53 full-time (51 women), 2 part-time (both women); includes 3 minority (1 African American, 1 Asian American or Pacific Islander, 1 Hispanic American). Average age 24. 84 applicants, 57% accepted, 30 enrolled. In 2009, 27 master's awarded. *Degree requirements:* For master's, comprehensive exam, thesis (for some programs). *Entrance requirements:* For master's, GRE, minimum GPA of 3.0; 3 letters of reference; personal essay, resume. Additional exam requirements/recommendations for international students: Required—TOEFL (minimum score 550 paper-based; 213 computer-based; 79 iBT). *Application deadline:* For fall admission, 2/1 priority date for domestic students, 12/1 for international students; for spring admission, 7/1 for international students. Applications are processed on a rolling basis. Application fee: $50. Electronic applications accepted. *Expenses:* Tuition, state resident: full-time $5086; part-time $211 per credit hour. Tuition, nonresident: full-time $12,608; part-time $525 per credit hour. Required fees: $2508; $105 per credit hour. *Financial support:* In 2009–10, 28 students received support, including 22 research assistantships with partial tuition reimbursements available (averaging $8,000 per year), 4 teaching assistantships with partial tuition reimbursements available (averaging $8,700 per year); career-related intern-

ships or fieldwork, Federal Work-Study, institutionally sponsored loans, scholarships/grants, and unspecified assistantships also available. Financial award application deadline: 3/1; financial award applicants required to submit FAFSA. *Unit head:* Dr. Claire Waldron, Chair, 540-831-7636, Fax: 540-831-7699, E-mail: cwaldron@radford.edu. *Application contact:* Graduate Admissions, 540-831-5431, Fax: 540-831-6061, E-mail: gradcollege@radford.edu.

Rockhurst University, School of Graduate and Professional Studies, Program in Communication Sciences and Disorders, Kansas City, MO 64110-2561. Offers MS. *Accreditation:* ASHA. Part-time and evening/weekend programs available. *Faculty:* 5 full-time (all women), 1 part-time/adjunct (0 women). *Students:* 68 full-time (67 women), 7 part-time (6 women); includes 9 minority (4 African Americans, 1 American Indian/Alaska Native, 4 Hispanic Americans). Average age 25. 140 applicants, 45% accepted, 33 enrolled. In 2009, 25 master's awarded. *Entrance requirements:* For master's, GRE General Test, interview, minimum GPA of 3.0, letters of recommendation. Additional exam requirements/recommendations for international students: Required—TOEFL (minimum score 550 paper-based; 213 computer-based; 79 iBT). *Application deadline:* Applications are processed on a rolling basis. Application fee: $25. Electronic applications accepted. *Financial support:* Career-related internships or fieldwork, institutionally sponsored loans, and unspecified assistantships available. Financial award applicants required to submit FAFSA. *Faculty research:* Bioacoustics, physiology, applied speech science, pediatric nutrition/dysphagia, communication/cognition. *Unit head:* Carol Koch, Chair, 816-501-4518, Fax: 816-501-4169, E-mail: carol.koch@rockhurst.edu. *Application contact:* Cheryl Hooper, Director of Graduate Admission, 816-501-4097, Fax: 816-501-4241, E-mail: cherly.hooper@rockhurst.edu.

Rush University, College of Health Sciences, Department of Communication Disorders and Sciences, Chicago, IL 60612-3832. Offers audiology (Au D); speech-language pathology (MS). *Accreditation:* ASHA (one or more programs are accredited). Part-time programs available. *Degree requirements:* For master's, comprehensive exam, thesis optional; for doctorate, comprehensive exam, investigative project. *Entrance requirements:* For master's and doctorate, GRE General Test, minimum GPA of 3.0. Additional exam requirements/recommendations for international students: Required—TOEFL. Electronic applications accepted. *Expenses:* Contact institution. *Faculty research:* Electrostimulation of subthalamic nucleus, sensory feedback in speech modulation, sentence complexity in children's writing, velopharyngeal function, adult neurology.

St. Cloud State University, School of Graduate Studies, College of Fine Arts and Humanities, Department of Communication Sciences and Disorders, St. Cloud, MN 56301-4498. Offers MS. *Accreditation:* ASHA. *Faculty:* 5 full-time (4 women), 1 (woman) part-time/adjunct. *Students:* 33 full-time (32 women), 2 part-time (both women); includes 1 minority (Asian American or Pacific Islander), 2 international. 64 applicants, 75% accepted. In 2009, 19 master's awarded. *Degree requirements:* For master's, comprehensive exam (for some programs), thesis or alternative. *Entrance requirements:* For master's, GRE General Test, minimum GPA of 2.75. Additional exam requirements/recommendations for international students: Required—Michigan English Language Assessment Battery; Recommended—TOEFL (minimum score 550 paper-based; 213 computer-based), IELTS (minimum score 6.5). *Application deadline:* For fall admission, 2/1 for domestic and international students. Application fee: $35. Electronic applications accepted. *Financial support:* Federal Work-Study, scholarships/grants, and unspecified assistantships available. Financial award application deadline: 3/1. *Unit head:* Dr. G. N. Rangamani, Chairperson, 320-308-5769, E-mail: ghrangamuni@stcloudstate.edu. *Application contact:* Linda Lou Krueger, School of Graduate Studies, 320-308-2113, Fax: 320-308-5371, E-mail: lekrueger@stcloudstate.edu.

St. John's University, St. John's College of Liberal Arts and Sciences, Department of Communication Sciences and Disorders, Queens, NY 11439. Offers MA, Au D, Advanced Diploma. *Accreditation:* ASHA. Evening/weekend programs available. *Students:* 98 full-time (94 women), 55 part-time (51 women); includes 35 minority (8 African Americans, 8 Asian Americans or Pacific Islanders, 19 Hispanic Americans), 2 international. Average age 27. 484 applicants, 25% accepted, 45 enrolled. In 2009, 63 master's, 1 doctorate awarded. *Degree requirements:* For master's, comprehensive exam, thesis optional, internship. *Entrance requirements:* For master's, minimum GPA of 3.0. Additional exam requirements/recommendations for international students: Required—TOEFL (minimum score 500 paper-based; 173 computer-based; 61 iBT), IELTS (minimum score 5.5). *Application deadline:* For fall admission, 2/1 for domestic students, 2/1 priority date for international students; for spring admission, 10/1 for domestic students, 10/1 priority date for international students. Applications are processed on a rolling basis. Application fee: $70. Electronic applications accepted. *Expenses:* Contact institution. *Financial support:* Research assistantships, career-related internships or fieldwork and scholarships/grants available. Support available to part-time students. Financial award application deadline: 3/1; financial award applicants required to submit FAFSA. *Faculty research:* Bilingualism and adult and child language disorders, dementia, dysphagia, speech motor control, electrophysiological measurement of hearing, central auditory processing disorders, auditory habilitation and rehabilitation, scholarship of teaching and learning, evidence-based education. *Unit head:* Dr. Fredericka Bell-Berti, Chair, 718-990-6452, E-mail: bellf@stjohns.edu. *Application contact:* Kathleen Davis, Director of Graduate Admission, 718-990-2790, Fax: 718-990-5686, E-mail: gradhelp@stjohns.edu.

Saint Louis University, Graduate School, College of Arts and Sciences and Graduate School, Department of Communication Sciences and Disorders, St. Louis, MO 63103-2097. Offers MA, MA-R. *Accreditation:* ASHA (one or more programs are accredited). *Degree requirements:* For master's, thesis optional, comprehensive oral and written exams. *Entrance requirements:* For master's, GRE General Test, letters of recommendation, resume. Additional exam requirements/recommendations for international students: Required—TOEFL (minimum score 525 paper-based; 194 computer-based). Electronic applications accepted. *Faculty research:* Communication disorders in culturally and linguistically diverse populations, disability study-specific to World Health Organization classifications, early intervention in communication disorders and literacy skills, communication difficulties in internationally adopted children, voice and swallowing disorders secondary to cancer treatments.

Saint Xavier University, Graduate Studies, School of Arts and Sciences, Department of Speech-Language Pathology, Chicago, IL 60655-3105. Offers MS. *Accreditation:* ASHA. *Entrance requirements:* For master's, GRE General Test, minimum GPA of 3.0, undergraduate course work in speech. *Expenses:* Contact institution.

Salus University, George S. Osborne College of Audiology, Elkins Park, PA 19027-1598. Offers Au D. *Faculty:* 4 full-time (3 women). *Students:* 52 full-time (45 women); includes 18 minority (8 African Americans, 6 Asian Americans or Pacific Islanders, 4 Hispanic Americans). Average age 26. 60 applicants, 63% accepted, 20 enrolled. In 2009, 11 doctorates awarded. *Entrance requirements:* Additional exam requirements/recommendations for international students: Required—TOEFL. *Application deadline:* For fall admission, 6/5 for domestic and international students. Applications are processed on a rolling basis. Application fee: $50. Electronic applications accepted. *Expenses:* Tuition: Full-time $31,700. Required fees: $550. Full-time tuition and fees vary according to degree level and program. *Unit head:* Dr. Victor Bray, Dean of Audiology, E-mail: VBray@Salus.edu. *Application contact:* Robert E. Horne, Dean of Student Affairs, 215-780-1312, Fax: 215-780-1396, E-mail: rhorne@Salus.edu.

San Diego State University, Graduate and Research Affairs, College of Health and Human Services, School of Speech, Language, and Hearing Sciences, San Diego, CA 92182. Offers audiology (Au D); communicative disorders (MA); language and communicative disorders (PhD). *Accreditation:* ASHA (one or more programs are accredited). Part-time programs available. *Degree requirements:* For master's, comprehensive exam (for some programs), thesis (for some programs); for doctorate, thesis/dissertation. *Entrance requirements:* For master's and doctorate, GRE General Test. Additional exam requirements/recommendations for international students: Required—TOEFL. Electronic applications accepted. *Faculty research:* Brain/behavior relationships in language development, grammatical processing and language disorders, interdisciplinary training of bilingual speech pathologists.

San Francisco State University, Division of Graduate Studies, College of Education, Department of Special Education, Program in Communicative Disorders, San Francisco, CA 94132-1722. Offers MS. *Accreditation:* ASHA.

San Jose State University, Graduate Studies and Research, Connie L. Lurie College of Education, Department of Communicative Disorders and Sciences, San Jose, CA 95192-0001. Offers speech-language pathology (MA). *Accreditation:* ASHA. Evening/weekend programs available. *Students:* 110 full-time (103 women), 2 part-time (both women); includes 33 minority (4 African Americans, 19 Asian Americans or Pacific Islanders, 10 Hispanic Americans), 3 international. Average age 30. 274 applicants, 17% accepted, 40 enrolled. In 2009, 51 master's awarded. *Entrance requirements:* For master's, MAT. *Application deadline:* For fall admission, 6/29 for domestic students; for spring admission, 11/30 for domestic students. Applications are processed on a rolling basis. Application fee: $59. Electronic applications accepted. *Financial support:* Career-related internships or fieldwork available. Financial award applicants required to submit FAFSA. *Unit head:* Dr. Michael L. Kimbarow, Chair, 408-924-3691, Fax: 408-924-3641, E-mail: michael.kimbarow@sjsu.edu. *Application contact:* Dr. Michael L. Kimbarow, Chair, 408-924-3691, Fax: 408-924-3641, E-mail: michael.kimbarow@sjsu.edu.

Seton Hall University, School of Health and Medical Sciences, Program in Speech-Language Pathology, South Orange, NJ 07079-2697. Offers MS. *Accreditation:* ASHA. *Entrance requirements:* For master's, GRE, bachelor's degree, clinical experience; minimum GPA of 3.0, undergraduate preprofessional coursework in communication sciences and disorders. Electronic applications accepted. *Faculty research:* Child language disorders, motor speech control, voice disorders, dysphagia, early intervention/teaming.

South Carolina State University, School of Graduate Studies, Department of Health Sciences, Orangeburg, SC 29117-0001. Offers speech/language pathology (MA). *Accreditation:* ASHA. Part-time and evening/weekend programs available. *Degree requirements:* For master's, thesis optional, departmental qualifying exam. *Entrance requirements:* For master's, GRE or NTE, minimum GPA of 3.0. Electronic applications accepted. *Expenses:* Tuition, state resident: part-time $470 per credit hour. Tuition, nonresident: part-time $924 per credit hour.

Southeastern Louisiana University, College of Nursing and Health Sciences, Department of Communication Sciences and Disorders, Hammond, LA 70402. Offers MS. *Accreditation:* ASHA; NCATE. *Faculty:* 10 full-time (9 women). *Students:* 41 full-time (39 women), 19 part-time (all women); includes 3 minority (1 African American, 1 Asian American or Pacific Islander, 1 Hispanic American). Average age 27. 37 applicants, 97% accepted, 21 enrolled. In 2009, 14 master's awarded. *Degree requirements:* For master's, comprehensive exam (for some programs), thesis optional. *Entrance requirements:* For master's, GRE (verbal and quantitative), 3 letters of reference. Additional exam requirements/recommendations for international students: Required—TOEFL (minimum score 500 paper-based; 173 computer-based; 61 iBT). *Application deadline:* For fall admission, 7/15 priority date for domestic students, 6/1 priority date for international students; for spring admission, 12/1 priority date for domestic students, 10/1 priority date for international students. Applications are processed on a rolling basis. Application fee: $20 ($30 for international students). Electronic applications accepted. *Expenses:* Tuition, state resident: full-time $3086; part-time $225 per credit hour. Tuition, nonresident: part-time $529 per credit hour. Required fees: $1195. Tuition and fees vary according to course level and course load. *Financial support:* In 2009–10, 2 students received support. Federal Work-Study, institutionally sponsored loans, scholarships/grants, and administrative assistantships available. Support available to part-time students. Financial award application deadline: 5/1; financial award applicants required to submit FAFSA. *Faculty research:* Conversational analysis in standard and communication disordered population, educational needs of children with cochlear implants, autism, acoustic characteristics of American English linguistics stress patterns, languages disorders and literacy. *Unit head:* Dr. Paula Currie, Department Head, 985-549-2214, Fax: 985-549-5030, E-mail: pcurrie@selu.edu. *Application contact:* Sandra Meyers, Graduate Admissions Analyst, 985-549-5620, Fax: 985-549-5632, E-mail: admissions@selu.edu.

Southeast Missouri State University, School of Graduate Studies, Department of Communication Disorders, Cape Girardeau, MO 63701-4799. Offers MA. *Accreditation:* ASHA. *Degree requirements:* For master's, comprehensive exam, thesis or alternative. *Entrance requirements:* For master's, GRE, minimum undergraduate GPA of 3.0. Additional exam requirements/recommendations for international students: Required—TOEFL (minimum score 550 paper-based; 213 computer-based); Recommended—IELTS (minimum score 6). *Expenses:* Tuition, state resident: full-time $4266; part-time $237 per credit hour. Tuition, nonresident: full-time $7506; part-time $417 per credit hour. Required fees: $427; $427.

Southern Connecticut State University, School of Graduate Studies, School of Health and Human Services, Department of Communication Disorders, New Haven, CT 06515-1355. Offers speech pathology (MS). *Accreditation:* ASHA. Part-time programs available. *Faculty:* 12 full-time, 2 part-time/adjunct. *Students:* 115 full-time (113 women), 14 part-time (13 women); includes 19 minority (7 African Americans, 12 Hispanic Americans), 1 international. 163 applicants, 61% accepted, 30 enrolled. In 2009, 38 master's awarded. *Degree requirements:* For master's, thesis or alternative, clinical experience. *Entrance requirements:* For master's, GRE, interview, minimum QPA of 3.0. *Application deadline:* For fall admission, 3/1 for domestic students. Application fee: $50. Electronic applications accepted. Tuition and fees vary according to program. *Financial support:* Career-related internships or fieldwork available. Financial award application deadline: 4/15; financial award applicants required to submit FAFSA. *Unit head:* Dr. James Dempsey, Chairperson, 203-392-5962, Fax: 203-392-5968, E-mail: dempsey@southernct.edu. *Application contact:* Dr. Deborah Weiss, Graduate Coordinator, 203-392-6615, Fax: 203-392-5968, E-mail: weissd1@southernct.edu.

Southern Illinois University Carbondale, Graduate School, College of Education, Rehabilitation Institute, Department of Communication Disorders and Sciences, Carbondale, IL 62901-4701. Offers MS. *Accreditation:* ASHA. *Degree requirements:* For master's, thesis. *Entrance requirements:* For master's, GRE, minimum GPA of 3.0. Additional exam requirements/recommendations for international students: Required—TOEFL. *Faculty research:* Neurolinguistics, language processing, child language, fluency, phonology.

Southern Illinois University Edwardsville, Graduate Studies and Research, School of Education, Department of Special Education and Communication Disorders, Program in Speech-Language Pathology, Edwardsville, IL 62026-0001. Offers MS. *Accreditation:* ASHA. Part-time and evening/weekend programs available. *Students:* 59 full-time (58 women); includes 3 minority (all African Americans). Average age 26. 164 applicants, 37% accepted. In 2009, 25 master's awarded. *Degree requirements:* For master's, thesis or alternative, final exam. *Entrance requirements:* For master's, GRE, minimum GPA of 3.0. Additional exam requirements/recommendations for international students: Required—TOEFL (minimum score 550 paper-based; 213 computer-based; 79 iBT), IELTS (minimum score 6.5). *Application deadline:* For fall admission, 2/1 for domestic and international students. Application fee: $30. Electronic applications accepted. *Expenses:* Tuition, state resident: part-time $1252.50 per semester. Tuition, nonresident: part-time $3131.25 per semester. Required fees: $586.85 per semester. Tuition and fees vary according to course load. *Financial support:* In 2009–10, 1 fellowship with full tuition reimbursement (averaging $8,370 per year), 1 research assistantship with full tuition reimbursement (averaging $8,064 per year), 20 teaching assistantships with full tuition reimbursements (averaging $8,064 per year) were awarded; career-related internships or fieldwork, Federal Work-Study, institutionally sponsored loans, scholarships/grants, traineeships, and unspecified assistantships also available. Support available to part-time students. Financial award application deadline: 3/1; financial award applicants required to submit FAFSA. *Unit head:* Dr. James Panico, Chair, 618-650-5838, E-mail: jpanico@siue.edu. *Application contact:* Dr. James Panico, Chair, 618-650-5838, E-mail: jpanico@siue.edu.

State University of New York at Fredonia, Graduate Studies, Department of Speech Pathology and Audiology, Fredonia, NY 14063-1136. Offers MS, MS Ed. *Accreditation:* ASHA. Part-time and evening/weekend programs available. *Degree requirements:* For master's, thesis optional,

Communication Disorders

State University of New York at Fredonia (continued)
clinical practice. *Expenses:* Tuition, state resident: full-time $8370; part-time $349 per credit. Tuition, nonresident: full-time $13,250; part-time $552 per credit. Required fees: $1289; $53.55 per credit.

State University of New York at New Paltz, Graduate School, School of Liberal Arts and Sciences, Department of Communication Disorders, New Paltz, NY 12561. Offers communication disorders (MS), including speech-language disabilities, speech-language pathology. *Accreditation:* ASHA. Part-time and evening/weekend programs available. *Faculty:* 8 full-time (all women), 6 part-time/adjunct (1 woman). *Students:* 44 full-time (43 women), 5 part-time (all women); includes 4 minority (2 African Americans, 2 Hispanic Americans). Average age 30. 136 applicants, 26% accepted, 15 enrolled. In 2009, 25 master's awarded. *Degree requirements:* For master's, comprehensive exam, thesis. *Entrance requirements:* For master's, GRE General Test or MAT, minimum GPA of 3.0. Additional exam requirements/recommendations for international students: Required—TOEFL (minimum score 550 paper-based; 213 computer-based; 80 iBT), IELTS (minimum score 6.5). *Application deadline:* For fall admission, 3/1 for domestic and international students. Application fee: $50. Electronic applications accepted. *Financial support:* In 2009–10, 5 students received support, including 2 fellowships (averaging $9,000 per year), 3 teaching assistantships with partial tuition reimbursements available (averaging $5,000 per year); Federal Work-Study, institutionally sponsored loans, scholarships/grants, health care benefits, and unspecified assistantships also available. Financial award application deadline: 8/1; financial award applicants required to submit FAFSA. *Unit head:* Dr. Stella Turk, Chairman, 845-257-3603, E-mail: turks@newpaltz.edu. *Application contact:* Dr. Elizabeth Hester, Coordinator, 845-257-3465, E-mail: hestere@newpaltz.edu.

State University of New York at Plattsburgh, Division of Education, Health, and Human Services, Department of Communication Disorders, Plattsburgh, NY 12901-2681. Offers speech-language pathology (MA). *Accreditation:* ASHA. Part-time programs available. *Faculty:* 11 full-time (7 women), 8 part-time/adjunct (all women). *Students:* 30 full-time (28 women), 1 (woman) part-time; includes 2 minority (1 African American, 1 Asian American or Pacific Islander), 3 international. Average age 28. 59 applicants, 36% accepted, 16 enrolled. In 2009, 17 master's awarded. *Degree requirements:* For master's, thesis, PRAXIS II. *Entrance requirements:* For master's, GRE General Test, minimum GPA of 3.0. Additional exam requirements/recommendations for international students: Required—TOEFL (minimum score 550 paper-based; 213 computer-based; 79 iBT). *Application deadline:* For fall admission, 2/15 priority date for domestic students. Applications are processed on a rolling basis. Application fee: $75. *Expenses:* Tuition, state resident: full-time $8370; part-time $349 per credit hour. Tuition, nonresident: full-time $13,250; part-time $552 per credit hour. Required fees: $1130. *Financial support:* Career-related internships or fieldwork and Federal Work-Study available. Support available to part-time students. Financial award application deadline: 4/15; financial award applicants required to submit FAFSA. *Faculty research:* Ototoxins and noise effects on hearing, language impairment in Alzheimer's disease, attitudes on stuttering, diagnostic audiology. *Unit head:* Dr. Raymond Domenico, Chair, 518-564-3154, E-mail: domenira@plattsburgh.edu. *Application contact:* Marguerite Adelman, Assistant Director, Graduate Admissions, 518-564-4723, Fax: 518-564-4722, E-mail: adelmaml@plattsburgh.edu.

State University of New York College at Geneseo, Graduate Studies, Department of Communicative Disorders and Sciences, Geneseo, NY 14454-1401. Offers MA. *Accreditation:* ASHA. *Faculty:* 5 full-time (2 women), 7 part-time/adjunct (6 women). *Students:* 24 full-time (23 women), 10 part-time (all women); includes 2 minority (1 African American, 1 Asian American or Pacific Islander). Average age 25. 85 applicants, 21% accepted, 11 enrolled. In 2009, 25 master's awarded. *Degree requirements:* For master's, comprehensive exam, thesis optional. *Entrance requirements:* For master's, GRE General Test, interview, letters of reference. *Application deadline:* For fall admission, 2/1 for domestic students; for spring admission, 10/1 for domestic students. Application fee: $50. *Expenses:* Tuition, state resident: full-time $8370; part-time $349 per credit hour. Tuition, nonresident: full-time $13,250; part-time $552 per credit hour. Required fees: $700.52; $29 per credit hour. *Financial support:* Career-related internships or fieldwork and institutionally sponsored loans available. Financial award application deadline: 4/1; financial award applicants required to submit FAFSA. *Unit head:* Dr. Linda House, Chairperson, 585-245-5328, Fax: 585-245-5434, E-mail: house@geneseo.edu. *Application contact:* Dr. Douglas J. MacKenzie, Associate Professor/Director of the Graduate Program in Speech-Language Pathology, 585-245-5328, Fax: 585-245-5434, E-mail: mackenzie@geneseo.edu.

Stephen F. Austin State University, Graduate School, College of Education, Department of Human Services, Nacogdoches, TX 75962. Offers counseling (MA); school psychology (MA); special education (M Ed); speech pathology (MS). *Accreditation:* ACA (one or more programs are accredited); ASHA (one or more programs are accredited); CORE; NCATE. *Degree requirements:* For master's, comprehensive exam, thesis (for some programs). *Entrance requirements:* For master's, GRE General Test, minimum GPA of 2.8. Additional exam requirements/recommendations for international students: Required—TOEFL.

Syracuse University, College of Arts and Sciences, Program in Audiology, Syracuse, NY 13244. Offers Au D, PhD. *Accreditation:* ASHA. Part-time programs available. *Students:* 14 full-time (13 women), 4 part-time (3 women); includes 3 minority (2 African Americans, 1 Asian American or Pacific Islander), 5 international. Average age 26. 29 applicants, 52% accepted, 7 enrolled. In 2009, 4 doctorates awarded. *Degree requirements:* For doctorate, thesis/dissertation. *Entrance requirements:* For doctorate, GRE General Test. Additional exam requirements/recommendations for international students: Required—TOEFL (minimum score 100 iBT). *Application deadline:* For fall admission, 2/1 priority date for domestic and international students. Application fee: $75. Electronic applications accepted. *Expenses:* Tuition: Full-time $26,808; part-time $1117 per credit. Required fees: $1024. *Financial support:* Fellowships, research assistantships, teaching assistantships available. Financial award application deadline: 1/1. *Unit head:* Dr. Linda Milosky, Department Chair, 315-443-9637. *Application contact:* Jennifer Steigerwald, Information Contact, 315-443-9615, E-mail: jssteige@syr.edu.

Syracuse University, College of Arts and Sciences, Program in Speech Language Pathology, Syracuse, NY 13244. Offers MS, PhD. *Accreditation:* ASHA. Part-time programs available. *Students:* 47 full-time (46 women), 3 part-time (all women); includes 6 minority (2 African Americans, 2 Asian Americans or Pacific Islanders, 2 Hispanic Americans), 4 international. Average age 25. 114 applicants, 56% accepted, 21 enrolled. In 2009, 30 master's, 1 doctorate awarded. *Degree requirements:* For master's, thesis or alternative; for doctorate, thesis/dissertation. *Entrance requirements:* For master's and doctorate, GRE. Additional exam requirements/recommendations for international students: Required—TOEFL (minimum score 100 iBT). *Application deadline:* For fall admission, 2/1 priority date for domestic and international students. Application fee: $75. Electronic applications accepted. *Expenses:* Tuition: Full-time $26,808; part-time $1117 per credit. Required fees: $1024. *Financial support:* Application deadline: 1/1. *Unit head:* Dr. Linda Milosky, Chair, 315-443-9637, E-mail: csd@syr.edu. *Application contact:* Jennifer Steigerwald, Information Contact, 315-443-9615.

Teachers College, Columbia University, Graduate Faculty of Education, Department of Biobehavioral Studies, Program in Speech-Language Pathology, New York, NY 10027-6696. Offers Ed M, MS, Ed D, PhD. *Accreditation:* ASHA. *Faculty:* 5 full-time (3 women). *Students:* 86 full-time (85 women), 59 part-time (56 women); includes 36 minority (8 African Americans, 11 Asian Americans or Pacific Islanders, 17 Hispanic Americans), 10 international. Average age 28. 479 applicants, 28% accepted, 55 enrolled. In 2009, 50 master's awarded. Terminal master's awarded for partial completion of doctoral program. *Degree requirements:* For doctorate, thesis/dissertation. *Application deadline:* For fall admission, 2/1 priority date for domestic students. Application fee: $75. *Financial support:* Fellowships, teaching assistantships, career-related internships or fieldwork, Federal Work-Study, institutionally sponsored loans, and tuition waivers (full and partial) available. Support available to part-time students. Financial award application deadline: 2/1. *Faculty research:* Neuropathology of speech, stuttering, language disorders in children and adults, motor speech. *Unit head:* John H. Saxman, Chair, 212-678-3895, E-mail: jhs37@columbia.edu. *Application contact:* Debbie Lesperance, Assistant Director of Admission, 212-678-3710, Fax: 212-678-4171.

Teachers College, Columbia University, Graduate Faculty of Education, Department of Health and Behavioral Studies, Program in Hearing Impairment, New York, NY 10027-6696. Offers MA, Ed D. *Faculty:* 1 full-time (0 women), 2 part-time/adjunct. *Students:* 10 full-time (all women), 16 part-time (15 women); includes 3 minority (1 African American, 2 Asian Americans or Pacific Islanders), 1 international. Average age 27. 16 applicants, 94% accepted, 10 enrolled. In 2009, 23 master's awarded. *Degree requirements:* For doctorate, thesis/dissertation. *Application deadline:* For fall admission, 5/15 for domestic students; for spring admission, 12/1 for domestic students. Application fee: $65. *Financial support:* Fellowships, career-related internships or fieldwork, Federal Work-Study, institutionally sponsored loans, and tuition waivers (full and partial) available. Support available to part-time students. Financial award application deadline: 2/1. *Faculty research:* Language development, reading/writing, cognitive abilities, text analysis, auditory streaming. *Unit head:* Dr. Chuck Basch, Chair, 212-678-3964, E-mail: ceb35@columbia.edu. *Application contact:* Peter Shon, Assistant Director of Admission, 212-678-3305, Fax: 212-678-4171, E-mail: shon@exchange.tc.columbia.edu.

Teachers College, Columbia University, Graduate Faculty of Education, Department of Health and Behavioral Studies, Program in Teaching of Sign Language, New York, NY 10027-6696. Offers MA. *Accreditation:* NCATE. *Students:* 3 full-time (all women), 6 part-time (4 women); includes 1 minority (Hispanic American). Average age 25. 6 applicants, 83% accepted, 3 enrolled. In 2009, 7 master's awarded. Application fee: $65. *Unit head:* Dr. Chuck Basch, Chair, 212-678-3964, E-mail: ceb35@columbia.edu. *Application contact:* Peter Shon, Assistant Director of Admission, 212-678-3305, Fax: 212-678-4171, E-mail: shon@exchange.tc.columbia.edu.

Temple University, Health Sciences Center and Graduate School, College of Health Professions, Department of Communication Sciences, Program in Speech-Language-Hearing, Philadelphia, PA 19122-6096. Offers MA. *Entrance requirements:* For master's, GRE General Test, minimum GPA of 3.0. Additional exam requirements/recommendations for international students: Required—TOEFL (minimum score 550 paper-based; 213 computer-based; 79 iBT). Electronic applications accepted.

Tennessee State University, The School of Graduate Studies and Research, College of Health Sciences, Department of Speech Pathology and Audiology, Nashville, TN 37209-1561. Offers speech and hearing science (MS). Part-time programs available. Postbaccalaureate distance learning degree programs offered (minimal on-campus study). *Degree requirements:* For master's, comprehensive exam, thesis optional. *Entrance requirements:* For master's, GRE General Test, MAT, minimum GPA of 3.5. Additional exam requirements/recommendations for international students: Required—TOEFL. *Faculty research:* Auditory dunction to sickle cell disease, assessment and management of dysphagia, early intervention language disorders, multicultural diversity.

Texas A&M University–Kingsville, College of Graduate Studies, College of Arts and Sciences, Department of Communication, Kingsville, TX 78363. Offers MS. *Accreditation:* ASHA. *Degree requirements:* For master's, comprehensive exam, thesis or alternative. *Entrance requirements:* For master's, GRE General Test. Additional exam requirements/recommendations for international students: Required—TOEFL.

Texas Christian University, Harris College of Nursing and Health Sciences, Department of Communication Sciences and Disorders, Fort Worth, TX 76129-0002. Offers speech-language pathology (MS). *Accreditation:* ASHA. *Degree requirements:* For master's, comprehensive exam. *Entrance requirements:* For master's, GRE General Test, previous course work in speech-language pathology. Additional exam requirements/recommendations for international students: Required—TOEFL. *Application deadline:* For fall admission, 2/1 for domestic students. Application fee: $0. *Expenses:* Tuition: Full-time $17,640; part-time $980 per credit hour. Tuition and fees vary according to program. *Financial support:* In 2009–10, 25 students received support, including 25 teaching assistantships; unspecified assistantships also available. Financial award application deadline: 2/1; financial award applicants required to submit FAFSA. *Unit head:* Dr. Christopher Watts, Chairperson, 817-257-7621, E-mail: c.watts@tcu.edu. *Application contact:* Admissions, TCU Graduate Studies Office, 817-257-7515, Fax: 817-257-7484, E-mail: frogmail@tcu.edu.

Texas State University–San Marcos, Graduate School, College of Health Professions, Department of Communication Disorders, San Marcos, TX 78666. Offers MA, MSCD. *Accreditation:* ASHA (one or more programs are accredited). Part-time programs available. *Faculty:* 7 full-time (6 women). *Students:* 43 full-time (all women), 12 part-time (11 women); includes 17 minority (2 African Americans, 2 Asian Americans or Pacific Islanders, 13 Hispanic Americans). Average age 26. 178 applicants, 19% accepted, 31 enrolled. In 2009, 20 master's awarded. *Degree requirements:* For master's, comprehensive exam, thesis (for some programs), practicum. *Entrance requirements:* For master's, minimum GPA of 3.0 in communications disorders and in last 60 hours of course work; 25 hours of observation; 2 letters of recommendation from professors in previous major; resume on form provided by department. Additional exam requirements/recommendations for international students: Required—TOEFL (minimum score 550 paper-based; 213 computer-based). *Application deadline:* For fall admission, 2/1 for domestic and international students. Applications are processed on a rolling basis. Application fee: $40 ($90 for international students). Electronic applications accepted. *Expenses:* Tuition, state resident: full-time $5784; part-time $241 per credit hour. Tuition, nonresident: full-time $13,224; part-time $551 per credit hour. Required fees: $1728; $48 per credit hour. $306. Tuition and fees vary according to course load. *Financial support:* In 2009–10, 43 students received support, including 6 research assistantships (averaging $1,269 per year), 5 teaching assistantships (averaging $1,255 per year); fellowships, career-related internships or fieldwork, Federal Work-Study, institutionally sponsored loans, and scholarships/grants also available. Support available to part-time students. Financial award application deadline: 4/1; financial award applicants required to submit FAFSA. *Unit head:* Dr. Maria Dianna Gonzales, Chair, 512-245-2330, Fax: 512-245-2029, E-mail: mg29@txstate.edu. *Application contact:* Dr. J. Michael Willoughby, Dean of Graduate School, 512-245-2581, Fax: 512-245-8365, E-mail: gradcollege@txstate.edu.

Texas Tech University Health Sciences Center, School of Allied Health Sciences, Program in Speech, Language and Hearing Sciences, Lubbock, TX 79430. Offers MS, Au D, PhD. *Accreditation:* ASHA (one or more programs are accredited). *Faculty:* 24 full-time (18 women). *Students:* 112 full-time (107 women), 6 part-time (5 women); includes 14 minority (2 African Americans, 1 American Indian/Alaska Native, 1 Asian American or Pacific Islander, 10 Hispanic Americans). Average age 26. 114 applicants, 42% accepted, 48 enrolled. In 2009, 24 master's, 9 doctorates awarded. *Degree requirements:* For master's, comprehensive exam, thesis optional; for doctorate, comprehensive exam, thesis/dissertation. *Entrance requirements:* For master's, GRE General Test, GRE Writing Test; for doctorate, GRE. Additional exam requirements/recommendations for international students: Required—TOEFL, IELTS. *Application deadline:* For fall admission, 11/1 for domestic students; for spring admission, 2/1 for domestic students. Application fee: $35. Electronic applications accepted. *Financial support:* In 2009–10, 15 students received support, including 6 research assistantships, 5 teaching assistantships; career-related internships or fieldwork, institutionally sponsored loans, and scholarships/grants also available. Financial award application deadline: 9/1; financial award applicants required to submit FAFSA. *Faculty research:* Craniofacial anomalies, evoked potentials, neurolinguistics, language simulations, vocal fold burns. Total annual research expenditures: $150,000. *Unit head:* Dr. Rajinder Koul, Chairperson, 806-743-5660 Ext. 227, Fax: 806-742-0907, E-mail: rajinder.koul@ttuhsc.edu. *Application contact:* Lindsay Johnson, Assistant Dean for Admissions and Student Affairs, 806-743-3220, Fax: 806-742-2994, E-mail: lindsay.johnson@ttuhsc.edu.

Texas Woman's University, Graduate School, College of Health Sciences, Department of Communication Sciences and Disorders, Denton, TX 76201. Offers education of the deaf (MS); speech-language pathology (MS). *Accreditation:* ASHA. Part-time programs available.

Postbaccalaureate distance learning degree programs offered (no on-campus study). *Faculty:* 19 full-time (16 women). *Students:* 177 full-time (173 women), 49 part-time (47 women); includes 74 minority (16 African Americans, 1 American Indian/Alaska Native, 6 Asian Americans or Pacific Islanders, 51 Hispanic Americans), 3 international. Average age 30. 37 applicants, 97% accepted, 13 enrolled. In 2009, 51 master's awarded. *Degree requirements:* For master's, comprehensive exam, thesis. *Entrance requirements:* For master's, GRE General Test, 2 letters of reference. Additional exam requirements/recommendations for international students: Required—TOEFL (minimum score 550 paper-based; 213 computer-based; 79 iBT). *Application deadline:* For fall admission, 2/1 priority date for domestic and international students. Applications are processed on a rolling basis. Application fee: $50. Electronic applications accepted. *Expenses:* Tuition, state resident: full-time $3564; part-time $198 per credit hour. Tuition, nonresident: full-time $8550; part-time $475 per credit hour. Required fees: $69.26 per credit hour. Tuition and fees vary according to course load. *Financial support:* In 2009–10, 67 students received support, including 10 research assistantships (averaging $9,504 per year); career-related internships or fieldwork, Federal Work-Study, institutionally sponsored loans, scholarships/grants, traineeships, health care benefits, and unspecified assistantships also available. Support available to part-time students. Financial award application deadline: 3/1; financial award applicants required to submit FAFSA. *Faculty research:* Stroke, language assessment auditory processing and relationship between speech and language, effectiveness of distance education learning, neuromodulation of recovery of aphasia. *Unit head:* Dr. Dorothy Grant, Chair, 940-898-2025, Fax: 940-898-2070, E-mail: coms@twu.edu. *Application contact:* Samuel Wheeler, Assistant Director of Admissions, 940-898-3188, Fax: 940-898-3081, E-mail: wheelersr@twu.edu.

Touro College, School of Health Sciences, Bay Shore, NY 11706. Offers acupuncture (MS); occupational therapy (MS); oriental medicine (MSOM); physical therapy (DPT); public health (MPH); speech-language pathology (MS). *Expenses:* Contact institution.

Towson University, College of Graduate Studies and Research, Program in Audiology, Towson, MD 21252-0001. Offers Au D. *Accreditation:* ASHA. *Entrance requirements:* For doctorate, GRE, 3 letters of recommendation, minimum GPA of 3.0. Additional exam requirements/recommendations for international students: Required—TOEFL (minimum score 600 paper-based). Electronic applications accepted. *Faculty research:* Auditory processing, cortical potentials, otoacoustic emissions, electrophysiology, cochlear implants.

Towson University, College of Graduate Studies and Research, Program in Speech-Language Pathology, Towson, MD 21252-0001. Offers MS. *Accreditation:* ASHA. *Degree requirements:* For master's, thesis (for some programs), exam. *Entrance requirements:* For master's, GRE, minimum GPA of 3.0 in major, undergraduate coursework in speech-language pathology with 42 hours clinical observation or 33 units in pathology. Additional exam requirements/recommendations for international students: Required—TOEFL (minimum score 600 paper-based). Electronic applications accepted. *Faculty research:* Oral-literate issues, narratives, localization in noise, cross-language assessment, temporal processing of speech.

Truman State University, Graduate School, School of Health Sciences and Education, Program in Communication Disorders, Kirksville, MO 63501-4221. Offers MA. *Accreditation:* ASHA. *Degree requirements:* For master's, comprehensive exam, thesis optional. *Entrance requirements:* For master's, GRE General Test, minimum GPA of 3.0. Additional exam requirements/recommendations for international students: Required—TOEFL (minimum score 550 paper-based; 213 computer-based). Electronic applications accepted. *Expenses:* Tuition, state resident: part-time $291 per credit. Tuition, nonresident: part-time $499 per credit hour. Tuition and fees vary according to course load.

Universidad del Turabo, Graduate Programs, School of Health Sciences, Program in Speech and Language Pathology, Gurabo, PR 00778-3030. Offers MS. *Students:* 61 full-time (57 women), 5 part-time (4 women); includes 63 Hispanic Americans. Average age 28. 55 applicants, 73% accepted, 25 enrolled. In 2009, 24 master's awarded. *Unit head:* David Mendez, Head, 787-743-7979. *Application contact:* Virginia Gonzalez, Admissions Officer, 787-746-3009.

Université de Montréal, Faculty of Medicine, School of Speech Therapy and Audiology, Montréal, QC H3C 3J7, Canada. Offers audiology (PMS); speach therapy (PMS, DESS). *Faculty:* 14 full-time (9 women), 5 part-time/adjunct (4 women). *Students:* 63 full-time (all women), 26 part-time (23 women). 81 applicants, 77% accepted, 61 enrolled. In 2009, 84 master's awarded. *Degree requirements:* For master's, thesis. *Entrance requirements:* For master's, B Sc in speech-language pathology and audiology, proficiency in French. *Application deadline:* For fall admission, 2/1 for domestic students. Application fee: $100. Electronic applications accepted. *Faculty research:* Aphasia in adults, dysarthria, speech and hearing-impaired children, noise-induced hearing impairment, computerized audiometry. *Unit head:* Louise Getty, Director, 514-343-7672, Fax: 514-343-2115. *Application contact:* Ana Ines Ansaldo, Responsible for Graduate Studies, 514-343-6111 Ext. 47490, Fax: 514-343-2115, E-mail: ana.ines.ansaldo@umontreal.ca.

Université Laval, Faculty of Medicine, Graduate Programs in Medicine, Program in Speech Therapy, Québec, QC G1K 7P4, Canada. Offers M Sc. *Entrance requirements:* For master's, knowledge of French, interview. Electronic applications accepted.

University at Buffalo, the State University of New York, Graduate School, College of Arts and Sciences, Department of Communicative Disorders, Buffalo, NY 14260. Offers audiology (Au D); communicative disorders and sciences (MA, PhD). *Accreditation:* ASHA (one or more programs are accredited). *Faculty:* 20 full-time (14 women), 2 part-time/adjunct (1 woman). *Students:* 97 full-time (92 women), 6 part-time (5 women); includes 7 minority (1 African American, 6 Asian Americans or Pacific Islanders), 25 international. 206 applicants, 33% accepted. In 2009, 38 master's, 1 doctorate awarded. *Degree requirements:* For master's, thesis or alternative, exam; for doctorate, thesis/dissertation, exams. *Entrance requirements:* For master's and doctorate, GRE General Test, minimum GPA of 3.0. Additional exam requirements/recommendations for international students: Required—TOEFL (minimum score 550 paper-based; 213 computer-based; 79 iBT). *Application deadline:* For fall admission, 1/15 priority date for domestic and international students. Application fee: $50. Electronic applications accepted. *Financial support:* In 2009–10, 22 students received support, including 3 fellowships with full tuition reimbursements available (averaging $3,000 per year), 19 teaching assistantships with full tuition reimbursements available (averaging $6,464 per year); career-related internships or fieldwork, Federal Work-Study, institutionally sponsored loans, scholarships/grants, health care benefits, tuition waivers (partial), and unspecified assistantships also available. Financial award applicants required to submit FAFSA. *Faculty research:* Hearing and speech science, child and adult language disorders, augmentative communication, cochlear implants, tinnitis. Total annual research expenditures: $2.7 million. *Unit head:* Dr. Joan Sussman, Chairperson, 716-829-5551, Fax: 716-829-3979, E-mail: jsussman@acsu.buffalo.edu. *Application contact:* Linda L. Mehnert, Graduate Admissions Coordinator, 716-829-5570, Fax: 716-829-3979, E-mail: lmehnert@buffalo.edu.

The University of Akron, Graduate School, College of Health Sciences and Human Services, School of Speech-Language Pathology and Audiology, Program in Audiology, Akron, OH 44325. Offers Au D. *Accreditation:* ASHA. *Students:* 40 full-time (35 women), 3 international. Average age 25. 36 applicants, 47% accepted, 10 enrolled. In 2009, 8 doctorates awarded. *Degree requirements:* For doctorate, 2000 clock hours of clinical experience, academic and competency-based exams. *Entrance requirements:* For doctorate, GRE, minimum GPA of 3.0, letters of recommendation. Additional exam requirements/recommendations for international students: Required—TOEFL (minimum score 550 paper-based; 213 computer-based; 79 iBT). *Application deadline:* For fall admission, 1/15 for domestic and international students. Application fee: $30 ($40 for international students). Electronic applications accepted. *Expenses:* Tuition, state resident: full-time $6570; part-time $365 per credit hour. Tuition, nonresident: full-time $11,250; part-time $625 per credit hour. *Unit head:* Dr. Sharon Lesner, Coordinator, 330-972-6118, E-mail: lesner@uakron.edu. *Application contact:* Dr. Sharon Lesner, Coordinator, 330-972-6118, E-mail: lesner@uakron.edu.

The University of Akron, Graduate School, College of Health Sciences and Human Services, School of Speech-Language Pathology and Audiology, Program in Speech-Language Pathology, Akron, OH 44325. Offers MA. *Accreditation:* ASHA. *Students:* 81 full-time (79 women), 39 part-time (38 women); includes 7 minority (3 African Americans, 2 Asian Americans or Pacific Islanders, 2 Hispanic Americans). Average age 28. 156 applicants, 32% accepted, 39 enrolled. In 2009, 25 master's awarded. *Degree requirements:* For master's, thesis optional. *Entrance requirements:* For master's, GRE, baccalaureate degree in speech-language pathology, minimum GPA of 2.75, letters of recommendation, resume. Additional exam requirements/recommendations for international students: Required—TOEFL (minimum score 550 paper-based; 213 computer-based; 79 iBT). *Application deadline:* For fall admission, 1/15 for domestic and international students. Application fee: $30 ($40 for international students). Electronic applications accepted. *Expenses:* Tuition, state resident: full-time $6570; part-time $365 per credit hour. Tuition, nonresident: full-time $11,250; part-time $625 per credit hour. *Unit head:* Dr. Yvonne Gillette, Coordinator, 330-972-6115, E-mail: ygillette@uakron.edu. *Application contact:* Dr. Yvonne Gillette, Coordinator, 330-972-6115, E-mail: ygillette@uakron.edu.

The University of Alabama, Graduate School, College of Arts and Sciences, Department of Communicative Disorders, Tuscaloosa, AL 35487. Offers speech language pathology (MS). *Accreditation:* ASHA. *Faculty:* 10 full-time (8 women), 2 part-time/adjunct (both women). *Students:* 52 full-time (48 women), 10 part-time (all women); includes 7 minority (6 African Americans, 1 American Indian/Alaska Native). Average age 23. 122 applicants, 38% accepted, 27 enrolled. In 2009, 23 degrees awarded. *Degree requirements:* For master's, comprehensive exam, thesis optional. *Entrance requirements:* For master's, MAT or GRE, minimum GPA of 3.0. Additional exam requirements/recommendations for international students: Required—TOEFL, English grammar and articulation departmental exam. *Application deadline:* For fall and spring admission, 2/1 for domestic and international students. Applications are processed on a rolling basis. Application fee: $50 ($60 for international students). Electronic applications accepted. *Expenses:* Tuition, state resident: full-time $7000. Tuition, nonresident: full-time $19,200. *Financial support:* In 2009–10, 12 students received support, including 3 fellowships with full tuition reimbursements available (averaging $15,000 per year), 10 research assistantships (averaging $7,000 per year); career-related internships or fieldwork, Federal Work-Study, scholarships/grants, traineeships, health care benefits, and unspecified assistantships also available. Financial award application deadline: 2/10. *Faculty research:* Aphasia, cochlear implants, autism, voice, balance, multicultural, administrative. Total annual research expenditures: $336,426. *Unit head:* Dr. Karen F. Steckol, Professor, Chair and Clinic Director, 205-348-7131, Fax: 205-348-1845, E-mail: ksteckol@bama.ua.edu. *Application contact:* Mary Durrett, Secretary, 205-348-7131, Fax: 205-348-1845, E-mail: mdurrett@cd.as.ua.edu.

University of Alberta, Faculty of Graduate Studies and Research, Department of Speech Pathology and Audiology, Edmonton, AB T6G 2E1, Canada. Offers speech pathology and audiology (PhD); speech-language pathology (M Sc). *Faculty:* 7 full-time (5 women), 2 part-time/adjunct (both women). *Students:* 61 full-time (59 women), 17 part-time (all women). Average age 26. 175 applicants, 21% accepted. In 2009, 36 master's awarded. *Degree requirements:* For master's, thesis (for some programs), clinical practicum (MSLP). *Entrance requirements:* For master's, GRE, minimum GPA of 6.5 on a 9.0 scale. Additional exam requirements/recommendations for international students: Required—TOEFL. *Application deadline:* For fall admission, 2/15 for domestic students. Application fee: $60. Tuition and fees charges are reported in Canadian dollars. *Expenses:* Tuition, area resident: Full-time $4626 Canadian dollars; part-time $99.72 Canadian dollars per unit. International tuition: $8216 Canadian dollars full-time. Required fees: $3590 Canadian dollars; $99.72 Canadian dollars per unit. $215 Canadian dollars per term. *Financial support:* Research assistantships, teaching assistantships, career-related internships or fieldwork, institutionally sponsored loans, and scholarships/grants also available. *Faculty research:* Clinical education, hearing conservation, motor speech disorders, child language, voice resonance. *Unit head:* Dr. Karen Pollock, Chair, 780-492-0840, Fax: 403-492-9333, E-mail: karen.pollock@ualberta.ca. *Application contact:* Anita Moore, Administrative Assistant, 403-492-0840, Fax: 403-492-9333, E-mail: mscslp.info@rehabmed.ualberta.ca.

The University of Arizona, Graduate College, College of Science, Department of Speech, Language, and Hearing Sciences, Tucson, AZ 85721. Offers MS, Au D, PhD. *Accreditation:* ASHA (one or more programs are accredited). *Faculty:* 11. *Students:* 72 full-time (66 women), 11 part-time (7 women); includes 13 minority (1 American Indian/Alaska Native, 4 Asian Americans or Pacific Islanders, 8 Hispanic Americans), 4 international. Average age 33. 205 applicants, 17% accepted, 27 enrolled. In 2009, 19 master's, 2 doctorates awarded. *Degree requirements:* For master's, thesis optional; for doctorate, thesis/dissertation. *Entrance requirements:* For master's, GRE General Test, 3 letters of recommendation; for doctorate, GRE General Test, 3 letters of recommendation, personal statement, writing sample. Additional exam requirements/recommendations for international students: Required—TOEFL (minimum score 550 paper-based; 213 computer-based; 79 iBT). *Application deadline:* Applications are processed on a rolling basis. Application fee: $75. Electronic applications accepted. *Expenses:* Tuition, state resident: full-time $9028. Tuition, nonresident: full-time $24,890. *Financial support:* In 2009–10, 8 research assistantships with full tuition reimbursements (averaging $14,229 per year), 12 teaching assistantships with full tuition reimbursements (averaging $11,729 per year) were awarded; career-related internships or fieldwork, Federal Work-Study, institutionally sponsored loans, scholarships/grants, health care benefits, tuition waivers (full and partial), and unspecified assistantships also available. Financial award application deadline: 2/1. *Faculty research:* Alzheimer's disease, speech motor control, auditory-evoked potentials, analyzing pathological speech. Total annual research expenditures: $1.8 million. *Unit head:* Dr. Elena Plante, Head, 520-621-1644, Fax: 520-621-9901, E-mail: eplante@email.arizona.edu. *Application contact:* Pamela Adams, Information Contact, 520-621-1644, Fax: 520-621-9901, E-mail: adamsp@email.arizona.edu.

University of Arkansas, Graduate School, College of Education and Health Professions, Department of Rehabilitation, Human Resources and Communication Disorders, Program in Communication Disorders, Fayetteville, AR 72701-1201. Offers MS. *Accreditation:* ASHA. Part-time programs available. *Students:* 38 full-time (37 women); includes 3 minority (1 African American, 2 Hispanic Americans), 1 international. In 2009, 18 master's awarded. *Degree requirements:* For master's, thesis optional, 8 week externship. *Entrance requirements:* For master's, GRE General Test. Application fee: $40 ($50 for international students). *Expenses:* Tuition, state resident: full-time $7355; part-time $356.58 per hour. Tuition, nonresident: full-time $17,401; part-time $775.17 per hour. Required fees: $1203. *Financial support:* In 2009–10, 5 research assistantships were awarded; fellowships, teaching assistantships, career-related internships or fieldwork and Federal Work-Study also available. Support available to part-time students. Financial award application deadline: 4/1; financial award applicants required to submit FAFSA. *Unit head:* Dr. Fran Hagstrom, Head, 479-575-4758, E-mail: fhagstr@uark.edu. *Application contact:* Dr. Brent Williams, Program Coordinator, 479-575-4758, E-mail: btwilli@uark.edu.

University of Arkansas for Medical Sciences, Graduate School, Program in Communicative Disorders, Little Rock, AR 72205-7199. Offers MS, PhD. Part-time programs available. *Faculty:* 15 full-time (11 women). *Students:* 40 full-time, 5 part-time. In 2009, 19 master's, 1 doctorate awarded. *Degree requirements:* For master's, thesis or alternative. *Entrance requirements:* For master's, GRE General Test. Additional exam requirements/recommendations for international students: Required—TOEFL. *Application deadline:* For fall admission, 2/15 for domestic and international students. Application fee: $0. *Financial support:* Research assistantships available. Support available to part-time students. *Unit head:* Dr. Thomas Guyette, Chair, 501-569-3155. *Application contact:* Terri Hutton, Program Director, 501-569-3155, E-mail: huttonterrij@uams.edu.

The University of British Columbia, Faculty of Medicine, School of Audiology and Speech Sciences, Vancouver, BC V6T 1Z3, Canada. Offers M Sc, PhD. *Accreditation:* ASHA. *Degree requirements:* For master's, thesis or alternative, externship; for doctorate, comprehensive exam, thesis/dissertation. *Entrance requirements:* Additional exam requirements/recommendations for international students: Required—TOEFL (minimum score 600 paper-

Communication Disorders

The University of British Columbia (continued)
based; 250 computer-based; 100 iBT), IELTS (minimum score 7). Electronic applications accepted. *Faculty research:* Language development, experimental phonetics, linguistic aphasiology, amplification, auditory physiology.

University of California, San Diego, Office of Graduate Studies, Interdisciplinary Program in Language and Communicative Disorders, La Jolla, CA 92093. Offers PhD. *Accreditation:* ASHA. Electronic applications accepted.

University of California, San Diego, School of Medicine, Program in Audiology, La Jolla, CA 92093. Offers Au D.

University of Central Arkansas, Graduate School, College of Health and Behavioral Sciences, Department of Speech-Language Pathology, Conway, AR 72035-0001. Offers communication sciences and disorders (PhD); speech-language pathology (MS). *Accreditation:* ASHA (one or more programs are accredited). *Faculty:* 8 full-time (5 women), 3 part-time/adjunct (2 women). *Students:* 96 full-time (94 women), 7 part-time (all women); includes 7 minority (6 African Americans, 1 Asian American or Pacific Islander). Average age 24. 27 applicants, 93% accepted, 22 enrolled. In 2009, 49 master's awarded. *Degree requirements:* For master's, comprehensive exam, thesis optional, portfolio, internship. *Entrance requirements:* For master's, GRE General Test, NTE, minimum GPA of 2.7. Additional exam requirements/recommendations for international students: Required—TOEFL (minimum score 550 paper-based; 213 computer-based). *Application deadline:* For fall admission, 3/1 priority date for domestic students; for spring admission, 10/1 for domestic students. Applications are processed on a rolling basis. Application fee: $25 ($50 for international students). *Expenses:* Contact institution. *Financial support:* In 2009–10, 3 research assistantships with full and partial tuition reimbursements (averaging $4,000 per year), 3 teaching assistantships (averaging $3,000 per year) were awarded; career-related internships or fieldwork, Federal Work-Study, scholarships/grants, traineeships, and unspecified assistantships also available. Financial award application deadline: 2/15; financial award applicants required to submit FAFSA. *Unit head:* Dr. John Lowe, Chairperson, 501-450-3176, Fax: 501-450-5474, E-mail: jlowe@uca.edu. *Application contact:* Sharon Ross, Graduate Advisor, 501-450-5489, Fax: 501-450-5474, E-mail: sharonr@uca.edu.

University of Central Florida, College of Education, Education PhD Program, Orlando, FL 32816. Offers communication sciences and disorders (PhD); counselor education (PhD); elementary education (PhD); exceptional education (PhD); higher education (PhD); hospitality education (PhD); instructional technology (PhD); mathematics education (PhD); science education (PhD); social science education (PhD). *Students:* 99 full-time (70 women), 14 part-time (9 women); includes 28 minority (17 African Americans, 2 Asian Americans or Pacific Islanders, 9 Hispanic Americans), 20 international. In 2009, 15 doctorates awarded. Application fee: $30. Electronic applications accepted. *Expenses:* Tuition, state resident: part-time $306.31 per credit hour. Tuition, nonresident: part-time $1099.01 per credit hour. Part-time tuition and fees vary according to degree level and program. *Financial support:* In 2009–10, 40 fellowships with partial tuition reimbursements (averaging $9,200 per year), 61 research assistantships with partial tuition reimbursements (averaging $7,800 per year), 18 teaching assistantships with partial tuition reimbursements (averaging $6,500 per year) were awarded. *Unit head:* Dr. B. Grant Hayes, Associate Dean, 407-823-5391, E-mail: ghayes@mail.ucf.edu. *Application contact:* Dr. B. Grant Hayes, Associate Dean, 407-823-5391, E-mail: ghayes@mail.ucf.edu.

University of Central Florida, College of Health and Public Affairs, Department of Communication Sciences and Disorders, Orlando, FL 32816. Offers child language disorders (Certificate); communication sciences and disorders (MA); medical speech-language pathology (Certificate). *Accreditation:* ASHA (one or more programs are accredited). Part-time and evening/weekend programs available. *Faculty:* 23 full-time (15 women), 20 part-time/adjunct (16 women). *Students:* 179 full-time (175 women), 29 part-time (26 women); includes 51 minority (14 African Americans, 8 Asian Americans or Pacific Islanders, 29 Hispanic Americans), 2 international. Average age 26. 134 applicants, 62% accepted, 26 enrolled. In 2009, 68 master's awarded. *Degree requirements:* For master's, thesis or alternative, NESPH exam or comprehensive exam. *Entrance requirements:* For master's, GRE General Test, minimum GPA of 3.0 in last 60 hours. Additional exam requirements/recommendations for international students: Required—TOEFL. *Application deadline:* For fall admission, 4/1 for domestic students; for spring admission, 11/1 for domestic students. Electronic applications accepted. *Expenses:* Tuition, state resident: part-time $306.31 per credit hour. Tuition, nonresident: part-time $1099.01 per credit hour. Part-time tuition and fees vary according to degree level and program. *Financial support:* In 2009–10, 23 students received support, including 19 fellowships with partial tuition reimbursements available (averaging $6,700 per year), 2 research assistantships with partial tuition reimbursements available (averaging $8,000 per year), 3 teaching assistantships with partial tuition reimbursements available (averaging $6,400 per year); career-related internships or fieldwork, Federal Work-Study, institutionally sponsored loans, and unspecified assistantships also available. Financial award application deadline: 3/1; financial award applicants required to submit FAFSA. *Unit head:* Dr. R. Jane Lieberman, Chair, 407-249-4798, E-mail: jlieberm@mail.ucf.edu. *Application contact:* Dr. R. Jane Lieberman, Chair, 407-249-4798, E-mail: jlieberm@mail.ucf.edu.

University of Central Missouri, The Graduate School, College of Health and Human Services, Warrensburg, MO 64093. Offers criminal justice (MS); industrial hygiene (MS); occupational safety management (MS); physical education/exercise and sport science (MS); rural family nursing (MS); social gerontology (MS); sociology (MA); speech language pathology and audiology (MS). *Accreditation:* NCATE. Part-time programs available. Postbaccalaureate distance learning degree programs offered. *Faculty:* 53. *Students:* 169 full-time (107 women), 364 part-time (210 women); includes 65 minority (46 African Americans, 1 American Indian/Alaska Native, 5 Asian Americans or Pacific Islanders, 13 Hispanic Americans), 27 international. Average age 32. 236 applicants, 92% accepted, 211 enrolled. In 2009, 153 master's awarded. *Entrance requirements:* Additional exam requirements/recommendations for international students: Required—TOEFL (minimum score 550 paper-based; 79 computer-based). *Application deadline:* For fall admission, 6/1 priority date for domestic students, 5/1 for international students; for spring admission, 10/1 priority date for domestic students, 10/1 for international students. Applications are processed on a rolling basis. Application fee: $30 ($75 for international students). Electronic applications accepted. *Expenses:* Tuition, area resident: Part-time $245.80 per credit hour. Tuition, nonresident: part-time $491.60 per credit hour. Required fees: $24.20 per credit hour. Full-time tuition and fees vary according to course load, degree level, campus/location and reciprocity agreements. *Financial support:* Research assistantships with full and partial tuition reimbursements, teaching assistantships with full and partial tuition reimbursements, career-related internships or fieldwork, Federal Work-Study, scholarships/grants, and administrative and laboratory assistantships available. Support available to part-time students. Financial award application deadline: 3/1; financial award applicants required to submit FAFSA. *Unit head:* Dr. Rick Sluder, Dean, 660-543-4245, Fax: 660-543-4167, E-mail: sluder@ucmo.edu. *Application contact:* Laurie Delap, Admissions Coordinator, 660-543-4621, Fax: 660-543-4778, E-mail: gradinfo@ucmo.edu.

University of Central Oklahoma, College of Graduate Studies and Research, College of Education, Department of Special Services, Program in Speech-Language Pathology, Edmond, OK 73034-5209. Offers M Ed. *Accreditation:* ASHA. Part-time programs available. *Faculty:* 3 full-time (1 woman), 3 part-time/adjunct (2 women). *Students:* 36 full-time (35 women), 13 part-time (all women); includes 4 minority (1 African American, 1 Asian American or Pacific Islander, 2 Hispanic Americans). Average age 26. 19 applicants, 100% accepted. In 2009, 22 master's awarded. *Entrance requirements:* For master's, GRE General Test. Additional exam requirements/recommendations for international students: Required—TOEFL (minimum score 550 paper-based; 213 computer-based). *Application deadline:* For fall admission, 7/1 for international students; for spring admission, 11/1 for international students. Applications are processed on a rolling basis. Application fee: $25. Electronic applications accepted. *Expenses:* Tuition, state resident: full-time $4128; part-time $172 per credit hour. Tuition, nonresident: full-time $10,373; part-time $432.20 per credit hour. Required fees: $433.20; $18.05 per credit

hour. *Financial support:* Unspecified assistantships available. Financial award application deadline: 3/31; financial award applicants required to submit FAFSA. *Unit head:* Dr. Barbara Green, Director, 405-974-5283, Fax: 405-974-3822, E-mail: smclaughlin@uco.edu. *Application contact:* Dr. Richard Bernard, Dean, Graduate College, 405-974-3493, Fax: 405-974-3852, E-mail: gradcoll@uco.edu.

University of Cincinnati, Graduate School, College of Allied Health Sciences, Department of Communication Sciences and Disorders, Cincinnati, OH 45221. Offers MA, Au D, PhD. *Accreditation:* ASHA (one or more programs are accredited). *Degree requirements:* For master's, thesis optional; for doctorate, comprehensive exam, thesis/dissertation. *Entrance requirements:* For master's and doctorate, GRE General Test, minimum GPA of 3.0. Additional exam requirements/recommendations for international students: Required—TOEFL (minimum score 600 paper-based; 250 computer-based). Electronic applications accepted. *Faculty research:* Neurogenic speech and language disorders, speech science, linguistics, swallowing disorders, speech-language pathology.

University of Cincinnati, Graduate School, College of Education, Criminal Justice, and Human Services, Division of Teacher Education, Cincinnati, OH 45221. Offers curriculum and instruction (M Ed, Ed D); deaf studies (Certificate); early childhood education (M Ed); middle childhood education (M Ed); postsecondary literacy instruction (Certificate); reading/literacy (M Ed, Ed D); secondary education (M Ed); special education (M Ed, Ed D); teaching English as a second language (M Ed, Ed D, Certificate); teaching science (MS). Part-time programs available. *Degree requirements:* For doctorate, thesis/dissertation. *Entrance requirements:* For master's, GRE General Test. Electronic applications accepted.

University of Colorado at Boulder, Graduate School, College of Arts and Sciences, Department of Speech, Language and Hearing Sciences, Boulder, CO 80309. Offers audiology (Au D, PhD); clinical research and practice in audiology (PhD); speech, language and hearing science (MA); speech-language pathology (MA, PhD); speech-language-hearing sciences (PhD). *Accreditation:* ASHA (one or more programs are accredited). *Faculty:* 10 full-time (8 women). *Students:* 104 full-time (88 women), 11 part-time (9 women); includes 10 minority (2 African Americans, 4 Asian Americans or Pacific Islanders, 4 Hispanic Americans), 2 international. Average age 29. 317 applicants, 15% accepted, 41 enrolled. In 2009, 30 master's, 4 doctorates awarded. Terminal master's awarded for partial completion of doctoral program. *Degree requirements:* For master's, comprehensive exam, thesis or alternative; for doctorate, one foreign language, thesis/dissertation. *Entrance requirements:* For master's, GRE General Test, minimum undergraduate GPA of 3.25; for doctorate, GRE General Test. *Application deadline:* For fall admission, 2/1 priority date for domestic students, 2/1 for international students. Applications are processed on a rolling basis. Application fee: $50 ($60 for international students). *Financial support:* In 2009–10, 49 fellowships (averaging $4,004 per year), 8 research assistantships (averaging $8,846 per year) were awarded; tuition waivers (full) also available. Financial award application deadline: 2/1. *Faculty research:* Speech-language pathology. Total annual research expenditures: $1.2 million.

University of Connecticut, Graduate School, College of Liberal Arts and Sciences, Department of Communication Sciences, Program in Audiology, Storrs, CT 06269. Offers Au D, PhD, Au D/PhD. *Accreditation:* ASHA. *Students:* 28 full-time (23 women), 2 part-time (both women), 1 international. Average age 26. 51 applicants, 22% accepted, 8 enrolled. In 2009, 8 doctorates awarded. *Degree requirements:* For doctorate, thesis/dissertation. *Entrance requirements:* For doctorate, GRE General Test. Additional exam requirements/recommendations for international students: Required—TOEFL (minimum score 550 paper-based; 213 computer-based). *Application deadline:* For fall admission, 2/1 priority date for domestic and international students; for spring admission, 11/1 for domestic and international students. Applications are processed on a rolling basis. Electronic applications accepted. *Expenses:* Tuition, state resident: full-time $4725; part-time $525 per credit. Tuition, nonresident: full-time $12,267; part-time $1363 per credit. Required fees: $346 per semester. Tuition and fees vary according to course load. *Financial support:* In 2009–10, 3 research assistantships, 2 teaching assistantships were awarded; Federal Work-Study, scholarships/grants, health care benefits, and unspecified assistantships also available. Financial award application deadline: 2/1. *Unit head:* Carl A. Coelho, Chair, 860-486-2628. *Application contact:* Sue Kiss, Administrative Assistant, 860-486-2628, Fax: 860-486-5422, E-mail: susan.kiss@uconn.edu.

University of Connecticut, Graduate School, College of Liberal Arts and Sciences, Department of Communication Sciences, Program in Speech-Language Pathology, Storrs, CT 06269. Offers MA, PhD. *Accreditation:* ASHA. *Faculty:* 10 full-time (3 women). *Students:* 54 full-time (49 women), 2 part-time (both women); includes 6 minority (2 African Americans, 1 Asian American or Pacific Islander, 3 Hispanic Americans), 2 international. Average age 26. 145 applicants, 19% accepted, 14 enrolled. In 2009, 21 master's, 2 doctorates awarded. Terminal master's awarded for partial completion of doctoral program. *Degree requirements:* For master's, comprehensive exam, thesis optional; for doctorate, thesis/dissertation. *Entrance requirements:* For master's and doctorate, GRE General Test. Additional exam requirements/recommendations for international students: Required—TOEFL (minimum score 550 paper-based; 213 computer-based). *Application deadline:* For fall admission, 2/1 priority date for domestic and international students; for spring admission, 11/1 for domestic students, 10/1 for international students. Applications are processed on a rolling basis. Application fee: $55. Electronic applications accepted. *Expenses:* Tuition, state resident: full-time $4725; part-time $525 per credit. Tuition, nonresident: full-time $12,267; part-time $1363 per credit. Required fees: $346 per semester. Tuition and fees vary according to course load. *Financial support:* In 2009–10, 5 research assistantships with full tuition reimbursements, 7 teaching assistantships with full tuition reimbursements were awarded; fellowships, Federal Work-Study, scholarships/grants, health care benefits, and unspecified assistantships also available. Financial award application deadline: 2/1; financial award applicants required to submit FAFSA. *Unit head:* Carl A. Coelho, Chair, 860-486-2628. *Application contact:* Sue Kiss, Administrative Assistant, 860-486-2628, Fax: 860-486-5422, E-mail: susan.kiss@uconn.edu.

University of Florida, Graduate School, College of Liberal Arts and Sciences, Department of Communication Sciences and Disorders, Gainesville, FL 32611. Offers MA, Au D, PhD. *Accreditation:* ASHA (one or more programs are accredited). *Degree requirements:* For master's, thesis optional; for doctorate, variable foreign language requirement, thesis/dissertation. *Entrance requirements:* For master's and doctorate, GRE General Test, minimum GPA of 3.0. Additional exam requirements/recommendations for international students: Required—TOEFL (minimum score 550 paper-based; 213 computer-based). Electronic applications accepted. *Faculty research:* Phonetic science, cochlear implant, dyslexia, auditory development, voice.

University of Florida, Graduate School, College of Public Health and Health Professions and College of Liberal Arts and Sciences, Program in Audiology, Gainesville, FL 32611. Offers Au D. *Accreditation:* ASHA. Postbaccalaureate distance learning degree programs offered. *Entrance requirements:* For doctorate, GRE General Test, minimum GPA of 3.0. Additional exam requirements/recommendations for international students: Required—TOEFL (minimum score 550 paper-based; 213 computer-based). Electronic applications accepted.

University of Georgia, Graduate School, College of Education, Department of Communication Sciences and Special Education, Athens, GA 30602. Offers communication science and disorders (M Ed, MA, PhD, Ed S); special education (M Ed, Ed D, PhD, Ed S). *Accreditation:* ASHA (one or more programs are accredited). *Faculty:* 13 full-time (7 women). *Students:* 77 full-time (72 women), 33 part-time (31 women); includes 20 minority (6 African Americans, 1 American Indian/Alaska Native, 9 Asian Americans or Pacific Islanders, 4 Hispanic Americans), 1 international. Average age 24. 190 applicants, 50% accepted, 42 enrolled. In 2009, 31 master's, 2 doctorates, 4 other advanced degrees awarded. Terminal master's awarded for partial completion of doctoral program. *Degree requirements:* For master's, comprehensive exam (for some programs), thesis (for some programs); for doctorate, thesis/dissertation. *Entrance requirements:* For master's, doctorate, and Ed S, GRE General Test. Additional exam requirements/recommendations for international students: Required—TOEFL. *Application deadline:* For fall admission, 7/1 priority date for domestic students; for spring admission, 11/15 for domestic students. Application fee: $50. Electronic applications accepted. *Expenses:*

Tuition, state resident: full-time $6000; part-time $250 per credit hour. Tuition, nonresident: full-time $20,904; part-time $871 per credit hour. Required fees: $730 per semester. *Financial support:* Fellowships, research assistantships, teaching assistantships, unspecified assistantships available. *Unit head:* Dr. Anne C. Bothe, Interim Head, 706-542-0436, Fax: 706-542-5348, E-mail: abothe@.uga.edu. *Application contact:* Dr. Rebecca S. Marshall, Graduate Coordinator, 706-542-0737, E-mail: rshisler@uga.edu.

University of Hawaii at Manoa, John A. Burns School of Medicine, Department of Communication Sciences and Disorders, Honolulu, HI 96822. Offers MS. *Accreditation:* ASHA. Part-time programs available. *Students:* 19 full-time (16 women), 1 (woman) part-time; includes 17 minority (all Asian Americans or Pacific Islanders). Average age 28. 46 applicants, 30% accepted, 11 enrolled. In 2009, 13 master's awarded. *Degree requirements:* For master's, thesis optional. *Entrance requirements:* For master's, GRE General Test, minimum GPA of 3.0. Additional exam requirements/recommendations for international students: Required—TOEFL (minimum score 580 paper-based; 237 computer-based; 92 iBT), IELTS (minimum score 5). *Application deadline:* For fall admission, 3/1 for domestic and international students; for spring admission, 9/1 for domestic and international students. Application fee: $60. *Expenses:* Tuition, state resident: full-time $8900; part-time $372 per credit. Tuition, nonresident: full-time $21,400; part-time $898 per credit. Required fees: $207 per semester. *Financial support:* In 2009–10, 6 fellowships (averaging $2,175 per year), 1 research assistantship (averaging $16,824 per year) were awarded; career-related internships or fieldwork, Federal Work-Study, institutionally sponsored loans, and tuition waivers (full and partial) also available. Support available to part-time students. *Faculty research:* Emerging language (child phonology and special populations), central auditory function, developmental phonology, processing in the aging. Total annual research expenditures: $750,000. *Application contact:* Dorothy Craven, Graduate Chair, 808-956-5483, Fax: 808-956-5482, E-mail: dorothy@hawaii.edu.

University of Houston, College of Liberal Arts and Social Sciences, Department of Communication Sciences and Disorders, Houston, TX 77204. Offers speech language pathology (MA). *Accreditation:* ASHA. Part-time programs available. *Faculty:* 5 full-time (4 women), 9 part-time/adjunct (all women). *Students:* 73 full-time (72 women); includes 21 minority (5 African Americans, 2 American Indian/Alaska Native, 7 Asian Americans or Pacific Islanders, 7 Hispanic Americans), 1 international. Average age 26. 145 applicants, 28% accepted, 38 enrolled. In 2009, 21 master's awarded. *Degree requirements:* For master's, comprehensive exam, thesis optional. *Entrance requirements:* For master's, GRE General Test, minimum GPA of 3.0 in last 60 hours. Additional exam requirements/recommendations for international students: Required—TOEFL (minimum score 550 paper-based; 79 computer-based; 79 iBT). *Application deadline:* For fall admission, 2/15 for domestic and international students. Applications are processed on a rolling basis. Application fee: $25 ($75 for international students). Electronic applications accepted. *Expenses:* Tuition, state resident: full-time $7676; part-time $320 per credit hour. Tuition, nonresident: full-time $14,324; part-time $597 per credit hour. Required fees: $3034. *Financial support:* Career-related internships or fieldwork, Federal Work-Study, institutionally sponsored loans, scholarships/grants, health care benefits, and unspecified assistantships available. Support available to part-time students. Financial award application deadline: 2/1. *Faculty research:* Stuttering, voice disorders, language disorders, phonological processing, cognition. *Unit head:* Lynn Maher, Chairperson, 713-743-2896, Fax: 713-743-2926, E-mail: lmmaher@uh.edu. *Application contact:* Dr. Margaret L. Blake, Associate Professor, 713-743-2894, Fax: 713-743-2926, E-mail: mtblake@uh.edu.

University of Illinois at Urbana–Champaign, Graduate College, College of Applied Health Sciences, Department of Speech and Hearing Science, Champaign, IL 61820. Offers audiology (Au D); speech and hearing science (MA, PhD). *Accreditation:* ASHA (one or more programs are accredited). *Faculty:* 16 full-time (9 women), 1 part-time/adjunct (0 women). *Students:* 78 full-time (69 women), 8 part-time (all women); includes 3 minority (1 African American, 1 Asian American or Pacific Islander, 1 Hispanic American), 10 international. 278 applicants, 9% accepted, 23 enrolled. In 2009, 21 master's, 9 doctorates awarded. *Entrance requirements:* For master's, GRE General Test, minimum GPA of 3.0. Additional exam requirements/recommendations for international students: Required—TOEFL (minimum score 550 paper-based; 213 computer-based; 79 iBT). *Application deadline:* Applications are processed on a rolling basis. Application fee: $60 ($75 for international students). Electronic applications accepted. *Financial support:* In 2009–10, 6 fellowships, 15 research assistantships, 18 teaching assistantships were awarded; tuition waivers (full and partial) also available. *Unit head:* Adrienne L. Perlman, Head, 217-244-2545, Fax: 217-244-2235, E-mail: aperlman@illinois.edu. *Application contact:* Patricia K. Hawkins, Office Support Associate, 217-244-2565, Fax: 217-244-2235, E-mail: phawkins@illinois.edu.

The University of Iowa, Graduate College, College of Liberal Arts and Sciences, Department of Communication Sciences and Disorders, Program in Professional Speech Pathology and Audiology, Iowa City, IA 52242-1316. Offers MA, Au D, Au D/PhD. *Accreditation:* ASHA. *Degree requirements:* For master's, thesis optional, exam; for doctorate, practicum. *Entrance requirements:* For master's and doctorate, GRE General Test, minimum GPA of 3.0. Additional exam requirements/recommendations for international students: Required—TOEFL (minimum score 550 paper-based; 213 computer-based; 81 iBT). Electronic applications accepted.

The University of Iowa, Graduate College, College of Liberal Arts and Sciences, Department of Communication Sciences and Disorders, Program in Speech and Hearing Science, Iowa City, IA 52242-1316. Offers PhD, Au D/PhD. *Degree requirements:* For doctorate, comprehensive exam, thesis/dissertation. *Entrance requirements:* For doctorate, GRE General Test, minimum GPA of 3.0. Additional exam requirements/recommendations for international students: Required—TOEFL (minimum score 600 paper-based; 250 computer-based; 100 iBT). Electronic applications accepted.

The University of Kansas, Graduate Studies, College of Liberal Arts and Sciences, Department of Speech-Language-Hearing: Sciences and Disorders, Lawrence, KS 66045. Offers audiology (PhD); speech-language pathology (MA, PhD). Offered jointly with the Department of Hearing and Speech at the Kansas City campus. *Accreditation:* ASHA. Part-time programs available. *Students:* 81 full-time (78 women), 9 part-time (6 women); includes 5 minority (1 African American, 2 Asian Americans or Pacific Islanders, 2 Hispanic Americans), 11 international. Average age 28. 130 applicants, 55% accepted, 31 enrolled. In 2009, 36 master's, 3 doctorates awarded. *Degree requirements:* For master's, comprehensive exam, thesis optional; for doctorate, comprehensive exam, thesis/dissertation. *Entrance requirements:* For master's and doctorate, GRE General Test, MAT, minimum GPA of 3.0. Additional exam requirements/recommendations for international students: Required—TOEFL. *Application deadline:* For fall admission, 1/15 for domestic and international students; for spring admission, 10/1 for domestic and international students. Application fee: $45 ($55 for international students). Electronic applications accepted. *Expenses:* Tuition, state resident: full-time $6492; part-time $270.50 per credit hour. Tuition, nonresident: full-time $15,510; part-time $646.25 per credit hour. Required fees: $847; $70.56 per credit hour. Tuition and fees vary according to course load and program. *Financial support:* Fellowships with full tuition reimbursements, research assistantships, teaching assistantships with full and partial tuition reimbursements, career-related internships or fieldwork, Federal Work-Study, institutionally sponsored loans, and unspecified assistantships available. Support available to part-time students. Financial award application deadline: 3/1; financial award applicants required to submit FAFSA. *Faculty research:* Reading disorders, language acquisition, auditory electrophysiology, genetics of language, phonological development. *Unit head:* Hugh W. Catts, Chair, 785-864-0630, Fax: 785-864-3974, E-mail: catts@ku.edu. *Application contact:* Wanda Lowe, Administrative Professional, 785-864-0634, E-mail: wlowe@ku.edu.

The University of Kansas, University of Kansas Medical Center, School of Allied Health, Intercampus Program in Communicative Disorders, Lawrence, KS 66045. Offers audiology (MA, Au D, PhD); speech-language pathology (MA, PhD). *Faculty:* 19 full-time, 15 part-time/adjunct. *Students:* 22 full-time (20 women), 10 part-time (9 women); includes 2 minority (1 African American, 1 Asian American or Pacific Islander), 1 international. Average age 26. 32 applicants, 50% accepted, 11 enrolled. In 2009, 9 doctorates awarded. Terminal master's awarded for partial completion of doctoral program. *Degree requirements:* For master's, thesis optional, formative and summative exams; for doctorate, comprehensive exam, thesis/dissertation. *Entrance requirements:* For master's, GRE, bachelor's degree. Additional exam requirements/recommendations for international students: Required—TOEFL. *Application deadline:* For fall admission, 1/15 for domestic and international students. Application fee: $60. *Expenses:* Tuition, state resident: full-time $6492; part-time $270.50 per credit hour. Tuition, nonresident: full-time $15,510; part-time $646.25 per credit hour. Required fees: $847; $70.56 per credit hour. Tuition and fees vary according to course load and program. *Financial support:* In 2009–10, 17 students received support, including 5 research assistantships with partial tuition reimbursements available, 6 teaching assistantships with partial tuition reimbursements available; institutionally sponsored loans, scholarships/grants, traineeships, and unspecified assistantships also available. Financial award application deadline: 1/15. *Faculty research:* Child language development, diagnosis and treatment of language disorders; newborn/pediatric hearing testing and treatment of hearing loss in children; voice disorders; auditory physiology and applied electrophysiology; diagnosis and treatment for adult speech and language disorders. Total annual research expenditures: $100,996. *Unit head:* Dr. John A. Ferraro, Chair, Hearing and Speech/Co-Director of the Intercampus Program, 913-588-5937, Fax: 913-588-5923, E-mail: jferraro@kumc.edu. *Application contact:* Diane Wright-Cook, Coordinator, 913-588-5937, Fax: 913-588-5923, E-mail: dswright@kumc.edu.

University of Kentucky, Graduate School, College of Health Sciences, Program in Communication Disorders, Lexington, KY 40506-0032. Offers MSCD. *Accreditation:* ASHA. *Degree requirements:* For master's, comprehensive exam. *Entrance requirements:* For master's, GRE General Test, minimum undergraduate GPA of 2.75. Additional exam requirements/recommendations for international students: Required—TOEFL (minimum score 550 paper-based; 213 computer-based). Electronic applications accepted. *Faculty research:* Swallowing disorders, infant speech development, child language intervention, augmentative communication.

University of Louisiana at Lafayette, College of Liberal Arts, Department of Communicative Disorders, Lafayette, LA 70504. Offers MS, PhD. *Accreditation:* ASHA (one or more programs are accredited). *Degree requirements:* For master's, thesis or alternative. *Entrance requirements:* For master's, GRE General Test, minimum GPA of 2.75. Additional exam requirements/recommendations for international students: Required—TOEFL (minimum score 550 paper-based; 213 computer-based).

University of Louisiana at Monroe, Graduate School, College of Health Sciences, Department of Speech-Language Pathology, Monroe, LA 71209-0001. Offers speech-language pathology (MS). *Accreditation:* ASHA. *Faculty:* 4 full-time (all women), 3 part-time/adjunct (all women). *Students:* 22 full-time (all women), 10 part-time (9 women); includes 5 minority (1 African American, 1 American Indian/Alaska Native, 3 Asian Americans or Pacific Islanders). Average age 27. In 2009, 15 master's awarded. *Degree requirements:* For master's, thesis. *Entrance requirements:* For master's, GRE, minimum GPA of 2.5. Additional exam requirements/recommendations for international students: Required—TOEFL (minimum score 500 paper-based; 173 computer-based; 61 iBT). *Application deadline:* For fall admission, 8/24 priority date for domestic students, 7/1 for international students; for winter admission, 12/14 priority date for domestic students; for spring admission, 1/19 for domestic students, 11/1 for international students. Applications are processed on a rolling basis. Application fee: $20 ($30 for international students). Electronic applications accepted. *Expenses:* Tuition, state resident: part-time $159 per credit hour. Tuition, nonresident: part-time $159 per credit hour. Required fees: $1300 per year. Tuition and fees vary according to course load. *Financial support:* In 2009–10, 7 research assistantships with full tuition reimbursements (averaging $2,500 per year) were awarded; career-related internships or fieldwork, Federal Work-Study, and unspecified assistantships also available. Financial award application deadline: 4/1; financial award applicants required to submit FAFSA. *Faculty research:* Child language, stuttering, multicultural issues, ethics. *Unit head:* Dr. Johanna Rose Boult, Department Head, 318-342-1390, Fax: 318-342-1687, E-mail: boult@ulm.edu. *Application contact:* Dr. Johanna Rose Boult, Department Head, 318-342-1390, Fax: 318-342-1687, E-mail: boult@ulm.edu.

University of Louisville, School of Medicine, Department of Surgery, Louisville, KY 40292-0001. Offers audiology (Au D); communicative disorders (MS). *Students:* 88 full-time (73 women), 3 part-time (all women); includes 1 minority (African American). Average age 26. 145 applicants, 59% accepted, 34 enrolled. In 2009, 18 master's, 8 doctorates awarded. Application fee: $50. *Unit head:* Dr. Edward C. Halperin, Dean, 502-852-1499, Fax: 502-852-1484, E-mail: edward.halperin@louisville.edu. *Application contact:* Director of Admissions, 502-852-5793, Fax: 502-852-6849.

University of Maine, Graduate School, College of Liberal Arts and Sciences, Department of Communication Sciences and Disorders, Orono, ME 04469. Offers MA. *Accreditation:* ASHA. *Faculty:* 6 full-time (5 women), 5 part-time/adjunct (4 women). *Students:* 21 full-time (5 women), 4 part-time (2 women), 4 international. Average age 28. 55 applicants, 47% accepted, 21 enrolled. In 2009, 10 master's awarded. *Entrance requirements:* For master's, GRE General Test. Additional exam requirements/recommendations for international students: Required—TOEFL. *Application deadline:* For fall admission, 2/1 priority date for domestic students. Applications are processed on a rolling basis. Application fee: $65. Electronic applications accepted. *Financial support:* In 2009–10, 2 teaching assistantships with tuition reimbursements (averaging $12,790 per year) were awarded; career-related internships or fieldwork, Federal Work-Study, institutionally sponsored loans, and tuition waivers (full and partial) also available. Support available to part-time students. Financial award application deadline: 3/1. *Faculty research:* Interpersonal communication between supervisor and supervised, clinicians and clients; language and voice impairments; children's pragmatics. *Unit head:* Dr. Judy Walker, Chair, 207-581-2006, Fax: 207-581-1953. *Application contact:* Scott G. Delcourt, Associate Dean of the Graduate School, 207-581-3291, Fax: 207-581-3232, E-mail: graduate@maine.edu.

University of Maryland, College Park, Academic Affairs, College of Behavioral and Social Sciences, Department of Hearing and Speech Sciences, College Park, MD 20742. Offers audiology (MA, PhD); hearing and speech sciences (Au D); language pathology (MA, PhD); neuroscience (PhD); speech (MA, PhD). *Accreditation:* ASHA (one or more programs are accredited). *Faculty:* 19 full-time (18 women), 13 part-time/adjunct (11 women). *Students:* 82 full-time (76 women), 18 part-time (all women); includes 20 minority (9 African Americans, 8 Asian Americans or Pacific Islanders, 3 Hispanic Americans), 2 international. 260 applicants, 46% accepted, 36 enrolled. In 2009, 23 master's, 11 doctorates awarded. *Degree requirements:* For master's, thesis optional; for doctorate, thesis/dissertation, written and oral exams. *Entrance requirements:* For master's, GRE General Test, minimum GPA of 3.5, 3 letters of recommendation; for doctorate, GRE General Test, minimum GPA of 3.5. Additional exam requirements/recommendations for international students: Required—TOEFL. *Application deadline:* For fall admission, 1/15 for domestic and international students. Applications are processed on a rolling basis. Application fee: $60. Electronic applications accepted. *Expenses:* Tuition, area resident: Part-time $471 per credit hour. Tuition, state resident: part-time $471 per credit hour. Tuition, nonresident: part-time $1016 per credit hour. Required fees: $337.04 per term. *Financial support:* In 2009–10, 3 fellowships with partial tuition reimbursements (averaging $10,848 per year), 2 research assistantships (averaging $15,614 per year), 34 teaching assistantships with tuition reimbursements (averaging $15,709 per year) were awarded; career-related internships or fieldwork, Federal Work-Study, scholarships/grants, and health care benefits also available. Support available to part-time students. Financial award applicants required to submit FAFSA. *Faculty research:* Speech perception, language acquisition, bilingualism, hearing loss. Total annual research expenditures: $491,296. *Unit head:* Dr. Nan B. Bernstein-Ratner, Chair, 301-405-4217, Fax: 301-314-2023, E-mail: nratner@umd.edu. *Application contact:* Dean of Graduate School, 301-405-0358, Fax: 301-314-9305.

University of Massachusetts Amherst, Graduate School, School of Public Health and Health Sciences, Department of Communication Disorders, Amherst, MA 01003. Offers MA, Au D, PhD. *Accreditation:* ASHA (one or more programs are accredited). Part-time programs available. *Faculty:* 14 full-time (12 women). *Students:* 74 full-time (71 women), 12 part-time (11

Communication Disorders

University of Massachusetts Amherst (continued)
women); includes 7 minority (3 African Americans, 1 Asian American or Pacific Islander, 3 Hispanic Americans), 1 international. Average age 28. 278 applicants, 36% accepted, 36 enrolled. In 2009, 24 master's, 2 doctorates awarded. Terminal master's awarded for partial completion of doctoral program. *Degree requirements:* For master's, thesis optional; for doctorate, comprehensive exam, thesis/dissertation. *Entrance requirements:* For master's and doctorate, GRE General Test. Additional exam requirements/recommendations for international students: Required—TOEFL (minimum score 550 paper-based; 213 computer-based; 80 iBT), IELTS (minimum score 6.5). *Application deadline:* For fall admission, 2/1 for domestic and international students; for spring admission, 10/1 for domestic and international students. Applications are processed on a rolling basis. Application fee: $50 ($65 for international students). Electronic applications accepted. *Expenses:* Tuition, state resident: full-time $2640; part-time $110 per credit. Tuition, nonresident: full-time $9936; part-time $414 per credit. Tuition and fees vary according to course load. *Financial support:* In 2009–10, 10 research assistantships with full tuition reimbursements (averaging $7,354 per year), 9 teaching assistantships with full tuition reimbursements (averaging $6,381 per year) were awarded; fellowships, career-related internships or fieldwork, Federal Work-Study, scholarships/grants, traineeships, health care benefits, tuition waivers (full), and unspecified assistantships also available. Support available to part-time students. Financial award application deadline: 2/1. *Unit head:* Dr. Karen S. Helfer, Graduate Program Director, 413-545-0131, Fax: 413-545-0803. *Application contact:* Jean M. Ames, Supervisor of Admissions, 413-545-0722, Fax: 413-577-0010, E-mail: gradadm@grad.umass.edu.

University of Memphis, Graduate School, School of Audiology and Speech-Language Pathology, Memphis, TN 38152. Offers MA, Au D, PhD. *Accreditation:* ASHA. Part-time programs available. *Faculty:* 14 full-time (6 women), 1 (woman) part-time/adjunct. *Students:* 76 full-time (71 women), 11 part-time (all women); includes 5 minority (2 African Americans, 3 Asian Americans or Pacific Islanders), 3 international. Average age 26. 203 applicants, 37% accepted, 37 enrolled. In 2009, 22 master's, 2 doctorates awarded. Terminal master's awarded for partial completion of doctoral program. *Degree requirements:* For master's, comprehensive exam, thesis or alternative; for doctorate, thesis/dissertation, qualifying exam. *Entrance requirements:* For master's, GRE General Test or MAT, minimum GPA of 3.0, ASHA certification; for doctorate, GRE General Test, minimum GPA of 3.5, letters of recommendation. *Application deadline:* For fall admission, 2/1 for domestic students. Application fee: $35 ($60 for international students). *Expenses:* Tuition, state resident: full-time $6246; part-time $347 per credit hour. Tuition, nonresident: full-time $15,894; part-time $883 per credit hour. Required fees: $1160. Full-time tuition and fees vary according to course load, degree level and program. *Financial support:* In 2009–10, 64 students received support; research assistantships with full tuition reimbursements available, Federal Work-Study, scholarships/grants, and unspecified assistantships available. Financial award application deadline: 2/15; financial award applicants required to submit FAFSA. *Faculty research:* Hearing aid characteristic selection, language acquisition, speech disorders, characteristics of the aging voice, hearing science. Total annual research expenditures: $1.5 million. *Unit head:* Dr. Maurice Mendel, Dean, 901-678-5800, Fax: 901-525-1282, E-mail: dlluna@memphis.edu. *Application contact:* Dr. David J. Wark, Coordinator of Graduate Studies, 901-678-5891, E-mail: dwark@memphis.edu.

University of Minnesota, Duluth, Graduate School, College of Education and Human Service Professions, Department of Communication Sciences and Disorders, Duluth, MN 55812-2496. Offers MA. *Accreditation:* ASHA. Part-time programs available. *Degree requirements:* For master's, research project, oral exam. *Entrance requirements:* For master's, minimum GPA of 3.0, undergraduate degree in communication sciences and disorders. Additional exam requirements/recommendations for international students: Required—TOEFL (minimum score 550 paper-based; 213 computer-based). *Faculty research:* Clinical supervision, augmentative communication, speech understanding, fluency, developmental apraxia of speech.

University of Minnesota, Twin Cities Campus, Graduate School, College of Liberal Arts, Department of Speech-Language-Hearing Sciences, Minneapolis, MN 55455. Offers audiology (Au D); speech-language pathology (MA); speech-language-hearing sciences (PhD). *Accreditation:* ASHA (one or more programs are accredited). Terminal master's awarded for partial completion of doctoral program. *Degree requirements:* For master's, thesis, 375 client contact hours; for doctorate, comprehensive exam, thesis/dissertation. *Entrance requirements:* For master's and doctorate, GRE General Test, minimum GPA of 3.0. Additional exam requirements/recommendations for international students: Required—TOEFL. Electronic applications accepted. *Faculty research:* Normal and disordered child phonology, specific language impairment, bilingual and multicultural aspects of language, TBI, AAC.

University of Mississippi, Graduate School, School of Applied Sciences, Department of Communicative Disorders, Oxford, University, MS 38677. Offers MS. *Accreditation:* ASHA. *Faculty:* 8 full-time (7 women). *Students:* 55 full-time (48 women); includes 7 minority (all African Americans), 3 international. In 2009, 21 master's awarded. *Entrance requirements:* For master's, GRE General Test, minimum GPA of 3.0. Additional exam requirements/recommendations for international students: Required—TOEFL. *Application deadline:* For fall admission, 2/1 for domestic students; for spring admission, 10/1 for domestic students. Applications are processed on a rolling basis. Application fee: $25. Electronic applications accepted. *Financial support:* Scholarships/grants available. Financial award application deadline: 3/1; financial award applicants required to submit FAFSA. *Unit head:* Dr. Carolyn Wiles Higdon, Chair, 662-915-7652, Fax: 662-915-5717, E-mail: chigdon@olemiss.edu. *Application contact:* Dr. Christy M. Wyandt, Associate Dean, 662-915-7474, Fax: 662-915-7577, E-mail: cwyandt@olemiss.edu.

University of Missouri, School of Health Professions, Program in Communication Science and Disorders, Columbia, MO 65211. Offers MHS. *Accreditation:* ASHA. *Entrance requirements:* For master's, GRE General Test, minimum GPA of 3.0. Additional exam requirements/recommendations for international students: Required—TOEFL (minimum score 600 paper-based; 250 computer-based; 100 iBT).

University of Montevallo, College of Arts and Sciences, Department of Communication Science and Disorders, Montevallo, AL 35115. Offers speech-language pathology (MS). *Accreditation:* ASHA. *Students:* 39 full-time (38 women); includes 4 minority (1 African American, 2 Asian Americans or Pacific Islanders, 1 Hispanic American). In 2009, 13 master's awarded. *Degree requirements:* For master's, comprehensive exam. *Entrance requirements:* For master's, GRE General Test, MAT. Additional exam requirements/recommendations for international students: Required—TOEFL (minimum score 550 paper-based). *Application deadline:* For fall admission, 7/15 for domestic students; for spring admission, 11/15 for domestic students. Application fee: $25. *Expenses:* Tuition, state resident: full-time $5592; part-time $233 per credit. Tuition, nonresident: full-time $11,184; part-time $466 per credit hour. Required fees: $482; $241 per semester. One-time fee: $25 part-time. *Financial support:* Federal Work-Study, scholarships/grants, and unspecified assistantships available. *Unit head:* Dr. Marlene Salas-Provance, Chair, 205-665-6725, E-mail: provancem@montevallo.edu. *Application contact:* Dr. Margaret L. Johnson, Graduate Program Coordinator, 205-665-6717, E-mail: johnsonm@montevallo.edu.

University of Nebraska at Kearney, College of Graduate Study, College of Education, Department of Communication Disorders, Kearney, NE 68849-0001. Offers speech pathology (MS Ed). *Accreditation:* ASHA. Part-time programs available. *Entrance requirements:* For master's, GRE General Test. Electronic applications accepted. *Faculty research:* Neurogenic, communication disorders in adults, phonological development and disorders, orofacial anomalies, audiologic rehabilitation of the elderly.

University of Nebraska at Omaha, Graduate Studies, College of Education, Department of Special Education and Communication Disorders, Omaha, NE 68182. Offers special education (MS); speech-language pathology (MA, MS). *Accreditation:* ASHA (one or more programs are accredited); NCATE. Part-time and evening/weekend programs available. *Faculty:* 10 full-time (6 women). *Students:* 34 full-time (32 women), 64 part-time (52 women); includes 5 minority (1 African American, 2 American Indian/Alaska Native, 1 Asian American or Pacific Islander, 1 Hispanic American), 1 international. Average age 30. 101 applicants, 49% accepted, 17 enrolled. In 2009, 26 master's awarded. *Degree requirements:* For master's, comprehensive exam, thesis (for some programs). *Entrance requirements:* For master's, GRE General Test or MAT, minimum GPA of 3.0. Additional exam requirements/recommendations for international students: Required—TOEFL (minimum score 500 paper-based; 173 computer-based; 61 iBT). *Application deadline:* For fall admission, 2/1 for domestic students; for spring admission, 9/1 for domestic students. Applications are processed on a rolling basis. Application fee: $45. Electronic applications accepted. *Financial support:* In 2009–10, 64 students received support; fellowships, research assistantships with tuition reimbursements available, career-related internships or fieldwork, Federal Work-Study, institutionally sponsored loans, scholarships/grants, tuition waivers (partial), and unspecified assistantships available. Support available to part-time students. Financial award application deadline: 3/1; financial award applicants required to submit FAFSA. *Unit head:* Dr. Mary Friehe, Chairperson, 402-554-2201. *Application contact:* Dr. Mary Friehe, Chairperson, 402-554-2201.

University of Nebraska–Lincoln, Graduate College, College of Education and Human Sciences, Department of Special Education and Communication Disorders, Program in Speech-Language Pathology and Audiology, Lincoln, NE 68588. Offers audiology and hearing science (Au D); speech-language pathology and audiology (MS). *Accreditation:* ASHA. *Degree requirements:* For master's, thesis optional. *Entrance requirements:* For master's, GRE. Additional exam requirements/recommendations for international students: Required—TOEFL (minimum score 500 paper-based; 173 computer-based). Electronic applications accepted.

University of Nevada, Reno, Graduate School, Division of Health Sciences, Department of Speech Pathology and Audiology, Reno, NV 89557. Offers speech pathology (PhD); speech pathology and audiology (MS). *Accreditation:* ASHA (one or more programs are accredited). Terminal master's awarded for partial completion of doctoral program. *Degree requirements:* For master's, thesis optional; for doctorate, thesis/dissertation. *Entrance requirements:* For master's, GRE General Test, minimum GPA of 2.75; for doctorate, GRE General Test, minimum GPA of 3.0. Additional exam requirements/recommendations for international students: Required—TOEFL (minimum score 500 paper-based; 173 computer-based; 61 iBT), IELTS (minimum score 6). Electronic applications accepted. *Faculty research:* Language impairment in children, voice disorders, stuttering.

University of New Hampshire, Graduate School, School of Health and Human Services, Department of Communication Sciences and Disorders, Durham, NH 03824. Offers communication sciences and disorders (Postbaccalaureate Certificate); early childhood intervention (MS); language and literature disabilities (MS). Program offered in fall only. *Accreditation:* ASHA (one or more programs are accredited). Part-time programs available. *Faculty:* 7 full-time (3 women). *Students:* 44 full-time (43 women), 1 (woman) part-time; includes 1 minority (Asian American or Pacific Islander), 1 international. Average age 28. 115 applicants, 30% accepted, 18 enrolled. In 2009, 25 master's awarded. *Degree requirements:* For master's, thesis or alternative. *Entrance requirements:* For master's, GRE General Test or MAT. Additional exam requirements/recommendations for international students: Required—TOEFL (minimum score 550 paper-based; 213 computer-based; 80 iBT). *Application deadline:* For fall admission, 1/15 priority date for domestic students, 4/1 for international students. Applications are processed on a rolling basis. Application fee: $65. Electronic applications accepted. *Expenses:* Tuition, state resident: full-time $10,380; part-time $577 per credit hour. Tuition, nonresident: full-time $24,350; part-time $1002 per credit hour. Required fees: $1550; $387.50 per semester. Tuition and fees vary according to course load and program. *Financial support:* In 2009–10, 20 students received support, including 6 teaching assistantships; fellowships, research assistantships, career-related internships or fieldwork, Federal Work-Study, scholarships/grants, and tuition waivers (full and partial) also available. Support available to part-time students. Financial award application deadline: 2/15. *Faculty research:* Speech pathology. *Unit head:* Dr. Stephen Calculator, Chairperson, 603-862-3836. *Application contact:* Maria Russell, Administrative Assistant, 603-862-0144, E-mail: communication.disorders@unh.edu.

University of New Mexico, Graduate School, College of Arts and Sciences, Department of Speech and Hearing Sciences, Albuquerque, NM 87131-2039. Offers speech-language pathology (MS). *Accreditation:* ASHA. *Faculty:* 7 full-time (6 women), 1 part-time/adjunct (0 women). *Students:* 31 full-time (30 women), 4 part-time (all women); includes 9 minority (1 American Indian/Alaska Native, 8 Hispanic Americans). Average age 32. 54 applicants, 24% accepted, 12 enrolled. In 2009, 16 master's awarded. *Degree requirements:* For master's, comprehensive exam, thesis optional. *Entrance requirements:* For master's, GRE General Test, minimum GPA of 3.2 during previous 2 years. Additional exam requirements/recommendations for international students: Required—TOEFL (minimum score 550 paper-based; 213 computer-based). *Application deadline:* For fall admission, 2/1 for domestic students, 1/1 for international students. Application fee: $50. Electronic applications accepted. *Expenses:* Tuition, state resident: full-time $2099; part-time $233.20 per credit hour. Tuition, nonresident: full-time $6650. Required fees: $25 per semester. Tuition and fees vary according to course load, program and reciprocity agreements. *Financial support:* In 2009–10, 8 research assistantships with partial tuition reimbursements (averaging $6,100 per year) were awarded; career-related internships or fieldwork, Federal Work-Study, scholarships/grants, health care benefits, and unspecified assistantships also available. Financial award application deadline: 2/15; financial award applicants required to submit FAFSA. *Faculty research:* AAC (Augmentative and Alternative Communication), behavioral genetic studies of language, child language assessment, cultural influences on language acquisition, speech perception, swallowing disorders, transition from oral language to literacy. Total annual research expenditures: $99,569. *Unit head:* Dr. Philip S. Dale, Chair, 505-277-5338, Fax: 505-277-0968, E-mail: dalep@unm.edu. *Application contact:* Maria C. Pearson, Administrative Assistant, 505-277-4454, Fax: 505-277-0968, E-mail: mpearson@unm.edu.

The University of North Carolina at Chapel Hill, School of Medicine and Graduate School, Graduate Programs in Medicine, Chapel Hill, NC 27599. Offers allied health sciences (MPT, MS, Au D, DPT, PhD), including human movement science (MS, PhD), occupational science (MS, PhD), physical therapy (MPT, MS, DPT), rehabilitation counseling and psychology (MS), speech and hearing sciences (MS, Au D, PhD); biochemistry and biophysics (MS, PhD); biomedical engineering (MS, PhD); cell and developmental biology (PhD); cell and molecular physiology (PhD); genetics and molecular biology (PhD); microbiology and immunology (MS, PhD), including immunology, microbiology; neurobiology (PhD); pathology and laboratory medicine (PhD), including experimental pathology; pharmacology (PhD); MD/PhD. Post-baccalaureate distance learning degree programs offered. Terminal master's awarded for partial completion of doctoral program. *Degree requirements:* For master's, comprehensive exam; for doctorate, thesis/dissertation. Electronic applications accepted. *Expenses:* Contact institution.

The University of North Carolina at Chapel Hill, School of Medicine and Graduate School, Graduate Programs in Medicine, Department of Allied Health Sciences, Division of Speech and Hearing Sciences, Chapel Hill, NC 27599. Offers audiology (Au D); speech and hearing sciences (MS, PhD). *Accreditation:* ASHA (one or more programs are accredited). Post-baccalaureate distance learning degree programs offered (no on-campus study). *Faculty:* 17 full-time (15 women), 11 part-time/adjunct (4 women). *Students:* 93 full-time (89 women), 1 (woman) part-time; includes 13 minority (6 African Americans, 3 Asian Americans or Pacific Islanders, 4 Hispanic Americans). Average age 27. 218 applicants, 29% accepted, 35 enrolled. In 2009, 25 master's, 4 doctorates awarded. *Degree requirements:* For master's, comprehensive exam, thesis optional; for doctorate, comprehensive exam, thesis/dissertation. *Entrance requirements:* For master's, GRE General Test, minimum GPA of 3.0; for doctorate, GRE, minimum GPA of 3.0. Additional exam requirements/recommendations for international students: Required—TOEFL (minimum score 550 paper-based; 79 computer-based). *Application deadline:* For fall admission, 1/1 for domestic and international students. Application fee: $75. Electronic applications accepted. *Financial support:* In 2009–10, 62 students received support, including 15 research assistantships with partial tuition reimbursements available (averaging $1,747 per year); fellowships with full tuition reimbursements available, teaching assistantships, career-

related internships or fieldwork, Federal Work-Study, scholarships/grants, traineeships, health care benefits, and unspecified assistantships also available. Financial award application deadline: 1/1. *Faculty research:* Child language and literacy, family participation in early intervention, child and adult hearing loss and treatment, vocal characteristics of African-American speakers and aging populations, adult apraxia of speech. Total annual research expenditures: $1.4 million. *Unit head:* Dr. Jackson Roush, Director, 919-966-9467, Fax: 919-966-0100, E-mail: jroush@med.unc.edu. *Application contact:* Ina Diana, Admission Assistant, 919-966-1007, Fax: 919-966-0100.

The University of North Carolina at Greensboro, Graduate School, School of Health and Human Performance, Department of Communication Sciences and Disorders, Greensboro, NC 27412-5001. Offers speech language pathology (PhD); speech pathology and audiology (MA). *Accreditation:* ASHA. *Degree requirements:* For master's, thesis or alternative. *Entrance requirements:* For master's, GRE General Test. Additional exam requirements/recommendations for international students: Required—TOEFL. Electronic applications accepted.

University of North Dakota, Graduate School, College of Arts and Sciences, Department of Communication Disorders and Speech-Language Pathology, Grand Forks, ND 58202. Offers communication sciences and disorders (PhD); speech-language pathology (MS). *Accreditation:* ASHA (one or more programs are accredited). Part-time programs available. *Degree requirements:* For master's, comprehensive exam, thesis or alternative; for doctorate, comprehensive exam, thesis/dissertation, final exam. *Entrance requirements:* For master's and doctorate, GRE General Test, minimum GPA of 3.0. Additional exam requirements/recommendations for international students: Required—TOEFL (minimum score 550 paper-based; 213 computer-based; 79 iBT), IELTS (minimum score 6.5). Electronic applications accepted. *Faculty research:* Mass communications, journalism, community law, international communications, cultural studies.

University of Northern Colorado, Graduate School, College of Natural and Health Sciences, School of Human Sciences, Program in Audiology and Speech Language Sciences, Greeley, CO 80639. Offers audiology (Au D); speech language pathology (MA). *Accreditation:* ASHA (one or more programs are accredited). Part-time and evening/weekend programs available. Postbaccalaureate distance learning degree programs offered (no on-campus study). *Faculty:* 9 full-time (8 women). *Students:* 62 full-time (59 women), 1 (woman) part-time; includes 3 minority (1 Asian American or Pacific Islander, 2 Hispanic Americans), 1 international. Average age 28. 295 applicants, 38% accepted, 25 enrolled. In 2009, 18 master's, 5 doctorates awarded. *Degree requirements:* For master's, comprehensive exam, thesis or alternative; for doctorate, comprehensive exam, thesis/dissertation. *Entrance requirements:* For master's and doctorate, GRE General Test. *Application deadline:* Applications are processed on a rolling basis. Application fee: $50 ($60 for international students). Electronic applications accepted. *Expenses:* Tuition, state resident: full-time $5770; part-time $320.55 per credit hour. Tuition, nonresident: full-time $13,847; part-time $769.27 per credit hour. Required fees: $948.78; $52.72 per credit. *Financial support:* In 2009–10, 4 research assistantships (averaging $5,525 per year) were awarded; fellowships, teaching assistantships, unspecified assistantships also available. Financial award application deadline: 3/1; financial award applicants required to submit FAFSA. *Unit head:* Dr. Katie Bright, Program Coordinator, 970-351-2734. *Application contact:* Linda Sisson, Graduate Student Admission Coordinator, 970-351-1807, Fax: 970-351-2371, E-mail: linda.sisson@unco.edu.

University of Northern Iowa, Graduate College, College of Humanities and Fine Arts, Department of Communicative Sciences and Disorders, Cedar Falls, IA 50614. Offers audiology (MA); speech pathology (MA). *Accreditation:* ASHA. Part-time and evening/weekend programs available. *Students:* 66 full-time (64 women); includes 6 minority (4 African Americans, 2 Hispanic Americans). 78 applicants, 56% accepted, 24 enrolled. In 2009, 23 master's awarded. *Degree requirements:* For master's, comprehensive exam, thesis or alternative. *Entrance requirements:* For master's, GRE, minimum GPA of 3.0. Additional exam requirements/recommendations for international students: Required—TOEFL (minimum score 500 paper-based; 180 computer-based; 61 iBT). *Application deadline:* For fall admission, 8/1 priority date for domestic students. Applications are processed on a rolling basis. Application fee: $30 ($50 for international students). *Financial support:* Career-related internships or fieldwork, Federal Work-Study, scholarships/grants, and tuition waivers (full and partial) available. Financial award application deadline: 2/1. *Unit head:* Dr. Carlin Hageman, Department Head/Professor, 319-273-2497, Fax: 319-273-6384, E-mail: carlin.hageman@uni.edu. *Application contact:* Laurie S. Russell, Record Analyst, 319-273-2623, Fax: 319-273-6792, E-mail: laurie.russell@uni.edu.

University of North Florida, College of Education and Human Services, Department of Exceptional Student and Deaf Education, Jacksonville, FL 32224. Offers American sign language/English interpreting (M Ed); applied behavior analysis (M Ed); deaf education (M Ed); disability services (M Ed); exceptional student education (M Ed). *Accreditation:* NCATE. Part-time and evening/weekend programs available. *Faculty:* 11 full-time (9 women). *Students:* 34 full-time (all women), 33 part-time (28 women); includes 8 minority (2 African Americans, 3 Asian Americans or Pacific Islanders, 3 Hispanic Americans). Average age 31. 23 applicants, 61% accepted, 8 enrolled. In 2009, 34 master's awarded. *Entrance requirements:* For master's, GRE General Test, minimum GPA of 3.0 in last 60 hours, interview, 3 letters of recommendation. Additional exam requirements/recommendations for international students: Required—TOEFL (minimum score 500 paper-based; 173 computer-based). *Application deadline:* For fall admission, 7/1 priority date for domestic students, 5/1 for international students; for spring admission, 11/1 priority date for domestic students, 10/1 for international students. Applications are processed on a rolling basis. Application fee: $30. Electronic applications accepted. *Expenses:* Tuition, state resident: full-time $6649.20; part-time $277.05 per credit hour. Tuition, nonresident: full-time $22,970; part-time $957.08 per credit hour. Required fees: $985; $41.03 per credit hour. *Financial support:* In 2009–10, 40 students received support; research assistantships, teaching assistantships, career-related internships or fieldwork, Federal Work-Study, and tuition waivers (partial) available. Support available to part-time students. Financial award application deadline: 4/1; financial award applicants required to submit FAFSA. *Faculty research:* Transition, integrating technology into teacher education, written language development, professional school development, learning strategies. Total annual research expenditures: $1 million. *Unit head:* Dr. Karen Patterson, Chair, 904-620-2930, Fax: 904-620-3895, E-mail: karen.patterson@unf.edu. *Application contact:* Kiersten Jarvis, Graduate Admissions Coordinator, 904-620-2530, Fax: 904-620-1135, E-mail: kiersten.jarvis@unf.edu.

University of North Texas, Robert B. Toulouse School of Graduate Studies, College of Arts and Sciences, Department of Speech and Hearing Sciences, Denton, TX 76203. Offers audiology (Au D); speech-language pathology (MA, MS). *Accreditation:* ASHA. Part-time programs available. *Degree requirements:* For master's, comprehensive exam, thesis optional, internship; for doctorate, comprehensive exam, thesis/dissertation, internship/externship. *Entrance requirements:* For master's, GRE General Test, minimum GPA of 3.0 in major, 2.8 overall; 15 hours of course work in communication disorders; for doctorate, GRE General Test. Additional exam requirements/recommendations for international students: Required—proof of English language proficiency required for non-native English speakers; Recommended—TOEFL (minimum score 550 paper-based; 213 computer-based; 79 iBT). *Application deadline:* Applications are processed on a rolling basis. Application fee: $50 ($75 for international students). Electronic applications accepted. *Expenses:* Tuition, state resident: full-time $4298; part-time $239 per contact hour. Tuition, nonresident: full-time $9878; part-time $549 per contact hour. Required fees: $265 per contact hour. *Financial support:* Fellowships, research assistantships, teaching assistantships, career-related internships or fieldwork, Federal Work-Study, institutionally sponsored loans, and unspecified assistantships available. Financial award applicants required to submit FAFSA. *Faculty research:* Cognition and hearing aids, assessment of noise technology, meta analysis on adaptive testing and binaural listening in cochlear implant language literacy for school aged children, tissue specificity in culture using corticle and non-corticle neuronal networks growing on microelectrode arrays. *Application contact:* Director of Graduate Studies, 940-565-7367, Fax: 940-565-4058.

University of Oklahoma Health Sciences Center, Graduate College, College of Allied Health, Department of Communication Sciences and Disorders, Oklahoma City, OK 73190.

Offers audiology (MS, Au D, PhD); communication sciences and disorders (Certificate), including reading, speech-language pathology; education of the deaf (MS); speech-language pathology (MS, PhD). *Accreditation:* ASHA (one or more programs are accredited). Part-time programs available. *Faculty:* 13 full-time (10 women), 2 part-time/adjunct (1 woman). *Students:* 67 full-time (66 women), 4 part-time (3 women); includes 10 minority (8 American Indian/Alaska Native, 1 Asian American or Pacific Islander, 1 Hispanic American). Average age 25. 92 applicants, 49% accepted, 25 enrolled. In 2009, 24 master's, 7 doctorates awarded. Terminal master's awarded for partial completion of doctoral program. *Degree requirements:* For master's, comprehensive exam, thesis optional; for doctorate, one foreign language, comprehensive exam, thesis/dissertation. *Entrance requirements:* For master's and doctorate, GRE General Test, 3 letters of recommendation. Additional exam requirements/recommendations for international students: Required—TOEFL (minimum score 550 paper-based). *Application deadline:* For fall admission, 2/1 for domestic students. Applications are processed on a rolling basis. Application fee: $50. *Expenses:* Tuition, state resident: full-time $3120; part-time $156 per credit hour. Tuition, nonresident: full-time $11,314; part-time $409.70 per credit hour. Required fees: $1471; $51.20 per credit hour. $223.25 per term. *Financial support:* In 2009–10, 8 research assistantships (averaging $16,000 per year) were awarded; fellowships, career-related internships or fieldwork, Federal Work-Study, institutionally sponsored loans, and traineeships also available. Support available to part-time students. *Faculty research:* Event-related potentials, cleft palate, fluency disorders, language disorders, hearing and speech science. *Unit head:* Dr. Stephen Painton, Chair, 405-271-4214, E-mail: stephen-painton@ouhsc.edu. *Application contact:* Dr. Sarah Christman, Graduate Liaison, 405-271-4214, Fax: 405-271-1153, E-mail: sarah-christman@ouhsc.edu.

University of Ottawa, Faculty of Graduate and Postdoctoral Studies, Faculty of Health Sciences, School of Rehabilitation Sciences, Ottawa, ON K1N 6N5, Canada. Offers audiology (M Sc); orthophony (M Sc). Part-time and evening/weekend programs available. *Entrance requirements:* For master's, honors degree or equivalent, minimum B average. Electronic applications accepted.

University of Pittsburgh, School of Health and Rehabilitation Sciences, Department of Communication Science and Disorders, Pittsburgh, PA 15260. Offers MA, MS, Au D, CScD, PhD. *Accreditation:* ASHA (one or more programs are accredited). *Faculty:* 18 full-time (13 women), 9 part-time/adjunct (4 women). *Students:* 110 full-time (109 women), 34 part-time (27 women); includes 9 minority (3 African Americans, 4 Asian Americans or Pacific Islanders, 2 Hispanic Americans), 15 international. Average age 28. 252 applicants, 45% accepted, 45 enrolled. In 2009, 42 master's, 10 doctorates awarded. *Degree requirements:* For master's, comprehensive exam, thesis (for some programs); for doctorate, comprehensive exam, thesis/dissertation. *Entrance requirements:* For master's and doctorate, GRE General Test. Additional exam requirements/recommendations for international students: Required—TOEFL (minimum score 550 paper-based; 213 computer-based; 80 iBT), IELTS (minimum score 6.5). *Application deadline:* For fall admission, 2/1 for domestic students, 1/31 for international students. Applications are processed on a rolling basis. Application fee: $50. Electronic applications accepted. *Expenses:* Contact institution. *Financial support:* In 2009–10, 10 research assistantships with full tuition reimbursements (averaging $13,758 per year), 2 teaching assistantships with full tuition reimbursements (averaging $15,675 per year) were awarded; fellowships, career-related internships or fieldwork, Federal Work-Study, scholarships/grants, and traineeships also available. Financial award applicants required to submit FAFSA. *Faculty research:* Pediatric and geriatric neurogenic speech and language, pediatric hearing disorders, hearing aids, language development, speech motor control. *Unit head:* Dr. Malcolm R. McNeil, Chairman, 412-383-6541, Fax: 412-383-6555, E-mail: mcneil@pitt.edu. *Application contact:* Theresa Niecgorski, Admissions Secretary, 412-383-6540, Fax: 412-383-6555, E-mail: thn49@pitt.edu.

University of Puerto Rico, Medical Sciences Campus, School of Health Professions, Program in Audiology, San Juan, PR 00936-5067. Offers Au D. *Faculty research:* Hearing, auditory brainstem responses, otoacoustic emissions.

University of Puerto Rico, Medical Sciences Campus, School of Health Professions, Program in Speech-Language Pathology, San Juan, PR 00936-5067. Offers MS. *Accreditation:* ASHA. *Degree requirements:* For master's, one foreign language, comprehensive exam, thesis or alternative. *Entrance requirements:* For master's, EXADEP, interview; previous course work in linguistics, statistics, human development, and basic concepts in speech-language pathology; minimum GPA of 2.5. *Faculty research:* Aphasia, autism, language, aphasia, assistive technology.

University of Redlands, College of Arts and Sciences, Department of Communicative Disorders, Redlands, CA 92373-0999. Offers MS. *Accreditation:* ASHA. *Degree requirements:* For master's, final exam. *Entrance requirements:* For master's, GMAT or GRE, minimum GPA of 3.0, 3 letters of recommendation. Additional exam requirements/recommendations for international students: Required—TOEFL (minimum score 550 paper-based; 213 computer-based). Electronic applications accepted. *Expenses:* Contact institution. *Faculty research:* Neuropathy.

University of Rhode Island, Graduate School, College of Human Science and Services, Department of Communicative Disorders, Kingston, RI 02881. Offers speech-language pathology (MS). *Accreditation:* ASHA. Part-time programs available. *Faculty:* 7 full-time (5 women), 2 part-time/adjunct (1 woman). *Students:* 37 full-time (34 women), 11 part-time (all women); includes 1 minority (American Indian/Alaska Native). In 2009, 18 master's awarded. *Degree requirements:* For master's, comprehensive exam (for some programs), thesis optional. *Entrance requirements:* For master's, GRE or MAT, 2 letters of recommendation. Additional exam requirements/recommendations for international students: Required—TOEFL (minimum score 550 paper-based; 213 computer-based). *Application deadline:* For fall admission, 3/1 for domestic students, 2/1 for international students; for spring admission, 10/15 for domestic students, 7/15 for international students. Application fee: $65. Electronic applications accepted. *Expenses:* Tuition, state resident: full-time $8828; part-time $490 per credit hour. Tuition, nonresident: full-time $22,100; part-time $1228 per credit hour. Required fees: $1118; $57 per semester. Tuition and fees vary according to program. *Financial support:* In 2009–10, 3 teaching assistantships with full and partial tuition reimbursements (averaging $6,451 per year) were awarded. Financial award application deadline: 3/1; financial award applicants required to submit FAFSA. *Faculty research:* Efficacy of treatment for acquired alexia in individuals with aphasia, application of principles of neuroplasticity to individuals with motor speech disorders secondary to neurological deficits, study of the conversation factors that promote fluency or exacerbate stuttering in young children who stutter. Total annual research expenditures: $73,118. *Unit head:* Dr. Jay Singer, Chair, 401-874-4742, Fax: 401-874-4404, E-mail: drjay@uri.edu. *Application contact:* Dr. Jay Singer, Chair, 401-874-4742, Fax: 401-874-4404, E-mail: drjay@uri.edu.

University of San Diego, School of Leadership and Education Sciences, Department of Learning and Teaching, San Diego, CA 92110-2492. Offers curriculum and instruction (M Ed); mathematics, science and technology education (M Ed); special education (M Ed); special education with deaf and hard of hearing (M Ed); teaching (MAT); TESOL, literacy and culture (M Ed). Part-time and evening/weekend programs available. *Faculty:* 13 full-time (9 women), 24 part-time/adjunct (21 women). *Students:* 77 full-time (63 women), 92 part-time (74 women); includes 46 minority (13 African Americans, 12 Asian Americans or Pacific Islanders, 21 Hispanic Americans), 6 international. Average age 31. 142 applicants, 75% accepted, 59 enrolled. In 2009, 64 master's awarded. *Degree requirements:* For master's, thesis (for some programs). *Entrance requirements:* For master's, minimum GPA of 3.0. Additional exam requirements/recommendations for international students: Required—TOEFL (minimum score 580 paper-based; 237 computer-based; 83 iBT), TWE. *Application deadline:* For fall admission, 7/15 for domestic and international students; for spring admission, 12/1 for domestic and international students. Applications are processed on a rolling basis. Application fee: $45. Electronic applications accepted. *Expenses:* Tuition: Full-time $21,042; part-time $1169 per unit. Required fees: $224. Full-time tuition and fees vary according to course load and degree level. *Financial support:* In 2009–10, 113 students received support. Career-related internships or fieldwork, Federal Work-Study, institutionally sponsored loans, and stipends available.

Communication Disorders

University of San Diego (continued)
Support available to part-time students. Financial award application deadline: 4/1; financial award applicants required to submit FAFSA. *Faculty research:* Action research methodology, cultural studies, instructional theories and practices, second language acquisition, school reform. *Unit head:* Dr. Judy Mantle, Director, 619-260-7879, Fax: 619-260-6835, E-mail: jmantle@sandiego.edu. *Application contact:* Dr. John Mosby, Associate Director of Graduate Admissions, 619-260-4524, Fax: 619-260-4158, E-mail: grads@sandiego.edu.

University of South Alabama, Graduate School, College of Allied Health Professions, Department of Speech Pathology and Audiology, Mobile, AL 36688-0002. Offers audiology (Au D); communication sciences and disorders (PhD); speech and hearing sciences (MS). *Accreditation:* ASHA. *Degree requirements:* For master's, thesis optional, externship; for doctorate, thesis/dissertation, clinical internship. *Entrance requirements:* For master's, GRE, bachelor's degree in communication sciences and disorders; for doctorate, GRE. *Expenses:* Tuition, state resident: part-time $218 per contact hour. Required fees: $1102 per year. *Faculty research:* Computer applications to speech and hearing science, telecommunications and clinical research in articulation and languages.

University of South Carolina, The Graduate School, Arnold School of Public Health, Department of Communication Sciences and Disorders, Columbia, SC 29208. Offers MCD, MSP, PhD. *Accreditation:* ASHA (one or more programs are accredited). Postbaccalaureate distance learning degree programs offered. *Degree requirements:* For master's, thesis optional; for doctorate, comprehensive exam, thesis/dissertation. *Entrance requirements:* For master's, GRE General Test, minimum GPA of 3.0; for doctorate, GRE General Test. Electronic applications accepted. *Faculty research:* Noise-induced hearing loss, recurrent laryngeal nerve regeneration, cleft palate, child language-phonology, epidemiology of craniofacial anomalies.

The University of South Dakota, Graduate School, College of Arts and Sciences, Department of Communication Disorders, Vermillion, SD 57069-2390. Offers audiology (Au D); communications disorders (MA); speech-language pathology (MA). *Accreditation:* ASHA (one or more programs are accredited). Part-time programs available. *Degree requirements:* For master's, comprehensive exam; for doctorate, comprehensive exam, thesis/dissertation. *Entrance requirements:* For master's, GRE General Test, minimum GPA of 3.0. Additional exam requirements/recommendations for international students: Required—TOEFL (minimum score 550 paper-based; 213 computer-based; 79 iBT). Electronic applications accepted. *Faculty research:* Craniofacial anomalies, central auditory processing, phonological disorders.

University of Southern Mississippi, Graduate School, College of Health, Department of Speech and Hearing Sciences, Hattiesburg, MS 39406-0001. Offers MA, MS, Au D. *Accreditation:* ASHA (one or more programs are accredited). *Faculty:* 10 full-time (4 women). *Students:* 65 full-time (63 women), 4 part-time (3 women); includes 5 minority (2 African Americans, 2 Asian Americans or Pacific Islanders, 1 Hispanic American), 1 international. Average age 27. 77 applicants, 42% accepted, 12 enrolled. In 2009, 20 master's, 3 doctorates awarded. *Degree requirements:* For master's, comprehensive exam, thesis or alternative; for doctorate, comprehensive exam, thesis/dissertation. *Entrance requirements:* For master's, GRE General Test, minimum GPA of 3.0 in field of study, 2.75 in last 2 years; for doctorate, GRE General Test, minimum GPA of 3.5. Additional exam requirements/recommendations for international students: Required—TOEFL. *Application deadline:* For fall admission, 3/1 for domestic and international students. Application fee: $35. Electronic applications accepted. *Expenses:* Tuition, state resident: full-time $5096; part-time $284 per hour. Tuition, nonresident: full-time $13,052; part-time $726 per hour. Required fees: $402. Tuition and fees vary according to course level and course load. *Financial support:* In 2009–10, 9 research assistantships with full and partial tuition reimbursements (averaging $6,000 per year) were awarded; teaching assistantships with full and partial tuition reimbursements, career-related internships or fieldwork, Federal Work-Study, institutionally sponsored loans, and tuition waivers (full) also available. Financial award application deadline: 3/15; financial award applicants required to submit FAFSA. *Faculty research:* Voice disorders, auditory-evoked responses, acoustic analysis of speech, child language, parent-child interaction. *Unit head:* Dr. Brett Kemker, Interim Chair, 601-266-5216. *Application contact:* Shonna Breland, Manager of Graduate Admissions, 601-266-6563, Fax: 601-266-5138.

University of South Florida, Graduate School, College of Behavioral and Community Sciences, Department of Communication Sciences and Disorders, Tampa, FL 33620. Offers audiology (Au D); hearing science (PhD); language and speech science (PhD); neurocommunicative science (PhD); speech-language pathology (MS). *Accreditation:* ASHA (one or more programs are accredited). Part-time and evening/weekend programs available. Postbaccalaureate distance learning degree programs offered (minimal on-campus study). *Faculty:* 30 full-time (23 women), 43 part-time/adjunct (42 women). *Students:* 187 full-time (174 women), 8 part-time (all women); includes 42 minority (10 African Americans, 7 Asian Americans or Pacific Islanders, 25 Hispanic Americans). Average age 24. 354 applicants, 48% accepted, 98 enrolled. In 2009, 67 master's, 112 doctorates awarded. *Degree requirements:* For master's, comprehensive exam, thesis (for some programs); for doctorate, comprehensive exam, thesis/dissertation. *Entrance requirements:* For master's, GRE; for doctorate, GRE. Additional exam requirements/recommendations for international students: Required—TOEFL (minimum score 550 paper-based; 213 computer-based). *Application deadline:* For fall admission, 12/1 for domestic and international students; for spring admission, 2/1 for domestic and international students. Application fee: $30. Electronic applications accepted. *Financial support:* In 2009–10, 25 students received support, including 14 teaching assistantships with full and partial tuition reimbursements available (averaging $15,000 per year); career-related internships or fieldwork, traineeships, health care benefits, and unspecified assistantships also available. Financial award application deadline: 2/1; financial award applicants required to submit FAFSA. *Faculty research:* Speech perception, motor speech, neurogenic communication disorder, oncology, speech acoustics. Total annual research expenditures: $305,551. *Unit head:* Dr. Theresa Chisolm, Professor/Chair, 813-974-9826, E-mail: tchisolm@bcs.usf.edu. *Application contact:* Vivian Maldando, Academic Program Specialist, 813-974-2006, Fax: 813-974-0822, E-mail: frisch@cas.usf.edu.

The University of Tennessee, Graduate School, College of Arts and Sciences, Department of Audiology and Speech Pathology, Program in Audiology, Knoxville, TN 37996. Offers MA. *Accreditation:* ASHA. *Degree requirements:* For master's, thesis or alternative. *Entrance requirements:* For master's, GRE General Test, minimum GPA of 2.7. Additional exam requirements/recommendations for international students: Required—TOEFL. Electronic applications accepted. *Expenses:* Tuition, state resident: full-time $6826; part-time $380 per semester hour. Tuition, nonresident: full-time $21,844; part-time $1147 per semester hour. Tuition and fees vary according to program.

The University of Tennessee, Graduate School, College of Arts and Sciences, Department of Audiology and Speech Pathology, Program in Speech and Hearing Science, Knoxville, TN 37996. Offers audiology (PhD); hearing science (PhD); speech and language pathology (PhD); speech and language science (PhD). *Accreditation:* ASHA. *Degree requirements:* For doctorate, thesis/dissertation. *Entrance requirements:* For doctorate, GRE General Test, minimum GPA of 2.7. Additional exam requirements/recommendations for international students: Required—TOEFL. Electronic applications accepted. *Expenses:* Tuition, state resident: full-time $6826; part-time $380 per semester hour. Tuition, nonresident: full-time $21,844; part-time $1147 per semester hour. Tuition and fees vary according to program.

The University of Tennessee, Graduate School, College of Arts and Sciences, Department of Audiology and Speech Pathology, Program in Speech Pathology, Knoxville, TN 37996. Offers MA. *Accreditation:* ASHA. *Degree requirements:* For master's, thesis or alternative. *Entrance requirements:* For master's, GRE General Test, minimum GPA of 2.7. Additional exam requirements/recommendations for international students: Required—TOEFL. Electronic applications accepted. *Expenses:* Tuition, state resident: full-time $6826; part-time $380 per semester hour. Tuition, nonresident: full-time $21,844; part-time $1147 per semester hour. Tuition and fees vary according to program.

The University of Tennessee, Graduate School, College of Education, Health and Human Sciences, Program in Education, Knoxville, TN 37996. Offers art education (MS); counseling education (PhD); cultural studies in education (PhD); curriculum (MS, Ed S); curriculum, educational research and evaluation (Ed D, PhD); early childhood education (PhD); early childhood special education (MS); education of deaf and hard of hearing (MS); educational administration and policy studies (Ed D, PhD); educational administration and supervision (Ed S); educational psychology (Ed D, PhD); elementary education (MS, Ed S); elementary teaching (MS); English education (MS, Ed S); exercise science (PhD); foreign language/ESL education (MS, Ed S); instructional technology (MS, Ed D, PhD, Ed S); literacy, language and ESL education (PhD); literacy, language education, and ESL education (Ed D); mathematics education (MS, Ed S); modified and comprehensive special education (MS); reading education (MS, Ed S); school counseling (Ed S); school psychology (PhD, Ed S); science education (MS, Ed S); secondary teaching (MS); social foundations (MS); social science education (MS, Ed S); socio-cultural foundations of sports and education (PhD); special education (Ed S); teacher education (Ed D, PhD). *Accreditation:* NCATE. Part-time and evening/weekend programs available. *Degree requirements:* For master's and Ed S, thesis optional; for doctorate, variable foreign language requirement, thesis/dissertation. *Entrance requirements:* For master's, minimum GPA of 2.7; for doctorate and Ed S, GRE General Test, minimum GPA of 2.7. Additional exam requirements/recommendations for international students: Required—TOEFL. Electronic applications accepted. *Expenses:* Tuition, state resident: full-time $6826; part-time $380 per semester hour. Tuition, nonresident: full-time $21,844; part-time $1147 per semester hour. Tuition and fees vary according to program.

The University of Texas at Austin, Graduate School, College of Communication, Department of Communication Sciences and Disorders, Austin, TX 78712-1111. Offers audiology (Au D, PhD); speech language pathology (MA, PhD). *Accreditation:* ASHA (one or more programs are accredited). *Entrance requirements:* For master's and doctorate, GRE General Test.

The University of Texas at Dallas, School of Behavioral and Brain Sciences, Program in Audiology, Richardson, TX 75080. Offers Au D. *Accreditation:* ASHA. *Faculty:* 6 full-time (2 women), 3 part-time/adjunct (2 women). *Students:* 32 full-time (24 women), 2 part-time (both women); includes 6 minority (1 African American, 3 Asian Americans or Pacific Islanders, 2 Hispanic Americans), 2 international. Average age 26. 64 applicants, 27% accepted, 9 enrolled. *Degree requirements:* For doctorate, thesis/dissertation. *Entrance requirements:* Additional exam requirements/recommendations for international students: Required—TOEFL (minimum score 550 paper-based; 213 computer-based). *Application deadline:* For fall admission, 7/15 for domestic students, 5/1 priority date for international students; for spring admission, 11/15 for domestic students, 9/1 priority date for international students. Applications are processed on a rolling basis. Application fee: $50 ($100 for international students). Electronic applications accepted. *Expenses:* Tuition, state resident: full-time $11,068; part-time $461 per credit hour. Tuition, nonresident: full-time $21,178; part-time $882 per credit hour. Tuition and fees vary according to course load. *Financial support:* Fellowships, research assistantships, teaching assistantships, career-related internships or fieldwork, Federal Work-Study, institutionally sponsored loans, scholarships/grants, and unspecified assistantships available. Support available to part-time students. Financial award application deadline: 4/30; financial award applicants required to submit FAFSA. *Faculty research:* Cochlear implants, auditory electrophysiology, psychoacoustics. *Unit head:* Dr. Lee Wilson, Head, 214-905-3036, E-mail: pwilson@utdallas.edu. *Application contact:* Dr. Robert D. Stillman, Head, 972-883-3106, Fax: 972-883-3022, E-mail: stillman@utdallas.edu.

The University of Texas at Dallas, School of Behavioral and Brain Sciences, Program in Communication Sciences and Disorders, Richardson, TX 75080. Offers communication disorders (MS); communication sciences (PhD). Part-time and evening/weekend programs available. *Faculty:* 19 full-time (10 women), 2 part-time/adjunct (both women). *Students:* 221 full-time (216 women), 15 part-time (13 women); includes 35 minority (7 African Americans, 1 American Indian/Alaska Native, 15 Asian Americans or Pacific Islanders, 12 Hispanic Americans), 7 international. Average age 25. 295 applicants, 28% accepted, 65 enrolled. In 2009, 96 master's, 4 doctorates awarded. *Degree requirements:* For doctorate, thesis/dissertation. *Entrance requirements:* For master's and doctorate, GRE General Test, minimum GPA of 3.0 in upper-level course work in field. Additional exam requirements/recommendations for international students: Required—TOEFL (minimum score 550 paper-based; 213 computer-based). *Application deadline:* For fall admission, 7/15 for domestic students, 5/1 priority date for international students; for spring admission, 11/15 for domestic students, 9/1 priority date for international students. Applications are processed on a rolling basis. Application fee: $50 ($100 for international students). Electronic applications accepted. *Expenses:* Tuition, state resident: full-time $11,068; part-time $461 per credit hour. Tuition, nonresident: full-time $21,178; part-time $882 per credit hour. Tuition and fees vary according to course load. *Financial support:* In 2009–10, 6 research assistantships with full tuition reimbursements (averaging $18,317 per year), 11 teaching assistantships with full tuition reimbursements (averaging $10,681 per year) were awarded; fellowships, Federal Work-Study, institutionally sponsored loans, scholarships/grants, and unspecified assistantships also available. Support available to part-time students. Financial award application deadline: 4/30; financial award applicants required to submit FAFSA. *Faculty research:* Speech perception, auditory processing, language acquisition by young children, language development. *Unit head:* Dr. Robert D. Stillman, Program Head, 972-883-3106, Fax: 972-883-3022, E-mail: stillman@utdallas.edu. *Application contact:* Dr. Robert D. Stillman, Program Head, 972-883-3106, Fax: 972-883-3022, E-mail: stillman@utdallas.edu.

The University of Texas at El Paso, Graduate School, College of Health Sciences, Department of Speech-Language Pathology, El Paso, TX 79968-0001. Offers MS. *Accreditation:* ASHA. *Students:* 32 (29 women); includes 25 minority (all Hispanic Americans), 2 international. Average age 34. In 2009, 10 master's awarded. *Degree requirements:* For master's, thesis optional. *Entrance requirements:* For master's, GRE, minimum GPA of 3.0, resume, letters of recommendation. Additional exam requirements/recommendations for international students: Required—TOEFL; Recommended—IELTS. *Application deadline:* For fall admission, 8/1 for domestic students, 3/1 for international students; for spring admission, 11/1 for domestic students, 9/1 for international students. Applications are processed on a rolling basis. Application fee: $45 ($80 for international students). Electronic applications accepted. *Financial support:* In 2009–10, research assistantships with partial tuition reimbursements (averaging $18,825 per year), teaching assistantships with partial tuition reimbursements (averaging $18,000 per year) were awarded; fellowships with partial tuition reimbursements, institutionally sponsored loans, scholarships/grants, health care benefits, tuition waivers (partial), and unspecified assistantships also available. Support available to part-time students. Financial award application deadline: 3/15; financial award applicants required to submit FAFSA. *Faculty research:* Cleft palate, bilingual language disorders, clinical supervision, hearing loss. *Unit head:* Dr. Anthony Salvatore, Chair, 915-747-7250, Fax: 915-747-7207, E-mail: asalvatore@utep.edu. *Application contact:* Dr. Patricia D. Witherspoon, Dean of the Graduate School, 915-747-5491, Fax: 915-747-5788, E-mail: withersp@utep.edu.

The University of Texas Health Science Center at San Antonio, School of Allied Health Sciences, San Antonio, TX 78229-3900. Offers clinical laboratory sciences (MS); deaf education and hearing science (MED); dental hygiene (MS); occupational therapy (MOT); physical therapy (MPT); physician assistant studies (MS). *Accreditation:* AOTA; APTA; ARC-PA. *Expenses:* Tuition, state resident: full-time $2832; part-time $118 per credit hour. Tuition, nonresident: full-time $10,896; part-time $454 per credit hour. Required fees: $884 per semester. One-time fee: $70.

The University of Texas–Pan American, College of Health Sciences and Human Services, Department of Communication Sciences and Disorders, Edinburg, TX 78539. Offers MS. *Accreditation:* ASHA. *Degree requirements:* For master's, comprehensive exam, thesis optional, NESPA exam (national exam). *Entrance requirements:* For master's, GRE General Test, minimum GPA of 3.0 in major, 3 letters of recommendation, resume. Additional exam requirements/recommendations for international students: Required—TOEFL (minimum score 550 paper-based). Electronic applications accepted. *Expenses:* Tuition, state resident: full-time

$3630.60; part-time $201.70 per credit hour. Tuition, nonresident: full-time $8617; part-time $478.70 per credit hour. Required fees: $806.50. *Faculty research:* Bilingual/bicultural language development/disorders, elementary-age language disorders, voice disorders.

University of the District of Columbia, College of Arts and Sciences, Department of Language and Communication Disorders, Program in Speech and Language Pathology, Washington, DC 20008-1175. Offers MS. *Accreditation:* ASHA. Part-time programs available. *Students:* 27 full-time (25 women), 8 part-time (all women); includes 16 minority (13 African Americans, 2 Asian Americans or Pacific Islanders, 1 Hispanic American). Average age 31. 37 applicants, 81% accepted, 19 enrolled. In 2009, 15 master's awarded. *Degree requirements:* For master's, comprehensive exam, thesis optional. *Entrance requirements:* For master's, GRE General Test, writing proficiency exam. *Application deadline:* For fall admission, 6/15 priority date for domestic students; for spring admission, 11/1 for domestic students. Applications are processed on a rolling basis. Application fee: $20. *Expenses:* Tuition, state resident: full-time $7580. Tuition, nonresident: full-time $14,580. Required fees: $620. *Financial support:* Fellowships, research assistantships available. Financial award application deadline: 6/10. *Faculty research:* Child language, dialect variation, English as a second language. *Unit head:* Prof. Maxine LeGall, Chair, 202-274-7405. *Application contact:* Ann Marie Waterman, Associate Vice President of Admission, Recruitment and Financial Aid, 202-274-6069.

University of the Pacific, School of Pharmacy and Health Sciences, Department of Speech-Language Pathology, Stockton, CA 95211-0197. Offers MS. *Accreditation:* ASHA. *Faculty:* 8 full-time (4 women), 12 part-time/adjunct (all women). *Students:* 55 full-time (52 women), 2 part-time (both women); includes 10 minority (4 Asian Americans or Pacific Islanders, 6 Hispanic Americans). Average age 26. 130 applicants, 35% accepted, 29 enrolled. In 2009, 41 master's awarded. *Entrance requirements:* For master's, GRE General Test. Additional exam requirements/recommendations for international students: Required—TOEFL (minimum score 475 paper-based; 150 computer-based). *Application deadline:* For fall admission, 2/1 for domestic students. Application fee: $75. *Financial support:* Institutionally sponsored loans available. Support available to part-time students. Financial award application deadline: 2/1; financial award applicants required to submit FAFSA. *Unit head:* Dr. Robert Hanyak, Chairman, 209-946-3223, E-mail: rhanyak@pacific.edu. *Application contact:* Cyndi Porter, Outreach Officer, 209-946-3957, Fax: 209-946-2410, E-mail: cporter@pacific.edu.

The University of Toledo, College of Graduate Studies, College of Health Science and Human Service, Division of Human Services, Department of Public Health and Rehabilitative Services, Toledo, OH 43606-3390. Offers speech-language pathology (MA).

University of Toronto, School of Graduate Studies, Life Sciences Division, Department of Speech-Language Pathology, Toronto, ON M5S 1A1, Canada. Offers M Sc, MH Sc, PhD. Part-time programs available. *Degree requirements:* For master's, thesis (for some programs), clinical internship (MH Sc), oral thesis defense (M Sc); for doctorate, comprehensive exam, thesis/dissertation, oral thesis defense. *Entrance requirements:* For master's, minimum B+ average in last 2 years (MH Sc), B average in final year (M Sc); volunteer/work experience in a clinical setting (MH Sc); for doctorate, previous research experience or thesis, resumé, 3 writing samples, 3 letters of recommendation. Additional exam requirements/recommendations for international students: Recommended—TWE.

University of Tulsa, Graduate School, College of Arts and Sciences, Program in Speech-Language Pathology, Tulsa, OK 74104-3189. Offers MS. *Accreditation:* ASHA. Part-time programs available. *Faculty:* 7 full-time (all women), 1 (woman) part-time/adjunct. *Students:* 26 full-time (25 women), 1 (woman) part-time; includes 5 minority (4 American Indian/Alaska Native, 1 Hispanic American). Average age 24. 28 applicants, 82% accepted, 15 enrolled. In 2009, 16 master's awarded. *Degree requirements:* For master's, thesis optional. *Entrance requirements:* For master's, GRE General Test. Additional exam requirements/recommendations for international students: Required—TOEFL (minimum score 577 paper-based; 233 computer-based; 90 iBT), IELTS (minimum score 6.5). *Application deadline:* For fall admission, 2/1 priority date for domestic students. Application fee: $40. Electronic applications accepted. *Expenses:* Tuition: Full-time $16,182; part-time $899 per credit hour. Required fees: $4 per credit hour. Tuition and fees vary according to course load. *Financial support:* In 2009–10, 14 students received support, including 14 teaching assistantships with full and partial tuition reimbursements available (averaging $6,707 per year); fellowships, research assistantships with full tuition reimbursements available, career-related internships or fieldwork, Federal Work-Study, scholarships/grants, traineeships, health care benefits, tuition waivers (full and partial), and unspecified assistantships also available. Support available to part-time students. Financial award application deadline: 2/1; financial award applicants required to submit FAFSA. *Faculty research:* Disorders of fluency, delayed language and literacy, aphasia, voice, speech articulation, swallowing, cognition. Total annual research expenditures: $141,535. *Unit head:* Dr. Paula Cadogan, Chairperson, 918-631-2897, Fax: 918-631-3668, E-mail: paula-cadogan@utulsa.edu. *Application contact:* Dr. Paula Cadogan, Adviser, 918-631-2897, Fax: 918-631-3668, E-mail: paula-cadogan@utulsa.edu.

University of Utah, Graduate School, College of Education, Department of Special Education, Salt Lake City, UT 84112. Offers early childhood hearing impairments (M Ed, MS); early childhood special education (M Ed, PhD); early childhood vision impairments (M Ed, MS); hearing impairments (M Ed, MS); mild/moderate disabilities (M Ed, MS, PhD); professional practice (M Ed); research in special education (MS); severe disabilities (M Ed, MS, PhD); vision impairments (M Ed). Part-time and evening/weekend programs available. Post-baccalaureate distance learning degree programs offered (no on-campus study). *Faculty:* 17 full-time (12 women), 7 part-time/adjunct (5 women). *Students:* 41 full-time (40 women), 20 part-time (16 women); includes 5 minority (1 African American, 2 American Indian/Alaska Native, 2 Hispanic Americans), 3 international. Average age 35. 34 applicants, 65% accepted, 11 enrolled. In 2009, 27 master's, 2 doctorates awarded. Terminal master's awarded for partial completion of doctoral program. *Degree requirements:* For master's, comprehensive exam, thesis (for some programs), qualifying exam; for doctorate, thesis/dissertation, qualifying exam. *Entrance requirements:* For master's, GRE or Analytical/Writing portion of GRE plus PRAXIS I; Basic Skills Test, minimum GPA of 3.0; for doctorate, GRE General Test (minimum score: Verbal-600; Quantitative-600; Analytical/Writing-4), minimum GPA of 3.0, 3.5 (recommended). Additional exam requirements/recommendations for international students: Required—TOEFL (minimum score 600 paper-based; 250 computer-based; 100 iBT). *Application deadline:* For fall admission, 3/1 for domestic and international students; for spring admission, 11/1 for domestic and international students. Application fee: $55 ($65 for international students). *Expenses:* Contact institution. *Financial support:* In 2009–10, 44 students received support, including 44 fellowships with full and partial tuition reimbursements available (averaging $8,800 per year), 1 research assistantship (averaging $4,500 per year), 3 teaching assistantships (averaging $3,000 per year); career-related internships or fieldwork and scholarships/grants also available. Support available to part-time students. Financial award application deadline: 3/1; financial award applicants required to submit FAFSA. *Faculty research:* Inclusive education, positive behavior support, reading, instruction and intervention strategies. *Unit head:* Dr. Andrea P. McDonnell, Chair, 801-581-8121, Fax: 801-585-6476, E-mail: andrea.mcdonnell@utah.edu. *Application contact:* Patty Davis, Academic Advisor, 801-581-4764, Fax: 801-585-6476, E-mail: patty.davis@utah.edu.

University of Utah, Graduate School, College of Health, Department of Communication Sciences and Disorders, Salt Lake City, UT 84108. Offers audiology (Au D, PhD); speech-language pathology (MA, MS, PhD). *Accreditation:* ASHA (one or more programs are accredited). *Faculty:* 10 full-time (6 women). *Students:* 92 full-time (70 women), 3 part-time (all women); includes 7 minority (1 American Indian/Alaska Native, 1 Asian American or Pacific Islander, 5 Hispanic Americans), 3 international. Average age 26. 138 applicants, 62% accepted, 42 enrolled. In 2009, 22 master's, 1 doctorate awarded. Terminal master's awarded for partial completion of doctoral program. *Degree requirements:* For master's, thesis optional, written exam; for doctorate, thesis/dissertation, written and oral exams. *Entrance requirements:* For master's and doctorate, GRE General Test, minimum GPA of 3.0. Additional exam requirements/recommendations for international students: Required—TOEFL (minimum score 600 paper-based; 250 computer-based; 100 iBT), TSE. *Application deadline:* For fall admission, 2/15 priority date for domestic and international students; for spring admission, 11/1 priority date for domestic and international students. Application fee: $55 ($65 for international students). Electronic applications accepted. *Expenses:* Contact institution. *Financial support:* Research assistantships with partial tuition reimbursements, teaching assistantships with partial tuition reimbursements, career-related internships or fieldwork, Federal Work-Study, scholarships/grants, tuition waivers (partial), and unspecified assistantships available. Financial award application deadline: 2/15; financial award applicants required to submit FAFSA. *Faculty research:* Motor speech disorders, fluency disorders, language disorders, voice disorders, cochlear implants and speech perception. Total annual research expenditures: $153,206. *Unit head:* Dr. Michael Blomberg, Department Chair, E-mail: michael.blomberg@health.utah.edu. *Application contact:* Dr. Kathy Chapman, Director of Graduate Studies, 801-5887-9076, Fax: 801-581-7955, E-mail: kathy.chapman@health.utah.edu.

University of Virginia, Curry School of Education, Department of Human Services, Program in Communication Disorders, Charlottesville, VA 22903. Offers M Ed. *Accreditation:* ASHA. *Students:* 65 full-time (63 women), 2 part-time (both women); includes 7 minority (2 African Americans, 2 Asian Americans or Pacific Islanders, 3 Hispanic Americans). Average age 24. 141 applicants, 54% accepted, 28 enrolled. In 2009, 25 master's awarded. *Entrance requirements:* For master's, GRE General Test, 2 letters of recommendation. Additional exam requirements/recommendations for international students: Required—TOEFL (minimum score 600 paper-based; 250 computer-based; 90 iBT), IELTS (minimum score 7). *Application deadline:* Applications are processed on a rolling basis. Application fee: $60. Electronic applications accepted. *Financial support:* Applicants required to submit FAFSA. *Unit head:* Randall R. Robey, Director, 434-924-6351, E-mail: robey@virginia.edu. *Application contact:* Randall R. Robey, Director, 434-924-6351, E-mail: robey@virginia.edu.

University of Washington, Graduate School, College of Arts and Sciences, Department of Speech and Hearing Sciences, Seattle, WA 98195. Offers audiology (Au D); speech and hearing sciences (PhD); speech-language pathology (MS). *Accreditation:* ASHA (one or more programs are accredited). *Degree requirements:* For master's, comprehensive exam, thesis or alternative; for doctorate, thesis/dissertation. *Entrance requirements:* For master's and doctorate, GRE, minimum GPA of 3.0. Additional exam requirements/recommendations for international students: Required—TOEFL. Electronic applications accepted. *Faculty research:* Treatment of communication disorders across the life span, speech physiology, auditory perception, behavioral and physiologic audiology.

The University of Western Ontario, Faculty of Graduate Studies, Health Sciences Division, School of Communication Sciences and Disorders, London, ON N6A 5B8, Canada. Offers audiology (M Cl Sc, M Sc); speech-language pathology (M Cl Sc, M Sc). *Degree requirements:* For master's, thesis (for some programs), supervised clinical practicum. *Entrance requirements:* For master's, 14 hours volunteer experience in field of study, minimum B average during last 2 years, previous course work in developmental psychology and statistics, 4 year honors degree. Additional exam requirements/recommendations for international students: Required—TOEFL (minimum score 620 paper-based; 260 computer-based). *Faculty research:* Child language, voice, neurogenics; auditory function, stuttering.

University of West Georgia, Graduate School, College of Education, Department of Special Education and Speech-Language Pathology, Carrollton, GA 30118. Offers special education-general (M Ed, Ed S); speech-language pathology (M Ed). *Accreditation:* ASHA; NCATE. Part-time and evening/weekend programs available. *Faculty:* 8 full-time (6 women), 2 part-time/adjunct (both women). *Students:* 68 full-time (63 women), 222 part-time (190 women); includes 98 minority (93 African Americans, 5 Hispanic Americans), 2 international. Average age 36. 184 applicants, 48% accepted, 48 enrolled. In 2009, 42 master's, 20 Ed Ss awarded. *Degree requirements:* For Ed S, research project. *Entrance requirements:* For master's, GRE General Test, minimum GPA of 3.0 in speech-language pathology, 2.7 overall; for Ed S, GRE General Test, master's degree, minimum graduate GPA of 3.4. *Application deadline:* For fall admission, 7/17 for domestic students; for spring admission, 11/20 for domestic students. Applications are processed on a rolling basis. Application fee: $30. Electronic applications accepted. *Expenses:* Tuition, state resident: full-time $2952; part-time $164 per semester hour. Tuition, nonresident: full-time $11,808; part-time $656 per semester hour. Required fees: $42.90 per semester hour. $307 per semester. Tuition and fees vary according to course load. *Financial support:* In 2009–10, 4 research assistantships with full tuition reimbursements (averaging $12,000 per year) were awarded; career-related internships or fieldwork, scholarships/grants, and unspecified assistantships also available. Support available to part-time students. Financial award applicants required to submit FAFSA. *Faculty research:* Mentoring, inclusion, learning strategies, scaffolding strategies, applied behavior analysis. *Unit head:* Dr. John von Eschenbach, Interim Chair, 678-839-6149, Fax: 678-839-6162, E-mail: johnvone@westga.edu. *Application contact:* Dr. Charles W. Clark, Dean, 678-839-6508, E-mail: cclark@westga.edu.

University of Wisconsin–Eau Claire, College of Education and Human Sciences, Program in Communication Sciences and Disorders, Eau Claire, WI 54702-4004. Offers MS. *Accreditation:* ASHA. *Faculty:* 4 full-time (all women). *Students:* 31 full-time (all women), 2 part-time (both women); includes 3 minority (all Asian Americans or Pacific Islanders), 1 international. Average age 24. 139 applicants, 12% accepted, 17 enrolled. In 2009, 16 master's awarded. *Degree requirements:* For master's, thesis optional, written or oral exam with thesis, externship. *Entrance requirements:* For master's, GRE, Wisconsin residency; minimum GPA of 3.0 in communication disorders, 2.75 overall. Additional exam requirements/recommendations for international students: Required—TOEFL (minimum score 550 paper-based; 213 computer-based; 79 iBT). *Application deadline:* For fall admission, 2/1 priority date for domestic students, 6/1 priority date for international students; for spring admission, 11/1 priority date for international students. Applications are processed on a rolling basis. Application fee: $56. Electronic applications accepted. *Expenses:* Tuition, state resident: full-time $6705.90; part-time $372.55 per credit. Tuition, nonresident: full-time $16,771; part-time $931.74 per credit. Required fees: $925.50; $51.19 per credit. One-time fee: $56. *Financial support:* In 2009–10, 29 students received support, including 7 fellowships (averaging $2,500 per year); Federal Work-Study and unspecified assistantships also available. Financial award application deadline: 3/1; financial award applicants required to submit FAFSA. *Unit head:* Dr. Kristine Retherford, Chair, 715-836-4186, Fax: 715-836-4846, E-mail: retherk@uwec.edu. *Application contact:* Kristina Anderson, Director of Admissions, 715-836-5415, Fax: 715-836-2409, E-mail: admissions@uwec.edu.

University of Wisconsin–Madison, Graduate School, College of Letters and Science, Department of Communicative Disorders, Madison, WI 53706-1380. Offers normal aspects of speech, language and hearing (MS, PhD); speech-language pathology (MS, PhD); MS/PhD. *Accreditation:* ASHA (one or more programs are accredited). *Degree requirements:* For doctorate, thesis/dissertation. *Entrance requirements:* For master's and doctorate, GRE. Electronic applications accepted. *Expenses:* Tuition, state resident: part-time $594 per credit. Tuition, nonresident: part-time $1504 per credit. Required fees: $65 per credit. Tuition and fees vary according to course load, program and reciprocity agreements. *Faculty research:* Language disorders in children and adults, disorders of speech production, intelligibility, fluency, hearing impairment, deafness.

University of Wisconsin–Milwaukee, Graduate School, College of Health Sciences, Department of Communication Sciences and Disorders, Milwaukee, WI 53211. Offers communication sciences and disorders (MS). *Accreditation:* ASHA (one or more programs are accredited). Part-time programs available. *Faculty:* 5 full-time (all women). *Students:* 51 full-time (49 women), 4 part-time (all women). Average age 25. 113 applicants, 25% accepted, 18 enrolled. In 2009, 25 master's awarded. *Degree requirements:* For master's, comprehensive exam, thesis optional. *Entrance requirements:* For master's, GRE General Test, minimum GPA of 3.0. Additional exam requirements/recommendations for international students: Required—TOEFL (minimum score 550 paper-based; 79 iBT), IELTS (minimum score 6.5). *Application deadline:* For fall admission, 1/1 priority date for domestic students; for spring admission, 9/1 for domestic students. Applications are processed on a rolling basis. Application fee: $45 ($75

Communication Disorders

University of Wisconsin–Milwaukee (continued)
for international students). *Expenses:* Tuition, state resident: full-time $8800. Tuition, nonresident: full-time $20,760. Tuition and fees vary according to program and reciprocity agreements. *Financial support:* In 2009–10, 1 teaching assistantship was awarded; fellowships, research assistantships, career-related internships or fieldwork and unspecified assistantships also available. Support available to part-time students. Financial award application deadline: 4/15. Total annual research expenditures: $107,054. *Unit head:* Carol Seery, Representative, 414-229-4291, Fax: 414-906-3910, E-mail: cseery@uwm.edu. *Application contact:* General Information Contact, 414-229-4982, Fax: 414-229-6967, E-mail: gradschool@uwm.edu.

University of Wisconsin–River Falls, Outreach and Graduate Studies, College of Education and Professional Studies, Department of Communicative Disorders, River Falls, WI 54022. Offers communicative disorders (MS); secondary education-communicative disorders (MSE). *Accreditation:* ASHA (one or more programs are accredited). Part-time programs available. *Degree requirements:* For master's, comprehensive exam. *Entrance requirements:* For master's, minimum GPA of 2.75, 3 letters of reference. Additional exam requirements/recommendations for international students: Required—TOEFL (minimum score 500 paper-based; 65 iBT), IELTS (minimum score 5.5). *Faculty research:* SHRG, voice, language, audiology.

University of Wisconsin–Stevens Point, College of Professional Studies, School of Communicative Disorders, Stevens Point, WI 54481-3897. Offers audiology (Au D); speech-language pathology (MS). *Accreditation:* ASHA (one or more programs are accredited). *Students:* 46 full-time (all women); includes 1 minority (American Indian/Alaska Native). *Degree requirements:* For master's, thesis optional, clinical semester and capstone project; for doctorate, capstone project, full-time clinical externship. *Entrance requirements:* For master's, completion of specific course contents and practicum experiences at the undergraduate level. *Application deadline:* For fall admission, 1/10 for domestic students. Application fee: $45. *Expenses:* Tuition, state resident: full-time $7740; part-time $430 per credit hour. Tuition, nonresident: full-time $17,804; part-time $989 per credit hour. Tuition and fees vary according to course load and reciprocity agreements. *Financial support:* Research assistantships, teaching assistantships, Federal Work-Study and unspecified assistantships available. Financial award application deadline: 5/1; financial award applicants required to submit FAFSA. *Unit head:* Dr. Gary Cumley, Chair, 715-346-4699, Fax: 715-346-2157, E-mail: gcumley@uwsp.edu. *Application contact:* Leslie Plonsker, Information Contact, 715-346-4835, Fax: 715-346-2157, E-mail: lplonske@uwsp.edu.

University of Wisconsin–Whitewater, School of Graduate Studies, College of Education, Program in Communicative Disorders, Whitewater, WI 53190-1790. Offers MS. *Accreditation:* ASHA. Part-time and evening/weekend programs available. Postbaccalaureate distance learning degree programs offered (no on-campus study). *Degree requirements:* For master's, comprehensive exam, thesis or alternative. *Entrance requirements:* For master's, 2 letters of recommendation. Additional exam requirements/recommendations for international students: Required—TOEFL (minimum score 550 paper-based; 213 computer-based). Electronic applications accepted. *Faculty research:* Occupational hearing conservation.

University of Wyoming, College of Health Sciences, Division of Communication Disorders, Laramie, WY 82070. Offers speech-language pathology (MS). *Accreditation:* ASHA. Part-time programs available. Postbaccalaureate distance learning degree programs offered (minimal on-campus study). *Entrance requirements:* For master's, GRE General Test, minimum GPA of 3.0. Additional exam requirements/recommendations for international students: Required—TOEFL. Electronic applications accepted. *Faculty research:* Child language, visual reinforcement audiometry, voice, auditory brain response, TBI.

Utah State University, School of Graduate Studies, College of Education and Human Services, Department of Communicative Disorders and Deaf Education, Logan, UT 84322. Offers audiology (Au D, Ed S); communication disorders and deaf education (M Ed); communicative disorders and deaf education (MA, MS). *Accreditation:* ASHA (one or more programs are accredited). Evening/weekend programs available. Postbaccalaureate distance learning degree programs offered (minimal on-campus study). *Degree requirements:* For master's, thesis optional; for Ed S, thesis or alternative. *Entrance requirements:* For master's, GRE General Test, minimum GPA of 3.0, 3 recommendations; for doctorate, GRE General Test, interview, minimum GPA of 3.25. Additional exam requirements/recommendations for international students: Required—TOEFL. *Expenses:* Contact institution. *Faculty research:* Parent-infant intervention with hearing-impaired infants, voice disorders, language development and disorders, oto-accoustic emissions, deaf or hard-of-hearing infants.

Vanderbilt University, School of Medicine, Department of Hearing and Speech Sciences, Nashville, TN 37240-1001. Offers audiology (Au D, PhD); education of the deaf (MED); hearing and speech sciences (MS); speech-language-pathology (MS). *Degree requirements:* For master's, thesis optional; for doctorate, thesis/dissertation, final and qualifying exams. *Entrance requirements:* For master's and doctorate, GRE General Test. Additional exam requirements/recommendations for international students: Required—TOEFL. Electronic applications accepted. *Faculty research:* Audiology, speech-language pathology, child language.

Washington State University Spokane, Graduate Programs, Program in Speech and Hearing Sciences, Spokane, WA 99210. Offers MA. *Faculty:* 10. *Students:* 46 full-time (45 women), 2 part-time (both women); includes 3 minority (2 American Indian/Alaska Native, 1 Asian American or Pacific Islander), 1 international. In 2009, 23 master's awarded. *Degree requirements:* For master's, comprehensive exam, thesis (for some programs). *Entrance requirements:* For master's, GRE, minimum GPA of 3.0, 3 letters of recommendation. Additional exam requirements/recommendations for international students: Required—TOEFL (minimum score 550 paper-based; 213 computer-based). *Application deadline:* For fall admission, 1/10 priority date for domestic students, 1/10 for international students; for spring admission, 9/1 priority date for domestic students, 7/1 for international students. Application fee: $50. *Expenses:* Tuition, state resident: part-time $423 per credit. Tuition, nonresident: part-time $1032 per credit. *Financial support:* In 2009–10, research assistantships with full and partial tuition reimbursements (averaging $14,634 per year), teaching assistantships with full and partial tuition reimbursements (averaging $13,383 per year) were awarded; Federal Work-Study, scholarships/grants, health care benefits, tuition waivers (partial), and unspecified assistantships also available. Financial award application deadline: 2/15. *Faculty research:* Central auditory processing disorders, articulation, cleft palate. Total annual research expenditures: $1.6 million. *Unit head:* Dr. Chuck Madison, Professor/Graduate Coordinator, 509-358-7602, E-mail: madisonc@wsu.edu. *Application contact:* Graduate School Admissions, 800-GRADWSU, Fax: 509-335-1949, E-mail: gradsch@wsu.edu.

Washington University in St. Louis, School of Medicine, Program in Audiology and Communication Sciences, St. Louis, MO 63110. Offers audiology (Au D); deaf education (MS); speech and hearing sciences (PhD). *Accreditation:* ASHA (one or more programs are accredited). *Faculty:* 22 full-time (12 women), 18 part-time/adjunct (12 women). *Students:* 74 full-time (72 women). Average age 24. 117 applicants, 21% accepted, 24 enrolled. In 2009, 14 master's, 9 doctorates awarded. *Degree requirements:* For master's, comprehensive exam, thesis, independent study project, oral exam; for doctorate, comprehensive exam, thesis/dissertation, capstone project, comprehensive exam. *Entrance requirements:* For master's, GRE General Test, minimum B average in undergraduate course work; for doctorate, GRE General Test, minimum B average. Additional exam requirements/recommendations for international students: Required—TOEFL (minimum score 600 paper-based; 250 computer-based; 100 iBT). *Application deadline:* For fall admission, 2/15 for domestic and international students. Application fee: $50 ($75 for international students). Electronic applications accepted. *Expenses:* Contact institution. *Financial support:* In 2009–10, 74 fellowships with tuition reimbursements were awarded; research assistantships with tuition reimbursements, teaching assistantships with tuition reimbursements, career-related internships or fieldwork, Federal Work-Study, institutionally sponsored loans, scholarships/grants, traineeships, health care benefits, tuition waivers (partial), and unspecified assistantships also available. Financial award application deadline: 2/15; financial award applicants required to submit FAFSA. *Faculty research:* Audiology, deaf

education, speech and hearing sciences, hearing aids and cochlear implants, sensory neuroscience. *Unit head:* Dr. William W. Clark, Program Director, 314-747-0104, Fax: 314-747-0105. *Application contact:* Elizabeth A. Elliott, Manager, Financial Operations and Admissions, 314-747-0104, Fax: 314-747-0105, E-mail: elliottb@wustl.edu.

Wayne State University, College of Liberal Arts and Sciences, Department of Communications Disorders and Sciences, Detroit, MI 48202. Offers audiology (MA, MS, Au D, PhD); communication disorders and science (MA, PhD); speech-language pathology (MA, PhD). *Accreditation:* ASHA (one or more programs are accredited). *Degree requirements:* For doctorate, thesis/dissertation. *Entrance requirements:* For master's, GRE, letters of recommendation, minimum GPA of 3.0; for doctorate, GRE, letters or recommendation; personal statement; interview; curriculum vitae. Additional exam requirements/recommendations for international students: Required—TOEFL (minimum score 550 paper-based; 213 computer-based); Recommended—TWE (minimum score 6). Electronic applications accepted. *Faculty research:* Language disorders in children and adults, speech perception and production, neuroimaging of speech and language, tinnitus and electrophysilogy; acquired brain damage.

West Chester University of Pennsylvania, Office of Graduate Studies, College of Health Sciences, Department of Communicative Disorders, West Chester, PA 19383. Offers communicative disorders (MA); speech correction (Teaching Certificate). *Accreditation:* ASHA (one or more programs are accredited). Part-time and evening/weekend programs available. *Students:* 38 full-time (all women), 47 part-time (46 women); includes 2 minority (both Hispanic Americans). Average age 28. 174 applicants, 44% accepted, 40 enrolled. In 2009, 34 master's awarded. *Degree requirements:* For master's, comprehensive exam, thesis optional. *Entrance requirements:* For master's, MAT or GRE , three letters of recommendation, personal statement of academic and professional goals, logs of clinical observation and practicum hours. Additional exam requirements/recommendations for international students: Required—TOEFL (minimum score 550 paper-based; 213 computer-based; 80 iBT). *Application deadline:* For fall admission, 4/15 priority date for domestic students, 3/15 for international students; for spring admission, 10/15 for domestic students, 9/1 for international students. Applications are processed on a rolling basis. Application fee: $35. Electronic applications accepted. *Expenses:* Tuition, state resident: full-time $6666; part-time $370 per credit. Tuition, nonresident: full-time $10,666; part-time $593 per credit. Required fees: $122.56 per credit. *Financial support:* In 2009–10, 13 research assistantships with full and partial tuition reimbursements (averaging $5,000 per year) were awarded; unspecified assistantships also available. Support available to part-time students. Financial award application deadline: 2/15; financial award applicants required to submit FAFSA. *Faculty research:* Identification/interaction with students with communicative disorders. *Unit head:* Dr. Michael Weiss, Chair, 610-436-3401, E-mail: mweiss@wcupa.edu. *Application contact:* Dr. Mareile Koenig, Graduate Coordinator, 610-436-3218, E-mail: mkoenig@wcupa.edu.

Western Carolina University, Graduate School, College of Health and Human Sciences, Department of Communication Sciences and Disorders, Cullowhee, NC 28723. Offers MS. *Accreditation:* ASHA. Part-time programs available. *Students:* 52 full-time (50 women). Average age 26. 102 applicants, 50% accepted, 26 enrolled. In 2009, 15 master's awarded. *Degree requirements:* For master's, comprehensive exam, thesis or alternative. *Entrance requirements:* For master's, GRE, appropriate undergraduate degree with minimum GPA of 3.0, 3 letters of recommendation. Additional exam requirements/recommendations for international students: Required—TOEFL (minimum score 550 paper-based; 270 computer-based; 79 iBT). *Application deadline:* For fall admission, 2/15 for domestic students. Application fee: $45. *Financial support:* In 2009–10, 20 students received support, including 20 research assistantships (averaging $3,500 per year); fellowships, teaching assistantships, institutionally sponsored loans, traineeships, and unspecified assistantships also available. Financial award application deadline: 3/31; financial award applicants required to submit FAFSA. *Faculty research:* Early assessment and intervention in language, stuttering, school-family partnerships, voice and organic disorders, accent reduction. *Unit head:* Dr. Bill Ogletree, Head, 828-227-3379, Fax: 828-227-3312, E-mail: ogletree@email.wcu.edu. *Application contact:* Admissions Specialist for Communication Sciences and Disorders, 828-227-7398, Fax: 828-227-7480, E-mail: gradsch@email.wcu.edu.

Western Illinois University, School of Graduate Studies, College of Fine Arts and Communication, Department of Communication Sciences and Disorders, Macomb, IL 61455-1390. Offers MS. *Accreditation:* ASHA. Part-time programs available. *Students:* 32 full-time (all women); includes 2 minority (1 African American, 1 Asian American or Pacific Islander), 2 international. Average age 24. 103 applicants, 15% accepted. In 2009, 18 master's awarded. *Degree requirements:* For master's, comprehensive exam, thesis or alternative. *Entrance requirements:* For master's, GRE, minimum GPA of 3.0. Additional exam requirements/recommendations for international students: Required—TOEFL (minimum score 550 paper-based; 213 computer-based; 80 iBT). *Application deadline:* For fall admission, 2/1 priority date for domestic students. Applications are processed on a rolling basis. Application fee: $30. Electronic applications accepted. *Expenses:* Tuition, state resident: full-time $4486; part-time $249.21 per credit hour. Tuition, nonresident: full-time $8972; part-time $498.42 per credit hour. Required fees: $72.62 per credit hour. *Financial support:* In 2009–10, 13 students received support, including 13 research assistantships with full tuition reimbursements available (averaging $7,280 per year). Financial award applicants required to submit FAFSA. *Unit head:* Dr. Maureen Marx, Chairperson, 309-298-1955. *Application contact:* Evelyn Hoing, Assistant Director of Graduate Studies, 309-298-1806, Fax: 309-298-2345, E-mail: grad-office@wiu.edu.

Western Kentucky University, Graduate Studies, College of Health and Human Services, Department of Communication Disorders, Bowling Green, KY 42101. Offers MS. *Accreditation:* ASHA. Part-time and evening/weekend programs available. Postbaccalaureate distance learning degree programs offered (no on-campus study). *Degree requirements:* For master's, comprehensive exam, written exam. *Entrance requirements:* For master's, GRE General Test, 3 letters of recommendation. Additional exam requirements/recommendations for international students: Required—TOEFL (minimum score 555 paper-based; 213 computer-based; 79 iBT). *Expenses:* Tuition, state resident: full-time $4160; part-time $416 per credit hour. Tuition, nonresident: full-time $9550; part-time $506 per credit hour. Tuition and fees vary according to campus/location and reciprocity agreements.

Western Michigan University, Graduate College, College of Health and Human Services, Department of Speech Pathology and Audiology, Kalamazoo, MI 49008. Offers audiology (Au D); speech-language pathology (MA). *Accreditation:* ASHA. *Faculty:* 14 full-time (9 women). *Students:* 59 full-time (55 women), 1 (woman) part-time; includes 2 minority (both Hispanic Americans), 3 international. 110 applicants, 66% accepted, 26 enrolled. In 2009, 33 master's awarded. *Degree requirements:* For master's, thesis optional, clinical practicum. *Entrance requirements:* For master's, GRE General Test. *Application deadline:* For fall admission, 3/15 priority date for domestic students. Applications are processed on a rolling basis. Application fee: $25. *Financial support:* Fellowships, research assistantships, teaching assistantships, Federal Work-Study available. Financial award application deadline: 2/15; financial award applicants required to submit FAFSA. *Unit head:* Dr. Ann A. Tyler, Chair, 269-387-8049. *Application contact:* Admissions and Orientation, 269-387-2000, Fax: 269-387-2355.

Western Washington University, Graduate School, College of Humanities and Social Sciences, Department of Communication Sciences and Disorders, Bellingham, WA 98225-5996. Offers MA. *Accreditation:* ASHA. Part-time programs available. *Degree requirements:* For master's, comprehensive exam, thesis optional. *Entrance requirements:* For master's, GRE General Test, minimum GPA of 3.0 in last 60 semester hours or last 90 quarter hours. Additional exam requirements/recommendations for international students: Required—TOEFL (minimum score 567 paper-based; 227 computer-based). Electronic applications accepted. *Faculty research:* Autism, stroke and stroke perception, aural rehabilitation and cochlear implants, auditory processing, speech in individuals with Parkinson's disease.

West Texas A&M University, College of Fine Arts and Humanities, Department of Art, Communication, and Theater, Program in Communication Disorders, Canyon, TX 79016-0001. Offers MS. *Accreditation:* ASHA. Part-time programs available. *Degree requirements:* For master's, comprehensive exam, thesis optional. *Entrance requirements:* For master's, GRE

General Test, minimum B average in all clinical courses, liability insurance, first aid card, immunizations. Additional exam requirements/recommendations for international students: Required—TOEFL (minimum score 550 paper-based).

West Virginia University, College of Human Resources and Education, Department of Speech Pathology and Audiology, Morgantown, WV 26506. Offers audiology (Au D); speech-language pathology (MS). *Accreditation:* ASHA. *Degree requirements:* For master's, thesis optional, PRAXIS; for doctorate, thesis/dissertation or alternative, PRAXIS. *Entrance requirements:* For master's, GRE General Test, minimum GPA of 3.0, letter of recommendation; for doctorate, GRE General Test, letters of recommendation, minimum GPA of 3.0. Additional exam requirements/recommendations for international students: Required—TOEFL. Electronic applications accepted. *Faculty research:* Speech perception, language disorders in children, auditory skills, fluency disorders, phonological disorders in children.

Wichita State University, Graduate School, College of Health Professions, Department of Communication Sciences and Disorders, Wichita, KS 67260. Offers MA, Au D, PhD. *Accreditation:* ASHA (one or more programs are accredited). *Expenses:* Tuition, state resident: full-time $4247; part-time $235.95 per credit hour. Tuition, nonresident: full-time $11,171; part-time $620.60 per credit hour. Required fees: $34; $3.60 per credit hour. $17 per term. Tuition and fees vary according to campus/location and program. *Financial support:* Teaching assistantships available. *Unit head:* Dr. Kathy Coufal, Chairperson, 316-978-3240, Fax: 316-978-3302, E-mail: kathy.coufal@wichita.edu. *Application contact:* Dr. Kathy Coufal, Chairperson, 316-978-3240, Fax: 316-978-3302, E-mail: kathy.coufal@wichita.edu.

William Paterson University of New Jersey, College of Science and Health, Wayne, NJ 07470-8420. Offers biotechnology (MS); communication disorders (MS); general biology (MS); nursing (MSN). Part-time and evening/weekend programs available. *Students:* 53 full-time (48 women), 135 part-time (126 women); includes 27 minority (7 African Americans, 11 Asian Americans or Pacific Islanders, 9 Hispanic Americans), 4 international. *Entrance requirements:* For master's, GRE General Test, minimum GPA of 2.75. *Application deadline:* Applications are processed on a rolling basis. Application fee: $50. Electronic applications accepted. *Financial support:* Research assistantships with full tuition reimbursements, career-related internships or fieldwork and unspecified assistantships available. Support available to part-time students. Financial award application deadline: 4/1; financial award applicants required to submit FAFSA. *Faculty research:* Plant tissue culture, DNA cloning, cellular structure, language development, speech and hearing science. *Unit head:* Dr. Sandra DeYoung, Dean, 973-720-2432, E-mail: deyoungs@wpunj.edu. *Application contact:* Christina Aiello, Assistant Director, Graduate Admissions, 973-720-2506, Fax: 973-720-2035, E-mail: aielloc@wpunj.edu.

Worcester State College, Graduate Studies, Program in Speech-Language Pathology, Worcester, MA 01602-2597. Offers MS. *Accreditation:* ASHA. Part-time and evening/weekend programs available. *Faculty:* 8 full-time (6 women). *Students:* 52 full-time (49 women), 36 part-time (all women); includes 4 minority (1 American Indian/Alaska Native, 1 Asian American or Pacific Islander, 2 Hispanic Americans). Average age 28. 175 applicants, 26% accepted, 32 enrolled. In 2009, 24 master's awarded. *Degree requirements:* For master's, comprehensive exam, thesis, national licensing exam. *Entrance requirements:* For master's, GRE General Test or MAT, 15 credits of course work in human communication. Additional exam requirements/recommendations for international students: Required—TOEFL (minimum score 550 paper-based; 213 computer-based; 79 iBT). *Application deadline:* For fall admission, 2/15 for domestic and international students. Application fee: $30. *Expenses:* Contact institution. *Financial support:* In 2009–10, 8 students received support, including 8 research assistantships with full tuition reimbursements available (averaging $4,400 per year); career-related internships or fieldwork, scholarships/grants, and unspecified assistantships also available. Financial award application deadline: 3/1; financial award applicants required to submit FAFSA. *Faculty research:* Hearing threshold norms, language learning disabilities. *Unit head:* Dr. Maryann Power, Coordinator, 508-929-8629, Fax: 508-929-8475, E-mail: mpower@worcester.edu. *Application contact:* Nicole Brown, Assistant Dean of Graduate and Continuing Education, 508-929-8787, Fax: 508-929-8100, E-mail: nbrown@worcester.edu.

Dental Hygiene

Boston University, Goldman School of Dental Medicine, Graduate Programs in Dentistry, Boston, MA 02215. Offers advanced general dentistry (CAGS); dental public health (MS, MSD, D Sc D, CAGS); dentistry (DMD); endodontics (MSD, D Sc D, CAGS); implantology (CAGS); operative dentistry (MSD, D Sc D, CAGS); oral and maxillofacial surgery (MSD, D Sc D, CAGS); oral biology (MSD, D Sc, D Sc D, PhD); orthodontics (MSD, D Sc D, CAGS); pediatric dentistry (MSD, D Sc D, CAGS); periodontology (MSD, D Sc D, CAGS); prosthodontics (MSD, D Sc D, CAGS). *Students:* 606 full-time (295 women); includes 149 minority (7 African Americans, 3 American Indian/Alaska Native, 113 Asian Americans or Pacific Islanders, 26 Hispanic Americans), 209 international. Average age 26. In 2009, 175 first professional degrees awarded. *Degree requirements:* For master's, thesis; for doctorate, thesis/dissertation; for CAGS, thesis (for some programs). *Entrance requirements:* For DMD, DAT, minimum GPA of 3.0; for CAGS, dental degree. *Application deadline:* For fall admission, 5/1 for domestic students. Applications are processed on a rolling basis. Application fee: $60. *Expenses:* Contact institution. *Financial support:* Career-related internships or fieldwork and institutionally sponsored loans available. Financial award application deadline: 4/15; financial award applicants required to submit CSS PROFILE or FAFSA. *Faculty research:* Defensive mechanisms, bone-cell regulation, protein biochemistry, molecular biology, biomaterials. *Unit head:* Dr. Jeffrey W. Hutter, Interim Dean, 617-638-4780. *Application contact:* 617-638-4787, Fax: 617-638-4798.

Eastern Washington University, Graduate Studies, College of Science, Health and Engineering, Department of Dental Hygiene, Cheney, WA 99004-2431. Offers MS. *Expenses:* Tuition, state resident: full-time $7476; part-time $249 per quarter hour. Tuition, nonresident: full-time $18,030; part-time $601 per quarter hour. Required fees: $3.50 per quarter hour. $142 per quarter.

Idaho State University, Office of Graduate Studies, Kasiska College of Health Professions, Department of Dental Hygiene, Pocatello, ID 83209-8048. Offers MS. Part-time programs available. *Faculty:* 5 full-time (all women). *Students:* 35 part-time (all women); includes 6 minority (3 Asian Americans or Pacific Islanders, 3 Hispanic Americans), 1 international. Average age 41. In 2009, 2 master's awarded. *Degree requirements:* For master's, comprehensive exam, thesis, thesis defense, practicum experience, oral exam. *Entrance requirements:* For master's, GRE, MAT, baccalaureate degree in dental hygiene, minimum GPA of 3.0 in upper-division and dental hygiene coursework, current dental hygiene licensure in good standing. Additional exam requirements/recommendations for international students: Required—TOEFL (minimum score 600 paper-based; 213 computer-based; 80 iBT). *Application deadline:* For fall admission, 7/1 for domestic students, 6/1 for international students; for spring admission, 12/1 for domestic students, 11/1 for international students. Applications are processed on a rolling basis. Application fee: $55. Electronic applications accepted. *Expenses:* Tuition, state resident: full-time $3318; part-time $297 per credit hour. Tuition, nonresident: full-time $13,120; part-time $437 per credit hour. Required fees: $2530. Tuition and fees vary according to program. *Financial support:* Teaching assistantships with full and partial tuition reimbursements, career-related internships or fieldwork, Federal Work-Study, institutionally sponsored loans, scholarships/grants, traineeships, health care benefits, tuition waivers (full and partial), and unspecified assistantships available. Support available to part-time students. Financial award application deadline: 1/1; financial award applicants required to submit FAFSA. *Unit head:* Kathleen Hodges, Chair, 208-282-2744, Fax: 208-282-5834, E-mail: hodgkat1@isu.edu. *Application contact:* Tami Carson, Graduate School Technical Records Specialist, 208-282-2150, Fax: 208-282-4847, E-mail: carstami@isu.edu.

Missouri Southern State University, Program in Dental Hygiene, Joplin, MO 64801-1595. Offers MS. Part-time programs available. *Degree requirements:* For master's, project. *Entrance requirements:* For master's, copy of current dental hygiene license. Electronic applications accepted.

Old Dominion University, College of Health Sciences, School of Dental Hygiene, Norfolk, VA 23529. Offers MS. Part-time programs available. *Faculty:* 8 full-time (all women). *Students:* 7 full-time (all women), 13 part-time (all women); includes 5 minority (4 African Americans, 1 Asian American or Pacific Islander), 3 international. Average age 32. 5 applicants, 80% accepted, 4 enrolled. In 2009, 4 master's awarded. *Degree requirements:* For master's, comprehensive exam, thesis optional, writing proficiency exam. *Entrance requirements:* For master's, Dental Hygiene National Board Examination, BS or certificate in dental hygiene or related area, minimum GPA of 2.8 (3.0 in major), letters of recommendation. Additional exam requirements/recommendations for international students: Required—TOEFL (minimum score 550 paper-based; 213 computer-based; 79 iBT). *Application deadline:* For fall admission, 7/1 for domestic students, 4/15 for international students; for spring admission, 12/1 for domestic students, 10/1 for international students. Applications are processed on a rolling basis. Application fee: $40. Electronic applications accepted. *Expenses:* Tuition, state resident: full-time $8112; part-time $338 per credit. Tuition, nonresident: full-time $20,256; part-time $844 per credit. Required fees: $119 per semester. One-time fee: $50. *Financial support:* In 2009–10, 4 students received support, including 3 teaching assistantships with partial tuition reimbursements available (averaging $10,000 per year); fellowships, research assistantships, career-related internships or fieldwork, scholarships/grants, tuition waivers, and unspecified assistantships also available. Support available to part-time students. Financial award application deadline: 2/15; financial award applicants required to submit CSS PROFILE or FAFSA. *Faculty research:* Clinical dental hygiene practice, dental hygiene client health behaviors, dental hygiene education interventions, oral product testing. Total annual research expenditures: $93,714. *Unit head:* Prof. Michele L. Darby, Graduate Program Director, 757-683-5232, Fax: 757-683-5329, E-mail: mdarby@odu.edu. *Application contact:* Prof. Michele L. Darby, Graduate Program Director, 757-683-5232, Fax: 757-683-5329, E-mail: mdarby@odu.edu.

Texas A&M Health Science Center, Baylor College of Dentistry, Graduate Division, Department of Dental Hygiene, College Station, TX 77840. Offers MS. Part-time programs available. *Degree requirements:* For master's, thesis (for some programs). *Entrance requirements:* For master's, GRE General Test, National Dental Hygiene Board Examination, minimum GPA of 3.0 in dental hygiene course work, 2.7 overall. *Faculty research:* Assessment of outcomes, dental materials, educational research, HIV patients, underserved patient populations, handicapped patients.

Université de Montréal, Faculty of Dental Medicine, Program in Stomatology Residency, Montréal, QC H3C 3J7, Canada. Offers Certificate. *Students:* 1 full-time (0 women). *Unit head:* Gilles Lavigne, Dean, 514-343-6005, Fax: 514-343-2233, E-mail: gilles.lavigne@umontreal.ca. *Application contact:* Anne Charbonneau, Associate Dean for Graduate Studies, 514-343-5761, Fax: 514-343-2233, E-mail: anne.charbonneau@umontreal.ca.

University of Alberta, Faculty of Medicine and Dentistry, Department of Dentistry, Program in Dental Hygiene, Edmonton, AB T6G 2E1, Canada. Offers Diploma. *Faculty:* 7 full-time (all women), 26 part-time/adjunct. *Students:* 84 full-time (83 women). 154 applicants, 32% accepted, 42 enrolled. *Application deadline:* For fall admission, 11/1 for domestic students. Application fee: $75. Electronic applications accepted. Tuition and fees charges are reported in Canadian dollars. *Expenses:* Tuition, area resident: Full-time $4626 Canadian dollars; part-time $99.72 Canadian dollars per unit. International tuition: $8216 Canadian dollars full-time. Required fees: $3590 Canadian dollars; $99.72 Canadian dollars per unit. $215 Canadian dollars per term. *Unit head:* Dr. Sharon Compton, Director, 780-492-4479, Fax: 780-492-8552. *Application contact:* Melanie Grams, Administrative Assistant, 780-492-6437, Fax: 780-492-7536, E-mail: melanie.grams@ualberta.ca.

University of Bridgeport, Fones School of Dental Hygiene, Bridgeport, CT 06604. Offers MS. Part-time and evening/weekend programs available. Postbaccalaureate distance learning degree programs offered (no on-campus study). *Degree requirements:* For master's, thesis. *Entrance requirements:* For master's, Dental Hygiene National Board Examination. Additional exam requirements/recommendations for international students: Recommended—TOEFL (minimum score 550 paper-based; 213 computer-based; 80 iBT), IELTS (minimum score 6.5).

University of Maryland, Baltimore, Graduate School, Graduate Programs in Dentistry, Department of Dental Hygiene, Baltimore, MD 21201. Offers MS. *Students:* 2 full-time (both women), 7 part-time (all women); includes 2 minority (both Asian Americans or Pacific Islanders). Average age 36. 11 applicants, 64% accepted, 5 enrolled. In 2009, 2 master's awarded. *Degree requirements:* For master's, thesis or alternative. *Entrance requirements:* For master's, GRE General Test, minimum GPA of 3.0. Additional exam requirements/recommendations for international students: Required—TOEFL (minimum score 550 paper-based; 80 iBT), or IELTS (minimum score 7). *Application deadline:* For fall admission, 6/30 for domestic students, 1/15 for international students; for spring admission, 11/30 for domestic students. Application fee: $50. Electronic applications accepted. *Expenses:* Tuition, state resident: full-time $7290; part-time $405 per credit hour. Tuition, nonresident: full-time $12,780; part-time $710 per credit hour. Required fees: $774; $10 per credit hour. $297 per semester. Tuition and fees vary according to course load, degree level and program. *Financial support:* Fellowships available. Support available to part-time students. Financial award application deadline: 2/15. *Faculty research:* Dental hygiene education, health care management, health system theory and policy development, hospital dental hygiene, clinical practice. *Unit head:* Jacqueline Fried, Chairperson, 410-706-7773, Fax: 410-706-0349. *Application contact:* Kathryn Battani, Graduate Program Director, 410-706-7773, E-mail: kbattani@umaryland.edu.

University of Michigan, School of Dentistry and Horace H. Rackham School of Graduate Studies, Graduate Programs in Dentistry, Dental Hygiene Program, Ann Arbor, MI 48109-1078. Offers MS. Part-time and evening/weekend programs available. Postbaccalaureate distance learning degree programs offered (minimal on-campus study). Terminal master's awarded for partial completion of doctoral program. *Degree requirements:* For master's, thesis. *Entrance requirements:* For master's, bachelor's degree in dental hygiene. Additional exam requirements/recommendations for international students: Required—TOEFL (minimum score 84 iBT). Electronic applications accepted. *Expenses:* Tuition, state resident: full-time $17,286; part-time $1099 per credit hour. Tuition, nonresident: full-time $34,944; part-time $2080 per credit hour. Required fees: $95 per semester. Tuition and fees vary according to course load, degree level and program.

University of Missouri–Kansas City, School of Dentistry, Kansas City, MO 64110-2499. Offers advanced education in dentistry (Graduate Dental Certificate); dental hygiene education (MS); dental specialties (Graduate Dental Certificate); dentistry (DDS); diagnostic sciences (Graduate Dental Certificate); oral and maxillofacial surgery (Graduate Dental Certificate); oral biology (MS, PhD); orthodontics and dentofacial orthopedics (Graduate Dental Certificate);

Dental Hygiene

University of Missouri–Kansas City (continued)
pediatric dentistry (Graduate Dental Certificate); periodontics (Graduate Dental Certificate); prosthodontics (Graduate Dental Certificate). PhD (interdisciplinary) offered through the School of Graduate Studies. *Accreditation:* ADA (one or more programs are accredited). *Faculty:* 101 full-time (40 women), 77 part-time/adjunct (25 women). *Students:* 402 full-time (177 women), 50 part-time (28 women); includes 54 minority (8 African Americans, 3 American Indian/Alaska Native, 29 Asian Americans or Pacific Islanders, 14 Hispanic Americans), 1 international. Average age 27. 536 applicants, 24% accepted, 126 enrolled. In 2009, 102 first professional degrees, 9 master's awarded. *Degree requirements:* For master's, thesis; for doctorate, thesis/dissertation. *Entrance requirements:* For DDS, DAT; for master's, DAT, letters of evaluation, personal interview; for Graduate Dental Certificate, DDS. Additional exam requirements/recommendations for international students: Required—TOEFL (minimum score 550 paper-based; 213 computer-based; 80 iBT). *Application deadline:* For fall admission, 2/1 for domestic and international students. Application fee: $45 ($50 for international students). *Expenses:* Contact institution. *Financial support:* In 2009–10, 4 fellowships (averaging $60,500 per year), 3 research assistantships (averaging $17,728 per year) were awarded; career-related internships or fieldwork, Federal Work-Study, institutionally sponsored loans, and tuition waivers (full and partial) also available. Support available to part-time students. Financial award application deadline: 3/1; financial award applicants required to submit FAFSA. *Faculty research:* Biomaterials, dental use of lasers, effectiveness of periodontal treatments, temporomandibular joint dysfunction. Total annual research expenditures: $5.9 million. *Unit head:* Dr. Marsha Pyle, Dean, 816-235-2010. *Application contact:* 816-235-2080.

University of New Mexico, School of Medicine, Program in Dental Hygiene, Albuquerque, NM 87131-2039. Offers MS. *Expenses:* Tuition, state resident: full-time $2099; part-time $233.20 per credit hour. Tuition, nonresident: full-time $6650. Required fees: $25 per semester. Tuition and fees vary according to course load, program and reciprocity agreements.

The University of North Carolina at Chapel Hill, School of Dentistry and Graduate School, Graduate Programs in Dentistry, Chapel Hill, NC 27599. Offers dental hygiene (MS); endodontics (MS); epidemiology (PhD); operative dentistry (MS); oral and maxillofacial pathology (MS); oral and maxillofacial radiology (MS); oral biology (PhD); orthodontics (MS); pediatric dentistry (MS); periodontology (MS); prosthodontics (MS). *Degree requirements:* For master's, thesis; for doctorate, thesis/dissertation. *Entrance requirements:* For master's, dental degree; for doctorate, GRE General Test. Additional exam requirements/recommendations for international students: Required—TOEFL (minimum score 550 paper-based; 213 computer-based). Electronic applications accepted. *Expenses:* Contact institution. *Faculty research:* Inflammation, cell biology, immunology, microbiology, neuroscience, molecular biology.

The University of Texas Health Science Center at San Antonio, School of Allied Health Sciences, San Antonio, TX 78229-3900. Offers clinical laboratory sciences (MS); deaf education and hearing science (MED); dental hygiene (MS); occupational therapy (MOT); physical therapy (MPT); physician assistant studies (MS). *Accreditation:* AOTA; APTA; ARC-PA. *Expenses:* Tuition, state resident: full-time $2832; part-time $118 per credit hour. Tuition, nonresident: full-time $10,896; part-time $454 per credit hour. Required fees: $884 per semester. One-time fee: $70.

Emergency Medical Services

Baylor University, Graduate School, Military Programs, Program in Emergency Medicine, Waco, TX 76798. Offers D Sc PA. *Students:* 16 full-time (2 women); includes 4 minority (1 African American, 1 American Indian/Alaska Native, 1 Asian American or Pacific Islander, 1 Hispanic American). In 2009, 10 doctorates awarded. *Unit head:* Maj. Larry Lindsay, Graduate Program Director, 210-916-4542, Fax: 210-221-7306, E-mail: larry.lindsay1@us.army.mil. *Application contact:* Maj. Sue Love, 210-916-4542, Fax: 254-710-3870, E-mail: sue.love@us.army.mil.

Drexel University, College of Nursing and Health Professions, Emergency and Public Safety Services Program, Philadelphia, PA 19104-2875. Offers MS. Part-time and evening/weekend programs available. *Degree requirements:* For master's, comprehensive exam. *Entrance requirements:* For master's, GRE General Test, minimum GPA of 2.75.

San Diego State University, Graduate and Research Affairs, College of Health and Human Services, Graduate School of Public Health, San Diego, CA 92182. Offers environmental health (MPH); epidemiology (MPH, PhD), including biostatistics (MPH); global emergency preparedness and response (MS); global health (PhD); health behavior (PhD); health promotion (MPH); health services administration (MPH); toxicology (MS); MPH/MA; MSW/MPH. *Accreditation:* ABET (one or more programs are accredited); CAHME (one or more programs are accredited); CEPH (one or more programs are accredited). Part-time programs available. *Degree requirements:* For master's, comprehensive exam (for some programs), thesis (for some programs); for doctorate, thesis/dissertation. *Entrance requirements:* For master's, GMAT (MPH in health services administration), GRE General Test; for doctorate, GRE General Test. Additional exam requirements/recommendations for international students: Required—TOEFL. *Faculty research:* Evaluation of tobacco, AIDS prevalence and prevention, mammography, infant death project, Alzheimer's in elderly Chinese.

Université Laval, Faculty of Medicine, Post-Professional Programs in Medical Studies, Québec, QC G1K 7P4, Canada. Offers anatomy–pathology (DESS); anesthesiology (DESS); cardiology (DESS); care of older people (Diploma); clinical research (DESS); community health (DESS); dermatology (DESS); diagnostic radiology (DESS); emergency medicine (Diploma); family medicine (DESS); general surgery (DESS); geriatrics (DESS); hematology (DESS); internal medicine (DESS); maternal and fetal medicine (Diploma); medical biochemistry (DESS); medical microbiology and infectious diseases (DESS); medical oncology (DESS); nephrology (DESS); neurology (DESS); neurosurgery (DESS); obstetrics and gynecology (DESS); ophthalmology (DESS); orthopedic surgery (DESS); oto-rhino-laryngology (DESS); palliative medicine (Diploma); pediatrics (DESS); plastic surgery (DESS); psychiatry (DESS); pulmonary medicine (DESS); radiology–oncology (DESS); thoracic surgery (DESS); urology (DESS). *Degree requirements:* For other advanced degree, comprehensive exam. *Entrance requirements:* For degree, knowledge of French. Electronic applications accepted.

University of Guelph, Ontario Veterinary College and Graduate Program Services, Graduate Programs in Veterinary Sciences, Department of Clinical Studies, Guelph, ON N1G 2W1, Canada. Offers anesthesiology (M Sc, DV Sc); cardiology (DV Sc, Diploma); clinical studies (Diploma); dermatology (M Sc); diagnostic imaging (M Sc, DV Sc); emergency/critical care (M Sc, DV Sc, Diploma); medicine (M Sc, DV Sc); neurology (M Sc, DV Sc); ophthalmology (M Sc, DV Sc); surgery (M Sc, DV Sc). *Degree requirements:* For master's, thesis; for doctorate, comprehensive exam, thesis/dissertation. *Entrance requirements:* Additional exam requirements/recommendations for international students: Required—TOEFL (minimum score 550 paper-based; 213 computer-based), IELTS (minimum score 6.5). Electronic applications accepted. *Faculty research:* Orthopedics, respirology, oncology, exercise physiology, cardiology.

Occupational Therapy

Alvernia University, Graduate Studies, Program in Occupational Therapy, Reading, PA 19607-1799. Offers MSOT. *Accreditation:* AOTA. Part-time and evening/weekend programs available. *Degree requirements:* For master's, thesis optional. Electronic applications accepted.

American International College, School of Health Sciences, Program in Occupational Therapy, Springfield, MA 01109-3189. Offers MSOT. *Accreditation:* AOTA. *Degree requirements:* For master's, comprehensive exam, thesis (for some programs), clinical observation. *Entrance requirements:* Additional exam requirements/recommendations for international students: Required—TOEFL. Electronic applications accepted. *Expenses:* Contact institution.

A.T. Still University of Health Sciences, Arizona School of Health Sciences, Mesa, AZ 85206. Offers advanced occupational therapy (MS); advanced physician assistant (MS); athletic training (MS); audiology (Au D); health sciences (DHSc); human movement (MS); occupational therapy (MS); physical therapy (MS, DPT); physician assistant (MS); transitional audiology (Au D); transitional physical therapy (DPT). *Accreditation:* AOTA (one or more programs are accredited); ASHA. Postbaccalaureate distance learning degree programs offered (no on-campus study). *Faculty:* 53 full-time (30 women), 205 part-time/adjunct (117 women). *Students:* 491 full-time (353 women), 1,251 part-time (874 women); includes 319 minority (70 African Americans, 11 American Indian/Alaska Native, 176 Asian Americans or Pacific Islanders, 62 Hispanic Americans), 3 international. Average age 31. 2,697 applicants, 22% accepted, 420 enrolled. In 2009, 225 master's, 523 doctorates awarded. *Degree requirements:* For master's, thesis (for some programs); for doctorate, thesis/dissertation (for some programs). *Entrance requirements:* For master's, GRE General Test; for doctorate, GRE, Evaluation of Practicing Audiologists Capabilities (Au D), Physical Therapy Evaluation Tool (DPT), current state licensure, master's degree or equivalent (Au D), minimum GPA of 2.7. Additional exam requirements/recommendations for international students: Recommended—TOEFL (minimum score 550 paper-based; 213 computer-based; 80 iBT). *Application deadline:* For fall admission, 2/1 priority date for domestic and international students. Applications are processed on a rolling basis. Application fee: $60. *Expenses:* Contact institution. *Financial support:* In 2009–10, 651 students received support. Federal Work-Study and scholarships/grants available. Financial award application deadline: 5/1; financial award applicants required to submit FAFSA. *Faculty research:* Adolescent health-related quality of life, clinical outcomes following sport related injury, pediatric concussion, shoulder stability and neuromuscular control, sport conditioning, exercise and sport psychology, geriatric exercise and wellness. Total annual research expenditures: $61,527. *Unit head:* Dr. Randy Danielsen, Dean, 480-219-6000, Fax: 480-219-6110, E-mail: rdanielsen@atsu.edu. *Application contact:* Donna Sparks, Associate Director for Admissions, 660-626-2237, Fax: 660-626-2969, E-mail: admissions@atsu.edu.

Barry University, College of Health Sciences, Program in Occupational Therapy, Miami Shores, FL 33161-6695. Offers MS. *Accreditation:* AOTA. Electronic applications accepted.

Bay Path College, Program in Occupational Therapy, Longmeadow, MA 01106-2292. Offers MOT, MS. *Accreditation:* AOTA. Part-time and evening/weekend programs available. *Entrance requirements:* Additional exam requirements/recommendations for international students: Recommended—TOEFL (minimum score 500 paper-based). Electronic applications accepted.

Belmont University, College of Health Sciences, School of Occupational Therapy, Nashville, TN 37212-3757. Offers MSOT, OTD. *Accreditation:* AOTA. Evening/weekend programs available. *Degree requirements:* For master's, thesis, 6 months of supervised clinical work; for doctorate, comprehensive exam, thesis/dissertation, 6 months of supervised clinical work. *Entrance requirements:* For master's, GRE General Test, 50 observation hours, 1 year experience as licensed healthcare professional; for doctorate, GRE General Test, 50 observation hours. Additional exam requirements/recommendations for international students: Required—TOEFL (minimum score 500 paper-based; 173 computer-based). Electronic applications accepted. *Expenses:* Contact institution. *Faculty research:* Rehabilitation outcomes, pediatrics, low vision, assistive technology.

Boston University, College of Health and Rehabilitation Sciences—Sargent College, Department of Occupational Therapy, Boston, MA 02215. Offers occupational therapy (MS, MSOT, OTD); rehabilitation sciences (D Sc). *Accreditation:* AOTA (one or more programs are accredited). Postbaccalaureate distance learning degree programs offered (minimal on-campus study). *Faculty:* 13 full-time (all women), 2 part-time/adjunct (both women). *Students:* 124 full-time (123 women), 1 (woman) part-time; includes 20 minority (1 African American, 12 Asian Americans or Pacific Islanders, 7 Hispanic Americans). Average age 28. 89 applicants, 69% accepted, 26 enrolled. In 2009, 31 master's, 3 doctorates awarded. *Degree requirements:* For master's, thesis optional, full-time internship; for doctorate, thesis/dissertation. *Entrance requirements:* For master's, minimum GPA of 3.0; BS in occupational therapy; for doctorate, GRE General Test. Additional exam requirements/recommendations for international students: Required—TOEFL (minimum score 550 paper-based; 84 computer-based), TWE (minimum score 5). *Application deadline:* For fall admission, 1/15 priority date for domestic and international students. Applications are processed on a rolling basis. Application fee: $70. Electronic applications accepted. *Expenses:* Tuition: Full-time $37,910; part-time $1184 per credit hour. Required fees: $386; $40 per semester. Part-time tuition and fees vary according to class time, course level, degree level and program. *Financial support:* In 2009–10, 64 students received support, including 11 fellowships (averaging $14,000 per year); career-related internships or fieldwork, Federal Work-Study, institutionally sponsored loans, scholarships/grants, and tuition waivers (partial) also available. Financial award application deadline: 4/15; financial award applicants required to submit FAFSA. *Faculty research:* Sensory integration, outcomes measurement, impact of Parkinson's disease, families of people with autism. *Unit head:* Dr. Wendy J. Coster, Department Chair, 617-353-2727, Fax: 617-353-2926, E-mail: wjcoster@bu.edu. *Application contact:* Sharon Sankey, Director, Student Services, 617-353-2713, Fax: 617-353-7500, E-mail: ssankey@bu.edu.

Brenau University, Graduate Programs, School of Health and Science, Gainesville, GA 30501. Offers family nurse practitioner (MSN); nurse educator (MSN); nursing management (MSN); occupational therapy (MS); psychology (MS). *Accreditation:* AOTA; NLN. Part-time and

evening/weekend programs available. *Faculty:* 14 full-time (12 women), 6 part-time/adjunct (5 women). *Students:* 97 full-time (92 women), 92 part-time (84 women); includes 46 minority (37 African Americans, 2 American Indian/Alaska Native, 2 Asian Americans or Pacific Islanders, 5 Hispanic Americans), 2 international. Average age 34. 168 applicants, 50% accepted, 68 enrolled. In 2009, 35 master's awarded. *Degree requirements:* For master's, comprehensive exam (for some programs), thesis (for some programs), clinical practicum hours. *Entrance requirements:* For master's, GRE General Test or MAT (for some programs), interview, writing sample, references (for some programs). Additional exam requirements/recommendations for international students: Required—TOEFL (minimum score 500 paper-based). *Application deadline:* Applications are processed on a rolling basis. Application fee: $35. Electronic applications accepted. *Expenses:* Contact institution. *Financial support:* In 2009–10, 32 students received support. Scholarships/grants and traineeships available. Support available to part-time students. Financial award application deadline: 7/15; financial award applicants required to submit FAFSA. *Unit head:* Dr. Gale Starich, Dean, 777-718-5305, Fax: 770-297-5929, E-mail: gstarich@brenau.edu. *Application contact:* Christina White, Admissions Coordinator, 770-718-5320, Fax: 770-770-5338, E-mail: cwhite@brenau.edu.

California State University, Dominguez Hills, College of Professional Studies, School of Health and Human Services, Program in Occupational Therapy, Carson, CA 90747-0001. Offers MS. *Accreditation:* AOTA. *Faculty:* 5 full-time (4 women), 6 part-time/adjunct (all women). *Students:* 117 full-time (102 women), 1 (woman) part-time; includes 57 minority (5 African Americans, 38 Asian Americans or Pacific Islanders, 14 Hispanic Americans), 2 international. Average age 28. 3 applicants, 0% accepted, 0 enrolled. In 2009, 38 master's awarded. *Degree requirements:* For master's, comprehensive exam. *Entrance requirements:* For master's, GRE. Additional exam requirements/recommendations for international students: Required—TOEFL, TWE. *Application deadline:* For fall admission, 9/15 priority date for domestic students. Electronic applications accepted. *Expenses:* Tuition, nonresident: full-time $6696; part-time $372 per unit. Required fees: $5946; $1752 per semester. *Faculty research:* Child school functioning, assessment, lifespan occupational development, low vision occupational therapy intervention. *Unit head:* Dr. Claudia Peyton, Director, 310-243-3067, E-mail: cpayton@csudh.edu. *Application contact:* Dr. Gayle Ball-Parker, Director of Admissions, 310-243-3645, E-mail: gball@csudh.edu.

Chatham University, Program in Occupational Therapy, Pittsburgh, PA 15232-2826. Offers MOT, OTD. *Accreditation:* AOTA. *Students:* 80 full-time (69 women), 11 part-time (10 women). Average age 32. 127 applicants, 59% accepted, 50 enrolled. *Entrance requirements:* For master's, recommendation letter, community service, volunteer service. Additional exam requirements/recommendations for international students: Required—TOEFL (minimum score 600 paper-based; 250 computer-based; 100 iBT), IELTS (minimum score 6.5), TWE. *Application deadline:* For fall admission, 5/1 priority date for domestic and international students. Applications are processed on a rolling basis. Application fee: $45. Electronic applications accepted. *Expenses:* Contact institution. *Financial support:* Applicants required to submit FAFSA. *Unit head:* Dr. Joyce Salls, Director, 412-365-1177, E-mail: salls@chatham.edu. *Application contact:* Dory Perry, Associate Director of Graduate Admissions, 412-365-2758, Fax: 412-365-1609, E-mail: gradadmissions@chatham.edu.

Cleveland State University, College of Graduate Studies, College of Science, Department of Health Sciences, Program in Occupational Therapy, Cleveland, OH 44115. Offers MOT. *Accreditation:* AOTA. *Degree requirements:* For master's, completion of fieldwork, capstone research project. *Entrance requirements:* For master's, GRE (if overall GPA less than 3.0). Additional exam requirements/recommendations for international students: Recommended—TOEFL (minimum score 525 paper-based; 197 computer-based; 14 iBT), IELTS (minimum score 6). Electronic applications accepted. *Faculty research:* Pediatrics, psychology, daily living, exercise physiology, neuromuscular disorders.

College of Saint Mary, Program in Occupational Therapy, Omaha, NE 68106. Offers MOT.

The College of St. Scholastica, Graduate Studies, Department of Occupational Therapy, Duluth, MN 55811-4199. Offers MA. *Accreditation:* AOTA. Part-time programs available. *Degree requirements:* For master's, thesis. *Entrance requirements:* For master's, interview, minimum GPA of 2.7. Additional exam requirements/recommendations for international students: Required—TOEFL (minimum score 550 paper-based; 213 computer-based; 79 iBT). Electronic applications accepted. *Faculty research:* Gerontology, occupational therapy administration, neurorehabilitation, occupational therapy in nontraditional settings, clinical fieldwork issues.

Colorado State University, Graduate School, College of Applied Human Sciences, Department of Occupational Therapy, Fort Collins, CO 80523-1573. Offers MS. *Accreditation:* AOTA. *Faculty:* 8 full-time (6 women). *Students:* 123 full-time (121 women), 3 part-time (all women); includes 14 minority (1 African American, 3 American Indian/Alaska Native, 5 Asian Americans or Pacific Islanders, 5 Hispanic Americans), 2 international. Average age 27. 177 applicants, 33% accepted, 45 enrolled. In 2009, 40 master's awarded. *Degree requirements:* For master's, thesis optional, group research project. *Entrance requirements:* For master's, GRE Analytical Writing Test (minimum score 4.0), minimum GPA of 3.0, 3 letters of reference, resume, experience with people who have disabilities. Additional exam requirements/recommendations for international students: Required—TOEFL (minimum score 550 paper-based; 240 computer-based; 94 iBT). *Application deadline:* For fall admission, 1/15 for domestic and international students; for spring admission, 10/15 for domestic and international students. Application fee: $50. *Expenses:* Tuition, state resident: full-time $6434; part-time $359.10 per credit. Tuition, nonresident: full-time $18,116; part-time $1006.45 per credit. Required fees: $1496; $83 per credit. *Financial support:* In 2009–10, 3 students received support, including 3 teaching assistantships with partial tuition reimbursements available (averaging $9,647 per year); fellowships, research assistantships with partial tuition reimbursements available also available. Financial award application deadline: 4/30; financial award applicants required to submit FAFSA. *Faculty research:* Geriatrics, school-based service, traumatic brain injury, neurorehabilitation, neurobehavioral development. Total annual research expenditures: $630,661. *Unit head:* Dr. Wendy Wood, Department Head, 970-491-1882, Fax: 970-491-6920, E-mail: wwood@cahs.colostate.edu. *Application contact:* Linda McDowell, Admissions Coordinator, 970-491-6243, Fax: 970-491-6290, E-mail: mcdowell@cahs.colostate.edu.

Columbia University, College of Physicians and Surgeons, Programs in Occupational Therapy, New York, NY 10032. Offers movement science (Ed D), including occupational therapy; occupational therapy (professional) (MS); occupational therapy administration or education (post-professional) (MS); MPH/MS. *Accreditation:* AOTA. *Faculty:* 10 full-time (9 women), 7 part-time/adjunct (4 women). *Students:* 98 full-time (91 women), 4 part-time (all women); includes 17 minority (3 African Americans, 9 Asian Americans or Pacific Islanders, 5 Hispanic Americans). Average age 26. In 2009, 48 master's awarded. *Degree requirements:* For master's, project, 6 months of fieldwork, thesis (for post-professional students); for doctorate, comprehensive exam, thesis/dissertation. *Entrance requirements:* For master's, undergraduate course work in anatomy, physiology, statistics, psychology, social sciences, humanities, English composition; NBCOT eligibility; for doctorate, NBCOT certification, MS. Additional exam requirements/recommendations for international students: Required—TOEFL (minimum score 250 computer-based; 100 iBT), TWE (minimum score 4). *Application deadline:* For fall admission, 1/3 for domestic and international students. Application fee: $75. Electronic applications accepted. *Expenses:* Contact institution. *Financial support:* In 2009–10, 80 students received support. Career-related internships or fieldwork, Federal Work-Study, institutionally sponsored loans, and scholarships/grants available. Financial award application deadline: 4/15; financial award applicants required to submit FAFSA. *Faculty research:* Community mental health, developmental tasks of late life, infant play, cognition, obesity, motor learning. Total annual research expenditures: $35,000. *Unit head:* Dr. Janet Falk-Kessler, Director, 212-305-5267, Fax: 212-305-4569, E-mail: jf6@columbia.edu. *Application contact:* Marilyn Harper, Administrative Assistant, 212-305-5267, Fax: 212-305-4569, E-mail: mh15@columbia.edu.

Concordia University Wisconsin, Graduate Programs, School of Health and Human Services, Program in Occupational Therapy, Mequon, WI 53097-2402. Offers MOT. *Accreditation:* AOTA. *Degree requirements:* For master's, comprehensive exam, thesis or alternative. *Entrance*

requirements: Additional exam requirements/recommendations for international students: Required—TOEFL.

Creighton University, School of Pharmacy and Health Professions, Program in Occupational Therapy, Omaha, NE 68178-0001. Offers OTD. *Accreditation:* AOTA. Postbaccalaureate distance learning degree programs offered (minimal on-campus study). Electronic applications accepted. *Expenses:* Tuition: Full-time $11,700; part-time $650 per credit hour. Required fees: $126 per semester. *Faculty research:* Patient safety in health services research, health information technology and health services research, health care services in minority and underserved populations, occupational therapy in school-based programs, educational technology use in the classroom.

Dalhousie University, Faculty of Health Professions, School of Occupational Therapy, Halifax, NS B3H3J5, Canada. Offers occupational therapy (entry to profession) (M Sc); occupational therapy (post-professional) (M Sc). Part-time and evening/weekend programs available. Postbaccalaureate distance learning degree programs offered (no on-campus study). *Faculty:* 2 full-time (both women), 9 part-time/adjunct (7 women). *Students:* 2 full-time (1 woman), 4 part-time (all women). Average age 25. 6 applicants, 67% accepted. *Degree requirements:* For master's, thesis. *Entrance requirements:* Additional exam requirements/recommendations for international students: Required—TOEFL, IELTS, CANTEST, CAEL, or Michigan English Language Assessment Battery. *Application deadline:* Applications are processed on a rolling basis. Application fee: $70. Electronic applications accepted. *Financial support:* In 2009–10, 1 student received support, including 1 teaching assistantship; psychiatry practicum award also available. *Faculty research:* Gender, health systems, design, geriatrics power and empowerment. *Unit head:* Dr. Joan Versnel, Director, 902-494-2601, Fax: 902-494-1229, E-mail: occupational.therapy@dal.ca. *Application contact:* Pauline Fitzgerald, Graduate and Alumni Secretary, 902-494-6351, Fax: 902-494-1229, E-mail: p.fitzgerald@dal.ca.

Dominican College, Division of Allied Health, Department of Occupational Therapy, Orangeburg, NY 10962-1210. Offers MS. Students enter program as undergraduates. *Accreditation:* AOTA. Part-time and evening/weekend programs available. *Degree requirements:* For master's, 2 clinical affiliations. *Entrance requirements:* For master's, minimum GPA of 3.0, writing sample, 3 letters of recommendation. Additional exam requirements/recommendations for international students: Required—TOEFL (minimum score 550 paper-based; 213 computer-based).

Dominican University of California, Graduate Programs, School of Health and Natural Sciences, Program in Occupational Therapy, San Rafael, CA 94901-2298. Offers MS. *Accreditation:* AOTA. Part-time programs available. *Degree requirements:* For master's, thesis. *Entrance requirements:* For master's, minimum GPA of 3.0, clinical experience, course work in nursing research and statistics, CPR certification, professional liability and malpractice insurance, interview. Additional exam requirements/recommendations for international students: Required—TOEFL (minimum score 550 paper-based; 213 computer-based). Electronic applications accepted.

Duquesne University, John G. Rangos, Sr. School of Health Sciences, Pittsburgh, PA 15282-0001. Offers health management systems (MHMS); occupational therapy (MS); physical therapy (DPT); physician assistant studies (MPAS); rehabilitation science (MS, PhD); speech-language pathology (MS); MBA/MHMS. *Accreditation:* AOTA (one or more programs are accredited); APTA (one or more programs are accredited); ASHA. *Faculty:* 35 full-time (23 women), 17 part-time/adjunct (10 women). *Students:* 309 full-time (258 women), 11 part-time (7 women); includes 11 minority (5 African Americans, 5 Asian Americans or Pacific Islanders, 1 Hispanic American), 6 international. Average age 23. 454 applicants, 20% accepted, 20 enrolled. In 2009, 92 master's, 23 doctorates awarded. *Degree requirements:* For doctorate, thesis/dissertation. *Entrance requirements:* For master's, GRE General Test (speech-language pathology), 3 letters of recommendation; minimum GPA of 2.75 (health management systems, occupational therapy), minimum GPA of 3.0 (speech-language pathology); for doctorate, GRE General Test (for physical therapy), 3 letters of recommendation, minimum GPA of 3.0, personal interview. Additional exam requirements/recommendations for international students: Required—TOEFL (minimum score 550 paper-based; 233 computer-based; 90 iBT). *Application deadline:* Applications are processed on a rolling basis. Electronic applications accepted. *Expenses:* Contact institution. *Financial support:* Federal Work-Study available. *Faculty research:* Neuronal processing, electrical stimulation on peripheral neuropathy, CNS stimulatory and inhibitory signals, behavioral genetic methodologies to development disorders of speech, neurogenic communication disorders. Total annual research expenditures: $338,404. *Unit head:* Dr. Gregory H. Frazer, Dean, 412-396-5303, Fax: 412-396-5554, E-mail: frazer@duq.edu. *Application contact:* Christopher R. Hilf, Recruiter/Academic Advisor, 412-396-5653, Fax: 412-396-5554, E-mail: hilfc@duq.edu.

D'Youville College, Occupational Therapy Department, Buffalo, NY 14201-1084. Offers MS. *Accreditation:* AOTA. *Degree requirements:* For master's, research project. *Entrance requirements:* For master's, minimum undergraduate GPA of 3.0; successful completion of degrees. Additional exam requirements/recommendations for international students: Required—TOEFL (minimum score 500 paper-based; 173 computer-based). Electronic applications accepted. *Faculty research:* Learning styles, range of motion in the elderly, hospice care, culture, health, differences in education and performance of Afro-American children, autistic spectrum disorder and social stories, autistic disorders and listening programs.

East Carolina University, Graduate School, School of Allied Health Sciences, Department of Occupational Therapy, Greenville, NC 27858-4353. Offers MSOT. *Accreditation:* AOTA. Part-time programs available. Postbaccalaureate distance learning degree programs offered (minimal on-campus study). *Degree requirements:* For master's, comprehensive exam, thesis or research project. *Entrance requirements:* For master's, GRE General Test. Additional exam requirements/recommendations for international students: Required—TOEFL. Electronic applications accepted. *Faculty research:* Quality of life, assistive technology, environmental contributions, modifications of occupation to health, therapeutic activities.

East Carolina University, Graduate School, School of Allied Health Sciences, Program in Rehabilitation Studies, Greenville, NC 27858-4353. Offers rehabilitation counseling (MS); substance abuse and clinical counseling (MS); vocational evaluation (MS). *Accreditation:* CORE. Part-time and evening/weekend programs available. *Degree requirements:* For master's, comprehensive exam, thesis or alternative, internship. *Entrance requirements:* For master's, GRE General Test or MAT. Additional exam requirements/recommendations for international students: Required—TOEFL.

Eastern Kentucky University, The Graduate School, College of Health Sciences, Department of Occupational Therapy, Richmond, KY 40475-3102. Offers MS. *Accreditation:* AOTA. Part-time programs available. *Degree requirements:* For master's, thesis optional. *Entrance requirements:* For master's, GRE General Test, minimum GPA of 3.0. *Faculty research:* Rehabilitation, pediatrics, leadership issues.

Eastern Michigan University, Graduate School, College of Health and Human Services, School of Health Sciences, Program in Occupational Therapy, Ypsilanti, MI 48197. Offers MOT, MS. Part-time and evening/weekend programs available. Postbaccalaureate distance learning degree programs offered (minimal on-campus study). *Students:* 40 full-time (35 women), 23 part-time (22 women); includes 3 minority (1 African American, 1 Asian American or Pacific Islander, 1 Hispanic American), 1 international. Average age 29. In 2009, 24 master's awarded. *Entrance requirements:* Additional exam requirements/recommendations for international students: Required—TOEFL. *Application deadline:* Applications are processed on a rolling basis. Application fee: $35. Tuition and fees vary according to course level. *Financial support:* Fellowships, research assistantships with full tuition reimbursements, teaching assistantships with full tuition reimbursements, career-related internships or fieldwork, Federal Work-Study, institutionally sponsored loans, scholarships/grants, tuition waivers (partial), and unspecified assistantships available. Support available to part-time students. Financial award applicants required to submit FAFSA. *Unit head:* Dr. Valerie Howells, Program Director, 734-487-3227, Fax: 734-487-4095, E-mail: valerie.howells@emich.edu. *Application contact:*

Occupational Therapy

Eastern Michigan University (continued)
Dr. Valerie Howells, Program Director, 734-487-3227, Fax: 734-487-4095, E-mail: valerie. howells@emich.edu.

Eastern Washington University, Graduate Studies, College of Science, Health and Engineering, Department of Occupational Therapy, Cheney, WA 99004-2431. Offers MOT. *Accreditation:* AOTA. *Degree requirements:* For master's, comprehensive exam. *Expenses:* Tuition, state resident: full-time $7476; part-time $249 per quarter hour. Tuition, nonresident: full-time $18,030; part-time $601 per quarter hour. Required fees: $3.50 per quarter hour. $142 per quarter.

Elizabethtown College, Department of Occupational Therapy, Elizabethtown, PA 17022-2298. Offers MS. *Accreditation:* AOTA.

Florida Gulf Coast University, College of Health Professions, Department of Occupational Therapy, Fort Myers, FL 33965-6565. Offers MS. *Faculty:* 42 full-time (33 women), 30 part-time/adjunct (20 women). *Students:* 22 full-time (18 women), 23 part-time (18 women); includes 6 minority (1 African American, 1 American Indian/Alaska Native, 1 Asian American or Pacific Islander, 3 Hispanic Americans). Average age 27. 55 applicants, 44% accepted, 20 enrolled. In 2009, 13 master's awarded. *Entrance requirements:* For master's, GRE General Test, MAT, minimum GPA 3.0. Additional exam requirements/recommendations for international students: Required—TOEFL (minimum score 550 paper-based; 213 computer-based). *Application deadline:* For fall admission, 2/1 for domestic students. Applications are processed on a rolling basis. Application fee: $30. Electronic applications accepted. *Unit head:* Dr. Linda Martin, Head, 239-590-7556, Fax: 239-590-7474, E-mail: lmartin@fgcu.edu. *Application contact:* Lynn O'Hare, Administrative Assistant, 239-590-7451, Fax: 239-590-7474, E-mail: lohare@fgcu.edu.

Florida International University, College of Nursing and Health Sciences, Department of Occupational Therapy, Miami, FL 33199. Offers entry level professional (MS). *Accreditation:* AOTA. Part-time programs available. *Faculty:* 5 full-time (4 women). *Students:* 123 full-time (110 women), 25 part-time (23 women); includes 105 minority (15 African Americans, 6 Asian Americans or Pacific Islanders, 84 Hispanic Americans), 4 international. Average age 31. 92 applicants, 39% accepted, 36 enrolled. In 2009, 41 master's awarded. *Degree requirements:* For master's, thesis or alternative. *Entrance requirements:* For master's, minimum undergraduate GPA of 3.0 in upper-level course work, letter of intent, 3 letters of recommendation, resume. Additional exam requirements/recommendations for international students: Required—TOEFL (minimum score 550 paper-based; 80 iBT). *Application deadline:* For fall admission, 2/15 for domestic and international students. Applications are processed on a rolling basis. Application fee: $30. Electronic applications accepted. *Expenses:* Contact institution. *Financial support:* In 2009–10, 58 students received support. Career-related internships or fieldwork, Federal Work-Study, institutionally sponsored loans, scholarships/grants, and unspecified assistantships available. Financial award application deadline: 3/1; financial award applicants required to submit FAFSA. *Faculty research:* Senior transportation and driving; foster care, adolescent transitions, independent living skills development; family and patient centered care; aging, quality of life, social justice, cognition. *Unit head:* Dr. Alma Abdel-Moty, Chair, 305-348-6068, Fax: 305-348-1240, E-mail: abdela@fiu.edu. *Application contact:* Prof. Pamela Shaffner, Graduate Program Director, 305-348-6068, Fax: 305-348-1240, E-mail: pamela.shaffner@fiu.edu.

Gannon University, School of Graduate Studies, Morosky College of Health Professions and Sciences, School of Health Professions, Program in Occupational Therapy, Erie, PA 16541-0001. Offers MS. Offered as five-year program. *Accreditation:* AOTA. *Students:* 38 full-time (35 women); includes 2 minority (1 African American, 1 Asian American or Pacific Islander), 3 international. Average age 23. 34 applicants, 71% accepted, 10 enrolled. In 2009, 25 master's awarded. *Degree requirements:* For master's, thesis, research project. *Entrance requirements:* Additional exam requirements/recommendations for international students: Required—TOEFL (minimum score 79 iBT). *Application deadline:* For fall admission, 1/15 for domestic students. Application fee: $25. Electronic applications accepted. *Expenses:* Contact institution. *Financial support:* Scholarships/grants and unspecified assistantships available. Financial award application deadline: 7/1; financial award applicants required to submit FAFSA. *Unit head:* Jeff Boss, Director, 814-871-5670, E-mail: boss001@gannon.edu. *Application contact:* Kara Morgan, Assistant Director of Graduate Admissions, 814-871-5831, Fax: 814-871-5827, E-mail: graduate@gannon.edu.

Governors State University, College of Health Professions, Program in Occupational Therapy, University Park, IL 60466-0975. Offers MOT. *Accreditation:* AOTA. *Degree requirements:* For master's, thesis or alternative. *Entrance requirements:* For master's, minimum GPA of 3.0 in field, 2.75 overall.

Grand Valley State University, College of Health Professions, Occupational Therapy Program, Allendale, MI 49401-9403. Offers MS. *Accreditation:* AOTA. *Faculty:* 5 full-time (4 women). *Students:* 49 full-time (44 women), 1 (woman) part-time; includes 1 minority (Hispanic American). Average age 24. 54 applicants, 48% accepted, 26 enrolled. In 2009, 17 master's awarded. *Degree requirements:* For master's, thesis or alternative, fieldwork, project. *Entrance requirements:* For master's, interview, volunteer work, writing sample. Additional exam requirements/recommendations for international students: Required—TOEFL (minimum score 610 paper-based; 253 computer-based). *Application deadline:* For winter admission, 1/15 priority date for domestic students. Applications are processed on a rolling basis. Application fee: $30. Electronic applications accepted. *Expenses:* Tuition, state resident: part-time $471 per credit hour. Tuition, nonresident: part-time $646 per credit hour. Tuition and fees vary according to course level. *Financial support:* In 2009–10, 4 students received support, including 4 fellowships (averaging $3,725 per year), 1 research assistantship with full and partial tuition reimbursement available (averaging $8,000 per year); unspecified assistantships also available. Financial award application deadline: 2/15. *Faculty research:* Teaching/learning methods, continuing professional education, clinical reasoning, geriatrics, performing artists. *Unit head:* Dr. Cynthia Grapczynski, Director, 616-331-2734, Fax: 616-331-3350, E-mail: grapczyc@gvsu.edu. *Application contact:* Darlene Zwart, Student Services Coordinator, 616-331-3958, E-mail: zwartda@gvsu.edu.

Husson University, School of Graduate and Professional Studies, Program in Occupational Therapy, Bangor, ME 04401-2999. Offers MSOT. *Accreditation:* AOTA.

Idaho State University, Office of Graduate Studies, Kasiska College of Health Professions, Department of Physical and Occupational Therapy, Program in Occupational Therapy, Pocatello, ID 83209-8045. Offers MOT. *Accreditation:* AOTA. *Students:* 17 full-time (12 women); includes 2 minority (1 Asian American or Pacific Islander, 1 Hispanic American). Average age 29. In 2009, 6 master's awarded. *Degree requirements:* For master's, comprehensive exam, thesis, oral and written exam. *Entrance requirements:* For master's, GRE General Test, minimum GPA of 3.0, 80 hours in 2 practice settings of occupational therapy. Additional exam requirements/recommendations for international students: Required—TOEFL (minimum score 600 paper-based; 213 computer-based). *Application deadline:* For fall admission, 7/1 for domestic students, 6/1 for international students; for spring admission, 12/1 for domestic students, 11/1 for international students. Applications are processed on a rolling basis. Application fee: $55. Electronic applications accepted. *Expenses:* Contact institution. *Financial support:* Teaching assistantships with full and partial tuition reimbursements, career-related internships or fieldwork, Federal Work-Study, institutionally sponsored loans, scholarships/grants, traineeships, health care benefits, tuition waivers (full and partial), and unspecified assistantships available. Support available to part-time students. Financial award application deadline: 1/1; financial award applicants required to submit FAFSA. *Faculty research:* Human movement, health care. *Unit head:* Dr. Kevin Helgeson, Department Chair, 208-282-4095, Fax: 208-282-4962, E-mail: helgkevi@isu.edu. *Application contact:* Tami Carson, Graduate School Technical Records Specialist, 208-282-2150, Fax: 208-282-4847, E-mail: carstami@isu.edu.

Indiana University–Purdue University Indianapolis, Indiana University School of Medicine, School of Health and Rehabilitation Sciences, Indianapolis, IN 46202-2896. Offers health sciences education (MS); nutrition and dietetics (MS); occupational therapy (MS); physical therapy (DPT). Part-time and evening/weekend programs available. *Faculty:* 8 full-time (5 women). *Students:* 206 full-time (161 women), 11 part-time (8 women); includes 16 minority (5 African Americans, 1 American Indian/Alaska Native, 8 Asian Americans or Pacific Islanders, 2 Hispanic Americans), 1 international. Average age 26. 23 applicants, 83% accepted, 18 enrolled. In 2009, 9 master's, 32 doctorates awarded. *Degree requirements:* For master's, thesis (for some programs). *Entrance requirements:* For master's, GRE General Test, minimum GPA of 3.0. Additional exam requirements/recommendations for international students: Required—TOEFL. *Application deadline:* For fall admission, 1/15 priority date for domestic students; for spring admission, 10/15 for domestic students. Application fee: $55 ($65 for international students). *Financial support:* In 2009–10, 10 fellowships (averaging $2,485 per year), 1 teaching assistantship (averaging $3,600 per year) were awarded; research assistantships, Federal Work-Study, institutionally sponsored loans, and scholarships/grants also available. Support available to part-time students. Financial award applicants required to submit FAFSA. *Unit head:* Dr. Mark S. Sothmann, Dean, 317-274-4702, E-mail: msothman@iupui.edu. *Application contact:* Dr. Mark S. Sothmann, Dean, 317-274-4702, E-mail: msothman@iupui.edu.

Ithaca College, Division of Graduate and Professional Studies, School of Health Sciences and Human Performance, Program in Occupational Therapy, Ithaca, NY 14850. Offers MS. Students enter the program as freshmen. *Accreditation:* AOTA. *Faculty:* 7 full-time (all women). *Students:* 29 full-time (28 women); includes 1 minority (African American). Average age 22. In 2009, 16 master's awarded. *Degree requirements:* For master's, thesis optional, clinical fieldwork. *Entrance requirements:* Additional exam requirements/recommendations for international students: Required—TOEFL (minimum score 550 paper-based; 213 computer-based; 80 iBT). *Expenses:* Tuition: Full-time $18,960; part-time $632 per credit hour. *Financial support:* In 2009–10, 22 students received support. Career-related internships or fieldwork, Federal Work-Study, and scholarships/grants available. Support available to part-time students. Financial award applicants required to submit CSS PROFILE or FAFSA. *Faculty research:* Sensory integration intervention, therapeutic listening, motor control intervention for pediatrics and adults, adult neuromuscular facilitation for individuals with neurological impairments, school-aged handwriting assessment, psychosocial community, intervention and assessment, virtual reality and robotic training for children with neurological and or sensory disorders, clinical reasoning, aging and human occupations. *Unit head:* Dr. Melinda Cozzolino, Chairperson, 607-274-3527, Fax: 607-274-1263, E-mail: gps@ithaca.edu. *Application contact:* Dr. Rob Gearhart, Dean, Graduate and Professional Studies, 607-274-3527, Fax: 607-274-1263, E-mail: gps@ithaca.edu.

James Madison University, The Graduate School, College of Integrated Science and Technology, Department of Health Sciences, Program in Occupational Therapy, Harrisonburg, VA 22807. Offers MOT. *Accreditation:* AOTA. Part-time programs available. *Students:* 46 full-time (44 women); includes 5 minority (1 African American, 2 Asian Americans or Pacific Islanders, 2 Hispanic Americans). Average age 27. In 2009, 20 master's awarded. *Entrance requirements:* For master's, GRE General Test, GRE Subject Test, 3 reference forms, evidence of one instructional experience, documentation of competency in computer technology and information seeking skills. *Application deadline:* For fall admission, 2/1 priority date for domestic students. Application fee: $55. *Expenses:* Tuition, area resident: Part-time $305 per credit hour. Tuition, state resident: part-time $305 per credit hour. Tuition, nonresident: part-time $890 per credit hour. *Financial support:* Application deadline: 3/1. *Unit head:* Dr. Jeff Loveland, Graduate Coordinator, 540-568-2399. *Application contact:* Lynette M. Bible, Director of Graduate Admissions, 540-568-6395, Fax: 540-568-7860, E-mail: biblelm@jmu.edu.

Jefferson College of Health Sciences, Program in Occupational Therapy, Roanoke, VA 24031-3186. Offers MS. *Accreditation:* AOTA. Part-time programs available. *Faculty:* 14 full-time (5 women), 3 part-time/adjunct (2 women). *Students:* 26 full-time (24 women), 2 part-time (both women). Average age 29. 60 applicants, 38% accepted, 13 enrolled. *Entrance requirements:* For master's, GRE. Additional exam requirements/recommendations for international students: Required—TOEFL (minimum score 550 paper-based; 213 computer-based; 80 iBT). *Application deadline:* Applications are processed on a rolling basis. Application fee: $35. Electronic applications accepted. *Financial support:* Career-related internships or fieldwork, Federal Work-Study, scholarships/grants, traineeships, and tuition waivers (full and partial) available. Support available to part-time students. Financial award applicants required to submit FAFSA. *Unit head:* Dr. David Haynes, Program Director, 540-985-4020, E-mail: dahaynes@jchs.edu. *Application contact:* Judith McKeon, Director of Admissions, 540-985-9083, Fax: 540-985-9773, E-mail: jomckeon@jchs.edu.

Kean University, Nathan Weiss Graduate College, Program in Occupational Therapy, Union, NJ 07083. Offers MS. *Accreditation:* AOTA. Part-time and evening/weekend programs available. *Faculty:* 3 full-time (all women). *Students:* 50 full-time (44 women), 27 part-time (26 women); includes 15 minority (4 African Americans, 5 Asian Americans or Pacific Islanders, 6 Hispanic Americans). Average age 27. 140 applicants, 19% accepted, 18 enrolled. In 2009, 28 master's awarded. *Degree requirements:* For master's, 6 months of field work, final project. *Entrance requirements:* For master's, minimum GPA of 3.0, 3 letters of recommendation, interview, document observation of occupational therapy service in 2 or more settings of a total of 40 hours. *Application deadline:* For fall admission, 2/1 for domestic students. Application fee: $60 ($150 for international students). Electronic applications accepted. *Expenses:* Tuition, state resident: full-time $10,440; part-time $435 per credit. Tuition, nonresident: full-time $14,160; part-time $590 per credit. Required fees: $2642; $110 per credit. Part-time tuition and fees vary according to course load and degree level. *Financial support:* In 2009–10, 4 research assistantships with full tuition reimbursements (averaging $3,263 per year) were awarded; unspecified assistantships also available. *Unit head:* Dr. Laurie Knis-Matthews, Program Coordinator, 908-737-3380, E-mail: ot@kean.edu. *Application contact:* Steven Koch, Pre-Admissions Coordinator, 908-737-5924, Fax: 908-737-5965, E-mail: skoch@kean.edu.

Keuka College, Program in Occupational Therapy, Keuka Park, NY 14478-0098. Offers MS. *Accreditation:* AOTA. *Faculty:* 5 full-time (3 women). *Students:* 20 full-time (18 women). Average age 23. 15 applicants, 100% accepted. In 2009, 13 master's awarded. *Degree requirements:* For master's, thesis or alternative, clinical internships. *Entrance requirements:* For master's, minimum GPA of 3.0, BS in occupational therapy at Keuka College. Additional exam requirements/recommendations for international students: Required—TOEFL (minimum score 550 paper-based; 213 computer-based). *Application deadline:* For fall admission, 8/15 priority date for domestic students; for winter admission, 12/15 priority date for domestic students; for spring admission, 4/15 priority date for domestic students. Applications are processed on a rolling basis. Application fee: $30. *Expenses:* Contact institution. *Unit head:* Dr. Vicki Smith, Associate Professor and Chair, 315-279-5666, Fax: 315-279-5439, E-mail: vlsmith@mail.keuka.edu. *Application contact:* Claudine Ninestine, Director of Admissions, 315-279-5413, Fax: 315-279-5386, E-mail: admissions@mail.keuka.edu.

Lenoir-Rhyne University, Graduate Programs, School of Occupational Therapy, Hickory, NC 28601. Offers MS. *Accreditation:* AOTA. *Entrance requirements:* For master's, GRE or MAT, minimum GPA of 2.7.

Loma Linda University, School of Allied Health Professions, Department of Occupational Therapy, Loma Linda, CA 92350. Offers MOT, OTD.

Louisiana State University Health Sciences Center, School of Allied Health Professions, Department of Occupational Therapy, New Orleans, LA 70112-2223. Offers MOT. *Accreditation:* AOTA. *Entrance requirements:* For master's, GRE (minimum combined score 800).

Maryville University of Saint Louis, School of Health Professions, Occupational Therapy Program, St. Louis, MO 63141-7299. Offers MOT. *Accreditation:* AOTA. In 2009, 29 master's awarded. *Entrance requirements:* For master's, minimum ACT composite score of 21 or SAT-I combined score of 990 (unless applicant has completed more than 30 college credits), minimum cumulative GPA of 3.0, resume, interview, writing sample. Additional exam requirements/recommendations for international students: Required—TOEFL (minimum score 550 paper-based). *Application deadline:* Applications are processed on a rolling basis. Application

fee: $40 ($60 for international students). Electronic applications accepted. *Expenses:* Contact institution. *Financial support:* Career-related internships or fieldwork, Federal Work-Study, and campus employment available. Financial award application deadline: 3/1; financial award applicants required to submit FAFSA. *Faculty research:* Older driver safety rehabilitation options, adaptive equipment and training remediation, injured workers disability interventions. *Unit head:* Dr. Paula Bohr, Director, 314-529-9682, Fax: 314-529-9191, E-mail: pbohr@maryville.edu. *Application contact:* 314-529-9350, Fax: 314-529-9927, E-mail: admissions@maryville.edu.

McMaster University, Faculty of Health Sciences, Professional Program in Occupational Therapy, Hamilton, ON L8S 4M2, Canada. Offers M Sc. *Degree requirements:* For master's, fieldwork and independent research project. *Entrance requirements:* For master's, minimum B average over last 60 undergraduate units. Additional exam requirements/recommendations for international students: Required—TOEFL (minimum score 600 paper-based; 250 computer-based).

Medical University of South Carolina, College of Health Professions, Department of Health Professions, Program in Occupational Therapy, Charleston, SC 29425. Offers MS. *Accreditation:* AOTA. *Faculty:* 6 full-time (3 women), 3 part-time/adjunct (all women). *Students:* 79 full-time (76 women); includes 7 minority (1 African American, 1 American Indian/Alaska Native, 2 Asian Americans or Pacific Islanders, 3 Hispanic Americans). Average age 24. 99 applicants, 55% accepted, 39 enrolled. In 2009, 33 master's awarded. *Degree requirements:* For master's, thesis or alternative, research project. *Entrance requirements:* For master's, GRE General Test, interview, minimum GPA of 3.0, references. Additional exam requirements/recommendations for international students: Required—TOEFL (minimum score 600 paper-based; 250 computer-based). *Application deadline:* For fall admission, 1/15 priority date for domestic and international students; for spring admission, 11/1 for international students. Application fee: $85. Electronic applications accepted. *Financial support:* Federal Work-Study and scholarships/grants available. Support available to part-time students. Financial award application deadline: 3/10; financial award applicants required to submit FAFSA. *Faculty research:* Therapeutic interventions for children with cerebral palsy; function, well being, quality of life for adults with chronic conditions and health disparities; driving interventions for adults with head and neck cancer; oral health for adults with tetraplegia; interprofessional education. Total annual research expenditures: $458,634. *Unit head:* Dr. Maralynne Mitcham, Director, 843-792-9734, Fax: 843-792-0710, E-mail: mitchamm@musc.edu. *Application contact:* Susan Johnson, Student Services Program Coordinator, 843-792-5377, Fax: 843-792-0710, E-mail: johnsoss@musc.edu.

Mercy College, School of Health and Natural Sciences, Program in Occupational Therapy, Dobbs Ferry, NY 10522-1189. Offers MS. *Accreditation:* AOTA. Evening/weekend programs available. *Students:* 63 full-time (53 women), 31 part-time (25 women); includes 44 minority (18 African Americans, 1 American Indian/Alaska Native, 10 Asian Americans or Pacific Islanders, 15 Hispanic Americans), 1 international. Average age 34. 144 applicants, 24% accepted, 32 enrolled. In 2009, 32 master's awarded. *Degree requirements:* For master's, thesis, fieldwork. *Entrance requirements:* For master's, minimum GPA of 3.0, 3 references, resume. Additional exam requirements/recommendations for international students: Required—TOEFL (minimum score 600 paper-based; 250 computer-based; 100 iBT). *Application deadline:* For fall admission, 12/1 for domestic students. Application fee: $65. *Expenses:* Contact institution. *Financial support:* Career-related internships or fieldwork, Federal Work-Study, scholarships/grants, and unspecified assistantships available. Financial award applicants required to submit FAFSA. *Unit head:* Joan Toglia, Director, 914-674-7815, Fax: 914-674-7840, E-mail: jtoglia@mercy.edu. *Application contact:* Joan Toglia, Director, 914-674-7815, Fax: 914-674-7840, E-mail: jtoglia@mercy.edu.

Midwestern University, Downers Grove Campus, College of Health Sciences, Illinois Campus, Program in Occupational Therapy, Downers Grove, IL 60515-1235. Offers MOT. *Accreditation:* AOTA. *Faculty:* 8 full-time (all women). *Students:* 108 full-time (99 women); includes 19 minority (3 African Americans, 12 Asian Americans or Pacific Islanders, 4 Hispanic Americans). Average age 25. 114 applicants, 66% accepted, 37 enrolled. In 2009, 14 master's awarded. *Entrance requirements:* For master's, GRE General Test. *Application deadline:* Applications are processed on a rolling basis. Application fee: $50. *Expenses:* Contact institution. *Financial support:* Federal Work-Study and scholarships/grants available. Financial award applicants required to submit FAFSA. *Unit head:* Kimberly A. Bryze, Director, 630-515-7226, E-mail: kbryze@midwestern.edu. *Application contact:* Michael Laken, Director of Admissions, 630-515-6171, Fax: 630-971-6086, E-mail: admissil@midwestern.edu.

Midwestern University, Glendale Campus, College of Health Sciences, Arizona Campus, Program in Occupational Therapy, Glendale, AZ 85308. Offers MOT. *Accreditation:* AOTA. *Faculty:* 5 full-time (all women). *Students:* 82 full-time (74 women); includes 11 minority (3 African Americans, 6 Asian Americans or Pacific Islanders, 2 Hispanic Americans). Average age 26. 100 applicants, 41% accepted, 30 enrolled. In 2009, 8 master's awarded. *Entrance requirements:* For master's, GRE. *Application deadline:* Applications are processed on a rolling basis. Application fee: $50. *Expenses:* Contact institution. *Unit head:* Christine R. Merchant, Director, 623-572-3638, E-mail: cmerch@midwestern.edu. *Application contact:* James Walter, Director of Admissions, 888-247-9277, Fax: 623-572-3229, E-mail: admissaz@midwestern.edu.

Milligan College, Program in Occupational Therapy, Milligan College, TN 37682. Offers MSOT. *Accreditation:* AOTA. *Degree requirements:* For master's, thesis. *Entrance requirements:* For master's, GRE. Additional exam requirements/recommendations for international students: Required—TOEFL (minimum score 550 paper-based; 213 computer-based; 80 iBT). Electronic applications accepted. *Expenses:* Contact institution. *Faculty research:* Handwriting, creativity, leadership in health care and rehabilitation, prevention and rehabilitation of work related musculoskeletal disorders, parent-child interaction therapy.

Misericordia University, College of Health Sciences, Program in Occupational Therapy, Dallas, PA 18612-1098. Offers MSOT, OTD. *Accreditation:* AOTA. *Faculty:* 5 full-time (4 women), 8 part-time/adjunct (5 women). *Students:* 18 full-time (all women), 17 part-time (14 women). Average age 29. In 2009, 30 master's awarded. *Application deadline:* Applications are processed on a rolling basis. Application fee: $25. Electronic applications accepted. *Financial support:* In 2009–10, 22 students received support; teaching assistantships, career-related internships or fieldwork and scholarships/grants available. Support available to part-time students. Financial award application deadline: 6/30; financial award applicants required to submit FAFSA. *Unit head:* Dr. Grace Fisher, Department Chair, 570-674-8015, E-mail: gfisher@misericordia.edu. *Application contact:* Dr. Grace Fisher, Department Chair, 570-674-8015, E-mail: gfisher@misericordia.edu.

Mount Mary College, Graduate Programs, Program in Occupational Therapy, Milwaukee, WI 53222-4597. Offers MS. *Accreditation:* AOTA. Part-time and evening/weekend programs available. *Faculty:* 4 full-time (all women), 13 part-time/adjunct (11 women). *Students:* 96 full-time (95 women), 4 part-time (2 women); includes 8 minority (3 African Americans, 4 Asian Americans or Pacific Islanders, 1 Hispanic American). Average age 31. 66 applicants, 67% accepted, 32 enrolled. In 2009, 18 master's awarded. *Degree requirements:* For master's, comprehensive exam, thesis or alternative, professional development portfolio. *Entrance requirements:* For master's, minimum GPA of 2.75, occupational therapy license, 1 year of work experience. Additional exam requirements/recommendations for international students: Required—TOEFL (minimum score 500 paper-based; 173 computer-based). *Application deadline:* For fall admission, 10/15 priority date for domestic and international students; for spring admission, 3/15 for domestic and international students. Application fee: $35 ($100 for international students). *Expenses:* Tuition: Part-time $595 per credit. Tuition and fees vary according to program. *Financial support:* In 2009–10, 11 students received support. Career-related internships or fieldwork and Federal Work-Study available. Support available to part-time students. Financial award application deadline: 5/1; financial award applicants required to submit FAFSA. *Faculty research:* Clinical reasoning, occupational science, sensory integration. *Unit head:* Dr. Jane Olson, Director, 414-258-4810 Ext. 348, E-mail: olsonj@mtmary.edu. *Application contact:* Dr. Jane Olson, Director, 414-258-4810 Ext. 348, E-mail: olsonj@mtmary.edu.

New York Institute of Technology, Graduate Division, School of Health Professions, Program in Occupational Therapy, Old Westbury, NY 11568-8000. Offers MS. *Accreditation:* AOTA. *Students:* 62 full-time (47 women); includes 26 minority (3 African Americans, 17 Asian Americans or Pacific Islanders, 6 Hispanic Americans), 1 international. Average age 26. In 2009, 11 master's awarded. *Degree requirements:* For master's, thesis. *Entrance requirements:* For master's, minimum GPA of 2.0 in science or mathematics, 2.5 overall; 100 hours of supervised volunteer work; interview; 2 professional letters of recommendation. Additional exam requirements/recommendations for international students: Required—TOEFL (minimum score 550 paper-based; 213 computer-based). *Application deadline:* For fall admission, 7/1 priority date for domestic students; for spring admission, 12/1 priority date for domestic students. Applications are processed on a rolling basis. Application fee: $50. Electronic applications accepted. *Expenses:* Tuition: Part-time $825 per credit. *Financial support:* Research assistantships with partial tuition reimbursements available. Financial award applicants required to submit FAFSA. *Unit head:* Hermine Plotnick, Director, 516-686-3865, Fax: 516-686-3795, E-mail: hplotnic@nyit.edu. *Application contact:* Dr. Jacquelyn Nealon, Vice President for Enrollment Services, 516-686-7925, Fax: 516-686-7597, E-mail: jnealon@nyit.edu.

New York University, Steinhardt School of Culture, Education, and Human Development, Department of Occupational Therapy, New York, NY 10012. Offers advanced occupational therapy (MA); occupational therapy (MS, DPS); research in occupational therapy (PhD). *Accreditation:* AOTA (one or more programs are accredited). Part-time programs available. *Faculty:* 11 full-time (8 women), 21 part-time/adjunct (16 women). *Students:* 168 full-time (161 women), 29 part-time (27 women); includes 26 minority (4 African Americans, 13 Asian Americans or Pacific Islanders, 9 Hispanic Americans), 21 international. Average age 26. 275 applicants, 60% accepted, 66 enrolled. In 2009, 62 master's, 8 doctorates awarded. *Degree requirements:* For master's, thesis (for some programs), project; for doctorate, thesis/dissertation. *Entrance requirements:* For doctorate, GRE General Test, interview. Additional exam requirements/recommendations for international students: Required—TOEFL. *Application deadline:* For fall admission, 12/15 priority date for domestic and international students. Applications are processed on a rolling basis. Application fee: $75. Electronic applications accepted. *Expenses:* Tuition: Full-time $30,528; part-time $1272 per credit. Required fees: $2177. *Financial support:* Fellowships with full and partial tuition reimbursements, teaching assistantships with full and partial tuition reimbursements, career-related internships or fieldwork, Federal Work-Study, institutionally sponsored loans, scholarships/grants, traineeships, tuition waivers (partial), and unspecified assistantships available. Support available to part-time students. Financial award application deadline: 2/1; financial award applicants required to submit FAFSA. *Faculty research:* Pediatrics, assistive rehabilitation technology, adaptive computer technology for children with disabilities, cognitive bases of adult disablement, upper limb rehabilitation. *Unit head:* Dr. Jane Bear-Lehman, Chairperson, 212-998-5846, Fax: 212-995-4044, E-mail: occupational.therapy@nyu.edu. *Application contact:* 212-998-5030, Fax: 212-995-4328, E-mail: steinhardt.gradadmissions@nyu.edu.

Nova Southeastern University, Health Professions Division, College of Allied Health and Nursing, Department of Occupational Therapy, Fort Lauderdale, FL 33314-7796. Offers MOT, OTD, PhD. *Accreditation:* AOTA (one or more programs are accredited). Postbaccalaureate distance learning degree programs offered. *Faculty:* 11 full-time (9 women), 6 part-time/adjunct (3 women). *Students:* 104 full-time (91 women), 38 part-time (36 women); includes 49 minority (17 African Americans, 10 Asian Americans or Pacific Islanders, 22 Hispanic Americans), 1 international. Average age 27. 96 applicants, 75% accepted, 47 enrolled. In 2009, 28 master's, 5 doctorates awarded. *Degree requirements:* For master's, thesis or alternative; for doctorate, comprehensive exam (for some programs), thesis/dissertation (for some programs). *Entrance requirements:* For master's and doctorate, GRE General Test. *Application deadline:* Applications are processed on a rolling basis. Application fee: $50. Electronic applications accepted. *Financial support:* Federal Work-Study and institutionally sponsored loans available. *Faculty research:* Older adult falls prevention, sensory integration, diabetes, autism, literacy. *Unit head:* Dr. Sandee M. Dunbar, Chair, 954-262-1243, Fax: 954-262-2290, E-mail: sdunbar@nova.edu. *Application contact:* Corinne Kessler, Admissions Counselor, 954-262-1110, Fax: 954-262-2282, E-mail: kcorinne@nsu.nova.edu.

The Ohio State University, College of Medicine, School of Allied Medical Professions, Program in Occupational Therapy, Columbus, OH 43210. Offers MOT. *Accreditation:* AOTA. *Entrance requirements:* For master's, GRE General Test. Additional exam requirements/recommendations for international students: Required—TOEFL (paper-based 550; computer-based 213) or Michigan English Language Assessment Battery (82). Electronic applications accepted. *Expenses:* Tuition, state resident: full-time $10,683. Tuition, nonresident: full-time $25,923. Tuition and fees vary according to course load and program.

Pacific University, School of Occupational Therapy, Forest Grove, OR 97116-1797. Offers MOT. *Accreditation:* AOTA. *Degree requirements:* For master's, research project, professional project. Electronic applications accepted. *Expenses:* Contact institution. *Faculty research:* Cultural competency development, disability policy, scholarship of teaching and learning, driver rehabilitation and older adult visual perception, neurorehabilitation and motor learning.

Philadelphia University, School of Science and Health, Program in Occupational Therapy, Philadelphia, PA 19144. Offers MS. *Accreditation:* AOTA. Evening/weekend programs available. *Degree requirements:* For master's, practicum. *Entrance requirements:* For master's, GRE or MAT. Additional exam requirements/recommendations for international students: Required—TOEFL (minimum score 550 paper-based; 213 computer-based; 79 iBT). Electronic applications accepted.

Queen's University at Kingston, School of Graduate Studies and Research, Faculty of Health Sciences, School of Rehabilitation Therapy, Kingston, ON K7L 3N6, Canada. Offers occupational therapy (M Sc OT); physical therapy (M Sc PT); rehabilitation science (M Sc, PhD). Part-time programs available. *Degree requirements:* For master's, thesis; for doctorate, comprehensive exam, thesis/dissertation. *Entrance requirements:* Additional exam requirements/recommendations for international students: Required—TOEFL. *Faculty research:* Disability, community, motor performance, rehabilitation, treatment efficiency.

Quinnipiac University, School of Health Sciences, Program in Occupational Therapy, Hamden, CT 06518-1940. Offers MOT. Students are admitted to the program as undergraduates. *Faculty:* 5 full-time (all women), 7 part-time/adjunct (all women). *Students:* 97 full-time (90 women), 27 part-time (25 women); includes 10 minority (3 African Americans, 1 Asian American or Pacific Islander, 6 Hispanic Americans), 1 international. Average age 24. 55 applicants, 100% accepted, 55 enrolled. In 2009, 39 master's awarded. *Entrance requirements:* Additional exam requirements/recommendations for international students: Required—TOEFL (minimum score 575 paper-based; 233 computer-based; 90 iBT). *Expenses:* Tuition: Full-time $16,030; part-time $770 per credit. Required fees: $630; $35 per credit. *Financial support:* Scholarships/grants and unspecified assistantships available. Financial award application deadline: 4/15; financial award applicants required to submit FAFSA. *Unit head:* Kimberly Hartmann, Chairperson, 203-582-8679, E-mail: kim.hartmann@quinnipiac.edu. *Application contact:* 800-462-1944, E-mail: admissions@quinnipiac.edu.

Radford University, College of Graduate and Professional Studies, Waldron College of Health and Human Services, Department of Occupational Therapy, Radford, VA 24142. Offers MOT. Part-time and evening/weekend programs available. *Faculty:* 4 full-time (3 women). *Students:* 11 full-time (8 women); includes 1 minority (African American). Average age 31. 17 applicants, 94% accepted, 11 enrolled. *Degree requirements:* For master's, comprehensive exam. *Entrance requirements:* For master's, GRE, minimum GPA of 3.25, minimum C grade in prerequisite courses, 2 letters of recommendation, professional resume, 40 hours of observation. Additional exam requirements/recommendations for international students: Required—TOEFL (minimum score 550 paper-based; 213 computer-based; 79 iBT). *Application deadline:* For fall

Occupational Therapy

Radford University (continued)
admission, 5/15 priority date for domestic students, 12/1 for international students. Applications are processed on a rolling basis. Application fee: $50. Electronic applications accepted. *Expenses:* Tuition, state resident: full-time $5086; part-time $211 per credit hour. Tuition, nonresident: full-time $12,608; part-time $525 per credit hour. Required fees: $2508; $105 per credit hour. *Financial support:* Career-related internships or fieldwork, Federal Work-Study, institutionally sponsored loans, scholarships/grants, and unspecified assistantships available. Financial award application deadline: 3/1; financial award applicants required to submit FAFSA. *Unit head:* Dr. Douglas Mitchell, Chair, 540-831-7643, E-mail: dmmitchell@radford.edu. *Application contact:* Graduate Admissions Office, 540-831-5431, Fax: 540-831-6061, E-mail: gradcollege@radford.edu.

The Richard Stockton College of New Jersey, School of Graduate and Continuing Education, Program in Occupational Therapy, Pomona, NJ 08240-0195. Offers MSOT. *Accreditation:* AOTA. *Degree requirements:* For master's, fieldwork, research project. *Entrance requirements:* For master's, minimum GPA of 3.0, 120 hours of work, volunteer or community service. Additional exam requirements/recommendations for international students: Required—TOEFL. *Expenses:* Tuition, state resident: part-time $497.36 per credit hour. Tuition, nonresident: part-time $765.61 per credit hour. Required fees: $129.12 per credit hour. Tuition and fees vary according to degree level. *Faculty research:* Home health based occupational therapy for women with HIV/AIDS.

Rockhurst University, School of Graduate and Professional Studies, Program in Occupational Therapy, Kansas City, MO 64110-2561. Offers MOT. *Accreditation:* AOTA. Part-time programs available. *Faculty:* 3 full-time (all women), 7 part-time/adjunct (all women). *Students:* 65 full-time (56 women), 6 part-time (all women); includes 4 minority (1 African American, 1 American Indian/Alaska Native, 2 Asian Americans or Pacific Islanders). Average age 26. 99 applicants, 49% accepted, 35 enrolled. In 2009, 27 master's awarded. *Entrance requirements:* For master's, minimum GPA of 3.0. Additional exam requirements/recommendations for international students: Required—TOEFL (minimum score 550 paper-based; 213 computer-based; 79 iBT). *Application deadline:* Applications are processed on a rolling basis. Application fee: $25. Electronic applications accepted. *Financial support:* In 2009–10, 5 research assistantships, 10 teaching assistantships were awarded; career-related internships or fieldwork, institutionally sponsored loans, and unspecified assistantships also available. Financial award applicants required to submit FAFSA. *Faculty research:* Problem-based learning, cognitive rehabilitation behavioral state in infants and children, adult neurological defects and prosthetics. *Unit head:* Dr. Kris Vacek, Chair, 816-501-4635, Fax: 816-501-4643, E-mail: kris.vacek@rockhurst.edu. *Application contact:* Cheryl Hooper, Director of Graduate Recruitment Admission, 816-501-4097, Fax: 816-501-4241, E-mail: cheryl.hooper@rockhurst.edu.

Rush University, College of Health Sciences, Department of Occupational Therapy, Chicago, IL 60612-3832. Offers MS. *Accreditation:* AOTA. *Degree requirements:* For master's, thesis optional. *Entrance requirements:* For master's, GRE General Test. Electronic applications accepted. *Faculty research:* Intervention and practice strategies in the stroke population and the impact of evidenced based interventions.

Sacred Heart University, Graduate Programs, College of Education and Health Professions, Program in Occupational Therapy, Fairfield, CT 06825-1000. Offers MSOT. *Accreditation:* AOTA. *Faculty:* 5 full-time (all women), 15 part-time/adjunct (13 women). *Students:* 29 full-time (28 women), 32 part-time (28 women); includes 4 minority (2 African Americans, 2 Asian Americans or Pacific Islanders). Average age 27. 57 applicants, 88% accepted, 26 enrolled. In 2009, 15 master's awarded. *Entrance requirements:* For master's, minimum GPA of 3.0. Additional exam requirements/recommendations for international students: Required—TOEFL (minimum score 550 paper-based; 213 computer-based). *Application deadline:* For fall admission, 1/15 priority date for domestic students. Applications are processed on a rolling basis. Application fee: $50 ($100 for international students). Electronic applications accepted. *Expenses:* Contact institution. *Financial support:* Career-related internships or fieldwork, institutionally sponsored loans, and unspecified assistantships available. Support available to part-time students. Financial award applicants required to submit FAFSA. *Unit head:* Dr. Jody Bortone, Director, 203-396-8023, Fax: 203-365-7508, E-mail: gradstudies@sacredheart.edu. *Application contact:* Kathy Dilks, Assistant Dean of Graduate Admissions, Health Professions, 203-396-8259, Fax: 203-365-4732, E-mail: gradstudies@sacredheart.edu.

Sage Graduate School, Graduate School, School of Health Sciences, Program in Occupational Therapy, Troy, NY 12180-4115. Offers MS. *Accreditation:* AOTA. Part-time and evening/weekend programs available. *Faculty:* 8 full-time (all women), 9 part-time/adjunct (8 women). *Students:* 55 full-time (54 women), 25 part-time (24 women); includes 4 minority (2 Asian Americans or Pacific Islanders, 2 Hispanic Americans). Average age 25. 3 applicants, 100% accepted, 3 enrolled. In 2009, 24 master's awarded. *Entrance requirements:* For master's, baccalaureate degree, minimum undergraduate GPA of 3.0, completion of program prerequisites with minimum C grade, completion of 20 hours of clinical observation. Additional exam requirements/recommendations for international students: Required—TOEFL (minimum score 550 paper-based; 213 computer-based). *Application deadline:* For fall admission, 2/1 for domestic students. Applications are processed on a rolling basis. Application fee: $40. *Expenses:* Tuition: Full-time $10,620; part-time $590 per credit hour. *Financial support:* Fellowships, research assistantships, Federal Work-Study, scholarships/grants, and unspecified assistantships available. Support available to part-time students. *Unit head:* Nancy Ranft, Director, 518-244-2056, E-mail: ranftn@sage.edu. *Application contact:* Wendy D. Diefendorf, Director of Graduate and Adult Admission, 518-244-2443, Fax: 518-244-6880, E-mail: diefew@sage.edu.

Saginaw Valley State University, Crystal M. Lange College of Nursing and Health Sciences, Program in Occupational Therapy, University Center, MI 48710. Offers MSOT. *Accreditation:* AOTA. *Students:* 81 full-time (64 women), 35 part-time (29 women); includes 5 minority (1 African American, 1 Asian American or Pacific Islander, 3 Hispanic Americans), 5 international. Average age 25. 3 applicants, 100% accepted, 2 enrolled. In 2009, 22 master's awarded. *Entrance requirements:* Additional exam requirements/recommendations for international students: Required—TOEFL (minimum score 525 paper-based; 197 computer-based; 71 iBT). *Financial support:* Federal Work-Study and scholarships/grants available. Support available to part-time students. *Unit head:* Dr. Donald Earley, Associate Professor, 989-964-4689, E-mail: dwe@svsu.edu. *Application contact:* Dr. Donald Earley, Associate Professor, 989-964-4689, E-mail: dwe@svsu.edu.

St. Ambrose University, College of Education and Health Sciences, Program in Occupational Therapy, Davenport, IA 52803-2898. Offers MOT. *Accreditation:* AOTA. *Faculty:* 9 full-time (8 women), 1 part-time/adjunct (0 women). *Students:* 47 full-time (46 women), 2 part-time (both women); includes 1 minority (American Indian/Alaska Native), 1 international. Average age 25. 27 applicants, 96% accepted, 18 enrolled. In 2009, 25 master's awarded. *Degree requirements:* For master's, board exams. *Entrance requirements:* For master's, 50 hours of volunteer experience in 2 occupational therapy settings, minimum GPA of 2.7, essay or interview on campus, 3 letters of reference. Additional exam requirements/recommendations for international students: Required—TOEFL. *Application deadline:* For fall admission, 1/31 for domestic students. Application fee: $25. Electronic applications accepted. *Expenses:* Tuition: Part-time $702 per credit hour. Tuition and fees vary according to degree level, program and reciprocity agreements. *Financial support:* In 2009–10, 47 students received support, including 10 research assistantships with partial tuition reimbursements available (averaging $3,500 per year); career-related internships or fieldwork, scholarships/grants, tuition waivers (partial), and unspecified assistantships also available. Financial award application deadline: 8/15; financial award applicants required to submit FAFSA. *Unit head:* Phyllis J. Wenthe, Director, 563-333-6276, Fax: 563-333-6243, E-mail: wenthephyllisj@sau.edu. *Application contact:* Lori J. Parker, Administrative Assistant, 563-333-6413, Fax: 563-333-6243, E-mail: parkerlorij@sau.edu.

St. Catherine University, Graduate Programs, Program in Occupational Therapy, St. Paul, MN 55105. Offers MA. *Accreditation:* AOTA. Part-time and evening/weekend programs available. *Faculty:* 17 full-time (16 women). *Students:* 114 full-time (113 women), 10 part-time (all women); includes 4 minority (2 Asian Americans or Pacific Islanders, 2 Hispanic Americans). Average age 29. 126 applicants, 53% accepted, 57 enrolled. In 2009, 40 master's awarded. *Degree requirements:* For master's, thesis. *Entrance requirements:* For master's, GRE, minimum GPA of 3.0. Additional exam requirements/recommendations for international students: Required—Michigan English Language Assessment Battery or TOEFL. *Application deadline:* For fall admission, 2/1 priority date for domestic students. Applications are processed on a rolling basis. Application fee: $35. Tuition and fees vary according to program. *Financial support:* In 2009–10, 106 students received support. Career-related internships or fieldwork and institutionally sponsored loans available. Support available to part-time students. Financial award application deadline: 4/1; financial award applicants required to submit FAFSA. *Unit head:* Dr. Kathleen Matuska, Director, 651-690-6606, Fax: 651-690-8804. *Application contact:* 651-690-6933, Fax: 651-690-6064.

Saint Francis University, Department of Occupational Therapy, Loretto, PA 15940-0600. Offers MOT. *Accreditation:* AOTA. *Faculty:* 6 full-time (4 women). *Students:* 23 full-time (21 women). Average age 22. 23 applicants, 100% accepted, 23 enrolled. In 2009, 29 master's awarded. *Degree requirements:* For master's, one foreign language, thesis. *Expenses:* Tuition: Part-time $765 per credit. Part-time tuition and fees vary according to course load and program. *Faculty research:* Retention, technology, work injury, distance learning. *Unit head:* Dr. Donald Walkovich, Chair, 814-472-3899, Fax: 814-472-3950, E-mail: dwalkovich@francis.edu. *Application contact:* Dr. Peter Raymond Skoner, Associate Vice President for Academic Affairs, 814-472-3085, Fax: 814-472-3365, E-mail: pskoner@francis.edu.

Saint Louis University, Graduate School, Doisy College of Health Sciences, Department of Occupational Science and Occupational Therapy, St. Louis, MO 63103-2097. Offers MOT. *Accreditation:* AOTA. *Degree requirements:* For master's, project. *Entrance requirements:* For master's, minimum GPA of 2.8. Additional exam requirements/recommendations for international students: Required—TOEFL (minimum score 525 paper-based; 194 computer-based; 55 iBT). Electronic applications accepted. *Faculty research:* Autism spectrum and Asperger's disease, early intervention with children of homeless families, disability awareness program development of developing countries, environmental adaptations and universal design for persons who are disabled and/or aging, physical activity models for persons with dementia.

Salem State College, School of Graduate Studies, Program in Occupational Therapy, Salem, MA 01970-5353. Offers MS. *Accreditation:* AOTA. Part-time and evening/weekend programs available. *Students:* 1 (woman) full-time, 18 part-time (17 women). Average age 35. 9 applicants, 100% accepted, 9 enrolled. In 2009, 12 master's awarded. *Entrance requirements:* For master's, GRE or MAT. Additional exam requirements/recommendations for international students: Required—TOEFL (minimum score 550 paper-based; 80 iBT), IELTS (minimum score 5.5). *Application deadline:* For fall admission, 5/31 for domestic students. Application fee: $50. *Expenses:* Tuition, state resident: full-time $2520; part-time $275 per credit hour. Tuition, nonresident: full-time $4140; part-time $365 per credit hour. Required fees: $2430. *Financial support:* In 2009–10, 15 students received support. Career-related internships or fieldwork, Federal Work-Study, scholarships/grants, and unspecified assistantships available. Support available to part-time students. Financial award application deadline: 5/1; financial award applicants required to submit FAFSA. *Unit head:* Jeramie Silveria, Associate Professor, 978-542-6075, E-mail: jsilveria@salemstate.edu. *Application contact:* Dr. Lee A. Brossoit, Assistant Dean of Graduate Admissions, 978-542-6675, Fax: 978-542-7215, E-mail: lbrossoit@salemstate.edu.

Samuel Merritt University, Department of Occupational Therapy, Oakland, CA 94609-3108. Offers MOT. *Accreditation:* AOTA. *Degree requirements:* For master's, project. *Entrance requirements:* For master's, GRE General Test, minimum GPA of 2.6 in science, 2.8 overall; 40-70 hours of volunteer or professional occupational therapy experience; interview. Additional exam requirements/recommendations for international students: Required—TOEFL. *Expenses:* Contact institution.

San Jose State University, Graduate Studies and Research, College of Applied Sciences and Arts, Department of Occupational Therapy, San Jose, CA 95192-0001. Offers MS. *Accreditation:* AOTA. *Students:* 118 full-time (104 women), 3 part-time (all women); includes 44 minority (1 African American, 1 American Indian/Alaska Native, 29 Asian Americans or Pacific Islanders, 13 Hispanic Americans), 2 international. Average age 29. 213 applicants, 40% accepted, 77 enrolled. In 2009, 88 master's awarded. *Degree requirements:* For master's, thesis or alternative. *Entrance requirements:* For master's, GRE, minimum GPA of 3.0. *Application deadline:* For fall admission, 6/29 for domestic students; for spring admission, 11/30 for domestic students. Applications are processed on a rolling basis. Application fee: $59. Electronic applications accepted. *Financial support:* Career-related internships or fieldwork, Federal Work-Study, and institutionally sponsored loans available. Financial award applicants required to submit FAFSA. *Faculty research:* Generic occupational therapy, psychosocial rehabilitation, physical rehabilitation, organizational development, occupational performance. *Unit head:* Heidi McHugh Pendleton, Chair, 408-924-3072, Fax: 408-924-3088. *Application contact:* Heidi McHugh Pendleton, Chair, 408-924-3072, Fax: 408-924-3088.

Seton Hall University, School of Health and Medical Sciences, Program in Occupational Therapy, South Orange, NJ 07079-2697. Offers MS. *Accreditation:* AOTA. *Entrance requirements:* For master's, health care experience, minimum GPA of 3.0, 50 hours of occupational therapy volunteer work, pre-requisite courses. Additional exam requirements/recommendations for international students: Required—TOEFL. Electronic applications accepted. *Faculty research:* Occupational genesis, occupational technology, pediatric OT, community practice, families of children with special needs; family routines; complementary medicine and wellness.

Shawnee State University, Program in Occupational Therapy, Portsmouth, OH 45662-4344. Offers MOT. *Accreditation:* AOTA.

Shenandoah University, School of Health Professions, Division of Occupational Therapy, Winchester, VA 22601-5195. Offers MS. *Accreditation:* AOTA. *Faculty:* 4 full-time (all women), 12 part-time/adjunct (all women). *Students:* 54 full-time (49 women), 14 part-time (all women); includes 2 minority (1 Asian American or Pacific Islander, 1 Hispanic American). Average age 30. 72 applicants, 47% accepted, 28 enrolled. In 2009, 13 master's awarded. *Degree requirements:* For master's, comprehensive exam, thesis, fieldwork. *Entrance requirements:* For master's, GRE (minimum score 480 quantitative), 24 hours of clinical exposure, 2 references, writing sample, minimum GPA of 3.0. Additional exam requirements/recommendations for international students: Required—TOEFL (minimum score 550 paper-based; 213 computer-based; 79 iBT), IELTS (minimum score 6.5). *Application deadline:* For fall admission, 7/1 for domestic students. Applications are processed on a rolling basis. Application fee: $30. Electronic applications accepted. *Expenses:* Contact institution. *Financial support:* Application deadline: 3/15. *Unit head:* Dr. Deborah A. Marr, Director, 540-678-4312, Fax: 540-665-5564, E-mail: dmarr@su.edu. *Application contact:* David Anthony, Dean of Admissions, 540-665-4581, Fax: 540-665-4627, E-mail: admit@su.edu.

Spalding University, Graduate Studies, College of Health and Natural Sciences, Auerbach School of Occupational Therapy, Louisville, KY 40203-2188. Offers occupational therapy (advanced-level) (MS); occupational therapy (entry-level) (MS). *Accreditation:* AOTA. *Faculty:* 6 full-time (4 women), 5 part-time/adjunct (all women). *Students:* 62 full-time (60 women), 36 part-time (33 women); includes 4 minority (1 African American, 3 Asian Americans or Pacific Islanders). Average age 29. 17 applicants, 94% accepted, 13 enrolled. In 2009, 29 master's awarded. *Degree requirements:* For master's, project. *Entrance requirements:* For master's, interview, letters of recommendation. Additional exam requirements/recommendations for international students: Required—TOEFL (minimum score 535 paper-based; 203 computer-based). *Application deadline:* For fall admission, 9/1 priority date for domestic and international students. Application fee: $30 ($400 for international students). Electronic applications accepted. *Expenses:* Tuition: Full-time $11,340; part-time $630 per credit hour. Tuition and fees vary according to program. *Financial support:* In 2009–10, 72 students received support, including

10 research assistantships with partial tuition reimbursements available (averaging $3,273 per year); unspecified assistantships also available. Financial award applicants required to submit FAFSA. *Faculty research:* High-risk youth, community-dwelling older adults, assistive technology, mother-infant relationships, community accessibility. *Unit head:* Dr. Laura Schluter Strickland, Associate Professor/Chairperson, 502-585-9911 Ext. 2324, Fax: 502-585-7149, E-mail: lstrickland@spalding.edu. *Application contact:* Admissions Office, 502-585-7111, E-mail: admissions@spalding.edu.

Springfield College, Graduate Programs, Program in Occupational Therapy, Springfield, MA 01109-3797. Offers M Ed, MS, CAGS. *Accreditation:* AOTA (one or more programs are accredited). Part-time programs available. *Degree requirements:* For master's, comprehensive exam. *Entrance requirements:* For master's, prerequisite courses for accreditation. Additional exam requirements/recommendations for international students: Required—TOEFL (minimum score 550 paper-based; 213 computer-based). Electronic applications accepted. *Expenses:* Tuition: Full-time $19,800; part-time $825 per credit hour. Required fees: $150.

Stony Brook University, State University of New York, Stony Brook University Medical Center, Health Sciences Center, School of Health Technology and Management, Stony Brook, NY 11794. Offers health care management (Advanced Certificate); health care policy and management (MS); occupational therapy (MS); physical therapy (DPT); physician assistant (MS). *Accreditation:* APTA. Part-time programs available. *Faculty:* 33 full-time (25 women), 25 part-time/adjunct (12 women). *Students:* 217 full-time (162 women), 130 part-time (93 women); includes 87 minority (21 African Americans, 1 American Indian/Alaska Native, 46 Asian Americans or Pacific Islanders, 19 Hispanic Americans), 8 international. 54 applicants, 91% accepted. In 2009, 89 master's, 77 doctorates, 15 other advanced degrees awarded. *Degree requirements:* For master's, thesis. *Entrance requirements:* For master's, GRE General Test, minimum GPA of 3.0, work experience in field. *Application deadline:* For fall admission, 1/15 for domestic students. Application fee: $60. *Expenses:* Tuition, state resident: full-time $8370; part-time $349 per credit. Tuition, nonresident: full-time $13,250; part-time $552 per credit. Required fees: $933. *Financial support:* In 2009–10, 2 research assistantships, 1 teaching assistantship were awarded; fellowships, career-related internships or fieldwork, Federal Work-Study, and institutionally sponsored loans also available. Financial award application deadline: 3/15. *Faculty research:* Health promotion and disease prevention. Total annual research expenditures: $842,937. *Unit head:* Dr. Craig A. Lehmann, Dean, 631-444-2251, Fax: 631-444-7621. *Application contact:* Richard W. Johnson, Associate Dean for Graduate Studies, 631-444-3251.

Temple University, Health Sciences Center and Graduate School, College of Health Professions, Department of Occupational Therapy, Philadelphia, PA 19122-6096. Offers MOT, MS. *Accreditation:* AOTA. Part-time programs available. *Degree requirements:* For master's, comprehensive exam (for some programs), thesis. *Entrance requirements:* For master's, GRE General Test or MAT, minimum GPA of 3.0, interview. Additional exam requirements/recommendations for international students: Required—TOEFL (minimum score 550 paper-based; 213 computer-based; 79 iBT). Electronic applications accepted. *Expenses:* Contact institution. *Faculty research:* Pediatrics, elderly, sensory integration, education, participation.

Texas Tech University Health Sciences Center, School of Allied Health Sciences, Program in Occupational Therapy, Lubbock, TX 79430. Offers MOT. *Accreditation:* AOTA. *Faculty:* 5 full-time (3 women). *Students:* 101 full-time (90 women); includes 25 minority (6 African Americans, 3 Asian Americans or Pacific Islanders, 16 Hispanic Americans). Average age 25. 144 applicants, 24% accepted, 35 enrolled. In 2009, 35 master's awarded. *Entrance requirements:* Additional exam requirements/recommendations for international students: Required—TOEFL, IELTS. *Application deadline:* For fall admission, 10/15 priority date for domestic students; for spring admission, 1/15 priority date for domestic students. Application fee: $35. Electronic applications accepted. *Financial support:* Career-related internships or fieldwork, institutionally sponsored loans, and scholarships/grants available. Financial award application deadline: 9/1; financial award applicants required to submit FAFSA. *Unit head:* Dr. Steve Sawyer, Chair, 806-743-3226, Fax: 806-743-3249, E-mail: steve.sawyer@ttuhsc.edu. *Application contact:* Jeri Moravcik, Assistant Director of Admissions and Student Affairs, 806-743-3220, Fax: 806-743-2994, E-mail: jeri.moravcik@ttuhsc.edu.

Texas Woman's University, Graduate School, College of Health Sciences, School of Occupational Therapy, Denton, TX 76201. Offers MA, MOT, PhD. *Accreditation:* AOTA (one or more programs are accredited). Part-time and evening/weekend programs available. Postbaccalaureate distance learning degree programs offered. *Faculty:* 23 full-time (all women), 11 part-time/adjunct (all women). *Students:* 271 full-time (258 women), 82 part-time (74 women); includes 109 minority (23 African Americans, 3 American Indian/Alaska Native, 30 Asian Americans or Pacific Islanders, 53 Hispanic Americans), 6 international. Average age 30. 291 applicants, 88% accepted, 80 enrolled. In 2009, 118 master's, 2 doctorates awarded. *Degree requirements:* For master's, thesis; for doctorate, comprehensive exam, thesis/dissertation. *Entrance requirements:* For master's, minimum GPA of 3.0, interview, recommendation based on 20 hours of observation with one supervising OTR; for doctorate, GRE General Test, essay, interview, 3 letters of reference, certification and master's degree in occupational therapy or related field. Additional exam requirements/recommendations for international students: Required—TOEFL (minimum score 550 paper-based; 213 computer-based; 79 iBT). *Application deadline:* For fall admission, 10/15 priority date for domestic and international students. Applications are processed on a rolling basis. Application fee: $50. Electronic applications accepted. *Expenses:* Tuition, state resident: full-time $3564; part-time $198 per credit hour. Tuition, nonresident: full-time $8550; part-time $475 per credit hour. Required fees: $69.26 per credit hour. Tuition and fees vary according to course load. *Financial support:* In 2009–10, 131 students received support, including 8 research assistantships (averaging $10,440 per year); career-related internships or fieldwork, Federal Work-Study, institutionally sponsored loans, scholarships/grants, traineeships, health care benefits, and unspecified assistantships also available. Support available to part-time students. Financial award application deadline: 3/1; financial award applicants required to submit FAFSA. *Faculty research:* Quality of life/wellness, Alzheimer's disease, hand rehabilitation, psychosocial dysfunction, adaptation/chronic disability, long term care. *Unit head:* Dr. Catherine Candler, Interim Director, 940-898-2801, Fax: 940-898-2806, E-mail: ot@twu.edu. *Application contact:* Samuel Wheeler, Assistant Director of Admissions, 940-898-3188, Fax: 940-898-3081, E-mail: wheelersr@twu.edu.

Thomas Jefferson University, Jefferson College of Health Professions, Program in Occupational Therapy, Philadelphia, PA 19107. Offers MS. *Accreditation:* AOTA. Part-time programs available. *Degree requirements:* For master's, thesis (for some programs). *Entrance requirements:* For master's, GRE General Test or MAT. Additional exam requirements/recommendations for international students: Required—TOEFL (minimum score 213 computer-based). Electronic applications accepted. *Expenses:* Contact institution. *Faculty research:* Functional outcomes in traumatic brain injury, clinical reasoning in therapist/patient interactions, gerontology, sensory integration in pediatrics, effective intervention for homeless.

Touro College, School of Health Sciences, Occupational Therapy Program, New York, NY 10010. Offers MS. *Accreditation:* AOTA. *Entrance requirements:* For master's, interview, minimum GPA of 2.8.

Towson University, College of Graduate Studies and Research, Program in Occupational Therapy, Towson, MD 21252-0001. Offers MS. *Accreditation:* AOTA. Part-time and evening/weekend programs available. *Degree requirements:* For master's, thesis optional, exam. *Entrance requirements:* For master's, minimum GPA of 3.0, 3 letters of recommendation, 30 hours of human service activity. *Faculty research:* Issues of the aging, training caregivers, hand function in children, family studies, community programs/collaboration.

Tufts University, Graduate School of Arts and Sciences, Department of Occupational Therapy, Medford, MA 02155. Offers MA, MS, OTD. *Accreditation:* AOTA. *Faculty:* 6 full-time, 9 part-time/adjunct. *Students:* 120 (115 women); includes 17 minority (1 African American, 8 Asian Americans or Pacific Islanders, 8 Hispanic Americans), 13 international. Average age 27. 114 applicants, 76% accepted, 40 enrolled. In 2009, 38 master's, 2 doctorates awarded. *Degree requirements:* For master's, thesis (for some programs); for doctorate, leadership project. *Entrance requirements:* For master's and doctorate, GRE General Test. Additional exam requirements/recommendations for international students: Required—TOEFL (minimum score 550 paper-based; 213 computer-based; 80 iBT). *Application deadline:* For fall admission, 2/15 for domestic students, 12/15 for international students; for spring admission, 10/15 for domestic students, 9/15 for international students. Applications are processed on a rolling basis. Application fee: $75. Electronic applications accepted. *Expenses:* Contact institution. *Financial support:* Teaching assistantships with partial tuition reimbursements, Federal Work-Study, scholarships/grants, and tuition waivers (partial) available. Support available to part-time students. Financial award application deadline: 2/15; financial award applicants required to submit FAFSA. *Unit head:* Linda Tickle-Degnen, 617-627-5720. *Application contact:* Elizabeth Owen, Staff Assistant, 617-627-5720.

Tufts University, Graduate School of Arts and Sciences, Graduate Certificate Programs, Advanced Professional Study in Occupational Therapy Program, Medford, MA 02155. Offers Certificate. Part-time and evening/weekend programs available. Electronic applications accepted. *Expenses:* Contact institution.

Université de Montréal, Faculty of Medicine, Programs in Ergonomics, Montréal, QC H3C 3J7, Canada. Offers occupational therapy (DESS). In 2009, 4 DESSs awarded. *Application deadline:* For fall admission, 2/1 priority date for domestic students; for winter admission, 11/1 priority date for domestic students; for spring admission, 2/1 priority date for domestic students. Applications are processed on a rolling basis. Application fee: $100. *Unit head:* Daniel Bourbonnais, Director, 514-343-6417, E-mail: daniel.bourbonnais@umontreal.ca. *Application contact:* Elaine Chapman, Professor responsible for graduate studies, 514-343-2304, E-mail: c.elaine.chapman@umontreal.ca.

University at Buffalo, the State University of New York, Graduate School, School of Public Health and Health Professions, Department of Rehabilitation Science, Program in Occupational Therapy, Buffalo, NY 14260. Offers MS. *Accreditation:* AOTA. *Faculty:* 21 full-time (15 women), 14 part-time/adjunct (9 women). *Students:* 30 full-time (28 women), 2 part-time (both women); includes 3 minority (2 African Americans, 1 Hispanic American), 2 international. Average age 23. 41 applicants, 78% accepted. In 2009, 31 master's awarded. *Degree requirements:* For master's, thesis, project. *Entrance requirements:* For master's, GRE, BS in occupational therapy. Additional exam requirements/recommendations for international students: Required—TOEFL (minimum score 550 paper-based; 213 computer-based; 79 iBT). *Application deadline:* For fall admission, 6/1 priority date for domestic students, 4/1 for international students; for spring admission, 11/1 priority date for domestic students, 9/1 for international students. Application fee: $50. Electronic applications accepted. *Financial support:* In 2009–10, 5 students received support, including 2 teaching assistantships with partial tuition reimbursements available (averaging $6,023 per year); unspecified assistantships also available. Financial award application deadline: 3/1; financial award applicants required to submit FAFSA. *Faculty research:* Sensory integration, assistive technology, aging and technology, transition for students with emotional/behavioral problems. Total annual research expenditures: $485,000. *Unit head:* Dr. Susan Nochajski, Graduate Program Director, 716-829-6942, Fax: 716-829-3217, E-mail: nochajsk@buffalo.edu. *Application contact:* Dr. Susan Nochajski, Graduate Program Director, 716-829-6942, Fax: 716-829-3217, E-mail: nochajsk@buffalo.edu.

The University of Alabama at Birmingham, School of Health Professions, Program in Occupational Therapy, Birmingham, AL 35294. Offers MS.

University of Alberta, Faculty of Graduate Studies and Research, Department of Occupational Therapy, Edmonton, AB T6G 2E1, Canada. Offers M Sc, PhD. Part-time programs available. *Faculty:* 13 full-time (10 women). *Students:* 3 full-time (2 women), 8 part-time (5 women). Average age 28. 4 applicants, 25% accepted. In 2009, 3 master's awarded. *Degree requirements:* For master's, thesis. *Entrance requirements:* For master's, bachelor's degree in occupational therapy, minimum GPA of 6.9 on a 9.0 scale. Additional exam requirements/recommendations for international students: Required—TOEFL. *Application deadline:* For fall admission, 5/15 for domestic students, 3/15 for international students; for winter admission, 10/15 for domestic students, 7/15 for international students. Applications are processed on a rolling basis. Application fee: $0. Electronic applications accepted. Tuition and fees charges are reported in Canadian dollars. *Expenses:* Tuition, area resident: Full-time $4626 Canadian dollars; part-time $99.72 Canadian dollars per unit. International tuition: $8216 Canadian dollars full-time. Required fees: $3590 Canadian dollars; $99.72 Canadian dollars per unit. $215 Canadian dollars per term. *Financial support:* In 2009–10, 1 research assistantship (averaging $2,721 per year), 1 teaching assistantship (averaging $2,535 per year) were awarded; career-related internships or fieldwork, institutionally sponsored loans, and scholarships/grants also available. Financial award application deadline: 1/1. *Faculty research:* Work evaluation, pediatrics, geriatrics, program evaluation, community-based rehabilitation. *Unit head:* L. Liu, Graduate Program Coordinator, 780-492-1595, Fax: 780-492-1626. *Application contact:* Angela Libutti, Administrative Assistant, Graduate Studies, 780-492-1595, Fax: 780-492-1626, E-mail: mscot.info@rehabmed.ualberta.ca.

The University of British Columbia, Faculty of Medicine, Department of Occupational Science and Occupational Therapy, Vancouver, BC V6T 1Z1, Canada. Offers MOT.

University of Central Arkansas, Graduate School, College of Health and Behavioral Sciences, Department of Occupational Therapy, Conway, AR 72035-0001. Offers MS. *Accreditation:* AOTA. *Faculty:* 7 full-time (6 women). *Students:* 93 full-time (85 women), 1 (woman) part-time; includes 4 minority (2 African Americans, 1 Asian American or Pacific Islander, 1 Hispanic American). Average age 24. 42 applicants, 100% accepted, 42 enrolled. In 2009, 51 master's awarded. *Degree requirements:* For master's, thesis optional, internship. *Entrance requirements:* For master's, GRE General Test, minimum GPA of 2.7. Additional exam requirements/recommendations for international students: Required—TOEFL (minimum score 550 paper-based; 213 computer-based). *Application deadline:* For fall admission, 3/1 priority date for domestic students; for spring admission, 10/1 for domestic students. Applications are processed on a rolling basis. Application fee: $25 ($50 for international students). *Expenses:* Contact institution. *Financial support:* In 2009–10, 6 research assistantships (averaging $2,200 per year) were awarded; Federal Work-Study, scholarships/grants, and unspecified assistantships also available. Financial award application deadline: 2/15; financial award applicants required to submit FAFSA. *Unit head:* Dr. Linda Musselman, Chair, 501-450-3192, Fax: 501-450-5503, E-mail: lindam@uca.edu. *Application contact:* Patti Hornor, Administrative Assistant, 501-450-5063, Fax: 501-450-5678, E-mail: pattih@uca.edu.

The University of Findlay, Graduate and Professional Studies, College of Health Professions, Master of Occupational Therapy Program, Findlay, OH 45840-3653. Offers MOT. *Accreditation:* AOTA. Part-time and evening/weekend programs available. *Entrance requirements:* For master's, 50 hours of observation, 3 letters of recommendation, minimum GPA of 3.0. Additional exam requirements/recommendations for international students: Required—TOEFL (minimum score 550 paper-based; 213 computer-based; 80 iBT). Electronic applications accepted.

University of Florida, Graduate School, College of Public Health and Health Professions, Department of Occupational Therapy, Gainesville, FL 32611. Offers MHS, MOT. *Accreditation:* AOTA. Postbaccalaureate distance learning degree programs offered. *Degree requirements:* For master's, research project. *Entrance requirements:* For master's, GRE General Test, minimum GPA of 3.0. Additional exam requirements/recommendations for international students: Required—TOEFL (minimum score 550 paper-based; 213 computer-based). Electronic applications accepted. *Faculty research:* Occupational therapy related to ergonomics, body image, pediatrics, HIV, and hand therapy.

University of Illinois at Chicago, Graduate College, College of Applied Health Sciences, Department of Occupational Therapy, Chicago, IL 60607-7128. Offers MS, OTD. *Accreditation:* AOTA. Part-time programs available. *Degree requirements:* For master's, thesis. *Entrance requirements:* For master's, GRE General Test, minimum GPA of 2.75, previous course work in statistics. Additional exam requirements/recommendations for international students: Required—

Occupational Therapy

University of Illinois at Chicago (continued)
TOEFL. Electronic applications accepted. *Faculty research:* Sensory integration, perception, play, treatment efficacy, instrument development.

University of Indianapolis, Graduate Programs, School of Occupational Therapy, Indianapolis, IN 46227-3697. Offers MHS, MOT, DHS. *Accreditation:* AOTA. Part-time and evening/weekend programs available. *Faculty:* 6 full-time (all women), 3 part-time/adjunct (1 woman). *Students:* 108 full-time (96 women), 75 part-time (67 women); includes 17 minority (5 African Americans, 7 Asian Americans or Pacific Islanders, 5 Hispanic Americans), 1 international. Average age 27. *Degree requirements:* For master's, thesis. *Entrance requirements:* For master's, minimum GPA of 3.0, interview; for doctorate, minimum GPA of 3.3, BA/BS or MAIMS from occupational therapy program, current state license, currently in practice as occupational therapist or have 1000 hours of practice in last 5 years. Additional exam requirements/recommendations for international students: Required—TOEFL (minimum score 550 paper-based; 237 computer-based; 92 iBT), TWE (minimum score 5). *Application deadline:* For fall admission, 11/1 for domestic students, 2/1 for international students. Application fee: $55. *Expenses:* Contact institution. *Financial support:* Career-related internships or fieldwork, Federal Work-Study, tuition waivers (full and partial), and unspecified assistantships available. Financial award application deadline: 5/1; financial award applicants required to submit FAFSA. *Unit head:* Dr. Stephanie Kelly, Acting Dean, College of Health Sciences, 317-788-3500, Fax: 317-788-3542, E-mail: spkelly@ulndy.edu. *Application contact:* Kelly Wilson, Director, Admissions, 317-788-3457, Fax: 317-788-3542, E-mail: kwilson@uindy.edu.

The University of Kansas, University of Kansas Medical Center, School of Allied Health, Department of Occupational Therapy Education, Kansas City, KS 66160. Offers occupational therapy (MOT, MS, OTD); therapeutic science (PhD). *Accreditation:* AOTA. Part-time programs available. *Faculty:* 8 full-time, 3 part-time/adjunct. *Students:* 45 full-time (43 women), 39 part-time (32 women); includes 5 minority (2 African Americans, 1 American Indian/Alaska Native, 1 Asian American or Pacific Islander, 1 Hispanic American), 16 international. Average age 28. 13 applicants, 69% accepted, 9 enrolled. In 2009, 31 master's awarded. *Degree requirements:* For doctorate, comprehensive exam, thesis/dissertation, oral defense. *Entrance requirements:* For master's, 1 year of experience in a field related to disability; for doctorate, 24 hours of master's level research. Additional exam requirements/recommendations for international students: Required—TOEFL. *Application deadline:* For fall admission, 6/15 for domestic students, 4/1 for international students. Applications are processed on a rolling basis. Application fee: $60. Electronic applications accepted. *Expenses:* Tuition, state resident: full-time $6492; part-time $270.50 per credit hour. Tuition, nonresident: full-time $15,510; part-time $646.25 per credit hour. Required fees: $847; $70.56 per credit hour. Tuition and fees vary according to course load and program. *Financial support:* In 2009–10, 36 students received support, including 3 teaching assistantships with full and partial tuition reimbursements available (averaging $41,288 per year); research assistantships with partial tuition reimbursements available, traineeships and unspecified assistantships also available. Financial award applicants required to submit FAFSA. *Faculty research:* The impact of sensory processing in everyday life; brain activity in various disorders and conditions; home and work modifications; cognition, executive function and problem solving in everyday life; best practices in serving children, families and schools. Total annual research expenditures: $99,220. *Unit head:* Dr. Winifred W. Dunn, Professor and Chair, 913-588-7195, Fax: 913-588-4568, E-mail: wdunn@kumc.edu. *Application contact:* Laura Neely, Coordinator, 913-588-7174, Fax: 913-588-4568, E-mail: lneely@kumc.edu.

University of Manitoba, Faculty of Graduate Studies, School of Medical Rehabilitation, Winnipeg, MB R3T 2N2, Canada. Offers applied health sciences (PhD); occupational therapy (MOT); physical therapy (MPT); rehabilitation (M Sc).

University of Mary, Department of Occupational Therapy, Bismarck, ND 58504-9652. Offers entry level (MSOT); post professional (MSOT). *Accreditation:* AOTA. Part-time programs available. Postbaccalaureate distance learning degree programs offered (minimal on-campus study). *Degree requirements:* For master's, thesis or alternative, practicum. *Entrance requirements:* For master's, ACT or equivalent, minimum GPA of 2.75, 48 hours of volunteer experience. Additional exam requirements/recommendations for international students: Required—TOEFL (minimum score 550 paper-based). Electronic applications accepted. *Expenses:* Contact institution. *Faculty research:* Safe homes for well elderly, occupation and spirituality, professional development in the spiritual domain, case method instruction, ergonomics, assistive technology.

University of Mississippi Medical Center, School of Health Related Professions, Department of Occupational Therapy, Jackson, MS 39216-4505. Offers MOT. *Accreditation:* AOTA.

University of Missouri, School of Health Professions, Program in Occupational Therapy, Columbia, MO 65211. Offers MOT. *Accreditation:* AOTA. *Entrance requirements:* Additional exam requirements/recommendations for international students: Required—TOEFL (minimum score 500 paper-based; 173 computer-based; 61 iBT).

University of New England, Westbrook College of Health Professions, Program in Occupational Therapy, Biddeford, ME 04005-9526. Offers occupational therapy (MS); post professional occupational therapy (MS). *Accreditation:* AOTA. *Faculty:* 8 full-time (7 women). *Students:* 35 full-time (all women), 3 part-time (all women); includes 2 minority (1 Asian American or Pacific Islander, 1 Hispanic American). In 2009, 32 master's awarded. *Degree requirements:* For master's, research project. *Entrance requirements:* For master's, minimum undergraduate GPA of 3.0, 1 level II clinical. *Application deadline:* Applications are processed on a rolling basis. Application fee: $40. *Expenses:* Contact institution. *Financial support:* Application deadline: 5/1. *Faculty research:* Aging and cognition, neurobehavioral basis of motor control, post breast surgery syndrome, sensory modulation, ergonomics. *Unit head:* Regi Robnett, Director, 207-602-2233, Fax: 207-602-5963, E-mail: rrobnett@une.edu. *Application contact:* Stacy Gato, Assistant Director of Graduate Admissions, 207-221-4225, Fax: 207-221-4898, E-mail: gradadmissions@une.edu.

University of New Hampshire, Graduate School, School of Health and Human Services, Department of Occupational Therapy, Durham, NH 03824. Offers MS, Postbaccalaureate Certificate. Degree offered in professional and post-professional tracks. *Accreditation:* AOTA. Part-time programs available. *Faculty:* 6 full-time (5 women). *Students:* 66 full-time (63 women), 7 part-time (6 women); includes 3 minority (1 Asian American or Pacific Islander, 2 Hispanic Americans). Average age 35. 69 applicants, 59% accepted, 36 enrolled. In 2009, 61 master's, 9 other advanced degrees awarded. *Degree requirements:* For master's, thesis or alternative. *Entrance requirements:* For master's, GRE General Test, current certification as an OTR from the American Occupational Therapy Board or World Federation of Occupational Therapy. Additional exam requirements/recommendations for international students: Required—TOEFL (minimum score 550 paper-based; 213 computer-based; 80 iBT). *Application deadline:* For fall admission, 4/1 for domestic and international students. Applications are processed on a rolling basis. Application fee: $65. Electronic applications accepted. *Expenses:* Tuition, state resident: full-time $10,380; part-time $577 per credit hour. Tuition, nonresident: full-time $24,350; part-time $1002 per credit hour. Required fees: $1550; $387.50 per semester. Tuition and fees vary according to course load and program. *Financial support:* In 2009–10, 2 students received support; fellowships, research assistantships, teaching assistantships, career-related internships or fieldwork, Federal Work-Study, and scholarships/grants available. Support available to part-time students. Financial award application deadline: 2/15. *Unit head:* Dr. Shelly Mulligan, Chairperson, 603-862-3528. *Application contact:* Renate Jurden, Administrative Assistant, 603-862-2168, E-mail: ot.dept@unh.edu.

University of New Mexico, School of Medicine, Program in Occupational Therapy, Albuquerque, NM 87131-5196. Offers MOT. *Accreditation:* AOTA. Part-time programs available. *Degree requirements:* For master's, thesis, clinical fieldwork. *Entrance requirements:* For master's, interview, writing sample, volunteer experience. Additional exam requirements/recommendations for international students: Required—TOEFL. Electronic applications accepted. *Expenses:* Tuition, state resident: full-time $2099; part-time $233.20 per credit hour. Tuition, nonresident:

full-time $6650. Required fees: $25 per semester. Tuition and fees vary according to course load, program and reciprocity agreements. *Faculty research:* Gait analysis.

The University of North Carolina at Chapel Hill, School of Medicine and Graduate School, Graduate Programs in Medicine, Chapel Hill, NC 27599. Offers allied health sciences (MPT, MS, Au D, DPT, PhD), including human movement science (MS, PhD), occupational science (MS, PhD), physical therapy (MPT, MS, DPT), rehabilitation counseling and psychology (MS), speech and hearing sciences (MS, Au D, PhD); biochemistry and biophysics (MS, PhD); biomedical engineering (MS, PhD); cell and developmental biology (PhD); cell and molecular physiology (PhD); genetics and molecular biology (PhD); microbiology and immunology (MS, PhD), including immunology, microbiology; neurobiology (PhD); pathology and laboratory medicine (PhD), including experimental pathology; pharmacology (PhD); MD/PhD. Postbaccalaureate distance learning degree programs offered. Terminal master's awarded for partial completion of doctoral program. *Degree requirements:* For master's, comprehensive exam; for doctorate, thesis/dissertation. Electronic applications accepted. *Expenses:* Contact institution.

The University of North Carolina at Chapel Hill, School of Medicine and Graduate School, Graduate Programs in Medicine, Department of Allied Health Sciences, Division of Occupational Science, Chapel Hill, NC 27599. Offers occupational science (MS, PhD). *Accreditation:* AOTA. *Faculty:* 9 full-time (7 women), 1 (woman) part-time/adjunct. *Students:* 53 full-time (46 women), 3 part-time (all women); includes 9 minority (6 African Americans, 2 Asian Americans or Pacific Islanders, 1 Hispanic American). Average age 27. 102 applicants, 25% accepted, 25 enrolled. In 2009, 18 master's awarded. *Degree requirements:* For master's, comprehensive exam, thesis optional, collaborative research project; for doctorate, thesis/dissertation. *Entrance requirements:* For master's, GRE General Test; for doctorate, GRE, master's degree in occupational therapy, relevant social behavioral sciences or health field. Additional exam requirements/recommendations for international students: Required—TOEFL (minimum score 550 paper-based; 79 computer-based). *Application deadline:* For fall admission, 1/1 for domestic and international students. Application fee: $75. Electronic applications accepted. *Financial support:* In 2009–10, 38 students received support; fellowships with full tuition reimbursements available, research assistantships, teaching assistantships, institutionally sponsored loans, scholarships/grants, traineeships, and unspecified assistantships available. Financial award application deadline: 1/1; financial award applicants required to submit FAFSA. *Faculty research:* Parents and infants in co-occupations, psychosocial dysfunction, predictors of autism, factors influencing the occupation of primates, factors influencing occupations of people with dementia, occupational development of young children. Total annual research expenditures: $645,274. *Unit head:* Virginia Dickie, Director, 919-966-2452, Fax: 919-966-9007, E-mail: virginia_dickie@med.unc.edu. *Application contact:* Jenny Womack, Admissions Co-Chair, 919-843-4463, Fax: 919-966-9007, E-mail: jwomack@med.unc.edu.

University of North Dakota, School of Medicine and Health Sciences and Graduate School, Graduate Programs in Medicine, Department of Occupational Therapy, Grand Forks, ND 58202. Offers MOT. *Accreditation:* AOTA. *Entrance requirements:* For master's, letter of reference; volunteer or work experience, preferably from health-related field; interview; minimum GPA of 2.7. Additional exam requirements/recommendations for international students: Required—TOEFL (minimum score 550 paper-based; 213 computer-based; 79 iBT), IELTS (minimum score 6.5).

University of Oklahoma Health Sciences Center, Graduate College, College of Allied Health, Department of Occupational Therapy, Oklahoma City, OK 73190. Offers MOT. *Accreditation:* AOTA. *Faculty:* 3 full-time (2 women). *Students:* 62 full-time (58 women), 8 part-time (4 women); includes 11 minority (1 African American, 5 American Indian/Alaska Native, 3 Asian Americans or Pacific Islanders, 2 Hispanic Americans). Average age 25. 44 applicants, 66% accepted, 21 enrolled. In 2009, 20 master's awarded. *Application deadline:* For fall admission, 6/1 for domestic students; for winter admission, 4/1 for domestic students; for spring admission, 10/1 for domestic students. *Expenses:* Tuition, state resident: full-time $3120; part-time $156 per credit hour. Tuition, nonresident: full-time $11,314; part-time $409.70 per credit hour. Required fees: $1471; $51.20 per credit hour. $223.25 per term. *Unit head:* Dr. Carole Sullivan, Dean, 405-271-2288, Fax: 405-271-1190, E-mail: carole-sullivan@ouhsc.edu. *Application contact:* Jenielle Greenlee, Associate Dean for Finance, 405-271-2288, Fax: 405-271-1190, E-mail: jenielle-greenlee@ouhse.edu.

University of Pittsburgh, School of Health and Rehabilitation Sciences, Master of Occupational Therapy Program, Pittsburgh, PA 15260. Offers MOT. *Accreditation:* AOTA. *Faculty:* 5 full-time (all women), 3 part-time/adjunct (all women). *Students:* 77 full-time (65 women), 8 part-time (7 women); includes 5 minority (3 African Americans, 2 Asian Americans or Pacific Islanders), 2 international. Average age 26. 120 applicants, 58% accepted, 48 enrolled. In 2009, 32 master's awarded. *Entrance requirements:* For master's, GRE General Test, volunteer experience. Additional exam requirements/recommendations for international students: Required—TOEFL (minimum score 550 paper-based; 213 computer-based; 80 iBT), IELTS (minimum score 6.5). *Application deadline:* Applications are processed on a rolling basis. Application fee: $50. Electronic applications accepted. *Expenses:* Contact institution. *Financial support:* Fellowships, research assistantships, teaching assistantships, Federal Work-Study available. *Faculty research:* Expertise in evidence-based practice, measuring occupational performance, ergonomics, geriatrics, mental health, neurorehabilitation, research. Total annual research expenditures: $573,070. *Unit head:* Dr. Joan Rogers, Chairperson, 412-383-6620, Fax: 412-383-6613, E-mail: admissions@shrs.pitt.edu. *Application contact:* Shameem Gangjee, Director of Admissions, 412-383-6558, Fax: 412-383-6535, E-mail: admissions@shrs.pitt.edu.

University of Pittsburgh, School of Health and Rehabilitation Sciences, Master's Programs in Health and Rehabilitation Sciences, Pittsburgh, PA 15260. Offers health and rehabilitation sciences (MS), including clinical dietetics and nutrition, health care supervision and management, health information systems, occupational therapy, physical therapy, rehabilitation counseling, rehabilitation science and technology, sports medicine, wellness and human performance. *Accreditation:* APTA. Part-time and evening/weekend programs available. *Faculty:* 30 full-time (14 women), 4 part-time/adjunct (3 women). *Students:* 81 full-time (47 women), 54 part-time (27 women); includes 10 minority (6 African Americans, 4 Asian Americans or Pacific Islanders), 44 international. Average age 29. 326 applicants, 65% accepted, 130 enrolled. In 2009, 93 master's awarded. *Degree requirements:* For master's, comprehensive exam (for some programs), thesis optional. *Entrance requirements:* For master's, minimum GPA of 3.0. Additional exam requirements/recommendations for international students: Required—TOEFL, IELTS. *Application deadline:* For fall admission, 1/31 for international students; for spring admission, 7/31 for international students. Applications are processed on a rolling basis. Application fee: $50. Electronic applications accepted. *Expenses:* Contact institution. *Financial support:* In 2009–10, 3 research assistantships with full tuition reimbursements (averaging $18,450 per year) were awarded; teaching assistantships, Federal Work-Study, institutionally sponsored loans, traineeships, and unspecified assistantships also available. Financial award applicants required to submit FAFSA. *Faculty research:* Assistive technology, seating and wheeled mobility, cellular neurophysiology, low back syndrome, augmentative communication. Total annual research expenditures: $6.5 million. *Unit head:* Dr. Clifford E. Brubaker, Dean, 412-383-6560, Fax: 412-383-6535, E-mail: cliffb@pitt.edu. *Application contact:* Shameem Gangjee, Director of Admissions, 412-383-6558, Fax: 412-383-6535, E-mail: admissions@shrs.pitt.edu.

University of Puerto Rico, Medical Sciences Campus, School of Health Professions, Program in Occupational Therapy, San Juan, PR 00936-5067. Offers MS. *Accreditation:* AOTA.

University of Puget Sound, Graduate Studies, School of Occupational Therapy and Physical Therapy, Occupational Therapy Program, Tacoma, WA 98416. Offers MOT, MSOT. *Accreditation:* AOTA. *Faculty:* 7 full-time (5 women). *Students:* 88 full-time (82 women), 7 part-time (6 women); includes 16 minority (2 African Americans, 11 Asian Americans or Pacific Islanders, 3 Hispanic Americans), 1 international. Average age 29. 78 applicants, 86% accepted, 38 enrolled. In 2009, 24 master's awarded. *Degree requirements:* For master's, thesis, publishable paper or program development project. *Entrance requirements:* For master's, GRE General

Test, minimum GPA of 3.0. Additional exam requirements/recommendations for international students: Required—TOEFL (minimum score 550 paper-based; 213 computer-based; 80 iBT). *Application deadline:* For fall admission, 1/15 priority date for domestic and international students. Application fee: $75. Electronic applications accepted. Tuition and fees vary according to course load, degree level and program. *Financial support:* In 2009–10, 23 students received support, including 21 fellowships (averaging $9,000 per year); career-related internships or fieldwork and scholarships/grants also available. Financial award application deadline: 3/31; financial award applicants required to submit FAFSA. *Faculty research:* Scope of practice for school-based occupational therapy, family occupational adaptation to autism, clinical decision making, low vision adaptation, assistive technology. *Unit head:* Dr. George S. Tomlin, Professor and Program Director, 253-879-3522, Fax: 253-879-2933, E-mail: tomlin@pugetsound.edu. *Application contact:* Dr. George H. Mills, Vice President for Enrollment, 253-879-3211, Fax: 253-879-3993, E-mail: admission@pugetsound.edu.

University of St. Augustine for Health Sciences, Graduate Programs, Division of Occupational Therapy, St. Augustine, FL 32086. Offers MOT, OTD. *Accreditation:* AOTA. *Entrance requirements:* For master's, GRE General Test.

The University of Scranton, College of Graduate and Continuing Education, Program in Occupational Therapy, Scranton, PA 18510. Offers MS. *Accreditation:* AOTA. *Faculty:* 6 full-time (5 women). *Students:* 41 full-time (all women), 1 part-time (0 women); includes 2 minority (both Hispanic Americans). Average age 23. 1 applicant, 0% accepted. In 2009, 30 master's awarded. *Degree requirements:* For master's, thesis, capstone experience. *Entrance requirements:* For master's, minimum GPA of 2.75. Additional exam requirements/recommendations for international students: Required—TOEFL (minimum score 500 paper-based; 173 computer-based), IELTS (minimum score 5.5). *Application deadline:* Applications are processed on a rolling basis. Application fee: $0. *Financial support:* In 2009–10, 2 students received support, including 2 teaching assistantships with full tuition reimbursements available (averaging $6,600 per year); career-related internships or fieldwork, Federal Work-Study, and unspecified assistantships also available. Support available to part-time students. Financial award application deadline: 3/1. *Unit head:* Dr. Marlene Joy Morgan, Director, 570-941-5789, Fax: 570-941-4380. *Application contact:* Joseph M. Roback, Director of Admissions, 570-941-4385, Fax: 570-941-5928, E-mail: roback j2@scranton.edu.

University of South Alabama, Graduate School, College of Allied Health Professions, Department of Occupational Therapy, Mobile, AL 36688-0002. Offers MS. *Accreditation:* AOTA. *Entrance requirements:* For master's, GRE, minimum GPA of 3.0. *Expenses:* Tuition, state resident: part-time $218 per contact hour. Required fees: $1102 per year.

The University of South Dakota, School of Medicine and Health Sciences and Graduate School, Graduate Programs in Health Sciences, Department of Occupational Therapy, Vermillion, SD 57069-2390. Offers MS. *Accreditation:* AOTA. Part-time programs available. *Degree requirements:* For master's, thesis optional, 6 months of supervised fieldwork. *Entrance requirements:* For master's, courses in human anatomy, human physiology, general psychology, abnormal psychology, lifespan development, statistics. Additional exam requirements/recommendations for international students: Required—TOEFL (minimum score 550 paper-based; 213 computer-based). *Expenses:* Contact institution. *Faculty research:* Low vision in youth and adults, agricultural/rural, health, childhood obesity, adolescent mental health, elder health and well being.

University of Southern California, Graduate School, School of Dentistry, Division of Occupational Science and Occupational Therapy, Graduate Program in Occupational Science, Los Angeles, CA 90089. Offers PhD. Part-time programs available. *Faculty:* 33 full-time (29 women), 30 part-time/adjunct (28 women). *Students:* 21 full-time (17 women), 1 part-time (0 women); includes 2 minority (1 Asian American or Pacific Islander, 1 Hispanic American), 2 international. 9 applicants. In 2009, 3 doctorates awarded. *Degree requirements:* For doctorate, thesis/dissertation, qualifying exam. *Entrance requirements:* For doctorate, GRE (minimum combined score of 1100), minimum GPA of 3.0. Additional exam requirements/recommendations for international students: Required—TOEFL (minimum score 600 paper-based; 250 computer-based; 100 iBT). *Application deadline:* Applications are processed on a rolling basis. Application fee: $85. Electronic applications accepted. *Expenses:* Tuition: Full-time $25,980; part-time $1315 per unit. Required fees: $554. One-time fee: $35 full-time. Full-time tuition and fees vary according to degree level and program. *Financial support:* In 2009–10, 19 students received support, including 5 research assistantships with full tuition reimbursements available (averaging $28,000 per year); scholarships/grants and tuition waivers also available. Support available to part-time students. Financial award application deadline: 2/15; financial award applicants required to submit FAFSA. *Faculty research:* Rehabilitation science, prevention of chronic disease and disability in vulnerable populations, health disparities and cultural boundaries that impact health care, sensory processing and integration including their impact on autism, innovative technology. *Unit head:* Dr. Florence Clark, Associate Dean and Chair, 323-442-2850, Fax: 323-442-1590, E-mail: fclark@usc.edu. *Application contact:* Sarah Kelly, Director of Admissions, 323-442-2822, Fax: 323-442-1590, E-mail: skelly@usc.edu.

University of Southern California, Graduate School, School of Dentistry, Division of Occupational Science and Occupational Therapy, Graduate Programs in Occupational Therapy, Los Angeles, CA 90089. Offers MA, OTD. *Accreditation:* AOTA. Part-time programs available. *Faculty:* 33 full-time (29 women), 30 part-time/adjunct (28 women). *Students:* 263 full-time (238 women), 5 part-time (all women); includes 121 minority (5 African Americans, 90 Asian Americans or Pacific Islanders, 26 Hispanic Americans), 12 international. 276 applicants, 78% accepted, 144 enrolled. In 2009, 116 master's, 116 doctorates awarded. *Degree requirements:* For master's, comprehensive exam (for some programs), thesis or alternative; for doctorate, residency, portfolio. *Entrance requirements:* For master's and doctorate, GRE (minimim score 1000), minimum cumulative GPA of 3.0. Additional exam requirements/recommendations for international students: Required—TOEFL (minimum score 600 paper-based; 250 computer-based; 100 iBT). *Application deadline:* Applications are processed on a rolling basis. Application fee: $85. Electronic applications accepted. *Expenses:* Tuition: Full-time $25,980; part-time $1315 per unit. Required fees: $554. One-time fee: $35 full-time. Full-time tuition and fees vary according to degree level and program. *Financial support:* In 2009–10, 116 students received support, including 42 teaching assistantships with partial tuition reimbursements available (averaging $9,500 per year); Federal Work-Study, scholarships/grants, traineeships, and tuition waivers also available. Financial award application deadline: 2/15; financial award applicants required to submit FAFSA. *Faculty research:* Rehabilitation science, prevention of chronic disease and disability in vulnerable populations, health disparities and cultural boundaries that impact health care, sensory processing and integration including their impact on autism, innovative technology. *Unit head:* Dr. Florence Clark, Associate Dean and Chair, 323-442-2850, Fax: 323-442-1590, E-mail: fclark@usc.edu. *Application contact:* Sarah Kelly, Director of Admissions, 323-442-2822, Fax: 323-442-1590, E-mail: skelly@usc.edu.

University of Southern Indiana, Graduate Studies, College of Nursing and Health Professions, Program in Occupational Therapy, Evansville, IN 47712-3590. Offers MSOT. *Accreditation:* AOTA. Part-time programs available. Postbaccalaureate distance learning degree programs offered (minimal on-campus study). *Faculty:* 2 full-time (both women). *Students:* 27 part-time (26 women). Average age 26. In 2009, 28 master's awarded. *Entrance requirements:* Additional exam requirements/recommendations for international students: Required—TOEFL (minimum score 550 paper-based; 213 computer-based; 79 iBT), IELTS (minimum score 6). *Application deadline:* For fall admission, 8/15 priority date for domestic students, 3/1 priority date for international students. Applications are processed on a rolling basis. Application fee: $25. Electronic applications accepted. *Expenses:* Tuition, state resident: full-time $4592; part-time $255 per credit hour. Tuition, nonresident: full-time $9060; part-time $503 per credit hour. Required fees: $220; $22.75 per term. Tuition and fees vary according to course load and reciprocity agreements. *Financial support:* In 2009–10, 20 students received support. Federal Work-Study, scholarships/grants, tuition waivers (full and partial), and unspecified assistantships available. Financial award application deadline: 3/1; financial award applicants required to submit FAFSA. *Unit head:* Dr. Barbara Williams, Director, 812-461-5396, E-mail: bjwilliams4@usi.edu. *Application contact:* Dr. Peggy F. Harrel, Director, Graduate Studies, 812-465-7015, Fax: 812-464-1956, E-mail: pharrel@usi.edu.

University of Southern Maine, Program in Occupational Therapy, Lewiston, ME 04240. Offers MOT. *Accreditation:* AOTA. *Faculty:* 3 full-time (all women), 4 part-time/adjunct (3 women). *Students:* 40 full-time (37 women), 20 part-time (18 women); includes 1 minority (African American), 1 international. Average age 35. 31 applicants, 90% accepted, 20 enrolled. In 2009, 20 master's awarded. *Degree requirements:* For master's, fieldwork, original research. *Entrance requirements:* For master's, minimum GPA of 3.0, writing sample, interview, reference letters, job shadow observation. *Application deadline:* Applications are processed on a rolling basis. Application fee: $50. Electronic applications accepted. *Financial support:* In 2009–10, 3 students received support, including 1 research assistantship (averaging $2,400 per year), 1 teaching assistantship (averaging $2,400 per year); fellowships with partial tuition reimbursements available, Federal Work-Study, scholarships/grants, tuition waivers (partial), and unspecified assistantships also available. Financial award application deadline: 3/1; financial award applicants required to submit FAFSA. *Faculty research:* Multicultural curricula, cultural competence, parents responses to fussy infants, chronic pain, early childhood eating disorders. *Unit head:* Dr. Roxie M. Black, Professor and Program Director, 207-753-6515, Fax: 207-753-6555, E-mail: rblack@usm.maine.edu. *Application contact:* Luisa Scott, Administrative Assistant, 207-753-6523, Fax: 207-753-6555, E-mail: lscott@usm.maine.edu.

The University of Texas at El Paso, Graduate School, College of Health Sciences, Program in Occupational Therapy, El Paso, TX 79968-0001. Offers MOT. *Accreditation:* AOTA. *Students:* 44 (29 women); includes 36 minority (2 African Americans, 34 Hispanic Americans), 1 international. Average age 34. In 2009, 7 master's awarded. *Degree requirements:* For master's, thesis optional. *Entrance requirements:* For master's, GRE. Additional exam requirements/recommendations for international students: Required—TOEFL; Recommended—IELTS. *Application deadline:* For fall admission, 8/1 for domestic students, 3/1 for international students; for spring admission, 11/1 for domestic students, 9/1 for international students. Application fee: $45 ($80 for international students). *Financial support:* Fellowships with partial tuition reimbursements, research assistantships with partial tuition reimbursements, teaching assistantships with partial tuition reimbursements, institutionally sponsored loans, scholarships/grants, health care benefits, tuition waivers (partial), and unspecified assistantships available. Support available to part-time students. Financial award application deadline: 3/15; financial award applicants required to submit FAFSA. *Unit head:* Dr. Stephanie Capshaw, Chair, 915-747-8207, Fax: 915-747-8211, E-mail: scapshaw@utep.edu. *Application contact:* Dr. Patricia D. Witherspoon, Dean of the Graduate School, 915-747-5491, Fax: 915-747-5788, E-mail: withersp@utep.edu.

The University of Texas Health Science Center at San Antonio, School of Allied Health Sciences, San Antonio, TX 78229-3900. Offers clinical laboratory sciences (MS); deaf education and hearing science (MED); dental hygiene (MS); occupational therapy (MOT); physical therapy (MPT); physician assistant studies (MS). *Accreditation:* AOTA; APTA; ARC-PA. *Expenses:* Tuition, state resident: full-time $2832; part-time $118 per credit hour. Tuition, nonresident: full-time $10,896; part-time $454 per credit hour. Required fees: $884 per semester. One-time fee: $70.

The University of Texas Medical Branch, School of Health Professions, Department of Occupational Therapy, Galveston, TX 77555. Offers MOT. *Accreditation:* AOTA. *Students:* 103 full-time (94 women), 4 part-time (all women); includes 40 minority (12 African Americans, 3 American Indian/Alaska Native, 14 Asian Americans or Pacific Islanders, 11 Hispanic Americans), 1 international. Average age 26. In 2009, 28 master's awarded. *Entrance requirements:* For master's, MAT, 20 volunteer hours, telephone interview, 2 references. Application fee: $30. *Financial support:* Applicants required to submit FAFSA. *Unit head:* Dr. Gretchen Stone, Chair and Associate Professor, 409-772-3061, Fax: 409-747-1615, E-mail: gestone@utmb.edu. *Application contact:* Sharon G. McEachern, Special Programs Coordinator II, 409-772-3062, Fax: 409-747-1615, E-mail: smceache@utmb.edu.

The University of Texas–Pan American, College of Health Sciences and Human Services, Department of Occupational Therapy, Edinburg, TX 78539. Offers MS. *Accreditation:* AOTA. Evening/weekend programs available. *Entrance requirements:* For master's, Health Occupations Aptitude Examination. *Expenses:* Tuition, state resident: full-time $3630.60; part-time $201.70 per credit hour. Tuition, nonresident: full-time $8617; part-time $478.70 per credit hour. Required fees: $806.50. *Faculty research:* Parenting of children with disabilities, effects of healing touch on student stress, impact of RGV culture on women's roles.

The University of Toledo, College of Graduate Studies, College of Health Science and Human Service, Division of Health, Program in Occupational Therapy, Toledo, OH 43606-3390. Offers OTD. *Accreditation:* AOTA. *Expenses:* Contact institution. *Faculty research:* Therapeutic occupation, pediatric neuroscience, grief/loss, motor control.

University of Utah, Graduate School, College of Health, Division of Occupational Therapy, Salt Lake City, UT 84108. Offers MOT, OTD. *Accreditation:* AOTA. Postbaccalaureate distance learning degree programs offered (no on-campus study). *Faculty:* 8 full-time (7 women). *Students:* 73 full-time (47 women); includes 6 minority (1 African American, 1 American Indian/Alaska Native, 1 Asian American or Pacific Islander, 3 Hispanic Americans). Average age 28. 30 applicants, 63% accepted, 18 enrolled. In 2009, 18 master's awarded. *Degree requirements:* For master's, thesis or alternative, project; for doctorate, thesis/dissertation or alternative, capstone. *Entrance requirements:* For master's and doctorate, GRE General Test. Additional exam requirements/recommendations for international students: Required—TOEFL (minimum score 575 paper-based; 233 computer-based). *Application deadline:* For fall admission, 1/15 for domestic and international students. Application fee: $75. *Expenses:* Contact institution. *Financial support:* In 2009–10, 10 students received support, including 4 research assistantships with full and partial tuition reimbursements available (averaging $16,500 per year); career-related internships or fieldwork, Federal Work-Study, institutionally sponsored loans, scholarships/grants, and unspecified assistantships also available. Financial award application deadline: 2/15; financial award applicants required to submit FAFSA. *Faculty research:* Community-based practice, occupational science, obesity, refugee, resilience, low vision, traumatic brain injury. Total annual research expenditures: $6,679. *Unit head:* Dr. JoAnne Wright, Chairperson, 801-585-9135, Fax: 801-585-1001, E-mail: joanne.wright@hsc.utah.edu. *Application contact:* Kelly C. Brown, Academic Advisor, 801-585-0555, Fax: 801-585-1001, E-mail: kelly.brown@hsc.utah.edu.

University of Washington, Graduate School, School of Medicine and Graduate School, Graduate Programs in Medicine, Department of Rehabilitation Medicine, Seattle, WA 98195-6490. Offers occupational therapy (MOT); physical therapy (DPT); rehabilitation science (PhD). *Faculty:* 56. *Students:* 150. Average age 25. In 2009, 25 master's, 30 doctorates awarded. *Degree requirements:* For doctorate, comprehensive exam (for some programs), thesis/dissertation (for some programs). *Entrance requirements:* For master's and doctorate, GRE. Additional exam requirements/recommendations for international students: Required—TOEFL. Application fee: $65. *Financial support:* In 2009–10, 1 fellowship (averaging $5,000 per year) was awarded. Financial award applicants required to submit FAFSA. *Faculty research:* Biomechanics, balance, brain injury, spinal cord injury, pain, degenerative diseases. *Unit head:* Dr. Peter C. Esselman, Professor and Chair, 206-543-3600, Fax: 206-685-3244, E-mail: esselman@u.washington.edu. *Application contact:* Dr. Deborah Kartin, Graduate Program Coordinator, 206-598-5338, Fax: 206-685-3244, E-mail: kartin@u.washington.edu.

The University of Western Ontario, Faculty of Graduate Studies, Health Sciences Division, School of Occupational Therapy, London, ON N6A 5B8, Canada. Offers M Sc. Part-time programs available. *Degree requirements:* For master's, thesis. *Entrance requirements:* For master's, Canadian BA in occupational therapy or equivalent, minimum B+ average in last 2 years of 4 year degree. Additional exam requirements/recommendations for international students: Required—TOEFL (minimum score 570 paper-based; 250 computer-based). *Faculty research:* Human occupation, clumsy children, biomechanics, learning disabilities, ergonomics.

University of Wisconsin–La Crosse, Office of University Graduate Studies, College of Science and Health, Department of Health Professions, Program in Occupational Therapy, La

Occupational Therapy

University of Wisconsin–La Crosse (continued)
Crosse, WI 54601-3742. Offers MS. *Accreditation:* AOTA. *Students:* 48 full-time (46 women), 18 part-time (all women); includes 2 minority (1 Asian American or Pacific Islander, 1 Hispanic American). Average age 24. 64 applicants, 53% accepted, 27 enrolled. In 2009, 16 master's awarded. *Degree requirements:* For master's, 6 month clinical internship. *Entrance requirements:* For master's, minimum GPA of 3.0, job shadowing. *Application deadline:* For fall admission, 1/15 priority date for domestic students. Application fee: $56. Electronic applications accepted. *Unit head:* Dr. Peggy Denton, Director, 608-785-8470, E-mail: otprogram@uwlax.edu. *Application contact:* Kathryn Kiefer, Director of Admissions, 608-785-8939, E-mail: admissions@uwlax.edu.

University of Wisconsin–Madison, Graduate School, School of Education, Department of Kinesiology, Occupational Therapy Program, Madison, WI 53706-1380. Offers MS, PhD. *Degree requirements:* For doctorate, thesis/dissertation. Application fee: $56. *Expenses:* Tuition, state resident: part-time $594 per credit. Tuition, nonresident: part-time $1504 per credit. Required fees: $65 per credit. Tuition and fees vary according to course load, program and reciprocity agreements. *Financial support:* Fellowships with full tuition reimbursements, research assistantships with full tuition reimbursements, teaching assistantships with full tuition reimbursements, traineeships and project assistantships available. *Unit head:* Dr. Mary Schneider, Coordinator, 608-262-2936, E-mail: schneider@education.wisc.edu. *Application contact:* Admissions Coordinator.

University of Wisconsin–Milwaukee, Graduate School, College of Health Sciences, Department of Occupational Therapy, Milwaukee, WI 53201-0413. Offers ergonomics (Certificate); occupational therapy (MS); therapeutic recreation (Certificate). *Accreditation:* AOTA. *Faculty:* 7 full-time (3 women). *Students:* 40 full-time (37 women), 3 part-time (all women), 6 international. Average age 25. 19 applicants, 37% accepted, 1 enrolled. In 2009, 38 master's awarded. *Degree requirements:* For master's, thesis or alternative. *Entrance requirements:* Additional exam requirements/recommendations for international students: Required—TOEFL (minimum score 550 paper-based; 79 iBT), IELTS (minimum score 6.5). *Application deadline:* For fall admission, 1/1 priority date for domestic students; for spring admission, 9/1 for domestic students. Applications are processed on a rolling basis. Application fee: $45 ($75 for international students). *Expenses:* Tuition, state resident: full-time $8800. Tuition, nonresident: full-time $20,760. Tuition and fees vary according to program and reciprocity agreements. *Financial support:* Fellowships, research assistantships, teaching assistantships, unspecified assistantships available. Support available to part-time students. Financial award application deadline: 4/15. Total annual research expenditures: $778,000. *Unit head:* Virginia Stoffel, Chair, 414-229-5583, Fax: 414-229-5100, E-mail: stoffelv@uwm.edu. *Application contact:* Virginia Stoffel, Chair, 414-229-5583, Fax: 414-229-5100, E-mail: stoffelv@uwm.edu.

Utica College, Program in Occupational Therapy, Utica, NY 13502-4892. Offers MS. *Accreditation:* AOTA. Part-time and evening/weekend programs available. *Faculty:* 7 full-time (all women). *Students:* 65 full-time (59 women), 21 part-time (19 women); includes 10 minority (4 African Americans, 3 Asian Americans or Pacific Islanders, 3 Hispanic Americans), 5 international. Average age 30. In 2009, 21 master's awarded. *Degree requirements:* For master's, thesis. *Entrance requirements:* For master's, physical health exam, CPR certification, 60 hours of volunteer experience, minimum GPA of 3.0. Additional exam requirements/recommendations for international students: Required—TOEFL (minimum score 525 paper-based; 195 computer-based). *Application deadline:* Applications are processed on a rolling basis. Application fee: $50. Electronic applications accepted. *Expenses:* Contact institution. *Financial support:* Career-related internships or fieldwork, scholarships/grants, tuition waivers (partial), and unspecified assistantships available. Support available to part-time students. Financial award application deadline: 3/15; financial award applicants required to submit FAFSA. *Unit head:* Sally Townsend, Director, 315-792-3239, E-mail: stownsend@utica.edu. *Application contact:* John D. Rowe, Director of Graduate Admissions, 315-792-3824, Fax: 315-792-3003, E-mail: jrowe@utica.edu.

Virginia Commonwealth University, Graduate School, School of Allied Health Professions, Department of Health Administration, Doctoral Program in Health Related Sciences, Richmond, VA 23284-9005. Offers clinical laboratory sciences (PhD); gerontology (PhD); health administration (PhD); nurse anesthesia (PhD); occupational therapy (PhD); physical therapy (PhD); radiation sciences (PhD); rehabilitation leadership (PhD).

Virginia Commonwealth University, Graduate School, School of Allied Health Professions, Department of Occupational Therapy, Richmond, VA 23284-9005. Offers MS, MSOT. *Accreditation:* AOTA (one or more programs are accredited). *Degree requirements:* For master's, fieldwork. *Entrance requirements:* For master's, GRE General Test. *Faculty research:* Children with complex care needs, instrument development, carpal tunnel syndrome, development of oral-motor feeding programs, school system practice.

Washington University in St. Louis, School of Medicine, Graduate Programs in Medicine, Program in Occupational Therapy, St. Louis, MO 63108. Offers MSOT, OTD. *Accreditation:* AOTA. *Faculty:* 16 full-time (10 women), 7 part-time/adjunct (5 women). *Students:* 225 full-time (216 women); includes 35 minority (11 African Americans, 1 American Indian/Alaska Native, 17 Asian Americans or Pacific Islanders, 6 Hispanic Americans), 1 international. Average age 23. 153 applicants, 82% accepted, 75 enrolled. In 2009, 43 master's, 17 doctorates awarded. Terminal master's awarded for partial completion of doctoral program. *Degree requirements:* For master's and doctorate, fieldwork experiences. *Entrance requirements:* For master's, GRE General Test, bachelor's degree in another field or enrollment in an affiliated 3/2 institution; for doctorate, GRE General Test, bachelor's degree in another field or enrollment in an affiliated institution. Additional exam requirements/recommendations for international students: Required—TOEFL (minimum score 250 computer-based), TWE (minimum score 5). *Application deadline:* For fall admission, 1/31 priority date for domestic and international students. Applications are processed on a rolling basis. Application fee: $55. Electronic applications accepted. *Financial support:* In 2009–10, 16 research assistantships with partial tuition reimbursements (averaging $4,000 per year), 23 teaching assistantships with partial tuition reimbursements (averaging $3,750 per year) were awarded; Federal Work-Study, scholarships/grants, and health care benefits also available. Support available to part-time students. Financial award application deadline: 1/31; financial award applicants required to submit FAFSA. *Faculty research:* Brain injury, ergonomics, work performance, caregiving, quality of life, rehabilitation. Total annual research expenditures: $1.8 million. *Unit head:* Dr. Carolyn Baum, Director, 314-286-1600 Ext. 1619, Fax: 314-286-1601, E-mail: wuotinfo@wustl.edu. *Application contact:* Elaine Halley, Recruitment Manager, 314-286-1600 Ext. 1613, Fax: 314-286-1601, E-mail: halleye@wusm.wustl.edu.

Wayne State University, Eugene Applebaum College of Pharmacy and Health Sciences, Department of Health Care Sciences, Program in Occupational Therapy, Detroit, MI 48202. Offers MOT, MS. *Accreditation:* AOTA. Part-time programs available. *Degree requirements:* For master's, thesis optional. *Entrance requirements:* For master's, personal resume; 20 contact hours under supervision of an OTR; recommendations; interview. Additional exam requirements/recommendations for international students: Required—TOEFL (minimum score 550 paper-based; 213 computer-based); Recommended—TWE (minimum score 6). Electronic applications accepted. *Faculty research:* Assistive technology, education and fieldwork innovation, gerontology, motor control, rehabilitation outcomes.

Western Michigan University, Graduate College, College of Health and Human Services, Department of Occupational Therapy, Kalamazoo, MI 49008. Offers MS. *Accreditation:* AOTA. *Faculty:* 11 full-time (7 women). *Students:* 41 full-time (36 women), 24 part-time (19 women); includes 9 minority (7 African Americans, 1 Asian American or Pacific Islander, 1 Hispanic American), 2 international. 32 applicants, 94% accepted, 14 enrolled. In 2009, 19 master's awarded. *Entrance requirements:* For master's, GRE General Test. *Application deadline:* For fall admission, 3/15 priority date for domestic students. Applications are processed on a rolling basis. Application fee: $25. *Financial support:* Fellowships, research assistantships, teaching assistantships, Federal Work-Study available. Financial award application deadline: 2/15; financial award applicants required to submit FAFSA. *Unit head:* Dr. Joseph M. Pellerito, Chair, 269-387-7260. *Application contact:* Admissions and Orientation, 269-387-2000, Fax: 269-387-2355.

Western New Mexico University, Graduate Division, Program in Occupational Therapy, Silver City, NM 88062-0680. Offers MOT. Part-time programs available. Postbaccalaureate distance learning degree programs offered.

West Virginia University, School of Medicine, Graduate Programs in Human Performance, Division of Occupational Therapy, Morgantown, WV 26506. Offers MOT. Students enter program as undergraduates. *Accreditation:* AOTA. Postbaccalaureate distance learning degree programs offered. *Degree requirements:* For master's, clinical rotation. *Entrance requirements:* For master's, interview, 2 reference forms, minimum GPA of 3.0, 60 hours of volunteer experience with people with disabilities. *Expenses:* Contact institution.

Winston-Salem State University, Department of Occupational Therapy, Winston-Salem, NC 27110-0003. Offers MS. *Accreditation:* AOTA. *Entrance requirements:* For master's, GRE, 3 letters of recommendation (one from a licensed occupational therapist where volunteer or work experiences were performed; the other two from former professors or persons acquainted with academic potential); writing sample. Additional exam requirements/recommendations for international students: Required—TOEFL. Electronic applications accepted. *Faculty research:* Assistive technology, environmental adaptations, comprehensive performance evaluations.

Worcester State College, Graduate Studies, Program in Occupational Therapy, Worcester, MA 01602-2597. Offers MOT. *Accreditation:* AOTA. *Faculty:* 4 full-time (all women). *Students:* 44 full-time (41 women), 3 part-time (all women); includes 2 minority (1 Asian American or Pacific Islander, 1 Hispanic American). Average age 29. 66 applicants, 44% accepted, 28 enrolled. In 2009, 16 master's awarded. *Degree requirements:* For master's, comprehensive exam (for some programs), thesis optional. *Entrance requirements:* For master's, GRE General Test or MAT, minimum undergraduate GPA of 3.2. Additional exam requirements/recommendations for international students: Required—TOEFL (minimum score 550 paper-based; 213 computer-based; 79 iBT). *Application deadline:* For fall admission, 3/1 priority date for domestic and international students. Application fee: $30. *Expenses:* Contact institution. *Financial support:* In 2009–10, 7 students received support, including 7 research assistantships with full tuition reimbursements available (averaging $4,800 per year); career-related internships or fieldwork, scholarships/grants, and unspecified assistantships also available. Financial award application deadline: 3/1; financial award applicants required to submit FAFSA. *Unit head:* Dr. Margaret Hart, Coordinator, 508-929-8785, Fax: 508-929-8178, E-mail: mhart@worcester.edu. *Application contact:* Nicole Brown, Assistant Dean of Continuing Education, 508-929-8787, Fax: 508-929-8100, E-mail: nbrown@worcester.edu.

Xavier University, College of Social Sciences, Health and Education, Occupational Therapy Program, Cincinnati, OH 45207. Offers MOT. *Accreditation:* AOTA. *Faculty:* 5 full-time (all women), 2 part-time/adjunct (both women). *Students:* 32 full-time (30 women), 20 part-time (all women); includes 2 minority (1 African American, 1 Asian American or Pacific Islander), 1 international. Average age 26. 32 applicants, 88% accepted, 28 enrolled. In 2009, 19 master's awarded. *Degree requirements:* For master's, one foreign language. *Entrance requirements:* For master's, GRE, minimum GPA of 2.8, completion of 40 volunteer hours, completion of all prerequisite courses with no more than 2 grades of C or lower. Additional exam requirements/recommendations for international students: Required—TOEFL or IELTS. *Application deadline:* For winter admission, 6/1 for domestic and international students. Application fee: $35. Electronic applications accepted. *Expenses:* Tuition: Part-time $697 per credit hour. One-time fee: $35 part-time. *Financial support:* In 2009–10, 25 students received support. Scholarships/grants and tuition waivers (partial) available. Financial award application deadline: 5/23; financial award applicants required to submit FAFSA. *Faculty research:* Occupation, ethics, pediatric, occupational therapy interventions, pediatric occupational therapy assessment. *Unit head:* Dr. Carol Scheerer, Chair, 513-745-3310, Fax: 513-745-3261, E-mail: scheerer@xavier.edu. *Application contact:* Georganna Miller, Academic Advisor, 513-745-3104, Fax: 513-745-3261, E-mail: millerg@xavier.edu.

Perfusion

Long Island University, C.W. Post Campus, School of Health Professions and Nursing, Department of Biomedical Sciences, Brookville, NY 11548-1300. Offers cardiovascular perfusion (MS); clinical laboratory management (MS); medical biology (MS), including hematology, immunology, medical biology, medical chemistry, medical microbiology. Part-time and evening/weekend programs available. Postbaccalaureate distance learning degree programs offered. *Degree requirements:* For master's, thesis. *Entrance requirements:* For master's, minimum GPA of 2.75 in major. Electronic applications accepted.

Milwaukee School of Engineering, Department of Electrical Engineering and Computer Science, Program in Perfusion, Milwaukee, WI 53202-3109. Offers MS. Part-time and evening/weekend programs available. *Faculty:* 1 full-time (0 women), 4 part-time/adjunct (1 woman). *Students:* 10 full-time (2 women); includes 2 minority (both Asian Americans or Pacific Islanders). Average age 33. 31 applicants, 32% accepted, 7 enrolled. In 2009, 1 master's awarded. *Degree requirements:* For master's, comprehensive exam, thesis. *Entrance requirements:* For master's, GRE General Test or GMAT, BS in appropriate discipline, undergraduate work in human physiology or anatomy, 3 letters of recommendation, interview, observation of 2 perfusion cases. Additional exam requirements/recommendations for international students: Required—TOEFL (minimum score 79 iBT). *Application deadline:* Applications are processed on a rolling basis. Application fee: $30. Electronic applications accepted. *Expenses:* Tuition: Part-time $603 per credit. *Financial support:* In 2009–10, 8 students received support. Career-related internships or fieldwork available. Support available to part-time students. Financial award applicants required to submit FAFSA. *Faculty research:* Heart medicine. *Unit head:* Dr. Ronald Gerrits, Director, 414-277-7561, Fax: 414-277-7494, E-mail: gerrits@msoe.edu. *Application contact:* David E. Tietyen, Graduate Admissions Director, 800-332-6763, Fax: 414-277-7475, E-mail: wp@msoe.edu.

Quinnipiac University, School of Health Sciences, Program in Cardiovascular Perfusion, Hamden, CT 06518-1940. Offers MHS. *Faculty:* 1 full-time (0 women), 4 part-time/adjunct (0 women). *Students:* 8 full-time (2 women), 3 part-time (0 women); includes 3 minority (1 African American, 2 Asian Americans or Pacific Islanders), 1 international. Average age 36. 15 applicants, 67% accepted, 8 enrolled. In 2009, 2 master's awarded. *Entrance requirements:* For master's, bachelor's degree in science or health-related discipline from an accredited American or Canadian college or university; 2 years health care work experience; interview. Additional exam requirements/recommendations for international students: Required—TOEFL (minimum score 575 paper-based; 233 computer-based; 90 iBT), IELTS (minimum score 6.5). *Application deadline:* For fall admission, 7/30 priority date for domestic students, 4/30 priority

date for international students. Applications are processed on a rolling basis. Application fee: $45. Electronic applications accepted. *Expenses:* Tuition: Full-time $16,030; part-time $770 per credit. Required fees: $630; $35 per credit. *Financial support:* Career-related internships or fieldwork, tuition waivers, and unspecified assistantships available. Financial award application deadline: 4/15; financial award applicants required to submit FAFSA. *Unit head:* Michael Smith, Director, 203-582-3427, Fax: 203-582-8706, E-mail: michael.smith@quinnipiac.edu. *Application contact:* Kristin Parent, Assistant Director of Graduate Health Sciences Admissions, 800-462-1944, Fax: 208-582-3443, E-mail: kristin.parent@quinnipiac.edu.

The University of Arizona, Graduate College, College of Pharmacy, Department of Pharmacology and Toxicology, Graduate Program in Medical Pharmacology, Tucson, AZ 85721. Offers medical pharmacology (PhD); perfusion science (MS). *Faculty:* 11 full-time (3 women). *Students:* 31 full-time (19 women), 1 part-time (0 women); includes 4 minority (1 Asian American or Pacific Islander, 3 Hispanic Americans), 11 international. Average age 28. 40 applicants, 13% accepted, 5 enrolled. In 2009, 7 master's, 4 doctorates awarded. *Degree requirements:* For master's, thesis; for doctorate, comprehensive exam, thesis/dissertation. *Entrance requirements:* For master's, GRE General Test, 3 letters of recommendation; for doctorate, GRE General Test, personal statement, 3 letters of recommendation. Additional exam requirements/recommendations for international students: Required—TOEFL (minimum score 550 paper-

based; 213 computer-based; 79 iBT). *Application deadline:* For fall admission, 1/1 for domestic and international students. Applications are processed on a rolling basis. Application fee: $65. Electronic applications accepted. *Expenses:* Tuition, state resident: full-time $9028. Tuition, nonresident: full-time $24,890. *Financial support:* In 2009–10, 17 research assistantships with full tuition reimbursements (averaging $23,929 per year) were awarded; institutionally sponsored loans and tuition waivers (partial) also available. Financial award applicants required to submit FAFSA. *Faculty research:* Immunopharmacology, pharmacogenetics, pharmacogenomics, clinical pharmacology, ocularpharmacology and neuropharmacology. *Unit head:* Dr. I. Glenn Sipes, Head, 520-626-7123, Fax: 520-626-2204, E-mail: sipes@email.arizona.edu. *Application contact:* Trisha Stanley, Coordinator, 520-626-7218, Fax: 520-626-2204, E-mail: stanley@email.arizona.edu.

University of Nebraska Medical Center, School of Allied Health Professions, Program in Clinical Perfusion Education, Omaha, NE 68198-4144. Offers distance education perfusion education (MPS); perfusion science (MPS). *Accreditation:* NAACLS. Postbaccalaureate distance learning degree programs offered. *Degree requirements:* For master's, comprehensive exam, thesis. *Entrance requirements:* For master's, GRE. Electronic applications accepted. *Faculty research:* Platelet gel, hemoconcentrators.

Physical Therapy

Alabama State University, School of Graduate Studies, College of Health Sciences, Department of Physical Therapy, Montgomery, AL 36101-0271. Offers DPT. *Accreditation:* APTA. Terminal master's awarded for partial completion of doctoral program. *Entrance requirements:* Additional exam requirements/recommendations for international students: Required—TOEFL (minimum score 500 paper-based; 173 computer-based).

American International College, School of Health Sciences, Program in Physical Therapy, Springfield, MA 01109-3189. Offers DPT. *Accreditation:* APTA. *Entrance requirements:* For doctorate, minimum GPA of 3.2. Additional exam requirements/recommendations for international students: Required—TOEFL. Electronic applications accepted. *Expenses:* Contact institution.

Andrews University, School of Graduate Studies, College of Arts and Sciences, Department of Physical Therapy, Postprofessional Physical Therapy Program, Berrien Springs, MI 49104. Offers Dr Sc PT, TDPT. *Accreditation:* APTA. *Expenses:* Contact institution. *Faculty research:* Home health patient profile, clinical education, breeding success of marine birds, trends in home health care for physical therapy, patient motivation in acute rehabilitation.

Angelo State University, College of Graduate Studies, College of Nursing and Allied Health, Department of Physical Therapy, San Angelo, TX 76909. Offers DPT. *Accreditation:* APTA. *Faculty:* 7 full-time (4 women), 1 part-time/adjunct (0 women). *Students:* 56 full-time (38 women); includes 12 minority (4 African Americans, 2 Asian Americans or Pacific Islanders, 6 Hispanic Americans). Average age 25. 20 applicants, 100% accepted, 20 enrolled. *Entrance requirements:* Additional exam requirements/recommendations for international students: Required—TOEFL or IELTS. *Application deadline:* For fall admission, 2/1 for domestic students, 3/10 for international students. Applications are processed on a rolling basis. Application fee: $40 ($50 for international students). Electronic applications accepted. *Expenses:* Tuition, state resident: full-time $3396; part-time $142 per credit hour. Tuition, nonresident: full-time $10,152; part-time $423 per credit hour. Required fees: $1786; $36.25 per credit hour. $494 per semester. Full-time tuition and fees vary according to course load, degree level and program. *Financial support:* In 2009–10, 50 students received support. Scholarships/grants available. Financial award application deadline: 3/1; financial award applicants required to submit FAFSA. *Faculty research:* Women and lipoproteins, international distance education, quadriceps femoris and the VMO, ergonomics, children and obesity. *Unit head:* Dr. Scott Hasson, Department Head, 325-942-2581 Ext. 278, Fax: 325-942-2548, E-mail: ptdept@angelo.edu. *Application contact:* Dr. Scott Hasson, Department Head, 325-942-2581 Ext. 278, Fax: 325-942-2548, E-mail: ptdept@angelo.edu.

Arcadia University, Graduate Studies, Department of Physical Therapy, Glenside, PA 19038-3295. Offers DPT. *Accreditation:* APTA. *Faculty:* 6 full-time (4 women), 20 part-time/adjunct (15 women). *Students:* 157 full-time (106 women), 24 part-time (17 women); includes 6 minority (2 African Americans, 4 Asian Americans or Pacific Islanders). Average age 26. In 2009, 56 doctorates awarded. *Application deadline:* For fall admission, 1/31 for domestic students. Application fee: $50. *Expenses:* Contact institution. *Financial support:* In 2009–10, 15 students received support. Career-related internships or fieldwork, tuition waivers (partial), and unspecified assistantships available. *Unit head:* Dr. Rebecca L. Craik, Chair, 215-572-2143. *Application contact:* 215-572-2910, Fax: 215-572-4049, E-mail: admiss@arcadia.edu.

Arkansas State University—Jonesboro, Graduate School, College of Nursing and Health Professions, Department of Physical Therapy, Jonesboro, State University, AR 72467. Offers aging studies (Certificate); health sciences (MS); health sciences education (Certificate); physical therapy (DPT). *Accreditation:* APTA. Part-time programs available. *Faculty:* 8 full-time (4 women), 1 (woman) part-time/adjunct. *Students:* 49 full-time (31 women), 26 part-time (19 women); includes 12 minority (all African Americans), 5 international. Average age 28. 53 applicants, 70% accepted, 32 enrolled. In 2009, 22 master's awarded. *Degree requirements:* For master's, comprehensive exam; for doctorate, comprehensive exam, thesis/dissertation. *Entrance requirements:* For master's, GRE General Test, Allied Health Profession Admissions Test, writing exam, appropriate bachelor's degree, letters of reference, resume, writing sample; for doctorate, GRE, Allied Health Professions Admissions Test, appropriate bachelor's or master's degree, letters of reference, resume, official transcript, volunteer experience, criminal background check, immunization records. Additional exam requirements/recommendations for international students: Required—TOEFL (minimum score 550 paper-based; 213 computer-based; 79 iBT), IELTS (minimum score 6). *Application deadline:* For fall admission, 3/1 for domestic and international students. Applications are processed on a rolling basis. Application fee: $50. Electronic applications accepted. *Expenses:* Contact institution. *Financial support:* In 2009–10, 7 students received support; fellowships, career-related internships or fieldwork, scholarships/grants, and unspecified assistantships available. Financial award application deadline: 7/1; financial award applicants required to submit FAFSA. *Unit head:* Dr. Patricia King, Chair, 870-972-3591, Fax: 870-972-3652, E-mail: pking@astate.edu. *Application contact:* Dr. Andrew Sustich, Dean of the Graduate School, 870-972-3029, Fax: 870-972-3857, E-mail: sustich@astate.edu.

Armstrong Atlantic State University, School of Graduate Studies, Program in Physical Therapy, Savannah, GA 31419-1997. Offers DPT. *Accreditation:* APTA. *Entrance requirements:* Additional exam requirements/recommendations for international students: Required—TOEFL (minimum score 523 paper-based; 193 computer-based). Electronic applications accepted. *Faculty research:* Exercise modalities, physical agents, magnetic therapy, leadership development, perception of physical therapists.

A.T. Still University of Health Sciences, Arizona School of Health Sciences, Mesa, AZ 85206. Offers advanced occupational therapy (MS); advanced physician assistant (MS); athletic training (MS); audiology (Au D); health sciences (DHSc); human movement (MS); occupational therapy (MS); physical therapy (MS, DPT); physician assistant (MS); transitional audiology (Au D); transitional physical therapy (DPT). *Accreditation:* AOTA (one or more programs are accredited); ASHA. Postbaccalaureate distance learning degree programs offered (no on-campus

study). *Faculty:* 53 full-time (30 women), 205 part-time/adjunct (117 women). *Students:* 491 full-time (353 women), 1,251 part-time (874 women); includes 319 minority (70 African Americans, 11 American Indian/Alaska Native, 176 Asian Americans or Pacific Islanders, 62 Hispanic Americans), 3 international. Average age 31. 2,697 applicants, 22% accepted, 420 enrolled. In 2009, 225 master's, 523 doctorates awarded. *Degree requirements:* For master's, thesis (for some programs); for doctorate, thesis/dissertation (for some programs). *Entrance requirements:* For master's, GRE General Test; for doctorate, GRE, Evaluation of Practicing Audiologists Capabilities (Au D), Physical Therapy Evaluation Tool (DPT), current state licensure, master's degree or equivalent (Au D), minimum GPA of 2.7. Additional exam requirements/recommendations for international students: Recommended—TOEFL (minimum score 550 paper-based; 213 computer-based; 80 iBT). *Application deadline:* For fall admission, 2/1 priority date for domestic and international students. Applications are processed on a rolling basis. Application fee: $60. *Expenses:* Contact institution. *Financial support:* In 2009–10, 651 students received support. Federal Work-Study and scholarships/grants available. Financial award application deadline: 5/1; financial award applicants required to submit FAFSA. *Faculty research:* Adolescent health-related quality of life, clinical outcomes following sport related injury, pediatric concussion, shoulder stability and neuromuscular control, sport conditioning, exercise and sport psychology, geriatric exercise and wellness. Total annual research expenditures: $61,527. *Unit head:* Dr. Randy Danielsen, Dean, 480-219-6000, Fax: 480-219-6110, E-mail: rdanielsen@atsu.edu. *Application contact:* Donna Sparks, Associate Director for Admissions, 660-626-2237, Fax: 660-626-2969, E-mail: admissions@atsu.edu.

Azusa Pacific University, School of Behavioral and Applied Sciences, Department of Physical Therapy, Azusa, CA 91702-7000. Offers entry-level (DPT); transitional (DPT). *Accreditation:* APTA. *Faculty:* 7 full-time (4 women). *Students:* 106 full-time (74 women); includes 35 minority (1 African American, 2 American Indian/Alaska Native, 24 Asian Americans or Pacific Islanders, 8 Hispanic Americans). Average age 24. 250 applicants, 16% accepted, 39 enrolled. In 2009, 32 doctorates awarded. *Degree requirements:* For doctorate, thesis/dissertation. *Entrance requirements:* For doctorate, GRE General Test. Additional exam requirements/recommendations for international students: Required—TOEFL (minimum score 600 paper-based; 250 computer-based). *Application deadline:* For fall admission, 10/1 for domestic and international students. Applications are processed on a rolling basis. Application fee: $0. Electronic applications accepted. *Expenses:* Contact institution. *Financial support:* Career-related internships or fieldwork available. Financial award applicants required to submit FAFSA. *Faculty research:* FES and spinal cord injury, electromyogram and muscle pathology, thermal regulation and body composition. *Unit head:* Dr. Michael Laymon, Chair, 626-815-5020, Fax: 626-815-5017, E-mail: mlaymon@apu.edu. *Application contact:* Anel Herrera, Administrative Manager, 626-815-5014, Fax: 626-815-5017, E-mail: aherrera@apu.edu.

Baylor University, Graduate School, Military Programs, Program in Clinical Orthopedics, Waco, TX 76798. Offers D Sc. *Students:* 8 full-time (2 women). In 2009, 13 doctorates awarded. *Unit head:* Maj. Craig Paige, Graduate Program Director, 915-443-4215, Fax: 210-221-7306, E-mail: craig.v.paige@us.army.mil. *Application contact:* Lori McNamara, Administrative Assistant, 254-710-3588, Fax: 254-710-3870.

Baylor University, Graduate School, Military Programs, Program in Physical Therapy, Waco, TX 76798. Offers MPT, DPT. Offered jointly with the U. S. Army. *Accreditation:* APTA. *Students:* 47 full-time (21 women); includes 5 minority (2 African Americans, 2 Asian Americans or Pacific Islanders, 1 Hispanic American). In 2009, 40 doctorates awarded. *Degree requirements:* For master's, comprehensive exam, research paper. *Entrance requirements:* For master's, GRE General Test. *Application deadline:* For fall admission, 2/1 for domestic students. Applications are processed on a rolling basis. Application fee: $25. *Faculty research:* Effect of electrical stimulation on normal and immobilized muscle, effects of inversion traction. *Unit head:* Col. Josef Moore, Graduate Program Director, 210-221-8410, Fax: 210-221-7585, E-mail: josef.moore@cen.amedd.army.mil. *Application contact:* Cindy Quiroz, Training Technician, 210-221-8410, E-mail: cynthia.quiroz@cen.amedd.army.mil.

Bellarmine University, Donna and Allan Lansing School of Nursing and Health Sciences, Louisville, KY 40205-0671. Offers family nurse practitioner (MSN); nursing administration (MSN); nursing education (MSN); nursing practice (DNP); physical therapy (DPT). *Accreditation:* AACN; APTA. Part-time and evening/weekend programs available. *Faculty:* 16 full-time (11 women), 7 part-time/adjunct (6 women). *Students:* 126 full-time (94 women), 50 part-time (48 women); includes 4 minority (1 African American, 3 Asian Americans or Pacific Islanders). Average age 30. 350 applicants, 48 enrolled. In 2009, 9 master's, 41 doctorates awarded. *Degree requirements:* For doctorate, comprehensive exam, thesis/dissertation. *Entrance requirements:* For master's, GRE General Test, RN license; for doctorate, GRE General Test, Physical Therapist Centralized Application Service (for DPT). Additional exam requirements/recommendations for international students: Required—TOEFL (minimum score 550 paper-based; 213 computer-based; 80 iBT). Application fee: $25. Electronic applications accepted. *Expenses:* Contact institution. *Financial support:* Career-related internships or fieldwork and scholarships/grants available. *Faculty research:* Nursing: pain, empathy, leadership styles, control; physical therapy: service learning; exercise in chronic and pre-operative conditions, and athletes; women's health; aging. *Unit head:* Dr. Susan H. Davis, Dean, 800-274-4723 Ext. 8217, E-mail: sdavis@bellarmine.edu. *Application contact:* Julie Armstrong-Binnix, Health Science Recruiter, 800-274-4723 Ext. 8364, E-mail: julieab@bellarmine.edu.

Belmont University, College of Health Sciences, School of Physical Therapy, Nashville, TN 37212-3757. Offers DPT. *Accreditation:* APTA. *Entrance requirements:* For doctorate, GRE General Test, minimum GPA of 3.0, 50 observation hours, 2 recommendations (1 from licensed physical therapist), prerequisite courses. Additional exam requirements/recommendations for international students: Required—TOEFL (minimum score 550 paper-based; 213 computer-based; 80 iBT). Electronic applications accepted. *Expenses:* Contact institution. *Faculty research:* Electrophysiology, orthopedic neuromuscular functions, assessment of whole body vibration, pediatric balance scale, motion analysis.

Physical Therapy

Boston University, College of Health and Rehabilitation Sciences—Sargent College, Department of Physical Therapy and Athletic Training, Boston, MA 02215. Offers physical therapy (DPT); rehabilitation sciences (D Sc). *Accreditation:* APTA (one or more programs are accredited). Postbaccalaureate distance learning degree programs offered (minimal on-campus study). *Faculty:* 13 full-time (10 women), 26 part-time/adjunct (12 women). *Students:* 142 full-time (116 women); includes 20 minority (1 African American, 14 Asian Americans or Pacific Islanders, 5 Hispanic Americans). Average age 26. 177 applicants, 46% accepted, 31 enrolled. In 2009, 93 doctorates awarded. *Degree requirements:* For doctorate, comprehensive exam (for some programs), thesis/dissertation (for some programs). *Entrance requirements:* For doctorate, GRE General Test, master's degree (for ScD), bachelor's degree (for DPT). Additional exam requirements/recommendations for international students: Required—TOEFL (minimum score 550 paper-based; 84 computer-based). *Application deadline:* For fall admission, 1/7 priority date for domestic students. Applications are processed on a rolling basis. Application fee: $70. Electronic applications accepted. *Expenses:* Tuition: Full-time $37,910; part-time $1184 per credit hour. Required fees: $386; $40 per semester. Part-time tuition and fees vary according to class time, course level, degree level and program. *Financial support:* In 2009–10, 125 students received support, including 14 fellowships (averaging $16,000 per year), 10 teaching assistantships with partial tuition reimbursements available (averaging $3,000 per year); career-related internships or fieldwork, Federal Work-Study, institutionally sponsored loans, scholarships/grants, and tuition waivers (partial) also available. Financial award application deadline: 4/15; financial award applicants required to submit FAFSA. *Faculty research:* Gait, balance, motor control, dynamical systems. *Unit head:* Dr. Wendy Coster, Chairman, 617-353-2720, E-mail: wjcoster@bu.edu. *Application contact:* Sharon Sankey, Director, Student Services, 617-353-2713, Fax: 617-353-7500, E-mail: ssankey@bu.edu.

Bradley University, Graduate School, College of Education and Health Sciences, Department of Physical Therapy and Health Science, Peoria, IL 61625-0002. Offers physical therapy (DPT). *Accreditation:* APTA. *Entrance requirements:* For doctorate, GRE, 2 letters of recommendation. Additional exam requirements/recommendations for international students: Required—TOEFL (minimum score 600 paper-based; 250 computer-based; 100 iBT). *Expenses:* Contact institution.

California State University, Fresno, Division of Graduate Studies, College of Health and Human Services, Department of Physical Therapy, Fresno, CA 93740-8027. Offers MPT, DPT. *Accreditation:* APTA. *Degree requirements:* For master's, comprehensive exam. *Entrance requirements:* For master's, GRE General Test, minimum GPA of 3.0. Additional exam requirements/recommendations for international students: Required—TOEFL. Electronic applications accepted. *Faculty research:* Dance, occupational health, ethics.

California State University, Long Beach, Graduate Studies, College of Health and Human Services, Department of Physical Therapy, Long Beach, CA 90840. Offers MPT. *Accreditation:* APTA. *Faculty:* 8 full-time (4 women), 1 (woman) part-time/adjunct. *Students:* 104 full-time (68 women), 14 part-time (10 women); includes 46 minority (5 African Americans, 1 American Indian/Alaska Native, 31 Asian Americans or Pacific Islanders, 9 Hispanic Americans), 3 international. Average age 27. 175 applicants, 43% accepted, 39 enrolled. *Degree requirements:* For master's, comprehensive exam, thesis, project or directive studies. *Entrance requirements:* For master's, GRE General Test, minimum GPA of 3.0 in upper-division prerequisites. Additional exam requirements/recommendations for international students: Required—TOEFL. *Application deadline:* For fall admission, 1/15 for domestic students. Applications are processed on a rolling basis. Application fee: $55. Electronic applications accepted. *Expenses:* Required fees: $1802 per semester. Part-time tuition and fees vary according to course load. *Financial support:* Federal Work-Study, institutionally sponsored loans, and scholarships/grants available. Financial award application deadline: 3/2; financial award applicants required to submit FAFSA. *Unit head:* Dr. Kay Cerny, Chair, 562-985-4072, Fax: 562-985-4069, E-mail: kcerny@csulb.edu. *Application contact:* Dr. Kay Cerny, Chair, 562-985-4072, Fax: 562-985-4069, E-mail: kcerny@csulb.edu.

California State University, Northridge, Graduate Studies, College of Health and Human Development, Department of Physical Therapy, Northridge, CA 91330. Offers MPT. *Accreditation:* APTA. *Faculty:* 7 full-time (6 women), 7 part-time/adjunct (5 women). *Students:* 113 full-time (73 women); includes 2 African Americans, 15 Asian Americans or Pacific Islanders, 13 Hispanic Americans, 4 international. Average age 28. 234 applicants, 15% accepted, 33 enrolled. In 2009, 27 master's awarded. *Entrance requirements:* For master's, GRE General Test or minimum GPA of 3.0. Additional exam requirements/recommendations for international students: Required—TOEFL. *Application deadline:* For fall admission, 11/30 for domestic students. Application fee: $55. *Financial support:* Application deadline: 3/1. *Unit head:* Dr. Sheryl Low, Chair, 818-677-2203. *Application contact:* Dr. Sheryl Low, Chair, 818-677-2203.

Carroll University, Program in Physical Therapy, Waukesha, WI 53186-5593. Offers MPT, DPT. *Accreditation:* APTA. *Faculty:* 7 full-time (5 women), 3 part-time/adjunct (all women). *Students:* 66 full-time (49 women); includes 3 minority (1 Asian American or Pacific Islander, 2 Hispanic Americans), 1 international. Average age 24. 71 applicants, 79% accepted, 37 enrolled. In 2009, 28 doctorates awarded. *Degree requirements:* For master's, thesis (for some programs). *Entrance requirements:* For master's, GRE General Test, recommendations, clinical observation. Additional exam requirements/recommendations for international students: Required—TOEFL. *Application deadline:* For fall admission, 7/14 for domestic students. Applications are processed on a rolling basis. Application fee: $25. *Expenses:* Contact institution. *Financial support:* Available to part-time students. Application deadline: 3/15. *Faculty research:* Physical therapy education, geriatrics, neural control of movement, wellness and prevention in apparently healthy individuals with disease and disability. *Unit head:* Dr. Jane F. Hopp, Dean, Natural and Health Sciences, 262-524-7294, E-mail: jhopp@carrollu.edu. *Application contact:* Tami Bartunek, Graduate Admission Counselor, 262-524-7643, E-mail: tbartune@carrollu.edu.

Central Michigan University, College of Graduate Studies, The Herbert H. and Grace A. Dow College of Health Professions, School of Rehabilitation and Medical Sciences, Mount Pleasant, MI 48859. Offers physical therapy (DPT); physician assistant (MS). *Accreditation:* APTA; ARC-PA. *Degree requirements:* For master's, thesis or alternative; for doctorate, thesis/dissertation or alternative. *Entrance requirements:* For master's and doctorate, GRE. Electronic applications accepted.

Chapman University, Graduate Studies, Schmid College of Science, Department of Physical Therapy, Orange, CA 92866. Offers DPT. *Accreditation:* APTA. *Faculty:* 9 full-time (7 women), 3 part-time/adjunct (1 woman). *Students:* 97 full-time (66 women), 43 part-time (32 women); includes 33 minority (2 African Americans, 2 American Indian/Alaska Native, 26 Asian Americans or Pacific Islanders, 3 Hispanic Americans), 4 international. Average age 25. 617 applicants, 39% accepted, 49 enrolled. In 2009, 37 doctorates awarded. *Entrance requirements:* For doctorate, GRE, minimum undergraduate GPA of 3.0, 40 hours of physical therapy observation (or paid work). Additional exam requirements/recommendations for international students: Required—TOEFL (minimum score 550 paper-based; 213 computer-based; 80 iBT). *Application deadline:* For fall admission, 11/14 priority date for domestic students. Applications are processed on a rolling basis. Application fee: $65. Electronic applications accepted. *Expenses:* Contact institution. *Financial support:* Fellowships, Federal Work-Study and scholarships/grants available. Financial award application deadline: 6/30; financial award applicants required to submit FAFSA. *Unit head:* Dr. Jacki Brechter, Chair, 714-744-7649, E-mail: brechter@chapman.edu. *Application contact:* Serena Healey, Admissions Coordinator, 714-744-7620, Fax: 714-744-7621, E-mail: healey@chapman.edu.

Chatham University, Program in Physical Therapy, Pittsburgh, PA 15232-2826. Offers DPT, TDPT. *Accreditation:* APTA. *Students:* 89 full-time (58 women), 40 part-time (23 women). Average age 30. 227 applicants, 32% accepted, 48 enrolled. In 2009, 28 doctorates awarded. *Entrance requirements:* For doctorate, GRE, community service, interview, minimum GPA of 3.0, writing sample, volunteer/work experience, 3 references. Additional exam requirements/recommendations for international students: Required—TOEFL (minimum score 600 paper-based; 250 computer-based; 100 iBT), IELTS (minimum score 6.5), TWE. *Application deadline:* For fall admission, 12/1 priority date for domestic and international students. Application fee: $45. *Expenses:* Contact institution. *Financial support:* Career-related internships or fieldwork available. Financial award applicants required to submit FAFSA. *Faculty research:* Stroke rehabilitation, osteoporosis and fall prevention, physical therapy for children with disabilities, evidence-based practice and decision making, low back pain in children and adolescents. *Unit head:* Dr. Patricia Downey, Director, 412-365-1199, Fax: 412-365-1505, E-mail: downey@chatham.edu. *Application contact:* Maureen Stokan, Assistant Director of Graduate Admissions, 412-365-2988, Fax: 412-365-1609, E-mail: gradadmissions@chatham.edu.

Clarke College, Physical Therapy Program, Dubuque, IA 52001-3198. Offers DPT. Freshman-entry master's degree program. Entry to the MSPT is determined after junior year of BS program. *Accreditation:* APTA. *Faculty:* 6 full-time (2 women). *Students:* 66 full-time (49 women). Average age 22. 59 applicants, 69% accepted, 32 enrolled. In 2009, 19 doctorates awarded. *Application deadline:* For spring admission, 3/31 for domestic students. Application fee: $0. *Expenses:* Tuition: Full-time $10,836; part-time $602 per credit hour. Required fees: $30 per credit hour. *Financial support:* In 2009–10, 4 students received support. Career-related internships or fieldwork available. Support available to part-time students. Financial award applicants required to submit FAFSA. *Faculty research:* Qualitative research, occupational health, discontinuous anaerobic studies, low back dysfunction. *Unit head:* Dr. Andrew Priest, Chair, 319-588-6382, Fax: 319-588-8684. *Application contact:* Joan Coates, Information Contact, 563-588-6354, Fax: 563-588-6789, E-mail: graduate@clarke.edu.

Clarkson University, Graduate School, Division of Health Sciences, Department of Physical Therapy, Potsdam, NY 13699. Offers DPT. *Accreditation:* APTA. *Faculty:* 9 full-time (6 women), 6 part-time/adjunct (4 women). *Students:* 46 full-time (37 women), 1 (woman) part-time; includes 3 minority (all Hispanic Americans), 2 international. Average age 25. 172 applicants, 15% accepted, 16 enrolled. *Entrance requirements:* For doctorate, GRE, 3 letters of recommendation. Additional exam requirements/recommendations for international students: Required—TOEFL. *Application deadline:* For fall admission, 1/30 priority date for domestic and international students; for spring admission, 9/1 priority date for domestic and international students. Applications are processed on a rolling basis. Application fee: $25 ($35 for international students). Electronic applications accepted. *Expenses:* Tuition: Part-time $1074 per credit hour. *Financial support:* In 2009–10, 46 students received support. Tuition waivers (partial) available. *Faculty research:* Membrane transport, community-based health, gerontology, muscle structure or function, fibromyalgia. Total annual research expenditures: $102,886. *Unit head:* Mary Alice D. Minor, Interim Chair, 315-268-3786, Fax: 315-268-1539, E-mail: minora@clarkson.edu. *Application contact:* Jennifer E. Reed, Graduate School Coordinator for School of Arts and Sciences, 315-268-3802, Fax: 315-268-3989, E-mail: jreed@clarkson.edu.

Cleveland State University, College of Graduate Studies, College of Science, Department of Health Sciences, Program in Physical Therapy, Cleveland, OH 44115. Offers DPT. *Accreditation:* APTA. *Entrance requirements:* Additional exam requirements/recommendations for international students: Required—TOEFL (minimum score 550 paper-based; 220 computer-based). Electronic applications accepted. *Faculty research:* Biomechanics, exercise physiology, motor control, neurological disorders, physical dysfunctions.

College of Mount St. Joseph, Physical Therapy Program, Cincinnati, OH 45233-1670. Offers DPT. *Accreditation:* APTA. *Faculty:* 5 full-time (2 women), 1 (woman) part-time/adjunct. *Students:* 65 full-time (46 women), 19 part-time (16 women); includes 6 minority (1 African American, 1 American Indian/Alaska Native, 4 Asian Americans or Pacific Islanders). Average age 24. 63 applicants, 71% accepted, 38 enrolled. In 2009, 14 doctorates awarded. *Degree requirements:* For doctorate, clinical internship. *Entrance requirements:* For doctorate, GRE, minimum GPA of 3.0, prerequisite coursework in sciences, humanities, social sciences, and statistics, 80 observation hours. Additional exam requirements/recommendations for international students: Required—TOEFL (minimum score 560 paper-based; 220 computer-based; 83 iBT). Application fee: $50. Electronic applications accepted. *Expenses:* Contact institution. *Financial support:* In 2009–10, 3 students received support. Applicants required to submit FAFSA. *Faculty research:* Utilizing technology in learning, neurobiology, assessment of student learning, critical thinking, effectiveness of distance education methods. *Unit head:* Dr. Karen Holtgrefe, Chair, 513-244-3299, Fax: 513-451-2547, E-mail: karen_holtgrefe@mail.msj.edu. *Application contact:* Marilyn Hoskins, Assistant Director of Graduate Recruitment, 513-244-4723, Fax: 513-244-4629, E-mail: marilyn_hoskins@mail.msj.edu.

The College of St. Scholastica, Graduate Studies, Department of Physical Therapy, Duluth, MN 55811-4199. Offers DPT. *Accreditation:* APTA. *Entrance requirements:* For doctorate, GRE, minimum GPA of 3.0, interview. Additional exam requirements/recommendations for international students: Required—TOEFL (minimum score 550 paper-based; 213 computer-based; 79 iBT). Electronic applications accepted. *Faculty research:* Postural control, reliability and validity of spinal assessment tools, biomechanics of golf swing and low back pain, gait assessment and treatment, ethical issues.

Columbia University, College of Physicians and Surgeons, Program in Physical Therapy, New York, NY 10032. Offers DPT. *Accreditation:* APTA. *Degree requirements:* For doctorate, fieldwork, capstone project. *Entrance requirements:* For doctorate, GRE General Test, undergraduate course work in biology, chemistry, physics, psychology, statistics and humanities. Additional exam requirements/recommendations for international students: Required—TOEFL. Electronic applications accepted. *Expenses:* Contact institution. *Faculty research:* Motor control, motion analysis, back assessment, recovery of function following neurological injury, women's health, disability awareness, pediatrics, orthopedics.

Concordia University Wisconsin, Graduate Programs, School of Health and Human Services, Program in Physical Therapy, Mequon, WI 53097-2402. Offers MSPT, DPT. *Accreditation:* APTA. *Degree requirements:* For master's, comprehensive exam, thesis or alternative. *Entrance requirements:* Additional exam requirements/recommendations for international students: Required—TOEFL. *Expenses:* Contact institution.

Creighton University, School of Pharmacy and Health Professions, Program in Physical Therapy, Omaha, NE 68178-0001. Offers DPT. *Accreditation:* APTA. *Entrance requirements:* For doctorate, GRE. Electronic applications accepted. *Expenses:* Tuition: Full-time $11,700; part-time $650 per credit hour. Required fees: $126 per semester. *Faculty research:* Patient safety in health services research, health information technology and health services research, Parkinson's rigidity and rehabilitation sciences, prion disease transmission, outcomes research in the rehabilitation sciences.

Daemen College, Department of Physical Therapy, Amherst, NY 14226-3592. Offers orthopedic manual physical therapy (Advanced Certificate); physical therapy-direct entry (DPT). *Accreditation:* APTA. Part-time programs available. *Faculty:* 9 full-time (5 women), 4 part-time/adjunct (1 woman). *Students:* 74 full-time (58 women), 8 part-time (3 women); includes 6 minority (2 American Indian/Alaska Native, 2 Asian Americans or Pacific Islanders, 2 Hispanic Americans), 1 international. Average age 25. 97 applicants, 13% accepted, 9 enrolled. In 2009, 51 doctorates awarded. *Entrance requirements:* For doctorate, baccalaureate degree with minimum GPA of 2.8 in science coursework; letter of intent; resume; 2 letters of reference; 120 hours of physical therapy exposure. Additional exam requirements/recommendations for international students: Required—TOEFL (minimum score 500 paper-based; 173 computer-based; 61 iBT). *Application deadline:* For fall admission, 3/1 priority date for domestic and international students; for spring admission, 10/1 priority date for domestic and international students. Applications are processed on a rolling basis. Application fee: $25. Electronic applications accepted. *Expenses:* Tuition: Part-time $770 per credit hour. Tuition and fees vary according to course load, program and reciprocity agreements. *Financial support:* In 2009–10, 2 students received support; teaching assistantships, institutionally sponsored loans and scholarships/grants available. Financial award application deadline: 2/15; financial award applicants required to submit FAFSA. *Faculty research:* Athletic injuries, myofacial pain syndrome, electrical stimulation and tissue healing, lumbar spine dysfunction, temporomandibular joint syndrome. *Unit head:* Dr. Sharon L. Held, Chair, 716-839-8344, Fax: 716-839-8537, E-mail: sheld@daemen.edu. *Application contact:* Scott Rowe, Associate Director of Graduate Programs, 716-839-8225, Fax: 716-839-8229, E-mail: srowe@daemen.edu.

Dalhousie University, Faculty of Health Professions, School of Physiotherapy, Halifax, NS B3H 3J5, Canada. Offers physiotherapy (entry to profession) (M Sc); physiotherapy (rehabilitation research) (M Sc). *Entrance requirements:* Additional exam requirements/recommendations for international students: Required—TOEFL, IELTS, CANTEST, CAEL, or Michigan English Language Assessment Battery. *Application deadline:* For fall admission, 1/31 priority date for domestic and international students. Application fee: $70. Electronic applications accepted. *Unit head:* Dr. Anne Fenety, Head, 902-494-2634, Fax: 902-494-1941, E-mail: physiotherapy@dal.ca. *Application contact:* Kelly Underwood, Admissions Assistant, 902-494-1947, Fax: 902-494-1941, E-mail: kelly.underwood@dal.ca.

Des Moines University, College of Health Sciences, Program in Physical Therapy, Des Moines, IA 50312-4104. Offers DPT. *Accreditation:* APTA. *Faculty:* 8 full-time (6 women). *Students:* 150 full-time (100 women), 161 part-time (98 women); includes 70 minority (7 African Americans, 60 Asian Americans or Pacific Islanders, 3 Hispanic Americans). Average age 24. 505 applicants, 37% accepted, 136 enrolled. *Entrance requirements:* Additional exam requirements/recommendations for international students: Required—TOEFL. *Application deadline:* For fall admission, 1/31 priority date for domestic students. Applications are processed on a rolling basis. Electronic applications accepted. *Expenses:* Contact institution. *Financial support:* In 2009–10, 9 students received support. Career-related internships or fieldwork, institutionally sponsored loans, scholarships/grants, and university employment available. Support available to part-time students. Financial award application deadline: 4/15; financial award applicants required to submit FAFSA. *Unit head:* Traci Bush, Director, 515-271-1432, E-mail: traci.bush@dmu.edu. *Application contact:* Josh Kvinlaug, Admissions Coordinator, 515-271-7854, Fax: 515-271-7145.

Dominican College, Division of Allied Health, Department of Physical Therapy, Orangeburg, NY 10962-1210. Offers MS, DPT. *Accreditation:* APTA. Part-time and evening/weekend programs available. *Degree requirements:* For master's, 3 clinical affiliations. *Entrance requirements:* For master's, minimum GPA of 3.0. Additional exam requirements/recommendations for international students: Required—TOEFL (minimum score 550 paper-based; 213 computer-based).

Drexel University, College of Nursing and Health Professions, Department of Physical Therapy and Rehabilitation Sciences, Philadelphia, PA 19102. Offers hand and upper quarter rehabilitation (MHS, Certificate, PPDPT); movement science (PhD); orthopedics (MHS, PhD, PPDPT); pediatrics (MHS, PhD, PPDPT); physical therapy (DPT). *Accreditation:* APTA. Part-time programs available. Terminal master's awarded for partial completion of doctoral program. *Degree requirements:* For master's, comprehensive exam; for doctorate, thesis/dissertation, qualifying exam. *Entrance requirements:* For master's and doctorate, GRE General Test. Additional exam requirements/recommendations for international students: Required—TOEFL. Electronic applications accepted. *Faculty research:* Cerebral palsy, chronic low back pain, shoulder dysfunction, early intervention/community programs.

Duke University, School of Medicine, Physical Therapy Division, Durham, NC 27708. Offers DPT. *Accreditation:* APTA. *Faculty:* 18 full-time (11 women), 6 part-time/adjunct (2 women). *Students:* 180 full-time (147 women); includes 22 minority (8 African Americans, 7 Asian Americans or Pacific Islanders, 7 Hispanic Americans). 239 applicants, 50% accepted, 78 enrolled. In 2009, 60 doctorates awarded. *Degree requirements:* For doctorate, comprehensive exam, scholarly project. *Entrance requirements:* For doctorate, GRE, previous course work in anatomy, physiology, biological sciences, chemistry, physics, psychology, and statistics. Additional exam requirements/recommendations for international students: Required—TOEFL. *Application deadline:* For fall admission, 12/1 priority date for domestic and international students. Applications are processed on a rolling basis. Application fee: $75. Electronic applications accepted. *Expenses:* Contact institution. *Financial support:* In 2009–10, 161 students received support; fellowships, research assistantships, teaching assistantships, Federal Work-Study available. Financial award application deadline: 5/1; financial award applicants required to submit FAFSA. *Faculty research:* Geriatrics, visual plasticity, educational outcomes, orthopaedics, neurology. *Unit head:* Victoria Kaprielian, Interim Chief, 919-681-4380, Fax: 919-684-1846, E-mail: kapri001@mc.duke.edu. *Application contact:* Anita Aiken, Admissions Coordinator, 919-668-5206, Fax: 919-688-3024, E-mail: anita.aiken@duke.edu.

Duquesne University, John G. Rangos, Sr. School of Health Sciences, Pittsburgh, PA 15282-0001. Offers health management systems (MHMS); occupational therapy (MS); physical therapy (DPT); physician assistant studies (MPAS); rehabilitation science (MS, PhD); speech–language pathology (MS); MBA/MHMS. *Accreditation:* AOTA (one or more programs are accredited); APTA (one or more programs are accredited); ASHA. *Faculty:* 35 full-time (23 women), 17 part-time/adjunct (10 women). *Students:* 309 full-time (258 women), 11 part-time (7 women); includes 11 minority (5 African Americans, 5 Asian Americans or Pacific Islanders, 1 Hispanic American), 6 international. Average age 23. 454 applicants, 20% accepted, 20 enrolled. In 2009, 92 master's, 23 doctorates awarded. *Degree requirements:* For doctorate, thesis/dissertation. *Entrance requirements:* For master's, GRE General Test (speech-language pathology), 3 letters of recommendation; minimum GPA of 2.75 (health management systems, occupational therapy), minimum GPA of 3.0 (speech-language pathology); for doctorate, GRE General Test (for physical therapy), 3 letters of recommendation, minimum GPA of 3.0, personal interview. Additional exam requirements/recommendations for international students: Required—TOEFL (minimum score 550 paper-based; 233 computer-based; 90 iBT). *Application deadline:* Applications are processed on a rolling basis. Electronic applications accepted. *Expenses:* Contact institution. *Financial support:* Federal Work-Study available. *Faculty research:* Neuronal processing, electrical stimulation on peripheral neuropathy, CNS stimulatory and inhibitory signals, behavioral genetic methodologies to development disorders of speech, neurogenic communication disorders. Total annual research expenditures: $338,404. *Unit head:* Dr. Gregory H. Frazer, Dean, 412-396-5303, Fax: 412-396-5554, E-mail: frazer@duq.edu. *Application contact:* Christopher R. Hilf, Recruiter/Academic Advisor, 412-396-5653, Fax: 412-396-5554, E-mail: hilfc@duq.edu.

D'Youville College, Department of Physical Therapy, Buffalo, NY 14201-1084. Offers advanced orthopedic physical therapy (Certificate); manual physical therapy (Certificate); physical therapy (MPT, MS, DPT). *Accreditation:* APTA. Part-time programs available. Postbaccalaureate distance learning degree programs offered (minimal on-campus study). *Degree requirements:* For master's, comprehensive exam, thesis or alternative, project or thesis; for doctorate, comprehensive exam, project or thesis. *Entrance requirements:* For doctorate, bachelor's degree, minimum GPA of 3.0. Additional exam requirements/recommendations for international students: Required—TOEFL (minimum score 500 paper-based; 173 computer-based). Electronic applications accepted. *Faculty research:* Therapeutic effects of Tai Chi, selected topics in orthopedics, health promotion in type 2 diabetes, athletic performance in youth and college sports, behavioral determinants in childhood obesity.

East Carolina University, Graduate School, School of Allied Health Sciences, Department of Physical Therapy, Greenville, NC 27858-4353. Offers MPT, DPT. *Accreditation:* APTA. *Degree requirements:* For master's, comprehensive exam. *Entrance requirements:* For master's, GRE General Test. Additional exam requirements/recommendations for international students: Required—TOEFL. *Faculty research:* Diabetes and obesity, diabetic foot, ACL injury.

Eastern Washington University, Graduate Studies, College of Science, Health and Engineering, Department of Physical Therapy, Cheney, WA 99004-2431. Offers DPT. *Accreditation:* APTA. *Degree requirements:* For doctorate, comprehensive exam, thesis/dissertation or final project. *Entrance requirements:* For doctorate, GRE General Test, minimum GPA of 3.0, 75 hours of experience, 3 letters of recommendation. *Expenses:* Tuition, state resident: full-time $7476; part-time $249 per quarter hour. Tuition, nonresident: full-time $18,030; part-time $601 per quarter hour. Required fees: $3.50 per quarter hour. $142 per quarter.

East Tennessee State University, School of Graduate Studies, College of Public and Allied Health, Department of Physical Therapy, Johnson City, TN 37614. Offers DPT. *Accreditation:* APTA. *Entrance requirements:* Additional exam requirements/recommendations for international students: Required—TOEFL (minimum score 550 paper-based; 213 computer-based). *Faculty research:* Adult developmental delay, vestibular dysflaction, iontophoresis, musculoskeletal dysfunction, educational technology.

Elon University, Program in Physical Therapy, Elon, NC 27244-2010. Offers DPT. *Accreditation:* APTA. *Faculty:* 13 full-time (9 women), 7 part-time/adjunct (4 women). *Students:* 114 full-time (83 women); includes 5 minority (2 African Americans, 1 American Indian/Alaska Native, 1 Asian American or Pacific Islander, 1 Hispanic American). Average age 23. 300 applicants, 24% accepted, 38 enrolled. *Entrance requirements:* For doctorate, GRE General Test. Additional exam requirements/recommendations for international students: Required—TOEFL (minimum score 550 paper-based; 213 computer-based; 79 iBT). *Application deadline:* For winter admission, 12/1 priority date for domestic students. Applications are processed on a rolling basis. Application fee: $50. Electronic applications accepted. *Expenses:* Contact institution. *Financial support:* In 2009–10, 9 students received support. Federal Work-Study and scholarships/grants available. Financial award application deadline: 10/1; financial award applicants required to submit FAFSA. *Faculty research:* Safety in the anatomy laboratory related to formaldehyde, physical therapy management of persons with spinal pain, effects of exercise on persons in drug rehabilitation, effects of aquatic therapy in a young person with cerebral palsy, use of Wii Fit for balance rehabilitation in the elderly. *Unit head:* Dr. Elizabeth A. Rogers, Chair, 336-278-6400, Fax: 336-278-6414, E-mail: rogers@elon.edu. *Application contact:* Art Fadde, Director of Graduate Admissions, 800-334-8448 Ext. 3, Fax: 336-278-7699, E-mail: afadde@elon.edu.

Emory University, School of Medicine, Programs in Allied Health Professions, Physical Therapy Program, Atlanta, GA 30322-1100. Offers DPT. *Accreditation:* APTA. *Faculty:* 19 full-time (13 women), 5 part-time/adjunct (3 women). *Students:* 147 full-time (120 women), 2 part-time (both women); includes 29 minority (22 African Americans, 4 Asian Americans or Pacific Islanders, 3 Hispanic Americans), 3 international. Average age 24. 210 applicants, 45% accepted, 57 enrolled. In 2009, 41 doctorates awarded. *Entrance requirements:* For doctorate, GRE General Test. *Application deadline:* For fall admission, 10/1 priority date for domestic and international students. Applications are processed on a rolling basis. Application fee: $60. Electronic applications accepted. *Expenses:* Contact institution. *Financial support:* In 2009–10, 107 students received support. Institutionally sponsored loans and scholarships/grants available. Financial award application deadline: 3/1; financial award applicants required to submit FAFSA. *Faculty research:* Constraint induced recovery in stroke exercise in patients with vestibular hypofunction, immune response to exercise in aging, functional electrical stimulation and spinal cord injury. *Unit head:* Dr. Zoher F. Kapasi, Director, 404-712-5683, Fax: 404-712-4130, E-mail: pt_admissions@learnlink.emory.edu. *Application contact:* Monica George-Komi, Admission Coordinator, 404-712-5657, Fax: 404-712-4130, E-mail: mgeorg2@emory.edu.

Florida Agricultural and Mechanical University, Division of Graduate Studies, Research, and Continuing Education, School of Allied Health Sciences, Division of Physical Therapy, Tallahassee, FL 32307-3200. Offers MPT. *Accreditation:* APTA. *Faculty:* 7 full-time (2 women). *Students:* 69 full-time (47 women), 6 part-time (4 women); includes 66 minority (65 African Americans, 1 Asian American or Pacific Islander), 2 international. In 2009, 8 master's awarded. *Entrance requirements:* For master's, GRE General Test or GMAT, minimum GPA of 3.0. Additional exam requirements/recommendations for international students: Required—TOEFL. *Application deadline:* For fall admission, 5/18 for domestic students, 12/18 for international students; for spring admission, 11/12 for domestic students, 5/12 for international students. *Unit head:* Dr. Eric J. Toran, Interim Chairperson, 850-599-3820, Fax: 850-561-2457. *Application contact:* Dr. Chanta M. Haywood, Dean of Graduate Studies, Research, and Continuing Education, 850-599-3315, Fax: 850-599-3727.

Florida Gulf Coast University, College of Health Professions, Department of Physical Therapy, Fort Myers, FL 33965-6565. Offers MS, DPT. *Accreditation:* APTA. Part-time programs available. Postbaccalaureate distance learning degree programs offered (minimal on-campus study). *Faculty:* 42 full-time (33 women), 30 part-time/adjunct (20 women). *Students:* 51 full-time (32 women), 16 part-time (14 women); includes 13 minority (4 African Americans, 7 Asian Americans or Pacific Islanders, 2 Hispanic Americans), 1 international. Average age 26. 68 applicants, 35% accepted, 23 enrolled. In 2009, 7 master's awarded. *Degree requirements:* For master's, thesis or alternative. *Entrance requirements:* For master's, GRE General Test or MAT, minimum GPA of 3.0. Additional exam requirements/recommendations for international students: Required—TOEFL (minimum score 550 paper-based; 213 computer-based). *Application deadline:* For fall admission, 1/15 priority date for domestic students. Applications are processed on a rolling basis. Application fee: $30. Electronic applications accepted. *Financial support:* Career-related internships or fieldwork, Federal Work-Study, and institutionally sponsored loans available. *Faculty research:* Physical therapy practice and education. *Unit head:* Sharon Bevins, Chair, 239-590-7533, Fax: 239-590-7474, E-mail: sbevins@fgcu.edu. *Application contact:* Sharon Bevins, Chair, 239-590-7533, Fax: 239-590-7474, E-mail: sbevins@fgcu.edu.

Florida International University, College of Nursing and Health Sciences, Department of Physical Therapy, Miami, FL 33199. Offers DPT. *Accreditation:* APTA. Part-time programs available. *Faculty:* 8 full-time (4 women). *Students:* 147 full-time (105 women), 1 (woman) part-time; includes 106 minority (18 African Americans, 11 Asian Americans or Pacific Islanders, 77 Hispanic Americans), 8 international. Average age 29. 311 applicants, 17% accepted, 52 enrolled. *Degree requirements:* For doctorate, comprehensive exam. *Entrance requirements:* For doctorate, minimum undergraduate GPA of 3.0 in upper-level coursework; letter of intent; resume; at least 40 hours of observation within physical therapy clinic or facility. Additional exam requirements/recommendations for international students: Required—TOEFL (minimum score 550 paper-based; 80 iBT). *Application deadline:* For fall admission, 1/15 for domestic and international students. Application fee: $30. Electronic applications accepted. *Expenses:* Tuition, state resident: full-time $8008; part-time $4004 per year. Tuition, nonresident: full-time $20,104; part-time $10,052 per year. Required fees: $298; $149 per term. *Financial support:* Institutionally sponsored loans, scholarships/grants, and unspecified assistantships available. Financial award application deadline: 3/1; financial award applicants required to submit FAFSA. *Faculty research:* Isokinetic test results and gait abnormalities after knee arthroscopy. *Unit head:* Dr. Denis Brundt, Chair, 305-348-3647, Fax: 305-348-1979, E-mail: dbrunt@fiu.edu. *Application contact:* Nanett Rojas, Assistant Director of Graduate Admissions, 305-348-7442, Fax: 305-348-7441, E-mail: gradadm@fiu.edu.

Franklin Pierce University, Graduate Studies, Rindge, NH 03461-0060. Offers emerging network technology (Graduate Certificate); health practice management (MBA, Graduate Certificate); human resource management (MBA); human resources management (Graduate Certificate); information technology management (MS); leadership (MBA, DA), including transformational leadership (DA); nursing (MS); physical therapy (DPT); physician assistant (MPAS); sports facilities management (MS); teacher education (M Ed). *Accreditation:* APTA. Part-time programs available. Postbaccalaureate distance learning degree programs offered (no on-campus study). *Faculty:* 27 full-time (16 women), 18 part-time/adjunct (4 women). *Students:* 296 full-time (172 women), 249 part-time (165 women); includes 18 minority (5 African Americans, 7 Asian Americans or Pacific Islanders, 6 Hispanic Americans), 31 international. Average age 38. 227 applicants, 97% accepted, 185 enrolled. In 2009, 76 master's, 46 doctorates awarded. *Degree requirements:* For master's, concentrated original research projects; student teaching; fieldwork and/or internship; leadership project; for doctorate, concentrated original research projects, clinical fieldwork and/or internship, leadership project. *Entrance requirements:* For master's, minimum GPA of 2.5, 3 letters of recommendation; for doctorate, demonstrated success at previous academic institutions (minimum GPA of 2.5), 3 letters of recommendation, personal mission statement, interview; writing sample (for DA program). Additional exam requirements/recommendations for international students: Required—TOEFL (minimum score 550 paper-based; 195 computer-based). *Application deadline:* Applications are processed on a rolling basis. Application fee: $0. Electronic applications accepted. *Expenses:* Tuition: Part-time $1560 per course. Part-time tuition and fees vary according to degree level, campus/location and program. *Financial support:* In 2009–10, 36 students received support, including 22 teaching assistantships with full and partial tuition reimbursements available; career-related internships or fieldwork and unspecified assistantships also available. Support available to part-time students. Financial award applicants required to submit FAFSA.

Physical Therapy

Franklin Pierce University (continued)
Faculty research: Evidence based practice in sports physical therapy, human resource management in economic crisis, leadership in nursing, innovation in sports facility management, differentiated learning and understanding by design. *Unit head:* Dr. Robert G. Goddard, Assistant Dean, 603-899-4361, Fax: 603-229-4580, E-mail: goddardr@franklinpierce.edu. *Application contact:* 800-325-1090, Fax: 603-898-0827, E-mail: gpsadmin@franklinpierce.edu.

Gannon University, School of Graduate Studies, Morosky College of Health Professions and Sciences, School of Health Professions, Program in Physical Therapy, Erie, PA 16541-0001. Offers DPT. *Accreditation:* APTA. *Students:* 118 full-time (78 women), 1 part-time (0 women); includes 5 minority (3 African Americans, 1 Asian American or Pacific Islander, 1 Hispanic American), 7 international. Average age 24. 179 applicants, 70% accepted, 42 enrolled. In 2009, 45 doctorates awarded. *Entrance requirements:* For doctorate, interview, minimum GPA of 3.0 in prerequisite course work. Additional exam requirements/recommendations for international students: Required—TOEFL (minimum score 79 iBT). *Application deadline:* For fall admission, 1/15 for domestic students. Application fee: $50. Electronic applications accepted. *Expenses:* Contact institution. *Financial support:* Federal Work-Study, scholarships/grants, and unspecified assistantships available. Financial award application deadline: 7/1; financial award applicants required to submit FAFSA. *Unit head:* Kristine Legters, Chair, 814-871-5641, E-mail: legters001@gannon.edu. *Application contact:* Kara Morgan, Assistant Director of Graduate Admissions, 814-871-5831, Fax: 814-871-5827, E-mail: graduate@gannon.edu.

The George Washington University, School of Medicine and Health Sciences, Health Sciences Programs, Program in Physical Therapy, Washington, DC 20052. Offers DPT. *Accreditation:* APTA. *Students:* 97 full-time (80 women), 1 (woman) part-time; includes 20 minority (7 African Americans, 1 American Indian/Alaska Native, 6 Asian Americans or Pacific Islanders, 6 Hispanic Americans), 1 international. Average age 25. 227 applicants, 52% accepted, 35 enrolled. In 2009, 22 doctorates awarded. *Entrance requirements:* Additional exam requirements/recommendations for international students: Required—TOEFL (minimum score 550 paper-based; 213 computer-based). *Application deadline:* For spring admission, 7/31 priority date for domestic students. Applications are processed on a rolling basis. Application fee: $60. *Unit head:* Dr. Margaret Plack, Director, 202-994-7763, E-mail: hspmxp@gwumc.edu. *Application contact:* Marsha White, Information Contact, 202-994-8184, E-mail: hspmkw@gwumc.edu.

Georgia State University, College of Health and Human Sciences, School of Health Professions, Division of Physical Therapy, Atlanta, GA 30302-3083. Offers DPT. *Accreditation:* APTA. *Entrance requirements:* Additional exam requirements/recommendations for international students: Required—TOEFL (minimum score 550 paper-based; 213 computer-based). Electronic applications accepted. *Expenses:* Contact institution. *Faculty research:* Myofacial trigger points, myofacial pain, muscle injury, wellness programs.

Governors State University, College of Health Professions, Program in Physical Therapy, University Park, IL 60466-0975. Offers MPT, DPT. *Accreditation:* APTA. *Degree requirements:* For master's, thesis or alternative. *Entrance requirements:* For master's, minimum GPA of 3.0 in field, 2.75 overall.

Graduate School and University Center of the City University of New York, Graduate Studies, Program in Physical Therapy, New York, NY 10016-4039. Offers DPT. *Accreditation:* APTA. *Students:* 124 full-time (92 women); includes 17 minority (2 African Americans, 11 Asian Americans or Pacific Islanders, 4 Hispanic Americans), 3 international. Average age 28. 217 applicants, 24% accepted, 28 enrolled. In 2009, 41 doctorates awarded. *Degree requirements:* For doctorate, exams, publishable research project. *Entrance requirements:* For doctorate, GRE, CPR certification, 100 hours clinical experience, minimum undergraduate GPA of 3.0. Additional exam requirements/recommendations for international students: Required—TOEFL. *Application deadline:* For spring admission, 11/1 for domestic students. Application fee: $125. *Financial support:* In 2009–10, 57 students received support, including 23 fellowships. *Unit head:* Dr. Barbara Weinstein, Executive Officer, 212-817-7980, E-mail: bweinstein@gc.cuny.edu. *Application contact:* Les Gribben, Director of Admissions, 212-817-7470, Fax: 212-817-1624, E-mail: lgribben@gc.cuny.edu.

Grand Valley State University, College of Health Professions, Physical Therapy Program, Allendale, MI 49401-9403. Offers DPT. *Accreditation:* APTA. *Faculty:* 13 full-time (7 women), 13 part-time/adjunct (7 women). *Students:* 122 full-time (98 women), 122 part-time (98 women); includes 6 minority (1 African American, 1 American Indian/Alaska Native, 2 Asian Americans or Pacific Islanders, 2 Hispanic Americans), 1 international. Average age 24. 152 applicants, 31% accepted, 42 enrolled. In 2009, 42 doctorates awarded. *Entrance requirements:* For doctorate, GRE, minimum GPA of 3.0 in most recent 60 hours and in prerequisites, 50 hours of volunteer work, interview, writing sample. Additional exam requirements/recommendations for international students: Required—TOEFL (minimum score 610 paper-based; 253 computer-based). *Application deadline:* For winter admission, 1/15 priority date for domestic and international students. Applications are processed on a rolling basis. Application fee: $30. Electronic applications accepted. *Expenses:* Tuition, state resident: part-time $471 per credit hour. Tuition, nonresident: part-time $646 per credit hour. Tuition and fees vary according to course level. *Financial support:* In 2009–10, 46 students received support, including 19 fellowships (averaging $3,874 per year), 37 research assistantships with full and partial tuition reimbursements available (averaging $4,000 per year); career-related internships or fieldwork, Federal Work-Study, institutionally sponsored loans, and unspecified assistantships also available. Financial award application deadline: 2/15. *Faculty research:* Balance deficits, motion analysis, nutritional knowledge of female athletes, trust in athletic performance, spinal functions dysfunction. *Unit head:* Dr. John Peck, Director, 616-331-3356, Fax: 616-331-3350, E-mail: peckj@gvsu.edu. *Application contact:* Darlene Zwart, Student Services Coordinator, 616-331-3958, E-mail: zwartda@gvsu.edu.

Hampton University, Graduate College, Program in Physical Therapy, Hampton, VA 23668. Offers DPT. *Accreditation:* APTA. *Degree requirements:* For doctorate, thesis/dissertation, oral defense, qualifying exam. *Entrance requirements:* For doctorate, GRE General Test, minimum GPA of 3.0 or master's degree in physics or related field.

Hardin-Simmons University, Graduate School, Holland School of Sciences and Mathematics, Doctoral Program in Physical Therapy, Abilene, TX 79698. Offers DPT. *Accreditation:* APTA. *Faculty:* 8 full-time (4 women), 1 part-time/adjunct (0 women). *Students:* 79 full-time (56 women); includes 5 minority (1 Asian American or Pacific Islander, 4 Hispanic Americans). Average age 23. 115 applicants, 30% accepted, 28 enrolled. In 2009, 25 doctorates awarded. *Degree requirements:* For doctorate, comprehensive exam, thesis/dissertation or alternative. *Entrance requirements:* For doctorate, letters of recommendation, interview, writing sample. Additional exam requirements/recommendations for international students: Required—TOEFL (minimum score 550 paper-based; 213 computer-based; 75 iBT). *Application deadline:* For fall admission, 10/1 priority date for domestic and international students; for spring admission, 2/1 for domestic and international students. Applications are processed on a rolling basis. Application fee: $50 ($100 for international students). *Expenses:* Contact institution. *Financial support:* In 2009–10, 79 students received support. Scholarships/grants available. Financial award application deadline: 3/1; financial award applicants required to submit FAFSA. *Faculty research:* Neuraltension testing, gait parameters, health promotion for seniors, vastus medialis recruitment, spirituality, vibration platforms, sensory integration, postural stability. *Unit head:* Dr. Janelle K. O'Connell, Department Head and Professor, 325-670-5860, Fax: 325-670-5868, E-mail: ptoffice@hsutx.edu. *Application contact:* Dr. Janelle K. O'Connell, Department Head, 325-670-5860, Fax: 325-670-5868, E-mail: ptoffice@hsutx.edu.

Humboldt State University, Graduate Studies, College of Professional Studies, Department of Kinesiology, Arcata, CA 95521-8299. Offers athletic training education (MS); exercise science/wellness management (MS); pre-physical therapy (MS); teaching/coaching (MS). *Students:* 24 full-time (13 women), 8 part-time (5 women); includes 5 minority (2 African Americans, 1 American Indian/Alaska Native, 2 Hispanic Americans). Average age 30. 25 applicants, 80% accepted, 15 enrolled. In 2009, 4 master's awarded. *Degree requirements:* For master's, thesis or alternative. *Entrance requirements:* For master's, GMAT, minimum GPA of 2.5. Additional exam requirements/recommendations for international students: Required—TOEFL. *Application deadline:* For fall admission, 6/1 for domestic students; for spring admission, 12/2 for domestic students. Applications are processed on a rolling basis. Application fee: $55. *Expenses:* Tuition, nonresident: full-time $8928. Required fees: $6102. Tuition and fees vary according to program. *Financial support:* Teaching assistantships, career-related internships or fieldwork, Federal Work-Study, and institutionally sponsored loans available. Financial award application deadline: 3/1; financial award applicants required to submit FAFSA. *Faculty research:* Human performance, adapted physical education, physical therapy. *Unit head:* Dr. Kathy Munoz, Chair, 707-826-3840, Fax: 707-826-5451, E-mail: kdm1@humboldt.edu. *Application contact:* Dr. T. K. Koesterer, Coordinator, 707-826-5967, Fax: 707-826-5451, E-mail: tjk17@humboldt.edu.

Husson University, School of Graduate and Professional Studies, Program in Physical Therapy, Bangor, ME 04401-2999. Offers DPT. *Accreditation:* APTA. Part-time and evening/weekend programs available.

Idaho State University, Office of Graduate Studies, Kasiska College of Health Professions, Department of Physical and Occupational Therapy, Program in Physical Therapy, Pocatello, ID 83209-8045. Offers DPT. *Accreditation:* APTA. *Students:* 73 full-time (25 women), 1 part-time (0 women); includes 5 minority (1 African American, 3 Asian Americans or Pacific Islanders, 1 Hispanic American), 1 international. Average age 27. In 2009, 25 doctorates awarded. *Degree requirements:* For doctorate, comprehensive exam, thesis/dissertation, oral and written exam. *Entrance requirements:* For doctorate, GRE General Test, minimum GPA of 3.0, 80 hours in 2 practice settings of physical therapy. Additional exam requirements/recommendations for international students: Required—TOEFL (minimum score 600 paper-based; 213 computer-based). *Application deadline:* For fall admission, 7/1 for domestic students, 6/1 for international students; for spring admission, 12/1 for domestic students, 11/1 for international students. Applications are processed on a rolling basis. Application fee: $55. Electronic applications accepted. *Expenses:* Contact institution. *Financial support:* Teaching assistantships with full and partial tuition reimbursements, career-related internships or fieldwork, Federal Work-Study, institutionally sponsored loans, scholarships/grants, traineeships, health care benefits, tuition waivers (full), and unspecified assistantships available. Support available to part-time students. Financial award application deadline: 1/1; financial award applicants required to submit FAFSA. *Faculty research:* Cardiovascular/pulmonary balance, neural plasticity, orthopedics, geriatrics, hypertension. *Unit head:* Dr. Kevin Helgeson, Chairperson, 208-282-4459, Fax: 208-282-4962, E-mail: helgkevi@isu.edu. *Application contact:* Tami Carson, Graduate School Technical Records Specialist, 208-282-2150, Fax: 208-282-4847, E-mail: carstami@isu.edu.

Indiana University–Purdue University Indianapolis, Indiana University School of Medicine, School of Health and Rehabilitation Sciences, Indianapolis, IN 46202-2896. Offers health sciences education (MS); nutrition and dietetics (MS); occupational therapy (MS); physical therapy (DPT). Part-time and evening/weekend programs available. *Faculty:* 8 full-time (5 women). *Students:* 206 full-time (161 women), 11 part-time (8 women); includes 16 minority (5 African Americans, 1 American Indian/Alaska Native, 8 Asian Americans or Pacific Islanders, 2 Hispanic Americans), 1 international. Average age 26. 23 applicants, 83% accepted, 18 enrolled. In 2009, 9 master's, 32 doctorates awarded. *Degree requirements:* For master's, thesis (for some programs). *Entrance requirements:* For master's, GRE General Test, minimum GPA of 3.0. Additional exam requirements/recommendations for international students: Required—TOEFL. *Application deadline:* For fall admission, 1/15 priority date for domestic students; for spring admission, 10/15 for domestic students. Application fee: $55 ($65 for international students). *Financial support:* In 2009–10, 10 fellowships (averaging $2,485 per year), 1 teaching assistantship (averaging $3,600 per year) were awarded; research assistantships, Federal Work-Study, institutionally sponsored loans, and scholarships/grants also available. Support available to part-time students. Financial award applicants required to submit FAFSA. *Unit head:* Dr. Mark S. Sothmann, Dean, 317-274-4702, E-mail: msothman@iupui.edu. *Application contact:* Dr. Mark S. Sothmann, Dean, 317-274-4702, E-mail: msothman@iupui.edu.

Ithaca College, Division of Graduate and Professional Studies, School of Health Sciences and Human Performance, Program in Physical Therapy, Ithaca, NY 14850. Offers MS, DPT. Students enter the program as freshmen. *Accreditation:* APTA. *Faculty:* 13 full-time (7 women), 5 part-time/adjunct (4 women). *Students:* 146 full-time (104 women); includes 12 minority (1 African American, 1 American Indian/Alaska Native, 4 Asian Americans or Pacific Islanders, 6 Hispanic Americans). Average age 23. In 2009, 65 master's, 58 doctorates awarded. *Degree requirements:* For doctorate, thesis/dissertation optional. *Entrance requirements:* Additional exam requirements/recommendations for international students: Required—TOEFL (minimum score 550 paper-based; 213 computer-based; 80 iBT). *Expenses:* Tuition: Full-time $18,960; part-time $632 per credit hour. *Financial support:* In 2009–10, 132 students received support. Career-related internships or fieldwork, Federal Work-Study, and scholarships/grants available. Support available to part-time students. Financial award applicants required to submit CSS PROFILE or FAFSA. *Unit head:* Dr. Ernest Nalette, Chairperson, 607-274-3527, Fax: 607-274-1263, E-mail: gps@ithaca.edu. *Application contact:* Rob Gearhart, Dean, Graduate and Professional Studies, 607-274-3527, Fax: 607-274-1263, E-mail: gps@ithaca.edu.

Langston University, School of Physical Therapy, Langston, OK 73050. Offers DPT. *Accreditation:* APTA.

Lebanon Valley College, Physical Therapy Department, Annville, PA 17003-1400. Offers DPT. *Accreditation:* APTA. *Faculty:* 8 full-time (4 women). *Students:* 62 full-time (45 women); includes 1 minority (Hispanic American). 43 applicants, 40% accepted, 11 enrolled. In 2009, 16 doctorates awarded. Application fee: $30. Electronic applications accepted. *Expenses:* Tuition: Full-time $32,740; part-time $410 per credit hour. Required fees: $610. *Financial support:* In 2009–10, 62 students received support. Scholarships/grants available. Financial award application deadline: 5/1; financial award applicants required to submit FAFSA. *Unit head:* Dr. Stan M. Dacko, Chairperson/Associate Professor, 717-867-6843, Fax: 717-867-6849, E-mail: dacko@lvc.edu. *Application contact:* Susan Jones, Director of Admission, 866-582-4236, Fax: 717-867-6026, E-mail: sjones@lvc.edu.

Loma Linda University, School of Allied Health Professions, Department of Physical Therapy, Loma Linda, CA 92350. Offers MPT, D Sc, DPT, DPTSc. *Accreditation:* APTA. *Entrance requirements:* Additional exam requirements/recommendations for international students: Required—TOEFL (minimum score 550 paper-based; 213 computer-based). Electronic applications accepted.

Long Island University, Brooklyn Campus, School of Health Professions, Division of Physical Therapy, Brooklyn, NY 11201-8423. Offers DPT, TDPT. *Accreditation:* APTA. Part-time and evening/weekend programs available. *Entrance requirements:* Additional exam requirements/recommendations for international students: Required—TOEFL (minimum score 500 paper-based; 173 computer-based). Electronic applications accepted.

Louisiana State University Health Sciences Center, School of Allied Health Professions, Department of Physical Therapy, New Orleans, LA 70112-2223. Offers DPT. *Accreditation:* APTA. *Entrance requirements:* For doctorate, GRE General Test (minimum combined score: 900), 60 hours experience, 3.0 GPA min—Bachelor's Degree. *Faculty research:* Wound healing, spinal cord injury, pain management, geriatrics, muscle physiology, muscle damage, motor control, balance.

Lynchburg College, Graduate Studies, School of Health Sciences and Human Performance, Lynchburg, VA 24501-3199. Offers clinical nurse leader (MSN); nursing education (MSN); physical therapy (DPT). *Expenses:* Tuition: Full-time $7020; part-time $390 per credit hour.

Marquette University, Graduate School, College of Health Sciences, Department of Physical Therapy, Milwaukee, WI 53201-1881. Offers DPT. *Accreditation:* APTA. *Faculty:* 11 full-time (6 women), 22 part-time/adjunct (14 women). *Students:* 92 full-time (77 women); includes 11

minority (4 African Americans, 3 Asian Americans or Pacific Islanders, 4 Hispanic Americans), 1 international. Average age 24. 103 applicants, 21% accepted, 15 enrolled. In 2009, 66 doctorates awarded. *Entrance requirements:* Additional exam requirements/recommendations for international students: Required—TOEFL. Application fee: $40. *Financial support:* Application deadline: 2/15. *Unit head:* Dr. Lawrence G. Pan, Chair, 414-288-7161, Fax: 414-288-5987. *Application contact:* Erin Fox, Assistant Director for Recruitment, 414-288-5319, Fax: 414-288-1902, E-mail: erin.fox@marquette.edu.

Marymount University, School of Health Professions, Program in Physical Therapy, Arlington, VA 22207-4299. Offers DPT. *Accreditation:* APTA. *Faculty:* 6 full-time (5 women). *Students:* 88 full-time (68 women), 2 part-time (both women); includes 24 minority (13 African Americans, 6 Asian Americans or Pacific Islanders, 5 Hispanic Americans), 2 international. Average age 26. 349 applicants, 36% accepted, 33 enrolled. In 2009, 127 doctorates awarded. *Degree requirements:* For doctorate, comprehensive exam, thesis/dissertation. *Entrance requirements:* For doctorate, GRE, 2 letters of recommendation, interview, resume, 40 hours of clinical work experience, essay, minimum GPA of 3.0 from previous university coursework. Additional exam requirements/recommendations for international students: Required—TOEFL (minimum score 600 paper-based; 250 computer-based; 96 iBT), IELTS (minimum score 6.5). *Application deadline:* For fall admission, 12/15 for domestic and international students. Applications are processed on a rolling basis. Application fee: $40. Electronic applications accepted. *Expenses:* Contact institution. *Financial support:* In 2009–10, 10 students received support; research assistantships with full tuition reimbursements available, career-related internships or fieldwork, Federal Work-Study, scholarships/grants, and unspecified assistantships available. Financial award applicants required to submit FAFSA. *Unit head:* Dr. Rita Wong, Chair, 703-284-5982, Fax: 703-284-5981, E-mail: rita.wong@marymount.edu. *Application contact:* Francesca Reed, Director, Graduate Admissions, 703-284-5901, Fax: 703-527-3815, E-mail: grad.admissions@marymount.edu.

Maryville University of Saint Louis, School of Health Professions, Physical Therapy Program, St. Louis, MO 63141-7299. Offers DPT. *Accreditation:* APTA. *Students:* 39 full-time (28 women); includes 1 Hispanic American. Average age 22. *Degree requirements:* For doctorate, clinical rotations. *Entrance requirements:* For doctorate, minimum cumulative GPA of 3.0, 2 letters of recommendation, interview. Additional exam requirements/recommendations for international students: Required—TOEFL (minimum score 560 paper-based). *Application deadline:* Applications are processed on a rolling basis. Application fee: $40 ($60 for international students). Electronic applications accepted. *Expenses:* Tuition: Full-time $20,384; part-time $627.50 per credit hour. Required fees: $100 per semester. *Financial support:* Career-related internships or fieldwork, Federal Work-Study, and campus employment available. Financial award application deadline: 3/1; financial award applicants required to submit FAFSA. *Faculty research:* Memory and exercise. *Unit head:* Dr. Michelle Unterberg, Director, 314-529-9590, Fax: 314-529-9946, E-mail: munterberg@maryville.edu. *Application contact:* 314-529-9350, Fax: 314-529-9927, E-mail: admissions@maryville.edu.

Mayo School of Health Sciences, Program in Physical Therapy, Rochester, MN 55905. Offers DPT. *Accreditation:* APTA. *Entrance requirements:* Additional exam requirements/recommendations for international students: Required—TOEFL. Electronic applications accepted. *Faculty research:* Biomechanics, gait analysis, growth factor-mediated plasticity in muscle, musculoskeletal clinical tests and measures, Parkinson's disease.

McMaster University, Faculty of Health Sciences, Professional Program in Physiotherapy, Hamilton, ON L8S 4M2, Canada. Offers M Sc. *Degree requirements:* For master's, clinical placements, independent research project. *Entrance requirements:* For master's, minimum B average over last 60 undergraduate units. Additional exam requirements/recommendations for international students: Required—TOEFL (minimum score 600 paper-based; 250 computer-based).

Medical University of South Carolina, College of Health Professions, Department of Health Professions, Program in Physical Therapy, Charleston, SC 29425. Offers DPT. *Accreditation:* APTA. Postbaccalaureate distance learning degree programs offered (minimal on-campus study). *Faculty:* 9 full-time (5 women), 8 part-time/adjunct (6 women). *Students:* 174 full-time (131 women); includes 13 minority (5 African Americans, 2 American Indian/Alaska Native, 3 Asian Americans or Pacific Islanders, 3 Hispanic Americans). Average age 25. 309 applicants, 37% accepted, 65 enrolled. In 2009, 55 doctorates awarded. *Entrance requirements:* For doctorate, GRE, references, minimum GPA of 3.0, volunteer hours. Additional exam requirements/recommendations for international students: Required—TOEFL (minimum score 600 paper-based; 250 computer-based). *Application deadline:* For fall admission, 1/15 priority date for domestic and international students. Application fee: $85. Electronic applications accepted. *Financial support:* Federal Work-Study and scholarships/grants available. Support available to part-time students. Financial award application deadline: 3/10; financial award applicants required to submit FAFSA. *Faculty research:* Low back pain; spinal cord injury. Total annual research expenditures: $58,231. *Unit head:* Dr. David Morrisette, Interim Program Director, 843-792-2940, Fax: 843-792-0710, E-mail: morrisdc@musc.edu. *Application contact:* Susan Johnson, Student Services Program Coordinator, 843-792-5377, Fax: 843-792-0710, E-mail: johnsoss@musc.edu.

Mercy College, School of Health and Natural Sciences, Program in Physical Therapy, Dobbs Ferry, NY 10522-1189. Offers MS, DPT. *Accreditation:* APTA. Evening/weekend programs available. *Students:* 81 full-time (49 women), 22 part-time (12 women); includes 16 African Americans, 14 Asian Americans or Pacific Islanders, 15 Hispanic Americans, 2 international. Average age 33. 210 applicants, 18% accepted, 35 enrolled. In 2009, 1 master's, 16 doctorates awarded. *Degree requirements:* For master's, completion of research or educational externship. *Entrance requirements:* For doctorate, interview, two letters of reference, official college transcripts, minimum GPA of 3.0, two-page typewritten essay on reasons for pursuing career in physical therapy, volunteer/work experience forms demonstrating at least eighty hours of volunteer work or work-related experience. Additional exam requirements/recommendations for international students: Required—TOEFL (minimum score 600 paper-based; 250 computer-based; 100 iBT). *Application deadline:* For fall admission, 1/15 for domestic students. Application fee: $65. *Expenses:* Contact institution. *Financial support:* In 2009–10, 1 student received support. Career-related internships or fieldwork, Federal Work-Study, scholarships/grants, and unspecified assistantships available. *Unit head:* Dr. Nannette Hyland, Director, 914-674-7825, E-mail: nhyland@mercy.edu. *Application contact:* Dr. Nannette Hyland, Director, 914-674-7825, E-mail: nhyland@mercy.edu.

MGH Institute of Health Professions, Graduate Programs, School of Health and Rehabilitation Sciences, Post-Professional Graduate Program in Physical Therapy, Boston, MA 02129. Offers MS, DPT, Certificate. Part-time and evening/weekend programs available. *Faculty:* 11 full-time (9 women), 8 part-time/adjunct (all women). *Students:* 19 full-time (15 women), 106 part-time (86 women); includes 22 minority (2 African Americans, 20 Asian Americans or Pacific Islanders). Average age 35. 94 applicants, 72% accepted, 42 enrolled. In 2009, 22 master's, 84 doctorates, 1 other advanced degree awarded. *Degree requirements:* For master's, thesis, clinical preceptorship. *Entrance requirements:* For master's, GRE General Test, graduation from an approved program in physical therapy, 1 year of work experience as a physical therapist. Additional exam requirements/recommendations for international students: Required—TOEFL (minimum score 550 paper-based; 213 computer-based; 80 iBT). *Application deadline:* For fall admission, 7/1 priority date for domestic students, 3/1 for international students; for winter admission, 11/1 priority date for domestic students, 7/1 for international students; for spring admission, 3/1 priority date for domestic students, 11/1 for international students. Applications are processed on a rolling basis. Application fee: $50. Electronic applications accepted. *Expenses:* Tuition: Part-time $943 per credit. Required fees: $943 per credit. Tuition and fees vary according to course load. *Financial support:* In 2009–10, 10 students received support. Career-related internships or fieldwork, scholarships/grants, tuition waivers (partial), and unspecified assistantships available. Support available to part-time students. Financial award application deadline: 3/1; financial award applicants required to submit FAFSA. *Faculty research:* Disability in the elderly; gait, balance and posture; cardiac rehabilitation; relationship of impairment to disability; effect of muscle strengthening in the elderly. *Unit head:* Dr. Leslie G. Portney, Interim Dean/Department Chair, 617-726-3170, Fax: 617-724-6321, E-mail: lportney@mghihp.edu. *Application contact:* Maureen Rika Judd, Manager of Admissions, 617-726-6069, Fax: 617-726-8010, E-mail: admissions@mghihp.edu.

MGH Institute of Health Professions, Graduate Programs, School of Health and Rehabilitation Sciences, Professional Graduate Program in Physical Therapy, Boston, MA 02129. Offers DPT. *Accreditation:* APTA. *Faculty:* 11 full-time (9 women), 2 part-time/adjunct (both women). *Students:* 100 full-time (74 women), 42 part-time (31 women); includes 14 minority (1 African American, 1 American Indian/Alaska Native, 10 Asian Americans or Pacific Islanders, 2 Hispanic Americans). Average age 26. 373 applicants, 28% accepted, 66 enrolled. In 2009, 46 doctorates awarded. *Degree requirements:* For doctorate, thesis/dissertation or alternative, research project. *Entrance requirements:* For doctorate, GRE General Test, interview, minimum of 10 physical therapy observation hours. Additional exam requirements/recommendations for international students: Required—TOEFL (minimum score 550 paper-based; 213 computer-based; 80 iBT). *Application deadline:* For spring admission, 12/31 for domestic and international students. Application fee: $50. Electronic applications accepted. *Expenses:* Tuition: Part-time $943 per credit. Required fees: $943 per credit. Tuition and fees vary according to course load. *Financial support:* In 2009–10, 133 students received support; research assistantships, teaching assistantships, career-related internships or fieldwork, scholarships/grants, tuition waivers (full and partial), and unspecified assistantships available. Support available to part-time students. Financial award application deadline: 3/1; financial award applicants required to submit FAFSA. *Faculty research:* Disability in the elderly; gait, balance, and posture; cardiac rehabilitation: relationship of impairment to disability. *Unit head:* Dr. Leslie G. Portney, Director, 617-726-3170, Fax: 617-724-6321, E-mail: lportney@mghihp.edu. *Application contact:* Maureen Rika Judd, Manager of Admissions, 617-726-6069, Fax: 617-726-8010, E-mail: admissions@mghihp.edu.

Midwestern University, Downers Grove Campus, College of Health Sciences, Illinois Campus, Program in Physical Therapy, Downers Grove, IL 60515-1235. Offers DPT. *Accreditation:* APTA. *Faculty:* 10 full-time (7 women). *Students:* 141 full-time (106 women), 1 part-time (0 women); includes 16 minority (12 Asian Americans or Pacific Islanders, 4 Hispanic Americans). Average age 24. 431 applicants, 25% accepted, 48 enrolled. In 2009, 28 doctorates awarded. *Entrance requirements:* For doctorate, GRE General Test. *Application deadline:* Applications are processed on a rolling basis. Application fee: $50. *Expenses:* Contact institution. *Financial support:* In 2009–10, 87 students received support. Federal Work-Study available. *Unit head:* Donna Cech, Director, 630-515-7221, E-mail: dcechx@midwestern.edu. *Application contact:* Michael Laken, Director of Admissions, 630-515-6171, Fax: 630-971-6086, E-mail: admissil@midwestern.edu.

Misericordia University, College of Health Sciences, Program in Physical Therapy, Dallas, PA 18612-1098. Offers MSPT, DPT. *Accreditation:* APTA. *Faculty:* 7 full-time (5 women), 1 (woman) part-time/adjunct. *Students:* 48 full-time (35 women), 50 part-time (38 women); includes 1 minority (Hispanic American). Average age 25. In 2009, 33 master's, 11 doctorates awarded. *Degree requirements:* For master's, thesis optional. *Entrance requirements:* For master's, GRE General Test or MAT. *Application deadline:* For fall admission, 12/15 priority date for domestic students. Applications are processed on a rolling basis. Application fee: $25. Electronic applications accepted. *Financial support:* In 2009–10, 49 students received support; teaching assistantships, career-related internships or fieldwork, scholarships/grants, and tuition waivers (partial) available. Support available to part-time students. Financial award application deadline: 6/30; financial award applicants required to submit FAFSA. *Faculty research:* Wound care, computer-assisted instruction, instruction in applied physiology, isokinetics, prosthetics. *Unit head:* Dr. Susan Barker, Department Chair, 570-674-6422, E-mail: sbarker@misericordia.edu. *Application contact:* Dr. Susan Barker, Department Chair, 570-674-6422, E-mail: sbarker@misericordia.edu.

Missouri State University, Graduate College, College of Health and Human Services, Department of Physical Therapy, Springfield, MO 65897. Offers DPT. *Accreditation:* APTA. *Faculty:* 8 full-time (4 women), 3 part-time/adjunct (1 woman). *Students:* 68 full-time (40 women); includes 2 minority (1 Asian American or Pacific Islander, 1 Hispanic American), 2 international. Average age 25. 94 applicants, 35% accepted, 29 enrolled. In 2009, 25 doctorates awarded. *Degree requirements:* For doctorate, comprehensive exam, thesis/dissertation or alternative. *Entrance requirements:* For doctorate, GRE, minimum GPA of 3.0, interview. Additional exam requirements/recommendations for international students: Required—TOEFL (minimum score 550 paper-based; 213 computer-based; 79 iBT). *Application deadline:* For fall admission, 11/15 for domestic and international students. Application fee: $35 ($50 for international students). Electronic applications accepted. *Expenses:* Tuition, state resident: full-time $3852; part-time $214 per credit hour. Tuition, nonresident: full-time $7524; part-time $418 per credit hour. Required fees: $696; $172 per semester. Tuition and fees vary according to course level, course load, degree level and program. *Financial support:* Federal Work-Study, institutionally sponsored loans, and unspecified assistantships available. Financial award application deadline: 3/31; financial award applicants required to submit FAFSA. *Faculty research:* Complex regional pain syndrome (CRPS), posture and the temporomandibular joint, clinical orthopedics, aging of the motor system. *Unit head:* Dr. Akinniran Oladehin, Head, 417-836-8728, E-mail: physicaltherapy@missouristate.edu. *Application contact:* Eric Eckert, Coordinator of Admissions and Recruitment, 417-836-5331, Fax: 417-836-6200, E-mail: ericeckert@missouristate.edu.

Mount St. Mary's College, Graduate Division, Department of Physical Therapy, Los Angeles, CA 90007. Offers DPT. *Accreditation:* APTA. *Faculty:* 5 full-time (4 women), 27 part-time/adjunct (15 women). *Students:* 87 full-time (62 women), 3 part-time (2 women); includes 19 minority (5 African Americans, 1 American Indian/Alaska Native, 9 Asian Americans or Pacific Islanders, 4 Hispanic Americans). Average age 26. In 2009, 24 doctorates awarded. *Entrance requirements:* For doctorate, GRE General Test, minimum GPA of 3.0. Additional exam requirements/recommendations for international students: Required—TOEFL (minimum score 550 iBT). *Application deadline:* For fall admission, 12/1 priority date for domestic and international students. *Expenses:* Contact institution. *Financial support:* Application deadline: 3/15. *Unit head:* Dr. Deborah Lowe, Chair, 213-477-2601, Fax: 213-477-2609, E-mail: dlowe@msmc.la.edu.

Nazareth College of Rochester, Graduate Studies, Department of Physical Therapy, Doctoral Program in Physical Therapy, Rochester, NY 14618-3790. Offers DPT. *Entrance requirements:* For doctorate, minimum GPA of 3.0.

Nazareth College of Rochester, Graduate Studies, Department of Physical Therapy, Master's Program in Physical Therapy, Rochester, NY 14618-3790. Offers MS. *Accreditation:* APTA. *Entrance requirements:* For master's, minimum GPA of 3.0.

Neumann University, Program in Physical Therapy, Aston, PA 19014-1298. Offers DPT. *Accreditation:* APTA. Evening/weekend programs available. *Faculty:* 6 full-time (4 women), 6 part-time/adjunct (5 women). *Students:* 73 full-time (42 women), 8 part-time (6 women); includes 8 minority (4 African Americans, 2 Asian Americans or Pacific Islanders, 2 Hispanic Americans). Average age 34. 96 applicants, 47% accepted, 35 enrolled. In 2009, 33 doctorates awarded. *Entrance requirements:* Additional exam requirements/recommendations for international students: Required—TOEFL. *Application deadline:* For fall admission, 12/1 for domestic students. Application fee: $50. Electronic applications accepted. *Expenses:* Contact institution. *Financial support:* Available to part-time students. Application deadline: 3/15. *Unit head:* Dr. Robert Post, Director, 610-558-5233, Fax: 610-459-1370, E-mail: postr@neumann.edu. *Application contact:* Kittie D. Pain, Associate Director of Admissions, Graduate and Adult Programs, 610-558-5613, Fax: 610-558-5652, E-mail: paink@neumann.edu.

New York Institute of Technology, Graduate Division, School of Health Professions, Program in Physical Therapy, Old Westbury, NY 11568-8000. Offers MS, DPT. *Accreditation:* APTA. *Students:* 103 full-time (47 women), 13 part-time (5 women); includes 31 minority (5 African Americans, 21 Asian Americans or Pacific Islanders, 5 Hispanic Americans), 2 international.

Physical Therapy

New York Institute of Technology (continued)
Average age 26. In 2009, 14 master's, 40 doctorates awarded. *Degree requirements:* For master's, thesis. *Entrance requirements:* For master's, minimum GPA of 3.0, interview, 100 hours of volunteer work, 2 letters of recommendation. Additional exam requirements/recommendations for international students: Required—TOEFL (minimum score 550 paper-based; 213 computer-based). *Application deadline:* For fall admission, 7/1 priority date for domestic students; for spring admission, 12/1 priority date for domestic students. Application fee: $50. *Expenses:* Tuition: Part-time $825 per credit. *Financial support:* Research assistantships with partial tuition reimbursements available. Financial award applicants required to submit FAFSA. *Unit head:* Dr. Karen Friel, Chair, 516-686-7651, Fax: 516-686-7699, E-mail: kfriel@nyit.edu. *Application contact:* Dr. Jacquelyn Nealon, Vice President for Enrollment Services, 516-686-7925, Fax: 516-686-7597, E-mail: jnealon@nyit.edu.

New York Medical College, School of Health Sciences and Practice, Department of Physical Therapy, Valhalla, NY 10595-1691. Offers DPT. *Accreditation:* APTA. *Faculty:* 5 full-time, 15 part-time/adjunct. *Students:* 80 full-time. Average age 27. 85 applicants, 42% accepted, 30 enrolled. *Degree requirements:* For doctorate, comprehensive exam, final project. *Entrance requirements:* For doctorate, GRE, minimum GPA of 3.0. Additional exam requirements/recommendations for international students: Required—TOEFL (minimum score 637 paper-based; 250 computer-based; 117 iBT), IELTS (minimum score 7). *Application deadline:* For winter admission, 3/1 priority date for domestic students, 1/30 priority date for international students. Applications are processed on a rolling basis. Application fee: $75 ($100 for international students). Electronic applications accepted. *Expenses:* Contact institution. *Financial support:* Applicants required to submit FAFSA. *Unit head:* Dr. Michael Majsak, Chair, 914-594-4916, Fax: 914-594-4292, E-mail: michael_majsak@nymc.edu. *Application contact:* Pamela Suett, Director of Recruitment, 914-594-4510, Fax: 914-594-4292, E-mail: shsp_admissions@nymc.edu.

New York University, Steinhardt School of Culture, Education, and Human Development, Department of Physical Therapy, New York, NY 10010-5615. Offers orthopedic physical therapy (Advanced Certificate); physical therapy (MA, DPT), including pathokinesiology (MA); physical therapy for practicing physical therapists (DPT); research in physical therapy (PhD). *Accreditation:* APTA (one or more programs are accredited). Part-time programs available. *Faculty:* 12 full-time (6 women), 14 part-time/adjunct (8 women). *Students:* 124 full-time (93 women), 7 part-time (5 women); includes 43 minority (10 African Americans, 23 Asian Americans or Pacific Islanders, 10 Hispanic Americans), 15 international. Average age 27. 125 applicants, 70% accepted, 41 enrolled. In 2009, 3 master's, 42 doctorates awarded. *Degree requirements:* For master's, thesis (for some programs); for doctorate, thesis/dissertation. *Entrance requirements:* For master's, physical therapy certificate; for doctorate, GRE General Test, interview, physical therapy certificate. Additional exam requirements/recommendations for international students: Required—TOEFL. *Application deadline:* For fall admission, 12/1 priority date for domestic and international students; for spring admission, 11/1 for domestic and international students. Applications are processed on a rolling basis. Application fee: $75. Electronic applications accepted. *Expenses:* Tuition: Full-time $30,528; part-time $1272 per credit. Required fees: $2177. *Financial support:* Fellowships with full and partial tuition reimbursements, research assistantships with full and partial tuition reimbursements, career-related internships or fieldwork, Federal Work-Study, scholarships/grants, tuition waivers (partial), and unspecified assistantships available. Support available to part-time students. Financial award application deadline: 2/1; financial award applicants required to submit FAFSA. *Faculty research:* Motor learning and control, neuromuscular disorders, biomechanics and ergonomics, movement analysis, exercise physiology; neurocognitive function in joint instability; pathomechanics. *Unit head:* Dr. Wen K. Ling, Chairperson, 212-998-9400, Fax: 212-995-4190. *Application contact:* 212-998-5030, Fax: 212-995-4328, E-mail: steinhardt.gradadmissions@nyu.edu.

Northeastern University, Bouvé College of Health Sciences Graduate School, Program in Physical Therapy (Direct Entry), Boston, MA 02115-5096. Offers DPT. *Students:* 18 full-time (15 women); includes 2 Asian Americans or Pacific Islanders, 1 Hispanic American, 1 international. *Entrance requirements:* Additional exam requirements/recommendations for international students: Required—TOEFL (minimum score 100 iBT). *Application deadline:* For fall admission, 12/1 for domestic students, 3/1 for international students. Applications are processed on a rolling basis. Application fee: $50. Electronic applications accepted. *Financial support:* Scholarships/grants available. *Application contact:* Dr. Maura Iverson, Director, 617-373-2708.

Northern Arizona University, Graduate College, College of Health and Human Services, Department of Physical Therapy, Flagstaff, AZ 86011. Offers DPT, PPDPT. *Accreditation:* APTA. *Faculty:* 14 full-time (9 women). *Students:* 143 full-time (98 women), 3 part-time (2 women); includes 20 minority (4 African Americans, 4 American Indian/Alaska Native, 4 Asian Americans or Pacific Islanders, 8 Hispanic Americans). Average age 30. 502 applicants, 12% accepted, 52 enrolled. In 2009, 41 doctorates awarded. *Entrance requirements:* Additional exam requirements/recommendations for international students: Required—TOEFL (minimum score 550 paper-based; 213 computer-based; 80 iBT), IELTS (minimum score 7), or a bachelor's degree from an English-speaking university and demonstrated proficiency. *Application deadline:* For fall admission, 11/3 priority date for domestic students, 9/1 priority date for international students. Applications are processed on a rolling basis. Application fee: $65. Electronic applications accepted. *Expenses:* Contact institution. *Financial support:* Teaching assistantships, career-related internships or fieldwork, Federal Work-Study, tuition waivers, and unspecified assistantships available. Financial award application deadline: 3/30. *Unit head:* Dr. Mark Cornwall, Chair, 928-523-1606, Fax: 928-523-0148, E-mail: mark.cornwall@nau.edu. *Application contact:* Dr. Mark Cornwall, Chair, 928-523-1606, Fax: 928-523-0148, E-mail: mark.cornwall@nau.edu.

Northern Illinois University, Graduate School, College of Health and Human Sciences, School of Allied Health and Communicative Disorders, Program in Physical Therapy, De Kalb, IL 60115-2854. Offers physical therapy (MPT). Admission to MPT program as undergraduate only. *Accreditation:* APTA; CEPH. Part-time programs available. *Faculty:* 9 full-time (6 women). *Students:* 36 full-time (20 women), 2 part-time (both women); includes 4 minority (1 African American, 1 Asian American or Pacific Islander, 2 Hispanic Americans), 1 international. Average age 27. 125 applicants, 39% accepted, 17 enrolled. In 2009, 29 master's awarded. *Degree requirements:* For master's, comprehensive exam, thesis optional, internship, research paper in public health. *Entrance requirements:* For master's, GRE General Test, minimum GPA of 2.75. Additional exam requirements/recommendations for international students: Required—TOEFL (minimum score 550 paper-based; 213 computer-based). *Application deadline:* For fall admission, 6/1 for domestic students, 5/1 for international students; for spring admission, 11/1 for domestic students, 10/1 for international students. Applications are processed on a rolling basis. Application fee: $30. Electronic applications accepted. *Expenses:* Tuition, state resident: full-time $6576; part-time $274 per credit hour. Tuition, nonresident: full-time $13,152; part-time $548 per credit hour. Required fees: $1813; $75.53 per credit hour. Part-time tuition and fees vary according to course load. *Financial support:* In 2009–10, 30 research assistantships with full tuition reimbursements were awarded; fellowships with full tuition reimbursements, teaching assistantships with full tuition reimbursements, career-related internships or fieldwork, Federal Work-Study, scholarships/grants, tuition waivers (full), and unspecified assistantships also available. Support available to part-time students. Financial award applicants required to submit FAFSA. *Faculty research:* Stroke rehabilitation, radon exposure prevention, environmental causes of cancer, body image in young girls. *Unit head:* Dr. Sue Ouellette, Interim Chair, 815-753-1486, Fax: 815-753-0720, E-mail: soupllette@niu.edu. *Application contact:* Graduate School Office, 815-753-0395, E-mail: gradsch@niu.edu.

North Georgia College & State University, Graduate Studies, Department of Physical Therapy, Dahlonega, GA 30597. Offers DPT. *Accreditation:* APTA. *Entrance requirements:* For doctorate, interview. Electronic applications accepted. *Faculty research:* Ergonomics, spinal mobility measurements, electrophysiology, orthopedic physical therapy.

Northwestern University, Northwestern University Feinberg School of Medicine, Department of Physical Therapy and Human Movement Sciences, Chicago, IL 60611-2814. Offers movement and rehabilitation science (PhD); physical therapy (DPT). *Accreditation:* APTA. *Faculty:* 22 full-time (13 women), 4 part-time/adjunct (3 women). *Students:* 209 full-time (172 women); includes 16 minority (7 African Americans, 5 Asian Americans or Pacific Islanders, 4 Hispanic Americans). Average age 24. 375 applicants, 42% accepted, 64 enrolled. *Degree requirements:* For doctorate, synthesis project. *Entrance requirements:* Additional exam requirements/recommendations for international students: Required—TOEFL (minimum score 265 computer-based). *Application deadline:* For fall admission, 10/15 for domestic students. Applications are processed on a rolling basis. Application fee: $40. Electronic applications accepted. *Expenses:* Contact institution. *Financial support:* In 2009–10, 184 students received support. Federal Work-Study, institutionally sponsored loans, and scholarships/grants available. Financial award application deadline: 2/15; financial award applicants required to submit FAFSA. *Faculty research:* Neuromuscular control, student performance (academic/professional), clinical outcomes, human performance. Total annual research expenditures: $2.8 million. *Unit head:* Dr. Julius P. A. Dewald, Associate Professor and Chair, 312-908-6788, Fax: 312-908-0741, E-mail: j-dewald@northwestern.edu. *Application contact:* Dr. Jane Sullivan, Assistant Professor and Assistant Chair for Recruitment and Admissions, 312-908-6789, Fax: 312-908-0741, E-mail: j-sullivan@northwestern.edu.

Nova Southeastern University, Health Professions Division, College of Allied Health and Nursing, Department of Physical Therapy, Fort Lauderdale, FL 33314-7796. Offers DPT, PhD, TDPT. *Accreditation:* APTA. Part-time programs available. Postbaccalaureate distance learning degree programs offered (minimal on-campus study). *Faculty:* 13 full-time (9 women), 9 part-time/adjunct (5 women). *Students:* 146 full-time (106 women), 157 part-time (101 women); includes 85 minority (32 African Americans, 1 American Indian/Alaska Native, 21 Asian Americans or Pacific Islanders, 31 Hispanic Americans), 2 international. Average age 25. 121 applicants, 37% accepted, 45 enrolled. In 2009, 95 doctorates awarded. *Degree requirements:* For doctorate, comprehensive exam, thesis/dissertation. *Entrance requirements:* For doctorate, GRE General Test. Additional exam requirements/recommendations for international students: Required—TOEFL. *Application deadline:* For spring admission, 2/1 priority date for domestic students. Applications are processed on a rolling basis. Application fee: $50. *Expenses:* Contact institution. *Faculty research:* Therapeutic exercise. *Unit head:* Dr. Stanley H. Wilson, Associate Professor and Chair, 954-262-1266, Fax: 954-262-1783, E-mail: swilson@nsu.nova.edu. *Application contact:* Corinne Kessler, Admissions Counselor, 954-262-1110, Fax: 954-262-2282, E-mail: kcorinne@nsu.nova.edu.

Oakland University, Graduate Study and Lifelong Learning, School of Health Sciences, Program in Physical Therapy, Rochester, MI 48309-4401. Offers neurological rehabilitation (Certificate); orthopedic manual physical therapy (Certificate); orthopedic physical therapy (Certificate); pediatric rehabilitation (Certificate); physical therapy (MSPT, DPT, Dr Sc PT); teaching and learning for rehabilitation professionals (Certificate). *Accreditation:* APTA. *Degree requirements:* For master's, thesis (for some programs). *Entrance requirements:* For master's, acceptance in the 2-year preparatory post-baccalaureate program, minimum GPA of 3.0; for doctorate, GRE General Test. Additional exam requirements/recommendations for international students: Required—TOEFL (minimum score 550 paper-based; 213 computer-based). *Expenses:* Contact institution.

The Ohio State University, College of Medicine, School of Allied Medical Professions, Program in Physical Therapy, Columbus, OH 43210. Offers MPT. *Accreditation:* APTA. *Entrance requirements:* For master's, GRE General Test. Additional exam requirements/recommendations for international students: Required—TOEFL (paper-based 550; computer-based 213) or Michigan English Language Assessment Battery (82). Electronic applications accepted. *Expenses:* Tuition, state resident: full-time $10,683. Tuition, nonresident: full-time $25,923. Tuition and fees vary according to course load and program.

Ohio University, Graduate College, College of Health and Human Services, School of Physical Therapy, Athens, OH 45701-2979. Offers DPT. *Accreditation:* APTA. *Faculty:* 6 full-time (2 women), 1 (woman) part-time/adjunct. *Students:* 106 full-time (69 women), 6 part-time (2 women); includes 9 minority (2 African Americans, 2 American Indian/Alaska Native, 3 Asian Americans or Pacific Islanders, 2 Hispanic Americans). In 2009, 28 doctorates awarded. *Entrance requirements:* For doctorate, GRE. Additional exam requirements/recommendations for international students: Required—TOEFL (minimum score 550 paper-based; 80 iBT) or IELTS Academic (minimum score 6.5). Application fee: $50 ($55 for international students). Electronic applications accepted. *Expenses:* Tuition, state resident: full-time $7839; part-time $323 per quarter hour. Tuition, nonresident: full-time $15,831; part-time $654 per quarter hour. Required fees: $2931. *Financial support:* In 2009–10, 26 students received support; research assistantships with full tuition reimbursements available, teaching assistantships with full tuition reimbursements available, Federal Work-Study, institutionally sponsored loans, scholarships/grants, tuition waivers (full), and unspecified assistantships available. *Faculty research:* Motor control, muscle architecture, postural control, morphonetrics, sensory integration. *Unit head:* Dr. Averell S. Overby, Director, 740-593-1224, Fax: 740-593-0292, E-mail: overby@ohio.edu. *Application contact:* Janice Carnahan, Administrative Associate, 740-593-1224, Fax: 740-593-0292, E-mail: carnahan@ohio.edu.

Old Dominion University, College of Health Sciences, School of Physical Therapy, Norfolk, VA 23529. Offers DPT. *Accreditation:* APTA. *Faculty:* 9 full-time (6 women), 6 part-time/adjunct (4 women). *Students:* 126 full-time (97 women), 2 part-time (both women); includes 20 minority (10 African Americans, 5 Asian Americans or Pacific Islanders, 5 Hispanic Americans). Average age 24. 400 applicants, 20% accepted, 45 enrolled. In 2009, 38 doctorates awarded. *Degree requirements:* For doctorate, comprehensive exam, clinical internships. *Entrance requirements:* For doctorate, GRE, 3 letters of recommendation (1 of which is from a physical therapist); 80 hours of volunteer experience. Additional exam requirements/recommendations for international students: Required—TOEFL. *Application deadline:* For fall admission, 11/1 for domestic and international students. Application fee: $50. Electronic applications accepted. *Expenses:* Contact institution. *Financial support:* In 2009–10, 4 students received support, including 1 fellowship (averaging $15,000 per year), 4 teaching assistantships with partial tuition reimbursements available (averaging $7,500 per year); career-related internships or fieldwork and unspecified assistantships also available. Financial award applicants required to submit FAFSA. *Faculty research:* Virtual reality and rehabilitation, rehabilitation for amputees, electromyography, biomechanics, gait and balance. Total annual research expenditures: $103,022. *Unit head:* Dr. Martha Walker, Graduate Program Director, 757-683-4519, Fax: 757-683-4410, E-mail: ptgpd@odu.edu. *Application contact:* Dr. Martha Walker, Graduate Program Director, 757-683-4519, Fax: 757-683-4410, E-mail: ptgpd@odu.edu.

Pacific University, School of Physical Therapy, Forest Grove, OR 97116-1797. Offers entry level (DPT); post-professional (DPT). *Accreditation:* APTA. *Degree requirements:* For doctorate, evidence-based capstone project thesis. *Entrance requirements:* For doctorate, 100 hours of volunteer/observational hours, minimum cumulative GPA of 3.0, prerequisite courses with a C grade or better, minimum GPA of 2.5 in science/statistics. Additional exam requirements/recommendations for international students: Required—TOEFL (minimum score 600 paper-based; 250 computer-based). Electronic applications accepted. *Expenses:* Contact institution. *Faculty research:* Balance disorders, geriatrics, orthopedic treatment outcomes, obesity, women's health.

Queen's University at Kingston, School of Graduate Studies and Research, Faculty of Health Sciences, School of Rehabilitation Therapy, Kingston, ON K7L 3N6, Canada. Offers occupational therapy (M Sc OT); physical therapy (M Sc PT); rehabilitation science (M Sc, PhD). Part-time programs available. *Degree requirements:* For master's, thesis; for doctorate, comprehensive exam, thesis/dissertation. *Entrance requirements:* Additional exam requirements/recommendations for international students: Required—TOEFL. *Faculty research:* Disability, community, motor performance, rehabilitation, treatment efficiency.

Quinnipiac University, School of Health Sciences, Program in Physical Therapy, Hamden, CT 06518-1940. Offers MPT, DPT. 6½-year program, students are admitted as undergraduates. *Accreditation:* APTA. *Faculty:* 13 full-time (11 women), 8 part-time/adjunct (2 women). *Students:* 178 full-time (133 women); includes 8 minority (4 Asian Americans or Pacific Islanders, 4

Hispanic Americans), 1 international. 57 applicants, 100% accepted, 57 enrolled. In 2009, 20 master's, 19 doctorates awarded. *Degree requirements:* For doctorate, capstone research project. *Entrance requirements:* For doctorate, BS in health science studies with minor in biology. *Expenses:* Tuition: Full-time $16,030; part-time $770 per credit. Required fees: $630; $35 per credit. *Financial support:* Scholarships/grants, tuition waivers (partial), and unspecified assistantships available. Financial award application deadline: 4/15; financial award applicants required to submit FAFSA. *Unit head:* Donald Kowalsky, Chairperson, 203-582-8681, E-mail: donald.kowalsky@quinnipiac.edu. *Application contact:* 800-462-1944, Fax: 203-582-8901, E-mail: admission@quinnipiac.edu.

Regis University, Rueckert-Hartman School for Health Professions, Denver, CO 80221-1099. Offers clinical leadership for physician assistants (MS); family nurse practitioner (MSN); health informatics (Postbaccalaureate Certificate); health services administration (MS); healthcare education (Certificate); leadership in healthcare systems (MSN); neonatal nurse practitioner (MSN); nursing (MSN); pharmacy (Pharm D); physical therapy (DPT, TDPT). *Entrance requirements:* Additional exam requirements/recommendations for international students: Required—TOEFL (minimum score 550 paper-based; 213 computer-based; 82 iBT). Electronic applications accepted. *Expenses:* Contact institution. *Faculty research:* Normal and pathological balance and gait research, normal/pathological upper limb motor control/biomechanics, exercise energy/metabolism research, optical treatment protocols for therapeutic modalities.

The Richard Stockton College of New Jersey, School of Graduate and Continuing Education, Program in Physical Therapy, Pomona, NJ 08240-0195. Offers DPT. *Accreditation:* APTA. *Entrance requirements:* Additional exam requirements/recommendations for international students: Required—TOEFL. *Expenses:* Tuition, state resident: part-time $497.36 per credit hour. Tuition, nonresident: part-time $765.61 per credit hour. Required fees: $129.12 per credit hour. Tuition and fees vary according to degree level. *Faculty research:* Spinal flexibility in the well elderly, use of traditional Chinese medicine concepts in physical therapy, computerized vs. traditional study in human gross anatomy.

Rockhurst University, School of Graduate and Professional Studies, Program in Physical Therapy, Kansas City, MO 64110-2561. Offers DPT. *Accreditation:* APTA. *Faculty:* 10 full-time (5 women), 13 part-time/adjunct (10 women). *Students:* 132 full-time (92 women); includes 9 minority (2 Asian Americans or Pacific Islanders, 7 Hispanic Americans). Average age 25. 410 applicants, 21% accepted, 50 enrolled. In 2009, 39 doctorates awarded. *Entrance requirements:* For doctorate, 3 letters of recommendation, interview, minimum GPA of 3.0, physical therapy experience. Additional exam requirements/recommendations for international students: Required—TOEFL (minimum score 550 paper-based; 213 computer-based; 79 iBT). *Application deadline:* Applications are processed on a rolling basis. Application fee: $25. Electronic applications accepted. *Financial support:* In 2009–10, 5 research assistantships, 10 teaching assistantships were awarded; career-related internships or fieldwork, institutionally sponsored loans, and unspecified assistantships also available. Financial award application deadline: 4/1; financial award applicants required to submit FAFSA. *Faculty research:* Clinical decision making, geriatrics, balance in persons with neurological disorders, physical rehabilitation following total joint replacement, clinical education. *Unit head:* Dr. Brian McKiernan, Chair, 816-501-4059, Fax: 816-501-4169, E-mail: brian.mckiernan@rockhurst.edu. *Application contact:* Cheryl Hooper, Director of Graduate Admission, 816-501-4097, Fax: 816-501-4241, E-mail: cheryl.hooper@rockhurst.edu.

Rosalind Franklin University of Medicine and Science, College of Health Professions, Department of Physical Therapy, North Chicago, IL 60064-3095. Offers MS, DPT, TDPT. *Accreditation:* APTA. Postbaccalaureate distance learning degree programs offered (minimal on-campus study). *Faculty:* 7 full-time (6 women), 4 part-time/adjunct (3 women). *Students:* 112 full-time (85 women), 25 part-time (24 women); includes 19 minority (3 African Americans, 2 American Indian/Alaska Native, 9 Asian Americans or Pacific Islanders, 5 Hispanic Americans), 3 international. 436 applicants, 20% accepted, 40 enrolled. *Degree requirements:* For master's, thesis. *Entrance requirements:* For master's, physical therapy license. Additional exam requirements/recommendations for international students: Required—TOEFL. *Application deadline:* For fall admission, 10/15 for domestic students; for winter admission, 12/1 for domestic students. Applications are processed on a rolling basis. Application fee: $50. *Financial support:* Federal Work-Study available. Financial award application deadline: 2/1; financial award applicants required to submit FAFSA. *Faculty research:* Clinical research, development/analysis of tests, measures, education. *Unit head:* Dr. Roberta J. Henderson, Chair, 847-578-3307, Fax: 847-578-8816, E-mail: roberta.henderson@rosalindfranklin.edu. *Application contact:* Melissa Knox, Admissions Officer, 847-578-8772, Fax: 847-775-6559, E-mail: melissa.knox@rosalindfranklin.edu.

Rutgers, The State University of New Jersey, Camden, Graduate School of Arts and Sciences, Program in Physical Therapy, Camden, NJ 08102-1401. Offers DPT. *Accreditation:* APTA. *Entrance requirements:* For doctorate, GRE, physical therapy experience, 3 letters of recommendation, resume. Additional exam requirements/recommendations for international students: Required—TOEFL, IELTS. Electronic applications accepted. *Faculty research:* Clinical education, migrant workers, biomechanical constraints on motor control, high intensity strength training and the elderly, posture and ergonomics.

Sacred Heart University, Graduate Programs, College of Education and Health Professions, Department of Physical Therapy and Human Movement and Sports Science, Fairfield, CT 06825-1000. Offers exercise science and nutrition (MS); physical therapy (DPT). *Accreditation:* APTA. *Faculty:* 9 full-time (5 women). *Students:* 146 full-time (95 women); includes 17 minority (4 African Americans, 1 American Indian/Alaska Native, 7 Asian Americans or Pacific Islanders, 5 Hispanic Americans), 2 international. Average age 25. 205 applicants, 58% accepted, 63 enrolled. *Entrance requirements:* Additional exam requirements/recommendations for international students: Required—TOEFL (minimum score 550 paper-based; 213 computer-based). *Application deadline:* For fall admission, 1/15 priority date for domestic students. Applications are processed on a rolling basis. Application fee: $50 ($100 for international students). Electronic applications accepted. *Expenses:* Contact institution. *Financial support:* Career-related internships or fieldwork, institutionally sponsored loans, and unspecified assistantships available. Support available to part-time students. Financial award applicants required to submit FAFSA. *Unit head:* Dr. Michael Emery, Director, 203-365-7656. *Application contact:* Kathy Dilks, Assistant Dean of Graduate Admissions, Health Professions, 203-396-8259, Fax: 203-365-4732, E-mail: gradstudies@sacredheart.edu.

Sage Graduate School, Graduate School, School of Health Sciences, Program in Physical Therapy, Troy, NY 12180-4115. Offers DPT. *Accreditation:* APTA. *Faculty:* 11 full-time (10 women), 10 part-time/adjunct (9 women). *Students:* 87 full-time (66 women), 21 part-time (18 women); includes 9 minority (3 African Americans, 5 Asian Americans or Pacific Islanders, 1 Hispanic American), 1 international. Average age 27. 7 applicants, 100% accepted, 7 enrolled. In 2009, 40 doctorates awarded. *Entrance requirements:* For doctorate, current resume; 2 letters of recommendation; minimum GPA of 3.0 overall and in science prerequisites; completion of 40 hours of physical therapy observation. Additional exam requirements/recommendations for international students: Required—TOEFL (minimum score 550 paper-based; 213 computer-based). *Application deadline:* Applications are processed on a rolling basis. Application fee: $40. *Expenses:* Tuition: Full-time $10,620; part-time $590 per credit hour. *Financial support:* Federal Work-Study, scholarships/grants, and unspecified assistantships available. Support available to part-time students. Financial award application deadline: 3/1; financial award applicants required to submit FAFSA. *Unit head:* Marjane Selleck, Chair, 518-244-2060. *Application contact:* Wendy D. Diefendorf, Director of Graduate and Adult Admission, 518-244-2443, Fax: 518-244-6880, E-mail: diefew@sage.edu.

St. Ambrose University, College of Education and Health Sciences, Department of Physical Therapy, Davenport, IA 52803-2898. Offers DPT. *Accreditation:* APTA. *Faculty:* 10 full-time (5 women). *Students:* 78 full-time (63 women), 23 part-time (14 women). Average age 31. 284 applicants, 15% accepted, 42 enrolled. In 2009, 61 doctorates awarded. *Degree requirements:* For doctorate, board exams. *Entrance requirements:* For doctorate, GRE, interview. Additional exam requirements/recommendations for international students: Required—TOEFL. *Application*

deadline: For fall admission, 1/15 priority date for domestic students. Application fee: $25. *Expenses:* Tuition: Part-time $702 per credit hour. Tuition and fees vary according to degree level, program and reciprocity agreements. *Financial support:* In 2009–10, 69 students received support, including 8 research assistantships with partial tuition reimbursements available (averaging $3,600 per year); career-related internships or fieldwork, scholarships/grants, tuition waivers (partial), and unspecified assistantships also available. Financial award application deadline: 3/15; financial award applicants required to submit FAFSA. *Faculty research:* Human motor control, orthopedic physical therapy, cardiopulmonary physical therapy, kinesiology/biomechanics. *Unit head:* Dr. Sandra L. Cassady, Director, 563-333-6409, Fax: 563-333-6410, E-mail: cassadysandral@sau.edu. *Application contact:* Carrie Meador-Bliss, Office Administrator, 563-333-6401, Fax: 563-333-6410, E-mail: meador-blisscarrie@sau.edu.

St. Catherine University, Graduate Programs, Program in Physical Therapy, St. Paul, MN 55105. Offers DPT. Offered at Minneapolis campus only. *Accreditation:* APTA. *Faculty:* 9 full-time (6 women). *Students:* 15 full-time (0 women), 82 part-time (0 women); includes 3 minority (2 Asian Americans or Pacific Islanders, 1 Hispanic American), 1 international. Average age 27. 160 applicants, 38% accepted, 25 enrolled. In 2009, 38 doctorates awarded. *Degree requirements:* For doctorate, research project. *Entrance requirements:* For doctorate, GRE, minimum GPA of 3.0, coursework in biology/zoology, anatomy, physiology, chemistry, physics, psychology, statistics, mathematics and medical terminology. Additional exam requirements/recommendations for international students: Required—Michigan English Language Assessment Battery or TOEFL (minimum score 600 paper-based; 250 computer-based; 100 iBT). *Application deadline:* For fall admission, 1/20 priority date for domestic students. Application fee: $35. *Expenses:* Contact institution. *Financial support:* In 2009–10, 80 students received support. Institutionally sponsored loans available. Financial award application deadline: 4/1; financial award applicants required to submit FAFSA. *Unit head:* Cort Cieminski, Director, 651-690-7825, Fax: 651-690-7876. *Application contact:* 651-690-7800, Fax: 651-690-6064.

Saint Francis University, Department of Physical Therapy, Loretto, PA 15940-0600. Offers DPT. *Accreditation:* APTA. *Faculty:* 7 full-time (3 women), 10 part-time/adjunct (4 women). *Students:* 108 full-time (73 women); includes 1 African American. Average age 23. 50 applicants, 38% accepted, 8 enrolled. *Entrance requirements:* Additional exam requirements/recommendations for international students: Required—TOEFL. *Application deadline:* For winter admission, 1/15 for domestic and international students. Application fee: $30. Electronic applications accepted. *Expenses:* Tuition: Part-time $765 per credit. Part-time tuition and fees vary according to course load and program. *Financial support:* In 2009–10, 8 students received support, including 8 teaching assistantships with partial tuition reimbursements available; unspecified assistantships also available. *Faculty research:* Childhood obesity, athletic performance, energy expenditure, sports injuries. *Unit head:* Dr. Kay Malek, Department Chair/Assistant Professor, 814-472-3123, Fax: 814-472-3140, E-mail: kmalek@francis.edu. *Application contact:* Dr. Kay Malek, Department Chair/Assistant Professor, 814-472-3123, Fax: 814-472-3140, E-mail: kmalek@francis.edu.

Saint Louis University, Graduate School, Doisy College of Health Sciences, Department of Physical Therapy, St. Louis, MO 63103-2097. Offers athletic training (MAT); physical therapy (DPT). *Accreditation:* APTA. Part-time programs available. *Entrance requirements:* Additional exam requirements/recommendations for international students: Required—TOEFL (minimum score 525 paper-based; 194 computer-based; 55 iBT). Electronic applications accepted. *Faculty research:* Patellofemoral pain and associated risk factors; prevalence of disordered eating in physical therapy students; effects of selected interventions for children with cerebral palsy on gait and posture: hippotherapy, ankle strengthening, supported treadmill training, spirituality in physical therapy/patient care, risk factors for exercise-related leg pain in running athletes.

Samuel Merritt University, Department of Physical Therapy, Oakland, CA 94609-3108. Offers DPT. *Accreditation:* APTA. *Entrance requirements:* Additional exam requirements/recommendations for international students: Required—TOEFL. *Expenses:* Contact institution. *Faculty research:* Human movement, motor control, falls prevention in the elderly.

San Francisco State University, Division of Graduate Studies, College of Health and Human Services, Program in Physical Therapy, San Francisco, CA 94132-1722. Offers MS, DPT, Dr Sc PT.

Seton Hall University, School of Health and Medical Sciences, Program in Physical Therapy, South Orange, NJ 07079-2697. Offers professional physical therapy (DPT). *Accreditation:* APTA. *Degree requirements:* For doctorate, research project. *Entrance requirements:* Additional exam requirements/recommendations for international students: Required—TOEFL. Electronic applications accepted. *Faculty research:* Electrical stimulation, motor learning, backpacks, gait and balance, orthopedic injury, women's health, pediatric obesity.

Shenandoah University, School of Health Professions, Division of Physical Therapy, Winchester, VA 22601-5195. Offers physical therapy and non-traditional physical therapy (DPT). *Accreditation:* APTA. Part-time programs available. Postbaccalaureate distance learning degree programs offered. *Faculty:* 7 full-time (4 women), 5 part-time/adjunct (2 women). *Students:* 115 full-time (85 women), 125 part-time (96 women); includes 20 minority (4 African Americans, 7 Asian Americans or Pacific Islanders, 9 Hispanic Americans), 5 international. Average age 34. 483 applicants, 32% accepted, 109 enrolled. In 2009, 84 doctorates awarded. *Entrance requirements:* For doctorate, GRE General Test, minimum GPA of 2.8, 3 letters of recommendation, 100 hours of clinical experience (2 places). Additional exam requirements/recommendations for international students: Required—TOEFL (minimum score 550 paper-based; 213 computer-based; 79 iBT), IELTS (minimum score 6.5). *Application deadline:* For fall admission, 7/31 for domestic students; for spring admission, 5/15 for domestic students. Applications are processed on a rolling basis. Application fee: $30. Electronic applications accepted. *Expenses:* Contact institution. *Financial support:* Application deadline: 3/15. *Unit head:* Dr. Karen Abraham-Justice, Director, 540-665-5520, Fax: 540-545-7387, E-mail: kabraham@su.edu. *Application contact:* David Anthony, Dean of Admissions, 540-665-4581, Fax: 540-665-4627, E-mail: admit@su.edu.

Simmons College, School of Health Sciences, Program in Physical Therapy, Boston, MA 02115. Offers DPT. *Accreditation:* APTA. *Faculty:* 11 full-time (7 women), 30 part-time/adjunct (26 women). *Students:* 45 full-time (39 women), 98 part-time (84 women); includes 8 minority (1 African American, 5 Asian Americans or Pacific Islanders, 2 Hispanic Americans), 3 international. Average age 22. 113 applicants, 78% accepted, 53 enrolled. In 2009, 58 doctorates awarded. *Degree requirements:* For doctorate, 30 volunteer hours at clinic. *Entrance requirements:* For doctorate, GRE, courses in biology, chemistry, exercise physiology, physics, psychology, statistics, anatomy, and physiology; paid or volunteer healthcare experience for at least 30 hours. Additional exam requirements/recommendations for international students: Required—TOEFL (minimum score 570 paper-based; 230 computer-based; 88 iBT). *Application deadline:* For fall admission, 6/1 for domestic and international students; for winter admission, 12/1 for domestic and international students; for spring admission, 3/1 for domestic and international students. Applications are processed on a rolling basis. Application fee: $100. Electronic applications accepted. *Expenses:* Contact institution. *Financial support:* Teaching assistantships available. Financial award application deadline: 3/1; financial award applicants required to submit FAFSA. *Unit head:* Dr. Z. Annette Iglarsh, Department Chair. *Application contact:* Carmen Fortin, Assistant Dean/Director of Admission, School of Health Sciences, 617-521-2654, E-mail: shs@simmons.edu.

Slippery Rock University of Pennsylvania, Graduate Studies (Recruitment), College of Health, Environment, and Science, School of Physical Therapy, Slippery Rock, PA 16057-1383. Offers DPT. *Accreditation:* APTA. *Degree requirements:* For doctorate, comprehensive exam (for some programs), thesis/dissertation (for some programs), clinical residency. *Entrance requirements:* For doctorate, GRE General Test, minimum GPA of 2.75. Additional exam requirements/recommendations for international students: Required—TOEFL (minimum score 550 paper-based; 213 computer-based). *Application deadline:* For fall admission, 11/1 priority date for domestic and international students. Applications are processed on a rolling basis. Application fee: $35. Electronic applications accepted. *Expenses:* Contact institution. *Financial*

Physical Therapy

Slippery Rock University of Pennsylvania (continued)
support: Career-related internships or fieldwork, Federal Work-Study, scholarships/grants, and unspecified assistantships available. Financial award application deadline: 5/1; financial award applicants required to submit FAFSA. Unit head: Dr. Carol Martin-Elkins, Graduate Coordinator, 724-738-2916, Fax: 724-738-2113, E-mail: carol.martin-elkins@sru.edu. Application contact: Angela Piverotto, Interim Director of Graduate Studies, 724-738-2051, Fax: 724-738-2146, E-mail: graduate.admissions@sru.edu.

Southwest Baptist University, Program in Physical Therapy, Bolivar, MO 65613-2597. Offers DPT. Accreditation: APTA. Degree requirements: For doctorate, comprehensive exam, 3-4 clinical education experiences. Entrance requirements: Additional exam requirements/recommendations for international students: Required—TOEFL (minimum score 550 paper-based; 213 computer-based). Expenses: Contact institution. Faculty research: Balance and falls prevention, distance and web based learning, foot and ankle intervention, pediatrics, musculoskeletal management.

Springfield College, Graduate Programs, Program in Physical Therapy, Springfield, MA 01109-3797. Offers DPT. Accreditation: APTA. Part-time programs available. Degree requirements: For doctorate, comprehensive exam, thesis/dissertation, research project. Entrance requirements: For doctorate, GRE General Test, prerequisite courses. Additional exam requirements/recommendations for international students: Required—TOEFL (minimum score 550 paper-based; 213 computer-based). Electronic applications accepted. Expenses: Tuition: Full-time $19,800; part-time $825 per credit hour. Required fees: $150.

State University of New York Upstate Medical University, Department of Physical Therapy, Syracuse, NY 13210-2334. Offers DPT. Accreditation: APTA. Part-time and evening/weekend programs available. Postbaccalaureate distance learning degree programs offered (minimal on-campus study). Faculty: 12 full-time (7 women), 6 part-time/adjunct (3 women). Students: 94 full-time (72 women), 45 part-time (28 women); includes 18 minority (3 African Americans, 14 Asian Americans or Pacific Islanders, 1 Hispanic American), 2 international. Average age 30. 206 applicants, 31% accepted, 42 enrolled. In 2009, 73 doctorates awarded. Application deadline: For fall admission, 2/1 for domestic students. Applications are processed on a rolling basis. Application fee: $50. Electronic applications accepted. Financial support: In 2009–10, 84 students received support. Federal Work-Study and scholarships/grants available. Support available to part-time students. Financial award application deadline: 3/1; financial award applicants required to submit FAFSA. Unit head: Dr. Susan Miller, Chair, 315-464-5101, Fax: 315-464-4608. Application contact: Donna Vavonese, Associate Director of Admissions, 315-464-4570, Fax: 315-464-8867, E-mail: vavonesd@upstate.edu.

Stony Brook University, State University of New York, Stony Brook University Medical Center, Health Sciences Center, School of Health Technology and Management, Stony Brook, NY 11794. Offers health care management (Advanced Certificate); health care policy and management (MS); occupational therapy (MS); physical therapy (DPT); physician assistant (MS). Accreditation: APTA. Part-time programs available. Faculty: 33 full-time (25 women), 25 part-time/adjunct (12 women). Students: 217 full-time (162 women), 130 part-time (93 women); includes 87 minority (21 African Americans, 1 American Indian/Alaska Native, 46 Asian Americans or Pacific Islanders, 19 Hispanic Americans), 8 international. 54 applicants, 91% accepted. In 2009, 89 master's, 77 doctorates, 15 other advanced degrees awarded. Degree requirements: For master's, thesis. Entrance requirements: For master's, GRE General Test, minimum GPA of 3.0, work experience in field. Application deadline: For fall admission, 1/15 for domestic students. Application fee: $60. Expenses: Tuition, state resident: full-time $8370; part-time $349 per credit. Tuition, nonresident: full-time $13,250; part-time $552 per credit. Required fees: $933. Financial support: In 2009–10, 2 research assistantships, 1 teaching assistantship were awarded; fellowships, career-related internships or fieldwork, Federal Work-Study, and institutionally sponsored loans also available. Financial award application deadline: 3/15. Faculty research: Health promotion and disease prevention. Total annual research expenditures: $842,937. Unit head: Dr. Craig A. Lehmann, Dean, 631-444-2251, Fax: 631-444-7621. Application contact: Richard W. Johnson, Associate Dean for Graduate Studies, 631-444-3251.

Temple University, Health Sciences Center and Graduate School, College of Health Professions, Department of Physical Therapy, Philadelphia, PA 19122-6096. Offers DPT, PhD. Accreditation: APTA (one or more programs are accredited). Part-time and evening/weekend programs available. Degree requirements: For doctorate, thesis/dissertation. Entrance requirements: For doctorate, GRE General Test, interview. Additional exam requirements/recommendations for international students: Required—TOEFL (minimum score 550 paper-based; 213 computer-based; 79 iBT). Electronic applications accepted. Faculty research: Balance dysfunction, biomechanics, development, qualitative research, developmental neuroscience, health services.

Tennessee State University, The School of Graduate Studies and Research, College of Health Sciences, Department of Physical Therapy, Nashville, TN 37209-1561. Offers MPT, DPT. Accreditation: APTA. Part-time programs available. Postbaccalaureate distance learning degree programs offered (minimal on-campus study). Degree requirements: For master's, comprehensive exam, thesis optional. Entrance requirements: For master's, GRE General Test, MAT. Electronic applications accepted. Faculty research: Evidence-based research clinical research case studies/reports qualitative research education assessment total knee anthroplasty; ergonomics; childhood obesity.

Texas State University–San Marcos, Graduate School, College of Health Professions, Department of Physical Therapy, San Marcos, TX 78666. Offers DPT. Applicants accepted in summer only. Accreditation: APTA. Faculty: 9 full-time (6 women), 4 part-time/adjunct (1 woman). Students: 80 full-time (48 women); includes 22 minority (1 African American, 1 American Indian/Alaska Native, 2 Asian Americans or Pacific Islanders, 18 Hispanic Americans), 1 international. Average age 26. 337 applicants, 22% accepted, 40 enrolled. Degree requirements: For doctorate, comprehensive exam. Entrance requirements: For doctorate, GRE General Test (minimum combined score of 1000 Verbal and Quantitative), bachelor's degree in physical therapy; minimum GPA of 3.0 on last 60 hours of undergraduate and science courses. Additional exam requirements/recommendations for international students: Required—TOEFL (minimum score 550 paper-based; 213 computer-based). Application deadline: For fall admission, 10/15 for domestic students. Applications are processed on a rolling basis. Application fee: $65 ($115 for international students). Electronic applications accepted. Expenses: Tuition, state resident: full-time $5784; part-time $241 per credit hour. Tuition, nonresident: full-time $13,224; part-time $551 per credit hour. Required fees: $1728; $48 per credit hour. $306. Tuition and fees vary according to course load. Financial support: In 2009–10, 78 students received support, including 9 teaching assistantships (averaging $1,739 per year); research assistantships, career-related internships or fieldwork, Federal Work-Study, and institutionally sponsored loans also available. Support available to part-time students. Financial award application deadline: 4/1; financial award applicants required to submit FAFSA. Unit head: Dr. Barbara Sanders, Chair, 512-245-8351, Fax: 512-245-8736, E-mail: bs04@txstate.edu. Application contact: Dr. J. Michael Willoughby, Dean of Graduate School, 512-245-2581, Fax: 512-245-8365, E-mail: gradcollege@txstate.edu.

Texas Tech University Health Sciences Center, School of Allied Health Sciences, Program in Physical Therapy, Lubbock, TX 79430. Offers MPT, DPT, Sc D. Accreditation: APTA. Faculty: 20 full-time (4 women). Students: 194 full-time (120 women), 64 part-time (32 women); includes 59 minority (9 African Americans, 20 Asian Americans or Pacific Islanders, 30 Hispanic Americans), 2 international. Average age 29. 307 applicants, 26% accepted, 81 enrolled. In 2009, 73 doctorates awarded. Entrance requirements: Additional exam requirements/recommendations for international students: Required—TOEFL, IELTS. Application deadline: For fall admission, 9/15 priority date for domestic students; for winter admission, 1/15 priority date for domestic students. Application fee: $35. Electronic applications accepted. Financial support: Career-related internships or fieldwork, institutionally sponsored loans, and scholarships/grants available. Financial award application deadline: 9/1; financial award applicants required

to submit FAFSA. Faculty research: Closed chain proprioception; effects of unloading; retrospective studies including ACL, hippotherapy, orthopedic/sports medicine injuries. Unit head: Dr. Steve Sawyer, Chair, 806-743-3226, Fax: 806-743-3249, E-mail: steve.sawyer@ttuhsc.edu. Application contact: Jeri Moravcik, Assistant Director of Admissions and Student Affairs, 806-743-3220, Fax: 806-743-2994, E-mail: jeri.moravcik@ttuhsc.edu.

Texas Woman's University, Graduate School, College of Health Sciences, School of Physical Therapy, Denton, TX 76201. Offers physical therapy (MS, DPT, PhD), including clinical level (MS), entry level (MS). Accreditation: APTA (one or more programs are accredited). Part-time and evening/weekend programs available. Faculty: 21 full-time (17 women), 3 part-time/adjunct (0 women). Students: 281 full-time (219 women), 87 part-time (71 women); includes 97 minority (28 African Americans, 1 American Indian/Alaska Native, 35 Asian Americans or Pacific Islanders, 33 Hispanic Americans), 10 international. Average age 27. 527 applicants, 97% accepted, 97 enrolled. In 2009, 1 master's, 25 doctorates awarded. Degree requirements: For master's, thesis; for doctorate, thesis/dissertation. Entrance requirements: For master's, GRE General Test, resume, 3 recommendations on department forms, licensure eligibility; for doctorate, interview, resume, eligibility for licensure, 2 letters of recommendation, essay. Additional exam requirements/recommendations for international students: Required—TOEFL (minimum score 550 paper-based; 213 computer-based; 79 iBT). Application deadline: For fall admission, 11/1 priority date for domestic and international students. Applications are processed on a rolling basis. Application fee: $50. Electronic applications accepted. Expenses: Tuition, state resident: full-time $3564; part-time $198 per credit hour. Tuition, nonresident: full-time $8550; part-time $475 per credit hour. Required fees: $69.26 per credit hour. Tuition and fees vary according to course load. Financial support: In 2009–10, 202 students received support, including 2 research assistantships (averaging $10,440 per year); career-related internships or fieldwork, Federal Work-Study, institutionally sponsored loans, scholarships/grants, traineeships, health care benefits, and unspecified assistantships also available. Support available to part-time students. Financial award application deadline: 3/1; financial award applicants required to submit FAFSA. Faculty research: Improving ambulation post stroke with robotic training, women's exercise injuries, rehabilitative ultrasound imaging biofeedback on urinary incontinence in women, walk tests in persons with amputations, multiple sclerosis aerobic exercises. Unit head: Dr. Sharon Olson, Director, 713-794-2070, Fax: 713-794-2361, E-mail: pt@twu.edu. Application contact: Samuel Wheeler, Assistant Director of Admissions, 940-898-3188, Fax: 940-898-3081, E-mail: wheelersr@twu.edu.

Thomas Jefferson University, Jefferson College of Health Professions, Program in Physical Therapy, Philadelphia, PA 19107. Offers MS, DPT. Accreditation: APTA. Degree requirements: For master's, thesis or alternative. Entrance requirements: For master's, minimum GPA of 3.0. Additional exam requirements/recommendations for international students: Required—TOEFL (minimum score 213 computer-based). Electronic applications accepted. Expenses: Contact institution. Faculty research: Gait and motion analysis, motor control and learning, single motor unit discharge in human muscle, musculoskeletal injuries, cancer rehabilitation.

Touro College, School of Health Sciences, Physical Therapy Program, New York, NY 10010. Offers MS, DPT. Accreditation: APTA. Degree requirements: For master's, thesis, community service project. Entrance requirements: For master's, interview, minimum GPA of 2.8, 100 hours of physical therapy work experience.

Touro University, Graduate Programs, Vallejo, CA 94592. Offers education (MA); osteopathic medicine (DO); pharmacy (Pharm D); physical therapy (DPT); physician assistant studies (MS); public health (MPH). Accreditation: AOsA; ARC-PA. Part-time and evening/weekend programs available. Faculty: 91 full-time (52 women), 51 part-time/adjunct (28 women). Students: 1,439 full-time (891 women). 6,914 applicants, 12% accepted, 503 enrolled. In 2009, 229 first professional degrees, 103 master's awarded. Degree requirements: For master's, comprehensive exam, thesis; for first professional degree, comprehensive exam. Entrance requirements: BS/BA. Application deadline: For fall admission, 3/15 for domestic students; for winter admission, 12/1 for domestic students. Applications are processed on a rolling basis. Application fee: $100. Electronic applications accepted. Financial support: In 2009–10, 1,236 students received support, including 119 fellowships (averaging $1,535 per year), 24 research assistantships (averaging $3,686 per year), 13 teaching assistantships (averaging $4,058 per year); Federal Work-Study and scholarships/grants also available. Support available to part-time students. Financial award applicants required to submit FAFSA. Faculty research: Cancer, heart disease. Application contact: Steve Davis, Associate Director of Admissions, 707-638-5270, Fax: 707-638-5250, E-mail: steven.davis@tu.edu.

Université de Montréal, Faculty of Medicine, Program in Specialized Studies, Montréal, QC H3C 3J7, Canada. Offers anesthesia (DES); diagnostic radiology (DES); family medicine (DES); gastroenterology (DES); geriatry (DES); intensive care (DES); medical biochemistry (DES); medical genetics (DES); medicine (DES); microbiology and infectious diseases (DES); nuclear medicine (DES); obstetrics and gynecology (DES); ophthalmology (DES); pediatrics (DES); pneumology (DES); psychiatry (DES); radiology-oncology (DES); rheumatology (DES); surgery (DES). Faculty: 154 full-time (40 women), 333 part-time/adjunct (100 women). Students: 930 full-time (580 women), 7 part-time (all women). 74 applicants, 77% accepted, 29 enrolled. Application deadline: For fall admission, 2/1 priority date for domestic students; for winter admission, 11/1 priority date for domestic students; for spring admission, 2/1 priority date for domestic students. Application fee: $100. Electronic applications accepted. Unit head: Lorraine Locas, Assistant to the Vice Dean of Graduate Studies, 514-343-6269, Fax: 514-343-5751, E-mail: lorraine.locas@umontreal.ca. Application contact: Dr. Andre Ferron, Vice Dean Graduate Studies, 514-343-6111 Ext. 0933, Fax: 514-343-5751, E-mail: andre.ferron@umontreal.ca.

University at Buffalo, the State University of New York, Graduate School, School of Public Health and Health Professions, Department of Rehabilitation Science, Program in Physical Therapy, Buffalo, NY 14260. Offers DPT. Accreditation: APTA. Faculty: 15 full-time (9 women), 5 part-time/adjunct (4 women). Students: 134 full-time (74 women); includes 23 minority (9 African Americans, 1 American Indian/Alaska Native, 11 Asian Americans or Pacific Islanders, 2 Hispanic Americans), 1 international. Average age 31. 94 applicants, 48% accepted. In 2009, 36 doctorates awarded. Entrance requirements: For doctorate, GRE. Additional exam requirements/recommendations for international students: Required—TOEFL (minimum score 79 iBT). Application deadline: For fall admission, 11/1 for domestic and international students. Application fee: $50. Electronic applications accepted. Financial support: Career-related internships or fieldwork and Federal Work-Study available. Faculty research: Biomechanics of gait and balance, balance retraining, electrotherapy for inflammation, physical therapy education outcomes. Unit head: Dr. Kirkwood Personious, Program Director, 716-829-6742, Fax: 716-829-3217, E-mail: kep7@buffalo.edu. Application contact: MaryAnne Venezia, Program Coordinator, 716-829-6742, Fax: 716-829-3217, E-mail: venezia3@buffalo.edu.

The University of Alabama at Birmingham, School of Health Professions, Program in Physical Therapy, Birmingham, AL 35294. Offers DPT. Accreditation: APTA. Electronic applications accepted. Faculty research: Geriatrics, exercise physiology, aquatic therapy, industrial rehabilitation, outcome measurement.

University of Alberta, Faculty of Graduate Studies and Research, Department of Physical Therapy, Edmonton, AB T6G 2E1, Canada. Offers M Sc, PhD. Part-time programs available. Faculty: 12 full-time (6 women). Students: 7 full-time (5 women), 6 part-time (4 women). Average age 28. 10 applicants, 50% accepted. In 2009, 2 master's awarded. Degree requirements: For master's, thesis. Entrance requirements: For master's, bachelor's degree in physical therapy, minimum GPA of 6.5 on a 9.0 scale. Additional exam requirements/recommendations for international students: Required—TOEFL. Application deadline: For fall admission, 3/1 for domestic and international students; for winter admission, 7/1 for domestic and international students. Applications are processed on a rolling basis. Application fee: $0. Electronic applications accepted. Tuition and fees charges are reported in Canadian dollars. Expenses: Tuition, area resident: Full-time $4626 Canadian dollars; part-time $99.72 Canadian dollars per unit. International tuition: $8216 Canadian dollars full-time. Required fees: $3590 Canadian dollars; $99.72 Canadian dollars per unit. $215 Canadian dollars per term. Financial support: In 2009–10, 2 research assistantships, 2 teaching assistantships were awarded;

scholarships/grants also available. Financial award application deadline: 1/1. *Faculty research:* Spinal disorders, musculoskeletal disorders, ergonomics, sports therapy, motor development, cardiac rehabilitation/therapeutic exercise. *Unit head:* Dr. J. Yang, Graduate Program Coordinator, 780-492-1595, Fax: 780-492-1626. *Application contact:* Angela Libutti, Administrative Assistant, Graduate Studies, 780-492-1595, Fax: 780-492-1626, E-mail: mscpt.info@rehabmed.ualberta.ca.

University of California, San Francisco, Graduate Division, Program in Physical Therapy, San Francisco, CA 94143. Offers MS, DPT, DPTSc. *Accreditation:* APTA. *Entrance requirements:* For master's, GRE General Test.

University of Central Arkansas, Graduate School, College of Health and Behavioral Sciences, Department of Physical Therapy, Conway, AR 72035-0001. Offers DPT, PhD. *Accreditation:* APTA. *Faculty:* 17 full-time (10 women). *Students:* 166 full-time (108 women); includes 10 minority (4 African Americans, 3 Asian Americans or Pacific Islanders, 3 Hispanic Americans). Average age 24. 73 applicants, 78% accepted, 56 enrolled. In 2009, 44 doctorates awarded. *Degree requirements:* For doctorate, comprehensive exam, thesis/dissertation. *Entrance requirements:* Additional exam requirements/recommendations for international students: Required—TOEFL (minimum score 550 paper-based; 213 computer-based). *Application deadline:* For fall admission, 3/1 priority date for domestic students; for spring admission, 10/1 for domestic students. Applications are processed on a rolling basis. Application fee: $25 ($50 for international students). *Expenses:* Contact institution. *Financial support:* In 2009–10, 4 research assistantships with partial tuition reimbursements (averaging $6,000 per year) were awarded; Federal Work-Study, scholarships/grants, and unspecified assistantships also available. Financial award application deadline: 2/15; financial award applicants required to submit FAFSA. *Unit head:* Dr. Nancy Reese, Chairperson, 501-450-3611, Fax: 501-450-5822, E-mail: nancyr@uca.edu. *Application contact:* Patti Hornor, Administrative Assistant, 501-450-5063, Fax: 501-450-5678, E-mail: pattih@uca.edu.

University of Central Florida, College of Health and Public Affairs, Department of Health Professions, Program in Physical Therapy, Orlando, FL 32816. Offers DPT. *Accreditation:* APTA. *Faculty:* 18 full-time (9 women), 7 part-time/adjunct (2 women). *Students:* 91 full-time (55 women); includes 13 minority (2 African Americans, 5 Asian Americans or Pacific Islanders, 6 Hispanic Americans). Average age 26.Application fee: $30. Electronic applications accepted. *Expenses:* Contact institution. *Financial support:* In 2009–10, 5 students received support, including 1 fellowship with tuition reimbursement available (averaging $10,000 per year), 4 teaching assistantships with tuition reimbursements available (averaging $6,400 per year); career-related internships or fieldwork, institutionally sponsored loans, scholarships/grants, tuition waivers (partial), and unspecified assistantships also available. *Unit head:* Dr. Gerald Smith, Program Director, 407-882-0094, E-mail: gesmith@mail.ucf.edu. *Application contact:* Dr. Gerald Smith, Program Director, 407-882-0094, E-mail: gesmith@mail.ucf.edu.

University of Colorado Denver, School of Medicine, Program in Physical Therapy, Denver, CO 80217-3364. Offers DPT. *Accreditation:* APTA. *Students:* 150 full-time (119 women); includes 7 minority (1 African American, 1 American Indian/Alaska Native, 3 Asian Americans or Pacific Islanders, 2 Hispanic Americans), 1 international. *Entrance requirements:* For doctorate, GRE, minimum GPA of 3.0, 3 letters of reference, CPR certification, 45 hours of field work. Additional exam requirements/recommendations for international students: Required—TOEFL (minimum score 550 paper-based; 213 computer-based). *Application deadline:* For spring admission, 12/15 for domestic students. Application fee: $50. *Financial support:* Research assistantships, teaching assistantships, Federal Work-Study and scholarships/grants available. Financial award application deadline: 3/15; financial award applicants required to submit FAFSA. *Faculty research:* Interventions for early and mid-stages of Parkinson's disease, physical therapy for individuals with recurrent lower back pain. *Unit head:* Margaret Schenkman, Program Director, 303-724-9375, E-mail: margaret.schenkman@ucdenver.edu. *Application contact:* Nancey Bookstein, Admissions Advisor, 303-724-9133, E-mail: nancey.bookstein@ucdenver.edu.

University of Connecticut, Graduate School, Neag School of Education, Department of Physical Therapy, Storrs, CT 06269. Offers DPT. *Accreditation:* APTA. *Faculty:* 12 full-time (6 women). *Students:* 49 full-time (29 women); includes 4 minority (2 Asian Americans or Pacific Islanders, 2 Hispanic Americans), 1 international. Average age 24. 115 applicants, 1% accepted, 0 enrolled. *Entrance requirements:* Additional exam requirements/recommendations for international students: Required—TOEFL (minimum score 550 paper-based; 213 computer-based). *Application deadline:* For fall admission, 2/1 priority date for domestic and international students; for spring admission, 11/1 for domestic students, 10/1 for international students. Applications are processed on a rolling basis. Application fee: $55. Electronic applications accepted. *Expenses:* Tuition, state resident: full-time $4725; part-time $525 per credit. Tuition, nonresident: full-time $12,267; part-time $1363 per credit. Required fees: $346 per semester. Tuition and fees vary according to course load. *Financial support:* Research assistantships, Federal Work-Study available. Financial award application deadline: 2/1; financial award applicants required to submit FAFSA. *Unit head:* Craig Denegar, Head, 860-486-0052, Fax: 860-486-1588, E-mail: craig.denegar@uconn.edu. *Application contact:* Katrease Gerace, Assistant, 860-486-0049, Fax: 860-486-1588, E-mail: katrease.gerace@uconn.edu.

University of Dayton, Graduate School, School of Education and Allied Professions, Department of Health and Sport Science, Dayton, OH 45469-1300. Offers exercise science (MS Ed); physical therapy (DPT). Part-time and evening/weekend programs available. *Faculty:* 16 full-time (7 women). *Students:* 116 full-time (79 women), 3 part-time (all women); includes 9 minority (5 African Americans, 3 Asian Americans or Pacific Islanders, 1 Hispanic American), 2 international. Average age 25. 200 applicants, 37% accepted, 43 enrolled. In 2009, 3 master's awarded. *Degree requirements:* For master's, thesis; for doctorate, thesis/dissertation. *Entrance requirements:* For master's, GRE General Test, MAT,.minimum GPA of 2.75; for doctorate, GRE General Test, minimum GPA of 3.0, 80 observation hours. Additional exam requirements/recommendations for international students: Required—TOEFL (minimum score 550 paper-based; 213 computer-based; 80 iBT). *Application deadline:* For fall admission, 2/15 priority date for domestic students, 3/1 priority date for international students; for winter admission, 7/1 priority date for international students; for spring admission, 1/1 priority date for international students. Applications are processed on a rolling basis. Application fee: $0 ($50 for international students). Electronic applications accepted. *Expenses:* Tuition: Full-time $8412; part-time $701 per credit hour. Required fees: $325; $65 per course. $25 per semester. Tuition and fees vary according to course load, degree level and program. *Financial support:* In 2009–10, 4 students received support, including 4 teaching assistantships with tuition reimbursements available (averaging $8,000 per year); research assistantships, career-related internships or fieldwork, institutionally sponsored loans, health care benefits, and unspecified assistantships also available. Financial award applicants required to submit FAFSA. *Faculty research:* Energy expenditure, strength, training, teaching nutrition and calcium intake of children and families in Head-Start. *Unit head:* Dr. Lloyd Laubach, Interim Chair, 937-229-4240, Fax: 937-229-4244, E-mail: lloyd.laubach@notes.udayton.edu. *Application contact:* Graduate Admissions, 937-229-4411, Fax: 937-229-4729, E-mail: gradadmission@udayton.edu.

University of Delaware, College of Arts and Sciences, Department of Physical Therapy, Newark, DE 19716. Offers DPT. *Accreditation:* APTA. *Entrance requirements:* For doctorate, GRE, 100 hours clinical experience, 3 letters of recommendation. Additional exam requirements/recommendations for international students: Required—TOEFL (minimum score 550 paper-based; 213 computer-based). Electronic applications accepted. *Faculty research:* Movement sciences, applied physiology, physical rehabilitation.

University of Evansville, College of Education and Health Sciences, Department of Physical Therapy, Evansville, IN 47722. Offers DPT. *Accreditation:* APTA. *Faculty:* 9 full-time (6 women), 3 part-time/adjunct (2 women). *Students:* 72 full-time (58 women), 2 international. Average age 24. 79 applicants, 65% accepted, 36 enrolled. In 2009, 28 doctorates awarded. *Degree requirements:* For doctorate, case study, 30 weeks of full-time clinical internships (20 credit hours). *Entrance requirements:* For doctorate, achelor's degree, science and math prerequisite courses, minimum GPA of 2.75, interview, recommendations. Additional exam requirements/recommendations for international students: Required—TOEFL (minimum score 570 paper-

based; 228 computer-based; 88 iBT). *Application deadline:* For fall admission, 10/1 for domestic and international students. Applications are processed on a rolling basis. Application fee: $65. *Expenses:* Contact institution. *Financial support:* In 2009–10, 72 students received support. Scholarships/grants available. Financial award application deadline: 4/1; financial award applicants required to submit FAFSA. *Faculty research:* Selective functional movement screen, pediatric services, school based physical therapy services, functional movement analysis, gait, interventions for lower extremity injuries, low back pain, lumbar multifidus, typical motor development, cultural competence. *Unit head:* Mary Kessler, Chair, 812-488-2579, Fax: 812-488-2717, E-mail: mk43@evansville.edu. *Application contact:* Sherri Chambliss, Operations Administrator, 812-488-2345, Fax: 812-488-2717, E-mail: sc9@evansville.edu.

The University of Findlay, Graduate and Professional Studies, College of Health Professions, Master of Physical Therapy Program, Findlay, OH 45840-3653. Offers MPT. *Accreditation:* APTA. Part-time and evening/weekend programs available. *Entrance requirements:* For master's, 2 letters of recommendation, 100 hours of observation, minimum GPA of 3.0. Additional exam requirements/recommendations for international students: Required—TOEFL (minimum score 550 paper-based; 213 computer-based; 80 iBT). Electronic applications accepted.

University of Florida, Graduate School, College of Public Health and Health Professions, Department of Physical Therapy, Gainesville, FL 32611. Offers DPT. *Accreditation:* APTA. *Entrance requirements:* Additional exam requirements/recommendations for international students: Required—TOEFL (minimum score 515 paper-based; 213 computer-based). Electronic applications accepted. *Faculty research:* Exercise physiology, motor control, rehabilitation, geriatrics.

University of Hartford, College of Education, Nursing, and Health Professions, Program in Physical Therapy, West Hartford, CT 06117-1599. Offers MSPT, DPT. *Accreditation:* APTA. *Entrance requirements:* For master's, GRE, 3 letters of recommendation. Additional exam requirements/recommendations for international students: Required—TOEFL (minimum score 550 paper-based; 213 computer-based).

University of Illinois at Chicago, Graduate College, College of Applied Health Sciences, Department of Physical Therapy, Chicago, IL 60607-7128. Offers MS, DPT. *Accreditation:* APTA. *Degree requirements:* For master's, thesis. *Entrance requirements:* For master's, GRE General Test, minimum GPA of 2.75. Additional exam requirements/recommendations for international students: Required—TOEFL. Electronic applications accepted.

University of Indianapolis, Graduate Programs, Krannert School of Physical Therapy, Indianapolis, IN 46227-3697. Offers MHS, DHS, DPT, TDPT. *Accreditation:* APTA (one or more programs are accredited). Part-time and evening/weekend programs available. *Faculty:* 10 full-time (5 women), 6 part-time/adjunct (5 women). *Students:* 120 full-time (95 women), 91 part-time (66 women); includes 7 minority (2 African Americans, 4 Asian Americans or Pacific Islanders, 1 Hispanic American), 47 international. Average age 28. *Entrance requirements:* For doctorate, GRE General Test (DPT), minimum GPA of 3.0 (DPT), 3 letters of recommendation (for physical therapist). Additional exam requirements/recommendations for international students: Required—TOEFL (minimum score 250 computer-based; 100 iBT), TWE (minimum score 5). *Application deadline:* For fall admission, 10/12 for domestic students. Application fee: $50. Electronic applications accepted. *Expenses:* Contact institution. *Financial support:* Teaching assistantships, career-related internships or fieldwork, Federal Work-Study, scholarships/grants, tuition waivers (full and partial), and unspecified assistantships available. Support available to part-time students. Financial award application deadline: 5/1; financial award applicants required to submit FAFSA. *Faculty research:* Patella positioning, reaction time, allocation of physical therapy resources. *Unit head:* Dr. Stephanie Kelly, Acting Dean, College of Health Sciences, 317-788-3500, Fax: 317-788-3542, E-mail: huerm@ulndy.edu. *Application contact:* Kelly Wilson, Admissions Counselor, 317-788-4909, Fax: 317-788-3542, E-mail: kwilson@uindy.edu.

The University of Iowa, Roy J. and Lucille A. Carver College of Medicine and Graduate College, Biosciences Program, Iowa City, IA 52242-1316. Offers anatomy and biology (PhD); biochemistry (PhD); biology (PhD); biomedical engineering (PhD); chemistry (PhD); free radical and radiation biology (PhD); genetics (PhD); human toxicology (PhD); immunology (PhD); microbiology (PhD); molecular and cellular biology (PhD); molecular physiology and biophysics (PhD); neuroscience (PhD); pharmacology (PhD); physical therapy and rehabilitation science (PhD); speech and hearing (PhD). *Faculty:* 310 full-time. *Students:* 25 full-time (13 women); includes 1 African American, 2 Asian Americans or Pacific Islanders, 4 international. 225 applicants. *Degree requirements:* For doctorate, thesis/dissertation. *Entrance requirements:* For doctorate, GRE General Test, minimum GPA of 3.0. Additional exam requirements/recommendations for international students: Required—TOEFL (minimum score 600 paper-based; 250 computer-based; 100 iBT). *Application deadline:* For fall admission, 1/15 priority date for domestic and international students. Applications are processed on a rolling basis. Application fee: $60 ($100 for international students). Electronic applications accepted. *Expenses:* Contact institution. *Financial support:* In 2009–10, 25 students received support, including 25 research assistantships with full tuition reimbursements available (averaging $24,250 per year); fellowships, teaching assistantships, health care benefits also available. *Unit head:* Dr. Andrew F. Russo, Director, 319-335-7872, Fax: 319-335-7656, E-mail: andrew-russo@uiowa.edu. *Application contact:* Jodi M. Graff, Program Associate, 319-335-8305, Fax: 319-335-7656, E-mail: biosciences-admissions@uiowa.edu.

The University of Iowa, Roy J. and Lucille A. Carver College of Medicine and Graduate College, Graduate Programs in Medicine, Graduate Program in Physical Therapy and Rehabilitation Science, Iowa City, IA 52242-1316. Offers physical therapy (DPT); rehabilitation science (PhD). *Accreditation:* APTA (one or more programs are accredited). *Faculty:* 7 full-time (3 women), 45 part-time/adjunct (23 women). *Students:* 110 full-time (77 women), 7 part-time (5 women); includes 2 minority (1 African American, 1 Hispanic American), 3 international. Average age 24. 298 applicants, 17% accepted, 37 enrolled. In 2009, 3 doctorates awarded. Terminal master's awarded for partial completion of doctoral program. *Degree requirements:* For doctorate, thesis/dissertation (for some programs). *Entrance requirements:* For doctorate, GRE. Additional exam requirements/recommendations for international students: Required—TOEFL. *Application deadline:* For fall admission, 12/1 priority date for domestic students, 5/15 for international students; for winter admission, 10/15 for international students; for spring admission, 3/15 for international students. Application fee: $60 ($85 for international students). Electronic applications accepted. *Expenses:* Contact institution. *Financial support:* In 2009–10, 94 students received support, including 1 fellowship with partial tuition reimbursement available (averaging $9,000 per year), 6 research assistantships with partial tuition reimbursements available (averaging $10,129 per year), teaching assistantships with partial tuition reimbursements available (averaging $10,129 per year); Federal Work-Study, institutionally sponsored loans, scholarships/grants, health care benefits, and unspecified assistantships also available. Support available to part-time students. Financial award application deadline: 6/30; financial award applicants required to submit FAFSA. *Faculty research:* Muscle fatigue, motor control, pain mechanisms, body composition, sports medicine, occupational safety, neuromuscular physiology, neural control of movement. Total annual research expenditures: $1.4 million. *Unit head:* Dr. Richard K. Shields, Director, 319-335-9791, Fax: 319-335-9707, E-mail: physical-therapy@uiowa.edu. *Application contact:* Dr. Richard K. Shields, Director, 319-335-9791, Fax: 319-335-9707, E-mail: physical-therapy@uiowa.edu.

The University of Kansas, University of Kansas Medical Center, School of Allied Health, Department of Physical Therapy and Rehabilitation Science, Kansas City, KS 66160. Offers DPT, PhD. *Accreditation:* APTA. *Faculty:* 17 full-time, 8 part-time/adjunct. *Students:* 107 full-time (83 women), 53 part-time (31 women); includes 9 minority (2 African Americans, 2 American Indian/Alaska Native, 5 Asian Americans or Pacific Islanders), 30 international. Average age 28. 170 applicants, 38% accepted, 59 enrolled. In 2009, 50 doctorates awarded. *Degree requirements:* For doctorate, comprehensive exam, research project with paper. *Entrance requirements:* For doctorate, GRE General Test, minimum GPA of 3.0. Additional exam requirements/recommendations for international students: Required—TOEFL. *Application deadline:* For fall admission, 12/31 for domestic students. Applications are processed on a

Physical Therapy

The University of Kansas *(continued)*
rolling basis. Application fee: $60. *Expenses:* Contact institution. *Financial support:* In 2009–10, 84 students received support; research assistantships with tuition reimbursements available, teaching assistantships with full and partial tuition reimbursements available, career-related internships or fieldwork, Federal Work-Study, institutionally sponsored loans, scholarships/grants, traineeships, and unspecified assistantships available. Financial award application deadline: 3/30; financial award applicants required to submit FAFSA. *Faculty research:* Stroke rehabilitation and the effects on balance and coordination; deep brain stimulation and Parkinson's Disease; peripheral neuropathies, pain and the effects of exercise; islet transplants for Type 1 diabetes; cardiac disease associated with diabetes. Total annual research expenditures: $202,053. *Unit head:* Dr. Lisa Stehno-Bittel, Chair, 913-588-6733, Fax: 913-588-4568, E-mail: lbittel@kumc.edu. *Application contact:* Robert Bagley, Admission Coordinator, 913-588-6799, Fax: 913-588-4568, E-mail: rbagley@kumc.edu.

University of Kentucky, Graduate School, College of Health Sciences, Program in Physical Therapy, Lexington, KY 40506-0032. Offers MSPT. *Accreditation:* APTA. *Degree requirements:* For master's, comprehensive exam, thesis optional. *Entrance requirements:* For master's, GRE General Test, minimum undergraduate GPA of 2.75, U.S. physical therapist license. Additional exam requirements/recommendations for international students: Required—TOEFL (minimum score 550 paper-based; 213 computer-based). Electronic applications accepted. *Faculty research:* Orthopedics, biomechanics, electrophysiological stimulation, neural plasticity, brain damage and mechanism.

University of Manitoba, Faculty of Graduate Studies, School of Medical Rehabilitation, Winnipeg, MB R3T 2N2, Canada. Offers applied health sciences (PhD); occupational therapy (MOT); physical therapy (MPT); rehabilitation (M Sc).

University of Mary, Department of Physical Therapy, Bismarck, ND 58504-9652. Offers DPT. *Accreditation:* APTA. *Degree requirements:* For doctorate, comprehensive exam, professional paper. *Entrance requirements:* For doctorate, minimum GPA of 3.0 in core requirements, 40 hours of paid/volunteer experience. Additional exam requirements/recommendations for international students: Required—TOEFL (minimum score 550 paper-based). Electronic applications accepted. *Expenses:* Contact institution. *Faculty research:* Proprioception, falls and elderly, clinical biomechanics, admission predictors, electromyography and muscle performance, wellness.

University of Maryland, Baltimore, School of Medicine, Department of Physical Therapy and Rehabilitation Science, Baltimore, MD 21201. Offers physical rehabilitation science (PhD); physical therapy and rehabilitation science (DPT). *Accreditation:* APTA. *Students:* 102 full-time (71 women), 74 part-time (59 women); includes 27 minority (7 African Americans, 16 Asian Americans or Pacific Islanders, 4 Hispanic Americans), 4 international. Average age 27. 362 applicants, 57% accepted, 57 enrolled. In 2009, 62 doctorates awarded. *Entrance requirements:* For doctorate, GRE General Test. Additional exam requirements/recommendations for international students: Required—TOEFL (minimum score 80 iBT). Application fee: $50. Electronic applications accepted. *Expenses:* Contact institution. *Financial support:* Application deadline: 3/1. *Unit head:* Dr. Mary Rodgers, Chair, 410-706-5216, Fax: 410-706-4903, E-mail: mrodgers@som.umaryland.edu. *Application contact:* Dr. Jill Whitall, Program Director, 410-706-7720, Fax: 410-706-6387, E-mail: ptadmissions@som.umaryland.edu.

University of Maryland Eastern Shore, Graduate Programs, Department of Physical Therapy, Princess Anne, MD 21853-1299. Offers DPT. *Accreditation:* APTA. *Degree requirements:* For doctorate, thesis/dissertation, clinical practicum, research project. *Entrance requirements:* For doctorate, minimum GPA of 3.0, course work in science and mathematics, interview, knowledge of the physical therapy field. Additional exam requirements/recommendations for international students: Required—TOEFL (minimum score 213 computer-based; 80 iBT). Electronic applications accepted. *Faculty research:* Allied health projects.

University of Massachusetts Lowell, School of Health and Environment, Department of Physical Therapy, Lowell, MA 01854-2881. Offers DPT. *Accreditation:* APTA. *Entrance requirements:* For doctorate, GRE General Test, minimum GPA of 3.0, 3 letters of recommendation. Additional exam requirements/recommendations for international students: Required—TOEFL (minimum score 560 paper-based; 220 computer-based). *Faculty research:* Orthopedics, pediatrics, electrophysiology, cardiopulmonary, neurology.

University of Medicine and Dentistry of New Jersey, School of Health Related Professions, Department of Interdisciplinary Studies, Program in Health Sciences, Newark, NJ 07107-1709. Offers cardiopulmonary sciences (PhD); clinical laboratory sciences (PhD); health sciences (MS); interdisciplinary studies (PhD); nutrition (PhD); physical therapy/movement science (PhD). *Degree requirements:* For doctorate, thesis/dissertation. *Entrance requirements:* For doctorate, interview, writing sample. Additional exam requirements/recommendations for international students: Required—TOEFL. Electronic applications accepted.

University of Medicine and Dentistry of New Jersey, School of Health Related Professions, Department of Rehabilitation and Movement Sciences, Program in Physical Therapy (Entry Level) –Newark, Newark, NJ 07107-1709. Offers DPT. *Accreditation:* APTA. *Entrance requirements:* Additional exam requirements/recommendations for international students: Required—TOEFL. Electronic applications accepted.

University of Medicine and Dentistry of New Jersey, School of Health Related Professions, Department of Rehabilitation and Movement Sciences, Program in Physical Therapy (Post-Professional Level) –Newark, Newark, NJ 07107-1709. Offers DPT. *Accreditation:* APTA. *Entrance requirements:* Additional exam requirements/recommendations for international students: Required—TOEFL. Electronic applications accepted.

University of Medicine and Dentistry of New Jersey, School of Health Related Professions, Department of Rehabilitation and Movement Sciences, Program in Physical Therapy–Stratford, Newark, NJ 07107-1709. Offers MPT. *Accreditation:* APTA. *Entrance requirements:* For master's, GRE General Test, related work or volunteer experience. Additional exam requirements/recommendations for international students: Required—TOEFL. Electronic applications accepted.

University of Miami, Graduate School, Miller School of Medicine, Graduate Programs in Medicine, Department of Physical Therapy, Coral Gables, FL 33124. Offers DPT, PhD. *Accreditation:* APTA (one or more programs are accredited). *Degree requirements:* For doctorate, comprehensive exam, thesis/dissertation. *Entrance requirements:* For doctorate, GRE General Test. Additional exam requirements/recommendations for international students: Required—TOEFL. Electronic applications accepted. *Expenses:* Contact institution. *Faculty research:* Central pattern generators in SCI balance and vestibular function in children, amputee rehabilitation.

University of Michigan–Flint, School of Health Professions and Studies, Program in Physical Therapy, Flint, MI 48502-1950. Offers online transitional (DPT); traditional entry-level (DPT). *Accreditation:* APTA. Part-time programs available. Postbaccalaureate distance learning degree programs offered. *Faculty:* 11 full-time (7 women), 6 part-time/adjunct (3 women). *Students:* 113 full-time (81 women), 58 part-time (43 women); includes 12 minority (3 African Americans, 7 Asian Americans or Pacific Islanders, 2 Hispanic Americans), 6 international. Average age 33. 196 applicants, 47% accepted, 40 enrolled. In 2009, 31 doctorates awarded. *Degree requirements:* For doctorate, comprehensive exam, thesis/dissertation or alternative. *Entrance requirements:* For doctorate, GRE (Verbal score between 340-480; Quantitative 370-710), minimum GPA of 3.16. Additional exam requirements/recommendations for international students: Required—TOEFL (minimum score 560 paper-based; 220 computer-based; 84 iBT), IELTS (minimum score 6.5). Application deadline: For fall admission, 8/1 priority date for domestic students, 5/1 priority date for international students; for winter admission, 11/15 priority date for domestic students, 9/1 priority date for international students; for spring admission, 3/15 priority date for domestic students, 1/1 priority date for international students. Applications are processed on a rolling basis. Application fee: $55. Electronic applications accepted. *Expenses:*

Contact institution. *Financial support:* Career-related internships or fieldwork, Federal Work-Study, scholarships/grants, and unspecified assistantships available. Support available to part-time students. Financial award application deadline: 6/1; financial award applicants required to submit FAFSA. *Faculty research:* Cumulative trauma disorders, oncology rehabilitation, neurological rehabilitation, musculoskeletal rehabilitation, cardiopulmonary rehabilitation. *Unit head:* Dr. Donna Fry, Interim Director, 810-762-3373, E-mail: donnafry@umflint.edu. *Application contact:* Reva Kidd, Business Administrator, 810-762-3373, Fax: 810-766-6668, E-mail: rpeariso@umflint.edu.

University of Minnesota, Twin Cities Campus, Medical School, Department of Physical Medicine and Rehabilitation, Program in Physical Therapy, Minneapolis, MN 55455. Offers DPT. *Accreditation:* APTA. *Degree requirements:* For doctorate, research project. *Entrance requirements:* For doctorate, GRE. Additional exam requirements/recommendations for international students: Required—TOEFL (minimum score 79 iBT). Electronic applications accepted. *Expenses:* Contact institution. *Faculty research:* Aging, stroke, muscle, balance, spine, Parkinson's disease, dystonia, biomechanics, ergonomics.

University of Mississippi Medical Center, School of Health Related Professions, Department of Physical Therapy, Jackson, MS 39216-4505. Offers MPT. *Accreditation:* APTA. *Faculty research:* Pain, acupressure, seating, patient satisfaction, physical therapy educational issues.

University of Missouri, School of Health Professions, Program in Physical Therapy, Columbia, MO 65211. Offers MPT. *Accreditation:* APTA. *Entrance requirements:* For master's, GRE General Test, minimum GPA of 3.0. Additional exam requirements/recommendations for international students: Required—TOEFL (minimum score 600 paper-based; 250 computer-based; 100 iBT).

The University of Montana, Graduate School, College of Health Professions and Biomedical Sciences, School of Physical Therapy and Rehabilitation Science, Missoula, MT 59812-0002. Offers physical therapy (DPT). *Accreditation:* APTA. *Degree requirements:* For doctorate, professional paper. *Entrance requirements:* For doctorate, GRE General Test. Additional exam requirements/recommendations for international students: Required—TOEFL. Electronic applications accepted. *Expenses:* Contact institution. *Faculty research:* Muscle stiffness, fitness with a disability, psychosocial aspects of disability, clinical learning, motion analysis.

University of Nebraska Medical Center, School of Allied Health Professions, Division of Physical Therapy Education, Omaha, NE 68198. Offers DPT. *Accreditation:* APTA. *Faculty:* 9 full-time (5 women), 1 (woman) part-time/adjunct. *Students:* 130 full-time (82 women); includes 5 minority (2 African Americans, 3 Hispanic Americans). Average age 25. 229 applicants, 22% accepted. *Entrance requirements:* For doctorate, GRE General Test. Additional exam requirements/recommendations for international students: Required—TOEFL. *Application deadline:* For fall admission, 10/15 for domestic students. Application fee: $45. Electronic applications accepted. *Financial support:* Applicants required to submit FAFSA. *Faculty research:* Aquatics effects on MS, balance control-age, performance in physical therapy with COPD, wheelchair use in nursing homes, human activity profile. Total annual research expenditures: $104,741. *Unit head:* Dr. Gilbert M. Willett, Interim Director, 402-559-4259. *Application contact:* Rita Parks-Agnew, Administrative and Admissions Coordinator, 402-559-4259, E-mail: rparks@unmc.edu.

University of Nevada, Las Vegas, Graduate College, School of Allied Health Sciences, Department of Physical Therapy, Las Vegas, NV 89154-3029. Offers DPT. *Accreditation:* APTA. *Faculty:* 7 full-time (2 women). *Students:* 74 full-time (37 women), 10 part-time (2 women); includes 4 minority (3 Asian Americans or Pacific Islanders, 1 Hispanic American). Average age 28. 5 applicants, 0% accepted, 0 enrolled. In 2009, 30 doctorates awarded. *Entrance requirements:* Additional exam requirements/recommendations for international students: Required—TOEFL (minimum score 550 paper-based; 213 computer-based; 80 iBT), IELTS (minimum score 7). *Application deadline:* Applications are processed on a rolling basis. Application fee: $60 ($95 for international students). Electronic applications accepted. *Financial support:* In 2009–10, 6 students received support, including 6 teaching assistantships with partial tuition reimbursements available (averaging $12,000 per year); institutionally sponsored loans, scholarships/grants, health care benefits, and unspecified assistantships also available. Financial award application deadline: 3/1. *Faculty research:* Balance, childhood obesity, exercise performance, Parkinson's disease, the spine. *Unit head:* Dr. Harvey Wallmann, Chair/Associate Professor, 702-895-3003, Fax: 702-895-4883, E-mail: harvey.wallmann@unlv.edu. *Application contact:* Graduate College Admissions Evaluator, 702-895-3320, Fax: 702-895-4180, E-mail: gradcollege@unlv.edu.

University of New England, Westbrook College of Health Professions, Program in Physical Therapy, Biddeford, ME 04005-9526. Offers physical therapy (DPT); post professional physical therapy (DPT). *Accreditation:* APTA. *Faculty:* 7 full-time (3 women), 5 part-time/adjunct (2 women). *Students:* 136 full-time (88 women); includes 4 Asian Americans or Pacific Islanders. *Entrance requirements:* Additional exam requirements/recommendations for international students: Required—TOEFL. *Application deadline:* For fall admission, 2/1 for domestic students. Applications are processed on a rolling basis. Application fee: $40. Electronic applications accepted. *Expenses:* Contact institution. *Financial support:* Scholarships/grants available. Financial award application deadline: 5/1; financial award applicants required to submit FAFSA. *Faculty research:* Biomechanics, motor control, clinical education, functional outcomes, health policy. *Unit head:* Michael Sheldon, Director, 207-221-4591, E-mail: msheldon@une.edu. *Application contact:* Stacy Gato, Director of Graduate Admissions, 207-221-4225, Fax: 207-221-4898, E-mail: gradadmissions@une.edu.

University of New Mexico, School of Medicine, Program in Physical Therapy, Albuquerque, NM 87131-2039. Offers MPT. *Accreditation:* APTA. *Degree requirements:* For master's, comprehensive exam, thesis or alternative. *Entrance requirements:* For master's, GRE General Test, GRE writing assessment test, interview, minimum GPA of 3.0. Additional exam requirements/recommendations for international students: Required—TOEFL (minimum score 580 paper-based; 237 computer-based). *Expenses:* Tuition, state resident: full-time $2099; part-time $233.20 per credit hour. Tuition, nonresident: full-time $6650. Required fees: $25 per semester. Tuition and fees vary according to course load, program and reciprocity agreements. *Faculty research:* Gait analysis, motion analysis, balance, articular cartilage, quality of life.

The University of North Carolina at Chapel Hill, School of Medicine and Graduate School, Graduate Programs in Medicine, Chapel Hill, NC 27599. Offers allied health sciences (MPT, MS, Au D, DPT, PhD), including human movement science (MS, PhD), occupational science (MS, PhD), physical therapy (MPT, MS, DPT), rehabilitation counseling and psychology (MS), speech and hearing sciences (MS, Au D, PhD); biochemistry and biophysics (MS, PhD); biomedical engineering (MS, PhD); cell and developmental biology (PhD); cell and molecular physiology (PhD); genetics and molecular biology (PhD); microbiology and immunology (MS, PhD), including immunology, microbiology; neurobiology (PhD); pathology and laboratory medicine (PhD), including experimental pathology; pharmacology (PhD); MD/PhD. Post-baccalaureate distance learning degree programs offered. Terminal master's awarded for partial completion of doctoral program. *Degree requirements:* For master's, comprehensive exam; for doctorate, thesis/dissertation. Electronic applications accepted. *Expenses:* Contact institution.

The University of North Carolina at Chapel Hill, School of Medicine and Graduate School, Graduate Programs in Medicine, Department of Allied Health Sciences, Program in Physical Therapy, Chapel Hill, NC 27599. Offers physical therapy—off campus (DPT); physical therapy—on campus (DPT). *Accreditation:* APTA. Part-time and evening/weekend programs available. Postbaccalaureate distance learning degree programs offered (no on-campus study). *Faculty:* 24 full-time (17 women), 7 part-time/adjunct (6 women). *Students:* 103 full-time (78 women), 22 part-time (20 women); includes 17 minority (10 African Americans, 7 Asian Americans or Pacific Islanders). Average age 30. 268 applicants, 18% accepted, 39 enrolled. In 2009, 4 doctorates awarded. *Degree requirements:* For doctorate, thesis/dissertation or alternative. *Entrance requirements:* For doctorate, physical therapy license. Additional exam requirements/recommendations for international students: Required—TOEFL (minimum score

550 paper-based; 79 computer-based). *Application deadline:* For fall admission, 11/1 for domestic and international students. Application fee: $75. Electronic applications accepted. *Financial support:* In 2009–10, 49 students received support; fellowships with tuition reimbursements available, research assistantships with tuition reimbursements available, career-related internships or fieldwork and institutionally sponsored loans available. Financial award application deadline: 11/1; financial award applicants required to submit FAFSA. *Faculty research:* Traumatic brain injury, quality of life after heart and/or lung transplant, cultural diversity, life care planning, rehabilitation education and supervision. Total annual research expenditures: $432,028. *Unit head:* Rick Segal, Associate Professor, Director, 919-843-8660, Fax: 919-966-3678, E-mail: richard_segal@med.unc.edu. *Application contact:* Shauni Lowrance, Registrar, 919-966-4708, Fax: 919-966-3678, E-mail: shauni-lowrance@med.unc.edu.

University of North Dakota, School of Medicine and Health Sciences and Graduate School, Graduate Programs in Medicine, Department of Physical Therapy, Grand Forks, ND 58202. Offers MPT, DPT. *Accreditation:* APTA. *Degree requirements:* For master's, comprehensive exam, thesis or alternative. *Entrance requirements:* For master's and doctorate, minimum GPA of 3.0, pre-physical therapy program. Additional exam requirements/recommendations for international students: Required—TOEFL (minimum score 550 paper-based; 213 computer-based; 79 iBT), IELTS (minimum score 6.5). *Faculty research:* Practice-based program.

University of North Florida, Brooks College of Health, Department of Athletic Training and Physical Therapy, Jacksonville, FL 32224. Offers DPT. *Accreditation:* APTA. Part-time and evening/weekend programs available. *Faculty:* 15 full-time (8 women). *Students:* 113 full-time (81 women), 17 part-time (10 women); includes 12 minority (7 African Americans, 1 Asian American or Pacific Islander, 4 Hispanic Americans), 1 international. Average age 27. 238 applicants, 22% accepted, 17 enrolled. In 2009, 20 doctorates awarded. *Entrance requirements:* Additional exam requirements/recommendations for international students: Required—TOEFL (minimum score 500 paper-based; 173 computer-based). *Application deadline:* For fall admission, 2/16 for domestic students, 1/16 for international students. Application fee: $30. Electronic applications accepted. *Expenses:* Tuition, state resident: full-time $6649.20; part-time $277.05 per credit hour. Tuition, nonresident: full-time $22,970; part-time $957.08 per credit hour. Required fees: $985; $41.03 per credit hour. *Financial support:* In 2009–10, 96 students received support; teaching assistantships, career-related internships or fieldwork, Federal Work-Study, scholarships/grants, and tuition waivers (partial) available. Support available to part-time students. Financial award application deadline: 4/1; financial award applicants required to submit FAFSA. *Faculty research:* Clinical outcomes related to orthopedic physical therapy interventions, instructional multimedia in physical therapy education, effect of functional electrical stimulation orthostatic hypotension in acute complete spinal cord injury individuals. Total annual research expenditures: $300,825. *Unit head:* Dr. Rusty Smith, Chair, 904-620-2841, E-mail: arsmith@unf.edu. *Application contact:* Heather Kenney, Director of Advising, 904-620-2810, Fax: 904-620-1030, E-mail: heather.kenney@unf.edu.

University of Oklahoma Health Sciences Center, Graduate College, College of Allied Health, Department of Physical Therapy, Oklahoma City, OK 73190. Offers MPT. *Accreditation:* APTA. *Faculty:* 10 full-time (7 women). *Students:* 170 full-time (132 women), 9 part-time (all women); includes 27 minority (3 African Americans, 14 American Indian/Alaska Native, 7 Asian Americans or Pacific Islanders, 3 Hispanic Americans), 1 international. Average age 24. 226 applicants, 35% accepted, 60 enrolled. In 2009, 53 master's awarded. *Expenses:* Tuition, state resident: full-time $3120; part-time $156 per credit hour. Tuition, nonresident: full-time $11,314; part-time $409.70 per credit hour. Required fees: $1471; $51.20 per credit hour. $223.25 per term. *Unit head:* Dr. Carole Sullivan, Dean, 405-271-2288, Fax: 405-271-1190, E-mail: carole-sullivan@ouhsc.edu. *Application contact:* Jenielle Greenlee, Associate Dean for Finance, 405-271-2288, Fax: 405-271-1190, E-mail: jenielle-greenlee@ouhse.edu.

University of Pittsburgh, School of Health and Rehabilitation Sciences, Doctor of Physical Therapy Program, Pittsburgh, PA 15260. Offers DPT. *Accreditation:* APTA. *Faculty:* 9 full-time (5 women), 2 part-time/adjunct (0 women). *Students:* 156 full-time (110 women), 10 part-time (4 women); includes 9 minority (6 African Americans, 2 Asian Americans or Pacific Islanders, 1 Hispanic American), 2 international. Average age 26. 396 applicants, 36% accepted, 55 enrolled. In 2009, 42 doctorates awarded. *Degree requirements:* For doctorate, clinical practice. *Entrance requirements:* For doctorate, GRE, volunteer work in physical therapy. Additional exam requirements/recommendations for international students: Required—TOEFL (minimum score 550 paper-based; 213 computer-based; 80 iBT), IELTS (minimum score 6.5). *Application deadline:* For fall admission, 1/31 for domestic students. Applications are processed on a rolling basis. Electronic applications accepted. *Expenses:* Contact institution. *Financial support:* Federal Work-Study, scholarships/grants, and traineeships available. Support available to part-time students. Financial award applicants required to submit FAFSA. *Faculty research:* Biomechanics, neuromuscular system, sports medicine, movement analysis, validity/outcomes of clinical procedures. Total annual research expenditures: $535,640. *Unit head:* Dr. Anthony Delitto, Chairman, 412-383-6630, Fax: 412-383-6629, E-mail: delitto@pitt.edu. *Application contact:* Shameem Gangjee, Director of Admissions, 412-383-6558, Fax: 412-383-6535, E-mail: admissions@shrs.pitt.edu.

University of Pittsburgh, School of Health and Rehabilitation Sciences, Master's Programs in Health and Rehabilitation Sciences, Pittsburgh, PA 15260. Offers health and rehabilitation sciences (MS), including clinical dietetics and nutrition, health care supervision and management, health information systems, occupational therapy, physical therapy, rehabilitation counseling, rehabilitation science and technology, sports medicine, wellness and human performance. *Accreditation:* APTA. Part-time and evening/weekend programs available. *Faculty:* 30 full-time (14 women), 4 part-time/adjunct (3 women). *Students:* 81 full-time (47 women), 54 part-time (27 women); includes 10 minority (6 African Americans, 4 Asian Americans or Pacific Islanders), 44 international. Average age 29. 326 applicants, 65% accepted, 130 enrolled. In 2009, 93 master's awarded. *Degree requirements:* For master's, comprehensive exam (for some programs), thesis optional. *Entrance requirements:* For master's, minimum GPA of 3.0. Additional exam requirements/recommendations for international students: Required—TOEFL, IELTS. *Application deadline:* For fall admission, 1/31 for international students; for spring admission, 7/31 for international students. Applications are processed on a rolling basis. Application fee: $50. Electronic applications accepted. *Expenses:* Contact institution. *Financial support:* In 2009–10, 3 research assistantships with full tuition reimbursements (averaging $18,450 per year) were awarded; teaching assistantships, Federal Work-Study, institutionally sponsored loans, traineeships, and unspecified assistantships also available. Financial award applicants required to submit FAFSA. *Faculty research:* Assistive technology, seating and wheeled mobility, cellular neurophysiology, low back syndrome, augmentative communication. Total annual research expenditures: $6.5 million. *Unit head:* Dr. Clifford E. Brubaker, Dean, 412-383-6560, Fax: 412-383-6535, E-mail: cliffb@pitt.edu. *Application contact:* Shameem Gangjee, Director of Admissions, 412-383-6558, Fax: 412-383-6535, E-mail: admissions@shrs.pitt.edu.

University of Puerto Rico, Medical Sciences Campus, School of Health Professions, Program in Physical Therapy, San Juan, PR 00936-5067. Offers MS. *Accreditation:* APTA. Part-time and evening/weekend programs available. *Degree requirements:* For master's, one foreign language, thesis. *Entrance requirements:* For master's, EXADEP, minimum GPA of 2.8, interview, first aid training and CPR certification.

University of Puget Sound, Graduate Studies, School of Occupational Therapy and Physical Therapy, Program in Physical Therapy, Tacoma, WA 98416. Offers DPT. *Accreditation:* APTA. *Faculty:* 7 full-time (4 women), 8 part-time/adjunct (5 women). *Students:* 104 full-time (73 women), 3 part-time (all women); includes 17 minority (14 Asian Americans or Pacific Islanders, 3 Hispanic Americans). Average age 26. 544 applicants, 24% accepted, 35 enrolled. *Entrance requirements:* Additional exam requirements/recommendations for international students: Required—TOEFL (minimum score 550 paper-based; 213 computer-based; 80 iBT). *Application deadline:* For fall admission, 12/15 priority date for domestic and international students. Application fee: $145. Electronic applications accepted. Tuition and fees vary according to course load, degree level and program. *Financial support:* In 2009–10, 21 students received support, including 15 fellowships (averaging $12,300 per year); career-related internships or fieldwork and scholarships/grants also available. Financial award application deadline: 3/31; financial award applicants required to submit FAFSA. *Faculty research:* Manual therapy, assessment of chronic pain, movement assessment of children, pediatric gait. *Unit head:* Dr. Kathleen Hummel-Berry, Director, 253-879-3531, Fax: 253-879-2933, E-mail: hummel@pugetsound.edu. *Application contact:* Dr. George H. Mills, Vice President for Enrollment, 253-879-3211, Fax: 253-879-3993, E-mail: admission@pugetsound.edu.

University of Rhode Island, Graduate School, College of Human Science and Services, Physical Therapy Department, Kingston, RI 02881. Offers DPT. *Accreditation:* APTA. Part-time programs available. *Faculty:* 6 full-time (4 women), 1 (woman) part-time/adjunct. *Students:* 85 full-time (64 women); includes 5 minority (3 African Americans, 2 Hispanic Americans), 1 international. In 2009, 20 doctorates awarded. *Degree requirements:* For doctorate, comprehensive exam. *Entrance requirements:* For doctorate, GRE, 2 letters of recommendation. Additional exam requirements/recommendations for international students: Required—TOEFL (minimum score 550 paper-based; 213 computer-based). *Application deadline:* For fall admission, 12/15 for domestic and international students. Application fee: $65. Electronic applications accepted. *Expenses:* Tuition, state resident: full-time $8828; part-time $490 per credit hour. Tuition, nonresident: full-time $22,100; part-time $1228 per credit hour. Required fees: $1118; $57 per semester. Tuition and fees vary according to program. *Financial support:* In 2009–10, 2 teaching assistantships with partial tuition reimbursements (averaging $3,474 per year) were awarded. Financial award application deadline: 12/15; financial award applicants required to submit FAFSA. Total annual research expenditures: $292,330. *Unit head:* Dr. Beth Marcoux, Chair, 401-574-5001, E-mail: bmarcoux@mail.uri.edu. *Application contact:* Dr. Susan E. Roush, Chair, Admissions Committee, 401-874-5626, E-mail: roush@uri.edu.

University of St. Augustine for Health Sciences, Graduate Programs, Division of Advanced Studies, St. Augustine, FL 32086. Offers MH Sc, DH Sc, TDPT. Part-time programs available. Postbaccalaureate distance learning degree programs offered (minimal on-campus study). *Entrance requirements:* For master's, GRE General Test, BS in physical therapy or equivalent; for doctorate, GRE General Test, master's degree in related field. Additional exam requirements/recommendations for international students: Required—TOEFL.

University of St. Augustine for Health Sciences, Graduate Programs, Division of Entry-Level Physical Therapy, St. Augustine, FL 32086. Offers DPT. *Accreditation:* APTA.

University of St. Augustine for Health Sciences, Graduate Programs, Division of Physical Therapy, St. Augustine, FL 32086. Offers DPT, Certificate. *Accreditation:* APTA. *Entrance requirements:* Additional exam requirements/recommendations for international students: Required—TOEFL.

The University of Scranton, College of Graduate and Continuing Education, Department of Physical Therapy, Scranton, PA 18510. Offers MPT, DPT. *Accreditation:* APTA. Part-time programs available. Postbaccalaureate distance learning degree programs offered (no on-campus study). *Faculty:* 7 full-time (3 women). *Students:* 74 full-time (44 women), 45 part-time (37 women); includes 9 minority (4 African Americans, 4 Asian Americans or Pacific Islanders, 1 Hispanic American). Average age 28. 65 applicants, 77% accepted. In 2009, 1 master's, 35 doctorates awarded. *Degree requirements:* For master's, thesis (for some programs), capstone experience. *Entrance requirements:* For master's, minimum GPA of 3.0; for doctorate, physical therapist license. Additional exam requirements/recommendations for international students: Required—TOEFL (minimum score 500 paper-based; 173 computer-based), IELTS (minimum score 5.5). *Application deadline:* Applications are processed on a rolling basis. Application fee: $0. *Financial support:* In 2009–10, 14 students received support, including 14 teaching assistantships (averaging $4,557 per year); career-related internships or fieldwork, Federal Work-Study, and unspecified assistantships also available. Support available to part-time students. Financial award application deadline: 3/1. *Unit head:* Dr. John P. Sanko, Chair, 570-941-7934, Fax: 570-941-7940, E-mail: sankoi1@scranton.edu. *Application contact:* Joseph M. Roback, Director of Admissions, 570-941-4385, Fax: 570-941-5928, E-mail: robackj2@scranton.edu.

University of South Alabama, Graduate School, College of Allied Health Professions, Department of Physical Therapy, Mobile, AL 36688-0002. Offers DPT. *Accreditation:* APTA. *Entrance requirements:* For doctorate, GRE, minimum GPA of 3.0. *Expenses:* Tuition, state resident: part-time $218 per credit hour. Required fees: $1102 per year.

The University of South Dakota, School of Medicine and Health Sciences and Graduate School, Graduate Programs in Health Sciences, Department of Physical Therapy, Vermillion, SD 57069-2390. Offers DPT. *Accreditation:* APTA. *Entrance requirements:* For doctorate, GRE General Test. Additional exam requirements/recommendations for international students: Required—TOEFL. *Expenses:* Contact institution. *Faculty research:* Physical therapy, knee rehabilitation, pediatric intervention, wound care, motion analysis.

University of Southern California, Graduate School, School of Dentistry, Division of Biokinesiology and Physical Therapy, Graduate Program in Physical Therapy, Los Angeles, CA 90089. Offers DPT. *Accreditation:* APTA. *Faculty:* 26 full-time (15 women), 48 part-time/adjunct (29 women). *Students:* 284 full-time (188 women); includes 134 minority (12 African Americans, 3 American Indian/Alaska Native, 95 Asian Americans or Pacific Islanders, 24 Hispanic Americans), 3 international. 328 applicants, 58% accepted, 95 enrolled. *Entrance requirements:* Additional exam requirements/recommendations for international students: Required—TOEFL (minimum score 600 paper-based; 250 computer-based; 100 iBT). *Application deadline:* For fall admission, 12/1 for domestic students. Application fee: $85. Electronic applications accepted. *Expenses:* Contact institution. *Financial support:* In 2009–10, 250 students received support. Federal Work-Study, institutionally sponsored loans, and scholarships/grants available. Financial award application deadline: 2/15; financial award applicants required to submit FAFSA. *Unit head:* Kathy Sullivan, Program Chair, 213-442-2651, Fax: 323-442-1515, E-mail: kasulliv@usc.edu. *Application contact:* Jesus Dominguez, Director of Admissions/Assistant Professor, Clinical Physical Therapy, 323-442-2907, Fax: 323-442-1515, E-mail: jdomingu@usc.edu.

University of South Florida, College of Medicine, School of Physical Therapy, Tampa, FL 33620-9951. Offers MS, DPT. *Accreditation:* APTA. *Students:* 108 full-time (91 women); includes 24 minority (9 African Americans, 1 American Indian/Alaska Native, 9 Asian Americans or Pacific Islanders, 5 Hispanic Americans). Average age 32. 36 applicants, 100% accepted, 36 enrolled. In 2009, 31 master's awarded. *Entrance requirements:* For master's, GRE General Test, minimum GPA of 3.0 in last 60 hours of coursework. Additional exam requirements/recommendations for international students: Required—TOEFL (minimum score 600 paper-based; 250 computer-based). *Application deadline:* For fall admission, 9/1 for domestic students, 2/1 for international students. Application fee: $30. *Financial support:* Applicants required to submit FAFSA. Total annual research expenditures: $597,405. *Unit head:* David Newman, Coordinator, 813-974-1326, Fax: 813-974-8614, E-mail: dnewman1@health.usf.edu. *Application contact:* David Newman, Coordinator, 813-974-1326, Fax: 813-974-8614, E-mail: dnewman1@health.usf.edu.

The University of Tennessee at Chattanooga, Graduate School, College of Health, Education and Professional Studies, Department of Physical Therapy, Chattanooga, TN 37403. Offers physical therapy (DPT); post professional (DPT). *Accreditation:* APTA. *Faculty:* 8 full-time (4 women), 8 part-time/adjunct (6 women). *Students:* 73 full-time (52 women), 19 part-time (11 women); includes 6 minority (4 African Americans, 2 Asian Americans or Pacific Islanders). Average age 33. 181 applicants, 18% accepted, 28 enrolled. In 2009, 45 doctorates awarded. *Degree requirements:* For doctorate, qualifying exams, internship. *Entrance requirements:* For doctorate, interview, minimum GPA of 3.0 in science and overall. Additional exam requirements/recommendations for international students: Required—TOEFL (minimum score 550 paper-based; 213 computer-based; 79 iBT); Recommended—IELTS (minimum score 6). *Application deadline:* For fall admission, 8/1 priority date for domestic students, 6/1 for international students; for spring admission, 12/1 priority date for domestic students, 10/1 for international students. Applications are processed on a rolling basis. Application fee: $35. Electronic applications accepted. *Expenses:* Tuition, state resident: full-time $5404; part-time $300 per credit

Physical Therapy

The University of Tennessee at Chattanooga (continued)

hour. Tuition, nonresident: full-time $16,702; part-time $928 per credit hour. Required fees: $1150; $130 per credit hour. *Financial support:* In 2009–10, 5 research assistantships with full and partial tuition reimbursements (averaging $5,500 per year) were awarded; career-related internships or fieldwork, scholarships/grants, and unspecified assistantships also available. Support available to part-time students. *Faculty research:* Diabetes and round management, disabilities, animal physical therapy and rehabilitation, orthopedics. Total annual research expenditures: $8,167. *Unit head:* Dr. Randy Walker, Acting Head, 423-425-4747, Fax: 423-425-2215, E-mail: randy-walker@utc.edu. *Application contact:* Dr. Stephanie Bellar, Dean of Graduate Studies, 423-425-4666, Fax: 423-425-5223, E-mail: stephanie-bellar@utc.edu.

The University of Tennessee Health Science Center, College of Allied Health Sciences, Memphis, TN 38163-0002. Offers MCP, MDH, MHIIM, MOT, MSCLS, MSPT, DPT, ScDPT, TDPT. *Accreditation:* AOTA; APTA. Part-time and evening/weekend programs available. Postbaccalaureate distance learning degree programs offered (minimal on-campus study). Terminal master's awarded for partial completion of doctoral program. *Degree requirements:* For master's, comprehensive exam, thesis; for doctorate, comprehensive exam, residency. *Entrance requirements:* For master's, GRE (MOT, MSCLS), minimum GPA of 3.0, 3 letters of reference, state license (MDH), national accreditation (MSCLS), GRE if GPA is less than 3.0 (MCP); for doctorate, GRE. Additional exam requirements/recommendations for international students: Required—TOEFL (minimum score 550 paper-based; 213 computer-based; 80 iBT). Electronic applications accepted. *Expenses:* Contact institution. *Faculty research:* Gait deviation, muscular dystrophy and strength, hemophilia and exercise, pediatric neurology, self-efficacy.

The University of Texas at El Paso, Graduate School, College of Health Sciences, Program in Physical Therapy, El Paso, TX 79968-0001. Offers MPT. *Accreditation:* APTA. *Entrance requirements:* For master's, GRE General Test. Additional exam requirements/recommendations for international students: Required—TOEFL. Electronic applications accepted.

The University of Texas Health Science Center at San Antonio, School of Allied Health Sciences, San Antonio, TX 78229-3900. Offers clinical laboratory sciences (MS); deaf education and hearing science (MED); dental hygiene (MS); occupational therapy (MOT); physical therapy (MPT); physician assistant studies (MS). *Accreditation:* AOTA; APTA; ARC-PA. *Expenses:* Tuition, state resident: full-time $2832; part-time $118 per credit hour. Tuition, nonresident: full-time $10,896; part-time $454 per credit hour. Required fees: $884 per semester. One-time fee: $70.

The University of Texas Medical Branch, School of Health Professions, Department of Physical Therapy, Galveston, TX 77555. Offers MPT, DPT. *Accreditation:* APTA. *Students:* 142 full-time (103 women), 11 part-time (8 women); includes 53 minority (9 African Americans, 13 Asian Americans or Pacific Islanders, 31 Hispanic Americans), 1 international. Average age 26. In 2009, 34 master's, 21 doctorates awarded. *Degree requirements:* For master's, thesis or alternative. *Entrance requirements:* For master's and doctorate, GRE, documentation of 40 hours' experience. *Application deadline:* For fall admission, 11/1 for domestic and international students. Applications are processed on a rolling basis. Application fee: $30. Electronic applications accepted. *Financial support:* Federal Work-Study, institutionally sponsored loans, and scholarships/grants available. Financial award applicants required to submit FAFSA. *Unit head:* Dr. Carolyn J. Utsey, Chair, 409-772-9497, Fax: 409-772-3014, E-mail: cutsey@utmb.edu. *Application contact:* Dr. Carolyn J. Utsey, Chair, 409-772-9497, Fax: 409-772-3014, E-mail: cutsey@utmb.edu.

The University of Texas Southwestern Medical Center at Dallas, Southwestern School of Health Professions, Physical Therapy Program, Dallas, TX 75390. Offers DPT. *Accreditation:* APTA. *Faculty:* 85 full-time (58 women). *Students:* 107 full-time (85 women); includes 19 minority (3 African Americans, 8 Asian Americans or Pacific Islanders, 8 Hispanic Americans), 1 international. Average age 26. 330 applicants, 17% accepted, 38 enrolled. *Entrance requirements:* For doctorate, GRE, minimum GPA of 3.0. Additional exam requirements/recommendations for international students: Required—TOEFL (minimum score 600 paper-based; 220 computer-based). *Application deadline:* For spring admission, 9/1 priority date for domestic students. Application fee: $10. Electronic applications accepted. *Financial support:* Application deadline: 3/1. *Unit head:* Dr. Patricia Winchester, Chair, 214-648-1551, Fax: 214-648-1511, E-mail: patricia.winchester@utsouthwestern.edu. *Application contact:* Billy Crawford, Education Coordinator, 214-648-1566, Fax: 214-648-1511, E-mail: billy.crawford@utsouthwestern.edu.

University of the Pacific, School of Pharmacy and Health Sciences, Department of Physical Therapy, Stockton, CA 95211-0197. Offers MS, DPT. *Accreditation:* APTA. *Faculty:* 8 full-time (6 women), 9 part-time/adjunct (7 women). *Students:* 67 full-time (43 women); includes 18 minority (1 American Indian/Alaska Native, 13 Asian Americans or Pacific Islanders, 4 Hispanic Americans), 1 international. Average age 24. 193 applicants, 38% accepted, 37 enrolled. In 2009, 32 doctorates awarded. *Entrance requirements:* For master's, GRE General Test, minimum GPA of 3.0. Additional exam requirements/recommendations for international students: Required—TOEFL (minimum score 475 paper-based; 150 computer-based). *Application deadline:* For fall admission, 1/4 for domestic students. Application fee: $75. *Financial support:* Federal Work-Study available. Financial award application deadline: 3/1; financial award applicants required to submit FAFSA. *Unit head:* Dr. Cathy Peterson, Chair, 209-946-2947, Fax: 209-946-2410. *Application contact:* Cyndi Porter, Outreach Officer, 209-946-3957, Fax: 209-946-2410, E-mail: cporter@pacific.edu.

The University of Toledo, College of Graduate Studies, College of Health Science and Human Service, Division of Health, Program in Physical Therapy, Toledo, OH 43606-3390. Offers DPT. *Accreditation:* APTA.

The University of Toledo, College of Graduate Studies, College of Medicine, Biomedical Science Programs, Program in Orthopedic Science, Toledo, OH 43606-3390. Offers MSBS. *Degree requirements:* For master's, thesis, qualifying exam. *Entrance requirements:* For master's, GRE General Test, minimum undergraduate GPA of 3.0.

University of Utah, Graduate School, College of Health, Department of Physical Therapy, Salt Lake City, UT 84112-1290. Offers DPT, PPDPT. *Accreditation:* APTA. *Faculty:* 13 full-time (7 women), 1 (woman) part-time/adjunct. *Students:* 130 full-time (58 women), 36 part-time (21 women); includes 5 minority (1 Asian American or Pacific Islander, 4 Hispanic Americans), 4 international. Average age 31. 88 applicants, 22% accepted, 18 enrolled. *Degree requirements:* For doctorate, clinical project; for PPDPT, Physical Therapist Evaluation Tool (PTET), physical therapy license. *Entrance requirements:* For doctorate, minimum GPA of 3.0, volunteer work. Additional exam requirements/recommendations for international students: Required—TOEFL (minimum score 575 paper-based; 233 computer-based). *Application deadline:* For fall admission, 11/1 priority date for domestic students, 11/1 for international students. Application fee: $55 ($65 for international students). Electronic applications accepted. *Expenses:* Contact institution. *Financial support:* In 2009–10, 20 students received support. Federal Work-Study, institutionally sponsored loans, scholarships/grants, and tuition waivers available. Financial award application deadline: 9/30; financial award applicants required to submit FAFSA. *Faculty research:* Rehabilitation and Parkinson's Disease, motor control and musculoskeletal dysfunction, burns/wound care, rehabilitation and multiple sclerosis, cancer. Total annual research expenditures: $616,707. *Unit head:* Dr. R. Scott Ward, Chair, 801-581-8681, Fax: 801-585-5629, E-mail: scott.ward@hsc.utah.edu. *Application contact:* Joyce Bawden, Administrative Assistant, 801-585-3122, Fax: 801-585-5629, E-mail: joyce.bawden@hsc.utah.edu.

University of Vermont, Graduate College, College of Nursing and Health Sciences, Program in Physical Therapy, Burlington, VT 05405. Offers DPT. *Accreditation:* APTA. *Students:* 93 (67 women); includes 8 minority (1 African American, 1 American Indian/Alaska Native, 4 Asian Americans or Pacific Islanders, 2 Hispanic Americans), 1 international. 116 applicants, 59% accepted, 0 enrolled. In 2009, 18 doctorates awarded. *Entrance requirements:* For doctorate, GRE General Test. Additional exam requirements/recommendations for international students: Required—TOEFL (minimum score 550 paper-based; 213 computer-based; 80 iBT). *Application deadline:* For fall admission, 12/15 priority date for domestic students. Applications are processed on a rolling basis. Application fee: $40. Electronic applications accepted. *Expenses:* Tuition, state resident: part-time $508 per credit hour. Tuition, nonresident: part-time $1281 per credit hour. *Financial support:* Fellowships, research assistantships, teaching assistantships, Federal Work-Study available. Financial award application deadline: 3/1. *Unit head:* Dr. Diane Jette, Coordinator, 802-656-3252. *Application contact:* Dr. Diane Jette, Coordinator, 802-656-3252.

University of Washington, Graduate School, School of Medicine and Graduate School, Graduate Programs in Medicine, Department of Rehabilitation Medicine, Seattle, WA 98195-6490. Offers occupational therapy (MOT); physical therapy (DPT); rehabilitation science (PhD). *Faculty:* 56. *Students:* 150. Average age 25. In 2009, 25 master's, 30 doctorates awarded. *Degree requirements:* For doctorate, comprehensive exam (for some programs), thesis/dissertation (for some programs). *Entrance requirements:* For master's and doctorate, GRE. Additional exam requirements/recommendations for international students: Required—TOEFL. Application fee: $65. *Financial support:* In 2009–10, 1 fellowship (averaging $5,000 per year) was awarded. Financial award applicants required to submit FAFSA. *Faculty research:* Biomechanics, balance, brain injury, spinal cord injury, pain, degenerative diseases. *Unit head:* Dr. Peter C. Esselman, Professor and Chair, 206-543-3600, Fax: 206-685-3244, E-mail: esselman@u.washington.edu. *Application contact:* Dr. Deborah Kartin, Graduate Program Coordinator, 206-598-5338, Fax: 206-685-3244, E-mail: kartin@u.washington.edu.

The University of Western Ontario, Faculty of Graduate Studies, Biosciences Division, School of Physical Therapy, London, ON N6A 5B8, Canada. Offers manipulative therapy (CAS); physical therapy (MPT); wound healing (CAS). *Accreditation:* APTA. Part-time programs available. *Degree requirements:* For master's, thesis. *Entrance requirements:* For master's, B Sc in physical therapy. Additional exam requirements/recommendations for international students: Required—TOEFL. *Faculty research:* Muscle strength, wound healing, motor control, respiratory physiology, exercise physiology.

University of Wisconsin–La Crosse, Office of University Graduate Studies, College of Science and Health, Department of Health Professions, Program in Physical Therapy, La Crosse, WI 54601-3742. Offers MSPT, DPT. *Accreditation:* APTA. *Students:* 84 full-time (62 women), 43 part-time (22 women); includes 4 minority (1 African American, 2 Asian Americans or Pacific Islanders, 1 Hispanic American). Average age 25. 230 applicants, 31% accepted, 45 enrolled. In 2009, 41 doctorates awarded. *Entrance requirements:* Additional exam requirements/recommendations for international students: Required—TOEFL (minimum score 550 paper-based; 213 computer-based; 79 iBT). *Application deadline:* For fall admission, 1/15 priority date for domestic students. Application fee: $56. Electronic applications accepted. *Financial support:* Research assistantships with partial tuition reimbursements, career-related internships or fieldwork, scholarships/grants, traineeships, health care benefits, and grant/contract-funded assistantships available. Financial award application deadline: 11/1. *Unit head:* Dr. Michele Thorman, Director, 608-785-8466, E-mail: thorman.mich@uwlax.edu. *Application contact:* Kathryn Kiefer, Director of Admissions, 608-785-8939, E-mail: admissions@uwlax.edu.

University of Wisconsin–Milwaukee, Graduate School, College of Health Sciences, Doctor of Physical Therapy (DPT) Program, Milwaukee, WI 53201-0413. Offers DPT. *Faculty:* 3 full-time (all women). *Students:* 55 full-time (38 women); includes 1 minority (Asian American or Pacific Islander). Average age 26. 11 applicants, 9% accepted, 1 enrolled. In 2009, 1 doctorate awarded. *Degree requirements:* For doctorate, thesis/dissertation optional. *Entrance requirements:* For doctorate, GRE General Test, minimum GPA of 3.0. Additional exam requirements/recommendations for international students: Required—TOEFL (minimum score 550 paper-based; 79 iBT), IELTS (minimum score 6.5). *Expenses:* Tuition, state resident: full-time $8800. Tuition, nonresident: full-time $20,760. Tuition and fees vary according to program and reciprocity agreements. *Unit head:* Tracy Turner, Representative, 414-229-3360, E-mail: turnertj@uwm.edu. *Application contact:* General Information Contact, 414-229-4982, Fax: 414-229-6967, E-mail: gradschool@uwm.edu.

Utica College, Department of Physical Therapy, Utica, NY 13502-4892. Offers DPT, TDPT. *Accreditation:* APTA. *Faculty:* 8 full-time (4 women). *Students:* 85 full-time (54 women), 89 part-time (45 women); includes 45 minority (6 African Americans, 36 Asian Americans or Pacific Islanders, 3 Hispanic Americans), 17 international. Average age 32. *Degree requirements:* For doctorate, comprehensive exam, thesis/dissertation (for some programs). *Entrance requirements:* For doctorate, GRE, MCAT, DAT or OPT, BS, minimum GPA of 3.0. Additional exam requirements/recommendations for international students: Required—TOEFL (minimum score 525 paper-based; 195 computer-based). *Application deadline:* Applications are processed on a rolling basis. Application fee: $50. Electronic applications accepted. *Expenses:* Contact institution. *Financial support:* Career-related internships or fieldwork, scholarships/grants, tuition waivers (partial), and unspecified assistantships available. Support available to part-time students. Financial award application deadline: 3/15; financial award applicants required to submit FAFSA. *Unit head:* Dr. Shauna Malta, Director, 315-792-3313, E-mail: smalta@utica.edu. *Application contact:* John D. Rowe, Director of Graduate Admissions, 315-792-3824, Fax: 315-792-3003, E-mail: jrowe@utica.edu.

Virginia Commonwealth University, Graduate School, School of Allied Health Professions, Department of Physical Therapy, Richmond, VA 23284-9005. Offers advanced physical therapy (MS); entry-level physical therapy (MS); physiology (PhD). *Accreditation:* APTA (one or more programs are accredited). *Degree requirements:* For doctorate, thesis/dissertation. *Entrance requirements:* For master's and doctorate, GRE General Test. *Faculty research:* Eye movement, bilabyrinthectomy on ferret muscle fiber typing, neck disability index, cost-effective care, training effect on muscle.

Virginia Commonwealth University, Medical College of Virginia-Professional Programs, School of Medicine, School of Medicine Graduate Programs, Department of Anatomy and Neurobiology, Richmond, VA 23284-9005. Offers anatomy (MS, PhD); anatomy and neurobiology (PhD); anatomy and physical therapy (PhD); neuroscience (MS, PhD). *Degree requirements:* For master's, thesis; for doctorate, thesis/dissertation, comprehensive oral and written exams. *Entrance requirements:* For master's, DAT, GRE General Test, or MCAT; for doctorate, DAT, GRE General Test, MCAT.

Walsh University, Graduate Studies, Program in Physical Therapy, North Canton, OH 44720-3396. Offers DPT. *Accreditation:* APTA. *Faculty:* 7 full-time (5 women), 2 part-time/adjunct (1 woman). *Students:* 62 full-time (48 women); includes 2 minority (1 African American, 1 American Indian/Alaska Native), 3 international. Average age 24. 114 applicants, 48% accepted, 25 enrolled. In 2009, 33 doctorates awarded. *Degree requirements:* For doctorate, comprehensive exam, research project, 3 clinical placements. *Entrance requirements:* For doctorate, GRE General Test, previous coursework in anatomy, physiology, chemistry, statistics, psychology, biology, and physics; minimum GPA of 3.0. Additional exam requirements/recommendations for international students: Required—TOEFL (minimum score 500 paper-based; 173 computer-based; 61 iBT). *Application deadline:* For fall admission, 5/1 for domestic students. Applications are processed on a rolling basis. Application fee: $25. Electronic applications accepted. *Expenses:* Contact institution. *Financial support:* In 2009–10, 6 fellowships (averaging $1,833 per year), 7 research assistantships with partial tuition reimbursements (averaging $2,163 per year) were awarded; tuition waivers (partial) and unspecified assistantships also available. Financial award application deadline: 12/31. *Faculty research:* Physical therapy practice management, intervention studies, biomechanics, motor control, mobilization/manipulation. *Unit head:* Dr. Chris Petrosino, Chair of Physical Therapy Division, 330-490-7362, Fax: 330-490-7371, E-mail: cpetrosino@walsh.edu. *Application contact:* Stephanie Wheeler, Director of Graduate and Transfer Admissions, 330-490-7181, Fax: 330-490-7182, E-mail: swheeler@walsh.edu.

Washington University in St. Louis, School of Medicine, Graduate Programs in Medicine, Program in Physical Therapy, St. Louis, MO 63130-4899. Offers movement science (PhD); physical therapy (DPT, PPDPT). *Accreditation:* APTA (one or more programs are accredited). Part-time and evening/weekend programs available. Postbaccalaureate distance learning degree programs offered (minimal on-campus study). *Faculty:* 22 full-time (15 women), 16 part-time/

adjunct (15 women). *Students:* 243 full-time (187 women), 42 part-time (22 women); includes 42 minority (10 African Americans, 1 American Indian/Alaska Native, 23 Asian Americans or Pacific Islanders, 8 Hispanic Americans). Average age 24. 447 applicants, 49% accepted, 83 enrolled. In 2009, 70 doctorates awarded. *Degree requirements:* For doctorate, thesis/dissertation (for some programs). *Entrance requirements:* For doctorate, GRE, sample of written work (PhD); for PPDPT, GRE, professional degree in physical therapy, clinical experience. Additional exam requirements/recommendations for international students: Required—TOEFL (minimum score 600 paper-based; 250 computer-based; 100 iBT), TWE (minimum score 5). *Application deadline:* For fall admission, 11/15 priority date for domestic and international students; for winter admission, 3/1 priority date for domestic and international students; for spring admission, 3/31 for domestic and international students. Applications are processed on a rolling basis. Application fee: $120. Electronic applications accepted. *Expenses:* Contact institution. *Financial support:* In 2009–10, 206 students received support, including 3 fellowships with full tuition reimbursements available (averaging $22,772 per year), 15 research assistantships (averaging $4,000 per year); Federal Work-Study, institutionally sponsored loans, and scholarships/grants also available. Support available to part-time students. Financial award application deadline: 3/1; financial award applicants required to submit CSS PROFILE or FAFSA. *Faculty research:* Movement and movement dysfunction. Total annual research expenditures: $2 million. *Unit head:* Dr. Susan S. Deusinger, Director, 314-286-1400, Fax: 314-286-1410. *Application contact:* Sarah J. Rands, Admissions and Student Affairs Coordinator, 314-286-1402, Fax: 314-286-1410, E-mail: rands@wustl.edu.

Wayne State University, Eugene Applebaum College of Pharmacy and Health Sciences, Department of Health Care Sciences, Program in Physical Therapy, Detroit, MI 48202. Offers MPT. *Accreditation:* APTA. *Entrance requirements:* For master's, personal resume, recommendations; interview. Additional exam requirements/recommendations for international students: Required—TOEFL (minimum score 550 paper-based; 213 computer-based); Recommended—TWE (minimum score 6). Electronic applications accepted.

Western Carolina University, Graduate School, College of Health and Human Sciences, Department of Physical Therapy, Cullowhee, NC 28723. Offers MPT. *Accreditation:* APTA. *Students:* 61 full-time (40 women). Average age 27. 127 applicants, 37% accepted, 31 enrolled. In 2009, 30 master's awarded. *Degree requirements:* For master's, comprehensive exam. *Entrance requirements:* For master's, GRE General Test, appropriate undergraduate degree with minimum GPA of 3.0, 3 letters of recommendation. Additional exam requirements/recommendations for international students: Required—TOEFL (minimum score 550 paper-based; 270 computer-based; 79 iBT). *Application deadline:* For fall admission, 2/1 for domestic students. Applications are processed on a rolling basis. Application fee: $45. *Financial support:* In 2009–10, 22 students received support, including 1 fellowship (averaging $6,000 per year), 21 research assistantships with full tuition reimbursements available (averaging $3,500 per year); teaching assistantships with full tuition reimbursements available, Federal Work-Study, institutionally sponsored loans, scholarships/grants, and unspecified assistantships also available. Financial award application deadline: 3/31; financial award applicants required to submit FAFSA. *Faculty research:* Bone density, disability in older adults, neuroanatomy, intervention of musculoskeletal conditions. *Unit head:* Dr. Karen Lunnen, Head, 828-227-7070, Fax: 828-227-7071, E-mail: klunnen@email.wcu.edu. *Application contact:* Admissions Specialist for Physical Therapy, 828-227-7398, Fax: 828-227-7480, E-mail: gradsch@email.wcu.edu.

Western University of Health Sciences, College of Allied Health Professions, Program in Physical Therapy, Pomona, CA 91766-1854. Offers DPT. *Accreditation:* APTA. *Entrance requirements:* For doctorate, GRE General Test, minimum GPA of 2.8, letters of recommendation, interview. *Expenses:* Contact institution.

West Virginia University, School of Medicine, Graduate Programs in Human Performance, Division of Physical Therapy, Morgantown, WV 26506. Offers DPT. *Accreditation:* APTA. Evening/weekend programs available. Postbaccalaureate distance learning degree programs offered (minimal on-campus study). *Entrance requirements:* For doctorate, GRE, minimum cumulative GPA and prerequisite science GPA of 3.0; volunteer/work experience in physical therapy; letters of recommendation. *Expenses:* Contact institution.

Wheeling Jesuit University, Department of Physical Therapy, Wheeling, WV 26003-6295. Offers DPT. *Accreditation:* APTA. *Faculty:* 6 full-time (3 women), 7 part-time/adjunct (2 women). *Students:* 80 full-time (43 women); includes 5 minority (1 African American, 3 Asian Americans or Pacific Islanders, 1 Hispanic American). Average age 24. 94 applicants, 84% accepted, 44 enrolled. In 2009, 30 doctorates awarded. *Degree requirements:* For doctorate, comprehensive exam, thesis/dissertation. *Entrance requirements:* For doctorate, GRE, minimum GPA of 3.0. Additional exam requirements/recommendations for international students: Required—TOEFL (minimum score 650 paper-based; 250 computer-based). *Application deadline:* For fall admission, 12/15 priority date for domestic and international students. Applications are processed on a rolling basis. Application fee: $25. Electronic applications accepted. *Expenses:* Contact institution. *Financial support:* In 2009–10, 74 students received support. Unspecified assistantships available. Financial award application deadline: 8/1; financial award applicants required to submit FAFSA. *Faculty research:* Problem-based learning versus traditional education outcomes, anterior cruciate ligament injuries in women athletes, prevention of disease and wellness, pediatrics. *Unit head:* Dr. Mark Drnach, Acting Director, 304-243-2432, Fax: 304-243-2042, E-mail: wjupt@wju.edu. *Application contact:* Dr. Mark Drnach, Acting Director, 304-243-2432, Fax: 304-243-2042, E-mail: wjupt@wju.edu.

Wichita State University, Graduate School, College of Health Professions, Department of Physical Therapy, Wichita, KS 67260. Offers DPT. *Accreditation:* APTA. *Expenses:* Tuition, state resident: full-time $4247; part-time $235.95 per credit hour. Tuition, nonresident: full-time $11,171; part-time $620.60 per credit hour. Required fees: $34; $3.60 per credit hour. $17 per term. Tuition and fees vary according to campus/location and program. *Unit head:* Dr. Camilla Wilson, Chair, 316-978-5780, Fax: 316-978-3025, E-mail: camilla.wilson@wichita.edu. *Application contact:* Dr. Camilla Wilson, Chair, 316-978-5780, Fax: 316-978-3025, E-mail: camilla.wilson@wichita.edu.

Widener University, School of Human Service Professions, Institute for Physical Therapy Education, Chester, PA 19013-5792. Offers MS, DPT. *Accreditation:* APTA. *Faculty:* 8 full-time (5 women), 1 (woman) part-time/adjunct. *Students:* 109 full-time (67 women), 14 part-time (3 women); includes 5 minority (1 African American, 4 Asian Americans or Pacific Islanders), 1 international. Average age 25. 82 applicants, 93% accepted. In 2009, 53 doctorates awarded. *Degree requirements:* For master's, thesis. *Entrance requirements:* For master's, GRE. *Application deadline:* For fall admission, 1/30 for domestic students. Applications are processed on a rolling basis. Application fee: $40. *Expenses:* Contact institution. *Financial support:* Teaching assistantships, Federal Work-Study, institutionally sponsored loans, and scholarships/grants available. Financial award application deadline: 5/1; financial award applicants required to submit FAFSA. *Faculty research:* Social support, aquatics, children and adults with movement dysfunction, physical therapy modalities. *Unit head:* Dr. Robin L. Dole, Associate Dean and Director, 610-499-1159, Fax: 610-499-1231, E-mail: robin.l.dole@widener.edu. *Application contact:* Dr. Robin L. Dole, Associate Dean and Director, 610-499-1159, Fax: 610-499-1231, E-mail: robin.l.dole@widener.edu.

Winston-Salem State University, Department of Physical Therapy, Winston-Salem, NC 27110-0003. Offers MPT. *Accreditation:* APTA. *Entrance requirements:* For master's, GRE, 3 letters of recommendation. Electronic applications accepted. *Faculty research:* Tissue healing; neuro-imaging with functional recovery; visual, proprioceptive and vestibular sensor inputs roles.

Youngstown State University, Graduate School, Bitonte College of Health and Human Services, Department of Physical Therapy, Youngstown, OH 44555-0001. Offers DPT. *Accreditation:* APTA. *Entrance requirements:* Additional exam requirements/recommendations for international students: Required—TOEFL.

Physician Assistant Studies

Albany Medical College, Center for Physician Assistant Studies, Albany, NY 12208-3479. Offers MS. *Accreditation:* ARC-PA. *Faculty:* 8 full-time (5 women), 17 part-time/adjunct (10 women). *Students:* 92 full-time (77 women); includes 8 minority (5 African Americans, 3 Asian Americans or Pacific Islanders), 1 international. Average age 27. 681 applicants, 11% accepted, 30 enrolled. In 2009, 32 master's awarded. *Degree requirements:* For master's, comprehensive exam, thesis. *Entrance requirements:* For master's, GRE. Additional exam requirements/recommendations for international students: Required—TOEFL. *Application deadline:* For winter admission, 11/1 for domestic and international students. Applications are processed on a rolling basis. Application fee: $50. *Expenses:* Contact institution. *Financial support:* In 2009–10, 89 students received support. Scholarships/grants available. Financial award application deadline: 10/1; financial award applicants required to submit FAFSA. *Faculty research:* Genetics, education, informatics. *Unit head:* Dr. David F. Irvine, Director, 518-262-5251, Fax: 518-262-6698, E-mail: irvined@mail.amc.edu. *Application contact:* Rosalyn Green, Admissions Coordinator, 518-262-5251, Fax: 518-262-6698, E-mail: greenr@mail.amc.edu.

Alderson-Broaddus College, Program in Physician Assistant Studies, Philippi, WV 26416. Offers MPAS. *Degree requirements:* For master's, comprehensive exam, thesis. *Entrance requirements:* For master's, minimum 60 semester hours plus specific science. Electronic applications accepted.

A.T. Still University of Health Sciences, Arizona School of Health Sciences, Mesa, AZ 85206. Offers advanced occupational therapy (MS); advanced physician assistant (MS); athletic training (MS); audiology (Au D); health sciences (DHSc); human movement (MS); occupational therapy (MS); physical therapy (MS, DPT); physician assistant (MS); transitional audiology (Au D); transitional physical therapy (DPT). *Accreditation:* AOTA (one or more programs are accredited); ASHA. Postbaccalaureate distance learning degree programs offered (no on-campus study). *Faculty:* 53 full-time (30 women), 205 part-time/adjunct (117 women). *Students:* 491 full-time (353 women), 1,251 part-time (874 women); includes 319 minority (70 African Americans, 11 American Indian/Alaska Native, 176 Asian Americans or Pacific Islanders, 62 Hispanic Americans), 3 international. Average age 31. 2,697 applicants, 22% accepted, 420 enrolled. In 2009, 225 master's, 523 doctorates awarded. *Degree requirements:* For master's, thesis (for some programs); for doctorate, thesis/dissertation (for some programs). *Entrance requirements:* For master's, GRE General Test; for doctorate, GRE, Evaluation of Practicing Audiologists Capabilities (Au D), Physical Therapy Evaluation Tool (DPT), current state licensure, master's degree or equivalent (Au D), minimum GPA of 2.7. Additional exam requirements/recommendations for international students: Recommended—TOEFL (minimum score 550 paper-based; 213 computer-based; 80 iBT). *Application deadline:* For fall admission, 2/1 priority date for domestic and international students. Applications are processed on a rolling basis. Application fee: $60. *Expenses:* Contact institution. *Financial support:* In 2009–10, 651 students received support. Federal Work-Study and scholarships/grants available. Financial award application deadline: 5/1; financial award applicants required to submit FAFSA. *Faculty research:* Adolescent health-related quality of life, clinical outcomes following sport related injury, pediatric concussion, shoulder stability and neuromuscular control, sport conditioning, exercise and sport psychology, geriatric exercise and wellness. Total annual research expenditures: $61,527. *Unit head:* Dr. Randy Danielsen, Dean, 480-219-6000, Fax: 480-219-6110, E-mail: rdanielsen@atsu.edu. *Application contact:* Donna Sparks, Associate Director for Admissions, 660-626-2237, Fax: 660-626-2969, E-mail: admissions@atsu.edu.

Augsburg College, Program in Physicians Assistant Studies, Minneapolis, MN 55454-1351. Offers MS. *Accreditation:* ARC-PA. *Expenses:* Tuition: Full-time $16,713; part-time $1857 per course. Required fees: $450; $50 per course. Tuition and fees vary according to course load and program.

Barry University, School of Graduate Medical Sciences, Physician Assistant Program, Miami Shores, FL 33161-6695. Offers MCMS. *Accreditation:* ARC-PA. *Entrance requirements:* For master's, GRE General Test. Electronic applications accepted.

Baylor College of Medicine, School of Allied Health Sciences, Physician Assistant Program, Houston, TX 77030-3498. Offers MS. *Accreditation:* ARC-PA. *Faculty:* 5 full-time (4 women), 5 part-time/adjunct (3 women). *Students:* 107 full-time (96 women); includes 20 minority (4 African Americans, 10 Asian Americans or Pacific Islanders, 6 Hispanic Americans). Average age 26. 703 applicants, 8% accepted, 40 enrolled. In 2009, 34 master's awarded. *Degree requirements:* For master's, comprehensive exam, thesis. *Entrance requirements:* For master's, GRE General Test, bachelor's degree. Additional exam requirements/recommendations for international students: Required—TOEFL. *Application deadline:* For fall admission, 10/1 for domestic students. Application fee: $35. Electronic applications accepted. *Expenses:* Contact institution. *Financial support:* In 2009–10, 87 students received support. Career-related internships or fieldwork, Federal Work-Study, institutionally sponsored loans, and scholarships/grants available. Financial award application deadline: 5/11; financial award applicants required to submit FAFSA. *Faculty research:* Cancer education, physician assistant studies, multiculturalism, alcoholism prevention, women's health. *Unit head:* Carl E. Fasser, Director, 713-798-5405, Fax: 713-798-6128, E-mail: cfasser@bcm.tmc.edu. *Application contact:* Dr. Florence Eddins-Folensbee, Associate Dean of Admissions, 713-798-4842, Fax: 713-798-5563, E-mail: wthomas@bcm.edu.

Butler University, College of Pharmacy, Indianapolis, IN 46208-3485. Offers pharmaceutical science (Pharm D, MS); physician assistance studies (MS). *Accreditation:* ACPE (one or more programs are accredited). Part-time and evening/weekend programs available. *Faculty:* 24 full-time (11 women), 2 part-time/adjunct (1 woman). *Students:* 274 full-time (194 women), 10 part-time (6 women); includes 19 minority (4 African Americans, 9 Asian Americans or Pacific Islanders, 6 Hispanic Americans), 11 international. Average age 24. 107 applicants, 6% accepted, 6 enrolled. In 2009, 129 first professional degrees, 51 master's awarded. *Degree requirements:* For master's, research paper or thesis. *Application deadline:* For fall admission, 8/1 priority date for domestic students; for spring admission, 12/15 for domestic students. Applications are processed on a rolling basis. Application fee: $35. Electronic applications accepted. *Expenses:* Contact institution. *Financial support:* Applicants required to submit FAFSA. *Faculty research:* Anti-seizure drugs, casein kinase inhibitors, speech recognition interface for prescribing drugs, pharmacoeconomics. Total annual research expenditures: $92,000. *Unit head:* Dr. Mary Andritz, Dean, 317-940-9451, Fax: 317-940-6172, E-mail: mandritz@butler.edu. *Application contact:* Dr. Bruce Clayton, Professor, 317-940-9830, E-mail: bclayton@butler.edu.

California State University, Dominguez Hills, College of Professional Studies, School of Health and Human Services, Division of Health Sciences, Carson, CA 90747-0001. Offers MS. Part-time programs available. *Students:* 3 full-time (2 women), 8 part-time (6 women); includes 7 minority (4 African Americans, 3 Hispanic Americans). Average age 43. 1 applicant, 0%

Physician Assistant Studies

California State University, Dominguez Hills (continued)
accepted, 0 enrolled. In 2009, 14 master's awarded. *Degree requirements:* For master's, comprehensive exam. *Entrance requirements:* Additional exam requirements/recommendations for international students: Required—TOEFL, TWE. *Application deadline:* For fall admission, 8/15 priority date for domestic students. Applications are processed on a rolling basis. Electronic applications accepted. *Expenses:* Tuition, nonresident: full-time $6696; part-time $372 per unit. Required fees: $5946; $1752 per semester. *Faculty research:* International health, health promotion and disease prevention, public health. *Unit head:* Dr. Mitchell T. Maki, Dean, 310-243-2046, Fax: 310-217-6800, E-mail: mmaki@csudh.edu. *Application contact:* Dr. Gayle Ball-Parker, Director of Admissions, 310-243-3645, E-mail: gball@csudh.edu.

Central Michigan University, College of Graduate Studies, The Herbert H. and Grace A. Dow College of Health Professions, School of Rehabilitation and Medical Sciences, Mount Pleasant, MI 48859. Offers physical therapy (DPT); physician assistant (MS). *Accreditation:* APTA; ARC-PA. *Degree requirements:* For master's, thesis or alternative; for doctorate, thesis/dissertation or alternative. *Entrance requirements:* For master's and doctorate, GRE. Electronic applications accepted.

Chatham University, Program in Physician Assistant Studies, Pittsburgh, PA 15232-2826. Offers MPAS. *Accreditation:* ARC-PA. *Students:* 133 full-time (109 women). Average age 27. 760 applicants, 15% accepted, 71 enrolled. In 2009, 43 master's awarded. *Degree requirements:* For master's, thesis, clinical experience, research project. *Entrance requirements:* For master's, community service, minimum GPA of 3.0, health science work or shadowing, volunteer work experience, PA shadowing form, 3 references. Additional exam requirements/recommendations for international students: Required—TOEFL (minimum score 600 paper-based; 250 computer-based; 100 iBT), IELTS (minimum score 6.5), TWE. *Application deadline:* For fall admission, 10/1 priority date for domestic and international students. Application fee: $45. *Expenses:* Contact institution. *Financial support:* Career-related internships or fieldwork available. Financial award applicants required to submit FAFSA. *Faculty research:* Complementary and alternative medicine, education methods, physician assistant practice. *Unit head:* Luis Ramos, Director, 412-365-1314, Fax: 412-365-1213, E-mail: lramos@chatham.edu. *Application contact:* Maureen Stokan, Assistant Director of Graduate Admissions, 412-365-2988, Fax: 412-365-1609, E-mail: gradadmissions@chatham.edu.

Cleveland State University, College of Graduate Studies, College of Science, Department of Health Sciences, Cleveland, OH 44115. Offers health sciences (MS), including health sciences, online health sciences; occupational therapy (MOT); physical therapy (DPT); physician's assistant (MS); speech pathology and audiology (MA). Part-time programs available. Postbaccalaureate distance learning degree programs offered (no on-campus study). *Degree requirements:* For master's, comprehensive exam (for some programs), thesis optional, clinical/fieldwork education. *Entrance requirements:* For master's, GRE, minimum cumulative GPA of 3.0; for doctorate, GRE, BA, minimum cumulative GPA of 3.0. Additional exam requirements/recommendations for international students: Required—TOEFL (minimum score 523 paper-based; 197 computer-based), IELTS (minimum score 6). *Faculty research:* Psychosocial needs of children, use of technology with disabilities, effects of stroke on gait, communication variables with accentedness, grasp patterns of possums.

Daemen College, Physician Assistant Department, Amherst, NY 14226-3592. Offers MS. *Accreditation:* ARC-PA. *Faculty:* 4 full-time (1 woman), 2 part-time/adjunct (1 woman). *Students:* 77 full-time (69 women); includes 6 minority (3 Asian Americans or Pacific Islanders, 3 Hispanic Americans). Average age 25. 208 applicants, 13% accepted, 24 enrolled. In 2009, 30 master's awarded. *Entrance requirements:* For master's, minimum GPA of 3.0 overall and in math and science prerequisites; 120 hours of direct patient contact. Additional exam requirements/recommendations for international students: Required—TOEFL (minimum score 500 paper-based; 173 computer-based; 61 iBT). *Application deadline:* For fall admission, 3/1 priority date for domestic and international students; for spring admission, 10/1 priority date for domestic and international students. Applications are processed on a rolling basis. Application fee: $25. Electronic applications accepted. *Expenses:* Tuition: Part-time $770 per credit hour. Tuition and fees vary according to course load, program and reciprocity agreements. *Financial support:* Institutionally sponsored loans and scholarships/grants available. Financial award application deadline: 2/15; financial award applicants required to submit FAFSA. *Unit head:* Gregg L. Shutts, Director, 716-839-8316, Fax: 716-839-8252, E-mail: shutts@daemen.edu. *Application contact:* Marcy Moore, Director of Graduate Admissions, 716-839-8383, Fax: 716-839-8252, E-mail: mmoore@daemen.edu.

DeSales University, Graduate Division, Program in Physician Assistant Studies, Center Valley, PA 18034-9568. Offers MSPAS. *Accreditation:* ARC-PA. Part-time and evening/weekend programs available. Postbaccalaureate distance learning degree programs offered (minimal on-campus study). *Faculty:* 6 full-time (4 women). *Students:* 46 full-time. 656 applicants, 5% accepted, 16 enrolled. In 2009, 218 master's awarded. *Degree requirements:* For master's, comprehensive exam. *Entrance requirements:* For master's, GRE General Test/MCAT. Additional exam requirements/recommendations for international students: Required—TOEFL (minimum score 600 paper-based). *Application deadline:* For fall admission, 1/15 for domestic and international students. Electronic applications accepted. *Expenses:* Tuition: Full-time $17,500; part-time $665 per credit. Full-time tuition and fees vary according to program. Part-time tuition and fees vary according to course load. *Financial support:* Applicants required to submit FAFSA. *Unit head:* Christine Bruce, Director, 610-282-1100 Ext. 1289, Fax: 610-282-0525, E-mail: christine.bruce@desales.edu. *Application contact:* Caryn Stopper, Director of Graduate Admissions, 610-282-1100 Ext. 1768, Fax: 610-282-0525, E-mail: caryn.stopper@desales.edu.

Des Moines University, College of Health Sciences, Physician Assistant Program, Des Moines, IA 50312-4104. Offers MS. *Accreditation:* ARC-PA. *Faculty:* 6 full-time (2 women). *Students:* 93 full-time (71 women); includes 3 minority (1 African American, 2 Hispanic Americans). Average age 25. 503 applicants, 16% accepted, 48 enrolled. In 2009, 44 master's awarded. *Degree requirements:* For master's, research project. *Entrance requirements:* For master's, GRE, interview, minimum GPA of 2.8, related work experience. *Application deadline:* For fall admission, 12/1 for domestic students. Applications are processed on a rolling basis. Electronic applications accepted. *Expenses:* Contact institution. *Financial support:* In 2009–10, 8 students received support. Career-related internships or fieldwork, institutionally sponsored loans, scholarships/grants, and university employment available. Support available to part-time students. Financial award application deadline: 4/1; financial award applicants required to submit FAFSA. *Unit head:* Jolene Kelly, Director, 515-271-1685, E-mail: jolene.kelly@dmu.edu. *Application contact:* Josh Kvinlaug, Admissions Coordinator, 515-271-7875, Fax: 515-271-7145, E-mail: paadmit@dmu.edu.

Drexel University, College of Nursing and Health Professions, Program in Physician Assistant Studies, Philadelphia, PA 19104-2875. Offers MHS. *Accreditation:* ARC-PA. Electronic applications accepted.

Duke University, School of Medicine, Physician Assistant Program, Durham, NC 27701. Offers MHS. *Accreditation:* ARC-PA. *Faculty:* 15 full-time (13 women), 17 part-time/adjunct (13 women). *Students:* 139 full-time (103 women); includes 37 minority (10 African Americans, 2 American Indian/Alaska Native, 15 Asian Americans or Pacific Islanders, 10 Hispanic Americans). Average age 28. 684 applicants, 13% accepted, 72 enrolled. In 2009, 57 master's awarded. *Entrance requirements:* For master's, GRE, minimum of 5 courses in biological sciences with courses in anatomy, physiology and microbiology, 8 undergraduate hours in chemistry and statistics, patient care experience. *Application deadline:* For fall admission, 10/1 for domestic students. Application fee: $0. Electronic applications accepted. *Expenses:* Contact institution. *Financial support:* In 2009–10, 133 students received support; fellowships, research assistantships, teaching assistantships, institutionally sponsored loans and scholarships/grants available. Financial award application deadline: 5/1; financial award applicants required to submit FAFSA. *Unit head:* Patricia M. Dieter, Director/Assistant Clinical Professor, 919-681-3161, Fax: 919-681-9666, E-mail: patricia.dieter@duke.edu. *Application contact:* Wendy Z. Elwell, Program Coordinator, 919-681-3154, Fax: 919-681-9666, E-mail: wendy.elwell@duke.edu.

Duquesne University, John G. Rangos, Sr. School of Health Sciences, Pittsburgh, PA 15282-0001. Offers health management systems (MHMS); occupational therapy (MS); physical therapy (DPT); physician assistant studies (MPAS); rehabilitation science (MS, PhD); speech–language pathology (MS); MBA/MHMS. *Accreditation:* AOTA (one or more programs are accredited); APTA (one or more programs are accredited); ASHA. *Faculty:* 35 full-time (23 women), 17 part-time/adjunct (10 women). *Students:* 309 full-time (258 women), 11 part-time (7 women); includes 11 minority (5 African Americans, 5 Asian Americans or Pacific Islanders, 1 Hispanic American), 6 international. Average age 23. 454 applicants, 20% accepted, 20 enrolled. In 2009, 92 master's, 23 doctorates awarded. *Degree requirements:* For doctorate, thesis/dissertation. *Entrance requirements:* For master's, GRE General Test (speech-language pathology), 3 letters of recommendation; minimum GPA of 2.75 (health management systems, occupational therapy), minimum GPA of 3.0 (speech-language pathology); for doctorate, GRE General Test (for physical therapy), 3 letters of recommendation, minimum GPA of 3.0, personal interview. Additional exam requirements/recommendations for international students: Required—TOEFL (minimum score 550 paper-based; 233 computer-based; 90 iBT). *Application deadline:* Applications are processed on a rolling basis. Electronic applications accepted. *Expenses:* Contact institution. *Financial support:* Federal Work-Study available. *Faculty research:* Neuronal processing, electrical stimulation on peripheral neuropathy, CNS stimulatory and inhibitory signals, behavioral genetic methodologies to development disorders of speech, neurogenic communication disorders. Total annual research expenditures: $338,404. *Unit head:* Dr. Gregory H. Frazer, Dean, 412-396-5303, Fax: 412-396-5554, E-mail: frazer@duq.edu. *Application contact:* Christopher R. Hilf, Recruiter/Academic Advisor, 412-396-5653, Fax: 412-396-5554, E-mail: hilfc@duq.edu.

D'Youville College, Physician Assistant Department, Buffalo, NY 14201-1084. Offers MS. *Accreditation:* ARC-PA. *Entrance requirements:* For master's, BS, patient contact, 3 letters of recommendation. Additional exam requirements/recommendations for international students: Required—TOEFL (minimum score 500 paper-based; 173 computer-based). Electronic applications accepted.

East Carolina University, Graduate School, School of Allied Health Sciences, Department of Physician Assistant Studies, Greenville, NC 27858-4353. Offers MS. *Accreditation:* ARC-PA.

Eastern Virginia Medical School, Master of Physician Assistant Program, Norfolk, VA 23501-1980. Offers MPA. *Accreditation:* ARC-PA. *Faculty:* 9 full-time (3 women). *Students:* 149 full-time (106 women); includes 11 African Americans, 1 Asian American or Pacific Islander, 3 Hispanic Americans. 624 applicants, 9% accepted, 50 enrolled. In 2009, 47 master's awarded. *Entrance requirements:* Additional exam requirements/recommendations for international students: Required—TOEFL. *Application deadline:* For spring admission, 3/1 for domestic students. Applications are processed on a rolling basis. Application fee: $60. Electronic applications accepted. *Expenses:* Contact institution. *Financial support:* Applicants required to submit FAFSA. *Unit head:* Dr. Thomas Parish, Director, 757-446-7126, Fax: 757-446-7403, E-mail: parishtg@evms.edu. *Application contact:* Rose Mwayungu, Director of Health Professions Enrollment, 757-446-7158, Fax: 757-446-8915, E-mail: mwayunra@evms.edu.

Emory University, School of Medicine, Programs in Allied Health Professions, Physician Assistant Program, Atlanta, GA 30322-1100. Offers MM Sc. *Accreditation:* ARC-PA. Postbaccalaureate distance learning degree programs offered (minimal on-campus study). *Faculty:* 9 full-time (6 women), 3 part-time/adjunct (2 women). *Students:* 155 full-time (115 women), 1 part-time (0 women); includes 35 minority (14 African Americans, 1 American Indian/Alaska Native, 10 Asian Americans or Pacific Islanders, 10 Hispanic Americans), 2 international. Average age 29. 857 applicants, 8% accepted, 54 enrolled. In 2009, 53 master's awarded. *Entrance requirements:* For master's, GRE General Test. Additional exam requirements/recommendations for international students: Required—TOEFL (minimum score 250 computer-based). *Application deadline:* For fall admission, 10/1 for domestic and international students. Applications are processed on a rolling basis. Application fee: $30. Electronic applications accepted. *Expenses:* Contact institution. *Financial support:* In 2009–10, 99 students received support. Institutionally sponsored loans and scholarships/grants available. Financial award application deadline: 3/1; financial award applicants required to submit FAFSA. *Faculty research:* Cultural competency in medical education, farmworker health, computer-assisted learning, physician assistants in primary care, geriatric functional assessment. *Unit head:* Dana Sayre-Stanhope, Director, 404-727-2762, Fax: 404-727-7836, E-mail: dsayre@emory.edu. *Application contact:* Kaye Johnson, Assistant Director of Admissions, 404-727-7857, Fax: 404-727-7836, E-mail: ljohn07@learnlink.emory.edu.

Franklin Pierce University, Graduate Studies, Rindge, NH 03461-0060. Offers emerging network technology (Graduate Certificate); health practice management (MBA, Graduate Certificate); human resource management (MBA); human resources management (Graduate Certificate); information technology management (MS); leadership (MBA, DA), including transformational leadership (DA); nursing (MS); physical therapy (DPT); physician assistant (MPAS); sports facilities management (MS); teacher education (M Ed). *Accreditation:* APTA. Part-time programs available. Postbaccalaureate distance learning degree programs offered (no on-campus study). *Faculty:* 27 full-time (16 women), 18 part-time/adjunct (4 women). *Students:* 296 full-time (172 women), 249 part-time (165 women); includes 18 minority (5 African Americans, 7 Asian Americans or Pacific Islanders, 6 Hispanic Americans), 31 international. Average age 38. 227 applicants, 97% accepted, 185 enrolled. In 2009, 76 master's, 46 doctorates awarded. *Degree requirements:* For master's, concentrated original research projects; student teaching; fieldwork and/or internship; leadership project; for doctorate, concentrated original research projects, clinical fieldwork and/or internship, leadership project. *Entrance requirements:* For master's, minimum GPA of 2.5, 3 letters of recommendation; for doctorate, demonstrated success at previous academic institutions (minimum GPA of 2.5), 3 letters of recommendation, personal mission statement, interview; writing sample (for DA program). Additional exam requirements/recommendations for international students: Required—TOEFL (minimum score 550 paper-based; 195 computer-based). *Application deadline:* Applications are processed on a rolling basis. Application fee: $0. Electronic applications accepted. *Expenses:* Tuition: Part-time $1560 per course. Part-time tuition and fees vary according to degree level, campus/location and program. *Financial support:* In 2009–10, 36 students received support, including 22 teaching assistantships with full and partial tuition reimbursements available; career-related internships or fieldwork and unspecified assistantships also available. Support available to part-time students. Financial award applicants required to submit FAFSA. *Faculty research:* Evidence based practice in sports physical therapy, human resource management in economic crisis, leadership in nursing, innovation in sports facility management, differentiated learning and understanding by design. *Unit head:* Dr. Robert G. Goddard, Assistant Dean, 603-899-4361, Fax: 603-229-4580, E-mail: goddardr@franklinpierce.edu. *Application contact:* 800-325-1090, Fax: 603-898-0827, E-mail: gpsadmin@franklinpierce.edu.

Gannon University, School of Graduate Studies, Morosky College of Health Professions and Sciences, School of Health Professions, Program in Physician Assistant, Erie, PA 16541-0001. Offers MPAS. Program requires five years to complete. *Accreditation:* ARC-PA. *Students:* 55 full-time (46 women); includes 3 minority (1 Asian American or Pacific Islander, 2 Hispanic Americans). Average age 23. 78 applicants, 21% accepted, 10 enrolled. In 2009, 40 master's awarded. *Degree requirements:* For master's, thesis or alternative, research project. *Entrance requirements:* For master's, interview, bachelor's degree, minimum QPA of 3.0. Additional exam requirements/recommendations for international students: Required—TOEFL (minimum score 79 iBT). *Application deadline:* For fall admission, 1/15 for domestic students. Application fee: $25. Electronic applications accepted. *Expenses:* Contact institution. *Financial support:* Scholarships/grants available. Financial award application deadline: 7/1; financial award applicants required to submit FAFSA. *Unit head:* Michele Roth-Kauffman, Chair, 814-871-5643, E-mail: rothkauf001@gannon.edu. *Application contact:* Kara Morgan, Assistant Director of Graduate Admissions, 814-871-5831, Fax: 814-871-5827, E-mail: graduate@gannon.edu.

The George Washington University, School of Medicine and Health Sciences, Health Sciences Programs, Physician Assistant Program, Washington, DC 20052. Offers MSHS, MSHS/MPH. *Accreditation:* ARC-PA. *Students:* 137 full-time (112 women), 5 part-time (all

women); includes 16 minority (4 African Americans, 7 Asian Americans or Pacific Islanders, 5 Hispanic Americans). Average age 28. 491 applicants, 24% accepted, 63 enrolled. In 2009, 59 master's awarded. *Entrance requirements:* For master's, GRE General Test, BA/BS with clinical experience. *Application deadline:* For fall admission, 10/15 for domestic students. Applications are processed on a rolling basis. Application fee: $60. Electronic applications accepted. *Unit head:* Venetia L. Orcutt, Director, 202-994-6670, E-mail: vorcutt@gwu.edu. *Application contact:* Jamie Lewis, Executive Assistant, 202-994-6661, E-mail: npajsl@gwumc.edu.

Grand Valley State University, College of Health Professions, Physician Assistant Studies Program, Allendale, MI 49401-9403. Offers MPAS. *Accreditation:* ARC-PA. *Faculty:* 8 full-time (2 women), 8 part-time/adjunct (2 women). *Students:* 90 full-time (66 women), 90 part-time (66 women); includes 5 minority (1 American Indian/Alaska Native, 4 Asian Americans or Pacific Islanders). Average age 26. 166 applicants, 23% accepted, 33 enrolled. In 2009, 28 master's awarded. *Degree requirements:* For master's, thesis, clinical rotations, project. *Entrance requirements:* For master's, interview, 250 hours of health care experience. Additional exam requirements/recommendations for international students: Required—TOEFL (minimum score 610 paper-based; 253 computer-based). *Application deadline:* For fall admission, 11/1 for domestic and international students. Application fee: $30. Electronic applications accepted. *Expenses:* Tuition, state resident: part-time $471 per credit hour. Tuition, nonresident: part-time $646 per credit hour. Tuition and fees vary according to course level. *Financial support:* In 2009–10, 4 students received support, including 2 fellowships (averaging $1,500 per year), 2 research assistantships (averaging $2,877 per year); institutionally sponsored loans also available. Financial award application deadline: 2/15. *Faculty research:* Women's health, pain management, PA practice issues, hematology/hemostasis, patient education. *Unit head:* Wallace Boeve, Director, 616-331-3356, Fax: 616-331-5999, E-mail: boevew@gvsu.edu. *Application contact:* Darlene Zwart, Student Services Coordinator, 616-331-3958, E-mail: zwartdo@gvsu.edu.

Harding University, College of Sciences, Searcy, AR 72149-0001. Offers physician assistant studies (MS). *Faculty:* 5 full-time (1 woman), 2 part-time/adjunct (1 woman). *Students:* 64 full-time (51 women); includes 8 minority (1 African American, 4 American Indian/Alaska Native, 2 Asian Americans or Pacific Islanders, 1 Hispanic American). Average age 26. 300 applicants, 11% accepted, 32 enrolled. In 2009, 32 master's awarded. *Degree requirements:* For master's, project. *Entrance requirements:* For master's, GRE. *Application deadline:* For fall admission, 11/1 for domestic students. Applications are processed on a rolling basis. Application fee: $25. Electronic applications accepted. *Expenses:* Contact institution. *Financial support:* Applicants required to submit FAFSA. *Unit head:* Michael Murphy, Director, 501-279-5642, E-mail: mmurphy1@harding.edu. *Application contact:* Marcia Murphy, Admissions Director, Physician Assistant Program, 501-279-5642, Fax: 501-279-4188, E-mail: paprogram@harding.edu.

Idaho State University, Office of Graduate Studies, Kasiska College of Health Professions, Program in Physician Assistant Studies, Pocatello, ID 83209-8253. Offers MPAS. *Accreditation:* ARC-PA. *Faculty:* 2 full-time (1 woman). *Students:* 109 full-time (73 women), 1 part-time (0 women); includes 10 minority (3 Asian Americans or Pacific Islanders, 7 Hispanic Americans), 1 international. Average age 28. In 2009, 28 master's awarded. *Degree requirements:* For master's, comprehensive exam, thesis (for some programs), portfolio, clinical year, oral case presentation. *Entrance requirements:* For master's, GRE General Test, minimum GPA of 3.0, letters of reference. Additional exam requirements/recommendations for international students: Required—TOEFL (minimum score 500 paper-based; 213 computer-based). *Application deadline:* For fall admission, 1/15 for domestic and international students. Applications are processed on a rolling basis. Application fee: $55. Electronic applications accepted. *Expenses:* Contact institution. *Financial support:* Teaching assistantships with full and partial tuition reimbursements, career-related internships or fieldwork, Federal Work-Study, institutionally sponsored loans, scholarships/grants, traineeships, health care benefits, tuition waivers, and unspecified assistantships available. Support available to part-time students. Financial award application deadline: 1/1; financial award applicants required to submit FAFSA. *Unit head:* Dr. John M. Schroeder, Director, 208-282-4726, Fax: 208-282-4969, E-mail: schrjohn@isu.edu. *Application contact:* Tami Carson, Graduate School Technical Records Specialist, 208-282-2150, Fax: 208-282-4847, E-mail: carstami@isu.edu.

James Madison University, The Graduate School, College of Integrated Science and Technology, Department of Health Sciences, Program in Physician Assistant Studies, Harrisonburg, VA 22807. Offers MPAS. *Accreditation:* ARC-PA. Part-time programs available. *Students:* 52 full-time (35 women); includes 4 minority (2 African Americans, 1 Asian American or Pacific Islander, 1 Hispanic American). Average age 27. In 2009, 20 master's awarded. *Entrance requirements:* For master's, GRE General Test. *Application deadline:* For fall admission, 1/15 priority date for domestic students. Application fee: $55. *Expenses:* Tuition, area resident: Part-time $305 per credit hour. Tuition, state resident: part-time $305 per credit hour. Tuition, nonresident: part-time $890 per credit hour. *Financial support:* Application deadline: 3/1. *Unit head:* James Hammond, Graduate Coordinator, 540-568-2395. *Application contact:* Lynette M. Bible, Director of Graduate Admissions, 540-568-6395, Fax: 540-568-7860, E-mail: biblelm@jmu.edu.

Jefferson College of Health Sciences, Program in Physician Assistant, Roanoke, VA 24031-3186. Offers MS. *Accreditation:* ARC-PA. *Faculty:* 15 full-time (7 women), 3 part-time/adjunct (1 woman). *Students:* 78 full-time (63 women); includes 1 American Indian/Alaska Native, 3 Asian Americans or Pacific Islanders, 3 Hispanic Americans. Average age 26. 548 applicants, 11% accepted, 40 enrolled. *Degree requirements:* For master's, rotations. *Entrance requirements:* For master's, GRE. Additional exam requirements/recommendations for international students: Required—TOEFL (minimum score 550 paper-based; 213 computer-based; 80 iBT). *Application deadline:* Applications are processed on a rolling basis. Application fee: $35. Electronic applications accepted. *Financial support:* Career-related internships or fieldwork, Federal Work-Study, scholarships/grants, traineeships, health care benefits, and tuition waivers (full and partial) available. Support available to part-time students. Financial award applicants required to submit FAFSA. *Faculty research:* Community health, chronic disease management, geriatrics, rheumatology, medically underserved populations. *Unit head:* Dr. Wilton Kennedy, Program Director, 540-985-8256, E-mail: wkennedy@jchs.edu. *Application contact:* Judith McKeon, Director of Admissions, 540-985-9083, Fax: 540-985-9773, E-mail: jomckeon@jchs.edu.

Keiser University, MS in Physician Assistant Program, Fort Lauderdale, FL 33309. Offers MS. *Unit head:* Helen Martin, Program Director, 888-7-KEISER. *Application contact:* Manuel Christiansen, Associate Director of Admissions, 954-318-1620 Ext. 309, E-mail: mchristiansen@keiseruniversity.edu.

King's College, Program in Physician Assistant Studies, Wilkes-Barre, PA 18711-0801. Offers MSPAS. *Accreditation:* ARC-PA. *Degree requirements:* For master's, thesis. *Entrance requirements:* Additional exam requirements/recommendations for international students: Required—TOEFL (minimum score 600 paper-based; 250 computer-based). Electronic applications accepted.

Le Moyne College, Department of Physician Assistant Studies, Syracuse, NY 13214. Offers MS. *Accreditation:* ARC-PA. *Faculty:* 6 full-time (4 women), 9 part-time/adjunct (2 women). *Students:* 76 full-time (60 women); includes 6 minority (2 African Americans, 3 Asian Americans or Pacific Islanders, 1 Hispanic American). Average age 27. 360 applicants, 15% accepted, 45 enrolled. In 2009, 34 master's awarded. *Degree requirements:* For master's, project. *Entrance requirements:* For master's, minimum GPA of 3.0, patient contact, interview, writing sample, 3 letters of recommendation. Additional exam requirements/recommendations for international students: Required—TOEFL (minimum score 550 paper-based; 213 computer-based; 79 iBT). *Application deadline:* For fall admission, 10/1 priority date for domestic and international students. Electronic applications accepted. *Expenses:* Contact institution. *Financial support:* In 2009–10, 8 students received support. Career-related internships or fieldwork and health care benefits available. Financial award applicants required to submit FAFSA. *Faculty research:*

Cultural competence, educational outcomes, HIV AIDS, occupational choice. *Unit head:* Mary E. Springston, Clinical Assistant Professor/Director, 315-445-4163, Fax: 315-445-4602, E-mail: springme@lemoyne.edu. *Application contact:* Kristen P. Trapasso, Director of Graduate Admission, 315-445-4265, Fax: 315-445-6027, E-mail: trapaskp@lemoyne.edu.

Lock Haven University of Pennsylvania, Department of Health Science, Lock Haven, PA 17745-2390. Offers physician assistant in rural primary care (MHS). *Accreditation:* ARC-PA. *Entrance requirements:* For master's, minimum undergraduate GPA of 3.0. Additional exam requirements/recommendations for international students: Required—TOEFL. Electronic applications accepted. *Expenses:* Tuition, state resident: full-time $6666; part-time $370 per credit hour. Tuition, nonresident: full-time $10,666; part-time $593 per credit hour. Required fees: $1988; $112 per credit hour. One-time fee: $25. Tuition and fees vary according to course load, campus/location and program.

Loma Linda University, School of Allied Health Professions, Department of Physician Assistant, Loma Linda, CA 92350. Offers MS. *Accreditation:* ARC-PA. *Entrance requirements:* For master's, minimum GPA of 3.0. Additional exam requirements/recommendations for international students: Required—TOEFL (minimum score 550 paper-based; 213 computer-based).

Marietta College, Program in Physician Assistant Studies, Marietta, OH 45750-4000. Offers MS. *Accreditation:* ARC-PA.

Marquette University, Graduate School, College of Health Sciences, Department of Physician Assistant Studies, Milwaukee, WI 53201-1881. Offers MS. Students enter the program as undergraduates. *Accreditation:* ARC-PA. *Faculty:* 6 full-time (4 women), 1 (woman) part-time/adjunct. *Students:* 98 full-time (86 women); includes 7 minority (1 African American, 1 American Indian/Alaska Native, 3 Asian Americans or Pacific Islanders, 2 Hispanic Americans), 1 international. Average age 24. 188 applicants, 34% accepted, 58 enrolled. In 2009, 35 master's awarded. *Entrance requirements:* Additional exam requirements/recommendations for international students: Required—TOEFL. Application fee: $40. *Financial support:* Application deadline: 2/15. *Unit head:* Timothy Gengembre, Chair, 414-288-5688, Fax: 414-288-7951. *Application contact:* Erin Fox, Assistant Director for Recruitment, 414-288-5319, Fax: 414-288-1902, E-mail: erin.fox@marquette.edu.

Marywood University, Academic Affairs, College of Health and Human Services, Department of Physician Assistant Studies, Clinical Physician Assistant Track, Scranton, PA 18509-1598. Offers MS. *Entrance requirements:* Additional exam requirements/recommendations for international students: Required—TOEFL (minimum score 550 paper-based; 213 computer-based; 79 iBT). Application fee: $35. Electronic applications accepted. *Expenses:* Tuition: Part-time $715 per credit. Required fees: $270 per semester. Tuition and fees vary according to degree level, campus/location and program. *Financial support:* Career-related internships or fieldwork, scholarships/grants, and unspecified assistantships available. Support available to part-time students. Financial award application deadline: 6/30; financial award applicants required to submit FAFSA. *Application contact:* Tammy Manka, Assistant Director of Graduate Admissions, 866-279-9663, E-mail: tmanka@marywood.edu.

Marywood University, Academic Affairs, College of Health and Human Services, Department of Physician Assistant Studies, Physician Assistant Studies Program, Scranton, PA 18509-1598. Offers MS. Part-time and evening/weekend programs available. *Students:* 45 full-time (31 women); includes 3 minority (1 African American, 2 Hispanic Americans). Average age 28. In 2009, 27 master's awarded. *Entrance requirements:* Additional exam requirements/recommendations for international students: Required—TOEFL (minimum score 550 paper-based; 213 computer-based; 79 iBT). Application fee: $35. Electronic applications accepted. *Expenses:* Contact institution. *Financial support:* Career-related internships or fieldwork, scholarships/grants, and unspecified assistantships available. Support available to part-time students. Financial award application deadline: 6/30; financial award applicants required to submit FAFSA. *Unit head:* Dr. Karen E. Arscott, Director, 570-348-6211 Ext. 2175, E-mail: arscott@es.marywood.edu. *Application contact:* Tammy Manka, Assistant Director of Graduate Admissions, 866-279-9663, E-mail: tmanka@marywood.edu.

Massachusetts College of Pharmacy and Health Sciences, Graduate Studies, School of Physician Assistant Studies, Program in Physician Assistant Studies (Manchester/Worcester), Boston, MA 02115-5896. Offers MPAS. *Accreditation:* ARC-PA. *Students:* 140 full-time (109 women), 3 part-time (1 woman); includes 17 minority (4 African Americans, 12 Asian Americans or Pacific Islanders, 1 Hispanic American), 1 international. Average age 28. 391 applicants, 28% accepted, 61 enrolled. *Entrance requirements:* Additional exam requirements/recommendations for international students: Required—TOEFL (minimum score 550 paper-based; 213 computer-based; 79 iBT). *Application deadline:* For spring admission, 10/1 priority date for domestic and international students. Application fee: $70. Electronic applications accepted. *Expenses:* Tuition: Full-time $28,000; part-time $875 per credit hour. Required fees: $750; $190 per semester. Part-time tuition and fees vary according to course load, campus/location, program and student level. *Financial support:* Application deadline: 3/15. *Unit head:* Dr. Scott Massey, Assistant Dean of Graduate Studies, 617-314-1708, E-mail: scott.massey@mcphs.edu. *Application contact:* Barbara Jellie, Admission Counselor, 603-314-1701, E-mail: barbara.jellie@mcphs.edu.

Medical University of South Carolina, College of Health Professions, Department of Health Professions, Physician Assistant Program, Charleston, SC 29425. Offers MS. *Accreditation:* ARC-PA. *Faculty:* 6 full-time (2 women), 14 part-time/adjunct (7 women). *Students:* 128 full-time (108 women), 8 part-time (7 women); includes 19 minority (10 African Americans, 5 Asian Americans or Pacific Islanders, 4 Hispanic Americans), 1 international. Average age 27. 494 applicants, 17% accepted, 69 enrolled. In 2009, 69 master's awarded. *Degree requirements:* For master's, clinical clerkship, research project. *Entrance requirements:* For master's, GRE General Test, interview, minimum GPA of 3.0, 3 references. Additional exam requirements/recommendations for international students: Required—TOEFL (minimum score 600 paper-based; 250 computer-based). *Application deadline:* For fall admission, 12/1 for domestic and international students. Application fee: $85. Electronic applications accepted. *Financial support:* Federal Work-Study available. Support available to part-time students. Financial award application deadline: 3/10; financial award applicants required to submit FAFSA. *Faculty research:* Oral health, pediatric emergency medicine, simulation technology in education, health manpower needs, cultural competency. Total annual research expenditures: $280,111. *Unit head:* Dr. Reamer L. Bushardt, Program Director, 843-792-9570, Fax: 843-792-0506, E-mail: busharr@musc.edu. *Application contact:* Kelly K. Long, Student Services Program Coordinator, 843-792-3775, Fax: 843-792-0506, E-mail: longkk@musc.edu.

Mercy College, School of Health and Natural Sciences, Program in Physician Assistant, Dobbs Ferry, NY 10522-1189. Offers physician assistant studies (MS). *Accreditation:* ARC-PA. Evening/weekend programs available. *Students:* 102 full-time (81 women), 1 (woman) part-time; includes 9 African Americans, 14 Asian Americans or Pacific Islanders, 4 Hispanic Americans, 3 international. Average age 26. In 2009, 23 master's awarded. *Degree requirements:* For master's, project. *Entrance requirements:* For master's, interview, two letters of reference, personal statement stating reason for pursuing degree in physician assistant studies, official transcripts, minimum GPA of 3.0, completed Medical and Community Experience Verification forms. Additional exam requirements/recommendations for international students: Required—TOEFL (minimum score 600 paper-based; 250 computer-based; 100 iBT). *Application deadline:* For fall admission, 12/1 for domestic students. Application fee: $65. *Expenses:* Tuition: Full-time $13,158; part-time $731 per credit. Required fees: $500. Tuition and fees vary according to degree level and program. *Financial support:* Career-related internships or fieldwork, Federal Work-Study, scholarships/grants, and unspecified assistantships available. Financial award applicants required to submit FAFSA. *Unit head:* Lorraine Cashin, Director, 914-674-7635, E-mail: lcashin@mercy.edu. *Application contact:* Lorraine Cashin, Director, 914-674-7635, E-mail: lcashin@mercy.edu.

Methodist University, School of Graduate Studies, Program in Physician Assistant Studies, Fayetteville, NC 28311-1498. Offers MMS. *Accreditation:* ARC-PA. *Faculty:* 6 full-time (1 woman), 5 part-time/adjunct (1 woman). *Students:* 96 full-time (68 women); includes 6 minority

Physician Assistant Studies

Methodist University (continued)

(2 African Americans, 1 Asian American or Pacific Islander, 3 Hispanic Americans). 699 applicants, 6% accepted, 34 enrolled. In 2009, 31 master's awarded. *Degree requirements:* For master's, comprehensive exam. *Entrance requirements:* For master's, GRE, bachelor's degree from four-year, regionally-accredited college or university; minimum of 500 hours' clinical experience with direct patient contact; minimum GPA of 3.0 on all college level work attempted, 3.2 on medical core prerequisites (recommended). Additional exam requirements/recommendations for international students: Required—TOEFL (minimum score 500 paper-based; 173 computer-based; 60 iBT). *Application deadline:* For fall admission, 3/1 for domestic and international students. Application fee: $100. *Expenses:* Tuition: Full-time $26,895; part-time $698 per course. Required fees: $110; $600 per year. One-time fee: $1125 full-time; $175 part-time. Full-time tuition and fees vary according to program. Part-time tuition and fees vary according to campus/location. *Financial support:* In 2009–10, 80 students received support. Scholarships/grants available. Financial award application deadline: 8/10; financial award applicants required to submit FAFSA. *Unit head:* Dr. Sekhar Kommu, Director, 800-488-7110 Ext. 7216, E-mail: skommu@methodist.edu. *Application contact:* Jennifer Mish, Director for Physician Assistant Admissions, 800-488-7110 Ext. 7615, E-mail: jmish@methodist.edu.

Midwestern University, Downers Grove Campus, College of Health Sciences, Illinois Campus, Program in Physician Assistant Studies, Downers Grove, IL 60515-1235. Offers MMS. *Accreditation:* ARC-PA. *Faculty:* 8 full-time (5 women). *Students:* 157 full-time (136 women), 5 part-time (3 women); includes 10 minority (5 Asian Americans or Pacific Islanders, 5 Hispanic Americans), 1 international. Average age 25. 1,035 applicants, 17% accepted, 84 enrolled. In 2009, 53 master's awarded. *Entrance requirements:* For master's, GRE General Test. *Application deadline:* Applications are processed on a rolling basis. Application fee: $50. *Expenses:* Contact institution. *Financial support:* In 2009–10, 65 students received support. Federal Work-Study available. *Unit head:* Dr. Alyson Smith, Director, 630-515-7609. *Application contact:* Michael Laken, Director of Admissions, 630-515-6171, Fax: 630-971-6086, E-mail: admissil@midwestern.edu.

Midwestern University, Glendale Campus, College of Health Sciences, Arizona Campus, Program in Physician Assistant Studies, Glendale, AZ 85308. Offers MMS. *Accreditation:* ARC-PA. *Faculty:* 7 full-time (3 women), 3 part-time/adjunct (all women). *Students:* 173 full-time (123 women), 5 part-time (4 women); includes 11 minority (1 American Indian/Alaska Native, 4 Asian Americans or Pacific Islanders, 6 Hispanic Americans), 1 international. Average age 27. 805 applicants, 19% accepted, 87 enrolled. In 2009, 53 master's awarded. *Entrance requirements:* For master's, GRE. *Application deadline:* Applications are processed on a rolling basis. Application fee: $50. *Expenses:* Contact institution. *Financial support:* Applicants required to submit FAFSA. *Unit head:* Kevin Lohenry, Director, 623-572-3611. *Application contact:* James Walter, Director of Admissions, 888-247-9277, Fax: 623-572-3229, E-mail: admissaz@midwestern.edu.

Missouri State University, Graduate College, College of Health and Human Services, Department of Physician Assistant Studies, Springfield, MO 65897. Offers MS. *Accreditation:* ARC-PA. *Faculty:* 3 full-time (0 women), 49 part-time/adjunct (12 women). *Students:* 49 full-time (24 women); includes 5 minority (1 African American, 2 Asian Americans or Pacific Islanders, 2 Hispanic Americans), 1 international. Average age 28. In 2009, 23 master's awarded. *Degree requirements:* For master's, comprehensive exam, thesis or alternative. *Entrance requirements:* For master's, GRE General Test, minimum GPA of 3.0. Additional exam requirements/recommendations for international students: Required—TOEFL (minimum score 550 paper-based; 213 computer-based; 79 iBT). *Application deadline:* For spring admission, 9/1 for domestic and international students. Application fee: $35 ($50 for international students). *Expenses:* Tuition, state resident: full-time $3852; part-time $214 per credit hour. Tuition, nonresident: full-time $7524; part-time $418 per credit hour. Required fees: $696; $172 per semester. Tuition and fees vary according to course level, course load, degree level and program. *Financial support:* Application deadline: 3/31. *Unit head:* Dr. Steven Dodge, Head, 417-836-6151, Fax: 417-836-6406, E-mail: physicianasststudies@missouristate.edu. *Application contact:* Eric Eckert, Coordinator of Admissions and Recruitment, 417-836-5331, Fax: 417-836-6200, E-mail: ericeckert@missouristate.edu.

Mountain State University, Graduate Studies, Physician Assistant Program, Beckley, WV 25802-9003. Offers MSPA. Admittance in junior year only. *Accreditation:* ARC-PA. *Faculty:* 4 full-time (3 women), 6 part-time/adjunct (1 woman). *Students:* 137 full-time (75 women); includes 12 minority (3 African Americans, 3 Asian Americans or Pacific Islanders, 6 Hispanic Americans), 3 international. Average age 26. 231 applicants, 22% accepted, 51 enrolled. In 2009, 25 master's awarded. *Degree requirements:* For master's, comprehensive exam, thesis or alternative. *Entrance requirements:* Additional exam requirements/recommendations for international students: Required—TOEFL (minimum score 550 paper-based; 213 computer-based); Recommended—IELTS (minimum score 6.5). *Application deadline:* For fall admission, 5/31 priority date for domestic and international students. Applications are processed on a rolling basis. Application fee: $25 ($50 for international students). Electronic applications accepted. *Expenses:* Contact institution. *Financial support:* Career-related internships or fieldwork, Federal Work-Study, and scholarships/grants available. Support available to part-time students. Financial award application deadline: 3/1; financial award applicants required to submit FAFSA. *Unit head:* Dr. Judith Halle, Dean, School of Health Science, 304-929-1327, Fax: 304-256-5571, E-mail: jhalle@mountainstate.edu. *Application contact:* Debra Campbell, Graduate Program Director, 304-929-1451, Fax: 304-256-5571, E-mail: dcampbell@mountainstate.edu.

New York Institute of Technology, Graduate Division, School of Health Professions, Program in Physician Assistant, Old Westbury, NY 11568-8000. Offers MS. *Accreditation:* ARC-PA. *Students:* 149 full-time (112 women), 2 part-time (1 woman); includes 16 minority (8 African Americans, 4 Asian Americans or Pacific Islanders, 4 Hispanic Americans). Average age 26. In 2009, 51 master's awarded. *Degree requirements:* For master's, thesis. *Entrance requirements:* For master's, minimum GPA of 3.0, interview, 100 hours of volunteer work, 2 letters of recommendation. Additional exam requirements/recommendations for international students: Required—TOEFL (minimum score 550 paper-based; 213 computer-based). *Application deadline:* For fall admission, 7/1 priority date for domestic students; for spring admission, 12/1 priority date for domestic students. Application fee: $50. *Expenses:* Tuition: Part-time $825 per credit. *Financial support:* Research assistantships with partial tuition reimbursements available. Financial award applicants required to submit FAFSA. *Unit head:* Dr. Salvatore Barese, Chair, 516-686-3804, Fax: 516-686-3795, E-mail: sbarese@nyit.edu. *Application contact:* Dr. Jacquelyn Nealon, Vice President for Enrollment Services, 516-686-7925, Fax: 516-686-7597, E-mail: jnealon@nyit.edu.

Northeastern University, Bouvé College of Health Sciences Graduate School, Physician Assistant Program, Boston, MA 02115-5096. Offers MS. *Accreditation:* ARC-PA. *Faculty:* 6 full-time (all women). *Entrance requirements:* For master's, minimum undergraduate GPA of 3.0; 2 semesters each of general biology plus lab and general chemistry plus lab; coursework in human anatomy, physiology, and statistics with minimum B average in each; 2,000 hours of hands-on patient care experience; interview; curriculum vitae. Additional exam requirements/recommendations for international students: Required—TOEFL (minimum score 600 paper-based; 250 computer-based; 100 iBT). *Application deadline:* For fall admission, 9/1 for domestic students. Application fee: $25. Electronic applications accepted. *Expenses:* Contact institution. *Financial support:* Federal Work-Study and institutionally sponsored loans available. Financial award application deadline: 3/1; financial award applicants required to submit FAFSA. *Faculty research:* Education and training, reimbursement. *Unit head:* Dr. Rosann M. Ippolito, Program Director, 617-373-3195, E-mail: r.ippolito@neu.edu. *Application contact:* Carol G. Goldberg, Assistant Director, 617-373-3195, E-mail: c.goldberg@neu.edu.

Nova Southeastern University, Health Professions Division, College of Allied Health and Nursing, Department of Physician Assistant Studies, Fort Lauderdale, FL 33314-7796. Offers medical science/physician assistant (MMS). Students enter program as undergraduates. *Accreditation:* ARC-PA. *Faculty:* 15 full-time (4 women). *Students:* 449 full-time (335 women), 9 part-time (6 women); includes 102 minority (14 African Americans, 2 American Indian/Alaska Native, 30 Asian Americans or Pacific Islanders, 56 Hispanic Americans), 4 international. Average age 25. 769 applicants, 17% accepted, 87 enrolled. In 2009, 128 master's awarded. *Entrance requirements:* For master's, GRE, minimum GPA of 2.9. *Application deadline:* Applications are processed on a rolling basis. Application fee: $170. Electronic applications accepted. *Expenses:* Contact institution. *Financial support:* In 2009–10, 130 students received support. *Unit head:* Bill Marquardt, Chair and Program Director, 954-262-1252, E-mail: marquard@nsu.nova.edu. *Application contact:* Judy Dickman, Admissions Counselor, 954-262-1109, E-mail: dickman@nsu.nova.edu.

Our Lady of the Lake College, School of Arts, Sciences and Health Professions, Baton Rouge, LA 70808. Offers physician associate studies (MMS).

Pace University, Dyson College of Arts and Sciences, Program in Physician Assistant, New York, NY 10038. Offers MS. *Accreditation:* ARC-PA. *Students:* 97 full-time (80 women); includes 8 Asian Americans or Pacific Islanders, 6 Hispanic Americans. Average age 25. 1,329 applicants, 7% accepted, 52 enrolled. *Entrance requirements:* Additional exam requirements/recommendations for international students: Required—TOEFL. *Application deadline:* For spring admission, 10/1 priority date for domestic students. *Expenses:* Tuition: Part-time $954 per credit. Tuition and fees vary according to course load, degree level and program. *Unit head:* Kathleen Roche, Program Director, 212-346-1357, E-mail: paprogram@pace.edu. *Application contact:* Susan Ford-Goldschein, Director of Admissions, 212-346-1652, Fax: 212-346-1585, E-mail: gradnyc@pace.edu.

Pacific University, School of Physician Assistant Studies, Forest Grove, OR 97116-1797. Offers MHS, MS. *Accreditation:* ARC-PA. *Degree requirements:* For master's, comprehensive exam, thesis, clinical project. *Entrance requirements:* For master's, minimum of 1000 hours of direct clinical patient care, prerequisite coursework in science with minimum C average. Additional exam requirements/recommendations for international students: Required—TOEFL (minimum score 600 paper-based; 250 computer-based). *Expenses:* Contact institution. *Faculty research:* Public health, evidenced based medicine.

Philadelphia College of Osteopathic Medicine, Graduate and Professional Programs, Physician Assistant Program, Philadelphia, PA 19131-1694. Offers health sciences (MS). *Accreditation:* ARC-PA. *Faculty:* 7 full-time (4 women), 42 part-time/adjunct (12 women). *Students:* 110 full-time (92 women); includes 22 minority (2 African Americans, 20 Asian Americans or Pacific Islanders). Average age 25. 1,701 applicants, 5% accepted, 54 enrolled. In 2009, 45 master's awarded. *Degree requirements:* For master's, thesis. *Entrance requirements:* For master's, minimum GPA of 3.0; course work in biology, chemistry, health science, math, social science; 200 hours patient contact. *Application deadline:* For fall admission, 12/1 for domestic students. *Unit head:* Dr. John M. Cavenagh, Chair, 215-871-6772, Fax: 215-871-6702, E-mail: johnca@pcom.edu. *Application contact:* Carol A. Fox, Associate Vice President for Enrollment Management, 215-871-6700, Fax: 215-871-6719, E-mail: carolf@pcom.edu.

See Close-Up on page 1429.

Philadelphia University, School of Science and Health, Program in Physician Assistant Studies, Philadelphia, PA 19144. Offers MS. *Accreditation:* ARC-PA. *Entrance requirements:* For master's, MCAT, GRE, or MAT. Additional exam requirements/recommendations for international students: Required—TOEFL (minimum score 550 paper-based; 213 computer-based; 79 iBT).

Quinnipiac University, School of Health Sciences, Program for Pathologists' Assistant, Hamden, CT 06518-1940. Offers MHS. *Accreditation:* NAACLS. *Faculty:* 2 full-time (0 women), 3 part-time/adjunct (1 woman). *Students:* 37 full-time (31 women); includes 5 minority (1 African American, 3 Asian Americans or Pacific Islanders, 1 Hispanic American), 5 international. Average age 27. 109 applicants, 19% accepted, 18 enrolled. In 2009, 18 master's awarded. *Degree requirements:* For master's, residency. *Entrance requirements:* For master's, interview, coursework in biological and health sciences, minimum GPA of 2.8. Additional exam requirements/recommendations for international students: Required—TOEFL (minimum score 575 paper-based; 233 computer-based; 90 iBT), IELTS (minimum score 6.5). *Application deadline:* For fall admission, 12/15 for domestic students. Applications are processed on a rolling basis. Application fee: $45. Electronic applications accepted. *Expenses:* Tuition: Full-time $16,030; part-time $770 per credit. Required fees: $630; $35 per credit. *Financial support:* Career-related internships or fieldwork, tuition waivers (partial), and unspecified assistantships available. Financial award application deadline: 4/15; financial award applicants required to submit FAFSA. *Unit head:* Dr. Kenneth Kaloustian, Director, 203-582-8676, Fax: 203-582-3443, E-mail: ken.kaloustian@quinnipiac.edu. *Application contact:* Kristin Parent, Assistant Director of Graduate Health Sciences Admissions, 800-462-1944, Fax: 203-582-3443, E-mail: kristin.parent@quinnipiac.edu.

Quinnipiac University, School of Health Sciences, Program for Physician Assistant, Hamden, CT 06518-1940. Offers MHS. *Accreditation:* ARC-PA. *Faculty:* 7 full-time (4 women), 19 part-time/adjunct (7 women). *Students:* 111 full-time (81 women), 5 part-time (4 women); includes 18 minority (4 African Americans, 9 Asian Americans or Pacific Islanders, 5 Hispanic Americans). 826 applicants, 10% accepted, 55 enrolled. In 2009, 41 master's awarded. *Degree requirements:* For master's, comprehensive exam. *Entrance requirements:* For master's, minimum GPA of 3.0; course work in biological, physical, and behavioral sciences; interviews; 2000 hours direct patient care experience. *Application deadline:* For fall admission, 9/1 for domestic students. *Expenses:* Tuition: Full-time $16,030; part-time $770 per credit. Required fees: $630; $35 per credit. *Financial support:* Career-related internships or fieldwork, Federal Work-Study, tuition waivers (partial), and unspecified assistantships available. Financial award application deadline: 4/15; financial award applicants required to submit FAFSA. *Unit head:* Cynthia Booth-Lord, Director, 203-582-5297, Fax: 203-582-8706, E-mail: cynthia.lord@quinnipiac.edu. *Application contact:* Kristin Parent, Office of Graduate Admissions, 800-462-1944, Fax: 203-582-3443, E-mail: kristin.parent@quinnipiac.edu.

Regis University, Rueckert-Hartman School for Health Professions, Denver, CO 80221-1099. Offers clinical leadership for physician assistants (MS); family nurse practitioner (MSN); health informatics (Postbaccalaureate Certificate); health services administration (MS); healthcare education (Certificate); leadership in healthcare systems (MSN); neonatal nurse practitioner (MSN); nursing (MSN); pharmacy (Pharm D); physical therapy (DPT, TDPT). *Entrance requirements:* Additional exam requirements/recommendations for international students: Required—TOEFL (minimum score 550 paper-based; 213 computer-based; 82 iBT). Electronic applications accepted. *Expenses:* Contact institution. *Faculty research:* Normal and pathological balance and gait research, normal/pathological upper limb motor control/biomechanics, exercise energy/metabolism research, optical treatment protocols for therapeutic modalities.

Rocky Mountain College, Graduate Programs, Billings, MT 59102-1796. Offers accounting (M Acc); educational leadership (M Ed); physician assistant studies (MPAS). Part-time programs available. *Faculty:* 10 full-time (3 women), 12 part-time/adjunct (4 women). *Students:* 65 full-time (34 women), 1 part-time (0 women). Average age 28. In 2009, 55 master's awarded. *Entrance requirements:* Additional exam requirements/recommendations for international students: Required—TOEFL (minimum score 570 paper-based; 230 computer-based; 88 iBT), IELTS (minimum score 6.5). *Application deadline:* Applications are processed on a rolling basis. Application fee: $35 ($40 for international students). Electronic applications accepted. *Expenses:* Tuition: Full-time $25,070. Required fees: $450. Full-time tuition and fees vary according to program. *Financial support:* In 2009–10, 65 students received support. Federal Work-Study and scholarships/grants available. Financial award applicants required to submit FAFSA. *Unit head:* Anthony Piltz, Academic Vice President, 406-657-1020, Fax: 406-259-9751, E-mail: piltza@rocky.edu. *Application contact:* Kelly Edwards, Director of Admissions, 406-657-1026, Fax: 406-657-1189, E-mail: admissions@rocky.edu.

Rosalind Franklin University of Medicine and Science, College of Health Professions, Physician Assistant Department, North Chicago, IL 60064-3095. Offers MS. *Accreditation:* ARC-PA. *Faculty:* 7 full-time (5 women), 2 part-time/adjunct (0 women). *Students:* 123 full-time

(96 women); includes 9 minority (1 African American, 5 Asian Americans or Pacific Islanders, 3 Hispanic Americans), 2 international. Average age 27. 1,215 applicants, 10% accepted, 64 enrolled. *Degree requirements:* For master's, thesis. *Entrance requirements:* For master's, GRE, writing sample. Additional exam requirements/recommendations for international students: Required—TOEFL. *Application deadline:* For fall admission, 12/1 for domestic students. Applications are processed on a rolling basis. Application fee: $50. Electronic applications accepted. *Financial support:* Applicants required to submit FAFSA. *Faculty research:* Ortho-spine, diabetes education, cultural competency, interprofessional medical education. *Unit head:* Dr. Patrick T. Knott, Associate Professor and Chair, 847-578-8689, Fax: 847-578-8690, E-mail: patrick.knott@rosalindfranklin.edu. *Application contact:* Melissa Knox, Admissions Officer, 847-578-8772, Fax: 847-775-6559, E-mail: melissa.knox@rosalindfranklin.edu.

Saint Francis University, Department of Physician Assistant Sciences, Loretto, PA 15940-0600. Offers health science (MHS); medical science (MMS); physician assistant sciences (MPAS). *Accreditation:* ARC-PA. *Faculty:* 11 full-time (9 women), 3 part-time/adjunct (0 women). *Students:* 110 full-time (84 women); includes 5 minority (2 American Indian/Alaska Native, 2 Asian Americans or Pacific Islanders, 1 Hispanic American). Average age 25. 744 applicants, 9% accepted, 17 enrolled. In 2009, 57 master's awarded. *Degree requirements:* For master's, capstone, summative evaluation. *Entrance requirements:* For master's, interview. Additional exam requirements/recommendations for international students: Required—TOEFL (minimum score 550 paper-based; 213 computer-based; 70 iBT). *Application deadline:* For fall admission, 10/1 for domestic and international students. Applications are processed on a rolling basis. Application fee: $170. Electronic applications accepted. *Expenses:* Tuition: Part-time $765 per credit. Part-time tuition and fees vary according to course load and program. *Financial support:* Applicants required to submit FAFSA. *Unit head:* Donna L. Yeisley, Director, 814-472-3131, Fax: 814-472-3137, E-mail: dyeisley@francis.edu. *Application contact:* Marie S. Link, Director of Research and MPAS Graduate Admission, 814-472-3138, Fax: 814-472-3137, E-mail: mlink@francis.edu.

Saint Louis University, Graduate School, Doisy College of Health Sciences, Department of Physician Assistant Education, St. Louis, MO 63103-2097. Offers MMS. *Accreditation:* ARC-PA. *Entrance requirements:* Additional exam requirements/recommendations for international students: Required—TOEFL (minimum score 86 iBT). Electronic applications accepted.

Salus University, College of Health Sciences, Elkins Park, PA 19027-1598. Offers MS. *Accreditation:* ARC-PA. *Faculty:* 5 full-time (3 women), 2 part-time/adjunct. *Students:* 87 full-time (63 women); includes 11 minority (1 African American, 8 Asian Americans or Pacific Islanders, 2 Hispanic Americans). Average age 25. 929 applicants, 7% accepted, 37 enrolled. In 2009, 20 master's awarded. *Entrance requirements:* For master's, GRE, recommended. Additional exam requirements/recommendations for international students: Required—TOEFL. *Application deadline:* For fall admission, 1/15 for domestic and international students. Applications are processed on a rolling basis. Electronic applications accepted. *Expenses:* Tuition: Full-time $31,700. Required fees: $550. Full-time tuition and fees vary according to degree level and program. *Unit head:* Dr. Richard Vause, Director, Physician Assistant Program, 215-780-1519. *Application contact:* Dr. James Caldwell, Director of Admissions, 215-780-1300, Fax: 215-780-1336, E-mail: JCaldwell@salus.edu.

Samuel Merritt University, Department of Physician Assistant Studies, Oakland, CA 94609-3108. Offers MPA. *Accreditation:* ARC-PA. *Entrance requirements:* For master's, health care experience, minimum GPA of 3.0, previous course work in statistics.

Seton Hall University, School of Health and Medical Sciences, Physician Assistant Program, South Orange, NJ 07079-2697. Offers MS. *Accreditation:* ARC-PA. *Entrance requirements:* For master's, GRE, health care experience, interview, minimum GPA of 3.0. Additional exam requirements/recommendations for international students: Required—TOEFL. Electronic applications accepted.

Seton Hill University, Program in Physician Assistant, Greensburg, PA 15601. Offers MS. *Accreditation:* ARC-PA. *Faculty:* 6 full-time (3 women), 25 part-time/adjunct (10 women). *Students:* 46 full-time (35 women); includes 3 minority (2 Asian Americans or Pacific Islanders, 1 Hispanic American). Average age 26. In 2009, 18 master's awarded. *Entrance requirements:* For master's, minimum GPA of 3.0, 23 credits of prerequisite coursework, 350 hours of experience in healthcare setting, interview. Additional exam requirements/recommendations for international students: Required—TOEFL (minimum score 600 paper-based; 250 computer-based), IELTS (minimum score 6.5). *Application deadline:* For spring admission, 3/1 for domestic and international students. Application fee: $110. Electronic applications accepted. *Expenses:* Contact institution. *Financial support:* Application deadline: 8/15. *Faculty research:* Underserved populations, women's health, healthcare for elderly. *Unit head:* Cathy Shallenberger, Director, 724-838-2455, Fax: 724-838-7843, E-mail: shallenberger@setonhill.edu. *Application contact:* Tracey Bartos, Director of Graduate and Adult Studies, 724-838-4283, Fax: 724-830-1891, E-mail: bartos@setonhill.edu.

Shenandoah University, School of Health Professions, Division of Physician Assistant Studies, Winchester, VA 22601-5195. Offers MS. *Accreditation:* ARC-PA. *Faculty:* 6 full-time (5 women). *Students:* 102 full-time (82 women), 3 part-time (all women); includes 11 minority (2 African Americans, 7 Asian Americans or Pacific Islanders, 2 Hispanic Americans), 1 international. Average age 28. 517 applicants, 13% accepted, 35 enrolled. In 2009, 31 master's awarded. *Degree requirements:* For master's, project. *Entrance requirements:* For master's, GRE General Test, minimum GPA of 3.0, 3 letters of reference, medical terminology proficiency, writing sample. Additional exam requirements/recommendations for international students: Required—TOEFL (minimum score 550 paper-based; 213 computer-based; 79 iBT), IELTS (minimum score 6.5). *Application deadline:* For fall admission, 1/15 for domestic students. Applications are processed on a rolling basis. Application fee: $30. Electronic applications accepted. *Expenses:* Contact institution. *Financial support:* Application deadline: 3/15. *Unit head:* Anthony A. Miller, Director, 540-545-7257, Fax: 540-542-6210, E-mail: amiller@su.edu. *Application contact:* David Anthony, Dean of Admissions, 540-665-4581, Fax: 540-665-4627, E-mail: admit@su.edu.

Southern Illinois University Carbondale, Graduate School, College of Applied Science, Program in Physician Assistant Studies, Carbondale, IL 62901-4701. Offers MSPA. *Accreditation:* ARC-PA.

South University, Graduate Programs, College of Health Professions, Program in Physician Assistant Studies, Savannah, GA 31406. Offers MS. *Accreditation:* ARC-PA.

See Close-Up on page 1433.

Springfield College, Graduate Programs, Program in Physician Assistant, Springfield, MA 01109-3797. Offers MS. *Accreditation:* ARC-PA. Part-time programs available. *Degree requirements:* For master's, comprehensive exam. *Entrance requirements:* For master's, prerequisite courses. Additional exam requirements/recommendations for international students: Required—TOEFL (minimum score 550 paper-based; 213 computer-based). Electronic applications accepted. *Expenses:* Tuition: Full-time $19,800; part-time $825 per credit hour. Required fees: $150.

Stony Brook University, State University of New York, Stony Brook University Medical Center, Health Sciences Center, School of Health Technology and Management, Stony Brook, NY 11794. Offers health care management (Advanced Certificate); health care policy and management (MS); occupational therapy (MS); physical therapy (DPT); physician assistant (MS). *Accreditation:* APTA. Part-time programs available. *Faculty:* 33 full-time (25 women), 25 part-time/adjunct (12 women). *Students:* 217 full-time (162 women), 130 part-time (93 women); includes 87 minority (21 African Americans, 1 American Indian/Alaska Native, 46 Asian Americans or Pacific Islanders, 19 Hispanic Americans), 8 international. 54 applicants, 91% accepted. In 2009, 89 master's, 77 doctorates, 15 other advanced degrees awarded. *Degree requirements:* For master's, thesis. *Entrance requirements:* For master's, GRE General Test, minimum GPA of 3.0, work experience in field. *Application deadline:* For fall admission, 1/15 for domestic students. Application fee: $60. *Expenses:* Tuition, state resident: full-time $8370; part-time $349 per credit. Tuition, nonresident: full-time $13,250; part-time $552 per credit. Required fees: $933. *Financial support:* In 2009–10, 2 research assistantships, 1 teaching assistantship were awarded; fellowships, career-related internships or fieldwork, Federal Work-Study, and institutionally sponsored loans also available. Financial award application deadline: 3/15. *Faculty research:* Health promotion and disease prevention. Total annual research expenditures: $842,937. *Unit head:* Dr. Craig A. Lehmann, Dean, 631-444-2251, Fax: 631-444-7621. *Application contact:* Richard W. Johnson, Associate Dean for Graduate Studies, 631-444-3251.

Texas Tech University Health Sciences Center, School of Allied Health Sciences, Program in Physician Assistant Studies, Lubbock, TX 79430. Offers MPAS. *Accreditation:* ARC-PA. *Faculty:* 8 full-time (3 women). *Students:* 108 full-time (76 women); includes 28 minority (5 African Americans, 2 American Indian/Alaska Native, 4 Asian Americans or Pacific Islanders, 17 Hispanic Americans). Average age 27. 755 applicants, 7% accepted, 54 enrolled. In 2009, 41 master's awarded. *Entrance requirements:* Additional exam requirements/recommendations for international students: Required—TOEFL, IELTS. *Application deadline:* For fall admission, 12/1 for domestic students. Application fee: $35. Electronic applications accepted. *Financial support:* Career-related internships or fieldwork, institutionally sponsored loans, and scholarships/grants available. Financial award applicants required to submit FAFSA. *Unit head:* Dr. Hal Larsen, Chair, 806-743-3223, E-mail: hal.larsen@ttuhsc.edu. *Application contact:* Jeri Moravcik, Assistant Director of Admissions and Student Affairs, 806-743-3220, Fax: 806-743-2994, E-mail: jeri.moravcik@ttuhsc.edu.

Touro University, Graduate Programs, Vallejo, CA 94592. Offers education (MA); osteopathic medicine (DO); pharmacy (Pharm D); physical therapy (DPT); physician assistant studies (MS); public health (MPH). *Accreditation:* AOsA; ARC-PA. Part-time and evening/weekend programs available. *Faculty:* 91 full-time (52 women), 51 part-time/adjunct (28 women). *Students:* 1,439 full-time (891 women). 6,914 applicants, 12% accepted, 503 enrolled. In 2009, 229 first professional degrees, 103 master's awarded. *Degree requirements:* For master's, comprehensive exam, thesis; for first professional degree, comprehensive exam. *Entrance requirements:* BS/BA. *Application deadline:* For fall admission, 3/15 for domestic students; for winter admission, 12/1 for domestic students. Applications are processed on a rolling basis. Application fee: $100. Electronic applications accepted. *Financial support:* In 2009–10, 1,236 students received support, including 119 fellowships (averaging $1,535 per year), 24 research assistantships (averaging $3,686 per year), 13 teaching assistantships (averaging $4,058 per year); Federal Work-Study and scholarships/grants also available. Support available to part-time students. Financial award applicants required to submit FAFSA. *Faculty research:* Cancer, heart disease. *Application contact:* Steve Davis, Associate Director of Admissions, 707-638-5270, Fax: 707-638-5250, E-mail: steven.davis@tu.edu.

Towson University, College of Graduate Studies and Research, Program in Physician Assistant Studies, Towson, MD 21252-0001. Offers MS. *Accreditation:* ARC-PA. *Entrance requirements:* For master's, supplemental materials for CCBC, completion of prerequisites. Additional exam requirements/recommendations for international students: Required—TOEFL. *Expenses:* Contact institution.

Trevecca Nazarene University, Graduate Division, Graduate Physician Assistant Program, Nashville, TN 37210-2877. Offers MS. *Accreditation:* ARC-PA. *Faculty:* 5 full-time (2 women), 6 part-time/adjunct (3 women). *Students:* 69 full-time (55 women); includes 1 minority (African American). Average age 26. In 2009, 33 master's awarded. *Degree requirements:* For master's, comprehensive exam, professional assessment, qualifying exam. *Entrance requirements:* For master's, GRE General Test, health care experience, minimum GPA of 3.25, 3 letters of recommendation. Additional exam requirements/recommendations for international students: Required—TOEFL (minimum score 550 paper-based; 213 computer-based). *Application deadline:* For fall admission, 11/1 for domestic students. Application fee: $45. *Expenses:* Contact institution. *Financial support:* Applicants required to submit FAFSA. *Unit head:* Dr. Mike Moredock, Director, 615-248-1261, Fax: 615-248-1622, E-mail: mmoredock@trevecca.edu. *Application contact:* Admissions Coordinator, 615-248-1621, Fax: 615-248-1622, E-mail: admissions_pa@trevecca.edu.

Union College, Physician Assistant Program, Lincoln, NE 68506-4300. Offers MPAS. *Accreditation:* ARC-PA. *Faculty:* 4 full-time (1 woman), 5 part-time/adjunct (2 women). *Students:* 75 full-time (57 women); includes 2 African Americans, 2 Asian Americans or Pacific Islanders, 8 Hispanic Americans. Average age 28. 220 applicants, 11% accepted, 25 enrolled. In 2009, 22 master's awarded. *Entrance requirements:* Additional exam requirements/recommendations for international students: Required—TOEFL (minimum score 600 paper-based; 100 iBT). *Application deadline:* For fall admission, 11/1 for domestic and international students. Applications are processed on a rolling basis. Electronic applications accepted. *Expenses:* Tuition: Full-time $19,440. Required fees: $1830. One-time fee: $540 full-time. *Financial support:* In 2009–10, 75 students received support. Applicants required to submit FAFSA. *Faculty research:* Servant leadership, cultural competency. *Application contact:* Jan Lemon, Physician Assistant Program, 402-486-2527, Fax: 402-486-2559, E-mail: jalemon@ucollege.edu.

The University of Alabama at Birmingham, School of Health Professions, Program in Physician Assistant Studies, Birmingham, AL 35294. Offers MSPAS. *Accreditation:* ARC-PA.

University of Colorado Denver, School of Medicine, Physician Assistant Program, Denver, CO 80217-3364. Offers MPAS. *Accreditation:* ARC-PA. *Students:* 120 full-time (103 women), 10 part-time (8 women); includes 6 minority (1 African American, 2 American Indian/Alaska Native, 2 Asian Americans or Pacific Islanders, 1 Hispanic American). In 2009, 11 master's awarded. *Entrance requirements:* For master's, GRE General Test, minimum GPA of 2.8, 3 letters of recommendation. Additional exam requirements/recommendations for international students: Required—TOEFL (minimum score 550 paper-based; 213 computer-based). *Application deadline:* For fall admission, 10/15 for domestic students. Application fee: $85. *Expenses:* Contact institution. *Financial support:* Career-related internships or fieldwork, Federal Work-Study, and institutionally sponsored loans available. Support available to part-time students. Financial award application deadline: 3/15; financial award applicants required to submit FAFSA. *Unit head:* Dr. Anita Glicken, Director, 303-724-1338, E-mail: anita.glicken@ucdenver.edu. *Application contact:* Melinda Sogo, Admissions and Course Support, 303-724-1340, E-mail: melinda.sogo@ucdenver.edu.

University of Detroit Mercy, College of Health Professions, Physician Assistant Program, Detroit, MI 48221. Offers MS. *Accreditation:* ARC-PA. *Degree requirements:* For master's, thesis or alternative. *Entrance requirements:* For master's, GRE General Test, minimum GPA of 3.0. *Expenses:* Contact institution. *Faculty research:* Substance abuse prevention, international health care, public health.

University of Florida, College of Medicine, Program in Physician Assistant, Gainesville, FL 32611. Offers MPAS. *Accreditation:* ARC-PA. *Entrance requirements:* For master's, GRE General Test, interview. Electronic applications accepted.

The University of Iowa, Roy J. and Lucille A. Carver College of Medicine and Graduate College, Graduate Programs in Medicine, Program in Physician Assistant, Iowa City, IA 52242-1316. Offers MPAS. *Accreditation:* ARC-PA. *Faculty:* 3 full-time (2 women), 2 part-time/adjunct (1 woman). *Students:* 49 full-time (31 women), 2 part-time (0 women); includes 8 minority (1 African American, 1 American Indian/Alaska Native, 5 Asian Americans or Pacific Islanders, 1 Hispanic American). Average age 25. 510 applicants, 5% accepted, 25 enrolled. In 2009, 23 master's awarded. *Degree requirements:* For master's, comprehensive clinical exam, master's clinical presentation. *Entrance requirements:* For master's, GRE General Test or MCAT, health care/research experience. *Application deadline:* For spring admission, 11/1 for domestic students. Applications are processed on a rolling basis. Application fee: $60. Electronic applications accepted. *Financial support:* In 2009–10, 48 students received support. Institutionally sponsored loans and scholarships/grants available. Financial award application deadline: 3/1; financial award applicants required to submit FAFSA. *Unit head:* Dr. David P. Asprey, Director, 319-335-8922, Fax: 319-335-8923, E-mail: david-asprey@uiowa.edu.

Physician Assistant Studies

The University of Iowa (continued)

Application contact: Janet L. Steenlage, Program Assistant, 319-353-5956, Fax: 319-335-8923, E-mail: janet-steenlage@uiowa.edu.

University of Kentucky, Graduate School, College of Health Sciences, Program in Physician Assistant Studies, Lexington, KY 40506-0032. Offers MSPAS. *Accreditation:* ARC-PA. *Degree requirements:* For master's, comprehensive exam. *Entrance requirements:* For master's, GRE General Test, minimum undergraduate GPA of 2.75. Additional exam requirements/recommendations for international students: Required—TOEFL (minimum score 550 paper-based; 213 computer-based). Electronic applications accepted.

University of Medicine and Dentistry of New Jersey, School of Health Related Professions, Department of Primary Care, Physician Assistant Program–Piscataway, Newark, NJ 07107-1709. Offers MS. *Accreditation:* ARC-PA. *Degree requirements:* For master's, internship. *Entrance requirements:* For master's, interview, minimum GPA of 3.0. Additional exam requirements/recommendations for international students: Required—TOEFL. Electronic applications accepted.

University of Nebraska Medical Center, School of Allied Health Professions, Division of Physician Assistant Education, Omaha, NE 68198-4300. Offers MPAS. *Accreditation:* ARC-PA. *Faculty:* 7 full-time (3 women), 298 part-time/adjunct (73 women). *Students:* 123 full-time (99 women); includes 6 minority (1 American Indian/Alaska Native, 2 Asian Americans or Pacific Islanders, 3 Hispanic Americans). Average age 23. 270 applicants, 19% accepted, 43 enrolled. In 2009, 38 master's awarded. *Degree requirements:* For master's, comprehensive exam, research paper. *Entrance requirements:* For master's, GRE General Test, 16 undergraduate hours of course work in both biology and chemistry, 3 undergraduate hours of course work in math, 6 undergraduate hours of course work in English, 9 undergraduate hours of course work in psychology, minimum GPA of 3.0. Additional exam requirements/recommendations for international students: Required—TOEFL (minimum score 600 paper-based; 250 computer-based; 100 iBT). *Application deadline:* For fall admission, 10/1 for domestic students. Application fee: $120. Electronic applications accepted. *Financial support:* In 2009–10, 120 students received support. Institutionally sponsored loans and scholarships/grants available. Financial award applicants required to submit FAFSA. *Faculty research:* Substance abuse, mental health, women's health, geriatrics. *Unit head:* Dr. James E. Somers, Director, 402-559-9495. *Application contact:* Diane K. Landon, Program Coordinator, 402-559-2232, Fax: 402-559-7996, E-mail: dklandon@unmc.edu.

University of New England, Westbrook College of Health Professions, Program in Physician Assistant, Biddeford, ME 04005-9526. Offers MS. *Accreditation:* ARC-PA. *Faculty:* 4 full-time (2 women), 1 part-time/adjunct (0 women). *Students:* 91 full-time (57 women); includes 3 minority (1 African American, 1 Asian American or Pacific Islander, 1 Hispanic American). In 2009, 41 master's awarded. *Degree requirements:* For master's, 12 month rotations. *Entrance requirements:* For master's, minimum GPA of 2.5. Additional exam requirements/recommendations for international students: Required—TOEFL. *Application deadline:* For fall admission, 11/1 for domestic students. Applications are processed on a rolling basis. Application fee: $40. *Expenses:* Contact institution. *Financial support:* Scholarships/grants available. Financial award application deadline: 5/1; financial award applicants required to submit FAFSA. *Unit head:* George S. Bottomley, Program Director, 207-221-4527, Fax: 207-221-4711, E-mail: gbottomley@une.edu. *Application contact:* Stacy Gato, Assistant Director of Graduate Admissions, 207-221-4225, Fax: 207-221-4898, E-mail: gradadmissions@une.edu.

University of North Dakota, School of Medicine and Health Sciences and Graduate School, Graduate Programs in Medicine, Physician Assistant Program, Grand Forks, ND 58202. Offers MPAS. *Accreditation:* ARC-PA. *Entrance requirements:* For master's, current RN licensure, minimum of 4 years of clinical experience, current ACLS certification, interview, letters of recommendation. Additional exam requirements/recommendations for international students: Required—TOEFL (minimum score 550 paper-based; 213 computer-based; 79 iBT), IELTS (minimum score 6.5).

University of North Texas Health Science Center at Fort Worth, Texas College of Osteopathic Medicine, School of Health Professions, Fort Worth, TX 76107-2699. Offers MPAS. *Accreditation:* ARC-PA. *Degree requirements:* For master's, thesis or alternative, research paper. *Entrance requirements:* For master's, minimum GPA of 2.85. *Faculty research:* Impact of mid-level providers on medical treatment, curriculum development, pain in geriatric patients, biopsychosocial risk factors.

University of Oklahoma—Tulsa, Physician Assistant Program, Tulsa, OK 74135-2512. Offers MHS. *Entrance requirements:* For master's, GRE General Test, minimum GPA of 2.75, 3 letters of reference, personal resume. Electronic applications accepted.

University of Pittsburgh, School of Health and Rehabilitation Sciences, Physician Assistant Studies Program, Pittsburgh, PA 15260. Offers MS. *Expenses:* Contact institution. *Unit head:* Dr. Deborah A. Opacic, Program Director, 412-647-4646, E-mail: dopacic@pitt.edu. *Application contact:* Shameem Gangjee, Director of Admissions, 412-383-6558, Fax: 412-383-6535, E-mail: admissions@shrs.pitt.edu.

University of St. Francis, College of Arts and Sciences, Joliet, IL 60435-6169. Offers physician assistant practice (MS); social work (MSW). *Faculty:* 9 full-time (7 women). *Students:* 78 full-time (58 women), 9 part-time (all women); includes 24 minority (11 African Americans, 2 American Indian/Alaska Native, 2 Asian Americans or Pacific Islanders, 9 Hispanic Americans). Average age 31. 50 applicants, 44% accepted, 10 enrolled. In 2009, 44 master's awarded. *Entrance requirements:* Additional exam requirements/recommendations for international students: Required—TOEFL (minimum score 550 paper-based; 213 computer-based). *Application deadline:* Applications are processed on a rolling basis. Application fee: $30. Electronic applications accepted. *Expenses:* Tuition: Part-time $589 per credit hour. Tuition and fees vary according to degree level, campus/location and program. *Financial support:* In 2009–10, 86 students received support. Federal Work-Study, scholarships/grants, and tuition waivers (partial) available. Support available to part-time students. Financial award applicants required to submit FAFSA. *Unit head:* Dr. Robert Kase, Dean, 815-740-3367, Fax: 815-740-6366. *Application contact:* Sandra Sloka, Director of Admissions for Graduate and Degree Completion Programs, 800-735-7500, Fax: 815-740-5032, E-mail: ssloka@stfrancis.edu.

University of Saint Francis, Graduate School, Department of Allied Health, Fort Wayne, IN 46808-3994. Offers physician assistant studies (MS). *Accreditation:* ARC-PA. *Entrance requirements:* For master's, GRE or MCAT, previous courses in biology, chemistry, and psychology, previous direct patient care.

University of South Alabama, Graduate School, College of Allied Health Professions, Department of Physician Assistant Studies, Mobile, AL 36688-0002. Offers MHS. *Accreditation:* ARC-PA. *Degree requirements:* For master's, thesis optional, externship. *Entrance requirements:* For master's, GRE General Test, minimum GPA of 3.0. *Expenses:* Tuition, state resident: part-time $218 per contact hour. Required fees: $1102 per year.

The University of South Dakota, School of Medicine and Health Sciences and Graduate School, Graduate Programs in Health Sciences, Department of Physician Assistant Studies, Vermillion, SD 57069-2390. Offers MS. *Accreditation:* ARC-PA. *Entrance requirements:* Additional exam requirements/recommendations for international students: Required—TOEFL (minimum score 550 paper-based; 213 computer-based). Electronic applications accepted. *Expenses:* Contact institution. *Faculty research:* Neuroscience, teaching techniques in physician assistant education.

University of Southern California, Keck School of Medicine and Graduate School, Graduate Programs in Medicine, Primary Care Physician Assistant Program, Los Angeles, CA 90089. Offers MPAP. *Accreditation:* ARC-PA. *Faculty:* 6 full-time (4 women), 3 part-time/adjunct (2 women). *Students:* 129 full-time (107 women); includes 71 minority (3 African Americans, 5 American Indian/Alaska Native, 32 Asian Americans or Pacific Islanders, 31 Hispanic Americans). Average age 27. 770 applicants, 8% accepted, 45 enrolled. In 2009, 49 master's awarded. *Degree requirements:* For master's, clinical training. *Entrance requirements:* For master's, GRE or MCAT, minimum GPA of 3.0. Additional exam requirements/recommendations for international students: Required—TOEFL (minimum score 600 paper-based; 200 computer-based; 100 iBT). *Application deadline:* For fall admission, 12/1 for domestic and international students. Applications are processed on a rolling basis. Application fee: $85. Electronic applications accepted. *Expenses:* Contact institution. *Financial support:* Institutionally sponsored loans and scholarships/grants available. Financial award application deadline: 5/5; financial award applicants required to submit FAFSA. *Unit head:* Dr. Rosslyn S. Byous, Director, 626-457-4262, Fax: 626-457-4245, E-mail: byous@usc.edu. *Application contact:* Janice Tramel, Chair, PA Admissions, 626-457-4250, Fax: 626-457-4245, E-mail: jtramel@usc.edu.

The University of Texas Health Science Center at San Antonio, School of Allied Health Sciences, San Antonio, TX 78229-3900. Offers clinical laboratory sciences (MS); deaf education and hearing science (MED); dental hygiene (MS); occupational therapy (MOT); physical therapy (MPT); physician assistant studies (MS). *Accreditation:* AOTA; APTA; ARC-PA. *Expenses:* Tuition, state resident: full-time $2832; part-time $118 per credit hour. Tuition, nonresident: full-time $10,896; part-time $454 per credit hour. Required fees: $884 per semester. One-time fee: $70.

The University of Texas Medical Branch, School of Health Professions, Department of Physician Assistant Studies, Galveston, TX 77555. Offers MPAS. *Accreditation:* ARC-PA. *Students:* 178 full-time (159 women); includes 45 minority (5 African Americans, 20 Asian Americans or Pacific Islanders, 20 Hispanic Americans). Average age 27. In 2009, 47 master's awarded. *Entrance requirements:* For master's, GRE, interview. Electronic applications accepted. *Financial support:* Applicants required to submit FAFSA. *Unit head:* Dr. Richard Rahr, Chair, 409-772-3047, Fax: 409-772-9710, E-mail: rrahr@utmb.edu. *Application contact:* Karen S. Stephenson, Admissions Coordinator, 409-772-9564, Fax: 409-772-9710, E-mail: kstephen@utmb.edu.

The University of Texas Southwestern Medical Center at Dallas, Southwestern School of Health Professions, Physician Assistant Studies Program, Dallas, TX 75390. Offers MPAS. *Accreditation:* ARC-PA. *Faculty:* 85 full-time (58 women). *Students:* 104 full-time (87 women); includes 26 minority (1 African American, 1 American Indian/Alaska Native, 10 Asian Americans or Pacific Islanders, 14 Hispanic Americans). Average age 26. 834 applicants, 6% accepted, 35 enrolled. In 2009, 35 master's awarded. *Entrance requirements:* For master's, GRE, minimum GPA of 3.0. *Application deadline:* For spring admission, 10/1 for domestic students. Electronic applications accepted. *Financial support:* Application deadline: 3/1. *Unit head:* Dr. Eugene Jones, Chair, 214-648-1701, Fax: 214-648-1003, E-mail: pa.sahss@utsouthwestern.edu. *Application contact:* Isela Perez, Education Coordinator, 214-648-1701, Fax: 214-648-1003, E-mail: isela.perez@utsouthwestern.edu.

The University of Toledo, College of Graduate Studies, College of Health Science and Human Service, Division of Health, Physician Assistant Studies Program, Toledo, OH 43606-3390. Offers MSBS. *Accreditation:* ARC-PA. *Degree requirements:* For master's, scholarly project. *Entrance requirements:* For master's, GRE, interview, minimum undergraduate GPA of 3.0, writing sample. *Expenses:* Contact institution.

University of Utah, School of Medicine and Graduate School, Graduate Programs in Medicine, Department of Family and Preventive Medicine, Utah Physician Assistant Program, Salt Lake City, UT 84112-1107. Offers MPAS. *Accreditation:* ARC-PA. *Degree requirements:* For master's, comprehensive exam, thesis or alternative. *Entrance requirements:* Additional exam requirements/recommendations for international students: Required—TOEFL (minimum score 550 paper-based). Electronic applications accepted. *Expenses:* Contact institution. *Faculty research:* Physical assistant education, evidence–based medicine, technology and education, international medicine education.

University of Wisconsin–La Crosse, Office of University Graduate Studies, College of Science and Health, Department of Health Professions, Program in Physician Assistant Studies, La Crosse, WI 54601-3742. Offers MS. *Accreditation:* ARC-PA. *Students:* 27 full-time (23 women); includes 1 minority (Asian American or Pacific Islander). Average age 25. 226 applicants, 6% accepted, 13 enrolled. In 2009, 13 master's awarded. *Degree requirements:* For master's, comprehensive exam. *Entrance requirements:* For master's, GRE, minimum GPA of 3.0 overall and in science. Additional exam requirements/recommendations for international students: Required—TOEFL (minimum score 550 paper-based; 213 computer-based; 79 iBT). *Application deadline:* For fall admission, 9/1 priority date for domestic students. Application fee: $56. Electronic applications accepted. *Unit head:* Dr. Edward Malone, Director, 608-785-8470, E-mail: malone.edwa@uwlax.edu. *Application contact:* Kathryn Kiefer, Director of Admissions, 608-785-8939, E-mail: admissions@uwlax.edu.

Wagner College, Division of Graduate Studies, Department of Biological Sciences, Program in Advanced Physician Assistant Studies, Staten Island, NY 10301-4495. Offers MS. *Accreditation:* ARC-PA. Part-time programs available. *Degree requirements:* For master's, comprehensive exam, thesis. *Entrance requirements:* For master's, minimum GPA of 3.0; bachelor's degree in one of the biological sciences, chemistry or physician assistant studies; physician assistant certification. Additional exam requirements/recommendations for international students: Required—TOEFL (minimum score 550 paper-based; 217 computer-based). *Expenses:* Tuition: Full-time $15,570; part-time $865 per credit. Required fees: $2.

Wayne State University, Eugene Applebaum College of Pharmacy and Health Sciences, Department of Health Care Sciences, Program in Physician Assistant Studies, Detroit, MI 48202. Offers MS. *Accreditation:* ARC-PA. *Entrance requirements:* For master's, GRE General Test, minimum GPA of 3.0, course work in science, 500 hours of work experience in health services; recommendations, interview. Additional exam requirements/recommendations for international students: Required—TOEFL (minimum score 550 paper-based; 213 computer-based); Recommended—TWE (minimum score 6). Electronic applications accepted. *Faculty research:* Medical treatment outcomes, learning and performance evaluation, service-learning research.

Western Michigan University, Graduate College, College of Health and Human Services, Department of Physician Assistant, Kalamazoo, MI 49008. Offers MS. *Accreditation:* ARC-PA. Part-time programs available. *Faculty:* 6 full-time (3 women). *Students:* 69 full-time (51 women); includes 4 minority (1 African American, 2 Asian Americans or Pacific Islanders, 1 Hispanic American). 129 applicants, 54% accepted, 28 enrolled. In 2009, 31 master's awarded. Application fee: $25. *Financial support:* Fellowships, research assistantships, teaching assistantships, Federal Work-Study available. Financial award application deadline: 2/15; financial award applicants required to submit FAFSA. *Unit head:* Dr. Eric Vangsnes, Chair, 269-387-5314. *Application contact:* Admissions and Orientation, 269-387-2000, Fax: 269-387-2355.

Western University of Health Sciences, College of Allied Health Professions, Program in Physician Assistant Studies, Pomona, CA 91766-1854. Offers MS. *Accreditation:* ARC-PA. *Entrance requirements:* For master's, minimum GPA of 2.5, letters of recommendation, interview. *Expenses:* Contact institution.

Wichita State University, Graduate School, College of Health Professions, Department of Physician Assistant, Wichita, KS 67260. Offers MPA. *Accreditation:* ARC-PA. *Expenses:* Tuition, state resident: full-time $4247; part-time $235.95 per credit hour. Tuition, nonresident: full-time $11,171; part-time $620.60 per credit hour. Required fees: $34; $3.60 per credit hour. $17 per term. Tuition and fees vary according to campus/location and program.

Yale University, School of Medicine, Physician Associate Program, New Haven, CT 06510. Offers MM Sc, MM Sc/MPH. *Accreditation:* ARC-PA. *Faculty:* 6 full-time (4 women), 17 part-time/adjunct (7 women). *Students:* 106 full-time (81 women); includes 14 minority (1 American Indian/Alaska Native, 7 Asian Americans or Pacific Islanders, 6 Hispanic Americans). 390 applicants, 12% accepted, 38 enrolled. In 2009, 31 master's awarded. *Degree requirements:* For master's, thesis. *Entrance requirements:* For master's, GRE General Test. Additional exam requirements/recommendations for international students: Required—TOEFL. *Application deadline:* For fall admission, 9/1 for domestic and international students. Electronic applica-

tions accepted. *Expenses:* Contact institution. *Financial support:* Institutionally sponsored loans and scholarships/grants available. Financial award application deadline: 5/1; financial award applicants required to submit FAFSA. *Faculty research:* Correlation of GRE scores and program performance, relationship of PA programs and pharmaceutical companies, career patterns in physician assistants, PA utilization and satisfaction with care, factors influencing PAs in their decision to pursue postgraduate residencies. Total annual research expenditures: $10,000. *Unit head:* Mary L. Warner, Director/Associate Dean, 203-785-2860, Fax: 203-785-3601, E-mail: mary.warner@yale.edu. *Application contact:* Susan de Guardiola, Assistant Director for Student Affairs, 203-737-1003, Fax: 203-785-3601, E-mail: susan.deguardiola@yale.edu.

Rehabilitation Sciences

Boston University, College of Health and Rehabilitation Sciences—Sargent College, Department of Physical Therapy and Athletic Training, Boston, MA 02215. Offers physical therapy (DPT); rehabilitation sciences (D Sc). *Accreditation:* APTA (one or more programs are accredited). Postbaccalaureate distance learning degree programs offered (minimal on-campus study). *Faculty:* 13 full-time (10 women), 26 part-time/adjunct (12 women). *Students:* 142 full-time (116 women); includes 20 minority (1 African American, 14 Asian Americans or Pacific Islanders, 5 Hispanic Americans). Average age 26. 177 applicants, 46% accepted, 31 enrolled. In 2009, 93 doctorates awarded. *Degree requirements:* For doctorate, comprehensive exam (for some programs), thesis/dissertation (for some programs). *Entrance requirements:* For doctorate, GRE General Test, master's degree (for ScD), bachelor's degree (for DPT). Additional exam requirements/recommendations for international students: Required—TOEFL (minimum score 550 paper-based; 84 computer-based). *Application deadline:* For fall admission, 1/7 priority date for domestic students. Applications are processed on a rolling basis. Application fee: $70. Electronic applications accepted. *Expenses:* Tuition: Full-time $37,910; part-time $1184 per credit hour. Required fees: $386; $40 per semester. Part-time tuition and fees vary according to class time, course level, degree level and program. *Financial support:* In 2009–10, 125 students received support, including 14 fellowships (averaging $16,000 per year), 10 teaching assistantships with partial tuition reimbursements available (averaging $3,000 per year); career-related internships or fieldwork, Federal Work-Study, institutionally sponsored loans, scholarships/grants, and tuition waivers (partial) also available. Financial award application deadline: 4/15; financial award applicants required to submit FAFSA. *Faculty research:* Gait, balance, motor control, dynamical systems. *Unit head:* Dr. Wendy Coster, Chairman, 617-353-2720, E-mail: wjcoster@bu.edu. *Application contact:* Sharon Sankey, Director, Student Services, 617-353-2713, Fax: 617-353-7500, E-mail: ssankey@bu.edu.

California University of Pennsylvania, School of Graduate Studies and Research, School of Education, Department of Athletic Training, Program in Exercise Science and Health Promotion, California, PA 15419-1394. Offers fitness and wellness (MS); performance enhancement and injury prevention (MS); rehabilitation sciences (MS); sport management (MS); sport psychology (MS). Part-time and evening/weekend programs available. Postbaccalaureate distance learning degree programs offered (no on-campus study). *Degree requirements:* For master's, comprehensive exam, thesis optional. *Entrance requirements:* For master's, minimum QPA of 3.0. Additional exam requirements/recommendations for international students: Required—TOEFL (minimum score 550 paper-based; 213 computer-based; 80 iBT). Electronic applications accepted. *Expenses:* Contact institution. *Faculty research:* Reducing obesity in children, sport performance, creating unique biomechanical assessment techniques, Web-based training for fitness professionals, Webcams.

Canisius College, Graduate Division, School of Education and Human Services, Department of Health and Human Performance, Buffalo, NY 14208-1098. Offers MS. Part-time and evening/weekend programs available. *Faculty:* 3 full-time (0 women), 3 part-time/adjunct (1 woman). *Students:* 13 full-time (10 women), 10 part-time (8 women); includes 1 minority (African American). Average age 24. 26 applicants, 81% accepted, 12 enrolled. In 2009, 9 master's awarded. *Degree requirements:* For master's, thesis, project internship. Application fee: $25. *Financial support:* In 2009–10, 9 students received support, including 1 research assistantship with tuition reimbursement available (averaging $6,000 per year); career-related internships or fieldwork, institutionally sponsored loans, health care benefits, and unspecified assistantships also available. *Faculty research:* Delayed onset of muscle soreness, exercising muscle blood flow, aging. Total annual research expenditures: $13,000. *Unit head:* Dr. Peter M. Koehneke, Chair, 716-888-2954, E-mail: koehneke@canisius.edu. *Application contact:* James D. Bagwell, Director of Graduate Recruitment and Admissions, 716-888-2544, Fax: 716-888-3290, E-mail: bagwellj@canisius.edu.

Central Michigan University, College of Graduate Studies, The Herbert H. and Grace A. Dow College of Health Professions, School of Rehabilitation and Medical Sciences, Mount Pleasant, MI 48859. Offers physical therapy (DPT); physician assistant (MS). *Accreditation:* APTA; ARC-PA. *Degree requirements:* For master's, thesis or alternative; for doctorate, thesis/dissertation or alternative. *Entrance requirements:* For master's and doctorate, GRE. Electronic applications accepted.

Clarion University of Pennsylvania, Office of Research and Graduate Studies, College of Education and Human Services, Department of Special Education and Rehabilitative Sciences, Program in Rehabilitative Sciences, Clarion, PA 16214. Offers MS. *Degree requirements:* For master's, thesis or alternative. *Entrance requirements:* For master's, GRE General Test or MAT, minimum QPA of 3.0. Additional exam requirements/recommendations for international students: Required—TOEFL (minimum score 550 paper-based; 213 computer-based; 80 iBT). Electronic applications accepted.

Concordia University Wisconsin, Graduate Programs, School of Health and Human Services, Program in Rehabilitation Science, Mequon, WI 53097-2402. Offers MSRS.

Duquesne University, John G. Rangos, Sr. School of Health Sciences, Pittsburgh, PA 15282-0001. Offers health management systems (MHMS); occupational therapy (MS); physical therapy (DPT); physician assistant studies (MPAS); rehabilitation science (MS, PhD); speech–language pathology (MS); MBA/MHMS. *Accreditation:* AOTA (one or more programs are accredited); APTA (one or more programs are accredited); ASHA. *Faculty:* 35 full-time (23 women), 17 part-time/adjunct (10 women). *Students:* 309 full-time (258 women), 11 part-time (7 women); includes 11 minority (5 African Americans, 5 Asian Americans or Pacific Islanders, 1 Hispanic American), 6 international. Average age 23. 454 applicants, 20% accepted, 20 enrolled. In 2009, 92 master's, 23 doctorates awarded. *Degree requirements:* For doctorate, thesis/dissertation. *Entrance requirements:* For master's, GRE General Test (speech-language pathology), 3 letters of recommendation; minimum GPA of 2.75 (health management systems, occupational therapy), minimum GPA of 3.0 (speech-language pathology); for doctorate, GRE General Test (for physical therapy), 3 letters of recommendation, minimum GPA of 3.0, personal interview. Additional exam requirements/recommendations for international students: Required—TOEFL (minimum score 550 paper-based; 233 computer-based; 90 iBT). *Application deadline:* Applications are processed on a rolling basis. Electronic applications accepted. *Expenses:* Contact institution. *Financial support:* Federal Work-Study available. *Faculty research:* Neuronal processing, electrical stimulation on peripheral neuropathy, CNS stimulatory and inhibitory signals, behavioral genetic methodologies to development disorders of speech, neurogenic communication disorders. Total annual research expenditures: $338,404. *Unit head:* Dr. Gregory H. Frazer, Dean, 412-396-5303, Fax: 412-396-5554, E-mail: frazer@duq.edu. *Application contact:* Christopher R. Hilf, Recruiter/Academic Advisor, 412-396-5653, Fax: 412-396-5554, E-mail: hilfc@duq.edu.

East Carolina University, Graduate School, School of Allied Health Sciences, Program in Rehabilitation Studies, Greenville, NC 27858-4353. Offers rehabilitation counseling (MS); substance abuse and clinical counseling (MS); vocational evaluation (MS). *Accreditation:* CORE. Part-time and evening/weekend programs available. *Degree requirements:* For master's, comprehensive exam, thesis or alternative, internship. *Entrance requirements:* For master's, GRE General Test or MAT. Additional exam requirements/recommendations for international students: Required—TOEFL.

East Stroudsburg University of Pennsylvania, Graduate School, College of Health Sciences, Department of Exercise Science, East Stroudsburg, PA 18301-2999. Offers cardiac rehabilitation and exercise science (MS). Part-time and evening/weekend programs available. *Faculty:* 3 full-time (1 woman). *Students:* 38 full-time (18 women), 3 part-time (2 women); includes 1 minority (Hispanic American), 4 international. Average age 25. In 2009, 35 master's awarded. *Degree requirements:* For master's, comprehensive exam, thesis or alternative, computer literacy. *Entrance requirements:* Additional exam requirements/recommendations for international students: Required—TOEFL (minimum score 560 paper-based; 220 computer-based; 83 iBT). *Application deadline:* For fall admission, 7/31 priority date for domestic students, 5/1 priority date for international students; for spring admission, 11/30 for domestic students, 10/1 for international students. Applications are processed on a rolling basis. Application fee: $50. *Expenses:* Tuition, state resident: full-time $9942; part-time $387 per credit. Tuition, nonresident: full-time $14,240; part-time $619 per credit. *Financial support:* In 2009–10, 57 research assistantships with full and partial tuition reimbursements (averaging $1,749 per year) were awarded; Federal Work-Study and institutionally sponsored loans also available. Financial award application deadline: 3/1. *Unit head:* Dr. Shala Davis, Graduate Coordinator, 570-422-3302, Fax: 570-422-3616, E-mail: sdavis@po-box.esu.edu. *Application contact:* Kevin Quintero, Graduate Admissions Coordinator, 570-422-3890, Fax: 570-422-2711, E-mail: kquintero@po-box.esu.edu.

George Mason University, College of Health and Human Services, Department of Global and Community Health, Fairfax, VA 22030. Offers biostatistics (Certificate); epidemiology (Certificate); epidemiology and biostatistics (MS); gerontology (Certificate); global health (MS, Certificate); nutrition (Certificate); public health (MPH, Certificate); rehabilitation science (Certificate). *Faculty:* 14 full-time (8 women), 12 part-time/adjunct (8 women). *Students:* 93 full-time (75 women), 106 part-time (92 women); includes 87 minority (46 African Americans, 1 American Indian/Alaska Native, 31 Asian Americans or Pacific Islanders, 9 Hispanic Americans), 22 international. Average age 31. 269 applicants, 69% accepted, 146 enrolled. In 2009, 17 master's, 2 other advanced degrees awarded. *Degree requirements:* For master's, comprehensive exam (for some programs), thesis or practicum. *Entrance requirements:* For master's, GRE, BA with minimum GPA of 3.0, 2 letters of recommendation. Additional exam requirements/recommendations for international students: Required—TOEFL. *Application deadline:* For fall admission, 4/1 priority date for domestic students, 4/1 for international students; for spring admission, 11/1 for domestic and international students. Applications are processed on a rolling basis. Application fee: $75. Electronic applications accepted. *Expenses:* Tuition, state resident: full-time $7568; part-time $315.33 per credit hour. Tuition, nonresident: full-time $21,704; part-time $904.33 per credit hour. Required fees: $2184; $91 per credit hour. *Financial support:* In 2009–10, 4 students received support, including 2 research assistantships with full and partial tuition reimbursements available (averaging $3,500 per year), 2 teaching assistantships with full and partial tuition reimbursements available (averaging $2,790 per year); Federal Work-Study, scholarships/grants, unspecified assistantships, and research awards, health care benefits health care benefits (full-time research or teaching assistantship recipients) also available. Support available to part-time students. Financial award application deadline: 3/1. *Faculty research:* Providing introductory and advanced degrees in health-related disciplines centered in global and community issues, health issues and the needs of affected populations at the regional and global level. *Unit head:* Dr. Shirley S. Travis, Dean, 703-993-1918. *Application contact:* Allan Weiss, Office Manager, 703-993-3126, E-mail: aweiss2@gmu.edu.

Indiana University–Purdue University Indianapolis, Indiana University School of Medicine, School of Health and Rehabilitation Sciences, Indianapolis, IN 46202-2896. Offers health sciences education (MS); nutrition and dietetics (MS); occupational therapy (MS); physical therapy (DPT). Part-time and evening/weekend programs available. *Faculty:* 8 full-time (5 women). *Students:* 206 full-time (161 women), 11 part-time (8 women); includes 16 minority (5 African Americans, 1 American Indian/Alaska Native, 8 Asian Americans or Pacific Islanders, 2 Hispanic Americans), 1 international. Average age 26. 23 applicants, 83% accepted, 18 enrolled. In 2009, 9 master's, 32 doctorates awarded. *Degree requirements:* For master's, thesis (for some programs). *Entrance requirements:* For master's, GRE General Test, minimum GPA of 3.0. Additional exam requirements/recommendations for international students: Required—TOEFL. *Application deadline:* For fall admission, 1/15 priority date for domestic students; for spring admission, 10/15 for domestic students. Application fee: $55 ($65 for international students). *Financial support:* In 2009–10, 10 fellowships (averaging $2,485 per year), 1 teaching assistantship (averaging $3,600 per year) were awarded; research assistantships, Federal Work-Study, institutionally sponsored loans, and scholarships/grants also available. Support available to part-time students. Financial award applicants required to submit FAFSA. *Unit head:* Dr. Mark S. Sothmann, Dean, 317-274-4702, E-mail: msothman@iupui.edu. *Application contact:* Dr. Mark S. Sothmann, Dean, 317-274-4702, E-mail: msothman@iupui.edu.

McGill University, Faculty of Graduate and Postdoctoral Studies, Faculty of Medicine, School of Physical and Occupational Therapy, Montréal, QC H3A 2T5, Canada. Offers assessing driving capability (PGC); rehabilitation science (M Sc, PhD).

McMaster University, Faculty of Health Sciences and School of Graduate Studies, Program in Rehabilitation Science (course-based), Hamilton, ON L8S 4M2, Canada. Offers M Sc. Part-time programs available. *Degree requirements:* For master's, online courses and scholarly paper. *Entrance requirements:* For master's, minimum B+ average in final year of a 4-year undergraduate health professional program or other relevant program. Additional exam requirements/recommendations for international students: Required—TOEFL (minimum score 600 paper-based; 250 computer-based).

McMaster University, Faculty of Health Sciences and School of Graduate Studies, Program in Rehabilitation Science (Thesis Option), Hamilton, ON L8S 4M2, Canada. Offers M Sc, PhD. Part-time programs available. *Degree requirements:* For master's, thesis. *Entrance requirements:* For master's, minimum B+ average in final year of a 4-year undergraduate health professional program or other relevant program. Additional exam requirements/recommendations for international students: Required—TOEFL (minimum score 600 paper-based; 250 computer-based).

Medical University of South Carolina, College of Health Professions, Department of Health Sciences and Research, PhD Program in Health and Rehabilitation Science, Charleston, SC 29425. Offers PhD. *Faculty:* 12 full-time (5 women). *Students:* 5 full-time (4 women), 1 part-time (0 women); includes 3 minority (1 African American, 2 Hispanic Americans). Average age 35. 8 applicants, 75% accepted, 6 enrolled. *Degree requirements:* For doctorate,

Rehabilitation Sciences

Medical University of South Carolina (continued)
comprehensive exam, thesis/dissertation. *Entrance requirements:* Additional exam requirements/recommendations for international students: Required—TOEFL (minimum score 600 paper-based; 250 computer-based). Application fee: $85. Electronic applications accepted. *Financial support:* Career-related internships or fieldwork, Federal Work-Study, scholarships/grants, and tuition waivers (partial) available. Support available to part-time students. Financial award application deadline: 3/10; financial award applicants required to submit FAFSA. *Faculty research:* Spinal cord injury, geriatrics, health economics, health psychology, behavioral medicine. *Unit head:* Dr. Bonnie Martin-Harris, Director, 843-792-7162, E-mail: harrisbm@musc.edu. *Application contact:* Susan Johnson, Student Services Program Coordinator, 843-792-5377, Fax: 843-792-0710, E-mail: johnsoss@musc.edu.

Northwestern Health Sciences University, School of Massage Therapy, Bloomington, MN 55431-1599. Offers Professional Certificate.

Northwestern University, Northwestern University Feinberg School of Medicine, Department of Physical Therapy and Human Movement Sciences, Chicago, IL 60611-2814. Offers movement and rehabilitation science (PhD); physical therapy (DPT). *Accreditation:* APTA. *Faculty:* 22 full-time (13 women), 4 part-time/adjunct (3 women). *Students:* 209 full-time (172 women); includes 16 minority (7 African Americans, 5 Asian Americans or Pacific Islanders, 4 Hispanic Americans). Average age 24. 375 applicants, 42% accepted, 64 enrolled. *Degree requirements:* For doctorate, synthesis project. *Entrance requirements:* Additional exam requirements/recommendations for international students: Required—TOEFL (minimum score 265 computer-based). *Application deadline:* For fall admission, 10/15 for domestic students. Applications are processed on a rolling basis. Application fee: $40. Electronic applications accepted. *Expenses:* Contact institution. *Financial support:* In 2009–10, 184 students received support. Federal Work-Study, institutionally sponsored loans, and scholarships/grants available. Financial award application deadline: 2/15; financial award applicants required to submit FAFSA. *Faculty research:* Neuromuscular control, student performance (academic/professional), clinical outcomes, human performance. Total annual research expenditures: $2.8 million. *Unit head:* Dr. Julius P. A. Dewald, Associate Professor and Chair, 312-908-6788, Fax: 312-908-0741, E-mail: j-dewald@northwestern.edu. *Application contact:* Dr. Jane Sullivan, Assistant Professor and Assistant Chair for Recruitment and Admissions, 312-908-6789, Fax: 312-908-0741, E-mail: j-sullivan@northwestern.edu.

Queen's University at Kingston, School of Graduate Studies and Research, Faculty of Health Sciences, School of Rehabilitation Therapy, Kingston, ON K7L 3N6, Canada. Offers occupational therapy (M Sc OT); physical therapy (M Sc PT); rehabilitation science (M Sc, PhD). Part-time programs available. *Degree requirements:* For master's, thesis; for doctorate, comprehensive exam, thesis/dissertation. *Entrance requirements:* Additional exam requirements/recommendations for international students: Required—TOEFL. *Faculty research:* Disability, community, motor performance, rehabilitation, treatment efficiency.

Salus University, Graduate Studies in Vision Impairment and Audiology, Elkins Park, PA 19027-1598. Offers education of children and youth with visual and multiple impairments (M Ed, Certificate); low vision rehabilitation (MS, Certificate); orientation and mobility therapy (MS, Certificate); vision rehabilitation therapy (MS, Certificate); OD/MS. Part-time programs available. Postbaccalaureate distance learning degree programs offered. *Faculty:* 8 full-time (7 women), 1 (woman) part-time/adjunct. *Students:* 4 full-time (all women), 64 part-time (58 women); includes 7 minority (5 African Americans, 1 American Indian/Alaska Native, 1 Hispanic American). Average age 37. In 2009, 14 master's, 12 other advanced degrees awarded. *Entrance requirements:* For master's, GRE or MAT, letters of reference (3), interviews (2). Additional exam requirements/recommendations for international students: Required—TOEFL, TWE. *Application deadline:* For fall admission, 6/1 for domestic students. Applications are processed on a rolling basis. *Expenses:* Contact institution. *Financial support:* Federal Work-Study and scholarships/grants available. Financial award applicants required to submit FAFSA. *Faculty research:* Knowledge utilization, technology transfer. *Unit head:* Dr. Audrey Smith, Associate Dean, 215-780-1361, Fax: 215-780-1357, E-mail: ASmith@Salus.edu. *Application contact:* Dr. Audrey Smith, Associate Dean, 215-780-1361, Fax: 215-780-1357, E-mail: ASmith@Salus.edu.

Texas Tech University Health Sciences Center, School of Allied Health Sciences, Program in Rehabilitation Sciences, Lubbock, TX 79430. Offers PhD. Part-time programs available. *Faculty:* 5 full-time (4 women). *Students:* 14 full-time (7 women), 4 part-time (1 woman); includes 3 minority (all Hispanic Americans). Average age 34. 4 applicants, 50% accepted, 2 enrolled. *Entrance requirements:* Additional exam requirements/recommendations for international students: Required—TOEFL, IELTS. *Application deadline:* For spring admission, 3/1 for domestic students. Application fee: $35. *Financial support:* Application deadline: 9/1. *Unit head:* Lindsay E. Roberts. *Application contact:* Jeri Moravcik, Assistant Director of Admissions and Student Affairs, 806-743-3220, Fax: 806-743-2994, E-mail: jeri.moravcik@ttuhsc.edu.

University at Buffalo, the State University of New York, Graduate School, School of Public Health and Health Professions, Department of Rehabilitation Science, Buffalo, NY 14260. Offers assistive and rehabilitation technology (Certificate); occupational therapy (MS); physical therapy (DPT). *Faculty:* 21 full-time (15 women), 14 part-time/adjunct (9 women). *Students:* 188 full-time (125 women), 11 part-time (10 women); includes 37 minority (15 African Americans, 20 Asian Americans or Pacific Islanders, 2 Hispanic Americans), 27 international. Average age 24. 128 applicants, 59% accepted, 59 enrolled. In 2009, 29 master's, 42 doctorates, 1 other advanced degree awarded. *Degree requirements:* For doctorate, comprehensive exam, thesis/dissertation. *Entrance requirements:* For master's, BS in occupational therapy; for doctorate, GRE General Test. Additional exam requirements/recommendations for international students: Required—TOEFL (minimum score 550 paper-based; 213 computer-based; 79 iBT). Application fee: $50. Electronic applications accepted. *Financial support:* In 2009–10, 4 students received support, including 2 research assistantships with full and partial tuition reimbursements available (averaging $15,000 per year), 2 teaching assistantships with full and partial tuition reimbursements available (averaging $11,198 per year); scholarships/grants and unspecified assistantships also available. *Faculty research:* Communicative disorders, nursing, occupational therapy, physical therapy, exercise physiology. Total annual research expenditures: $489,000. *Unit head:* Dr. Robert Burkard, Chair, 716-829-3141 Ext. 120, Fax: 716-829-2317, E-mail: phhpadv@buffalo.edu. *Application contact:* Cassandra Walker-Whiteside, Director, Student Advisement and Recruitment Services, 716-829-6769.

University of Alberta, Faculty of Graduate Studies and Research, Faculty of Rehabilitation Medicine, Edmonton, AB T6G 2E1, Canada. Offers PhD. *Faculty:* 28 full-time (17 women). *Students:* 11 full-time (6 women), 4 part-time (2 women). Average age 32. 10 applicants, 50% accepted, 5 enrolled. In 2009, 2 doctorates awarded. *Degree requirements:* For doctorate, thesis/dissertation. *Entrance requirements:* For doctorate, GRE, minimum GPA of 7.0 on a 9.0 scale. Additional exam requirements/recommendations for international students: Required—TOEFL. *Application deadline:* For fall admission, 3/1 for domestic and international students; for winter admission, 7/1 for domestic and international students. Applications are processed on a rolling basis. Application fee: $0. Electronic applications accepted. Tuition and fees charges are reported in Canadian dollars. *Expenses:* Tuition, area resident: Full-time $4626 Canadian dollars; part-time $99.72 Canadian dollars per unit. International tuition: $8216 Canadian dollars full-time. Required fees: $3590 Canadian dollars; $99.72 Canadian dollars per unit. $215 Canadian dollars per term. *Financial support:* In 2009–10, 1 fellowship (averaging $16,000 per year), 7 research assistantships (averaging $2,721 per year), 1 teaching assistantship (averaging $2,535 per year) were awarded; institutionally sponsored loans, scholarships/grants, and traineeships also available. Financial award application deadline: 1/1. *Faculty research:* Musculoskeletal disorders, neuromotor control, exercise physiology, motor speech disorders, assistive technologies, cardiac rehabilitation/therapeutic exercise. *Unit head:* Dr. P. Hagler, Associate Dean, 780-492-1595, Fax: 780-492-1626, E-mail: paul.hagler@ualberta.ca. *Application contact:* Angela Libutti, Administrative Assistant, Graduate Studies, 780-492-1595, Fax: 780-492-1626, E-mail: thesis.info@rehabmed.ualberta.ca.

The University of British Columbia, Faculty of Medicine, School of Rehabilitation Sciences, Vancouver, BC V6T 1Z1, Canada. Offers M Sc, MOT, MPT, MRSc, PhD. *Degree requirements:* For master's, thesis; for doctorate, comprehensive exam, thesis/dissertation. *Entrance requirements:* For master's, minimum B+ average; for doctorate, minimum B+ average, master's degree. Additional exam requirements/recommendations for international students: Required—TOEFL (minimum score 600 paper-based; 250 computer-based), GRE. Electronic applications accepted. *Faculty research:* Disability, rehabilitation and society, exercise science and rehabilitation, neurorehabilitation and motor control.

University of Cincinnati, Graduate School, College of Allied Health Sciences, Department of Rehabilitation Science, Cincinnati, OH 45221. Offers DPT. *Accreditation:* APTA. *Entrance requirements:* For doctorate, GRE General Test, bachelor's degree with minimum GPA of 3.0, 50 hours volunteer/work in physical therapy setting. Additional exam requirements/recommendations for international students: Required—TOEFL. Electronic applications accepted. *Faculty research:* Biomechanics, sports-related injuries, motor learning, stroke rehabilitation.

University of Florida, Graduate School, College of Public Health and Health Professions, Program in Rehabilitation Science, Gainesville, FL 32611. Offers PhD. *Degree requirements:* For doctorate, thesis/dissertation. *Entrance requirements:* For doctorate, GRE General Test, minimum GPA of 3.0. Additional exam requirements/recommendations for international students: Required—TOEFL (minimum score 550 paper-based; 213 computer-based). Electronic applications accepted.

University of Illinois at Urbana–Champaign, Graduate College, College of Applied Health Sciences, Department of Kinesiology and Community Health, Champaign, IL 61820. Offers community health (MS, MSPH, PhD); kinesiology (MS, PhD); public health (MPH); rehabilitation (MS). *Faculty:* 31 full-time (16 women). *Students:* 110 full-time (62 women), 17 part-time (9 women); includes 26 minority (15 African Americans, 1 American Indian/Alaska Native, 8 Asian Americans or Pacific Islanders, 2 Hispanic Americans), 23 international. 139 applicants, 28% accepted, 26 enrolled. In 2009, 26 master's, 9 doctorates awarded. *Entrance requirements:* For master's, GRE, minimum GPA of 3.0; for doctorate, GRE, minimum graduate GPA of 3.5. Additional exam requirements/recommendations for international students: Required—TOEFL. *Application deadline:* Applications are processed on a rolling basis. Application fee: $60 ($75 for international students). Electronic applications accepted. *Financial support:* In 2009–10, 13 fellowships, 55 research assistantships, 71 teaching assistantships were awarded; tuition waivers (full and partial) also available. *Unit head:* Wojciech Chodzko-Zajko, Head, 217-244-0823, Fax: 217-244-7322, E-mail: wojtek@illinois.edu. *Application contact:* Tina M. Candler, Office Manager, 217-333-1083, Fax: 217-244-7322, E-mail: tcandler@illinois.edu.

The University of Iowa, Roy J. and Lucille A. Carver College of Medicine and Graduate College, Graduate Programs in Medicine, Graduate Program in Physical Therapy and Rehabilitation Science, Iowa City, IA 52242-1316. Offers physical therapy (DPT); rehabilitation science (PhD). *Accreditation:* APTA (one or more programs are accredited). *Faculty:* 7 full-time (3 women), 45 part-time/adjunct (23 women). *Students:* 110 full-time (77 women), 7 part-time (5 women); includes 2 minority (1 African American, 1 Hispanic American), 3 international. Average age 24. 298 applicants, 17% accepted, 37 enrolled. In 2009, 3 doctorates awarded. Terminal master's awarded for partial completion of doctoral program. *Degree requirements:* For doctorate, thesis/dissertation (for some programs). *Entrance requirements:* For doctorate, GRE. Additional exam requirements/recommendations for international students: Required—TOEFL. *Application deadline:* For fall admission, 12/1 priority date for domestic students, 5/15 for international students; for winter admission, 10/15 for international students; for spring admission, 3/15 for international students. Application fee: $60 ($85 for international students). Electronic applications accepted. *Expenses:* Contact institution. *Financial support:* In 2009–10, 94 students received support, including 1 fellowship with partial tuition reimbursement available (averaging $9,000 per year), 6 research assistantships with partial tuition reimbursements available (averaging $10,129 per year), teaching assistantships with partial tuition reimbursements available (averaging $10,129 per year); Federal Work-Study, institutionally sponsored loans, scholarships/grants, health care benefits, and unspecified assistantships also available. Support available to part-time students. Financial award application deadline: 6/30; financial award applicants required to submit FAFSA. *Faculty research:* Muscle fatigue, motor control, pain mechanisms, body composition, sports medicine, occupational safety, neuromuscular physiology, neural control of movement. Total annual research expenditures: $1.4 million. *Unit head:* Dr. Richard K. Shields, Director, 319-335-9791, Fax: 319-335-9707, E-mail: physical-therapy@uiowa.edu. *Application contact:* Dr. Richard K. Shields, Director, 319-335-9791, Fax: 319-335-9707, E-mail: physical-therapy@uiowa.edu.

The University of Kansas, University of Kansas Medical Center, School of Allied Health, Department of Occupational Therapy Education, Kansas City, KS 66160. Offers occupational therapy (MOT, MS, OTD); therapeutic science (PhD). *Accreditation:* AOTA. Part-time programs available. *Faculty:* 8 full-time, 3 part-time/adjunct. *Students:* 45 full-time (43 women), 39 part-time (32 women); includes 5 minority (2 African Americans, 1 American Indian/Alaska Native, 1 Asian American or Pacific Islander, 1 Hispanic American), 16 international. Average age 28. 13 applicants, 69% accepted, 9 enrolled. In 2009, 31 master's awarded. *Degree requirements:* For doctorate, comprehensive exam, thesis/dissertation, oral defense. *Entrance requirements:* For master's, 1 year of experience in a field related to disability; for doctorate, 24 hours of master's level research. Additional exam requirements/recommendations for international students: Required—TOEFL. *Application deadline:* For fall admission, 6/15 for domestic students, 4/1 for international students. Applications are processed on a rolling basis. Application fee: $60. Electronic applications accepted. *Expenses:* Tuition, state resident: full-time $6492; part-time $270.50 per credit hour. Tuition, nonresident: full-time $15,510; part-time $646.25 per credit hour. Required fees: $847; $70.56 per credit hour. Tuition and fees vary according to course load and program. *Financial support:* In 2009–10, 36 students received support, including 3 teaching assistantships with full and partial tuition reimbursements available (averaging $41,288 per year); research assistantships with partial tuition reimbursements available, traineeships and unspecified assistantships also available. Financial award applicants required to submit FAFSA. *Faculty research:* The impact of sensory processing in everyday life; brain activity in various disorders and conditions; home and work modifications; cognition, executive function and problem solving in everyday life; best practices in serving children, families and schools. Total annual research expenditures: $99,220. *Unit head:* Dr. Winifred W. Dunn, Professor and Chair, 913-588-7195, Fax: 913-588-4568, E-mail: wdunn@kumc.edu. *Application contact:* Laura Neely, Coordinator, 913-588-7174, Fax: 913-588-4568, E-mail: lneely@kumc.edu.

University of Kentucky, Graduate School, College of Health Sciences, Program in Rehabilitation Sciences, Lexington, KY 40506-0032. Offers PhD. *Degree requirements:* For doctorate, comprehensive exam, thesis/dissertation. *Entrance requirements:* For doctorate, GRE General Test, minimum undergraduate GPA of 2.75. Additional exam requirements/recommendations for international students: Required—TOEFL (minimum score 550 paper-based; 213 computer-based). Electronic applications accepted.

University of Manitoba, Faculty of Graduate Studies, School of Medical Rehabilitation, Winnipeg, MB R3T 2N2, Canada. Offers applied health sciences (PhD); occupational therapy (MOT); physical therapy (MPT); rehabilitation (M Sc).

University of Manitoba, Faculty of Medicine and Faculty of Graduate Studies, Graduate Programs in Medicine, Department of Medical Rehabilitation, Winnipeg, MB R3T 2N2, Canada. Offers rehabilitation (M Sc). Part-time programs available. *Faculty research:* Understanding of human dynamics, motor control and neurological dysfunction, exercise physiology, functional motion of the upper extremity and effects of musculoskeletal disorders.

University of Maryland, Baltimore, Graduate School, Graduate Program in Life Sciences, Program in Physical Rehabilitation Science, Baltimore, MD 21201. Offers PhD. *Students:* 6 full-time (2 women), 2 part-time (1 woman); includes 2 minority (both Asian Americans or Pacific Islanders), 3 international. Average age 32. 13 applicants, 23% accepted, 1 enrolled. In 2009, 2 doctorates awarded. *Entrance requirements:* For doctorate, GRE. Additional exam

requirements/recommendations for international students: Required—TOEFL (minimum score 550 paper-based; 80 iBT); Recommended—IELTS (minimum score 7). *Application deadline:* For fall admission, 1/15 for domestic and international students. Application fee: $50. Electronic applications accepted. *Expenses:* Tuition, state resident: full-time $7290; part-time $405 per credit hour. Tuition, nonresident: full-time $12,780; part-time $710 per credit hour. Required fees: $774; $10 per credit hour. $297 per semester. Tuition and fees vary according to course load, degree level and program. *Financial support:* In 2009–10, research assistantships with partial tuition reimbursements (averaging $25,000 per year); health care benefits and unspecified assistantships also available. Financial award application deadline: 3/1. *Faculty research:* Applied physiology, biomechanics, epidemiology of disability, neuromotor control. *Unit head:* Dr. Mark Rogers, Program Director, 410-706-0841, Fax: 410-706-4903, E-mail: mrogers@som. umaryland.edu. *Application contact:* Terry Heron, Academic Coordinator, 410-706-7721, E-mail: theron@som.umaryland.edu.

University of Maryland, Baltimore, School of Medicine, Department of Physical Therapy and Rehabilitation Science, Baltimore, MD 21201. Offers physical rehabilitation science (PhD); physical therapy and rehabilitation science (DPT). *Accreditation:* APTA. *Students:* 102 full-time (71 women), 74 part-time (59 women); includes 27 minority (7 African Americans, 16 Asian Americans or Pacific Islanders, 4 Hispanic Americans), 4 international. Average age 27. 362 applicants, 57% accepted, 57 enrolled. In 2009, 62 doctorates awarded. *Entrance requirements:* For doctorate, GRE General Test. Additional exam requirements/recommendations for international students: Required—TOEFL (minimum score 80 iBT). Application fee: $50. Electronic applications accepted. *Expenses:* Contact institution. *Financial support:* Application deadline: 3/1. *Unit head:* Dr. Mary Rodgers, Chair, 410-706-5216, Fax: 410-706-4903, E-mail: mrodgers@ som.umaryland.edu. *Application contact:* Dr. Jill Whitall, Program Director, 410-706-7720, Fax: 410-706-6387, E-mail: ptadmissions@som.umaryland.edu.

University of Maryland Eastern Shore, Graduate Programs, Department of Rehabilitation Services, Princess Anne, MD 21853-1299. Offers rehabilitation counseling (MS). *Accreditation:* CORE. Part-time and evening/weekend programs available. *Degree requirements:* For master's, internship. *Entrance requirements:* For master's, interview. Additional exam requirements/ recommendations for international students: Required—TOEFL (minimum score 213 computer-based; 80 iBT). Electronic applications accepted. *Faculty research:* Long-term rehabilitation training.

University of Northern Iowa, Graduate College, College of Education, School of Health, Physical Education, and Leisure Services, Cedar Falls, IA 50614. Offers community health education (Ed D); health education (MA, Ed D); leisure services (MA, Ed D), including leisure services (Ed D), program administration (MA), youth/human services administration (MA); physical education (MA), including physical education, scientific basis of physical education, teaching/coaching; rehabilitation studies (Ed D). Part-time and evening/weekend programs available. *Students:* 79 full-time (43 women), 39 part-time (16 women); includes 23 minority (18 African Americans, 2 Asian Americans or Pacific Islanders, 3 Hispanic Americans), 13 international. 89 applicants, 71% accepted, 43 enrolled. In 2009, 29 master's, 1 doctorate awarded. *Degree requirements:* For master's, comprehensive exam, thesis or alternative; for doctorate, thesis/dissertation. *Entrance requirements:* For master's, minimum GPA of 3.0; for doctorate, GRE, minimum GPA of 3.5. Additional exam requirements/recommendations for international students: Required—TOEFL (minimum score 500 paper-based; 180 computer-based; 61 iBT). *Application deadline:* Applications are processed on a rolling basis. Application fee: $30 ($50 for international students). *Financial support:* Career-related internships or fieldwork, Federal Work-Study, institutionally sponsored loans, scholarships/grants, tuition waivers (full and partial), and unspecified assistantships available. Support available to part-time students. Financial award application deadline: 2/1. *Unit head:* Dr. Christopher R. Edginton, Director, 319-273-2840, Fax: 319-273-5958, E-mail: christopher.edginton@uni.edu. *Application contact:* Laurie S. Russell, Record Analyst, 319-273-2623, Fax: 319-273-6792, E-mail: laurie. russell@uni.edu.

University of North Texas, Robert B. Toulouse School of Graduate Studies, College of Public Affairs and Community Service, Department of Rehabilitation, Social Work, and Addictions, Denton, TX 76203. Offers rehabilitation counseling (MS). *Accreditation:* CORE. Part-time and evening/weekend programs available. Postbaccalaureate distance learning degree programs offered (no on-campus study). *Degree requirements:* For master's, comprehensive exam, thesis optional, 100 hour practicum, 600 hour internship. *Entrance requirements:* For master's, GRE General Test or 2 years experience, minimum overall GPA of 2.8, 3.0 in last 60 hours. Additional exam requirements/recommendations for international students: Required—proof of English language proficiency required for non-native English speakers; Recommended—TOEFL (minimum score 550 paper-based; 213 computer-based; 79 iBT). *Application deadline:* Applications are processed on a rolling basis. Application fee: $50 ($75 for international students). Electronic applications accepted. *Expenses:* Tuition, state resident: full-time $4298; part-time $239 per contact hour. Tuition, nonresident: full-time $9878; part-time $549 per contact hour. Required fees: $265 per contact hour. *Financial support:* Career-related internships or fieldwork, Federal Work-Study, institutionally sponsored loans, and scholarships/ grants available. Financial award application deadline: 4/15; financial award applicants required to submit FAFSA. *Faculty research:* Resiliency, multiculturalism, substance abuse and co-existing disabilities, social work pedagogy, spiritual aspects of disability and aging. *Application contact:* Program Coordinator, 940-565-4054, Fax: 940-369-8649.

University of Oklahoma Health Sciences Center, Graduate College, College of Allied Health, Department of Rehabilitation Sciences, Oklahoma City, OK 73190. Offers MS. *Faculty:* 6 full-time (5 women), 1 (woman) part-time/adjunct. *Students:* 27 part-time (all women); includes 2 minority (1 American Indian/Alaska Native, 1 Hispanic American). Average age 40. 28 applicants, 46% accepted, 9 enrolled. In 2009, 8 master's awarded. *Degree requirements:* For master's, comprehensive exam, thesis optional. *Entrance requirements:* For master's, GRE General Test, 2 years clinical experience, 3 letters of reference. Additional exam requirements/recommendations for international students: Required—TOEFL (minimum score 550 paper-based). *Application deadline:* For fall admission, 7/1 for domestic students; for winter admission, 5/1 for domestic students; for spring admission, 12/1 for domestic students. Application fee: $50. *Expenses:* Tuition, state resident: full-time $3120; part-time $156 per credit hour. Tuition, nonresident: full-time $11,314; part-time $409.70 per credit hour. Required fees: $1471; $51.20 per credit hour. $223.25 per term. *Financial support:* In 2009–10, 2 research assistantships (averaging $8,000 per year) were awarded. *Unit head:* Martha Ferretti, Chair, 405-271-2131, E-mail: martha-ferretti@ouhsc.edu. *Application contact:* Dr. Irene McEwen, Graduate Liaison, 405-271-2131, E-mail: irene-mcewen@ouhsc.edu.

University of Ottawa, Faculty of Graduate and Postdoctoral Studies, Faculty of Health Sciences, School of Rehabilitation Sciences, Ottawa, ON K1N 6N5, Canada. Offers audiology (M Sc); orthophony (M Sc). Part-time and evening/weekend programs available. *Entrance requirements:* For master's, honors degree or equivalent, minimum B average. Electronic applications accepted.

University of Pittsburgh, School of Health and Rehabilitation Sciences, Department of Rehabilitation Science and Technology, Pittsburgh, PA 15260. Offers assistive rehabilitation technology (Certificate). *Accreditation:* CORE. *Students:* 10 full-time (7 women), 1 part-time (0 women). Average age 27. *Entrance requirements:* Additional exam requirements/ recommendations for international students: Required—TOEFL (minimum score 550 paper-based; 213 computer-based; 80 iBT). Application fee: $50. *Expenses:* Tuition, state resident: full-time $16,402; part-time $665 per credit. Tuition, nonresident: full-time $28,694; part-time $1175 per credit. Required fees: $690; $175 per term. Tuition and fees vary according to program. *Financial support:* Applicants required to submit FAFSA. *Unit head:* Dr. Rory Cooper, Chair and Distinguished Professor, 412-383-6596, E-mail: rcooper@pitt.edu. *Application contact:* Shameem Gangjee, Director of Admissions, 412-383-6557, Fax: 412-383-6535, E-mail: admissions@shrs.pitt.edu.

University of Pittsburgh, School of Health and Rehabilitation Sciences, Master's Programs in Health and Rehabilitation Sciences, Pittsburgh, PA 15260. Offers health and rehabilitation

sciences (MS), including clinical dietetics and nutrition, health care supervision and management, health information systems, occupational therapy, physical therapy, rehabilitation counseling, rehabilitation science and technology, sports medicine, wellness and human performance. *Accreditation:* APTA. Part-time and evening/weekend programs available. *Faculty:* 30 full-time (14 women), 4 part-time/adjunct (3 women). *Students:* 81 full-time (47 women), 54 part-time (27 women); includes 10 minority (6 African Americans, 4 Asian Americans or Pacific Islanders), 44 international. Average age 29. 326 applicants, 65% accepted, 130 enrolled. In 2009, 93 master's awarded. *Degree requirements:* For master's, comprehensive exam (for some programs), thesis optional. *Entrance requirements:* For master's, minimum GPA of 3.0. Additional exam requirements/recommendations for international students: Required—TOEFL, IELTS. *Application deadline:* For fall admission, 1/31 for international students; for spring admission, 7/31 for international students. Applications are processed on a rolling basis. Application fee: $50. Electronic applications accepted. *Expenses:* Contact institution. *Financial support:* In 2009–10, 3 research assistantships with full tuition reimbursements (averaging $18,450 per year) were awarded; teaching assistantships, Federal Work-Study, institutionally sponsored loans, traineeships, and unspecified assistantships also available. Financial award applicants required to submit FAFSA. *Faculty research:* Assistive technology, seating and wheeled mobility, cellular neurophysiology, low back syndrome, augmentative communication. Total annual research expenditures: $6.5 million. *Unit head:* Dr. Clifford E. Brubaker, Dean, 412-383-6560, Fax: 412-383-6535, E-mail: cliffb@pitt.edu. *Application contact:* Shameem Gangjee, Director of Admissions, 412-383-6558, Fax: 412-383-6535, E-mail: admissions@shrs.pitt.edu.

University of Pittsburgh, School of Health and Rehabilitation Sciences, PhD Program in Rehabilitation Science, Pittsburgh, PA 15260. Offers PhD. Part-time programs available. *Faculty:* 32 full-time (14 women), 14 part-time/adjunct (5 women). *Students:* 25 full-time (10 women), 40 part-time (23 women); includes 1 minority (African American), 31 international. Average age 35. 48 applicants, 56% accepted, 23 enrolled. In 2009, 4 doctorates awarded. *Degree requirements:* For doctorate, comprehensive exam, thesis/dissertation. *Entrance requirements:* For doctorate, GRE General Test. Additional exam requirements/recommendations for international students: Required—TOEFL (minimum score 550 paper-based; 213 computer-based; 80 iBT), IELTS (minimum score 6.5). *Application deadline:* For fall admission, 1/31 for international students; for spring admission, 7/31 for international students. Applications are processed on a rolling basis. Application fee: $50. Electronic applications accepted. *Expenses:* Tuition, state resident: full-time $16,402; part-time $665 per credit. Tuition, nonresident: full-time $28,694; part-time $1175 per credit. Required fees: $690; $175 per term. Tuition and fees vary according to program. *Financial support:* In 2009–10, 42 research assistantships with full and partial tuition reimbursements (averaging $18,331 per year) were awarded. *Faculty research:* Measurement and study of motion, balance disorders, human performance, neuropsychological parameters, telerehabilitation, wheelchair performance and design, injury prevention and treatment, nutrition, data mining. Total annual research expenditures: $2.3 million. *Unit head:* Dr. George Carvell, Associate Dean of Graduate Studies, 412-383-6639, Fax: 412-383-6629, E-mail: gcarvell@pitt.edu. *Application contact:* Shameem Gangjee, Director of Admissions, 412-383-6558, Fax: 412-383-6535, E-mail: admissions@shrs.pitt.edu.

University of Pittsburgh, School of Health and Rehabilitation Sciences, Prosthetics and Orthotics Program, Pittsburgh, PA 15260. Offers MS. *Faculty:* 1 full-time (0 women). *Students:* 13 full-time (9 women); includes 1 minority (Asian American or Pacific Islander), 1 international. Average age 25. 18 applicants, 100% accepted, 13 enrolled. *Entrance requirements:* Additional exam requirements/recommendations for international students: Required—TOEFL (minimum score 550 paper-based; 213 computer-based; 80 iBT), IELTS (minimum score 6.5). Application fee: $50. *Expenses:* Contact institution. *Unit head:* Dr. Ray Burdett, Director. *Application contact:* Shameem Gangjee, Director of Admissions, 412-383-6558, Fax: 412-383-6535, E-mail: admissions@shrs.pitt.edu.

University of South Carolina, School of Medicine and The Graduate School, Graduate Programs in Medicine, Program in Rehabilitation Counseling, Columbia, SC 29208. Offers psychiatric rehabilitation (Certificate); rehabilitation counseling (MRC). *Accreditation:* CORE. Part-time and evening/weekend programs available. *Degree requirements:* For master's, comprehensive exam, internship, practicum. *Entrance requirements:* For master's and Certificate, GRE General Test or GMAT. Electronic applications accepted. *Expenses:* Contact institution. *Faculty research:* Quality of life, alcohol dependency, technology for disabled, psychiatric rehabilitation, women with disabilities.

University of Toronto, School of Graduate Studies, Life Sciences Division, Department of Rehabilitation Science, Toronto, ON M5S 1A1, Canada. Offers M Sc, PhD. *Degree requirements:* For master's, thesis. *Entrance requirements:* For master's, B Sc or equivalent; specialization in occupational therapy, physical therapy, or a related field; minimum B+ average in final 2 years.

University of Washington, Graduate School, School of Medicine and Graduate School, Graduate Programs in Medicine, Department of Rehabilitation Medicine, Seattle, WA 98195-6490. Offers occupational therapy (MOT); physical therapy (DPT); rehabilitation science (PhD). *Faculty:* 56. *Students:* 150. Average age 25. In 2009, 25 master's, 30 doctorates awarded. *Degree requirements:* For doctorate, comprehensive exam (for some programs), thesis/dissertation (for some programs). *Entrance requirements:* For master's and doctorate, GRE. Additional exam requirements/recommendations for international students: Required—TOEFL. Application fee: $65. *Financial support:* In 2009–10, 1 fellowship (averaging $5,000 per year) was awarded. Financial award applicants required to submit FAFSA. *Faculty research:* Biomechanics, balance, brain injury, spinal cord injury, pain, degenerative diseases. *Unit head:* Dr. Peter C. Esselman, Professor and Chair, 206-543-3600, Fax: 206-685-3244, E-mail: esselman@u.washington.edu. *Application contact:* Dr. Deborah Kartin, Graduate Program Coordinator, 206-598-5338, Fax: 206-685-3244, E-mail: kartin@u.washington.edu.

University of Wisconsin–La Crosse, Office of University Graduate Studies, College of Science and Health, Department of Exercise and Sport Science, Program in Clinical Exercise Physiology, La Crosse, WI 54601-3742. Offers MS. *Students:* 15 full-time (10 women); includes 1 minority (African American). Average age 23. 45 applicants, 44% accepted. In 2009, 15 master's awarded. *Degree requirements:* For master's, thesis optional. *Entrance requirements:* Additional exam requirements/recommendations for international students: Required—TOEFL (minimum score 550 paper-based; 213 computer-based; 79 iBT). *Application deadline:* For fall admission, 2/1 priority date for domestic students. Application fee: $56. Electronic applications accepted. *Financial support:* Research assistantships, career-related internships or fieldwork, Federal Work-Study, institutionally sponsored loans, health care benefits, tuition waivers (full and partial), and unspecified assistantships available. Financial award application deadline: 2/1; financial award applicants required to submit FAFSA. *Unit head:* Dr. John Porcari, Director, 608-785-8684, Fax: 608-785-8686, E-mail: porcari.john@uwlax.edu. *Application contact:* Kathryn Kiefer, Director of Admissions, 608-785-8939, E-mail: admissions@uwlax.edu.

University of Wisconsin–Madison, Graduate School, School of Education, Department of Kinesiology, Therapeutic Science Program, Madison, WI 53706-1380. Offers MS. *Accreditation:* AOTA. *Entrance requirements:* For master's, GRE General Test. Application fee: $56. *Expenses:* Tuition, state resident: part-time $594 per credit. Tuition, nonresident: part-time $1504 per credit. Required fees: $65 per credit. Tuition and fees vary according to course load, program and reciprocity agreements. *Financial support:* Fellowships with full tuition reimbursements, research assistantships with full tuition reimbursements, teaching assistantships with full tuition reimbursements, traineeships and project assistantships available. *Unit head:* Dr. Dorothy Edwards, Chair, 608-262-0048. *Application contact:* Dr. Dorothy Edwards, Chair, 608-262-0048.

Virginia Commonwealth University, Graduate School, School of Education, Department of Health and Human Performance, Program in Rehabilitation and Movement Science, Richmond, VA 23284-9005. Offers PhD.

Wayne State University, School of Medicine, Graduate Programs in Medicine, Department of Physical Medicine and Rehabilitation, Detroit, MI 48202. Offers rehabilitation science administration (Certificate); rehabilitation sciences (MS). *Entrance requirements:* For master's,

Rehabilitation Sciences

Wayne State University *(continued)*
MD or DO. Additional exam requirements/recommendations for international students: Required—TOEFL (minimum score 550 paper-based; 213 computer-based); Recommended—TWE (minimum score 6). Electronic applications accepted.

Western Michigan University, Graduate College, College of Health and Human Services, Department of Blindness and Low Vision Studies, Kalamazoo, MI 49008. Offers orientation and mobility (MA); orientation and mobility of children (MA); vision rehabilitation teaching (MA). *Accreditation:* CORE. *Faculty:* 8 full-time (4 women). *Students:* 46 full-time (34 women), 25 part-time (20 women); includes 4 minority (1 African American, 1 Asian American or Pacific Islander, 2 Hispanic Americans), 3 international. 39 applicants, 87% accepted, 33 enrolled. In 2009, 31 master's awarded. *Application deadline:* For fall admission, 2/15 priority date for domestic students. Applications are processed on a rolling basis. Application fee: $25. *Financial support:* Fellowships, research assistantships, teaching assistantships, Federal Work-Study available. Financial award application deadline: 2/15; financial award applicants required to submit FAFSA. *Unit head:* Dr. James Leja, Chair, 269-387-3453. *Application contact:* Admissions and Orientation, 269-387-2000, Fax: 269-387-2355.

NORTHWESTERN UNIVERSITY

The Roxelyn and Richard Pepper Department of Communication Sciences and Disorders
Programs in Audiology and Hearing Sciences, Learning Disabilities,
and Speech and Language Pathology

Programs of Study

The Department of Communication Sciences and Disorders offers graduate study in audiology and hearing sciences, learning disabilities, and speech and language pathology at the M.A. and Ph.D. degree levels. An Au.D. degree in clinical audiology is available. Opportunities for postdoctoral study exist across all areas.

Beginning in the 2010–11 academic year, the M.A. in speech and language pathology program will be integrated with the M.A. in learning disabilities program into the M.A. in speech, language, and learning program. Students choosing to concentrate in speech and language pathology will still be eligible for certification by ASHA as speech and language pathologists. It will also be possible for students seeking certification as a learning behavior specialist (LBS-1) to do so in this program.

Normal/developmental aspects of communication and learning are covered, along with courses on disorders of articulation, language, hearing, learning, swallowing, memory, fluency, attention, perception, voice, symbolization, and other related topics.

Clinical/educational setting practice is provided on site and in area schools, hospitals, clinics, rehabilitation agencies, and industrial and private practice locations. Courses at the M.A. level may lead to professional certification and/or preparation for advanced study in the field and in related areas. Study in the Au.D. degree program meets academic and clinical requirements for independent practice in audiology. Programs of study at the Ph.D. level include courses taken within the Department as well as other departments (e.g., bioengineering, cognitive science, linguistics, medicine, neuroscience, physiology, psychology, and others) and are tailored to the individual's experience and interest in basic or applied/clinical research. Independent study and research are encouraged, and small-group seminars are offered. Courses, laboratory work, and field activities offer opportunities to learn research methods and use scientific instrumentation. Doctoral students have opportunities for supervised research and teaching.

Students are prepared for careers as speech and language pathologists, clinical audiologists, learning disabilities specialists, teacher-investigators, and researchers. Graduates are employed in schools; hospitals; rehabilitation centers and clinics; special education centers; industry; local, state, and federal agencies; universities; research centers; private medical, educational, and clinical facilities; and other settings.

Faculty teaching and research interest areas are identified in the Department Faculty and Their Research section of this description. Further information is available on the Department's Web site at http://www.communication.northwestern.edu/departments/csd/.

Research Facilities

The Department maintains research laboratories that study how speech sounds are generated, speech sound characteristics in different languages, and the relationship between speech sounds and linguistic units; how speech elements are processed, interpreted, and decoded into linguistic units; speech synthesis, speech and voice recognition, and speech coding; electromyographic signals from speech muscles; electroencephalographic signals from the brain; speech articulator and laryngeal system activity; swallow behavior; word-finding deficits in children; language abilities in children; language processing in bilinguals and language and memory using eye-tracking, functional neuroimaging techniques, and narrative analysis; sentence processing in aphasic persons using functional magnetic resonance imaging techniques; verb structure in aphasia; language decline in dementia; perceptual, orthographic, phonological, semantic, and syntactic processes in development of oral language and reading; development and disorders of written language; cognitive, linguistic, and academic problems of adults with learning disabilities; cognitive processing in children; acoustic properties of speech signals; psychological and social effects of hearing loss in aging adults; molecular, cellular, physiological, and psychological bases of audition; and function of normal and abnormal auditory systems. Additional information about these laboratories and others can be found on the Department's Web site.

Financial Aid

The Graduate School and University provide fellowships and scholarships; the Department selects fellowship and scholarship awardees and recommends the awarding of teaching assistantships. In addition, principal investigators may provide financial assistance for a limited number of students. Students seeking loans must apply to a financial aid officer in the Graduate School.

Cost of Study

Tuition in 2010–11 is $13,280 per quarter. This cost is reduced to $3320 per quarter for Ph.D. students who are admitted to candidacy. Reduced tuition is available to Au.D. students; prospective students should contact the Au.D. program assistant for further information.

Living and Housing Costs

The University has a limited number of living units for single and married students on the Evanston and Chicago campuses. Many students find satisfactory accommodations in private homes and in apartments near the campuses; rents vary widely.

Student Group

An average of 45 students begin master's study in speech and language pathology each fall, and up to 10 new students begin master's study in learning disabilities. At the doctoral level, approximately 10 students begin study in the Au.D. degree program and about 7 new students begin study in the Ph.D. degree program. Students from within the disciplines and from other disciplines are encouraged to apply for graduate study. There are approximately 19,000 full-time students enrolled on the Evanston and Chicago campuses annually; approximately 40 percent are in graduate and professional programs.

Location

The main campus of the University is located in Evanston on the shore of Lake Michigan. The Chicago campus, about 12 miles south of Evanston, is also on the lakeshore near the center of the business district, one of Chicago's most attractive areas. An immense variety of cultural, social, and recreational activities can be found on and near each campus.

The University

Northwestern University, one of the nation's largest private universities, was founded in 1851. The College of Arts and Sciences (Weinberg); the Technological Institute (McCormick); the Schools of Education and Social Policy, Journalism, Music, and Communication; and the Graduate School of Management (Kellogg) are located on the Evanston campus. The Medical and Law Schools are located on the Chicago campus. There is a continuing expansion of facilities and programs, much of it in science and medicine, which will continue during the next ten years thanks to a vigorous program of financial contributions.

Applying

Applications are sought from highly qualified students from many fields. The Department typically admits students to begin in the fall quarter. Application deadlines are as follows: December 31, Ph.D. Program in Communication Sciences and Disorders, and January 15 to be considered for funding, M.A. Programs in Speech and Language Pathology, Learning Disabilities, and the Au.D. Clinical Doctorate Program. Applicants to the Au.D. program should submit a paper application (available at http://www.communication.northwestern.edu/programs/doctor_audiology), transcripts, and letters of recommendation to the Doctor of Audiology Program, 2240 Campus Drive, Evanston, Illinois 60208-3540. GRE scores should be submitted to Institution Code 2550. Applicants to programs other than the Au.D. should submit an online application, available at http://www.northwestern.edu/graduate; GRE scores to Institution Code 1565; and transcripts to the graduate application coordinator. Letters of recommendation may either be submitted as part of the online application or via mail, also to the graduate application coordinator.

Correspondence and Information

Graduate Application Coordinator
Department of Communication Sciences
and Disorders
2240 Campus Drive
Evanston, Illinois 60208-3540
Phone: 847-491-5073
E-mail: ccoy@northwestern.edu
Web site: http://www.communication.
northwestern.edu

Au.D. Program Assistant
Department of Communication Sciences
and Disorders
2240 Campus Drive
Evanston, Illinois 60208-3540
Phone: 847-491-4541
E-mail: c-lee6@northwestern.edu
Web site: http://www.communication.
northwestern.edu

Graduate Admissions
The Graduate School
Northwestern University
Evanston, Illinois 60208
Phone: 847-491-7265

Northwestern University

THE DEPARTMENT FACULTY AND THEIR RESEARCH

Amy Booth, Ph.D., Pittsburgh. Cognitive development, infancy, learning, memory and social cognition.
James Booth, Ph.D., Maryland. Neural bases of the development of language, reading, and attention.
Mary Ann Cheatham, Ph.D., Northwestern. Cochlear physiology and functional genomics.
Peter Dallos, Ph.D., Northwestern. Biophysics and physiology of the cochlea.
Sumit Dhar, Ph.D., Purdue. Applied auditory physiology.
Dean C. Garstecki, Ph.D., Illinois at Urbana-Champaign. Hearing loss and aging.
Nina Kraus, Ph.D., Northwestern. Neurobiology of speech and music.
Charles R. Larson, Chairman; Ph.D., Washington (Seattle). Voice physiology.
Jerilyn Ann Logemann, Ph.D., Northwestern. Structural anomalies of the vocal tract, dysphagia.
Molly C. Losh, Ph.D., Berkeley. Genetics of autism.
Viorica Marian, Ph.D., Cornell. Psycholinguistics, bilingualism, memory and language.
Sazzad M. Nasir, Ph.D., Cambridge. Computational neuroscience.
Barbara Roa Pauloski, Ph.D., Northwestern. Voice, speech, and swallowing.
Claus-Peter Richter, M.D., Ph.D., Frankfurt (Germany). Physiology of the cochlea.
Mario A. Ruggero, Ph.D., Chicago. Biophysics and physiology of the middle and inner ears.
Jonathan Siegel, Ph.D., Washington (St. Louis). Biophysics and physiology of the cochlea.
Pamela Souza, Ph.D., Syracuse. Speech recognition, amplification, auditory aging.
Cynthia Thompson, Ph.D., Kansas. Neurological disorders of language and cognition.
Catherine Warrier, Ph.D., McGill. Lateralization of auditory processes.
Patrick Wong, Ph.D., Texas at Austin. Functional neuroanatomy of speech perception.
Beverly Wright, Ph.D., Texas at Austin. Perceptual learning, auditory perception in individuals, psychoacoustics.
Dongsun Yim, Ph.D., Minnesota. Child language disorders.
Steven Zecker, Ph.D., Wayne State. Auditory processing and learning.

Lecturers and Clinical Faculty

Molly Aceves, M.A., Northwestern. Language-based learning disabilities, bilingual speech-language pathology.
Christopher Atkins, M.A., Northwestern. Voice and voice disorders, dysphagia, accent modification.
Tracy Cafferty, M.S., Eastern Illinois. Autism, early intervention.
Frances Block, M.A., Northwestern. Supervision, language disorders in older children.
Jill Eltanal, M.S., Arizona State. Articulation and language in school-age children.
Susan Erler, Ph.D., Northwestern. Audiologic rehabilitation.
Belma Hadziselimovic, M.S., Columbia. Aphasia, acquired disorders of cognition.
Tracy A. Hagan, M.A., Michigan State. Pediatrics.
Michelle A. Jones, M.A., Minnesota. Pediatric speech and language disorders, fluency disorders.
Kristen Larsen, M.A., Northwestern. Dysphagia, neurological speech and language disorders in adults.
Paula McGuire, Ph.D., Northwestern. Articulatory/phonological development and disorders.
Lowery Mayo, Au.D., Florida. Hearing devices and tinnitus treatment.
Susan Mulhern, M.A., Northwestern. Articulation and language problems in children.
Elizabeth Cook Musto, M.A., Northwestern; CCC-SLP. Dysphagia, motor speech, voice, adult neurologicial disorders (aphasia, TBI), cognitive communication problems, accent modification.
Diane Novak, M.S., Gallaudet. Hearing devices, aural rehabilitation.
Jane Rankin, Ph.D., Colorado. Parenting and communication, adolescent self-consciousness.
Megan Schliep, M.A., Northwestern. Dysphagia, neurological speech and language disorders in adults.
Lynda Thill, M.A., Northern Illinois. Early intervention, pediatric feeding and swallowing disorders, motor speech disorders.
Frank W. Van Santen, M.A., Northwestern. Learning disabilities assessment and remediation, behavior disorders.
Sharon Veis, M.A., Northwestern. Swallowing disorders, language disorders after neurosurgery.
Aaron Wilkins, M.S., Saint Xavier. Adult neurological disorders and dysphagia.

Adjunct Faculty

Joanne Bregman, Ph.D., Northwestern. High-risk infants and their families.
Martha Burns, Ph.D., Northwestern. Aphasia and adult neurological disorders.
Leora Cherney, Ph.D., Northwestern. Aphasia and neurological disorders.
Dawn B. Koch, Ph.D., Northwestern. Cochlear implantation.
Harold Pelzer, M.D., Northwestern. Treatment for head and neck cancer.

Emeritus Faculty

Elaine Brown-Grant, M.A., Northwestern. Clinical supervision.
Doris J. Johnson, Ph.D., Northwestern. Relationship between auditory disorders and higher levels of learning.
Laura Ann Wilber, Ph.D., Northwestern. Pediatric audiology, audiologic instrumentation.

PHILADELPHIA COLLEGE OF OSTEOPATHIC MEDICINE

Physician Assistant Program

Program of Study

The Physician Assistant (PA) Program is a twenty-six-month program that leads to a Master of Science degree in health sciences. Students are prepared for clinical practice, using a variety of learning strategies: formal lectures, practical laboratory classes, clinical education, and clinical research. Students develop patient communication skills and advanced clinical problem-solving skills in addition to acquiring technical proficiency in areas related to professional practice. Graduates of the program develop and implement clinical treatment plans with their supervising physician. The program is highly intensive. Most of the program is provided by physicians in order to ensure that patient-care functions provided by the Physician Assistant Program graduates are of the highest quality.

There are also two five-year cooperative programs with Philadelphia College of Osteopathic Medicine (PCOM) and either University of the Sciences in Philadelphia (USP) or Brenau University in Gainesville, Georgia. The programs consist of two distinct phases: the preprofessional phase and the professional phase. After successful completion of the fourth year, students earn a B.S. in health science from USP or Brenau and an M.S. from PCOM after completion of the fifth year. The B.S. degree does not qualify the student as a PA. Students must complete the entire professional phase of the program (years four and five) and obtain an M.S. from PCOM to become eligible to be certified as a PA. PCOM has the ultimate responsibility for granting the M.S. degree.

This unique program provides students with the ability to positively affect the lives of their patients, their families, their employers, and their communities. Students become lifelong learners, developing a baseline of analytic and critical thinking skills that prepare them for the challenges of caring for the entire patient, young or old, from the emergency room to the operating room.

Research Facilities

PCOM's library features both a well-developed collection of medical journals and texts and new capabilities for access to online medical references and Internet searching in a facility that provides individual student stations, Internet terminals, advanced audiovisual resources, and a large student computer lab.

Financial Aid

The Financial Aid Office at PCOM offers financial assistance to students through the Federal Direct Loan program, institutional grants, and various alternative private loan programs.

Cost of Study

In 2010–11, the tuition cost to attend PCOM was approximately $29,640 annually.

Living and Housing Costs

Students live off campus within the Philadelphia metropolitan and suburban areas, as there is no on-campus housing. Room and board costs vary by each student's individual preferences.

Student Group

Admission to the PA Program is competitive and selective. The College looks for academically and socially well-rounded individuals who are committed to caring for patients. The class of 2011 totaled 54 students, 44 women and 10 men, ranging in age from 20 to 34. Twenty-seven were residents of Pennsylvania.

Location

Philadelphia College of Osteopathic Medicine is the second largest of twenty-three osteopathic colleges in the United States, with campuses in both Philadelphia and suburban Atlanta. The PA studies program is offered only on the Philadelphia campus, which is located in a suburban setting on City Avenue, minutes away from Fairmount Park, Philadelphia's historic district, art museums, theaters, restaurants, and professional sports complexes. PCOM's renovated facilities include two large lecture halls, small classrooms, labs for teaching and research, and a state-of-the-art library.

The College

PCOM, chartered in 1899, enrolls approximately 2,200 students in its various programs and is committed to educating community-responsive, primary-care–oriented physicians and physician assistants to practice medicine in the twenty-first century. Supported by the latest in medical and educational technology, PCOM emphasizes treating the whole person, not merely the symptoms. The Department of Physician Assistant Studies coordinates the PA Program between USP or Brenau and PCOM and offers an early hands-on medical education experience during the professional phase. Students have a committed, professional, humanistic faculty who are leaders in the osteopathic and physician assistant national health-care community. The PA Program provides a thorough foundation in health-care delivery that focuses on comprehensive, humanistic health care.

Applying

Selection for the Physician Assistant Program is very competitive. Applicants must complete a baccalaureate degree at a regionally accredited college or university in the United States, Canada, or the United Kingdom with a minimum GPA of 2.8 (on a 4.0 scale), document 200 hours of experience in volunteer or employment in or related to the health-care industry, and fulfill the following course requirements: five semesters of biology, three semesters of chemistry, one semester of physics or another health related science, two semesters of mathematics, and three semesters of social science courses. All requirements must have been completed within the last ten years, unless the applicant has completed an advanced degree or has extensive experience in the field of patient care. Selected applicants are invited to interview on campus. Application and deadline information is available online at http://www.caspaonline.org and http://www.pcom.edu/Admissions/admissions.html.

Correspondence and Information

Office of Admissions
Philadelphia College of Osteopathic Medicine
4170 City Avenue
Philadelphia, Pennsylvania 19131
Phone: 215-871-6700
     800-999-6998 (toll-free)
Fax: 215-871-6719
E-mail: PAAdmissions@pcom.edu
Web site: http://www.pcom.edu

Philadelphia College of Osteopathic Medicine

THE FACULTY AND THEIR RESEARCH

Full-Time Faculty

Gregory McDonald, D.O., Philadelphia College of Osteopathic Medicine. Medical Director, Department of Physician Assistant Studies. Pathology.

John Cavenagh, Ph.D., Union (Ohio); PA-C. Professor, Chairman, Department of Physician Assistant Studies. Emergency medicine.

Patrick Coughlin, Ph.D., Cincinnati. Professor, Department of Anatomy. Human anatomy.

Jill Cunningham, M.H.S., Drexel; PA-C. Assistant Professor, Department of Physician Assistant Studies. Internal medicine.

Marilyn DeFeliciantonio, M.S.L.S., Villanova; PA-C. Assistant Professor, Department of Physician Assistant Studies. Hematology and oncology.

Sean Guinane, M.S., Philadelphia College of Osteopathic Medicine. Assistant Professor, Department of Physician Assistant Studies. Family medicine.

Paul Krajewski, M.S., Philadelphia College of Osteopathic Medicine; PA-C. Associate Professor, Department of Physician Assistant Studies. Orthopedic surgery, emergency medicine.

Laura Molloy, M.M.S., Saint Francis (Pennsylvania); PA-C. Associate Professor, Assistant Program Director, Department of Physician Assistant Studies. Family medicine, women's health.

Christine Mount, M.S., University of Medicine and Dentistry of New Jersey; PA-C. Assistant Professor, Department of Physician Assistant Studies. Neurology, emergency medicine, trauma.

Jennifer Windstein, M.S., Wagner; PA-C. Assistant Professor, Department of Physician Assistant Studies. Family practice, internal medicine.

Adjunct Faculty

Patrick Auth, Ph.D., Drexel; PA-C. Emergency medicine, orthopedics.

Matt Baker, D.H.Sc., Nova Southeastern; PA-C. Geriatrics and gerontology.

Robert Cuzzolino, Ed.D., Temple. Academic policy.

Daniel DuPont, D.O., Philadelphia College of Osteopathic Medicine. Pulmonology.

Leonard Finkelstein, D.O., Philadelphia College of Osteopathic Medicine. Urology.

Melissa Guarino, M.S., Philadelphia College of Osteopathic Medicine; PA-C. General surgery.

Jeff Gutting, M.S., Philadelphia College of Osteopathic Medicine; PA-C. Cardiology.

Matthew Hay, M.S., Philadelphia College of Osteopathic Medicine; PA-C. General surgery.

Robert D. Howard, M.D., Hahnemann. Emergency medicine.

Michael Kirifides, Ph.D., Maryland. Human physiology.

Colleen Maguire, M.H.S., Hahnemann; PA-C. Obstetrics and gynecology, emergency medicine.

Burton Mark, D.O., Kirksville College of Osteopathic Medicine. Psychiatry.

Richard Pascucci, D.O., Philadelphia College of Osteopathic Medicine; FACOI. Rheumatology.

Margaret Reinhart, M.M.A.; M.T., Penn State; ASCP. Laboratory diagnostics.

Gary Sloskey, Pharm.D., University of the Sciences in Philadelphia. Pharmacology.

Rosemary Vickers, D.O., Philadelphia College of Osteopathic Medicine. Pediatrics.

SouthUniversity℠

SOUTH UNIVERSITY

Savannah Campus
Anesthesiologist Assistant Program

Program of Study

The Master of Medical Science (M.M.Sc.) in anesthesiologist science program is designed to provide classroom, laboratory, and clinical experiences that prepare graduates to deliver anesthesia care to patients of all ages and severities of illness for the full spectrum of surgical procedures.

A career as an anesthesiologist assistant offers both challenges and rewards, and the University's program emphasizes both classroom and practical learning. In addition to the experienced faculty members, students have access to industry-relevant learning tools. The school maintains a fully equipped mock operating room and student lab, where students obtain experience that prepares them for clinical rotations and, ultimately, a full-time position as a member of an anesthesia care team.

In the first year of this intensive twenty-eight-month program curriculum, students are focused on the scientific foundations of anesthesia practice through classroom simulation, laboratory work, and clinical experience. As the year progresses, the amount of time that students spend at clinical sites steadily increases. The senior year comprises full-time clinical experience in four-week blocks, plus weekly senior seminar meetings in which students deliver presentations on various topics related to anesthesia care, sharing best practices from their experiences across the country. Students have the opportunity to complete their clinical rotations at some of the nation's most prominent health-care institutions, ranging from major hospitals to regional health-care centers.

Research Facilities

Facilities for the anesthesiologist assistant program include a sophisticated mock operating room with SimMan, a lifelike simulator that provides students with the opportunity to practice real-world scenarios before stepping into a hospital. A unique fully equipped anesthesia learning laboratory was built specifically for the program and features industry-standard technology and equipment.

The campus library, constructed in 2007, provides comfortable study space for students, wireless Internet capabilities for laptop network connectivity, a computer lab, and reference and interlibrary loan services. The open-stack book collection includes access to reference, reserve, and circulating materials, along with tutorial aides and program-specific resources for class assignments. The periodical collection also supports the curricula by way of authoritative journals in both print and electronic formats. The adjoining research center, which is furnished with ten computer workstations, offers students access to the Internet, online database services such as the MEDLINE office suite, tutorials, and class-support software.

Financial Aid

A wide range of financial aid options is available to students who qualify. The Savannah campus of South University offers access to federal and state aid, including grants, loans, and work-study programs. Eligible students may apply for veterans' educational benefits and are encouraged to investigate the availability of grants and scholarships through community resources. As a first step, students should complete the Free Application for Federal Student Aid (FAFSA). Students may apply electronically at http://www.fafsa.ed.gov or at the campus Student Financial Services Department. Applications should be submitted promptly to receive consideration for the maximum amount of aid.

Cost of Study

Tuition information for the anesthesiologist assistant program may be obtained by contacting the anesthesiologist assistant program via the South University Web site at http://www.southuniversity.edu/anesthesiologistassistant.

Living and Housing Costs

South University offers school-sponsored student housing at its Savannah, Georgia, campus in conjunction with several local apartment complexes. Due to the full-time nature of the program, anesthesiologist assistant program students typically live in rental homes, town homes, or apartments in the Savannah area. More information is available by contacting the Director of Student Housing at 912-201-8000.

Student Group

The Savannah campus of South University has a diverse student body enrolled in both day and evening classes.

Location

Located on the south side of the historic city of Savannah, the campus is situated on 9 acres of land. It is convenient to the city's bustling midtown section and a full range of educational and cultural activities. The Atlantic Ocean and recreational amenities of Tybee Island, including beaches and numerous outdoor activities, are just a short drive away. In addition, the campus is located just a short drive from Hilton Head Island and Charleston, South Carolina.

The University

South University is accredited by the Commission on Colleges of the Southern Association of Colleges and Schools (SACS) to award associate, bachelor's, master's, and doctoral degrees. Students should contact the Commission on Colleges at 1866 Southern Lane, Decatur, Georgia 30033-4097 or call 404-679-4500 with questions about the accreditation of South University. The anesthesiologist assistant program is accredited by the Commission for Accreditation of Allied Health Education Programs (CAAHEP; 1361 Park Street, Clearwater, Florida 33756; phone: 727-210-2350).

Applying

Students are accepted into the anesthesiologist assistant program once each year, with classes beginning in June and commencement taking place in mid-September two years later. Entrance into the program is gained through a formal application review and assessment of the applicant's potential for professional and academic achievement. Prospective students must complete premedical course work at a regionally accredited U.S. college or university, as described on the program's Web site. The admissions process requires official transcripts from all colleges and universities attended, scores from the Graduate Record Examinations (GRE) or the Medical College Admission Test (MCAT) that are not more than five years old, three letters of recommendation, proof of at least 8 hours spent with an anesthesiologist or anesthetist in an operating room, and a summary of an article published in a current anesthesia journal. For the GRE, the program must receive official score reports directly from the Educational Testing Service. The code for South University is 5157.

Correspondence and Information

Applications for admission to the South University anesthesiologist assistant program are available by contacting:

Anesthesiologist Assistant Program
South University
709 Mall Boulevard
Savannah, Georgia 31406-4805

Phone: 912-201-8080
Fax: 912-201-8070
E-mail: aaprograminfo@southuniversity.edu
Web site: http://www.southuniversity.edu/aa

South University

THE FACULTY

One of the most outstanding aspects of South University's anesthesiologist assistant program is the dedication of the faculty members and their ability to cultivate a supportive learning environment. Faculty members are committed to their roles as mentors, teachers, and colearners. They are also dedicated to the training of students who can assume positions of leadership within the field of anesthesiology. A current list of program faculty members is available at the South University Web site (http://www.southuniversity.edu/aa).

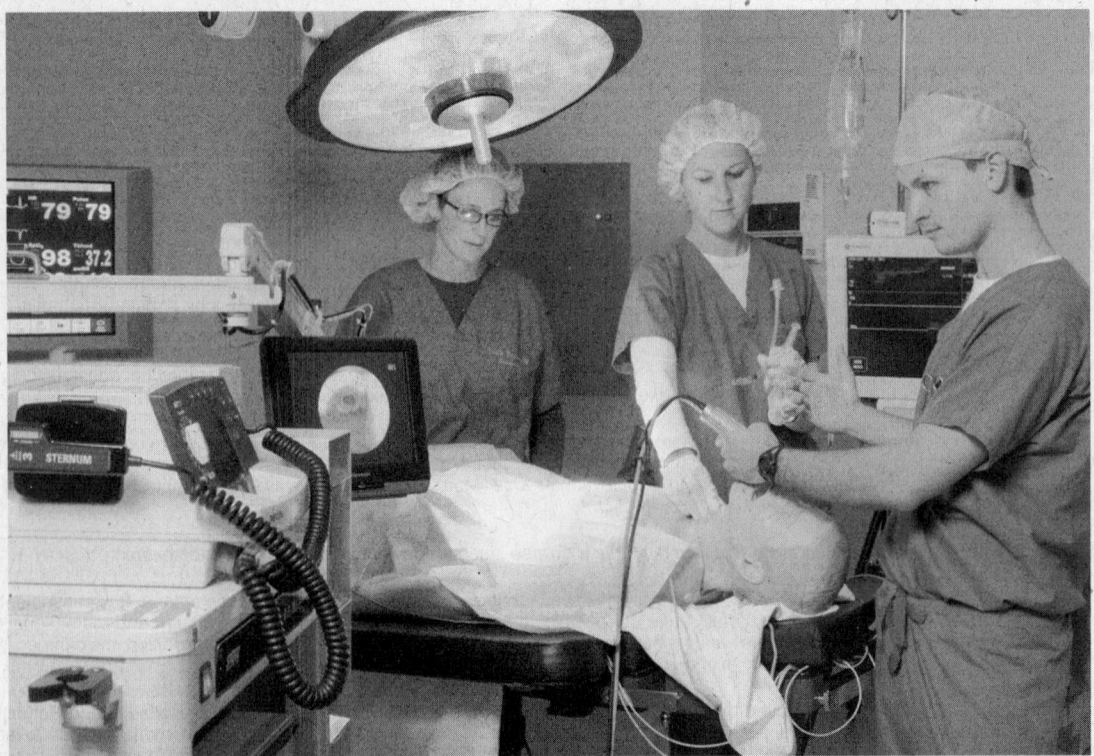

One of the main features of South University's anesthesiologist assistant program is its mock operating room. Modeled after actual operating rooms, the room is complete with current anesthesia equipment and SimMan, a model patient that is used to simulate real-life scenarios.

SouthUniversity℠

SOUTH UNIVERSITY

Savannah Campus
School of Health Professions
Physician Assistant Studies Program

Program of Study

The Master of Science in Physician Assistant Studies (M.S.P.A.S.) degree program at South University is an intensive twenty-seven-month curriculum structured around full-time course work. With students applying from across the country through the national Central Application Service for Physician Assistants (CASPA) system, South University routinely attracts students who have received their undergraduate education at major public universities. The program focuses on the study of pathology, physiology, epidemiology, pharmacology, diagnosis, patient management, and treatment. Students learn in small groups with on-site laboratories where individualized attention is delivered by faculty members who have a variety of both professional and teaching experience.

Within the first months of the program, students begin to gain experience in clinical and surgical settings. Program graduates are qualified to take the National Commission on the Certification of Physician Assistants (NCCPA) exam.

Once certified, graduates are prepared to work in internal medicine and family practice or specialty areas such as OB/GYN, pediatrics, surgery, orthopedics, postoperative care, cardiology, and many other specialties. In these areas, graduates may examine and treat patients, order and interpret lab results and X-rays, make diagnoses, prescribe medications, and take medical histories. They also may treat minor injuries, counsel patients, and carry out therapy instructions.

Research Facilities

The Physician Assistant (PA) Studies Program is housed in the School of Health Professions building at South University's campus in historic Savannah, Georgia. The campus features dedicated PA classrooms and lab facilities. The University recently opened a new on-campus library, more than doubling its previous library space. The new facility features comfortable study space for students, wireless Internet capabilities for laptop network connectivity, separate computer labs, and reference and interlibrary loan services.

Financial Aid

A wide range of financial aid options is available to students who qualify. The Savannah campus of South University offers access to federal and state programs, loans, and work-study programs. Eligible students may apply for veterans' educational benefits and are encouraged to investigate the availability of grants and scholarships through community resources. As a first step, students should complete the Free Application for Federal Student Aid (FAFSA). Students may apply electronically at http://www.fafsa.ed. gov or with the campus Director of Student Financial Services. Applications should be submitted promptly to receive consideration for the maximum amount of aid.

Cost of Study

Tuition information for the Physician Assistant Studies Program may be obtained by contacting Physician Assistant Studies Program Admissions at South University's Savannah campus.

Living and Housing Costs

South University offers a variety of school-sponsored student housing options at its Savannah, Georgia, campus in conjunction with local apartment complexes. Due to the full-time nature of the program, PA students typically live in rental homes or apartments in the Savannah area. More information is available by contacting the Director of Student Housing at 912-201-8000.

Student Group

The Savannah campus of South University has a diverse student body enrolled in both day and evening classes. Students are primarily commuters who live within 50 miles of the city.

Location

Located on the south side of the historic city of Savannah, the campus is situated on 9 acres of land. It is convenient to the city's bustling midtown section and a full range of educational and cultural activities. The Atlantic Ocean and recreational amenities of Tybee Island, including beaches and numerous outdoor activities, are just a short drive away. In addition, the campus is located just a short drive from Hilton Head Island and Charleston, South Carolina.

The Program

Accreditation for South University's Physician Assistant Studies Program has been granted by the Accreditation Review Commission on Education for the Physician Assistant Programs (ARC-PA). The program is also a member of the Physician Assistant Education Association, the national organization representing physician assistant education programs. South University is accredited by the Commission on Colleges of the Southern Association of Colleges and Schools (SACS) to award associate, bachelor's, master's, and doctoral degrees. Students should contact the Commission on Colleges at 1866 Southern Lane, Decatur, Georgia 30033-4097 or call 404-679-4500 with questions about the accreditation of South University.

Applying

Students are accepted into the Master of Science in Physician Assistant Studies degree program on an annual basis. Candidates may choose to qualify for early admission or general admission. Entrance into the program is gained through a formal application review and interview process. Acceptance is competitive and based on the admission committee's evaluation of the applicant's academic background (completed bachelor's degree with overall minimum GPA of 2.6 and recommended science GPA of 3.0 or better), scores on the Graduate Record Examination (GRE), personal motivation, clinical experience, and ability to be self-supporting throughout the rigors of the program. No transfer credit is accepted for this program. The South University Physician Assistant Studies Program utilizes CASPA (http://www.caspaonline.org); students who wish to do so may apply online through CASPA.

The South University Physician Assistant Studies Program is accepting applications for the class beginning January 2010. All applications for this class must be complete by September 1, 2009.

Correspondence and Information

Applications for admission to the South University Master of Science in Physician Assistant Studies degree program are available by contacting:

Physician Assistant Studies Program
South University
709 Mall Boulevard
Savannah, Georgia 31406-4805
Phone: 912-201-8025
         866-629-2901 (toll-free)
Fax: 912-790-4199
E-mail: paprogram@southuniversity.edu
Web site: http://www.southuniversity.edu/pa

South University

THE FACULTY

One of the most outstanding aspects of South University's Physician Assistant Studies Program is the dedication of the faculty members and their ability to cultivate a supportive learning environment. Faculty members are committed to their roles as mentors, teachers, and colearners. They are also dedicated to the training of students who can assume positions of leadership within the medical field. A current list of program faculty members is available in the South University catalog, which is located on the South University Web site (http://www.southuniversity.edu/pa).

South University PA students celebrate the completion of their first year of study and the beginning of clinical rotations.

Section 28
Health Sciences

This section contains a directory of institutions offering graduate work in health sciences, followed by an in-depth entry submitted by an institution that chose to prepare a detailed program description. Additional information about programs listed in the directory but not augmented by an in-depth entry may be obtained by writing directly to the dean of a graduate school or chair of a department at the address given in the directory.

For programs offering related work, see also in this book *Dentistry and Dental Sciences, Health Services, Medicine, Nursing,* and *Public Health.* In the other guides in this series:

Graduate Programs in the Biological Sciences
See *Biological and Biomedical Sciences* and *Biophysics (Radiation Biology)*

Graduate Programs in the Physical Sciences, Mathematics, Agricultural Sciences, the Environment & Natural Resources
See *Physics*

Graduate Programs in Engineering & Applied Sciences
See *Agricultural Engineering and Bioengineering (Bioengineering), Biomedical Engineering and Biotechnology,* and *Energy and Power Engineering (Nuclear Engineering)*

CONTENTS

Program Directories

Close-Up

Health Physics/Radiological Health

Bloomsburg University of Pennsylvania, School of Graduate Studies, College of Science and Technology, Department of Biological and Allied Health Sciences, Radiologist Assistant Program, Bloomsburg, PA 17815-1301. Offers MS. *Entrance requirements:* For master's, ARRT certificate and Regis in radiography receptor agreement, curriculum vitae, 3 letters of recommendation. Additional exam requirements/recommendations for international students: Required—TOEFL (minimum score 550 paper-based; 213 computer-based; 79 iBT).

Emory University, Graduate School of Arts and Sciences, Department of Physics, Atlanta, GA 30322-1100. Offers biophysics (PhD); condensed matter physics (PhD); non-linear physics (PhD); radiological physics (PhD); soft condensed matter physics (PhD); solid-state physics (PhD); statistical physics (PhD); MS/PhD. *Degree requirements:* For doctorate, thesis/dissertation, qualifier proposal (PhD). *Entrance requirements:* For doctorate, GRE General Test, minimum GPA of 3.0. Additional exam requirements/recommendations for international students: Required—TOEFL (minimum score 600 paper-based). Electronic applications accepted. *Faculty research:* Experimental studies of the structure and function of metalloproteins, soft condensed matter, granular materials, biophotonics and fluorescence correlation spectroscopy, single molecule studies of DNA-protein systems.

Georgetown University, Graduate School of Arts and Sciences, Programs in Biomedical Sciences, Department of Health Physics, Washington, DC 20057. Offers health physics (MS); radiobiology (MS). *Degree requirements:* For master's, thesis. *Entrance requirements:* Additional exam requirements/recommendations for international students: Required—TOEFL.

Georgia Institute of Technology, Graduate Studies and Research, College of Engineering, George W. Woodruff School of Mechanical Engineering, Nuclear and Radiological Engineering and Medical Physics Programs, Atlanta, GA 30332-0001. Offers medical physics (MS); nuclear and radiological engineering (MSNE, PhD). Part-time programs available. Postbaccalaureate distance learning degree programs offered (no on-campus study). Terminal master's awarded for partial completion of doctoral program. *Degree requirements:* For master's, thesis optional; for doctorate, comprehensive exam, thesis/dissertation. *Entrance requirements:* For master's and doctorate, GRE General Test, minimum GPA of 3.0. Additional exam requirements/recommendations for international students: Required—TOEFL (minimum score 580 paper-based; 240 computer-based). *Faculty research:* Reactor physics, nuclear materials, plasma physics, radiation detection, radiological assessment.

Idaho State University, Office of Graduate Studies, College of Arts and Sciences, Department of Physics, Pocatello, ID 83209-8106. Offers applied physics (PhD); health physics (MS); physics (MNS). Part-time programs available. *Faculty:* 7 full-time (1 woman), 1 part-time/adjunct (0 women). *Students:* 43 full-time (8 women), 28 part-time (5 women); includes 3 minority (1 African American, 2 Hispanic Americans), 27 international. Average age 32. In 2009, 2 doctorates awarded. *Degree requirements:* For master's, comprehensive exam, thesis (for some programs), oral exam (for some programs); for doctorate, comprehensive exam, thesis/dissertation (for some programs), oral exam, written qualifying exam in physics or health physics after 1st year. *Entrance requirements:* For master's, GRE General Test, 3 letters of recommendation, BS or BA in physics, teaching certificate (MNS); for doctorate, GRE General Test (minimum 50th percentile), 3 letters of recommendation, statement of career goals. Additional exam requirements/recommendations for international students: Required—TOEFL (minimum score 550 paper-based; 213 computer-based; 80 iBT). *Application deadline:* For fall admission, 7/1 for domestic students, 6/1 for international students; for spring admission, 12/1 for domestic students, 11/1 for international students. Applications are processed on a rolling basis. Application fee: $55. Electronic applications accepted. *Expenses:* Tuition, state resident: full-time $3318; part-time $297 per credit hour. Tuition, nonresident: full-time $13,120; part-time $437 per credit hour. Required fees: $2530. Tuition and fees vary according to program. *Financial support:* In 2009–10, 38 research assistantships with full and partial tuition reimbursements (averaging $13,169 per year), 7 teaching assistantships with full and partial tuition reimbursements (averaging $10,841 per year) were awarded; fellowships with full and partial tuition reimbursements, career-related internships or fieldwork, Federal Work-Study, institutionally sponsored loans, scholarships/grants, health care benefits, tuition waivers (full), and unspecified assistantships also available. Support available to part-time students. Financial award application deadline: 1/1; financial award applicants required to submit FAFSA. *Faculty research:* Ion beam applications, low-energy nuclear physics, relativity and cosmology, observational astronomy. *Unit head:* Dr. Richard Brey, Interim Chair, 208-282-3467, Fax: 208-282-4649, E-mail: brey@physics.isu.edu. *Application contact:* Tami Carson, Graduate School Technical Records Specialist, 208-282-2150, Fax: 208-282-4847, E-mail: carstami@isu.edu.

Illinois Institute of Technology, Graduate College, College of Science and Letters, Department of Biological, Chemical and Physical Sciences, Physics Division, Chicago, IL 60616-3793. Offers health physics (MHP); physics (MS, PhD). Part-time programs available. Postbaccalaureate distance learning degree programs offered. *Faculty:* 16 full-time (1 woman), 4 part-time/adjunct (1 woman). *Students:* 14 full-time (3 women), 56 part-time (11 women); includes 8 minority (1 American Indian/Alaska Native, 7 Asian Americans or Pacific Islanders), 14 international. Average age 35. 120 applicants, 45% accepted, 24 enrolled. In 2009, 11 master's, 2 doctorates awarded. Terminal master's awarded for partial completion of doctoral program. *Degree requirements:* For master's, comprehensive exam, thesis (for some programs); for doctorate, comprehensive exam, thesis/dissertation. *Entrance requirements:* For master's and doctorate, GRE General Test, minimum undergraduate GPA of 3.0. Additional exam requirements/recommendations for international students: Required—TOEFL (minimum score 550 paper-based; 213 computer-based; 80 iBT). *Application deadline:* For fall admission, 5/1 for domestic and international students; for spring admission, 1/5 for domestic and international students. Applications are processed on a rolling basis. Application fee: $40. Electronic applications accepted. *Expenses:* Tuition: Full-time $17,550; part-time $888 per credit hour. Required fees: $850; $7.50 per credit hour. One-time fee: $50 full-time. Full-time tuition and fees vary according to program. *Financial support:* In 2009–10, 1 fellowship with full tuition reimbursement (averaging $17,000 per year), 12 research assistantships with full tuition reimbursements (averaging $17,000 per year), 11 teaching assistantships with full tuition reimbursements (averaging $15,500 per year) were awarded; Federal Work-Study, institutionally sponsored loans, scholarships/grants, health care benefits, and unspecified assistantships also available. Support available to part-time students. Financial award applicants required to submit FAFSA. *Faculty research:* Elementary particle physics, accelerator physics, synchrotron radiation, research on materials and biological systems, XANES and XAFS, computational simulation of membranes. Total annual research expenditures: $2.1 million. *Application contact:* Morgan Frederick, Assistant Director of Graduate Communications, 866-472-3448, Fax: 312-567-3138, E-mail: inquiry.grad@iit.edu.

McMaster University, School of Graduate Studies, Faculty of Science, Department of Medical Physics and Applied Radiation Sciences, Hamilton, ON L8S 4M2, Canada. Offers health and radiation physics (M Sc); medical physics (M Sc, PhD). Part-time programs available. *Degree requirements:* For master's, thesis or alternative. *Entrance requirements:* For master's, minimum B+ average. Additional exam requirements/recommendations for international students: Required—TOEFL (minimum score 550 paper-based; 213 computer-based). *Faculty research:* Imaging, toxicology, dosimetry, body composition, medical lasers.

Midwestern State University, Graduate Studies, College of Health Sciences and Human Services, Program in Radiology, Wichita Falls, TX 76308. Offers radiologic administration (MSR); radiologic education (MSR); radiologic sciences (MSR); radiologist assistant (MSR). Part-time and evening/weekend programs available. Postbaccalaureate distance learning degree programs offered (minimal on-campus study). *Degree requirements:* For master's, comprehensive exam, thesis optional. *Entrance requirements:* For master's, GRE General Test, MAT or GMAT, credentials in one of the medical imaging modalities or radiation therapy; 1 year of experience; 3 letters of recommendation from past and/or present educators and employers. Additional exam requirements/recommendations for international students: Required—TOEFL (minimum score 550 paper-based; 213 computer-based). Electronic applications accepted. *Expenses:* Tuition, state resident: full-time $1620; part-time $90 per credit hour. Tuition, nonresident: full-time $2160; part-time $120 per credit hour. International tuition: $7506 full-time. Required fees: $3068.80; $145.60 per credit hour. $179 per semester.

New York Chiropractic College, Program in Diagnostic Imaging, Seneca Falls, NY 13148-0800. Offers MS. *Faculty:* 2 full-time (0 women). *Students:* 4 full-time (all women). 2 applicants, 50% accepted, 1 enrolled. In 2009, 1 master's awarded. *Degree requirements:* For master's, thesis. *Entrance requirements:* For master's, DC degree, minimum GPA of 3.0. *Application deadline:* Applications are processed on a rolling basis. Application fee: $0. *Expenses:* Tuition: Full-time $18,320; part-time $426 per credit hour. Required fees: $680. Tuition and fees vary according to course load and program. *Financial support:* In 2009–10, 3 fellowships (averaging $31,000 per year) were awarded. Financial award applicants required to submit FAFSA. *Unit head:* Dr. Jean-Nicolas Poirier, Director, 315-568-3197, E-mail: npoirier@nycc.edu. *Application contact:* Director of Admissions.

Oregon State University, Graduate School, College of Engineering, Department of Nuclear Engineering and Radiation Health Physics, Corvallis, OR 97331. Offers nuclear engineering (M Eng, MS, PhD); radiation health physics (MA, MHP, MS, PhD). Part-time programs available. *Faculty:* 11 full-time (2 women). *Students:* 89 full-time (34 women), 27 part-time (16 women); includes 13 minority (1 African American, 7 Asian Americans or Pacific Islanders, 5 Hispanic Americans), 8 international. Average age 33. 51 applicants, 61% accepted, 12 enrolled. In 2009, 7 master's, 1 doctorate awarded. Terminal master's awarded for partial completion of doctoral program. *Degree requirements:* For master's, thesis; for doctorate, thesis/dissertation. *Entrance requirements:* For master's and doctorate, GRE General Test, minimum GPA of 3.0 in last 90 hours. Additional exam requirements/recommendations for international students: Required—TOEFL (minimum score 550 paper-based; 213 computer-based). *Application deadline:* For fall admission, 6/15 for domestic students. Applications are processed on a rolling basis. Application fee: $50. *Expenses:* Tuition, state resident: full-time $9774; part-time $362 per credit. Tuition, nonresident: full-time $15,849; part-time $587 per credit. Required fees: $1639. Full-time tuition and fees vary according to course load and program. *Financial support:* In 2009–10, 3 fellowships with full tuition reimbursements (averaging $16,650 per year), 14 research assistantships with partial tuition reimbursements (averaging $12,627 per year), 6 teaching assistantships with full tuition reimbursements (averaging $12,627 per year) were awarded; institutionally sponsored loans also available. Support available to part-time students. Financial award application deadline: 2/1. *Faculty research:* Reactor thermal hydraulics and safety, applications of radiation and nuclear techniques, computational methods development, environmental transport of radioactive materials. Total annual research expenditures: $2.5 million. *Unit head:* Dr. Jose N. Reyes, Head, 541-737-2343, Fax: 541-737-0480, E-mail: nuc_engr@engr.orst.edu. *Application contact:* Dr. Kristie Marsh, Academic Program Assistant, 541-737-7066, Fax: 541-737-0480, E-mail: nuc_engr@engr.orst.edu.

Quinnipiac University, School of Health Sciences, Radiologist Assistant Program, Hamden, CT 06518-1940. Offers MHS. *Faculty:* 2 full-time (1 woman), 2 part-time/adjunct (0 women). *Students:* 9 full-time (2 women), 5 part-time (1 woman); includes 1 minority (African American). 18 applicants, 67% accepted, 9 enrolled. *Entrance requirements:* For master's, proof of certification from American Registry of Radiologic Technologists; 2000 hours of direct patient care; CPR certification. Additional exam requirements/recommendations for international students: Required—TOEFL (minimum score 575 paper-based; 233 computer-based; 90 iBT), IELTS (minimum score 6.5). *Application deadline:* For fall admission, 4/30 priority date for domestic and international students. Applications are processed on a rolling basis. Application fee: $45. Electronic applications accepted. *Expenses:* Tuition: Full-time $16,030; part-time $770 per credit. Required fees: $630; $35 per credit. *Financial support:* Career-related internships or fieldwork, tuition waivers (partial), and unspecified assistantships available. Financial award application deadline: 4/15; financial award applicants required to submit FAFSA. *Unit head:* Dr. Ramon Gonzalez, Director, 203-582-3765, Fax: 203-582-8706, E-mail: ramon.gonzalez@quinnipiac.edu. *Application contact:* Kristin Parent, Assistant Director of Graduate Health Sciences Admissions, 800-462-1944, Fax: 203-582-3443, E-mail: kristin.parent@quinnipiac.edu.

San Diego State University, Graduate and Research Affairs, College of Sciences, Department of Physics, Program in Radiological Physics, San Diego, CA 92182. Offers MS. Part-time programs available. *Degree requirements:* For master's, thesis optional, oral or written exam. *Entrance requirements:* For master's, GRE General Test, GRE Subject Test (physics), 2 letters of recommendation. Additional exam requirements/recommendations for international students: Required—TOEFL. Electronic applications accepted. *Faculty research:* Computational radiological physics, medical physics.

Texas A&M University, College of Engineering, Department of Nuclear Engineering, College Station, TX 77843. Offers health physics (MS); nuclear engineering (M Eng, MS, PhD). *Faculty:* 19. *Students:* 93 full-time (14 women), 18 part-time (4 women); includes 13 minority (2 African Americans, 6 Asian Americans or Pacific Islanders, 5 Hispanic Americans), 24 international. Average age 28. In 2009, 13 master's, 8 doctorates awarded. *Degree requirements:* For master's, thesis or alternative; for doctorate, thesis/dissertation, departmental qualifying exams. *Entrance requirements:* For master's and doctorate, GRE General Test, 3 letters of recommendation. Additional exam requirements/recommendations for international students: Required—TOEFL. *Application deadline:* For fall admission, 3/1 for domestic and international students; for spring admission, 8/1 for domestic and international students. Applications are processed on a rolling basis. Application fee: $50 ($75 for international students). Electronic applications accepted. *Expenses:* Tuition, state resident: full-time $3991; part-time $221.74 per credit hour. Tuition, nonresident: full-time $9049; part-time $502.74 per credit hour. *Financial support:* Fellowships, research assistantships, career-related internships or fieldwork, scholarships/grants, and unspecified assistantships available. Financial award application deadline: 4/1; financial award applicants required to submit FAFSA. *Faculty research:* Accelerators, aerosols, computational transport, fission, fusion. Total annual research expenditures: $4.2 million. *Unit head:* Dr. Yassin Hassan, Head, 979-845-1956, E-mail: y-hassan@tamu.edu. *Application contact:* Graduate Coordinator, 979-845-7090.

Université de Montréal, Faculty of Medicine, Program in Specialized Studies, Montréal, QC H3C 3J7, Canada. Offers anesthesia (DES); diagnostic radiology (DES); family medicine (DES); gastroenterology (DES); geriatry (DES); intensive care (DES); medical biochemistry (DES); medical genetics (DES); medicine (DES); microbiology and infectious diseases (DES); nuclear medicine (DES); obstetrics and gynecology (DES); ophthalmology (DES); pediatrics (DES); pneumology (DES); psychiatry (DES); radiology-oncology (DES); rheumatology (DES); surgery (DES). *Faculty:* 154 full-time (40 women), 333 part-time/adjunct (100 women). *Students:* 930 full-time (580 women), 7 part-time (all women). 74 applicants, 77% accepted, 29 enrolled. *Application deadline:* For fall admission, 2/1 priority date for domestic students; for winter admission, 11/1 priority date for domestic students; for spring admission, 2/1 priority date for domestic students. Application fee: $100. Electronic applications accepted. *Unit head:* Lorraine Locas, Assistant to the Vice Dean of Graduate Studies, 514-343-6269, Fax: 514-343-5751, E-mail: lorraine.locas@umontreal.ca. *Application contact:* Dr. Andre Ferron, Vice Dean Graduate Studies, 514-343-6111 Ext. 0933, Fax: 514-343-5751, E-mail: andre.ferron@umontreal.ca.

Université Laval, Faculty of Medicine, Post-Professional Programs in Medical Studies, Québec, QC G1K 7P4, Canada. Offers anatomy–pathology (DESS); anesthesiology (DESS); cardiology (DESS); care of older people (Diploma); clinical research (DESS); community health (DESS); dermatology (DESS); diagnostic radiology (DESS); emergency medicine (Diploma); family medicine (DESS); general surgery (DESS); geriatrics (DESS); hematology (DESS); internal medicine (DESS); maternal and fetal medicine (Diploma); medical biochemistry (DESS); medical microbiology and infectious diseases (DESS); medical oncology (DESS); nephrology (DESS); neurology (DESS); neurosurgery (DESS); obstetrics and gynecology (DESS);

ophthalmology (DESS); orthopedic surgery (DESS); oto-rhino-laryngology (DESS); palliative medicine (Diploma); pediatrics (DESS); plastic surgery (DESS); psychiatry (DESS); pulmonary medicine (DESS); radiology–oncology (DESS); thoracic surgery (DESS); urology (DESS). *Degree requirements:* For other advanced degree, comprehensive exam. *Entrance requirements:* For degree, knowledge of French. Electronic applications accepted.

University of Alberta, Faculty of Medicine and Dentistry and Faculty of Graduate Studies and Research, Graduate Programs in Medicine, Department of Radiology and Diagnostic Imaging, Edmonton, AB T6G 2E1, Canada. Offers medical sciences (PhD); radiology and diagnostic imaging (M Sc). *Faculty:* 2 part-time/adjunct (0 women). *Students:* 2 full-time (0 women). Average age 25. 50 applicants, 2% accepted. In 2009, 1 doctorate awarded. Terminal master's awarded for partial completion of doctoral program. *Degree requirements:* For master's, thesis; for doctorate, thesis/dissertation. *Entrance requirements:* For master's, minimum GPA of 6.5 on a 9.0 scale; for doctorate, M Sc. *Application deadline:* For fall admission, 4/1 priority date for domestic students; for winter admission, 7/1 priority date for domestic students. Application fee: $60. Tuition and fees charges are reported in Canadian dollars. *Expenses:* Tuition, area resident: Full-time $4626 Canadian dollars; part-time $99.72 Canadian dollars per unit. International tuition: $8216 Canadian dollars full-time. Required fees: $3590 Canadian dollars; $99.72 Canadian dollars per unit. $215 Canadian dollars per term. *Financial support:* In 2009–10, 2 fellowships, 1 research assistantship, 1 teaching assistantship were awarded; career-related internships or fieldwork also available. Financial award application deadline: 3/31. *Faculty research:* Spectroscopic attenuation correction, nuclear medicine technology, monoclonal antibody labeling, bone mineral analysis using ultrasound. Total annual research expenditures: $325,000. *Unit head:* Dr. Robert Lambert, Academic Chair, 780-407-6907, Fax: 780-407-1202, E-mail: rglambert@cha.ab.ca. *Application contact:* Dr. L. J. Filipow, Graduate Coordinator, 780-407-6907, Fax: 780-407-1202, E-mail: filipow@shaw.ca.

University of Cincinnati, Graduate School, College of Engineering, Department of Mechanical, Industrial and Nuclear Engineering, Program in Health Physics, Cincinnati, OH 45221. Offers MS. *Degree requirements:* For master's, thesis or alternative. *Entrance requirements:* For master's, GRE General Test. Additional exam requirements/recommendations for international students: Required—TOEFL (minimum score 575 paper-based; 233 computer-based). Electronic applications accepted.

University of Cincinnati, Graduate School, College of Medicine, Graduate Programs in Biomedical Sciences, Department of Radiological Sciences, Cincinnati, OH 45267. Offers medical physics (MS). Part-time programs available. *Degree requirements:* For master's, comprehensive exam, project. *Entrance requirements:* For master's, GRE General Test. Additional exam requirements/recommendations for international students: Required—TOEFL (minimum score 575 paper-based). Electronic applications accepted. *Faculty research:* Radiation oncology, radiologic imaging, dosimetry, radiation biology, radiation therapy.

University of Kentucky, Graduate School, College of Health Sciences, Program in Radiation Sciences, Lexington, KY 40506-0032. Offers health physics (MSHP); radiological medical physics (MSRMP). Offered in cooperation with Graduate Programs in Medicine. Part-time programs available. *Degree requirements:* For master's, comprehensive exam, thesis. *Entrance requirements:* For master's, GRE General Test, minimum undergraduate GPA of 2.75. Additional exam requirements/recommendations for international students: Required—TOEFL (minimum score 550 paper-based; 213 computer-based). Electronic applications accepted. *Faculty research:* Dosimetry, manpower studies, diagnostic imaging physics, shielding.

University of Massachusetts Lowell, College of Arts and Sciences, Department of Physics and Applied Physics, Program in Radiological Science and Protection, Lowell, MA 01854-2881. Offers MS. *Degree requirements:* For master's, one foreign language, thesis. *Entrance requirements:* For master's, GRE General Test, 3 letters of reference. Additional exam requirements/recommendations for international students: Required—TOEFL. Electronic applications accepted.

University of Medicine and Dentistry of New Jersey, School of Health Related Professions, Department of Medical Imaging Sciences, Newark, NJ 07107-1709. Offers radiologist assistant (MS). *Entrance requirements:* Additional exam requirements/recommendations for international students: Required—TOEFL. Electronic applications accepted.

University of Michigan, Horace H. Rackham School of Graduate Studies, College of Engineering, Department of Nuclear Engineering and Radiological Sciences, Ann Arbor, MI 48109. Offers nuclear engineering (Nuc E); nuclear engineering and radiological sciences (MSE, PhD); nuclear science (MS, PhD). *Faculty:* 20 full-time (2 women). *Students:* 106 full-time (16 women), 3 part-time (1 woman); includes 11 minority (6 Asian Americans or Pacific Islanders, 5 Hispanic Americans), 22 international. 140 applicants, 49% accepted, 31 enrolled. In 2009, 21 master's, 5 doctorates awarded. Terminal master's awarded for partial completion of doctoral program. *Degree requirements:* For master's, thesis optional; for doctorate, thesis/dissertation, oral defense of dissertation, preliminary exams. *Entrance requirements:* For master's and doctorate, GRE General Test. Additional exam requirements/recommendations for international students: Required—TOEFL (minimum score 560 paper-based; 220 computer-based). *Application deadline:* Applications are processed on a rolling basis. Application fee: $60 ($75 for international students). Electronic applications accepted. *Expenses:* Tuition, state resident: full-time $17,286; part-time $1099 per credit hour. Tuition, nonresident: full-time $34,944; part-time $2080 per credit hour. Required fees: $95 per semester. Tuition and fees vary according to course load, degree level and program. *Financial support:* Fellowships, research assistantships, teaching assistantships, career-related internships or fieldwork, institutionally sponsored loans, scholarships/grants, traineeships, health care benefits, and unspecified assistantships available. *Faculty research:* Radiation safety, environmental sciences, medical physics, fission systems and radiation transport, materials, plasmas and fusion, radiation measurements and imaging. *Unit head:* Dr. William R. Martin, Chair, 734-764-4260, Fax: 734-763-4540, E-mail: wrm@umich.edu. *Application contact:* Peggy Jo Gramer, Graduate Program Coordinator, 734-615-8810, Fax: 734-763-4540, E-mail: pjgramer@umich.edu.

University of Missouri, Graduate School, Nuclear Science and Engineering Institute, Columbia, MO 65211. Offers nuclear power engineering (MS, PhD), including health physics (MS), medical physics (MS), nuclear power engineering (MS). *Degree requirements:* For master's, research project; for doctorate, thesis/dissertation. *Entrance requirements:* For master's and doctorate, GRE General Test. Additional exam requirements/recommendations for international students: Required—TOEFL (minimum score 500 paper-based; 173 computer-based; 61 iBT).

University of Missouri, School of Health Professions, Program in Cardiopulmonary and Diagnostic Sciences, Columbia, MO 65211. Offers diagnostic medical ultrasound (MHS). *Entrance requirements:* Additional exam requirements/recommendations for international students: Required—TOEFL (minimum score 500 paper-based; 173 computer-based; 61 iBT).

University of Nevada, Las Vegas, Graduate College, School of Allied Health Sciences, Department of Health Physics, Las Vegas, NV 89154-3037. Offers MS. *Accreditation:* ABET. Part-time programs available. *Faculty:* 11 full-time (4 women), 1 (woman) part-time/adjunct. *Students:* 8 full-time (4 women), 6 part-time (1 woman); includes 1 minority (Asian American or Pacific Islander), 1 international. Average age 32. 7 applicants, 57% accepted, 2 enrolled. In 2009, 3 master's awarded. *Degree requirements:* For master's, thesis optional, professional paper, oral exam. *Entrance requirements:* Additional exam requirements/recommendations for international students: Required—TOEFL (minimum score 550 paper-based; 213 computer-based; 80 iBT), IELTS (minimum score 7). *Application deadline:* For fall admission, 6/15 priority date for domestic students, 5/1 for international students; for spring admission, 11/15 priority date for domestic students, 10/1 for international students. Applications are processed on a rolling basis. Application fee: $60 ($95 for international students). Electronic applications accepted. *Financial support:* In 2009–10, 6 students received support, including 6 research assistantships with partial tuition reimbursements available (averaging $10,000 per year); institutionally sponsored loans, scholarships/grants, health care benefits, and unspecified assistantships also available. Financial award application deadline: 3/1. *Faculty research:* Laser-based therapeutics and diagnostics, functional magnetic resonance imaging, fast automated radiochemistry analysis and nuclear forensics, nuclear waste management, immunological effects of environmental toxins. *Unit head:* Dr. Steen Madsen, Chair/ Associate Professor, 702-895-1805, Fax: 702-895-4819, E-mail: steen.madsen@unlv.edu. *Application contact:* Graduate College Admissions Evaluator, 702-895-3320, Fax: 702-895-4180, E-mail: gradcollege@unlv.edu.

University of Oklahoma Health Sciences Center, College of Medicine and Graduate College, Graduate Programs in Medicine, Department of Radiological Sciences, Oklahoma City, OK 73190. Offers medical radiation physics (MS, PhD), including diagnostic radiology, nuclear medicine, radiation therapy, ultrasound. Part-time programs available. *Faculty:* 10 full-time (4 women). *Students:* 11 part-time (2 women), 2 international. Average age 28. 53 applicants, 19% accepted, 3 enrolled. In 2009, 4 master's awarded. Terminal master's awarded for partial completion of doctoral program. *Degree requirements:* For master's, thesis; for doctorate, thesis/dissertation. *Entrance requirements:* For master's, GRE General Test; for doctorate, GRE General Test, 3 letters of recommendation. Additional exam requirements/recommendations for international students: Required—TOEFL. *Application deadline:* For fall admission, 4/1 priority date for domestic students; for spring admission, 10/1 for domestic students. Applications are processed on a rolling basis. Application fee: $50. *Expenses:* Tuition, state resident: full-time $3120; part-time $156 per credit hour. Tuition, nonresident: full-time $11,314; part-time $409.70 per credit hour. Required fees: $1471; $51.20 per credit hour. $223.25 per term. *Financial support:* In 2009–10, 2 research assistantships (averaging $17,000 per year) were awarded; fellowships, career-related internships or fieldwork and institutionally sponsored loans also available. Support available to part-time students. Financial award application deadline: 7/1. *Faculty research:* Monte Carlo applications in radiation therapy, observer-performed studies in diagnostic radiology, error analysis in gated cardiac nuclear medicine studies, nuclear medicine absorbed fraction determinations. *Unit head:* Dr. Susan Edwards, Chair, 405-271-5132, E-mail: susan-edwards@ouhsc.edu. *Application contact:* Dr. Dee Wu, Graduate Liaison, 405-270-8001, E-mail: dee-wu@ouhsc.edu.

The University of Toledo, College of Graduate Studies, College of Medicine, Biomedical Science Programs, Program in Radiation Oncology, Toledo, OH 43606-3390. Offers medical physics-clinical radiation oncology (MSBS). Part-time programs available. *Degree requirements:* For master's, thesis, qualifying exam. *Entrance requirements:* For master's, GRE General Test, minimum undergraduate GPA of 3.0. *Faculty research:* 3-D treatment planning, stereotactic radiosurgery.

The University of Toledo, College of Graduate Studies, College of Medicine, Program in Diagnostic Radiology, Toledo, OH 43606-3390. Offers MSBS. Part-time programs available. *Degree requirements:* For master's, thesis, qualifying exam. *Entrance requirements:* For master's, GRE General Test, minimum undergraduate GPA of 3.0. *Faculty research:* Radiation dosimetry, digital image processing, mathematical modeling, magnetic resonance imaging.

Virginia Commonwealth University, Graduate School, School of Allied Health Professions, Department of Health Administration, Doctoral Program in Health Related Sciences, Richmond, VA 23284-9005. Offers clinical laboratory sciences (PhD); gerontology (PhD); health administration (PhD); nurse anesthesia (PhD); occupational therapy (PhD); physical therapy (PhD); radiation sciences (PhD); rehabilitation leadership (PhD).

Wayne State University, School of Medicine, Graduate Programs in Medicine, Department of Radiation Oncology, Detroit, MI 48202. Offers medical physics (PhD); radiological physics (MS). Part-time and evening/weekend programs available. Terminal master's awarded for partial completion of doctoral program. *Degree requirements:* For master's, thesis, essay, exit exam; for doctorate, thesis/dissertation, qualifying exam. *Entrance requirements:* For master's, GRE General Test, BS in physics or related area; for doctorate, GRE General Test, GRE Subject Test, BS in physics or related area. Additional exam requirements/recommendations for international students: Required—TOEFL (minimum score 550 paper-based; 213 computer-based); Recommended—TWE (minimum score 6). Electronic applications accepted. *Faculty research:* Radiotherapy physics, hyperthermia, magnetic resonance imaging and spectroscopy, clinical ultrasound, x-ray physics.

Wayne State University, School of Medicine, Graduate Programs in Medicine, Department of Radiology, Detroit, MI 48202. Offers medical physics (PhD); radiological physics (MS). Part-time and evening/weekend programs available. *Degree requirements:* For master's, essay, exam; for doctorate, thesis/dissertation. *Entrance requirements:* For master's, GRE General Test, BS in physics or related area; for doctorate, GRE. Additional exam requirements/recommendations for international students: Required—TOEFL (minimum score 550 paper-based; 213 computer-based); Recommended—TWE (minimum score 6). Electronic applications accepted. *Faculty research:* Interventional radiology; magnetic resonance imaging; neuroimaging; pediatric imaging; emergency radiology.

Medical Imaging

The Catholic University of America, School of Engineering, Department of Biomedical Engineering, Washington, DC 20064. Offers bioinstrumentation (MBE, MSE, D Engr); biomechanics (MBE, D Engr, PhD); biosignal processing and medical imaging (MBE, MSE, PhD); home care technologies (MBE, MSE, D Engr); rehabilitation engineering (MBE, MSE, D Engr); telemedicine (MBE, MSE, D Engr). Part-time programs available. *Faculty:* 6 full-time (1 woman), 1 part-time/adjunct (0 women). *Students:* 13 full-time (6 women), 10 part-time (4 women); includes 6 minority (3 African Americans, 3 Hispanic Americans), 6 international. Average age 29. 30 applicants, 63% accepted, 12 enrolled. In 2009, 15 master's awarded. *Degree requirements:* For master's, thesis or alternative; for doctorate, comprehensive exam, thesis/dissertation, oral exams. *Entrance requirements:* For master's, GRE (minimum score: 1250), minimum GPA of 3.0, statement of purpose, official copies of academic transcripts, three letters of recommendation; for doctorate, GRE (minimum score 1300), minimum GPA of 3.5, 3 letters of recommendation. Additional exam requirements/recommendations for international students: Required—TOEFL (minimum score 580 paper-based; 237 computer-based). *Application deadline:* For fall admission, 8/1 priority date for domestic students, 7/15 for international students; for spring admission, 12/1 priority date for domestic students, 10/15 for international students. Applications are processed on a rolling basis. Application fee: $55. Electronic applications accepted. *Expenses:* Contact institution. *Financial support:* Fellowships, research assistantships, teaching assistantships, Federal Work-Study, scholarships/grants, tuition waivers (full and partial), and unspecified assistantships available. Financial

Medical Imaging

The Catholic University of America (continued)
award application deadline: 2/1; financial award applicants required to submit FAFSA. *Faculty research:* Cardiopulmonary biomechanics, robotics and human motor control, cell and tissue engineering, biomechanics, rehabilitation engineering. Total annual research expenditures: $780,403. *Unit head:* Dr. Binh Q. Tran, Chair, 202-319-5181, Fax: 202-319-4287, E-mail: tran@cua.edu. *Application contact:* Julie Schwing, Director of Graduate Admissions, 202-319-5057, Fax: 202-319-6533, E-mail: cua-admissions@cua.edu.

Cleveland State University, College of Graduate Studies, College of Science, Department of Physics, Cleveland, OH 44115. Offers applied optics (MS); condensed matter physics (MS); medical physics (MS); optics and materials (MS); optics and medical imaging (MS). Part-time and evening/weekend programs available. *Entrance requirements:* For master's, undergraduate degree in engineering, physics, chemistry or mathematics. Additional exam requirements/recommendations for international students: Required—TOEFL (minimum score 525 paper-based; 197 computer-based), GRE. Electronic applications accepted. *Faculty research:* Statistical physics, experimental solid-state physics, theoretical optics, experimental biological physics (macromolecular crystallography), experimental optics.

Illinois Institute of Technology, Graduate College, Armour College of Engineering, Department of Electrical and Computer Engineering, Chicago, IL 60616-3793. Offers biomedical imaging and signals (MBMI); computer engineering (MS, PhD); electrical and computer engineering (MECE); electrical engineering (MS, PhD); electricity markets (MEM); manufacturing engineering (MME, MS); network engineering (MNE); power engineering (MPE); telecommunications and software engineering (MTSE); VLSI and microelectronics (MVM). Part-time and evening/weekend programs available. *Faculty:* 23 full-time (2 women), 7 part-time/adjunct (0 women). *Students:* 383 full-time (66 women), 215 part-time (26 women); includes 27 minority (4 African Americans, 17 Asian Americans or Pacific Islanders, 6 Hispanic Americans), 492 international. Average age 26. 1,548 applicants, 61% accepted, 208 enrolled. In 2009, 175 master's, 8 doctorates awarded. Terminal master's awarded for partial completion of doctoral program. *Degree requirements:* For master's, comprehensive exam, thesis (for some programs); for doctorate, comprehensive exam, thesis/dissertation. *Entrance requirements:* For master's and doctorate, GRE General Test, minimum undergraduate GPA of 3.0. Additional exam requirements/recommendations for international students: Required—TOEFL (minimum score 523 paper-based; 70 iBT). *Application deadline:* For fall admission, 5/1 for domestic and international students; for spring admission, 10/15 for domestic and international students. Applications are processed on a rolling basis. Application fee: $50. Electronic applications accepted. *Expenses:* Tuition: Full-time $17,550; part-time $888 per credit hour. Required fees: $850; $7.50 per credit hour. One-time fee: $50 full-time. Full-time tuition and fees vary according to program. *Financial support:* In 2009–10, 5 fellowships with full tuition reimbursements (averaging $20,000 per year), 35 research assistantships with full tuition reimbursements (averaging $18,000 per year), 22 teaching assistantships with full tuition reimbursements (averaging $16,000 per year) were awarded; career-related internships or fieldwork, Federal Work-Study, institutionally sponsored loans, scholarships/grants, health care benefits, tuition waivers (full), and unspecified assistantships also available. Support available to part-time students. Financial award applicants required to submit FAFSA. *Faculty research:* Communications and signal processing, computers and digital systems, electronics and electromagnetics, power and control systems. Total annual research expenditures: $1.6 million. *Unit head:* Dr. Geoffrey Williamson, Interim Chair, 312-567-5960, Fax: 312-567-8976, E-mail: williamson@iit.edu. *Application contact:* Dr. Geoffrey Williamson, Interim Chair, 312-567-5960, Fax: 312-567-8976, E-mail: williamson@iit.edu.

Medical University of South Carolina, College of Graduate Studies, Program in Molecular and Cellular Biology and Pathobiology, Charleston, SC 29425. Offers cancer biology (PhD); cardiovascular biology (PhD); cardiovascular imaging (PhD); cell regulation (PhD); craniofacial biology (PhD); genetics and development (PhD); marine biomedicine (PhD); DMD/PhD; MD/PhD. *Faculty:* 137 full-time (33 women). *Students:* 39 full-time (25 women); includes 6 minority (4 African Americans, 1 Asian American or Pacific Islander, 1 Hispanic American), 9 international. Average age 28. In 2009, 16 doctorates awarded. *Degree requirements:* For doctorate, thesis/dissertation, oral and written exams. *Entrance requirements:* For doctorate, GRE General Test, interview, minimum GPA of 3.0. Additional exam requirements/recommendations for international students: Required—TOEFL (minimum score 600 paper-based; 250 computer-based; 100 iBT). *Application deadline:* For fall admission, 1/15 priority date for domestic and international students. Applications are processed on a rolling basis. Application fee: $0 ($85 for international students). Electronic applications accepted. *Financial support:* In 2009–10, 39 students received support, including 39 research assistantships with partial tuition reimbursements available (averaging $23,000 per year); Federal Work-Study and scholarships/grants also available. Support available to part-time students. Financial award application deadline: 3/10; financial award applicants required to submit FAFSA. *Unit head:* Dr. Donald R. Menick, Director, 843-876-5045, Fax: 843-792-6590, E-mail: menickd@musc.edu. *Application contact:* Dr. Cynthia F. Wright, Associate Dean for Admissions and Career Development, 843-792-2564, Fax: 843-792-6590, E-mail: wrightcf@musc.edu.

MGH Institute of Health Professions, Graduate Programs, School of Health and Rehabilitation Sciences, Graduate Program in Medical Imaging, Boston, MA 02129. Offers Certificate. Postbaccalaureate distance learning degree programs offered (minimal on-campus study). *Faculty:* 1 (woman) full-time, 1 (woman) part-time/adjunct. *Students:* 19 full-time (13 women), 13 part-time (7 women); includes 2 minority (1 African American, 1 Hispanic American). Average age 34. 74 applicants, 62% accepted, 21 enrolled. In 2009, 13 Certificates awarded. *Entrance requirements:* For degree, job shadow experience, self-assessment form, interview. Additional exam requirements/recommendations for international students: Required—TOEFL (minimum score 550 paper-based; 213 computer-based; 80 iBT). *Application deadline:* For fall admission, 4/15 for domestic students, 3/1 for international students. Application fee: $50. Electronic applications accepted. *Expenses:* Tuition: Part-time $943 per credit. Required fees: $943 per credit. Tuition and fees vary according to course load. *Financial support:* In 2009–10, 24 students received support. Application deadline: 3/1. *Unit head:* Richard Terrass, Director, 617-726-0781. *Application contact:* Maureen Rika Judd, Manager of Admissions, 617-726-6069, Fax: 617-726-8010, E-mail: admissions@mghihp.edu.

New York University, School of Medicine, New York, NY 10012-1019. Offers biomedical sciences (PhD), including biomedical imaging, cellular and molecular biology, computational biology, developmental genetics, medical and molecular parasitology, microbiology, molecular oncobiology and immunology, neuroscience and physiology, pathobiology, pharmacology, structural biology; clinical investigation (MS); medicine (MD); MD/MA; MD/MPA; MD/MS; MD/PhD. *Accreditation:* LCME/AMA (one or more programs are accredited). *Faculty:* 1,493 full-time (558 women), 327 part-time/adjunct (122 women). *Students:* 747 full-time (360 women); includes 275 minority (23 African Americans, 5 American Indian/Alaska Native, 199 Asian Americans or Pacific Islanders, 48 Hispanic Americans), 2 international. Average age 24. 7,568 applicants, 7% accepted, 213 enrolled. In 2009, 164 first professional degrees, 13 master's, 50 doctorates awarded. *Degree requirements:* For master's, comprehensive exam, thesis; for doctorate, comprehensive exam, thesis/dissertation. *Entrance requirements:* MCAT. Additional exam requirements/recommendations for international students: Required—TOEFL. *Application deadline:* For fall admission, 10/15 for domestic students; for winter admission, 12/18 for domestic students, 12/15 for international students. Application fee: $100. *Expenses:* Contact institution. *Financial support:* In 2009–10, 524 students received support, including 29 fellowships with full tuition reimbursements available (averaging $31,000 per year), 47 research assistantships with full tuition reimbursements available (averaging $31,000 per year); teaching assistantships, Federal Work-Study, institutionally sponsored loans, and health care benefits also available. Financial award application deadline: 3/1; financial award applicants required to submit FAFSA. *Faculty research:* AIDS, cancer, neuroscience, molecular biology, neuroscience, cell biology and molecular genetics, structural biology, microbial pathogenesis and host defense, pharmacology, molecular oncology and immunology. Total annual research expenditures: $201.1 million. *Unit head:* Dr. Robert Grossman, Dean, 212-263-3269, Fax: 212-263- 1828. *Application contact:* Dr. Nancy Genieser, Associate Dean, Admissions, 212-263-5290, Fax: 212-263-0720, E-mail: nancy.genieser@nyumc.org.

University of Cincinnati, Graduate School, College of Engineering, Department of Biomedical Engineering, Cincinnati, OH 45221. Offers bioinformatics (PhD); biomechanics (PhD); medical imaging (PhD); tissue engineering (PhD). Part-time programs available. *Degree requirements:* For doctorate, one foreign language, thesis/dissertation. *Entrance requirements:* For doctorate, GRE General Test. Additional exam requirements/recommendations for international students: Required—TOEFL (minimum score 600 paper-based; 250 computer-based).

University of Florida, College of Medicine, Department of Biochemistry and Molecular Biology, Gainesville, FL 32611. Offers biochemistry and molecular biology (MS, PhD); imaging science and technology (MS, PhD). *Degree requirements:* For doctorate, thesis/dissertation. *Entrance requirements:* For doctorate, GRE General Test, minimum GPA of 3.0. Additional exam requirements/recommendations for international students: Required—TOEFL. Electronic applications accepted. *Faculty research:* Gene expression, metabolic regulation, structural biology, enzyme mechanism, membrane transporters.

University of Guelph, Ontario Veterinary College and Graduate Program Services, Graduate Programs in Veterinary Sciences, Department of Clinical Studies, Guelph, ON N1G 2W1, Canada. Offers anesthesiology (M Sc, DV Sc); cardiology (DV Sc, Diploma); clinical studies (Diploma); dermatology (M Sc); diagnostic imaging (M Sc, DV Sc); emergency/critical care (M Sc, DV Sc, Diploma); medicine (M Sc, DV Sc); neurology (M Sc, DV Sc); ophthalmology (M Sc, DV Sc); surgery (M Sc, DV Sc). *Degree requirements:* For master's, thesis; for doctorate, comprehensive exam, thesis/dissertation. *Entrance requirements:* Additional exam requirements/recommendations for international students: Required—TOEFL (minimum score 550 paper-based; 213 computer-based), IELTS (minimum score 6.5). Electronic applications accepted. *Faculty research:* Orthopedics, respirology, oncology, exercise physiology, cardiology.

University of Medicine and Dentistry of New Jersey, School of Health Related Professions, Department of Medical Imaging Sciences, Newark, NJ 07107-1709. Offers radiologist assistant (MS). *Entrance requirements:* Additional exam requirements/recommendations for international students: Required—TOEFL. Electronic applications accepted.

University of Southern California, Graduate School, Viterbi School of Engineering, Department of Biomedical Engineering, Los Angeles, CA 90089. Offers biomedical engineering (MS, PhD), including medical imaging and imaging informatics (MS); medical device and diagnostic engineering (MS). Postbaccalaureate distance learning degree programs offered. *Faculty:* 11 full-time (1 woman), 13 part-time/adjunct (2 women). *Students:* 186 full-time (65 women), 44 part-time (14 women); includes 70 minority (4 African Americans, 1 American Indian/Alaska Native, 56 Asian Americans or Pacific Islanders, 9 Hispanic Americans), 110 international. 339 applicants, 51% accepted, 69 enrolled. In 2009, 61 master's, 18 doctorates awarded. *Degree requirements:* For doctorate, thesis/dissertation. *Entrance requirements:* For master's and doctorate, GRE General Test. *Application deadline:* For fall admission, 3/1 priority date for domestic and international students; for spring admission, 10/1 priority date for domestic and international students. Applications are processed on a rolling basis. Application fee: $85. Electronic applications accepted. *Expenses:* Tuition: Full-time $25,980; part-time $1315 per unit. Required fees: $554. One-time fee: $35 full-time. Full-time tuition and fees vary according to degree level and program. *Financial support:* In 2009–10, fellowships with full tuition reimbursements (averaging $30,000 per year), research assistantships with full tuition reimbursements (averaging $19,250 per year), teaching assistantships with full tuition reimbursements (averaging $19,250 per year) were awarded; career-related internships or fieldwork, scholarships/grants, health care benefits, and unspecified assistantships also available. Financial award application deadline: 12/1; financial award applicants required to submit CSS PROFILE or FAFSA. *Faculty research:* Medical ultrasound, BioMEMS, neural prosthetics, computational bioengineering, bioengineering of vision, medical devices. Total annual research expenditures: $11.4 million. *Unit head:* Dr. Michael C. K. Khoo, Chair, 213-740-0347, Fax: 213-740-0343, E-mail: khoo@bmsr.usc.edu. *Application contact:* Mischal C. Diasanta, Graduate Student Affairs Advisor, 213-740-0344, Fax: 213-821-3897, E-mail: diasanta@usc.edu.

Medical Physics

Cleveland State University, College of Graduate Studies, College of Science, Department of Physics, Cleveland, OH 44115. Offers applied optics (MS); condensed matter physics (MS); medical physics (MS); optics and materials (MS); optics and medical imaging (MS). Part-time and evening/weekend programs available. *Entrance requirements:* For master's, undergraduate degree in engineering, physics, chemistry or mathematics. Additional exam requirements/recommendations for international students: Required—TOEFL (minimum score 525 paper-based; 197 computer-based), GRE. Electronic applications accepted. *Faculty research:* Statistical physics, experimental solid-state physics, theoretical optics, experimental biological physics (macromolecular crystallography), experimental optics.

Columbia University, Fu Foundation School of Engineering and Applied Science, Department of Applied Physics and Applied Mathematics, New York, NY 10027. Offers applied physics (Eng Sc D); applied physics and applied mathematics (MS, PhD, Engr); materials science and engineering (MS, Eng Sc D, PhD); medical physics (MS). Part-time programs available. Postbaccalaureate distance learning degree programs offered (no on-campus study). *Faculty:* 19 full-time (1 woman), 3 part-time/adjunct (1 woman). *Students:* 127 full-time (24 women), 44 part-time (7 women); includes 12 minority (2 African Americans, 1 American Indian/Alaska Native, 8 Asian Americans or Pacific Islanders, 1 Hispanic American), 73 international. Average age 27. 300 applicants, 35% accepted, 45 enrolled. In 2009, 31 master's, 10 doctorates awarded. Terminal master's awarded for partial completion of doctoral program. *Degree requirements:* For master's, comprehensive exam; for doctorate, thesis/dissertation, qualifying exam. *Entrance requirements:* For master's, GRE General Test, GRE Subject Test (strongly recommended); for doctorate, GRE General Test, GRE Subject Test (physics); for Engr, GRE General Test. Additional exam requirements/recommendations for international students: Required—TOEFL. *Application deadline:* For fall admission, 12/1 priority date for domestic and international students; for spring admission, 10/1 priority date for domestic and international students. Application fee: $70. Electronic applications accepted. *Financial support:* In 2009–10, 70 students received support, including 4 fellowships with full and partial tuition reimbursements available, 50 research assistantships with full tuition reimbursements available (averaging $30,000 per year), 18 teaching assistantships with full tuition reimbursements available (averaging $30,000 per year); health care benefits and unspecified assistantships also available. Financial award application deadline: 12/1; financial award applicants required to submit FAFSA. *Faculty research:* Plasma, solid state, optical and laser physics; atmospheric,

oceanic and earth physics; computational math and applied mathematics; materials science and engineering. *Unit head:* Dr. Irving P. Herman, Professor and Chair, 212-854-4457, E-mail: seasinfo.apam@columbia.edu. *Application contact:* Montserrat Fernandez-Pinkley, Student Services Coordinator, 212-854-4457, Fax: 212-854-8257, E-mail: mf2157@columbia.edu.

East Carolina University, Graduate School, Thomas Harriot College of Arts and Sciences, Department of Physics, Greenville, NC 27858-4353. Offers applied and biomedical physics (MS); medical physics (MS); physics (PhD). Part-time programs available. *Degree requirements:* For master's, one foreign language, comprehensive exam. *Entrance requirements:* For master's, GRE General Test. Additional exam requirements/recommendations for international students: Required—TOEFL.

Georgia Institute of Technology, Graduate Studies and Research, College of Engineering, George W. Woodruff School of Mechanical Engineering, Nuclear and Radiological Engineering and Medical Physics Programs, Atlanta, GA 30332-0001. Offers medical physics (MS); nuclear and radiological engineering (MSNE, PhD). Part-time programs available. Postbaccalaureate distance learning degree programs offered (no on-campus study). Terminal master's awarded for partial completion of doctoral program. *Degree requirements:* For master's, thesis optional; for doctorate, comprehensive exam, thesis/dissertation. *Entrance requirements:* For master's and doctorate, GRE General Test, minimum GPA of 3.0. Additional exam requirements/recommendations for international students: Required—TOEFL (minimum score 580 paper-based; 240 computer-based). *Faculty research:* Reactor physics, nuclear materials, plasma physics, radiation detection, radiological assessment.

Hampton University, Graduate College, Department of Physics, Hampton, VA 23668. Offers atmospheric physics (MS, PhD); medical physics (MS, PhD); nuclear physics (MS, PhD); optical physics (MS, PhD). Part-time and evening/weekend programs available. Terminal master's awarded for partial completion of doctoral program. *Degree requirements:* For master's, thesis optional; for doctorate, thesis/dissertation, oral defense, qualifying exam. *Entrance requirements:* For master's, GRE General Test; for doctorate, GRE General Test, minimum GPA of 3.0 or master's degree in physics or related field. *Faculty research:* Laser optics, remote sensing.

Harvard University, Graduate School of Arts and Sciences, Department of Physics, Cambridge, MA 02138. Offers experimental physics (PhD); medical engineering/medical physics (PhD), including applied physics, engineering sciences, physics; theoretical physics (PhD). *Degree requirements:* For doctorate, thesis/dissertation, final exams, laboratory experience. *Entrance requirements:* For doctorate, GRE General Test, GRE Subject Test. Additional exam requirements/recommendations for international students: Required—TOEFL. *Expenses:* Tuition: Full-time $33,696. Required fees: $1126. Full-time tuition and fees vary according to program. *Faculty research:* Particle physics, condensed matter physics, atomic physics.

Harvard University, Harvard Medical School and Graduate School of Arts and Sciences, Division of Health Sciences and Technology and Department of Physics and School of Engineering and Applied Sciences, Program in Medical Engineering/Medical Physics, Cambridge, MA 02138. Offers medical engineering (PhD); medical engineering/medical physics (Sc D); medical physics (PhD). *Students:* 118 full-time (38 women); includes 31 minority (5 African Americans, 21 Asian Americans or Pacific Islanders, 5 Hispanic Americans), 35 international. Average age 26. 240 applicants, 11% accepted, 21 enrolled. In 2009, 17 doctorates awarded. *Degree requirements:* For doctorate, comprehensive exam, thesis/dissertation, oral and written qualifying exams. *Entrance requirements:* For doctorate, GRE, bachelor's degree in engineering or science. Additional exam requirements/recommendations for international students: Required—TOEFL; Recommended—IELTS. *Application deadline:* For fall admission, 12/15 for domestic and international students. Application fee: $70. *Expenses:* Contact institution. *Financial support:* In 2009–10, 96 students received support, including 61 fellowships with full and partial tuition reimbursements available (averaging $48,526 per year), 47 research assistantships with full and partial tuition reimbursements available (averaging $42,576 per year), 9 teaching assistantships with full and partial tuition reimbursements available (averaging $15,463 per year); career-related internships or fieldwork, institutionally sponsored loans, traineeships, health care benefits, and unspecified assistantships also available. Financial award application deadline: 12/15; financial award applicants required to submit FAFSA. *Faculty research:* Regenerative biomedical technologies, biomedical imaging and optics, biophysics, systems physiology, bioinstrumentation, biomedical informatics/integrative genomics. *Unit head:* Dr. Ram Sasisekharan, Director, 617-258-7282. *Application contact:* Laurie Ward, Graduate Administrator, 617-253-3609, Fax: 617-253-6692, E-mail: laurie@mit.edu.

Louisiana State University and Agricultural and Mechanical College, Graduate School, College of Basic Sciences, Department of Physics and Astronomy, Baton Rouge, LA 70803. Offers astronomy (PhD); astrophysics (PhD); medical physics (MS); physics (MS, PhD). *Faculty:* 45 full-time (4 women), 1 part-time/adjunct (0 women). *Students:* 97 full-time (24 women), 5 part-time (1 woman); includes 5 minority (1 African American, 2 Asian Americans or Pacific Islanders, 2 Hispanic Americans), 42 international. Average age 27. 127 applicants, 20% accepted, 21 enrolled. In 2009, 9 master's, 8 doctorates awarded. Terminal master's awarded for partial completion of doctoral program. *Degree requirements:* For master's, thesis or alternative; for doctorate, thesis/dissertation. *Entrance requirements:* For master's and doctorate, GRE General Test, minimum GPA of 3.0. Additional exam requirements/recommendations for international students: Required—TOEFL (minimum score 550 paper-based; 213 computer-based; 79 iBT) or IELTS (minimum score 6.5). *Application deadline:* For fall admission, 1/25 priority date for domestic students, 5/15 for international students; for spring admission, 10/15 for international students. Applications are processed on a rolling basis. Application fee: $50 ($70 for international students). Electronic applications accepted. *Financial support:* In 2009–10, 16 fellowships with full tuition reimbursements (averaging $24,969 per year), 53 research assistantships with full and partial tuition reimbursements (averaging $20,101 per year), 37 teaching assistantships with full and partial tuition reimbursements (averaging $17,943 per year) were awarded; Federal Work-Study, institutionally sponsored loans, health care benefits, tuition waivers (full and partial), and unspecified assistantships also available. Financial award application deadline: 3/15; financial award applicants required to submit FAFSA. *Faculty research:* Experimentation and numerical relativity, condensed matter astrophysics, quantum computing, medical physics. Total annual research expenditures: $7.5 million. *Unit head:* Dr. Michael Cherry, Chair, 225-578-2261, Fax: 225-578-5855, E-mail: cherry@phys.lsu.edu. *Application contact:* Arnell Dangerfield, Administrative Coordinator, 225-578-1193, Fax: 225-578-5855, E-mail: adanger@lsu.edu.

Massachusetts Institute of Technology, Harvard-MIT Division of Health Sciences and Technology, Medical Engineering/Medical Physics Program, Cambridge, MA 02139-4307. Offers medical engineering (PhD); medical engineering and medical physics (Sc D); medical physics (PhD). *Students:* 118 full-time (38 women); includes 33 minority (5 African Americans, 1 American Indian/Alaska Native, 21 Asian Americans or Pacific Islanders, 6 Hispanic Americans), 35 international. Average age 26. 240 applicants, 11% accepted, 21 enrolled. In 2009, 17 doctorates awarded. *Degree requirements:* For doctorate, comprehensive exam, thesis/dissertation, oral and written departmental qualifying exams. *Entrance requirements:* For doctorate, GRE, bachelor's degree in engineering or science. Additional exam requirements/recommendations for international students: Required—TOEFL; Recommended—IELTS. *Application deadline:* For fall admission, 12/15 for domestic and international students. Application fee: $70. Electronic applications accepted. *Expenses:* Contact institution. *Financial support:* In 2009–10, 96 students received support, including 61 fellowships with full and partial tuition reimbursements available (averaging $48,526 per year), 47 research assistantships with full and partial tuition reimbursements available (averaging $42,576 per year), 9 teaching assistantships with full and partial tuition reimbursements available (averaging $15,463 per year); career-related internships or fieldwork, institutionally sponsored loans, traineeships, health care benefits, and unspecified assistantships also available. Financial award application deadline: 12/15. *Faculty research:* Regenerative biomedical technologies, biomedical imaging and optics, biophysics, systems physiology, bioinstrumentation, biomedical informatics/integrative genomics. *Unit head:* Dr. Ram Sasisekharan, Director, E-mail: mgray@mit.edu. *Application contact:* Laurie Ward, Graduate Administrator, 617-253-3609, Fax: 617-253-6692, E-mail: laurie@mit.edu.

McGill University, Faculty of Graduate and Postdoctoral Studies, Faculty of Medicine, Medical Physics Unit, Montréal, QC H3A 2T5, Canada. Offers M Sc, PhD. *Entrance requirements:* Additional exam requirements/recommendations for international students: Required—TOEFL.

McMaster University, School of Graduate Studies, Faculty of Science, Department of Medical Physics and Applied Radiation Sciences, Hamilton, ON L8S 4M2, Canada. Offers health and radiation physics (M Sc); medical physics (M Sc, PhD). Part-time programs available. *Degree requirements:* For master's, thesis or alternative. *Entrance requirements:* For master's, minimum B+ average. Additional exam requirements/recommendations for international students: Required—TOEFL (minimum score 550 paper-based; 213 computer-based). *Faculty research:* Imaging, toxicology, dosimetry, body composition, medical lasers.

Oakland University, Graduate Study and Lifelong Learning, College of Arts and Sciences, Department of Physics, Rochester, MI 48309-4401. Offers medical physics (PhD); physics (MS). *Degree requirements:* For doctorate, thesis/dissertation. *Entrance requirements:* For master's, minimum GPA of 3.0 for unconditional admission; for doctorate, GRE Subject Test, GRE General Test, minimum GPA of 3.0 for unconditional admission. Additional exam requirements/recommendations for international students: Required—TOEFL (minimum score 550 paper-based; 213 computer-based). Electronic applications accepted. *Expenses:* Contact institution. *Faculty research:* Quantitative molecular imagings of articular cartilage, multifunctional ferrite-ferroelectric layered structures for microwave and millimeter wave devices, magnoelectric materials for antenna structures.

Rosalind Franklin University of Medicine and Science, College of Health Professions, Department of Medical Radiation Physics, North Chicago, IL 60064-3095. Offers MS. *Faculty:* 1 full-time (0 women), 10 part-time/adjunct (2 women). *Students:* 18 full-time (6 women); includes 7 minority (3 African Americans, 4 Asian Americans or Pacific Islanders). 20 applicants, 85% accepted, 11 enrolled. Terminal master's awarded for partial completion of doctoral program. *Entrance requirements:* For master's, GRE General Test. Additional exam requirements/recommendations for international students: Required—TOEFL. *Application deadline:* For fall admission, 6/1 for domestic students. Applications are processed on a rolling basis. Application fee: $50. *Expenses:* Contact institution. *Financial support:* Career-related internships or fieldwork and tuition waivers (partial) available. Financial award application deadline: 7/10; financial award applicants required to submit FAFSA. *Unit head:* Dr. Alexander Markovic, Director, 847-578-8322, Fax: 847-578-8536, E-mail: alexander.markovic@rosalindfranklin.edu. *Application contact:* Melissa Knox, Admissions Officer, 847-578-8772, Fax: 847-775-6559, E-mail: melissa.knox@rosalindfranklin.edu.

Rush University, Graduate College, Division of Medical Physics, Chicago, IL 60612-3832. Offers MS, PhD. Terminal master's awarded for partial completion of doctoral program. *Degree requirements:* For master's, thesis, qualifying exam; for doctorate, thesis/dissertation, preliminary and qualifying exams. *Entrance requirements:* For master's, GRE General Test, BS in physics or physical science; for doctorate, GRE General Test, GRE Subject Test. Additional exam requirements/recommendations for international students: Required—TOEFL. Electronic applications accepted. *Faculty research:* Radiation therapy treatment planning, dosimetry, diagnostic radiology and nuclear imaging.

Stony Brook University, State University of New York, Graduate School, College of Engineering and Applied Sciences, Department of Biomedical Engineering, Program in Medical Physics, Stony Brook, NY 11794. Offers MS, PhD. *Expenses:* Tuition, state resident: full-time $8370; part-time $349 per credit. Tuition, nonresident: full-time $13,250; part-time $552 per credit. Required fees: $933. *Application contact:* Anne Marie Dusatko, Administrative Secretary, 631-444-2303, Fax: 631-444-6646, E-mail: ann.dusatko@sunysb.edu.

University of Alberta, Faculty of Graduate Studies and Research, Department of Physics, Edmonton, AB T6G 2E1, Canada. Offers astrophysics (M Sc, PhD); condensed matter (M Sc, PhD); geophysics (M Sc, PhD); medical physics (M Sc, PhD); subatomic physics (M Sc, PhD). *Faculty:* 36 full-time (3 women), 7 part-time/adjunct (0 women). *Students:* 56 full-time (6 women), 16 part-time (2 women). 85 applicants, 35% accepted. In 2009, 7 master's, 10 doctorates awarded. *Degree requirements:* For master's, thesis; for doctorate, thesis/dissertation. *Entrance requirements:* For master's and doctorate, minimum GPA of 7.0 on a 9.0 scale. Additional exam requirements/recommendations for international students: Required—TOEFL. *Application deadline:* For fall admission, 2/15 priority date for domestic students. Applications are processed on a rolling basis. Tuition and fees charges are reported in Canadian dollars. *Expenses:* Tuition, area resident: Full-time $4626 Canadian dollars; part-time $99.72 Canadian dollars per unit. International tuition: $8216 Canadian dollars full-time. Required fees: $3590 Canadian dollars; $99.72 Canadian dollars per unit. $215 Canadian dollars per term. *Financial support:* In 2009–10, 6 fellowships with partial tuition reimbursements, 40 teaching assistantships were awarded; research assistantships, career-related internships or fieldwork, institutionally sponsored loans, and scholarships/grants also available. Financial award application deadline: 2/15. *Faculty research:* Cosmology, astroparticle physics, high-intermediate energy, magnetism, superconductivity. Total annual research expenditures: $3.1 million. *Unit head:* Dr. R. Marchand, Associate Chair, 780-492-1072, E-mail: assoc-chair@phys.ualberta.ca. *Application contact:* Lynn Chandler, Program Advisor, 780-492-1072, Fax: 780-492-0714, E-mail: grad.program@phys.ualberta.ca.

University of California, Los Angeles, David Geffen School of Medicine and Graduate Division, Graduate Programs in Medicine, Program in Biomedical Physics, Los Angeles, CA 90095. Offers MS, PhD. *Degree requirements:* For master's, comprehensive exam or thesis; for doctorate, thesis/dissertation, oral and written qualifying exams. *Entrance requirements:* For master's and doctorate, GRE General Test. Additional exam requirements/recommendations for international students: Required—TOEFL.

University of Central Arkansas, Graduate School, College of Health and Behavioral Sciences, Department of Health Sciences, Conway, AR 72035-0001. Offers health education (MS); health systems (MS). *Faculty:* 9 full-time (5 women), 1 part-time/adjunct (0 women). *Students:* 10 full-time (8 women), 17 part-time (12 women); includes 8 minority (7 African Americans, 1 Asian American or Pacific Islander). Average age 27. 14 applicants, 100% accepted, 11 enrolled. In 2009, 9 master's awarded. *Degree requirements:* For master's, comprehensive exam, thesis optional. *Entrance requirements:* For master's, GRE General Test, minimum GPA of 2.7. Additional exam requirements/recommendations for international students: Required—TOEFL (minimum score 550 paper-based; 213 computer-based). *Application deadline:* For fall admission, 3/1 priority date for domestic students; for spring admission, 10/1 for domestic students. Applications are processed on a rolling basis. Application fee: $25 ($50 for international students). *Expenses:* Tuition, state resident: full-time $5136; part-time $214 per credit hour. Required fees: $379.50; $127 per term. Tuition and fees vary according to course level, course load and campus/location. *Financial support:* In 2009–10, 4 research assistantships (averaging $5,700 per year) were awarded; Federal Work-Study, scholarships/grants, tuition waivers (partial), and unspecified assistantships also available. Financial award application deadline: 2/15; financial award applicants required to submit FAFSA. *Unit head:* Emogene Fox, Chairperson, 501-450-5508, Fax: 501-450-5515, E-mail: emogenef@uca.edu. *Application contact:* Patti Hornor, Administrative Assistant, 501-450-5063, Fax: 501-450-5678, E-mail: pattih@uca.edu.

University of Chicago, Division of the Biological Sciences, Committee on Medical Physics, Chicago, IL 60637-1513. Offers PhD. *Students:* 30 full-time (6 women); includes 12 minority (9 Asian Americans or Pacific Islanders, 3 Hispanic Americans). Average age 28. 40 applicants, 18% accepted, 4 enrolled. In 2009, 2 doctorates awarded. *Degree requirements:* For doctorate, thesis/dissertation, ethics class, 2 teaching assistantships. *Entrance requirements:* For doctorate, GRE General Test, GRE Subject Test. Additional exam requirements/recommendations for international students: Required—TOEFL (minimum score 600 paper-based; 250 computer-based; 104 iBT), IELTS (minimum score 7). *Application deadline:* For fall admission, 12/1

Medical Physics

University of Chicago (continued)
priority date for domestic and international students. Application fee: $55. Electronic applications accepted. *Financial support:* In 2009–10, 30 students received support, including fellowships with full tuition reimbursements available (averaging $29,781 per year), research assistantships with full tuition reimbursements available (averaging $29,781 per year). Financial award applicants required to submit FAFSA. *Unit head:* Dr. Maryellen Lissak Giger, Professor, 773-702-6778, Fax: 773-702-0371. *Application contact:* Parag M. Shah, Associate Dean of Students and Graduate Affairs, 773-702-5853, Fax: 773-834-1618, E-mail: pshah@bsd.uchicago.edu.

University of Cincinnati, Graduate School, College of Medicine, Graduate Programs in Biomedical Sciences, Department of Radiological Sciences, Cincinnati, OH 45267. Offers medical physics (MS). Part-time programs available. *Degree requirements:* For master's, comprehensive exam, project. *Entrance requirements:* For master's, GRE General Test. Additional exam requirements/recommendations for international students: Required—TOEFL (minimum score 575 paper-based). Electronic applications accepted. *Faculty research:* Radiation oncology, radiologic imaging, dosimetry, radiation biology, radiation therapy.

University of Colorado at Boulder, Graduate School, College of Arts and Sciences, Department of Physics, Boulder, CO 80309. Offers chemical physics (PhD); geophysics (PhD); liquid crystal science and technology (PhD); mathematical physics (PhD); medical physics (PhD); optical sciences and engineering (PhD); physics (MS, PhD). *Faculty:* 48 full-time (6 women). *Students:* 160 full-time (24 women), 47 part-time (8 women); includes 9 minority (6 Asian Americans or Pacific Islanders, 3 Hispanic Americans), 65 international. Average age 27. 548 applicants, 5% accepted, 27 enrolled. In 2009, 17 master's, 23 doctorates awarded. Terminal master's awarded for partial completion of doctoral program. *Degree requirements:* For master's, comprehensive exam, thesis or alternative; for doctorate, comprehensive exam, thesis/dissertation. *Entrance requirements:* For master's and doctorate, GRE General Test, GRE Subject Test, minimum undergraduate GPA of 3.0. Additional exam requirements/recommendations for international students: Required—TOEFL. *Application deadline:* For fall admission, 1/15 priority date for domestic students, 1/15 for international students. Applications are processed on a rolling basis. Application fee: $50 ($60 for international students). Electronic applications accepted. *Financial support:* In 2009–10, 21 fellowships with full tuition reimbursements (averaging $15,999 per year), 146 research assistantships with full tuition reimbursements (averaging $16,586 per year) were awarded; scholarships/grants also available. Financial award application deadline: 1/15. *Faculty research:* Atomic and molecular physics, nuclear physics, condensed matter, elementary particle physics, laser or optical physics, plasma physics, geophysics, astrophysics and chemical physics. Total annual research expenditures: $14.2 million.

University of Kentucky, Graduate School, College of Health Sciences, Program in Radiation Sciences, Lexington, KY 40506-0032. Offers health physics (MSHP); radiological medical physics (MSRMP). Offered in cooperation with Graduate Programs in Medicine. Part-time programs available. *Degree requirements:* For master's, comprehensive exam, thesis. *Entrance requirements:* For master's, GRE General Test, minimum undergraduate GPA of 2.75. Additional exam requirements/recommendations for international students: Required—TOEFL (minimum score 550 paper-based; 213 computer-based). Electronic applications accepted. *Faculty research:* Dosimetry, manpower studies, diagnostic imaging physics, shielding.

University of Massachusetts Worcester, Graduate School of Biomedical Sciences, Program in Biomedical Engineering and Medical Physics, Worcester, MA 01655-0115. Offers PhD. *Degree requirements:* For doctorate, comprehensive exam, thesis/dissertation. *Entrance requirements:* For doctorate, GRE General Test. Additional exam requirements/recommendations for international students: Required—TOEFL (minimum score 600 paper-based; 250 computer-based). Electronic applications accepted. *Faculty research:* Tissue engineering, imaging, bioinstrumentation.

University of Minnesota, Twin Cities Campus, Graduate School, Program in Biophysical Sciences and Medical Physics, Minneapolis, MN 55455-0213. Offers MS, PhD. Part-time programs available. *Degree requirements:* For master's, thesis optional, research paper, oral exam; for doctorate, thesis/dissertation, oral/written preliminary exam, oral final exam. *Faculty research:* Theoretical biophysics, radiological physics, cellular and molecular biophysics.

See Close-Up on page 1443.

University of Missouri, Graduate School, Nuclear Science and Engineering Institute, Columbia, MO 65211. Offers nuclear power engineering (MS, PhD), including health physics (MS), medical physics (MS), nuclear power engineering (MS). *Degree requirements:* For master's, research project; for doctorate, thesis/dissertation. *Entrance requirements:* For master's and doctorate, GRE General Test. Additional exam requirements/recommendations for international students: Required—TOEFL (minimum score 500 paper-based; 173 computer-based; 61 iBT).

University of Oklahoma Health Sciences Center, College of Medicine and Graduate College, Graduate Programs in Medicine, Department of Radiological Sciences, Oklahoma City, OK 73190. Offers medical radiation physics (MS, PhD), including diagnostic radiology, nuclear medicine, radiation therapy, ultrasound. Part-time programs available. *Faculty:* 10 full-time (4 women). *Students:* 11 part-time (2 women), 2 international. Average age 28. 53 applicants, 19% accepted, 3 enrolled. In 2009, 4 master's awarded. Terminal master's awarded for partial completion of doctoral program. *Degree requirements:* For master's, thesis; for doctorate, thesis/dissertation. *Entrance requirements:* For master's, GRE General Test; for doctorate, GRE General Test, 3 letters of recommendation. Additional exam requirements/recommendations for international students: Required—TOEFL. *Application deadline:* For fall admission, 4/1 priority date for domestic students; for spring admission, 10/1 for domestic students. Applications are processed on a rolling basis. Application fee: $50. *Expenses:* Tuition, state resident: full-time $3120; part-time $156 per credit hour. Tuition, nonresident: full-time $11,314; part-time $409.70 per credit hour. Required fees: $1471; $51.20 per credit hour. $223.25 per term. *Financial support:* In 2009–10, 2 research assistantships (averaging $17,000 per year) were awarded; fellowships, career-related internships or fieldwork and institutionally sponsored loans also available. Support available to part-time students. Financial award application deadline: 7/1. *Faculty research:* Monte Carlo applications in radiation therapy, observer-performed studies in diagnostic radiology, error analysis in gated cardiac nuclear medicine studies, nuclear medicine absorbed fraction determinations. *Unit head:* Dr. Susan Edwards, Chair, 405-271-5132, E-mail: susan-edwards@ouhsc.edu. *Application contact:* Dr. Dee Wu, Graduate Liaison, 405-270-8001, E-mail: dee-wu@ouhsc.edu.

University of Pennsylvania, School of Arts and Sciences, Graduate Group in Physics and Astronomy, Philadelphia, PA 19104. Offers medical physics (MS); physics (PhD). Part-time programs available. *Faculty:* 48 full-time (5 women), 14 part-time/adjunct (1 woman). *Students:* 103 full-time (30 women), 2 part-time (0 women); includes 7 minority (5 Asian Americans or Pacific Islanders, 2 Hispanic Americans), 22 international. 336 applicants, 15% accepted, 21 enrolled. In 2009, 4 master's, 17 doctorates awarded. *Degree requirements:* For doctorate, thesis/dissertation, oral, preliminary, and final exams. *Entrance requirements:* For doctorate, GRE General Test, GRE Subject Test (recommended). Additional exam requirements/recommendations for international students: Required—TOEFL. *Application deadline:* For fall admission, 12/1 priority date for domestic students. Application fee: $70. Electronic applications accepted. *Expenses:* Tuition: Full-time $25,660; part-time $4758 per course. Required fees: $2152; $270 per course. Tuition and fees vary according to course load, degree level and program. *Financial support:* Fellowships, research assistantships, teaching assistantships, institutionally sponsored loans, scholarships/grants, traineeships, health care benefits, and unspecified assistantships available. Financial award application deadline: 12/15. *Faculty research:* Astrophysics, condensed matter experiment, condensed matter theory, particle experiment, particle theory. Total annual research expenditures: $7.3 million.

The University of Texas Health Science Center at Houston, Graduate School of Biomedical Sciences, Program in Medical Physics, Houston, TX 77225-0036. Offers MS, PhD, MD/PhD. *Degree requirements:* For master's, thesis; for doctorate, thesis/dissertation. *Entrance requirements:* For master's and doctorate, GRE General Test. Additional exam requirements/recommendations for international students: Required—TOEFL. Electronic applications accepted. *Faculty research:* Medical physics, radiation oncology physics, diagnostic imaging physics, medical nuclear physics, image-guided therapy.

The University of Texas Health Science Center at San Antonio, Graduate School of Biomedical Sciences, Radiological Sciences Graduate Program, San Antonio, TX 78229-3900. Offers MS, PhD. *Faculty:* 29 full-time (4 women), 46 part-time/adjunct (8 women). *Students:* 45 full-time (15 women), 7 part-time (2 women); includes 6 minority (3 African Americans, 3 Hispanic Americans), 21 international. Average age 28. 158 applicants, 6% accepted, 9 enrolled. In 2009, 2 master's, 3 doctorates awarded. *Degree requirements:* For master's, thesis; for doctorate, thesis/dissertation. *Entrance requirements:* For master's and doctorate, GRE. Additional exam requirements/recommendations for international students: Required—TOEFL (minimum score 550 paper-based; 213 computer-based). *Application deadline:* For fall admission, 3/1 for domestic and international students. Applications are processed on a rolling basis. Application fee: $0. Electronic applications accepted. *Expenses:* Tuition, state resident: full-time $2832; part-time $118 per credit hour. Tuition, nonresident: full-time $10,896; part-time $454 per credit hour. Required fees: $884 per semester. One-time fee: $70. *Financial support:* In 2009–10, teaching assistantships (averaging $24,783 per year); scholarships/grants and NIH training grants also available. Financial award application deadline: 7/1. Total annual research expenditures: $16.8 million. *Unit head:* Dr. Geoffery D. Clarke, Chair, Committee on Graduate Studies, 210-567-5550, Fax: 210-567-5541, E-mail: clarkeg@uthscsa.edu. *Application contact:* Loretta M. Edwards, Academic Programs Coordinator, 210-567-5550, Fax: 210-567-5541, E-mail: edwards@uthscsa.edu.

The University of Toledo, College of Graduate Studies, College of Medicine, Biomedical Science Programs, Program in Medical Physics, Toledo, OH 43606-3390. Offers MSBS.

The University of Toledo, College of Graduate Studies, College of Medicine, Biomedical Science Programs, Program in Radiation Oncology, Toledo, OH 43606-3390. Offers medical physics-clinical radiation oncology (MSBS). Part-time programs available. *Degree requirements:* For master's, thesis, qualifying exam. *Entrance requirements:* For master's, GRE General Test, minimum undergraduate GPA of 3.0. *Faculty research:* 3-D treatment planning, stereotactic radiosurgery.

University of Utah, Graduate School, College of Science, Department of Physics and Astronomy, Program in Medical Physics, Salt Lake City, UT 84112-1107. Offers PhD. *Students:* 12 full-time (1 woman), 2 international. Average age 25. 10 applicants, 20% accepted, 0 enrolled. *Degree requirements:* For doctorate, comprehensive exam, thesis/dissertation. *Entrance requirements:* For doctorate, GRE General and Subject Tests, minimum GPA of 3.0. Additional exam requirements/recommendations for international students: Required—TOEFL (minimum score 500 paper-based; 173 computer-based; 69 iBT). *Application deadline:* For fall admission, 2/1 for domestic and international students. Application fee: $55 ($65 for international students). *Expenses:* Tuition, state resident: full-time $4004; part-time $1674 per semester. Tuition, nonresident: full-time $14,134; part-time $5915 per semester. Required fees: $324 per semester. Tuition and fees vary according to course load, degree level and program. *Financial support:* Research assistantships with full tuition reimbursements, teaching assistantships with full tuition reimbursements available. *Unit head:* Brian Saam, Program Director, 801-581-6958, Fax: 801-585-3169, E-mail: sokolsky@science.utah.edu. *Application contact:* Jackie Hadley, Information Contact, 801-581-6861, Fax: 801-581-4801, E-mail: jackie@physic.utah.edu.

University of Victoria, Faculty of Graduate Studies, Faculty of Science, Department of Physics and Astronomy, Victoria, BC V8W 2Y2, Canada. Offers astronomy and astrophysics (M Sc, PhD); condensed matter physics (M Sc, PhD); experimental particle physics (M Sc, PhD); medical physics (M Sc, PhD); ocean physics (M Sc, PhD); theoretical physics (M Sc, PhD). *Degree requirements:* For master's, thesis; for doctorate, comprehensive exam, thesis/dissertation, candidacy exam. *Entrance requirements:* For master's and doctorate, GRE. Additional exam requirements/recommendations for international students: Required—TOEFL (minimum score 575 paper-based; 233 computer-based), IELTS (minimum score 7). Electronic applications accepted. *Faculty research:* Old stellar populations; observational cosmology and large scale structure; cp violation; atlas.

University of Wisconsin–Madison, School of Medicine and Public Health and Graduate School, Graduate Programs in Medicine, Department of Medical Physics, Madison, WI 53705-2275. Offers health physics (MS); medical physics (MS, PhD). Part-time programs available. *Faculty:* 29 full-time (2 women), 13 part-time/adjunct (1 woman). *Students:* 110 full-time (33 women); includes 9 minority (3 African Americans, 3 American Indian/Alaska Native, 3 Hispanic Americans), 27 international. Average age 27. 196 applicants, 22% accepted, 23 enrolled. In 2009, 24 master's, 15 doctorates awarded. Terminal master's awarded for partial completion of doctoral program. *Degree requirements:* For master's, comprehensive exam; for doctorate, comprehensive exam, thesis/dissertation. *Entrance requirements:* For master's and doctorate, GRE General Test, GRE Subject Test (physics), minimum GPA of 3.0. Additional exam requirements/recommendations for international students: Required—TOEFL. *Application deadline:* For fall admission, 12/1 priority date for domestic students, 11/15 for international students. Application fee: $54. Electronic applications accepted. *Expenses:* Tuition, state resident: part-time $594 per credit. Tuition, nonresident: part-time $1504 per credit. Required fees: $65 per credit. Tuition and fees vary according to course load, program and reciprocity agreements. *Financial support:* In 2009–10, 100 students received support, including 12 fellowships with full tuition reimbursements available (averaging $24,221 per year), 75 research assistantships with full tuition reimbursements available (averaging $21,224 per year), 5 teaching assistantships with full tuition reimbursements available (averaging $28,175 per year); traineeships, health care benefits, and unspecified assistantships also available. Financial award application deadline: 11/15. *Faculty research:* Biomagnetism: imaging and physiology, medical imaging processing, radiation therapy and radiation physics. Total annual research expenditures: $4.7 million. *Unit head:* Dr. James A. Zagzebski, Chair, 608-262-2171, Fax: 608-262-2413, E-mail: jazagzeb@wisc.edu. *Application contact:* Debra A. Torgerson, Graduate Coordinator, 608-265-6504, Fax: 608-262-2413, E-mail: datorger@wisc.edu.

Vanderbilt University, School of Medicine, Program in Medical Physics, Nashville, TN 37240-1001. Offers MS. Part-time programs available. *Degree requirements:* For master's, comprehensive exam, thesis optional. *Entrance requirements:* For master's, GRE General Test, physics major, physics minor or physics minor equivalent. Additional exam requirements/recommendations for international students: Required—TOEFL. Electronic applications accepted. *Faculty research:* MRI Imaging, PET Imaging, Nuclear Medicine Dosimetry, Monte Carlo Dosimetry, IGRT.

Virginia Commonwealth University, Graduate School, College of Humanities and Sciences, Department of Physics, Program in Medical Physics, Richmond, VA 23284-9005. Offers MS, PhD.

Wayne State University, School of Medicine, Graduate Programs in Medicine, Department of Radiation Oncology, Detroit, MI 48202. Offers medical physics (PhD); radiological physics (MS). Part-time and evening/weekend programs available. Terminal master's awarded for partial completion of doctoral program. *Degree requirements:* For master's, thesis, essay, exit exam; for doctorate, thesis/dissertation, qualifying exam. *Entrance requirements:* For master's, GRE General Test, BS in physics or related area; for doctorate, GRE General Test, GRE Subject Test, BS in physics or related area. Additional exam requirements/recommendations for international students: Required—TOEFL (minimum score 550 paper-based; 213 computer-based); Recommended—TWE (minimum score 6). Electronic applications accepted. *Faculty research:* Radiotherapy physics, hyperthermia, magnetic resonance imaging and spectroscopy, clinical ultrasound, x-ray physics.

Wayne State University, School of Medicine, Graduate Programs in Medicine, Department of Radiology, Detroit, MI 48202. Offers medical physics (PhD); radiological physics (MS). Part-time

and evening/weekend programs available. *Degree requirements:* For master's, essay, exam; for doctorate, thesis/dissertation. *Entrance requirements:* For master's, GRE General Test, BS in physics or related area; for doctorate, GRE. Additional exam requirements/recommendations for international students: Required—TOEFL (minimum score 550 paper-based; 213 computer-based); Recommended—TWE (minimum score 6). Electronic applications accepted. *Faculty research:* Interventional radiology; magnetic resonance imaging; neuroimaging; pediatric imaging; emergency radiology.

Wright State University, School of Graduate Studies, College of Science and Mathematics, Department of Physics, Program in Physics, Dayton, OH 45435. Offers geophysics (MS); medical physics (MS). Part-time and evening/weekend programs available. *Degree requirements:* For master's, thesis. *Entrance requirements:* Additional exam requirements/recommendations for international students: Required—TOEFL. *Faculty research:* Solid-state physics, optics, geophysics.

UNIVERSITY
OF MINNESOTA

UNIVERSITY OF MINNESOTA

Graduate Program in Biophysical Sciences and Medical Physics

Programs of Study

The Graduate Program in Biophysical Sciences and Medical Physics is interdisciplinary, with faculty members having primary appointments in departments that include radiology, physics, engineering, computer science, physiology, dentistry, genetics, and biochemistry. Programs lead to the M.S. and Ph.D. degrees. Students concentrate in research areas that include molecular biophysics, medical imaging, magnetic resonance imaging and spectroscopy, radiobiology, radiation therapy physics, and mathematical biophysics and computation. A limited number of students prepare for employment as hospital-based medical physicists through a program that includes opportunities for course work, laboratories, and directed study to provide experience in areas such as purchase specification, acceptance testing, quality assurance, and radiation safety. The majority of students prepare for research careers.

Candidates for the M.S. degree may pursue either thesis or nonthesis plans of study. The thesis plan is considered suitable for students with full-time employment if their thesis can be related to their work assignments. The nonthesis plan is more suitable for students planning to work in government or hospital settings where technical knowledge is more germane than research experience. Students in the nonthesis plan perform a research project under the direction of a faculty member and present the work to their faculty committee in an oral exam.

Candidates for the Ph.D. take preliminary written exams at the end of the first year of study or as soon as possible after completing the core course sequence—topics in physics for medicine and biology. An oral preliminary exam focuses on the plan for thesis research and the student's grasp of related information and is taken by the fall of the third year of full-time registration or its equivalent.

The program reports to the Basic Science Policy and Review Council of the Graduate School and receives a small amount of funding in the form of block grants from the Graduate School. However, graduate student support is almost exclusively obtained through grants and contracts held by the faculty members.

Research Facilities

Students have access to personal computers and workstations as well as the facilities of the Minnesota Supercomputer Institute. Separate research facilities exist for the Center for Magnetic Resonance Research, the Center for Immunotherapy, Radiobiology, Radiation Therapy, Diagnostic Radiology, and the School of Dentistry.

Financial Aid

The majority of students receive some sort of financial aid, typically a 50-percent-time research assistantship with full tuition waiver. The sources of funds are NIH awards, departmental grants and contracts, and Graduate School block grants. For details on need-based awards, students should contact the Office of Student Financial Aid, 210 Fraser Hall, University of Minnesota, 106 Pleasant Street, SE, Minneapolis, Minnesota 55455-0422 (phone: 612-624-1665). Applications as early as January for the following fall quarter are encouraged.

Cost of Study

Tuition per semester for full-time students (6–14 semester credits) was $5223 for residents and $8772 for nonresidents in 2007–08. On average, tuition increases about 5 percent annually and is usually determined in July. A per-semester student services fee covers basic outpatient health care, student organization fees, and the student newspaper.

Living and Housing Costs

The cost of living is comparable to that of other Midwestern urban areas. The University offers dormitory housing for single and married graduate students. Information about housing in the Twin Cities area may be obtained from University of Minnesota Housing Services, Comstock Hall–East, 210 Delaware Street Southeast, Minneapolis, Minnesota 55455-0307.

Student Group

The graduate program typically has 20–25 students. One to 5 are M.S. students and the rest are Ph.D. students. In recent years, 23 percent have been women and 31 percent have been international students. Four to 6 new students are admitted each year. The total Graduate School enrollment is 9,000 students in 170 fields of study.

Location

The Graduate School of the University of Minnesota is located on the banks of the Mississippi River in the Twin Cities of Minneapolis (the largest city in Minnesota) and St. Paul (the state capital). The Twin Cities area, with a population of 2.3 million, provides an unusual combination of the personal and the cosmopolitan. It is home to the Tyrone Guthrie Theatre and the St. Paul Chamber orchestra, as well as a rich array of locally cherished theater, music, and arts organizations. It is also a thriving center of commerce, with major corporate headquarters in electronics and computers, food processing, retailing, and transportation. The area consistently ranks near the top on quality-of-life and residential satisfaction ratings, thanks in part to an extensive park system that covers 12,500 acres and includes more than 200 lakes. Residents may also drive a few hours north to the Boundary Waters Canoe Area Wilderness, one of the most unsullied wilderness areas in the nation.

The University and The Program

The University of Minnesota awarded its first Ph.D. in 1888. The biophysical sciences program, dating back to the early 1950s, is administered by the Graduate School of the University of Minnesota but involves collaborative teaching and research efforts from the Medical School. The program offers opportunities for interdisciplinary research and collaboration among clinical faculty members from the Fairview University Hospital, basic sciences departments, engineering, statistics, and computer science. Faculty members and students interact in Hospital, Medical School, and Graduate School projects. The Hospital and Medical School are internationally known for programs in bone marrow transplant, artificial organ development, and functional neurological imaging.

Applying

Applicants are required to possess strong backgrounds in physics and math with some course work in chemistry, biology or anatomy, and physiology. GRE General Test scores and three letters of recommendation are required to apply. International applicants must receive TOEFL scores above 550. Applicants are encouraged to submit materials early for fall consideration.

Correspondence and Information

E. Russell Ritenour
Department of Radiology, Box 292 UMHC
University of Minnesota School of Medicine
420 Delaware Street, SE
Minneapolis, Minnesota 55455

Phone: 612-626-0131
Fax: 612-626-1951
E-mail: riten001@tc.umn.edu
Web site: http://www.drad.umn.edu/faculty/geise/BPHY2.htm

University of Minnesota

THE FACULTY AND THEIR RESEARCH

Dwight L. Anderson, Ph.D. Structure and assembly of bacterial viruses.

Vincent Barnett, Ph.D. Correlation of mechanical response and molecular dynamics of muscle proteins, studies of the biochemical and physiological interaction of myosin and actin and the elasticity of titin. Techniques include electron paramagnetic resonance spectroscopy (EPR), measurement of muscle stiffness, and force generation.

Victor A. Bloomfield, Ph.D. Ion-induced transition in DNA, hydrodynamic theory, quasi-electric light scattering, dynamics of concentrated biopolymer solutions.

Bianca M. Conti-Fine, M.D. Neurobiochemistry and neuropharmacology.

Ralph DeLong, Ph.D. Robotics as applied to reproducing mandibular movement, three-dimensional digitalization of anatomic structures and computer graphics, wear of dental materials and oral anatomic structures, computer modeling of the masticatory system.

William H. Douglas, Ph.D. Robotics as applied to reproducing mandibular movement, three-dimensional digitalization of anatomic structures and computer graphics, wear of dental materials and oral anatomic structures, computer modeling of masticatory system.

Stanley M. Finkelstein, Ph.D. Hemodynamic impedance properties of peripheral vasculature, respiratory and cardiovascular simulation, monitoring of long-term care for chronic diseases, biomedical signal processing.

John E. Foker, M.D., Ph.D. Myocardial metabolism.

Michael G. Garwood, Ph.D. Magnetic resonance imaging and spectroscopy methods, the design of improved radio frequency pulses, pulse sequences to localize spectroscopic signals to specific tissues or organs of interest, fast imaging, application of these methods to investigate brain tumor metabolism in animals and humans.

Richard A. Geise, Ph.D. Radiation dose determination, particularly bone dosimetry from high-dose interventional procedures; evaluation of radiologic equipment performance, particularly mammography and computer tomography systems; dosimetry and performance evaluation of shock wave lithotripters, particularly by measurement of cavitation.

Bruce J. Gerbi, Ph.D. Ionization chamber response characteristics in high-energy proton and electron beams, electron contamination determination in high-energy proton beams, deposition of radiation dose for obliquely incident photon beams.

Rolf Gruetter, Ph.D. Study of biochemical pathways and physiology using NMR spectroscopy (MRI); interdisciplinary approaches to study regulation of metabolism in health and disease, such as combining MRS with PET, MRS with functional anatomic imaging, and MRS with molecular biology/gene therapy.

Bruce Hammer, Ph.D. Nuclear magnetic resonance imaging and spectroscopy.

Bruce E. Hasselquist, Ph.D. Computer modeling of imaging in nuclear medicine, including the effects of attenuation and scatter in single photon emission computed tomography; simultaneous dual isotope imaging in nuclear medicine.

Patrick Higgins, Ph.D. Radiation dosimetry, basic mechanisms of radiation interaction with matter using measurements and computer models, quantification of dose distributions in tissues against biological or clinical endpoints, thermal dosimetry and heat transport modeling for hyperthermia.

Russell K. Hobbie, Ph.D. Radiological physics.

James Holte, Ph.D. Technologies that support the delivery of high-quality health care at lower costs, including instrumentation, biological system modeling, and the creation of readily searchable database structures; flow of information, material, and people in the medical enterprise, using sensors, signal analysis, information capture, and storage (real-time measurement and long-term archiving).

Xiaoping Hu, Ph.D. Acquisition, reconstruction, processing, and visualization of medical imaging data and application of medical imaging techniques, with emphasis on magnetic resonance imaging and spectroscopy.

Michael Jerosch-Herold, Ph.D. Magnetic resonance imaging methods for functional evaluation of tissues or organs, in particular the heart; magnetic resonance perfusion imaging; tracer kinetic modeling for quantification of tissue blood flow; image processing for evaluation of heart function; application of MRI methods to experimental models of coronary artery disease.

Faiz M. Khan, Ph.D. Dosimetry of electron and photon beams radiotherapy treatment planning, portal electron imaging.

Seong-Gi Kim, Ph.D. Mapping the development and plasticity of the columnar organization in the mammalian cortex; development and application of columnar-resolution fMRI methods and their verification using single-unit and optical-imaging techniques.

Jeih-San Liow, Ph.D. Optimization of data acquisition, image reconstruction/processing, compartmental modeling and statistical analysis techniques for quantitative positron emission tomography (PET).

Merle K. Loken, M.D., Ph.D. Development and evaluation of radiopharmaceutical and instrumentation (including use of computers) for establishing new procedures in the practice of nuclear medicine.

Rex E. Lovrien, Ph.D. Enzymology, calorimetry, thermochemistry of biochemical reactions, development of new legends and methods for separations, protection, confirmation control, cocrystallization of proteins.

Robert Margolis, Ph.D. Biophysics of the middle ear: measuring the impedance in the ear canal of human and animal subjects with normal auditory function and with various ear pathologies; inner ear electrophysiology: auditory-evoked potentials that originate in the inner ear and auditory neural pathway.

Scott M. O'Grady, M.D. Mechanisms and regulation of electrolyte transport across epithelial tissues, role of electroneutral cotransport and exchange mechanisms in vectorial salt and water transport in epithelia, regulation of cell volume and intracellular pH.

Richard E. Poppele, Ph.D. Mammalian muscle spindles, mechanical properties of muscle, the nature of the transduction mechanism, encoding of muscle receptor information within the central nervous system.

Kelly Rehm, Ph.D. Digital image processing and evaluation; analysis and visualization of three-dimensional brain image volumes acquired by PET, MRI, and fMRI.

Stephen J. Riederer, Ph.D. The physics and engineering of diagnostic medical imaging systems, especially magnetic resonance imaging (MRI); high-speed MR image acquisition and reconstruction, vascular MRI and MR angiography, compensation for motion during MR image acquisition.

E. Russell Ritenour, Ph.D. Performance evaluation of radiologic imaging systems, specific absorption rate calculation for magnetic resonance imaging (MRI), ultrasound-induced mutation in mammalian cells, ultrasound dosimetry.

Andreas Rosenberg, Ph.D. Dynamics of protein structure, studies by methods such as fluorescence quenching and isotope exchange kinetics, structure-function relationships in red-cell cytoskeleton, studies by partial reconstruction of membrane structures.

Chang W. Song, Ph.D. Biological effects of radiation, vascular function in tumors and normal tissues, radiosensitization and radioprotection, microelectrode method to measure tissue pH and p02, ion transport through the cell membrane.

Arthur E. Stillman, M.D., Ph.D. Proton magnetic resonance spectroscopy of the brain for following treatment effects, functional magnetic resonance imaging of the brain for therapy planning.

Stephen Strother, Ph.D. Medical imaging, particularly positron emission tomography (PET) and magnetic resonance imaging (MRI), with emphasis on parameter estimation, optimal model selection, and artificial neural networks for functional activation studies of the brain.

David D. Thomas, Ph.D. Spectroscopic studies of molecular dynamics in energy transducing ATPase of muscle; myosin, actin, muscle fibers, sarcoplasmic reticulum, calcium transport, ATPase; electron paramagnetic resonance (EPR), phosphorescence, fluorescence.

Kamil Ugurbil, Ph.D. Development of magnetic resonance methods and their applications in vivo for obtaining physiological, functional, anatomical, and biochemical information noninvasively; functional mapping in the human brain; cardiac bioenergetics.

Warren J. Warwick, Ph.D. New models of the function of the lung, noninvasive measurements of physiologic functions, integration of computer technology in the practice of medicine, mucous transport in the airway, water balance in the lungs, total body water and body composition analysis, allometric effects seen in physiologic tests during growth.

Clare K. Woodward, Ph.D. Protein structure and dynamics, protein folding, construction and physical-chemical characterization of protein variants produced by site-directed mutagenesis, NMR, hydrogen exchange, colorimetry, protein engineering, computer-based molecular modeling of proteins, molecular graphics of proteins.

Section 29
Health Services

This section contains a directory of institutions offering graduate work in health services. Additional information about programs listed in the directory may be obtained by writing directly to the dean of a graduate school or chair of a department at the address given in the directory.

For programs offering related work, see also in this book *Allied Health, Business Administration and Management, Nursing,* and *Public Health.*

CONTENTS

Program Directories

Close-Ups

Health Services Management and Hospital Administration

Alaska Pacific University, Graduate Programs, Business Administration Department, Program in Business Administration, Anchorage, AK 99508-4672. Offers business administration (MBA); health services administration (MBA). Part-time and evening/weekend programs available. *Degree requirements:* For master's, capstone course. *Entrance requirements:* For master's, GMAT or GRE General Test, minimum GPA of 3.0.

Albany State University, College of Arts and Humanities, Department of History, Political Science and Public Administration, Albany, GA 31705-2717. Offers community and economic development administration (MPA); criminal justice administration (MPA); fiscal management (MPA); general management (MPA); health administration and policy (MPA); human resources management (MPA); public policy (MPA); water resource management and policy (MPA). *Accreditation:* NASPAA. *Students:* 17 full-time (11 women), 43 part-time (29 women); includes 57 minority (56 African Americans, 1 Asian American or Pacific Islander). Average age 34. 21 applicants, 100% accepted, 17 enrolled. In 2009, 17 master's awarded. *Entrance requirements:* For master's, GRE or MAT. *Application deadline:* For fall admission, 11/16 for domestic students, 9/16 for international students; for spring admission, 4/19 for domestic students, 2/19 for international students. Applications are processed on a rolling basis. Application fee: $20. Electronic applications accepted. *Expenses:* Tuition, state resident: full-time $2970; part-time $162 per credit hour. Tuition, nonresident: full-time $12,168; part-time $676 per credit hour. Required fees: $962; $75 per credit hour. *Financial support:* Application deadline: 6/30. *Faculty research:* Public policy, strategic public human resources and human capital management, diversity management in the public sector and collective bargaining and labor relations in the public sector, e-government and public sector information systems, public administration pedagogy and business process modeling simulation, funded research- community development, non profit organizations, civic engagement and civic participation, health care disparities among minorities and poverty. Total annual research expenditures: $26,000. *Unit head:* Dr. Peter Ngwafu, Director, 229-430-4873, Fax: 229-430-7895, E-mail: peter.ngwafu@asurams.edu. *Application contact:* Nicole Lane, Interim Graduate Admissions Officer, 229-430-4862, Fax: 229-430-6398, E-mail: nicole.lane@asurams.edu.

American InterContinental University Online, Program in Business Administration, Hoffman Estates, IL 60192. Offers accounting and finance (MBA); finance (MBA); healthcare management (MBA); human resource management (MBA); international business (MBA); management (MBA); marketing (MBA); operations management (MBA); organizational psychology and development (MBA); project management (MBA). Evening/weekend programs available. Postbaccalaureate distance learning degree programs offered (no on-campus study). *Entrance requirements:* Additional exam requirements/recommendations for international students: Required—TOEFL (minimum score 550 paper-based; 213 computer-based). Electronic applications accepted.

American Sentinel University, Graduate Programs, Englewood, CO 80112. Offers business administration (MBA); business intelligence (MS); computer science (MSCS); health information management (MS); healthcare (MBA); information systems (MSIS); nursing (MSN). Part-time and evening/weekend programs available. Postbaccalaureate distance learning degree programs offered (no on-campus study). *Entrance requirements:* Additional exam requirements/recommendations for international students: Required—TOEFL (minimum score 600 paper-based; 215 computer-based). Electronic applications accepted.

The American University in Dubai, Master in Business Administration Program, Dubai, United Arab Emirates. Offers general (MBA); healthcare management (MBA); international finance (MBA); international marketing (MBA); management of construction enterprises (MBA). Part-time and evening/weekend programs available. *Degree requirements:* For master's, thesis optional. *Entrance requirements:* For master's, GMAT, Interview. Additional exam requirements/recommendations for international students: Required—TOEFL (minimum score 550 paper-based; 213 computer-based; 79 iBT). Electronic applications accepted.

Andrew Jackson University, Brian Tracy College of Business and Entrepreneurship, Birmingham, AL 35244. Offers entrepreneurship (MBA); finance (MBA); health services management (MBA); hospitality and tourism management (MBA); human resource management (MBA); international business (MBA); management (MBA); marketing (MBA). Part-time and evening/weekend programs available. Postbaccalaureate distance learning degree programs offered (no on-campus study). *Entrance requirements:* For master's, course work in calculus, statistics, macroeconomics. Additional exam requirements/recommendations for international students: Required—TOEFL (minimum score 550 paper-based; 213 computer-based). Electronic applications accepted.

Aquinas Institute of Theology, Graduate and Professional Programs, St. Louis, MO 63108. Offers biblical studies (Certificate); health care mission (MAHCM); ministry (M Div); pastoral care (Certificate); pastoral ministry (MAPM); pastoral studies (MAPS); preaching (D Min); spiritual direction (Certificate); theology (M Div, MA); Thomistic studies (Certificate); M Div/MA; MAPS/MSW. *Accreditation:* ATS (one or more programs are accredited). Part-time and evening/weekend programs available. Postbaccalaureate distance learning degree programs offered (minimal on-campus study). *Faculty:* 17 full-time (10 women), 4 part-time/adjunct (2 women). *Students:* 65 full-time (21 women), 179 part-time (108 women); includes 37 minority (16 African Americans, 1 American Indian/Alaska Native, 8 Asian Americans or Pacific Islanders, 12 Hispanic Americans), 7 international. Average age 41. 39 applicants, 87% accepted, 27 enrolled. In 2009, 31 master's, 11 doctorates awarded. *Degree requirements:* For master's, one foreign language, comprehensive exam, thesis or major paper; for doctorate, thesis/dissertation. *Entrance requirements:* For M Div, master's, and Certificate, MAT; for doctorate, 3 years of ministerial experience, 6 hours of graduate course work in homiletics, M Div or the equivalent, minimum GPA of 3.0. Additional exam requirements/recommendations for international students: Required—TOEFL. *Application deadline:* For fall admission, 3/15 priority date for domestic and international students; for spring admission, 11/15 priority date for domestic and international students. Applications are processed on a rolling basis. Application fee: $50. *Expenses:* Tuition: Full-time $14,784; part-time $616 per credit hour. Required fees: $195 per semester. *Financial support:* Career-related internships or fieldwork, scholarships/grants, health care benefits, and tuition waivers (partial) available. Support available to part-time students. Financial award application deadline: 3/15; financial award applicants required to submit CSS PROFILE or FAFSA. *Faculty research:* Theology of preaching, hermeneutics, lay ecclesial ministry, pastoral and practical theology. *Unit head:* Fr. Gregory Heille, Academic Dean, 314-256-8800, Fax: 314-256-8888, E-mail: heille@ai.edu. *Application contact:* David Werthmann, Director of Admissions, 314-256-8806, Fax: 314-256-8888, E-mail: admissions@ai.edu.

Argosy University, Atlanta, College of Business, Atlanta, GA 30328. Offers accounting (DBA); corporate compliance (MBA); customized professional concentration (MBA, DBA); finance (MBA); healthcare administration (MBA); information systems (DBA); information systems management (MBA); international business (MBA, DBA); management (MBA, MSM, DBA); marketing (MBA, DBA).

See Close-Up on page 197.

Argosy University, Chicago, College of Business, Chicago, IL 60601. Offers accounting (DBA); customized professional concentration (MBA, DBA); finance (MBA); fraud examination (MBA); global business sustainability (DBA); healthcare administration (MBA); information systems (DBA); information systems management (MBA); international business (MBA, DBA); management (MBA, MSM, DBA); marketing (MBA, DBA); organizational leadership (Ed D); public administration (MBA); sustainable management (MBA). Postbaccalaureate distance learning degree programs offered (minimal on-campus study).

See Close-Up on page 199.

Argosy University, Dallas, College of Business, Farmers Branch, TX 75244. Offers accounting (DBA, AGC); corporate compliance (MBA, Graduate Certificate); customized professional concentration (MBA); finance (MBA, Graduate Certificate); fraud examination (MBA, Graduate Certificate); global business sustainability (DBA, AGC); healthcare administration (Graduate Certificate); healthcare management (MBA); information systems (MBA, DBA, AGC); information systems management (Graduate Certificate); international business (MBA, DBA, AGC, Graduate Certificate); management (MBA, DBA, AGC, Graduate Certificate); marketing (MBA, DBA, AGC, Graduate Certificate); public administration (MBA, Graduate Certificate); sustainable management (MBA, Graduate Certificate).

See Close-Up on page 201.

Argosy University, Denver, College of Business, Denver, CO 80231. Offers accounting (DBA); corporate compliance (MBA); customized professional concentration (MBA, DBA); finance (MBA); fraud examination (MBA); global business sustainability (DBA); healthcare administration (MBA); information systems (DBA); information systems management (MBA); international business (MBA, DBA); management (MBA, MSM, DBA); marketing (MBA, DBA); organizational leadership (Ed D); public administration (MBA); sustainable management (MBA).

See Close-Up on page 203.

Argosy University, Hawai'i, College of Business, Honolulu, HI 96813. Offers accounting (DBA); corporate compliance (MBA); customized professional concentration (MBA, DBA); finance (MBA, Certificate); fraud examination (MBA); global business sustainability (DBA); healthcare administration (MBA, Certificate); information systems (DBA); information systems management (MBA, Certificate); international business (MBA, DBA, Certificate); management (MBA, MSM, DBA); marketing (MBA, DBA, Certificate); organizational leadership (Ed D); public administration (MBA); sustainable management (MBA).

See Close-Up on page 205.

Argosy University, Inland Empire, College of Business, San Bernardino, CA 92408. Offers accounting (DBA); corporate compliance (MBA); customized professional concentration (MBA, DBA); finance (MBA); fraud examination (MBA); global business sustainability (DBA); healthcare administration (MBA); information systems (DBA); information systems management (MBA); international business (MBA, DBA); management (MBA, MSM, DBA); marketing (MBA, DBA); organizational leadership (Ed D); public administration (MBA); sustainable management (MBA).

See Close-Up on page 207.

Argosy University, Los Angeles, College of Business, Santa Monica, CA 90045. Offers accounting (DBA); corporate compliance (MBA); customized professional concentration (MBA, DBA); finance (MBA); fraud examination (MBA); global business sustainability (DBA); healthcare administration (MBA); information systems (DBA); information systems management (MBA); international business (MBA, DBA); management (MBA, MSM, DBA); marketing (MBA, DBA); organizational leadership (Ed D); public administration (MBA); sustainable management (MBA).

See Close-Up on page 209.

Argosy University, Nashville, College of Business, Nashville, TN 37214. Offers accounting (DBA); customized professional concentration (MBA, DBA); finance (MBA); healthcare administration (MBA); information systems (MBA, DBA); international business (MBA, DBA); management (MBA, MSM, DBA); marketing (MBA, DBA).

See Close-Up on page 211.

Argosy University, Orange County, College of Business, Orange, CA 92868. Offers accounting (DBA, Adv C); corporate compliance (MBA); customized professional concentration (MBA, DBA); finance (MBA, Certificate); fraud examination (MBA); global business sustainability (DBA); healthcare administration (MBA, Certificate); information systems (DBA, Adv C, Certificate); information systems management (MBA); international business (MBA, DBA, Adv C, Certificate); management (MBA, MSM, DBA, Adv C); marketing (MBA, DBA, Adv C, Certificate); organizational leadership (Ed D); public administration (MBA, Certificate); sustainable management (MBA).

See Close-Up on page 213.

Argosy University, Phoenix, College of Business, Phoenix, AZ 85021. Offers accounting (DBA); corporate compliance (MBA); customized professional concentration (MBA, DBA); finance (MBA); fraud examination (MBA); global business sustainability (DBA); healthcare administration (MBA); information systems (DBA); information systems management (MBA); international business (MBA, DBA); management (MBA, DBA); marketing (MBA, DBA); public administration (MBA); sustainable management (MBA).

See Close-Up on page 215.

Argosy University, Salt Lake City, College of Business, Draper, UT 84020. Offers accounting (DBA); corporate compliance (MBA); customized professional concentration (MBA, DBA); finance (MBA); fraud examination (MBA); global business sustainability (DBA); healthcare administration (MBA); information systems (DBA); information systems management (MBA); international business (MBA, DBA); management (MBA, DBA); marketing (MBA, DBA); public administration (MBA); sustainable management (MBA).

See Close-Up on page 217.

Argosy University, San Francisco Bay Area, College of Business, Alameda, CA 94501. Offers accounting (DBA); corporate compliance (MBA); customized professional concentration (MBA, DBA); finance (MBA); fraud examination (MBA); global business sustainability (DBA); healthcare administration (MBA); information systems (DBA); information systems management (MBA); international business (MBA, DBA); management (MBA, MSM, DBA); marketing (MBA, DBA); organizational leadership (Ed D); public administration (MBA); sustainable management (MBA).

See Close-Up on page 221.

Argosy University, Sarasota, College of Business, Sarasota, FL 34235. Offers accounting (DBA, Adv C); corporate compliance (MBA, DBA, Certificate); customized professional concentration (MBA, DBA); finance (MBA, Certificate); fraud examination (MBA, Certificate); global business sustainability (DBA, Adv C); healthcare administration (MBA, Certificate); information systems (DBA, Adv C, Certificate); information systems management (MBA); international business (MBA, DBA, Adv C, Certificate); management (MBA, MSM, DBA, Adv C, Certificate); marketing (MBA, DBA, Adv C, Certificate); organizational leadership (Ed D); public administration (MBA, Certificate); sustainable management (MBA, Certificate).

See Close-Up on page 223.

Argosy University, Schaumburg, College of Business, Schaumburg, IL 60173-5403. Offers accounting (DBA, Adv C); customized professional concentration (MBA, DBA); finance (MBA, Certificate); fraud examination (MBA); global business sustainability (DBA); healthcare administration (MBA, Certificate); information systems (DBA, Adv C, Certificate); information systems management (MBA); international business (MBA, DBA, Adv C, Certificate); management (MBA, MSM, DBA, Adv C, Certificate); marketing (MBA, DBA, Adv C, Certificate); organizational leadership (Ed D); public administration (MBA); sustainable management (MBA).

See Close-Up on page 225.

Argosy University, Seattle, College of Business, Seattle, WA 98121. Offers accounting (DBA); corporate compliance (MBA); customized professional concentration (MBA, DBA); finance (MBA); fraud examination (MBA); global business sustainability (DBA); healthcare administration (MBA); information systems (DBA); information systems management (MBA); international business (MBA, DBA); management (MBA, MSM, DBA); marketing (MBA, DBA); organizational leadership (Ed D); public administration (MBA); sustainable management (MBA).

See Close-Up on page 227.

Argosy University, Tampa, College of Business, Tampa, FL 33607. Offers accounting (DBA); corporate compliance (MBA); customized professional concentration (MBA, DBA); finance (MBA); fraud examination (MBA); global business sustainability (DBA); healthcare administration (MBA); information systems (DBA); information systems management (MBA); international business (MBA, DBA); management (MBA, MSM, DBA); marketing (MBA, DBA); organizational leadership (Ed D); public administration (MBA); sustainable management (MBA).

See Close-Up on page 229.

Argosy University, Twin Cities, College of Business, Eagan, MN 55121. Offers accounting (DBA); customized professional concentration (MBA, DBA); finance (MBA); fraud examination (MBA); global business sustainability (DBA); healthcare administration (MBA); information systems (DBA); information systems management (MBA); international business (MBA, DBA); management (MBA, MSM, DBA); marketing (MBA, DBA); organizational leadership (Ed D); public administration (MBA); sustainable management (MBA).

See Close-Up on page 231.

Argosy University, Twin Cities, College of Health Sciences, Eagan, MN 55121. Offers health services management (MS).

Argosy University, Washington DC, College of Business, Arlington, VA 22209. Offers accounting (DBA); customized professional concentration (MBA, DBA); finance (MBA); fraud examination (MBA); global business sustainability (DBA); healthcare administration (MBA); information systems (DBA); information systems management (MBA); international business (MBA, DBA, Certificate); management (MBA, MSM, DBA); marketing (MBA, DBA, Certificate); organizational leadership (Ed D); public administration (MBA); sustainable management (MBA).

See Close-Up on page 233.

Arizona State University, Graduate College, College of Design, Program in Design, Tempe, AZ 85287. Offers arts/media/engineering (MSD); healthcare and healing environments (MSD); industrial design (MSD); interaction design (MSD); interior design (MSD); new product innovation (MSD); visual communication design (MSD). *Accreditation:* NASAD. *Degree requirements:* For master's, thesis optional. *Entrance requirements:* For master's, GRE General Test, design portfolio.

Arizona State University, Graduate College, W.P. Carey School of Business, Program in Business Administration, Tempe, AZ 85287. Offers agribusiness (PhD); business administration (MBA); finance (MBA, PhD); health sector management (MBA); information systems (PhD); management (MBA, PhD); marketing (MBA, PhD); supply chain management (MBA, PhD); JD/MBA; MBA/M Arch; MBA/MHSM. *Accreditation:* AACSB. *Degree requirements:* For master's, thesis optional; for doctorate, thesis/dissertation. *Entrance requirements:* For master's, GMAT.

Arizona State University, Graduate College, W.P. Carey School of Business, School of Health Management and Policy, Tempe, AZ 85287. Offers health sector management (MHSM); urban health (MPH); MBA/MHSM. *Accreditation:* CAHME. *Entrance requirements:* For master's, GMAT.

Armstrong Atlantic State University, School of Graduate Studies, Program in Health Science, Savannah, GA 31419-1997. Offers health services administration (MHSA); public health (MPH). *Accreditation:* CAHME; CEPH. Part-time and evening/weekend programs available. Postbaccalaureate distance learning degree programs offered (no on-campus study). *Degree requirements:* For master's, comprehensive exam, thesis optional, internship. *Entrance requirements:* For master's, GMAT or GRE General Test, MAT, minimum GPA of 2.6. Additional exam requirements/recommendations for international students: Required—TOEFL (minimum score 523 paper-based; 193 computer-based). Electronic applications accepted. *Faculty research:* Health administration, community health, health education.

A.T. Still University of Health Sciences, School of Health Management, Kirksville, MO 63501. Offers geriatric healthcare (MGH); health administration (MHA); health education (MH Ed, DH Ed); public health (MPH). Part-time and evening/weekend programs available. Postbaccalaureate distance learning degree programs offered (minimal on-campus study). *Faculty:* 12 full-time (6 women), 31 part-time/adjunct (12 women). *Students:* 84 full-time (59 women), 503 part-time (340 women); includes 179 minority (103 African Americans, 11 American Indian/Alaska Native, 37 Asian Americans or Pacific Islanders, 28 Hispanic Americans). Average age 32. 179 applicants, 100% accepted, 98 enrolled. In 2009, 98 master's, 22 doctorates awarded. *Degree requirements:* For master's, thesis (for some programs), integrated terminal project; for doctorate, thesis/dissertation. *Entrance requirements:* For master's, minimum GPA of 2.5, bachelor's degree or equivalent from U.S. institution; for doctorate, minimum GPA of 2.5, master's or terminal degree, employment. Additional exam requirements/recommendations for international students: Required—TOEFL (minimum score 550 paper-based; 213 computer-based; 80 iBT). *Application deadline:* For fall admission, 8/7 for domestic and international students; for winter admission, 10/23 for domestic and international students; for spring admission, 2/5 for domestic and international students. Applications are processed on a rolling basis. Application fee: $60. Electronic applications accepted. *Expenses:* Contact institution. *Financial support:* In 2009–10, 408 students received support. Application deadline: 5/1. *Unit head:* Dr. Kimberly O'Reilly, Interim Dean, 660-626-2820, Fax: 660-626-2826, E-mail: koreilley@atsu.edu. *Application contact:* Sarah Spencer, Director of Recruitment, 660-626-2820 Ext. 2669, Fax: 660-626-2826, E-mail: sbartlett@atsu.edu.

Avila University, School of Business, Kansas City, MO 64145-1698. Offers accounting (MBA); finance (MBA); general management (MBA); health care administration (MBA); international business (MBA); management information systems (MBA); marketing (MBA). Part-time and evening/weekend programs available. *Faculty:* 9 full-time (3 women), 24 part-time/adjunct (5 women). *Students:* 148 full-time (71 women), 86 part-time (47 women); includes 56 minority (36 African Americans, 2 American Indian/Alaska Native, 13 Asian Americans or Pacific Islanders, 5 Hispanic Americans), 63 international. Average age 32. 53 applicants, 75% accepted, 40 enrolled. In 2009, 93 master's awarded. *Degree requirements:* For master's, comprehensive exam, capstone course. *Entrance requirements:* For master's, GMAT, minimum GPA of 3.0, interview. Additional exam requirements/recommendations for international students: Required—TOEFL (minimum score 550 paper-based). *Application deadline:* For fall admission, 7/30 priority date for domestic students, 7/30 for international students; for winter admission, 11/30 priority date for domestic students, 11/30 for international students; for spring admission, 2/28 priority date for domestic students, 2/28 for international students. Applications are processed on a rolling basis. Application fee: $0. Electronic applications accepted. *Expenses:* Contact institution. *Financial support:* In 2009–10, 102 students received support. Career-related internships or fieldwork available. Support available to part-time students. Financial award applicants required to submit FAFSA. *Faculty research:* Leadership characteristics, financial hedging, group dynamics. *Unit head:* Dr. Richard Woodall, Dean, 816-501-3720, Fax: 816-501-2463, E-mail: richard.woodall@avila.edu. *Application contact:* JoAnna Giffin, MBA Admissions Director, 816-501-3601, Fax: 816-501-2463, E-mail: joanna.giffin@avila.edu.

Baker College Center for Graduate Studies—Online, Graduate Programs—Online, Flint, MI 48507-9843. Offers accounting (MBA); business administration (DBA); finance (MBA); general business (MBA); health care management (MBA); human resources management (MBA); information management (MBA); leadership studies (MBA); management information systems (MSIS); marketing (MBA). Part-time and evening/weekend programs available. Postbaccalaureate distance learning degree programs offered. *Faculty:* 750. *Students:* 500 full-time, 500 part-time. Average age 37. *Degree requirements:* For master's, portfolio. *Entrance requirements:* For master's, 3 years of work experience, minimum undergraduate GPA of 2.5, writing sample, 3 letters of recommendation; for doctorate, MBA or acceptable related master's degree from accredited association, 5 years work experience, minimum graduate GPA of 3.25, writing sample, 3 professional references. Additional exam requirements/recommendations for international students: Required—TOEFL (minimum score 550 paper-based; 213 computer-based). *Application deadline:* For fall admission, 8/6 priority date for domestic students; for winter admission, 12/15 priority date for domestic students; for spring admission, 2/15 priority date for domestic students. Applications are processed on a rolling basis. Application fee: $25. Electronic applications accepted. *Expenses:* Tuition: Part-time $330 per credit hour. Tuition and fees vary according to degree level. *Financial support:* Scholarships/grants available. Support available to part-time students. Financial award applicants required to submit FAFSA. *Unit head:* Dr. Julia Teahen, President, 810-766-4023, Fax: 810-766-4399, E-mail: julia@baker.edu. *Application contact:* Chuck J. Gurden, Vice President for Graduate and Online Admissions, 800-469-3165, Fax: 810-766-4399, E-mail: adm-ol@baker.edu.

Baldwin-Wallace College, Graduate Programs, Division of Business, Program in Health Care Management, Berea, OH 44017-2088. Offers MBA. Part-time and evening/weekend programs available. *Students:* 34 full-time (22 women), 13 part-time (7 women); includes 4 minority (3 African Americans, 1 Asian American or Pacific Islander). Average age 37. 14 applicants, 71% accepted, 8 enrolled. In 2009, 17 master's awarded. *Entrance requirements:* For master's, GMAT, interview, work experience, bachelor's degree in any field. Additional exam requirements/recommendations for international students: Required—TOEFL (minimum score 523 paper-based; 193 computer-based; 70 iBT). *Application deadline:* For fall admission, 7/23 priority date for domestic students, 4/30 priority date for international students; for spring admission, 12/10 priority date for domestic students, 9/30 priority date for international students. Applications are processed on a rolling basis. Application fee: $25. Electronic applications accepted. *Expenses:* Tuition: Full-time $14,174; part-time $682 per credit. Tuition and fees vary according to program. *Financial support:* Career-related internships or fieldwork available. Support available to part-time students. Financial award application deadline: 5/1; financial award applicants required to submit FAFSA. *Unit head:* Tom Campanella, Director, 440-826-3818, Fax: 440-826-3868, E-mail: tcampane@bw.edu. *Application contact:* Barbara Peterson, Graduate Business Coordinator, 440-826-2064, Fax: 440-826-3868, E-mail: bpeterson@bw.edu.

Barry University, Andreas School of Business, Graduate Certificate Programs, Miami Shores, FL 33161-6695. Offers finance (Certificate); health services administration (Certificate); international business (Certificate); management (Certificate); management information systems (Certificate); marketing (Certificate).

Barry University, College of Health Sciences, Graduate Certificate Programs, Miami Shores, FL 33161-6695. Offers health care leadership (Certificate); health care planning and informatics (Certificate); histotechnology (Certificate); long term care management (Certificate); medical group practice management (Certificate); quality improvement and outcomes management (Certificate).

Barry University, College of Health Sciences, Program in Health Services Administration, Miami Shores, FL 33161-6695. Offers MS. Part-time and evening/weekend programs available. *Degree requirements:* For master's, comprehensive exam. *Entrance requirements:* For master's, GMAT or GRE General Test, 2 years of experience in the health field, minimum GPA of 3.0, 1 semester of course work in computer applications or the equivalent (business). Electronic applications accepted.

Baylor University, Graduate School, Military Programs, Program in Health Care Administration, Waco, TX 76798. Offers MHA. Offered jointly with the U. S. Army. *Accreditation:* CAHME. *Students:* 76 full-time (30 women); includes 15 minority (6 African Americans, 5 Asian Americans or Pacific Islanders, 4 Hispanic Americans). In 2009, 40 master's awarded. *Entrance requirements:* For master's, GRE General Test. *Application deadline:* For fall admission, 6/15 for domestic students. Applications are processed on a rolling basis. Application fee: $25. *Faculty research:* Data quality, public health policy, organizational behavior, AIDS. *Unit head:* Lt. Cdr. Lee Bewley, Graduate Program Director, 210-221-8857 Ext. 6443, E-mail: lee.bewley@us.army.mil. *Application contact:* Rene Pryor, Program Administrator, 210-221-6443, Fax: 210-221-6010, E-mail: rene.pryor@cen.amedd.army.mil.

Bellevue University, Graduate School, Programs in Healthcare Administration, Bellevue, NE 68005-3098. Offers healthcare administration (MHA); human services (MA, MS). Postbaccalaureate distance learning degree programs offered.

Benedictine University, Graduate Programs, Program in Business Administration, Lisle, IL 60532-0900. Offers accounting (MBA); entrepreneurship and managing innovation (MBA); financial management (MBA); health administration (MBA); human resource management (MBA); information systems security (MBA); international business (MBA); management consulting (MBA); management information systems (MBA); marketing management (MBA); operations management and logistics (MBA); organizational leadership (MBA); MBA/MPH; MBA/MS. Part-time and evening/weekend programs available. Postbaccalaureate distance learning degree programs offered (minimal on-campus study). *Faculty:* 4 full-time (2 women), 24 part-time/adjunct (3 women). *Students:* 247 full-time (141 women), 644 part-time (339 women); includes 223 minority (134 African Americans, 5 American Indian/Alaska Native, 44 Asian Americans or Pacific Islanders, 40 Hispanic Americans), 25 international. Average age 34. 287 applicants, 92% accepted, 229 enrolled. In 2009, 219 master's awarded. *Entrance requirements:* For master's, GMAT. Additional exam requirements/recommendations for international students: Required—TOEFL (minimum score 550 paper-based; 213 computer-based). *Application deadline:* For fall admission, 9/1 for domestic students; for winter admission, 12/1 for domestic students; for spring admission, 2/15 for domestic students. Applications are processed on a rolling basis. Application fee: $40. Electronic applications accepted. *Expenses:* Tuition: Part-time $750 per credit hour. Tuition and fees vary according to campus/location and program. *Financial support:* Career-related internships or fieldwork and health care benefits available. Support available to part-time students. *Faculty research:* Strategic leadership in professional organizations, sociology of professions, organizational change, social identity theory, applications to change management. *Unit head:* Dr. Sharon Borowicz, Director, 630-829-6219, E-mail: sborowicz@ben.edu. *Application contact:* Kari Gibbons, Director, Admissions, 630-829-6200, Fax: 630-829-6584, E-mail: kgibbons@ben.edu.

Benedictine University, Graduate Programs, Program in Public Health, Lisle, IL 60532-0900. Offers administration of health care institutions (MPH); dietetics (MPH); disaster management (MPH); health education (MPH); health information systems (MPH); MBA/MPH; MPH/MS. Part-time and evening/weekend programs available. Postbaccalaureate distance learning degree programs offered. *Faculty:* 2 full-time (0 women), 8 part-time/adjunct (3 women). *Students:* 132 full-time (92 women), 354 part-time (286 women); includes 171 minority (112 African Americans, 1 American Indian/Alaska Native, 35 Asian Americans or Pacific Islanders, 23 Hispanic Americans), 14 international. Average age 33. 247 applicants, 94% accepted, 180 enrolled. In 2009, 77 master's awarded. *Entrance requirements:* For master's, MAT, GRE, or GMAT. Additional exam requirements/recommendations for international students: Required—TOEFL (minimum score 550 paper-based; 213 computer-based). *Application deadline:* For fall admission, 9/1 for domestic students; for winter admission, 12/1 for domestic students; for spring admission, 2/15 for domestic students. Application fee: $40. *Expenses:* Tuition: Part-time $750 per credit hour. Tuition and fees vary according to campus/location and program. *Financial support:* Career-related internships or fieldwork and health care benefits available. Support available to part-time students. *Unit head:* Dr. Alan Gorr, Director, 630-829-6566, Fax: 630-960-1126, E-mail: agorr@ben.edu. *Application contact:* Kari Gibbons, Director, Admissions, 630-829-6200, Fax: 630-829-6584, E-mail: kgibbons@ben.edu.

Bernard M. Baruch College of the City University of New York, Zicklin School of Business, Zicklin Executive Programs, Baruch/Mt. Sinai Program in Health Care Administration, New York, NY 10010-5585. Offers MBA. *Accreditation:* CAHME. Part-time and evening/weekend programs available. *Entrance requirements:* For master's, GMAT, personal interview, work experience in health care. Additional exam requirements/recommendations for international

Health Services Management and Hospital Administration

Bernard M. Baruch College of the City University of New York *(continued)*
students: Required—TOEFL. Electronic applications accepted. *Expenses:* Contact institution. *Faculty research:* Economics of reproductive health, multivariate point estimation.

Boston University, School of Management, Master of Business Administration Program, Boston, MA 02215. Offers entrepreneurship (MBA); finance (MBA); health sector management (MBA); international management (MBA); marketing (MBA); operations and technology management (MBA); public and nonprofit management (MBA); strategy and business analysis (MBA); JD/MBA; MBA/MA; MBA/MPH; MBA/MS; MBA/MSIS; MS/MBA. Part-time and evening/weekend programs available. *Faculty:* 119 full-time (31 women), 99 part-time/adjunct (30 women). *Students:* 326 full-time (138 women), 677 part-time (257 women); includes 149 minority (13 African Americans, 119 Asian Americans or Pacific Islanders, 17 Hispanic Americans), 149 international. Average age 30. 1,617 applicants, 38% accepted, 317 enrolled. In 2009, 284 master's awarded. *Entrance requirements:* For master's, GMAT, resume, 2 letters of recommendation. Additional exam requirements/recommendations for international students: Required—TOEFL or IELTS. *Application deadline:* For fall admission, 3/15 for domestic and international students; for spring admission, 11/15 for domestic students. Application fee: $125. Electronic applications accepted. *Expenses:* Tuition: Full-time $37,910; part-time $1184 per credit hour. Required fees: $386; $40 per semester. Part-time tuition and fees vary according to class time, course level, degree level and program. *Financial support:* Career-related internships or fieldwork, Federal Work-Study, institutionally sponsored loans, and scholarships/grants available. Support available to part-time students. Financial award applicants required to submit FAFSA. *Unit head:* Katherine Nolan, Assistant Dean, Graduate Programs, 617-353-4157, Fax: 617-353-5003, E-mail: mba@bu.edu. *Application contact:* Hayden Estrada, Assistant Dean, Admissions, 617-353-2670, Fax: 617-353-7368, E-mail: mba@bu.edu.

Boston University, School of Public Health, Health Policy and Management Department, Boston, MA 02215. Offers health policy and management (MPH); health services research (M Sc, PhD). *Accreditation:* CAHME. Part-time and evening/weekend programs available. *Entrance requirements:* For master's, GRE, MCAT, LSAT, GMAT, or DAT; for doctorate, GRE, MCAT, GMAT, LSAT. Additional exam requirements/recommendations for international students: Required—TOEFL (minimum score 600 paper-based; 250 computer-based; 100 iBT) or IELTS (minimum score 6). *Application deadline:* For fall admission, 2/1 priority date for domestic and international students; for spring admission, 10/15 priority date for domestic and international students. Applications are processed on a rolling basis. Application fee: $95. Electronic applications accepted. *Expenses:* Tuition: Full-time $37,910; part-time $1184 per credit hour. Required fees: $386; $40 per semester. Part-time tuition and fees vary according to class time, course level, degree level and program. *Financial support:* Career-related internships or fieldwork, Federal Work-Study, institutionally sponsored loans, scholarships/grants, and tuition waivers (partial) available. Support available to part-time students. Financial award application deadline: 3/1; financial award applicants required to submit FAFSA. *Unit head:* Dr. Gary Young, Chair, 617-638-5042, E-mail: hlthserv@bu.edu. *Application contact:* LePhan Quan, Assistant Director of Admissions, 617-638-4640, Fax: 617-638-5299, E-mail: asksph@bu.edu.

Brandeis University, The Heller School for Social Policy and Management, Program in Nonprofit Management, Waltham, MA 02454-9110. Offers aging services management (MBA); child, youth, and family management (MBA); health care management (MBA); social impact management (MBA); social policy and management (MBA); sustainable development (MBA); MBA/MA. *Accreditation:* AACSB. Part-time and evening/weekend programs available. *Degree requirements:* For master's, team consulting project. *Entrance requirements:* For master's, GMAT. Additional exam requirements/recommendations for international students: Required—TOEFL (minimum score 600 paper-based). Electronic applications accepted. *Expenses:* Contact institution. *Faculty research:* Health care, child and family, elder and disabled services, general human services.

Brenau University, Graduate Programs, School of Business and Mass Communication, Gainesville, GA 30501. Offers accounting (MBA); business administration (MBA); healthcare management (MBA); organizational leadership (MS); project management (MBA). Part-time and evening/weekend programs available. Postbaccalaureate distance learning degree programs offered (no on-campus study). *Faculty:* 11 full-time (6 women), 22 part-time/adjunct (6 women). *Students:* 116 full-time (74 women), 256 part-time (181 women); includes 113 minority (98 African Americans, 6 Asian Americans or Pacific Islanders, 9 Hispanic Americans), 20 international. Average age 35. 278 applicants, 90% accepted, 185 enrolled. In 2009, 125 master's awarded. *Entrance requirements:* For master's, resume, minimum undergraduate GPA of 3.5. Additional exam requirements/recommendations for international students: Required—TOEFL (minimum score 500 paper-based). *Application deadline:* Applications are processed on a rolling basis. Electronic applications accepted. *Expenses:* Contact institution. *Financial support:* In 2009–10, 1 student received support. Application deadline: 7/15. *Unit head:* Dr. William S. Lightfoot, Dean, 770-538-5330, Fax: 770-537-4701, E-mail: wlightfoot@brenau.edu. *Application contact:* Christina White, Graduate Admissions Specialist, 770-718-5320, Fax: 770-718-5338, E-mail: cwhite@brenau.edu.

Brooklyn College of the City University of New York, Division of Graduate Studies, Department of Health and Nutrition Science, Program in Community Health, Brooklyn, NY 11210-2889. Offers community health education (MA); computer science and health science (MS); health care management (MPH); health care policy and administration (MPH); thanatology (MA). *Accreditation:* CEPH. *Students:* 5 full-time (3 women), 46 part-time (38 women); includes 39 minority (32 African Americans, 5 Asian Americans or Pacific Islanders, 2 Hispanic Americans), 2 international. Average age 36. 22 applicants, 95% accepted, 15 enrolled. In 2009, 9 master's awarded. *Degree requirements:* For master's, thesis or alternative. *Entrance requirements:* For master's, 18 credits, 2 letters of recommendation, essay. Additional exam requirements/recommendations for international students: Required—TOEFL. *Application deadline:* For fall admission, 3/1 priority date for domestic students, 2/1 priority date for international students; for spring admission, 11/1 priority date for domestic students, 10/1 priority date for international students. Applications are processed on a rolling basis. Application fee: $125. Electronic applications accepted. *Expenses:* Tuition, state resident: full-time $7360; part-time $310 per credit hour. Tuition, nonresident: full-time $13,800; part-time $575 per credit hour. Required fees: $140.10 per semester. *Financial support:* Federal Work-Study, institutionally sponsored loans, and scholarships/grants available. Support available to part-time students. Financial award application deadline: 5/1; financial award applicants required to submit FAFSA. *Faculty research:* Diet restriction, religious practices in bereavement, diabetes, stress management, palliative care. *Unit head:* Dr. Elizabeth Eastwood, Graduate Deputy Chairperson, 718-951-5026, Fax: 718-951-4670, E-mail: eastwood@brooklyn.cuny.edu. *Application contact:* Hernan Sierra, Graduate Admissions Coordinator, 718-951-4536, Fax: 718-951-4506, E-mail: grads@brooklyn.cuny.edu.

California Intercontinental University, School of Healthcare, Diamond Bar, CA 91765. Offers healthcare management and leadership (MBA, DBA).

California State University, Bakersfield, Division of Graduate Studies, School of Business and Public Administration, Program in Health Care Management, Bakersfield, CA 93311. Offers MSA. *Entrance requirements:* For master's, GRE.

California State University, Chico, Graduate School, College of Behavioral and Social Sciences, Department of Political Science, Program in Public Administration, Chico, CA 95929-0722. Offers health administration (MPA); local government management (MPA); public administration (MPA). *Accreditation:* NASPAA. Part-time programs available. *Students:* 21 full-time (7 women), 26 part-time (13 women); includes 18 minority (4 African Americans, 1 American Indian/Alaska Native, 5 Asian Americans or Pacific Islanders, 8 Hispanic Americans), 4 international. Average age 31. 44 applicants, 91% accepted, 19 enrolled. In 2009, 10 master's awarded. *Entrance requirements:* For master's, 2 letters of recommendation. Additional exam requirements/recommendations for international students: Required—TOEFL (minimum score 550 paper-based; 213 computer-based; 80 iBT), IELTS (minimum score 6.5). *Application deadline:* For fall admission, 3/1 priority date for domestic students, 3/1 for international

students; for spring admission, 9/15 priority date for domestic students, 9/15 for international students. Applications are processed on a rolling basis. Application fee: $55. Electronic applications accepted. *Financial support:* Fellowships, career-related internships or fieldwork available. *Unit head:* Dr. Donna Kemp, Graduate Coordinator, 530-898-5734. *Application contact:* Dr. Donna Kemp, Graduate Coordinator, 530-898-5734.

California State University, East Bay, Graduate Programs, College of Letters, Arts, and Social Sciences, Department of Public Affairs and Administration, Hayward, CA 94542-3000. Offers health care administration (MS); public administration (MPA). Part-time and evening/weekend programs available. *Faculty:* 8 full-time (4 women), 9 part-time/adjunct (1 woman). *Students:* 48 full-time (30 women), 241 part-time (162 women); includes 147 minority (54 African Americans, 1 American Indian/Alaska Native, 67 Asian Americans or Pacific Islanders, 25 Hispanic Americans), 38 international. Average age 34. 266 applicants, 58% accepted, 100 enrolled. In 2009, 92 master's awarded. *Degree requirements:* For master's, comprehensive exam or thesis. *Entrance requirements:* For master's, minimum GPA of 2.5. Additional exam requirements/recommendations for international students: Required—TOEFL (minimum score 550 paper-based; 213 computer-based). *Application deadline:* For fall admission, 4/15 for domestic students. Application fee: $55. Electronic applications accepted. *Financial support:* Fellowships, teaching assistantships, career-related internships or fieldwork, Federal Work-Study, institutionally sponsored loans, and scholarships/grants available. Support available to part-time students. Financial award application deadline: 3/1; financial award applicants required to submit FAFSA. *Unit head:* Prof. Toni Fogarty, Chair, 510-885-2268, Fax: 510-885-3726, E-mail: toni.fogarty@csueastbay.edu. *Application contact:* Donna Wiley, Interim Associate Director, 510-885-2928, Fax: 510-885-4777, E-mail: donna.wiley@csueastbay.edu.

California State University, Fresno, Division of Graduate Studies, College of Health and Human Services, Department of Public Health, Fresno, CA 93740-8027. Offers health policy and management (MPH); health promotion (MPH). *Accreditation:* CEPH. Part-time and evening/weekend programs available. *Degree requirements:* For master's, thesis or alternative. *Entrance requirements:* For master's, GRE General Test, minimum GPA of 2.5. Additional exam requirements/recommendations for international students: Required—TOEFL. Electronic applications accepted. *Faculty research:* Foster parent training, geriatrics, tobacco control.

California State University, Long Beach, Graduate Studies, College of Health and Human Services, Program in Health Care Administration, Long Beach, CA 90840. Offers MS. *Accreditation:* CAHME. Part-time programs available. *Faculty:* 1 (woman) full-time. *Students:* 20 full-time (14 women), 29 part-time (17 women); includes 23 minority (6 African Americans, 10 Asian Americans or Pacific Islanders, 7 Hispanic Americans), 17 international. Average age 30. 81 applicants, 60% accepted, 7 enrolled. *Degree requirements:* For master's, comprehensive exam or thesis. *Entrance requirements:* For master's, minimum GPA of 3.0. *Application deadline:* For fall admission, 6/15 for domestic students; for spring admission, 11/15 for domestic students. Applications are processed on a rolling basis. Application fee: $55. Electronic applications accepted. *Expenses:* Required fees: $1802 per semester. Part-time tuition and fees vary according to course load. *Financial support:* Federal Work-Study, institutionally sponsored loans, and scholarships/grants available. Financial award application deadline: 3/2. *Faculty research:* Long-term care, Immigration Reform Act and health care, physician reimbursement. *Unit head:* Dr. C. Kevin Malotte, Chair, 562-985-2177, Fax: 562-985-2180, E-mail: kmalotte@csulb.edu. *Application contact:* Dr. Tony Sinay, Program Director, 562-985-5304.

California State University, Los Angeles, Graduate Studies, College of Business and Economics, Department of Management, Los Angeles, CA 90032-8530. Offers health care management (MS); management (MBA, MS). *Accreditation:* AACSB. Part-time and evening/weekend programs available. *Faculty:* 4 full-time (3 women), 2 part-time/adjunct (0 women). *Students:* 10 full-time (5 women), 47 part-time (28 women); includes 21 minority (4 African Americans, 9 Asian Americans or Pacific Islanders, 8 Hispanic Americans), 18 international. Average age 33. 29 applicants, 93% accepted, 8 enrolled. In 2009, 24 master's awarded. *Entrance requirements:* For master's, GMAT, minimum GPA of 2.5 during previous 2 years of course work. Additional exam requirements/recommendations for international students: Required—TOEFL (minimum score 550 paper-based; 213 computer-based). *Application deadline:* For fall admission, 5/1 for domestic and international students. Applications are processed on a rolling basis. Application fee: $55. Electronic applications accepted. *Financial support:* Application deadline: 3/1. *Unit head:* Dr. Paul Washburn, Chair, 323-343-2890, Fax: 323-343-6461, E-mail: pwashbu@calstatela.edu. *Application contact:* Dr. Cheryl L. Ney, Associate Vice President for Academic Affairs and Dean of Graduate Studies, 323-343-3820 Ext. 3827, Fax: 323-343-5653, E-mail: cney@cslanet.calstatela.edu.

California State University, Northridge, Graduate Studies, College of Health and Human Development, Department of Health Sciences, Northridge, CA 91330. Offers health administration (MS); public health (MPH). *Accreditation:* CEPH. *Faculty:* 14 full-time (7 women), 54 part-time/adjunct (34 women). *Students:* 89 full-time (65 women), 65 part-time (49 women); includes 73 minority (16 African Americans, 32 Asian Americans or Pacific Islanders, 25 Hispanic Americans), 18 international. Average age 30. 659 applicants, 61% accepted, 99 enrolled. In 2009, 36 master's awarded. *Entrance requirements:* For master's, GRE General Test or minimum GPA of 3.0. Additional exam requirements/recommendations for international students: Required—TOEFL. *Application deadline:* For fall admission, 11/30 for domestic students. Application fee: $55. *Financial support:* Teaching assistantships available. Financial award application deadline: 3/1. *Faculty research:* Labor market needs assessment, health education products, dental hygiene, independent practice prototype. *Unit head:* Dr. Brian Malec, Chair, 818-677-3101. *Application contact:* Dr. Janet T. Reagan, Graduate Coordinator, 818-677-2298, E-mail: janet.reagan@csun.edu.

California State University, San Bernardino, Graduate Studies, College of Natural Sciences, Program in Health Services Administration, San Bernardino, CA 92407-2397. Offers MS. *Students:* 40 full-time (24 women), 14 part-time (11 women); includes 25 minority (11 African Americans, 1 American Indian/Alaska Native, 1 Asian American or Pacific Islander, 12 Hispanic Americans), 6 international. Average age 32. 57 applicants, 74% accepted, 27 enrolled. In 2009, 16 master's awarded. *Degree requirements:* For master's, thesis or alternative. *Entrance requirements:* For master's, GRE, writing exam, minimum GPA of 3.0. *Application deadline:* For fall admission, 8/31 priority date for domestic students. Application fee: $55. *Financial support:* Fellowships, research assistantships, teaching assistantships available. *Faculty research:* Smoking and health, oral hygiene, menopause, health services research. *Unit head:* Dr. Cynthia Paxton, Assistant Dean, 909-537-5343, Fax: 909-537-7037, E-mail: cpaxton@csusb.edu. *Application contact:* Olivia Rosas, Director of Admissions, 909-537-7577, Fax: 909-537-7034, E-mail: orosas@csusb.edu.

Cambridge College, School of Management, Cambridge, MA 02138-5304. Offers business negotiation and conflict resolution (M Mgt); general business (M Mgt); health care informatics (M Mgt); health care management (M Mgt); leadership in human and organizational dynamics (M Mgt); non-profit and public organization management (M Mgt); small business development (M Mgt); technology management (M Mgt). Part-time and evening/weekend programs available. *Faculty:* 4 full-time (3 women), 65 part-time/adjunct (32 women). *Students:* 297 full-time (178 women), 234 part-time (155 women); includes 217 minority (122 African Americans, 53 Asian Americans or Pacific Islanders, 42 Hispanic Americans), 135 international. Average age 39. In 2009, 259 master's awarded. *Degree requirements:* For master's, thesis, seminars. *Entrance requirements:* For master's, resume, 2 professional references. Additional exam requirements/recommendations for international students: Required—TOEFL (minimum score 550 paper-based; 213 computer-based; 79 iBT); Recommended—IELTS (minimum score 6). *Application deadline:* Applications are processed on a rolling basis. Application fee: $30. Electronic applications accepted. *Expenses:* Contact institution. *Financial support:* In 2009–10, 170 students received support. Career-related internships or fieldwork, Federal Work-Study, and scholarships/grants available. Financial award applicants required to submit FAFSA. *Faculty research:* Negotiation, mediation and conflict resolution; leadership; management of diverse organizations; case studies and simulation methodologies for management education, digital

as a second language: social networking for digital immigrants. *Unit head:* Dr. Mary Ann Joseph, Acting Dean, 617-873-0227, E-mail: maryann.joseph@cambridgecollege.edu. *Application contact:* Stephen Lyons, Director of Enrollment, Graduate and N.I.T.E. Programs, 617-868-1000, Fax: 617-349-3561, E-mail: stephen.lyons@cambridgecollege.edu.

Capella University, School of Business and Technology, Minneapolis, MN 55402. Offers accounting (MBA), including system design and programming; business (Certificate), including human resource management (MS, PhD, Certificate), information technology management (MS, PhD, Certificate), leadership (MBA, MS, PhD, Certificate); finance (MBA); general business (MBA); health care management (MBA); information technology (MS, Certificate), including general information technology (MS), information security, network architecture and design (MS), professional projects management (Certificate), project management and leadership (MS), system design and development (MS),); information technology management (MBA); marketing (MBA); organization and management (MBA, MS, PhD), including general business (PhD), general organization and management (MBA, MS), human resource management (MS, PhD, Certificate), information technology management (MS, PhD, Certificate), leadership (MBA, MS, PhD, Certificate); project management (MBA). Part-time and evening/weekend programs available. Postbaccalaureate distance learning degree programs offered (minimal on-campus study). Terminal master's awarded for partial completion of doctoral program. *Degree requirements:* For master's, thesis optional, integrative project; for doctorate, comprehensive exam, thesis/dissertation. *Entrance requirements:* Additional exam requirements/ recommendations for international students: Required—TOEFL (minimum score 550 paper-based; 213 computer-based), TWE (minimum score 4). Electronic applications accepted. *Faculty research:* Business policies: strategic, corporate, and financial management; interplay of technological, organizational and social change.

Capella University, School of Human Services, Minneapolis, MN 55402. Offers addictions counseling (Certificate); counseling studies (MS, PhD); criminal justice (MS, PhD, Certificate); diversity studies (Certificate); general human services (MS, PhD); health care administration (MS, PhD, Certificate); management of nonprofit agencies (MS, PhD, Certificate); marital, couple and family counseling/therapy (MS); marriage and family services (Certificate); mental health counseling (MS); professional counseling (Certificate); social and community services (MS, PhD, Certificate). Part-time and evening/weekend programs available. Postbaccalaureate distance learning degree programs offered (minimal on-campus study). Terminal master's awarded for partial completion of doctoral program. *Degree requirements:* For master's, thesis optional, integrative project; for doctorate, comprehensive exam, thesis/dissertation. *Entrance requirements:* Additional exam requirements/recommendations for international students: Required—TOEFL (minimum score 550 paper-based; 213 computer-based), TWE (minimum score 4). Electronic applications accepted. *Faculty research:* Compulsive and addictive behaviors, substance abuse, assessment of psychopathology and neuropsychology.

Capella University, School of Public Service Leadership, Minneapolis, MN 55402. Offers criminal justice (MS, PhD); emergency management (MS, PhD); general human services (MS, PhD); general public administration (MPA, DPA); gerontology (MS); health care administration (MS, PhD); health management and policy (MSPH); management of nonprofit agencies (MS, PhD); nurse educator (MS); public safety leadership (MS, PhD); social and community services (MS, PhD); social behavioral sciences (MSPH).

Carnegie Mellon University, H. John Heinz III College, School of Public Policy and Management, Programs in Health Care Policy and Management, Pittsburgh, PA 15213-3891. Offers MSHCPM. Part-time and evening/weekend programs available. *Degree requirements:* For master's, internship. Electronic applications accepted.

Carnegie Mellon University, H. John Heinz III College, School of Public Policy and Management, Programs in Medical Management, Pittsburgh, PA 15213-3891. Offers MMM.

Central Michigan University, Central Michigan University Off-Campus Programs, Program in Administration, Mount Pleasant, MI 48859. Offers acquisitions administration (MSA, Certificate); general administration (MSA, Certificate); health services administration (MSA, Certificate); human resources administration (MSA, Certificate); information resource management (MSA, Certificate); international administration (MSA, Certificate); leadership (MSA, Certificate); public administration (MSA, Certificate); vehicle design and manufacturing administration (MSA, Certificate). Part-time and evening/weekend programs available. Postbaccalaureate distance learning degree programs offered (no on-campus study). *Students:* Average age 38. *Entrance requirements:* For master's, minimum GPA of 2.7 in major. *Application deadline:* Applications are processed on a rolling basis. Application fee: $50. Electronic applications accepted. *Financial support:* Scholarships/grants available. Support available to part-time students. Financial award applicants required to submit FAFSA. *Unit head:* Dr. Nana Korsah, Director, MSA Programs, 989-774-6525, E-mail: korsa1na@cmich.edu. *Application contact:* 877-268-4636, E-mail: cmuoffcampus@cmich.edu.

Central Michigan University, Central Michigan University Off-Campus Programs, Program in Health Administration, Mount Pleasant, MI 48859. Offers health administration (DHA); international health (Certificate). Part-time and evening/weekend programs available. Postbaccalaureate distance learning degree programs offered (minimal on-campus study). Electronic applications accepted. *Financial support:* Scholarships/grants available. Support available to part-time students. Financial award applicants required to submit FAFSA. *Unit head:* Steven D. Berkshire, Director, 989-774-1640, E-mail: berks1sd@cmich.edu. *Application contact:* Off-Campus Programs Call Center, E-mail: cmuoffcampus@cmich.edu.

Central Michigan University, College of Graduate Studies, The Herbert H. and Grace A. Dow College of Health Professions, School of Health Sciences, Mount Pleasant, MI 48859. Offers DHA. Part-time and evening/weekend programs available. Postbaccalaureate distance learning degree programs offered (no on-campus study). *Degree requirements:* For doctorate, comprehensive exam, thesis/dissertation. *Entrance requirements:* For doctorate, accredited master's or doctoral degree, 5 years related work experience. Electronic applications accepted.

Central Michigan University, College of Graduate Studies, Interdisciplinary Administration Programs, Mount Pleasant, MI 48859. Offers acquisitions administration (MSA, Graduate Certificate); general administration (MSA, Graduate Certificate); health services administration (MSA, Graduate Certificate); human resource administration (Graduate Certificate); human resources administration (MSA); information resource management (MSA, Graduate Certificate); international administration (MSA, Graduate Certificate); leadership (MSA); organizational communication (MSA, Graduate Certificate); public administration (MSA, Graduate Certificate); recreation and park administration (MSA); sport administration (MSA). *Accreditation:* AACSB. Part-time and evening/weekend programs available. Postbaccalaureate distance learning degree programs offered (no on-campus study). *Degree requirements:* For master's, thesis or alternative. *Entrance requirements:* For master's, bachelor's degree with minimum GPA of 2.7. Electronic applications accepted. *Faculty research:* Interdisciplinary studies in acquisitions administration, health services administration, sport administration, recreation and park administration, and international administration.

Charleston Southern University, Program in Business, Charleston, SC 29423-8087. Offers accounting (MBA); finance (MBA); health care administration (MBA); information systems (MBA); organizational development (MBA). Part-time and evening/weekend programs available. *Faculty:* 14 full-time (1 woman), 6 part-time/adjunct (1 woman). *Students:* 316 part-time (157 women); includes 67 minority (53 African Americans, 1 American Indian/Alaska Native, 7 Asian Americans or Pacific Islanders, 6 Hispanic Americans), 7 international. Average age 32. 173 applicants, 85% accepted, 97 enrolled. In 2009, 69 master's awarded. *Degree requirements:* For master's, thesis optional. *Entrance requirements:* For master's, GMAT. Additional exam requirements/recommendations for international students: Required—TOEFL (minimum score 550 paper-based; 213 computer-based; 79 iBT). *Application deadline:* Applications are processed on a rolling basis. Application fee: $30. *Expenses:* Tuition: Part-time $350 per credit hour. Required fees: $40 per semester. Tuition and fees vary according to program. *Financial support:* Research assistantships with full tuition reimbursements available. Financial award application deadline: 4/15; financial award applicants required to submit FAFSA. *Unit head:* Dr. Scott Pearson, Director of the MBA Program, 843-863-7038, Fax: 843-863-7922, E-mail: spearson@csuniv.edu. *Application contact:* Alison Harrison, Graduate Enrollment Counselor, 843-863-7534, Fax: 843-863-7070, E-mail: aharrison@csuniv.edu.

Clark University, Graduate School, Graduate School of Management, Business Administration Program, Worcester, MA 01610-1477. Offers accounting (MBA); finance (MBA); global business (MBA); health care management (MBA); management (MBA); management of information technology (MBA); marketing (MBA). *Accreditation:* AACSB. Part-time and evening/weekend programs available. *Students:* 148 full-time (67 women), 120 part-time (52 women); includes 27 minority (12 African Americans, 2 American Indian/Alaska Native, 9 Asian Americans or Pacific Islanders, 4 Hispanic Americans), 108 international. Average age 29. 340 applicants, 57% accepted, 63 enrolled. In 2009, 118 master's awarded. *Degree requirements:* For master's, thesis optional. *Application deadline:* For fall admission, 6/1 priority date for domestic students; for spring admission, 12/1 priority date for domestic students. Applications are processed on a rolling basis. Application fee: $50. Electronic applications accepted. *Expenses:* Tuition: Full-time $34,900; part-time $4362.50 per course. *Financial support:* In 2009–10, research assistantships with partial tuition reimbursements (averaging $4,800 per year), teaching assistantships with partial tuition reimbursements (averaging $4,800 per year) were awarded; fellowships, career-related internships or fieldwork, Federal Work-Study, institutionally sponsored loans, and tuition waivers (partial) also available. Support available to part-time students. Financial award application deadline: 5/31. *Faculty research:* Organizational development, accounting, marketing, finance, human resource management. *Application contact:* Lynn Davis, Enrollment and Marketing Director, 508-793-7406, Fax: 508-793-8822, E-mail: clarkmba@clarku.edu.

Clayton State University, School of Graduate Studies, Program in Health Administration, Morrow, GA 30260-0285. Offers MHA. Part-time and evening/weekend programs available. *Students:* 21 full-time (13 women), 17 part-time (14 women); includes 26 minority (21 African Americans, 2 Asian Americans or Pacific Islanders, 3 Hispanic Americans), 2 international. Average age 34. 12 applicants, 83% accepted, 8 enrolled. *Degree requirements:* For master's, comprehensive exam, thesis. *Entrance requirements:* For master's, GRE. Additional exam requirements/recommendations for international students: Required—TOEFL (minimum score 550 paper-based; 213 computer-based; 80 iBT). *Application deadline:* For fall admission, 7/15 for domestic students, 5/1 for international students; for spring admission, 4/15 for domestic students, 2/1 for international students. Application fee: $50. Electronic applications accepted. *Expenses:* Contact institution. *Financial support:* Application deadline: 7/1. *Unit head:* Dr. Thomas McIlwain, Dean, School of Graduate Studies/Director, 678-466-4500, Fax: 678-466-4669, E-mail: thomasmcilwain@clayton.edu. *Application contact:* Michelle Terrell, Program Manager, 678-466-4500, Fax: 678-466-4669, E-mail: michelleterrell@clayton.edu.

Cleveland State University, College of Graduate Studies, Nance College of Business Administration, MBA Programs, Cleveland, OH 44115. Offers business administration (AMBA, MBA); executive business administration (EMBA); health care administration (MBA); off-campus programs (MBA); JD/MBA; MSN/MBA. *Accreditation:* AACSB. Part-time and evening/weekend programs available. *Entrance requirements:* For master's, GMAT or GRE. Additional exam requirements/recommendations for international students: Required—TOEFL (minimum score 550 paper-based; 213 computer-based; 79 iBT).

The College at Brockport, State University of New York, School of Education and Human Services, Department of Public Administration, Brockport, NY 14420-2997. Offers arts administration (AGC); nonprofit management (AGC); public administration (MPA), including general public administration, health care management, nonprofit management, public safety. *Accreditation:* NASPAA. Part-time and evening/weekend programs available. *Students:* 25 full-time (18 women), 91 part-time (72 women); includes 18 minority (12 African Americans, 3 Asian Americans or Pacific Islanders, 3 Hispanic Americans). 42 applicants, 95% accepted, 33 enrolled. In 2009, 30 master's awarded. *Degree requirements:* For master's, thesis or alternative. *Entrance requirements:* For master's, GRE or minimum GPA of 3.0, letters of recommendation, statement of objectives. Additional exam requirements/recommendations for international students: Required—TOEFL (minimum score 550 paper-based; 213 computer-based; 79 iBT). *Application deadline:* For fall admission, 3/1 priority date for domestic and international students; for spring admission, 10/1 priority date for domestic and international students. Application fee: $50. Electronic applications accepted. *Expenses:* Tuition, state resident: full-time $8370; part-time $349 per credit. Tuition, nonresident: full-time $13,250; part-time $522 per credit. *Financial support:* In 2009–10, 1 fellowship with full tuition reimbursement (averaging $7,500 per year) was awarded; Federal Work-Study, scholarships/ grants, and unspecified assistantships also available. Support available to part-time students. Financial award application deadline: 3/15; financial award applicants required to submit FAFSA. *Faculty research:* E-government, performance management, nonprofits and policy implementation, Medicaid and disabilities. *Unit head:* Dr. James Fatula, Chairperson, 585-395-2375, Fax: 585-395-2172, E-mail: jfatula@brockport.edu. *Application contact:* Dr. James Fatual, Chairperson, 585-395-2375, Fax: 585-395-2172, E-mail: jfatula@brockport.edu.

College of Saint Elizabeth, Department of Health Professions and Related Sciences, Morristown, NJ 07960-6989. Offers health care management (MS). Part-time and evening/ weekend programs available. *Faculty:* 2 full-time (both women), 8 part-time/adjunct (5 women). *Students:* 4 full-time (all women), 122 part-time (94 women); includes 29 minority (13 African Americans, 1 American Indian/Alaska Native, 7 Asian Americans or Pacific Islanders, 8 Hispanic Americans), 1 international. Average age 45. 17 applicants, 88% accepted, 12 enrolled. In 2009, 5 master's awarded. *Degree requirements:* For master's, thesis optional, culminating experience. *Entrance requirements:* For master's, minimum GPA of 3.0. *Application deadline:* Applications are processed on a rolling basis. Application fee: $35. Electronic applications accepted. *Expenses:* Tuition: Part-time $797 per credit hour. Required fees: $65 per credit hour. *Financial support:* Career-related internships or fieldwork, tuition waivers (partial), and unspecified assistantships available. Support available to part-time students. Financial award application deadline: 3/15; financial award applicants required to submit FAFSA. *Faculty research:* Consumer protection in health care. *Unit head:* Linda Hunter, Director of the Graduate Program in Health Care Management, 973-290-4040, Fax: 973-290-4167, E-mail: lhunter@cse.edu. *Application contact:* Donna Tatarka, Dean of Admission, 973-290-4705, Fax: 973-290-4710, E-mail: dtatarka@cse.edu.

Colorado Technical University Sioux Falls, Programs in Business Administration and Management, Sioux Falls, SD 57108. Offers business administration (MBA); business management (MSM); health science management (MSM); human resources management (MSM); information technology (MSM); organizational leadership (MSM); project management (MBA); technology management (MBA). Evening/weekend programs available. *Degree requirements:* For master's, thesis optional. *Entrance requirements:* For master's, minimum 2 years work experience, resume.

Columbia Southern University, MBA Program, Orange Beach, AL 36561. Offers electronic business and technology (MBA); finance (MBA); general (MBA); healthcare management (MBA); hospitality and tourism (MBA); human resources management (MBA); international management (MBA); marketing (MBA); project management (MBA); public administration (MBA); sport management (MBA). Part-time and evening/weekend programs available. Postbaccalaureate distance learning degree programs offered (no on-campus study). *Entrance requirements:* For master's, bachelor's degree from accredited/approved institution. Additional exam requirements/recommendations for international students: Required—TOEFL. Electronic applications accepted.

Columbia University, Columbia University Mailman School of Public Health, Division of Health Policy and Management, New York, NY 10032. Offers Exec MPH, MPH. *Accreditation:* CAHME. Evening/weekend programs available. *Students:* 138 full-time (104 women), 141 part-time (90 women); includes 88 minority (25 African Americans, 2 American Indian/Alaska Native, 47 Asian Americans or Pacific Islanders, 14 Hispanic Americans), 37 international. Average age 31. 379 applicants, 69% accepted, 110 enrolled. In 2009, 93 master's awarded. *Degree requirements:* For master's, thesis optional. *Entrance requirements:* For master's, GRE General Test. Additional exam requirements/recommendations for international students:

Health Services Management and Hospital Administration

Columbia University (continued)

Required—TOEFL (minimum score 600 paper-based; 250 computer-based; 100 iBT). *Application deadline:* For fall admission, 1/5 for domestic students. Application fee: $60. Electronic applications accepted. *Financial support:* Research assistantships, teaching assistantships, career-related internships or fieldwork and Federal Work-Study available. Support available to part-time students. Financial award application deadline: 2/1; financial award applicants required to submit FAFSA. *Faculty research:* Health care reform, health care disparities, state and national and cross national health policy, health care quality, organization structure and performance. *Unit head:* Dr. Sherry Glied, 212-305-0299. *Application contact:* Dr. Sherry Glied, 212-305-0299.

Columbus State University, Graduate Studies, College of Education and Health Professions, Department of Teacher Education, Columbus, GA 31907-5645. Offers accomplished teaching (M Ed); early childhood education (M Ed, Ed S); health administration (MPA); instructional technology (MS); middle grades education (M Ed, Ed S); physical education (M Ed); secondary education (M Ed, MAT, Ed S), including English/language arts (M Ed, Ed S), general science (M Ed), mathematics (M Ed), social science (M Ed); special education (M Ed), including behavior disorders, mental retardation. *Accreditation:* NCATE. Part-time and evening/weekend programs available. Postbaccalaureate distance learning degree programs offered (minimal on-campus study). *Faculty:* 18 full-time (15 women), 14 part-time/adjunct (10 women). *Students:* 146 full-time (113 women), 312 part-time (261 women); includes 142 minority (120 African Americans, 1 American Indian/Alaska Native, 8 Asian Americans or Pacific Islanders, 13 Hispanic Americans), 2 international. Average age 31. 248 applicants, 64% accepted, 114 enrolled. In 2009, 103 master's, 22 other advanced degrees awarded. *Degree requirements:* For master's, thesis, exit exam; for Ed S, thesis or alternative. *Entrance requirements:* For master's, GRE General Test, minimum GPA of 2.75; for Ed S, GRE General Test. Additional exam requirements/recommendations for international students: Required—TOEFL (minimum score 550 paper-based; 213 computer-based; 79 iBT). *Application deadline:* For fall admission, 5/1 priority date for domestic students, 5/1 for international students; for spring admission, 11/1 for domestic and international students. Applications are processed on a rolling basis. Application fee: $30. Electronic applications accepted. *Financial support:* In 2009–10, 305 students received support, including 36 research assistantships with partial tuition reimbursements available (averaging $3,000 per year); career-related internships or fieldwork, Federal Work-Study, institutionally sponsored loans, scholarships/grants, tuition waivers (partial), and unspecified assistantships also available. Support available to part-time students. Financial award application deadline: 5/1; financial award applicants required to submit FAFSA. *Unit head:* Dr. Deborah Gober, Acting Chair, 706-568-2255, Fax: 706-568-3134, E-mail: gober_deborah@colstate.edu. *Application contact:* Katie Thornton, Graduate Admissions Specialist, 706-568-2035, Fax: 706-568-2462, E-mail: thornton_katie@colstate.edu.

Columbus State University, Graduate Studies, College of Letters and Sciences, Master of Public Administration Program, Columbus, GA 31907-5645. Offers public administration (MPA), including government administration, health services administration, justice administration. Part-time and evening/weekend programs available. *Faculty:* 12 full-time (4 women), 12 part-time/adjunct (0 women). *Students:* 113 full-time (43 women), 209 part-time (63 women); includes 98 minority (86 African Americans, 4 American Indian/Alaska Native, 1 Asian American or Pacific Islander, 7 Hispanic Americans), 1 international. Average age 41. 84 applicants, 88% accepted, 58 enrolled. In 2009, 130 master's awarded. *Entrance requirements:* For master's, GRE General Test, minimum GPA of 2.75. Additional exam requirements/recommendations for international students: Required—TOEFL (minimum score 550 paper-based; 213 computer-based; 79 iBT). *Application deadline:* For fall admission, 5/1 priority date for domestic students, 5/1 for international students; for spring admission, 11/1 for domestic and international students. Applications are processed on a rolling basis. Application fee: $30. Electronic applications accepted. *Financial support:* In 2009–10, 71 students received support, including 6 research assistantships with partial tuition reimbursements available (averaging $3,000 per year); career-related internships or fieldwork, Federal Work-Study, institutionally sponsored loans, scholarships/grants, tuition waivers (partial), and unspecified assistantships also available. Support available to part-time students. Financial award application deadline: 5/1; financial award applicants required to submit FAFSA. *Unit head:* Dr. William Chappell, Program Director, 706-569-2891, E-mail: chappell_bill@colstate.edu. *Application contact:* Katie Thornton, Graduate Admissions Specialist, 706-568-2035, Fax: 706-568-2462, E-mail: thornton_katie@colstate.edu.

Concordia University, School of Graduate Studies, John Molson School of Business, Montréal, QC H3G 1M8, Canada. Offers administration (M Sc, Diploma); aviation management (Certificate, Diploma); business administration (MBA, UA Undergraduate Associate, PhD), including international aviation (UA Undergraduate Associate); chartered accountancy (Diploma); community organizational development (Certificate); event management and fundraising (Certificate); executive business administration (EMBA); investment management (Diploma); investment management option (MBA); management accounting (Certificate); management of healthcare organizations (Certificate); sport administration (Diploma). *Accreditation:* AACSB. Part-time and evening/weekend programs available. *Degree requirements:* For master's, one foreign language, thesis (for some programs), research project; for doctorate, one foreign language, thesis/dissertation; for other advanced degree, one foreign language. *Entrance requirements:* For master's and doctorate, GMAT. Additional exam requirements/recommendations for international students: Required—TOEFL. *Expenses:* Contact institution. *Faculty research:* General business, capital markets, international business.

Concordia University, St. Paul, College of Business and Organizational Leadership, St. Paul, MN 55104-5494. Offers business and organizational leadership (MBA); criminal justice leadership (MA); health care management (MBA); human resources management (MA); leadership and management (MA). *Accreditation:* ACBSP. Evening/weekend programs available. Postbaccalaureate distance learning degree programs offered (minimal on-campus study). *Faculty:* 10 full-time (5 women), 19 part-time/adjunct (4 women). *Students:* 295 full-time (169 women), 3 part-time (2 women); includes 30 minority (19 African Americans, 2 American Indian/Alaska Native, 5 Asian Americans or Pacific Islanders, 4 Hispanic Americans), 3 international. Average age 32. In 2009, 114 master's awarded. *Application deadline:* Applications are processed on a rolling basis. Application fee: $50. Electronic applications accepted. *Financial support:* Applicants required to submit FAFSA. *Unit head:* Dr. Bruce Corrie, Dean, 651-641-8226, Fax: 651-641-8807, E-mail: corrie@csp.edu. *Application contact:* Kimberly Craig, Director of Graduate and Cohort Admission, 651-603-6223, Fax: 651-603-6320, E-mail: craig@csp.edu.

Concordia University Wisconsin, Graduate Programs, School of Business and Legal Studies, MBA Program, Mequon, WI 53097-2402. Offers finance (MBA); health care administration (MBA); human resource management (MBA); international business (MBA); international business-bilingual English/Chinese (MBA); management (MBA); management information systems (MBA); managerial communications (MBA); marketing (MBA); public administration (MBA); risk management (MBA). Postbaccalaureate distance learning degree programs offered (minimal on-campus study). *Degree requirements:* For master's, comprehensive exam, thesis or alternative. *Entrance requirements:* Additional exam requirements/recommendations for international students: Required—TOEFL. *Expenses:* Contact institution.

Cornell University, Graduate School, Graduate Fields of Human Ecology, Field of Policy Analysis and Management, Ithaca, NY 14853-0001. Offers consumer policy (PhD); evaluation (PhD); family and social welfare policy (PhD); health administration (MHA); health management and policy (PhD). *Faculty:* 40 full-time (17 women). *Students:* 51 full-time (27 women); includes 13 minority (4 African Americans, 8 Asian Americans or Pacific Islanders, 1 Hispanic American), 7 international. Average age 26. 130 applicants, 38% accepted, 31 enrolled. In 2009, 25 master's, 5 doctorates awarded. *Degree requirements:* For master's, thesis; for doctorate, thesis/dissertation. *Entrance requirements:* For master's, GRE General Test or GMAT, 2 letters of recommendation; for doctorate, GRE General Test, 2 letters of recommendation. Additional exam requirements/recommendations for international students: Required—TOEFL (minimum score 550 paper-based; 213 computer-based; 77 iBT). *Application deadline:* For fall admission, 1/15 for domestic students. Application fee: $70. Electronic applications accepted. *Expenses:* Tuition: Full-time $29,500. Required fees: $70. Full-time tuition and fees vary according to degree level, program and student level. *Financial support:* In 2009–10, 17 students received support, including 1 fellowship with full and partial tuition reimbursement available, 8 teaching assistantships with full and partial tuition reimbursements available; research assistantships with full and partial tuition reimbursements available, institutionally sponsored loans, scholarships/grants, health care benefits, tuition waivers (full and partial), and unspecified assistantships also available. Financial award applicants required to submit FAFSA. *Faculty research:* Health policy, family policy, social welfare policy, program evaluation, consumer policy. *Unit head:* Director of Graduate Studies, 607-255-7772. *Application contact:* Graduate Field Assistant, 607-255-7772, Fax: 607-255-4071, E-mail: pam_phd@cornell.edu.

Dalhousie University, Faculty of Health Professions, School of Health Administration, Halifax, NS B3H 1R2, Canada. Offers MAHSR, MHA, MPH, PhD, LL B/MHA, MBA/MHA, MHA/MN. *Accreditation:* CAHME. Part-time programs available. Postbaccalaureate distance learning degree programs offered (minimal on-campus study). *Faculty:* 5 full-time (1 woman), 15 part-time/adjunct (8 women). *Students:* 33 full-time (27 women), 22 part-time (18 women); includes 9 minority (1 African American, 8 Asian Americans or Pacific Islanders). Average age 30. 31 applicants, 71% accepted. In 2009, 12 master's awarded. *Entrance requirements:* For master's, GMAT. Additional exam requirements/recommendations for international students: Required—TOEFL, IELTS, CANTEST, CAEL, or Michigan English Language Assessment Battery. *Application deadline:* For fall admission, 6/1 for domestic and international students. Applications are processed on a rolling basis. Application fee: $70. Electronic applications accepted. *Expenses:* Contact institution. *Financial support:* In 2009–10, 13 students received support, including fellowships (averaging $2,000 per year), 5 teaching assistantships (averaging $630 per year). *Faculty research:* Hospital, nursing, long-term, public, and community health administration; government administration in health areas. *Unit head:* Dr. Joesph Byrne, Graduate Coordinator, 902-494-7097, Fax: 902-494-6849, E-mail: healthadmin@dal.ca. *Application contact:* Sandra Drew, Administrative Officer, 902-494-1547, Fax: 902-494-6849, E-mail: sandra.drew@dal.ca.

Dallas Baptist University, College of Business, Business Administration Program, Dallas, TX 75211-9299. Offers accounting (MBA); business communication (MBA); conflict resolution management (MBA); e-business (MBA); entrepreneurship (MBA); finance (MBA); health care management (MBA); international business (MBA); leading the non-profit organization (MBA); management (MBA); management information systems (MBA); marketing (MBA); project management (MBA); technology and engineering management (MBA). *Accreditation:* ACBSP. Part-time and evening/weekend programs available. *Entrance requirements:* For master's, GMAT, minimum GPA of 3.0. Additional exam requirements/recommendations for international students: Required—TOEFL, IELTS. Electronic applications accepted. *Expenses:* Tuition: Full-time $10,674; part-time $593 per credit hour. *Faculty research:* Sports management, services marketing, retailing, strategic management, financial planning/investments.

Dallas Baptist University, College of Business, Management Program, Dallas, TX 75211-9299. Offers business communication (MA); conflict resolution management (MA); general management (MA); health care management (MA); human resource management (MA); performance management (MA). Part-time and evening/weekend programs available. *Entrance requirements:* For master's, GRE General Test, minimum GPA of 3.0. Additional exam requirements/recommendations for international students: Required—TOEFL, IELTS. Electronic applications accepted. *Expenses:* Tuition: Full-time $10,674; part-time $593 per credit hour. *Faculty research:* Organizational behavior, conflict personalities.

Dartmouth College, The Dartmouth Institute, Program in Health Policy and Clinical Practice, Hanover, NH 03755. Offers evaluative clinical sciences (MS, PhD). Part-time programs available. *Faculty:* 32 full-time (17 women), 9 part-time/adjunct (6 women). *Students:* 26 full-time (12 women), 25 part-time (15 women); includes 4 minority (1 American Indian/Alaska Native, 2 Asian Americans or Pacific Islanders, 1 Hispanic American), 2 international. Average age 37. 73 applicants, 66% accepted, 22 enrolled. In 2009, 5 master's, 9 doctorates awarded. *Degree requirements:* For master's, research project or practicum; for doctorate, thesis/dissertation. *Entrance requirements:* For master's and doctorate, GRE or MCAT, 3 letters of recommendation. Additional exam requirements/recommendations for international students: Required—TOEFL. *Application deadline:* For fall admission, 1/15 for domestic students. Applications are processed on a rolling basis. Application fee: $50. *Financial support:* In 2009–10, 5 students received support; fellowships with tuition reimbursements available, research assistantships, teaching assistantships with tuition reimbursements available, institutionally sponsored loans and scholarships/grants available. Financial award application deadline: 6/1; financial award applicants required to submit FAFSA. *Faculty research:* Prevention and treatment of cardiovascular diseases, health care cost containment, variation of delivery of care, health care improvement, decision evaluation. *Unit head:* Dr. Gerald T. O'Connor, Director, 603-650-1782, Fax: 603-650-1900. *Application contact:* Susan M. Benson, Academic Programs Director, 603-650-1782, Fax: 603-650-1900.

Davenport University, Sneden Graduate School, Grand Rapids, MI 49503. Offers accounting (MBA); business administration (EMBA); finance (MBA); health care management (MBA); human resources (MBA); information assurance (MS); public health (MPH); strategic management (MBA). Evening/weekend programs available. *Entrance requirements:* For master's, GMAT, minimum undergraduate GPA of 2.75. Additional exam requirements/recommendations for international students: Required—TOEFL. Electronic applications accepted. *Faculty research:* Leadership, management, marketing, organizational culture.

Davenport University, Sneden Graduate School, Warren, MI 48092-5209. Offers accounting (MBA); business administration (EMBA); finance (MBA); health care management (MBA); human resources management (MBA); information assurance (MS); public health (MPH); strategic management (MBA). *Entrance requirements:* For master's, minimum undergraduate GPA of 2.7.

Davenport University, Sneden Graduate School, Dearborn, MI 48126-3799. Offers accounting (MBA); business administration (EMBA); finance (MBA); health care management (MBA); human resources management (MBA); information assurance (MS); marketing (MBA); public health (MPH); strategic management (MBA). Part-time and evening/weekend programs available. Postbaccalaureate distance learning degree programs offered (no on-campus study). *Entrance requirements:* For master's, minimum GPA of 2.7, previous course work in accounting and statistics. *Faculty research:* Accounting, international accounting, social and environmental accounting, finance.

Defiance College, Program in Business Administration, Defiance, OH 43512-1610. Offers criminal justice (MBA); health care (MBA); leadership (MBA). Part-time and evening/weekend programs available. *Degree requirements:* For master's, thesis. *Entrance requirements:* For master's, minimum GPA of 2.5.

Delta State University, Graduate Programs, School of Nursing, Cleveland, MS 38733-0001. Offers family nurse practitioner (MSN); nurse administrator (MSN); nurse educator (MSN). *Accreditation:* AACN. Part-time programs available. *Degree requirements:* For master's, thesis optional. *Entrance requirements:* For master's, GRE General Test. Electronic applications accepted. *Expenses:* Tuition, state resident: full-time $4450; part-time $247 per credit hour. Tuition, nonresident: full-time $11,520; part-time $640 per credit hour.

DePaul University, Charles H. Kellstadt Graduate School of Business, Department of Management, Chicago, IL 60604-2287. Offers entrepreneurship (MBA); health sector management (MBA); human resource management (MBA, MSHR); leadership/change management (MBA); management planning and strategy (MBA); operations management (MBA). Part-time and evening/weekend programs available. *Faculty:* 36 full-time (7 women), 35 part-time/adjunct (16 women). *Students:* 284 full-time (115 women), 147 part-time (69 women); includes 75 minority (20 African Americans, 1 American Indian/Alaska Native, 37 Asian Americans or Pacific Islanders, 17 Hispanic Americans), 18 international. In 2009, 112 master's awarded. *Entrance requirements:* For master's, GMAT, GRE (MSHR), 2 letters of recommendation,

resume. Additional exam requirements/recommendations for international students: Required—TOEFL (minimum score 550 paper-based; 213 computer-based). *Application deadline:* For fall admission, 7/1 for domestic students; for winter admission, 10/1 for domestic students; for spring admission, 2/1 for domestic students. Applications are processed on a rolling basis. Application fee: $60. Electronic applications accepted. *Expenses:* Tuition: Full-time $37,525; part-time $620 per credit hour. *Financial support:* Research assistantships available. Financial award application deadline: 4/1. *Faculty research:* Growth management, creativity and innovation, quality management and business process design, entrepreneurship. *Application contact:* Christopher E. Kinsella, Director of Cohort MBA Programs, 312-362-8810, Fax: 312-362-6677, E-mail: kgsb@depaul.edu.

DePaul University, School of Public Service, Chicago, IL 60604. Offers financial administration management (Certificate); health administration (Certificate); health law and policy (MS); international public services (MS); leadership and policy studies (MS); metropolitan planning (Certificate); public administration (MPA); public service management (MS), including association management, fundraising and philanthropy, healthcare administration, higher education administration, metropolitan planning; public services (Certificate); JD/MS. Part-time and evening/weekend programs available. Postbaccalaureate distance learning degree programs offered (minimal on-campus study). *Faculty:* 14 full-time (3 women), 43 part-time/adjunct (24 women). *Students:* 283 full-time (206 women), 298 part-time (208 women); includes 196 minority (112 African Americans, 1 American Indian/Alaska Native, 30 Asian Americans or Pacific Islanders, 53 Hispanic Americans), 18 international. Average age 26. 162 applicants, 100% accepted, 94 enrolled. In 2009, 108 master's awarded. *Degree requirements:* For master's, thesis or integrative seminar. *Entrance requirements:* For master's, minimum GPA of 2.7. Additional exam requirements/recommendations for international students: Required—TOEFL (minimum score 550 paper-based; 213 computer-based; 80 iBT), IELTS (minimum score 6.5). *Application deadline:* Applications are processed on a rolling basis. Application fee: $40. Electronic applications accepted. *Expenses:* Tuition: Full-time $37,525; part-time $620 per credit hour. *Financial support:* In 2009–10, 60 students received support, including 3 research assistantships with full tuition reimbursements available (averaging $7,000 per year); career-related internships or fieldwork, Federal Work-Study, institutionally sponsored loans, scholarships/grants, tuition waivers (partial), and unspecified assistantships also available. Support available to part-time students. Financial award application deadline: 7/1; financial award applicants required to submit FAFSA. *Faculty research:* Government financing, transportation, leadership, health care, volunteerism and organizational behavior, non-profit organizations. Total annual research expenditures: $20,000. *Unit head:* Dr. J. Patrick Murphy, Director, 312-362-5608, Fax: 312-362-5506, E-mail: jpmurphy@depaul.edu. *Application contact:* Megan B. Balderston, Director of Admissions and Marketing, 312-362-5565, Fax: 312-362-5506, E-mail: pubserv@depaul.edu.

DeSales University, Graduate Division, Program in Business Administration, Center Valley, PA 18034-9568. Offers accounting (MBA); business administration (MBA); computer information systems (MBA); finance (MBA); health care systems management (MBA); management (MBA); marketing (MBA); project management (MBA); self-design (MBA); MSN/MBA. *Accreditation:* ACBSP. Part-time programs available. Postbaccalaureate distance learning degree programs offered (no on-campus study). *Students:* 433 part-time. In 2009, 218 master's awarded. *Entrance requirements:* For master's, minimum GPA of 3.0, 2 years of work experience. Additional exam requirements/recommendations for international students: Required—TOEFL. *Application deadline:* Applications are processed on a rolling basis. Application fee: $35. Electronic applications accepted. *Expenses:* Tuition: Full-time $17,500; part-time $665 per credit. Full-time tuition and fees vary according to program. Part-time tuition and fees vary according to course load. *Faculty research:* Quality improvement, executive development, productivity, cross-cultural managerial differences, leadership. *Unit head:* Dr. David Gilfoil, Director, 610-282-1100 Ext. 1828, Fax: 610-282-2869, E-mail: david.gilfoil@desales.edu. *Application contact:* Caryn Stopper, Director of Graduate Admissions, 610-282-1100 Ext. 1768, Fax: 610-282-0525, E-mail: caryn.stopper@desales.edu.

Des Moines University, College of Health Sciences, Program in Healthcare Administration, Des Moines, IA 50312-4104. Offers MHA. Part-time and evening/weekend programs available. *Faculty:* 1 (woman) full-time, 2 part-time/adjunct (0 women). *Students:* 138 part-time (95 women); includes 20 minority (2 African Americans, 2 American Indian/Alaska Native, 11 Asian Americans or Pacific Islanders, 5 Hispanic Americans). 181 applicants, 50% accepted. In 2009, 20 master's awarded. *Entrance requirements:* For master's, minimum GPA of 3.0. Additional exam requirements/recommendations for international students: Required—TOEFL (minimum score 600 paper-based). *Application deadline:* For fall admission, 7/1 for domestic and international students; for winter admission, 11/1 for domestic and international students; for spring admission, 3/1 for domestic and international students. Applications are processed on a rolling basis. Application fee: $50. Electronic applications accepted. *Expenses:* Contact institution. *Financial support:* In 2009–10, 1 student received support. Career-related internships or fieldwork, institutionally sponsored loans, scholarships/grants, and university employment available. Support available to part-time students. Financial award applicants required to submit FAFSA. *Faculty research:* Quality improvement, rural sociology, women's health, health promotion, patient education. *Unit head:* Dr. Carla Stebbins, Director, 515-271-1497. *Application contact:* Lisa Vroegh, Admissions Coordinator, 515-271-1364, Fax: 515-271-7162, E-mail: hmadmit@dmu.edu.

Dowling College, School of Business, Oakdale, NY 11769-1999. Offers aviation management (MBA, Certificate); banking and finance (MBA, Certificate); financial planning (Certificate); general management (MBA); health care management (MBA, Certificate); human resource management (Certificate); management and leadership (MBA); marketing (Certificate); project management (Certificate); public management (MBA, Certificate); total quality management (MBA, Certificate); JD/MBA. Part-time and evening/weekend programs available. *Faculty:* 14 full-time (5 women), 58 part-time/adjunct (5 women). *Students:* 324 full-time (142 women), 479 part-time (237 women); includes 238 minority (82 African Americans, 1 American Indian/Alaska Native, 117 Asian Americans or Pacific Islanders, 38 Hispanic Americans), 2 international. Average age 33. 457 applicants, 91% accepted, 153 enrolled. In 2009, 341 master's, 2 other advanced degrees awarded. *Degree requirements:* For master's, comprehensive exam, thesis optional. *Entrance requirements:* For master's, minimum GPA of 2.8, 2 letters of recommendation, courses in accounting and finance or seminar in accounting/finance, resume. Additional exam requirements/recommendations for international students: Required—TOEFL (minimum score 550 paper-based). *Application deadline:* For fall admission, 9/1 priority date for domestic students; for winter admission, 1/1 priority date for domestic students; for spring admission, 2/1 priority date for domestic students. Applications are processed on a rolling basis. Application fee: $50. Electronic applications accepted. *Expenses:* Tuition: Full-time $14,490; part-time $805 per credit. Required fees: $346 per term. *Financial support:* Career-related internships or fieldwork and Federal Work-Study available. Support available to part-time students. Financial award application deadline: 6/30; financial award applicants required to submit FAFSA. *Faculty research:* International finance, computer applications, labor relations, executive development. *Unit head:* Mathew Cordaro, Dean, 631-244-3162, Fax: 631-244-1018, E-mail: cordarom@dowling.edu. *Application contact:* Glenn M. Berman, Director of Admissions Operations, 631-244-3357, Fax: 631-244-1059, E-mail: glenn.berman@dowling.edu.

Duke University, The Fuqua School of Business, Concentration in Health Sector Management for Full-Time Programs, Durham, NC 27708-0586. Offers Certificate. Program must be taken while pursuing MBA. *Entrance requirements:* Additional exam requirements/recommendations for international students: Required—TOEFL. Electronic applications accepted. *Faculty research:* Health information technology, venture capital in health care, new business development, impact of genetics on practice of medicine, economics of the pharmaceutical innovation.

Duke University, The Fuqua School of Business, Concentration in Health Sector Management for Weekend and Global Programs, Durham, NC 27708-0586. Offers Certificate. Program must be taken while pursuibg WEMBA or GEMBA.

Duquesne University, John G. Rangos, Sr. School of Health Sciences, Pittsburgh, PA 15282-0001. Offers health management systems (MHMS); occupational therapy (MS); physical therapy (DPT); physician assistant studies (MPAS); rehabilitation science (MS, PhD); speech-language pathology (MS); MBA/MHMS. *Accreditation:* AOTA (one or more programs are accredited); APTA (one or more programs are accredited); ASHA. *Faculty:* 35 full-time (23 women), 17 part-time/adjunct (10 women). *Students:* 309 full-time (258 women), 11 part-time (7 women); includes 11 minority (5 African Americans, 5 Asian Americans or Pacific Islanders, 1 Hispanic American), 6 international. Average age 23. 454 applicants, 20% accepted, 20 enrolled. In 2009, 92 master's, 23 doctorates awarded. *Degree requirements:* For doctorate, thesis/dissertation. *Entrance requirements:* For master's, GRE General Test (speech-language pathology), 3 letters of recommendation; minimum GPA of 2.75 (health management systems, occupational therapy), minimum GPA of 3.0 (speech-language pathology); for doctorate, GRE General Test (for physical therapy), 3 letters of recommendation, minimum GPA of 3.0, personal interview. Additional exam requirements/recommendations for international students: Required—TOEFL (minimum score 550 paper-based; 233 computer-based; 90 iBT). *Application deadline:* Applications are processed on a rolling basis. Electronic applications accepted. *Expenses:* Contact institution. *Financial support:* Federal Work-Study available. *Faculty research:* Neuronal processing, electrical stimulation on peripheral neuropathy, CNS stimulatory and inhibitory signals, behavioral genetic methodologies to development disorders of speech, neurogenic communication disorders. Total annual research expenditures: $338,404. *Unit head:* Dr. Gregory H. Frazer, Dean, 412-396-5303, Fax: 412-396-5554, E-mail: frazer@duq.edu. *Application contact:* Christopher R. Hilf, Recruiter/Academic Advisor, 412-396-5653, Fax: 412-396-5554, E-mail: hilfc@duq.edu.

D'Youville College, Department of Health Services Administration, Buffalo, NY 14201-1084. Offers clinical research associate (Certificate); health services administration (MS, Certificate); long term care administration (Certificate). Part-time and evening/weekend programs available. *Degree requirements:* For master's, project or thesis. *Entrance requirements:* For master's, minimum GPA of 3.0 in major. Additional exam requirements/recommendations for international students: Required—TOEFL (minimum score 500 paper-based; 173 computer-based). Electronic applications accepted. *Faculty research:* Outcomes research in rehabilitation medicine, cost/benefit analysis of prospective payment systems.

D'Youville College, Doctoral Programs, Buffalo, NY 14201-1084. Offers educational leadership (Ed D); health education (Ed D); health policy (Ed D). Part-time and evening/weekend programs available. *Degree requirements:* For doctorate, comprehensive exam, thesis/dissertation, fieldwork. *Entrance requirements:* For doctorate, MS/MA; professional experience. *Faculty research:* Educational assessment, assessment reform, culture and education, market-based reform, men's health, electronic records.

Eastern Kentucky University, The Graduate School, College of Arts and Sciences, Department of Government, Program in General Public Administration, Richmond, KY 40475-3102. Offers community development (MPA); community health administration (MPA); general public administration (MPA). *Accreditation:* NASPAA. Part-time and evening/weekend programs available. *Entrance requirements:* For master's, GRE General Test, minimum GPA of 2.5.

Eastern Michigan University, Graduate School, College of Arts and Sciences, Department of Political Science, Programs in Public Administration, Ypsilanti, MI 48197. Offers local government management (Graduate Certificate); management of public healthcare services (Graduate Certificate); public administration (MPA, Graduate Certificate); public budget management (Graduate Certificate); public land planning (Graduate Certificate); public management (Graduate Certificate); public personnel management (Graduate Certificate); public policy analysis (Graduate Certificate). *Accreditation:* NASPAA. *Students:* 18 full-time (7 women), 130 part-time (72 women); includes 53 minority (46 African Americans, 2 American Indian/Alaska Native, 1 Asian American or Pacific Islander, 4 Hispanic Americans), 5 international. Average age 34. In 2009, 17 master's, 37 other advanced degrees awarded. Application fee: $35. Tuition and fees vary according to course level. *Unit head:* Dr. Joseph Ohren, Program Director, 734-487-2522, Fax: 734-487-3340, E-mail: joseph.ohren@emich.edu. *Application contact:* Dr. Sukru Koyluoglu, Program Coordinator, 734-487-0063, Fax: 734-487-3340, E-mail: sukru.koyuoglu@emich.edu.

Eastern Michigan University, Graduate School, College of Health and Human Services, Interdisciplinary Program in Health and Human Services, Ypsilanti, MI 48197. Offers community building (Graduate Certificate); nonprofit management (Graduate Certificate). Part-time and evening/weekend programs available. In 2009, 1 other advanced degree awarded. *Entrance requirements:* Additional exam requirements/recommendations for international students: Required—TOEFL. Application fee: $35. Tuition and fees vary according to course level. *Unit head:* Dr. Marcia Bombyk, Program Coordinator, 734-487-4173, Fax: 734-487-8536, E-mail: marcia.bombyk@emich.edu. *Application contact:* Dr. Marcia Bombyk, Program Coordinator, 734-487-4173, Fax: 734-487-8536, E-mail: marcia.bombyk@emich.edu.

Eastern Michigan University, Graduate School, College of Health and Human Services, School of Health Sciences, Program in Health Administration, Ypsilanti, MI 48197. Offers MHA, MS, Graduate Certificate. *Students:* 4 full-time (2 women), 37 part-time (23 women); includes 20 minority (18 African Americans, 2 Asian Americans or Pacific Islanders). Average age 37. In 2009, 5 master's, 1 other advanced degree awarded. Application fee: $35. Tuition and fees vary according to course level. *Unit head:* Dr. Colleen Croxall, Program Director, 734-487-2072, Fax: 734-487-4095, E-mail: colleen.croxall@emich.edu. *Application contact:* Dr. Colleen Croxall, Program Director, 734-487-2072, Fax: 734-487-4095, E-mail: colleen.croxall@emich.edu.

Eastern Michigan University, Graduate School, College of Health and Human Services, School of Nursing, Ypsilanti, MI 48197. Offers nursing (MSN); quality improvement in health care systems (Graduate Certificate); teaching in health care systems (MSN, Graduate Certificate). *Accreditation:* AACN. Part-time and evening/weekend programs available. Postbaccalaureate distance learning degree programs offered (minimal on-campus study). *Faculty:* 21 full-time (19 women). *Students:* 14 full-time (all women), 45 part-time (38 women); includes 17 minority (14 African Americans, 3 Asian Americans or Pacific Islanders), 3 international. Average age 42. 23 applicants, 65% accepted, 11 enrolled. In 2009, 15 master's, 19 other advanced degrees awarded. *Degree requirements:* For master's, thesis optional. *Entrance requirements:* For master's, GRE General Test, Michigan RN license. Additional exam requirements/recommendations for international students: Required—TOEFL. *Application deadline:* Applications are processed on a rolling basis. Application fee: $35. Tuition and fees vary according to course level. *Financial support:* In 2009–10, 2 research assistantships with full tuition reimbursements (averaging $8,400 per year) were awarded; fellowships, teaching assistantships with full tuition reimbursements, career-related internships or fieldwork, Federal Work-Study, institutionally sponsored loans, scholarships/grants, tuition waivers (partial), and unspecified assistantships also available. Support available to part-time students. Financial award applicants required to submit FAFSA. *Unit head:* Dr. Betty Beard, Director, 734-487-2310, Fax: 734-487-9646, E-mail: bbeard@emich.edu. *Application contact:* Dr. Barbara Scheffer, MSN Coordinator, 734-487-2310, Fax: 734-487-9646, E-mail: bscheffer@emich.edu.

Eastern University, School of Management Studies, St. Davids, PA 19087-3696. Offers health administration (MBA); management (MBA).

East Tennessee State University, School of Graduate Studies, College of Business and Technology, Department of Management and Marketing, Johnson City, TN 37614. Offers business administration (MBA, Certificate); health care management (Certificate). Part-time and evening/weekend programs available. *Degree requirements:* For master's, comprehensive exam. *Entrance requirements:* For master's, GMAT, minimum GPA of 2.5. Additional exam requirements/recommendations for international students: Required—TOEFL (minimum score 550 paper-based; 213 computer-based).

East Tennessee State University, School of Graduate Studies, College of Nursing, Johnson City, TN 37614. Offers advanced nursing practice (Post Master's Certificate); health care management (Certificate); nursing (MSN, DSN). *Accreditation:* AACN. Part-time programs available. *Degree requirements:* For master's, comprehensive exam, thesis optional. *Entrance*

Health Services Management and Hospital Administration

East Tennessee State University (continued)
requirements: For master's, GRE General Test, minimum GPA of 3.0, bachelor's degree in nursing, current RN license. Additional exam requirements/recommendations for international students: Required—TOEFL (minimum score 550 paper-based; 213 computer-based). *Faculty research:* Rural primary care, health care for the homeless, community health problems across the lifespan, nursing education research, school health services.

East Tennessee State University, School of Graduate Studies, College of Public and Allied Health, Department of Public Health, Johnson City, TN 37614. Offers community health (MPH); epidemiology (Certificate); gerontology (Certificate); health care management (Certificate); public health (MPH); public health administration (MPH). *Accreditation:* CEPH. Part-time programs available. *Degree requirements:* For master's, comprehensive exam, thesis optional. *Entrance requirements:* For master's, GRE General Test, 2 years of community health experience. Additional exam requirements/recommendations for international students: Required—TOEFL (minimum score 550 paper-based; 213 computer-based). *Faculty research:* Rural health issues, youth and adolescent health, health of the elderly, environmental epidemiology, spatial analysis of data.

Emory University, Rollins School of Public Health, Department of Health Policy and Management, Atlanta, GA 30322-1100. Offers health policy (MPH); health policy research (MSPH); health services management (MPH). Part-time programs available. *Degree requirements:* For master's, thesis (for some programs), practicum, capstone course. *Entrance requirements:* For master's, GRE General Test. Additional exam requirements/recommendations for international students: Required—TOEFL (minimum score 550 paper-based; 215 computer-based; 80 iBT). Electronic applications accepted. *Faculty research:* U.S. health policy and financing, healthcare organization and financing.

Emory University, Rollins School of Public Health, Online Program in Public Health, Atlanta, GA 30322-1100. Offers applied epidemiology (MPH); healthcare outcomes (MPH); prevention science (MPH). Part-time and evening/weekend programs available. Postbaccalaureate distance learning degree programs offered (minimal on-campus study). *Degree requirements:* For master's, thesis, practicum. *Entrance requirements:* For master's, GRE (may be waived). Additional exam requirements/recommendations for international students: Required—TOEFL (minimum score 550 paper-based; 213 computer-based; 80 iBT). Electronic applications accepted.

Fairfield University, School of Nursing, Fairfield, CT 06824-5195. Offers clinical nurse leader (MSN); family nurse practitioner (MSN, PMC); healthcare management (MSN); nurse anesthesia (MSN); psychiatric nurse practitioner (MSN, PMC). *Accreditation:* AACN; AANA/CANAEP. Part-time programs available. *Degree requirements:* For master's, capstone project. *Entrance requirements:* For master's, GRE (nurse anesthesia applicants only), minimum QPA of 3.0, RN license, resume, 2 recommendations; for PMC, 1 year of work experience as a registered nurse. Additional exam requirements/recommendations for international students: Required—TOEFL (minimum score 550 paper-based; 213 computer-based; 80 iBT). Electronic applications accepted. *Expenses:* Contact institution. *Faculty research:* Care of older adults, palliative care, spirituality and innovative partnerships, diabetes.

Fairleigh Dickinson University, College at Florham, Silberman College of Business, Executive MBA Programs, Executive MBA Program for Health Care and Life Sciences Professionals, Madison, NJ 07940-1099. Offers EMBA.

Fairleigh Dickinson University, Metropolitan Campus, Silberman College of Business, Program in Healthcare and Life Sciences, Teaneck, NJ 07666-1914. Offers EMBA. *Students:* 13 full-time (3 women), 4 part-time (2 women), 1 international. Average age 39. 13 applicants, 100% accepted, 9 enrolled. In 2009, 6 master's awarded. Application fee: $40. *Application contact:* Susan Brooman, University Director of Graduate Admissions, 201-692-2554, Fax: 201-692-2560, E-mail: globaleducation@fdu.edu.

Florida Institute of Technology, Graduate Programs, College of Business, Online Programs, Melbourne, FL 32901-6975. Offers accounting and finance (MBA); healthcare management (MBA); information technology (MS); information technology management (MBA); management (MBA); marketing (MBA); project management (MBA). Part-time and evening/weekend programs available. Postbaccalaureate distance learning degree programs offered (no on-campus study). *Faculty:* 30 part-time/adjunct (6 women). *Students:* 6 full-time (2 women), 875 part-time (387 women); includes 290 minority (194 African Americans, 6 American Indian/Alaska Native, 44 Asian Americans or Pacific Islanders, 46 Hispanic Americans), 32 international. Average age 37. 329 applicants, 64% accepted, 177 enrolled. In 2009, 33 master's awarded. *Entrance requirements:* For master's, GMAT or resume showing 8 years of supervised experience, 2 letters of recommendation, resume, competency in math past college algebra. Additional exam requirements/recommendations for international students: Required—TOEFL (minimum score 550 paper-based; 213 computer-based; 79 iBT). *Application deadline:* For fall admission, 4/1 for international students; for spring admission, 9/30 for international students. Applications are processed on a rolling basis. Application fee: $50. Electronic applications accepted. *Expenses:* Tuition: Part-time $1015 per credit. Tuition and fees vary according to campus/location and program. *Financial support:* Available to part-time students. Application deadline: 3/1. *Unit head:* Dr. Mary S. Bonhomme, Dean, Florida Tech Online/Associate Provost for Online Learning, 321-674-8883, Fax: 321-674-8216, E-mail: bonhomme@fit.edu. *Application contact:* Carolyn Farrior, Director of Graduate Admissions Online Learning and Off Campus Programs, 321-674-7118, Fax: 321-674-8216, E-mail: cfarrior@fit.edu.

Florida International University, Stempel College of Public Health and Social Work, Department of Health Policy and Management, Miami, FL 33199. Offers MHSA. Part-time and evening/weekend programs available. *Faculty:* 4 full-time (2 women). *Students:* 15 full-time (9 women), 12 part-time (7 women); includes 23 minority (10 African Americans, 1 Asian American or Pacific Islander, 12 Hispanic Americans), 3 international. Average age 29. 28 applicants, 0% accepted, 0 enrolled. In 2009, 12 master's awarded. *Entrance requirements:* For master's, GRE General Test, minimum GPA of 3.0. Additional exam requirements/recommendations for international students: Required—TOEFL (minimum score 550 paper-based; 80 iBT). *Application deadline:* For fall admission, 6/1 for domestic students, 4/1 for international students; for spring admission, 10/1 for domestic students, 9/1 for international students. Applications are processed on a rolling basis. Application fee: $30. Electronic applications accepted. *Expenses:* Tuition, state resident: full-time $8008; part-time $4004 per year. Tuition, nonresident: full-time $20,104; part-time $10,052 per year. Required fees: $298; $149 per term. *Financial support:* Institutionally sponsored loans and scholarships/grants available. Financial award application deadline: 3/1; financial award applicants required to submit FAFSA. *Unit head:* Dr. H. Virginia McCoy, Director, 305-348-3777, Fax: 305-348-5848, E-mail: ph@fiu.edu. *Application contact:* Nanett Rojas, Assistant Director of Graduate Admissions, 305-348-7442, Fax: 305-348-7441, E-mail: gradadm@fiu.edu.

Florida International University, Stempel College of Public Health and Social Work, Programs in Public Health, Miami, FL 33199. Offers biostatistics (MPH); environmental and occupational health (MPH, PhD); epidemiology (MPH, PhD); health policy and management (MPH); health promotion and disease prevention (PhD); health promotion and diseases prevention (MPH). PhD only admits in Fall. *Accreditation:* CEPH. Part-time and evening/weekend programs available. Postbaccalaureate distance learning degree programs offered (no on-campus study). *Faculty:* 18 full-time (6 women). *Students:* 249 full-time (186 women), 185 part-time (144 women); includes 309 minority (154 African Americans, 2 American Indian/Alaska Native, 26 Asian Americans or Pacific Islanders, 127 Hispanic Americans), 48 international. Average age 35. 484 applicants, 29% accepted, 123 enrolled. In 2009, 79 master's, 1 doctorate awarded. *Degree requirements:* For master's, thesis optional; for doctorate, comprehensive exam, thesis/dissertation. *Entrance requirements:* For master's, minimum GPA of 3.0, letters of recommendation; for doctorate, GRE, resume, minimum GPA of 3.0, letters of recommendation, letter of intent. Additional exam requirements/recommendations for international students: Required—TOEFL (minimum score 550 paper-based; 80 iBT). *Application deadline:* For fall admission, 6/1 for domestic students, 4/1 for international students; for spring admission, 10/1 for domestic students, 9/1 for international students. Applications are processed on a rolling basis. Application fee: $30. Electronic applications accepted. *Expenses:* Contact institution. *Financial support:* Institutionally sponsored loans, scholarships/grants, and tuition waivers (full) available. Financial award application deadline: 3/1; financial award applicants required to submit FAFSA. *Faculty research:* Drugs/AIDS intervention among migrant workers, provision of services for active/recovering drug users with HIV. *Unit head:* Dr. Gilbert Ramirez, Associate Dean for Academic and Student Affairs, 305-348-7442, E-mail: ph@fiu.edu. *Application contact:* Nanett Rojas, Assistant Director of Graduate Admissions, 305-348-7442, Fax: 305-348-7441, E-mail: gradadm@fiu.edu.

Florida State University, The Graduate School, College of Nursing, Tallahassee, FL 32312. Offers family nurse practitioner (MSN, DNP); health systems leadership (DNP); nurse educator (MSN, Certificate). *Accreditation:* AACN. Part-time programs available. Postbaccalaureate distance learning degree programs offered (no on-campus study). *Faculty:* 13 full-time (12 women). *Students:* 13 full-time (4 women), 102 part-time (100 women); includes 13 minority (7 African Americans, 3 Asian Americans or Pacific Islanders, 3 Hispanic Americans). Average age 35. 42 applicants, 71% accepted, 29 enrolled. In 2009, 25 master's, 3 other advanced degrees awarded. *Degree requirements:* For master's, thesis optional. *Entrance requirements:* For master's, GRE General Test, MAT, minimum GPA of 3.0, BSN, Florida RN license; for doctorate, GRE General Test, MAT, minimum GPA of 3.0, BSN or MSN, Florida RN license. Additional exam requirements/recommendations for international students: Required—TOEFL (minimum score 550 paper-based). *Application deadline:* For fall admission, 7/1 for domestic and international students. Application fee: $30. Electronic applications accepted. *Expenses:* Tuition, state resident: full-time $7413. Tuition, nonresident: full-time $22,567. *Financial support:* In 2009–10, 101 students received support, including fellowships with partial tuition reimbursements available (averaging $6,300 per year), research assistantships with partial tuition reimbursements available (averaging $3,000 per year), 3 teaching assistantships with partial tuition reimbursements available (averaging $3,000 per year); career-related internships or fieldwork, Federal Work-Study, institutionally sponsored loans, scholarships/grants, traineeships, and tuition waivers (partial) also available. Financial award application deadline: 4/15; financial award applicants required to submit FAFSA. *Faculty research:* Distance learning, gerontology, health promotion, educational strategies, rehabilitation of brain injured patients. *Unit head:* Dr. Lisa Ann Plowfield, Dean, 850-644-3297, Fax: 850-644-7660, E-mail: lplowfield@nursing.fsu.edu. *Application contact:* Brenda Pereira, Graduate Program Coordinator, 850-644-5638, Fax: 850-645-7249, E-mail: bpereira@fsu.edu.

Framingham State University, Division of Graduate and Continuing Education, Program in Health Care Administration, Framingham, MA 01701-9101. Offers MA. Part-time and evening/weekend programs available.

Francis Marion University, Graduate Programs, School of Business, Florence, SC 29502-0547. Offers business (MBA); health management (MBA). *Accreditation:* AACSB. Part-time and evening/weekend programs available. *Faculty:* 16 full-time (2 women), 1 part-time/adjunct (0 women). *Students:* 7 full-time (3 women), 35 part-time (16 women); includes 12 minority (10 African Americans, 2 Asian Americans or Pacific Islanders), 2 international. Average age 38. 32 applicants, 28% accepted, 9 enrolled. In 2009, 10 degrees awarded. *Degree requirements:* For master's, comprehensive exam. *Entrance requirements:* For master's, GMAT. *Application deadline:* For fall admission, 3/15 priority date for domestic students; for spring admission, 10/15 priority date for domestic students. Applications are processed on a rolling basis. Application fee: $30. *Expenses:* Tuition, state resident: full-time $8345; part-time $417.25 per semester hour. Tuition, nonresident: full-time $16,690; part-time $814.50 per semester hour. Required fees: $335; $12.25 per semester hour. $30 per semester. *Financial support:* In 2009–10, 2 research assistantships (averaging $1,500 per year) were awarded; unspecified assistantships also available. Support available to part-time students. Financial award application deadline: 3/1; financial award applicants required to submit FAFSA. *Faculty research:* Ethics, directions of MBA, international business, regional economics, environmental issues. *Unit head:* Dr. M. Barry O'Brien, Dean, 843-661-1419, Fax: 843-661-1432, E-mail: mbobrien@fmarion.edu. *Application contact:* Dr. M. Barry O'Brien, Dean, 843-661-1419, Fax: 843-661-1432, E-mail: mbobrien@fmarion.edu.

Franklin Pierce University, Graduate Studies, Rindge, NH 03461-0060. Offers emerging network technology (Graduate Certificate); health practice management (MBA, Graduate Certificate); human resource management (MBA); human resources management (Graduate Certificate); information technology management (MS); leadership (MBA, DA), including transformational leadership (DA); nursing (MS); physical therapy (DPT); physician assistant (MPAS); sports facilities management (MS); teacher education (M Ed). *Accreditation:* APTA. Part-time programs available. Postbaccalaureate distance learning degree programs offered (no on-campus study). *Faculty:* 27 full-time (16 women), 18 part-time/adjunct (4 women). *Students:* 296 full-time (172 women), 249 part-time (165 women); includes 18 minority (5 African Americans, 7 Asian Americans or Pacific Islanders, 6 Hispanic Americans), 31 international. Average age 38. 227 applicants, 97% accepted, 185 enrolled. In 2009, 76 master's, 46 doctorates awarded. *Degree requirements:* For master's, concentrated original research projects; student teaching; fieldwork and/or internship; leadership project; for doctorate, concentrated original research projects, clinical fieldwork and/or internship, leadership project. *Entrance requirements:* For master's, minimum GPA of 2.5, 3 letters of recommendation; for doctorate, demonstrated success at previous academic institutions (minimum GPA of 2.5), 3 letters of recommendation, personal mission statement, interview; writing sample (for DA program). Additional exam requirements/recommendations for international students: Required—TOEFL (minimum score 550 paper-based; 195 computer-based). *Application deadline:* Applications are processed on a rolling basis. Application fee: $0. Electronic applications accepted. *Expenses:* Tuition: Part-time $1560 per course. Part-time tuition and fees vary according to degree level, campus/location and program. *Financial support:* In 2009–10, 36 students received support, including 22 teaching assistantships with full and partial tuition reimbursements available; career-related internships or fieldwork and unspecified assistantships also available. Support available to part-time students. Financial award applicants required to submit FAFSA. *Faculty research:* Evidence based practice in sports physical therapy, human resource management in economic crisis, leadership in nursing, innovation in sports facility management, differentiated learning and understanding by design. *Unit head:* Dr. Robert G. Goddard, Assistant Dean, 603-899-4361, Fax: 603-229-4580, E-mail: goddardr@franklinpierce.edu. *Application contact:* 800-325-1090, Fax: 603-898-0827, E-mail: gpsadmin@franklinpierce.edu.

Friends University, Graduate School, Division of Business, Technology, and Leadership, Program in Health Care Leadership, Wichita, KS 67213. Offers MHCL. Evening/weekend programs available. *Entrance requirements:* Additional exam requirements/recommendations for international students: Required—TOEFL (minimum score 560 paper-based; 220 computer-based).

The George Washington University, College of Professional Studies, Program in Healthcare Corporate Compliance, Washington, DC 20052. Offers Graduate Certificate. Postbaccalaureate distance learning degree programs offered. *Students:* 26 part-time (17 women); includes 1 minority (African American). Average age 44. 40 applicants, 100% accepted, 25 enrolled. In 2009, 36 Graduate Certificates awarded. *Application deadline:* For fall admission, 8/31 for domestic students. *Unit head:* Phyllis C. Borzi, Director, 202-530-2312, E-mail: borziph@gwu.edu. *Application contact:* Kristin Williams, Assistant Vice President for Graduate and Special Enrollment Management, 202-994-0467, Fax: 202-994-0371, E-mail: ksw@gwu.edu.

The George Washington University, School of Medicine and Health Sciences, Health Sciences Programs, Washington, DC 20052. Offers adult nurse practitioner (MSN, Post Master's Certificate); clinical practice management (MSHS); clinical research administration (MSHS); clinical research administration for nurses (MSN); emergency services management (MSHS); end-of-life care (MSHS, MSN); family nurse practitioner (MSN, Post Master's Certificate); immunohematology (MSHS); nursing (DNP); nursing leadership and management (MSN); physical therapy (DPT); physician assistant (MSHS); MSHS/MPH. Postbaccalaureate distance learning degree programs offered (no on-campus study). *Students:* 270 full-time (220 women),

491 part-time (406 women); includes 176 minority (83 African Americans, 5 American Indian/Alaska Native, 62 Asian Americans or Pacific Islanders, 26 Hispanic Americans), 26 international. Average age 35. 1,059 applicants, 47% accepted, 292 enrolled. In 2009, 155 master's, 22 doctorates, 75 other advanced degrees awarded. *Entrance requirements:* Additional exam requirements/recommendations for international students: Required—TOEFL (minimum score 550 paper-based; 213 computer-based). *Application deadline:* Applications are processed on a rolling basis. Application fee: $60. *Expenses:* Contact institution. *Unit head:* Jean E. Johnson, Senior Associate Dean, 202-994-3725, E-mail: jejohns@gwu.edu. *Application contact:* Joke Ogundiran, Director of Admission, 202-994-1668, Fax: 202-994-0870, E-mail: jokeogun@gwu.edu.

The George Washington University, School of Public Health and Health Services, Department of Health Policy, Washington, DC 20052. Offers MPH, MS. *Faculty:* 98 part-time/adjunct (44 women). *Students:* 116 full-time (93 women), 102 part-time (80 women); includes 78 minority (31 African Americans, 2 American Indian/Alaska Native, 36 Asian Americans or Pacific Islanders, 9 Hispanic Americans), 14 international. Average age 29. 155 applicants, 91% accepted, 58 enrolled. In 2009, 48 master's awarded. *Degree requirements:* For master's, case study or special project. *Entrance requirements:* For master's, GMAT, GRE General Test, or MCAT. Additional exam requirements/recommendations for international students: Required—TOEFL. *Application deadline:* For fall admission, 4/15 priority date for domestic students, 4/15 for international students; for spring admission, 11/1 for domestic and international students. Applications are processed on a rolling basis. Application fee: $60. *Financial support:* In 2009–10, 10 students received support. Tuition waivers available. Financial award application deadline: 2/15. *Unit head:* Sara Rosenbaum, Chair, 202-994-4230, Fax: 202-296-0025, E-mail: sarar@gwu.edu. *Application contact:* Jane Smith, Director of Admissions, 202-994-0248, Fax: 202-994-1860, E-mail: sphhsinfo@gwumc.edu.

The George Washington University, School of Public Health and Health Services, Department of Health Services Management and Leadership, Washington, DC 20052. Offers health management and leadership (MHSA); health policy (MHSA); health services administration (Specialist); public health management (MPH). *Accreditation:* CAHME (one or more programs are accredited). *Degree requirements:* For master's, internship or residency. *Entrance requirements:* For master's, GMAT or GRE; for Specialist, GMAT or GRE, master's degree in related field. Additional exam requirements/recommendations for international students: Required—TOEFL. *Faculty research:* Hospital administration, ambulatory health care, social gerontology, health care financing, health care ethics.

Georgia College & State University, Graduate School, The J. Whitney Bunting School of Business, Milledgeville, GA 31061. Offers accountancy (MACCT); accounting (MBA); business (MBA); health services administration (MBA); information systems (MIS); management information services (MBA). *Accreditation:* AACSB. Part-time and evening/weekend programs available. Postbaccalaureate distance learning degree programs offered (no on-campus study). *Faculty:* 43 full-time (17 women). *Students:* 70 full-time (32 women), 166 part-time (63 women); includes 29 minority (20 African Americans, 7 Asian Americans or Pacific Islanders, 2 Hispanic Americans), 23 international. Average age 29. 134 applicants, 84% accepted, 78 enrolled. In 2009, 75 master's awarded. *Entrance requirements:* For master's, GMAT. Additional exam requirements/recommendations for international students: Recommended—TOEFL (minimum score 550 paper-based; 213 computer-based; 79 iBT). *Application deadline:* For fall admission, 7/1 priority date for domestic students; for spring admission, 11/15 priority date for domestic students. Applications are processed on a rolling basis. Application fee: $40. Electronic applications accepted. *Expenses:* Tuition, area resident: Part-time $241 per credit hour. Tuition, state resident: full-time $4338. Tuition, nonresident: full-time $17,352; part-time $964 per credit hour. Required fees: $609 per semester. Tuition and fees vary according to course load and campus/location. *Financial support:* In 2009–10, 30 research assistantships with full tuition reimbursements were awarded; career-related internships or fieldwork and unspecified assistantships also available. Support available to part-time students. Financial award application deadline: 3/1; financial award applicants required to submit FAFSA. *Unit head:* Dr. Dale Young, Interim Dean, 478-445-5497, E-mail: dale.young@gcsu.edu. *Application contact:* Lynn Hanson, Director of Graduate Programs, 478-445-5115, E-mail: lynn.hanson@gcsu.edu.

Georgia Institute of Technology, Graduate Studies and Research, College of Engineering, School of Industrial and Systems Engineering, Program in Health Systems, Atlanta, GA 30332-0001. Offers MSHS. *Entrance requirements:* For master's, GRE General Test, minimum GPA of 3.0. Additional exam requirements/recommendations for international students: Required—TOEFL. Electronic applications accepted. *Faculty research:* Emergency medical services, health development planning, health services evaluations.

Georgia Southern University, Jack N. Averitt College of Graduate Studies, Jiann-Ping Hsu College of Public Health, Program in Healthcare Administration, Statesboro, GA 30460. Offers MHA. Part-time and evening/weekend programs available. *Students:* 11 full-time (6 women), 3 part-time (1 woman); includes 2 African Americans, 1 international. Average age 26. 8 applicants, 75% accepted, 5 enrolled. *Degree requirements:* For master's, practicum. *Entrance requirements:* For master's, GRE, GMAT, personal statement, minimum cumulative undergraduate GPA of 2.75, resume, 3 letters of recommendation. Additional exam requirements/recommendations for international students: Required—TOEFL (minimum score 550 paper-based; 213 computer-based; 80 iBT). *Application deadline:* For fall admission, 3/1 priority date for domestic and international students; for spring admission, 10/1 priority date for domestic students, 10/1 for international students. Applications are processed on a rolling basis. Electronic applications accepted. *Expenses:* Contact institution. *Financial support:* In 2009–10, 12 students received support, including research assistantships with partial tuition reimbursements available (averaging $7,200 per year); unspecified assistantships also available. Financial award application deadline: 4/15; financial award applicants required to submit FAFSA. *Unit head:* Dr. James Stephens, Program Director, 912-478-5958, Fax: 912-478-0171, E-mail: jstephens@georgiasouthern.edu. *Application contact:* Dr. Charles Ziglar, Coordinator for Graduate Student Recruitment, 912-478-5635, Fax: 912-478-0740, E-mail: gradadmissions@georgiasouthern.edu.

Georgia Southern University, Jack N. Averitt College of Graduate Studies, Jiann-Ping Hsu College of Public Health, Program in Health Services Administration, Statesboro, GA 30460. Offers MHSA. Part-time programs available. *Students:* 3 part-time (2 women); includes 1 minority (African American). Average age 26. In 2009, 2 master's awarded. *Degree requirements:* For master's, managerial residency in health service or thesis. *Entrance requirements:* For master's, GRE General Test, GMAT, minimum GPA of 2.75, resume. Additional exam requirements/recommendations for international students: Required—TOEFL (minimum score 550 paper-based; 213 computer-based). *Application deadline:* For fall admission, 3/1 priority date for domestic and international students; for spring admission, 10/1 priority date for domestic students, 10/1 for international students. Applications are processed on a rolling basis. Application fee: $50. Electronic applications accepted. *Expenses:* Tuition, state resident: full-time $5040; part-time $210 per credit hour. Tuition, nonresident: full-time $20,136; part-time $839 per credit hour. Required fees: $1644. *Financial support:* In 2009–10, 3 students received support, including research assistantships with partial tuition reimbursements available (averaging $6,850 per year), teaching assistantships with partial tuition reimbursements available (averaging $6,850 per year); career-related internships or fieldwork, Federal Work-Study, scholarships/grants, tuition waivers (partial), and unspecified assistantships also available. Support available to part-time students. Financial award applicants required to submit FAFSA. *Faculty research:* Health care delivery systems, rural health care, health policy and health care financing. *Unit head:* Dr. Cassandra Arroyo, Coordinator, 912-478-1253, Fax: 912-478-5811, E-mail: carroyo@georgiasouthern.edu. *Application contact:* 912-478-5384, Fax: 912-478-0740, E-mail: gradadmissions@georgiasouthern.edu.

Georgia Southern University, Jack N. Averitt College of Graduate Studies, Jiann-Ping Hsu College of Public Health, Program in Public Health, Statesboro, GA 30460. Offers biostatistics (MPH, Dr PH); community health behavior and education (Dr PH); community health education (MPH); environmental health sciences (MPH); epidemiology (MPH); health services policy management (MPH); public health leadership (Dr PH). Part-time programs available. *Students:* 75 full-time (47 women), 23 part-time (15 women); includes 39 minority (36 African Americans, 3 Asian Americans or Pacific Islanders), 24 international. Average age 30. 50 applicants, 80% accepted, 20 enrolled. In 2009, 20 master's awarded. *Degree requirements:* For master's, thesis optional, practicum; for doctorate, comprehensive exam, thesis/dissertation, practicum. *Entrance requirements:* For master's, GRE General Test, minimum GPA of 2.75, resume, 3 letters of reference; for doctorate, GRE, GMAT, MCAT, LSAT, 3 letters of reference, statement of purpose, resume or curriculum vitae. Additional exam requirements/recommendations for international students: Required—TOEFL (minimum score 550 paper-based; 213 computer-based; 80 iBT). *Application deadline:* For fall admission, 3/1 priority date for domestic and international students; for spring admission, 10/1 priority date for domestic students, 10/1 for international students. Applications are processed on a rolling basis. Application fee: $50. Electronic applications accepted. *Expenses:* Contact institution. *Financial support:* In 2009–10, 83 students received support, including research assistantships with partial tuition reimbursements available (averaging $7,200 per year), teaching assistantships with partial tuition reimbursements available (averaging $7,200 per year); career-related internships or fieldwork, Federal Work-Study, scholarships/grants, tuition waivers (partial), and unspecified assistantships also available. Support available to part-time students. Financial award application deadline: 4/15; financial award applicants required to submit FAFSA. *Faculty research:* Biostatistics, community health, environmental health sciences, epidemiology, health policy and management, community health behavior and education, public health leadership. *Unit head:* Dr. Charles Hardy, Dean, 912-478-2674, Fax: 912-478-5811, E-mail: chardy@georgiasouthern.edu. *Application contact:* Dr. Charles Ziglar, Coordinator for Graduate Student Recruitment, 912-478-5635, Fax: 912-478-0740, E-mail: gradadmissions@georgiasouthern.edu.

Georgia State University, J. Mack Robinson College of Business, Institute of Health Administration, Atlanta, GA 30302-3083. Offers MBA, MHA, MSHA. *Accreditation:* CAHME. *Entrance requirements:* For master's, GMAT. Additional exam requirements/recommendations for international students: Required—TOEFL (minimum score 610 paper-based; 255 computer-based; 101 iBT). Electronic applications accepted.

Globe University, Minnesota School of Business, Woodbury, MN 55125. Offers business administration (MBA); health care management (MSM); information technology (MSM); managerial leadership (MSM).

Goldfarb School of Nursing at Barnes-Jewish College, Goldfarb School of Nursing at Barnes-Jewish College, St Louis, MO 63110. Offers adult acute care nurse practitioner (MSN); adult nurse practitioner (MSN); neonatal nurse practitioner (MSN); nurse anesthesia (MSN); nurse educator (MSN); nurse executive (MSN). *Accreditation:* AACN; AANA/CANAEP. Part-time and evening/weekend programs available. Postbaccalaureate distance learning degree programs offered (minimal on-campus study). *Faculty:* 18 full-time (16 women), 3 part-time/adjunct (2 women). *Students:* 28 full-time (25 women), 81 part-time (73 women); includes 34 minority (27 African Americans, 6 Asian Americans or Pacific Islanders, 1 Hispanic American), 3 international. Average age 38. 60 applicants, 75% accepted, 40 enrolled. In 2009, 26 master's awarded. *Degree requirements:* For master's, thesis or alternative. *Entrance requirements:* For master's, minimum GPA of 3.0, 2 references, statistics course. Additional exam requirements/recommendations for international students: Required—TOEFL (minimum score 550 paper-based; 213 computer-based). *Application deadline:* For fall admission, 2/1 priority date for international students; for spring admission, 10/1 priority date for international students. Applications are processed on a rolling basis. Application fee: $150. *Financial support:* In 2009–10, 60 students received support, including 20 fellowships (averaging $4,000 per year), 4 research assistantships (averaging $5,000 per year); Federal Work-Study, institutionally sponsored loans, and scholarships/grants also available. Support available to part-time students. Financial award applicants required to submit FAFSA. *Faculty research:* HIV Stigma, HIV symptom management, palliative care with children and their families, heart disease prevention in Hispanic women, depression in the well elderly, alternative therapies in pre-term infants. *Unit head:* Dr. Michael L. Evans, Dean, 314-362-6289, Fax: 314-362-0984, E-mail: mevans@bjc.org. *Application contact:* Dr. Michael Ward, Associate Dean for Student Programs, 314-362-9155, Fax: 314-362-9250, E-mail: mward@bjc.org.

Governors State University, College of Health Professions, Program in Health Administration, University Park, IL 60466-0975. Offers MHA. *Accreditation:* CAHME. *Degree requirements:* For master's, comprehensive exam, field experience or internship. *Entrance requirements:* For master's, minimum GPA of 3.0 in last 60 hours of undergraduate course work or 9 hours of graduate course work.

Grambling State University, School of Graduate Studies and Research, College of Arts and Sciences, Program in Public Administration, Grambling, LA 71270. Offers health service administration (MPA); human resource management (MPA); public management (MPA); state and local government (MPA). *Accreditation:* NASPAA. Part-time programs available. *Faculty:* 5 full-time (2 women), 2 part-time/adjunct (0 women). *Students:* 25 full-time (16 women), 14 part-time (12 women); includes 32 minority (all African Americans), 5 international. Average age 29. 30 applicants, 53% accepted, 11 enrolled. In 2009, 12 master's awarded. *Degree requirements:* For master's, comprehensive exam (for some programs), thesis optional. *Entrance requirements:* For master's, GRE, minimum GPA of 2.75 on last degree. Additional exam requirements/recommendations for international students: Required—TOEFL (minimum score 500 paper-based; 173 computer-based; 61 iBT). *Application deadline:* For fall admission, 7/1 for domestic and international students; for spring admission, 12/1 for domestic and international students. Applications are processed on a rolling basis. Application fee: $20 ($30 for international students). Electronic applications accepted. *Expenses:* Tuition, state resident: full-time $2610. Tuition, nonresident: full-time $2610. *Financial support:* In 2009–10, 6 research assistantships (averaging $5,958 per year) were awarded; health care benefits, tuition waivers (full), and unspecified assistantships also available. Financial award application deadline: 5/31. *Unit head:* Dr. Rose Harris, Director, 318-274-2310, Fax: 318-274-3427, E-mail: harrisr@gram.edu. *Application contact:* Sarah Dennis, Admissions Coordinator, 318-274-2319, Fax: 318-274-3427, E-mail: denniss@alpha0.gram.edu.

Grand Canyon University, College of Business, Phoenix, AZ 85017-1097. Offers accounting (MBA); executive fire service leadership (MS); finance (MBA); general management (MBA); health systems management (MBA); leadership (MBA, MS); management of information system (MBA); marketing (MBA); six sigma (MBA). *Accreditation:* ACBSP. Part-time and evening/weekend programs available. Postbaccalaureate distance learning degree programs offered (no on-campus study). *Entrance requirements:* For master's, equivalent of two years full-time professional work experience. Additional exam requirements/recommendations for international students: Required—TOEFL (minimum score 575 paper-based; 233 computer-based; 90 iBT), IELTS (minimum score 7). Electronic applications accepted.

Grand Valley State University, College of Community and Public Service, School of Public and Nonprofit Administration, Program in Health Administration, Allendale, MI 49401-9403. Offers MHA. Part-time and evening/weekend programs available. *Faculty:* 6 full-time (2 women), 3 part-time/adjunct (1 woman). *Students:* 16 full-time (12 women), 31 part-time (18 women); includes 8 minority (4 African Americans, 3 American Indian/Alaska Native, 1 Asian American or Pacific Islander). Average age 33. 15 applicants, 67% accepted, 5 enrolled. In 2009, 15 master's awarded. *Entrance requirements:* Additional exam requirements/recommendations for international students: Required—TOEFL. *Application deadline:* For fall admission, 5/1 priority date for domestic students; for winter admission, 11/1 priority date for domestic students. Applications are processed on a rolling basis. Application fee: $30. Electronic applications accepted. *Expenses:* Tuition, state resident: part-time $471 per credit hour. Tuition, nonresident: part-time $646 per credit hour. Tuition and fees vary according to course level. *Financial support:* In 2009–10, 10 students received support, including 1 fellowship (averaging $1,062 per year), 4 research assistantships with full and partial tuition reimbursements available (averaging $8,000 per year). Financial award application deadline: 5/1. *Faculty research:* Long-term care and aging, Medicare and Medicaid finance and administration, health economics. *Unit head:* Dr. Mark Hoffman, Director, 616-331-6575, Fax: 616-331-7120, E-mail: hoffman@

Health Services Management and Hospital Administration

Grand Valley State University (continued)

gvsu.edu. *Application contact:* Dr. Stephen Borders, Graduate Program Director, 616-331-8569, E-mail: borders@gvsu.edu.

Grand Valley State University, Kirkhof College of Nursing, Allendale, MI 49401-9403. Offers advanced practice (MSN); case management (MSN); nursing administration (MSN); nursing education (MSN); nursing practice (DNP); MSN/MBA. *Accreditation:* AACN. Part-time programs available. *Faculty:* 17 full-time (all women), 3 part-time/adjunct (all women). *Students:* 6 full-time (5 women), 69 part-time (61 women); includes 3 minority (all African Americans). Average age 39. 18 applicants, 100% accepted, 18 enrolled. In 2009, 23 master's awarded. *Degree requirements:* For master's, thesis optional. *Entrance requirements:* For master's, GRE, minimum GPA of 3.0 in upper-division course work, course work in statistics, Michigan RN license. Additional exam requirements/recommendations for international students: Required—TOEFL. *Application deadline:* For fall admission, 3/15 priority date for domestic students. Applications are processed on a rolling basis. Application fee: $30. Electronic applications accepted. *Expenses:* Tuition, state resident: part-time $471 per credit hour. Tuition, nonresident: part-time $646 per credit hour. Tuition and fees vary according to course level. *Financial support:* In 2009–10, 23 students received support, including 14 fellowships (averaging $3,207 per year), 9 research assistantships with full and partial tuition reimbursements available (averaging $8,053 per year); career-related internships or fieldwork, Federal Work-Study, institutionally sponsored loans, and traineeships also available. Financial award application deadline: 2/15. *Faculty research:* Multigenerational health promotion, chronic disease prevention, end-of-life issues, nursing workload, family caregiver health. Total annual research expenditures: $36,000. *Unit head:* Dr. Cynthia McCurren, Dean, 616-331-7161, Fax: 616-331-7362. *Application contact:* Dr. Jean Martin, Director of Graduate Programs, 616-331-7167, Fax: 616-331-7362, E-mail: martinj@gvsu.edu.

Grantham University, College of Arts and Sciences, Kansas City, MO 64153. Offers case management (MSN); health systems management (MS); healthcare administration (MHA); nursing (MSN); nursing education (MSN); nursing informatics (MSN); nursing management and organizational leadership (MSN). Part-time and evening/weekend programs available. Postbaccalaureate distance learning degree programs offered (no on-campus study). In 2009, 48 master's awarded. *Degree requirements:* For master's, thesis (for some programs), capstone project. *Entrance requirements:* For master's, bachelor's degree from accredited degree-granting institution. Additional exam requirements/recommendations for international students: Required—TOEFL (minimum score 500 paper-based; 213 computer-based; 61 iBT). *Application deadline:* Applications are processed on a rolling basis. Electronic applications accepted. *Expenses:* Tuition: Part-time $265 per credit hour. One-time fee: $30 part-time. *Financial support:* Institutionally sponsored loans and scholarships/grants available. *Unit head:* Dr. Kim Humerickhouse, Dean, 800-955-2527, Fax: 816-595-5757, E-mail: admissions@grantham.edu. *Application contact:* Matthew Hawes, Vice President of Enrollment Management, 800-955-2527, Fax: 816-595-5757, E-mail: admissions@grantham.edu.

Harding University, College of Business Administration, Searcy, AR 72149-0001. Offers accounting (MBA); health care management (MBA); information technology management (MBA); international business (MBA); leadership and organizational management (MBA). *Accreditation:* ACBSP. Part-time and evening/weekend programs available. Postbaccalaureate distance learning degree programs offered (no on-campus study). *Faculty:* 27 part-time/adjunct (6 women). *Students:* 105 full-time (46 women), 140 part-time (66 women); includes 31 minority (18 African Americans, 3 American Indian/Alaska Native, 6 Asian Americans or Pacific Islanders, 4 Hispanic Americans), 43 international. Average age 31. 82 applicants, 96% accepted, 66 enrolled. In 2009, 130 master's awarded. *Degree requirements:* For master's, portfolio. *Entrance requirements:* For master's, minimum GPA of 3.0, 2 letters of recommendation, resume. Additional exam requirements/recommendations for international students: Required—TOEFL (minimum score 550 paper-based; 213 computer-based; 80 iBT). *Application deadline:* For fall admission, 8/1 priority date for domestic and international students; for spring admission, 12/1 priority date for domestic and international students. Applications are processed on a rolling basis. Application fee: $35. *Expenses:* Tuition: Full-time $9720; part-time $540 per credit hour. Required fees: $22 per credit hour. Tuition and fees vary according to course load and program. *Financial support:* In 2009–10, 27 students received support. Unspecified assistantships available. Financial award application deadline: 7/30; financial award applicants required to submit FAFSA. *Unit head:* Glen Metheny, Director of Graduate Studies, 501-279-5851, Fax: 501-279-4805, E-mail: gmetheny@harding.edu. *Application contact:* Melanie Kiihnl, Recruiting Manager/Director of Marketing, 501-279-4523, Fax: 501-279-4805, E-mail: mba@harding.edu.

Harrisburg University of Science and Technology, Program in Information Systems Engineering and Management, Harrisburg, PA 17101. Offers digital government specialization (MS); digital health specialization (MS); entrepreneurship specialization (MS). Part-time programs available. *Faculty:* 1 full-time (0 women), 2 part-time/adjunct (0 women). *Degree requirements:* For master's, comprehensive exam, thesis optional. *Entrance requirements:* Additional exam requirements/recommendations for international students: Required—TOEFL (minimum score 520 paper-based; 200 computer-based; 80 iBT). *Application deadline:* For fall admission, 8/1 priority date for domestic students, 7/1 priority date for international students. Applications are processed on a rolling basis. Application fee: $0. Electronic applications accepted. *Expenses:* Tuition: Full-time $18,000; part-time $650 per semester hour. *Financial support:* Scholarships/grants available. Financial award applicants required to submit FAFSA. *Unit head:* Dr. Amjad Umar, Director and Professor, 717-901-5141, Fax: 717-901-3141, E-mail: aumar@harrisburgu.edu. *Application contact:* Julie Cullings, Information Contact, 717-901-5163, Fax: 717-901-3163, E-mail: admissions@harrisburgu.edu.

Harvard University, Graduate School of Arts and Sciences, Committee on Higher Degrees in Health Policy, Cambridge, MA 02138. Offers PhD. *Degree requirements:* For doctorate, thesis/dissertation. *Entrance requirements:* For doctorate, GMAT, GRE General Test, or MCAT. Additional exam requirements/recommendations for international students: Required—TOEFL. *Expenses:* Tuition: Full-time $33,696. Required fees: $1126. Full-time tuition and fees vary according to program.

Harvard University, Harvard Business School, Doctoral Programs in Management, Boston, MA 02163. Offers accounting and management (DBA); business economics (PhD); health policy management (PhD); management (DBA); marketing (DBA); organizational behavior (PhD); science, technology and management (PhD); strategy (DBA); technology and operations management (DBA). *Degree requirements:* For doctorate, comprehensive exam (for some programs), thesis/dissertation. *Entrance requirements:* For doctorate, GRE General Test or GMAT. Additional exam requirements/recommendations for international students: Required—TOEFL. *Expenses:* Tuition: Full-time $33,696. Required fees: $1126. Full-time tuition and fees vary according to program.

Harvard University, School of Public Health, Department of Health Policy and Management, Boston, MA 02115-6096. Offers health policy (PhD); health policy and management (SM, SD). Part-time programs available. *Faculty:* 43 full-time (12 women), 36 part-time/adjunct (14 women). *Students:* 109 full-time, 43 part-time; includes 29 minority (9 African Americans, 2 American Indian/Alaska Native, 14 Asian Americans or Pacific Islanders, 4 Hispanic Americans), 34 international. Average age 35. 123 applicants, 34% accepted, 23 enrolled. In 2009, 32 master's, 9 doctorates awarded. *Degree requirements:* For doctorate, thesis/dissertation, qualifying exam. *Entrance requirements:* For master's, GRE, GMAT; for doctorate, GRE. Additional exam requirements/recommendations for international students: Required—TOEFL (minimum score 595 paper-based; 240 computer-based; 95 iBT); Recommended—IELTS (minimum score 7). *Application deadline:* For fall admission, 12/15 for domestic and international students. Application fee: $115. *Expenses:* Tuition: Full-time $33,696. Required fees: $1126. Full-time tuition and fees vary according to program. *Financial support:* Fellowships, research assistantships, teaching assistantships, Federal Work-Study, scholarships/grants, traineeships, tuition waivers (partial), and unspecified assistantships available. Support available to part-time students. Financial award application deadline: 2/8; financial award applicants required to submit FAFSA. *Faculty research:* Environmental science and risk management.

Unit head: Dr. Arnold Epstein, Chair, 617-432-3895, Fax: 617-432-4494, E-mail: aepstein@hsph.harvard.edu. *Application contact:* Vincent W. James, Director of Admissions, 617-432-1031, Fax: 617-432-7080, E-mail: admisofc@hsph.harvard.edu.

Hofstra University, Frank G. Zarb School of Business, Department of Management, Entrepreneurship and General Management, Hempstead, NY 11549. Offers business administration (MBA), including health services management, management, sports and entertainment management; human resource management (MS). Part-time and evening/weekend programs available. *Faculty:* 6 full-time (2 women), 4 part-time/adjunct (0 women). *Students:* 75 full-time (35 women), 185 part-time (72 women); includes 55 minority (19 African Americans, 24 Asian Americans or Pacific Islanders, 12 Hispanic Americans), 26 international. Average age 33. 215 applicants, 61% accepted, 71 enrolled. In 2009, 53 master's awarded. *Degree requirements:* For master's, capstone course (MBA), thesis (MS). *Entrance requirements:* For master's, GMAT or GRE, 2 letters of recommendation, resume. Additional exam requirements/recommendations for international students: Required—TOEFL (minimum score 550 paper-based; 213 computer-based; 80 iBT); Recommended—IELTS (minimum score 6). *Application deadline:* Applications are processed on a rolling basis. Application fee: $60. Electronic applications accepted. *Expenses:* Contact institution. *Financial support:* In 2009–10, 23 students received support, including 20 fellowships with full and partial tuition reimbursements available (averaging $10,251 per year), 2 research assistantships with full and partial tuition reimbursements available (averaging $20,788 per year); career-related internships or fieldwork, Federal Work-Study, institutionally sponsored loans, scholarships/grants, tuition waivers (full and partial), and unspecified assistantships also available. Support available to part-time students. Financial award applicants required to submit FAFSA. *Faculty research:* Business/personal ethics; emotion in workplace; gender issues; learning and pedagogical issues; family business. *Unit head:* Dr. Mamdouh I. Farid, Chairperson, 516-463-5735, Fax: 516-463-4834, E-mail: mgbmif@hofstra.edu. *Application contact:* Carol Drummer, Dean of Graduate Admissions, 516-463-4876, Fax: 516-463-4664, E-mail: gradstudent@hofstra.edu.

Hofstra University, School of Education, Health, and Human Services, Department of Health Professions and Family Studies, Program in Health Administration, Hempstead, NY 11549. Offers MHA. Part-time programs available. *Students:* 46 full-time (35 women), 79 part-time (60 women); includes 51 minority (42 African Americans, 5 Asian Americans or Pacific Islanders, 4 Hispanic Americans), 7 international. Average age 33. 88 applicants, 82% accepted, 42 enrolled. In 2009, 22 master's awarded. *Degree requirements:* For master's, internship. *Entrance requirements:* For master's, interview, 2 letters of recommendation, resume. Additional exam requirements/recommendations for international students: Required—TOEFL (minimum score 550 paper-based; 213 computer-based; 80 iBT). *Application deadline:* Applications are processed on a rolling basis. Application fee: $60. Electronic applications accepted. *Expenses:* Tuition: Full-time $16,200; part-time $900 per credit hour. Required fees: $970; $145 per term. Tuition and fees vary according to program. *Financial support:* In 2009–10, 33 students received support, including 4 fellowships with full and partial tuition reimbursements available (averaging $2,688 per year); research assistantships with full and partial tuition reimbursements available, career-related internships or fieldwork, Federal Work-Study, institutionally sponsored loans, scholarships/grants, tuition waivers (full and partial), and unspecified assistantships also available. Support available to part-time students. Financial award applicants required to submit FAFSA. *Faculty research:* Health care policy; cost benefit analyses in health care settings; health and disease; chronic illness management; long term care policy reform. *Unit head:* Dr. Debra Tennyson-Feinstein, Program Director, 516-463-5224, Fax: 516-463-4810, E-mail: hprdht@hofstra.edu. *Application contact:* Carol Drummer, Dean of Graduate Admissions, 516-463-4876, Fax: 516-463-4664, E-mail: gradstudent@hofstra.edu.

Holy Family University, Division of Extended Learning, Philadelphia, PA 19114. Offers business administration (MBA); finance (MBA); health care administration (MBA). Part-time and evening/weekend programs available. *Faculty:* 78 part-time/adjunct (32 women). *Students:* 116 part-time (71 women); includes 18 minority (10 African Americans, 6 Asian Americans or Pacific Islanders, 2 Hispanic Americans). Average age 35. 46 applicants, 93% accepted, 41 enrolled. In 2009, 47 master's awarded. *Entrance requirements:* For master's, interview, essay. Additional exam requirements/recommendations for international students: Required—TOEFL. *Application deadline:* Applications are processed on a rolling basis. Application fee: $50. Electronic applications accepted. *Expenses:* Tuition: Part-time $600 per credit. Required fees: $58 per semester. *Financial support:* Applicants required to submit FAFSA. *Unit head:* Honour Moore, Associate Vice President, 267-341-5008, Fax: 215-633-0558, E-mail: hmoore@holyfamily.edu. *Application contact:* Don Reinmold, Director of Admissions, 267-341-5001 Ext. 3230, Fax: 215-633-0558, E-mail: dreinmold@holyfamily.edu.

Houston Baptist University, College of Business and Economics, Program in Health Administration, Houston, TX 77074-3298. Offers MSHA. Part-time and evening/weekend programs available. *Entrance requirements:* For master's, GMAT, minimum GPA of 2.5. Additional exam requirements/recommendations for international students: Required—TOEFL (minimum score 550 paper-based; 213 computer-based).

Hunter College of the City University of New York, Graduate School, Schools of the Health Professions, School of Health Sciences, Programs in Urban Public Health, Program in Health Policy Management, New York, NY 10021-5085. Offers MPH. Part-time and evening/weekend programs available. *Faculty:* 27 full-time (17 women), 3 part-time/adjunct (2 women). *Students:* 4 full-time (1 woman), 32 part-time (26 women); includes 13 minority (6 African Americans, 4 Asian Americans or Pacific Islanders, 3 Hispanic Americans). Average age 32. 49 applicants, 69% accepted, 22 enrolled. *Degree requirements:* For master's, comprehensive exam, thesis optional, internship. *Entrance requirements:* For master's, GRE General Test, previous course work in calculus and statistics. Additional exam requirements/recommendations for international students: Required—TOEFL. *Application deadline:* For fall admission, 4/1 for domestic students; for spring admission, 11/1 for domestic students. Application fee: $125. *Expenses:* Tuition, state resident: full-time $7360; part-time $310 per credit. Required fees: $250 per semester. *Financial support:* In 2009–10, 6 fellowships were awarded; career-related internships or fieldwork, Federal Work-Study, institutionally sponsored loans, and tuition waivers (partial) also available. Support available to part-time students. *Unit head:* Stacey Plichta, Coordinator, 212-481-7674, Fax: 212-481-5260, E-mail: splichta@hunter.cuny.edu. *Application contact:* Milena Solo, Director for Graduate Admissions, 212-772-4288, Fax: 212-650-3336, E-mail: milena.solo@hunter.cuny.edu.

Husson University, School of Graduate and Professional Studies, Program in Business, Bangor, ME 04401-2999. Offers health care management (MSB); nonprofit management (MSB). Part-time and evening/weekend programs available. *Degree requirements:* For master's, thesis optional. *Entrance requirements:* For master's, GMAT, minimum GPA of 2.5.

Independence University, Program in Business Administration in Health Care, Salt Lake City, UT 84107. Offers health care administration (MBA). Part-time and evening/weekend programs available. Postbaccalaureate distance learning degree programs offered (no on-campus study). *Degree requirements:* For master's, fieldwork/internship. *Expenses:* Required fees: $475 per credit. One-time fee: $100 part-time.

Independence University, Program in Health Care Administration, Salt Lake City, UT 84107. Offers MSHCA. Part-time and evening/weekend programs available. Postbaccalaureate distance learning degree programs offered (no on-campus study). *Degree requirements:* For master's, fieldwork, internship. *Entrance requirements:* For master's, previous course work in psychology. *Expenses:* Required fees: $475 per credit. One-time fee: $100 part-time.

Independence University, Program in Health Services, Salt Lake City, UT 84107. Offers community health (MSHS); wellness promotion (MSHS). Part-time and evening/weekend programs available. Postbaccalaureate distance learning degree programs offered (no on-campus study). *Degree requirements:* For master's, fieldwork, internship, final project (wellness promotion). *Entrance requirements:* For master's, previous course work in psychology. *Expenses:* Required fees: $475 per credit. One-time fee: $100 part-time.

Indiana Tech, Program in Business Administration, Fort Wayne, IN 46803-1297. Offers accounting (MBA); health care administration (MBA); human resources (MBA); management (MBA); marketing (MBA). Part-time and evening/weekend programs available. Postbaccalaureate distance learning degree programs offered (no on-campus study). *Students:* 202 full-time (97 women), 37 part-time (18 women); includes 60 minority (45 African Americans, 2 American Indian/Alaska Native, 7 Asian Americans or Pacific Islanders, 6 Hispanic Americans), 5 international. Average age 38. *Entrance requirements:* For master's, GMAT, minimum undergraduate GPA of 2.5, 3 letters of recommendation. *Application deadline:* Applications are processed on a rolling basis. Application fee: $25. Electronic applications accepted. *Expenses:* Tuition: Full-time $5160; part-time $430 per credit hour. Tuition and fees vary according to degree level and program. *Financial support:* Applicants required to submit FAFSA. *Unit head:* Dr. Andrew Nwanne, Associate Dean of College of Professional Studies, 260-422-5561 Ext. 2214, E-mail: ainwanne@indianatech.edu. *Application contact:* Steve Herendeen, Manager of Campus Development and Support, 260-422-5561 Ext. 2121, E-mail: saherendeen@indianatech.edu.

Indiana University Northwest, School of Public and Environmental Affairs, Gary, IN 46408-1197. Offers criminal justice (MPA); environmental affairs (Graduate Certificate); health services administration (MPA); human services administration (MPA); nonprofit management (Graduate Certificate); public management (MPA, Graduate Certificate). *Accreditation:* NASPAA (one or more programs are accredited). Part-time programs available. *Faculty:* 5 full-time (3 women). *Students:* 19 full-time (14 women), 121 part-time (100 women); includes 100 minority (84 African Americans, 1 American Indian/Alaska Native, 1 Asian American or Pacific Islander, 14 Hispanic Americans). Average age 39. In 2009, 29 master's, 27 other advanced degrees awarded. *Entrance requirements:* For master's, GRE General Test or GMAT, letters of recommendation. *Application deadline:* For fall admission, 8/15 priority date for domestic students. Applications are processed on a rolling basis. Application fee: $25. *Financial support:* Career-related internships or fieldwork, Federal Work-Study, and tuition waivers (partial) available. Support available to part-time students. Financial award application deadline: 3/1. *Faculty research:* Employment in income security policies, evidence in criminal justice, equal employment law, social welfare policy and welfare reform, public finance in developing countries. *Unit head:* George Assibey-Mensah, Interim Dean/Division Director, 219-980-6695, Fax: 219-980-6737. *Application contact:* Sandra Hall Smith, Secretary, 219-980-6695, Fax: 219-980-6737, E-mail: shsmith@iun.edu.

Indiana University of Pennsylvania, School of Graduate Studies and Research, College of Health and Human Services, Department of Nursing and Allied Health, Indiana, PA 15705-1087. Offers health service administration (MS); nursing (MS, PhD). Part-time programs available. *Faculty:* 6 full-time (5 women), 1 (woman) part-time/adjunct. *Students:* 3 full-time (all women), 73 part-time (68 women); includes 2 minority (1 African American, 1 Hispanic American), 1 international. Average age 41. 41 applicants, 51% accepted, 11 enrolled. In 2009, 14 master's awarded. *Degree requirements:* For master's, thesis optional. *Entrance requirements:* For master's, 2 letters of recommendation. Additional exam requirements/recommendations for international students: Required—TOEFL. *Application deadline:* For fall admission, 7/1 priority date for domestic students; for spring admission, 11/1 for domestic students. Applications are processed on a rolling basis. Application fee: $40. *Expenses:* Tuition, state resident: full-time $6666; part-time $370 per credit hour. Tuition, nonresident: full-time $10,666; part-time $593 per credit hour. Required fees: $813 per semester. *Financial support:* In 2009–10, 4 fellowships (averaging $875 per year), 5 research assistantships with full and partial tuition reimbursements (averaging $2,190 per year), 2 teaching assistantships (averaging $16,153 per year) were awarded; Federal Work-Study also available. Support available to part-time students. Financial award application deadline: 3/15; financial award applicants required to submit FAFSA. *Unit head:* Dr. Michele Gerwick, Chairperson, 724-357-2557, E-mail: mgerwick@iup.edu. *Application contact:* Dr. Nashat Zuraikat, Graduate Coordinator, 724-357-3262, E-mail: zuraikat@iup.edu.

Indiana University–Purdue University Indianapolis, Indiana University School of Medicine, Department of Public Health, Indianapolis, IN 46202-2896. Offers behavioral health science (MPH); epidemiology (MPH); health policy and management (MPH). *Students:* 62 full-time (47 women), 71 part-time (54 women); includes 37 minority (24 African Americans, 12 Asian Americans or Pacific Islanders, 1 Hispanic American), 15 international. Average age 31. 17 applicants, 65% accepted, 6 enrolled.Application fee: $55 ($65 for international students). *Expenses:* Contact institution. *Financial support:* In 2009–10, 1 teaching assistantship (averaging $14,058 per year) was awarded. *Unit head:* Dr. Carole Kacius, Director, 317-274-3126. *Application contact:* Robert M. Stump, Director of Admissions, 317-274-3772, E-mail: inmedadm@iupui.edu.

Indiana University–Purdue University Indianapolis, School of Public and Environmental Affairs, Indianapolis, IN 46202-2896. Offers health administration (MHA); public affairs (MPA), including criminal justice, environmental management, nonprofit management, policy analysis, public management; JD/MHA; MBA/MHA; MLS/NMC; MLS/PMC; MSN/MHA. *Accreditation:* CAHME (one or more programs are accredited); NASPAA. Part-time and evening/weekend programs available. *Faculty:* 17 full-time (6 women). *Students:* 126 full-time (71 women), 283 part-time (164 women); includes 58 minority (29 African Americans, 1 American Indian/Alaska Native, 17 Asian Americans or Pacific Islanders, 11 Hispanic Americans), 20 international. Average age 33. 255 applicants, 77% accepted, 136 enrolled. In 2009, 77 master's awarded. *Entrance requirements:* For master's, GRE General Test, minimum GPA of 3.0 (preferred). Additional exam requirements/recommendations for international students: Required—TOEFL. *Application deadline:* For fall admission, 7/15 priority date for domestic students; for spring admission, 11/15 for domestic students. Applications are processed on a rolling basis. Application fee: $55 ($65 for international students). *Financial support:* In 2009–10, 11 fellowships with full and partial tuition reimbursements (averaging $5,890 per year), 10 teaching assistantships (averaging $9,900 per year) were awarded; research assistantships with full and partial tuition reimbursements, career-related internships or fieldwork, Federal Work-Study, institutionally sponsored loans, and scholarships/grants also available. Support available to part-time students. Financial award application deadline: 3/1. *Faculty research:* Economic development, water and air quality, ethics, financing, organization design and structure. Total annual research expenditures: $1.9 million. *Unit head:* Dr. Greg Lindsey, Associate Dean, 317-274-4656, Fax: 317-274-5153. *Application contact:* 317-274-4656, Fax: 317-274-5153, E-mail: speainfo@speanet.iupui.edu.

Indiana University South Bend, School of Public and Environmental Affairs, South Bend, IN 46634-7111. Offers health systems administration and policy (MPA); health systems management (Certificate); nonprofit management (Certificate); public and community services administration and policy (MPA); public management (Certificate); urban affairs (Certificate). *Accreditation:* NASPAA. Part-time and evening/weekend programs available. *Faculty:* 4 full-time (1 woman). *Students:* 18 part-time (13 women); includes 3 minority (2 African Americans, 1 Hispanic American). Average age 40. In 2009, 9 master's awarded. *Entrance requirements:* For master's, GRE General Test, minimum undergraduate GPA of 2.5. *Application deadline:* For fall admission, 7/1 priority date for domestic students; for spring admission, 11/1 for domestic students. Applications are processed on a rolling basis. Application fee: $46 ($58 for international students). *Financial support:* Fellowships, research assistantships, career-related internships or fieldwork, Federal Work-Study, and institutionally sponsored loans available. Support available to part-time students. Financial award application deadline: 3/1; financial award applicants required to submit FAFSA. *Unit head:* Leda M. Hall, Dean, 574-520-4803. *Application contact:* Leda M. Hall, Dean, 574-520-4803.

Institute of Public Administration, Programs in Public Administration, Dublin, Ireland. Offers healthcare management (MA); local government management (MA); public management (MA, Diploma).

Iona College, Hagan School of Business, Department of Management, New Rochelle, NY 10801-1890. Offers business administration (MBA); health care management (MBA); human resource management (MBA, PMC); management (MBA, PMC). Part-time and evening/weekend programs available. *Faculty:* 7 full-time (2 women), 4 part-time/adjunct (2 women). *Students:* 23 full-time (12 women), 133 part-time (76 women); includes 19 minority (7 African Americans, 1 American Indian/Alaska Native, 3 Asian Americans or Pacific Islanders, 8 Hispanic Americans), 4 international. Average age 33. 71 applicants, 75% accepted, 34 enrolled. In 2009, 57 master's, 1 other advanced degree awarded. *Entrance requirements:* For master's, GMAT, 2 letters of recommendation; for PMC, GMAT. Additional exam requirements/recommendations for international students: Required—TOEFL (minimum score 550 paper-based; 213 computer-based). *Application deadline:* Applications are processed on a rolling basis. Application fee: $50. Electronic applications accepted. *Expenses:* Contact institution. *Financial support:* Scholarships/grants, tuition waivers (partial), and unspecified assistantships available. Support available to part-time students. Financial award application deadline: 4/15; financial award applicants required to submit FAFSA. *Faculty research:* Information systems, strategic management, corporate values and ethics. *Unit head:* Dr. Fredrica Rudell, Acting Chair, 914-637-2748, E-mail: frudell@iona.edu. *Application contact:* Jude Fleurismond, Director of MBA Admissions, 914-633-2289, Fax: 914-637-2708, E-mail: jfleurismond@iona.edu.

The Johns Hopkins University, Bloomberg School of Public Health, Department of Health Policy and Management, Baltimore, MD 21205-1996. Offers bioethics and policy (PhD); health and public policy (PhD); health care management and leadership (Dr PH); health economics (MHS); health economics and policy (PhD); health finance and management (MHA); health policy (MHS); health services research and policy (PhD). *Accreditation:* CAHME (one or more programs are accredited). Part-time programs available. *Faculty:* 60 full-time (32 women), 178 part-time/adjunct (66 women). *Students:* 136 full-time (95 women), 55 part-time (21 women); includes 53 minority (14 African Americans, 36 Asian Americans or Pacific Islanders, 3 Hispanic Americans), 48 international. Average age 32. 299 applicants, 39% accepted, 64 enrolled. In 2009, 49 master's, 19 doctorates awarded. *Degree requirements:* For master's, thesis (for some programs), internship (for some programs); for doctorate, comprehensive exam, thesis/dissertation, 1 year full-time residency (for some programs), oral and written exams. *Entrance requirements:* For master's, GRE General Test or GMAT, 3 letters of recommendation, curriculum vitae/resume; for doctorate, GRE General Test or GMAT, 3 letters of recommendation, curriculum vitae, transcripts. Additional exam requirements/recommendations for international students: Recommended—TOEFL (minimum score 600 paper-based; 250 computer-based; 100 iBT), IELTS. *Application deadline:* For fall admission, 12/1 for domestic and international students. Applications are processed on a rolling basis. Application fee: $45. Electronic applications accepted. *Financial support:* In 2009–10, 145 students received support; fellowships, research assistantships, teaching assistantships, career-related internships or fieldwork, Federal Work-Study, institutionally sponsored loans, scholarships/grants, traineeships, and stipends available. Support available to part-time students. Financial award application deadline: 3/15; financial award applicants required to submit FAFSA. *Faculty research:* Quality of care and health outcomes, health care finance and technology, health disparities and vulnerable populations, injury prevention, health policy and health care policy. Total annual research expenditures: $14.2 million. *Unit head:* Dr. Ellen J. MacKenzie, Chairman, 410-955-3625, E-mail: emackenz@jhsph.edu. *Application contact:* Mary Sewell, Coordinator, 410-955-2489, Fax: 410-614-9152, E-mail: msewell@jhsph.edu.

The Johns Hopkins University, Bloomberg School of Public Health, Department of International Health, Baltimore, MD 21205. Offers global disease epidemiology and control (MHS, PhD); health systems (MHS, PhD); human nutrition (MHS, PhD); international health (Dr PH); social and behavioral interventions (MHS, PhD). *Faculty:* 137 full-time (82 women), 185 part-time/adjunct (63 women). *Students:* 242 full-time (189 women), 1 (woman) part-time; includes 61 minority (9 African Americans, 41 Asian Americans or Pacific Islanders, 11 Hispanic Americans), 71 international. Average age 28. 494 applicants, 48% accepted, 100 enrolled. In 2009, 66 master's, 15 doctorates awarded. *Degree requirements:* For master's, comprehensive exam, thesis (for some programs), 1 year full-time residency, 4-9 month internship; for doctorate, comprehensive exam, thesis/dissertation or alternative, 1.5 years full-time residency, oral and written exams. *Entrance requirements:* For master's, GRE General Test or MCAT, 3 letters of recommendation, resume; for doctorate, GRE General Test or MCAT, 3 letters of recommendation, resume, transcripts. Additional exam requirements/recommendations for international students: Required—TOEFL (minimum score 600 paper-based; 250 computer-based; 100 iBT); Recommended—IELTS (minimum score 7). *Application deadline:* For fall admission, 1/2 priority date for domestic and international students. Applications are processed on a rolling basis. Application fee: $45. Electronic applications accepted. *Financial support:* In 2009–10, 188 students received support, including 15 fellowships (averaging $50,000 per year); Federal Work-Study, institutionally sponsored loans, scholarships/grants, traineeships, and stipends also available. Financial award application deadline: 1/2. *Faculty research:* Nutrition, infectious diseases, health systems, health economics, humanitarian emergencies. Total annual research expenditures: $72 million. *Unit head:* Dr. Robert E. Black, Chairman, 410-955-3934, Fax: 410-955-7159, E-mail: rblack@jhsph.edu. *Application contact:* Cristina G. Salazar, Academic Program Manager, 410-955-3734, Fax: 410-955-7159, E-mail: csalazar@jhsph.edu.

The Johns Hopkins University, Carey Business School, Business of Health Program, Baltimore, MD 21218-2699. Offers business of medicine (Certificate); business of nursing (Certificate); leadership and management in the life sciences (MBA); medical services management (MBA); MBA/MPH; MBA/MS; MBA/MSN. Part-time and evening/weekend programs available. *Faculty:* 29 full-time (6 women), 135 part-time/adjunct (29 women). *Students:* 24 full-time (9 women), 119 part-time (46 women); includes 43 minority (19 African Americans, 19 Asian Americans or Pacific Islanders, 5 Hispanic Americans), 20 international. Average age 40. 121 applicants, 82% accepted, 67 enrolled. In 2009, 69 master's, 1 other advanced degree awarded. *Degree requirements:* For master's, 54 credits including capstone project. *Entrance requirements:* For master's, GMAT or GRE, minimum GPA of 3.0, resume, work experience, two letters of recommendation; for Certificate, minimum GPA of 3.0, resume, work experience, two letters of recommendation. Additional exam requirements/recommendations for international students: Required—TOEFL (minimum score 600 paper-based; 250 computer-based; 100 iBT). *Application deadline:* For fall admission, 5/1 for international students; for spring admission, 10/15 for international students. Applications are processed on a rolling basis. Application fee: $100. Electronic applications accepted. *Financial support:* Scholarships/grants available. Support available to part-time students. Financial award application deadline: 4/1; financial award applicants required to submit FAFSA. *Faculty research:* Clinical practice optimization, operations management, supply chain risk management. *Unit head:* Dr. Dipankar Chakravarti, Vice Dean of Programs, 410-516-8561, E-mail: dipankar.chakravarti@jhu.edu. *Application contact:* Robin Greenberg, Admissions Coordinator, 410-516-4234, Fax: 410-516-0826, E-mail: carey.admissions@jhu.edu.

Jones International University, School of Business, Centennial, CO 80112. Offers accounting (MBA); business communication (MABC); entrepreneurship (MABC, MBA); finance (MBA); global enterprise management (MBA); health care management (MBA); information security management (MBA); information technology management (MBA); leadership and influence (MABC); leading the customer-driven organization (MABC); negotiation and conflict management (MBA); project management (MABC, MBA). Program only offered online. Part-time and evening/weekend programs available. Postbaccalaureate distance learning degree programs offered (no on-campus study). *Degree requirements:* For master's, capstone project. *Entrance requirements:* For master's, minimum cumulative GPA of 2.5. Additional exam requirements/recommendations for international students: Recommended—TOEFL (minimum score 550 paper-based; 213 computer-based). Electronic applications accepted.

Kaplan University, Davenport Campus, School of Business, Davenport, IA 52807-2095. Offers business administration (MBA); change leadership (MS); entrepreneurship (MBA); finance (MBA); health care management (MBA, MS); human resource (MBA); international business (MBA); management (MS); marketing (MBA); project management (MBA, MS); supply chain management and logistics (MBA, MS). Part-time and evening/weekend programs available. Postbaccalaureate distance learning degree programs offered (no on-campus study). *Entrance requirements:* Additional exam requirements/recommendations for international

Health Services Management and Hospital Administration

Kaplan University, Davenport Campus (continued)
students: Required—TOEFL (minimum score 550 paper-based; 218 computer-based; 80 iBT). Electronic applications accepted.

Kaplan University, Davenport Campus, School of Legal Studies, Davenport, IA 52807-2095. Offers health care delivery (MS); pathway to paralegal (Postbaccalaureate Certificate); state and local government (MS). Part-time and evening/weekend programs available. Postbaccalaureate distance learning degree programs offered (no on-campus study). *Entrance requirements:* Additional exam requirements/recommendations for international students: Required—TOEFL (minimum score 550 paper-based; 218 computer-based; 80 iBT).

Kean University, College of Business and Public Administration, Program in Public Administration, Union, NJ 07083. Offers environmental management (MPA); health services administration (MPA); non-profit management (MPA); public administration (MPA). *Accreditation:* NASPAA. Part-time and evening/weekend programs available. *Faculty:* 8 full-time (4 women). *Students:* 48 full-time (33 women), 92 part-time (53 women); includes 85 minority (62 African Americans, 9 Asian Americans or Pacific Islanders, 14 Hispanic Americans), 9 international. Average age 31. 80 applicants, 74% accepted, 34 enrolled. In 2009, 49 master's awarded. *Degree requirements:* For master's, thesis, internship, research seminar. *Entrance requirements:* For master's, minimum GPA of 3.0, 2 letters of recommendation, interview. *Application deadline:* For fall admission, 5/1 for domestic students; for spring admission, 11/1 for domestic students. Application fee: $60 ($150 for international students). Electronic applications accepted. *Expenses:* Tuition, state resident: full-time $10,440; part-time $435 per credit. Tuition, nonresident: full-time $14,160; part-time $590 per credit. Required fees: $2642; $110 per credit. Part-time tuition and fees vary according to course load and degree level. *Financial support:* In 2009–10, 10 research assistantships with full tuition reimbursements (averaging $3,263 per year) were awarded; unspecified assistantships also available. *Unit head:* Dr. Patricia Moore, Program Coordinator, 908-737-4300, E-mail: pmoore@kean.edu. *Application contact:* Steven Koch, Pre-Admissions Coordinator, 908-737-5924, Fax: 908-737-5965, E-mail: skoch@kean.edu.

Kennesaw State University, College of Health and Human Services, Program in Advanced Care Management and Leadership, Kennesaw, GA 30144-5591. Offers MSN. Part-time and evening/weekend programs available. Postbaccalaureate distance learning degree programs offered (minimal on-campus study). *Students:* 14 full-time (all women), 2 part-time (both women); includes 6 minority (5 African Americans, 1 Asian American or Pacific Islander), 2 international. Average age 36. 26 applicants, 58% accepted, 12 enrolled. In 2009, 1 master's awarded. *Entrance requirements:* For master's, GRE General Test, minimum GPA of 3.0, 3 years experience, RN license. Additional exam requirements/recommendations for international students: Required—TOEFL (minimum score 550 paper-based; 213 computer-based; 80 iBT), IELTS (minimum score 6). *Application deadline:* For fall admission, 6/1 for domestic and international students. Application fee: $60. Electronic applications accepted. *Expenses:* Tuition, state resident: full-time $2341; part-time $196 per credit hour. Tuition, nonresident: full-time $9396; part-time $783 per credit hour. Required fees: $573 per semester. *Financial support:* In 2009–10, research assistantships with tuition reimbursements (averaging $4,000 per year); unspecified assistantships also available. *Unit head:* Dr. Marilyn King, Director, 770-423-6172, Fax: 770-423-6870, E-mail: mking71@kennesaw.edu. *Application contact:* Vilma Marquez, Admissions Counselor, 770-420-4377, Fax: 770-423-6885, E-mail: ksugrad@kennesaw.edu.

King's College, William G. McGowan School of Business, Wilkes-Barre, PA 18711-0801. Offers health care administration (MS). *Accreditation:* AACSB. Part-time programs available. *Entrance requirements:* Additional exam requirements/recommendations for international students: Required—TOEFL (minimum score 600 paper-based; 250 computer-based).

Lake Erie College, Division of Management Studies, Painesville, OH 44077-3389. Offers general management (MBA); management healthcare administration (MBA). Part-time and evening/weekend programs available. *Entrance requirements:* For master's, GMAT or minimum GPA of 3.0, resume, references. Additional exam requirements/recommendations for international students: Required—TOEFL (minimum score 590 paper-based). Electronic applications accepted. *Faculty research:* Organizational effectiveness.

Lakeland College, Graduate Studies Division, Program in Business Administration, Sheboygan, WI 53082-0359. Offers accounting (MBA); finance (MBA); healthcare management (MBA); project management (MBA). *Entrance requirements:* For master's, GMAT. *Expenses:* Contact institution.

Lamar University, College of Graduate Studies, College of Business, Beaumont, TX 77710. Offers accounting (MBA); experiential business and entrepreneurship (MBA); financial management (MBA); healthcare administration (MBA); information systems (MBA); management (MBA). *Accreditation:* AACSB. Part-time and evening/weekend programs available. *Faculty:* 18 full-time (4 women), 4 part-time/adjunct (0 women). *Students:* 62 full-time (27 women), 59 part-time (16 women); includes 19 minority (8 African Americans, 6 Asian Americans or Pacific Islanders, 5 Hispanic Americans), 19 international. Average age 29. 210 applicants, 34% accepted, 33 enrolled. In 2009, 41 master's awarded. *Degree requirements:* For master's, comprehensive exam (for some programs), thesis optional. *Entrance requirements:* For master's, GMAT. Additional exam requirements/recommendations for international students: Required—TOEFL (minimum score 525 paper-based; 197 computer-based). *Application deadline:* For fall admission, 3/15 priority date for domestic students; for spring admission, 10/1 priority date for domestic students. Applications are processed on a rolling basis. Application fee: $25 ($50 for international students). *Financial support:* In 2009–10, 12 students received support, including 4 research assistantships with partial tuition reimbursements available; fellowships with tuition reimbursements available, career-related internships or fieldwork, Federal Work-Study, institutionally sponsored loans, scholarships/grants, and tuition waivers (partial) also available. Support available to part-time students. Financial award application deadline: 4/1; financial award applicants required to submit FAFSA. *Faculty research:* Marketing, finance, quantitative methods, management information systems, legal, environmental. *Unit head:* Dr. Enrique R. Venta, Dean, 409-880-8604, Fax: 409-880-8088, E-mail: henry.venta@lamar.edu. *Application contact:* Dr. Brad Mayer, Professor and Associate Dean, 409-880-2383, Fax: 409-880-8605, E-mail: bradley.mayer@lamar.edu.

Lewis University, College of Business, Graduate School of Management, Program in Business Administration, Romeoville, IL 60446. Offers accounting (MBA); custom elective option (MBA); e-business (MBA); finance (MBA); healthcare management (MBA); human resources management (MBA); information security (MBA); international business (MBA); management information systems (MBA); marketing (MBA); project management (MBA); technology and operations management (MBA). Part-time and evening/weekend programs available. *Faculty:* 15 full-time (2 women), 18 part-time/adjunct (4 women). *Students:* 120 full-time (64 women), 222 part-time (103 women); includes 97 minority (62 African Americans, 4 Asian Americans or Pacific Islanders, 31 Hispanic Americans), 9 international. Average age 31. In 2009, 84 master's awarded. *Entrance requirements:* For master's, interview, bachelor's degree, resume, 2 recommendations. Additional exam requirements/recommendations for international students: Required—TOEFL (minimum score 550 paper-based; 213 computer-based). *Application deadline:* For fall admission, 8/15 priority date for domestic students, 5/1 priority date for international students; for spring admission, 11/15 priority date for international students. Applications are processed on a rolling basis. Application fee: $40. Electronic applications accepted. *Expenses:* Tuition: Full-time $6480; part-time $720 per credit. One-time fee: $40. Tuition and fees vary according to course load, degree level and program. *Financial support:* Career-related internships or fieldwork, Federal Work-Study, scholarships/grants, and unspecified assistantships available. Financial award application deadline: 5/1; financial award applicants required to submit FAFSA. *Unit head:* Dr. Maureen Culleeney, Academic Program Director, 815-838-0500 Ext. 5631, E-mail: culleema@lewisu.edu. *Application contact:* Michele King, Director of Admission, 815-838-0500 Ext. 5384, E-mail: gsm@lewisu.edu.

Lindenwood University, Graduate Programs, College of Individualized Education, St. Charles, MO 63301-1695. Offers administration (MSA); business administration (MBA); communications (MA); criminal justice and administration (MS); gerontology (MA); health management (MS); human resource management (MS); information technology (MBA, Certificate); management (MSA); managing information technology (MS); marketing (MSA); writing (MFA). Part-time and evening/weekend programs available. *Faculty:* 15 full-time (8 women), 128 part-time/adjunct (53 women). *Students:* 679 full-time (432 women), 90 part-time (57 women); includes 138 minority (121 African Americans, 2 American Indian/Alaska Native, 5 Asian Americans or Pacific Islanders, 10 Hispanic Americans), 18 international. Average age 34. 223 applicants, 44% accepted, 87 enrolled. In 2009, 478 master's awarded. *Degree requirements:* For master's, thesis (for some programs), 1 colloquium per term. *Entrance requirements:* For master's, interview, minimum GPA of 3.0. Additional exam requirements/recommendations for international students: Required—TOEFL (minimum score 550 paper-based; 213 computer-based; 80 iBT). *Application deadline:* For fall admission, 10/2 priority date for domestic and international students; for winter admission, 1/8 priority date for domestic and international students; for spring admission, 4/8 priority date for domestic and international students. Applications are processed on a rolling basis. Application fee: $30 ($100 for international students). *Expenses:* Tuition: Full-time $12,960; part-time $370 per credit hour. Required fees: $340. One-time fee: $30 full-time. Tuition and fees vary according to course level and course load. *Financial support:* In 2009–10, 631 students received support. Career-related internships or fieldwork, institutionally sponsored loans, tuition waivers (partial), and unspecified assistantships available. Financial award application deadline: 6/30; financial award applicants required to submit FAFSA. *Unit head:* Dan Kemper, Dean, 636-949-4501, Fax: 636-949-4505, E-mail: dkemper@lindenwood.edu. *Application contact:* Brett Barger, Dean of Evening Admissions and Extension Campuses, 636-949-4934, Fax: 636-949-4109, E-mail: adultadmissions@lindenwood.edu.

Lipscomb University, MBA Program, Nashville, TN 37204-3951. Offers accounting (MBA); business administration (general) (MBA); conflict management (MBA); financial services (MBA); healthcare management (MBA); leadership (MBA); nonprofit management (MBA); sports administration (MBA); sustainable practice (MBA). *Accreditation:* ACBSP. Part-time and evening/weekend programs available. *Faculty:* 10 full-time (1 woman), 7 part-time/adjunct (2 women). *Students:* 43 full-time (23 women), 86 part-time (38 women); includes 23 minority (18 African Americans, 1 Asian American or Pacific Islander, 4 Hispanic Americans), 1 international. Average age 31. 95 applicants, 64% accepted, 35 enrolled. In 2009, 59 master's awarded. *Entrance requirements:* For master's, GMAT, interview, 2 references, resume. Additional exam requirements/recommendations for international students: Required—TOEFL (minimum score 570 paper-based; 230 computer-based). *Application deadline:* For fall admission, 2/1 for international students; for winter admission, 6/1 for international students. Applications are processed on a rolling basis. Application fee: $50 ($75 for international students). Electronic applications accepted. *Expenses:* Contact institution. *Financial support:* Career-related internships or fieldwork, Federal Work-Study, scholarships/grants, tuition waivers (partial), and unspecified assistantships available. Support available to part-time students. Financial award application deadline: 7/1; financial award applicants required to submit FAFSA. *Faculty research:* Impact of spirituality on organization commitment, leadership, psychological empowerment, training. *Unit head:* Dr. Mike Kendrick, Interim Chair of Graduate Business Studies, 615-966-1833, Fax: 615-966-1818, E-mail: mikekendrick@lipscomb.edu. *Application contact:* Emily Landsdell, 615-966-5284, E-mail: emily.lansdell@lipscomb.edu.

Loma Linda University, School of Public Health, Programs in Health Administration, Loma Linda, CA 92350. Offers MBA, MHA, MPH. *Entrance requirements:* For master's, GMAT (MHA). Additional exam requirements/recommendations for international students: Required—Michigan Test of English Language Proficiency or TOEFL.

Long Island University, Brooklyn Campus, School of Health Professions, Department of Community Health, Brooklyn, NY 11201-8423. Offers community mental health (MS); family health (MS); health management (MS). Part-time and evening/weekend programs available. *Entrance requirements:* For master's, 2 letters of recommendation. Additional exam requirements/recommendations for international students: Required—TOEFL (minimum score 500 paper-based; 173 computer-based). Electronic applications accepted.

Long Island University, C.W. Post Campus, College of Management, Department of Health Care and Public Administration, Brookville, NY 11548-1300. Offers gerontology (Certificate); health care administration (MPA); health care administration/gerontology (MPA); nonprofit management (MPA, Certificate); public administration (MPA). *Accreditation:* NASPAA (one or more programs are accredited). Part-time and evening/weekend programs available. *Degree requirements:* For master's, thesis. *Entrance requirements:* For master's, GMAT, minimum GPA of 2.5; for Certificate, minimum GPA of 2.5. Electronic applications accepted. *Faculty research:* Critical issues in sexuality, social work in religious communities, gerontological social work.

Long Island University, Rockland Graduate Campus, Graduate School, Programs in Health and Public Administration, Orangeburg, NY 10962. Offers gerontology (Advanced Certificate); health administration (MPA); public administration (MPA). *Faculty:* 1 full-time (0 women), 5 part-time/adjunct (3 women). *Students:* 2 full-time (1 woman), 25 part-time (19 women). In 2009, 8 master's awarded. *Entrance requirements:* For master's, GRE General Test. *Application deadline:* Applications are processed on a rolling basis. Application fee: $30. *Expenses:* Tuition: Part-time $930 per credit. Required fees: $200 per semester. *Financial support:* Applicants required to submit FAFSA. *Unit head:* Prof. Patricia Latona, Program Director, 845-359-7200 Ext. 5410, Fax: 845-359-7248, E-mail: patricia.latona@liu.edu. *Application contact:* Peter S. Reiner, Director of Admissions and Marketing, 845-359-7200, Fax: 845-359-7248, E-mail: peter.reiner@liu.edu.

Louisiana State University in Shreveport, College of Business Administration, Program in Health Administration, Shreveport, LA 71115-2399. Offers MHA. Part-time and evening/weekend programs available. *Students:* 9 full-time (6 women), 17 part-time (9 women); includes 6 minority (all African Americans), 2 international. Average age 33. 18 applicants, 83% accepted, 8 enrolled. In 2009, 13 master's awarded. *Entrance requirements:* For master's, GRE or GMAT, minimum GPA of 3.0, recommendations. Additional exam requirements/recommendations for international students: Required—TOEFL (minimum score 550 paper-based; 173 computer-based; 61 iBT). *Application deadline:* For fall admission, 6/30 for domestic and international students; for spring admission, 11/30 for domestic and international students. Applications are processed on a rolling basis. Application fee: $10 ($20 for international students). *Financial support:* In 2009–10, 3 students received support, including 3 research assistantships with partial tuition reimbursements available (averaging $10,000 per year). *Faculty research:* Healthcare marketing, law and ethics, leadership. *Unit head:* Dr. John Fortenberry, Program Director, 318-795-4208, E-mail: john.fortenberry@lsus.edu. *Application contact:* Yvonne Yarbrough, Secretary, Graduate Studies, 318-797-5247, Fax: 318-798-4120, E-mail: yyarbrou@lsus.edu.

Loyola University Chicago, Graduate School, Marcella Niehoff School of Nursing, Health Systems Management Program, Chicago, IL 60660. Offers MSN, Certificate. Part-time and evening/weekend programs available. Postbaccalaureate distance learning degree programs offered (minimal on-campus study). *Students:* 4 full-time (all women), 35 part-time (32 women); includes 6 minority (2 African Americans, 3 Asian Americans or Pacific Islanders, 1 Hispanic American). Average age 37. 8 applicants, 63% accepted, 4 enrolled. In 2009, 10 master's awarded. *Degree requirements:* For master's, comprehensive exam or oral thesis defense. *Entrance requirements:* For master's, BSN, minimum nursing GPA of 3.0, IL nursing license, 1000 hours experience before starting clincial. *Application deadline:* Applications are processed on a rolling basis. Application fee: $50. Electronic applications accepted. *Expenses:* Tuition: Full-time $14,220; part-time $790 per credit hour. Required fees: $60 per semester hour. Tuition and fees vary according to program. *Financial support:* Traineeships available. Financial award application deadline: 3/1. *Faculty research:* Patient classification systems, career/job mobility. *Unit head:* Dr. Ida Androwich, Professor, 708-216-9276, Fax: 708-216-9555, E-mail: iandrow@luc.edu. *Application contact:* Dr. Vicki A. Keough, Associate Professor/Master's Program Director, 708-216-3582, Fax: 708-216-9555, E-mail: vkeough@luc.edu.

Loyola University New Orleans, College of Social Sciences, School of Nursing, New Orleans, LA 70118-6195. Offers adult nurse practitioner (MSN); family nurse practitioner (MSN); health care systems management (MSN); nursing (MSN, DNP). *Accreditation:* NLN. Part-time and evening/weekend programs available. Postbaccalaureate distance learning degree programs offered. *Students:* 60 full-time (56 women), 543 part-time (490 women); includes 147 minority (116 African Americans, 4 American Indian/Alaska Native, 13 Asian Americans or Pacific Islanders, 14 Hispanic Americans), 1 international. Average age 43. 296 applicants, 97% accepted, 206 enrolled. In 2009, 153 master's awarded. *Degree requirements:* For doctorate, capstone project. *Entrance requirements:* For master's, BSN, Louisiana nursing license, 1 year of work experience in clinical nursing, minimum undergraduate GPA of 2.8, interview, resume. Additional exam requirements/recommendations for international students: Required—TOEFL (minimum score 550 paper-based; 213 computer-based). *Application deadline:* For fall admission, 8/1 priority date for domestic and international students; for winter admission, 12/15 priority date for domestic and international students; for spring admission, 5/15 priority date for domestic and international students. Applications are processed on a rolling basis. Application fee: $20. Electronic applications accepted. *Financial support:* Traineeships and Incumbent Workers Training Program grants available. Financial award application deadline: 5/1; financial award applicants required to submit FAFSA. *Faculty research:* Increasing compliance with treatment, patient satisfaction with care provided by nurse practitioners. *Unit head:* Ann H. Cary, Director, 800-488-6257, Fax: 504-865-3254, E-mail: nursing@loyno.edu. *Application contact:* Deborah Smith, Assistant to the Director, 504-865-2823, Fax: 504-865-3254, E-mail: dhsmith@loyno.edu.

Madonna University, Program in Health Services, Livonia, MI 48150-1173. Offers MSHS. Part-time programs available. *Degree requirements:* For master's, thesis or alternative. *Entrance requirements:* For master's, GRE General Test or minimum GPA of 3.25. Additional exam requirements/recommendations for international students: Required—TOEFL, TWE. Electronic applications accepted.

Marlboro College, Graduate School, Program in (Management) Healthcare Administration, Brattleboro, VT 05301. Offers MS. Part-time and evening/weekend programs available. Postbaccalaureate distance learning degree programs offered (minimal on-campus study). *Faculty:* 8 part-time/adjunct (4 women). *Students:* 7 part-time (3 women). Average age 44. *Degree requirements:* For master's, capstone project. *Entrance requirements:* For master's, 2 letters of recommendation. *Application deadline:* Applications are processed on a rolling basis. Application fee: $0. Electronic applications accepted. *Expenses:* Tuition: Full-time $9520; part-time $680 per credit. Tuition and fees vary according to course load and program. *Financial support:* Available to part-time students. Applicants required to submit FAFSA. *Application contact:* Joe Heslin, Associate Director of Admissions, 802-258-9209, Fax: 802-258-9201, E-mail: jheslin@gradcenter.marlboro.edu.

Marshall University, Academic Affairs Division, Lewis College of Business, Graduate School of Management, Program in Health Care Administration, Huntington, WV 25755. Offers MS, DMPNA. Part-time and evening/weekend programs available. *Students:* 21 full-time (15 women), 24 part-time (14 women); includes 5 minority (2 African Americans, 2 Asian Americans or Pacific Islanders, 1 Hispanic American), 2 international. Average age 31. In 2009, 44 master's awarded. *Degree requirements:* For master's, comprehensive assessment. *Entrance requirements:* For master's, GMAT or GRE General Test. *Application deadline:* Applications are processed on a rolling basis. Application fee: $40. *Financial support:* Career-related internships or fieldwork and tuition waivers (full) available. Support available to part-time students. Financial award applicants required to submit FAFSA. *Unit head:* Dr. Andrew Sikula, Associate Dean, 304-746-1956, E-mail: sikula@marshall.edu. *Application contact:* Steven Shumlas, Academic Advisor, 304-746-8964, Fax: 304-746-1902, E-mail: shumlas@marshall.edu.

Marylhurst University, Department of Business Administration, Marylhurst, OR 97036-0261. Offers finance (MBA); general management (MBA); government policy and administration (MBA); green development (MBA); health care management (MBA); marketing (MBA); natural and organic resources (MBA); nonprofit management (MBA); organizational behavior (MBA); real estate (MBA); renewable energy (MBA); sustainable business (MBA). Part-time and evening/weekend programs available. Postbaccalaureate distance learning degree programs offered (no on-campus study). *Faculty:* 2 full-time (1 woman), 28 part-time/adjunct (5 women). *Students:* 30 full-time (12 women), 627 part-time (323 women); includes 79 minority (28 African Americans, 3 American Indian/Alaska Native, 17 Asian Americans or Pacific Islanders, 31 Hispanic Americans), 9 international. Average age 37. 299 applicants, 80% accepted, 209 enrolled. In 2009, 193 master's awarded. *Degree requirements:* For master's, comprehensive exam, capstone course. *Entrance requirements:* For master's, GMAT (if GPA less than 3.0 and fewer than 5 years of work experience), interview, resume, 2 letters of recommendation. Additional exam requirements/recommendations for international students: Recommended—TOEFL (minimum score 550 paper-based; 213 computer-based; 80 iBT). *Application deadline:* For fall admission, 9/11 priority date for domestic and international students; for winter admission, 12/15 priority date for domestic and international students; for spring admission, 3/17 priority date for domestic and international students. Applications are processed on a rolling basis. Application fee: $40 ($50 for international students). Electronic applications accepted. *Financial support:* Scholarships/grants available. Support available to part-time students. Financial award applicants required to submit FAFSA. *Unit head:* Bob Hanks, Director of Business and Real Estate Programs, 503-636-8141, Fax: 503-697-5597, E-mail: mba@marylhurst.edu. *Application contact:* Kathleen Schneff, Admissions Specialist, 800-634-9982 Ext. 3322, Fax: 503-635-6585, E-mail: admissions@marylhurst.edu.

Marymount University, Educational Partnerships Program, Arlington, VA 22207-4299. Offers business administration (MBA); health care management (MS); management studies (Certificate); organization development (Certificate). Part-time and evening/weekend programs available. *Students:* 25 part-time (17 women); includes 12 minority (11 African Americans, 1 Asian American or Pacific Islander), 1 international. Average age 43. *Entrance requirements:* For master's, GRE or GMAT, resume; for Certificate, resume. Additional exam requirements/recommendations for international students: Required—TOEFL (minimum score 600 paper-based; 250 computer-based; 96 iBT), IELTS (minimum score 6.5). *Application deadline:* For fall admission, 7/1 for international students; for spring admission, 10/15 for international students. Applications are processed on a rolling basis. Application fee: $40. Electronic applications accepted. *Expenses:* Tuition: Full-time $13,050; part-time $725 per credit hour. Required fees: $135; $7.50 per credit hour. *Financial support:* Career-related internships or fieldwork, Federal Work-Study, scholarships/grants, and unspecified assistantships available. Support available to part-time students. Financial award applicants required to submit FAFSA. *Unit head:* Dr. Sherri Hughes, Vice President for Academic Affairs and Provost, 703-284-1550, E-mail: sherri.hughes@marymount.edu. *Application contact:* Francesca Reed, Director, Graduate Admissions, 703-284-5901, Fax: 703-527-3815, E-mail: grad.admissions@marymount.edu.

Marymount University, School of Business Administration, Program in Health Care Management, Arlington, VA 22207-4299. Offers MS. *Accreditation:* CAHME. Part-time and evening/weekend programs available. *Students:* 24 full-time (10 women), 17 part-time (9 women); includes 16 minority (12 African Americans, 3 Asian Americans or Pacific Islanders, 1 Hispanic American), 6 international. Average age 33. 54 applicants, 96% accepted, 36 enrolled. In 2009, 31 master's awarded. *Degree requirements:* For master's, thesis or alternative. *Entrance requirements:* For master's, GMAT or GRE General Test, resume. Additional exam requirements/recommendations for international students: Required—TOEFL (minimum score 600 paper-based; 250 computer-based; 96 iBT), IELTS (minimum score 6.5). *Application deadline:* For fall admission, 7/15 for domestic students, 7/1 for international students; for spring admission, 11/15 for domestic students, 10/15 for international students. Applications are processed on a rolling basis. Application fee: $40. Electronic applications accepted. *Expenses:* Tuition: Full-time $13,050; part-time $725 per credit hour. Required fees: $135; $7.50 per credit hour. *Financial support:* In 2009–10, 3 students received support; research assistantships with full tuition reimbursements available, career-related internships or fieldwork, Federal Work-Study, scholarships/grants, and unspecified assistantships available. Support available to part-time students. Financial award applicants required to submit FAFSA. *Unit head:* Dr. Alyson Eisenhardt, Interim Director, 703-284-4984, Fax: 703-527-3830, E-mail: alyson.eisenhardt@marymount.edu. *Application contact:* Francesca Reed, Director, Graduate Admissions, 703-284-5901, Fax: 703-527-3815, E-mail: grad.admissions@marymount.edu.

Marywood University, Academic Affairs, College of Health and Human Services, Department of Nursing and Public Administration, Program in Health Services Administration, Scranton, PA 18509-1598. Offers MHSA. *Students:* 6 full-time (0 women), 18 part-time (16 women); includes 1 minority (Hispanic American), 5 international. Average age 35. In 2009, 6 master's awarded. *Entrance requirements:* Additional exam requirements/recommendations for international students: Required—TOEFL (minimum score 550 paper-based; 213 computer-based; 79 iBT). *Application deadline:* For fall admission, 4/1 priority date for domestic students, 3/31 priority date for international students; for spring admission, 11/1 priority date for domestic students, 8/31 priority date for international students. Applications are processed on a rolling basis. Application fee: $35. Electronic applications accepted. *Expenses:* Tuition: Part-time $715 per credit. Required fees: $270 per semester. Tuition and fees vary according to degree level, campus/location and program. *Financial support:* Career-related internships or fieldwork, scholarships/grants, and unspecified assistantships available. Support available to part-time students. Financial award application deadline: 6/30; financial award applicants required to submit FAFSA. *Application contact:* Tammy Manka, Assistant Director of Graduate Admissions, 866-279-9663, E-mail: tmanka@marywood.edu.

Massachusetts College of Pharmacy and Health Sciences, Graduate Studies, Program in Drug Regulatory Affairs and Health Policy, Boston, MA 02115-5896. Offers MS. Part-time and evening/weekend programs available. *Students:* 10 full-time (4 women), 17 part-time (13 women); includes 6 minority (2 African Americans, 4 Asian Americans or Pacific Islanders), 8 international. Average age 31. 25 applicants, 76% accepted, 9 enrolled. In 2009, 2 master's awarded. *Degree requirements:* For master's, thesis, oral defense of thesis. *Entrance requirements:* For master's, GRE General Test, minimum GPA of 3.0. Additional exam requirements/recommendations for international students: Required—TOEFL (minimum score 550 paper-based; 213 computer-based; 79 iBT). *Application deadline:* For fall admission, 7/1 priority date for domestic students, 2/1 for international students. Application fee: $70. Electronic applications accepted. *Expenses:* Tuition: Full-time $28,000; part-time $875 per credit hour. Required fees: $750; $190 per semester. Part-time tuition and fees vary according to course load, campus/location, program and student level. *Financial support:* Application deadline: 3/15. *Faculty research:* Epidemiology, drug policy, drug regulation, ethics. *Unit head:* Josephine Babiarz, Director, 617-732-2939. *Application contact:* Tara Hennesey, Coordinator of Graduate Admission, 617-732-2850, E-mail: admissions@mcphs.edu.

McGill University, Faculty of Graduate and Postdoctoral Studies, Faculty of Medicine, Department of Epidemiology and Biostatistics, Montréal, QC H3A 2T5, Canada. Offers community health (M Sc); environmental health (M Sc); epidemiology and biostatistics (M Sc, PhD, Diploma); health care evaluation (M Sc); medical statistics (M Sc). *Accreditation:* CEPH (one or more programs are accredited).

Medical University of South Carolina, College of Health Professions, Department of Health Professions, Program in Health Administration-Executive, Charleston, SC 29425. Offers MHA. Part-time programs available. Postbaccalaureate distance learning degree programs offered (no on-campus study). *Faculty:* 6 full-time (3 women), 7 part-time/adjunct (3 women). *Students:* 21 full-time (17 women), 27 part-time (19 women); includes 7 African Americans, 3 Asian Americans or Pacific Islanders, 3 Hispanic Americans. Average age 36. 24 applicants, 83% accepted, 20 enrolled. In 2009, 19 master's awarded. *Degree requirements:* For master's, 20 hours of community service. *Entrance requirements:* For master's, GRE General Test or GMAT, minimum GPA of 3.0. Additional exam requirements/recommendations for international students: Required—TOEFL (minimum score 600 paper-based; 250 computer-based). *Application deadline:* For fall admission, 2/1 priority date for domestic and international students; for spring admission, 11/15 priority date for domestic and international students. Application fee: $85. Electronic applications accepted. *Financial support:* Federal Work-Study and scholarships/grants available. Support available to part-time students. Financial award application deadline: 3/10; financial award applicants required to submit FAFSA. *Faculty research:* Electronic health records; telemedicine; fraud prediction and prevention; decision modeling; continuous quality improvement; empathy, caring, patient-centered health care and health outcomes; heath policy. Total annual research expenditures: $38,131. *Unit head:* Dr. Andrea W. White, Program Director, 843-792-4493, Fax: 843-792-3327, E-mail: whiteand@musc.edu. *Application contact:* Ann Brown, Student Services Program Coordinator, 843-792-2115, Fax: 843-792-3327, E-mail: brownah@musc.edu.

Medical University of South Carolina, College of Health Professions, Department of Health Professions, Program in Health Administration-Global, Charleston, SC 29425. Offers MHA. *Entrance requirements:* Additional exam requirements/recommendations for international students: Required—TOEFL. *Unit head:* Dr. Emily L. Moore, Program Director, 843-792-4840, E-mail: mooreemi@musc.edu. *Application contact:* Laura Mewbourn, Student Services Coordinator, 843-792-2926, Fax: 843-792-3327, E-mail: mewbourn@musc.edu.

Medical University of South Carolina, College of Health Professions, Department of Health Professions, Program in Health Administration-Residential, Charleston, SC 29425. Offers MHA. *Accreditation:* CAHME. Part-time programs available. Postbaccalaureate distance learning degree programs offered (minimal on-campus study). *Faculty:* 6 full-time (3 women), 6 part-time/adjunct (3 women). *Students:* 66 full-time (48 women); includes 7 minority (6 African Americans, 1 Hispanic American). Average age 24. 61 applicants, 75% accepted, 41 enrolled. In 2009, 32 master's awarded. *Degree requirements:* For master's, 20 hours of community service, internship or field project. *Entrance requirements:* For master's, GRE General Test, GMAT, minimum GPA of 3.0, 3 references, interview. Additional exam requirements/recommendations for international students: Required—TOEFL (minimum score 550 paper-based; 213 computer-based). *Application deadline:* For fall admission, 3/1 priority date for domestic and international students. Application fee: $85. *Financial support:* Federal Work-Study and scholarships/grants available. Support available to part-time students. Financial award application deadline: 3/10; financial award applicants required to submit FAFSA. *Faculty research:* Electronic health records; telemedicine; fraud prediction and prevention; decision modeling; continuous quality improvement; empathy, caring, patient-centered health care; health policy; health outcomes. Total annual research expenditures: $38,131. *Unit head:* Dr. Andrea W. White, Program Director, 843-792-4493, Fax: 843-792-3327, E-mail: whiteand@musc.edu. *Application contact:* Ann Brown, Student Services Program Coordinator, 843-792-2115, Fax: 843-792-3327, E-mail: brownah@musc.edu.

Medical University of South Carolina, College of Health Professions, Department of Health Sciences and Research, Doctoral Program in Health Administration, Charleston, SC 29425. Offers DHA. *Faculty:* 2 full-time (1 woman), 6 part-time/adjunct (3 women). *Students:* 42 full-time (20 women); includes 12 minority (11 African Americans, 1 Hispanic American). Average age 45. 21 applicants, 95% accepted, 18 enrolled. In 2009, 15 doctorates awarded. *Degree requirements:* For doctorate, comprehensive exam, thesis/dissertation. *Entrance requirements:* For doctorate, experience in health care, interview, master's degree in relevant field, resume, 3 references. Additional exam requirements/recommendations for international students: Required—TOEFL (minimum score 600 paper-based; 250 computer-based). *Application deadline:* For fall admission, 8/15 for domestic and international students. Applications are processed on a rolling basis. Application fee: $85. *Financial support:* Federal Work-Study and scholarships/grants available. Support available to part-time students. Financial award application deadline: 3/10; financial award applicants required to submit FAFSA. *Unit head:* Dr. James S. Zoller, Program Director, 843-792-3849, E-mail: zollerjs@musc.edu. *Application contact:* Melissa Freeland, Director of Student Services, 843-792-8510, Fax: 843-792-3327, E-mail: freelan@musc.edu.

Meharry Medical College, School of Graduate Studies, Division of Community Health Sciences, Nashville, TN 37208-9989. Offers occupational medicine (MSPH); public health administration (MSPH). *Accreditation:* CEPH. Part-time and evening/weekend programs available. *Degree requirements:* For master's, thesis, externship. *Entrance requirements:* For

Health Services Management and Hospital Administration

Meharry Medical College *(continued)*
master's, GRE General Test, GMAT. *Expenses:* Contact institution. *Faculty research:* Policy and management, health care financing, health education and promotion.

Mercy College, School of Social and Behavioral Sciences, Program in Health Services Management, Dobbs Ferry, NY 10522-1189. Offers MPA, MS. Part-time and evening/weekend programs available. Postbaccalaureate distance learning degree programs offered (no on-campus study). *Students:* 7 full-time (5 women), 47 part-time (36 women); includes 20 African Americans, 5 Asian Americans or Pacific Islanders, 11 Hispanic Americans, 1 international. Average age 36. 60 applicants, 42% accepted, 14 enrolled. In 2009, 11 master's awarded. *Entrance requirements:* For master's, interview, letters of recommendation from two instructors in the major area of study or professional letters from employers, minimum GPA of 3.0, 3- to 5-page essay on reason for pursuing master's degree in health services management, 8 years of work experience in health care (MS). Additional exam requirements/recommendations for international students: Required—TOEFL (minimum score 600 paper-based; 250 computer-based; 100 iBT). *Application deadline:* For fall admission, 8/1 for international students. Applications are processed on a rolling basis. Application fee: $40. Electronic applications accepted. *Expenses:* Tuition: Full-time $13,158; part-time $731 per credit. Required fees: $500. Tuition and fees vary according to degree level and program. *Financial support:* Career-related internships or fieldwork, Federal Work-Study, scholarships/grants, and unspecified assistantships available. Support available to part-time students. Financial award applicants required to submit FAFSA. *Unit head:* Dr. Mary C. Kraetzer, Program Director, 914-674-7341, E-mail: mkraetzer@mercy.edu. *Application contact:* Dr. Mary C. Kraetzer, Program Director, 914-674-7341, E-mail: mkraetzer@mercy.edu.

Meritus University, School of Business, Fredericton, NB E3C 2R2, Canada. Offers global management (MBA); health care management (MBA); human resources management (MBA); information technology management (MBA); marketing (MBA); technology management (MBA). Evening/weekend programs available. Postbaccalaureate distance learning degree programs offered (no on-campus study). *Faculty:* 5 full-time (1 woman), 50 part-time/adjunct (15 women). *Students:* 77 full-time (29 women). Average age 35. *Entrance requirements:* For master's, undergraduate degree or comparable equivalent with minimum cumulative GPA of 2.5; minimum equivalent of two years of full-time, post high-school work experience; current employment. Additional exam requirements/recommendations for international students: Required—TOEFL (minimum score 213 computer-based; 79 iBT), IELTS (minimum score 6.5), or TOEIC (minimum score 750) or Berlitz (minimum score 550). *Application deadline:* Applications are processed on a rolling basis. Application fee: $45. Electronic applications accepted. Tuition and fees charges are reported in Canadian dollars. *Expenses:* Tuition: Full-time $14,400 Canadian dollars. Required fees: $720 Canadian dollars. *Unit head:* Dr. Albert K. S. Wong, Program Chair, Business Administration, 604-657-5465, Fax: 602-643-4624, E-mail: albert.wong@staff.meritusu.ca. *Application contact:* Jeremy S. DeMerchant, Enrolment Manager, 506-443-8413, Fax: 602-759-3688, E-mail: jeremy.demerchant@staff.meritusu.ca.

Middle Tennessee State University, College of Graduate Studies, Program in Health Care Management, Murfreesboro, TN 37132. Offers Graduate Certificate. *Students:* 7 part-time (5 women); includes 4 minority (all African Americans). *Entrance requirements:* Additional exam requirements/recommendations for international students: Required—TOEFL (minimum score 525 paper-based; 195 computer-based; 71 iBT) or IELTS (minimum score 6). *Expenses:* Tuition, state resident: full-time $4404. Tuition, nonresident: full-time $10,956. *Financial support:* Application deadline: 5/1. *Unit head:* Dr. Millicent Nelson, Program Director, 615-898-2033, E-mail: mnelson@mtsu.edu. *Application contact:* Dr. Michael Allen, Dean and Vice Provost for Research, 615-898-2840, Fax: 615-904-8020, E-mail: mallen@mtsu.edu.

Midwestern State University, Graduate Studies, College of Business Administration, Wichita Falls, TX 76308. Offers business administration (MBA); health services administration (MBA). *Accreditation:* ACBSP. Part-time and evening/weekend programs available. *Degree requirements:* For master's, comprehensive exam, thesis optional. *Entrance requirements:* For master's, GMAT. Additional exam requirements/recommendations for international students: Required—TOEFL (minimum score 550 paper-based; 213 computer-based). Electronic applications accepted. *Expenses:* Tuition, state resident: full-time $1620; part-time $90 per credit hour. Tuition, nonresident: full-time $2160; part-time $120 per credit hour. International tuition: $7506 full-time. Required fees: $3068.80; $145.60 per credit hour. $179 per semester. *Faculty research:* Small business management, health care personnel administration, Pacific Rim trade, AIDS in the workplace, technology transfer.

Midwestern State University, Graduate Studies, College of Health Sciences and Human Services, Nursing Program, Wichita Falls, TX 76308. Offers family nurse practitioner (MSN); health services administration (MSN); nurse educator (MSN). *Accreditation:* AACN. Part-time and evening/weekend programs available. *Degree requirements:* For master's, comprehensive exam, thesis optional. *Entrance requirements:* For master's, GRE General Test or MAT. Additional exam requirements/recommendations for international students: Required—TOEFL (minimum score 550 paper-based; 213 computer-based). Electronic applications accepted. *Expenses:* Tuition, state resident: full-time $1620; part-time $90 per credit hour. Tuition, nonresident: full-time $2160; part-time $120 per credit hour. International tuition: $7506 full-time. Required fees: $3068.80; $145.60 per credit hour. $179 per semester.

Midwestern State University, Graduate Studies, College of Health Sciences and Human Services, Program in Health Services and Public Administration, Wichita Falls, TX 76308. Offers health services administration (MHA); public administration (MPA); public administration (administrative justice) (MPA); public administration (health services administration) with certificate (MPA); public administration (health services) (MPA). Part-time and evening/weekend programs available. *Degree requirements:* For master's, comprehensive exam, thesis. *Entrance requirements:* For master's, GRE. Additional exam requirements/recommendations for international students: Required—TOEFL (minimum score 550 paper-based; 213 computer-based). Electronic applications accepted. *Expenses:* Tuition, state resident: full-time $1620; part-time $90 per credit hour. Tuition, nonresident: full-time $2160; part-time $120 per credit hour. International tuition: $7506 full-time. Required fees: $3068.80; $145.60 per credit hour. $179 per semester.

Mississippi College, Graduate School, Program in Health Services Administration, Clinton, MS 39058. Offers MHSA. Part-time programs available. *Faculty:* 1 (woman) full-time, 7 part-time/adjunct (4 women). *Students:* 12 full-time (8 women), 25 part-time (16 women); includes 9 minority (all African Americans), 15 international. Average age 30. In 2009, 30 master's awarded. *Degree requirements:* For master's, comprehensive exam. *Entrance requirements:* For master's, GRE General Test, minimum GPA of 2.5. Additional exam requirements/recommendations for international students: Recommended—IELTS. *Application deadline:* For fall admission, 8/15 priority date for domestic students. Applications are processed on a rolling basis. Application fee: $30. Electronic applications accepted. *Expenses:* Tuition: Part-time $452 per credit hour. Required fees: $101 per semester. Tuition and fees vary according to degree level, campus/location, program and student level. *Financial support:* Career-related internships or fieldwork, Federal Work-Study, and unspecified assistantships available. Support available to part-time students. Financial award application deadline: 4/1; financial award applicants required to submit FAFSA. *Unit head:* Jeannie Lane, Adviser, 601-925-3891, Fax: 601-925-3889, E-mail: jlane@mc.edu. *Application contact:* Elnora Lewis, Secretary, 601-925-3225, Fax: 601-925-3889, E-mail: lewis09@mc.edu.

Missouri State University, Graduate College, College of Business Administration, Department of Management, Springfield, MO 65897. Offers health administration (MHA). Part-time and evening/weekend programs available. *Faculty:* 10 full-time (3 women). *Students:* 21 full-time (13 women), 19 part-time (9 women); includes 3 minority (1 African American, 2 Asian Americans or Pacific Islanders), 2 international. Average age 32. 17 applicants, 59% accepted, 6 enrolled. In 2009, 13 master's awarded. *Degree requirements:* For master's, thesis optional. *Entrance requirements:* For master's, GMAT or GRE, minimum GPA of 2.75. Additional exam requirements/recommendations for international students: Required—TOEFL (minimum score

550 paper-based; 213 computer-based; 79 iBT), IELTS (minimum score 6). *Application deadline:* For fall admission, 7/20 priority date for domestic students, 5/1 for international students; for spring admission, 12/20 priority date for domestic students, 9/1 for international students. Applications are processed on a rolling basis. Application fee: $35 ($50 for international students). Electronic applications accepted. *Expenses:* Tuition, state resident: full-time $3852; part-time $214 per credit hour. Tuition, nonresident: full-time $7524; part-time $418 per credit hour. Required fees: $696; $172 per semester. Tuition and fees vary according to course level, course load, degree level and program. *Financial support:* Career-related internships or fieldwork, institutionally sponsored loans, scholarships/grants, tuition waivers, and unspecified assistantships available. Support available to part-time students. Financial award application deadline: 3/31; financial award applicants required to submit FAFSA. *Faculty research:* Health care management, human resource management, strategic management. *Unit head:* Dr. Barry Wisdom, Head, 417-836-5415, E-mail: barrywisdom@missouristate.edu. *Application contact:* Dr. Robert Lunn, Program Director, 417-836-5647, E-mail: robertlunn@missouristate.edu.

Monmouth University, Graduate School, Leon Hess Business School, West Long Branch, NJ 07764-1898. Offers accounting (Post-Master's Certificate); healthcare management (MBA, Post-Master's Certificate). *Accreditation:* AACSB. Part-time and evening/weekend programs available. *Faculty:* 31 full-time (10 women), 4 part-time/adjunct (0 women). *Students:* 81 full-time (24 women), 153 part-time (63 women); includes 19 minority (7 African Americans, 6 Asian Americans or Pacific Islanders, 6 Hispanic Americans), 18 international. Average age 29. 183 applicants, 76% accepted, 80 enrolled. In 2009, 70 master's awarded. *Degree requirements:* For master's, capstone course. *Entrance requirements:* For master's, GMAT, minimum GPA of 3.0 in major, 2.75 overall. Additional exam requirements/recommendations for international students: Required—TOEFL (minimum score 550 paper-based; 213 computer-based; 79 iBT), IELTS (minimum score 5), Michigan English Language Assessment Battery (minimum score 77), Cambridge A, B, C. *Application deadline:* For fall admission, 7/15 priority date for domestic students, 6/1 for international students; for spring admission, 11/15 priority date for domestic students, 11/1 for international students. Applications are processed on a rolling basis. Application fee: $50. Electronic applications accepted. *Expenses:* Tuition: Part-time $773 per credit. Required fees: $157 per semester. *Financial support:* In 2009–10, 154 students received support, including 128 fellowships (averaging $1,796 per year), 19 research assistantships (averaging $8,633 per year); career-related internships or fieldwork, scholarships/grants, and unspecified assistantships also available. Support available to part-time students. Financial award applicants required to submit FAFSA. *Faculty research:* Information technology and marketing, behavioral research in accounting, human resources, management of technology. *Unit head:* Donald Smith, Program Director, 732-571-7536, Fax: 732-263-5517, E-mail: dsmith@monmouth.edu. *Application contact:* Kevin Roane, Director, Office of Graduate Admission, 732-571-3452, Fax: 732-263-5123, E-mail: gradadm@monmouth.edu.

Montana State University Billings, College of Allied Health Professions, Department of Health Administration, Billings, MT 59101-0298. Offers MHA. Postbaccalaureate distance learning degree programs offered (minimal on-campus study). *Degree requirements:* For master's, thesis or professional paper and/or field experience. *Entrance requirements:* For master's, GRE General Test or GMAT, minimum undergraduate GPA of 3.0, graduate 3.25; 3 years' clinical or administrative experience in health care delivery or 5 years' experience in business or industry management.

Morehouse School of Medicine, Master of Public Health Program, Atlanta, GA 30310-1495. Offers epidemiology (MPH); health administration, management and policy (MPH); health education/health promotion (MPH); international health (MPH). *Accreditation:* CEPH. Part-time programs available. *Faculty:* 4 full-time (1 woman), 36 part-time/adjunct (21 women). *Students:* 54 full-time (37 women), 3 part-time (2 women); includes 34 minority (33 African Americans, 1 American Indian/Alaska Native). Average age 28. 62 applicants, 48% accepted, 29 enrolled. In 2009, 13 master's awarded. *Degree requirements:* For master's, thesis, practicum, public health leadership seminar. *Entrance requirements:* For master's, GRE General Test, writing test, public health or human service experience. Additional exam requirements/recommendations for international students: Required—TOEFL (minimum score 550 paper-based; 200 computer-based). *Application deadline:* For fall admission, 3/1 for domestic and international students. Application fee: $50. Electronic applications accepted. *Expenses:* Contact institution. *Financial support:* In 2009–10, 32 students received support, including 6 research assistantships with partial tuition reimbursements available (averaging $10,000 per year); fellowships, teaching assistantships, career-related internships or fieldwork, Federal Work-Study, institutionally sponsored loans, scholarships/grants, and unspecified assistantships also available. Support available to part-time students. Financial award application deadline: 5/1; financial award applicants required to submit FAFSA. *Faculty research:* Women's and adolescent health, violence prevention, cancer epidemiology/disparities, substance abuse prevention. Total annual research expenditures: $640,176. *Unit head:* Dr. Patricia Rodney, Director/Assistant Dean for Public Health Education, 404-752-1944, Fax: 404-752-1051, E-mail: prodney@msm.edu. *Application contact:* Dr. Sterling Roaf, Director of Admissions, 404-752-1650, Fax: 404-752-1512, E-mail: mphadmissions@msm.edu.

National University, Academic Affairs, School of Health and Human Services, Department of Health Sciences, La Jolla, CA 92037-1011. Offers integrative health (MIH). Part-time and evening/weekend programs available. Postbaccalaureate distance learning degree programs offered. *Faculty:* 2 full-time (1 woman), 2 part-time/adjunct (both women). *Students:* 12 full-time (7 women), 50 part-time (37 women); includes 23 minority (6 African Americans, 9 Asian Americans or Pacific Islanders, 8 Hispanic Americans), 20 international. Average age 31. 75 applicants, 100% accepted, 55 enrolled. In 2009, 6 master's awarded. *Degree requirements:* For master's, thesis. *Entrance requirements:* For master's, interview, minimum GPA of 2.5. Additional exam requirements/recommendations for international students: Required—TOEFL (minimum score 550 paper-based; 213 computer-based; 79 iBT). Application fee: $60 ($65 for international students). *Expenses:* Tuition: Part-time $338 per quarter hour. *Financial support:* Career-related internships or fieldwork, institutionally sponsored loans, and scholarships/grants available. Support available to part-time students. Financial award application deadline: 6/30; financial award applicants required to submit FAFSA. *Unit head:* Dr. Patric Schiltz, Lead Faculty, 858-309-3476, Fax: 858-309-3480, E-mail: pschiltz@nu.edu. *Application contact:* Dominick Giovanniello, Associate Regional Dean—San Diego, 800-NAT-UNIV, Fax: 858-541-7792, E-mail: dgiovann@nu.edu.

Nebraska Methodist College, Program in Medical Group Administration, Omaha, NE 68114. Offers MS. Evening/weekend programs available. Postbaccalaureate distance learning degree programs offered (no on-campus study). *Faculty:* 9 part-time/adjunct (2 women). *Students:* 11 full-time (3 women); includes 1 Asian American or Pacific Islander. Average age 39. 8 applicants, 75% accepted, 6 enrolled. In 2009, 5 master's awarded. *Degree requirements:* For master's, thesis or alternative, capstone. *Entrance requirements:* Additional exam requirements/recommendations for international students: Required—TOEFL (minimum score 550 paper-based; 213 computer-based; 80 iBT). Application fee: $25. *Expenses:* Tuition: Full-time $6552; part-time $546 per credit hour. Required fees: $300; $25 per credit hour. *Financial support:* In 2009–10, 3 students received support. Scholarships/grants available. Financial award applicants required to submit FAFSA. *Unit head:* Beth Pernie, Program Development Officer, 402-354-7138, Fax: 402-354-7020, E-mail: beth.pernie@methodistcollege.edu. *Application contact:* Sara Bonney, Director of Admissions, 402-354-7111, Fax: 402-354-7020, E-mail: admissions@methodistcollege.edu.

New England College, Program in Management, Henniker, NH 03242-3293. Offers accounting (MSA); healthcare administration (MS); international relations (MA); marketing management (MS); nonprofit leadership (MS); project management (MS); strategic leadership (MS). Part-time and evening/weekend programs available. *Degree requirements:* For master's, independent research project. Electronic applications accepted.

New Jersey City University, Graduate Studies and Continuing Education, College of Professional Studies, Department of Health Sciences, Jersey City, NJ 07305-1597. Offers community health education (MS); health administration (MS); school health education (MS). Part-time

and evening/weekend programs available. *Faculty:* 3. *Students:* 8 full-time (6 women), 42 part-time (32 women); includes 18 minority (10 African Americans, 1 American Indian/Alaska Native, 3 Asian Americans or Pacific Islanders, 4 Hispanic Americans), 3 international. Average age 41. In 2009, 21 master's awarded. *Degree requirements:* For master's, thesis or alternative, internship. *Entrance requirements:* For master's, GRE General Test or MAT. Additional exam requirements/recommendations for international students: Required—TOEFL. *Application deadline:* For fall admission, 8/1 priority date for domestic students; for spring admission, 12/1 for domestic students. Applications are processed on a rolling basis. Application fee: $0. *Expenses:* Tuition, area resident: Part-time $456.75 per credit. Tuition, nonresident: part-time $842.55 per credit. Required fees: $65 per term. *Financial support:* Career-related internships or fieldwork and unspecified assistantships available. *Unit head:* Dr. Gail Gordon, Chairperson, 201-200-3431, E-mail: ggordon@njcu.edu. *Application contact:* Dr. Gail Gordon, Chairperson, 201-200-3431, E-mail: ggordon@njcu.edu.

New York Medical College, School of Health Sciences and Practice, Department of Health Policy and Management, Valhalla, NY 10595-1691. Offers emergency preparedness (Graduate Certificate); global health (Graduate Certificate); health policy and management (MPH, Dr PH). Part-time and evening/weekend programs available. *Faculty:* 5 full-time, 23 part-time/adjunct. *Students:* 45 full-time, 81 part-time. Average age 32. 120 applicants, 65% accepted, 59 enrolled. *Degree requirements:* For master's, thesis; for doctorate, comprehensive exam, thesis/dissertation. *Entrance requirements:* For master's, minimum GPA of 3.0, some work experience; for doctorate, GRE, minimum graduate GPA of 3.4. Additional exam requirements/recommendations for international students: Required—TOEFL (minimum score 600 paper-based; 250 computer-based; 100 iBT), IELTS (minimum score 7). *Application deadline:* For fall admission, 8/1 priority date for domestic students, 5/15 for international students; for spring admission, 12/1 priority date for domestic students, 10/15 for international students. Applications are processed on a rolling basis. Application fee: $50 ($100 for international students). Electronic applications accepted. *Expenses:* Tuition: Full-time $18,170; part-time $790 per credit. Required fees: $790 per credit. $20 per semester. One-time fee: $100. Tuition and fees vary according to class time, course level, course load, degree level, program, student level and student's religious affiliation. *Financial support:* Research assistantships, teaching assistantships, career-related internships or fieldwork, Federal Work-Study, institutionally sponsored loans, health care benefits, and tuition reimbursements available. Support available to part-time students. Financial award applicants required to submit FAFSA. *Unit head:* Annette Choolfaian, Chair, 914-594-4250, Fax: 914-594-4292, E-mail: annette_choolfaian@nymc.edu. *Application contact:* Pamela Suett, Director of Recruitment, 914-594-4510, Fax: 914-594-4292, E-mail: shsp_admissions@nymc.edu.

New York University, Robert F. Wagner Graduate School of Public Service, Program in Health Policy and Management, New York, NY 10012-1019. Offers health finance (MPA); health policy analysis (MPA); health policy and management (Advanced Certificate); health services management (MPA); international health (MPA); MBA/MPA; MD/MPA. *Accreditation:* CAHME (one or more programs are accredited). Part-time and evening/weekend programs available. *Faculty:* 11 full-time (3 women), 6 part-time/adjunct (5 women). *Students:* 65 full-time (49 women), 84 part-time (61 women); includes 43 minority (10 African Americans, 24 Asian Americans or Pacific Islanders, 9 Hispanic Americans), 16 international. Average age 28. 223 applicants, 45% accepted, 38 enrolled. In 2009, 49 master's awarded. *Degree requirements:* For master's, thesis or alternative, residency (internship) or capstone end event. *Entrance requirements:* For master's, minimum undergraduate GPA of 3.0. Additional exam requirements/recommendations for international students: Required—TOEFL (minimum score 600 paper-based; 250 computer-based; 100 iBT), TWE (minimum score 4). *Application deadline:* For fall admission, 6/1 for domestic students, 1/15 for international students; for spring admission, 11/15 for domestic students, 10/1 for international students. Applications are processed on a rolling basis. Application fee: $80. Electronic applications accepted. *Expenses:* Contact institution. *Financial support:* In 2009–10, 26 students received support, including 25 fellowships (averaging $11,186 per year), 1 research assistantship with full tuition reimbursement available (averaging $22,440 per year); career-related internships or fieldwork, Federal Work-Study, institutionally sponsored loans, scholarships/grants, health care benefits, and unspecified assistantships also available. Support available to part-time students. Financial award application deadline: 1/15; financial award applicants required to submit FAFSA. *Unit head:* Prof. Jan Blustein, Director, 212-998-7440, Fax: 212-995-4162. *Application contact:* Christopher Alexander, Administrative Aide, Enrollment, 212-998-7414, Fax: 212-995-4611, E-mail: wagner.admissions@nyu.edu.

Northeastern University, College of Social Sciences and Humanities, Department of Political Science, Boston, MA 02115-5096. Offers political science (MA); public administration (MPA, Certificate), including development administration (MPA), health administration and policy (MPA), state and local government (MPA), urban studies (Certificate); public and international affairs (PhD). Part-time and evening/weekend programs available. *Faculty:* 22 full-time (4 women), 10 part-time/adjunct (1 woman). *Students:* 10 full-time (3 women), 62 part-time (28 women); includes 7 minority (2 African Americans, 2 American Indian/Alaska Native, 2 Asian Americans or Pacific Islanders, 1 Hispanic American), 11 international. Average age 30. 129 applicants, 69% accepted, 24 enrolled. In 2009, 28 master's, 3 doctorates awarded. *Degree requirements:* For master's, thesis optional; for doctorate, thesis/dissertation. *Entrance requirements:* For master's, GRE General Test. Additional exam requirements/recommendations for international students: Required—TOEFL. *Application deadline:* Applications are processed on a rolling basis. Application fee: $50. *Financial support:* In 2009–10, 12 fellowships, 3 research assistantships with tuition reimbursements, 18 teaching assistantships with tuition reimbursements (averaging $14,035 per year) were awarded; career-related internships or fieldwork, Federal Work-Study, tuition waivers (full and partial), and unspecified assistantships also available. Support available to part-time students. Financial award application deadline: 2/1; financial award applicants required to submit FAFSA. *Faculty research:* Presidency, public opinion, Congress, democratization, national identity. *Unit head:* Dr. John Portz, Chair, 617-373-2796, Fax: 617-373-5311, E-mail: gradpolisci@neu.edu. *Application contact:* Brynn Thompson, Graduate Programs Assistant, 617-373-4404, Fax: 617-373-5311, E-mail: gradpolisci@neu.edu.

Northeastern University, College of Social Sciences and Humanities, Program in Public Administration, Boston, MA 02115-5096. Offers development administration (MPA); health administration and policy (MPA); state and local government (MPA); urban studies (Certificate). *Accreditation:* NASPAA (one or more programs are accredited). Part-time and evening/weekend programs available. *Faculty:* 22 full-time (4 women), 10 part-time/adjunct (1 woman). *Students:* 49 full-time (26 women), 28 part-time (18 women); includes 8 African Americans, 1 Asian American or Pacific Islander, 1 Hispanic American, 14 international. 102 applicants, 52% accepted, 26 enrolled. In 2009, 11 master's awarded. *Degree requirements:* For master's, thesis optional. *Entrance requirements:* For master's, GRE General Test. Additional exam requirements/recommendations for international students: Required—TOEFL. *Application deadline:* For fall admission, 2/1 priority date for domestic students, 5/1 for international students. Applications are processed on a rolling basis. Application fee: $50. *Financial support:* In 2009–10, 2 research assistantships with tuition reimbursements (averaging $14,035 per year) were awarded; teaching assistantships with tuition reimbursements, career-related internships or fieldwork, Federal Work-Study, tuition waivers (full and partial), and unspecified assistantships also available. Support available to part-time students. Financial award application deadline: 2/1; financial award applicants required to submit FAFSA. *Faculty research:* National health care, Third World development, leadership and ethics, science and technology, budgeting. *Unit head:* Dr. Ronald D. Hedlund, Graduate Coordinator, 617-373-2796, Fax: 617-373-5311, E-mail: gradpolisci@neu.edu. *Application contact:* Brynn Thompson, Graduate Programs Assistant, 617-373-4404, Fax: 617-373-5311, E-mail: gradpolisci@neu.edu.

Northern Arizona University, Graduate College, College of Health and Human Services, Program in Interdisciplinary Health Policy, Flagstaff, AZ 86011. Offers Certificate.

Northwest Missouri State University, Graduate School, Melvin and Valorie Booth College of Business and Professional Studies, Program in Health Management, Maryville, MO 64468-6001. Offers MBA. Part-time programs available. In 2009, 2 master's awarded. *Degree requirements:* For master's, comprehensive exam. *Entrance requirements:* For master's, GMAT, minimum GPA of 2.5. Additional exam requirements/recommendations for international students: Required—TOEFL (minimum score 550 paper-based; 213 computer-based). *Application deadline:* For fall admission, 7/1 for domestic and international students; for spring admission, 12/1 for domestic students, 11/15 for international students. Applications are processed on a rolling basis. Application fee: $0 ($50 for international students). Electronic applications accepted. *Expenses:* Tuition, state resident: part-time $296.34 per credit hour. Tuition, nonresident: part-time $510.43 per credit hour. *Financial support:* Application deadline: 4/1. *Unit head:* Dr. Mark Jelavich, Director, 660-562-1763. *Application contact:* Dr. Gregory Haddock, Dean of Graduate School, 660-562-1145, Fax: 660-562-1096, E-mail: gradsch@nwmissouri.edu.

OGI School of Science & Engineering at Oregon Health & Science University, Graduate Studies, Department of Management in Science and Technology, Beaverton, OR 97006-8921. Offers health care management (Certificate); management in science and technology (MS, Certificate). Part-time and evening/weekend programs available. *Degree requirements:* For master's, thesis. *Entrance requirements:* For master's, 2 years of work experience. Additional exam requirements/recommendations for international students: Recommended—TOEFL (minimum score 625 paper-based; 263 computer-based). Electronic applications accepted.

The Ohio State University, College of Public Health, Columbus, OH 43210. Offers MHA, MPH, MS, PhD, JD/MHA, MHA/MBA, MHA/MD, MHA/MPA, MHA/MS, MPH/JD, MPH/MD, OD/MPH. *Accreditation:* CAHME; CEPH. *Students:* 434 full-time (260 women), 97 part-time (55 women); includes 79 minority (25 African Americans, 1 American Indian/Alaska Native, 44 Asian Americans or Pacific Islanders, 9 Hispanic Americans), 22 international. Average age 28. In 2009, 116 master's, 6 doctorates awarded. *Degree requirements:* For master's, thesis optional, practicum. *Entrance requirements:* For master's, GRE. Additional exam requirements/recommendations for international students: Required—TOEFL. *Application deadline:* Applications are processed on a rolling basis. Application fee: $40 ($50 for international students). Electronic applications accepted. *Expenses:* Tuition, state resident: full-time $10,683. Tuition, nonresident: full-time $25,923. Tuition and fees vary according to course load and program. *Financial support:* Fellowships, research assistantships available. *Unit head:* Stanley Lemeshow, Dean, 614-293-3913, Fax: 614-293-3937, E-mail: lemeshow.1@osu.edu. *Application contact:* Graduate Admissions, 614-292-9444, Fax: 614-292-3895, E-mail: domestic.grad@osu.edu.

Ohio University, Graduate College, College of Health and Human Services, School of Health Sciences, Athens, OH 45701-2979. Offers MHA, MPH. Part-time and evening/weekend programs available. Postbaccalaureate distance learning degree programs offered (no on-campus study). *Faculty:* 10 full-time (3 women), 3 part-time/adjunct (all women). *Students:* 12 full-time (8 women), 185 part-time (155 women); includes 16 minority (8 African Americans, 1 American Indian/Alaska Native, 7 Asian Americans or Pacific Islanders), 7 international. 92 applicants, 80% accepted, 55 enrolled. In 2009, 10 master's awarded. *Degree requirements:* For master's, capstone (MPH). *Entrance requirements:* For master's, GMAT, GRE General Test, previous course work in accounting, management, and statistics, previous public health background (MHA, MPH). Additional exam requirements/recommendations for international students: Required—TOEFL (minimum score 550 paper-based; 80 iBT) or IELTS Academic (minimum score 6.5). *Application deadline:* Applications are processed on a rolling basis. Application fee: $50 ($55 for international students). Electronic applications accepted. *Expenses:* Contact institution. *Financial support:* Research assistantships with full tuition reimbursements, career-related internships or fieldwork, Federal Work-Study, institutionally sponsored loans, and unspecified assistantships available. Financial award applicants required to submit FAFSA. *Faculty research:* Health care management, health policy, managed care, health behavior, disease prevention. *Unit head:* Dr. Matthew Adeyanju, Director, 740-593-1849, Fax: 740-593-0555, E-mail: adeyanju@ohio.edu. *Application contact:* Dr. Ruth Ann Althaus, Graduate Coordinator, Master of Health Administration Program, 740-597-2981, E-mail: althaus@ohio.edu.

Oklahoma City University, Meinders School of Business, Program in Business Administration, Oklahoma City, OK 73106-1402. Offers finance (MBA); health administration (MBA); information technology (MBA); integrated marketing communications (MBA); international business (MBA); marketing (MBA); JD/MBA. *Accreditation:* ACBSP. Part-time and evening/weekend programs available. *Faculty:* 24 full-time (7 women), 11 part-time/adjunct (1 woman). *Students:* 268 full-time (91 women), 180 part-time (62 women); includes 51 minority (20 African Americans, 7 American Indian/Alaska Native, 11 Asian Americans or Pacific Islanders, 13 Hispanic Americans), 257 international. Average age 30. 158 applicants, 90% accepted, 35 enrolled. In 2009, 236 master's awarded. *Degree requirements:* For master's, comprehensive exam. *Entrance requirements:* Additional exam requirements/recommendations for international students: Required—TOEFL (minimum score 560 paper-based; 220 computer-based; 83 iBT). *Application deadline:* For fall admission, 8/20 for domestic students; for spring admission, 1/6 for domestic students. Applications are processed on a rolling basis. Application fee: $50 ($70 for international students). *Expenses:* Tuition: Full-time $15,930; part-time $885 per hour. *Financial support:* Fellowships with partial tuition reimbursements, career-related internships or fieldwork, Federal Work-Study, institutionally sponsored loans, and tuition waivers (partial) available. Support available to part-time students. Financial award application deadline: 8/1. *Faculty research:* Management information systems, international business strategies. *Unit head:* Dr. Mahmood Shandiz, Senior Associate Dean, 405-208-5130, Fax: 405-208-5098, E-mail: mshandiz@okcu.edu. *Application contact:* Michelle Lockhart, Director, Graduate Admissions, 800-633-7242, Fax: 405-208-5916, E-mail: gadmissions@okcu.edu.

Oregon State University, Graduate School, College of Health and Human Sciences, Department of Public Health, Program in Health Management and Policy, Corvallis, OR 97331. Offers MS, PhD. Application fee: $50. *Expenses:* Tuition, state resident: full-time $9774; part-time $362 per credit. Tuition, nonresident: full-time $15,849; part-time $587 per credit. Required fees: $1639. Full-time tuition and fees vary according to course load and program. *Unit head:* Dr. Leonard H. Friedman, Coordinator, 541-737-2323, Fax: 541-737-4001, E-mail: leonard.friedman@oregonstate.edu. *Application contact:* Dr. Leonard H. Friedman, Coordinator, 541-737-2323, Fax: 541-737-4001, E-mail: leonard.friedman@oregonstate.edu.

Our Lady of the Lake University of San Antonio, School of Business and Leadership, Program in Healthcare Management, San Antonio, TX 78207-4689. Offers MBA. Part-time and evening/weekend programs available. *Students:* 2 full-time (1 woman), 42 part-time (24 women); includes 31 minority (6 African Americans, 1 Asian American or Pacific Islander, 24 Hispanic Americans), 1 international. Average age 33. In 2009, 19 master's awarded. *Expenses:* Tuition: Full-time $12,330; part-time $685 per contact hour. Required fees: $139; $12 per contact hour. $57 per semester. Tuition and fees vary according to campus/location. *Unit head:* Dr. Robert Bisking, Dean, 210-434-6711 Ext. 2281, Fax: 210-434-0821, E-mail: rbisking@ollusa.edu. *Application contact:* Dr. Robert Bisking, Dean, 210-434-6711 Ext. 2281, Fax: 210-434-0821, E-mail: rbisking@ollusa.edu.

Pace University, Dyson College of Arts and Sciences, Department of Public Administration, New York, NY 10038. Offers environmental management (MPA); government management (MPA); health care administration (MPA); management for public safety and homeland security (MA); nonprofit management (MPA); JD/MPA. Offered at White Plains, NY location only. Part-time and evening/weekend programs available. *Faculty:* 4 full-time, 6 part-time/adjunct. *Students:* 52 full-time (31 women), 75 part-time (49 women); includes 47 minority (28 African Americans, 1 American Indian/Alaska Native, 1 Asian American or Pacific Islander, 17 Hispanic Americans), 8 international. Average age 30. 75 applicants, 100% accepted, 43 enrolled. In 2009, 38 master's awarded. *Degree requirements:* For master's, capstone project. *Entrance requirements:* For master's, GRE General Test. Additional exam requirements/recommendations for international students: Required—TOEFL. *Application deadline:* For fall admission, 8/1 priority date for domestic students; for spring admission, 12/1 priority date for domestic students. Applications are processed on a rolling basis. Application fee: $70. Electronic applications accepted. *Expenses:* Tuition: Part-time $954 per credit. Tuition and fees vary according to course load, degree level and program. *Financial support:* Research assistantships, career-

Health Services Management and Hospital Administration

Pace University (continued)
related internships or fieldwork, Federal Work-Study, and tuition waivers (partial) available. Support available to part-time students. Financial award applicants required to submit FAFSA. *Unit head:* Dr. Farrokh Hormozi, Chairperson, 914-422-4285, E-mail: fhormozi@pace.edu. *Application contact:* Joanna Broda, Director of Admissions, 914-422-4283, Fax: 914-422-4287, E-mail: gradwp@pace.edu.

Pacific University, Healthcare Administration Program, Forest Grove, OR 97116-1797. Offers MHA.

Park University, College of Graduate and Professional Studies, Kansas City, MO 54105. Offers adult education (M Ed); at-risk students (M Ed); disaster and emergency management (MPA); educational administration (M Ed); entrepreneurship (MBA); general business (MBA); general education (M Ed); government/business relations (MPA); healthcare/services management (MBA, MPA); international business (MBA); K-12 certification (MAT); management information systems (MBA); management of information systems (MPA); middle school certification (MAT); multi-cultural education (M Ed); nonprofit management (MPA); public management (MPA); school law (M Ed); secondary school certification (MAT); special education (M Ed). Part-time and evening/weekend programs available. Postbaccalaureate distance learning degree programs offered (no on-campus study). *Degree requirements:* For master's, comprehensive exam, thesis (for some programs). *Entrance requirements:* For master's, GRE, GMAT, teacher certification (M Ed). Additional exam requirements/recommendations for international students: Required—TOEFL (minimum score 550 paper-based). Electronic applications accepted. *Faculty research:* Literacy, leadership, brain based research, multicultural education, diversity.

Penn State University Park, Graduate School, College of Health and Human Development, Department of Health Policy and Administration, State College, University Park, PA 16802-1503. Offers MHA, MS, PhD. *Accreditation:* CAHME.

Pfeiffer University, Program in Health Administration, Misenheimer, NC 28109-0960. Offers MHA, MBA/MHA.

Philadelphia University, School of Business Administration, Program in Business Administration, Philadelphia, PA 19144. Offers business administration (MBA); finance (MBA); health care management (MBA); international business (MBA); marketing (MBA); MBA/MS. Part-time and evening/weekend programs available. Postbaccalaureate distance learning degree programs offered (no on-campus study). *Entrance requirements:* For master's, GMAT. Additional exam requirements/recommendations for international students: Required—TOEFL (minimum score 550 paper-based; 213 computer-based; 79 iBT).

Portland State University, Graduate Studies, College of Urban and Public Affairs, School of Community Health, Program in Health Studies, Portland, OR 97207-0751. Offers health administration (MPA, MPH). Part-time and evening/weekend programs available. *Degree requirements:* For master's, internship (MPA), practicum (MPH). *Entrance requirements:* For master's, minimum GPA of 3.0 in upper-division course work or 2.75 overall, resume, 3 recommendation forms. Additional exam requirements/recommendations for international students: Required—TOEFL (minimum score 550 paper-based; 213 computer-based).

Queen's University at Kingston, School of Graduate Studies and Research, Faculty of Health Sciences, Department of Community Health and Epidemiology, Kingston, ON K7L 3N6, Canada. Offers epidemiology (PhD); epidemiology and population health (M Sc); health services (M Sc); policy research and clinical epidemiology (M Sc); public health (MPH). Part-time programs available. *Degree requirements:* For master's, thesis. *Entrance requirements:* For master's, GRE General Test (strongly recommended). Additional exam requirements/recommendations for international students: Required—TOEFL (minimum score 600 paper-based; 250 computer-based). *Faculty research:* Cancer epidemiology, clinical trials, biostatistics health services research, health policy.

Quinnipiac University, School of Business, Program in Health Care Management, Hamden, CT 06518-1940. Offers MBA, JD/MBA. Part-time and evening/weekend programs available. *Faculty:* 24 full-time (6 women), 12 part-time/adjunct (4 women). *Students:* 7 full-time (2 women), 23 part-time (14 women); includes 7 minority (1 African American, 4 Asian Americans or Pacific Islanders, 2 Hispanic Americans), 2 international. Average age 31. 20 applicants, 70% accepted, 14 enrolled. In 2009, 13 master's awarded. *Degree requirements:* For master's, thesis or alternative, internship. *Entrance requirements:* For master's, GMAT, minimum GPA of 3.0. Additional exam requirements/recommendations for international students: Required—TOEFL (minimum score 575 paper-based; 233 computer-based; 90 iBT), IELTS (minimum score 6.5). *Application deadline:* For fall admission, 7/30 priority date for domestic students, 4/30 priority date for international students; for spring admission, 12/15 priority date for domestic students, 9/15 priority date for international students. Applications are processed on a rolling basis. Application fee: $45. Electronic applications accepted. *Expenses:* Tuition: Full-time $16,030; part-time $770 per credit. Required fees: $630; $35 per credit. *Financial support:* Career-related internships or fieldwork, tuition waivers (partial), and unspecified assistantships available. Support available to part-time students. Financial award application deadline: 4/15; financial award applicants required to submit FAFSA. *Faculty research:* Health care financing, health policy, health care marketing, health economics, health care management information systems. *Unit head:* Dr. Kimberly McKeage, MBA Director, 203-582-3676, Fax: 203-582-8664, E-mail: kim.mckeage@quinnipiac.edu. *Application contact:* Jennifer Boutin, Associate Director of Graduate Admissions, 800-462-1944, Fax: 203-582-3443, E-mail: jennifer.boutin@quinnipiac.edu.

Regent University, Graduate School, Robertson School of Government, Virginia Beach, VA 23464. Offers American government (MA); global politics (MA); health care policy and administration (MA); international politics (MA); law and public policy (MA); Mid-East politics (MA); political leadership and management (MA); political management (MA); political theory (MA); public administration (MA); public policy (MA); terrorism and homeland defense (MA); world economies and political development (MA); JD/MA; M Div/MA; M Ed/MA; MBA/MA. Part-time and evening/weekend programs available. Postbaccalaureate distance learning degree programs offered (minimal on-campus study). *Faculty:* 6 full-time (2 women), 11 part-time/adjunct (1 woman). *Students:* 77 full-time (55 women), 65 part-time (36 women); includes 47 minority (38 African Americans, 2 Asian Americans or Pacific Islanders, 7 Hispanic Americans), 4 international. Average age 30. 131 applicants, 65% accepted, 54 enrolled. In 2009, 51 master's awarded. *Degree requirements:* For master's, thesis optional, internship. *Entrance requirements:* For master's, GRE General Test or LSAT, minimum undergraduate GPA of 3.0, writing sample, resume, interview, references. Additional exam requirements/recommendations for international students: Required—TOEFL (minimum score 577 paper-based; 233 computer-based). *Application deadline:* For fall admission, 5/1 priority date for domestic students; for spring admission, 11/1 priority date for domestic students. Applications are processed on a rolling basis. Application fee: $50. Electronic applications accepted. *Expenses:* Contact institution. *Financial support:* In 2009–10, 130 students received support. Career-related internships or fieldwork, scholarships/grants, tuition waivers (full and partial), and unspecified assistantships available. Support available to part-time students. Financial award application deadline: 9/1; financial award applicants required to submit FAFSA. *Faculty research:* Education reform, political character issues, social capital concerns, administrative ethics, Biblical law and public policy. *Unit head:* Dr. Charles W. Dunn, Dean, 757-352-4322, Fax: 757-352-4643, E-mail: cwdunn@regent.edu. *Application contact:* Matthew Chadwick, Director of Admissions, 800-373-5504, Fax: 757-352-4381, E-mail: admissions@regent.edu.

Regis College, School of Nursing and Health Professions, Weston, MA 02493. Offers health administration (MS); nurse educator (Certificate); nurse practitioner (Certificate); nursing (MS, DNP). *Accreditation:* NLN. Part-time and evening/weekend programs available. *Faculty:* 18 full-time (all women), 12 part-time/adjunct (all women). *Students:* 158 full-time (147 women), 324 part-time (299 women); includes 50 minority (29 African Americans, 1 American Indian/Alaska Native, 15 Asian Americans or Pacific Islanders, 5 Hispanic Americans). Average age 38. 320 applicants, 63% accepted, 155 enrolled. In 2009, 47 master's, 7 other advanced degrees awarded. *Degree requirements:* For master's, thesis. *Entrance requirements:* For master's, GRE General Test or MAT, minimum GPA of 3.0; for doctorate, MAT or GRE if GPA from master's lower than 3.5. Additional exam requirements/recommendations for international students: Required—TOEFL (minimum score 550 paper-based; 213 computer-based). *Application deadline:* Applications are processed on a rolling basis. Application fee: $50. Electronic applications accepted. *Expenses:* Tuition: Full-time $29,000; part-time $800 per credit. Tuition and fees vary according to course load, degree level and program. *Financial support:* In 2009–10, 28 students received support, including 13 research assistantships; Federal Work-Study, scholarships/grants, traineeships, and unspecified assistantships also available. Support available to part-time students. Financial award applicants required to submit FAFSA. *Faculty research:* Health policy, education, aging, job satisfaction, psychiatric nursing, critical thinking. *Unit head:* Dr. Antoinette Hays, Dean, 781-768-7091, Fax: 781-768-8339, E-mail: antoinette.hays@regiscollege.edu. *Application contact:* Christine Petherick, Administrative Coordinator, Graduate Admission, 866-438-7344, Fax: 781-768-7071, E-mail: christine.petherick@regiscollege.edu.

Regis University, Rueckert-Hartman School for Health Professions, Denver, CO 80221-1099. Offers clinical leadership for physician assistants (MS); family nurse practitioner (MSN); health informatics (Postbaccalaureate Certificate); health services administration (MS); healthcare education (Certificate); leadership in healthcare systems (MSN); neonatal nurse practitioner (MSN); nursing (MSN); pharmacy (Pharm D); physical therapy (DPT, TDPT). *Entrance requirements:* Additional exam requirements/recommendations for international students: Required—TOEFL (minimum score 550 paper-based; 213 computer-based; 82 iBT). Electronic applications accepted. *Expenses:* Contact institution. *Faculty research:* Normal and pathological balance and gait research, normal/pathological upper limb motor control/biomechanics, exercise energy/metabolism research, optical treatment protocols for therapeutic modalities.

Roberts Wesleyan College, Division of Adult Professional Studies, Rochester, NY 14624-1997. Offers health administration (MS). Evening/weekend programs available. *Degree requirements:* For master's, thesis or alternative. *Entrance requirements:* For master's, minimum GPA of 3.0, verifiable work experience or recommendation. *Faculty research:* Small business entrepreneurship, church management.

Rochester Institute of Technology, Graduate Enrollment Services, College of Applied Science and Technology, Department of Hospitality and Service Management, Program in Health Systems Administration, Rochester, NY 14623-5603. Offers elements of health care leadership (AC); health information resources (AC); health systems administration (MS); health systems administration executive leader (MS); health systems-finance (AC). Part-time and evening/weekend programs available. Postbaccalaureate distance learning degree programs offered (no on-campus study). *Students:* 4 full-time (3 women), 23 part-time (14 women); includes 3 African Americans, 2 American Indian/Alaska Native, 1 Hispanic American. Average age 43. 32 applicants, 38% accepted, 4 enrolled. In 2009, 12 master's, 2 other advanced degrees awarded. *Degree requirements:* For master's, thesis. *Entrance requirements:* For master's, minimum GPA of 3.0; related professional work experience; for AC, minimum GPA of 3.0. Additional exam requirements/recommendations for international students: Required—TOEFL (minimum score 550 paper-based; 213 computer-based; 79 iBT), or IELTS (minimum score 6.5). *Application deadline:* For fall admission, 2/15 priority date for domestic and international students; for winter admission, 11/1 priority date for domestic students; for spring admission, 2/1 priority date for domestic students. Applications are processed on a rolling basis. Application fee: $50. Electronic applications accepted. *Expenses:* Tuition: Full-time $31,533; part-time $876 per credit hour. Required fees: $210. *Financial support:* In 2009–10, 26 students received support; research assistantships with partial tuition reimbursements available, teaching assistantships with partial tuition reimbursements available, career-related internships or fieldwork, scholarships/grants, and unspecified assistantships available. Support available to part-time students. Financial award applicants required to submit FAFSA. *Unit head:* Dr. Linda Underhill, Program Chair, 585-475-7359, E-mail: lmuism@rit.edu. *Application contact:* Diane Ellison, Assistant Vice President, Graduate Enrollment Services, 585-475-2229, Fax: 585-475-7164, E-mail: gradinfo@rit.edu.

Rosalind Franklin University of Medicine and Science, College of Health Professions, Department of Interprofessional Healthcare Studies, Healthcare Administration and Management Program, North Chicago, IL 60064-3095. Offers MS, Certificate. Part-time and evening/weekend programs available. Postbaccalaureate distance learning degree programs offered (no on-campus study). *Faculty:* 2 full-time (both women), 5 part-time/adjunct (4 women). *Students:* 95; includes 29 minority (9 African Americans, 18 Asian Americans or Pacific Islanders, 2 Hispanic Americans), 5 international. Average age 27. 81 applicants, 98% accepted, 76 enrolled. *Degree requirements:* For master's, capstone portfolio. *Entrance requirements:* For master's, minimum GPA of 2.75, BS/BA from accredited college or university. Additional exam requirements/recommendations for international students: Required—TOEFL. *Application deadline:* For fall admission, 8/6 for domestic students; for winter admission, 10/29 for domestic students; for spring admission, 2/5 for domestic students. Applications are processed on a rolling basis. Application fee: $50. *Financial support:* In 2009–10, 39 students received support. Institutionally sponsored loans and tuition waivers available. Support available to part-time students. Financial award application deadline: 7/3; financial award applicants required to submit FAFSA. *Unit head:* Diane Bridges, Director/Assistant Professor, 847-578-8479, Fax: 847-578-8623, E-mail: diane.bridges@rosalindfranklin.edu. *Application contact:* Melissa Knox, Admissions Officer, 847-578-8772, Fax: 847-775-6559, E-mail: melissa.knox@rosalindfranklin.edu.

Royal Roads University, Graduate Studies, Applied Leadership and Management Program, Victoria, BC V9B 5Y2, Canada. Offers executive coaching (Graduate Certificate); health systems leadership (Graduate Certificate); project management (Graduate Certificate); public relations management (Graduate Certificate); strategic human resources management (Graduate Certificate).

Rush University, College of Health Sciences, Department of Health Systems Management, Chicago, IL 60612-3832. Offers MS, DHSc. *Accreditation:* CAHME. Part-time and evening/weekend programs available. *Degree requirements:* For master's, thesis; for doctorate, thesis/dissertation. *Entrance requirements:* For master's, GMAT or GRE General Test, previous undergraduate course work in accounting and statistics; for doctorate, GRE General Test, master's degree preferably in a health discipline. Additional exam requirements/recommendations for international students: Required—TOEFL. Electronic applications accepted. *Faculty research:* Organizational performance, occupational health, quality of care indicators, leadership development, entrepreneurship, health insurance and disability, managed care.

Rutgers, The State University of New Jersey, Newark, Graduate School, Program in Public Administration, Newark, NJ 07102. Offers health care administration (MPA); human resources administration (MPA); public administration (PhD); public management (MPA); public policy analysis (MPA); urban systems and issues (MPA). *Accreditation:* NASPAA (one or more programs are accredited). Part-time and evening/weekend programs available. *Degree requirements:* For master's, comprehensive exam, thesis or alternative; for doctorate, thesis/dissertation. *Entrance requirements:* For master's, GRE, minimum undergraduate B average; for doctorate, GRE, MPA, minimum B average. Electronic applications accepted. *Faculty research:* Government finance, municipal and state government, public productivity.

Sacred Heart University, Graduate Programs, College of Education and Health Professions, Department of Nursing, Fairfield, CT 06825-1000. Offers clinical nurse leader (MSN); clinical practice in health care (DNP); family nurse practitioner (MSN); leadership in health care (DNP); nursing (DN Sc); patient care services administration (MSN). *Accreditation:* AACN. Part-time and evening/weekend programs available. Postbaccalaureate distance learning degree programs offered (minimal on-campus study). *Faculty:* 12 full-time (all women). *Students:* 7 full-time (6 women), 155 part-time (146 women); includes 27 minority (9 African Americans, 11 Asian Americans or Pacific Islanders, 7 Hispanic Americans), 1 international. Average age 39. 72 applicants, 93% accepted, 28 enrolled. In 2009, 13 master's awarded. *Entrance requirements:* For master's, BSN, minimum GPA of 3.0. Additional exam requirements/recommendations for

international students: Required—TOEFL (minimum score 550 paper-based; 213 computer-based). *Application deadline:* Applications are processed on a rolling basis. Application fee: $50 ($100 for international students). Electronic applications accepted. *Expenses:* Contact institution. *Financial support:* Career-related internships or fieldwork, institutionally sponsored loans, and unspecified assistantships available. Support available to part-time students. Financial award applicants required to submit FAFSA. *Unit head:* Dr. Dori Sullivan, Chair, 203-371-7715. *Application contact:* Kathy Dilks, Assistant Dean of Graduate Admissions, Health Professions, 203-396-8259, Fax: 203-365-4732, E-mail: gradstudies@sacredheart.edu.

Sage Graduate School, Graduate School, School of Health Sciences, Department of Nursing, Troy, NY 12180-4115. Offers adult health (MS); adult nurse practitioner (MS, Post Master's Certificate); clinical nurse leader/specialist (Post Master's Certificate); community health (MS); education and leadership (DNS); family nurse practitioner (MS, Post Master's Certificate); gerontological nurse practitioner (Post Master's Certificate); nurse administrator/executive (Post Master's Certificate); nursing (Post Master's Certificate); psychiatric mental health nurse practitioner (MS, Post Master's Certificate), including psychiatric mental health. *Accreditation:* AACN. Part-time and evening/weekend programs available. *Faculty:* 5 full-time (all women), 8 part-time/adjunct (all women). *Students:* 23 full-time (22 women), 134 part-time (129 women); includes 16 minority (6 African Americans, 1 American Indian/Alaska Native, 8 Asian Americans or Pacific Islanders, 1 Hispanic American), 1 international. Average age 42. 97 applicants, 64% accepted, 49 enrolled. In 2009, 25 master's, 3 other advanced degrees awarded. *Degree requirements:* For master's, thesis or alternative. *Entrance requirements:* For master's, BS in nursing, minimum GPA of 2.75, resume, 2 letters of recommendation. Additional exam requirements/recommendations for international students: Required—TOEFL (minimum score 550 paper-based; 213 computer-based). *Application deadline:* Applications are processed on a rolling basis. Application fee: $40. *Expenses:* Tuition: Full-time $10,620; part-time $590 per credit hour. *Financial support:* Fellowships, research assistantships, Federal Work-Study, scholarships/grants, and unspecified assistantships available. Support available to part-time students. Financial award application deadline: 3/1; financial award applicants required to submit FAFSA. *Unit head:* Dr. Glenda Kelman, Chair, 518-244-2001, E-mail: kelmag@sage.edu. *Application contact:* Wendy D. Diefendorf, Director of Graduate and Adult Admission, 518-244-2443, Fax: 518-244-6880, E-mail: diefew@sage.edu.

Sage Graduate School, Graduate School, School of Management, Program in Health Services Administration, Troy, NY 12180-4115. Offers dietetic internship (Certificate); gerontology (MS). Part-time and evening/weekend programs available. *Faculty:* 4 full-time (2 women), 6 part-time/adjunct (0 women). *Students:* 7 full-time (6 women), 19 part-time (15 women); includes 4 minority (2 African Americans, 2 Hispanic Americans). Average age 29. 16 applicants. In 2009, 5 master's awarded. *Entrance requirements:* For master's, minimum GPA of 2.75, resume, 2 letters of recommendation. Additional exam requirements/recommendations for international students: Required—TOEFL (minimum score 550 paper-based; 213 computer-based). Application fee: $40. *Expenses:* Tuition: Full-time $10,620; part-time $590 per credit hour. *Financial support:* Fellowships, research assistantships, Federal Work-Study, scholarships/grants, and unspecified assistantships available. Support available to part-time students. Financial award application deadline: 3/1; financial award applicants required to submit FAFSA. *Unit head:* Dr. Kimberly Fredricks, Program Director, 518-292-1700, Fax: 518-292-5414, E-mail: fredek1@sage.edu. *Application contact:* Wendy D. Diefendorf, Director of Graduate and Adult Admission, 518-244-2443, Fax: 518-244-6880, E-mail: diefew@sage.edu.

Saginaw Valley State University, Crystal M. Lange College of Nursing and Health Sciences, Program in Health Leadership, University Center, MI 48710. Offers MS. *Students:* 11 full-time (7 women), 15 part-time (12 women); includes 3 minority (1 African American, 2 Asian Americans or Pacific Islanders), 6 international. Average age 38. 31 applicants, 100% accepted, 11 enrolled. *Financial support:* Federal Work-Study and scholarships/grants available. Support available to part-time students. *Unit head:* Dr. Janalou Blecke, Dean, 989-964-4145, Fax: 989-964-4024, E-mail: blecke@svsu.edu. *Application contact:* Dr. Janalou Blecke, Dean, 989-964-4145, Fax: 989-964-4024, E-mail: blecke@svsu.edu.

St. Ambrose University, College of Business, Program in Business Administration, Davenport, IA 52803-2898. Offers business administration (DBA); health care (MBA); human resources (MBA). *Accreditation:* ACBSP. Part-time and evening/weekend programs available. *Faculty:* 19 full-time (4 women), 8 part-time/adjunct (3 women). *Students:* 29 full-time (11 women), 279 part-time (146 women); includes 16 minority (6 African Americans, 3 Asian Americans or Pacific Islanders, 7 Hispanic Americans). Average age 36. 95 applicants, 86% accepted, 82 enrolled. In 2009, 146 master's, 3 doctorates awarded. *Degree requirements:* For master's, comprehensive exam (for some programs), thesis or alternative, capstone seminar; for doctorate, comprehensive exam, thesis/dissertation, oral and written exams. *Entrance requirements:* For master's, GMAT; for doctorate, GMAT, master's degree. Additional exam requirements/recommendations for international students: Required—TOEFL. *Application deadline:* For fall admission, 8/15 priority date for domestic students; for winter admission, 12/15 for domestic students; for spring admission, 1/1 for domestic students. Applications are processed on a rolling basis. Application fee: $25. Electronic applications accepted. *Expenses:* Contact institution. *Financial support:* In 2009–10, 48 students received support, including 5 research assistantships with partial tuition reimbursements available (averaging $3,600 per year); career-related internships or fieldwork, scholarships/grants, tuition waivers (partial), and unspecified assistantships also available. Financial award application deadline: 3/15; financial award applicants required to submit FAFSA. *Unit head:* Joseph L. Kehoe, Director of MBA, 563-322-1142, Fax: 563-333-6268, E-mail: kehoejosephl@sau.edu. *Application contact:* Erin E. Leifker, Assistant MBA Director, 563-322-1165, Fax: 563-333-6268, E-mail: leifkererine@sau.edu.

St. Joseph's College, Long Island Campus, Program in Management, Patchogue, NY 11772-2399. Offers health care (AC); health care management (MS); human resource management (AC); human resources management (MS); organizational management (MS).

St. Joseph's College, New York, Graduate Programs, Program in Health Care Management, Brooklyn, NY 11205-3688. Offers MBA.

Saint Joseph's College of Maine, Program in Health Services Administration, Standish, ME 04084. Offers MHSA. Degree program is external; available only by correspondence and online. Part-time programs available. Postbaccalaureate distance learning degree programs offered (minimal on-campus study). *Degree requirements:* For master's, summer residency. *Entrance requirements:* For master's, 2 years of health-related experience. Electronic applications accepted. *Faculty research:* Health care organization, policy, and management; long-term care.

Saint Joseph's University, College of Arts and Sciences, Department of Health Services, Philadelphia, PA 19131-1395. Offers health administration (MS, Post-Master's Certificate); health care ethics (Post-Master's Certificate); health education (MS, Post-Master's Certificate); health informatics (Post-Master's Certificate); healthcare ethics (MS); nurse anesthesia (MS); school nurse certification (MS). Part-time and evening/weekend programs available. *Students:* 10 full-time (5 women), 180 part-time (135 women); includes 67 minority (50 African Americans, 11 Asian Americans or Pacific Islanders, 6 Hispanic Americans), 8 international. Average age 36. In 2009, 72 master's awarded. *Entrance requirements:* For master's, GRE (if GPA less than 2.75), 2 letters of recommendation, minimum GPA of 2.75, resume. Additional exam requirements/recommendations for international students: Required—TOEFL (minimum score 550 paper-based; 213 computer-based; 79 iBT). *Application deadline:* For fall admission, 7/15 priority date for domestic students, 4/15 for international students; for winter admission, 1/15 for international students; for spring admission, 11/15 priority date for domestic students, 10/15 for international students. Applications are processed on a rolling basis. Application fee: $35. Electronic applications accepted. *Expenses:* Tuition: Part-time $729 per credit hour. Tuition and fees vary according to degree level and program. *Financial support:* Career-related internships or fieldwork and unspecified assistantships available. Financial award applicants required to submit FAFSA. *Unit head:* Nakia Henderson, Director, 610-660-2952, E-mail: nakia.henderson@sju.edu. *Application contact:* Kate McConnell, Director, Graduate College of Arts and Sciences Admissions and Retention, 610-660-3184, Fax: 610-660-3230, E-mail: kate.mcconnell@sju.edu.

Saint Joseph's University, Erivan K. Haub School of Business, Professional MBA Program, Philadelphia, PA 19131-1395. Offers accounting (MBA); finance (MBA), including finance; general business (MBA); health and medical services administration (MBA); human resource management (MBA); international business (MBA); international marketing (MBA); management (MBA); marketing (MBA); DO/MBA. Part-time and evening/weekend programs available. *Students:* 51 full-time (24 women), 480 part-time (184 women); includes 71 minority (32 African Americans, 1 American Indian/Alaska Native, 30 Asian Americans or Pacific Islanders, 8 Hispanic Americans), 38 international. Average age 30. In 2009, 190 master's awarded. *Entrance requirements:* For master's, GMAT or GRE, 2 letters of recommendation, resume. Additional exam requirements/recommendations for international students: Required—TOEFL (minimum score 550 paper-based; 213 computer-based; 79 iBT) or IELTS (minimum score 6.5). *Application deadline:* For fall admission, 7/15 priority date for domestic students, 4/15 priority date for international students; for spring admission, 11/15 priority date for domestic students, 10/15 priority date for international students. Applications are processed on a rolling basis. Application fee: $35. Electronic applications accepted. *Expenses:* Tuition: Part-time $729 per credit hour. Tuition and fees vary according to degree level and program. *Financial support:* Scholarships/grants and unspecified assistantships available. Financial award application deadline: 5/1. *Unit head:* Adele C. Foley, Associate Dean/Director, Graduate Business Programs, 610-660-1691, Fax: 610-660-1599, E-mail: afoley@sju.edu. *Application contact:* Janine N. Guerra, Esq., Assistant Director, MBA Program, 610-660-1695, Fax: 610-660-1599, E-mail: jguerra@sju.edu.

Saint Leo University, Graduate Business Studies, Saint Leo, FL 33574-6665. Offers accounting (MBA); business (MBA); criminal justice (MBA); health services management (MBA); human resource administration (MBA); information security management (MBA); marketing (MBA); sport business (MBA). Part-time and evening/weekend programs available. Postbaccalaureate distance learning degree programs offered (no on-campus study). *Faculty:* 31 full-time (5 women), 48 part-time/adjunct (17 women). *Students:* 1,433 full-time (856 women), 3 part-time (1 woman); includes 601 minority (429 African Americans, 8 American Indian/Alaska Native, 75 Asian Americans or Pacific Islanders, 89 Hispanic Americans), 11 international. Average age 37. In 2009, 405 master's awarded. *Entrance requirements:* For master's, GMAT (minimum score 500 if applicant does not have 5 years of professional work experience), bachelor's degree from regionally-accredited college or university with minimum GPA of 3.0 in the last 60 hours of coursework; 5 years of professional work experience; resume; 2 letters of recommendation. Additional exam requirements/recommendations for international students: Required—TOEFL (minimum score 550 paper-based; 213 computer-based; 80 iBT). *Application deadline:* For fall admission, 7/1 priority date for domestic students; for spring admission, 11/12 priority date for domestic students. Applications are processed on a rolling basis. Application fee: $75. Electronic applications accepted. *Expenses:* Contact institution. *Financial support:* In 2009–10, 1 student received support. Career-related internships or fieldwork, Federal Work-Study, and health care benefits available. Financial award application deadline: 3/1; financial award applicants required to submit FAFSA. *Unit head:* Dr. Robert Robertson, Director, 352-588-7390, Fax: 352-588-8585, E-mail: mba@saintleo.edu. *Application contact:* Jared Welling, Director, Graduate/Weekend and Evening Admission, 800-707-8846, Fax: 352-588-7873, E-mail: grad.admissions@saintleo.edu.

Saint Louis University, Graduate School, School of Public Health and Graduate School, Department of Health Management and Policy, St. Louis, MO 63103-2097. Offers health administration (MHA); health policy (MPH); public health studies (PhD). *Accreditation:* CAHME. Part-time programs available. *Degree requirements:* For master's, comprehensive exam, internship. *Entrance requirements:* For master's, GMAT or GRE General Test, LSAT, MCAT, letters of recommendation, resume. Additional exam requirements/recommendations for international students: Required—TOEFL (minimum score 525 paper-based; 194 computer-based). *Faculty research:* Management of HIV/AIDS, rural health services, prevention of asthma, genetics and health services use, health insurance and access to care.

Saint Mary's University of Minnesota, Schools of Graduate and Professional Programs, Graduate School of Health and Human Services, Health and Human Services Administration Program, Winona, MN 55987-1399. Offers MA. *Unit head:* Carolyn Bell, Director, 507-285-1410, E-mail: cbell@smumn.edu. *Application contact:* Yasin Alsaidi, Director of Admissions for Graduate and Professional Programs, 612-728-5207, Fax: 612-728-5121, E-mail: yalsaidi@smumn.edu.

Saint Peter's College, Graduate Business Programs, MBA Program, Jersey City, NJ 07306-5997. Offers finance (MBA); health care administration (MBA); international business (MBA); management (MBA); management information systems (MBA); marketing (MBA); MBA/MS. Part-time and evening/weekend programs available. *Entrance requirements:* Additional exam requirements/recommendations for international students: Required—TOEFL. *Application deadline:* Applications are processed on a rolling basis. Electronic applications accepted. *Expenses:* Tuition: Part-time $971 per credit. *Financial support:* Career-related internships or fieldwork, Federal Work-Study, and institutionally sponsored loans available. *Faculty research:* Finance, health care management, human resource management, international business, management, management information systems, marketing, risk management.

St. Thomas University, School of Business, Department of Management, Miami Gardens, FL 33054-6459. Offers accounting (MBA); general management (MSM, Certificate); health management (MBA, MSM, Certificate); human resource management (MBA, MSM, Certificate); international business (MBA, MIB, MSM, Certificate); justice administration (MSM, Certificate); management accounting (MSM, Certificate); public management (MSM, Certificate); sports administration (MS). Part-time and evening/weekend programs available. *Degree requirements:* For master's, comprehensive exam. *Entrance requirements:* For master's, interview, minimum GPA of 3.0 or GMAT. Additional exam requirements/recommendations for international students: Required—TOEFL (minimum score 550 paper-based; 213 computer-based; 79 iBT). Electronic applications accepted.

Saint Xavier University, Graduate Studies, Graham School of Management, Chicago, IL 60655-3105. Offers e-commerce (MBA); employee health benefits (Certificate); finance (MBA, MS); financial analysis and investments (MBA); financial planning (MBA, Certificate); financial trading and practice (MBA, Certificate); generalist/administration (MBA); health administration (MBA, MS); managed care (Certificate); management (MBA, MS); marketing (MBA); public and non-profit management (MBA); public health (MPH); service management (MBA); training and performance management (MBA); MBA/MS. *Accreditation:* ACBSP. Part-time and evening/weekend programs available. *Entrance requirements:* For master's, GMAT, minimum GPA of 3.0, 2 years of work experience. Electronic applications accepted. *Expenses:* Contact institution.

Salve Regina University, Graduate Studies, Program in Healthcare Administration and Management, Newport, RI 02840-4192. Offers MS, Certificate. Part-time and evening/weekend programs available. *Faculty:* 2 full-time (1 woman), 4 part-time/adjunct (0 women). *Students:* 6 full-time (all women), 52 part-time (39 women); includes 3 minority (2 African Americans, 1 Hispanic American), 1 international. Average age 45. 20 applicants, 80% accepted, 15 enrolled. In 2009, 12 master's awarded. *Degree requirements:* For master's, internship. *Entrance requirements:* For master's, GMAT, GRE General Test, or MAT, health care work experience or 250 internship hours. Additional exam requirements/recommendations for international students: Required—TOEFL (minimum score 600 paper-based; 250 computer-based; 100 iBT), or IELTS. *Application deadline:* For fall admission, 3/15 priority date for domestic and international students; for spring admission, 9/15 priority date for domestic and international students. Applications are processed on a rolling basis. Application fee: $60. Electronic applications accepted. *Expenses:* Tuition: Part-time $395 per credit. Part-time tuition and fees vary according to degree level. *Financial support:* Career-related internships or fieldwork and Federal Work-Study available. Support available to part-time students. Financial award application deadline: 3/1; financial award applicants required to submit FAFSA. *Unit head:* Mark Hough, Director, 401-341-3123, E-mail: mark.hough@salve.edu. *Application contact:*

Health Services Management and Hospital Administration

Salve Regina University (continued)
Kelly Alverson, Graduate Admissions Counselor, 401-341-2153, Fax: 401-341-2973, E-mail: kelly.alverson@salve.edu.

San Diego State University, Graduate and Research Affairs, College of Health and Human Services, Graduate School of Public Health, San Diego, CA 92182. Offers environmental health (MPH); epidemiology (MPH, PhD), including biostatistics (MPH); global emergency preparedness and response (MS); global health (PhD); health behavior (PhD); health promotion (MPH); health services administration (MPH); toxicology (MS); MPH/MA; MSW/MPH. *Accreditation:* ABET (one or more programs are accredited); CAHME (one or more programs are accredited); CEPH (one or more programs are accredited). Part-time programs available. *Degree requirements:* For master's, comprehensive exam (for some programs), thesis (for some programs); for doctorate, thesis/dissertation. *Entrance requirements:* For master's, GMAT (MPH in health services administration), GRE General Test; for doctorate, GRE General Test. Additional exam requirements/recommendations for international students: Required—TOEFL. *Faculty research:* Evaluation of tobacco, AIDS prevalence and prevention, mammography, infant death project, Alzheimer's in elderly Chinese.

Seton Hall University, College of Arts and Sciences, Department of Public and Healthcare Administration, South Orange, NJ 07079-2697. Offers healthcare administration (MHA, Graduate Certificate); public administration (MPA, Graduate Certificate), including health policy and management (MPA), nonprofit organization management, public service: leadership, governance, and policy. *Accreditation:* NASPAA. Part-time and evening/weekend programs available. Postbaccalaureate distance learning degree programs offered (minimal on-campus study). *Faculty:* 7 full-time (4 women), 6 part-time/adjunct (2 women). *Students:* 60 full-time (35 women), 100 part-time (60 women); includes 58 minority (36 African Americans, 2 American Indian/Alaska Native, 16 Asian Americans or Pacific Islanders, 4 Hispanic Americans), 5 international. Average age 32. 95 applicants, 88% accepted, 51 enrolled. In 2009, 33 master's awarded. *Degree requirements:* For master's, thesis or alternative, internship or practicum. *Entrance requirements:* Additional exam requirements/recommendations for international students: Required—TOEFL. *Application deadline:* For fall admission, 7/1 priority date for domestic and international students; for spring admission, 11/1 priority date for domestic and international students. Applications are processed on a rolling basis. Application fee: $50. Electronic applications accepted. *Financial support:* Research assistantships, career-related internships or fieldwork, Federal Work-Study, scholarships/grants, and unspecified assistantships available. Financial award applicants required to submit FAFSA. *Unit head:* Dr. Matthew Hale, Chair, 973-761-9510, Fax: 973-275-2463, E-mail: halematt@shu.edu. *Application contact:* Dr. Matthew Hale, Chair, 973-761-9510, Fax: 973-275-2463, E-mail: halematt@shu.edu.

Seton Hall University, College of Nursing, South Orange, NJ 07079-2697. Offers advanced practice in primary health care (MSN), including adult nurse practitioner, gerontological nurse practitioner, pediatric nurse practitioner; entry into practice (MSN); health systems administration (MSN, DNP); nursing (PhD); nursing case management (MSN); nursing education (MA); school nurse (MSN); MSN/MA. *Accreditation:* AACN. Part-time programs available. Postbaccalaureate distance learning degree programs offered (minimal on-campus study). *Faculty:* 10 full-time (all women), 3 part-time/adjunct (1 woman). *Students:* 46 full-time (35 women), 94 part-time (90 women); includes 22 minority (8 African Americans, 5 Asian Americans or Pacific Islanders, 9 Hispanic Americans). 92 applicants, 88% accepted, 55 enrolled. *Degree requirements:* For master's, research project; for doctorate, dissertation or scholarly project. *Entrance requirements:* For doctorate, GRE. Additional exam requirements/recommendations for international students: Required—TOEFL. *Application deadline:* For fall admission, 6/15 priority date for domestic students. Applications are processed on a rolling basis. Electronic applications accepted. *Financial support:* Institutionally sponsored loans, scholarships/grants, traineeships, tuition waivers (partial), and unspecified assistantships available. Support available to part-time students. Financial award applicants required to submit FAFSA. *Faculty research:* Parent/child, adult, and gerontological nursing; breast cancer; families of children with HIV; parish nursing. *Unit head:* Dr. Phyllis Shanley Hansell, Dean. *Application contact:* Kristyn Kent Wuillermin, Director of Strategic Alliances, Marketing and Enrollment, 973-761-9291, Fax: 973-761-9607, E-mail: kristyn.kent@shu.edu.

Simmons College, School of Management, Program in Health Care Administration, Boston, MA 02115. Offers MHA, CAGS. *Accreditation:* CAHME (one or more programs are accredited). Part-time programs available. Postbaccalaureate distance learning degree programs offered. *Students:* 3 full-time (1 woman), 65 part-time (59 women); includes 10 minority (7 African Americans, 1 Asian American or Pacific Islander, 2 Hispanic Americans), 1 international. In 2009, 10 master's, 1 CAGS awarded. *Expenses:* Contact institution. *Financial support:* Application deadline: 3/1. *Unit head:* Dr. John M. Lowe, Director, 617-521-2375, Fax: 617-521-3046, E-mail: john.lowe@simmons.edu. *Application contact:* Leslee DiGirolamo-Magee, Program Administrator, 617-521-2376, E-mail: digirola@simmons.edu.

Southeast Missouri State University, School of Graduate Studies, Harrison College of Business, Cape Girardeau, MO 63701-4799. Offers accounting (MBA); entrepreneurship (MBA); environmental management (MBA); financial management (MBA); general management (MBA); health administration (MBA); industrial management (MBA); international business (MBA); sport management (MBA). *Accreditation:* AACSB. Part-time and evening/weekend programs available. Postbaccalaureate distance learning degree programs offered (no on-campus study). *Degree requirements:* For master's, applied research project. *Entrance requirements:* For master's, GMAT, minimum undergraduate GPA of 2.5. Additional exam requirements/recommendations for international students: Required—TOEFL (minimum score 550 paper-based; 213 computer-based); Recommended—IELTS (minimum score 6). *Expenses:* Tuition, state resident: full-time $4266; part-time $237 per credit hour. Tuition, nonresident: full-time $7506; part-time $417 per credit hour. Required fees: $427; $427. *Faculty research:* Human resources, laws impacting accounting, advertising.

Southern Adventist University, School of Business and Management, Collegedale, TN 37315-0370. Offers accounting (MBA); church administration (MSA); church and nonprofit leadership (MBA); financial management (MFM); healthcare administration (MBA); management (MBA); marketing management (MBA); outdoor education (MSA); MFM. Part-time and evening/weekend programs available. Postbaccalaureate distance learning degree programs offered (no on-campus study). *Faculty:* 2 full-time (0 women), 8 part-time/adjunct (1 woman). *Students:* 55 full-time (32 women), 30 part-time (22 women); includes 23 minority (14 African Americans, 1 American Indian/Alaska Native, 1 Asian American or Pacific Islander, 7 Hispanic Americans). Average age 35. In 2009, 20 master's awarded. *Entrance requirements:* For master's, GMAT. Additional exam requirements/recommendations for international students: Required—TOEFL (minimum score 600 paper-based; 250 computer-based; 100 iBT). *Application deadline:* For fall admission, 8/1 priority date for domestic students, 7/1 for international students; for winter admission, 12/1 priority date for domestic students, 11/1 for international students; for spring admission, 4/1 priority date for domestic students, 3/1 for international students. Applications are processed on a rolling basis. Application fee: $25. Electronic applications accepted. *Expenses:* Tuition: Full-time $13,149; part-time $487 per credit hour. *Financial support:* In 2009–10, 32 students received support. Scholarships/grants and unspecified assistantships available. Financial award application deadline: 9/1; financial award applicants required to submit FAFSA. *Unit head:* Dr. Don Van Ornam, Dean, 423-236-2750, Fax: 423-236-1527, E-mail: dvanorna@southern.edu. *Application contact:* Linda Wilhelm, Admissions Coordinator, 423-236-2751, Fax: 423-236-1527, E-mail: sbm@southern.edu.

Southern Illinois University Carbondale, School of Law, Program in Legal Studies, Carbondale, IL 62901-4701. Offers general law (MLS); health law and policy (MLS).

South University, Program in Business Administration, Royal Palm Beach, FL 33411. Offers business administration (MBA); healthcare administration (MBA).

South University, Program in Business Administration, Montgomery, AL 36116-1120. Offers business administration (MBA); healthcare administration (MBA).

South University, Program in Business Administration, Columbia, SC 29203. Offers business administration (MBA); healthcare administration (MBA).

Southwest Baptist University, Program in Business, Bolivar, MO 65613-2597. Offers business administration (MBA); health administration (MBA). *Accreditation:* ACBSP. Part-time programs available. Postbaccalaureate distance learning degree programs offered (no on-campus study). *Degree requirements:* For master's, comprehensive exam. *Entrance requirements:* For master's, interviews, minimum GPA of 2.75. Additional exam requirements/recommendations for international students: Required—TOEFL (minimum score 550 paper-based; 213 computer-based).

Springfield College, Graduate Programs, Program in Health Care Management, Springfield, MA 01109-3797. Offers M Ed, MS. Part-time programs available. *Degree requirements:* For master's, comprehensive exam. *Entrance requirements:* Additional exam requirements/recommendations for international students: Required—TOEFL (minimum score 550 paper-based; 213 computer-based). Electronic applications accepted. *Expenses:* Tuition: Full-time $19,800; part-time $825 per credit hour. Required fees: $150.

State University of New York at Binghamton, Graduate School, School of Management, Program in Business Administration, Binghamton, NY 13902-6000. Offers business administration (MBA, PhD); health care professional executive (MBA). *Accreditation:* AACSB. *Students:* 170 full-time (60 women), 21 part-time (6 women); includes 28 minority (2 African Americans, 18 Asian Americans or Pacific Islanders, 8 Hispanic Americans), 73 international. Average age 28. 353 applicants, 47% accepted, 91 enrolled. In 2009, 115 master's, 2 doctorates awarded. *Degree requirements:* For doctorate, thesis/dissertation. *Entrance requirements:* For master's and doctorate, GMAT. Additional exam requirements/recommendations for international students: Required—TOEFL (minimum score 550 paper-based; 213 computer-based; 80 iBT). *Application deadline:* For fall admission, 3/1 priority date for domestic and international students; for spring admission, 10/15 priority date for domestic and international students. Applications are processed on a rolling basis. Application fee: $60. Electronic applications accepted. *Financial support:* Fellowships, research assistantships, teaching assistantships, career-related internships or fieldwork, Federal Work-Study, institutionally sponsored loans, scholarships/grants, health care benefits, and unspecified assistantships available. Financial award application deadline: 2/15; financial award applicants required to submit FAFSA. *Unit head:* Dr. George Bobinski, Associate Dean, 607-777-2315, E-mail: gbobins@binghamton.edu. *Application contact:* Victoria Williams, Recruiting and Admissions Coordinator, 607-777-2151, Fax: 607-777-2501, E-mail: vwilliam@binghamton.edu.

State University of New York Institute of Technology, School of Business, Program in Health Services Administration, Utica, NY 13504-3050. Offers MS. Part-time and evening/weekend programs available. Postbaccalaureate distance learning degree programs offered (no on-campus study). *Degree requirements:* For master's, capstone or project. *Entrance requirements:* For master's, GMAT or GRE, minimum GPA of 3.0. Additional exam requirements/recommendations for international students: Required—TOEFL (minimum score 550 paper-based; 213 computer-based). *Faculty research:* Institutional utilization, health policy, health finance.

Stony Brook University, State University of New York, Graduate School, College of Business, Program in Business Administration, Stony Brook, NY 11794. Offers finance (MBA, Certificate); health care management (MBA, Certificate); human resource management (Certificate); human resources (MBA); information systems management (MBA, Certificate); management (MBA); marketing (MBA). *Faculty:* 17 full-time (2 women), 25 part-time/adjunct (5 women). *Students:* 134 full-time (64 women), 112 part-time (44 women); includes 54 minority (8 African Americans, 1 American Indian/Alaska Native, 35 Asian Americans or Pacific Islanders, 10 Hispanic Americans), 56 international. 222 applicants, 55% accepted. In 2009, 134 master's, 5 other advanced degrees awarded. Application fee: $60. *Expenses:* Tuition, state resident: full-time $8370; part-time $349 per credit. Tuition, nonresident: full-time $13,250; part-time $552 per credit. Required fees: $933. *Financial support:* In 2009–10, 2 teaching assistantships were awarded. *Unit head:* Joseph McDonnell, Interim Dean, 631-632-7180. *Application contact:* Dr. Aristotle Lekacos, Director, Graduate Program, 631-632-7171, E-mail: aristotle.lekacost@notes.cc.sunysb.edu.

Stony Brook University, State University of New York, Stony Brook University Medical Center, Health Sciences Center, School of Health Technology and Management, Stony Brook, NY 11794. Offers health care management (Advanced Certificate); health care policy and management (MS); occupational therapy (MS); physical therapy (DPT); physician assistant (MS). *Accreditation:* APTA. Part-time programs available. *Faculty:* 33 full-time (25 women), 25 part-time/adjunct (12 women). *Students:* 217 full-time (162 women), 130 part-time (93 women); includes 87 minority (21 African Americans, 1 American Indian/Alaska Native, 46 Asian Americans or Pacific Islanders, 19 Hispanic Americans), 8 international. 54 applicants, 91% accepted. In 2009, 89 master's, 77 doctorates, 15 other advanced degrees awarded. *Degree requirements:* For master's, thesis. *Entrance requirements:* For master's, GRE General Test, minimum GPA of 3.0, work experience in field. *Application deadline:* For fall admission, 1/15 for domestic students. Application fee: $60. *Expenses:* Tuition, state resident: full-time $8370; part-time $349 per credit. Tuition, nonresident: full-time $13,250; part-time $552 per credit. Required fees: $933. *Financial support:* In 2009–10, 2 research assistantships, 1 teaching assistantship were awarded; fellowships, career-related internships or fieldwork, Federal Work-Study, and institutionally sponsored loans also available. Financial award application deadline: 3/15. *Faculty research:* Health promotion and disease prevention. Total annual research expenditures: $842,937. *Unit head:* Dr. Craig A. Lehmann, Dean, 631-444-2251, Fax: 631-444-7621. *Application contact:* Richard W. Johnson, Associate Dean for Graduate Studies, 631-444-3251.

Stony Brook University, State University of New York, Stony Brook University Medical Center, Health Sciences Center, School of Nursing, Program in Nursing Practice, Stony Brook, NY 11794. Offers DNP. Postbaccalaureate distance learning degree programs offered. *Degree requirements:* For doctorate, project. *Entrance requirements:* For doctorate, minimum GPA of 3.0. Additional exam requirements/recommendations for international students: Required—TOEFL. *Application deadline:* For fall admission, 12/1 for domestic and international students. Application fee: $60. *Expenses:* Tuition, state resident: full-time $8370; part-time $349 per credit. Tuition, nonresident: full-time $13,250; part-time $552 per credit. Required fees: $933. *Unit head:* Dr. Lee Xippolitos, Interim Dean, 631-444-3200, Fax: 631-444-6628. *Application contact:* Dr. Marie Ann Marino, Coordinator, 631-444-3295, Fax: 631-444-3074, E-mail: marie.marino@stonybrook.edu.

Strayer University, Graduate Studies, Washington, DC 20005-2603. Offers accounting (MS); acquisition (MBA); business administration (MBA); communications technology (MS); educational management (M Ed); finance (MBA); health services administration (MHSA); hospitality and tourism management (MBA); human resource management (MBA); information systems (MS), including computer security management, decision support system management, enterprise resource management, network management, software engineering management, systems development management; management (MBA); management information systems (MS); marketing (MBA); professional accounting (MS), including accounting information systems, controllership, taxation; public administration (MPA); supply chain management (MBA); technology in education (M Ed). Programs also offered at campus locations in Birmingham, AL; Chamblee, GA; Cobb County, GA; Morrow, GA; White Marsh, MD; Charleston, SC; Columbia, SC; Greensboro, NC; Greenville, SC; Lexington, KY; Louisville, KY; Nashville, TN; North Raleigh, NC; Washington, DC. Part-time and evening/weekend programs available. Postbaccalaureate distance learning degree programs offered (minimal on-campus study). *Degree requirements:* For master's, thesis. *Entrance requirements:* For master's, GMAT, GRE General Test, bachelor's degree from an accredited college or university, minimum undergraduate GPA of 2.75. Electronic applications accepted.

Suffolk University, Sawyer Business School, Master of Business Administration Program, Boston, MA 02108-2770. Offers accounting (MBA); business administration (APC); corporate

financial executive track (MBA); entrepreneurship (MBA); executive business administration (EMBA); finance (MBA); global business administration (GMBA); health administration (MBA); international business (MBA); marketing (MBA); organizational behavior (MBA); strategic management (MBA); taxation (MBA); JD/MBA; MBA/GDPA; MBA/MHA; MBA/MSA; MBA/MSF; MBA/MST. *Accreditation:* AACSB. Part-time and evening/weekend programs available. Postbaccalaureate distance learning degree programs offered (no on-campus study). *Faculty:* 103 full-time (30 women), 63 part-time/adjunct (19 women). *Students:* 173 full-time (68 women), 406 part-time (178 women); includes 51 minority (16 African Americans, 3 American Indian/Alaska Native, 22 Asian Americans or Pacific Islanders, 10 Hispanic Americans), 90 international. Average age 29. 460 applicants, 72% accepted, 157 enrolled. In 2009, 245 master's awarded. *Entrance requirements:* For master's, GMAT, minimum undergraduate GPA of 2.75 (MBA), 5 years of managerial experience (EMBA). Additional exam requirements/recommendations for international students: Required—TOEFL (minimum score 550 paper-based; 213 computer-based). *Application deadline:* For fall admission, 6/15 priority date for domestic students, 6/15 for international students; for spring admission, 11/1 priority date for domestic students, 11/1 for international students. Applications are processed on a rolling basis. Application fee: $50. Electronic applications accepted. *Expenses:* Tuition: Full-time $33,000; part-time $1100 per credit. Required fees: $20. Tuition and fees vary according to program. *Financial support:* In 2009–10, 284 students received support, including 99 fellowships with full and partial tuition reimbursements available (averaging $13,599 per year); career-related internships or fieldwork, Federal Work-Study, and institutionally sponsored loans also available. Support available to part-time students. Financial award application deadline: 4/1; financial award applicants required to submit FAFSA. *Faculty research:* Foreign investments; career strategies and boundaryless careers; corporate ethics codes; interest rates, inflation, and growth options; innovation and product development performance. *Unit head:* Lillian Hallberg, Assistant Dean of Graduate Programs/Director of MBA Programs, 617-573-8306, E-mail: lhallber@suffolk.edu. *Application contact:* Judith Reynolds, Director of Graduate Admissions, 617-573-8302, Fax: 617-305-1733, E-mail: grad.admission@suffolk.edu.

Suffolk University, Sawyer Business School, Program in Health Administration, Boston, MA 02108-2770. Offers MBAH, MHA. Part-time and evening/weekend programs available. *Faculty:* 3 full-time (1 woman). *Students:* 18 full-time (14 women), 37 part-time (21 women); includes 7 minority (3 African Americans, 1 American Indian/Alaska Native, 2 Asian Americans or Pacific Islanders, 1 Hispanic American), 11 international. Average age 29. 47 applicants, 83% accepted, 19 enrolled. In 2009, 9 master's awarded. *Entrance requirements:* Additional exam requirements/recommendations for international students: Required—TOEFL (minimum score 550 paper-based; 213 computer-based; 80 iBT). *Application deadline:* For fall admission, 6/15 priority date for domestic students, 6/15 for international students; for spring admission, 11/1 priority date for domestic students, 11/1 for international students. Applications are processed on a rolling basis. Application fee: $50. Electronic applications accepted. *Expenses:* Contact institution. *Financial support:* In 2009–10, 33 students received support, including 17 fellowships with full and partial tuition reimbursements available (averaging $11,868 per year); career-related internships or fieldwork, Federal Work-Study, and institutionally sponsored loans also available. Support available to part-time students. Financial award application deadline: 4/1; financial award applicants required to submit FAFSA. *Faculty research:* Mental health, federal policy, health care. *Unit head:* Richard Gregg, Director, 617-994-4246, E-mail: rgregg@suffolk.edu. *Application contact:* Judith Reynolds, Director of Graduate Admissions, 617-573-8302, Fax: 617-305-1733, E-mail: grad.admission@suffolk.edu.

Syracuse University, Maxwell School of Citizenship and Public Affairs, Program in Health Services Management and Policy, Syracuse, NY 13244. Offers CAS. Part-time and evening/weekend programs available. *Students:* 1 part-time (0 women). Average age 50. 6 applicants, 100% accepted, 1 enrolled. In 2009, 7 CASs awarded. *Entrance requirements:* For degree, 7 years of mid-career experience. Additional exam requirements/recommendations for international students: Required—TOEFL (minimum score 100 iBT). *Application deadline:* For fall admission, 2/1 priority date for domestic and international students; for spring admission, 8/15 priority date for domestic and international students. Application fee: $75. Electronic applications accepted. *Expenses:* Tuition: Full-time $26,808; part-time $1117 per credit. Required fees: $1024. *Financial support:* Application deadline: 1/1. *Unit head:* Dr. Thomas Dennison, Head, 315-443-9215, Fax: 315-443-9721, E-mail: thdennis@syr.edu. *Application contact:* Dr. Thomas Dennison, Head, 315-443-9215, Fax: 315-443-9721, E-mail: thdennis@syr.edu.

Temple University, Graduate School, Fox School of Business, MBA Programs, Philadelphia, PA 19122-6096. Offers accounting (MBA); business management (MBA); financial management (MBA); healthcare and life sciences innovation (MBA); human resource management (MBA); international business (IMBA); IT management (MBA); marketing management (MBA); pharmaceutical management (MBA); strategic management (EMBA, MBA). EMBA offered in Philadelphia, PA and Tokyo, Japan. *Accreditation:* AACSB. Part-time and evening/weekend programs available. Postbaccalaureate distance learning degree programs offered (minimal on-campus study). *Entrance requirements:* For master's, GMAT, minimum undergraduate GPA of 3.0. Additional exam requirements/recommendations for international students: Required—TOEFL (minimum score 600 paper-based; 250 computer-based; 100 iBT), IELTS (minimum score 7.5).

Temple University, Graduate School, Fox School of Business, Specialized Master's Programs, Philadelphia, PA 19122-6096. Offers accounting and financial management (MS); actuarial science (MS); finance (MS); financial engineering (MS); healthcare financial management (MS); healthcare management (MHM); human resource management (MS); management information systems (MS); marketing (MS); statistics (MS). *Accreditation:* AACSB. Part-time programs available. *Entrance requirements:* For master's, GRE General Test or GMAT, minimum undergraduate GPA of 3.0. Additional exam requirements/recommendations for international students: Required—TOEFL (minimum score 600 paper-based; 250 computer-based; 100 iBT), IELTS (minimum score 7.5).

Texas A&M Health Science Center, School of Rural Public Health, College Station, TX 77840. Offers environmental/occupational health (MPH); epidemiology/biostatistics (MPH); health policy/management (MPH); social and behavioral health (MPH). *Accreditation:* CEPH. Part-time programs available. Postbaccalaureate distance learning degree programs offered (no on-campus study). *Degree requirements:* For master's, thesis optional. *Entrance requirements:* For master's, GRE General Test, minimum undergraduate GPA of 3.0. Electronic applications accepted. *Faculty research:* Tobacco cessation, youth health risk.

Texas A&M University–Corpus Christi, Graduate Studies and Research, College of Business, Corpus Christi, TX 78412-5503. Offers accounting (M Acc); health care administration (MBA); international business (MBA). *Accreditation:* AACSB. Part-time and evening/weekend programs available. *Degree requirements:* For master's, comprehensive exam, thesis (for some programs). *Entrance requirements:* For master's, GMAT. Additional exam requirements/recommendations for international students: Required—TOEFL. Electronic applications accepted.

Texas A&M University–Corpus Christi, Graduate Studies and Research, College of Nursing and Health Sciences, Corpus Christi, TX 78412-5503. Offers clinical nurse specialist (MSN); family nurse practitioner (MSN); health care administration (MSN); leadership in nursing systems (MSN). *Accreditation:* AACN. Part-time and evening/weekend programs available. *Degree requirements:* For master's, comprehensive exam, thesis (for some programs). *Entrance requirements:* For master's, GRE General Test. Additional exam requirements/recommendations for international students: Required—TOEFL. Electronic applications accepted.

Texas State University–San Marcos, Graduate School, College of Health Professions, School of Health Administration, Program in Healthcare Administration, San Marcos, TX 78666. Offers MHA. Part-time and evening/weekend programs available. *Faculty:* 9 full-time (2 women). *Students:* 33 full-time (18 women), 23 part-time (13 women); includes 23 minority (6 African Americans, 1 American Indian/Alaska Native, 4 Asian Americans or Pacific Islanders, 12 Hispanic Americans), 1 international. Average age 27. 49 applicants, 69% accepted, 26 enrolled. In 2009, 28 master's awarded. *Degree requirements:* For master's, comprehensive exam, thesis optional, committee review. *Entrance requirements:* For master's, GRE General Test, 3 letters of reference; resume; interview. Additional exam requirements/recommendations for international students: Required—TOEFL (minimum score 550 paper-based; 213 computer-based). *Application deadline:* For fall admission, 6/1 priority date for domestic students, 6/1 for international students; for spring admission, 10/1 priority date for domestic students, 10/1 for international students. Applications are processed on a rolling basis. Application fee: $40 ($90 for international students). Electronic applications accepted. *Expenses:* Tuition, state resident: full-time $5784; part-time $241 per credit hour. Tuition, nonresident: full-time $13,224; part-time $551 per credit hour. Required fees: $1728; $48 per credit hour. $306. Tuition and fees vary according to course load. *Financial support:* In 2009–10, 46 students received support, including 5 teaching assistantships (averaging $4,315 per year); research assistantships, career-related internships or fieldwork, Federal Work-Study, and institutionally sponsored loans also available. Support available to part-time students. Financial award application deadline: 4/1; financial award applicants required to submit FAFSA. *Faculty research:* Computer applications, quantitative management science technology, philosophy and methodology of research, evaluation. *Unit head:* Dr. Michael Nowicki, Advisor, 512-245-3556, E-mail: mn03@txstate.edu. *Application contact:* Dr. J. Michael Willoughby, Dean of Graduate School, 512-245-2581, Fax: 512-245-8365, E-mail: gradcollege@txstate.edu.

Texas State University–San Marcos, Graduate School, College of Health Professions, School of Health Administration, Program in Healthcare Human Resources, San Marcos, TX 78666. Offers MS. *Accreditation:* CAHME. Part-time and evening/weekend programs available. *Faculty:* 5 full-time (1 woman). *Students:* 4 full-time (2 women), 11 part-time (8 women); includes 4 minority (2 African Americans, 1 Asian American or Pacific Islander, 1 Hispanic American). Average age 31. 6 applicants, 100% accepted, 3 enrolled. In 2009, 7 master's awarded. *Degree requirements:* For master's, comprehensive exam, thesis optional, committee review. *Entrance requirements:* For master's, GRE General Test, department interview; 3 letters of reference; resume. Additional exam requirements/recommendations for international students: Required—TOEFL (minimum score 550 paper-based; 213 computer-based). *Application deadline:* For fall admission, 6/15 priority date for domestic students, 6/1 for international students; for spring admission, 10/15 priority date for domestic students, 10/1 for international students. Applications are processed on a rolling basis. Application fee: $40 ($90 for international students). Electronic applications accepted. *Expenses:* Tuition, state resident: full-time $5784; part-time $241 per credit hour. Tuition, nonresident: full-time $13,224; part-time $551 per credit hour. Required fees: $1728; $48 per credit hour. $306. Tuition and fees vary according to course load. *Financial support:* In 2009–10, 11 students received support; research assistantships, teaching assistantships, career-related internships or fieldwork, Federal Work-Study, and institutionally sponsored loans available. Support available to part-time students. Financial award application deadline: 4/1; financial award applicants required to submit FAFSA. *Unit head:* Dr. Michael Nowicki, Program Advisor, 512-245-3556, Fax: 512-245-8712, E-mail: mn03@txstate.edu. *Application contact:* Dr. J. Michael Willoughby, Dean of Graduate School, 512-245-2581, Fax: 512-245-8365, E-mail: gradcollege@txstate.edu.

Texas Tech University, Jerry S. Rawls College of Business Administration, Area of Information Systems and Quantitative Sciences, Lubbock, TX 79409. Offers business statistics (MS, PhD); healthcare management (MS); management information systems (MS, PhD); production and operations management (MS, PhD); risk management (MS). Part-time programs available. *Faculty:* 14 full-time (0 women). *Students:* 61 full-time (14 women), 5 part-time (1 woman); includes 2 minority (1 African American, 1 Asian American or Pacific Islander), 52 international. Average age 27. 94 applicants, 84% accepted, 35 enrolled. In 2009, 6 master's, 6 doctorates awarded. Terminal master's awarded for partial completion of doctoral program. *Degree requirements:* For master's, comprehensive exam or capstone course; for doctorate, thesis/dissertation, qualifying exams. *Entrance requirements:* For master's and doctorate, GMAT, holistic profile of academic credentials. Additional exam requirements/recommendations for international students: Required—TOEFL (minimum score 550 paper-based; 213 computer-based; 79 iBT). *Application deadline:* For fall admission, 4/1 priority date for domestic students, 1/15 priority date for international students; for spring admission, 9/1 priority date for domestic students, 7/15 priority date for international students. Applications are processed on a rolling basis. Application fee: $50 ($75 for international students). Electronic applications accepted. *Expenses:* Tuition, state resident: full-time $5100; part-time $213 per credit hour. Tuition, nonresident: full-time $11,748; part-time $490 per credit hour. Required fees: $2298; $50 per credit hour. $555 per semester. *Financial support:* In 2009–10, 4 research assistantships (averaging $8,000 per year), 8 teaching assistantships (averaging $17,000 per year) were awarded; Federal Work-Study, scholarships/grants, and unspecified assistantships also available. *Faculty research:* Database management systems, systems management and engineering, expert systems and adaptive knowledge-based sciences, statistical analysis and design. *Unit head:* Dr. Bradley Ewing, Area Coordinator, 806-742-3939, Fax: 806-742-3193, E-mail: bradley.ewing@ttu.edu. *Application contact:* Cynthia D. Barnes, Director, Graduate Services Center, 806-742-3184, Fax: 806-742-3958, E-mail: ba_grad@ttu.edu.

Texas Tech University, Jerry S. Rawls College of Business Administration, Programs in Business Administration, Lubbock, TX 79409. Offers agricultural business (MBA); business administration (IMBA); entrepreneurship (MBA); finance (MBA); general business (MBA); health organization management (MBA); international business (MBA); management and leadership skills (MBA); management information systems (MBA); marketing (MBA); statistics (MBA); JD/MBA; MBA/M Arch; MBA/MA; MBA/MD; MBA/MS; MBA/Pharm D. Part-time and evening/weekend programs available. *Faculty:* 54 full-time (9 women), 5 part-time/adjunct (0 women). *Students:* 59 full-time (15 women), 487 part-time (148 women); includes 107 minority (24 African Americans, 4 American Indian/Alaska Native, 30 Asian Americans or Pacific Islanders, 49 Hispanic Americans), 51 international. Average age 30. 477 applicants, 81% accepted, 302 enrolled. In 2009, 185 degrees awarded. *Degree requirements:* For master's, capstone course. *Entrance requirements:* For master's, GMAT, holistic review of academic credentials. Additional exam requirements/recommendations for international students: Required—TOEFL (minimum score 550 paper-based; 213 computer-based; 79 iBT). *Application deadline:* For fall admission, 4/1 priority date for domestic students, 1/15 priority date for international students; for spring admission, 9/1 priority date for domestic students, 7/15 priority date for international students. Applications are processed on a rolling basis. Application fee: $50 ($75 for international students). Electronic applications accepted. *Expenses:* Tuition, state resident: full-time $5100; part-time $213 per credit hour. Tuition, nonresident: full-time $11,748; part-time $490 per credit hour. Required fees: $2298; $50 per credit hour. $555 per semester. *Financial support:* In 2009–10, 13 research assistantships (averaging $8,000 per year) were awarded; teaching assistantships, career-related internships or fieldwork, Federal Work-Study, scholarships/grants, health care benefits, and unspecified assistantships also available. Support available to part-time students. Financial award applicants required to submit FAFSA. *Unit head:* Dr. W. Jay Conover, Director, 806-742-1546, Fax: 806-742-3958, E-mail: jay.conover@ttu.edu. *Application contact:* Cynthia D. Barnes, Director, Graduate Services Center, 806-742-3184, Fax: 806-742-3958, E-mail: ba_grad@ttu.edu.

Texas Tech University Health Sciences Center, School of Allied Health Sciences, Program in Clinical Practice Management, Lubbock, TX 79430. Offers MS. *Accreditation:* CORE. Part-time programs available. *Faculty:* 4 full-time (0 women). *Students:* 65 full-time (39 women), 21 part-time (12 women); includes 29 minority (8 African Americans, 1 American Indian/Alaska Native, 5 Asian Americans or Pacific Islanders, 15 Hispanic Americans). Average age 36. 90 applicants, 76% accepted, 68 enrolled. In 2009, 12 master's awarded. *Entrance requirements:* Additional exam requirements/recommendations for international students: Required—TOEFL, IELTS. *Application deadline:* For fall admission, 8/1 for domestic students; for spring admission, 12/1 for domestic students. Applications are processed on a rolling basis. Application fee: $35. Electronic applications accepted. *Financial support:* Institutionally sponsored loans available. *Unit head:* Dr. Robin Satterwhite, Chair, 806-743-2263, Fax: 806-743-3249, E-mail: robin.satterwhite@ttuhsc.edu. *Application contact:* Jeri Moravcik, Assistant Director of Admissions and Student Affairs, 806-743-3220, Fax: 806-743-2994, E-mail: jeri.moravcik@ttuhsc.edu.

Texas Wesleyan University, Graduate Programs, Graduate Business Programs, Fort Worth, TX 76105-1536. Offers business administration (MBA); health services administration (MS);

Health Services Management and Hospital Administration

Texas Wesleyan University (continued)

management (MiM). *Accreditation:* ACBSP. Part-time and evening/weekend programs available. *Faculty:* 16 full-time (6 women), 6 part-time/adjunct (4 women). *Students:* 16 full-time (4 women), 36 part-time (20 women); includes 15 minority (11 African Americans, 1 American Indian/Alaska Native, 3 Hispanic Americans), 8 international. Average age 32. 27 applicants, 74% accepted, 15 enrolled. In 2009, 18 master's awarded. *Degree requirements:* For master's, capstone course. *Entrance requirements:* For master's, GMAT, 3 letters of recommendation. *Application deadline:* For fall admission, 7/7 priority date for domestic students; for spring admission, 11/1 priority date for domestic students. Applications are processed on a rolling basis. Application fee: $50. *Expenses:* Contact institution. *Financial support:* Federal Work-Study, scholarships/grants, and tuition waivers (full and partial) available. Support available to part-time students. Financial award application deadline: 3/15; financial award applicants required to submit FAFSA. *Unit head:* Dr. Hector Quintanilla, Dean, 817-531-4840, Fax: 817-531-6585. *Application contact:* Dr. Hector Quintanilla, Dean, 817-531-4840, Fax: 817-531-6585.

Texas Woman's University, Graduate School, College of Arts and Sciences, School of Management, Denton, TX 76201. Offers business administration (EMBA, MBA); health systems management (MHSM). Part-time programs available. *Faculty:* 17 full-time (8 women), 3 part-time/adjunct (all women). *Students:* 543 full-time (444 women), 384 part-time (312 women); includes 547 minority (353 African Americans, 3 American Indian/Alaska Native, 98 Asian Americans or Pacific Islanders, 93 Hispanic Americans), 45 international. Average age 36. 471 applicants, 86% accepted, 326 enrolled. In 2009, 369 master's awarded. *Degree requirements:* For master's, thesis optional. *Entrance requirements:* For master's, 3 letters of reference, resume, minimum GPA of 3.0; 5 years relevant experience (EMBA). Additional exam requirements/recommendations for international students: Required—TOEFL (minimum score 550 paper-based; 213 computer-based; 79 iBT). *Application deadline:* For fall admission, 8/1 priority date for domestic students, 3/1 for international students; for spring admission, 12/1 priority date for domestic students, 7/1 for international students. Applications are processed on a rolling basis. Application fee: $50. Electronic applications accepted. *Expenses:* Tuition, state resident: full-time $3564; part-time $198 per credit hour. Tuition, nonresident: full-time $8550; part-time $475 per credit hour. Required fees: $69.26 per credit hour. Tuition and fees vary according to course load. *Financial support:* In 2009–10, 441 students received support, including 15 research assistantships (averaging $9,684 per year), teaching assistantships (averaging $9,684 per year); career-related internships or fieldwork, Federal Work-Study, institutionally sponsored loans, scholarships/grants, traineeships, health care benefits, and unspecified assistantships also available. Support available to part-time students. Financial award application deadline: 3/1; financial award applicants required to submit FAFSA. *Faculty research:* Leadership, tax, women in management, sales, job satisfaction. *Unit head:* Dr. P. Ann Hughes, Director, 940-898-2458, Fax: 940-898-2120, E-mail: som@twu.edu. *Application contact:* Samuel Wheeler, Assistant Director of Admissions, 940-898-3188, Fax: 940-898-3081, E-mail: wheelersr@twu.edu.

Texas Woman's University, Graduate School, College of Health Sciences, Program in Health Care Administration-Houston Center, Denton, TX 76201. Offers MHA. *Accreditation:* CAHME. Part-time and evening/weekend programs available. *Faculty:* 4 full-time (1 woman). *Students:* 39 full-time (31 women), 66 part-time (56 women); includes 72 minority (34 African Americans, 1 American Indian/Alaska Native, 27 Asian Americans or Pacific Islanders, 10 Hispanic Americans), 13 international. Average age 31. 61 applicants, 56% accepted, 22 enrolled. In 2009, 27 master's awarded. *Degree requirements:* For master's, comprehensive exam, thesis or alternative. *Entrance requirements:* For master's, GMAT (minimum score 450) or GRE General Test (minimum score 350 verbal, 450 quantitative), interview, resume, 3 letters of reference. Additional exam requirements/recommendations for international students: Required—TOEFL (minimum score 550 paper-based; 213 computer-based; 79 iBT). *Application deadline:* For fall admission, 6/30 priority date for domestic students, 3/1 for international students; for spring admission, 10/30 priority date for domestic students, 7/1 for international students. Applications are processed on a rolling basis. Application fee: $30 ($50 for international students). Electronic applications accepted. *Expenses:* Tuition, state resident: full-time $3564; part-time $198 per credit hour. Tuition, nonresident: full-time $8550; part-time $475 per credit hour. Required fees: $69.26 per credit hour. Tuition and fees vary according to course load. *Financial support:* In 2009–10, 13 students received support, including 1 research assistantship (averaging $9,504 per year); career-related internships or fieldwork, Federal Work-Study, institutionally sponsored loans, scholarships/grants, traineeships, health care benefits, and unspecified assistantships also available. Support available to part-time students. Financial award application deadline: 3/1; financial award applicants required to submit FAFSA. *Faculty research:* Organizational culture, medical errors, ethical analysis in health care, leadership and professional development, strategic management, recruitment and retention issues in elderly health care. *Unit head:* Dr. Kelley Moseley, Program Director, 713-794-2061, Fax: 713-794-2350, E-mail: kmoseley@twu.edu. *Application contact:* Samuel Wheeler, Assistant Director of Admissions, 940-898-3188, Fax: 940-898-3081, E-mail: wheelersr@twu.edu.

Texas Woman's University, Graduate School, College of Nursing, Denton, TX 76201. Offers acute care nurse practitioner (MS); adult health clinical nurse specialist (MS); adult health nurse practitioner (MS); child health clinical nurse specialist (MS); clinical nurse leader (MS); community health (MS); family nurse practitioner (MS); health systems management (MS); nursing education (MS); nursing practice (DNP); nursing science (PhD); pediatric nurse practitioner (MS); women's health clinical nurse specialist (MS); women's health nurse practitioner (MS). *Accreditation:* AACN. Part-time programs available. Postbaccalaureate distance learning degree programs offered. *Faculty:* 85 full-time (80 women), 6 part-time/adjunct (all women). *Students:* 81 full-time (76 women), 602 part-time (571 women); includes 293 minority (154 African Americans, 3 American Indian/Alaska Native, 90 Asian Americans or Pacific Islanders, 46 Hispanic Americans), 19 international. Average age 39. 259 applicants, 81% accepted, 166 enrolled. In 2009, 100 master's, 22 doctorates awarded. *Degree requirements:* For master's, thesis or alternative; for doctorate, comprehensive exam, thesis/dissertation. *Entrance requirements:* For master's, GRE or MAT, minimum GPA of 3.0, RN license, BS in nursing, basic statistics course; for doctorate, GRE (Verbal 460, Quantitative 500) or MAT (50), MS in nursing, minimum GPA of 3.5, RN license, coursework in statistics, 2 letters of reference, curriculum vitae, nursing-theory course, graduate research course, letter stating professional and research goals. Additional exam requirements/recommendations for international students: Required—TOEFL (minimum score 550 paper-based; 213 computer-based; 79 iBT). *Application deadline:* For fall admission, 5/1 priority date for domestic students, 3/1 for international students; for spring admission, 9/15 priority date for domestic students, 7/1 for international students. Applications are processed on a rolling basis. Application fee: $50. Electronic applications accepted. *Expenses:* Tuition, state resident: full-time $3564; part-time $198 per credit hour. Tuition, nonresident: full-time $8550; part-time $475 per credit hour. Required fees: $69.26 per credit hour. Tuition and fees vary according to course load. *Financial support:* In 2009–10, 99 students received support, including 16 fellowships (averaging $17,325 per year), 5 research assistantships (averaging $11,484 per year), 5 teaching assistantships (averaging $11,484 per year); career-related internships or fieldwork, Federal Work-Study, institutionally sponsored loans, scholarships/grants, traineeships, health care benefits, and unspecified assistantships also available. Support available to part-time students. Financial award application deadline: 3/1; financial award applicants required to submit FAFSA. *Faculty research:* Evaluation of pre-natal care, screening for intimate partner violence, stressors and nursing success, breast surgery, breast feeding, adolescent needs during childbirth. *Unit head:* Dr. Patricia Holden-Huchton, Interim Dean, 940-898-2401, Fax: 940-898-2437, E-mail: pholdenhuchton@twu.edu. *Application contact:* Samuel Wheeler, Assistant Director of Admissions, 940-898-3188, Fax: 940-898-3081, E-mail: wheelersr@twu.edu.

Thomas Jefferson University, Jefferson School of Population Health, Program in Healthcare Quality and Safety, Philadelphia, PA 19107. Offers MS. Postbaccalaureate distance learning degree programs offered. *Expenses:* Tuition: Full-time $26,858; part-time $879 per credit. Required fees: $525.

Thomas Jefferson University, Jefferson School of Population Health, Program in Health Policy, Philadelphia, PA 19107. Offers MS. Postbaccalaureate distance learning degree programs offered. *Expenses:* Tuition: Full-time $26,858; part-time $879 per credit. Required fees: $525.

Towson University, College of Graduate Studies and Research, Program in Clinician-Administrator Transition, Towson, MD 21252-0001. Offers Certificate. *Entrance requirements:* For degree, minimum GPA of 3.0; bachelor's or master's degree in a clinical field; licensure, licensure eligibility, or certificate in a clinical field. Electronic applications accepted.

Trinity University, Department of Health Care Administration, San Antonio, TX 78212-7200. Offers MS. *Accreditation:* CAHME. Part-time programs available. Postbaccalaureate distance learning degree programs offered (minimal on-campus study). *Degree requirements:* For master's, research projects. *Entrance requirements:* For master's, GMAT, GRE General Test, previous course work in accounting, economics, and statistics.

Trinity Western University, School of Graduate Studies, Program in Leadership, Langley, BC V2Y 1Y1, Canada. Offers business (MA, Certificate); Christian ministry (MA); education (MA, Certificate); healthcare (MA, Certificate); non-profit (MA, Certificate). Postbaccalaureate distance learning degree programs offered (minimal on-campus study). *Degree requirements:* For master's, major project. *Entrance requirements:* For master's, minimum GPA of 2.7. Additional exam requirements/recommendations for international students: Required—TOEFL (minimum score 620 paper-based; 260 computer-based; 105 iBT). Electronic applications accepted. *Expenses:* Contact institution. *Faculty research:* Servant leadership.

Troy University, Graduate School, College of Arts and Sciences, Program in Public Administration, Troy, AL 36082. Offers education (MPA); environmental management (MPA); government contracting (MPA); health care administration (MPA); justice administration (MPA); management information systems (MPA); national security affairs (MPA); nonprofit management (MPA); public human resources management (MPA); public management (MPA). *Accreditation:* NASPAA. Part-time and evening/weekend programs available. Postbaccalaureate distance learning degree programs offered (no on-campus study). *Students:* 239 full-time (161 women), 652 part-time (416 women); includes 596 minority (547 African Americans, 11 American Indian/Alaska Native, 6 Asian Americans or Pacific Islanders, 32 Hispanic Americans). Average age 34. 415 applicants, 80% accepted. In 2009, 247 master's awarded. *Degree requirements:* For master's, capstone course, research methodologies course. *Entrance requirements:* For master's, GRE, MAT or GMAT, minimum undergraduate GPA of 2.5, letter of recommendation. Additional exam requirements/recommendations for international students: Required—TOEFL (minimum score 523 paper-based; 193 computer-based; 70 iBT), IELTS (minimum score 6). *Application deadline:* Applications are processed on a rolling basis. Application fee: $50. Electronic applications accepted. *Financial support:* Available to part-time students. Applicants required to submit FAFSA. *Unit head:* Dr. Ellen Rosell, Chairman, 334-670-3758, Fax: 334-670-5647, E-mail: erosell@troy.edu. *Application contact:* Brenda K. Campbell, Director of Graduate Admissions, 334-670-3178, Fax: 334-670-3733, E-mail: bcamp@troy.edu.

Troy University, Graduate School, College of Business, Program in Business Administration, Troy, AL 36082. Offers accounting (EMBA, MBA); criminal justice (EMBA); finance (MBA); general management (EMBA); healthcare management (EMBA); information systems (EMBA, MBA); international economic development (MBA). *Accreditation:* ACBSP. Part-time and evening/weekend programs available. *Students:* 382 full-time (196 women), 732 part-time (457 women); includes 616 minority (483 African Americans, 14 American Indian/Alaska Native, 96 Asian Americans or Pacific Islanders, 23 Hispanic Americans). Average age 29. 869 applicants, 61% accepted. In 2009, 296 master's awarded. *Degree requirements:* For master's, thesis or alternative. *Entrance requirements:* For master's, GMAT (minimum score 500) or GRE General Test (minimum score 900), minimum GPA of 2.5; letter of recommendation. Additional exam requirements/recommendations for international students: Required—TOEFL (minimum score 523 paper-based; 193 computer-based; 70 iBT), IELTS (minimum score 6), or ACT Compass ESL (minimum score 270 on Listening, Reading, and Grammar with no individual score below 85 and a minimum score of 8 out of 12 on writing test). *Application deadline:* Applications are processed on a rolling basis. Application fee: $50. *Unit head:* Dr. Henry M. Findley, Interim Chair/Professor, 334-670-3271, Fax: 334-670-3599, E-mail: hfindley@troy.edu. *Application contact:* Brenda K. Campbell, Director of Graduate Admissions, 334-670-3178, Fax: 334-670-3733, E-mail: bcamp@troy.edu.

Troy University, Graduate School, College of Business, Program in Management, Troy, AL 36082. Offers healthcare management (MSM); human resources management (MSM); information systems (MSM); international hospitality management (MSM); international management (MSM); leadership and organizational effectiveness (MSM); public management (MS, MSM). *Accreditation:* ACBSP. Evening/weekend programs available. *Students:* 193 full-time (130 women), 575 part-time (374 women); includes 473 minority (417 African Americans, 12 American Indian/Alaska Native, 20 Asian Americans or Pacific Islanders, 24 Hispanic Americans). Average age 35. 275 applicants, 91% accepted. In 2009, 332 master's awarded. *Degree requirements:* For master's, thesis or alternative. *Entrance requirements:* For master's, GMAT (minimum score 500) or GRE General Test (minimum score 900), minimum GPA of 2.5; letter of recommendation. Additional exam requirements/recommendations for international students: Required—TOEFL (minimum score 523 paper-based; 193 computer-based; 70 iBT), IELTS, or ACT Compass ESL (minimum score 270 on Listening, Reading, and Grammar with no individual score below 85 and a minimum score of 8 out of 12 on writing test). *Application deadline:* Applications are processed on a rolling basis. Application fee: $50. Electronic applications accepted. *Expenses:* Contact institution. *Unit head:* Dr. Henry M. Findley, Interim Chair/Professor, 334-670-3271, Fax: 334-670-3599, E-mail: hfindley@troy.edu. *Application contact:* Brenda K. Campbell, Director of Graduate Admissions, 334-670-3178, Fax: 334-670-3733, E-mail: bcamp@troy.edu.

TUI University, College of Health Sciences, Cypress, CA 90630. Offers MS, PhD, Certificate. Part-time and evening/weekend programs available. Postbaccalaureate distance learning degree programs offered (no on-campus study). *Degree requirements:* For doctorate, comprehensive exam, thesis/dissertation. *Entrance requirements:* For master's, minimum GPA of 2.5 (students with GPA 3.0 or greater may transfer up to 30% of graduate level credits); for doctorate, minimum GPA of 3.4. Additional exam requirements/recommendations for international students: Required—TOEFL. Electronic applications accepted.

Tulane University, School of Public Health and Tropical Medicine, Department of Health Systems Management, New Orleans, LA 70118-5669. Offers MHA, MMM, MPH, PhD, Sc D, JD/MHA, MD/MPH. *Accreditation:* CAHME (one or more programs are accredited). *Degree requirements:* For doctorate, comprehensive exam, thesis/dissertation. *Entrance requirements:* For master's, GMAT, GRE General Test; for doctorate, GRE General Test. Additional exam requirements/recommendations for international students: Required—TOEFL. Electronic applications accepted. *Faculty research:* Health policy, organizational governance, international health administration.

Union Graduate College, Center for Bioethics and Clinical Leadership, Schenectady, NY 12308-3107. Offers bioethics (MS); clinical ethics (AC); clinical leadership in health management (MS); health, policy and law (AC). Part-time and evening/weekend programs available. Postbaccalaureate distance learning degree programs offered (minimal on-campus study). *Faculty:* 9 full-time (1 woman), 13 part-time/adjunct (6 women). *Students:* 7 full-time (3 women), 53 part-time (38 women); includes 20 minority (all Asian Americans or Pacific Islanders), 4 international. Average age 32. 69 applicants, 91% accepted, 57 enrolled. In 2009, 21 master's awarded. *Entrance requirements:* For master's, MCAT, letters of recommendation. Additional exam requirements/recommendations for international students: Required—TOEFL (minimum score 550 paper-based; 213 computer-based). *Application deadline:* Applications are processed on a rolling basis. Application fee: $60. Electronic applications accepted. *Expenses:* Contact institution. *Financial support:* Federal Work-Study, scholarships/grants, health care benefits, and tuition waivers (partial) available. Support available to part-time students. Financial award applicants required to submit FAFSA. *Faculty research:* Bioethics education, clinical ethics consultation, research ethics, history of biomedical ethics, international bioethics/research

ethics. *Unit head:* Dr. Robert B. Baker, Director, 518-631-9860, Fax: 518-631-9903, E-mail: bakerr@union.edu. *Application contact:* Ann Nolte, Assistant Director, 518-631-9860, Fax: 518-631-9903, E-mail: noltea@uniongraduatecollege.edu.

Union Graduate College, School of Management, Schenectady, NY 12308-3107. Offers Business Administration (MBA); Financial Management (Certificate); General Management (Certificate); Health Systems Administration (MBA, Certificate); Human Resources (Certificate). *Accreditation:* AACSB. Part-time and evening/weekend programs available. *Faculty:* 9 full-time (1 woman), 25 part-time/adjunct (9 women). *Students:* 112 full-time (53 women), 86 part-time (38 women); includes 24 minority (4 African Americans, 16 Asian Americans or Pacific Islanders, 4 Hispanic Americans), 13 international. Average age 26. 173 applicants, 61% accepted, 93 enrolled. In 2009, 76 master's, 15 other advanced degrees awarded. *Degree requirements:* For master's, internship, capstone course. *Entrance requirements:* For master's, GMAT, minimum GPA of 3.0, 3 letters of recommendation. Additional exam requirements/recommendations for international students: Required—TOEFL (minimum score 550 paper-based; 213 computer-based). *Application deadline:* Applications are processed on a rolling basis. Application fee: $60. *Financial support:* Research assistantships, career-related internships or fieldwork, Federal Work-Study, scholarships/grants, health care benefits, and tuition waivers (partial) available. Support available to part-time students. Financial award applicants required to submit FAFSA. *Unit head:* Dr. Eric Lewis, Dean, 518-631-9890, Fax: 518-631-9902, E-mail: lewise@uniongraduatecollege.edu. *Application contact:* Diane Trzaskos, Admissions Coordinator, 518-631-9837, Fax: 518-631-9901, E-mail: trzaskod@uniongraduatecollege.edu.

Universidad de Ciencias Medicas, Graduate Programs, San Jose, Costa Rica. Offers dermatology (SP); family health (MS); health service center administration (MHA); human anatomy (MS); medical and surgery (MD); occupational medicine (MS); pharmacy (Pharm D). Part-time programs available. *Degree requirements:* For master's, thesis; for first professional degree and SP, comprehensive exam. *Entrance requirements:* For first professional degree, admissions test; for master's, MD or bachelors degree; for SP, admissions test, MD degree.

Universidad de Iberoamerica, Graduate School, San Jose, Costa Rica. Offers clinical neuropsychology (PhD); clinical psychology (M Psych); educational psychology (M Psych); forensic psychology (M Psych); hospital management (MHA); intensive care nursing (MN); medicine (MD). *Entrance requirements:* For master's, 2 letters of recommendation, interview.

Université de Montréal, Faculty of Medicine, Department of Health Administration, Montréal, QC H3C 3J7, Canada. Offers M Sc, DESS. *Accreditation:* CAHME. *Faculty:* 33 full-time (15 women), 17 part-time/adjunct (2 women). *Students:* 64 full-time (34 women), 178 part-time (107 women). 194 applicants, 50% accepted, 77 enrolled. In 2009, 41 master's, 36 DESSs awarded. *Degree requirements:* For master's, thesis. *Entrance requirements:* For master's, proficiency in French. *Application deadline:* For fall admission, 2/1 priority date for domestic students; for winter admission, 11/1 priority date for domestic students; for spring admission, 2/1 priority date for domestic students. Applications are processed on a rolling basis. Application fee: $100. Electronic applications accepted. *Financial support:* Career-related internships or fieldwork and institutionally sponsored loans available. *Unit head:* R??gis Blais, Chairperson, 514-343-5907, Fax: 514-343-2448, E-mail: regis.blais@umonteal.ca. *Application contact:* Lise Lamothe, Responsible for Graduate Studies, 514-343-7983, Fax: 514-343-2448, E-mail: lise.lamothe@umontreal.ca.

University at Albany, State University of New York, School of Public Health, Department of Health Policy, Management, and Behavior, Albany, NY 12222-0001. Offers MS. *Degree requirements:* For master's, thesis. *Entrance requirements:* For master's, GRE General Test. Additional exam requirements/recommendations for international students: Required—TOEFL (minimum score 550 paper-based; 213 computer-based). Electronic applications accepted.

The University of Akron, Graduate School, College of Business Administration, Department of Management, Program in Management-Health Services Administration, Akron, OH 44325. Offers MSM. *Students:* 9 full-time (1 woman), 9 part-time (6 women); includes 1 minority (African American), 3 international. Average age 30. 14 applicants, 79% accepted, 7 enrolled. In 2009, 4 master's awarded. *Entrance requirements:* For master's, GMAT, minimum GPA of 2.75, letters of recommendation, resume. Additional exam requirements/recommendations for international students: Required—TOEFL (minimum score 550 paper-based; 213 computer-based; 79 iBT). *Application deadline:* For fall admission, 8/1 for domestic and international students; for spring admission, 12/1 for domestic and international students. Electronic applications accepted. *Expenses:* Tuition, state resident: full-time $6570; part-time $365 per credit hour. Tuition, nonresident: full-time $11,250; part-time $625 per credit hour. *Unit head:* Dr. Ravi Krovi, Chair, 330-972-8108, E-mail: krovi@uakron.edu. *Application contact:* Dr. Susan Hanlon, Director of Graduate Business Programs, 330-972-7043, Fax: 330-972-6588, E-mail: shanlon@uakron.edu.

The University of Alabama at Birmingham, School of Business, Program in Administrative Health Sciences, Birmingham, AL 35294. Offers PhD.

The University of Alabama at Birmingham, School of Health Professions, Program in Administration/Health Services, Birmingham, AL 35294. Offers D Sc, PhD. *Degree requirements:* For doctorate, thesis/dissertation. *Entrance requirements:* For doctorate, GMAT or GRE General Test. Electronic applications accepted. *Faculty research:* Healthcare strategic management, marketing, and organization studies.

The University of Alabama at Birmingham, School of Health Professions, Program in Health Administration, Birmingham, AL 35294. Offers MSHA. *Accreditation:* CAHME. *Degree requirements:* For master's, administrative residency. *Entrance requirements:* For master's, GMAT, GRE General Test, minimum GPA of 3.0 in final 60 hours of undergraduate course work. Electronic applications accepted.

The University of Alabama in Huntsville, School of Graduate Studies, College of Nursing, Huntsville, AL 35899. Offers family nurse practitioner (Certificate); nursing (MSN, DNP), including acute care nurse practitioner (MSN), adult clinical nursing specialist (MSN), clinical nurse leader (MSN), family nurse practitioner (MSN), leadership in health care systems (MSN); nursing education (Certificate). *Accreditation:* AACN. Part-time and evening/weekend programs available. Postbaccalaureate distance learning degree programs offered (minimal on-campus study). *Faculty:* 13 full-time (11 women), 3 part-time/adjunct (2 women). *Students:* 45 full-time (43 women), 121 part-time (111 women); includes 25 minority (17 African Americans, 5 American Indian/Alaska Native, 3 Asian Americans or Pacific Islanders), 3 international. Average age 39. 151 applicants, 68% accepted, 74 enrolled. In 2009, 52 master's, 5 other advanced degrees awarded. *Degree requirements:* For master's, comprehensive exam, thesis or alternative, oral and written exams; for doctorate, comprehensive exam, thesis/dissertation or alternative, oral and written exams. *Entrance requirements:* For master's, MAT or GRE, Alabama RN license, BSN, minimum GPA of 3.0; for doctorate, master's degree in nursing in an advanced practice area; for Certificate, MAT or GRE, minimum GPA of 3.0. Additional exam requirements/recommendations for international students: Required—TOEFL (minimum score 500 paper-based; 173 computer-based; 62 iBT). *Application deadline:* For fall admission, 7/15 for domestic students, 4/1 for international students; for spring admission, 11/30 for domestic students, 9/1 for international students. Applications are processed on a rolling basis. Application fee: $40 ($50 for international students). Electronic applications accepted. *Expenses:* Tuition, state resident: part-time $355.75 per credit hour. Tuition, nonresident: part-time $847.10 per credit hour. Required fees: $210.80 per semester. Tuition and fees vary according to course load and program. *Financial support:* In 2009–10, 11 students received support, including 11 teaching assistantships with full and partial tuition reimbursements available (averaging $9,996 per year); career-related internships or fieldwork, Federal Work-Study, institutionally sponsored loans, scholarships/grants, traineeships, health care benefits, and unspecified assistantships also available. Support available to part-time students. Financial award application deadline: 4/1; financial award applicants required to submit FAFSA. *Faculty research:* Home health care, gerontology, pediatric nursing, family nurse practitioner, adult acute care administration. *Unit head:* Dr. Fay Raines, Dean, 256-824-6345, Fax: 256-824-6026, E-mail: rainesc@uah.edu. *Application contact:* Charles Davis, Associate Director of Nursing Student Affairs Graduate Programs, 256-824-6669, Fax: 256-824-6026, E-mail: charles.davis@uah.edu.

University of Alberta, School of Public Health, Department of Public Health Sciences, Edmonton, AB T6G 2E1, Canada. Offers clinical epidemiology (M Sc, MPH); environmental and occupational health (MPH); environmental health sciences (M Sc); epidemiology (M Sc); global health (M Sc, MPH); health policy and management (MPH); health policy research (M Sc); health technology assessment (MPH); occupational health (M Sc); population health (M Sc); public health leadership (MPH); public health sciences (PhD); quantitative methods (MPH). *Accreditation:* CEPH (one or more programs are accredited). *Faculty:* 24 full-time (5 women), 59 part-time/adjunct (13 women). *Students:* 49 full-time, 49 part-time. 81 applicants, 31% accepted. In 2009, 28 master's awarded. Terminal master's awarded for partial completion of doctoral program. *Degree requirements:* For master's, thesis (for some programs); for doctorate, thesis/dissertation. *Entrance requirements:* For master's, GMAT or GRE General Test. Additional exam requirements/recommendations for international students: Required—TOEFL (minimum score 550 paper-based; 213 computer-based) or IELTS (minimum score 6). *Application deadline:* For fall admission, 3/15 for domestic students, 7/1 for international students; for winter admission, 11/1 for international students; for spring admission, 3/1 for international students. Applications are processed on a rolling basis. Application fee: $0. Electronic applications accepted. Tuition and fees charges are reported in Canadian dollars. *Expenses:* Tuition, area resident: Full-time $4626 Canadian dollars; part-time $99.72 Canadian dollars per unit. International tuition: $8216 Canadian dollars full-time. Required fees: $3590 Canadian dollars; $99.72 Canadian dollars per unit. $215 Canadian dollars per term. *Financial support:* In 2009–10, 11 students received support, including 6 research assistantships with tuition reimbursements available (averaging $2,200 per year); fellowships, teaching assistantships, career-related internships or fieldwork and tuition waivers (partial) also available. Financial award application deadline: 2/1. *Faculty research:* Biostatistics, health promotion and socio-behavioral health science. Total annual research expenditures: $5.7 million. *Unit head:* L. Duncan Saunders, Acting Chair, 780-492-6814, Fax: 780-492-0364. *Application contact:* Felicity R. Hey, Graduate Programs Administrator, 780-492-6407, Fax: 780-492-0364, E-mail: felicity.hey@ualberta.ca.

University of Atlanta, Graduate Programs, Atlanta, GA 30360. Offers business (MS); business administration (Exec MBA, MBA); computer science (MS); educational leadership (MS, Ed D); healthcare administration (MS, D Sc, Graduate Certificate); information technology for management (Graduate Certificate); international project management (Graduate Certificate); law (JD); managerial science (DBA); project management (Graduate Certificate); social science (MS). Postbaccalaureate distance learning degree programs offered. *Faculty:* 54 part-time/adjunct (10 women). *Students:* 251 full-time. *Entrance requirements:* For master's, minimum cumulative GPA of 2.5. *Expenses:* Tuition: Part-time $1000 per course. Part-time tuition and fees vary according to course load and degree level.

University of Baltimore, Graduate School, The Yale Gordon College of Liberal Arts, Program in Health Systems Management, Baltimore, MD 21201-5779. Offers MS. Part-time and evening/weekend programs available. *Entrance requirements:* For master's, minimum undergraduate GPA of 3.0. Additional exam requirements/recommendations for international students: Required—TOEFL (minimum score 550 paper-based; 213 computer-based).

The University of British Columbia, Faculty of Medicine, School of Population and Public Health, Vancouver, BC V6T 1Z3, Canada. Offers health administration (MHA); health care and epidemiology (MH Sc, PhD); public health (MPH). *Accreditation:* CEPH (one or more programs are accredited). Postbaccalaureate distance learning degree programs offered (minimal on-campus study). *Degree requirements:* For master's, thesis (for some programs), major paper (MH Sc), research project (MHA); for doctorate, thesis/dissertation. *Entrance requirements:* For master's, GRE General Test or GMAT, PCAT, MCAT (MHA), MD or equivalent (for MH Sc); 4-year undergraduate degree from accredited university with minimum B+ overall academic average and in math or statistics course at undergraduate level (for MPH); 4-year undergraduate degree from accredited university with minimum B+ overall academic average plus work experience (for MHA); for doctorate, master's degree from accredited university with minimum B+ overall academic average and in math or statistics course at undergraduate level. Additional exam requirements/recommendations for international students: Required—TOEFL. Electronic applications accepted. *Faculty research:* Population and public health, clinical epidemiology, epidemiology and biostatistics, global health and vulnerable populations, health care services and systems, occupational and environmental health, public health emerging threats and rapid response, social and life course determinants of health, health administration.

University of California, Berkeley, Graduate Division, School of Public Health, Group in Health Services and Policy Analysis, Berkeley, CA 94720-1500. Offers PhD. *Students:* 20 full-time (13 women). Average age 33. 50 applicants, 3 enrolled. In 2009, 4 doctorates awarded. *Degree requirements:* For doctorate, thesis/dissertation, qualifying exam. *Entrance requirements:* For doctorate, GRE General Test, minimum GPA of 3.0, 3 letters of recommendation. *Application deadline:* For fall admission, 12/1 for domestic students. Applications are processed on a rolling basis. Application fee: $70 ($90 for international students). *Financial support:* Fellowships, research assistantships, teaching assistantships, unspecified assistantships available. *Unit head:* Prof. William Dow, Chair, 510-643-8571, E-mail: hspa_phd@berkeley.edu. *Application contact:* Dion Shimatsu-ong, Graduate Assistant for Admission, 510-643-8571, Fax: 510-643-6981, E-mail: hspa_phd@berkeley.edu.

University of California, Los Angeles, Graduate Division, School of Public Health, Department of Health Services, Los Angeles, CA 90095. Offers MPH, MS, Dr PH, PhD, JD/MPH, MBA/MPH, MD/MPH. *Degree requirements:* For master's, comprehensive exam or thesis; for doctorate, thesis/dissertation, oral and written qualifying exams. *Entrance requirements:* For master's, GRE General Test, minimum GPA of 3.0; for doctorate, GRE General Test, minimum undergraduate GPA of 3.0. Electronic applications accepted.

University of California, San Diego, Office of Graduate Studies, Program in Health Law, La Jolla, CA 92093. Offers MAS. Part-time programs available. *Degree requirements:* For master's, capstone project. *Entrance requirements:* For master's, undergraduate degree in healthcare, law, or related field; 3 years work experience; 3 letters of recommendation; resume.

University of California, San Diego, School of Medicine, Program in Leadership in Healthcare Organizations, La Jolla, CA 92093. Offers MAS.

University of Central Florida, College of Health and Public Affairs, Program in Health Services Administration, Orlando, FL 32816. Offers health sciences (MS); health services administration (Certificate). *Accreditation:* CAHME. Part-time and evening/weekend programs available. *Students:* 119 full-time (81 women), 76 part-time (54 women); includes 63 minority (32 African Americans, 12 Asian Americans or Pacific Islanders, 19 Hispanic Americans), 11 international. Average age 28. 191 applicants, 82% accepted, 111 enrolled. In 2009, 37 master's awarded. *Degree requirements:* For master's, comprehensive exam, thesis or alternative, research report. *Entrance requirements:* For master's, GRE General Test. Additional exam requirements/recommendations for international students: Required—TOEFL. *Application deadline:* For fall admission, 7/15 for domestic students; for spring admission, 10/1 for domestic students. Application fee: $30. Electronic applications accepted. *Expenses:* Tuition, state resident: part-time $306.31 per credit hour. Tuition, nonresident: part-time $1099.01 per credit hour. Part-time tuition and fees vary according to degree level and program. *Financial support:* In 2009–10, 1 student received support, including 1 fellowship with partial tuition reimbursement available (averaging $10,000 per year); career-related internships or fieldwork, Federal Work-Study, institutionally sponsored loans, and unspecified assistantships also available. Financial award application deadline: 3/1; financial award applicants required to submit FAFSA. *Unit head:* Dr. Dawn Oetjen, Program Director, 407-823-3729, E-mail: doetjen@mail.ucf.edu. *Application contact:* Dr. Dawn Oetjen, Program Director, 407-823-3729, E-mail: doetjen@mail.ucf.edu.

University of Colorado Denver, Business School, Program in Health Administration, Denver, CO 80217-3364. Offers MS. *Accreditation:* CAHME. Part-time and evening/weekend programs

Health Services Management and Hospital Administration

University of Colorado Denver (continued)
available. *Students:* 3 full-time (2 women), 5 part-time (2 women); includes 3 minority (1 African American, 1 American Indian/Alaska Native, 1 Asian American or Pacific Islander). 28 applicants, 32% accepted, 3 enrolled. In 2009, 4 master's awarded. *Entrance requirements:* For master's, GMAT. Additional exam requirements/recommendations for international students: Required—TOEFL (minimum score 525 paper-based; 197 computer-based). *Application deadline:* For fall admission, 6/1 for domestic students, 3/15 for international students; for spring admission, 11/1 priority date for domestic students, 10/1 for international students. Applications are processed on a rolling basis. Application fee: $50 ($75 for international students). Electronic applications accepted. *Financial support:* Federal Work-Study, institutionally sponsored loans, and traineeships available. Support available to part-time students. Financial award application deadline: 4/1; financial award applicants required to submit FAFSA. *Faculty research:* Cost containment, financial management, governance, rural health-care delivery systems. *Unit head:* Errol Biggs, Director, 303-556-5845, Fax: 303-556-5899, E-mail: errolbriggs@aol.com. *Application contact:* Shelly Townley, Admissions Coordinator, 303-556-5956, Fax: 303-556-5904, E-mail: shelly.townley@ucdenver.edu.

University of Connecticut, Graduate School, School of Business, Storrs, CT 06269. Offers accounting (MS, PhD); business administration (Exec MBA, MBA, PhD); finance (PhD); health care management and insurance studies (MBA); management (PhD); management consulting (MBA); marketing (PhD); marketing intelligence (MBA); MA/MBA; MBA/MSW. *Accreditation:* AACSB. *Faculty:* 75 full-time (14 women). *Students:* 405 full-time (134 women), 999 part-time (364 women); includes 198 minority (43 African Americans, 3 American Indian/Alaska Native, 102 Asian Americans or Pacific Islanders, 50 Hispanic Americans), 136 international. Average age 31. 956 applicants, 20% accepted, 187 enrolled. In 2009, 413 master's, 6 doctorates awarded. *Degree requirements:* For master's, comprehensive exam; for doctorate, thesis/dissertation. *Entrance requirements:* For master's and doctorate, GMAT. Additional exam requirements/recommendations for international students: Required—TOEFL (minimum score 550 paper-based; 213 computer-based). *Application deadline:* For fall admission, 2/1 priority date for domestic and international students; for spring admission, 11/1 for domestic students, 10/1 for international students. Applications are processed on a rolling basis. Electronic applications accepted. *Expenses:* Tuition, state resident: full-time $4725; part-time $525 per credit. Tuition, nonresident: full-time $12,267; part-time $1363 per credit. Required fees: $346 per semester. Tuition and fees vary according to course load. *Financial support:* In 2009–10, 76 research assistantships with full tuition reimbursements, 41 teaching assistantships with full tuition reimbursements were awarded; fellowships, career-related internships or fieldwork, Federal Work-Study, scholarships/grants, health care benefits, and unspecified assistantships also available. Financial award application deadline: 2/1; financial award applicants required to submit FAFSA. *Unit head:* P. Christopher Earley, Dean, 860-486-2317, Fax: 860-846-0889, E-mail: paul.earley@uconn.edu. *Application contact:* Richard Dino, Admissions Chairperson, 860-486-4483, E-mail: rich.dino@uconn.edu.

See Close-Up on page 263.

University of Dallas, Graduate School of Management, Irving, TX 75062-4736. Offers accounting (MBA, MM, MS); business management (MBA, MM); corporate finance (MBA, MM); financial services (MBA); global business (MBA, MM); health services management (MBA, MM); human resource management (MBA, MM); information assurance (MBA, MM, MS); information technology (MBA, MM, MS); information technology service management (MBA, MM, MS); marketing management (MBA, MM); organization development (MBA, MM); project management (MBA, MM); sports and entertainment management (MBA, MM); strategic leadership (MBA, MM); supply chain management (MBA); supply chain management and market logistics (MM). *Accreditation:* ACBSP. Part-time and evening/weekend programs available. Postbaccalaureate distance learning degree programs offered (no on-campus study). *Faculty:* 25 full-time (6 women), 31 part-time/adjunct (6 women). *Students:* 232 full-time (95 women), 923 part-time (365 women); includes 462 minority (184 African Americans, 14 American Indian/Alaska Native, 153 Asian Americans or Pacific Islanders, 111 Hispanic Americans), 184 international. Average age 34. 474 applicants, 85% accepted, 237 enrolled. In 2009, 399 master's awarded. *Entrance requirements:* Additional exam requirements/recommendations for international students: Required—TOEFL. *Application deadline:* Applications are processed on a rolling basis. Application fee: $50. Electronic applications accepted. *Expenses:* Contact institution. *Financial support:* In 2009–10, 399 students received support. Scholarships/grants and unspecified assistantships available. Financial award application deadline: 2/15; financial award applicants required to submit FAFSA. *Unit head:* Alounda Joseph, Director of Enrollment Processes, 972-721-5356, E-mail: admiss@gsm.udallas.edu. *Application contact:* Alounda Joseph, Director of Enrollment Processes, 972-721-5356, E-mail: admiss@gsm.udallas.edu.

University of Detroit Mercy, College of Health Professions, Program in Health Services Administration, Detroit, MI 48221. Offers MHSA. *Degree requirements:* For master's, thesis. *Entrance requirements:* For master's, GRE General Test, minimum GPA of 3.0. *Faculty research:* Health systems issues, organizational theory.

University of Detroit Mercy, College of Health Professions, Program in Health Systems Management, Detroit, MI 48221. Offers MSN.

University of Evansville, College of Education and Health Sciences, Department of Nursing and Health Sciences, Evansville, IN 47722. Offers health services administration (MS). Part-time and evening/weekend programs available. *Faculty:* 1 full-time (0 women), 4 part-time/adjunct (2 women). *Students:* 8 full-time (2 women), 6 part-time (4 women), 8 international. Average age 30. 7 applicants, 86% accepted, 6 enrolled. In 2009, 10 master's awarded. *Entrance requirements:* For master's, GRE or GMAT, 2 letters of reference, interview. Additional exam requirements/recommendations for international students: Required—TOEFL (minimum score 530 paper-based; 71 iBT), IELTS (minimum score 6). *Application deadline:* For fall admission, 7/1 priority date for domestic and international students; for spring admission, 10/1 priority date for domestic students. Applications are processed on a rolling basis. Application fee: $35 ($50 for international students). *Expenses:* Contact institution. *Financial support:* In 2009–10, 2 students received support. Application deadline: 6/1. *Faculty research:* International health systems, health care ethics, health care marketing. *Unit head:* Dr. Amy Hall, Chair, 812-488-2343, Fax: 812-488-2717, E-mail: ah169@evansville.edu. *Application contact:* Dr. William Stroube, Professor and Director, Health Services Administration Program, 812-488-2343, Fax: 812-488-2717, E-mail: hsa@evansville.edu.

University of Florida, College of Pharmacy and Graduate School, Graduate Programs in Pharmacy, Department of Pharmacy Health Care Administration, Gainesville, FL 32611. Offers MSP, PhD. Part-time programs available. *Degree requirements:* For doctorate, thesis/dissertation. *Entrance requirements:* For master's, minimum GPA of 3.0; for doctorate, GRE General Test, minimum GPA of 3.0. Additional exam requirements/recommendations for international students: Required—TOEFL. Electronic applications accepted. *Faculty research:* Pharmaceutical care, drug use systems, drug-related morbidity, pharmacy law.

University of Florida, Graduate School, College of Public Health and Health Professions, Department of Health Services Research, Management and Policy, Gainesville, FL 32611. Offers health administration (MHA); health services research (PhD). *Accreditation:* CAHME. Part-time programs available. *Entrance requirements:* For master's, GRE General Test, minimum GPA of 3.0. Additional exam requirements/recommendations for international students: Required—TOEFL (minimum score 550 paper-based; 213 computer-based). Electronic applications accepted. *Faculty research:* Hospital profitability, indigent care, rural health care systems, AIDS education, managed care, outcomes.

University of Florida, Graduate School, Warrington College of Business Administration, Hough Graduate School of Business, Programs in Business Administration, Gainesville, FL 32611. Offers accounting (MBA); arts administration (MBA); business strategy and public policy (MBA); competitive strategy (MBA); decision and information sciences (MBA); electronic commerce (MBA); finance (MBA); general business (MBA); global management (MBA); Graham-Buffett security analysis (MBA); health administration (MBA); human resources management (MBA); international studies (MBA); Latin American business (MBA); management (MBA); marketing (MBA); sports administration (MBA); JD/MBA; MBA/MS; MBA/PhD; MBA/Pharm D; MD/MBA. *Accreditation:* AACSB. Part-time and evening/weekend programs available. Post-baccalaureate distance learning degree programs offered. *Entrance requirements:* For master's, GMAT, minimum GPA of 3.0, interview. Additional exam requirements/recommendations for international students: Required—TOEFL (minimum score 550 paper-based; 213 computer-based). Electronic applications accepted. *Faculty research:* Accounting, finance, insurance, management, real estate and urban analysis marketing.

University of Houston–Clear Lake, School of Business, Program in Healthcare Administration, Houston, TX 77058-1098. Offers MHA, MHA/MBA. *Degree requirements:* For master's, thesis optional. *Entrance requirements:* For master's, GMAT. Additional exam requirements/recommendations for international students: Required—TOEFL (minimum score 550 paper-based; 213 computer-based).

University of Illinois at Chicago, Graduate College, School of Public Health, Division of Health Policy and Administration, Chicago, IL 60607-7128. Offers clinical translational science (MS); health policy (PhD); health policy and administration (Dr PH); health services research (PhD); healthcare (MHA); public health policy management (MPH). Part-time programs available. Terminal master's awarded for partial completion of doctoral program. *Degree requirements:* For master's, thesis, field practicum; for doctorate, thesis/dissertation, independent research, internship. *Entrance requirements:* For master's and doctorate, GRE General Test, minimum GPA of 2.75. Additional exam requirements/recommendations for international students: Required—TOEFL. Electronic applications accepted.

The University of Iowa, Graduate College, College of Public Health, Department of Health Management and Policy, Iowa City, IA 52242-1316. Offers MHA, PhD, JD/MHA, MBA/MHA, MHA/MA, MHA/MS. *Accreditation:* CAHME (one or more programs are accredited). *Degree requirements:* For doctorate, comprehensive exam, thesis/dissertation. *Entrance requirements:* For master's, GRE General Test or equivalent, minimum GPA of 3.0; for doctorate, GRE General Test, minimum GPA of 3.0. Additional exam requirements/recommendations for international students: Required—TOEFL (minimum score 550 paper-based; 213 computer-based; 81 iBT). Electronic applications accepted. *Expenses:* Contact institution.

The University of Kansas, University of Kansas Medical Center, School of Medicine, Department of Health Policy and Management, Kansas City, KS 66160. Offers MHSA, PhD, JD/MHSA, MBA/MHSA, MD/MHSA, MHSA/MS. *Accreditation:* CAHME. Part-time programs available. *Faculty:* 8 full-time, 6 part-time/adjunct. *Students:* 33 full-time (19 women), 29 part-time (21 women); includes 8 minority (1 African American, 1 American Indian/Alaska Native, 5 Asian Americans or Pacific Islanders, 1 Hispanic American), 7 international. Average age 30. 59 applicants, 78% accepted, 34 enrolled. In 2009, 31 master's awarded. *Degree requirements:* For master's, internship or research practicum; for doctorate, comprehensive exam, thesis/dissertation. *Entrance requirements:* For master's, college-level statistics; for doctorate, GRE, course work in health delivery system, healthcare finance, health behavior/organizations, healthcare economics, healthcare management, health policy, graduate statistics. Additional exam requirements/recommendations for international students: Required—TOEFL (minimum score 570 paper-based; 90 iBT). *Application deadline:* For fall admission, 4/15 for domestic and international students. Applications are processed on a rolling basis. Application fee: $60. Electronic applications accepted. *Expenses:* Tuition, state resident: full-time $6492; part-time $270.50 per credit hour. Tuition, nonresident: full-time $15,510; part-time $646.25 per credit hour. Required fees: $847; $70.56 per credit hour. Tuition and fees vary according to course load and program. *Financial support:* In 2009–10, 15 students received support. Career-related internships or fieldwork and departmental scholarships available. Support available to part-time students. Financial award applicants required to submit FAFSA. *Faculty research:* Economic analysis of long-term care facilities, healthcare workforce supply and demand, the impact of disaster preparedness on individuals with developmental disabilities, policy analysis and readiness for biological outbreaks, gender issues in health roles and functions. Total annual research expenditures: $184,633. *Unit head:* Dr. Glendon G. Cox, Chair, 913-588-0357, Fax: 913-588-8236, E-mail: gcox@kumc.edu. *Application contact:* Deborah S. Lewis, Student Support Manager, 913-588-3763, Fax: 913-588-8236, E-mail: dlewis4@kumc.edu.

University of Kentucky, Graduate School, Program in Health Administration, Lexington, KY 40506-0032. Offers MHA. *Accreditation:* CAHME. *Degree requirements:* For master's, comprehensive exam. *Entrance requirements:* For master's, GRE General Test, minimum undergraduate GPA of 2.75. Additional exam requirements/recommendations for international students: Required—TOEFL (minimum score 550 paper-based; 213 computer-based). Electronic applications accepted. *Faculty research:* Health economy, health finance, health policy.

University of La Verne, College of Business and Public Management, Graduate Programs in Business Administration, La Verne, CA 91750-4443. Offers accounting (MBA); executive management (MBA-EP); finance (MBA, MBA-EP); health services management (MBA); information technology (MBA, MBA-EP); international business (MBA, MBA-EP); leadership (MBA-EP); managed care (MBA); management (MBA, MBA-EP); marketing (MBA, MBA-EP). Part-time and evening/weekend programs available. *Faculty:* 22 full-time (11 women), 41 part-time/adjunct (8 women). *Students:* 409 full-time (213 women), 156 part-time (74 women); includes 371 minority (23 African Americans, 7 American Indian/Alaska Native, 259 Asian Americans or Pacific Islanders, 82 Hispanic Americans), 9 international. Average age 29. In 2009, 356 master's awarded. *Entrance requirements:* For master's, minimum undergraduate GPA of 3.0, 2 letters of recommendation, resume. Additional exam requirements/recommendations for international students: Required—TOEFL (minimum score 550 paper-based; 213 computer-based). *Application deadline:* Applications are processed on a rolling basis. Application fee: $50. *Expenses:* Contact institution. *Financial support:* Career-related internships or fieldwork, institutionally sponsored loans, and scholarships/grants available. Financial award application deadline: 3/2; financial award applicants required to submit FAFSA. *Unit head:* Dr. Abe Helou, Chairperson, 909-593-3511 Ext. 4211, Fax: 909-392-2704, E-mail: ihelou@laverne.edu. *Application contact:* Rina Lazarian, Program and Admission Specialist, 909-593-3511 Ext. 4819, Fax: 909-392-2704, E-mail: cbpm@ulv.edu.

University of La Verne, College of Business and Public Management, Program in Gerontology, La Verne, CA 91750-4443. Offers gerontology (Certificate); gerontology administration (MS). Part-time programs available. *Faculty:* 22 full-time (11 women), 41 part-time/adjunct (8 women). *Students:* 13 full-time (11 women), 25 part-time (24 women); includes 16 minority (9 African Americans, 3 Asian Americans or Pacific Islanders, 4 Hispanic Americans). Average age 43. In 2009, 11 master's awarded. *Entrance requirements:* For master's, minimum GPA of 2.5. Additional exam requirements/recommendations for international students: Required—TOEFL (minimum score 550 paper-based; 213 computer-based). *Application deadline:* Applications are processed on a rolling basis. Application fee: $50. *Expenses:* Contact institution. *Financial support:* Institutionally sponsored loans available. Financial award application deadline: 3/2; financial award applicants required to submit FAFSA. *Unit head:* Joan Branin, Chairperson, 909-593-3511 Ext. 4247, E-mail: jbranin@laverne.edu. *Application contact:* Barbara Cox, Program and Admissions Specialist, 909-593-3511 Ext. 4004, Fax: 909-392-2761, E-mail: bcox@laverne.edu.

University of La Verne, College of Business and Public Management, Program in Health Administration, La Verne, CA 91750-4443. Offers financial management (MHA); health administration (MHA); human resources (MHA); information management (MHA); leadership and management (MHA); managed care (MHA); marketing and business development (MHA). Part-time programs available. *Faculty:* 22 full-time (11 women), 41 part-time/adjunct (8 women). *Students:* 32 full-time (19 women), 21 part-time (16 women); includes 25 minority (9 African Americans, 10 Asian Americans or Pacific Islanders, 6 Hispanic Americans). Average age 34. In 2009, 19 master's awarded. *Entrance requirements:* For master's, minimum undergraduate GPA of 2.5, 3 letters of reference, curriculum vitae or resume, writing sample. Additional exam requirements/recommendations for international students: Required—TOEFL (minimum score 550 paper-based; 213 computer-based). *Application deadline:* Applications are processed on

a rolling basis. Application fee: $50. *Expenses:* Contact institution. *Financial support:* Application deadline: 3/2. *Unit head:* Joan Branin, Chairperson, 909-593-3511 Ext. 4247, E-mail: jbranin@laverne.edu. *Application contact:* Barbara Cox, Program and Admissions Specialist, 909-593-3511 Ext. 4004, Fax: 909-392-2761, E-mail: bcox@laverne.edu.

University of La Verne, Regional Campus Administration, Graduate Programs, Central Coast/Vandenberg Air Force Base Campuses, La Verne, CA 91750-4443. Offers business (MBA-EP), including health services management, information technology; health administration (MHA); leadership and management (MS). *Faculty:* 18 part-time/adjunct (6 women). *Students:* 19 full-time (12 women), 35 part-time (14 women); includes 20 minority (7 African Americans, 2 American Indian/Alaska Native, 2 Asian Americans or Pacific Islanders, 9 Hispanic Americans). Average age 36. In 2009, 20 master's awarded. *Entrance requirements:* For master's, 2 letters of recommendation, resume. *Application deadline:* Applications are processed on a rolling basis. Application fee: $50. *Expenses:* Contact institution. *Financial support:* Institutionally sponsored loans available. Financial award application deadline: 3/2; financial award applicants required to submit FAFSA. *Unit head:* Kitt Vincent, Director, Central Coast Campus, 805-542-9690 Ext. 6043, Fax: 805-542-9735, E-mail: kvincent@laverne.edu. *Application contact:* Kitt Vincent, Director, Central Coast Campus, 805-542-9690 Ext. 6043, Fax: 805-542-9735, E-mail: kvincent@laverne.edu.

University of La Verne, Regional Campus Administration, Graduate Programs, Inland Empire Campus, Rancho Cucamonga, CA 91730. Offers business (MBA-EP), including health services management, information technology, management, marketing; leadership and management (MS). *Faculty:* 2 full-time (both women), 12 part-time/adjunct (2 women). *Students:* 20 full-time (13 women), 61 part-time (41 women); includes 50 minority (10 African Americans, 11 Asian Americans or Pacific Islanders, 29 Hispanic Americans). Average age 37. In 2009, 24 master's awarded. *Entrance requirements:* For master's, 2 letters of recommendation, resume. *Application deadline:* Applications are processed on a rolling basis. Application fee: $50. *Expenses:* Contact institution. *Financial support:* Institutionally sponsored loans available. Financial award application deadline: 3/2; financial award applicants required to submit FAFSA. *Unit head:* Allan Stout, Director, 909-484-3858 Ext. 6002, Fax: 909-484-9469, E-mail: astout@laverne.edu. *Application contact:* Allan Stout, Director, 909-484-3858 Ext. 6002, Fax: 909-484-9469, E-mail: astout@laverne.edu.

University of La Verne, Regional Campus Administration, Graduate Programs, Kern County Campus, Bakersfield, CA 93301. Offers business (MBA-EP); health administration (MHA); leadership and management (MS). *Faculty:* 1 part-time/adjunct (0 women). *Students:* 10 part-time (5 women); includes 5 minority (2 Asian Americans or Pacific Islanders, 3 Hispanic Americans). Average age 32. In 2009, 2 master's awarded. *Entrance requirements:* For master's, 2 letters of recommendation, resume. *Application deadline:* Applications are processed on a rolling basis. Application fee: $50. *Expenses:* Contact institution. *Financial support:* Institutionally sponsored loans available. Financial award application deadline: 3/2; financial award applicants required to submit FAFSA. *Unit head:* Nora Dominguez, Interim Director, 661-328-1430 Ext. 6024, E-mail: ndominguez@laverne.edu. *Application contact:* Nora Dominguez, Interim Director, 661-328-1430 Ext. 6024, E-mail: ndominguez@laverne.edu.

University of La Verne, Regional Campus Administration, Graduate Programs, Orange County Campus, Garden Grove, CA 92840. Offers business (MBA); health administration (MHA); leadership and management (MS). *Faculty:* 3 full-time (1 woman), 11 part-time/adjunct (2 women). *Students:* 11 full-time (6 women), 64 part-time (30 women); includes 41 minority (3 African Americans, 4 American Indian/Alaska Native, 18 Asian Americans or Pacific Islanders, 16 Hispanic Americans). Average age 40. In 2009, 35 master's awarded. *Entrance requirements:* For master's, 2 letters of recommendation, resume. *Application deadline:* Applications are processed on a rolling basis. Application fee: $50. *Expenses:* Contact institution. *Financial support:* Institutionally sponsored loans available. Financial award application deadline: 3/2; financial award applicants required to submit FAFSA. *Unit head:* Pamela Bergovoy, Director, 714-505-1682 Ext. 6900, E-mail: pbergovoy@laverne.edu. *Application contact:* Pamela Bergovoy, Director, 714-505-1682 Ext. 6900, E-mail: pbergovoy@laverne.edu.

University of Louisville, Graduate School, School of Public Health and Information Sciences, Louisville, KY 40292-0001. Offers bioinformatics and biostatistics (MS, PhD), including biostatistics (MPH, MS, PhD), decision science (MS); clinical investigation sciences (Certificate); population health and epidemiology (MS, PhD), including epidemiology (MPH, MS, PhD), public health sciences (PhD); public health (MPH), including biostatistics (MPH, MS, PhD), environmental and occupational health, epidemiology (MPH, MS, PhD), health management (MPH, PhD), health promotion and behavior; public health sciences (PhD), including environmental health, epidemiology (MPH, MS, PhD), health management (MPH, PhD), health promotion. Part-time and evening/weekend programs available. *Faculty:* 39 full-time (13 women), 1 part-time/adjunct (0 women). *Students:* 92 full-time (52 women), 72 part-time (47 women); includes 36 minority (15 African Americans, 19 Asian Americans or Pacific Islanders, 2 Hispanic Americans), 21 international. Average age 33. 194 applicants, 47% accepted, 65 enrolled. In 2009, 35 master's, 4 doctorates awarded. *Degree requirements:* For master's, thesis; for doctorate, thesis/dissertation. *Entrance requirements:* For master's, GRE General Test, GMAT, DAT, MCAT, minimum of 2 letters of recommendation; for doctorate, GRE General Test, minimum of 2 letters of recommendation. Additional exam requirements/recommendations for international students: Required—TOEFL (minimum score 600 paper-based; 250 computer-based; 100 iBT). *Application deadline:* For fall admission, 2/1 for domestic and international students. Applications are processed on a rolling basis. Application fee: $50. Electronic applications accepted. *Financial support:* In 2009–10, 30 students received support, including 11 research assistantships with full tuition reimbursements available (averaging $20,000 per year); unspecified assistantships also available. Financial award application deadline: 5/1; financial award applicants required to submit FAFSA. *Faculty research:* Clinical research training, cancer and environmental exposure, health effects of air pollution, occupational injuries and illness, network science applications in health. Total annual research expenditures: $3.2 million. *Unit head:* Dr. Pete Walton, Associate Dean for Academic Affairs, 502-852-4493, Fax: 502-852-3291, E-mail: pete.walton@gwise.louisville.edu. *Application contact:* Vicki Lewis, Administrative Assistant, 502-852-1798, Fax: 502-852-3294, E-mail: vicki.lewis@louisville.edu.

University of Mary, Gary Tharaldson School of Business, Bismarck, ND 58504-9652. Offers health care (MBA); human resource management (MBA); management (MBA); project management (MPM); strategic leadership (MSSL). Part-time and evening/weekend programs available. *Degree requirements:* For master's, strategic planning seminar. *Entrance requirements:* For master's, minimum GPA of 2.5. Additional exam requirements/recommendations for international students: Required—TOEFL. *Expenses:* Tuition: Full-time $10,062; part-time $430 per credit. Tuition and fees vary according to course load, degree level, program and student level.

University of Maryland, Baltimore County, Graduate School, College of Arts, Humanities and Social Sciences, Department of Emergency Health Services, Baltimore, MD 21250. Offers administration, planning, and policy (MS); education (MS); emergency health services (MS); emergency management (Postbaccalaureate Certificate); preventive medicine and epidemiology (MS). Part-time and evening/weekend programs available. Postbaccalaureate distance learning degree programs offered (no on-campus study). *Faculty:* 4 full-time (0 women), 7 part-time/adjunct (1 woman). *Students:* 20 full-time (8 women), 21 part-time (10 women); includes 2 minority (both African Americans), 6 international. Average age 32. 13 applicants, 85% accepted, 10 enrolled. In 2009, 13 master's awarded. *Degree requirements:* For master's, comprehensive exam, thesis (for some programs). *Entrance requirements:* For master's, GRE General Test, minimum GPA of 3.0. Additional exam requirements/recommendations for international students: Required—TOEFL (minimum score 550 paper-based; 213 computer-based; 80 iBT). *Application deadline:* For fall admission, 7/1 for domestic students, 4/1 for international students. Applications are processed on a rolling basis. Application fee: $45. Electronic applications accepted. *Financial support:* In 2009–10, 2 students received support, including fellowships with tuition reimbursements available (averaging $70,000 per year), research assistantships with tuition reimbursements available (averaging $21,000 per year); career-related internships or fieldwork, Federal Work-Study, health care benefits, and unspecified assistantships also available. Financial award application deadline: 5/30; financial award applicants required to submit FAFSA. *Faculty research:* EMS management, disaster health services, emergency management. Total annual research expenditures: $50,000. *Unit head:* Dr. Bruce Walz, Chairman, 410-455-3223. *Application contact:* Dr. Rick Bissell, Program Director, 410-455-3776, Fax: 410-455-3045, E-mail: bissell@umbc.edu.

University of Maryland, Baltimore County, Graduate School, College of Arts, Humanities and Social Sciences, Department of Public Policy, Program in Public Policy, Baltimore, MD 21250. Offers economics (PhD); education (MPP, PhD); evaluation (MPP); health (MPP, PhD); legal (MPP, PhD); management (MPP, PhD); urban (MPP, PhD). Part-time and evening/weekend programs available. *Faculty:* 40 full-time (12 women), 2 part-time/adjunct (1 woman). *Students:* 57 full-time (34 women), 114 part-time (61 women); includes 47 minority (26 African Americans, 21 Hispanic Americans). Average age 33. 89 applicants, 47% accepted, 24 enrolled. In 2009, 12 master's, 5 doctorates awarded. Terminal master's awarded for partial completion of doctoral program. *Degree requirements:* For master's, thesis optional, public analysis paper; for doctorate, comprehensive exam, thesis/dissertation, comprehensive and field qualifying exams. *Entrance requirements:* For master's, GRE General Test, 3 academic letters of reference, transcripts, resume; for doctorate, GRE General Test, 3 academic letters of reference, transcripts, resume, research paper. Additional exam requirements/recommendations for international students: Required—TOEFL (minimum score 550 paper-based; 213 computer-based; 80 iBT). *Application deadline:* For fall admission, 1/15 priority date for domestic students, 1/1 priority date for international students; for spring admission, 11/1 priority date for domestic students, 5/1 priority date for international students. Applications are processed on a rolling basis. Application fee: $50. Electronic applications accepted. *Financial support:* In 2009–10, 32 students received support, including 1 fellowship (averaging $3,000 per year), 17 research assistantships with full tuition reimbursements available (averaging $17,400 per year); career-related internships or fieldwork, Federal Work-Study, scholarships/grants, health care benefits, and unspecified assistantships also available. Support available to part-time students. Financial award application deadline: 2/1; financial award applicants required to submit FAFSA. *Faculty research:* Health policy, education policy, urban policy, public management, evaluation and analytical method. *Unit head:* Dr. Donald Norris, Chair, 410-455-1455, E-mail: norris@umbc.edu. *Application contact:* Sally F. Helms, Administrator of Academic Affairs, 410-455-3202, Fax: 410-455-1172, E-mail: gradposi@umbc.edu.

University of Maryland, Baltimore County, Graduate School, Erickson School of Aging Studies, Baltimore, MD 21228. Offers management of aging services (MA). *Faculty:* 3 full-time (1 woman), 16 part-time/adjunct (6 women). *Students:* 25 full-time (21 women), 11 part-time (7 women); includes 5 African Americans, 2 Hispanic Americans. Average age 43. 28 applicants, 46% accepted, 13 enrolled. In 2009, 23 master's awarded. *Application deadline:* Applications are processed on a rolling basis. Electronic applications accepted. *Financial support:* Applicants required to submit FAFSA. *Unit head:* Dr. Janet C. Rutledge, Interim Vice Provost for Graduate Education, 410-455-2199. *Application contact:* Kathryn Nee, Coordinator of Domestic Admissions, 410-455-2944, E-mail: nee@umbc.edu.

University of Maryland, College Park, Academic Affairs, School of Public Health, Department of Health Services Administration, College Park, MD 20742. Offers MHA, PhD. *Faculty:* 18 full-time (10 women), 4 part-time/adjunct (2 women). *Students:* 8 full-time (7 women), 4 part-time (1 woman); includes 5 minority (3 African Americans, 2 Asian Americans or Pacific Islanders), 3 international. 47 applicants, 26% accepted, 4 enrolled. In 2009, 2 master's awarded. *Application deadline:* For fall admission, 1/15 for domestic and international students; for spring admission, 6/1 for international students. *Expenses:* Tuition, area resident: Part-time $471 per credit hour. Tuition, state resident: part-time $471 per credit hour. Tuition, nonresident: part-time $1016 per credit hour. Required fees: $337.04 per term. *Financial support:* In 2009–10, 4 research assistantships (averaging $15,742 per year), 1 teaching assistantship with tuition reimbursement (averaging $16,099 per year) were awarded; fellowships also available. Total annual research expenditures: $1.3 million. *Unit head:* Dr. Laura Wilson, Chair, 301-405-2469, E-mail: lwilson@umd.edu. *Application contact:* Dean of Graduate School, 301-405-0358.

University of Maryland University College, Graduate School of Management and Technology, Program in Health Care Administration, Adelphi, MD 20783. Offers MS, Certificate. Part-time and evening/weekend programs available. Postbaccalaureate distance learning degree programs offered (no on-campus study). *Students:* 23 full-time (18 women), 464 part-time (343 women); includes 267 minority (226 African Americans, 2 American Indian/Alaska Native, 15 Asian Americans or Pacific Islanders, 24 Hispanic Americans), 8 international. Average age 36. 121 applicants, 100% accepted, 98 enrolled. In 2009, 98 master's awarded. *Degree requirements:* For master's, thesis or alternative. *Application deadline:* Applications are processed on a rolling basis. Application fee: $50. Electronic applications accepted. *Expenses:* Tuition, state resident: full-time $7704; part-time $428 per credit hour. Tuition, nonresident: full-time $11,862; part-time $659 per credit hour. *Financial support:* Federal Work-Study and scholarships/grants available. Support available to part-time students. Financial award application deadline: 6/1; financial award applicants required to submit FAFSA. *Unit head:* Dr. Diane Bartoo, Head, 240-684-2400, Fax: 240-684-2401, E-mail: dbartoo@umuc.edu. *Application contact:* Coordinator, Graduate Admissions, 800-888-UMUC, Fax: 240-684-2151, E-mail: newgrad@umuc.edu.

University of Massachusetts Amherst, Graduate School, School of Public Health and Health Sciences, Department of Public Health, Amherst, MA 01003. Offers biostatistics (MS, PhD); community health education (MS); environmental health sciences (MPH, MS); epidemiology (MPH, MS); health policy and management (MPH, MS); nutrition (PhD); public health practice (MPH). *Accreditation:* CEPH (one or more programs are accredited). Part-time and evening/weekend programs available. Postbaccalaureate distance learning degree programs offered (no on-campus study). *Faculty:* 38 full-time (23 women). *Students:* 96 full-time (71 women), 232 part-time (153 women); includes 41 minority (14 African Americans, 17 Asian Americans or Pacific Islanders, 10 Hispanic Americans), 65 international. Average age 36. 316 applicants, 61% accepted, 79 enrolled. In 2009, 91 master's, 5 doctorates awarded. Terminal master's awarded for partial completion of doctoral program. *Degree requirements:* For master's, thesis (for some programs); for doctorate, comprehensive exam, thesis/dissertation. *Entrance requirements:* For master's and doctorate, GRE General Test. Additional exam requirements/recommendations for international students: Required—TOEFL (minimum score 550 paper-based; 213 computer-based; 80 iBT), IELTS (minimum score 6.5). *Application deadline:* For fall admission, 2/1 for domestic and international students. Applications are processed on a rolling basis. Application fee: $40 ($65 for international students). Electronic applications accepted. *Expenses:* Tuition, state resident: full-time $2640; part-time $110 per credit. Tuition, nonresident: full-time $9936; part-time $414 per credit. Tuition and fees vary according to course load. *Financial support:* In 2009–10, 3 fellowships with full tuition reimbursements (averaging $2,791 per year), 32 research assistantships with full tuition reimbursements (averaging $9,196 per year), 24 teaching assistantships with full tuition reimbursements (averaging $5,789 per year) were awarded; career-related internships or fieldwork, Federal Work-Study, scholarships/grants, traineeships, health care benefits, tuition waivers (full), and unspecified assistantships also available. Support available to part-time students. Financial award application deadline: 2/1. *Unit head:* Dr. Paula Stamps, Graduate Program Director, 413-545-2861, Fax: 413-545-0964. *Application contact:* Jean M. Ames, Supervisor of Admissions, 413-545-0722, Fax: 413-577-0010, E-mail: gradadm@grad.umass.edu.

University of Massachusetts Boston, Office of Graduate Studies, John W. McCormack Graduate School of Policy Studies, Program in Gerontology, Boston, MA 02125-3393. Offers gerontology (MS, PhD, Certificate); gerontology research (MA); management in aging services (MA). Part-time programs available. *Degree requirements:* For doctorate, comprehensive exam, thesis/dissertation. *Entrance requirements:* For doctorate, GRE General Test, minimum GPA of 3.0. *Faculty research:* Aging with a chronic disability, pension policy and social security system, elderly minorities, health services research, living arrangements.

University of Massachusetts Lowell, School of Health and Environment, Department of Community Health and Sustainability, Lowell, MA 01854-2881. Offers health management and

Health Services Management and Hospital Administration

University of Massachusetts Lowell (continued)
policy (MS, Graduate Certificate). Part-time programs available. *Degree requirements:* For master's, thesis optional. *Entrance requirements:* For master's, GRE General Test. *Faculty research:* Alzheimer's disease, total quality management systems, information systems, market analysis.

University of Medicine and Dentistry of New Jersey, School of Health Related Professions, Department of Interdisciplinary Studies, Program in Health Systems, Newark, NJ 07107-1709. Offers MS. *Entrance requirements:* For master's, minimum GPA of 2.75. Additional exam requirements/recommendations for international students: Required—TOEFL. Electronic applications accepted.

University of Memphis, Graduate School, School of Public Health, Memphis, TN 38152. Offers biostatistics (MPH); environmental health (MPH); epidemiology (MPH); health systems management (MPH); public health (MHA); social and behavioral sciences (MPH). Part-time and evening/weekend programs available. Postbaccalaureate distance learning degree programs offered. *Faculty:* 5 full-time (2 women), 4 part-time/adjunct (2 women). *Students:* 45 full-time (23 women), 29 part-time (14 women); includes 19 African Americans, 6 Asian Americans or Pacific Islanders, 2 Hispanic Americans, 7 international. Average age 32. 57 applicants, 70% accepted, 22 enrolled. In 2009, 17 master's awarded. *Degree requirements:* For master's, comprehensive exam, thesis. *Entrance requirements:* For master's, GRE, MAT, DAT, GMAT or LSAT, letters of recommendation. Additional exam requirements/recommendations for international students: Required—TOEFL. *Application deadline:* For fall admission, 11/1 for domestic students; for spring admission, 4/1 for domestic students. Application fee: $35 ($60 for international students). Electronic applications accepted. *Expenses:* Tuition, state resident: full-time $6246; part-time $347 per credit hour. Tuition, nonresident: full-time $15,894; part-time $883 per credit hour. Required fees: $1160. Full-time tuition and fees vary according to course load, degree level and program. *Financial support:* In 2009–10, 46 students received support; research assistantships with full tuition reimbursements available, Federal Work-Study, scholarships/grants, and unspecified assistantships available. Financial award application deadline: 2/15; financial award applicants required to submit FAFSA. *Faculty research:* Health and medical savings accounts, adoption rates, health informatics, Telehealth technologies, biostatistics, environmental health, epidemiology, health systems management, social and behavioral sciences. *Unit head:* Dr. Lisa M. Klesges, Director, 901-678-4637, E-mail: lmklsges@memphis.edu. *Application contact:* Dr. Lisa M. Klesges, Director, 901-678-4637, E-mail: lmklsges@memphis.edu.

University of Michigan, School of Public Health, Department of Health Management and Policy, Ann Arbor, MI 48109. Offers health management and policy (MHSA, MPH, MS); health services organization and policy (PhD); JD/MHSA; MD/MPH; MHSA/MBA; MHSA/MNA; MHSA/MPP; MHSA/MSIOE; MPH/JD; MPH/MBA; MPH/MPP. PhD and MS offered through the Horace H. Rackham School of Graduate Studies. *Accreditation:* CAHME (one or more programs are accredited). *Degree requirements:* For doctorate, thesis/dissertation, oral defense of dissertation, preliminary exam. *Entrance requirements:* For master's, GMAT, GRE General Test; for doctorate, GRE General Test. Additional exam requirements/recommendations for international students: Required—TOEFL (minimum score 600 paper-based; 250 computer-based; 100 iBT). Electronic applications accepted. *Expenses:* Tuition, state resident: full-time $17,286; part-time $1099 per credit hour. Tuition, nonresident: full-time $34,944; part-time $2080 per credit hour. Required fees: $95 per semester. Tuition and fees vary according to course load, degree level and program. *Faculty research:* Economics, long term care and aging, women's health, healthcare finance, understanding organization.

University of Minnesota, Twin Cities Campus, Carlson School of Management, Carlson Full-Time MBA Program, Minneapolis, MN 55455. Offers finance (MBA); information technology (MBA); management (MBA); marketing (MBA); medical industry orientation (MBA); supply chain and operations (MBA); JD/MBA; MBA/MPP; MD/MBA; MHA/MBA; Pharm D/MBA. *Accreditation:* AACSB. *Faculty:* 60 full-time (11 women), 15 part-time/adjunct (7 women). *Students:* 217 full-time (78 women); includes 23 minority (6 African Americans, 1 American Indian/Alaska Native, 14 Asian Americans or Pacific Islanders, 2 Hispanic Americans), 41 international. Average age 28. 548 applicants, 41% accepted, 104 enrolled. In 2009, 91 master's awarded. *Entrance requirements:* For master's, GMAT. Additional exam requirements/recommendations for international students: Required—TOEFL (minimum score 580 paper-based; 240 computer-based; 82 iBT), or IELTS (minimum score 7), or Pearson Test of English (PTE). *Application deadline:* For fall admission, 4/1 for domestic students, 2/1 for international students. Application fee: $60 ($90 for international students). Electronic applications accepted. *Expenses:* Contact institution. *Financial support:* In 2009–10, 107 students received support, including 107 fellowships with full and partial tuition reimbursements available (averaging $22,174 per year); research assistantships with partial tuition reimbursements available, teaching assistantships with partial tuition reimbursements available, career-related internships or fieldwork, Federal Work-Study, institutionally sponsored loans, scholarships/grants, health care benefits, and unspecified assistantships also available. Financial award application deadline: 2/1; financial award applicants required to submit FAFSA. *Unit head:* Kathryn J. Carlson, Assistant Dean, MBA Programs and Graduate Business Career Center, 612-625-5555, Fax: 612-625-1012, E-mail: mba@umn.edu. *Application contact:* Tracy J. Keeling, Associate Director of Admissions, Full-Time and Part-Time MBA Programs, 612-625-5555, Fax: 612-625-1012, E-mail: mba@umn.edu.

University of Minnesota, Twin Cities Campus, Graduate School, Program in Health Informatics, Minneapolis, MN 55455-0213. Offers MHI, MS, PhD, MD/MHI. Part-time programs available. *Faculty:* 20 full-time (6 women), 8 part-time/adjunct (2 women). *Students:* 36 full-time (15 women), 17 part-time (7 women); includes 27 minority (4 African Americans, 23 Asian Americans or Pacific Islanders). Average age 34. 24 applicants, 58% accepted, 9 enrolled. In 2009, 4 master's, 3 doctorates awarded. *Degree requirements:* For master's, thesis or alternative; for doctorate, thesis/dissertation. *Entrance requirements:* For master's and doctorate, GRE General Test, previous course work in life sciences, programming, calculus. Additional exam requirements/recommendations for international students: Required—TOEFL (minimum score 550 paper-based; 237 computer-based). *Application deadline:* For fall admission, 6/15 for domestic and international students; for winter admission, 10/15 for domestic and international students; for spring admission, 3/15 for domestic and international students. Applications are processed on a rolling basis. Application fee: $75. Electronic applications accepted. *Financial support:* In 2009–10, 18 students received support, including 8 fellowships with full tuition reimbursements available (averaging $40,905 per year), 9 research assistantships with full and partial tuition reimbursements available (averaging $16,868 per year), 1 teaching assistantship with full and partial tuition reimbursement available (averaging $16,868 per year); Federal Work-Study, scholarships/grants, traineeships, and tuition waivers (full and partial) also available. Financial award application deadline: 1/15. *Faculty research:* Medical decision making, physiological control systems, population studies, clinical information systems, telemedicine. Total annual research expenditures: $1.4 million. *Unit head:* Dr. Terrence Adam, Director of Graduate Studies, 612-625-5825, Fax: 612-625-7166, E-mail: adamx004@umn.edu. *Application contact:* Jessica Whitcombe-Trance, Executive Administrative Specialist, 612-626-3348, Fax: 612-626-7227, E-mail: jwhitcom@umn.edu.

University of Minnesota, Twin Cities Campus, School of Public Health, Major in Health Services Research, Policy, and Administration, Minneapolis, MN 55455-0213. Offers MS, PhD, JD/MS, JD/PhD, MD/PhD, MPP/MS. Part-time programs available. Terminal master's awarded for partial completion of doctoral program. *Degree requirements:* For master's, thesis, internship, final oral exam; for doctorate, thesis/dissertation, teaching experience, written preliminary exam, final oral exam, dissertation. *Entrance requirements:* For master's, GRE General Test, course work in mathematics; for doctorate, GRE General Test, prerequisite courses in calculus and statistics. Additional exam requirements/recommendations for international students: Required—TOEFL (minimum score 600 paper-based; 250 computer-based; 100 iBT). *Faculty research:* Outcomes, economics and statistics, sociology, health care management.

University of Minnesota, Twin Cities Campus, School of Public Health, Major in Public Health Administration and Policy, Minneapolis, MN 55455-0213. Offers MPH, MPH/JD, MPH/MSN. Part-time programs available. *Degree requirements:* For master's, thesis, field experience. *Entrance requirements:* For master's, GRE General Test. Additional exam requirements/recommendations for international students: Required—TOEFL. Electronic applications accepted. *Faculty research:* Community health service organizations, nursing services, dental services, the elderly, insurance coverage.

University of Minnesota, Twin Cities Campus, School of Public Health, Program in Healthcare Administration, Minneapolis, MN 55455-0213. Offers MHA. *Accreditation:* AACSB; CAHME. Part-time and evening/weekend programs available. Postbaccalaureate distance learning degree programs offered (minimal on-campus study). *Degree requirements:* For master's, thesis, project. *Entrance requirements:* For master's, GMAT or GRE General Test, minimum GPA of 3.0. Additional exam requirements/recommendations for international students: Required—TOEFL (minimum score 600 paper-based; 250 computer-based; 100 iBT). Electronic applications accepted. *Expenses:* Contact institution. *Faculty research:* Managed care, physician payment, structure and performance of healthcare systems, long-term care.

University of Missouri, Graduate School, Department of Health Management and Informatics, Columbia, MO 65211. Offers health administration (MHA); health informatics (MHA); health services management (MHA). *Accreditation:* CAHME. Part-time programs available. *Entrance requirements:* For master's, GRE General Test or GMAT, minimum GPA of 3.0. Additional exam requirements/recommendations for international students: Required—TOEFL (minimum score 500 paper-based; 173 computer-based; 61 iBT).

University of Missouri–St. Louis, College of Arts and Sciences, Program in Gerontology, St. Louis, MO 63121. Offers gerontology (MS, Certificate); long term care administration (Certificate). Part-time and evening/weekend programs available. *Faculty:* 5 full-time (3 women), 8 part-time/adjunct (6 women). *Students:* 6 full-time (2 women), 13 part-time (12 women); includes 3 minority (all African Americans), 1 international. Average age 40. In 2009, 6 master's awarded. *Entrance requirements:* For master's, 3 letters of recommendation. Additional exam requirements/recommendations for international students: Required—TOEFL (minimum score 550 paper-based; 213 computer-based). *Application deadline:* For fall admission, 7/1 priority date for domestic and international students; for spring admission, 12/1 priority date for domestic and international students. Applications are processed on a rolling basis. Application fee: $35 ($40 for international students). Electronic applications accepted. *Expenses:* Tuition, state resident: full-time $5377; part-time $297.70 per credit hour. Tuition, nonresident: full-time $13,882; part-time $771.20 per credit hour. Required fees: $220; $12.20 per credit hour. One-time fee: $12. Tuition and fees vary according to course level, campus/location and program. *Financial support:* In 2009–10, 1 research assistantship with full and partial tuition reimbursement (averaging $5,625 per year) was awarded; career-related internships or fieldwork and Federal Work-Study also available. Financial award applicants required to submit FAFSA. *Faculty research:* Health care policy, social support and stress, retirement policy health behavior, ethnic differences in aging. *Unit head:* Thomas Meuser, Director, 314-516-5421, Fax: 314-516-5210, E-mail: meusert@umsl.edu. *Application contact:* 314-516-5458, Fax: 314-516-6996, E-mail: gradadm@umsl.edu.

University of Missouri–St. Louis, Graduate School, Program in Public Policy Administration, St. Louis, MO 63121. Offers health policy (MPPA); local government management (MPPA); managing human resources and organization (MPPA); nonprofit organization management (MPPA); nonprofit organization management and leadership (Certificate); policy research and analysis (MPPA). *Accreditation:* NASPAA. Part-time and evening/weekend programs available. *Faculty:* 7 full-time (4 women), 6 part-time/adjunct (1 woman). *Students:* 20 full-time (8 women), 69 part-time (45 women); includes 13 minority (11 African Americans, 2 Hispanic Americans), 8 international. Average age 31. 85 applicants, 58% accepted, 28 enrolled. In 2009, 12 master's, 34 Certificates awarded. *Degree requirements:* For master's, exit project. *Entrance requirements:* For master's, 3 letters of recommendation. Additional exam requirements/recommendations for international students: Required—TOEFL (minimum score 550 paper-based; 213 computer-based). *Application deadline:* For fall admission, 7/1 priority date for domestic and international students; for spring admission, 12/1 priority date for domestic and international students. Applications are processed on a rolling basis. Application fee: $35 ($40 for international students). Electronic applications accepted. *Expenses:* Tuition, state resident: full-time $5377; part-time $297.70 per credit hour. Tuition, nonresident: full-time $13,882; part-time $771.20 per credit hour. Required fees: $220; $12.20 per credit hour. One-time fee: $12. Tuition and fees vary according to course level, campus/location and program. *Financial support:* In 2009–10, 2 research assistantships with full and partial tuition reimbursements (averaging $12,000 per year) were awarded; career-related internships or fieldwork also available. Financial award application deadline: 4/1; financial award applicants required to submit FAFSA. *Faculty research:* Urban policy, public finance, evaluation. *Unit head:* Dr. Brady Baybeck, Director, 314-516-5145, Fax: 314-516-5210, E-mail: baybeck@umsl.edu. *Application contact:* 314-516-5458, Fax: 314-516-6996, E-mail: gradadm@umsl.edu.

University of Nevada, Las Vegas, Graduate College, School of Community Health Sciences, Department of Health Care Administration, Las Vegas, NV 89154-3023. Offers MHA. *Faculty:* 4 full-time (0 women). *Students:* 15 full-time (10 women), 20 part-time (17 women); includes 4 minority (1 African American, 2 Asian Americans or Pacific Islanders, 1 Hispanic American), 2 international. Average age 36. 47 applicants, 60% accepted, 19 enrolled. In 2009, 3 master's awarded. *Entrance requirements:* Additional exam requirements/recommendations for international students: Required—TOEFL (minimum score 550 paper-based; 213 computer-based; 80 iBT), IELTS (minimum score 7). *Application deadline:* For fall admission, 6/1 priority date for domestic students, 5/1 for international students; for spring admission, 11/1 priority date for domestic students, 10/1 for international students. Applications are processed on a rolling basis. Application fee: $60 ($95 for international students). Electronic applications accepted. *Financial support:* In 2009–10, 3 students received support, including 3 research assistantships with partial tuition reimbursements available (averaging $10,000 per year); institutionally sponsored loans, scholarships/grants, health care benefits, and unspecified assistantships also available. Financial award application deadline: 3/1. *Faculty research:* Health care for the uninsured, quality improvement for health care delivery, health services planning and marketing, health care economics. *Unit head:* Dr. Charles Moseley, Chair/ Associate Professor, 702-895-4413, Fax: 702-895-5573, E-mail: charles.moseley@unlv.edu. *Application contact:* Graduate College Admissions Evaluator, 702-895-3320, Fax: 702-895-4180, E-mail: gradcollege@unlv.edu.

University of New Haven, Graduate School, School of Business, Program in Health Care Administration, West Haven, CT 06516-1916. Offers health care management (Certificate); health care marketing (MS); health policy and finance (MS); human resource management in health care (MS); long-term care (MS); long-term health care (Certificate); managed care (MS); medical group management (MS). Part-time and evening/weekend programs available. *Faculty:* 5 full-time (2 women), 11 part-time/adjunct (4 women). *Students:* 42 full-time (27 women), 25 part-time (20 women); includes 16 minority (9 African Americans, 5 Asian Americans or Pacific Islanders, 2 Hispanic Americans), 28 international. Average age 29. 121 applicants, 96% accepted, 23 enrolled. In 2009, 32 master's, 2 other advanced degrees awarded. *Degree requirements:* For master's, thesis or alternative. *Entrance requirements:* Additional exam requirements/recommendations for international students: Required—TOEFL (minimum score 520 paper-based; 190 computer-based; 70 iBT), IELTS (minimum score 5.5). *Application deadline:* For fall admission, 5/31 for international students; for winter admission, 10/15 for international students; for spring admission, 1/15 for international students. Applications are processed on a rolling basis. Application fee: $50. Electronic applications accepted. *Expenses:* Tuition: Part-time $700 per credit. Required fees: $45 per term. One-time fee: $390 part-time. *Financial support:* Research assistantships with partial tuition reimbursements, teaching assistantships with partial tuition reimbursements, career-related internships or fieldwork, Federal Work-Study, scholarships/grants, tuition waivers, and unspecified assistantships available. Support available to part-time students. Financial award applicants required to submit FAFSA. *Unit head:* Charles Coleman, Chairman, 203-932-7375. *Application contact:*

Eloise Gormley, Director of Graduate Admissions, 203-932-7449, Fax: 203-932-7137, E-mail: gradinfo@newhaven.edu.

University of New Haven, Graduate School, School of Business, Program in Public Administration, West Haven, CT 06516-1916. Offers personnel and labor relations (MPA); public administration (MPA, Certificate), including city management (MPA), community-clinical services (MPA), health care management (MPA), long-term health care (MPA), personnel and labor relations (MPA), public administration (Certificate), public management (Certificate), public personnel management (Certificate); MBA/MPA. Part-time and evening/weekend programs available. *Faculty:* 3 full-time (1 woman), 11 part-time/adjunct (5 women). *Students:* 17 full-time (9 women), 26 part-time (14 women); includes 11 minority (9 African Americans, 1 Asian American or Pacific Islander, 1 Hispanic American), 1 international. Average age 35. 35 applicants, 94% accepted, 8 enrolled. In 2009, 9 master's, 12 other advanced degrees awarded. *Degree requirements:* For master's, thesis or alternative. *Entrance requirements:* Additional exam requirements/recommendations for international students: Required—TOEFL (minimum score 520 paper-based; 190 computer-based; 70 iBT); Recommended—IELTS (minimum score 5.5). *Application deadline:* For fall admission, 5/31 for international students; for winter admission, 10/15 for international students; for spring admission, 1/15 for international students. Applications are processed on a rolling basis. Application fee: $50. Electronic applications accepted. *Expenses:* Contact institution. *Financial support:* Research assistantships with partial tuition reimbursements, teaching assistantships with partial tuition reimbursements, career-related internships or fieldwork, Federal Work-Study, scholarships/grants, tuition waivers, and unspecified assistantships available. Support available to part-time students. Financial award application deadline: 5/1; financial award applicants required to submit FAFSA. *Unit head:* Charles Coleman, Chairman, 203-932-7375. *Application contact:* Eloise Gormley, Director of Graduate Admissions, 203-932-7449, Fax: 203-932-7137, E-mail: gradinfo@newhaven.edu.

University of New Orleans, Graduate School, College of Business Administration, Program in Health Care Management, New Orleans, LA 70148. Offers MS. *Degree requirements:* For master's, thesis optional. *Entrance requirements:* For master's, GRE or GMAT. Additional exam requirements/recommendations for international students: Required—TOEFL (minimum score 550 paper-based; 213 computer-based; 79 iBT). Electronic applications accepted.

The University of North Carolina at Chapel Hill, Graduate School, School of Public Health, Department of Health Policy and Administration, Chapel Hill, NC 27599. Offers MHA, MPH, MSPH, Dr PH, PhD, DDS/MPH, JD/MPH, MBA/MHA, MD/MPH, MHA/MBA, MHA/MSIS, MHA/MSLS. *Accreditation:* CAHME (one or more programs are accredited). Part-time programs available. Postbaccalaureate distance learning degree programs offered (minimal on-campus study). *Degree requirements:* For master's, comprehensive exam, capstone course or paper; for doctorate, comprehensive exam, thesis/dissertation. *Entrance requirements:* For master's and doctorate, GRE General Test, minimum GPA of 3.0. Additional exam requirements/recommendations for international students: Required—TOEFL. Electronic applications accepted. *Faculty research:* Organizational behavior; human resource management in healthcare; health services finance; mental health economics, service, and research; strategic planning and marketing.

The University of North Carolina at Charlotte, Graduate School, College of Health and Human Services, Department of Health Behavior and Administration, Charlotte, NC 28223-0001. Offers health care administration (MHA); public health (MSPH). *Accreditation:* CAHME. *Faculty:* 15 full-time (9 women), 18 part-time/adjunct (10 women). *Students:* 23 full-time (19 women), 8 part-time (6 women); includes 8 minority (6 African Americans, 1 Asian American or Pacific Islander, 1 Hispanic American), 4 international. Average age 28. 42 applicants, 71% accepted, 13 enrolled. In 2009, 8 master's awarded. *Degree requirements:* For master's, thesis or comprehensive exam. *Entrance requirements:* For master's, GRE or MAT (public health), GRE or GMAT (health administration), minimum GPA of 3.0 during previous 2 years, 2.75 overall. Additional exam requirements/recommendations for international students: Required—TOEFL (minimum score 557 paper-based; 220 computer-based; 83 iBT). *Application deadline:* For fall admission, 7/1 for domestic students, 5/1 for international students; for spring admission, 11/1 for domestic students, 10/1 for international students. Applications are processed on a rolling basis. Application fee: $55. Electronic applications accepted. *Financial support:* Career-related internships or fieldwork, Federal Work-Study, institutionally sponsored loans, scholarships/grants, and unspecified assistantships available. Support available to part-time students. Financial award application deadline: 4/1; financial award applicants required to submit FAFSA. *Faculty research:* Pediatric asthma self-management, reproductive epidemiology, social aspects of injury prevention, chronic illness self-care, competency-based professional education. Total annual research expenditures: $649,694. *Unit head:* Dr. Andrew R. Harver, Chair, 704-687-8680, Fax: 704-687-6122, E-mail: arharver@uncc.edu. *Application contact:* Kathy B. Giddings, Director of Graduate Admissions, 704-687-5503, Fax: 704-687-3279, E-mail: gradadm@uncc.edu.

University of North Florida, Brooks College of Health, Department of Public Health, Jacksonville, FL 32224. Offers community health (MPH); geriatric management (MSH); health administration (MHA); health behavior research and evaluation (Certificate); nutrition (MSH); rehabilitation counseling (MS). *Accreditation:* CEPH. Part-time and evening/weekend programs available. *Faculty:* 23 full-time (17 women). *Students:* 118 full-time (91 women), 82 part-time (61 women); includes 42 minority (23 African Americans, 8 Asian Americans or Pacific Islanders, 11 Hispanic Americans), 9 international. Average age 31. 192 applicants, 26% accepted, 23 enrolled. In 2009, 69 master's awarded. *Degree requirements:* For master's, thesis optional. *Entrance requirements:* For master's, GRE General Test (MSH, MS, MPH); GMAT or GRE General Test (MHA), minimum GPA of 3.0 in last 60 hours. Additional exam requirements/recommendations for international students: Required—TOEFL (minimum score 500 paper-based; 173 computer-based). *Application deadline:* For fall admission, 7/1 priority date for domestic students, 5/1 for international students; for spring admission, 11/1 priority date for domestic students, 10/1 for international students. Applications are processed on a rolling basis. Application fee: $30. Electronic applications accepted. *Expenses:* Tuition, state resident: full-time $6649.20; part-time $277.05 per credit hour. Tuition, nonresident: full-time $22,970; part-time $957.08 per credit hour. Required fees: $985; $41.03 per credit hour. *Financial support:* In 2009–10, 99 students received support, including 1 teaching assistantship (averaging $1,004 per year); research assistantships, career-related internships or fieldwork, Federal Work-Study, scholarships/grants, and tuition waivers (partial) also available. Support available to part-time students. Financial award application deadline: 4/1; financial award applicants required to submit FAFSA. *Faculty research:* Dietary supplements; alcohol, tobacco, and other drug use prevention; turnover among health professionals; aging; psychosocial aspects of disabilities. Total annual research expenditures: $335,106. *Unit head:* Dr. JoAnn Nolin, Chair, 904-620-2840, Fax: 904-620-2848, E-mail: jnolin@unf.edu. *Application contact:* Heather Kenney, Director of Advising, 904-620-2810, Fax: 904-620-1030, E-mail: heather.kenney@unf.edu.

University of North Texas Health Science Center at Fort Worth, School of Public Health, Fort Worth, TX 76107-2699. Offers biostatistics (MPH); community health (MPH); disease control and prevention (Dr PH); environmental and occupational health sciences (MPH); epidemiology (MPH); health administration (MHA); health policy and management (MPH, Dr PH); DO/MPH; MS/MPH; MSN/MPH. *Accreditation:* CEPH. Part-time and evening/weekend programs available. *Degree requirements:* For master's, thesis or alternative, supervised internship; for doctorate, thesis/dissertation, supervised internship. *Entrance requirements:* For master's, GRE General Test. Additional exam requirements/recommendations for international students: Required—TOEFL. Electronic applications accepted.

University of Oklahoma, Graduate College, College of Liberal Studies, Norman, OK 73019-0390. Offers administrative leadership (MLS); integrated studies (MLS); interprofessional human and health services (MLS); museum studies (MLS). Part-time programs available. Postbaccalaureate distance learning degree programs offered (no on-campus study). *Faculty:* 15 full-time (8 women), 26 part-time/adjunct (16 women). *Students:* 17 full-time (11 women), 326 part-time (169 women); includes 71 minority (33 African Americans, 24 American Indian/Alaska Native, 4 Asian Americans or Pacific Islanders, 10 Hispanic Americans). 126 applicants, 90% accepted, 75 enrolled. In 2009, 94 master's awarded. *Degree requirements:* For master's, thesis, research project, internship. *Entrance requirements:* For master's, minimum GPA of 3.0 in last 60 hours, writing sample. Additional exam requirements/recommendations for international students: Required—TOEFL (minimum score 550 paper-based; 213 computer-based). *Application deadline:* For fall admission, 7/15 priority date for domestic students, 4/1 for international students; for spring admission, 12/1 for domestic students, 9/1 for international students. Applications are processed on a rolling basis. Application fee: $40 ($90 for international students). Electronic applications accepted. *Expenses:* Tuition, state resident: full-time $3744; part-time $156 per credit hour. Tuition, nonresident: full-time $13,577; part-time $565.70 per credit hour. Required fees: $2415; $90.10 per credit hour. *Financial support:* In 2009–10, 163 students received support. Career-related internships or fieldwork, scholarships/grants, and tuition waivers (partial) available. Support available to part-time students. Financial award applicants required to submit FAFSA. *Faculty research:* Distance education, adult learning processes, student satisfaction, administrative leadership, organizations, museum studies. *Unit head:* Dr. James Pappas, Dean and Vice President for University Outreach, 405-325-6361, Fax: 405-325-7196, E-mail: jpappas@ou.edu. *Application contact:* Dr. Julie Raadschelders, MA Program Coordinator, 405-325-1061, Fax: 405-325-9632, E-mail: jraadschelders@ou.edu.

University of Oklahoma Health Sciences Center, Graduate College, College of Public Health, Department of Health Administration and Policy, Oklahoma City, OK 73190. Offers MHA, MPH, MS, Dr PH, PhD, JD/MPH, MBA/MPH. *Accreditation:* CAHME. Part-time programs available. *Faculty:* 7 full-time (3 women), 1 part-time/adjunct (0 women). *Students:* 26 full-time (15 women), 15 part-time (10 women); includes 9 minority (4 African Americans, 3 American Indian/Alaska Native, 1 Asian American or Pacific Islander, 1 Hispanic American), 4 international. Average age 31. 18 applicants, 83% accepted, 9 enrolled. In 2009, 29 master's awarded. *Degree requirements:* For master's, comprehensive exam, thesis (for some programs); for doctorate, 2 foreign languages, comprehensive exam, thesis/dissertation. *Entrance requirements:* For master's, 3 letters of recommendation, resume; for doctorate, GRE General Test, letters of recommendation. Additional exam requirements/recommendations for international students: Required—TOEFL (minimum score 570 paper-based; 230 computer-based). *Application deadline:* For fall admission, 7/1 for domestic students; for winter admission, 4/1 for domestic students; for spring admission, 12/1 for domestic students. Applications are processed on a rolling basis. Application fee: $50. *Expenses:* Tuition, state resident: full-time $3120; part-time $156 per credit hour. Tuition, nonresident: full-time $11,314; part-time $409.70 per credit hour. Required fees: $1471; $51.20 per credit hour. $223.25 per term. *Financial support:* In 2009–10, 3 research assistantships (averaging $13,000 per year) were awarded; fellowships, career-related internships or fieldwork, institutionally sponsored loans, traineeships, and tuition waivers (partial) also available. Support available to part-time students. Financial award application deadline: 5/1. *Faculty research:* Public health administration, health institutions management, public policy and the aged, injury control. *Unit head:* Dr. Peter Budetti, Chair, 405-271-2114, E-mail: peter-budetti@ouhsc.edu. *Application contact:* Robin Howell, Information Contact, 405-271-2308, E-mail: robin_howell@ouhsc.edu.

University of Oklahoma—Tulsa, College of Public Health, Tulsa, OK 74135-2512. Offers general public health (MPH); health administration and policy (MPH); public health preparedness and terrorism (MPH).

University of Ottawa, Faculty of Graduate and Postdoctoral Studies, Telfer School of Management, Health Administration Program, Ottawa, ON K1N 6N5, Canada. Offers MHA. Part-time programs available. *Degree requirements:* For master's, thesis optional, residency. *Entrance requirements:* For master's, GMAT, bachelor's degree or equivalent, minimum B average. Additional exam requirements/recommendations for international students: Recommended—TOEFL (minimum score 237 computer-based). Electronic applications accepted.

University of Pennsylvania, Wharton School, Health Care Management Department, Philadelphia, PA 19104. Offers MBA, PhD. *Accreditation:* CAHME (one or more programs are accredited). *Degree requirements:* For doctorate, comprehensive exam, thesis/dissertation. *Entrance requirements:* For master's, GMAT; for doctorate, GMAT or GRE. Electronic applications accepted. *Expenses:* Tuition: Full-time $25,660; part-time $4758 per course. Required fees: $2152; $270 per course. Tuition and fees vary according to course load, degree level and program. *Faculty research:* Health economics, health policy, health care management, health insurance and financing.

University of Phoenix, School of Advanced Studies, Phoenix, AZ 85034-7209. Offers business administration (DBA); education (Ed D); educational leadership (Ed D), including curriculum and instruction, educational leadership, educational technology; health administration (DHA); higher education administration (PhD); industrial/organizational psychology (PhD); nursing (PhD); organizational leadership (DM), including information systems and technology, organizational leadership. Evening/weekend programs available. *Faculty:* 83 full-time (47 women), 540 part-time/adjunct (264 women). *Students:* 7,749 full-time (5,032 women); includes 3,180 minority (2,473 African Americans, 61 American Indian/Alaska Native, 221 Asian Americans or Pacific Islanders, 425 Hispanic Americans), 490 international. Average age 44. In 2009, 467 doctorates awarded. *Degree requirements:* For doctorate, thesis/dissertation. *Entrance requirements:* For doctorate, 3 letters of recommendation, minimum master's GPA of 3.0, 3 years professional work experience. Additional exam requirements/recommendations for international students: Required—TOEFL (minimum score 550 paper-based; 213 computer-based; 79 iBT). *Application deadline:* Applications are processed on a rolling basis. Application fee: $45. Electronic applications accepted. *Expenses:* Tuition: Full-time $13,272. Required fees: $660. Full-time tuition and fees vary according to course level, degree level and program. *Financial support:* Institutionally sponsored loans and scholarships/grants available. Financial award applicants required to submit FAFSA. *Unit head:* Dr. Jeremy Moreland, Dean/Executive Director, 480-557-3231, E-mail: jeremy.moreland@phoenix.edu. *Application contact:* Information Contact, 800-697-8223.

University of Phoenix–Atlanta Campus, The Artemis School, College of Health and Human Services, Sandy Springs, GA 30350-4153. Offers administration of justice and security (MS); health administration (MHA); health care management (MBA); nursing (MSN); nursing/health care education (MSN); MSN/MBA; MSN/MHA. Evening/weekend programs available. Postbaccalaureate distance learning degree programs offered. *Degree requirements:* For master's, thesis (for some programs). *Entrance requirements:* For master's, minimum undergraduate GPA of 2.5, 3 years of work experience. Additional exam requirements/recommendations for international students: Required—TOEFL (minimum score 550 paper-based; 213 computer-based; 79 iBT). Electronic applications accepted.

University of Phoenix–Augusta Campus, College of Health and Human Services, Augusta, GA 30909-4583. Offers health administration (MHA); health care management (MBA); nursing (MSN); nursing/health care education (MSN); MSN/MBA; MSN/MHA. Postbaccalaureate distance learning degree programs offered.

University of Phoenix–Austin Campus, College of Health and Human Services, Austin, TX 78759. Offers health administration (MHA); health care management (MBA). Postbaccalaureate distance learning degree programs offered.

University of Phoenix–Bay Area Campus, The Artemis School, College of Health and Human Services, Pleasanton, CA 94588-3677. Offers administration of justice and security (MS); family nurse practitioner (MSN); health care management (MBA); marriage, family and child therapy (MSC); nursing (MSN); nursing/health care education (MSN); MSN/MBA. Evening/weekend programs available. Postbaccalaureate distance learning degree programs offered (no on-campus study). *Degree requirements:* For master's, thesis (for some programs). *Entrance requirements:* For master's, minimum undergraduate GPA of 2.5, 3 years of work experience, RN license. Additional exam requirements/recommendations for international students: Required—TOEFL (minimum score 550 paper-based; 213 computer-based; 79 iBT). Electronic applications accepted.

Health Services Management and Hospital Administration

University of Phoenix–Birmingham Campus, College of Health and Human Services, Birmingham, AL 35244. Offers education (MHA); gerontology (MHA); health administration (MHA); health care management (MBA); informatics (MHA); nursing (MSN); nursing/health care education (MSN); MSN/MBA; MSN/MHA.

University of Phoenix–Central Florida Campus, The Artemis School, College of Health and Human Services, Maitland, FL 32751-7057. Offers health administration (MHA); health and human services (MSN); health care management (MBA); nursing (MSN); nursing/health care education (MSN); MSN/MBA; MSN/MHA. Evening/weekend programs available. *Degree requirements:* For master's, thesis (for some programs). *Entrance requirements:* For master's, minimum undergraduate GPA of 2.5, 3 years work experience, RN license. Additional exam requirements/recommendations for international students: Required—TOEFL (minimum score 550 paper-based; 213 computer-based; 79 iBT). Electronic applications accepted.

University of Phoenix–Central Valley Campus, College of Health and Human Services, Fresno, CA 93720-1562. Offers education (MHA); gerontology (MHA); health administration (MHA); health care management (MBA); nursing (MSN); MSN/MBA.

University of Phoenix–Chattanooga Campus, College of Health and Human Services, Chattanooga, TN 37421-3707. Offers education (MHA); gerontology (MHA); health administration (MHA); health care management (MBA).

University of Phoenix–Cheyenne Campus, College of Health and Human Services, Cheyenne, WY 82009. Offers health administration (MHA); health care management (MBA); nursing (MSN); nursing/health care education (MSN); MSN/MBA; MSN/MHA. Postbaccalaureate distance learning degree programs offered.

University of Phoenix–Cincinnati Campus, The Artemis School, College of Health and Human Services, West Chester, OH 45069-4875. Offers administration of justice and security (MS); health care management (MBA); nursing (MSN); psychology (MS). Evening/weekend programs available. Postbaccalaureate distance learning degree programs offered. *Degree requirements:* For master's, thesis (for some programs). *Entrance requirements:* For master's, minimum undergraduate GPA of 2.5, 3 years of work experience. Additional exam requirements/recommendations for international students: Required—TOEFL (minimum score 550 paper-based; 79 iBT). Electronic applications accepted.

University of Phoenix–Cleveland Campus, The Artemis School, College of Health and Human Services, Independence, OH 44131-2194. Offers administration of justice and security (MS); health care management (MBA); nursing (MSN); psychology (MS). Evening/weekend programs available. Postbaccalaureate distance learning degree programs offered. *Degree requirements:* For master's, thesis (for some programs). *Entrance requirements:* For master's, minimum undergraduate GPA of 2.5, 3 years of work experience. Additional exam requirements/recommendations for international students: Required—TOEFL (minimum score 550 paper-based; 213 computer-based; 79 iBT). Electronic applications accepted.

University of Phoenix–Columbus Georgia Campus, The Artemis School, College of Health and Human Services, Columbus, GA 31904-6321. Offers administration of justice and security (MS); health administration (MHA); health care management (MBA); nursing (MSN). Postbaccalaureate distance learning degree programs offered. *Degree requirements:* For master's, thesis (for some programs). *Entrance requirements:* For master's, minimum undergraduate GPA of 2.5, 3 years of work experience. Additional exam requirements/recommendations for international students: Required—TOEFL (minimum score 550 paper-based; 213 computer-based; 79 iBT). Electronic applications accepted.

University of Phoenix–Columbus Ohio Campus, The Artemis School, College of Health and Human Services, Columbus, OH 43240-4032. Offers administration of justice and security (MS); health care management (MBA); nursing (MSN); psychology (MS). Evening/weekend programs available. Postbaccalaureate distance learning degree programs offered. *Degree requirements:* For master's, thesis (for some programs). *Entrance requirements:* For master's, minimum undergraduate GPA of 2.5, 3 years work experience. Additional exam requirements/recommendations for international students: Required—TOEFL (minimum score 550 paper-based; 213 computer-based; 79 iBT). Electronic applications accepted.

University of Phoenix–Dallas Campus, The Artemis School, College of Health and Human Services, Dallas, TX 75251-2009. Offers administration of justice and security (MS); health administration (MHA); health care management (MBA); psychology (MS). Postbaccalaureate distance learning degree programs offered. *Degree requirements:* For master's, thesis (for some programs). *Entrance requirements:* For master's, minimum undergraduate GPA of 2.5, 3 years of work experience. Additional exam requirements/recommendations for international students: Required—TOEFL (minimum score 550 paper-based; 213 computer-based; 79 iBT). Electronic applications accepted.

University of Phoenix–Denver Campus, The Artemis School, College of Health and Human Services, Lone Tree, CO 80124-5453. Offers administration of justice and security (MS); community counseling (MSC); health administration (MHA); health care management (MBA); marriage, family and child therapy (MSC); nursing (MSN); psychology (MS); MSN/MBA; MSN/MHA. Evening/weekend programs available. Postbaccalaureate distance learning degree programs offered. *Degree requirements:* For master's, thesis (for some programs). *Entrance requirements:* For master's, minimum undergraduate GPA of 2.5, 3 years work experience, RN license. Additional exam requirements/recommendations for international students: Required—TOEFL (minimum score 550 paper-based; 213 computer-based; 79 iBT). Electronic applications accepted.

University of Phoenix–Des Moines Campus, College of Health and Human Services, Des Moines, IA 50266. Offers health care management (MBA).

University of Phoenix–Eastern Washington Campus, The Artemis School, College of Health and Human Services, Spokane Valley, WA 99212-2531. Offers health care management (MBA). Evening/weekend programs available. *Degree requirements:* For master's, thesis (for some programs). *Entrance requirements:* For master's, minimum undergraduate GPA of 2.5, 3 years of work experience. Additional exam requirements/recommendations for international students: Required—TOEFL (minimum score 550 paper-based; 213 computer-based; 79 iBT). Electronic applications accepted.

University of Phoenix–Harrisburg Campus, College of Health and Human Services, Harrisburg, PA 17112. Offers health administration (MHA); health care management (MBA); nursing (MSN); nursing/health care education (MSN); MSN/MBA; MSN/MHA. Postbaccalaureate distance learning degree programs offered.

University of Phoenix–Hawaii Campus, The Artemis School, College of Health and Human Services, Honolulu, HI 96813-4317. Offers administration of justice and security (MS); community counseling (MSC); education (MHA); family nurse practitioner (MSN); gerontology (MHA); health administration (MHA); health care management (MBA); marriage, family and child therapy (MSC); nursing (MSN); nursing/health care education (MSN); psychology (MS); MSN/MBA. Evening/weekend programs available. *Degree requirements:* For master's, thesis (for some programs). *Entrance requirements:* For master's, minimum undergraduate GPA of 2.5, 3 years of work experience, RN license. Additional exam requirements/recommendations for international students: Required—TOEFL (minimum score 550 paper-based; 213 computer-based; 79 iBT). Electronic applications accepted.

University of Phoenix–Houston Campus, The Artemis School, College of Health and Human Services, Houston, TX 77079-2004. Offers administration of justice and security (MS); health administration (MHA); health care management (MBA); psychology (MS). Postbaccalaureate distance learning degree programs offered. *Degree requirements:* For master's, thesis (for some programs). *Entrance requirements:* For master's, minimum undergraduate GPA of 2.5, 3 years of work experience. Additional exam requirements/recommendations for international students: Required—TOEFL (minimum score 550 paper-based; 213 computer-based; 79 iBT). Electronic applications accepted.

University of Phoenix–Idaho Campus, The Artemis School, College of Health and Human Services, Meridian, ID 83642-3014. Offers administration of justice and security (MS); health administration (MHA); health care management (MBA); nursing (MSN); nursing/health care education (MSN); psychology (MS); MSN/MBA. Evening/weekend programs available. Postbaccalaureate distance learning degree programs offered. *Degree requirements:* For master's, thesis (for some programs). *Entrance requirements:* For master's, minimum undergraduate GPA of 2.5, 3 years of work experience. Additional exam requirements/recommendations for international students: Required—TOEFL (minimum score 550 paper-based; 213 computer-based). Electronic applications accepted.

University of Phoenix–Indianapolis Campus, The Artemis School, College of Health and Human Services, Indianapolis, IN 46250-932. Offers administration of justice and security (MS); health administration (MHA); health care management (MBA); nursing (MSN); nursing/health care education (MSN); psychology (MS); MSN/MBA; MSN/MHA. Evening/weekend programs available. Postbaccalaureate distance learning degree programs offered. *Degree requirements:* For master's, thesis. *Entrance requirements:* For master's, 3 years work experience, minimum undergraduate GPA of 2.5. Additional exam requirements/recommendations for international students: Required—TOEFL (minimum score 500 paper-based; 213 computer-based). Electronic applications accepted.

University of Phoenix–Jersey City Campus, College of Health and Human Services, Jersey City, NJ 07310. Offers health care management (MBA). Postbaccalaureate distance learning degree programs offered.

University of Phoenix–Kansas City Campus, The Artemis School, College of Health and Human Services, Kansas City, MO 64131-4517. Offers administration of justice and security (MS); community counseling (MSC); health administration (MHA); health care management (MBA); nursing (MSN); MSN/MBA. Evening/weekend programs available. Postbaccalaureate distance learning degree programs offered. *Degree requirements:* For master's, thesis (for some programs). *Entrance requirements:* For master's, 3 years work experience, minimum undergraduate GPA of 2.5. Additional exam requirements/recommendations for international students: Required—TOEFL (minimum score 550 paper-based; 213 computer-based).

University of Phoenix–Las Vegas Campus, The Artemis School, College of Health and Human Services, Las Vegas, NV 89128. Offers administration of justice and security (MS); health administration (MHA); health care management (MBA); marriage, family, and child therapy (MSC); mental health counseling (MSC); nursing (MSN); nursing/health care education (MSN); psychology (MS); MSN/MBA; MSN/MHA. Postbaccalaureate distance learning degree programs offered. *Entrance requirements:* For master's, minimum undergraduate GPA of 2.5, 3 years of work experience. Additional exam requirements/recommendations for international students: Required—TOEFL (minimum score 550 paper-based; 213 computer-based; 79 iBT). Electronic applications accepted.

University of Phoenix–Louisiana Campus, The Artemis School, College of Health and Human Services, Metairie, LA 70001-2082. Offers administration of justice and security (MS); health administration (MHA); health care management (MBA); nursing (MSN); psychology (MS); MSN/MBA. Evening/weekend programs available. Postbaccalaureate distance learning degree programs offered (no on-campus study). *Degree requirements:* For master's, thesis (for some programs). *Entrance requirements:* For master's, minimum undergraduate GPA of 2.5, 3 years work experience, RN license. Additional exam requirements/recommendations for international students: Required—TOEFL (minimum score 550 paper-based; 213 computer-based; 79 iBT). Electronic applications accepted.

University of Phoenix–Louisville Campus, College of Health and Human Services, Louisville, KY 40223-3839. Offers health care management (MBA). Postbaccalaureate distance learning degree programs offered.

University of Phoenix–Madison Campus, The Artemis School, College of Health and Human Services, Madison, WI 53718-2416. Offers healthcare management (MBA). Evening/weekend programs available. *Degree requirements:* For master's, thesis (for some programs). *Entrance requirements:* Additional exam requirements/recommendations for international students: Required—TOEFL (minimum score 550 paper-based; 213 computer-based; 79 iBT). Electronic applications accepted.

University of Phoenix–Madison Campus, College of Health and Human Services, Madison, WI 53718-2416. Offers health care management (MBA).

University of Phoenix–Maryland Campus, The Artemis School, College of Health and Human Services, Columbia, MD 21045-5424. Offers administration of justice and security (MS); health administration (MHA); health care education (MSN); health care management (MBA); nursing (MSN); psychology (MS); MSN/MBA; MSN/MHA. Evening/weekend programs available. *Degree requirements:* For master's, thesis (for some programs). *Entrance requirements:* For master's, minimum undergraduate GPA of 2.5, 3 years work experience. Additional exam requirements/recommendations for international students: Required—TOEFL (minimum score 550 paper-based; 213 computer-based; 79 iBT). Electronic applications accepted.

University of Phoenix–Memphis Campus, College of Health and Human Services, Cordova, TN 38018. Offers health administration (MHA); health care management (MBA).

University of Phoenix–Minneapolis/St. Louis Park Campus, College of Health and Human Services, St. Louis Park, MN 55426. Offers community counseling (MSC); family nurse practitioner (MSN); health care education (MSN); health care management (MBA); nursing (MSN).

University of Phoenix–Nashville Campus, The Artemis School, College of Health and Human Services, Nashville, TN 37214-5048. Offers health administration (MHA); health care management (MBA). Evening/weekend programs available. *Degree requirements:* For master's, thesis (for some programs). *Entrance requirements:* For master's, minimum undergraduate GPA of 2.5, 3 years of work experience. Additional exam requirements/recommendations for international students: Required—TOEFL (minimum score 550 paper-based; 213 computer-based). Electronic applications accepted.

University of Phoenix–New Mexico Campus, The Artemis School, College of Health and Human Services, Albuquerque, NM 87113-1570. Offers administration of justice and security (MS); health administration (MHA); health care education (MSN); health care management (MBA); marriage and family therapy (MSC); nursing (MSN); psychology (MS); MSN/MBA. Evening/weekend programs available. *Degree requirements:* For master's, thesis (for some programs). *Entrance requirements:* For master's, minimum undergraduate GPA of 2.5, 3 years of work experience, RN license. Additional exam requirements/recommendations for international students: Required—TOEFL (minimum score 550 paper-based; 213 computer-based; 79 iBT). Electronic applications accepted.

University of Phoenix–Northern Nevada Campus, College of Health and Human Services, Reno, NV 89521-5862. Offers health administration (MHA); health care education (MSN); health care management (MBA); nursing (MSN); MSN/MBA; MSN/MHA.

University of Phoenix–Northern Virginia Campus, College of Health and Human Services, Reston, VA 20190. Offers health administration (MHA); health care management (MBA); nursing (MSN).

University of Phoenix–North Florida Campus, The Artemis School, College of Health and Human Services, Jacksonville, FL 32216-0959. Offers health administration (MHA); health care education (MSN); health care management (MBA); nursing (MSN); MSN/MBA; MSN/MHA. Evening/weekend programs available. *Degree requirements:* For master's, thesis (for some programs). *Entrance requirements:* For master's, minimum undergraduate GPA of 2.5, 3 years work experience, RN license. Additional exam requirements/recommendations for international students: Required—TOEFL (minimum score 550 paper-based; 213 computer-based; 79 iBT). Electronic applications accepted.

University of Phoenix–Northwest Arkansas Campus, College of Health and Human Services, Rogers, AR 72756-9615. Offers health administration (MHA); health care education (MSN); health care management (MBA); nursing (MSN); MSN/MBA.

University of Phoenix–Oklahoma City Campus, College of Health and Human Services, Oklahoma City, OK 73116-8244. Offers administration of justice and security (MS); health care management (MBA); nursing (MSN); psychology (MS).

University of Phoenix–Omaha Campus, College of Health and Human Services, Omaha, NE 68154-5240. Offers health administration (MHA); health care management (MBA).

University of Phoenix–Oregon Campus, The Artemis School, College of Health and Human Services, Tigard, OR 97223. Offers administration of justice and security (MS); health administration (MHA); health care management (MBA); nursing (MSN); psychology (MS); MSN/MBA. Evening/weekend programs available. *Degree requirements:* For master's, thesis (for some programs). *Entrance requirements:* For master's, minimum undergraduate GPA of 2.5, 3 years of work experience, current RN license (nursing). Additional exam requirements/recommendations for international students: Required—TOEFL (minimum score 550 paper-based; 213 computer-based; 79 iBT). Electronic applications accepted.

University of Phoenix–Philadelphia Campus, The Artemis School, College of Health and Human Services, Wayne, PA 19087-2121. Offers administration of justice and security (MS); health administration (MHA); health care education (MSN); health care management (MBA); nursing (MSN); psychology (MS); MSN/MBA. Evening/weekend programs available. *Degree requirements:* For master's, thesis (for some programs). *Entrance requirements:* For master's, minimum undergraduate GPA of 2.5, 3 years work experience. Additional exam requirements/recommendations for international students: Required—TOEFL (minimum score 550 paper-based; 213 computer-based; 79 iBT). Electronic applications accepted.

University of Phoenix–Phoenix Campus, School of Business, College of Natural Sciences, Phoenix, AZ 85040-1958. Offers education (MHA); gerontology (MHA); health administration (MHA); informatics (MHA). Evening/weekend programs available. *Students:* 18 full-time (17 women); includes 16 minority (1 African American, 12 American Indian/Alaska Native, 2 Asian Americans or Pacific Islanders, 1 Hispanic American), 2 international. Average age 41. In 2009, 1 master's awarded. *Degree requirements:* For master's, thesis (for some programs). *Entrance requirements:* For master's, 3 years of work experience, minimum undergraduate GPA of 3.0. Additional exam requirements/recommendations for international students: Required—TOEFL (minimum score 550 paper-based; 213 computer-based; 79 iBT). *Application deadline:* Applications are processed on a rolling basis. Application fee: $45. Electronic applications accepted. *Expenses:* Tuition: Full-time $10,272. Required fees: $760. *Financial support:* Institutionally sponsored loans and scholarships/grants available. Financial award applicants required to submit FAFSA. *Unit head:* Dr. Hinrich Eyers, Dean/Executive Director, 480-557-7278, Fax: 602-557-7428, E-mail: hinrich.eyers@phoenix.edu. *Application contact:* Campus College Chair, 866-766-0766, Fax: 480-557-2320.

University of Phoenix–Pittsburgh Campus, The Artemis School, College of Health and Human Services, Pittsburgh, PA 15276. Offers administration of justice and security (MS); health administration (MHA); health care education (MSN); health care management (MBA); nursing (MSN); psychology (MS); MSN/MBA; MSN/MHA. Evening/weekend programs available. *Degree requirements:* For master's, thesis (for some programs). *Entrance requirements:* For master's, minimum undergraduate GPA of 2.5, 3 years work experience, current RN license (nursing). Additional exam requirements/recommendations for international students: Required—TOEFL (minimum score 550 paper-based; 213 computer-based; 79 iBT). Electronic applications accepted.

University of Phoenix–Puerto Rico Campus, The Artemis School, College of Health and Human Services, Guaynabo, PR 00968. Offers marriage and family counseling (MSC); mental health counseling (MSC). Evening/weekend programs available. *Degree requirements:* For master's, thesis (for some programs). *Entrance requirements:* For master's, Counselor Preparation Comprehensive Examination, minimum undergraduate GPA of 2.5, 3 years work experience. Additional exam requirements/recommendations for international students: Required—TOEFL (minimum score 550 paper-based; 213 computer-based; 79 iBT). Electronic applications accepted.

University of Phoenix–Raleigh Campus, College of Health and Human Services, Raleigh, NC 27606. Offers health care management (MBA).

University of Phoenix–Richmond Campus, The Artemis School, College of Health and Human Services, Richmond, VA 23230. Offers administration of justice and security (MS); health administration (MHA); health care education (MSN); health care management (MBA); nursing (MSN); psychology (MS); MSN/MBA; MSN/MHA. Evening/weekend programs available. *Degree requirements:* For master's, thesis (for some programs). *Entrance requirements:* For master's, minimum undergraduate GPA of 2.5, 3 years work experience, current RN license for nursing programs. Additional exam requirements/recommendations for international students: Required—TOEFL (minimum score 500 paper-based; 213 computer-based; 79 iBT). Electronic applications accepted.

University of Phoenix–Sacramento Valley Campus, The Artemis School, College of Health and Human Services, Sacramento, CA 95833-3632. Offers administration of justice and security (MS); community counseling (MSC); family nurse practitioner (MSN); health administration (MHA); health care education (MSN); health care management (MBA); marriage, family and child counseling (MSC); nursing (MSN); psychology (MS); MSN/MBA. Evening/weekend programs available. *Degree requirements:* For master's, thesis (for some programs). *Entrance requirements:* For master's, RN license, minimum undergraduate GPA of 2.5, 3 years work experience. Additional exam requirements/recommendations for international students: Required—TOEFL (minimum score 550 paper-based; 213 computer-based; 79 iBT). Electronic applications accepted.

University of Phoenix–St. Louis Campus, The Artemis School, College of Health and Human Services, St. Louis, MO 63043-4828. Offers administration of justice and security (MS); health administration (MHA); health care management (MBA); nursing (MSN); MSN/MBA; MSN/MHA. Evening/weekend programs available. *Degree requirements:* For master's, thesis (for some programs). *Entrance requirements:* For master's, minimum undergraduate GPA of 2.5, 3 years work experience. Additional exam requirements/recommendations for international students: Required—TOEFL (minimum score 550 paper-based; 213 computer-based; 79 iBT). Electronic applications accepted.

University of Phoenix–San Antonio Campus, College of Health and Human Services, San Antonio, TX 78230. Offers health administration (MHA); health care management (MBA).

University of Phoenix–San Diego Campus, The Artemis School, College of Health and Human Services, San Diego, CA 92123. Offers administration of justice and security (MS); health care education (MSN); health care management (MBA); marriage, family and child counseling (MSC); marriage, family and child therapy (MSC); nursing (MSN); MSN/MBA. Evening/weekend programs available. *Degree requirements:* For master's, thesis (for some programs). *Entrance requirements:* For master's, minimum undergraduate GPA of 2.5, 3 years work experience, RN license. Additional exam requirements/recommendations for international students: Required—TOEFL (minimum score 550 paper-based; 213 computer-based; 79 iBT). Electronic applications accepted.

University of Phoenix–Savannah Campus, College of Health and Human Services, Savannah, GA 31405-7400. Offers health administration (MHA); health care management (MBA); nursing (MSN); nursing/health care education (MSN); MSN/MBA; MSN/MHA.

University of Phoenix–Southern Arizona Campus, The Artemis School, College of Health and Human Services, Tucson, AZ 85711. Offers administration of justice and security (MS); family nurse practitioner (MSN, Certificate); health administration (MHA); health care management (MBA); marriage, family and child therapy (MSC); nursing (MSN); psychology (MS). Evening/weekend programs available. *Degree requirements:* For master's, thesis (for some programs). *Entrance requirements:* For master's, minimum undergraduate GPA of 2.5, 3 years of work experience, RN license. Additional exam requirements/recommendations for international students: Required—TOEFL (minimum score 550 paper-based; 213 computer-based; 79 iBT). Electronic applications accepted.

University of Phoenix–Southern Colorado Campus, The Artemis School, College of Health and Human Services, Colorado Springs, CO 80919-2335. Offers administration of justice and security (MS); community counseling (MSC); education (MHA); gerontology (MHA); health administration (MHA); health care management (MBA); marriage, family and child therapy (MSC); nursing (MSN); psychology (MS); MSN/MBA. Evening/weekend programs available. *Degree requirements:* For master's, thesis (for some programs). *Entrance requirements:* For master's, minimum undergraduate GPA of 2.5, 3 years of work experience, RN license. Additional exam requirements/recommendations for international students: Required—TOEFL (minimum score 550 paper-based; 213 computer-based; 79 iBT). Electronic applications accepted.

University of Phoenix–South Florida Campus, The Artemis School, College of Health and Human Services, Fort Lauderdale, FL 33309. Offers health administration (MHA); health care education (MSN); health care management (MBA); nursing (MSN); MSN/MBA; MSN/MHA. Evening/weekend programs available. *Degree requirements:* For master's, thesis (for some programs). *Entrance requirements:* For master's, minimum undergraduate GPA of 2.5, 3 years work experience, RN license. Additional exam requirements/recommendations for international students: Required—TOEFL (minimum score 550 paper-based; 213 computer-based; 79 iBT). Electronic applications accepted.

University of Phoenix–Springfield Campus, College of Health and Human Services, Springfield, MO 65804-7211. Offers health administration (MHA); health care management (MBA); nursing (MSN); MSN/MBA; MSN/MHA.

University of Phoenix–Tulsa Campus, College of Health and Human Services, Tulsa, OK 74134-1412. Offers administration of justice and security (MS); health care management (MBA); nursing (MSN); psychology (MS).

University of Phoenix–Utah Campus, The Artemis School, College of Health and Human Services, Salt Lake City, UT 84123-4617. Offers health care management (MBA); healthcare education (MSN); mental health counseling (MSC); nursing (MSN); MSN/MBA. Evening/weekend programs available. *Degree requirements:* For master's, thesis (for some programs). *Entrance requirements:* For master's, minimum undergraduate GPA of 2.5, 3 years work experience, RN license. Additional exam requirements/recommendations for international students: Required—TOEFL (minimum score 550 paper-based; 213 computer-based; 79 iBT). Electronic applications accepted.

University of Phoenix–Vancouver Campus, The Artemis School, College of Health and Human Services, Burnaby, BC V5C 6G9, Canada. Offers health care management (MBA). Evening/weekend programs available. *Degree requirements:* For master's, thesis (for some programs). *Entrance requirements:* For master's, minimum undergraduate GPA of 2.5, 3 years work experience. Additional exam requirements/recommendations for international students: Required—TOEFL (minimum score 550 paper-based; 213 computer-based; 79 iBT). Electronic applications accepted.

University of Phoenix–Western Washington Campus, College of Health and Human Services, Tukwila, WA 98188. Offers health administration (MHA); health care education (MSN); health care management (MBA); nursing (MSN); MSN/MBA; MSN/MHA. Evening/weekend programs available. *Degree requirements:* For master's, thesis (for some programs). *Entrance requirements:* For master's, minimum undergraduate GPA of 2.5, 3 years of work experience. Additional exam requirements/recommendations for international students: Required—TOEFL (minimum score 550 paper-based; 213 computer-based; 79 iBT). Electronic applications accepted.

University of Phoenix–West Florida Campus, The Artemis School, College of Health and Human Services, Temple Terrace, FL 33637. Offers health administration (MHA); health care education (MSN); health care management (MBA); nursing (MSN); MSN/MBA; MSN/MHA. Evening/weekend programs available. Postbaccalaureate distance learning degree programs offered. *Degree requirements:* For master's, thesis (for some programs). *Entrance requirements:* For master's, minimum undergraduate GPA of 2.5, RN license, 3 years work experience. Additional exam requirements/recommendations for international students: Required—TOEFL (minimum score 550 paper-based; 213 computer-based; 79 iBT). Electronic applications accepted.

University of Pittsburgh, Graduate School of Public Health, Department of Behavioral and Community Health Science, Pittsburgh, PA 15260. Offers behavioral and community health sciences (MPH, Dr PH); lesbian, gay, bisexual and transgender health and wellness (Certificate); minority health and health disparities (Certificate); program evaluation (Certificate); public health and aging (Certificate); public health preparedness (Certificate); MID/MPH; MPH/MPA; MPH/MSW; MPH/PhD. *Accreditation:* CAHME (one or more programs are accredited). Part-time programs available. *Faculty:* 17 full-time (8 women), 13 part-time/adjunct (3 women). *Students:* 86 full-time (66 women), 46 part-time (37 women); includes 27 minority (20 African Americans, 1 American Indian/Alaska Native, 4 Asian Americans or Pacific Islanders, 2 Hispanic Americans), 7 international. Average age 30. 235 applicants, 74% accepted, 46 enrolled. In 2009, 30 master's, 5 doctorates awarded. *Degree requirements:* For master's, thesis; for doctorate, comprehensive exam, thesis/dissertation, preliminary exams. *Entrance requirements:* For master's and Certificate, GRE; for doctorate, GRE, master's degree in public health or related field. Additional exam requirements/recommendations for international students: Required—TOEFL (minimum score 550 paper-based; 213 computer-based; 80 iBT). *Application deadline:* For fall admission, 5/1 priority date for domestic students, 4/1 for international students; for winter admission, 9/1 for international students; for spring admission, 10/1 priority date for domestic students, 2/1 for international students. Applications are processed on a rolling basis. Application fee: $95. Electronic applications accepted. *Expenses:* Tuition, state resident: full-time $16,402; part-time $665 per credit. Tuition, nonresident: full-time $28,694; part-time $1175 per credit. Required fees: $690; $175 per term. Tuition and fees vary according to program. *Financial support:* In 2009–10, 21 students received support, including 1 fellowship with full tuition reimbursement available (averaging $20,976 per year), 19 research assistantships with full and partial tuition reimbursements available (averaging $12,300 per year), 2 teaching assistantships with full tuition reimbursements available (averaging $15,065 per year); unspecified assistantships also available. *Faculty research:* Maternal and child health, program evaluation, community-based participatory research, minority health and health disparities, aging. Total annual research expenditures: $1.7 million. *Unit head:* Dr. Ronald D. Stall, Chairman, 412-624-7933, Fax: 412-648-5975, E-mail: rstall@pitt.edu. *Application contact:* Natalie C. Arnold, Recruitment and Academic Affairs Administrator, 412-624-3107, Fax: 412-624-5510, E-mail: narnold@pitt.edu.

University of Pittsburgh, Graduate School of Public Health, Department of Health Policy and Management, Pittsburgh, PA 15260. Offers MHA, MPH, JD/MPH. *Accreditation:* CAHME. Part-time programs available. *Faculty:* 15 full-time (7 women), 17 part-time/adjunct (5 women). *Students:* 48 full-time (38 women), 22 part-time (12 women); includes 15 minority (4 African Americans, 9 Asian Americans or Pacific Islanders, 2 Hispanic Americans), 8 international. Average age 28. 219 applicants, 58% accepted, 32 enrolled. In 2009, 22 master's awarded. *Degree requirements:* For master's, essay. *Entrance requirements:* For master's, GRE, 3 credits each of course work in mathematics and biology, 6 in social science. Additional exam requirements/recommendations for international students: Required—TOEFL (minimum score 550 paper-based; 213 computer-based; 80 iBT). *Application deadline:* For fall admission, 4/30 priority date for domestic students, 4/1 for international students; for winter admission, 9/1 for international students; for spring admission, 10/30 priority date for domestic students, 2/1 for international students. Applications are processed on a rolling basis. Application fee: $95. Electronic applications accepted. *Expenses:* Tuition, state resident: full-time $16,402; part-time

Health Services Management and Hospital Administration

University of Pittsburgh (continued)

$665 per credit. Tuition, nonresident: full-time $28,694; part-time $1175 per credit. Required fees: $690; $175 per term. Tuition and fees vary according to program. *Financial support:* In 2009–10, 14 students received support, including 6 fellowships with partial tuition reimbursements available (averaging $4,705 per year), 8 research assistantships with full and partial tuition reimbursements available (averaging $12,300 per year); scholarships/grants, health care benefits, and unspecified assistantships also available. Support available to part-time students. *Faculty research:* Health care financing/insurance, long-term care, health policy, health law, nursing homes, quality. Total annual research expenditures: $1.1 million. *Unit head:* Dr. Mark S. Roberts, Chair, 412-383-7049, Fax: 412-624-3146, E-mail: mroberts@pitt.edu. *Application contact:* Donna Schultz, Administrative Assistant, 412-624-3123, Fax: 412-624-3146, E-mail: dschultz@pitt.edu.

University of Pittsburgh, School of Health and Rehabilitation Sciences, Master's Programs in Health and Rehabilitation Sciences, Pittsburgh, PA 15260. Offers health and rehabilitation sciences (MS), including clinical dietetics and nutrition, health care supervision and management, health information systems, occupational therapy, physical therapy, rehabilitation counseling, rehabilitation science and technology, sports medicine, wellness and human performance. *Accreditation:* APTA. Part-time and evening/weekend programs available. *Faculty:* 30 full-time (14 women), 4 part-time/adjunct (3 women). *Students:* 81 full-time (47 women), 54 part-time (27 women); includes 10 minority (6 African Americans, 4 Asian Americans or Pacific Islanders), 44 international. Average age 29. 326 applicants, 65% accepted, 130 enrolled. In 2009, 93 master's awarded. *Degree requirements:* For master's, comprehensive exam (for some programs), thesis optional. *Entrance requirements:* For master's, minimum GPA of 3.0. Additional exam requirements/recommendations for international students: Required—TOEFL, IELTS. *Application deadline:* For fall admission, 1/31 for international students; for spring admission, 7/31 for international students. Applications are processed on a rolling basis. Application fee: $50. Electronic applications accepted. *Expenses:* Contact institution. *Financial support:* In 2009–10, 3 research assistantships with full tuition reimbursements (averaging $18,450 per year) were awarded; teaching assistantships, Federal Work-Study, institutionally sponsored loans, traineeships, and unspecified assistantships also available. Financial award applicants required to submit FAFSA. *Faculty research:* Assistive technology, seating and wheeled mobility, cellular neurophysiology, low back syndrome, augmentative communication. Total annual research expenditures: $6.5 million. *Unit head:* Dr. Clifford E. Brubaker, Dean, 412-383-6560, Fax: 412-383-6535, E-mail: cliffb@pitt.edu. *Application contact:* Shameem Gangjee, Director of Admissions, 412-383-6558, Fax: 412-383-6535, E-mail: admissions@shrs.pitt.edu.

University of Puerto Rico, Medical Sciences Campus, Graduate School of Public Health, Program in Health Services Administration, San Juan, PR 00936-5067. Offers MHSA. *Accreditation:* CAHME. Part-time programs available. *Degree requirements:* For master's, thesis. *Entrance requirements:* For master's, GRE, previous course work in accounting, statistics, economics, algebra, and managerial finance.

University of Rochester, School of Nursing, Rochester, NY 14642. Offers acute care nurse practitioner (MS); adult nurse practitioner (MS); adult psychiatric mental health nurse practitioner (MS); adult/geriatric nurse practitioner (MS); care of children and families/pediatric nurse practitioner (MS); care of children and families/pediatric nurse practitioner with pediatric behavioral health (MS); care of children and families/pediatric nurse practitioner/neonatal nurse practitioner (MS); child and adolescent psychiatric mental health nurse practitioner (MS); clinical nurse leader (MS); disaster response and emergency preparedness (MS); family nurse practitioner (MS); health care organization management and leadership (MS); health practice research (PhD); health promotion, education and technology (MS); nursing (Certificate). *Accreditation:* AACN; NLN (one or more programs are accredited). Part-time programs available. Postbaccalaureate distance learning degree programs offered (minimal on-campus study). *Faculty:* 26 full-time (24 women), 20 part-time/adjunct (15 women). *Students:* 50 full-time (45 women), 178 part-time (165 women); includes 33 minority (17 African Americans, 2 American Indian/Alaska Native, 10 Asian Americans or Pacific Islanders, 4 Hispanic Americans), 11 international. Average age 35. 56 applicants, 80% accepted, 35 enrolled. In 2009, 53 master's, 5 doctorates awarded. Terminal master's awarded for partial completion of doctoral program. *Degree requirements:* For master's, comprehensive exam or thesis; for doctorate, thesis/dissertation. *Entrance requirements:* For master's, BS in nursing, minimum GPA of 3.0, course work in statistics; for doctorate, GRE General Test, MS in nursing, minimum GPA of 3.5; for Certificate, MS in nursing. Additional exam requirements/recommendations for international students: Recommended—TOEFL (minimum score 560 paper-based; 230 computer-based; 88 iBT). *Application deadline:* For fall admission, 11/1 priority date for domestic and international students. Application fee: $50. *Financial support:* In 2009–10, 53 students received support, including 14 fellowships with full and partial tuition reimbursements available (averaging $17,497 per year); scholarships/grants, traineeships, health care benefits, tuition waivers (partial), and unspecified assistantships also available. Support available to part-time students. Financial award application deadline: 6/30. *Faculty research:* Clinical research in aging, managing asthma in children, interventions to improve outcomes in critically ill children and their mothers, nurse home visitation studies, medical device evaluation, critical care clinical studies, high risk behavior and prevention, palliative care, pregnancy-related weight gain. Total annual research expenditures: $4.8 million. *Unit head:* Dr. Kathy P. Parker, Dean, 585-273-5639, Fax: 585-273-1268, E-mail: kathy_parker@urmc.rochester.edu. *Application contact:* Elaine Andolina, Director of Admissions, 585-275-2375, Fax: 585-756-8299, E-mail: elaine_andolina@urmc.rochester.edu.

University of St. Francis, College of Business and Health Administration, School of Health Administration, Joliet, IL 60435-6169. Offers MS. Part-time and evening/weekend programs available. Postbaccalaureate distance learning degree programs offered (no on-campus study). *Faculty:* 3 full-time (0 women), 32 part-time/adjunct (13 women). *Students:* 107 full-time (90 women), 414 part-time (331 women); includes 483 minority (53 African Americans, 1 American Indian/Alaska Native, 14 Asian Americans or Pacific Islanders, 415 Hispanic Americans). Average age 44. 176 applicants, 73% accepted, 100 enrolled. In 2009, 176 master's awarded. *Entrance requirements:* For master's, minimum undergraduate GPA of 2.75, computer competency, 2 letters of recommendation, 2 years of work experience. Additional exam requirements/recommendations for international students: Required—TOEFL (minimum score 550 paper-based; 213 computer-based). *Application deadline:* Applications are processed on a rolling basis. Application fee: $30. Electronic applications accepted. *Expenses:* Tuition: Part-time $589 per credit hour. Tuition and fees vary according to degree level, campus/location and program. *Financial support:* In 2009–10, 202 students received support. Tuition waivers (partial) available. Support available to part-time students. Financial award applicants required to submit FAFSA. *Unit head:* Dr. Michael LaRocco, Dean, 815-740-5025, Fax: 815-774-2920, E-mail: mlarocco@stfrancis.edu. *Application contact:* Sandra Sloka, Director of Admissions for Graduate and Degree Completion Programs, 800-735-7500, Fax: 815-740-5032, E-mail: ssloka@stfrancis.edu.

University of St. Thomas, Graduate Studies, Opus College of Business, Health Care UST MBA Program, Minneapolis, MN 55403. Offers MBA. *Accreditation:* CAHME. Postbaccalaureate distance learning degree programs offered (minimal on-campus study). *Students:* 62 part-time (32 women); includes 9 minority (2 African Americans, 5 Asian Americans or Pacific Islanders, 2 Hispanic Americans). Average age 40. 25 applicants, 100% accepted, 23 enrolled. In 2009, 12 master's awarded. *Entrance requirements:* For master's, GMAT or master's degree (or request for waiver of GMAT for experience and undergraduate performance), minimum 5 years of work experience in health care related field. Additional exam requirements/recommendations for international students: Required—TOEFL, IELTS or Michigan English Language Assessment Battery. *Application deadline:* For fall admission, 6/1 for domestic students. Applications are processed on a rolling basis. Application fee: $75. *Expenses:* Contact institution. *Financial support:* Institutionally sponsored loans and scholarships/grants available. Financial award application deadline: 7/1; financial award applicants required to submit FAFSA. *Unit head:* Dr. Jack Militello, Director, 651-962-4135, Fax: 651-962-8810. *Application contact:* Cindy Lorah, Manager of Marketing and Recruitment, 651-962-4135, Fax: 651-962-8810, E-mail: medmba@stthomas.edu.

University of San Francisco, School of Business and Professional Studies, Program in Public Administration, Concentration in Health Services Administration, San Francisco, CA 94117-1080. Offers MPA. Part-time and evening/weekend programs available. *Faculty:* 4 full-time (1 woman), 3 part-time/adjunct (1 woman). *Students:* 33 full-time (27 women); includes 13 minority (3 African Americans, 3 Asian Americans or Pacific Islanders, 7 Hispanic Americans), 1 international. Average age 33. 20 applicants, 75% accepted, 9 enrolled. In 2009, 29 master's awarded. *Degree requirements:* For master's, thesis optional. *Entrance requirements:* For master's, minimum GPA of 3.0. Application fee: $55 ($65 for international students). *Expenses:* Tuition: Full-time $19,710; part-time $1095 per unit. Part-time tuition and fees vary according to degree level, campus/location and program. *Financial support:* In 2009–10, 22 students received support. Application deadline: 3/2. *Unit head:* Dr. Maurice Penner. *Application contact:* 415-422-6000, E-mail: graduate@usfca.edu.

University of Saskatchewan, College of Graduate Studies and Research, Edwards School of Business, Program in Business Administration, Saskatoon, SK S7N 5A2, Canada. Offers agribusiness management (MBA); biotechnology management (MBA); health services management (MBA); indigenous management (MBA); international business management (MBA). Tuition and fees charges are reported in Canadian dollars. *Expenses:* Tuition, area resident: Full-time $3000 Canadian dollars; part-time $500 Canadian dollars per term. Required fees: $700 Canadian dollars; $100 Canadian dollars per term.

The University of Scranton, College of Graduate and Continuing Education, Department of Health Administration and Human Resources, Program in Health Administration, Scranton, PA 18510. Offers MHA. *Accreditation:* CAHME. Part-time and evening/weekend programs available. *Students:* 45 full-time (23 women), 4 part-time (3 women); includes 6 minority (2 American Indian/Alaska Native, 3 Asian Americans or Pacific Islanders, 1 Hispanic American), 17 international. Average age 27. 63 applicants, 89% accepted. In 2009, 12 master's awarded. *Degree requirements:* For master's, capstone experience. *Entrance requirements:* For master's, minimum GPA of 2.75. Additional exam requirements/recommendations for international students: Required—TOEFL (minimum score 550 paper-based; 173 computer-based), IELTS (minimum score 5.5). *Application deadline:* For fall admission, 4/15 priority date for domestic students. Applications are processed on a rolling basis. Application fee: $0. *Financial support:* Fellowships, teaching assistantships, career-related internships or fieldwork and unspecified assistantships also available. Financial award application deadline: 3/1. *Unit head:* Steven J. Szydlowski, Director, 570-941-4367, Fax: 570-941-4201, E-mail: sjs14@scranton.edu. *Application contact:* Joseph M. Roback, Director of Admissions, 570-941-4385, Fax: 570-941-5928, E-mail: robackj2@scranton.edu.

The University of Scranton, College of Graduate and Continuing Education, Program in Business Administration, Scranton, PA 18510. Offers accounting (MBA); finance (MBA); general business administration (MBA); health care management (MBA); international business (MBA); management information systems (MBA); marketing (MBA); operations management (MBA). *Accreditation:* AACSB. Part-time and evening/weekend programs available. Postbaccalaureate distance learning degree programs offered (no on-campus study). *Faculty:* 34 full-time (8 women). *Students:* 92 full-time (38 women), 137 part-time (58 women); includes 27 minority (15 African Americans, 5 Asian Americans or Pacific Islanders, 7 Hispanic Americans), 21 international. Average age 31. 255 applicants, 79% accepted. In 2009, 33 master's awarded. *Degree requirements:* For master's, capstone experience. *Entrance requirements:* For master's, GMAT, minimum GPA of 2.75. Additional exam requirements/recommendations for international students: Required—TOEFL (minimum score 500 paper-based; 173 computer-based), IELTS (minimum score 5.5). *Application deadline:* Applications are processed on a rolling basis. Application fee: $0. *Financial support:* In 2009–10, 10 students received support, including 10 teaching assistantships with full and partial tuition reimbursements available (averaging $6,600 per year); fellowships, career-related internships or fieldwork, Federal Work-Study, and unspecified assistantships also available. Support available to part-time students. Financial award application deadline: 3/1. *Faculty research:* Financial markets, strategic impact of total quality management, internal accounting controls, consumer preference, information systems and the Internet. *Unit head:* Dr. Murli Rajan, Director, 570-941-4043, Fax: 570-941-4342. *Application contact:* Joseph M. Roback, Director of Admissions, 570-941-4385, Fax: 570-941-5928, E-mail: robackj2@scranton.edu.

University of South Africa, College of Human Sciences, Pretoria, South Africa. Offers adult education (M Ed); African languages (MA, PhD); African politics (MA, PhD); Afrikaans (MA, PhD); ancient history (MA, PhD); ancient Near Eastern studies (MA, PhD); anthropology (MA, PhD); applied linguistics (MA); Arabic (MA, PhD); archaeology (MA); art history (MA); Biblical archaeology (MA); Biblical studies (M Th, D Th, PhD); Christian spirituality (M Th, D Th); church history (M Th, D Th); classical studies (MA, PhD); clinical psychology (MA); communication (MA, PhD); comparative education (M Ed, Ed D); consulting psychology (D Admin, D Com, PhD); curriculum studies (M Ed, Ed D); development studies (M Admin, MA, D Admin, PhD); didactics (M Ed, Ed D); education (M Tech); education management (M Ed, Ed D); educational psychology (M Ed); English (MA); environmental education (M Ed); French (MA, PhD); German (MA, PhD); Greek (MA); guidance and counseling (M Ed); health studies (MA, PhD), including health sciences education (MA), health services management (MA), medical and surgical nursing science (critical care general) (MA), midwifery and neonatal nursing science (MA), trauma and emergency care (MA); history (MA, PhD); history of education (Ed D); inclusive education (M Ed, Ed D); information and communications technology policy and regulation (MA); information science (MA, MIS, PhD); international politics (MA, PhD); Islamic studies (MA, PhD); Italian (MA, PhD); Judaica (MA, PhD); linguistics (MA, PhD); mathematical education (M Ed); mathematics education (MA); missiology (M Th, D Th); modern Hebrew (MA, PhD); musicology (MA, MMus, D Mus, PhD); natural science education (M Ed); New Testament (M Th, D Th); Old Testament (D Th); pastoral therapy (M Th, D Th); philosophy (MA); philosophy of education (M Ed, Ed D); politics (MA, PhD); Portuguese (MA, PhD); practical theology (M Th, D Th); psychology (MA, MS, PhD); psychology of education (M Ed, Ed D); public health (MA); religious studies (MA, D Th, PhD); Romance languages (MA); Russian (MA, PhD); Semitic languages (MA, PhD); social behavior studies in HIV/AIDS (MA); social science (mental health) (MA); social science in development studies (MA); social science in psychology (MA); social science in social work (MA); social science in sociology (MA); social work (MSW, DSW, PhD); socio-education (M Ed, Ed D); sociolinguistics (MA); sociology (MA, PhD); Spanish (MA, PhD); systematic theology (M Th, D Th); TESOL (teaching English to speakers of other languages) (MA); theological ethics (M Th, D Th); theory of literature (MA, PhD); urban ministries (D Th); urban ministry (M Th).

University of South Carolina, The Graduate School, Arnold School of Public Health, Department of Health Services Policy and Management, Columbia, SC 29208. Offers MHA, MPH, Dr PH, PhD, JD/MHA, MPH/MSN, MSW/MPH. *Accreditation:* CAHME (one or more programs are accredited). Part-time and evening/weekend programs available. *Degree requirements:* For master's, comprehensive exam, thesis or alternative, internship (MHA); for doctorate, comprehensive exam, thesis/dissertation. *Entrance requirements:* For master's, GMAT (MHA), GRE General Test (MPH); for doctorate, GRE General Test. Additional exam requirements/recommendations for international students: Required—TOEFL (minimum score 570 paper-based; 230 computer-based). Electronic applications accepted. *Faculty research:* Health systems management, evaluation, and planning; forecast applications in health care; Medicaid process to health care services.

University of Southern California, Graduate School, School of Policy, Planning, and Development, Executive Master of Health Administration Program, Los Angeles, CA 90089. Offers EMHA. Part-time and evening/weekend programs available. *Faculty:* 51 full-time (12 women), 74 part-time/adjunct (26 women). *Students:* 5 full-time (3 women), 49 part-time (23 women); includes 32 minority (6 African Americans, 16 Asian Americans or Pacific Islanders, 10 Hispanic Americans), 2 international. 37 applicants, 76% accepted, 24 enrolled. In 2009, 29 master's awarded. *Entrance requirements:* Additional exam requirements/recommendations for international students: Required—TOEFL (minimum score 600 paper-based; 250 computer-based; 100 iBT). *Application deadline:* For fall admission, 2/1 priority date for domestic and international students. Application fee: $85. Electronic applications accepted. *Expenses:* Contact

institution. *Faculty research:* Health management and policy, health care systems, health care economics and financing, health care access, community health, healthy communities. Total annual research expenditures: $5 million. *Unit head:* Dr. Michael B. Nichol, Director, Graduate Programs in Health, 213-740-2355, Fax: 213-740-0001, E-mail: mnichol@usc.edu. *Application contact:* Marisol R. Gonzalez, Director of Recruitment and Admission, 213-740-0550, Fax: 213-740-7573, E-mail: marisolr@usc.edu.

University of Southern California, Graduate School, School of Policy, Planning, and Development, Master of Health Administration Program, Los Angeles, CA 90089. Offers health administration (MHA); MHA/MS. *Accreditation:* CAHME. Part-time and evening/weekend programs available. *Faculty:* 51 full-time (12 women), 74 part-time/adjunct (26 women). *Students:* 77 full-time (49 women), 14 part-time (8 women); includes 38 minority (4 African Americans, 1 American Indian/Alaska Native, 24 Asian Americans or Pacific Islanders, 9 Hispanic Americans), 17 international. 93 applicants, 84% accepted, 37 enrolled. In 2009, 34 master's awarded. *Degree requirements:* For master's, residency placement. *Entrance requirements:* For master's, GRE or GMAT. Additional exam requirements/recommendations for international students: Required—TOEFL (minimum score 600 paper-based; 250 computer-based; 100 iBT). *Application deadline:* For fall admission, 12/15 priority date for domestic and international students; for spring admission, 11/1 for domestic and international students. Applications are processed on a rolling basis. Application fee: $85. Electronic applications accepted. *Expenses:* Tuition: Full-time $25,980; part-time $1315 per unit. Required fees: $554. One-time fee: $35 full-time. Full-time tuition and fees vary according to degree level and program. *Financial support:* In 2009–10, 27 students received support, including 1 research assistantship with full tuition reimbursement available (averaging $4,783 per year); scholarships/grants and tuition waivers (full and partial) also available. Financial award application deadline: 12/15. *Faculty research:* Health administration, health management and policy, health care economics and financing, health care access, community health, healthy communities. Total annual research expenditures: $5 million. *Unit head:* Dr. Michael B. Nichol, Director, 213-740-0550, Fax: 213-740-7573, E-mail: mnichol@usc.edu. *Application contact:* Marisol R. Gonzalez, Director of Recruitment and Admission, 213-740-0550, Fax: 213-740-7573, E-mail: marisolr@usc.edu.

University of Southern Indiana, Graduate Studies, College of Nursing and Health Professions, Program in Health Administration, Evansville, IN 47712-3590. Offers MHA. Part-time programs available. Postbaccalaureate distance learning degree programs offered (minimal on-campus study). *Faculty:* 1 full-time (0 women). *Students:* 33 part-time (21 women); includes 2 minority (1 African American, 1 Asian American or Pacific Islander). Average age 31. 13 applicants, 100% accepted, 13 enrolled. In 2009, 8 master's awarded. *Entrance requirements:* For master's, GRE or GMAT, minimum GPA of 3.0. Additional exam requirements/recommendations for international students: Required—TOEFL (minimum score 550 paper-based; 213 computer-based; 79 iBT), IELTS (minimum score 6). *Application deadline:* For fall admission, 6/1 for domestic students, 1/1 priority date for international students. Applications are processed on a rolling basis. Application fee: $25. Electronic applications accepted. *Expenses:* Tuition, state resident: full-time $4592; part-time $255 per credit hour. Tuition, nonresident: full-time $9060; part-time $503 per credit hour. Required fees: $220; $22.75 per term. Tuition and fees vary according to course load and reciprocity agreements. *Financial support:* In 2009–10, 16 students received support. Federal Work-Study, scholarships/grants, tuition waivers (full and partial), and unspecified assistantships available. Financial award application deadline: 3/1; financial award applicants required to submit FAFSA. *Unit head:* Dr. Kevin Valadares, Director, 812-461-5277, E-mail: kvaladar@usi.edu. *Application contact:* Dr. Peggy F. Harrel, Director, Graduate Studies, 812-465-7015, Fax: 812-464-1956, E-mail: pharrel@usi.edu.

University of Southern Maine, Edmund S. Muskie School of Public Service, Program in Health Policy and Management, Portland, ME 04104-9300. Offers MS, Certificate, JD/MS. *Accreditation:* CAHME. Part-time and evening/weekend programs available. Postbaccalaureate distance learning degree programs offered (minimal on-campus study). *Degree requirements:* For master's, thesis, capstone project, field experience. *Entrance requirements:* For master's, GRE General Test. Additional exam requirements/recommendations for international students: Required—TOEFL. Electronic applications accepted. *Faculty research:* Health care, child welfare, social services, aging, substance abuse, health policy.

University of Southern Mississippi, Graduate School, College of Health, Department of Community Health Sciences, Hattiesburg, MS 39406-0001. Offers epidemiology and biostatistics (MPH); health education (MPH); health policy/administration (MPH); occupational/environmental health (MPH); public health nutrition (MPH). *Accreditation:* CEPH. Part-time and evening/weekend programs available. *Faculty:* 8 full-time (4 women), 1 part-time/adjunct (0 women). *Students:* 92 full-time (59 women), 20 part-time (14 women); includes 40 minority (36 African Americans, 1 Asian American or Pacific Islander, 3 Hispanic Americans), 13 international. Average age 32. 90 applicants, 73% accepted, 47 enrolled. In 2009, 4 master's awarded. *Degree requirements:* For master's, comprehensive exam, thesis (for some programs). *Entrance requirements:* For master's, GRE General Test, minimum GPA of 2.75 in last 60 hours. Additional exam requirements/recommendations for international students: Required—TOEFL. *Application deadline:* For fall admission, 3/1 for domestic and international students. Applications are processed on a rolling basis. Application fee: $35. *Expenses:* Tuition, state resident: full-time $5096; part-time $284 per hour. Tuition, nonresident: full-time $13,052; part-time $726 per hour. Required fees: $402. Tuition and fees vary according to course level and course load. *Financial support:* In 2009–10, 5 research assistantships with full tuition reimbursements (averaging $7,000 per year), 1 teaching assistantship with full tuition reimbursement (averaging $8,263 per year) were awarded; career-related internships or fieldwork and Federal Work-Study also available. Financial award application deadline: 3/15; financial award applicants required to submit FAFSA. *Faculty research:* Rural health care delivery, school health, nutrition of pregnant teens, risk factor reduction, sexually transmitted diseases. *Unit head:* Dr. James McGuire, Chair, 601-266-5437, Fax: 601-266-5043. *Application contact:* Shonna Breland, Manager of Graduate Admissions, 601-266-6563, Fax: 601-266-5138.

University of South Florida, Graduate School, College of Public Health, Department of Health Policy and Management, Tampa, FL 33620-9951. Offers MHA, MPH, MSPH, PhD. Part-time and evening/weekend programs available. *Faculty:* 5 full-time (2 women), 5 part-time/adjunct (1 woman). *Students:* 52 full-time (39 women), 51 part-time (38 women); includes 39 minority (19 African Americans, 8 Asian Americans or Pacific Islanders, 12 Hispanic Americans), 15 international. Average age 31. 130 applicants, 56% accepted, 26 enrolled. In 2009, 24 master's awarded. *Degree requirements:* For master's, comprehensive exam, thesis (for some programs); for doctorate, comprehensive exam, thesis/dissertation. *Entrance requirements:* For master's, GRE General Test or GMAT, minimum GPA of 3.0 in upper-level course work, 3 professional letters of recommendation, resume/curriculum vitae; for doctorate, GRE General Test, minimum GPA of 3.0 in upper-level course work, goal statement letter, three professional letters of recommendation, resume/curriculum vitae, writing sample. Additional exam requirements/recommendations for international students: Required—TOEFL (minimum score 550 paper-based; 213 computer-based; 79 iBT). *Application deadline:* For fall admission, 6/1 for domestic students, 1/2 for international students; for spring admission, 10/15 for domestic students, 7/1 for international students. Applications are processed on a rolling basis. Application fee: $30. Electronic applications accepted. *Financial support:* In 2009–10, 3 fellowships with full tuition reimbursements (averaging $6,964 per year), 5 research assistantships with full and partial tuition reimbursements (averaging $2,432 per year), 4 teaching assistantships (averaging $3,680 per year) were awarded; career-related internships or fieldwork, Federal Work-Study, institutionally sponsored loans, scholarships/grants, traineeships, and unspecified assistantships also available. Support available to part-time students. Financial award applicants required to submit FAFSA. *Faculty research:* Tracking community health, inpatient care, discharge policies, stroke education, leadership practices. Total annual research expenditures: $13,882. *Unit head:* Dr. Barbara L. Orban, Chairperson, 813-974-7701, Fax: 813-974-6741. *Application contact:* Michelle Hodge, Academic Advisor, 813-974-6665, Fax: 813-974-8121, E-mail: mhodge1@health.usf.edu.

The University of Tennessee, Graduate School, College of Education, Health and Human Sciences, Program in Public Health, Knoxville, TN 37996. Offers community health education (MPH); gerontology (MPH); health planning/administration (MPH); MS/MPH. *Accreditation:* CEPH. *Degree requirements:* For master's, thesis optional. *Entrance requirements:* For master's, minimum GPA of 2.7. Additional exam requirements/recommendations for international students: Required—TOEFL. Electronic applications accepted. *Expenses:* Tuition, state resident: full-time $6826; part-time $380 per semester hour. Tuition, nonresident: full-time $21,844; part-time $1147 per semester hour. Tuition and fees vary according to program.

The University of Texas at Arlington, Graduate School, College of Business, Program in Health Care Administration, Arlington, TX 76019. Offers MS. Part-time and evening/weekend programs available. *Students:* 8 full-time (6 women), 147 part-time (86 women); includes 79 minority (35 African Americans, 22 Asian Americans or Pacific Islanders, 22 Hispanic Americans), 17 international. 81 applicants, 94% accepted, 43 enrolled. In 2009, 62 master's awarded. *Degree requirements:* For master's, thesis optional. *Entrance requirements:* For master's, GRE General Test or GMAT, minimum GPA of 3.0. Additional exam requirements/recommendations for international students: Required—TOEFL (minimum score 550 paper-based; 213 computer-based; 79 iBT). *Application deadline:* For fall admission, 6/5 for domestic students, 4/1 for international students; for spring admission, 10/15 for domestic students, 8/1 for international students. Application fee: $35 ($50 for international students). *Financial support:* In 2009–10, 1 fellowship (averaging $1,000 per year) was awarded. Financial award application deadline: 6/1; financial award applicants required to submit FAFSA. *Unit head:* Dr. David Gray, Associate Dean, 817-272-2881, Fax: 817-272-2073, E-mail: gray@uta.edu. *Application contact:* Demetria Wilhiste, Program Director, 817-272-0698, Fax: 817-272-5799, E-mail: demetria@uta.edu.

The University of Texas at Dallas, School of Management, Program in Business Administration, Richardson, TX 75080. Offers cohort (MBA); executive business administration (EMBA); global leadership (EMBA); global online (MBA); healthcare management (EMBA); professional business administration (MBA); project management (EMBA). *Accreditation:* AACSB. Part-time and evening/weekend programs available. Postbaccalaureate distance learning degree programs offered. *Faculty:* 79 full-time (13 women), 29 part-time/adjunct (9 women). *Students:* 314 full-time (104 women), 857 part-time (244 women); includes 377 minority (52 African Americans, 5 American Indian/Alaska Native, 231 Asian Americans or Pacific Islanders, 89 Hispanic Americans), 211 international. Average age 32. 712 applicants, 48% accepted, 317 enrolled. In 2009, 409 master's awarded. *Degree requirements:* For master's, thesis optional. *Entrance requirements:* For master's, GMAT, 10 years of business experience (EMBA), minimum GPA of 3.0. Additional exam requirements/recommendations for international students: Required—TOEFL (minimum score 550 paper-based; 213 computer-based). *Application deadline:* For fall admission, 7/15 for domestic students, 5/1 priority date for international students; for spring admission, 11/15 for domestic students, 9/1 priority date for international students. Applications are processed on a rolling basis. Application fee: $50 ($100 for international students). Electronic applications accepted. *Expenses:* Contact institution. *Financial support:* In 2009–10, 5 research assistantships with full tuition reimbursements (averaging $10,692 per year), 23 teaching assistantships with full tuition reimbursements (averaging $10,050 per year) were awarded; fellowships, career-related internships or fieldwork, Federal Work-Study, institutionally sponsored loans, scholarships/grants, and unspecified assistantships also available. Support available to part-time students. Financial award application deadline: 4/30; financial award applicants required to submit FAFSA. *Faculty research:* Production scheduling, trade and finance, organizational decision making, life/work planning. *Unit head:* Lisa Shatz, Director, 972-883-6191, E-mail: mba@utdallas.edu. *Application contact:* James Parker, Assistant Director, 972-883-5842, E-mail: jparker@utdallas.edu.

The University of Texas at Dallas, School of Management, Program in Information Systems and Operations Management, Richardson, TX 75080. Offers information technology management (MS), including enterprise systems, health care systems, information security; supply chain management (MS). Part-time and evening/weekend programs available. *Faculty:* 23 full-time (1 woman), 1 (woman) part-time/adjunct. *Students:* 153 full-time (54 women), 129 part-time (51 women); includes 36 minority (4 African Americans, 28 Asian Americans or Pacific Islanders, 4 Hispanic Americans), 212 international. Average age 27. 352 applicants, 74% accepted, 105 enrolled. In 2009, 67 master's awarded. *Degree requirements:* For master's, thesis optional. *Entrance requirements:* For master's, GMAT. Additional exam requirements/recommendations for international students: Required—TOEFL (minimum score 550 paper-based; 213 computer-based). *Application deadline:* For fall admission, 7/15 for domestic students, 5/1 priority date for international students; for spring admission, 11/15 for domestic students, 9/1 priority date for international students. Applications are processed on a rolling basis. Application fee: $50 ($100 for international students). Electronic applications accepted. *Expenses:* Tuition, state resident: full-time $11,068; part-time $461 per credit hour. Tuition, nonresident: full-time $21,178; part-time $882 per credit hour. Tuition and fees vary according to course load. *Financial support:* In 2009–10, 7 research assistantships with full tuition reimbursements (averaging $10,933 per year), 5 teaching assistantships with full tuition reimbursements (averaging $10,050 per year) were awarded; career-related internships or fieldwork, Federal Work-Study, institutionally sponsored loans, scholarships/grants, and unspecified assistantships also available. Support available to part-time students. Financial award application deadline: 4/30; financial award applicants required to submit FAFSA. *Faculty research:* Technology marketing, measuring information work productivity, electronic commerce, decision support systems, data quality. *Unit head:* Dr. Mark Thouin, Director, 972-883-4011, E-mail: mark.thouin@utdallas.edu. *Application contact:* James Parker, Assistant Director, 972-883-5842, E-mail: jparker@utdallas.edu.

The University of Texas at Dallas, School of Management, Program in Management and Administrative Sciences, Richardson, TX 75080. Offers e-commerce (MS); health care management (MS); innovation and entrepreneurship (MS); organizations and strategy (MS). *Accreditation:* AACSB. Part-time and evening/weekend programs available. *Faculty:* 12 full-time (3 women), 13 part-time/adjunct (3 women). *Students:* 46 full-time (29 women), 103 part-time (47 women); includes 53 minority (12 African Americans, 34 Asian Americans or Pacific Islanders, 7 Hispanic Americans), 32 international. Average age 33. 156 applicants, 66% accepted, 47 enrolled. In 2009, 83 master's awarded. *Degree requirements:* For master's, thesis optional. *Entrance requirements:* For master's, GMAT. Additional exam requirements/recommendations for international students: Required—TOEFL (minimum score 550 paper-based; 213 computer-based). *Application deadline:* For fall admission, 7/15 for domestic students, 5/1 priority date for international students; for spring admission, 11/15 for domestic students, 9/1 priority date for international students. Applications are processed on a rolling basis. Application fee: $50 ($100 for international students). Electronic applications accepted. *Expenses:* Tuition, state resident: full-time $11,068; part-time $461 per credit hour. Tuition, nonresident: full-time $21,178; part-time $882 per credit hour. Tuition and fees vary according to course load. *Financial support:* In 2009–10, 25 teaching assistantships with full tuition reimbursements (averaging $14,400 per year) were awarded; fellowships, research assistantships, career-related internships or fieldwork, Federal Work-Study, institutionally sponsored loans, scholarships/grants, and unspecified assistantships also available. Support available to part-time students. Financial award application deadline: 4/30; financial award applicants required to submit FAFSA. *Faculty research:* Integrated and detailed knowledge of functional areas of management, analytical tools for effective appraisal and decision making. *Unit head:* Dr. Doug Eckel, Assistant Dean, 972-883-5923, E-mail: dogb.eckel@utdallas.edu. *Application contact:* James Parker, Assistant Director, 972-883-5842, E-mail: jparker@utdallas.edu.

The University of Texas at El Paso, Graduate School, School of Nursing, El Paso, TX 79968-0001. Offers evidence-based practice (Certificate); family nurse practitioner (MSN); health care leadership and management (Certificate); interdisciplinary health sciences (PhD); nurse clinical specialist (MSN); nursing (Post-Master's Certificate); nursing systems management (MSN). *Accreditation:* AACN. *Students:* 153 (124 women); includes 100 minority (11 African Americans, 1 American Indian/Alaska Native, 6 Asian Americans or Pacific Islanders, 82 Hispanic Americans), 5 international. Average age 34. 91 applicants, 49% accepted. In 2009, 33 master's awarded. *Degree requirements:* For master's, thesis optional; for doctorate, thesis/dissertation. *Entrance requirements:* For master's, GRE, minimum GPA of 3.0, course

Health Services Management and Hospital Administration

The University of Texas at El Paso (continued)

work in statistics, resume; for doctorate, GRE, letters of reference, relevant personal/professional experience, master's degree in health. Additional exam requirements/recommendations for international students: Required—TOEFL; Recommended—IELTS. *Application deadline:* For fall admission, 8/1 for domestic students, 3/1 for international students; for spring admission, 11/1 for domestic students, 9/1 for international students. Applications are processed on a rolling basis. Application fee: $45 ($80 for international students). Electronic applications accepted. *Financial support:* In 2009–10, research assistantships with partial tuition reimbursements (averaging $18,825 per year), teaching assistantships with partial tuition reimbursements (averaging $18,000 per year) were awarded; fellowships with partial tuition reimbursements, institutionally sponsored loans, scholarships/grants, health care benefits, tuition waivers (partial), and unspecified assistantships also available. Support available to part-time students. Financial award application deadline: 3/15; financial award applicants required to submit FAFSA. *Unit head:* Dr. Elias Provencio-Vasquez, Dean, 915-747-7273, Fax: 915-747-8266, E-mail: eprovenciovasquez@utep.edu. *Application contact:* Dr. Patricia D. Witherspoon, Dean of the Graduate School, 915-747-5491, Fax: 915-747-5788, E-mail: withersp@utep.edu.

The University of Texas at Tyler, College of Business and Technology, School of Business Administration, Tyler, TX 75799-0001. Offers business administration (MBA); general management (MBA); health care (MBA). Part-time programs available. Postbaccalaureate distance learning degree programs offered (no on-campus study). *Faculty:* 14 full-time (8 women). *Students:* 33 full-time (13 women), 116 part-time (44 women); includes 25 minority (12 African Americans, 2 American Indian/Alaska Native, 3 Asian Americans or Pacific Islanders, 8 Hispanic Americans), 7 international. Average age 29. 73 applicants, 96% accepted, 35 enrolled. In 2009, 37 master's awarded. *Entrance requirements:* Additional exam requirements/recommendations for international students: Required—TOEFL (minimum score 550 paper-based; 79 computer-based). *Application deadline:* For fall admission, 8/17 priority date for domestic students, 7/1 priority date for international students; for spring admission, 12/21 priority date for domestic students, 11/1 priority date for international students. Application fee: $25 ($50 for international students). *Expenses:* Tuition, state resident: part-time $665 per semester hour. Tuition, nonresident: part-time $942 per semester hour. Part-time tuition and fees vary according to degree level and program. *Faculty research:* General business, inventory control, institutional markets, service marketing, product distribution, accounting fraud, financial reporting and recognition. *Unit head:* Dr. Mary Fischer, Associate Dean/Interim Chair/Professor of Accounting, 903-566-7433, Fax: 903-566-7372. *Application contact:* Dr. Mary Fischer.

University of the Incarnate Word, School of Graduate Studies and Research, H-E-B School of Business and Administration, Program in Health Administration, San Antonio, TX 78209-6397. Offers MHA. *Expenses:* Tuition: Full-time $12,150; part-time $675 per credit hour. Required fees: $83 per credit hour. *Unit head:* Dr. Dan Dominguez, Director, 210-829-3180, E-mail: domingue@uiwtx.edu. *Application contact:* Andrea Cyterski-Acosta, Dean of Enrollment, 210-829-6005, Fax: 210-829-3921, E-mail: admis@uiwtx.edu.

University of the Incarnate Word, School of Graduate Studies and Research, H-E-B School of Business and Administration, Programs in Administration, San Antonio, TX 78209-6397. Offers adult education (MAA); applied administration (MAA); communication arts (MAA); healthcare administration (MAA); instructional technology (MAA); international business (Certificate); nutrition (MAA); organizational development (MAA, Certificate); project management (Certificate); sports management (MAA). Part-time and evening/weekend programs available. Postbaccalaureate distance learning degree programs offered (no on-campus study). *Students:* 30 full-time (17 women), 163 part-time (114 women); includes 128 minority (18 African Americans, 3 Asian Americans or Pacific Islanders, 107 Hispanic Americans), 8 international. Average age 35. In 2009, 68 master's awarded. *Degree requirements:* For master's, capstone. *Entrance requirements:* For master's, GRE, GMAT, undergraduate degree, minimum GPA of 2.5. Additional exam requirements/recommendations for international students: Required—TOEFL (minimum score 560 paper-based; 220 computer-based; 83 iBT). *Application deadline:* Applications are processed on a rolling basis. Application fee: $20. Electronic applications accepted. *Expenses:* Tuition: Full-time $12,150; part-time $675 per credit hour. Required fees: $83 per credit hour. *Financial support:* Federal Work-Study and scholarships/grants available. Financial award applicants required to submit FAFSA. *Unit head:* Dr. Daniel Dominguez, MAA Director, 210-829-3180, Fax: 210-805-3564, E-mail: domingue@uiwtx.edu. *Application contact:* Andrea Cyterski-Acosta, Dean of Enrollment, 210-829-6005, Fax: 210-829-3921, E-mail: admis@uiwtx.edu.

University of the Sciences in Philadelphia, College of Graduate Studies, Mayes College of Healthcare Business and Policy, Program in Public Health, Philadelphia, PA 19104-4495. Offers MPH. *Expenses:* Tuition: Full-time $22,230; part-time $1235 per credit. Tuition and fees vary according to program.

University of the Sciences in Philadelphia, College of Graduate Studies, Program in Health Policy and Public Health, Philadelphia, PA 19104-4495. Offers health policy (MPH, MS); public health (MPH). Part-time and evening/weekend programs available. *Degree requirements:* For doctorate, comprehensive exam, thesis/dissertation. *Entrance requirements:* For master's and doctorate, GRE General Test. Additional exam requirements/recommendations for international students: Required—TOEFL, TWE. *Expenses:* Contact institution. *Faculty research:* Managed care, pharmacoeconomics, health law and regulation, rehabilitation, genetic technologies.

The University of Toledo, College of Graduate Studies, College of Arts and Sciences, Department of Political Science and Public Administration, Program in Public Administration, Toledo, OH 43606-3390. Offers health care policy (MPA); healthcare policy (Certificate); municipal administration (MPA, Certificate); public administration (MPA). *Accreditation:* NASPAA. *Degree requirements:* For master's, internship. *Entrance requirements:* For master's, GRE General Test, minimum GPA of 3.0. Electronic applications accepted. *Faculty research:* Economic development, health administration, personnel, budgeting, urban administration.

University of Utah, Graduate School, David Eccles School of Business, Program in Healthcare Administration, Salt Lake City, UT 84112-1107. Offers MS. Part-time and evening/weekend programs available. *Students:* 3 full-time (2 women). Average age 32. 4 applicants, 75% accepted, 2 enrolled. *Entrance requirements:* For master's, GMAT, statistics course with minimum B grade; minimum undergraduate GPA of 3.0. Additional exam requirements/recommendations for international students: Required—TOEFL (minimum score 600 paper-based; 250 computer-based; 100 iBT), IELTS (minimum score 7). *Application deadline:* For fall admission, 2/15 priority date for domestic and international students. Applications are processed on a rolling basis. Application fee: $55. Electronic applications accepted. *Expenses:* Tuition, state resident: full-time $4004; part-time $1674 per semester. Tuition, nonresident: full-time $14,134; part-time $5915 per semester. Required fees: $324 per semester. Tuition and fees vary according to course load, degree level and program. *Financial support:* Scholarships/grants and unspecified assistantships available. Financial award application deadline: 2/15; financial award applicants required to submit FAFSA. *Unit head:* Dr. Don Wardell, 801-581-8774, Fax: 801-581-3666, E-mail: don.wardell@utah.edu. *Application contact:* Andrea Chmelik, Admissions Coordinator, 801-585-1719, Fax: 801-587-3666, E-mail: andrea.chmelik@business.utah.edu.

University of Virginia, School of Medicine, Department of Public Health Sciences, Charlottesville, VA 22903. Offers clinical research (MS), including clinical investigation and patient-oriented research, informatics in medicine; public health (MPH). Part-time programs available. *Faculty:* 30 full-time (15 women), 3 part-time/adjunct (1 woman). *Students:* 22 full-time (13 women), 20 part-time (13 women); includes 11 minority (3 African Americans, 5 Asian Americans or Pacific Islanders, 3 Hispanic Americans). Average age 32. 89 applicants, 48% accepted, 26 enrolled. In 2009, 27 master's awarded. *Entrance requirements:* For master's, GRE General Test or MCAT. Additional exam requirements/recommendations for international students: Required—TOEFL. *Application deadline:* Applications are processed on a rolling basis. Application fee: $60. Electronic applications accepted. *Financial support:* Career-related internships or fieldwork available. Financial award applicants required to submit FAFSA. *Unit head:* Dr. William A. Knaus, Chair, 434-924-8430, Fax: 434-924-8437. *Application contact:* Tracey L. Brookman, Academic Programs Administrator, 434-924-8430, Fax: 434-924-8437, E-mail: ms-hes@virginia.edu.

University of Washington, Graduate School, School of Public Health, Department of Health Services, Programs in Health Services Administration, Seattle, WA 98195. Offers EMHA, MHA, MHA/MBA, MHA/MD, MHA/MPA. *Accreditation:* CAHME. *Faculty:* 18 full-time (6 women), 2 part-time/adjunct (both women). *Students:* 81 full-time (39 women), 33 part-time (24 women); includes 39 minority (6 African Americans, 1 American Indian/Alaska Native, 24 Asian Americans or Pacific Islanders, 8 Hispanic Americans), 3 international. Average age 34. 156 applicants, 57% accepted, 68 enrolled. In 2009, 46 master's awarded. *Degree requirements:* For master's, capstone project. *Entrance requirements:* For master's, GRE General Test, GMAT (preferred), minimum GPA of 3.0, program-specified tutorial in accounting, economics, and statistics. Additional exam requirements/recommendations for international students: Required—TOEFL (minimum score 580 paper-based; 237 computer-based; 70 iBT). *Application deadline:* For fall admission, 1/15 for domestic students, 11/1 for international students. Application fee: $50. Electronic applications accepted. *Financial support:* In 2009–10, 75 students received support, including 1 research assistantship (averaging $15,720 per year), 5 teaching assistantships with partial tuition reimbursements available (averaging $18,300 per year); scholarships/grants and tuition waivers (partial) also available. Financial award application deadline: 2/28; financial award applicants required to submit FAFSA. *Faculty research:* Organizational analysis and behavior, quality assurance, cost and outcomes of health care, management and leadership development, strategic management, health law, health policy. *Unit head:* William E. Welton, Director, 206-543-8778, Fax: 206-543-3964, E-mail: wwelton@u.washington.edu. *Application contact:* Karen L. Wetterhahn, Program Coordinator, 206-543-8878, Fax: 206-543-3964, E-mail: karenlw@u.washington.edu.

The University of Western Ontario, Richard Ivey School of Business, London, ON N6A 3K7, Canada. Offers business (EMBA, PhD); corporate strategy and leadership elective (MBA); entrepreneurship elective (MBA); finance elective (MBA); health sector stream (MBA); international management elective (MBA); marketing elective (MBA); JD/MBA. *Faculty:* 61 full-time (13 women). *Students:* 164 full-time (50 women). Average age 29. In 2009, 167 master's awarded. *Degree requirements:* For master's, thesis (for some programs); for doctorate, thesis/dissertation. *Entrance requirements:* For master's, GMAT, 2 years of full-time work experience, interview. Additional exam requirements/recommendations for international students: Required—TOEFL (minimum score 100 computer-based; 100 iBT), IELTS (minimum score 6), IELTS or TOEFL. *Application deadline:* For fall admission, 10/12 for domestic students, 8/16 for international students; for winter admission, 12/16 for domestic students, 10/12 for international students; for spring admission, 1/10 priority date for domestic students, 12/16 for international students. Applications are processed on a rolling basis. Application fee: $150 Canadian dollars. Electronic applications accepted. *Financial support:* Scholarships/grants and health care benefits available. Financial award application deadline: 1/10. *Faculty research:* Strategy, organizational behavior, international business, finance, operations management. *Unit head:* Carol Stephenson, Dean, 519-661-3285, Fax: 519-661-4126, E-mail: cstephenson@ivey.ca. *Application contact:* Niki da Silva, Director, MBA Program Services, 519-661-3419, Fax: 519-661-3431, E-mail: ndasilva@ivey.ca.

University of West Georgia, Graduate School, School of Nursing, Carrollton, GA 30118. Offers health systems leadership (Post-Master's Certificate); nursing (MSN); nursing education (Post-Master's Certificate). *Accreditation:* AACN. Part-time programs available. *Faculty:* 23 full-time (all women), 8 part-time/adjunct (all women). *Students:* 17 full-time (all women), 12 part-time (all women); includes 4 minority (all African Americans), 5 international. Average age 36. 30 applicants, 70% accepted, 10 enrolled. In 2009, 11 master's awarded. *Degree requirements:* For master's, comprehensive exam, thesis or alternative. *Entrance requirements:* For master's, GRE or MAT, BSN, Georgia RN license, minimum GPA of 3.0 for upper-division nursing courses, completion of basic undergraduate statistics course. *Application deadline:* For fall admission, 7/17 for domestic students; for spring admission, 11/20 for domestic students. Applications are processed on a rolling basis. Application fee: $30. Electronic applications accepted. *Expenses:* Tuition, state resident: full-time $2952; part-time $164 per semester hour. Tuition, nonresident: full-time $11,808; part-time $656 per semester hour. Required fees: $42.90 per semester hour. $307 per semester. Tuition and fees vary according to course load. *Financial support:* In 2009–10, 1 research assistantship with full tuition reimbursement (averaging $6,000 per year) was awarded. Financial award application deadline: 7/1; financial award applicants required to submit FAFSA. *Faculty research:* Caring in nursing education, pain assessment in older adults, pain outcomes. *Unit head:* Dr. Kathryn Mary Grams, Dean, 678-839-6552, Fax: 678-839-6553, E-mail: kgrams@westga.edu. *Application contact:* Dr. Charles W. Clark, Dean, 678-839-6508, E-mail: cclark@westga.edu.

University of Wisconsin–Oshkosh, The Office of Graduate Studies, College of Letters and Science, Department of Public Administration, Oshkosh, WI 54901. Offers general agency (MPA); health care (MPA). Part-time and evening/weekend programs available. *Degree requirements:* For master's, thesis or alternative. *Entrance requirements:* For master's, public service-related experience, resume, sample of written work. Additional exam requirements/recommendations for international students: Required—TOEFL (minimum score 550 paper-based; 213 computer-based; 79 iBT). Electronic applications accepted. *Faculty research:* Drug policy, local government state revenues and expenditures, health care regulation.

Utica College, Program in Health Care Administration, Utica, NY 13502-4892. Offers MS. *Students:* 31 part-time (26 women); includes 3 minority (1 African American, 1 American Indian/Alaska Native, 1 Hispanic American). Average age 34. *Expenses:* Tuition: Full-time $24,880; part-time $670 per credit hour. Required fees: $50; $50 per course. Tuition and fees vary according to course load and program. *Unit head:* Dr. Dana Hart, Head, 315-792-3375, E-mail: dhart@utica.edu. *Application contact:* John D. Rowe, Director of Graduate Admissions, 315-792-3824, Fax: 315-792-3003, E-mail: jrowe@utica.edu.

Villanova University, College of Nursing, Villanova, PA 19085-1699. Offers adult nurse practitioner (MSN, Post Master's Certificate); family nurse practitioner (MSN, Post Master's Certificate); health care administration (MSN); nurse anesthetist (MSN, Post Master's Certificate); nursing (PhD); nursing education (MSN, Post Master's Certificate); pediatric nurse practitioner (MSN, Post Master's Certificate). *Accreditation:* AACN; AANA/CANAEP. Part-time programs available. Postbaccalaureate distance learning degree programs offered (minimal on-campus study). *Faculty:* 15 full-time (all women), 3 part-time/adjunct (2 women). *Students:* 58 full-time (53 women), 188 part-time (164 women); includes 29 minority (13 African Americans, 1 American Indian/Alaska Native, 13 Asian Americans or Pacific Islanders, 2 Hispanic Americans), 3 international. Average age 33. 171 applicants, 70% accepted, 89 enrolled. In 2009, 32 master's, 1 doctorate awarded. *Degree requirements:* For master's, independent study project; for doctorate, comprehensive exam, thesis/dissertation. *Entrance requirements:* For master's, GRE or MAT, BSN, 1 year of recent nursing experience, physical assessment, course work in statistics; for doctorate, GRE, MSN. Additional exam requirements/recommendations for international students: Required—TOEFL. *Application deadline:* For fall admission, 7/1 priority date for domestic students, 7/1 for international students; for spring admission, 11/1 priority date for domestic students, 11/1 for international students. Applications are processed on a rolling basis. Application fee: $50. *Expenses:* Contact institution. *Financial support:* In 2009–10, 53 students received support, including 5 teaching assistantships with full tuition reimbursements available (averaging $13,100 per year); institutionally sponsored loans, scholarships/grants, traineeships, tuition waivers (full), and unspecified assistantships also available. Financial award application deadline: 3/1; financial award applicants required to submit FAFSA. *Faculty research:* Genetics, ethics, cognitive development of students, women with disabilities, nursing leadership. *Unit head:* Dr. Marguerite K. Schlag, Assistant Dean and Director, Graduate Program, 610-519-4907, Fax: 610-519-7650, E-mail: marguerite.schlag@villanova.edu. *Application contact:* Dean, Graduate School of Liberal Arts and Sciences.

Virginia Commonwealth University, Graduate School, School of Allied Health Professions, Department of Health Administration, Doctoral Program in Health Related Sciences, Richmond, VA 23284-9005. Offers clinical laboratory sciences (PhD); gerontology (PhD); health administration (PhD); nurse anesthesia (PhD); occupational therapy (PhD); physical therapy (PhD); radiation sciences (PhD); rehabilitation leadership (PhD).

Virginia Commonwealth University, Graduate School, School of Allied Health Professions, Department of Health Administration, Doctoral Program in Health Services Organization and Research, Richmond, VA 23284-9005. Offers PhD. *Degree requirements:* For doctorate, thesis/dissertation, residency. *Entrance requirements:* For doctorate, GMAT or GRE General Test.

Virginia Commonwealth University, Graduate School, School of Allied Health Professions, Department of Health Administration, Master's Program in Health Administration, Richmond, VA 23284-9005. Offers MHA, JD/MHA, MD/MHA. *Accreditation:* CAHME. *Degree requirements:* For master's, residency. *Entrance requirements:* For master's, GMAT or GRE General Test, course work in accounting, economics, and statistics.

Virginia Commonwealth University, Graduate School, School of Allied Health Professions, Department of Health Administration, Professional Online Master's Program in Health Administration, Richmond, VA 23284-9005. Offers MSHA. *Accreditation:* CAHME. *Degree requirements:* For master's, residency. *Entrance requirements:* For master's, GMAT or GRE General Test.

Virginia International University, Business Programs Department, Fairfax, VA 22030. Offers accounting (MBA); executive management (Graduate Certificate); global logistics (MBA); health care management (MBA); human resources management (MBA); international business management (MBA); international finance (MBA); marketing management (MBA). Part-time programs available. *Faculty:* 12 part-time/adjunct (1 woman). *Students:* 138 full-time (63 women), 7 part-time (5 women); includes 7 minority (1 African American, 5 Asian Americans or Pacific Islanders, 1 Hispanic American), 136 international. Average age 27. 331 applicants, 31% accepted, 40 enrolled. In 2009, 42 master's awarded. *Entrance requirements:* For master's and Graduate Certificate, bachelor's degree. Additional exam requirements/recommendations for international students: Required—TOEFL (minimum score 550 paper-based; 213 computer-based; 80 iBT), IELTS (minimum score 6). *Application deadline:* For fall admission, 7/31 for domestic students, 7/3 for international students; for spring admission, 12/18 for domestic students, 11/20 for international students. Applications are processed on a rolling basis. Application fee: $100. Electronic applications accepted. *Expenses:* Tuition: Full-time $10,044; part-time $569 per credit. One-time fee: $75. Tuition and fees vary according to degree level. *Financial support:* In 2009–10, 10 students received support. Scholarships/grants available. Financial award application deadline: 7/1. *Unit head:* Dr. Gail Whitaker, Chair, 703-591-7042 Ext. 346, Fax: 703-591-7046, E-mail: gwhitaker@viu.edu. *Application contact:* Emily L. Kraus, Director of Admissions, 703-591-7042 Ext. 309, Fax: 703-591-7048, E-mail: admissions@viu.edu.

Wagner College, Division of Graduate Studies, Department of Business Administration, Program in Health Care Administration, Staten Island, NY 10301-4495. Offers MBA. *Degree requirements:* For master's, thesis optional. *Entrance requirements:* For master's, GMAT, minimum GPA of 2.6. Additional exam requirements/recommendations for international students: Required—TOEFL (minimum score 550 paper-based; 217 computer-based). *Expenses:* Tuition: Full-time $15,570; part-time $865 per credit. Required fees: $2.

Wake Forest University, Babcock Graduate School of Management, Full-time MBA Program, Winston-Salem, NC 27106. Offers consulting/general management (MBA); entrepreneurship (MBA); finance (MBA); health (MBA); marketing (MBA); operations management (MBA); JD/MBA; MBA/MSA; MD/MBA. *Accreditation:* AACSB. *Faculty:* 62 full-time (13 women), 36 part-time/adjunct (14 women). *Students:* 144 full-time (36 women); includes 17 minority (8 African Americans, 9 Asian Americans or Pacific Islanders), 22 international. Average age 28. In 2009, 81 master's awarded. *Entrance requirements:* For master's, GMAT or GRE, letters of recommendation, official transcripts, current resume or curriculum vitae, 2 years of work experience with the exception of joint-degree candidates. Additional exam requirements/recommendations for international students: Required—TOEFL (minimum score 600 paper-based; 250 computer-based; 100 iBT), Pearson Test of English (PTE). *Application deadline:* For fall admission, 6/1 for domestic and international students. Applications are processed on a rolling basis. Application fee: $75. Electronic applications accepted. *Expenses:* Contact institution. *Financial support:* In 2009–10, 95 students received support. Career-related internships or fieldwork, scholarships/grants, and unspecified assistantships available. Financial award application deadline: 3/1; financial award applicants required to submit FAFSA. *Faculty research:* The influence of personal relationships on business decision making and management of change; drivers of perceived value and consumer behavior; impact of accounting on auditing, financial, managerial, systems and taxation stakeholders; corporate governance and executive compensation; impact of operations strategies on competitiveness. *Unit head:* Sherry Moss, Director, Full-time MBA Program, 336-758-5422, Fax: 336-758-5830, E-mail: admissions@mba.wfu.edu. *Application contact:* LaKesha Alston, Administrative Assistant, 336-758-5422, Fax: 336-758-5830, E-mail: admissions@mba.wfu.edu.

Walden University, Graduate Programs, School of Health Sciences, Minneapolis, MN 55401. Offers clinical research administration (MS); health informatics (MS); health services (PhD), including community health promotion and education, general program, health management and policy; healthcare administration (MHA); public health (MPH, PhD), including community health promotion and education (PhD), epidemiology (PhD). Part-time and evening/weekend programs available. Postbaccalaureate distance learning degree programs offered (minimal on-campus study). *Faculty:* 14 full-time, 136 part-time/adjunct. *Students:* 2,121 full-time (1,670 women), 724 part-time (568 women); includes 1,370 minority (1,149 African Americans, 20 American Indian/Alaska Native, 95 Asian Americans or Pacific Islanders, 106 Hispanic Americans), 134 international. Average age 40. In 2009, 232 master's, 24 doctorates awarded. *Degree requirements:* For doctorate, thesis/dissertation, residency. *Entrance requirements:* For master's, bachelor's degree or equivalent in related field, minimum GPA of 2.5; for doctorate, master's degree or equivalent in related field; minimum GPA of 3.0; official transcripts; three years of related professional/academic experience (preferred); access to computer and Internet. Additional exam requirements/recommendations for international students: Required—TOEFL (minimum score 550 paper-based; 213 computer-based), IELTS (minimum score 6.5), or Michigan English Language Assessment Battery (minimum score 82). *Application deadline:* Applications are processed on a rolling basis. Application fee: $50. Electronic applications accepted. *Expenses:* Tuition: Full-time $13,665; part-time $560 per credit. Required fees: $1375. Tuition and fees vary according to course load, degree level and program. *Financial support:* In 2009–10, 152 students received support; fellowships, Federal Work-Study, scholarships/grants, unspecified assistantships, and family tuition reduction, active duty/veteran tuition reduction, group tuition reduction, interest-free payment plans available. Support available to part-time students. Financial award applicants required to submit FAFSA. *Unit head:* Dr. Jorg Westermann, Interim Associate Dean, 800-925-3368. *Application contact:* Jennifer Hall, Director of Enrollment, 866-4-WALDEN, E-mail: info@waldenu.edu.

Walden University, Graduate Programs, School of Management, Minneapolis, MN 55401. Offers applied management and decision sciences (PhD), including accounting, engineering management, finance, general applied management and decision sciences, information systems management, knowledge management, leadership and organizational change, learning management, operations research, self-designed program in applied management and design sciences; business information management (MISM); enterprise information security (MISM); entrepreneurship (MBA, DBA); finance (MBA, DBA); global supply chain management (DBA); healthcare management (MBA); healthcare system improvement (MBA); human resource management (MBA); information systems management (DBA); international business (MBA, DBA); IT strategy and governance (MISM); leadership (MBA, MS, DBA), including entrepreneurship (MS), general management (MS), human resources leadership (MS), innovation and technology (MS), leader development (MS), project management (MS), self-designed (MS), sustainable futures (MS); managing global software and service supply chains (MISM); marketing (MBA, DBA); project management (MBA, MS); risk management (MBA); self-designed (MBA, DBA); social impact management (DBA); sustainable futures (MBA); technology (MBA); technology entrepreneurship (DBA). Part-time and evening/weekend programs available. Postbaccalaureate distance learning degree programs offered (minimal on-campus study). *Faculty:* 17 full-time, 211 part-time/adjunct. *Students:* 3,389 full-time (1,774 women), 815 part-time (482 women); includes 1,969 minority (1,640 African Americans, 36 American Indian/Alaska Native, 123 Asian Americans or Pacific Islanders, 170 Hispanic Americans), 95 international. Average age 41. In 2009, 699 master's, 42 doctorates awarded. *Degree requirements:* For doctorate, thesis/dissertation (for some programs), residency. *Entrance requirements:* For master's, bachelor's degree or equivalent in related field; minimum GPA of 2.5; official transcripts; goal statement; access to computer and Internet; for doctorate, master's degree or equivalent in related field; minimum GPA of 3.0; 3 years of related professional/academic experience (preferred). Additional exam requirements/recommendations for international students: Required—TOEFL (minimum score 550 paper-based; 213 computer-based), IELTS (minimum score 6.5), TOEFL, IELTS, or Michigan English Language Assessment Battery (minimum score 82). *Application deadline:* Applications are processed on a rolling basis. Application fee: $50. Electronic applications accepted. *Expenses:* Tuition: Full-time $13,665; part-time $560 per credit. Required fees: $1375. Tuition and fees vary according to course load, degree level and program. *Financial support:* In 2009–10, 466 students received support; fellowships, Federal Work-Study, scholarships/grants, unspecified assistantships, and family tuition reduction, active duty/veteran tuition reduction, group tuition reduction, interest-free payment plans available. Support available to part-time students. Financial award applicants required to submit FAFSA. *Unit head:* William Schulz, Interim Associate Dean, 800-925-3368. *Application contact:* Jennifer Hall, Director of Enrollment, 866-4-WALDEN, E-mail: info@waldenu.edu.

Walden University, Graduate Programs, School of Public Policy and Administration, Minneapolis, MN 55401. Offers government management (Postbaccalaureate Certificate); health policy (MPA); homeland security policy (MPA); interdisciplinary policy studies (MPA); law and public policy (MPA); local government management for sustainable communities (MPA); nonprofit management (Postbaccalaureate Certificate); nonprofit management and leadership (MPA, MS); policy analysis (MPA); public management and leadership (MPA); public policy and administration (MPA, PhD), including criminal justice (PhD), health services (PhD), homeland security policy and coordination (PhD), international nongovernmental organizations (PhD), law and public policy (PhD), local government management for sustainable communities (PhD), nonprofit management and leadership (PhD), public management and leadership (PhD), public policy (PhD), public safety management (PhD), terrorism, mediation, and peace (PhD); terrorism, mediation, and peace (MPA). Part-time and evening/weekend programs available. Postbaccalaureate distance learning degree programs offered (minimal on-campus study). *Faculty:* 7 full-time, 62 part-time/adjunct. *Students:* 1,468 full-time (941 women), 233 part-time (162 women); includes 852 minority (761 African Americans, 9 American Indian/Alaska Native, 19 Asian Americans or Pacific Islanders, 63 Hispanic Americans), 53 international. Average age 40. In 2009, 173 master's, 13 doctorates awarded. *Degree requirements:* For doctorate, thesis/dissertation, residency. *Entrance requirements:* For master's, bachelor's degree or equivalent in related field, minimum GPA of 2.5; for doctorate, master's degree or equivalent in related field; minimum GPA of 3.0; official transcripts; three years of related professional/academic experience (preferred); access to computer and Internet. Additional exam requirements/recommendations for international students: Required—TOEFL (minimum score 550 paper-based; 213 computer-based), IELTS (minimum score 6.5), or Michigan English Language Assessment Battery (minimum score 82). *Application deadline:* Applications are processed on a rolling basis. Application fee: $50. Electronic applications accepted. *Expenses:* Tuition: Full-time $13,665; part-time $560 per credit. Required fees: $1375. Tuition and fees vary according to course load, degree level and program. *Financial support:* In 2009–10, 207 students received support; fellowships with tuition reimbursements available, Federal Work-Study, scholarships/grants, unspecified assistantships, and family tuition reduction, active duty/veteran tuition reduction, group tuition reduction, interest-free payment plans available. Support available to part-time students. Financial award applicants required to submit FAFSA. *Unit head:* Dr. Mark Gordon, Associate Dean, 800-925-3368. *Application contact:* Jennifer Hall, Director of Enrollment, 866-4-WALDEN, E-mail: info@waldenu.edu.

Washington State University, Graduate School, College of Pharmacy, Department of Health Policy and Administration, Pullman, WA 99164. Offers MHPA. Part-time programs available. *Faculty:* 5. *Students:* 20 full-time (8 women), 2 part-time (1 woman), 4 international. 64 applicants, 55% accepted, 14 enrolled. In 2009, 10 master's awarded. *Entrance requirements:* For master's, GMAT, GRE, official copies of all college transcripts, letter of intent and introduction, three letters of recommendation. Additional exam requirements/recommendations for international students: Required—TOEFL or IELTS. *Application deadline:* For fall admission, 1/10 for domestic and international students; for spring admission, 9/1 for domestic and international students. Application fee: $50. *Financial support:* Application deadline: 2/15. *Unit head:* Dr. Joseph Coyne, Interim Chair, 509-358-7983, Fax: 509-358-7984, E-mail: jsc@wsu.edu. *Application contact:* Graduate School Admissions, 800-GRADWSU, Fax: 509-335-1949, E-mail: gradsch@wsu.edu.

Washington State University Spokane, Graduate Programs, Program in Health Policy and Administration, Spokane, WA 99210. Offers MHPA. *Accreditation:* CAHME. Part-time and evening/weekend programs available. *Faculty:* 8. *Students:* 20 full-time (8 women), 2 part-time (1 woman), 4 international. In 2009, 9 master's awarded. *Degree requirements:* For master's, comprehensive exam (for some programs), thesis (for some programs), oral exam. *Entrance requirements:* For master's, GRE General Test or GMAT, minimum GPA of 3.0, 3 letters of recommendation. Additional exam requirements/recommendations for international students: Required—TOEFL (minimum score 550 paper-based; 213 computer-based) or IELTS (minimum score 7). *Application deadline:* For fall admission, 1/10 priority date for domestic students, 1/10 for international students; for spring admission, 7/1 priority date for domestic students, 7/1 for international students. Application fee: $50. *Expenses:* Tuition, state resident: part-time $423 per credit. Tuition, nonresident: part-time $1032 per credit. *Financial support:* In 2009–10, research assistantships with full and partial tuition reimbursements (averaging $14,634 per year), teaching assistantships (averaging $13,383 per year) were awarded; career-related internships or fieldwork also available. Support available to part-time students. Financial award application deadline: 2/15. Total annual research expenditures: $1.1 million. *Unit head:* Dr. Joseph Coyne, Interim Chair and Professor, 509-358-7981, E-mail: jsc@wsu.edu. *Application contact:* Graduate School Admissions, 800-GRADWSU, Fax: 509-335-1949, E-mail: gradsch@wsu.edu.

Wayland Baptist University, Graduate Programs, Programs in Business Administration/Management, Plainview, TX 79072-6998. Offers general business (MBA); health care administration (MBA); human resource management (MBA); international management (MBA); management (MA, MBA), including health care administration (MA), human resource management (MA), organization management (MA); management information systems (MBA). Part-time and evening/weekend programs available. Postbaccalaureate distance learning degree programs offered (no on-campus study). *Faculty:* 10 full-time (3 women). *Students:* 6 full-time (1 woman), 55 part-time (31 women); includes 24 minority (9 African Americans, 1 American Indian/Alaska Native, 14 Hispanic Americans). Average age 34. 25 applicants, 76% accepted, 10 enrolled. In 2009, 8 master's awarded. *Degree requirements:* For master's, capstone course. *Entrance requirements:* For master's, GMAT, GRE or MAT. Additional exam requirements/recommendations for international students: Required—TOEFL (minimum score 500 paper-based; 173 computer-based; 61 iBT). *Application deadline:* Applications are processed on a rolling basis. Application fee: $50. Electronic applications accepted. *Expenses:* Tuition: Full-time $5796; part-time $322 per credit hour. Required fees: $782; $9 per credit hour. $60 per semester. Tuition and fees vary according to course load and campus/location. *Financial support:* Federal Work-Study, institutionally sponsored loans, and scholarships/grants available. Support available to part-time students. Financial award application deadline: 5/1; financial award applicants required to submit FAFSA. *Unit head:* Dr. Otto Schacht, Chairman, 806-291-

Health Services Management and Hospital Administration

Wayland Baptist University (continued)

1020, Fax: 806-291-1957. *Application contact:* Amanda Stanton, Graduate Studies, 806-291-3423, Fax: 806-291-1950, E-mail: stanton@wbu.edu.

Waynesburg University, Graduate and Professional Studies, Waynesburg, PA 15370-1222. Offers business (MBA), including finance, health systems, human resources, leadership, market development; counseling (MA), including addictions counseling, clinical mental health; education (MAT); nursing (MSN), including administration, education, informatics, palliative care; nursing practice (DNP); special education (M Ed); technology (M Ed); MSN/MBA. *Accreditation:* AACN. Part-time and evening/weekend programs available. *Faculty:* 11 full-time (5 women), 136 part-time/adjunct (80 women). *Students:* 116 full-time (85 women), 984 part-time (682 women). 711 applicants, 80% accepted, 485 enrolled. In 2009, 320 master's, 41 doctorates awarded. *Degree requirements:* For doctorate, thesis/dissertation. *Entrance requirements:* Additional exam requirements/recommendations for international students: Required—TOEFL. *Application deadline:* For fall admission, 8/1 priority date for domestic students. Applications are processed on a rolling basis. Electronic applications accepted. *Expenses:* Tuition: Part-time $520 per credit. *Financial support:* Available to part-time students. Application deadline: 5/1. *Unit head:* David Mariner, Dean, 724-743-4420, Fax: 724-743-4425, E-mail: dmariner@waynesburg.edu. *Application contact:* Michael Bednarski, Director of Admissions, 724-743-4420, Fax: 724-743-4425, E-mail: mbednars@waynesburg.edu.

Weber State University, College of Health Professions, Program of Health Administration, Ogden, UT 84408-1001. Offers MHA. Part-time and evening/weekend programs available. *Entrance requirements:* For master's, GMAT or GRE. Additional exam requirements/recommendations for international students: Required—TOEFL.

Webster University, College of Arts and Sciences, Department of Nursing, St. Louis, MO 63119-3194. Offers healthcare leadership (Certificate); nursing (MSN). *Accreditation:* NLN. *Faculty:* 4 full-time, 4 part-time/adjunct. *Students:* 70 part-time (68 women); includes 9 minority (8 African Americans, 1 Hispanic American). Average age 44. In 2009, 19 master's, 5 other advanced degrees awarded. *Degree requirements:* For master's, comprehensive exam. *Entrance requirements:* For master's, 1 year of clinical experience, BSN, interview, minimum C+ average in statistics and physical assessment, minimum GPA of 3.0, RN license. Additional exam requirements/recommendations for international students: Required—TOEFL. *Application deadline:* Applications are processed on a rolling basis. Application fee: $25 ($50 for international students). *Expenses:* Tuition: Part-time $565 per credit hour. Tuition and fees vary according to degree level, campus/location and program. *Financial support:* Federal Work-Study available. Support available to part-time students. Financial award application deadline: 4/1; financial award applicants required to submit FAFSA. *Faculty research:* Health teaching. *Unit head:* Jennifer Broeder, Coordinator, 314-968-7486, Fax: 314-968-6101. *Application contact:* Matt Nolan, Associate Vice President for Enrollment Management/Dean of Admissions, Fax: 314-968-7116, E-mail: gadmit@webste.edu.

Webster University, George Herbert Walker School of Business and Technology, Department of Business, St. Louis, MO 63119-3194. Offers business (MA); business and organizational security management (MBA); computer resources and information management (MBA); environmental management (MBA); finance (MA, MBA); health services management (MBA); human resources development (MBA); human resources management (MBA); international business (MA, MBA); management and leadership (MBA); marketing (MBA); procurement and acquisitions management (MBA); telecommunications management (MBA). *Accreditation:* ACBSP. Part-time and evening/weekend programs available. Postbaccalaureate distance learning degree programs offered (no on-campus study). *Faculty:* 9 full-time, 430 part-time/adjunct. *Students:* 1,190 full-time (543 women), 4,226 part-time (2,159 women). Average age 34. In 2009, 2,021 master's awarded. *Degree requirements:* For master's, comprehensive exam (for some programs), thesis (for some programs). *Entrance requirements:* Additional exam requirements/recommendations for international students: Required—TOEFL. *Application deadline:* Applications are processed on a rolling basis. Application fee: $35 ($50 for international students). *Expenses:* Tuition: Part-time $565 per credit hour. Tuition and fees vary according to degree level, campus/location and program. *Financial support:* Federal Work-Study available. Support available to part-time students. Financial award application deadline: 4/1; financial award applicants required to submit FAFSA. *Unit head:* Dr. Debbie Psihountas, Chair, 314-246-7553 Ext. 7017, Fax: 314-968-7077, E-mail: buschair@webster.edu. *Application contact:* Matt Nolan, Associate Vice President for Enrollment Management/Dean of Admissions, Fax: 314-968-7116, E-mail: gadmit@webster.edu.

Webster University, George Herbert Walker School of Business and Technology, Department of Management, St. Louis, MO 63119-3194. Offers business and organizational security management (MA); computer resources and information management (MA); environmental management (MS); government contracting (Certificate); health care management (MA); health services management (MA); human resources development (MA); human resources management (MA); management (DM); management and leadership (MA); marketing (MA); nonprofit management (Certificate); procurement and acquisitions management (MA); public administration (MA); quality management (MA); space systems operations management (MS); telecommunications management (MA). *Accreditation:* ACBSP. Part-time and evening/weekend programs available. Postbaccalaureate distance learning degree programs offered (no on-campus study). *Faculty:* 16 full-time, 781 part-time/adjunct. *Students:* 1,369 full-time (610 women), 5,182 part-time (3,047 women); includes 3,460 minority (2,835 African Americans, 38 American Indian/Alaska Native, 169 Asian Americans or Pacific Islanders, 418 Hispanic Americans), 80 international. Average age 37. In 2009, 2,491 master's, 13 doctorates, 68 other advanced degrees awarded. *Degree requirements:* For master's, thesis (for some programs); for doctorate, thesis/dissertation, written exam. *Entrance requirements:* For doctorate, GMAT, 3 years of work experience, MBA. Additional exam requirements/recommendations for international students: Required—TOEFL. *Application deadline:* Applications are processed on a rolling basis. Application fee: $25 ($50 for international students). *Expenses:* Tuition: Part-time $565 per credit hour. Tuition and fees vary according to degree level, campus/location and program. *Financial support:* Federal Work-Study available. Support available to part-time students. Financial award application deadline: 4/1; financial award applicants required to submit FAFSA. *Unit head:* Jim Brasfield, Chair, 314-961-2660 Ext. 7063, Fax: 314-968-7077, E-mail: mgtchair@webster.edu. *Application contact:* Matt Nolan, Associate Vice President for Enrollment Management/Dean of Admissions, Fax: 314-968-7116, E-mail: gadmit@webster.edu.

West Chester University of Pennsylvania, Office of Graduate Studies, College of Health Sciences, Department of Health, West Chester, PA 19383. Offers emergency preparedness (Certificate); health care administration (Certificate); integrative health (Certificate); public health (MPH), including administration, community, environment, integrative, nutrition; school health (M Ed). *Accreditation:* CEPH. Part-time and evening/weekend programs available. *Students:* 15 full-time (9 women), 128 part-time (91 women); includes 41 minority (34 African Americans, 2 American Indian/Alaska Native, 5 Asian Americans or Pacific Islanders), 22 international. Average age 30. 83 applicants, 88% accepted, 41 enrolled. In 2009, 45 master's, 8 other advanced degrees awarded. *Degree requirements:* For master's, thesis (for some programs). *Entrance requirements:* For master's, one-page statement of career objectives, two letters of reference. Additional exam requirements/recommendations for international students: Required—TOEFL (minimum score 550 paper-based; 213 computer-based; 80 iBT). *Application deadline:* For fall admission, 4/15 priority date for domestic students, 3/15 for international students; for spring admission, 10/15 for domestic students, 9/1 for international students. Applications are processed on a rolling basis. Application fee: $35. Electronic applications accepted. *Expenses:* Tuition, state resident: full-time $6666; part-time $370 per credit. Tuition, nonresident: full-time $10,666; part-time $593 per credit. Required fees: $122.56 per credit. *Financial support:* In 2009–10, 11 research assistantships with full and partial tuition reimbursements (averaging $5,000 per year) were awarded; unspecified assistantships also available. Support available to part-time students. Financial award application deadline: 2/15; financial award applicants required to submit FAFSA. *Faculty research:* HIV/AIDS education, teacher preparation, water quality. *Unit head:* Dr. Roger Mustalish, Chair, 610-436-2931, E-mail: rmustalish@wcupa.edu. *Application contact:* Dr. Bethann Cinelli, Graduate Coordinator, 610-436-2267, E-mail: bcinelli@wcupa.edu.

Western Carolina University, Graduate School, College of Health and Human Sciences, School of Health Sciences, Cullowhee, NC 28723. Offers MHS. Part-time and evening/weekend programs available. *Students:* 24 full-time (19 women), 46 part-time (31 women). Average age 34. 39 applicants, 95% accepted, 28 enrolled. In 2009, 8 master's awarded. *Degree requirements:* For master's, thesis or alternative. *Entrance requirements:* For master's, GRE General Test, appropriate undergraduate degree with minimum GPA of 3.0, 3 letters of recommendation. Additional exam requirements/recommendations for international students: Required—TOEFL (minimum score 550 paper-based; 270 computer-based; 79 iBT). *Application deadline:* For fall admission, 5/1 priority date for domestic students; for spring admission, 9/1 priority date for domestic students. Applications are processed on a rolling basis. Application fee: $45. *Financial support:* In 2009–10, 4 students received support, including 4 research assistantships with full and partial tuition reimbursements available (averaging $7,000 per year); fellowships, teaching assistantships with full and partial tuition reimbursements available, institutionally sponsored loans, scholarships/grants, and unspecified assistantships also available. Financial award application deadline: 3/31; financial award applicants required to submit FAFSA. *Faculty research:* Epidemiology, dietetics, public health, environmental technology, water quality, occupational health. *Unit head:* Dr. Marianne Hollis, Director, 828-227-2660, Fax: 828-227-7446, E-mail: mhollis@email.wcu.edu. *Application contact:* Admissions Specialist for Health Sciences, 828-227-7398, Fax: 828-227-7480, E-mail: gradsch@email.wcu.edu.

Western Connecticut State University, Division of Graduate Studies, Ancell School of Business, Program in Health Administration, Danbury, CT 06810-6885. Offers MHA. Part-time programs available. *Students:* 1 (woman) full-time, 22 part-time (14 women); includes 2 minority (1 African American, 1 Hispanic American). Average age 37. 32 applicants, 69% accepted, 17 enrolled. In 2009, 6 master's awarded. *Degree requirements:* For master's, comprehensive exam, completion of program within 6 years. *Entrance requirements:* For master's, GMAT, GRE, or MAT, minimum GPA of 2.5. Additional exam requirements/recommendations for international students: Recommended—TOEFL (minimum score 550 paper-based; 213 computer-based; 79 iBT), IELTS (minimum score 6). *Application deadline:* For fall admission, 8/5 priority date for domestic students; for spring admission, 1/5 priority date for domestic students. Applications are processed on a rolling basis. Application fee: $50. *Expenses:* Tuition, state resident: full-time $5012; part-time $278 per credit hour. Tuition, nonresident: full-time $13,962; part-time $284 per credit hour. Required fees: $3886; $139 per credit hour. Full-time tuition and fees vary according to course load and program. Part-time tuition and fees vary according to course level, degree level and program. *Financial support:* Application deadline: 5/1. *Unit head:* Dr. Neil Dworkin, MHA Coordinator, 203-837-8475, Fax: 203-837-8527. *Application contact:* Chris Shankle, Associate Director of Graduate Studies, 203-837-9005, Fax: 203-837-8326, E-mail: shanklec@wcsu.edu.

Western Illinois University, School of Graduate Studies, College of Education and Human Services, Department of Health Sciences, Macomb, IL 61455-1390. Offers health education (MS); health services administration (Certificate). *Accreditation:* NCATE. Part-time programs available. *Students:* 18 full-time (7 women), 33 part-time (27 women); includes 1 minority (African American), 14 international. Average age 33. 33 applicants, 79% accepted. In 2009, 19 master's awarded. *Degree requirements:* For master's, comprehensive exam, thesis or alternative. *Entrance requirements:* Additional exam requirements/recommendations for international students: Required—TOEFL (minimum score 550 paper-based; 213 computer-based; 80 iBT). *Application deadline:* Applications are processed on a rolling basis. Application fee: $30. Electronic applications accepted. *Expenses:* Tuition, state resident: full-time $4486; part-time $249.21 per credit hour. Tuition, nonresident: full-time $8972; part-time $498.42 per credit hour. Required fees: $72.62 per credit hour. *Financial support:* In 2009–10, 10 students received support, including 10 research assistantships with full tuition reimbursements available (averaging $7,280 per year). Financial award applicants required to submit FAFSA. *Unit head:* Dr. R. Mark Kelley, Chairperson, 309-298-1076. *Application contact:* Evelyn Hoing, Assistant Director of Graduate Studies, 309-298-1806, Fax: 309-298-2345, E-mail: grad-office@wiu.edu.

Western Kentucky University, Graduate Studies, College of Health and Human Services, Department of Public Health, Bowling Green, KY 42101. Offers healthcare administration (MHA); public health (MPH). *Accreditation:* CEPH. Part-time and evening/weekend programs available. *Degree requirements:* For master's, comprehensive exam, thesis or alternative. *Entrance requirements:* For master's, GRE General Test, minimum GPA of 2.75. Additional exam requirements/recommendations for international students: Required—TOEFL (minimum score 555 paper-based; 213 computer-based; 79 iBT). *Expenses:* Tuition, state resident: full-time $4160; part-time $416 per credit hour. Tuition, nonresident: full-time $9550; part-time $506 per credit hour. Tuition and fees vary according to campus/location and reciprocity agreements. *Faculty research:* Health education training, driver traffic safety, community readiness, occupational injuries, local health departments.

Western Michigan University, Graduate College, College of Arts and Sciences, School of Public Affairs and Administration, Kalamazoo, MI 49008. Offers health care administration (Graduate Certificate); nonprofit leadership and administration (Graduate Certificate); public administration (MPA, PhD). *Accreditation:* NASPAA (one or more programs are accredited). *Faculty:* 6 full-time (1 woman). *Students:* 100 full-time (57 women), 189 part-time (100 women); includes 59 minority (50 African Americans, 2 American Indian/Alaska Native, 5 Asian Americans or Pacific Islanders, 2 Hispanic Americans), 2 international. 85 applicants, 85% accepted, 30 enrolled. In 2009, 81 master's, 2 doctorates awarded. *Degree requirements:* For doctorate, thesis/dissertation, oral exams. *Entrance requirements:* For doctorate, GRE General Test. *Application deadline:* For fall admission, 2/15 priority date for domestic students. Application fee: $25. *Financial support:* Fellowships, research assistantships, teaching assistantships, Federal Work-Study available. Financial award application deadline: 2/15; financial award applicants required to submit FAFSA. *Unit head:* Barbara S. Liggett, Interim Director, 269-387-8943. *Application contact:* Admissions and Orientation, 269-387-2000, Fax: 269-387-2355.

Widener University, School of Business Administration, Program in Health and Medical Services Administration, Chester, PA 19013-5792. Offers MBA, MHA, MD/MBA, MD/MHA, Psy D/MBA, Psy D/MHA. *Accreditation:* CAHME (one or more programs are accredited). Part-time and evening/weekend programs available. *Faculty:* 3 full-time (1 woman), 6 part-time/adjunct (1 woman). *Students:* 30 applicants, 80% accepted. In 2009, 1 master's awarded. *Degree requirements:* For master's, clerkship, residency. *Entrance requirements:* For master's, GMAT, interview, minimum GPA of 2.5. *Application deadline:* For fall admission, 8/1 priority date for domestic students; for spring admission, 12/1 for domestic students. Applications are processed on a rolling basis. Application fee: $25 ($300 for international students). Electronic applications accepted. *Financial support:* Research assistantships, career-related internships or fieldwork and traineeships available. Support available to part-time students. Financial award application deadline: 5/1. *Faculty research:* Cost containment in health care, reimbursement of hospitals, strategic behavior. *Unit head:* Dr. Caryl Carpenter, Director, 610-499-4109. *Application contact:* Ann Seltzer, Graduate Enrollment Administrator, 610-499-4305, E-mail: apseltzer@widener.edu.

Widener University, School of Human Service Professions, Institute for Graduate Clinical Psychology, Program in Clinical Psychology and Health and Medical Services Administration, Chester, PA 19013-5792. Offers Psy D/MBA, Psy D/MHA. *Accreditation:* APA (one or more programs are accredited); CAHME. *Faculty:* 15 full-time (6 women), 18 part-time/adjunct (10 women). *Students:* 6 full-time (4 women), 1 part-time (0 women); includes 1 minority (African American). Average age 28. *Application deadline:* For fall admission, 12/31 for domestic students. Application fee: $75. Electronic applications accepted. *Financial support:* Career-related internships or fieldwork, Federal Work-Study, and institutionally sponsored loans available. Financial award application deadline: 5/31. *Faculty research:* Psychosocial competence, family systems, medical care systems and financing. *Unit head:* Dr. Hal Shorey, Director, 610-499-4598, Fax: 610-499-4625. *Application contact:* Admissions Coordinator.

William Woods University, Graduate and Adult Studies, Fulton, MO 65251-1098. Offers administration (Ed S); agriculture (MBA); athletic/activities administration (M Ed); curriculum and instruction (M Ed); curriculum leadership (Ed S); elementary administration (M Ed); health management (MBA); human resources (MBA); principalship (Ed S); secondary administration (M Ed); special education director (M Ed). Evening/weekend programs available. *Degree requirements:* For master's, capstone course (MBA), action research (M Ed); for Ed S, field experience. *Entrance requirements:* For master's, 2 recommendations, resumé, BA/BS; teaching certification (M Ed); course work in economics and accounting (MBA); for Ed S, M Ed, 2 letters of recommendation, resume, teaching certification. Additional exam requirements/recommendations for international students: Required—TOEFL (minimum score 550 paper-based). Electronic applications accepted.

Wilmington University, College of Business, New Castle, DE 19720-6491. Offers business administration (MBA); finance (MBA); health care administration (MBA, MS); homeland security (MBA, MS); human resource management (MS); management (MS); management information systems (MBA); organizational leadership (MS); public administration (MS); transportation and logistics (MBA, MS). Part-time and evening/weekend programs available. *Entrance requirements:* Additional exam requirements/recommendations for international students: Required—TOEFL (minimum score 500 paper-based; 173 computer-based). Electronic applications accepted.

Worcester State College, Graduate Studies, Program in Health Care Administration, Worcester, MA 01602-2597. Offers MS. *Faculty:* 1 (woman) full-time, 2 part-time/adjunct (both women). *Students:* 12 part-time (6 women). Average age 32. 27 applicants, 81% accepted, 5 enrolled. In 2009, 11 master's awarded. *Degree requirements:* For master's, comprehensive exam (for some programs), thesis optional. *Entrance requirements:* For master's, MAT, GRE. Additional exam requirements/recommendations for international students: Required—TOEFL (minimum score 550 paper-based; 213 computer-based; 79 iBT). *Application deadline:* Applications are processed on a rolling basis. Application fee: $30. *Expenses:* Tuition, area resident: Part-time $150 per credit. Tuition, state resident: part-time $150 per credit. Tuition, nonresident: part-time $150 per credit. Required fees: $85. *Financial support:* In 2009–10, 1 student received support, including 1 research assistantship with full tuition reimbursement available (averaging $4,800 per year); career-related internships or fieldwork, scholarships/grants, and unspecified assistantships also available. Financial award application deadline: 3/1; financial award applicants required to submit FAFSA. *Unit head:* Robert Shafner, Coordinator, 508-929-8739, Fax: 508-929-8175, E-mail: rshafner@worcester.edu. *Application contact:* Nicole Brown, Assistant Dean of Graduate and Continuing Education, 508-929-8787, Fax: 508-929-8100, E-mail: nbrown@worcester.edu.

Wright State University, School of Graduate Studies, Raj Soin College of Business, Department of Management, Dayton, OH 45435. Offers flexible business (MBA); health care management (MBA); international business (MBA); management, innovation and change (MBA); project management (MBA); supply chain management (MBA); MBA/MS. *Entrance requirements:* For master's, GMAT, minimum AACSB index of 1000. Additional exam requirements/recommendations for international students: Required—TOEFL.

Xavier University, College of Social Sciences, Health and Education, Program in Health Services Administration, Cincinnati, OH 45207. Offers MHSA, MBA/MHSA. *Accreditation:* CAHME. Part-time and evening/weekend programs available. *Faculty:* 6 full-time (2 women), 5 part-time/adjunct (0 women). *Students:* 62 full-time (27 women), 52 part-time (26 women); includes 16 minority (10 African Americans, 1 American Indian/Alaska Native, 4 Asian Americans or Pacific Islanders, 1 Hispanic American), 3 international. Average age 28. 113 applicants, 56% accepted, 41 enrolled. In 2009, 7 master's awarded. *Degree requirements:* For master's, thesis. *Entrance requirements:* For master's, GMAT or GRE, resume, 2 letters of recommendation. Additional exam requirements/recommendations for international students: Required—TOEFL (minimum score 550 paper-based; 213 computer-based; 80 iBT). *Application deadline:* For fall admission, 6/1 priority date for domestic students, 1/1 for international students. Applications are processed on a rolling basis. Application fee: $35. Electronic applications accepted. *Expenses:* Tuition: Part-time $697 per credit hour. One-time fee: $35 part-time. *Financial support:* In 2009–10, 17 students received support. Tuition waivers and unspecified assistantships available. Financial award application deadline: 4/30; financial award applicants required to submit FAFSA. *Faculty research:* Ethics and leadership, early hospital readmission and quality, health and labor economics, clinical emergency medicine and uncompensated care. *Unit head:* Dr. Ida Critelli Schick, Director/Chair, 513-745-3716, Fax: 513-745-4301, E-mail: schicki@xavier.edu. *Application contact:* Christina E. Swift, Recruitment/Promotions Coordinator, 513-745-3687, Fax: 513-745-4301, E-mail: swiftce@xavier.edu.

Yale University, School of Medicine, School of Public Health, Division of Health Policy and Administration, New Haven, CT 06520. Offers MPH, PhD. PhD offered through the Graduate School. *Accreditation:* CAHME. Part-time programs available. *Degree requirements:* For master's, thesis, internship. *Entrance requirements:* For master's, GMAT, GRE, or MCAT, previous undergraduate course work in mathematics and science. Additional exam requirements/recommendations for international students: Required—TOEFL. Electronic applications accepted. *Faculty research:* Health politics, policy, and regulation; mental health and substance abuse; consumer choice and decision making; determinants of clinical decision making.

Youngstown State University, Graduate School, Bitonte College of Health and Human Services, Department of Health Professions, Youngstown, OH 44555-0001. Offers health and human services (MHHS); public health (MPH). *Accreditation:* NAACLS. Part-time and evening/weekend programs available. *Degree requirements:* For master's, thesis optional. *Entrance requirements:* For master's, GRE General Test, minimum GPA of 3.0. Additional exam requirements/recommendations for international students: Required—TOEFL. *Faculty research:* Drug prevention, multiskilling in health care, organizational behavior, health care management, health behaviors, research management.

Health Services Research

Albany College of Pharmacy and Health Sciences, Program in Pharmacy, Albany, NY 12208. Offers health outcomes research (MS); pharmaceutical sciences (MS); pharmacy (Pharm D); pharmacy administration (MS). *Accreditation:* ACPE. *Faculty:* 60 full-time (24 women), 10 part-time/adjunct (6 women). *Students:* 452 full-time (245 women); includes 78 minority (21 African Americans, 54 Asian Americans or Pacific Islanders, 3 Hispanic Americans), 46 international. Average age 26. 1,223 applicants, 12% accepted, 79 enrolled. In 2009, 211 first professional degrees awarded. *Degree requirements:* For master's, thesis (for some programs); for Pharm D, comprehensive exam (for some programs), practice experience. *Entrance requirements:* For Pharm D, PCAT, minimum GPA of 3.0; for master's, GRE, minimum GPA of 3.0. Additional exam requirements/recommendations for international students: Required—TOEFL (minimum score 600 paper-based; 250 computer-based; 100 iBT). *Application deadline:* For fall admission, 2/1 for domestic and international students. Applications are processed on a rolling basis. Application fee: $75. Electronic applications accepted. *Expenses:* Tuition: Full-time $23,260; part-time $775 per credit hour. Required fees: $1150. *Financial support:* In 2009–10, 185 students received support, including 1 fellowship (averaging $40,000 per year); Federal Work-Study and scholarships/grants also available. Support available to part-time students. Financial award application deadline: 3/1; financial award applicants required to submit FAFSA. *Faculty research:* Therapeutic use of drugs, pharmacokinetics, pharmaceutical care, health outcomes, drug delivery. *Unit head:* Dr. Mehdi Boroujerdi, Dean, 518-694-7212, Fax: 518-694-7063. *Application contact:* Donna Myers, Pharmacy and Graduate Admissions Counselor, 518-694-7186, Fax: 518-694-7063.

See Close-Up on page 1789.

Brown University, Graduate School, Division of Biology and Medicine, Department of Community Health, Program in Health Services Research, Providence, RI 02912. Offers MS, PhD.

Case Western Reserve University, School of Medicine and School of Graduate Studies, Graduate Programs in Medicine, Department of Epidemiology and Biostatistics, Program in Health Services Research, Cleveland, OH 44106. Offers MS, PhD. *Degree requirements:* For master's, comprehensive exam, thesis; for doctorate, comprehensive exam, thesis/dissertation. *Entrance requirements:* For master's and doctorate, GRE. Additional exam requirements/recommendations for international students: Required—TOEFL (minimum score 550 paper-based; 213 computer-based).

Cornell University, Joan and Sanford I. Weill Medical College and Graduate School of Medical Sciences, Weill Cornell Graduate School of Medical Sciences, Program in Clinical Epidemiology and Health Services Research, New York, NY 10021. Offers MS. *Faculty:* 22 full-time (8 women). *Students:* 22 full-time (12 women); includes 6 minority (2 African Americans, 3 Asian Americans or Pacific Islanders, 1 Hispanic American), 3 international. Average age 35. 14 applicants, 50% accepted, 7 enrolled. In 2009, 3 master's awarded. *Degree requirements:* For master's, thesis. *Entrance requirements:* For master's, 3 years of work experience, MD or RN certificate. *Application deadline:* For fall admission, 12/15 for domestic students. Application fee: $60. *Expenses:* Tuition: Full-time $44,650. Required fees: $2805. *Financial support:* Scholarships/grants available. *Faculty research:* Research methodology, biostatistical techniques, data management, decision analysis, health economics. *Unit head:* Dr. Carol Mancuso, Director, 212-746-5454. *Application contact:* Alison Kenny, Administrator of Clinical and Educational Programs, 212-746-1608, Fax: 212-746-7443, E-mail: alh2006@med.cornell.edu.

Dartmouth College, The Dartmouth Institute, Hanover, NH 03755. Offers MPH, MS, PhD. Part-time programs available. *Faculty:* 32 full-time (17 women), 10 part-time/adjunct (7 women). *Students:* 34 full-time (19 women), 85 part-time (56 women); includes 21 minority (2 African Americans, 1 American Indian/Alaska Native, 14 Asian Americans or Pacific Islanders, 4 Hispanic Americans), 6 international. Average age 34. 243 applicants, 79% accepted, 82 enrolled. In 2009, 56 master's, 5 doctorates awarded. *Degree requirements:* For master's, research project or practicum; for doctorate, thesis/dissertation. *Entrance requirements:* For master's and doctorate, GRE or MCAT, 3 letters of recommendation. *Application deadline:* For fall admission, 1/15 for domestic students. Application fee: $50. *Financial support:* In 2009–10, 5 students received support. *Unit head:* Dr. Gerald T. O'Connor, Director, 603-650-1782, Fax: 603-650-1900. *Application contact:* Susan Benson, Academic Programs Director, 603-650-1782, Fax: 603-650-1900.

Emory University, Rollins School of Public Health, Department of Health Policy and Management, Atlanta, GA 30322-1100. Offers health policy (MPH); health policy research (MSPH); health services management (MPH). Part-time programs available. *Degree requirements:* For master's, thesis (for some programs), practicum, capstone course. *Entrance requirements:* For master's, GRE General Test. Additional exam requirements/recommendations for international students: Required—TOEFL (minimum score 550 paper-based; 215 computer-based; 80 iBT). Electronic applications accepted. *Faculty research:* U.S. health policy and financing, healthcare organization and financing.

The George Washington University, School of Medicine and Health Sciences, Health Sciences Programs, Washington, DC 20052. Offers adult nurse practitioner (MSN, Post Master's Certificate); clinical practice management (MSHS); clinical research administration (MSHS); clinical research administration for nurses (MSN); emergency services management (MSHS); end-of-life care (MSHS, MSN); family nurse practitioner (MSN, Post Master's Certificate); immunohematology (MSHS); nursing (DNP); nursing leadership and management (MSN); physical therapy (DPT); physician assistant (MSHS); MSHS/MPH. Postbaccalaureate distance learning degree programs offered (no on-campus study). *Students:* 270 full-time (220 women), 491 part-time (406 women); includes 176 minority (83 African Americans, 5 American Indian/Alaska Native, 62 Asian Americans or Pacific Islanders, 26 Hispanic Americans), 26 international. Average age 35. 1,059 applicants, 47% accepted, 292 enrolled. In 2009, 155 master's, 22 doctorates, 75 other advanced degrees awarded. *Entrance requirements:* Additional exam requirements/recommendations for international students: Required—TOEFL (minimum score 550 paper-based; 213 computer-based). *Application deadline:* Applications are processed on a rolling basis. Application fee: $60. *Expenses:* Contact institution. *Unit head:* Jean E. Johnson, Senior Associate Dean, 202-994-3725, E-mail: jejohns@gwu.edu. *Application contact:* Joke Ogundiran, Director of Admission, 202-994-1668, Fax: 202-994-0870, E-mail: jokeogun@gwu.edu.

The Johns Hopkins University, Bloomberg School of Public Health, Department of Health Policy and Management, Baltimore, MD 21205-1996. Offers bioethics and policy (PhD); health and public policy (PhD); health care management and leadership (Dr PH); health economics (MHS); health economics and policy (PhD); health finance and management (MHA); health policy (MHS); health services research and policy (PhD). *Accreditation:* CAHME (one or more programs are accredited). Part-time programs available. *Faculty:* 60 full-time (32 women), 178 part-time/adjunct (66 women). *Students:* 136 full-time (95 women), 55 part-time (21 women); includes 53 minority (14 African Americans, 36 Asian Americans or Pacific Islanders, 3 Hispanic Americans), 48 international. Average age 32. 299 applicants, 39% accepted, 64 enrolled. In 2009, 49 master's, 19 doctorates awarded. *Degree requirements:* For master's, thesis (for some programs), internship (for some programs); for doctorate, comprehensive exam, thesis/dissertation, 1 year full-time residency (for some programs), oral and written exams. *Entrance requirements:* For master's, GRE General Test or GMAT, 3 letters of recommendation, curriculum vitae/resume; for doctorate, GRE General Test or GMAT, 3 letters of recommendation, curriculum vitae, transcripts. Additional exam requirements/recommendations for international students: Recommended—TOEFL (minimum score 600 paper-based; 250 computer-based; 100 iBT), IELTS. *Application deadline:* For fall admission, 12/1 for domestic and international students. Applications are processed on a rolling basis. Application fee: $45. Electronic applications accepted. *Financial support:* In 2009–10, 145 students received support; fellowships, research assistantships, teaching assistantships, career-related internships or fieldwork, Federal Work-Study, institutionally sponsored loans, scholarships/grants, traineeships, and stipends available. Support available to part-time students. Financial award application deadline: 3/15; financial award applicants required to submit FAFSA. *Faculty research:* Quality of care and health outcomes, health care finance and technology, health disparities and vulnerable populations, injury prevention, health policy and health care policy. Total annual research expenditures: $14.2 million. *Unit head:* Dr. Ellen J. MacKenzie, Chairman, 410-955-3625, E-mail: emackenz@jhsph.edu. *Application contact:* Mary Sewell, Coordinator, 410-955-2489, Fax: 410-614-9152, E-mail: msewell@jhsph.edu.

Lakehead University, Graduate Studies, Faculty of Social Sciences and Humanities, Department of Sociology, Thunder Bay, ON P7B 5E1, Canada. Offers gerontology (MA); health services and policy research (MA); sociology (MA); women's studies (MA). Part-time and evening/weekend programs available. *Degree requirements:* For master's, research project or thesis. *Entrance requirements:* For master's, minimum B average. Additional exam requirements/recommendations for international students: Required—TOEFL. *Faculty research:*

Health Services Research

Lakehead University (continued)
Sociology of medicine, cultural and social change, health human resources, gerontology, women's studies.

McMaster University, Faculty of Health Sciences and School of Graduate Studies, Program in Health Research Methodology (course-based), Hamilton, ON L8S 4M2, Canada. Offers M Sc. Part-time programs available. *Degree requirements:* For master's, research internship, scholarly paper courses. *Entrance requirements:* For master's, 4 year honors degree, minimum B+ average in last year of course work. Additional exam requirements/recommendations for international students: Required—TOEFL (minimum score 580 paper-based; 237 computer-based).

McMaster University, Faculty of Health Sciences and School of Graduate Studies, Program in Health Research Methodology (thesis), Hamilton, ON L8S 4M2, Canada. Offers M Sc, PhD. Part-time programs available. *Degree requirements:* For master's, thesis; for doctorate, comprehensive exam, thesis/dissertation. *Entrance requirements:* For master's, honors degree, minimum B+ average in last year of undergraduate course work; for doctorate, M Sc, minimum B+ average. Additional exam requirements/recommendations for international students: Required—TOEFL (minimum score 580 paper-based; 237 computer-based; 92 iBT).

Medical University of South Carolina, College of Health Professions, Department of Health Sciences and Research, Program in Research Administration, Charleston, SC 29425. Offers MRA. Part-time programs available. *Faculty:* 1 full-time (0 women), 5 part-time/adjunct (3 women). *Students:* 2 full-time (both women), 5 part-time (3 women); includes 1 minority (Hispanic American). Average age 36. 8 applicants, 100% accepted, 7 enrolled. *Entrance requirements:* For master's, GRE. Additional exam requirements/recommendations for international students: Required—TOEFL (minimum score 600 paper-based; 250 computer-based). Application fee: $85. Electronic applications accepted. *Financial support:* Career-related internships or fieldwork, Federal Work-Study, scholarships/grants, and tuition waivers (partial) available. Support available to part-time students. Financial award application deadline: 3/10; financial award applicants required to submit FAFSA. *Unit head:* Dr. James S. Zoller, Program Director, 843-792-3849, E-mail: zollerjs@musc.edu. *Application contact:* Ann Brown, Student Services Program Coordinator, 843-792-2115, Fax: 843-792-3327, E-mail: brownah@musc.edu.

Old Dominion University, College of Health Sciences, Program in Health Services Research, Norfolk, VA 23529. Offers PhD. Evening/weekend programs available. *Faculty:* 12 full-time (8 women), 12 part-time/adjunct (10 women). *Students:* 12 full-time (7 women), 17 part-time (12 women); includes 12 minority (10 African Americans, 2 Asian Americans or Pacific Islanders), 5 international. Average age 44. 10 applicants, 60% accepted, 5 enrolled. In 2009, 3 doctorates awarded. *Degree requirements:* For doctorate, comprehensive exam, thesis/dissertation. *Entrance requirements:* For doctorate, GRE, minimum GPA of 3.25, master's degree. Additional exam requirements/recommendations for international students: Required—TOEFL (minimum score 550 paper-based). *Application deadline:* For fall admission, 7/1 for domestic students, 6/1 for international students. Applications are processed on a rolling basis. Application fee: $50. Electronic applications accepted. *Expenses:* Tuition, state resident: full-time $8112; part-time $338 per credit. Tuition, nonresident: full-time $20,256; part-time $844 per credit. Required fees: $119 per semester. One-time fee: $50. *Financial support:* In 2009–10, 8 students received support, including 3 fellowships with full tuition reimbursements available (averaging $15,000 per year), 2 research assistantships with tuition reimbursements available (averaging $15,000 per year), 2 teaching assistantships with tuition reimbursements available (averaging $15,000 per year); career-related internships or fieldwork, scholarships/grants, and tuition waivers (partial) also available. Financial award application deadline: 7/1; financial award applicants required to submit FAFSA. *Faculty research:* Access to health services, women's health, domestic violence, health policy and planning, economics of obesity, substance abuse, health disparities. Total annual research expenditures: $150,133. *Unit head:* Dr. George Maihafer, Graduate Program Director, 757-683-3830, Fax: 757-683-6333, E-mail: chpgpd@odu.edu. *Application contact:* Dr. George Maihafer, Graduate Program Director, 757-683-3830, Fax: 757-683-6333, E-mail: chpgpd@odu.edu.

Penn State Hershey Medical Center, College of Medicine, Graduate School Programs in the Biomedical Sciences, Graduate Program in Public Health Sciences, Hershey, PA 17033. Offers MS. Part-time programs available. *Students:* 9 applicants, 67% accepted, 6 enrolled. *Degree requirements:* For master's, thesis or alternative. *Entrance requirements:* Additional exam requirements/recommendations for international students: Required—TOEFL (minimum score 550 paper-based). *Application deadline:* For fall admission, 1/31 priority date for domestic students, 2/1 priority date for international students. Applications are processed on a rolling basis. Application fee: $65. Electronic applications accepted. *Expenses:* Tuition, state resident: part-time $644 per credit. Tuition, nonresident: part-time $1142 per credit. Required fees: $22 per semester. *Financial support:* Fellowships available. Financial award applicants required to submit FAFSA. *Faculty research:* Clinical trials, statistical methods in genetic epidemiology, genetic factors in nicotine dependence and dementia syndromes, health economics, cancer. *Unit head:* Dr. Christopher Hollenbeak, Chair, 717-531-5890, Fax: 717-531-5779, E-mail: hes-grad-hmc@psu.edu. *Application contact:* Mardi Sawyer, Program Administrator, 717-531-7178, Fax: 717-531-5779, E-mail: hes-grad-hmc@psu.edu.

Stanford University, School of Medicine, Graduate Programs in Medicine, Division of Health Services Research, Stanford, CA 94305-9991. Offers MS. Division accepts internal applicants only. *Degree requirements:* For master's, thesis. Electronic applications accepted. *Expenses:* Tuition: Full-time $37,380; part-time $2760 per quarter. Required fees: $501. *Faculty research:* Cost and quality of life in cardiovascular disease, technology assessment, physician decision making.

Texas State University–San Marcos, Graduate School, College of Health Professions, School of Health Administration, Program in Health Services Research, San Marcos, TX 78666. Offers MS. Part-time and evening/weekend programs available. *Faculty:* 5 full-time (1 woman). *Students:* 7 full-time (6 women), 8 part-time (7 women); includes 5 minority (1 Asian American or Pacific Islander, 4 Hispanic Americans), 3 international. Average age 28. 3 applicants, 100% accepted, 3 enrolled. In 2009, 5 master's awarded. *Degree requirements:* For master's, comprehensive exam, thesis optional, committee review. *Entrance requirements:* For master's, GRE General Test, 3 letters of reference, resume, department interview. Additional exam requirements/recommendations for international students: Required—TOEFL (minimum score 550 paper-based; 213 computer-based). *Application deadline:* For fall admission, 6/15 priority date for domestic students, 6/1 for international students; for spring admission, 10/15 priority date for domestic students, 10/1 for international students. Applications are processed on a rolling basis. Application fee: $40 ($90 for international students). Electronic applications accepted. *Expenses:* Tuition, state resident: full-time $5784; part-time $241 per credit hour. Tuition, nonresident: full-time $13,224; part-time $551 per credit hour. Required fees: $1728; $48 per credit hour. $306. Tuition and fees vary according to course load. *Financial support:* In 2009–10, 8 students received support, including 2 research assistantships (averaging $4,928 per year), 3 teaching assistantships (averaging $5,177 per year); career-related internships or fieldwork, Federal Work-Study, and institutionally sponsored loans also available. Support available to part-time students. Financial award application deadline: 4/1; financial award applicants required to submit FAFSA. *Faculty research:* Human resource development, biostatistics, long-term care. *Unit head:* Dr. Michael Nowicki, Program Advisor, 512-245-3556, E-mail: mn03@txstate.edu. *Application contact:* Dr. J. Michael Willoughby, Dean of Graduate School, 512-245-2581, Fax: 512-245-8365, E-mail: gradcollege@txstate.edu.

Thomas Jefferson University, Jefferson College of Graduate Studies, Program in Clinical Research, Public Health, and Research Management, Philadelphia, PA 19107. Offers Certificate. *Students:* 17 part-time (14 women); includes 8 minority (4 African Americans, 4 Asian Americans or Pacific Islanders), 2 international. 17 applicants, 94% accepted, 13 enrolled. In 2009, 5 Certificates awarded. *Entrance requirements:* For degree, GRE General Test (recommended). Additional exam requirements/recommendations for international students: Required—TOEFL (minimum score 250 computer-based; 100 iBT), or IELTS. *Application deadline:* For fall admission, 8/1 priority date for domestic students, 3/1 priority date for international students; for winter admission, 12/1 priority date for domestic students, 6/1 priority date for international students; for spring admission, 4/1 priority date for domestic students. Applications are processed on a rolling basis. Application fee: $50. Electronic applications accepted. *Expenses:* Tuition: Full-time $26,858; part-time $879 per credit. Required fees: $525. *Financial support:* Federal Work-Study and institutionally sponsored loans available. Support available to part-time students. Financial award applicants required to submit FAFSA. *Faculty research:* Pharmacoeconomics, epidemiology, clinical research, performance improvement, statistics. *Unit head:* Dr. Dennis M. Gross, Associate Dean, 215-503-0156, Fax: 215-503-3433, E-mail: dennis.gross@jefferson.edu. *Application contact:* Eleanor M. Gorman, Assistant Coordinator, Graduate Center Programs, 215-503-5799, Fax: 215-503-3433, E-mail: eleanor.gorman@jefferson.edu.

University of Alberta, School of Public Health, Department of Public Health Sciences, Edmonton, AB T6G 2E1, Canada. Offers clinical epidemiology (M Sc, MPH); environmental and occupational health (MPH); environmental health sciences (M Sc); epidemiology (M Sc); global health (M Sc, MPH); health policy and management (MPH); health policy research (M Sc); health technology assessment (MPH); occupational health (M Sc); population health (M Sc); public health leadership (MPH); public health sciences (PhD); quantitative methods (MPH). *Accreditation:* CEPH (one or more programs are accredited). *Faculty:* 24 full-time (5 women), 59 part-time/adjunct (13 women). *Students:* 49 full-time, 49 part-time. 81 applicants, 31% accepted. In 2009, 28 master's awarded. Terminal master's awarded for partial completion of doctoral program. *Degree requirements:* For master's, thesis (for some programs); for doctorate, thesis/dissertation. *Entrance requirements:* For master's, GMAT or GRE General Test. Additional exam requirements/recommendations for international students: Required—TOEFL (minimum score 550 paper-based; 213 computer-based) or IELTS (minimum score 6). *Application deadline:* For fall admission, 3/15 for domestic students, 7/1 for international students; for winter admission, 11/1 for international students; for spring admission, 3/1 for international students. Applications are processed on a rolling basis. Application fee: $0. Electronic applications accepted. Tuition and fees charges are reported in Canadian dollars. *Expenses:* Tuition, area resident: Full-time $4626 Canadian dollars; part-time $99.72 Canadian dollars per unit. International tuition: $8216 Canadian dollars full-time. Required fees: $3590 Canadian dollars; $99.72 Canadian dollars per unit. $215 Canadian dollars per term. *Financial support:* In 2009–10, 11 students received support, including 6 research assistantships with tuition reimbursements available (averaging $2,200 per year); fellowships, teaching assistantships, career-related internships or fieldwork and tuition waivers (partial) also available. Financial award application deadline: 2/1. *Faculty research:* Biostatistics, health promotion and socio-behavioral health science. Total annual research expenditures: $5.7 million. *Unit head:* L. Duncan Saunders, Acting Chair, 780-492-6814, Fax: 780-492-0364. *Application contact:* Felicity R. Hey, Graduate Programs Administrator, 780-492-6407, Fax: 780-492-0364, E-mail: felicity.hey@ualberta.ca.

University of Arkansas for Medical Sciences, Graduate School, Program in Health Systems Research, Little Rock, AR 72205-7199. Offers PhD. *Faculty:* 17 full-time (8 women). *Students:* 3 full-time, 5 part-time. *Degree requirements:* For doctorate, thesis/dissertation. *Entrance requirements:* For doctorate, GRE. Additional exam requirements/recommendations for international students: Required—TOEFL. *Faculty research:* Health economics, quality and health outcomes research. *Unit head:* Dr. Glen Mays, Chair, Health Policy and Management and Program Director, 501-526-6647, E-mail: gpmays@uams.edu. *Application contact:* Dr. Glen Mays, Chair, Health Policy and Management and Program Director, 501-526-6647, E-mail: gpmays@uams.edu.

University of Colorado Denver, Colorado School of Public Health, Health Services Research Program, Denver, CO 80217-3364. Offers computational bioscience (PhD); epidemiology (PhD); health services research (PhD). *Students:* 35 full-time (17 women), 3 part-time (all women); includes 3 minority (all Hispanic Americans), 3 international. In 2009, 3 doctorates awarded. *Degree requirements:* For doctorate, comprehensive exam, thesis/dissertation. *Entrance requirements:* For doctorate, GRE, interview, 3 letters of recommendation. Additional exam requirements/recommendations for international students: Required—TOEFL (minimum score 550 paper-based; 213 computer-based). *Application deadline:* For fall admission, 2/1 for domestic students. Application fee: $50. *Financial support:* Application deadline: 3/1. *Faculty research:* Biochemical functions of proteins, description and classification of enzymatic functions, optimization of genome-shuffling in gram negative bacteria. *Application contact:* Information Contact, 303-724-4613, Fax: 303-724-4620, E-mail: colorado.sph@ucdenver.edu.

University of Florida, Graduate School, College of Public Health and Health Professions, Department of Health Services Research, Management and Policy, Gainesville, FL 32611. Offers health administration (MHA); health services research (PhD). *Accreditation:* CAHME. Part-time programs available. *Entrance requirements:* For master's, GRE General Test, minimum GPA of 3.0. Additional exam requirements/recommendations for international students: Required—TOEFL (minimum score 550 paper-based; 213 computer-based). Electronic applications accepted. *Faculty research:* Hospital profitability, indigent care, rural health care systems, AIDS education, managed care, outcomes.

University of Illinois at Chicago, Graduate College, School of Public Health, Division of Health Policy and Administration, Chicago, IL 60607-7128. Offers clinical translational science (MS); health policy (PhD); health policy and administration (Dr PH); health services research (PhD); healthcare (MHA); public health policy management (MPH). Part-time programs available. Terminal master's awarded for partial completion of doctoral program. *Degree requirements:* For master's, thesis, field practicum; for doctorate, thesis/dissertation, independent research, internship. *Entrance requirements:* For master's and doctorate, GRE General Test, minimum GPA of 2.75. Additional exam requirements/recommendations for international students: Required—TOEFL. Electronic applications accepted.

University of La Verne, College of Business and Public Management, Program in Health Administration, La Verne, CA 91750-4443. Offers financial management (MHA); health administration (MHA); human resources (MHA); information management (MHA); leadership and management (MHA); managed care (MHA); marketing and business development (MHA). Part-time programs available. *Faculty:* 22 full-time (11 women), 41 part-time/adjunct (8 women). *Students:* 32 full-time (19 women), 21 part-time (16 women); includes 25 minority (9 African Americans, 10 Asian Americans or Pacific Islanders, 6 Hispanic Americans). Average age 34. In 2009, 19 master's awarded. *Entrance requirements:* For master's, minimum undergraduate GPA of 2.5, 3 letters of reference, curriculum vitae or resume, writing sample. Additional exam requirements/recommendations for international students: Required—TOEFL (minimum score 550 paper-based; 213 computer-based). *Application deadline:* Applications are processed on a rolling basis. Application fee: $50. *Expenses:* Contact institution. *Financial support:* Application deadline: 3/2. *Unit head:* Joan Branin, Chairperson, 909-593-3511 Ext. 4247, E-mail: jbranin@laverne.edu. *Application contact:* Barbara Cox, Program and Admissions Specialist, 909-593-3511 Ext. 4004, Fax: 909-392-2761, E-mail: bcox@laverne.edu.

University of Maryland, Baltimore, Graduate School, Graduate Programs in Pharmacy, Department of Pharmaceutical Health Service Research, Baltimore, MD 21201. Offers epidemiology (MS); pharmacy administration (PhD); Pharm D/PhD. *Degree requirements:* For doctorate, comprehensive exam, thesis/dissertation. *Entrance requirements:* For doctorate, GRE General Test. Additional exam requirements/recommendations for international students: Required—TOEFL, IELTS. Electronic applications accepted. *Expenses:* Tuition, state resident: full-time $7290; part-time $405 per credit hour. Tuition, nonresident: full-time $12,780; part-time $710 per credit hour. Required fees: $774; $10 per credit hour. $297 per semester. Tuition and fees vary according to course load, degree level and program. *Faculty research:* Pharmacoeconomics, outcomes research, public health policy, drug therapy and aging.

University of Massachusetts Worcester, Graduate School of Biomedical Sciences, Program in Clinical and Population Health Research, Worcester, MA 01655-0115. Offers PhD. *Degree requirements:* For doctorate, comprehensive exam, thesis/dissertation. *Entrance requirements:* For doctorate, GRE General Test, master's degree in public health, clinical research, or in one

of the social, psychological, physical, or biological sciences, with adequate introductory course work in biostatistics and epidemiology; 3 letters of recommendation. Additional exam requirements/recommendations for international students: Required—TOEFL (minimum score 600 paper-based; 250 computer-based; 100 iBT). Electronic applications accepted.

University of Minnesota, Twin Cities Campus, School of Public Health, Major in Health Services Research, Policy, and Administration, Minneapolis, MN 55455-0213. Offers MS, PhD, JD/MS, JD/PhD, MD/PhD, MPP/MS. Part-time programs available. Terminal master's awarded for partial completion of doctoral program. *Degree requirements:* For master's, thesis, internship, final oral exam; for doctorate, thesis/dissertation, teaching experience, written preliminary exam, final oral exam, dissertation. *Entrance requirements:* For master's, GRE General Test, course work in mathematics; for doctorate, GRE General Test, prerequisite courses in calculus and statistics. Additional exam requirements/recommendations for international students: Required—TOEFL (minimum score 600 paper-based; 250 computer-based; 100 iBT). *Faculty research:* Outcomes, economics and statistics, sociology, health care management.

University of New Brunswick Fredericton, School of Graduate Studies, Applied Health Services Research Program, Fredericton, NB E3B 5A3, Canada. Offers MAHSR. Part-time programs available. Postbaccalaureate distance learning degree programs offered. *Students:* 6 full-time (all women), 3 part-time (all women). In 2009, 1 master's awarded. *Degree requirements:* For master's, thesis. *Entrance requirements:* For master's, honours BA, minimum GPA of 3.0. Additional exam requirements/recommendations for international students: Required—TOEFL (minimum score 600 paper-based; 250 computer-based; 100 iBT), TWE (minimum score 4), or IELTS (minimum score 7). *Application deadline:* For winter admission, 3/31 for domestic and international students. Application fee: $50 Canadian dollars. Tuition and fees charges are reported in Canadian dollars. *Expenses:* Tuition, area resident: Full-time $5562 Canadian dollars; part-time $2781 Canadian dollars per year. Required fees: $49.75 Canadian dollars per term. *Financial support:* In 2009–10, 2 research assistantships with tuition reimbursements (averaging $9,000 per year) were awarded. *Unit head:* Dr. Linda Eyre, Associate Dean of Graduate Studies, 506-447-3044, Fax: 506-453-4817, E-mail: gradidst@unb.ca. *Application contact:* Janet Amurault, Graduate Secretary, 506-458-7558, Fax: 506-453-4817, E-mail: jamiraul@unb.ca.

The University of North Carolina at Charlotte, Graduate School, College of Health and Human Services, Program in Health Services Research, Charlotte, NC 28223-0001. Offers PhD. *Faculty:* 37 full-time (25 women). *Students:* 13 full-time (12 women), 11 part-time (10 women); includes 4 African Americans, 2 Hispanic Americans, 3 international. Average age 38. 12 applicants, 50% accepted, 5 enrolled. In 2009, 1 doctorate awarded. *Degree requirements:* For doctorate, thesis/dissertation. *Entrance requirements:* For doctorate, GRE. Additional exam requirements/recommendations for international students: Required—TOEFL (minimum score 557 paper-based; 220 computer-based; 83 iBT). *Application deadline:* For fall admission, 7/1 for domestic students, 5/1 for international students; for spring admission, 11/1 for domestic students, 10/1 for international students. Application fee: $55. *Financial support:* In 2009–10, 18 students received support, including 8 research assistantships (averaging $13,219 per year), 10 teaching assistantships (averaging $8,601 per year); career-related internships or fieldwork, Federal Work-Study, institutionally sponsored loans, scholarships/grants, traineeships, and unspecified assistantships also available. Support available to part-time students. Financial award application deadline: 4/1; financial award applicants required to submit FAFSA. Total annual research expenditures: $649,694. *Unit head:* Dr. James Laditka, Director, 704-687-7035, E-mail: jladitka@uncc.edu. *Application contact:* Kathy B. Giddings, Director of Graduate Admissions, 704-687-5503, Fax: 704-687-3279, E-mail: gradadm@uncc.edu.

University of North Florida, Brooks College of Health, Department of Public Health, Jacksonville, FL 32224. Offers community health (MPH); geriatric management (MSH); health administration (MHA); health behavior research and evaluation (Certificate); nutrition (MSH); rehabilitation counseling (MS). *Accreditation:* CEPH. Part-time and evening/weekend programs available. *Faculty:* 23 full-time (17 women). *Students:* 118 full-time (91 women), 82 part-time (61 women); includes 42 minority (23 African Americans, 8 Asian Americans or Pacific Islanders, 11 Hispanic Americans), 9 international. Average age 31. 192 applicants, 26% accepted, 23 enrolled. In 2009, 69 master's awarded. *Degree requirements:* For master's, thesis optional. *Entrance requirements:* For master's, GRE General Test (MSH, MS, MPH); GMAT or GRE General Test (MHA), minimum GPA of 3.0 in last 60 hours. Additional exam requirements/recommendations for international students: Required—TOEFL (minimum score 500 paper-based; 173 computer-based). *Application deadline:* For fall admission, 7/1 priority date for domestic students, 5/1 for international students; for spring admission, 11/1 priority date for domestic students, 10/1 for international students. Applications are processed on a rolling basis. Application fee: $30. Electronic applications accepted. *Expenses:* Tuition, state resident: full-time $6649.20; part-time $277.05 per credit hour. Tuition, nonresident: full-time $22,970; part-time $957.08 per credit hour. Required fees: $985; $41.03 per credit hour. *Financial support:* In 2009–10, 99 students received support, including 1 teaching assistantship (averaging $1,004 per year); research assistantships, career-related internships or fieldwork, Federal Work-Study, scholarships/grants, and tuition waivers (partial) also available. Support available to part-time students. Financial award application deadline: 4/1; financial award applicants required to submit FAFSA. *Faculty research:* Dietary supplements; alcohol, tobacco, and other drug use prevention; turnover among health professionals; aging; psychosocial aspects of disabilities. Total annual research expenditures: $335,106. *Unit head:* Dr. JoAnn Nolin, Chair, 904-620-2840, Fax: 904-620-2848, E-mail: jnolin@unf.edu. *Application contact:* Heather Kenney, Director of Advising, 904-620-2810, Fax: 904-620-1030, E-mail: heather.kenney@unf.edu.

University of Ottawa, Faculty of Graduate and Postdoctoral Studies, Interdisciplinary Programs, Ottawa, ON K1N 6N5, Canada. Offers e-business (Certificate); e-commerce (Certificate); finance (Certificate); health services and policies research (Diploma); population health (PhD); population health risk assessment and management (Certificate); public management and governance (Certificate); systems science (Certificate).

University of Puerto Rico, Medical Sciences Campus, Graduate School of Public Health, Program in Evaluative Research of Health Systems, San Juan, PR 00936-5067. Offers MS. Part-time programs available. *Degree requirements:* For master's, thesis. *Entrance requirements:* For master's, GRE, previous course work in algebra and statistics. *Expenses:* Contact institution.

University of Rochester, School of Medicine and Dentistry, Graduate Programs in Medicine and Dentistry, Department of Community and Preventive Medicine, Program in Health Services Research and Policy, Rochester, NY 14627. Offers PhD, MPH/PhD. *Degree requirements:* For doctorate, thesis/dissertation, qualifying exam. *Entrance requirements:* For doctorate, GRE General Test.

University of Rochester, School of Nursing, Rochester, NY 14642. Offers acute care nurse practitioner (MS); adult nurse practitioner (MS); adult psychiatric mental health nurse practitioner (MS); adult/geriatric nurse practitioner (MS); care of children and families/pediatric nurse practitioner (MS); care of children and families/pediatric nurse practitioner with pediatric behavioral health (MS); care of children and families/pediatric nurse practitioner/neonatal nurse practitioner (MS); child and adolescent psychiatric mental health nurse practitioner (MS); clinical nurse leader (MS); disaster response and emergency preparedness (MS); family nurse practitioner (MS); health care organization management and leadership (MS); health practice research (PhD); health promotion, education and technology (MS); nursing (Certificate). *Accreditation:* AACN; NLN (one or more programs are accredited). Part-time programs available. Postbaccalaureate distance learning degree programs offered (minimal on-campus study). *Faculty:* 26 full-time (24 women), 20 part-time/adjunct (15 women). *Students:* 50 full-time (45 women), 178 part-time (165 women); includes 33 minority (17 African Americans, 2 American Indian/Alaska Native, 10 Asian Americans or Pacific Islanders, 4 Hispanic Americans), 11 international. Average age 35. 56 applicants, 80% accepted, 35 enrolled. In 2009, 53 master's, 5 doctorates awarded. Terminal master's awarded for partial completion of doctoral program. *Degree requirements:* For master's, comprehensive exam or thesis; for doctorate, thesis/dissertation. *Entrance requirements:* For master's, BS in nursing, minimum GPA of 3.0, course work in statistics; for doctorate, GRE General Test, MS in nursing, minimum GPA of 3.5; for Certificate, MS in nursing. Additional exam requirements/recommendations for international students: Recommended—TOEFL (minimum score 560 paper-based; 230 computer-based; 88 iBT). *Application deadline:* For fall admission, 11/1 priority date for domestic and international students. Application fee: $50. *Financial support:* In 2009–10, 53 students received support, including 14 fellowships with full and partial tuition reimbursements available (averaging $17,497 per year); scholarships/grants, traineeships, health care benefits, tuition waivers (partial), and unspecified assistantships also available. Support available to part-time students. Financial award application deadline: 6/30. *Faculty research:* Clinical research in aging, managing asthma in children, interventions to improve outcomes in critically ill children and their mothers, nurse home visitation studies, medical device evaluation, critical care clinical studies, high risk behavior and prevention, palliative care, pregnancy-related weight gain. Total annual research expenditures: $4.8 million. *Unit head:* Dr. Kathy P. Parker, Dean, 585-273-5639, Fax: 585-273-1268, E-mail: kathy_parker@urmc.rochester.edu. *Application contact:* Elaine Andolina, Director of Admissions, 585-275-2375, Fax: 585-756-8299, E-mail: elaine_andolina@urmc.rochester.edu.

University of Southern California, Keck School of Medicine and Graduate School, Graduate Programs in Medicine, Department of Preventive Medicine, Program in Health Behavior Research, Los Angeles, CA 90089. Offers PhD. *Faculty:* 20 full-time (12 women). *Students:* 26 full-time (23 women); includes 10 minority (2 African Americans, 1 American Indian/Alaska Native, 6 Asian Americans or Pacific Islanders, 1 Hispanic American), 2 international. Average age 29. 35 applicants, 26% accepted, 6 enrolled. In 2009, 7 doctorates awarded. *Degree requirements:* For doctorate, comprehensive exam, thesis/dissertation. *Entrance requirements:* For doctorate, GRE General Test, minimum GPA of 3.0. Additional exam requirements/recommendations for international students: Required—TOEFL (minimum score 600 paper-based; 250 computer-based; 100 iBT). *Application deadline:* For fall admission, 12/1 priority date for domestic and international students. Application fee: $85. Electronic applications accepted. *Expenses:* Tuition: Full-time $25,980; part-time $1315 per unit. Required fees: $554. One-time fee: $35 full-time. Full-time tuition and fees vary according to degree level and program. *Financial support:* In 2009–10, 8 fellowships with full tuition reimbursements (averaging $27,060 per year), 17 research assistantships with full tuition reimbursements (averaging $27,060 per year), 8 teaching assistantships with full and partial tuition reimbursements (averaging $27,060 per year) were awarded; institutionally sponsored loans, scholarships/grants, traineeships, health care benefits, and unspecified assistantships also available. Financial award application deadline: 12/1; financial award applicants required to submit CSS PROFILE or FAFSA. *Faculty research:* Obesity prevention, etiology and prevention of substance abuse and chronic diseases, health disparities, translational research. Total annual research expenditures: $2.8 million. *Unit head:* Dr. Louise Ann Rohrbach, Director, 626-457-6642, Fax: 626-457-4012, E-mail: rohrbac@usc.edu. *Application contact:* Marny Barovich, Program Manager, 626-457-6648, Fax: 626-457-4012, E-mail: barovich@hsc.usc.edu.

University of Virginia, School of Medicine, Department of Public Health Sciences, Charlottesville, VA 22903. Offers clinical research (MS), including clinical investigation and patient-oriented research, informatics in medicine; public health (MPH). Part-time programs available. *Faculty:* 30 full-time (15 women), 3 part-time/adjunct (1 woman). *Students:* 22 full-time (13 women), 20 part-time (13 women); includes 11 minority (3 African Americans, 5 Asian Americans or Pacific Islanders, 3 Hispanic Americans). Average age 32. 89 applicants, 48% accepted, 26 enrolled. In 2009, 27 master's awarded. *Entrance requirements:* For master's, GRE General Test or MCAT. Additional exam requirements/recommendations for international students: Required—TOEFL. *Application deadline:* Applications are processed on a rolling basis. Application fee: $60. Electronic applications accepted. *Financial support:* Career-related internships or fieldwork available. Financial award applicants required to submit FAFSA. *Unit head:* Dr. William A. Knaus, Chair, 434-924-8430, Fax: 434-924-8437. *Application contact:* Tracey L. Brookman, Academic Programs Administrator, 434-924-8430, Fax: 434-924-8437, E-mail: ms-hes@virginia.edu.

University of Washington, Graduate School, School of Public Health, Department of Health Services, Seattle, WA 98195. Offers bioinformatics (PhD); cancer prevention and control (PhD); clinical research (MS); community oriented public health practice (MPH); economics or finance (PhD); evaluation sciences (PhD); executive program (MHA); health behavior and health promotion (PhD); health care and population health research (MPH); health policy analysis and process (PhD); health policy and analysis and process (MPH); health services (MS, PhD); health services administration (EMHA, MHA); in residence program (MHA); occupational health (PhD); population health and social determinants (PhD); social and behavioral sciences (MPH); sociology and demography (PhD); JD/MHA; MHA/MBA; MHA/MD; MHA/MPA; MPH/JD; MPH/MD; MPH/MN; MPH/MPA; MPH/MSD; MPH/MSW; MPH/PhD. Part-time and evening/weekend programs available. Postbaccalaureate distance learning degree programs offered (minimal on-campus study). *Faculty:* 52 full-time (24 women), 60 part-time/adjunct (28 women). *Students:* 104 full-time (83 women), 100 part-time (76 women); includes 21 minority (6 African Americans, 1 American Indian/Alaska Native, 11 Asian Americans or Pacific Islanders, 3 Hispanic Americans), 6 international. Average age 34. 375 applicants, 17% accepted, 24 enrolled. In 2009, 33 master's awarded. Terminal master's awarded for partial completion of doctoral program. *Degree requirements:* For master's, thesis (for some programs), practicum (MPH); for doctorate, comprehensive exam, thesis/dissertation. *Entrance requirements:* For master's and doctorate, GRE General Test, minimum GPA of 3.0. Additional exam requirements/recommendations for international students: Required—TOEFL. *Application deadline:* For fall admission, 1/15 for domestic students, 11/1 for international students. Application fee: 50 Albanian leks. Electronic applications accepted. *Financial support:* In 2009–10, 64 students received support, including 10 fellowships with full and partial tuition reimbursements available (averaging $21,000 per year), 10 research assistantships with full and partial tuition reimbursements available (averaging $18,000 per year), 3 teaching assistantships with full and partial tuition reimbursements available (averaging $18,000 per year); career-related internships or fieldwork, Federal Work-Study, institutionally sponsored loans, and traineeships also available. Financial award application deadline: 2/28; financial award applicants required to submit FAFSA. *Faculty research:* Health promotion and disease prevention, maternal and child health, health services research design, program evaluation, health policy. Total annual research expenditures: $10.5 million. *Unit head:* Dr. Larry Kessler, Chair, 206-543-616-2930. *Application contact:* Kitty A. Andert, Program Manager, 206-616-2926, Fax: 206-543-3964, E-mail: kitander@u.washington.edu.

University of Wisconsin–Madison, School of Medicine and Public Health and Graduate School, Graduate Programs in Medicine, Department of Population Health Sciences, Madison, WI 53726. Offers clinical research (MS, PhD); epidemiology (MS, PhD); health services research (MS, PhD); population health sciences (MPH); social and behavioral health sciences (MS, PhD); DPT/MPH; DVM/MPH; MD/MPH; MPA/MPH; MS/MPH; Pharm D/MPH. *Accreditation:* CEPH. Part-time programs available. *Faculty:* 104 full-time (54 women), 2 part-time/adjunct (0 women). *Students:* 105 full-time (76 women), 38 part-time (31 women); includes 19 minority (8 African Americans, 8 Asian Americans or Pacific Islanders, 3 Hispanic Americans), 15 international. Average age 30. 126 applicants, 75% accepted, 58 enrolled. In 2009, 13 master's, 8 doctorates awarded. Terminal master's awarded for partial completion of doctoral program. *Degree requirements:* For master's, thesis, defense; for doctorate, comprehensive exam, thesis/dissertation, qualifying exam, preliminary exam, dissertation defense. *Entrance requirements:* For master's and doctorate, GRE (separate guidelines for those with doctoral degrees), minimum GPA of 3.0, quantitative preparation (calculus, statistics, or other) with minimum B average. Additional exam requirements/recommendations for international students: Required—TOEFL (minimum score 600 paper-based; 250 computer-based; 100 iBT). *Application deadline:* For fall admission, 1/15 for domestic and international students. Application fee: $56. Electronic applications accepted. *Expenses:* Tuition, state resident: part-time $594 per credit. Tuition, nonresident: part-time $1504 per credit. Required fees: $65 per credit. Tuition and fees vary according to course load, program and reciprocity agreements. *Financial support:* In 2009–10, 73 students received support, including 16 fellowships with full tuition reimbursements available (averaging $21,000 per year), 38 research assistantships with full tuition reimbursements available (averaging $17,300 per year), 7 teaching assistantships with full tuition reimbursements available (averaging $17,300 per year); scholarships/grants, trainee-

Health Services Research

University of Wisconsin–Madison (continued)
ships, health care benefits, and unspecified assistantships also available. Support available to part-time students. *Faculty research:* Epidemiology (cancer, environmental, aging, infectious disease and genetic), determinants of population health, health services research, social and behavioral health sciences, biostatistics. Total annual research expenditures: $11.4 million. *Unit head:* Dr. F. Javier Nieto, Chair, 608-265-5242, Fax: 608-263-2820, E-mail: fjnieto@wisc.edu. *Application contact:* Kelly Haslam, Graduate Program Coordinator, 608-265-8108, Fax: 608-263-2820, E-mail: haslam@wisc.edu.

Virginia Commonwealth University, Graduate School, School of Allied Health Professions, Department of Health Administration, Doctoral Program in Health Services Organization and Research, Richmond, VA 23284-9005. Offers PhD. *Degree requirements:* For doctorate, thesis/dissertation, residency. *Entrance requirements:* For doctorate, GMAT or GRE General Test.

Wake Forest University, School of Medicine and Graduate School of Arts and Sciences, Graduate Programs in Medicine, Program in Health Sciences Research, Winston-Salem, NC 27109. Offers MS. *Degree requirements:* For master's, thesis. *Entrance requirements:* For master's, GRE General Test. Additional exam requirements/recommendations for international students: Required—TOEFL. Electronic applications accepted. *Faculty research:* Research methodologies, statistical methods, measurement of health outcomes, health economics.

Section 30
Nursing

This section contains a directory of institutions offering graduate work in nursing, followed by in-depth entries submitted by institutions that chose to prepare detailed program descriptions. Additional information about programs listed in the directory but not augmented by an in-depth entry may be obtained by writing directly to the dean of a graduate school or chair of a department at the address given in the directory.

For programs offering related work, see also in this book *Health Services* and *Public Health*.

In another guide in this series: **Graduate Programs in the Humanities, Arts & Social Sciences**, see *Family and Consumer Sciences (Gerontology)*

CONTENTS

Nursing—General

Abilene Christian University, Graduate School, School of Nursing, Abilene, TX 79699-9100. Offers education and administration (MSN); family nurse practitioner (MSN). *Accreditation:* AACN. Part-time programs available. *Faculty:* 6 part-time/adjunct (all women). *Students:* 3 full-time (all women), 4 part-time (2 women); includes 4 minority (1 American Indian/Alaska Native, 2 Asian Americans or Pacific Islanders, 1 Hispanic American). 11 applicants, 36% accepted, 4 enrolled. In 2009, 5 master's, 1 other advanced degree awarded. *Entrance requirements:* For master's, GRE General Test. *Application deadline:* For fall admission, 4/1 priority date for domestic students; for spring admission, 11/1 for domestic students. Applications are processed on a rolling basis. Application fee: $40. Electronic applications accepted. *Expenses:* Tuition: Full-time $11,520; part-time $640 per hour. Required fees: $1090; $53.50 per hour. $10 per term. Tuition and fees vary according to program. *Financial support:* In 2009–10, 6 students received support. Application deadline: 4/1. *Unit head:* Dr. Amy Toone, Graduate Director, 325-671-2361, Fax: 325-671-2386, E-mail: atoone@phssn.edu. *Application contact:* William Horn, Graduate Admissions Counselor, 325-674-2656, Fax: 325-674-6717, E-mail: gradinfo@acu.edu.

Adelphi University, School of Nursing, Garden City, NY 11530-0701. Offers MS, PhD, Certificate. *Accreditation:* AACN. Part-time and evening/weekend programs available. *Faculty:* 36 full-time (34 women), 100 part-time/adjunct (94 women). *Students:* 137 part-time (120 women); includes 74 minority (52 African Americans, 17 Asian Americans or Pacific Islanders, 5 Hispanic Americans). Average age 42. 78 applicants, 53% accepted, 38 enrolled. In 2009, 54 master's, 2 other advanced degrees awarded. *Degree requirements:* For master's, thesis or alternative. *Entrance requirements:* For master's, BSN, clinical experience, 1 course in basic statistics, minimum GPA of 3.0, 2 letters of recommendation, resume or curriculum vitae; for doctorate, GRE, licensure as RN in New York, professional writing sample (scholarly writing), 3 letters of recommendation, resume or curriculum vitae; for Certificate, MSN. Additional exam requirements/recommendations for international students: Required—TOEFL (minimum score 550 paper-based; 213 computer-based; 80 iBT). *Application deadline:* For fall admission, 3/15 for domestic students, 4/1 for international students; for spring admission, 11/1 for international students. Application fee: $50. Electronic applications accepted. *Expenses:* Tuition: Full-time $28,340; part-time $830 per credit. Required fees: $600; $250 per credit. Full-time tuition and fees vary according to course load and program. *Financial support:* In 2009–10, 15 teaching assistantships (averaging $4,512 per year) were awarded; career-related internships or fieldwork, unspecified assistantships, and graduate achievement awards also available. Support available to part-time students. Financial award application deadline: 2/15; financial award applicants required to submit FAFSA. *Faculty research:* Social practices in healthcare, bereavement, family grief, historiography, gerontology. *Unit head:* Dr. Patrick Coonan, Dean, 516-877-4511, E-mail: coonan@adelphi.edu. *Application contact:* Christine Murphy, Director of Admissions, 516-877-3050, Fax: 516-877-3039, E-mail: graduateadmissions@adelphi.edu.

Albany State University, College of Sciences and Health Professions, Department of Nursing, Albany, GA 31705-2717. Offers RN to MSN family nurse practitioner (MSN); RN to MSN nurse educator (MSN). Part-time and evening/weekend programs available. Postbaccalaureate distance learning degree programs offered. *Students:* 12 full-time (11 women), 49 part-time (45 women); includes 32 minority (30 African Americans, 2 Asian Americans or Pacific Islanders). Average age 39. 20 applicants, 95% accepted, 16 enrolled. In 2009, 21 master's awarded. *Degree requirements:* For master's, comprehensive exam, thesis or major research project. *Entrance requirements:* For master's, GRE or MAT, baccalaureate degree in nursing, minimum GPA of 3.0, current Georgia RN practicing license, personal interview with the Coordinator of the Graduate Nursing Program, two letters of reference regarding professional accomplishments and academic potential, ASU medical and immunization forms. Additional exam requirements/recommendations for international students: Required—TOEFL. *Application deadline:* For fall admission, 11/16 for domestic students, 9/16 for international students; for spring admission, 4/19 for domestic students, 2/19 for international students. Applications are processed on a rolling basis. Application fee: $20. Electronic applications accepted. *Expenses:* Tuition, state resident: full-time $2970; part-time $162 per credit hour. Tuition, nonresident: full-time $12,168; part-time $676 per credit hour. Required fees: $962; $75 per credit hour. *Financial support:* Application deadline: 6/30. *Faculty research:* HIV issues, cancer-specifically breast, prostate, and lung, cultural diversity, health promotion, smoking cessation. *Unit head:* Linda Grimsley, Chairperson, 229-430-4724, Fax: 229-430-3937, E-mail: lgrimsl@asurams.edu. *Application contact:* Linda Grimsley, Chairperson, 229-430-4724, Fax: 229-430-3937, E-mail: linda.grimsley@asurams.edu.

Alcorn State University, School of Graduate Studies, School of Nursing, Natchez, MS 39122-8399. Offers rural nursing (MSN). *Accreditation:* NLN.

Allen College, Program in Nursing, Waterloo, IA 50703. Offers acute care nurse practitioner (MSN); adult nurse practitioner (MSN); adult psychiatric-mental health nurse practitioner (MSN); family nurse practitioner (MSN); gerontological nurse practitioner (MSN); health education (MSN); leadership in health care delivery (MSN). *Accreditation:* AACN; NLN. Part-time programs available. *Faculty:* 2 full-time (both women), 8 part-time/adjunct (all women). *Students:* 37 full-time (35 women), 103 part-time (99 women); includes 1 minority (Asian American or Pacific Islander). Average age 38. *Degree requirements:* For master's, thesis optional. *Entrance requirements:* For master's, minimum GPA of 3.0. Additional exam requirements/recommendations for international students: Required—TOEFL (minimum score 550 paper-based). *Application deadline:* For fall admission, 7/15 priority date for domestic students; for spring admission, 12/1 priority date for domestic students. Applications are processed on a rolling basis. Application fee: $50. Electronic applications accepted. *Expenses:* Tuition: Full-time $12,550; part-time $651 per credit hour. Required fees: $826; $65 per credit hour. One-time fee: $425. Tuition and fees vary according to course load. *Financial support:* Teaching assistantships, institutionally sponsored loans, scholarships/grants, and traineeships available. Support available to part-time students. Financial award application deadline: 8/15; financial award applicants required to submit FAFSA. *Faculty research:* Pain and aged, congestive heart failure. *Unit head:* Nancy Kramer, Dean, School of Nursing, 319-226-2040, Fax: 319-226-2070, E-mail: kramerna@ihs.org. *Application contact:* Michelle Koehn, Admissions Counselor, 319-226-2002, Fax: 319-226-2051, E-mail: koehnml@ihs.org.

Alverno College, School of Nursing, Milwaukee, WI 53234-3922. Offers MSN. *Accreditation:* AACN. Part-time and evening/weekend programs available. *Faculty:* 7 full-time (all women), 2 part-time/adjunct (both women). *Students:* 13 full-time (all women), 35 part-time (all women); includes 7 minority (4 African Americans, 1 Asian American or Pacific Islander, 2 Hispanic Americans), 1 international. Average age 40. 32 applicants, 66% accepted, 17 enrolled. In 2009, 11 master's awarded. *Degree requirements:* For master's, 500 clinical hours, capstone. *Entrance requirements:* For master's, BSN, current license. Additional exam requirements/recommendations for international students: Required—TOEFL. *Application deadline:* For fall admission, 7/15 priority date for domestic and international students; for spring admission, 12/15 priority date for domestic and international students. Applications are processed on a rolling basis. Application fee: $50. Electronic applications accepted. *Expenses:* Contact institution. *Financial support:* In 2009–10, 21 students received support. Federal Work-Study available. Support available to part-time students. Financial award application deadline: 4/15. *Faculty research:* Impact of stroke on sexuality, children's asthma management factors affecting baccalaureate student success. *Unit head:* Julie Millenbruch, Program Director, Fax: 414-382-6354, E-mail: julie.millenbruch@alverno.edu. *Application contact:* Carolyn Wise, Graduate Recruiter, 414-382-6045, Fax: 414-382-6354, E-mail: carolyn.wise@alverno.edu.

American International College, School of Health Sciences, Department of Nursing, Springfield, MA 01109-3189. Offers nursing administration (MSN); nursing education (MSN). *Accreditation:* AACN. *Entrance requirements:* For master's, BSN. Additional exam requirements/recommendations for international students: Required—TOEFL. Electronic applications accepted. *Expenses:* Tuition: Full-time $12,510; part-time $695 per credit hour. Required fees: $35 per term.

American Sentinel University, Graduate Programs, Englewood, CO 80112. Offers business administration (MBA); business intelligence (MS); computer science (MSCS); health information management (MS); healthcare (MBA); information systems (MSIS); nursing (MSN). Part-time and evening/weekend programs available. Postbaccalaureate distance learning degree programs offered (no on-campus study). *Entrance requirements:* Additional exam requirements/recommendations for international students: Required—TOEFL (minimum score 600 paper-based; 215 computer-based). Electronic applications accepted.

American University of Beirut, Graduate Programs, School of Nursing, Beirut, Lebanon. Offers MSN. *Accreditation:* AACN. Part-time programs available. *Degree requirements:* For master's, comprehensive exam, thesis optional. *Entrance requirements:* For master's, GRE, letter of recommendation. Additional exam requirements/recommendations for international students: Required—TOEFL (minimum score 600 paper-based; 250 computer-based; 100 iBT), IELTS (minimum score 7.5). *Faculty research:* Pain management and palliative care, stress and post-traumatic stress disorder, health benefits and chronic illness, health promotion and community interventions.

Andrews University, School of Graduate Studies, College of Arts and Sciences, Department of Nursing, Berrien Springs, MI 49104. Offers MS. *Accreditation:* NLN. Part-time and evening/weekend programs available. *Faculty:* 4 full-time (all women). *Students:* 7 full-time (all women); includes 3 minority (all African Americans), 1 international. Average age 44. 5 applicants, 0% accepted, 0 enrolled. In 2009, 4 master's awarded. *Degree requirements:* For master's, thesis. *Entrance requirements:* For master's, GRE, minimum GPA of 2.5, 1 year of nursing experience, RN license. Additional exam requirements/recommendations for international students: Required—TOEFL (minimum score 550 paper-based). *Application deadline:* Applications are processed on a rolling basis. Application fee: $40. *Financial support:* Institutionally sponsored loans available. *Faculty research:* Theory for nursing, salary equitability. *Unit head:* Dr. Karen A. Allen, Chairperson, 269-471-3364. *Application contact:* Carolyn Hurst, Supervisor of Graduate Admission, 800-253-2874, Fax: 269-471-6321, E-mail: graduate@andrews.edu.

Arizona State University, Graduate College, College of Nursing and Healthcare Innovation, Tempe, AZ 85287. Offers child and adolescent mental health intervention specialist (Graduate Certificate); community and public health practice (Graduate Certificate); community health (MS); evidence-based practice in nursing (Graduate Certificate); exercise and wellness (MS, PhD), including exercise and wellness (MS), physical activity, nutrition and wellness (PhD); healthcare innovation (MHI); nurse education in academic and practice settings (Graduate Certificate); nurse educator (MS); nursing (MS); nursing and healthcare innovation (PhD); nursing practice (DNP); nutrition (MS). *Accreditation:* AACN. Postbaccalaureate distance learning degree programs offered.

Arkansas State University—Jonesboro, Graduate School, College of Nursing and Health Professions, School of Nursing, Jonesboro, State University, AR 72467. Offers nurse anesthesia (MSN); nursing (MSN). *Accreditation:* AANA/CANAEP; NLN. Part-time programs available. *Faculty:* 7 full-time (6 women), 5 part-time/adjunct (4 women). *Students:* 110 full-time (45 women), 83 part-time (78 women); includes 22 minority (19 African Americans, 1 American Indian/Alaska Native, 2 Asian Americans or Pacific Islanders). Average age 33. 52 applicants, 38% accepted, 15 enrolled. In 2009, 70 master's awarded. *Degree requirements:* For master's, comprehensive exam, thesis or alternative. *Entrance requirements:* For master's, GRE General Test or MAT, appropriate bachelor's degree, current Arkansas nursing license, CPR certification, physical examination, professional liability insurance, critical care experience, ACLS Certification, PALS Certification, interview, immunization records. Additional exam requirements/recommendations for international students: Required—TOEFL (minimum score 550 paper-based; 213 computer-based; 79 iBT), IELTS (minimum score 6). *Application deadline:* For spring admission, 10/15 for domestic and international students. Applications are processed on a rolling basis. Application fee: $30 ($40 for international students). Electronic applications accepted. *Expenses:* Contact institution. *Financial support:* In 2009–10, 4 students received support. Career-related internships or fieldwork, scholarships/grants, and unspecified assistantships available. Financial award application deadline: 7/1; financial award applicants required to submit FAFSA. *Unit head:* Dr. Sue McLarry, Chair, 870-972-3074, Fax: 870-972-2954, E-mail: smclarry@astate.edu. *Application contact:* Dr. Andrew Sustich, Dean of the Graduate School, 870-972-3029, Fax: 870-972-3857, E-mail: sustich@astate.edu.

Arkansas Tech University, Graduate College, College of Natural and Health Sciences, Russellville, AR 72801. Offers fisheries and wildlife biology (MS); health informatics (MS); nursing (MSN). *Students:* 6 full-time (5 women), 12 part-time (6 women). Average age 31. In 2009, 1 master's awarded. *Degree requirements:* For master's, thesis, project. *Entrance requirements:* For master's, GRE General Test. Additional exam requirements/recommendations for international students: Required—TOEFL (minimum score 550 paper-based; 213 computer-based; 79 iBT), IELTS (minimum score 6). *Application deadline:* For fall admission, 3/1 priority date for domestic students, 5/1 priority date for international students; for spring admission, 10/1 priority date for domestic and international students. Applications are processed on a rolling basis. Application fee: $0 ($30 for international students). Electronic applications accepted. *Expenses:* Tuition, state resident: full-time $3438; part-time $191 per hour. Tuition, nonresident: full-time $6876; part-time $382 per hour. Required fees: $482; $9 per credit hour. $140 per semester. Tuition and fees vary according to course load. *Financial support:* In 2009–10, teaching assistantships with full tuition reimbursements (averaging $4,000 per year); research assistantships, career-related internships or fieldwork, Federal Work-Study, scholarships/grants, health care benefits, and unspecified assistantships also available. Support available to part-time students. Financial award application deadline: 4/15; financial award applicants required to submit FAFSA. *Faculty research:* Fisheries, warblers, fish movement, darter populations, bob white studies. *Unit head:* Dr. Richard Cohoon, Dean, 479-964-0816, E-mail: richard.cohoon@atu.edu. *Application contact:* Dr. Mary B. Gunter, Dean of Graduate College, 479-968-0398, Fax: 479-964-0542, E-mail: graduate.school@atu.edu.

Armstrong Atlantic State University, School of Graduate Studies, Program in Nursing, Savannah, GA 31419-1997. Offers MSN. *Accreditation:* AACN. Part-time and evening/weekend programs available. *Degree requirements:* For master's, comprehensive exam, thesis optional, project. *Entrance requirements:* For master's, GRE General Test or MAT, minimum GPA of 2.5, letter of recommendation, Georgia RN license, BS in nursing, letter of intent. Additional exam requirements/recommendations for international students: Required—TOEFL (minimum score 523 paper-based; 193 computer-based). Electronic applications accepted. *Faculty research:* Osteoporosis, cancer, tai chi, heart disease.

Athabasca University, Centre for Nursing and Health Studies, Athabasca, AB T9S 3A3, Canada. Offers advanced nursing practice (MN, Advanced Diploma); generalist (MN); health studies-leadership (MHS). Part-time programs available. Postbaccalaureate distance learning degree programs offered. *Faculty:* 11 full-time (all women), 1 (woman) part-time/adjunct. *Students:* 542 part-time. Average age 38. 428 applicants, 51 enrolled. In 2009, 181 master's, 6 other advanced degrees awarded. *Degree requirements:* For master's, comprehensive exam (for some programs). *Entrance requirements:* For master's, bachelor's degree in health-related field, 2 years professional health service experience (MHS), bachelor's degree in nursing, 2 years nursing experience (MN), minimum GPA of 3.0 in final 30 credits; for Advanced Diploma, RN license, 2 years health care experience. *Application deadline:* For fall admission, 3/1 for domestic and international students. Application fee: $80. Electronic applications accepted. *Expenses:* Contact institution. *Unit head:* Dr. Donna Romyn, Dean, 800-788-9041 Ext. 6794, Fax: 780-675-6468, E-mail: dromyn@athabascau.ca. *Application contact:* Donna Dunn Hart, Academic Student Advisor—Graduate Programs, 800-788-9041 Ext. 6300, Fax: 780-675-6468, E-mail: donnad@athabascau.ca.

Auburn University, Graduate School, School of Nursing, Auburn University, AL 36849. Offers MSN. *Accreditation:* AACN. *Expenses:* Tuition, state resident: full-time $6240. Tuition,

nonresident: full-time $18,720. International tuition: $18,938 full-time. Required fees: $492. Tuition and fees vary according to course load, program and reciprocity agreements.

Augsburg College, Program in Transcultural Community Health Nursing, Minneapolis, MN 55454-1351. Offers MA. *Accreditation:* AACN. *Degree requirements:* For master's, thesis or alternative. *Expenses:* Tuition: Full-time $16,713; part-time $1857 per course. Required fees: $450; $50 per course. Tuition and fees vary according to course load and program.

Augustana College, Program in Advanced Nursing Practice in Emerging Health Systems, Sioux Falls, SD 57197. Offers MA. *Accreditation:* AACN. Part-time programs available. Postbaccalaureate distance learning degree programs offered (minimal on-campus study). *Degree requirements:* For master's, portfolio, oral exam, paper. *Entrance requirements:* For master's, current licensure, minimum GPA of 3.0, previous course work in statistics, bachelor's degree in nursing. Additional exam requirements/recommendations for international students: Required—TOEFL. *Application deadline:* For fall admission, 6/1 priority date for domestic students. Applications are processed on a rolling basis. Application fee: $50. *Expenses:* Tuition: Full-time $25,422; part-time $427 per credit hour. Required fees: $274. Part-time tuition and fees vary according to course load and program. *Financial support:* Career-related internships or fieldwork, Federal Work-Study, institutionally sponsored loans, and scholarships/grants available. *Faculty research:* HIV infected persons, nursing theory development, nursing workforce development. *Application contact:* Graduate Coordinator, 274-274-4043, Fax: 274-274-4450, E-mail: graduate@augie.edu.

Austin Peay State University, College of Graduate Studies, College of Behavioral and Health Sciences, School of Nursing, Clarksville, TN 37044. Offers advanced practice (MSN); nursing administration (MSN); nursing education (MSN); nursing informatics (MSN). Part-time programs available. Postbaccalaureate distance learning degree programs offered. *Faculty:* 7 full-time (all women). *Students:* 15 full-time (14 women), 62 part-time (57 women); includes 6 minority (3 African Americans, 1 American Indian/Alaska Native, 2 Asian Americans or Pacific Islanders). Average age 39. 31 applicants, 100% accepted, 22 enrolled. In 2009, 9 master's awarded. *Degree requirements:* For master's, comprehensive exam. *Entrance requirements:* For master's, GRE General Test, minimum GPA of 3.0, RN license eligibility, 3 letters of recommendation. Additional exam requirements/recommendations for international students: Required—TOEFL (minimum score 600 paper-based). *Application deadline:* For fall admission, 7/27 priority date for domestic students; for spring admission, 12/17 priority date for domestic students. Applications are processed on a rolling basis. Application fee: $25. Electronic applications accepted. *Expenses:* Tuition, state resident: full-time $6160; part-time $608 per credit hour. Tuition, nonresident: full-time $17,080; part-time $854 per credit hour. Required fees: $1224; $61.20 per credit hour. *Financial support:* In 2009–10, 1 student received support, including 1 research assistantship with full tuition reimbursement available (averaging $5,184 per year); career-related internships or fieldwork, Federal Work-Study, institutionally sponsored loans, scholarships/grants, and unspecified assistantships also available. Support available to part-time students. *Unit head:* Dr. Francisca Ann Farrar, Director, 931-221-7737, Fax: 931-221-6490, E-mail: farrarf@apsu.edu. *Application contact:* Dr. Doris Davenport, Associate Professor, 931-221-7467, Fax: 931-221-7595, E-mail: davenportd@apsu.edu.

Azusa Pacific University, School of Nursing, Azusa, CA 91702-7000. Offers nursing (MSN); nursing education (PhD). *Accreditation:* AACN. Part-time and evening/weekend programs available. *Degree requirements:* For master's, thesis optional. *Entrance requirements:* For master's, BSN. *Faculty research:* Family adaptation to illness and crisis, bioethical issues in nursing, self-care activities, quality of life issues, home health.

Ball State University, Graduate School, College of Applied Science and Technology, School of Nursing, Muncie, IN 47306-1099. Offers MS. *Accreditation:* AACN. Part-time programs available. *Entrance requirements:* For master's, bachelor's degree in nursing, minimum GPA of 2.8 in upper-level course work, interview, resume.

Barry University, School of Nursing, Miami Shores, FL 33161-6695. Offers MSN, PhD, Certificate, MSN/MBA. Part-time and evening/weekend programs available. *Degree requirements:* For master's, research project or thesis; for doctorate, thesis/dissertation. *Entrance requirements:* For master's, GRE General Test or MAT, BSN, minimum GPA of 3.0, course work in statistics and research, Florida RN license; for doctorate, GRE General Test or MAT, minimum GPA of 3.3, MSN. Electronic applications accepted. *Faculty research:* Adult education, nurse practitioner, stress reduction in pregnancy, prevention of cardiac problems, in children, level of school age children.

Baylor University, Graduate School, Louise Herrington School of Nursing, Dallas, TX 75246. Offers family nurse practitioner (MSN); neonatal nurse practitioner (MSN); nursing administration and management (MSN). *Accreditation:* AACN. *Students:* 32 full-time (31 women), 26 part-time (25 women); includes 12 minority (4 African Americans, 1 American Indian/Alaska Native, 3 Asian Americans or Pacific Islanders, 4 Hispanic Americans), 1 international. In 2009, 17 master's awarded. *Entrance requirements:* For master's, GRE General Test. *Application deadline:* For fall admission, 8/1 for domestic students; for spring admission, 12/1 for domestic students. Applications are processed on a rolling basis. Application fee: $25. *Unit head:* Dr. Mary Brucker, Graduate Program Director, 214-820-4111, Fax: 214-818-8692, E-mail: mary_brucker@baylor.edu. *Application contact:* Beverly Kurfees, Administrative Assistant, 214-820-4111, Fax: 254-710-3870, E-mail: beverly_kurfees@baylor.edu.

Bellarmine University, Donna and Allan Lansing School of Nursing and Health Sciences, Louisville, KY 40205-0671. Offers family nurse practitioner (MSN); nursing administration (MSN); nursing education (MSN); nursing practice (DNP); physical therapy (DPT). *Accreditation:* AACN; APTA. Part-time and evening/weekend programs available. *Faculty:* 16 full-time (11 women), 7 part-time/adjunct (6 women). *Students:* 126 full-time (94 women), 50 part-time (48 women); includes 4 minority (1 African American, 3 Asian Americans or Pacific Islanders). Average age 30. 350 applicants, 48 enrolled. In 2009, 9 master's, 41 doctorates awarded. *Degree requirements:* For doctorate, comprehensive exam, thesis/dissertation. *Entrance requirements:* For master's, GRE General Test, RN license; for doctorate, GRE General Test, Physical Therapist Centralized Application Service (for DPT). Additional exam requirements/recommendations for international students: Required—TOEFL (minimum score 550 paper-based; 213 computer-based; 80 iBT). Application fee: $25. Electronic applications accepted. *Expenses:* Contact institution. *Financial support:* Career-related internships or fieldwork and scholarships/grants available. *Faculty research:* Nursing: pain, empathy, leadership styles, control; physical therapy: service learning; exercise in chronic and pre-operative conditions, and athletes; women's health; aging. *Unit head:* Dr. Susan H. Davis, Dean, 800-274-4723 Ext. 8217, E-mail: sdavis@bellarmine.edu. *Application contact:* Julie Armstrong-Binnix, Health Science Recruiter, 800-274-4723 Ext. 8364, E-mail: julieab@bellarmine.edu.

Bellin College, Program in Nursing, Green Bay, WI 54305. Offers administrator (MSN); educator (MSN). *Accreditation:* AACN.

Belmont University, College of Health Sciences, School of Nursing, Nashville, TN 37212-3757. Offers MSN. *Accreditation:* AACN. Part-time programs available. *Degree requirements:* For master's, comprehensive exam. *Entrance requirements:* For master's, GRE, BSN, minimum GPA of 3.0. Additional exam requirements/recommendations for international students: Required—TOEFL (minimum score 550 paper-based; 213 computer-based). Electronic applications accepted. *Expenses:* Contact institution. *Faculty research:* Postpartum post-operative care, adherence/compliance behavior in chronic illness, women's health in primary care, geriatrics.

Bethel College, Division of Graduate Studies, Program in Nursing, Mishawaka, IN 46545-5591. Offers MSN. *Accreditation:* NLN. Part-time and evening/weekend programs available. *Faculty:* 1 (woman) full-time, 5 part-time/adjunct (4 women). *Students:* 23 part-time (all women). 18 applicants, 94% accepted, 14 enrolled. In 2009, 5 master's awarded. *Degree requirements:* For master's, thesis. *Entrance requirements:* Additional exam requirements/recommendations for international students: Required—TOEFL (minimum score 540 paper-based; 207 computer-based). *Application deadline:* For fall admission, 8/15 for domestic students, 5/1 for international students; for spring admission, 10/1 for international students. Application fee: $25. Electronic applications accepted. *Financial support:* Career-related internships or fieldwork available. Financial award applicants required to submit FAFSA. *Unit head:* Dr. Karon Schwartz, Director, 574-257-3382, E-mail: schwark@bethelcollege.edu. *Application contact:* Dr. Karon Schwartz, Director, 574-257-3382, E-mail: schwark@bethelcollege.edu.

Bethel University, Graduate School, Department of Nursing, St. Paul, MN 55112-6999. Offers healthcare leadership (MA); nursing education (MA, Certificate). *Accreditation:* AACN. Evening/weekend programs available. *Faculty:* 12 full-time (10 women), 2 part-time/adjunct (both women). *Students:* 60 full-time (58 women), 11 part-time (9 women); includes 7 minority (4 African Americans, 3 Hispanic Americans), 3 international. Average age 42. 31 applicants, 84% accepted, 23 enrolled. In 2009, 13 master's awarded. *Degree requirements:* For master's, comprehensive exam, thesis, internship. *Entrance requirements:* For master's, MAT, interview, minimum GPA of 3.0, RN experience, bachelor's degree in nursing, letters of reference, course in statistics, current RN license. Additional exam requirements/recommendations for international students: Required—TOEFL (minimum score 550 paper-based; 213 computer-based; 80 iBT). *Application deadline:* For spring admission, 1/31 priority date for domestic students. Applications are processed on a rolling basis. Application fee: $25. Electronic applications accepted. *Expenses:* Contact institution. *Financial support:* Applicants required to submit FAFSA. *Unit head:* Dr. Diane Dahl, Assistant Dean, 651-635-8000, Fax: 651-635-8004, E-mail: diane-dahl@bethel.edu. *Application contact:* Michael Price, Director of Admissions, 651-635-8000, Fax: 651-635-8004, E-mail: m-price@bethel.edu.

Blessing-Rieman College of Nursing, Program in Nursing, Quincy, IL 62305-7005. Offers MSN. Part-time programs available. *Faculty:* 9 full-time (all women). *Students:* 9 part-time (all women). Average age 30. 15 applicants, 73% accepted, 9 enrolled. In 2009, 9 master's awarded. *Degree requirements:* For master's, thesis. *Entrance requirements:* For master's, proof of RN license. *Application deadline:* For fall admission, 4/1 for domestic students. *Expenses:* Tuition: Part-time $542.50 per credit hour. Required fees: $180 per course. Tuition and fees vary according to course load and program. *Unit head:* Dr. Karen Mayville, Administrative Coordinator, Program Evaluation and Instructional Design/Program Director, 217-228-5520 Ext. 6968, Fax: 217-223-4661, E-mail: kmayville@brcn.edu. *Application contact:* Heather Mutter, Admissions Counselor, 217-228-5520 Ext. 6964, Fax: 217-223-4661, E-mail: hmutter@brcn.edu.

Bloomsburg University of Pennsylvania, School of Graduate Studies, College of Professional Studies, School of Health Sciences, Department of Nursing, Bloomsburg, PA 17815-1301. Offers adult and family nurse practitioner (MSN); adult health and illness (MSN); community health (MSN); nursing (MSN); nursing administration (MSN). *Accreditation:* AACN; AANA/CANAEP. *Degree requirements:* For master's, thesis. *Entrance requirements:* For master's, minimum QPA of 3.0. Additional exam requirements/recommendations for international students: Required—TOEFL. Electronic applications accepted. *Faculty research:* Cardiopulmonary nursing, cancer topics, women's health.

Boston College, William F. Connell School of Nursing, Chestnut Hill, MA 02467-3800. Offers adult health nursing (MS); community health nursing (MS); family health (MS); forensic nursing (MS); gerontology (MS); maternal/child health nursing (MS), including pediatric and women's health; nurse anesthesia (MS); nursing (PhD); palliative care (MS), including adult and pediatric; psychiatric-mental health nursing (MS); MBA/MS; MS/MA; MS/PhD. *Accreditation:* AACN; AANA/CANAEP (one or more programs are accredited). Part-time programs available. *Faculty:* 48 full-time (46 women), 31 part-time/adjunct (29 women). *Students:* 183 full-time (169 women), 147 part-time (140 women); includes 36 minority (15 African Americans, 2 American Indian/Alaska Native, 17 Asian Americans or Pacific Islanders, 2 Hispanic Americans), 7 international. Average age 29. 347 applicants, 53% accepted, 103 enrolled. In 2009, 79 master's, 7 doctorates awarded. *Degree requirements:* For master's, comprehensive exam, research project; for doctorate, comprehensive exam, thesis/dissertation, computer literacy exam or foreign language. *Entrance requirements:* For master's, bachelor's degree in nursing; for doctorate, GRE General Test, master's degree in nursing. Additional exam requirements/recommendations for international students: Required—TOEFL (minimum score 550 paper-based; 213 computer-based). *Application deadline:* For fall admission, 11/1 for domestic and international students; for winter admission, 12/31 for domestic and international students; for spring admission, 9/15 for domestic and international students. Applications are processed on a rolling basis. Application fee: $40. Electronic applications accepted. *Financial support:* In 2009–10, 83 students received support, including 12 fellowships with partial tuition reimbursements available (averaging $15,000 per year), 5 teaching assistantships (averaging $13,746 per year); research assistantships, Federal Work-Study, institutionally sponsored loans, scholarships/grants, traineeships, health care benefits, and tuition waivers (partial) also available. Support available to part-time students. Financial award application deadline: 3/1; financial award applicants required to submit FAFSA. *Faculty research:* Ethics, reduction of risk behaviors, support during chronic illness, violence, gerontology. Total annual research expenditures: $1.4 million. *Unit head:* Dr. Susan Gennaro, Dean, 617-552-4251, Fax: 617-552-0931, E-mail: susan.gennaro@bc.edu. *Application contact:* MaryBeth Crowley, Graduate Programs Assistant, 617-552-4928, Fax: 617-552-2121, E-mail: csongrad@bc.edu.

Bowie State University, Graduate Programs, Department of Nursing, Bowie, MD 20715-9465. Offers administration of nursing services (MS); family nurse practitioner (MS); nursing education (MS). *Accreditation:* NLN. Part-time programs available. *Degree requirements:* For master's, comprehensive exam, thesis, research paper. *Entrance requirements:* For master's, minimum GPA of 2.5. Electronic applications accepted. *Faculty research:* Minority health, women's health, gerontology, leadership management.

Bradley University, Graduate School, College of Education and Health Sciences, Department of Nursing, Peoria, IL 61625-0002. Offers nurse administered anesthesia (MSN); nursing administration (MSN). *Accreditation:* AANA/CANAEP; NLN. Part-time and evening/weekend programs available. *Degree requirements:* For master's, comprehensive exam, thesis optional. *Entrance requirements:* For master's, GRE General Test or MAT, interview, Illinois RN license, advanced cardiac life support certification, pediatric advanced life support certification, 3 letters of recommendation. Additional exam requirements/recommendations for international students: Required—TOEFL (minimum score 550 paper-based; 213 computer-based; 79 iBT).

Briar Cliff University, Program in Nursing, Sioux City, IA 51104-0100. Offers MSN. *Accreditation:* NLN. Part-time and evening/weekend programs available. *Faculty:* 3 full-time (2 women), 5 part-time/adjunct (4 women). *Students:* 1 (woman) full-time, 41 part-time (40 women); includes 1 minority (Asian American or Pacific Islander). Average age 42. In 2009, 7 master's awarded. *Degree requirements:* For master's, thesis optional. *Entrance requirements:* For master's, minimum undergraduate GPA of 3.0; completion of course work in ethics, health assessment, statistics, and research. *Application deadline:* For fall admission, 8/1 for domestic students. Application fee: $25. *Expenses:* Contact institution. *Financial support:* Application deadline: 8/1. *Faculty research:* The process/experience of trying something new (or change), the experience of taking a risk. *Unit head:* Dr. Richard Peterson, Director, 712-279-1662, Fax: 712-279-1698, E-mail: richard.petersen@briarcliff.edu. *Application contact:* Cheryl Olson, Continuing Studies Admissions Representative, 712-279-1777, Fax: 712-279-1632, E-mail: cheryl.olson@briarcliff.edu.

Brigham Young University, Graduate Studies, College of Nursing, Provo, UT 84602. Offers family nurse practitioner (MS). *Accreditation:* AACN. *Faculty:* 26 full-time (24 women). *Students:* 28 full-time (18 women); includes 4 minority (1 African American, 3 Asian Americans or Pacific Islanders). Average age 36. 23 applicants, 65% accepted, 15 enrolled. In 2009, 13 master's awarded. *Degree requirements:* For master's, thesis. *Entrance requirements:* For master's, GRE, minimum GPA of 3.0 in last 60 hours, interview, BS in nursing, pathophysiology class within undergraduate program, course work in basic statistics. Additional exam requirements/recommendations for international students: Required—TOEFL; Recommended—IELTS. *Application deadline:* For spring admission, 12/1 for domestic students. Applications are processed on a rolling basis. Application fee: $50. Electronic applications accepted. *Expenses:* Tuition: Full-time $5580; part-time $301 per credit hour. Tuition and fees vary according to

Nursing—General

Brigham Young University (continued)

student's religious affiliation. *Financial support:* In 2009–10, 28 students received support, including 2 research assistantships with full and partial tuition reimbursements available (averaging $10,000 per year), 3 teaching assistantships with full and partial tuition reimbursements available (averaging $10,000 per year); institutionally sponsored loans, scholarships/grants, tuition waivers (full), and unspecified assistantships also available. Support available to part-time students. Financial award application deadline: 2/1; financial award applicants required to submit FAFSA. *Faculty research:* Cardiovascular risk factors, stroke patients, nutrition, stress among children, family response to life-threatening illness. Total annual research expenditures: $1,200. *Unit head:* Dr. Beth Vaughan Cole, Dean, 801-422-8296, Fax: 801-422-0536, E-mail: beth-cole@byu.edu. *Application contact:* Denise Gibbons Davis, Graduate Secretary, 801-422-4142, Fax: 801-422-0538, E-mail: denise_gibbons@byu.edu.

See Close-Up on page 1607.

California Baptist University, Program in Nursing, Riverside, CA 92504-3206. Offers MS. Part-time programs available. *Faculty:* 3 full-time (all women). *Students:* 20 full-time (16 women), 7 part-time (all women); includes 13 minority (2 African Americans, 7 Asian Americans or Pacific Islanders, 4 Hispanic Americans), 1 international. 32 applicants, 34% accepted, 10 enrolled. *Degree requirements:* For master's, comprehensive exam (for some programs), thesis optional. *Entrance requirements:* For master's, GRE or CCTT, and TEAS, minimum GPA of 3.0, health clearance, health insurance, CPR certification, vehicle insurance. Additional exam requirements/recommendations for international students: Required—TOEFL (minimum score 575 paper-based; 230 computer-based; 89 iBT). *Application deadline:* For fall admission, 8/1 for domestic students; for spring admission, 12/1 for domestic students. Application fee: $45. Electronic applications accepted. *Expenses:* Tuition: Full-time $8352; part-time $464 per semester hour. Required fees: $125 per semester. Tuition and fees vary according to course load, campus/location and program. *Financial support:* Federal Work-Study and scholarships/grants available. Support available to part-time students. Financial award applicants required to submit FAFSA. *Unit head:* Dr. Constance Milton, Dean, School of Nursing, 951-343-4700, E-mail: cmilton@calbaptist.edu. *Application contact:* Gail Ronveaux, Dean of Graduate Enrollment, 951-343-5045, Fax: 951-343-5095, E-mail: graduateadmissions@calbaptist.edu.

California State University, Bakersfield, Division of Graduate Studies, School of Natural Sciences and Mathematics, Program in Nursing, Bakersfield, CA 93311. Offers MS. *Accreditation:* AACN. *Degree requirements:* For master's, thesis, project. *Entrance requirements:* For master's, MAT, BSN from NLN-accredited program. Electronic applications accepted. *Faculty research:* AIDS, gerontological nursing, cultural health beliefs.

California State University, Chico, Graduate School, College of Natural Sciences, School of Nursing, Chico, CA 95929-0722. Offers MS. *Accreditation:* AACN. Part-time programs available. Postbaccalaureate distance learning degree programs offered. *Faculty:* 13 full-time (all women), 5 part-time/adjunct (all women). *Students:* 5 full-time (4 women), 10 part-time (8 women); includes 5 minority (2 African Americans, 2 Asian Americans or Pacific Islanders, 1 Hispanic American). Average age 35. In 2009, 4 master's awarded. *Degree requirements:* For master's, thesis, oral exam. *Entrance requirements:* For master's, GRE, course work in statistics, California nursing license. Additional exam requirements/recommendations for international students: Required—TOEFL (minimum score 550 paper-based; 213 computer-based; 80 iBT), IELTS (minimum score 6.5). *Application deadline:* For fall admission, 3/1 for domestic and international students. Applications are processed on a rolling basis. Application fee: $55. Electronic applications accepted. *Financial support:* Career-related internships or fieldwork available. *Unit head:* Dr. Sherry D. Fox, Director, 530-898-5891. *Application contact:* Dr. Irene Morgan, Graduate Coordinator, 530-898-6207.

California State University, Dominguez Hills, College of Professional Studies, School of Health and Human Services, Program in Nursing, Carson, CA 90747-0001. Offers MSN. *Accreditation:* AACN. Part-time programs available. Postbaccalaureate distance learning degree programs offered. *Faculty:* 14 full-time (13 women), 30 part-time/adjunct (28 women). *Students:* 135 full-time (120 women), 434 part-time (390 women); includes 278 minority (84 African Americans, 1 American Indian/Alaska Native, 117 Asian Americans or Pacific Islanders, 76 Hispanic Americans). Average age 40. 285 applicants, 80% accepted, 127 enrolled. In 2009, 151 master's awarded. *Degree requirements:* For master's, comprehensive exam. *Entrance requirements:* For master's, minimum GPA of 2.5, 3.0 in prior coursework in statistics, research, pathophysiology and assessment. Additional exam requirements/recommendations for international students: Required—TOEFL. *Application deadline:* For fall admission, 6/1 for domestic students; for spring admission, 11/1 for domestic students. Applications are processed on a rolling basis. Application fee: $55. Electronic applications accepted. *Expenses:* Tuition, nonresident: full-time $6696; part-time $372 per unit. Required fees: $5946; $1752 per semester. *Faculty research:* AIDS/HIV, health promotion, elderly. *Unit head:* Dr. Carole Shea, Director, 310-243-2059, E-mail: cshea@csudh.edu. *Application contact:* 310-243-3426.

California State University, Fresno, Division of Graduate Studies, College of Health and Human Services, Department of Nursing, Fresno, CA 93740-8027. Offers nursing (MS), including clinical nurse, primary care nurse practitioner, specialist/nurse educator. *Accreditation:* AACN. Part-time and evening/weekend programs available. *Degree requirements:* For master's, thesis or alternative. *Entrance requirements:* For master's, GRE General Test, 1 year of clinical practice, previous course work in statistics, BSN, minimum GPA of 3.0 in nursing. Additional exam requirements/recommendations for international students: Required—TOEFL. Electronic applications accepted. *Faculty research:* Training grant, HIV assessment.

California State University, Fullerton, Graduate Studies, College of Health and Human Development, Department of Nursing, Fullerton, CA 92834-9480. Offers MS. *Accreditation:* AACN; AANA/CANAEP. Part-time programs available. *Students:* 201 full-time (142 women), 190 part-time (181 women); includes 178 minority (22 African Americans, 2 American Indian/Alaska Native, 109 Asian Americans or Pacific Islanders, 45 Hispanic Americans), 4 international. Average age 35. 680 applicants, 24% accepted, 143 enrolled. In 2009, 70 master's awarded. Application fee: $55. *Expenses:* Tuition, nonresident: full-time $11,160; part-time $373 per credit. Required fees: $1440 per term. Tuition and fees vary according to course load, degree level and program. *Financial support:* Career-related internships or fieldwork, Federal Work-Study, institutionally sponsored loans, scholarships/grants, and traineeships available. Support available to part-time students. Financial award application deadline: 3/1; financial award applicants required to submit FAFSA. *Unit head:* Dr. Paula Herberg, Chair, 657-278-5570. *Application contact:* Admissions/Applications, 657-278-2371.

California State University, Long Beach, Graduate Studies, College of Health and Human Services, Department of Nursing, Long Beach, CA 90840. Offers MSN, MSN/MPH. *Accreditation:* AACN. Part-time programs available. *Faculty:* 28 full-time (26 women), 13 part-time/adjunct (all women). *Students:* 134 full-time (120 women), 122 part-time (110 women); includes 150 minority (25 African Americans, 5 American Indian/Alaska Native, 82 Asian Americans or Pacific Islanders, 38 Hispanic Americans), 6 international. Average age 37. 189 applicants, 73% accepted, 126 enrolled. *Degree requirements:* For master's, thesis optional. *Entrance requirements:* For master's, minimum GPA of 3.0. *Application deadline:* For fall admission, 7/1 for domestic students. Applications are processed on a rolling basis. Application fee: $55. Electronic applications accepted. *Expenses:* Required fees: $1802 per semester. Part-time tuition and fees vary according to course load. *Financial support:* Federal Work-Study, institutionally sponsored loans, and scholarships/grants available. Financial award application deadline: 3/2. *Faculty research:* Newborns of drug-dependent mothers, abuse of residents in nursing homes, interventions in care of Alzheimer's patients. *Unit head:* Dr. Lucy Huckabay, Director, 562-985-4582, Fax: 562-985-2382, E-mail: huckabay@csulb.edu. *Application contact:* Dr. David Kumrow, Graduate Advisor, 562-985-8082, Fax: 562-985-2382, E-mail: dkumrow@csulb.edu.

California State University, Los Angeles, Graduate Studies, College of Health and Human Services, School of Nursing, Los Angeles, CA 90032-8530. Offers health science (MA); nursing (MS). *Accreditation:* AACN. Part-time and evening/weekend programs available. *Faculty:* 17 part-time/adjunct (15 women). *Students:* 92 full-time (76 women), 130 part-time (114 women); includes 133 minority (18 African Americans, 89 Asian Americans or Pacific Islanders, 26 Hispanic Americans), 8 international. Average age 37. 149 applicants, 79% accepted, 53 enrolled. In 2009, 51 master's awarded. *Degree requirements:* For master's, comprehensive exam, project or thesis. *Entrance requirements:* For master's, minimum GPA of 3.0 in nursing, course work in nursing and statistics. Additional exam requirements/recommendations for international students: Required—TOEFL (minimum score 500 paper-based; 173 computer-based). *Application deadline:* For fall admission, 5/1 for domestic and international students. Applications are processed on a rolling basis. Application fee: $55. *Financial support:* Federal Work-Study available. Support available to part-time students. Financial award application deadline: 3/1. *Faculty research:* Family stress, geripsychiatric nursing, self-care counseling, holistic nursing, adult health. *Unit head:* Dr. Cynthia Hughes, Director, 323-343-4700, Fax: 323-343-6454, E-mail: chughes2@calstatela.edu. *Application contact:* Dr. Cheryl L. Ney, Associate Vice President for Academic Affairs and Dean of Graduate Studies, 323-343-3820, Fax: 323-343-5653, E-mail: cney@cslanet.calstatela.edu.

California State University, Sacramento, Graduate Studies, College of Health and Human Services, Division of Nursing, Sacramento, CA 95819. Offers MS. *Accreditation:* AACN. Part-time programs available. *Degree requirements:* For master's, thesis or alternative, writing proficiency exam. *Entrance requirements:* For master's, GRE, bachelor's degree in nursing, minimum GPA of 3.0. Additional exam requirements/recommendations for international students: Required—TOEFL. Electronic applications accepted.

California State University, San Bernardino, Graduate Studies, College of Natural Sciences, Department of Nursing, San Bernardino, CA 92407-2397. Offers MS. *Faculty:* 3 full-time (all women). *Students:* 34 full-time (26 women), 23 part-time (18 women); includes 28 minority (9 African Americans, 9 Asian Americans or Pacific Islanders, 10 Hispanic Americans). Average age 34. 16 applicants, 81% accepted, 6 enrolled. In 2009, 4 master's awarded. *Degree requirements:* For master's, thesis optional. *Entrance requirements:* For master's, writing exam, BSN or BS, minimum GPA of 3.0, California RN license. Application fee: $55. *Unit head:* J. Paul Vicknair, Interim Chair, 909-537-5385, Fax: 909-537-7089, E-mail: vicknai@csusb.edu. *Application contact:* Olivia Rosas, Director of Admissions, 909-537-7577, Fax: 909-537-7034, E-mail: orosas@csusb.edu.

Capital University, School of Nursing, Columbus, OH 43209-2394. Offers administration (MSN); legal studies (MSN); theological studies (MSN); JD/MSN; MBA/MSN; MSN/MTS. *Accreditation:* AACN. Part-time and evening/weekend programs available. *Degree requirements:* For master's, thesis or alternative. *Entrance requirements:* For master's, BSN, current RN license, minimum GPA of 3.0, undergraduate courses in statistics and research. Additional exam requirements/recommendations for international students: Required—TOEFL (minimum score 550 paper-based). *Expenses:* Contact institution. *Faculty research:* Bereavement, wellness/health promotion, emergency cardiac care, critical thinking, complementary and alternative healthcare.

Cardinal Stritch University, College of Nursing, Milwaukee, WI 53217-3985. Offers MSN. *Accreditation:* NLN. Part-time and evening/weekend programs available. *Degree requirements:* For master's, thesis. *Entrance requirements:* For master's, interview; minimum GPA of 3.0; RN license; 3 letters of recommendation; undergraduate coursework in statistics and nursing research; computer literacy; curriculum vitae. Electronic applications accepted. *Expenses:* Contact institution.

Carlow University, School of Nursing, Pittsburgh, PA 15213-3165. Offers family nurse practitioner (MSN); home health advanced practice nursing (MSN); nursing (DNP); nursing case management/leadership (MSN); nursing leadership (MSN). *Accreditation:* AACN. Part-time and evening/weekend programs available. Postbaccalaureate distance learning degree programs offered (minimal on-campus study). *Degree requirements:* For master's, thesis or alternative. *Entrance requirements:* Additional exam requirements/recommendations for international students: Required—TOEFL (minimum score 550 paper-based; 213 computer-based). Electronic applications accepted. *Expenses:* Tuition: Full-time $11,250; part-time $625 per credit. Tuition and fees vary according to course load, degree level and program. *Faculty research:* Research utilization, community and home health, medically underserved.

Carson-Newman College, Department of Nursing, Jefferson City, TN 37760. Offers family nurse practitioner (MSN); nurse educator (MSN). *Accreditation:* AACN. *Faculty:* 2 full-time (both women), 10 part-time/adjunct (9 women). *Students:* 21 full-time (19 women), 27 part-time (23 women); includes 3 minority (2 Asian Americans or Pacific Islanders, 1 Hispanic American). Average age 32. In 2009, 11 master's awarded. *Application deadline:* For fall admission, 7/15 priority date for domestic students. Applications are processed on a rolling basis. Application fee: $50. *Expenses:* Tuition: Full-time $5490; part-time $305 per semester hour. Required fees: $200. *Unit head:* Dr. Patricia Kraft, Dean and Chair, 865-471-3426. *Application contact:* Graduate Admissions and Services Adviser, 865-473-3468, Fax: 865-472-3475.

Case Western Reserve University, Frances Payne Bolton School of Nursing, Doctoral Program in Nursing, Cleveland, OH 44106. Offers PhD. *Degree requirements:* For doctorate, thesis/dissertation. *Entrance requirements:* For doctorate, GRE General Test. *Faculty research:* Acute care nursing, parent-child gerontology, information systems, clinical decisions.

Case Western Reserve University, Frances Payne Bolton School of Nursing, Doctor of Nursing Practice Program, Cleveland, OH 44106. Offers acute care nurse practitioner (DNP); adult nurse practitioner (DNP); family nurse practitioner (DNP); gerontological nurse practitioner (DNP); graduate entry/pre-licensure option (DNP); medical-surgical nursing (DNP); midwifery/family nursing (DNP); neonatal nurse practitioner (DNP); pediatric nurse practitioner (DNP); post-licensure option (DNP); psychiatric-mental health nurse practitioner (DNP); women's health nurse practitioner (DNP). Graduate entry option allows baccalaureate-prepared college graduates from non-nursing backgrounds to earn certificate and MSN in addition to ND. Terminal master's awarded for partial completion of doctoral program. *Degree requirements:* For doctorate, thesis/dissertation. *Entrance requirements:* For doctorate, GRE General Test or MAT. *Faculty research:* Clinical nursing, acute care, gerontology, mental health, critical care.

Case Western Reserve University, Frances Payne Bolton School of Nursing, Master's Programs in Nursing, Cleveland, OH 44106. Offers community health nursing (MSN); medical-surgical nursing (MSN); nurse anesthesia (MSN); nurse midwifery (MSN); nurse practitioner (MSN), including acute care cardiovascular nursing, acute care nurse practitioner, acute care/flight nurse, adult nurse practitioner, family nurse practitioner, gerontological nurse practitioner, neonatal nurse practitioner, pediatric nurse practitioner, psychiatric-mental health nurse practitioner, women's health nurse practitioner; nursing informatics (MSN). *Accreditation:* NLN. Part-time programs available. Postbaccalaureate distance learning degree programs offered (minimal on-campus study). *Degree requirements:* For master's, thesis optional. *Entrance requirements:* For master's, GRE General Test or MAT. *Faculty research:* Preterm skin contact effects on electrophysiologic sleep, intergenerational caregiving to at risk youth, maintaining exercise in cardiac rehabilitation, left ventricular function and duration of mechanical ventilation.

Case Western Reserve University, Frances Payne Bolton School of Nursing and Department of Anthropology, Nursing/Anthropology Program, Cleveland, OH 44106. Offers MSN/MA.

Case Western Reserve University, Frances Payne Bolton School of Nursing, Nursing/Bioethics Program, Cleveland, OH 44106. Offers MSN/MA.

Case Western Reserve University, Frances Payne Bolton School of Nursing, Nursing/Public Health Program, Cleveland, OH 44106. Offers MSN/MPH.

The Catholic University of America, School of Nursing, Washington, DC 20064. Offers adult health specialist with functional role as nurse educator (MSN); adult nurse practitioner (MSN); community/public health nurse specialist educator (MSN); family nurse practitioner (MSN); geriatric nurse practitioner (MSN); immigrant, refugee, and global health clinical nurse specialist (MSN); nursing (DNP, PhD, Certificate); pediatric nurse practitioner (MSN); promoting healthy families in vulnerable communities (MSN); psychiatric-mental health nursing (MSN).

Accreditation: AACN. Part-time programs available. *Faculty:* 15 full-time (all women), 43 part-time/adjunct (41 women). *Students:* 28 full-time (26 women), 75 part-time (73 women); includes 37 minority (27 African Americans, 6 Asian Americans or Pacific Islanders, 4 Hispanic Americans), 4 international. Average age 42. 84 applicants, 64% accepted, 30 enrolled. In 2009, 23 master's, 7 doctorates, 3 other advanced degrees awarded. *Degree requirements:* For master's, comprehensive exam, thesis optional; for doctorate, comprehensive exam, thesis/dissertation, minimum GPA of 3.0, oral proposal defense. *Entrance requirements:* For master's, 3 letters of recommendation, BA in nursing, RN registration, official copies of academic transcripts, some post-baccalaureate nursing experience; for doctorate, GRE General Test, BA in nursing, professional portfolio (including statements, resume, copy of RN license, 3 letters of recommendation, narrative description of clinical practice, proposal), copy of research/scholarly paper related to clinical nursing. Additional exam requirements/recommendations for international students: Required—TOEFL (minimum score 580 paper-based; 237 computer-based). *Application deadline:* For fall admission, 8/1 priority date for domestic students, 7/15 for international students; for spring admission, 12/1 priority date for domestic students, 10/15 for international students. Applications are processed on a rolling basis. Application fee: $55. Electronic applications accepted. *Expenses:* Tuition: Full-time $31,740; part-time $1245 per credit hour. Required fees: $50; $25 per semester hour. One-time fee: $425. *Financial support:* Fellowships, research assistantships, teaching assistantships, Federal Work-Study, scholarships/grants, tuition waivers (full and partial), and unspecified assistantships available. Financial award application deadline: 2/1; financial award applicants required to submit FAFSA. *Faculty research:* Community involvement in health care services, primary health care services, pediatrics, chronic illness, cardiovascular disease. Total annual research expenditures: $311,172. *Unit head:* Dr. Nalini N. Jairath, Dean, 202-319-5403, Fax: 202-319-6485, E-mail: cua-deanschoolofnursing@cua.edu. *Application contact:* Julie Schwing, Director of Graduate Admissions, 202-319-5057, Fax: 202-319-6533, E-mail: cua-admissions@cua.edu.

Central Methodist University, College of Graduate and Extended Studies, Fayette, MO 65248-1198. Offers clinical counseling (MS); clinical nurse leader (MSN); education (M Ed). Part-time and evening/weekend programs available. Postbaccalaureate distance learning degree programs offered (no on-campus study). *Degree requirements:* For master's, thesis. *Entrance requirements:* For master's, GRE General Test, minimum GPA of 2.75. Electronic applications accepted.

Chatham University, Program in Nursing, Pittsburgh, PA 15232-2826. Offers education/leadership (MSN); nursing (DNP). *Accreditation:* AACN. *Students:* 48 full-time (41 women), 79 part-time (70 women). Average age 45. 139 applicants, 90% accepted, 69 enrolled. *Entrance requirements:* For master's and doctorate, RN license. Additional exam requirements/recommendations for international students: Required—TOEFL (minimum score 600 paper-based; 250 computer-based; 100 iBT), IELTS (minimum score 6.5), TWE. *Application deadline:* For fall admission, 5/1 priority date for domestic and international students. Applications are processed on a rolling basis. Application fee: $45. Electronic applications accepted. *Financial support:* Applicants required to submit FAFSA. *Unit head:* Dr. Elizabeth Gazza, Director, 412-365-2746, E-mail: egazza@chatham.edu. *Application contact:* David Vey, Admissions Support Specialist, 412-365-1498, Fax: 412-365-1720, E-mail: dvey@chatham.edu.

Clarion University of Pennsylvania, Office of Research and Graduate Studies, School of Nursing, Program in Nursing, Clarion, PA 16214. Offers MSN. *Accreditation:* NLN. *Degree requirements:* For master's, comprehensive exam, thesis. *Entrance requirements:* For master's, minimum QPA of 2.75. Additional exam requirements/recommendations for international students: Required—TOEFL (minimum score 550 paper-based; 213 computer-based; 80 iBT).

Clarke College, Department of Nursing and Health, Dubuque, IA 52001-3198. Offers administration of nursing systems (MSN); advanced practice nursing (MSN); education (MSN); family nurse practitioner (MSN, PMC). *Accreditation:* AACN. Part-time programs available. *Faculty:* 4 full-time (all women), 2 part-time/adjunct (1 woman). *Students:* 35 full-time (34 women), 19 part-time (all women). Average age 35. 48 applicants, 83% accepted, 25 enrolled. In 2009, 13 master's awarded. *Entrance requirements:* For master's, GRE General Test or MAT, BSN, minimum GPA of 3.0. *Application deadline:* For fall admission, 2/15 priority date for domestic students; for spring admission, 12/15 priority date for domestic students. Applications are processed on a rolling basis. Application fee: $25. Electronic applications accepted. *Expenses:* Tuition: Full-time $10,836; part-time $602 per credit hour. Required fees: $30 per credit hour. *Financial support:* In 2009–10, 6 students received support. Career-related internships or fieldwork available. Support available to part-time students. Financial award applicants required to submit FAFSA. *Faculty research:* Narrative pedagogy, ethics, end-of-life care, pedagogy, family systems. *Unit head:* Dr. Susan DeCrane, Chair, 800-224-2736, Fax: 319-584-8684. *Application contact:* Carrie Kirk, Information Contact, 563-588-6635, Fax: 563-588-6789, E-mail: graduate@clarke.edu.

Clarkson College, Master of Science in Nursing Program, Omaha, NE 68131. Offers adult nurse practitioner (MSN, Post-Master's Certificate); family nurse practitioner (MSN, Post-Master's Certificate); nursing education (MSN, Post-Master's Certificate); nursing health care leadership (MSN, Post-Master's Certificate). *Accreditation:* NLN. Part-time and evening/weekend programs available. Postbaccalaureate distance learning degree programs offered (minimal on-campus study). *Degree requirements:* For master's, on-campus skills assessment (family nurse practitioner, adult nurse practitioner), comprehensive exam or thesis. *Entrance requirements:* For master's, minimum GPA of 3.0, 2 references, resume. Additional exam requirements/recommendations for international students: Required—TOEFL (minimum score 600 paper-based; 250 computer-based; 100 iBT). Electronic applications accepted.

Clayton State University, School of Graduate Studies, Program in Nursing, Morrow, GA 30260-0285. Offers MSN. *Accreditation:* AACN. *Students:* 6 full-time (3 women), 11 part-time (8 women); includes 12 minority (11 African Americans, 1 Asian American or Pacific Islander). Average age 40. 5 applicants, 100% accepted, 4 enrolled. *Degree requirements:* For master's, thesis. *Entrance requirements:* For master's, GRE. Additional exam requirements/recommendations for international students: Required—TOEFL (minimum score 550 paper-based; 213 computer-based; 80 iBT). *Application deadline:* For fall admission, 7/15 for domestic students, 5/1 for international students; for spring admission, 4/15 for domestic students, 2/1 for international students. Application fee: $50. Electronic applications accepted. *Expenses:* Contact institution. *Financial support:* Application deadline: 7/1. *Unit head:* Dr. Katherine Willock, Director, 678-466-4959, Fax: 678-466-4999, E-mail: katherinewillock@clayton.edu. *Application contact:* Christy Hicks, Coordinator, 678-466-4959, Fax: 678-466-4999, E-mail: christyhicks@clayton.edu.

Clemson University, Graduate School, College of Health, Education, and Human Development, School of Nursing, Clemson, SC 29634. Offers healthcare genetics (PhD); nursing (MS). *Accreditation:* AACN. Part-time programs available. Postbaccalaureate distance learning degree programs offered. *Faculty:* 15 full-time (all women), 1 (woman) part-time/adjunct. *Students:* 44 full-time (42 women), 37 part-time (34 women); includes 7 minority (4 African Americans, 2 Asian Americans or Pacific Islanders, 1 Hispanic American), 3 international. Average age 34. 39 applicants, 38% accepted, 10 enrolled. In 2009, 32 master's awarded. *Degree requirements:* For master's, thesis or alternative; for doctorate, comprehensive exam, thesis/dissertation. *Entrance requirements:* For master's, GRE General Test, RN license; for doctorate, GRE General Test. Additional exam requirements/recommendations for international students: Required—TOEFL. *Application deadline:* For fall admission, 4/1 for domestic students; for spring admission, 10/1 for domestic students. Applications are processed on a rolling basis. Application fee: $70 ($80 for international students). Electronic applications accepted. *Expenses:* Contact institution. *Financial support:* In 2009–10, 24 students received support, including 1 research assistantship with partial tuition reimbursement available (averaging $15,600 per year), 20 teaching assistantships with partial tuition reimbursements available (averaging $10,341 per year); fellowships with full and partial tuition reimbursements available, career-related internships or fieldwork, institutionally sponsored loans, scholarships/grants, health care benefits, and unspecified assistantships also available. Support available to part-time students. Financial award applicants required to submit FAFSA. *Faculty research:* Risk behaviors and chronic risk-taking in early adolescents, stress in older caregivers, home care of elderly, cancer awareness, pain. Total annual research expenditures: $414,950. *Unit head:* Dr. Rosanne Pruitt, Director, 864-656-7622, Fax: 864-656-5488, E-mail: prosan@clemson.edu. *Application contact:* Dr. Margaret Ann Wetsel, Graduate Studies Coordinator, 864-656-5527, Fax: 864-656-5488, E-mail: mwetsel@clemson.edu.

Cleveland State University, College of Graduate Studies, College of Education and Human Services, School of Nursing, Cleveland, OH 44115. Offers clinical nursing leader (MSN); executive track (MSN); forensic nursing (MSN); nursing education (MSN); population health nursing (MSN); MSN/MBA. *Accreditation:* AACN. Part-time programs available. *Degree requirements:* For master's, thesis or alternative, portfolio, population health project. *Entrance requirements:* For master's, RN license, BSN, course work in statistics. Additional exam requirements/recommendations for international students: Required—TOEFL (minimum score 525 paper-based; 197 computer-based), IELTS (minimum score 6). Electronic applications accepted. *Faculty research:* Diabetes management, African-American elders medication compliance, risk in home visiting, suffering, COPD and stress.

College of Mount St. Joseph, Master of Nursing Program, Cincinnati, OH 45233-1670. Offers MN. *Accreditation:* AACN. *Faculty:* 5 full-time (3 women), 9 part-time/adjunct (all women). *Students:* 43 full-time (41 women); includes 7 minority (all African Americans). Average age 27. 61 applicants, 97% accepted. In 2009, 17 master's awarded. *Degree requirements:* For master's, evidence-based project. *Entrance requirements:* For master's, GRE (or minimum GPA of 3.0), minimum GPA of 3.0 (or GRE); interview; course work in chemistry, anatomy, physiology, microbiology, psychology, sociology, statistics, life span development, and nutrition; non-nursing bachelor's degree; statement of goals. Additional exam requirements/recommendations for international students: Required—TOEFL (minimum score 560 paper-based; 220 computer-based; 83 iBT). *Application deadline:* Applications are processed on a rolling basis. Application fee: $50. Electronic applications accepted. *Expenses:* Contact institution. *Financial support:* In 2009–10, 1 student received support. Scholarships/grants available. Financial award applicants required to submit FAFSA. *Faculty research:* Utilizing technology in learning, assessment of student learning, critical thinking, women's health and nursing education. *Unit head:* Dr. Mary Kishman, Chair of Graduate Nursing, 513-244-4726, Fax: 513-451-2547, E-mail: mary_kishman@mail.msj.edu. *Application contact:* Marilyn Hoskins, Assistant Director of Graduate Recruitment, 513-244-4723, Fax: 513-244-4629, E-mail: marilyn_hoskins@mail.msj.edu.

College of Mount Saint Vincent, School of Professional and Continuing Studies, Department of Nursing, Riverdale, NY 10471-1093. Offers adult nurse practitioner (MSN, PMC); family nurse practitioner (MSN, PMC); nurse educator (PMC); nursing administration (MSN); nursing for the adult and aged (MSN). *Accreditation:* AACN. Part-time programs available. *Entrance requirements:* For master's, BSN, interview, RN license, minimum GPA of 3.0, letters of reference. Additional exam requirements/recommendations for international students: Required—TOEFL. *Expenses:* Contact institution.

The College of New Jersey, Graduate Division, School of Nursing, Health and Exercise Science, Program in Nursing, Ewing, NJ 08628. Offers MSN, Certificate. *Accreditation:* AACN. Part-time programs available. *Students:* 2 full-time (both women), 35 part-time (all women); includes 11 minority (7 African Americans, 3 Asian Americans or Pacific Islanders, 1 Hispanic American), 2 international. 36 applicants, 64% accepted. In 2009, 7 master's, 3 other advanced degrees awarded. *Degree requirements:* For master's, comprehensive exam. *Entrance requirements:* For master's, GRE, minimum GPA of 3.0 in field or 2.75 overall. Additional exam requirements/recommendations for international students: Required—TOEFL. *Application deadline:* For fall admission, 2/1 priority date for domestic students; for spring admission, 10/1 priority date for domestic students. Application fee: $70. Electronic applications accepted. *Expenses:* Tuition, state resident: part-time $573.70 per credit. Tuition, nonresident: part-time $887.75 per credit. Required fees: $140.85 per credit. One-time fee: $10 part-time. *Financial support:* Tuition waivers (partial) and unspecified assistantships available. Financial award application deadline: 5/1; financial award applicants required to submit FAFSA. *Application contact:* Susan L. Hydro, Assistant Dean, Office of Graduate Studies, 609-771-2300, Fax: 609-637-5105, E-mail: graduate@tcnj.edu.

The College of New Rochelle, Graduate School, Program in Nursing, New Rochelle, NY 10805-2308. Offers acute care nurse practitioner (MS, Certificate); clinical specialist in holistic nursing (MS, Certificate); family nurse practitioner (MS, Certificate); nursing and health care management (MS); nursing education (Certificate). *Accreditation:* AACN. Part-time programs available. *Entrance requirements:* For master's, GRE General Test or MAT, BSN, malpractice insurance, minimum GPA of 3.0, RN license. *Expenses:* Contact institution. *Faculty research:* Holistic modalities, academic success variables.

College of Saint Elizabeth, Department of Nursing, Morristown, NJ 07960-6989. Offers MSN. *Accreditation:* NLN. *Faculty:* 2 full-time (both women), 2 part-time/adjunct (0 women). *Students:* 42 part-time (40 women); includes 13 minority (5 African Americans, 6 Asian Americans or Pacific Islanders, 2 Hispanic Americans). Average age 49. 35 applicants, 91% accepted, 28 enrolled. In 2009, 12 master's awarded. Application fee: $35. *Expenses:* Tuition: Part-time $797 per credit hour. Required fees: $65 per credit hour. *Unit head:* Dr. Sharon Hellwig, Director of Graduate Program, 973-290-1074, E-mail: shellwig@cse.edu. *Application contact:* Donna Tatarka, Dean of Admission, 973-290-4705, Fax: 973-290-4710, E-mail: dtatarka@cse.edu.

College of Saint Mary, Program in Nursing, Omaha, NE 68106. Offers MSN. *Accreditation:* NLN. Part-time programs available. *Entrance requirements:* For master's, bachelor's degree in nursing, Nebraska RN license, essay or scholarly writing, minimum cumulative GPA of 3.0, 2 references. Additional exam requirements/recommendations for international students: Required—TOEFL.

The College of St. Scholastica, Graduate Studies, Department of Nursing, Duluth, MN 55811-4199. Offers MA, PMC. *Accreditation:* AACN. Part-time programs available. *Degree requirements:* For master's, thesis. *Entrance requirements:* For master's, GRE General Test or MAT, bachelor's degree in nursing, interview, RN license, minimum GPA of 3.0. Additional exam requirements/recommendations for international students: Required—TOEFL (minimum score 550 paper-based; 213 computer-based; 79 iBT). Electronic applications accepted. *Faculty research:* Critical thinking and professional development, social organization of responsibility, rural health HIV/AIDS prevention, web-based instruction in nursing.

College of Staten Island of the City University of New York, Graduate Programs, Department of Nursing, Staten Island, NY 10314-6600. Offers adult health nursing (MS, 6th Year Certificate); cultural competence (6th Year Certificate); gerontological nursing (MS, 6th Year Certificate); nursing education (6th Year Certificate). *Accreditation:* NLN. *Students:* 34 part-time (32 women); includes 11 minority (5 African Americans, 4 Asian Americans or Pacific Islanders, 2 Hispanic Americans), 2 international. Average age 38. 30 applicants, 77% accepted, 16 enrolled. In 2009, 10 master's, 1 other advanced degree awarded. *Entrance requirements:* Additional exam requirements/recommendations for international students: Required—TOEFL (minimum score 550 paper-based; 213 computer-based; 79 iBT). *Application deadline:* Applications are processed on a rolling basis. Application fee: $125. Electronic applications accepted. *Expenses:* Tuition, state resident: full-time $7360; part-time $310 per credit. Tuition, nonresident: part-time $575 per credit. Required fees: $378; $113 per semester. *Financial support:* In 2009–10, 1 student received support. Applicants required to submit FAFSA. *Unit head:* Dr. Mary O'Donnell, Chairperson, 718-982-3812, Fax: 718-982-3813, E-mail: odonnellm@mail.csi.cuny.edu. *Application contact:* Sasha Spence, Assistant Director of Graduate Recruitment and Admissions, 718-982-2699, Fax: 718-982-2500, E-mail: sasha.spence@csi.cuny.edu.

Colorado State University–Pueblo, College of Education, Engineering and Professional Studies, Nursing Department, Pueblo, CO 81001-4901. Offers MS. *Accreditation:* NLN. *Degree requirements:* For master's, comprehensive exam or thesis. *Entrance requirements:* Additional exam requirements/recommendations for international students: Required—TOEFL, NCLEX exam.

Nursing—General

Columbia University, School of Nursing, New York, NY 10032. Offers MS, DN Sc, DNP, Adv C, MBA/MS, MPH/MS. *Accreditation:* AACN. Part-time programs available. *Degree requirements:* For doctorate, thesis/dissertation. *Entrance requirements:* For master's, GRE General Test, BSN, 1 year of clinical experience (preferred); for doctorate, GRE General Test, MSN; course work in statistics, research, and theory. Additional exam requirements/recommendations for international students: Required—TOEFL. Electronic applications accepted. *Expenses:* Contact institution. *Faculty research:* HIV/AIDS, health promotion/disease prevention, health policies, advanced practice, urban health.

See Close-Up on page 1609.

Concordia University Wisconsin, Graduate Programs, School of Health and Human Services, Program in Nursing, Mequon, WI 53097-2402. Offers family nurse practitioner (MSN); geriatric nurse practitioner (MSN); nurse educator (MSN). *Accreditation:* AACN. Postbaccalaureate distance learning degree programs offered (minimal on-campus study). *Degree requirements:* For master's, comprehensive exam, thesis or alternative. *Entrance requirements:* Additional exam requirements/recommendations for international students: Required—TOEFL. *Expenses:* Contact institution.

Coppin State University, Division of Graduate Studies, Helene Fuld School of Nursing, Baltimore, MD 21216-3698. Offers family nurse practitioner (PMC); nursing (MSN). *Accreditation:* NLN. Part-time and evening/weekend programs available. *Degree requirements:* For master's, comprehensive exam, thesis, clinical internship. *Entrance requirements:* For master's, GRE, bachelor's degree in nursing, interview, minimum GPA of 3.0, RN license. Additional exam requirements/recommendations for international students: Required—TOEFL (minimum score 550 paper-based).

Creighton University, School of Nursing, Omaha, NE 68178-0001. Offers MS, DNP. *Accreditation:* AACN. Part-time programs available. Postbaccalaureate distance learning degree programs offered (minimal on-campus study). *Faculty:* 27 full-time (26 women), 1 (woman) part-time/adjunct. *Students:* 39 full-time (38 women), 35 part-time (33 women); includes 4 minority (2 African Americans, 2 Hispanic Americans). Average age 33. 63 applicants, 92% accepted, 49 enrolled. In 2009, 31 master's, 1 doctorate awarded. *Degree requirements:* For master's, thesis optional, capstone project; for doctorate, thesis/dissertation, scholarly research project. *Entrance requirements:* For master's, BSN, minimum GPA of 3.0, RN license; for doctorate, BSN or MSN, minimum GPA of 3.0, RN license. Additional exam requirements/recommendations for international students: Required—TOEFL (minimum score 600 paper-based; 250 computer-based; 100 iBT). *Application deadline:* For fall admission, 3/15 priority date for domestic and international students; for spring admission, 10/15 priority date for domestic and international students. Applications are processed on a rolling basis. Application fee: $50. Electronic applications accepted. *Expenses:* Tuition: Full-time $11,700; part-time $650 per credit hour. Required fees: $126 per semester. *Financial support:* Career-related internships or fieldwork, Federal Work-Study, institutionally sponsored loans, and traineeships available. Financial award applicants required to submit FAFSA. *Faculty research:* Hereditary cancer family adaptation, osteoporosis prevention, partnering with high-risk clients, obesity prevention in children, participatory action research with a Native American tribe, evaluation of simulated clinical experiences. *Unit head:* Dr. Eleanor V. Howell, Dean, 402-280-2004, Fax: 402-280-2045, E-mail: howell@creighton.edu. *Application contact:* Dr. Mary Kunes-Connell, Associate Dean for Academic and Clinical Affairs, 402-280-2024, Fax: 402-280-2045, E-mail: mkc@creighton.edu.

Daemen College, Department of Nursing, Amherst, NY 14226-3592. Offers adult nurse practitioner (MS); nursing education (MS, Post Master's Certificate); nursing executive leadership (MS); nursing practice (DNP); palliative care nursing (MS, Post Master's Certificate). *Accreditation:* NLN. Part-time programs available. *Faculty:* 3 full-time (all women), 6 part-time/adjunct (all women). *Students:* 8 full-time (all women), 105 part-time (98 women); includes 17 minority (10 African Americans, 1 American Indian/Alaska Native, 3 Asian Americans or Pacific Islanders, 3 Hispanic Americans), 1 international. Average age 42. 66 applicants, 79% accepted, 37 enrolled. In 2009, 24 master's, 4 other advanced degrees awarded. *Degree requirements:* For master's, thesis or alternative. *Entrance requirements:* For master's, BN, 1 year medical/surgical experience, RN license and state registration, 1 course in statistics with minimum grade of 'C', 3 letters of recommendation, minimum GPA of 3.25, interview; for doctorate, MS in advance nursing practice; New York state RN license; personal goal statement; resume; interview; statistics course with minimum grade of 'C'; for Post Master's Certificate, master's degree in clinical area; RN license and current registration; one year of clinical experience; statistics course with minimum grade of 'C'. Additional exam requirements/recommendations for international students: Required—TOEFL (minimum score 500 paper-based; 173 computer-based; 61 iBT). *Application deadline:* For fall admission, 3/1 priority date for domestic and international students; for spring admission, 10/1 priority date for domestic and international students. Applications are processed on a rolling basis. Application fee: $25. Electronic applications accepted. *Expenses:* Tuition: Part-time $770 per credit hour. Tuition and fees vary according to course load, program and reciprocity agreements. *Financial support:* In 2009–10, 1 student received support. Institutionally sponsored loans and scholarships/grants available. Financial award application deadline: 2/15; financial award applicants required to submit FAFSA. *Faculty research:* Professional stress, client behavior, drug therapy, treatment modalities and pulmonary cancers, chemical dependency. *Unit head:* Dr. Mary Lou Rusin, Chair, 716-839-8387, Fax: 716-839-8403, E-mail: mrusin@daemen.edu. *Application contact:* Scott Rowe, Associate Director of Graduate Programs, 716-839-8225, Fax: 716-839-8229, E-mail: srowe@daemen.edu.

Dalhousie University, Faculty of Health Professions, School of Nursing, Halifax, NS B3H 3J5, Canada. Offers MN, PhD, MN/MHSA. Part-time programs available. Postbaccalaureate distance learning degree programs offered (minimal on-campus study). *Faculty:* 16 full-time (15 women). *Students:* 16 full-time (15 women), 73 part-time (all women). Average age 32. 31 applicants, 94% accepted. In 2009, 20 master's awarded. *Degree requirements:* For master's, thesis optional. *Entrance requirements:* For master's, minimum GPA of 3.0; for doctorate, written support of faculty member who has agreed to be thesis supervisor. Additional exam requirements/recommendations for international students: Required—TOEFL, IELTS, CANTEST, CAEL, or Michigan English Language Assessment Battery. *Application deadline:* For fall admission, 2/1 priority date for domestic students, 2/1 for international students. Applications are processed on a rolling basis. Application fee: $70. Electronic applications accepted. *Financial support:* Fellowships, research assistantships, teaching assistantships available. *Faculty research:* Coping, social support, health promotion, aging, feminist studies. *Unit head:* Dr. Ruth Martin-Misener, Graduate Coordinator, 902-494-2143, Fax: 902-494-3487, E-mail: ruth.martin-misener@dal.ca. *Application contact:* Jackie Gilby, Graduate Programs Secretary, 902-494-2397, Fax: 902-494-3487, E-mail: nursing@dal.ca.

Delaware State University, Graduate Programs, Department of Nursing, Dover, DE 19901-2277. Offers MS. *Accreditation:* AACN. *Entrance requirements:* Additional exam requirements/recommendations for international students: Required—TOEFL (minimum score 550 paper-based). Electronic applications accepted.

Delta State University, Graduate Programs, School of Nursing, Cleveland, MS 38733-0001. Offers family nurse practitioner (MSN); nurse administrator (MSN); nurse educator (MSN). *Accreditation:* AACN. Part-time programs available. *Degree requirements:* For master's, thesis optional. *Entrance requirements:* For master's, GRE General Test. Electronic applications accepted. *Expenses:* Tuition, state resident: full-time $4450; part-time $247 per credit hour. Tuition, nonresident: full-time $11,520; part-time $640 per credit hour.

DePaul University, College of Liberal Arts and Sciences, Department of Nursing, Chicago, IL 60614. Offers adult nursing (MS); family nursing (MS); generalist nursing (MS); nurse anesthesia (MS). MS in nurse anesthesia offered jointly with Ravenswood Hospital Medical Center. *Accreditation:* AACN; AANA/CANAEP. Part-time and evening/weekend programs available. *Faculty:* 13 full-time (11 women), 12 part-time/adjunct (11 women). *Students:* 195 full-time (167 women), 43 part-time (41 women); includes 43 minority (9 African Americans, 1 American Indian/Alaska Native, 19 Asian Americans or Pacific Islanders, 14 Hispanic Americans), 2 international. Average age 39. 238 applicants, 46% accepted, 74 enrolled. In 2009, 70 master's awarded. *Degree requirements:* For master's, comprehensive exam (for some programs), thesis optional. *Entrance requirements:* For master's, GRE (if bachelor's GPA less than 3.2). Additional exam requirements/recommendations for international students: Required—TOEFL (minimum score 590 paper-based; 243 computer-based; 96 iBT) or IELTS (minimum score 7.5), Pearson Test of English (PTE). *Application deadline:* For fall admission, 3/1 priority date for domestic and international students; for winter admission, 8/15 priority date for domestic and international students. Application fee: $40. Electronic applications accepted. *Expenses:* Tuition: Full-time $37,525; part-time $620 per credit hour. *Financial support:* In 2009–10, 5 students received support, including 6 fellowships (averaging $1,500 per year); traineeships also available. Financial award applicants required to submit FAFSA. *Faculty research:* Children's health, women's health, health promotion. *Unit head:* Dr. Kay Thurn, Chair. *Application contact:* Ann Spittle, Director of Graduate Admissions, 773-325-7315, Fax: 773-325-7315, E-mail: graduatelas@depaul.edu.

DeSales University, Graduate Division, Programs in Nursing, Center Valley, PA 18034-9568. Offers adult advanced practice nurse specialist (MSN); certified nurse midwives (MSN); certified nurse practitioners (MSN); family nurse practitioner (MSN); nurse educator (MSN); MSN/MBA. *Accreditation:* NLN. Part-time programs available. *Students:* 67 part-time. In 2009, 218 master's awarded. *Degree requirements:* For master's, thesis optional. *Entrance requirements:* For master's, GRE General Test, MAT, minimum B average in undergraduate course work, health assessment course or equivalent, course work in statistics. Additional exam requirements/recommendations for international students: Required—TOEFL. *Application deadline:* Applications are processed on a rolling basis. Application fee: $35. Electronic applications accepted. *Expenses:* Tuition: Full-time $17,500; part-time $665 per credit. Full-time tuition and fees vary according to program. Part-time tuition and fees vary according to course load. *Financial support:* Applicants required to submit FAFSA. *Faculty research:* Women's health, theory validation, needs of homeless, behavior risk evaluation, wound healing. *Unit head:* Dr. Carol Gullo Mest, Director, 610-282-1100 Ext. 1394, Fax: 610-282-2091, E-mail: carol.mest@desales.edu. *Application contact:* Caryn Stopper, Director of Graduate Admissions, 610-282-1100 Ext. 1768, Fax: 610-282-2254, E-mail: caryn.stopper@desales.edu.

Dominican College, Division of Nursing, Department of Nursing, Orangeburg, NY 10962-1210. Offers family nurse practitioner (MSN). *Accreditation:* AACN. Part-time and evening/weekend programs available. *Degree requirements:* For master's, guided research project, 750 hours clinical practice with a final written project. *Entrance requirements:* For master's, bachelor's degree in nursing, minimum GPA of 3.0, RN license, 1 year of nursing experience, 3 letters of recommendation. Additional exam requirements/recommendations for international students: Required—TOEFL (minimum score 550 paper-based; 213 computer-based).

Dominican University of California, Graduate Programs, School of Health and Natural Sciences, Program in Nursing, San Rafael, CA 94901-2298. Offers geriatric and nurse educator (MS); integrated health practices (clinical nursing specialist) (MS). *Accreditation:* AACN. Part-time and evening/weekend programs available. *Degree requirements:* For master's, thesis. *Entrance requirements:* For master's, minimum GPA of 3.0; clinical experience; course work in nursing research and statistics; CPR certification; professional liability and malpractice insurance; interview. Additional exam requirements/recommendations for international students: Required—TOEFL (minimum score 550 paper-based; 213 computer-based). Electronic applications accepted.

Drexel University, College of Nursing and Health Professions, Graduate Nursing Program, Philadelphia, PA 19104-2875. Offers MSN. *Accreditation:* AACN; NLN. Electronic applications accepted.

Duke University, School of Nursing, Program in Nursing, Durham, NC 27708-0586. Offers PhD. *Faculty:* 31 full-time (27 women). *Students:* 15 full-time (12 women); includes 4 minority (1 African American, 1 American Indian/Alaska Native, 1 Asian American or Pacific Islander, 1 Hispanic American). Average age 34. 21 applicants, 24% accepted, 5 enrolled. *Degree requirements:* For doctorate, comprehensive exam, thesis/dissertation. *Entrance requirements:* For doctorate, GRE General Test. Additional exam requirements/recommendations for international students: Required—TOEFL (minimum score 550 paper-based; 213 computer-based; 83 iBT), IELTS (minimum score 7). *Application deadline:* For fall admission, 12/15 for domestic and international students. Application fee: $75. Electronic applications accepted. *Financial support:* In 2009–10, 4 students received support, including 13 fellowships (averaging $19,988 per year); institutionally sponsored loans, scholarships/grants, and health care benefits also available. *Faculty research:* Nursing management practices, adolescents and families undergoing intense treatments, psychosocial and chronic disease. Total annual research expenditures: $3.5 million. *Unit head:* Dr. Linda L. Davis, Director of Graduate Studies, 919-684-0343, Fax: 919-681-8899, E-mail: linda.davis@duke.edu. *Application contact:* Revonda P. Huppert, Program Coordinator, 919-668-4797, Fax: 919-681-8899, E-mail: huppert@duke.edu.

Duquesne University, School of Nursing, Doctor of Nursing Practice Program, Pittsburgh, PA 15282-0001. Offers DNP. Part-time and evening/weekend programs available. Postbaccalaureate distance learning degree programs offered (minimal on-campus study). *Faculty:* 11 full-time (10 women). *Students:* 32 full-time (31 women), 3 part-time (all women); includes 4 minority (3 African Americans, 1 American Indian/Alaska Native), 1 international. 60 applicants, 43% accepted, 22 enrolled. *Degree requirements:* For doctorate, thesis/dissertation, capstone project. *Entrance requirements:* For doctorate, current RN license; BSN; MSN with minimum GPA of 3.0; current certifications; phone interview. Additional exam requirements/recommendations for international students: Required—TOEFL (minimum score 600 paper-based; 80 iBT). *Application deadline:* For fall admission, 3/1 for domestic and international students. Application fee: $0. *Expenses:* Tuition: Part-time $851 per credit. Required fees: $81 per credit. *Financial support:* In 2009–10, 22 students received support, including 4 research assistantships with partial tuition reimbursements available (averaging $2,250 per year), 1 teaching assistantship with partial tuition reimbursement available (averaging $1,075 per year); institutionally sponsored loans, traineeships, and unspecified assistantships also available. Support available to part-time students. Financial award application deadline: 7/1; financial award applicants required to submit FAFSA. *Faculty research:* Vulnerable populations, social justice, cultural competence, health disparities, wellness within chronic illness. *Unit head:* Dr. Joan Such Lockhart, Professor and Associate Dean of Academic Affairs, 412-396-6540, Fax: 412-396-1821, E-mail: lockhart@duq.edu. *Application contact:* Susan Hardner, Nurse Recruiter, 412-396-4945, Fax: 412-396-6346, E-mail: nursing@duq.edu.

Duquesne University, School of Nursing, Doctor of Philosophy in Nursing Program, Pittsburgh, PA 15282-0001. Offers PhD. Part-time and evening/weekend programs available. Postbaccalaureate distance learning degree programs offered (minimal on-campus study). *Faculty:* 13 full-time (11 women), 2 part-time/adjunct (1 woman). *Students:* 21 full-time (20 women), 30 part-time (28 women); includes 7 minority (4 African Americans, 1 Asian American or Pacific Islander, 2 Hispanic Americans), 2 international. 28 applicants, 36% accepted, 8 enrolled. In 2009, 6 doctorates awarded. *Degree requirements:* For doctorate, thesis/dissertation, preliminary exam. *Entrance requirements:* For doctorate, GRE General Test, current RN license; BSN; master's degree with minimum GPA of 3.5; phone interview. Additional exam requirements/recommendations for international students: Required—TOEFL (minimum score 600 paper-based; 80 iBT). *Application deadline:* For fall admission, 2/1 for domestic and international students. *Expenses:* Tuition: Part-time $851 per credit. Required fees: $81 per credit. *Financial support:* In 2009–10, 25 students received support, including 6 research assistantships with partial tuition reimbursements available (averaging $2,250 per year), 3 teaching assistantships with partial tuition reimbursements available (averaging $1,075 per year); institutionally sponsored loans, scholarships/grants, traineeships, and unspecified assistantships also available. Support available to part-time students. Financial award application deadline: 7/1; financial award applicants required to submit FAFSA. *Faculty research:* Vulnerable populations, social justice, cultural competence, health disparities, wellness within chronic illness. *Unit head:* Dr. Joan Such Lockhart, Professor and Associate Dean of Academic Affairs, 412-396-6540, Fax: 412-

396-1821, E-mail: lockhart@duq.edu. *Application contact:* Susan Hardner, Nurse Recruiter, 412-396-4945, Fax: 412-396-6346, E-mail: nursing@duq.edu.

Duquesne University, School of Nursing, Master of Science in Nursing Program, Pittsburgh, PA 15282-0001. Offers family nurse practitioner (MSN); forensic nursing (MSN); nursing education (MSN). *Accreditation:* AACN. Part-time and evening/weekend programs available. Postbaccalaureate distance learning degree programs offered (minimal on-campus study). *Faculty:* 15 full-time (13 women), 4 part-time/adjunct (all women). *Students:* 73 full-time (69 women), 43 part-time (42 women); includes 8 minority (6 African Americans, 2 Asian Americans or Pacific Islanders). 131 applicants, 32% accepted, 36 enrolled. In 2009, 39 master's awarded. *Degree requirements:* For master's, culminating paper. *Entrance requirements:* For master's, current RN license; BSN with minimum GPA of 3.0; minimum of 1 year full-time work experience as RN prior to registration in clinical or specialty course. Additional exam requirements/recommendations for international students: Required—TOEFL (minimum score 600 paper-based; 80 iBT). *Application deadline:* For fall admission, 4/1 for domestic and international students. *Expenses:* Tuition: Part-time $851 per credit. Required fees: $81 per credit. *Financial support:* In 2009–10, 38 students received support, including 4 research assistantships with partial tuition reimbursements available (averaging $2,250 per year), 4 teaching assistantships with partial tuition reimbursements available (averaging $1,075 per year); institutionally sponsored loans, scholarships/grants, traineeships, and tuition waivers (partial) also available. Support available to part-time students. Financial award application deadline: 7/1. *Faculty research:* Vulnerable populations, social justice, cultural competence, health disparities, wellness within chronic illness. Total annual research expenditures: $457,857. *Unit head:* Dr. Joan Such Lockhart, Professor and Associate Dean of Academic Affairs, 412-396-6540, Fax: 412-396-1821, E-mail: lockhart@duq.edu. *Application contact:* Susan Hardner, Nurse Recruiter, 412-396-4945, Fax: 412-396-6346, E-mail: nursing@duq.edu.

Duquesne University, School of Nursing, Post Master's Certificate Program, Pittsburgh, PA 15282-0001. Offers family nurse practitioner (Post-Master's Certificate); forensic nursing (Post-Master's Certificate); transcultural/international nursing (Post-Master's Certificate). Part-time and evening/weekend programs available. Postbaccalaureate distance learning degree programs offered (minimal on-campus study). *Faculty:* 9 full-time (8 women), 1 (woman) part-time/adjunct. *Students:* 1 full-time (0 women), 5 part-time (all women). 18 applicants, 39% accepted, 5 enrolled. In 2009, 4 Post-Master's Certificates awarded. *Entrance requirements:* For degree, current RN license, BSN, MSN. Additional exam requirements/recommendations for international students: Required—TOEFL (minimum score 600 paper-based; 80 iBT). *Application deadline:* For fall admission, 4/1 for domestic and international students. *Expenses:* Tuition: Part-time $851 per credit. Required fees: $81 per credit. *Financial support:* In 2009–10, 3 students received support. Institutionally sponsored loans, scholarships/grants, traineeships, and tuition waivers (partial) available. Support available to part-time students. Financial award application deadline: 7/1. *Faculty research:* Vulnerable populations, social justice, cultural competence, health disparities, wellness within chronic illness. *Unit head:* Dr. Joan Such Lockhart, Professor and Associate Dean of Academic Affairs, 412-396-6540, Fax: 412-396-1821, E-mail: lockhart@duq.edu. *Application contact:* Susan Hardner, Nurse Recruiter, 412-396-4945, Fax: 412-396-6346, E-mail: nursing@duq.edu.

D'Youville College, Department of Nursing, Buffalo, NY 14201-1084. Offers community health nursing/education (MSN); community health nursing/high risk parents and children (MSN); community health nursing/management (MSN); family nurse practitioner (MS, Post-Master's Certificate); nursing and health-related professions (Certificate); nursing with clinical focus choice (MSN). *Accreditation:* AACN. Part-time and evening/weekend programs available. *Degree requirements:* For master's, thesis optional, membership on board of community agency, publishable paper. *Entrance requirements:* For master's, BS in nursing, minimum GPA of 3.0, course work in statistics and computers. Additional exam requirements/recommendations for international students: Required—TOEFL (minimum score 500 paper-based; 173 computer-based). Electronic applications accepted. *Faculty research:* Nursing curriculum, nursing theory-testing, wellness research, communication and socialization patterns.

See Display below and Close-Up on page 1611.

East Carolina University, Graduate School, College of Nursing, Greenville, NC 27858-4353. Offers MSN, PhD. *Accreditation:* AACN; AANA/CANAEP (one or more programs are accredited); ACNM/DOA (one or more programs are accredited); NLN. Part-time programs available. *Degree requirements:* For master's, comprehensive exam, thesis optional. *Entrance requirements:* For master's, GRE General Test or MAT, bachelor's degree in nursing, professional license, minimum B average in nursing.

Eastern Kentucky University, The Graduate School, College of Health Sciences, Department of Nursing, Richmond, KY 40475-3102. Offers rural community health care (MSN); rural health family nurse practitioner (MSN). *Accreditation:* AACN. *Entrance requirements:* For master's, GRE General Test, minimum GPA of 2.75.

Eastern Washington University, Graduate Studies, Intercollegiate College of Nursing, Cheney, WA 99004-2431. Offers MN. *Degree requirements:* For master's, comprehensive exam, thesis. *Entrance requirements:* For master's, GRE General Test, minimum GPA of 3.0. *Expenses:* Tuition, state resident: full-time $7476; part-time $249 per quarter hour. Tuition, nonresident: full-time $18,030; part-time $601 per quarter hour. Required fees: $3.50 per quarter hour. $142 per quarter.

East Tennessee State University, School of Graduate Studies, College of Nursing, Johnson City, TN 37614. Offers advanced nursing practice (Post Master's Certificate); health care management (Certificate); nursing (MSN, DSN). *Accreditation:* AACN. Part-time programs available. *Degree requirements:* For master's, comprehensive exam, thesis optional. *Entrance requirements:* For master's, GRE General Test, minimum GPA of 3.0, bachelor's degree in nursing, current RN license. Additional exam requirements/recommendations for international students: Required—TOEFL (minimum score 550 paper-based; 213 computer-based). *Faculty research:* Rural primary care, health care for the homeless, community health problems across the lifespan, nursing education research, school health services.

Edgewood College, Program in Nursing, Madison, WI 53711-1997. Offers MS. *Accreditation:* AACN. *Students:* 1 (woman) full-time, 34 part-time (32 women); includes 1 minority (Asian American or Pacific Islander). Average age 38. In 2009, 13 master's awarded. *Degree requirements:* For master's, practicum, research project. *Entrance requirements:* For master's, minimum GPA of 3.0, 2 letters of reference, current license. Additional exam requirements/recommendations for international students: Required—TOEFL. *Application deadline:* For fall admission, 8/24 priority date for domestic students, 8/1 for international students; for spring admission, 1/10 priority date for domestic students, 10/1 for international students. Applications are processed on a rolling basis. Application fee: $25. Electronic applications accepted. *Expenses:* Tuition: Part-time $688 per credit hour. *Unit head:* Dr. Margaret Noreuil, Dean, 608-663-2820, Fax: 608-663-3291, E-mail: mnoreuil@edgewood.edu. *Application contact:* Joann Eastman, Admissions Counselor, 608-663-3250, Fax: 608-663-2214, E-mail: gps@edgewood.edu.

Edinboro University of Pennsylvania, School of Graduate Studies and Research, School of Science, Management and Technology, Department of Nursing, Edinboro, PA 16444. Offers family nurse practitioner (MSN); nurse educator (Certificate); nursing (MSN); palliative and end-of-life care (Certificate). *Accreditation:* NLN. Part-time and evening/weekend programs available. *Faculty:* 5 full-time (all women). *Students:* 47 part-time (42 women); includes 4 minority (3 African Americans, 1 Hispanic American). Average age 40. In 2009, 26 master's, 3 other advanced degrees awarded. *Degree requirements:* For master's, thesis, competency exam. *Entrance requirements:* For master's, GRE or MAT, minimum QPA of 2.5. *Application deadline:* Applications are processed on a rolling basis. Application fee: $30. Electronic applications accepted. *Expenses:* Tuition, state resident: full-time $6666; part-time $370 per credit. Tuition, nonresident: full-time $10,666; part-time $593 per credit. Required fees: $2206.28. One-time fee: $204 part-time. *Financial support:* In 2009–10, 2 research assistantships with full and partial tuition reimbursements (averaging $4,050 per year) were awarded; career-related internships or fieldwork, Federal Work-Study, scholarships/grants, and unspecified assistantships also available. Support available to part-time students. Financial award application deadline: 2/15; financial award applicants required to submit FAFSA. *Unit head:* Dr. Alice

Nursing—General

Edinboro University of Pennsylvania (continued)
Conway, Program Head, 814-732-2285, E-mail: aconwayt@edinboro.edu. *Application contact:* Dr. Alice Conway, Program Head, 814-732-2285, E-mail: aconwayt@edinboro.edu.

Elmhurst College, Graduate Programs, Program in Nursing, Elmhurst, IL 60126-3296. Offers MSN. *Accreditation:* AACN. Part-time and evening/weekend programs available. *Faculty:* 3 full-time (all women). *Students:* 22 part-time (21 women); includes 2 minority (1 African American, 1 Asian American or Pacific Islander). Average age 46. 25 applicants, 80% accepted, 14 enrolled. In 2009, 18 master's awarded. *Entrance requirements:* For master's, 3 recommendations. Additional exam requirements/recommendations for international students: Required—TOEFL (minimum score 550 paper-based; 213 computer-based). *Application deadline:* Applications are processed on a rolling basis. Application fee: $25. Electronic applications accepted. *Expenses:* Contact institution. *Financial support:* In 2009–10, 1 student received support. Federal Work-Study and scholarships/grants available. Support available to part-time students. Financial award application deadline: 6/1; financial award applicants required to submit FAFSA. *Unit head:* Dr. Ted E. Lerud, Associate Dean of the Faculty, 630-617-3661, Fax: 630-617-6415, E-mail: gradadm@elmhurst.edu. *Application contact:* Elizabeth D. Kuebler, Director of Adult and Graduate Admission, 630-617-3069, Fax: 630-617-5501, E-mail: betsyk@elmhurst.edu.

Elms College, Division of Nursing, Chicopee, MA 01013-2839. Offers nursing and health services management (MSN); nursing education (MSN). *Accreditation:* AACN. Part-time and evening/weekend programs available. *Faculty:* 5 full-time (4 women), 3 part-time/adjunct (all women). *Students:* 8 full-time (all women), 27 part-time (26 women); includes 1 minority (African American). 11 applicants, 82% accepted, 8 enrolled. *Entrance requirements:* Additional exam requirements/recommendations for international students:;Required—TOEFL. *Application deadline:* For fall admission, 7/1 priority date for domestic students; for spring admission, 11/1 priority date for domestic students. Applications are processed on a rolling basis. Application fee: $30. *Financial support:* Applicants required to submit FAFSA. *Unit head:* Dr. Kathleen Scoble, Director, 413-265-2204, E-mail: scoblek@elms.edu. *Application contact:* Dr. Cynthia L. Dakin, Assistant Director of Graduate Studies, 413-265-2455, Fax: 413-265-2335, E-mail: dakinc@elms.edu.

Emory University, Graduate School of Arts and Sciences, Program in Nursing, Atlanta, GA 30322-1100. Offers PhD. *Accreditation:* AACN. *Degree requirements:* For doctorate, comprehensive exam, thesis/dissertation. *Entrance requirements:* For doctorate, GRE General Test. Additional exam requirements/recommendations for international students: Required—TOEFL. Electronic applications accepted. *Faculty research:* Symptoms, self management, care-giving, biobehavioral approaches, women's health.

Emory University, Nell Hodgson Woodruff School of Nursing, Atlanta, GA 30322-1100. Offers adult and elder health advanced practice nursing (MSN), including acute care, adult nurse practitioner, gerontological nurse practitioner; emergency nurse practitioner (MSN); family nurse practitioner (MSN); family nurse-midwife (MSN); nurse midwifery (MSN); pediatric nurse practitioner acute and primary care (MSN); public health nursing leadership (MSN); women's health nurse practitioner (MSN); women's health title x (MSN); women's health/adult health nurse practitioner (MSN); MSN/MPH. *Accreditation:* AACN; ACNM/DOA (one or more programs are accredited). Part-time programs available. *Faculty:* 30 full-time (29 women), 11 part-time/adjunct (10 women). *Students:* 110 full-time (106 women), 53 part-time (51 women); includes 49 minority (35 African Americans, 2 American Indian/Alaska Native, 10 Asian Americans or Pacific Islanders, 2 Hispanic Americans), 4 international. Average age 32. 182 applicants, 63% accepted, 86 enrolled. In 2009, 81 master's awarded. *Entrance requirements:* For master's, GRE General Test or MAT, minimum GPA of 3.0, BS in nursing from an accredited institution, RN license and additional course work, 3 letters of recommendation. Additional exam requirements/recommendations for international students: Required—TOEFL (minimum score 600 paper-based; 100 iBT). *Application deadline:* For fall admission, 1/15 priority date for domestic and international students; for spring admission, 10/1 priority date for domestic and international students. Applications are processed on a rolling basis. Application fee: $50. Electronic applications accepted. *Expenses:* Contact institution. *Financial support:* In 2009–10, 14 fellowships (averaging $28,000 per year) were awarded; career-related internships or fieldwork, Federal Work-Study, institutionally sponsored loans, and scholarships/grants also available. Support available to part-time students. Financial award application deadline: 3/1; financial award applicants required to submit CSS PROFILE or FAFSA. *Faculty research:* Older adult falls and injuries, minority health issues, cardiac symptoms and quality of life, bio-ethics and decision making, menopausal issues. *Unit head:* Dr. Linda McCauley, Dean, 404-727-7976, Fax: 404-727-9800, E-mail: linda.mccauley@emory.edu. *Application contact:* Katie Kennedy, Associate Director for Admission and Financial Aid, 404-727-7980, Fax: 404-727-8509, E-mail: admit@nursing.emory.edu.

See Close-Up on page 1613.

Excelsior College, School of Nursing, Albany, NY 12203-5159. Offers clinical systems management (MS); nursing (MS). *Accreditation:* NLN. Part-time and evening/weekend programs available. Postbaccalaureate distance learning degree programs offered (no on-campus study). *Entrance requirements:* For master's, RN license. Electronic applications accepted. *Faculty research:* Leadership development, test anxiety, use of technology in online learning.

Fairfield University, School of Nursing, Fairfield, CT 06824-5195. Offers clinical nurse leader (MSN); family nurse practitioner (MSN, PMC); healthcare management (MSN); nurse anesthesia (MSN); psychiatric nurse practitioner (MSN, PMC). *Accreditation:* AACN; AANA/CANAEP. Part-time programs available. *Degree requirements:* For master's, capstone project. *Entrance requirements:* For master's, GRE (nurse anesthesia applicants only), minimum QPA of 3.0, RN license, resume, 2 recommendations; for PMC, 1 year of work experience as a registered nurse. Additional exam requirements/recommendations for international students: Required—TOEFL (minimum score 550 paper-based; 213 computer-based; 80 iBT). Electronic applications accepted. *Expenses:* Contact institution. *Faculty research:* Care of older adults, palliative care, spirituality and innovative partnerships, diabetes.

Fairleigh Dickinson University, Metropolitan Campus, University College: Arts, Sciences, and Professional Studies, Henry P. Becton School of Nursing and Allied Health, Program in Nursing, Teaneck, NJ 07666-1914. Offers MSN, Certificate. *Accreditation:* AACN. *Students:* 3 full-time (2 women), 97 part-time (87 women), 1 international. Average age 39. 64 applicants, 83% accepted, 36 enrolled. In 2009, 18 master's awarded. *Application deadline:* Applications are processed on a rolling basis. Application fee: $40. *Application contact:* Susan Brooman, University Director of Graduate Admissions, 201-692-2554, Fax: 201-692-2560, E-mail: globaleducation@fdu.edu.

Fairleigh Dickinson University, Metropolitan Campus, University College: Arts, Sciences, and Professional Studies, Henry P. Becton School of Nursing and Allied Health, Program in Nursing Practice, Teaneck, NJ 07666-1914. Offers DNP. *Students:* 44 full-time (38 women). Average age 51. 22 applicants, 100% accepted, 15 enrolled. In 2009, 5 doctorates awarded. Application fee: $40. *Application contact:* Susan Brooman, University Director of Graduate Admissions, 201-692-2554, Fax: 201-692-2560, E-mail: globaleducation@fdu.edu.

Fairmont State University, Graduate Studies, Program in Nursing, Fairmont, WV 26554. Offers nursing administration (MS); nursing education (MS).

Felician College, Program in Nursing, Lodi, NJ 07644-2117. Offers adult health nurse (MSN, PMC); family practice nurse (MSN, PMC); nursing (MSN); nursing education (MSN). *Accreditation:* AACN. Part-time and evening/weekend programs available. Postbaccalaureate distance learning degree programs offered (no on-campus study). *Students:* 4 full-time (all women), 74 part-time (64 women); includes 18 minority (10 African Americans, 5 Asian Americans or Pacific Islanders, 3 Hispanic Americans). Average age 42. 29 applicants, 90% accepted, 24 enrolled. *Degree requirements:* For master's, scholarly project. *Entrance requirements:* For master's, BS in nursing or equivalent, minimum GPA of 3.0, 2 letters of recommendation, RN license; for PMC, RN license, minimum GPA of 2.75. Additional exam

requirements/recommendations for international students: Recommended—TOEFL (minimum score 550 paper-based; 213 computer-based). *Application deadline:* Applications are processed on a rolling basis. Application fee: $40. *Financial support:* In 2009–10, 10 students received support. Traineeships available. Financial award applicants required to submit FAFSA. *Faculty research:* Anxiety and fear, curriculum innovation, health promotion. *Unit head:* Dr. Muriel Shore, Dean, Division of Health Sciences, 201-559-6030, E-mail: shorem@felician.edu. *Application contact:* Dr. Wendy Lin-Cook, Director of Adult and Graduate Admission, 201-559-6077, Fax: 201-559-6138, E-mail: adultandgraduate@felician.edu.

See Close-Up on page 1615.

Ferris State University, College of Allied Health Sciences, School of Nursing, Big Rapids, MI 49307. Offers nursing (MS); nursing administration (MS); nursing education (MS); nursing informatics (MS). *Accreditation:* NLN. Part-time and evening/weekend programs available. Postbaccalaureate distance learning degree programs offered (minimal on-campus study). *Faculty:* 1 (woman) full-time, 69 part-time/adjunct (63 women). *Students:* 1 (woman) full-time, 64 part-time (58 women). Average age 42. 30 applicants, 53% accepted, 11 enrolled. In 2009, 9 master's awarded. *Degree requirements:* For master's, comprehensive exam, practicum, scholarly project. *Entrance requirements:* For master's, BS in nursing, writing sample, letters of reference, 2 years clinical experience. Additional exam requirements/recommendations for international students: Required—TOEFL (minimum score 550 paper-based). *Application deadline:* For fall admission, 7/15 priority date for domestic students. Applications are processed on a rolling basis. Application fee: $30. Electronic applications accepted. *Financial support:* In 2009–10, 4 students received support; fellowships, research assistantships, teaching assistantships, scholarships/grants available. Financial award application deadline: 4/15. *Faculty research:* Nursing education-minority student focus, student attitudes toward aging. *Unit head:* Dr. Julie A. Coon, Director, 231-591-2267, Fax: 231-591-2325, E-mail: coonj@ferris.edu. *Application contact:* Debby Buck, Off Campus Program Secretary, 231-591-2270, Fax: 231-591-3788, E-mail: buckd@ferris.edu.

Florida Agricultural and Mechanical University, Division of Graduate Studies, Research, and Continuing Education, School of Nursing, Tallahassee, FL 32307-3200. Offers MS. *Accreditation:* NLN. *Faculty:* 15 full-time (14 women). *Students:* 12 full-time (11 women), 1 part-time (0 women); includes 12 African Americans. In 2009, 2 master's awarded. *Entrance requirements:* Additional exam requirements/recommendations for international students: Required—TOEFL. *Application deadline:* For fall admission, 5/18 for domestic students, 12/18 for international students; for spring admission, 11/12 for domestic students, 5/12 for international students. Application fee: $30. *Unit head:* Dr. Cornelia P. Porter, Dean, 850-599-3017, Fax: 850-599-3508. *Application contact:* Dr. Doris E. Ballard-Ferguson, Graduate Coordinator, 850-412-7067.

Florida Atlantic University, Christine E. Lynn College of Nursing, Boca Raton, FL 33431-0991. Offers MS, DNP, PhD, Post Master's Certificate. *Accreditation:* AACN. Part-time programs available. *Faculty:* 41 full-time (38 women), 17 part-time/adjunct (all women). *Students:* 26 full-time (25 women), 304 part-time (281 women); includes 133 minority (80 African Americans, 2 American Indian/Alaska Native, 17 Asian Americans or Pacific Islanders, 34 Hispanic Americans), 1 international. Average age 41. 222 applicants, 30% accepted, 42 enrolled. In 2009, 118 master's, 6 doctorates awarded. *Degree requirements:* For master's, thesis or alternative; for doctorate, comprehensive exam, thesis/dissertation. *Entrance requirements:* For master's, GRE General Test, bachelor's degree in nursing, Florida RN license, minimum GPA of 3.0; for doctorate, GRE General Test, curriculum vitae, Florida RN license, minimum GPA of 3.5, MS in nursing. *Application deadline:* For fall admission, 6/1 for domestic students, 2/15 for international students; for spring admission, 10/1 for domestic students, 7/15 for international students. Applications are processed on a rolling basis. Application fee: $30. *Expenses:* Tuition, state resident: full-time $7055; part-time $293.94 per credit hour. Tuition, nonresident: full-time $22,096; part-time $920.66 per credit hour. *Financial support:* Research assistantships with partial tuition reimbursements, teaching assistantships with partial tuition reimbursements, career-related internships or fieldwork, Federal Work-Study, institutionally sponsored loans, scholarships/grants, and traineeships available. Support available to part-time students. *Faculty research:* Econometrics of nurse-patient relationship, Alzheimer's disease, community-based programs, falls, self-healing. *Unit head:* Dr. Anne J. Boykin, Dean, 561-297-3206, Fax: 561-297-3687, E-mail: boykina@fau.edu. *Application contact:* Carol Kruse, Graduate Coordinator, 561-297-3261, Fax: 561-297-0088, E-mail: ckruse@fau.edu.

Florida Gulf Coast University, College of Health Professions, School of Nursing, Fort Myers, FL 33965-6565. Offers MSN. *Accreditation:* AACN; AANA/CANAEP. Part-time programs available. *Faculty:* 42 full-time (33 women), 30 part-time/adjunct (20 women). *Students:* 49 full-time (42 women); includes 7 minority (5 African Americans, 2 Asian Americans or Pacific Islanders). Average age 38. 42 applicants, 36% accepted, 9 enrolled. In 2009, 7 master's awarded. *Degree requirements:* For master's, thesis or alternative. *Entrance requirements:* For master's, GRE General Test, MAT, minimum GPA of 3.0. Additional exam requirements/recommendations for international students: Required—TOEFL (minimum score 550 paper-based; 213 computer-based). *Application deadline:* For fall admission, 4/15 priority date for domestic students; for spring admission, 6/1 for domestic students. Applications are processed on a rolling basis. Application fee: $30. Electronic applications accepted. *Faculty research:* Gerontology, community health, ethical and legal aspects of health care, critical care. Total annual research expenditures: $181,623. *Unit head:* Dr. Marianne Rodgers, Director, 239-590-7454, Fax: 239-590-7474, E-mail: mrodgers@fgcu.edu. *Application contact:* Lynn O'Hare, Administrative Assistant, 239-590-7451, Fax: 239-590-7474, E-mail: lohare@fgcu.edu.

Florida International University, College of Nursing and Health Sciences, Nursing Program, Miami, FL 33199. Offers MSN, PhD. *Accreditation:* AACN; AANA/CANAEP. Part-time and evening/weekend programs available. *Faculty:* 28 full-time (26 women), 3 part-time/adjunct (all women). *Students:* 140 full-time (106 women), 193 part-time (162 women); includes 237 minority (83 African Americans, 28 Asian Americans or Pacific Islanders, 126 Hispanic Americans), 2 international. Average age 37. 216 applicants, 25% accepted, 51 enrolled. In 2009, 113 master's awarded. *Degree requirements:* For master's, thesis or alternative; for doctorate, comprehensive exam, thesis/dissertation. *Entrance requirements:* For master's, bachelor's degree in nursing, minimum undergraduate GPA of 3.0 in upper-level coursework, letters of recommendation; for doctorate, GRE, letters of recommendation, minimum undergraduate GPA of 3.0 in upper-level coursework, interview. Additional exam requirements/recommendations for international students: Required—TOEFL (minimum score 550 paper-based; 213 computer-based; 80 iBT). *Application deadline:* For fall admission, 6/1 for domestic students, 4/1 for international students; for spring admission, 10/1 for domestic students, 9/1 for international students. Applications are processed on a rolling basis. Application fee: $30. Electronic applications accepted. *Expenses:* Tuition, state resident: full-time $8008; part-time $4004 per year. Tuition, nonresident: full-time $20,104; part-time $10,052 per year. Required fees: $298; $149 per term. *Financial support:* Institutionally sponsored loans and scholarships/grants available. Financial award application deadline: 3/1; financial award applicants required to submit FAFSA. *Faculty research:* Adult health nursing. *Unit head:* Dr. Anahid Kulwicki, Interim Director, 305-348-7703, Fax: 305-348-7764, E-mail: anahid.kulwicki@fiu.edu. *Application contact:* Nanett Rojas, Assistant Director of Graduate Admissions, 305-348-7442, Fax: 305-348-7441, E-mail: gradadm@fiu.edu.

Florida Southern College, Program in Nursing, Lakeland, FL 33801-5698. Offers MSN. *Accreditation:* AACN. Part-time and evening/weekend programs available. *Entrance requirements:* For master's, Florida RN license. Additional exam requirements/recommendations for international students: Required—TOEFL (minimum score 550 paper-based). *Expenses:* Contact institution. *Faculty research:* End of life care, dementia, health promotion.

Florida State University, The Graduate School, College of Nursing, Tallahassee, FL 32312. Offers family nurse practitioner (MSN, DNP); health systems leadership (DNP); nurse educator (MSN, Certificate). *Accreditation:* AACN. Part-time programs available. Postbaccalaureate distance learning degree programs offered (no on-campus study). *Faculty:* 13 full-time (12 women). *Students:* 13 full-time (4 women), 102 part-time (100 women); includes 13 minority (7

African Americans, 3 Asian Americans or Pacific Islanders, 3 Hispanic Americans). Average age 35. 42 applicants, 71% accepted, 29 enrolled. In 2009, 25 master's, 3 other advanced degrees awarded. *Degree requirements:* For master's, thesis optional. *Entrance requirements:* For master's, GRE General Test, MAT, minimum GPA of 3.0, BSN, Florida RN license; for doctorate, GRE General Test, MAT, minimum GPA of 3.0, BSN or MSN, Florida RN license. Additional exam requirements/recommendations for international students: Required—TOEFL (minimum score 550 paper-based). *Application deadline:* For fall admission, 7/1 for domestic and international students. Application fee: $30. Electronic applications accepted. *Expenses:* Tuition, state resident: full-time $7413. Tuition, nonresident: full-time $22,567. *Financial support:* In 2009–10, 101 students received support, including fellowships with partial tuition reimbursements available (averaging $6,300 per year), research assistantships with partial tuition reimbursements available (averaging $3,000 per year), 3 teaching assistantships with partial tuition reimbursements available (averaging $3,000 per year); career-related internships or fieldwork, Federal Work-Study, institutionally sponsored loans, scholarships/grants, traineeships, and tuition waivers (partial) also available. Financial award application deadline: 4/15; financial award applicants required to submit FAFSA. *Faculty research:* Distance learning, gerontology, health promotion, educational strategies, rehabilitation of brain injured patients. *Unit head:* Dr. Lisa Ann Plowfield, Dean, 850-644-3297, Fax: 850-644-7660, E-mail: lplowfield@nursing.fsu.edu. *Application contact:* Brenda Pereira, Graduate Program Coordinator, 850-644-5638, Fax: 850-645-7249, E-mail: bpereira@fsu.edu.

Fort Hays State University, Graduate School, College of Health and Life Sciences, Department of Nursing, Hays, KS 67601-4099. Offers MSN. *Accreditation:* AACN. *Degree requirements:* For master's, comprehensive exam, thesis optional. *Entrance requirements:* For master's, GRE General Test or MAT. Additional exam requirements/recommendations for international students: Required—TOEFL (minimum score 550 paper-based; 213 computer-based). Electronic applications accepted.

Framingham State University, Division of Graduate and Continuing Education, Program in Nursing, Framingham, MA 01701-9101. Offers nursing education (MSN); nursing leadership (MSN). *Accreditation:* AACN. *Entrance requirements:* For master's, BSN; minimum cumulative undergraduate GPA of 3.0, 3.25 in nursing courses; coursework in statistics; 2 letters of recommendation; interview. Electronic applications accepted.

Franciscan University of Steubenville, Graduate Programs, Department of Nursing, Steubenville, OH 43952-1763. Offers MSN. *Accreditation:* NLN. Part-time and evening/weekend programs available. *Degree requirements:* For master's, thesis. *Entrance requirements:* For master's, GRE General Test, MAT.

Franklin Pierce University, Graduate Studies, Rindge, NH 03461-0060. Offers emerging network technology (Graduate Certificate); health practice management (MBA, Graduate Certificate); human resource management (MBA); human resources management (Graduate Certificate); information technology management (MS); leadership (MBA, DA), including transformational leadership (DA); nursing (MS); physical therapy (DPT); physician assistant (MPAS); sports facilities management (MS); teacher education (M Ed). *Accreditation:* APTA. Part-time programs available. Postbaccalaureate distance learning degree programs offered (no on-campus study). *Faculty:* 27 full-time (16 women), 18 part-time/adjunct (4 women). *Students:* 296 full-time (172 women), 249 part-time (165 women); includes 18 minority (5 African Americans, 7 Asian Americans or Pacific Islanders, 6 Hispanic Americans), 31 international. Average age 38. 227 applicants, 97% accepted, 185 enrolled. In 2009, 76 master's, 46 doctorates awarded. *Degree requirements:* For master's, concentrated original research projects; student teaching; fieldwork and/or internship; leadership project; for doctorate, concentrated original research projects, clinical fieldwork and/or internship, leadership project. *Entrance requirements:* For master's, minimum GPA of 2.5, 3 letters of recommendation; for doctorate, demonstrated success at previous academic institutions (minimum GPA of 2.5), 3 letters of recommendation, personal mission statement, interview; writing sample (for DA program). Additional exam requirements/recommendations for international students: Required—TOEFL (minimum score 550 paper-based; 195 computer-based). *Application deadline:* Applications are processed on a rolling basis. Application fee: $0. Electronic applications accepted. *Expenses:* Tuition: Part-time $1560 per course. Part-time tuition and fees vary according to degree level, campus/location and program. *Financial support:* In 2009–10, 36 students received support, including 22 teaching assistantships with full and partial tuition reimbursements available; career-related internships or fieldwork and unspecified assistantships also available. Support available to part-time students. Financial award applicants required to submit FAFSA. *Faculty research:* Evidence based practice in sports physical therapy, human resource management in economic crisis, leadership in nursing, innovation in sports facility management, differentiated learning and understanding by design. *Unit head:* Dr. Robert G. Goddard, Assistant Dean, 603-899-4361, Fax: 603-229-4580, E-mail: goddardr@franklinpierce.edu. *Application contact:* 800-325-1090, Fax: 603-898-0827, E-mail: gpsadmin@franklinpierce.edu.

Frontier School of Midwifery and Family Nursing, Graduate Programs, Hyden, KY 41749. Offers community-based family nurse practitioner (MSN, Post Master's Certificate); community-based nurse-midwifery education (MSN, Post Master's Certificate); community-based women[0092]s health care nurse practitioner (MSN, Post Master's Certificate). *Accreditation:* ACNM; NLN.

Gannon University, School of Graduate Studies, Morosky College of Health Professions and Sciences, School of Health Professions, Villa Maria School of Nursing, Erie, PA 16541-0001. Offers anesthesia (MSN); business administration (MSN); family nurse practitioner (Certificate); medical-surgical nursing (MSN); nurse anesthesia (Certificate); nursing rural practitioner (MSN). *Accreditation:* AACN; AANA/CANAEP (one or more programs are accredited). Part-time and evening/weekend programs available. *Students:* 19 full-time (11 women), 59 part-time (45 women); includes 2 minority (both African Americans). Average age 36. 16 applicants, 81% accepted, 0 enrolled. In 2009, 19 master's awarded. *Degree requirements:* For master's, thesis. *Entrance requirements:* For master's, GRE General Test, degree in nursing. Additional exam requirements/recommendations for international students: Required—TOEFL (minimum score 79 iBT). *Application deadline:* For spring admission, 8/1 for domestic students. Application fee: $25. Electronic applications accepted. *Expenses:* Tuition: Full-time $13,590; part-time $755 per credit. Required fees: $524; $17 per credit. Tuition and fees vary according to course load, degree level, campus/location and program. *Financial support:* Scholarships/grants available. Financial award application deadline: 7/1; financial award applicants required to submit FAFSA. *Unit head:* Dr. Sharon Thompson, Director, 814-871-5345, E-mail: thompson001@gannon.edu. *Application contact:* Kara Morgan, Assistant Director of Graduate Admissions, 814-871-5831, Fax: 814-871-5827, E-mail: graduate@gannon.edu.

Gardner-Webb University, Graduate School, School of Nursing, Boiling Springs, NC 28017. Offers MSN, PMC. *Accreditation:* NLN. *Faculty:* 5 full-time (all women). *Students:* 3 full-time (all women), 100 part-time (94 women); includes 12 African Americans, 1 American Indian/Alaska Native, 1 Hispanic American. Average age 42. In 2009, 23 master's awarded. *Expenses:* Tuition: Part-time $305 per credit hour. *Unit head:* Dr. Gayle B. Price, Dean, 704-406-4723, Fax: 704-406-4329, E-mail: gradschool@gardner-webb.edu. *Application contact:* Dr. Jackson Rainer, Dean, Graduate School, 704-406-4724, Fax: 704-406-4329, E-mail: gradschool@gardner-webb.edu.

George Mason University, College of Health and Human Services, School of Nursing, Fairfax, VA 22030. Offers forensic nursing (Certificate); nursing (MSN, PhD); nursing administration (Certificate); nursing education (Certificate); nursing practice (DNP). *Faculty:* 36 full-time (all women), 52 part-time/adjunct (49 women). *Students:* 47 full-time (46 women), 275 part-time (259 women); includes 90 minority (43 African Americans, 3 American Indian/Alaska Native, 33 Asian Americans or Pacific Islanders, 11 Hispanic Americans), 10 international. Average age 42. 176 applicants, 66% accepted, 77 enrolled. In 2009, 72 master's, 8 doctorates, 3 other advanced degrees awarded. *Degree requirements:* For master's, comprehensive exam (for some programs), thesis in clinical classes; for doctorate, comprehensive exam (for some programs), thesis/dissertation (for some programs). *Entrance requirements:* For master's, resume, 2 recommendation letters, transcripts, nursing license, goal statement, at least 1 year working in the nursing field; for doctorate, resume, 3 recommendation letters, nursing license, at least 1 year of work in the nursing field. Additional exam requirements/recommendations for international students: Required—TOEFL. *Application deadline:* For fall admission, 4/1 priority date for domestic students; for spring admission, 11/1 priority date for domestic students. Applications are processed on a rolling basis. Application fee: $75. Electronic applications accepted. *Expenses:* Tuition, state resident: full-time $7568; part-time $315.33 per credit hour. Tuition, nonresident: full-time $21,704; part-time $904.33 per credit hour. Required fees: $2184; $91 per credit hour. *Financial support:* In 2009–10, 2 students received support, including 2 research assistantships with full and partial tuition reimbursements available (averaging $4,186 per year); Federal Work-Study, scholarships/grants, unspecified assistantships, and nurse faculty loan, health care benefits (full-time research or teaching assistantship recipients) also available. Support available to part-time students. Financial award application deadline: 3/1; financial award applicants required to submit FAFSA. Total annual research expenditures: $270,863. *Unit head:* Dr. Shirley S. Travis, Dean, 703-993-1918. *Application contact:* Janice Lee-Beverly, Program Support, 703-993-1947, E-mail: jleebev1@gmu.edu.

Georgetown University, Graduate School of Arts and Sciences, School of Nursing and Health Studies, Washington, DC 20057. Offers acute care nurse practitioner (MS); clinical nurse specialist (MS); family nurse practitioner (MS); nurse anesthesia (MS); nurse-midwifery (MS); nursing education (MS). *Accreditation:* AACN; AANA/CANAEP; ACNM/DOA. *Degree requirements:* For master's, thesis optional. *Entrance requirements:* For master's, GRE General Test or MAT, bachelor's degree in nursing from NLN-accredited school, minimum undergraduate GPA of 3.0. Additional exam requirements/recommendations for international students: Required—TOEFL.

The George Washington University, School of Medicine and Health Sciences, Health Sciences Programs, Washington, DC 20052. Offers adult nurse practitioner (MSN, Post Master's Certificate); clinical practice management (MSHS); clinical research administration (MSHS); clinical research administration for nurses (MSN); emergency services management (MSHS); end-of-life care (MSHS, MSN); family nurse practitioner (MSN, Post Master's Certificate); immunohematology (MSHS); nursing (DNP); nursing leadership and management (MSN); physical therapy (DPT); physician assistant (MSHS); MSHS/MPH. Postbaccalaureate distance learning degree programs offered (no on-campus study). *Students:* 270 full-time (220 women), 491 part-time (406 women); includes 176 minority (83 African Americans, 5 American Indian/Alaska Native, 62 Asian Americans or Pacific Islanders, 26 Hispanic Americans), 26 international. Average age 35. 1,059 applicants, 47% accepted, 292 enrolled. In 2009, 155 master's, 22 doctorates, 75 other advanced degrees awarded. *Entrance requirements:* Additional exam requirements/recommendations for international students: Required—TOEFL (minimum score 550 paper-based; 213 computer-based). *Application deadline:* Applications are processed on a rolling basis. Application fee: $60. *Expenses:* Contact institution. *Unit head:* Jean E. Johnson, Senior Associate Dean, 202-994-3725, E-mail: jejohns@gwu.edu. *Application contact:* Joke Ogundiran, Director of Admission, 202-994-1668, Fax: 202-994-0870, E-mail: jokeogun@gwu.edu.

Georgia College & State University, Graduate School, College of Health Sciences, Graduate Nursing Program, Milledgeville, GA 31061. Offers adult health (MSN); family nurse practitioner (MSN); nursing administration (MSN); MSN/MBA. *Accreditation:* NLN. Part-time and evening/weekend programs available. *Faculty:* 22 full-time (21 women). *Students:* 13 full-time (all women), 44 part-time (42 women); includes 8 minority (all African Americans), 1 international. Average age 35. 22 applicants, 91% accepted, 18 enrolled. In 2009, 18 master's awarded. *Degree requirements:* For master's, comprehensive exam, thesis optional. *Entrance requirements:* For master's, GMAT, GRE General Test, or MAT, bachelor's degree in nursing, RN license. Additional exam requirements/recommendations for international students: Recommended—TOEFL (minimum score 550 paper-based; 213 computer-based; 79 iBT). *Application deadline:* For fall admission, 7/1 priority date for domestic students. Applications are processed on a rolling basis. Application fee: $40. Electronic applications accepted. *Expenses:* Tuition, area resident: Part-time $241 per credit hour. Tuition, state resident: full-time $4338. Tuition, nonresident: full-time $17,352; part-time $964 per credit hour. Required fees: $609 per semester. Tuition and fees vary according to course load and campus/location. *Financial support:* In 2009–10, 1 research assistantship with full tuition reimbursement was awarded; unspecified assistantships also available. Financial award applicants required to submit FAFSA. *Unit head:* Dr. Judith Malachowski, Director, School of Nursing, 478-445-5122, E-mail: judith.malachowski@gcsu.edu. *Application contact:* Lora Crowe, Coordinator, 478-445-5122, E-mail: lora.crowe@gcsu.edu.

Georgia Southern University, Jack N. Averitt College of Graduate Studies, College of Health and Human Sciences, School of Nursing, Program in Clinical Nurse Specialist, Statesboro, GA 30460. Offers MSN, Certificate. Part-time programs available. Postbaccalaureate distance learning degree programs offered. *Students:* 4 part-time (all women). Average age 45. *Entrance requirements:* For master's, GRE General Test or MAT, minimum GPA of 3.0, Georgia nursing license, 2 years of clinical experience, CPR certification. Additional exam requirements/recommendations for international students: Required—TOEFL (minimum score 550 paper-based; 213 computer-based; 80 iBT). *Expenses:* Tuition, state resident: full-time $5040; part-time $210 per credit hour. Tuition, nonresident: full-time $20,136; part-time $839 per credit hour. Required fees: $1644. *Financial support:* In 2009–10, research assistantships with partial tuition reimbursements (averaging $6,850 per year), teaching assistantships with partial tuition reimbursements (averaging $6,850 per year) were awarded; career-related internships or fieldwork, Federal Work-Study, scholarships/grants, traineeships, health care benefits, tuition waivers (partial), and unspecified assistantships also available. Support available to part-time students. Financial award application deadline: 4/15. *Unit head:* Dr. Donna Hodnicki, Coordinator, 912-478-5056, E-mail: dhodnicki@georgiasouthern.edu. *Application contact:* Office of Graduate Admission, 912-478-5384, Fax: 912-478-0740, E-mail: gradadmissino@georgiasouthern.edu.

Georgia Southern University, Jack N. Averitt College of Graduate Studies, College of Health and Human Sciences, School of Nursing, Program in Nursing Science, Statesboro, GA 30460. Offers DNP. Part-time programs available. Postbaccalaureate distance learning degree programs offered. *Students:* 21 part-time (17 women); includes 2 minority (both African Americans). Average age 46. 14 applicants, 64% accepted, 5 enrolled. *Entrance requirements:* Additional exam requirements/recommendations for international students: Required—TOEFL (minimum score 550 paper-based; 213 computer-based; 80 iBT). *Application deadline:* For fall admission, 3/1 priority date for domestic and international students; for spring admission, 10/1 priority date for domestic students, 10/1 for international students. Applications are processed on a rolling basis. Application fee: $50. Electronic applications accepted. *Expenses:* Tuition, state resident: full-time $5040; part-time $210 per credit hour. Tuition, nonresident: full-time $20,136; part-time $839 per credit hour. Required fees: $1644. *Financial support:* In 2009–10, 12 students received support, including research assistantships (averaging $6,850 per year), teaching assistantships (averaging $6,850 per year); career-related internships or fieldwork, Federal Work-Study, scholarships/grants, traineeships, tuition waivers, and unspecified assistantships also available. Support available to part-time students. Financial award application deadline: 4/15; financial award applicants required to submit FAFSA. *Unit head:* Dr. Jean Bartels, Chair, 912-478-5479, Fax: 912-478-0536, E-mail: jbartels@georgiasouthern.edu. *Application contact:* Dr. Jean Bartels, Chair, 912-478-5479, Fax: 912-478-0536, E-mail: jbartels@georgiasouthern.edu.

Georgia State University, College of Health and Human Sciences, Byrdine F. Lewis School of Nursing, Atlanta, GA 30302-3083. Offers adult health (MS); adult health nursing (Certificate); child health (MS); family nurse practitioner (MS, Certificate); health promotion, protection and restoration (PhD); perinatal/women's health (MS); psychiatric mental health nursing (Certificate); psychiatric/mental health (MS); women's health nursing (Certificate). *Accreditation:* AACN. Part-time and evening/weekend programs available. Postbaccalaureate distance learning degree programs offered (minimal on-campus study). *Degree requirements:* For master's, research activity; for doctorate, comprehensive exam, thesis/dissertation. *Entrance requirements:* For master's, MAT (preferred) or GRE, interview, RN license; for doctorate, GRE General Test. Additional exam requirements/recommendations for international students: Required—TOEFL

Nursing—General

Georgia State University (continued)
(minimum score 550 paper-based; 213 computer-based). Electronic applications accepted. *Expenses:* Contact institution. *Faculty research:* Breast cancer prevention, sexually compulsive behaviors, health risks in minority youth, asthma treatment strategies, adolescent alcohol-related issues.

Goldfarb School of Nursing at Barnes-Jewish College, Goldfarb School of Nursing at Barnes-Jewish College, St Louis, MO 63110. Offers adult acute care nurse practitioner (MSN); adult nurse practitioner (MSN); neonatal nurse practitioner (MSN); nurse anesthesia (MSN); nurse educator (MSN); nurse executive (MSN). *Accreditation:* AACN; AANA/CANAEP. Part-time and evening/weekend programs available. Postbaccalaureate distance learning degree programs offered (minimal on-campus study). *Faculty:* 18 full-time (16 women), 3 part-time/adjunct (2 women). *Students:* 28 full-time (25 women), 81 part-time (73 women); includes 34 minority (27 African Americans, 6 Asian Americans or Pacific Islanders, 1 Hispanic American), 3 international. Average age 38. 60 applicants, 75% accepted, 40 enrolled. In 2009, 26 master's awarded. *Degree requirements:* For master's, thesis or alternative. *Entrance requirements:* For master's, minimum GPA of 3.0, 2 references, statistics course. Additional exam requirements/recommendations for international students: Required—TOEFL (minimum score 550 paper-based; 213 computer-based). *Application deadline:* For fall admission, 2/1 priority date for international students; for spring admission, 10/1 priority date for international students. Applications are processed on a rolling basis. Application fee: $150. *Financial support:* In 2009–10, 60 students received support, including 20 fellowships (averaging $4,000 per year), 4 research assistantships (averaging $5,000 per year); Federal Work-Study, institutionally sponsored loans, and scholarships/grants also available. Support available to part-time students. Financial award applicants required to submit FAFSA. *Faculty research:* HIV Stigma, HIV symptom management, palliative care with children and their families, heart disease prevention in Hispanic women, depression in the well elderly, alternative therapies in pre-term infants. *Unit head:* Dr. Michael L. Evans, Dean, 314-362-6289, Fax: 314-362-0984, E-mail: mevans@bjc.org. *Application contact:* Dr. Michael Ward, Associate Dean for Student Programs, 314-362-9155, Fax: 314-362-9250, E-mail: mward@bjc.org.

Gonzaga University, School of Professional Studies, Department of Nursing, Spokane, WA 99258. Offers MSN. *Accreditation:* AACN. Postbaccalaureate distance learning degree programs offered. *Faculty:* 17 full-time (15 women), 5 part-time/adjunct (all women). *Students:* 20 full-time (14 women), 224 part-time (199 women); includes 23 minority (6 African Americans, 1 American Indian/Alaska Native, 9 Asian Americans or Pacific Islanders, 7 Hispanic Americans), 2 international. Average age 39. In 2009, 85 master's awarded. *Entrance requirements:* For master's, MAT, minimum B average in undergraduate course work. Additional exam requirements/recommendations for international students: Required—TOEFL. *Application deadline:* For fall admission, 7/20 priority date for domestic students; for spring admission, 11/1 for domestic students. Applications are processed on a rolling basis. Application fee: $50. Tuition and fees vary according to course level, course load, degree level, campus/location and program. *Financial support:* Application deadline: 3/1. *Unit head:* Mary Sue Gorski, Head, 509-328-4220 Ext. 3587. *Application contact:* Dr. Joseph Albert, Application Contact, 509-328-4220 Ext. 3564.

Goshen College, Program in Nursing, Goshen, IN 46526-4794. Offers clinical nurse leader (MSN); family nurse practitioner (MSN). *Accreditation:* AACN. Part-time and evening/weekend programs available. *Faculty:* 1 (woman) full-time, 7 part-time/adjunct (all women). *Students:* 35 part-time (32 women), 2 international. Average age 39. 17 applicants, 88% accepted, 14 enrolled. *Degree requirements:* For master's, comprehensive exam (for some programs). *Entrance requirements:* Additional exam requirements/recommendations for international students: Required—TOEFL (minimum score 213 paper-based; 79 computer-based; 6 iBT). *Application deadline:* Applications are processed on a rolling basis. Application fee: $50. *Expenses:* Contact institution. *Financial support:* In 2009–10, 10 students received support. Scholarships/grants available. Financial award applicants required to submit FAFSA. *Unit head:* Dr. Brenda Srof, Director, 574-535-7375, E-mail: brendajs@goshen.edu. *Application contact:* Dr. Brenda Srof, 574-535-7375, E-mail: brendajs@goshen.edu.

Governors State University, College of Health Professions, Program in Nursing, University Park, IL 60466-0975. Offers MSN. *Accreditation:* NLN. *Degree requirements:* For master's, comprehensive exam, thesis or alternative, practicum. *Entrance requirements:* For master's, GRE General Test, minimum GPA of 3.0 in upper-division nursing course work, 2.5 overall; BSN verification of AAS or employment as registered nurse; Illinois licensure; BSN from NLN-accredited institution.

Graceland University, School of Nursing, Independence, MO 64050-3434. Offers family nurse practitioner (MSN, PMC); nurse educator (MSN, PMC). Part-time programs available. Postbaccalaureate distance learning degree programs offered (minimal on-campus study). *Faculty:* 9 full-time (all women), 9 part-time/adjunct (7 women). *Students:* 138 full-time (128 women), 146 part-time (126 women); includes 14 minority (8 African Americans, 1 American Indian/Alaska Native, 4 Asian Americans or Pacific Islanders, 1 Hispanic American). Average age 40. 251 applicants, 51% accepted, 90 enrolled. In 2009, 44 master's, 2 other advanced degrees awarded. *Degree requirements:* For master's, comprehensive exam (for some programs), thesis optional. *Entrance requirements:* For master's, BSN from nationally accredited program, portfolio, RN license, minimum GPA of 3.0. *Application deadline:* For fall admission, 6/1 priority date for domestic students; for winter admission, 10/1 priority date for domestic students; for spring admission, 3/1 priority date for domestic students. Application fee: $50. Electronic applications accepted. *Expenses:* Contact institution. *Financial support:* In 2009–10, 117 students received support. Institutionally sponsored loans and traineeships available. Support available to part-time students. Financial award applicants required to submit FAFSA. *Faculty research:* International nursing, family care-giving, health promotion. *Unit head:* Dr. Claudia D. Horton, Dean, 816-833-0524 Ext. 4214, Fax: 816-833-2990, E-mail: horton@graceland.edu. *Application contact:* Abbey Riley, Program Consultant, 816-833-0524 Ext. 4803, Fax: 816-833-2990, E-mail: ajriley@graceland.edu.

Graduate School and University Center of the City University of New York, Graduate Studies, Program in Nursing Science, New York, NY 10016-4039. Offers DNS. *Faculty:* 5 full-time (4 women), 1 (woman) part-time/adjunct. *Students:* 47 full-time (44 women); includes 10 African Americans, 1 Asian American or Pacific Islander, 4 Hispanic Americans. Average age 49. 29 applicants, 48% accepted, 14 enrolled. *Degree requirements:* For doctorate, thesis/dissertation, exams. *Entrance requirements:* For doctorate, GRE, 2 letters of recommendation. Additional exam requirements/recommendations for international students: Required—TOEFL. *Application deadline:* For fall admission, 2/15 for domestic students. Application fee: $125. Electronic applications accepted. *Financial support:* In 2009–10, 2 students received support. *Unit head:* Dr. Barbara Weinstein, Executive Officer, 212-817-7980, E-mail: bweinstein@gc.cuny.edu. *Application contact:* Les Gribben, Director of Admissions, 212-817-7470, Fax: 212-817-1624, E-mail: lgribben@gc.cuny.edu.

Grambling State University, School of Graduate Studies and Research, College of Professional Studies, School of Nursing, Grambling, LA 71245. Offers family nurse practitioner (MSN, PMC); nurse educator (MSN). *Accreditation:* NLN. Part-time programs available. *Faculty:* 8 full-time (all women). *Students:* 40 full-time (37 women), 15 part-time (13 women); includes 20 minority (19 African Americans, 1 Asian American or Pacific Islander), 1 international. Average age 38. 9 applicants, 67% accepted, 5 enrolled. In 2009, 17 master's awarded. *Degree requirements:* For master's, comprehensive exam (for some programs), thesis (for some programs). *Entrance requirements:* For master's, GRE, minimum GPA of 3.0 on last degree, interview, 2 years experience as RN. Additional exam requirements/recommendations for international students: Required—TOEFL (minimum score 500 paper-based; 173 computer-based; 61 iBT). *Application deadline:* For fall admission, 7/1 for domestic and international students; for spring admission, 12/1 for domestic and international students. Applications are processed on a rolling basis. Application fee: $20 ($30 for international students). Electronic applications accepted. *Expenses:* Tuition, state resident: full-time $2610. Tuition, nonresident: full-time $2610. *Financial support:* Health care benefits and tuition waivers (full and partial) available. Financial award application deadline: 5/31; financial award applicants required to submit FAFSA. *Unit head:* Dr. Rhonda Hensley, MSN Program Director, 318-274-2897, Fax: 318-274-3491, E-mail: hensleyr@gram.edu. *Application contact:* Katina Crowe, Special Assistant to Associate Vice President/Dean, 318-274-2158, Fax: 318-274-7373, E-mail: croweks@gram.edu.

Grand Canyon University, College of Nursing and Health Sciences, Phoenix, AZ 85017-1097. Offers addiction counseling (MS); nursing (MS), including adult clinical nurse specialist, family nurse practitioner, nursing education, nursing leadership in health care system; professional counseling (MS). Part-time and evening/weekend programs available. Postbaccalaureate distance learning degree programs offered (no on-campus study). *Entrance requirements:* Additional exam requirements/recommendations for international students: Required—TOEFL (minimum score 575 paper-based; 233 computer-based; 90 iBT), IELTS (minimum score 7).

Grand Valley State University, Kirkhof College of Nursing, Allendale, MI 49401-9403. Offers advanced practice (MSN); case management (MSN); nursing administration (MSN); nursing education (MSN); nursing practice (DNP); MSN/MBA. *Accreditation:* AACN. Part-time programs available. *Faculty:* 17 full-time (all women), 3 part-time/adjunct (all women). *Students:* 6 full-time (5 women), 69 part-time (61 women); includes 3 minority (all African Americans). Average age 39. 18 applicants, 100% accepted, 18 enrolled. In 2009, 23 master's awarded. *Degree requirements:* For master's, thesis optional. *Entrance requirements:* For master's, GRE, minimum GPA of 3.0 in upper-division course work, course work in statistics, Michigan RN license. Additional exam requirements/recommendations for international students: Required—TOEFL. *Application deadline:* For fall admission, 3/15 priority date for domestic students. Applications are processed on a rolling basis. Application fee: $30. Electronic applications accepted. *Expenses:* Tuition, state resident: part-time $471 per credit hour. Tuition, nonresident: part-time $646 per credit hour. Tuition and fees vary according to course level. *Financial support:* In 2009–10, 23 students received support, including 14 fellowships (averaging $3,207 per year), 9 research assistantships with full and partial tuition reimbursements available (averaging $8,053 per year); career-related internships or fieldwork, Federal Work-Study, institutionally sponsored loans, and traineeships also available. Financial award application deadline: 2/15. *Faculty research:* Multigenerational health promotion, chronic disease prevention, end-of-life issues, nursing workload, family caregiver health. Total annual research expenditures: $36,000. *Unit head:* Dr. Cynthia McCurren, Dean, 616-331-7161, Fax: 616-331-7362. *Application contact:* Dr. Jean Martin, Director of Graduate Programs, 616-331-7167, Fax: 616-331-7362, E-mail: martinj@gvsu.edu.

Grand View University, Program in Innovative Leadership, Des Moines, IA 50316-1599. Offers business (MS); education (MS); nursing (MS). *Entrance requirements:* For master's, GRE or GMAT, minimum undergraduate GPA of 3.0, professional resume, 3 letters of recommendation, interview. Additional exam requirements/recommendations for international students: Required—TOEFL (minimum score 550 paper-based; 210 computer-based). Electronic applications accepted.

Gwynedd-Mercy College, School of Nursing, Gwynedd Valley, PA 19437-0901. Offers clinical nurse specialist (MSN), including gerontology, oncology, pediatrics; nurse practitioner (MSN), including adult health, pediatric health. *Accreditation:* NLN. *Degree requirements:* For master's, thesis optional. *Entrance requirements:* For master's, GRE General Test or MAT, current nursing experience, physical assessment, course work in statistics, BSN from an NLNAC accredited program, 2 letters of recommendation, personal interview. Additional exam requirements/recommendations for international students: Required—TOEFL (minimum score 575 paper-based). Electronic applications accepted. *Expenses:* Contact institution. *Faculty research:* Critical thinking, primary care, domestic violence, multiculturalism, nursing centers.

Hampton University, Graduate College, School of Nursing, Hampton, VA 23668. Offers advanced adult nursing (MS); community health nursing (MS); community mental health/psychiatric nursing (MS); family nursing (MS); gerontological nursing for the nurse practitioner (MS); pediatric nursing (MS); women's health nursing (MS). *Accreditation:* AACN; NLN. Part-time and evening/weekend programs available. *Degree requirements:* For master's, thesis optional. *Entrance requirements:* For master's, GRE General Test. *Faculty research:* Curriculum development, physical and mental assessment.

Hardin-Simmons University, Graduate School, Patty Hanks Shelton School of Nursing, Abilene, TX 79698-0001. Offers advanced healthcare delivery (MSN); family nurse practitioner (MSN). *Accreditation:* AACN. Part-time programs available. *Faculty:* 3 full-time (all women), 1 (woman) part-time/adjunct. *Students:* 5 full-time (all women), 13 part-time (12 women); includes 2 minority (both Hispanic Americans). Average age 37. 5 applicants, 100% accepted, 4 enrolled. In 2009, 6 master's awarded. *Degree requirements:* For master's, comprehensive exam, thesis or alternative. *Entrance requirements:* For master's, GRE, minimum undergraduate GPA of 3.0 in major, 2.8 overall; interview; upper-level course work in statistics; CPR certification; letters of recommendation. Additional exam requirements/recommendations for international students: Required—TOEFL (minimum score 550 paper-based; 213 computer-based; 75 iBT). *Application deadline:* For fall admission, 8/15 priority date for domestic students, 4/1 for international students; for spring admission, 1/5 priority date for domestic students, 9/1 for international students. Applications are processed on a rolling basis. Application fee: $50. *Expenses:* Contact institution. *Financial support:* In 2009–10, 2 students received support. Career-related internships or fieldwork and scholarships/grants available. Support available to part-time students. Financial award application deadline: 6/30; financial award applicants required to submit FAFSA. *Faculty research:* Child abuse, alternative medicine, pediatric chronic disease, health promotion. *Unit head:* Dr. Amy Toone, Director, 325-671-2361, Fax: 325-671-2386, E-mail: atoone@phssn.edu. *Application contact:* Dr. Gary Stanlake, Dean of Graduate Studies, 325-670-1298, Fax: 325-670-1564, E-mail: gradoff@hsutx.edu.

Hawai'i Pacific University, College of Nursing and Health Sciences, Honolulu, HI 96813. Offers community clinical nurse specialist (MSN); community clinical nurse specialist educator option (MSN); family nurse practitioner (MSN). *Accreditation:* NLN. Part-time and evening/weekend programs available. *Faculty:* 5 full-time (4 women), 2 part-time/adjunct (1 woman). *Students:* 26 full-time (23 women), 13 part-time (all women); includes 18 minority (3 African Americans, 2 American Indian/Alaska Native, 12 Asian Americans or Pacific Islanders, 1 Hispanic American), 7 international. Average age 38. 22 applicants, 68% accepted, 10 enrolled. In 2009, 11 master's awarded. *Degree requirements:* For master's, practicum, professional paper. *Entrance requirements:* For master's, bachelor's degree in nursing, minimum GPA of 3.0. Additional exam requirements/recommendations for international students: Recommended—TOEFL (minimum score 550 paper-based; 213 computer-based; 80 iBT), TWE (minimum score 5). *Application deadline:* Applications are processed on a rolling basis. Application fee: $50. Electronic applications accepted. *Expenses:* Tuition: Full-time $12,600; part-time $700 per credit hour. Tuition and fees vary according to program. *Financial support:* In 2009–10, 17 students received support. Career-related internships or fieldwork, Federal Work-Study, scholarships/grants, and traineeships available. Support available to part-time students. Financial award application deadline: 3/1; financial award applicants required to submit FAFSA. *Faculty research:* Hawaiian elders, traditional healing and nursing center. *Unit head:* Dr. Patricia Lange-Otsuka, Associate Dean of Nursing for Administration, 808-236-5812, Fax: 808-236-5818, E-mail: potsuka@hpu.edu. *Application contact:* Danny Lam, Assistant Director of Graduate Admissions, 808-544-1135, Fax: 808-544-0280, E-mail: graduate@hpu.edu.

Holy Family University, Graduate School, School of Nursing, Philadelphia, PA 19114. Offers community health nursing (MSN); nursing administration (MSN); nursing education (MSN). *Accreditation:* AACN. Part-time and evening/weekend programs available. *Faculty:* 1 (woman) full-time, 1 (woman) part-time/adjunct. *Students:* 1 (woman) full-time, 46 part-time (all women); includes 7 minority (5 African Americans, 2 Asian Americans or Pacific Islanders). Average age 41. 17 applicants, 76% accepted, 11 enrolled. In 2009, 3 master's awarded. *Degree requirements:* For master's, thesis or alternative. *Entrance requirements:* For master's, bachelor's degree in nursing, RN license, minimum GPA of 3.0, 2 letters of reference. *Application deadline:* For fall admission, 7/1 priority date for domestic students; for winter admission, 11/1 priority date for domestic students. Applications are processed on a rolling basis. Application

fee: $25. *Expenses:* Tuition: Part-time $600 per credit. Required fees: $58 per semester. *Financial support:* Federal Work-Study available. Support available to part-time students. Financial award application deadline: 2/15; financial award applicants required to submit FAFSA. *Unit head:* Dr. Christine Rosner, Dean, 267-341-3292, Fax: 215-637-6598, E-mail: crosner@holyfamily.edu. *Application contact:* Gidget Matie Montelibano, Graduate Admissions Counselor, 267-341-3558, Fax: 215-637-1478, E-mail: gmontelibano@holyfamily.edu.

Holy Names University, Graduate Division, Department of Nursing, Oakland, CA 94619-1699. Offers administration/management (MS, Certificate); clinical faculty (MS, Certificate); community health nursing/case manager (MS); family nurse practitioner (MS, Certificate); MSN/Certificate; MSN/MBA. *Accreditation:* AACN. Part-time and evening/weekend programs available. *Entrance requirements:* For master's, bachelor's degree in nursing or related field, California RN license or eligibility, minimum GPA of 3.0, previous course work in research or statistics. Additional exam requirements/recommendations for international students: Required—TOEFL (minimum score 500 paper-based). *Faculty research:* Women's reproductive health, gerontology, attitudes about aging, schizophrenic families, international health issues.

Howard University, College of Pharmacy, Nursing and Allied Health Sciences, Division of Nursing, Washington, DC 20059-0002. Offers nurse practitioner (Certificate); primary family health nursing (MSN). *Accreditation:* AACN. Part-time programs available. *Degree requirements:* For master's, comprehensive exam, thesis optional. *Entrance requirements:* For master's, RN license, minimum GPA of 3.0, BS in nursing. *Faculty research:* Urinary incontinence, breast cancer prevention, depression in the elderly, adolescent pregnancy.

Hunter College of the City University of New York, Graduate School, Schools of the Health Professions, Hunter-Bellevue School of Nursing, New York, NY 10021-5085. Offers MS, AC, MS/MPH. *Accreditation:* AACN. Part-time programs available. *Faculty:* 15 full-time (11 women). *Students:* 1 (woman) full-time, 187 part-time (163 women); includes 62 minority (28 African Americans, 27 Asian Americans or Pacific Islanders, 7 Hispanic Americans). Average age 35. 152 applicants, 70% accepted, 78 enrolled. In 2009, 118 master's, 2 other advanced degrees awarded. *Degree requirements:* For master's, practicum, portfolio. *Entrance requirements:* For master's, BSN, minimum GPA of 3.0, New York RN license, course work in basic statistics, resume; for AC, MSN, minimum GPA of 3.0. Additional exam requirements/recommendations for international students: Required—TOEFL. *Application deadline:* For fall admission, 4/1 for domestic students; for spring admission, 11/1 for domestic students. Applications are processed on a rolling basis. Application fee: $125. *Expenses:* Tuition, state resident: full-time $7360; part-time $310 per credit. Required fees: $250 per semester. *Financial support:* In 2009–10, 9 students received support. Federal Work-Study, scholarships/grants, traineeships, and tuition waivers (partial) available. Support available to part-time students. Financial award application deadline: 5/1; financial award applicants required to submit FAFSA. *Faculty research:* Aging, high-risk mothers and babies, adolescent health, care of HIV/AIDS clients, critical care nursing. *Unit head:* Dr. Diane Rendon, Director, 212-481-7596, Fax: 212-481-5078, E-mail: drendon@hunter.cuny.edu. *Application contact:* Milena Solo, Director for Graduate Admissions, 212-772-4482, Fax: 212-650-3336, E-mail: milena.solo@hunter.cuny.edu.

Husson University, School of Graduate and Professional Studies, Program in Nursing, Bangor, ME 04401-2999. Offers advanced practice psychiatric nursing (MSN, PMC); family and community nurse practitioner (MSN, PMC). *Accreditation:* AACN. *Entrance requirements:* For master's, MAT, BSN. *Expenses:* Contact institution.

Idaho State University, Office of Graduate Studies, Kasiska College of Health Professions, Department of Nursing, Pocatello, ID 83209-8101. Offers nursing (MS, Post-Master's Certificate). *Accreditation:* AACN. Part-time programs available. *Faculty:* 4 full-time (all women). *Students:* 63 full-time (54 women), 65 part-time (53 women); includes 6 minority (2 Asian Americans or Pacific Islanders, 4 Hispanic Americans). Average age 37. In 2009, 32 master's awarded. *Degree requirements:* For master's, comprehensive exam, thesis optional, practicum and/or clinical hours; for Post-Master's Certificate, comprehensive exam, thesis optional, practicum. *Entrance requirements:* For master's, GRE General Test, interview, 3 letters of reference, active RN license; for Post-Master's Certificate, GRE General Test, 3 letters of reference, practicum or nursing license, graduate degree. Additional exam requirements/recommendations for international students: Required—TOEFL (minimum score 600 paper-based; 213 computer-based). *Application deadline:* For fall admission, 7/1 for domestic students, 6/1 for international students; for spring admission, 12/1 for domestic students, 11/1 for international students. Applications are processed on a rolling basis. Application fee: $55. Electronic applications accepted. *Expenses:* Tuition, state resident: full-time $3318; part-time $297 per credit hour. Tuition, nonresident: full-time $13,120; part-time $437 per credit hour. Required fees: $2530. Tuition and fees vary according to program. *Financial support:* In 2009–10, 1 research assistantship with full and partial tuition reimbursement (averaging $9,401 per year), 4 teaching assistantships with full and partial tuition reimbursements (averaging $10,841 per year) were awarded; career-related internships or fieldwork, Federal Work-Study, institutionally sponsored loans, scholarships/grants, health care benefits, tuition waivers (full and partial), and unspecified assistantships also available. Support available to part-time students. Financial award application deadline: 1/1; financial award applicants required to submit FAFSA. *Faculty research:* Health promotions, health of homeless, exercise and elderly, student stress, midwifery. *Unit head:* Dr. Carol Ashton, Chair, 208-282-2443, Fax: 208-282-4476, E-mail: ashtcaro@isu.edu. *Application contact:* Tami Carson, Graduate School Technical Records Specialist, 208-282-2150, Fax: 208-282-4847, E-mail: carstami@isu.edu.

Illinois State University, Graduate School, Mennonite College of Nursing, Normal, IL 61790. Offers family nurse practitioner (PMC); nursing (MSN, PhD). *Accreditation:* AACN. *Faculty research:* Expanding the teaching-nursing home culture in the state of Illinois, advanced education nursing traineeship program, collaborative doctoral program-caring for older adults.

Immaculata University, College of Graduate Studies, Department of Nursing, Immaculata, PA 19345. Offers MSN. *Accreditation:* AACN. *Entrance requirements:* For master's, MAT or GRE, BSN. Additional exam requirements/recommendations for international students: Required—TOEFL.

Independence University, Program in Nursing, Salt Lake City, UT 84107. Offers community health (MSN); gerontology (MSN); nursing administration (MSN); wellness promotion (MSN). *Expenses:* Required fees: $475 per credit. One-time fee: $100 part-time.

Indiana State University, School of Graduate Studies, College of Nursing, Health and Human Services, Department of Nursing, Terre Haute, IN 47809. Offers MS. *Accreditation:* NLN. Part-time programs available. *Degree requirements:* For master's, thesis or alternative. *Entrance requirements:* For master's, BSN, RN license, minimum undergraduate GPA of 3.0. Electronic applications accepted. *Faculty research:* Nursing faculty-student interactions, clinical evaluation, program evaluation, sexual dysfunction, faculty attitudes.

Indiana University of Pennsylvania, School of Graduate Studies and Research, College of Health and Human Services, Department of Nursing and Allied Health, Program in Nursing, Indiana, PA 15705-1087. Offers MS. *Accreditation:* AACN. Part-time programs available. *Faculty:* 6 full-time (5 women), 1 (woman) part-time/adjunct. *Students:* 2 full-time (both women), 44 part-time (42 women). Average age 39. 23 applicants, 52% accepted, 11 enrolled. In 2009, 13 master's awarded. *Degree requirements:* For master's, thesis optional. *Entrance requirements:* For master's, 2 letters of recommendation. Additional exam requirements/recommendations for international students: Required—TOEFL. *Application deadline:* For fall admission, 7/1 priority date for domestic students; for spring admission, 11/1 for domestic students. Applications are processed on a rolling basis. Application fee: $40. *Expenses:* Tuition, state resident: full-time $6666; part-time $370 per credit hour. Tuition, nonresident: full-time $10,666; part-time $593 per credit hour. Required fees: $813 per semester. *Financial support:* In 2009–10, 3 research assistantships with full and partial tuition reimbursements (averaging $1,360 per year) were awarded; Federal Work-Study also available. Support available to part-time students. Financial award application deadline: 3/15; financial award applicants required to submit FAFSA. *Unit head:* Dr. Kristy Chunta, Graduate Coordinator, 724-357-3262, E-mail: kristy.chunta@iup.edu. *Application contact:* Dr. Nashat Zuraikat, Graduate Coordinator, 724-357-3262, E-mail: zuraikat@iup.edu.

Indiana University–Purdue University Fort Wayne, College of Health and Human Services, Department of Nursing, Fort Wayne, IN 46805-1499. Offers adult nursing practice (MS); nursing administration (MS, Certificate); nursing education (MS); women's health nursing practice (MS). Part-time programs available. *Faculty:* 7 full-time (all women), 1 (woman) part-time/adjunct. *Students:* 5 full-time (all women), 34 part-time (32 women); includes 4 minority (3 African Americans, 1 American Indian/Alaska Native). Average age 37. 15 applicants, 93% accepted, 11 enrolled. *Entrance requirements:* For master's, GRE Writing Test (if GPA below 3.0), BS in nursing, eligibility for Indiana RN license, minimum GPA of 3.0, essay, copy of resume, three references, undergraduate course work in research and statistics within last 5 years. Additional exam requirements/recommendations for international students: Required—TOEFL (minimum score 550 paper-based; 213 computer-based; 77 iBT); Recommended—TWE. *Application deadline:* For fall admission, 5/1 priority date for domestic and international students. Applications are processed on a rolling basis. Application fee: $55 ($60 for international students). Electronic applications accepted. *Expenses:* Tuition, state resident: full-time $4595; part-time $255 per credit. Tuition, nonresident: full-time $10,963; part-time $609 per credit. Required fees: $528; $29.35 per credit. Tuition and fees vary according to course load. *Financial support:* In 2009–10, 11 teaching assistantships with partial tuition reimbursements (averaging $12,740 per year) were awarded; scholarships/grants also available. Support available to part-time students. Financial award application deadline: 3/1; financial award applicants required to submit FAFSA. *Unit head:* Dr. Carol Sternberger, Chair, 260-481-6816, Fax: 260-481-5767, E-mail: sternber@ipfw.edu. *Application contact:* Dr. Susan Ahrens, Graduate Program Director, 260-481-6816, Fax: 260-481-5767, E-mail: ahrenss@ipfw.edu.

Indiana University–Purdue University Indianapolis, School of Nursing, Indianapolis, IN 46202-2896. Offers acute care nurse practitioner (MSN); adult health clinical nurse specialist (MSN); adult health nursing (MSN), including adult clinical nurse specialist, adult nurse practitioner (MSN); adult psychiatric/mental health nursing (MSN); child psychiatric/mental health nursing (MSN); community health nursing (MSN); family nurse practitioner (MSN); neonatal nurse practitioner (MSN); nursing science (PhD); pediatric clinical nurse specialist (MSN); women's health nurse practitioner (MSN); MSN/MPA; MSN/MPH. *Accreditation:* AACN; NLN (one or more programs are accredited). Part-time programs available. *Faculty:* 85 full-time (82 women), 60 part-time/adjunct (all women). *Students:* 46 full-time (43 women), 369 part-time (354 women); includes 30 minority (21 African Americans, 6 Asian Americans or Pacific Islanders, 3 Hispanic Americans), 5 international. Average age 39. 121 applicants, 82% accepted, 67 enrolled. In 2009, 106 master's, 3 doctorates awarded. Terminal master's awarded for partial completion of doctoral program. *Degree requirements:* For master's, thesis; for doctorate, thesis/dissertation. *Entrance requirements:* For master's, minimum GPA of 3.0, RN license; for doctorate, GRE General Test, minimum GPA of 3.0, MSN, RN license, graduate statistics course with B grade or better (not older than 3 years). Additional exam requirements/recommendations for international students: Required—TOEFL. *Application deadline:* For fall admission, 2/15 for domestic students; for spring admission, 9/15 for domestic students. Application fee: $55 ($65 for international students). *Financial support:* In 2009–10, 93 students received support, including 9 fellowships with full tuition reimbursements available (averaging $7,039 per year), 7 teaching assistantships with full tuition reimbursements available (averaging $5,300 per year); research assistantships with full tuition reimbursements available, Federal Work-Study, institutionally sponsored loans, scholarships/grants, and tuition waivers (full) also available. Support available to part-time students. Financial award application deadline: 5/1. *Faculty research:* Clinical science, health systems. Total annual research expenditures: $3 million. *Unit head:* Associate Dean for Graduate Programs, 317-274-2806, E-mail: nursing@iupui.edu. *Application contact:* Information Contact, 317-274-2806.

Indiana Wesleyan University, College of Graduate Studies, School of Nursing, Marion, IN 46953-4974. Offers community health nursing (MS); nursing (Post Master's Certificate); nursing administration (MS); nursing education (MS); primary care nursing (MS). *Accreditation:* AACN. Part-time programs available. Postbaccalaureate distance learning degree programs offered (minimal on-campus study). *Degree requirements:* For master's, capstone project or thesis. *Entrance requirements:* For master's, writing sample, RN license, 1 year of related experience, graduate statistics course. Additional exam requirements/recommendations for international students: Required—TOEFL. *Expenses:* Contact institution. *Faculty research:* Primary health care with international emphasis, international nursing.

Inter American University of Puerto Rico, Arecibo Campus, Program in Nursing, Arecibo, PR 00614-4050. Offers community nursing (MS); critical care nursing (MS); primary care nursing (MS); surgical nursing (MS). *Entrance requirements:* For master's, EXADEP or GRE General Test or MAT, 2 letters of recommendation, bachelor's degree in nursing, minimum GPA of 2.5 in last 60 credits, minimum 1 year nursing experience, nursing license.

Jacksonville State University, College of Graduate Studies and Continuing Education, College of Nursing, Jacksonville, AL 36265-1602. Offers MSN. *Accreditation:* AACN. Part-time and evening/weekend programs available. *Degree requirements:* For master's, comprehensive exam, thesis (for some programs). *Entrance requirements:* For master's, GRE General Test or MAT. Additional exam requirements/recommendations for international students: Required—TOEFL (minimum score 500 paper-based; 173 computer-based; 61 iBT). Electronic applications accepted.

Jacksonville University, College of Arts and Sciences, School of Nursing, Jacksonville, FL 32211. Offers MSN. *Accreditation:* AACN. Part-time programs available. *Degree requirements:* For master's, thesis. *Entrance requirements:* For master's, GRE General Test, BS in nursing from an accredited program, course work in statistics within last 5 years, Florida nursing license. Additional exam requirements/recommendations for international students: Required—TOEFL (minimum score 550 paper-based). *Expenses:* Contact institution.

James Madison University, The Graduate School, College of Integrated Science and Technology, Department of Nursing, Harrisonburg, VA 22807. Offers MSN. *Accreditation:* AACN. *Faculty:* 6 full-time (all women). *Students:* 13 full-time (12 women), 29 part-time (26 women); includes 3 minority (2 African Americans, 1 American Indian/Alaska Native). Average age 27. In 2009, 12 master's awarded. *Entrance requirements:* For master's, GRE General Test. *Application deadline:* For fall admission, 4/1 priority date for domestic students; for spring admission, 4/1 priority date for domestic students. Application fee: $55. *Expenses:* Tuition, area resident: Part-time $305 per credit hour. Tuition, state resident: part-time $305 per credit hour. Tuition, nonresident: part-time $890 per credit hour. *Financial support:* In 2009–10, 1 student received support. Application deadline: 3/1. *Unit head:* Dr. Merle E. Mast, Academic Unit Head, 540-568-6314. *Application contact:* Dr. Patty Hale, Graduate Program Coordinator, 540-568-6314.

Jefferson College of Health Sciences, Program in Nursing, Roanoke, VA 24031-3186. Offers nursing education (MSN); nursing management (MSN). *Accreditation:* AACN. Part-time programs available. *Faculty:* 16 full-time (9 women), 1 part-time/adjunct (0 women). *Students:* 31 full-time (28 women), 10 part-time (9 women); includes 6 minority (3 African Americans, 2 Asian Americans or Pacific Islanders, 1 Hispanic American). Average age 43. 63 applicants, 59% accepted, 21 enrolled. In 2009, 13 master's awarded. *Degree requirements:* For master's, project. *Entrance requirements:* For master's, MAT. Additional exam requirements/recommendations for international students: Required—TOEFL (minimum score 550 paper-based; 213 computer-based; 80 iBT). *Application deadline:* Applications are processed on a rolling basis. Application fee: $35. Electronic applications accepted. *Financial support:* Career-related internships or fieldwork, Federal Work-Study, scholarships/grants, traineeships, health care benefits, and tuition waivers (full) available. Support available to part-time students. Financial award applicants required to submit FAFSA. *Faculty research:* Nursing, teaching and learning techniques, cultural competence, spirituality and nursing. *Unit head:* Dr. Ava Porter, Department Chair, 540-985-8531, E-mail: agporter@jchs.edu. *Application contact:* Judith McKeon, Director of Admissions, 540-985-9083, Fax: 540-985-9773, E-mail: jomckeon@jchs.edu.

Nursing—General

The Johns Hopkins University, School of Nursing, Baltimore, MD 21218-2699. Offers MSN, DNP, PhD, Certificate, MSN/MBA, MSN/MPH. *Accreditation:* AACN; NLN (one or more programs are accredited). Part-time programs available. *Faculty:* 31 full-time (27 women), 23 part-time/adjunct (21 women). *Students:* 131 full-time (123 women), 175 part-time (163 women); includes 76 minority (32 African Americans, 6 American Indian/Alaska Native, 32 Asian Americans or Pacific Islanders, 6 Hispanic Americans), 5 international. Average age 36. 405 applicants, 78% accepted, 94 enrolled. In 2009, 80 master's, 3 doctorates awarded. *Degree requirements:* For master's, thesis optional, portfolio or scholarly project; for doctorate, thesis/dissertation. *Entrance requirements:* For master's, GRE, interview, minimum GPA of 3.0, BSN, RN license; for doctorate, GRE, interview, minimum GPA of 3.0, resume, RN license, writing sample; for Certificate, interview, minimum GPA of 3.0, MSN, resume, RN license. Additional exam requirements/recommendations for international students: Required—TOEFL (minimum score 550 paper-based; 213 computer-based). *Application deadline:* For fall admission, 3/1 priority date for domestic and international students; for winter admission, 7/1 priority date for domestic and international students; for spring admission, 7/1 priority date for domestic and international students. Applications are processed on a rolling basis. Application fee: $75. Electronic applications accepted. *Expenses:* Contact institution. *Financial support:* In 2009–10, 79 students received support, including 6 fellowships with partial tuition reimbursements available (averaging $23,272 per year); research assistantships with full tuition reimbursements available, teaching assistantships with full tuition reimbursements available, career-related internships or fieldwork, Federal Work-Study, scholarships/grants, traineeships, and tuition waivers (partial) also available. Support available to part-time students. Financial award application deadline: 3/1; financial award applicants required to submit FAFSA. *Faculty research:* Hypertension, violence, cardiovascular risk symptom management, symptom management, health disparities. *Unit head:* Dr. Martha N. Hill, Dean, 410-955-7544, Fax: 410-955-4890, E-mail: mnhill@son.jhmi.edu. *Application contact:* Mary O'Rourke, Director of Admissions and Student Services, 410-955-7548, Fax: 410-614-7086, E-mail: orourke@son.jhmi.edu.

Kaplan University, Davenport Campus, School of Nursing, Davenport, IA 52807-2095. Offers nurse administrator (MS); nurse educator (MS). Part-time and evening/weekend programs available. Postbaccalaureate distance learning degree programs offered (no on-campus study). *Entrance requirements:* For master's, RN. Additional exam requirements/recommendations for international students: Required—TOEFL (minimum score 550 paper-based; 80 computer-based).

Kean University, College of Natural, Applied and Health Sciences, Program in Nursing, Union, NJ 07083. Offers clinical management (MSN), including transcultural focus; community health nursing (MSN); school nursing (MSN). *Accreditation:* NLN. Part-time and evening/weekend programs available. *Faculty:* 7 full-time (all women). *Students:* 12 full-time (all women), 78 part-time (74 women); includes 46 minority (31 African Americans, 10 Asian Americans or Pacific Islanders, 5 Hispanic Americans). Average age 44. 44 applicants, 98% accepted, 26 enrolled. In 2009, 36 master's awarded. *Degree requirements:* For master's, thesis or alternative, clinical field experience. *Entrance requirements:* For master's, minimum GPA of 3.0; BS in nursing; RN license; 2 letters of recommendation; interview; 1 completed course of the following: Basic Health Assessment and Human Growth and Development across the life span. *Application deadline:* For fall admission, 5/1 for domestic students; for spring admission, 11/1 for domestic students. Application fee: $60 ($150 for international students). Electronic applications accepted. *Expenses:* Tuition, state resident: full-time $10,440; part-time $435 per credit. Tuition, nonresident: full-time $14,160; part-time $590 per credit. Required fees: $2642; $110 per credit. Part-time tuition and fees vary according to course load and degree level. *Financial support:* In 2009–10, 1 research assistantship with full tuition reimbursement (averaging $3,263 per year) was awarded; unspecified assistantships also available. *Unit head:* Dr. Cheryl Krause-Parello, Program Coordinator, 908-737-3390, E-mail: ckrausep@kean.edu. *Application contact:* Dorothy Rowe, Pre-Admissions Coordinator, 908-737-5928, Fax: 908-737-5965, E-mail: drowe@kean.edu.

Kean University, College of Natural, Applied and Health Sciences, Program in Nursing and Public Administration, Union, NJ 07083. Offers MSN/MPA. *Accreditation:* NLN. Part-time and evening/weekend programs available. *Faculty:* 7 full-time (all women). *Students:* 6 part-time (5 women); includes 5 minority (all African Americans). Average age 40. 8 applicants, 88% accepted, 3 enrolled. *Application deadline:* For fall admission, 5/1 for domestic students; for spring admission, 11/1 for domestic students. Application fee: $60 ($150 for international students). Electronic applications accepted. *Expenses:* Tuition, state resident: full-time $10,440; part-time $435 per credit. Tuition, nonresident: full-time $14,160; part-time $590 per credit. Required fees: $2642; $110 per credit. Part-time tuition and fees vary according to course load and degree level. *Financial support:* Research assistantships with full tuition reimbursements, unspecified assistantships available. *Unit head:* Dr. Estelle Pisani, Program Coordinator, 908-737-3390, E-mail: episani@kean.edu. *Application contact:* Dorothy Rowe, Pre-Admissions Coordinator, 908-737-5928, Fax: 908-737-5965, E-mail: drowe@kean.edu.

Kennesaw State University, College of Health and Human Services, Doctor of Nursing Science Program, Kennesaw, GA 30144-5591. Offers DNS. Part-time programs available. *Students:* 5 full-time (all women). Average age 44. 13 applicants, 46% accepted, 3 enrolled. *Degree requirements:* For doctorate, thesis/dissertation. *Entrance requirements:* For doctorate, GRE. Additional exam requirements/recommendations for international students: Required—TOEFL (minimum score 550 paper-based; 213 computer-based; 80 iBT), IELTS (minimum score 6). *Application deadline:* For fall admission, 3/1 for domestic and international students. Applications are processed on a rolling basis. Application fee: $60. Electronic applications accepted. *Expenses:* Tuition, state resident: full-time $2341; part-time $196 per credit hour. Tuition, nonresident: full-time $9396; part-time $783 per credit hour. Required fees: $573 per semester. *Unit head:* Tommie Nelms, Director, 678-797-2088, E-mail: tnelms1@kennesaw.edu. *Application contact:* Vilma Marquez, Admissions Counselor, 770-420-4377, Fax: 770-423-6885, E-mail: ksugrad@kennesaw.edu.

Kennesaw State University, College of Health and Human Services, Program in Primary Care Nurse Practitioner, Kennesaw, GA 30144-5591. Offers MSN. *Accreditation:* AACN. Part-time and evening/weekend programs available. *Faculty:* 7 full-time (6 women), 15 part-time/adjunct (10 women). *Students:* 77 full-time (64 women), 17 part-time (12 women); includes 30 minority (13 African Americans, 10 Asian Americans or Pacific Islanders, 7 Hispanic Americans), 2 international. Average age 40. 82 applicants, 51% accepted, 37 enrolled. In 2009, 37 master's awarded. *Entrance requirements:* For master's, GRE General Test, minimum GPA of 2.5, RN license, 3 years of professional experience. Additional exam requirements/recommendations for international students: Required—TOEFL (minimum score 550 paper-based; 213 computer-based), IELTS (minimum score 6). *Application deadline:* For fall admission, 6/1 for domestic and international students. Application fee: $60. Electronic applications accepted. *Expenses:* Tuition, state resident: full-time $2341; part-time $196 per credit hour. Tuition, nonresident: full-time $9396; part-time $783 per credit hour. Required fees: $573 per semester. *Financial support:* In 2009–10, 2 research assistantships with full tuition reimbursements (averaging $15,000 per year) were awarded; Federal Work-Study and unspecified assistantships also available. Support available to part-time students. Financial award application deadline: 6/15; financial award applicants required to submit FAFSA. *Unit head:* Dr. Marilyn King, Director, 770-423-6172, Fax: 770-423-6627, E-mail: mking71@kennesaw.edu. *Application contact:* Vilma Marquez, Admissions Counselor, 770-420-4377, Fax: 770-423-6885, E-mail: ksugrad@kennesaw.edu.

Kent State University, College of Nursing, Kent, OH 44242-0001. Offers adult nurse practitioner (MSN); family nurse practitioner (MSN); geriatric nurse practitioner (MSN); nursing (PhD); nursing and health care management (MSN); nursing of adults (clinical nurse specialist) (MSN); pediatric nurse practitioner (MSN); psychiatric/mental health nursing (MSN); women's health nursing (MSN). *Accreditation:* AACN. Part-time programs available. *Degree requirements:* For master's, thesis optional; for doctorate, comprehensive exam, thesis/dissertation. *Entrance requirements:* For master's, GRE (if undergraduate GPA less than 3.0), minimum GPA of 2.75; for doctorate, GRE, MSN. Additional exam requirements/recommendations for international students: Required—TOEFL. Electronic applications accepted. *Expenses:* Contact institution.

Faculty research: Women and violence, methodological specialties, osteoporosis in women, new caregivers and the elderly.

Keuka College, Program in Nursing, Keuka Park, NY 14478-0098. Offers MS. *Expenses:* Tuition: Part-time $600 per contact hour.

Lamar University, College of Graduate Studies, College of Arts and Sciences, Department of Nursing, Beaumont, TX 77710. Offers nursing administration (MSN); nursing education (MSN); MSN/MBA. *Accreditation:* NLN. Part-time and evening/weekend programs available. Postbaccalaureate distance learning degree programs offered. *Faculty:* 4 full-time (all women). *Students:* 3 full-time (2 women), 8 part-time (7 women); includes 2 minority (1 African American, 1 Hispanic American). Average age 41. 15 applicants. In 2009, 3 master's awarded. *Degree requirements:* For master's, comprehensive exam, practicum project presentation, evidence-based project. *Entrance requirements:* For master's, GRE General Test, MAT, criminal background check, RN license, NLN-accredited BSN, college course work in graduate statistics in past 5 years, letters of recommendation, minimum undergraduate GPA of 3.0. Additional exam requirements/recommendations for international students: Required—TOEFL. *Application deadline:* For fall admission, 8/1 priority date for domestic students; for spring admission, 12/1 priority date for domestic students. Applications are processed on a rolling basis. Application fee: $25 ($50 for international students). *Financial support:* In 2009–10, 3 students received support, including 2 teaching assistantships (averaging $24,000 per year); scholarships/grants and traineeships also available. Financial award application deadline: 4/1. *Faculty research:* Student retention, theory, caregiving, online course and research. *Unit head:* Dr. Nancy Blume, Director of Graduate Nursing Studies, 409-880-8820, Fax: 409-880-8698, E-mail: nancy.blume@lamar.edu. *Application contact:* Shelly R. Belk, Administrative Associate, 409-880-7720.

La Roche College, School of Graduate Studies and Adult Education, Program in Nursing, Pittsburgh, PA 15237-5898. Offers nursing education (MSN); nursing management (MSN). *Accreditation:* AANA/CANAEP; NLN. Part-time and evening/weekend programs available. Postbaccalaureate distance learning degree programs offered (minimal on-campus study). *Faculty:* 2 full-time (both women), 1 part-time/adjunct (0 women). *Students:* 8 full-time (all women), 3 part-time (all women), 6 international. Average age 36. 5 applicants, 80% accepted, 4 enrolled. In 2009, 3 master's awarded. *Degree requirements:* For master's, thesis optional, internship, practicum. *Entrance requirements:* For master's, GRE General Test, BSN, nursing license, work experience. Additional exam requirements/recommendations for international students: Recommended—TOEFL (minimum score 550 paper-based; 220 computer-based). *Application deadline:* For fall admission, 8/15 priority date for domestic students, 8/15 for international students; for spring admission, 12/15 priority date for domestic students, 12/15 for international students. Applications are processed on a rolling basis. Application fee: $50. Electronic applications accepted. *Expenses:* Contact institution. *Financial support:* Application deadline: 3/31. *Faculty research:* Patient education, perception. *Unit head:* Dr. Kathleen Sullivan, Division Chair, 412-536-1173, Fax: 412-536-1175, E-mail: sullivk1@laroche.edu. *Application contact:* Hope Schiffgens, Director of Graduate Studies and Adult Education, 412-536-1266, Fax: 412-536-1283, E-mail: schombh1@laroche.edu.

La Salle University, School of Nursing and Health Sciences, Program in Nursing, Philadelphia, PA 19141-1199. Offers MSN, Certificate. *Accreditation:* AANA/CANAEP. Part-time programs available. Postbaccalaureate distance learning degree programs offered (minimal on-campus study). *Entrance requirements:* For master's, GRE or MAT, 1 year of professional work experience, BSN, Pennsylvania RN license. *Expenses:* Contact institution. *Faculty research:* Medication errors, wound care, metacognition, education of RN students.

Laurentian University, School of Graduate Studies and Research, Programme in Nursing, Sudbury, ON P3E 2C6, Canada. Offers M Sc N.

Lehman College of the City University of New York, Division of Natural and Social Sciences, Department of Nursing, Bronx, NY 10468-1589. Offers adult health nursing (MS); nursing of older adults (MS); parent-child nursing (MS); pediatric nurse practitioner (MS). *Accreditation:* AACN. Part-time and evening/weekend programs available. *Entrance requirements:* For master's, bachelor's degree in nursing, New York RN license.

Le Moyne College, Department of Nursing, Syracuse, NY 13214. Offers nursing administration (MS, CAS); nursing education (MS, CAS). *Accreditation:* AACN. Part-time and evening/weekend programs available. *Faculty:* 2 full-time (both women), 6 part-time/adjunct (5 women). *Students:* 25 part-time (24 women); includes 2 minority (both African Americans). Average age 43. 14 applicants, 100% accepted, 14 enrolled. In 2009, 2 master's awarded. *Degree requirements:* For master's, scholarly project. *Entrance requirements:* For master's, interview, minimum GPA of 3.0, New York RN license, 2 letters of recommendation, writing sample. Additional exam requirements/recommendations for international students: Required—TOEFL (minimum score 550 paper-based; 213 computer-based; 79 iBT). *Application deadline:* For fall admission, 6/1 priority date for domestic and international students; for spring admission, 11/1 priority date for domestic and international students. Applications are processed on a rolling basis. Application fee: $50. *Expenses:* Contact institution. *Financial support:* In 2009–10, 7 students received support. Career-related internships or fieldwork, scholarships/grants, health care benefits, and unspecified assistantships available. Support available to part-time students. Financial award applicants required to submit FAFSA. *Faculty research:* Patient and staff education, inter-profession education, eldercare, utilization of free healthcare services by the insured, faculty perceptions of transgender nursing students. *Unit head:* Dr. Susan B. Bastable, Chair/Professor, 315-445-5436, Fax: 315-445-6024, E-mail: bastabsb@lemoyne.edu. *Application contact:* Kristen P. Trapasso, Director of Graduate Admission, 315-445-4265, Fax: 315-445-6027, E-mail: trapaskp@lemoyne.edu.

Lewis University, College of Nursing and Health Professions, Program in Nursing, Romeoville, IL 60446. Offers adult nurse practitioner (MSN); nursing administration (MSN); nursing education (MSN). *Accreditation:* AACN. Part-time and evening/weekend programs available. Postbaccalaureate distance learning degree programs offered (no on-campus study). *Students:* 20 full-time (19 women), 172 part-time (169 women); includes 53 minority (32 African Americans, 11 Asian Americans or Pacific Islanders, 10 Hispanic Americans), 3 international. Average age 41. In 2009, 46 master's awarded. *Degree requirements:* For master's, clinical practicum. *Entrance requirements:* For master's, minimum undergraduate GPA of 2.75, degree in nursing, RN license, letter of recommendation, interview, resume or curriculum vitae. Additional exam requirements/recommendations for international students: Required—TOEFL (minimum score 550 paper-based; 213 computer-based). *Application deadline:* For fall admission, 5/1 priority date for international students; for spring admission, 11/15 priority date for international students. Applications are processed on a rolling basis. Application fee: $40. Electronic applications accepted. *Expenses:* Tuition: Full-time $6480; part-time $720 per credit. One-time fee: $40. Tuition and fees vary according to course load, degree level and program. *Financial support:* Federal Work-Study, scholarships/grants, tuition waivers (full and partial), and unspecified assistantships available. Financial award application deadline: 5/1; financial award applicants required to submit FAFSA. *Faculty research:* Cancer prevention, phenomenological methods, public policy analysis. Total annual research expenditures: $1,000. *Unit head:* Dr. Nan Yancey, Director, 815-838-0500 Ext. 5878, E-mail: yanceyna@lewisu.edu. *Application contact:* Kathy Lisak, Information Contact, 815-838-0500 Ext. 5355, E-mail: lisakka@lewisu.edu.

Lewis University, College of Nursing and Health Professions and College of Business, Program in Nursing/Business, Romeoville, IL 60446. Offers MSN/MBA. Part-time and evening/weekend programs available. *Students:* 12 full-time (11 women), 32 part-time (all women); includes 18 minority (12 African Americans, 3 Asian Americans or Pacific Islanders, 3 Hispanic Americans), 1 international. Average age 38. 13 applicants, 69% accepted, 8 enrolled. *Entrance requirements:* Additional exam requirements/recommendations for international students: Required—TOEFL (minimum score 550 paper-based; 213 computer-based). *Application deadline:* For fall admission, 5/1 priority date for international students; for spring admission, 11/15 priority date for international students. Applications are processed on a rolling basis. Electronic applications accepted. *Expenses:* Tuition: Full-time $6480; part-time $720 per credit. One-time fee: $40. Tuition and fees vary according to course load, degree level and

program. *Financial support:* Scholarships/grants, tuition waivers (full and partial), and unspecified assistantships available. Financial award application deadline: 5/1; financial award applicants required to submit FAFSA. *Faculty research:* Cancer prevention, phenomenological methods, public policy analysis. Total annual research expenditures: $1,000. *Unit head:* Dr. Nan Yancey, Director, 815-838-0500 Ext. 5878, E-mail: yanceyna@lewisu.edu. *Application contact:* Kathy Lisak, Information Contact, 815-838-0500 Ext. 5355, E-mail: lisakka@lewisu.edu.

Liberty University, College of Arts and Sciences, Lynchburg, VA 24502. Offers counseling (MA); nursing (MSN); pastoral care and counseling (PhD); professional counseling (PhD). *Accreditation:* AACN. Part-time programs available. Postbaccalaureate distance learning degree programs offered (minimal on-campus study). *Degree requirements:* For master's, comprehensive exam (for some programs); for doctorate, comprehensive exam, thesis/dissertation. *Entrance requirements:* For master's, GRE General Test (MSN), minimum undergraduate GPA of 3.0; for doctorate, GRE General Test, minimum master's GPA of 3.25. Additional exam requirements/recommendations for international students: Required—TOEFL (minimum score 600 paper-based; 250 computer-based). Electronic applications accepted. *Expenses:* Tuition: Full-time $7110; part-time $415 per credit hour. Required fees: $150 per semester. Tuition and fees vary according to course load, degree level, campus/location and program. *Faculty research:* God concept and adult attachment, building marital strength, image of God and gender, breastfeeding behavior among adolescent mothers, osteoporosis.

Lincoln Memorial University, Caylor School of Nursing, Harrogate, TN 37752-1901. Offers family nurse practitioner (MSN); nurse anesthesia (MSN). *Accreditation:* AANA/CANAEP; NLN. Part-time programs available. *Faculty:* 5 full-time (3 women), 2 part-time/adjunct (both women). *Students:* 40 full-time (33 women), 3 part-time (2 women). Average age 30. 66 applicants, 91% accepted, 43 enrolled. In 2009, 6 master's awarded. *Entrance requirements:* For master's, GRE. *Application deadline:* For fall admission, 2/1 for domestic students. Application fee: $25. *Expenses:* Tuition: Full-time $11,700; part-time $390 per hour. *Financial support:* Applicants required to submit FAFSA. *Unit head:* Dr. Mary Anne Modrcin, Dean, 423-869-6319, Fax: 423-869-6244, E-mail: maryanne.modrcin@lmunet.edu. *Application contact:* Sherry Pearman, Director of Nursing Recruitment and Advising, 423-869-6283, E-mail: sherry.pearman@lmunet.edu.

Loma Linda University, Department of Graduate Nursing, Loma Linda, CA 92350. Offers adult and aging family nursing (MS); growing family nursing (MS); nursing administration (MS). *Accreditation:* AACN. Part-time programs available. *Degree requirements:* For master's, thesis or alternative. *Entrance requirements:* For master's, GRE General Test, BSN, minimum GPA of 3.0, RN license. Additional exam requirements/recommendations for international students: Required—TOEFL (minimum score 550 paper-based; 213 computer-based). Electronic applications accepted.

Long Island University, Brooklyn Campus, School of Nursing, Brooklyn, NY 11201-8423. Offers MS, Certificate. *Accreditation:* AACN. *Entrance requirements:* For master's, New York RN license, 2 letters of recommendation. Additional exam requirements/recommendations for international students: Required—TOEFL (minimum score 500 paper-based; 173 computer-based). Electronic applications accepted.

Long Island University, C.W. Post Campus, School of Health Professions and Nursing, Department of Nursing, Brookville, NY 11548-1300. Offers clinical nurse specialist (MS); family nurse practitioner (MS, Certificate). *Accreditation:* AACN. Part-time and evening/weekend programs available. *Degree requirements:* For master's, thesis. *Entrance requirements:* For master's, minimum GPA of 3.0 in major, bachelor's degree in nursing, NYS registered nurse, interview. Electronic applications accepted. *Faculty research:* Lactation/breast cancer, early discharge in maternity.

Louisiana State University Health Sciences Center, School of Nursing, New Orleans, LA 70112-2223. Offers advanced public/community health nursing (MN); clinical nurse specialist (MN); nurse anesthesia (MN); nurse practitioner (MN); nursing (DNS). *Accreditation:* AACN; AANA/CANAEP (one or more programs are accredited). Part-time programs available. *Degree requirements:* For master's, thesis optional; for doctorate, thesis/dissertation. *Entrance requirements:* For master's, GRE General Test, MAT, minimum GPA of 3.0; for doctorate, GRE General Test, minimum GPA of 3.5. Additional exam requirements/recommendations for international students: Required—TOEFL. *Faculty research:* Advanced clinical practice, nursing education, health, social support, nursing administration.

Loyola University Chicago, Graduate School, Marcella Niehoff School of Nursing, Doctor of Nursing Practice Program, Maywood, IL 60153. Offers DNP. Evening/weekend programs available. Postbaccalaureate distance learning degree programs offered (minimal on-campus study). *Faculty:* 45 full-time (44 women). *Students:* 10 part-time (8 women); includes 1 minority (African American). Average age 46. 13 applicants, 77% accepted, 10 enrolled. *Degree requirements:* For doctorate, capstone project. *Entrance requirements:* For doctorate, BSN or MSN, minimum GPA of 3.25, Illinois nursing license, 3 letters of recommendation, 1000 hours experience and certification in area of specialty, curriculum vitae. Additional exam requirements/recommendations for international students: Required—TOEFL. *Expenses:* Tuition: Full-time $14,220; part-time $790 per credit hour. Required fees: $60 per semester hour. Tuition and fees vary according to program. *Unit head:* Dr. Mary K. Walker, Dean, Marcella Niehoff School of Nursing, 708-216-5448, Fax: 708-216-9555, E-mail: mwalker@luc.edu. *Application contact:* Dr. Vicki A. Keough, Associate Dean, Master's and Doctor of Nursing Practice Programs, 708-216-3582, Fax: 708-216-9555, E-mail: vkeough@luc.edu.

Loyola University Chicago, Graduate School, Marcella Niehoff School of Nursing, PhD Program in Nursing, Chicago, IL 60660. Offers PhD. *Faculty:* 21 full-time (20 women). *Students:* 37 full-time (34 women), 7 part-time (5 women); includes 3 minority (1 African American, 1 Asian American or Pacific Islander, 1 Hispanic American). Average age 47. 14 applicants, 43% accepted, 5 enrolled. In 2009, 4 doctorates awarded. *Degree requirements:* For doctorate, comprehensive exam, thesis/dissertation, research internship. *Entrance requirements:* For doctorate, GRE General Test, master's degree in nursing or related field, minimum GPA of 3.0, active nursing license, 3 letters of recommendation. Additional exam requirements/recommendations for international students: Required—TOEFL (minimum score 650 paper-based; 280 computer-based; 114 iBT), or IELTS. *Application deadline:* For fall admission, 3/15 priority date for domestic students, 3/15 for international students. Applications are processed on a rolling basis. Application fee: $0. *Expenses:* Tuition: Full-time $14,220; part-time $790 per credit hour. Required fees: $60 per semester hour. Tuition and fees vary according to program. *Financial support:* In 2009–10, 3 students received support, including 3 research assistantships with full tuition reimbursements available (averaging $18,000 per year). Financial award application deadline: 5/1; financial award applicants required to submit FAFSA. *Faculty research:* Women's health, adolescent health and chronic illness, psychoneuroimmunology, grief and bereavement, nurse staffing and outcomes. *Unit head:* Dr. Lee Schmidt, Director, 708-216-3573, Fax: 708-216-9555, E-mail: lschm3@luc.edu. *Application contact:* Dr. Lee Schmidt, Director, 708-216-3573, Fax: 708-216-9555, E-mail: lschm3@luc.edu.

Loyola University Chicago, Graduate School, Marcella Niehoff School of Nursing, Program in Emergency Nurse Practitioner, Chicago, IL 60660. Offers MSN. *Entrance requirements:* For master's, Illinois nursing license, 3 letters of recommendation, minimum nursing GPA of 3.0, 1000 hours experience before starting clinical. Application fee: $50. *Expenses:* Tuition: Full-time $14,220; part-time $790 per credit hour. Required fees: $60 per semester hour. Tuition and fees vary according to program. *Financial support:* Traineeships available. *Unit head:* Dr. Vicki A. Keough, Associate Professor/Master's Program Director, 708-216-3582, Fax: 708-216-9555, E-mail: vkeough@luc.edu. *Application contact:* Dr. Vicki A. Keough, Associate Professor/Master's Program Director, 708-216-3582, Fax: 708-216-9555, E-mail: vkeough@luc.edu.

Loyola University New Orleans, College of Social Sciences, School of Nursing, New Orleans, LA 70118-6195. Offers adult nurse practitioner (MSN); family nurse practitioner (MSN); health care systems management (MSN); nursing (MSN, DNP). *Accreditation:* NLN. Part-time and evening/weekend programs available. Postbaccalaureate distance learning degree programs offered. *Students:* 60 full-time (56 women), 543 part-time (490 women); includes 147 minority (116 African Americans, 4 American Indian/Alaska Native, 13 Asian Americans or Pacific Islanders, 14 Hispanic Americans), 1 international. Average age 43. 296 applicants, 97% accepted, 206 enrolled. In 2009, 153 master's awarded. *Degree requirements:* For doctorate, capstone project. *Entrance requirements:* For master's, BSN, Louisiana nursing license, 1 year of work experience in clinical nursing, minimum undergraduate GPA of 2.8, interview, resume. Additional exam requirements/recommendations for international students: Required—TOEFL (minimum score 550 paper-based; 213 computer-based). *Application deadline:* For fall admission, 8/1 priority date for domestic and international students; for winter admission, 12/15 priority date for domestic and international students; for spring admission, 5/15 priority date for domestic and international students. Applications are processed on a rolling basis. Application fee: $20. Electronic applications accepted. *Financial support:* Traineeships and Incumbent Workers Training Program grants available. Financial award application deadline: 5/1; financial award applicants required to submit FAFSA. *Faculty research:* Increasing compliance with treatment, patient satisfaction with care provided by nurse practitioners. *Unit head:* Ann H. Cary, Director, 800-488-6257, Fax: 504-865-3254, E-mail: nursing@loyno.edu. *Application contact:* Deborah Smith, Assistant to the Director, 504-865-2823, Fax: 504-865-3254, E-mail: dhsmith@loyno.edu.

Lynchburg College, Graduate Studies, School of Health Sciences and Human Performance, Lynchburg, VA 24501-3199. Offers clinical nurse leader (MSN); nursing education (MSN); physical therapy (DPT). *Expenses:* Tuition: Full-time $7020; part-time $390 per credit hour.

Madonna University, Program in Nursing, Livonia, MI 48150-1173. Offers adult health: chronic health conditions (MSN); adult nurse practitioner (MSN); nursing administration (MSN); MSN/MSBA. *Accreditation:* AACN. Part-time programs available. *Degree requirements:* For master's, thesis or alternative. *Entrance requirements:* For master's, GRE General Test, Michigan nursing license. Electronic applications accepted. *Faculty research:* Coping, caring.

Malone University, Graduate Program in Nursing, Canton, OH 44709. Offers clinical nurse specialist (MSN); family nurse practitioner (MSN). *Accreditation:* AACN. Part-time and evening/weekend programs available. *Faculty:* 9 full-time (all women), 13 part-time/adjunct (8 women). *Students:* 50 part-time (45 women); includes 2 minority (both African Americans). Average age 35. 49 applicants, 73% accepted, 27 enrolled. In 2009, 20 master's awarded. *Degree requirements:* For master's, thesis. *Entrance requirements:* For master's, minimum GPA of 3.0 from BSN program, interview, Ohio RN license. Additional exam requirements/recommendations for international students: Required—TOEFL (minimum score 550 paper-based; 213 computer-based; 79 iBT). *Application deadline:* Applications are processed on a rolling basis. Application fee: $25. *Expenses:* Contact institution. *Financial support:* Tuition waivers (partial) available. Support available to part-time students. Financial award application deadline: 6/30. *Faculty research:* Periparticum cardiomyopathy in women of childbearing age; direct observation of nurse practitioner care; prevalence of Hepatitis B in pregnant women in Mali, West Africa; breast cancer knowledge of Amish women in northeast Ohio, gender issues in the Hispanic population. *Unit head:* Dr. Sharon M. Weyer, Director, 330-471-8612, Fax: 330-471-8607, E-mail: sweyer@malone.edu. *Application contact:* David L. Kleffman, Assistant Director of Enrollment, 330-471-8447, Fax: 330-471-8343, E-mail: dkleffman@malone.edu.

Mansfield University of Pennsylvania, Graduate Studies, Program in Nursing, Mansfield, PA 16933. Offers MSN. *Accreditation:* NLN. Part-time and evening/weekend programs available. Postbaccalaureate distance learning degree programs offered. *Faculty:* 2 full-time (both women), 1 (woman) part-time/adjunct. *Students:* 44 part-time (40 women); includes 1 minority (Hispanic American). Average age 39. In 2009, 8 master's awarded. *Degree requirements:* For master's, comprehensive exam, thesis optional. *Entrance requirements:* For master's, minimum GPA of 3.0. Additional exam requirements/recommendations for international students: Required—TOEFL (minimum score 550 paper-based; 220 computer-based). *Application deadline:* For fall admission, 8/1 priority date for domestic students, 6/1 priority date for international students; for spring admission, 11/1 priority date for domestic students, 9/1 priority date for international students. Applications are processed on a rolling basis. Application fee: $25. Electronic applications accepted. *Expenses:* Tuition, state resident: full-time $6666; part-time $370 per credit. Tuition, nonresident: full-time $10,666; part-time $593 per credit. Required fees: $1388. *Financial support:* Unspecified assistantships available. *Faculty research:* Women's health, gyniatrics, art therapy, nursing empowerment. *Unit head:* Dr. Janeen Sheehe, Chairperson, 570-662-4522, E-mail: jsheehe@mansfield.edu. *Application contact:* Christina Hale, Assistant Director of Enrollment Services/Graduate Admissions, 570-662-4812, Fax: 570-662-4121, E-mail: chale@mansfield.edu.

Marian University, School of Nursing, Fond du Lac, WI 54935-4699. Offers adult nurse practitioner (MSN); nurse educator (MSN). *Accreditation:* AACN. Part-time and evening/weekend programs available. *Faculty:* 6 full-time (5 women), 5 part-time/adjunct (4 women). *Students:* 40 full-time (37 women), 25 part-time (all women); includes 4 minority (3 Asian Americans or Pacific Islanders, 1 Hispanic American). Average age 39. 28 applicants, 89% accepted, 25 enrolled. In 2009, 21 master's awarded. *Degree requirements:* For master's, thesis, 675 clinical practicum hours. *Entrance requirements:* For master's, 3 letters of professional recommendation; undergraduate work in nursing research, statistics, health assessment. Additional exam requirements/recommendations for international students: Required—TOEFL (minimum score 525 paper-based). *Application deadline:* Applications are processed on a rolling basis. Application fee: $50. Electronic applications accepted. *Expenses:* Contact institution. *Financial support:* In 2009–10, 25 students received support. Institutionally sponsored loans and scholarships/grants available. Support available to part-time students. Financial award application deadline: 3/1; financial award applicants required to submit FAFSA. *Unit head:* Greta Kostac, Interim Assistant Dean, 920-923-8094, Fax: 920-923-8770, E-mail: gmkostac@marianuniversity.edu. *Application contact:* Dr. Greta Kostac, Director, 920-923-7603, Fax: 920-923-8770, E-mail: gmkostac@marianuniversity.edu.

Marquette University, Graduate School, College of Nursing, Milwaukee, WI 53201-1881. Offers adult nurse practitioner (Certificate); advanced practice nursing (MSN), including adult, children, neonatal nurse practitioner, nurse-midwifery, older adult; gerontological nurse practitioner (Certificate); neonatal nurse practitioner (Certificate); nurse-midwifery (Certificate); nursing (PhD); pediatric nurse practitioner (Certificate). *Accreditation:* AACN. Part-time and evening/weekend programs available. *Faculty:* 29 full-time (27 women), 43 part-time/adjunct (all women). *Students:* 115 full-time (105 women), 209 part-time (197 women); includes 28 minority (13 African Americans, 2 American Indian/Alaska Native, 8 Asian Americans or Pacific Islanders, 5 Hispanic Americans), 1 international. Average age 32. 143 applicants, 91% accepted, 86 enrolled. In 2009, 64 master's, 10 doctorates awarded. *Degree requirements:* For master's, comprehensive exam, thesis or alternative. *Entrance requirements:* For master's, GRE General Test, BSN, Wisconsin RN license. Additional exam requirements/recommendations for international students: Required—TOEFL. Application fee: $40. *Financial support:* In 2009–10, 6 research assistantships, 1 teaching assistantship were awarded; career-related internships or fieldwork, Federal Work-Study, institutionally sponsored loans, scholarships/grants, and tuition waivers (full and partial) also available. Support available to part-time students. Financial award application deadline: 2/15. *Faculty research:* Psychosocial adjustment to chronic illness, gerontology, reminiscence, health policy: uninsured and access, hospital care delivery systems. *Unit head:* Dr. Lea Acord, Dean, 414-288-3812, Fax: 414-288-1578. *Application contact:* Dr. Judy Miller, Director of Graduate Studies, 414-288-3810, Fax: 414-288-1578.

Marshall University, Academic Affairs Division, College of Health Professions, Department of Nursing, Huntington, WV 25755. Offers MSN. *Faculty:* 21 full-time (20 women), 12 part-time/adjunct (10 women). *Students:* 21 full-time (all women), 121 part-time (108 women); includes 5 minority (3 African Americans, 1 American Indian/Alaska Native, 1 Asian American or Pacific Islander). Average age 35. In 2009, 32 master's awarded. *Entrance requirements:* For master's, GRE General Test. Application fee: $40. *Unit head:* Dr. Denise Landry, Chairperson, 304-696-2630, E-mail: landry@marshall.edu. *Application contact:* Information Contact, 304-746-1900, Fax: 304-746-1902, E-mail: services@marshall.edu.

Marymount University, School of Health Professions, Program in Nursing, Arlington, VA 22207-4299. Offers family nurse practitioner (MSN, Certificate); nursing (DNP); nursing education

Nursing—General

Marymount University *(continued)*

(MSN, Certificate); RN to MSN (MSN). *Accreditation:* AACN. Part-time and evening/weekend programs available. *Faculty:* 5 full-time (all women), 2 part-time/adjunct (both women). *Students:* 13 full-time (12 women), 66 part-time (60 women); includes 38 minority (26 African Americans, 9 Asian Americans or Pacific Islanders, 3 Hispanic Americans), 4 international. Average age 38. 56 applicants, 79% accepted, 30 enrolled. In 2009, 17 master's awarded. *Degree requirements:* For master's, comprehensive exam; for doctorate, thesis/dissertation or alternative. *Entrance requirements:* For master's, 2 letters of recommendation, interview, resume, RN license; for doctorate, 2 letters of recommendation, interview, resume, RN license, minimum MSN GPA of 3.5 or BSN GPA of 3.3; for Certificate, interview, master's degree in nursing. Additional exam requirements/recommendations for international students: Required—TOEFL (minimum score 600 paper-based; 250 computer-based; 96 iBT), IELTS (minimum score 6.5). *Application deadline:* For fall admission, 7/1 for international students; for spring admission, 10/15 for international students. Applications are processed on a rolling basis. Application fee: $40. Electronic applications accepted. *Expenses:* Tuition: Full-time $13,050; part-time $725 per credit hour. Required fees: $135; $7.50 per credit hour. *Financial support:* In 2009–10, 8 students received support; research assistantships with partial tuition reimbursements available, career-related internships or fieldwork, Federal Work-Study, scholarships/grants, and unspecified assistantships available. Support available to part-time students. Financial award applicants required to submit FAFSA. *Unit head:* Dr. Susan Bidwell, Chair, 703-284-1593, Fax: 703-284-3819, E-mail: susan.bidwell@marymount.edu. *Application contact:* Francesca Reed, Director, Graduate Admissions, 703-284-5901, Fax: 703-527-3815, E-mail: grad.admissions@marymount.edu.

Maryville University of Saint Louis, School of Health Professions, Nursing Program, St. Louis, MO 63141-7299. Offers accelerated RN to MSN (MSN); adult nurse practitioner (MSN); advanced practice nursing (DNP); family nurse practitioner (MSN); nursing education (MSN). *Accreditation:* AACN. Postbaccalaureate distance learning degree programs offered. *Students:* 23 full-time (22 women), 96 part-time (92 women); includes 6 African Americans, 6 Asian Americans or Pacific Islanders, 2 Hispanic Americans. Average age 36. In 2009, 23 master's awarded. *Degree requirements:* For master's, practicum. *Entrance requirements:* For master's, BSN, current licensure, minimum GPA of 3.0, 3 letters of recommendation, curriculum vitae. Additional exam requirements/recommendations for international students: Required—TOEFL (minimum score 550 paper-based). *Application deadline:* Applications are processed on a rolling basis. Application fee: $40 ($60 for international students). Electronic applications accepted. *Expenses:* Tuition: Full-time $20,384; part-time $627.50 per credit hour. Required fees: $100 per semester. *Financial support:* Federal Work-Study and campus employment available. Support available to part-time students. Financial award application deadline: 3/1; financial award applicants required to submit FAFSA. *Unit head:* Dr. Mary Curtis, Director, 314-529-9478, Fax: 314-529-9139, E-mail: mcurtis@maryville.edu. *Application contact:* Dr. Mary Curtis, Director, 314-529-9478, Fax: 314-529-9139, E-mail: mcurtis@maryville.edu.

Massachusetts College of Pharmacy and Health Sciences, Graduate Studies, Program in Nursing, Boston, MA 02115-5896. Offers MS. Part-time programs available. Postbaccalaureate distance learning degree programs offered (minimal on-campus study). *Students:* 8 part-time (all women); includes 2 Asian Americans or Pacific Islanders. Average age 35. 9 applicants, 89% accepted, 8 enrolled. *Entrance requirements:* For master's, BSN. Additional exam requirements/recommendations for international students: Required—TOEFL (minimum score 550 paper-based; 213 computer-based; 79 iBT). *Application deadline:* Applications are processed on a rolling basis. Electronic applications accepted. *Expenses:* Tuition: Full-time $28,000; part-time $875 per credit hour. Required fees: $750; $190 per semester. Part-time tuition and fees vary according to course load, campus/location, program and student level. *Unit head:* Carol Eliadi, Assistant Dean/Chief Nurse Administrator, School of Nursing, 508-373-5680, E-mail: carol.eliadi@mcphs.edu. *Application contact:* Bryan Witham, Director of Admission, Worcester/Manchester, 508-373-5623, E-mail: bryan.witham@mcphs.edu.

McGill University, Faculty of Graduate and Postdoctoral Studies, Faculty of Medicine, School of Nursing, Montréal, QC H3A 2T5, Canada. Offers nurse practitioner (Graduate Diploma); nursing (M Sc A, PhD).

McKendree University, Graduate Programs, Master of Science in Nursing Program, Lebanon, IL 62254-1299. Offers nursing education (MSN); nursing management/administration (MSN). *Accreditation:* AACN. Part-time and evening/weekend programs available. Postbaccalaureate distance learning degree programs offered (no on-campus study). *Faculty:* 5 full-time (all women), 3 part-time/adjunct (2 women). *Students:* 1 full-time (0 women), 86 part-time (82 women); includes 6 minority (5 African Americans, 1 Hispanic American), 1 international. Average age 44. 80 applicants, 84% accepted, 52 enrolled. In 2009, 47 master's awarded. *Degree requirements:* For master's, research project or thesis. *Entrance requirements:* For master's, resume, references, valid Professional Registered Nurse license. Additional exam requirements/recommendations for international students: Required—TOEFL. *Application deadline:* Applications are processed on a rolling basis. Application fee: $0. Electronic applications accepted. *Expenses:* Tuition: Full-time $6300; part-time $350 per credit hour. One-time fee: $125. *Financial support:* Applicants required to submit FAFSA. *Unit head:* Dr. Richelle Rennegarbe, Division Chair, 618-537-2148, E-mail: rarennegarbe@mckendree.edu. *Application contact:* Kim Eichelberger, Director of Nursing Admission, 618-537-6411, Fax: 618-537-6410, E-mail: kaeichelberger@mckendree.edu.

McMaster University, Faculty of Health Sciences and School of Graduate Studies, Program in Nursing (course-based), Hamilton, ON L8S 4M2, Canada. Offers M Sc. *Degree requirements:* For master's, scholarly paper. *Entrance requirements:* For master's, 4 year honors BSCN, minimum B+ average in last 60 units. Additional exam requirements/recommendations for international students: Required—TOEFL (minimum score 580 paper-based; 237 computer-based; 92 iBT).

McMaster University, Faculty of Health Sciences and School of Graduate Studies, Program in Nursing (thesis), Hamilton, ON L8S 4M2, Canada. Offers M Sc, PhD. *Degree requirements:* For master's, thesis; for doctorate, comprehensive exam, thesis/dissertation. *Entrance requirements:* For master's, honors B Sc N, B+ average in last 60 units; for doctorate, M Sc, minimum B+ average. Additional exam requirements/recommendations for international students: Required—TOEFL (minimum score 580 paper-based; 237 computer-based; 92 iBT).

McNeese State University, Doré School of Graduate Studies, College of Nursing, Lake Charles, LA 70609. Offers clinical nurse specialist (MSN); nurse educator (MSN); nurse practitioner (MSN); nursing leadership and administration (MSN). *Accreditation:* AACN. *Faculty:* 4 full-time (all women), 1 part-time/adjunct (0 women). *Students:* 17 full-time (9 women), 72 part-time (56 women); includes 14 minority (12 African Americans, 2 Asian Americans or Pacific Islanders). In 2009, 21 master's awarded. *Degree requirements:* For master's, comprehensive exam. *Entrance requirements:* For master's, GRE, eligibility for unencumbered licensure as RN in Louisiana. *Application deadline:* For fall admission, 5/15 priority date for domestic and international students; for spring admission, 10/15 priority date for domestic and international students. Applications are processed on a rolling basis. Application fee: $20 ($30 for international students). *Expenses:* Tuition, area resident: Full-time $2556. Tuition, state resident: full-time $2556. Required fees: $1031. Tuition and fees vary according to course load. *Financial support:* Application deadline: 5/1. *Unit head:* Dr. Peggy L. Wolfe, Dean, 337-475-5820, Fax: 337-475-5924, E-mail: pwolfe@mcneese.edu. *Application contact:* Valarie Waldmeier, Coordinator of Graduate Nursing, 337-475-5285, Fax: 337-475-5707, E-mail: vwaldmeier@mcneese.edu.

Medical College of Georgia, School of Graduate Studies, Doctor of Nursing Practice Program, Augusta, GA 30912. Offers DNP. *Degree requirements:* For doctorate, thesis/dissertation or alternative. *Entrance requirements:* For doctorate, GRE General Test or MAT, master's degree in nursing or related field, current professional nurse licensure. Additional exam requirements/recommendations for international students: Required—TOEFL (minimum score 600 paper-based; 250 computer-based; 100 iBT). Electronic applications accepted. Full-time tuition and fees vary according to campus/location, program and student level.

Medical College of Georgia, School of Graduate Studies, Nursing PhD Program, Augusta, GA 30912. Offers PhD. *Degree requirements:* For doctorate, thesis/dissertation. *Entrance requirements:* For doctorate, GRE General Test, current GA nurse licensure. Additional exam requirements/recommendations for international students: Required—TOEFL (minimum score 550 paper-based; 213 computer-based; 79 iBT). Electronic applications accepted. Full-time tuition and fees vary according to campus/location, program and student level.

Medical University of South Carolina, College of Graduate Studies, PhD in Nursing Program, Charleston, SC 29425. Offers PhD. *Accreditation:* AACN. Part-time programs available. Postbaccalaureate distance learning degree programs offered (minimal on-campus study). *Faculty:* 11 full-time (all women), 2 part-time/adjunct (1 woman). *Students:* 26 full-time (25 women), 21 part-time (18 women); includes 3 minority (2 African Americans, 1 American Indian/Alaska Native). Average age 44. 20 applicants, 85% accepted, 15 enrolled. In 2009, 3 doctorates awarded. *Degree requirements:* For doctorate, comprehensive exam, thesis/dissertation, mentored teaching and research seminar. *Entrance requirements:* For doctorate, interview, minimum GPA of 3.5, BSN/MSN, RN license, curriculum vitae. Additional exam requirements/recommendations for international students: Required—TOEFL (minimum score 600 paper-based; 250 computer-based). *Application deadline:* For fall admission, 2/1 priority date for domestic and international students. Applications are processed on a rolling basis. Application fee: $85. Electronic applications accepted. *Financial support:* Federal Work-Study and scholarships/grants available. Support available to part-time students. Financial award application deadline: 3/10; financial award applicants required to submit FAFSA. *Faculty research:* Health disparities, community partnerships, ethics, skin temperature in venous disease, spinal cord injury, smoking cessation. *Unit head:* Dr. Gail A. Gilden, Director, 843-792-3815, Fax: 843-792-9258, E-mail: barbosag@musc.edu. *Application contact:* Yolanda M. Long, Administrative Coordinator, 843-792-3815, Fax: 843-792-9258, E-mail: morrisym@musc.edu.

Medical University of South Carolina, College of Nursing, Doctor of Nursing Practice Program, Charleston, SC 29425. Offers adult nurse practitioner (DNP); family nurse practitioner (DNP); pediatric nurse practitioner (DNP); post-master's for advanced practice nurses (DNP). Part-time programs available. Postbaccalaureate distance learning degree programs offered (minimal on-campus study). *Faculty:* 20 full-time (19 women), 2 part-time/adjunct (1 woman). *Students:* 28 full-time (all women), 17 part-time (16 women); includes 7 minority (5 African Americans, 1 American Indian/Alaska Native, 1 Hispanic American). Average age 32. 99 applicants, 54% accepted, 45 enrolled. *Degree requirements:* For doctorate, thesis/dissertation (for some programs), practice inquiry project. *Entrance requirements:* For doctorate, BSN or MSN, minimum GPA of 3.0, course work in statistics, RN license, 3 references, interview (if requested). Additional exam requirements/recommendations for international students: Required—TOEFL (minimum score 600 paper-based; 250 computer-based). *Application deadline:* For fall admission, 2/1 priority date for domestic and international students. Application fee: $85. Electronic applications accepted. *Financial support:* Federal Work-Study and scholarships/grants available. Support available to part-time students. Financial award applicants required to submit FAFSA. *Faculty research:* Community partnerships, smoking cessation, gerontology, lateral violence in the workplace. *Unit head:* Dr. Robin L. Bissinger, Director of Graduate Programs, 843-792-0531, Fax: 843-792-9258, E-mail: bissinrl@musc.edu. *Application contact:* Carolyn F. Page, Director, Student Services, 843-792-3844, Fax: 843-792-5395, E-mail: pagecf@musc.edu.

Memorial University of Newfoundland, School of Graduate Studies, School of Nursing, St. John's, NL A1C 5S7, Canada. Offers MN, PMD. Part-time programs available. *Degree requirements:* For master's, thesis optional; for PMD, clinical placement. *Entrance requirements:* For master's, bachelor's degree in nursing, 1 year experience in nursing practice, practicing license; for PMD, 2 years clinical nursing experience, practicing license (Canada) or proof of registration as a practicing nurse (international), letter from a health care agency guaranteeing clinical placement. Electronic applications accepted. *Faculty research:* Women's health, infant feeding practices, nursing management, care of the elderly, children's health.

Mercer University, Graduate Studies, Cecil B. Day Campus, Georgia Baptist College of Nursing, Macon, GA 31207-0003. Offers nurse education (Certificate); nursing (MSN, PhD). *Accreditation:* AACN; AANA/CANAEP. Part-time programs available. *Faculty:* 11 full-time (10 women). *Students:* 15 full-time (14 women), 7 part-time (all women); includes 4 minority (all African Americans). Average age 43. In 2009, 7 master's awarded. *Degree requirements:* For master's, thesis or alternative; for doctorate, comprehensive exam, thesis/dissertation. *Entrance requirements:* For master's, MAT or GRE, bachelor's degree from an accredited nursing program, registered GA nursing license (unencumbered); for doctorate, GRE, master's degree from accredited nursing program, RN licensure. Additional exam requirements/recommendations for international students: Required—TOEFL (minimum score 80 iBT). *Application deadline:* For fall admission, 6/1 for domestic students, 4/1 for international students; for winter admission, 11/1 for domestic students, 9/1 for international students; for spring admission, 4/1 for domestic students, 2/1 for international students. Applications are processed on a rolling basis. Application fee: $50. *Expenses:* Contact institution. *Financial support:* Institutionally sponsored loans, scholarships/grants, and traineeships available. Support available to part-time students. Financial award application deadline: 5/1; financial award applicants required to submit FAFSA. *Faculty research:* Osteoporosis, honor system, women and alcoholism, nursing assessment measures. *Unit head:* Dr. Linda Streit, Dean/Professor, 678-547-6793, Fax: 678-547-6796, E-mail: gunby_ss@mercer.edu. *Application contact:* Lynn Vines, Director of Admissions, 678-547-6700, Fax: 678-547-6794, E-mail: vines_ml@mercer.edu.

Mercy College, School of Health and Natural Sciences, Program in Nursing, Dobbs Ferry, NY 10522-1189. Offers nursing administration (MS); nursing education (MS). *Accreditation:* AACN. Part-time and evening/weekend programs available. Postbaccalaureate distance learning degree programs offered (no on-campus study). *Students:* 28 full-time (20 women), 113 part-time (108 women); includes 45 African Americans, 14 Asian Americans or Pacific Islanders, 8 Hispanic Americans, 16 international. Average age 42. 97 applicants, 48% accepted, 38 enrolled. In 2009, 33 master's awarded. *Degree requirements:* For master's, written comprehensive exam or the production of a comprehensive project. *Entrance requirements:* For master's, bachelor's degree, two letters of reference, interview/assessment, RN registration in the U.S. Additional exam requirements/recommendations for international students: Required—TOEFL (minimum score 600 paper-based; 250 computer-based; 100 iBT). *Application deadline:* For fall admission, 8/1 for international students. Applications are processed on a rolling basis. Application fee: $40. Electronic applications accepted. *Expenses:* Tuition: Full-time $13,158; part-time $731 per credit. Required fees: $500. Tuition and fees vary according to degree level and program. *Financial support:* Career-related internships or fieldwork, Federal Work-Study, scholarships/grants, and unspecified assistantships available. Support available to part-time students. Financial award applicants required to submit FAFSA. *Unit head:* Ellen Beatty, Director, 914-674-7548, E-mail: ebeatty@mercy.edu. *Application contact:* Mildred Burns, Administrative Assistant, 914-674-7865, Fax: 914-674-7623, E-mail: mburns@mercy.edu.

Mesa State College, Department of Health Sciences, Grand Junction, CO 81501-3122. Offers MSN, DNP. *Expenses:* Tuition, state resident: full-time $5400; part-time $300 per credit hour. Tuition, nonresident: full-time $16,200; part-time $900 per credit hour. Required fees: $460; $25 per credit hour. Tuition and fees vary according to program.

Metropolitan State University, College of Nursing and Health Sciences, St. Paul, MN 55106-5000. Offers adult/geriatric nurse practitioner (MSN); family nurse practitioner (MSN); leadership and management (MSN); nursing (MSN, DNP); oral health care practitioner (MS); public health nursing leadership (MSN); women's health care nurse practitioner (MSN). *Accreditation:* AACN. Part-time programs available. *Degree requirements:* For master's, thesis or alternative; for doctorate, thesis/dissertation or alternative. *Entrance requirements:* For master's, GRE General Test, minimum GPA of 3.0, RN license, B.S./BAN degree; for doctorate, minimum GPA of 3.0; RN licensure, MSN degree. Additional exam requirements/recommendations for international students: Required—TOEFL (minimum score 550 paper-based; 213 computer-

based). *Expenses:* Tuition, state resident: full-time $5520; part-time $276 per credit hour. Tuition, nonresident: full-time $11,040; part-time $552 per credit hour. Required fees: $209; $10 per credit hour. Tuition and fees vary according to degree level. *Faculty research:* Women's health, gerontology.

MGH Institute of Health Professions, Graduate Programs, School of Nursing, Boston, MA 02129. Offers advanced practice nursing (MSN); gerontological nursing (MSN); nursing (DNP); pediatric nursing (MSN); psychiatric nursing (MSN); teaching and learning for health care education (Certificate); women's health nursing (MSN). *Accreditation:* AACN; NLN (one or more programs are accredited). *Faculty:* 37 full-time (33 women), 11 part-time/adjunct (10 women). *Students:* 325 full-time (275 women), 72 part-time (59 women); includes 48 minority (22 African Americans, 1 American Indian/Alaska Native, 18 Asian Americans or Pacific Islanders, 7 Hispanic Americans). Average age 31. 840 applicants, 53% accepted, 221 enrolled. In 2009, 78 master's, 12 doctorates, 45 other advanced degrees awarded. *Degree requirements:* For master's, thesis or alternative. *Entrance requirements:* For master's, GRE General Test. Additional exam requirements/recommendations for international students: Required—TOEFL (minimum score 550 paper-based; 213 computer-based; 80 iBT). *Application deadline:* For fall admission, 1/10 for domestic and international students. Application fee: $50. Electronic applications accepted. *Expenses:* Tuition: Part-time $943 per credit. Required fees: $943 per credit. Tuition and fees vary according to course load. *Financial support:* In 2009–10, 292 students received support, including 1 research assistantship (averaging $1,200 per year), 2 teaching assistantships (averaging $1,200 per year); career-related internships or fieldwork, scholarships/grants, traineeships, tuition waivers (full and partial), and unspecified assistantships also available. Support available to part-time students. Financial award application deadline: 3/1; financial award applicants required to submit FAFSA. *Faculty research:* Biobehavioral nursing, HIV/AIDS, gerontological nursing, women's health, vulnerable populations, health systems. *Unit head:* Margery Chisholm, Dean, 617-724-0480, Fax: 617-726-8022, E-mail: mchisholm@mghihp.edu. *Application contact:* Maureen Rika Judd, Manager of Admissions, 617-726-6069, Fax: 617-726-8010, E-mail: admissions@mghihp.edu.

Michigan State University, The Graduate School, College of Nursing, East Lansing, MI 48824. Offers MSN, PhD. *Accreditation:* AACN; AANA/CANAEP. Part-time programs available. Postbaccalaureate distance learning degree programs offered (no on-campus study). *Faculty:* 21 full-time (19 women). *Students:* 69 full-time (62 women), 147 part-time (136 women); includes 15 minority (4 African Americans, 2 American Indian/Alaska Native, 5 Asian Americans or Pacific Islanders, 4 Hispanic Americans), 4 international. Average age 37. 174 applicants, 41% accepted. In 2009, 51 master's, 1 doctorate awarded. *Entrance requirements:* Additional exam requirements/recommendations for international students: Required—TOEFL (minimum score 580 paper-based; 213 computer-based), Michigan State University ELT (minimum score 85), Michigan Michigan English Language Assessment Battery (minimum score 83). *Application deadline:* For fall admission, 11/1 priority date for domestic students. Electronic applications accepted. *Expenses:* Tuition, state resident: part-time $478.25 per credit hour. Tuition, nonresident: part-time $966.50 per credit hour. Part-time tuition and fees vary according to program. *Financial support:* In 2009–10, 1 research assistantship with tuition reimbursement (averaging $6,110 per year), 2 teaching assistantships with tuition reimbursements (averaging $7,076 per year) were awarded. *Faculty research:* Hormone replacement therapy, end of life research, human-animal bond, chronic disease, family home care for cancer. Total annual research expenditures: $1.6 million. *Unit head:* Dr. Mary Mundt, Dean, 517-355-6527, Fax: 517-353-9553, E-mail: mary.mundt@hc.msu.edu. *Application contact:* Application Contact, 517-353-4827, Fax: 517-432-8251, E-mail: nurse@hc.msu.edu.

Middle Tennessee State University, College of Graduate Studies, College of Basic and Applied Sciences, School of Nursing, Murfreesboro, TN 37132. Offers MSN, Graduate Certificate. Part-time and evening/weekend programs available. Postbaccalaureate distance learning degree programs offered. *Faculty:* 11 full-time (10 women). *Students:* 1 (woman) full-time, 74 part-time (67 women); includes 10 minority (8 African Americans, 2 Asian Americans or Pacific Islanders). Average age 35. 48 applicants, 63% accepted, 30 enrolled. In 2009, 14 master's awarded. *Entrance requirements:* Additional exam requirements/recommendations for international students: Required—TOEFL (minimum score 525 paper-based; 195 computer-based; 71 iBT) or IELTS (minimum score 6). *Application deadline:* For fall admission, 6/1 for domestic and international students. Applications are processed on a rolling basis. Application fee: $25 ($30 for international students). Electronic applications accepted. *Expenses:* Tuition, state resident: full-time $4404. Tuition, nonresident: full-time $10,956. *Financial support:* In 2009–10, 2 students received support. Institutionally sponsored loans available. Support available to part-time students. Financial award application deadline: 5/1. *Unit head:* Dr. Lynn Parsons, Director, 615-898-5340. *Application contact:* Dr. Michael Allen, Dean and Vice Provost for Research, 615-898-2840, Fax: 615-904-8020, E-mail: mallen@mtsu.edu.

Midwestern State University, Graduate Studies, College of Health Sciences and Human Services, Nursing Program, Wichita Falls, TX 76308. Offers family nurse practitioner (MSN); health services administration (MSN); nurse educator (MSN). *Accreditation:* AACN. Part-time and evening/weekend programs available. *Degree requirements:* For master's, comprehensive exam, thesis optional. *Entrance requirements:* For master's, GRE General Test or MAT. Additional exam requirements/recommendations for international students: Required—TOEFL (minimum score 550 paper-based; 213 computer-based). Electronic applications accepted. *Expenses:* Tuition, state resident: full-time $1620; part-time $90 per credit hour. Tuition, nonresident: full-time $2160; part-time $120 per credit hour. International tuition: $7506 full-time. Required fees: $3068.80; $145.60 per credit hour. $179 per semester.

Millersville University of Pennsylvania, College of Graduate and Professional Studies, School of Science and Mathematics, Department of Nursing, Millersville, PA 17551-0302. Offers MSN. *Accreditation:* NLN. Part-time and evening/weekend programs available. *Faculty:* 5 full-time (all women), 4 part-time/adjunct (all women). *Students:* 57 part-time (54 women); includes 2 minority (1 African American, 1 Hispanic American). Average age 40. 30 applicants, 90% accepted, 25 enrolled. In 2009, 12 master's awarded. *Entrance requirements:* For master's, 3 letters of recommendation; interview; resume. Additional exam requirements/recommendations for international students: Required—TOEFL (minimum score 500 paper-based; 183 computer-based; 65 iBT) or IELTS (minimum score 6). *Application deadline:* For fall admission, 1/15 priority date for domestic and international students; for winter admission, 10/1 priority date for domestic and international students; for spring admission, 10/1 priority date for domestic and international students. Applications are processed on a rolling basis. Application fee: $40 ($50 for international students). Electronic applications accepted. *Expenses:* Tuition, state resident: full-time $6666; part-time $370 per credit. Tuition, nonresident: full-time $10,666; part-time $593 per credit. Required fees: $1578.50; $76.25 per credit. One-time fee: $60 part-time. Tuition and fees vary according to course load. *Financial support:* In 2009–10, 3 students received support, including 3 research assistantships with partial tuition reimbursements available (averaging $1,578 per year); institutionally sponsored loans and unspecified assistantships also available. Support available to part-time students. Financial award application deadline: 3/15; financial award applicants required to submit FAFSA. *Unit head:* Dr. Deborah T. Castellucci, Chairperson, 717-871-5341, Fax: 717-871-4877, E-mail: deborah.castellucci@millersville.edu. *Application contact:* Dr. Victor S. DeSantis, Dean of Graduate and Professional Studies, 717-872-3099, Fax: 717-872-3453, E-mail: victor.desantis@millersville.edu.

Millikin University, School of Nursing, Decatur, IL 62522-2084. Offers clinical nurse leader (MSN); entry into nursing practice: pre-licensure (MSN); nurse educator (MSN). *Accreditation:* AACN. Part-time programs available. *Faculty:* 9 full-time (8 women). *Students:* 4 full-time (all women), 11 part-time (10 women); includes 1 minority (African American). Average age 41. 9 applicants, 100% accepted, 6 enrolled. In 2009, 3 master's awarded. *Degree requirements:* For master's, thesis or alternative, research project. *Entrance requirements:* For master's, GRE, official academic transcript(s), written essay, immunizations, statistics course, 2 letters of recommendation, CPR certification, professional liability insurance/malpractice insurance. Additional exam requirements/recommendations for international students: Required—TOEFL (minimum score 550 paper-based; 79 iBT). *Application deadline:* For spring admission, 11/1 priority date for domestic students. Applications are processed on a rolling basis. Application fee: $0. Electronic applications accepted. *Expenses:* Tuition: Full-time $24,890; part-time $655 per credit hour. *Financial support:* In 2009–10, 1 student received support. Institutionally sponsored loans available. Financial award applicants required to submit FAFSA. *Faculty research:* Congestive heart failure, quality of life, transcultural nursing issues, teaching/learning strategies, maternal—newborn. *Unit head:* Dr. Deborah Slayton, Director, 217-424-6348, Fax: 217-420-6731, E-mail: dslayton@millikin.edu. *Application contact:* Michelle Whitehead, Administrative Assistant, Master of Science in Nursing Program, 800-373-7733 Ext. 5034, Fax: 217-420-6677, E-mail: mwhitehead@millikin.edu.

Milwaukee School of Engineering, Department of Nursing, Program in Clinical Nurse Leadership, Milwaukee, WI 53202-3109. Offers MS. Application fee: $30. *Expenses:* Tuition: Part-time $603 per credit. *Unit head:* Dr. Debra Jenks, Director, 414-277-4516. *Application contact:* David E. Tietyen, Graduate Admissions Director, 800-332-6763, Fax: 414-277-7475, E-mail: wp@msoe.edu.

Minnesota State University Mankato, College of Graduate Studies, College of Allied Health and Nursing, School of Nursing, Mankato, MN 56001. Offers family nursing (MSN), including family nurse practitioner; nursing (DNP). *Accreditation:* AACN; NLN. *Students:* 9 full-time (all women), 87 part-time (81 women). *Degree requirements:* For master's, comprehensive exam, internships, research project or thesis; for doctorate, capstone project. *Entrance requirements:* For master's, GRE General Test or on-campus essay, minimum GPA of 3.0 during previous 2 years, BSN or equivalent references; for doctorate, master's degree in nursing. Additional exam requirements/recommendations for international students: Required—TOEFL. *Application deadline:* For fall admission, 1/15 priority date for domestic students. Applications are processed on a rolling basis. Application fee: $40. Electronic applications accepted. *Expenses:* Tuition, state resident: full-time $5364. Tuition, nonresident: full-time $8314. *Financial support:* Research assistantships with full tuition reimbursements, teaching assistantships with full tuition reimbursements available. Financial award application deadline: 3/15; financial award applicants required to submit FAFSA. *Faculty research:* Psychosocial nursing, computers in nursing, family adaptation. *Unit head:* Dr. Sue Ellen Bell, Graduate Coordinator, 507-389-6814. *Application contact:* Collaborative MSN Program Admissions, 507-389-6022.

Minnesota State University Moorhead, Graduate Studies, College of Education and Human Services, Moorhead, MN 56563-0002. Offers counseling and student affairs (MS); curriculum and instruction (MS); educational leadership (MS, Ed S); nursing (MS); reading (MS); special education (MS); speech-language pathology (MS). *Accreditation:* NCATE. Part-time and evening/weekend programs available. *Degree requirements:* For master's, comprehensive exam, final oral exam, project or thesis. *Entrance requirements:* Additional exam requirements/recommendations for international students: Required—TOEFL. Electronic applications accepted.

Misericordia University, College of Health Sciences, Department of Nursing, Dallas, PA 18612-1098. Offers MSN. *Accreditation:* AACN. Part-time and evening/weekend programs available. *Faculty:* 3 full-time (all women), 3 part-time/adjunct (all women). *Students:* 59 part-time (56 women). Average age 37. In 2009, 4 master's awarded. *Degree requirements:* For master's, thesis optional, practicum. *Entrance requirements:* For master's, GRE General Test or MAT (minimum 35th percentile), interview, minimum GPA of 2.5, physical assessment, course work in statistics. *Application deadline:* For fall admission, 8/7 priority date for domestic students; for spring admission, 1/3 for domestic students. Applications are processed on a rolling basis. Application fee: $25. Electronic applications accepted. *Expenses:* Contact institution. *Financial support:* In 2009–10, 32 students received support; teaching assistantships, career-related internships or fieldwork, scholarships/grants, traineeships, tuition waivers (partial), and unspecified assistantships available. Support available to part-time students. Financial award application deadline: 6/30; financial award applicants required to submit FAFSA. *Faculty research:* Quality of life, maternal-child, spirituality, critical thinking, adult health. *Unit head:* Dr. Brenda Hage, Coordinator of Graduate Nursing, 570-674-6760, E-mail: bhage@misericordia.edu. *Application contact:* Larree Brown, Coordinator of Part-Time Undergraduate and Graduate Programs, 570-674-6451, Fax: 570-674-6232, E-mail: lbrown@misericordia.edu.

Mississippi University for Women, Graduate School, College of Nursing and Speech-Language Pathology, Columbus, MS 39701-9998. Offers nursing (MSN, PMC); speech/language pathology (MS). *Accreditation:* AACN. Part-time programs available. *Degree requirements:* For master's, comprehensive exam, thesis. *Entrance requirements:* For master's, GRE General Test, bachelor's degree in nursing, previous course work in statistics, proficiency in English.

Missouri Southern State University, Program in Nursing, Joplin, MO 64801-1595. Offers MSN. *Accreditation:* AACN. Part-time programs available. *Entrance requirements:* For master's, minimum cumulative GPA of 3.2, resume, RN licensure, CPR certification, course work in statistics and health assessment. Electronic applications accepted.

Missouri State University, Graduate College, College of Health and Human Services, Department of Nursing, Springfield, MO 65897. Offers nursing (MSN), including family nurse practitioner, nurse educator. *Accreditation:* AACN. *Faculty:* 7 full-time (all women), 3 part-time/adjunct (all women). *Students:* 20 full-time (19 women), 22 part-time (19 women); includes 1 minority (Asian American or Pacific Islander), 1 international. Average age 37. 2 applicants, 50% accepted, 1 enrolled. In 2009, 6 master's awarded. *Degree requirements:* For master's, comprehensive exam, thesis or alternative. *Entrance requirements:* For master's, GRE General Test, minimum GPA of 3.0, RN license (MSN), 1 year work experience (MPH). Additional exam requirements/recommendations for international students: Required—TOEFL (minimum score 550 paper-based; 213 computer-based; 79 iBT). *Application deadline:* For fall admission, 7/20 priority date for domestic students, 5/1 for international students; for spring admission, 12/20 priority date for domestic students, 9/1 for international students. Applications are processed on a rolling basis. Application fee: $35 ($50 for international students). Electronic applications accepted. *Expenses:* Tuition, state resident: full-time $3852; part-time $214 per credit hour. Tuition, nonresident: full-time $7524; part-time $418 per credit hour. Required fees: $696; $172 per semester. Tuition and fees vary according to course level, course load, degree level and program. *Financial support:* Federal Work-Study, institutionally sponsored loans, scholarships/grants, and unspecified assistantships available. Financial award application deadline: 3/31; financial award applicants required to submit FAFSA. *Faculty research:* Preconceptual health, women's health, nursing satisfaction, nursing education. *Unit head:* Dr. Kathryn Hope, Head, 417-836-5310, Fax: 417-836-5484, E-mail: nursing@missouristate.edu. *Application contact:* Eric Eckert, Coordinator of Admissions and Recruitment, 417-836-5331, Fax: 417-836-6200, E-mail: tobinbushman@missouristate.edu.

Molloy College, Graduate Nursing Program, Rockville Centre, NY 11571-5002. Offers adult nurse practitioner (Advanced Certificate); clinical nurse specialist: adult health (Advanced Certificate); family nurse practitioner (Advanced Certificate); nurse practitioner psychiatry (Advanced Certificate); nursing (MS); nursing administration (Advanced Certificate); nursing administration with informatics (Advanced Certificate); nursing education (Advanced Certificate); nursing informatics (Advanced Certificate); pediatric nurse practitioner (Advanced Certificate). *Accreditation:* AACN. Part-time and evening/weekend programs available. *Faculty:* 23 full-time (22 women), 5 part-time/adjunct (4 women). *Students:* 11 full-time (10 women), 405 part-time (377 women); includes 206 minority (124 African Americans, 52 Asian Americans or Pacific Islanders, 30 Hispanic Americans), 2 international. Average age 39. In 2009, 64 master's awarded. *Degree requirements:* For master's, thesis optional. *Entrance requirements:* For master's, 3 letters of reference, BS in nursing, minimum undergraduate GPA of 3.0; for Advanced Certificate, 3 letters of reference, master's degree in nursing. *Application deadline:* For fall admission, 9/2 priority date for domestic students; for spring admission, 1/20 priority date for domestic students. Applications are processed on a rolling basis. Application fee: $60. *Expenses:* Tuition: Part-time $765 per credit. Required fees: $340 per semester. *Financial support:* Research assistantships with partial tuition reimbursements, teaching assistantships with partial tuition reimbursements, institutionally sponsored loans, scholarships/grants, and unspecified assistantships available. Support available to part-time students. Financial award application deadline: 4/1; financial award applicants required to submit FAFSA. *Unit head:* Dr. Mary T. O'Shaughnessy, Acting Director, 516-678-5000, Fax: 516-678-9718, E-mail:

Nursing—General

Molloy College (continued)

moshaughnessy@molloy.edu. *Application contact:* Alina Haitz, Assistant Director of Graduate Admissions, 516-678-5000 Ext. 6399, Fax: 516-256-2247, E-mail: ahaitz@molloy.edu.

Monmouth University, Graduate School, The Marjorie K. Unterberg School of Nursing and Health Studies, West Long Branch, NJ 07764-1898. Offers adult nurse practitioner (MSN); adult psychiatric and mental health advanced practice nursing (MSN, Post-Master's Certificate); advanced practice nursing (Post-Master's Certificate); family nurse practitioner (MSN, Post-Master's Certificate); forensic nursing (MSN, Certificate); nursing (MSN); nursing administration (MSN, Post-Master's Certificate); nursing education (MSN, Post-Master's Certificate); school nursing (MSN, Certificate). *Accreditation:* AACN. Part-time and evening/weekend programs available. *Faculty:* 11 full-time (all women), 2 part-time/adjunct (both women). *Students:* 15 full-time (14 women), 183 part-time (178 women); includes 51 minority (14 African Americans, 3 American Indian/Alaska Native, 26 Asian Americans or Pacific Islanders, 8 Hispanic Americans), 1 international. Average age 41. 95 applicants, 99% accepted, 44 enrolled. In 2009, 36 master's awarded. *Degree requirements:* For master's, practicum (for some tracks). *Entrance requirements:* For master's, GRE General Test, RN license, 1 year of work experience, minimum undergraduate GPA of 2.75. Additional exam requirements/recommendations for international students: Required—TOEFL (minimum score 550 paper-based; 213 computer-based; 79 iBT), IELTS (minimum score 5), Michigan English Language Assessment Battery (minimum score 77), Cambridge A, B, C. *Application deadline:* For fall admission, 7/15 priority date for domestic students, 6/1 for international students; for spring admission, 11/15 priority date for domestic students, 11/1 for international students. Applications are processed on a rolling basis. Application fee: $50. Electronic applications accepted. *Expenses:* Tuition: Part-time $773 per credit. Required fees: $157 per semester. *Financial support:* In 2009–10, 118 students received support, including 96 fellowships (averaging $1,308 per year), 4 research assistantships (averaging $3,610 per year); career-related internships or fieldwork, scholarships/grants, and unspecified assistantships also available. Support available to part-time students. Financial award applicants required to submit FAFSA. *Faculty research:* Relationship of undergraduate GPA and GRE to succeed in a graduate nursing program. *Unit head:* Dr. Janet Mahoney, Dean, 732-571-3443, Fax: 732-263-5131, E-mail: jmahoney@monmouth.edu. *Application contact:* Kevin Roane, Director, Office of Graduate Admission, 732-571-3452, Fax: 732-263-5123, E-mail: gradadm@monmouth.edu.

Montana State University, College of Graduate Studies, College of Nursing, Bozeman, MT 59717. Offers clinical nurse specialist (CNS) (MN, Post-Master's Certificate); family nurse practitioner (MN, Post-Master's Certificate); nursing education (Certificate); psychiatric mental health nurse practitioner (MN). *Accreditation:* AACN. Part-time programs available. Postbaccalaureate distance learning degree programs offered (no on-campus study). *Faculty:* 49 full-time (46 women), 25 part-time/adjunct (all women). *Students:* 41 full-time (39 women), 24 part-time (23 women); includes 8 minority (7 American Indian/Alaska Native, 1 Hispanic American). Average age 38. 54 applicants, 33% accepted, 16 enrolled. In 2009, 13 master's awarded. *Degree requirements:* For master's, comprehensive exam, thesis (for some programs). *Entrance requirements:* For master's, GRE General Test. Additional exam requirements/recommendations for international students: Required—TOEFL (minimum score 580 paper-based; 213 computer-based). *Application deadline:* For fall admission, 7/15 priority date for domestic students, 5/15 priority date for international students; for spring admission, 12/1 priority date for domestic students, 10/1 priority date for international students. Applications are processed on a rolling basis. Application fee: $30. Electronic applications accepted. *Expenses:* Tuition, state resident: full-time $5635; part-time $3492 per year. Tuition, nonresident: full-time $17,212; part-time $7865.10 per year. Required fees: $1441; $153.15 per credit. Tuition and fees vary according to course load and program. *Financial support:* In 2009–10, 16 students received support, including 3 fellowships with full tuition reimbursements available (averaging $15,000 per year), 1 research assistantship (averaging $7,000 per year), 8 teaching assistantships with partial tuition reimbursements available (averaging $7,050 per year); traineeships and tuition waivers (partial) also available. Financial award application deadline: 3/1; financial award applicants required to submit FAFSA. *Faculty research:* Environmental exposures, chronic illness, sleep habits, oral health, pressure ulcers. Total annual research expenditures: $2.3 million. *Unit head:* Dr. Elizabeth Kinion, Dean, 406-994-2725, Fax: 406-994-6020, E-mail: ekinion@montana.edu. *Application contact:* Dr. Carl A. Fox, Vice Provost for Graduate Education, 406-994-4145, Fax: 406-994-7433, E-mail: gradstudy@montana.edu.

Moravian College, Moravian College Comenius Center, St. Luke's School of Nursing, Bethlehem, PA 18018-6650. Offers nurse administrator (MS); nurse educator (MS); nurse leadership (MS). Part-time and evening/weekend programs available. *Faculty:* 2 full-time (both women). *Students:* 31 part-time (all women); includes 2 minority (1 African American, 1 Asian American or Pacific Islander). 34 applicants, 94% accepted, 31 enrolled. *Degree requirements:* For master's, comprehensive exam (for some programs), evidence-based practice project. *Entrance requirements:* For master's, GRE or MAT. Additional exam requirements/recommendations for international students: Required—TOEFL (minimum score 550 paper-based; 260 computer-based; 90 iBT). *Application deadline:* Applications are processed on a rolling basis. Application fee: $40. *Expenses:* Tuition: Part-time $1132 per course. Required fees: $40 per term. One-time fee: $30 part-time. *Unit head:* Dr. Lori Hoffman, Director, Master of Science Program in Nursing, 610-861-1400, Fax: 610-861-1466, E-mail: comenius@moravian.edu. *Application contact:* Dr. Lori Hoffman, Director, Master of Science Program in Nursing, 610-861-1400, Fax: 610-861-1466, E-mail: comenius@moravian.edu.

Morgan State University, School of Graduate Studies, School of Community Health and Policy, Department of Nursing, Baltimore, MD 21251. Offers MS, PhD.

Mountain State University, Graduate Studies, Program in Nursing, Beckley, WV 25802-9003. Offers administration/education (MSN); family nurse practitioner (MSN); nurse anesthesia (MSN); registered nurse anesthetist (Certificate). *Accreditation:* AANA/CANAEP; NLN. Part-time programs available. Postbaccalaureate distance learning degree programs offered (minimal on-campus study). *Faculty:* 4 full-time (all women), 10 part-time/adjunct (9 women). *Students:* 117 full-time (102 women); includes 10 minority (6 African Americans, 1 American Indian/Alaska Native, 3 Asian Americans or Pacific Islanders), 1 international. Average age 37. 46 applicants, 80% accepted, 37 enrolled. In 2009, 35 master's awarded. *Degree requirements:* For master's, comprehensive exam, thesis or alternative. *Entrance requirements:* For master's, GRE. Additional exam requirements/recommendations for international students: Required—TOEFL (minimum score 550 paper-based; 213 computer-based); Recommended—IELTS (minimum score 6.5). *Application deadline:* For spring admission, 6/30 for domestic and international students. Applications are processed on a rolling basis. Application fee: $25 ($50 for international students). Electronic applications accepted. *Expenses:* Contact institution. *Financial support:* Federal Work-Study, scholarships/grants, and unspecified assistantships available. Support available to part-time students. Financial award applicants required to submit FAFSA. *Unit head:* Dr. Judith Halle, Dean, School of Health Sciences, 304-929-1327, Fax: 304-929-1601, E-mail: jhalle@mountainstate.edu. *Application contact:* Melody Tilley, Program Specialist, 304-929-1576, Fax: 304-929-1601, E-mail: mtilley@mountainstate.edu.

Mount Carmel College of Nursing, Nursing Program, Columbus, OH 43222. Offers adult health CNS (clinical nurse specialist) (MS); nursing administration (MS); nursing education (MS). *Accreditation:* AACN. Part-time programs available. *Degree requirements:* For master's, professional manuscript. *Entrance requirements:* For master's, letters of recommendation, current resume, baccalaureate degree in nursing, current Ohio RN license, minimum cumulative GPA of 3.0. Additional exam requirements/recommendations for international students: Required—TOEFL (minimum score 550 paper-based; 213 computer-based; 80 iBT).

Mount Saint Mary College, Division of Nursing, Newburgh, NY 12550-3494. Offers adult nurse practitioner (MS), including nursing education, nursing management; clinical nurse specialist-adult health (MS), including nursing education, nursing management; family nurse practitioner (Advanced Certificate). *Accreditation:* AACN. Part-time and evening/weekend programs available. *Faculty:* 3 full-time (all women), 2 part-time/adjunct (both women). *Students:* 1 full-time (0 women), 53 part-time (50 women); includes 17 minority (8 African Americans, 4 Asian Americans or Pacific Islanders, 5 Hispanic Americans). Average age 39. 16 applicants, 100% accepted, 6 enrolled. In 2009, 5 master's awarded. *Degree requirements:* For master's, research utilization project. *Entrance requirements:* For master's, BSN, minimum GPA of 3.0, RN license. *Application deadline:* For fall admission, 6/3 priority date for domestic students; for spring admission, 10/31 priority date for domestic students. Applications are processed on a rolling basis. Application fee: $45. *Expenses:* Tuition: Full-time $13,356; part-time $742 per credit. Required fees: $50 per semester. *Financial support:* In 2009–10, 2 students received support. Unspecified assistantships available. Financial award application deadline: 4/15; financial award applicants required to submit FAFSA. *Unit head:* Dr. Karen Baldwin, Coordinator, 845-569-3512, Fax: 845-562-6762, E-mail: baldwin@msmc.edu. *Application contact:* Graduate Coordinator, 845-561-0800, Fax: 845-562-6762.

Mount St. Mary's College, Graduate Division, Program in Nursing, Los Angeles, CA 90049-1599. Offers clinical nurse specialist/adult health (MS); community health (MS); educator (MS); leadership and administration (MS); nursing (MS). *Accreditation:* AACN. *Faculty:* 2 full-time (both women), 11 part-time/adjunct (9 women). *Students:* 31 full-time (29 women), 8 part-time (6 women); includes 24 minority (5 African Americans, 12 Asian Americans or Pacific Islanders, 7 Hispanic Americans), 1 international. Average age 41. In 2009, 22 master's awarded. *Entrance requirements:* Additional exam requirements/recommendations for international students: Required—TOEFL (minimum score 550 iBT). *Application deadline:* For fall admission, 7/15 priority date for domestic students; for spring admission, 11/15 priority date for domestic students. *Expenses:* Tuition: Part-time $730 per unit. Part-time tuition and fees vary according to degree level and program. *Unit head:* Dr. Marsha Sato, Chair, 213-477-2980, E-mail: msato@msmc.la.edu. *Application contact:* Director of Graduate Admission.

Murray State University, College of Health Sciences and Human Services, Program in Nursing, Murray, KY 42071. Offers clinical nurse specialist (MSN); family nurse practitioner (MSN); nurse anesthesia (MSN). *Accreditation:* AACN; AANA/CANAEP. *Degree requirements:* For master's, research project. *Entrance requirements:* For master's, GRE General Test, BSN, interview, RN licensure. Additional exam requirements/recommendations for international students: Required—TOEFL (minimum score 550 paper-based). *Faculty research:* Fibromyalgis, primary care, rural health.

Nazareth College of Rochester, Graduate Studies, Department of Nursing, Rochester, NY 14618-3790. Offers gerontological nurse practitioner (MS). *Accreditation:* AACN. Part-time programs available. *Entrance requirements:* For master's, minimum GPA of 3.0, RN license.

Nebraska Methodist College, Program in Nursing, Omaha, NE 68114. Offers MSN. *Accreditation:* AACN. Evening/weekend programs available. Postbaccalaureate distance learning degree programs offered (no on-campus study). *Faculty:* 1 (woman) full-time, 5 part-time/adjunct (all women). *Students:* 23 full-time (all women), 24 part-time (23 women); includes 3 minority (all African Americans). Average age 41. 17 applicants, 41% accepted, 7 enrolled. In 2009, 19 master's awarded. *Degree requirements:* For master's, thesis or alternative, Evidence Based Practice (EBP) project. *Entrance requirements:* For master's, interview. Additional exam requirements/recommendations for international students: Required—TOEFL (minimum score 550 paper-based; 213 computer-based; 80 iBT). *Application deadline:* For spring admission, 11/1 for domestic and international students. Applications are processed on a rolling basis. Application fee: $25. *Expenses:* Tuition: Full-time $6552; part-time $546 per credit hour. Required fees: $300; $25 per credit hour. *Financial support:* In 2009–10, 12 students received support; research assistantships with full and partial tuition reimbursements available, scholarships/grants available. Support available to part-time students. Financial award applicants required to submit FAFSA. *Faculty research:* Spirituality, student outcomes, service learning, leadership and administration, women's issues. *Unit head:* Linda Foley, Coordinator, 402-354-7050, Fax: 402-354-7020, E-mail: linda.foley@methodistcollege.edu. *Application contact:* Sara Bonney, Director of Admissions, 402-354-7111, Fax: 402-354-7020, E-mail: admissions@methodistcollege.edu.

Nebraska Wesleyan University, University College, Program in Nursing, Lincoln, NE 68504-2796. Offers MSN. *Accreditation:* NLN. Part-time programs available.

Neumann University, Program in Nursing and Health Sciences, Aston, PA 19014-1298. Offers MS. *Accreditation:* NLN. Part-time programs available. *Faculty:* 6 full-time (all women), 1 (woman) part-time/adjunct. *Students:* 18 part-time (all women). Average age 46. 10 applicants, 100% accepted, 8 enrolled. In 2009, 2 master's awarded. *Entrance requirements:* For master's, GRE or MAT. Additional exam requirements/recommendations for international students: Required—TOEFL. *Application deadline:* Applications are processed on a rolling basis. Application fee: $50. *Expenses:* Contact institution. *Financial support:* Available to part-time students. Application deadline: 3/15. *Unit head:* Dr. Kathleen Hoover, Dean, Division of Nursing and Health Services, 610-558-5560, Fax: 610-459-1370, E-mail: hooverk@neumann.edu. *Application contact:* Kittie D. Pain, Associate Director of Admissions, Graduate and Adult Programs, 610-558-5613, Fax: 610-558-5652, E-mail: paink@neumann.edu.

New Mexico State University, Graduate School, College of Health and Social Services, School of Nursing, Las Cruces, NM 88003-8001. Offers community/public health (MSN); medical-surgical (adult health) (MSN); nursing (PhD); nursing administration (MSN); psychiatric/mental health (MSN). *Accreditation:* AACN. Part-time programs available. Postbaccalaureate distance learning degree programs offered (minimal on-campus study). *Faculty:* 10 full-time (all women), 5 part-time/adjunct (all women). *Students:* 59 full-time (48 women), 70 part-time (61 women); includes 47 minority (9 African Americans, 3 American Indian/Alaska Native, 5 Asian Americans or Pacific Islanders, 30 Hispanic Americans). Average age 43. 82 applicants, 96% accepted, 63 enrolled. In 2009, 32 master's, 1 doctorate awarded. *Degree requirements:* For master's, comprehensive exam, thesis optional, clinical practice; for doctorate, comprehensive exam, thesis/dissertation, clinical practice. *Entrance requirements:* For master's, NCLEX exam, BSN, minimum GPA of 3.0, course work in statistics, 3 letters of reference, writing sample, RN license, CPR certification, proof of liability, immunizations, criminal background check; for doctorate, NCLEX exam, MSN, minimum GPA of 3.0, 3 letters of reference, writing sample, RN license, CPR certification, proof of liability, immunizations, criminal background check. Additional exam requirements/recommendations for international students: Required—TOEFL (minimum score 550 paper-based). *Application deadline:* For fall admission, 3/1 priority date for domestic students; for spring admission, 10/1 priority date for domestic students. Applications are processed on a rolling basis. Application fee: $30 ($50 for international students). Electronic applications accepted. *Expenses:* Tuition, state resident: full-time $4080; part-time $223 per credit. Tuition, nonresident: full-time $14,256; part-time $647 per credit. Required fees: $1278; $639 per semester. *Financial support:* In 2009–10, 14 students received support, including 2 teaching assistantships (averaging $18,380 per year); fellowships, research assistantships, career-related internships or fieldwork, Federal Work-Study, scholarships/grants, traineeships, and health care benefits also available. Financial award application deadline: 3/1. *Faculty research:* Public policy, community health, health disparities, self efficacy and self management, psychiatric mental health. *Unit head:* Dr. Pamela Schultz, Director, 575-646-3812, Fax: 575-646-2167, E-mail: pschultz@nmsu.edu. *Application contact:* Dr. Kathleen Huttlinger, Associate Director for Graduate Studies, 575-646-4386, Fax: 575-646-2167.

New York University, College of Nursing, Advanced Programs in Nursing, New York, NY 10012-1019. Offers nursing (DNP); research and theory development in nursing science (PhD). Part-time and evening/weekend programs available. *Faculty:* 5 full-time (all women). *Students:* 7 full-time (5 women), 31 part-time (28 women); includes 11 minority (5 African Americans, 6 Asian Americans or Pacific Islanders). Average age 43. 14 applicants, 71% accepted, 8 enrolled. In 2009, 3 doctorates awarded. *Degree requirements:* For doctorate, thesis/dissertation. *Entrance requirements:* For doctorate, GRE General Test, interview. Additional exam requirements/recommendations for international students: Required—TOEFL. *Application deadline:* For fall admission, 3/1 priority date for domestic students, 3/1 for international students. Applications are processed on a rolling basis. Application fee: $75. *Expenses:* Tuition: Full-time $30,528; part-time $1272 per credit. Required fees: $2177. *Financial support:* Fellowships with full and partial tuition reimbursements, research assistantships with full and partial tuition reimbursements, institutionally sponsored loans, scholarships/grants, and tuition

waivers (partial) available. Support available to part-time students. Financial award application deadline: 2/1; financial award applicants required to submit FAFSA. *Faculty research:* Geriatrics, infectious diseases global health, chronic illnesses prevention management, healthcare workforce/education. *Unit head:* Dr. Deborah Chyun, Director, 212-998-5264, Fax: 212-995-4561. *Application contact:* Amy Knowles, Assistant Dean for Student Affairs and Admissions, 212-998-5333, Fax: 212-995-4302, E-mail: ak96@nyu.edu.

New York University, College of Nursing, Programs in Advanced Practice Nursing, New York, NY 10012-1019. Offers advanced practice nursing: adult acute care (MS, Advanced Certificate); advanced practice nursing: adult nurse practictioner/palliative care nursing (MS); advanced practice nursing: adult nurse practitioner/holistic nurse practitioner (Advanced Certificate); advanced practice nursing: adult nurse practitioner/holistic nursing (MS); advanced practice nursing: adult nurse practitioner/palliative care nurse practitioner (Advanced Certificate); advanced practice nursing: adult primary care (MS, Advanced Certificate); advanced practice nursing: adult primary care/geriatrics (MS); advanced practice nursing: geriatrics (MS, Advanced Certificate); advanced practice nursing: mental health (MS); advanced practice nursing: mental health nursing (Advanced Certificate); advanced practice nursing: pediatrics (MS, Advanced Certificate); advanced practice nursing:adult primary care and geriatrics (Advanced Certificate); nurse midwifery (MS, Advanced Certificate); nursing administration (MS, Advanced Certificate); nursing education (MS, Advanced Certificate); nursing informatics (MS, Advanced Certificate); MS/MPH; MS/MS. *Accreditation:* AACN; ACNM/DOA. Part-time and evening/weekend programs available. *Faculty:* 17 full-time (all women), 22 part-time/adjunct (19 women). *Students:* 18 full-time (17 women), 524 part-time (485 women); includes 238 minority (90 African Americans, 119 Asian Americans or Pacific Islanders, 29 Hispanic Americans). Average age 33. 191 applicants, 89% accepted, 120 enrolled. In 2009, 117 master's, 2 other advanced degrees awarded. *Degree requirements:* For master's, thesis (for some programs). *Entrance requirements:* For master's, BS in nursing, AS in nursing with another BS/BA, interview; for Advanced Certificate, master's degree. Additional exam requirements/recommendations for international students: Required—TOEFL. *Application deadline:* For fall admission, 7/1 priority date for domestic students, 7/1 for international students; for spring admission, 12/1 for domestic and international students. Applications are processed on a rolling basis. Application fee: $75. *Expenses:* Tuition: Full-time $30,528; part-time $1272 per credit. Required fees: $2177. *Financial support:* Career-related internships or fieldwork, institutionally sponsored loans, scholarships/grants, traineeships, and tuition waivers (partial) available. Support available to part-time students. Financial award application deadline: 2/1; financial award applicants required to submit FAFSA. *Faculty research:* Elderly black diabetics, families and illness, public health nursing, parent-child nursing, health policy costs. *Unit head:* Dr. Judith Haber, Associate Dean for Graduate Programs, 212-998-9020, Fax: 212-995-3143. *Application contact:* Amy Knowles, Assistant Dean for Student Affairs and Admissions, 212-998-5333, Fax: 212-995-4302, E-mail: ak96@nyu.edu.

North Dakota State University, College of Graduate and Interdisciplinary Studies, College of Pharmacy, Nursing and Allied Sciences, Graduate Nursing Program, Fargo, ND 58108. Offers MS, DNP. *Accreditation:* AACN. Part-time programs available. Postbaccalaureate distance learning degree programs offered (minimal on-campus study). *Faculty:* 1 full-time (0 women), 5 part-time/adjunct (all women). *Students:* 28 full-time (26 women), 11 part-time (10 women); includes 2 minority (1 American Indian/Alaska Native, 1 Asian American or Pacific Islander), 2 international. Average age 35. 12 applicants, 100% accepted, 11 enrolled. In 2009, 3 master's, 7 doctorates awarded. *Degree requirements:* For master's, thesis or alternative, oral defense; for doctorate, thesis/dissertation or alternative, oral defense. *Entrance requirements:* For master's, bachelor's degree with nursing major, minimum GPA of 3.0 in nursing courses, RN license; for doctorate, bachelor's or master's degree with a nursing major, minimum GPA of 3.0 in nursing courses, RN license. Additional exam requirements/recommendations for international students: Required—TOEFL, IELTS. *Application deadline:* For fall admission, 7/15 priority date for domestic students; for winter admission, 2/1 priority date for domestic students; for spring admission, 11/15 priority date for domestic students. Applications are processed on a rolling basis. Application fee: $45 ($60 for international students). Electronic applications accepted. *Expenses:* Contact institution. *Financial support:* In 2009–10, 1 research assistantship with full tuition reimbursement (averaging $1,600 per year), 6 teaching assistantships with full tuition reimbursements (averaging $4,668 per year) were awarded; traineeships and unspecified assistantships also available. Financial award application deadline: 8/15; financial award applicants required to submit CSS PROFILE or FAFSA. *Faculty research:* Prevention of farmers' hearing loss, breast cancer in Native American women, colon cancer, quality improvement in a wellness center. Total annual research expenditures: $142,500. *Unit head:* Dr. Mary Wright, Associate Dean, 701-231-7943, Fax: 701-231-7606. *Application contact:* Dr. Jonathan Sheng, Assistant Professor, 701-231-6140, Fax: 701-231-8333, E-mail: jonathan.sheng@ndsu.edu.

Northeastern University, Bouvé College of Health Sciences Graduate School, School of Nursing, Program in Primary Care Nursing, Boston, MA 02115-5096. Offers MS, CAGS, CAS. *Accreditation:* AACN. *Students:* 27 full-time (25 women), 15 part-time (13 women); includes 3 African Americans, 1 American Indian/Alaska Native, 1 Asian American or Pacific Islander, 1 international. 22 applicants, 77% accepted, 10 enrolled. In 2009, 10 master's awarded. *Entrance requirements:* For master's, GRE General Test; for other advanced degree, MS in nursing. Additional exam requirements/recommendations for international students: Required—TOEFL (minimum score 100 iBT). *Application deadline:* For fall admission, 7/1 for domestic students. Applications are processed on a rolling basis. Application fee: $50. Electronic applications accepted. *Financial support:* Research assistantships with tuition reimbursements, teaching assistantships with tuition reimbursements, scholarships/grants, traineeships, and tuition waivers (partial) available. Financial award application deadline: 7/1; financial award applicants required to submit FAFSA. *Unit head:* Dr. Susan Jo Roberts, Director, 617-373-3130, Fax: 617-373-3050, E-mail: s.roberts@neu.edu. *Application contact:* Margaret Schnabel, Director of Graduate Admissions, 617-373-2708, E-mail: bouvegrad@neu.edu.

Northern Arizona University, Graduate College, College of Health and Human Services, School of Nursing, Flagstaff, AZ 86011. Offers family nurse practitioner (MSN, Certificate); nurse educator (MSN); nurse generalist (MSN); nursing (MSN). *Accreditation:* AACN. *Faculty:* 19 full-time (all women). *Students:* 17 full-time (14 women), 32 part-time (29 women); includes 4 minority (1 American Indian/Alaska Native, 3 Hispanic Americans). Average age 30. 43 applicants, 19% accepted, 4 enrolled. In 2009, 7 master's awarded. *Degree requirements:* For master's, project or thesis. *Entrance requirements:* For master's, GRE General Test or minimum GPA of 3.0, undergraduate statistics or health assessment with minimum grade of B in last 5 years or 3 years of RN experience (nursing education). Additional exam requirements/recommendations for international students: Required—TOEFL (minimum score 550 paper-based; 213 computer-based; 80 iBT), IELTS (minimum score 7), or a bachelor's degree from an English-speaking university and demonstrated proficiency. *Application deadline:* For fall admission, 1/15 priority date for domestic students, 9/1 priority date for international students. Application fee: $65. Electronic applications accepted. *Financial support:* In 2009–10, 4 teaching assistantships with partial tuition reimbursements were awarded; career-related internships or fieldwork, Federal Work-Study, traineeships, health care benefits, tuition waivers, and unspecified assistantships also available. Support available to part-time students. Financial award application deadline: 3/30; financial award applicants required to submit FAFSA. *Unit head:* Debera Thomas, Chair, 928-523-2656, Fax: 928-523-7171, E-mail: debera.thomas@nau.edu. *Application contact:* Penny Susan Walior, Student Academic Specialist, 928-523-6717, Fax: 928-523-9155, E-mail: penny.walior@nau.edu.

Northern Illinois University, Graduate School, College of Health and Human Sciences, School of Nursing and Health Studies, De Kalb, IL 60115-2854. Offers nursing (MS); public health (MPH). *Accreditation:* AACN. Part-time programs available. *Faculty:* 12 full-time (11 women), 1 (woman) part-time/adjunct. *Students:* 28 full-time (22 women), 184 part-time (170 women); includes 38 minority (11 African Americans, 18 Asian Americans or Pacific Islanders, 9 Hispanic Americans), 14 international. Average age 36. 77 applicants, 68% accepted, 35 enrolled. In 2009, 46 master's awarded. *Degree requirements:* For master's, thesis optional, internship. *Entrance requirements:* For master's, minimum GPA of 3.0 in last 60 hours, BA in nursing, nursing license. Additional exam requirements/recommendations for international students: Required—TOEFL (minimum score 550 paper-based; 213 computer-based). *Application deadline:* For fall admission, 6/1 for domestic students, 5/1 for international students; for spring admission, 11/1 for domestic students, 10/1 for international students. Applications are processed on a rolling basis. Application fee: $30. Electronic applications accepted. *Expenses:* Tuition, state resident: full-time $6576; part-time $274 per credit hour. Tuition, nonresident: full-time $13,152; part-time $548 per credit hour. Required fees: $1813; $75.53 per credit hour. Part-time tuition and fees vary according to course load. *Financial support:* In 2009–10, 13 research assistantships with full tuition reimbursements, 7 teaching assistantships with full tuition reimbursements were awarded; fellowships with full tuition reimbursements, career-related internships or fieldwork, Federal Work-Study, scholarships/grants, tuition waivers (full), and unspecified assistantships also available. Support available to part-time students. Financial award applicants required to submit FAFSA. *Faculty research:* Neonatal intensive care, stress and coping, refugee and immigrant issues, older adults, autoimmune disorders. *Unit head:* Dr. Brigid Lusk, Chair, 815-753-0663, Fax: 815-753-0814, E-mail: blusk@niu.edu. *Application contact:* Graduate School Office, 815-753-0395, E-mail: gradsch@niu.edu.

Northern Kentucky University, Office of Graduate Programs, School of Nursing and Health Professions, Program in Nursing, Highland Heights, KY 41099. Offers nursing (MSN, Post-Master's Certificate). *Accreditation:* NLN. Part-time and evening/weekend programs available. Postbaccalaureate distance learning degree programs offered (no on-campus study). *Students:* 18 full-time (all women), 224 part-time (205 women); includes 17 minority (10 African Americans, 1 American Indian/Alaska Native, 4 Asian Americans or Pacific Islanders, 2 Hispanic Americans). Average age 38. 174 applicants, 37% accepted, 58 enrolled. In 2009, 44 master's, 17 other advanced degrees awarded. *Degree requirements:* For master's, comprehensive exam. *Entrance requirements:* For master's, minimum cumulative GPA of 2.75; one year of experience as RN; college courses in statistics, nursing research, physical assessment and nursing theory, proof of current nursing licensure, updated resume. Additional exam requirements/recommendations for international students: Required—TOEFL (minimum score 550 paper-based; 213 computer-based; 79 iBT); Recommended—IELTS (minimum score 6.5). *Application deadline:* For fall admission, 2/1 for domestic and international students; for spring admission, 10/15 for domestic and international students. Application fee: $40. Electronic applications accepted. *Expenses:* Tuition, state resident: full-time $6912; part-time $384 per credit hour. Tuition, nonresident: full-time $12,150; part-time $675 per credit hour. Tuition and fees vary according to course load, program and reciprocity agreements. *Financial support:* Unspecified assistantships available. Financial award applicants required to submit FAFSA. *Faculty research:* Lead poisoning in children, career planning for middle school students, technology skills for workforce. *Unit head:* Dr. Marilyn Schleyer, Program Director, 859-572-5240, Fax: 859-572-1934, E-mail: schleyerm1@nku.edu. *Application contact:* Dr. Peg Griffin, Director of Graduate Programs, 859-572-6934, Fax: 859-572-6670, E-mail: griffinp@nku.edu.

Northern Michigan University, College of Graduate Studies, College of Professional Studies, School of Nursing, Marquette, MI 49855-5301. Offers MSN. *Accreditation:* AACN. Part-time and evening/weekend programs available. *Degree requirements:* For master's, thesis or alternative. *Entrance requirements:* For master's, GRE General Test, minimum GPA of 3.0.

North Park University, School of Nursing, Chicago, IL 60625-4895. Offers advanced practice nursing (MS); leadership and management (MS); MBA/MS; MM/MSN; MS/MHR; MS/MNA. *Accreditation:* AACN. Part-time and evening/weekend programs available. *Degree requirements:* For master's, thesis. *Entrance requirements:* For master's, GMAT, MAT. *Faculty research:* Aging, consultation roles, critical thinking skills, family breakdown, science of caring.

Northwestern State University of Louisiana, Graduate Studies and Research, College of Nursing, Shreveport, LA 71101-4653. Offers MSN. *Accreditation:* AACN. Part-time programs available. *Degree requirements:* For master's, comprehensive exam, thesis or alternative. *Entrance requirements:* For master's, GRE General Test, 6 months of clinical nursing experience, BS in nursing, minimum GPA of 3.0.

Nova Southeastern University, Health Professions Division, College of Allied Health and Nursing, Department of Nursing, Fort Lauderdale, FL 33314-7796. Offers MSN, PhD. *Accreditation:* AACN. Part-time and evening/weekend programs available. Postbaccalaureate distance learning degree programs offered (no on-campus study). *Faculty:* 4 full-time (all women). *Students:* 1 (woman) full-time, 109 part-time (99 women); includes 45 minority (31 African Americans, 5 Asian Americans or Pacific Islanders, 9 Hispanic Americans). 70 applicants, 54% accepted, 38 enrolled. In 2009, 23 master's awarded. *Degree requirements:* For doctorate, comprehensive exam. *Entrance requirements:* For master's, minimum GPA of 3.0, RN, BSN; for doctorate, minimum GPA of 3.5, BSN, RN. *Application deadline:* For fall admission, 3/1 for domestic and international students; for winter admission, 11/1 for domestic and international students. Applications are processed on a rolling basis. Application fee: $50. Electronic applications accepted. *Faculty research:* Nursing education, curriculum, clinical research, interdisciplinary research. *Unit head:* Dr. Diane Whitehead, Professor, 954-262-1962, E-mail: dwhitehe@nova.edu. *Application contact:* Dr. Patricia Dittman, Application Contact, 954-262-1991, E-mail: pdittman@nova.edu.

Oakland University, Graduate Study and Lifelong Learning, School of Nursing, Rochester, MI 48309-4401. Offers MSN, DNP, Certificate. *Accreditation:* AACN. Part-time and evening/weekend programs available. *Entrance requirements:* For master's, GRE General Test, minimum GPA of 3.0 for unconditional admission. Electronic applications accepted. *Faculty research:* Accelerated Health Care Career Training Initiative.

The Ohio State University, Graduate School, College of Nursing, Columbus, OH 43210. Offers MS, PhD. *Accreditation:* AACN; ACNM/DOA. Part-time programs available. *Faculty:* 31. *Students:* 191 full-time (162 women), 165 part-time (148 women); includes 27 minority (13 African Americans, 1 American Indian/Alaska Native, 8 Asian Americans or Pacific Islanders, 5 Hispanic Americans), 1 international. Average age 33. In 2009, 100 master's, 7 doctorates awarded. *Degree requirements:* For master's, thesis optional; for doctorate, thesis/dissertation. *Entrance requirements:* Additional exam requirements/recommendations for international students: Required—TOEFL (minimum score 600 paper-based; 250 computer-based). *Application deadline:* For fall admission, 8/15 priority date for domestic students, 7/1 priority date for international students; for winter admission, 12/1 priority date for domestic students, 11/1 priority date for international students; for spring admission, 3/1 priority date for domestic students, 2/1 priority date for international students. Applications are processed on a rolling basis. Application fee: $40 ($50 for international students). Electronic applications accepted. *Expenses:* Tuition, state resident: full-time $10,683. Tuition, nonresident: full-time $25,923. Tuition and fees vary according to course load and program. *Financial support:* Fellowships, research assistantships, teaching assistantships, Federal Work-Study, institutionally sponsored loans, and unspecified assistantships available. Support available to part-time students. *Unit head:* Dr. Elizabeth R. Lenz, Dean, 614-292-8900, Fax: 614-292-4535, E-mail: lenz.23@osu.edu. *Application contact:* 614-292-9444, Fax: 614-292-3895, E-mail: domestic.grad@osu.edu.

The Ohio State University at Marion, Graduate Programs, Marion, OH 43302-5695. Offers early childhood education (pre-K to grade 3) (M Ed); integrated teaching and learning (MA); middle childhood education (grades 4-9) (M Ed); nursing (MS, PhD); social work (MSW); MS/PhD. Part-time programs available. *Students:* 49 full-time (38 women), 34 part-time (25 women); includes 2 minority (both African Americans). Average age 31. *Degree requirements:* For master's, comprehensive exam (for some programs), thesis (for some programs). *Entrance requirements:* For master's and doctorate, GRE, minimum undergraduate GPA of 3.0. Additional exam requirements/recommendations for international students: Required—TOEFL, IELTS or Michigan English Language Assessment Battery. *Application deadline:* For fall admission, 8/15 priority date for domestic students, 7/1 priority date for international students; for winter admission, 12/1 priority date for domestic students, 11/1 priority date for international students; for spring admission, 3/1 priority date for domestic students, 2/1 priority date for international

Nursing—General

The Ohio State University at Marion (continued)

students. Applications are processed on a rolling basis. Application fee: $40 ($50 for international students). Electronic applications accepted. *Expenses:* Tuition, state resident: full-time $10,155. Tuition, nonresident: full-time $25,395. Tuition and fees vary according to course load. *Unit head:* Gregory S. Rose, Dean/Director, 740-389-6786 Ext. 6218, E-mail: rose.9@osu.edu. *Application contact:* Graduate Admissions, 614-292-9444, Fax: 614-292-3895, E-mail: domestic.grad@osu.edu.

Ohio University, Graduate College, College of Health and Human Services, School of Nursing, Athens, OH 45701-2979. Offers family nurse practitioner (MSN); nurse administrator (MSN); nurse educator (MSN). *Accreditation:* AACN. *Faculty:* 8 full-time (all women). *Students:* 24 full-time (23 women), 31 part-time (25 women); includes 1 African American, 2 American Indian/Alaska Native. 36 applicants, 92% accepted, 25 enrolled. In 2009, 12 master's awarded. *Degree requirements:* For master's, capstone project. *Entrance requirements:* For master's, GRE, bachelor's degree in nursing from an accredited college or university, minimum overall undergraduate GPA of 3.0, official transcripts, statement of goals and objectives, resume, 3 letters of recommendation. Additional exam requirements/recommendations for international students: Required—TOEFL (minimum score 550 paper-based; 80 iBT) or IELTS Academic (minimum score 6.5). *Application deadline:* For fall admission, 3/1 priority date for domestic students, 2/1 priority date for international students. Applications are processed on a rolling basis. Application fee: $50 ($55 for international students). Electronic applications accepted. *Expenses:* Tuition, state resident: full-time $7839; part-time $323 per quarter hour. Tuition, nonresident: full-time $15,831; part-time $654 per quarter hour. Required fees: $2931. *Financial support:* Research assistantships, Federal Work-Study, institutionally sponsored loans, and unspecified assistantships available. Financial award application deadline: 3/1. *Unit head:* Mary Bowen, Director, 740-593-9134, E-mail: bowenm2@ohio.edu. *Application contact:* Cheryl Branham, Administrative Associate, 740-593-4494, E-mail: branhamc@ohio.edu.

Oklahoma City University, Kramer School of Nursing, Oklahoma City, OK 73106-1402. Offers MSN, DNP, PhD. *Accreditation:* NLN. *Faculty:* 2 full-time (both women), 3 part-time/adjunct (2 women). *Students:* 15 full-time (14 women), 24 part-time (21 women); includes 11 minority (5 African Americans, 4 American Indian/Alaska Native, 1 Asian American or Pacific Islander, 1 Hispanic American), 2 international. Average age 44. 26 applicants, 100% accepted, 19 enrolled. In 2009, 4 master's awarded. *Degree requirements:* For master's, thesis; for doctorate, comprehensive exam, thesis/dissertation. *Entrance requirements:* For master's, registered nurse licensure, minimum undergraduate GPA of 3.0, BSN from nationally accredited nursing program, completion of courses in health assessment and statistics. Additional exam requirements/recommendations for international students: Required—TOEFL (minimum score 550 paper-based). *Application deadline:* For fall admission, 8/20 for domestic students; for spring admission, 1/6 for domestic students. Applications are processed on a rolling basis. Application fee: $50 ($70 for international students). *Expenses:* Tuition: Full-time $15,930; part-time $885 per hour. *Financial support:* Applicants required to submit FAFSA. *Unit head:* Dr. Marvel L. Williamson, Dean, 405-208-5900, Fax: 405-208-5914, E-mail: mwilliamson@okcu.edu. *Application contact:* Michelle Lockhart, Director, Admissions, 405-208-5340, Fax: 405-208-5916, E-mail: gadmissions@okcu.edu.

Old Dominion University, College of Health Sciences, Doctor of Nursing Practice Program, Norfolk, VA 23529. Offers DNP. Part-time programs available. Postbaccalaureate distance learning degree programs offered (minimal on-campus study). *Faculty:* 10 full-time (9 women), 3 part-time/adjunct (all women). *Students:* 19 full-time (18 women), 22 part-time (21 women); includes 6 minority (4 African Americans, 1 American Indian/Alaska Native, 1 Hispanic American), 1 international. Average age 46. 50 applicants, 94% accepted. *Degree requirements:* For doctorate, comprehensive exam. *Entrance requirements:* For doctorate, GRE, MAT. Additional exam requirements/recommendations for international students: Required—TOEFL. *Application deadline:* For spring admission, 11/15 priority date for domestic students. Application fee: $50. Electronic applications accepted. *Expenses:* Tuition, state resident: full-time $8112; part-time $338 per credit. Tuition, nonresident: full-time $20,256; part-time $844 per credit. Required fees: $119 per semester. One-time fee: $50. *Financial support:* In 2009–10, 2 students received support, including 2 fellowships with full tuition reimbursements available (averaging $15,000 per year); scholarships/grants, traineeships, and unspecified assistantships also available. *Faculty research:* Cultural competency, sleep disorders, self-care in HIV positive African-American women, ethical decision making in pediatric cases. *Unit head:* Dr. Laurel S. Garzon, Graduate Program Director, 757-683-5250, Fax: 757-683-5253, E-mail: lgarzon@odu.edu. *Application contact:* Rosa Herron, Administrative Assistant, 757-683-5068, Fax: 757-683-5124, E-mail: rherron@odu.edu.

Old Dominion University, College of Health Sciences, School of Nursing, Norfolk, VA 23529. Offers family nurse practitioner (MSN); nurse anesthesia (MSN); nurse educator (MSN); nurse midwifery (MSN); women's health nurse practitioner (MSN). *Accreditation:* AACN; AANA/CANAEP. Part-time programs available. Postbaccalaureate distance learning degree programs offered (no on-campus study). *Faculty:* 11 full-time (10 women), 15 part-time/adjunct (14 women). *Students:* 122 full-time (113 women), 101 part-time (97 women); includes 49 minority (23 African Americans, 2 American Indian/Alaska Native, 19 Asian Americans or Pacific Islanders, 5 Hispanic Americans). Average age 37. 169 applicants, 81% accepted, 122 enrolled. In 2009, 77 master's awarded. *Degree requirements:* For master's, comprehensive exam. *Entrance requirements:* For master's, GRE or MAT, BSN, minimum GPA of 3.0 in nursing and overall. Additional exam requirements/recommendations for international students: Required—TOEFL. *Application deadline:* For fall admission, 5/1 for domestic students. Applications are processed on a rolling basis. Application fee: $40. Electronic applications accepted. *Expenses:* Tuition, state resident: full-time $8112; part-time $338 per credit. Tuition, nonresident: full-time $20,256; part-time $844 per credit. Required fees: $119 per semester. One-time fee: $50. *Financial support:* In 2009–10, 18 students received support, including 2 research assistantships with tuition reimbursements available (averaging $10,000 per year); teaching assistantships, career-related internships or fieldwork, scholarships/grants, traineeships, and tuition waivers (partial) also available. Support available to part-time students. Financial award application deadline: 2/15; financial award applicants required to submit FAFSA. *Faculty research:* Health and culture, cardiovascular health, transition of military families, genetics, cultural diversity. Total annual research expenditures: $231,117. *Unit head:* Dr. Karen Karlowicz, Chair, 757-683-5262, Fax: 757-683-5253, E-mail: nursgpd@odu.edu. *Application contact:* Sue Parker, Coordinator, Graduate Student Services, 757-683-4298, Fax: 757-683-5253, E-mail: sparker@odu.edu.

Oregon Health & Science University, School of Nursing, Portland, OR 97239-3098. Offers MN, MPH, MS, DNP, PhD, Post Master's Certificate. *Accreditation:* AACN; ACNM/DOA (one or more programs are accredited). Part-time programs available. *Degree requirements:* For master's, thesis optional; for doctorate, thesis/dissertation. *Entrance requirements:* For master's, GRE General Test, bachelor's degree in nursing, minimum undergraduate GPA of 3.0, previous course work in statistics; for doctorate, GRE General Test, master's degree in nursing; minimum undergraduate GPA of 3.0, 3.5 graduate; for Post Master's Certificate, master's degree in nursing. Electronic applications accepted. *Expenses:* Contact institution. *Faculty research:* Nursing care of older persons; families in health, illness, and transition; family caregiving; end of life care/decision making; mother-infant interactions; pregnancy outcomes; enteral feeding; psychoactive drugs in long-term care.

Otterbein University, Department of Nursing, Westerville, OH 43081. Offers adult nurse practitioner (MSN, Certificate); clinical nurse leader (MSN); family nurse practitioner (MSN, Certificate); nurse service administration (MSN). *Accreditation:* AACN; NLN. Part-time and evening/weekend programs available. Postbaccalaureate distance learning degree programs offered (minimal on-campus study). *Degree requirements:* For master's, comprehensive exam (for some programs), thesis (for some programs). *Entrance requirements:* For master's, 2 reference forms, resume; for Certificate, official transcripts, 2 reference forms, essay, resumé. Additional exam requirements/recommendations for international students: Required—TOEFL (minimum score 550 paper-based; 213 computer-based; 79 iBT). *Faculty research:* Patient education, women's health, trauma curriculum development, administration.

Our Lady of the Lake College, School of Nursing, Baton Rouge, LA 70808. Offers nurse anesthesia (MS); nursing (MS), including administration, education. *Accreditation:* NLN.

Pace University, Lienhard School of Nursing, New York, NY 10038. Offers family nurse practitioner (MS); nursing education (MA); nursing leadership (Advanced Certificate); nursing practice (DNP). *Accreditation:* AACN. Part-time and evening/weekend programs available. *Faculty:* 9 full-time (all women), 18 part-time/adjunct (14 women). *Students:* 41 full-time (37 women), 333 part-time (303 women); includes 140 minority (63 African Americans, 41 Asian Americans or Pacific Islanders, 36 Hispanic Americans), 12 international. Average age 36. 459 applicants, 66% accepted, 125 enrolled. In 2009, 79 master's, 3 other advanced degrees awarded. *Degree requirements:* For master's, thesis. *Entrance requirements:* For master's, GRE General Test or MAT, RN license, resume, personal statement, 2 letters of recommendation, official transcripts; for doctorate, RN license, resume, personal statement, 2 letters of recommendation, official transcripts, accredited master's degree in nursing, minimum GPA of 3.3, advanced experience, state certification; for Advanced Certificate, RN license, completion of 2nd degree in nursing. Additional exam requirements/recommendations for international students: Required—TOEFL. *Application deadline:* For fall admission, 7/31 priority date for domestic students, 4/30 priority date for international students; for spring admission, 10/14 for domestic students, 9/14 for international students. Applications are processed on a rolling basis. Application fee: $70. Electronic applications accepted. *Expenses:* Contact institution. *Financial support:* Research assistantships, career-related internships or fieldwork, Federal Work-Study, and tuition waivers (partial) available. Support available to part-time students. Financial award applicants required to submit FAFSA. *Unit head:* Dr. Harriet Feldman, Dean, 914-773-3341. *Application contact:* Joanna Broda, Director of Graduate Admissions, 914-422-4283, Fax: 914-422-4287, E-mail: gradwp@pace.edu.

Pacific Lutheran University, Division of Graduate Studies, School of Nursing, Tacoma, WA 98447. Offers MSN. *Accreditation:* AACN. Part-time and evening/weekend programs available. *Degree requirements:* For master's, thesis or alternative. *Entrance requirements:* For master's, GRE General Test, minimum undergraduate GPA of 3.0. Additional exam requirements/recommendations for international students: Required—TOEFL (minimum score 550 paper-based; 213 computer-based).

Penn State University Park, Graduate School, College of Health and Human Development, School of Nursing, State College, University Park, PA 16802-1503. Offers MS, PhD. *Accreditation:* AACN; NLN.

Pittsburg State University, Graduate School, College of Arts and Sciences, Department of Nursing, Pittsburg, KS 66762. Offers MSN. *Accreditation:* AACN. *Entrance requirements:* For master's, GRE General Test. *Expenses:* Tuition, state resident: full-time $4212; part-time $176 per credit. Tuition, nonresident: full-time $11,530; part-time $480 per credit. Required fees: $940; $43 per credit. Tuition and fees vary according to course level, course load, degree level, campus/location, reciprocity agreements and student level.

Point Loma Nazarene University, Program in Nursing, San Diego, CA 92106-2899. Offers MSN, Post-MSN Certificate. *Accreditation:* AACN. Part-time programs available. *Faculty:* 9 full-time (8 women). *Students:* 39 full-time (34 women), 8 part-time (7 women); includes 17 minority (4 African Americans, 11 Asian Americans or Pacific Islanders, 2 Hispanic Americans). Average age 40. In 2009, 10 master's awarded. *Entrance requirements:* For master's, MAT, BS in nursing, interview, minimum GPA of 3.0, RN license. *Application deadline:* Applications are processed on a rolling basis. Application fee: $35. *Unit head:* Dr. Barb Taylor, Dean of the School of Nursing, 619-849-2766, E-mail: bataylor@pointloma.edu. *Application contact:* Lauren Kaplan, Graduate Admissions Enrollment Counselor, 619-563-2821, E-mail: laurenkaplan@pointloma.edu.

Pontifical Catholic University of Puerto Rico, College of Sciences, Department of Nursing, Ponce, PR 00717-0777. Offers medical-surgical nursing (MS); mental health and psychiatric nursing (MS). *Accreditation:* NLN. Part-time and evening/weekend programs available. *Degree requirements:* For master's, comprehensive exam (for some programs), thesis, clinical research paper. *Entrance requirements:* For master's, GRE General Test, 2 letters of recommendation, interview, minimum GPA of 2.5. Electronic applications accepted.

Prairie View A&M University, College of Nursing, Houston, TX 77030. Offers family nurse practitioner (MSN); nursing administration (MSN); nursing education (MSN). *Accreditation:* AACN; NLN. Part-time programs available. *Faculty:* 6 full-time (all women), 6 part-time/adjunct (all women). *Students:* 100 part-time (93 women); includes 82 minority (74 African Americans, 1 American Indian/Alaska Native, 4 Asian Americans or Pacific Islanders, 3 Hispanic Americans), 7 international. Average age 37. 37 applicants, 100% accepted, 32 enrolled. In 2009, 7 master's awarded. *Degree requirements:* For master's, comprehensive exam, thesis. *Entrance requirements:* For master's, MAT or GRE, BS in nursing; 2 years of experience as a registered nurse; 1 course each in statistics, basic health and assessment. *Application deadline:* For fall admission, 6/1 priority date for domestic students; for spring admission, 11/1 priority date for domestic students. Applications are processed on a rolling basis. Application fee: $50. *Expenses:* Tuition, state resident: full-time $2200. Tuition, nonresident: full-time $5600. Required fees: $1720. Tuition and fees vary according to course load. *Financial support:* In 2009–10, 17 students received support. Career-related internships or fieldwork, Federal Work-Study, institutionally sponsored loans, scholarships/grants, and traineeships available. Support available to part-time students. Financial award application deadline: 4/1; financial award applicants required to submit FAFSA. *Faculty research:* Software development and violence prevention, health promotion and disease prevention. Total annual research expenditures: $350,000. *Unit head:* Dr. Betty N. Adams, Dean, 713-797-7009, Fax: 713-797-7013, E-mail: bnadams@pvamu.edu. *Application contact:* Dr. Forest Smith, Director of Student Services and Admissions, 713-797-7031, Fax: 713-797-7012, E-mail: pcwillson@pvamu.edu.

Purdue University Calumet, Graduate School, School of Nursing, Hammond, IN 46323-2094. Offers MS. *Accreditation:* NLN. Part-time programs available. Postbaccalaureate distance learning degree programs offered (minimal on-campus study). *Entrance requirements:* For master's, BSN. Additional exam requirements/recommendations for international students: Required—TOEFL. Electronic applications accepted. *Faculty research:* Adult health, cardiovascular and pulmonary nursing.

Queen's University at Kingston, School of Graduate Studies and Research, Faculty of Health Sciences, School of Nursing, Kingston, ON K7L 3N6, Canada. Offers health and chronic illness (M Sc); nurse scientist (PhD); primary health care nurse practitioner (Certificate); women's and children's health (M Sc). *Degree requirements:* For master's, thesis. *Entrance requirements:* For master's, RN license. Additional exam requirements/recommendations for international students: Required—TOEFL. *Faculty research:* Women and children's health, health and chronic illness.

Queens University of Charlotte, Presbyterian School of Nursing, Charlotte, NC 28274-0002. Offers nursing management (MSN). *Accreditation:* AACN. *Degree requirements:* For master's, research project. *Entrance requirements:* For master's, minimum GPA of 3.0. Additional exam requirements/recommendations for international students: Required—TOEFL. Electronic applications accepted. *Expenses:* Contact institution.

Quinnipiac University, School of Health Sciences, Nursing Program, Hamden, CT 06518-1940. Offers adult nurse practitioner (MSN, Post Master's Certificate); family nurse practitioner (MSN, Post Master's Certificate). Part-time programs available. *Faculty:* 7 full-time (5 women), 8 part-time/adjunct (4 women). *Students:* 35 full-time (31 women), 85 part-time (78 women); includes 22 minority (8 African Americans, 8 Asian Americans or Pacific Islanders, 6 Hispanic Americans), 1 international. 57 applicants, 77% accepted, 40 enrolled. In 2009, 33 master's awarded. *Degree requirements:* For master's, thesis optional, clinical practicum. *Entrance requirements:* For master's, RN license, minimum GPA of 3.0. Additional exam requirements/recommendations for international students: Required—TOEFL (minimum score 575 paper-

based; 233 computer-based; 90 iBT), IELTS (minimum score 6.5). *Application deadline:* For fall admission, 5/15 priority date for domestic students, 4/30 priority date for international students; for spring admission, 12/1 priority date for domestic students, 9/15 priority date for international students. Applications are processed on a rolling basis. Application fee: $45. Electronic applications accepted. *Expenses:* Tuition: Full-time $16,030; part-time $770 per credit. Required fees: $630; $35 per credit. *Financial support:* Traineeships, tuition waivers (partial), and unspecified assistantships available. Support available to part-time students. Financial award application deadline: 4/15; financial award applicants required to submit FAFSA. *Unit head:* Dr. Jeanne LeVasseur, Director of Graduate Admissions, 203-582-3484, Fax: 203-582-3230, E-mail: jeanne.levasseur@quinnipiac.edu. *Application contact:* Kristin Parent, Assistant Director of Graduate Health Sciences Admissions, 800-462-1944, Fax: 203-582-3443, E-mail: kristin.parent@quinnipiac.edu.

Radford University, College of Graduate and Professional Studies, Waldron College of Health and Human Services, School of Nursing, Radford, VA 24142. Offers adult clinical nurse specialist (MSN); family nurse practitioner (MSN); gerontology clinical nurse specialist (MSN); nurse midwifery (MSN). *Accreditation:* AACN. Part-time programs available. *Faculty:* 15 full-time (14 women), 3 part-time/adjunct (2 women). *Students:* 15 full-time (all women), 17 part-time (all women); includes 1 minority (Asian American or Pacific Islander). Average age 35. 17 applicants, 76% accepted, 8 enrolled. In 2009, 11 master's awarded. *Degree requirements:* For master's, comprehensive exam, thesis optional. *Entrance requirements:* For master's, GRE, minimum GPA of 3.0; 3 letters of reference from professional contacts, letter of intent, resume. Additional exam requirements/recommendations for international students: Required—TOEFL (minimum score 550 paper-based; 213 computer-based; 79 iBT). *Application deadline:* For fall admission, 2/1 priority date for domestic students, 12/1 for international students. Applications are processed on a rolling basis. Application fee: $50. Electronic applications accepted. *Expenses:* Tuition, state resident: full-time $5086; part-time $211 per credit hour. Tuition, nonresident: full-time $12,608; part-time $525 per credit hour. Required fees: $2508; $105 per credit hour. *Financial support:* In 2009–10, 5 students received support, including 4 teaching assistantships with partial tuition reimbursements available (averaging $8,700 per year); career-related internships or fieldwork, Federal Work-Study, institutionally sponsored loans, scholarships/grants, and unspecified assistantships also available. Financial award application deadline: 3/1; financial award applicants required to submit FAFSA. *Unit head:* Dr. Kimberly F. Carter, Director, 540-831-7700, Fax: 540-831-7716, E-mail: kcarter@radford.edu. *Application contact:* Graduate Admissions, 540-831-5431, Fax: 540-831-6061, E-mail: gradcollege@radford.edu.

Ramapo College of New Jersey, Master of Science in Nursing Program, Mahwah, NJ 07430. Offers nursing education (MSN). *Accreditation:* NLN. Part-time programs available. Postbaccalaureate distance learning degree programs offered (minimal on-campus study). *Faculty:* 7 part-time/adjunct (5 women). *Students:* 34 full-time (32 women), 4 part-time (all women); includes 6 minority (4 African Americans, 2 Asian Americans or Pacific Islanders). Average age 42. 30 applicants, 100% accepted, 12 enrolled. In 2009, 16 master's awarded. *Degree requirements:* For master's, capstone project. *Entrance requirements:* For master's, minimum GPA of 3.0, current RN licensure, 2 letters of recommendation. Additional exam requirements/recommendations for international students: Required—TOEFL (minimum score 550 paper-based; 213 computer-based; 95 iBT). *Application deadline:* Applications are processed on a rolling basis. Application fee: $60. *Expenses:* Tuition, state resident: part-time $525.30 per credit. Tuition, nonresident: part-time $675.20 per credit. Required fees: $53.55 per credit. *Financial support:* In 2009–10, 10 students received support, including 10 fellowships with partial tuition reimbursements available (averaging $1,992 per year); traineeships also available. Financial award applicants required to submit FAFSA. *Unit head:* Dr. Kathleen M. Burke, Assistant Dean, 201-684-7737, E-mail: kmburke@ramapo.edu. *Application contact:* Ulysses Simpkins, Program Assistant, 201-684-7749, E-mail: usimpkin@ramapo.edu.

Regis College, School of Nursing and Health Professions, Weston, MA 02493. Offers health administration (MS); nurse educator (Certificate); nurse practitioner (Certificate); nursing (MS, DNP). *Accreditation:* NLN. Part-time and evening/weekend programs available. *Faculty:* 18 full-time (all women), 12 part-time/adjunct (all women). *Students:* 158 full-time (147 women), 324 part-time (299 women); includes 50 minority (29 African Americans, 1 American Indian/Alaska Native, 15 Asian Americans or Pacific Islanders, 5 Hispanic Americans). Average age 38. 320 applicants, 63% accepted, 155 enrolled. In 2009, 47 master's, 7 other advanced degrees awarded. *Degree requirements:* For master's, thesis. *Entrance requirements:* For master's, GRE General Test or MAT, minimum GPA of 3.0; for doctorate, MAT or GRE if GPA from master's lower than 3.5. Additional exam requirements/recommendations for international students: Required—TOEFL (minimum score 550 paper-based; 213 computer-based). *Application deadline:* Applications are processed on a rolling basis. Application fee: $50. Electronic applications accepted. *Expenses:* Tuition: Full-time $29,000; part-time $800 per credit. Tuition and fees vary according to course load, degree level and program. *Financial support:* In 2009–10, 28 students received support, including 13 research assistantships; Federal Work-Study, scholarships/grants, traineeships, and unspecified assistantships also available. Support available to part-time students. Financial award applicants required to submit FAFSA. *Faculty research:* Health policy, education, aging, job satisfaction, psychiatric nursing, critical thinking. *Unit head:* Dr. Antoinette Hays, Dean, 781-768-7091, Fax: 781-768-8339, E-mail: antoinette.hays@regiscollege.edu. *Application contact:* Christine Petherick, Administrative Coordinator, Graduate Admission, 866-438-7344, Fax: 781-768-7071, E-mail: christine.petherick@regiscollege.edu.

Regis University, Rueckert-Hartman School for Health Professions, Denver, CO 80221-1099. Offers clinical leadership for physician assistants (MS); family nurse practitioner (MSN); health informatics (Postbaccalaureate Certificate); health services administration (MS); healthcare education (Certificate); leadership in healthcare systems (MSN); neonatal nurse practitioner (MSN); nursing (MSN); pharmacy (Pharm D); physical therapy (DPT, TDPT). *Entrance requirements:* Additional exam requirements/recommendations for international students: Required—TOEFL (minimum score 550 paper-based; 213 computer-based; 82 iBT). Electronic applications accepted. *Expenses:* Contact institution. *Faculty research:* Normal and pathological balance and gait research, normal/pathological upper limb motor control/biomechanics, exercise energy/metabolism research, optical treatment protocols for therapeutic modalities.

Research College of Nursing, Nursing Program, Kansas City, MO 64132. Offers executive nurse practitioner (MSN); family nurse practitioner (MSN); nursing education (MSN). *Accreditation:* AACN. Part-time programs available. Postbaccalaureate distance learning degree programs offered (no on-campus study). *Degree requirements:* For master's, research project. *Entrance requirements:* For master's, minimum GPA of 3.0, interview, 3 letters of recommendation. Additional exam requirements/recommendations for international students: Required—TOEFL (minimum score 550 paper-based; 213 computer-based), TWE. *Expenses:* Tuition: Part-time $400 per credit hour. Required fees: $25 per credit hour. $50 per semester.

Rhode Island College, School of Graduate Studies, School of Nursing, Providence, RI 02908-1991. Offers MSN. *Accreditation:* AACN. Part-time programs available. *Faculty:* 6 full-time (all women), 5 part-time/adjunct (all women). *Students:* 41 part-time (37 women); includes 3 minority (2 African Americans, 1 Hispanic American). Average age 46. *Entrance requirements:* For master's, GRE, undergraduate transcripts; minimum undergraduate GPA of 3.0; 3 letters of recommendation; evidence of current unrestricted Rhode Island RN licensure; professional resume; letter of intent. Additional exam requirements/recommendations for international students: Recommended—TOEFL (minimum score 550 paper-based; 213 computer-based; 79 iBT). *Application deadline:* For fall admission, 2/15 for domestic students. Applications are processed on a rolling basis. Application fee: $50. *Expenses:* Tuition, state resident: full-time $7440; part-time $310 per credit hour. Tuition, nonresident: full-time $14,784; part-time $616 per credit hour. Required fees: $552; $20 per credit. $70 per term. *Financial support:* In 2009–10, 1 teaching assistantship with full tuition reimbursement (averaging $4,550 per year) was awarded; Federal Work-Study, scholarships/grants, health care benefits, and unspecified assistantships also available. Support available to part-time students. Financial award application deadline: 5/15; financial award applicants required to submit FAFSA. *Unit head:* Dr. Jane Williams, Dean, 401-456-8013, Fax: 401-456-9608, E-mail: jwilliams@ric.edu. *Application contact:* Graduate Studies, 401-456-8700.

The Richard Stockton College of New Jersey, School of Graduate and Continuing Education, Program in Nursing, Pomona, NJ 08240-0195. Offers MSN. *Accreditation:* AACN. Part-time programs available. *Degree requirements:* For master's, 300 clinical hours. *Entrance requirements:* For master's, GRE General Test, CPR certification, minimum GPA of 3.0, RN license. Additional exam requirements/recommendations for international students: Required—TOEFL. *Expenses:* Tuition, state resident: part-time $497.36 per credit hour. Tuition, nonresident: part-time $765.61 per credit hour. Required fees: $129.12 per credit hour. Tuition and fees vary according to degree level. *Faculty research:* Psychoneuroimmunology, relationship of nutrition and disease, mental health as affected by chronic disease states, home care for elderly relatives.

Rivier College, School of Graduate Studies, Division of Nursing, Nashua, NH 03060. Offers family nurse practitioner (MS); nursing education (MS). *Accreditation:* NLN. Part-time and evening/weekend programs available. *Faculty:* 4 full-time (3 women). *Students:* 4 full-time (3 women), 37 part-time (36 women); includes 4 minority (1 African American, 2 Asian Americans or Pacific Islanders, 1 Hispanic American). Average age 36. 29 applicants, 52% accepted, 4 enrolled. In 2009, 12 master's awarded. *Entrance requirements:* For master's, GRE, MAT. *Application deadline:* Applications are processed on a rolling basis. Application fee: $25. Electronic applications accepted. *Expenses:* Tuition: Part-time $447 per credit. *Financial support:* Available to part-time students. Application deadline: 2/1. *Unit head:* Dr. Paula Williams, Head, 603-897-8529. *Application contact:* Mathew Kittredge, Director of Graduate Admissions, 603-897-8129, Fax: 603-897-8810, E-mail: mkittredge@rivier.edu.

Robert Morris University, Graduate Studies, School of Nursing and Health Sciences, Moon Township, PA 15108-1189. Offers MS, DNP. *Accreditation:* AACN. Part-time and evening/weekend programs available. *Faculty:* 7 full-time (3 women), 4 part-time/adjunct (3 women). *Students:* 159 part-time (140 women); includes 10 minority (5 African Americans, 3 Asian Americans or Pacific Islanders, 2 Hispanic Americans), 2 international. Average age 38. 87 applicants, 100% accepted, 70 enrolled. In 2009, 10 master's awarded. *Entrance requirements:* For master's, letters of recommendation. Additional exam requirements/recommendations for international students: Required—TOEFL (minimum score 550 paper-based; 213 computer-based; 79 iBT). *Application deadline:* For fall admission, 7/1 priority date for domestic and international students; for spring admission, 11/1 priority date for domestic and international students. Applications are processed on a rolling basis. Application fee: $35. Electronic applications accepted. *Expenses:* Contact institution. *Financial support:* Federal Work-Study, institutionally sponsored loans, and unspecified assistantships available. Financial award application deadline: 5/1; financial award applicants required to submit FAFSA. *Unit head:* Dr. Lynda J. Davidson, Dean, 412-397-3859, Fax: 412-397-3277, E-mail: davidson@rmu.edu. *Application contact:* Deborah Roach, Assistant Dean, Graduate Admissions, 412-397-5200, Fax: 412-397-2425, E-mail: graduateadmissions@rmu.edu.

Roberts Wesleyan College, Division of Nursing, Rochester, NY 14624-1997. Offers nursing administration (MSN); nursing education (MSN). *Accreditation:* AACN. *Entrance requirements:* For master's, minimum GPA of 3.0; BS in nursing; interview; RN license; resume; course work in statistics and health assessment. Additional exam requirements/recommendations for international students: Required—TOEFL.

Rush University, College of Nursing, Chicago, IL 60612-3832. Offers MSN, DNP, PhD, Post-Master's Certificate. *Accreditation:* AACN; AANA/CANAEP (one or more programs are accredited). Part-time programs available. Postbaccalaureate distance learning degree programs offered (minimal on-campus study). Terminal master's awarded for partial completion of doctoral program. *Degree requirements:* For master's, capstone project; for doctorate, thesis/dissertation, DNP leadership project. *Entrance requirements:* For master's, GRE General Test (waived if nursing GPA is greater than 3.0 or cumulative GPA is greater than 3.25), interview; for doctorate, GRE General Test. Additional exam requirements/recommendations for international students: Required—TOEFL, TWE. Electronic applications accepted. *Faculty research:* Parenting intervention, immigrant mental health, caregiver interventions, immune function, cardiac risk reduction.

Rutgers, The State University of New Jersey, Newark, Graduate School, Program in Nursing, Newark, NJ 07102. Offers nursing (MS), including acute care of adults and aged, advanced practice in pediatric nursing, advanced practice with childbearing families, community health nursing, family nurse practitioner, primary care of adults and aged, psychiatric/mental health nursing. *Accreditation:* AACN. Part-time programs available. *Degree requirements:* For master's, comprehensive exam. *Entrance requirements:* For master's, GRE General Test, RN license, minimum B average, BS in nursing. Additional exam requirements/recommendations for international students: Required—TOEFL. Electronic applications accepted. *Faculty research:* HIV/AIDS, quality of life—MS and breast cancer, sleep patterns of cardiac patients.

Sacred Heart University, Graduate Programs, College of Education and Health Professions, Department of Nursing, Fairfield, CT 06825-1000. Offers clinical nurse leader (MSN); clinical practice in health care (DNP); family nurse practitioner (MSN); leadership in health care (DNP); nursing (DN Sc); patient care services administration (MSN). *Accreditation:* AACN. Part-time and evening/weekend programs available. Postbaccalaureate distance learning degree programs offered (minimal on-campus study). *Faculty:* 12 full-time (all women). *Students:* 7 full-time (6 women), 155 part-time (146 women); includes 27 minority (9 African Americans, 11 Asian Americans or Pacific Islanders, 7 Hispanic Americans), 1 international. Average age 39. 72 applicants, 93% accepted, 28 enrolled. In 2009, 13 master's awarded. *Entrance requirements:* For master's, BSN, minimum GPA of 3.0. Additional exam requirements/recommendations for international students: Required—TOEFL (minimum score 550 paper-based; 213 computer-based). *Application deadline:* Applications are processed on a rolling basis. Application fee: $50 ($100 for international students). Electronic applications accepted. *Expenses:* Contact institution. *Financial support:* Career-related internships or fieldwork, institutionally sponsored loans, and unspecified assistantships available. Support available to part-time students. Financial award applicants required to submit FAFSA. *Unit head:* Dr. Dori Sullivan, Chair, 203-371-7715. *Application contact:* Kathy Dilks, Assistant Dean of Graduate Admissions, Health Professions, 203-396-8259, Fax: 203-365-4732, E-mail: gradstudies@sacredheart.edu.

Sage Graduate School, Graduate School, School of Health Sciences, Department of Nursing, Troy, NY 12180-4115. Offers adult health (MS); adult nurse practitioner (MS, Post Master's Certificate); clinical nurse leader/specialist (Post Master's Certificate); community health (MS); education and leadership (DNS); family nurse practitioner (MS, Post Master's Certificate); gerontological nurse practitioner (Post Master's Certificate); nurse administrator/executive (Post Master's Certificate); nursing (Post Master's Certificate); psychiatric mental health nurse practitioner (MS, Post Master's Certificate), including psychiatric mental health. *Accreditation:* AACN. Part-time and evening/weekend programs available. *Faculty:* 5 full-time (all women), 8 part-time/adjunct (all women). *Students:* 23 full-time (22 women), 134 part-time (129 women); includes 16 minority (6 African Americans, 1 American Indian/Alaska Native, 8 Asian Americans or Pacific Islanders, 1 Hispanic American), 1 international. Average age 42. 97 applicants, 64% accepted, 49 enrolled. In 2009, 25 master's, 3 other advanced degrees awarded. *Degree requirements:* For master's, thesis or alternative. *Entrance requirements:* For master's, BS in nursing, minimum GPA of 2.75, resume, 2 letters of recommendation. Additional exam requirements/recommendations for international students: Required—TOEFL (minimum score 550 paper-based; 213 computer-based). *Application deadline:* Applications are processed on a rolling basis. Application fee: $40. *Expenses:* Tuition: Full-time $10,620; part-time $590 per credit hour. *Financial support:* Fellowships, research assistantships, Federal Work-Study, scholarships/grants, and unspecified assistantships available. Support available to part-time students. Financial award application deadline: 3/1; financial award applicants required to submit FAFSA. *Unit head:* Dr. Glenda Kelman, Chair, 518-244-2001, E-mail: kelmag@sage.edu. *Application contact:* Wendy D. Diefendorf, Director of Graduate and Adult Admission, 518-244-2443, Fax: 518-244-6880, E-mail: diefew@sage.edu.

Nursing—General

Saginaw Valley State University, Crystal M. Lange College of Nursing and Health Sciences, Program in Clinical Nurse Specialist, University Center, MI 48710. Offers MSN. *Accreditation:* AACN. Part-time and evening/weekend programs available. *Students:* 2 part-time (both women). Average age 36. *Degree requirements:* For master's, thesis optional. *Entrance requirements:* For master's, GRE. Additional exam requirements/recommendations for international students: Required—TOEFL (minimum score 525 paper-based; 237 computer-based; 92 iBT). *Application deadline:* Applications are processed on a rolling basis. Application fee: $25. Electronic applications accepted. *Financial support:* Federal Work-Study and scholarships/grants available. Support available to part-time students. Financial award application deadline: 4/1; financial award applicants required to submit FAFSA. *Unit head:* Dr. Sally Decker, Professor of Nursing, 989-964-4098, E-mail: decker@svsu.edu. *Application contact:* Dr. Sally Decker, Professor of Nursing, 989-964-4098, E-mail: decker@svsu.edu.

Saginaw Valley State University, Crystal M. Lange College of Nursing and Health Sciences, Program in Nursing, University Center, MI 48710. Offers MSN. *Accreditation:* AACN. *Students:* 5 part-time (4 women); includes 1 minority (African American). Average age 41. 2 applicants, 100% accepted, 2 enrolled. *Financial support:* Federal Work-Study and scholarships/grants available. Support available to part-time students. *Unit head:* Dr. Sally Decker, Professor, 989-964-4098, E-mail: decker@svsu.edu. *Application contact:* Dr. Sally Decker, Professor, 989-964-4098, E-mail: decker@svsu.edu.

St. Ambrose University, College of Education and Health Sciences, Program in Nursing, Davenport, IA 52803-2898. Offers MSN. *Accreditation:* AACN. Part-time and evening/weekend programs available. *Faculty:* 1 (woman) full-time, 1 (woman) part-time/adjunct. *Students:* 16 part-time (all women). Average age 42. 14 applicants, 79% accepted, 10 enrolled. In 2009, 10 master's awarded. *Entrance requirements:* Additional exam requirements/recommendations for international students: Required—TOEFL. *Application deadline:* Applications are processed on a rolling basis. Application fee: $25. Electronic applications accepted. *Expenses:* Tuition: Part-time $702 per credit hour. Tuition and fees vary according to degree level, program and reciprocity agreements. *Financial support:* In 2009–10, 5 students received support. Career-related internships or fieldwork, scholarships/grants, tuition waivers (partial), and unspecified assistantships available. *Unit head:* Kathryn M. McKnight, Director, 563-333-6069, Fax: 563-333-6063, E-mail: mcknightkathrynm@sau.edu. *Application contact:* Laura R. Hudson, Academic Advisor and Recruiter, 563-333-6082, Fax: 563-333-6063, E-mail: hudsonlaurar@sau.edu.

Saint Anthony College of Nursing, Graduate Program, Rockford, IL 61108-2468. Offers MSN. *Accreditation:* AACN. Part-time programs available.

St. Catherine University, Graduate Programs, Program in Nursing, St. Paul, MN 55105. Offers MA, DNP. *Accreditation:* NLN. Part-time and evening/weekend programs available. *Faculty:* 9 full-time (8 women). *Students:* 54 full-time (50 women), 66 part-time (63 women); includes 8 minority (6 African Americans, 1 Asian American or Pacific Islander, 1 Hispanic American), 2 international. Average age 38. 108 applicants, 69% accepted, 54 enrolled. In 2009, 22 master's awarded. *Degree requirements:* For master's, thesis. *Entrance requirements:* For master's, GRE General Test, bachelor's degree in nursing, current nursing license, 2 years of recent clinical practice; for doctorate, master's degree in nursing, RN license, advanced nursing position. Additional exam requirements/recommendations for international students: Required—TOEFL (minimum score 600 paper-based; 250 computer-based; 100 iBT). *Application deadline:* For fall admission, 1/15 priority date for domestic students. Application fee: $35. Tuition and fees vary according to program. *Financial support:* In 2009–10, 61 students received support. Career-related internships or fieldwork and institutionally sponsored loans available. Support available to part-time students. Financial award application deadline: 4/1; financial award applicants required to submit FAFSA. *Unit head:* Alice Swan, Associate Dean, 651-690-6583, Fax: 651-690-6941. *Application contact:* 651-690-6933, Fax: 651-690-6064.

Saint Francis Medical Center College of Nursing, Graduate Program, Peoria, IL 61603-3783. Offers child and family nursing (MSN); clinical nurse leader (MSN); medical-surgical nursing (MSN); neonatal nurse practitioner (MSN); nurse clinician (Post-Graduate Certificate); nurse educator (Post-Graduate Certificate); nursing (DNP). *Accreditation:* NLN. Part-time programs available. Postbaccalaureate distance learning degree programs offered (minimal on-campus study). *Faculty:* 3 full-time (all women), 9 part-time/adjunct (all women). *Students:* 8 full-time (all women), 135 part-time (122 women); includes 6 minority (1 African American, 4 Asian Americans or Pacific Islanders, 1 Hispanic American). Average age 28. 19 applicants, 100% accepted, 19 enrolled. In 2009, 24 master's awarded. *Degree requirements:* For master's, research experience, portfolio, practicum. *Entrance requirements:* For master's, nursing research, health assessment, graduate course work in statistics, RN license. Additional exam requirements/recommendations for international students: Required—TOEFL. *Application deadline:* For fall admission, 6/1 priority date for domestic and international students; for spring admission, 11/15 priority date for domestic and international students. Applications are processed on a rolling basis. Application fee: $50. Electronic applications accepted. *Expenses:* Tuition: Part-time $472 per semester hour. Required fees: $130 per semester. *Financial support:* In 2009–10, 6 students received support. Scholarships/grants and tuition waivers (partial) available. Support available to part-time students. Financial award application deadline: 6/15; financial award applicants required to submit FAFSA. *Faculty research:* Outcome and curriculum planning, health promotion, NCLEX-RN results, decision making program evaluation. *Unit head:* Dr. Lois J. Hamilton, Dean, 309-655-2201, Fax: 309-624-8973, E-mail: lois.j.hamilton@osfhealthcare.org. *Application contact:* Dr. Janice F. Boundy, Associate Dean, 309-655-2230, Fax: 309-624-8973, E-mail: jan.f.boundy@osfhealthcare.org.

St. John Fisher College, Wegmans School of Nursing, Advanced Practice Nursing Program, Rochester, NY 14618-3597. Offers advanced practice nursing (MS); clinical nurse specialist (Certificate); family nurse practitioner (Certificate); nurse educator (Certificate). *Accreditation:* AACN. Part-time and evening/weekend programs available. *Faculty:* 9 full-time (all women). *Students:* 5 full-time (4 women), 88 part-time (83 women); includes 7 minority (all African Americans), 1 international. Average age 38. 60 applicants, 87% accepted, 30 enrolled. In 2009, 9 master's awarded. *Degree requirements:* For master's, clinical practice, project; for Certificate, clinical practice. *Entrance requirements:* For master's, BSN; undergraduate course work in statistics, health assessment, and nursing research; current New York State RN License; 2 letters of recommendation; current resume. Additional exam requirements/recommendations for international students: Required—TOEFL (minimum score 575 paper-based; 233 computer-based; 80 iBT). *Application deadline:* Applications are processed on a rolling basis. Application fee: $30. Electronic applications accepted. *Expenses:* Tuition: Part-time $680 per credit hour. Required fees: $25 per semester. Tuition and fees vary according to degree level and program. *Financial support:* In 2009–10, 64 students received support. Federal Work-Study, scholarships/grants, and traineeships available. Financial award applicants required to submit FAFSA. *Faculty research:* Chronic illness, pediatric injury, women's health, public health policy, health care teams. *Unit head:* Dr. Cynthia McCloskey, Graduate Director, 585-385-8471, Fax: 585-385-8466, E-mail: cmccloskey@sjfc.edu. *Application contact:* Jose Perales, Director of Graduate Admissions, 585-385-8067, E-mail: jperales@sjfc.edu.

St. John Fisher College, Wegmans School of Nursing, Doctor of Nursing Practice Program, Rochester, NY 14618-3597. Offers DNP. Part-time and evening/weekend programs available. *Faculty:* 9 full-time (all women), 1 (woman) part-time/adjunct. *Students:* 20 full-time (all women), 3 part-time (all women); includes 3 minority (2 African Americans, 1 Hispanic American). Average age 46. 10 applicants, 100% accepted, 9 enrolled. *Degree requirements:* For doctorate, 1,000 hours of clinical practice, clinical scholarship project. *Entrance requirements:* For doctorate, New York State RN License; New York State Certificate as advanced practice nurse or eligibility and National Professional Certification in advanced practice nurse (APN) specialty; currently practicing as APN; 2 letters of recommendation; writing sample. *Application deadline:* For fall admission, 8/1 for domestic students; for spring admission, 12/1 for domestic students. Applications are processed on a rolling basis. Application fee: $0. Electronic applications accepted. *Expenses:* Contact institution. *Financial support:* In 2009–10, 18 students received support. Scholarships/grants available. Financial award applicants required to submit FAFSA. *Unit head:* Dr. Mary S. Collins, Program Director, 585-385-8397, E-mail: mscollins@sjfc.edu. *Application contact:* Jose Perales, Director of Graduate Admissions, 585-385-8067, E-mail: jperales@sjfc.edu.

Saint Joseph College, Department of Nursing, West Hartford, CT 06117-2700. Offers MS. *Accreditation:* AACN. Part-time and evening/weekend programs available. *Students:* 5 full-time (4 women), 59 part-time (55 women); includes 16 minority (6 African Americans, 5 Asian Americans or Pacific Islanders, 5 Hispanic Americans). *Degree requirements:* For master's, thesis. *Entrance requirements:* For master's, 2 letters of recommendation. *Application deadline:* Applications are processed on a rolling basis. Application fee: $50. Electronic applications accepted. *Expenses:* Tuition: Part-time $595 per credit. Required fees: $30 per credit. Tuition and fees vary according to program. *Financial support:* Career-related internships or fieldwork and unspecified assistantships available. Support available to part-time students. Financial award applicants required to submit FAFSA. *Application contact:* Graduate Admissions Office, 860-231-5261, E-mail: graduate@sjc.edu.

St. Joseph's College, Long Island Campus, Program in Nursing, Patchogue, NY 11772-2399. Offers MS.

St. Joseph's College, New York, Graduate Programs, Program in Nursing, Brooklyn, NY 11205-3688. Offers MS. *Accreditation:* NLN.

See Close-Up on page 1617.

Saint Joseph's College of Maine, Department of Nursing, Standish, ME 04084. Offers nursing (MS); nursing administration and leadership (Certificate); nursing and health care education (Certificate). MS degree offered only through faculty-directed independent study. *Accreditation:* AACN. Part-time programs available. Postbaccalaureate distance learning degree programs offered (minimal on-campus study). *Degree requirements:* For master's, summer residency. *Entrance requirements:* For master's, MAT. Electronic applications accepted.

Saint Louis University, Graduate School, Doisy College of Health Sciences, School of Nursing, St. Louis, MO 63104-1099. Offers MSN, MSN-R, DNP, PhD, Certificate. *Accreditation:* AACN. Part-time programs available. Postbaccalaureate distance learning degree programs offered (minimal on-campus study). *Degree requirements:* For master's, comprehensive exam, thesis optional; for doctorate, comprehensive exam, thesis/dissertation, preliminary exams. *Entrance requirements:* For master's, 3 letters of recommendation, resumé, transcripts; for doctorate, GRE General Test, 3 letters of recommendation, curriculum vitae; for Certificate, 3 letters of recommendation, resumé, transcripts, copy of RN license, personal statement. Additional exam requirements/recommendations for international students: Required—TOEFL (minimum score 525 paper-based; 194 computer-based). Electronic applications accepted. *Faculty research:* Sensory enhancement to the elderly, fall prevention in elderly, tube feeding placement and gastroenterology, patient outcomes, exercise behavior in the older adult.

Saint Peter's College, School of Nursing, Nursing Program, Jersey City, NJ 07306-5997. Offers adult nurse practitioner (MSN); case management (MSN); nursing (DNP); RN to MSN bridge (MSN). *Accreditation:* AACN. Part-time and evening/weekend programs available. *Entrance requirements:* Additional exam requirements/recommendations for international students: Required—TOEFL. *Application deadline:* Applications are processed on a rolling basis. Electronic applications accepted. *Expenses:* Tuition: Part-time $971 per credit. *Financial support:* Federal Work-Study and institutionally sponsored loans available. *Unit head:* Dr. Ann Tritak, Director, 201-761-6270. *Application contact:* Dr. Ann Tritak, Director, 201-761-6270.

Saint Xavier University, Graduate Studies, School of Nursing, Chicago, IL 60655-3105. Offers adult health clinical nurse specialist (MS); family nurse practitioner (MS, PMC); leadership in community health nursing (MS); psychiatric-mental health clinical nurse specialist (MS); psychiatric-mental health clinical specialist (PMC); MBA/MS. *Accreditation:* AACN. Part-time and evening/weekend programs available. *Entrance requirements:* For master's, GRE General Test or MAT, minimum GPA of 3.0, RN license. *Expenses:* Tuition: Part-time $743 per credit hour. Required fees: $135 per semester.

Salem State College, School of Graduate Studies, Program in Nursing, Salem, MA 01970-5353. Offers direct entry nursing (MSN); MBA/MSN. *Accreditation:* AACN; NLN. Part-time and evening/weekend programs available. *Students:* 24 full-time (20 women), 70 part-time (67 women); includes 3 minority (1 African American, 1 Asian American or Pacific Islander, 1 Hispanic American), 4 international. Average age 39. 19 applicants, 89% accepted, 17 enrolled. In 2009, 20 master's awarded. *Entrance requirements:* For master's, GRE or MAT. Additional exam requirements/recommendations for international students: Required—TOEFL (minimum score 550 paper-based; 80 iBT), or IELTS (minimum score 5.5). *Application deadline:* For fall admission, 5/1 for domestic students; for spring admission, 10/1 for domestic students. Applications are processed on a rolling basis. Application fee: $50. *Expenses:* Tuition, state resident: full-time $2520; part-time $275 per credit hour. Tuition, nonresident: full-time $4140; part-time $365 per credit hour. Required fees: $2430. *Financial support:* In 2009–10, 40 students received support. Career-related internships or fieldwork, Federal Work-Study, scholarships/grants, and unspecified assistantships available. Support available to part-time students. Financial award application deadline: 5/1; financial award applicants required to submit FAFSA. *Unit head:* Kathleen Skrabat, Program Coordinator, 978-542-6075, Fax: 978-542-7215, E-mail: kskrabat@salemstate.edu. *Application contact:* Dr. Lee A. Brossoit, Assistant Dean of Graduate Admissions, 978-542-6675, Fax: 978-542-7215, E-mail: lbrossoit@salemstate.edu.

Salisbury University, Graduate Division, Program in Nursing, Salisbury, MD 21801-6837. Offers MS. *Accreditation:* AACN. Part-time programs available. *Faculty:* 6 full-time (all women), 1 (woman) part-time/adjunct. *Students:* 5 full-time (4 women), 22 part-time (20 women); includes 4 minority (2 African Americans, 1 Asian American or Pacific Islander, 1 Hispanic American). Average age 34. 24 applicants, 54% accepted, 5 enrolled. In 2009, 4 master's awarded. *Degree requirements:* For master's, thesis or capstone project. *Entrance requirements:* For master's, minimum GPA of 3.0, interview, resume, CPR certification, proof of immunizations. Additional exam requirements/recommendations for international students: Required—TOEFL (minimum score 550 paper-based; 213 computer-based). *Application deadline:* For fall admission, 2/15 for domestic students; for spring admission, 10/15 for domestic students. Applications are processed on a rolling basis. Application fee: $45. Electronic applications accepted. *Expenses:* Tuition, area resident: Part-time $278 per credit hour. Tuition, state resident: part-time $278 per credit hour. Tuition, nonresident: part-time $574 per credit hour. Required fees: $57 per credit hour. *Financial support:* In 2009–10, 8 students received support. Career-related internships or fieldwork, scholarships/grants, and unspecified assistantships available. Support available to part-time students. Financial award applicants required to submit FAFSA. *Faculty research:* Female health and maternity, adolescent health, family health, school health. *Unit head:* Dr. Mary Parsons, Director, 410-543-6416, Fax: 410-548-3313, E-mail: mtparsons@salisbury.edu. *Application contact:* Carmel Boger, Administrative Assistant, 410-543-6420, Fax: 410-548-3313, E-mail: ciboger@salisbury.edu.

Samford University, Ida V. Moffett School of Nursing, Birmingham, AL 35229. Offers advance practice (DNP); anesthesia (MSN); family nurse practitioner (MSN); nurse educator (MSN); nurse executive (DNP); nurse manager (MSN); MBA/MSN. *Accreditation:* AACN; AANA/CANAEP (one or more programs are accredited). Part-time programs available. Postbaccalaureate distance learning degree programs offered (minimal on-campus study). *Faculty:* 10 full-time (all women), 1 part-time/adjunct (0 women). *Students:* 149 full-time (102 women), 31 part-time (24 women); includes 21 minority (14 African Americans, 4 Asian Americans or Pacific Islanders, 3 Hispanic Americans), 1 international. Average age 31. 56 applicants, 98% accepted, 52 enrolled. In 2009, 58 master's awarded. *Degree requirements:* For master's and doctorate, capstone project with oral presentation. *Entrance requirements:* For master's, GRE General Test or MAT. Additional exam requirements/recommendations for international students: Required—TOEFL (minimum score 550 paper-based; 213 computer-based; 80 iBT). *Application deadline:* For fall admission, 7/1 priority date for domestic and international students; for spring admission, 11/1 priority date for domestic and international students. Applications are processed on a rolling basis. Application fee: $35. *Expenses:* Contact institution. *Financial support:* Institutionally sponsored loans, scholarships/grants, and traineeships available. Financial award

application deadline: 3/1; financial award applicants required to submit FAFSA. *Faculty research:* Issues in rural health care, vulnerable populations, genetics and disabilities in pediatrics, geriatrics, Parrish nursing research. *Unit head:* Dr. Nena F. Sanders, Dean, 205-726-2629, E-mail: nfsander@samford.edu. *Application contact:* Marian Carter, Director of Graduate Student Services, 205-726-2047, Fax: 205-726-4269, E-mail: mwcarter@samford.edu.

Samuel Merritt University, School of Nursing, Oakland, CA 94609-3108. Offers case management (MSN); family nurse practitioner (MSN, Certificate); nurse anesthetist (MSN, Certificate); nursing (MSN). *Accreditation:* AACN; AANA/CANAEP (one or more programs are accredited). Part-time and evening/weekend programs available. *Degree requirements:* For master's, thesis or alternative. *Entrance requirements:* For master's, minimum GPA of 2.5 in science, 3.0 overall; previous course work in statistics; current RN license. Additional exam requirements/recommendations for international students: Required—TOEFL. *Faculty research:* Gerontology, community health, maternal-child health, sexually transmitted diseases, substance abuse, oncology.

San Diego State University, Graduate and Research Affairs, College of Health and Human Services, School of Nursing, San Diego, CA 92182. Offers MS. *Accreditation:* AACN; ACNM/DOA. Part-time and evening/weekend programs available. *Entrance requirements:* For master's, GRE General Test, previous course work in statistics and physical assessment, 3 letters of recommendation, California RN license. Additional exam requirements/recommendations for international students: Required—TOEFL. Electronic applications accepted. *Faculty research:* Health promotion, nursing systems and leadership, maternal-child nursing, advanced practice nursing, child oral health.

San Francisco State University, Division of Graduate Studies, College of Health and Human Services, School of Nursing, San Francisco, CA 94132-1722. Offers case management (MS), including long-term care, primary care/family nurse practitioner; nursing administration (MS); nursing education (MS). *Accreditation:* AACN. Part-time programs available.

San Jose State University, Graduate Studies and Research, College of Applied Sciences and Arts, School of Nursing, San Jose, CA 95192-0001. Offers gerontology nurse practitioner (MS); nursing (Certificate); nursing administration (MS); nursing education (MS). *Accreditation:* AACN. Part-time and evening/weekend programs available. *Students:* 8 full-time (7 women), 45 part-time (42 women); includes 20 minority (3 African Americans, 2 American Indian/Alaska Native, 12 Asian Americans or Pacific Islanders, 3 Hispanic Americans), 2 international. Average age 43. 35 applicants, 40% accepted, 8 enrolled. In 2009, 24 master's awarded. *Degree requirements:* For master's, thesis. *Entrance requirements:* For master's, BS in nursing, RN license. *Application deadline:* For fall admission, 6/29 for domestic students; for spring admission, 11/30 for domestic students. Applications are processed on a rolling basis. Application fee: $59. Electronic applications accepted. *Financial support:* Career-related internships or fieldwork, institutionally sponsored loans, and scholarships/grants available. Support available to part-time students. Financial award applicants required to submit FAFSA. *Faculty research:* Nurse-managed clinics, computers in nursing. *Unit head:* Jayne Cohen, Director, 408-924-3132, Fax: 408-924-3135. *Application contact:* Dr. Phyllis Connolly, Graduate Coordinator, 408-924-3144.

Seattle Pacific University, MS in Nursing Program, Seattle, WA 98119-1997. Offers administration (MSN); adult/gerontology nurse practitioner (MSN); clinical nurse specialist (MSN); family nurse practitioner (MSN, Certificate); informatics (MSN); nurse educator (MSN). *Accreditation:* AACN. Part-time programs available. *Faculty:* 3 full-time (all women), 7 part-time/adjunct (6 women). *Students:* 9 full-time (8 women), 63 part-time (57 women); includes 9 minority (1 American Indian/Alaska Native, 7 Asian Americans or Pacific Islanders, 1 Hispanic American), 1 international. Average age 46. 60 applicants, 45% accepted, 27 enrolled. In 2009, 12 master's awarded. *Degree requirements:* For master's, thesis. *Application deadline:* For fall admission, 2/1 priority date for domestic students. Applications are processed on a rolling basis. Application fee: $50. Electronic applications accepted. *Expenses:* Contact institution. *Financial support:* In 2009–10, 41 students received support; fellowships, scholarships/grants available. Financial award applicants required to submit FAFSA. *Unit head:* Dr. Susan Casey, Director, 206-281-2769, Fax: 206-281-2767, E-mail: caseys@spu.edu. *Application contact:* The Grad Center, 206-281-2091.

Seattle University, College of Nursing, Program in Advanced Practice Nursing Immersion, Seattle, WA 98122-1090. Offers MSN.

Seattle University, College of Nursing, Program in Nursing, Seattle, WA 98122-1090. Offers leadership in community nursing (MSN), including program development, spirituality and health; primary care nurse practitioner (MSN), including family nurse practitioner, psychiatric mental health nurse practitioner.

Seton Hall University, College of Nursing, South Orange, NJ 07079-2697. Offers advanced practice in primary health care (MSN), including adult nurse practitioner, gerontological nurse practitioner, pediatric nurse practitioner; entry into practice (MSN); health systems administration (MSN, DNP); nursing (PhD); nursing case management (MSN); nursing education (MA); school nurse (MSN); MSN/MA. *Accreditation:* AACN. Part-time programs available. Postbaccalaureate distance learning degree programs offered (minimal on-campus study). *Faculty:* 10 full-time (all women), 3 part-time/adjunct (1 woman). *Students:* 46 full-time (35 women), 94 part-time (90 women); includes 22 minority (8 African Americans, 5 Asian Americans or Pacific Islanders, 9 Hispanic Americans). 92 applicants, 88% accepted, 55 enrolled. *Degree requirements:* For master's, research project; for doctorate, dissertation or scholarly project. *Entrance requirements:* For doctorate, GRE. Additional exam requirements/recommendations for international students: Required—TOEFL. *Application deadline:* For fall admission, 6/15 priority date for domestic students. Applications are processed on a rolling basis. Electronic applications accepted. *Financial support:* Institutionally sponsored loans, scholarships/grants, traineeships, tuition waivers (partial), and unspecified assistantships available. Support available to part-time students. Financial award applicants required to submit FAFSA. *Faculty research:* Parent/child, adult, and gerontological nursing; breast cancer; families of children with HIV; parish nursing. *Unit head:* Dr. Phyllis Shanley Hansell, Dean. *Application contact:* Kristyn Kent Wuillermin, Director of Strategic Alliances, Marketing and Enrollment, 973-761-9291, Fax: 973-761-9607, E-mail: kristyn.kent@shu.edu.

Shenandoah University, School of Health Professions, Division of Nursing, Winchester, VA 22601-5195. Offers family nurse practitioner (Certificate); nurse-midwifery (Certificate); nurse-midwifery endorsement (Certificate); nursing (MSN, DNP); post-master's in nursing education (Certificate); psychiatric mental health nurse practitioner (Certificate). *Accreditation:* AACN; ACNM/DOA. Part-time programs available. *Faculty:* 11 full-time (all women), 4 part-time/adjunct (all women). *Students:* 21 full-time (20 women), 67 part-time (64 women); includes 11 minority (7 African Americans, 2 Asian Americans or Pacific Islanders, 2 Hispanic Americans). Average age 39. 71 applicants, 97% accepted, 53 enrolled. In 2009, 8 master's, 6 other advanced degrees awarded. *Degree requirements:* For master's, research project, clinical hours; for doctorate and Certificate, clinical hours. *Entrance requirements:* For master's, GRE General Test, previous course work in statistics, community nursing, and physical assessment; RN license; BSN; minimum undergraduate GPA of 3.0; appropriate clinical experience; curriculum vitae; 3 letters of recommendation; for Certificate, MSN, minimum GPA of 3.0, 3 letters of recommendation. Additional exam requirements/recommendations for international students: Required—TOEFL (minimum score 550 paper-based; 213 computer-based; 79 iBT), IELTS (minimum score 6.5). *Application deadline:* For fall admission, 6/15 priority date for domestic and international students. Applications are processed on a rolling basis. Application fee: $30. Electronic applications accepted. *Expenses:* Tuition: Full-time $11,925; part-time $695 per credit. Required fees: $400 per semester. *Financial support:* Application deadline: 3/15. *Unit head:* Dr. Kathryn Ganske, Director, 540-678-4381, Fax: 540-665-5519. *Application contact:* David Anthony, Dean of Admissions, 540-665-4581, Fax: 540-665-4627, E-mail: admit@su.edu.

Simmons College, School of Health Sciences, Graduate Nursing Program, Boston, MA 02115. Offers health professions education (PhD, CAGS); nursing (MSN, DNP); nursing practice (PhD); primary health care nursing (MS, CAGS). *Accreditation:* AACN. Part-time programs available. Postbaccalaureate distance learning degree programs offered (minimal on-campus study). *Faculty:* 37 full-time (31 women), 42 part-time/adjunct (31 women). *Students:* 99 full-time (97 women), 116 part-time (107 women); includes 22 minority (5 African Americans, 11 Asian Americans or Pacific Islanders, 6 Hispanic Americans). Average age 38. 306 applicants, 52% accepted, 72 enrolled. In 2009, 29 master's, 2 doctorates, 2 other advanced degrees awarded. *Degree requirements:* For master's, research project; for doctorate, capstone project (for DNP only). *Entrance requirements:* For master's, courses in statistics and health assessment; for CAGS, previous coursework in microbiology, statistics, developmental psychology, organic and inorganic chemistry. Additional exam requirements/recommendations for international students: Required—TOEFL (minimum score 570 paper-based; 230 computer-based; 88 iBT). *Application deadline:* For fall admission, 6/1 for domestic and international students; for spring admission, 11/1 for domestic students. Application fee: $50. *Expenses:* Contact institution. *Financial support:* Scholarships/grants available. Financial award application deadline: 3/1; financial award applicants required to submit FAFSA. *Faculty research:* Environmental effects on DNA, nursing care of the developmentally disabled, ethical decision-making, depression and grief of the elderly, cultural impressions of dementia. *Unit head:* Dr. Judy A. Beal, Chairperson, 617-521-2139, Fax: 617-521-3045, E-mail: judy.beal@simmons.edu. *Application contact:* Carmen Fortin, Assistant Dean/Director of Admission, 617-521-2605, Fax: 617-521-3137, E-mail: shs@simmons.edu.

South Dakota State University, Graduate School, College of Nursing, Brookings, SD 57007. Offers MS, PhD. *Accreditation:* AACN. Part-time and evening/weekend programs available. Postbaccalaureate distance learning degree programs offered. *Degree requirements:* For master's, comprehensive exam, thesis (for some programs), oral exam. *Entrance requirements:* For master's, nurse registration; for doctorate, nurse registration, MS. Additional exam requirements/recommendations for international students: Required—TOEFL (minimum score 525 paper-based; 197 computer-based; 71 iBT). *Expenses:* Contact institution. *Faculty research:* Rural health, aging, health promotion, Native American health, woman's health, underserved populations, quality of life.

Southeastern Louisiana University, College of Nursing and Health Sciences, School of Nursing, Hammond, LA 70402. Offers MSN. *Accreditation:* AACN. Part-time programs available. *Faculty:* 10 full-time (9 women), 3 part-time/adjunct (2 women). *Students:* 7 full-time (all women), 81 part-time (66 women); includes 9 minority (7 African Americans, 1 American Indian/Alaska Native, 1 Asian American or Pacific Islander), 1 international. Average age 37. 14 applicants, 86% accepted, 12 enrolled. In 2009, 16 master's awarded. *Degree requirements:* For master's, thesis or alternative. *Entrance requirements:* For master's, GRE (verbal and quantitative). Additional exam requirements/recommendations for international students: Required—TOEFL (minimum score 500 paper-based; 173 computer-based; 61 iBT). *Application deadline:* For fall admission, 7/15 priority date for domestic students, 6/1 priority date for international students; for spring admission, 12/1 priority date for domestic students, 10/1 priority date for international students. Applications are processed on a rolling basis. Application fee: $20 ($30 for international students). Electronic applications accepted. *Expenses:* Tuition, state resident: full-time $3086; part-time $225 per credit hour. Tuition, nonresident: part-time $529 per credit hour. Required fees: $1195. Tuition and fees vary according to course level and course load. *Financial support:* In 2009–10, 4 students received support, including 1 teaching assistantship (averaging $9,000 per year); career-related internships or fieldwork, Federal Work-Study, institutionally sponsored loans, scholarships/grants, and administrative assistantship also available. Support available to part-time students. Financial award application deadline: 5/1; financial award applicants required to submit FAFSA. *Faculty research:* Healthy farm families-intervention outcomes, motivational interviewing in client teaching, migrant worker health, novice to expert in the nursing faculty role, effectiveness of and satisfaction with distance learning. Total annual research expenditures: $62,630. *Unit head:* Dr. Cynthia Logan, Interim Department Head, 985-549-2156, Fax: 985-549-2869, E-mail: cynthia.logan@selu.edu. *Application contact:* Sandra Meyers, Graduate Admissions Analyst, 985-549-5620, Fax: 985-549-5632, E-mail: admissions@selu.edu.

Southeast Missouri State University, School of Graduate Studies, Department of Nursing, Cape Girardeau, MO 63701-4799. Offers MSN. *Accreditation:* AACN. Part-time programs available. *Degree requirements:* For master's, research project or thesis. *Entrance requirements:* For master's, minimum GPA of 3.25, current Missouri nursing license, CPR certification, BSN, professional liability insurance, grade of B or higher in one health assessment and one basic statistics course. Additional exam requirements/recommendations for international students: Required—TOEFL (minimum score 550 paper-based; 213 computer-based); Recommended—IELTS (minimum score 6). *Expenses:* Contact institution. *Faculty research:* Gerontology, teaching methodology, addictions, student transition into leadership, health outcomes.

Southern Adventist University, School of Nursing, Collegedale, TN 37315-0370. Offers acute care nurse practitioner (MSN); adult nurse practitioner (MSN); family nurse practitioner (MSN); nurse educator (MSN); MSN/MSBA. *Accreditation:* NLN. Part-time programs available. *Faculty:* 6 full-time (5 women). *Students:* 69 full-time (50 women), 28 part-time (25 women); includes 9 minority (6 African Americans, 1 American Indian/Alaska Native, 1 Asian American or Pacific Islander, 1 Hispanic American). Average age 35. 40 applicants, 95% accepted, 31 enrolled. In 2009, 21 master's awarded. *Degree requirements:* For master's, thesis or project. *Entrance requirements:* For master's, RN license. Additional exam requirements/recommendations for international students: Required—TOEFL (minimum score 600 paper-based; 250 computer-based). *Application deadline:* For fall admission, 7/1 for domestic and international students; for winter admission, 12/1 for domestic and international students. Applications are processed on a rolling basis. Application fee: $25. Electronic applications accepted. *Expenses:* Tuition: Full-time $13,149; part-time $487 per credit hour. *Financial support:* In 2009–10, 1 teaching assistantship with partial tuition reimbursement (averaging $5,000 per year) was awarded. *Faculty research:* Pain management, ethics, corporate wellness, caring spirituality, stress. *Unit head:* Dr. Barbara James, Dean, 423-236-2940, Fax: 423-236-1940, E-mail: bjames@southern.edu. *Application contact:* Diane Proffitt, Enrollment Counselor, 423-236-2941, Fax: 423-236-1940, E-mail: dproffitt@southern.edu.

Southern Connecticut State University, School of Graduate Studies, School of Health and Human Services, Department of Nursing, New Haven, CT 06515-1355. Offers nursing administration (MSN); nursing education (MSN). *Accreditation:* AACN; AANA/CANAEP. Part-time and evening/weekend programs available. *Faculty:* 6 full-time, 1 part-time/adjunct. *Students:* 2 full-time (both women), 29 part-time (27 women); includes 4 minority (3 African Americans, 1 Hispanic American). 33 applicants, 21% accepted, 7 enrolled. In 2009, 14 master's awarded. *Degree requirements:* For master's, thesis. *Entrance requirements:* For master's, GRE, MAT, interview, minimum QPA of 2.8, RN license, minimum 1 year of professional nursing experience. *Application deadline:* For fall admission, 7/15 priority date for domestic students. Applications are processed on a rolling basis. Application fee: $50. Electronic applications accepted. Tuition and fees vary according to program. *Financial support:* Application deadline: 4/15. *Unit head:* Dr. Lisa Rebeschi, Chairperson, 203-392-6485. *Application contact:* Dr. Antonia Nelson, Graduate Coordinator, 203-392-6480, Fax: 203-392-6493, E-mail: nelsona13@southernct.edu.

Southern Illinois University Edwardsville, Graduate Studies and Research, School of Nursing, Edwardsville, IL 62026-0001. Offers MS, Post-Master's Certificate. *Accreditation:* AACN. *Faculty:* 30 full-time (28 women). *Students:* 56 full-time (35 women), 134 part-time (124 women); includes 9 minority (1 African American, 6 Asian Americans or Pacific Islanders, 2 Hispanic Americans). Average age 26. 122 applicants, 29% accepted. In 2009, 57 master's, 2 other advanced degrees awarded. *Degree requirements:* For master's, comprehensive exam. *Entrance requirements:* For master's, appropriate bachelor's degree, RN license. Additional exam requirements/recommendations for international students: Required—TOEFL (minimum score 550 paper-based; 213 computer-based; 79 iBT), IELTS (minimum score 6.5). *Application deadline:* For fall admission, 3/1 for domestic and international students. Application fee: $30. Electronic applications accepted. *Expenses:* Tuition, state resident: part-time $1252.50 per semester. Tuition, nonresident: part-time $3131.25 per semester. Required fees: $586.85 per semester. Tuition and fees vary according to course load. *Financial support:* In 2009–10, 2

Nursing—General

Southern Illinois University Edwardsville *(continued)*
fellowships with full tuition reimbursements (averaging $8,370 per year), 1 teaching assistantship with full tuition reimbursement (averaging $8,064 per year) were awarded; research assistantships, career-related internships or fieldwork, Federal Work-Study, institutionally sponsored loans, scholarships/grants, traineeships, and unspecified assistantships also available. Support available to part-time students. Financial award application deadline: 3/1; financial award applicants required to submit FAFSA. *Unit head:* Dr. Marcia Maurer, Dean, 618-650-3959, E-mail: mamaure@siue.edu. *Application contact:* Dr. Jacquelyn Clement, Director, 618-650-3923, E-mail: jclemen@siue.edu.

Southern Nazarene University, Graduate College, School of Nursing, Bethany, OK 73008. Offers nursing education (MS); nursing leadership (MS). *Accreditation:* AACN. Part-time and evening/weekend programs available.

Southern University and Agricultural and Mechanical College, School of Nursing, Baton Rouge, LA 70813. Offers educator/administrator (PhD); family health nursing (MSN); family nurse practitioner (Post Master's Certificate); geriatric nurse practitioner/gerontology (PhD). *Accreditation:* AACN. Part-time programs available. *Degree requirements:* For master's, comprehensive exam, thesis; for doctorate, comprehensive exam, thesis/dissertation. *Entrance requirements:* For master's, GRE General Test, BSN, minimum GPA of 2.7; for doctorate, GRE General Test; for Post Master's Certificate, MSN. Additional exam requirements/recommendations for international students: Required—TOEFL (minimum score 525 paper-based; 193 computer-based). *Faculty research:* Health promotions, vulnerable populations, (community-based) cardiovascular participating research, health disparities chronic diseases, care of the elderly.

Spalding University, Graduate Studies, College of Health and Natural Sciences, School of Nursing, Louisville, KY 40203-2188. Offers adult nurse practitioner (MSN); family nurse practitioner (MSN); leadership in nursing and healthcare (MSN); pediatric nurse practitioner (MSN). *Accreditation:* AACN. Part-time and evening/weekend programs available. *Faculty:* 6 full-time (all women), 7 part-time/adjunct (all women). *Students:* 41 full-time (38 women), 36 part-time (34 women); includes 12 minority (9 African Americans, 3 Hispanic Americans), 2 international. Average age 38. 27 applicants, 70% accepted, 18 enrolled. In 2009, 25 master's awarded. *Degree requirements:* For master's, comprehensive exam (for some programs), thesis. *Entrance requirements:* For master's, GRE General Test, BSN or bachelor's degree and RN licensure. Additional exam requirements/recommendations for international students: Required—TOEFL (minimum score 535 paper-based; 203 computer-based). *Application deadline:* Applications are processed on a rolling basis. Application fee: $30. *Expenses:* Tuition: Full-time $11,340; part-time $630 per credit hour. Tuition and fees vary according to program. *Financial support:* In 2009–10, 53 students received support, including 2 research assistantships with partial tuition reimbursements available (averaging $4,020 per year); career-related internships or fieldwork, scholarships/grants, and traineeships also available. Support available to part-time students. Financial award application deadline: 3/15; financial award applicants required to submit FAFSA. *Faculty research:* Nurse educational administration, gerontology, bioterrorism, healthcare ethics, leadership. *Unit head:* Dr. Carolyn Lewis, Interim Chair, 502-585-9911 Ext. 2331, E-mail: clewis@spalding.edu. *Application contact:* Dr. Carolyn Lewis, Interim Chair, 502-585-9911 Ext. 2331, E-mail: clewis@spalding.edu.

Spring Arbor University, School of Graduate and Professional Studies, Spring Arbor, MI 49283-9799. Offers counseling (MAC); family studies (MAFS); nursing (MSN); organizational management (MAOM). Part-time and evening/weekend programs available. Postbaccalaureate distance learning degree programs offered (no on-campus study). *Faculty:* 8 full-time (3 women), 99 part-time/adjunct (45 women). *Students:* 412 full-time (327 women), 420 part-time (351 women); includes 215 minority (182 African Americans, 2 American Indian/Alaska Native, 10 Asian Americans or Pacific Islanders, 21 Hispanic Americans), 3 international. Average age 40. In 2009, 257 master's awarded. *Entrance requirements:* For master's, minimum GPA of 3.0, interview, writing sample, 2 professional references. Additional exam requirements/recommendations for international students: Required—TOEFL (minimum score 550 paper-based; 220 computer-based). *Application deadline:* Applications are processed on a rolling basis. Application fee: $40. Electronic applications accepted. *Expenses:* Tuition: Full-time $5400; part-time $450 per credit hour. Required fees: $240; $150 per year. Tuition and fees vary according to course load and program. *Financial support:* Scholarships/grants available. Support available to part-time students. Financial award applicants required to submit FAFSA. *Unit head:* Dr. Robert Hamill, Dean of Graduate and Professional Studies, 517-750-1200 Ext. 1343, Fax: 517-750-6602, E-mail: rhamill@arbor.edu. *Application contact:* Greg Bentle, Coordinator of Graduate Recruitment, 517-750-6763, Fax: 517-750-6624, E-mail: gbentle@arbor.edu.

Spring Hill College, Graduate Programs, Program in Nursing, Mobile, AL 36608-1791. Offers clinical nurse leader (MSN). *Accreditation:* AACN. Part-time and evening/weekend programs available. Postbaccalaureate distance learning degree programs offered (no on-campus study). *Faculty:* 4 full-time (all women). *Students:* 5 full-time (all women), 29 part-time (26 women); includes 9 minority (all African Americans). Average age 40. 28 applicants, 57% accepted, 12 enrolled. In 2009, 21 master's awarded. *Degree requirements:* For master's, comprehensive exam, capstone courses, completion of program within 6 calendar years. *Entrance requirements:* For master's, RN license; 1 year of clinical nursing experience; work in clinical setting or access to health care facility for clinical integration/research; 3 written references; employer verification; resume. Additional exam requirements/recommendations for international students: Required—TOEFL (minimum score 550 paper-based; 213 computer-based; 80 iBT), IELTS (minimum score 6.5). *Application deadline:* For fall admission, 8/1 priority date for domestic and international students; for spring admission, 12/1 priority date for domestic and international students. Applications are processed on a rolling basis. Application fee: $25 ($35 for international students). Electronic applications accepted. *Expenses:* Contact institution. *Financial support:* In 2009–10, 31 students received support. Institutionally sponsored loans and scholarships/grants available. Support available to part-time students. Financial award applicants required to submit FAFSA. *Unit head:* Dr. Ola H. Fox, Director, 251-380-4486, Fax: 251-460-4495, E-mail: ofox@shc.edu. *Application contact:* Donna B. Tarasavage, Director of Marketing and Recruiting, Graduate and Continuing Studies, 251-380-3067, Fax: 251-460-2190, E-mail: dtarasavage@shc.edu.

State University of New York at Binghamton, Graduate School, Decker School of Nursing, Binghamton, NY 13902-6000. Offers MS, PhD, Certificate. *Accreditation:* AACN. Part-time and evening/weekend programs available. *Faculty:* 30 full-time (28 women), 9 part-time/adjunct (8 women). *Students:* 60 full-time (56 women), 61 part-time (58 women); includes 15 minority (9 African Americans, 4 Asian Americans or Pacific Islanders, 2 Hispanic Americans), 5 international. Average age 37. 54 applicants, 98% accepted, 46 enrolled. In 2009, 37 master's, 4 doctorates, 33 other advanced degrees awarded. *Degree requirements:* For master's, comprehensive exam, thesis; for doctorate, thesis/dissertation. *Entrance requirements:* For master's, GRE General Test. Additional exam requirements/recommendations for international students: Required—TOEFL. *Application deadline:* For fall admission, 4/15 priority date for domestic students, 1/15 priority date for international students; for spring admission, 11/1 for domestic students, 10/1 priority date for international students. Applications are processed on a rolling basis. Application fee: $60. Electronic applications accepted. *Financial support:* In 2009–10, 25 students received support, including 14 fellowships with partial tuition reimbursements available (averaging $8,250 per year), 2 research assistantships with full tuition reimbursements available (averaging $10,000 per year), 6 teaching assistantships with full tuition reimbursements available (averaging $10,000 per year); career-related internships or fieldwork, Federal Work-Study, institutionally sponsored loans, traineeships, health care benefits, and unspecified assistantships also available. Financial award application deadline: 2/15; financial award applicants required to submit FAFSA. *Unit head:* Dr. Joyce Ferrario, Dean, 607-777-2311, Fax: 607-777-4440, E-mail: jferrari@binghamton.edu. *Application contact:* Theresa Grabo, Director of Graduate Studies, 607-777-6163, Fax: 607-777-4440, E-mail: tgrabo@binghamton.edu.

State University of New York Downstate Medical Center, College of Nursing, Graduate Program in Nursing, Brooklyn, NY 11203-2098. Offers clinical nurse specialist (MS, Post Master's Certificate); nurse anesthesia (MS); nurse midwifery (MS, Post Master's Certificate); nurse practitioner (MS, Post Master's Certificate); nursing (MS). *Accreditation:* AACN. Part-time programs available. *Degree requirements:* For master's, thesis optional, clinical research project. *Entrance requirements:* For master's, GRE, BSN; minimum GPA of 3.0; previous undergraduate course work in statistics, health assessment, and nursing research; RN license; for Post Master's Certificate, BSN; minimum GPA of 3.0; RN license; previous undergraduate course work in statistics, health assessment, and nursing research. *Faculty research:* AIDS, continuity of care, case management, self-care.

State University of New York Institute of Technology, School of Nursing and Health Systems, Utica, NY 13504-3050. Offers adult nurse practitioner (MS, CAS); family nurse practitioner (MS, CAS); gerontological nurse practitioner (MS, CAS); nursing administration (MS, CAS); nursing education (MS, CAS). *Accreditation:* AACN. Part-time programs available. *Degree requirements:* For master's, thesis or project. *Entrance requirements:* For master's, GRE General Test (if undergraduate GPA less than 3.3), minimum GPA of 3.0 in last 30 hours of undergraduate course work, bachelor's degree in nursing, 1 year of professional experience, RN license, interview, 2 letters of recommendation. Additional exam requirements/recommendations for international students: Required—TOEFL (minimum score 550 paper-based; 213 computer-based). *Faculty research:* Evidence-based practice, gerontological health issues, nursing informatics, nursing education, healthcare in minority populations.

State University of New York Upstate Medical University, College of Nursing, Syracuse, NY 13210-2334. Offers nurse practitioner (Post Master's Certificate); nursing (MS). *Accreditation:* AACN. Part-time programs available. Postbaccalaureate distance learning degree programs offered (no on-campus study). *Faculty:* 14 full-time (all women), 7 part-time/adjunct (6 women). *Students:* 61 full-time (50 women), 120 part-time (115 women); includes 17 minority (9 African Americans, 1 American Indian/Alaska Native, 4 Asian Americans or Pacific Islanders, 3 Hispanic Americans), 3 international. Average age 42. 108 applicants, 82% accepted, 73 enrolled. In 2009, 29 master's, 9 other advanced degrees awarded. *Degree requirements:* For master's, thesis or alternative. *Entrance requirements:* For master's, 3 years of work experience. *Application deadline:* For fall admission, 3/1 priority date for domestic and international students; for spring admission, 11/1 for domestic and international students. Applications are processed on a rolling basis. Application fee: $40. Electronic applications accepted. *Financial support:* In 2009–10, 134 students received support. Federal Work-Study, institutionally sponsored loans, scholarships/grants, and traineeships available. Support available to part-time students. Financial award application deadline: 3/1; financial award applicants required to submit FAFSA. *Unit head:* Dr. Elvira Szigeti, Dean, 315-464-4276, Fax: 315-464-5168. *Application contact:* Donna Vavonese, Associate Director of Admissions, 315-464-4570, Fax: 315-464-8867, E-mail: vavonesd@upstate.edu.

Stony Brook University, State University of New York, Stony Brook University Medical Center, Health Sciences Center, School of Nursing, Stony Brook, NY 11794. Offers MS, DNP, Certificate. *Accreditation:* AACN; ACNM/DOA. Postbaccalaureate distance learning degree programs offered. *Faculty:* 35 full-time (29 women), 12 part-time/adjunct (all women). *Students:* 84 full-time (80 women), 442 part-time (409 women); includes 127 minority (64 African Americans, 38 Asian Americans or Pacific Islanders, 25 Hispanic Americans), 3 international. Average age 30. 82 applicants, 61% accepted. In 2009, 114 master's, 12 other advanced degrees awarded. *Degree requirements:* For master's, thesis. *Entrance requirements:* For master's, BSN, minimum GPA of 3.0, course work in statistics. *Application deadline:* For fall admission, 1/15 for domestic students. Application fee: $60. *Expenses:* Tuition, state resident: full-time $8370; part-time $349 per credit. Tuition, nonresident: full-time $13,250; part-time $552 per credit. Required fees: $933. *Financial support:* Fellowships, research assistantships, teaching assistantships, career-related internships or fieldwork, Federal Work-Study, institutionally sponsored loans, and traineeships available. Financial award application deadline: 3/15. Total annual research expenditures: $533,457. *Unit head:* Dr. Lee Anne Xippolitos, Dean, 631-444-3200, Fax: 631-444-6628, E-mail: lee.xippolitos@stonybrook.edu. *Application contact:* Dr. Kent Marks, Assistant Dean, Admissions and Records, 631-632-4723, Fax: 631-632-7243, E-mail: kmarks@notes.cc.sunysb.edu.

Temple University, Health Sciences Center and Graduate School, College of Health Professions, Department of Nursing, Philadelphia, PA 19122-6096. Offers MSN. *Accreditation:* AACN. Part-time programs available. *Degree requirements:* For master's, thesis or research project. *Entrance requirements:* For master's, GRE General Test, current RN license, interview. Additional exam requirements/recommendations for international students: Required—TOEFL (minimum score 550 paper-based; 213 computer-based; 79 iBT). Electronic applications accepted. *Faculty research:* Osteoporosis, sensory deprivation in elderly, child abuse, attitudes towards AIDS, management styles.

Tennessee State University, The School of Graduate Studies and Research, School of Nursing, Nashville, TN 37209-1561. Offers family nurse practitioner (MSN); holistic nursing (MSN); nursing administration (MSN); nursing education (MSN); nursing informatics (MSN). *Accreditation:* NLN. *Entrance requirements:* For master's, GRE General Test or MAT, BSN, current RN license, minimum GPA of 3.0.

Tennessee Technological University, School of Nursing, Cookeville, TN 38505. Offers family nurse practitioner (MSN); informatics (MSN); nursing administration (MSN); nursing education (MSN). *Students:* 11 full-time (10 women), 30 part-time (27 women); includes 2 minority (1 African American, 1 Hispanic American). 40 applicants, 35% accepted, 10 enrolled. In 2009, 14 master's awarded. *Degree requirements:* For master's, comprehensive exam, thesis or alternative. *Entrance requirements:* Additional exam requirements/recommendations for international students: Required—TOEFL (minimum score 550 paper-based; 79 iBT), IELTS (minimum score 5.5). *Application deadline:* For fall admission, 8/1 for domestic students, 5/1 for international students; for spring admission, 12/1 for domestic students, 10/1 for international students. Application fee: $25 ($30 for international students). Electronic applications accepted. *Expenses:* Tuition, state resident: full-time $7034; part-time $368 per credit hour. *Financial support:* Application deadline: 4/1. *Unit head:* Dr. Sheila Green, Interim Dean, 931-372-3203, Fax: 931-372-6244, E-mail: sgreen@tntech.edu. *Application contact:* Shelia K. Kendrick, Coordinator of Graduate Studies, 931-372-3808, Fax: 931-372-3497, E-mail: skendrick@tntech.edu.

Texas A&M International University, Office of Graduate Studies and Research, College of Nursing and Health Sciences, Laredo, TX 78041-1900. Offers MSN. *Accreditation:* NLN. *Faculty:* 3 full-time (all women), 3 part-time/adjunct (all women). *Students:* 30 part-time (19 women); includes 28 minority (1 Asian American or Pacific Islander, 27 Hispanic Americans). Average age 36. In 2009, 17 master's awarded. Application fee: $25. *Financial support:* In 2009–10, 12 students received support, including 1 fellowship. *Unit head:* Regina Aune, Dean, 956-326-2574, E-mail: regina.aune@tamiu.edu. *Application contact:* Rosie Espinoza, Director, Office of Admissions, 956-326-2200, Fax: 956-326-2269, E-mail: enroll@tamiu.edu.

Texas A&M University–Corpus Christi, Graduate Studies and Research, College of Nursing and Health Sciences, Corpus Christi, TX 78412-5503. Offers clinical nurse specialist (MSN); family nurse practitioner (MSN); health care administration (MSN); leadership in nursing systems (MSN). *Accreditation:* AACN. Part-time and evening/weekend programs available. *Degree requirements:* For master's, comprehensive exam, thesis (for some programs). *Entrance requirements:* For master's, GRE General Test. Additional exam requirements/recommendations for international students: Required—TOEFL. Electronic applications accepted.

Texas Christian University, Harris College of Nursing and Health Sciences, Program in Nursing, Fort Worth, TX 76129-0002. Offers adult nursing (CNS) (MSN); nursing (DNP); pediatric nursing (CNS) (MSN). *Accreditation:* AACN; AANA/CANAEP (one or more programs are accredited). Part-time programs available. Postbaccalaureate distance learning degree programs offered (minimal on-campus study). *Degree requirements:* For master's and doctorate, professional project. *Entrance requirements:* For master's, GRE General Test or MAT, 3 letters

of reference, 2 years full-time experience in nursing, current nursing licensure. Additional exam requirements/recommendations for international students: Required—TOEFL. *Application deadline:* For fall admission, 2/1 for domestic students. Application fee: $0. *Expenses:* Tuition: Full-time $17,640; part-time $980 per credit hour. Tuition and fees vary according to program. *Financial support:* Application deadline: 2/1. *Unit head:* Dr. Pamela Frable, Director, 817-257-5840, E-mail: p.frable@tcu.edu. *Application contact:* Dr. Kathleen Baldwin, Director of Graduate Studies, 817-257-6756, E-mail: k.baldwin@tcu.edu.

Texas Tech University Health Sciences Center, School of Nursing, Lubbock, TX 79430. Offers acute care nurse practitioner (MSN, Certificate); administration (MSN); advanced practice (DNP); education (MSN); executive leadership (DNP); family nurse practitioner (MSN, Certificate); geriatric nurse practitioner (MSN, Certificate); pediatric nurse practitioner (MSN, Certificate). *Accreditation:* AACN. Part-time programs available. Postbaccalaureate distance learning degree programs offered (minimal on-campus study). *Degree requirements:* For master's, thesis optional. *Entrance requirements:* For master's, minimum GPA of 3.0, 3 letters of reference, BSN, RN license; for Certificate, minimum GPA of 3.0, 3 letters of reference, RN license. Additional exam requirements/recommendations for international students: Required—TOEFL (minimum score 550 paper-based; 213 computer-based). *Faculty research:* Diabetes/obesity, nurse competency, disease management, intervention and measurements, health disparities.

Texas Woman's University, Graduate School, College of Nursing, Denton, TX 76201. Offers acute care nurse practitioner (MS); adult health clinical nurse specialist (MS); adult health nurse practitioner (MS); child health clinical nurse specialist (MS); clinical nurse leader (MS); community health (MS); family nurse practitioner (MS); health systems management (MS); nursing education (MS); nursing practice (DNP); nursing science (PhD); pediatric nurse practitioner (MS); women's health clinical nurse specialist (MS); women's health nurse practitioner (MS). *Accreditation:* AACN. Part-time programs available. Postbaccalaureate distance learning degree programs offered. *Faculty:* 85 full-time (80 women), 6 part-time/adjunct (all women). *Students:* 81 full-time (76 women), 602 part-time (571 women); includes 293 minority (154 African Americans, 3 American Indian/Alaska Native, 90 Asian Americans or Pacific Islanders, 46 Hispanic Americans), 19 international. Average age 39. 259 applicants, 81% accepted, 166 enrolled. In 2009, 100 master's, 22 doctorates awarded. *Degree requirements:* For master's, thesis or alternative; for doctorate, comprehensive exam, thesis/dissertation. *Entrance requirements:* For master's, GRE or MAT, minimum GPA of 3.0, RN license, BS in nursing, basic statistics course; for doctorate, GRE (Verbal 460, Quantitative 500) or MAT (50), MS in nursing, minimum GPA of 3.5, RN license, coursework in statistics, 2 letters of reference, curriculum vitae, nursing-theory course, graduate research course, letter stating professional and research goals. Additional exam requirements/recommendations for international students: Required—TOEFL (minimum score 550 paper-based; 213 computer-based; 79 iBT). *Application deadline:* For fall admission, 5/1 priority date for domestic students, 3/1 for international students; for spring admission, 9/15 priority date for domestic students, 7/1 for international students. Applications are processed on a rolling basis. Application fee: $50. Electronic applications accepted. *Expenses:* Tuition, state resident: full-time $3564; part-time $198 per credit hour. Tuition, nonresident: full-time $8550; part-time $475 per credit hour. Required fees: $69.26 per credit hour. Tuition and fees vary according to course load. *Financial support:* In 2009–10, 99 students received support, including 16 fellowships (averaging $17,325 per year), 5 research assistantships (averaging $11,484 per year), 5 teaching assistantships (averaging $11,484 per year); career-related internships or fieldwork, Federal Work-Study, institutionally sponsored loans, scholarships/grants, traineeships, health care benefits, and unspecified assistantships also available. Support available to part-time students. Financial award application deadline: 3/1; financial award applicants required to submit FAFSA. *Faculty research:* Evaluation of pre-natal care, screening for intimate partner violence, stressors and nursing success, breast surgery, breast feeding, adolescent needs during childbirth. *Unit head:* Dr. Patricia Holden-Huchton, Interim Dean, 940-898-2401, Fax: 940-898-2437, E-mail: pholdenhuchton@twu.edu. *Application contact:* Samuel Wheeler, Assistant Director of Admissions, 940-898-3188, Fax: 940-898-3081, E-mail: wheelersr@twu.edu.

Thomas Edison State College, School of Nursing, Program in Nursing, Trenton, NJ 08608-1176. Offers MSN. *Accreditation:* AACN. Part-time programs available. Postbaccalaureate distance learning degree programs offered (no on-campus study). *Students:* 219 part-time (203 women); includes 45 minority (31 African Americans, 1 American Indian/Alaska Native, 6 Asian Americans or Pacific Islanders, 7 Hispanic Americans), 1 international. Average age 46. In 2009, 6 master's awarded. *Degree requirements:* For master's, nursing education seminar, onground practicum, online practicum. *Entrance requirements:* For master's, BSN. Additional exam requirements/recommendations for international students: Required—TOEFL (minimum score 550 paper-based; 213 computer-based; 79 iBT). *Application deadline:* For fall admission, 8/15 for domestic and international students; for winter admission, 11/15 for domestic and international students; for spring admission, 2/15 for domestic and international students. Application fee: $75. Electronic applications accepted. *Expenses:* Tuition, area resident: Part-time $479 per credit. Tuition, state resident: part-time $479 per credit. Tuition, nonresident: part-time $479 per credit. *Financial support:* Applicants required to submit FAFSA. *Unit head:* Dr. Susan O'Brien, Dean, School of Nursing, 609-633-6460, Fax: 609-292-8279, E-mail: nursing@tesc.edu. *Application contact:* David Hoftiezer, Director of Admissions, 888-442-8372, Fax: 609-984-8447, E-mail: admissions@tesc.edu.

Thomas Jefferson University, Jefferson College of Health Professions, Program in Nursing, Philadelphia, PA 19107. Offers MS. *Accreditation:* AACN; AANA/CANAEP. Part-time programs available. Postbaccalaureate distance learning degree programs offered (no on-campus study). *Entrance requirements:* For master's, GRE or MAT, BSN or equivalent, CPR certification, professional RN license, previous undergraduate course work in statistics and nursing research, minimum GPA of 3.0. Additional exam requirements/recommendations for international students: Required—TOEFL (minimum score 213 computer-based). Electronic applications accepted. *Expenses:* Contact institution. *Faculty research:* Interdisciplinary primary care, women and HIV, health promotion and disease prevention, psychosocial impact of disability, ethical decision making.

Thomas University, Department of Nursing, Thomasville, GA 31792-7499. Offers MSN. *Accreditation:* NLN. Part-time programs available. *Entrance requirements:* For master's, resume, 3 academic/professional references. Additional exam requirements/recommendations for international students: Required—TOEFL (minimum score 600 paper-based; 250 computer-based). Electronic applications accepted.

Towson University, College of Graduate Studies and Research, Program in Nursing, Towson, MD 21252-0001. Offers nursing (MS); nursing education (Certificate). *Accreditation:* AACN. Part-time programs available. *Degree requirements:* For master's, thesis optional. *Entrance requirements:* For master's, minimum GPA of 3.0, copy of current nursing license, bachelor's degree in nursing, curriculum vitae; for Certificate, minimum GPA of 3.0, copy of current nursing license, curriculum vitae, bachelor's degree in nursing. Electronic applications accepted. *Faculty research:* End of life care, caring, health policy, parish nursing.

Troy University, Graduate School, College of Health and Human Services, Program in Nursing, Troy, AL 36082. Offers adult health (MSN); clinical nurse specialist adult health (DNP); clinical nurse specialist nurse practitioner (DNP); family nurse practitioner (MSN); informatics specialist (MSN); maternal infant (MSN). *Accreditation:* NLN. Part-time and evening/weekend programs available. *Students:* 28 full-time (all women), 102 part-time (93 women); includes 49 minority (48 African Americans, 1 American Indian/Alaska Native). Average age 37. 76 applicants, 86% accepted. In 2009, 25 master's awarded. *Degree requirements:* For master's, comprehensive exam, thesis optional. *Entrance requirements:* For master's, MAT (minimum score 396) or GRE (minimum score 850), minimum GPA of 2.5, BSN. Additional exam requirements/recommendations for international students: Required—TOEFL (minimum score 523 paper-based; 193 computer-based; 70 iBT), IELTS (minimum score 6), TOEFL or IELTS or ACT Compass ESL (minimum score 270 on Listening, Reading, and Grammar with no individual score below 85 and minimum score of 8 out of 12 on writing test). *Application deadline:* Applications are processed on a rolling basis. Application fee: $50. Electronic applications accepted. *Financial support:* Available to part-time students. Applicants required to submit FAFSA. *Application contact:* Brenda K. Campbell, Director of Graduate Admissions, 334-670-3178, Fax: 334-670-3733, E-mail: bcamp@troy.edu.

Uniformed Services University of the Health Sciences, Graduate School of Nursing, Bethesda, MD 20814-4799. Offers family nurse practitioner (MSN); nurse anesthesia (MSN); perioperative clinical nurse specialty (MSN); psychiatric mental health nurse practitioner (MSN). Available to military officers only. *Accreditation:* AACN; NLN. Postbaccalaureate distance learning degree programs offered (no on-campus study). *Faculty:* 27 full-time (18 women), 2 part-time/adjunct (both women). *Students:* 75 full-time (32 women), 3 part-time (all women); includes 20 minority (8 African Americans, 5 Asian Americans or Pacific Islanders, 7 Hispanic Americans). Average age 36. 108 applicants, 72% accepted, 78 enrolled. In 2009, 54 master's awarded. *Degree requirements:* For master's, thesis or alternative. *Entrance requirements:* For master's, GRE, BSN, clinical experience, minimum GPA of 3.0, previous course work in science. *Application deadline:* For fall admission, 7/1 for domestic students; for winter admission, 2/15 for domestic students. Application fee: $0. Electronic applications accepted. *Faculty research:* Prenatal care, military health care, military readiness, distance learning. *Unit head:* Col. Bruce A. Schoneboom, Associate Dean for Academic Affairs, 301-295-1180, Fax: 301-295-1707, E-mail: bschoneboom@usuhs.mil. *Application contact:* Terry Lynn Malavakis, Recording Secretary for Admissions Committee, 301-295-1055, Fax: 301-295-1707, E-mail: tmalavakis@usuhs.mil.

Union University, School of Nursing, Jackson, TN 38305-3697. Offers executive leadership (DNP); nurse anesthesia (DNP); nurse anesthetist (PMC); nurse practitioner (DNP); nursing education (MSN, PMC). *Accreditation:* AACN; AANA/CANAEP. *Degree requirements:* For master's, thesis or alternative. *Entrance requirements:* For master's, GRE, 3 letters of reference, bachelor's degree in nursing, minimum GPA of 3.0. Additional exam requirements/recommendations for international students: Required—TOEFL (minimum score 560 paper-based; 220 computer-based). Electronic applications accepted. *Faculty research:* Children's health, occupational rehabilitation, informatics, health promotion.

Universidad del Turabo, Graduate Programs, School of Health Sciences, Programs in Nursing, Program in Clinical Nurse Leader, Gurabo, PR 00778-3030. Offers MSN. *Accreditation:* AACN. *Students:* 3 applicants, 67% accepted, 0 enrolled. In 2009, 2 master's awarded. *Unit head:* Dr. Maria Rosa, Dean, 787-743-7979. *Application contact:* Virginia Gonzalez, Admissions Officer, 787-746-3009.

Université de Montréal, Faculty of Nursing, Montréal, QC H3C 3J7, Canada. Offers M Sc, PhD, Certificate, DESS. Part-time programs available. *Faculty:* 32 full-time (26 women), 24 part-time/adjunct (20 women). *Students:* 153 full-time (140 women), 201 part-time (188 women). 308 applicants, 55% accepted, 149 enrolled. In 2009, 32 master's, 2 doctorates, 11 other advanced degrees awarded. *Degree requirements:* For master's, one foreign language, thesis optional; for doctorate, thesis/dissertation, general exam; for other advanced degree, one foreign language. *Entrance requirements:* For master's, doctorate, and other advanced degree, proficiency in French. *Application deadline:* For fall admission, 2/1 priority date for domestic students; for winter admission, 11/1 priority date for domestic students; for spring admission, 2/1 priority date for domestic students. Applications are processed on a rolling basis. Application fee: $100. Electronic applications accepted. *Financial support:* Fellowships, research assistantships, teaching assistantships, career-related internships or fieldwork, Federal Work-Study, and institutionally sponsored loans available. *Faculty research:* Mental and physical care of chronic patients, care of the hospitalized aged, cancer nursing, home care of caregivers, AIDS patients. *Unit head:* Francine Girard, Dean, 514-343-6436, Fax: 514-343-2306, E-mail: francine.d.girard@umontreal.ca. *Application contact:* Chantal Cara, Vice Dean of Graduate Studies, 514-343-5835, Fax: 514-343-2306, E-mail: chantal.cara@umontreal.ca.

Université du Québec à Rimouski, Graduate Programs, Program in Nursing Studies, Rimouski, QC G5L 3A1, Canada. Offers M Sc, Diploma.

Université du Québec à Trois-Rivières, Graduate Programs, Program in Nursing Sciences, Trois-Rivières, QC G9A 5H7, Canada. Offers M Sc, DESS. Part-time programs available.

Université du Québec en Outaouais, Graduate Programs, Program in Nursing, Gatineau, QC J8X 3X7, Canada. Offers M Sc, Diploma.

Université Laval, Faculty of Nursing, Programs in Nursing, Québec, QC G1K 7P4, Canada. Offers M Sc, PhD, DESS, Diploma. *Degree requirements:* For master's, thesis (for some programs). *Entrance requirements:* For master's, French exam, knowledge of English; for other advanced degree, knowledge of French. Electronic applications accepted.

University at Buffalo, the State University of New York, Graduate School, School of Nursing, Buffalo, NY 14260. Offers adult health nursing (MS); family nursing (MS); nurse anesthetist (MS); nursing (PhD); nursing education (Certificate); psychiatric/mental health nursing (MS). *Accreditation:* AACN; AANA/CANAEP (one or more programs are accredited). Part-time programs available. Postbaccalaureate distance learning degree programs offered (minimal on-campus study). *Faculty:* 42 full-time (38 women), 16 part-time/adjunct (all women). *Students:* 128 full-time (102 women), 69 part-time (58 women); includes 27 minority (7 African Americans, 1 American Indian/Alaska Native, 12 Asian Americans or Pacific Islanders, 7 Hispanic Americans), 15 international. Average age 34. 375 applicants, 25% accepted, 65 enrolled. In 2009, 58 master's, 3 doctorates, 4 other advanced degrees awarded. Terminal master's awarded for partial completion of doctoral program. *Degree requirements:* For master's, thesis optional, comprehensive exams or project; for doctorate, comprehensive exam, thesis/dissertation. *Entrance requirements:* For master's, GRE General Test (if overall GPA less than 3.0), interview, minimum GPA of 3.0, RN license, 3 references; for doctorate, GRE General Test, MAT, minimum GPA of 3.25, RN license, BS or MS in nursing, 3 references, writing sample; for Certificate, interview, minimum GPA of 3.0 or GRE General Test, RN license, MS in nursing. Additional exam requirements/recommendations for international students: Required—TOEFL (minimum score 550 paper-based; 213 computer-based; 79 iBT), IELTS (minimum score 6.5). *Application deadline:* For fall admission, 6/1 priority date for domestic students, 4/1 priority date for international students; for spring admission, 11/1 for domestic students, 10/1 priority date for international students. Applications are processed on a rolling basis. Application fee: $75. Electronic applications accepted. *Financial support:* In 2009–10, 78 students received support, including 14 fellowships with full tuition reimbursements available (averaging $8,200 per year), 5 research assistantships with full tuition reimbursements available (averaging $16,794 per year), 13 teaching assistantships with full tuition reimbursements available (averaging $10,636 per year); scholarships/grants, traineeships, health care benefits, and unspecified assistantships also available. Financial award application deadline: 3/15; financial award applicants required to submit FAFSA. *Faculty research:* Oncology symptom management, end of life decision making, changing behaviors using the transtheoretical model, addictions, nursing workforce. Total annual research expenditures: $1.3 million. *Unit head:* Dr. Jean K. Brown, Dean and Professor, 716-829-2533, Fax: 716-829-2566, E-mail: ubnursingdean@buffalo.edu. *Application contact:* Dr. David J. Lang, Director of Student Affairs, 716-829-2537, Fax: 716-829-2021, E-mail: langdj@buffalo.edu.

The University of Akron, Graduate School, College of Nursing, Akron, OH 44325. Offers nursing (MSN, PhD); public health (MPH). *Accreditation:* AACN; AANA/CANAEP (one or more programs are accredited). Part-time programs available. *Faculty:* 48 full-time (46 women), 55 part-time/adjunct (54 women). *Students:* 75 full-time (68 women), 265 part-time (225 women); includes 32 minority (23 African Americans, 1 American Indian/Alaska Native, 5 Asian Americans or Pacific Islanders, 3 Hispanic Americans), 8 international. Average age 35. 101 applicants, 88% accepted, 54 enrolled. In 2009, 76 master's, 1 doctorate awarded. *Degree requirements:* For doctorate, one foreign language, thesis/dissertation, qualifying exam. *Entrance requirements:* For master's, GRE, interview, letters of recommendation, minimum GPA of 3.0, current license to practice nursing; for doctorate, GRE, minimum GPA of 3.0, MSN, nursing license or eligibility for licensure, writing sample, letters of recommendation, interview, resume, personal statement. Additional exam requirements/recommendations for international students: Required—TOEFL (minimum score 550 paper-based; 213 computer-based; 79 iBT). *Application deadline:*

Nursing—General

The University of Akron (continued)

Applications are processed on a rolling basis. Application fee: $30 ($40 for international students). Electronic applications accepted. *Expenses:* Tuition, state resident: full-time $6570; part-time $365 per credit hour. Tuition, nonresident: full-time $11,250; part-time $625 per credit hour. *Financial support:* In 2009–10, 7 research assistantships with full tuition reimbursements, 8 teaching assistantships with full tuition reimbursements were awarded; career-related internships or fieldwork and Federal Work-Study also available. *Faculty research:* Health promotion and chronic disease prevention; mental health and psychosocial resilience; gerontological health, trauma and violence; gut oxygenation during shock and trauma, simulation and the pedagogy of teaching and learning. Total annual research expenditures: $728,561. *Unit head:* Dr. Margaret Wineman, Dean, 330-972-7551, E-mail: wineman@uakron.edu. *Application contact:* Dr. Marlene Huff, Graduate Director, 330-972-7555, E-mail: mhuff@uakron.edu.

The University of Alabama, Graduate School, Capstone College of Nursing, Tuscaloosa, AL 35487. Offers MSN, DNP, Ed D, MSN/Ed D. *Accreditation:* AACN. Part-time programs available. Postbaccalaureate distance learning degree programs offered (no on-campus study). *Faculty:* 15 full-time (14 women). *Students:* 43 full-time (42 women), 126 part-time (118 women); includes 47 minority (41 African Americans, 2 American Indian/Alaska Native, 1 Asian American or Pacific Islander, 3 Hispanic Americans). Average age 44. 119 applicants, 76% accepted, 80 enrolled. In 2009, 42 degrees awarded. *Degree requirements:* For doctorate, comprehensive exam, thesis/dissertation. *Entrance requirements:* For master's, GRE or MAT (if GPA is below 3.0), BSN, RN licensure, minimum GPA of 3.0; for doctorate, GRE or MAT, MSN, RN licensure, minimum GPA of 3.0, references, writing sample, curriculum vitae (EdD). *Application deadline:* For fall admission, 6/1 priority date for domestic students; for winter admission, 1/1 priority date for domestic students; for spring admission, 4/15 priority date for domestic students. Applications are processed on a rolling basis. Application fee: $50 ($60 for international students). Electronic applications accepted. *Expenses:* Tuition, state resident: full-time $7000. Tuition, nonresident: full-time $19,200. *Financial support:* In 2009–10, 2 fellowships with full tuition reimbursements (averaging $14,000 per year) were awarded; scholarships/grants and traineeships also available. Financial award application deadline: 8/1; financial award applicants required to submit FAFSA. *Faculty research:* Diabetes education, childhood asthma, HIV/AIDS prevention and care, breast cancer in rural minority women, nursing labor cost, nursing case management, sleep. Total annual research expenditures: $28,512. *Unit head:* Dr. Sara E. Barger, Dean, 205-348-1040, Fax: 205-348-5559, E-mail: sbarger@bama.ua.edu. *Application contact:* Dr. Marietta Stanton, Assistant Dean, Graduate Programs, 205-348-1020, Fax: 205-348-5559, E-mail: mstanton@bama.ua.edu.

The University of Alabama at Birmingham, School of Nursing, Birmingham, AL 35294. Offers MSN, DNP, PhD. *Accreditation:* AACN. Terminal master's awarded for partial completion of doctoral program. *Degree requirements:* For doctorate, thesis/dissertation, research mentorship experience. *Entrance requirements:* For master's, GRE General Test, BS in nursing, interview; for doctorate, GRE General Test, computer literacy, course work in statistics, interview, minimum GPA of 3.0, MS in nursing. Additional exam requirements/recommendations for international students: Required—TOEFL. Electronic applications accepted. *Expenses:* Contact institution.

The University of Alabama in Huntsville, School of Graduate Studies, College of Nursing, Huntsville, AL 35899. Offers family nurse practitioner (Certificate); nursing (MSN, DNP), including acute care nurse practitioner (MSN), adult clinical nursing specialist (MSN), clinical nurse leader (MSN), family nurse practitioner (MSN), leadership in health care systems (MSN); nursing education (Certificate). *Accreditation:* AACN. Part-time and evening/weekend programs available. Postbaccalaureate distance learning degree programs offered (minimal on-campus study). *Faculty:* 13 full-time (11 women), 3 part-time/adjunct (2 women). *Students:* 45 full-time (43 women), 121 part-time (111 women); includes 25 minority (17 African Americans, 5 American Indian/Alaska Native, 3 Asian Americans or Pacific Islanders), 3 international. Average age 39. 151 applicants, 68% accepted, 74 enrolled. In 2009, 52 master's, 5 other advanced degrees awarded. *Degree requirements:* For master's, comprehensive exam, thesis or alternative, oral and written exams; for doctorate, comprehensive exam, thesis/dissertation or alternative, oral and written exams. *Entrance requirements:* For master's, MAT or GRE, Alabama RN license, BSN, minimum GPA of 3.0; for doctorate, master's degree in nursing in an advanced practice area; for Certificate, MAT or GRE, minimum GPA of 3.0. Additional exam requirements/recommendations for international students: Required—TOEFL (minimum score 500 paper-based; 173 computer-based; 62 iBT). *Application deadline:* For fall admission, 7/15 for domestic students, 4/1 for international students; for spring admission, 11/30 for domestic students, 9/1 for international students. Applications are processed on a rolling basis. Application fee: $40 ($50 for international students). Electronic applications accepted. *Expenses:* Tuition, state resident: part-time $355.75 per credit hour. Tuition, nonresident: part-time $847.10 per credit hour. Required fees: $210.80 per semester. Tuition and fees vary according to course load and program. *Financial support:* In 2009–10, 11 students received support, including 11 teaching assistantships with full and partial tuition reimbursements available (averaging $9,996 per year); career-related internships or fieldwork, Federal Work-Study, institutionally sponsored loans, scholarships/grants, traineeships, health care benefits, and unspecified assistantships also available. Support available to part-time students. Financial award application deadline: 4/1; financial award applicants required to submit FAFSA. *Faculty research:* Home health care, gerontology, pediatric nursing, family nurse practitioner, adult acute care administration. *Unit head:* Dr. Fay Raines, Dean, 256-824-6345, Fax: 256-824-6026, E-mail: rainesc@uah.edu. *Application contact:* Charles Davis, Associate Director of Nursing Student Affairs Graduate Programs, 256-824-6669, Fax: 256-824-6026, E-mail: charles.davis@uah.edu.

University of Alaska Anchorage, College of Health and Social Welfare, School of Nursing, Anchorage, AK 99508. Offers family nurse practitioner (Certificate); nursing (MS); nursing education (Certificate); psychiatric nurse practitioner (Certificate). *Accreditation:* NLN. Part-time and evening/weekend programs available. *Degree requirements:* For master's, comprehensive exam, individual project. *Entrance requirements:* For master's, GRE or MAT, BS in nursing, interview, minimum GPA of 3.0, RN license, 1 year of part-time or 6 months of full-time clinical experience. Additional exam requirements/recommendations for international students: Required—TOEFL (minimum score 550 paper-based; 213 computer-based).

University of Alberta, Faculty of Graduate Studies and Research, Faculty of Nursing, Edmonton, AB T6G 2E1, Canada. Offers MN, PhD. Part-time programs available. *Faculty:* 58 full-time (all women), 1 part-time/adjunct (0 women). *Students:* 39 full-time (37 women), 154 part-time (149 women). 48 applicants, 88% accepted, 40 enrolled. In 2009, 13 master's, 6 doctorates awarded. *Degree requirements:* For master's, thesis optional, clinical practice; for doctorate, thesis/dissertation. *Entrance requirements:* For master's, B Sc N, 1 year of clinical nursing experience in specialty area; for doctorate, MN. Additional exam requirements/recommendations for international students: Required—TOEFL (minimum score 550 paper-based; 213 computer-based). *Application deadline:* For fall admission, 6/1 for domestic and international students; for winter admission, 10/1 for domestic and international students; for spring admission, 2/1 for domestic and international students. Applications are processed on a rolling basis. Tuition and fees charges are reported in Canadian dollars. *Expenses:* Tuition, area resident: Full-time $4626 Canadian dollars; part-time $99.72 Canadian dollars per unit. International tuition: $8216 Canadian dollars full-time. Required fees: $3590 Canadian dollars; $99.72 Canadian dollars per unit. $215 Canadian dollars per term. *Financial support:* In 2009–10, 12 fellowships with partial tuition reimbursements (averaging $23,868 per year), 27 research assistantships with partial tuition reimbursements (averaging $6,186 per year), 12 teaching assistantships with partial tuition reimbursements (averaging $2,365 per year) were awarded; institutionally sponsored loans and scholarships/grants also available. *Faculty research:* Symptom management, healthy human development, health policy, teaching excellence and information. Total annual research expenditures: $3.2 million. *Unit head:* Dr. M. Allen, Associate Dean, 780-492-4338, Fax: 780-492-2551. *Application contact:* Elaine Carswell, Administrative Assistant, 403-492-6251, Fax: 403-492-2551, E-mail: ecarswel@ua-nursing.ualberta.ca.

The University of Arizona, College of Nursing, Tucson, AZ 85721. Offers health care informatics (Certificate); nurse practitioner (MS, Certificate); nursing (DNP, PhD); rural health (Certificate). *Accreditation:* AACN. Part-time programs available. Postbaccalaureate distance learning degree programs offered (minimal on-campus study). *Faculty:* 19. *Students:* 63 full-time (58 women), 81 part-time (71 women); includes 3 minority (all Hispanic Americans), 9 international. Average age 41. In 2009, 25 master's, 19 doctorates awarded. Terminal master's awarded for partial completion of doctoral program. *Degree requirements:* For master's, thesis optional; for doctorate, comprehensive exam, thesis/dissertation. *Entrance requirements:* For master's, BSN, eligibility for RN license; for doctorate, BSN; for Certificate, GRE General Test, Arizona RN license, BSN, minimum GPA of 3.0. Additional exam requirements/recommendations for international students: Required—TOEFL (minimum score 550 paper-based; 213 computer-based; 79 iBT). *Application deadline:* For fall admission, 1/15 for domestic and international students. Applications are processed on a rolling basis. Application fee: $75. Electronic applications accepted. *Expenses:* Contact institution. *Financial support:* In 2009–10, 6 research assistantships with full tuition reimbursements (averaging $15,552 per year) were awarded; teaching assistantships, career-related internships or fieldwork, institutionally sponsored loans, scholarships/grants, traineeships, health care benefits, tuition waivers (full), and unspecified assistantships also available. Financial award application deadline: 6/1. *Faculty research:* Vulnerable populations, injury mechanisms and biobehavioral responses, health care systems, informatics, rural health. Total annual research expenditures: $4.9 million. *Unit head:* Dr. Carolyn Murdaugh, Associate Dean, 520-626-7124, Fax: 520-626-6424, E-mail: cmurdaugh@nursing.arizona.edu. *Application contact:* Sally J. Reel, Assistant Dean, Student Affairs, 520-626-6767, Fax: 520-626-6424, E-mail: sreel@nursing.arizona.edu.

University of Arkansas, Graduate School, College of Education and Health Professions, Eleanor Mann School of Nursing, Fayetteville, AR 72701-1201. Offers MSN. *Accreditation:* AACN. Postbaccalaureate distance learning degree programs offered. *Students:* 6 full-time (all women), 6 part-time (all women); includes 3 minority (1 African American, 1 American Indian/Alaska Native, 1 Hispanic American). In 2009, 5 master's awarded. Application fee: $40 ($50 for international students). *Expenses:* Tuition, state resident: full-time $7355; part-time $356.58 per hour. Tuition, nonresident: full-time $17,401; part-time $775.17 per hour. Required fees: $1203. *Financial support:* Fellowships, research assistantships, teaching assistantships available. *Unit head:* Dr. Nan A. Smith-Blair, Director, 479-575-3904, Fax: 479-575-3218, E-mail: nsblair@uark.edu. *Application contact:* Dr. Kathleen Barta, Graduate Admissions, 479-575-5871, E-mail: kbarta@uark.edu.

University of Arkansas for Medical Sciences, Graduate School, College of Nursing, Little Rock, AR 72205-7199. Offers PhD. *Accreditation:* AACN. Part-time programs available. *Faculty:* 77 full-time (71 women). *Students:* 1 full-time, 27 part-time. *Entrance requirements:* For doctorate, GRE. Additional exam requirements/recommendations for international students: Required—TOEFL. *Application deadline:* For fall admission, 1/2 for domestic and international students. Application fee: $0. *Financial support:* Career-related internships or fieldwork and traineeships available. Support available to part-time students. *Unit head:* Dr. Claudia P. Barone, Dean, 501-686-5374. *Application contact:* Dr. Elaine Souder, Information Contact, 501-296-1893, E-mail: esouder@uams.edu.

The University of British Columbia, Faculty of Applied Science, Program in Nursing, Vancouver, BC V6T 1Z1, Canada. Offers MSN, PhD. Part-time programs available. *Degree requirements:* For master's, essay or thesis; for doctorate, comprehensive exam, thesis/dissertation. *Entrance requirements:* For master's, GRE, bachelor's degree in nursing; for doctorate, GRE, master's degree in nursing. Additional exam requirements/recommendations for international students: Required—TOEFL. Electronic applications accepted. *Faculty research:* Women and children, aging, critical care, cross-cultural.

University of Calgary, Faculty of Graduate Studies, Faculty of Nursing, Calgary, AB T2N 1N4, Canada. Offers MN, PhD, PMD. Part-time programs available. *Degree requirements:* For master's, comprehensive exam (for some programs), thesis (for some programs); for doctorate, thesis/dissertation; for PMD, comprehensive exam. *Entrance requirements:* For master's and PMD, nursing experience, nursing registration; for doctorate, nursing registration. Additional exam requirements/recommendations for international students: Required—TOEFL (minimum score 600 paper-based; 250 computer-based). Electronic applications accepted. *Expenses:* Contact institution. *Faculty research:* Health outcomes across multiple populations and multiple settings includes patients and families with chronic health problems, culturally diverse and vulnerable populations; family health; core processes; professional, educational and health services delivery.

University of California, Los Angeles, Graduate Division, School of Nursing, Los Angeles, CA 90095. Offers MSN, PhD, MBA/MSN. *Accreditation:* AACN. *Students:* 344 full-time (310 women); includes 138 minority (23 African Americans, 2 American Indian/Alaska Native, 61 Asian Americans or Pacific Islanders, 52 Hispanic Americans), 1 international. Average age 32. 684 applicants, 28% accepted, 136 enrolled. In 2009, 180 master's, 5 doctorates awarded. *Degree requirements:* For master's, comprehensive exam; for doctorate, thesis/dissertation, oral and written qualifying exams. *Entrance requirements:* For master's, minimum GPA of 3.0, bachelor's degree in nursing; for doctorate, GRE General Test, minimum undergraduate GPA of 3.5, bachelor's or master's degree in nursing, licensed as registered nurse. Additional exam requirements/recommendations for international students: Required—TOEFL, Commission on Graduates of Foreign Nursing Schools exam. *Application deadline:* For fall admission, 12/1 priority date for domestic and international students. Application fee: $70 ($90 for international students). Electronic applications accepted. *Financial support:* In 2009–10, 185 fellowships with full and partial tuition reimbursements, 10 research assistantships with full and partial tuition reimbursements, 34 teaching assistantships with full and partial tuition reimbursements were awarded; Federal Work-Study, institutionally sponsored loans, scholarships/grants, health care benefits, tuition waivers (full and partial), and unspecified assistantships also available. Financial award application deadline: 3/1; financial award applicants required to submit FAFSA. *Faculty research:* AIDS, adolescents, gerontology, homeless, activity/mobility. *Unit head:* Prof. Courtney H. Lyder, Dean, 310-825-9621. *Application contact:* Department Office, 310-825-7181, E-mail: sonsaff@sonnet.ucla.edu.

University of California, San Francisco, Graduate Division, School of Nursing, Program in Nursing, San Francisco, CA 94143. Offers MS, PhD. *Accreditation:* AACN; ACNM/DOA (one or more programs are accredited). *Degree requirements:* For master's, comprehensive exam, thesis or alternative; for doctorate, thesis/dissertation. *Entrance requirements:* For master's and doctorate, GRE General Test. *Expenses:* Contact institution.

University of Central Arkansas, Graduate School, College of Health and Behavioral Sciences, Department of Nursing, Conway, AR 72035-0001. Offers clinical nurse specialist (MSN); nurse practitioner (MSN). *Accreditation:* AACN. *Faculty:* 7 full-time (all women). *Students:* 12 full-time (11 women), 134 part-time (128 women); includes 14 minority (9 African Americans, 4 American Indian/Alaska Native, 1 Asian American or Pacific Islander), 1 international. Average age 34. 40 applicants, 93% accepted, 32 enrolled. In 2009, 19 master's awarded. *Degree requirements:* For master's, comprehensive exam, thesis optional, clinicals. *Entrance requirements:* For master's, GRE General Test, minimum GPA of 2.7. Additional exam requirements/recommendations for international students: Required—TOEFL (minimum score 550 paper-based; 213 computer-based). *Application deadline:* For fall admission, 3/1 priority date for domestic students; for spring admission, 10/1 for domestic students. Applications are processed on a rolling basis. Application fee: $25 ($50 for international students). *Expenses:* Contact institution. *Financial support:* Federal Work-Study, traineeships, and unspecified assistantships available. Financial award application deadline: 2/15; financial award applicants required to submit FAFSA. Total annual research expenditures: $216,643. *Unit head:* Dr. Barbara Williams, Chairperson, 501-450-3119, Fax: 501-450-5503, E-mail: barbaraw@uca.edu. *Application contact:* Patti Hornor, Administrative Assistant, 501-450-5063, Fax: 501-450-5678, E-mail: pattih@uca.edu.

University of Central Florida, College of Nursing, Orlando, FL 32816. Offers adult nurse practitioner (MSN, Post-Master's Certificate); clinical nurse leader (MSN, Post-Master's Certificate); clinical nurse specialist (MSN, Post-Master's Certificate); family nurse practitioner (MSN, Post-Master's Certificate); leadership and management (MSN); nurse educator (MSN);

nursing (PhD); nursing education (Post-Master's Certificate); nursing practice (DNP); pediatric nurse practitioner (MSN, Post-Master's Certificate). *Accreditation:* AACN. Part-time and evening/weekend programs available. *Faculty:* 38 full-time (34 women), 49 part-time/adjunct (47 women). *Students:* 98 full-time (93 women), 371 part-time (350 women); includes 132 minority (63 African Americans, 2 American Indian/Alaska Native, 29 Asian Americans or Pacific Islanders, 38 Hispanic Americans), 9 international. Average age 39. 363 applicants, 49% accepted, 139 enrolled. In 2009, 72 master's, 3 doctorates, 8 other advanced degrees awarded. *Degree requirements:* For master's, thesis or alternative. *Entrance requirements:* For master's, GRE General Test, minimum GPA of 3.0 in last 60 hours. Additional exam requirements/recommendations for international students: Required—TOEFL. *Application deadline:* For fall admission, 2/15 for domestic students; for spring admission, 9/15 for domestic students. Application fee: $30. Electronic applications accepted. *Expenses:* Tuition, state resident: part-time $306.31 per credit hour. Tuition, nonresident: part-time $1099.01 per credit hour. Part-time tuition and fees vary according to degree level and program. *Financial support:* In 2009–10, 30 students received support, including 30 fellowships with partial tuition reimbursements available (averaging $3,200 per year), 1 teaching assistantship with partial tuition reimbursement available (averaging $13,440 per year); research assistantships with partial tuition reimbursements available, career-related internships or fieldwork, Federal Work-Study, institutionally sponsored loans, traineeships, and unspecified assistantships also available. Financial award application deadline: 3/1; financial award applicants required to submit FAFSA. *Unit head:* Dr. Jean D. Leuner, Dean, 407-823-5496, Fax: 407-823-5675, E-mail: jleuner@mail.ucf.edu. *Application contact:* Dr. Jean D. Leuner, Dean, 407-823-5496, Fax: 407-823-5675, E-mail: jleuner@mail.ucf.edu.

University of Central Missouri, The Graduate School, College of Health and Human Services, Warrensburg, MO 64093. Offers criminal justice (MS); industrial hygiene (MS); occupational safety management (MS); physical education/exercise and sport science (MS); rural family nursing (MS); social gerontology (MS); sociology (MA); speech language pathology and audiology (MS). *Accreditation:* NCATE. Part-time programs available. Postbaccalaureate distance learning degree programs offered. *Faculty:* 53. *Students:* 169 full-time (107 women), 364 part-time (210 women); includes 65 minority (46 African Americans, 1 American Indian/Alaska Native, 5 Asian Americans or Pacific Islanders, 13 Hispanic Americans), 27 international. Average age 32. 236 applicants, 92% accepted, 211 enrolled. In 2009, 153 master's awarded. *Entrance requirements:* Additional exam requirements/recommendations for international students: Required—TOEFL (minimum score 550 paper-based; 79 computer-based). *Application deadline:* For fall admission, 6/1 priority date for domestic students, 5/1 for international students; for spring admission, 10/1 priority date for domestic students, 10/1 for international students. Applications are processed on a rolling basis. Application fee: $30 ($75 for international students). Electronic applications accepted. *Expenses:* Tuition, area resident: Part-time $245.80 per credit hour. Tuition, nonresident: part-time $491.60 per credit hour. Required fees: $24.20 per credit hour. Full-time tuition and fees vary according to course load, degree level, campus/location and reciprocity agreements. *Financial support:* Research assistantships with full and partial tuition reimbursements, teaching assistantships with full and partial tuition reimbursements, career-related internships or fieldwork, Federal Work-Study, scholarships/grants, and administrative and laboratory assistantships available. Support available to part-time students. Financial award application deadline: 3/1; financial award applicants required to submit FAFSA. *Unit head:* Dr. Rick Sluder, Dean, 660-543-4245, Fax: 660-543-4167, E-mail: sluder@ucmo.edu. *Application contact:* Laurie Delap, Admissions Coordinator, 660-543-4621, Fax: 660-543-4778, E-mail: gradinfo@ucmo.edu.

University of Cincinnati, Graduate School, College of Nursing, Cincinnati, OH 45221-0038. Offers clinical nurse specialist (MSN), including adult health, community health, neonatal, nursing administration, occupational health, pediatric health, psychiatric nursing, women's health; nurse anesthesia (MSN); nurse midwifery (MSN); nurse practitioner (MSN), including acute care, ambulatory care, family, family/psychiatric, women's health; nursing (PhD); MBA/MSN. *Accreditation:* AACN; AANA/CANAEP (one or more programs are accredited); ACNM/DOA. Part-time programs available. Postbaccalaureate distance learning degree programs offered (no on-campus study). Terminal master's awarded for partial completion of doctoral program. *Degree requirements:* For master's, thesis or alternative; for doctorate, comprehensive exam, thesis/dissertation. *Entrance requirements:* For master's and doctorate, GRE General Test. Additional exam requirements/recommendations for international students: Required—TOEFL (minimum score 520 paper-based; 190 computer-based). Electronic applications accepted. *Faculty research:* Substance abuse, injury and violence, symptom management.

University of Colorado at Colorado Springs, Graduate School, Beth-El College of Nursing and Health Sciences, Colorado Springs, CO 80933-7150. Offers adult health nurse practitioner and clinical specialist (MSN); family practitioner (MSN), including community clinical specialist, forensic clinical specialist, holistic clinical specialist; neonatal nurse practitioner and clinical specialist (MSN); nursing administration (MSN); nursing practice (DNP); women nurse practitioner (MSN). *Accreditation:* AACN. Part-time programs available. Postbaccalaureate distance learning degree programs offered (minimal on-campus study). *Faculty:* 26 full-time (21 women), 3 part-time/adjunct (all women). *Students:* 132 full-time (112 women), 81 part-time (71 women); includes 35 minority (6 African Americans, 2 American Indian/Alaska Native, 6 Asian Americans or Pacific Islanders, 21 Hispanic Americans), 3 international. Average age 36. 245 applicants, 47% accepted, 58 enrolled. In 2009, 33 master's awarded. *Degree requirements:* For master's, comprehensive exam, thesis optional; for doctorate, capstone project. *Entrance requirements:* For master's, GRE General Test or MAT, BSN, minimum GPA of 3.0, unrestricted RN license; for doctorate, interview; active RN license; MA; minimum GPA of 3.3; National Certification as NP or CNS; portfolio. Additional exam requirements/recommendations for international students: Required—TOEFL. *Application deadline:* For fall admission, 6/1 priority date for domestic students; for spring admission, 11/15 for domestic students. Application fee: $60 ($75 for international students). Electronic applications accepted. *Expenses:* Contact institution. *Financial support:* Fellowships, career-related internships or fieldwork, Federal Work-Study, and scholarships/grants available. Support available to part-time students. Financial award application deadline: 3/1; financial award applicants required to submit FAFSA. *Faculty research:* Women's health, uncertainty, empowerment, family experience in chronic illness. Total annual research expenditures: $703,545. *Unit head:* Dr. Nancy Smith, Dean, 719-255-4411, Fax: 719-255-4416, E-mail: nsmith2@uccs.edu. *Application contact:* Jackie Crouch, Graduate Recruitment Coordinator, 719-255-4493, Fax: 719-255-4416, E-mail: jcrouch@uccs.edu.

University of Colorado Denver, College of Nursing, Doctor of Nursing Practice Program, Denver, CO 80217-3364. Offers DNP. *Accreditation:* AACN; NLN. Postbaccalaureate distance learning degree programs offered. *Students:* 19 full-time (all women), 29 part-time (27 women); includes 6 minority (1 African American, 1 Asian American or Pacific Islander, 4 Hispanic Americans), 1 international. *Degree requirements:* For doctorate, comprehensive exam, thesis/dissertation. *Entrance requirements:* For doctorate, GRE General Test, minimum GPA of 3.0, portfolio, resume or curriculum vitae. Additional exam requirements/recommendations for international students: Required—TOEFL (minimum score 550 paper-based; 213 computer-based). *Application deadline:* For fall admission, 12/1 for domestic students. Application fee: $50. Electronic applications accepted. *Financial support:* Career-related internships or fieldwork, Federal Work-Study, and institutionally sponsored loans available. Support available to part-time students. Financial award application deadline: 3/15; financial award applicants required to submit FAFSA. *Unit head:* Dr. Kathy Magilvy, Assistant Dean, 303-724-8507, E-mail: kathy.magilvy@ucdenver.edu. *Application contact:* Dr. Kathy Magilvy, Assistant Dean, 303-724-8507, E-mail: kathy.magilvy@ucdenver.edu.

University of Connecticut, Graduate School, School of Nursing, Storrs, CT 06269. Offers MS, PhD, Post-Master's Certificate. *Accreditation:* AACN. *Faculty:* 37 full-time (29 women). *Students:* 59 full-time (53 women), 134 part-time (119 women); includes 30 minority (12 African Americans, 1 American Indian/Alaska Native, 6 Asian Americans or Pacific Islanders, 11 Hispanic Americans), 1 international. Average age 39. 89 applicants, 71% accepted, 34 enrolled. In 2009, 32 master's, 4 doctorates, 2 other advanced degrees awarded. *Degree requirements:* For master's, comprehensive exam; for doctorate, thesis/dissertation. *Entrance requirements:* Additional exam requirements/recommendations for international students: Required—TOEFL (minimum score 550 paper-based; 213 computer-based). *Application deadline:* For fall admission, 2/1 priority date for domestic and international students; for spring admission, 11/1 for domestic students, 10/1 for international students. Applications are processed on a rolling basis. Application fee: $55. Electronic applications accepted. *Expenses:* Tuition, state resident: full-time $4725; part-time $525 per credit. Tuition, nonresident: full-time $12,267; part-time $1363 per credit. Required fees: $346 per semester. Tuition and fees vary according to course load. *Financial support:* In 2009–10, 9 research assistantships with full tuition reimbursements, 12 teaching assistantships with full tuition reimbursements were awarded; fellowships, Federal Work-Study, scholarships/grants, health care benefits, and unspecified assistantships also available. Financial award application deadline: 2/1; financial award applicants required to submit FAFSA. *Unit head:* Anne R. Bavier, Dean, 860-486-0537, Fax: 860-486-0001, E-mail: anne.bavier@uconn.edu. *Application contact:* Elizabeth Anderson, Chairperson, 860-486-0577, E-mail: elizabeth.anderson@uconn.edu.

University of Delaware, College of Health Sciences, School of Nursing, Newark, DE 19716. Offers adult nurse practitioner (MSN, PMC); cardiopulmonary clinical nurse specialist (MSN, PMC); cardiopulmonary clinical nurse specialist/adult nurse practitioner (MSN, PMC); family nurse practitioner (MSN, PMC); gerontology clinical nurse specialist (MSN, PMC); gerontology clinical nurse specialist geriatric nurse practitioner (PMC); gerontology clinical nurse specialist/geriatric nurse practitioner (MSN); health services administration (MSN, PMC); nursing of children clinical nurse specialist (MSN, PMC); nursing of children clinical nurse specialist/pediatric nurse practitioner (MSN, PMC); oncology/immune deficiency clinical nurse specialist (MSN, PMC); oncology/immune deficiency clinical nurse specialist/adult nurse practitioner (MSN, PMC); perinatal/women's health clinical nurse specialist (MSN, PMC); perinatal/women's health clinical nurse specialist/women's health nurse practitioner (MSN, PMC); psychiatric nursing clinical nurse specialist (MSN, PMC). *Accreditation:* AACN; NLN (one or more programs are accredited). Part-time and evening/weekend programs available. Postbaccalaureate distance learning degree programs offered (minimal on-campus study). *Degree requirements:* For master's, thesis optional. *Entrance requirements:* For master's, BSN, interview, RN license. Electronic applications accepted. *Faculty research:* Marriage and chronic illness, health promotion, congestive heart failure patient outcomes, school nursing, diabetes in children, culture, health disparities, cardiovascular, prison nursing, oncology, public policy, child obesity, smoking and teen pregnancy, blood pressure measurements, men's health.

University of Evansville, College of Education and Health Sciences, Department of Nursing and Health Sciences, Evansville, IN 47722. Offers health services administration (MS). Part-time and evening/weekend programs available. *Faculty:* 1 full-time (0 women), 4 part-time/adjunct (2 women). *Students:* 8 full-time (2 women), 6 part-time (4 women), 8 international. Average age 30. 7 applicants, 86% accepted, 6 enrolled. In 2009, 10 master's awarded. *Entrance requirements:* For master's, GRE or GMAT, 2 letters of reference, interview. Additional exam requirements/recommendations for international students: Required—TOEFL (minimum score 530 paper-based; 71 iBT), IELTS (minimum score 6). *Application deadline:* For fall admission, 7/1 priority date for domestic and international students; for spring admission, 10/1 priority date for domestic students. Applications are processed on a rolling basis. Application fee: $35 ($50 for international students). *Expenses:* Contact institution. *Financial support:* In 2009–10, 2 students received support. Application deadline: 6/1. *Faculty research:* International health systems, health care ethics, health care marketing. *Unit head:* Dr. Amy Hall, Chair, 812-488-2343, Fax: 812-488-2717, E-mail: ah169@evansville.edu. *Application contact:* Dr. William Stroube, Professor and Director, Health Services Administration Program, 812-488-2343, Fax: 812-488-2717, E-mail: hsa@evansville.edu.

University of Florida, Graduate School, College of Nursing, Gainesville, FL 32611. Offers nursing (MSN); nursing sciences (PhD). *Accreditation:* AACN; ACNM/DOA (one or more programs are accredited). Part-time programs available. *Degree requirements:* For master's, thesis optional; for doctorate, thesis/dissertation. *Entrance requirements:* For master's and doctorate, GRE General Test, minimum GPA of 3.0. Additional exam requirements/recommendations for international students: Required—TOEFL (minimum score 550 paper-based; 213 computer-based). Electronic applications accepted. *Faculty research:* Wellness in the elderly, women's health, sleep patterns, immune competence, hypertension.

University of Hartford, College of Education, Nursing, and Health Professions, Program in Nursing, West Hartford, CT 06117-1599. Offers community/public health nursing (MSN); nursing education (MSN); nursing management (MSN). *Accreditation:* AACN. Part-time and evening/weekend programs available. *Degree requirements:* For master's, research project. *Entrance requirements:* For master's, BSN, Connecticut RN license. Additional exam requirements/recommendations for international students: Required—TOEFL (minimum score 550 paper-based; 213 computer-based). Electronic applications accepted. *Expenses:* Contact institution. *Faculty research:* Child development, women in doctoral study, applying feminist theory in teaching methods, near death experience, grandmothers as primary care providers.

University of Hawaii at Manoa, Graduate Division, School of Nursing and Dental Hygiene, Honolulu, HI 96822. Offers clinical nurse specialist (MS), including adult health, community mental health; nurse practitioner (MS), including adult health, community mental health, family nurse practitioner; nursing (PhD, Graduate Certificate); nursing administration (MS). *Accreditation:* AACN; NLN (one or more programs are accredited). Part-time programs available. Postbaccalaureate distance learning degree programs offered (minimal on-campus study). *Faculty:* 20 full-time (18 women), 16 part-time/adjunct (15 women). *Students:* 81 full-time (69 women), 135 part-time (121 women); includes 115 minority (4 African Americans, 2 American Indian/Alaska Native, 105 Asian Americans or Pacific Islanders, 4 Hispanic Americans), 2 international. Average age 38. 189 applicants, 52% accepted, 79 enrolled. In 2009, 25 master's, 4 doctorates awarded. *Degree requirements:* For master's, thesis optional; for doctorate, comprehensive exam, thesis/dissertation. *Entrance requirements:* For master's, Hawaii RN license. Additional exam requirements/recommendations for international students: Required—TOEFL (minimum score 580 paper-based; 237 computer-based; 92 iBT), IELTS (minimum score 5). *Application deadline:* For fall admission, 2/1 for domestic and international students. Application fee: $60. *Expenses:* Contact institution. *Financial support:* In 2009–10, 6 students received support, including 28 fellowships (averaging $960 per year), 7 research assistantships (averaging $18,080 per year). Total annual research expenditures: $1.8 million. *Unit head:* Mary Boland, Dean, 808-956-8522, Fax: 808-956-3257, E-mail: mgboland@hawaii.edu. *Application contact:* Kristine Qureshi, Graduate Chair, 808-956-8744, Fax: 808-956-3257, E-mail: kqureshi@hawaii.edu.

University of Houston–Victoria, School of Nursing, Victoria, TX 77901-4450. Offers MSN. *Accreditation:* AACN. *Entrance requirements:* For master's, GRE or MAT, BSN degree from an accredited bachelor's degree or diploma program, minimum GPA of 3.0 in last 60 hours of academic course work, valid Texas RN licensure, 2 letters of recommendation.

University of Illinois at Chicago, Graduate College, College of Nursing, Chicago, IL 60607-7128. Offers MS, DNP, PhD, MBA/MS, MPH/MS. *Accreditation:* AACN. Part-time programs available. *Degree requirements:* For master's, thesis or alternative; for doctorate, thesis/dissertation. *Entrance requirements:* For master's and doctorate, GRE General Test, minimum GPA of 2.75. Additional exam requirements/recommendations for international students: Required—TOEFL. Electronic applications accepted. *Expenses:* Contact institution.

University of Indianapolis, Graduate Programs, School of Nursing, Indianapolis, IN 46227-3697. Offers family practice (post-RN) (MSN); gerontological nurse practitioner (MSN); nurse-midwifery (MSN); nursing (MSN); nursing administration (MSN); nursing education (MSN); MBA/MSN. *Accreditation:* AACN; ACNM. *Faculty:* 4 full-time (3 women), 2 part-time/adjunct (both women). *Students:* 27 full-time (26 women), 118 part-time (109 women); includes 10 minority (6 African Americans, 1 American Indian/Alaska Native, 1 Asian American or Pacific Islander, 2 Hispanic Americans), 2 international. Average age 38. *Entrance requirements:* For master's, minimum GPA of 3.0, interview, letters of recommendation, resume, IN nursing license, 1 year professional practice. Additional exam requirements/recommendations for

Nursing—General

University of Indianapolis (continued)
international students: Required—TOEFL (minimum score 550 paper-based; 213 computer-based). *Application deadline:* For fall admission, 8/1 for domestic students; for winter admission, 12/15 for domestic students; for spring admission, 4/15 for domestic students. Applications are processed on a rolling basis. Application fee: $50. *Financial support:* Federal Work-Study available. *Unit head:* Dr. Anne Thomas, Dean, 317-788-3206, E-mail: athomas@uindy.edu. *Application contact:* T. C. Crum, Information Contact, 317-788-2128, Fax: 317-788-3542, E-mail: tcrum@uindy.edu.

The University of Iowa, Graduate College, College of Nursing, Iowa City, IA 52242-1316. Offers MSN, DNP, PhD, MBA/MSN, MSN/MPH. *Accreditation:* AACN; AANA/CANAEP (one or more programs are accredited). *Degree requirements:* For master's, thesis optional, portfolio, project; for doctorate, comprehensive exam, thesis/dissertation. *Entrance requirements:* For master's, minimum GPA of 3.0; for doctorate, GRE General Test, minimum GPA of 3.0. Additional exam requirements/recommendations for international students: Required—TOEFL (minimum score 550 paper-based; 213 computer-based; 81 iBT). Electronic applications accepted. *Expenses:* Contact institution.

The University of Kansas, University of Kansas Medical Center, School of Nursing, Kansas City, KS 66160. Offers clinical research management (PMC); family nurse practitioner (PMC); health care informatics (PMC); health professions educator (PMC); nurse midwife (PMC); nursing (MS, DNP, PhD); organizational leadership (PMC); psychiatric/mental health nurse practitioner (PMC); public health nursing (PMC). *Accreditation:* AACN; ACNM/DOA. Part-time programs available. Postbaccalaureate distance learning degree programs offered (minimal on-campus study). *Faculty:* 65. *Students:* 59 full-time (56 women), 309 part-time (285 women); includes 37 minority (17 African Americans, 4 American Indian/Alaska Native, 7 Asian Americans or Pacific Islanders, 9 Hispanic Americans), 10 international. Average age 38. 138 applicants, 59% accepted, 82 enrolled. In 2009, 78 master's, 3 doctorates awarded. Terminal master's awarded for partial completion of doctoral program. *Degree requirements:* For master's, thesis optional, general oral exam; for doctorate, one foreign language, thesis/dissertation, comprehensive oral and written exam. *Entrance requirements:* For master's, bachelor's degree in nursing, minimum GPA of 3.0, RN license, 1 year of clinical experience; for doctorate, GRE General Test, master's degree in nursing, minimum GPA of 3.5. Additional exam requirements/recommendations for international students: Required—TOEFL. *Application deadline:* For fall admission, 4/1 for domestic students; for spring admission, 9/1 for domestic students. Application fee: $60. Electronic applications accepted. *Expenses:* Tuition, state resident: full-time $6492; part-time $270.50 per credit hour. Tuition, nonresident: full-time $15,510; part-time $646.25 per credit hour. Required fees: $847; $70.56 per credit hour. Tuition and fees vary according to course load and program. *Financial support:* In 2009–10, 93 students received support, including 7 research assistantships (averaging $24,000 per year), 23 teaching assistantships with full and partial tuition reimbursements available (averaging $24,000 per year); traineeships also available. Financial award application deadline: 2/14; financial award applicants required to submit FAFSA. *Faculty research:* Breastfeeding practices of teen mothers, national database of nursing quality indicators, caregiving of families of patients using technology in the home, self care talk intervention partnership between caregivers of stroke survivors and nurses, smoking cessation. Total annual research expenditures: $5 million. *Unit head:* Dr. Karen L. Miller, Dean, 913-588-1601, Fax: 913-588-1660, E-mail: kmiller@kumc.edu. *Application contact:* Dr. Rita K. Clifford, Associate Dean, Student Affairs, 913-588-1619, Fax: 913-588-1615, E-mail: rcliffor@kumc.edu.

University of Kentucky, Graduate School, Graduate School Programs in the College of Nursing, Program in Nursing, Lexington, KY 40506-0032. Offers MSN, PhD. *Accreditation:* AACN. *Degree requirements:* For master's, comprehensive exam, thesis optional, research project; for doctorate, comprehensive exam, thesis/dissertation. *Entrance requirements:* For master's, GRE General Test, minimum undergraduate GPA of 2.75; for doctorate, GRE General Test, minimum undergraduate GPA of 2.75, graduate 3.0. Additional exam requirements/recommendations for international students: Required—TOEFL (minimum score 550 paper-based; 213 computer-based). Electronic applications accepted.

University of Lethbridge, School of Graduate Studies, Lethbridge, AB T1K 3M4, Canada. Offers accounting (MScM); addictions counseling (M Sc); agricultural biotechnology (M Sc); agricultural studies (M Sc, MA); anthropology (MA); archaeology (MA); art (MA, MFA); biochemistry (M Sc); biological sciences (M Sc); biomolecular science (PhD); biosystems and biodiversity (PhD); Canadian studies (MA); chemistry (M Sc); computer science (M Sc); computer science and geographical information science (M Sc); counseling psychology (M Ed); dramatic arts (MA); earth, space, and physical science (PhD); economics (MA); educational leadership (M Ed); English (MA); environmental science (M Sc); evolution and behavior (PhD); exercise science (M Sc); finance (MScM); French (MA); French/German (MA); French/Spanish (MA); general education (M Ed); general management (MScM); geography (M Sc, MA); German (MA); health science (M Sc); health sciences (MA); history (MA); human resource management and labour relations (MScM); individualized multidisciplinary (M Sc, MA); information systems (MScM); international management (MScM); kinesiology (M Sc, MA); management (M Sc, MA); marketing (MScM); mathematics (M Sc); music (M Mus, MA); Native American studies (MA); neuroscience (M Sc, PhD); new media (MA); nursing (M Sc); philosophy (MA); physics (M Sc); policy and strategy (MScM); political science (MA); psychology (M Sc, MA); religious studies (MA); social sciences (MA); sociology (MA); theatre and dramatic arts (MFA); theoretical and computational science (PhD); urban and regional studies (MA); women's studies (MA). Part-time and evening/weekend programs available. *Degree requirements:* For doctorate, comprehensive exam, thesis/dissertation. *Entrance requirements:* For master's, GMAT (M Sc in management), bachelor's degree in related field, minimum GPA of 3.0 during previous 20 graded semester courses, 2 years teaching or related experience (M Ed); for doctorate, master's degree, minimum graduate GPA of 3.5. Additional exam requirements/recommendations for international students: Required—TOEFL. *Faculty research:* Movement and brain plasticity, gibberellin physiology, photosynthesis, carbon cycling, molecular properties of main-group ring components.

University of Louisiana at Lafayette, College of Nursing, Lafayette, LA 70504. Offers MSN. *Accreditation:* AACN. *Degree requirements:* For master's, thesis or alternative. *Entrance requirements:* For master's, GRE General Test, minimum GPA of 2.75. Additional exam requirements/recommendations for international students: Required—TOEFL (minimum score 550 paper-based; 213 computer-based). Electronic applications accepted.

University of Louisville, Graduate School, School of Nursing, Louisville, KY 40202. Offers adult nurse practitioner (MSN); family nurse practitioner (MSN); health professions education (MSN); neonatal nurse practitioner (MSN); nursing research (PhD); psychiatric mental health nurse practitioner (MSN). *Accreditation:* AACN. Part-time programs available. *Faculty:* 28 full-time (25 women), 4 part-time/adjunct (3 women). *Students:* 72 full-time (66 women), 57 part-time (52 women); includes 15 minority (11 African Americans, 3 Asian Americans or Pacific Islanders, 1 Hispanic American), 4 international. Average age 35. 45 applicants, 82% accepted, 31 enrolled. In 2009, 28 master's, 3 doctorates awarded. Terminal master's awarded for partial completion of doctoral program. *Degree requirements:* For master's, thesis optional; for doctorate, comprehensive exam, thesis/dissertation. *Entrance requirements:* For master's, GRE General Test, bachelor's degree in nursing, minimum GPA of 3.0, RN license; for doctorate, GRE General Test, BSN and MSN with recommended minimum GPA of 3.0. Additional exam requirements/recommendations for international students: Required—TOEFL. *Application deadline:* For fall admission, 4/1 priority date for domestic students, 4/1 for international students; for spring admission, 10/1 priority date for domestic students, 10/1 for international students. Applications are processed on a rolling basis. Application fee: $50. Electronic applications accepted. *Financial support:* In 2009–10, 45 students received support, including 2 fellowships with full tuition reimbursements available (averaging $20,000 per year), 5 research assistantships with full tuition reimbursements available (averaging $18,000 per year), 5 teaching assistantships with full tuition reimbursements available (averaging $18,000 per year); institutionally sponsored loans, scholarships/grants, traineeships, health care benefits, and unspecified assistantships also available. Support available to part-time students. Financial award application deadline: 4/15; financial award applicants required to submit FAFSA. *Faculty research:* Maternal-child/family stress after pregnancy loss, postpartum depression, access to healthcare (underserved populations), quality of life issues, physical activity (impact on chronic/acute conditions). Total annual research expenditures: $363,876. *Unit head:* Dr. Marcia J. Hern, Dean, 502-852-8300, Fax: 502-852-5044, E-mail: m.hern@gwise.louisville.edu. *Application contact:* Dr. Rosalie O'Dell Mainous, Associate Dean for Graduate Academic Affairs, 502-852-8387, Fax: 502-852-8783, E-mail: romain01@louisville.edu.

University of Maine, Graduate School, College of Natural Sciences, Forestry, and Agriculture, School of Nursing, Orono, ME 04469. Offers MS, CAS. *Accreditation:* AACN. *Faculty:* 16 full-time (15 women), 20 part-time/adjunct (18 women). *Students:* 7 full-time (all women), 11 part-time (all women); includes 1 minority (Hispanic American). Average age 38. 10 applicants, 40% accepted, 4 enrolled. In 2009, 12 master's awarded. *Entrance requirements:* For master's, GRE General Test. Additional exam requirements/recommendations for international students: Required—TOEFL. *Application deadline:* Applications are processed on a rolling basis. Application fee: $65. Electronic applications accepted. *Financial support:* Career-related internships or fieldwork, Federal Work-Study, institutionally sponsored loans, and tuition waivers (full and partial) available. Support available to part-time students. Financial award application deadline: 3/1. *Unit head:* Dr. Nancy Fishwick, Director, 207-581-2505, Fax: 207-581-2585. *Application contact:* Scott G. Delcourt, Associate Dean of the Graduate School, 207-581-3291, Fax: 207-581-3232, E-mail: graduate@maine.edu.

University of Manitoba, Faculty of Graduate Studies, Faculty of Nursing, Winnipeg, MB R3T 2N2, Canada. Offers cancer nursing (MN); nursing (MN). *Degree requirements:* For master's, thesis.

University of Mary, Division of Nursing, Bismarck, ND 58504-9652. Offers family nurse practitioner (MSN); nurse administrator (MSN); nursing educator (MSN). *Accreditation:* AACN. Part-time and evening/weekend programs available. Postbaccalaureate distance learning degree programs offered (minimal on-campus study). *Degree requirements:* For master's, comprehensive exam, thesis (for some programs), internship (family nurse practitioner), teaching practice. *Entrance requirements:* For master's, minimum GPA of 3.0 in nursing, interview, letters of recommendation. Additional exam requirements/recommendations for international students: Required—TOEFL. Electronic applications accepted. *Expenses:* Tuition: Full-time $10,062; part-time $430 per credit. Tuition and fees vary according to course load, degree level, program and student level. *Faculty research:* Gerontology issues, rural nursing, health policy, primary care, women's health.

University of Mary Hardin-Baylor, Graduate Studies in Nursing, Belton, TX 76513. Offers MSN. *Accreditation:* AACN. Part-time and evening/weekend programs available. *Degree requirements:* For master's, practicum. *Entrance requirements:* For master's, GRE General Test, RN, BSN. Electronic applications accepted.

University of Maryland, Baltimore, Graduate School, School of Nursing, Doctoral Program in Nursing, Baltimore, MD 21201. Offers direct nursing (PhD); indirect nursing (PhD). *Students:* 24 full-time (21 women), 29 part-time (26 women); includes 17 minority (9 African Americans, 5 Asian Americans or Pacific Islanders, 3 Hispanic Americans), 6 international. Average age 41. 34 applicants, 41% accepted, 6 enrolled. In 2009, 13 doctorates awarded. *Degree requirements:* For doctorate, thesis/dissertation. *Entrance requirements:* For doctorate, GRE General Test, minimum GPA of 3.0, MS in nursing. Additional exam requirements/recommendations for international students: Required—TOEFL (minimum score 550 paper-based; 80 iBT); Recommended—IELTS. *Application deadline:* For fall admission, 1/15 for domestic and international students. Application fee: $50. Electronic applications accepted. *Expenses:* Tuition, state resident: full-time $7290; part-time $405 per credit hour. Tuition, nonresident: full-time $12,780; part-time $710 per credit hour. Required fees: $774; $10 per credit hour. $297 per semester. Tuition and fees vary according to course load, degree level and program. *Financial support:* Fellowships, research assistantships, teaching assistantships available. Financial award application deadline: 2/15; financial award applicants required to submit FAFSA. *Unit head:* Dr. Susan Thomas, Director, 410-706-3716, Fax: 410-706-3769. *Application contact:* Janice Anarino, Program Coordinator.

University of Maryland, Baltimore, Graduate School, School of Nursing, Master's Program in Nursing, Baltimore, MD 21201. Offers community health nursing (MS); gerontological nursing (MS); maternal-child nursing (MS); medical-surgical nursing (MS); nurse-midwifery education (MS); nursing administration (MS); nursing education (MS); nursing health policy (MS); primary care nursing (MS); psychiatric nursing (MS); MS/MBA. *Accreditation:* AACN; AANA/CANAEP; ACNM/DOA; NLN (one or more programs are accredited). Part-time programs available. *Students:* 387 full-time (338 women), 528 part-time (491 women); includes 330 minority (230 African Americans, 3 American Indian/Alaska Native, 81 Asian Americans or Pacific Islanders, 16 Hispanic Americans), 10 international. Average age 36. 849 applicants, 40% accepted, 255 enrolled. In 2009, 264 master's awarded. *Degree requirements:* For master's, comprehensive exam (for some programs), thesis or alternative. *Entrance requirements:* For master's, GRE General Test, minimum GPA of 2.75, course work in statistics, BS in nursing. Additional exam requirements/recommendations for international students: Required—TOEFL (minimum score 550 paper-based; 80 iBT), or IELTS (minimum score 7). *Application deadline:* For fall admission, 1/15 for international students. Application fee: $50. Electronic applications accepted. *Expenses:* Tuition, state resident: full-time $7290; part-time $405 per credit hour. Tuition, nonresident: full-time $12,780; part-time $710 per credit hour. Required fees: $774; $10 per credit hour. $297 per semester. Tuition and fees vary according to course load, degree level and program. *Financial support:* Fellowships, research assistantships, teaching assistantships, career-related internships or fieldwork and traineeships available. Support available to part-time students. Financial award application deadline: 2/15; financial award applicants required to submit FAFSA. *Unit head:* Dr. Jane Kapustin, Assistant Dean, 410-706-6741, Fax: 410-706-4231. *Application contact:* Marjorie Fass, Admissions Director, 410-706-0501, Fax: 410-706-7238.

University of Massachusetts Amherst, Graduate School, School of Nursing, Amherst, MA 01003. Offers MS, DNP, PhD. *Accreditation:* AACN. Part-time programs available. Postbaccalaureate distance learning degree programs offered (minimal on-campus study). *Faculty:* 18 full-time (all women). *Students:* 54 full-time (50 women), 132 part-time (122 women); includes 42 minority (21 African Americans, 5 Asian Americans or Pacific Islanders, 16 Hispanic Americans), 8 international. Average age 43. 146 applicants, 77% accepted, 82 enrolled. In 2009, 6 master's, 9 doctorates awarded. Terminal master's awarded for partial completion of doctoral program. *Degree requirements:* For master's, thesis optional; for doctorate, comprehensive exam, thesis/dissertation. *Entrance requirements:* For master's and doctorate, GRE General Test. Additional exam requirements/recommendations for international students: Required—TOEFL (minimum score 550 paper-based; 213 computer-based; 80 iBT), IELTS (minimum score 6.5). *Application deadline:* For fall admission, 2/1 for domestic and international students. Applications are processed on a rolling basis. Application fee: $50 ($65 for international students). Electronic applications accepted. *Expenses:* Tuition, state resident: full-time $2640; part-time $110 per credit. Tuition, nonresident: full-time $9936; part-time $414 per credit. Tuition and fees vary according to course load. *Financial support:* In 2009–10, 8 fellowships with full tuition reimbursements (averaging $5,175 per year), 1 research assistantship with full tuition reimbursement (averaging $8,911 per year), 27 teaching assistantships with full tuition reimbursements (averaging $7,250 per year) were awarded; career-related internships or fieldwork, Federal Work-Study, scholarships/grants, traineeships, health care benefits, tuition waivers (full), and unspecified assistantships also available. Support available to part-time students. Financial award application deadline: 2/1. *Faculty research:* Health of older adults and their caretakers, mental health of individuals and families, health of children and adolescents, power and decision making, transcultural health. *Unit head:* Dr. M. Christine King, Graduate Program Director, 413-577-2322, Fax: 413-577-2550. *Application contact:* Jean M. Ames, Supervisor of Admissions, 413-545-0722, Fax: 413-577-0010, E-mail: gradadm@grad.umass.edu.

University of Massachusetts Boston, Office of Graduate Studies, College of Nursing and Health Sciences, Boston, MA 02125-3393. Offers MS, PhD, MS/MBA. *Accreditation:* AACN. Part-time and evening/weekend programs available. *Degree requirements:* For master's, comprehensive exam; for doctorate, comprehensive exam, thesis/dissertation. *Entrance requirements:* For master's, minimum GPA of 2.75; for doctorate, GRE General Test, master's degree, minimum GPA of 3.3. *Faculty research:* Domestic abuse and pregnancy, health policy and home health care, caregiving burdens of families, the chronically ill, health care delivery models and their impact on outcomes, health promotion and disease prevention among the elderly.

University of Massachusetts Dartmouth, Graduate School, College of Nursing, Graduate Nursing Programs, North Dartmouth, MA 02747-2300. Offers adult health/adult nurse practitioner (MS); adult health/advanced practice (MS); adult nurse practitioner (PMC); community nursing/advanced practice (MS); individualized nursing (PMC); nursing (PhD). Part-time programs available. *Faculty:* 29 full-time (all women), 26 part-time/adjunct (25 women). *Students:* 13 full-time (all women), 62 part-time (57 women); includes 4 minority (1 African American, 1 American Indian/Alaska Native, 2 Hispanic Americans), 1 international. Average age 40. 24 applicants, 100% accepted, 20 enrolled. In 2009, 17 master's, 2 other advanced degrees awarded. *Degree requirements:* For master's, thesis; for doctorate, thesis/dissertation. *Entrance requirements:* For master's, GRE General Test, BSN, minimum undergraduate GPA of 3.0, RN license, 3 letters of recommendation, 1 year experience as registered nurse; for doctorate, GRE General Test, minimum undergraduate GPA of 3.0, graduate 3.3; 3 letters of recommendation; personal statement; current Massachusetts RN license or eligibility for licensure in Massachusetts; 1 year professional nursing experience; example of scholarly writing. Additional exam requirements/recommendations for international students: Required—TOEFL (minimum score 500 paper-based). *Application deadline:* For fall admission, 4/20 for domestic students, 2/20 for international students; for spring admission, 10/15 for domestic students, 8/15 for international students. Application fee: $40 ($60 for international students). Electronic applications accepted. *Expenses:* Tuition, state resident: full-time $2071; part-time $86.29 per credit. Tuition, nonresident: full-time $8099; part-time $337.46 per credit. Required fees: $9446. Tuition and fees vary according to class time, course load and reciprocity agreements. *Financial support:* In 2009–10, 11 teaching assistantships with full tuition reimbursements (averaging $3,359 per year) were awarded; Federal Work-Study also available. Support available to part-time students. Financial award application deadline: 3/1; financial award applicants required to submit FAFSA. *Faculty research:* Chronic illness management, quality of life, diabetes care and education, environmental health, quantitative methodologies. Total annual research expenditures: $44,000. *Unit head:* Dr. Gail Russell, Director, 508-999-8251, Fax: 508-999-9127, E-mail: grussell@umassd.edu. *Application contact:* Elan Turcotte-Shamski, Graduate Admissions Officer, 508-999-8604, Fax: 508-999-8183, E-mail: graduate@umassd.edu.

University of Massachusetts Lowell, School of Health and Environment, Department of Nursing, Lowell, MA 01854-2881. Offers adult psychiatric and mental health nursing (MS, Graduate Certificate); family health nursing (MS); gerontological nursing (MS, Graduate Certificate); geropsychiatric nursing (Graduate Certificate); nursing (PhD); nursing education (Graduate Certificate); palliative and end-of-life nursing care (Graduate Certificate). *Accreditation:* AACN. *Degree requirements:* For master's, thesis optional; for doctorate, thesis/dissertation. *Entrance requirements:* For master's and doctorate, GRE General Test. *Faculty research:* Gerontology, women's health issues, long-term care, alcoholism, health promotion.

University of Massachusetts Worcester, Graduate School of Nursing, Worcester, MA 01655-0115. Offers adult acute/critical care nurse practitioner (MS, Post Master's Certificate); adult acute/critical care nurse practitioner and gerontological nurse practitioner (MS, Post Master's Certificate); adult primary care nurse practitioner (MS, Post Master's Certificate); adult primary care nurse practitioner and gerontological nurse practitioner (MS, Post Master's Certificate); family nurse practitioner (MS); gerontological nurse practitioner (Post Master's Certificate); nurse educator (MS); nursing (PhD). *Accreditation:* AACN. *Faculty:* 15 full-time (13 women), 31 part-time/adjunct (29 women). *Students:* 151 full-time (131 women), 6 part-time (all women); includes 14 minority (5 African Americans, 1 American Indian/Alaska Native, 5 Asian Americans or Pacific Islanders, 3 Hispanic Americans). Average age 37. 206 applicants, 34% accepted, 61 enrolled. In 2009, 62 master's, 3 doctorates awarded. *Degree requirements:* For doctorate, comprehensive exam, thesis/dissertation. *Entrance requirements:* For master's, GRE General Test, bachelor's degree, course work in statistics; for doctorate, GRE General Test, bachelor's or master's degree, RN licensure; for Post Master's Certificate, MS in nursing. Additional exam requirements/recommendations for international students: Required—TOEFL. *Application deadline:* For fall admission, 3/15 for domestic students. Applications are processed on a rolling basis. Application fee: $40 ($60 for international students). *Expenses:* Contact institution. *Financial support:* In 2009–10, 130 students received support. Scholarships/grants and traineeships available. Support available to part-time students. Financial award application deadline: 5/18; financial award applicants required to submit FAFSA. *Faculty research:* Symptom management, interventions, individual and family adjustment to chronic illness, women's health. *Unit head:* Dr. Paulette Seymour-Route, Dean, 508-856-5801, Fax: 508-856-6552, E-mail: paulette.seymour-route@umassmed.edu. *Application contact:* Diane Brescia, Admissions Coordinator, 508-856-3488, Fax: 508-856-5851, E-mail: diane.brescia@umassmed.edu.

University of Medicine and Dentistry of New Jersey, School of Nursing, Program in Advanced Practice Nursing, Newark, NJ 07107-1709. Offers MSN, Post Master's Certificate. *Entrance requirements:* Additional exam requirements/recommendations for international students: Required—TOEFL. Electronic applications accepted.

University of Memphis, Loewenberg School of Nursing, Memphis, TN 38152. Offers MSN, Graduate Certificate. *Accreditation:* AACN. *Faculty:* 15 full-time (all women), 3 part-time/adjunct (all women). *Students:* 20 full-time (all women), 226 part-time (217 women); includes 81 minority (71 African Americans, 6 Asian Americans or Pacific Islanders, 4 Hispanic Americans), 2 international. Average age 35. 111 applicants, 80% accepted, 20 enrolled. In 2009, 47 master's, 2 other advanced degrees awarded. *Degree requirements:* For master's, thesis or alternative. *Entrance requirements:* For master's, NCLEX Exam, interview. *Application fee:* $35 ($60 for international students). *Expenses:* Tuition, state resident: full-time $6246; part-time $347 per credit hour. Tuition, nonresident: full-time $15,894; part-time $883 per credit hour. Required fees: $1160. Full-time tuition and fees vary according to course load, degree level and program. *Financial support:* In 2009–10, 147 students received support. Federal Work-Study and scholarships/grants available. Financial award application deadline: 2/15; financial award applicants required to submit FAFSA. *Faculty research:* Technology in nursing, nurse retention, cultural competence, health policy, health access. Total annual research expenditures: $560,619. *Unit head:* Dr. Marjorie Luttrell, Dean, 901-678-2003, Fax: 901-678-4906, E-mail: mluttrel@memphis.edu. *Application contact:* Dr. Robert Koch, Associate Dean/Director of Graduate Studies, 901-678-2003, Fax: 901-678-4906, E-mail: rkoch@memphis.edu.

University of Miami, Graduate School, School of Nursing and Health Studies, Coral Gables, FL 33124. Offers acute care (MSN), including acute care nurse practitioner, nurse anesthesia; nursing (PhD); primary care (MSN), including adult nurse practitioner, family nurse practitioner, nurse midwifery, women's health practitioner. *Accreditation:* AACN; AANA/CANAEP; ACNM/DOA (one or more programs are accredited). Part-time programs available. *Degree requirements:* For master's, thesis optional; for doctorate, thesis/dissertation. *Entrance requirements:* For master's, GRE General Test, BSN, minimum GPA of 3.0, Florida RN license; for doctorate, GRE General Test, BSN or MSN, minimum GPA of 3.0. Additional exam requirements/recommendations for international students: Required—TOEFL (minimum score 550 paper-based; 213 computer-based). Electronic applications accepted. *Faculty research:* Transcultural nursing, exercise and depression in Alzheimer's disease, infectious diseases/HIV–AIDS, postpartum depression, outcomes assessment.

University of Michigan, Horace H. Rackham School of Graduate Studies, School of Nursing, Ann Arbor, MI 48109. Offers MS, PhD, Post Master's Certificate, MBA/MS, MHSA/MS, MS/MSI. *Accreditation:* AACN; ACNM/DOA (one or more programs are accredited). Part-time programs available. Postbaccalaureate distance learning degree programs offered (minimal on-campus

study). Terminal master's awarded for partial completion of doctoral program. *Degree requirements:* For doctorate, thesis/dissertation, oral defense of dissertation, preliminary exam. *Entrance requirements:* For master's, GRE General Test (if undergraduate GPA less than 3.25), minimum B average, nursing license; for doctorate, GRE General Test, nursing license, minimum B average, 2 original papers. Electronic applications accepted. *Expenses:* Tuition, state resident: full-time $17,286; part-time $1099 per credit hour. Tuition, nonresident: full-time $34,944; part-time $2080 per credit hour. Required fees: $95 per semester. Tuition and fees vary according to course load, degree level and program. *Faculty research:* Preparation of clinical nurse researchers, biobehavior, women's health, health promotion, substance abuse, psychobiology of menopause, fertility, obesity, health care systems.

University of Michigan–Flint, School of Health Professions and Studies, Program in Nursing, Flint, MI 48502-1950. Offers DNP. *Accreditation:* AACN. Part-time programs available. *Faculty:* 8 full-time (all women), 6 part-time/adjunct (all women). *Students:* 75 full-time (5 women), 7 part-time (0 women); includes 9 minority (5 African Americans, 1 Asian American or Pacific Islander, 3 Hispanic Americans), 1 international. Average age 42. 94 applicants, 32% accepted, 22 enrolled. *Entrance requirements:* Additional exam requirements/recommendations for international students: Required—TOEFL (minimum score 560 paper-based; 220 computer-based), IELTS (minimum score 6.5). *Application deadline:* For fall admission, 8/1 priority date for domestic students, 5/1 priority date for international students; for winter admission, 11/15 priority date for domestic students, 9/1 priority date for international students; for spring admission, 3/15 priority date for domestic students, 1/1 priority date for international students. Applications are processed on a rolling basis. Application fee: $55. Electronic applications accepted. *Expenses:* Contact institution. *Financial support:* Federal Work-Study, scholarships/grants, and unspecified assistantships available. Support available to part-time students. Financial award application deadline: 6/1; financial award applicants required to submit FAFSA. *Faculty research:* Family system stress, self breast exam, family roads evaluation, causal model testing for psychosocial development, basic needs. *Unit head:* Dr. Margaret Andrews, Director, 810-762-3420, Fax: 810-766-6851, E-mail: mmandrew@umflint.edu. *Application contact:* Bradley T. Maki, Director of Graduate Admissions, 810-762-3171, Fax: 810-766-6789, E-mail: bmaki@umflint.edu.

University of Minnesota, Twin Cities Campus, Graduate School, School of Nursing, Minneapolis, MN 55455-0213. Offers MN, MS, DNP, PhD. *Accreditation:* AACN; AANA/CANAEP; ACNM/DOA (one or more programs are accredited). Part-time programs available. Postbaccalaureate distance learning degree programs offered (minimal on-campus study). Terminal master's awarded for partial completion of doctoral program. *Degree requirements:* For master's, final oral exam, project or thesis; for doctorate, thesis/dissertation. *Entrance requirements:* For master's and doctorate, GRE General Test. Additional exam requirements/recommendations for international students: Required—TOEFL (minimum score 586 paper-based; 240 computer-based). *Expenses:* Contact institution. *Faculty research:* Child and family health promotion, nursing research on elders.

University of Mississippi Medical Center, School of Graduate Studies in the Health Sciences, Program in Nursing, Jackson, MS 39216-4505. Offers MSN, PhD. *Accreditation:* AACN. Part-time and evening/weekend programs available. *Degree requirements:* For master's, thesis optional; for doctorate, comprehensive exam, thesis/dissertation, publishable paper. *Entrance requirements:* For master's, GRE, 1 year of clinical experience, RN license; for doctorate, GRE, RN license, professional nursing experience. Electronic applications accepted. *Expenses:* Contact institution. *Faculty research:* Quality of life, neuroscience nursing, adult learning, gerontology, child birthing/parenting education.

University of Missouri, Graduate School, Sinclair School of Nursing, Columbia, MO 65211. Offers MS, PhD. *Accreditation:* AACN. Part-time programs available. *Degree requirements:* For master's, thesis, non-thesis, or practicum; oral exam; for doctorate, thesis/dissertation. *Entrance requirements:* For master's, GRE General Test, BSN, minimum GPA of 3.0 during last 60 hours, nursing license. Additional exam requirements/recommendations for international students: Required—TOEFL (minimum score 550 paper-based; 213 computer-based; 79 iBT). *Faculty research:* Pain, stepfamilies, chemotherapy-related nausea and vomiting, stress management, self-care deficit theory.

University of Missouri–Kansas City, School of Nursing, Kansas City, MO 64110-2499. Offers adult clinical nurse specialist (MSN), including adult nurse practitioner, women's health nurse practitioner; family nurse practitioner (MSN); neonatal nurse practitioner (MSN); nurse educator (MSN); nurse executive (MSN); nursing (PhD); nursing practice (DNP); pediatric nurse practitioner (MSN). *Accreditation:* AACN. Part-time programs available. Postbaccalaureate distance learning degree programs offered (minimal on-campus study). *Faculty:* 36 full-time (30 women), 40 part-time/adjunct (all women). *Students:* 31 full-time (26 women), 310 part-time (287 women); includes 38 minority (17 African Americans, 2 American Indian/Alaska Native, 10 Asian Americans or Pacific Islanders, 9 Hispanic Americans). Average age 36. 151 applicants, 72% accepted, 109 enrolled. In 2009, 57 master's, 10 doctorates awarded. *Degree requirements:* For master's, thesis or alternative. *Entrance requirements:* For master's, minimum undergraduate GPA of 3.2; for doctorate, GRE, 3 letters of reference, interview by invitation. Additional exam requirements/recommendations for international students: Required—TOEFL (minimum score 550 paper-based; 213 computer-based; 80 iBT). *Application deadline:* For fall admission, 2/1 priority date for domestic and international students; for spring admission, 9/1 priority date for domestic and international students. Application fee: $45 ($50 for international students). *Expenses:* Tuition, state resident: full-time $5378; part-time $299 per credit hour. Tuition, nonresident: full-time $13,881; part-time $771 per credit hour. Required fees: $641; $71 per credit hour. Tuition and fees vary according to course load and program. *Financial support:* In 2009–10, 6 teaching assistantships with partial tuition reimbursements (averaging $4,402 per year) were awarded; fellowships, research assistantships, career-related internships or fieldwork, Federal Work-Study, institutionally sponsored loans, and tuition waivers (full and partial) also available. Support available to part-time students. Financial award application deadline: 3/1; financial award applicants required to submit FAFSA. *Faculty research:* Geriatrics/gerontology, children's pain, neonatology, Alzheimer's care, cancer caregivers. Total annual research expenditures: $2.1 million. *Unit head:* Dr. Lora Lacey-Haun, Dean, 816-235-1700, Fax: 816-235-1701, E-mail: lacey-haunc@umkc.edu. *Application contact:* Leah Wilder, Coordinator for Admissions and Recruitment, 816-235-5768, Fax: 816-235-1701, E-mail: wilderl@umkc.edu.

University of Missouri–St. Louis, College of Nursing, St. Louis, MO 63121. Offers nurse educator (MSN); nurse practitioner (MSN, Post Master's Certificate); nursing (DNP, PhD). *Accreditation:* AACN. Part-time programs available. *Faculty:* 14 full-time (13 women), 19 part-time/adjunct (18 women). *Students:* 9 full-time (all women), 216 part-time (203 women); includes 31 minority (29 African Americans, 1 American Indian/Alaska Native, 1 Asian American or Pacific Islander). Average age 37. In 2009, 47 master's, 3 doctorates, 1 other advanced degree awarded. *Degree requirements:* For doctorate, comprehensive exam, thesis/dissertation; for Post Master's Certificate, thesis. *Entrance requirements:* For master's, GRE, 2 recommendation letters; minimum GPA of 3.0; BSN; nursing licensure; statement of purpose; for doctorate, GRE, 2 letters of recommendation, MSN, minimum GPA of 3.2; for Post Master's Certificate, 2 recommendation letters; MSN; advanced practice certificate; minimum GPA of 3.0; essay. Additional exam requirements/recommendations for international students: Required—TOEFL (minimum score 550 paper-based; 213 computer-based). *Application deadline:* For fall admission, 4/1 for domestic and international students; for spring admission, 10/1 for domestic and international students. Application fee: $35 ($40 for international students). Electronic applications accepted. *Expenses:* Tuition, state resident: full-time $5377; part-time $297.70 per credit hour. Tuition, nonresident: full-time $13,882; part-time $771.20 per credit hour. Required fees: $220; $12.20 per credit hour. One-time fee: $12. Tuition and fees vary according to course level, campus/location and program. *Financial support:* In 2009–10, 1 research assistantship with full and partial tuition reimbursement (averaging $12,339 per year), 4 teaching assistantships with full and partial tuition reimbursements (averaging $12,339 per year) were awarded. Financial award application deadline: 4/1; financial award applicants required to submit FAFSA. *Faculty research:* Health promotion and restoration, family disruption,

Nursing—General

University of Missouri–St. Louis (continued)

violence, abuse, battered women, health survey methods. *Unit head:* Dean Juliann Sebastian, Dean, 314-516-6066. *Application contact:* 314-516-5458, Fax: 314-516-6996, E-mail: gradadm@umsl.edu.

University of Mobile, Graduate Programs, Program in Nursing, Mobile, AL 36613. Offers MSN. *Accreditation:* AACN. Part-time and evening/weekend programs available. *Faculty:* 2 full-time (1 woman), 2 part-time/adjunct (1 woman). *Students:* 9 full-time (all women), 7 part-time (6 women); includes 7 minority (6 African Americans, 1 American Indian/Alaska Native). Average age 38. 11 applicants, 100% accepted, 8 enrolled. In 2009, 4 master's awarded. *Degree requirements:* For master's, comprehensive exam, thesis or alternative. *Entrance requirements:* For master's, GRE or MAT. Additional exam requirements/recommendations for international students: Required—TOEFL (minimum score 550 paper-based; 213 computer-based; 80 iBT). *Application deadline:* For fall admission, 8/3 priority date for domestic students; for spring admission, 12/23 for domestic students. Applications are processed on a rolling basis. Application fee: $40 ($50 for international students). *Financial support:* Application deadline: 8/1. *Faculty research:* Nursing management, transcultural nursing, spiritual aspects, educational expectations. *Unit head:* Dr. Richard McElhaney, Dean, School of Nursing, 251-442-2256, Fax: 251-442-2520, E-mail: rmcelhaney@umobile.edu. *Application contact:* Tammy C. Eubanks, Administrative Assistant to Dean of Graduate Programs, 251-442-2270, Fax: 251-442-2523, E-mail: teubanks@umobile.edu.

University of Nebraska Medical Center, Graduate Studies, Program in Nursing, Omaha, NE 68198. Offers MSN, PhD. *Accreditation:* AACN. Part-time programs available. Postbaccalaureate distance learning degree programs offered. *Degree requirements:* For master's, comprehensive exam, research project or thesis; for doctorate, comprehensive exam, thesis/dissertation. *Entrance requirements:* For master's, minimum GPA of 3.0; for doctorate, GRE General Test, minimum GPA of 3.2. Additional exam requirements/recommendations for international students: Required—TOEFL (minimum score 550 paper-based; 213 computer-based). Electronic applications accepted. *Expenses:* Contact institution. *Faculty research:* Health promotion, sleep and fatigue in cancer patients, symptoms management in cardiovascular disease, prevention of osteoporosis in breast cancer survivors, impact of quality end of life care in nursing homes.

University of Nevada, Las Vegas, Graduate College, School of Nursing, Las Vegas, NV 89154-3018. Offers family nurse practitioner (Advanced Certificate); nursing (MS, PhD); nursing education (Advanced Certificate). *Accreditation:* AACN; NLN. Part-time programs available. Postbaccalaureate distance learning degree programs offered (minimal on-campus study). *Faculty:* 35 full-time (30 women), 5 part-time/adjunct (all women). *Students:* 68 full-time (56 women), 94 part-time (83 women); includes 30 minority (3 African Americans, 1 American Indian/Alaska Native, 18 Asian Americans or Pacific Islanders, 8 Hispanic Americans), 19 international. Average age 41. 147 applicants, 46% accepted, 51 enrolled. In 2009, 50 master's, 4 doctorates, 1 other advanced degree awarded. *Entrance requirements:* For doctorate, GRE General Test. Additional exam requirements/recommendations for international students: Recommended—TOEFL (minimum score 550 paper-based; 213 computer-based; 80 iBT), IELTS (minimum score 7). *Application deadline:* For fall admission, 3/1 priority date for domestic and international students. Applications are processed on a rolling basis. Application fee: $60 ($95 for international students). Electronic applications accepted. *Financial support:* In 2009–10, 9 students received support, including 8 research assistantships with partial tuition reimbursements available (averaging $14,275 per year), 1 teaching assistantship (averaging $12,000 per year); institutionally sponsored loans, scholarships/grants, health care benefits, and unspecified assistantships also available. Financial award application deadline: 3/1. *Faculty research:* Obesity, weight loss maintenance; eukocyte response to exercise-related skeletal muscle injury; smoke-free policy, smoking cessation; exercise, health promotion; community-based participatory research, occupational health/injury, low-back pain. *Unit head:* Dr. Carolyn Yucha, Interim Dean, 702-895-3906, Fax: 702-895-5050, E-mail: carolyn.yucha@unlv.edu. *Application contact:* Graduate College Admissions Evaluator, 702-895-3320, Fax: 702-895-4180, E-mail: gradcollege@unlv.edu.

University of Nevada, Reno, Graduate School, Division of Health Sciences, Orvis School of Nursing, Reno, NV 89557. Offers MSN, MPH/MSN. *Accreditation:* AACN. *Degree requirements:* For master's, thesis optional. *Entrance requirements:* For master's, minimum GPA of 3.0 in bachelor's degree from accredited school. Additional exam requirements/recommendations for international students: Required—TOEFL (minimum score 500 paper-based; 173 computer-based; 61 iBT), IELTS (minimum score 6). Electronic applications accepted. *Faculty research:* Analysis and evaluation of nursing theory, strategies for nursing applications.

University of New Brunswick Fredericton, School of Graduate Studies, Faculty of Nursing, Fredericton, NB E3B 5A3, Canada. Offers nurse educator (MN); nurse practitioner (MN); nursing (MN). Part-time programs available. Postbaccalaureate distance learning degree programs offered. *Faculty:* 27 full-time (all women), 5 part-time/adjunct (4 women). *Students:* 15 full-time (13 women), 32 part-time (all women). In 2009, 13 master's awarded. *Degree requirements:* For master's, comprehensive exam (for some programs), thesis (for some programs). *Entrance requirements:* For master's, undergraduate coursework in statistics and nursing research, minimum GPA of 3.3, registration as a nurse in New Brunswick (or eligibility). Additional exam requirements/recommendations for international students: Required—TOEFL (minimum score 600 paper-based; 250 computer-based). *Application deadline:* For winter admission, 2/5 for domestic students. Application fee: $50 Canadian dollars. Electronic applications accepted. Tuition and fees charges are reported in Canadian dollars. *Expenses:* Tuition, area resident: Full-time $5562 Canadian dollars; part-time $2781 Canadian dollars per year. Required fees: $49.75 Canadian dollars per term. *Faculty research:* Violence and abuse; healthy child development, chronic illness and addiction; rural populations access to health care and primary healthcare; teaching and learning in classroom, clinical lab, and by distance. *Unit head:* Gail Storr, Director of Graduate Studies, 506-458-7643, Fax: 506-447-3057, E-mail: storr@unb.ca. *Application contact:* Francis Perry, Graduate Secretary, 506-451-6844, Fax: 506-447-3057, E-mail: fperry@unb.ca.

University of New Hampshire, Graduate School, School of Health and Human Services, Department of Nursing, Durham, NH 03824. Offers MS, Postbaccalaureate Certificate. *Accreditation:* AACN. Part-time programs available. *Faculty:* 12 full-time (11 women). *Students:* 34 full-time (28 women), 58 part-time (54 women); includes 7 minority (3 African Americans, 2 Asian Americans or Pacific Islanders, 2 Hispanic Americans), 1 international. Average age 37. 35 applicants, 86% accepted, 15 enrolled. In 2009, 40 master's awarded. *Degree requirements:* For master's, thesis or alternative. *Entrance requirements:* For master's, GRE General Test or MAT. Additional exam requirements/recommendations for international students: Required—TOEFL (minimum score 550 paper-based; 213 computer-based; 80 iBT). *Application deadline:* For fall admission, 4/1 priority date for domestic students, 4/1 for international students; for spring admission, 11/1 for domestic students. Applications are processed on a rolling basis. Application fee: $65. Electronic applications accepted. *Expenses:* Tuition, state resident: full-time $10,380; part-time $577 per credit hour. Tuition, nonresident: full-time $24,350; part-time $1002 per credit hour. Required fees: $1550; $387.50 per semester. Tuition and fees vary according to course load and program. *Financial support:* In 2009–10, 2 students received support, including 1 teaching assistantship; fellowships, research assistantships, Federal Work-Study, scholarships/grants, and tuition waivers (full and partial) also available. Financial award application deadline: 2/15. *Faculty research:* Adult health, nursing administration, family nurse practitioner. *Unit head:* Dr. Lynette Hamlin, Chairperson, 603-862-2390. *Application contact:* Jane Dufresne, Administrative Assistant, 603-862-2299, E-mail: nursing.department@unh.edu.

University of New Mexico, Graduate School, College of Nursing, Albuquerque, NM 87131-2039. Offers MSN, PhD, MSN/MA. *Accreditation:* AACN; ACNM/DOA (one or more programs are accredited). Part-time programs available. Postbaccalaureate distance learning degree programs offered (minimal on-campus study). *Faculty:* 46 full-time (42 women), 5 part-time/adjunct (4 women). *Students:* 52 full-time (50 women), 165 part-time (152 women); includes 57 minority (4 African Americans, 6 American Indian/Alaska Native, 5 Asian Americans or Pacific Islanders, 42 Hispanic Americans), 9 international. Average age 43. 55 applicants, 47%

accepted, 26 enrolled. In 2009, 45 master's, 1 doctorate awarded. *Degree requirements:* For master's, comprehensive exam, thesis optional; for doctorate, comprehensive exam, thesis/dissertation. *Entrance requirements:* For master's, minimum GPA of 3.0, course work in statistics (recommended), interview (for some concentrations), BSN or RN with BA; for doctorate, interview, minimum GPA of 3.0, writing sample, MSN or BSN with MA. Additional exam requirements/recommendations for international students: Required—TOEFL. Application fee: $50. Electronic applications accepted. *Expenses:* Tuition, state resident: full-time $2099; part-time $233.20 per credit hour. Tuition, nonresident: full-time $6650. Required fees: $25 per semester. Tuition and fees vary according to course load, program and reciprocity agreements. *Financial support:* In 2009–10, 64 students received support, including 5 teaching assistantships with partial tuition reimbursements available (averaging $6,750 per year); research assistantships with partial tuition reimbursements available, scholarships/grants and traineeships also available. Financial award application deadline: 3/1; financial award applicants required to submit FAFSA. *Faculty research:* Women's and children's health, pregnancy prevention in teens, vulnerable populations, nursing education, chronic illness, symptom appraisal and management. *Unit head:* Dr. Jean Giddens, Executive Dean, 505-272-0716, Fax: 505-272-4343, E-mail: jgiddens@salud.unm.edu. *Application contact:* Karen Wells, Student Academic Advisor, 505-272-4223, Fax: 505-272-3970, E-mail: kwells@salud.unm.edu.

University of North Alabama, College of Nursing and Allied Health, Florence, AL 35632-0001. Offers MSN. *Accreditation:* AACN. *Faculty:* 2 full-time (both women), 1 (woman) part-time/adjunct. *Students:* 18 full-time (16 women), 32 part-time (all women); includes 8 minority (7 African Americans, 1 American Indian/Alaska Native). Average age 39. In 2009, 15 master's awarded. *Expenses:* Tuition, state resident: full-time $5040; part-time $210 per credit hour. Tuition, nonresident: full-time $10,080; part-time $420 per credit hour. Required fees: $906. *Unit head:* Dr. Birdie Bailey, Dean, 256-765-4984, E-mail: bibailey@una.edu. *Application contact:* Kim Mauldin, Director of Admissions, 256-465-4608, Fax: 256-765-4960, E-mail: komauldin@una.edu.

The University of North Carolina at Chapel Hill, School of Nursing, Chapel Hill, NC 27599-7460. Offers nursing (MSN, PhD, PMC), including adult nurse practitioner (MSN, PMC), children's health advanced practice (MSN, PMC), family nurse practitioner (MSN, PMC), health care systems (MSN, PMC), psychiatric/mental health nursing (MSN, PMC), women's health nursing (MSN, PMC). *Accreditation:* AACN; NLN (one or more programs are accredited). Part-time programs available. *Degree requirements:* For master's, comprehensive exam, thesis; for doctorate, thesis/dissertation, 3 exams. *Entrance requirements:* For master's and doctorate, GRE General Test. *Faculty research:* Chronic illness, parenting, cardiovascular health in children, elderly, HIV-AIDS.

The University of North Carolina at Charlotte, Graduate School, College of Health and Human Services, School of Nursing, Charlotte, NC 28223-0001. Offers nursing advanced clinical (MSN); nursing anesthesia (MSN); nursing systems population (MSN). *Accreditation:* AACN. *Faculty:* 21 full-time (20 women), 5 part-time/adjunct (all women). *Students:* 77 full-time (65 women), 142 part-time (130 women); includes 26 African Americans, 6 Asian Americans or Pacific Islanders, 4 Hispanic Americans, 1 international. Average age 36. 163 applicants, 52% accepted, 78 enrolled. In 2009, 40 master's awarded. *Entrance requirements:* For master's, GRE General Test, minimum GPA of 3.0 in undergraduate major. Additional exam requirements/recommendations for international students: Required—TOEFL (minimum score 570 paper-based; 220 computer-based; 83 iBT). *Application deadline:* For fall admission, 7/15 for domestic students, 5/1 for international students; for spring admission, 11/15 for domestic students, 10/1 for international students. Application fee: $55. *Financial support:* In 2009–10, 7 students received support, including 1 research assistantship (averaging $12,872 per year), 6 teaching assistantships (averaging $6,171 per year); career-related internships or fieldwork, Federal Work-Study, institutionally sponsored loans, scholarships/grants, traineeships, and unspecified assistantships also available. Support available to part-time students. Financial award application deadline: 4/1; financial award applicants required to submit FAFSA. Total annual research expenditures: $717,259. *Unit head:* Dr. Lucille L. Travis, Director, 704-687-7959, Fax: 704-687-6017, E-mail: ltravis1@uncc.edu. *Application contact:* Kathy B. Giddings, Director of Graduate Admissions, 704-687-5503, Fax: 704-687-3279, E-mail: gradadm@uncc.edu.

The University of North Carolina at Greensboro, Graduate School, School of Nursing, Greensboro, NC 27412-5001. Offers adult clinical nurse specialist (MSN, PMC); adult/gerontological nurse practitioner (MSN, PMC); nurse anesthesia (MSN, PMC); nursing (PhD); nursing administration (MSN); nursing education (MSN); MSN/MBA. *Accreditation:* AACN; AANA/CANAEP; NLN. *Degree requirements:* For master's, thesis or alternative. *Entrance requirements:* For master's, GRE General Test or MAT, BSN, clinical experience, liability insurance, RN license; for PMC, liability insurance, MSN, RN license. Additional exam requirements/recommendations for international students: Required—TOEFL. Electronic applications accepted.

The University of North Carolina Wilmington, School of Nursing, Wilmington, NC 28403-3297. Offers family nurse practitioner (MSN); nurse educator (MSN). *Accreditation:* AACN; NLN. *Degree requirements:* For master's, comprehensive exam, thesis or project. *Entrance requirements:* For master's, GRE General Test, bachelor's degree in nursing. Additional exam requirements/recommendations for international students: Required—TOEFL (minimum score 550 paper-based; 217 computer-based; 79 iBT), IELTS (minimum score 6.5). Electronic applications accepted.

University of North Dakota, Graduate School, College of Nursing, Grand Forks, ND 58202. Offers MS, PhD. *Accreditation:* AACN; AANA/CANAEP (one or more programs are accredited). Part-time and evening/weekend programs available. Postbaccalaureate distance learning degree programs offered (minimal on-campus study). *Degree requirements:* For master's, thesis or alternative. *Entrance requirements:* For master's, minimum GPA of 3.0; for doctorate, GRE or MAT, minimum GPA of 3.0. Additional exam requirements/recommendations for international students: Required—TOEFL (minimum score 550 paper-based; 213 computer-based; 79 iBT), IELTS (minimum score 6.5). Electronic applications accepted. *Faculty research:* Adult health, anesthesia, rural health, health administration, family nurse practitioner.

University of Northern Colorado, Graduate School, College of Natural and Health Sciences, School of Nursing, Greeley, CO 80639. Offers clinical nurse specialist in chronic illness (MS); family nurse practitioner (MS); nursing education (MS, PhD). *Accreditation:* AACN. Postbaccalaureate distance learning degree programs offered. *Faculty:* 9 full-time (all women). *Students:* 35 part-time (34 women); includes 2 minority (both Hispanic Americans). Average age 35. 84 applicants, 64% accepted, 13 enrolled. In 2009, 27 master's, 2 doctorates awarded. *Degree requirements:* For master's, comprehensive exam, thesis or alternative; for doctorate, comprehensive exam, thesis/dissertation. *Entrance requirements:* For master's and doctorate, GRE General Test, minimum GPA of 3.0 in last 60 hours, BS in nursing, 2 letters of recommendation. *Application deadline:* Applications are processed on a rolling basis. Application fee: $50 ($60 for international students). Electronic applications accepted. *Expenses:* Tuition, state resident: full-time $5770; part-time $320.55 per credit hour. Tuition, nonresident: full-time $13,847; part-time $769.27 per credit hour. Required fees: $948.78; $52.72 per credit. *Financial support:* In 2009–10, 7 research assistantships (averaging $6,183 per year), 1 teaching assistantship (averaging $2,849 per year) were awarded; fellowships, unspecified assistantships also available. Financial award application deadline: 3/1; financial award applicants required to submit FAFSA. *Unit head:* Dr. Kathleen Bradshaw-LaSala, Director, 970-351-2293, Fax: 970-351-1707. *Application contact:* Linda Sisson, Graduate Student Admission Coordinator, 970-351-1807, Fax: 970-351-2371, E-mail: linda.sisson@unco.edu.

University of North Florida, Brooks College of Health, School of Nursing, Jacksonville, FL 32224. Offers advanced practice nursing (MSN); nursing (DNP); primary care nurse practitioner (Certificate). *Accreditation:* AACN; AANA/CANAEP. *Faculty:* 26 full-time (19 women). *Students:* 91 full-time (69 women), 64 part-time (56 women); includes 35 minority (13 African Americans, 2 American Indian/Alaska Native, 13 Asian Americans or Pacific Islanders, 7 Hispanic Americans). Average age 37. 146 applicants, 21% accepted, 16 enrolled. In 2009, 37 master's, 8 doctorates awarded. *Degree requirements:* For master's, thesis optional. *Entrance*

requirements: For master's, GRE General Test, minimum GPA of 3.0 in last 60 hours of course work, BSN, clinical experience, resume. Additional exam requirements/recommendations for international students: Required—TOEFL (minimum score 500 paper-based; 173 computer-based). *Application deadline:* For fall admission, 6/1 for domestic students, 5/1 for international students. Applications are processed on a rolling basis. Application fee: $30. Electronic applications accepted. *Expenses:* Tuition, state resident: full-time $6649.20; part-time $277.05 per credit hour. Tuition, nonresident: full-time $22,970; part-time $957.08 per credit hour. Required fees: $985; $41.03 per credit hour. *Financial support:* In 2009–10, 87 students received support; research assistantships available. Financial award application deadline: 4/1; financial award applicants required to submit FAFSA. *Faculty research:* Teen pregnancy, diabetes, ethical decision making, family caregivers. Total annual research expenditures: $538,202. *Unit head:* Dr. Lillia Loriz, Chair, 904-620-2684, E-mail: lloriz@unf.edu. *Application contact:* Beth Dibble, 904-620-2684, E-mail: bdibble@unf.edu.

University of Oklahoma Health Sciences Center, Graduate College, College of Nursing, Oklahoma City, OK 73190. Offers MS, MS/MBA. *Accreditation:* NLN. Part-time programs available. *Faculty:* 35 full-time (33 women), 2 part-time/adjunct (both women). *Students:* 40 full-time (32 women), 99 part-time (91 women); includes 40 minority (8 African Americans, 21 American Indian/Alaska Native, 6 Asian Americans or Pacific Islanders, 5 Hispanic Americans), 1 international. Average age 38. 43 applicants, 63% accepted, 21 enrolled. In 2009, 74 master's awarded. *Degree requirements:* For master's, comprehensive exam, thesis optional. *Entrance requirements:* For master's, 3 letters of recommendation, Oklahoma RN license, statistics course, research methods, computer course or completion of a computer literacy test. *Application deadline:* For fall admission, 6/1 for domestic students; for winter admission, 4/1 for domestic students; for spring admission, 11/1 for domestic students. Applications are processed on a rolling basis. Application fee: $50. *Expenses:* Tuition, state resident: full-time $3120; part-time $156 per credit hour. Tuition, nonresident: full-time $11,314; part-time $409.70 per credit hour. Required fees: $1471; $51.20 per credit hour. $223.25 per term. *Financial support:* In 2009–10, 6 research assistantships (averaging $6,000 per year) were awarded; teaching assistantships, institutionally sponsored loans, scholarships/grants, and traineeships also available. Support available to part-time students. Financial award application deadline: 8/1. *Faculty research:* Parenting and Native Americans, elderly reminiscence, diabetes in Native Americans. *Unit head:* Dr. Carol Kenner, Dean, 405-271-2420, E-mail: carol-kenner@ouhsc.edu. *Application contact:* Dr. Francene Weatherby, Information Contact, 405-271-2420, Fax: 405-271-3443, E-mail: francene-weatherby@ouhsc.edu.

University of Oklahoma—Tulsa, Program in Nursing, Tulsa, OK 74135-2512. Offers MS, MSN, Post Master's Certificate.

University of Ottawa, Faculty of Graduate and Postdoctoral Studies, Faculty of Health Sciences, School of Nursing, Ottawa, ON K1N 6N5, Canada. Offers nurse practitioner (Certificate); nursing (M Sc, PhD); nursing/primary health care (M Sc). Part-time and evening/weekend programs available. *Degree requirements:* For master's, thesis or alternative. *Entrance requirements:* For master's, honors degree or equivalent, minimum B average. Electronic applications accepted. *Faculty research:* Decision making in nursing, evaluating complete nursing interventions.

University of Pennsylvania, School of Nursing, Philadelphia, PA 19104. Offers MSN, PhD, Certificate, MBA/MSN, MBA/PhD, MSN/PhD. *Accreditation:* AACN; AANA/CANAEP. Part-time programs available. Postbaccalaureate distance learning degree programs offered. *Faculty:* 55 full-time (50 women), 50 part-time/adjunct (45 women). *Students:* 238 full-time (216 women), 250 part-time (232 women); includes 76 minority (29 African Americans, 2 American Indian/Alaska Native, 34 Asian Americans or Pacific Islanders, 11 Hispanic Americans), 13 international. 383 applicants, 55% accepted, 173 enrolled. In 2009, 157 master's, 8 doctorates, 10 other advanced degrees awarded. Terminal master's awarded for partial completion of doctoral program. *Degree requirements:* For doctorate, thesis/dissertation. *Entrance requirements:* For master's, GRE General Test, BSN, minimum GPA of 3.0; for doctorate, GRE General Test, BSN or MSN, minimum GPA of 3.0. Additional exam requirements/recommendations for international students: Required—TOEFL. *Application deadline:* For fall admission, 2/15 priority date for domestic students. Applications are processed on a rolling basis. Application fee: $70. *Expenses:* Contact institution. *Financial support:* In 2009–10, 71 students received support; fellowships, research assistantships, teaching assistantships, institutionally sponsored loans, scholarships/grants, traineeships, health care benefits, and unspecified assistantships available. Financial award application deadline: 12/15. *Faculty research:* Nursing and patient outcomes research. *Unit head:* Assistant Dean of Admissions and Financial Aid, 866-867-6877, Fax: 215-573-8439, E-mail: admissions@nursing.upenn.edu. *Application contact:* Sylvia V. J. English, Enrollment Management Coordinator, 866-867-6877, Fax: 215-573-8439, E-mail: admissions@nursing.upenn.edu.

University of Phoenix, College of Natural Sciences, College of Nursing, Phoenix, AZ 85034-7209. Offers education (MHA); gerontology (MHA); informatics (MHA, MSN); nursing (MSN); MSN/MBA; MSN/MHA. *Accreditation:* AACN. Evening/weekend programs available. Postbaccalaureate distance learning degree programs offered. *Faculty:* 13 full-time (11 women), 327 part-time/adjunct (252 women). *Students:* 5,797 full-time (5,365 women); includes 1,337 minority (831 African Americans, 46 American Indian/Alaska Native, 292 Asian Americans or Pacific Islanders, 168 Hispanic Americans), 302 international. Average age 40. In 2009, 1,646 master's awarded. *Degree requirements:* For master's, thesis (for some programs). *Entrance requirements:* For master's, 3 years of work experience, minimum undergraduate GPA of 2.5, RN license. Additional exam requirements/recommendations for international students: Required—TOEFL (minimum score 550 paper-based; 213 computer-based; 79 iBT). *Application deadline:* Applications are processed on a rolling basis. Application fee: $45. Electronic applications accepted. *Expenses:* Tuition: Full-time $13,272. Required fees: $660. Full-time tuition and fees vary according to course level, degree level and program. *Financial support:* Institutionally sponsored loans and scholarships/grants available. Financial award applicants required to submit FAFSA. *Unit head:* Dr. Pam Fuller, Dean/Executive Director, 480-557-1140, Fax: 480-929-7164, E-mail: pam.fuller@phoenix.edu. *Application contact:* Chair, 866-766-0766, Fax: 602-387-6020.

University of Phoenix, School of Advanced Studies, Phoenix, AZ 85034-7209. Offers business administration (DBA); education (Ed D); educational leadership (Ed D), including curriculum and instruction, educational leadership, educational technology; health administration (DHA); higher education administration (PhD); industrial/organizational psychology (PhD); nursing (PhD); organizational leadership (DM), including information systems and technology, organizational leadership. Evening/weekend programs available. *Faculty:* 83 full-time (47 women), 540 part-time/adjunct (264 women). *Students:* 7,749 full-time (5,032 women); includes 3,180 minority (2,473 African Americans, 61 American Indian/Alaska Native, 221 Asian Americans or Pacific Islanders, 425 Hispanic Americans), 490 international. Average age 44. In 2009, 467 doctorates awarded. *Degree requirements:* For doctorate, thesis/dissertation. *Entrance requirements:* For doctorate, 3 letters of recommendation, minimum master's GPA of 3.0, 3 years professional work experience. Additional exam requirements/recommendations for international students: Required—TOEFL (minimum score 550 paper-based; 213 computer-based; 79 iBT). *Application deadline:* Applications are processed on a rolling basis. Application fee: $45. Electronic applications accepted. *Expenses:* Tuition: Full-time $13,272. Required fees: $660. Full-time tuition and fees vary according to course level, degree level and program. *Financial support:* Institutionally sponsored loans and scholarships/grants available. Financial award applicants required to submit FAFSA. *Unit head:* Dr. Jeremy Moreland, Dean/Executive Director, 480-557-3231, E-mail: jeremy.moreland@phoenix.edu. *Application contact:* Information Contact, 800-697-8223.

University of Phoenix–Atlanta Campus, The Artemis School, College of Health and Human Services, Sandy Springs, GA 30350-4153. Offers administration of justice and security (MS); health administration (MHA); health care management (MBA); nursing (MSN); nursing/health care education (MSN); MSN/MBA; MSN/MHA. Evening/weekend programs available. Postbaccalaureate distance learning degree programs offered. *Degree requirements:* For master's,

thesis (for some programs). *Entrance requirements:* For master's, minimum undergraduate GPA of 2.5, 3 years of work experience. Additional exam requirements/recommendations for international students: Required—TOEFL (minimum score 550 paper-based; 213 computer-based; 79 iBT). Electronic applications accepted.

University of Phoenix–Augusta Campus, College of Health and Human Services, Augusta, GA 30909-4583. Offers health administration (MHA); health care management (MBA); nursing (MSN); nursing/health care education (MSN); MSN/MBA; MSN/MHA. Postbaccalaureate distance learning degree programs offered.

University of Phoenix–Bay Area Campus, The Artemis School, College of Health and Human Services, Pleasanton, CA 94588-3677. Offers administration of justice and security (MS); family nurse practitioner (MSN); health care management (MBA); marriage, family and child therapy (MSC); nursing (MSN); nursing/health care education (MSN); MSN/MBA. Evening/weekend programs available. Postbaccalaureate distance learning degree programs offered (no on-campus study). *Degree requirements:* For master's, thesis (for some programs). *Entrance requirements:* For master's, minimum undergraduate GPA of 2.5, 3 years of work experience, RN license. Additional exam requirements/recommendations for international students: Required—TOEFL (minimum score 550 paper-based; 213 computer-based; 79 iBT). Electronic applications accepted.

University of Phoenix–Birmingham Campus, College of Health and Human Services, Birmingham, AL 35244. Offers education (MHA); gerontology (MHA); health administration (MHA); health care management (MBA); informatics (MHA); nursing (MSN); nursing/health care education (MSN); MSN/MBA; MSN/MHA.

University of Phoenix–Central Florida Campus, The Artemis School, College of Health and Human Services, Maitland, FL 32751-7057. Offers health administration (MHA); health and human services (MSN); health care management (MBA); nursing (MSN); nursing/health care education (MSN); MSN/MBA; MSN/MHA. Evening/weekend programs available. *Degree requirements:* For master's, thesis (for some programs). *Entrance requirements:* For master's, minimum undergraduate GPA of 2.5, 3 years work experience, RN license. Additional exam requirements/recommendations for international students: Required—TOEFL (minimum score 550 paper-based; 213 computer-based; 79 iBT). Electronic applications accepted.

University of Phoenix–Central Valley Campus, College of Health and Human Services, Fresno, CA 93720-1562. Offers education (MHA); gerontology (MHA); health administration (MHA); health care management (MBA); nursing (MSN); MSN/MBA.

University of Phoenix–Charlotte Campus, The Artemis School, College of Health and Human Services, Charlotte, NC 28273-3409. Offers health care management (MBA). Evening/weekend programs available. *Degree requirements:* For master's, thesis (for some programs). *Entrance requirements:* For master's, minimum undergraduate GPA of 2.5, 3 years work experience. Additional exam requirements/recommendations for international students: Required—TOEFL (minimum score 550 paper-based; 213 computer-based; 79 iBT). Electronic applications accepted.

University of Phoenix–Cheyenne Campus, College of Health and Human Services, Cheyenne, WY 82009. Offers health administration (MHA); health care management (MBA); nursing (MSN); nursing/health care education (MSN); MSN/MBA; MSN/MHA. Postbaccalaureate distance learning degree programs offered.

University of Phoenix–Cincinnati Campus, The Artemis School, College of Health and Human Services, West Chester, OH 45069-4875. Offers administration of justice and security (MS); health care management (MBA); nursing (MSN); psychology (MS). Evening/weekend programs available. Postbaccalaureate distance learning degree programs offered. *Degree requirements:* For master's, thesis (for some programs). *Entrance requirements:* For master's, minimum undergraduate GPA of 2.5, 3 years of work experience. Additional exam requirements/recommendations for international students: Required—TOEFL (minimum score 550 paper-based; 79 iBT). Electronic applications accepted.

University of Phoenix–Cleveland Campus, The Artemis School, College of Health and Human Services, Independence, OH 44131-2194. Offers administration of justice and security (MS); health care management (MBA); nursing (MSN); psychology (MS). Evening/weekend programs available. Postbaccalaureate distance learning degree programs offered. *Degree requirements:* For master's, thesis (for some programs). *Entrance requirements:* For master's, minimum undergraduate GPA of 2.5, 3 years of work experience. Additional exam requirements/recommendations for international students: Required—TOEFL (minimum score 550 paper-based; 213 computer-based; 79 iBT). Electronic applications accepted.

University of Phoenix–Columbus Georgia Campus, The Artemis School, College of Health and Human Services, Columbus, GA 31904-6321. Offers administration of justice and security (MS); health administration (MHA); health care management (MBA); nursing (MSN). Postbaccalaureate distance learning degree programs offered. *Degree requirements:* For master's, thesis (for some programs). *Entrance requirements:* For master's, minimum undergraduate GPA of 2.5, 3 years of work experience. Additional exam requirements/recommendations for international students: Required—TOEFL (minimum score 550 paper-based; 213 computer-based; 79 iBT). Electronic applications accepted.

University of Phoenix–Columbus Ohio Campus, The Artemis School, College of Health and Human Services, Columbus, OH 43240-4032. Offers administration of justice and security (MS); health care management (MBA); nursing (MSN); psychology (MS). Evening/weekend programs available. Postbaccalaureate distance learning degree programs offered. *Degree requirements:* For master's, thesis (for some programs). *Entrance requirements:* For master's, minimum undergraduate GPA of 2.5, 3 years work experience. Additional exam requirements/recommendations for international students: Required—TOEFL (minimum score 550 paper-based; 213 computer-based; 79 iBT). Electronic applications accepted.

University of Phoenix–Denver Campus, The Artemis School, College of Health and Human Services, Lone Tree, CO 80124-5453. Offers administration of justice and security (MS); community counseling (MSC); health administration (MHA); health care management (MBA); marriage, family and child therapy (MSC); nursing (MSN); psychology (MS); MSN/MBA; MSN/MHA. Evening/weekend programs available. Postbaccalaureate distance learning degree programs offered. *Degree requirements:* For master's, thesis (for some programs). *Entrance requirements:* For master's, minimum undergraduate GPA of 2.5, 3 years work experience, RN license. Additional exam requirements/recommendations for international students: Required—TOEFL (minimum score 550 paper-based; 213 computer-based; 79 iBT). Electronic applications accepted.

University of Phoenix–Harrisburg Campus, College of Health and Human Services, Harrisburg, PA 17112. Offers health administration (MHA); health care management (MBA); nursing (MSN); nursing/health care education (MSN); MSN/MBA; MSN/MHA. Postbaccalaureate distance learning degree programs offered.

University of Phoenix–Hawaii Campus, The Artemis School, College of Health and Human Services, Honolulu, HI 96813-4317. Offers administration of justice and security (MS); community counseling (MSC); education (MHA); family nurse practitioner (MSN); gerontology (MHA); health administration (MHA); health care management (MBA); marriage, family and child therapy (MSC); nursing (MSN); nursing/health care education (MSN); psychology (MS); MSN/MBA. Evening/weekend programs available. *Degree requirements:* For master's, thesis (for some programs). *Entrance requirements:* For master's, minimum undergraduate GPA of 2.5, 3 years of work experience, RN license. Additional exam requirements/recommendations for international students: Required—TOEFL (minimum score 550 paper-based; 213 computer-based; 79 iBT). Electronic applications accepted.

University of Phoenix–Idaho Campus, The Artemis School, College of Health and Human Services, Meridian, ID 83642-3014. Offers administration of justice and security (MS); health administration (MHA); health care management (MBA); nursing (MSN); nursing/health care

Nursing—General

University of Phoenix–Idaho Campus (continued)
education (MSN); psychology (MS); MSN/MBA. Evening/weekend programs available. Post-baccalaureate distance learning degree programs offered. *Degree requirements:* For master's, thesis (for some programs). *Entrance requirements:* For master's, minimum undergraduate GPA of 2.5, 3 years of work experience. Additional exam requirements/recommendations for international students: Required—TOEFL (minimum score 550 paper-based; 213 computer-based). Electronic applications accepted.

University of Phoenix–Indianapolis Campus, The Artemis School, College of Health and Human Services, Indianapolis, IN 46250-932. Offers administration of justice and security (MS); health administration (MHA); health care management (MBA); nursing (MSN); nursing/health care education (MSN); psychology (MS); MSN/MBA; MSN/MHA. Evening/weekend programs available. Postbaccalaureate distance learning degree programs offered. *Degree requirements:* For master's, thesis. *Entrance requirements:* For master's, 3 years work experience, minimum undergraduate GPA of 2.5. Additional exam requirements/recommendations for international students: Required—TOEFL (minimum score 500 paper-based; 213 computer-based). Electronic applications accepted.

University of Phoenix–Kansas City Campus, The Artemis School, College of Health and Human Services, Kansas City, MO 64131-4517. Offers administration of justice and security (MS); community counseling (MSC); health administration (MHA); health care management (MBA); nursing (MSN); MSN/MBA. Evening/weekend programs available. Postbaccalaureate distance learning degree programs offered. *Degree requirements:* For master's, thesis (for some programs). *Entrance requirements:* For master's, 3 years work experience, minimum undergraduate GPA of 2.5. Additional exam requirements/recommendations for international students: Required—TOEFL (minimum score 550 paper-based; 213 computer-based).

University of Phoenix–Las Vegas Campus, The Artemis School, College of Health and Human Services, Las Vegas, NV 89128. Offers administration of justice and security (MS); health administration (MHA); health care management (MBA); marriage, family, and child therapy (MSC); mental health counseling (MSC); nursing (MSN); nursing/health care education (MSN); psychology (MS); MSN/MBA; MSN/MHA. Postbaccalaureate distance learning degree programs offered. *Entrance requirements:* For master's, minimum undergraduate GPA of 2.5, 3 years of work experience. Additional exam requirements/recommendations for international students: Required—TOEFL (minimum score 550 paper-based; 213 computer-based; 79 iBT). Electronic applications accepted.

University of Phoenix–Louisiana Campus, The Artemis School, College of Health and Human Services, Metairie, LA 70001-2082. Offers administration of justice and security (MS); health administration (MHA); health care management (MBA); nursing (MSN); psychology (MS); MSN/MBA. Evening/weekend programs available. Postbaccalaureate distance learning degree programs offered (no on-campus study). *Degree requirements:* For master's, thesis (for some programs). *Entrance requirements:* For master's, minimum undergraduate GPA of 2.5, 3 years work experience, RN license. Additional exam requirements/recommendations for international students: Required—TOEFL (minimum score 550 paper-based; 213 computer-based; 79 iBT). Electronic applications accepted.

University of Phoenix–Maryland Campus, The Artemis School, College of Health and Human Services, Columbia, MD 21045-5424. Offers administration of justice and security (MS); health administration (MHA); health care education (MSN); health care management (MBA); nursing (MSN); psychology (MS); MSN/MBA; MSN/MHA. Evening/weekend programs available. *Degree requirements:* For master's, thesis (for some programs). *Entrance requirements:* For master's, minimum undergraduate GPA of 2.5, 3 years work experience. Additional exam requirements/recommendations for international students: Required—TOEFL (minimum score 550 paper-based; 213 computer-based; 79 iBT). Electronic applications accepted.

University of Phoenix–Metro Detroit Campus, College of Nursing, Southfield, MI 48076. Offers health care education (MSN); nursing (MSN). Evening/weekend programs available. *Faculty:* 1 (woman) full-time, 3 part-time/adjunct (all women). *Students:* 4 full-time (all women), 1 international. Average age 49. In 2009, 8 master's awarded. *Degree requirements:* For master's, thesis (for some programs). *Entrance requirements:* For master's, minimum undergraduate GPA of 2.5, 3 years of work experience, RN license. Additional exam requirements/recommendations for international students: Required—TOEFL (minimum score 550 paper-based; 213 computer-based; 79 iBT). *Application deadline:* Applications are processed on a rolling basis. Application fee: $45. Electronic applications accepted. *Expenses:* Tuition: Full-time $14,136. Required fees: $660. *Financial support:* Institutionally sponsored loans and scholarships/grants available. Financial award applicants required to submit FAFSA. *Unit head:* Dr. Pam Fuller, Dean/Executive Director, 480-557-1140, E-mail: pam.fuller@phoenix.edu. *Application contact:* Chair, 800-834-2438, Fax: 248-267-0147.

University of Phoenix–Minneapolis/St. Louis Park Campus, College of Health and Human Services, St. Louis Park, MN 55426. Offers community counseling (MSC); family nurse practitioner (MSN); health care education (MSN); health care management (MBA); nursing (MSN).

University of Phoenix–New Mexico Campus, The Artemis School, College of Health and Human Services, Albuquerque, NM 87113-1570. Offers administration of justice and security (MS); health administration (MHA); health care education (MSN); health care management (MBA); marriage and family therapy (MSC); nursing (MSN); psychology (MS); MSN/MBA. Evening/weekend programs available. *Degree requirements:* For master's, thesis (for some programs). *Entrance requirements:* For master's, minimum undergraduate GPA of 2.5, 3 years of work experience, RN license. Additional exam requirements/recommendations for international students: Required—TOEFL (minimum score 550 paper-based; 213 computer-based; 79 iBT). Electronic applications accepted.

University of Phoenix–Northern Nevada Campus, College of Health and Human Services, Reno, NV 89521-5862. Offers health administration (MHA); health care education (MSN); health care management (MBA); nursing (MSN); MSN/MBA; MSN/MHA.

University of Phoenix–Northern Virginia Campus, College of Health and Human Services, Reston, VA 20190. Offers health administration (MHA); health care management (MBA); nursing (MSN).

University of Phoenix–North Florida Campus, The Artemis School, College of Health and Human Services, Jacksonville, FL 32216-0959. Offers health administration (MHA); health care education (MSN); health care management (MBA); nursing (MSN); MSN/MBA; MSN/MHA. Evening/weekend programs available. *Degree requirements:* For master's, thesis (for some programs). *Entrance requirements:* For master's, minimum undergraduate GPA of 2.5, 3 years work experience, RN license. Additional exam requirements/recommendations for international students: Required—TOEFL (minimum score 550 paper-based; 213 computer-based; 79 iBT). Electronic applications accepted.

University of Phoenix–Northwest Arkansas Campus, College of Health and Human Services, Rogers, AR 72756-9615. Offers health administration (MHA); health care education (MSN); health care management (MBA); nursing (MSN); MSN/MBA.

University of Phoenix–Oklahoma City Campus, College of Health and Human Services, Oklahoma City, OK 73116-8244. Offers administration of justice and security (MS); health care management (MBA); nursing (MSN); psychology (MS).

University of Phoenix–Philadelphia Campus, The Artemis School, College of Health and Human Services, Wayne, PA 19087-2121. Offers administration of justice and security (MS); health administration (MHA); health care education (MSN); health care management (MBA); nursing (MSN); psychology (MS); MSN/MBA. Evening/weekend programs available. *Degree requirements:* For master's, thesis (for some programs). *Entrance requirements:* For master's, minimum undergraduate GPA of 2.5, 3 years work experience. Additional exam requirements/

recommendations for international students: Required—TOEFL (minimum score 550 paper-based; 213 computer-based; 79 iBT). Electronic applications accepted.

University of Phoenix–Phoenix Campus, College of Social Sciences, College of Nursing, Phoenix, AZ 85040-1958. Offers health care education (MSN); nursing (MSN). Evening/weekend programs available. *Faculty:* 45 full-time (20 women), 510 part-time/adjunct (308 women). *Students:* 148 full-time (136 women); includes 22 minority (8 African Americans, 1 American Indian/Alaska Native, 8 Asian Americans or Pacific Islanders, 5 Hispanic Americans), 5 international. Average age 38. In 2009, 54 master's awarded. *Degree requirements:* For master's, thesis (for some programs). *Entrance requirements:* For master's, 3 years of work experience in field, minimum undergraduate GPA of 2.5, RN license. Additional exam requirements/recommendations for international students: Required—TOEFL (minimum score 550 paper-based; 213 computer-based; 79 iBT). *Application deadline:* Applications are processed on a rolling basis. Application fee: $45. Electronic applications accepted. *Expenses:* Tuition: Full-time $10,272. Required fees: $760. *Financial support:* Institutionally sponsored loans and scholarships/grants available. Financial award applicants required to submit FAFSA. *Unit head:* Dr. Pam Fuller, Dean/Executive Director, 480-557-1140, Fax: 480-929-7164, E-mail: pam.fuller@phoenix.edu. *Application contact:* Chair, 800-866-0766.

University of Phoenix–Richmond Campus, The Artemis School, College of Health and Human Services, Richmond, VA 23230. Offers administration of justice and security (MS); health administration (MHA); health care education (MSN); health care management (MBA); nursing (MSN); psychology (MS); MSN/MBA; MSN/MHA. Evening/weekend programs available. *Degree requirements:* For master's, thesis (for some programs). *Entrance requirements:* For master's, minimum undergraduate GPA of 2.5; 3 years work experience, current RN license for nursing programs. Additional exam requirements/recommendations for international students: Required—TOEFL (minimum score 500 paper-based; 213 computer-based; 79 iBT). Electronic applications accepted.

University of Phoenix–Sacramento Valley Campus, The Artemis School, College of Health and Human Services, Sacramento, CA 95833-3632. Offers administration of justice and security (MS); community counseling (MSC); family nurse practitioner (MSN); health administration (MHA); health care education (MSN); health care management (MBA); marriage, family and child counseling (MSC); nursing (MSN); psychology (MS); MSN/MBA. Evening/weekend programs available. *Degree requirements:* For master's, thesis (for some programs). *Entrance requirements:* For master's, RN license, minimum undergraduate GPA of 2.5, 3 years work experience. Additional exam requirements/recommendations for international students: Required—TOEFL (minimum score 550 paper-based; 213 computer-based; 79 iBT). Electronic applications accepted.

University of Phoenix–St. Louis Campus, The Artemis School, College of Health and Human Services, St. Louis, MO 63043-4828. Offers administration of justice and security (MS); health administration (MHA); health care management (MBA); nursing (MSN); MSN/MBA; MSN/MHA. Evening/weekend programs available. *Degree requirements:* For master's, thesis (for some programs). *Entrance requirements:* For master's, minimum undergraduate GPA of 2.5, 3 years work experience. Additional exam requirements/recommendations for international students: Required—TOEFL (minimum score 550 paper-based; 213 computer-based; 79 iBT). Electronic applications accepted.

University of Phoenix–San Diego Campus, The Artemis School, College of Health and Human Services, San Diego, CA 92123. Offers administration of justice and security (MS); health care education (MSN); health care management (MBA); marriage, family and child counseling (MSC); marriage, family and child therapy (MSC); nursing (MSN); MSN/MBA. Evening/weekend programs available. *Degree requirements:* For master's, thesis (for some programs). *Entrance requirements:* For master's, minimum undergraduate GPA of 2.5, 3 years work experience, RN license. Additional exam requirements/recommendations for international students: Required—TOEFL (minimum score 550 paper-based; 213 computer-based; 79 iBT). Electronic applications accepted.

University of Phoenix–Savannah Campus, College of Health and Human Services, Savannah, GA 31405-7400. Offers health administration (MHA); health care management (MBA); nursing (MSN); nursing/health care education (MSN); MSN/MBA; MSN/MHA.

University of Phoenix–Southern California Campus, College of Nursing, Costa Mesa, CA 92626. Offers family nurse practitioner (MSN); health care education (MSN); nursing (MSN); MSN/MBA; MSN/MHA. Evening/weekend programs available. *Faculty:* 3 full-time (all women), 41 part-time/adjunct (32 women). *Students:* 79 full-time (42 women); includes 155 minority (48 African Americans, 1 American Indian/Alaska Native, 76 Asian Americans or Pacific Islanders, 30 Hispanic Americans), 27 international. Average age 44. In 2009, 154 master's awarded. *Degree requirements:* For master's, thesis (for some programs). *Entrance requirements:* For master's, minimum undergraduate GPA of 2.5, 3 years work experience, RN license. Additional exam requirements/recommendations for international students: Required—TOEFL (minimum score 550 paper-based; 213 computer-based; 79 iBT). *Application deadline:* Applications are processed on a rolling basis. Application fee: $45. Electronic applications accepted. *Expenses:* Tuition: Full-time $15,120. Required fees: $660. *Financial support:* Institutionally sponsored loans and scholarships/grants available. Financial award applicants required to submit FAFSA. *Unit head:* Dr. Pam Fuller, Dean/Executive Director, 480-557-1140, E-mail: pam.fuller@phoenix.edu. *Application contact:* Campus College Chair, 714-398-1878, Fax: 714-378-5856.

University of Phoenix–Southern Colorado Campus, The Artemis School, College of Health and Human Services, Colorado Springs, CO 80919-2335. Offers administration of justice and security (MS); community counseling (MSC); education (MHA); gerontology (MHA); health administration (MHA); health care management (MBA); marriage, family and child therapy (MSC); nursing (MSN); psychology (MS); MSN/MBA. Evening/weekend programs available. *Degree requirements:* For master's, thesis (for some programs). *Entrance requirements:* For master's, minimum undergraduate GPA of 2.5, 3 years of work experience, RN license. Additional exam requirements/recommendations for international students: Required—TOEFL (minimum score 550 paper-based; 213 computer-based; 79 iBT). Electronic applications accepted.

University of Phoenix–South Florida Campus, The Artemis School, College of Health and Human Services, Fort Lauderdale, FL 33309. Offers health administration (MHA); health care education (MSN); health care management (MBA); nursing (MSN); MSN/MBA; MSN/MHA. Evening/weekend programs available. *Degree requirements:* For master's, thesis (for some programs). *Entrance requirements:* For master's, minimum undergraduate GPA of 2.5, 3 years work experience, RN license. Additional exam requirements/recommendations for international students: Required—TOEFL (minimum score 550 paper-based; 213 computer-based; 79 iBT). Electronic applications accepted.

University of Phoenix–Springfield Campus, College of Health and Human Services, Springfield, MO 65804-7211. Offers health administration (MHA); health care management (MBA); nursing (MSN); MSN/MBA; MSN/MHA.

University of Phoenix–Tulsa Campus, College of Health and Human Services, Tulsa, OK 74134-1412. Offers administration of justice and security (MS); health care management (MBA); nursing (MSN); psychology (MS).

University of Phoenix–Utah Campus, The Artemis School, College of Health and Human Services, Salt Lake City, UT 84123-4617. Offers health care management (MBA); healthcare education (MSN); mental health counseling (MSC); nursing (MSN); MSN/MBA. Evening/weekend programs available. *Degree requirements:* For master's, thesis (for some programs). *Entrance requirements:* For master's, minimum undergraduate GPA of 2.5, 3 years work experience, RN license. Additional exam requirements/recommendations for international students: Required—TOEFL (minimum score 550 paper-based; 213 computer-based; 79 iBT). Electronic applications accepted.

University of Phoenix–Vancouver Campus, The Artemis School, College of Health and Human Services, Burnaby, BC V5C 6G9, Canada. Offers health care management (MBA). Evening/weekend programs available. *Degree requirements:* For master's, thesis (for some programs). *Entrance requirements:* For master's, minimum undergraduate GPA of 2.5, 3 years work experience. Additional exam requirements/recommendations for international students: Required—TOEFL (minimum score 550 paper-based; 213 computer-based; 79 iBT). Electronic applications accepted.

University of Phoenix–Western Washington Campus, College of Health and Human Services, Tukwila, WA 98188. Offers health administration (MHA); health care education (MSN); health care management (MBA); nursing (MSN); MSN/MBA; MSN/MHA. Evening/weekend programs available. *Degree requirements:* For master's, thesis (for some programs). *Entrance requirements:* For master's, minimum undergraduate GPA of 2.5, 3 years of work experience. Additional exam requirements/recommendations for international students: Required—TOEFL (minimum score 550 paper-based; 213 computer-based; 79 iBT). Electronic applications accepted.

University of Phoenix–West Florida Campus, The Artemis School, College of Health and Human Services, Temple Terrace, FL 33637. Offers health administration (MHA); health care education (MSN); health care management (MBA); nursing (MSN); MSN/MBA; MSN/MHA. Evening/weekend programs available. Postbaccalaureate distance learning degree programs offered. *Degree requirements:* For master's, thesis (for some programs). *Entrance requirements:* For master's, minimum undergraduate GPA of 2.5, RN license, 3 years work experience. Additional exam requirements/recommendations for international students: Required—TOEFL (minimum score 550 paper-based; 213 computer-based; 79 iBT). Electronic applications accepted.

University of Pittsburgh, School of Nursing, Clinical Nurse Specialist Program, Pittsburgh, PA 15260. Offers medical/surgical clinical nurse specialist (MSN, DNP); psychiatric and mental health clinical nurse specialist (MSN, DNP). *Accreditation:* AACN. Part-time programs available. *Students:* 3 full-time (2 women), 17 part-time (16 women); includes 1 minority (Asian American or Pacific Islander). Average age 39. 8 applicants, 75% accepted, 6 enrolled. In 2009, 9 master's awarded. *Degree requirements:* For master's, comprehensive exam, thesis optional. *Entrance requirements:* For master's, GRE or MAT, BSN, RN license, letters of recommendation, resume, course work in statistics, 1-3 years of nursing experience. Additional exam requirements/recommendations for international students: Required—TOEFL (minimum score 550 paper-based; 213 computer-based; 80 iBT). *Application deadline:* For fall admission, 8/1 priority date for domestic students; for spring admission, 12/1 priority date for domestic students. Applications are processed on a rolling basis. Application fee: $50. Electronic applications accepted. *Expenses:* Tuition, state resident: full-time $16,402; part-time $665 per credit. Tuition, nonresident: full-time $28,694; part-time $1175 per credit. Required fees: $690; $175 per term. Tuition and fees vary according to program. *Unit head:* Dr. Helen Burns, Associate Dean for Clinical Education, 412-624-6616, Fax: 412-624-2401, E-mail: burnsh@pitt.edu. *Application contact:* Laurie Lapsley, Administrator of Graduate Student Services, 412-624-9670, Fax: 412-624-2409, E-mail: lapsleyl@pitt.edu.

University of Pittsburgh, School of Nursing, Nurse Specialty Role Program, Pittsburgh, PA 15260. Offers clinical nurse leader (MSN); nursing administration (MSN, DNP); nursing education (MSN); nursing informatics (MSN); nursing research (MSN). *Accreditation:* AACN. Part-time programs available. *Students:* 8 full-time (all women), 47 part-time (46 women); includes 5 minority (1 African American, 4 Asian Americans or Pacific Islanders). Average age 42. 16 applicants, 94% accepted, 13 enrolled. In 2009, 12 master's awarded. *Degree requirements:* For master's, comprehensive exam, thesis optional. *Entrance requirements:* For master's, GRE or MAT, BSN, RN license, letters of recommendation, resume, course work in statistics, 1-3 years of nursing experience. Additional exam requirements/recommendations for international students: Required—TOEFL (minimum score 550 paper-based; 213 computer-based; 80 iBT). *Application deadline:* For fall admission, 8/1 priority date for domestic students; for spring admission, 12/1 priority date for domestic students. Applications are processed on a rolling basis. Application fee: $50. Electronic applications accepted. *Expenses:* Tuition, state resident: full-time $16,402; part-time $665 per credit. Tuition, nonresident: full-time $28,694; part-time $1175 per credit. Required fees: $690; $175 per term. Tuition and fees vary according to program. *Unit head:* Dr. Helen Burns, Associate Dean for Clinical Education, 412-624-6616, Fax: 412-624-2401, E-mail: burnsh@pitt.edu. *Application contact:* Laurie Lapsley, Administrator of Graduate Student Services, 412-624-9670, Fax: 412-624-2409, E-mail: lapsleyl@pitt.edu.

University of Pittsburgh, School of Nursing, PhD Program in Nursing, Pittsburgh, PA 15261. Offers PhD. Part-time programs available. *Students:* 16 full-time (14 women), 7 part-time (all women); includes 5 minority (1 African American, 4 Asian Americans or Pacific Islanders), 3 international. Average age 39. 13 applicants, 31% accepted, 3 enrolled. In 2009, 12 doctorates awarded. *Degree requirements:* For doctorate, comprehensive exam, thesis/dissertation. *Entrance requirements:* For doctorate, GRE General Test. Additional exam requirements/recommendations for international students: Required—TOEFL (minimum score 550 paper-based; 213 computer-based; 79 iBT) or IELTS (minimum score 6.5). *Application deadline:* For fall admission, 8/1 priority date for domestic students, 2/1 priority date for international students. Applications are processed on a rolling basis. Application fee: $50. Electronic applications accepted. *Expenses:* Tuition, state resident: full-time $16,402; part-time $665 per credit. Tuition, nonresident: full-time $28,694; part-time $1175 per credit. Required fees: $690; $175 per term. Tuition and fees vary according to program. *Financial support:* In 2009–10, 12 fellowships with partial tuition reimbursements (averaging $21,000 per year), 12 research assistantships with full tuition reimbursements (averaging $19,000 per year), teaching assistantships with full tuition reimbursements (averaging $12,000 per year) were awarded; scholarships/grants, traineeships, health care benefits, and unspecified assistantships also available. Support available to part-time students. *Faculty research:* Adolescent health, critical care, chronic disorders, genetics, technology-informatics, women-health. *Unit head:* Dr. Judith Erlen, Coordinator, 412-624-1905, Fax: 412-624-2401, E-mail: jae001@pitt.edu. *Application contact:* Laurie Lapsley, Administrator of Graduate Student Services, 412-624-9670, Fax: 412-624-2409, E-mail: lapsleyl@pitt.edu.

University of Portland, School of Nursing, Portland, OR 97203-5798. Offers clinical nurse leader (MS); nursing (DNP). *Accreditation:* AACN. Part-time and evening/weekend programs available. Postbaccalaureate distance learning degree programs offered (minimal on-campus study). *Faculty:* 11 full-time (10 women). *Students:* 53 full-time (41 women), 39 part-time (37 women); includes 5 minority (2 African Americans, 2 Asian Americans or Pacific Islanders, 1 Hispanic American), 2 international. Average age 34. In 2009, 16 master's awarded. *Entrance requirements:* For master's, GRE General Test or MAT, Oregon RN license, BSN, course work in statistics, resume, letters of recommendation, writing sample; for doctorate, GRE General Test or MAT, Oregon RN license, BSN or MSN, 2 letters of recommendation, resume, writing sample, official transcripts. Additional exam requirements/recommendations for international students: Required—TOEFL (minimum score 550 paper-based; 80 iBT), IELTS (minimum score 7). *Application deadline:* For fall admission, 11/2 priority date for domestic and international students; for spring admission, 1/7 priority date for domestic and international students. Applications are processed on a rolling basis. Application fee: $50. *Expenses:* Contact institution. *Financial support:* Fellowships, research assistantships, Federal Work-Study and scholarships/grants available. Support available to part-time students. Financial award application deadline: 3/1; financial award applicants required to submit FAFSA. *Unit head:* Dr. Joanne Warner, Fax: 503-943-7729, E-mail: warner@up.edu. *Application contact:* Dr. Susan Mascato, Associate Dean, 503-943-7211, E-mail: mascato@up.edu.

University of Puerto Rico, Medical Sciences Campus, School of Nursing, San Juan, PR 00936-5067. Offers anesthesia (MSN); critical care nursing (MSN); family and community nursing (MSN); family nurse practitioner (MSN); mental health and psychiatric nursing (MSN); nursing (MSN). *Accreditation:* AACN; AANA/CANAEP. *Entrance requirements:* For master's, GRE or EXADEP, interview, Puerto Rico RN license or professional license for international students, general and specific point average, article analysis. Electronic applications accepted. *Faculty research:* HIV, health disparities, teen violence, women and violence, neurological disorders.

University of Rhode Island, Graduate School, College of Nursing, Kingston, RI 02881. Offers administration (MS); clinical nurse leader (MS); clinical specialist in gerontology (MS); clinical specialist in psychiatric/mental health (MS); family nurse practitioner (MS); gerontological nurse practitioner (MS); nursing (DNP, PhD); nursing education (MS). *Accreditation:* AACN; ACNM/DOA (one or more programs are accredited). Part-time programs available. *Faculty:* 28 full-time (27 women), 3 part-time/adjunct (all women). *Students:* 21 full-time (20 women), 74 part-time (71 women); includes 3 minority (1 African American, 2 Asian Americans or Pacific Islanders), 5 international. In 2009, 29 master's, 2 doctorates awarded. *Degree requirements:* For master's, comprehensive exam; for doctorate, comprehensive exam, thesis/dissertation. *Entrance requirements:* For master's, GRE or MAT, 2 letters of recommendation, scholarly papers; for doctorate, GRE, 3 letters of recommendation, scholarly papers. Additional exam requirements/recommendations for international students: Required—TOEFL (minimum score 550 paper-based; 213 computer-based). *Application deadline:* For fall admission, 4/15 for domestic students, 2/1 for international students; for spring admission, 11/15 for domestic students, 7/15 for international students. Application fee: $65. Electronic applications accepted. *Expenses:* Tuition, state resident: full-time $8828; part-time $490 per credit hour. Tuition, nonresident: full-time $22,100; part-time $1228 per credit hour. Required fees: $1118; $57 per semester. Tuition and fees vary according to program. *Financial support:* In 2009–10, 3 teaching assistantships with full and partial tuition reimbursements (averaging $8,428 per year) were awarded. Financial award application deadline: 4/15; financial award applicants required to submit FAFSA. *Faculty research:* Group intervention for grieving women in prison, translating Best Practice in non-drug interventions for postoperative pain management, further development and testing of the pain assessment inventory, preschool motor and functional performance of two cohorts, neuroactivation of brain motor areas in preterm children. Total annual research expenditures: $926,949. *Unit head:* Dr. Dayle Joseph, Dean, 401-874-2766, Fax: 401-874-2061, E-mail: dayle@uri.edu. *Application contact:* Dr. Mary C. Sullivan, Director of Graduate Studies, 401-874-5339, Fax: 401-874-2061, E-mail: mcsullivan@uri.edu.

University of Rochester, School of Nursing, Rochester, NY 14642. Offers acute care nurse practitioner (MS); adult nurse practitioner (MS); adult psychiatric mental health nurse practitioner (MS); adult/geriatric nurse practitioner (MS); care of children and families/pediatric nurse practitioner (MS); care of children and families/pediatric nurse practitioner with pediatric behavioral health (MS); care of children and families/pediatric nurse practitioner/neonatal nurse practitioner (MS); child and adolescent psychiatric mental health nurse practitioner (MS); clinical nurse leader (MS); disaster response and emergency preparedness (MS); family nurse practitioner (MS); health care organization management and leadership (MS); health practice research (PhD); health promotion, education and technology (MS); nursing (Certificate). *Accreditation:* AACN; NLN (one or more programs are accredited). Part-time programs available. Postbaccalaureate distance learning degree programs offered (minimal on-campus study). *Faculty:* 26 full-time (24 women), 20 part-time/adjunct (15 women). *Students:* 50 full-time (45 women), 178 part-time (165 women); includes 33 minority (17 African Americans, 2 American Indian/Alaska Native, 10 Asian Americans or Pacific Islanders, 4 Hispanic Americans), 11 international. Average age 35. 56 applicants, 80% accepted, 35 enrolled. In 2009, 53 master's, 5 doctorates awarded. Terminal master's awarded for partial completion of doctoral program. *Degree requirements:* For master's, comprehensive exam or thesis; for doctorate, thesis/dissertation. *Entrance requirements:* For master's, BS in nursing, minimum GPA of 3.0, course work in statistics; for doctorate, GRE General Test, MS in nursing, minimum GPA of 3.5; for Certificate, MS in nursing. Additional exam requirements/recommendations for international students: Recommended—TOEFL (minimum score 560 paper-based; 230 computer-based; 88 iBT). *Application deadline:* For fall admission, 11/1 priority date for domestic and international students. Application fee: $50. *Financial support:* In 2009–10, 53 students received support, including 14 fellowships with full and partial tuition reimbursements available (averaging $17,497 per year); scholarships/grants, traineeships, health care benefits, tuition waivers (partial), and unspecified assistantships also available. Support available to part-time students. Financial award application deadline: 6/30. *Faculty research:* Clinical research in aging, managing asthma in children, interventions to improve outcomes in critically ill children and their mothers, nurse home visitation studies, medical device evaluation, critical care clinical studies, high risk behavior and prevention, palliative care, pregnancy-related weight gain. Total annual research expenditures: $4.8 million. *Unit head:* Dr. Kathy P. Parker, Dean, 585-273-5639, Fax: 585-273-1268, E-mail: kathy_parker@urmc.rochester.edu. *Application contact:* Elaine Andolina, Director of Admissions, 585-275-2375, Fax: 585-756-8299, E-mail: elaine_andolina@urmc.rochester.edu.

University of St. Francis, College of Nursing and Allied Health, Joliet, IL 60435-6169. Offers nursing (MSN), including adult health clinical nurse specialist, adult nurse practitioner, family nurse practitioner; nursing practice (DNP). *Accreditation:* AACN. Part-time and evening/weekend programs available. Postbaccalaureate distance learning degree programs offered. *Faculty:* 10 full-time (all women), 11 part-time/adjunct (10 women). *Students:* 13 full-time (10 women), 164 part-time (153 women); includes 41 minority (22 African Americans, 1 American Indian/Alaska Native, 6 Asian Americans or Pacific Islanders, 12 Hispanic Americans). Average age 40. 161 applicants, 43% accepted, 56 enrolled. In 2009, 10 master's awarded. *Entrance requirements:* For master's, GRE General Test (MS), minimum GPA of 2.75, 2 years of work experience in clinical nursing, CPR certification, computer competency, 3 letters of recommendation, interview, RN license, current licensure, immunizations, liability insurance, resume, work history (MSN); for doctorate, master's degree in nursing with minimum GPA of 3.0, national certification as nurse practitioner or clinical nurse specialist, current RN licensure, interview, computer competency, CPR certification, immunizations, medical history, physical form, drug screen, criminal background check, liability insurance, letter of recommendation, resume. Additional exam requirements/recommendations for international students: Required—TOEFL (minimum score 550 paper-based; 213 computer-based). *Application deadline:* Applications are processed on a rolling basis. Application fee: $30. Electronic applications accepted. *Expenses:* Contact institution. *Financial support:* In 2009–10, 135 students received support. Scholarships/grants, traineeships, and tuition waivers (partial) available. Support available to part-time students. Financial award applicants required to submit FAFSA. *Unit head:* Dr. Maria Connolly, Dean, 815-740-3840, Fax: 815-740-4243, E-mail: mconnolly@stfrancis.edu. *Application contact:* Sandra Sloka, Director of Admissions for Graduate and Degree Completion Programs, 800-735-7500, Fax: 815-740-5032, E-mail: ssloka@stfrancis.edu.

University of Saint Francis, Graduate School, Department of Nursing, Fort Wayne, IN 46808-3994. Offers MSN. *Accreditation:* AACN. Part-time and evening/weekend programs available. Postbaccalaureate distance learning degree programs offered (no on-campus study). *Degree requirements:* For master's, research project. *Entrance requirements:* For master's, GRE, minimum GPA of 3.2, Indiana RN license.

University of San Diego, Hahn School of Nursing and Health Science, San Diego, CA 92110-2492. Offers adult nurse practitioner/family nurse practitioner (MSN); adult-gerontology clinical nurse specialist (MSN); clinical nursing (MSN); entry-level nursing (for non-RNs) (MSN); executive nurse leader (MSN); family nurse practitioner (MSN); nursing (PhD); nursing practice (DNP); pediatric nurse practitioner/family nurse practitioner (MSN); psychiatric-mental health nurse practitioner (MSN). *Accreditation:* AACN. Part-time and evening/weekend programs available. *Faculty:* 18 full-time (17 women), 25 part-time/adjunct (22 women). *Students:* 141 full-time (117 women), 173 part-time (152 women); includes 95 minority (20 African Americans, 9 American Indian/Alaska Native, 45 Asian Americans or Pacific Islanders, 21 Hispanic Americans), 7 international. Average age 38. 404 applicants, 50% accepted, 132 enrolled. In 2009, 103 master's, 10 doctorates awarded. *Degree requirements:* For doctorate, thesis/dissertation (for some programs), residency (DNP). *Entrance requirements:* For master's, GRE General Test (entry-level nursing), BSN, current California RN licensure (except for entry-level nursing); minimum GPA of 3.0; for doctorate, minimum GPA of 3.5, MSN, current California RN licensure. Additional exam requirements/recommendations for international students: Required—TOEFL (minimum score 580 paper-based; 237 computer-based; 83 iBT),

Nursing—General

University of San Diego *(continued)*
TWE. *Application deadline:* For fall admission, 3/1 priority date for domestic students, 3/1 for international students; for spring admission, 11/1 priority date for domestic students, 11/1 for international students. Applications are processed on a rolling basis. Application fee: $45. Electronic applications accepted. *Expenses:* Tuition: Full-time $21,042; part-time $1169 per unit. Required fees: $224. Full-time tuition and fees vary according to course load and degree level. *Financial support:* In 2009–10, 270 students received support. Scholarships/grants and traineeships available. Support available to part-time students. Financial award application deadline: 4/1; financial award applicants required to submit FAFSA. *Faculty research:* Health promotion, decision making, psychogeriatric nursing, historical nursing, leadership behavior. *Unit head:* Dr. Sally Hardin, Dean, 619-260-4550, Fax: 619-260-6814. *Application contact:* Dr. John Mosby, Associate Director of Graduate Admissions, 619-260-4524, Fax: 619-260-4158, E-mail: grads@sandiego.edu.

University of San Francisco, School of Nursing, San Francisco, CA 94117-1080. Offers clinical nurse leader (MSN); healthcare systems leadership (MSN); nursing practice (DNP), including family nurse practitioner, healthcare systems leadership; MSN/MBA; MSN/MPA; MSN/MSIS. *Accreditation:* AACN. Part-time programs available. *Faculty:* 7 full-time (all women), 31 part-time/adjunct (30 women). *Students:* 216 full-time (185 women), 53 part-time (49 women); includes 101 minority (16 African Americans, 3 American Indian/Alaska Native, 62 Asian Americans or Pacific Islanders, 20 Hispanic Americans), 3 international. Average age 38. 320 applicants, 38% accepted, 72 enrolled. In 2009, 56 master's, 9 doctorates awarded. *Entrance requirements:* For master's, minimum GPA of 3.0. *Application deadline:* Applications are processed on a rolling basis. Application fee: $40. *Expenses:* Tuition: Full-time $19,710; part-time $1095 per unit. Part-time tuition and fees vary according to degree level, campus/location and program. *Financial support:* In 2009–10, 189 students received support. Institutionally sponsored loans available. Financial award application deadline: 3/2. *Faculty research:* Direct patient/client care, providers of health care. *Unit head:* Dr. Judith Karshmer, Dean, 415-422-6681, Fax: 415-422-6877, E-mail: nursing@usfca.edu. *Application contact:* Information Contact, 415-422-4723, Fax: 415-422-2217.

University of Saskatchewan, College of Graduate Studies and Research, College of Nursing, Saskatoon, SK S7N 5E5, Canada. Offers MN. Part-time programs available. *Entrance requirements:* Additional exam requirements/recommendations for international students: Required—TOEFL. Tuition and fees charges are reported in Canadian dollars. *Expenses:* Tuition, area resident: Full-time $3000 Canadian dollars; part-time $500 Canadian dollars per term. Required fees: $700 Canadian dollars; $100 Canadian dollars per term.

The University of Scranton, College of Graduate and Continuing Education, Department of Nursing, Scranton, PA 18510. Offers adult health nursing (MSN); family nurse practitioner (MSN, PMC); nurse anesthesia (MSN, PMC). Applicants accepted in odd-numbered years only. *Accreditation:* AACN; AANA/CANAEP. Part-time and evening/weekend programs available. *Faculty:* 13 full-time (all women), 2 part-time/adjunct (both women). *Students:* 40 full-time (37 women), 35 part-time (25 women); includes 6 minority (5 African Americans, 1 Asian American or Pacific Islander). Average age 35. 74 applicants, 85% accepted. In 2009, 34 master's awarded. *Degree requirements:* For master's, thesis (for some programs), capstone experience. *Entrance requirements:* For master's, BSN, minimum GPA of 3.0, Pennsylvania RN license. Additional exam requirements/recommendations for international students: Required—TOEFL (minimum score 500 paper-based; 173 computer-based), IELTS (minimum score 5.5). *Application deadline:* For fall admission, 9/1 for domestic students. Applications are processed on a rolling basis. Application fee: $0. *Financial support:* In 2009–10, 8 students received support, including 8 teaching assistantships with full and partial tuition reimbursements available (averaging $6,600 per year); career-related internships or fieldwork, Federal Work-Study, and unspecified assistantships also available. Support available to part-time students. Financial award application deadline: 3/1. *Faculty research:* Home care, doctoral education, health care of women and children, pain, health promotion and adolescence. *Unit head:* Dr. Patricia Harrington, Chair, 570-941-7673, Fax: 570-941-4201, E-mail: harringtonp1@uofs.edu. *Application contact:* Dr. Mary Jane Hanson, Director, 570-941-4060, Fax: 570-941-4201, E-mail: hansonm2@scranton.edu.

University of South Alabama, Graduate School, College of Nursing, Mobile, AL 36688-0002. Offers adult health nursing (MSN); community/mental health nursing (MSN); maternal/child nursing (MSN); nursing (DNP). *Accreditation:* AACN. *Degree requirements:* For master's, thesis optional. *Entrance requirements:* For master's, BSN, RN licensure, minimum GPA of 3.0, resume documenting clinical experience, background check, drug screening; for doctorate, GRE. *Expenses:* Tuition, state resident: part-time $218 per contact hour. Required fees: $1102 per year.

University of South Carolina, The Graduate School, College of Nursing, Program in Advanced Practice Clinical Nursing, Columbia, SC 29208. Offers acute care nurse practitioner (Certificate); advanced practice clinical nursing (MSN). *Accreditation:* AACN. Part-time programs available. Postbaccalaureate distance learning degree programs offered (minimal on-campus study). *Entrance requirements:* For master's, master's degree in nursing, RN license; for Certificate, MSN. Additional exam requirements/recommendations for international students: Required—TOEFL (minimum score 570 paper-based; 213 computer-based). Electronic applications accepted. *Faculty research:* Systems research, evidence based practice, breast cancer, violence.

University of South Carolina, The Graduate School, College of Nursing, Program in Advanced Practice Nursing in Primary Care, Columbia, SC 29208. Offers MSN, Certificate. *Accreditation:* AACN. *Entrance requirements:* For master's, master's degree in nursing, RN license; for Certificate, MSN. Additional exam requirements/recommendations for international students: Required—TOEFL (minimum score 570 paper-based; 230 computer-based). Electronic applications accepted. *Faculty research:* Systems research, evidence based practice, breast cancer, violence.

University of Southern Indiana, Graduate Studies, College of Nursing and Health Professions, Program in Nursing, Evansville, IN 47712-3590. Offers MSN, DNP. Part-time programs available. Postbaccalaureate distance learning degree programs offered (minimal on-campus study). *Faculty:* 2 full-time (both women), 1 (woman) part-time/adjunct. *Students:* 11 full-time (10 women), 300 part-time (287 women); includes 13 minority (6 African Americans, 5 Asian Americans or Pacific Islanders, 2 Hispanic Americans), 2 international. Average age 37. 115 applicants, 99% accepted, 75 enrolled. In 2009, 57 master's awarded. *Entrance requirements:* For master's, minimum GPA of 3.0, licensure or eligibility for licensure in Indiana, 1 year or 2000 hours of clinical practice, bachelor's degree in nursing from accredited school. Additional exam requirements/recommendations for international students: Required—TOEFL (minimum score 550 paper-based; 213 computer-based; 79 iBT), IELTS (minimum score 6). *Application deadline:* For fall admission, 2/1 for domestic students, 1/1 priority date for international students. Applications are processed on a rolling basis. Application fee: $25. Electronic applications accepted. *Expenses:* Tuition, state resident: full-time $4592; part-time $255 per credit hour. Tuition, nonresident: full-time $9060; part-time $503 per credit hour. Required fees: $220; $22.75 per term. Tuition and fees vary according to course load and reciprocity agreements. *Financial support:* In 2009–10, 93 students received support. Federal Work-Study, scholarships/grants, tuition waivers (full and partial), and unspecified assistantships available. Financial award application deadline: 3/1; financial award applicants required to submit FAFSA. *Unit head:* Dr. Ann H. White, Director, 812-465-1154, E-mail: awhite@usi.edu. *Application contact:* Dr. Peggy F. Harrel, Director, Graduate Studies, 812-465-7015, Fax: 812-464-1956, E-mail: pharrel@usi.edu.

University of Southern Maine, College of Nursing and Health Professions, Portland, ME 04104-9300. Offers adult health nursing (PMC); clinical nurse leader (MS); clinical nurse specialist psychiatric-mental health nursing (MS); family nursing (PMC); medical/surgical nursing (MS); nurse practitioner adult health nursing (MS); nurse practitioner family nursing (MS); nurse practitioner psychiatric/mental health nursing (MS); psychiatric-mental health nursing (PMC); MBA/MSN. *Accreditation:* AACN. Part-time programs available. *Faculty:* 15 full-time

(13 women), 4 part-time/adjunct (2 women). *Students:* 51 full-time (40 women), 54 part-time (49 women); includes 4 minority (1 American Indian/Alaska Native, 2 Asian Americans or Pacific Islanders, 1 Hispanic American). Average age 36. 95 applicants, 52% accepted, 27 enrolled. In 2009, 34 master's awarded. *Degree requirements:* For master's, thesis optional. *Entrance requirements:* For master's, GRE General Test or MAT, minimum GPA of 3.0. Additional exam requirements/recommendations for international students: Required—TOEFL (minimum score 550 paper-based; 213 computer-based). *Application deadline:* For fall admission, 4/1 for domestic and international students; for spring admission, 10/1 for domestic and international students. Application fee: $50. Electronic applications accepted. *Financial support:* In 2009–10, 10 students received support, including 5 research assistantships with tuition reimbursements available (averaging $3,375 per year), 3 teaching assistantships with tuition reimbursements available (averaging $3,375 per year); career-related internships or fieldwork, Federal Work-Study, scholarships/grants, traineeships, tuition waivers (full and partial), and unspecified assistantships also available. Support available to part-time students. Financial award application deadline: 2/15; financial award applicants required to submit FAFSA. *Faculty research:* Women's health, nursing history, weight control, community services, substance abuse. *Unit head:* Krista M. Meinersmann, Director of Nursing Program, 207-780-4505, Fax: 207-228-8177, E-mail: kmeinersmann@usm.maine.edu. *Application contact:* Mary Sloan, Assistant Director, Office of Graduate Studies, 207-780-4386, Fax: 207-780-4969, E-mail: gradstudies@usm.maine.edu.

University of Southern Mississippi, Graduate School, College of Health, School of Nursing, Hattiesburg, MS 39406-0001. Offers adult health nursing (MSN); community health nursing (MSN); ethics (PhD); family nurse practitioner (MSN); leadership (PhD); nursing service administration (MSN); policy analysis (PhD); psychiatric nursing (MSN). *Accreditation:* AACN. Part-time and evening/weekend programs available. *Faculty:* 17 full-time (16 women), 1 part-time/adjunct (0 women). *Students:* 63 full-time (57 women), 40 part-time (36 women); includes 23 minority (all African Americans). Average age 40. 69 applicants, 59% accepted, 37 enrolled. In 2009, 28 master's, 2 doctorates awarded. *Degree requirements:* For master's, comprehensive exam, thesis optional; for doctorate, comprehensive exam, thesis/dissertation. *Entrance requirements:* For master's, GRE General Test, minimum GPA of 2.75, nursing license, BS in nursing; for doctorate, GRE General Test, master's degree in nursing, minimum GPA of 3.5. Additional exam requirements/recommendations for international students: Required—TOEFL. *Application deadline:* For fall admission, 3/15 priority date for domestic students, 5/1 for international students. Applications are processed on a rolling basis. Application fee: $35. Electronic applications accepted. *Expenses:* Tuition, state resident: full-time $5096; part-time $284 per hour. Tuition, nonresident: full-time $13,052; part-time $726 per hour. Required fees: $402. Tuition and fees vary according to course level and course load. *Financial support:* In 2009–10, 14 research assistantships with full tuition reimbursements (averaging $12,577 per year) were awarded; teaching assistantships, Federal Work-Study and traineeships also available. Financial award application deadline: 3/15; financial award applicants required to submit FAFSA. *Faculty research:* Gerontology, caregivers, HIV, bereavement, pain, nursing leadership. *Unit head:* Dr. Katherine Nugent, Director and Associate Dean, 601-266-5500, Fax: 601-266-5927. *Application contact:* Dr. Anne Brock, Graduate Coordinator, 601-266-5500, Fax: 601-266-5927.

University of South Florida, Graduate School, College of Nursing, Tampa, FL 33620-9951. Offers MS, DNP, PhD. *Accreditation:* AACN; AANA/CANAEP; NLN (one or more programs are accredited). Part-time programs available. *Faculty:* 25 full-time (21 women), 6 part-time/adjunct (5 women). *Students:* 91 full-time (79 women), 627 part-time (568 women); includes 170 minority (84 African Americans, 3 American Indian/Alaska Native, 32 Asian Americans or Pacific Islanders, 51 Hispanic Americans), 10 international. Average age 34. 527 applicants, 29% accepted, 129 enrolled. In 2009, 154 master's, 10 doctorates awarded. *Degree requirements:* For master's, comprehensive exam, thesis optional; for doctorate, comprehensive exam, thesis/dissertation. *Entrance requirements:* For master's and doctorate, GRE General Test. Additional exam requirements/recommendations for international students: Required—TOEFL (minimum score 550 paper-based; 213 computer-based). *Application deadline:* For fall admission, 2/15 for domestic students, 1/2 for international students; for spring admission, 10/15 for domestic students, 6/1 for international students. Application fee: $30. Electronic applications accepted. *Financial support:* In 2009–10, teaching assistantships (averaging $24,202 per year); tuition waivers (partial) and unspecified assistantships also available. Financial award application deadline: 2/1; financial award applicants required to submit FAFSA. *Faculty research:* Women's health, palliative and end-of-life care, cardiac rehabilitation, complementary therapies for chronic illness and cancer. Total annual research expenditures: $2.1 million. *Application contact:* Mary Webb, Director, 813-974-3442, Fax: 813-974-3118, E-mail: mwebb@health.usf.edu.

The University of Tampa, Nursing Program, Tampa, FL 33606-1490. Offers adult nurse practitioner (MSN); family nurse practitioner (MSN). *Accreditation:* NLN. Part-time and evening/weekend programs available. *Faculty:* 10 full-time (all women), 2 part-time/adjunct (both women). *Students:* 4 full-time (all women), 87 part-time (80 women); includes 24 minority (10 African Americans, 1 American Indian/Alaska Native, 1 Asian American or Pacific Islander, 12 Hispanic Americans), 1 international. Average age 38. 64 applicants, 56% accepted, 28 enrolled. In 2009, 22 master's awarded. *Degree requirements:* For master's, comprehensive exam, thesis optional, oral exam, practicum. *Entrance requirements:* For master's, GRE General Test, minimum GPA of 3.0, RN license-Florida, bachelor's degree. Additional exam requirements/recommendations for international students: Required—TOEFL (minimum score 577 paper-based; 230 computer-based; 90 iBT), IELTS (minimum score 7). *Application deadline:* For fall admission, 7/15 for domestic students, 6/1 for international students. Applications are processed on a rolling basis. Application fee: $40. Electronic applications accepted. *Expenses:* Tuition: Part-time $488 per credit hour. *Financial support:* In 2009–10, 68 students received support, including 3 research assistantships with tuition reimbursements available (averaging $2,847 per year); career-related internships or fieldwork and unspecified assistantships also available. Support available to part-time students. Financial award applicants required to submit FAFSA. *Faculty research:* Domestic violence (assessment in emergency departments, changing demographics), trans-cultural health assessment, priorities in maintaining autonomy of elderly. *Unit head:* Dr. Maria Warda, Director, 813-257-3302, Fax: 813-258-7214, E-mail: mwarda@ut.edu. *Application contact:* Karen Full, Graduate Advisor and Recruiter, 813-257-3642, E-mail: kfull@ut.edu.

The University of Tennessee, Graduate School, College of Nursing, Knoxville, TN 37996. Offers MSN, PhD. *Accreditation:* AACN; AANA/CANAEP. Part-time programs available. *Degree requirements:* For master's, thesis or alternative; for doctorate, thesis/dissertation. *Entrance requirements:* For master's and doctorate, GRE General Test, minimum GPA of 2.7. Additional exam requirements/recommendations for international students: Required—TOEFL. Electronic applications accepted. *Expenses:* Tuition, state resident: full-time $6826; part-time $380 per semester hour. Tuition, nonresident: full-time $21,844; part-time $1147 per semester hour. Tuition and fees vary according to program.

The University of Tennessee at Chattanooga, Graduate School, College of Health, Education and Professional Studies, School of Nursing, Chattanooga, TN 37403. Offers administration (MSN); certified nurse anesthetist (Post-Master's Certificate); education (MSN); family nurse practitioner (MSN, Post-Master's Certificate); health care informatics (Post-Master's Certificate); nurse anesthesia (MSN); nurse education (Post-Master's Certificate). *Accreditation:* AACN; AANA/CANAEP (one or more programs are accredited). *Faculty:* 4 full-time (all women). *Students:* 42 full-time (33 women), 53 part-time (38 women); includes 10 minority (5 African Americans, 1 American Indian/Alaska Native, 2 Asian Americans or Pacific Islanders, 2 Hispanic Americans). Average age 35. 13 applicants, 31% accepted, 3 enrolled. In 2009, 36 master's, 5 other advanced degrees awarded. *Degree requirements:* For master's, thesis optional, qualifying exams, professional project; for Post-Master's Certificate, thesis or alternative, practicum, seminar. *Entrance requirements:* For master's, GRE General Test, MAT, BSN, minimum GPA of 3.0, eligibility for Tennessee RN license, 1 year direct patient care experience; for Post-Master's Certificate, GRE General Test, MAT, MSN, minimum GPA of 3.0, eligibility for

Tennessee RN license, one year of direct patient care experience. Additional exam requirements/recommendations for international students: Required—TOEFL (minimum score 550 paper-based; 213 computer-based; 79 iBT), IELTS (minimum score 6). *Application deadline:* For fall admission, 8/1 priority date for domestic students, 6/1 for international students; for spring admission, 12/1 priority date for domestic students, 10/1 for international students. Applications are processed on a rolling basis. Application fee: $35. Electronic applications accepted. *Expenses:* Tuition, state resident: full-time $5404; part-time $300 per credit hour. Tuition, nonresident: full-time $16,702; part-time $928 per credit hour. Required fees: $1150; $130 per credit hour. *Financial support:* Career-related internships or fieldwork and scholarships/grants available. Support available to part-time students. *Faculty research:* Diabetes in women, health care for elderly, alternative medicine, hypertension, nurse anesthesia. Total annual research expenditures: $1.5 million. *Unit head:* Dr. Kay R. Lindgren, Head, 423-425-4646, Fax: 423-425-4668, E-mail: kay-lindgren@utc.edu. *Application contact:* Dr. Stephanie Bellar, Dean of Graduate Studies, 423-425-4666, Fax: 423-425-5223, E-mail: stephanie-bellar@utc.edu.

The University of Tennessee Health Science Center, College of Graduate Health Sciences and College of Nursing, PhD Program in Nursing, Memphis, TN 38163-0002. Offers PhD. Part-time programs available. *Degree requirements:* For doctorate, thesis/dissertation, oral and written preliminary and comprehensive exams. *Entrance requirements:* For doctorate, GRE General Test, minimum GPA of 3.0. Additional exam requirements/recommendations for international students: Required—TOEFL. Electronic applications accepted. *Faculty research:* Obesity in children, genetic markers in transplantation, relative caregivers, quality of life, renal transplantation.

The University of Tennessee Health Science Center, College of Nursing, Memphis, TN 38163-0002. Offers MSN, DNP, PhD. *Accreditation:* AACN; AANA/CANAEP. Postbaccalaureate distance learning degree programs offered (minimal on-campus study). *Degree requirements:* For master's, thesis; for doctorate, thesis/dissertation. *Entrance requirements:* For master's, GRE General Test, BSN, minimum GPA of 3.0; for doctorate, minimum GPA of 3.0. Additional exam requirements/recommendations for international students: Required—TOEFL. Electronic applications accepted. *Expenses:* Contact institution.

The University of Texas at Arlington, Graduate School, School of Nursing, Arlington, TX 76019. Offers administration/supervision of nursing (MSN); nurse practitioner (MSN); nursing science (PhD); teaching of nursing (MSN). *Accreditation:* AACN. Part-time and evening/weekend programs available. *Faculty:* 12 full-time (all women), 8 part-time/adjunct (all women). *Students:* 59 full-time (52 women), 483 part-time (441 women); includes 151 minority (75 African Americans, 3 American Indian/Alaska Native, 32 Asian Americans or Pacific Islanders, 41 Hispanic Americans), 9 international. Average age 37. 227 applicants, 97% accepted, 130 enrolled. In 2009, 72 master's, 3 doctorates awarded. *Degree requirements:* For master's, comprehensive exam, thesis or project; for doctorate, comprehensive exam, thesis/dissertation, successful proposal defense. *Entrance requirements:* For master's, GRE General Test, minimum GPA of 3.0, Texas nursing license, minimum C in undergraduate statistics course, physical assessment course within last 3 years; for doctorate, GRE General Test, minimum undergraduate, graduate and statistics GPA of 3.0; Texas RN license; interview; 3 letters of reference, written statement of goals. Additional exam requirements/recommendations for international students: Required—TOEFL (minimum score 550 paper-based; 213 computer-based), IELTS (minimum score 7). *Application deadline:* For fall admission, 6/5 for domestic students, 4/3 for international students; for spring admission, 10/7 for domestic students, 9/5 for international students. Applications are processed on a rolling basis. Application fee: $40 ($70 for international students). *Financial support:* In 2009–10, 27 students received support, including 24 fellowships with partial tuition reimbursements available (averaging $3,000 per year), 6 research assistantships (averaging $7,992 per year), 7 teaching assistantships (averaging $10,080 per year); career-related internships or fieldwork and traineeships also available. Financial award application deadline: 6/1; financial award applicants required to submit FAFSA. *Faculty research:* Simulation in clinical education and practice, cultural diversity, vulnerable populations, substance abuse. *Unit head:* Dr. Elizabeth C. Poster, Dean, 817-272-2776, Fax: 817-272-5006, E-mail: poster@uta.edu. *Application contact:* Dr. Mary Schira, Graduate Advisor & Associate Dean, 817-272-2329, Fax: 817-272-2065, E-mail: schira@uta.edu.

The University of Texas at Austin, Graduate School, School of Nursing, Austin, TX 78712-1111. Offers MSN, PhD. *Accreditation:* AACN. Part-time programs available. *Degree requirements:* For master's, thesis optional; for doctorate, thesis/dissertation. *Entrance requirements:* For master's and doctorate, GRE General Test. Additional exam requirements/recommendations for international students: Required—TOEFL (minimum score 550 paper-based; 213 computer-based). Electronic applications accepted. *Faculty research:* Chronic illness management, memory and aging, health promotion, women's health, adolescent health.

The University of Texas at El Paso, Graduate School, School of Nursing, El Paso, TX 79968-0001. Offers evidence-based practice (Certificate); family nurse practitioner (MSN); health care leadership and management (Certificate); interdisciplinary health sciences (PhD); nurse clinical specialist (MSN); nursing (Post-Master's Certificate); nursing systems management (MSN). *Accreditation:* AACN. *Students:* 153 (124 women); includes 100 minority (11 African Americans, 1 American Indian/Alaska Native, 6 Asian Americans or Pacific Islanders, 82 Hispanic Americans), 5 international. Average age 34. 91 applicants, 49% accepted. In 2009, 33 master's awarded. *Degree requirements:* For master's, thesis optional; for doctorate, thesis/dissertation. *Entrance requirements:* For master's, GRE, minimum GPA of 3.0, course work in statistics, resume; for doctorate, GRE, letters of reference, relevant personal/professional experience, master's degree in health. Additional exam requirements/recommendations for international students: Required—TOEFL; Recommended—IELTS. *Application deadline:* For fall admission, 8/1 for domestic students, 3/1 for international students; for spring admission, 11/1 for domestic students, 9/1 for international students. Applications are processed on a rolling basis. Application fee: $45 ($80 for international students). Electronic applications accepted. *Financial support:* In 2009–10, research assistantships with partial tuition reimbursements (averaging $18,825 per year), teaching assistantships with partial tuition reimbursements (averaging $18,000 per year) were awarded; fellowships with partial tuition reimbursements, institutionally sponsored loans, scholarships/grants, health care benefits, tuition waivers (partial), and unspecified assistantships also available. Support available to part-time students. Financial award application deadline: 3/15; financial award applicants required to submit FAFSA. *Unit head:* Dr. Elias Provencio-Vasquez, Dean, 915-747-7273, Fax: 915-747-8266, E-mail: eprovenciovasquez@utep.edu. *Application contact:* Dr. Patricia D. Witherspoon, Dean of the Graduate School, 915-747-5491, Fax: 915-747-5788, E-mail: withersp@utep.edu.

The University of Texas at Tyler, College of Nursing and Health Sciences, Program in Nursing, Tyler, TX 75799-0001. Offers nurse practitioner (MSN); nursing (PhD); nursing administration (MSN); nursing education (MSN); MSN/MBA. *Accreditation:* AACN. Part-time and evening/weekend programs available. Postbaccalaureate distance learning degree programs offered (no on-campus study). *Faculty:* 15 full-time (all women). *Students:* 26 full-time (24 women), 158 part-time (139 women); includes 36 minority (17 African Americans, 3 American Indian/Alaska Native, 7 Asian Americans or Pacific Islanders, 9 Hispanic Americans). Average age 40. 51 applicants, 57% accepted, 15 enrolled. In 2009, 32 master's awarded. *Degree requirements:* For master's, comprehensive exam (for some programs), thesis (for some programs); for doctorate, thesis/dissertation. *Entrance requirements:* For master's, GRE General Test or MAT, GMAT, minimum undergraduate GPA of 3.0, course work in statistics, RN license, BSN. Additional exam requirements/recommendations for international students: Required—TOEFL (minimum score 79 computer-based). *Application deadline:* For fall admission, 8/17 priority date for domestic students, 7/1 priority date for international students; for spring admission, 12/21 priority date for domestic students, 11/1 priority date for international students. Applications are processed on a rolling basis. Application fee: $25 ($50 for international students). Electronic applications accepted. *Expenses:* Tuition, state resident: part-time $665 per semester hour. Tuition, nonresident: part-time $942 per semester hour. Part-time tuition and fees vary according to degree level and program. *Financial support:* In 2009–10, 15 students received support, including 1 fellowship (averaging $10,000 per year), 3 research assistantships (averaging $2,200 per year); institutionally sponsored loans and scholarships/grants also available. Financial award application deadline: 7/1; financial award applicants required to submit FAFSA. *Faculty research:* Psychosocial adjustment, aging, support/commitment of caregivers, psychological abuse and violence, hope/hopelessness, professional values, end of life care, suicidology, clinical supervision, workforce retention and issues, global health issues, health promotion. Total annual research expenditures: $258,200. *Unit head:* Dr. Susan Yarbrough, Assistant Dean, 903-566-1220, E-mail: syarbrou@mail.uttyl.edu. *Application contact:* Dr. Susan Yarbrough.

The University of Texas Health Science Center at Houston, School of Nursing, Houston, TX 77225-0036. Offers MSN, DNP, PhD, MSN/MPH. *Accreditation:* AACN; AANA/CANAEP. Part-time programs available. *Faculty:* 38 full-time (31 women). *Students:* 117 full-time (92 women), 230 part-time (203 women); includes 124 minority (46 African Americans, 2 American Indian/Alaska Native, 36 Asian Americans or Pacific Islanders, 40 Hispanic Americans), 6 international. Average age 35. 318 applicants, 48% accepted, 128 enrolled. In 2009, 104 master's, 15 doctorates awarded. *Degree requirements:* For master's, thesis, research project, or clinical project; for doctorate, thesis/dissertation. *Entrance requirements:* For master's, GRE or MAT, BSN, Texas RN license, related work experience, interview, writing sample; for doctorate, GRE, interview, Texas RN license, portfolio, master's degree. Additional exam requirements/recommendations for international students: Required—TOEFL (minimum score 550 paper-based; 213 computer-based; 86 iBT). *Application deadline:* For fall admission, 4/1 priority date for domestic students. Applications are processed on a rolling basis. Application fee: $30. Electronic applications accepted. *Financial support:* In 2009–10, 125 students received support; research assistantships with tuition reimbursements available, teaching assistantships with tuition reimbursements available, institutionally sponsored loans, scholarships/grants, traineeships, and tuition waivers (full) available. Support available to part-time students. Financial award applicants required to submit FAFSA. *Faculty research:* Malnutrition in institutionalized elderly, defining nursing, sensitive outcome measures, substance abuse in mothers during pregnancy, psychoeducational intervention among caregivers of stroke patients. Total annual research expenditures: $150,000. *Unit head:* Dr. Patricia L. Starck, Dean, 713-500-2100, Fax: 713-500-2107. *Application contact:* Laurie G. Rutherford, Student Affairs, 713-500-2101, Fax: 713-500-2107, E-mail: soninfo@uth.tmc.edu.

The University of Texas Health Science Center at San Antonio, Graduate School of Biomedical Sciences, School of Nursing, San Antonio, TX 78229-3900. Offers MSN, PhD. *Accreditation:* AACN. Part-time programs available. *Faculty:* 39 full-time (38 women), 2 part-time/adjunct (0 women). *Students:* 46 full-time (32 women), 166 part-time (143 women); includes 106 minority (17 African Americans, 3 American Indian/Alaska Native, 17 Asian Americans or Pacific Islanders, 69 Hispanic Americans). Average age 39. 134 applicants, 46% accepted, 56 enrolled. In 2009, 78 master's, 4 doctorates awarded. Terminal master's awarded for partial completion of doctoral program. *Degree requirements:* For master's, thesis optional; for doctorate, comprehensive exam, thesis/dissertation. *Entrance requirements:* For master's, minimum GPA of 3.0, work experience, personal interview; for doctorate, GRE, MAT, minimum GPA of 3.0, personal interview. Additional exam requirements/recommendations for international students: Required—TOEFL (minimum score 560 paper-based; 220 computer-based; 83 iBT). *Application deadline:* For fall admission, 2/1 for domestic students; for spring admission, 9/1 for domestic students. Application fee: $45. Electronic applications accepted. *Expenses:* Tuition, state resident: full-time $2832; part-time $118 per credit hour. Tuition, nonresident: full-time $10,896; part-time $454 per credit hour. Required fees: $884 per semester. One-time fee: $70. *Financial support:* In 2009–10, 51 students received support, including 2 fellowships with full tuition reimbursements available (averaging $30,000 per year); research assistantships, teaching assistantships, institutionally sponsored loans and scholarships/grants also available. Financial award application deadline: 4/1; financial award applicants required to submit FAFSA. *Faculty research:* Pain, organizational structure, aging, quality and safety. Total annual research expenditures: $2.4 million. *Unit head:* Eileen T. Breslin, Dean, 210-567-5800, Fax: 210-567-5929, E-mail: breslin@uthscsa.edu. *Application contact:* Beverly Robinson, Associate Dean for Graduate Nursing Program and Director of Doctoral Studies, 210-567-5815, Fax: 210-567-3813, E-mail: robinsonb@uthscsa.edu.

The University of Texas Medical Branch, Graduate School of Biomedical Sciences, Doctoral Program in Nursing, Galveston, TX 77555. Offers PhD. *Students:* 20 full-time (18 women), 16 part-time (14 women); includes 15 minority (6 African Americans, 3 American Indian/Alaska Native, 3 Asian Americans or Pacific Islanders, 3 Hispanic Americans). Average age 48. In 2009, 8 doctorates awarded. *Degree requirements:* For doctorate, comprehensive exam, thesis/dissertation. *Entrance requirements:* For doctorate, GRE General Test, minimum GPA of 3.0, BSN and MSN or equivalent advanced degree, 2 writing samples, 3 letters of reference, curriculum vitae or resume. Additional exam requirements/recommendations for international students: Required—TOEFL (minimum score 550 paper-based; 213 computer-based). *Application deadline:* For fall admission, 3/1 for domestic students, 3/1 priority date for international students. Applications are processed on a rolling basis. Application fee: $30 ($75 for international students). Electronic applications accepted. *Financial support:* In 2009–10, 2 teaching assistantships (averaging $25,000 per year) were awarded; scholarships/grants and unspecified assistantships also available. Financial award applicants required to submit FAFSA. *Unit head:* Dr. Alice T. Hill, Director, 409-772-8251, Fax: 409-747-1550, E-mail: ahill@utmb.edu. *Application contact:* Denise Reed, Administrative Associate, 409-772-8206, Fax: 409-747-1550, E-mail: djreed@utmb.edu.

The University of Texas Medical Branch, School of Nursing, Master's Program in Nursing, Galveston, TX 77555. Offers MSN. Part-time programs available. Postbaccalaureate distance learning degree programs offered. *Students:* 26 full-time (22 women), 218 part-time (193 women); includes 87 minority (29 African Americans, 1 American Indian/Alaska Native, 21 Asian Americans or Pacific Islanders, 36 Hispanic Americans), 1 international. Average age 37. In 2009, 74 master's awarded. *Entrance requirements:* For master's, GRE General Test or MAT, minimum BSN GPA of 3.0, 3 references, interview, 1 year nursing experience. Additional exam requirements/recommendations for international students: Required—TOEFL (minimum score 550 paper-based). *Unit head:* Dr. Kathryn Fiandt, Professor and Associate Dean for Graduate Programs and Clinical Affairs, 409-772-8297, Fax: 409-772-8215, E-mail: klfiandt@utmb.edu. *Application contact:* Diane Sierra, Administrative Associate, 409-772-4855, Fax: 409-772-8215, E-mail: dvsierra@utmb.edu.

The University of Texas–Pan American, College of Health Sciences and Human Services, Department of Nursing, Edinburg, TX 78539. Offers adult health nursing (MSN); family nurse practitioner (MSN); pediatric nurse practitioner (MSN). *Accreditation:* AACN. Part-time and evening/weekend programs available. *Degree requirements:* For master's, thesis optional. *Entrance requirements:* For master's, Texas RN licensure, undergraduate physical statistic course. Additional exam requirements/recommendations for international students: Required—TOEFL (minimum score 550 paper-based). Electronic applications accepted. *Expenses:* Contact institution. *Faculty research:* Health promotion, adolescent pregnancy, herbal and nontraditional approaches, healing touch stress.

University of the Incarnate Word, School of Graduate Studies and Research, School of Nursing and Health Professions, Program in Nursing, San Antonio, TX 78209-6397. Offers MSN. *Accreditation:* AACN. Part-time and evening/weekend programs available. *Students:* 3 full-time (all women), 62 part-time (54 women); includes 21 minority (7 African Americans, 3 Asian Americans or Pacific Islanders, 11 Hispanic Americans), 34 international. Average age 40. In 2009, 5 master's awarded. *Degree requirements:* For master's, capstone, clinical hours. *Entrance requirements:* For master's, baccalaureate degree in nursing from CCNE- or NLN-accredited program including courses in statistics and health assessment; minimum undergraduate cumulative GPA of 2.5, 3.0 in upper-division nursing courses; three professional references; license to practice nursing in Texas or recognized state. Additional exam requirements/recommendations for international students: Required—TOEFL (minimum score 560 paper-based; 220 computer-based; 83 iBT). *Application deadline:* Applications are processed on a rolling basis. Application fee: $20. Electronic applications accepted. *Expenses:* Tuition:

Nursing—General

University of the Incarnate Word (continued)
Full-time $12,150; part-time $675 per credit hour. Required fees: $83 per credit hour. *Financial support:* Federal Work-Study, scholarships/grants, and traineeships available. Support available to part-time students. Financial award applicants required to submit FAFSA. *Unit head:* Dr. Sandra Strickland, Chair, 210-829-3988, Fax: 210-829-3174, E-mail: strickla@uiwtx.edu. *Application contact:* Andrea Cyterski-Acosta, Dean of Enrollment, 210-829-6005, Fax: 210-829-3921, E-mail: admis@uiwtx.edu.

The University of Toledo, College of Graduate Studies, College of Nursing, Toledo, OH 43606-3390. Offers adult health practitioner/clinical nurse specialist (MSN); adult nurse practitioner (Certificate); entry-level nursing initiative (GEMINI) (MSN); family nurse practitioner (MSN, Certificate); nursing education (Certificate); pediatric nurse practitioner (Certificate); pediatric nurse practitioner/clinical nurse specialist (MSN); RN to MSN (MSN). *Accreditation:* AACN. Part-time programs available. *Degree requirements:* For master's, thesis or scholarly project. *Entrance requirements:* For master's, GRE General Test, BS in nursing, minimum undergraduate GPA of 3.0. *Expenses:* Contact institution. *Faculty research:* Sexuality issues, prenatal testing, health care of homeless, nursing education, chronic/acute pain, eating disorders, low birth weight infants.

University of Toronto, School of Graduate Studies, Life Sciences Division, Department of Nursing Science, Toronto, ON M5S 1A1, Canada. Offers MN, PhD. Part-time programs available. *Degree requirements:* For doctorate, thesis/dissertation, departmental and final oral exam/thesis defense. *Entrance requirements:* For master's, B Sc N or equivalent, minimum B average in next-to-final year, resume, (MN), 3 letters of reference (MN); for doctorate, minimum B+ average, master's degree in nursing or a related area, resumé, 2 letters of recommendation. *Expenses:* Contact institution.

University of Utah, Graduate School, College of Nursing, Program in Nursing, Salt Lake City, UT 84112. Offers MS, DNP, PhD. Part-time programs available. *Faculty:* 52 full-time (43 women), 9 part-time/adjunct (8 women). *Students:* 169 full-time (134 women), 109 part-time (93 women); includes 22 minority (4 African Americans, 2 American Indian/Alaska Native, 10 Asian Americans or Pacific Islanders, 6 Hispanic Americans), 6 international. Average age 40. 188 applicants, 56% accepted, 91 enrolled. In 2009, 62 master's, 7 doctorates awarded. *Degree requirements:* For master's, thesis or project; for doctorate, comprehensive exam, thesis/dissertation. *Entrance requirements:* For master's, GRE General Test (if BSN GPA less than 3.25), Utah RN license; for doctorate, GRE General Test, interview, Utah RN license, curriculum vitae/resume, goal statement, professional references. Additional exam requirements/recommendations for international students: Required—TOEFL (minimum score 500 paper-based; 173 computer-based; 85 iBT). *Application deadline:* For fall admission, 7/1 for domestic and international students. Application fee: $55 ($65 for international students). Electronic applications accepted. *Expenses:* Contact institution. *Financial support:* In 2009–10, 32 fellowships (averaging $7,250 per year), 13 teaching assistantships (averaging $9,000 per year) were awarded. Financial award application deadline: 3/15; financial award applicants required to submit FAFSA. *Faculty research:* Symptom management, patient-provider communication, patient safety/informatics, gerontology/geriatric nursing, end-of-life bereavement. Total annual research expenditures: $2.1 million. *Unit head:* Dr. Maureen Keefe, Dean, 801-581-8262, Fax: 801-581-4642, E-mail: maureen.keefe@nurs.utah.edu. *Application contact:* Carrie L. Radmall, Director, Academic Programs and Student Services, 801-581-8798, Fax: 801-585-9705, E-mail: carrie.radmall@nurs.utah.edu.

University of Vermont, Graduate College, College of Nursing and Health Sciences, Department of Nursing, Burlington, VT 05405. Offers MS. *Accreditation:* AACN. *Students:* 88 (81 women); includes 10 minority (3 African Americans, 2 American Indian/Alaska Native, 5 Asian Americans or Pacific Islanders), 1 international. 154 applicants, 32% accepted, 11 enrolled. In 2009, 4 master's awarded. *Entrance requirements:* For master's, GRE General Test. Additional exam requirements/recommendations for international students: Required—TOEFL (minimum score 550 paper-based; 213 computer-based; 80 iBT). *Application deadline:* For fall admission, 4/1 priority date for domestic students. Applications are processed on a rolling basis. Application fee: $40. Electronic applications accepted. *Expenses:* Tuition, state resident: part-time $508 per credit hour. Tuition, nonresident: part-time $1281 per credit hour. *Financial support:* Application deadline: 3/1. *Unit head:* Dr. Jeanine Carr, Coordinator, 802-656-3830. *Application contact:* Dr. Jeanine Carr, Coordinator, 802-656-3830.

University of Victoria, Faculty of Graduate Studies, Faculty of Human and Social Development, School of Nursing, Victoria, BC V8W 2Y2, Canada. Offers advanced nursing practice (advanced practice leadership option) (MN); advanced nursing practice (nurse educator option) (MN); advanced nursing practice (nurse practitioner option) (MN); nursing (PhD). Part-time programs available. Postbaccalaureate distance learning degree programs offered (no on-campus study). *Entrance requirements:* Additional exam requirements/recommendations for international students: Required—TOEFL (minimum score 575 paper-based; 233 computer-based), IELTS (minimum score 7). Electronic applications accepted.

University of Virginia, School of Nursing, Charlottesville, VA 22903. Offers acute and specialty care (MSN); acute care nurse practitioner (MSN); clinical nurse leadership (MSN); community-public health leadership (MSN); nursing (DNP, PhD); psychiatric mental health counseling (MSN); MSN/MBA. *Accreditation:* AACN. Part-time programs available. *Faculty:* 50 full-time (47 women), 4 part-time/adjunct (3 women). *Students:* 158 full-time (135 women), 118 part-time (117 women); includes 41 minority (30 African Americans, 1 American Indian/Alaska Native, 4 Asian Americans or Pacific Islanders, 6 Hispanic Americans), 4 international. Average age 36. 302 applicants, 48% accepted, 106 enrolled. In 2009, 84 master's, 12 doctorates awarded. *Degree requirements:* For doctorate, comprehensive exam (for some programs), capstone project (DNP), dissertation (PhD). *Entrance requirements:* For master's, GRE General Test, MAT; for doctorate, GRE General Test. Additional exam requirements/recommendations for international students: Required—TOEFL, IELTS. *Application deadline:* Applications are processed on a rolling basis. Application fee: $60. Electronic applications accepted. *Expenses:* Contact institution. *Financial support:* Fellowships, research assistantships, teaching assistantships, Federal Work-Study and scholarships/grants available. Financial award applicants required to submit FAFSA. *Unit head:* Dorrie K. Fontaine, Dean, 434-924-0141, Fax: 434-982-1809. *Application contact:* Clay Hysell, Assistant Dean for Graduate Student Services, 434-924-0141, Fax: 434-982-1809, E-mail: nur-osa@virginia.edu.

University of Washington, Graduate School, School of Nursing, Seattle, WA 98195. Offers MN, MS, DNP, PhD, Graduate Certificate, MN/MPH. *Accreditation:* AACN; ACNM/DOA (one or more programs are accredited). Part-time programs available. *Degree requirements:* For master's, thesis (for some programs); for doctorate, thesis/dissertation. *Entrance requirements:* For master's, GRE, minimum GPA of 3.0, resume; for doctorate, GRE, minimum GPA of 3.0. Additional exam requirements/recommendations for international students: Required—TOEFL. *Faculty research:* High risk youth, pain management, women's health, oncology, sleep.

University of Washington, Bothell, Program in Nursing, Bothell, WA 98011-8246. Offers MN. Part-time programs available. *Faculty:* 8 full-time (all women). *Students:* 2 full-time (1 woman), 76 part-time (69 women); includes 11 minority (4 African Americans, 4 Asian Americans or Pacific Islanders, 3 Hispanic Americans), 2 international. Average age 44. 45 applicants, 62% accepted, 27 enrolled. In 2009, 24 master's awarded. *Degree requirements:* For master's, thesis. *Entrance requirements:* Additional exam requirements/recommendations for international students: Required—TOEFL. *Application deadline:* For fall admission, 3/1 priority date for domestic and international students. Applications are processed on a rolling basis. Application fee: $65. Electronic applications accepted. *Expenses:* Tuition, state resident: full-time $10,160; part-time $484 per credit hour. Tuition, nonresident: full-time $23,500; part-time $1120 per credit hour. Required fees: $567; $21.50 per credit hour. Tuition and fees vary according to course load and program. *Financial support:* Federal Work-Study and unspecified assistantships available. *Faculty research:* Health of special populations, nursing education, higher education technology, healing through patient's narratives, women's health care issues, end of life issues in nursing. *Unit head:* Prof. Mary Baroni, Director, 425-352-3543, Fax: 425-352-3237, E-mail: mbaroni@uwb.edu. *Application contact:* Judy Lynn, Administrative Coordinator, 425-352-5376, Fax: 425-352-3237, E-mail: jlynn@uwb.edu.

University of Washington, Tacoma, Graduate Programs, Program in Nursing, Tacoma, WA 98402-3100. Offers MN. *Faculty:* 9 full-time (all women), 3 part-time/adjunct (all women). *Students:* 2 full-time (both women), 80 part-time (73 women); includes 22 minority (9 African Americans, 1 American Indian/Alaska Native, 10 Asian Americans or Pacific Islanders, 2 Hispanic Americans). Average age 43. *Expenses:* Tuition, state resident: full-time $10,660; part-time $484 per credit. Tuition, nonresident: full-time $24,000; part-time $1119 per credit. Required fees: $150 per term. Tuition and fees vary according to course load and program. *Faculty research:* Psychological adaptation in death and dying and related tool development; health care and decision making, including cancer clinical trial; participation; community health, especially as related to race, gender and class, and health disparities and community health; environmental health and policy; health care delivery. *Unit head:* Dr. Patricia Spakes, Chancellor, 253-692-5646, E-mail: pspakes@u.washington.edu. *Application contact:* Joan Abe, Director, The University of Washington Graduate School, 253-543-5929, E-mail: uwgrad@u.washington.edu.

The University of Western Ontario, Faculty of Graduate Studies, Health Sciences Division, School of Nursing, London, ON N6A 5B8, Canada. Offers M Sc N, MN NP, PhD. Part-time programs available. *Degree requirements:* For master's, thesis; for doctorate, thesis/dissertation. *Entrance requirements:* Additional exam requirements/recommendations for international students: Required—TOEFL. *Faculty research:* Empowerment, self-efficacy, family health, community health, gerontology.

University of West Georgia, Graduate School, School of Nursing, Carrollton, GA 30118. Offers health systems leadership (Post-Master's Certificate); nursing (MSN); nursing education (Post-Master's Certificate). *Accreditation:* AACN. Part-time programs available. *Faculty:* 23 full-time (all women), 8 part-time/adjunct (all women). *Students:* 17 full-time (all women), 12 part-time (all women); includes 4 minority (all African Americans), 5 international. Average age 36. 30 applicants, 70% accepted, 10 enrolled. In 2009, 11 master's awarded. *Degree requirements:* For master's, comprehensive exam, thesis or alternative. *Entrance requirements:* For master's, GRE or MAT, BSN, Georgia RN license, minimum GPA of 3.0 for upper-division nursing courses, completion of basic undergraduate statistics course. *Application deadline:* For fall admission, 7/17 for domestic students; for spring admission, 11/20 for domestic students. Applications are processed on a rolling basis. Application fee: $30. Electronic applications accepted. *Expenses:* Tuition, state resident: full-time $2952; part-time $164 per semester hour. Tuition, nonresident: full-time $11,808; part-time $656 per semester hour. Required fees: $42.90 per semester hour. $307 per semester. Tuition and fees vary according to course load. *Financial support:* In 2009–10, 1 research assistantship with full tuition reimbursement (averaging $6,000 per year) was awarded. Financial award application deadline: 7/1; financial award applicants required to submit FAFSA. *Faculty research:* Caring in nursing education, pain assessment in older adults, pain outcomes. *Unit head:* Dr. Kathryn Mary Grams, Dean, 678-839-6552, Fax: 678-839-6553, E-mail: kgrams@westga.edu. *Application contact:* Dr. Charles W. Clark, Dean, 678-839-6508, E-mail: cclark@westga.edu.

University of Windsor, Faculty of Graduate Studies, Faculty of Nursing, Windsor, ON N9B 3P4, Canada. Offers M Sc, MN. *Degree requirements:* For master's, thesis or alternative. *Entrance requirements:* For master's, minimum B average, certificate of competence (nurse registration). Additional exam requirements/recommendations for international students: Required—TOEFL (minimum score 560 paper-based; 220 computer-based). Electronic applications accepted.

University of Wisconsin–Eau Claire, College of Nursing and Health Sciences, Program in Nursing, Eau Claire, WI 54702-4004. Offers adult health clinical nurse specialist (MSN); adult health in administration (MSN); adult health in education (MSN); adult health nurse practitioner (MSN); family health in administration (MSN); family health in education (MSN); family health nurse practitioner (MSN). Part-time programs available. *Faculty:* 15 full-time (14 women). *Students:* 34 full-time (32 women), 55 part-time (51 women); includes 1 minority (Asian American or Pacific Islander). Average age 35. 58 applicants, 59% accepted, 2 enrolled. In 2009, 32 master's awarded. Terminal master's awarded for partial completion of doctoral program. *Degree requirements:* For master's, thesis optional, 500-600 hours clinical practicum, oral and written exams. *Entrance requirements:* For master's, Wisconsin RN license, minimum GPA of 3.0, undergraduate statistics, course work in health assessment. Additional exam requirements/recommendations for international students: Required—TOEFL (minimum score 550 paper-based; 213 computer-based; 79 iBT). *Application deadline:* For fall admission, 1/15 priority date for domestic students, 6/1 priority date for international students; for spring admission, 11/1 priority date for international students. Applications are processed on a rolling basis. Application fee: $56. Electronic applications accepted. *Expenses:* Tuition, state resident: full-time $6705.90; part-time $372.55 per credit. Tuition, nonresident: full-time $16,771; part-time $931.74 per credit. Required fees: $925.50; $51.19 per credit. One-time fee: $56. *Financial support:* In 2009–10, 50 students received support, including 2 fellowships (averaging $500 per year); Federal Work-Study and unspecified assistantships also available. Financial award application deadline: 3/1; financial award applicants required to submit FAFSA. *Unit head:* Dr. Mary Zwygart-Stauffacher, Interim Dean, 715-836-5287, Fax: 715-836-5925, E-mail: zwygarmc@uwec.edu. *Application contact:* Kristina Anderson, Director of Admissions, 715-836-5415, Fax: 715-836-2409, E-mail: admissions@uwec.edu.

University of Wisconsin–Madison, School of Nursing, Madison, WI 53706-1380. Offers DNP, PhD, MS/MPH. *Accreditation:* AACN. Part-time programs available. *Faculty:* 19 full-time (all women). *Students:* 55 full-time (52 women), 146 part-time (137 women); includes 17 minority (7 African Americans, 2 American Indian/Alaska Native, 3 Asian Americans or Pacific Islanders, 5 Hispanic Americans), 3 international. Average age 37. 23 applicants, 43% accepted, 8 enrolled. In 2009, 3 doctorates awarded. *Degree requirements:* For doctorate, comprehensive exam, thesis/dissertation. *Entrance requirements:* For doctorate, GRE General Test, 2 samples of scholarly written work, BS in nursing from an accredited program, minimum undergraduate GPA of 3.0 in last 60 credits. Additional exam requirements/recommendations for international students: Required—TOEFL (minimum score 550 paper-based; 213 computer-based). *Application deadline:* For fall admission, 2/1 priority date for domestic and international students. Application fee: $45. Electronic applications accepted. *Expenses:* Tuition, state resident: part-time $594 per credit. Tuition, nonresident: part-time $1504 per credit. Required fees: $65 per credit. Tuition and fees vary according to course load, program and reciprocity agreements. *Financial support:* In 2009–10, 12 fellowships with full tuition reimbursements (averaging $22,000 per year), 6 research assistantships with full tuition reimbursements (averaging $21,000 per year), 7 teaching assistantships with full tuition reimbursements (averaging $14,000 per year) were awarded; career-related internships or fieldwork, Federal Work-Study, institutionally sponsored loans, scholarships/grants, traineeships, health care benefits, and unspecified assistantships also available. Support available to part-time students. Financial award application deadline: 3/1; financial award applicants required to submit FAFSA. *Faculty research:* Nursing informatics to promote self-care and disease management skills among patients and caregivers; quality of care to frail, vulnerable, and chronically ill populations; study of health-related and health-seeking behaviors; eliminating health disparities; pain and symptom management for patients with cancer. Total annual research expenditures: $3 million. *Unit head:* Dr. Katharyn A. May, Dean, 608-263-5155, Fax: 608-263-5323, E-mail: kamay@wisc.edu. *Application contact:* Marcia L. Voss, Program Coordinator, 608-263-5258, Fax: 608-263-5332, E-mail: mlvoss@wisc.edu.

University of Wisconsin–Milwaukee, Graduate School, College of Nursing, Milwaukee, WI 53201-0413. Offers family nursing practitioner (Post Master's Certificate); health professional education (Certificate); nursing (MS, PhD); public health (Certificate). *Accreditation:* AACN. Part-time programs available. *Faculty:* 34 full-time (33 women). *Students:* 159 full-time (148 women), 118 part-time (100 women); includes 32 minority (15 African Americans, 1 American Indian/Alaska Native, 11 Asian Americans or Pacific Islanders, 5 Hispanic Americans), 6 international. Average age 40. 123 applicants, 54% accepted, 37 enrolled. In 2009, 53 master's,

13 doctorates awarded. *Degree requirements:* For master's, thesis; for doctorate, thesis/dissertation. *Entrance requirements:* For master's, GRE General Test or MAT, autobiographical sketch; for doctorate, GRE, minimum GPA of 3.2. Additional exam requirements/recommendations for international students: Required—TOEFL (minimum score 550 paper-based; 79 iBT), IELTS (minimum score 6.5). *Application deadline:* For fall admission, 1/1 priority date for domestic students; for spring admission, 9/1 for domestic students. Applications are processed on a rolling basis. Application fee: $45 ($75 for international students). *Expenses:* Tuition, state resident: full-time $8800. Tuition, nonresident: full-time $20,760. Tuition and fees vary according to program and reciprocity agreements. *Financial support:* In 2009–10, 8 teaching assistantships were awarded; career-related internships or fieldwork, Federal Work-Study, and unspecified assistantships also available. Support available to part-time students. Financial award application deadline: 4/15. Total annual research expenditures: $3.4 million. *Unit head:* Dr. Sally Lundeen, Dean, 414-229-4189, E-mail: slundeen@uwm.edu. *Application contact:* Ellen K. Murphy, Representative, 414-229-5468.

University of Wisconsin–Oshkosh, The Office of Graduate Studies, College of Nursing, Oshkosh, WI 54901. Offers adult health and illness (MSN); family nurse practitioner (MSN). *Accreditation:* AACN. Part-time programs available. *Degree requirements:* For master's, thesis or alternative, clinical paper. *Entrance requirements:* For master's, RN license, BSN, previous course work in statistics and health assessment, minimum undergraduate GPA of 3.0, letters of recommendation. Additional exam requirements/recommendations for international students: Required—TOEFL (minimum score 550 paper-based; 213 computer-based; 79 iBT). Electronic applications accepted. *Faculty research:* Adult health and illness, nurse practitioners practice, health care service, advanced practitioner roles, natural alternative complementary healthcare.

University of Wyoming, College of Health Sciences, Fay W. Whitney School of Nursing, Laramie, WY 82070. Offers MS. *Accreditation:* AACN. Part-time programs available. Postbaccalaureate distance learning degree programs offered (no on-campus study). *Degree requirements:* For master's, thesis. *Entrance requirements:* For master's, GRE General Test, BSN from CCNE or NCN-accredited school, minimum GPA of 3.0. Additional exam requirements/recommendations for international students: Required—TOEFL. *Faculty research:* Support systems for the elderly, fetal alcohol syndrome, teen pregnancy, rehabilitation with chronic mental illness, global peace building among women.

Urbana University, College of Nursing and Allied Health, Urbana, OH 43078-2091. Offers nursing (MSN). *Accreditation:* AACN. *Entrance requirements:* For master's, baccalaureate degree in nursing with cumulative undergraduate GPA of 3.0, official transcripts, Ohio RN license, background check, statement of goals and objectives, resume, 3 letters of recommendation, interview. Application fee: $25. *Expenses:* Tuition: Full-time $8550; part-time $475 per semester hour. Required fees: $950; $475 per semester. One-time fee: $25. *Unit head:* Nancy Sweeney, Dean, 937-328-9661, E-mail: nsweeney@urbana.edu. *Application contact:* Brian Kesse, Director of Admissions, 937-484-1370, Fax: 937-484-1389, E-mail: bkesse@urbana.edu.

Ursuline College, School of Graduate Studies, Programs in Nursing, Pepper Pike, OH 44124-4398. Offers care management (MSN); nurse practitioner (MSN); nursing (DNP); nursing education (MSN); palliative care (MSN). *Accreditation:* AACN. Part-time programs available. *Faculty:* 2 full-time (both women), 2 part-time/adjunct (both women). *Students:* 1 (woman) full-time, 94 part-time (88 women); includes 12 minority (11 African Americans, 1 Asian American or Pacific Islander). Average age 39. 68 applicants, 78% accepted, 40 enrolled. In 2009, 22 master's awarded. *Degree requirements:* For master's, comprehensive exam. *Entrance requirements:* For master's, minimum undergraduate GPA of 3.0, bachelor's degree in nursing, eligibility for or current Ohio RN license. Additional exam requirements/recommendations for international students: Required—TOEFL (minimum score 500 paper-based; 173 computer-based). *Application deadline:* For fall admission, 8/1 priority date for domestic students. Applications are processed on a rolling basis. Application fee: $25. *Expenses:* Tuition: Full-time $14,544; part-time $808 per credit hour. Required fees: $230; $75 per semester. *Financial support:* In 2009–10, 11 students received support. Federal Work-Study available. Financial award application deadline: 3/1. *Unit head:* Dr. Janet Baker, Director, 440-864-8172, Fax: 440-684-6053. *Application contact:* Melanie Steele, Secretary, 440-646-8199, Fax: 440-684-6138, E-mail: gradsch@ursuline.edu.

Utah Valley University, Program in Nursing, Orem, UT 84058-5999. Offers MSN. Part-time programs available. *Faculty:* 4 full-time (all women). *Students:* 5 full-time (4 women), 1 international. Average age 41. 8 applicants, 88% accepted, 5 enrolled.Terminal master's awarded for partial completion of doctoral program. *Degree requirements:* For master's, project or thesis. *Entrance requirements:* For master's, GRE, baccalaureate degree in nursing, nurse licensure, undergraduate course in statistics, minimum GPA of 3.2, 3 letters of recommendation. Additional exam requirements/recommendations for international students: Required—TOEFL (minimum score 83 iBT). *Application deadline:* For fall admission, 4/1 for domestic and international students. Application fee: $45 ($100 for international students). Electronic applications accepted. *Expenses:* Tuition, state resident: full-time $5805; part-time $325 per credit. Tuition, nonresident: full-time $18,792; part-time $1044 per credit. Required fees: $292 per semester. Tuition and fees vary according to course load and program. *Financial support:* Application deadline: 5/1. *Unit head:* Sam Rushforth, Dean of the College of Science and Health, 801-863-6441. *Application contact:* Sam Rushforth, Dean of the College of Science and Health, 801-863-6441.

Valparaiso University, Graduate School, College of Nursing, Valparaiso, IN 46383. Offers management (Certificate); nursing education (MSN, Certificate); MSN/MBA. *Accreditation:* AACN. Part-time and evening/weekend programs available. *Faculty:* 7 part-time/adjunct (all women). *Students:* 26 full-time (23 women), 46 part-time (all women); includes 7 minority (4 African Americans, 1 Asian American or Pacific Islander, 2 Hispanic Americans), 1 international. Average age 42. In 2009, 16 master's, 12 other advanced degrees awarded. *Entrance requirements:* For master's, minimum GPA of 3.0, undergraduate major in nursing, Indiana registered nursing license, undergraduate courses in research and statistics. Additional exam requirements/recommendations for international students: Required—TOEFL (minimum score 550 paper-based; 213 computer-based; 80 iBT). *Application deadline:* Applications are processed on a rolling basis. Application fee: $30 ($50 for international students). Electronic applications accepted. *Expenses:* Contact institution. *Financial support:* Scholarships/grants available. Support available to part-time students. Financial award applicants required to submit FAFSA. *Unit head:* Dr. Janet Brown, Dean, 219-464-5289, Fax: 219-464-5425, E-mail: janet.brown@valpo.edu. *Application contact:* Jamie Haney, Coordinator of Graduate Admission, 219-464-5313, Fax: 219-464-5381, E-mail: jamie.haney@valpo.edu.

Vanderbilt University, Graduate School, Program in Nursing Science, Nashville, TN 37240-1001. Offers PhD. *Faculty:* 15 full-time (12 women). *Students:* 20 full-time (15 women), 1 (woman) part-time; includes 2 minority (both African Americans), 1 international. Average age 42. 17 applicants, 35% accepted, 4 enrolled. In 2009, 1 doctorate awarded. *Degree requirements:* For doctorate, comprehensive exam, thesis/dissertation, final and qualifying exams. *Entrance requirements:* For doctorate, GRE General Test. Additional exam requirements/recommendations for international students: Required—TOEFL (minimum score 570 paper-based; 230 computer-based; 88 iBT). *Application deadline:* For fall admission, 1/15 for domestic and international students. Application fee: $0. Electronic applications accepted. *Financial support:* Fellowships with full tuition reimbursements, research assistantships with full tuition reimbursements, teaching assistantships with full tuition reimbursements, career-related internships or fieldwork, Federal Work-Study, institutionally sponsored loans, scholarships/grants, health care benefits, and tuition waivers (full and partial) available. Financial award application deadline: 1/15; financial award applicants required to submit CSS PROFILE or FAFSA. *Faculty research:* Adaptation to chronic illness/conditions, health problems related to stress and coping, vulnerable childbearing and child rearing families. *Unit head:* Ann F. Minnick, Co-Director, 615-322-3800, Fax: 615-343-8204, E-mail: ann.minnick@vanderbilt.edu. *Application contact:* Irene McKirgan, Administrative Manager, 615-322-7410, Fax: 615-343-7505, E-mail: irene.mckirgan@vanderbilt.edu.

Vanderbilt University, School of Nursing, Nashville, TN 37240. Offers adult acute care nurse practitioner (MSN); adult nurse practitioner/cardiovascular disease management and prevention (MSN); adult nurse practitioner/palliative care (MSN); clinical management (clinical nurse leader/specialist) (MSN); emergency nurse practitioner (MSN); family nurse practitioner (MSN); gerontology nurse practitioner (MSN); health systems management (MSN); neonatal nurse practitioner (MSN); nurse midwifery (MSN); nurse midwifery/family nurse practitioner (MSN); nursing informatics (MSN); nursing practice (DNP); nursing science (PhD); nutrition (MS); pediatric acute care nurse practitioner (MSN); pediatric primary care nurse practitioner (MSN); psychiatric-mental health nurse practitioner (MSN); women's health nurse practitioner (MSN), including urogynecology; women's health nurse practitioner/adult nurse practitioner (MSN); MSN/M Div; MSN/MTS. *Accreditation:* ACNM/DOA; NLN (one or more programs are accredited). Part-time programs available. Postbaccalaureate distance learning degree programs offered (minimal on-campus study). *Faculty:* 118 full-time (102 women), 429 part-time/adjunct (309 women). *Students:* 484 full-time (435 women), 319 part-time (284 women); includes 84 minority (55 African Americans, 4 American Indian/Alaska Native, 10 Asian Americans or Pacific Islanders, 15 Hispanic Americans), 16 international. Average age 32. 900 applicants, 65% accepted, 433 enrolled. In 2009, 303 master's, 1 doctorate awarded. *Degree requirements:* For doctorate, comprehensive exam, thesis/dissertation. *Entrance requirements:* For master's, GRE General Test, minimum B average in undergraduate course work, 3 letters of recommendation; for doctorate, GRE General Test, interview, 3 letters of recommendation from doctorally-prepared faculty, MSN, essay. Additional exam requirements/recommendations for international students: Required—TOEFL. *Application deadline:* For fall admission, 12/1 priority date for domestic and international students. Applications are processed on a rolling basis. Application fee: $50. *Expenses:* Contact institution. *Financial support:* In 2009–10, 389 students received support, including 1 research assistantship (averaging $5,000 per year); teaching assistantships, scholarships/grants, health care benefits, and tuition waivers also available. Support available to part-time students. Financial award application deadline: 3/15; financial award applicants required to submit FAFSA. *Faculty research:* Lymphedema, palliative care and bereavement, health services research including workforce, safety and quality of care, gerontology, better birth outcomes including nutrition. Total annual research expenditures: $1.4 million. *Unit head:* Dr. Colleen Conway-Welch, Dean, 615-343-8776, Fax: 615-343-7711, E-mail: colleen.conway-welch@vanderbilt.edu. *Application contact:* Cheryl Feldner, Assistant Director of Admissions, 615-322-3800, Fax: 615-343-0333, E-mail: cheryl.feldner@vanderbilt.edu.

Villanova University, College of Nursing, Villanova, PA 19085-1699. Offers adult nurse practitioner (MSN, Post Master's Certificate); family nurse practitioner (MSN, Post Master's Certificate); health care administration (MSN); nurse anesthetist (MSN, Post Master's Certificate); nursing (PhD); nursing education (MSN, Post Master's Certificate); pediatric nurse practitioner (MSN, Post Master's Certificate). *Accreditation:* AACN; AANA/CANAEP. Part-time programs available. Postbaccalaureate distance learning degree programs offered (minimal on-campus study). *Faculty:* 15 full-time (all women), 3 part-time/adjunct (2 women). *Students:* 58 full-time (53 women), 188 part-time (164 women); includes 29 minority (13 African Americans, 1 American Indian/Alaska Native, 13 Asian Americans or Pacific Islanders, 2 Hispanic Americans), 3 international. Average age 33. 171 applicants, 70% accepted, 89 enrolled. In 2009, 32 master's, 1 doctorate awarded. *Degree requirements:* For master's, independent study project; for doctorate, comprehensive exam, thesis/dissertation. *Entrance requirements:* For master's, GRE or MAT, BSN, 1 year of recent nursing experience, physical assessment, course work in statistics; for doctorate, GRE, MSN. Additional exam requirements/recommendations for international students: Required—TOEFL. *Application deadline:* For fall admission, 7/1 priority date for domestic students, 7/1 for international students; for spring admission, 11/1 priority date for domestic students, 11/1 for international students. Applications are processed on a rolling basis. Application fee: $50. *Expenses:* Contact institution. *Financial support:* In 2009–10, 53 students received support, including 5 teaching assistantships with full tuition reimbursements available (averaging $13,100 per year); institutionally sponsored loans, scholarships/grants, traineeships, tuition waivers (full), and unspecified assistantships also available. Financial award application deadline: 3/1; financial award applicants required to submit FAFSA. *Faculty research:* Genetics, ethics, cognitive development of students, women with disabilities, nursing leadership. *Unit head:* Dr. Marguerite K. Schlag, Assistant Dean and Director, Graduate Program, 610-519-4907, Fax: 610-519-7650, E-mail: marguerite.schlag@villanova.edu. *Application contact:* Dean, Graduate School of Liberal Arts and Sciences.

Virginia Commonwealth University, Graduate School, School of Nursing, Richmond, VA 23284-9005. Offers adult health nursing (MS); child health nursing (MS); family health nursing (MS); health system (PhD); immunocompetence (PhD); nurse practitioner (MS, Certificate); nursing administration (MS), including clinical nurse manager, nurse executive; psychiatric-mental health nursing (MS); risk and resilience (PhD); women's health nursing (MS). *Accreditation:* NLN (one or more programs are accredited). Part-time and evening/weekend programs available. *Degree requirements:* For master's, thesis optional; for doctorate, thesis/dissertation. *Entrance requirements:* For master's, GRE General Test, BSN, minimum GPA of 2.8; for doctorate, GRE General Test.

Viterbo University, Graduate Program in Nursing, La Crosse, WI 54601-4797. Offers MSN. *Accreditation:* AACN. Part-time programs available. Postbaccalaureate distance learning degree programs offered (minimal on-campus study). *Faculty:* 5 full-time, 5 part-time/adjunct. *Students:* 28 full-time (26 women), 32 part-time (all women); includes 3 minority (2 Asian Americans or Pacific Islanders, 1 Hispanic American). Average age 37. *Entrance requirements:* For master's, GRE General Test or MAT, bachelor's degree in nursing, minimum GPA of 3.0, RN license. *Application deadline:* For spring admission, 2/1 priority date for domestic students. Applications are processed on a rolling basis. Application fee: $50. *Expenses:* Contact institution. *Financial support:* In 2009–10, 9 students received support. Institutionally sponsored loans, scholarships/grants, and traineeships available. Financial award application deadline: 6/1; financial award applicants required to submit FAFSA. *Unit head:* Dr. Bonnie Nesbitt, Assistant Dean, 608-796-3688, Fax: 608-796-3668, E-mail: bjnesbitt@viterbo.edu. *Application contact:* 608-796-3671.

Wagner College, Division of Graduate Studies, Department of Nursing, Program in Nursing, Staten Island, NY 10301-4495. Offers MS. *Accreditation:* NLN. Part-time and evening/weekend programs available. *Degree requirements:* For master's, thesis optional. *Entrance requirements:* For master's, BS in nursing, current clinical experience, minimum GPA of 2.75. *Expenses:* Tuition: Full-time $15,570; part-time $865 per credit. Required fees: $2.

Walden University, Graduate Programs, School of Nursing, Minneapolis, MN 55401. Offers education (MSN); informatics (MSN); leadership and management (MSN); nursing (Post-Master's Certificate), including nursing education, nursing informatics, nursing leadership and management. *Accreditation:* AACN. Part-time and evening/weekend programs available. Postbaccalaureate distance learning degree programs offered (no on-campus study). *Faculty:* 5 full-time, 105 part-time/adjunct. *Students:* 2,644 full-time (2,468 women), 805 part-time (755 women); includes 660 minority (430 African Americans, 23 American Indian/Alaska Native, 122 Asian Americans or Pacific Islanders, 85 Hispanic Americans), 34 international. Average age 44. In 2009, 624 master's, 1 other advanced degree awarded. *Entrance requirements:* For master's, bachelor's degree or equivalent in related field or RN; minimum GPA of 2.5. Additional exam requirements/recommendations for international students: Required—TOEFL (minimum score 550 paper-based; 213 computer-based), IELTS (minimum score 6.5), or Michigan English Language Assessment Battery (minimum score 82). *Application deadline:* Applications are processed on a rolling basis. Application fee: $50. Electronic applications accepted. *Expenses:* Tuition: Full-time $13,665; part-time $560 per credit. Required fees: $1375. Tuition and fees vary according to course load, degree level and program. *Financial support:* In 2009–10, 273 students received support; fellowships, Federal Work-Study, scholarships/grants, unspecified assistantships, and family tuition reduction, active duty/veteran tuition reduction, group tuition reduction, interest-free payment plans available. Support available to part-time students. Financial award applicants required to submit FAFSA. *Unit head:* Dr. Sara Torres, Associate Dean, 800-925-3368. *Application contact:* Jennifer Hall, Director of Enrollment, 866-4-WALDEN, E-mail: info@walden.edu.

Nursing—General

Washington Adventist University, Program in Nursing—Business Leadership, Takoma Park, MD 20912. Offers MSN. Part-time programs available. *Students:* 1 (woman) full-time, 9 part-time (8 women); includes 8 minority (6 African Americans, 2 Asian Americans or Pacific Islanders). Average age 38. *Application deadline:* Applications are processed on a rolling basis. *Financial support:* Applicants required to submit FAFSA. *Unit head:* Dr. Davenia Lea, Dean of School of Graduate and Professional Studies, E-mail: dlea@wau.edu. *Application contact:* Rahneeka Hazelton, Director, 301-891-4092, E-mail: rhazelto@wau.edu.

Washington State University Spokane, Graduate Programs, Intercollegiate College of Nursing, Spokane, WA 99210. Offers MN. *Accreditation:* AACN. *Faculty:* 30. *Students:* 39 full-time (33 women), 51 part-time (46 women); includes 7 minority (2 American Indian/Alaska Native, 2 Asian Americans or Pacific Islanders, 3 Hispanic Americans), 1 international. In 2009, 26 master's awarded. *Degree requirements:* For master's, comprehensive exam (for some programs), thesis (for some programs), oral exam, research project. *Entrance requirements:* For master's, minimum GPA of 3.0, Washington state RN license, physical assessment skills, course work in statistics, recommendations, written interview (nurse practitioner). *Application deadline:* For fall admission, 1/10 priority date for domestic students, 1/10 for international students; for spring admission, 7/1 priority date for domestic students, 7/1 for international students. Application fee: $50. *Expenses:* Tuition, state resident: part-time $423 per credit. Tuition, nonresident: part-time $1032 per credit. *Financial support:* Teaching assistantships with tuition reimbursements available. Financial award application deadline: 4/1. *Faculty research:* Cardiovascular and type 2 diabetes in children, evaluation of strategies to increase physical activity in sedentary people. Total annual research expenditures: $2.1 million. *Unit head:* Dr. Patricia Butterfield, Dean, 509-324-7292, Fax: 509-858-7336. *Application contact:* Graduate School Admissions, 800-GRADWSU, Fax: 509-335-1949, E-mail: gradsch@wsu.edu.

Washington State University Tri-Cities, Graduate Programs, Intercollegiate College of Nursing, Richland, WA 99354. Offers MN. Part-time programs available. Postbaccalaureate distance learning degree programs offered (minimal on-campus study). *Faculty:* 30. *Students:* 10 full-time (9 women), 19 part-time (18 women); includes 1 minority (American Indian/Alaska Native). *Degree requirements:* For master's, comprehensive exam (for some programs), thesis (for some programs), oral exam, research project. *Entrance requirements:* For master's, current Washington state RN license; minimum cumulative GPA of 2.5, 2.0 in each nursing course. Additional exam requirements/recommendations for international students: Required—TOEFL. *Application deadline:* For fall admission, 1/10 priority date for domestic students, 1/10 for international students; for spring admission, 7/1 priority date for domestic students, 7/1 for international students. Application fee: $50. *Expenses:* Tuition, state resident: part-time $423 per credit. Tuition, nonresident: part-time $1032 per credit. *Financial support:* In 2009–10, 24 students received support, including fellowships (averaging $4,050 per year), teaching assistantships with tuition reimbursements available (averaging $13,056 per year). Financial award application deadline: 4/1; financial award applicants required to submit FAFSA. *Unit head:* Phyllis Morris, Interim Director, 509-372-7196, Fax: 509-372-7116, E-mail: pmorris@tricity.wsu.edu. *Application contact:* Graduate School Admissions, 800-GRADWSU, Fax: 509-335-1949, E-mail: gradsch@wsu.edu.

Washington State University Vancouver, Graduate Programs, Intercollegiate College of Nursing, Vancouver, WA 98686. Offers MN. *Faculty:* 30. *Students:* 11 full-time (all women), 92 part-time (82 women); includes 7 minority (6 Asian Americans or Pacific Islanders, 1 Hispanic American). In 2009, 34 master's awarded. *Degree requirements:* For master's, comprehensive exam (for some programs), thesis (for some programs), research project. *Entrance requirements:* For master's, Washington RN license, minimum GPA of 3.0. Additional exam requirements/recommendations for international students: Required—TOEFL. *Application deadline:* For fall admission, 1/10 priority date for domestic students, 1/10 for international students; for spring admission, 7/1 priority date for domestic students, 7/1 for international students. Applications are processed on a rolling basis. Application fee: $50. Electronic applications accepted. *Expenses:* Tuition, state resident: full-time $4228; part-time $423 per credit. Tuition, nonresident: full-time $10,322; part-time $1032 per credit. *Financial support:* In 2009–10, research assistantships (averaging $14,634 per year), teaching assistantships with tuition reimbursements (averaging $13,383 per year) were awarded. Financial award application deadline: 2/15. *Faculty research:* Cultural competence in nursing, prescribing controlled substances by Advanced Registered Nurse Practitioners, decreasing health disparities, workforce diversity. Total annual research expenditures: $1.5 million. *Unit head:* Dr. Ginny Guido, Regional Director, 360-546-9244, Fax: 360-546-9038, E-mail: ginny_guido@vancouver.wsu.edu. *Application contact:* Tami Kelly, Principal Assistant, 509-324-7334, E-mail: kelleyt@wsu.edu.

Waynesburg University, Graduate and Professional Studies, Waynesburg, PA 15370-1222. Offers business (MBA), including finance, health systems, human resources, leadership, market development; counseling (MA), including addictions counseling, clinical mental health; education (MAT); nursing (MSN), including administration, education, informatics, palliative care; nursing practice (DNP); special education (M Ed); technology (M Ed); MSN/MBA. *Accreditation:* AACN. Part-time and evening/weekend programs available. *Faculty:* 11 full-time (5 women), 136 part-time/adjunct (80 women). *Students:* 116 full-time (85 women), 984 part-time (682 women). 711 applicants, 80% accepted, 485 enrolled. In 2009, 320 master's, 41 doctorates awarded. *Degree requirements:* For doctorate, thesis/dissertation. *Entrance requirements:* Additional exam requirements/recommendations for international students: Required—TOEFL. *Application deadline:* For fall admission, 8/1 priority date for domestic students. Applications are processed on a rolling basis. Electronic applications accepted. *Expenses:* Tuition: Part-time $520 per credit. *Financial support:* Available to part-time students. Application deadline: 5/1. *Unit head:* David Mariner, Dean, 724-743-4420, Fax: 724-743-4425, E-mail: dmariner@waynesburg.edu. *Application contact:* Michael Bednarski, Director of Admissions, 724-743-4420, Fax: 724-743-4425, E-mail: mbednars@waynesburg.edu.

Wayne State University, College of Nursing, Program in Nursing, Detroit, MI 48202. Offers PhD. Part-time programs available. *Degree requirements:* For doctorate, thesis/dissertation. *Entrance requirements:* For doctorate, GRE General Test, minimum GPA of 3.3. Additional exam requirements/recommendations for international students: Required—TOEFL (minimum score 550 paper-based; 213 computer-based); Recommended—TWE (minimum score 6). Electronic applications accepted. *Faculty research:* Self-care, transcultural care, adaptation to acute and chronic illness, urban health and health care systems.

Webster University, College of Arts and Sciences, Department of Nursing, St. Louis, MO 63119-3194. Offers healthcare leadership (Certificate); nursing (MSN). *Accreditation:* NLN. *Faculty:* 4 full-time, 4 part-time/adjunct. *Students:* 70 part-time (68 women); includes 9 minority (8 African Americans, 1 Hispanic American). Average age 44. In 2009, 19 master's, 5 other advanced degrees awarded. *Degree requirements:* For master's, comprehensive exam. *Entrance requirements:* For master's, 1 year of clinical experience, BSN, interview, minimum C+ average in statistics and physical assessment, minimum GPA of 3.0, RN license. Additional exam requirements/recommendations for international students: Required—TOEFL. *Application deadline:* Applications are processed on a rolling basis. Application fee: $25 ($50 for international students). *Expenses:* Tuition: Part-time $565 per credit hour. Tuition and fees vary according to degree level, campus/location and program. *Financial support:* Federal Work-Study available. Support available to part-time students. Financial award application deadline: 4/1; financial award applicants required to submit FAFSA. *Faculty research:* Health teaching. *Unit head:* Jennifer Broeder, Coordinator, 314-968-7486, Fax: 314-968-6101. *Application contact:* Matt Nolan, Associate Vice President for Enrollment Management/Dean of Admissions, Fax: 314-968-7116, E-mail: gadmit@webste.edu.

Wesley College, Nursing Program, Dover, DE 19901-3875. Offers MSN. *Accreditation:* NLN. Part-time and evening/weekend programs available. *Degree requirements:* For master's, thesis optional, portfolio. *Entrance requirements:* For master's, GRE or MAT. Electronic applications accepted. *Faculty research:* Childhood obesity, organizational behavior, health promotion and wellness.

West Chester University of Pennsylvania, Office of Graduate Studies, College of Health Sciences, Department of Nursing, West Chester, PA 19383. Offers administration (MSN); integrative health (MSN); nursing education (MSN, Certificate); school nursing (Teaching Certificate). *Accreditation:* AACN. Part-time and evening/weekend programs available. *Students:* 3 full-time (all women), 34 part-time (33 women); includes 2 minority (1 African American, 1 Asian American or Pacific Islander). Average age 42. 15 applicants, 100% accepted, 10 enrolled. In 2009, 10 master's awarded. *Entrance requirements:* For master's, RN license, BSN, minimum GPA of 2.8, two years' full-time experience as a clinical care nurse, three letters of recommendation; for other advanced degree, BSN, RN license, minimum GPA of 3.0 in last 48 nursing credits. Additional exam requirements/recommendations for international students: Required—TOEFL (minimum score 550 paper-based; 213 computer-based; 80 iBT). *Application deadline:* For fall admission, 4/15 priority date for domestic students, 3/15 for international students; for spring admission, 10/15 for domestic students, 9/1 for international students. Applications are processed on a rolling basis. Application fee: $35. Electronic applications accepted. *Expenses:* Tuition, state resident: full-time $6666; part-time $370 per credit. Tuition, nonresident: full-time $10,666; part-time $593 per credit. Required fees: $122.56 per credit. *Financial support:* In 2009–10, 1 research assistantship with full and partial tuition reimbursement (averaging $5,000 per year) was awarded; unspecified assistantships also available. Support available to part-time students. Financial award application deadline: 2/15; financial award applicants required to submit FAFSA. *Faculty research:* Violence against women. *Unit head:* Dr. Charlotte Mackey, Chair, 610-436-3474, E-mail: cmackey@wcupa.edu. *Application contact:* Ann Coghlan Stowe, Graduate Coordinator, 610-436-2331, E-mail: astowe@wcupa.edu.

Western Carolina University, Graduate School, College of Health and Human Sciences, School of Nursing, Cullowhee, NC 28723. Offers nurse educator (PMC); nursing (MSN). *Accreditation:* AACN; AANA/CANAEP. Part-time and evening/weekend programs available. *Students:* 31 full-time (20 women), 61 part-time (51 women). Average age 38. 51 applicants, 76% accepted, 26 enrolled. In 2009, 13 master's awarded. *Degree requirements:* For master's, comprehensive exam, thesis or alternative. *Entrance requirements:* For master's, GRE General Test, BSN with minimum GPA of 3.0, 3 references, 1 year of clinical experience. Additional exam requirements/recommendations for international students: Required—TOEFL (minimum score 550 paper-based; 270 computer-based; 79 iBT). *Application deadline:* For fall admission, 2/15 for domestic students; for spring admission, 6/15 for domestic students. Applications are processed on a rolling basis. Application fee: $45. *Financial support:* In 2009–10, 1 student received support; fellowships, research assistantships with full and partial tuition reimbursements available, teaching assistantships with full and partial tuition reimbursements available, career-related internships or fieldwork, institutionally sponsored loans, scholarships/grants, and unspecified assistantships available. Financial award application deadline: 3/31; financial award applicants required to submit FAFSA. *Unit head:* Dr. Vincent Hall, Head, 828-227-3511, Fax: 828-227-7052, E-mail: hallv@email.wcu.edu. *Application contact:* Admissions Specialist for Nursing, 828-227-7398, Fax: 828-227-7480, E-mail: gradsch@email.wcu.edu.

Western Connecticut State University, Division of Graduate Studies, School of Professional Studies, Nursing Department, Danbury, CT 06810-6885. Offers adult nurse practitioner (MSN); clinical nurse specialist (MSN). *Accreditation:* AACN. Part-time programs available. *Faculty:* 3 full-time (all women), 1 (woman) part-time/adjunct. *Students:* 32 part-time (all women); includes 3 minority (2 African Americans, 1 Asian American or Pacific Islander). Average age 41. 24 applicants, 71% accepted, 13 enrolled. *Degree requirements:* For master's, clinical component, thesis or research project, completion of program in 6 years. *Entrance requirements:* For master's, MAT (if GPA less than 3.0), bachelor's degree in nursing, minimum GPA of 3.0, previous course work in statistics and nursing research, RN license. Additional exam requirements/recommendations for international students: Recommended—TOEFL (minimum score 550 paper-based; 213 computer-based; 79 iBT), IELTS (minimum score 6). *Application deadline:* For fall admission, 8/5 priority date for domestic students; for spring admission, 1/5 for domestic students. Applications are processed on a rolling basis. Application fee: $50. *Expenses:* Tuition, state resident: full-time $5012; part-time $278 per credit hour. Tuition, nonresident: full-time $13,962; part-time $284 per credit hour. Required fees: $3886; $139 per credit hour. Full-time tuition and fees vary according to course load and program. Part-time tuition and fees vary according to course level, degree level and program. *Financial support:* In 2009–10, 4 students received support. Scholarships/grants available. Financial award application deadline: 5/1; financial award applicants required to submit FAFSA. *Unit head:* Dr. Patricia Z. Lund, Professor, 203-837-8567, Fax: 203-837-8550, E-mail: lundp@wcsu.edu. *Application contact:* Chris Shankle, Associate Director of Graduate Studies, 203-837-9005, Fax: 203-837-8326, E-mail: shanklec@wcsu.edu.

Western Kentucky University, Graduate Studies, College of Health and Human Services, Department of Nursing, Bowling Green, KY 42101. Offers MSN. *Accreditation:* AACN. Part-time and evening/weekend programs available. *Degree requirements:* For master's, comprehensive exam, thesis optional. *Entrance requirements:* For master's, GRE General Test, minimum GPA of 2.75. Additional exam requirements/recommendations for international students: Required—TOEFL (minimum score 555 paper-based; 213 computer-based; 79 iBT). *Expenses:* Tuition, state resident: full-time $4160; part-time $416 per credit hour. Tuition, nonresident: full-time $9550; part-time $506 per credit hour. Tuition and fees vary according to campus/location and reciprocity agreements. *Faculty research:* Folic acid, disease and injury prevention, rural mobile health, mental health issues.

Western Michigan University, Graduate College, College of Health and Human Services, Bronson School of Nursing, Kalamazoo, MI 49008. Offers MSN. *Accreditation:* AACN. *Unit head:* Dr. Linda Zoeller, Director, 269-387-8162, E-mail: linda.zoeller@wmich.edu. *Application contact:* Admissions and Orientation, 269-387-2000, Fax: 269-387-2355.

Western University of Health Sciences, College of Graduate Nursing, Pomona, CA 91766-1854. Offers family nurse practitioner (MSN). *Accreditation:* AACN. Part-time and evening/weekend programs available. Postbaccalaureate distance learning degree programs offered. *Degree requirements:* For master's, culminating project. *Entrance requirements:* For master's, GRE General Test, BSN or bachelor's degree in related field, nurse practitioner certificate, minimum GPA of 3.0, interview, letters of recommendation. Additional exam requirements/recommendations for international students: Required—TOEFL. *Expenses:* Contact institution.

Westminster College, School of Nursing and Health Sciences, Salt Lake City, UT 84105-3697. Offers family nurse practitioner (MSN); nurse anesthesia (MSNA); nurse education (MSNED); nursing (MSN); public health (MPH). *Accreditation:* AACN; AANA/CANAEP. *Faculty:* 11 full-time (6 women), 12 part-time/adjunct (6 women). *Students:* 77 full-time (54 women), 49 part-time (16 women); includes 11 minority (3 African Americans, 6 Asian Americans or Pacific Islanders, 2 Hispanic Americans), 2 international. Average age 34. 152 applicants, 57% accepted, 48 enrolled. In 2009, 23 master's awarded. *Degree requirements:* For master's, clinical practicum, 504 clinical practice hours. *Entrance requirements:* For master's, GRE, resume, Utah RN license in good standing, minimum GPA of 3.0, 3 letters of reference, BSN from accredited nursing program, proof of clear state and federal background check, drug test results, personal interview, current PALS certification, current ACLS certification. Additional exam requirements/recommendations for international students: Required—TOEFL (minimum score 600 paper-based; 250 computer-based; 100 iBT). *Application deadline:* Applications are processed on a rolling basis. Application fee: $40. Electronic applications accepted. *Expenses:* Contact institution. *Financial support:* In 2009–10, 60 students received support. Career-related internships or fieldwork and tuition reimbursement, tuition remission available. Support available to part-time students. Financial award applicants required to submit FAFSA. *Faculty research:* Emotional intelligence, graduate faculty mentorship, parish nursing roles in women's disease prevention, psychiatric nursing students' self-assessment of therapeutic relationships, psychosocial nurse practitioner's self-assessment of therapeutic relationships, curriculum simulation. *Unit head:* Dr. Sheryl Steadman, Dean, 801-832-2164, Fax: 801-832-3110, E-mail: ssteadman@westminstercollege.edu. *Application contact:* Joel Bauman, Vice President of Enrollment Services, 801-832-2200, Fax: 801-832-3101, E-mail: admission@westminstercollege.edu.

West Suburban College of Nursing, Nursing Program, Oak Park, IL 60302. Offers MSN. *Entrance requirements:* For master's, letter of recommendation.

West Texas A&M University, College of Agriculture, Nursing, and Natural Sciences, Division of Nursing, Canyon, TX 79016-0001. Offers MSN. *Accreditation:* AACN. Part-time programs available. Postbaccalaureate distance learning degree programs offered (minimal on-campus study). *Degree requirements:* For master's, comprehensive exam, thesis optional. *Entrance requirements:* For master's, GRE General Test, bachelor's degree in nursing, minimum GPA of 3.0 in last 60 hours. Additional exam requirements/recommendations for international students: Required—TOEFL (minimum score 550 paper-based). Electronic applications accepted. *Faculty research:* Family-focused nursing, nursing traineeship, professional nursing.

West Virginia University, School of Nursing, Morgantown, WV 26506. Offers nurse practitioner (Certificate); nursing (MSN, DNP, PhD). *Accreditation:* AACN. Part-time programs available. Postbaccalaureate distance learning degree programs offered (minimal on-campus study). *Degree requirements:* For master's, thesis or alternative; for doctorate, comprehensive exam, thesis/dissertation. *Entrance requirements:* For master's, minimum GPA of 3.0, current U.S. RN license, BSN, course work in statistics and physical assessment, GRE General Test; for doctorate, GRE General Test (PhD), minimum graduate GPA of 3.0, minimum grade of B in graduate statistics course work. Additional exam requirements/recommendations for international students: Required—TOEFL. Electronic applications accepted. *Expenses:* Contact institution. *Faculty research:* Rural primary health/health promotion, parent/child/women's health, cardiovascular risk reduction, complementary health modalities, breast cancer detection-care.

West Virginia Wesleyan College, Department of Nursing, Buckhannon, WV 26201. Offers MS. *Expenses:* Tuition: Part-time $360 per credit hour.

Wheeling Jesuit University, Department of Nursing, Wheeling, WV 26003-6295. Offers MSN. *Accreditation:* AACN. Part-time and evening/weekend programs available. Postbaccalaureate distance learning degree programs offered (minimal on-campus study). *Faculty:* 6 full-time (all women), 1 part-time/adjunct (0 women). *Students:* 16 full-time (15 women), 102 part-time (95 women); includes 2 minority (both African Americans). Average age 39. 40 applicants, 95% accepted, 36 enrolled. In 2009, 22 master's awarded. *Entrance requirements:* For master's, GRE General Test, BSN, minimum GPA of 3.0, course work in research and statistics, US nursing license. Additional exam requirements/recommendations for international students: Required—TOEFL (minimum score 600 paper-based; 250 computer-based; 80 iBT). *Application deadline:* For fall admission, 8/1 priority date for domestic students, 7/15 for international students; for spring admission, 12/15 priority date for domestic students, 12/1 for international students. Applications are processed on a rolling basis. Application fee: $25. Electronic applications accepted. *Expenses:* Tuition: Full-time $9000; part-time $500 per credit hour. Required fees: $195 per semester. One-time fee: $375. Tuition and fees vary according to program. *Financial support:* In 2009–10, 83 students received support. Scholarships/grants and unspecified assistantships available. Financial award application deadline: 8/1; financial award applicants required to submit FAFSA. *Faculty research:* Low income and uninsured women, public policy, spirituality and aging, delivery of online education, quality of life, heart failure. *Unit head:* Dr. Rose M. Kutlenios, Chair, 304-243-2227, Fax: 304-243-4441, E-mail: rosekut@wju.edu. *Application contact:* Melissa Rataiczak, Director of Admissions, Professional and Graduate Studies, 304-243-2250, Fax: 304-243-4441, E-mail: mrataiczak@wju.edu.

Wichita State University, Graduate School, College of Health Professions, School of Nursing, Wichita, KS 67260. Offers clinical nurse specialist (MSN); nurse midwifery (MSN); nurse practitioner (MSN); nursing and healthcare systems administration (MSN); nursing practice (DNP); MSN/MBA. *Accreditation:* AACN. Part-time programs available. *Expenses:* Tuition, state resident: full-time $4247; part-time $235.95 per credit hour. Tuition, nonresident: full-time $11,171; part-time $620.60 per credit hour. Required fees: $34; $3.60 per credit hour. $17 per term. Tuition and fees vary according to campus/location and program. *Faculty research:* Adolescent pregnancy, alcoholism, arthritis and chronic disease, health practices of elderly, diabetes. *Unit head:* Dr. Mary Koehn, Chairperson, 316-978-3610, Fax: 316-978-3025, E-mail: mary.koehn@wichita.edu. *Application contact:* Dr. Mary Koehn, Chairperson, 316-978-3610, Fax: 316-978-3025, E-mail: mary.koehn@wichita.edu.

Widener University, School of Nursing, Chester, PA 19013-5792. Offers MSN, DN Sc, PhD, PMC. *Accreditation:* AACN; NLN (one or more programs are accredited). Part-time and evening/weekend programs available. *Faculty:* 12 full-time (all women), 4 part-time/adjunct (3 women). *Students:* 24 full-time (all women), 128 part-time (116 women); includes 8 minority (5 African Americans, 2 American Indian/Alaska Native, 1 Asian American or Pacific Islander), 1 international. Average age 33. 77 applicants, 79% accepted. In 2009, 34 master's, 11 doctorates awarded. *Degree requirements:* For doctorate, thesis/dissertation. *Entrance requirements:* For master's, GRE General Test, BSN, undergraduate course in statistics; for doctorate, GRE General Test, MSN, undergraduate course in statistics. *Application deadline:* For fall admission, 7/1 for domestic students; for winter admission, 3/1 for domestic students; for spring admission, 11/1 for domestic students. Applications are processed on a rolling basis. Application fee: $25 ($300 for international students). Electronic applications accepted. *Expenses:* Contact institution. *Financial support:* Career-related internships or fieldwork, Federal Work-Study, and traineeships available. Support available to part-time students. Financial award application deadline: 4/1. *Faculty research:* Women's health leadership, nursing education, research utilization, program evaluation, health promotion. *Unit head:* Dr. Mary B. Walker, Assistant Dean for Graduate Studies, 610-499-4208, Fax: 610-499-4216, E-mail: mary.b.walker@widener.edu. *Application contact:* Betty A. Boyles, Information Contact, 610-499-4207, Fax: 610-499-4216, E-mail: betty.a.boyles@widener.edu.

Wilkes University, College of Graduate and Professional Studies, Nesbitt College of Pharmacy and Nursing, Department of Nursing, Wilkes-Barre, PA 18766-0002. Offers MSN. *Accreditation:* AACN. Part-time and evening/weekend programs available. *Students:* 14 full-time (11 women), 26 part-time (all women); includes 3 minority (2 African Americans, 1 Asian American or Pacific Islander). Average age 39. In 2009, 18 master's awarded. *Entrance requirements:* For master's, GRE General Test, MAT. Additional exam requirements/recommendations for international students: Required—TOEFL (minimum score 500 paper-based; 173 computer-based; 79 iBT). *Application deadline:* Applications are processed on a rolling basis. Application fee: $45. *Financial support:* Federal Work-Study and unspecified assistantships available. Financial award application deadline: 3/1; financial award applicants required to submit FAFSA. *Unit head:* Dr. Mary Ann Merrigan, Chair, 570-408-4070, Fax: 570-408-7807, E-mail: maryann.merrigan@wilkes.edu. *Application contact:* Kathleen Houlihan, Director of Graduate Studies, 570-408-3235, Fax: 570-408-7846, E-mail: kathleen.houlihan@wilkes.edu.

William Carey University, School of Nursing, Hattiesburg, MS 39401-5499. Offers MSN. *Accreditation:* AACN. Part-time programs available. *Degree requirements:* For master's, thesis or alternative. *Entrance requirements:* For master's, GRE, minimum GPA of 3.0, RN license. Additional exam requirements/recommendations for international students: Required—TOEFL (minimum score 500 paper-based; 213 computer-based).

William Paterson University of New Jersey, College of Science and Health, Wayne, NJ 07470-8420. Offers biotechnology (MS); communication disorders (MS); general biology (MS); nursing (MSN). Part-time and evening/weekend programs available. *Students:* 53 full-time (48 women), 135 part-time (126 women); includes 27 minority (7 African Americans, 11 Asian Americans or Pacific Islanders, 9 Hispanic Americans), 4 international. *Entrance requirements:* For master's, GRE General Test, minimum GPA of 2.75. *Application deadline:* Applications are processed on a rolling basis. Application fee: $50. Electronic applications accepted. *Financial support:* Research assistantships with full tuition reimbursements, career-related internships or fieldwork and unspecified assistantships available. Support available to part-time students. Financial award application deadline: 4/1; financial award applicants required to submit FAFSA.

Faculty research: Plant tissue culture, DNA cloning, cellular structure, language development, speech and hearing science. *Unit head:* Dr. Sandra DeYoung, Dean, 973-720-2432, E-mail: deyoungs@wpunj.edu. *Application contact:* Christina Aiello, Assistant Director, Graduate Admissions, 973-720-2506, Fax: 973-720-2035, E-mail: aielloc@wpunj.edu.

Wilmington University, College of Health Professions, New Castle, DE 19720-6491. Offers adult nurse practitioner (MSN); family nurse practitioner (MSN); gerontology (MSN); leadership (MSN); nursing (MSN); women's nurse practitioner (MSN). *Accreditation:* AACN. Part-time programs available. *Degree requirements:* For master's, thesis. *Entrance requirements:* For master's, BSN, RN license, interview, 3 letters of recommendation. Additional exam requirements/recommendations for international students: Required—TOEFL (minimum score 500 paper-based; 173 computer-based). Electronic applications accepted. *Faculty research:* Outcomes assessment, student writing ability.

Winona State University, College of Nursing and Health Sciences, Winona, MN 55987-5838. Offers adult nurse practitioner (MS, Post Master's Certificate); clinical nurse specialist (MS, Post Master's Certificate); family nurse practitioner (MS, Post Master's Certificate); nurse administrator (MS); nurse educator (MS, Post Master's Certificate); nursing (DNP). *Accreditation:* AACN. Part-time programs available. Postbaccalaureate distance learning degree programs offered (no on-campus study). *Degree requirements:* For master's, thesis; for doctorate, capstone. *Entrance requirements:* For master's, GRE (if GPA less than 3.0). Additional exam requirements/recommendations for international students: Required—TOEFL (minimum score 550 paper-based). *Faculty research:* Job satisfaction; nursing diagnoses; dehydration among elderly; correlates to functional status in elderly.

Winston-Salem State University, Program in Nursing, Winston-Salem, NC 27110-0003. Offers MSN. *Accreditation:* AACN. Part-time and evening/weekend programs available. Postbaccalaureate distance learning degree programs offered. *Entrance requirements:* For master's, GRE, MAT, resume, NC or state compact license, 3 letters of recommendation. Electronic applications accepted. *Faculty research:* Elimination of health care disparities.

Wright State University, School of Graduate Studies, College of Nursing and Health, Program in Nursing, Dayton, OH 45435. Offers acute care nurse practitioner (MS); administration of nursing and health care systems (MS); adult health (MS); child and adolescent health (MS); community health (MS); family nurse practitioner (MS); nurse practitioner (MS); school nurse (MS); MBA/MS. *Accreditation:* AACN. Part-time and evening/weekend programs available. *Degree requirements:* For master's, thesis or alternative. *Entrance requirements:* For master's, GRE General Test, BSN from NLN-accredited college, Ohio RN license. Additional exam requirements/recommendations for international students: Required—TOEFL. *Faculty research:* Clinical nursing and health, teaching, caring, pain administration, informatics and technology.

Xavier University, College of Social Sciences, Health and Education, School of Nursing, Cincinnati, OH 45207. Offers clinical nurse leader (MSN); education (MSN); forensic nursing (MSN); healthcare law (MSN); informatics (MSN); nursing administration (MSN); school nursing (MSN); MSN/M Ed; MSN/MBA; MSN/MS. *Accreditation:* AACN. Part-time and evening/weekend programs available. Postbaccalaureate distance learning degree programs offered (no on-campus study). *Faculty:* 10 full-time (all women), 10 part-time/adjunct (9 women). *Students:* 64 full-time (55 women), 148 part-time (146 women); includes 19 minority (17 African Americans, 1 Asian American or Pacific Islander, 1 Hispanic American), 2 international. Average age 38. 141 applicants, 88% accepted, 110 enrolled. In 2009, 48 master's awarded. *Degree requirements:* For master's, thesis, scholarly project. *Entrance requirements:* For master's, GRE. Additional exam requirements/recommendations for international students: Required—TOEFL. *Application deadline:* Applications are processed on a rolling basis. Application fee: $35. Electronic applications accepted. *Expenses:* Tuition: Part-time $697 per credit hour. One-time fee: $35 part-time. *Financial support:* In 2009–10, 68 students received support. Applicants required to submit FAFSA. *Faculty research:* Clinical nurse leader, simulation, employment satisfaction, nontraditional students, holistic nursing. *Unit head:* Dr. Susan M. Schmidt, Director, 513-745-3815, Fax: 513-745-1087, E-mail: schmidt@xavier.edu. *Application contact:* Marilyn Volk Gomez, Director of Nursing Student Services, 513-745-4392, Fax: 513-745-1087, E-mail: gomez@xavier.edu.

Yale University, School of Nursing, New Haven, CT 06536. Offers MSN, PhD, Post Master's Certificate, MAR/MSN, MSN/M Div, MSN/MPH. *Accreditation:* AACN. Part-time programs available. Postbaccalaureate distance learning degree programs offered (minimal on-campus study). *Faculty:* 54 full-time (51 women), 95 part-time/adjunct (90 women). *Students:* 279 full-time (261 women), 50 part-time (45 women); includes 53 minority (17 African Americans, 3 American Indian/Alaska Native, 22 Asian Americans or Pacific Islanders, 11 Hispanic Americans), 13 international. Average age 28. 537 applicants, 38% accepted, 115 enrolled. In 2009, 80 master's, 3 doctorates, 2 other advanced degrees awarded. Terminal master's awarded for partial completion of doctoral program. *Degree requirements:* For master's, thesis; for doctorate, comprehensive exam, thesis/dissertation. *Entrance requirements:* For master's, GRE General Test, bachelor's degree; for doctorate, GRE General Test, MSN; for Post Master's Certificate, MSN. Additional exam requirements/recommendations for international students: Required—TOEFL or IELTS. *Application deadline:* For fall admission, 11/1 priority date for domestic students. Application fee: $65. Electronic applications accepted. *Expenses:* Contact institution. *Financial support:* In 2009–10, 265 students received support, including 239 fellowships (averaging $5,905 per year), 13 research assistantships with tuition reimbursements available (averaging $28,450 per year); Federal Work-Study, scholarships/grants, traineeships, and health care benefits also available. Support available to part-time students. Financial award application deadline: 2/1; financial award applicants required to submit FAFSA. *Faculty research:* Family-based care, chronic illness, primary care, development, policy. Total annual research expenditures: $6.4 million. *Unit head:* Dr. Margaret Grey, Dean, 203-785-2393, Fax: 203-785-6455, E-mail: margaret.grey@yale.edu. *Application contact:* Angela Kuhne, Director, Admissions, 203-737-1793, Fax: 203-737-5409, E-mail: angela.kunhe@yale.edu.

York College of Pennsylvania, Department of Nursing, York, PA 17405-7199. Offers MS. *Accreditation:* AACN; AANA/CANAEP. Part-time and evening/weekend programs available. *Faculty:* 6 full-time (all women), 4 part-time/adjunct (2 women). *Students:* 26 full-time (20 women), 36 part-time (33 women); includes 3 minority (1 African American, 2 Asian Americans or Pacific Islanders). Average age 37. 41 applicants, 68% accepted, 18 enrolled. In 2009, 10 master's awarded. *Entrance requirements:* For master's, GRE General Test, minimum GPA of 3.0 with NLNAC or CCNE major. Additional exam requirements/recommendations for international students: Required—TOEFL (minimum score 530 paper-based; 200 computer-based; 72 iBT). *Application deadline:* For fall admission, 7/15 priority date for domestic students; for spring admission, 11/15 priority date for domestic students. Applications are processed on a rolling basis. Application fee: $60. Electronic applications accepted. *Expenses:* Tuition: Full-time $10,980; part-time $610 per credit hour. Required fees: $320 per semester. *Financial support:* Federal Work-Study available. *Faculty research:* Employer and faculty beliefs about concepts in RN-BS education, evaluating effectiveness of mental health partnerships in psychiatric settings. *Unit head:* Lynn Warner, Coordinator, 717-815-1212, E-mail: lwarner@ycp.edu. *Application contact:* Nancy Spataro, Director of Admissions, 717-815-1600, Fax: 717-849-1607, E-mail: admissions@ycp.edu.

York University, Faculty of Graduate Studies, Faculty of Health, Program in Nursing, Toronto, ON M3J 1P3, Canada. Offers M Sc N.

Youngstown State University, Graduate School, Bitonte College of Health and Human Services, Department of Nursing, Youngstown, OH 44555-0001. Offers MSN. *Accreditation:* NLN. Part-time and evening/weekend programs available. *Degree requirements:* For master's, thesis optional. *Entrance requirements:* For master's, GRE General Test, BSN, CPR certification. Additional exam requirements/recommendations for international students: Required—TOEFL.

Acute Care/Critical Care Nursing

Allen College, Program in Nursing, Waterloo, IA 50703. Offers acute care nurse practitioner (MSN); adult nurse practitioner (MSN); adult psychiatric-mental health nurse practitioner (MSN); family nurse practitioner (MSN); gerontological nurse practitioner (MSN); health education (MSN); leadership in health care delivery (MSN). *Accreditation:* AACN; NLN. Part-time programs available. *Faculty:* 2 full-time (both women), 8 part-time/adjunct (all women). *Students:* 37 full-time (35 women), 103 part-time (99 women); includes 1 minority (Asian American or Pacific Islander). Average age 38. *Degree requirements:* For master's, thesis optional. *Entrance requirements:* For master's, minimum GPA of 3.0. Additional exam requirements/recommendations for international students: Required—TOEFL (minimum score 550 paper-based). *Application deadline:* For fall admission, 7/15 priority date for domestic students; for spring admission, 12/1 priority date for domestic students. Applications are processed on a rolling basis. Application fee: $50. Electronic applications accepted. *Expenses:* Tuition: Full-time $12,550; part-time $651 per credit hour. Required fees: $826; $65 per credit hour. One-time fee: $425. Tuition and fees vary according to course load. *Financial support:* Teaching assistantships, institutionally sponsored loans, scholarships/grants, and traineeships available. Support available to part-time students. Financial award application deadline: 8/15; financial award applicants required to submit FAFSA. *Faculty research:* Pain and aged, congestive heart failure. *Unit head:* Nancy Kramer, Dean, School of Nursing, 319-226-2040, Fax: 319-226-2070, E-mail: kramerna@ihs.org. *Application contact:* Michelle Koehn, Admissions Counselor, 319-226-2002, Fax: 319-226-2051, E-mail: koehnml@ihs.org.

Barry University, School of Nursing, Program in Nurse Practitioner, Miami Shores, FL 33161-6695. Offers acute care nurse practitioner (MSN); family nurse practitioner (MSN); nurse practitioner (Certificate). *Accreditation:* AACN. Part-time and evening/weekend programs available. *Degree requirements:* For master's, research project or thesis. *Entrance requirements:* For master's, GRE General Test or MAT, BSN, minimum GPA of 3.0, course work in statistics. Electronic applications accepted. *Faculty research:* Child abuse, health beliefs, teenage pregnancy, cultural and clinical studies across the lifespan.

Case Western Reserve University, Frances Payne Bolton School of Nursing, Doctor of Nursing Practice Program, Cleveland, OH 44106. Offers acute care nurse practitioner (DNP); adult nurse practitioner (DNP); family nurse practitioner (DNP); gerontological nurse practitioner (DNP); graduate entry/pre-licensure option (DNP); medical-surgical nursing (DNP); midwifery/family nursing (DNP); neonatal nurse practitioner (DNP); pediatric nurse practitioner (DNP); post-licensure option (DNP); psychiatric-mental health nurse practitioner (DNP); women's health nurse practitioner (DNP). Graduate entry option allows baccalaureate-prepared college graduates from non-nursing backgrounds to earn certificate and MSN in addition to ND. Terminal master's awarded for partial completion of doctoral program. *Degree requirements:* For doctorate, thesis/dissertation. *Entrance requirements:* For doctorate, GRE General Test or MAT. *Faculty research:* Clinical nursing, acute care, gerontology, mental health, critical care.

Case Western Reserve University, Frances Payne Bolton School of Nursing, Master's Programs in Nursing, Nurse Practitioner Program, Cleveland, OH 44106. Offers acute care cardiovascular nursing (MSN); acute care nurse practitioner (MSN); acute care/flight nurse (MSN); adult nurse practitioner (MSN); family nurse practitioner (MSN); gerontological nurse practitioner (MSN); neonatal nurse practitioner (MSN); pediatric nurse practitioner (MSN); psychiatric-mental health nurse practitioner (MSN); women's health nurse practitioner (MSN). *Accreditation:* NLN. Part-time programs available. Postbaccalaureate distance learning degree programs offered (minimal on-campus study). *Degree requirements:* For master's, thesis optional. *Entrance requirements:* For master's, GRE General Test or MAT. Additional exam requirements/recommendations for international students: Required—TOEFL. *Faculty research:* Positive and negative mood states in parents of twins, effect of a carepath on chronic obstructive pulmonary disease home care.

The College of New Rochelle, Graduate School, Program in Nursing, New Rochelle, NY 10805-2308. Offers acute care nurse practitioner (MS, Certificate); clinical specialist in holistic nursing (MS, Certificate); family nurse practitioner (MS, Certificate); nursing and health care management (MS); nursing education (Certificate). *Accreditation:* AACN. Part-time programs available. *Entrance requirements:* For master's, GRE General Test or MAT, BSN, malpractice insurance, minimum GPA of 3.0, RN license. *Expenses:* Contact institution. *Faculty research:* Holistic modalities, academic success variables.

Columbia University, School of Nursing, Program in Acute Care Nurse Practitioner, New York, NY 10032. Offers MS, Adv C. *Accreditation:* AACN. Part-time programs available. *Entrance requirements:* For master's, GRE General Test, 1 year of clinical experience (preferred), BSN; for Adv C, MSN. Electronic applications accepted.

Duke University, School of Nursing, Durham, NC 27708-0586. Offers adult acute care (Certificate); adult cardiovascular (Certificate); adult oncology (Certificate); adult primary care (Certificate); clinical nurse specialist (MSN), including adult oncology, gerontology, neonatal, pediatric; clinical research management (MSN, Certificate); family (Certificate); gerontology (Certificate); health and nursing ministries (MSN, Certificate); health systems leadership and outcomes (Certificate); neonatal (Certificate); neonatal/pediatric in rural health (MSN, Certificate); nurse anesthetist (MSN, Certificate); nurse practitioner (MSN), including adult acute care, adult cardiovascular, adult oncology, adult primary care, family, gerontology, neonatal, pediatric, pediatric acute care; nursing (DNP, PhD); nursing and healthcare leadership (MSN); nursing education (MSN); nursing informatics (MSN, Certificate); pediatric (Certificate); pediatric acute care (Certificate); MBA/MSN; MSN/MCM. *Accreditation:* AACN; AANA/CANAEP. Part-time programs available. Postbaccalaureate distance learning degree programs offered (minimal on-campus study). *Faculty:* 45 full-time (41 women), 169 part-time/adjunct (150 women). *Students:* 213 full-time (179 women), 116 part-time (105 women); includes 37 minority (17 African Americans, 13 Asian Americans or Pacific Islanders, 7 Hispanic Americans), 9 international. Average age 36. 234 applicants, 53% accepted, 97 enrolled. In 2009, 142 master's, 24 other advanced degrees awarded. Terminal master's awarded for partial completion of doctoral program. *Degree requirements:* For master's, thesis optional; for doctorate, Capstone Project. *Entrance requirements:* For master's, GRE General Test, 1 year of nursing experience, BSN, minimum GPA of 3.0, previous course work in statistics; for doctorate, GRE for BSN prepared, BSN or MSN, minimum GPA of 3.0. Portfolio; for Certificate, MSN. Additional exam requirements/recommendations for international students: Required—TOEFL (minimum score 550 paper-based; 213 computer-based), Commission on Graduates of Foreign Nursing Schools exam. *Application deadline:* For fall admission, 7/2 priority date for domestic and international students; for spring admission, 11/15 priority date for domestic and international students. Applications are processed on a rolling basis. Application fee: $50. Electronic applications accepted. *Expenses:* Contact institution. *Financial support:* Career-related internships or fieldwork, institutionally sponsored loans, scholarships/grants, traineeships, and tuition waivers (partial) available. Support available to part-time students. Financial award application deadline: 4/1; financial award applicants required to submit FAFSA. *Faculty research:* Cardiovascular disease, caregiver skill training, data mining, prostate cancer, neonatal immune system. Total annual research expenditures: $3.5 million. *Unit head:* Dr. Catherine L. Gilliss, Dean/Vice Chancellor for Nursing Affairs, 919-684-9444, Fax: 919-684-9414, E-mail: gilli025@mc.duke.edu. *Application contact:* Bebe T. Mills, Director of Admissions, 919-684-9151, Fax: 919-668-4693, E-mail: mills031@mc.duke.edu.

Emory University, Nell Hodgson Woodruff School of Nursing, Atlanta, GA 30322-1100. Offers adult and elder health advanced practice nursing (MSN), including acute care, adult nurse practitioner, gerontological nurse practitioner; emergency nurse practitioner (MSN); family nurse practitioner (MSN); family nurse-midwife (MSN); nurse midwifery (MSN); pediatric nurse practitioner acute and primary care (MSN); public health nursing leadership (MSN); women's health nurse practitioner (MSN); women's health title x (MSN); women's health/adult health nurse practitioner (MSN); MSN/MPH. *Accreditation:* AACN; ACNM/DOA (one or more programs are accredited). Part-time programs available. *Faculty:* 30 full-time (29 women), 11 part-time/adjunct (10 women). *Students:* 110 full-time (106 women), 53 part-time (51 women); includes 49 minority (35 African Americans, 2 American Indian/Alaska Native, 10 Asian Americans or Pacific Islanders, 2 Hispanic Americans), 4 international. Average age 32. 182 applicants, 63% accepted, 86 enrolled. In 2009, 81 master's awarded. *Entrance requirements:* For master's, GRE General Test or MAT, minimum GPA of 3.0, BS in nursing from an accredited institution, RN license and additional course work, 3 letters of recommendation. Additional exam requirements/recommendations for international students: Required—TOEFL (minimum score 600 paper-based; 100 iBT). *Application deadline:* For fall admission, 1/15 priority date for domestic and international students; for spring admission, 10/1 priority date for domestic and international students. Applications are processed on a rolling basis. Application fee: $50. Electronic applications accepted. *Expenses:* Contact institution. *Financial support:* In 2009–10, 14 fellowships (averaging $28,000 per year) were awarded; career-related internships or fieldwork, Federal Work-Study, institutionally sponsored loans, and scholarships/grants also available. Support available to part-time students. Financial award application deadline: 3/1; financial award applicants required to submit CSS PROFILE or FAFSA. *Faculty research:* Older adult falls and injuries, minority health issues, cardiac symptoms and quality of life, bio-ethics and decision making, menopausal issues. *Unit head:* Dr. Linda McCauley, Dean, 404-727-7976, Fax: 404-727-9800, E-mail: linda.mccauley@emory.edu. *Application contact:* Katie Kennedy, Associate Director for Admission and Financial Aid, 404-727-7980, Fax: 404-727-8509, E-mail: admit@nursing.emory.edu.

See Close-Up on page 1613.

Georgetown University, Graduate School of Arts and Sciences, School of Nursing and Health Studies, Washington, DC 20057. Offers acute care nurse practitioner (MS); clinical nurse specialist (MS); family nurse practitioner (MS); nurse anesthesia (MS); nurse-midwifery (MS); nursing education (MS). *Accreditation:* AACN; AANA/CANAEP; ACNM/DOA. *Degree requirements:* For master's, thesis optional. *Entrance requirements:* For master's, GRE General Test or MAT, bachelor's degree in nursing from NLN-accredited school, minimum undergraduate GPA of 3.0. Additional exam requirements/recommendations for international students: Required—TOEFL.

Indiana University–Purdue University Indianapolis, School of Nursing, Indianapolis, IN 46202-2896. Offers acute care nurse practitioner (MSN); adult health clinical nurse specialist (MSN); adult health nursing (MSN), including adult clinical nurse specialist; adult nurse practitioner (MSN); adult psychiatric/mental health nursing (MSN); child psychiatric/mental health nursing (MSN); community health nursing (MSN); family nurse practitioner (MSN); neonatal nurse practitioner (MSN); nursing science (PhD); pediatric clinical nurse specialist (MSN); women's health nurse practitioner (MSN); MSN/MPA; MSN/MPH. *Accreditation:* AACN; NLN (one or more programs are accredited). Part-time programs available. *Faculty:* 85 full-time (82 women), 60 part-time/adjunct (all women). *Students:* 46 full-time (43 women), 369 part-time (354 women); includes 30 minority (21 African Americans, 6 Asian Americans or Pacific Islanders, 3 Hispanic Americans), 5 international. Average age 39. 121 applicants, 82% accepted, 67 enrolled. In 2009, 106 master's, 3 doctorates awarded. Terminal master's awarded for partial completion of doctoral program. *Degree requirements:* For master's, thesis; for doctorate, thesis/dissertation. *Entrance requirements:* For master's, minimum GPA of 3.0, RN license; for doctorate, GRE General Test, minimum GPA of 3.0, MSN, RN license, graduate statistics course with B grade or better (not older than 3 years). Additional exam requirements/recommendations for international students: Required—TOEFL. *Application deadline:* For fall admission, 2/15 for domestic students; for spring admission, 9/15 for domestic students. Application fee: $55 ($65 for international students). *Financial support:* In 2009–10, 93 students received support, including 9 fellowships with full tuition reimbursements available (averaging $7,039 per year), 7 teaching assistantships with full tuition reimbursements available (averaging $5,300 per year); research assistantships with full tuition reimbursements available, Federal Work-Study, institutionally sponsored loans, scholarships/grants, and tuition waivers (full) also available. Support available to part-time students. Financial award application deadline: 5/1. *Faculty research:* Clinical science, health systems. Total annual research expenditures: $3 million. *Unit head:* Associate Dean for Graduate Programs, 317-274-2806, E-mail: nursing@iupui.edu. *Application contact:* Information Contact, 317-274-2806.

Inter American University of Puerto Rico, Arecibo Campus, Program in Nursing, Arecibo, PR 00614-4050. Offers community nursing (MS); critical care nursing (MS); primary care nursing (MS); surgical nursing (MS). *Entrance requirements:* For master's, EXADEP or GRE General Test or MAT, 2 letters of recommendation, bachelor's degree in nursing, minimum GPA of 2.5 in last 60 credits, minimum 1 year nursing experience, nursing license.

The Johns Hopkins University, School of Nursing, Nurse Practitioner Program, Baltimore, MD 21218-2699. Offers adult acute/critical care (MSN, Certificate); adult and pediatric primary care (MSN); adult or pediatric primary care (Certificate); emergency preparedness/disaster response (Certificate); family primary care (MSN, Certificate); women's health (Certificate). *Accreditation:* AACN; NLN (one or more programs are accredited). Part-time programs available. *Faculty:* 9 full-time (all women), 10 part-time/adjunct (all women). *Students:* 28 full-time (27 women), 75 part-time (73 women); includes 33 minority (14 African Americans, 16 Asian Americans or Pacific Islanders, 3 Hispanic Americans), 3 international. Average age 31. 223 applicants, 80% accepted, 29 enrolled. In 2009, 37 master's awarded. *Degree requirements:* For master's, thesis optional, scholarly project or portfolio. *Entrance requirements:* For master's, GRE, interview, minimum GPA of 3.0, BSN, Maryland RN license. Additional exam requirements/recommendations for international students: Required—TOEFL (minimum score 550 paper-based; 213 computer-based). *Application deadline:* For fall admission, 3/1 priority date for domestic and international students; for spring admission, 7/1 priority date for domestic and international students. Application fee: $75. Electronic applications accepted. *Expenses:* Contact institution. *Financial support:* In 2009–10, 25 students received support. Federal Work-Study, scholarships/grants, traineeships, and tuition waivers (partial) available. Support available to part-time students. Financial award application deadline: 3/1; financial award applicants required to submit FAFSA. *Faculty research:* Community outreach, primary care of underserved populations, substance abusing individuals, childhood violence, women's health. *Unit head:* Dr. Julie A. Stanik-Hutt, Director, Master's Programs, 410-502-0184, Fax: 410-955-7463, E-mail: jstanik1@son.jhmi.edu. *Application contact:* Mary O'Rourke, Director of Admissions and Student Services, 410-955-7548, Fax: 410-614-7086, E-mail: orourke@son.jhmi.edu.

Loyola University Chicago, Graduate School, Marcella Niehoff School of Nursing, Acute Care Clinical Nurse Specialist Program, Chicago, IL 60660. Offers acute care clinical nurse specialist (MSN), including cardiovascular health. *Accreditation:* AACN. Part-time and evening/weekend programs available. *Degree requirements:* For master's, comprehensive exam or oral thesis defense. *Entrance requirements:* For master's, BSN, Illinois nursing license, 3 letters of recommendation, 1000 hours experience in acute care before starting clinical. *Application deadline:* Applications are processed on a rolling basis. Electronic applications accepted. *Expenses:* Tuition: Full-time $14,220; part-time $790 per credit hour. Required fees: $60 per semester hour. Tuition and fees vary according to program. *Financial support:* Teaching assistantships, traineeships and unspecified assistantships available. Financial award application deadline: 3/1. *Unit head:* Dr. Judith Jennrich, Associate Professor, 708-216-3813, E-mail: jjrennri@luc.edu. *Application contact:* Dr. Vicki A. Keough, Associate Professor/Master's Program Director, 708-216-3582, Fax: 708-216-9555, E-mail: vkeough@luc.edu.

Loyola University Chicago, Graduate School, Marcella Niehoff School of Nursing, Acute Care Nurse Practitioner Program, Chicago, IL 60660. Offers acute care (Certificate); acute care nurse practitioner (MSN); emergency nurse practitioner (Certificate). *Accreditation:* AACN. Part-time and evening/weekend programs available. *Students:* 16 full-time (14 women), 44 part-time (39 women); includes 13 minority (1 African American, 9 Asian Americans or Pacific Islanders, 3 Hispanic Americans). Average age 34. 33 applicants, 70% accepted, 13 enrolled. In 2009, 13 master's awarded. *Degree requirements:* For master's, comprehensive exam or oral thesis defense. *Entrance requirements:* For master's, Illinois nursing license, BSN, minimum

nursing GPA of 3.0, 3 letters of recommendation, 1,000 hours experience in acute care prior to clinical. *Application deadline:* Applications are processed on a rolling basis. Application fee: $40. Electronic applications accepted. *Expenses:* Tuition: Full-time $14,220; part-time $790 per credit hour. Required fees: $60 per semester hour. Tuition and fees vary according to program. *Financial support:* Traineeships available. Financial award application deadline: 3/1. *Unit head:* Dr. Judith Jennrich, Associate Professor, 708-216-3813, E-mail: jjrennri@luc.edu. *Application contact:* Dr. Vicki A. Keough, Associate Professor/Master's Program Director, 708-216-3582, Fax: 708-216-9555, E-mail: vkeough@luc.edu.

Loyola University Chicago, Graduate School, Marcella Niehoff School of Nursing, Program in Critical Care/Trauma, Chicago, IL 60660. Offers MSN. Application fee: $50. *Expenses:* Tuition: Full-time $14,220; part-time $790 per credit hour. Required fees: $60 per semester hour. Tuition and fees vary according to program. *Unit head:* Dr. Mary K. Walker, Dean, 773-508-3275, E-mail: mwalker1@luc.edu. *Application contact:* Dr. Vicki A. Keough, Associate Professor/Master's Program Director, 708-216-3582, Fax: 708-216-9555, E-mail: vkeough@luc.edu.

Medical College of Georgia, School of Graduate Studies, Adult Acute/Critical Care Advanced Practice Nursing Program, Augusta, GA 30912. Offers MSN. *Entrance requirements:* For master's, GRE General Test or MAT, Georgia professional registered nurse licensure, 1 year RN experience. Additional exam requirements/recommendations for international students: Required—TOEFL (minimum score 550 paper-based; 213 computer-based; 79 iBT). Electronic applications accepted. Full-time tuition and fees vary according to campus/location, program and student level.

New York University, College of Nursing, Programs in Advanced Practice Nursing, New York, NY 10012-1019. Offers advanced practice nursing: adult acute care (MS, Advanced Certificate); advanced practice nursing: adult nurse practitioner/palliative care nursing (MS); advanced practice nursing: adult nurse practitioner/holistic nurse practitioner (Advanced Certificate); advanced practice nursing: adult nurse practitioner/holistic nursing (MS); advanced practice nursing: adult nurse practitioner/palliative care nurse practitioner (Advanced Certificate); advanced practice nursing: adult primary care (MS, Advanced Certificate); advanced practice nursing: adult primary care/geriatrics (MS); advanced practice nursing: geriatrics (MS, Advanced Certificate); advanced practice nursing: mental health (MS); advanced practice nursing: mental health nursing (Advanced Certificate); advanced practice nursing: pediatrics (MS, Advanced Certificate); advanced practice nursing:adult primary care and geriatrics (Advanced Certificate); nurse midwifery (MS, Advanced Certificate); nursing administration (MS, Advanced Certificate); nursing education (MS, Advanced Certificate); nursing informatics (MS, Advanced Certificate); MS/MPH; MS/MS. *Accreditation:* AACN; ACNM/DOA. Part-time and evening/weekend programs available. *Faculty:* 17 full-time (all women), 22 part-time/adjunct (19 women). *Students:* 18 full-time (17 women), 524 part-time (485 women); includes 238 minority (90 African Americans, 119 Asian Americans or Pacific Islanders, 29 Hispanic Americans). Average age 33. 191 applicants, 89% accepted, 120 enrolled. In 2009, 117 master's, 2 other advanced degrees awarded. *Degree requirements:* For master's, thesis (for some programs). *Entrance requirements:* For master's, BS in nursing, AS in nursing with another BS/BA, interview; for Advanced Certificate, master's degree. Additional exam requirements/recommendations for international students: Required—TOEFL. *Application deadline:* For fall admission, 7/1 priority date for domestic students, 7/1 for international students; for spring admission, 12/1 for domestic and international students. Applications are processed on a rolling basis. Application fee: $75. *Expenses:* Tuition: Full-time $30,528; part-time $1272 per credit. Required fees: $2177. *Financial support:* Career-related internships or fieldwork, institutionally sponsored loans, scholarships/grants, traineeships, and tuition waivers (partial) available. Support available to part-time students. Financial award application deadline: 2/1; financial award applicants required to submit FAFSA. *Faculty research:* Elderly black diabetics, families and illness, public health nursing, parent-child nursing, health policy costs. *Unit head:* Dr. Judith Haber, Associate Dean for Graduate Programs, 212-998-9020, Fax: 212-995-3143. *Application contact:* Amy Knowles, Assistant Dean for Student Affairs and Admissions, 212-998-5333, Fax: 212-995-4302, E-mail: ak96@nyu.edu.

Northeastern University, Bouvé College of Health Sciences Graduate School, School of Nursing, Program in Critical Care-Acute Care Nurse Practitioner, Boston, MA 02115-5096. Offers MS, CAGS, CAS. *Accreditation:* AACN. *Students:* 10 full-time (8 women), 17 part-time (14 women); includes 3 Asian Americans or Pacific Islanders. 5 applicants, 100% accepted, 5 enrolled. In 2009, 5 master's awarded. *Degree requirements:* For master's, thesis or alternative. *Entrance requirements:* For master's, GRE General Test; for other advanced degree, MS in nursing. Additional exam requirements/recommendations for international students: Required—TOEFL (minimum score 100 iBT). *Application deadline:* For fall admission, 7/1 for domestic students. Applications are processed on a rolling basis. Application fee: $50. Electronic applications accepted. *Financial support:* Research assistantships with tuition reimbursements, teaching assistantships with tuition reimbursements, scholarships/grants, traineeships, and tuition waivers (partial) available. Financial award application deadline: 7/1; financial award applicants required to submit FAFSA. *Unit head:* Prof. John Kenna, Director, 617-373-6543, Fax: 617-373-6543, E-mail: j.kenna@neu.edu. *Application contact:* Margaret Schnabel, Director of Graduate Admissions, 617-373-2708, E-mail: bouvegrad@neu.edu.

Northeastern University, Bouvé College of Health Sciences Graduate School, School of Nursing, Program in Critical Care-Neonatal Nurse Practitioner, Boston, MA 02115-5096. Offers MS, CAS. *Accreditation:* AACN. *Students:* 1 (woman) part-time. 1 applicant, 100% accepted, 1 enrolled. In 2009, 7 master's awarded. *Degree requirements:* For master's, thesis or alternative. *Entrance requirements:* For master's, GRE General Test, minimum GPA of 3.0, previous course work in statistics, 1-2 years of nursing experience, RN license, ICU experience. Additional exam requirements/recommendations for international students: Required—TOEFL (minimum score 100 iBT). *Application deadline:* For fall admission, 7/1 for domestic students. Application fee: $50. Electronic applications accepted. *Financial support:* Research assistantships, teaching assistantships, scholarships/grants, traineeships, and tuition waivers (partial) available. Financial award application deadline: 7/1; financial award applicants required to submit FAFSA. *Unit head:* Prof. Gretchen R. Hamn, Director, E-mail: g.hamn@neu.edu. *Application contact:* Margaret Schnabel, Director of Graduate Admissions, 617-373-2708, E-mail: bouvegrad@neu.edu.

Rush University, College of Nursing, Department of Adult Health Nursing, Chicago, IL 60612-3832. Offers acute care nurse practitioner (MSN, Post-Master's Certificate); adult health nursing (DNP, PhD); adult nurse practitioner (MSN, Post-Master's Certificate); adult/gerontological nurse practitioner (MSN); anesthesia nurse practitioner (MSN, Post-Master's Certificate); critical care clinical specialist (MSN); gerontological nurse practitioner (MSN, Post-Master's Certificate); medical surgical clinical specialist (MSN). *Accreditation:* AACN; AANA/CANAEP (one or more programs are accredited). Part-time programs available. Postbaccalaureate distance learning degree programs offered (minimal on-campus study). Terminal master's awarded for partial completion of doctoral program. *Degree requirements:* For master's, capstone project; for doctorate, thesis/dissertation, DNP leadership project. *Entrance requirements:* For master's, GRE General Test (waived if nursing GPA is above 3.0 or cumulative GPA is above 3.25), interview; for doctorate, GRE General Test, interview, course work in statistics (PhD). Additional exam requirements/recommendations for international students: Required—TOEFL, TWE. Electronic applications accepted. *Faculty research:* Complementary/alternative medicine, critical care outcomes, cardiac risk reduction, Alzheimer's Disease, telehealth monitoring.

Rush University, College of Nursing, Department of Women's and Children's Health Nursing, Chicago, IL 60612-3832. Offers neonatal nurse practitioner (MSN, Post-Master's Certificate); pediatric acute/chronic care nurse practitioner (MSN); pediatric clinical nurse specialist (MSN); pediatric nurse practitioner (MSN, Post-Master's Certificate); women's and children's health nursing (DNP, PhD). *Accreditation:* AACN. Part-time programs available. Postbaccalaureate distance learning degree programs offered (minimal on-campus study). Terminal master's awarded for partial completion of doctoral program. *Degree requirements:* For master's,

capstone project; for doctorate, thesis/dissertation, DNP leadership project. *Entrance requirements:* For master's, GRE General Test (waived if nursing GPA is above 3.0 or cumulative GPA is above 3.25), interview; for doctorate, GRE General Test, interview, course work in statistics (PhD). Additional exam requirements/recommendations for international students: Required—TOEFL, TWE. Electronic applications accepted. *Faculty research:* Family-centered care, women's health, health outcomes of human milk feeding for VhBW infants.

Southern Adventist University, School of Nursing, Collegedale, TN 37315-0370. Offers acute care nurse practitioner (MSN); adult nurse practitioner (MSN); family nurse practitioner (MSN); nurse educator (MSN); MSN/MSBA. *Accreditation:* NLN. Part-time programs available. *Faculty:* 6 full-time (5 women). *Students:* 69 full-time (50 women), 28 part-time (25 women); includes 9 minority (6 African Americans, 1 American Indian/Alaska Native, 1 Asian American or Pacific Islander, 1 Hispanic American). Average age 35. 40 applicants, 95% accepted, 31 enrolled. In 2009, 21 master's awarded. *Degree requirements:* For master's, thesis or project. *Entrance requirements:* For master's, RN license. Additional exam requirements/recommendations for international students: Required—TOEFL (minimum score 600 paper-based; 250 computer-based). *Application deadline:* For fall admission, 7/1 for domestic and international students; for winter admission, 12/1 for domestic and international students. Applications are processed on a rolling basis. Application fee: $25. Electronic applications accepted. *Expenses:* Tuition: Full-time $13,149; part-time $487 per credit hour. *Financial support:* In 2009–10, 1 teaching assistantship with partial tuition reimbursement (averaging $5,000 per year) was awarded. *Faculty research:* Pain management, ethics, corporate wellness, caring spirituality, stress. *Unit head:* Dr. Barbara James, Dean, 423-236-2940, Fax: 423-236-1940, E-mail: bjames@southern.edu. *Application contact:* Diane Proffitt, Enrollment Counselor, 423-236-2941, Fax: 423-236-1940, E-mail: dproffitt@southern.edu.

Texas Tech University Health Sciences Center, School of Nursing, Lubbock, TX 79430. Offers acute care nurse practitioner (MSN, Certificate); administration (MSN); advanced practice (DNP); education (MSN); executive leadership (DNP); family nurse practitioner (MSN, Certificate); geriatric nurse practitioner (MSN, Certificate); pediatric nurse practitioner (MSN, Certificate). *Accreditation:* AACN. Part-time programs available. Postbaccalaureate distance learning degree programs offered (minimal on-campus study). *Degree requirements:* For master's, thesis optional. *Entrance requirements:* For master's, minimum GPA of 3.0, 3 letters of reference, BSN, RN license; for Certificate, minimum GPA of 3.0, 3 letters of reference, RN license. Additional exam requirements/recommendations for international students: Required—TOEFL (minimum score 550 paper-based; 213 computer-based). *Faculty research:* Diabetes/obesity, nurse competency, disease management, intervention and measurements, health disparities.

Texas Woman's University, Graduate School, College of Nursing, Denton, TX 76201. Offers acute care nurse practitioner (MS); adult health clinical nurse specialist (MS); adult health nurse practitioner (MS); child health clinical nurse specialist (MS); clinical nurse leader (MS); community health (MS); family nurse practitioner (MS); health systems management (MS); nursing education (MS); nursing practice (DNP); nursing science (PhD); pediatric nurse practitioner (MS); women's health clinical nurse specialist (MS); women's health nurse practitioner (MS). *Accreditation:* AACN. Part-time programs available. Postbaccalaureate distance learning degree programs offered. *Faculty:* 85 full-time (80 women), 6 part-time/adjunct (all women). *Students:* 81 full-time (76 women), 602 part-time (571 women); includes 293 minority (154 African Americans, 3 American Indian/Alaska Native, 90 Asian Americans or Pacific Islanders, 46 Hispanic Americans), 19 international. Average age 39. 259 applicants, 81% accepted, 166 enrolled. In 2009, 100 master's, 22 doctorates awarded. *Degree requirements:* For master's, thesis or alternative; for doctorate, comprehensive exam, thesis/dissertation. *Entrance requirements:* For master's, GRE or MAT, minimum GPA of 3.0, RN license, BS in nursing, basic statistics course; for doctorate, GRE (Verbal 460, Quantitative 500) or MAT (50), MS in nursing, minimum GPA of 3.5, RN license, coursework in statistics, 2 letters of reference, curriculum vitae, nursing-theory course, graduate research course, letter stating professional and research goals. Additional exam requirements/recommendations for international students: Required—TOEFL (minimum score 550 paper-based; 213 computer-based; 79 iBT). *Application deadline:* For fall admission, 5/1 priority date for domestic students, 3/1 for international students; for spring admission, 9/15 priority date for domestic students, 7/1 for international students. Applications are processed on a rolling basis. Application fee: $50. Electronic applications accepted. *Expenses:* Tuition, state resident: full-time $3564; part-time $198 per credit hour. Tuition, nonresident: full-time $8550; part-time $475 per credit hour. Required fees: $69.26 per credit hour. Tuition and fees vary according to course load. *Financial support:* In 2009–10, 99 students received support, including 16 fellowships (averaging $17,325 per year), 5 research assistantships (averaging $11,484 per year), 5 teaching assistantships (averaging $11,484 per year); career-related internships or fieldwork, Federal Work-Study, institutionally sponsored loans, scholarships/grants, traineeships, health care benefits, and unspecified assistantships also available. Support available to part-time students. Financial award application deadline: 3/1; financial award applicants required to submit FAFSA. *Faculty research:* Evaluation of pre-natal care, screening for intimate partner violence, stressors and nursing success, breast surgery, breast feeding, adolescent needs during childbirth. *Unit head:* Dr. Patricia Holden-Huchton, Interim Dean, 940-898-2401, Fax: 940-898-2437, E-mail: pholdenhuchton@twu.edu. *Application contact:* Samuel Wheeler, Assistant Director of Admissions, 940-898-3188, Fax: 940-898-3081, E-mail: wheelersr@twu.edu.

Universidad de Iberoamerica, Graduate School, San Jose, Costa Rica. Offers clinical neuropsychology (PhD); clinical psychology (M Psych); educational psychology (M Psych); forensic psychology (M Psych); hospital management (MHA); intensive care nursing (MN); medicine (MD). *Entrance requirements:* For master's, 2 letters of recommendation, interview.

Université de Montréal, Faculty of Medicine, Program in Specialized Studies, Montréal, QC H3C 3J7, Canada. Offers anesthesia (DES); diagnostic radiology (DES); family medicine (DES); gastroenterology (DES); geriatry (DES); intensive care (DES); medical biochemistry (DES); medical genetics (DES); medicine (DES); microbiology and infectious diseases (DES); nuclear medicine (DES); obstetrics and gynecology (DES); ophthalmology (DES); pediatrics (DES); pneumology (DES); psychiatry (DES); radiology-oncology (DES); rheumatology (DES); surgery (DES). *Faculty:* 154 full-time (40 women), 333 part-time/adjunct (100 women). *Students:* 930 full-time (580 women), 7 part-time (all women). 74 applicants, 77% accepted, 29 enrolled. *Application deadline:* For fall admission, 2/1 priority date for domestic students; for winter admission, 11/1 priority date for domestic students; for spring admission, 2/1 priority date for domestic students. Application fee: $100. Electronic applications accepted. *Unit head:* Lorraine Locas, Assistant to the Vice Dean of Graduate Studies, 514-343-6269, Fax: 514-343-5751, E-mail: lorraine.locas@umontreal.ca. *Application contact:* Dr. Andre Ferron, Vice Dean Graduate Studies, 514-343-6111 Ext. 0933, Fax: 514-343-5751, E-mail: andre.ferron@umontreal.ca.

The University of Alabama in Huntsville, School of Graduate Studies, College of Nursing, Huntsville, AL 35899. Offers family nurse practitioner (Certificate); nursing (MSN, DNP), including acute care nurse practitioner (MSN), adult clinical nursing specialist (MSN), clinical nurse leader (MSN), family nurse practitioner (MSN), leadership in health care systems (MSN); nursing education (Certificate). *Accreditation:* AACN. Part-time and evening/weekend programs available. Postbaccalaureate distance learning degree programs offered (minimal on-campus study). *Faculty:* 13 full-time (11 women), 3 part-time/adjunct (2 women). *Students:* 45 full-time (43 women), 121 part-time (111 women); includes 25 minority (17 African Americans, 5 American Indian/Alaska Native, 3 Asian Americans or Pacific Islanders), 3 international. Average age 39. 151 applicants, 68% accepted, 74 enrolled. In 2009, 52 master's, 5 other advanced degrees awarded. *Degree requirements:* For master's, comprehensive exam, thesis or alternative, oral and written exams; for doctorate, comprehensive exam, thesis/dissertation or alternative, oral and written exams. *Entrance requirements:* For master's, MAT or GRE, Alabama RN license, BSN, minimum GPA of 3.0; for doctorate, master's degree in nursing in an advanced practice area; for Certificate, MAT or GRE, minimum GPA of 3.0. Additional exam requirements/recommendations for international students: Required—TOEFL (minimum score 500 paper-based; 173 computer-based; 62 iBT). *Application deadline:* For fall admission, 7/15 for domestic students, 4/1 for international students; for spring admission, 11/30 for domestic students, 9/1 for international students. Applications are processed on a rolling basis. Application

Acute Care/Critical Care Nursing

The University of Alabama in Huntsville (continued)
fee: $40 ($50 for international students). Electronic applications accepted. *Expenses:* Tuition, state resident: part-time $355.75 per credit hour. Tuition, nonresident: part-time $847.10 per credit hour. Required fees: $210.80 per semester. Tuition and fees vary according to course load and program. *Financial support:* In 2009–10, 11 students received support, including 11 teaching assistantships with full and partial tuition reimbursements available (averaging $9,996 per year); career-related internships or fieldwork, Federal Work-Study, institutionally sponsored loans, scholarships/grants, traineeships, health care benefits, and unspecified assistantships also available. Support available to part-time students. Financial award application deadline: 4/1; financial award applicants required to submit FAFSA. *Faculty research:* Home health care, gerontology, pediatric nursing, family nurse practitioner, adult acute care administration. *Unit head:* Dr. Fay Raines, Dean, 256-824-6345, Fax: 256-824-6026, E-mail: rainesc@uah.edu. *Application contact:* Charles Davis, Associate Director of Nursing Student Affairs Graduate Programs, 256-824-6669, Fax: 256-824-6026, E-mail: charles.davis@uah.edu.

University of Cincinnati, Graduate School, College of Nursing, Cincinnati, OH 45221-0038. Offers clinical nurse specialist (MSN), including adult health, community health, neonatal, nursing administration, occupational health, pediatric health, psychiatric nursing, women's health; nurse anesthesia (MSN); nurse midwifery (MSN); nurse practitioner (MSN), including acute care, ambulatory care, family, family/psychiatric, women's health; nursing (PhD); MBA/MSN. *Accreditation:* AACN; AANA/CANAEP (one or more programs are accredited); ACNM/DOA. Part-time programs available. Postbaccalaureate distance learning degree programs offered (no on-campus study). Terminal master's awarded for partial completion of doctoral program. *Degree requirements:* For master's, thesis or alternative; for doctorate, comprehensive exam, thesis/dissertation. *Entrance requirements:* For master's and doctorate, GRE General Test. Additional exam requirements/recommendations for international students: Required—TOEFL (minimum score 520 paper-based; 190 computer-based). Electronic applications accepted. *Faculty research:* Substance abuse, injury and violence, symptom management.

University of Guelph, Ontario Veterinary College and Graduate Program Services, Graduate Programs in Veterinary Sciences, Department of Clinical Studies, Guelph, ON N1G 2W1, Canada. Offers anesthesiology (M Sc, DV Sc); cardiology (DV Sc, Diploma); clinical studies (Diploma); dermatology (M Sc); diagnostic imaging (M Sc, DV Sc); emergency/critical care (M Sc, DV Sc, Diploma); medicine (M Sc, DV Sc); neurology (M Sc, DV Sc); ophthalmology (M Sc, DV Sc); surgery (M Sc, DV Sc). *Degree requirements:* For master's, thesis; for doctorate, comprehensive exam, thesis/dissertation. *Entrance requirements:* Additional exam requirements/recommendations for international students: Required—TOEFL (minimum score 550 paper-based; 213 computer-based), IELTS (minimum score 6.5). Electronic applications accepted. *Faculty research:* Orthopedics, respirology, oncology, exercise physiology, cardiology.

University of Illinois at Chicago, Graduate College, College of Nursing, Program in Nursing, Chicago, IL 60607-7128. Offers acute care clinical nurse specialist (MS); acute care nurse practitioner (MS); administrative studies in nursing (MS); adult nurse practitioner (MS); adult/geriatric nurse practitioner (MS); advanced community health nurse specialist (MS); family nurse practitioner (MS); geriatric clinical nurse specialist (MS); geriatric nurse practitioner (MS); mental health clinical nurse specialist (MS); mental health nurse practitioner (MS); nurse midwifery (MS); occupational health/advanced community health nurse specialist (MS); occupational health/family nurse practitioner (MS); pediatric clinical nurse specialist (MS); pediatric nurse practitioner (MS); perinatal clinical nurse specialist (MS); school/advanced community health nurse specialist (MS); school/family nurse practitioner (MS); women's health nurse practitioner (MS). *Accreditation:* AACN. Part-time programs available. *Degree requirements:* For master's, thesis or alternative. *Entrance requirements:* For master's, GRE General Test, minimum GPA of 2.75. Additional exam requirements/recommendations for international students: Required—TOEFL. Electronic applications accepted.

University of Massachusetts Worcester, Graduate School of Nursing, Worcester, MA 01655-0115. Offers adult acute/critical care nurse practitioner (MS, Post Master's Certificate); adult acute/critical care nurse practitioner and gerontological nurse practitioner (MS, Post Master's Certificate); adult primary care nurse practitioner (MS, Post Master's Certificate); adult primary care nurse practitioner and gerontological nurse practitioner (MS, Post Master's Certificate); family nurse practitioner (MS); gerontological nurse practitioner (Post Master's Certificate); nurse educator (MS); nursing (PhD). *Accreditation:* AACN. *Faculty:* 15 full-time (13 women), 31 part-time/adjunct (29 women). *Students:* 151 full-time (131 women), 6 part-time (all women); includes 14 minority (5 African Americans, 1 American Indian/Alaska Native, 5 Asian Americans or Pacific Islanders, 3 Hispanic Americans). Average age 37. 206 applicants, 34% accepted, 61 enrolled. In 2009, 62 master's, 3 doctorates awarded. *Degree requirements:* For doctorate, comprehensive exam, thesis/dissertation. *Entrance requirements:* For master's, GRE General Test, bachelor's degree, course work in statistics; for doctorate, GRE General Test, bachelor's or master's degree, RN licensure; for Post Master's Certificate, MS in nursing. Additional exam requirements/recommendations for international students: Required—TOEFL. *Application deadline:* For fall admission, 3/15 for domestic students. Applications are processed on a rolling basis. Application fee: $40 ($60 for international students). *Expenses:* Contact institution. *Financial support:* In 2009–10, 130 students received support. Scholarships/grants and traineeships available. Support available to part-time students. Financial award application deadline: 5/18; financial award applicants required to submit FAFSA. *Faculty research:* Symptom management, interventions, individual and family adjustment to chronic illness, women's health. *Unit head:* Dr. Paulette Seymour-Route, Dean, 508-856-5801, Fax: 508-856-6552, E-mail: paulette.seymour-route@umassmed.edu. *Application contact:* Diane Brescia, Admissions Coordinator, 508-856-3488, Fax: 508-856-5851, E-mail: diane.brescia@umassmed.edu.

University of Miami, Graduate School, School of Nursing and Health Studies, Coral Gables, FL 33124. Offers acute care (MSN), including acute care nurse practitioner, nurse anesthesia; nursing (PhD); primary care (MSN), including adult nurse practitioner, family nurse practitioner, nurse midwifery, women's health practitioner. *Accreditation:* AACN; AANA/CANAEP; ACNM/DOA (one or more programs are accredited). Part-time programs available. *Degree requirements:* For master's, thesis optional; for doctorate, thesis/dissertation. *Entrance requirements:* For master's, GRE General Test, BSN, minimum GPA of 3.0, Florida RN license; for doctorate, GRE General Test, BSN or MSN, minimum GPA of 3.0. Additional exam requirements/recommendations for international students: Required—TOEFL (minimum score 550 paper-based; 213 computer-based). Electronic applications accepted. *Faculty research:* Transcultural nursing, exercise and depression in Alzheimer's disease, infectious diseases/HIV–AIDS, postpartum depression, outcomes assessment.

University of Michigan, Horace H. Rackham School of Graduate Studies, School of Nursing, Division of Acute, Critical and Long-term Care, Program in Adult Acute Care Nurse Practitioner, Ann Arbor, MI 48109. Offers MS. *Accreditation:* AACN. Part-time programs available. *Degree requirements:* For master's, thesis. *Entrance requirements:* For master's, GRE General Test (if BSN GPA less than 3.25), Michigan licensure, minimum of B average in BSN program. Additional exam requirements/recommendations for international students: Required—TOEFL (minimum score 560 paper-based; 220 computer-based). Electronic applications accepted. *Expenses:* Tuition, state resident: full-time $17,286; part-time $1099 per credit hour. Tuition, nonresident: full-time $34,944; part-time $2080 per credit hour. Required fees: $95 per semester. Tuition and fees vary according to course load, degree level and program. *Faculty research:* The functional outcomes and quality of life in women with breast cancer, hypertension.

University of Pennsylvania, School of Nursing, Adult Acute Care Nurse Practitioner Program, Philadelphia, PA 19104. Offers acute care nurse practitioner (MSN). *Accreditation:* AACN. Part-time programs available. *Students:* 35 full-time (30 women), 69 part-time (63 women); includes 15 minority (5 African Americans, 1 American Indian/Alaska Native, 7 Asian Americans or Pacific Islanders, 2 Hispanic Americans), 6 international. In 2009, 24 master's awarded. *Entrance requirements:* For master's, GRE General Test, BSN, minimum GPA of 3.0, previous course work in statistics. *Application deadline:* For fall admission, 2/15 priority date for domestic students. Applications are processed on a rolling basis. Application fee: $70. *Expenses:* Contact institution. *Financial support:* Fellowships, research assistantships, teaching assistantships, Federal Work-Study and institutionally sponsored loans available. Support available to part-time students. Financial award application deadline: 4/1. *Faculty research:* Post-injury disability, bereavement and attributions in fire survivors, stress in staff nurses.

University of Pennsylvania, School of Nursing, Pediatric Acute/Chronic Care Nurse Practitioner Program, Philadelphia, PA 19104. Offers MSN. *Accreditation:* AACN. Part-time programs available. Postbaccalaureate distance learning degree programs offered. *Students:* 12 full-time (all women), 13 part-time (all women); includes 1 minority (Hispanic American). In 2009, 11 master's awarded. *Entrance requirements:* For master's, GRE General Test, 1 year of clinical course work, BSN, minimum GPA of 3.0, previous course work in statistics. Additional exam requirements/recommendations for international students: Required—TOEFL. *Application deadline:* For fall admission, 2/15 priority date for domestic students. Applications are processed on a rolling basis. Application fee: $70. *Expenses:* Contact institution. *Financial support:* Research assistantships, teaching assistantships, career-related internships or fieldwork and institutionally sponsored loans available. Support available to part-time students. Financial award application deadline: 4/1. *Faculty research:* Hispanic health, bereavement, pediatric AIDS, chronically ill children and their families.

University of Pennsylvania, School of Nursing, Pediatric Critical Care Nurse Practitioner Program, Philadelphia, PA 19104. Offers MSN. *Accreditation:* AACN. *Students:* 7 full-time (all women), 8 part-time (7 women); includes 3 minority (all Asian Americans or Pacific Islanders). In 2009, 7 master's awarded. *Entrance requirements:* For master's, GRE General Test, BSN, minimum GPA of 3.0, previous course work in statistics, 1 year of clinical course work. Additional exam requirements/recommendations for international students: Required—TOEFL. *Application deadline:* For fall admission, 2/15 priority date for domestic students. Applications are processed on a rolling basis. Application fee: $70. *Expenses:* Contact institution. *Financial support:* Application deadline: 4/1.

University of Pittsburgh, School of Nursing, Nurse Practitioner Program, Pittsburgh, PA 15260. Offers acute care nurse practitioner (MSN, DNP); adult nurse practitioner (MSN, DNP); family nurse practitioner (MSN, DNP); neonatal (MSN, DNP); nursing practice (DNP); pediatric nurse practitioner (MSN, DNP); psychiatric primary care nurse practitioner (MSN, DNP). *Accreditation:* AACN. Part-time programs available. *Students:* 27 full-time (26 women), 89 part-time (84 women); includes 6 minority (5 African Americans, 1 Asian American or Pacific Islander). Average age 34. 44 applicants, 64% accepted, 25 enrolled. In 2009, 28 master's awarded. *Degree requirements:* For master's, comprehensive exam, thesis optional. *Entrance requirements:* For master's, GRE General Test or MAT, BSN, RN license, letters of recommendation, resume, course work in statistics, 1-3 years of nursing experience; for doctorate, GRE General Test, BSN, RN license, minimum GPA of 3.5, 3 letters of recommendation. Additional exam requirements/recommendations for international students: Required—TOEFL (minimum score 550 paper-based; 213 computer-based; 80 iBT). *Application deadline:* For fall admission, 8/1 priority date for domestic students, 8/1 for international students; for spring admission, 12/1 priority date for domestic students, 12/1 for international students. Applications are processed on a rolling basis. Application fee: $50. Electronic applications accepted. *Expenses:* Tuition, state resident: full-time $16,402; part-time $665 per credit. Tuition, nonresident: full-time $28,694; part-time $1175 per credit. Required fees: $690; $175 per term. Tuition and fees vary according to program. *Unit head:* Dr. Helen Burns, Associate Dean for Clinical Education, 412-624-6616, Fax: 412-624-2401, E-mail: burnsh@pitt.edu. *Application contact:* Laurie Lapsley, Administrator of Graduate Student Services, 412-624-9670, Fax: 412-624-2409, E-mail: lapsleyl@pitt.edu.

University of Puerto Rico, Medical Sciences Campus, School of Nursing, San Juan, PR 00936-5067. Offers anesthesia (MSN); critical care nursing (MSN); family and community nursing (MSN); family nurse practitioner (MSN); mental health and psychiatric nursing (MSN); nursing (MSN). *Accreditation:* AACN; AANA/CANAEP. *Entrance requirements:* For master's, GRE or EXADEP, interview, Puerto Rico RN license or professional license for international students, general and specific point average, article analysis. Electronic applications accepted. *Faculty research:* HIV, health disparities, teen violence, women and violence, neurological disorders.

University of Rochester, School of Nursing, Rochester, NY 14642. Offers acute care nurse practitioner (MS); adult nurse practitioner (MS); adult psychiatric mental health nurse practitioner (MS); adult/geriatric nurse practitioner (MS); care of children and families/pediatric nurse practitioner (MS); care of children and families/pediatric nurse practitioner with pediatric behavioral health (MS); care of children and families/pediatric nurse practitioner/neonatal nurse practitioner (MS); child and adolescent psychiatric mental health nurse practitioner (MS); clinical nurse leader (MS); disaster response and emergency preparedness (MS); family nurse practitioner (MS); health care organization management and leadership (MS); health practice research (PhD); health promotion, education and technology (MS); nursing (Certificate). *Accreditation:* AACN; NLN (one or more programs are accredited). Part-time programs available. Postbaccalaureate distance learning degree programs offered (minimal on-campus study). *Faculty:* 26 full-time (24 women), 20 part-time/adjunct (15 women). *Students:* 50 full-time (45 women), 178 part-time (165 women); includes 33 minority (17 African Americans, 2 American Indian/Alaska Native, 10 Asian Americans or Pacific Islanders, 4 Hispanic Americans), 11 international. Average age 35. 56 applicants, 80% accepted, 35 enrolled. In 2009, 53 master's, 5 doctorates awarded. Terminal master's awarded for partial completion of doctoral program. *Degree requirements:* For master's, comprehensive exam or thesis; for doctorate, thesis/dissertation. *Entrance requirements:* For master's, BS in nursing, minimum GPA of 3.0, course work in statistics; for doctorate, GRE General Test, MS in nursing, minimum GPA of 3.5; for Certificate, MS in nursing. Additional exam requirements/recommendations for international students: Recommended—TOEFL (minimum score 560 paper-based; 230 computer-based; 88 iBT). *Application deadline:* For fall admission, 11/1 priority date for domestic and international students. Application fee: $50. *Financial support:* In 2009–10, 53 students received support, including 14 fellowships with full and partial tuition reimbursements available (averaging $17,497 per year); scholarships/grants, traineeships, health care benefits, tuition waivers (partial), and unspecified assistantships also available. Support available to part-time students. Financial award application deadline: 6/30. *Faculty research:* Clinical research in aging, managing asthma in children, interventions to improve outcomes in critically ill children and their mothers, nurse home visitation studies, medical device evaluation, critical care clinical studies, high risk behavior and prevention, palliative care, pregnancy-related weight gain. Total annual research expenditures: $4.8 million. *Unit head:* Dr. Kathy P. Parker, Dean, 585-273-5639, Fax: 585-273-1268, E-mail: kathy_parker@urmc.rochester.edu. *Application contact:* Elaine Andolina, Director of Admissions, 585-275-2375, Fax: 585-756-8299, E-mail: elaine_andolina@urmc.rochester.edu.

University of South Africa, College of Human Sciences, Pretoria, South Africa. Offers adult education (M Ed); African languages (MA, PhD); African politics (MA, PhD); Afrikaans (MA, PhD); ancient history (MA, PhD); ancient Near Eastern studies (MA, PhD); anthropology (MA, PhD); applied linguistics (MA, PhD); Arabic (MA, PhD); archaeology (MA); art history (MA); Biblical archaeology (MA); Biblical studies (M Th, D Th, PhD); Christian spirituality (M Th, D Th); church history (M Th, D Th); classical studies (MA, PhD); clinical psychology (MA); communication (MA, PhD); comparative education (M Ed, Ed D); consulting psychology (D Admin, D Com, PhD); curriculum studies (M Ed, Ed D); development studies (M Admin, MA, D Admin, PhD); didactics (M Ed, Ed D); education (M Tech); education management (M Ed, Ed D); educational psychology (M Ed); English (MA); environmental education (M Ed); French (MA, PhD); German (MA, PhD); Greek (MA); guidance and counseling (M Ed); health studies (MA, PhD), including health sciences education (MA), health services management (MA), medical and surgical nursing science (critical care general) (MA), midwifery and neonatal nursing science (MA), trauma and emergency care (MA); history (MA, PhD); history of education (Ed D); inclusive education (M Ed, Ed D); information and communications technology policy and regulation (MA); information science (MA, MIS, PhD); international politics (MA, PhD); Islamic studies (MA, PhD); Italian (MA, PhD); Judaica (MA, PhD); linguistics (MA, PhD); mathematical education (M Ed); mathematics education (MA); missiology (M Th, D Th); modern Hebrew (MA, PhD); musicology (MA, MMus, D Mus, PhD); natural science education (M Ed); New Testament (M Th, D Th); Old Testament (D Th); pastoral therapy (M Th, D Th); philosophy

(MA); philosophy of education (M Ed, Ed D); politics (MA, PhD); Portuguese (MA, PhD); practical theology (M Th, D Th); psychology (MA, MS, PhD); psychology of education (M Ed, Ed D); public health (MA); religious studies (MA, D Th, PhD); Romance languages (MA); Russian (MA, PhD); Semitic languages (MA, PhD); social behavior studies in HIV/AIDS (MA); social science (mental health) (MA); social science in development studies (MA); social science in psychology (MA); social science in social work (MA); social science in sociology (MA); social work (MSW, DSW, PhD); socio-education (M Ed, Ed D); sociolinguistics (MA); sociology (MA, PhD); Spanish (MA, PhD); systematic theology (M Th, D Th); TESOL (teaching English to speakers of other languages) (MA); theological ethics (M Th, D Th); theory of literature (MA, PhD); urban ministries (D Th); urban ministry (M Th).

University of South Carolina, The Graduate School, College of Nursing, Program in Advanced Practice Clinical Nursing, Columbia, SC 29208. Offers acute care nurse practitioner (Certificate); advanced practice clinical nursing (MSN). *Accreditation:* AACN. Part-time programs available. Postbaccalaureate distance learning degree programs offered (minimal on-campus study). *Entrance requirements:* For master's, master's degree in nursing, RN license; for Certificate, MSN. Additional exam requirements/recommendations for international students: Required—TOEFL (minimum score 570 paper-based; 213 computer-based). Electronic applications accepted. *Faculty research:* Systems research, evidence based practice, breast cancer, violence.

University of South Carolina, The Graduate School, College of Nursing, Program in Clinical Nursing, Columbia, SC 29208. Offers acute care clinical specialist (MSN); acute care nurse practitioner (MSN); women's health nurse practitioner (MSN). *Accreditation:* AACN. Part-time programs available. *Degree requirements:* For master's, thesis or alternative. *Entrance requirements:* For master's, GRE General Test or MAT, BS in nursing, RN licensure. Additional exam requirements/recommendations for international students: Required—TOEFL (minimum score 570 paper-based; 230 computer-based). Electronic applications accepted. *Faculty research:* Systems research, evidence based practice, breast cancer, violence.

University of Virginia, School of Nursing, Charlottesville, VA 22903. Offers acute and specialty care (MSN); acute care nurse practitioner (MSN); clinical nurse leadership (MSN); community-public health leadership (MSN); nursing (DNP, PhD); psychiatric mental health counseling (MSN); MSN/MBA. *Accreditation:* AACN. Part-time programs available. *Faculty:* 50 full-time (47 women), 4 part-time/adjunct (3 women). *Students:* 158 full-time (135 women), 118 part-time (117 women); includes 41 minority (30 African Americans, 1 American Indian/Alaska Native, 4 Asian Americans or Pacific Islanders, 6 Hispanic Americans), 4 international. Average age 36. 302 applicants, 48% accepted, 106 enrolled. In 2009, 84 master's, 12 doctorates awarded. *Degree requirements:* For doctorate, comprehensive exam (for some programs), capstone project (DNP), dissertation (PhD). *Entrance requirements:* For master's, GRE General Test, MAT; for doctorate, GRE General Test. Additional exam requirements/recommendations for international students: Required—TOEFL, IELTS. *Application deadline:* Applications are processed on a rolling basis. Application fee: $60. Electronic applications accepted. *Expenses:* Contact institution. *Financial support:* Fellowships, research assistantships, teaching assistantships, Federal Work-Study and scholarships/grants available. Financial award applicants required to submit FAFSA. *Unit head:* Dorrie K. Fontaine, Dean, 434-924-0141, Fax: 434-982-1809. *Application contact:* Clay Hysell, Assistant Dean for Graduate Student Services, 434-924-0141, Fax: 434-982-1809, E-mail: nur-osa@virginia.edu.

Vanderbilt University, School of Nursing, Nashville, TN 37240. Offers adult acute care nurse practitioner (MSN); adult nurse practitioner/cardiovascular disease management and prevention (MSN); adult nurse practitioner/palliative care (MSN); clinical management (clinical nurse leader/specialist) (MSN); emergency nurse practitioner (MSN); family nurse practitioner (MSN); gerontology nurse practitioner (MSN); health systems management (MSN); neonatal nurse practitioner (MSN); nurse midwifery (MSN); nurse midwifery/family nurse practitioner (MSN); nursing informatics (MSN); nursing practice (DNP); nursing science (PhD); nutrition (MS); pediatric acute care nurse practitioner (MSN); pediatric primary care nurse practitioner (MSN); psychiatric-mental health nurse practitioner (MSN); women's health nurse practitioner (MSN), including urogynecology; women's health nurse practitioner/adult nurse practitioner (MSN); MSN/M Div; MSN/MTS. *Accreditation:* ACNM/DOA; NLN (one or more programs are accredited). Part-time programs available. Postbaccalaureate distance learning degree programs offered (minimal on-campus study). *Faculty:* 118 full-time (102 women), 429 part-time/adjunct (309 women). *Students:* 484 full-time (435 women), 319 part-time (284 women); includes 84 minority (55 African Americans, 4 American Indian/Alaska Native, 10 Asian Americans or

Pacific Islanders, 15 Hispanic Americans), 16 international. Average age 32. 900 applicants, 65% accepted, 433 enrolled. In 2009, 303 master's, 1 doctorate awarded. *Degree requirements:* For doctorate, comprehensive exam, thesis/dissertation. *Entrance requirements:* For master's, GRE General Test, minimum B average in undergraduate course work, 3 letters of recommendation; for doctorate, GRE General Test, interview, 3 letters of recommendation from doctorally-prepared faculty, MSN, essay. Additional exam requirements/recommendations for international students: Required—TOEFL. *Application deadline:* For fall admission, 12/1 priority date for domestic and international students. Applications are processed on a rolling basis. Application fee: $50. *Expenses:* Contact institution. *Financial support:* In 2009–10, 389 students received support, including 1 research assistantship (averaging $5,000 per year); teaching assistantships, scholarships/grants, health care benefits, and tuition waivers also available. Support available to part-time students. Financial award application deadline: 3/15; financial award applicants required to submit FAFSA. *Faculty research:* Lymphedema, palliative care and bereavement, health services research including workforce, safety and quality of care, gerontology, better birth outcomes including nutrition. Total annual research expenditures: $1.4 million. *Unit head:* Dr. Colleen Conway-Welch, Dean, 615-343-8776, Fax: 615-343-7711, E-mail: colleen.conway-welch@vanderbilt.edu. *Application contact:* Cheryl Feldner, Assistant Director of Admissions, 615-322-3800, Fax: 615-343-0333, E-mail: cheryl.feldner@vanderbilt.edu.

Virginia Polytechnic Institute and State University, Graduate School, College of Agriculture and Life Sciences, Department of Agricultural and Applied Economics, Blacksburg, VA 24061. Offers agribusiness (MS); agricultural economics (MS, PhD); applied economics (MS); developmental and international economics (PhD); econometrics (PhD); macro and micro economics (PhD); markets and industrial organizations (PhD); public and regional/urban economics (PhD); resource and environmental economics (PhD). *Faculty:* 22 full-time (5 women). *Students:* 33 full-time (18 women); includes 18 American Indian/Alaska Native, 1 Asian American or Pacific Islander, 1 international. Average age 28. 47 applicants, 43% accepted, 12 enrolled. In 2009, 13 master's, 3 doctorates awarded. *Entrance requirements:* For master's and doctorate, GRE, GMAT. Additional exam requirements/recommendations for international students: Required—TOEFL (minimum score 575 paper-based; 213 computer-based). *Application deadline:* For fall admission, 5/15 for international students; for spring admission, 10/15 for international students. Applications are processed on a rolling basis. Application fee: $65. Electronic applications accepted. *Expenses:* Tuition, area resident: Full-time $10,228; part-time $459 per credit hour. Tuition, nonresident: full-time $17,892; part-time $865 per credit hour. Required fees: $1966; $451 per semester. *Financial support:* In 2009–10, 1 fellowship with full tuition reimbursement (averaging $20,000 per year), 21 research assistantships with full tuition reimbursements (averaging $21,611 per year), 8 teaching assistantships with full tuition reimbursements (averaging $13,481 per year) were awarded; career-related internships or fieldwork, Federal Work-Study, scholarships/grants, and unspecified assistantships also available. Financial award application deadline: 1/15. *Faculty research:* Rural development. Total annual research expenditures: $2.3 million. *Unit head:* Dr. Kevin Boyle, Dean, 540-231-6301, Fax: 540-231-7417, E-mail: kjboyle@vt.edu. *Application contact:* Bradford Mills, Contact, 540-231-6461, Fax: 540-231-7417, E-mail: bfmills@vt.edu.

Wayne State University, College of Nursing, Program in Adult Acute Care Nursing, Detroit, MI 48202. Offers MSN. *Accreditation:* AACN. Part-time programs available. *Degree requirements:* For master's, thesis or alternative. *Entrance requirements:* For master's, GRE General Test, minimum GPA of 2.8. Additional exam requirements/recommendations for international students: Required—TOEFL (minimum score 550 paper-based; 213 computer-based); Recommended—TWE (minimum score 6). Electronic applications accepted. *Faculty research:* Cardiovascular nursing with vulnerable populations, wound healing, symptom management.

Wright State University, School of Graduate Studies, College of Nursing and Health, Program in Nursing, Dayton, OH 45435. Offers acute care nurse practitioner (MS); administration of nursing and health care systems (MS); adult health (MS); child and adolescent health (MS); community health (MS); family nurse practitioner (MS); nurse practitioner (MS); school nurse (MS); MBA/MS. *Accreditation:* AACN. Part-time and evening/weekend programs available. *Degree requirements:* For master's, thesis or alternative. *Entrance requirements:* For master's, GRE General Test, BSN from NLN-accredited college, Ohio RN license. Additional exam requirements/recommendations for international students: Required—TOEFL. *Faculty research:* Clinical nursing and health, teaching, caring, pain administration, informatics and technology.

Adult Nursing

Allen College, Program in Nursing, Waterloo, IA 50703. Offers acute care nurse practitioner (MSN); adult nurse practitioner (MSN); adult psychiatric-mental health nurse practitioner (MSN); family nurse practitioner (MSN); gerontological nurse practitioner (MSN); health education (MSN); leadership in health care delivery (MSN). *Accreditation:* AACN; NLN. Part-time programs available. *Faculty:* 2 full-time (both women), 8 part-time/adjunct (all women). *Students:* 37 full-time (35 women), 103 part-time (99 women); includes 1 minority (Asian American or Pacific Islander). Average age 38. *Degree requirements:* For master's, thesis optional. *Entrance requirements:* For master's, minimum GPA of 3.0. Additional exam requirements/recommendations for international students: Required—TOEFL (minimum score 550 paper-based). *Application deadline:* For fall admission, 7/15 priority date for domestic students; for spring admission, 12/1 priority date for domestic students. Applications are processed on a rolling basis. Application fee: $50. Electronic applications accepted. *Expenses:* Tuition: Full-time $12,550; part-time $651 per credit hour. Required fees: $826; $65 per credit hour. One-time fee: $425. Tuition and fees vary according to course load. *Financial support:* Teaching assistantships, institutionally sponsored loans, scholarships/grants, and traineeships available. Support available to part-time students. Financial award application deadline: 8/15; financial award applicants required to submit FAFSA. *Faculty research:* Pain and aged, congestive heart failure. *Unit head:* Nancy Kramer, Dean, School of Nursing, 319-226-2040, Fax: 319-226-2070, E-mail: kramerna@ihs.org. *Application contact:* Michelle Koehn, Admissions Counselor, 319-226-2002, Fax: 319-226-2051, E-mail: koehnml@ihs.org.

Angelo State University, College of Graduate Studies, College of Nursing and Allied Health, Department of Nursing, San Angelo, TX 76909. Offers advanced practice registered nurse (MSN); nurse educator (MSN); nursing—RN to MSN (MSN). *Accreditation:* NLN. Part-time and evening/weekend programs available. *Faculty:* 7 full-time (all women). *Students:* 11 full-time (9 women), 41 part-time (38 women); includes 13 minority (3 African Americans, 4 Asian Americans or Pacific Islanders, 6 Hispanic Americans). Average age 41. 29 applicants, 93% accepted, 21 enrolled. In 2009, 13 master's awarded. *Degree requirements:* For master's, comprehensive exam. *Entrance requirements:* For master's, GRE General Test. Additional exam requirements/recommendations for international students: Required—TOEFL or IELTS. *Application deadline:* For fall admission, 7/15 priority date for domestic students, 6/10 for international students; for spring admission, 12/1 priority date for domestic students, 11/1 for international students. Applications are processed on a rolling basis. Application fee: $40 ($50 for international students). Electronic applications accepted. *Expenses:* Tuition, state resident: full-time $3396; part-time $142 per credit hour. Tuition, nonresident: full-time $10,152; part-time $423 per credit hour. Required fees: $1786; $36.25 per credit hour. $494 per semester. Full-time tuition and fees vary according to course load, degree level and program. *Financial support:* In 2009–10, 24 students received support. Career-related internships or fieldwork, Federal Work-Study, and scholarships/grants available. Support available to part-time students. Financial award application deadline: 3/1. *Unit head:* Dr. Susan S. Wilkinson, Department Head, 325-942-2060

Ext. 290, Fax: 325-942-2236, E-mail: susan.wilkinson@angelo.edu. *Application contact:* Dr. Molly J. Walker, Graduate Advisor, 325-942-2060 Ext. 246, Fax: 325-942-2236, E-mail: molly.walker@angelo.edu.

Bloomsburg University of Pennsylvania, School of Graduate Studies, College of Professional Studies, School of Health Sciences, Department of Nursing, Bloomsburg, PA 17815-1301. Offers adult and family nurse practitioner (MSN); adult health and illness (MSN); community health (MSN); nursing (MSN); nursing administration (MSN). *Accreditation:* AACN; AANA/CANAEP. *Degree requirements:* For master's, thesis. *Entrance requirements:* For master's, minimum QPA of 3.0. Additional exam requirements/recommendations for international students: Required—TOEFL. Electronic applications accepted. *Faculty research:* Cardiopulmonary nursing, cancer topics, women's health.

Boston College, William F. Connell School of Nursing, Chestnut Hill, MA 02467-3800. Offers adult health nursing (MS); community health nursing (MS); family health (MS); forensic nursing (MS); gerontology (MS); maternal/child health nursing (MS), including pediatric and women's health; nurse anesthesia (MS); nursing (PhD); palliative care (MS), including adult and pediatric; psychiatric-mental health nursing (MS); MBA/MS; MS/MA; MS/PhD. *Accreditation:* AACN; AANA/CANAEP (one or more programs are accredited). Part-time programs available. *Faculty:* 48 full-time (46 women), 31 part-time/adjunct (29 women). *Students:* 183 full-time (169 women), 147 part-time (140 women); includes 36 minority (15 African Americans, 2 American Indian/Alaska Native, 17 Asian Americans or Pacific Islanders, 2 Hispanic Americans), 7 international. Average age 29. 347 applicants, 53% accepted, 103 enrolled. In 2009, 79 master's, 7 doctorates awarded. *Degree requirements:* For master's, comprehensive exam, research project; for doctorate, comprehensive exam, thesis/dissertation, computer literacy exam or foreign language. *Entrance requirements:* For master's, bachelor's degree in nursing; for doctorate, GRE General Test, master's degree in nursing. Additional exam requirements/recommendations for international students: Required—TOEFL (minimum score 550 paper-based; 213 computer-based). *Application deadline:* For fall admission, 11/1 for domestic and international students; for winter admission, 12/31 for domestic and international students; for spring admission, 9/15 for domestic and international students. Applications are processed on a rolling basis. Application fee: $40. Electronic applications accepted. *Financial support:* In 2009–10, 83 students received support, including 12 fellowships with partial tuition reimbursements available (averaging $15,000 per year), 5 teaching assistantships (averaging $13,746 per year); research assistantships, Federal Work-Study, institutionally sponsored loans, scholarships/grants, traineeships, health care benefits, and tuition waivers (partial) also available. Support available to part-time students. Financial award application deadline: 3/1; financial award applicants required to submit FAFSA. *Faculty research:* Ethics, reduction of risk behaviors, support during chronic illness, violence, gerontology. Total annual research expenditures: $1.4 million. *Unit head:* Dr. Susan Gennaro, Dean, 617-552-4251, Fax: 617-552-0931, E-mail: susan.gennaro@bc.edu.

Adult Nursing

Boston College *(continued)*
Application contact: MaryBeth Crowley, Graduate Programs Assistant, 617-552-4928, Fax: 617-552-2121, E-mail: csongrad@bc.edu.

Case Western Reserve University, Frances Payne Bolton School of Nursing, Doctor of Nursing Practice Program, Cleveland, OH 44106. Offers acute care nurse practitioner (DNP); adult nurse practitioner (DNP); family nurse practitioner (DNP); gerontological nurse practitioner (DNP); graduate entry/pre-licensure option (DNP); medical-surgical nursing (DNP); midwifery/family nursing (DNP); neonatal nurse practitioner (DNP); pediatric nurse practitioner (DNP); post-licensure option (DNP); psychiatric-mental health nurse practitioner (DNP); women's health nurse practitioner (DNP). Graduate entry option allows baccalaureate-prepared college graduates from non-nursing backgrounds to earn certificate and MSN in addition to ND. Terminal master's awarded for partial completion of doctoral program. *Degree requirements:* For doctorate, thesis/dissertation. *Entrance requirements:* For doctorate, GRE General Test or MAT. *Faculty research:* Clinical nursing, acute care, gerontology, mental health, critical care.

Case Western Reserve University, Frances Payne Bolton School of Nursing, Master's Programs in Nursing, Nurse Practitioner Program, Cleveland, OH 44106. Offers acute care cardiovascular nursing (MSN); acute care nurse practitioner (MSN); acute care/flight nurse (MSN); adult nurse practitioner (MSN); family nurse practitioner (MSN); gerontological nurse practitioner (MSN); neonatal nurse practitioner (MSN); pediatric nurse practitioner (MSN); psychiatric-mental health nurse practitioner (MSN); women's health nurse practitioner (MSN). *Accreditation:* NLN. Part-time programs available. Postbaccalaureate distance learning degree programs offered (minimal on-campus study). *Degree requirements:* For master's, thesis optional. *Entrance requirements:* For master's, GRE General Test or MAT. Additional exam requirements/recommendations for international students: Required—TOEFL. *Faculty research:* Positive and negative mood states in parents of twins, effect of a carepath on chronic obstructive pulmonary disease home care.

The Catholic University of America, School of Nursing, Washington, DC 20064. Offers adult health specialist with functional role as nurse educator (MSN); adult nurse practitioner (MSN); community/public health nurse specialist educator (MSN); family nurse practitioner (MSN); geriatric nurse practitioner (MSN); immigrant, refugee, and global health clinical nurse specialist (MSN); nursing (DNP, PhD, Certificate); pediatric nurse practitioner (MSN); promoting healthy families in vulnerable communities (MSN); psychiatric-mental health nursing (MSN). *Accreditation:* AACN. Part-time programs available. *Faculty:* 15 full-time (all women), 43 part-time/adjunct (41 women). *Students:* 28 full-time (26 women), 75 part-time (73 women); includes 37 minority (27 African Americans, 6 Asian Americans or Pacific Islanders, 4 Hispanic Americans), 4 international. Average age 42. 84 applicants, 64% accepted, 30 enrolled. In 2009, 23 master's, 7 doctorates, 3 other advanced degrees awarded. *Degree requirements:* For master's, comprehensive exam, thesis optional; for doctorate, comprehensive exam, thesis/dissertation, minimum GPA of 3.0, oral proposal defense. *Entrance requirements:* For master's, 3 letters of recommendation, BA in nursing, RN registration, official copies of academic transcripts, some post-baccalaureate nursing experience; for doctorate, GRE General Test, BA in nursing, professional portfolio (including statements, resume, copy of RN license, 3 letters of recommendation, narrative description of clinical practice, proposal), copy of research/scholarly paper related to clinical nursing. Additional exam requirements/recommendations for international students: Required—TOEFL (minimum score 580 paper-based; 237 computer-based). *Application deadline:* For fall admission, 8/1 priority date for domestic students, 7/15 for international students; for spring admission, 12/1 priority date for domestic students, 10/15 for international students. Applications are processed on a rolling basis. Application fee: $55. Electronic applications accepted. *Expenses:* Tuition: Full-time $31,740; part-time $1245 per credit hour. Required fees: $50; $25 per semester hour. One-time fee: $425. *Financial support:* Fellowships, research assistantships, teaching assistantships, Federal Work-Study, scholarships/grants, tuition waivers (full and partial), and unspecified assistantships available. Financial award application deadline: 2/1; financial award applicants required to submit FAFSA. *Faculty research:* Community involvement in health care services, primary health care services, pediatrics, chronic illness, cardiovascular disease. Total annual research expenditures: $311,172. *Unit head:* Dr. Nalini N. Jairath, Dean, 202-319-5403, Fax: 202-319-6485, E-mail: cua-deanschoolofnursing@cua.edu. *Application contact:* Julie Schwing, Director of Graduate Admissions, 202-319-5057, Fax: 202-319-6533, E-mail: cua-admissions@cua.edu.

Clarkson College, Master of Science in Nursing Program, Omaha, NE 68131. Offers adult nurse practitioner (MSN, Post-Master's Certificate); family nurse practitioner (MSN, Post-Master's Certificate); nursing education (MSN, Post-Master's Certificate); nursing health care leadership (MSN, Post-Master's Certificate). *Accreditation:* NLN. Part-time and evening/weekend programs available. Postbaccalaureate distance learning degree programs offered (minimal on-campus study). *Degree requirements:* For master's, on-campus skills assessment (family nurse practitioner, adult nurse practitioner), comprehensive exam or thesis. *Entrance requirements:* For master's, minimum GPA of 3.0, 2 references, resume. Additional exam requirements/recommendations for international students: Required—TOEFL (minimum score 600 paper-based; 250 computer-based; 100 iBT). Electronic applications accepted.

College of Mount Saint Vincent, School of Professional and Continuing Studies, Department of Nursing, Riverdale, NY 10471-1093. Offers adult nurse practitioner (MSN, PMC); family nurse practitioner (MSN, PMC); nurse educator (PMC); nursing administration (MSN); nursing for the adult and aged (MSN). *Accreditation:* AACN. Part-time programs available. *Entrance requirements:* For master's, BSN, interview, RN license, minimum GPA of 3.0, letters of reference. Additional exam requirements/recommendations for international students: Required—TOEFL. *Expenses:* Contact institution.

College of Staten Island of the City University of New York, Graduate Programs, Department of Nursing, Program in Adult Health Nursing, Staten Island, NY 10314-6600. Offers MS, 6th Year Certificate. Part-time and evening/weekend programs available. *Faculty:* 4 full-time (all women), 4 part-time/adjunct (3 women). *Students:* 27 part-time (25 women); includes 8 minority (3 African Americans, 3 Asian Americans or Pacific Islanders, 2 Hispanic Americans), 2 international. Average age 36. 25 applicants, 100% accepted, 13 enrolled. In 2009, 7 master's, 1 other advanced degree awarded. *Degree requirements:* For master's, thesis optional. *Entrance requirements:* For master's, minimum undergraduate GPA of 3.0 in nursing courses, New York RN license, 2 professional references; for 6th Year Certificate, master's degree in nursing. Additional exam requirements/recommendations for international students: Required—TOEFL (minimum score 550 paper-based; 213 computer-based; 79 iBT). *Application deadline:* Applications are processed on a rolling basis. Application fee: $125. Electronic applications accepted. *Expenses:* Tuition, state resident: full-time $7360; part-time $310 per credit. Tuition, nonresident: part-time $575 per credit. Required fees: $378; $113 per semester. *Financial support:* In 2009–10, 1 student received support. Career-related internships or fieldwork, Federal Work-Study, scholarships/grants, and traineeships available. Support available to part-time students. Financial award applicants required to submit FAFSA. *Unit head:* Dr. Margaret Lunney, Coordinator, 718-982-3823, Fax: 718-982-3813, E-mail: lunney@mail.csi.cuny.edu. *Application contact:* Sasha Spence, Assistant Director of Graduate Recruitment and Admissions, 718-982-2699, Fax: 718-982-2500, E-mail: spence@mail.csi.cuny.edu.

Columbia University, School of Nursing, Program in Adult Nurse Practitioner, New York, NY 10032. Offers MS, Adv C. *Accreditation:* AACN. Part-time programs available. *Entrance requirements:* For master's, GRE General Test, BSN, 1 year of clinical experience (preferred); for Adv C, MSN. Electronic applications accepted.

Daemen College, Department of Nursing, Amherst, NY 14226-3592. Offers adult nurse practitioner (MS); nursing education (MS, Post Master's Certificate); nursing executive leadership (MS); nursing practice (DNP); palliative care nursing (MS, Post Master's Certificate). *Accreditation:* NLN. Part-time programs available. *Faculty:* 3 full-time (all women), 6 part-time/adjunct (all women). *Students:* 8 full-time (all women), 105 part-time (98 women); includes 17 minority (10 African Americans, 1 American Indian/Alaska Native, 3 Asian Americans or Pacific Islanders, 3 Hispanic Americans), 1 international. Average age 42. 66 applicants, 79% accepted,

37 enrolled. In 2009, 24 master's, 4 other advanced degrees awarded. *Degree requirements:* For master's, thesis or alternative. *Entrance requirements:* For master's, BN, 1 year medical/surgical experience, RN license and state registration, 1 course in statistics with minimum grade of 'C', 3 letters of recommendation, minimum GPA of 3.25, interview; for doctorate, MS in advance nursing practice; New York state RN license; personal goal statement; resume; interview; statistics course with minimum grade of 'C'; for Post Master's Certificate, master's degree in clinical area; RN license and current registration; one year of clinical experience; statistics course with minimum grade of 'C'. Additional exam requirements/recommendations for international students: Required—TOEFL (minimum score 500 paper-based; 173 computer-based; 61 iBT). *Application deadline:* For fall admission, 3/1 priority date for domestic and international students; for spring admission, 10/1 priority date for domestic and international students. Applications are processed on a rolling basis. Application fee: $25. Electronic applications accepted. *Expenses:* Tuition: Part-time $770 per credit hour. Tuition and fees vary according to course load, program and reciprocity agreements. *Financial support:* In 2009–10, 1 student received support. Institutionally sponsored loans and scholarships/grants available. Financial award application deadline: 2/15; financial award applicants required to submit FAFSA. *Faculty research:* Professional stress, client behavior, drug therapy, treatment modalities and pulmonary cancers, chemical dependency. *Unit head:* Dr. Mary Lou Rusin, Chair, 716-839-8387, Fax: 716-839-8403, E-mail: mrusin@daemen.edu. *Application contact:* Scott Rowe, Associate Director of Graduate Programs, 716-839-8225, Fax: 716-839-8229, E-mail: srowe@daemen.edu.

DePaul University, College of Liberal Arts and Sciences, Department of Nursing, Chicago, IL 60614. Offers adult nursing (MS); family nursing (MS); generalist nursing (MS); nurse anesthesia (MS). MS in nurse anesthesia offered jointly with Ravenswood Hospital Medical Center. *Accreditation:* AACN; AANA/CANAEP. Part-time and evening/weekend programs available. *Faculty:* 13 full-time (11 women), 12 part-time/adjunct (11 women). *Students:* 195 full-time (167 women), 43 part-time (41 women); includes 43 minority (9 African Americans, 1 American Indian/Alaska Native, 19 Asian Americans or Pacific Islanders, 14 Hispanic Americans), 2 international. Average age 39. 238 applicants, 46% accepted, 74 enrolled. In 2009, 70 master's awarded. *Degree requirements:* For master's, comprehensive exam (for some programs), thesis optional. *Entrance requirements:* For master's, GRE (if bachelor's GPA less than 3.2). Additional exam requirements/recommendations for international students: Required—TOEFL (minimum score 590 paper-based; 243 computer-based; 96 iBT) or IELTS (minimum score 7.5), Pearson Test of English (PTE). *Application deadline:* For fall admission, 3/1 priority date for domestic and international students; for winter admission, 8/15 priority date for domestic and international students. Application fee: $40. Electronic applications accepted. *Expenses:* Tuition: Full-time $37,525; part-time $620 per credit hour. *Financial support:* In 2009–10, 5 students received support, including 6 fellowships (averaging $1,500 per year); traineeships also available. Financial award applicants required to submit FAFSA. *Faculty research:* Children's health, women's health, health promotion. *Unit head:* Dr. Kay Thurn, Chair. *Application contact:* Ann Spittle, Director of Graduate Admissions, 773-325-7315, Fax: 773-325-7315, E-mail: graduatelas@depaul.edu.

DeSales University, Graduate Division, Programs in Nursing, Center Valley, PA 18034-9568. Offers adult advanced practice nurse specialist (MSN); certified nurse midwives (MSN); certified nurse practitioners (MSN); family nurse practitioner (MSN); nurse educator (MSN); MSN/MBA. *Accreditation:* NLN. Part-time programs available. *Students:* 67 part-time. In 2009, 218 master's awarded. *Degree requirements:* For master's, thesis optional. *Entrance requirements:* For master's, GRE General Test, MAT, minimum B average in undergraduate course work, health assessment course or equivalent, course work in statistics. Additional exam requirements/recommendations for international students: Required—TOEFL. *Application deadline:* Applications are processed on a rolling basis. Application fee: $35. Electronic applications accepted. *Expenses:* Tuition: Full-time $17,500; part-time $665 per credit. Full-time tuition and fees vary according to program. Part-time tuition and fees vary according to course load. *Financial support:* Applicants required to submit FAFSA. *Faculty research:* Women's health, theory validation, needs of homeless, behavior risk evaluation, wound healing. *Unit head:* Dr. Carol Gullo Mest, Director, 610-282-1100 Ext. 1394, Fax: 610-282-2091, E-mail: carol.mest@desales.edu. *Application contact:* Caryn Stopper, Director of Graduate Admissions, 610-282-1100 Ext. 1768, Fax: 610-282-2254, E-mail: caryn.stopper@desales.edu.

Duke University, School of Nursing, Durham, NC 27708-0586. Offers adult acute care (Certificate); adult cardiovascular (Certificate); adult oncology (Certificate); adult primary care (Certificate); clinical nurse specialist (MSN), including adult oncology, gerontology, neonatal, pediatric; clinical research management (MSN, Certificate); family (Certificate); gerontology (Certificate); health and nursing ministries (MSN, Certificate); health systems leadership and outcomes (Certificate); neonatal (Certificate); neonatal/pediatric in rural health (MSN, Certificate); nurse anesthetist (MSN, Certificate); nurse practitioner (MSN), including adult acute care, adult cardiovascular, adult oncology, adult primary care, family, gerontology, neonatal, pediatric, pediatric acute care; nursing (DNP, PhD); nursing and healthcare leadership (MSN); nursing education (MSN); nursing informatics (MSN, Certificate); pediatric (Certificate); pediatric acute care (Certificate); MBA/MSN; MSN/MCM. *Accreditation:* AACN; AANA/CANAEP. Part-time programs available. Postbaccalaureate distance learning degree programs offered (minimal on-campus study). *Faculty:* 45 full-time (41 women), 169 part-time/adjunct (150 women). *Students:* 213 full-time (179 women), 116 part-time (105 women); includes 37 minority (17 African Americans, 13 Asian Americans or Pacific Islanders, 7 Hispanic Americans), 9 international. Average age 36. 234 applicants, 53% accepted, 97 enrolled. In 2009, 142 master's, 24 other advanced degrees awarded. Terminal master's awarded for partial completion of doctoral program. *Degree requirements:* For master's, thesis optional; for doctorate, Capstone Project. *Entrance requirements:* For master's, GRE General Test, 1 year of nursing experience, BSN, minimum GPA of 3.0, previous course work in statistics; for doctorate, GRE for BSN prepared, BSN or MSN, minimum GPA of 3.0. Portfolio; for Certificate, MSN. Additional exam requirements/recommendations for international students: Required—TOEFL (minimum score 550 paper-based; 213 computer-based), Commission on Graduates of Foreign Nursing Schools exam. *Application deadline:* For fall admission, 7/2 priority date for domestic and international students; for spring admission, 11/15 priority date for domestic and international students. Applications are processed on a rolling basis. Application fee: $50. Electronic applications accepted. *Expenses:* Contact institution. *Financial support:* Career-related internships or fieldwork, institutionally sponsored loans, scholarships/grants, traineeships, and tuition waivers (partial) available. Support available to part-time students. Financial award application deadline: 4/1; financial award applicants required to submit FAFSA. *Faculty research:* Cardiovascular disease, caregiver skill training, data mining, prostate cancer, neonatal immune system. Total annual research expenditures: $3.5 million. *Unit head:* Dr. Catherine L. Gilliss, Dean/Vice Chancellor for Nursing Affairs, 919-684-9444, Fax: 919-684-9414, E-mail: gilli025@mc.duke.edu. *Application contact:* Bebe T. Mills, Director of Admissions, 919-684-9151, Fax: 919-668-4693, E-mail: mills031@mc.duke.edu.

Eastern Michigan University, Graduate School, College of Health and Human Services, School of Nursing, Ypsilanti, MI 48197. Offers nursing (MSN); quality improvement in health care systems (Graduate Certificate); teaching in health care systems (MSN, Graduate Certificate). *Accreditation:* AACN. Part-time and evening/weekend programs available. Postbaccalaureate distance learning degree programs offered (minimal on-campus study). *Faculty:* 21 full-time (19 women). *Students:* 14 full-time (all women), 45 part-time (38 women); includes 17 minority (14 African Americans, 3 Asian Americans or Pacific Islanders), 3 international. Average age 42. 23 applicants, 65% accepted, 11 enrolled. In 2009, 15 master's, 19 other advanced degrees awarded. *Degree requirements:* For master's, thesis optional. *Entrance requirements:* For master's, GRE General Test, Michigan RN license. Additional exam requirements/recommendations for international students: Required—TOEFL. *Application deadline:* Applications are processed on a rolling basis. Application fee: $35. Tuition and fees vary according to course level. *Financial support:* In 2009–10, 2 research assistantships with full tuition reimbursements (averaging $8,400 per year) were awarded; fellowships, teaching assistantships with full tuition reimbursements, career-related internships or fieldwork, Federal Work-Study, institutionally sponsored loans, scholarships/grants, tuition waivers (partial), and

unspecified assistantships also available. Support available to part-time students. Financial award applicants required to submit FAFSA. *Unit head:* Dr. Betty Beard, Director, 734-487-2310, Fax: 734-487-9646, E-mail: bbeard@emich.edu. *Application contact:* Dr. Barbara Scheffer, MSN Coordinator, 734-487-2310, Fax: 734-487-9646, E-mail: bscheffer@emich.edu.

Emory University, Nell Hodgson Woodruff School of Nursing, Atlanta, GA 30322-1100. Offers adult and elder health advanced practice nursing (MSN), including acute care, adult nurse practitioner, gerontological nurse practitioner; emergency nurse practitioner (MSN); family nurse practitioner (MSN); family nurse-midwife (MSN); nurse midwifery (MSN); pediatric nurse practitioner acute and primary care (MSN); public health nursing leadership (MSN); women's health nurse practitioner (MSN); women's health title x (MSN); women's health/adult health nurse practitioner (MSN); MSN/MPH. *Accreditation:* AACN; ACNM/DOA (one or more programs are accredited). Part-time programs available. *Faculty:* 30 full-time (29 women), 11 part-time/adjunct (10 women). *Students:* 110 full-time (106 women), 53 part-time (51 women); includes 49 minority (35 African Americans, 2 American Indian/Alaska Native, 10 Asian Americans or Pacific Islanders, 2 Hispanic Americans), 4 international. Average age 32. 182 applicants, 63% accepted, 86 enrolled. In 2009, 81 master's awarded. *Entrance requirements:* For master's, GRE General Test or MAT, minimum GPA of 3.0, BS in nursing from an accredited institution, RN license and additional course work, 3 letters of recommendation. Additional exam requirements/recommendations for international students: Required—TOEFL (minimum score 600 paper-based; 100 iBT). *Application deadline:* For fall admission, 1/15 priority date for domestic and international students; for spring admission, 10/1 priority date for domestic and international students. Applications are processed on a rolling basis. Application fee: $50. Electronic applications accepted. *Expenses:* Contact institution. *Financial support:* In 2009–10, 14 fellowships (averaging $28,000 per year) were awarded; career-related internships or fieldwork, Federal Work-Study, institutionally sponsored loans, and scholarships/grants also available. Support available to part-time students. Financial award application deadline: 3/1; financial award applicants required to submit CSS PROFILE or FAFSA. *Faculty research:* Older adult falls and injuries, minority health issues, cardiac symptoms and quality of life, bio-ethics and decision making, menopausal issues. *Unit head:* Dr. Linda McCauley, Dean, 404-727-7976, Fax: 404-727-9800, E-mail: linda.mccauley@emory.edu. *Application contact:* Katie Kennedy, Associate Director for Admission and Financial Aid, 404-727-7980, Fax: 404-727-8509, E-mail: admit@nursing.emory.edu.

See Close-Up on page 1613.

Felician College, Program in Nursing, Lodi, NJ 07644-2117. Offers adult health nurse (MSN, PMC); family practice nurse (MSN, PMC); nursing (MSN); nursing education (MSN). *Accreditation:* AACN. Part-time and evening/weekend programs available. Postbaccalaureate distance learning degree programs offered (no on-campus study). *Students:* 4 full-time (all women), 74 part-time (64 women); includes 18 minority (10 African Americans, 5 Asian Americans or Pacific Islanders, 3 Hispanic Americans). Average age 42. 29 applicants, 90% accepted, 24 enrolled. *Degree requirements:* For master's, scholarly project. *Entrance requirements:* For master's, BS in nursing or equivalent, minimum GPA of 3.0, 2 letters of recommendation, RN license; for PMC, RN license, minimum GPA of 2.75. Additional exam requirements/recommendations for international students: Recommended—TOEFL (minimum score 550 paper-based; 213 computer-based). *Application deadline:* Applications are processed on a rolling basis. Application fee: $40. *Financial support:* In 2009–10, 10 students received support. Traineeships available. Financial award applicants required to submit FAFSA. *Faculty research:* Anxiety and fear, curriculum innovation, health promotion. *Unit head:* Dr. Muriel Shore, Dean, Division of Health Sciences, 201-559-6030, E-mail: shorem@felician.edu. *Application contact:* Dr. Wendy Lin-Cook, Director of Adult and Graduate Admission, 201-559-6077, Fax: 201-559-6138, E-mail: adultandgraduate@felician.edu.

See Close-Up on page 1615.

The George Washington University, School of Medicine and Health Sciences, Health Sciences Programs, Washington, DC 20052. Offers adult nurse practitioner (MSN, Post Master's Certificate); clinical practice management (MSHS); clinical research administration (MSHS); clinical research administration for nurses (MSN); emergency services management (MSHS); end-of-life care (MSHS, MSN); family nurse practitioner (MSN, Post Master's Certificate); immunohematology (MSHS); nursing (DNP); nursing leadership and management (MSN); physical therapy (DPT); physician assistant (MSHS); MSHS/MPH. Postbaccalaureate distance learning degree programs offered (no on-campus study). *Students:* 270 full-time (220 women), 491 part-time (406 women); includes 176 minority (83 African Americans, 5 American Indian/Alaska Native, 62 Asian Americans or Pacific Islanders, 26 Hispanic Americans), 26 international. Average age 35. 1,059 applicants, 47% accepted, 292 enrolled. In 2009, 155 master's, 22 doctorates, 75 other advanced degrees awarded. *Entrance requirements:* Additional exam requirements/recommendations for international students: Required—TOEFL (minimum score 550 paper-based; 213 computer-based). *Application deadline:* Applications are processed on a rolling basis. Application fee: $60. *Expenses:* Contact institution. *Unit head:* Jean E. Johnson, Senior Associate Dean, 202-994-3725, E-mail: jejohns@gwu.edu. *Application contact:* Joke Ogundiran, Director of Admission, 202-994-1668, Fax: 202-994-0870, E-mail: jokeogun@gwu.edu.

Georgia College & State University, Graduate School, College of Health Sciences, Graduate Nursing Program, Milledgeville, GA 31061. Offers adult health (MSN); family nurse practitioner (MSN); nursing administration (MSN); MSN/MBA. *Accreditation:* NLN. Part-time and evening/weekend programs available. *Faculty:* 22 full-time (21 women). *Students:* 13 full-time (all women), 44 part-time (42 women); includes 8 minority (all African Americans), 1 international. Average age 35. 22 applicants, 91% accepted, 18 enrolled. In 2009, 18 master's awarded. *Degree requirements:* For master's, comprehensive exam, thesis optional. *Entrance requirements:* For master's, GMAT, GRE General Test, or MAT, bachelor's degree in nursing, RN license. Additional exam requirements/recommendations for international students: Recommended—TOEFL (minimum score 550 paper-based; 213 computer-based; 79 iBT). *Application deadline:* For fall admission, 7/1 priority date for domestic students. Applications are processed on a rolling basis. Application fee: $40. Electronic applications accepted. *Expenses:* Tuition, area resident: Part-time $241 per credit hour. Tuition, state resident: full-time $4338. Tuition, nonresident: full-time $17,352; part-time $964 per credit hour. Required fees: $609 per semester. Tuition and fees vary according to course load and campus/location. *Financial support:* In 2009–10, 1 research assistantship with full tuition reimbursement was awarded; unspecified assistantships also available. Financial award applicants required to submit FAFSA. *Unit head:* Dr. Judith Malachowski, Director, School of Nursing, 478-445-5122, E-mail: judith.malachowski@gcsu.edu. *Application contact:* Lora Crowe, Coordinator, 478-445-5122, E-mail: lora.crowe@gcsu.edu.

Georgia State University, College of Health and Human Sciences, Byrdine F. Lewis School of Nursing, Atlanta, GA 30302-3083. Offers adult health (MS); adult health nursing (Certificate); child health (MS); family nurse practitioner (MS, Certificate); health promotion, protection and restoration (PhD); perinatal/women's health (MS); psychiatric mental health nursing (Certificate); psychiatric/mental health (MS); women's health nursing (Certificate). *Accreditation:* AACN. Part-time and evening/weekend programs available. Postbaccalaureate distance learning degree programs offered (minimal on-campus study). *Degree requirements:* For master's, research activity; for doctorate, comprehensive exam, thesis/dissertation. *Entrance requirements:* For master's, MAT (preferred) or GRE, interview, RN license; for doctorate, GRE General Test. Additional exam requirements/recommendations for international students: Required—TOEFL (minimum score 550 paper-based; 213 computer-based). Electronic applications accepted. *Expenses:* Contact institution. *Faculty research:* Breast cancer prevention, sexually compulsive behaviors, health risks in minority youth, asthma treatment strategies, adolescent alcohol-related issues.

Goldfarb School of Nursing at Barnes-Jewish College, Goldfarb School of Nursing at Barnes-Jewish College, St Louis, MO 63110. Offers adult acute care nurse practitioner (MSN); adult nurse practitioner (MSN); neonatal nurse practitioner (MSN); nurse anesthesia (MSN); nurse educator (MSN); nurse executive (MSN). *Accreditation:* AACN; AANA/CANAEP. Part-time and evening/weekend programs available. Postbaccalaureate distance learning degree programs offered (minimal on-campus study). *Faculty:* 18 full-time (16 women), 3 part-time/adjunct (2 women). *Students:* 28 full-time (25 women), 81 part-time (73 women); includes 34 minority (27 African Americans, 6 Asian Americans or Pacific Islanders, 1 Hispanic American), 3 international. Average age 38. 60 applicants, 75% accepted, 40 enrolled. In 2009, 26 master's awarded. *Degree requirements:* For master's, thesis or alternative. *Entrance requirements:* For master's, minimum GPA of 3.0, 2 references, statistics course. Additional exam requirements/recommendations for international students: Required—TOEFL (minimum score 550 paper-based; 213 computer-based). *Application deadline:* For fall admission, 2/1 priority date for international students; for spring admission, 10/1 priority date for international students. Applications are processed on a rolling basis. Application fee: $150. *Financial support:* In 2009–10, 60 students received support, including 20 fellowships (averaging $4,000 per year), 4 research assistantships (averaging $5,000 per year); Federal Work-Study, institutionally sponsored loans, and scholarships/grants also available. Support available to part-time students. Financial award applicants required to submit FAFSA. *Faculty research:* HIV Stigma, HIV symptom management, palliative care with children and their families, heart disease prevention in Hispanic women, depression in the well elderly, alternative therapies in pre-term infants. *Unit head:* Dr. Michael L. Evans, Dean, 314-362-6289, Fax: 314-362-0984, E-mail: mevans@bjc.org. *Application contact:* Dr. Michael Ward, Associate Dean for Student Programs, 314-362-9155, Fax: 314-362-9250, E-mail: mward@bjc.org.

Grand Canyon University, College of Nursing and Health Sciences, Phoenix, AZ 85017-1097. Offers addiction counseling (MS); nursing (MS), including adult clinical nurse specialist, family nurse practitioner, nursing education, nursing leadership in health care system; professional counseling (MS). Part-time and evening/weekend programs available. Postbaccalaureate distance learning degree programs offered (no on-campus study). *Entrance requirements:* Additional exam requirements/recommendations for international students: Required—TOEFL (minimum score 575 paper-based; 233 computer-based; 90 iBT), IELTS (minimum score 7).

Grantham University, College of Arts and Sciences, Kansas City, MO 64153. Offers case management (MSN); health systems management (MSN); healthcare administration (MHA); nursing (MSN); nursing education (MSN); nursing informatics (MSN); nursing management and organizational leadership (MSN). Part-time and evening/weekend programs available. Postbaccalaureate distance learning degree programs offered (no on-campus study). In 2009, 48 master's awarded. *Degree requirements:* For master's, thesis (for some programs), capstone project. *Entrance requirements:* For master's, bachelor's degree from accredited degree-granting institution. Additional exam requirements/recommendations for international students: Required—TOEFL (minimum score 500 paper-based; 213 computer-based; 61 iBT). *Application deadline:* Applications are processed on a rolling basis. Electronic applications accepted. *Expenses:* Tuition: Part-time $265 per credit hour. One-time fee: $30 part-time. *Financial support:* Institutionally sponsored loans and scholarships/grants available. *Unit head:* Dr. Kim Humerickhouse, Dean, 800-955-2527, Fax: 816-595-5757, E-mail: admissions@grantham.edu. *Application contact:* Matthew Hawes, Vice President of Enrollment Management, 800-955-2527, Fax: 816-595-5757, E-mail: admissions@grantham.edu.

Gwynedd-Mercy College, School of Nursing, Gwynedd Valley, PA 19437-0901. Offers clinical nurse specialist (MSN), including gerontology, oncology, pediatrics; nurse practitioner (MSN), including adult health, pediatric health. *Accreditation:* NLN. *Degree requirements:* For master's, thesis optional. *Entrance requirements:* For master's, GRE General Test or MAT, current nursing experience, physical assessment, course work in statistics, BSN from an NLNAC accredited program, 2 letters of recommendation, personal interview. Additional exam requirements/recommendations for international students: Required—TOEFL (minimum score 575 paper-based). Electronic applications accepted. *Expenses:* Contact institution. *Faculty research:* Critical thinking, primary care, domestic violence, multiculturalism, nursing centers.

Hampton University, Graduate College, School of Nursing, Hampton, VA 23668. Offers advanced adult nursing (MS); community health nursing (MS); community mental health/psychiatric nursing (MS); family nursing (MS); gerontological nursing for the nurse practitioner (MS); pediatric nursing (MS); women's health nursing (MS). *Accreditation:* AACN; NLN. Part-time and evening/weekend programs available. *Degree requirements:* For master's, thesis optional. *Entrance requirements:* For master's, GRE General Test. *Faculty research:* Curriculum development, physical and mental assessment.

Hunter College of the City University of New York, Graduate School, Schools of the Health Professions, Hunter-Bellevue School of Nursing, Program in Adult Nurse Practitioner, New York, NY 10021-5085. Offers MS. *Accreditation:* AACN. *Faculty:* 11 full-time (10 women), 19 part-time/adjunct (2 women). *Students:* 1 (woman) full-time, 74 part-time (61 women); includes 25 minority (4 African Americans, 1 American Indian/Alaska Native, 14 Asian Americans or Pacific Islanders, 6 Hispanic Americans). Average age 34. 78 applicants, 62% accepted, 24 enrolled. In 2009, 30 master's awarded. *Degree requirements:* For master's, practicum. *Entrance requirements:* For master's, minimum GPA of 3.0, New York RN license, 2 years of professional practice experience, BSN. Additional exam requirements/recommendations for international students: Required—TOEFL. *Application deadline:* For fall admission, 4/1 for domestic students, 2/1 for international students; for spring admission, 11/1 for domestic students, 9/1 for international students. Applications are processed on a rolling basis. Application fee: $125. *Expenses:* Tuition, state resident: full-time $7360; part-time $310 per credit. Required fees: $250 per semester. *Financial support:* Federal Work-Study, scholarships/grants, and traineeships available. Support available to part-time students. Financial award application deadline: 5/1. *Faculty research:* Adult primary care, critical care. *Unit head:* Dr. Joanna Hofmann, Graduate Advisor, 212-481-4454, Fax: 212-481-5078, E-mail: jhofmann@hunter.cuny.edu. *Application contact:* William Zlata, Director for Graduate Admissions, 212-772-4482, Fax: 212-650-3336, E-mail: admissions@hunter.cuny.edu.

Indiana University–Purdue University Fort Wayne, College of Health and Human Services, Department of Nursing, Fort Wayne, IN 46805-1499. Offers adult nursing practice (MS); nursing administration (MS, Certificate); nursing education (MS); women's health nursing practice (MS). Part-time programs available. *Faculty:* 7 full-time (all women), 1 (woman) part-time/adjunct. *Students:* 5 full-time (all women), 34 part-time (32 women); includes 4 minority (3 African Americans, 1 American Indian/Alaska Native). Average age 37. 15 applicants, 93% accepted, 11 enrolled. *Entrance requirements:* For master's, GRE Writing Test (if GPA below 3.0), BS in nursing, eligibility for Indiana RN license, minimum GPA of 3.0, essay, copy of resume, three references, undergraduate course work in research and statistics within last 5 years. Additional exam requirements/recommendations for international students: Required—TOEFL (minimum score 550 paper-based; 213 computer-based; 77 iBT); Recommended—TWE. *Application deadline:* For fall admission, 5/1 priority date for domestic and international students. Applications are processed on a rolling basis. Application fee: $55 ($60 for international students). Electronic applications accepted. *Expenses:* Tuition, state resident: full-time $4595; part-time $255 per credit. Tuition, nonresident: full-time $10,963; part-time $609 per credit. Required fees: $528; $29.35 per credit. Tuition and fees vary according to course load. *Financial support:* In 2009–10, 11 teaching assistantships with partial tuition reimbursements (averaging $12,740 per year) were awarded; scholarships/grants also available. Support available to part-time students. Financial award application deadline: 3/1; financial award applicants required to submit FAFSA. *Unit head:* Dr. Carol Sternberger, Chair, 260-481-6816, Fax: 260-481-5767, E-mail: sternber@ipfw.edu. *Application contact:* Dr. Susan Ahrens, Graduate Program Director, 260-481-6816, Fax: 260-481-5767, E-mail: ahrenss@ipfw.edu.

Indiana University–Purdue University Indianapolis, School of Nursing, Indianapolis, IN 46202-2896. Offers acute care nurse practitioner (MSN); adult health clinical nurse specialist (MSN); adult health nursing (MSN), including adult clinical nurse specialist; adult nurse practitioner (MSN); adult psychiatric/mental health nursing (MSN); child psychiatric/mental health nursing (MSN); community health nursing (MSN); family nurse practitioner (MSN); neonatal nurse practitioner (MSN); nursing science (PhD); pediatric clinical nurse specialist (MSN); women's health nurse practitioner (MSN); MSN/MPA; MSN/MPH. *Accreditation:* AACN; NLN (one or more programs are accredited). Part-time programs available. *Faculty:* 85 full-time (82 women), 60 part-time/adjunct (all women). *Students:* 46 full-time (43 women), 369 part-time

Adult Nursing

Indiana University–Purdue University Indianapolis (continued)
(354 women); includes 30 minority (21 African Americans, 6 Asian Americans or Pacific Islanders, 3 Hispanic Americans), 5 international. Average age 39. 121 applicants, 82% accepted, 67 enrolled. In 2009, 106 master's, 3 doctorates awarded. Terminal master's awarded for partial completion of doctoral program. *Degree requirements:* For master's, thesis; for doctorate, thesis/dissertation. *Entrance requirements:* For master's, minimum GPA of 3.0, RN license; for doctorate, GRE General Test, minimum GPA of 3.0, MSN, RN license, graduate statistics course with B grade or better (not older than 3 years). Additional exam requirements/recommendations for international students: Required—TOEFL. *Application deadline:* For fall admission, 2/15 for domestic students; for spring admission, 9/15 for domestic students. Application fee: $55 ($65 for international students). *Financial support:* In 2009–10, 93 students received support, including 9 fellowships with full tuition reimbursements available (averaging $7,039 per year), 7 teaching assistantships with full tuition reimbursements available (averaging $5,300 per year); research assistantships with full tuition reimbursements available, Federal Work-Study, institutionally sponsored loans, scholarships/grants, and tuition waivers (full) also available. Support available to part-time students. Financial award application deadline: 5/1. *Faculty research:* Clinical science, health systems. Total annual research expenditures: $3 million. *Unit head:* Associate Dean for Graduate Programs, 317-274-2806, E-mail: nursing@iupui.edu. *Application contact:* Information Contact, 317-274-2806.

Inter American University of Puerto Rico, Arecibo Campus, Program in Nursing, Arecibo, PR 00614-4050. Offers community nursing (MS); critical care nursing (MS); primary care nursing (MS); surgical nursing (MS). *Entrance requirements:* For master's, EXADEP or GRE General Test or MAT, 2 letters of recommendation, bachelor's degree in nursing, minimum GPA of 2.5 in last 60 credits, minimum 1 year nursing experience, nursing license.

The Johns Hopkins University, School of Nursing, Nurse Practitioner Program, Baltimore, MD 21218-2699. Offers adult acute/critical care (MSN, Certificate); adult and pediatric primary care (MSN); adult or pediatric primary care (Certificate); emergency preparedness/disaster response (Certificate); family primary care (MSN, Certificate); women's health (Certificate). *Accreditation:* AACN; NLN (one or more programs are accredited). Part-time programs available. *Faculty:* 9 full-time (all women), 10 part-time/adjunct (all women). *Students:* 28 full-time (27 women), 75 part-time (73 women); includes 33 minority (14 African Americans, 16 Asian Americans or Pacific Islanders, 3 Hispanic Americans), 3 international. Average age 31. 223 applicants, 80% accepted, 29 enrolled. In 2009, 37 master's awarded. *Degree requirements:* For master's, thesis optional, scholarly project or portfolio. *Entrance requirements:* For master's, GRE, interview, minimum GPA of 3.0, BSN, Maryland RN license. Additional exam requirements/recommendations for international students: Required—TOEFL (minimum score 550 paper-based; 213 computer-based). *Application deadline:* For fall admission, 3/1 priority date for domestic and international students; for spring admission, 7/1 priority date for domestic and international students. Application fee: $75. Electronic applications accepted. *Expenses:* Contact institution. *Financial support:* In 2009–10, 25 students received support. Federal Work-Study, scholarships/grants, traineeships, and tuition waivers (partial) available. Support available to part-time students. Financial award application deadline: 3/1; financial award applicants required to submit FAFSA. *Faculty research:* Community outreach, primary care of underserved populations, substance abusing individuals, childhood violence, women's health. *Unit head:* Dr. Julie A. Stanik-Hutt, Director, Master's Programs, 410-502-0184, Fax: 410-955-7463, E-mail: jstanik1@son.jhmi.edu. *Application contact:* Mary O'Rourke, Director of Admissions and Student Services, 410-955-7548, Fax: 410-614-7086, E-mail: orourke@son.jhmi.edu.

Kent State University, College of Nursing, Kent, OH 44242-0001. Offers adult nurse practitioner (MSN); family nurse practitioner (MSN); geriatric nurse practitioner (MSN); nursing (PhD); nursing and health care management (MSN); nursing of adults (clinical nurse specialist) (MSN); pediatric nurse practitioner (MSN); psychiatric/mental health nursing (MSN); women's health nursing (MSN). *Accreditation:* AACN. Part-time programs available. *Degree requirements:* For master's, thesis optional; for doctorate, comprehensive exam, thesis/dissertation. *Entrance requirements:* For master's, GRE (if undergraduate GPA less than 3.0), minimum GPA of 2.75; for doctorate, GRE, MSN. Additional exam requirements/recommendations for international students: Required—TOEFL. Electronic applications accepted. *Expenses:* Contact institution. *Faculty research:* Women and violence, methodological specialties, osteoporosis in women, new caregivers and the elderly.

Lehman College of the City University of New York, Division of Natural and Social Sciences, Department of Nursing, Bronx, NY 10468-1589. Offers adult health nursing (MS); nursing of older adults (MS); parent-child nursing (MS); pediatric nurse practitioner (MS). *Accreditation:* AACN. Part-time and evening/weekend programs available. *Entrance requirements:* For master's, bachelor's degree in nursing, New York RN license.

Lewis University, College of Nursing and Health Professions, Program in Nursing, Romeoville, IL 60446. Offers adult nurse practitioner (MSN); nursing administration (MSN); nursing education (MSN). *Accreditation:* AACN. Part-time and evening/weekend programs available. Postbaccalaureate distance learning degree programs offered (no on-campus study). *Students:* 20 full-time (19 women), 172 part-time (169 women); includes 53 minority (32 African Americans, 11 Asian Americans or Pacific Islanders, 10 Hispanic Americans), 3 international. Average age 41. In 2009, 46 master's awarded. *Degree requirements:* For master's, clinical practicum. *Entrance requirements:* For master's, minimum undergraduate GPA of 2.75, degree in nursing, RN license, letter of recommendation, interview, resume or curriculum vitae. Additional exam requirements/recommendations for international students: Required—TOEFL (minimum score 550 paper-based; 213 computer-based). *Application deadline:* For fall admission, 5/1 priority date for international students; for spring admission, 11/15 priority date for international students. Applications are processed on a rolling basis. Application fee: $40. Electronic applications accepted. *Expenses:* Tuition: Full-time $6480; part-time $720 per credit. One-time fee: $40. Tuition and fees vary according to course load, degree level and program. *Financial support:* Federal Work-Study, scholarships/grants, tuition waivers (full and partial), and unspecified assistantships available. Financial award application deadline: 5/1; financial award applicants required to submit FAFSA. *Faculty research:* Cancer prevention, phenomenological methods, public policy analysis. Total annual research expenditures: $1,000. *Unit head:* Dr. Nan Yancey, Director, 815-838-0500 Ext. 5878, E-mail: yanceyna@lewisu.edu. *Application contact:* Kathy Lisak, Information Contact, 815-838-0500 Ext. 5355, E-mail: lisakka@lewisu.edu.

Loma Linda University, Department of Graduate Nursing, Program in Adult and Aging Family Nursing, Loma Linda, CA 92350. Offers MS. *Accreditation:* AACN. Part-time programs available. *Degree requirements:* For master's, thesis or alternative. *Entrance requirements:* For master's, GRE General Test, BSN, minimum GPA of 3.0, RN license. Additional exam requirements/recommendations for international students: Required—TOEFL. Electronic applications accepted. *Faculty research:* Coping, integration of research.

Long Island University, Brooklyn Campus, School of Nursing, Department of Adult Nurse Practitioner, Brooklyn, NY 11201-8423. Offers MS, Certificate. *Accreditation:* AACN. *Entrance requirements:* For master's, New York RN license, 2 letters of recommendation. Additional exam requirements/recommendations for international students: Required—TOEFL (minimum score 500 paper-based; 173 computer-based). Electronic applications accepted.

Louisiana State University Health Sciences Center, School of Nursing, New Orleans, LA 70112-2223. Offers advanced public/community health nursing (MN); clinical nurse specialist (MN); nurse anesthesia (MN); nurse practitioner (MN); nursing (DNS). *Accreditation:* AACN; AANA/CANAEP (one or more programs are accredited). Part-time programs available. *Degree requirements:* For master's, thesis optional; for doctorate, thesis/dissertation. *Entrance requirements:* For master's, GRE General Test, MAT, minimum GPA of 3.0; for doctorate, GRE General Test, minimum GPA of 3.5. Additional exam requirements/recommendations for international students: Required—TOEFL. *Faculty research:* Advanced clinical practice, nursing education, health, social support, nursing administration.

Loyola University Chicago, Graduate School, Marcella Niehoff School of Nursing, Adult Clinical Nurse Specialist Program, Chicago, IL 60660. Offers adult clinical nurse specialist (MSN, Certificate); cardiovascular health (Certificate); oncology nursing (Certificate). Part-time and evening/weekend programs available. Postbaccalaureate distance learning degree programs offered (minimal on-campus study). In 2009, 1 master's awarded. *Entrance requirements:* For master's, Illinois nursing license, BSN, minimum nursing GPA of 3.0, 3 letters of recommendation, 1,000 hours experience in area of specialty. *Expenses:* Tuition: Full-time $14,220; part-time $790 per credit hour. Required fees: $60 per semester hour. Tuition and fees vary according to program. *Unit head:* Dr. Meg Gulanick, Professor, 708-216-9687, Fax: 708-216-9555, E-mail: mgulani@luc.edu. *Application contact:* Dr. Vicki A. Keough, Associate Professor/Master's Program Director, 708-216-3582, Fax: 708-216-9555, E-mail: vkeough@luc.edu.

Loyola University Chicago, Graduate School, Marcella Niehoff School of Nursing, Adult Nurse Practitioner Program, Chicago, IL 60660. Offers adult nurse practitioner (MSN); cardiac health (Certificate). *Accreditation:* AACN. Part-time and evening/weekend programs available. *Students:* 5 full-time (all women), 53 part-time (52 women); includes 8 minority (3 African Americans, 3 Asian Americans or Pacific Islanders, 2 Hispanic Americans). Average age 36. 15 applicants, 53% accepted, 6 enrolled. In 2009, 18 master's awarded. *Degree requirements:* For master's, comprehensive exam or oral thesis defense. *Entrance requirements:* For master's, BSN, minimum nursing GPA of 3.0, Illinois nursing license, 3 letters of recommendation, 1000 hours experience before starting clinical. *Application deadline:* Applications are processed on a rolling basis. Application fee: $50. Electronic applications accepted. *Expenses:* Tuition: Full-time $14,220; part-time $790 per credit hour. Required fees: $60 per semester hour. Tuition and fees vary according to program. *Financial support:* Traineeships available. *Faculty research:* Menopause. *Unit head:* Dr. Marijo Letizia, Associate Professor, 708-216-9325, Fax: 708-216-9555, E-mail: mletizi@luc.edu. *Application contact:* Dr. Vicki A. Keough, Associate Professor/Master's Program Director, 708-216-3582, Fax: 708-216-9555, E-mail: vkeough@luc.edu.

Loyola University Chicago, Graduate School, Marcella Niehoff School of Nursing, Cardiovascular Health and Disease Management Clinical Nurse Specialist Program, Chicago, IL 60660. Offers MSN, Certificate. *Accreditation:* AACN. Part-time and evening/weekend programs available. *Students:* 4 full-time (all women), 24 part-time (23 women); includes 3 minority (2 African Americans, 1 Asian American or Pacific Islander). Average age 37. 4 applicants, 50% accepted, 2 enrolled. In 2009, 4 master's, 1 other advanced degree awarded. *Degree requirements:* For master's, comprehensive exam or oral thesis defense. *Entrance requirements:* For master's, Illinois nursing license, 3 letters of recommendation, minimum nursing GPA of 3.0, 1000 hours experience before starting clinical. *Application deadline:* Applications are processed on a rolling basis. Application fee: $50. Electronic applications accepted. *Expenses:* Tuition: Full-time $14,220; part-time $790 per credit hour. Required fees: $60 per semester hour. Tuition and fees vary according to program. *Financial support:* Traineeships available. Financial award application deadline: 3/1. *Faculty research:* Cardiac exercise. *Unit head:* Dr. Meg Gulanick, Professor, 708-216-9687, Fax: 708-216-9555, E-mail: mgulani@luc.edu. *Application contact:* Dr. Vicki A. Keough, Associate Professor/Master's Program Director, 708-216-3582, Fax: 708-216-9555, E-mail: vkeough@luc.edu.

Loyola University New Orleans, College of Social Sciences, School of Nursing, New Orleans, LA 70118-6195. Offers adult nurse practitioner (MSN); family nurse practitioner (MSN); health care systems management (MSN); nursing (MSN, DNP). *Accreditation:* NLN. Part-time and evening/weekend programs available. Postbaccalaureate distance learning degree programs offered. *Students:* 60 full-time (56 women), 543 part-time (490 women); includes 147 minority (116 African Americans, 4 American Indian/Alaska Native, 13 Asian Americans or Pacific Islanders, 14 Hispanic Americans), 1 international. Average age 43. 296 applicants, 97% accepted, 206 enrolled. In 2009, 153 master's awarded. *Degree requirements:* For doctorate, capstone project. *Entrance requirements:* For master's, BSN, Louisiana nursing license, 1 year of work experience in clinical nursing, minimum undergraduate GPA of 2.8, interview, resume. Additional exam requirements/recommendations for international students: Required—TOEFL (minimum score 550 paper-based; 213 computer-based). *Application deadline:* For fall admission, 8/1 priority date for domestic and international students; for winter admission, 12/15 priority date for domestic and international students; for spring admission, 5/15 priority date for domestic and international students. Applications are processed on a rolling basis. Application fee: $20. Electronic applications accepted. *Financial support:* Traineeships and Incumbent Workers Training Program grants available. Financial award application deadline: 5/1; financial award applicants required to submit FAFSA. *Faculty research:* Increasing compliance with treatment, patient satisfaction with care provided by nurse practitioners. *Unit head:* Ann H. Cary, Director, 800-488-6257, Fax: 504-865-3254, E-mail: nursing@loyno.edu. *Application contact:* Deborah Smith, Assistant to the Director, 504-865-2823, Fax: 504-865-3254, E-mail: dhsmith@loyno.edu.

Madonna University, Program in Nursing, Livonia, MI 48150-1173. Offers adult health: chronic health conditions (MSN); adult nurse practitioner (MSN); nursing administration (MSN); MSN/MSBA. *Accreditation:* AACN. Part-time programs available. *Degree requirements:* For master's, thesis or alternative. *Entrance requirements:* For master's, GRE General Test, Michigan nursing license. Electronic applications accepted. *Faculty research:* Coping, caring.

Marian University, School of Nursing, Fond du Lac, WI 54935-4699. Offers adult nurse practitioner (MSN); nurse educator (MSN). *Accreditation:* AACN. Part-time and evening/weekend programs available. *Faculty:* 6 full-time (5 women), 5 part-time/adjunct (4 women). *Students:* 40 full-time (37 women), 25 part-time (all women); includes 4 minority (3 Asian Americans or Pacific Islanders, 1 Hispanic American). Average age 39. 28 applicants, 89% accepted, 25 enrolled. In 2009, 21 master's awarded. *Degree requirements:* For master's, thesis, 675 clinical practicum hours. *Entrance requirements:* For master's, 3 letters of professional recommendation; undergraduate work in nursing research, statistics, health assessment. Additional exam requirements/recommendations for international students: Required—TOEFL (minimum score 525 paper-based). *Application deadline:* Applications are processed on a rolling basis. Application fee: $50. Electronic applications accepted. *Expenses:* Contact institution. *Financial support:* In 2009–10, 25 students received support. Institutionally sponsored loans and scholarships/grants available. Support available to part-time students. Financial award application deadline: 3/1; financial award applicants required to submit FAFSA. *Unit head:* Greta Kostac, Interim Assistant Dean, 920-923-8094, Fax: 920-923-8770, E-mail: gmkostac@marianuniversity.edu. *Application contact:* Dr. Greta Kostac, Director, 920-923-7603, Fax: 920-923-8770, E-mail: gmkostac@marianuniversity.edu.

Marquette University, Graduate School, College of Nursing, Milwaukee, WI 53201-1881. Offers adult nurse practitioner (Certificate); advanced practice nursing (MSN), including adult, children, neonatal nurse practitioner, nurse-midwifery, older adult; gerontological nurse practitioner (Certificate); neonatal nurse practitioner (Certificate); nurse-midwifery (Certificate); nursing (PhD); pediatric nurse practitioner (Certificate). *Accreditation:* AACN. Part-time and evening/weekend programs available. *Faculty:* 29 full-time (27 women), 43 part-time/adjunct (all women). *Students:* 115 full-time (105 women), 209 part-time (197 women); includes 28 minority (13 African Americans, 2 American Indian/Alaska Native, 8 Asian Americans or Pacific Islanders, 5 Hispanic Americans), 1 international. Average age 32. 143 applicants, 91% accepted, 86 enrolled. In 2009, 64 master's, 10 doctorates awarded. *Degree requirements:* For master's, comprehensive exam, thesis or alternative. *Entrance requirements:* For master's, GRE General Test, BSN, Wisconsin RN license. Additional exam requirements/recommendations for international students: Required—TOEFL. Application fee: $40. *Financial support:* In 2009–10, 6 research assistantships, 1 teaching assistantship were awarded; career-related internships or fieldwork, Federal Work-Study, institutionally sponsored loans, scholarships/grants, and tuition waivers (full and partial) also available. Support available to part-time students. Financial award application deadline: 2/15. *Faculty research:* Psychosocial adjustment to chronic illness, gerontology, reminiscence, health policy: uninsured and access, hospital care delivery systems. *Unit head:* Dr. Lea Acord, Dean, 414-288-3812, Fax: 414-288-1578. *Application contact:* Dr. Judy Miller, Director of Graduate Studies, 414-288-3810, Fax: 414-288-1578.

Maryville University of Saint Louis, School of Health Professions, Nursing Program, St. Louis, MO 63141-7299. Offers accelerated RN to MSN (MSN); adult nurse practitioner (MSN);

advanced practice nursing (DNP); family nurse practitioner (MSN); nursing education (MSN). *Accreditation:* AACN. Postbaccalaureate distance learning degree programs offered. *Students:* 23 full-time (22 women), 96 part-time (92 women); includes 6 African Americans, 6 Asian Americans or Pacific Islanders, 2 Hispanic Americans. Average age 36. In 2009, 23 master's awarded. *Degree requirements:* For master's, practicum. *Entrance requirements:* For master's, BSN, current licensure, minimum GPA of 3.0, 3 letters of recommendation, curriculum vitae. Additional exam requirements/recommendations for international students: Required—TOEFL (minimum score 550 paper-based). *Application deadline:* Applications are processed on a rolling basis. Application fee: $40 ($60 for international students). Electronic applications accepted. *Expenses:* Tuition: Full-time $20,384; part-time $627.50 per credit hour. Required fees: $100 per semester. *Financial support:* Federal Work-Study and campus employment available. Support available to part-time students. Financial award application deadline: 3/1; financial award applicants required to submit FAFSA. *Unit head:* Dr. Mary Curtis, Director, 314-529-9478, Fax: 314-529-9139, E-mail: mcurtis@maryville.edu. *Application contact:* Dr. Mary Curtis, Director, 314-529-9478, Fax: 314-529-9139, E-mail: mcurtis@maryville.edu.

Medical College of Georgia, School of Graduate Studies, Adult Acute/Critical Care Advanced Practice Nursing Program, Augusta, GA 30912. Offers MSN. *Entrance requirements:* For master's, GRE General Test or MAT, Georgia professional registered nurse licensure, 1 year RN experience. Additional exam requirements/recommendations for international students: Required—TOEFL (minimum score 550 paper-based; 213 computer-based; 79 iBT). Electronic applications accepted. Full-time tuition and fees vary according to campus/location, program and student level.

Medical University of South Carolina, College of Nursing, Adult Nurse Practitioner Program, Charleston, SC 29425. Offers MSN. Part-time programs available. Postbaccalaureate distance learning degree programs offered (minimal on-campus study). *Faculty:* 10 full-time (all women), 3 part-time/adjunct (2 women). *Students:* 5 full-time (all women), 6 part-time (all women); includes 1 minority (African American). Average age 36. 9 applicants, 89% accepted, 5 enrolled. In 2009, 4 master's awarded. *Degree requirements:* For master's, comprehensive exam (for some programs), thesis optional. *Entrance requirements:* For master's, BSN, course work in statistics, nursing license, minimum GPA of 3.0. Additional exam requirements/recommendations for international students: Required—TOEFL (minimum score 600 paper-based; 250 computer-based). *Application deadline:* For fall admission, 2/1 priority date for domestic and international students. Application fee: $85. Electronic applications accepted. *Financial support:* Federal Work-Study, scholarships/grants, and traineeships available. Support available to part-time students. Financial award application deadline: 3/10; financial award applicants required to submit FAFSA. *Faculty research:* Primary and palliative care, use of PDAs, diabetes. *Unit head:* Dr. Barbara J. Edlund, Lead Faculty, 843-792-4653, Fax: 843-792-2104, E-mail: edlundb@musc.edu. *Application contact:* Carolyn F. Page, Director, Student Services, 843-792-3844, Fax: 843-792-5395, E-mail: pagecf@musc.edu.

Medical University of South Carolina, College of Nursing, Doctor of Nursing Practice Program, Charleston, SC 29425. Offers adult nurse practitioner (DNP); family nurse practitioner (DNP); pediatric nurse practitioner (DNP); post-master's for advanced practice nurses (DNP). Part-time programs available. Postbaccalaureate distance learning degree programs offered (minimal on-campus study). *Faculty:* 20 full-time (19 women), 2 part-time/adjunct (1 woman). *Students:* 28 full-time (all women), 17 part-time (16 women); includes 7 minority (5 African Americans, 1 American Indian/Alaska Native, 1 Hispanic American). Average age 32. 99 applicants, 54% accepted, 45 enrolled. *Degree requirements:* For doctorate, thesis/dissertation (for some programs), practice inquiry project. *Entrance requirements:* For doctorate, BSN or MSN, minimum GPA of 3.0, course work in statistics, RN license, 3 references, interview (if requested). Additional exam requirements/recommendations for international students: Required—TOEFL (minimum score 600 paper-based; 250 computer-based). *Application deadline:* For fall admission, 2/1 priority date for domestic and international students. Application fee: $85. Electronic applications accepted. *Financial support:* Federal Work-Study and scholarships/grants available. Support available to part-time students. Financial award applicants required to submit FAFSA. *Faculty research:* Community partnerships, smoking cessation, gerontology, lateral violence in the workplace. *Unit head:* Dr. Robin L. Bissinger, Director of Graduate Programs, 843-792-0531, Fax: 843-792-9258, E-mail: bissinrl@musc.edu. *Application contact:* Carolyn F. Page, Director, Student Services, 843-792-3844, Fax: 843-792-5395, E-mail: pagecf@musc.edu.

Metropolitan State University, College of Nursing and Health Sciences, St. Paul, MN 55106-5000. Offers adult/geriatric nurse practitioner (MSN); family nurse practitioner (MSN); leadership and management (MSN); nursing (MSN, DNP); oral health care practitioner (MS); public health nursing leadership (MSN); women's health care nurse practitioner (MSN). *Accreditation:* AACN. Part-time programs available. *Degree requirements:* For master's, thesis or alternative; for doctorate, thesis/dissertation or alternative. *Entrance requirements:* For master's, GRE General Test, minimum GPA of 3.0, RN license, B.S./BAN degree; for doctorate, minimum GPA of 3.0; RN licensure, MSN degree. Additional exam requirements/recommendations for international students: Required—TOEFL (minimum score 550 paper-based; 213 computer-based). *Expenses:* Tuition, state resident: full-time $5520; part-time $276 per credit hour. Tuition, nonresident: full-time $11,040; part-time $552 per credit hour. Required fees: $209; $10 per credit hour. Tuition and fees vary according to degree level. *Faculty research:* Women's health, gerontology.

Molloy College, Graduate Nursing Program, Rockville Centre, NY 11571-5002. Offers adult nurse practitioner (Advanced Certificate); clinical nurse specialist: adult health (Advanced Certificate); family nurse practitioner (Advanced Certificate); nurse practitioner psychiatry (Advanced Certificate); nursing (MS); nursing administration (Advanced Certificate); nursing administration with informatics (Advanced Certificate); nursing education (Advanced Certificate); nursing informatics (Advanced Certificate); pediatric nurse practitioner (Advanced Certificate). *Accreditation:* AACN. Part-time and evening/weekend programs available. *Faculty:* 23 full-time (22 women), 5 part-time/adjunct (4 women). *Students:* 11 full-time (10 women), 405 part-time (377 women); includes 206 minority (124 African Americans, 52 Asian Americans or Pacific Islanders, 30 Hispanic Americans), 2 international. Average age 39. In 2009, 64 master's awarded. *Degree requirements:* For master's, thesis optional. *Entrance requirements:* For master's, 3 letters of reference, BS in nursing, minimum undergraduate GPA of 3.0; for Advanced Certificate, 3 letters of reference, master's degree in nursing. *Application deadline:* For fall admission, 9/2 priority date for domestic students; for spring admission, 1/20 priority date for domestic students. Applications are processed on a rolling basis. Application fee: $60. *Expenses:* Tuition: Part-time $765 per credit. Required fees: $340 per semester. *Financial support:* Research assistantships with partial tuition reimbursements, teaching assistantships with partial tuition reimbursements, institutionally sponsored loans, scholarships/grants, and unspecified assistantships available. Support available to part-time students. Financial award application deadline: 4/1; financial award applicants required to submit FAFSA. *Unit head:* Dr. Mary T. O'Shaughnessy, Acting Director, 516-678-5000, Fax: 516-678-9718, E-mail: moshaughnessy@molloy.edu. *Application contact:* Alina Haitz, Assistant Director of Graduate Admissions, 516-678-5000 Ext. 6399, Fax: 516-256-2247, E-mail: ahaitz@molloy.edu.

Monmouth University, Graduate School, The Marjorie K. Unterberg School of Nursing and Health Studies, West Long Branch, NJ 07764-1898. Offers adult nurse practitioner (MSN); adult psychiatric and mental health advanced practice nursing (MSN, Post-Master's Certificate); advanced practice nursing (Post-Master's Certificate); family nurse practitioner (MSN, Post-Master's Certificate); forensic nursing (MSN, Certificate); nursing (MSN); nursing administration (MSN, Post-Master's Certificate); nursing education (MSN, Post-Master's Certificate); school nursing (MSN, Certificate). *Accreditation:* AACN. Part-time and evening/weekend programs available. *Faculty:* 11 full-time (all women), 2 part-time/adjunct (both women). *Students:* 15 full-time (14 women), 183 part-time (178 women); includes 51 minority (14 African Americans, 3 American Indian/Alaska Native, 26 Asian Americans or Pacific Islanders, 8 Hispanic Americans), 1 international. Average age 41. 95 applicants, 99% accepted, 44 enrolled. In 2009, 36 master's awarded. *Degree requirements:* For master's, practicum (for some tracks). *Entrance requirements:* For master's, GRE General Test, RN license, 1 year of work experience,

minimum undergraduate GPA of 2.75. Additional exam requirements/recommendations for international students: Required—TOEFL (minimum score 550 paper-based; 213 computer-based; 79 iBT), IELTS (minimum score 5), Michigan English Language Assessment Battery (minimum score 77), Cambridge A, B, C. *Application deadline:* For fall admission, 7/15 priority date for domestic students, 6/1 for international students; for spring admission, 11/15 priority date for domestic students, 11/1 for international students. Applications are processed on a rolling basis. Application fee: $50. Electronic applications accepted. *Expenses:* Tuition: Part-time $773 per credit. Required fees: $157 per semester. *Financial support:* In 2009–10, 118 students received support, including 96 fellowships (averaging $1,308 per year), 4 research assistantships (averaging $3,610 per year); career-related internships or fieldwork, scholarships/grants, and unspecified assistantships also available. Support available to part-time students. Financial award applicants required to submit FAFSA. *Faculty research:* Relationship of undergraduate GPA and GRE to succeed in a graduate nursing program. *Unit head:* Dr. Janet Mahoney, Dean, 732-571-3443, Fax: 732-263-5131, E-mail: jmahoney@monmouth.edu. *Application contact:* Kevin Roane, Director, Office of Graduate Admission, 732-571-3452, Fax: 732-263-5123, E-mail: gradadm@monmouth.edu.

Mount Carmel College of Nursing, Nursing Program, Columbus, OH 43222. Offers adult health CNS (clinical nurse specialist) (MS); nursing administration (MS); nursing education (MS). *Accreditation:* AACN. Part-time programs available. *Degree requirements:* For master's, professional manuscript. *Entrance requirements:* For master's, letters of recommendation, current resume, baccalaureate degree in nursing, current Ohio RN license, minimum cumulative GPA of 3.0. Additional exam requirements/recommendations for international students: Required—TOEFL (minimum score 550 paper-based; 213 computer-based; 80 iBT).

Mount Saint Mary College, Division of Nursing, Newburgh, NY 12550-3494. Offers adult nurse practitioner (MS), including nursing education, nursing management; clinical nurse specialist-adult health (MS), including nursing education, nursing management; family nurse practitioner (Advanced Certificate). *Accreditation:* AACN. Part-time and evening/weekend programs available. *Faculty:* 3 full-time (all women), 2 part-time/adjunct (both women). *Students:* 1 full-time (0 women), 53 part-time (50 women); includes 17 minority (8 African Americans, 4 Asian Americans or Pacific Islanders, 5 Hispanic Americans). Average age 39. 16 applicants, 100% accepted, 6 enrolled. In 2009, 5 master's awarded. *Degree requirements:* For master's, research utilization project. *Entrance requirements:* For master's, BSN, minimum GPA of 3.0, RN license. *Application deadline:* For fall admission, 6/3 priority date for domestic students; for spring admission, 10/31 priority date for domestic students. Applications are processed on a rolling basis. Application fee: $45. *Expenses:* Tuition: Full-time $13,356; part-time $742 per credit. Required fees: $50 per semester. *Financial support:* In 2009–10, 2 students received support. Unspecified assistantships available. Financial award application deadline: 4/15; financial award applicants required to submit FAFSA. *Unit head:* Dr. Karen Baldwin, Coordinator, 845-569-3512, Fax: 845-562-6762, E-mail: baldwin@msmc.edu. *Application contact:* Graduate Coordinator, 845-561-0800, Fax: 845-562-6762.

Mount St. Mary's College, Graduate Division, Program in Nursing, Los Angeles, CA 90049-1599. Offers clinical nurse specialist/adult health (MS); community health (MS); educator (MS); leadership and administration (MS); nursing (MS). *Accreditation:* AACN. *Faculty:* 2 full-time (both women), 11 part-time/adjunct (9 women). *Students:* 31 full-time (29 women), 8 part-time (6 women); includes 24 minority (5 African Americans, 12 Asian Americans or Pacific Islanders, 7 Hispanic Americans), 1 international. Average age 41. In 2009, 22 master's awarded. *Entrance requirements:* Additional exam requirements/recommendations for international students: Required—TOEFL (minimum score 550 iBT). *Application deadline:* For fall admission, 7/15 priority date for domestic students; for spring admission, 11/15 priority date for domestic students. *Expenses:* Tuition: Part-time $730 per unit. Part-time tuition and fees vary according to degree level and program. *Unit head:* Dr. Marsha Sato, Chair, 213-477-2980, E-mail: msato@msmc.la.edu. *Application contact:* Director of Graduate Admission.

New Mexico State University, Graduate School, College of Health and Social Services, School of Nursing, Las Cruces, NM 88003-8001. Offers community/public health (MSN); medical-surgical (adult health) (MSN); nursing (PhD); nursing administration (MSN); psychiatric/mental health (MSN). *Accreditation:* AACN. Part-time programs available. Postbaccalaureate distance learning degree programs offered (minimal on-campus study). *Faculty:* 10 full-time (all women), 5 part-time/adjunct (all women). *Students:* 59 full-time (48 women), 70 part-time (61 women); includes 47 minority (9 African Americans, 3 American Indian/Alaska Native, 5 Asian Americans or Pacific Islanders, 30 Hispanic Americans). Average age 43. 82 applicants, 96% accepted, 63 enrolled. In 2009, 32 master's, 1 doctorate awarded. *Degree requirements:* For master's, comprehensive exam, thesis optional, clinical practice; for doctorate, comprehensive exam, thesis/dissertation, clinical practice. *Entrance requirements:* For master's, NCLEX exam, BSN, minimum GPA of 3.0, course work in statistics, 3 letters of reference, writing sample, RN license, CPR certification, proof of liability, immunizations, criminal background check; for doctorate, NCLEX exam, MSN, minimum GPA of 3.0, 3 letters of reference, writing sample, RN license, CPR certification, proof of liability, immunizations, criminal background check. Additional exam requirements/recommendations for international students: Required—TOEFL (minimum score 550 paper-based). *Application deadline:* For fall admission, 3/1 priority date for domestic students; for spring admission, 10/1 priority date for domestic students. Applications are processed on a rolling basis. Application fee: $30 ($50 for international students). Electronic applications accepted. *Expenses:* Tuition, state resident: full-time $4080; part-time $223 per credit. Tuition, nonresident: full-time $14,256; part-time $647 per credit. Required fees: $1278; $639 per semester. *Financial support:* In 2009–10, 14 students received support, including 2 teaching assistantships (averaging $18,380 per year); fellowships, research assistantships, career-related internships or fieldwork, Federal Work-Study, scholarships/grants, traineeships, and health care benefits also available. Financial award application deadline: 3/1. *Faculty research:* Public policy, community health, health disparities, self efficacy and self management, psychiatric mental health. *Unit head:* Dr. Pamela Schultz, Director, 575-646-3812, Fax: 575-646-2167, E-mail: pschultz@nmsu.edu. *Application contact:* Dr. Kathleen Huttlinger, Associate Director for Graduate Studies, 575-646-4386, Fax: 575-646-2167.

New York University, College of Nursing, Programs in Advanced Practice Nursing, New York, NY 10012-1019. Offers advanced practice nursing: adult acute care (MS, Advanced Certificate); advanced practice nursing: adult nurse practitioner/palliative care nursing (MS); advanced practice nursing: adult nurse practitioner/holistic nurse practitioner (Advanced Certificate); advanced practice nursing: adult nurse practitioner/holistic nursing (MS); advanced practice nursing: adult nurse practitioner/palliative care nurse practitioner (Advanced Certificate); advanced practice nursing: adult primary care (MS, Advanced Certificate); advanced practice nursing: adult primary care/geriatrics (MS); advanced practice nursing: geriatrics (MS, Advanced Certificate); advanced practice nursing: mental health (MS); advanced practice nursing: mental health nursing (Advanced Certificate); advanced practice nursing: pediatrics (MS, Advanced Certificate); advanced practice nursing:adult primary care and geriatrics (Advanced Certificate); nurse midwifery (MS, Advanced Certificate); nursing administration (MS, Advanced Certificate); nursing education (MS, Advanced Certificate); nursing informatics (MS, Advanced Certificate); MS/MPH; MS/MS. *Accreditation:* AACN; ACNM/DOA. Part-time and evening/weekend programs available. *Faculty:* 17 full-time (all women), 22 part-time/adjunct (19 women). *Students:* 18 full-time (17 women), 524 part-time (485 women); includes 238 minority (90 African Americans, 119 Asian Americans or Pacific Islanders, 29 Hispanic Americans). Average age 33. 191 applicants, 89% accepted, 120 enrolled. In 2009, 117 master's, 2 other advanced degrees awarded. *Degree requirements:* For master's, thesis (for some programs). *Entrance requirements:* For master's, BS in nursing, AS in nursing with another BS/BA, interview; for Advanced Certificate, master's degree. Additional exam requirements/recommendations for international students: Required—TOEFL. *Application deadline:* For fall admission, 7/1 priority date for domestic students, 7/1 for international students; for spring admission, 12/1 for domestic and international students. Applications are processed on a rolling basis. Application fee: $75. *Expenses:* Tuition: Full-time $30,528; part-time $1272 per credit. Required fees: $2177. *Financial support:* Career-related internships or fieldwork, institutionally sponsored loans, scholarships/grants, traineeships, and tuition waivers (partial) available. Support available

Adult Nursing

New York University (continued)
to part-time students. Financial award application deadline: 2/1; financial award applicants required to submit FAFSA. *Faculty research:* Elderly black diabetics, families and illness, public health nursing, parent-child nursing, health policy costs. *Unit head:* Dr. Judith Haber, Associate Dean for Graduate Programs, 212-998-9020, Fax: 212-995-3143. *Application contact:* Amy Knowles, Assistant Dean for Student Affairs and Admissions, 212-998-5333, Fax: 212-995-4302, E-mail: ak96@nyu.edu.

North Park University, School of Nursing, Chicago, IL 60625-4895. Offers advanced practice nursing (MS); leadership and management (MS); MBA/MS; MM/MSN; MS/MHR; MS/MNA. *Accreditation:* AACN. Part-time and evening/weekend programs available. *Degree requirements:* For master's, thesis. *Entrance requirements:* For master's, GMAT, MAT. *Faculty research:* Aging, consultation roles, critical thinking skills, family breakdown, science of caring.

Oakland University, Graduate Study and Lifelong Learning, School of Nursing, Program in Adult Health, Rochester, MI 48309-4401. Offers MSN. *Accreditation:* AACN. *Degree requirements:* For master's, thesis (for some programs). *Entrance requirements:* For master's, GRE General Test, minimum GPA of 3.0 for unconditional admission. Electronic applications accepted.

Otterbein University, Department of Nursing, Westerville, OH 43081. Offers adult nurse practitioner (MSN, Certificate); clinical nurse leader (MSN); family nurse practitioner (MSN, Certificate); nurse service administration (MSN). *Accreditation:* AACN; NLN. Part-time and evening/weekend programs available. Postbaccalaureate distance learning degree programs offered (minimal on-campus study). *Degree requirements:* For master's, comprehensive exam (for some programs), thesis (for some programs). *Entrance requirements:* For master's, 2 reference forms, resume; for Certificate, official transcripts, 2 reference forms, essay, resumé. Additional exam requirements/recommendations for international students: Required—TOEFL (minimum score 550 paper-based; 213 computer-based; 79 iBT). *Faculty research:* Patient education, women's health, trauma curriculum development, administration.

Quinnipiac University, School of Health Sciences, Nursing Program, Adult Nurse Practitioner Track, Hamden, CT 06518-1940. Offers MSN, Post Master's Certificate. *Accreditation:* NLN. Part-time programs available. *Faculty:* 7 full-time (5 women), 8 part-time/adjunct (4 women). *Students:* Average age 30. *Degree requirements:* For master's, thesis optional, clinical practicum. *Entrance requirements:* For master's, RN license, minimum GPA of 3.0. Additional exam requirements/recommendations for international students: Required—TOEFL (minimum score 575 paper-based; 233 computer-based; 90 iBT), IELTS (minimum score 6.5). *Application deadline:* For fall admission, 6/1 priority date for domestic students, 4/30 for international students. Applications are processed on a rolling basis. Application fee: $45. Electronic applications accepted. *Expenses:* Tuition: Full-time $16,030; part-time $770 per credit. Required fees: $630; $35 per credit. *Financial support:* Traineeships, tuition waivers (partial), and unspecified assistantships available. Support available to part-time students. Financial award application deadline: 4/15; financial award applicants required to submit FAFSA. *Unit head:* Dr. Jeanne LeVasseur, Professor of Nursing, 203-582-5397, Fax: 203-582-3230, E-mail: jeanne.levasseur@quinnipiac.edu. *Application contact:* Kristin Parent, Assistant Director of Graduate Health Sciences Admissions, 800-462-1944, Fax: 203-582-3443, E-mail: kristin.parent@quinnipiac.edu.

Radford University, College of Graduate and Professional Studies, Waldron College of Health and Human Services, School of Nursing, Radford, VA 24142. Offers adult clinical nurse specialist (MSN); family nurse practitioner (MSN); gerontology clinical nurse specialist (MSN); nurse midwifery (MSN). *Accreditation:* AACN. Part-time programs available. *Faculty:* 15 full-time (14 women), 3 part-time/adjunct (2 women). *Students:* 15 full-time (all women), 17 part-time (all women); includes 1 minority (Asian American or Pacific Islander). Average age 35. 17 applicants, 76% accepted, 8 enrolled. In 2009, 11 master's awarded. *Degree requirements:* For master's, comprehensive exam, thesis optional. *Entrance requirements:* For master's, GRE, minimum GPA of 3.0; 3 letters of reference from professional contacts, letter of intent, resume. Additional exam requirements/recommendations for international students: Required—TOEFL (minimum score 550 paper-based; 213 computer-based; 79 iBT). *Application deadline:* For fall admission, 2/1 priority date for domestic students, 12/1 for international students. Applications are processed on a rolling basis. Application fee: $50. Electronic applications accepted. *Expenses:* Tuition, state resident: full-time $5086; part-time $211 per credit hour. Tuition, nonresident: full-time $12,608; part-time $525 per credit hour. Required fees: $2508; $105 per credit hour. *Financial support:* In 2009–10, 5 students received support, including 4 teaching assistantships with partial tuition reimbursements available (averaging $8,700 per year); career-related internships or fieldwork, Federal Work-Study, institutionally sponsored loans, scholarships/grants, and unspecified assistantships also available. Financial award application deadline: 3/1; financial award applicants required to submit FAFSA. *Unit head:* Dr. Kimberly F. Carter, Director, 540-831-7700, Fax: 540-831-7716, E-mail: kcarter@radford.edu. *Application contact:* Graduate Admissions, 540-831-5431, Fax: 540-831-6061, E-mail: gradcollege@radford.edu.

Rush University, College of Nursing, Department of Adult Health Nursing, Chicago, IL 60612-3832. Offers acute care nurse practitioner (MSN, Post-Master's Certificate); adult health nursing (DNP, PhD); adult nurse practitioner (MSN, Post-Master's Certificate); adult/gerontological nurse practitioner (MSN); anesthesia nurse practitioner (MSN, Post-Master's Certificate); critical care clinical specialist (MSN); gerontological nurse practitioner (MSN, Post-Master's Certificate); medical surgical clinical specialist (MSN). *Accreditation:* AACN; AANA/CANAEP (one or more programs are accredited). Part-time programs available. Postbaccalaureate distance learning degree programs offered (minimal on-campus study). Terminal master's awarded for partial completion of doctoral program. *Degree requirements:* For master's, capstone project; for doctorate, thesis/dissertation, DNP leadership project. *Entrance requirements:* For master's, GRE General Test (waived if nursing GPA is above 3.0 or cumulative GPA is above 3.25), interview; for doctorate, GRE General Test, interview, course work in statistics (PhD). Additional exam requirements/recommendations for international students: Required—TOEFL, TWE. Electronic applications accepted. *Faculty research:* Complementary/alternative medicine, critical care outcomes, cardiac risk reduction, Alzheimer's Disease, telehealth monitoring.

Rush University, College of Nursing, Department of Community Systems and Mental Health Nursing, Chicago, IL 60612-3832. Offers community and mental health nursing (DNP, PhD); family nurse practitioner (MSN, Post-Master's Certificate); psychiatric clinical specialist (MSN); psychiatric nurse practitioner—adult (MSN); psychiatric nurse practitioner—family (MSN); psychiatric-mental health clinical specialist (Post-Master's Certificate); psychiatric-mental health nurse practitioner (Post-Master's Certificate); public health nursing (MSN). *Accreditation:* AACN. Part-time programs available. Postbaccalaureate distance learning degree programs offered (minimal on-campus study). Terminal master's awarded for partial completion of doctoral program. *Degree requirements:* For master's, capstone project; for doctorate, thesis/dissertation, DNP leadership project. *Entrance requirements:* For master's, GRE General Test (waived if nursing GPA is above 3.0 or cumulative GPA is above 3.25), interview; for doctorate, GRE General Test, interview, course work in statistics (DN Sc). Electronic applications accepted. *Faculty research:* Immigrant mental health, de-escalation strategies, caregiver interventions, parent-teacher training, restraint use.

Rutgers, The State University of New Jersey, Newark, Graduate School, Program in Nursing, Newark, NJ 07102. Offers nursing (MS), including acute care of adults and aged, advanced practice in pediatric nursing, advanced practice with childbearing families, community health nursing, family nurse practitioner, primary care of adults and aged, psychiatric/mental health nursing. *Accreditation:* AACN. Part-time programs available. *Degree requirements:* For master's, comprehensive exam. *Entrance requirements:* For master's, GRE General Test, RN license, minimum B average, BS in nursing. Additional exam requirements/recommendations for international students: Required—TOEFL. Electronic applications accepted. *Faculty research:* HIV/AIDS, quality of life—MS and breast cancer, sleep patterns of cardiac patients.

Sage Graduate School, Graduate School, School of Health Sciences, Department of Nursing, Program in Adult Health, Troy, NY 12180-4115. Offers MS. *Accreditation:* AACN. Part-time and evening/weekend programs available. *Faculty:* 5 full-time (all women), 8 part-time/adjunct (all women). *Students:* 2 full-time (both women), 30 part-time (29 women); includes 4 minority (2 African Americans, 2 Asian Americans or Pacific Islanders). Average age 40. 18 applicants, 72% accepted, 10 enrolled. In 2009, 6 master's awarded. *Degree requirements:* For master's, thesis or alternative. *Entrance requirements:* For master's, BS in nursing, minimum GPA of 2.75, resume, 2 letters of recommendation. Additional exam requirements/recommendations for international students: Required—TOEFL (minimum score 550 paper-based; 213 computer-based). *Application deadline:* Applications are processed on a rolling basis. Application fee: $40. *Expenses:* Tuition: Full-time $10,620; part-time $590 per credit hour. *Financial support:* Fellowships, research assistantships, Federal Work-Study, scholarships/grants, and unspecified assistantships available. Support available to part-time students. Financial award application deadline: 3/1; financial award applicants required to submit FAFSA. *Unit head:* Arlene Pericak, Director, 518-244-2012, E-mail: perica@sage.edu. *Application contact:* Wendy D. Diefendorf, Director of Graduate and Adult Admission, 518-244-2443, Fax: 518-244-6880, E-mail: diefew@sage.edu.

Sage Graduate School, Graduate School, School of Health Sciences, Department of Nursing, Program in Adult Nurse Practitioner, Troy, NY 12180-4115. Offers MS, Post Master's Certificate. *Accreditation:* AACN. Part-time and evening/weekend programs available. *Faculty:* 5 full-time (all women), 8 part-time/adjunct (all women). *Students:* 4 full-time (all women), 20 part-time (19 women); includes 2 minority (both Asian Americans or Pacific Islanders). Average age 40. 13 applicants. In 2009, 35 master's, 2 other advanced degrees awarded. *Degree requirements:* For master's, thesis or alternative. *Entrance requirements:* For master's, BS in nursing, minimum GPA of 2.75, resume, 2 letters of recommendation. Additional exam requirements/recommendations for international students: Required—TOEFL (minimum score 550 paper-based; 213 computer-based). *Application deadline:* Applications are processed on a rolling basis. Application fee: $40. *Expenses:* Tuition: Full-time $10,620; part-time $590 per credit hour. *Financial support:* Fellowships, research assistantships, Federal Work-Study, scholarships/grants, and unspecified assistantships available. Support available to part-time students. Financial award application deadline: 3/1; financial award applicants required to submit FAFSA. *Unit head:* Arlene Pericak, Director, 518-244-2012, E-mail: perica@sage.edu. *Application contact:* Wendy D. Diefendorf, Director of Graduate and Adult Admission, 518-244-2443, Fax: 518-244-6880, E-mail: diefew@sage.edu.

Saint Peter's College, School of Nursing, Nursing Program, Jersey City, NJ 07306-5997. Offers adult nurse practitioner (MSN); case management (MSN); nursing (DNP); RN to MSN bridge (MSN). *Accreditation:* AACN. Part-time and evening/weekend programs available. *Entrance requirements:* Additional exam requirements/recommendations for international students: Required—TOEFL. *Application deadline:* Applications are processed on a rolling basis. Electronic applications accepted. *Expenses:* Tuition: Part-time $971 per credit. *Financial support:* Federal Work-Study and institutionally sponsored loans available. *Unit head:* Dr. Ann Tritak, Director, 201-761-6270. *Application contact:* Dr. Ann Tritak, Director, 201-761-6270.

Saint Xavier University, Graduate Studies, School of Nursing, Chicago, IL 60655-3105. Offers adult health clinical nurse specialist (MS); family nurse practitioner (MS, PMC); leadership in community health nursing (MS); psychiatric-mental health clinical nurse specialist (MS); psychiatric-mental health clinical specialist (PMC); MBA/MS. *Accreditation:* AACN. Part-time and evening/weekend programs available. *Entrance requirements:* For master's, GRE General Test or MAT, minimum GPA of 3.0, RN license. *Expenses:* Tuition: Part-time $743 per credit hour. Required fees: $135 per semester.

Seattle Pacific University, MS in Nursing Program, Seattle, WA 98119-1997. Offers administration (MSN); adult/gerontology nurse practitioner (MSN); clinical nurse specialist (MSN); family nurse practitioner (MSN, Certificate); informatics (MSN); nurse educator (MSN). *Accreditation:* AACN. Part-time programs available. *Faculty:* 3 full-time (all women), 7 part-time/adjunct (6 women). *Students:* 9 full-time (8 women), 63 part-time (57 women); includes 9 minority (1 American Indian/Alaska Native, 7 Asian Americans or Pacific Islanders, 1 Hispanic American), 1 international. Average age 46. 60 applicants, 45% accepted, 27 enrolled. In 2009, 12 master's awarded. *Degree requirements:* For master's, thesis. *Application deadline:* For fall admission, 2/1 priority date for domestic students. Applications are processed on a rolling basis. Application fee: $50. Electronic applications accepted. *Expenses:* Contact institution. *Financial support:* In 2009–10, 41 students received support; fellowships, scholarships/grants available. Financial award applicants required to submit FAFSA. *Unit head:* Dr. Susan Casey, Director, 206-281-2769, Fax: 206-281-2767, E-mail: caseys@spu.edu. *Application contact:* The Grad Center, 206-281-2091.

Seton Hall University, College of Nursing, South Orange, NJ 07079-2697. Offers advanced practice in primary health care (MSN), including adult nurse practitioner, gerontological nurse practitioner, pediatric nurse practitioner; entry into practice (MSN); health systems administration (MSN, DNP); nursing (PhD); nursing case management (MSN); nursing education (MA); school nurse (MSN); MSN/MA. *Accreditation:* AACN. Part-time programs available. Post-baccalaureate distance learning degree programs offered (minimal on-campus study). *Faculty:* 10 full-time (all women), 3 part-time/adjunct (1 woman). *Students:* 46 full-time (35 women), 94 part-time (90 women); includes 22 minority (8 African Americans, 5 Asian Americans or Pacific Islanders, 9 Hispanic Americans). 92 applicants, 88% accepted, 55 enrolled. *Degree requirements:* For master's, research project; for doctorate, dissertation or scholarly project. *Entrance requirements:* For doctorate, GRE. Additional exam requirements/recommendations for international students: Required—TOEFL. *Application deadline:* For fall admission, 6/15 priority date for domestic students. Applications are processed on a rolling basis. Electronic applications accepted. *Financial support:* Institutionally sponsored loans, scholarships/grants, traineeships, tuition waivers (partial), and unspecified assistantships available. Support available to part-time students. Financial award applicants required to submit FAFSA. *Faculty research:* Parent/child, adult, and gerontological nursing; breast cancer; families of children with HIV; parish nursing. *Unit head:* Dr. Phyllis Shanley Hansell, Dean. *Application contact:* Kristyn Kent Wuillermin, Director of Strategic Alliances, Marketing and Enrollment, 973-761-9291, Fax: 973-761-9607, E-mail: kristyn.kent@shu.edu.

Southern Adventist University, School of Nursing, Collegedale, TN 37315-0370. Offers acute care nurse practitioner (MSN); adult nurse practitioner (MSN); family nurse practitioner (MSN); nurse educator (MSN); MSN/MSBA. *Accreditation:* NLN. Part-time programs available. *Faculty:* 6 full-time (5 women). *Students:* 69 full-time (50 women), 28 part-time (25 women); includes 9 minority (6 African Americans, 1 American Indian/Alaska Native, 1 Asian American or Pacific Islander, 1 Hispanic American). Average age 35. 40 applicants, 95% accepted, 31 enrolled. In 2009, 21 master's awarded. *Degree requirements:* For master's, thesis or project. *Entrance requirements:* For master's, RN license. Additional exam requirements/recommendations for international students: Required—TOEFL (minimum score 600 paper-based; 250 computer-based). *Application deadline:* For fall admission, 7/1 for domestic and international students; for winter admission, 12/1 for domestic and international students. Applications are processed on a rolling basis. Application fee: $25. Electronic applications accepted. *Expenses:* Tuition: Full-time $13,149; part-time $487 per credit hour. *Financial support:* In 2009–10, 1 teaching assistantship with partial tuition reimbursement (averaging $5,000 per year) was awarded. *Faculty research:* Pain management, ethics, corporate wellness, caring spirituality, stress. *Unit head:* Dr. Barbara James, Dean, 423-236-2940, Fax: 423-236-1940, E-mail: bjames@southern.edu. *Application contact:* Diane Proffitt, Enrollment Counselor, 423-236-2941, Fax: 423-236-1940, E-mail: dproffitt@southern.edu.

Spalding University, Graduate Studies, College of Health and Natural Sciences, School of Nursing, Louisville, KY 40203-2188. Offers adult nurse practitioner (MSN); family nurse practitioner (MSN); leadership in nursing and healthcare (MSN); pediatric nurse practitioner (MSN). *Accreditation:* AACN. Part-time and evening/weekend programs available. *Faculty:* 6 full-time (all women), 7 part-time/adjunct (all women). *Students:* 41 full-time (38 women), 36 part-time (34 women); includes 12 minority (9 African Americans, 3 Hispanic Americans), 2 international.

Average age 38. 27 applicants, 70% accepted, 18 enrolled. In 2009, 25 master's awarded. *Degree requirements:* For master's, comprehensive exam (for some programs), thesis. *Entrance requirements:* For master's, GRE General Test, BSN or bachelor's degree and RN licensure. Additional exam requirements/recommendations for international students: Required—TOEFL (minimum score 535 paper-based; 203 computer-based). *Application deadline:* Applications are processed on a rolling basis. Application fee: $30. *Expenses:* Tuition: Full-time $11,340; part-time $630 per credit hour. Tuition and fees vary according to program. *Financial support:* In 2009–10, 53 students received support, including 2 research assistantships with partial tuition reimbursements available (averaging $4,020 per year); career-related internships or fieldwork, scholarships/grants, and traineeships also available. Support available to part-time students. Financial award application deadline: 3/15; financial award applicants required to submit FAFSA. *Faculty research:* Nurse educational administration, gerontology, bioterrorism, healthcare ethics, leadership. *Unit head:* Dr. Carolyn Lewis, Interim Chair, 502-585-9911 Ext. 2331, E-mail: clewis@spalding.edu. *Application contact:* Dr. Carolyn Lewis, Interim Chair, 502-585-9911 Ext. 2331, E-mail: clewis@spalding.edu.

State University of New York Institute of Technology, School of Nursing and Health Systems, Program in Adult Nurse Practitioner, Utica, NY 13504-3050. Offers MS, CAS. *Accreditation:* AACN. Part-time programs available. *Degree requirements:* For master's, thesis or project. *Entrance requirements:* For master's, GRE General Test (if undergraduate GPA less than 3.3), minimum GPA of 3.0 in last 30 hours of undergraduate coursework, BS in nursing, 1 year of RN experience, RN license, interview, 2 letters of recommendation. Additional exam requirements/recommendations for international students: Required—TOEFL (minimum score 550 paper-based; 213 computer-based). *Faculty research:* Adult health care, critical thinking, epidemiology, ethics, moral reasoning.

Stony Brook University, State University of New York, Stony Brook University Medical Center, Health Sciences Center, School of Nursing, Program in Adult Health/Primary Care Nursing, Stony Brook, NY 11794. Offers adult health nurse practitioner (Certificate); adult health/primary care nursing (MS). *Accreditation:* AACN. Postbaccalaureate distance learning degree programs offered. *Students:* 21 full-time (20 women), 191 part-time (174 women); includes 51 minority (23 African Americans, 17 Asian Americans or Pacific Islanders, 11 Hispanic Americans). In 2009, 44 master's, 3 other advanced degrees awarded. *Degree requirements:* For master's, thesis. *Entrance requirements:* For master's, BSN, minimum GPA of 3.0, course work in statistics. *Application deadline:* For fall admission, 1/15 for domestic students. Application fee: $60. *Expenses:* Tuition, state resident: full-time $8370; part-time $349 per credit. Tuition, nonresident: full-time $13,250; part-time $552 per credit. Required fees: $933. *Financial support:* Application deadline: 3/15. *Unit head:* Prof. Mary Anne Dumas, Chair, 631-444-3297, Fax: 631-444-3136, E-mail: mary.dumas@stonybrook.edu. *Application contact:* Dr. Kent Marks, Assistant Dean, Admissions and Records, 631-632-4723, Fax: 631-632-7243, E-mail: kmarks@notes.cc.sunysb.edu.

Texas Christian University, Harris College of Nursing and Health Sciences, Program in Nursing, Fort Worth, TX 76129-0002. Offers adult nursing (CNS) (MSN); nursing (DNP); pediatric nursing (CNS) (MSN). *Accreditation:* AACN; AANA/CANAEP (one or more programs are accredited). Part-time programs available. Postbaccalaureate distance learning degree programs offered (minimal on-campus study). *Degree requirements:* For master's and doctorate, professional project. *Entrance requirements:* For master's, GRE General Test or MAT, 3 letters of reference, 2 years full-time experience in nursing, current nursing licensure. Additional exam requirements/recommendations for international students: Required—TOEFL. *Application deadline:* For fall admission, 2/1 for domestic students. Application fee: $0. *Expenses:* Tuition: Full-time $17,640; part-time $980 per credit hour. Tuition and fees vary according to program. *Financial support:* Application deadline: 2/1. *Unit head:* Dr. Pamela Frable, Director, 817-257-5840, E-mail: p.frable@tcu.edu. *Application contact:* Dr. Kathleen Baldwin, Director of Graduate Studies, 817-257-6756, E-mail: k.baldwin@tcu.edu.

Texas Woman's University, Graduate School, College of Nursing, Denton, TX 76201. Offers acute care nurse practitioner (MS); adult health clinical nurse specialist (MS); adult health nurse practitioner (MS); child health clinical nurse specialist (MS); clinical nurse leader (MS); community health (MS); family nurse practitioner (MS); health systems management (MS); nursing education (MS); nursing practice (DNP); nursing science (PhD); pediatric nurse practitioner (MS); women's health clinical nurse specialist (MS); women's health nurse practitioner (MS). *Accreditation:* AACN. Part-time programs available. Postbaccalaureate distance learning degree programs offered. *Faculty:* 85 full-time (80 women), 6 part-time/adjunct (all women). *Students:* 81 full-time (76 women), 602 part-time (571 women); includes 293 minority (154 African Americans, 3 American Indian/Alaska Native, 90 Asian Americans or Pacific Islanders, 46 Hispanic Americans), 19 international. Average age 39. 259 applicants, 81% accepted, 166 enrolled. In 2009, 100 master's, 22 doctorates awarded. *Degree requirements:* For master's, thesis or alternative; for doctorate, comprehensive exam, thesis/dissertation. *Entrance requirements:* For master's, GRE or MAT, minimum GPA of 3.0, RN license, BS in nursing, basic statistics course; for doctorate, GRE (Verbal 460, Quantitative 500) or MAT (50), MS in nursing, minimum GPA of 3.5, RN license, coursework in statistics, 2 letters of reference, curriculum vitae, nursing-theory course, graduate research course, letter stating professional and research goals. Additional exam requirements/recommendations for international students: Required—TOEFL (minimum score 550 paper-based; 213 computer-based; 79 iBT). *Application deadline:* For fall admission, 5/1 priority date for domestic students, 3/1 for international students; for spring admission, 9/15 priority date for domestic students, 7/1 for international students. Applications are processed on a rolling basis. Application fee: $50. Electronic applications accepted. *Expenses:* Tuition, state resident: full-time $3564; part-time $198 per credit hour. Tuition, nonresident: full-time $8550; part-time $475 per credit hour. Required fees: $69.26 per credit hour. Tuition and fees vary according to course load. *Financial support:* In 2009–10, 99 students received support, including 16 fellowships (averaging $17,325 per year), 5 research assistantships (averaging $11,484 per year), 5 teaching assistantships (averaging $11,484 per year); career-related internships or fieldwork, Federal Work-Study, institutionally sponsored loans, scholarships/grants, traineeships, health care benefits, and unspecified assistantships also available. Support available to part-time students. Financial award application deadline: 3/1; financial award applicants required to submit FAFSA. *Faculty research:* Evaluation of pre-natal care, screening for intimate partner violence, stressors and nursing success, breast surgery, breast feeding, adolescent needs during childbirth. *Unit head:* Dr. Patricia Holden-Huchton, Interim Dean, 940-898-2401, Fax: 940-898-2437, E-mail: pholdenhuchton@twu.edu. *Application contact:* Samuel Wheeler, Assistant Director of Admissions, 940-898-3188, Fax: 940-898-3081, E-mail: wheelersr@twu.edu.

Troy University, Graduate School, College of Health and Human Services, Program in Nursing, Troy, AL 36082. Offers adult health (MSN); clinical nurse specialist adult health (DNP); clinical nurse specialist nurse practitioner (DNP); family nurse practitioner (MSN); informatics specialist (MSN); maternal infant (MSN). *Accreditation:* NLN. Part-time and evening/weekend programs available. *Students:* 28 full-time (all women), 102 part-time (93 women); includes 49 minority (48 African Americans, 1 American Indian/Alaska Native). Average age 37. 76 applicants, 86% accepted. In 2009, 25 master's awarded. *Degree requirements:* For master's, comprehensive exam, thesis optional. *Entrance requirements:* For master's, MAT (minimum score 396) or GRE (minimum score 850), minimum GPA of 2.5, BSN. Additional exam requirements/recommendations for international students: Required—TOEFL (minimum score 523 paper-based; 193 computer-based; 70 iBT), IELTS (minimum score 6), TOEFL or IELTS or ACT Compass ESL (minimum score 270 on Listening, Reading, and Grammar with no individual score below 85 and minimum score of 8 out of 12 on writing test). *Application deadline:* Applications are processed on a rolling basis. Application fee: $50. Electronic applications accepted. *Financial support:* Available to part-time students. Applicants required to submit FAFSA. *Application contact:* Brenda K. Campbell, Director of Graduate Admissions, 334-670-3178, Fax: 334-670-3733, E-mail: bcamp@troy.edu.

Universidad del Turabo, Graduate Programs, School of Health Sciences, Programs in Nursing, Program in Family Nurse Practitioner—Adult Nursing, Gurabo, PR 00778-3030. Offers MSN. *Students:* 2 full-time (both women), 2 part-time (1 woman); includes 3 minority (all Hispanic Americans). Average age 42. In 2009, 2 master's awarded. *Unit head:* David Mendez, Head, 787-743-7979. *Application contact:* Virginia Gonzalez, Admissions Officer, 787-746-3009.

University at Buffalo, the State University of New York, Graduate School, School of Nursing, Buffalo, NY 14260. Offers adult health nursing (MS); family nursing (MS); nurse anesthetist (MS); nursing (PhD); nursing education (Certificate); psychiatric/mental health nursing (MS). *Accreditation:* AACN; AANA/CANAEP (one or more programs are accredited). Part-time programs available. Postbaccalaureate distance learning degree programs offered (minimal on-campus study). *Faculty:* 42 full-time (38 women), 16 part-time/adjunct (all women). *Students:* 128 full-time (102 women), 69 part-time (58 women); includes 27 minority (7 African Americans, 1 American Indian/Alaska Native, 12 Asian Americans or Pacific Islanders, 7 Hispanic Americans), 15 international. Average age 34. 375 applicants, 25% accepted, 65 enrolled. In 2009, 58 master's, 3 doctorates, 4 other advanced degrees awarded. Terminal master's awarded for partial completion of doctoral program. *Degree requirements:* For master's, thesis optional, comprehensive exams or project; for doctorate, comprehensive exam, thesis/dissertation. *Entrance requirements:* For master's, GRE General Test (if overall GPA less than 3.0), interview, minimum GPA of 3.0, RN license, 3 references; for doctorate, GRE General Test, MAT, minimum GPA of 3.25, RN license, BS or MS in nursing, 3 references, writing sample; for Certificate, interview, minimum GPA of 3.0 or GRE General Test, RN license, MS in nursing. Additional exam requirements/recommendations for international students: Required—TOEFL (minimum score 550 paper-based; 213 computer-based; 79 iBT), IELTS (minimum score 6.5). *Application deadline:* For fall admission, 6/1 priority date for domestic students, 4/1 priority date for international students; for spring admission, 11/1 for domestic students, 10/1 priority date for international students. Applications are processed on a rolling basis. Application fee: $75. Electronic applications accepted. *Financial support:* In 2009–10, 78 students received support, including 14 fellowships with full tuition reimbursements available (averaging $8,200 per year), 5 research assistantships with full tuition reimbursements available (averaging $16,794 per year), 13 teaching assistantships with full tuition reimbursements available (averaging $10,636 per year); scholarships/grants, traineeships, health care benefits, and unspecified assistantships also available. Financial award application deadline: 3/15; financial award applicants required to submit FAFSA. *Faculty research:* Oncology symptom management, end of life decision making, changing behaviors using the transtheoretical model, addictions, nursing workforce. Total annual research expenditures: $1.3 million. *Unit head:* Dr. Jean K. Brown, Dean and Professor, 716-829-2533, Fax: 716-829-2566, E-mail: ubnursingdean@buffalo.edu. *Application contact:* Dr. David J. Lang, Director of Student Affairs, 716-829-2537, Fax: 716-829-2021, E-mail: langdj@buffalo.edu.

University of Central Florida, College of Nursing, Orlando, FL 32816. Offers adult nurse practitioner (MSN, Post-Master's Certificate); clinical nurse leader (MSN, Post-Master's Certificate); clinical nurse specialist (MSN, Post-Master's Certificate); family nurse practitioner (MSN, Post-Master's Certificate); leadership and management (MSN); nurse educator (MSN); nursing (PhD); nursing education (Post-Master's Certificate); nursing practice (DNP); pediatric nurse practitioner (MSN, Post-Master's Certificate). *Accreditation:* AACN. Part-time and evening/weekend programs available. *Faculty:* 38 full-time (34 women), 49 part-time/adjunct (47 women). *Students:* 98 full-time (93 women), 371 part-time (350 women); includes 132 minority (63 African Americans, 2 American Indian/Alaska Native, 29 Asian Americans or Pacific Islanders, 38 Hispanic Americans), 9 international. Average age 39. 363 applicants, 49% accepted, 139 enrolled. In 2009, 72 master's, 3 doctorates, 8 other advanced degrees awarded. *Degree requirements:* For master's, thesis or alternative. *Entrance requirements:* For master's, GRE General Test, minimum GPA of 3.0 in last 60 hours. Additional exam requirements/recommendations for international students: Required—TOEFL. *Application deadline:* For fall admission, 2/15 for domestic students; for spring admission, 9/15 for domestic students. Application fee: $30. Electronic applications accepted. *Expenses:* Tuition, state resident: part-time $306.31 per credit hour. Tuition, nonresident: part-time $1099.01 per credit hour. Part-time tuition and fees vary according to degree level and program. *Financial support:* In 2009–10, 30 students received support, including 30 fellowships with partial tuition reimbursements available (averaging $3,200 per year), 1 teaching assistantship with partial tuition reimbursement available (averaging $13,440 per year); research assistantships with partial tuition reimbursements available, career-related internships or fieldwork, Federal Work-Study, institutionally sponsored loans, traineeships, and unspecified assistantships also available. Financial award application deadline: 3/1; financial award applicants required to submit FAFSA. *Unit head:* Dr. Jean D. Leuner, Dean, 407-823-5496, Fax: 407-823-5675, E-mail: jleuner@mail.ucf.edu. *Application contact:* Dr. Jean D. Leuner, Dean, 407-823-5496, Fax: 407-823-5675, E-mail: jleuner@mail.ucf.edu.

University of Cincinnati, Graduate School, College of Nursing, Cincinnati, OH 45221-0038. Offers clinical nurse specialist (MSN), including adult health, community health, neonatal, nursing administration, occupational health, pediatric health, psychiatric nursing, women's health; nurse anesthesia (MSN); nurse midwifery (MSN); nurse practitioner (MSN), including acute care, ambulatory care, family, family/psychiatric, women's health; nursing (PhD); MBA/MSN. *Accreditation:* AACN; AANA/CANAEP (one or more programs are accredited); ACNM/DOA. Part-time programs available. Postbaccalaureate distance learning degree programs offered (no on-campus study). Terminal master's awarded for partial completion of doctoral program. *Degree requirements:* For master's, thesis or alternative; for doctorate, comprehensive exam, thesis/dissertation. *Entrance requirements:* For master's and doctorate, GRE General Test. Additional exam requirements/recommendations for international students: Required—TOEFL (minimum score 520 paper-based; 190 computer-based). Electronic applications accepted. *Faculty research:* Substance abuse, injury and violence, symptom management.

University of Colorado at Colorado Springs, Graduate School, Beth-El College of Nursing and Health Sciences, Colorado Springs, CO 80933-7150. Offers adult health nurse practitioner and clinical specialist (MSN); family practitioner (MSN), including community clinical specialist, forensic clinical specialist, holistic clinical specialist; neonatal nurse practitioner and clinical specialist (MSN); nursing administration (MSN); nursing practice (DNP); women nurse practitioner (MSN). *Accreditation:* AACN. Part-time programs available. Postbaccalaureate distance learning degree programs offered (minimal on-campus study). *Faculty:* 26 full-time (21 women), 3 part-time/adjunct (all women). *Students:* 132 full-time (112 women), 81 part-time (71 women); includes 35 minority (6 African Americans, 2 American Indian/Alaska Native, 6 Asian Americans or Pacific Islanders, 21 Hispanic Americans), 3 international. Average age 36. 245 applicants, 47% accepted, 58 enrolled. In 2009, 33 master's awarded. *Degree requirements:* For master's, comprehensive exam, thesis optional; for doctorate, capstone project. *Entrance requirements:* For master's, GRE General Test or MAT, BSN, minimum GPA of 3.0, unrestricted RN license; for doctorate, interview; active RN license; MA; minimum GPA of 3.3; National Certification as NP or CNS; portfolio. Additional exam requirements/recommendations for international students: Required—TOEFL. *Application deadline:* For fall admission, 6/1 priority date for domestic students; for spring admission, 11/15 for domestic students. Application fee: $60 ($75 for international students). Electronic applications accepted. *Expenses:* Contact institution. *Financial support:* Fellowships, career-related internships or fieldwork, Federal Work-Study, and scholarships/grants available. Support available to part-time students. Financial award application deadline: 3/1; financial award applicants required to submit FAFSA. *Faculty research:* Women's health, uncertainty, empowerment, family experience in chronic illness. Total annual research expenditures: $703,545. *Unit head:* Dr. Nancy Smith, Dean, 719-255-4411, Fax: 719-255-4416, E-mail: nsmith2@uccs.edu. *Application contact:* Jackie Crouch, Graduate Recruitment Coordinator, 719-255-4493, Fax: 719-255-4416, E-mail: jcrouch@uccs.edu.

University of Delaware, College of Health Sciences, School of Nursing, Newark, DE 19716. Offers adult nurse practitioner (MSN, PMC); cardiopulmonary clinical nurse specialist (MSN, PMC); cardiopulmonary clinical nurse specialist/adult nurse practitioner (MSN, PMC); family nurse practitioner (MSN, PMC); gerontology clinical nurse specialist (MSN, PMC); gerontology clinical nurse specialist geriatric nurse practitioner (PMC); gerontology clinical nurse specialist/geriatric nurse practitioner (MSN); health services administration (MSN, PMC); nursing of children clinical nurse specialist (MSN, PMC); nursing of children clinical nurse specialist/

Adult Nursing

University of Delaware (continued)
pediatric nurse practitioner (MSN, PMC); oncology/immune deficiency clinical nurse specialist (MSN, PMC); oncology/immune deficiency clinical nurse specialist/adult nurse practitioner (MSN, PMC); perinatal/women's health clinical nurse specialist (MSN, PMC); perinatal/women's health clinical nurse specialist/women's health nurse practitioner (MSN, PMC); psychiatric nursing clinical nurse specialist (MSN, PMC). *Accreditation:* AACN; NLN (one or more programs are accredited). Part-time and evening/weekend programs available. Postbaccalaureate distance learning degree programs offered (minimal on-campus study). *Degree requirements:* For master's, thesis optional. *Entrance requirements:* For master's, BSN, interview, RN license. Electronic applications accepted. *Faculty research:* Marriage and chronic illness, health promotion, congestive heart failure patient outcomes, school nursing, diabetes in children, culture, health disparities, cardiovascular, prison nursing, oncology, public policy, child obesity, smoking and teen pregnancy, blood pressure measurements, men's health.

University of Hawaii at Manoa, Graduate Division, School of Nursing and Dental Hygiene, Honolulu, HI 96822. Offers clinical nurse specialist (MS), including adult health, community mental health; nurse practitioner (MS), including adult health, community mental health, family nurse practitioner; nursing (PhD, Graduate Certificate); nursing administration (MS). *Accreditation:* AACN; NLN (one or more programs are accredited). Part-time programs available. Postbaccalaureate distance learning degree programs offered (minimal on-campus study). *Faculty:* 20 full-time (18 women), 16 part-time/adjunct (15 women). *Students:* 81 full-time (69 women), 135 part-time (121 women); includes 115 minority (4 African Americans, 2 American Indian/Alaska Native, 105 Asian Americans or Pacific Islanders, 4 Hispanic Americans), 2 international. Average age 38. 189 applicants, 52% accepted, 79 enrolled. In 2009, 25 master's, 4 doctorates awarded. *Degree requirements:* For master's, thesis optional; for doctorate, comprehensive exam, thesis/dissertation. *Entrance requirements:* For master's, Hawaii RN license. Additional exam requirements/recommendations for international students: Required—TOEFL (minimum score 580 paper-based; 237 computer-based; 92 iBT), IELTS (minimum score 5). *Application deadline:* For fall admission, 2/1 for domestic and international students. Application fee: $60. *Expenses:* Contact institution. *Financial support:* In 2009–10, 6 students received support, including 28 fellowships (averaging $960 per year), 7 research assistantships (averaging $18,080 per year). Total annual research expenditures: $1.8 million. *Unit head:* Mary Boland, Dean, 808-956-8522, Fax: 808-956-3257, E-mail: mgboland@hawaii.edu. *Application contact:* Kristine Qureshi, Graduate Chair, 808-956-8744, Fax: 808-956-3257, E-mail: kqureshi@hawaii.edu.

University of Illinois at Chicago, Graduate College, College of Nursing, Program in Nursing, Chicago, IL 60607-7128. Offers acute care clinical nurse specialist (MS); acute care nurse practitioner (MS); administrative studies in nursing (MS); adult nurse practitioner (MS); adult/geriatric nurse practitioner (MS); advanced community health nurse specialist (MS); family nurse practitioner (MS); geriatric clinical nurse specialist (MS); geriatric nurse practitioner (MS); mental health clinical nurse specialist (MS); mental health nurse practitioner (MS); nurse midwifery (MS); occupational health/advanced community health nurse specialist (MS); occupational health/family nurse practitioner (MS); pediatric clinical nurse specialist (MS); pediatric nurse practitioner (MS); perinatal clinical nurse specialist (MS); school/advanced community health nurse specialist (MS); school/family nurse practitioner (MS); women's health nurse practitioner (MS). *Accreditation:* AACN. Part-time programs available. *Degree requirements:* For master's, thesis or alternative. *Entrance requirements:* For master's, GRE General Test, minimum GPA of 2.75. Additional exam requirements/recommendations for international students: Required—TOEFL. Electronic applications accepted.

University of Louisville, Graduate School, School of Nursing, Louisville, KY 40202. Offers adult nurse practitioner (MSN); family nurse practitioner (MSN); health professions education (MSN); neonatal nurse practitioner (MSN); nursing research (PhD); psychiatric mental health nurse practitioner (MSN). *Accreditation:* AACN. Part-time programs available. *Faculty:* 28 full-time (25 women), 4 part-time/adjunct (3 women). *Students:* 72 full-time (66 women), 57 part-time (52 women); includes 15 minority (11 African Americans, 3 Asian Americans or Pacific Islanders, 1 Hispanic American), 4 international. Average age 35. 45 applicants, 82% accepted, 31 enrolled. In 2009, 28 master's, 3 doctorates awarded. Terminal master's awarded for partial completion of doctoral program. *Degree requirements:* For master's, thesis optional; for doctorate, comprehensive exam, thesis/dissertation. *Entrance requirements:* For master's, GRE General Test, bachelor's degree in nursing, minimum GPA of 3.0, RN license; for doctorate, GRE General Test, BSN and MSN with recommended minimum GPA of 3.0. Additional exam requirements/recommendations for international students: Required—TOEFL. *Application deadline:* For fall admission, 4/1 priority date for domestic students, 4/1 for international students; for spring admission, 10/1 priority date for domestic students, 10/1 for international students. Applications are processed on a rolling basis. Application fee: $50. Electronic applications accepted. *Financial support:* In 2009–10, 45 students received support, including 2 fellowships with full tuition reimbursements available (averaging $20,000 per year), 5 research assistantships with full tuition reimbursements available (averaging $18,000 per year), 5 teaching assistantships with full tuition reimbursements available (averaging $18,000 per year); institutionally sponsored loans, scholarships/grants, traineeships, health care benefits, and unspecified assistantships also available. Support available to part-time students. Financial award application deadline: 4/15; financial award applicants required to submit FAFSA. *Faculty research:* Maternal-child/family stress after pregnancy loss, postpartum depression, access to healthcare (underserved populations), quality of life issues, physical activity (impact on chronic/acute conditions). Total annual research expenditures: $363,876. *Unit head:* Dr. Marcia J. Hern, Dean, 502-852-8300, Fax: 502-852-5044, E-mail: m.hern@gwise.louisville.edu. *Application contact:* Dr. Rosalie O'Dell Mainous, Associate Dean for Graduate Academic Affairs, 502-852-8387, Fax: 502-852-8783, E-mail: romain01@louisville.edu.

University of Massachusetts Dartmouth, Graduate School, College of Nursing, Graduate Nursing Programs, North Dartmouth, MA 02747-2300. Offers adult health/adult nurse practitioner (MS); adult health/advanced practice (MS); adult nurse practitioner (PMC); community nursing/advanced practice (MS); individualized nursing (PMC); nursing (PhD). Part-time programs available. *Faculty:* 29 full-time (all women), 26 part-time/adjunct (25 women). *Students:* 13 full-time (all women), 62 part-time (57 women); includes 4 minority (1 African American, 1 American Indian/Alaska Native, 2 Hispanic Americans), 1 international. Average age 40. 24 applicants, 100% accepted, 20 enrolled. In 2009, 17 master's, 2 other advanced degrees awarded. *Degree requirements:* For master's, thesis; for doctorate, thesis/dissertation. *Entrance requirements:* For master's, GRE General Test, BSN, minimum undergraduate GPA of 3.0, RN license, 3 letters of recommendation, 1 year experience as registered nurse; for doctorate, GRE General Test, minimum undergraduate GPA of 3.0, graduate 3.3; 3 letters of recommendation; personal statement; current Massachusetts RN license or eligibility for licensure in Massachusetts; 1 year professional nursing experience; example of scholarly writing. Additional exam requirements/recommendations for international students: Required—TOEFL (minimum score 500 paper-based). *Application deadline:* For fall admission, 4/20 for domestic students, 2/20 for international students; for spring admission, 10/15 for domestic students, 8/15 for international students. Application fee: $40 ($60 for international students). Electronic applications accepted. *Expenses:* Tuition, state resident: full-time $2071; part-time $86.29 per credit. Tuition, nonresident: full-time $8099; part-time $337.46 per credit. Required fees: $9446. Tuition and fees vary according to class time, course load and reciprocity agreements. *Financial support:* In 2009–10, 11 teaching assistantships with full tuition reimbursements (averaging $3,359 per year) were awarded; Federal Work-Study also available. Support available to part-time students. Financial award application deadline: 3/1; financial award applicants required to submit FAFSA. *Faculty research:* Chronic illness management, quality of life, diabetes care and education, environmental health, quantitative methodologies. Total annual research expenditures: $44,000. *Unit head:* Dr. Gail Russell, Director, 508-999-8251, Fax: 508-999-9127, E-mail: grussell@umassd.edu. *Application contact:* Elan Turcotte-Shamski, Graduate Admissions Officer, 508-999-8604, Fax: 508-999-8183, E-mail: graduate@umassd.edu.

University of Massachusetts Worcester, Graduate School of Nursing, Worcester, MA 01655-0115. Offers adult acute/critical care nurse practitioner (MS, Post Master's Certificate); adult acute/critical care nurse practitioner and gerontological nurse practitioner (MS, Post Master's Certificate); adult primary care nurse practitioner (MS, Post Master's Certificate); adult primary care nurse practitioner and gerontological nurse practitioner (MS, Post Master's Certificate); family nurse practitioner (MS); gerontological nurse practitioner (Post Master's Certificate); nurse educator (MS); nursing (PhD). *Accreditation:* AACN. *Faculty:* 15 full-time (13 women), 31 part-time/adjunct (29 women). *Students:* 151 full-time (131 women), 6 part-time (all women); includes 14 minority (5 African Americans, 1 American Indian/Alaska Native, 5 Asian Americans or Pacific Islanders, 3 Hispanic Americans). Average age 37. 206 applicants, 34% accepted, 61 enrolled. In 2009, 62 master's, 3 doctorates awarded. *Degree requirements:* For doctorate, comprehensive exam, thesis/dissertation. *Entrance requirements:* For master's, GRE General Test, bachelor's degree, course work in statistics; for doctorate, GRE General Test, bachelor's or master's degree, RN licensure; for Post Master's Certificate, MS in nursing. Additional exam requirements/recommendations for international students: Required—TOEFL. *Application deadline:* For fall admission, 3/15 for domestic students. Applications are processed on a rolling basis. Application fee: $40 ($60 for international students). *Expenses:* Contact institution. *Financial support:* In 2009–10, 130 students received support. Scholarships/grants and traineeships available. Support available to part-time students. Financial award application deadline: 5/18; financial award applicants required to submit FAFSA. *Faculty research:* Symptom management, interventions, individual and family adjustment to chronic illness, women's health. *Unit head:* Dr. Paulette Seymour-Route, Dean, 508-856-5801, Fax: 508-856-6552, E-mail: paulette.seymour-route@umassmed.edu. *Application contact:* Diane Brescia, Admissions Coordinator, 508-856-3488, Fax: 508-856-5851, E-mail: diane.brescia@umassmed.edu.

University of Medicine and Dentistry of New Jersey, School of Nursing, Newark, NJ 07107-3001. Offers adult health (MSN); adult occupational health (MSN); advanced practice nursing (MSN, Post Master's Certificate); family nurse practitioner (MSN); nurse anesthesia (MSN); nursing (MSN); nursing informatics (MSN); urban health (PhD); women's health practitioner (MSN). *Accreditation:* AANA/CANAEP; NLN (one or more programs are accredited). Part-time programs available. *Entrance requirements:* For master's, GRE, RN license; basic life support, statistics, and health assessment experience. Additional exam requirements/recommendations for international students: Required—TOEFL. Electronic applications accepted. *Expenses:* Contact institution. *Faculty research:* HIV/AIDS, diabetes education, learned helplessness, nursing science, psychoeducation.

University of Miami, Graduate School, School of Nursing and Health Studies, Coral Gables, FL 33124. Offers acute care (MSN), including acute care nurse practitioner, nurse anesthesia; nursing (PhD); primary care (MSN), including adult nurse practitioner, family nurse practitioner, nurse midwifery, women's health practitioner. *Accreditation:* AACN; AANA/CANAEP; ACNM/DOA (one or more programs are accredited). Part-time programs available. *Degree requirements:* For master's, thesis optional; for doctorate, thesis/dissertation. *Entrance requirements:* For master's, GRE General Test, BSN, minimum GPA of 3.0, Florida RN license; for doctorate, GRE General Test, BSN or MSN, minimum GPA of 3.0. Additional exam requirements/recommendations for international students: Required—TOEFL (minimum score 550 paper-based; 213 computer-based). Electronic applications accepted. *Faculty research:* Transcultural nursing, exercise and depression in Alzheimer's disease, infectious diseases/HIV–AIDS, postpartum depression, outcomes assessment.

University of Michigan, Horace H. Rackham School of Graduate Studies, School of Nursing, Division of Acute, Critical and Long-term Care, Program in Adult Acute Care Nurse Practitioner, Ann Arbor, MI 48109. Offers MS. *Accreditation:* AACN. Part-time programs available. *Degree requirements:* For master's, thesis. *Entrance requirements:* For master's, GRE General Test (if BSN GPA less than 3.25), Michigan licensure, minimum of B average in BSN program. Additional exam requirements/recommendations for international students: Required—TOEFL (minimum score 560 paper-based; 220 computer-based). Electronic applications accepted. *Expenses:* Tuition, state resident: full-time $17,286; part-time $1099 per credit hour. Tuition, nonresident: full-time $34,944; part-time $2080 per credit hour. Required fees: $95 per semester. Tuition and fees vary according to course load, degree level and program. *Faculty research:* The functional outcomes and quality of life in women with breast cancer, hypertension.

University of Michigan, Horace H. Rackham School of Graduate Studies, School of Nursing, Division of Health Promotion and Risk Reduction, Program in Community Health Nursing, Ann Arbor, MI 48109. Offers adult nurse practitioner (Post Master's Certificate); adult primary care/adult nurse practitioner (MS); community care (Post Master's Certificate); community care/home care (MS); family nurse practitioner (MS, Post Master's Certificate); occupational health nursing (MS). *Accreditation:* AACN. Part-time and evening/weekend programs available. *Degree requirements:* For master's, thesis. *Entrance requirements:* For master's, GRE General Test (if cumulative BSN GPA less than 3.25), licensure, minimum GPA of 3.0 in BSN program. Additional exam requirements/recommendations for international students: Required—TOEFL (minimum score 560 paper-based; 220 computer-based). *Expenses:* Tuition, state resident: full-time $17,286; part-time $1099 per credit hour. Tuition, nonresident: full-time $34,944; part-time $2080 per credit hour. Required fees: $95 per semester. Tuition and fees vary according to course load, degree level and program.

University of Minnesota, Twin Cities Campus, Graduate School, School of Nursing, Program in Adult Health Clinical Nurse Specialist, Minneapolis, MN 55455-0213. Offers MS. *Accreditation:* AACN. *Degree requirements:* For master's, final oral exam, project or thesis. *Entrance requirements:* Additional exam requirements/recommendations for international students: Required—TOEFL (minimum score 586 paper-based; 240 computer-based).

University of Missouri–Kansas City, School of Nursing, Kansas City, MO 64110-2499. Offers adult clinical nurse specialist (MSN), including adult nurse practitioner, women's health nurse practitioner; family nurse practitioner (MSN); neonatal nurse practitioner (MSN); nurse educator (MSN); nurse executive (MSN); nursing (PhD); nursing practice (DNP); pediatric nurse practitioner (MSN). *Accreditation:* AACN. Part-time programs available. Postbaccalaureate distance learning degree programs offered (minimal on-campus study). *Faculty:* 36 full-time (30 women), 40 part-time/adjunct (all women). *Students:* 31 full-time (26 women), 310 part-time (287 women); includes 38 minority (17 African Americans, 2 American Indian/Alaska Native, 10 Asian Americans or Pacific Islanders, 9 Hispanic Americans). Average age 36. 151 applicants, 72% accepted, 109 enrolled. In 2009, 57 master's, 10 doctorates awarded. *Degree requirements:* For master's, thesis or alternative. *Entrance requirements:* For master's, minimum undergraduate GPA of 3.2; for doctorate, GRE, 3 letters of reference, interview by invitation. Additional exam requirements/recommendations for international students: Required—TOEFL (minimum score 550 paper-based; 213 computer-based; 80 iBT). *Application deadline:* For fall admission, 2/1 priority date for domestic and international students; for spring admission, 9/1 priority date for domestic and international students. Application fee: $45 ($50 for international students). *Expenses:* Tuition, state resident: full-time $5378; part-time $299 per credit hour. Tuition, nonresident: full-time $13,881; part-time $771 per credit hour. Required fees: $641; $71 per credit hour. Tuition and fees vary according to course load and program. *Financial support:* In 2009–10, 6 teaching assistantships with partial tuition reimbursements (averaging $4,402 per year) were awarded; fellowships, research assistantships, career-related internships or fieldwork, Federal Work-Study, institutionally sponsored loans, and tuition waivers (full and partial) also available. Support available to part-time students. Financial award application deadline: 3/1; financial award applicants required to submit FAFSA. *Faculty research:* Geriatrics/gerontology, children's pain, neonatology, Alzheimer's care, cancer caregivers. Total annual research expenditures: $2.1 million. *Unit head:* Dr. Lora Lacey-Haun, Dean, 816-235-1700, Fax: 816-235-1701, E-mail: lacey-haunc@umkc.edu. *Application contact:* Leah Wilder, Coordinator for Admissions and Recruitment, 816-235-5768, Fax: 816-235-1701, E-mail: wilderl@umkc.edu.

The University of North Carolina at Chapel Hill, School of Nursing, Chapel Hill, NC 27599-7460. Offers nursing (MSN, PhD, PMC), including adult nurse practitioner (MSN, PMC), children's health advanced practice (MSN, PMC), family nurse practitioner (MSN, PMC), health care systems (MSN, PMC), psychiatric/mental health nursing (MSN, PMC), women's health nursing (MSN, PMC). *Accreditation:* AACN; NLN (one or more programs are accredited). Part-time programs available. *Degree requirements:* For master's, comprehensive exam, thesis;

for doctorate, thesis/dissertation, 3 exams. *Entrance requirements:* For master's and doctorate, GRE General Test. *Faculty research:* Chronic illness, parenting, cardiovascular health in children, elderly, HIV-AIDS.

The University of North Carolina at Charlotte, Graduate School, College of Health and Human Services, School of Nursing, Charlotte, NC 28223-0001. Offers nursing advanced clinical (MSN); nursing anesthesia (MSN); nursing systems population (MSN). *Accreditation:* AACN. *Faculty:* 21 full-time (20 women), 5 part-time/adjunct (all women). *Students:* 77 full-time (65 women), 142 part-time (130 women); includes 26 African Americans, 6 Asian Americans or Pacific Islanders, 4 Hispanic Americans, 1 international. Average age 36. 163 applicants, 52% accepted, 78 enrolled. In 2009, 40 master's awarded. *Entrance requirements:* For master's, GRE General Test, minimum GPA of 3.0 in undergraduate major. Additional exam requirements/recommendations for international students: Required—TOEFL (minimum score 570 paper-based; 220 computer-based; 83 iBT). *Application deadline:* For fall admission, 7/15 for domestic students, 5/1 for international students; for spring admission, 11/15 for domestic students, 10/1 for international students. Application fee: $55. *Financial support:* In 2009–10, 7 students received support, including 1 research assistantship (averaging 12,872 per year), 6 teaching assistantships (averaging $6,171 per year); career-related internships or fieldwork, Federal Work-Study, institutionally sponsored loans, scholarships/grants, traineeships, and unspecified assistantships also available. Support available to part-time students. Financial award application deadline: 4/1; financial award applicants required to submit FAFSA. Total annual research expenditures: $717,259. *Unit head:* Dr. Lucille L. Travis, Director, 704-687-7959, Fax: 704-687-6017, E-mail: ltravis1@uncc.edu. *Application contact:* Kathy B. Giddings, Director of Graduate Admissions, 704-687-5503, Fax: 704-687-3279, E-mail: gradadm@uncc.edu.

The University of North Carolina at Greensboro, Graduate School, School of Nursing, Greensboro, NC 27412-5001. Offers adult clinical nurse specialist (MSN, PMC); adult/gerontological nurse practitioner (MSN, PMC); nurse anesthesia (MSN, PMC); nursing (PhD); nursing administration (MSN); nursing education (MSN); MSN/MBA. *Accreditation:* AACN; AANA/CANAEP; NLN. *Degree requirements:* For master's, thesis or alternative. *Entrance requirements:* For master's, GRE General Test or MAT, BSN, clinical experience, liability insurance, RN license; for PMC, liability insurance, MSN, RN license. Additional exam requirements/recommendations for international students: Required—TOEFL. Electronic applications accepted.

University of Pennsylvania, School of Nursing, Adult Acute Care Nurse Practitioner Program, Philadelphia, PA 19104. Offers acute care nurse practitioner (MSN). *Accreditation:* AACN. Part-time programs available. *Students:* 35 full-time (30 women), 69 part-time (63 women); includes 15 minority (5 African Americans, 1 American Indian/Alaska Native, 7 Asian Americans or Pacific Islanders, 2 Hispanic Americans), 6 international. In 2009, 24 master's awarded. *Entrance requirements:* For master's, GRE General Test, BSN, minimum GPA of 3.0, previous course work in statistics. *Application deadline:* For fall admission, 2/15 priority date for domestic students. Applications are processed on a rolling basis. Application fee: $70. *Expenses:* Contact institution. *Financial support:* Fellowships, research assistantships, teaching assistantships, Federal Work-Study and institutionally sponsored loans available. Support available to part-time students. Financial award application deadline: 4/1. *Faculty research:* Post-injury disability, bereavement and attributions in fire survivors, stress in staff nurses.

University of Pennsylvania, School of Nursing, Adult Health Nurse Practitioner Program, Philadelphia, PA 19104. Offers MSN. *Accreditation:* AACN. Part-time programs available. *Students:* 13 full-time (all women), 9 part-time (8 women); includes 3 minority (1 African American, 2 Asian Americans or Pacific Islanders). In 2009, 10 master's awarded. *Entrance requirements:* For master's, GRE General Test, BSN, minimum GPA of 3.0, previous course work in basic statistics. Additional exam requirements/recommendations for international students: Required—TOEFL. *Application deadline:* For fall admission, 2/15 priority date for domestic students. Applications are processed on a rolling basis. Application fee: $70. *Expenses:* Contact institution. *Financial support:* Fellowships, research assistantships, teaching assistantships, career-related internships or fieldwork, Federal Work-Study, and institutionally sponsored loans available. Support available to part-time students. Financial award application deadline: 4/1. *Faculty research:* Restraints, incontinence, discharge planning, frail elders, quality of life across continuum of care.

University of Pennsylvania, School of Nursing, Adult Oncology Nurse Practitioner Program, Philadelphia, PA 19104. Offers MSN. *Accreditation:* AACN. Part-time programs available. *Students:* 2 full-time (both women), 15 part-time (all women), 1 international. In 2009, 4 master's awarded. *Entrance requirements:* For master's, GRE General Test, BSN, minimum GPA of 3.0, previous course work in statistics. Additional exam requirements/recommendations for international students: Required—TOEFL. *Application deadline:* For fall admission, 2/15 priority date for domestic students. Applications are processed on a rolling basis. Application fee: $70. *Expenses:* Contact institution. *Financial support:* Fellowships, research assistantships, teaching assistantships, career-related internships or fieldwork, Federal Work-Study, and institutionally sponsored loans available. Support available to part-time students. Financial award application deadline: 4/1. *Faculty research:* Randomized clinical trials to evaluate advanced nursing practice in oncology patients and their caregivers, symptoms management.

University of Pittsburgh, School of Nursing, Nurse Practitioner Program, Pittsburgh, PA 15260. Offers acute care nurse practitioner (MSN, DNP); adult nurse practitioner (MSN, DNP); family nurse practitioner (MSN, DNP); neonatal (MSN, DNP); nursing practice (DNP); pediatric nurse practitioner (MSN, DNP); psychiatric primary care nurse practitioner (MSN, DNP). *Accreditation:* AACN. Part-time programs available. *Students:* 27 full-time (26 women), 89 part-time (84 women); includes 6 minority (5 African Americans, 1 Asian American or Pacific Islander). Average age 34. 44 applicants, 64% accepted, 25 enrolled. In 2009, 28 master's awarded. *Degree requirements:* For master's, comprehensive exam, thesis optional. *Entrance requirements:* For master's, GRE General Test or MAT, BSN, RN license, letters of recommendation, resume, course work in statistics, 1-3 years of nursing experience; for doctorate, GRE General Test, BSN, RN license, minimum GPA of 3.5, 3 letters of recommendation. Additional exam requirements/recommendations for international students: Required—TOEFL (minimum score 550 paper-based; 213 computer-based; 80 iBT). *Application deadline:* For fall admission, 8/1 priority date for domestic students, 8/1 for international students; for spring admission, 12/1 priority date for domestic students, 12/1 for international students. Applications are processed on a rolling basis. Application fee: $50. Electronic applications accepted. *Expenses:* Tuition, state resident: full-time $16,402; part-time $665 per credit. Tuition, nonresident: full-time $28,694; part-time $1175 per credit. Required fees: $690; $175 per term. Tuition and fees vary according to program. *Unit head:* Dr. Helen Burns, Associate Dean for Clinical Education, 412-624-6616, Fax: 412-624-2401, E-mail: burnsh@pitt.edu. *Application contact:* Laurie Lapsley, Administrator of Graduate Student Services, 412-624-9670, Fax: 412-624-2409, E-mail: lapsleyl@pitt.edu.

University of Rochester, School of Nursing, Rochester, NY 14642. Offers acute care nurse practitioner (MS); adult nurse practitioner (MS); adult psychiatric mental health nurse practitioner (MS); adult/geriatric nurse practitioner (MS); care of children and families/pediatric nurse practitioner (MS); care of children and families/pediatric nurse practitioner with pediatric behavioral health (MS); care of children and families/pediatric nurse practitioner/neonatal nurse practitioner (MS); child and adolescent psychiatric mental health nurse practitioner (MS); clinical nurse leader (MS); disaster response and emergency preparedness (MS); family nurse practitioner (MS); health care organization management and leadership (MS); health practice research (PhD); health promotion, education and technology (MS); nursing (Certificate). *Accreditation:* AACN; NLN (one or more programs are accredited). Part-time programs available. Postbaccalaureate distance learning degree programs offered (minimal on-campus study). *Faculty:* 26 full-time (24 women), 20 part-time/adjunct (15 women). *Students:* 50 full-time (45 women), 178 part-time (165 women); includes 33 minority (17 African Americans, 2 American Indian/Alaska Native, 10 Asian Americans or Pacific Islanders, 4 Hispanic Americans), 11 international. Average age 35. 56 applicants, 80% accepted, 35 enrolled. In 2009, 53 master's, 5 doctorates awarded. Terminal master's awarded for partial completion of doctoral program.

Degree requirements: For master's, comprehensive exam or thesis; for doctorate, thesis/dissertation. *Entrance requirements:* For master's, BS in nursing, minimum GPA of 3.0, course work in statistics; for doctorate, GRE General Test, MS in nursing, minimum GPA of 3.5; for Certificate, MS in nursing. Additional exam requirements/recommendations for international students: Recommended—TOEFL (minimum score 560 paper-based; 230 computer-based; 88 iBT). *Application deadline:* For fall admission, 11/1 priority date for domestic and international students. Application fee: $50. *Financial support:* In 2009–10, 53 students received support, including 14 fellowships with full and partial tuition reimbursements available (averaging $17,497 per year); scholarships/grants, traineeships, health care benefits, tuition waivers (partial), and unspecified assistantships also available. Support available to part-time students. Financial award application deadline: 6/30. *Faculty research:* Clinical research in aging, managing asthma in children, interventions to improve outcomes in critically ill children and their mothers, nurse home visitation studies, medical device evaluation, critical care clinical studies, high risk behavior and prevention, palliative care, pregnancy-related weight gain. Total annual research expenditures: $4.8 million. *Unit head:* Dr. Kathy P. Parker, Dean, 585-273-5639, Fax: 585-273-1268, E-mail: kathy_parker@urmc.rochester.edu. *Application contact:* Elaine Andolina, Director of Admissions, 585-275-2375, Fax: 585-756-8299, E-mail: elaine_andolina@urmc.rochester.edu.

University of St. Francis, College of Nursing and Allied Health, Joliet, IL 60435-6169. Offers nursing (MSN), including adult health clinical nurse specialist, adult nurse practitioner, family nurse practitioner; nursing practice (DNP). *Accreditation:* AACN. Part-time and evening/weekend programs available. Postbaccalaureate distance learning degree programs offered. *Faculty:* 10 full-time (all women), 11 part-time/adjunct (10 women). *Students:* 13 full-time (10 women), 164 part-time (153 women); includes 41 minority (22 African Americans, 1 American Indian/Alaska Native, 6 Asian Americans or Pacific Islanders, 12 Hispanic Americans). Average age 40. 161 applicants, 43% accepted, 56 enrolled. In 2009, 10 master's awarded. *Entrance requirements:* For master's, GRE General Test (MS), minimum GPA of 2.75, 2 years of work experience in clinical nursing, CPR certification, computer competency, 3 letters of recommendation, interview, RN license, current licensure, immunizations, liability insurance, resume, work history (MSN); for doctorate, master's degree in nursing with minimum GPA of 3.0, national certification as nurse practitioner or clinical nurse specialist, current RN licensure, interview, computer competency, CPR certification, immunizations, medical history, physical form, drug screen, criminal background check, liability insurance, letter of recommendation, resume. Additional exam requirements/recommendations for international students: Required—TOEFL (minimum score 550 paper-based; 213 computer-based). *Application deadline:* Applications are processed on a rolling basis. Application fee: $30. Electronic applications accepted. *Expenses:* Contact institution. *Financial support:* In 2009–10, 135 students received support. Scholarships/grants, traineeships, and tuition waivers (partial) available. Support available to part-time students. Financial award applicants required to submit FAFSA. *Unit head:* Dr. Maria Connolly, Dean, 815-740-3840, Fax: 815-740-4243, E-mail: mconnolly@stfrancis.edu. *Application contact:* Sandra Sloka, Director of Admissions for Graduate and Degree Completion Programs, 800-735-7500, Fax: 815-740-5032, E-mail: ssloka@stfrancis.edu.

University of San Diego, Hahn School of Nursing and Health Science, San Diego, CA 92110-2492. Offers adult nurse practitioner/family nurse practitioner (MSN); adult-gerontology clinical nurse specialist (MSN); clinical nursing (MSN); entry-level nursing (for non-RNs) (MSN); executive nurse leader (MSN); family nurse practitioner (MSN); nursing (PhD); nursing practice (DNP); pediatric nurse practitioner/family nurse practitioner (MSN); psychiatric-mental health nurse practitioner (MSN). *Accreditation:* AACN. Part-time and evening/weekend programs available. *Faculty:* 18 full-time (17 women), 25 part-time/adjunct (22 women). *Students:* 141 full-time (117 women), 173 part-time (152 women); includes 95 minority (20 African Americans, 9 American Indian/Alaska Native, 45 Asian Americans or Pacific Islanders, 21 Hispanic Americans), 7 international. Average age 38. 404 applicants, 50% accepted, 132 enrolled. In 2009, 103 master's, 10 doctorates awarded. *Degree requirements:* For doctorate, thesis/dissertation (for some programs), residency (DNP). *Entrance requirements:* For master's, GRE General Test (entry-level nursing), BSN, current California RN licensure (except for entry-level nursing); minimum GPA of 3.0; for doctorate, minimum GPA of 3.5, MSN, current California RN licensure. Additional exam requirements/recommendations for international students: Required—TOEFL (minimum score 580 paper-based; 237 computer-based; 83 iBT), TWE. *Application deadline:* For fall admission, 3/1 priority date for domestic students, 3/1 for international students; for spring admission, 11/1 priority date for domestic students, 11/1 for international students. Applications are processed on a rolling basis. Application fee: $45. Electronic applications accepted. *Expenses:* Tuition: Full-time $21,042; part-time $1169 per unit. Required fees: $224. Full-time tuition and fees vary according to course load and degree level. *Financial support:* In 2009–10, 270 students received support. Scholarships/grants and traineeships available. Support available to part-time students. Financial award application deadline: 4/1; financial award applicants required to submit FAFSA. *Faculty research:* Health promotion, decision making, psychogeriatric nursing, historical nursing, leadership behavior. *Unit head:* Dr. Sally Hardin, Dean, 619-260-4550, Fax: 619-260-6814. *Application contact:* Dr. John Mosby, Associate Director of Graduate Admissions, 619-260-4524, Fax: 619-260-4158, E-mail: grads@sandiego.edu.

The University of Scranton, College of Graduate and Continuing Education, Department of Nursing, Scranton, PA 18510. Offers adult health nursing (MSN); family nurse practitioner (MSN, PMC); nurse anesthesia (MSN, PMC). Applicants accepted in odd-numbered years only. *Accreditation:* AACN; AANA/CANAEP. Part-time and evening/weekend programs available. *Faculty:* 13 full-time (all women), 2 part-time/adjunct (both women). *Students:* 40 full-time (37 women), 35 part-time (25 women); includes 6 minority (5 African Americans, 1 Asian American or Pacific Islander). Average age 35. 74 applicants, 85% accepted. In 2009, 34 master's awarded. *Degree requirements:* For master's, thesis (for some programs), capstone experience. *Entrance requirements:* For master's, BSN, minimum GPA of 3.0, Pennsylvania RN license. Additional exam requirements/recommendations for international students: Required—TOEFL (minimum score 500 paper-based; 173 computer-based), IELTS (minimum score 5.5). *Application deadline:* For fall admission, 9/1 for domestic students. Applications are processed on a rolling basis. Application fee: $0. *Financial support:* In 2009–10, 8 students received support, including 8 teaching assistantships with full and partial tuition reimbursements available (averaging $6,600 per year); career-related internships or fieldwork, Federal Work-Study, and unspecified assistantships also available. Support available to part-time students. Financial award application deadline: 3/1. *Faculty research:* Home care, doctoral education, health care of women and children, pain, health promotion and adolescence. *Unit head:* Dr. Patricia Harrington, Chair, 570-941-7673, Fax: 570-941-4201, E-mail: harringtonp1@uofs.edu. *Application contact:* Dr. Mary Jane Hanson, Director, 570-941-4060, Fax: 570-941-4201, E-mail: hansonm2@scranton.edu.

University of South Alabama, Graduate School, College of Nursing, Mobile, AL 36688-0002. Offers adult health nursing (MSN); community/mental health nursing (MSN); maternal/child nursing (MSN); nursing (DNP). *Accreditation:* AACN. *Degree requirements:* For master's, thesis optional. *Entrance requirements:* For master's, BSN, RN licensure, minimum GPA of 3.0, resume documenting clinical experience, background check, drug screening; for doctorate, GRE. *Expenses:* Tuition, state resident: part-time $218 per contact hour. Required fees: $1102 per year.

University of South Carolina, The Graduate School, College of Nursing, Program in Health Nursing, Columbia, SC 29208. Offers adult nurse practitioner (MSN); community/public health clinical nurse specialist (MSN); family nurse practitioner (MSN); pediatric nurse practitioner (MSN). *Accreditation:* AACN. Part-time programs available. *Degree requirements:* For master's, thesis or alternative. *Entrance requirements:* For master's, GRE General Test or MAT, BS in nursing, nursing license. Additional exam requirements/recommendations for international students: Required—TOEFL (minimum score 570 paper-based; 230 computer-based). Electronic applications accepted. *Faculty research:* System research, evidence based practice, breast cancer, violence.

University of Southern Maine, College of Nursing and Health Professions, Portland, ME 04104-9300. Offers adult health nursing (PMC); clinical nurse leader (MS); clinical nurse

Adult Nursing

University of Southern Maine (continued)

specialist psychiatric-mental health nursing (MS); family nursing (PMC); medical/surgical nursing (MS); nurse practitioner adult health nursing (MS); nurse practitioner family nursing (MS); nurse practitioner psychiatric/mental health nursing (MS); psychiatric-mental health nursing (PMC); MBA/MSN. *Accreditation:* AACN. Part-time programs available. *Faculty:* 15 full-time (13 women), 4 part-time/adjunct (2 women). *Students:* 51 full-time (40 women), 54 part-time (49 women); includes 4 minority (1 American Indian/Alaska Native, 2 Asian Americans or Pacific Islanders, 1 Hispanic American). Average age 36. 95 applicants, 52% accepted, 27 enrolled. In 2009, 34 master's awarded. *Degree requirements:* For master's, thesis optional. *Entrance requirements:* For master's, GRE General Test or MAT, minimum GPA of 3.0. Additional exam requirements/recommendations for international students: Required—TOEFL (minimum score 550 paper-based; 213 computer-based). *Application deadline:* For fall admission, 4/1 for domestic and international students; for spring admission, 10/1 for domestic and international students. Application fee: $50. Electronic applications accepted. *Financial support:* In 2009–10, 10 students received support, including 5 research assistantships with tuition reimbursements available (averaging $3,375 per year), 3 teaching assistantships with tuition reimbursements available (averaging $3,375 per year); career-related internships or fieldwork, Federal Work-Study, scholarships/grants, traineeships, tuition waivers (full and partial), and unspecified assistantships also available. Support available to part-time students. Financial award application deadline: 2/15; financial award applicants required to submit FAFSA. *Faculty research:* Women's health, nursing history, weight control, community services, substance abuse. *Unit head:* Krista M. Meinersmann, Director of Nursing Program, 207-780-4505, Fax: 207-228-8177, E-mail: kmeinersmann@usm.maine.edu. *Application contact:* Mary Sloan, Assistant Director, Office of Graduate Studies, 207-780-4386, Fax: 207-780-4969, E-mail: gradstudies@usm.maine.edu.

University of Southern Mississippi, Graduate School, College of Health, School of Nursing, Hattiesburg, MS 39406-0001. Offers adult health nursing (MSN); community health nursing (MSN); ethics (PhD); family nurse practitioner (MSN); leadership (PhD); nursing service administration (MSN); policy analysis (PhD); psychiatric nursing (MSN). *Accreditation:* AACN. Part-time and evening/weekend programs available. *Faculty:* 17 full-time (16 women), 1 part-time/adjunct (0 women). *Students:* 63 full-time (57 women), 40 part-time (36 women); includes 23 minority (all African Americans). Average age 40. 69 applicants, 59% accepted, 37 enrolled. In 2009, 28 master's, 2 doctorates awarded. *Degree requirements:* For master's, comprehensive exam, thesis optional; for doctorate, comprehensive exam, thesis/dissertation. *Entrance requirements:* For master's, GRE General Test, minimum GPA of 2.75, nursing license, BS in nursing; for doctorate, GRE General Test, master's degree in nursing, minimum GPA of 3.5. Additional exam requirements/recommendations for international students: Required—TOEFL. *Application deadline:* For fall admission, 3/15 priority date for domestic students, 5/1 for international students. Applications are processed on a rolling basis. Application fee: $35. Electronic applications accepted. *Expenses:* Tuition, state resident: full-time $5096; part-time $284 per hour. Tuition, nonresident: full-time $13,052; part-time $726 per hour. Required fees: $402. Tuition and fees vary according to course level and course load. *Financial support:* In 2009–10, 14 research assistantships with full tuition reimbursements (averaging $12,577 per year) were awarded; teaching assistantships, Federal Work-Study and traineeships also available. Financial award application deadline: 3/15; financial award applicants required to submit FAFSA. *Faculty research:* Gerontology, caregivers, HIV, bereavement, pain, nursing leadership. *Unit head:* Dr. Katherine Nugent, Director and Associate Dean, 601-266-5500, Fax: 601-266-5927. *Application contact:* Dr. Anne Brock, Graduate Coordinator, 601-266-5500, Fax: 601-266-5927.

The University of Tampa, Nursing Program, Tampa, FL 33606-1490. Offers adult nurse practitioner (MSN); family nurse practitioner (MSN). *Accreditation:* NLN. Part-time and evening/weekend programs available. *Faculty:* 10 full-time (all women), 2 part-time/adjunct (both women). *Students:* 4 full-time (all women), 87 part-time (80 women); includes 24 minority (10 African Americans, 1 American Indian/Alaska Native, 1 Asian American or Pacific Islander, 12 Hispanic Americans), 1 international. Average age 38. 64 applicants, 56% accepted, 28 enrolled. In 2009, 22 master's awarded. *Degree requirements:* For master's, comprehensive exam, thesis optional, oral exam, practicum. *Entrance requirements:* For master's, GRE General Test, minimum GPA of 3.0, RN license-Florida, bachelor's degree. Additional exam requirements/recommendations for international students: Required—TOEFL (minimum score 577 paper-based; 230 computer-based; 90 iBT), IELTS (minimum score 7). *Application deadline:* For fall admission, 7/15 for domestic students, 6/1 for international students. Applications are processed on a rolling basis. Application fee: $40. Electronic applications accepted. *Expenses:* Tuition: Part-time $488 per credit hour. *Financial support:* In 2009–10, 68 students received support, including 3 research assistantships with tuition reimbursements available (averaging $2,847 per year); career-related internships or fieldwork and unspecified assistantships also available. Support available to part-time students. Financial award applicants required to submit FAFSA. *Faculty research:* Domestic violence (assessment in emergency departments, changing demographics), trans-cultural health assessment, priorities in maintaining autonomy of elderly. *Unit head:* Dr. Maria Warda, Director, 813-257-3302, Fax: 813-258-7214, E-mail: mwarda@ut.edu. *Application contact:* Karen Full, Graduate Advisor and Recruiter, 813-257-3642, E-mail: kfull@ut.edu.

The University of Texas–Pan American, College of Health Sciences and Human Services, Department of Nursing, Edinburg, TX 78539. Offers adult health nursing (MSN); family nurse practitioner (MSN); pediatric nurse practitioner (MSN). *Accreditation:* AACN. Part-time and evening/weekend programs available. *Degree requirements:* For master's, thesis optional. *Entrance requirements:* For master's, Texas RN licensure, undergraduate physical statistic course. Additional exam requirements/recommendations for international students: Required—TOEFL (minimum score 550 paper-based). Electronic applications accepted. *Expenses:* Contact institution. *Faculty research:* Health promotion, adolescent pregnancy, herbal and nontraditional approaches, healing touch stress.

The University of Toledo, College of Graduate Studies, College of Nursing, Toledo, OH 43606-3390. Offers adult health practitioner/clinical nurse specialist (MSN); adult nurse practitioner (Certificate); entry-level nursing initiative (GEMINI) (MSN); family nurse practitioner (MSN, Certificate); nursing education (Certificate); pediatric nurse practitioner (Certificate); pediatric nurse practitioner/clinical nurse specialist (MSN); RN to MSN (MSN). *Accreditation:* AACN. Part-time programs available. *Degree requirements:* For master's, thesis or scholarly project. *Entrance requirements:* For master's, GRE General Test, BS in nursing, minimum undergraduate GPA of 3.0. *Expenses:* Contact institution. *Faculty research:* Sexuality issues, prenatal testing, health care of homeless, nursing education, chronic/acute pain, eating disorders, low birth weight infants.

University of Wisconsin–Eau Claire, College of Nursing and Health Sciences, Program in Nursing, Eau Claire, WI 54702-4004. Offers adult health clinical nurse specialist (MSN); adult health in administration (MSN); adult health in education (MSN); adult health nurse practitioner (MSN); family health in administration (MSN); family health in education (MSN); family health nurse practitioner (MSN). Part-time programs available. *Faculty:* 15 full-time (14 women). *Students:* 34 full-time (32 women), 55 part-time (51 women); includes 1 minority (Asian American or Pacific Islander). Average age 35. 58 applicants, 59% accepted, 2 enrolled. In 2009, 32 master's awarded. Terminal master's awarded for partial completion of doctoral program. *Degree requirements:* For master's, thesis optional, 500-600 hours clinical practicum, oral and written exams. *Entrance requirements:* For master's, Wisconsin RN license, minimum GPA of 3.0, undergraduate statistics, course work in health assessment. Additional exam requirements/recommendations for international students: Required—TOEFL (minimum score 550 paper-based; 213 computer-based; 79 iBT). *Application deadline:* For fall admission, 1/15 priority date for domestic students, 6/1 priority date for international students; for spring admission, 11/1 priority date for international students. Applications are processed on a rolling basis. Application fee: $56. Electronic applications accepted. *Expenses:* Tuition, state resident: full-time $6705.90; part-time $372.55 per credit. Tuition, nonresident: full-time $16,771; part-time $931.74 per credit. Required fees: $925.50; $51.19 per credit. One-time fee: $56. *Financial support:* In 2009–10, 50 students received support, including 2 fellowships (averaging $500 per year); Federal Work-Study and unspecified assistantships also available. Financial award application deadline: 3/1; financial award applicants required to submit FAFSA. *Unit head:* Dr. Mary Zwygart-Stauffacher, Interim Dean, 715-836-5287, Fax: 715-836-5925, E-mail: zwygarmc@uwec.edu. *Application contact:* Kristina Anderson, Director of Admissions, 715-836-5415, Fax: 715-836-2409, E-mail: admissions@uwec.edu.

University of Wisconsin–Oshkosh, The Office of Graduate Studies, College of Nursing, Oshkosh, WI 54901. Offers adult health and illness (MSN); family nurse practitioner (MSN). *Accreditation:* AACN. Part-time programs available. *Degree requirements:* For master's, thesis or alternative, clinical paper. *Entrance requirements:* For master's, RN license, BSN, previous course work in statistics and health assessment, minimum undergraduate GPA of 3.0, letters of recommendation. Additional exam requirements/recommendations for international students: Required—TOEFL (minimum score 550 paper-based; 213 computer-based; 79 iBT). Electronic applications accepted. *Faculty research:* Adult health and illness, nurse practitioners practice, health care service, advanced practitioner roles, natural alternative complementary healthcare.

Vanderbilt University, School of Nursing, Nashville, TN 37240. Offers adult acute care nurse practitioner (MSN); adult nurse practitioner/cardiovascular disease management and prevention (MSN); adult nurse practitioner/palliative care (MSN); clinical management (clinical nurse leader/specialist) (MSN); emergency nurse practitioner (MSN); family nurse practitioner (MSN); gerontology nurse practitioner (MSN); health systems management (MSN); neonatal nurse practitioner (MSN); nurse midwifery (MSN); nurse midwifery/family nurse practitioner (MSN); nursing informatics (MSN); nursing practice (DNP); nursing science (PhD); nutrition (MS); pediatric acute care nurse practitioner (MSN); pediatric primary care nurse practitioner (MSN); psychiatric-mental health nurse practitioner (MSN); women's health nurse practitioner (MSN), including urogynecology; women's health nurse practitioner/adult nurse practitioner (MSN); MSN/M Div; MSN/MTS. *Accreditation:* ACNM/DOA; NLN (one or more programs are accredited). Part-time programs available. Postbaccalaureate distance learning degree programs offered (minimal on-campus study). *Faculty:* 118 full-time (102 women), 429 part-time/adjunct (309 women). *Students:* 484 full-time (435 women), 319 part-time (284 women); includes 84 minority (55 African Americans, 4 American Indian/Alaska Native, 10 Asian Americans or Pacific Islanders, 15 Hispanic Americans), 16 international. Average age 32. 900 applicants, 65% accepted, 433 enrolled. In 2009, 303 master's, 1 doctorate awarded. *Degree requirements:* For doctorate, comprehensive exam, thesis/dissertation. *Entrance requirements:* For master's, GRE General Test, minimum B average in undergraduate course work, 3 letters of recommendation; for doctorate, GRE General Test, interview, 3 letters of recommendation from doctorally-prepared faculty, MSN, essay. Additional exam requirements/recommendations for international students: Required—TOEFL. *Application deadline:* For fall admission, 12/1 priority date for domestic and international students. Applications are processed on a rolling basis. Application fee: $50. *Expenses:* Contact institution. *Financial support:* In 2009–10, 389 students received support, including 1 research assistantship (averaging $5,000 per year); teaching assistantships, scholarships/grants, health care benefits, and tuition waivers also available. Support available to part-time students. Financial award application deadline: 3/15; financial award applicants required to submit FAFSA. *Faculty research:* Lymphedema, palliative care and bereavement, health services research including workforce, safety and quality of care, gerontology, better birth outcomes including nutrition. Total annual research expenditures: $1.4 million. *Unit head:* Dr. Colleen Conway-Welch, Dean, 615-343-8776, Fax: 615-343-7711, E-mail: colleen.conway-welch@vanderbilt.edu. *Application contact:* Cheryl Feldner, Assistant Director of Admissions, 615-322-3800, Fax: 615-343-0333, E-mail: cheryl.feldner@vanderbilt.edu.

Villanova University, College of Nursing, Villanova, PA 19085-1699. Offers adult nurse practitioner (MSN, Post Master's Certificate); family nurse practitioner (MSN, Post Master's Certificate); health care administration (MSN); nurse anesthetist (MSN, Post Master's Certificate); nursing (PhD); nursing education (MSN, Post Master's Certificate); pediatric nurse practitioner (MSN, Post Master's Certificate). *Accreditation:* AACN; AANA/CANAEP. Part-time programs available. Postbaccalaureate distance learning degree programs offered (minimal on-campus study). *Faculty:* 15 full-time (all women), 3 part-time/adjunct (2 women). *Students:* 58 full-time (53 women), 188 part-time (164 women); includes 29 minority (13 African Americans, 1 American Indian/Alaska Native, 13 Asian Americans or Pacific Islanders, 2 Hispanic Americans), 3 international. Average age 33. 171 applicants, 70% accepted, 89 enrolled. In 2009, 32 master's, 1 doctorate awarded. *Degree requirements:* For master's, independent study project; for doctorate, comprehensive exam, thesis/dissertation. *Entrance requirements:* For master's, GRE or MAT, BSN, 1 year of recent nursing experience, physical assessment, course work in statistics; for doctorate, GRE, MSN. Additional exam requirements/recommendations for international students: Required—TOEFL. *Application deadline:* For fall admission, 7/1 priority date for domestic students, 7/1 for international students; for spring admission, 11/1 priority date for domestic students, 11/1 for international students. Applications are processed on a rolling basis. Application fee: $50. *Expenses:* Contact institution. *Financial support:* In 2009–10, 53 students received support, including 5 teaching assistantships with full tuition reimbursements available (averaging $13,100 per year); institutionally sponsored loans, scholarships/grants, traineeships, tuition waivers (full), and unspecified assistantships also available. Financial award application deadline: 3/1; financial award applicants required to submit FAFSA. *Faculty research:* Genetics, ethics, cognitive development of students, women with disabilities, nursing leadership. *Unit head:* Dr. Marguerite K. Schlag, Assistant Dean and Director, Graduate Program, 610-519-4907, Fax: 610-519-7650, E-mail: marguerite.schlag@villanova.edu. *Application contact:* Dean, Graduate School of Liberal Arts and Sciences.

Virginia Commonwealth University, Graduate School, School of Nursing, Richmond, VA 23284-9005. Offers adult health nursing (MS); child health nursing (MS); family health nursing (MS); health system (PhD); immunocompetence (PhD); nurse practitioner (MS, Certificate); nursing administration (MS), including clinical nurse manager, nurse executive; psychiatric-mental health nursing (MS); risk and resilience (PhD); women's health nursing (MS). *Accreditation:* NLN (one or more programs are accredited). Part-time and evening/weekend programs available. *Degree requirements:* For master's, thesis optional; for doctorate, thesis/dissertation. *Entrance requirements:* For master's, GRE General Test, BSN, minimum GPA of 2.8; for doctorate, GRE General Test.

Wayne State University, College of Nursing, Program in Adult Acute Care Nursing, Detroit, MI 48202. Offers MSN. *Accreditation:* AACN. Part-time programs available. *Degree requirements:* For master's, thesis or alternative. *Entrance requirements:* For master's, GRE General Test, minimum GPA of 2.8. Additional exam requirements/recommendations for international students: Required—TOEFL (minimum score 550 paper-based; 213 computer-based); Recommended—TWE (minimum score 6). Electronic applications accepted. *Faculty research:* Cardiovascular nursing with vulnerable populations, wound healing, symptom management.

Wayne State University, College of Nursing, Program in Adult Primary Care Nursing, Detroit, MI 48202. Offers MSN. *Accreditation:* AACN. Part-time programs available. *Degree requirements:* For master's, thesis or alternative. *Entrance requirements:* For master's, GRE General Test, minimum GPA of 2.8. Additional exam requirements/recommendations for international students: Required—TOEFL (minimum score 550 paper-based; 213 computer-based); Recommended—TWE (minimum score 6). Electronic applications accepted. *Faculty research:* Smoking risk behaviors in adolescents, sleep disturbances in postmenopausal women, health disparities in urban environments, nurse practitioner interventions, caregiving and pain management.

Western Connecticut State University, Division of Graduate Studies, School of Professional Studies, Nursing Department, Danbury, CT 06810-6885. Offers adult nurse practitioner (MSN); clinical nurse specialist (MSN). *Accreditation:* AACN. Part-time programs available. *Faculty:* 3 full-time (all women), 1 (woman) part-time/adjunct. *Students:* 32 part-time (all women); includes 3 minority (2 African Americans, 1 Asian American or Pacific Islander). Average age 41. 24 applicants, 71% accepted, 13 enrolled. *Degree requirements:* For master's, clinical component, thesis or research project, completion of program in 6 years. *Entrance requirements:* For master's, MAT (if GPA less than 3.0), bachelor's degree in nursing, minimum GPA of 3.0,

previous course work in statistics and nursing research, RN license. Additional exam requirements/recommendations for international students: Recommended—TOEFL (minimum score 550 paper-based; 213 computer-based; 79 iBT), IELTS (minimum score 6). *Application deadline:* For fall admission, 8/5 priority date for domestic students; for spring admission, 1/5 for domestic students. Applications are processed on a rolling basis. Application fee: $50. *Expenses:* Tuition, state resident: full-time $5012; part-time $278 per credit hour. Tuition, nonresident: full-time $13,962; part-time $284 per credit hour. Required fees: $3886; $139 per credit hour. Full-time tuition and fees vary according to course load and program. Part-time tuition and fees vary according to course level, degree level and program. *Financial support:* In 2009–10, 4 students received support. Scholarships/grants available. Financial award application deadline: 5/1; financial award applicants required to submit FAFSA. *Unit head:* Dr. Patricia Z. Lund, Professor, 203-837-8567, Fax: 203-837-8550, E-mail: lundp@wcsu.edu. *Application contact:* Chris Shankle, Associate Director of Graduate Studies, 203-837-9005, Fax: 203-837-8326, E-mail: shanklec@wcsu.edu.

Wilmington University, College of Health Professions, New Castle, DE 19720-6491. Offers adult nurse practitioner (MSN); family nurse practitioner (MSN); gerontology (MSN); leadership (MSN); nursing (MSN); women's nurse practitioner (MSN). *Accreditation:* AACN. Part-time programs available. *Degree requirements:* For master's, thesis. *Entrance requirements:* For master's, BSN, RN license, interview, 3 letters of recommendation. Additional exam requirements/recommendations for international students: Required—TOEFL (minimum score 500 paper-based; 173 computer-based). Electronic applications accepted. *Faculty research:* Outcomes assessment, student writing ability.

Winona State University, College of Nursing and Health Sciences, Winona, MN 55987-5838. Offers adult nurse practitioner (MS, Post Master's Certificate); clinical nurse specialist (MS, Post Master's Certificate); family nurse practitioner (MS, Post Master's Certificate); nurse administrator (MS); nurse educator (MS, Post Master's Certificate); nursing (DNP). *Accreditation:* AACN. Part-time programs available. Postbaccalaureate distance learning degree programs offered (no on-campus study). *Degree requirements:* For master's, thesis; for doctorate, capstone. *Entrance requirements:* For master's, GRE (if GPA less than 3.0). Additional exam requirements/recommendations for international students: Required—TOEFL (minimum score 550 paper-based). *Faculty research:* Job satisfaction; nursing diagnoses; dehydration among elderly; correlates to functional status in elderly.

Wright State University, School of Graduate Studies, College of Nursing and Health, Program in Nursing, Dayton, OH 45435. Offers acute care nurse practitioner (MS); administration of nursing and health care systems (MS); adult health (MS); child and adolescent health (MS); community health (MS); family nurse practitioner (MS); nurse practitioner (MS); school nurse (MS); MBA/MS. *Accreditation:* AACN. Part-time and evening/weekend programs available. *Degree requirements:* For master's, thesis or alternative. *Entrance requirements:* For master's, GRE General Test, BSN from NLN-accredited college, Ohio RN license. Additional exam requirements/recommendations for international students: Required—TOEFL. *Faculty research:* Clinical nursing and health, teaching, caring, pain administration, informatics and technology.

Community Health Nursing

Arizona State University, Graduate College, College of Nursing and Healthcare Innovation, Tempe, AZ 85287. Offers child and adolescent mental health intervention specialist (Graduate Certificate); community and public health practice (Graduate Certificate); community health (MS); evidence-based practice in nursing (Graduate Certificate); exercise and wellness (MS, PhD), including exercise and wellness (MS), physical activity, nutrition and wellness (PhD); healthcare innovation (MHI); nurse education in academic and practice settings (Graduate Certificate); nurse educator (MS); nursing (MS); nursing and healthcare innovation (PhD); nursing practice (DNP); nutrition (MS). *Accreditation:* AACN. Postbaccalaureate distance learning degree programs offered.

Augsburg College, Program in Transcultural Community Health Nursing, Minneapolis, MN 55454-1351. Offers MA. *Accreditation:* AACN. *Degree requirements:* For master's, thesis or alternative. *Expenses:* Tuition: Full-time $16,713; part-time $1857 per course. Required fees: $450; $50 per course. Tuition and fees vary according to course load and program.

Boston College, William F. Connell School of Nursing, Chestnut Hill, MA 02467-3800. Offers adult health nursing (MS); community health nursing (MS); family health (MS); forensic nursing (MS); gerontology (MS); maternal/child health nursing (MS), including pediatric and women's health; nurse anesthesia (MS); nursing (PhD); palliative care (MS), including adult and pediatric; psychiatric-mental health nursing (MS); MBA/MS; MS/MA; MS/PhD. *Accreditation:* AACN; AANA/CANAEP (one or more programs are accredited). Part-time programs available. *Faculty:* 48 full-time (46 women), 31 part-time/adjunct (29 women). *Students:* 183 full-time (169 women), 147 part-time (140 women); includes 36 minority (15 African Americans, 2 American Indian/Alaska Native, 17 Asian Americans or Pacific Islanders, 2 Hispanic Americans), 7 international. Average age 29. 347 applicants, 53% accepted, 103 enrolled. In 2009, 79 master's, 7 doctorates awarded. *Degree requirements:* For master's, comprehensive exam, research project; for doctorate, comprehensive exam, thesis/dissertation, computer literacy exam or foreign language. *Entrance requirements:* For master's, bachelor's degree in nursing; for doctorate, GRE General Test, master's degree in nursing. Additional exam requirements/recommendations for international students: Required—TOEFL (minimum score 550 paper-based; 213 computer-based). *Application deadline:* For fall admission, 11/1 for domestic and international students; for winter admission, 12/31 for domestic and international students; for spring admission, 9/15 for domestic and international students. Applications are processed on a rolling basis. Application fee: $40. Electronic applications accepted. *Financial support:* In 2009–10, 83 students received support, including 12 fellowships with partial tuition reimbursements available (averaging $15,000 per year), 5 teaching assistantships (averaging $13,746 per year); research assistantships, Federal Work-Study, institutionally sponsored loans, scholarships/grants, traineeships, health care benefits, and tuition waivers (partial) also available. Support available to part-time students. Financial award application deadline: 3/1; financial award applicants required to submit FAFSA. *Faculty research:* Ethics, reduction of risk behaviors, support during chronic illness, violence, gerontology. Total annual research expenditures: $1.4 million. *Unit head:* Dr. Susan Gennaro, Dean, 617-552-4251, Fax: 617-552-0931, E-mail: susan.gennaro@bc.edu. *Application contact:* MaryBeth Crowley, Graduate Programs Assistant, 617-552-4928, Fax: 617-552-2121, E-mail: csongrad@bc.edu.

Case Western Reserve University, Frances Payne Bolton School of Nursing, Master's Programs in Nursing, Cleveland, OH 44106. Offers community health nursing (MSN); medical-surgical nursing (MSN); nurse anesthesia (MSN); nurse midwifery (MSN); nurse practitioner (MSN), including acute care cardiovascular nursing, acute care nurse practitioner, acute care/flight nurse, adult nurse practitioner, family nurse practitioner, gerontological nurse practitioner, neonatal nurse practitioner, pediatric nurse practitioner, psychiatric-mental health nurse practitioner, women's health nurse practitioner; nursing informatics (MSN). *Accreditation:* NLN. Part-time programs available. Postbaccalaureate distance learning degree programs offered (minimal on-campus study). *Degree requirements:* For master's, thesis optional. *Entrance requirements:* For master's, GRE General Test or MAT. *Faculty research:* Preterm skin contact effects on electrophysiologic sleep, intergenerational caregiving to at risk youth, maintaining exercise in cardiac rehabilitation, left ventricular function and duration of mechanical ventilation.

The Catholic University of America, School of Nursing, Washington, DC 20064. Offers adult health specialist with functional role as nurse educator (MSN); adult nurse practitioner (MSN); community/public health nurse specialist educator (MSN); family nurse practitioner (MSN); geriatric nurse practitioner (MSN); immigrant, refugee, and global health clinical nurse specialist (MSN); nursing (DNP, PhD, Certificate); pediatric nurse practitioner (MSN); promoting healthy families in vulnerable communities (MSN); psychiatric-mental health nursing (MSN). *Accreditation:* AACN. Part-time programs available. *Faculty:* 15 full-time (all women), 43 part-time/adjunct (41 women). *Students:* 28 full-time (26 women), 75 part-time (73 women); includes 37 minority (27 African Americans, 6 Asian Americans or Pacific Islanders, 4 Hispanic Americans), 4 international. Average age 42. 84 applicants, 64% accepted, 30 enrolled. In 2009, 23 master's, 7 doctorates, 3 other advanced degrees awarded. *Degree requirements:* For master's, comprehensive exam, thesis optional; for doctorate, comprehensive exam, thesis/dissertation, minimum GPA of 3.0, oral proposal defense. *Entrance requirements:* For master's, 3 letters of recommendation, BA in nursing, RN registration, official copies of academic transcripts, some post-baccalaureate nursing experience; for doctorate, GRE General Test, BA in nursing, professional portfolio (including statements, resume, copy of RN license, 3 letters of recommendation, narrative description of clinical practice, proposal), copy of research/scholarly paper related to clinical nursing. Additional exam requirements/recommendations for international students: Required—TOEFL (minimum score 580 paper-based; 237 computer-based). *Application deadline:* For fall admission, 8/1 priority date for domestic students, 7/15 for international students; for spring admission, 12/1 priority date for domestic students, 10/15 for international students. Applications are processed on a rolling basis. Application fee: $55. Electronic applications accepted. *Expenses:* Tuition: Full-time $31,740; part-time $1245 per credit hour. Required fees: $50; $25 per semester hour. One-time fee: $425. *Financial support:* Fellowships, research assistantships, teaching assistantships, Federal Work-Study, scholarships/grants, tuition waivers (full and partial), and unspecified assistantships available. Financial award application deadline: 2/1; financial award applicants required to submit FAFSA. *Faculty research:* Community involvement in health care services, primary health care services, pediatrics, chronic illness, cardiovascular disease. Total annual research expenditures: $311,172. *Unit head:* Dr. Nalini N. Jairath, Dean, 202-319-5403, Fax: 202-319-6485, E-mail: cua-deanschoolofnursing@cua.edu. *Application contact:* Julie Schwing, Director of Graduate Admissions, 202-319-5057, Fax: 202-319-6533, E-mail: cua-admissions@cua.edu.

Cleveland State University, College of Graduate Studies, College of Education and Human Services, School of Nursing, Cleveland, OH 44115. Offers clinical nursing leader (MSN); executive track (MSN); forensic nursing (MSN); nursing education (MSN); population health nursing (MSN); MSN/MBA. *Accreditation:* AACN. Part-time programs available. *Degree requirements:* For master's, thesis or alternative, portfolio, population health project. *Entrance requirements:* For master's, RN license, BSN, course work in statistics. Additional exam requirements/recommendations for international students: Required—TOEFL (minimum score 525 paper-based; 197 computer-based), IELTS (minimum score 6). Electronic applications accepted. *Faculty research:* Diabetes management, African-American elders medication compliance, risk in home visiting, suffering, COPD and stress.

D'Youville College, Department of Nursing, Buffalo, NY 14201-1084. Offers community health nursing/education (MSN); community health nursing/high risk parents and children (MSN); community health nursing/management (MSN); family nurse practitioner (MS, Post-Master's Certificate); nursing and health-related professions (Certificate); nursing with clinical focus choice (MSN). *Accreditation:* AACN. Part-time and evening/weekend programs available. *Degree requirements:* For master's, thesis optional, membership on board of community agency, publishable paper. *Entrance requirements:* For master's, BS in nursing, minimum GPA of 3.0, course work in statistics and computers. Additional exam requirements/recommendations for international students: Required—TOEFL (minimum score 500 paper-based; 173 computer-based). Electronic applications accepted. *Faculty research:* Nursing curriculum, nursing theory-testing, wellness research, communication and socialization patterns.

See Display on page 1487 and Close-Up on page 1611.

Georgia Southern University, Jack N. Averitt College of Graduate Studies, College of Health and Human Sciences, School of Nursing, Statesboro, GA 30460. Offers clinical nurse specialist (MSN, Certificate); nurse practitioner (MSN, Certificate); nursing science (DNP); rural community health nurse practitioner (MSN); rural community health nurse specialist (Certificate); rural family nurse practitioner (MSN, Certificate); women's health nurse practitioner (MSN, Certificate). *Accreditation:* AACN. Part-time programs available. Postbaccalaureate distance learning degree programs offered. *Students:* 12 full-time (all women), 89 part-time (80 women); includes 17 minority (11 African Americans, 1 American Indian/Alaska Native, 3 Asian Americans or Pacific Islanders, 2 Hispanic Americans). Average age 39. 34 applicants, 85% accepted, 24 enrolled. In 2009, 7 master's awarded. *Degree requirements:* For master's, comprehensive exam, thesis optional; for doctorate, clinical immersion project, capstone practicum. *Entrance requirements:* For master's, GRE General Test or MAT, minimum GPA of 3.0, Georgia nursing license, 2 years of clinical experience, CPR certification; for doctorate, GRE, MAT, portfolio, certification, RN licensure, clinical hours; for Certificate, MSN. Additional exam requirements/recommendations for international students: Required—TOEFL (minimum score 550 paper-based; 213 computer-based; 80 iBT). *Application deadline:* For fall admission, 3/1 priority date for domestic and international students; for spring admission, 10/1 priority date for domestic students, 10/1 for international students. Applications are processed on a rolling basis. Application fee: $50. Electronic applications accepted. *Expenses:* Tuition, state resident: full-time $5040; part-time $210 per credit hour. Tuition, nonresident: full-time $20,136; part-time $839 per credit hour. Required fees: $1644. *Financial support:* In 2009–10, 101 students received support, including research assistantships with partial tuition reimbursements available (averaging $7,200 per year), teaching assistantships with partial tuition reimbursements available (averaging $7,200 per year); career-related internships or fieldwork, Federal Work-Study, scholarships/grants, traineeships, tuition waivers (partial), and unspecified assistantships also available. Support available to part-time students. Financial award application deadline: 4/15; financial award applicants required to submit FAFSA. *Faculty research:* Obesity, cardiac disease, rural healthcare, nursing education, health literacy. Total annual research expenditures: $189,915. *Unit head:* Dr. Donna Hodnicki, Chair, 912-478-5056, Fax: 912-478-0536, E-mail: dhodnick@georgiasouthern.edu. *Application contact:* Dr. Charles Ziglar, Coordinator for Graduate Student Recruitment, 912-478-5635, Fax: 912-478-0740, E-mail: gradadmissionss@georgiasouthern.edu.

Hampton University, Graduate College, School of Nursing, Hampton, VA 23668. Offers advanced adult nursing (MS); community health nursing (MS); community mental health/psychiatric nursing (MS); family nursing (MS); gerontological nursing for the nurse practitioner (MS); pediatric nursing (MS); women's health nursing (MS). *Accreditation:* AACN; NLN. Part-time and evening/weekend programs available. *Degree requirements:* For master's, thesis optional. *Entrance requirements:* For master's, GRE General Test. *Faculty research:* Curriculum development, physical and mental assessment.

Hawai'i Pacific University, College of Nursing and Health Sciences, Honolulu, HI 96813. Offers community clinical nurse specialist (MSN); community clinical nurse specialist educator option (MSN); family nurse practitioner (MSN). *Accreditation:* NLN. Part-time and evening/weekend programs available. *Faculty:* 5 full-time (4 women), 2 part-time/adjunct (1 woman). *Students:* 26 full-time (23 women), 13 part-time (all women); includes 18 minority (3 African Americans, 2 American Indian/Alaska Native, 12 Asian Americans or Pacific Islanders, 1

Community Health Nursing

Hawai'i Pacific University *(continued)*

Hispanic American), 7 international. Average age 38. 22 applicants, 68% accepted, 10 enrolled. In 2009, 11 master's awarded. *Degree requirements:* For master's, practicum, professional paper. *Entrance requirements:* For master's, bachelor's degree in nursing, minimum GPA of 3.0. Additional exam requirements/recommendations for international students: Recommended—TOEFL (minimum score 550 paper-based; 213 computer-based; 80 iBT), TWE (minimum score 5). *Application deadline:* Applications are processed on a rolling basis. Application fee: $50. Electronic applications accepted. *Expenses:* Tuition: Full-time $12,600; part-time $700 per credit hour. Tuition and fees vary according to program. *Financial support:* In 2009–10, 17 students received support. Career-related internships or fieldwork, Federal Work-Study, scholarships/grants, and traineeships available. Support available to part-time students. Financial award application deadline: 3/1; financial award applicants required to submit FAFSA. *Faculty research:* Hawaiian elders, traditional healing and nursing center. *Unit head:* Dr. Patricia Lange-Otsuka, Associate Dean of Nursing for Administration, 808-236-5812, Fax: 808-236-5818, E-mail: potsuka@hpu.edu. *Application contact:* Danny Lam, Assistant Director of Graduate Admissions, 808-544-1135, Fax: 808-544-0280, E-mail: graduate@hpu.edu.

Holy Family University, Graduate School, School of Nursing, Philadelphia, PA 19114. Offers community health nursing (MSN); nursing administration (MSN); nursing education (MSN). *Accreditation:* AACN. Part-time and evening/weekend programs available. *Faculty:* 1 (woman) full-time, 1 (woman) part-time/adjunct. *Students:* 1 (woman) full-time, 46 part-time (all women); includes 7 minority (5 African Americans, 2 Asian Americans or Pacific Islanders). Average age 41. 17 applicants, 76% accepted, 11 enrolled. In 2009, 3 master's awarded. *Degree requirements:* For master's, thesis or alternative. *Entrance requirements:* For master's, bachelor's degree in nursing, RN license, minimum GPA of 3.0, 2 letters of reference. *Application deadline:* For fall admission, 7/1 priority date for domestic students; for winter admission, 11/1 priority date for domestic students. Applications are processed on a rolling basis. Application fee: $25. *Expenses:* Tuition: Part-time $600 per credit. Required fees: $58 per semester. *Financial support:* Federal Work-Study available. Support available to part-time students. Financial award application deadline: 2/15; financial award applicants required to submit FAFSA. *Unit head:* Dr. Christine Rosner, Dean, 267-341-3292, Fax: 215-637-6598, E-mail: crosner@holyfamily.edu. *Application contact:* Gidget Matie Montelibano, Graduate Admissions Counselor, 267-341-3558, Fax: 215-637-1478, E-mail: gmontelibano@holyfamily.edu.

Holy Names University, Graduate Division, Department of Nursing, Oakland, CA 94619-1699. Offers administration/management (MS, Certificate); clinical faculty (MS, Certificate); community health nursing/case manager (MS); family nurse practitioner (MS, Certificate); MSN/Certificate; MSN/MBA. *Accreditation:* AACN. Part-time and evening/weekend programs available. *Entrance requirements:* For master's, bachelor's degree in nursing or related field, California RN license or eligibility, minimum GPA of 3.0, previous course work in research or statistics. Additional exam requirements/recommendations for international students: Required—TOEFL (minimum score 500 paper-based). *Faculty research:* Women's reproductive health, gerontology, attitudes about aging, schizophrenic families, international health issues.

Hunter College of the City University of New York, Graduate School, Schools of the Health Professions, Hunter-Bellevue School of Nursing, Community Health Nursing Program, New York, NY 10021-5085. Offers MS. *Accreditation:* AACN. Part-time programs available. *Faculty:* 4 full-time (0 women), 11 part-time/adjunct (0 women). *Students:* 1 (woman) full-time, 20 part-time (17 women); includes 13 minority (7 African Americans, 3 Asian Americans or Pacific Islanders, 3 Hispanic Americans). Average age 34. 9 applicants, 78% accepted, 5 enrolled. In 2009, 30 master's awarded. *Degree requirements:* For master's, practicum. *Entrance requirements:* For master's, minimum GPA of 3.0, New York RN license, BSN. Additional exam requirements/recommendations for international students: Required—TOEFL. *Application deadline:* For fall admission, 4/1 for domestic students, 2/1 for international students; for spring admission, 11/1 for domestic students, 9/1 for international students. Applications are processed on a rolling basis. Application fee: $125. *Expenses:* Tuition, state resident: full-time $7360; part-time $310 per credit. Required fees: $250 per semester. *Financial support:* Federal Work-Study, scholarships/grants, traineeships, and tuition waivers (partial) available. Support available to part-time students. Financial award application deadline: 5/1; financial award applicants required to submit FAFSA. *Faculty research:* HIV/AIDS, health promotion with vulnerable populations. *Unit head:* Dr. Patricia Hill, Coordinator, 212-481-3478, E-mail: psthil@hunter.cuny.edu. *Application contact:* William Zlata, Director for Graduate Admissions, 212-772-4482, Fax: 212-650-3336, E-mail: admissions@hunter.cuny.edu.

Hunter College of the City University of New York, Graduate School, Schools of the Health Professions, Hunter-Bellevue School of Nursing, Community/Public Health Nursing/Urban Public Health Program, New York, NY 10021-5085. Offers MS/MPH. *Accreditation:* AACN. Part-time programs available. *Faculty:* 27 full-time (17 women), 3 part-time/adjunct (2 women). *Students:* 17 part-time (15 women); includes 12 minority (7 African Americans, 2 Asian Americans or Pacific Islanders, 3 Hispanic Americans). Average age 37. 14 applicants, 86% accepted, 9 enrolled. *Entrance requirements:* Additional exam requirements/recommendations for international students: Required—TOEFL. *Application deadline:* For fall admission, 4/1 for domestic students, 2/1 for international students; for spring admission, 11/1 for domestic students, 9/1 for international students. Applications are processed on a rolling basis. Application fee: $125. *Expenses:* Tuition, state resident: full-time $7360; part-time $310 per credit. Required fees: $250 per semester. *Financial support:* Federal Work-Study, scholarships/grants, traineeships, and tuition waivers (partial) available. Support available to part-time students. Financial award application deadline: 5/1; financial award applicants required to submit FAFSA. *Faculty research:* HIV/AIDS, health promotion with vulnerable populations, immigrant health. *Unit head:* Dr. Kathleen Nokes, Coordinator, 212-481-7594, Fax: 212-481-5078, E-mail: knokes@hejira.hunter.cuny.edu. *Application contact:* William Zlata, Director for Graduate Admissions, 212-772-4482, Fax: 212-650-3336, E-mail: admissions@hunter.cuny.edu.

Husson University, School of Graduate and Professional Studies, Program in Nursing, Bangor, ME 04401-2999. Offers advanced practice psychiatric nursing (MSN, PMC); family and community nurse practitioner (MSN, PMC). *Accreditation:* AACN. *Entrance requirements:* For master's, MAT, BSN. *Expenses:* Contact institution.

Independence University, Program in Nursing, Salt Lake City, UT 84107. Offers community health (MSN); gerontology (MSN); nursing administration (MSN); wellness promotion (MSN). *Expenses:* Required fees: $475 per credit. One-time fee: $100 part-time.

Indiana University–Purdue University Indianapolis, School of Nursing, Indianapolis, IN 46202-2896. Offers acute care nurse practitioner (MSN); adult health clinical nurse specialist (MSN); adult health nursing (MSN), including adult clinical nurse specialist; adult nurse practitioner (MSN); adult psychiatric/mental health nursing (MSN); child psychiatric/mental health nursing (MSN); community health nursing (MSN); family nurse practitioner (MSN); neonatal nurse practitioner (MSN); nursing science (PhD); pediatric clinical nurse specialist (MSN); women's health nurse practitioner (MSN); MSN/MPA; MSN/MPH. *Accreditation:* AACN; NLN (one or more programs are accredited). Part-time programs available. *Faculty:* 85 full-time (82 women), 60 part-time/adjunct (all women). *Students:* 46 full-time (43 women), 369 part-time (354 women); includes 30 minority (21 African Americans, 6 Asian Americans or Pacific Islanders, 3 Hispanic Americans), 5 international. Average age 39. 121 applicants, 82% accepted, 67 enrolled. In 2009, 106 master's, 3 doctorates awarded. Terminal master's awarded for partial completion of doctoral program. *Degree requirements:* For master's, thesis; for doctorate, thesis/dissertation. *Entrance requirements:* For master's, minimum GPA of 3.0, RN license; for doctorate, GRE General Test, minimum GPA of 3.0, MSN, RN license, graduate statistics course with B grade or better (not older than 3 years). Additional exam requirements/recommendations for international students: Required—TOEFL. *Application deadline:* For fall admission, 2/15 for domestic students; for spring admission, 9/15 for domestic students. Application fee: $55 ($65 for international students). *Financial support:* In 2009–10, 93 students received support, including 9 fellowships with full tuition reimbursements available (averaging $7,039 per year), 7 teaching assistantships with full tuition reimbursements available (averaging $5,300 per year); research assistantships with full tuition reimbursements available, Federal

Work-Study, institutionally sponsored loans, scholarships/grants, and tuition waivers (full) also available. Support available to part-time students. Financial award application deadline: 5/1. *Faculty research:* Clinical science, health systems. Total annual research expenditures: $3 million. *Unit head:* Associate Dean for Graduate Programs, 317-274-2806, E-mail: nursing@iupui.edu. *Application contact:* Information Contact, 317-274-2806.

Indiana Wesleyan University, College of Graduate Studies, School of Nursing, Marion, IN 46953-4974. Offers community health nursing (MS); nursing (Post Master's Certificate); nursing administration (MS); nursing education (MS); primary care nursing (MS). *Accreditation:* AACN. Part-time programs available. Postbaccalaureate distance learning degree programs offered (minimal on-campus study). *Degree requirements:* For master's, capstone project or thesis. *Entrance requirements:* For master's, writing sample, RN license, 1 year of related experience, graduate statistics course. Additional exam requirements/recommendations for international students: Required—TOEFL. *Expenses:* Contact institution. *Faculty research:* Primary health care with international emphasis, international nursing.

Inter American University of Puerto Rico, Arecibo Campus, Program in Nursing, Arecibo, PR 00614-4050. Offers community nursing (MS); critical care nursing (MS); primary care nursing (MS); surgical nursing (MS). *Entrance requirements:* For master's, EXADEP or GRE General Test or MAT, 2 letters of recommendation, bachelor's degree in nursing, minimum GPA of 2.5 in last 60 credits, minimum 1 year nursing experience, nursing license.

The Johns Hopkins University, School of Nursing and Bloomberg School of Public Health, Joint Degree Program in Nursing and Public Health, Baltimore, MD 21218-2699. Offers MSN/MPH. *Accreditation:* AACN; CEPH. Part-time programs available. *Faculty:* 4 full-time (all women), 2 part-time/adjunct (both women). *Students:* 10 full-time (9 women), 22 part-time (19 women); includes 11 minority (6 African Americans, 5 Asian Americans or Pacific Islanders). Average age 29. 37 applicants, 81% accepted, 7 enrolled. *Entrance requirements:* Additional exam requirements/recommendations for international students: Required—TOEFL (minimum score 550 paper-based; 213 computer-based). *Application deadline:* For fall admission, 3/1 priority date for domestic and international students; for spring admission, 1/31 priority date for domestic and international students. Applications are processed on a rolling basis. Application fee: $75. Electronic applications accepted. *Expenses:* Contact institution. *Financial support:* In 2009–10, 29 students received support. Federal Work-Study, scholarships/grants, traineeships, and tuition waivers (partial) available. Support available to part-time students. Financial award application deadline: 3/1; financial award applicants required to submit FAFSA. *Faculty research:* Asthma, tuberculosis control, injury, violence, international health, women's health, substance abuse. *Unit head:* Dr. Julie A. Stanik-Hutt, Director, Master's Programs, 410-502-0184, Fax: 410-955-7463, E-mail: jstanik1@son.jhmi.edu. *Application contact:* Mary O'Rourke, Director of Admissions and Student Services, 410-955-7548, Fax: 410-614-7086, E-mail: orourke@son.jhmi.edu.

The Johns Hopkins University, School of Nursing, Program in Public Health Nursing, Baltimore, MD 21218-2699. Offers MSN. *Accreditation:* AACN; NLN. Part-time programs available. *Faculty:* 3 full-time (all women), 2 part-time/adjunct (both women). *Students:* 1 (woman) full-time, 1 (woman) part-time; includes 1 minority (Asian American or Pacific Islander). Average age 44. 6 applicants, 83% accepted, 2 enrolled. In 2009, 7 master's awarded. *Degree requirements:* For master's, thesis optional, scholarly project or portfolio. *Entrance requirements:* For master's, interview, minimum GPA of 3.0, BSN, Maryland RN license. Additional exam requirements/recommendations for international students: Required—TOEFL (minimum score 550 paper-based; 213 computer-based). *Application deadline:* For fall admission, 3/1 priority date for domestic and international students; for spring admission, 7/1 priority date for domestic and international students. Applications are processed on a rolling basis. Application fee: $75. Electronic applications accepted. *Expenses:* Contact institution. *Financial support:* Career-related internships or fieldwork, Federal Work-Study, scholarships/grants, traineeships, and tuition waivers (partial) available. Support available to part-time students. Financial award application deadline: 3/1; financial award applicants required to submit FAFSA. *Faculty research:* Violence, community outreach, outcomes, asthma, HIV. *Unit head:* Dr. Julie A. Stanik-Hutt, Director, Master's Programs, 410-502-0184, Fax: 410-955-7463, E-mail: jstanik1@son.jhmi.edu. *Application contact:* Mary O'Rourke, Director of Admissions and Student Services, 410-955-7548, Fax: 410-614-7086, E-mail: orourke@son.jhmi.edu.

Kean University, College of Natural, Applied and Health Sciences, Program in Nursing, Union, NJ 07083. Offers clinical-management (MSN), including transcultural focus; community health nursing (MSN); school nursing (MSN). *Accreditation:* NLN. Part-time and evening/weekend programs available. *Faculty:* 7 full-time (all women). *Students:* 12 full-time (all women), 78 part-time (74 women); includes 46 minority (31 African Americans, 10 Asian Americans or Pacific Islanders, 5 Hispanic Americans). Average age 44. 44 applicants, 98% accepted, 26 enrolled. In 2009, 36 master's awarded. *Degree requirements:* For master's, thesis or alternative, clinical field experience. *Entrance requirements:* For master's, minimum GPA of 3.0; BS in nursing; RN license; 2 letters of recommendation; interview; 1 completed course of the following: Basic Health Assessment and Human Growth and Development across the life span. *Application deadline:* For fall admission, 5/1 for domestic students; for spring admission, 11/1 for domestic students. Application fee: $60 ($150 for international students). Electronic applications accepted. *Expenses:* Tuition, state resident: full-time $10,440; part-time $435 per credit. Tuition, nonresident: full-time $14,160; part-time $590 per credit. Required fees: $2642; $110 per credit. Part-time tuition and fees vary according to course load and degree level. *Financial support:* In 2009–10, 1 research assistantship with full tuition reimbursement (averaging $3,263 per year) was awarded; unspecified assistantships also available. *Unit head:* Dr. Cheryl Krause-Parello, Program Coordinator, 908-737-3390, E-mail: ckrausep@kean.edu. *Application contact:* Dorothy Rowe, Pre-Admissions Coordinator, 908-737-5928, Fax: 908-737-5965, E-mail: drowe@kean.edu.

Louisiana State University Health Sciences Center, School of Nursing, New Orleans, LA 70112-2223. Offers advanced public/community health nursing (MN); clinical nurse specialist (MN); nurse anesthesia (MN); nurse practitioner (MN); nursing (DNS). *Accreditation:* AACN; AANA/CANAEP (one or more programs are accredited). Part-time programs available. *Degree requirements:* For master's, thesis optional; for doctorate, thesis/dissertation. *Entrance requirements:* For master's, GRE General Test, MAT, minimum GPA of 3.0; for doctorate, GRE General Test, minimum GPA of 3.5. Additional exam requirements/recommendations for international students: Required—TOEFL. *Faculty research:* Advanced clinical practice, nursing education, health, social support, nursing administration.

Metropolitan State University, College of Nursing and Health Sciences, St. Paul, MN 55106-5000. Offers adult/geriatric nurse practitioner (MSN); family nurse practitioner (MSN); leadership and management (MSN); nursing (MSN, DNP); oral health care practitioner (MS); public health nursing leadership (MSN); women's health care nurse practitioner (MSN). *Accreditation:* AACN. Part-time programs available. *Degree requirements:* For master's, thesis or alternative; for doctorate, thesis/dissertation or alternative. *Entrance requirements:* For master's, GRE General Test, minimum GPA of 3.0, RN license, B.S./BAN degree; for doctorate, minimum GPA of 3.0; RN licensure, MSN degree. Additional exam requirements/recommendations for international students: Required—TOEFL (minimum score 550 paper-based; 213 computer-based). *Expenses:* Tuition, state resident: full-time $5520; part-time $276 per credit hour. Tuition, nonresident: full-time $11,040; part-time $552 per credit hour. Required fees: $209; $10 per credit hour. Tuition and fees vary according to degree level. *Faculty research:* Women's health, gerontology.

New Mexico State University, Graduate School, College of Health and Social Services, School of Nursing, Las Cruces, NM 88003-8001. Offers community/public health (MSN); medical-surgical (adult health) (MSN); nursing (PhD); nursing administration (MSN); psychiatric/mental health (MSN). *Accreditation:* AACN. Part-time programs available. Postbaccalaureate distance learning degree programs offered (minimal on-campus study). *Faculty:* 10 full-time (all women), 5 part-time/adjunct (all women). *Students:* 59 full-time (48 women), 70 part-time (61 women); includes 47 minority (9 African Americans, 3 American Indian/Alaska Native, 5 Asian Americans or Pacific Islanders, 30 Hispanic Americans). Average age 43. 82 applicants,

96% accepted, 63 enrolled. In 2009, 32 master's, 1 doctorate awarded. *Degree requirements:* For master's, comprehensive exam, thesis optional, clinical practice; for doctorate, comprehensive exam, thesis/dissertation, clinical practice. *Entrance requirements:* For master's, NCLEX exam, BSN, minimum GPA of 3.0, course work in statistics, 3 letters of reference, writing sample, RN license, CPR certification, proof of liability, immunizations, criminal background check; for doctorate, NCLEX exam, MSN, minimum GPA of 3.0, 3 letters of reference, writing sample, RN license, CPR certification, proof of liability, immunizations, criminal background check. Additional exam requirements/recommendations for international students: Required—TOEFL (minimum score 550 paper-based). *Application deadline:* For fall admission, 3/1 priority date for domestic students; for spring admission, 10/1 priority date for domestic students. Applications are processed on a rolling basis. Application fee: $30 ($50 for international students). Electronic applications accepted. *Expenses:* Tuition, state resident: full-time $4080; part-time $223 per credit. Tuition, nonresident: full-time $14,256; part-time $647 per credit. Required fees: $1278; $639 per semester. *Financial support:* In 2009–10, 14 students received support, including 2 teaching assistantships (averaging $18,380 per year); fellowships, research assistantships, career-related internships or fieldwork, Federal Work-Study, scholarships/grants, traineeships, and health care benefits also available. Financial award application deadline: 3/1. *Faculty research:* Public policy, community health, health disparities, self efficacy and self management, psychiatric mental health. *Unit head:* Dr. Pamela Schultz, Director, 575-646-3812, Fax: 575-646-2167, E-mail: pschultz@nmsu.edu. *Application contact:* Dr. Kathleen Huttlinger, Associate Director for Graduate Studies, 575-646-4386, Fax: 575-646-2167.

Oregon Health & Science University, School of Nursing, Program in Nursing Education, Portland, OR 97239-3098. Offers MN, MS, Post Master's Certificate. Tuition and fees vary according to course level, course load, degree level, program and reciprocity agreements.

Oregon Health & Science University, School of Nursing, Program in Public Health Nursing, Portland, OR 97239-3098. Offers primary care and disparities (MPH); public health (MPH, Post Master's Certificate). *Accreditation:* AACN. *Degree requirements:* For master's, thesis optional. *Entrance requirements:* For master's, GRE General Test, bachelor's degree in nursing, minimum undergraduate GPA of 3.0, previous course work in statistics. Tuition and fees vary according to course level, course load, degree level, program and reciprocity agreements.

Rush University, College of Nursing, Department of Community Systems and Mental Health Nursing, Chicago, IL 60612-3832. Offers community and mental health nursing (DNP, PhD); family nurse practitioner (MSN, Post-Master's Certificate); psychiatric clinical specialist (MSN); psychiatric nurse practitioner—adult (MSN); psychiatric nurse practitioner—family (MSN); psychiatric-mental health clinical specialist (Post-Master's Certificate); psychiatric-mental health nurse practitioner (Post-Master's Certificate); public health nursing (MSN). *Accreditation:* AACN. Part-time programs available. Postbaccalaureate distance learning degree programs offered (minimal on-campus study). Terminal master's awarded for partial completion of doctoral program. *Degree requirements:* For master's, capstone project; for doctorate, thesis/dissertation, DNP leadership project. *Entrance requirements:* For master's, GRE General Test (waived if nursing GPA is above 3.0 or cumulative GPA is above 3.25), interview; for doctorate, GRE General Test, interview, course work in statistics (DN Sc). Electronic applications accepted. *Faculty research:* Immigrant mental health, de-escalation strategies, caregiver interventions, parent-teacher training, restraint use.

Rutgers, The State University of New Jersey, Newark, Graduate School, Program in Nursing, Newark, NJ 07102. Offers nursing (MS), including acute care of adults and aged, advanced practice in pediatric nursing, advanced practice with childbearing families, community health nursing, family nurse practitioner, primary care of adults and aged, psychiatric/mental health nursing. *Accreditation:* AACN. Part-time programs available. *Degree requirements:* For master's, comprehensive exam. *Entrance requirements:* For master's, GRE General Test, RN license, minimum B average, BS in nursing. Additional exam requirements/recommendations for international students: Required—TOEFL. Electronic applications accepted. *Faculty research:* HIV/AIDS, quality of life—MS and breast cancer, sleep patterns of cardiac patients.

Sage Graduate School, Graduate School, School of Health Sciences, Department of Nursing, Program in Community Health, Troy, NY 12180-4115. Offers MS. *Accreditation:* AACN. Part-time programs available. *Faculty:* 5 full-time (all women), 8 part-time/adjunct (all women). *Students:* 1 (woman) full-time, 6 part-time (all women), 1 international. Average age 33. 5 applicants, 60% accepted, 2 enrolled. In 2009, 4 master's awarded. *Degree requirements:* For master's, thesis or alternative. *Entrance requirements:* For master's, BS in nursing, minimum GPA of 2.75, resume, 2 letters of recommendation. Additional exam requirements/recommendations for international students: Required—TOEFL (minimum score 550 paper-based; 213 computer-based). *Application deadline:* Applications are processed on a rolling basis. Application fee: $40. *Expenses:* Tuition: Full-time $10,620; part-time $590 per credit hour. *Financial support:* Fellowships, research assistantships, Federal Work-Study, scholarships/grants, and unspecified assistantships available. Support available to part-time students. Financial award application deadline: 3/1; financial award applicants required to submit FAFSA. *Unit head:* Arlene Pericak, Director, 518-244-2012, E-mail: perica@sage.edu. *Application contact:* Wendy D. Diefendorf, Director of Graduate and Adult Admission, 518-244-2443, Fax: 518-244-6880, E-mail: diefew@sage.edu.

Saint Xavier University, Graduate Studies, School of Nursing, Chicago, IL 60655-3105. Offers adult health clinical nurse specialist (MS); family nurse practitioner (MS, PMC); leadership in community health nursing (MS); psychiatric-mental health clinical nurse specialist (MS); psychiatric-mental health clinical specialist (PMC); MBA/MS. *Accreditation:* AACN. Part-time and evening/weekend programs available. *Entrance requirements:* For master's, GRE General Test or MAT, minimum GPA of 3.0, RN license. *Expenses:* Tuition: Part-time $743 per credit hour. Required fees: $135 per semester.

Seattle University, College of Nursing, Program in Nursing, Seattle, WA 98122-1090. Offers leadership in community nursing (MSN), including program development, spirituality and health; primary care nurse practitioner (MSN), including family nurse practitioner, psychiatric mental health nurse practitioner.

University of Cincinnati, Graduate School, College of Nursing, Cincinnati, OH 45221-0038. Offers clinical nurse specialist (MSN), including adult health, community health, neonatal, nursing administration, occupational health, pediatric health, psychiatric nursing, women's health; nurse anesthesia (MSN); nurse midwifery (MSN); nurse practitioner (MSN), including acute care, ambulatory care, family, family/psychiatric, women's health; nursing (PhD); MBA/MSN. *Accreditation:* AACN; AANA/CANAEP (one or more programs are accredited); ACNM/DOA. Part-time programs available. Postbaccalaureate distance learning degree programs offered (no on-campus study). Terminal master's awarded for partial completion of doctoral program. *Degree requirements:* For master's, thesis or alternative; for doctorate, comprehensive exam, thesis/dissertation. *Entrance requirements:* For master's and doctorate, GRE General Test. Additional exam requirements/recommendations for international students: Required—TOEFL (minimum score 520 paper-based; 190 computer-based). Electronic applications accepted. *Faculty research:* Substance abuse, injury and violence, symptom management.

University of Colorado at Colorado Springs, Graduate School, Beth-El College of Nursing and Health Sciences, Colorado Springs, CO 80933-7150. Offers adult health nurse practitioner and clinical specialist (MSN); family practitioner (MSN), including community clinical specialist, forensic clinical specialist, holistic clinical specialist; neonatal nurse practitioner and clinical specialist (MSN); nursing administration (MSN); nursing practice (DNP); women nurse practitioner (MSN). *Accreditation:* AACN. Part-time programs available. Postbaccalaureate distance learning degree programs offered (minimal on-campus study). *Faculty:* 26 full-time (21 women), 3 part-time/adjunct (all women). *Students:* 132 full-time (112 women), 81 part-time (71 women); includes 35 minority (6 African Americans, 2 American Indian/Alaska Native, 6 Asian Americans or Pacific Islanders, 21 Hispanic Americans), 3 international. Average age 36. 245 applicants, 47% accepted, 58 enrolled. In 2009, 33 master's awarded. *Degree requirements:* For master's, comprehensive exam, thesis optional; for doctorate, capstone project. *Entrance requirements:* For master's, GRE General Test or MAT, BSN, minimum GPA

of 3.0, unrestricted RN license; for doctorate, interview; active RN license; MA; minimum GPA of 3.3; National Certification as NP or CNS; portfolio. Additional exam requirements/recommendations for international students: Required—TOEFL. *Application deadline:* For fall admission, 6/1 priority date for domestic students; for spring admission, 11/15 for domestic students. Application fee: $60 ($75 for international students). Electronic applications accepted. *Expenses:* Contact institution. *Financial support:* Fellowships, career-related internships or fieldwork, Federal Work-Study, and scholarships/grants available. Support available to part-time students. Financial award application deadline: 3/1; financial award applicants required to submit FAFSA. *Faculty research:* Women's health, uncertainty, empowerment, family experience in chronic illness. Total annual research expenditures: $703,545. *Unit head:* Dr. Nancy Smith, Dean, 719-255-4411, Fax: 719-255-4416, E-mail: nsmith2@uccs.edu. *Application contact:* Jackie Crouch, Graduate Recruitment Coordinator, 719-255-4493, Fax: 719-255-4416, E-mail: jcrouch@uccs.edu.

University of Hartford, College of Education, Nursing, and Health Professions, Program in Nursing, West Hartford, CT 06117-1599. Offers community/public health nursing (MSN); nursing education (MSN); nursing management (MSN). *Accreditation:* AACN. Part-time and evening/weekend programs available. *Degree requirements:* For master's, research project. *Entrance requirements:* For master's, BSN, Connecticut RN license. Additional exam requirements/recommendations for international students: Required—TOEFL (minimum score 550 paper-based; 213 computer-based). Electronic applications accepted. *Expenses:* Contact institution. *Faculty research:* Child development, women in doctoral study, applying feminist theory in teaching methods, near death experience, grandmothers as primary care providers.

University of Hawaii at Manoa, Graduate Division, School of Nursing and Dental Hygiene, Honolulu, HI 96822. Offers clinical nurse specialist (MS), including adult health, community mental health; nurse practitioner (MS), including adult health, community mental health, family nurse practitioner; nursing (PhD, Graduate Certificate); nursing administration (MS). *Accreditation:* AACN; NLN (one or more programs are accredited). Part-time programs available. Postbaccalaureate distance learning degree programs offered (minimal on-campus study). *Faculty:* 20 full-time (18 women), 16 part-time/adjunct (15 women). *Students:* 81 full-time (69 women), 135 part-time (121 women); includes 115 minority (4 African Americans, 2 American Indian/Alaska Native, 105 Asian Americans or Pacific Islanders, 4 Hispanic Americans), 2 international. Average age 38. 189 applicants, 52% accepted, 79 enrolled. In 2009, 25 master's, 4 doctorates awarded. *Degree requirements:* For master's, thesis optional; for doctorate, comprehensive exam, thesis/dissertation. *Entrance requirements:* For master's, Hawaii RN license. Additional exam requirements/recommendations for international students: Required—TOEFL (minimum score 580 paper-based; 237 computer-based; 92 iBT), IELTS (minimum score 5). *Application deadline:* For fall admission, 2/1 for domestic and international students. Application fee: $60. *Expenses:* Contact institution. *Financial support:* In 2009–10, 6 students received support, including 28 fellowships (averaging $960 per year), 7 research assistantships (averaging $18,080 per year). Total annual research expenditures: $1.8 million. *Unit head:* Mary Boland, Dean, 808-956-8522, Fax: 808-956-3257, E-mail: mgboland@hawaii.edu. *Application contact:* Kristine Qureshi, Graduate Chair, 808-956-8744, Fax: 808-956-3257, E-mail: kqureshi@hawaii.edu.

University of Illinois at Chicago, Graduate College, College of Nursing, Program in Nursing, Chicago, IL 60607-7128. Offers acute care clinical nurse specialist (MS); acute care nurse practitioner (MS); administrative studies in nursing (MS); adult nurse practitioner (MS); adult/geriatric nurse practitioner (MS); advanced community health nurse specialist (MS); family nurse practitioner (MS); geriatric clinical nurse specialist (MS); geriatric nurse practitioner (MS); mental health clinical nurse specialist (MS); mental health nurse practitioner (MS); nurse midwifery (MS); occupational health/advanced community health nurse specialist (MS); occupational health/family nurse practitioner (MS); pediatric clinical nurse specialist (MS); pediatric nurse practitioner (MS); perinatal clinical nurse specialist (MS); school/advanced community health nurse specialist (MS); school/family nurse practitioner (MS); women's health nurse practitioner (MS). *Accreditation:* AACN. Part-time programs available. *Degree requirements:* For master's, thesis or alternative. *Entrance requirements:* For master's, GRE General Test, minimum GPA of 2.75. Additional exam requirements/recommendations for international students: Required—TOEFL. Electronic applications accepted.

The University of Kansas, University of Kansas Medical Center, School of Nursing, Kansas City, KS 66160. Offers clinical research management (PMC); family nurse practitioner (PMC); health care informatics (PMC); health professions educator (PMC); nurse midwife (PMC); nursing (MS, DNP, PhD); organizational leadership (PMC); psychiatric/mental health nurse practitioner (PMC); public health nursing (PMC). *Accreditation:* AACN; ACNM/DOA. Part-time programs available. Postbaccalaureate distance learning degree programs offered (minimal on-campus study). *Faculty:* 65. *Students:* 59 full-time (56 women), 309 part-time (285 women); includes 37 minority (17 African Americans, 4 American Indian/Alaska Native, 7 Asian Americans or Pacific Islanders, 9 Hispanic Americans), 10 international. Average age 38. 138 applicants, 59% accepted, 82 enrolled. In 2009, 78 master's, 3 doctorates awarded. Terminal master's awarded for partial completion of doctoral program. *Degree requirements:* For master's, thesis optional, general oral exam; for doctorate, one foreign language, thesis/dissertation, comprehensive oral and written exam. *Entrance requirements:* For master's, bachelor's degree in nursing, minimum GPA of 3.0, RN license, 1 year of clinical experience; for doctorate, GRE General Test, master's degree in nursing, minimum GPA of 3.5. Additional exam requirements/recommendations for international students: Required—TOEFL. *Application deadline:* For fall admission, 4/1 for domestic students; for spring admission, 9/1 for domestic students. Application fee: $60. Electronic applications accepted. *Expenses:* Tuition, state resident: full-time $6492; part-time $270.50 per credit hour. Tuition, nonresident: full-time $15,510; part-time $646.25 per credit hour. Required fees: $847; $70.56 per credit hour. Tuition and fees vary according to course load and program. *Financial support:* In 2009–10, 93 students received support, including 7 research assistantships (averaging $24,000 per year), 23 teaching assistantships with full and partial tuition reimbursements available (averaging $24,000 per year); traineeships also available. Financial award application deadline: 2/14; financial award applicants required to submit FAFSA. *Faculty research:* Breastfeeding practices of teen mothers, national database of nursing quality indicators, caregiving of families of patients using technology in the home, self care talk intervention partnership between caregivers of stroke survivors and nurses, smoking cessation. Total annual research expenditures: $5 million. *Unit head:* Dr. Karen L. Miller, Dean, 913-588-1601, Fax: 913-588-1660, E-mail: kmiller@kumc.edu. *Application contact:* Dr. Rita K. Clifford, Associate Dean, Student Affairs, 913-588-1619, Fax: 913-588-1615, E-mail: rcliffor@kumc.edu.

University of Maryland, Baltimore, Graduate School, School of Nursing, Master's Program in Nursing, Baltimore, MD 21201. Offers community health nursing (MS); gerontological nursing (MS); maternal-child nursing (MS); medical-surgical nursing (MS); nurse-midwifery education (MS); nursing administration (MS); nursing education (MS); nursing health policy (MS); primary care nursing (MS); psychiatric nursing (MS); MS/MBA. *Accreditation:* AACN; AANA/CANAEP; ACNM/DOA; NLN (one or more programs are accredited). Part-time programs available. *Students:* 387 full-time (338 women), 528 part-time (491 women); includes 330 minority (230 African Americans, 3 American Indian/Alaska Native, 81 Asian Americans or Pacific Islanders, 16 Hispanic Americans), 10 international. Average age 36. 849 applicants, 40% accepted, 255 enrolled. In 2009, 264 master's awarded. *Degree requirements:* For master's, comprehensive exam (for some programs), thesis or alternative. *Entrance requirements:* For master's, GRE General Test, minimum GPA of 2.75, course work in statistics, BS in nursing. Additional exam requirements/recommendations for international students: Required—TOEFL (minimum score 550 paper-based; 80 iBT), or IELTS (minimum score 7). *Application deadline:* For fall admission, 1/15 for international students. Application fee: $50. Electronic applications accepted. *Expenses:* Tuition, state resident: full-time $7290; part-time $405 per credit hour. Tuition, nonresident: full-time $12,780; part-time $710 per credit hour. Required fees: $774; $10 per credit hour. $297 per semester. Tuition and fees vary according to course load, degree level and program. *Financial support:* Fellowships, research assistantships, teaching assistantships, career-related internships or fieldwork and traineeships available. Support available to part-time

Community Health Nursing

University of Maryland, Baltimore (continued)

students. Financial award application deadline: 2/15; financial award applicants required to submit FAFSA. *Unit head:* Dr. Jane Kapustin, Assistant Dean, 410-706-6741, Fax: 410-706-4231. *Application contact:* Marjorie Fass, Admissions Director, 410-706-0501, Fax: 410-706-7238.

University of Massachusetts Dartmouth, Graduate School, College of Nursing, Graduate Nursing Programs, North Dartmouth, MA 02747-2300. Offers adult health/adult nurse practitioner (MS); adult health/advanced practice (MS); adult nurse practitioner (PMC); community nursing/advanced practice (MS); individualized nursing (PMC); nursing (PhD). Part-time programs available. *Faculty:* 29 full-time (all women), 26 part-time/adjunct (25 women). *Students:* 13 full-time (all women), 62 part-time (57 women); includes 4 minority (1 African American, 1 American Indian/Alaska Native, 2 Hispanic Americans), 1 international. Average age 40. 24 applicants, 100% accepted, 20 enrolled. In 2009, 17 master's, 2 other advanced degrees awarded. *Degree requirements:* For master's, thesis; for doctorate, thesis/dissertation. *Entrance requirements:* For master's, GRE General Test, BSN, minimum undergraduate GPA of 3.0, RN license, 3 letters of recommendation, 1 year experience as registered nurse; for doctorate, GRE General Test, minimum undergraduate GPA of 3.0, graduate 3.3; 3 letters of recommendation; personal statement; current Massachusetts RN license or eligibility for licensure in Massachusetts; 1 year professional nursing experience; example of scholarly writing. Additional exam requirements/recommendations for international students: Required—TOEFL (minimum score 500 paper-based). *Application deadline:* For fall admission, 4/20 for domestic students, 2/20 for international students; for spring admission, 10/15 for domestic students, 8/15 for international students. Application fee: $40 ($60 for international students). Electronic applications accepted. *Expenses:* Tuition, state resident: full-time $2071; part-time $86.29 per credit. Tuition, nonresident: full-time $8099; part-time $337.46 per credit. Required fees: $9446. Tuition and fees vary according to class time, course load and reciprocity agreements. *Financial support:* In 2009–10, 11 teaching assistantships with full tuition reimbursements (averaging $3,359 per year) were awarded; Federal Work-Study also available. Support available to part-time students. Financial award application deadline: 3/1; financial award applicants required to submit FAFSA. *Faculty research:* Chronic illness management, quality of life, diabetes care and education, environmental health, quantitative methodologies. Total annual research expenditures: $44,000. *Unit head:* Dr. Gail Russell, Director, 508-999-8251, Fax: 508-999-9127, E-mail: grussell@umassd.edu. *Application contact:* Elan Turcotte-Shamski, Graduate Admissions Officer, 508-999-8604, Fax: 508-999-8183, E-mail: graduate@umassd.edu.

University of Michigan, Horace H. Rackham School of Graduate Studies, School of Nursing, Division of Health Promotion and Risk Reduction, Program in Community Health Nursing, Ann Arbor, MI 48109. Offers adult nurse practitioner (Post Master's Certificate); adult primary care/adult nurse practitioner (MS); community care (Post Master's Certificate); community care/home care (MS); family nurse practitioner (MS, Post Master's Certificate); occupational health nursing (MS). *Accreditation:* AACN. Part-time and evening/weekend programs available. *Degree requirements:* For master's, thesis. *Entrance requirements:* For master's, GRE General Test (if cumulative BSN GPA less than 3.25), licensure, minimum GPA of 3.0 in BSN program. Additional exam requirements/recommendations for international students: Required—TOEFL (minimum score 560 paper-based; 220 computer-based). *Expenses:* Tuition, state resident: full-time $17,286; part-time $1099 per credit hour. Tuition, nonresident: full-time $34,944; part-time $2080 per credit hour. Required fees: $95 per semester. Tuition and fees vary according to course load, degree level and program.

University of Minnesota, Twin Cities Campus, Graduate School, School of Nursing, Program in Public Health Nursing, Minneapolis, MN 55455-0213. Offers MS. *Accreditation:* AACN. Part-time programs available. Postbaccalaureate distance learning degree programs offered (minimal on-campus study). *Degree requirements:* For master's, final oral exam, project or thesis. *Entrance requirements:* Additional exam requirements/recommendations for international students: Required—TOEFL (minimum score 586 paper-based; 240 computer-based).

The University of North Carolina at Chapel Hill, Graduate School, School of Public Health, Public Health Leadership Program, Chapel Hill, NC 27599. Offers health care and prevention (MPH); leadership (MPH); occupational health nursing (MPH); public health nursing (MS). Part-time programs available. Postbaccalaureate distance learning degree programs offered (minimal on-campus study). *Degree requirements:* For master's, comprehensive exam, thesis (MS), paper (MPH). *Entrance requirements:* For master's, GRE General Test, minimum GPA of 3.0, public health experience. Additional exam requirements/recommendations for international students: Required—TOEFL. Electronic applications accepted. *Faculty research:* Occupational health issues, clinical outcomes, prenatal and early childcare, adolescent health, effectiveness of home visiting, issues in occupational health nursing, community-based interventions.

University of Puerto Rico, Medical Sciences Campus, School of Nursing, San Juan, PR 00936-5067. Offers anesthesia (MSN); critical care nursing (MSN); family and community nursing (MSN); family nurse practitioner (MSN); mental health and psychiatric nursing (MSN); nursing (MSN). *Accreditation:* AACN; AANA/CANAEP. *Entrance requirements:* For master's, GRE or EXADEP, interview, Puerto Rico RN license or professional license for international students, general and specific point average, article analysis. Electronic applications accepted. *Faculty research:* HIV, health disparities, teen violence, women and violence, neurological disorders.

University of South Alabama, Graduate School, College of Nursing, Mobile, AL 36688-0002. Offers adult health nursing (MSN); community/mental health nursing (MSN); maternal/child nursing (MSN); nursing (DNP). *Accreditation:* AACN. *Degree requirements:* For master's, thesis optional. *Entrance requirements:* For master's, BSN, RN licensure, minimum GPA of 3.0, resume documenting clinical experience, background check, drug screening; for doctorate, GRE. *Expenses:* Tuition, state resident: part-time $218 per contact hour. Required fees: $1102 per year.

University of South Carolina, The Graduate School, College of Nursing, Program in Health Nursing, Columbia, SC 29208. Offers adult nurse practitioner (MSN); community/public health clinical nurse specialist (MSN); family nurse practitioner (MSN); pediatric nurse practitioner (MSN). *Accreditation:* AACN. Part-time programs available. *Degree requirements:* For master's, thesis or alternative. *Entrance requirements:* For master's, GRE General Test or MAT, BS in nursing, nursing license. Additional exam requirements/recommendations for international students: Required—TOEFL (minimum score 570 paper-based; 230 computer-based). Electronic applications accepted. *Faculty research:* System research, evidence based practice, breast cancer, violence.

University of South Carolina, The Graduate School, College of Nursing, Program in Nursing and Public Health, Columbia, SC 29208. Offers MPH/MSN. *Accreditation:* AACN; CEPH. Part-time programs available. *Entrance requirements:* Additional exam requirements/recommendations for international students: Required—TOEFL (minimum score 570 paper-based; 230 computer-based). Electronic applications accepted. *Faculty research:* System research, evidence based practice, breast cancer, violence.

University of Southern Mississippi, Graduate School, College of Health, School of Nursing, Hattiesburg, MS 39406-0001. Offers adult health nursing (MSN); community health nursing (MSN); ethics (PhD); family nurse practitioner (MSN); leadership (PhD); nursing service administration (MSN); policy analysis (PhD); psychiatric nursing (MSN). *Accreditation:* AACN. Part-time and evening/weekend programs available. *Faculty:* 17 full-time (16 women), 1 part-time/adjunct (0 women). *Students:* 63 full-time (57 women), 40 part-time (36 women); includes 23 minority (all African Americans). Average age 40. 69 applicants, 59% accepted, 37 enrolled. In 2009, 28 master's, 2 doctorates awarded. *Degree requirements:* For master's, comprehensive exam, thesis optional; for doctorate, comprehensive exam, thesis/dissertation. *Entrance requirements:* For master's, GRE General Test, minimum GPA of 2.75, nursing license, BS in nursing; for doctorate, GRE General Test, master's degree in nursing, minimum GPA of 3.5. Additional exam requirements/recommendations for international students: Required—TOEFL. *Application deadline:* For fall admission, 3/15 priority date for domestic students, 5/1 for international students. Applications are processed on a rolling basis. Application fee: $35. Electronic applications accepted. *Expenses:* Tuition, state resident: full-time $5096; part-time $284 per hour. Tuition, nonresident: full-time $13,052; part-time $726 per hour. Required fees: $402. Tuition and fees vary according to course level and course load. *Financial support:* In 2009–10, 14 research assistantships with full tuition reimbursements (averaging $12,577 per year) were awarded; teaching assistantships, Federal Work-Study and traineeships also available. Financial award application deadline: 3/15; financial award applicants required to submit FAFSA. *Faculty research:* Gerontology, caregivers, HIV, bereavement, pain, nursing leadership. *Unit head:* Dr. Katherine Nugent, Director and Associate Dean, 601-266-5500, Fax: 601-266-5927. *Application contact:* Dr. Anne Brock, Graduate Coordinator, 601-266-5500, Fax: 601-266-5927.

The University of Texas at Brownsville, Graduate Studies, School of Health Sciences, Brownsville, TX 78520-4991. Offers MSN. *Accreditation:* NLN. *Degree requirements:* For master's, comprehensive exam, thesis optional.

Wayne State University, College of Nursing, Program in Community Health Nursing, Detroit, MI 48202. Offers MSN. *Accreditation:* AACN. Part-time programs available. *Degree requirements:* For master's, thesis or alternative. *Entrance requirements:* For master's, minimum GPA of 2.8. Additional exam requirements/recommendations for international students: Required—TOEFL (minimum score 550 paper-based; 213 computer-based); Recommended—TWE (minimum score 6). Electronic applications accepted. *Faculty research:* Alternative therapies, end-of-life issues, health literacy communication, physical activity and exercise, quality of nursing care.

Worcester State College, Graduate Studies, Program in Community Health Nursing, Worcester, MA 01602-2597. Offers MS. *Accreditation:* AACN. *Faculty:* 1 (woman) full-time. *Students:* 6 full-time (5 women), 3 part-time (all women), 1 international. Average age 45. 7 applicants, 43% accepted, 2 enrolled. In 2009, 2 master's awarded. *Degree requirements:* For master's, comprehensive exam (for some programs), thesis optional. *Entrance requirements:* For master's, GRE, MAT. Additional exam requirements/recommendations for international students: Required—TOEFL (minimum score 550 paper-based; 213 computer-based; 79 iBT). *Application deadline:* Applications are processed on a rolling basis. Application fee: $30. *Expenses:* Contact institution. *Financial support:* Career-related internships or fieldwork, scholarships/grants, and unspecified assistantships available. Financial award application deadline: 3/1; financial award applicants required to submit FAFSA. *Unit head:* Dr. Stephanie Chalupka, Coordinator, 508-929-8680, Fax: 508-929-8168, E-mail: schalupka@worcester.edu. *Application contact:* Nicole Brown, Assistant Dean of Graduate and Continuing Education, 508-929-8787, Fax: 508-929-8100, E-mail: nbrown@worcester.edu.

Wright State University, School of Graduate Studies, College of Nursing and Health, Program in Nursing, Dayton, OH 45435. Offers acute care nurse practitioner (MS); administration of nursing and health care systems (MS); adult health (MS); child and adolescent health (MS); community health (MS); family nurse practitioner (MS); nurse practitioner (MS); school nurse (MS); MBA/MS. *Accreditation:* AACN. Part-time and evening/weekend programs available. *Degree requirements:* For master's, thesis or alternative. *Entrance requirements:* For master's, GRE General Test, BSN from NLN-accredited college, Ohio RN license. Additional exam requirements/recommendations for international students: Required—TOEFL. *Faculty research:* Clinical nursing and health, teaching, caring, pain administration, informatics and technology.

Family Nurse Practitioner Studies

Abilene Christian University, Graduate School, School of Nursing, Abilene, TX 79699-9100. Offers education and administration (MSN); family nurse practitioner (MSN). *Accreditation:* AACN. Part-time programs available. *Faculty:* 6 part-time/adjunct (all women). *Students:* 3 full-time (all women), 4 part-time (2 women); includes 4 minority (1 American Indian/Alaska Native, 2 Asian Americans or Pacific Islanders, 1 Hispanic American). 11 applicants, 36% accepted, 4 enrolled. In 2009, 5 master's, 1 other advanced degree awarded. *Entrance requirements:* For master's, GRE General Test. *Application deadline:* For fall admission, 4/1 priority date for domestic students; for spring admission, 11/1 for domestic students. Applications are processed on a rolling basis. Application fee: $40. Electronic applications accepted. *Expenses:* Tuition: Full-time $11,520; part-time $640 per hour. Required fees: $1090; $53.50 per hour. $10 per term. Tuition and fees vary according to program. *Financial support:* In 2009–10, 6 students received support. Application deadline: 4/1. *Unit head:* Dr. Amy Toone, Graduate Director, 325-671-2361, Fax: 325-671-2386, E-mail: atoone@phssn.edu. *Application contact:* William Horn, Graduate Admissions Counselor, 325-674-2656, Fax: 325-674-6717, E-mail: gradinfo@acu.edu.

Albany State University, College of Sciences and Health Professions, Department of Nursing, Albany, GA 31705-2717. Offers RN to MSN family nurse practitioner (MSN); RN to MSN nurse educator (MSN). Part-time and evening/weekend programs available. Postbaccalaureate distance learning degree programs offered. *Students:* 12 full-time (11 women), 49 part-time (45 women); includes 32 minority (30 African Americans, 2 Asian Americans or Pacific Islanders). Average age 39. 20 applicants, 95% accepted, 16 enrolled. In 2009, 21 master's awarded. *Degree requirements:* For master's, comprehensive exam, thesis or major research project. *Entrance requirements:* For master's, GRE or MAT, baccalaureate degree in nursing, minimum GPA of 3.0, current Georgia RN practicing license, personal interview with the Coordinator of the Graduate Nursing Program, two letters of reference regarding professional accomplishments and academic potential, ASU medical and immunization forms. Additional exam requirements/recommendations for international students: Required—TOEFL. *Application deadline:* For fall admission, 11/16 for domestic students, 9/16 for international students; for spring admission, 4/19 for domestic students, 2/19 for international students. Applications are processed on a rolling basis. Application fee: $20. Electronic applications accepted. *Expenses:* Tuition, state resident: full-time $2970; part-time $162 per credit hour. Tuition, nonresident: full-time $12,168; part-time $676 per credit hour. Required fees: $962; $75 per credit hour. *Financial support:* Application deadline: 6/30. *Faculty research:* HIV issues, cancer-specifically breast, prostate, and lung, cultural diversity, health promotion, smoking cessation. *Unit head:* Linda Grimsley, Chairperson, 229-430-4724, Fax: 229-430-3937, E-mail: lgrimsl@asurams.edu. *Application contact:* Linda Grimsley, Chairperson, 229-430-4724, Fax: 229-430-3937, E-mail: linda.grimsley@asurams.edu.

Allen College, Program in Nursing, Waterloo, IA 50703. Offers acute care nurse practitioner (MSN); adult nurse practitioner (MSN); adult psychiatric-mental health nurse practitioner (MSN); family nurse practitioner (MSN); gerontological nurse practitioner (MSN); health education

(MSN); leadership in health care delivery (MSN). *Accreditation:* AACN; NLN. Part-time programs available. *Faculty:* 2 full-time (both women), 8 part-time/adjunct (all women). *Students:* 37 full-time (35 women), 103 part-time (99 women); includes 1 minority (Asian American or Pacific Islander). Average age 38. *Degree requirements:* For master's, thesis optional. *Entrance requirements:* For master's, minimum GPA of 3.0. Additional exam requirements/recommendations for international students: Required—TOEFL (minimum score 550 paper-based). *Application deadline:* For fall admission, 7/15 priority date for domestic students; for spring admission, 12/1 priority date for domestic students. Applications are processed on a rolling basis. Application fee: $50. Electronic applications accepted. *Expenses:* Tuition: Full-time $12,550; part-time $651 per credit hour. Required fees: $826; $65 per credit hour. One-time fee: $425. Tuition and fees vary according to course load. *Financial support:* Teaching assistantships, institutionally sponsored loans, scholarships/grants, and traineeships available. Support available to part-time students. Financial award application deadline: 8/15; financial award applicants required to submit FAFSA. *Faculty research:* Pain and aged, congestive heart failure. *Unit head:* Nancy Kramer, Dean, School of Nursing, 319-226-2040, Fax: 319-226-2070, E-mail: kramerna@ihs.org. *Application contact:* Michelle Koehn, Admissions Counselor, 319-226-2002, Fax: 319-226-2051, E-mail: koehnml@ihs.org.

Barry University, School of Nursing, Program in Nurse Practitioner, Miami Shores, FL 33161-6695. Offers acute care nurse practitioner (MSN); family nurse practitioner (MSN); nurse practitioner (Certificate). *Accreditation:* AACN. Part-time and evening/weekend programs available. *Degree requirements:* For master's, research project or thesis. *Entrance requirements:* For master's, GRE General Test or MAT, BSN, minimum GPA of 3.0, course work in statistics. Electronic applications accepted. *Faculty research:* Child abuse, health beliefs, teenage pregnancy, cultural and clinical studies across the lifespan.

Baylor University, Graduate School, Louise Herrington School of Nursing, Dallas, TX 75246. Offers family nurse practitioner (MSN); neonatal nurse practitioner (MSN); nursing administration and management (MSN). *Accreditation:* AACN. *Students:* 32 full-time (31 women), 26 part-time (25 women); includes 12 minority (4 African Americans, 1 American Indian/Alaska Native, 3 Asian Americans or Pacific Islanders, 4 Hispanic Americans), 1 international. In 2009, 17 master's awarded. *Entrance requirements:* For master's, GRE General Test. *Application deadline:* For fall admission, 8/1 for domestic students; for spring admission, 12/1 for domestic students. Applications are processed on a rolling basis. Application fee: $25. *Unit head:* Dr. Mary Brucker, Graduate Program Director, 214-820-4111, Fax: 214-818-8692, E-mail: mary_brucker@baylor.edu. *Application contact:* Beverly Kurfees, Administrative Assistant, 214-820-4111, Fax: 254-710-3870, E-mail: beverly_kurfees@baylor.edu.

Bellarmine University, Donna and Allan Lansing School of Nursing and Health Sciences, Louisville, KY 40205-0671. Offers family nurse practitioner (MSN); nursing administration (MSN); nursing education (MSN); nursing practice (DNP); physical therapy (DPT). *Accreditation:* AACN; APTA. Part-time and evening/weekend programs available. *Faculty:* 16 full-time (11 women), 7 part-time/adjunct (6 women). *Students:* 126 full-time (94 women), 50 part-time (48 women); includes 4 minority (1 African American, 3 Asian Americans or Pacific Islanders). Average age 30. 350 applicants, 48 enrolled. In 2009, 9 master's, 41 doctorates awarded. *Degree requirements:* For doctorate, comprehensive exam, thesis/dissertation. *Entrance requirements:* For master's, GRE General Test, RN license; for doctorate, GRE General Test, Physical Therapist Centralized Application Service (for DPT). Additional exam requirements/recommendations for international students: Required—TOEFL (minimum score 550 paper-based; 213 computer-based; 80 iBT). Application fee: $25. Electronic applications accepted. *Expenses:* Contact institution. *Financial support:* Career-related internships or fieldwork and scholarships/grants available. *Faculty research:* Nursing: pain, empathy, leadership styles, control; physical therapy: service learning; exercise in chronic and pre-operative conditions, and athletes; women's health; aging. *Unit head:* Dr. Susan H. Davis, Dean, 800-274-4723 Ext. 8217, E-mail: sdavis@bellarmine.edu. *Application contact:* Julie Armstrong-Binnix, Health Science Recruiter, 800-274-4723 Ext. 8364, E-mail: julieab@bellarmine.edu.

Bloomsburg University of Pennsylvania, School of Graduate Studies, College of Professional Studies, School of Health Sciences, Department of Nursing, Bloomsburg, PA 17815-1301. Offers adult and family nurse practitioner (MSN); adult health and illness (MSN); community health (MSN); nursing (MSN); nursing administration (MSN). *Accreditation:* AACN; AANA/CANAEP. *Degree requirements:* For master's, thesis. *Entrance requirements:* For master's, minimum QPA of 3.0. Additional exam requirements/recommendations for international students: Required—TOEFL. Electronic applications accepted. *Faculty research:* Cardiopulmonary nursing, cancer topics, women's health.

Bowie State University, Graduate Programs, Department of Nursing, Bowie, MD 20715-9465. Offers administration of nursing services (MS); family nurse practitioner (MS); nursing education (MS). *Accreditation:* NLN. Part-time programs available. *Degree requirements:* For master's, comprehensive exam, thesis, research paper. *Entrance requirements:* For master's, minimum GPA of 2.5. Electronic applications accepted. *Faculty research:* Minority health, women's health, gerontology, leadership management.

Brenau University, Graduate Programs, School of Health and Science, Gainesville, GA 30501. Offers family nurse practitioner (MSN); nurse educator (MSN); nursing management (MSN); occupational therapy (MS); psychology (MS). *Accreditation:* AOTA; NLN. Part-time and evening/weekend programs available. *Faculty:* 14 full-time (12 women), 6 part-time/adjunct (5 women). *Students:* 97 full-time (92 women), 92 part-time (84 women); includes 46 minority (37 African Americans, 2 American Indian/Alaska Native, 2 Asian Americans or Pacific Islanders, 5 Hispanic Americans), 2 international. Average age 34. 168 applicants, 50% accepted, 68 enrolled. In 2009, 35 master's awarded. *Degree requirements:* For master's, comprehensive exam (for some programs), thesis (for some programs), clinical practicum hours. *Entrance requirements:* For master's, GRE General Test or MAT (for some programs), interview, writing sample, references (for some programs). Additional exam requirements/recommendations for international students: Required—TOEFL (minimum score 500 paper-based). *Application deadline:* Applications are processed on a rolling basis. Application fee: $35. Electronic applications accepted. *Expenses:* Contact institution. *Financial support:* In 2009–10, 32 students received support. Scholarships/grants and traineeships available. Support available to part-time students. Financial award application deadline: 7/15; financial award applicants required to submit FAFSA. *Unit head:* Dr. Gale Starich, Dean, 777-718-5305, Fax: 770-297-5929, E-mail: gstarich@brenau.edu. *Application contact:* Christina White, Admissions Coordinator, 770-718-5320, Fax: 770-770-5338, E-mail: cwhite@brenau.edu.

Brigham Young University, Graduate Studies, College of Nursing, Provo, UT 84602. Offers family nurse practitioner (MS). *Accreditation:* AACN. *Faculty:* 26 full-time (24 women). *Students:* 28 full-time (18 women); includes 4 minority (1 African American, 3 Asian Americans or Pacific Islanders). Average age 36. 23 applicants, 65% accepted, 15 enrolled. In 2009, 13 master's awarded. *Degree requirements:* For master's, thesis. *Entrance requirements:* For master's, GRE, minimum GPA of 3.0 in last 60 hours, interview, BS in nursing, pathophysiology class within undergraduate program, course work in basic statistics. Additional exam requirements/recommendations for international students: Required—TOEFL; Recommended—IELTS. *Application deadline:* For spring admission, 12/1 for domestic students. Applications are processed on a rolling basis. Application fee: $50. Electronic applications accepted. *Expenses:* Tuition: Full-time $5580; part-time $301 per credit hour. Tuition and fees vary according to student's religious affiliation. *Financial support:* In 2009–10, 28 students received support, including 2 research assistantships with full and partial tuition reimbursements available (averaging $10,000 per year), 3 teaching assistantships with full and partial tuition reimbursements available (averaging $10,000 per year); institutionally sponsored loans, scholarships/grants, tuition waivers (full), and unspecified assistantships also available. Support available to part-time students. Financial award application deadline: 2/1; financial award applicants required to submit FAFSA. *Faculty research:* Cardiovascular risk factors, stroke patients, nutrition, stress among children, family response to life-threatening illness. Total annual research expenditures: $1,200. *Unit head:* Dr. Beth Vaughan Cole, Dean, 801-422-8296, Fax: 801-422-0536, E-mail: beth-cole@byu.edu. *Application contact:* Denise Gibbons Davis, Graduate Secretary, 801-422-4142, Fax: 801-422-0538, E-mail: denise_gibbons@byu.edu.

See Close-Up on page 1607.

California State University, Fresno, Division of Graduate Studies, College of Health and Human Services, Department of Nursing, Fresno, CA 93740-8027. Offers nursing (MS), including clinical nurse, primary care nurse practitioner, specialist/nurse educator. *Accreditation:* AACN. Part-time and evening/weekend programs available. *Degree requirements:* For master's, thesis or alternative. *Entrance requirements:* For master's, GRE General Test, 1 year of clinical practice, previous course work in statistics, BSN, minimum GPA of 3.0 in nursing. Additional exam requirements/recommendations for international students: Required—TOEFL. Electronic applications accepted. *Faculty research:* Training grant, HIV assessment.

Carlow University, School of Nursing, Pittsburgh, PA 15213-3165. Offers family nurse practitioner (MSN); home health advanced practice nursing (MSN); nursing (DNP); nursing case management/leadership (MSN); nursing leadership (MSN). *Accreditation:* AACN. Part-time and evening/weekend programs available. Postbaccalaureate distance learning degree programs offered (minimal on-campus study). *Degree requirements:* For master's, thesis or alternative. *Entrance requirements:* Additional exam requirements/recommendations for international students: Required—TOEFL (minimum score 550 paper-based; 213 computer-based). Electronic applications accepted. *Expenses:* Tuition: Full-time $11,250; part-time $625 per credit. Tuition and fees vary according to course load, degree level and program. *Faculty research:* Research utilization, community and home health, medically underserved.

Carson-Newman College, Department of Nursing, Jefferson City, TN 37760. Offers family nurse practitioner (MSN); nurse educator (MSN). *Accreditation:* AACN. *Faculty:* 2 full-time (both women), 10 part-time/adjunct (9 women). *Students:* 21 full-time (19 women), 27 part-time (23 women); includes 3 minority (2 Asian Americans or Pacific Islanders, 1 Hispanic American). Average age 32. In 2009, 11 master's awarded. *Application deadline:* For fall admission, 7/15 priority date for domestic students. Applications are processed on a rolling basis. Application fee: $50. *Expenses:* Tuition: Full-time $5490; part-time $305 per semester hour. Required fees: $200. *Unit head:* Dr. Patricia Kraft, Dean and Chair, 865-471-3426. *Application contact:* Graduate Admissions and Services Adviser, 865-473-3468, Fax: 865-472-3475.

Case Western Reserve University, Frances Payne Bolton School of Nursing, Doctor of Nursing Practice Program, Cleveland, OH 44106. Offers acute care nurse practitioner (DNP); adult nurse practitioner (DNP); family nurse practitioner (DNP); gerontological nurse practitioner (DNP); graduate entry/pre-licensure option (DNP); medical-surgical nursing (DNP); midwifery/family nursing (DNP); neonatal nurse practitioner (DNP); pediatric nurse practitioner (DNP); post-licensure option (DNP); psychiatric-mental health nurse practitioner (DNP); women's health nurse practitioner (DNP). Graduate entry option allows baccalaureate-prepared college graduates from non-nursing backgrounds to earn certificate and MSN in addition to ND. Terminal master's awarded for partial completion of doctoral program. *Degree requirements:* For doctorate, thesis/dissertation. *Entrance requirements:* For doctorate, GRE General Test or MAT. *Faculty research:* Clinical nursing, acute care, gerontology, mental health, critical care.

Case Western Reserve University, Frances Payne Bolton School of Nursing, Master's Programs in Nursing, Nurse Practitioner Program, Cleveland, OH 44106. Offers acute care cardiovascular nursing (MSN); acute care nurse practitioner (MSN); acute care/flight nurse (MSN); adult nurse practitioner (MSN); family nurse practitioner (MSN); gerontological nurse practitioner (MSN); neonatal nurse practitioner (MSN); pediatric nurse practitioner (MSN); psychiatric-mental health nurse practitioner (MSN); women's health nurse practitioner (MSN). *Accreditation:* NLN. Part-time programs available. Postbaccalaureate distance learning degree programs offered (minimal on-campus study). *Degree requirements:* For master's, thesis optional. *Entrance requirements:* For master's, GRE General Test or MAT. Additional exam requirements/recommendations for international students: Required—TOEFL. *Faculty research:* Positive and negative mood states in parents of twins, effect of a carepath on chronic obstructive pulmonary disease home care.

The Catholic University of America, School of Nursing, Washington, DC 20064. Offers adult health specialist with functional role as nurse educator (MSN); adult nurse practitioner (MSN); community/public health nurse specialist educator (MSN); family nurse practitioner (MSN); geriatric nurse practitioner (MSN); immigrant, refugee, and global health clinical nurse specialist (MSN); nursing (DNP, PhD, Certificate); pediatric nurse practitioner (MSN); promoting healthy families in vulnerable communities (MSN); psychiatric-mental health nursing (MSN). *Accreditation:* AACN. Part-time programs available. *Faculty:* 15 full-time (all women), 43 part-time/adjunct (41 women). *Students:* 28 full-time (26 women), 75 part-time (73 women); includes 37 minority (27 African Americans, 6 Asian Americans or Pacific Islanders, 4 Hispanic Americans), 4 international. Average age 42. 84 applicants, 64% accepted, 30 enrolled. In 2009, 23 master's, 7 doctorates, 3 other advanced degrees awarded. *Degree requirements:* For master's, comprehensive exam, thesis optional; for doctorate, comprehensive exam, thesis/dissertation, minimum GPA of 3.0, oral proposal defense. *Entrance requirements:* For master's, 3 letters of recommendation, BA in nursing, RN registration, official copies of academic transcripts, some post-baccalaureate nursing experience; for doctorate, GRE General Test, BA in nursing, professional portfolio (including statements, resume, copy of RN license, 3 letters of recommendation, narrative description of clinical practice, proposal), copy of research/scholarly paper related to clinical nursing. Additional exam requirements/recommendations for international students: Required—TOEFL (minimum score 580 paper-based; 237 computer-based). *Application deadline:* For fall admission, 8/1 priority date for domestic students, 7/15 for international students; for spring admission, 12/1 priority date for domestic students, 10/15 for international students. Applications are processed on a rolling basis. Application fee: $55. Electronic applications accepted. *Expenses:* Tuition: Full-time $31,740; part-time $1245 per credit hour. Required fees: $50; $25 per semester hour. One-time fee: $425. *Financial support:* Fellowships, research assistantships, teaching assistantships, Federal Work-Study, scholarships/grants, tuition waivers (full and partial), and unspecified assistantships available. Financial award application deadline: 2/1; financial award applicants required to submit FAFSA. *Faculty research:* Community involvement in health care services, primary health care services, pediatrics, chronic illness, cardiovascular disease. Total annual research expenditures: $311,172. *Unit head:* Dr. Nalini N. Jairath, Dean, 202-319-5403, Fax: 202-319-6485, E-mail: cua-deanschoolofnursing@cua.edu. *Application contact:* Julie Schwing, Director of Graduate Admissions, 202-319-5057, Fax: 202-319-6533, E-mail: cua-admissions@cua.edu.

Clarke College, Department of Nursing and Health, Dubuque, IA 52001-3198. Offers administration of nursing systems (MSN); advanced practice nursing (MSN); education (MSN); family nurse practitioner (MSN, PMC). *Accreditation:* AACN. Part-time programs available. *Faculty:* 4 full-time (all women), 2 part-time/adjunct (1 woman). *Students:* 35 full-time (34 women), 19 part-time (all women). Average age 35. 48 applicants, 83% accepted, 25 enrolled. In 2009, 13 master's awarded. *Entrance requirements:* For master's, GRE General Test or MAT, BSN, minimum GPA of 3.0. *Application deadline:* For fall admission, 2/15 priority date for domestic students; for spring admission, 12/15 priority date for domestic students. Applications are processed on a rolling basis. Application fee: $25. Electronic applications accepted. *Expenses:* Tuition: Full-time $10,836; part-time $602 per credit hour. Required fees: $30 per credit hour. *Financial support:* In 2009–10, 6 students received support. Career-related internships or fieldwork available. Support available to part-time students. Financial award applicants required to submit FAFSA. *Faculty research:* Narrative pedagogy, ethics, end-of-life care, pedagogy, family systems. *Unit head:* Dr. Susan DeCrane, Chair, 800-224-2736, Fax: 319-584-8684. *Application contact:* Carrie Kirk, Information Contact, 563-588-6635, Fax: 563-588-6789, E-mail: graduate@clarke.edu.

Clarkson College, Master of Science in Nursing Program, Omaha, NE 68131. Offers adult nurse practitioner (MSN, Post-Master's Certificate); family nurse practitioner (MSN, Post-Master's Certificate); nursing education (MSN, Post-Master's Certificate); nursing health care leadership (MSN, Post-Master's Certificate). *Accreditation:* NLN. Part-time and evening/weekend programs available. Postbaccalaureate distance learning degree programs offered (minimal on-campus study). *Degree requirements:* For master's, on-campus skills assessment

Family Nurse Practitioner Studies

Clarkson College (continued)
(family nurse practitioner, adult nurse practitioner), comprehensive exam or thesis. *Entrance requirements:* For master's, minimum GPA of 3.0, 2 references, resume. Additional exam requirements/recommendations for international students: Required—TOEFL (minimum score 600 paper-based; 250 computer-based; 100 iBT). Electronic applications accepted.

College of Mount Saint Vincent, School of Professional and Continuing Studies, Department of Nursing, Riverdale, NY 10471-1093. Offers adult nurse practitioner (MSN, PMC); family nurse practitioner (MSN, PMC); nurse educator (PMC); nursing administration (MSN); nursing for the adult and aged (MSN). *Accreditation:* AACN. Part-time programs available. *Entrance requirements:* For master's, BSN, interview, RN license, minimum GPA of 3.0, letters of reference. Additional exam requirements/recommendations for international students: Required—TOEFL. *Expenses:* Contact institution.

The College of New Rochelle, Graduate School, Program in Nursing, New Rochelle, NY 10805-2308. Offers acute care nurse practitioner (MS, Certificate); clinical specialist in holistic nursing (MS, Certificate); family nurse practitioner (MS, Certificate); nursing and health care management (MS); nursing education (Certificate). *Accreditation:* AACN. Part-time programs available. *Entrance requirements:* For master's, GRE General Test or MAT, BSN, malpractice insurance, minimum GPA of 3.0, RN license. *Expenses:* Contact institution. *Faculty research:* Holistic modalities, academic success variables.

Columbia University, School of Nursing, Program in Family Nurse Practitioner, New York, NY 10032. Offers MS, Adv C. *Accreditation:* AACN. Part-time programs available. *Entrance requirements:* For master's, GRE General Test, BSN, 1 year of clinical experience (preferred); for Adv C, MSN. Electronic applications accepted.

Concordia University Wisconsin, Graduate Programs, School of Health and Human Services, Program in Nursing, Mequon, WI 53097-2402. Offers family nurse practitioner (MSN); geriatric nurse practitioner (MSN); nurse educator (MSN). *Accreditation:* AACN. Postbaccalaureate distance learning degree programs offered (minimal on-campus study). *Degree requirements:* For master's, comprehensive exam, thesis or alternative. *Entrance requirements:* Additional exam requirements/recommendations for international students: Required—TOEFL. *Expenses:* Contact institution.

Coppin State University, Division of Graduate Studies, Helene Fuld School of Nursing, Baltimore, MD 21216-3698. Offers family nurse practitioner (PMC); nursing (MSN). *Accreditation:* NLN. Part-time and evening/weekend programs available. *Degree requirements:* For master's, comprehensive exam, thesis, clinical internship. *Entrance requirements:* For master's, GRE, bachelor's degree in nursing, interview, minimum GPA of 3.0, RN license. Additional exam requirements/recommendations for international students: Required—TOEFL (minimum score 550 paper-based).

Delta State University, Graduate Programs, School of Nursing, Cleveland, MS 38733-0001. Offers family nurse practitioner (MSN); nurse administrator (MSN); nurse educator (MSN). *Accreditation:* AACN. Part-time programs available. *Degree requirements:* For master's, thesis optional. *Entrance requirements:* For master's, GRE General Test. Electronic applications accepted. *Expenses:* Tuition, state resident: full-time $4450; part-time $247 per credit hour. Tuition, nonresident: full-time $11,520; part-time $640 per credit hour.

DeSales University, Graduate Division, Programs in Nursing, Center Valley, PA 18034-9568. Offers adult advanced practice nurse specialist (MSN); certified nurse midwives (MSN); certified nurse practitioners (MSN); family nurse practitioner (MSN); nurse educator (MSN); MSN/MBA. *Accreditation:* NLN. Part-time programs available. *Students:* 67 part-time. In 2009, 218 master's awarded. *Degree requirements:* For master's, thesis optional. *Entrance requirements:* For master's, GRE General Test, MAT, minimum B average in undergraduate course work, health assessment course or equivalent, course work in statistics. Additional exam requirements/recommendations for international students: Required—TOEFL. *Application deadline:* Applications are processed on a rolling basis. Application fee: $35. Electronic applications accepted. *Expenses:* Tuition: Full-time $17,500; part-time $665 per credit. Full-time tuition and fees vary according to program. Part-time tuition and fees vary according to course load. *Financial support:* Applicants required to submit FAFSA. *Faculty research:* Women's health, theory validation, needs of homeless, behavior risk evaluation, wound healing. *Unit head:* Dr. Carol Gullo Mest, Director, 610-282-1100 Ext. 1394, Fax: 610-282-2091, E-mail: carol.mest@desales.edu. *Application contact:* Caryn Stopper, Director of Graduate Admissions, 610-282-1100 Ext. 1768, Fax: 610-282-2254, E-mail: caryn.stopper@desales.edu.

Dominican College, Division of Nursing, Department of Nursing, Orangeburg, NY 10962-1210. Offers family nurse practitioner (MSN). *Accreditation:* AACN. Part-time and evening/weekend programs available. *Degree requirements:* For master's, guided research project, 750 hours clinical practice with a final written project. *Entrance requirements:* For master's, bachelor's degree in nursing, minimum GPA of 3.0, RN license, 1 year of nursing experience, 3 letters of recommendation. Additional exam requirements/recommendations for international students: Required—TOEFL (minimum score 550 paper-based; 213 computer-based).

Duke University, School of Nursing, Durham, NC 27708-0586. Offers adult acute care (Certificate); adult cardiovascular (Certificate); adult oncology (Certificate); adult primary care (Certificate); clinical nurse specialist (MSN), including adult oncology, gerontology, neonatal, pediatric; clinical research management (MSN, Certificate); family (Certificate); gerontology (Certificate); health and nursing ministries (MSN, Certificate); health systems leadership and outcomes (Certificate); neonatal (Certificate); neonatal/pediatric in rural health (MSN, Certificate); nurse anesthetist (MSN, Certificate); nurse practitioner (MSN), including adult acute care, adult cardiovascular, adult oncology, adult primary care, family, gerontology, neonatal, pediatric, pediatric acute care; nursing (DNP, PhD); nursing and healthcare leadership (MSN); nursing education (MSN); nursing informatics (MSN, Certificate); pediatric (Certificate); pediatric acute care (Certificate); MBA/MSN; MSN/MCM. *Accreditation:* AACN; AANA/CANAEP. Part-time programs available. Postbaccalaureate distance learning degree programs offered (minimal on-campus study). *Faculty:* 45 full-time (41 women), 169 part-time/adjunct (150 women). *Students:* 213 full-time (179 women), 116 part-time (105 women); includes 37 minority (17 African Americans, 13 Asian Americans or Pacific Islanders, 7 Hispanic Americans), 9 international. Average age 36. 234 applicants, 53% accepted, 97 enrolled. In 2009, 142 master's, 24 other advanced degrees awarded. Terminal master's awarded for partial completion of doctoral program. *Degree requirements:* For master's, thesis optional; for doctorate, Capstone Project. *Entrance requirements:* For master's, GRE General Test, 1 year of nursing experience, BSN, minimum GPA of 3.0, previous course work in statistics; for doctorate, GRE for BSN prepared, BSN or MSN, minimum GPA of 3.0. Portfolio; for Certificate, MSN. Additional exam requirements/recommendations for international students: Required—TOEFL (minimum score 550 paper-based; 213 computer-based), Commission on Graduates of Foreign Nursing Schools exam. *Application deadline:* For fall admission, 7/2 priority date for domestic and international students; for spring admission, 11/15 priority date for domestic and international students. Applications are processed on a rolling basis. Application fee: $50. Electronic applications accepted. *Expenses:* Contact institution. *Financial support:* Career-related internships or fieldwork, institutionally sponsored loans, scholarships/grants, traineeships, and tuition waivers (partial) available. Support available to part-time students. Financial award application deadline: 4/1; financial award applicants required to submit FAFSA. *Faculty research:* Cardiovascular disease, caregiver skill training, data mining, prostate cancer, neonatal immune system. Total annual research expenditures: $3.5 million. *Unit head:* Dr. Catherine L. Gilliss, Dean/Vice Chancellor for Nursing Affairs, 919-684-9444, Fax: 919-684-9414, E-mail: gilli025@mc.duke.edu. *Application contact:* Bebe T. Mills, Director of Admissions, 919-684-9151, Fax: 919-668-4693, E-mail: mills031@mc.duke.edu.

Duquesne University, School of Nursing, Master of Science in Nursing Program, Pittsburgh, PA 15282-0001. Offers family nurse practitioner (MSN); forensic nursing (MSN); nursing education (MSN). *Accreditation:* AACN. Part-time and evening/weekend programs available. Postbaccalaureate distance learning degree programs offered (minimal on-campus study). *Faculty:* 15 full-time (13 women), 4 part-time/adjunct (all women). *Students:* 73 full-time (69 women), 43 part-time (42 women); includes 8 minority (6 African Americans, 2 Asian Americans or Pacific Islanders). 131 applicants, 32% accepted, 36 enrolled. In 2009, 39 master's awarded. *Degree requirements:* For master's, culminating paper. *Entrance requirements:* For master's, current RN license; BSN with minimum GPA of 3.0; minimum of 1 year full-time work experience as RN prior to registration in clinical or specialty course. Additional exam requirements/recommendations for international students: Required—TOEFL (minimum score 600 paper-based; 80 iBT). *Application deadline:* For fall admission, 4/1 for domestic and international students. *Expenses:* Tuition: Part-time $851 per credit. Required fees: $81 per credit. *Financial support:* In 2009–10, 38 students received support, including 4 research assistantships with partial tuition reimbursements available (averaging $2,250 per year), 4 teaching assistantships with partial tuition reimbursements available (averaging $1,075 per year); institutionally sponsored loans, scholarships/grants, traineeships, and tuition waivers (partial) also available. Support available to part-time students. Financial award application deadline: 7/1. *Faculty research:* Vulnerable populations, social justice, cultural competence, health disparities, wellness within chronic illness. Total annual research expenditures: $457,857. *Unit head:* Dr. Joan Such Lockhart, Professor and Associate Dean of Academic Affairs, 412-396-6540, Fax: 412-396-1821, E-mail: lockhart@duq.edu. *Application contact:* Susan Hardner, Nurse Recruiter, 412-396-4945, Fax: 412-396-6346, E-mail: nursing@duq.edu.

Duquesne University, School of Nursing, Post Master's Certificate Program, Pittsburgh, PA 15282-0001. Offers family nurse practitioner (Post-Master's Certificate); forensic nursing (Post-Master's Certificate); transcultural/international nursing (Post-Master's Certificate). Part-time and evening/weekend programs available. Postbaccalaureate distance learning degree programs offered (minimal on-campus study). *Faculty:* 9 full-time (8 women), 1 (woman) part-time/adjunct. *Students:* 1 full-time (0 women), 5 part-time (all women). 18 applicants, 39% accepted, 5 enrolled. In 2009, 4 Post-Master's Certificates awarded. *Entrance requirements:* For degree, current RN license, BSN, MSN. Additional exam requirements/recommendations for international students: Required—TOEFL (minimum score 600 paper-based; 80 iBT). *Application deadline:* For fall admission, 4/1 for domestic and international students. *Expenses:* Tuition: Part-time $851 per credit. Required fees: $81 per credit. *Financial support:* In 2009–10, 3 students received support. Institutionally sponsored loans, scholarships/grants, traineeships, and tuition waivers (partial) available. Support available to part-time students. Financial award application deadline: 7/1. *Faculty research:* Vulnerable populations, social justice, cultural competence, health disparities, wellness within chronic illness. *Unit head:* Dr. Joan Such Lockhart, Professor and Associate Dean of Academic Affairs, 412-396-6540, Fax: 412-396-1821, E-mail: lockhart@duq.edu. *Application contact:* Susan Hardner, Nurse Recruiter, 412-396-4945, Fax: 412-396-6346, E-mail: nursing@duq.edu.

D'Youville College, Department of Nursing, Buffalo, NY 14201-1084. Offers community health nursing/education (MSN); community health nursing/high risk parents and children (MSN); community health nursing/management (MSN); family nurse practitioner (MS, Post-Master's Certificate); nursing and health-related professions (Certificate); nursing with clinical focus choice (MSN). *Accreditation:* AACN. Part-time and evening/weekend programs available. *Degree requirements:* For master's, thesis optional, membership on board of community agency, publishable paper. *Entrance requirements:* For master's, BS in nursing, minimum GPA of 3.0, course work in statistics and computers. Additional exam requirements/recommendations for international students: Required—TOEFL (minimum score 500 paper-based; 173 computer-based). Electronic applications accepted. *Faculty research:* Nursing curriculum, nursing theory-testing, wellness research, communication and socialization patterns.

See Display on page 1487 and Close-Up on page 1611.

Eastern Kentucky University, The Graduate School, College of Health Sciences, Department of Nursing, Richmond, KY 40475-3102. Offers rural community health care (MSN); rural health family nurse practitioner (MSN). *Accreditation:* AACN. *Entrance requirements:* For master's, GRE General Test, minimum GPA of 2.75.

Edinboro University of Pennsylvania, School of Graduate Studies and Research, School of Science, Management and Technology, Department of Nursing, Edinboro, PA 16444. Offers family nurse practitioner (MSN); nurse educator (Certificate); nursing (MSN); palliative and end-of-life care (Certificate). *Accreditation:* NLN. Part-time and evening/weekend programs available. *Faculty:* 5 full-time (all women). *Students:* 47 part-time (42 women); includes 4 minority (3 African Americans, 1 Hispanic American). Average age 40. In 2009, 26 master's, 3 other advanced degrees awarded. *Degree requirements:* For master's, thesis, competency exam. *Entrance requirements:* For master's, GRE or MAT, minimum QPA of 2.5. *Application deadline:* Applications are processed on a rolling basis. Application fee: $30. Electronic applications accepted. *Expenses:* Tuition, state resident: full-time $6666; part-time $370 per credit. Tuition, nonresident: full-time $10,666; part-time $593 per credit. Required fees: $2206.28. One-time fee: $204 part-time. *Financial support:* In 2009–10, 2 research assistantships with full and partial tuition reimbursements (averaging $4,050 per year) were awarded; career-related internships or fieldwork, Federal Work-Study, scholarships/grants, and unspecified assistantships also available. Support available to part-time students. Financial award application deadline: 2/15; financial award applicants required to submit FAFSA. *Unit head:* Dr. Alice Conway, Program Head, 814-732-2285, E-mail: aconwayt@edinboro.edu. *Application contact:* Dr. Alice Conway, Program Head, 814-732-2285, E-mail: aconwayt@edinboro.edu.

Emory University, Nell Hodgson Woodruff School of Nursing, Atlanta, GA 30322-1100. Offers adult and elder health advanced practice nursing (MSN), including acute care, adult nurse practitioner, gerontological nurse practitioner; emergency nurse practitioner (MSN); family nurse practitioner (MSN); family nurse-midwife (MSN); nurse midwifery (MSN); pediatric nurse practitioner acute and primary care (MSN); public health nursing leadership (MSN); women's health nurse practitioner (MSN); women's health title x (MSN); women's health/adult health nurse practitioner (MSN); MSN/MPH. *Accreditation:* AACN; ACNM/DOA (one or more programs are accredited). Part-time programs available. *Faculty:* 30 full-time (29 women), 11 part-time/adjunct (10 women). *Students:* 110 full-time (106 women), 53 part-time (51 women); includes 49 minority (35 African Americans, 2 American Indian/Alaska Native, 10 Asian Americans or Pacific Islanders, 2 Hispanic Americans), 4 international. Average age 32. 182 applicants, 63% accepted, 86 enrolled. In 2009, 81 master's awarded. *Entrance requirements:* For master's, GRE General Test or MAT, minimum GPA of 3.0, BS in nursing from an accredited institution, RN license and additional course work, 3 letters of recommendation. Additional exam requirements/recommendations for international students: Required—TOEFL (minimum score 600 paper-based; 100 iBT). *Application deadline:* For fall admission, 1/15 priority date for domestic and international students; for spring admission, 10/1 priority date for domestic and international students. Applications are processed on a rolling basis. Application fee: $50. Electronic applications accepted. *Expenses:* Contact institution. *Financial support:* In 2009–10, 14 fellowships (averaging $28,000 per year) were awarded; career-related internships or fieldwork, Federal Work-Study, institutionally sponsored loans, and scholarships/grants also available. Support available to part-time students. Financial award application deadline: 3/1; financial award applicants required to submit CSS PROFILE or FAFSA. *Faculty research:* Older adult falls and injuries, minority health issues, cardiac symptoms and quality of life, bio-ethics and decision making, menopausal issues. *Unit head:* Dr. Linda McCauley, Dean, 404-727-7976, Fax: 404-727-9800, E-mail: linda.mccauley@emory.edu. *Application contact:* Katie Kennedy, Associate Director for Admission and Financial Aid, 404-727-7980, Fax: 404-727-8509, E-mail: admit@nursing.emory.edu.

See Close-Up on page 1613.

Fairfield University, School of Nursing, Fairfield, CT 06824-5195. Offers clinical nurse leader (MSN); family nurse practitioner (MSN, PMC); healthcare management (MSN); nurse anesthesia (MSN); psychiatric nurse practitioner (MSN, PMC). *Accreditation:* AACN; AANA/CANAEP. Part-time programs available. *Degree requirements:* For master's, capstone project. *Entrance requirements:* For master's, GRE (nurse anesthesia applicants only), minimum QPA of 3.0, RN license, resume, 2 recommendations; for PMC, 1 year of work experience as a registered nurse. Additional exam requirements/recommendations for international students: Required—TOEFL (minimum score 550 paper-based; 213 computer-based; 80 iBT). Electronic applica-

tions accepted. *Expenses:* Contact institution. *Faculty research:* Care of older adults, palliative care, spirituality and innovative partnerships, diabetes.

Felician College, Program in Nursing, Lodi, NJ 07644-2117. Offers adult health nurse (MSN, PMC); family practice nurse (MSN, PMC); nursing (MSN); nursing education (MSN). *Accreditation:* AACN. Part-time and evening/weekend programs available. Postbaccalaureate distance learning degree programs offered (no on-campus study). *Students:* 4 full-time (all women), 74 part-time (64 women); includes 18 minority (10 African Americans, 5 Asian Americans or Pacific Islanders, 3 Hispanic Americans). Average age 42. 29 applicants, 90% accepted, 24 enrolled. *Degree requirements:* For master's, scholarly project. *Entrance requirements:* For master's, BS in nursing or equivalent, minimum GPA of 3.0, 2 letters of recommendation, RN license; for PMC, RN license, minimum GPA of 2.75. Additional exam requirements/recommendations for international students: Recommended—TOEFL (minimum score 550 paper-based; 213 computer-based). *Application deadline:* Applications are processed on a rolling basis. Application fee: $40. *Financial support:* In 2009–10, 10 students received support. Traineeships available. Financial award applicants required to submit FAFSA. *Faculty research:* Anxiety and fear, curriculum innovation, health promotion. *Unit head:* Dr. Muriel Shore, Dean, Division of Health Sciences, 201-559-6030, E-mail: shorem@felician.edu. *Application contact:* Dr. Wendy Lin-Cook, Director of Adult and Graduate Admission, 201-559-6077, Fax: 201-559-6138, E-mail: adultandgraduate@felician.edu.

See Close-Up on page 1615.

Florida State University, The Graduate School, College of Nursing, Tallahassee, FL 32312. Offers family nurse practitioner (MSN, DNP); health systems leadership (DNP); nurse educator (MSN, Certificate). *Accreditation:* AACN. Part-time programs available. Postbaccalaureate distance learning degree programs offered (no on-campus study). *Faculty:* 13 full-time (12 women). *Students:* 13 full-time (4 women), 102 part-time (100 women); includes 13 minority (7 African Americans, 3 Asian Americans or Pacific Islanders, 3 Hispanic Americans). Average age 35. 42 applicants, 71% accepted, 29 enrolled. In 2009, 25 master's, 3 other advanced degrees awarded. *Degree requirements:* For master's, thesis optional. *Entrance requirements:* For master's, GRE General Test, MAT, minimum GPA of 3.0, BSN, Florida RN license; for doctorate, GRE General Test, MAT, minimum GPA of 3.0, BSN or MSN, Florida RN license. Additional exam requirements/recommendations for international students: Required—TOEFL (minimum score 550 paper-based). *Application deadline:* For fall admission, 7/1 for domestic and international students. Application fee: $30. Electronic applications accepted. *Expenses:* Tuition, state resident: full-time $7413. Tuition, nonresident: full-time $22,567. *Financial support:* In 2009–10, 101 students received support, including fellowships with partial tuition reimbursements available (averaging $6,300 per year), research assistantships with partial tuition reimbursements available (averaging $3,000 per year), 3 teaching assistantships with partial tuition reimbursements available (averaging $3,000 per year); career-related internships or fieldwork, Federal Work-Study, institutionally sponsored loans, scholarships/grants, traineeships, and tuition waivers (partial) also available. Financial award application deadline: 4/15; financial award applicants required to submit FAFSA. *Faculty research:* Distance learning, gerontology, health promotion, educational strategies, rehabilitation of brain injured patients. *Unit head:* Dr. Lisa Ann Plowfield, Dean, 850-644-3297, Fax: 850-644-7660, E-mail: lplowfield@nursing.fsu.edu. *Application contact:* Brenda Pereira, Graduate Program Coordinator, 850-644-5638, Fax: 850-645-7249, E-mail: bpereira@fsu.edu.

Frontier School of Midwifery and Family Nursing, Graduate Programs, Hyden, KY 41749. Offers community-based family nurse practitioner (MSN, Post Master's Certificate); community-based nurse-midwifery education (MSN, Post Master's Certificate); community-based women[0092]s health care nurse practitioner (MSN, Post Master's Certificate). *Accreditation:* ACNM; NLN.

Gannon University, School of Graduate Studies, Morosky College of Health Professions and Sciences, School of Health Professions, Villa Maria School of Nursing, Erie, PA 16541-0001. Offers anesthesia (MSN); business administration (MSN); family nurse practitioner (Certificate); medical-surgical nursing (MSN); nurse anesthesia (Certificate); nursing rural practitioner (MSN). *Accreditation:* AACN; AANA/CANAEP (one or more programs are accredited). Part-time and evening/weekend programs available. *Students:* 19 full-time (11 women), 59 part-time (45 women); includes 2 minority (both African Americans). Average age 36. 16 applicants, 81% accepted, 0 enrolled. In 2009, 19 master's awarded. *Degree requirements:* For master's, thesis. *Entrance requirements:* For master's, GRE General Test, degree in nursing. Additional exam requirements/recommendations for international students: Required—TOEFL (minimum score 79 iBT). *Application deadline:* For spring admission, 8/1 for domestic students. Application fee: $25. Electronic applications accepted. *Expenses:* Tuition: Full-time $13,590; part-time $755 per credit. Required fees: $524; $17 per credit. Tuition and fees vary according to course load, degree level, campus/location and program. *Financial support:* Scholarships/grants available. Financial award application deadline: 7/1; financial award applicants required to submit FAFSA. *Unit head:* Dr. Sharon Thompson, Director, 814-871-5345, E-mail: thompson001@gannon.edu. *Application contact:* Kara Morgan, Assistant Director of Graduate Admissions, 814-871-5831, Fax: 814-871-5827, E-mail: graduate@gannon.edu.

Georgetown University, Graduate School of Arts and Sciences, School of Nursing and Health Studies, Washington, DC 20057. Offers acute care nurse practitioner (MS); clinical nurse specialist (MS); family nurse practitioner (MS); nurse anesthesia (MS); nurse-midwifery (MS); nursing education (MS). *Accreditation:* AACN; AANA/CANAEP; ACNM/DOA. *Degree requirements:* For master's, thesis optional. *Entrance requirements:* For master's, GRE General Test or MAT, bachelor's degree in nursing from NLN-accredited school, minimum undergraduate GPA of 3.0. Additional exam requirements/recommendations for international students: Required—TOEFL.

The George Washington University, School of Medicine and Health Sciences, Health Sciences Programs, Washington, DC 20052. Offers adult nurse practitioner (MSN, Post Master's Certificate); clinical practice management (MSHS); clinical research administration (MSHS); clinical research administration for nurses (MSN); emergency services management (MSHS); end-of-life care (MSHS, MSN); family nurse practitioner (MSN, Post Master's Certificate); immunohematology (MSHS); nursing (DNP); nursing leadership and management (MSN); physical therapy (DPT); physician assistant (MSHS); MSHS/MPH. Postbaccalaureate distance learning degree programs offered (no on-campus study). *Students:* 270 full-time (220 women), 491 part-time (406 women); includes 176 minority (83 African Americans, 5 American Indian/Alaska Native, 62 Asian Americans or Pacific Islanders, 26 Hispanic Americans), 26 international. Average age 35. 1,059 applicants, 47% accepted, 292 enrolled. In 2009, 155 master's, 22 doctorates, 75 other advanced degrees awarded. *Entrance requirements:* Additional exam requirements/recommendations for international students: Required—TOEFL (minimum score 550 paper-based; 213 computer-based). *Application deadline:* Applications are processed on a rolling basis. Application fee: $60. *Expenses:* Contact institution. *Unit head:* Jean E. Johnson, Senior Associate Dean, 202-994-3725, E-mail: jejohns@gwu.edu. *Application contact:* Joke Ogundiran, Director of Admission, 202-994-1668, Fax: 202-994-0870, E-mail: jokeogun@gwu.edu.

Georgia College & State University, Graduate School, College of Health Sciences, Graduate Nursing Program, Milledgeville, GA 31061. Offers adult health (MSN); family nurse practitioner (MSN); nursing administration (MSN); MSN/MBA. *Accreditation:* NLN. Part-time and evening/weekend programs available. *Faculty:* 22 full-time (21 women). *Students:* 13 full-time (all women), 44 part-time (42 women); includes 8 minority (all African Americans), 1 international. Average age 35. 22 applicants, 91% accepted, 18 enrolled. In 2009, 18 master's awarded. *Degree requirements:* For master's, comprehensive exam, thesis optional. *Entrance requirements:* For master's, GMAT, GRE General Test, or MAT, bachelor's degree in nursing, RN license. Additional exam requirements/recommendations for international students: Recommended—TOEFL (minimum score 550 paper-based; 213 computer-based; 79 iBT). *Application deadline:* For fall admission, 7/1 priority date for domestic students. Applications are processed on a rolling basis. Application fee: $40. Electronic applications accepted. *Expenses:* Tuition, area resident: Part-time $241 per credit hour. Tuition, state resident: full-time $4338. Tuition, nonresident: full-time $17,352; part-time $964 per credit hour. Required fees: $609 per semester. Tuition and fees vary according to course load and campus/location. *Financial support:* In 2009–10, 1 research assistantship with full tuition reimbursement was awarded; unspecified assistantships also available. Financial award applicants required to submit FAFSA. *Unit head:* Dr. Judith Malachowski, Director, School of Nursing, 478-445-5122, E-mail: judith.malachowski@gcsu.edu. *Application contact:* Lora Crowe, Coordinator, 478-445-5122, E-mail: lora.crowe@gcsu.edu.

Georgia Southern University, Jack N. Averitt College of Graduate Studies, College of Health and Human Sciences, School of Nursing, Program in Nurse Practitioner, Statesboro, GA 30460. Offers MSN, Certificate. Part-time programs available. Postbaccalaureate distance learning degree programs offered. *Students:* 12 full-time (all women), 64 part-time (59 women); includes 15 minority (9 African Americans, 1 American Indian/Alaska Native, 3 Asian Americans or Pacific Islanders, 2 Hispanic Americans). Average age 36. 20 applicants, 100% accepted, 19 enrolled. In 2009, 7 master's awarded. *Entrance requirements:* For master's, GRE General Test or MAT, minimum GPA of 3.0, Georgia nursing license, 2 years of clinical experience, CPR certification. Additional exam requirements/recommendations for international students: Required—TOEFL (minimum score 550 paper-based; 213 computer-based; 80 iBT). *Application deadline:* For fall admission, 3/1 priority date for domestic and international students; for spring admission, 10/1 priority date for domestic students, 10/1 for international students. Applications are processed on a rolling basis. Application fee: $50. Electronic applications accepted. *Expenses:* Tuition, state resident: full-time $5040; part-time $210 per credit hour. Tuition, nonresident: full-time $20,136; part-time $839 per credit hour. Required fees: $1644. *Financial support:* In 2009–10, 62 students received support, including research assistantships with partial tuition reimbursements available (averaging $6,850 per year), teaching assistantships with partial tuition reimbursements available (averaging $6,850 per year); career-related internships or fieldwork, Federal Work-Study, scholarships/grants, traineeships, tuition waivers (partial), and unspecified assistantships also available. Support available to part-time students. Financial award application deadline: 4/15. *Unit head:* Dr. Donna Hodnicki, Coordinator, 912-478-5056, E-mail: dhodnicki@georgiasouthern.edu. *Application contact:* Office of Graduate Admissions, 912-478-5384, Fax: 912-478-0740, E-mail: gradadmissions@georgiasouthern.edu.

Georgia State University, College of Health and Human Sciences, Byrdine F. Lewis School of Nursing, Atlanta, GA 30302-3083. Offers adult health (MS); adult health nursing (Certificate); child health (MS); family nurse practitioner (MS, Certificate); health promotion, protection and restoration (PhD); perinatal/women's health (MS); psychiatric mental health nursing (Certificate); psychiatric/mental health (MS); women's health nursing (Certificate). *Accreditation:* AACN. Part-time and evening/weekend programs available. Postbaccalaureate distance learning degree programs offered (minimal on-campus study). *Degree requirements:* For master's, research activity; for doctorate, comprehensive exam, thesis/dissertation. *Entrance requirements:* For master's, MAT (preferred) or GRE, interview, RN license; for doctorate, GRE General Test. Additional exam requirements/recommendations for international students: Required—TOEFL (minimum score 550 paper-based; 213 computer-based). Electronic applications accepted. *Expenses:* Contact institution. *Faculty research:* Breast cancer prevention, sexually compulsive behaviors, health risks in minority youth, asthma treatment strategies, adolescent alcohol-related issues.

Goshen College, Program in Nursing, Goshen, IN 46526-4794. Offers clinical nurse leader (MSN); family nurse practitioner (MSN). *Accreditation:* AACN. Part-time and evening/weekend programs available. *Faculty:* 1 (woman) full-time, 7 part-time/adjunct (all women). *Students:* 35 part-time (32 women), 2 international. Average age 39. 17 applicants, 88% accepted, 14 enrolled. *Degree requirements:* For master's, comprehensive exam (for some programs). *Entrance requirements:* Additional exam requirements/recommendations for international students: Required—TOEFL (minimum score 213 paper-based; 79 computer-based; 6 iBT). *Application deadline:* Applications are processed on a rolling basis. Application fee: $50. *Expenses:* Contact institution. *Financial support:* In 2009–10, 10 students received support. Scholarships/grants available. Financial award applicants required to submit FAFSA. *Unit head:* Dr. Brenda Srof, Director, 574-535-7375, E-mail: brendajs@goshen.edu. *Application contact:* Dr. Brenda Srof, 574-535-7375, E-mail: brendajs@goshen.edu.

Graceland University, School of Nursing, Independence, MO 64050-3434. Offers family nurse practitioner (MSN, PMC); nurse educator (MSN, PMC). Part-time programs available. Postbaccalaureate distance learning degree programs offered (minimal on-campus study). *Faculty:* 9 full-time (all women), 9 part-time/adjunct (7 women). *Students:* 138 full-time (128 women), 146 part-time (126 women); includes 14 minority (8 African Americans, 1 American Indian/Alaska Native, 4 Asian Americans or Pacific Islanders, 1 Hispanic American). Average age 40. 251 applicants, 51% accepted, 90 enrolled. In 2009, 44 master's, 2 other advanced degrees awarded. *Degree requirements:* For master's, comprehensive exam (for some programs), thesis optional. *Entrance requirements:* For master's, BSN from nationally accredited program, portfolio, RN license, minimum GPA of 3.0. *Application deadline:* For fall admission, 6/1 priority date for domestic students; for winter admission, 10/1 priority date for domestic students; for spring admission, 3/1 priority date for domestic students. Application fee: $50. Electronic applications accepted. *Expenses:* Contact institution. *Financial support:* In 2009–10, 117 students received support. Institutionally sponsored loans and traineeships available. Support available to part-time students. Financial award applicants required to submit FAFSA. *Faculty research:* International nursing, family care-giving, health promotion. *Unit head:* Dr. Claudia D. Horton, Dean, 816-833-0524 Ext. 4214, Fax: 816-833-2990, E-mail: horton@graceland.edu. *Application contact:* Abbey Riley, Program Consultant, 816-833-0524 Ext. 4803, Fax: 816-833-2990, E-mail: ajriley@graceland.edu.

Grambling State University, School of Graduate Studies and Research, College of Professional Studies, School of Nursing, Grambling, LA 71245. Offers family nurse practitioner (MSN, PMC); nurse educator (MSN). *Accreditation:* NLN. Part-time programs available. *Faculty:* 8 full-time (all women). *Students:* 40 full-time (37 women), 15 part-time (13 women); includes 20 minority (19 African Americans, 1 Asian American or Pacific Islander), 1 international. Average age 38. 9 applicants, 67% accepted, 5 enrolled. In 2009, 17 master's awarded. *Degree requirements:* For master's, comprehensive exam (for some programs), thesis (for some programs). *Entrance requirements:* For master's, GRE, minimum GPA of 3.0 on last degree, interview, 2 years experience as RN. Additional exam requirements/recommendations for international students: Required—TOEFL (minimum score 500 paper-based; 173 computer-based; 61 iBT). *Application deadline:* For fall admission, 7/1 for domestic and international students; for spring admission, 12/1 for domestic and international students. Applications are processed on a rolling basis. Application fee: $20 ($30 for international students). Electronic applications accepted. *Expenses:* Tuition, state resident: full-time $2610. Tuition, nonresident: full-time $2610. *Financial support:* Health care benefits and tuition waivers (full and partial) available. Financial award application deadline: 5/31; financial award applicants required to submit FAFSA. *Unit head:* Dr. Rhonda Hensley, MSN Program Director, 318-274-2897, Fax: 318-274-3491, E-mail: hensleyr@gram.edu. *Application contact:* Katina Crowe, Special Assistant to Associate Vice President/Dean, 318-274-2158, Fax: 318-274-7373, E-mail: croweks@gram.edu.

Grand Canyon University, College of Nursing and Health Sciences, Phoenix, AZ 85017-1097. Offers addiction counseling (MS); nursing (MS), including adult clinical nurse specialist, family nurse practitioner, nursing education, nursing leadership in health care system; professional counseling (MS). Part-time and evening/weekend programs available. Postbaccalaureate distance learning degree programs offered (no on-campus study). *Entrance requirements:* Additional exam requirements/recommendations for international students: Required—TOEFL (minimum score 575 paper-based; 233 computer-based; 90 iBT), IELTS (minimum score 7).

Gwynedd-Mercy College, School of Nursing, Gwynedd Valley, PA 19437-0901. Offers clinical nurse specialist (MSN), including gerontology, oncology, pediatrics; nurse practitioner (MSN), including adult health, pediatric health. *Accreditation:* NLN. *Degree requirements:* For master's, thesis optional. *Entrance requirements:* For master's, GRE General Test or MAT, current nursing experience, physical assessment, course work in statistics, BSN from an NLNAC

Family Nurse Practitioner Studies

Gwynedd-Mercy College (continued)

accredited program, 2 letters of recommendation, personal interview. Additional exam requirements/recommendations for international students: Required—TOEFL (minimum score 575 paper-based). Electronic applications accepted. *Expenses:* Contact institution. *Faculty research:* Critical thinking, primary care, domestic violence, multiculturalism, nursing centers.

Hardin-Simmons University, Graduate School, Patty Hanks Shelton School of Nursing, Abilene, TX 79698-0001. Offers advanced healthcare delivery (MSN); family nurse practitioner (MSN). *Accreditation:* AACN. Part-time programs available. *Faculty:* 3 full-time (all women), 1 (woman) part-time/adjunct. *Students:* 5 full-time (all women), 13 part-time (12 women); includes 2 minority (both Hispanic Americans). Average age 37. 5 applicants, 100% accepted, 4 enrolled. In 2009, 6 master's awarded. *Degree requirements:* For master's, comprehensive exam, thesis or alternative. *Entrance requirements:* For master's, GRE, minimum undergraduate GPA of 3.0 in major, 2.8 overall; interview; upper-level course work in statistics; CPR certification; letters of recommendation. Additional exam requirements/recommendations for international students: Required—TOEFL (minimum score 550 paper-based; 213 computer-based; 75 iBT). *Application deadline:* For fall admission, 8/15 priority date for domestic students, 4/1 for international students; for spring admission, 1/5 priority date for domestic students, 9/1 for international students. Applications are processed on a rolling basis. Application fee: $50. *Expenses:* Contact institution. *Financial support:* In 2009–10, 2 students received support. Career-related internships or fieldwork and scholarships/grants available. Support available to part-time students. Financial award application deadline: 6/30; financial award applicants required to submit FAFSA. *Faculty research:* Child abuse, alternative medicine, pediatric chronic disease, health promotion. *Unit head:* Dr. Amy Toone, Director, 325-671-2361, Fax: 325-671-2386, E-mail: atoone@phssn.edu. *Application contact:* Dr. Gary Stanlake, Dean of Graduate Studies, 325-670-1298, Fax: 325-670-1564, E-mail: gradoff@hsutx.edu.

Hawai'i Pacific University, College of Nursing and Health Sciences, Honolulu, HI 96813. Offers community clinical nurse specialist (MSN); community clinical nurse specialist educator option (MSN); family nurse practitioner (MSN). *Accreditation:* NLN. Part-time and evening/weekend programs available. *Faculty:* 5 full-time (4 women), 2 part-time/adjunct (1 woman). *Students:* 26 full-time (23 women), 13 part-time (all women); includes 18 minority (3 African Americans, 2 American Indian/Alaska Native, 12 Asian Americans or Pacific Islanders, 1 Hispanic American), 7 international. Average age 38. 22 applicants, 68% accepted, 10 enrolled. In 2009, 11 master's awarded. *Degree requirements:* For master's, practicum, professional paper. *Entrance requirements:* For master's, bachelor's degree in nursing, minimum GPA of 3.0. Additional exam requirements/recommendations for international students: Recommended—TOEFL (minimum score 550 paper-based; 213 computer-based; 80 iBT), TWE (minimum score 5). *Application deadline:* Applications are processed on a rolling basis. Application fee: $50. Electronic applications accepted. *Expenses:* Tuition: Full-time $12,600; part-time $700 per credit hour. Tuition and fees vary according to program. *Financial support:* In 2009–10, 17 students received support. Career-related internships or fieldwork, Federal Work-Study, scholarships/grants, and traineeships available. Support available to part-time students. Financial award application deadline: 3/1; financial award applicants required to submit FAFSA. *Faculty research:* Hawaiian elders, traditional healing and nursing center. *Unit head:* Dr. Patricia Lange-Otsuka, Associate Dean of Nursing for Administration, 808-236-5812, Fax: 808-236-5818, E-mail: potsuka@hpu.edu. *Application contact:* Danny Lam, Assistant Director of Graduate Admissions, 808-544-1135, Fax: 808-544-0280, E-mail: graduate@hpu.edu.

Holy Names University, Graduate Division, Department of Nursing, Oakland, CA 94619-1699. Offers administration/management (MS, Certificate); clinical faculty (MS, Certificate); community health nursing/case manager (MS); family nurse practitioner (MS, Certificate); MSN/Certificate; MSN/MBA. *Accreditation:* AACN. Part-time and evening/weekend programs available. *Entrance requirements:* For master's, bachelor's degree in nursing or related field, California RN license or eligibility, minimum GPA of 3.0, previous course work in research or statistics. Additional exam requirements/recommendations for international students: Required—TOEFL (minimum score 500 paper-based). *Faculty research:* Women's reproductive health, gerontology, attitudes about aging, schizophrenic families, international health issues.

Howard University, College of Pharmacy, Nursing and Allied Health Sciences, Division of Nursing, Washington, DC 20059-0002. Offers nurse practitioner (Certificate); primary family health nursing (MSN). *Accreditation:* AACN. Part-time programs available. *Degree requirements:* For master's, comprehensive exam, thesis optional. *Entrance requirements:* For master's, RN license, minimum GPA of 3.0, BS in nursing. *Faculty research:* Urinary incontinence, breast cancer prevention, depression in the elderly, adolescent pregnancy.

Husson University, School of Graduate and Professional Studies, Program in Nursing, Bangor, ME 04401-2999. Offers advanced practice psychiatric nursing (MSN, PMC); family and community nurse practitioner (MSN, PMC). *Accreditation:* AACN. *Entrance requirements:* For master's, MAT, BSN. *Expenses:* Contact institution.

Illinois State University, Graduate School, Mennonite College of Nursing, Normal, IL 61790. Offers family nurse practitioner (PMC); nursing (MSN, PhD). *Accreditation:* AACN. *Faculty research:* Expanding the teaching-nursing home culture in the state of Illinois, advanced education nursing traineeship program, collaborative doctoral program-caring for older adults.

Indiana University–Purdue University Indianapolis, School of Nursing, Indianapolis, IN 46202-2896. Offers acute care nurse practitioner (MSN); adult health clinical nurse specialist (MSN); adult health nursing (MSN), including adult clinical nurse specialist; adult nurse practitioner (MSN); adult psychiatric/mental health nursing (MSN); child psychiatric/mental health nursing (MSN); community health nursing (MSN); family nurse practitioner (MSN); neonatal nurse practitioner (MSN); nursing science (PhD); pediatric clinical nurse specialist (MSN); women's health nurse practitioner (MSN); MSN/MPA; MSN/MPH. *Accreditation:* AACN; NLN (one or more programs are accredited). Part-time programs available. *Faculty:* 85 full-time (82 women), 60 part-time/adjunct (all women). *Students:* 46 full-time (43 women), 369 part-time (354 women); includes 30 minority (21 African Americans, 6 Asian Americans or Pacific Islanders, 3 Hispanic Americans), 5 international. Average age 39. 121 applicants, 82% accepted, 67 enrolled. In 2009, 106 master's, 3 doctorates awarded. Terminal master's awarded for partial completion of doctoral program. *Degree requirements:* For master's, thesis; for doctorate, thesis/dissertation. *Entrance requirements:* For master's, minimum GPA of 3.0, RN license; for doctorate, GRE General Test, minimum GPA of 3.0, MSN, RN license, graduate statistics course with B grade or better (not older than 3 years). Additional exam requirements/recommendations for international students: Required—TOEFL. *Application deadline:* For fall admission, 2/15 for domestic students; for spring admission, 9/15 for domestic students. Application fee: $55 ($65 for international students). *Financial support:* In 2009–10, 93 students received support, including 9 fellowships with full tuition reimbursements available (averaging $7,039 per year), 7 teaching assistantships with full tuition reimbursements available (averaging $5,300 per year); research assistantships with full tuition reimbursements available, Federal Work-Study, institutionally sponsored loans, scholarships/grants, and tuition waivers (full) also available. Support available to part-time students. Financial award application deadline: 5/1. *Faculty research:* Clinical science, health systems. Total annual research expenditures: $3 million. *Unit head:* Associate Dean for Graduate Programs, 317-274-2806, E-mail: nursing@iupui.edu. *Application contact:* Information Contact, 317-274-2806.

The Johns Hopkins University, School of Nursing, Nurse Practitioner Program, Baltimore, MD 21218-2699. Offers adult acute/critical care (MSN, Certificate); adult and pediatric primary care (MSN); adult or pediatric primary care (Certificate); emergency preparedness/disaster response (Certificate); family primary care (MSN, Certificate); women's health (Certificate). *Accreditation:* AACN; NLN (one or more programs are accredited). Part-time programs available. *Faculty:* 9 full-time (all women), 10 part-time/adjunct (all women). *Students:* 28 full-time (27 women), 75 part-time (73 women); includes 33 minority (14 African Americans, 16 Asian Americans or Pacific Islanders, 3 Hispanic Americans), 3 international. Average age 31. 223 applicants, 80% accepted, 29 enrolled. In 2009, 37 master's awarded. *Degree requirements:* For master's, thesis optional, scholarly project or portfolio. *Entrance requirements:* For master's, GRE, interview, minimum GPA of 3.0, BSN, Maryland RN license. Additional exam requirements/recommendations for international students: Required—TOEFL (minimum score 550 paper-based; 213 computer-based). *Application deadline:* For fall admission, 3/1 priority date for domestic and international students; for spring admission, 7/1 priority date for domestic and international students. Application fee: $75. Electronic applications accepted. *Expenses:* Contact institution. *Financial support:* In 2009–10, 25 students received support. Federal Work-Study, scholarships/grants, traineeships, and tuition waivers (partial) available. Support available to part-time students. Financial award application deadline: 3/1; financial award applicants required to submit FAFSA. *Faculty research:* Community outreach, primary care of underserved populations, substance abusing individuals, childhood violence, women's health. *Unit head:* Dr. Julie A. Stanik-Hutt, Director, Master's Programs, 410-502-0184, Fax: 410-955-7463, E-mail: jstanik1@son.jhmi.edu. *Application contact:* Mary O'Rourke, Director of Admissions and Student Services, 410-955-7548, Fax: 410-614-7086, E-mail: orourke@son.jhmi.edu.

Kent State University, College of Nursing, Kent, OH 44242-0001. Offers adult nurse practitioner (MSN); family nurse practitioner (MSN); geriatric nurse practitioner (MSN); nursing (PhD); nursing and health care management (MSN); nursing of adults (clinical nurse specialist) (MSN); pediatric nurse practitioner (MSN); psychiatric/mental health nursing (MSN); women's health nursing (MSN). *Accreditation:* AACN. Part-time programs available. *Degree requirements:* For master's, thesis optional; for doctorate, comprehensive exam, thesis/dissertation. *Entrance requirements:* For master's, GRE (if undergraduate GPA less than 3.0), minimum GPA of 2.75; for doctorate, GRE, MSN. Additional exam requirements/recommendations for international students: Required—TOEFL. Electronic applications accepted. *Expenses:* Contact institution. *Faculty research:* Women and violence, methodological specialties, osteoporosis in women, new caregivers and the elderly.

Lincoln Memorial University, Caylor School of Nursing, Harrogate, TN 37752-1901. Offers family nurse practitioner (MSN); nurse anesthesia (MSN). *Accreditation:* AANA/CANAEP; NLN. Part-time programs available. *Faculty:* 5 full-time (3 women), 2 part-time/adjunct (both women). *Students:* 40 full-time (33 women), 3 part-time (2 women). Average age 30. 66 applicants, 91% accepted, 43 enrolled. In 2009, 6 master's awarded. *Entrance requirements:* For master's, GRE. *Application deadline:* For fall admission, 2/1 for domestic students. Application fee: $25. *Expenses:* Tuition: Full-time $11,700; part-time $390 per hour. *Financial support:* Applicants required to submit FAFSA. *Unit head:* Dr. Mary Anne Modrcin, Dean, 423-869-6319, Fax: 423-869-6244, E-mail: maryanne.modrcin@lmunet.edu. *Application contact:* Sherry Pearman, Director of Nursing Recruitment and Advising, 423-869-6283, E-mail: sherry.pearman@lmunet.edu.

Long Island University, C.W. Post Campus, School of Health Professions and Nursing, Department of Nursing, Brookville, NY 11548-1300. Offers clinical nurse specialist (MS); family nurse practitioner (MS, Certificate). *Accreditation:* AACN. Part-time and evening/weekend programs available. *Degree requirements:* For master's, thesis. *Entrance requirements:* For master's, minimum GPA of 3.0 in major, bachelor's degree in nursing, NYS registered nurse, interview. Electronic applications accepted. *Faculty research:* Lactation/breast cancer, early discharge in maternity.

Loyola University Chicago, Graduate School, Marcella Niehoff School of Nursing, Family Nurse Practitioner Program, Chicago, IL 60660. Offers family nurse practitioner (MSN); family practice nurse practitioner (Certificate); informatics (Certificate); manager care (Certificate). Part-time and evening/weekend programs available. *Students:* 7 full-time (all women), 67 part-time (66 women); includes 18 minority (5 African Americans, 12 Asian Americans or Pacific Islanders, 1 Hispanic American). Average age 33. 38 applicants, 55% accepted, 15 enrolled. In 2009, 4 master's awarded. *Entrance requirements:* For master's, BSN, Illinois nursing license, minimum nursing GPA of 3.0, 1000 hours experience before starting clinical. *Application deadline:* Applications are processed on a rolling basis. Application fee: $50. Electronic applications accepted. *Expenses:* Tuition: Full-time $14,220; part-time $790 per credit hour. Required fees: $60 per semester hour. Tuition and fees vary according to program. *Financial support:* Traineeships available. Financial award applicants required to submit FAFSA. *Unit head:* Dr. Marijo Letizia, Associate Professor, 708-216-9325, Fax: 708-216-9555, E-mail: mletizi@luc.edu. *Application contact:* Dr. Vicki A. Keough, Associate Professor/Master's Program Director, 708-216-3582, Fax: 708-216-9555, E-mail: vkeough@luc.edu.

Loyola University New Orleans, College of Social Sciences, School of Nursing, New Orleans, LA 70118-6195. Offers adult nurse practitioner (MSN); family nurse practitioner (MSN); health care systems management (MSN); nursing (MSN, DNP). *Accreditation:* NLN. Part-time and evening/weekend programs available. Postbaccalaureate distance learning degree programs offered. *Students:* 60 full-time (56 women), 543 part-time (490 women); includes 147 minority (116 African Americans, 4 American Indian/Alaska Native, 13 Asian Americans or Pacific Islanders, 14 Hispanic Americans), 1 international. Average age 43. 296 applicants, 97% accepted, 206 enrolled. In 2009, 153 master's awarded. *Degree requirements:* For doctorate, capstone project. *Entrance requirements:* For master's, BSN, Louisiana nursing license, 1 year of work experience in clinical nursing, minimum undergraduate GPA of 2.8, interview, resume. Additional exam requirements/recommendations for international students: Required—TOEFL (minimum score 550 paper-based; 213 computer-based). *Application deadline:* For fall admission, 8/1 priority date for domestic and international students; for winter admission, 12/15 priority date for domestic and international students; for spring admission, 5/15 priority date for domestic and international students. Applications are processed on a rolling basis. Application fee: $20. Electronic applications accepted. *Financial support:* Traineeships and Incumbent Workers Training Program grants available. Financial award application deadline: 5/1; financial award applicants required to submit FAFSA. *Faculty research:* Increasing compliance with treatment, patient satisfaction with care provided by nurse practitioners. *Unit head:* Ann H. Cary, Director, 800-488-6257, Fax: 504-865-3254, E-mail: nursing@loyno.edu. *Application contact:* Deborah Smith, Assistant to the Director, 504-865-2823, Fax: 504-865-3254, E-mail: dhsmith@loyno.edu.

Malone University, Graduate Program in Nursing, Canton, OH 44709. Offers clinical nurse specialist (MSN); family nurse practitioner (MSN). *Accreditation:* AACN. Part-time and evening/weekend programs available. *Faculty:* 9 full-time (all women), 13 part-time/adjunct (8 women). *Students:* 50 part-time (45 women); includes 2 minority (both African Americans). Average age 35. 49 applicants, 73% accepted, 27 enrolled. In 2009, 20 master's awarded. *Degree requirements:* For master's, thesis. *Entrance requirements:* For master's, minimum GPA of 3.0 from BSN program, interview, Ohio RN license. Additional exam requirements/recommendations for international students: Required—TOEFL (minimum score 550 paper-based; 213 computer-based; 79 iBT). *Application deadline:* Applications are processed on a rolling basis. Application fee: $25. *Expenses:* Contact institution. *Financial support:* Tuition waivers (partial) available. Support available to part-time students. Financial award application deadline: 6/30. *Faculty research:* Peripartum cardiomyopathy in women of childbearing age; direct observation of nurse practitioner care; prevalence of Hepatitis B in pregnant women in Mali, West Africa; breast cancer knowledge of Amish women in northeast Ohio, gender issues in the Hispanic population. *Unit head:* Dr. Sharon M. Weyer, Director, 330-471-8612, Fax: 330-471-8607, E-mail: sweyer@malone.edu. *Application contact:* David L. Kleffman, Assistant Director of Enrollment, 330-471-8447, Fax: 330-471-8343, E-mail: dkleffman@malone.edu.

Marymount University, School of Health Professions, Program in Nursing, Arlington, VA 22207-4299. Offers family nurse practitioner (MSN, Certificate); nursing (DNP); nursing education (MSN, Certificate); RN to MSN (MSN). *Accreditation:* AACN. Part-time and evening/weekend programs available. *Faculty:* 5 full-time (all women), 2 part-time/adjunct (both women). *Students:* 13 full-time (12 women), 66 part-time (60 women); includes 38 minority (26 African Americans, 9 Asian Americans or Pacific Islanders, 3 Hispanic Americans), 4 international. Average age 38. 56 applicants, 79% accepted, 30 enrolled. In 2009, 17 master's awarded. *Degree requirements:* For master's, comprehensive exam; for doctorate, thesis/dissertation or alternative. *Entrance requirements:* For master's, 2 letters of recommendation, interview, resume, RN license; for doctorate, 2 letters of recommendation, interview, resume, RN license, minimum MSN GPA of 3.5 or BSN GPA of 3.3; for Certificate, interview, master's degree in nursing.

Additional exam requirements/recommendations for international students: Required—TOEFL (minimum score 600 paper-based; 250 computer-based; 96 iBT), IELTS (minimum score 6.5). *Application deadline:* For fall admission, 7/1 for international students; for spring admission, 10/15 for international students. Applications are processed on a rolling basis. Application fee: $40. Electronic applications accepted. *Expenses:* Tuition: Full-time $13,050; part-time $725 per credit hour. Required fees: $135; $7.50 per credit hour. *Financial support:* In 2009–10, 8 students received support; research assistantships with partial tuition reimbursements available, career-related internships or fieldwork, Federal Work-Study, scholarships/grants, and unspecified assistantships available. Support available to part-time students. Financial award applicants required to submit FAFSA. *Unit head:* Dr. Susan Bidwell, Chair, 703-284-1593, Fax: 703-284-3819, E-mail: susan.bidwell@marymount.edu. *Application contact:* Francesca Reed, Director, Graduate Admissions, 703-284-5901, Fax: 703-527-3815, E-mail: grad.admissions@marymount.edu.

Maryville University of Saint Louis, School of Health Professions, Nursing Program, St. Louis, MO 63141-7299. Offers accelerated RN to MSN (MSN); adult nurse practitioner (MSN); advanced practice nursing (DNP); family nurse practitioner (MSN); nursing education (MSN). *Accreditation:* AACN. Postbaccalaureate distance learning degree programs offered. *Students:* 23 full-time (22 women), 96 part-time (92 women); includes 6 African Americans, 6 Asian Americans or Pacific Islanders, 2 Hispanic Americans. Average age 36. In 2009, 23 master's awarded. *Degree requirements:* For master's, practicum. *Entrance requirements:* For master's, BSN, current licensure, minimum GPA of 3.0, 3 letters of recommendation, curriculum vitae. Additional exam requirements/recommendations for international students: Required—TOEFL (minimum score 550 paper-based). *Application deadline:* Applications are processed on a rolling basis. Application fee: $40 ($60 for international students). Electronic applications accepted. *Expenses:* Tuition: Full-time $20,384; part-time $627.50 per credit hour. Required fees: $100 per semester. *Financial support:* Federal Work-Study and campus employment available. Support available to part-time students. Financial award application deadline: 3/1; financial award applicants required to submit FAFSA. *Unit head:* Dr. Mary Curtis, Director, 314-529-9478, Fax: 314-529-9139, E-mail: mcurtis@maryville.edu. *Application contact:* Dr. Mary Curtis, Director, 314-529-9478, Fax: 314-529-9139, E-mail: mcurtis@maryville.edu.

McGill University, Faculty of Graduate and Postdoctoral Studies, Faculty of Medicine, School of Nursing, Montréal, QC H3A 2T5, Canada. Offers nurse practitioner (Graduate Diploma); nursing (M Sc A, PhD).

McNeese State University, Doré School of Graduate Studies, College of Nursing, Lake Charles, LA 70609. Offers clinical nurse specialist (MSN); nurse educator (MSN); nurse practitioner (MSN); nursing leadership and administration (MSN). *Accreditation:* AACN. *Faculty:* 4 full-time (all women), 1 part-time/adjunct (0 women). *Students:* 17 full-time (9 women), 72 part-time (56 women); includes 14 minority (12 African Americans, 2 Asian Americans or Pacific Islanders). In 2009, 21 master's awarded. *Degree requirements:* For master's, comprehensive exam. *Entrance requirements:* For master's, GRE, eligibility for unencumbered licensure as RN in Louisiana. *Application deadline:* For fall admission, 5/15 priority date for domestic and international students; for spring admission, 10/15 priority date for domestic and international students. Applications are processed on a rolling basis. Application fee: $20 ($30 for international students). *Expenses:* Tuition, area resident: Full-time $2556. Tuition, state resident: full-time $2556. Required fees: $1031. Tuition and fees vary according to course load. *Financial support:* Application deadline: 5/1. *Unit head:* Dr. Peggy L. Wolfe, Dean, 337-475-5820, Fax: 337-475-5924, E-mail: pwolfe@mcneese.edu. *Application contact:* Valarie Waldmeier, Coordinator of Graduate Nursing, 337-475-5285, Fax: 337-475-5707, E-mail: vwaldmeier@mcneese.edu.

Medical College of Georgia, School of Graduate Studies, Family Nurse Practitioner Program, Augusta, GA 30912. Offers MSN. *Entrance requirements:* For master's, GRE General Test or MAT, Georgia registered professional nurse license. Additional exam requirements/recommendations for international students: Required—TOEFL (minimum score 550 paper-based; 213 computer-based; 79 iBT). Electronic applications accepted. Full-time tuition and fees vary according to campus/location, program and student level.

Medical University of South Carolina, College of Nursing, Doctor of Nursing Practice Program, Charleston, SC 29425. Offers adult nurse practitioner (DNP); family nurse practitioner (DNP); pediatric nurse practitioner (DNP); post-master's for advanced practice nurses (DNP). Part-time programs available. Postbaccalaureate distance learning degree programs offered (minimal on-campus study). *Faculty:* 20 full-time (19 women), 2 part-time/adjunct (1 woman). *Students:* 28 full-time (all women), 17 part-time (16 women); includes 7 minority (5 African Americans, 1 American Indian/Alaska Native, 1 Hispanic American). Average age 32. 99 applicants, 54% accepted, 45 enrolled. *Degree requirements:* For doctorate, thesis/dissertation (for some programs), practice inquiry project. *Entrance requirements:* For doctorate, BSN or MSN, minimum GPA of 3.0, course work in statistics, RN license, 3 references, interview (if requested). Additional exam requirements/recommendations for international students: Required—TOEFL (minimum score 600 paper-based; 250 computer-based). *Application deadline:* For fall admission, 2/1 priority date for domestic and international students. Application fee: $85. Electronic applications accepted. *Financial support:* Federal Work-Study and scholarships/grants available. Support available to part-time students. Financial award applicants required to submit FAFSA. *Faculty research:* Community partnerships, smoking cessation, gerontology, lateral violence in the workplace. *Unit head:* Dr. Robin L. Bissinger, Director of Graduate Programs, 843-792-0531, Fax: 843-792-9258, E-mail: bissinrl@musc.edu. *Application contact:* Carolyn F. Page, Director, Student Services, 843-792-3844, Fax: 843-792-5395, E-mail: pagecf@musc.edu.

Medical University of South Carolina, College of Nursing, Family Nurse Practitioner Program, Charleston, SC 29425. Offers MSN. Part-time programs available. *Faculty:* 10 full-time (all women), 3 part-time/adjunct (2 women). *Students:* 28 full-time (all women), 14 part-time (all women); includes 4 minority (all African Americans). Average age 29. 64 applicants, 58% accepted, 29 enrolled. In 2009, 14 master's awarded. *Degree requirements:* For master's, thesis optional. *Entrance requirements:* For master's, BSN, course work in statistics, nursing license, minimum GPA of 3.0. Additional exam requirements/recommendations for international students: Required—TOEFL (minimum score 600 paper-based; 250 computer-based). *Application deadline:* For fall admission, 2/1 priority date for domestic and international students. Application fee: $85. Electronic applications accepted. *Financial support:* Fellowships, Federal Work-Study, scholarships/grants, and traineeships available. Support available to part-time students. Financial award application deadline: 3/10; financial award applicants required to submit FAFSA. *Faculty research:* Use of PDAs in clinical practice, palliative care, diabetes, smoking cessation, feeding with late stage dementia. *Unit head:* Margaret P. Spain, Lead Faculty, 843-792-2315, Fax: 843-792-2104, E-mail: spainm@musc.edu. *Application contact:* Carolyn F. Page, Director, Student Services, 843-792-3844, Fax: 843-792-5395, E-mail: pagecf@musc.edu.

Metropolitan State University, College of Nursing and Health Sciences, St. Paul, MN 55106-5000. Offers adult/geriatric nurse practitioner (MSN); family nurse practitioner (MSN); leadership and management (MSN); nursing (MSN, DNP); oral health care practitioner (MS); public health nursing leadership (MSN); women's health care nurse practitioner (MSN). *Accreditation:* AACN. Part-time programs available. *Degree requirements:* For master's, thesis or alternative; for doctorate, thesis/dissertation or alternative. *Entrance requirements:* For master's, GRE General Test, minimum GPA of 3.0, RN license, B.S./BAN degree; for doctorate, minimum GPA of 3.0; RN licensure, MSN degree. Additional exam requirements/recommendations for international students: Required—TOEFL (minimum score 550 paper-based; 213 computer-based). *Expenses:* Tuition, state resident: full-time $5520; part-time $276 per credit hour. Tuition, nonresident: full-time $11,040; part-time $552 per credit hour. Required fees: $209; $10 per credit hour. Tuition and fees vary according to degree level. *Faculty research:* Women's health, gerontology.

Middle Tennessee State University, College of Graduate Studies, College of Basic and Applied Sciences, School of Nursing, Program in Family Nurse Practitioner, Murfreesboro, TN 37132. Offers MSN, Graduate Certificate. Part-time and evening/weekend programs available. Postbaccalaureate distance learning degree programs offered. *Students:* 2 part-time (both women). *Entrance requirements:* Additional exam requirements/recommendations for international students: Required—TOEFL (minimum score 525 paper-based; 195 computer-based; 71 iBT) or IELTS (minimum score 6). *Expenses:* Tuition, state resident: full-time $4404. Tuition, nonresident: full-time $10,956. *Financial support:* Institutionally sponsored loans available. Support available to part-time students. Financial award application deadline: 5/1. *Unit head:* Dr. Lynn Parsons, Director, 615-898-5340. *Application contact:* Dr. Michael Allen, Dean and Vice Provost for Research, 615-898-2840, Fax: 615-904-8020, E-mail: mallen@mtsu.edu.

Midwestern State University, Graduate Studies, College of Health Sciences and Human Services, Nursing Program, Wichita Falls, TX 76308. Offers family nurse practitioner (MSN); health services administration (MSN); nurse educator (MSN). *Accreditation:* AACN. Part-time and evening/weekend programs available. *Degree requirements:* For master's, comprehensive exam, thesis optional. *Entrance requirements:* For master's, GRE General Test or MAT. Additional exam requirements/recommendations for international students: Required—TOEFL (minimum score 550 paper-based; 213 computer-based). Electronic applications accepted. *Expenses:* Tuition, state resident: full-time $1620; part-time $90 per credit hour. Tuition, nonresident: full-time $2160; part-time $120 per credit hour. International tuition: $7506 full-time. Required fees: $3068.80; $145.60 per credit hour. $179 per semester.

Minnesota State University Mankato, College of Graduate Studies, College of Allied Health and Nursing, School of Nursing, Mankato, MN 56001. Offers family nursing (MSN), including family nurse practitioner; nursing (DNP). *Accreditation:* AACN; NLN. *Students:* 9 full-time (all women), 87 part-time (81 women). *Degree requirements:* For master's, comprehensive exam, internships, research project or thesis; for doctorate, capstone project. *Entrance requirements:* For master's, GRE General Test or on-campus essay, minimum GPA of 3.0 during previous 2 years, BSN or equivalent references; for doctorate, master's degree in nursing. Additional exam requirements/recommendations for international students: Required—TOEFL. *Application deadline:* For fall admission, 1/15 priority date for domestic students. Applications are processed on a rolling basis. Application fee: $40. Electronic applications accepted. *Expenses:* Tuition, state resident: full-time $5364. Tuition, nonresident: full-time $8314. *Financial support:* Research assistantships with full tuition reimbursements, teaching assistantships with full tuition reimbursements available. Financial award application deadline: 3/15; financial award applicants required to submit FAFSA. *Faculty research:* Psychosocial nursing, computers in nursing, family adaptation. *Unit head:* Dr. Sue Ellen Bell, Graduate Coordinator, 507-389-6814. *Application contact:* Collaborative MSN Program Admissions, 507-389-6022.

Missouri State University, Graduate College, College of Health and Human Services, Department of Nursing, Springfield, MO 65897. Offers nursing (MSN), including family nurse practitioner, nurse educator. *Accreditation:* AACN. *Faculty:* 7 full-time (all women), 3 part-time/adjunct (all women). *Students:* 20 full-time (19 women), 22 part-time (19 women); includes 1 minority (Asian American or Pacific Islander), 1 international. Average age 37. 2 applicants, 50% accepted, 1 enrolled. In 2009, 6 master's awarded. *Degree requirements:* For master's, comprehensive exam, thesis or alternative. *Entrance requirements:* For master's, GRE General Test, minimum GPA of 3.0, RN license (MSN), 1 year work experience (MPH). Additional exam requirements/recommendations for international students: Required—TOEFL (minimum score 550 paper-based; 213 computer-based; 79 iBT). *Application deadline:* For fall admission, 7/20 priority date for domestic students, 5/1 for international students; for spring admission, 12/20 priority date for domestic students, 9/1 for international students. Applications are processed on a rolling basis. Application fee: $35 ($50 for international students). Electronic applications accepted. *Expenses:* Tuition, state resident: full-time $3852; part-time $214 per credit hour. Tuition, nonresident: full-time $7524; part-time $418 per credit hour. Required fees: $696; $172 per semester. Tuition and fees vary according to course level, course load, degree level and program. *Financial support:* Federal Work-Study, institutionally sponsored loans, scholarships/grants, and unspecified assistantships available. Financial award application deadline: 3/31; financial award applicants required to submit FAFSA. *Faculty research:* Preconceptual health, women's health, nursing satisfaction, nursing education. *Unit head:* Dr. Kathryn Hope, Head, 417-836-5310, Fax: 417-836-5484, E-mail: nursing@missouristate.edu. *Application contact:* Eric Eckert, Coordinator of Admissions and Recruitment, 417-836-5331, Fax: 417-836-6200, E-mail: tobinbushman@missouristate.edu.

Molloy College, Graduate Nursing Program, Rockville Centre, NY 11571-5002. Offers adult nurse practitioner (Advanced Certificate); clinical nurse specialist: adult health (Advanced Certificate); family nurse practitioner (Advanced Certificate); nurse practitioner psychiatry (Advanced Certificate); nursing (MS); nursing administration (Advanced Certificate); nursing administration with informatics (Advanced Certificate); nursing education (Advanced Certificate); nursing informatics (Advanced Certificate); pediatric nurse practitioner (Advanced Certificate). *Accreditation:* AACN. Part-time and evening/weekend programs available. *Faculty:* 23 full-time (22 women), 5 part-time/adjunct (4 women). *Students:* 11 full-time (10 women), 405 part-time (377 women); includes 206 minority (124 African Americans, 52 Asian Americans or Pacific Islanders, 30 Hispanic Americans), 2 international. Average age 39. In 2009, 64 master's awarded. *Degree requirements:* For master's, thesis optional. *Entrance requirements:* For master's, 3 letters of reference, BS in nursing, minimum undergraduate GPA of 3.0; for Advanced Certificate, 3 letters of reference, master's degree in nursing. *Application deadline:* For fall admission, 9/2 priority date for domestic students; for spring admission, 1/20 priority date for domestic students. Applications are processed on a rolling basis. Application fee: $60. *Expenses:* Tuition: Part-time $765 per credit. Required fees: $340 per semester. *Financial support:* Research assistantships with partial tuition reimbursements, teaching assistantships with partial tuition reimbursements, institutionally sponsored loans, scholarships/grants, and unspecified assistantships available. Support available to part-time students. Financial award application deadline: 4/1; financial award applicants required to submit FAFSA. *Unit head:* Dr. Mary T. O'Shaughnessy, Acting Director, 516-678-5000, Fax: 516-678-9718, E-mail: moshaughnessy@molloy.edu. *Application contact:* Alina Haitz, Assistant Director of Graduate Admissions, 516-678-5000 Ext. 6399, Fax: 516-256-2247, E-mail: ahaitz@molloy.edu.

Monmouth University, Graduate School, The Marjorie K. Unterberg School of Nursing and Health Studies, West Long Branch, NJ 07764-1898. Offers adult nurse practitioner (MSN); adult psychiatric and mental health advanced practice nursing (MSN, Post-Master's Certificate); advanced practice nursing (Post-Master's Certificate); family nurse practitioner (MSN, Post-Master's Certificate); forensic nursing (MSN, Certificate); nursing (MSN); nursing administration (MSN, Post-Master's Certificate); nursing education (MSN, Post-Master's Certificate); school nursing (MSN, Certificate). *Accreditation:* AACN. Part-time and evening/weekend programs available. *Faculty:* 11 full-time (all women), 2 part-time/adjunct (both women). *Students:* 15 full-time (14 women), 183 part-time (178 women); includes 51 minority (14 African Americans, 3 American Indian/Alaska Native, 26 Asian Americans or Pacific Islanders, 8 Hispanic Americans), 1 international. Average age 41. 95 applicants, 99% accepted, 44 enrolled. In 2009, 36 master's awarded. *Degree requirements:* For master's, practicum (for some tracks). *Entrance requirements:* For master's, GRE General Test, RN license, 1 year of work experience, minimum undergraduate GPA of 2.75. Additional exam requirements/recommendations for international students: Required—TOEFL (minimum score 550 paper-based; 213 computer-based; 79 iBT), IELTS (minimum score 5), Michigan English Language Assessment Battery (minimum score 77), Cambridge A, B, C. *Application deadline:* For fall admission, 7/15 priority date for domestic students, 6/1 for international students; for spring admission, 11/15 priority date for domestic students, 11/1 for international students. Applications are processed on a rolling basis. Application fee: $50. Electronic applications accepted. *Expenses:* Tuition: Part-time $773 per credit. Required fees: $157 per semester. *Financial support:* In 2009–10, 118 students received support, including 96 fellowships (averaging $1,308 per year), 4 research assistantships (averaging $3,610 per year); career-related internships or fieldwork, scholarships/grants, and unspecified assistantships also available. Support available to part-time students. Financial award applicants required to submit FAFSA. *Faculty research:* Relationship of undergraduate GPA and GRE to succeed in a graduate nursing program. *Unit head:* Dr. Janet Mahoney, Dean, 732-571-3443, Fax: 732-263-5131, E-mail: jmahoney@monmouth.edu.

Family Nurse Practitioner Studies

Monmouth University (continued)
Application contact: Kevin Roane, Director, Office of Graduate Admission, 732-571-3452, Fax: 732-263-5123, E-mail: gradadm@monmouth.edu.

Montana State University, College of Graduate Studies, College of Nursing, Bozeman, MT 59717. Offers clinical nurse specialist (CNS) (MN, Post-Master's Certificate); family nurse practitioner (MN, Post-Master's Certificate); nursing education (Certificate); psychiatric mental health nurse practitioner (MN). *Accreditation:* AACN. Part-time programs available. Post-baccalaureate distance learning degree programs offered (no on-campus study). *Faculty:* 49 full-time (46 women), 25 part-time/adjunct (all women). *Students:* 41 full-time (39 women), 24 part-time (23 women); includes 8 minority (7 American Indian/Alaska Native, 1 Hispanic American). Average age 38. 54 applicants, 33% accepted, 16 enrolled. In 2009, 13 master's awarded. *Degree requirements:* For master's, comprehensive exam, thesis (for some programs). *Entrance requirements:* For master's, GRE General Test. Additional exam requirements/ recommendations for international students: Required—TOEFL (minimum score 580 paper-based; 213 computer-based). *Application deadline:* For fall admission, 7/15 priority date for domestic students, 5/15 priority date for international students; for spring admission, 12/1 priority date for domestic students, 10/1 priority date for international students. Applications are processed on a rolling basis. Application fee: $30. Electronic applications accepted. *Expenses:* Tuition, state resident: full-time $5635; part-time $3492 per year. Tuition, nonresident: full-time $17,212; part-time $7865.10 per year. Required fees: $1441; $153.15 per credit. Tuition and fees vary according to course load and program. *Financial support:* In 2009–10, 16 students received support, including 3 fellowships with full tuition reimbursements available (averaging $15,000 per year), 1 research assistantship (averaging $7,000 per year), 8 teaching assistantships with partial tuition reimbursements available (averaging $7,050 per year); traineeships and tuition waivers (partial) also available. Financial award application deadline: 3/1; financial award applicants required to submit FAFSA. *Faculty research:* Environmental exposures, chronic illness, sleep habits, oral health, pressure ulcers. Total annual research expenditures: $2.3 million. *Unit head:* Dr. Elizabeth Kinion, Dean, 406-994-2725, Fax: 406-994-6020, E-mail: ekinion@montana.edu. *Application contact:* Dr. Carl A. Fox, Vice Provost for Graduate Education, 406-994-4145, Fax: 406-994-7433, E-mail: gradstudy@montana.edu.

Mountain State University, Graduate Studies, Program in Nursing, Beckley, WV 25802-9003. Offers administration/education (MSN); family nurse practitioner (MSN); nurse anesthesia (MSN); registered nurse anesthetist (Certificate). *Accreditation:* AANA/CANAEP; NLN. Part-time programs available. Postbaccalaureate distance learning degree programs offered (minimal on-campus study). *Faculty:* 4 full-time (all women), 10 part-time/adjunct (9 women). *Students:* 117 full-time (102 women); includes 10 minority (6 African Americans, 1 American Indian/ Alaska Native, 3 Asian Americans or Pacific Islanders), 1 international. Average age 37. 46 applicants, 80% accepted, 37 enrolled. In 2009, 35 master's awarded. *Degree requirements:* For master's, comprehensive exam, thesis or alternative. *Entrance requirements:* For master's, GRE. Additional exam requirements/recommendations for international students: Required— TOEFL (minimum score 550 paper-based; 213 computer-based); Recommended—IELTS (minimum score 6.5). *Application deadline:* For spring admission, 6/30 for domestic and international students. Applications are processed on a rolling basis. Application fee: $25 ($50 for international students). Electronic applications accepted. *Expenses:* Contact institution. *Financial support:* Federal Work-Study, scholarships/grants, and unspecified assistantships available. Support available to part-time students. Financial award applicants required to submit FAFSA. *Unit head:* Dr. Judith Halle, Dean, School of Health Sciences, 304-929-1327, Fax: 304-929-1601, E-mail: jhalle@mountainstate.edu. *Application contact:* Melody Tilley, Program Specialist, 304-929-1576, Fax: 304-929-1601, E-mail: mtilley@mountainstate.edu.

Mount Saint Mary College, Division of Nursing, Newburgh, NY 12550-3494. Offers adult nurse practitioner (MS), including nursing education, nursing management; clinical nurse specialist-adult health (MS), including nursing education, nursing management; family nurse practitioner (Advanced Certificate). *Accreditation:* AACN. Part-time and evening/weekend programs available. *Faculty:* 3 full-time (all women), 2 part-time/adjunct (both women). *Students:* 1 full-time (0 women), 53 part-time (50 women); includes 17 minority (8 African Americans, 4 Asian Americans or Pacific Islanders, 5 Hispanic Americans). Average age 39. 16 applicants, 100% accepted, 6 enrolled. In 2009, 5 master's awarded. *Degree requirements:* For master's, research utilization project. *Entrance requirements:* For master's, BSN, minimum GPA of 3.0, RN license. *Application deadline:* For fall admission, 6/3 priority date for domestic students; for spring admission, 10/31 priority date for domestic students. Applications are processed on a rolling basis. Application fee: $45. *Expenses:* Tuition: Full-time $13,356; part-time $742 per credit. Required fees: $50 per semester. *Financial support:* In 2009–10, 2 students received support. Unspecified assistantships available. Financial award application deadline: 4/15; financial award applicants required to submit FAFSA. *Unit head:* Dr. Karen Baldwin, Coordinator, 845-569-3512, Fax: 845-562-6762, E-mail: baldwin@msmc.edu. *Application contact:* Graduate Coordinator, 845-561-0800, Fax: 845-562-6762.

Murray State University, College of Health Sciences and Human Services, Program in Nursing, Murray, KY 42071. Offers clinical nurse specialist (MSN); family nurse practitioner (MSN); nurse anesthesia (MSN). *Accreditation:* AACN; AANA/CANAEP. *Degree requirements:* For master's, research project. *Entrance requirements:* For master's, GRE General Test, BSN, interview, RN licensure. Additional exam requirements/recommendations for international students: Required—TOEFL (minimum score 550 paper-based). *Faculty research:* Fibromyalgis, primary care, rural health.

Northern Arizona University, Graduate College, College of Health and Human Services, School of Nursing, Flagstaff, AZ 86011. Offers family nurse practitioner (MSN, Certificate); nurse educator (MSN); nurse generalist (MSN); nursing (MSN). *Accreditation:* AACN. *Faculty:* 19 full-time (all women). *Students:* 17 full-time (14 women), 32 part-time (29 women); includes 4 minority (1 American Indian/Alaska Native, 3 Hispanic Americans). Average age 30. 43 applicants, 19% accepted, 4 enrolled. In 2009, 7 master's awarded. *Degree requirements:* For master's, project or thesis. *Entrance requirements:* For master's, GRE General Test or minimum GPA of 3.0, undergraduate statistics or health assessment with minimum grade of B in last 5 years or 3 years of RN experience (nursing education). Additional exam requirements/ recommendations for international students: Required—TOEFL (minimum score 550 paper-based; 213 computer-based; 80 iBT), IELTS (minimum score 7), or a bachelor's degree from an English-speaking university and demonstrated proficiency. *Application deadline:* For fall admission, 1/15 priority date for domestic students, 9/1 priority date for international students. Application fee: $65. Electronic applications accepted. *Financial support:* In 2009–10, 4 teaching assistantships with partial tuition reimbursements were awarded; career-related internships or fieldwork, Federal Work-Study, traineeships, health care benefits, tuition waivers, and unspecified assistantships also available. Support available to part-time students. Financial award application deadline: 3/30; financial award applicants required to submit FAFSA. *Unit head:* Debera Thomas, Chair, 928-523-2656, Fax: 928-523-7171, E-mail: debera.thomas@nau.edu. *Application contact:* Penny Susan Walior, Student Academic Specialist, 928-523-6717, Fax: 928-523-9155, E-mail: penny.walior@nau.edu.

North Georgia College & State University, Graduate Studies, Department of Nursing, Dahlonega, GA 30597. Offers family nurse practitioner (MSN); nursing education (MSN). *Accreditation:* NLN. Part-time programs available. *Degree requirements:* For master's, one foreign language, comprehensive exam, thesis. *Entrance requirements:* For master's, GRE General Test or MAT, minimum GPA of 2.75, 3 letters of recommendation, current Georgia RN license, 1 year of post-licensure work, BSN. Electronic applications accepted.

Oakland University, Graduate Study and Lifelong Learning, School of Nursing, Program in Family Nurse Practitioner, Rochester, MI 48309-4401. Offers MSN, Certificate. *Accreditation:* AACN. *Degree requirements:* For master's, thesis. *Entrance requirements:* For master's, GRE General Test, minimum GPA of 3.0 for unconditional admission. Additional exam requirements/ recommendations for international students: Required—TOEFL (minimum score 550 paper-based; 213 computer-based). Electronic applications accepted. *Expenses:* Contact institution.

Ohio University, Graduate College, College of Health and Human Services, School of Nursing, Athens, OH 45701-2979. Offers family nurse practitioner (MSN); nurse administrator (MSN); nurse educator (MSN). *Accreditation:* AACN. *Faculty:* 8 full-time (all women). *Students:* 24 full-time (23 women), 31 part-time (25 women); includes 1 African American, 2 American Indian/Alaska Native. 36 applicants, 92% accepted, 25 enrolled. In 2009, 12 master's awarded. *Degree requirements:* For master's, capstone project. *Entrance requirements:* For master's, GRE, bachelor's degree in nursing from an accredited college or university, minimum overall undergraduate GPA of 3.0, official transcripts, statement of goals and objectives, resume, 3 letters of recommendation. Additional exam requirements/recommendations for international students: Required—TOEFL (minimum score 550 paper-based; 80 iBT) or IELTS Academic (minimum score 6.5). *Application deadline:* For fall admission, 3/1 priority date for domestic students, 2/1 priority date for international students. Applications are processed on a rolling basis. Application fee: $50 ($55 for international students). Electronic applications accepted. *Expenses:* Tuition, state resident: full-time $7839; part-time $323 per quarter hour. Tuition, nonresident: full-time $15,831; part-time $654 per quarter hour. Required fees: $2931. *Financial support:* Research assistantships, Federal Work-Study, institutionally sponsored loans, and unspecified assistantships available. Financial award application deadline: 3/1. *Unit head:* Mary Bowen, Director, 740-593-9134, E-mail: bowenm2@ohio.edu. *Application contact:* Cheryl Branham, Administrative Associate, 740-593-4494, E-mail: branhamc@ohio.edu.

Old Dominion University, College of Health Sciences, School of Nursing, Norfolk, VA 23529. Offers family nurse practitioner (MSN); nurse anesthesia (MSN); nurse educator (MSN); nurse midwifery (MSN); women's health nurse practitioner (MSN). *Accreditation:* AACN; AANA/ CANAEP. Part-time programs available. Postbaccalaureate distance learning degree programs offered (no on-campus study). *Faculty:* 11 full-time (10 women), 15 part-time/adjunct (14 women). *Students:* 122 full-time (113 women), 101 part-time (97 women); includes 49 minority (23 African Americans, 2 American Indian/Alaska Native, 19 Asian Americans or Pacific Islanders, 5 Hispanic Americans). Average age 37. 169 applicants, 81% accepted, 122 enrolled. In 2009, 77 master's awarded. *Degree requirements:* For master's, comprehensive exam. *Entrance requirements:* For master's, GRE or MAT, BSN, minimum GPA of 3.0 in nursing and overall. Additional exam requirements/recommendations for international students: Required— TOEFL. *Application deadline:* For fall admission, 5/1 for domestic students. Applications are processed on a rolling basis. Application fee: $40. Electronic applications accepted. *Expenses:* Tuition, state resident: full-time $8112; part-time $338 per credit. Tuition, nonresident: full-time $20,256; part-time $844 per credit. Required fees: $119 per semester. One-time fee: $50. *Financial support:* In 2009–10, 18 students received support, including 2 research assistantships with tuition reimbursements available (averaging $10,000 per year); teaching assistantships, career-related internships or fieldwork, scholarships/grants, traineeships, and tuition waivers (partial) also available. Support available to part-time students. Financial award application deadline: 2/15; financial award applicants required to submit FAFSA. *Faculty research:* Health and culture, cardiovascular health, transition of military families, genetics, cultural diversity. Total annual research expenditures: $231,117. *Unit head:* Dr. Karen Karlowicz, Chair, 757-683-5262, Fax: 757-683-5253, E-mail: nursgpd@odu.edu. *Application contact:* Sue Parker, Coordinator, Graduate Student Services, 757-683-4298, Fax: 757-683-5253, E-mail: sparker@odu.edu.

Oregon Health & Science University, School of Nursing, Family Nurse Practitioner Program, Portland, OR 97239-3098. Offers MN, MS, Post Master's Certificate. Tuition and fees vary according to course level, course load, degree level, program and reciprocity agreements.

Otterbein University, Department of Nursing, Westerville, OH 43081. Offers adult nurse practitioner (MSN, Certificate); clinical nurse leader (MSN); family nurse practitioner (MSN, Certificate); nurse service administration (MSN). *Accreditation:* AACN; NLN. Part-time and evening/weekend programs available. Postbaccalaureate distance learning degree programs offered (minimal on-campus study). *Degree requirements:* For master's, comprehensive exam (for some programs), thesis (for some programs). *Entrance requirements:* For master's, 2 reference forms, resume; for Certificate, official transcripts, 2 reference forms, essay, resumé. Additional exam requirements/recommendations for international students: Required—TOEFL (minimum score 550 paper-based; 213 computer-based; 79 iBT). *Faculty research:* Patient education, women's health, trauma curriculum development, administration.

Pace University, Lienhard School of Nursing, New York, NY 10038. Offers family nurse practitioner (MS); nursing education (MA); nursing leadership (Advanced Certificate); nursing practice (DNP). *Accreditation:* AACN. Part-time and evening/weekend programs available. *Faculty:* 9 full-time (all women), 18 part-time/adjunct (14 women). *Students:* 41 full-time (37 women), 333 part-time (303 women); includes 140 minority (63 African Americans, 41 Asian Americans or Pacific Islanders, 36 Hispanic Americans), 12 international. Average age 36. 459 applicants, 66% accepted, 125 enrolled. In 2009, 79 master's, 3 other advanced degrees awarded. *Degree requirements:* For master's, thesis. *Entrance requirements:* For master's, GRE General Test or MAT, RN license, resume, personal statement, 2 letters of recommendation, official transcripts; for doctorate, RN license, resume, personal statement, 2 letters of recommendation, official transcripts, accredited master's degree in nursing, minimum GPA of 3.3, advanced experience, state certification; for Advanced Certificate, RN license, completion of 2nd degree in nursing. Additional exam requirements/recommendations for international students: Required—TOEFL. *Application deadline:* For fall admission, 7/31 priority date for domestic students, 4/30 priority date for international students; for spring admission, 10/14 for domestic students, 9/14 for international students. Applications are processed on a rolling basis. Application fee: $70. Electronic applications accepted. *Expenses:* Contact institution. *Financial support:* Research assistantships, career-related internships or fieldwork, Federal Work-Study, and tuition waivers (partial) available. Support available to part-time students. Financial award applicants required to submit FAFSA. *Unit head:* Dr. Harriet Feldman, Dean, 914-773-3341. *Application contact:* Joanna Broda, Director of Graduate Admissions, 914-422-4283, Fax: 914-422-4287, E-mail: gradwp@pace.edu.

Pacific Lutheran University, Division of Graduate Studies, School of Nursing, Program in Family Nurse Practitioner, Tacoma, WA 98447. Offers MSN. *Accreditation:* AACN. Part-time and evening/weekend programs available. *Degree requirements:* For master's, thesis or alternative. *Entrance requirements:* For master's, GRE General Test, minimum undergraduate GPA of 3.0. Additional exam requirements/recommendations for international students: Required—TOEFL (minimum score 550 paper-based; 213 computer-based). *Expenses:* Contact institution.

Prairie View A&M University, College of Nursing, Houston, TX 77030. Offers family nurse practitioner (MSN); nursing administration (MSN); nursing education (MSN). *Accreditation:* AACN; NLN. Part-time programs available. *Faculty:* 6 full-time (all women), 6 part-time/adjunct (all women). *Students:* 100 part-time (93 women); includes 82 minority (74 African Americans, 1 American Indian/Alaska Native, 4 Asian Americans or Pacific Islanders, 3 Hispanic Americans), 7 international. Average age 37. 37 applicants, 100% accepted, 32 enrolled. In 2009, 7 master's awarded. *Degree requirements:* For master's, comprehensive exam, thesis. *Entrance requirements:* For master's, MAT or GRE, BS in nursing; 2 years of experience as a registered nurse; 1 course each in statistics, basic health and assessment. *Application deadline:* For fall admission, 6/1 priority date for domestic students; for spring admission, 11/1 priority date for domestic students. Applications are processed on a rolling basis. Application fee: $50. *Expenses:* Tuition, state resident: full-time $2200. Tuition, nonresident: full-time $5600. Required fees: $1720. Tuition and fees vary according to course load. *Financial support:* In 2009–10, 17 students received support. Career-related internships or fieldwork, Federal Work-Study, institutionally sponsored loans, scholarships/grants, and traineeships available. Support available to part-time students. Financial award application deadline: 4/1; financial award applicants required to submit FAFSA. *Faculty research:* Software development and violence prevention, health promotion and disease prevention. Total annual research expenditures: $350,000. *Unit head:* Dr. Betty N. Adams, Dean, 713-797-7009, Fax: 713-797-7013, E-mail: bnadams@pvamu.edu. *Application contact:* Dr. Forest Smith, Director of Student Services and Admissions, 713-797-7031, Fax: 713-797-7012, E-mail: pcwillson@pvamu.edu.

Queen's University at Kingston, School of Graduate Studies and Research, Faculty of Health Sciences, School of Nursing, Kingston, ON K7L 3N6, Canada. Offers health and chronic illness (M Sc); nurse scientist (PhD); primary health care nurse practitioner (Certificate); women's and children's health (M Sc). *Degree requirements:* For master's, thesis. *Entrance requirements:* For master's, RN license. Additional exam requirements/recommendations for international students: Required—TOEFL. *Faculty research:* Women and children's health, health and chronic illness.

Quinnipiac University, School of Health Sciences, Nursing Program, Family Nurse Practitioner Track, Hamden, CT 06518-1940. Offers MSN, Post Master's Certificate. *Accreditation:* NLN. *Faculty:* 7 full-time (5 women), 8 part-time/adjunct (4 women). *Degree requirements:* For master's, thesis optional, clinical practicum. *Entrance requirements:* For master's, RN license, minimum GPA of 3.0. Additional exam requirements/recommendations for international students: Required—TOEFL (minimum score 575 paper-based; 233 computer-based; 90 iBT), IELTS (minimum score 6.5). *Application deadline:* For fall admission, 6/1 priority date for domestic students, 4/30 priority date for international students; for spring admission, 9/15 for international students. Applications are processed on a rolling basis. Electronic applications accepted. *Expenses:* Tuition: Full-time $16,030; part-time $770 per credit. Required fees: $630; $35 per credit. *Financial support:* Traineeships and unspecified assistantships available. Support available to part-time students. Financial award application deadline: 4/15. *Unit head:* Dr. Jeanne LeVasseur, Professor of Nursing, 203-582-3483, Fax: 203-582-3230, E-mail: jeanne.levasseur@quinnipiac.edu. *Application contact:* Kristin Parent, Assistant Director of Graduate Health Sciences Admissions, 800-462-1944, Fax: 203-582-3443, E-mail: kristin.parent@quinnipiac.edu.

Radford University, College of Graduate and Professional Studies, Waldron College of Health and Human Services, School of Nursing, Radford, VA 24142. Offers adult clinical nurse specialist (MSN); family nurse practitioner (MSN); gerontology clinical nurse specialist (MSN); nurse midwifery (MSN). *Accreditation:* AACN. Part-time programs available. *Faculty:* 15 full-time (14 women), 3 part-time/adjunct (2 women). *Students:* 15 full-time (all women), 17 part-time (all women); includes 1 minority (Asian American or Pacific Islander). Average age 35. 17 applicants, 76% accepted, 8 enrolled. In 2009, 11 master's awarded. *Degree requirements:* For master's, comprehensive exam, thesis optional. *Entrance requirements:* For master's, GRE, minimum GPA of 3.0; 3 letters of reference from professional contacts, letter of intent, resume. Additional exam requirements/recommendations for international students: Required—TOEFL (minimum score 550 paper-based; 213 computer-based; 79 iBT). *Application deadline:* For fall admission, 2/1 priority date for domestic students, 12/1 for international students. Applications are processed on a rolling basis. Application fee: $50. Electronic applications accepted. *Expenses:* Tuition, state resident: full-time $5086; part-time $211 per credit hour. Tuition, nonresident: full-time $12,608; part-time $525 per credit hour. Required fees: $2508; $105 per credit hour. *Financial support:* In 2009–10, 5 students received support, including 4 teaching assistantships with partial tuition reimbursements available (averaging $8,700 per year); career-related internships or fieldwork, Federal Work-Study, institutionally sponsored loans, scholarships/grants, and unspecified assistantships also available. Financial award application deadline: 3/1; financial award applicants required to submit FAFSA. *Unit head:* Dr. Kimberly F. Carter, Director, 540-831-7700, Fax: 540-831-7716, E-mail: kcarter@radford.edu. *Application contact:* Graduate Admissions, 540-831-5431, Fax: 540-831-6061, E-mail: gradcollege@radford.edu.

Regis College, School of Nursing and Health Professions, Weston, MA 02493. Offers health administration (MS); nurse educator (Certificate); nurse practitioner (Certificate); nursing (MS, DNP). *Accreditation:* NLN. Part-time and evening/weekend programs available. *Faculty:* 18 full-time (all women), 12 part-time/adjunct (all women). *Students:* 158 full-time (147 women), 324 part-time (299 women); includes 50 minority (29 African Americans, 1 American Indian/Alaska Native, 15 Asian Americans or Pacific Islanders, 5 Hispanic Americans). Average age 38. 320 applicants, 63% accepted, 155 enrolled. In 2009, 47 master's, 7 other advanced degrees awarded. *Degree requirements:* For master's, thesis. *Entrance requirements:* For master's, GRE General Test or MAT, minimum GPA of 3.0; for doctorate, MAT or GRE if GPA from master's lower than 3.5. Additional exam requirements/recommendations for international students: Required—TOEFL (minimum score 550 paper-based; 213 computer-based). *Application deadline:* Applications are processed on a rolling basis. Application fee: $50. Electronic applications accepted. *Expenses:* Tuition: Full-time $29,000; part-time $800 per credit. Tuition and fees vary according to course load, degree level and program. *Financial support:* In 2009–10, 28 students received support, including 13 research assistantships; Federal Work-Study, scholarships/grants, traineeships, and unspecified assistantships also available. Support available to part-time students. Financial award applicants required to submit FAFSA. *Faculty research:* Health policy, education, aging, job satisfaction, psychiatric nursing, critical thinking. *Unit head:* Dr. Antoinette Hays, Dean, 781-768-7091, Fax: 781-768-8339, E-mail: antoinette.hays@regiscollege.edu. *Application contact:* Christine Petherick, Administrative Coordinator, Graduate Admission, 866-438-7344, Fax: 781-768-7071, E-mail: christine.petherick@regiscollege.edu.

Regis University, Rueckert-Hartman School for Health Professions, Denver, CO 80221-1099. Offers clinical leadership for physician assistants (MS); family nurse practitioner (MSN); health informatics (Postbaccalaureate Certificate); health services administration (MS); healthcare education (Certificate); leadership in healthcare systems (MSN); neonatal nurse practitioner (MSN); nursing (MSN); pharmacy (Pharm D); physical therapy (DPT, TDPT). *Entrance requirements:* Additional exam requirements/recommendations for international students: Required—TOEFL (minimum score 550 paper-based; 213 computer-based; 82 iBT). Electronic applications accepted. *Expenses:* Contact institution. *Faculty research:* Normal and pathological balance and gait research, normal/pathological upper limb motor control/biomechanics, exercise energy/metabolism research, optical treatment protocols for therapeutic modalities.

Research College of Nursing, Nursing Program, Kansas City, MO 64132. Offers executive nurse practitioner (MSN); family nurse practitioner (MSN); nursing education (MSN). *Accreditation:* AACN. Part-time programs available. Postbaccalaureate distance learning degree programs offered (no on-campus study). *Degree requirements:* For master's, research project. *Entrance requirements:* For master's, minimum GPA of 3.0, interview, 3 letters of recommendation. Additional exam requirements/recommendations for international students: Required—TOEFL (minimum score 550 paper-based; 213 computer-based), TWE. *Expenses:* Tuition: Part-time $400 per credit hour. Required fees: $25 per credit hour. $50 per semester.

Rivier College, School of Graduate Studies, Division of Nursing, Nashua, NH 03060. Offers family nurse practitioner (MS); nursing education (MS). *Accreditation:* NLN. Part-time and evening/weekend programs available. *Faculty:* 4 full-time (3 women). *Students:* 4 full-time (3 women), 37 part-time (36 women); includes 4 minority (1 African American, 2 Asian Americans or Pacific Islanders, 1 Hispanic American). Average age 36. 29 applicants, 52% accepted, 4 enrolled. In 2009, 12 master's awarded. *Entrance requirements:* For master's, GRE, MAT. *Application deadline:* Applications are processed on a rolling basis. Application fee: $25. Electronic applications accepted. *Expenses:* Tuition: Part-time $447 per credit. *Financial support:* Available to part-time students. Application deadline: 2/1. *Unit head:* Dr. Paula Williams, Head, 603-897-8529. *Application contact:* Mathew Kittredge, Director of Graduate Admissions, 603-897-8129, Fax: 603-897-8810, E-mail: mkittredge@rivier.edu.

Rush University, College of Nursing, Department of Community Systems and Mental Health Nursing, Chicago, IL 60612-3832. Offers community and mental health nursing (DNP, PhD); family nurse practitioner (MSN, Post-Master's Certificate); psychiatric clinical specialist (MSN); psychiatric nurse practitioner—adult (MSN); psychiatric nurse practitioner—family (MSN); psychiatric-mental health clinical specialist (Post-Master's Certificate); psychiatric-mental health nurse practitioner (Post-Master's Certificate); public health nursing (MSN). *Accreditation:* AACN. Part-time programs available. Postbaccalaureate distance learning degree programs offered (minimal on-campus study). Terminal master's awarded for partial completion of doctoral program. *Degree requirements:* For master's, capstone project; for doctorate, thesis/dissertation, DNP leadership project. *Entrance requirements:* For master's, GRE General Test (waived if nursing GPA is above 3.0 or cumulative GPA is above 3.25), interview; for doctorate, GRE General Test, interview, course work in statistics (DN Sc). Electronic applications accepted. *Faculty research:* Immigrant mental health, de-escalation strategies, caregiver interventions, parent-teacher training, restraint use.

Rutgers, The State University of New Jersey, Newark, Graduate School, Program in Nursing, Newark, NJ 07102. Offers nursing (MS), including acute care of adults and aged, advanced practice in pediatric nursing, advanced practice with childbearing families, community health nursing, family nurse practitioner, primary care of adults and aged, psychiatric/mental health nursing. *Accreditation:* AACN. Part-time programs available. *Degree requirements:* For master's, comprehensive exam. *Entrance requirements:* For master's, GRE General Test, RN license, minimum B average, BS in nursing. Additional exam requirements/recommendations for international students: Required—TOEFL. Electronic applications accepted. *Faculty research:* HIV/AIDS, quality of life—MS and breast cancer, sleep patterns of cardiac patients.

Sacred Heart University, Graduate Programs, College of Education and Health Professions, Department of Nursing, Fairfield, CT 06825-1000. Offers clinical nurse leader (MSN); clinical practice in health care (DNP); family nurse practitioner (MSN); leadership in health care (DNP); nursing (DN Sc); patient care services administration (MSN). *Accreditation:* AACN. Part-time and evening/weekend programs available. Postbaccalaureate distance learning degree programs offered (minimal on-campus study). *Faculty:* 12 full-time (all women). *Students:* 7 full-time (6 women), 155 part-time (146 women); includes 27 minority (9 African Americans, 11 Asian Americans or Pacific Islanders, 7 Hispanic Americans), 1 international. Average age 39. 72 applicants, 93% accepted, 28 enrolled. In 2009, 13 master's awarded. *Entrance requirements:* For master's, BSN, minimum GPA of 3.0. Additional exam requirements/recommendations for international students: Required—TOEFL (minimum score 550 paper-based; 213 computer-based). *Application deadline:* Applications are processed on a rolling basis. Application fee: $50 ($100 for international students). Electronic applications accepted. *Expenses:* Contact institution. *Financial support:* Career-related internships or fieldwork, institutionally sponsored loans, and unspecified assistantships available. Support available to part-time students. Financial award applicants required to submit FAFSA. *Unit head:* Dr. Dori Sullivan, Chair, 203-371-7715. *Application contact:* Kathy Dilks, Assistant Dean of Graduate Admissions, Health Professions, 203-396-8259, Fax: 203-365-4732, E-mail: gradstudies@sacredheart.edu.

Sage Graduate School, Graduate School, School of Health Sciences, Department of Nursing, Program in Family Nurse Practitioner, Troy, NY 12180-4115. Offers MS, Post Master's Certificate. *Accreditation:* AACN. Part-time and evening/weekend programs available. *Faculty:* 5 full-time (all women), 8 part-time/adjunct (all women). *Students:* 7 full-time (6 women), 25 part-time (24 women); includes 3 minority (1 African American, 1 Asian American or Pacific Islander, 1 Hispanic American). Average age 37. 24 applicants, 79% accepted, 13 enrolled. In 2009, 10 master's awarded. *Degree requirements:* For master's, thesis or alternative. *Entrance requirements:* For master's, BS in nursing, minimum GPA of 2.75, resume, 2 letters of recommendation. Additional exam requirements/recommendations for international students: Required—TOEFL (minimum score 550 paper-based; 213 computer-based). *Application deadline:* Applications are processed on a rolling basis. Application fee: $40. *Expenses:* Tuition: Full-time $10,620; part-time $590 per credit hour. *Financial support:* Fellowships, research assistantships, teaching assistantships, Federal Work-Study, scholarships/grants, and unspecified assistantships available. Support available to part-time students. Financial award application deadline: 3/1; financial award applicants required to submit FAFSA. *Unit head:* Arlene Pericak, Director, 518-244-2012, E-mail: perica@sage.edu. *Application contact:* Wendy D. Diefendorf, Director of Graduate and Adult Admission, 518-244-2443, Fax: 518-244-6880, E-mail: diefew@sage.edu.

Saginaw Valley State University, Crystal M. Lange College of Nursing and Health Sciences, Program in Nurse Practitioner, University Center, MI 48710. Offers MSN. *Accreditation:* AACN. Part-time and evening/weekend programs available. *Students:* 8 full-time (7 women), 39 part-time (36 women); includes 2 minority (1 African American, 1 Asian American or Pacific Islander), 5 international. Average age 37. 24 applicants, 100% accepted, 21 enrolled. In 2009, 13 master's awarded. *Degree requirements:* For master's, thesis optional. *Entrance requirements:* For master's, GRE. Additional exam requirements/recommendations for international students: Required—TOEFL (minimum score 525 paper-based; 237 computer-based; 92 iBT). *Application deadline:* Applications are processed on a rolling basis. Application fee: $25. Electronic applications accepted. *Financial support:* Federal Work-Study and scholarships/grants available. Support available to part-time students. Financial award application deadline: 4/1; financial award applicants required to submit FAFSA. *Unit head:* Dr. Sally Decker, Professor of Nursing, 989-964-4098, E-mail: decker@svsu.edu. *Application contact:* Dr. Sally Decker, Professor of Nursing, 989-964-4098, E-mail: decker@svsu.edu.

St. John Fisher College, Wegmans School of Nursing, Advanced Practice Nursing Program, Rochester, NY 14618-3597. Offers advanced practice nursing (MS); clinical nurse specialist (Certificate); family nurse practitioner (Certificate); nurse educator (Certificate). *Accreditation:* AACN. Part-time and evening/weekend programs available. *Faculty:* 9 full-time (all women). *Students:* 5 full-time (4 women), 88 part-time (83 women); includes 7 minority (all African Americans), 1 international. Average age 38. 60 applicants, 87% accepted, 30 enrolled. In 2009, 9 master's awarded. *Degree requirements:* For master's, clinical practice, project; for Certificate, clinical practice. *Entrance requirements:* For master's, BSN; undergraduate course work in statistics, health assessment, and nursing research; current New York State RN License; 2 letters of recommendation; current resume. Additional exam requirements/recommendations for international students: Required—TOEFL (minimum score 575 paper-based; 233 computer-based; 80 iBT). *Application deadline:* Applications are processed on a rolling basis. Application fee: $30. Electronic applications accepted. *Expenses:* Tuition: Part-time $680 per credit hour. Required fees: $25 per semester. Tuition and fees vary according to degree level and program. *Financial support:* In 2009–10, 64 students received support. Federal Work-Study, scholarships/grants, and traineeships available. Financial award applicants required to submit FAFSA. *Faculty research:* Chronic illness, pediatric injury, women's health, public health policy, health care teams. *Unit head:* Dr. Cynthia McCloskey, Graduate Director, 585-385-8471, Fax: 585-385-8466, E-mail: cmccloskey@sjfc.edu. *Application contact:* Jose Perales, Director of Graduate Admissions, 585-385-8067, E-mail: jperales@sjfc.edu.

Saint Xavier University, Graduate Studies, School of Nursing, Chicago, IL 60655-3105. Offers adult health clinical nurse specialist (MS); family nurse practitioner (MS, PMC); leadership in community health nursing (MS); psychiatric-mental health clinical nurse specialist (MS); psychiatric-mental health clinical specialist (PMC); MBA/MS. *Accreditation:* AACN. Part-time and evening/weekend programs available. *Entrance requirements:* For master's, GRE General Test or MAT, minimum GPA of 3.0, RN license. *Expenses:* Tuition: Part-time $743 per credit hour. Required fees: $135 per semester.

Samford University, Ida V. Moffett School of Nursing, Birmingham, AL 35229. Offers advance practice (DNP); anesthesia (MSN); family nurse practitioner (MSN); nurse educator (MSN); nurse executive (DNP); nurse manager (MSN); MBA/MSN. *Accreditation:* AACN; AANA/CANAEP (one or more programs are accredited). Part-time programs available. Postbaccalaureate distance learning degree programs offered (minimal on-campus study). *Faculty:* 10 full-time (all women), 1 part-time/adjunct (0 women). *Students:* 149 full-time (102 women), 31 part-time (24 women); includes 21 minority (14 African Americans, 4 Asian Americans or Pacific Islanders, 3 Hispanic Americans), 1 international. Average age 31. 56 applicants, 98% accepted, 52 enrolled. In 2009, 58 master's awarded. *Degree requirements:* For master's and doctorate, capstone project with oral presentation. *Entrance requirements:* For master's, GRE General Test or MAT. Additional exam requirements/recommendations for international students: Required—TOEFL (minimum score 550 paper-based; 213 computer-based; 80 iBT). *Application deadline:* For fall admission, 7/1 priority date for domestic and international students; for spring admission, 11/1 priority date for domestic and international students. Applications are processed on a rolling basis. Application fee: $35. *Expenses:* Contact institution. *Financial support:* Institutionally sponsored loans, scholarships/grants, and traineeships available. Financial award application deadline: 3/1; financial award applicants required to submit FAFSA. *Faculty research:* Issues in rural health care, vulnerable populations, genetics and disabilities in pediatrics,

Family Nurse Practitioner Studies

Samford University (continued)

geriatrics, Parrish nursing research. *Unit head:* Dr. Nena F. Sanders, Dean, 205-726-2629, E-mail: nfsander@samford.edu. *Application contact:* Marian Carter, Director of Graduate Student Services, 205-726-2047, Fax: 205-726-4269, E-mail: mwcarter@samford.edu.

Samuel Merritt University, School of Nursing, Oakland, CA 94609-3108. Offers case management (MSN); family nurse practitioner (MSN, Certificate); nurse anesthetist (MSN, Certificate); nursing (MSN). *Accreditation:* AACN; AANA/CANAEP (one or more programs are accredited). Part-time and evening/weekend programs available. *Degree requirements:* For master's, thesis or alternative. *Entrance requirements:* For master's, minimum GPA of 2.5 in science, 3.0 overall; previous course work in statistics; current RN license. Additional exam requirements/recommendations for international students: Required—TOEFL. *Faculty research:* Gerontology, community health, maternal-child health, sexually transmitted diseases, substance abuse, oncology.

San Francisco State University, Division of Graduate Studies, College of Health and Human Services, School of Nursing, San Francisco, CA 94132-1722. Offers case management (MS), including long-term care, primary care/family nurse practitioner; nursing administration (MS); nursing education (MS). *Accreditation:* AACN. Part-time programs available.

Seattle Pacific University, MS in Nursing Program, Seattle, WA 98119-1997. Offers administration (MSN); adult/gerontology nurse practitioner (MSN); clinical nurse specialist (MSN); family nurse practitioner (MSN, Certificate); informatics (MSN); nurse educator (MSN). *Accreditation:* AACN. Part-time programs available. *Faculty:* 3 full-time (all women), 7 part-time/adjunct (6 women). *Students:* 9 full-time (8 women), 63 part-time (57 women); includes 9 minority (1 American Indian/Alaska Native, 7 Asian Americans or Pacific Islanders, 1 Hispanic American), 1 international. Average age 46. 60 applicants, 45% accepted, 27 enrolled. In 2009, 12 master's awarded. *Degree requirements:* For master's, thesis. *Application deadline:* For fall admission, 2/1 priority date for domestic students. Applications are processed on a rolling basis. Application fee: $50. Electronic applications accepted. *Expenses:* Contact institution. *Financial support:* In 2009–10, 41 students received support; fellowships, scholarships/grants available. Financial award applicants required to submit FAFSA. *Unit head:* Dr. Susan Casey, Director, 206-281-2769, Fax: 206-281-2767, E-mail: caseys@spu.edu. *Application contact:* The Grad Center, 206-281-2091.

Shenandoah University, School of Health Professions, Division of Nursing, Winchester, VA 22601-5195. Offers family nurse practitioner (Certificate); nurse-midwifery (Certificate); nurse-midwifery endorsement (Certificate); nursing (MSN, DNP); post-master's in nursing education (Certificate); psychiatric mental health nurse practitioner (Certificate). *Accreditation:* AACN; ACNM/DOA. Part-time programs available. *Faculty:* 11 full-time (all women), 4 part-time/adjunct (all women). *Students:* 21 full-time (20 women), 67 part-time (64 women); includes 11 minority (7 African Americans, 2 Asian Americans or Pacific Islanders, 2 Hispanic Americans). Average age 39. 71 applicants, 97% accepted, 53 enrolled. In 2009, 8 master's, 6 other advanced degrees awarded. *Degree requirements:* For master's, research project, clinical hours; for doctorate and Certificate, clinical hours. *Entrance requirements:* For master's, GRE General Test, previous course work in statistics, community nursing, and physical assessment; RN license; BSN; minimum undergraduate GPA of 3.0; appropriate clinical experience; curriculum vitae; 3 letters of recommendation; for Certificate, MSN, minimum GPA of 3.0, 3 letters of recommendation. Additional exam requirements/recommendations for international students: Required—TOEFL (minimum score 550 paper-based; 213 computer-based; 79 iBT), IELTS (minimum score 6.5). *Application deadline:* For fall admission, 6/15 priority date for domestic and international students. Applications are processed on a rolling basis. Application fee: $30. Electronic applications accepted. *Expenses:* Tuition: Full-time $11,925; part-time $695 per credit. Required fees: $400 per semester. *Financial support:* Application deadline: 3/15. *Unit head:* Dr. Kathryn Ganske, Director, 540-678-4381, Fax: 540-665-5519. *Application contact:* David Anthony, Dean of Admissions, 540-665-4581, Fax: 540-665-4627, E-mail: admit@su.edu.

Sonoma State University, School of Science and Technology, Family Nurse Practitioner Program, Rohnert Park, CA 94928. Offers MS. *Accreditation:* NLN. Part-time programs available. *Faculty:* 4 full-time (all women), 5 part-time/adjunct (all women). *Students:* 7 full-time (6 women), 101 part-time (88 women); includes 13 minority (1 African American, 8 Asian Americans or Pacific Islanders, 4 Hispanic Americans), 1 international. Average age 41. 88 applicants, 65% accepted, 28 enrolled. In 2009, 41 master's awarded. *Degree requirements:* For master's, comprehensive exam, thesis or alternative, oral exams. *Entrance requirements:* For master's, GRE General Test, BSN, minimum GPA of 3.0, course work in statistics, physical assessment, RN license. Additional exam requirements/recommendations for international students: Required—TOEFL (minimum score 500 paper-based; 173 computer-based). *Application deadline:* For fall admission, 11/30 for domestic students. Application fee: $55. *Expenses:* Tuition, nonresident: full-time $11,160. Required fees: $6226. Full-time tuition and fees vary according to course load. *Financial support:* Fellowships, traineeships available. Financial award applicants required to submit FAFSA. *Faculty research:* Neonatal ethics. *Unit head:* Dr. Elizabeth Close, Chair, 707-664-2465, E-mail: elizabeth.close@sonoma.edu. *Application contact:* Dr. Melissa Vandeveer, Director, 707-664-2276, E-mail: vandeveer@sonoma.edu.

Southern Adventist University, School of Nursing, Collegedale, TN 37315-0370. Offers acute care nurse practitioner (MSN); adult nurse practitioner (MSN); family nurse practitioner (MSN); nurse educator (MSN); MSN/MSBA. *Accreditation:* NLN. Part-time programs available. *Faculty:* 6 full-time (5 women). *Students:* 69 full-time (50 women), 28 part-time (25 women); includes 9 minority (6 African Americans, 1 American Indian/Alaska Native, 1 Asian American or Pacific Islander, 1 Hispanic American). Average age 35. 40 applicants, 95% accepted, 31 enrolled. In 2009, 21 master's awarded. *Degree requirements:* For master's, thesis or project. *Entrance requirements:* For master's, RN license. Additional exam requirements/recommendations for international students: Required—TOEFL (minimum score 600 paper-based; 250 computer-based). *Application deadline:* For fall admission, 7/1 for domestic and international students; for winter admission, 12/1 for domestic and international students. Applications are processed on a rolling basis. Application fee: $25. Electronic applications accepted. *Expenses:* Tuition: Full-time $13,149; part-time $487 per credit hour. *Financial support:* In 2009–10, 1 teaching assistantship with partial tuition reimbursement (averaging $5,000 per year) was awarded. *Faculty research:* Pain management, ethics, corporate wellness, caring spirituality, stress. *Unit head:* Dr. Barbara James, Dean, 423-236-2940, Fax: 423-236-1940, E-mail: bjames@southern.edu. *Application contact:* Diane Proffitt, Enrollment Counselor, 423-236-2941, Fax: 423-236-1940, E-mail: dproffitt@southern.edu.

Southern Illinois University Edwardsville, Graduate Studies and Research, School of Nursing, Program in Family Nurse Practitioner, Edwardsville, IL 62026-0001. Offers MS, Post-Master's Certificate. *Accreditation:* AACN. Part-time programs available. *Students:* 65 part-time (59 women); includes 2 minority (1 African American, 1 Hispanic American), 1 international. Average age 26. 65 applicants, 34% accepted. In 2009, 20 master's, 2 other advanced degrees awarded. *Degree requirements:* For master's, comprehensive exam. *Entrance requirements:* For master's, appropriate bachelor's degree, RN license. Additional exam requirements/recommendations for international students: Required—TOEFL (minimum score 550 paper-based; 213 computer-based; 79 iBT), IELTS (minimum score 6.5). *Application deadline:* For fall admission, 3/1 for domestic and international students. Application fee: $30. Electronic applications accepted. *Expenses:* Tuition, state resident: part-time $1252.50 per semester. Tuition, nonresident: part-time $3131.25 per semester. Required fees: $586.85 per semester. Tuition and fees vary according to course load. *Financial support:* Fellowships with full tuition reimbursements, research assistantships, teaching assistantships, career-related internships or fieldwork, Federal Work-Study, institutionally sponsored loans, scholarships/grants, traineeships, and unspecified assistantships available. Support available to part-time students. Financial award application deadline: 3/1; financial award applicants required to submit FAFSA. *Unit head:* Dr. Jacquelyn Clement, Director, 618-650-3923, E-mail: jclemen@siue.edu. *Application contact:* Dr. Jacquelyn Clement, Director, 618-650-3923, E-mail: jclemen@siue.edu.

Southern University and Agricultural and Mechanical College, School of Nursing, Baton Rouge, LA 70813. Offers educator/administrator (PhD); family health nursing (MSN); family nurse practitioner (Post Master's Certificate); geriatric nurse practitioner/gerontology (PhD). *Accreditation:* AACN. Part-time programs available. *Degree requirements:* For master's, comprehensive exam, thesis; for doctorate, comprehensive exam, thesis/dissertation. *Entrance requirements:* For master's, GRE General Test, BSN, minimum GPA of 2.7; for doctorate, GRE General Test; for Post Master's Certificate, MSN. Additional exam requirements/recommendations for international students: Required—TOEFL (minimum score 525 paper-based; 193 computer-based). *Faculty research:* Health promotions, vulnerable populations, (community-based) cardiovascular participating research, health disparities chronic diseases, care of the elderly.

Spalding University, Graduate Studies, College of Health and Natural Sciences, School of Nursing, Louisville, KY 40203-2188. Offers adult nurse practitioner (MSN); family nurse practitioner (MSN); leadership in nursing and healthcare (MSN); pediatric nurse practitioner (MSN). *Accreditation:* AACN. Part-time and evening/weekend programs available. *Faculty:* 6 full-time (all women), 7 part-time/adjunct (all women). *Students:* 41 full-time (38 women), 36 part-time (34 women); includes 12 minority (9 African Americans, 3 Hispanic Americans), 2 international. Average age 38. 27 applicants, 70% accepted, 18 enrolled. In 2009, 25 master's awarded. *Degree requirements:* For master's, comprehensive exam (for some programs), thesis. *Entrance requirements:* For master's, GRE General Test, BSN or bachelor's degree and RN licensure. Additional exam requirements/recommendations for international students: Required—TOEFL (minimum score 535 paper-based; 203 computer-based). *Application deadline:* Applications are processed on a rolling basis. Application fee: $30. *Expenses:* Tuition: Full-time $11,340; part-time $630 per credit hour. Tuition and fees vary according to program. *Financial support:* In 2009–10, 53 students received support, including 2 research assistantships with partial tuition reimbursements available (averaging $4,020 per year); career-related internships or fieldwork, scholarships/grants, and traineeships also available. Support available to part-time students. Financial award application deadline: 3/15; financial award applicants required to submit FAFSA. *Faculty research:* Nurse educational administration, gerontology, bioterrorism, healthcare ethics, leadership. *Unit head:* Dr. Carolyn Lewis, Interim Chair, 502-585-9911 Ext. 2331, E-mail: clewis@spalding.edu. *Application contact:* Dr. Carolyn Lewis, Interim Chair, 502-585-9911 Ext. 2331, E-mail: clewis@spalding.edu.

State University of New York Downstate Medical Center, College of Nursing, Graduate Program in Nursing, Nurse Practitioner Program, Brooklyn, NY 11203-2098. Offers MS, Post Master's Certificate. *Accreditation:* AACN. Part-time programs available. *Degree requirements:* For master's, thesis optional. *Entrance requirements:* For master's, GRE, BSN; minimum GPA of 3.0; previous undergraduate course work in statistics, health assessment, and nursing research; RN license; for Post Master's Certificate, BSN; minimum GPA of 3.0; RN license; previous undergraduate course work in statistics, health assessment, and nursing research. *Faculty research:* Women's health.

State University of New York Institute of Technology, School of Nursing and Health Systems, Program in Family Nurse Practitioner, Utica, NY 13504-3050. Offers MS, CAS. *Accreditation:* AACN. Part-time programs available. *Degree requirements:* For master's, thesis or project. *Entrance requirements:* For master's, GRE (if undergraduate GPA less than 3.3), minimum GPA of 3.0 in last 30 undergraduate hours, bachelor's degree in nursing, 1 year professional experience, RN license, interview, 2 letters of recommendation. Additional exam requirements/recommendations for international students: Required—TOEFL (minimum score 550 paper-based; 213 computer-based). *Faculty research:* Adult and family healthcare, critical thinking, epidemiology, refugee and women's health, child obesity.

State University of New York Upstate Medical University, College of Nursing, Syracuse, NY 13210-2334. Offers nurse practitioner (Post Master's Certificate); nursing (MS). *Accreditation:* AACN. Part-time programs available. Postbaccalaureate distance learning degree programs offered (no on-campus study). *Faculty:* 14 full-time (all women), 7 part-time/adjunct (6 women). *Students:* 61 full-time (50 women), 120 part-time (115 women); includes 17 minority (9 African Americans, 1 American Indian/Alaska Native, 4 Asian Americans or Pacific Islanders, 3 Hispanic Americans), 3 international. Average age 42. 108 applicants, 82% accepted, 73 enrolled. In 2009, 29 master's, 9 other advanced degrees awarded. *Degree requirements:* For master's, thesis or alternative. *Entrance requirements:* For master's, 3 years of work experience. *Application deadline:* For fall admission, 3/1 priority date for domestic and international students; for spring admission, 11/1 for domestic and international students. Applications are processed on a rolling basis. Application fee: $40. Electronic applications accepted. *Financial support:* In 2009–10, 134 students received support. Federal Work-Study, institutionally sponsored loans, scholarships/grants, and traineeships available. Support available to part-time students. Financial award application deadline: 3/1; financial award applicants required to submit FAFSA. *Unit head:* Dr. Elvira Szigeti, Dean, 315-464-4276, Fax: 315-464-5168. *Application contact:* Donna Vavonese, Associate Director of Admissions, 315-464-4570, Fax: 315-464-8867, E-mail: vavonesd@upstate.edu.

Stony Brook University, State University of New York, Stony Brook University Medical Center, Health Sciences Center, School of Nursing, Program in Family Nurse Practitioner, Stony Brook, NY 11794. Offers MS, Certificate. *Accreditation:* AACN. Postbaccalaureate distance learning degree programs offered. *Students:* 6 full-time (5 women), 94 part-time (88 women); includes 28 minority (14 African Americans, 8 Asian Americans or Pacific Islanders, 6 Hispanic Americans). In 2009, 21 master's, 3 other advanced degrees awarded. *Degree requirements:* For master's, thesis. *Entrance requirements:* For master's, BSN, minimum GPA of 3.0, course work in statistics. *Application deadline:* For fall admission, 1/15 for domestic students. Application fee: $60. *Expenses:* Tuition, state resident: full-time $8370; part-time $349 per credit. Tuition, nonresident: full-time $13,250; part-time $552 per credit. Required fees: $933. *Financial support:* Application deadline: 3/15. *Application contact:* Irene Stern, Information Contact, 631-444-3286, E-mail: irene.stern@stonybrook.edu.

Stony Brook University, State University of New York, Stony Brook University Medical Center, Health Sciences Center, School of Nursing, Program in Perinatal Women's Health Nursing, Stony Brook, NY 11794. Offers MS, Certificate. *Accreditation:* AACN. Postbaccalaureate distance learning degree programs offered. *Students:* 2 full-time (both women), 25 part-time (all women); includes 6 minority (4 African Americans, 2 Hispanic Americans). In 2009, 2 master's awarded. *Degree requirements:* For master's, thesis. *Entrance requirements:* For master's, BSN, minimum GPA of 3.0, course work in statistics. *Application deadline:* For fall admission, 1/15 for domestic students. Application fee: $60. *Expenses:* Tuition, state resident: full-time $8370; part-time $349 per credit. Tuition, nonresident: full-time $13,250; part-time $552 per credit. Required fees: $933. *Financial support:* Application deadline: 3/15. *Unit head:* Prof. Arleen Steckel, Chair, 631-444-3298, Fax: 631-444-3136. *Application contact:* Dr. Kent Marks, Assistant Dean, Admissions and Records, 631-632-4723, Fax: 631-632-7243, E-mail: kmarks@notes.cc.sunysb.edu.

Tennessee State University, The School of Graduate Studies and Research, School of Nursing, Nashville, TN 37209-1561. Offers family nurse practitioner (MSN); holistic nursing (MSN); nursing administration (MSN); nursing education (MSN); nursing informatics (MSN). *Accreditation:* NLN. *Entrance requirements:* For master's, GRE General Test or MAT, BSN, current RN license, minimum GPA of 3.0.

Tennessee Technological University, School of Nursing, Cookeville, TN 38505. Offers family nurse practitioner (MSN); informatics (MSN); nursing administration (MSN); nursing education (MSN). *Students:* 11 full-time (10 women), 30 part-time (27 women); includes 2 minority (1 African American, 1 Hispanic American). 40 applicants, 35% accepted, 10 enrolled. In 2009, 14 master's awarded. *Degree requirements:* For master's, comprehensive exam, thesis or alternative. *Entrance requirements:* Additional exam requirements/recommendations for international students: Required—TOEFL (minimum score 550 paper-based; 79 iBT), IELTS (minimum score 5.5). *Application deadline:* For fall admission, 8/1 for domestic students, 5/1 for international students; for spring admission, 12/1 for domestic students, 10/1 for international students. Application fee: $25 ($30 for international students). Electronic applica-

tions accepted. *Expenses:* Tuition, state resident: full-time $7034; part-time $368 per credit hour. *Financial support:* Application deadline: 4/1. *Unit head:* Dr. Sheila Green, Interim Dean, 931-372-3203, Fax: 931-372-6244, E-mail: sgreen@tntech.edu. *Application contact:* Shelia K. Kendrick, Coordinator of Graduate Studies, 931-372-3808, Fax: 931-372-3497, E-mail: skendrick@tntech.edu.

Texas A&M University–Corpus Christi, Graduate Studies and Research, College of Nursing and Health Sciences, Corpus Christi, TX 78412-5503. Offers clinical nurse specialist (MSN); family nurse practitioner (MSN); health care administration (MSN); leadership in nursing systems (MSN). *Accreditation:* AACN. Part-time and evening/weekend programs available. *Degree requirements:* For master's, comprehensive exam, thesis (for some programs). *Entrance requirements:* For master's, GRE General Test. Additional exam requirements/recommendations for international students: Required—TOEFL. Electronic applications accepted.

Texas Tech University Health Sciences Center, School of Nursing, Lubbock, TX 79430. Offers acute care nurse practitioner (MSN, Certificate); administration (MSN); advanced practice (DNP); education (MSN); executive leadership (DNP); family nurse practitioner (MSN, Certificate); geriatric nurse practitioner (MSN, Certificate); pediatric nurse practitioner (MSN, Certificate). *Accreditation:* AACN. Part-time programs available. Postbaccalaureate distance learning degree programs offered (minimal on-campus study). *Degree requirements:* For master's, thesis optional. *Entrance requirements:* For master's, minimum GPA of 3.0, 3 letters of reference, BSN, RN license; for Certificate, minimum GPA of 3.0, 3 letters of reference, RN license. Additional exam requirements/recommendations for international students: Required—TOEFL (minimum score 550 paper-based; 213 computer-based). *Faculty research:* Diabetes/obesity, nurse competency, disease management, intervention and measurements, health disparities.

Texas Woman's University, Graduate School, College of Nursing, Denton, TX 76201. Offers acute care nurse practitioner (MS); adult health clinical nurse specialist (MS); adult health nurse practitioner (MS); child health clinical nurse specialist (MS); clinical nurse leader (MS); community health (MS); family nurse practitioner (MS); health systems management (MS); nursing education (MS); nursing practice (DNP); nursing science (PhD); pediatric nurse practitioner (MS); women's health clinical nurse specialist (MS); women's health nurse practitioner (MS). *Accreditation:* AACN. Part-time programs available. Postbaccalaureate distance learning degree programs offered. *Faculty:* 85 full-time (80 women), 6 part-time/adjunct (all women). *Students:* 81 full-time (76 women), 602 part-time (571 women); includes 293 minority (154 African Americans, 3 American Indian/Alaska Native, 90 Asian Americans or Pacific Islanders, 46 Hispanic Americans), 19 international. Average age 39. 259 applicants, 81% accepted, 166 enrolled. In 2009, 100 master's, 22 doctorates awarded. *Degree requirements:* For master's, thesis or alternative; for doctorate, comprehensive exam, thesis/dissertation. *Entrance requirements:* For master's, GRE or MAT, minimum GPA of 3.0, RN license, BS in nursing, basic statistics course; for doctorate, GRE (Verbal 460, Quantitative 500) or MAT (50), MS in nursing, minimum GPA of 3.5, RN license, coursework in statistics, 2 letters of reference, curriculum vitae, nursing-theory course, graduate research course, letter stating professional and research goals. Additional exam requirements/recommendations for international students: Required—TOEFL (minimum score 550 paper-based; 213 computer-based; 79 iBT). *Application deadline:* For fall admission, 5/1 priority date for domestic students, 3/1 for international students; for spring admission, 9/15 priority date for domestic students, 7/1 for international students. Applications are processed on a rolling basis. Application fee: $50. Electronic applications accepted. *Expenses:* Tuition, state resident: full-time $3564; part-time $198 per credit hour. Tuition, nonresident: full-time $8550; part-time $475 per credit hour. Required fees: $69.26 per credit hour. Tuition and fees vary according to course load. *Financial support:* In 2009–10, 99 students received support, including 16 fellowships (averaging $17,325 per year), 5 research assistantships (averaging $11,484 per year), 5 teaching assistantships (averaging $11,484 per year); career-related internships or fieldwork, Federal Work-Study, institutionally sponsored loans, scholarships/grants, traineeships, health care benefits, and unspecified assistantships also available. Support available to part-time students. Financial award application deadline: 3/1; financial award applicants required to submit FAFSA. *Faculty research:* Evaluation of pre-natal care, screening for intimate partner violence, stressors and nursing success, breast surgery, breast feeding, adolescent needs during childbirth. *Unit head:* Dr. Patricia Holden-Huchton, Interim Dean, 940-898-2401, Fax: 940-898-2437, E-mail: pholdenhuchton@twu.edu. *Application contact:* Samuel Wheeler, Assistant Director of Admissions, 940-898-3188, Fax: 940-898-3081, E-mail: wheelersr@twu.edu.

Troy University, Graduate School, College of Health and Human Services, Program in Nursing, Troy, AL 36082. Offers adult health (MSN); clinical nurse specialist adult health (DNP); clinical nurse specialist nurse practitioner (DNP); family nurse practitioner (MSN); informatics specialist (MSN); maternal infant (MSN). *Accreditation:* NLN. Part-time and evening/weekend programs available. *Students:* 28 full-time (all women), 102 part-time (93 women); includes 49 minority (48 African Americans, 1 American Indian/Alaska Native). Average age 37. 76 applicants, 86% accepted. In 2009, 25 master's awarded. *Degree requirements:* For master's, comprehensive exam, thesis optional. *Entrance requirements:* For master's, MAT (minimum score 396) or GRE (minimum score 850), minimum GPA of 2.5, BSN. Additional exam requirements/recommendations for international students: Required—TOEFL (minimum score 523 paper-based; 193 computer-based; 70 iBT), IELTS (minimum score 6), TOEFL or IELTS or ACT Compass ESL (minimum score 270 on Listening, Reading, and Grammar with no individual score below 85 and minimum score of 8 out of 12 on writing test). *Application deadline:* Applications are processed on a rolling basis. Application fee: $50. Electronic applications accepted. *Financial support:* Available to part-time students. Applicants required to submit FAFSA. *Application contact:* Brenda K. Campbell, Director of Graduate Admissions, 334-670-3178, Fax: 334-670-3733, E-mail: bcamp@troy.edu.

Uniformed Services University of the Health Sciences, Graduate School of Nursing, Bethesda, MD 20814-4799. Offers family nurse practitioner (MSN); nurse anesthesia (MSN); perioperative clinical nurse specialty (MSN); psychiatric mental health nurse practitioner (MSN). Available to military officers only. *Accreditation:* AACN; NLN. Postbaccalaureate distance learning degree programs offered (no on-campus study). *Faculty:* 27 full-time (18 women), 2 part-time/adjunct (both women). *Students:* 75 full-time (32 women), 3 part-time (all women); includes 20 minority (8 African Americans, 5 Asian Americans or Pacific Islanders, 7 Hispanic Americans). Average age 36. 108 applicants, 72% accepted, 78 enrolled. In 2009, 54 master's awarded. *Degree requirements:* For master's, thesis or alternative. *Entrance requirements:* For master's, GRE, BSN, clinical experience, minimum GPA of 3.0, previous course work in science. *Application deadline:* For fall admission, 7/1 for domestic students; for winter admission, 2/15 for domestic students. Application fee: $0. Electronic applications accepted. *Faculty research:* Prenatal care, military health care, military readiness, distance learning. *Unit head:* Col. Bruce A. Schoneboom, Associate Dean for Academic Affairs, 301-295-1180, Fax: 301-295-1707, E-mail: bschoneboom@usuhs.mil. *Application contact:* Terry Lynn Malavakis, Recording Secretary for Admissions Committee, 301-295-1055, Fax: 301-295-1707, E-mail: tmalavakis@usuhs.mil.

Union University, School of Nursing, Jackson, TN 38305-3697. Offers executive leadership (DNP); nurse anesthesia (DNP); nurse anesthetist (PMC); nurse practitioner (DNP); nursing education (MSN, PMC). *Accreditation:* AACN; AANA/CANAEP. *Degree requirements:* For master's, thesis or alternative. *Entrance requirements:* For master's, GRE, 3 letters of reference, bachelor's degree in nursing, minimum GPA of 3.0. Additional exam requirements/recommendations for international students: Required—TOEFL (minimum score 560 paper-based; 220 computer-based). Electronic applications accepted. *Faculty research:* Children's health, occupational rehabilitation, informatics, health promotion.

Universidad del Turabo, Graduate Programs, School of Health Sciences, Programs in Nursing, Program in Family Nurse Practitioner, Gurabo, PR 00778-3030. Offers MSN. *Students:* 8 full-time (4 women), 2 part-time (0 women); includes 9 Hispanic Americans. Average age 37. 12 applicants, 75% accepted, 6 enrolled. In 2009, 2 master's awarded. *Unit head:* Dr. Maria Rosa, Dean, 787-743-7979. *Application contact:* Virginia Gonzalez, Admissions Officer, 787-746-3009.

The University of Alabama in Huntsville, School of Graduate Studies, College of Nursing, Huntsville, AL 35899. Offers family nurse practitioner (Certificate); nursing (MSN, DNP), including acute care nurse practitioner (MSN), adult clinical nursing specialist (MSN), clinical nurse leader (MSN), family nurse practitioner (MSN), leadership in health care systems (MSN); nursing education (Certificate). *Accreditation:* AACN. Part-time and evening/weekend programs available. Postbaccalaureate distance learning degree programs offered (minimal on-campus study). *Faculty:* 13 full-time (11 women), 3 part-time/adjunct (2 women). *Students:* 45 full-time (43 women), 121 part-time (111 women); includes 25 minority (17 African Americans, 5 American Indian/Alaska Native, 3 Asian Americans or Pacific Islanders), 3 international. Average age 39. 151 applicants, 68% accepted, 74 enrolled. In 2009, 52 master's, 5 other advanced degrees awarded. *Degree requirements:* For master's, comprehensive exam, thesis or alternative, oral and written exams; for doctorate, comprehensive exam, thesis/dissertation or alternative, oral and written exams. *Entrance requirements:* For master's, MAT or GRE, Alabama RN license, BSN, minimum GPA of 3.0; for doctorate, master's degree in nursing in an advanced practice area; for Certificate, MAT or GRE, minimum GPA of 3.0. Additional exam requirements/recommendations for international students: Required—TOEFL (minimum score 500 paper-based; 173 computer-based; 62 iBT). *Application deadline:* For fall admission, 7/15 for domestic students, 4/1 for international students; for spring admission, 11/30 for domestic students, 9/1 for international students. Applications are processed on a rolling basis. Application fee: $40 ($50 for international students). Electronic applications accepted. *Expenses:* Tuition, state resident: part-time $355.75 per credit hour. Tuition, nonresident: part-time $847.10 per credit hour. Required fees: $210.80 per semester. Tuition and fees vary according to course load and program. *Financial support:* In 2009–10, 11 students received support, including 11 teaching assistantships with full and partial tuition reimbursements available (averaging $9,996 per year); career-related internships or fieldwork, Federal Work-Study, institutionally sponsored loans, scholarships/grants, traineeships, health care benefits, and unspecified assistantships also available. Support available to part-time students. Financial award application deadline: 4/1; financial award applicants required to submit FAFSA. *Faculty research:* Home health care, gerontology, pediatric nursing, family nurse practitioner, adult acute care administration. *Unit head:* Dr. Fay Raines, Dean, 256-824-6345, Fax: 256-824-6026, E-mail: rainesc@uah.edu. *Application contact:* Charles Davis, Associate Director of Nursing Student Affairs Graduate Programs, 256-824-6669, Fax: 256-824-6026, E-mail: charles.davis@uah.edu.

University of Alaska Anchorage, College of Health and Social Welfare, School of Nursing, Anchorage, AK 99508. Offers family nurse practitioner (Certificate); nursing (MS); nursing education (Certificate); psychiatric nurse practitioner (Certificate). *Accreditation:* NLN. Part-time and evening/weekend programs available. *Degree requirements:* For master's, comprehensive exam, individual project. *Entrance requirements:* For master's, GRE or MAT, BS in nursing, interview, minimum GPA of 3.0, RN license, 1 year of part-time or 6 months of full-time clinical experience. Additional exam requirements/recommendations for international students: Required—TOEFL (minimum score 550 paper-based; 213 computer-based).

The University of Arizona, College of Nursing, Tucson, AZ 85721. Offers health care informatics (Certificate); nurse practitioner (MS, Certificate); nursing (DNP, PhD); rural health (Certificate). *Accreditation:* AACN. Part-time programs available. Postbaccalaureate distance learning degree programs offered (minimal on-campus study). *Faculty:* 19. *Students:* 63 full-time (58 women), 81 part-time (71 women); includes 3 minority (all Hispanic Americans), 9 international. Average age 41. In 2009, 25 master's, 19 doctorates awarded. Terminal master's awarded for partial completion of doctoral program. *Degree requirements:* For master's, thesis optional; for doctorate, comprehensive exam, thesis/dissertation. *Entrance requirements:* For master's, BSN, eligibility for RN license; for doctorate, BSN; for Certificate, GRE General Test, Arizona RN license, BSN, minimum GPA of 3.0. Additional exam requirements/recommendations for international students: Required—TOEFL (minimum score 550 paper-based; 213 computer-based; 79 iBT). *Application deadline:* For fall admission, 1/15 for domestic and international students. Applications are processed on a rolling basis. Application fee: $75. Electronic applications accepted. *Expenses:* Contact institution. *Financial support:* In 2009–10, 6 research assistantships with full tuition reimbursements (averaging $15,552 per year) were awarded; teaching assistantships, career-related internships or fieldwork, institutionally sponsored loans, scholarships/grants, traineeships, health care benefits, tuition waivers (full), and unspecified assistantships also available. Financial award application deadline: 6/1. *Faculty research:* Vulnerable populations, injury mechanisms and biobehavioral responses, health care systems, informatics, rural health. Total annual research expenditures: $4.9 million. *Unit head:* Dr. Carolyn Murdaugh, Associate Dean, 520-626-7124, Fax: 520-626-6424, E-mail: cmurdaugh@nursing.arizona.edu. *Application contact:* Sally J. Reel, Assistant Dean, Student Affairs, 520-626-6767, Fax: 520-626-6424, E-mail: sreel@nursing.arizona.edu.

University of Central Arkansas, Graduate School, College of Health and Behavioral Sciences, Department of Nursing, Conway, AR 72035-0001. Offers clinical nurse specialist (MSN); nurse practitioner (MSN). *Accreditation:* AACN. *Faculty:* 7 full-time (all women). *Students:* 12 full-time (11 women), 134 part-time (128 women); includes 14 minority (9 African Americans, 4 American Indian/Alaska Native, 1 Asian American or Pacific Islander), 1 international. Average age 34. 40 applicants, 93% accepted, 32 enrolled. In 2009, 19 master's awarded. *Degree requirements:* For master's, comprehensive exam, thesis optional, clinicals. *Entrance requirements:* For master's, GRE General Test, minimum GPA of 2.7. Additional exam requirements/recommendations for international students: Required—TOEFL (minimum score 550 paper-based; 213 computer-based). *Application deadline:* For fall admission, 3/1 priority date for domestic students; for spring admission, 10/1 for domestic students. Applications are processed on a rolling basis. Application fee: $25 ($50 for international students). *Expenses:* Contact institution. *Financial support:* Federal Work-Study, traineeships, and unspecified assistantships available. Financial award application deadline: 2/15; financial award applicants required to submit FAFSA. Total annual research expenditures: $216,643. *Unit head:* Dr. Barbara Williams, Chairperson, 501-450-3119, Fax: 501-450-5503, E-mail: barbaraw@uca.edu. *Application contact:* Patti Hornor, Administrative Assistant, 501-450-5063, Fax: 501-450-5678, E-mail: pattih@uca.edu.

University of Central Florida, College of Nursing, Orlando, FL 32816. Offers adult nurse practitioner (MSN, Post-Master's Certificate); clinical nurse leader (MSN, Post-Master's Certificate); clinical nurse specialist (MSN, Post-Master's Certificate); family nurse practitioner (MSN, Post-Master's Certificate); leadership and management (MSN); nurse educator (MSN); nursing (PhD); nursing education (Post-Master's Certificate); nursing practice (DNP); pediatric nurse practitioner (MSN, Post-Master's Certificate). *Accreditation:* AACN. Part-time and evening/weekend programs available. *Faculty:* 38 full-time (34 women), 49 part-time/adjunct (47 women). *Students:* 98 full-time (93 women), 371 part-time (350 women); includes 132 minority (63 African Americans, 2 American Indian/Alaska Native, 29 Asian Americans or Pacific Islanders, 38 Hispanic Americans), 9 international. Average age 39. 363 applicants, 49% accepted, 139 enrolled. In 2009, 72 master's, 3 doctorates, 8 other advanced degrees awarded. *Degree requirements:* For master's, thesis or alternative. *Entrance requirements:* For master's, GRE General Test, minimum GPA of 3.0 in last 60 hours. Additional exam requirements/recommendations for international students: Required—TOEFL. *Application deadline:* For fall admission, 2/15 for domestic students; for spring admission, 9/15 for domestic students. Application fee: $30. Electronic applications accepted. *Expenses:* Tuition, state resident: part-time $306.31 per credit hour. Tuition, nonresident: part-time $1099.01 per credit hour. Part-time tuition and fees vary according to degree level and program. *Financial support:* In 2009–10, 30 students received support, including 30 fellowships with partial tuition reimbursements available (averaging $3,200 per year), 1 teaching assistantship with partial tuition reimbursement available (averaging $13,440 per year); research assistantships with partial tuition reimbursements available, career-related internships or fieldwork, Federal Work-Study, institutionally sponsored loans, traineeships, and unspecified assistantships also available. Financial award application deadline: 3/1; financial award applicants required to submit FAFSA. *Unit head:* Dr. Jean D. Leuner, Dean, 407-823-5496, Fax: 407-823-5675, E-mail: jleuner@mail.ucf.edu. *Application contact:* Dr. Jean D. Leuner, Dean, 407-823-5496, Fax: 407-823-5675, E-mail: jleuner@mail.ucf.edu.

Family Nurse Practitioner Studies

University of Colorado at Colorado Springs, Graduate School, Beth-El College of Nursing and Health Sciences, Colorado Springs, CO 80933-7150. Offers adult health nurse practitioner and clinical specialist (MSN); family practitioner (MSN), including community clinical specialist, forensic clinical specialist, holistic clinical specialist; neonatal nurse practitioner and clinical specialist (MSN); nursing administration (MSN); nursing practice (DNP); women nurse practitioner (MSN). *Accreditation:* AACN. Part-time programs available. Postbaccalaureate distance learning degree programs offered (minimal on-campus study). *Faculty:* 26 full-time (21 women), 3 part-time/adjunct (all women). *Students:* 132 full-time (112 women), 81 part-time (71 women); includes 35 minority (6 African Americans, 2 American Indian/Alaska Native, 6 Asian Americans or Pacific Islanders, 21 Hispanic Americans), 3 international. Average age 36. 245 applicants, 47% accepted, 58 enrolled. In 2009, 33 master's awarded. *Degree requirements:* For master's, comprehensive exam, thesis optional; for doctorate, capstone project. *Entrance requirements:* For master's, GRE General Test or MAT, BSN, minimum GPA of 3.0, unrestricted RN license; for doctorate, interview; active RN license; MA; minimum GPA of 3.3; National Certification as NP or CNS; portfolio. Additional exam requirements/recommendations for international students: Required—TOEFL. *Application deadline:* For fall admission, 6/1 priority date for domestic students; for spring admission, 11/15 for domestic students. Application fee: $60 ($75 for international students). Electronic applications accepted. *Expenses:* Contact institution. *Financial support:* Fellowships, career-related internships or fieldwork, Federal Work-Study, and scholarships/grants available. Support available to part-time students. Financial award application deadline: 3/1; financial award applicants required to submit FAFSA. *Faculty research:* Women's health, uncertainty, empowerment, family experience in chronic illness. Total annual research expenditures: $703,545. *Unit head:* Dr. Nancy Smith, Dean, 719-255-4411, Fax: 719-255-4416, E-mail: nsmith2@uccs.edu. *Application contact:* Jackie Crouch, Graduate Recruitment Coordinator, 719-255-4493, Fax: 719-255-4416, E-mail: jcrouch@uccs.edu.

University of Delaware, College of Health Sciences, School of Nursing, Newark, DE 19716. Offers adult nurse practitioner (MSN, PMC); cardiopulmonary clinical nurse specialist (MSN, PMC); cardiopulmonary clinical nurse specialist/adult nurse practitioner (MSN, PMC); family nurse practitioner (MSN, PMC); gerontology clinical nurse specialist (MSN, PMC); gerontology clinical nurse specialist geriatric nurse practitioner (PMC); gerontology clinical nurse specialist/geriatric nurse practitioner (MSN); health services administration (MSN, PMC); nursing of children clinical nurse specialist (MSN, PMC); nursing of children clinical nurse specialist/pediatric nurse practitioner (MSN, PMC); oncology/immune deficiency clinical nurse specialist (MSN, PMC); oncology/immune deficiency clinical nurse specialist/adult nurse practitioner (MSN, PMC); perinatal/women's health clinical nurse specialist (MSN, PMC); perinatal/women's health clinical nurse specialist/women's health nurse practitioner (MSN, PMC); psychiatric nursing clinical nurse specialist (MSN, PMC). *Accreditation:* AACN; NLN (one or more programs are accredited). Part-time and evening/weekend programs available. Postbaccalaureate distance learning degree programs offered (minimal on-campus study). *Degree requirements:* For master's, thesis optional. *Entrance requirements:* For master's, BSN, interview, RN license. Electronic applications accepted. *Faculty research:* Marriage and chronic illness, health promotion, congestive heart failure patient outcomes, school nursing, diabetes in children, culture, health disparities, cardiovascular, prison nursing, oncology, public policy, child obesity, smoking and teen pregnancy, blood pressure measurements, men's health.

University of Detroit Mercy, College of Health Professions, Program in Family Nurse Practitioner, Detroit, MI 48221. Offers MSN, Certificate. *Accreditation:* AACN.

University of Hawaii at Manoa, Graduate Division, School of Nursing and Dental Hygiene, Honolulu, HI 96822. Offers clinical nurse specialist (MS), including adult health, community mental health; nurse practitioner (MS), including adult health, community mental health, family nurse practitioner; nursing (PhD, Graduate Certificate); nursing administration (MS). *Accreditation:* AACN; NLN (one or more programs are accredited). Part-time programs available. Postbaccalaureate distance learning degree programs offered (minimal on-campus study). *Faculty:* 20 full-time (18 women), 16 part-time/adjunct (15 women). *Students:* 81 full-time (69 women), 135 part-time (121 women); includes 115 minority (4 African Americans, 2 American Indian/Alaska Native, 105 Asian Americans or Pacific Islanders, 4 Hispanic Americans), 2 international. Average age 38. 189 applicants, 52% accepted, 79 enrolled. In 2009, 25 master's, 4 doctorates awarded. *Degree requirements:* For master's, thesis optional; for doctorate, comprehensive exam, thesis/dissertation. *Entrance requirements:* For master's, Hawaii RN license. Additional exam requirements/recommendations for international students: Required—TOEFL (minimum score 580 paper-based; 237 computer-based; 92 iBT), IELTS (minimum score 5). *Application deadline:* For fall admission, 2/1 for domestic and international students. Application fee: $60. *Expenses:* Contact institution. *Financial support:* In 2009–10, 6 students received support, including 28 fellowships (averaging $960 per year), 7 research assistantships (averaging $18,080 per year). Total annual research expenditures: $1.8 million. *Unit head:* Mary Boland, Dean, 808-956-8522, Fax: 808-956-3257, E-mail: mgboland@hawaii.edu. *Application contact:* Kristine Qureshi, Graduate Chair, 808-956-8744, Fax: 808-956-3257, E-mail: kqureshi@hawaii.edu.

University of Illinois at Chicago, Graduate College, College of Nursing, Program in Nursing, Chicago, IL 60607-7128. Offers acute care clinical nurse specialist (MS); acute care nurse practitioner (MS); administrative studies in nursing (MS); adult nurse practitioner (MS); adult/geriatric nurse practitioner (MS); advanced community health nurse specialist (MS); family nurse practitioner (MS); geriatric clinical nurse specialist (MS); geriatric nurse practitioner (MS); mental health clinical nurse specialist (MS); mental health nurse practitioner (MS); nurse midwifery (MS); occupational health/advanced community health nurse specialist (MS); occupational health/family nurse practitioner (MS); pediatric clinical nurse specialist (MS); pediatric nurse practitioner (MS); perinatal clinical nurse specialist (MS); school/advanced community health nurse specialist (MS); school/family nurse practitioner (MS); women's health nurse practitioner (MS). *Accreditation:* AACN. Part-time programs available. *Degree requirements:* For master's, thesis or alternative. *Entrance requirements:* For master's, GRE General Test, minimum GPA of 2.75. Additional exam requirements/recommendations for international students: Required—TOEFL. Electronic applications accepted.

The University of Kansas, University of Kansas Medical Center, School of Nursing, Kansas City, KS 66160. Offers clinical research management (PMC); family nurse practitioner (PMC); health care informatics (PMC); health professions educator (PMC); nurse midwife (PMC); nursing (MS, DNP, PhD); organizational leadership (PMC); psychiatric/mental health nurse practitioner (PMC); public health nursing (PMC). *Accreditation:* AACN; ACNM/DOA. Part-time programs available. Postbaccalaureate distance learning degree programs offered (minimal on-campus study). *Faculty:* 65. *Students:* 59 full-time (56 women), 309 part-time (285 women); includes 37 minority (17 African Americans, 4 American Indian/Alaska Native, 7 Asian Americans or Pacific Islanders, 9 Hispanic Americans), 10 international. Average age 38. 138 applicants, 59% accepted, 82 enrolled. In 2009, 78 master's, 3 doctorates awarded. Terminal master's awarded for partial completion of doctoral program. *Degree requirements:* For master's, thesis optional, general oral exam; for doctorate, one foreign language, thesis/dissertation, comprehensive oral and written exam. *Entrance requirements:* For master's, bachelor's degree in nursing, minimum GPA of 3.0, RN license, 1 year of clinical experience; for doctorate, GRE General Test, master's degree in nursing, minimum GPA of 3.5. Additional exam requirements/recommendations for international students: Required—TOEFL. *Application deadline:* For fall admission, 4/1 for domestic students; for spring admission, 9/1 for domestic students. Application fee: $60. Electronic applications accepted. *Expenses:* Tuition, state resident: full-time $6492; part-time $270.50 per credit hour. Tuition, nonresident: full-time $15,510; part-time $646.25 per credit hour. Required fees: $847; $70.56 per credit hour. Tuition and fees vary according to course load and program. *Financial support:* In 2009–10, 93 students received support, including 7 research assistantships (averaging $24,000 per year), 23 teaching assistantships with full and partial tuition reimbursements available (averaging $24,000 per year); traineeships also available. Financial award application deadline: 2/14; financial award applicants required to submit FAFSA. *Faculty research:* Breastfeeding practices of teen mothers, national database of nursing quality indicators, caregiving of families of patients using technology in the home, self care talk intervention partnership between caregivers of stroke survivors and nurses, smoking cessation. Total annual research expenditures: $5 million. *Unit head:* Dr. Karen L. Miller, Dean, 913-588-1601, Fax: 913-588-1660, E-mail: kmiller@kumc.edu. *Application contact:* Dr. Rita K. Clifford, Associate Dean, Student Affairs, 913-588-1619, Fax: 913-588-1615, E-mail: rcliffor@kumc.edu.

University of Louisville, Graduate School, School of Nursing, Louisville, KY 40202. Offers adult nurse practitioner (MSN); family nurse practitioner (MSN); health professions education (MSN); neonatal nurse practitioner (MSN); nursing research (PhD); psychiatric mental health nurse practitioner (MSN). *Accreditation:* AACN. Part-time programs available. *Faculty:* 28 full-time (25 women), 4 part-time/adjunct (3 women). *Students:* 72 full-time (66 women), 57 part-time (52 women); includes 15 minority (11 African Americans, 3 Asian Americans or Pacific Islanders, 1 Hispanic American), 4 international. Average age 35. 45 applicants, 82% accepted, 31 enrolled. In 2009, 28 master's, 3 doctorates awarded. Terminal master's awarded for partial completion of doctoral program. *Degree requirements:* For master's, thesis optional; for doctorate, comprehensive exam, thesis/dissertation. *Entrance requirements:* For master's, GRE General Test, bachelor's degree in nursing, minimum GPA of 3.0, RN license; for doctorate, GRE General Test, BSN and MSN with recommended minimum GPA of 3.0. Additional exam requirements/recommendations for international students: Required—TOEFL. *Application deadline:* For fall admission, 4/1 priority date for domestic students, 4/1 for international students; for spring admission, 10/1 priority date for domestic students, 10/1 for international students. Applications are processed on a rolling basis. Application fee: $50. Electronic applications accepted. *Financial support:* In 2009–10, 45 students received support, including 2 fellowships with full tuition reimbursements available (averaging $20,000 per year), 5 research assistantships with full tuition reimbursements available (averaging $18,000 per year), 5 teaching assistantships with full tuition reimbursements available (averaging $18,000 per year); institutionally sponsored loans, scholarships/grants, traineeships, health care benefits, and unspecified assistantships also available. Support available to part-time students. Financial award application deadline: 4/15; financial award applicants required to submit FAFSA. *Faculty research:* Maternal-child/family stress after pregnancy loss, postpartum depression, access to healthcare (underserved populations), quality of life issues, physical activity (impact on chronic/acute conditions). Total annual research expenditures: $363,876. *Unit head:* Dr. Marcia J. Hern, Dean, 502-852-8300, Fax: 502-852-5044, E-mail: m.hern@gwise.louisville.edu. *Application contact:* Dr. Rosalie O'Dell Mainous, Associate Dean for Graduate Academic Affairs, 502-852-8387, Fax: 502-852-8783, E-mail: romain01@louisville.edu.

University of Mary, Division of Nursing, Bismarck, ND 58504-9652. Offers family nurse practitioner (MSN); nurse administrator (MSN); nursing educator (MSN). *Accreditation:* AACN. Part-time and evening/weekend programs available. Postbaccalaureate distance learning degree programs offered (minimal on-campus study). *Degree requirements:* For master's, comprehensive exam, thesis (for some programs), internship (family nurse practitioner), teaching practice. *Entrance requirements:* For master's, minimum GPA of 3.0 in nursing, interview, letters of recommendation. Additional exam requirements/recommendations for international students: Required—TOEFL. Electronic applications accepted. *Expenses:* Tuition: Full-time $10,062; part-time $430 per credit. Tuition and fees vary according to course load, degree level, program and student level. *Faculty research:* Gerontology issues, rural nursing, health policy, primary care, women's health.

University of Massachusetts Lowell, School of Health and Environment, Department of Nursing, Program in Family Health Nursing, Lowell, MA 01854-2881. Offers MS. *Accreditation:* AACN. *Degree requirements:* For master's, thesis optional. *Entrance requirements:* For master's, GRE General Test, minimum GPA of 3.0, MA nursing license, interview, 3 letters of recommendation.

University of Massachusetts Worcester, Graduate School of Nursing, Worcester, MA 01655-0115. Offers adult acute/critical care nurse practitioner (MS, Post Master's Certificate); adult acute/critical care nurse practitioner and gerontological nurse practitioner (MS, Post Master's Certificate); adult primary care nurse practitioner (MS, Post Master's Certificate); adult primary care nurse practitioner and gerontological nurse practitioner (MS, Post Master's Certificate); family nurse practitioner (MS); gerontological nurse practitioner (Post Master's Certificate); nurse educator (MS); nursing (PhD). *Accreditation:* AACN. *Faculty:* 15 full-time (13 women), 31 part-time/adjunct (29 women). *Students:* 151 full-time (131 women), 6 part-time (all women); includes 14 minority (5 African Americans, 1 American Indian/Alaska Native, 5 Asian Americans or Pacific Islanders, 3 Hispanic Americans). Average age 37. 206 applicants, 34% accepted, 61 enrolled. In 2009, 62 master's, 3 doctorates awarded. *Degree requirements:* For doctorate, comprehensive exam, thesis/dissertation. *Entrance requirements:* For master's, GRE General Test, bachelor's degree, course work in statistics; for doctorate, GRE General Test, bachelor's or master's degree, RN licensure; for Post Master's Certificate, MS in nursing. Additional exam requirements/recommendations for international students: Required—TOEFL. *Application deadline:* For fall admission, 3/15 for domestic students. Applications are processed on a rolling basis. Application fee: $40 ($60 for international students). *Expenses:* Contact institution. *Financial support:* In 2009–10, 130 students received support. Scholarships/grants and traineeships available. Support available to part-time students. Financial award application deadline: 5/18; financial award applicants required to submit FAFSA. *Faculty research:* Symptom management, interventions, individual and family adjustment to chronic illness, women's health. *Unit head:* Dr. Paulette Seymour-Route, Dean, 508-856-5801, Fax: 508-856-6552, E-mail: paulette.seymour-route@umassmed.edu. *Application contact:* Diane Brescia, Admissions Coordinator, 508-856-3488, Fax: 508-856-5851, E-mail: diane.brescia@umassmed.edu.

University of Medicine and Dentistry of New Jersey, School of Nursing, Newark, NJ 07107-3001. Offers adult health (MSN); adult occupational health (MSN); advanced practice nursing (MSN, Post Master's Certificate); family nurse practitioner (MSN); nurse anesthesia (MSN); nursing (MSN); nursing informatics (MSN); urban health (PhD); women's health practitioner (MSN). *Accreditation:* AANA/CANAEP; NLN (one or more programs are accredited). Part-time programs available. *Entrance requirements:* For master's, GRE, RN license; basic life support, statistics, and health assessment experience. Additional exam requirements/recommendations for international students: Required—TOEFL. Electronic applications accepted. *Expenses:* Contact institution. *Faculty research:* HIV/AIDS, diabetes education, learned helplessness, nursing science, psychoeducation.

University of Miami, Graduate School, School of Nursing and Health Studies, Coral Gables, FL 33124. Offers acute care (MSN), including acute care nurse practitioner, nurse anesthesia; nursing (PhD); primary care (MSN), including adult nurse practitioner, family nurse practitioner, nurse midwifery, women's health practitioner. *Accreditation:* AACN; AANA/CANAEP; ACNM/DOA (one or more programs are accredited). Part-time programs available. *Degree requirements:* For master's, thesis optional; for doctorate, thesis/dissertation. *Entrance requirements:* For master's, GRE General Test, BSN, minimum GPA of 3.0, Florida RN license; for doctorate, GRE General Test, BSN or MSN, minimum GPA of 3.0. Additional exam requirements/recommendations for international students: Required—TOEFL (minimum score 550 paper-based; 213 computer-based). Electronic applications accepted. *Faculty research:* Transcultural nursing, exercise and depression in Alzheimer's disease, infectious diseases/HIV–AIDS, postpartum depression, outcomes assessment.

University of Michigan, Horace H. Rackham School of Graduate Studies, School of Nursing, Division of Health Promotion and Risk Reduction, Program in Community Health Nursing, Ann Arbor, MI 48109. Offers adult nurse practitioner (Post Master's Certificate); adult primary care/adult nurse practitioner (MS); community care (Post Master's Certificate); community care/home care (MS); family nurse practitioner (MS, Post Master's Certificate); occupational health nursing (MS). *Accreditation:* AACN. Part-time and evening/weekend programs available. *Degree requirements:* For master's, thesis. *Entrance requirements:* For master's, GRE General Test (if cumulative BSN GPA less than 3.25), licensure, minimum GPA of 3.0 in BSN program. Additional exam requirements/recommendations for international students: Required—TOEFL (minimum score 560 paper-based; 220 computer-based). *Expenses:* Tuition, state resident: full-time $17,286; part-time $1099 per credit hour. Tuition, nonresident: full-time $34,944;

part-time $2080 per credit hour. Required fees: $95 per semester. Tuition and fees vary according to course load, degree level and program.

University of Minnesota, Twin Cities Campus, Graduate School, School of Nursing, Family Nurse Practitioner Program, Minneapolis, MN 55455-0213. Offers MS. *Accreditation:* AACN. *Degree requirements:* For master's, final oral exam, project or thesis. *Entrance requirements:* Additional exam requirements/recommendations for international students: Required—TOEFL (minimum score 586 paper-based; 240 computer-based).

University of Missouri–Kansas City, School of Nursing, Kansas City, MO 64110-2499. Offers adult clinical nurse specialist (MSN), including adult nurse practitioner, women's health nurse practitioner; family nurse practitioner (MSN); neonatal nurse practitioner (MSN); nurse educator (MSN); nurse executive (MSN); nursing (PhD); nursing practice (DNP); pediatric nurse practitioner (MSN). *Accreditation:* AACN. Part-time programs available. Postbaccalaureate distance learning degree programs offered (minimal on-campus study). *Faculty:* 36 full-time (30 women), 40 part-time/adjunct (all women). *Students:* 31 full-time (26 women), 310 part-time (287 women); includes 38 minority (17 African Americans, 2 American Indian/Alaska Native, 10 Asian Americans or Pacific Islanders, 9 Hispanic Americans). Average age 36. 151 applicants, 72% accepted, 109 enrolled. In 2009, 57 master's, 10 doctorates awarded. *Degree requirements:* For master's, thesis or alternative. *Entrance requirements:* For master's, minimum undergraduate GPA of 3.2; for doctorate, GRE, 3 letters of reference, interview by invitation. Additional exam requirements/recommendations for international students: Required—TOEFL (minimum score 550 paper-based; 213 computer-based; 80 iBT). *Application deadline:* For fall admission, 2/1 priority date for domestic and international students; for spring admission, 9/1 priority date for domestic and international students. Application fee: $45 ($50 for international students). *Expenses:* Tuition, state resident: full-time $5378; part-time $299 per credit hour. Tuition, nonresident: full-time $13,881; part-time $771 per credit hour. Required fees: $641; $71 per credit hour. Tuition and fees vary according to course load and program. *Financial support:* In 2009–10, 6 teaching assistantships with partial tuition reimbursements (averaging $4,402 per year) were awarded; fellowships, research assistantships, career-related internships or fieldwork, Federal Work-Study, institutionally sponsored loans, and tuition waivers (full and partial) also available. Support available to part-time students. Financial award application deadline: 3/1; financial award applicants required to submit FAFSA. *Faculty research:* Geriatrics/gerontology, children's pain, neonatology, Alzheimer's care, cancer caregivers. Total annual research expenditures: $2.1 million. *Unit head:* Dr. Lora Lacey-Haun, Dean, 816-235-1700, Fax: 816-235-1701, E-mail: lacey-haunc@umkc.edu. *Application contact:* Leah Wilder, Coordinator for Admissions and Recruitment, 816-235-5768, Fax: 816-235-1701, E-mail: wilderl@umkc.edu.

University of Missouri–St. Louis, College of Nursing, St. Louis, MO 63121. Offers nurse educator (MSN); nurse practitioner (MSN, Post Master's Certificate); nursing (DNP, PhD). *Accreditation:* AACN. Part-time programs available. *Faculty:* 14 full-time (13 women), 19 part-time/adjunct (18 women). *Students:* 9 full-time (all women), 216 part-time (203 women); includes 31 minority (29 African Americans, 1 American Indian/Alaska Native, 1 Asian American or Pacific Islander). Average age 37. In 2009, 47 master's, 3 doctorates, 1 other advanced degree awarded. *Degree requirements:* For doctorate, comprehensive exam, thesis/dissertation; for Post Master's Certificate, thesis. *Entrance requirements:* For master's, GRE, 2 recommendation letters; minimum GPA of 3.0; BSN; nursing licensure; statement of purpose; for doctorate, GRE, 2 letters of recommendation, MSN, minimum GPA of 3.2; for Post Master's Certificate, 2 recommendation letters; MSN; advanced practice certificate; minimum GPA of 3.0; essay. Additional exam requirements/recommendations for international students: Required—TOEFL (minimum score 550 paper-based; 213 computer-based). *Application deadline:* For fall admission, 4/1 for domestic and international students; for spring admission, 10/1 for domestic and international students. Application fee: $35 ($40 for international students). Electronic applications accepted. *Expenses:* Tuition, state resident: full-time $5377; part-time $297.70 per credit hour. Tuition, nonresident: full-time $13,882; part-time $771.20 per credit hour. Required fees: $220; $12.20 per credit hour. One-time fee: $12. Tuition and fees vary according to course level, campus/location and program. *Financial support:* In 2009–10, 1 research assistantship with full and partial tuition reimbursement (averaging $12,339 per year), 4 teaching assistantships with full and partial tuition reimbursements (averaging $12,339 per year) were awarded. Financial award application deadline: 4/1; financial award applicants required to submit FAFSA. *Faculty research:* Health promotion and restoration, family disruption, violence, abuse, battered women, health survey methods. *Unit head:* Dean Juliann Sebastian, Dean, 314-516-6066. *Application contact:* 314-516-5458, Fax: 314-516-6996, E-mail: gradadm@umsl.edu.

University of Nevada, Las Vegas, Graduate College, School of Nursing, Las Vegas, NV 89154-3018. Offers family nurse practitioner (Advanced Certificate); nursing (MS, PhD); nursing education (Advanced Certificate). *Accreditation:* AACN; NLN. Part-time programs available. Postbaccalaureate distance learning degree programs offered (minimal on-campus study). *Faculty:* 35 full-time (30 women), 5 part-time/adjunct (all women). *Students:* 68 full-time (56 women), 94 part-time (83 women); includes 30 minority (3 African Americans, 1 American Indian/Alaska Native, 18 Asian Americans or Pacific Islanders, 8 Hispanic Americans), 19 international. Average age 41. 147 applicants, 46% accepted, 51 enrolled. In 2009, 50 master's, 4 doctorates, 1 other advanced degree awarded. *Entrance requirements:* For doctorate, GRE General Test. Additional exam requirements/recommendations for international students: Recommended—TOEFL (minimum score 550 paper-based; 213 computer-based; 80 iBT), IELTS (minimum score 7). *Application deadline:* For fall admission, 3/1 priority date for domestic and international students. Applications are processed on a rolling basis. Application fee: $60 ($95 for international students). Electronic applications accepted. *Financial support:* In 2009–10, 9 students received support, including 8 research assistantships with partial tuition reimbursements available (averaging $14,275 per year), 1 teaching assistantship (averaging $12,000 per year); institutionally sponsored loans, scholarships/grants, health care benefits, and unspecified assistantships also available. Financial award application deadline: 3/1. *Faculty research:* Obesity, weight loss maintenance; eukocyte response to exercise-related skeletal muscle injury; smoke-free policy, smoking cessation; exercise, health promotion; community-based participatory research, occupational health/injury, low-back pain. *Unit head:* Dr. Carolyn Yucha, Interim Dean, 702-895-3906, Fax: 702-895-5050, E-mail: carolyn.yucha@unlv.edu. *Application contact:* Graduate College Admissions Evaluator, 702-895-3320, Fax: 702-895-4180, E-mail: gradcollege@unlv.edu.

The University of North Carolina at Chapel Hill, School of Nursing, Chapel Hill, NC 27599-7460. Offers nursing (MSN, PhD, PMC), including adult nurse practitioner (MSN, PMC), children's health advanced practice (MSN, PMC), family nurse practitioner (MSN, PMC), health care systems (MSN, PMC), psychiatric/mental health nursing (MSN, PMC), women's health nursing (MSN, PMC). *Accreditation:* AACN; NLN (one or more programs are accredited). Part-time programs available. *Degree requirements:* For master's, comprehensive exam, thesis; for doctorate, thesis/dissertation, 3 exams. *Entrance requirements:* For master's and doctorate, GRE General Test. *Faculty research:* Chronic illness, parenting, cardiovascular health in children, elderly, HIV-AIDS.

The University of North Carolina Wilmington, School of Nursing, Wilmington, NC 28403-3297. Offers family nurse practitioner (MSN); nurse educator (MSN). *Accreditation:* AACN; NLN. *Degree requirements:* For master's, comprehensive exam, thesis or project. *Entrance requirements:* For master's, GRE General Test, bachelor's degree in nursing. Additional exam requirements/recommendations for international students: Required—TOEFL (minimum score 550 paper-based; 217 computer-based; 79 iBT), IELTS (minimum score 6.5). Electronic applications accepted.

University of Northern Colorado, Graduate School, College of Natural and Health Sciences, School of Nursing, Greeley, CO 80639. Offers clinical nurse specialist in chronic illness (MS); family nurse practitioner (MS); nursing education (MS, PhD). *Accreditation:* AACN. Postbaccalaureate distance learning degree programs offered. *Faculty:* 9 full-time (all women). *Students:* 35 part-time (34 women); includes 2 minority (both Hispanic Americans). Average age 35. 84 applicants, 64% accepted, 13 enrolled. In 2009, 27 master's, 2 doctorates awarded.

Degree requirements: For master's, comprehensive exam, thesis or alternative; for doctorate, comprehensive exam, thesis/dissertation. *Entrance requirements:* For master's and doctorate, GRE General Test, minimum GPA of 3.0 in last 60 hours, BS in nursing, 2 letters of recommendation. *Application deadline:* Applications are processed on a rolling basis. Application fee: $50 ($60 for international students). Electronic applications accepted. *Expenses:* Tuition, state resident: full-time $5770; part-time $320.55 per credit hour. Tuition, nonresident: full-time $13,847; part-time $769.27 per credit hour. Required fees: $948.78; $52.72 per credit. *Financial support:* In 2009–10, 7 research assistantships (averaging $6,183 per year), 1 teaching assistantship (averaging $2,849 per year) were awarded; fellowships, unspecified assistantships also available. Financial award application deadline: 3/1; financial award applicants required to submit FAFSA. *Unit head:* Dr. Kathleen Bradshaw-LaSala, Director, 970-351-2293, Fax: 970-351-1707. *Application contact:* Linda Sisson, Graduate Student Admission Coordinator, 970-351-1807, Fax: 970-351-2371, E-mail: linda.sisson@unco.edu.

University of Pennsylvania, School of Nursing, Family Health Nurse Practitioner Program, Philadelphia, PA 19104. Offers MSN, Certificate. *Accreditation:* AACN. Part-time programs available. *Students:* 22 full-time (20 women), 38 part-time (37 women); includes 12 minority (5 African Americans, 6 Asian Americans or Pacific Islanders, 1 Hispanic American). In 2009, 20 master's, 1 other advanced degree awarded. *Entrance requirements:* For master's, GRE General Test, 1 year of clinical experience in area of interest, BSN, minimum GPA of 3.0, previous course work in statistics. Additional exam requirements/recommendations for international students: Required—TOEFL. *Application deadline:* For fall admission, 2/15 priority date for domestic students. Applications are processed on a rolling basis. Application fee: $70. *Expenses:* Contact institution. *Financial support:* Research assistantships, teaching assistantships, career-related internships or fieldwork, Federal Work-Study, and institutionally sponsored loans available. Support available to part-time students. Financial award application deadline: 4/1. *Faculty research:* Evaluation of primary care practitioner practice, access to primary care.

University of Phoenix–Bay Area Campus, The Artemis School, College of Health and Human Services, Pleasanton, CA 94588-3677. Offers administration of justice and security (MS); family nurse practitioner (MSN); health care management (MBA); marriage, family and child therapy (MSC); nursing (MSN); nursing/health care education (MSN); MSN/MBA. Evening/weekend programs available. Postbaccalaureate distance learning degree programs offered (no on-campus study). *Degree requirements:* For master's, thesis (for some programs). *Entrance requirements:* For master's, minimum undergraduate GPA of 2.5, 3 years of work experience, RN license. Additional exam requirements/recommendations for international students: Required—TOEFL (minimum score 550 paper-based; 213 computer-based; 79 iBT). Electronic applications accepted.

University of Phoenix–Hawaii Campus, The Artemis School, College of Health and Human Services, Honolulu, HI 96813-4317. Offers administration of justice and security (MS); community counseling (MSC); education (MHA); family nurse practitioner (MSN); gerontology (MHA); health administration (MHA); health care management (MBA); marriage, family and child therapy (MSC); nursing (MSN); nursing/health care education (MSN); psychology (MS); MSN/MBA. Evening/weekend programs available. *Degree requirements:* For master's, thesis (for some programs). *Entrance requirements:* For master's, minimum undergraduate GPA of 2.5, 3 years of work experience, RN license. Additional exam requirements/recommendations for international students: Required—TOEFL (minimum score 550 paper-based; 213 computer-based; 79 iBT). Electronic applications accepted.

University of Phoenix–Minneapolis/St. Louis Park Campus, College of Health and Human Services, St. Louis Park, MN 55426. Offers community counseling (MSC); family nurse practitioner (MSN); health care education (MSN); health care management (MBA); nursing (MSN).

University of Phoenix–Sacramento Valley Campus, The Artemis School, College of Health and Human Services, Sacramento, CA 95833-3632. Offers administration of justice and security (MS); community counseling (MSC); family nurse practitioner (MSN); health administration (MHA); health care education (MSN); health care management (MBA); marriage, family and child counseling (MSC); nursing (MSN); psychology (MS); MSN/MBA. Evening/weekend programs available. *Degree requirements:* For master's, thesis (for some programs). *Entrance requirements:* For master's, RN license, minimum undergraduate GPA of 2.5, 3 years work experience. Additional exam requirements/recommendations for international students: Required—TOEFL (minimum score 550 paper-based; 213 computer-based; 79 iBT). Electronic applications accepted.

University of Phoenix–Southern Arizona Campus, The Artemis School, College of Health and Human Services, Tucson, AZ 85711. Offers administration of justice and security (MS); family nurse practitioner (MSN, Certificate); health administration (MHA); health care management (MBA); marriage, family and child therapy (MSC); nursing (MSN); psychology (MS). Evening/weekend programs available. *Degree requirements:* For master's, thesis (for some programs). *Entrance requirements:* For master's, minimum undergraduate GPA of 2.5, 3 years of work experience, RN license. Additional exam requirements/recommendations for international students: Required—TOEFL (minimum score 550 paper-based; 213 computer-based; 79 iBT). Electronic applications accepted.

University of Phoenix–Southern California Campus, College of Nursing, Costa Mesa, CA 92626. Offers family nurse practitioner (MSN); health care education (MSN); nursing (MSN); MSN/MBA; MSN/MHA. Evening/weekend programs available. *Faculty:* 3 full-time (all women), 41 part-time/adjunct (32 women). *Students:* 79 full-time (42 women); includes 155 minority (48 African Americans, 1 American Indian/Alaska Native, 76 Asian Americans or Pacific Islanders, 30 Hispanic Americans), 27 international. Average age 44. In 2009, 154 master's awarded. *Degree requirements:* For master's, thesis (for some programs). *Entrance requirements:* For master's, minimum undergraduate GPA of 2.5, 3 years work experience, RN license. Additional exam requirements/recommendations for international students: Required—TOEFL (minimum score 550 paper-based; 213 computer-based; 79 iBT). *Application deadline:* Applications are processed on a rolling basis. Application fee: $45. Electronic applications accepted. *Expenses:* Tuition: Full-time $15,120. Required fees: $660. *Financial support:* Institutionally sponsored loans and scholarships/grants available. Financial award applicants required to submit FAFSA. *Unit head:* Dr. Pam Fuller, Dean/Executive Director, 480-557-1140, E-mail: pam.fuller@phoenix.edu. *Application contact:* Campus College Chair, 714-398-1878, Fax: 714-378-5856.

University of Pittsburgh, School of Nursing, Nurse Practitioner Program, Pittsburgh, PA 15260. Offers acute care nurse practitioner (MSN, DNP); adult nurse practitioner (MSN, DNP); family nurse practitioner (MSN, DNP); neonatal (MSN, DNP); nursing practice (DNP); pediatric nurse practitioner (MSN, DNP); psychiatric primary care nurse practitioner (MSN, DNP). *Accreditation:* AACN. Part-time programs available. *Students:* 27 full-time (26 women), 89 part-time (84 women); includes 6 minority (5 African Americans, 1 Asian American or Pacific Islander). Average age 34. 44 applicants, 64% accepted, 25 enrolled. In 2009, 28 master's awarded. *Degree requirements:* For master's, comprehensive exam, thesis optional. *Entrance requirements:* For master's, GRE General Test or MAT, BSN, RN license, letters of recommendation, resume, course work in statistics, 1-3 years of nursing experience; for doctorate, GRE General Test, BSN, RN license, minimum GPA of 3.5, 3 letters of recommendation. Additional exam requirements/recommendations for international students: Required—TOEFL (minimum score 550 paper-based; 213 computer-based; 80 iBT). *Application deadline:* For fall admission, 8/1 priority date for domestic students, 8/1 for international students; for spring admission, 12/1 priority date for domestic students, 12/1 for international students. Applications are processed on a rolling basis. Application fee: $50. Electronic applications accepted. *Expenses:* Tuition, state resident: full-time $16,402; part-time $665 per credit. Tuition, nonresident: full-time $28,694; part-time $1175 per credit. Required fees: $690; $175 per term. Tuition and fees vary according to program. *Unit head:* Dr. Helen Burns, Associate Dean for Clinical Education, 412-624-6616, Fax: 412-624-2401, E-mail: burnsh@pitt.edu. *Application contact:* Laurie Lapsley, Administrator of Graduate Student Services, 412-624-9670, Fax: 412-624-2409, E-mail: lapsleyl@pitt.edu.

Family Nurse Practitioner Studies

University of Puerto Rico, Medical Sciences Campus, School of Nursing, San Juan, PR 00936-5067. Offers anesthesia (MSN); critical care nursing (MSN); family and community nursing (MSN); family nurse practitioner (MSN); mental health and psychiatric nursing (MSN); nursing (MSN). *Accreditation:* AACN; AANA/CANAEP. *Entrance requirements:* For master's, GRE or EXADEP, interview, Puerto Rico RN license or professional license for international students, general and specific point average, article analysis. Electronic applications accepted. *Faculty research:* HIV, health disparities, teen violence, women and violence, neurological disorders.

University of Rhode Island, Graduate School, College of Nursing, Kingston, RI 02881. Offers administration (MS); clinical nurse leader (MS); clinical specialist in gerontology (MS); clinical specialist in psychiatric/mental health (MS); family nurse practitioner (MS); gerontological nurse practitioner (MS); nursing (DNP, PhD); nursing education (MS). *Accreditation:* AACN; ACNM/DOA (one or more programs are accredited). Part-time programs available. *Faculty:* 28 full-time (27 women), 3 part-time/adjunct (all women). *Students:* 21 full-time (20 women), 74 part-time (71 women); includes 3 minority (1 African American, 2 Asian Americans or Pacific Islanders), 5 international. In 2009, 29 master's, 2 doctorates awarded. *Degree requirements:* For master's, comprehensive exam; for doctorate, comprehensive exam, thesis/dissertation. *Entrance requirements:* For master's, GRE or MAT, 2 letters of recommendation, scholarly papers; for doctorate, GRE, 3 letters of recommendation, scholarly papers. Additional exam requirements/recommendations for international students: Required—TOEFL (minimum score 550 paper-based; 213 computer-based). *Application deadline:* For fall admission, 4/15 for domestic students, 2/1 for international students; for spring admission, 11/15 for domestic students, 7/15 for international students. Application fee: $65. Electronic applications accepted. *Expenses:* Tuition, state resident: full-time $8828; part-time $490 per credit hour. Tuition, nonresident: full-time $22,100; part-time $1228 per credit hour. Required fees: $1118; $57 per semester. Tuition and fees vary according to program. *Financial support:* In 2009–10, 3 teaching assistantships with full and partial tuition reimbursements (averaging $8,428 per year) were awarded. Financial award application deadline: 4/15; financial award applicants required to submit FAFSA. *Faculty research:* Group intervention for grieving women in prison, translating Best Practice in non-drug interventions for postoperative pain management, further development and testing of the pain assessment inventory, preschool motor and functional performance of two cohorts, neuroactivation of brain motor areas in preterm children. Total annual research expenditures: $926,949. *Unit head:* Dr. Dayle Joseph, Dean, 401-874-2766, Fax: 401-874-2061, E-mail: dayle@uri.edu. *Application contact:* Dr. Mary C. Sullivan, Director of Graduate Studies, 401-874-5339, Fax: 401-874-2061, E-mail: mcsullivan@uri.edu.

University of Rochester, School of Nursing, Rochester, NY 14642. Offers acute care nurse practitioner (MS); adult nurse practitioner (MS); adult psychiatric mental health nurse practitioner (MS); adult/geriatric nurse practitioner (MS); care of children and families/pediatric nurse practitioner (MS); care of children and families/pediatric nurse practitioner with pediatric behavioral health (MS); care of children and families/pediatric nurse practitioner/neonatal nurse practitioner (MS); child and adolescent psychiatric mental health nurse practitioner (MS); clinical nurse leader (MS); disaster response and emergency preparedness (MS); family nurse practitioner (MS); health care organization management and leadership (MS); health practice research (PhD); health promotion, education and technology (MS); nursing (Certificate). *Accreditation:* AACN; NLN (one or more programs are accredited). Part-time programs available. Postbaccalaureate distance learning degree programs offered (minimal on-campus study). *Faculty:* 26 full-time (24 women), 20 part-time/adjunct (15 women). *Students:* 50 full-time (45 women), 178 part-time (165 women); includes 33 minority (17 African Americans, 2 American Indian/Alaska Native, 10 Asian Americans or Pacific Islanders, 4 Hispanic Americans), 11 international. Average age 35. 56 applicants, 80% accepted, 35 enrolled. In 2009, 53 master's, 5 doctorates awarded. Terminal master's awarded for partial completion of doctoral program. *Degree requirements:* For master's, comprehensive exam or thesis; for doctorate, thesis/dissertation. *Entrance requirements:* For master's, BS in nursing, minimum GPA of 3.0, course work in statistics; for doctorate, GRE General Test, MS in nursing, minimum GPA of 3.5; for Certificate, MS in nursing. Additional exam requirements/recommendations for international students: Recommended—TOEFL (minimum score 560 paper-based; 230 computer-based; 88 iBT). *Application deadline:* For fall admission, 11/1 priority date for domestic and international students. Application fee: $50. *Financial support:* In 2009–10, 53 students received support, including 14 fellowships with full and partial tuition reimbursements available (averaging $17,497 per year); scholarships/grants, traineeships, health care benefits, tuition waivers (partial), and unspecified assistantships also available. Support available to part-time students. Financial award application deadline: 6/30. *Faculty research:* Clinical research in aging, managing asthma in children, interventions to improve outcomes in critically ill children and their mothers, nurse home visitation studies, medical device evaluation, critical care clinical studies, high risk behavior and prevention, palliative care, pregnancy-related weight gain. Total annual research expenditures: $4.8 million. *Unit head:* Dr. Kathy P. Parker, Dean, 585-273-5639, Fax: 585-273-1268, E-mail: kathy_parker@urmc.rochester.edu. *Application contact:* Elaine Andolina, Director of Admissions, 585-275-2375, Fax: 585-756-8299, E-mail: elaine_andolina@urmc.rochester.edu.

University of St. Francis, College of Nursing and Allied Health, Joliet, IL 60435-6169. Offers nursing (MSN), including adult health clinical nurse specialist, adult nurse practitioner, family nurse practitioner; nursing practice (DNP). *Accreditation:* AACN. Part-time and evening/weekend programs available. Postbaccalaureate distance learning degree programs offered. *Faculty:* 10 full-time (all women), 11 part-time/adjunct (10 women). *Students:* 13 full-time (10 women), 164 part-time (153 women); includes 41 minority (22 African Americans, 1 American Indian/Alaska Native, 6 Asian Americans or Pacific Islanders, 12 Hispanic Americans). Average age 40. 161 applicants, 43% accepted, 56 enrolled. In 2009, 10 master's awarded. *Entrance requirements:* For master's, GRE General Test (MS), minimum GPA of 2.75, 2 years of work experience in clinical nursing, CPR certification, computer competency, 3 letters of recommendation, interview, RN license, current licensure, immunizations, liability insurance, resume, work history (MSN); for doctorate, master's degree in nursing with minimum GPA of 3.0, national certification as nurse practitioner or clinical nurse specialist, current RN licensure, interview, computer competency, CPR certification, immunizations, medical history, physical form, drug screen, criminal background check, liability insurance, letter of recommendation, resume. Additional exam requirements/recommendations for international students: Required—TOEFL (minimum score 550 paper-based; 213 computer-based). *Application deadline:* Applications are processed on a rolling basis. Application fee: $30. Electronic applications accepted. *Expenses:* Contact institution. *Financial support:* In 2009–10, 135 students received support. Scholarships/grants, traineeships, and tuition waivers (partial) available. Support available to part-time students. Financial award applicants required to submit FAFSA. *Unit head:* Dr. Maria Connolly, Dean, 815-740-3840, Fax: 815-740-4243, E-mail: mconnolly@stfrancis.edu. *Application contact:* Sandra Sloka, Director of Admissions for Graduate and Degree Completion Programs, 800-735-7500, Fax: 815-740-5032, E-mail: ssloka@stfrancis.edu.

University of San Diego, Hahn School of Nursing and Health Science, San Diego, CA 92110-2492. Offers adult nurse practitioner/family nurse practitioner (MSN); adult-gerontology clinical nurse specialist (MSN); clinical nursing (MSN); entry-level nursing (for non-RNs) (MSN); executive nurse leader (MSN); family nurse practitioner (MSN); nursing (PhD); nursing practice (DNP); pediatric nurse practitioner/family nurse practitioner (MSN); psychiatric-mental health nurse practitioner (MSN). *Accreditation:* AACN. Part-time and evening/weekend programs available. *Faculty:* 18 full-time (17 women), 25 part-time/adjunct (22 women). *Students:* 141 full-time (117 women), 173 part-time (152 women); includes 95 minority (20 African Americans, 9 American Indian/Alaska Native, 45 Asian Americans or Pacific Islanders, 21 Hispanic Americans), 7 international. Average age 38. 404 applicants, 50% accepted, 132 enrolled. In 2009, 103 master's, 10 doctorates awarded. *Degree requirements:* For doctorate, thesis/dissertation (for some programs), residency (DNP). *Entrance requirements:* For master's, GRE General Test (entry-level nursing), BSN, current California RN licensure (except for entry-level nursing); minimum GPA of 3.0; for doctorate, minimum GPA of 3.5, MSN, current California RN licensure. Additional exam requirements/recommendations for international students: Required—TOEFL (minimum score 580 paper-based; 237 computer-based; 83 iBT), TWE. *Application deadline:* For fall admission, 3/1 priority date for domestic students, 3/1 for international students; for spring admission, 11/1 priority date for domestic students, 11/1 for international students. Applications are processed on a rolling basis. Application fee: $45. Electronic applications accepted. *Expenses:* Tuition: Full-time $21,042; part-time $1169 per unit. Required fees: $224. Full-time tuition and fees vary according to course load and degree level. *Financial support:* In 2009–10, 270 students received support. Scholarships/grants and traineeships available. Support available to part-time students. Financial award application deadline: 4/1; financial award applicants required to submit FAFSA. *Faculty research:* Health promotion, decision making, psychogeriatric nursing, historical nursing, leadership behavior. *Unit head:* Dr. Sally Hardin, Dean, 619-260-4550, Fax: 619-260-6814. *Application contact:* Dr. John Mosby, Associate Director of Graduate Admissions, 619-260-4524, Fax: 619-260-4158, E-mail: grads@sandiego.edu.

University of San Francisco, School of Nursing, Program in Nursing Practice, San Francisco, CA 94117-1080. Offers family nurse practitioner (DNP); healthcare systems leadership (DNP). *Faculty:* 2 full-time (both women), 5 part-time/adjunct (4 women). *Students:* 29 full-time (25 women), 24 part-time (22 women); includes 22 minority (7 African Americans, 12 Asian Americans or Pacific Islanders, 3 Hispanic Americans). Average age 47. 41 applicants, 59% accepted, 18 enrolled. In 2009, 9 doctorates awarded. *Entrance requirements:* For doctorate, nursing bachelor's degree, valid RN license in California. *Expenses:* Tuition: Full-time $19,710; part-time $1095 per unit. Part-time tuition and fees vary according to degree level, campus/location and program. *Financial support:* In 2009–10, 32 students received support. *Unit head:* Dr. Judith Karshmer, Dean, 415-422-6681, Fax: 415-422-6877, E-mail: nursing@usfca.edu. *Application contact:* Information Contact, 415-422-4723, Fax: 415-422-2217.

The University of Scranton, College of Graduate and Continuing Education, Department of Nursing, Scranton, PA 18510. Offers adult health nursing (MSN); family nurse practitioner (MSN, PMC); nurse anesthesia (MSN, PMC). Applicants accepted in odd-numbered years only. *Accreditation:* AACN; AANA/CANAEP. Part-time and evening/weekend programs available. *Faculty:* 13 full-time (all women), 2 part-time/adjunct (both women). *Students:* 40 full-time (37 women), 35 part-time (25 women); includes 6 minority (5 African Americans, 1 Asian American or Pacific Islander). Average age 35. 74 applicants, 85% accepted. In 2009, 34 master's awarded. *Degree requirements:* For master's, thesis (for some programs), capstone experience. *Entrance requirements:* For master's, BSN, minimum GPA of 3.0, Pennsylvania RN license. Additional exam requirements/recommendations for international students: Required—TOEFL (minimum score 500 paper-based; 173 computer-based), IELTS (minimum score 5.5). *Application deadline:* For fall admission, 9/1 for domestic students. Applications are processed on a rolling basis. Application fee: $0. *Financial support:* In 2009–10, 8 students received support, including 8 teaching assistantships with full and partial tuition reimbursements available (averaging $6,600 per year); career-related internships or fieldwork, Federal Work-Study, and unspecified assistantships also available. Support available to part-time students. Financial award application deadline: 3/1. *Faculty research:* Home care, doctoral education, health care of women and children, pain, health promotion and adolescence. *Unit head:* Dr. Patricia Harrington, Chair, 570-941-7673, Fax: 570-941-4201, E-mail: harringtonp1@uofs.edu. *Application contact:* Dr. Mary Jane Hanson, Director, 570-941-4060, Fax: 570-941-4201, E-mail: hansonm2@scranton.edu.

University of South Carolina, The Graduate School, College of Nursing, Program in Health Nursing, Columbia, SC 29208. Offers adult nurse practitioner (MSN); community/public health clinical nurse specialist (MSN); family nurse practitioner (MSN); pediatric nurse practitioner (MSN). *Accreditation:* AACN. Part-time programs available. *Degree requirements:* For master's, thesis or alternative. *Entrance requirements:* For master's, GRE General Test or MAT, BS in nursing, nursing license. Additional exam requirements/recommendations for international students: Required—TOEFL (minimum score 570 paper-based; 230 computer-based). Electronic applications accepted. *Faculty research:* System research, evidence based practice, breast cancer, violence.

University of Southern Maine, College of Nursing and Health Professions, Portland, ME 04104-9300. Offers adult health nursing (PMC); clinical nurse leader (MS); clinical nurse specialist psychiatric-mental health nursing (MS); family nursing (PMC); medical/surgical nursing (MS); nurse practitioner adult health nursing (MS); nurse practitioner family nursing (MS); nurse practitioner psychiatric/mental health nursing (MS); psychiatric-mental health nursing (PMC); MBA/MSN. *Accreditation:* AACN. Part-time programs available. *Faculty:* 15 full-time (13 women), 4 part-time/adjunct (2 women). *Students:* 51 full-time (40 women), 54 part-time (49 women); includes 4 minority (1 American Indian/Alaska Native, 2 Asian Americans or Pacific Islanders, 1 Hispanic American). Average age 36. 95 applicants, 52% accepted, 27 enrolled. In 2009, 34 master's awarded. *Degree requirements:* For master's, thesis optional. *Entrance requirements:* For master's, GRE General Test or MAT, minimum GPA of 3.0. Additional exam requirements/recommendations for international students: Required—TOEFL (minimum score 550 paper-based; 213 computer-based). *Application deadline:* For fall admission, 4/1 for domestic and international students; for spring admission, 10/1 for domestic and international students. Application fee: $50. Electronic applications accepted. *Financial support:* In 2009–10, 10 students received support, including 5 research assistantships with tuition reimbursements available (averaging $3,375 per year), 3 teaching assistantships with tuition reimbursements available (averaging $3,375 per year); career-related internships or fieldwork, Federal Work-Study, scholarships/grants, traineeships, tuition waivers (full and partial), and unspecified assistantships also available. Support available to part-time students. Financial award application deadline: 2/15; financial award applicants required to submit FAFSA. *Faculty research:* Women's health, nursing history, weight control, community services, substance abuse. *Unit head:* Krista M. Meinersmann, Director of Nursing Program, 207-780-4505, Fax: 207-228-8177, E-mail: kmeinersmann@usm.maine.edu. *Application contact:* Mary Sloan, Assistant Director, Office of Graduate Studies, 207-780-4386, Fax: 207-780-4969, E-mail: gradstudies@usm.maine.edu.

University of Southern Mississippi, Graduate School, College of Health, School of Nursing, Hattiesburg, MS 39406-0001. Offers adult health nursing (MSN); community health nursing (MSN); ethics (PhD); family nurse practitioner (MSN); leadership (PhD); nursing service administration (MSN); policy analysis (PhD); psychiatric nursing (MSN). *Accreditation:* AACN. Part-time and evening/weekend programs available. *Faculty:* 17 full-time (16 women), 1 part-time/adjunct (0 women). *Students:* 63 full-time (57 women), 40 part-time (36 women); includes 23 minority (all African Americans). Average age 40. 69 applicants, 59% accepted, 37 enrolled. In 2009, 28 master's, 2 doctorates awarded. *Degree requirements:* For master's, comprehensive exam, thesis optional; for doctorate, comprehensive exam, thesis/dissertation. *Entrance requirements:* For master's, GRE General Test, minimum GPA of 2.75, nursing license, BS in nursing; for doctorate, GRE General Test, master's degree in nursing, minimum GPA of 3.5. Additional exam requirements/recommendations for international students: Required—TOEFL. *Application deadline:* For fall admission, 3/15 priority date for domestic students, 5/1 for international students. Applications are processed on a rolling basis. Application fee: $35. Electronic applications accepted. *Expenses:* Tuition, state resident: full-time $5096; part-time $284 per hour. Tuition, nonresident: full-time $13,052; part-time $726 per hour. Required fees: $402. Tuition and fees vary according to course level and course load. *Financial support:* In 2009–10, 14 research assistantships with full tuition reimbursements (averaging $12,577 per year) were awarded; teaching assistantships, Federal Work-Study and traineeships also available. Financial award application deadline: 3/15; financial award applicants required to submit FAFSA. *Faculty research:* Gerontology, caregivers, HIV, bereavement, pain, nursing leadership. *Unit head:* Dr. Katherine Nugent, Director and Associate Dean, 601-266-5500, Fax: 601-266-5927. *Application contact:* Dr. Anne Brock, Graduate Coordinator, 601-266-5500, Fax: 601-266-5927.

The University of Tampa, Nursing Program, Tampa, FL 33606-1490. Offers adult nurse practitioner (MSN); family nurse practitioner (MSN). *Accreditation:* NLN. Part-time and evening/weekend programs available. *Faculty:* 10 full-time (all women), 2 part-time/adjunct (both women). *Students:* 4 full-time (all women), 87 part-time (80 women); includes 24 minority (10 African Americans, 1 American Indian/Alaska Native, 1 Asian American or Pacific Islander, 12 Hispanic Americans), 1 international. Average age 38. 64 applicants, 56% accepted, 28

enrolled. In 2009, 22 master's awarded. *Degree requirements:* For master's, comprehensive exam, thesis optional, oral exam, practicum. *Entrance requirements:* For master's, GRE General Test, minimum GPA of 3.0, RN license-Florida, bachelor's degree. Additional exam requirements/recommendations for international students: Required—TOEFL (minimum score 577 paper-based; 230 computer-based; 90 iBT), IELTS (minimum score 7). *Application deadline:* For fall admission, 7/15 for domestic students, 6/1 for international students. Applications are processed on a rolling basis. Application fee: $40. Electronic applications accepted. *Expenses:* Tuition: Part-time $488 per credit hour. *Financial support:* In 2009–10, 68 students received support, including 3 research assistantships with tuition reimbursements available (averaging $2,847 per year); career-related internships or fieldwork and unspecified assistantships also available. Support available to part-time students. Financial award applicants required to submit FAFSA. *Faculty research:* Domestic violence (assessment in emergency departments, changing demographics), trans-cultural health assessment, priorities in maintaining autonomy of elderly. *Unit head:* Dr. Maria Warda, Director, 813-257-3302, Fax: 813-258-7214, E-mail: mwarda@ut.edu. *Application contact:* Karen Full, Graduate Advisor and Recruiter, 813-257-3642, E-mail: kfull@ut.edu.

The University of Tennessee at Chattanooga, Graduate School, College of Health, Education and Professional Studies, School of Nursing, Chattanooga, TN 37403. Offers administration (MSN); certified nurse anesthetist (Post-Master's Certificate); education (MSN); family nurse practitioner (MSN, Post-Master's Certificate); health care informatics (Post-Master's Certificate); nurse anesthesia (MSN); nurse education (Post-Master's Certificate). *Accreditation:* AACN; AANA/CANAEP (one or more programs are accredited). *Faculty:* 4 full-time (all women). *Students:* 42 full-time (33 women), 53 part-time (38 women); includes 10 minority (5 African Americans, 1 American Indian/Alaska Native, 2 Asian Americans or Pacific Islanders, 2 Hispanic Americans). Average age 35. 13 applicants, 31% accepted, 3 enrolled. In 2009, 36 master's, 5 other advanced degrees awarded. *Degree requirements:* For master's, thesis optional, qualifying exams, professional project; for Post-Master's Certificate, thesis or alternative, practicum, seminar. *Entrance requirements:* For master's, GRE General Test, MAT, BSN, minimum GPA of 3.0, eligibility for Tennessee RN license, 1 year direct patient care experience; for Post-Master's Certificate, GRE General Test, MAT, MSN, minimum GPA of 3.0, eligibility for Tennessee RN license, one year of direct patient care experience. Additional exam requirements/recommendations for international students: Required—TOEFL (minimum score 550 paper-based; 213 computer-based; 79 iBT), IELTS (minimum score 6). *Application deadline:* For fall admission, 8/1 priority date for domestic students, 6/1 for international students; for spring admission, 12/1 priority date for domestic students, 10/1 for international students. Applications are processed on a rolling basis. Application fee: $35. Electronic applications accepted. *Expenses:* Tuition, state resident: full-time $5404; part-time $300 per credit hour. Tuition, nonresident: full-time $16,702; part-time $928 per credit hour. Required fees: $1150; $130 per credit hour. *Financial support:* Career-related internships or fieldwork and scholarships/grants available. Support available to part-time students. *Faculty research:* Diabetes in women, health care for elderly, alternative medicine, hypertension, nurse anesthesia. Total annual research expenditures: $1.5 million. *Unit head:* Dr. Kay R. Lindgren, Head, 423-425-4646, Fax: 423-425-4668, E-mail: kay-lindgren@utc.edu. *Application contact:* Dr. Stephanie Bellar, Dean of Graduate Studies, 423-425-4666, Fax: 423-425-5223, E-mail: stephanie-bellar@utc.edu.

The University of Texas at Arlington, Graduate School, School of Nursing, Arlington, TX 76019. Offers administration/supervision of nursing (MSN); nurse practitioner (MSN); nursing science (PhD); teaching of nursing (MSN). *Accreditation:* AACN. Part-time and evening/weekend programs available. *Faculty:* 12 full-time (all women), 8 part-time/adjunct (all women). *Students:* 59 full-time (52 women), 483 part-time (441 women); includes 151 minority (75 African Americans, 3 American Indian/Alaska Native, 32 Asian Americans or Pacific Islanders, 41 Hispanic Americans), 9 international. Average age 37. 227 applicants, 97% accepted, 130 enrolled. In 2009, 72 master's, 3 doctorates awarded. *Degree requirements:* For master's, comprehensive exam, thesis or project; for doctorate, comprehensive exam, thesis/dissertation, successful proposal defense. *Entrance requirements:* For master's, GRE General Test, minimum GPA of 3.0, Texas nursing license, minimum C in undergraduate statistics course, physical assessment course within last 3 years; for doctorate, GRE General Test, minimum undergraduate, graduate and statistics GPA of 3.0; Texas RN license; interview; 3 letters of reference, written statement of goals. Additional exam requirements/recommendations for international students: Required—TOEFL (minimum score 550 paper-based; 213 computer-based), IELTS (minimum score 7). *Application deadline:* For fall admission, 6/5 for domestic students, 4/3 for international students; for spring admission, 10/7 for domestic students, 9/5 for international students. Applications are processed on a rolling basis. Application fee: $40 ($70 for international students). *Financial support:* In 2009–10, 27 students received support, including 24 fellowships with partial tuition reimbursements available (averaging $3,000 per year), 6 research assistantships (averaging $7,992 per year), 7 teaching assistantships (averaging $10,080 per year); career-related internships or fieldwork and traineeships also available. Financial award application deadline: 6/1; financial award applicants required to submit FAFSA. *Faculty research:* Simulation in clinical education and practice, cultural diversity, vulnerable populations, substance abuse. *Unit head:* Dr. Elizabeth C. Poster, Dean, 817-272-2776, Fax: 817-272-5006, E-mail: poster@uta.edu. *Application contact:* Dr. Mary Schira, Graduate Advisor & Associate Dean, 817-272-2329, Fax: 817-272-2065, E-mail: schira@uta.edu.

The University of Texas at El Paso, Graduate School, School of Nursing, El Paso, TX 79968-0001. Offers evidence-based practice (Certificate); family nurse practitioner (MSN); health care leadership and management (Certificate); interdisciplinary health sciences (PhD); nurse clinical specialist (MSN); nursing (Post-Master's Certificate); nursing systems management (MSN). *Accreditation:* AACN. *Students:* 153 (124 women); includes 100 minority (11 African Americans, 1 American Indian/Alaska Native, 6 Asian Americans or Pacific Islanders, 82 Hispanic Americans), 5 international. Average age 34. 91 applicants, 49% accepted. In 2009, 33 master's awarded. *Degree requirements:* For master's, thesis optional; for doctorate, thesis/dissertation. *Entrance requirements:* For master's, GRE, minimum GPA of 3.0, course work in statistics, resume; for doctorate, GRE, letters of reference, relevant personal/professional experience, master's degree in health. Additional exam requirements/recommendations for international students: Required—TOEFL; Recommended—IELTS. *Application deadline:* For fall admission, 8/1 for domestic students, 3/1 for international students; for spring admission, 11/1 for domestic students, 9/1 for international students. Applications are processed on a rolling basis. Application fee: $45 ($80 for international students). Electronic applications accepted. *Financial support:* In 2009–10, research assistantships with partial tuition reimbursements (averaging $18,825 per year), teaching assistantships with partial tuition reimbursements (averaging $18,000 per year) were awarded; fellowships with partial tuition reimbursements, institutionally sponsored loans, scholarships/grants, health care benefits, tuition waivers (partial), and unspecified assistantships also available. Support available to part-time students. Financial award application deadline: 3/15; financial award applicants required to submit FAFSA. *Unit head:* Dr. Elias Provencio-Vasquez, Dean, 915-747-7273, Fax: 915-747-8266, E-mail: eprovenciovasquez@utep.edu. *Application contact:* Dr. Patricia D. Witherspoon, Dean of the Graduate School, 915-747-5491, Fax: 915-747-5788, E-mail: withersp@utep.edu.

The University of Texas at Tyler, College of Nursing and Health Sciences, Program in Nursing, Tyler, TX 75799-0001. Offers nurse practitioner (MSN); nursing (PhD); nursing administration (MSN); nursing education (MSN); MSN/MBA. *Accreditation:* AACN. Part-time and evening/weekend programs available. Postbaccalaureate distance learning degree programs offered (no on-campus study). *Faculty:* 15 full-time (all women). *Students:* 26 full-time (24 women), 158 part-time (139 women); includes 36 minority (17 African Americans, 3 American Indian/Alaska Native, 7 Asian Americans or Pacific Islanders, 9 Hispanic Americans). Average age 40. 51 applicants, 57% accepted, 15 enrolled. In 2009, 32 master's awarded. *Degree requirements:* For master's, comprehensive exam (for some programs), thesis (for some programs); for doctorate, thesis/dissertation. *Entrance requirements:* For master's, GRE General Test or MAT, GMAT, minimum undergraduate GPA of 3.0, course work in statistics, RN license, BSN. Additional exam requirements/recommendations for international students: Required—TOEFL (minimum score 79 computer-based). *Application deadline:* For fall admission, 8/17 priority date for domestic students, 7/1 priority date for international students; for spring admission, 12/21 priority date for domestic students, 11/1 priority date for international students. Applications are processed on a rolling basis. Application fee: $25 ($50 for international students). Electronic applications accepted. *Expenses:* Tuition, state resident: part-time $665 per semester hour. Tuition, nonresident: part-time $942 per semester hour. Part-time tuition and fees vary according to degree level and program. *Financial support:* In 2009–10, 15 students received support, including 1 fellowship (averaging $10,000 per year), 3 research assistantships (averaging $2,200 per year); institutionally sponsored loans and scholarships/grants also available. Financial award application deadline: 7/1; financial award applicants required to submit FAFSA. *Faculty research:* Psychosocial adjustment, aging, support/commitment of caregivers, psychological abuse and violence, hope/hopelessness, professional values, end of life care, suicidology, clinical supervision, workforce retention and issues, global health issues, health promotion. Total annual research expenditures: $258,200. *Unit head:* Dr. Susan Yarbrough, Assistant Dean, 903-566-1220, E-mail: syarbrou@mail.uttyl.edu. *Application contact:* Dr. Susan Yarbrough.

The University of Texas–Pan American, College of Health Sciences and Human Services, Department of Nursing, Edinburg, TX 78539. Offers adult health nursing (MSN); family nurse practitioner (MSN); pediatric nurse practitioner (MSN). *Accreditation:* AACN. Part-time and evening/weekend programs available. *Degree requirements:* For master's, thesis optional. *Entrance requirements:* For master's, Texas RN licensure, undergraduate physical statistic course. Additional exam requirements/recommendations for international students: Required—TOEFL (minimum score 550 paper-based). Electronic applications accepted. *Expenses:* Contact institution. *Faculty research:* Health promotion, adolescent pregnancy, herbal and nontraditional approaches, healing touch stress.

The University of Toledo, College of Graduate Studies, College of Nursing, Toledo, OH 43606-3390. Offers adult health practitioner/clinical nurse specialist (MSN); adult nurse practitioner (Certificate); entry-level nursing initiative (GEMINI) (MSN); family nurse practitioner (MSN, Certificate); nursing education (Certificate); pediatric nurse practitioner (Certificate); pediatric nurse practitioner/clinical nurse specialist (MSN); RN to MSN (MSN). *Accreditation:* AACN. Part-time programs available. *Degree requirements:* For master's, thesis or scholarly project. *Entrance requirements:* For master's, GRE General Test, BS in nursing, minimum undergraduate GPA of 3.0. *Expenses:* Contact institution. *Faculty research:* Sexuality issues, prenatal testing, health care of homeless, nursing education, chronic/acute pain, eating disorders, low birth weight infants.

University of Victoria, Faculty of Graduate Studies, Faculty of Human and Social Development, School of Nursing, Victoria, BC V8W 2Y2, Canada. Offers advanced nursing practice (advanced practice leadership option) (MN); advanced nursing practice (nurse educator option) (MN); advanced nursing practice (nurse practitioner option) (MN); nursing (PhD). Part-time programs available. Postbaccalaureate distance learning degree programs offered (no on-campus study). *Entrance requirements:* Additional exam requirements/recommendations for international students: Required—TOEFL (minimum score 575 paper-based; 233 computer-based), IELTS (minimum score 7). Electronic applications accepted.

University of Wisconsin–Eau Claire, College of Nursing and Health Sciences, Program in Nursing, Eau Claire, WI 54702-4004. Offers adult health clinical nurse specialist (MSN); adult health in administration (MSN); adult health in education (MSN); adult health nurse practitioner (MSN); family health in administration (MSN); family health in education (MSN); family health nurse practitioner (MSN). Part-time programs available. *Faculty:* 15 full-time (14 women). *Students:* 34 full-time (32 women), 55 part-time (51 women); includes 1 minority (Asian American or Pacific Islander). Average age 35. 58 applicants, 59% accepted, 2 enrolled. In 2009, 32 master's awarded. Terminal master's awarded for partial completion of doctoral program. *Degree requirements:* For master's, thesis optional, 500-600 hours clinical practicum, oral and written exams. *Entrance requirements:* For master's, Wisconsin RN license, minimum GPA of 3.0, undergraduate statistics, course work in health assessment. Additional exam requirements/recommendations for international students: Required—TOEFL (minimum score 550 paper-based; 213 computer-based; 79 iBT). *Application deadline:* For fall admission, 1/15 priority date for domestic students, 6/1 priority date for international students; for spring admission, 11/1 priority date for international students. Applications are processed on a rolling basis. Application fee: $56. Electronic applications accepted. *Expenses:* Tuition, state resident: full-time $6705.90; part-time $372.55 per credit. Tuition, nonresident: full-time $16,771; part-time $931.74 per credit. Required fees: $925.50; $51.19 per credit. One-time fee: $56. *Financial support:* In 2009–10, 50 students received support, including 2 fellowships (averaging $500 per year); Federal Work-Study and unspecified assistantships also available. Financial award application deadline: 3/1; financial award applicants required to submit FAFSA. *Unit head:* Dr. Mary Zwygart-Stauffacher, Interim Dean, 715-836-5287, Fax: 715-836-5925, E-mail: zwygarmc@uwec.edu. *Application contact:* Kristina Anderson, Director of Admissions, 715-836-5415, Fax: 715-836-2409, E-mail: admissions@uwec.edu.

University of Wisconsin–Milwaukee, Graduate School, College of Nursing, Milwaukee, WI 53201-0413. Offers family nursing practitioner (Post Master's Certificate); health professional education (Certificate); nursing (MS, PhD); public health (Certificate). *Accreditation:* AACN. Part-time programs available. *Faculty:* 34 full-time (33 women). *Students:* 159 full-time (148 women), 118 part-time (100 women); includes 32 minority (15 African Americans, 1 American Indian/Alaska Native, 11 Asian Americans or Pacific Islanders, 5 Hispanic Americans), 6 international. Average age 40. 123 applicants, 54% accepted, 37 enrolled. In 2009, 53 master's, 13 doctorates awarded. *Degree requirements:* For master's, thesis; for doctorate, thesis/dissertation. *Entrance requirements:* For master's, GRE General Test or MAT, autobiographical sketch; for doctorate, GRE, minimum GPA of 3.2. Additional exam requirements/recommendations for international students: Required—TOEFL (minimum score 550 paper-based; 79 iBT), IELTS (minimum score 6.5). *Application deadline:* For fall admission, 1/1 priority date for domestic students; for spring admission, 9/1 for domestic students. Applications are processed on a rolling basis. Application fee: $45 ($75 for international students). *Expenses:* Tuition, state resident: full-time $8800. Tuition, nonresident: full-time $20,760. Tuition and fees vary according to program and reciprocity agreements. *Financial support:* In 2009–10, 8 teaching assistantships were awarded; career-related internships or fieldwork, Federal Work-Study, and unspecified assistantships also available. Support available to part-time students. Financial award application deadline: 4/15. Total annual research expenditures: $3.4 million. *Unit head:* Dr. Sally Lundeen, Dean, 414-229-4189, E-mail: slundeen@uwm.edu. *Application contact:* Ellen K. Murphy, Representative, 414-229-5468.

University of Wisconsin–Oshkosh, The Office of Graduate Studies, College of Nursing, Oshkosh, WI 54901. Offers adult health and illness (MSN); family nurse practitioner (MSN). *Accreditation:* AACN. Part-time programs available. *Degree requirements:* For master's, thesis or alternative, clinical paper. *Entrance requirements:* For master's, RN license, BSN, previous course work in statistics and health assessment, minimum undergraduate GPA of 3.0, letters of recommendation. Additional exam requirements/recommendations for international students: Required—TOEFL (minimum score 550 paper-based; 213 computer-based; 79 iBT). Electronic applications accepted. *Faculty research:* Adult health and illness, nurse practitioners practice, health care service, advanced practitioner roles, natural alternative complementary healthcare.

Vanderbilt University, School of Nursing, Nashville, TN 37240. Offers adult acute care nurse practitioner (MSN); adult nurse practitioner/cardiovascular disease management and prevention (MSN); adult nurse practitioner/palliative care (MSN); clinical management (clinical nurse leader/specialist) (MSN); emergency nurse practitioner (MSN); family nurse practitioner (MSN); gerontology nurse practitioner (MSN); health systems management (MSN); neonatal nurse practitioner (MSN); nurse midwifery (MSN); nurse midwifery/family nurse practitioner (MSN); nursing informatics (MSN); nursing practice (DNP); nursing science (PhD); nutrition (MS); pediatric acute care nurse practitioner (MSN); pediatric primary care nurse practitioner (MSN); psychiatric-mental health nurse practitioner (MSN); women's health nurse practitioner (MSN), including urogynecology; women's health nurse practitioner/adult nurse practitioner (MSN);

Family Nurse Practitioner Studies

Vanderbilt University (continued)
MSN/M Div; MSN/MTS. *Accreditation:* ACNM/DOA; NLN (one or more programs are accredited). Part-time programs available. Postbaccalaureate distance learning degree programs offered (minimal on-campus study). *Faculty:* 118 full-time (102 women), 429 part-time/adjunct (309 women). *Students:* 484 full-time (435 women), 319 part-time (284 women); includes 84 minority (55 African Americans, 4 American Indian/Alaska Native, 10 Asian Americans or Pacific Islanders, 15 Hispanic Americans), 16 international. Average age 32. 900 applicants, 65% accepted, 433 enrolled. In 2009, 303 master's, 1 doctorate awarded. *Degree requirements:* For doctorate, comprehensive exam, thesis/dissertation. *Entrance requirements:* For master's, GRE General Test, minimum B average in undergraduate course work, 3 letters of recommendation; for doctorate, GRE General Test, interview, 3 letters of recommendation from doctorally-prepared faculty, MSN, essay. Additional exam requirements/recommendations for international students: Required—TOEFL. *Application deadline:* For fall admission, 12/1 priority date for domestic and international students. Applications are processed on a rolling basis. Application fee: $50. *Expenses:* Contact institution. *Financial support:* In 2009–10, 389 students received support, including 1 research assistantship (averaging $5,000 per year); teaching assistantships, scholarships/grants, health care benefits, and tuition waivers also available. Support available to part-time students. Financial award application deadline: 3/15; financial award applicants required to submit FAFSA. *Faculty research:* Lymphedema, palliative care and bereavement, health services research including workforce, safety and quality of care, gerontology, better birth outcomes including nutrition. Total annual research expenditures: $1.4 million. *Unit head:* Dr. Colleen Conway-Welch, Dean, 615-343-8776, Fax: 615-343-7711, E-mail: colleen.conway-welch@vanderbilt.edu. *Application contact:* Cheryl Feldner, Assistant Director of Admissions, 615-322-3800, Fax: 615-343-0333, E-mail: cheryl.feldner@vanderbilt.edu.

Villanova University, College of Nursing, Villanova, PA 19085-1699. Offers adult nurse practitioner (MSN, Post Master's Certificate); family nurse practitioner (MSN, Post Master's Certificate); health care administration (MSN); nurse anesthetist (MSN, Post Master's Certificate); nursing (PhD); nursing education (MSN, Post Master's Certificate); pediatric nurse practitioner (MSN, Post Master's Certificate). *Accreditation:* AACN; AANA/CANAEP. Part-time programs available. Postbaccalaureate distance learning degree programs offered (minimal on-campus study). *Faculty:* 15 full-time (all women), 3 part-time/adjunct (2 women). *Students:* 58 full-time (53 women), 188 part-time (164 women); includes 29 minority (13 African Americans, 1 American Indian/Alaska Native, 13 Asian Americans or Pacific Islanders, 2 Hispanic Americans), 3 international. Average age 33. 171 applicants, 70% accepted, 89 enrolled. In 2009, 32 master's, 1 doctorate awarded. *Degree requirements:* For master's, independent study project; for doctorate, comprehensive exam, thesis/dissertation. *Entrance requirements:* For master's, GRE or MAT, BSN, 1 year of recent nursing experience, physical assessment, course work in statistics; for doctorate, GRE, MSN. Additional exam requirements/recommendations for international students: Required—TOEFL. *Application deadline:* For fall admission, 7/1 priority date for domestic students, 7/1 for international students; for spring admission, 11/1 priority date for domestic students, 11/1 for international students. Applications are processed on a rolling basis. Application fee: $50. *Expenses:* Contact institution. *Financial support:* In 2009–10, 53 students received support, including 5 teaching assistantships with full tuition reimbursements available (averaging $13,100 per year); institutionally sponsored loans, scholarships/grants, traineeships, tuition waivers (full), and unspecified assistantships also available. Financial award application deadline: 3/1; financial award applicants required to submit FAFSA. *Faculty research:* Genetics, ethics, cognitive development of students, women with disabilities, nursing leadership. *Unit head:* Dr. Marguerite K. Schlag, Assistant Dean and Director, Graduate Program, 610-519-4907, Fax: 610-519-7650, E-mail: marguerite.schlag@villanova.edu. *Application contact:* Dean, Graduate School of Liberal Arts and Sciences.

Virginia Commonwealth University, Graduate School, School of Nursing, Nurse Practitioner Program, Richmond, VA 23284-9005. Offers MS, Certificate.

Wagner College, Division of Graduate Studies, Department of Nursing, Program in Family Nurse Practitioner, Staten Island, NY 10301-4495. Offers Certificate. Part-time and evening/weekend programs available. *Entrance requirements:* For degree, master's degree in nursing from an NLN-accredited program, minimum GPA of 3.0. *Expenses:* Tuition: Full-time $15,570; part-time $865 per credit. Required fees: $2.

Western University of Health Sciences, College of Graduate Nursing, Pomona, CA 91766-1854. Offers family nurse practitioner (MSN). *Accreditation:* AACN. Part-time and evening/weekend programs available. Postbaccalaureate distance learning degree programs offered. *Degree requirements:* For master's, culminating project. *Entrance requirements:* For master's, GRE General Test, BSN or bachelor's degree in related field, nurse practitioner certificate, minimum GPA of 3.0, interview, letters of recommendation. Additional exam requirements/recommendations for international students: Required—TOEFL. *Expenses:* Contact institution.

Westminster College, School of Nursing and Health Sciences, Salt Lake City, UT 84105-3697. Offers family nurse practitioner (MSN); nurse anesthesia (MSNA); nurse education (MSNED); nursing (MSN); public health (MPH). *Accreditation:* AACN; AANA/CANAEP. *Faculty:* 11 full-time (6 women), 12 part-time/adjunct (6 women). *Students:* 77 full-time (54 women), 49 part-time (16 women); includes 11 minority (3 African Americans, 6 Asian Americans or Pacific Islanders, 2 Hispanic Americans), 2 international. Average age 34. 152 applicants, 57% accepted, 48 enrolled. In 2009, 23 master's awarded. *Degree requirements:* For master's, clinical practicum, 504 clinical practice hours. *Entrance requirements:* For master's, GRE, resume, Utah RN license in good standing, minimum GPA of 3.0, 3 letters of reference, BSN from accredited nursing program, proof of clear state and federal background check, drug test results, personal interview, current PALS certification, current ACLS certification. Additional exam requirements/recommendations for international students: Required—TOEFL (minimum score 600 paper-based; 250 computer-based; 100 iBT). *Application deadline:* Applications are processed on a rolling basis. Application fee: $40. Electronic applications accepted. *Expenses:* Contact institution. *Financial support:* In 2009–10, 60 students received support. Career-related internships or fieldwork and tuition remission available. Support available to part-time students. Financial award applicants required to submit FAFSA. *Faculty research:* Emotional intelligence, graduate faculty mentorship, parish nursing roles in women's disease prevention, psychiatric nursing students' self-assessment of therapeutic relationships, psychosocial nurse practitioner's self-assessment of therapeutic relationships, curriculum simulation. *Unit head:* Dr. Sheryl Steadman, Dean, 801-832-2164, Fax: 801-832-3110, E-mail: ssteadman@westminstercollege.edu. *Application contact:* Joel Bauman, Vice President of Enrollment Services, 801-832-2200, Fax: 801-832-3101, E-mail: admission@westminstercollege.edu.

Wichita State University, Graduate School, College of Health Professions, School of Nursing, Wichita, KS 67260. Offers clinical nurse specialist (MSN); nurse midwifery (MSN); nurse practitioner (MSN); nursing and healthcare systems administration (MSN); nursing practice (DNP); MSN/MBA. *Accreditation:* AACN. Part-time programs available. *Expenses:* Tuition, state resident: full-time $4247; part-time $235.95 per credit hour. Tuition, nonresident: full-time $11,171; part-time $620.60 per credit hour. Required fees: $34; $3.60 per credit hour. $17 per term. Tuition and fees vary according to campus/location and program. *Faculty research:* Adolescent pregnancy, alcoholism, arthritis and chronic disease, health practices of elderly, diabetes. *Unit head:* Dr. Mary Koehn, Chairperson, 316-978-3610, Fax: 316-978-3025, E-mail: mary.koehn@wichita.edu. *Application contact:* Dr. Mary Koehn, Chairperson, 316-978-3610, Fax: 316-978-3025, E-mail: mary.koehn@wichita.edu.

Wilmington University, College of Health Professions, New Castle, DE 19720-6491. Offers adult nurse practitioner (MSN); family nurse practitioner (MSN); gerontology (MSN); leadership (MSN); nursing (MSN); women's nurse practitioner (MSN). *Accreditation:* AACN. Part-time programs available. *Degree requirements:* For master's, thesis. *Entrance requirements:* For master's, BSN, RN license, interview, 3 letters of recommendation. Additional exam requirements/recommendations for international students: Required—TOEFL (minimum score 500 paper-based; 173 computer-based). Electronic applications accepted. *Faculty research:* Outcomes assessment, student writing ability.

Winona State University, College of Nursing and Health Sciences, Winona, MN 55987-5838. Offers adult nurse practitioner (MS, Post Master's Certificate); clinical nurse specialist (MS, Post Master's Certificate); family nurse practitioner (MS, Post Master's Certificate); nurse administrator (MS); nurse educator (MS, Post Master's Certificate); nursing (DNP). *Accreditation:* AACN. Part-time programs available. Postbaccalaureate distance learning degree programs offered (no on-campus study). *Degree requirements:* For master's, thesis; for doctorate, capstone. *Entrance requirements:* For master's, GRE (if GPA less than 3.0). Additional exam requirements/recommendations for international students: Required—TOEFL (minimum score 550 paper-based). *Faculty research:* Job satisfaction; nursing diagnoses; dehydration among elderly; correlates to functional status in elderly.

Wright State University, School of Graduate Studies, College of Nursing and Health, Program in Nursing, Dayton, OH 45435. Offers acute care nurse practitioner (MS); administration of nursing and health care systems (MS); adult health (MS); child and adolescent health (MS); community health (MS); family nurse practitioner (MS); nurse practitioner (MS); school nurse (MS); MBA/MS. *Accreditation:* AACN. Part-time and evening/weekend programs available. *Degree requirements:* For master's, thesis or alternative. *Entrance requirements:* For master's, GRE General Test, BSN from NLN-accredited college, Ohio RN license. Additional exam requirements/recommendations for international students: Required—TOEFL. *Faculty research:* Clinical nursing and health, teaching, caring, pain administration, informatics and technology.

Forensic Nursing

Boston College, William F. Connell School of Nursing, Chestnut Hill, MA 02467-3800. Offers adult health nursing (MS); community health nursing (MS); family health (MS); forensic nursing (MS); gerontology (MS); maternal/child health nursing (MS), including pediatric and women's health; nurse anesthesia (MS); nursing (PhD); palliative care (MS), including adult and pediatric; psychiatric-mental health nursing (MS); MBA/MS; MS/MA; MS/PhD. *Accreditation:* AACN; AANA/CANAEP (one or more programs are accredited). Part-time programs available. *Faculty:* 48 full-time (46 women), 31 part-time/adjunct (29 women). *Students:* 183 full-time (169 women), 147 part-time (140 women); includes 36 minority (15 African Americans, 2 American Indian/Alaska Native, 17 Asian Americans or Pacific Islanders, 2 Hispanic Americans), 7 international. Average age 29. 347 applicants, 53% accepted, 103 enrolled. In 2009, 79 master's, 7 doctorates awarded. *Degree requirements:* For master's, comprehensive exam, research project; for doctorate, comprehensive exam, thesis/dissertation, computer literacy exam or foreign language. *Entrance requirements:* For master's, bachelor's degree in nursing; for doctorate, GRE General Test, master's degree in nursing. Additional exam requirements/recommendations for international students: Required—TOEFL (minimum score 550 paper-based; 213 computer-based). *Application deadline:* For fall admission, 11/1 for domestic and international students; for winter admission, 12/31 for domestic and international students; for spring admission, 9/15 for domestic and international students. Applications are processed on a rolling basis. Application fee: $40. Electronic applications accepted. *Financial support:* In 2009–10, 83 students received support, including 12 fellowships with partial tuition reimbursements available (averaging $15,000 per year), 5 teaching assistantships (averaging $13,746 per year); research assistantships, Federal Work-Study, institutionally sponsored loans, scholarships/grants, traineeships, health care benefits, and tuition waivers (partial) also available. Support available to part-time students. Financial award application deadline: 3/1; financial award applicants required to submit FAFSA. *Faculty research:* Ethics, reduction of risk behaviors, support during chronic illness, violence, gerontology. Total annual research expenditures: $1.4 million. *Unit head:* Dr. Susan Gennaro, Dean, 617-552-4251, Fax: 617-552-0931, E-mail: susan.gennaro@bc.edu. *Application contact:* MaryBeth Crowley, Graduate Programs Assistant, 617-552-4928, Fax: 617-552-2121, E-mail: csongrad@bc.edu.

Cleveland State University, College of Graduate Studies, College of Education and Human Services, School of Nursing, Cleveland, OH 44115. Offers clinical nursing leader (MSN); executive track (MSN); forensic nursing (MSN); nursing education (MSN); population health nursing (MSN); MSN/MBA. *Accreditation:* AACN. Part-time programs available. *Degree requirements:* For master's, thesis or alternative, portfolio, population health project. *Entrance requirements:* For master's, RN license, BSN, course work in statistics. Additional exam requirements/recommendations for international students: Required—TOEFL (minimum score 525 paper-based; 197 computer-based), IELTS (minimum score 6). Electronic applications accepted. *Faculty research:* Diabetes management, African-American elders medication compliance, risk in home visiting, suffering, COPD and stress.

Duquesne University, School of Nursing, Master of Science in Nursing Program, Pittsburgh, PA 15282-0001. Offers family nurse practitioner (MSN); forensic nursing (MSN); nursing education (MSN). *Accreditation:* AACN. Part-time and evening/weekend programs available. Postbaccalaureate distance learning degree programs offered (minimal on-campus study). *Faculty:* 15 full-time (13 women), 4 part-time/adjunct (all women). *Students:* 73 full-time (69 women), 43 part-time (42 women); includes 8 minority (6 African Americans, 2 Asian Americans or Pacific Islanders). 131 applicants, 32% accepted, 36 enrolled. In 2009, 39 master's awarded. *Degree requirements:* For master's, culminating paper. *Entrance requirements:* For master's, current RN license; BSN with minimum GPA of 3.0; minimum of 1 year full-time work experience as RN prior to registration in clinical or specialty course. Additional exam requirements/recommendations for international students: Required—TOEFL (minimum score 600 paper-based; 80 iBT). *Application deadline:* For fall admission, 4/1 for domestic and international students. *Expenses:* Tuition: Part-time $851 per credit. Required fees: $81 per credit. *Financial support:* In 2009–10, 38 students received support, including 4 research assistantships with partial tuition reimbursements available (averaging $2,250 per year), 4 teaching assistantships with partial tuition reimbursements available (averaging $1,075 per year); institutionally sponsored loans, scholarships/grants, traineeships, and tuition waivers (partial) also available. Support available to part-time students. Financial award application deadline: 7/1. *Faculty research:* Vulnerable populations, social justice, cultural competence, health disparities, wellness within chronic illness. Total annual research expenditures: $457,857. *Unit head:* Dr. Joan Such Lockhart, Professor and Associate Dean of Academic Affairs, 412-396-6540, Fax: 412-396-1821, E-mail: lockhart@duq.edu. *Application contact:* Susan Hardner, Nurse Recruiter, 412-396-4945, Fax: 412-396-6346, E-mail: nursing@duq.edu.

Duquesne University, School of Nursing, Post Master's Certificate Program, Pittsburgh, PA 15282-0001. Offers family nurse practitioner (Post-Master's Certificate); forensic nursing (Post-Master's Certificate); transcultural/international nursing (Post-Master's Certificate). Part-time and evening/weekend programs available. Postbaccalaureate distance learning degree programs offered (minimal on-campus study). *Faculty:* 9 full-time (8 women), 1 (woman) part-time/

adjunct. *Students:* 1 full-time (0 women), 5 part-time (all women). 18 applicants, 39% accepted, 5 enrolled. In 2009, 4 Post-Master's Certificates awarded. *Entrance requirements:* For degree, current RN license, BSN, MSN. Additional exam requirements/recommendations for international students: Required—TOEFL (minimum score 600 paper-based; 80 iBT). *Application deadline:* For fall admission, 4/1 for domestic and international students. *Expenses:* Tuition: Part-time $851 per credit. Required fees: $81 per credit. *Financial support:* In 2009–10, 3 students received support. Institutionally sponsored loans, scholarships/grants, traineeships, and tuition waivers (partial) available. Support available to part-time students. Financial award application deadline: 7/1. *Faculty research:* Vulnerable populations, social justice, cultural competence, health disparities, wellness within chronic illness. *Unit head:* Dr. Joan Such Lockhart, Professor and Associate Dean of Academic Affairs, 412-396-6540, Fax: 412-396-1821, E-mail: lockhart@duq.edu. *Application contact:* Susan Hardner, Nurse Recruiter, 412-396-4945, Fax: 412-396-6346, E-mail: nursing@duq.edu.

Fitchburg State University, Division of Graduate and Continuing Education, Program in Forensic Nursing, Fitchburg, MA 01420-2697. Offers MS, Certificate. *Accreditation:* AACN. Part-time and evening/weekend programs available. Postbaccalaureate distance learning degree programs offered (no on-campus study). *Students:* 25 part-time (all women); includes 2 African Americans. Average age 39. 9 applicants, 100% accepted, 7 enrolled. In 2009, 1 master's awarded. *Entrance requirements:* For master's, GRE General Test or MAT, bachelor's degree in nursing from accredited program, 1 year of clinical practice, nursing license, letters of recommendation, resume. Additional exam requirements/recommendations for international students: Required—TOEFL (minimum score 550 paper-based; 213 computer-based; 79 iBT). *Application deadline:* Applications are processed on a rolling basis. Application fee: $25 ($50 for international students). *Expenses:* Tuition, area resident: Part-time $150 per credit. Tuition, state resident: part-time $150 per credit. Tuition, nonresident: part-time $150 per credit. Required fees: $120 per credit. *Financial support:* In 2009–10, research assistantships with partial tuition reimbursements (averaging $5,500 per year); Federal Work-Study, scholarships/grants, and unspecified assistantships also available. Support available to part-time students. Financial award application deadline: 3/1; financial award applicants required to submit FAFSA. *Unit head:* Dr. Rachel Boersma, Chair, 978-665-3036, Fax: 978-665-3658, E-mail: gce@fsc.edu. *Application contact:* Director of Admissions, 978-665-3144, Fax: 978-665-4540, E-mail: admissions@fsc.edu.

George Mason University, College of Health and Human Services, School of Nursing, Fairfax, VA 22030. Offers forensic nursing (Certificate); nursing (MSN, PhD); nursing administration (Certificate); nursing education (Certificate); nursing practice (DNP). *Faculty:* 36 full-time (all women), 52 part-time/adjunct (49 women). *Students:* 47 full-time (46 women), 275 part-time (259 women); includes 90 minority (43 African Americans, 3 American Indian/Alaska Native, 33 Asian Americans or Pacific Islanders, 11 Hispanic Americans), 10 international. Average age 42. 176 applicants, 66% accepted, 77 enrolled. In 2009, 72 master's, 8 doctorates, 3 other advanced degrees awarded. *Degree requirements:* For master's, comprehensive exam (for some programs), thesis in clinical classes; for doctorate, comprehensive exam (for some programs), thesis/dissertation (for some programs). *Entrance requirements:* For master's, resume, 2 recommendation letters, transcripts, nursing license, goal statement, at least 1 year working in the nursing field; for doctorate, resume, 3 recommendation letters, nursing license, at least 1 year of work in the nursing field. Additional exam requirements/recommendations for international students: Required—TOEFL. *Application deadline:* For fall admission, 4/1 priority date for domestic students; for spring admission, 11/1 priority date for domestic students. Applications are processed on a rolling basis. Application fee: $75. Electronic applications accepted. *Expenses:* Tuition, state resident: full-time $7568; part-time $315.33 per credit hour. Tuition, nonresident: full-time $21,704; part-time $904.33 per credit hour. Required fees: $2184; $91 per credit hour. *Financial support:* In 2009–10, 2 students received support, including 2 research assistantships with full and partial tuition reimbursements available (averaging $4,186 per year); Federal Work-Study, scholarships/grants, unspecified assistantships, and nurse faculty loan, health care benefits (full-time research or teaching assistantship recipients) also available. Support available to part-time students. Financial award application deadline: 3/1; financial award applicants required to submit FAFSA. Total annual research expenditures: $270,863. *Unit head:* Dr. Shirley S. Travis, Dean, 703-993-1918. *Application contact:* Janice Lee-Beverly, Program Support, 703-993-1947, E-mail: jleebev1@gmu.edu.

Monmouth University, Graduate School, The Marjorie K. Unterberg School of Nursing and Health Studies, West Long Branch, NJ 07764-1898. Offers adult nurse practitioner (MSN); adult psychiatric and mental health advanced practice nursing (MSN, Post-Master's Certificate); advanced practice nursing (Post-Master's Certificate); family nurse practitioner (MSN, Post-Master's Certificate); forensic nursing (MSN, Certificate); nursing (MSN); nursing administration (MSN, Post-Master's Certificate); nursing education (MSN, Post-Master's Certificate); school nursing (MSN, Certificate). *Accreditation:* AACN. Part-time and evening/weekend programs available. *Faculty:* 11 full-time (all women), 2 part-time/adjunct (both women). *Students:* 15 full-time (14 women), 183 part-time (178 women); includes 51 minority (14 African Americans, 3 American Indian/Alaska Native, 26 Asian Americans or Pacific Islanders, 8 Hispanic Americans), 1 international. Average age 41. 95 applicants, 99% accepted, 44 enrolled. In 2009, 36 master's awarded. *Degree requirements:* For master's, practicum (for some tracks). *Entrance requirements:* For master's, GRE General Test, RN license, 1 year of work experience, minimum undergraduate GPA of 2.75. Additional exam requirements/recommendations for international students: Required—TOEFL (minimum score 550 paper-based; 213 computer-based; 79 iBT), IELTS (minimum score 5), Michigan English Language Assessment Battery (minimum score 77), Cambridge A, B, C. *Application deadline:* For fall admission, 7/15 priority date for domestic students, 6/1 for international students; for spring admission, 11/15 priority date for domestic students, 11/1 for international students. Applications are processed on a rolling basis. Application fee: $50. Electronic applications accepted. *Expenses:* Tuition: Part-time $773 per credit. Required fees: $157 per semester. *Financial support:* In 2009–10, 118 students received support, including 96 fellowships (averaging $1,308 per year), 4 research assistantships (averaging $3,610 per year); career-related internships or fieldwork, scholarships/grants, and unspecified assistantships also available. Support available to part-time students. Financial award applicants required to submit FAFSA. *Faculty research:* Relationship of undergraduate GPA and GRE to succeed in a graduate nursing program. *Unit head:* Dr. Janet Mahoney, Dean, 732-571-3443, Fax: 732-263-5131, E-mail: jmahoney@monmouth.edu. *Application contact:* Kevin Roane, Director, Office of Graduate Admission, 732-571-3452, Fax: 732-263-5123, E-mail: gradadm@monmouth.edu.

University of Colorado at Colorado Springs, Graduate School, Beth-El College of Nursing and Health Sciences, Colorado Springs, CO 80933-7150. Offers adult health nurse practitioner and clinical specialist (MSN); family practitioner (MSN), including community clinical specialist, forensic clinical specialist, holistic clinical specialist; neonatal nurse practitioner and clinical specialist (MSN); nursing administration (MSN); nursing practice (DNP); women nurse practitioner (MSN). *Accreditation:* AACN. Part-time programs available. Postbaccalaureate distance learning degree programs offered (minimal on-campus study). *Faculty:* 26 full-time (21 women), 3 part-time/adjunct (all women). *Students:* 132 full-time (112 women), 81 part-time (71 women); includes 35 minority (6 African Americans, 2 American Indian/Alaska Native, 6 Asian Americans or Pacific Islanders, 21 Hispanic Americans), 3 international. Average age 36. 245 applicants, 47% accepted, 58 enrolled. In 2009, 33 master's awarded. *Degree requirements:* For master's, comprehensive exam, thesis optional; for doctorate, capstone project. *Entrance requirements:* For master's, GRE General Test or MAT, BSN, minimum GPA of 3.0, unrestricted RN license; for doctorate, interview; active RN license; MA; minimum GPA of 3.3; National Certification as NP or CNS; portfolio. Additional exam requirements/recommendations for international students: Required—TOEFL. *Application deadline:* For fall admission, 6/1 priority date for domestic students; for spring admission, 11/15 for domestic students. Application fee: $60 ($75 for international students). Electronic applications accepted. *Expenses:* Contact institution. *Financial support:* Fellowships, career-related internships or fieldwork, Federal Work-Study, and scholarships/grants available. Support available to part-time students. Financial award application deadline: 3/1; financial award applicants required to submit FAFSA. *Faculty research:* Women's health, uncertainty, empowerment, family experience in chronic illness. Total annual research expenditures: $703,545. *Unit head:* Dr. Nancy Smith, Dean, 719-255-4411, Fax: 719-255-4416, E-mail: nsmith2@uccs.edu. *Application contact:* Jackie Crouch, Graduate Recruitment Coordinator, 719-255-4493, Fax: 719-255-4416, E-mail: jcrouch@uccs.edu.

Gerontological Nursing

Allen College, Program in Nursing, Waterloo, IA 50703. Offers acute care nurse practitioner (MSN); adult nurse practitioner (MSN); adult psychiatric-mental health nurse practitioner (MSN); family nurse practitioner (MSN); gerontological nurse practitioner (MSN); health education (MSN); leadership in health care delivery (MSN). *Accreditation:* AACN; NLN. Part-time programs available. *Faculty:* 2 full-time (both women), 8 part-time/adjunct (all women). *Students:* 37 full-time (35 women), 103 part-time (99 women); includes 1 minority (Asian American or Pacific Islander). Average age 38. *Degree requirements:* For master's, thesis optional. *Entrance requirements:* For master's, minimum GPA of 3.0. Additional exam requirements/recommendations for international students: Required—TOEFL (minimum score 550 paper-based). *Application deadline:* For fall admission, 7/15 priority date for domestic students; for spring admission, 12/1 priority date for domestic students. Applications are processed on a rolling basis. Application fee: $50. Electronic applications accepted. *Expenses:* Tuition: Full-time $12,550; part-time $651 per credit hour. Required fees: $826; $65 per credit hour. One-time fee: $425. Tuition and fees vary according to course load. *Financial support:* Teaching assistantships, institutionally sponsored loans, scholarships/grants, and traineeships available. Support available to part-time students. Financial award application deadline: 8/15; financial award applicants required to submit FAFSA. *Faculty research:* Pain and aged, congestive heart failure. *Unit head:* Nancy Kramer, Dean, School of Nursing, 319-226-2040, Fax: 319-226-2070, E-mail: kramerna@ihs.org. *Application contact:* Michelle Koehn, Admissions Counselor, 319-226-2002, Fax: 319-226-2051, E-mail: koehnml@ihs.org.

Boston College, William F. Connell School of Nursing, Chestnut Hill, MA 02467-3800. Offers adult health nursing (MS); community health nursing (MS); family health (MS); forensic nursing (MS); gerontology (MS); maternal/child health nursing (MS), including pediatric and women's health; nurse anesthesia (MS); nursing (PhD); palliative care (MS), including adult and pediatric; psychiatric-mental health nursing (MS); MBA/MS; MS/MA; MS/PhD. *Accreditation:* AACN; AANA/CANAEP (one or more programs are accredited). Part-time programs available. *Faculty:* 48 full-time (46 women), 31 part-time/adjunct (29 women). *Students:* 183 full-time (169 women), 147 part-time (140 women); includes 36 minority (15 African Americans, 2 American Indian/Alaska Native, 17 Asian Americans or Pacific Islanders, 2 Hispanic Americans), 7 international. Average age 29. 347 applicants, 53% accepted, 103 enrolled. In 2009, 79 master's, 7 doctorates awarded. *Degree requirements:* For master's, comprehensive exam, research project; for doctorate, comprehensive exam, thesis/dissertation, computer literacy exam or foreign language. *Entrance requirements:* For master's, bachelor's degree in nursing; for doctorate, GRE General Test, master's degree in nursing. Additional exam requirements/recommendations for international students: Required—TOEFL (minimum score 550 paper-based; 213 computer-based). *Application deadline:* For fall admission, 11/1 for domestic and international students; for winter admission, 12/31 for domestic and international students; for spring admission, 9/15 for domestic and international students. Applications are processed on a rolling basis. Application fee: $40. Electronic applications accepted. *Financial support:* In 2009–10, 83 students received support, including 12 fellowships with partial tuition reimbursements available (averaging $15,000 per year), 5 teaching assistantships (averaging $13,746 per year); research assistantships, Federal Work-Study, institutionally sponsored loans, scholarships/grants, traineeships, health care benefits, and tuition waivers (partial) also available. Support available to part-time students. Financial award application deadline: 3/1; financial award applicants required to submit FAFSA. *Faculty research:* Ethics, reduction of risk behaviors, support during chronic illness, violence, gerontology. Total annual research expenditures: $1.4 million. *Unit head:* Dr. Susan Gennaro, Dean, 617-552-4251, Fax: 617-552-0931, E-mail: susan.gennaro@bc.edu. *Application contact:* MaryBeth Crowley, Graduate Programs Assistant, 617-552-4928, Fax: 617-552-2121, E-mail: csongrad@bc.edu.

Caribbean University, Graduate School, Bayamón, PR 00960-0493. Offers administration and supervision (MA Ed); criminal justice (MA); curriculum and instruction (MA Ed), including elementary education, English education, history education, mathematics education, primary education, science education, Spanish education; education (PhD); gerontology (MSN); human resources (MBA); museology, archiving and art history (MA Ed); neonatal pediatrics (MSN); physical education (MA Ed); special education (MA Ed). *Entrance requirements:* For master's, interview, minimum GPA of 2.5.

Case Western Reserve University, Frances Payne Bolton School of Nursing, Doctor of Nursing Practice Program, Cleveland, OH 44106. Offers acute care nurse practitioner (DNP); adult nurse practitioner (DNP); family nurse practitioner (DNP); gerontological nurse practitioner (DNP); graduate entry/pre-licensure option (DNP); medical-surgical nursing (DNP); midwifery/family nursing (DNP); neonatal nurse practitioner (DNP); pediatric nurse practitioner (DNP); post-licensure option (DNP); psychiatric-mental health nurse practitioner (DNP); women's health nurse practitioner (DNP). Graduate entry option allows baccalaureate-prepared college graduates from non-nursing backgrounds to earn certificate and MSN in addition to ND. Terminal master's awarded for partial completion of doctoral program. *Degree requirements:* For doctorate, thesis/dissertation. *Entrance requirements:* For doctorate, GRE General Test or MAT. *Faculty research:* Clinical nursing, acute care, gerontology, mental health, critical care.

Case Western Reserve University, Frances Payne Bolton School of Nursing, Master's Programs in Nursing, Nurse Practitioner Program, Cleveland, OH 44106. Offers acute care cardiovascular nursing (MSN); acute care nurse practitioner (MSN); acute care/flight nurse (MSN); adult nurse practitioner (MSN); family nurse practitioner (MSN); gerontological nurse practitioner (MSN); neonatal nurse practitioner (MSN); pediatric nurse practitioner (MSN); psychiatric-mental health nurse practitioner (MSN); women's health nurse practitioner (MSN). *Accreditation:* NLN. Part-time programs available. Postbaccalaureate distance learning degree programs offered (minimal on-campus study). *Degree requirements:* For master's, thesis optional. *Entrance requirements:* For master's, GRE General Test or MAT. Additional exam requirements/recommendations for international students: Required—TOEFL. *Faculty research:* Positive and negative mood states in parents of twins, effect of a carepath on chronic obstructive pulmonary disease home care.

The Catholic University of America, School of Nursing, Washington, DC 20064. Offers adult health specialist with functional role as nurse educator (MSN); adult nurse practitioner (MSN); community/public health nurse specialist educator (MSN); family nurse practitioner (MSN);

Gerontological Nursing

The Catholic University of America (continued)
geriatric nurse practitioner (MSN); immigrant, refugee, and global health clinical nurse specialist (MSN); nursing (DNP, PhD, Certificate); pediatric nurse practitioner (MSN); promoting healthy families in vulnerable communities (MSN); psychiatric-mental health nursing (MSN). *Accreditation:* AACN. Part-time programs available. *Faculty:* 15 full-time (all women), 43 part-time/adjunct (41 women). *Students:* 28 full-time (26 women), 75 part-time (73 women); includes 37 minority (27 African Americans, 6 Asian Americans or Pacific Islanders, 4 Hispanic Americans), 4 international. Average age 42. 84 applicants, 64% accepted, 30 enrolled. In 2009, 23 master's, 7 doctorates, 3 other advanced degrees awarded. *Degree requirements:* For master's, comprehensive exam, thesis optional; for doctorate, comprehensive exam, thesis/dissertation, minimum GPA of 3.0, oral proposal defense. *Entrance requirements:* For master's, 3 letters of recommendation, BA in nursing, RN registration, official copies of academic transcripts, some post-baccalaureate nursing experience; for doctorate, GRE General Test, BA in nursing, professional portfolio (including statements, resume, copy of RN license, 3 letters of recommendation, narrative description of clinical practice, proposal), copy of research/scholarly paper related to clinical nursing. Additional exam requirements/recommendations for international students: Required—TOEFL (minimum score 580 paper-based; 237 computer-based). *Application deadline:* For fall admission, 8/1 priority date for domestic students, 7/15 for international students; for spring admission, 12/1 priority date for domestic students, 10/15 for international students. Applications are processed on a rolling basis. Application fee: $55. Electronic applications accepted. *Expenses:* Tuition: Full-time $31,740; part-time $1245 per credit hour. Required fees: $50; $25 per semester hour. One-time fee: $425. *Financial support:* Fellowships, research assistantships, teaching assistantships, Federal Work-Study, scholarships/grants, tuition waivers (full and partial), and unspecified assistantships available. Financial award application deadline: 2/1; financial award applicants required to submit FAFSA. *Faculty research:* Community involvement in health care services, primary health care services, pediatrics, chronic illness, cardiovascular disease. Total annual research expenditures: $311,172. *Unit head:* Dr. Nalini N. Jairath, Dean, 202-319-5403, Fax: 202-319-6485, E-mail: cua-deanschoolofnursing@cua.edu. *Application contact:* Julie Schwing, Director of Graduate Admissions, 202-319-5057, Fax: 202-319-6533, E-mail: cua-admissions@cua.edu.

College of Mount Saint Vincent, School of Professional and Continuing Studies, Department of Nursing, Riverdale, NY 10471-1093. Offers adult nurse practitioner (MSN, PMC); family nurse practitioner (MSN, PMC); nurse educator (PMC); nursing administration (MSN); nursing for the adult and aged (MSN). *Accreditation:* AACN. Part-time programs available. *Entrance requirements:* For master's, BSN, interview, RN license, minimum GPA of 3.0, letters of reference. Additional exam requirements/recommendations for international students: Required—TOEFL. *Expenses:* Contact institution.

College of Staten Island of the City University of New York, Graduate Programs, Department of Nursing, Program in Gerontological Nursing, Staten Island, NY 10314-6600. Offers MS, 6th Year Certificate. Part-time and evening/weekend programs available. *Faculty:* 4 full-time (all women), 4 part-time/adjunct (3 women). *Students:* 5 part-time (all women); includes 2 minority (1 African American, 1 Asian American or Pacific Islander). Average age 46. 2 applicants, 100% accepted, 2 enrolled. In 2009, 2 other advanced degrees awarded. *Degree requirements:* For master's, thesis optional. *Entrance requirements:* For master's, minimum undergraduate GPA of 3.0 in nursing courses, New York RN license, 2 professional references; for 6th Year Certificate, master's degree in nursing. Additional exam requirements/recommendations for international students: Required—TOEFL (minimum score 550 paper-based; 213 computer-based; 79 iBT). *Application deadline:* Applications are processed on a rolling basis. Application fee: $125. Electronic applications accepted. *Expenses:* Tuition, state resident: full-time $7360; part-time $310 per credit. Tuition, nonresident: part-time $575 per credit. Required fees: $378; $113 per semester. *Financial support:* Federal Work-Study and traineeships available. Support available to part-time students. Financial award applicants required to submit FAFSA. *Unit head:* Dr. Margaret Lunney, Coordinator, 718-982-3823, Fax: 718-982-3813, E-mail: lunney@mail.csi.cuny.edu. *Application contact:* Sasha Spence, Assistant Director of Graduate Recruitment and Admissions, 718-982-2699, Fax: 718-982-2500, E-mail: spence@mail.csi.cuny.edu.

Columbia University, School of Nursing, Program in Geriatric Nurse Practitioner, New York, NY 10032. Offers MS, Adv C. *Accreditation:* AACN. Part-time programs available. *Entrance requirements:* For master's, GRE General Test, BSN, 1 year of clinical experience (preferred); for Adv C, MSN. Electronic applications accepted.

Concordia University Wisconsin, Graduate Programs, School of Health and Human Services, Program in Nursing, Mequon, WI 53097-2402. Offers family nurse practitioner (MSN); geriatric nurse practitioner (MSN); nurse educator (MSN). *Accreditation:* AACN. Postbaccalaureate distance learning degree programs offered (minimal on-campus study). *Degree requirements:* For master's, comprehensive exam, thesis or alternative. *Entrance requirements:* Additional exam requirements/recommendations for international students: Required—TOEFL. *Expenses:* Contact institution.

Duke University, School of Nursing, Durham, NC 27708-0586. Offers adult acute care (Certificate); adult cardiovascular (Certificate); adult oncology (Certificate); adult primary care (Certificate); clinical nurse specialist (MSN), including adult oncology, gerontology, neonatal, pediatric; clinical research management (MSN, Certificate); family (Certificate); gerontology (Certificate); health and nursing ministries (MSN, Certificate); health systems leadership and outcomes (Certificate); neonatal (Certificate); neonatal/pediatric in rural health (MSN, Certificate); nurse anesthetist (MSN, Certificate); nurse practitioner (MSN), including adult acute care, adult cardiovascular, adult oncology, adult primary care, family, gerontology, neonatal, pediatric, pediatric acute care; nursing (DNP, PhD); nursing and healthcare leadership (MSN); nursing education (MSN); nursing informatics (MSN, Certificate); pediatric (Certificate); pediatric acute care (Certificate); MBA/MSN; MSN/MCM. *Accreditation:* AACN; AANA/CANAEP. Part-time programs available. Postbaccalaureate distance learning degree programs offered (minimal on-campus study). *Faculty:* 45 full-time (41 women), 169 part-time/adjunct (150 women). *Students:* 213 full-time (179 women), 116 part-time (105 women); includes 37 minority (17 African Americans, 13 Asian Americans or Pacific Islanders, 7 Hispanic Americans), 9 international. Average age 36. 234 applicants, 53% accepted, 97 enrolled. In 2009, 142 master's, 24 other advanced degrees awarded. Terminal master's awarded for partial completion of doctoral program. *Degree requirements:* For master's, thesis optional; for doctorate, Capstone Project. *Entrance requirements:* For master's, GRE General Test, 1 year of nursing experience, BSN, minimum GPA of 3.0, previous course work in statistics; for doctorate, GRE for BSN prepared, BSN or MSN, minimum GPA of 3.0. Portfolio; for Certificate, MSN. Additional exam requirements/recommendations for international students: Required—TOEFL (minimum score 550 paper-based; 213 computer-based), Commission on Graduates of Foreign Nursing Schools exam. *Application deadline:* For fall admission, 7/2 priority date for domestic and international students; for spring admission, 11/15 priority date for domestic and international students. Applications are processed on a rolling basis. Application fee: $50. Electronic applications accepted. *Expenses:* Contact institution. *Financial support:* Career-related internships or fieldwork, institutionally sponsored loans, scholarships/grants, traineeships, and tuition waivers (partial) available. Support available to part-time students. Financial award application deadline: 4/1; financial award applicants required to submit FAFSA. *Faculty research:* Cardiovascular disease, caregiver skill training, data mining, prostate cancer, neonatal immune system. Total annual research expenditures: $3.5 million. *Unit head:* Dr. Catherine L. Gilliss, Dean/Vice Chancellor for Nursing Affairs, 919-684-9444, Fax: 919-684-9414, E-mail: gilli025@mc.duke.edu. *Application contact:* Bebe T. Mills, Director of Admissions, 919-684-9151, Fax: 919-668-4693, E-mail: mills031@mc.duke.edu.

Emory University, Nell Hodgson Woodruff School of Nursing, Atlanta, GA 30322-1100. Offers adult and elder health advanced practice nursing (MSN), including acute care, adult nurse practitioner, gerontological nurse practitioner; emergency nurse practitioner (MSN); family nurse practitioner (MSN); family nurse-midwife (MSN); nurse midwifery (MSN); pediatric nurse practitioner acute and primary care (MSN); public health nursing leadership (MSN); women's health nurse practitioner (MSN); women's health title x (MSN); women's health/adult health nurse practitioner (MSN); MSN/MPH. *Accreditation:* AACN; ACNM/DOA (one or more programs are accredited). Part-time programs available. *Faculty:* 30 full-time (29 women), 11 part-time/adjunct (10 women). *Students:* 110 full-time (106 women), 53 part-time (51 women); includes 49 minority (35 African Americans, 2 American Indian/Alaska Native, 10 Asian Americans or Pacific Islanders, 2 Hispanic Americans), 4 international. Average age 32. 182 applicants, 63% accepted, 86 enrolled. In 2009, 81 master's awarded. *Entrance requirements:* For master's, GRE General Test or MAT, minimum GPA of 3.0, BS in nursing from an accredited institution, RN license and additional course work, 3 letters of recommendation. Additional exam requirements/recommendations for international students: Required—TOEFL (minimum score 600 paper-based; 100 iBT). *Application deadline:* For fall admission, 1/15 priority date for domestic and international students; for spring admission, 10/1 priority date for domestic and international students. Applications are processed on a rolling basis. Application fee: $50. Electronic applications accepted. *Expenses:* Contact institution. *Financial support:* In 2009–10, 14 fellowships (averaging $28,000 per year) were awarded; career-related internships or fieldwork, Federal Work-Study, institutionally sponsored loans, and scholarships/grants also available. Support available to part-time students. Financial award application deadline: 3/1; financial award applicants required to submit CSS PROFILE or FAFSA. *Faculty research:* Older adult falls and injuries, minority health issues, cardiac symptoms and quality of life, bio-ethics and decision making, menopausal issues. *Unit head:* Dr. Linda McCauley, Dean, 404-727-7976, Fax: 404-727-9800, E-mail: linda.mccauley@emory.edu. *Application contact:* Katie Kennedy, Associate Director for Admission and Financial Aid, 404-727-7980, Fax: 404-727-8509, E-mail: admit@nursing.emory.edu.

See Close-Up on page 1613.

Gwynedd-Mercy College, School of Nursing, Gwynedd Valley, PA 19437-0901. Offers clinical nurse specialist (MSN), including gerontology, oncology, pediatrics; nurse practitioner (MSN), including adult health, pediatric health. *Accreditation:* NLN. *Degree requirements:* For master's, thesis optional. *Entrance requirements:* For master's, GRE General Test or MAT, current nursing experience, physical assessment, course work in statistics, BSN from an NLNAC accredited program, 2 letters of recommendation, personal interview. Additional exam requirements/recommendations for international students: Required—TOEFL (minimum score 575 paper-based). Electronic applications accepted. *Expenses:* Contact institution. *Faculty research:* Critical thinking, primary care, domestic violence, multiculturalism, nursing centers.

Hampton University, Graduate College, School of Nursing, Hampton, VA 23668. Offers advanced adult nursing (MS); community health nursing (MS); community mental health/psychiatric nursing (MS); family nursing (MS); gerontological nursing for the nurse practitioner (MS); pediatric nursing (MS); women's health nursing (MS). *Accreditation:* AACN; NLN. Part-time and evening/weekend programs available. *Degree requirements:* For master's, thesis optional. *Entrance requirements:* For master's, GRE General Test. *Faculty research:* Curriculum development, physical and mental assessment.

Hunter College of the City University of New York, Graduate School, Schools of the Health Professions, Hunter-Bellevue School of Nursing, Gerontological Nurse Practitioner Program, New York, NY 10021-5085. Offers MS. *Accreditation:* AACN. Part-time programs available. *Faculty:* 15 full-time (11 women). *Students:* 57 part-time (44 women); includes 28 minority (7 African Americans, 20 Asian Americans or Pacific Islanders, 1 Hispanic American). Average age 33. 44 applicants, 59% accepted, 19 enrolled. *Degree requirements:* For master's, practicum. *Entrance requirements:* For master's, minimum GPA of 3.0, New York RN license, 2 years of professional practice experience, BSN. Additional exam requirements/recommendations for international students: Required—TOEFL. *Application deadline:* For fall admission, 4/1 for domestic students, 2/1 for international students; for spring admission, 11/1 for domestic students, 9/1 for international students. Applications are processed on a rolling basis. Application fee: $125. *Expenses:* Tuition, state resident: full-time $7360; part-time $310 per credit. Required fees: $250 per semester. *Financial support:* Federal Work-Study, scholarships/grants, traineeships, and tuition waivers (partial) available. Support available to part-time students. Financial award application deadline: 5/1; financial award applicants required to submit FAFSA. *Faculty research:* Primary care of older adults, lived experiences of elders. *Unit head:* Dr. Steven Baumann, Coordinator, 212-481-4457, Fax: 212-481-5078, E-mail: sbaumann@shiva.hunter.cuny.edu. *Application contact:* William Zlata, Director for Graduate Admissions, 212-772-4482, Fax: 212-650-3336, E-mail: admissions@hunter.cuny.edu.

Independence University, Program in Nursing, Salt Lake City, UT 84107. Offers community health (MSN); gerontology (MSN); nursing administration (MSN); wellness promotion (MSN). *Expenses:* Required fees: $475 per credit. One-time fee: $100 part-time.

Kent State University, College of Nursing, Kent, OH 44242-0001. Offers adult nurse practitioner (MSN); family nurse practitioner (MSN); geriatric nurse practitioner (MSN); nursing (PhD); nursing and health care management (MSN); nursing of adults (clinical nurse specialist) (MSN); pediatric nurse practitioner (MSN); psychiatric/mental health nursing (MSN); women's health nursing (MSN). *Accreditation:* AACN. Part-time programs available. *Degree requirements:* For master's, thesis optional; for doctorate, comprehensive exam, thesis/dissertation. *Entrance requirements:* For master's, GRE (if undergraduate GPA less than 3.0), minimum GPA of 2.75; for doctorate, GRE, MSN. Additional exam requirements/recommendations for international students: Required—TOEFL. Electronic applications accepted. *Expenses:* Contact institution. *Faculty research:* Women and violence, methodological specialties, osteoporosis in women, new caregivers and the elderly.

Lehman College of the City University of New York, Division of Natural and Social Sciences, Department of Nursing, Bronx, NY 10468-1589. Offers adult health nursing (MS); nursing of older adults (MS); parent-child nursing (MS); pediatric nurse practitioner (MS). *Accreditation:* AACN. Part-time and evening/weekend programs available. *Entrance requirements:* For master's, bachelor's degree in nursing, New York RN license.

Loma Linda University, Department of Graduate Nursing, Program in Adult and Aging Family Nursing, Loma Linda, CA 92350. Offers MS. *Accreditation:* AACN. Part-time programs available. *Degree requirements:* For master's, thesis or alternative. *Entrance requirements:* For master's, GRE General Test, BSN, minimum GPA of 3.0, RN license. Additional exam requirements/recommendations for international students: Required—TOEFL. Electronic applications accepted. *Faculty research:* Coping, integration of research.

Marquette University, Graduate School, College of Nursing, Milwaukee, WI 53201-1881. Offers adult nurse practitioner (Certificate); advanced practice nursing (MSN), including adult, children, neonatal nurse practitioner, nurse-midwifery, older adult; gerontological nurse practitioner (Certificate); neonatal nurse practitioner (Certificate); nurse-midwifery (Certificate); nursing (PhD); pediatric nurse practitioner (Certificate). *Accreditation:* AACN. Part-time and evening/weekend programs available. *Faculty:* 29 full-time (27 women), 43 part-time/adjunct (all women). *Students:* 115 full-time (105 women), 209 part-time (197 women); includes 28 minority (13 African Americans, 2 American Indian/Alaska Native, 8 Asian Americans or Pacific Islanders, 5 Hispanic Americans), 1 international. Average age 32. 143 applicants, 91% accepted, 86 enrolled. In 2009, 64 master's, 10 doctorates awarded. *Degree requirements:* For master's, comprehensive exam, thesis or alternative. *Entrance requirements:* For master's, GRE General Test, BSN, Wisconsin RN license. Additional exam requirements/recommendations for international students: Required—TOEFL. Application fee: $40. *Financial support:* In 2009–10, 6 research assistantships, 1 teaching assistantship were awarded; career-related internships or fieldwork, Federal Work-Study, institutionally sponsored loans, scholarships/grants, and tuition waivers (full and partial) also available. Support available to part-time students. Financial award application deadline: 2/15. *Faculty research:* Psychosocial adjustment to chronic illness, gerontology, reminiscence, health policy: uninsured and access, hospital care delivery systems. *Unit head:* Dr. Lea Acord, Dean, 414-288-3812, Fax: 414-288-1578. *Application contact:* Dr. Judy Miller, Director of Graduate Studies, 414-288-3810, Fax: 414-288-1578.

Metropolitan State University, College of Nursing and Health Sciences, St. Paul, MN 55106-5000. Offers adult/geriatric nurse practitioner (MSN); family nurse practitioner (MSN); leadership and management (MSN); nursing (MSN, DNP); oral health care practitioner (MS); public

health nursing leadership (MSN); women's health care nurse practitioner (MSN). *Accreditation:* AACN. Part-time programs available. *Degree requirements:* For master's, thesis or alternative; for doctorate, thesis/dissertation or alternative. *Entrance requirements:* For master's, GRE General Test, minimum GPA of 3.0, RN license, B.S./BAN degree; for doctorate, minimum GPA of 3.0; RN licensure, MSN degree. Additional exam requirements/recommendations for international students: Required—TOEFL (minimum score 550 paper-based; 213 computer-based). *Expenses:* Tuition, state resident: full-time $5520; part-time $276 per credit hour. Tuition, nonresident: full-time $11,040; part-time $552 per credit hour. Required fees: $209; $10 per credit hour. Tuition and fees vary according to degree level. *Faculty research:* Women's health, gerontology.

MGH Institute of Health Professions, Graduate Programs, School of Nursing, Boston, MA 02129. Offers advanced practice nursing (MSN); gerontological nursing (MSN); nursing (DNP); pediatric nursing (MSN); psychiatric nursing (MSN); teaching and learning for health care education (Certificate); women's health nursing (MSN). *Accreditation:* AACN; NLN (one or more programs are accredited). *Faculty:* 37 full-time (33 women), 11 part-time/adjunct (10 women). *Students:* 325 full-time (275 women), 72 part-time (59 women); includes 48 minority (22 African Americans, 1 American Indian/Alaska Native, 18 Asian Americans or Pacific Islanders, 7 Hispanic Americans). Average age 31. 840 applicants, 53% accepted, 221 enrolled. In 2009, 78 master's, 12 doctorates, 45 other advanced degrees awarded. *Degree requirements:* For master's, thesis or alternative. *Entrance requirements:* For master's, GRE General Test. Additional exam requirements/recommendations for international students: Required—TOEFL (minimum score 550 paper-based; 213 computer-based; 80 iBT). *Application deadline:* For fall admission, 1/10 for domestic and international students. Application fee: $50. Electronic applications accepted. *Expenses:* Tuition: Part-time $943 per credit. Required fees: $943 per credit. Tuition and fees vary according to course load. *Financial support:* In 2009–10, 292 students received support, including 1 research assistantship (averaging $1,200 per year), 2 teaching assistantships (averaging $1,200 per year); career-related internships or fieldwork, scholarships/grants, traineeships, tuition waivers (full and partial), and unspecified assistantships also available. Support available to part-time students. Financial award application deadline: 3/1; financial award applicants required to submit FAFSA. *Faculty research:* Biobehavioral nursing, HIV/AIDS, gerontological nursing, women's health, vulnerable populations, health systems. *Unit head:* Margery Chisholm, Dean, 617-724-0480, Fax: 617-726-8022, E-mail: mchisholm@mghihp.edu. *Application contact:* Maureen Rika Judd, Manager of Admissions, 617-726-6069, Fax: 617-726-8010, E-mail: admissions@mghihp.edu.

Nazareth College of Rochester, Graduate Studies, Department of Nursing, Gerontological Nurse Practitioner Program, Rochester, NY 14618-3790. Offers MS. *Accreditation:* AACN. Part-time programs available. *Entrance requirements:* For master's, minimum GPA of 3.0, RN license.

New York University, College of Nursing, Programs in Advanced Practice Nursing, New York, NY 10012-1019. Offers advanced practice nursing: adult acute care (MS, Advanced Certificate); advanced practice nursing: adult nurse practictioner/palliative care nursing (MS); advanced practice nursing: adult nurse practitioner/holistic nurse practitioner (Advanced Certificate); advanced practice nursing: adult nurse practitioner/holistic nursing (MS); advanced practice nursing: adult nurse practitioner/palliative care nurse practitioner (Advanced Certificate); advanced practice nursing: adult primary care (MS, Advanced Certificate); advanced practice nursing: adult primary care/geriatrics (MS); advanced practice nursing: geriatrics (MS, Advanced Certificate); advanced practice nursing: mental health (MS); advanced practice nursing: mental health nursing (Advanced Certificate); advanced practice nursing: pediatrics (MS, Advanced Certificate); advanced practice nursing:adult primary care and geriatrics (Advanced Certificate); nurse midwifery (MS, Advanced Certificate); nursing administration (MS, Advanced Certificate); nursing education (MS, Advanced Certificate); nursing informatics (MS, Advanced Certificate); MS/MPH; MS/MS. *Accreditation:* AACN; ACNM/DOA. Part-time and evening/weekend programs available. *Faculty:* 17 full-time (all women), 22 part-time/adjunct (19 women). *Students:* 18 full-time (17 women), 524 part-time (485 women); includes 238 minority (90 African Americans, 119 Asian Americans or Pacific Islanders, 29 Hispanic Americans). Average age 33. 191 applicants, 89% accepted, 120 enrolled. In 2009, 117 master's, 2 other advanced degrees awarded. *Degree requirements:* For master's, thesis (for some programs). *Entrance requirements:* For master's, BS in nursing, AS in nursing with another BS/BA, interview; for Advanced Certificate, master's degree. Additional exam requirements/recommendations for international students: Required—TOEFL. *Application deadline:* For fall admission, 7/1 priority date for domestic students, 7/1 for international students; for spring admission, 12/1 for domestic and international students. Applications are processed on a rolling basis. Application fee: $75. *Expenses:* Tuition: Full-time $30,528; part-time $1272 per credit. Required fees: $2177. *Financial support:* Career-related internships or fieldwork, institutionally sponsored loans, scholarships/grants, traineeships, and tuition waivers (partial) available. Support available to part-time students. Financial award application deadline: 2/1; financial award applicants required to submit FAFSA. *Faculty research:* Elderly black diabetics, families and illness, public health nursing, parent-child nursing, health policy costs. *Unit head:* Dr. Judith Haber, Associate Dean for Graduate Programs, 212-998-9020, Fax: 212-995-3143. *Application contact:* Amy Knowles, Assistant Dean for Student Affairs and Admissions, 212-998-5333, Fax: 212-995-4302, E-mail: ak96@nyu.edu.

Oakland University, Graduate Study and Lifelong Learning, School of Nursing, Adult Gerontological Nurse Practitioner Program, Rochester, MI 48309-4401. Offers MSN, Certificate.

Oregon Health & Science University, School of Nursing, Program in Gerontological Nursing, Portland, OR 97239-3098. Offers Post Master's Certificate. *Accreditation:* AACN. *Entrance requirements:* For degree, master's or associate's degree in nursing. Tuition and fees vary according to course level, course load, degree level, program and reciprocity agreements.

Radford University, College of Graduate and Professional Studies, Waldron College of Health and Human Services, School of Nursing, Radford, VA 24142. Offers adult clinical nurse specialist (MSN); family nurse practitioner (MSN); gerontology clinical nurse specialist (MSN); nurse midwifery (MSN). *Accreditation:* AACN. Part-time programs available. *Faculty:* 15 full-time (14 women), 3 part-time/adjunct (2 women). *Students:* 15 full-time (all women), 17 part-time (all women); includes 1 minority (Asian American or Pacific Islander). Average age 35. 17 applicants, 76% accepted, 8 enrolled. In 2009, 11 master's awarded. *Degree requirements:* For master's, comprehensive exam, thesis optional. *Entrance requirements:* For master's, GRE, minimum GPA of 3.0; 3 letters of reference from professional contacts, letter of intent, resume. Additional exam requirements/recommendations for international students: Required—TOEFL (minimum score 550 paper-based; 213 computer-based; 79 iBT). *Application deadline:* For fall admission, 2/1 priority date for domestic students, 12/1 for international students. Applications are processed on a rolling basis. Application fee: $50. Electronic applications accepted. *Expenses:* Tuition, state resident: full-time $5086; part-time $211 per credit hour. Tuition, nonresident: full-time $12,608; part-time $525 per credit hour. Required fees: $2508; $105 per credit hour. *Financial support:* In 2009–10, 5 students received support, including 4 teaching assistantships with partial tuition reimbursements available (averaging $8,700 per year); career-related internships or fieldwork, Federal Work-Study, institutionally sponsored loans, scholarships/grants, and unspecified assistantships also available. Financial award application deadline: 3/1; financial award applicants required to submit FAFSA. *Unit head:* Dr. Kimberly F. Carter, Director, 540-831-7700, Fax: 540-831-7716, E-mail: kcarter@radford.edu. *Application contact:* Graduate Admissions, 540-831-5431, Fax: 540-831-6061, E-mail: gradcollege@radford.edu.

Rush University, College of Nursing, Department of Adult Health Nursing, Chicago, IL 60612-3832. Offers acute care nurse practitioner (MSN, Post-Master's Certificate); adult health nursing (DNP, PhD); adult nurse practitioner (MSN, Post-Master's Certificate); adult/gerontological nurse practitioner (MSN); anesthesia nurse practitioner (MSN, Post-Master's Certificate); critical care clinical specialist (MSN); gerontological nurse practitioner (MSN, Post-Master's Certificate); medical surgical clinical specialist (MSN). *Accreditation:* AACN; AANA/CANAEP (one or more programs are accredited). Part-time programs available. Post-baccalaureate distance learning degree programs offered (minimal on-campus study). Terminal master's awarded for partial completion of doctoral program. *Degree requirements:* For master's, capstone project; for doctorate, thesis/dissertation, DNP leadership project. *Entrance requirements:* For master's, GRE General Test (waived if nursing GPA is above 3.0 or cumulative GPA is above 3.25), interview; for doctorate, GRE General Test, interview, course work in statistics (PhD). Additional exam requirements/recommendations for international students: Required—TOEFL, TWE. Electronic applications accepted. *Faculty research:* Complementary/alternative medicine, critical care outcomes, cardiac risk reduction, Alzheimer's Disease, telehealth monitoring.

Rutgers, The State University of New Jersey, Newark, Graduate School, Program in Nursing, Newark, NJ 07102. Offers nursing (MS), including acute care of adults and aged, advanced practice in pediatric nursing, advanced practice with childbearing families, community health nursing, family nurse practitioner, primary care of adults and aged, psychiatric/mental health nursing. *Accreditation:* AACN. Part-time programs available. *Degree requirements:* For master's, comprehensive exam. *Entrance requirements:* For master's, GRE General Test, RN license, minimum B average, BS in nursing. Additional exam requirements/recommendations for international students: Required—TOEFL. Electronic applications accepted. *Faculty research:* HIV/AIDS, quality of life—MS and breast cancer, sleep patterns of cardiac patients.

Sage Graduate School, Graduate School, School of Health Sciences, Department of Nursing, Troy, NY 12180-4115. Offers adult health (MS); adult nurse practitioner (MS, Post Master's Certificate); clinical nurse leader/specialist (Post Master's Certificate); community health (MS); education and leadership (DNS); family nurse practitioner (MS, Post Master's Certificate); gerontological nurse practitioner (Post Master's Certificate); nurse administrator/executive (Post Master's Certificate); nursing (Post Master's Certificate); psychiatric mental health nurse practitioner (MS, Post Master's Certificate), including psychiatric mental health. *Accreditation:* AACN. Part-time and evening/weekend programs available. *Faculty:* 5 full-time (all women), 8 part-time/adjunct (all women). *Students:* 23 full-time (22 women), 134 part-time (129 women); includes 16 minority (6 African Americans, 1 American Indian/Alaska Native, 8 Asian Americans or Pacific Islanders, 1 Hispanic American), 1 international. Average age 42. 97 applicants, 64% accepted, 49 enrolled. In 2009, 25 master's, 3 other advanced degrees awarded. *Degree requirements:* For master's, thesis or alternative. *Entrance requirements:* For master's, BS in nursing, minimum GPA of 2.75, resume, 2 letters of recommendation. Additional exam requirements/recommendations for international students: Required—TOEFL (minimum score 550 paper-based; 213 computer-based). *Application deadline:* Applications are processed on a rolling basis. Application fee: $40. *Expenses:* Tuition: Full-time $10,620; part-time $590 per credit hour. *Financial support:* Fellowships, research assistantships, Federal Work-Study, scholarships/grants, and unspecified assistantships available. Support available to part-time students. Financial award application deadline: 3/1; financial award applicants required to submit FAFSA. *Unit head:* Dr. Glenda Kelman, Chair, 518-244-2001, E-mail: kelmag@sage.edu. *Application contact:* Wendy D. Diefendorf, Director of Graduate and Adult Admission, 518-244-2443, Fax: 518-244-6880, E-mail: diefew@sage.edu.

San Jose State University, Graduate Studies and Research, College of Applied Sciences and Arts, School of Nursing, San Jose, CA 95192-0001. Offers gerontology nurse practitioner (MS); nursing (Certificate); nursing administration (MS); nursing education (MS). *Accreditation:* AACN. Part-time and evening/weekend programs available. *Students:* 8 full-time (7 women), 45 part-time (42 women); includes 20 minority (3 African Americans, 2 American Indian/Alaska Native, 12 Asian Americans or Pacific Islanders, 3 Hispanic Americans), 2 international. Average age 43. 35 applicants, 40% accepted, 8 enrolled. In 2009, 24 master's awarded. *Degree requirements:* For master's, thesis. *Entrance requirements:* For master's, BS in nursing, RN license. *Application deadline:* For fall admission, 6/29 for domestic students; for spring admission, 11/30 for domestic students. Applications are processed on a rolling basis. Application fee: $59. Electronic applications accepted. *Financial support:* Career-related internships or fieldwork, institutionally sponsored loans, and scholarships/grants available. Support available to part-time students. Financial award applicants required to submit FAFSA. *Faculty research:* Nurse-managed clinics, computers in nursing. *Unit head:* Jayne Cohen, Director, 408-924-3132, Fax: 408-924-3135. *Application contact:* Dr. Phyllis Connolly, Graduate Coordinator, 408-924-3144.

Seattle Pacific University, MS in Nursing Program, Seattle, WA 98119-1997. Offers administration (MSN); adult/gerontology nurse practitioner (MSN); clinical nurse specialist (MSN); family nurse practitioner (MSN, Certificate); informatics (MSN); nurse educator (MSN). *Accreditation:* AACN. Part-time programs available. *Faculty:* 3 full-time (all women), 7 part-time/adjunct (6 women). *Students:* 9 full-time (8 women), 63 part-time (57 women); includes 9 minority (1 American Indian/Alaska Native, 7 Asian Americans or Pacific Islanders, 1 Hispanic American), 1 international. Average age 46. 60 applicants, 45% accepted, 27 enrolled. In 2009, 12 master's awarded. *Degree requirements:* For master's, thesis. *Application deadline:* For fall admission, 2/1 priority date for domestic students. Applications are processed on a rolling basis. Application fee: $50. Electronic applications accepted. *Expenses:* Contact institution. *Financial support:* In 2009–10, 41 students received support; fellowships, scholarships/grants available. Financial award applicants required to submit FAFSA. *Unit head:* Dr. Susan Casey, Director, 206-281-2769, Fax: 206-281-2767, E-mail: caseys@spu.edu. *Application contact:* The Grad Center, 206-281-2091.

Seton Hall University, College of Nursing, South Orange, NJ 07079-2697. Offers advanced practice in primary health care (MSN), including adult nurse practitioner, gerontological nurse practitioner, pediatric nurse practitioner; entry into practice (MSN); health systems administration (MSN, DNP); nursing (PhD); nursing case management (MSN); nursing education (MA); school nurse (MSN); MSN/MA. *Accreditation:* AACN. Part-time programs available. Post-baccalaureate distance learning degree programs offered (minimal on-campus study). *Faculty:* 10 full-time (all women), 3 part-time/adjunct (1 woman). *Students:* 46 full-time (35 women), 94 part-time (90 women); includes 22 minority (8 African Americans, 5 Asian Americans or Pacific Islanders, 9 Hispanic Americans). 92 applicants, 88% accepted, 55 enrolled. *Degree requirements:* For master's, research project; for doctorate, dissertation or scholarly project. *Entrance requirements:* For doctorate, GRE. Additional exam requirements/recommendations for international students: Required—TOEFL. *Application deadline:* For fall admission, 6/15 priority date for domestic students. Applications are processed on a rolling basis. Electronic applications accepted. *Financial support:* Institutionally sponsored loans, scholarships/grants, traineeships, tuition waivers (partial), and unspecified assistantships available. Support available to part-time students. Financial award applicants required to submit FAFSA. *Faculty research:* Parent/child, adult, and gerontological nursing; breast cancer; families of children with HIV; parish nursing. *Unit head:* Dr. Phyllis Shanley Hansell, Dean. *Application contact:* Kristyn Kent Wuillermin, Director of Strategic Alliances, Marketing and Enrollment, 973-761-9291, Fax: 973-761-9607, E-mail: kristyn.kent@shu.edu.

Southern University and Agricultural and Mechanical College, School of Nursing, Baton Rouge, LA 70813. Offers educator/administrator (PhD); family health nursing (MSN); family nurse practitioner (Post Master's Certificate); geriatric nurse practitioner/gerontology (PhD). *Accreditation:* AACN. Part-time programs available. *Degree requirements:* For master's, comprehensive exam, thesis; for doctorate, comprehensive exam, thesis/dissertation. *Entrance requirements:* For master's, GRE General Test, BSN, minimum GPA of 2.7; for doctorate, GRE General Test; for Post Master's Certificate, MSN. Additional exam requirements/recommendations for international students: Required—TOEFL (minimum score 525 paper-based; 193 computer-based). *Faculty research:* Health promotions, vulnerable populations, (community-based) cardiovascular participating research, health disparities chronic diseases, care of the elderly.

State University of New York Institute of Technology, School of Nursing and Health Systems, Program in Gerontological Nurse Practitioner, Utica, NY 13504-3050. Offers MS, CAS. *Entrance requirements:* For master's, GRE General Test (if undergraduate GPA less than, minimum GPA of 3.0 in last 30 hours of undergraduate work, bachelor's degree in nursing, 1 year professional experience, RN license, interview, 2 letters of recommendation.

Gerontological Nursing

State University of New York Institute of Technology (continued)
Additional exam requirements/recommendations for international students: Required—TOEFL (minimum score 550 paper-based; 213 computer-based). *Faculty research:* Gerontological health issues, assessment of eldercare, nursing shortages, nursing faculty shortages.

Texas Tech University Health Sciences Center, School of Nursing, Lubbock, TX 79430. Offers acute care nurse practitioner (MSN, Certificate); administration (MSN); advanced practice (DNP); education (MSN); executive leadership (DNP); family nurse practitioner (MSN, Certificate); geriatric nurse practitioner (MSN, Certificate); pediatric nurse practitioner (MSN, Certificate). *Accreditation:* AACN. Part-time programs available. Postbaccalaureate distance learning degree programs offered (minimal on-campus study). *Degree requirements:* For master's, thesis optional. *Entrance requirements:* For master's, minimum GPA of 3.0, 3 letters of reference, BSN, RN license; for Certificate, minimum GPA of 3.0, 3 letters of reference, RN license. Additional exam requirements/recommendations for international students: Required—TOEFL (minimum score 550 paper-based; 213 computer-based). *Faculty research:* Diabetes/obesity, nurse competency, disease management, intervention and measurements, health disparities.

University of Delaware, College of Health Sciences, School of Nursing, Newark, DE 19716. Offers adult nurse practitioner (MSN, PMC); cardiopulmonary clinical nurse specialist (MSN, PMC); cardiopulmonary clinical nurse specialist/adult nurse practitioner (MSN, PMC); family nurse practitioner (MSN, PMC); gerontology clinical nurse specialist (MSN, PMC); gerontology clinical nurse specialist geriatric nurse practitioner (PMC); gerontology clinical nurse specialist/ geriatric nurse practitioner (MSN); health services administration (MSN, PMC); nursing of children clinical nurse specialist (MSN, PMC); nursing of children clinical nurse specialist/ pediatric nurse practitioner (MSN, PMC); oncology/immune deficiency clinical nurse specialist (MSN, PMC); oncology/immune deficiency clinical nurse specialist/adult nurse practitioner (MSN, PMC); perinatal/women's health clinical nurse specialist (MSN, PMC); perinatal/ women's health clinical nurse specialist/women's health nurse practitioner (MSN, PMC); psychiatric nursing clinical nurse specialist (MSN, PMC). *Accreditation:* AACN; NLN (one or more programs are accredited). Part-time and evening/weekend programs available. Postbaccalaureate distance learning degree programs offered (minimal on-campus study). *Degree requirements:* For master's, thesis optional. *Entrance requirements:* For master's, BSN, interview, RN license. Electronic applications accepted. *Faculty research:* Marriage and chronic illness, health promotion, congestive heart failure patient outcomes, school nursing, diabetes in children, culture, health disparities, cardiovascular, prison nursing, oncology, public policy, child obesity, smoking and teen pregnancy, blood pressure measurements, men's health.

University of Illinois at Chicago, Graduate College, College of Nursing, Program in Nursing, Chicago, IL 60607-7128. Offers acute care clinical nurse specialist (MS); acute care nurse practitioner (MS); administrative studies in nursing (MS); adult nurse practitioner (MS); adult/ geriatric nurse practitioner (MS); advanced community health nurse specialist (MS); family nurse practitioner (MS); geriatric clinical nurse specialist (MS); geriatric nurse practitioner (MS); mental health clinical nurse specialist (MS); mental health nurse practitioner (MS); nurse midwifery (MS); occupational health/advanced community health nurse specialist (MS); occupational health/family nurse practitioner (MS); pediatric clinical nurse specialist (MS); pediatric nurse practitioner (MS); perinatal clinical nurse specialist (MS); school/advanced community health nurse specialist (MS); school/family nurse practitioner (MS); women's health nurse practitioner (MS). *Accreditation:* AACN. Part-time programs available. *Degree requirements:* For master's, thesis or alternative. *Entrance requirements:* For master's, GRE General Test, minimum GPA of 2.75. Additional exam requirements/recommendations for international students: Required—TOEFL. Electronic applications accepted.

University of Maryland, Baltimore, Graduate School, School of Nursing, Master's Program in Nursing, Baltimore, MD 21201. Offers community health nursing (MS); gerontological nursing (MS); maternal-child nursing (MS); medical-surgical nursing (MS); nurse-midwifery education (MS); nursing administration (MS); nursing education (MS); nursing health policy (MS); primary care nursing (MS); psychiatric nursing (MS); MS/MBA. *Accreditation:* AACN; AANA/CANAEP; ACNM/DOA; NLN (one or more programs are accredited). Part-time programs available. *Students:* 387 full-time (338 women), 528 part-time (491 women); includes 330 minority (230 African Americans, 3 American Indian/Alaska Native, 81 Asian Americans or Pacific Islanders, 16 Hispanic Americans), 10 international. Average age 36. 849 applicants, 40% accepted, 255 enrolled. In 2009, 264 master's awarded. *Degree requirements:* For master's, comprehensive exam (for some programs), thesis or alternative. *Entrance requirements:* For master's, GRE General Test, minimum GPA of 2.75, course work in statistics, BS in nursing. Additional exam requirements/recommendations for international students: Required—TOEFL (minimum score 550 paper-based; 80 iBT), or IELTS (minimum score 7). *Application deadline:* For fall admission, 1/15 for international students. Application fee: $50. Electronic applications accepted. *Expenses:* Tuition, state resident: full-time $7290; part-time $405 per credit hour. Tuition, nonresident: full-time $12,780; part-time $710 per credit hour. Required fees: $774; $10 per credit hour. $297 per semester. Tuition and fees vary according to course load, degree level and program. *Financial support:* Fellowships, research assistantships, teaching assistantships, career-related internships or fieldwork and traineeships available. Support available to part-time students. Financial award application deadline: 2/15; financial award applicants required to submit FAFSA. *Unit head:* Dr. Jane Kapustin, Assistant Dean, 410-706-6741, Fax: 410-706-4231. *Application contact:* Marjorie Fass, Admissions Director, 410-706-0501, Fax: 410-706-7238.

University of Massachusetts Lowell, School of Health and Environment, Department of Nursing, Program in Gerontological Nursing, Lowell, MA 01854-2881. Offers MS, Graduate Certificate. *Accreditation:* AACN. *Degree requirements:* For master's, thesis optional. *Entrance requirements:* For master's, GRE General Test, minimum GPA of 3.0, MA nursing license, interview, 3 letters of recommendation.

University of Massachusetts Worcester, Graduate School of Nursing, Worcester, MA 01655-0115. Offers adult acute/critical care nurse practitioner (MS, Post Master's Certificate); adult acute/critical care nurse practitioner and gerontological nurse practitioner (MS, Post Master's Certificate); adult primary care nurse practitioner (MS, Post Master's Certificate); adult primary care nurse practitioner and gerontological nurse practitioner (MS, Post Master's Certificate); family nurse practitioner (MS); gerontological nurse practitioner (Post Master's Certificate); nurse educator (MS); nursing (PhD). *Accreditation:* AACN. *Faculty:* 15 full-time (13 women), 31 part-time/adjunct (29 women). *Students:* 151 full-time (131 women), 6 part-time (all women); includes 14 minority (5 African Americans, 1 American Indian/Alaska Native, 5 Asian Americans or Pacific Islanders, 3 Hispanic Americans). Average age 37. 206 applicants, 34% accepted, 61 enrolled. In 2009, 62 master's, 3 doctorates awarded. *Degree requirements:* For doctorate, comprehensive exam, thesis/dissertation. *Entrance requirements:* For master's, GRE General Test, bachelor's degree, course work in statistics; for doctorate, GRE General Test, bachelor's or master's degree, RN licensure; for Post Master's Certificate, MS in nursing. Additional exam requirements/recommendations for international students: Required—TOEFL. *Application deadline:* For fall admission, 3/15 for domestic students. Applications are processed on a rolling basis. Application fee: $40 ($60 for international students). *Expenses:* Contact institution. *Financial support:* In 2009–10, 130 students received support. Scholarships/grants and traineeships available. Support available to part-time students. Financial award application deadline: 5/18; financial award applicants required to submit FAFSA. *Faculty research:* Symptom management, interventions, individual and family adjustment to chronic illness, women's health. *Unit head:* Dr. Paulette Seymour-Route, Dean, 508-856-5801, Fax: 508-856-6552, E-mail: paulette.seymour-route@umassmed.edu. *Application contact:* Diane Brescia, Admissions Coordinator, 508-856-3488, Fax: 508-856-5851, E-mail: diane.brescia@umassmed.edu.

University of Michigan, Horace H. Rackham School of Graduate Studies, School of Nursing, Division of Acute, Critical and Long-term Care, Program in Gerontology Nursing, Ann Arbor, MI 48109. Offers gerontology nurse practitioner (MS); gerontology-clinical nurse specialist (MS). *Accreditation:* AACN. Part-time programs available. *Degree requirements:* For master's, thesis. *Entrance requirements:* For master's, GRE General Test (if BSN GPA less than 3.25), Michigan licensure, minimum of B average in BSN program. Additional exam requirements/ recommendations for international students: Required—TOEFL (minimum score 560 paper-based; 220 computer-based). Electronic applications accepted. *Expenses:* Tuition, state resident: full-time $17,286; part-time $1099 per credit hour. Tuition, nonresident: full-time $34,944; part-time $2080 per credit hour. Required fees: $95 per semester. Tuition and fees vary according to course load, degree level and program. *Faculty research:* Wandering in the elderly, Alzheimer's, clinical specialist and nurse practitioner roles, enhancement of cognitive function.

University of Minnesota, Twin Cities Campus, Graduate School, School of Nursing, Gerontological Nurse Practitioner Program, Minneapolis, MN 55455-0213. Offers MS. *Accreditation:* AACN. *Degree requirements:* For master's, final oral exam, project or thesis. *Entrance requirements:* Additional exam requirements/recommendations for international students: Required—TOEFL (minimum score 586 paper-based; 240 computer-based).

University of Minnesota, Twin Cities Campus, Graduate School, School of Nursing, Program in Gerontological Clinical Nurse Specialist, Minneapolis, MN 55455-0213. Offers advanced clinical specialist in gerontology (MS). *Accreditation:* AACN. Part-time programs available. *Degree requirements:* For master's, final oral exam, project or thesis. *Entrance requirements:* Additional exam requirements/recommendations for international students: Required—TOEFL (minimum score 586 paper-based; 240 computer-based).

The University of North Carolina at Greensboro, Graduate School, School of Nursing, Greensboro, NC 27412-5001. Offers adult clinical nurse specialist (MSN, PMC); adult/ gerontological nurse practitioner (MSN, PMC); nurse anesthesia (MSN, PMC); nursing (PhD); nursing administration (MSN); nursing education (MSN); MSN/MBA. *Accreditation:* AACN; AANA/CANAEP; NLN. *Degree requirements:* For master's, thesis or alternative. *Entrance requirements:* For master's, GRE General Test or MAT, BSN, clinical experience, liability insurance, RN license; for PMC, liability insurance, MSN, RN license. Additional exam requirements/recommendations for international students: Required—TOEFL. Electronic applications accepted.

University of Rhode Island, Graduate School, College of Nursing, Kingston, RI 02881. Offers administration (MS); clinical nurse leader (MS); clinical specialist in gerontology (MS); clinical specialist in psychiatric/mental health (MS); family nurse practitioner (MS); gerontological nurse practitioner (MS); nursing (DNP, PhD); nursing education (MS). *Accreditation:* AACN; ACNM/DOA (one or more programs are accredited). Part-time programs available. *Faculty:* 28 full-time (27 women), 3 part-time/adjunct (all women). *Students:* 21 full-time (20 women), 74 part-time (71 women); includes 3 minority (1 African American, 2 Asian Americans or Pacific Islanders), 5 international. In 2009, 29 master's, 2 doctorates awarded. *Degree requirements:* For master's, comprehensive exam; for doctorate, comprehensive exam, thesis/dissertation. *Entrance requirements:* For master's, GRE or MAT, 2 letters of recommendation, scholarly papers; for doctorate, GRE, 3 letters of recommendation, scholarly papers. Additional exam requirements/recommendations for international students: Required—TOEFL (minimum score 550 paper-based; 213 computer-based). *Application deadline:* For fall admission, 4/15 for domestic students, 2/1 for international students; for spring admission, 11/15 for domestic students, 7/15 for international students. Application fee: $65. Electronic applications accepted. *Expenses:* Tuition, state resident: full-time $8828; part-time $490 per credit hour. Tuition, nonresident: full-time $22,100; part-time $1228 per credit hour. Required fees: $1118; $57 per semester. Tuition and fees vary according to program. *Financial support:* In 2009–10, 3 teaching assistantships with full and partial tuition reimbursements (averaging $8,428 per year) were awarded. Financial award application deadline: 4/15; financial award applicants required to submit FAFSA. *Faculty research:* Group intervention for grieving women in prison, translating Best Practice in non-drug interventions for postoperative pain management, further development and testing of the pain assessment inventory, preschool motor and functional performance of two cohorts, neuroactivation of brain motor areas in preterm children. Total annual research expenditures: $926,949. *Unit head:* Dr. Dayle Joseph, Dean, 401-874-2766, Fax: 401-874-2061, E-mail: dayle@uri.edu. *Application contact:* Dr. Mary C. Sullivan, Director of Graduate Studies, 401-874-5339, Fax: 401-874-2061, E-mail: mcsullivan@uri.edu.

University of Rochester, School of Nursing, Rochester, NY 14642. Offers acute care nurse practitioner (MS); adult nurse practitioner (MS); adult psychiatric mental health nurse practitioner (MS); adult/geriatric nurse practitioner (MS); care of children and families/pediatric nurse practitioner (MS); care of children and families/pediatric nurse practitioner with pediatric behavioral health (MS); care of children and families/pediatric nurse practitioner/neonatal nurse practitioner (MS); child and adolescent psychiatric mental health nurse practitioner (MS); clinical nurse leader (MS); disaster response and emergency preparedness (MS); family nurse practitioner (MS); health care organization management and leadership (MS); health practice research (PhD); health promotion, education and technology (MS); nursing (Certificate). *Accreditation:* AACN; NLN (one or more programs are accredited). Part-time programs available. Postbaccalaureate distance learning degree programs offered (minimal on-campus study). *Faculty:* 26 full-time (24 women), 20 part-time/adjunct (15 women). *Students:* 50 full-time (45 women), 178 part-time (165 women); includes 33 minority (17 African Americans, 2 American Indian/Alaska Native, 10 Asian Americans or Pacific Islanders, 4 Hispanic Americans), 11 international. Average age 35. 56 applicants, 80% accepted, 35 enrolled. In 2009, 53 master's, 5 doctorates awarded. Terminal master's awarded for partial completion of doctoral program. *Degree requirements:* For master's, comprehensive exam or thesis; for doctorate, thesis/ dissertation. *Entrance requirements:* For master's, BS in nursing, minimum GPA of 3.0, course work in statistics; for doctorate, GRE General Test, MS in nursing, minimum GPA of 3.5; for Certificate, MS in nursing. Additional exam requirements/recommendations for international students: Recommended—TOEFL (minimum score 560 paper-based; 230 computer-based; 88 iBT). *Application deadline:* For fall admission, 11/1 priority date for domestic and international students. Application fee: $50. *Financial support:* In 2009–10, 53 students received support, including 14 fellowships with full and partial tuition reimbursements available (averaging $17,497 per year); scholarships/grants, traineeships, health care benefits, tuition waivers (partial), and unspecified assistantships also available. Support available to part-time students. Financial award application deadline: 6/30. *Faculty research:* Clinical research in aging, managing asthma in children, interventions to improve outcomes in critically ill children and their mothers, nurse home visitation studies, medical device evaluation, critical care clinical studies, high risk behavior and prevention, palliative care, pregnancy-related weight gain. Total annual research expenditures: $4.8 million. *Unit head:* Dr. Kathy P. Parker, Dean, 585-273-5639, Fax: 585-273-1268, E-mail: kathy_parker@urmc.rochester.edu. *Application contact:* Elaine Andolina, Director of Admissions, 585-275-2375, Fax: 585-756-8299, E-mail: elaine_andolina@urmc.rochester.edu.

University of San Diego, Hahn School of Nursing and Health Science, San Diego, CA 92110-2492. Offers adult nurse practitioner/family nurse practitioner (MSN); adult-gerontology clinical nurse specialist (MSN); clinical nursing (MSN); entry-level nursing (for non-RNs) (MSN); executive nurse leader (MSN); family nurse practitioner (MSN); nursing (PhD); nursing practice (DNP); pediatric nurse practitioner/family nurse practitioner (MSN); psychiatric-mental health nurse practitioner (MSN). *Accreditation:* AACN. Part-time and evening/weekend programs available. *Faculty:* 18 full-time (17 women), 25 part-time/adjunct (22 women). *Students:* 141 full-time (117 women), 173 part-time (152 women); includes 95 minority (20 African Americans, 9 American Indian/Alaska Native, 45 Asian Americans or Pacific Islanders, 21 Hispanic Americans), 7 international. Average age 38. 404 applicants, 50% accepted, 132 enrolled. In 2009, 103 master's, 10 doctorates awarded. *Degree requirements:* For doctorate, thesis/ dissertation (for some programs), residency (DNP). *Entrance requirements:* For master's, GRE General Test (entry-level nursing), BSN, current California RN licensure (except for entry-level nursing); minimum GPA of 3.0; for doctorate, minimum GPA of 3.5, MSN, current California RN licensure. Additional exam requirements/recommendations for international students: Required—TOEFL (minimum score 580 paper-based; 237 computer-based; 83 iBT), TWE. *Application deadline:* For fall admission, 3/1 priority date for domestic students, 3/1 for international students; for spring admission, 11/1 priority date for domestic students, 11/1 for international students. Applications are processed on a rolling basis. Application fee: $45. Electronic applications accepted. *Expenses:* Tuition: Full-time $21,042; part-time $1169 per unit. Required fees: $224. Full-time tuition and fees vary according to course load and degree

level. *Financial support:* In 2009–10, 270 students received support. Scholarships/grants and traineeships available. Support available to part-time students. Financial award application deadline: 4/1; financial award applicants required to submit FAFSA. *Faculty research:* Health promotion, decision making, psychogeriatric nursing, historical nursing, leadership behavior. *Unit head:* Dr. Sally Hardin, Dean, 619-260-4550, Fax: 619-260-6814. *Application contact:* Dr. John Mosby, Associate Director of Graduate Admissions, 619-260-4524, Fax: 619-260-4158, E-mail: grads@sandiego.edu.

University of Utah, Graduate School, College of Nursing, Gerontology Interdisciplinary Program, Salt Lake City, UT 84112. Offers MS, Certificate. *Accreditation:* AACN. Part-time programs available. *Faculty:* 2 full-time (0 women), 1 (woman) part-time/adjunct. *Students:* 3 full-time (all women), 12 part-time (9 women); includes 2 minority (1 Asian American or Pacific Islander, 1 Hispanic American), 1 international. Average age 38. 7 applicants, 57% accepted, 4 enrolled. In 2009, 5 master's awarded. *Degree requirements:* For master's, thesis optional. *Entrance requirements:* For master's, minimum undergraduate GPA of 3.0. Additional exam requirements/recommendations for international students: Required—TOEFL (minimum score 500 paper-based; 173 computer-based). *Application deadline:* For fall admission, 4/1 priority date for domestic and international students. Applications are processed on a rolling basis. Application fee: $75 ($85 for international students). Electronic applications accepted. *Expenses:* Contact institution. *Financial support:* In 2009–10, 10 students received support, including 20 fellowships with partial tuition reimbursements available, 2 research assistantships; teaching assistantships, scholarships/grants also available. Financial award application deadline: 4/1. *Faculty research:* Spousal bereavement, family caregiving, healthy promotion and self-care, environmental issues, geriatric care management, technology and aging. Total annual research expenditures: $104,232. *Unit head:* Dr. Scott D. Wright, Director, 801-793-5752, E-mail: scott. wright@nurs.utah.edu. *Application contact:* Mirela Rankovic, Administrative Assistant, 801-581-8273, Fax: 801-581-4642, E-mail: mirela.rankovic@nurs.utah.edu.

Vanderbilt University, School of Nursing, Nashville, TN 37240. Offers adult acute care nurse practitioner (MSN); adult nurse practitioner/cardiovascular disease management and prevention (MSN); adult nurse practitioner/palliative care (MSN); clinical management (clinical nurse leader/specialist) (MSN); emergency nurse practitioner (MSN); family nurse practitioner (MSN); gerontology nurse practitioner (MSN); health systems management (MSN); neonatal nurse practitioner (MSN); nurse midwifery (MSN); nurse midwifery/family nurse practitioner (MSN); nursing informatics (MSN); nursing practice (DNP); nursing science (PhD); nutrition (MS); pediatric acute care nurse practitioner (MSN); pediatric primary care nurse practitioner (MSN); psychiatric-mental health nurse practitioner (MSN); women's health nurse practitioner (MSN), including urogynecology; women's health nurse practitioner/adult nurse practitioner (MSN); MSN/M Div; MSN/MTS. *Accreditation:* ACNM/DOA; NLN (one or more programs are accredited). Part-time programs available. Postbaccalaureate distance learning degree programs offered (minimal on-campus study). *Faculty:* 118 full-time (102 women), 429 part-time/adjunct (309 women). *Students:* 484 full-time (435 women), 319 part-time (284 women); includes 84 minority (55 African Americans, 4 American Indian/Alaska Native, 10 Asian Americans or Pacific Islanders, 15 Hispanic Americans), 16 international. Average age 32. 900 applicants, 65% accepted, 433 enrolled. In 2009, 303 master's, 1 doctorate awarded. *Degree requirements:* For doctorate, comprehensive exam, thesis/dissertation. *Entrance requirements:* For master's, GRE General Test, minimum B average in undergraduate course work, 3 letters of recommendation; for doctorate, GRE General Test, interview, 3 letters of recommendation from doctorally-prepared faculty, MSN, essay. Additional exam requirements/recommendations for international students: Required—TOEFL. *Application deadline:* For fall admission, 12/1 priority date for domestic and international students. Applications are processed on a rolling basis. Application fee: $50. *Expenses:* Contact institution. *Financial support:* In 2009–10, 389 students received support, including 1 research assistantship (averaging $5,000 per year); teaching assistantships, scholarships/grants, health care benefits, and tuition waivers also available. Support available to part-time students. Financial award application deadline: 3/15; financial award applicants required to submit FAFSA. *Faculty research:* Lymphedema, palliative care and bereavement, health services research including workforce, safety and quality of care, gerontology, better birth outcomes including nutrition. Total annual research expenditures: $1.4 million. *Unit head:* Dr. Colleen Conway-Welch, Dean, 615-343-8776, Fax: 615-343-7711, E-mail: colleen.conway-welch@vanderbilt.edu. *Application contact:* Cheryl Feldner, Assistant Director of Admissions, 615-322-3800, Fax: 615-343-0333, E-mail: cheryl.feldner@vanderbilt.edu.

HIV/AIDS Nursing

University of Delaware, College of Health Sciences, School of Nursing, Newark, DE 19716. Offers adult nurse practitioner (MSN, PMC); cardiopulmonary clinical nurse specialist (MSN, PMC); cardiopulmonary clinical nurse specialist/adult nurse practitioner (MSN, PMC); family nurse practitioner (MSN, PMC); gerontology clinical nurse specialist (MSN, PMC); gerontology clinical nurse specialist geriatric nurse practitioner (PMC); gerontology clinical nurse specialist/ geriatric nurse practitioner (MSN); health services administration (MSN, PMC); nursing of children clinical nurse specialist (MSN, PMC); nursing of children clinical nurse specialist/ pediatric nurse practitioner (MSN, PMC); oncology/immune deficiency clinical nurse specialist (MSN, PMC); oncology/immune deficiency clinical nurse specialist/adult nurse practitioner (MSN, PMC); perinatal/women's health clinical nurse specialist (MSN, PMC); perinatal/ women's health clinical nurse specialist/women's health nurse practitioner (MSN, PMC); psychiatric nursing clinical nurse specialist (MSN, PMC). *Accreditation:* AACN; NLN (one or more programs are accredited). Part-time and evening/weekend programs available. Post-baccalaureate distance learning degree programs offered (minimal on-campus study). *Degree requirements:* For master's, thesis optional. *Entrance requirements:* For master's, BSN, interview, RN license. Electronic applications accepted. *Faculty research:* Marriage and chronic illness, health promotion, congestive heart failure patient outcomes, school nursing, diabetes in children, culture, health disparities, cardiovascular, prison nursing, oncology, public policy, child obesity, smoking and teen pregnancy, blood pressure measurements, men's health.

Hospice Nursing

Madonna University, Program in Hospice, Livonia, MI 48150-1173. Offers MSH. Part-time and evening/weekend programs available. *Degree requirements:* For master's, thesis or alternative. *Entrance requirements:* For master's, GRE General Test, minimum undergraduate GPA of 3.0, 2 letters of recommendation, interview. Electronic applications accepted.

Maternal and Child/Neonatal Nursing

Baylor University, Graduate School, Louise Herrington School of Nursing, Dallas, TX 75246. Offers family nurse practitioner (MSN); neonatal nurse practitioner (MSN); nursing administration and management (MSN). *Accreditation:* AACN. *Students:* 32 full-time (31 women), 26 part-time (25 women); includes 12 minority (4 African Americans, 1 American Indian/Alaska Native, 3 Asian Americans or Pacific Islanders, 4 Hispanic Americans), 1 international. In 2009, 17 master's awarded. *Entrance requirements:* For master's, GRE General Test. *Application deadline:* For fall admission, 8/1 for domestic students; for spring admission, 12/1 for domestic students. Applications are processed on a rolling basis. Application fee: $25. *Unit head:* Dr. Mary Brucker, Graduate Program Director, 214-820-4111, Fax: 214-818-8692, E-mail: mary_brucker@baylor.edu. *Application contact:* Beverly Kurfees, Administrative Assistant, 214-820-4111, Fax: 254-710-3870, E-mail: beverly_kurfees@baylor.edu.

Boston College, William F. Connell School of Nursing, Chestnut Hill, MA 02467-3800. Offers adult health nursing (MS); community health nursing (MS); family health (MS); forensic nursing (MS); gerontology (MS); maternal/child health nursing (MS), including pediatric and women's health; nurse anesthesia (MS); nursing (PhD); palliative care (MS), including adult and pediatric; psychiatric-mental health nursing (MS); MBA/MS; MS/MA; MS/PhD. *Accreditation:* AACN; AANA/CANAEP (one or more programs are accredited). Part-time programs available. *Faculty:* 48 full-time (46 women), 31 part-time/adjunct (29 women). *Students:* 183 full-time (169 women), 147 part-time (140 women); includes 36 minority (15 African Americans, 2 American Indian/ Alaska Native, 17 Asian Americans or Pacific Islanders, 2 Hispanic Americans), 7 international. Average age 29. 347 applicants, 53% accepted, 103 enrolled. In 2009, 79 master's, 7 doctorates awarded. *Degree requirements:* For master's, comprehensive exam, research project; for doctorate, comprehensive exam, thesis/dissertation, computer literacy exam or foreign language. *Entrance requirements:* For master's, bachelor's degree in nursing; for doctorate, GRE General Test, master's degree in nursing. Additional exam requirements/recommendations for international students: Required—TOEFL (minimum score 550 paper-based; 213 computer-based). *Application deadline:* For fall admission, 11/1 for domestic and international students; for winter admission, 12/31 for domestic and international students; for spring admission, 9/15 for domestic and international students. Applications are processed on a rolling basis. Application fee: $40. Electronic applications accepted. *Financial support:* In 2009–10, 83 students received support, including 12 fellowships with partial tuition reimbursements available (averaging $15,000 per year), 5 teaching assistantships (averaging $13,746 per year); research assistantships, Federal Work-Study, institutionally sponsored loans, scholarships/grants, traineeships, health care benefits, and tuition waivers (partial) also available. Support available to part-time students. Financial award application deadline: 3/1; financial award applicants required to submit FAFSA. *Faculty research:* Ethics, reduction of risk behaviors, support during chronic illness, violence, gerontology. Total annual research expenditures: $1.4 million. *Unit head:* Dr. Susan Gennaro, Dean, 617-552-4251, Fax: 617-552-0931, E-mail: susan.gennaro@bc.edu. *Application contact:* MaryBeth Crowley, Graduate Programs Assistant, 617-552-4928, Fax: 617-552-2121, E-mail: csongrad@bc.edu.

Case Western Reserve University, Frances Payne Bolton School of Nursing, Doctor of Nursing Practice Program, Cleveland, OH 44106. Offers acute care nurse practitioner (DNP); adult nurse practitioner (DNP); family nurse practitioner (DNP); gerontological nurse practitioner (DNP); graduate entry/pre-licensure option (DNP); medical-surgical nursing (DNP); midwifery/family nursing (DNP); neonatal nurse practitioner (DNP); pediatric nurse practitioner (DNP); post-licensure option (DNP); psychiatric-mental health nurse practitioner (DNP); women's health nurse practitioner (DNP). Graduate entry option allows baccalaureate-prepared college graduates from non-nursing backgrounds to earn certificate and MSN in addition to ND. Terminal master's awarded for partial completion of doctoral program. *Degree requirements:* For doctorate, thesis/dissertation. *Entrance requirements:* For doctorate, GRE General Test or MAT. *Faculty research:* Clinical nursing, acute care, gerontology, mental health, critical care.

Case Western Reserve University, Frances Payne Bolton School of Nursing, Master's Programs in Nursing, Nurse Practitioner Program, Cleveland, OH 44106. Offers acute care cardiovascular nursing (MSN); acute care nurse practitioner (MSN); acute care/flight nurse (MSN); adult nurse practitioner (MSN); family nurse practitioner (MSN); gerontological nurse practitioner (MSN); neonatal nurse practitioner (MSN); pediatric nurse practitioner (MSN); psychiatric-mental health nurse practitioner (MSN); women's health nurse practitioner (MSN). *Accreditation:* NLN. Part-time programs available. Postbaccalaureate distance learning degree programs offered (minimal on-campus study). *Degree requirements:* For master's, thesis optional. *Entrance requirements:* For master's, GRE General Test or MAT. Additional exam requirements/recommendations for international students: Required—TOEFL. *Faculty research:* Positive and negative mood states in parents of twins, effect of a carepath on chronic obstructive pulmonary disease home care.

Columbia University, School of Nursing, Program in Neonatal Nurse Practitioner, New York, NY 10032. Offers MS, Adv C. *Accreditation:* AACN. Part-time programs available. *Entrance requirements:* For master's, GRE General Test, BSN, 1 year of neonatal intensive care unit experience; for Adv C, MSN. Electronic applications accepted.

Duke University, School of Nursing, Durham, NC 27708-0586. Offers adult acute care (Certificate); adult cardiovascular (Certificate); adult oncology (Certificate); adult primary care

Maternal and Child/Neonatal Nursing

Duke University (continued)

(Certificate); clinical nurse specialist (MSN), including adult oncology, gerontology, neonatal, pediatric; clinical research management (MSN, Certificate); family (Certificate); gerontology (Certificate); health and nursing ministries (MSN, Certificate); health systems leadership and outcomes (Certificate); neonatal (Certificate); neonatal/pediatric in rural health (MSN, Certificate); nurse anesthetist (MSN, Certificate); nurse practitioner (MSN), including adult acute care, adult cardiovascular, adult oncology, adult primary care, family, gerontology, neonatal, pediatric, pediatric acute care; nursing (DNP, PhD); nursing and healthcare leadership (MSN); nursing education (MSN); nursing informatics (MSN, Certificate); pediatric (Certificate); pediatric acute care (Certificate); MBA/MSN; MSN/MCM. *Accreditation:* AACN; AANA/CANAEP. Part-time programs available. Postbaccalaureate distance learning degree programs offered (minimal on-campus study). *Faculty:* 45 full-time (41 women), 169 part-time/adjunct (150 women). *Students:* 213 full-time (179 women), 116 part-time (105 women); includes 37 minority (17 African Americans, 13 Asian Americans or Pacific Islanders, 7 Hispanic Americans), 9 international. Average age 36. 234 applicants, 53% accepted, 97 enrolled. In 2009, 142 master's, 24 other advanced degrees awarded. Terminal master's awarded for partial completion of doctoral program. *Degree requirements:* For master's, thesis optional; for doctorate, Capstone Project. *Entrance requirements:* For master's, GRE General Test, 1 year of nursing experience, BSN, minimum GPA of 3.0, previous course work in statistics; for doctorate, GRE for BSN prepared, BSN or MSN, minimum GPA of 3.0, Portfolio; for Certificate, MSN. Additional exam requirements/recommendations for international students: Required—TOEFL (minimum score 550 paper-based; 213 computer-based), Commission on Graduates of Foreign Nursing Schools exam. *Application deadline:* For fall admission, 7/2 priority date for domestic and international students; for spring admission, 11/15 priority date for domestic and international students. Applications are processed on a rolling basis. Application fee: $50. Electronic applications accepted. *Expenses:* Contact institution. *Financial support:* Career-related internships or fieldwork, institutionally sponsored loans, scholarships/grants, traineeships, and tuition waivers (partial) available. Support available to part-time students. Financial award application deadline: 4/1; financial award applicants required to submit FAFSA. *Faculty research:* Cardiovascular disease, caregiver skill training, data mining, prostate cancer, neonatal immune system. Total annual research expenditures: $3.5 million. *Unit head:* Dr. Catherine L. Gilliss, Dean/Vice Chancellor for Nursing Affairs, 919-684-9444, Fax: 919-684-9414, E-mail: gilli025@mc.duke.edu. *Application contact:* Bebe T. Mills, Director of Admissions, 919-684-9151, Fax: 919-668-4693, E-mail: mills031@mc.duke.edu.

Goldfarb School of Nursing at Barnes-Jewish College, Goldfarb School of Nursing at Barnes-Jewish College, St Louis, MO 63110. Offers adult acute care nurse practitioner (MSN); adult nurse practitioner (MSN); neonatal nurse practitioner (MSN); nurse anesthesia (MSN); nurse educator (MSN); nurse executive (MSN). *Accreditation:* AACN; AANA/CANAEP. Part-time and evening/weekend programs available. Postbaccalaureate distance learning degree programs offered (minimal on-campus study). *Faculty:* 18 full-time (16 women), 3 part-time/adjunct (2 women). *Students:* 28 full-time (25 women), 81 part-time (73 women); includes 34 minority (27 African Americans, 6 Asian Americans or Pacific Islanders, 1 Hispanic American), 3 international. Average age 38. 60 applicants, 75% accepted, 40 enrolled. In 2009, 26 master's awarded. *Degree requirements:* For master's, thesis or alternative. *Entrance requirements:* For master's, minimum GPA of 3.0, 2 references, statistics course. Additional exam requirements/recommendations for international students: Required—TOEFL (minimum score 550 paper-based; 213 computer-based). *Application deadline:* For fall admission, 2/1 priority date for international students; for spring admission, 10/1 priority date for international students. Applications are processed on a rolling basis. Application fee: $150. *Financial support:* In 2009–10, 60 students received support, including 20 fellowships (averaging $4,000 per year), 4 research assistantships (averaging $5,000 per year); Federal Work-Study, institutionally sponsored loans, and scholarships/grants also available. Support available to part-time students. Financial award applicants required to submit FAFSA. *Faculty research:* HIV Stigma, HIV symptom management, palliative care with children and their families, heart disease prevention in Hispanic women, depression in the well elderly, alternative therapies in pre-term infants. *Unit head:* Dr. Michael L. Evans, Dean, 314-362-6289, Fax: 314-362-0984, E-mail: mevans@bjc.org. *Application contact:* Dr. Michael Ward, Associate Dean for Student Programs, 314-362-9155, Fax: 314-362-9250, E-mail: mward@bjc.org.

Hardin-Simmons University, Graduate School, Patty Hanks Shelton School of Nursing, Abilene, TX 79698-0001. Offers advanced healthcare delivery (MSN); family nurse practitioner (MSN). *Accreditation:* AACN. Part-time programs available. *Faculty:* 3 full-time (all women), 1 (woman) part-time/adjunct. *Students:* 5 full-time (all women), 13 part-time (12 women); includes 2 minority (both Hispanic Americans). Average age 37. 5 applicants, 100% accepted, 4 enrolled. In 2009, 6 master's awarded. *Degree requirements:* For master's, comprehensive exam, thesis or alternative. *Entrance requirements:* For master's, GRE, minimum undergraduate GPA of 3.0 in major, 2.8 overall; interview; upper-level course work in statistics; CPR certification; letters of recommendation. Additional exam requirements/recommendations for international students: Required—TOEFL (minimum score 550 paper-based; 213 computer-based; 75 iBT). *Application deadline:* For fall admission, 8/15 priority date for domestic students, 4/1 for international students; for spring admission, 1/5 priority date for domestic students, 9/1 for international students. Applications are processed on a rolling basis. Application fee: $50. *Expenses:* Contact institution. *Financial support:* In 2009–10, 2 students received support. Career-related internships or fieldwork and scholarships/grants available. Support available to part-time students. Financial award application deadline: 6/30; financial award applicants required to submit FAFSA. *Faculty research:* Child abuse, alternative medicine, pediatric chronic disease, health promotion. *Unit head:* Dr. Amy Toone, Director, 325-671-2361, Fax: 325-671-2386, E-mail: atoone@phssn.edu. *Application contact:* Dr. Gary Stanlake, Dean of Graduate Studies, 325-670-1298, Fax: 325-670-1564, E-mail: gradoff@hsutx.edu.

Indiana University–Purdue University Indianapolis, School of Nursing, Indianapolis, IN 46202-2896. Offers acute care nurse practitioner (MSN); adult health clinical nurse specialist (MSN); adult health nursing (MSN), including adult clinical nurse specialist; adult nurse practitioner (MSN); adult psychiatric/mental health nursing (MSN); child psychiatric/mental health nursing (MSN); community health nursing (MSN); family nurse practitioner (MSN); neonatal nurse practitioner (MSN); nursing science (PhD); pediatric clinical nurse specialist (MSN); women's health nurse practitioner (MSN); MSN/MPA; MSN/MPH. *Accreditation:* AACN; NLN (one or more programs are accredited). Part-time programs available. *Faculty:* 85 full-time (82 women), 60 part-time/adjunct (all women). *Students:* 46 full-time (43 women), 369 part-time (354 women); includes 30 minority (21 African Americans, 6 Asian Americans or Pacific Islanders, 3 Hispanic Americans), 5 international. Average age 39. 121 applicants, 82% accepted, 67 enrolled. In 2009, 106 master's, 3 doctorates awarded. Terminal master's awarded for partial completion of doctoral program. *Degree requirements:* For master's, thesis; for doctorate, thesis/dissertation. *Entrance requirements:* For master's, minimum GPA of 3.0, RN license; for doctorate, GRE General Test, minimum GPA of 3.0, MSN, RN license, graduate statistics course with B grade or better (not older than 3 years). Additional exam requirements/recommendations for international students: Required—TOEFL. *Application deadline:* For fall admission, 2/15 for domestic students; for spring admission, 9/15 for domestic students. Application fee: $55 ($65 for international students). *Financial support:* In 2009–10, 93 students received support, including 9 fellowships with full tuition reimbursements available (averaging $7,039 per year), 7 teaching assistantships with full tuition reimbursements available (averaging $5,300 per year); research assistantships with full tuition reimbursements available, Federal Work-Study, institutionally sponsored loans, scholarships/grants, and tuition waivers (full) also available. Support available to part-time students. Financial award application deadline: 5/1. *Faculty research:* Clinical science, health systems. Total annual research expenditures: $3 million. *Unit head:* Associate Dean for Graduate Programs, 317-274-2806, E-mail: nursing@iupui.edu. *Application contact:* Information Contact, 317-274-2806.

Lehman College of the City University of New York, Division of Natural and Social Sciences, Department of Nursing, Bronx, NY 10468-1589. Offers adult health nursing (MS); nursing of older adults (MS); parent-child nursing (MS); pediatric nurse practitioner (MS);

Accreditation: AACN. Part-time and evening/weekend programs available. *Entrance requirements:* For master's, bachelor's degree in nursing, New York RN license.

Marquette University, Graduate School, College of Nursing, Milwaukee, WI 53201-1881. Offers adult nurse practitioner (Certificate); advanced practice nursing (MSN), including adult, children, neonatal nurse practitioner, nurse-midwifery, older adult; gerontological nurse practitioner (Certificate); neonatal nurse practitioner (Certificate); nurse-midwifery (Certificate); nursing (PhD); pediatric nurse practitioner (Certificate). *Accreditation:* AACN. Part-time and evening/weekend programs available. *Faculty:* 29 full-time (27 women), 43 part-time/adjunct (all women). *Students:* 115 full-time (105 women), 209 part-time (197 women); includes 28 minority (13 African Americans, 2 American Indian/Alaska Native, 8 Asian Americans or Pacific Islanders, 5 Hispanic Americans), 1 international. Average age 32. 143 applicants, 91% accepted, 86 enrolled. In 2009, 64 master's, 10 doctorates awarded. *Degree requirements:* For master's, comprehensive exam, thesis or alternative. *Entrance requirements:* For master's, GRE General Test, BSN, Wisconsin RN license. Additional exam requirements/recommendations for international students: Required—TOEFL. Application fee: $40. *Financial support:* In 2009–10, 6 research assistantships, 1 teaching assistantship were awarded; career-related internships or fieldwork, Federal Work-Study, institutionally sponsored loans, scholarships/grants, and tuition waivers (full and partial) also available. Support available to part-time students. Financial award application deadline: 2/15. *Faculty research:* Psychosocial adjustment to chronic illness, gerontology, reminiscence, health policy: uninsured and access, hospital care delivery systems. *Unit head:* Dr. Lea Acord, Dean, 414-288-3812, Fax: 414-288-1578. *Application contact:* Dr. Judy Miller, Director of Graduate Studies, 414-288-3810, Fax: 414-288-1578.

Medical University of South Carolina, College of Nursing, Pediatric Nurse Practitioner Program, Charleston, SC 29425. Offers MSN. *Accreditation:* AACN. Part-time programs available. *Faculty:* 7 full-time (all women), 3 part-time/adjunct (2 women). *Students:* 7 full-time (all women), 12 part-time (all women); includes 2 minority (1 African American, 1 Hispanic American). Average age 26. 21 applicants, 71% accepted, 13 enrolled. In 2009, 7 master's awarded. *Degree requirements:* For master's, comprehensive exam (for some programs), thesis optional. *Entrance requirements:* For master's, BSN, course work in statistics, nursing license, minimum GPA of 3.0. Additional exam requirements/recommendations for international students: Required—TOEFL (minimum score 600 paper-based; 250 computer-based). *Application deadline:* For fall admission, 2/1 priority date for domestic and international students. Application fee: $85. Electronic applications accepted. *Financial support:* Federal Work-Study, scholarships/grants, and traineeships available. Support available to part-time students. Financial award application deadline: 3/10; financial award applicants required to submit FAFSA. *Faculty research:* Epilepsy management, ADHD/ADD management, school-based clinics. *Unit head:* Dr. Dianna D. Inman, Lead Faculty, 843-792-7201, Fax: 843-792-1741, E-mail: inmandd@musc.edu. *Application contact:* Carolyn F. Page, Director, Student Services, 843-792-3844, Fax: 843-792-5395, E-mail: pagecf@musc.edu.

Northeastern University, Bouvé College of Health Sciences Graduate School, School of Nursing, Program in Critical Care-Neonatal Nurse Practitioner, Boston, MA 02115-5096. Offers MS, CAS. *Accreditation:* AACN. *Students:* 1 (woman) part-time. 1 applicant, 100% accepted, 1 enrolled. In 2009, 7 master's awarded. *Degree requirements:* For master's, thesis or alternative. *Entrance requirements:* For master's, GRE General Test, minimum GPA of 3.0, previous course work in statistics, 1-2 years of nursing experience, RN license, ICU experience. Additional exam requirements/recommendations for international students: Required—TOEFL (minimum score 100 iBT). *Application deadline:* For fall admission, 7/1 for domestic students. Application fee: $50. Electronic applications accepted. *Financial support:* Research assistantships, teaching assistantships, scholarships/grants, traineeships, and tuition waivers (partial) available. Financial award application deadline: 7/1; financial award applicants required to submit FAFSA. *Unit head:* Prof. Gretchen R. Hamn, Director, E-mail: g.hamn@neu.edu. *Application contact:* Margaret Schnabel, Director of Graduate Admissions, 617-373-2708, E-mail: bouvegrad@neu.edu.

Regis University, Rueckert-Hartman School for Health Professions, Denver, CO 80221-1099. Offers clinical leadership for physician assistants (MS); family nurse practitioner (MSN); health informatics (Postbaccalaureate Certificate); health services administration (MS); healthcare education (Certificate); leadership in healthcare systems (MSN); neonatal nurse practitioner (MSN); nursing (MSN); pharmacy (Pharm D); physical therapy (DPT, TDPT). *Entrance requirements:* Additional exam requirements/recommendations for international students: Required—TOEFL (minimum score 550 paper-based; 213 computer-based; 82 iBT). Electronic applications accepted. *Expenses:* Contact institution. *Faculty research:* Normal and pathological balance and gait research, normal/pathological upper limb motor control/biomechanics, exercise energy/metabolism research, optical treatment protocols for therapeutic modalities.

Rush University, College of Nursing, Department of Women's and Children's Health Nursing, Chicago, IL 60612-3832. Offers neonatal nurse practitioner (MSN, Post-Master's Certificate); pediatric acute/chronic care nurse practitioner (MSN); pediatric clinical nurse specialist (MSN); pediatric nurse practitioner (MSN, Post-Master's Certificate); women's and children's health nursing (DNP, PhD). *Accreditation:* AACN. Part-time programs available. Postbaccalaureate distance learning degree programs offered (minimal on-campus study). Terminal master's awarded for partial completion of doctoral program. *Degree requirements:* For master's, capstone project; for doctorate, thesis/dissertation, DNP leadership project. *Entrance requirements:* For master's, GRE General Test (waived if nursing GPA is above 3.0 or cumulative GPA is above 3.25), interview; for doctorate, GRE General Test, interview, course work in statistics (PhD). Additional exam requirements/recommendations for international students: Required—TOEFL, TWE. Electronic applications accepted. *Faculty research:* Family-centered care, women's health, health outcomes of human milk feeding for VhBW infants.

Rutgers, The State University of New Jersey, Newark, Graduate School, Program in Nursing, Newark, NJ 07102. Offers nursing (MS), including acute care of adults and aged, advanced practice in pediatric nursing, advanced practice with childbearing families, community health nursing, family nurse practitioner, primary care of adults and aged, psychiatric/mental health nursing. *Accreditation:* AACN. Part-time programs available. *Degree requirements:* For master's, comprehensive exam. *Entrance requirements:* For master's, GRE General Test, RN license, minimum B average, BS in nursing. Additional exam requirements/recommendations for international students: Required—TOEFL. Electronic applications accepted. *Faculty research:* HIV/AIDS, quality of life—MS and breast cancer, sleep patterns of cardiac patients.

Saint Francis Medical Center College of Nursing, Graduate Program, Peoria, IL 61603-3783. Offers child and family nursing (MSN); clinical nurse leader (MSN); medical-surgical nursing (MSN); neonatal nurse practitioner (MSN); nurse clinician (Post-Graduate Certificate); nurse educator (Post-Graduate Certificate); nursing (DNP). *Accreditation:* NLN. Part-time programs available. Postbaccalaureate distance learning degree programs offered (minimal on-campus study). *Faculty:* 3 full-time (all women), 9 part-time/adjunct (all women). *Students:* 8 full-time (all women), 135 part-time (122 women); includes 6 minority (1 African American, 4 Asian Americans or Pacific Islanders, 1 Hispanic American). Average age 28. 19 applicants, 100% accepted, 19 enrolled. In 2009, 24 master's awarded. *Degree requirements:* For master's, research experience, portfolio, practicum. *Entrance requirements:* For master's, nursing research, health assessment, graduate course work in statistics, RN license. Additional exam requirements/recommendations for international students: Required—TOEFL. *Application deadline:* For fall admission, 6/1 priority date for domestic and international students; for spring admission, 11/15 priority date for domestic and international students. Applications are processed on a rolling basis. Application fee: $50. Electronic applications accepted. *Expenses:* Tuition: Part-time $472 per semester hour. Required fees: $130 per semester. *Financial support:* In 2009–10, 6 students received support. Scholarships/grants and tuition waivers (partial) available. Support available to part-time students. Financial award application deadline: 6/15; financial award applicants required to submit FAFSA. *Faculty research:* Outcome and curriculum planning, health promotion, NCLEX-RN results, decision making program evaluation. *Unit head:* Dr. Lois J. Hamilton, Dean, 309-655-2201, Fax: 309-624-8973, E-mail: lois.j.hamilton@osfhealthcare.org.

Application contact: Dr. Janice F. Boundy, Associate Dean, 309-655-2230, Fax: 309-624-8973, E-mail: jan.f.boundy@osfhealthcare.org.

Stony Brook University, State University of New York, Stony Brook University Medical Center, Health Sciences Center, School of Nursing, Program in Neonatal Nursing, Stony Brook, NY 11794. Offers neonatal nurse practitioner (Certificate); neonatal nursing (MS). *Accreditation:* AACN. Postbaccalaureate distance learning degree programs offered. *Students:* 13 full-time (all women), 37 part-time (all women); includes 10 minority (5 Asian Americans or Pacific Islanders, 5 Hispanic Americans), 3 international. In 2009, 8 master's, 1 other advanced degree awarded. *Degree requirements:* For master's, thesis. *Entrance requirements:* For master's, BSN, minimum GPA of 3.0, course work in statistics. *Application deadline:* For fall admission, 1/15 for domestic students. Application fee: $60. *Expenses:* Tuition, state resident: full-time $8370; part-time $349 per credit. Tuition, nonresident: full-time $13,250; part-time $552 per credit. Required fees: $933. *Financial support:* Application deadline: 3/15. *Unit head:* Prof. Arleen Steckel, Chair, 631-444-3264, Fax: 631-444-3136, E-mail: arleen.steckel@stonybrook.edu. *Application contact:* Prof. Arleen Steckel, Chair, 631-444-3264, Fax: 631-444-3136, E-mail: arleen.steckel@stonybrook.edu.

Stony Brook University, State University of New York, Stony Brook University Medical Center, Health Sciences Center, School of Nursing, Program in Perinatal Women's Health Nursing, Stony Brook, NY 11794. Offers MS, Certificate. *Accreditation:* AACN. Postbaccalaureate distance learning degree programs offered. *Students:* 2 full-time (both women), 25 part-time (all women); includes 6 minority (4 African Americans, 2 Hispanic Americans). In 2009, 2 master's awarded. *Degree requirements:* For master's, thesis. *Entrance requirements:* For master's, BSN, minimum GPA of 3.0, course work in statistics. *Application deadline:* For fall admission, 1/15 for domestic students. Application fee: $60. *Expenses:* Tuition, state resident: full-time $8370; part-time $349 per credit. Tuition, nonresident: full-time $13,250; part-time $552 per credit. Required fees: $933. *Financial support:* Application deadline: 3/15. *Unit head:* Prof. Arleen Steckel, Chair, 631-444-3298, Fax: 631-444-3136. *Application contact:* Dr. Kent Marks, Assistant Dean, Admissions and Records, 631-632-4723, Fax: 631-632-7243, E-mail: kmarks@notes.cc.sunysb.edu.

Université de Montréal, Faculty of Medicine, Program in Specialized Studies, Montréal, QC H3C 3J7, Canada. Offers anesthesia (DES); diagnostic radiology (DES); family medicine (DES); gastroenterology (DES); geriatry (DES); intensive care (DES); medical biochemistry (DES); medical genetics (DES); medicine (DES); microbiology and infectious diseases (DES); nuclear medicine (DES); obstetrics and gynecology (DES); ophthalmology (DES); pediatrics (DES); pneumology (DES); psychiatry (DES); radiology-oncology (DES); rheumatology (DES); surgery (DES). *Faculty:* 154 full-time (40 women), 333 part-time/adjunct (100 women). *Students:* 930 full-time (580 women), 7 part-time (all women). 74 applicants, 77% accepted, 29 enrolled. *Application deadline:* For fall admission, 2/1 priority date for domestic students; for winter admission, 11/1 priority date for domestic students; for spring admission, 2/1 priority date for domestic students. Application fee: $100. Electronic applications accepted. *Unit head:* Lorraine Locas, Assistant to the Vice Dean of Graduate Studies, 514-343-6269, Fax: 514-343-5751, E-mail: lorraine.locas@umontreal.ca. *Application contact:* Dr. Andre Ferron, Vice Dean Graduate Studies, 514-343-6111 Ext. 0933; Fax: 514-343-5751, E-mail: andre.ferron@umontreal.ca.

University of Alberta, Faculty of Medicine and Dentistry and Faculty of Graduate Studies and Research, Graduate Programs in Medicine, Department of Obstetrics and Gynecology, Edmonton, AB T6G 2E1, Canada. Offers MD. *Faculty:* 3 full-time (1 woman). *Students:* 3 full-time (2 women). Average age 26. 1 applicant. *Entrance requirements:* Additional exam requirements/recommendations for international students: Required—TOEFL. *Application deadline:* Applications are processed on a rolling basis. Application fee: $60. Tuition and fees charges are reported in Canadian dollars. *Expenses:* Tuition, area resident: Full-time $4626 Canadian dollars; part-time $99.72 Canadian dollars per unit. International tuition: $8216 Canadian dollars full-time. Required fees: $3590 Canadian dollars; $99.72 Canadian dollars per unit. $215 Canadian dollars per term. *Financial support:* Fellowships, scholarships/grants, traineeships, tuition waivers (partial), and unspecified assistantships available. *Faculty research:* Parturition, fetal/neonatal lung development, nitric oxide, vascular reactivity, pre-eclampsia gestational diabetes. Total annual research expenditures: $650,000. *Unit head:* Dr. J. Wylam Faught, Chair, 780-735-4927, Fax: 780-477-4981. *Application contact:* Sharon Campbell, Information Contact, 780-407-3131, Fax: 780-407-3134.

University of Cincinnati, Graduate School, College of Nursing, Cincinnati, OH 45221-0038. Offers clinical nurse specialist (MSN), including adult health, community health, neonatal, nursing administration, occupational health, pediatric health, psychiatric nursing, women's health; nurse anesthesia (MSN); nurse midwifery (MSN); nurse practitioner (MSN), including acute care, ambulatory care, family, family/psychiatric, women's health; nursing (PhD); MBA/MSN. *Accreditation:* AACN; AANA/CANAEP (one or more programs are accredited); ACNM/DOA. Part-time programs available. Postbaccalaureate distance learning degree programs offered (no on-campus study). Terminal master's awarded for partial completion of doctoral program. *Degree requirements:* For master's, thesis or alternative; for doctorate, comprehensive exam, thesis/dissertation. *Entrance requirements:* For master's and doctorate, GRE General Test. Additional exam requirements/recommendations for international students: Required—TOEFL (minimum score 520 paper-based; 190 computer-based). Electronic applications accepted. *Faculty research:* Substance abuse, injury and violence, symptom management.

University of Colorado at Colorado Springs, Graduate School, Beth-El College of Nursing and Health Sciences, Colorado Springs, CO 80933-7150. Offers adult health nurse practitioner and clinical specialist (MSN); family practitioner (MSN), including community clinical specialist, forensic clinical specialist, holistic clinical specialist; neonatal nurse practitioner and clinical specialist (MSN); nursing administration (MSN); nursing practice (DNP); women nurse practitioner (MSN). *Accreditation:* AACN. Part-time programs available. Postbaccalaureate distance learning degree programs offered (minimal on-campus study). *Faculty:* 26 full-time (21 women), 3 part-time/adjunct (all women). *Students:* 132 full-time (112 women), 81 part-time (71 women); includes 35 minority (6 African Americans, 2 American Indian/Alaska Native, 6 Asian Americans or Pacific Islanders, 21 Hispanic Americans), 3 international. Average age 36. 245 applicants, 47% accepted, 58 enrolled. In 2009, 33 master's awarded. *Degree requirements:* For master's, comprehensive exam, thesis optional; for doctorate, capstone project. *Entrance requirements:* For master's, GRE General Test or MAT, BSN, minimum GPA of 3.0, unrestricted RN license; for doctorate, interview; active RN license; MA; minimum GPA of 3.3; National Certification as NP or CNS; portfolio. Additional exam requirements/recommendations for international students: Required—TOEFL. *Application deadline:* For fall admission, 6/1 priority date for domestic students; for spring admission, 11/15 for domestic students. Application fee: $60 ($75 for international students). Electronic applications accepted. *Expenses:* Contact institution. *Financial support:* Fellowships, career-related internships or fieldwork, Federal Work-Study, and scholarships/grants available. Support available to part-time students. Financial award application deadline: 3/1; financial award applicants required to submit FAFSA. *Faculty research:* Women's health, uncertainty, empowerment, family experience in chronic illness. Total annual research expenditures: $703,545. *Unit head:* Dr. Nancy Smith, Dean, 719-255-4411, Fax: 719-255-4416, E-mail: nsmith2@uccs.edu. *Application contact:* Jackie Crouch, Graduate Recruitment Coordinator, 719-255-4493, Fax: 719-255-4416, E-mail: jcrouch@uccs.edu.

University of Delaware, College of Health Sciences, School of Nursing, Newark, DE 19716. Offers adult nurse practitioner (MSN, PMC); cardiopulmonary clinical nurse specialist (MSN, PMC); cardiopulmonary clinical nurse specialist/adult nurse practitioner (MSN, PMC); family nurse practitioner (MSN, PMC); gerontology clinical nurse specialist (MSN, PMC); gerontology clinical nurse specialist geriatric nurse practitioner (PMC); gerontology clinical nurse specialist/ geriatric nurse practitioner (MSN); health services administration (MSN, PMC); nursing of children clinical nurse specialist (MSN, PMC); nursing of children clinical nurse specialist/ pediatric nurse practitioner (MSN, PMC); oncology/immune deficiency clinical nurse specialist (MSN, PMC); oncology/immune deficiency clinical nurse specialist/adult nurse practitioner (MSN, PMC); perinatal/women's health clinical nurse specialist (MSN, PMC); perinatal/

women's health clinical nurse specialist/women's health nurse practitioner (MSN, PMC); psychiatric nursing clinical nurse specialist (MSN, PMC). *Accreditation:* AACN; NLN (one or more programs are accredited). Part-time and evening/weekend programs available. Post-baccalaureate distance learning degree programs offered (minimal on-campus study). *Degree requirements:* For master's, thesis optional. *Entrance requirements:* For master's, BSN, interview, RN license. Electronic applications accepted. *Faculty research:* Marriage and chronic illness, health promotion, congestive heart failure patient outcomes, school nursing, diabetes in children, culture, health disparities, cardiovascular, prison nursing, oncology, public policy, child obesity, smoking and teen pregnancy, blood pressure measurements, men's health.

University of Illinois at Chicago, Graduate College, College of Nursing, Program in Nursing, Chicago, IL 60607-7128. Offers acute care clinical nurse specialist (MS); acute care nurse practitioner (MS); administrative studies in nursing (MS); adult nurse practitioner (MS); adult/ geriatric nurse practitioner (MS); advanced community health nurse specialist (MS); family nurse practitioner (MS); geriatric clinical nurse specialist (MS); geriatric nurse practitioner (MS); mental health clinical nurse specialist (MS); mental health nurse practitioner (MS); nurse midwifery (MS); occupational health/advanced community health nurse specialist (MS); occupational health/family nurse practitioner (MS); pediatric clinical nurse specialist (MS); pediatric nurse practitioner (MS); perinatal clinical nurse specialist (MS); school/advanced community health nurse specialist (MS); school/family nurse practitioner (MS); women's health nurse practitioner (MS). *Accreditation:* AACN. Part-time programs available. *Degree requirements:* For master's, thesis or alternative. *Entrance requirements:* For master's, GRE General Test, minimum GPA of 2.75. Additional exam requirements/recommendations for international students: Required—TOEFL. Electronic applications accepted.

University of Louisville, Graduate School, School of Nursing, Louisville, KY 40202. Offers adult nurse practitioner (MSN); family nurse practitioner (MSN); health professions education (MSN); neonatal nurse practitioner (MSN); nursing research (PhD); psychiatric mental health nurse practitioner (MSN). *Accreditation:* AACN. Part-time programs available. *Faculty:* 28 full-time (25 women), 4 part-time/adjunct (3 women). *Students:* 72 full-time (66 women), 57 part-time (52 women); includes 15 minority (11 African Americans, 3 Asian Americans or Pacific Islanders, 1 Hispanic American), 4 international. Average age 35. 45 applicants, 82% accepted, 31 enrolled. In 2009, 28 master's, 3 doctorates awarded. Terminal master's awarded for partial completion of doctoral program. *Degree requirements:* For master's, thesis optional; for doctorate, comprehensive exam, thesis/dissertation. *Entrance requirements:* For master's, GRE General Test, bachelor's degree in nursing, minimum GPA of 3.0, RN license; for doctorate, GRE General Test, BSN and MSN with recommended minimum GPA of 3.0. Additional exam requirements/recommendations for international students: Required—TOEFL. *Application deadline:* For fall admission, 4/1 priority date for domestic students, 4/1 for international students; for spring admission, 10/1 priority date for domestic students, 10/1 for international students. Applications are processed on a rolling basis. Application fee: $50. Electronic applications accepted. *Financial support:* In 2009–10, 45 students received support, including 2 fellowships with full tuition reimbursements available (averaging $20,000 per year), 5 research assistantships with full tuition reimbursements available (averaging $18,000 per year), 5 teaching assistantships with full tuition reimbursements available (averaging $18,000 per year); institutionally sponsored loans, scholarships/grants, traineeships, health care benefits, and unspecified assistantships also available. Support available to part-time students. Financial award application deadline: 4/15; financial award applicants required to submit FAFSA. *Faculty research:* Maternal-child/family stress after pregnancy loss, postpartum depression, access to healthcare (underserved populations), quality of life issues, physical activity (impact on chronic/ acute conditions). Total annual research expenditures: $363,876. *Unit head:* Dr. Marcia J. Hern, Dean, 502-852-8300, Fax: 502-852-5044, E-mail: m.hern@gwise.louisville.edu. *Application contact:* Dr. Rosalie O'Dell Mainous, Associate Dean for Graduate Academic Affairs, 502-852-8387, Fax: 502-852-8783, E-mail: romain01@louisville.edu.

University of Maryland, Baltimore, Graduate School, School of Nursing, Master's Program in Nursing, Baltimore, MD 21201. Offers community health nursing (MS); gerontological nursing (MS); maternal-child nursing (MS); medical-surgical nursing (MS); nurse-midwifery education (MS); nursing administration (MS); nursing education (MS); nursing health policy (MS); primary care nursing (MS); psychiatric nursing (MS); MS/MBA. *Accreditation:* AACN; AANA/CANAEP; ACNM/DOA; NLN (one or more programs are accredited). Part-time programs available. *Students:* 387 full-time (338 women), 528 part-time (491 women); includes 330 minority (230 African Americans, 3 American Indian/Alaska Native, 81 Asian Americans or Pacific Islanders, 16 Hispanic Americans), 10 international. Average age 36. 849 applicants, 40% accepted, 255 enrolled. In 2009, 264 master's awarded. *Degree requirements:* For master's, comprehensive exam (for some programs), thesis or alternative. *Entrance requirements:* For master's, GRE General Test, minimum GPA of 2.75, course work in statistics, BS in nursing. Additional exam requirements/recommendations for international students: Required—TOEFL (minimum score 550 paper-based; 80 iBT), or IELTS (minimum score 7). *Application deadline:* For fall admission, 1/15 for international students. Application fee: $50. Electronic applications accepted. *Expenses:* Tuition, state resident: full-time $7290; part-time $405 per credit hour. Tuition, nonresident: full-time $12,780; part-time $710 per credit hour. Required fees: $774; $10 per credit hour. $297 per semester. Tuition and fees vary according to course load, degree level and program. *Financial support:* Fellowships, research assistantships, teaching assistantships, career-related internships or fieldwork and traineeships available. Support available to part-time students. Financial award application deadline: 2/15; financial award applicants required to submit FAFSA. *Unit head:* Dr. Jane Kapustin, Assistant Dean, 410-706-6741, Fax: 410-706-4231. *Application contact:* Marjorie Fass, Admissions Director, 410-706-0501, Fax: 410-706-7238.

University of Missouri–Kansas City, School of Nursing, Kansas City, MO 64110-2499. Offers adult clinical nurse specialist (MSN), including adult nurse practitioner, women's health nurse practitioner; family nurse practitioner (MSN); neonatal nurse practitioner (MSN); nurse educator (MSN); nurse executive (MSN); nursing (PhD); nursing practice (DNP); pediatric nurse practitioner (MSN). *Accreditation:* AACN. Part-time programs available. Postbaccalaureate distance learning degree programs offered (minimal on-campus study). *Faculty:* 36 full-time (30 women), 40 part-time/adjunct (all women). *Students:* 31 full-time (26 women), 310 part-time (287 women); includes 38 minority (17 African Americans, 2 American Indian/Alaska Native, 10 Asian Americans or Pacific Islanders, 9 Hispanic Americans). Average age 36. 151 applicants, 72% accepted, 109 enrolled. In 2009, 57 master's, 10 doctorates awarded. *Degree requirements:* For master's, thesis or alternative. *Entrance requirements:* For master's, minimum undergraduate GPA of 3.2; for doctorate, GRE, 3 letters of reference, interview by invitation. Additional exam requirements/recommendations for international students: Required—TOEFL (minimum score 550 paper-based; 213 computer-based; 80 iBT). *Application deadline:* For fall admission, 2/1 priority date for domestic and international students; for spring admission, 9/1 priority date for domestic and international students. Application fee: $45 ($50 for international students). *Expenses:* Tuition, state resident: full-time $5378; part-time $299 per credit hour. Tuition, nonresident: full-time $13,881; part-time $771 per credit hour. Required fees: $641; $71 per credit hour. Tuition and fees vary according to course load and program. *Financial support:* In 2009–10, 6 teaching assistantships with partial tuition reimbursements (averaging $4,402 per year) were awarded; fellowships, research assistantships, career-related internships or fieldwork, Federal Work-Study, institutionally sponsored loans, and tuition waivers (full and partial) also available. Support available to part-time students. Financial award application deadline: 3/1; financial award applicants required to submit FAFSA. *Faculty research:* Geriatrics/gerontology, children's pain, neonatology, Alzheimer's care, cancer caregivers. Total annual research expenditures: $2.1 million. *Unit head:* Dr. Lora Lacey-Haun, Dean, 816-235-1700, Fax: 816-235-1701, E-mail: lacey-haunc@umkc.edu. *Application contact:* Leah Wilder, Coordinator for Admissions and Recruitment, 816-235-5768, Fax: 816-235-1701, E-mail: wilderl@umkc.edu.

University of Pennsylvania, School of Nursing, Family Health Nurse Practitioner Program, Philadelphia, PA 19104. Offers MSN, Certificate. *Accreditation:* AACN. Part-time programs available. *Students:* 22 full-time (20 women), 38 part-time (37 women); includes 12 minority (5 African Americans, 6 Asian Americans or Pacific Islanders, 1 Hispanic American). In 2009, 20

Maternal and Child/Neonatal Nursing

University of Pennsylvania (continued)
master's, 1 other advanced degree awarded. *Entrance requirements:* For master's, GRE General Test, 1 year of clinical experience in area of interest, BSN, minimum GPA of 3.0, previous course work in statistics. Additional exam requirements/recommendations for international students: Required—TOEFL. *Application deadline:* For fall admission, 2/15 priority date for domestic students. Applications are processed on a rolling basis. Application fee: $70. *Expenses:* Contact institution. *Financial support:* Research assistantships, teaching assistantships, career-related internships or fieldwork, Federal Work-Study, and institutionally sponsored loans available. Support available to part-time students. Financial award application deadline: 4/1. *Faculty research:* Evaluation of primary care practitioner practice, access to primary care.

University of Pennsylvania, School of Nursing, Neonatal Nurse Practitioner Program, Philadelphia, PA 19104. Offers MSN. *Accreditation:* AACN. Part-time programs available. *Students:* 1 (woman) full-time, 9 part-time (8 women). In 2009, 3 master's awarded. *Entrance requirements:* For master's, GRE General Test, BSN, minimum GPA of 3.0, previous course work in statistics, 1 year of experience in a neonatal intensive care unit. Additional exam requirements/recommendations for international students: Required—TOEFL. *Application deadline:* For fall admission, 2/15 priority date for domestic students. Applications are processed on a rolling basis. Application fee: $70. *Expenses:* Contact institution. *Financial support:* Fellowships, research assistantships, teaching assistantships, career-related internships or fieldwork, Federal Work-Study, and institutionally sponsored loans available. Support available to part-time students. Financial award application deadline: 4/1. *Faculty research:* Neurobehavioral development, temperament, newborn sucking behaviors, parenting pre-term infants.

University of Pennsylvania, School of Nursing, Perinatal Advanced Practice Nurse Specialist Program, Philadelphia, PA 19104. Offers MSN. *Accreditation:* AACN. Part-time programs available. *Students:* 4 full-time (all women), 17 part-time (all women); includes 4 minority (1 African American, 3 Asian Americans or Pacific Islanders). In 2009, 12 master's awarded. *Entrance requirements:* For master's, GRE General Test, BSN, minimum GPA of 3.0, previous course work in statistics. Additional exam requirements/recommendations for international students: Required—TOEFL. *Application deadline:* For fall admission, 2/15 priority date for domestic students. Applications are processed on a rolling basis. Application fee: $70. *Expenses:* Contact institution. *Financial support:* Fellowships, research assistantships, teaching assistantships, career-related internships or fieldwork, Federal Work-Study, and institutionally sponsored loans available. Support available to part-time students. Financial award application deadline: 4/1.

University of Pittsburgh, School of Nursing, Nurse Practitioner Program, Pittsburgh, PA 15260. Offers acute care nurse practitioner (MSN, DNP); adult nurse practitioner (MSN, DNP); family nurse practitioner (MSN, DNP); neonatal (MSN, DNP); nursing practice (DNP); pediatric nurse practitioner (MSN, DNP); psychiatric primary care nurse practitioner (MSN, DNP). *Accreditation:* AACN. Part-time programs available. *Students:* 27 full-time (26 women), 89 part-time (84 women); includes 6 minority (5 African Americans, 1 Asian American or Pacific Islander). Average age 34. 44 applicants, 64% accepted, 25 enrolled. In 2009, 28 master's awarded. *Degree requirements:* For master's, comprehensive exam, thesis optional. *Entrance requirements:* For master's, GRE General Test or MAT, BSN, RN license, letters of recommendation, resume, course work in statistics, 1-3 years of nursing experience; for doctorate, GRE General Test, BSN, RN license, minimum GPA of 3.5, 3 letters of recommendation. Additional exam requirements/recommendations for international students: Required—TOEFL (minimum score 550 paper-based; 213 computer-based; 80 iBT). *Application deadline:* For fall admission, 8/1 priority date for domestic students, 8/1 for international students; for spring admission, 12/1 priority date for domestic students, 12/1 for international students. Applications are processed on a rolling basis. Application fee: $50. Electronic applications accepted. *Expenses:* Tuition, state resident: full-time $16,402; part-time $665 per credit. Tuition, nonresident: full-time $28,694; part-time $1175 per credit. Required fees: $690; $175 per term. Tuition and fees vary according to program. *Unit head:* Dr. Helen Burns, Associate Dean for Clinical Education, 412-624-6616, Fax: 412-624-2401, E-mail: burnsh@pitt.edu. *Application contact:* Laurie Lapsley, Administrator of Graduate Student Services, 412-624-9670, Fax: 412-624-2409, E-mail: lapsleyl@pitt.edu.

University of Rochester, School of Nursing, Rochester, NY 14642. Offers acute care nurse practitioner (MS); adult nurse practitioner (MS); adult psychiatric mental health nurse practitioner (MS); adult/geriatric nurse practitioner (MS); care of children and families/pediatric nurse practitioner (MS); care of children and families/pediatric nurse practitioner with pediatric behavioral health (MS); care of children and families/pediatric nurse practitioner/neonatal nurse practitioner (MS); child and adolescent psychiatric mental health nurse practitioner (MS); clinical nurse leader (MS); disaster response and emergency preparedness (MS); family nurse practitioner (MS); health care organization management and leadership (MS); health practice research (PhD); health promotion, education and technology (MS); nursing (Certificate). *Accreditation:* AACN; NLN (one or more programs are accredited). Part-time programs available. Postbaccalaureate distance learning degree programs offered (minimal on-campus study). *Faculty:* 26 full-time (24 women), 20 part-time/adjunct (15 women). *Students:* 50 full-time (45 women), 178 part-time (165 women); includes 33 minority (17 African Americans, 2 American Indian/Alaska Native, 10 Asian Americans or Pacific Islanders, 4 Hispanic Americans), 11 international. Average age 35. 56 applicants, 80% accepted, 35 enrolled. In 2009, 53 master's, 5 doctorates awarded. Terminal master's awarded for partial completion of doctoral program. *Degree requirements:* For master's, comprehensive exam or thesis; for doctorate, thesis/dissertation. *Entrance requirements:* For master's, BS in nursing, minimum GPA of 3.0, course work in statistics; for doctorate, GRE General Test, MS in nursing, minimum GPA of 3.5; for Certificate, MS in nursing. Additional exam requirements/recommendations for international students: Recommended—TOEFL (minimum score 560 paper-based; 230 computer-based; 88 iBT). *Application deadline:* For fall admission, 11/1 priority date for domestic and international students. Application fee: $50. *Financial support:* In 2009–10, 53 students received support, including 14 fellowships with full and partial tuition reimbursements available (averaging $17,497 per year); scholarships/grants, traineeships, health care benefits, tuition waivers (partial), and unspecified assistantships also available. Support available to part-time students. Financial award application deadline: 6/30. *Faculty research:* Clinical research in aging, managing asthma in children, interventions to improve outcomes in critically ill children and their mothers, nurse home visitation studies, medical device evaluation, critical care clinical studies, high risk behavior and prevention, palliative care, pregnancy-related weight gain. Total annual research expenditures: $4.8 million. *Unit head:* Dr. Kathy P. Parker, Dean, 585-273-5639, Fax: 585-273-1268, E-mail: kathy_parker@urmc.rochester.edu. *Application contact:* Elaine Andolina, Director of Admissions, 585-275-2375, Fax: 585-756-8299, E-mail: elaine_andolina@urmc.rochester.edu.

University of South Africa, College of Human Sciences, Pretoria, South Africa. Offers adult education (M Ed); African languages (MA, PhD); African politics (MA, PhD); Afrikaans (MA, PhD); ancient history (MA, PhD); ancient Near Eastern studies (MA, PhD); anthropology (MA, PhD); applied linguistics (MA); Arabic (MA, PhD); archaeology (MA); art history (MA); Biblical archaeology (MA); Biblical studies (M Th, D Th, PhD); Christian spirituality (M Th, D Th); church history (M Th, D Th); classical studies (MA, PhD); clinical psychology (MA); communication (MA, PhD); comparative education (M Ed, Ed D); consulting psychology (D Admin, D Com, PhD); curriculum studies (M Ed, Ed D); development studies (M Admin, MA, D Admin, PhD); didactics (M Ed, Ed D); education (M Tech); education management (M Ed, Ed D); educational psychology (M Ed); English (MA); environmental education (M Ed); French (MA, PhD); German (MA, PhD); Greek (MA); guidance and counseling (M Ed); health studies (MA, PhD), including health sciences education (MA), health services management (MA), medical and surgical nursing science (critical care general) (MA), midwifery and neonatal nursing science (MA), trauma and emergency care (MA); history (MA, PhD); history of education (Ed D); inclusive education (M Ed, Ed D); information and communications technology policy and regulation (MA); information science (MA, MIS, PhD); international politics (MA, PhD); Islamic studies (MA, PhD); Italian (MA, PhD); Judaica (MA, PhD); linguistics (MA, PhD); mathematical education (M Ed); mathematics education (MA); missiology (M Th, D Th); modern Hebrew (MA, PhD); musicology (MA, MMus, D Mus, PhD); natural science education (M Ed); New Testament (M Th, D Th); Old Testament (D Th); pastoral therapy (M Th, D Th); philosophy (MA); philosophy of education (M Ed, Ed D); politics (MA, PhD); Portuguese (MA, PhD); practical theology (M Th, D Th); psychology (MA, MS, PhD); psychology of education (M Ed, Ed D); public health (MA); religious studies (MA, D Th, PhD); Romance languages (MA); Russian (MA, PhD); Semitic languages (MA, PhD); social behavior studies in HIV/AIDS (MA); social science (mental health) (MA); social science in development studies (MA); social science in psychology (MA); social science in social work (MA); social science in sociology (MA); social work (MSW, DSW, PhD); socio-education (M Ed, Ed D); sociolinguistics (MA); sociology (MA, PhD); Spanish (MA, PhD); systematic theology (M Th, D Th); TESOL (teaching English to speakers of other languages) (MA); theological ethics (M Th, D Th); theory of literature (MA, PhD); urban ministries (D Th); urban ministry (M Th).

University of South Alabama, Graduate School, College of Nursing, Mobile, AL 36688-0002. Offers adult health nursing (MSN); community/mental health nursing (MSN); maternal/child nursing (MSN); nursing (DNP). *Accreditation:* AACN. *Degree requirements:* For master's, thesis optional. *Entrance requirements:* For master's, BSN, RN licensure, minimum GPA of 3.0, resume documenting clinical experience, background check, drug screening; for doctorate, GRE. *Expenses:* Tuition, state resident: part-time $218 per contact hour. Required fees: $1102 per year.

University of Southern Mississippi, Graduate School, College of Health, School of Nursing, Hattiesburg, MS 39406-0001. Offers adult health nursing (MSN); community health nursing (MSN); ethics (PhD); family nurse practitioner (MSN); leadership (PhD); nursing service administration (MSN); policy analysis (PhD); psychiatric nursing (MSN). *Accreditation:* AACN. Part-time and evening/weekend programs available. *Faculty:* 17 full-time (16 women), 1 part-time/adjunct (0 women). *Students:* 63 full-time (57 women), 40 part-time (36 women); includes 23 minority (all African Americans). Average age 40. 69 applicants, 59% accepted, 37 enrolled. In 2009, 28 master's, 2 doctorates awarded. *Degree requirements:* For master's, comprehensive exam, thesis optional; for doctorate, comprehensive exam, thesis/dissertation. *Entrance requirements:* For master's, GRE General Test, minimum GPA of 2.75, nursing license, BS in nursing; for doctorate, GRE General Test, master's degree in nursing, minimum GPA of 3.5. Additional exam requirements/recommendations for international students: Required—TOEFL. *Application deadline:* For fall admission, 3/15 priority date for domestic students, 5/1 for international students. Applications are processed on a rolling basis. Application fee: $35. Electronic applications accepted. *Expenses:* Tuition, state resident: full-time $5096; part-time $284 per hour. Tuition, nonresident: full-time $13,052; part-time $726 per hour. Required fees: $402. Tuition and fees vary according to course level and course load. *Financial support:* In 2009–10, 14 research assistantships with full tuition reimbursements (averaging $12,577 per year) were awarded; teaching assistantships, Federal Work-Study and traineeships also available. Financial award application deadline: 3/15; financial award applicants required to submit FAFSA. *Faculty research:* Gerontology, caregivers, HIV, bereavement, pain, nursing leadership. *Unit head:* Dr. Katherine Nugent, Director and Associate Dean, 601-266-5500, Fax: 601-266-5927. *Application contact:* Dr. Anne Brock, Graduate Coordinator, 601-266-5500, Fax: 601-266-5927.

Vanderbilt University, School of Nursing, Nashville, TN 37240. Offers adult acute care nurse practitioner (MSN); adult nurse practitioner/cardiovascular disease management and prevention (MSN); adult nurse practitioner/palliative care (MSN); clinical management (clinical nurse leader/specialist) (MSN); emergency nurse practitioner (MSN); family nurse practitioner (MSN); gerontology nurse practitioner (MSN); health systems management (MSN); neonatal nurse practitioner (MSN); nurse midwifery (MSN); nurse midwifery/family nurse practitioner (MSN); nursing informatics (MSN); nursing practice (DNP); nursing science (PhD); nutrition (MS); pediatric acute care nurse practitioner (MSN); pediatric primary care nurse practitioner (MSN); psychiatric-mental health nurse practitioner (MSN); women's health nurse practitioner (MSN), including urogynecology; women's health nurse practitioner/adult nurse practitioner (MSN); MSN/M Div; MSN/MTS. *Accreditation:* ACNM/DOA; NLN (one or more programs are accredited). Part-time programs available. Postbaccalaureate distance learning degree programs offered (minimal on-campus study). *Faculty:* 118 full-time (102 women), 429 part-time/adjunct (309 women). *Students:* 484 full-time (435 women), 319 part-time (284 women); includes 84 minority (55 African Americans, 4 American Indian/Alaska Native, 10 Asian Americans or Pacific Islanders, 15 Hispanic Americans), 16 international. Average age 32. 900 applicants, 65% accepted, 433 enrolled. In 2009, 303 master's, 1 doctorate awarded. *Degree requirements:* For doctorate, comprehensive exam, thesis/dissertation. *Entrance requirements:* For master's, GRE General Test, minimum B average in undergraduate course work, 3 letters of recommendation; for doctorate, GRE General Test, interview, 3 letters of recommendation from doctorally-prepared faculty, MSN, essay. Additional exam requirements/recommendations for international students: Required—TOEFL. *Application deadline:* For fall admission, 12/1 priority date for domestic and international students. Applications are processed on a rolling basis. Application fee: $50. *Expenses:* Contact institution. *Financial support:* In 2009–10, 389 students received support, including 1 research assistantship (averaging $5,000 per year); teaching assistantships, scholarships/grants, health care benefits, and tuition waivers also available. Support available to part-time students. Financial award application deadline: 3/15; financial award applicants required to submit FAFSA. *Faculty research:* Lymphedema, palliative care and bereavement, health services research including workforce, safety and quality of care, gerontology, better birth outcomes including nutrition. Total annual research expenditures: $1.4 million. *Unit head:* Dr. Colleen Conway-Welch, Dean, 615-343-8776, Fax: 615-343-7711, E-mail: colleen.conway-welch@vanderbilt.edu. *Application contact:* Cheryl Feldner, Assistant Director of Admissions, 615-322-3800, Fax: 615-343-0333, E-mail: cheryl.feldner@vanderbilt.edu.

Wayne State University, College of Nursing, Program in Advanced Practice Nursing with Women, Neonates and Children, Detroit, MI 48202. Offers advanced practice nursing with women, neonates and children (MSN); neonatal nurse practitioner (Certificate). *Accreditation:* AACN. Part-time programs available. *Degree requirements:* For master's, thesis or alternative. *Entrance requirements:* For master's, minimum GPA of 2.8. Additional exam requirements/recommendations for international students: Required—TOEFL (minimum score 550 paper-based; 213 computer-based); Recommended—TWE (minimum score 6). Electronic applications accepted. *Faculty research:* Acculturation and parenting, domestic violence, evidence-based midwifery practice, pain in children, trauma and community violence.

Medical/Surgical Nursing

Angelo State University, College of Graduate Studies, College of Nursing and Allied Health, Department of Nursing, San Angelo, TX 76909. Offers advanced practice registered nurse (MSN); nurse educator (MSN); nursing—RN to MSN (MSN). *Accreditation:* NLN. Part-time and evening/weekend programs available. *Faculty:* 7 full-time (all women). *Students:* 11 full-time (9 women), 41 part-time (38 women); includes 13 minority (3 African Americans, 4 Asian Americans or Pacific Islanders, 6 Hispanic Americans). Average age 41. 29 applicants, 93% accepted, 21 enrolled. In 2009, 13 master's awarded. *Degree requirements:* For master's, comprehensive exam. *Entrance requirements:* For master's, GRE General Test. Additional exam requirements/recommendations for international students: Required—TOEFL or IELTS. *Application deadline:* For fall admission, 7/15 priority date for domestic students, 6/10 for international students; for spring admission, 12/1 priority date for domestic students, 11/1 for international students. Applications are processed on a rolling basis. Application fee: $40 ($50 for international students). Electronic applications accepted. *Expenses:* Tuition, state resident: full-time $3396; part-time $142 per credit hour. Tuition, nonresident: full-time $10,152; part-time $423 per credit hour. Required fees: $1786; $36.25 per credit hour. $494 per semester. Full-time tuition and fees vary according to course load, degree level and program. *Financial support:* In 2009–10, 24 students received support. Career-related internships or fieldwork, Federal Work-Study, and scholarships/grants available. Support available to part-time students. Financial award application deadline: 3/1. *Unit head:* Dr. Susan S. Wilkinson, Department Head, 325-942-2060 Ext. 290, Fax: 325-942-2236, E-mail: susan.wilkinson@angelo.edu. *Application contact:* Dr. Molly J. Walker, Graduate Advisor, 325-942-2060 Ext. 246, Fax: 325-942-2236, E-mail: molly.walker@angelo.edu.

Boston College, William F. Connell School of Nursing, Chestnut Hill, MA 02467-3800. Offers adult health nursing (MS); community health nursing (MS); family health (MS); forensic nursing (MS); gerontology (MS); maternal/child health nursing (MS), including pediatric and women's health; nurse anesthesia (MS); nursing (PhD); palliative care (MS), including adult and pediatric; psychiatric-mental health nursing (MS); MBA/MS; MS/MA; MS/PhD. *Accreditation:* AACN; AANA/CANAEP (one or more programs are accredited). Part-time programs available. *Faculty:* 48 full-time (46 women), 31 part-time/adjunct (29 women). *Students:* 183 full-time (169 women), 147 part-time (140 women); includes 36 minority (15 African Americans, 2 American Indian/Alaska Native, 17 Asian Americans or Pacific Islanders, 2 Hispanic Americans), 7 international. Average age 29. 347 applicants, 53% accepted, 103 enrolled. In 2009, 79 master's, 7 doctorates awarded. *Degree requirements:* For master's, comprehensive exam, research project; for doctorate, comprehensive exam, thesis/dissertation, computer literacy exam or foreign language. *Entrance requirements:* For master's, bachelor's degree in nursing; for doctorate, GRE General Test, master's degree in nursing. Additional exam requirements/recommendations for international students: Required—TOEFL (minimum score 550 paper-based; 213 computer-based). *Application deadline:* For fall admission, 11/1 for domestic and international students; for winter admission, 12/31 for domestic and international students; for spring admission, 9/15 for domestic and international students. Applications are processed on a rolling basis. Application fee: $40. Electronic applications accepted. *Financial support:* In 2009–10, 83 students received support, including 12 fellowships with partial tuition reimbursements available (averaging $15,000 per year), 5 teaching assistantships (averaging $13,746 per year); research assistantships, Federal Work-Study, institutionally sponsored loans, scholarships/grants, traineeships, health care benefits, and tuition waivers (partial) also available. Support available to part-time students. Financial award application deadline: 3/1; financial award applicants required to submit FAFSA. *Faculty research:* Ethics, reduction of risk behaviors, support during chronic illness, violence, gerontology. Total annual research expenditures: $1.4 million. *Unit head:* Dr. Susan Gennaro, Dean, 617-552-4251, Fax: 617-552-0931, E-mail: susan.gennaro@bc.edu. *Application contact:* MaryBeth Crowley, Graduate Programs Assistant, 617-552-4928, Fax: 617-552-2121, E-mail: csongrad@bc.edu.

Case Western Reserve University, Frances Payne Bolton School of Nursing, Doctor of Nursing Practice Program, Cleveland, OH 44106. Offers acute care nurse practitioner (DNP); adult nurse practitioner (DNP); family nurse practitioner (DNP); gerontological nurse practitioner (DNP); graduate entry/pre-licensure option (DNP); medical-surgical nursing (DNP); midwifery/family nursing (DNP); neonatal nurse practitioner (DNP); pediatric nurse practitioner (DNP); post-licensure option (DNP); psychiatric-mental health nurse practitioner (DNP); women's health nurse practitioner (DNP). Graduate entry option allows baccalaureate-prepared college graduates from non-nursing backgrounds to earn certificate and MSN in addition to ND. Terminal master's awarded for partial completion of doctoral program. *Degree requirements:* For doctorate, thesis/dissertation. *Entrance requirements:* For doctorate, GRE General Test or MAT. *Faculty research:* Clinical nursing, acute care, gerontology, mental health, critical care.

Case Western Reserve University, Frances Payne Bolton School of Nursing, Master's Programs in Nursing, Program in Medical-Surgical Nursing, Cleveland, OH 44106. Offers MSN. *Accreditation:* NLN. Part-time programs available. *Degree requirements:* For master's, thesis optional. *Entrance requirements:* For master's, GRE General Test or MAT. *Faculty research:* Clinical nursing, oncology, acute care, critical care, mobilization in the Intensive Care Unit.

Columbia University, School of Nursing, Program in Acute Care Nurse Practitioner, New York, NY 10032. Offers MS, Adv C. *Accreditation:* AACN. Part-time programs available. *Entrance requirements:* For master's, GRE General Test, 1 year of clinical experience (preferred), BSN; for Adv C, MSN. Electronic applications accepted.

Daemen College, Department of Nursing, Amherst, NY 14226-3592. Offers adult nurse practitioner (MS); nursing education (MS, Post Master's Certificate); nursing executive leadership (MS); nursing practice (DNP); palliative care nursing (MS, Post Master's Certificate). *Accreditation:* NLN. Part-time programs available. *Faculty:* 3 full-time (all women), 6 part-time/adjunct (all women). *Students:* 8 full-time (all women), 105 part-time (98 women); includes 17 minority (10 African Americans, 1 American Indian/Alaska Native, 3 Asian Americans or Pacific Islanders, 3 Hispanic Americans), 1 international. Average age 42. 66 applicants, 79% accepted, 37 enrolled. In 2009, 24 master's, 4 other advanced degrees awarded. *Degree requirements:* For master's, thesis or alternative. *Entrance requirements:* For master's, BN, 1 year medical/surgical experience, RN license and state registration, 1 course in statistics with minimum grade of 'C', 3 letters of recommendation, minimum GPA of 3.25, interview; for doctorate, MS in advance nursing practice; New York state RN license; personal goal statement; resume; interview; statistics course with minimum grade of 'C'; for Post Master's Certificate, master's degree in clinical area; RN license and current registration; one year of clinical experience; statistics course with minimum grade of 'C'. Additional exam requirements/recommendations for international students: Required—TOEFL (minimum score 500 paper-based; 173 computer-based; 61 iBT). *Application deadline:* For fall admission, 3/1 priority date for domestic and international students; for spring admission, 10/1 priority date for domestic and international students. Applications are processed on a rolling basis. Application fee: $25. Electronic applications accepted. *Expenses:* Tuition: Part-time $770 per credit hour. Tuition and fees vary according to course load, program and reciprocity agreements. *Financial support:* In 2009–10, 1 student received support. Institutionally sponsored loans and scholarships/grants available. Financial award application deadline: 2/15; financial award applicants required to submit FAFSA. *Faculty research:* Professional stress, client behavior, drug therapy, treatment modalities and pulmonary cancers, chemical dependency. *Unit head:* Dr. Mary Lou Rusin, Chair, 716-839-8387, Fax: 716-839-8403, E-mail: mrusin@daemen.edu. *Application contact:* Scott Rowe, Associate Director of Graduate Programs, 716-839-8225, Fax: 716-839-8229, E-mail: srowe@daemen.edu.

Eastern Virginia Medical School, Surgical Assistant Program, Norfolk, VA 23501-1980. Offers Certificate, Graduate Certificate. *Faculty:* 8. *Students:* 23 full-time (20 women); includes 1 African American, 2 Asian Americans or Pacific Islanders, 2 Hispanic Americans. 19 applicants, 79% accepted, 12 enrolled. *Application deadline:* For fall admission, 2/1 for domestic students. Applications are processed on a rolling basis. Application fee: $60. Electronic applications accepted. *Expenses:* Contact institution. *Unit head:* R. Clinton Crews, Program Director, 757-446-8961, Fax: 757-446-6179, E-mail: crewsrc@evms.edu. *Application contact:* Nancy Stromann, Health Professions Supervisor, 757-446-6100, Fax: 757-446-6179, E-mail: stromand@evms.edu.

Gannon University, School of Graduate Studies, Morosky College of Health Professions and Sciences, School of Health Professions, Villa Maria School of Nursing, Erie, PA 16541-0001. Offers anesthesia (MSN); business administration (MSN); family nurse practitioner (Certificate); medical-surgical nursing (MSN); nurse anesthesia (Certificate); nursing rural practitioner (MSN). *Accreditation:* AACN; AANA/CANAEP (one or more programs are accredited). Part-time and evening/weekend programs available. *Students:* 19 full-time (11 women), 59 part-time (45 women); includes 2 minority (both African Americans). Average age 36. 16 applicants, 81% accepted, 0 enrolled. In 2009, 19 master's awarded. *Degree requirements:* For master's, thesis. *Entrance requirements:* For master's, GRE General Test, degree in nursing. Additional exam requirements/recommendations for international students: Required—TOEFL (minimum score 79 iBT). *Application deadline:* For spring admission, 8/1 for domestic students. Application fee: $25. Electronic applications accepted. *Expenses:* Tuition: Full-time $13,590; part-time $755 per credit. Required fees: $524; $17 per credit. Tuition and fees vary according to course load, degree level, campus/location and program. *Financial support:* Scholarships/grants available. Financial award application deadline: 7/1; financial award applicants required to submit FAFSA. *Unit head:* Dr. Sharon Thompson, Director, 814-871-5345, E-mail: thompson001@gannon.edu. *Application contact:* Kara Morgan, Assistant Director of Graduate Admissions, 814-871-5831, Fax: 814-871-5827, E-mail: graduate@gannon.edu.

Inter American University of Puerto Rico, Arecibo Campus, Program in Nursing, Arecibo, PR 00614-4050. Offers community nursing (MS); critical care nursing (MS); primary care nursing (MS); surgical nursing (MS). *Entrance requirements:* For master's, EXADEP or GRE General Test or MAT, 2 letters of recommendation, bachelor's degree in nursing, minimum GPA of 2.5 in last 60 credits, minimum 1 year nursing experience, nursing license.

New Mexico State University, Graduate School, College of Health and Social Services, School of Nursing, Las Cruces, NM 88003-8001. Offers community/public health (MSN); medical-surgical (adult health) (MSN); nursing (PhD); nursing administration (MSN); psychiatric/mental health (MSN). *Accreditation:* AACN. Part-time programs available. Postbaccalaureate distance learning degree programs offered (minimal on-campus study). *Faculty:* 10 full-time (all women), 5 part-time/adjunct (all women). *Students:* 59 full-time (48 women), 70 part-time (61 women); includes 47 minority (9 African Americans, 3 American Indian/Alaska Native, 5 Asian Americans or Pacific Islanders, 30 Hispanic Americans). Average age 43. 82 applicants, 96% accepted, 63 enrolled. In 2009, 32 master's, 1 doctorate awarded. *Degree requirements:* For master's, comprehensive exam, thesis optional, clinical practice; for doctorate, comprehensive exam, thesis/dissertation, clinical practice. *Entrance requirements:* For master's, NCLEX exam, BSN, minimum GPA of 3.0, course work in statistics, 3 letters of reference, writing sample, RN license, CPR certification, proof of liability, immunizations, criminal background check; for doctorate, NCLEX exam, MSN, minimum GPA of 3.0, 3 letters of reference, writing sample, RN license, CPR certification, proof of liability, immunizations, criminal background check. Additional exam requirements/recommendations for international students: Required—TOEFL (minimum score 550 paper-based). *Application deadline:* For fall admission, 3/1 priority date for domestic students; for spring admission, 10/1 priority date for domestic students. Applications are processed on a rolling basis. Application fee: $30 ($50 for international students). Electronic applications accepted. *Expenses:* Tuition, state resident: full-time $4080; part-time $223 per credit. Tuition, nonresident: full-time $14,256; part-time $647 per credit. Required fees: $1278; $639 per semester. *Financial support:* In 2009–10, 14 students received support, including 2 teaching assistantships (averaging $18,380 per year); fellowships, research assistantships, career-related internships or fieldwork, Federal Work-Study, scholarships/grants, traineeships, and health care benefits also available. Financial award application deadline: 3/1. *Faculty research:* Public policy, community health, health disparities, self efficacy and self management, psychiatric mental health. *Unit head:* Dr. Pamela Schultz, Director, 575-646-3812, Fax: 575-646-2167, E-mail: pschultz@nmsu.edu. *Application contact:* Dr. Kathleen Huttlinger, Associate Director for Graduate Studies, 575-646-4386, Fax: 575-646-2167.

Pontifical Catholic University of Puerto Rico, College of Sciences, Department of Nursing, Program in Medical-Surgical Nursing, Ponce, PR 00717-0777. Offers MS. Part-time and evening/weekend programs available. *Degree requirements:* For master's, comprehensive exam (for some programs), thesis, clinical research paper. *Entrance requirements:* For master's, GRE General Test, 2 letters of recommendation, interview, minimum GPA of 2.75. Electronic applications accepted.

Rush University, College of Nursing, Department of Adult Health Nursing, Chicago, IL 60612-3832. Offers acute care nurse practitioner (MSN, Post-Master's Certificate); adult health nursing (DNP, PhD); adult nurse practitioner (MSN, Post-Master's Certificate); adult/gerontological nurse practitioner (MSN); anesthesia nurse practitioner (MSN, Post-Master's Certificate); critical care clinical specialist (MSN); gerontological nurse practitioner (MSN, Post-Master's Certificate); medical surgical clinical specialist (MSN). *Accreditation:* AACN; AANA/CANAEP (one or more programs are accredited). Part-time programs available. Postbaccalaureate distance learning degree programs offered (minimal on-campus study). Terminal master's awarded for partial completion of doctoral program. *Degree requirements:* For master's, capstone project; for doctorate, thesis/dissertation, DNP leadership project. *Entrance requirements:* For master's, GRE General Test (waived if nursing GPA is above 3.0 or cumulative GPA is above 3.25), interview; for doctorate, GRE General Test, interview, course work in statistics (PhD). Additional exam requirements/recommendations for international students: Required—TOEFL, TWE. Electronic applications accepted. *Faculty research:* Complementary/alternative medicine, critical care outcomes, cardiac risk reduction, Alzheimer's Disease, telehealth monitoring.

Saint Francis Medical Center College of Nursing, Graduate Program, Peoria, IL 61603-3783. Offers child and family nursing (MSN); clinical nurse leader (MSN); medical-surgical nursing (MSN); neonatal nurse practitioner (MSN); nurse clinician (Post-Graduate Certificate); nurse educator (Post-Graduate Certificate); nursing (DNP). *Accreditation:* NLN. Part-time programs available. Postbaccalaureate distance learning degree programs offered (minimal on-campus study). *Faculty:* 3 full-time (all women), 9 part-time/adjunct (all women). *Students:* 8 full-time (all women), 135 part-time (122 women); includes 6 minority (1 African American, 4 Asian Americans or Pacific Islanders, 1 Hispanic American). Average age 28. 19 applicants, 100% accepted, 19 enrolled. In 2009, 24 master's awarded. *Degree requirements:* For master's, research experience, portfolio, practicum. *Entrance requirements:* For master's, nursing research, health assessment, graduate course work in statistics, RN license. Additional exam requirements/recommendations for international students: Required—TOEFL. *Application deadline:* For fall admission, 6/1 priority date for domestic and international students; for spring admission, 11/15 priority date for domestic and international students. Applications are processed on a rolling basis. Application fee: $50. Electronic applications accepted. *Expenses:* Tuition: Part-time $472 per semester hour. Required fees: $130 per semester. *Financial support:* In 2009–10, 6 students received support. Scholarships/grants and tuition waivers (partial) available. Support available to part-time students. Financial award application deadline: 6/15; financial award applicants required to submit FAFSA. *Faculty research:* Outcome and curriculum planning, health promotion, NCLEX-RN results, decision making program evaluation. *Unit head:* Dr. Lois J. Hamilton, Dean, 309-655-2201, Fax: 309-624-8973, E-mail: lois.j.hamilton@osfhealthcare.org. *Application contact:* Dr. Janice F. Boundy, Associate Dean, 309-655-2230, Fax: 309-624-8973, E-mail: jan.f.boundy@osfhealthcare.org.

State University of New York Downstate Medical Center, College of Nursing, Graduate Program in Nursing, Program in Clinical Nurse Specialist, Brooklyn, NY 11203-2098. Offers MS, Post Master's Certificate.

Medical/Surgical Nursing

Uniformed Services University of the Health Sciences, Graduate School of Nursing, Bethesda, MD 20814-4799. Offers family nurse practitioner (MSN); nurse anesthesia (MSN); perioperative clinical nurse specialty (MSN); psychiatric mental health nurse practitioner (MSN). Available to military officers only. *Accreditation:* AACN; NLN. Postbaccalaureate distance learning degree programs offered (no on-campus study). *Faculty:* 27 full-time (18 women), 2 part-time/adjunct (both women). *Students:* 75 full-time (32 women), 3 part-time (all women); includes 20 minority (8 African Americans, 5 Asian Americans or Pacific Islanders, 7 Hispanic Americans). Average age 36. 108 applicants, 72% accepted, 78 enrolled. In 2009, 54 master's awarded. *Degree requirements:* For master's, thesis or alternative. *Entrance requirements:* For master's, GRE, BSN, clinical experience, minimum GPA of 3.0, previous course work in science. *Application deadline:* For fall admission, 7/1 for domestic students; for winter admission, 2/15 for domestic students. Application fee: $0. Electronic applications accepted. *Faculty research:* Prenatal care, military health care, military readiness, distance learning. *Unit head:* Col. Bruce A. Schoneboom, Associate Dean for Academic Affairs, 301-295-1180, Fax: 301-295-1707, E-mail: bschoneboom@usuhs.mil. *Application contact:* Terry Lynn Malavakis, Recording Secretary for Admissions Committee, 301-295-1055, Fax: 301-295-1707, E-mail: tmalavakis@usuhs.mil.

University of Maryland, Baltimore, Graduate School, School of Nursing, Master's Program in Nursing, Baltimore, MD 21201. Offers community health nursing (MS); gerontological nursing (MS); maternal-child nursing (MS); medical-surgical nursing (MS); nurse-midwifery education (MS); nursing administration (MS); nursing education (MS); nursing health policy (MS); primary care nursing (MS); psychiatric nursing (MS); MS/MBA. *Accreditation:* AACN; AANA/CANAEP; ACNM/DOA; NLN (one or more programs are accredited). Part-time programs available. *Students:* 387 full-time (338 women), 528 part-time (491 women); includes 330 minority (230 African Americans, 3 American Indian/Alaska Native, 81 Asian Americans or Pacific Islanders, 16 Hispanic Americans), 10 international. Average age 36. 849 applicants, 40% accepted, 255 enrolled. In 2009, 264 master's awarded. *Degree requirements:* For master's, comprehensive exam (for some programs), thesis or alternative. *Entrance requirements:* For master's, GRE General Test, minimum GPA of 2.75, course work in statistics, BS in nursing. Additional exam requirements/recommendations for international students: Required—TOEFL (minimum score 550 paper-based; 80 iBT), or IELTS (minimum score 7). *Application deadline:* For fall admission, 1/15 for international students. Application fee: $50. Electronic applications accepted. *Expenses:* Tuition, state resident: full-time $7290; part-time $405 per credit hour. Tuition, nonresident: full-time $12,780; part-time $710 per credit hour. Required fees: $774; $10 per credit hour. $297 per semester. Tuition and fees vary according to course load, degree level and program. *Financial support:* Fellowships, research assistantships, teaching assistantships, career-related internships or fieldwork and traineeships available. Support available to part-time students. Financial award application deadline: 2/15; financial award applicants required to submit FAFSA. *Unit head:* Dr. Jane Kapustin, Assistant Dean, 410-706-6741, Fax: 410-706-4231. *Application contact:* Marjorie Fass, Admissions Director, 410-706-0501, Fax: 410-706-7238.

University of Massachusetts Lowell, School of Health and Environment, Department of Nursing, Lowell, MA 01854-2881. Offers adult psychiatric and mental health nursing (MS, Graduate Certificate); family health nursing (MS); gerontological nursing (MS, Graduate Certificate); geropsychiatric nursing (Graduate Certificate); nursing (PhD); nursing education (Graduate Certificate); palliative and end-of-life nursing care (Graduate Certificate). *Accreditation:* AACN. *Degree requirements:* For master's, thesis optional; for doctorate, thesis/dissertation. *Entrance requirements:* For master's and doctorate, GRE General Test. *Faculty research:* Gerontology, women's health issues, long-term care, alcoholism, health promotion.

University of Michigan, Horace H. Rackham School of Graduate Studies, School of Nursing, Division of Acute, Critical and Long-term Care, Program in Medical-Surgical Clinical Nurse Specialist, Ann Arbor, MI 48109. Offers MS. *Accreditation:* AACN. Part-time programs available. *Degree requirements:* For master's, thesis. *Entrance requirements:* For master's, GRE General Test (if BSN GPA less than 3.25), Michigan licensure, B average in BSN. Additional exam requirements/recommendations for international students: Required—TOEFL (minimum score 560 paper-based; 220 computer-based). Electronic applications accepted. *Expenses:* Tuition, state resident: full-time $17,286; part-time $1099 per credit hour. Tuition, nonresident: full-time $34,944; part-time $2080 per credit hour. Required fees: $95 per semester. Tuition and fees vary according to course load, degree level and program. *Faculty research:* Clinical specialist and nurse practitioner roles, obesity, breast cancer, Alzheimer's, neurological disorders.

University of South Africa, College of Human Sciences, Pretoria, South Africa. Offers adult education (M Ed); African languages (MA, PhD); African politics (MA, PhD); Afrikaans (MA, PhD); ancient history (MA, PhD); ancient Near Eastern studies (MA, PhD); anthropology (MA, PhD); applied linguistics (MA, PhD); Arabic (MA, PhD); archaeology (MA); art history (MA); Biblical archaeology (MA); Biblical studies (M Th, D Th, PhD); Christian spirituality (M Th, D Th); church history (M Th, D Th); classical studies (MA, PhD); clinical psychology (MA); communication (MA, PhD); comparative education (M Ed, Ed D); consulting psychology (D Admin, D Com, PhD); curriculum studies (M Ed, Ed D); development studies (M Admin, MA, D Admin, PhD); didactics (M Ed, Ed D); education (M Tech); education management (M Ed, Ed D); educational psychology (M Ed); English (MA); environmental education (M Ed); French (MA, PhD); German (MA, PhD); Greek (MA); guidance and counseling (M Ed); health studies (MA, PhD), including health sciences education (MA), health services management (MA), medical and surgical nursing science (critical care general) (MA), midwifery and neonatal nursing science (MA), trauma and emergency care (MA); history (MA, PhD); history of education (Ed D); inclusive education (M Ed, Ed D); information and communications technology policy and regulation (MA); information science (MA, MIS, PhD); international politics (MA, PhD); Islamic studies (MA, PhD); Italian (MA, PhD); Judaica (MA, PhD); linguistics (MA, PhD); mathematical education (M Ed); mathematics education (MA); missiology (M Th, D Th); modern Hebrew (MA, PhD); musicology (MA, MMus, D Mus, PhD); natural science education (M Ed); New Testament (M Th, D Th); Old Testament (D Th); pastoral therapy (M Th, D Th); philosophy (MA); philosophy of education (M Ed, Ed D); politics (MA, PhD); Portuguese (MA, PhD); practical theology (M Th, D Th); psychology (MA, MS, PhD); psychology of education (M Ed, Ed D); public health (MA); religious studies (MA, D Th, PhD); Romance languages (MA); Russian (MA, PhD); Semitic languages (MA, PhD); social behavior studies in HIV/AIDS (MA); social science (mental health) (MA); social science in development studies (MA); social science in psychology (MA); social science in social work (MA); social science in sociology (MA); social work (MSW, DSW, PhD); socio-education (M Ed, Ed D); sociolinguistics (MA); sociology (MA, PhD); Spanish (MA, PhD); systematic theology (M Th, D Th); TESOL (teaching English to speakers of other languages) (MA); theological ethics (M Th, D Th); theory of literature (MA, PhD); urban ministries (D Th); urban ministry (M Th).

University of South Carolina, The Graduate School, College of Nursing, Program in Clinical Nursing, Columbia, SC 29208. Offers acute care clinical specialist (MSN); acute care nurse practitioner (MSN); women's health nurse practitioner (MSN). *Accreditation:* AACN. Part-time programs available. *Degree requirements:* For master's, thesis or alternative. *Entrance requirements:* For master's, GRE General Test or MAT, BS in nursing, RN licensure. Additional exam requirements/recommendations for international students: Required—TOEFL (minimum score 570 paper-based; 230 computer-based). Electronic applications accepted. *Faculty research:* Systems research, evidence based practice, breast cancer, violence.

University of Southern Maine, College of Nursing and Health Professions, Portland, ME 04104-9300. Offers adult health nursing (PMC); clinical nurse leader (MS); clinical nurse specialist psychiatric-mental health nursing (MS); family nursing (PMC); medical/surgical nursing (MS); nurse practitioner adult health nursing (MS); nurse practitioner family nursing (MS); nurse practitioner psychiatric/mental health nursing (MS); psychiatric-mental health nursing (PMC); MBA/MSN. *Accreditation:* AACN. Part-time programs available. *Faculty:* 15 full-time (13 women), 4 part-time/adjunct (2 women). *Students:* 51 full-time (40 women), 54 part-time (49 women); includes 4 minority (1 American Indian/Alaska Native, 2 Asian Americans or Pacific Islanders, 1 Hispanic American). Average age 36. 95 applicants, 52% accepted, 27 enrolled. In 2009, 34 master's awarded. *Degree requirements:* For master's, thesis optional. *Entrance requirements:* For master's, GRE General Test or MAT, minimum GPA of 3.0. Additional exam requirements/recommendations for international students: Required—TOEFL (minimum score 550 paper-based; 213 computer-based). *Application deadline:* For fall admission, 4/1 for domestic and international students; for spring admission, 10/1 for domestic and international students. Application fee: $50. Electronic applications accepted. *Financial support:* In 2009–10, 10 students received support, including 5 research assistantships with tuition reimbursements available (averaging $3,375 per year), 3 teaching assistantships with tuition reimbursements available (averaging $3,375 per year); career-related internships or fieldwork, Federal Work-Study, scholarships/grants, traineeships, tuition waivers (full and partial), and unspecified assistantships also available. Support available to part-time students. Financial award application deadline: 2/15; financial award applicants required to submit FAFSA. *Faculty research:* Women's health, nursing history, weight control, community services, substance abuse. *Unit head:* Krista M. Meinersmann, Director of Nursing Program, 207-780-4505, Fax: 207-228-8177, E-mail: kmeinersmann@usm.maine.edu. *Application contact:* Mary Sloan, Assistant Director, Office of Graduate Studies, 207-780-4386, Fax: 207-780-4969, E-mail: gradstudies@usm.maine.edu.

Ursuline College, School of Graduate Studies, Programs in Nursing, Pepper Pike, OH 44124-4398. Offers care management (MSN); nurse practitioner (MSN); nursing (DNP); nursing education (MSN); palliative care (MSN). *Accreditation:* AACN. Part-time programs available. *Faculty:* 2 full-time (both women), 2 part-time/adjunct (both women). *Students:* 1 (woman) full-time, 94 part-time (88 women); includes 12 minority (11 African Americans, 1 Asian American or Pacific Islander). Average age 39. 68 applicants, 78% accepted, 40 enrolled. In 2009, 22 master's awarded. *Degree requirements:* For master's, comprehensive exam. *Entrance requirements:* For master's, minimum undergraduate GPA of 3.0, bachelor's degree in nursing, eligibility for or current Ohio RN license. Additional exam requirements/recommendations for international students: Required—TOEFL (minimum score 500 paper-based; 173 computer-based). *Application deadline:* For fall admission, 8/1 priority date for domestic students. Applications are processed on a rolling basis. Application fee: $25. *Expenses:* Tuition: Full-time $14,544; part-time $808 per credit hour. Required fees: $230; $75 per semester. *Financial support:* In 2009–10, 11 students received support. Federal Work-Study available. Financial award application deadline: 3/1. *Unit head:* Dr. Janet Baker, Director, 440-864-8172, Fax: 440-684-6053. *Application contact:* Melanie Steele, Secretary, 440-646-8199, Fax: 440-684-6138, E-mail: gradsch@ursuline.edu.

Vanderbilt University, School of Nursing, Nashville, TN 37240. Offers adult acute care nurse practitioner (MSN); adult nurse practitioner/cardiovascular disease management and prevention (MSN); adult nurse practitioner/palliative care (MSN); clinical management (clinical nurse leader/specialist) (MSN); emergency nurse practitioner (MSN); family nurse practitioner (MSN); gerontology nurse practitioner (MSN); health systems management (MSN); neonatal nurse practitioner (MSN); nurse midwifery (MSN); nurse midwifery/family nurse practitioner (MSN); nursing informatics (MSN); nursing practice (DNP); nursing science (PhD); nutrition (MS); pediatric acute care nurse practitioner (MSN); pediatric primary care nurse practitioner (MSN); psychiatric-mental health nurse practitioner (MSN); women's health nurse practitioner (MSN), including urogynecology; women's health nurse practitioner/adult nurse practitioner (MSN); MSN/M Div; MSN/MTS. *Accreditation:* ACNM/DOA; NLN (one or more programs are accredited). Part-time programs available. Postbaccalaureate distance learning degree programs offered (minimal on-campus study). *Faculty:* 118 full-time (102 women), 429 part-time/adjunct (309 women). *Students:* 484 full-time (435 women), 319 part-time (284 women); includes 84 minority (55 African Americans, 4 American Indian/Alaska Native, 10 Asian Americans or Pacific Islanders, 15 Hispanic Americans), 16 international. Average age 32. 900 applicants, 65% accepted, 433 enrolled. In 2009, 303 master's, 1 doctorate awarded. *Degree requirements:* For doctorate, comprehensive exam, thesis/dissertation. *Entrance requirements:* For master's, GRE General Test, minimum B average in undergraduate course work, 3 letters of recommendation; for doctorate, GRE General Test, interview, 3 letters of recommendation from doctorally-prepared faculty, MSN, essay. Additional exam requirements/recommendations for international students: Required—TOEFL. *Application deadline:* For fall admission, 12/1 priority date for domestic and international students. Applications are processed on a rolling basis. Application fee: $50. *Expenses:* Contact institution. *Financial support:* In 2009–10, 389 students received support, including 1 research assistantship (averaging $5,000 per year); teaching assistantships, scholarships/grants, health care benefits, and tuition waivers also available. Support available to part-time students. Financial award application deadline: 3/15; financial award applicants required to submit FAFSA. *Faculty research:* Lymphedema, palliative care and bereavement, health services research including workforce, safety and quality of care, gerontology, better birth outcomes including nutrition. Total annual research expenditures: $1.4 million. *Unit head:* Dr. Colleen Conway-Welch, Dean, 615-343-8776, Fax: 615-343-7711, E-mail: colleen.conway-welch@vanderbilt.edu. *Application contact:* Cheryl Feldner, Assistant Director of Admissions, 615-322-3800, Fax: 615-343-0333, E-mail: cheryl.feldner@vanderbilt.edu.

Waynesburg University, Graduate and Professional Studies, Waynesburg, PA 15370-1222. Offers business (MBA), including finance, health systems, human resources, leadership, market development; counseling (MA), including addictions counseling, clinical mental health; education (MAT); nursing (MSN), including administration, education, informatics, palliative care; nursing practice (DNP); special education (M Ed); technology (M Ed); MSN/MBA. *Accreditation:* AACN. Part-time and evening/weekend programs available. *Faculty:* 11 full-time (5 women), 136 part-time/adjunct (80 women). *Students:* 116 full-time (85 women), 984 part-time (682 women). 711 applicants, 80% accepted, 485 enrolled. In 2009, 320 master's, 41 doctorates awarded. *Degree requirements:* For doctorate, thesis/dissertation. *Entrance requirements:* Additional exam requirements/recommendations for international students: Required—TOEFL. *Application deadline:* For fall admission, 8/1 priority date for domestic students. Applications are processed on a rolling basis. Electronic applications accepted. *Expenses:* Tuition: Part-time $520 per credit. *Financial support:* Available to part-time students. Application deadline: 5/1. *Unit head:* David Mariner, Dean, 724-743-4420, Fax: 724-743-4425, E-mail: dmariner@waynesburg.edu. *Application contact:* Michael Bednarski, Director of Admissions, 724-743-4420, Fax: 724-743-4425, E-mail: mbednars@waynesburg.edu.

Nurse Anesthesia

Albany Medical College, Center for Nurse Anesthesiology, Albany, NY 12208-3479. Offers MS. *Accreditation:* AANA/CANAEP. Postbaccalaureate distance learning degree programs offered (minimal on-campus study). *Faculty:* 5 full-time (all women). *Students:* 52 full-time (35 women); includes 4 minority (1 African American, 2 Asian Americans or Pacific Islanders, 1 Hispanic American). Average age 31. 59 applicants, 34% accepted, 19 enrolled. In 2009, 15 master's awarded. *Degree requirements:* For master's, thesis, thesis proposal/clinical research. *Entrance requirements:* For master's, GRE General Test, BSN or appropriate bachelor's degree, current RN license, critical care experience, organic chemistry, research methods. Additional exam requirements/recommendations for international students: Required—TOEFL. *Application deadline:* For fall admission, 3/15 priority date for domestic students. Applications are processed on a rolling basis. Application fee: $75. *Expenses:* Contact institution. *Financial support:* Scholarships/grants and traineeships available. Financial award applicants required to submit FAFSA. *Unit head:* Dr. Denise Martin-Sheridan, Center Director, 518-262-4303, Fax: 518-262-5170, E-mail: amcnap@mail.amc.edu. *Application contact:* Helene M. Gregory, Coordinator, 518-262-4303, Fax: 518-262-5170, E-mail: amcnap@mail.amc.edu.

Arkansas State University—Jonesboro, Graduate School, College of Nursing and Health Professions, School of Nursing, Jonesboro, State University, AR 72467. Offers nurse anesthesia (MSN); nursing (MSN). *Accreditation:* AANA/CANAEP; NLN. Part-time programs available. *Faculty:* 7 full-time (6 women), 5 part-time/adjunct (4 women). *Students:* 110 full-time (45 women), 83 part-time (78 women); includes 22 minority (19 African Americans, 1 American Indian/Alaska Native, 2 Asian Americans or Pacific Islanders). Average age 33. 52 applicants, 38% accepted, 15 enrolled. In 2009, 70 master's awarded. *Degree requirements:* For master's, comprehensive exam, thesis or alternative. *Entrance requirements:* For master's, GRE General Test or MAT, appropriate bachelor's degree, current Arkansas nursing license, CPR certification, physical examination, professional liability insurance, critical care experience, ACLS Certification, PALS Certification, interview, immunization records. Additional exam requirements/recommendations for international students: Required—TOEFL (minimum score 550 paper-based; 213 computer-based; 79 iBT), IELTS (minimum score 6). *Application deadline:* For spring admission, 10/15 for domestic and international students. Applications are processed on a rolling basis. Application fee: $30 ($40 for international students). Electronic applications accepted. *Expenses:* Contact institution. *Financial support:* In 2009–10, 4 students received support. Career-related internships or fieldwork, scholarships/grants, and unspecified assistantships available. Financial award application deadline: 7/1; financial award applicants required to submit FAFSA. *Unit head:* Dr. Sue McLarry, Chair, 870-972-3074, Fax: 870-972-2954, E-mail: smclarry@astate.edu. *Application contact:* Dr. Andrew Sustich, Dean of the Graduate School, 870-972-3029, Fax: 870-972-3857, E-mail: sustich@astate.edu.

Barry University, College of Health Sciences, Program in Anesthesiology, Miami Shores, FL 33161-6695. Offers MS. *Accreditation:* AANA/CANAEP. *Degree requirements:* For master's, comprehensive exam. *Entrance requirements:* For master's, GRE General Test, minimum GPA of 3.0; 2 courses in chemistry (1 with lab); minimum 1 year critical care experience; BSN or RN; 4-year bachelor's degree in health sciences, nursing, biology, or chemistry. Electronic applications accepted. *Faculty research:* Use of computers in education, psychological well-bring of health care providers.

Baylor College of Medicine, School of Allied Health Sciences, Graduate Program in Nurse Anesthesia, Houston, TX 77030-3498. Offers MS. *Accreditation:* AANA/CANAEP. *Faculty:* 11 full-time (4 women). *Students:* 43 full-time (26 women); includes 11 minority (2 African Americans, 2 American Indian/Alaska Native, 4 Asian Americans or Pacific Islanders, 3 Hispanic Americans). Average age 32. 120 applicants, 13% accepted, 15 enrolled. In 2009, 14 master's awarded. *Degree requirements:* For master's, comprehensive exam, thesis. *Entrance requirements:* For master's, GRE General Test, Texas nursing license, 1 year of work experience in acute care nursing, minimum GPA of 3.0, BSN. *Application deadline:* For fall admission, 9/1 for domestic students. Application fee: $85. Electronic applications accepted. *Expenses:* Contact institution. *Financial support:* In 2009–10, 43 students received support. Career-related internships or fieldwork, Federal Work-Study, institutionally sponsored loans, scholarships/grants, and traineeships available. Financial award application deadline: 5/1; financial award applicants required to submit FAFSA. *Unit head:* Dr. James R. Walker, Director, 713-798-8650, Fax: 713-798-2743, E-mail: jrwalker@bcm.edu. *Application contact:* Dr. James R. Walker, Director, 713-798-8650, Fax: 713-798-2743, E-mail: jrwalker@bcm.edu.

Boston College, William F. Connell School of Nursing, Chestnut Hill, MA 02467-3800. Offers adult health nursing (MS); community health nursing (MS); family health (MS); forensic nursing (MS); gerontology (MS); maternal/child health nursing (MS), including pediatric and women's health; nurse anesthesia (MS); nursing (PhD); palliative care (MS), including adult and pediatric; psychiatric-mental health nursing (MS); MBA/MS; MS/MA; MS/PhD. *Accreditation:* AACN; AANA/CANAEP (one or more programs are accredited). Part-time programs available. *Faculty:* 48 full-time (46 women), 31 part-time/adjunct (29 women). *Students:* 183 full-time (169 women), 147 part-time (140 women); includes 36 minority (15 African Americans, 2 American Indian/Alaska Native, 17 Asian Americans or Pacific Islanders, 2 Hispanic Americans), 7 international. Average age 29. 347 applicants, 53% accepted, 103 enrolled. In 2009, 79 master's, 7 doctorates awarded. *Degree requirements:* For master's, comprehensive exam, research project; for doctorate, comprehensive exam, thesis/dissertation, computer literacy exam or foreign language. *Entrance requirements:* For master's, bachelor's degree in nursing; for doctorate, GRE General Test, master's degree in nursing. Additional exam requirements/recommendations for international students: Required—TOEFL (minimum score 550 paper-based; 213 computer-based). *Application deadline:* For fall admission, 11/1 for domestic and international students; for winter admission, 12/31 for domestic and international students; for spring admission, 9/15 for domestic and international students. Applications are processed on a rolling basis. Application fee: $40. Electronic applications accepted. *Financial support:* In 2009–10, 83 students received support, including 12 fellowships with partial tuition reimbursements available (averaging $15,000 per year), 5 teaching assistantships (averaging $13,746 per year); research assistantships, Federal Work-Study, institutionally sponsored loans, scholarships/grants, traineeships, health care benefits, and tuition waivers (partial) also available. Support available to part-time students. Financial award application deadline: 3/1; financial award applicants required to submit FAFSA. *Faculty research:* Ethics, reduction of risk behaviors, support during chronic illness, violence, gerontology. Total annual research expenditures: $1.4 million. *Unit head:* Dr. Susan Gennaro, Dean, 617-552-4251, Fax: 617-552-0931, E-mail: susan.gennaro@bc.edu. *Application contact:* MaryBeth Crowley, Graduate Programs Assistant, 617-552-4928, Fax: 617-552-2121, E-mail: csongrad@bc.edu.

Bradley University, Graduate School, College of Education and Health Sciences, Department of Nursing, Peoria, IL 61625-0002. Offers nurse administered anesthesia (MSN); nursing administration (MSN). *Accreditation:* AANA/CANAEP; NLN. Part-time and evening/weekend programs available. *Degree requirements:* For master's, comprehensive exam, thesis optional. *Entrance requirements:* For master's, GRE General Test or MAT, interview, Illinois RN license, advanced cardiac life support certification, pediatric advanced life support certification, 3 letters of recommendation. Additional exam requirements/recommendations for international students: Required—TOEFL (minimum score 550 paper-based; 213 computer-based; 79 iBT).

Case Western Reserve University, Frances Payne Bolton School of Nursing, Master's Programs in Nursing, Program in Nurse Anesthesia, Cleveland, OH 44106. Offers MSN. *Accreditation:* AANA/CANAEP. *Degree requirements:* For master's, thesis optional. *Entrance requirements:* For master's, GRE General Test or MAT. *Faculty research:* Mechanical ventilation antioxidant trial; intravenous function and mechanical ventilation; impact of taxane on peripheral nerve function.

Central Connecticut State University, School of Graduate Studies, School of Arts and Sciences, Department of Biology, New Britain, CT 06050-4010. Offers biological sciences (MA, MS), including anesthesia (MS), ecology and environmental sciences (MA), general

biology (MA), health sciences specialization (MS), professional education program (MS); biology (Certificate). Part-time and evening/weekend programs available. *Faculty:* 13 full-time (4 women), 7 part-time/adjunct (4 women). *Students:* 99 full-time (58 women), 32 part-time (25 women); includes 29 minority (11 African Americans, 12 Asian Americans or Pacific Islanders, 6 Hispanic Americans), 1 international. Average age 32. 36 applicants, 28% accepted, 7 enrolled. In 2009, 37 master's, 5 other advanced degrees awarded. *Degree requirements:* For master's, comprehensive exam, thesis or alternative; for Certificate, qualifying exam. *Entrance requirements:* For master's, minimum undergraduate GPA of 2.7. Additional exam requirements/recommendations for international students: Required—TOEFL. *Application deadline:* For fall admission, 7/1 for domestic students; for spring admission, 12/1 for domestic students. Applications are processed on a rolling basis. Application fee: $50. Electronic applications accepted. *Expenses:* Tuition, area resident: Full-time $4662; part-time $440 per credit. Tuition, state resident: full-time $6994; part-time $440 per credit. Tuition, nonresident: full-time $12,988; part-time $440 per credit. Required fees: $3606. One-time fee: $62 part-time. *Financial support:* In 2009–10, 20 students received support, including 3 research assistantships; career-related internships or fieldwork, Federal Work-Study, scholarships/grants, and unspecified assistantships also available. Support available to part-time students. Financial award application deadline: 3/1; financial award applicants required to submit FAFSA. *Faculty research:* Environmental science, anesthesia, health sciences, zoology, animal behavior. *Unit head:* Dr. Jeremiah Jarrett, Chair, 860-832-2645. *Application contact:* Dr. Jeremiah Jarrett, Chair, 860-832-2645.

Columbia University, School of Nursing, Program in Nurse Anesthesia, New York, NY 10032. Offers MS, Adv C. *Accreditation:* AACN; AANA/CANAEP. *Entrance requirements:* For master's, GRE General Test, BSN, 1 year of intensive care unit experience; for Adv C, MSN, 1 year of intensive care unit experience. Electronic applications accepted.

DePaul University, College of Liberal Arts and Sciences, Department of Nursing, Chicago, IL 60614. Offers adult nursing (MS); family nursing (MS); generalist nursing (MS); nurse anesthesia (MS). MS in nurse anesthesia offered jointly with Ravenswood Hospital Medical Center. *Accreditation:* AACN; AANA/CANAEP. Part-time and evening/weekend programs available. *Faculty:* 13 full-time (11 women), 12 part-time/adjunct (11 women). *Students:* 195 full-time (167 women), 43 part-time (41 women); includes 43 minority (9 African Americans, 1 American Indian/Alaska Native, 19 Asian Americans or Pacific Islanders, 14 Hispanic Americans), 2 international. Average age 39. 238 applicants, 46% accepted, 74 enrolled. In 2009, 70 master's awarded. *Degree requirements:* For master's, comprehensive exam (for some programs), thesis optional. *Entrance requirements:* For master's, GRE (if bachelor's GPA less than 3.2). Additional exam requirements/recommendations for international students: Required—TOEFL (minimum score 590 paper-based; 243 computer-based; 96 iBT) or IELTS (minimum score 7.5), Pearson Test of English (PTE). *Application deadline:* For fall admission, 3/1 priority date for domestic and international students; for winter admission, 8/15 priority date for domestic and international students. Application fee: $40. Electronic applications accepted. *Expenses:* Tuition: Full-time $37,525; part-time $620 per credit hour. *Financial support:* In 2009–10, 5 students received support, including 6 fellowships (averaging $1,500 per year); traineeships also available. Financial award applicants required to submit FAFSA. *Faculty research:* Children's health, women's health, health promotion. *Unit head:* Dr. Kay Thurn, Chair. *Application contact:* Ann Spittle, Director of Graduate Admissions, 773-325-7315, Fax: 773-325-7315, E-mail: graduatelas@depaul.edu.

Drexel University, College of Nursing and Health Professions, Program in Nurse Anesthesia, Philadelphia, PA 19104-2875. Offers MSN. *Accreditation:* AACN; AANA/CANAEP. Electronic applications accepted.

Duke University, School of Nursing, Durham, NC 27708-0586. Offers adult acute care (Certificate); adult cardiovascular (Certificate); adult oncology (Certificate); adult primary care (Certificate); clinical nurse specialist (MSN), including adult oncology, gerontology, neonatal, pediatric; clinical research management (MSN, Certificate); family (Certificate); gerontology (Certificate); health and nursing ministries (MSN, Certificate); health systems leadership and outcomes (Certificate); neonatal (Certificate); neonatal/pediatric in rural health (MSN, Certificate); nurse anesthetist (MSN, Certificate); nurse practitioner (MSN), including adult acute care, adult cardiovascular, adult oncology, adult primary care, family, gerontology, neonatal, pediatric, pediatric acute care; nursing (DNP, PhD); nursing and healthcare leadership (MSN); nursing education (MSN); nursing informatics (MSN, Certificate); pediatric (Certificate); pediatric acute care (Certificate); MBA/MSN; MSN/MCM. *Accreditation:* AACN; AANA/CANAEP. Part-time programs available. Postbaccalaureate distance learning degree programs offered (minimal on-campus study). *Faculty:* 45 full-time (41 women), 169 part-time/adjunct (150 women). *Students:* 213 full-time (179 women), 116 part-time (105 women); includes 37 minority (17 African Americans, 13 Asian Americans or Pacific Islanders, 7 Hispanic Americans), 9 international. Average age 36. 234 applicants, 53% accepted, 97 enrolled. In 2009, 142 master's, 24 other advanced degrees awarded. Terminal master's awarded for partial completion of doctoral program. *Degree requirements:* For master's, thesis optional; for doctorate, Capstone Project. *Entrance requirements:* For master's, GRE General Test, 1 year of nursing experience, BSN, minimum GPA of 3.0, previous course work in statistics; for doctorate, GRE for BSN prepared, BSN or MSN, minimum GPA of 3.0. Portfolio; for Certificate, MSN. Additional exam requirements/recommendations for international students: Required—TOEFL (minimum score 550 paper-based; 213 computer-based), Commission on Graduates of Foreign Nursing Schools exam. *Application deadline:* For fall admission, 7/2 priority date for domestic and international students; for spring admission, 11/15 priority date for domestic and international students. Applications are processed on a rolling basis. Application fee: $50. Electronic applications accepted. *Expenses:* Contact institution. *Financial support:* Career-related internships or fieldwork, institutionally sponsored loans, scholarships/grants, traineeships, and tuition waivers (partial) available. Support available to part-time students. Financial award application deadline: 4/1; financial award applicants required to submit FAFSA. *Faculty research:* Cardiovascular disease, caregiver skill training, data mining, prostate cancer, neonatal immune system. Total annual research expenditures: $3.5 million. *Unit head:* Dr. Catherine L. Gilliss, Dean/Vice Chancellor for Nursing Affairs, 919-684-9444, Fax: 919-684-9414, E-mail: gilli025@mc.duke.edu. *Application contact:* Bebe T. Mills, Director of Admissions, 919-684-9151, Fax: 919-668-4693, E-mail: mills031@mc.duke.edu.

Emory University, School of Medicine, Programs in Allied Health Professions, Atlanta, GA 30322-1100. Offers anesthesiology (MM Sc); anesthesiology/patient monitoring systems (MM Sc); ophthalmic technology (MM Sc); physical therapy (DPT); physician assistant (MM Sc). Postbaccalaureate distance learning degree programs offered. *Faculty:* 29 full-time (19 women), 18 part-time/adjunct (8 women). *Students:* 381 full-time (273 women), 3 part-time (2 women); includes 80 minority (43 African Americans, 2 American Indian/Alaska Native, 20 Asian Americans or Pacific Islanders, 15 Hispanic Americans), 5 international. Average age 27. 1,299 applicants, 16% accepted, 149 enrolled. In 2009, 99 master's, 41 doctorates awarded. *Entrance requirements:* For master's, GRE or MCAT; for doctorate, GRE. *Application deadline:* Applications are processed on a rolling basis. Electronic applications accepted. *Expenses:* Contact institution. *Financial support:* In 2009–10, 275 students received support. Institutionally sponsored loans and scholarships/grants available. Financial award application deadline: 3/1; financial award applicants required to submit FAFSA. *Unit head:* Dr. J. Alan Otsuki, Assistant Dean, Office of Medical Education and Student Affairs, 404-727-5655, Fax: 404-727-0045, E-mail: jotsuki@emory.edu. *Application contact:* Marvell Nesmith, Associate Director of Registration and Student Affairs, 404-712-9921, Fax: 404-727-0045, E-mail: marvell.nesmith@emory.edu.

Fairfield University, School of Nursing, Fairfield, CT 06824-5195. Offers clinical nurse leader (MSN); family nurse practitioner (MSN, PMC); healthcare management (MSN); nurse anesthesia (MSN); psychiatric nurse practitioner (MSN, PMC). *Accreditation:* AACN; AANA/CANAEP. Part-time programs available. *Degree requirements:* For master's, capstone project. *Entrance requirements:* For master's, GRE (nurse anesthesia applicants only), minimum QPA of 3.0, RN license, resume, 2 recommendations; for PMC, 1 year of work experience as a registered

Nurse Anesthesia

Fairfield University (continued)

nurse. Additional exam requirements/recommendations for international students: Required—TOEFL (minimum score 550 paper-based; 213 computer-based; 80 iBT). Electronic applications accepted. *Expenses:* Contact institution. *Faculty research:* Care of older adults, palliative care, spirituality and innovative partnerships, diabetes.

Florida Hospital College of Health Sciences, Program in Nurse Anesthesia, Orlando, FL 32803. Offers MS. *Entrance requirements:* For master's, GRE or MAT, minimum undergraduate cumulative GPA of 3.0, 1 year of intensive critical care nursing experience, 3 recommendations, interview.

Gannon University, School of Graduate Studies, Morosky College of Health Professions and Sciences, School of Health Professions, Villa Maria School of Nursing, Erie, PA 16541-0001. Offers anesthesia (MSN); business administration (MSN); family nurse practitioner (Certificate); medical-surgical nursing (MSN); nurse anesthesia (Certificate); nursing rural practitioner (MSN). *Accreditation:* AACN; AANA/CANAEP (one or more programs are accredited). Part-time and evening/weekend programs available. *Students:* 19 full-time (11 women), 59 part-time (45 women); includes 2 minority (both African Americans). Average age 36. 16 applicants, 81% accepted, 0 enrolled. In 2009, 19 master's awarded. *Degree requirements:* For master's, thesis. *Entrance requirements:* For master's, GRE General Test, degree in nursing. Additional exam requirements/recommendations for international students: Required—TOEFL (minimum score 79 iBT). *Application deadline:* For spring admission, 8/1 for domestic students. Application fee: $25. Electronic applications accepted. *Expenses:* Tuition: Full-time $13,590; part-time $755 per credit. Required fees: $524; $17 per credit. Tuition and fees vary according to course load, degree level, campus/location and program. *Financial support:* Scholarships/grants available. Financial award application deadline: 7/1; financial award applicants required to submit FAFSA. *Unit head:* Dr. Sharon Thompson, Director, 814-871-5345, E-mail: thompson001@gannon.edu. *Application contact:* Kara Morgan, Assistant Director of Graduate Admissions, 814-871-5831, Fax: 814-871-5827, E-mail: graduate@gannon.edu.

Georgetown University, Graduate School of Arts and Sciences, School of Nursing and Health Studies, Washington, DC 20057. Offers acute care nurse practitioner (MS); clinical nurse specialist (MS); family nurse practitioner (MS); nurse anesthesia (MS); nurse-midwifery (MS); nursing education (MS). *Accreditation:* AACN; AANA/CANAEP; ACNM/DOA. *Degree requirements:* For master's, thesis optional. *Entrance requirements:* For master's, GRE General Test or MAT, bachelor's degree in nursing from NLN-accredited school, minimum undergraduate GPA of 3.0. Additional exam requirements/recommendations for international students: Required—TOEFL.

Goldfarb School of Nursing at Barnes-Jewish College, Goldfarb School of Nursing at Barnes-Jewish College, St Louis, MO 63110. Offers adult acute care nurse practitioner (MSN); adult nurse practitioner (MSN); neonatal nurse practitioner (MSN); nurse anesthesia (MSN); nurse educator (MSN); nurse executive (MSN). *Accreditation:* AACN; AANA/CANAEP. Part-time and evening/weekend programs available. Postbaccalaureate distance learning degree programs offered (minimal on-campus study). *Faculty:* 18 full-time (16 women), 3 part-time/adjunct (2 women). *Students:* 28 full-time (25 women), 81 part-time (73 women); includes 34 minority (27 African Americans, 6 Asian Americans or Pacific Islanders, 1 Hispanic American), 3 international. Average age 38. 60 applicants, 75% accepted, 40 enrolled. In 2009, 26 master's awarded. *Degree requirements:* For master's, thesis or alternative. *Entrance requirements:* For master's, minimum GPA of 3.0, 2 references, statistics course. Additional exam requirements/recommendations for international students: Required—TOEFL (minimum score 550 paper-based; 213 computer-based). *Application deadline:* For fall admission, 2/1 priority date for international students; for spring admission, 10/1 priority date for international students. Applications are processed on a rolling basis. Application fee: $150. *Financial support:* In 2009–10, 60 students received support, including 20 fellowships (averaging $4,000 per year), 4 research assistantships (averaging $5,000 per year); Federal Work-Study, institutionally sponsored loans, and scholarships/grants also available. Support available to part-time students. Financial award applicants required to submit FAFSA. *Faculty research:* HIV Stigma, HIV symptom management, palliative care with children and their families, heart disease prevention in Hispanic women, depression in the well elderly, alternative therapies in pre-term infants. *Unit head:* Dr. Michael L. Evans, Dean, 314-362-6289, Fax: 314-362-0984, E-mail: mevans@bjc.org. *Application contact:* Dr. Michael Ward, Associate Dean for Student Programs, 314-362-9155, Fax: 314-362-9250, E-mail: mward@bjc.org.

Gonzaga University, School of Education, Program in Anesthesiology Education, Spokane, WA 99258. Offers M Anesth Ed. *Accreditation:* AANA/CANAEP. *Faculty:* 3 full-time (2 women), 5 part-time/adjunct (2 women). *Students:* 8 full-time (6 women), 8 part-time (5 women); includes 1 minority (American Indian/Alaska Native). Average age 36. In 2009, 6 master's awarded. *Degree requirements:* For master's, comprehensive exam. *Entrance requirements:* For master's, GRE General Test or MAT. Additional exam requirements/recommendations for international students: Required—TOEFL. *Application deadline:* For fall admission, 12/1 for domestic students. Application fee: $50. Tuition and fees vary according to course level, course load, degree level, campus/location and program. *Financial support:* Application deadline: 3/1. *Unit head:* Dr. Dan Mahoney, University Program Director, 509-328-4220 Ext. 3584. *Application contact:* Julie McCulloh, Dean of Admissions, 509-313-6592, Fax: 509-313-5780, E-mail: mcculloh@gu.gonzaga.edu.

Gooding Institute of Nurse Anesthesia, Program in Nurse Anesthesia, Panama City, FL 32401. Offers MS. *Accreditation:* AANA/CANAEP. *Degree requirements:* For master's, comprehensive exam, thesis. *Entrance requirements:* For master's, GRE General Test, BSN or BA, RN license.

Inter American University of Puerto Rico, Arecibo Campus, Program in Anesthesia, Arecibo, PR 00614-4050. Offers MS. *Accreditation:* AANA/CANAEP. *Degree requirements:* For master's, comprehensive exam, thesis optional. *Entrance requirements:* For master's, GRE, EXADEP, 2 letters of recommendation, bachelor's degree in nursing, interview, minimum GPA of 3.0 in last 60 credits, minimum 1 year experience.

La Roche College, School of Graduate Studies and Adult Education, Program in Health Sciences, Pittsburgh, PA 15237-5898. Offers nurse anesthesia (MS). *Accreditation:* AANA/CANAEP. *Faculty:* 2 full-time (0 women), 1 part-time/adjunct (0 women). *Students:* 36 full-time (21 women). Average age 31. 17 applicants, 100% accepted, 17 enrolled. In 2009, 19 master's awarded. *Degree requirements:* For master's, thesis optional. *Entrance requirements:* For master's, GRE General Test, prior acceptance to the Allegheny Valley School of Anesthesia. *Application deadline:* For fall admission, 12/31 for domestic students. Application fee: $50. Electronic applications accepted. *Expenses:* Tuition: Full-time $10,350; part-time $575 per credit hour. *Financial support:* Application deadline: 3/31. *Unit head:* Dr. Don Fujito, Coordinator, 412-536-1157, Fax: 412-536-1175, E-mail: fujitod1@laroche.edu. *Application contact:* Hope Schiffgens, Director of Graduate Studies and Adult Education, 412-536-1266, Fax: 412-536-1283, E-mail: schombh1@laroche.edu.

Lincoln Memorial University, Caylor School of Nursing, Harrogate, TN 37752-1901. Offers family nurse practitioner (MSN); nurse anesthesia (MSN). *Accreditation:* AANA/CANAEP; NLN. Part-time programs available. *Faculty:* 5 full-time (3 women), 2 part-time/adjunct (both women). *Students:* 40 full-time (33 women), 3 part-time (2 women). Average age 30. 66 applicants, 91% accepted, 43 enrolled. In 2009, 6 master's awarded. *Entrance requirements:* For master's, GRE. *Application deadline:* For fall admission, 2/1 for domestic students. Application fee: $25. *Expenses:* Tuition: Full-time $11,700; part-time $390 per hour. *Financial support:* Applicants required to submit FAFSA. *Unit head:* Dr. Mary Anne Modrcin, Dean, 423-869-6319, Fax: 423-869-6244, E-mail: maryanne.modrcin@lmunet.edu. *Application contact:* Sherry Pearman, Director of Nursing Recruitment and Advising, 423-869-6283, E-mail: sherry.pearman@lmunet.edu.

Louisiana State University Health Sciences Center, School of Nursing, New Orleans, LA 70112-2223. Offers advanced public/community health nursing (MN); clinical nurse specialist (MN); nurse anesthesia (MN); nurse practitioner (MN); nursing (DNS). *Accreditation:* AACN; AANA/CANAEP (one or more programs are accredited). Part-time programs available. *Degree requirements:* For master's, thesis optional; for doctorate, thesis/dissertation. *Entrance requirements:* For master's, GRE General Test, MAT, minimum GPA of 3.0; for doctorate, GRE General Test, minimum GPA of 3.5. Additional exam requirements/recommendations for international students: Required—TOEFL. *Faculty research:* Advanced clinical practice, nursing education, health, social support, nursing administration.

Mayo School of Health Sciences, Program in Nurse Anesthesia, Rochester, MN 55905. Offers MNA. *Accreditation:* AANA/CANAEP. *Degree requirements:* For master's, comprehensive exam, research project. *Entrance requirements:* For master's, GRE General Test, minimum GPA of 3.0, minimum 1 year of critical care experience. Additional exam requirements/recommendations for international students: Required—TOEFL. Electronic applications accepted. *Expenses:* Contact institution.

Medical College of Georgia, School of Graduate Studies, Nursing Anesthesia Program, Augusta, GA 30912. Offers MSN. *Accreditation:* AACN; AANA/CANAEP. *Entrance requirements:* For master's, GRE General Test, Georgia RN license, at least 1 year of critical care RN experience. Additional exam requirements/recommendations for international students: Required—TOEFL (minimum score 550 paper-based; 213 computer-based; 79 iBT). Electronic applications accepted. Full-time tuition and fees vary according to campus/location, program and student level.

Medical University of South Carolina, College of Health Professions, Department of Health Professions, Anesthesia for Nurses Program, Charleston, SC 29425. Offers MS. *Accreditation:* AANA/CANAEP. *Faculty:* 1 full-time (0 women), 3 part-time/adjunct (1 woman). *Students:* 77 full-time (53 women); includes 5 minority (4 African Americans, 1 Hispanic American). Average age 30. 134 applicants, 22% accepted, 27 enrolled. In 2009, 24 master's awarded. *Degree requirements:* For master's, comprehensive exam, research project, clinical practica. *Entrance requirements:* For master's, GRE General Test, interview, minimum GPA of 3.0, 2 years of RN (ICU) experience, RN license. Additional exam requirements/recommendations for international students: Required—TOEFL (minimum score 600 paper-based; 250 computer-based). *Application deadline:* For fall admission, 11/30 priority date for domestic and international students. Application fee: $85. Electronic applications accepted. *Financial support:* In 2009–10, 2 students received support. Federal Work-Study, scholarships/grants, and tuition waivers (partial) available. Support available to part-time students. Financial award application deadline: 3/10; financial award applicants required to submit FAFSA. *Faculty research:* Stress in nurse anesthesia; economic changes and continuing education. *Unit head:* Dr. Anthony Chipas, Director, 843-792-3785, Fax: 843-792-1984, E-mail: chipas@musc.edu. *Application contact:* Ann H. Brown, Student Services Program Coordinator, 843-792-2115, Fax: 843-792-3327, E-mail: brownah@musc.edu.

Middle Tennessee School of Anesthesia, Program in Nurse Anesthesia, Madison, TN 37116. Offers MS. *Accreditation:* AANA/CANAEP. *Degree requirements:* For master's, project. *Entrance requirements:* For master's, GRE General Test, RN license, 1 year of critical-care nursing experience, BSN, general chemistry (3 semester hours minimum).

Midwestern University, Glendale Campus, College of Health Sciences, Arizona Campus, Program in Nurse Anesthesia, Glendale, AZ 85308. Offers MS. *Faculty:* 3 full-time (all women), 4 part-time/adjunct (2 women). *Students:* 38 full-time (15 women), 1 part-time (0 women); includes 11 minority (3 African Americans, 3 Asian Americans or Pacific Islanders, 5 Hispanic Americans). Average age 33. 151 applicants, 26% accepted, 23 enrolled. In 2009, 13 master's awarded. Application fee: $50. *Expenses:* Contact institution. *Unit head:* Mary Wojnakowski, Head, 623-572-3763. *Application contact:* James Walter, Director of Admissions, 888-247-9277, Fax: 623-572-3229, E-mail: admissaz@midwestern.edu.

Missouri State University, Graduate College, College of Health and Human Services, Department of Biomedical Sciences, Program in Nurse Anesthesia, Springfield, MO 65897. Offers MS. *Accreditation:* AANA/CANAEP. *Students:* 29 full-time (13 women), 1 (woman) part-time, 1 international. Average age 34. 6 applicants, 100% accepted, 5 enrolled. In 2009, 14 master's awarded. *Degree requirements:* For master's, comprehensive exam, thesis or alternative, oral exams. *Entrance requirements:* For master's, GRE General Test, 1 year of experience in acute care nursing, current RN license, interview, minimum GPA of 3.0 during final 60 hours of course work. Additional exam requirements/recommendations for international students: Required—TOEFL (minimum score 550 paper-based; 213 computer-based; 79 iBT). *Application deadline:* For fall admission, 11/1 priority date for domestic students, 11/1 for international students; for spring admission, 7/1 priority date for domestic students, 7/1 for international students. Application fee: $35. *Expenses:* Tuition, state resident: full-time $3852; part-time $214 per credit hour. Tuition, nonresident: full-time $7524; part-time $418 per credit hour. Required fees: $696; $172 per semester. Tuition and fees vary according to course level, course load, degree level and program. *Financial support:* Career-related internships or fieldwork and institutionally sponsored loans available. Support available to part-time students. Financial award application deadline: 3/31; financial award applicants required to submit FAFSA. *Unit head:* Benjamin Timson, Didactic Director, 417-838-4145, E-mail: bentimson@missouristate.edu. *Application contact:* Benjamin Timson, Didactic Director, 417-838-4145, E-mail: bentimson@missouristate.edu.

Mountain State University, Graduate Studies, Program in Nursing, Beckley, WV 25802-9003. Offers administration/education (MSN); family nurse practitioner (MSN); nurse anesthesia (MSN); registered nurse anesthetist (Certificate). *Accreditation:* AANA/CANAEP; NLN. Part-time programs available. Postbaccalaureate distance learning degree programs offered (minimal on-campus study). *Faculty:* 4 full-time (all women), 10 part-time/adjunct (9 women). *Students:* 117 full-time (102 women); includes 10 minority (6 African Americans, 1 American Indian/Alaska Native, 3 Asian Americans or Pacific Islanders), 1 international. Average age 37. 46 applicants, 80% accepted, 37 enrolled. In 2009, 35 master's awarded. *Degree requirements:* For master's, comprehensive exam, thesis or alternative. *Entrance requirements:* For master's, GRE. Additional exam requirements/recommendations for international students: Required—TOEFL (minimum score 550 paper-based; 213 computer-based); Recommended—IELTS (minimum score 6.5). *Application deadline:* For spring admission, 6/30 for domestic and international students. Applications are processed on a rolling basis. Application fee: $25 ($50 for international students). Electronic applications accepted. *Expenses:* Contact institution. *Financial support:* Federal Work-Study, scholarships/grants, and unspecified assistantships available. Support available to part-time students. Financial award applicants required to submit FAFSA. *Unit head:* Dr. Judith Halle, Dean, School of Health Sciences, 304-929-1327, Fax: 304-929-1601, E-mail: jhalle@mountainstate.edu. *Application contact:* Melody Tilley, Program Specialist, 304-929-1576, Fax: 304-929-1601, E-mail: mtilley@mountainstate.edu.

Mount Marty College, Graduate Studies Division, Yankton, SD 57078-3724. Offers business administration (MBA); nurse anesthesia (MS); pastoral ministries (MPM). *Accreditation:* AANA/CANAEP (one or more programs are accredited). *Degree requirements:* For master's, thesis or alternative. *Entrance requirements:* For master's, GRE General Test, minimum GPA of 3.0. Electronic applications accepted. *Faculty research:* Clinical anesthesia, professional characteristics, motivations of applicants.

Murray State University, College of Health Sciences and Human Services, Program in Nursing, Murray, KY 42071. Offers clinical nurse specialist (MSN); family nurse practitioner (MSN); nurse anesthesia (MSN). *Accreditation:* AACN; AANA/CANAEP. *Degree requirements:* For master's, research project. *Entrance requirements:* For master's, GRE General Test, BSN, interview, RN licensure. Additional exam requirements/recommendations for international students: Required—TOEFL (minimum score 550 paper-based). *Faculty research:* Fibromyalgis, primary care, rural health.

Newman University, School of Nursing and Allied Health, Wichita, KS 67213-2097. Offers nurse anesthesia (MS). *Accreditation:* AANA/CANAEP. *Faculty:* 3 full-time (2 women), 3 part-time/adjunct (2 women). *Students:* 37 full-time (19 women); includes 5 minority (1 African American, 1 American Indian/Alaska Native, 2 Asian Americans or Pacific Islanders, 1 Hispanic

American). Average age 33. 141 applicants, 16% accepted, 21 enrolled. In 2009, 18 master's awarded. *Degree requirements:* For master's, thesis optional. *Entrance requirements:* For master's, GRE General Test, registered professional nursing license in Kansas, 3 professional recommendations, BSN, statistics course, 1 year of employment, interview, minimum GPA of 3.0. Additional exam requirements/recommendations for international students: Required— TOEFL (minimum score 600 paper-based; 250 computer-based; 100 iBT). *Application deadline:* For fall admission, 11/15 for domestic and international students. Applications are processed on a rolling basis. Application fee: $25 ($40 for international students). Electronic applications accepted. *Expenses:* Contact institution. *Financial support:* Federal Work-Study available. Financial award application deadline: .8/15; financial award applicants required to submit FAFSA. *Unit head:* Prof. Sharon Niemann, Director, 316-942-4291 Ext. 2272, Fax: 316-942-4483, E-mail: niemanns@newmanu.edu. *Application contact:* Linda Kay Sabala, Director of Graduate Admissions, 316-942-4291 Ext. 2230, Fax: 316-942-4483, E-mail: sabalal@newmanu.edu.

Northeastern University, Bouvé College of Health Sciences Graduate School, School of Nursing, Program in Nurse Anesthesia, Boston, MA 02115-5096. Offers MS, CAGS. *Accreditation:* AACN; AANA/CANAEP. *Students:* 26 full-time (17 women); includes 1 African American, 1 Asian American or Pacific Islander, 1 Hispanic American. 99 applicants, 33% accepted, 23 enrolled. In 2009, 25 master's awarded. *Degree requirements:* For master's, thesis or alternative. *Entrance requirements:* For master's, GRE General Test. Additional exam requirements/recommendations for international students: Required—TOEFL (minimum score 100 iBT). *Application deadline:* For fall admission, 12/1 for domestic students. Application fee: $50. Electronic applications accepted. *Financial support:* Research assistantships, teaching assistantships, scholarships/grants, traineeships, and tuition waivers (partial) available. Financial award application deadline: 7/1; financial award applicants required to submit FAFSA. *Unit head:* Dr. Steve Alves, Director, 617-373-2985, Fax: 617-373-8672, E-mail: s.alves@neu.edu. *Application contact:* Margaret Schnabel, Director of Graduate Admissions, 617-373-2708, E-mail: bouvegrad@neu.edu.

Oakland University, Graduate Study and Lifelong Learning, School of Nursing, Program in Nurse Anesthetist, Rochester, MI 48309-4401. Offers MSN, Certificate. Programs offered jointly with Beaumont Hospital Corporation. *Accreditation:* AACN; AANA/CANAEP. *Degree requirements:* For master's, thesis (for some programs). *Entrance requirements:* For master's, GRE General Test. Additional exam requirements/recommendations for international students: Required—TOEFL (minimum score 550 paper-based; 213 computer-based). Electronic applications accepted. *Expenses:* Contact institution.

Old Dominion University, College of Health Sciences, School of Nursing, Norfolk, VA 23529. Offers family nurse practitioner (MSN); nurse anesthesia (MSN); nurse educator (MSN); nurse midwifery (MSN); women's health nurse practitioner (MSN). *Accreditation:* AACN; AANA/CANAEP. Part-time programs available. Postbaccalaureate distance learning degree programs offered (no on-campus study). *Faculty:* 11 full-time (10 women), 15 part-time/adjunct (14 women). *Students:* 122 full-time (113 women), 101 part-time (97 women); includes 49 minority (23 African Americans, 2 American Indian/Alaska Native, 19 Asian Americans or Pacific Islanders, 5 Hispanic Americans). Average age 37. 169 applicants, 81% accepted, 122 enrolled. In 2009, 77 master's awarded. *Degree requirements:* For master's, comprehensive exam. *Entrance requirements:* For master's, GRE or MAT, BSN, minimum GPA of 3.0 in nursing and overall. Additional exam requirements/recommendations for international students: Required— TOEFL. *Application deadline:* For fall admission, 5/1 for domestic students. Applications are processed on a rolling basis. Application fee: $40. Electronic applications accepted. *Expenses:* Tuition, state resident: full-time $8112; part-time $338 per credit. Tuition, nonresident: full-time $20,256; part-time $844 per credit. Required fees: $119 per semester. One-time fee: $50. *Financial support:* In 2009–10, 18 students received support, including 2 research assistantships with tuition reimbursements available (averaging $10,000 per year); teaching assistantships, career-related internships or fieldwork, scholarships/grants, traineeships, and tuition waivers (partial) also available. Support available to part-time students. Financial award application deadline: 2/15; financial award applicants required to submit FAFSA. *Faculty research:* Health and culture, cardiovascular health, transition of military families, genetics, cultural diversity. Total annual research expenditures: $231,117. *Unit head:* Dr. Karen Karlowicz, Chair, 757-683-5262, Fax: 757-683-5253, E-mail: nursgpd@odu.edu. *Application contact:* Sue Parker, Coordinator, Graduate Student Services, 757-683-4298, Fax: 757-683-5253, E-mail: sparker@odu.edu.

Oregon Health & Science University, School of Nursing, Program in Nurse Anesthesia, Portland, OR 97239-3098. Offers MN, MS. *Accreditation:* AANA/CANAEP. Tuition and fees vary according to course level, course load, degree level, program and reciprocity agreements.

Our Lady of the Lake College, School of Nursing, Program in Nurse Anesthesia, Baton Rouge, LA 70808. Offers MS. *Degree requirements:* For master's, clinical practicum. *Entrance requirements:* For master's, GRE, current RN license; baccalaureate degree in nursing; 1 year full-time experience (2 years preferred) as RN in adult critical care setting (adult intensive care unit preferred); minimum cumulative GPA of 3.0; one undergraduate or graduate chemistry course. Additional exam requirements/recommendations for international students: Required— TOEFL.

Rosalind Franklin University of Medicine and Science, College of Health Professions, Nurse Anesthesia Department, North Chicago, IL 60064-3095. Offers MS. *Accreditation:* AANA/CANAEP. *Faculty:* 2 full-time (both women), 4 part-time/adjunct (1 woman). *Students:* 35 full-time (21 women), 1 (woman) part-time; includes 6 minority (3 African Americans, 2 Asian Americans or Pacific Islanders, 1 Hispanic American), 1 international. Average age 32. 70 applicants, 26% accepted, 13 enrolled. *Entrance requirements:* For master's, GRE, RN license, ICU experience. Additional exam requirements/recommendations for international students: Required—TOEFL. *Application deadline:* For fall admission, 9/1 for domestic students. Application fee: $50. Electronic applications accepted. *Financial support:* Applicants required to submit FAFSA. *Faculty research:* Patient safety, pediatric anesthesia, instructional technology. *Unit head:* Lenore Litwin, Director, 847-578-3400, E-mail: lenore.litwin@rosalindfranklin.edu. *Application contact:* Melissa Knox, Admissions Officer, 847-578-8772, Fax: 847-775-6559, E-mail: melissa.knox@rosalindfranklin.edu.

Rush University, College of Nursing, Department of Adult Health Nursing, Chicago, IL 60612-3832. Offers acute care nurse practitioner (MSN, Post-Master's Certificate); adult health nursing (DNP, PhD); adult nurse practitioner (MSN, Post-Master's Certificate); adult/gerontological nurse practitioner (MSN); anesthesia nurse practitioner (MSN, Post-Master's Certificate); critical care clinical specialist (MSN); gerontological nurse practitioner (MSN, Post-Master's Certificate); medical surgical clinical specialist (MSN). *Accreditation:* AACN; AANA/CANAEP (one or more programs are accredited). Part-time programs available. Post-baccalaureate distance learning degree programs offered (minimal on-campus study). Terminal master's awarded for partial completion of doctoral program. *Degree requirements:* For master's, capstone project; for doctorate, thesis/dissertation, DNP leadership project. *Entrance requirements:* For master's, GRE General Test (waived if nursing GPA is above 3.0 or cumulative GPA is above 3.25), interview; for doctorate, GRE General Test, interview, course work in statistics (PhD). Additional exam requirements/recommendations for international students: Required—TOEFL, TWE. Electronic applications accepted. *Faculty research:* Complementary/alternative medicine, critical care outcomes, cardiac risk reduction, Alzheimer's Disease, telehealth monitoring.

Saint Joseph's University, College of Arts and Sciences, Department of Health Services, Philadelphia, PA 19131-1395. Offers health administration (MS, Post-Master's Certificate); health care ethics (Post-Master's Certificate); health education (MS, Post-Master's Certificate); health informatics (Post-Master's Certificate); healthcare ethics (MS); nurse anesthesia (MS); school nurse certification (MS). Part-time and evening/weekend programs available. *Students:* 10 full-time (5 women), 180 part-time (135 women); includes 67 minority (50 African Americans, 11 Asian Americans or Pacific Islanders, 6 Hispanic Americans), 8 international. Average age 36. In 2009, 72 master's awarded. *Entrance requirements:* For master's, GRE (if GPA less

than 2.75), 2 letters of recommendation, minimum GPA of 2.75, resume. Additional exam requirements/recommendations for international students: Required—TOEFL (minimum score 550 paper-based; 213 computer-based; 79 iBT). *Application deadline:* For fall admission, 7/15 priority date for domestic students, 4/15 for international students; for winter admission, 1/15 for international students; for spring admission, 11/15 priority date for domestic students, 10/15 for international students. Applications are processed on a rolling basis. Application fee: $35. Electronic applications accepted. *Expenses:* Tuition: Part-time $729 per credit hour. Tuition and fees vary according to degree level and program. *Financial support:* Career-related internships or fieldwork and unspecified assistantships available. Financial award applicants required to submit FAFSA. *Unit head:* Nakia Henderson, Director, 610-660-2952, E-mail: nakia.henderson@sju.edu. *Application contact:* Kate McConnell, Director, Graduate College of Arts and Sciences Admissions and Retention, 610-660-3184, Fax: 610-660-3230, E-mail: kate.mcconnell@sju.edu.

Saint Mary's University of Minnesota, Schools of Graduate and Professional Programs, Graduate School of Health and Human Services, Nurse Anesthesia Program, Winona, MN 55987-1399. Offers MS. Offered jointly with the Minneapolis School of Anesthesia. *Accreditation:* AANA/CANAEP. *Unit head:* Merri Moody, 612-728-5133. *Application contact:* Yasin Alsaidi, Director of Admissions for Graduate and Professional Programs, 612-728-5207, Fax: 612-728-5121, E-mail: yalsaidi@smumn.edu.

Saint Vincent College, Program in Health Services, Latrobe, PA 15650-2690. Offers nurse anesthesia (MS).

Samford University, Ida V. Moffett School of Nursing, Birmingham, AL 35229. Offers advance practice (DNP); anesthesia (MSN); family nurse practitioner (MSN); nurse educator (MSN); nurse executive (DNP); nurse manager (MSN); MBA/MSN. *Accreditation:* AACN; AANA/CANAEP (one or more programs are accredited). Part-time programs available. Post-baccalaureate distance learning degree programs offered (minimal on-campus study). *Faculty:* 10 full-time (all women), 1 part-time/adjunct (0 women). *Students:* 149 full-time (102 women), 31 part-time (24 women); includes 21 minority (14 African Americans, 4 Asian Americans or Pacific Islanders, 3 Hispanic Americans), 1 international. Average age 31. 56 applicants, 98% accepted, 52 enrolled. In 2009, 58 master's awarded. *Degree requirements:* For master's and doctorate, capstone project with oral presentation. *Entrance requirements:* For master's, GRE General Test or MAT. Additional exam requirements/recommendations for international students: Required—TOEFL (minimum score 550 paper-based; 213 computer-based; 80 iBT). *Application deadline:* For fall admission, 7/1 priority date for domestic and international students; for spring admission, 11/1 priority date for domestic and international students. Applications are processed on a rolling basis. Application fee: $35. *Expenses:* Contact institution. *Financial support:* Institutionally sponsored loans, scholarships/grants, and traineeships available. Financial award application deadline: 3/1; financial award applicants required to submit FAFSA. *Faculty research:* Issues in rural health care, vulnerable populations, genetics and disabilities in pediatrics, geriatrics, Parrish nursing research. *Unit head:* Dr. Nena F. Sanders, Dean, 205-726-2629, E-mail: nfsander@samford.edu. *Application contact:* Marian Carter, Director of Graduate Student Services, 205-726-2047, Fax: 205-726-4269, E-mail: mwcarter@samford.edu.

Samuel Merritt University, School of Nursing, Oakland, CA 94609-3108. Offers case management (MSN); family nurse practitioner (MSN, Certificate); nurse anesthetist (MSN, Certificate); nursing (MSN). *Accreditation:* AACN; AANA/CANAEP (one or more programs are accredited). Part-time and evening/weekend programs available. *Degree requirements:* For master's, thesis or alternative. *Entrance requirements:* For master's, minimum GPA of 2.5 in science, 3.0 overall; previous course work in statistics; current RN license. Additional exam requirements/recommendations for international students: Required—TOEFL. *Faculty research:* Gerontology, community health, maternal-child health, sexually transmitted diseases, substance abuse, oncology.

Southern Illinois University Edwardsville, Graduate Studies and Research, School of Nursing, Program in Nurse Anesthesia, Edwardsville, IL 62026-0001. Offers MS, Post-Master's Certificate. *Accreditation:* AANA/CANAEP. Part-time programs available. *Students:* 56 full-time (35 women), 12 part-time (10 women); includes 6 minority (5 Asian Americans or Pacific Islanders, 1 Hispanic American). Average age 26. 20 applicants, 5% accepted. In 2009, 23 master's awarded. *Degree requirements:* For master's, comprehensive exam. *Entrance requirements:* For master's, appropriate bachelor's degree, RN license. Additional exam requirements/recommendations for international students: Required—TOEFL (minimum score 550 paper-based; 213 computer-based; 79 iBT), IELTS (minimum score 6.5). *Application deadline:* For spring admission, 6/1 for domestic and international students. Application fee: $30. Electronic applications accepted. *Expenses:* Tuition, state resident: part-time $1252.50 per semester. Tuition, nonresident: part-time $3131.25 per semester. Required fees: $586.85 per semester. Tuition and fees vary according to course load. *Financial support:* Fellowships, research assistantships, teaching assistantships, career-related internships or fieldwork, Federal Work-Study, institutionally sponsored loans, scholarships/grants, traineeships, and unspecified assistantships available. Support available to part-time students. Financial award application deadline: 3/1; financial award applicants required to submit FAFSA. *Unit head:* Dr. Jacquelyn Clement, Director, 618-650-3923, E-mail: jclemen@siue.edu. *Application contact:* Dr. Jacquelyn Clement, Director, 618-650-3923, E-mail: jclemen@siue.edu.

State University of New York Downstate Medical Center, College of Nursing, Graduate Program in Nursing, Program in Nurse Anesthesia, Brooklyn, NY 11203-2098. Offers MS. *Accreditation:* AACN; AANA/CANAEP. *Degree requirements:* For master's, thesis optional. *Entrance requirements:* For master's, GRE, BSN; minimum GPA of 3.0; previous undergraduate course work in statistics, health assessment, and nursing research; RN license.

Texas Christian University, Harris College of Nursing and Health Sciences, School of Nurse Anesthesia, Fort Worth, TX 76129-0002. Offers MSNA. Postbaccalaureate distance learning degree programs offered (minimal on-campus study). *Entrance requirements:* For master's, CCRN, GRE, MAT. *Application deadline:* For fall admission, 10/1 for domestic and international students. Application fee: $50. *Expenses:* Contact institution. *Financial support:* Applicants required to submit FAFSA. *Unit head:* Dr. Kay K. Sanders, Director, 817-257-7887, E-mail: k.sanders@tcu.edu. *Application contact:* Admissions, TCU Graduate Studies Office, 817-257-7515, Fax: 817-257-7484, E-mail: frogmail@tcu.edu.

Texas Wesleyan University, Graduate Programs, Programs in Nurse Anesthesia, Fort Worth, TX 76105-1536. Offers MHS, MSNA, DNAP. *Accreditation:* AANA/CANAEP (one or more programs are accredited). *Faculty:* 11 full-time (5 women), 1 (woman) part-time/adjunct. *Students:* 420 full-time (245 women); includes 62 minority (13 African Americans, 4 American Indian/Alaska Native, 29 Asian Americans or Pacific Islanders, 16 Hispanic Americans). Average age 33. 496 applicants, 36% accepted, 152 enrolled. In 2009, 124 master's awarded. *Entrance requirements:* For master's, GRE General Test, master's degree; copy of current Council on Certification/Recertification card (all applicants must be Certified RN Anesthetists); minimum GPA of 3.0, science 2.75; undergraduate statistics course with minimum C grade; graduate statistics course with minimum B grade; graduate-level research course; current curriculum vitae; 3 letters of support; for doctorate, master's degree; copy of current Council on Certification/Recertification card (all applicants must be Certified RN Anesthetists); minimum GPA of 3.0, science 2.75; undergraduate statistics course with minimum C grade; graduate statistics course with minimum B grade, graduate-level research course; current curriculum vitae; 3 letters of support. *Application deadline:* For fall admission, 12/1 priority date for domestic students. Applications are processed on a rolling basis. Application fee: $50. *Expenses:* Contact institution. *Financial support:* Federal Work-Study, institutionally sponsored loans, scholarships/grants, and tuition waivers (full and partial) available. Support available to part-time students. Financial award application deadline: 3/15; financial award applicants required to submit FAFSA. *Unit head:* John Martin, Director, 817-531-4406, Fax: 817-531-6508. *Application contact:* Information Contact, 817-531-4406, Fax: 817-531-6508, E-mail: igriffin@txwes.edu.

Uniformed Services University of the Health Sciences, Graduate School of Nursing, Bethesda, MD 20814-4799. Offers family nurse practitioner (MSN); nurse anesthesia (MSN);

Nurse Anesthesia

Uniformed Services University of the Health Sciences *(continued)*
perioperative clinical nurse specialty (MSN); psychiatric mental health nurse practitioner (MSN). Available to military officers only. *Accreditation:* AACN; NLN. Postbaccalaureate distance learning degree programs offered (no on-campus study). *Faculty:* 27 full-time (18 women), 2 part-time/adjunct (both women). *Students:* 75 full-time (32 women), 3 part-time (all women); includes 20 minority (8 African Americans, 5 Asian Americans or Pacific Islanders, 7 Hispanic Americans). Average age 36. 108 applicants, 72% accepted, 78 enrolled. In 2009, 54 master's awarded. *Degree requirements:* For master's, thesis or alternative. *Entrance requirements:* For master's, GRE, BSN, clinical experience, minimum GPA of 3.0, previous course work in science. *Application deadline:* For fall admission, 7/1 for domestic students; for winter admission, 2/15 for domestic students. Application fee: $0. Electronic applications accepted. *Faculty research:* Prenatal care, military health care, military readiness, distance learning. *Unit head:* Col. Bruce A. Schoneboom, Associate Dean for Academic Affairs, 301-295-1180, Fax: 301-295-1707, E-mail: bschoneboom@usuhs.mil. *Application contact:* Terry Lynn Malavakis, Recording Secretary for Admissions Committee, 301-295-1055, Fax: 301-295-1707, E-mail: tmalavakis@usuhs.mil.

Union University, School of Nursing, Jackson, TN 38305-3697. Offers executive leadership (DNP); nurse anesthesia (DNP); nurse anesthetist (PMC); nurse practitioner (DNP); nursing education (MSN, PMC). *Accreditation:* AACN; AANA/CANAEP. *Degree requirements:* For master's, thesis or alternative. *Entrance requirements:* For master's, GRE, 3 letters of reference, bachelor's degree in nursing, minimum GPA of 3.0. Additional exam requirements/recommendations for international students: Required—TOEFL (minimum score 560 paper-based; 220 computer-based). Electronic applications accepted. *Faculty research:* Children's health, occupational rehabilitation, informatics, health promotion.

Université de Montréal, Faculty of Medicine, Program in Specialized Studies, Montréal, QC H3C 3J7, Canada. Offers anesthesia (DES); diagnostic radiology (DES); family medicine (DES); gastroenterology (DES); geriatry (DES); intensive care (DES); medical biochemistry (DES); medical genetics (DES); medicine (DES); microbiology and infectious diseases (DES); nuclear medicine (DES); obstetrics and gynecology (DES); ophthalmology (DES); pediatrics (DES); pneumology (DES); psychiatry (DES); radiology-oncology (DES); rheumatology (DES); surgery (DES). *Faculty:* 154 full-time (40 women), 333 part-time/adjunct (100 women). *Students:* 930 full-time (580 women), 7 part-time (all women). 74 applicants, 77% accepted, 29 enrolled. *Application deadline:* For fall admission, 2/1 priority date for domestic students; for winter admission, 11/1 priority date for domestic students; for spring admission, 2/1 priority date for domestic students. Application fee: $100. Electronic applications accepted. *Unit head:* Lorraine Locas, Assistant to the Vice Dean of Graduate Studies, 514-343-6269, Fax: 514-343-5751, E-mail: lorraine.locas@umontreal.ca. *Application contact:* Dr. Andre Ferron, Vice Dean Graduate Studies, 514-343-6111 Ext. 0933, Fax: 514-343-5751, E-mail: andre.ferron@umontreal.ca.

University at Buffalo, the State University of New York, Graduate School, School of Nursing, Buffalo, NY 14260. Offers adult health nursing (MS); family nursing (MS); nurse anesthetist (MS); nursing (PhD); nursing education (Certificate); psychiatric/mental health nursing (MS). *Accreditation:* AACN; AANA/CANAEP (one or more programs are accredited). Part-time programs available. Postbaccalaureate distance learning degree programs offered (minimal on-campus study). *Faculty:* 42 full-time (38 women), 16 part-time/adjunct (all women). *Students:* 128 full-time (102 women), 69 part-time (58 women); includes 27 minority (7 African Americans, 1 American Indian/Alaska Native, 12 Asian Americans or Pacific Islanders, 7 Hispanic Americans), 15 international. Average age 34. 375 applicants, 25% accepted, 65 enrolled. In 2009, 58 master's, 3 doctorates, 4 other advanced degrees awarded. Terminal master's awarded for partial completion of doctoral program. *Degree requirements:* For master's, thesis optional, comprehensive exams or project; for doctorate, comprehensive exam, thesis/dissertation. *Entrance requirements:* For master's, GRE General Test (if overall GPA less than 3.0), interview, minimum GPA of 3.0, RN license, 3 references; for doctorate, GRE General Test, MAT, minimum GPA of 3.25, RN license, BS or MS in nursing, 3 references, writing sample; for Certificate, interview, minimum GPA of 3.0 or GRE General Test, RN license, MS in nursing. Additional exam requirements/recommendations for international students: Required—TOEFL (minimum score 550 paper-based; 213 computer-based; 79 iBT), IELTS (minimum score 6.5). *Application deadline:* For fall admission, 6/1 priority date for domestic students, 4/1 priority date for international students; for spring admission, 11/1 for domestic students, 10/1 priority date for international students. Applications are processed on a rolling basis. Application fee: $75. Electronic applications accepted. *Financial support:* In 2009–10, 78 students received support, including 14 fellowships with full tuition reimbursements available (averaging $8,200 per year), 5 research assistantships with full tuition reimbursements available (averaging $16,794 per year), 13 teaching assistantships with full tuition reimbursements available (averaging $10,636 per year); scholarships/grants, traineeships, health care benefits, and unspecified assistantships also available. Financial award application deadline: 3/15; financial award applicants required to submit FAFSA. *Faculty research:* Oncology symptom management, end of life decision making, changing behaviors using the transtheoretical model, addictions, nursing workforce. Total annual research expenditures: $1.3 million. *Unit head:* Dr. Jean K. Brown, Dean and Professor, 716-829-2533, Fax: 716-829-2566, E-mail: ubnursingdean@buffalo.edu. *Application contact:* Dr. David J. Lang, Director of Student Affairs, 716-829-2537, Fax: 716-829-2021, E-mail: langdj@buffalo.edu.

The University of Alabama at Birmingham, School of Health Professions, Program in Nurse Anesthesia, Birmingham, AL 35294. Offers MNA. *Accreditation:* AACN; AANA/CANAEP. *Entrance requirements:* For master's, GRE, MAT, minimum GPA of 3.0, RN license, 1 year of critical care experience. Electronic applications accepted. *Faculty research:* Technology in health care, perioperative temperature control, outcome research.

The University of British Columbia, Faculty of Medicine, Department of Anesthesiology, Pharmacology and Therapeutics, Vancouver, BC V6T 1Z3, Canada. Offers M Sc, PhD. Terminal master's awarded for partial completion of doctoral program. *Degree requirements:* For master's, thesis; for doctorate, comprehensive exam, thesis/dissertation. *Entrance requirements:* For master's, MD or appropriate bachelor's degree; for doctorate, MD or M Sc. Additional exam requirements/recommendations for international students: Required—TOEFL (minimum score 600 paper-based; 250 computer-based; 100 iBT). Electronic applications accepted. *Faculty research:* Cellular, biochemical, autonomic, cardiovascular pharmacology; neuropharmacology and pulmonary pharmacology.

University of Cincinnati, Graduate School, College of Nursing, Cincinnati, OH 45221-0038. Offers clinical nurse specialist (MSN), including adult health, community health, neonatal, nursing administration, occupational health, pediatric health, psychiatric nursing, women's health; nurse anesthesia (MSN); nurse midwifery (MSN); nurse practitioner (MSN), including acute care, ambulatory care, family, family/psychiatric, women's health; nursing (PhD); MBA/MSN. *Accreditation:* AACN; AANA/CANAEP (one or more programs are accredited); ACNM/DOA. Part-time programs available. Postbaccalaureate distance learning degree programs offered (no on-campus study). Terminal master's awarded for partial completion of doctoral program. *Degree requirements:* For master's, thesis or alternative; for doctorate, comprehensive exam, thesis/dissertation. *Entrance requirements:* For master's and doctorate, GRE General Test. Additional exam requirements/recommendations for international students: Required—TOEFL (minimum score 520 paper-based; 190 computer-based). Electronic applications accepted. *Faculty research:* Substance abuse, injury and violence, symptom management.

University of Detroit Mercy, College of Health Professions, Program in Nurse Anesthesiology, Detroit, MI 48221. Offers MS. *Accreditation:* AANA/CANAEP. *Entrance requirements:* For master's, GRE General Test, minimum GPA of 3.0. *Expenses:* Contact institution.

The University of Kansas, University of Kansas Medical Center, School of Allied Health, Department of Nurse Anesthesia Education, Lawrence, KS 66045. Offers nurse anesthesia (MS). *Accreditation:* AANA/CANAEP. *Faculty:* 36 full-time, 36 part-time/adjunct. *Students:* 62 full-time (36 women); includes 12 minority (6 African Americans, 5 Asian Americans or Pacific Islanders, 1 Hispanic American). Average age 32. 89 applicants, 34% accepted, 22 enrolled.

In 2009, 19 master's awarded. *Degree requirements:* For master's, comprehensive exam, thesis or alternative. *Entrance requirements:* For master's, bachelor's degree in related field, RN license, 2 years of experience as an RN including 1 year of experience in ICU. Additional exam requirements/recommendations for international students: Required—TOEFL. *Application deadline:* For fall admission, 7/15 for domestic and international students. Application fee: $60. *Expenses:* Contact institution. *Financial support:* In 2009–10, 47 students received support. Traineeships available. Financial award application deadline: 2/1; financial award applicants required to submit FAFSA. *Faculty research:* Use of technology in education, simulation training, diaphragm fatigue, predicting student success. Total annual research expenditures: $16,248. *Unit head:* Donna S. Nyght, Chair, 913-588-6612, Fax: 913-588-3334, E-mail: dnyght@kumc.edu. *Application contact:* Ruth A. Lee, Administrative Officer, 913-588-6612, Fax: 913-588-3334, E-mail: na@kumc.edu.

University of Medicine and Dentistry of New Jersey, School of Nursing, Newark, NJ 07107-3001. Offers adult health (MSN); adult occupational health (MSN); advanced practice nursing (MSN, Post Master's Certificate); family nurse practitioner (MSN); nurse anesthesia (MSN); nursing (MSN); nursing informatics (MSN); urban health (PhD); women's health practitioner (MSN). *Accreditation:* AANA/CANAEP; NLN (one or more programs are accredited). Part-time programs available. *Entrance requirements:* For master's, GRE, RN license; basic life support, statistics, and health assessment experience. Additional exam requirements/recommendations for international students: Required—TOEFL. Electronic applications accepted. *Expenses:* Contact institution. *Faculty research:* HIV/AIDS, diabetes education, learned helplessness, nursing science, psychoeducation.

University of Miami, Graduate School, School of Nursing and Health Studies, Coral Gables, FL 33124. Offers acute care (MSN), including acute care nurse practitioner, nurse anesthesia; nursing (PhD); primary care (MSN), including adult nurse practitioner, family nurse practitioner, nurse midwifery, women's health practitioner. *Accreditation:* AACN; AANA/CANAEP; ACNM/DOA (one or more programs are accredited). Part-time programs available. *Degree requirements:* For master's, thesis optional; for doctorate, thesis/dissertation. *Entrance requirements:* For master's, GRE General Test, BSN, minimum GPA of 3.0, Florida RN license; for doctorate, GRE General Test, BSN or MSN, minimum GPA of 3.0. Additional exam requirements/recommendations for international students: Required—TOEFL (minimum score 550 paper-based; 213 computer-based). Electronic applications accepted. *Faculty research:* Transcultural nursing, exercise and depression in Alzheimer's disease, infectious diseases/HIV–AIDS, postpartum depression, outcomes assessment.

University of Michigan–Flint, School of Health Professions and Studies, Program in Anesthesia, Flint, MI 48502-1950. Offers MSA. *Accreditation:* AACN; AANA/CANAEP. Part-time programs available. *Faculty:* 2 full-time (both women), 3 part-time/adjunct (1 woman). *Students:* 35 full-time (31 women); includes 1 minority (African American), 2 international. Average age 33. 95 applicants, 26% accepted, 16 enrolled. In 2009, 14 master's awarded. *Degree requirements:* For master's, thesis. *Entrance requirements:* For master's, GRE, BSN or BS in science, critical care experience, RN license, minimum GPA of 3.0 in prerequisites. Additional exam requirements/recommendations for international students: Required—TOEFL (minimum score 560 paper-based; 220 computer-based; 84 iBT), IELTS (minimum score 6.5). *Application deadline:* For fall admission, 8/1 priority date for domestic students, 5/1 priority date for international students; for winter admission, 11/15 priority date for domestic students, 9/1 priority date for international students; for spring admission, 3/15 priority date for domestic students, 1/1 priority date for international students. Application fee: $55. *Expenses:* Contact institution. *Financial support:* Career-related internships or fieldwork, scholarships/grants, traineeships, and unspecified assistantships available. Support available to part-time students. Financial award application deadline: 6/1; financial award applicants required to submit FAFSA. *Faculty research:* CRNA expected retirement patterns, factors of importance in CENA selection of first job, lidocaine 4% in ETT cuff and reducing in coughing on emergence, orientation of spinal needle benel, length of time to discharge outpatients. *Unit head:* Dr. Lynn Lebeck, Director, 810-257-9264, Fax: 810-760-0839, E-mail: lynnlebeck@hurleymc.com. *Application contact:* Bradley T. Maki, Director of Graduate Admissions, 810-762-3171, Fax: 810-766-6789, E-mail: bmaki@umflint.edu.

University of Minnesota, Twin Cities Campus, Graduate School, School of Nursing, Program in Nurse Anesthetist, Minneapolis, MN 55455-0213. Offers MS. *Accreditation:* AANA/CANAEP. *Entrance requirements:* Additional exam requirements/recommendations for international students: Required—TOEFL (minimum score 586 paper-based; 240 computer-based).

University of New England, Westbrook College of Health Professions, Program in Nurse Anesthesia, Biddeford, ME 04005-9526. Offers MS. Offered in association with Eastern Maine Medical Center, St. Joseph Hospital, and Harlem Hospital. *Accreditation:* AANA/CANAEP. *Faculty:* 1 (woman) full-time, 3 part-time/adjunct (all women). *Students:* 91 full-time (59 women); includes 8 minority (2 African Americans, 1 American Indian/Alaska Native, 2 Asian Americans or Pacific Islanders, 3 Hispanic Americans). In 2009, 22 master's awarded. *Degree requirements:* For master's, thesis or alternative, practicum. *Entrance requirements:* For master's, GRE, RN license, 1 year of acute care experience, 3 letters of reference, recent completion of organic or biochemistry course. *Application deadline:* For fall admission, 2/1 for domestic and international students. Applications are processed on a rolling basis. Application fee: $40. Electronic applications accepted. *Expenses:* Contact institution. *Financial support:* Application deadline: 5/1. *Faculty research:* Evaluation, faculty perceptions of student characteristics and success during clinical practicum. *Unit head:* Catherine Hagerman, Interim Program Director, 207-221-4546, Fax: 207-221-4546, E-mail: chagerman@une.edu. *Application contact:* Stacy Gato, Assistant Director of Graduate Admissions, 207-221-4225, Fax: 207-221-4898, E-mail: gradadmissions@une.edu.

The University of North Carolina at Charlotte, Graduate School, College of Health and Human Services, School of Nursing, Charlotte, NC 28223-0001. Offers nursing advanced clinical (MSN); nursing anesthesia (MSN); nursing systems population (MSN). *Accreditation:* AACN. *Faculty:* 21 full-time (20 women), 5 part-time/adjunct (all women). *Students:* 77 full-time (65 women), 142 part-time (130 women); includes 26 African Americans, 6 Asian Americans or Pacific Islanders, 4 Hispanic Americans, 1 international. Average age 36. 163 applicants, 52% accepted, 78 enrolled. In 2009, 40 master's awarded. *Entrance requirements:* For master's, GRE General Test, minimum GPA of 3.0 in undergraduate major. Additional exam requirements/recommendations for international students: Required—TOEFL (minimum score 570 paper-based; 220 computer-based; 83 iBT). *Application deadline:* For fall admission, 7/15 for domestic students, 5/1 for international students; for spring admission, 11/15 for domestic students, 10/1 for international students. Application fee: $55. *Financial support:* In 2009–10, 7 students received support, including 1 research assistantship (averaging $12,872 per year), 6 teaching assistantships (averaging $6,171 per year); career-related internships or fieldwork, Federal Work-Study, institutionally sponsored loans, scholarships/grants, traineeships, and unspecified assistantships also available. Support available to part-time students. Financial award application deadline: 4/1; financial award applicants required to submit FAFSA. Total annual research expenditures: $717,259. *Unit head:* Dr. Lucille L. Travis, Director, 704-687-7959, Fax: 704-687-6017, E-mail: ltravis1@uncc.edu. *Application contact:* Kathy B. Giddings, Director of Graduate Admissions, 704-687-5503, Fax: 704-687-3279, E-mail: gradadm@uncc.edu.

The University of North Carolina at Greensboro, Graduate School, School of Nursing, Greensboro, NC 27412-5001. Offers adult clinical nurse specialist (MSN, PMC); adult/gerontological nurse practitioner (MSN, PMC); nurse anesthesia (MSN, PMC); nursing (PhD); nursing administration (MSN); nursing education (MSN); MSN/MBA. *Accreditation:* AACN; AANA/CANAEP; NLN. *Degree requirements:* For master's, thesis or alternative. *Entrance requirements:* For master's, GRE General Test or MAT, BSN, clinical experience, liability insurance, RN license; for PMC, liability insurance, MSN, RN license. Additional exam requirements/recommendations for international students: Required—TOEFL. Electronic applications accepted.

University of Pennsylvania, School of Nursing, Nurse Anesthetist Program, Philadelphia, PA 19104. Offers MSN. *Students:* 38 full-time (28 women), 4 part-time (all women); includes 9 minority (3 African Americans, 1 American Indian/Alaska Native, 5 Asian Americans or Pacific

Islanders). In 2009, 15 master's awarded. Application fee: $70. *Expenses:* Tuition: Full-time $25,660; part-time $4758 per course. Required fees: $2152; $270 per course. Tuition and fees vary according to course load, degree level and program.

University of Pittsburgh, School of Nursing, Nurse Anesthesia Program, Pittsburgh, PA 15260. Offers MSN, DNP. *Accreditation:* AACN; AANA/CANAEP. *Students:* 106 full-time (75 women), 18 part-time (13 women); includes 12 minority (5 African Americans, 5 Asian Americans or Pacific Islanders, 2 Hispanic Americans). Average age 29. 151 applicants, 36% accepted, 46 enrolled. In 2009, 52 master's awarded. *Degree requirements:* For master's, comprehensive exam, thesis optional. *Entrance requirements:* For master's, GRE General Test, BSN, RN license, 1-3 years nursing experience, letters of recommendation, resume, course work in statistics. Additional exam requirements/recommendations for international students: Required—TOEFL (minimum score 550 paper-based; 213 computer-based; 80 iBT). *Application deadline:* For fall admission, 1/2 for domestic students. Application fee: $50. Electronic applications accepted. *Expenses:* Tuition, state resident: full-time $16,402; part-time $665 per credit. Tuition, nonresident: full-time $28,694; part-time $1175 per credit. Required fees: $690; $175 per term. Tuition and fees vary according to program. *Unit head:* John O'Donnell, Director, 412-624-4860, Fax: 412-624-2401, E-mail: jod01@pitt.edu. *Application contact:* Laurie Lapsley, Administrator of Graduate Student Services, 412-624-9670, Fax: 412-624-2409, E-mail: lapsleyl@pitt.edu.

University of Puerto Rico, Medical Sciences Campus, School of Nursing, San Juan, PR 00936-5067. Offers anesthesia (MSN); critical care nursing (MSN); family and community nursing (MSN); family nurse practitioner (MSN); mental health and psychiatric nursing (MSN); nursing (MSN). *Accreditation:* AACN; AANA/CANAEP. *Entrance requirements:* For master's, GRE or EXADEP, interview, Puerto Rico RN license or professional license for international students, general and specific point average, article analysis. Electronic applications accepted. *Faculty research:* HIV, health disparities, teen violence, women and violence, neurological disorders.

The University of Scranton, College of Graduate and Continuing Education, Department of Nursing, Scranton, PA 18510. Offers adult health nursing (MSN); family nurse practitioner (MSN, PMC); nurse anesthesia (MSN, PMC). Applicants accepted in odd-numbered years only. *Accreditation:* AACN; AANA/CANAEP. Part-time and evening/weekend programs available. *Faculty:* 13 full-time (all women), 2 part-time/adjunct (both women). *Students:* 40 full-time (37 women), 35 part-time (25 women); includes 6 minority (5 African Americans, 1 Asian American or Pacific Islander). Average age 35. 74 applicants, 85% accepted. In 2009, 34 master's awarded. *Degree requirements:* For master's, thesis (for some programs), capstone experience. *Entrance requirements:* For master's, BSN, minimum GPA of 3.0, Pennsylvania RN license. Additional exam requirements/recommendations for international students: Required—TOEFL (minimum score 500 paper-based; 173 computer-based), IELTS (minimum score 5.5). *Application deadline:* For fall admission, 9/1 for domestic students. Applications are processed on a rolling basis. Application fee: $0. *Financial support:* In 2009–10, 8 students received support, including 8 teaching assistantships with full and partial tuition reimbursements available (averaging $6,600 per year); career-related internships or fieldwork, Federal Work-Study, and unspecified assistantships also available. Support available to part-time students. Financial award application deadline: 3/1. *Faculty research:* Home care, doctoral education, health care of women and children, pain, health promotion and adolescence. *Unit head:* Dr. Patricia Harrington, Chair, 570-941-7673, Fax: 570-941-4201, E-mail: harringtonp1@uofs.edu. *Application contact:* Dr. Mary Jane Hanson, Director, 570-941-4060, Fax: 570-941-4201, E-mail: hansonm2@scranton.edu.

University of South Carolina, School of Medicine and The Graduate School, Graduate Programs in Medicine, Program in Nurse Anesthesia, Columbia, SC 29208. Offers MNA. *Accreditation:* AACN; AANA/CANAEP. *Degree requirements:* For master's, comprehensive exam, practicum. *Entrance requirements:* For master's, GRE, 1 year of critical care experience, RN license. Electronic applications accepted. *Expenses:* Contact institution. *Faculty research:* Neuroscience, cardiovascular, hormones, stress, homeostasis.

The University of Tennessee at Chattanooga, Graduate School, College of Health, Education and Professional Studies, School of Nursing, Chattanooga, TN 37403. Offers administration (MSN); certified nurse anesthetist (Post-Master's Certificate); education (MSN); family nurse practitioner (MSN, Post-Master's Certificate); health care informatics (Post-Master's Certificate); nurse anesthesia (MSN); nurse education (Post-Master's Certificate). *Accreditation:* AACN; AANA/CANAEP (one or more programs are accredited). *Faculty:* 4 full-time (all women). *Students:* 42 full-time (33 women), 53 part-time (38 women); includes 10 minority (5 African Americans, 1 American Indian/Alaska Native, 2 Asian Americans or Pacific Islanders, 2 Hispanic Americans). Average age 35. 13 applicants, 31% accepted, 3 enrolled. In 2009, 36 master's, 5 other advanced degrees awarded. *Degree requirements:* For master's, thesis optional, qualifying exams, professional project; for Post-Master's Certificate, thesis or alternative, practicum, seminar. *Entrance requirements:* For master's, GRE General Test, MAT, BSN, minimum GPA of 3.0, eligibility for Tennessee RN license, 1 year direct patient care experience; for Post-Master's Certificate, GRE General Test, MAT, MSN, minimum GPA of 3.0, eligibility for Tennessee RN license, one year of direct patient care experience. Additional exam requirements/recommendations for international students: Required—TOEFL (minimum score 550 paper-based; 213 computer-based; 79 iBT), IELTS (minimum score 6). *Application deadline:* For fall admission, 8/1 priority date for domestic students, 6/1 for international students; for spring admission, 12/1 priority date for domestic students, 10/1 for international students. Applications are processed on a rolling basis. Application fee: $35. Electronic applications accepted. *Expenses:* Tuition, state resident: full-time $5404; part-time $300 per credit hour. Tuition, nonresident: full-time $16,702; part-time $928 per credit hour. Required fees: $1150; $130 per credit hour. *Financial support:* Career-related internships or fieldwork and scholarships/grants available. Support available to part-time students. *Faculty research:* Diabetes in women, health care for elderly, alternative medicine, hypertension, nurse anesthesia. Total annual research expenditures: $1.5 million. *Unit head:* Dr. Kay R. Lindgren, Head, 423-425-4646, Fax: 423-425-4668, E-mail: kay-lindgren@utc.edu. *Application contact:* Dr. Stephanie Bellar, Dean of Graduate Studies, 423-425-4666, Fax: 423-425-5223, E-mail: stephanie-bellar@utc.edu.

University of Wisconsin–La Crosse, Office of University Graduate Studies, College of Science and Health, Department of Biology, La Crosse, WI 54601-3742. Offers aquatic sciences (MS); biology (MS); cellular and molecular biology (MS); clinical microbiology (MS); microbiology (MS); nurse anesthesia (MS); physiology (MS). Part-time programs available. *Faculty:* 27 full-time (7 women). *Students:* 19 full-time (8 women), 35 part-time (20 women); includes 1 minority (Asian American or Pacific Islander), 2 international. Average age 28. 87 applicants, 32% accepted, 21 enrolled. In 2009, 18 master's awarded. *Degree requirements:* For master's, comprehensive exam, thesis. *Entrance requirements:* For master's, GRE General Test, minimum GPA of 2.85. Additional exam requirements/recommendations for international students: Required—TOEFL (minimum score 550 paper-based; 213 computer-based; 79 iBT). Application fee: $56. Electronic applications accepted. *Financial support:* In 2009–10, 19 research assistantships with partial tuition reimbursements (averaging $10,021 per year) were awarded; career-related internships or fieldwork, Federal Work-Study, health care benefits, unspecified assistantships, and grant-funded positions also available. Support available to part-time students. Financial award application deadline: 3/15; financial award applicants required to submit FAFSA. *Unit head:* Dr. David Howard, Chair, 608-785-6455, E-mail: howard.davi@uwlax.edu. *Application contact:* Kathryn Kiefer, Director of Admissions, 608-785-8939, E-mail: admissions@uwlax.edu.

Villanova University, College of Nursing, Villanova, PA 19085-1699. Offers adult nurse practitioner (MSN, Post Master's Certificate); family nurse practitioner (MSN, Post Master's Certificate); health care administration (MSN); nurse anesthetist (MSN, Post Master's Certificate); nursing (PhD); nursing education (MSN, Post Master's Certificate); pediatric nurse practitioner (MSN, Post Master's Certificate). *Accreditation:* AACN; AANA/CANAEP. Part-time programs available. Postbaccalaureate distance learning degree programs offered (minimal on-campus study). *Faculty:* 15 full-time (all women), 3 part-time/adjunct (2 women). *Students:* 58 full-time (53 women), 188 part-time (164 women); includes 29 minority (13 African Americans, 1 American Indian/Alaska Native, 13 Asian Americans or Pacific Islanders, 2 Hispanic Americans), 3 international. Average age 33. 171 applicants, 70% accepted, 89 enrolled. In 2009, 32 master's, 1 doctorate awarded. *Degree requirements:* For master's, independent study project; for doctorate, comprehensive exam, thesis/dissertation. *Entrance requirements:* For master's, GRE or MAT, BSN, 1 year of recent nursing experience, physical assessment, course work in statistics; for doctorate, GRE, MSN. Additional exam requirements/recommendations for international students: Required—TOEFL. *Application deadline:* For fall admission, 7/1 priority date for domestic students, 7/1 for international students; for spring admission, 11/1 priority date for domestic students, 11/1 for international students. Applications are processed on a rolling basis. Application fee: $50. *Expenses:* Contact institution. *Financial support:* In 2009–10, 53 students received support, including 5 teaching assistantships with full tuition reimbursements available (averaging $13,100 per year); institutionally sponsored loans, scholarships/grants, traineeships, tuition waivers (full), and unspecified assistantships also available. Financial award application deadline: 3/1; financial award applicants required to submit FAFSA. *Faculty research:* Genetics, ethics, cognitive development of students, women with disabilities, nursing leadership. *Unit head:* Dr. Marguerite K. Schlag, Assistant Dean and Director, Graduate Program, 610-519-4907, Fax: 610-519-7650, E-mail: marguerite.schlag@villanova.edu. *Application contact:* Dean, Graduate School of Liberal Arts and Sciences.

Virginia Commonwealth University, Graduate School, School of Allied Health Professions, Department of Health Administration, Doctoral Program in Health Related Sciences, Richmond, VA 23284-9005. Offers clinical laboratory sciences (PhD); gerontology (PhD); health administration (PhD); nurse anesthesia (PhD); occupational therapy (PhD); physical therapy (PhD); radiation sciences (PhD); rehabilitation leadership (PhD).

Virginia Commonwealth University, Graduate School, School of Allied Health Professions, Department of Nurse Anesthesia, Richmond, VA 23284-9005. Offers MSNA. *Accreditation:* AANA/CANAEP. *Degree requirements:* For master's, thesis. *Entrance requirements:* For master's, GRE General Test, 1 year experience in acute critical care nursing, BSN, current state RPN license. *Faculty research:* Obstetrical anesthesia, ambulatory anesthesia, regional anesthesia, practice profiles, clinical practice.

Wayne State University, Eugene Applebaum College of Pharmacy and Health Sciences, Department of Health Care Sciences, Program in Nursing Anesthesia, Detroit, MI 48202. Offers nurse anesthesia (MS); pediatric nurse anesthesia (Certificate). *Accreditation:* AACN; AANA/CANAEP. *Degree requirements:* For master's, thesis optional. *Entrance requirements:* For master's, GRE General Test, BSN, 1 year of ICU experience; current RN license, current advanced Cardiac Life Support. Additional exam requirements/recommendations for international students: Required—TOEFL (minimum score 550 paper-based; 213 computer-based); Recommended—TWE (minimum score 6). Electronic applications accepted. *Faculty research:* Maternal oxygen administration, re-activated epidural anesthesia, temperate monitoring modalities, sedation, anesthesia outcomes.

Webster University, College of Arts and Sciences, Department of Biological Sciences, Program in Nurse Anesthesia, St. Louis, MO 63119-3194. Offers MS. *Accreditation:* AANA/CANAEP. Postbaccalaureate distance learning degree programs offered. *Degree requirements:* For master's, thesis. *Entrance requirements:* For master's, 1 year of work-related experience, 75 hours of graduate course work, BSN, interview, minimum GPA of 3.0. Additional exam requirements/recommendations for international students: Required—TOEFL. *Expenses:* Tuition: Part-time $565 per credit hour. Tuition and fees vary according to degree level, campus/location and program. *Faculty research:* Clinical anesthesia, substance abuse education in the health professions, technology and education, clinical pharmacology.

Westminster College, School of Nursing and Health Sciences, Salt Lake City, UT 84105-3697. Offers family nurse practitioner (MSN); nurse anesthesia (MSNA); nurse education (MSNED); nursing (MSN); public health (MPH). *Accreditation:* AACN; AANA/CANAEP. *Faculty:* 11 full-time (6 women), 12 part-time/adjunct (6 women). *Students:* 77 full-time (54 women), 49 part-time (16 women); includes 11 minority (3 African Americans, 6 Asian Americans or Pacific Islanders, 2 Hispanic Americans), 2 international. Average age 34. 152 applicants, 57% accepted, 48 enrolled. In 2009, 23 master's awarded. *Degree requirements:* For master's, clinical practicum, 504 clinical practice hours. *Entrance requirements:* For master's, GRE, resume, Utah RN license in good standing, minimum GPA of 3.0, 3 letters of reference, BSN from accredited nursing program, proof of clear state and federal background check, drug test results, personal interview, current PALS certification, current ACLS certification. Additional exam requirements/recommendations for international students: Required—TOEFL (minimum score 600 paper-based; 250 computer-based; 100 iBT). *Application deadline:* Applications are processed on a rolling basis. Application fee: $40. Electronic applications accepted. *Expenses:* Contact institution. *Financial support:* In 2009–10, 60 students received support. Career-related internships or fieldwork and tuition reimbursement, tuition remission available. Support available to part-time students. Financial award applicants required to submit FAFSA. *Faculty research:* Emotional intelligence, graduate faculty mentorship, parish nursing roles in women's disease prevention, psychiatric nursing students' self-assessment of therapeutic relationships, psychosocial nurse practitioner's self-assessment of therapeutic relationships, curriculum simulation. *Unit head:* Dr. Sheryl Steadman, Dean, 801-832-2164, Fax: 801-832-3110, E-mail: ssteadman@westminstercollege.edu. *Application contact:* Joel Bauman, Vice President of Enrollment Services, 801-832-2200, Fax: 801-832-3101, E-mail: admission@westminstercollege.edu.

Nurse Midwifery

Case Western Reserve University, Frances Payne Bolton School of Nursing, Doctor of Nursing Practice Program, Cleveland, OH 44106. Offers acute care nurse practitioner (DNP); adult nurse practitioner (DNP); family nurse practitioner (DNP); gerontological nurse practitioner (DNP); graduate entry/pre-licensure option (DNP); medical-surgical nursing (DNP); midwifery/family nursing (DNP); neonatal nurse practitioner (DNP); pediatric nurse practitioner (DNP); post-licensure option (DNP); psychiatric-mental health nurse practitioner (DNP); women's health nurse practitioner (DNP). Graduate entry option allows baccalaureate-prepared college graduates from non-nursing backgrounds to earn certificate and MSN in addition to ND. Terminal master's awarded for partial completion of doctoral program. *Degree requirements:* For doctorate, thesis/dissertation. *Entrance requirements:* For doctorate, GRE General Test or MAT. *Faculty research:* Clinical nursing, acute care, gerontology, mental health, critical care.

Case Western Reserve University, Frances Payne Bolton School of Nursing, Master's Programs in Nursing, Program in Nurse Midwifery, Cleveland, OH 44106. Offers MSN. *Accreditation:* ACNM/DOA. *Degree requirements:* For master's, thesis optional. *Entrance*

Nurse Midwifery

Case Western Reserve University (continued)
requirements: For master's, GRE General Test or MAT. *Faculty research:* Clinical nursing, normal childbearing, descriptive studies of care, high risk pregnancy side effects of bedrest, strengthening and expanding nursing services.

Columbia University, School of Nursing, Program in Nurse Midwifery, New York, NY 10032. Offers MS. *Accreditation:* AACN; ACNM/DOA. Part-time programs available. *Entrance requirements:* For master's, GRE General Test, BSN, 1 year of clinical experience (preferred). Electronic applications accepted.

DeSales University, Graduate Division, Programs in Nursing, Center Valley, PA 18034-9568. Offers adult advanced practice nurse specialist (MSN); certified nurse midwives (MSN); certified nurse practitioners (MSN); family nurse practitioner (MSN); nurse educator (MSN); MSN/MBA. *Accreditation:* NLN. Part-time programs available. *Students:* 67 part-time. In 2009, 218 master's awarded. *Degree requirements:* For master's, thesis optional. *Entrance requirements:* For master's, GRE General Test, MAT, minimum B average in undergraduate course work, health assessment course or equivalent, course work in statistics. Additional exam requirements/recommendations for international students: Required—TOEFL. *Application deadline:* Applications are processed on a rolling basis. Application fee: $35. Electronic applications accepted. *Expenses:* Tuition: Full-time $17,500; part-time $665 per credit. Full-time tuition and fees vary according to program. Part-time tuition and fees vary according to course load. *Financial support:* Applicants required to submit FAFSA. *Faculty research:* Women's health, theory validation, needs of homeless, behavior risk evaluation, wound healing. *Unit head:* Dr. Carol Gullo Mest, Director, 610-282-1100 Ext. 1394, Fax: 610-282-2091, E-mail: carol.mest@desales.edu. *Application contact:* Caryn Stopper, Director of Graduate Admissions, 610-282-1100 Ext. 1768, Fax: 610-282-2254, E-mail: caryn.stopper@desales.edu.

Emory University, Nell Hodgson Woodruff School of Nursing, Atlanta, GA 30322-1100. Offers adult and elder health advanced practice nursing (MSN), including acute care, adult nurse practitioner, gerontological nurse practitioner; emergency nurse practitioner (MSN); family nurse practitioner (MSN); family nurse-midwife (MSN); nurse midwifery (MSN); pediatric nurse practitioner acute and primary care (MSN); public health nursing leadership (MSN); women's health nurse practitioner (MSN); women's health title x (MSN); women's health/adult health nurse practitioner (MSN); MSN/MPH. *Accreditation:* AACN; ACNM/DOA (one or more programs are accredited). Part-time programs available. *Faculty:* 30 full-time (29 women), 11 part-time/adjunct (10 women). *Students:* 110 full-time (106 women), 53 part-time (51 women); includes 49 minority (35 African Americans, 2 American Indian/Alaska Native, 10 Asian Americans or Pacific Islanders, 2 Hispanic Americans), 4 international. Average age 32. 182 applicants, 63% accepted, 86 enrolled. In 2009, 81 master's awarded. *Entrance requirements:* For master's, GRE General Test or MAT, minimum GPA of 3.0, BS in nursing from an accredited institution, RN license and additional course work, 3 letters of recommendation. Additional exam requirements/recommendations for international students: Required—TOEFL (minimum score 600 paper-based; 100 iBT). *Application deadline:* For fall admission, 1/15 priority date for domestic and international students; for spring admission, 10/1 priority date for domestic and international students. Applications are processed on a rolling basis. Application fee: $50. Electronic applications accepted. *Expenses:* Contact institution. *Financial support:* In 2009–10, 14 fellowships (averaging $28,000 per year) were awarded; career-related internships or fieldwork, Federal Work-Study, institutionally sponsored loans, and scholarships/grants also available. Support available to part-time students. Financial award application deadline: 3/1; financial award applicants required to submit CSS PROFILE or FAFSA. *Faculty research:* Older adult falls and injuries, minority health issues, cardiac symptoms and quality of life, bio-ethics and decision making, menopausal issues. *Unit head:* Dr. Linda McCauley, Dean, 404-727-7976, Fax: 404-727-9800, E-mail: linda.mccauley@emory.edu. *Application contact:* Katie Kennedy, Associate Director for Admission and Financial Aid, 404-727-7980, Fax: 404-727-8509, E-mail: admit@nursing.emory.edu.

See Close-Up on page 1613.

Frontier School of Midwifery and Family Nursing, Graduate Programs, Hyden, KY 41749. Offers community-based family nurse practitioner (MSN, Post Master's Certificate); community-based nurse-midwifery education (MSN, Post Master's Certificate); community-based women[0092]s health care nurse practitioner (MSN, Post Master's Certificate). *Accreditation:* ACNM; NLN.

Georgetown University, Graduate School of Arts and Sciences, School of Nursing and Health Studies, Washington, DC 20057. Offers acute care nurse practitioner (MS); clinical nurse specialist (MS); family nurse practitioner (MS); nurse anesthesia (MS); nurse-midwifery (MS); nursing education (MS). *Accreditation:* AACN; AANA/CANAEP; ACNM/DOA. *Degree requirements:* For master's, thesis optional. *Entrance requirements:* For master's, GRE General Test or MAT, bachelor's degree in nursing from NLN-accredited school, minimum undergraduate GPA of 3.0. Additional exam requirements/recommendations for international students: Required—TOEFL.

Marquette University, Graduate School, College of Nursing, Milwaukee, WI 53201-1881. Offers adult nurse practitioner (Certificate); advanced practice nursing (MSN), including adult, children, neonatal nurse practitioner, nurse-midwifery, older adult; gerontological nurse practitioner (Certificate); neonatal nurse practitioner (Certificate); nurse-midwifery (Certificate); nursing (PhD); pediatric nurse practitioner (Certificate). *Accreditation:* AACN. Part-time and evening/weekend programs available. *Faculty:* 29 full-time (27 women), 43 part-time/adjunct (all women). *Students:* 115 full-time (105 women), 209 part-time (197 women); includes 28 minority (13 African Americans, 2 American Indian/Alaska Native, 8 Asian Americans or Pacific Islanders, 5 Hispanic Americans), 1 international. Average age 32. 143 applicants, 91% accepted, 86 enrolled. In 2009, 64 master's, 10 doctorates awarded. *Degree requirements:* For master's, comprehensive exam, thesis or alternative. *Entrance requirements:* For master's, GRE General Test, BSN, Wisconsin RN license. Additional exam requirements/recommendations for international students: Required—TOEFL. Application fee: $40. *Financial support:* In 2009–10, 6 research assistantships, 1 teaching assistantship were awarded; career-related internships or fieldwork, Federal Work-Study, institutionally sponsored loans, scholarships/grants, and tuition waivers (full and partial) also available. Support available to part-time students. Financial award application deadline: 2/15. *Faculty research:* Psychosocial adjustment to chronic illness, gerontology, reminiscence, health policy: uninsured and access, hospital care delivery systems. *Unit head:* Dr. Lea Acord, Dean, 414-288-3812, Fax: 414-288-1578. *Application contact:* Dr. Judy Miller, Director of Graduate Studies, 414-288-3810, Fax: 414-288-1578.

Midwives College of Utah, Graduate Program, Salt Lake City, UT 84106. Offers MS. *Accreditation:* MEAC. *Degree requirements:* For master's, comprehensive exam (for some programs), thesis.

National College of Midwifery, Graduate Programs, Taos, NM 87571. Offers MS, PhD. *Accreditation:* MEAC. Part-time and evening/weekend programs available. Postbaccalaureate distance learning degree programs offered (no on-campus study). *Degree requirements:* For master's, thesis, publication; for doctorate, thesis/dissertation, presentation, publication. *Entrance requirements:* For master's and doctorate, midwifery license or certification. Electronic applications accepted.

New York University, College of Nursing, Programs in Advanced Practice Nursing, New York, NY 10012-1019. Offers advanced practice nursing: adult acute care (MS, Advanced Certificate); advanced practice nursing: adult nurse practitioner/palliative care nursing (MS); advanced practice nursing: adult nurse practitioner/holistic nurse practitioner (Advanced Certificate); advanced practice nursing: adult nurse practitioner/holistic nursing (MS); advanced practice nursing: adult nurse practitioner/palliative care nurse practitioner (Advanced Certificate); advanced practice nursing: adult primary care (MS, Advanced Certificate); advanced practice nursing: adult primary care/geriatrics (MS); advanced practice nursing: geriatrics (MS, Advanced Certificate); advanced practice nursing: mental health (MS); advanced practice nursing: mental health nursing (Advanced Certificate); advanced practice nursing: pediatrics (MS, Advanced Certificate); advanced practice nursing:adult primary care and geriatrics (Advanced Certificate); nurse midwifery (MS, Advanced Certificate); nursing administration (MS, Advanced Certificate); nursing education (MS, Advanced Certificate); nursing informatics (MS, Advanced Certificate); MS/MPH; MS/MS. *Accreditation:* AACN; ACNM/DOA. Part-time and evening/weekend programs available. *Faculty:* 17 full-time (all women), 22 part-time/adjunct (19 women). *Students:* 18 full-time (17 women), 524 part-time (485 women); includes 238 minority (90 African Americans, 119 Asian Americans or Pacific Islanders, 29 Hispanic Americans). Average age 33. 191 applicants, 89% accepted, 120 enrolled. In 2009, 117 master's, 2 other advanced degrees awarded. *Degree requirements:* For master's, thesis (for some programs). *Entrance requirements:* For master's, BS in nursing, AS in nursing with another BS/BA, interview; for Advanced Certificate, master's degree. Additional exam requirements/recommendations for international students: Required—TOEFL. *Application deadline:* For fall admission, 7/1 priority date for domestic students, 7/1 for international students; for spring admission, 12/1 for domestic and international students. Applications are processed on a rolling basis. Application fee: $75. *Expenses:* Tuition: Full-time $30,528; part-time $1272 per credit. Required fees: $2177. *Financial support:* Career-related internships or fieldwork, institutionally sponsored loans, scholarships/grants, traineeships, and tuition waivers (partial) available. Support available to part-time students. Financial award application deadline: 2/1; financial award applicants required to submit FAFSA. *Faculty research:* Elderly black diabetics, families and illness, public health nursing, parent-child nursing, health policy costs. *Unit head:* Dr. Judith Haber, Associate Dean for Graduate Programs, 212-998-9020, Fax: 212-995-3143. *Application contact:* Amy Knowles, Assistant Dean for Student Affairs and Admissions, 212-998-5333, Fax: 212-995-4302, E-mail: ak96@nyu.edu.

Old Dominion University, College of Health Sciences, School of Nursing, Norfolk, VA 23529. Offers family nurse practitioner (MSN); nurse anesthesia (MSN); nurse educator (MSN); nurse midwifery (MSN); women's health nurse practitioner (MSN). *Accreditation:* AACN; AANA/CANAEP. Part-time programs available. Postbaccalaureate distance learning degree programs offered (no on-campus study). *Faculty:* 11 full-time (10 women), 15 part-time/adjunct (14 women). *Students:* 122 full-time (113 women), 101 part-time (97 women); includes 49 minority (23 African Americans, 2 American Indian/Alaska Native, 19 Asian Americans or Pacific Islanders, 5 Hispanic Americans). Average age 37. 169 applicants, 81% accepted, 122 enrolled. In 2009, 77 master's awarded. *Degree requirements:* For master's, comprehensive exam. *Entrance requirements:* For master's, GRE or MAT, BSN, minimum GPA of 3.0 in nursing and overall. Additional exam requirements/recommendations for international students: Required—TOEFL. *Application deadline:* For fall admission, 5/1 for domestic students. Applications are processed on a rolling basis. Application fee: $40. Electronic applications accepted. *Expenses:* Tuition, state resident: full-time $8112; part-time $338 per credit. Tuition, nonresident: full-time $20,256; part-time $844 per credit. Required fees: $119 per semester. One-time fee: $50. *Financial support:* In 2009–10, 18 students received support, including 2 research assistantships with tuition reimbursements available (averaging $10,000 per year); teaching assistantships, career-related internships or fieldwork, scholarships/grants, traineeships, and tuition waivers (partial) also available. Support available to part-time students. Financial award application deadline: 2/15; financial award applicants required to submit FAFSA. *Faculty research:* Health and culture, cardiovascular health, transition of military families, genetics, cultural diversity. Total annual research expenditures: $231,117. *Unit head:* Dr. Karen Karlowicz, Chair, 757-683-5262, Fax: 757-683-5253, E-mail: nursgpd@odu.edu. *Application contact:* Sue Parker, Coordinator, Graduate Student Services, 757-683-4298, Fax: 757-683-5253, E-mail: sparker@odu.edu.

Oregon Health & Science University, School of Nursing, Program in Nurse Midwifery, Portland, OR 97239-3098. Offers MN, MS, Post Master's Certificate. *Accreditation:* AACN; ACNM/DOA (one or more programs are accredited). *Degree requirements:* For master's, thesis optional. *Entrance requirements:* For master's, GRE General Test, bachelor's degree in nursing, minimum undergraduate GPA of 3.0, previous course work in statistics; for Post Master's Certificate, master's degree in nursing. Tuition and fees vary according to course level, course load, degree level, program and reciprocity agreements.

Philadelphia University, School of Science and Health, Program in Midwifery, Philadelphia, PA 19144. Offers midwifery (MS); nurse midwifery (Postbaccalaureate Certificate). *Accreditation:* ACNM/DOA. Part-time and evening/weekend programs available. Postbaccalaureate distance learning degree programs offered (minimal on-campus study). *Entrance requirements:* For master's, GRE or MAT. Additional exam requirements/recommendations for international students: Required—TOEFL (minimum score 550 paper-based; 213 computer-based; 79 iBT). Electronic applications accepted.

Radford University, College of Graduate and Professional Studies, Waldron College of Health and Human Services, School of Nursing, Radford, VA 24142. Offers adult clinical nurse specialist (MSN); family nurse practitioner (MSN); gerontology clinical nurse specialist (MSN); nurse midwifery (MSN). *Accreditation:* AACN. Part-time programs available. *Faculty:* 15 full-time (14 women), 3 part-time/adjunct (2 women). *Students:* 15 full-time (all women), 17 part-time (all women); includes 1 minority (Asian American or Pacific Islander). Average age 35. 17 applicants, 76% accepted, 8 enrolled. In 2009, 11 master's awarded. *Degree requirements:* For master's, comprehensive exam, thesis optional. *Entrance requirements:* For master's, GRE, minimum GPA of 3.0; 3 letters of reference from professional contacts, letter of intent, resume. Additional exam requirements/recommendations for international students: Required—TOEFL (minimum score 550 paper-based; 213 computer-based; 79 iBT). *Application deadline:* For fall admission, 2/1 priority date for domestic students, 12/1 for international students. Applications are processed on a rolling basis. Application fee: $50. Electronic applications accepted. *Expenses:* Tuition, state resident: full-time $5086; part-time $211 per credit hour. Tuition, nonresident: full-time $12,608; part-time $525 per credit hour. Required fees: $2508; $105 per credit hour. *Financial support:* In 2009–10, 5 students received support, including 4 teaching assistantships with partial tuition reimbursements available (averaging $8,700 per year); career-related internships or fieldwork, Federal Work-Study, institutionally sponsored loans, scholarships/grants, and unspecified assistantships also available. Financial award application deadline: 3/1; financial award applicants required to submit FAFSA. *Unit head:* Dr. Kimberly F. Carter, Director, 540-831-7700, Fax: 540-831-7716, E-mail: kcarter@radford.edu. *Application contact:* Graduate Admissions, 540-831-5431, Fax: 540-831-6061, E-mail: gradcollege@radford.edu.

Shenandoah University, School of Health Professions, Division of Nursing, Winchester, VA 22601-5195. Offers family nurse practitioner (Certificate); nurse-midwifery (Certificate); nurse-midwifery endorsement (Certificate); nursing (MSN, DNP); post-master's in nursing education (Certificate); psychiatric mental health nurse practitioner (Certificate). *Accreditation:* AACN; ACNM/DOA. Part-time programs available. *Faculty:* 11 full-time (all women), 4 part-time/adjunct (all women). *Students:* 21 full-time (20 women), 67 part-time (64 women); includes 11 minority (7 African Americans, 2 Asian Americans or Pacific Islanders, 2 Hispanic Americans). Average age 39. 71 applicants, 97% accepted, 53 enrolled. In 2009, 8 master's, 6 other advanced degrees awarded. *Degree requirements:* For master's, research project, clinical hours; for doctorate and Certificate, clinical hours. *Entrance requirements:* For master's, GRE General Test, previous course work in statistics, community nursing, and physical assessment; RN license; BSN; minimum undergraduate GPA of 3.0; appropriate clinical experience; curriculum vitae; 3 letters of recommendation; for Certificate, MSN, minimum GPA of 3.0, 3 letters of recommendation. Additional exam requirements/recommendations for international students: Required—TOEFL (minimum score 550 paper-based; 213 computer-based; 79 iBT), IELTS (minimum score 6.5). *Application deadline:* For fall admission, 6/15 priority date for domestic and international students. Applications are processed on a rolling basis. Application fee: $30. Electronic applications accepted. *Expenses:* Tuition: Full-time $11,925; part-time $695 per credit. Required fees: $400 per semester. *Financial support:* Application deadline: 3/15. *Unit head:* Dr. Kathryn Ganske, Director, 540-678-4381, Fax: 540-665-5519. *Application contact:* David Anthony, Dean of Admissions, 540-665-4581, Fax: 540-665-4627, E-mail: admit@su.edu.

State University of New York Downstate Medical Center, College of Nursing, Graduate Program in Nursing, Program in Nurse Midwifery, Brooklyn, NY 11203-2098. Offers MS, Post Master's Certificate.

Stony Brook University, State University of New York, Stony Brook University Medical Center, Health Sciences Center, School of Nursing, Program in Nurse Midwifery, Stony Brook, NY 11794. Offers MS, Certificate. *Accreditation:* AACN; ACNM/DOA. Postbaccalaureate distance learning degree programs offered. *Students:* 11 full-time (all women), 16 part-time (all women); includes 2 minority (1 African American, 1 Asian American or Pacific Islander). In 2009, 7 master's awarded. *Degree requirements:* For master's, thesis. *Entrance requirements:* For master's, BSN, minimum GPA of 3.0, course work in statistics. *Application deadline:* For fall admission, 1/15 for domestic students. Application fee: $60. *Expenses:* Tuition, state resident: full-time $8370; part-time $349 per credit. Tuition, nonresident: full-time $13,250; part-time $552 per credit. Required fees: $933. *Financial support:* Fellowships, research assistantships, teaching assistantships available. Financial award application deadline: 3/15. *Unit head:* Prof. Arleen Steckel, Director, 631-444-3264, Fax: 631-444-3136, E-mail: arleen.steckel@stonybrook.edu. *Application contact:* Dr. Kent Marks, Assistant Dean, Admissions and Records, 631-632-4723, Fax: 631-632-7243, E-mail: kmarks@notes.cc.sunysb.edu.

University of Cincinnati, Graduate School, College of Nursing, Cincinnati, OH 45221-0038. Offers clinical nurse specialist (MSN), including adult health, community health, neonatal, nursing administration, occupational health, pediatric health, psychiatric nursing, women's health; nurse anesthesia (MSN); nurse midwifery (MSN); nurse practitioner (MSN), including acute care, ambulatory care, family, family/psychiatric, women's health; nursing (PhD); MBA/MSN. *Accreditation:* AACN; AANA/CANAEP (one or more programs are accredited); ACNM/DOA. Part-time programs available. Postbaccalaureate distance learning degree programs offered (no on-campus study). Terminal master's awarded for partial completion of doctoral program. *Degree requirements:* For master's, thesis or alternative; for doctorate, comprehensive exam, thesis/dissertation. *Entrance requirements:* For master's and doctorate, GRE General Test. Additional exam requirements/recommendations for international students: Required—TOEFL (minimum score 520 paper-based; 190 computer-based). Electronic applications accepted. *Faculty research:* Substance abuse, injury and violence, symptom management.

University of Illinois at Chicago, Graduate College, College of Nursing, Program in Nursing, Chicago, IL 60607-7128. Offers acute care clinical nurse specialist (MS); acute care nurse practitioner (MS); administrative studies in nursing (MS); adult nurse practitioner (MS); adult/geriatric nurse practitioner (MS); advanced community health nurse specialist (MS); family nurse practitioner (MS); geriatric clinical nurse specialist (MS); geriatric nurse practitioner (MS); mental health clinical nurse specialist (MS); mental health nurse practitioner (MS); nurse midwifery (MS); occupational health/advanced community health nurse specialist (MS); occupational health/family nurse practitioner (MS); pediatric clinical nurse specialist (MS); pediatric nurse practitioner (MS); perinatal clinical nurse specialist (MS); school/advanced community health nurse specialist (MS); school/family nurse practitioner (MS); women's health nurse practitioner (MS). *Accreditation:* AACN. Part-time programs available. *Degree requirements:* For master's, thesis or alternative. *Entrance requirements:* For master's, GRE General Test, minimum GPA of 2.75. Additional exam requirements/recommendations for international students: Required—TOEFL. Electronic applications accepted.

University of Indianapolis, Graduate Programs, School of Nursing, Indianapolis, IN 46227-3697. Offers family practice (post-RN) (MSN); gerontological nurse practitioner (MSN); nurse-midwifery (MSN); nursing (MSN); nursing administration (MSN); nursing education (MSN); MBA/MSN. *Accreditation:* AACN; ACNM. *Faculty:* 4 full-time (3 women), 2 part-time/adjunct (both women). *Students:* 27 full-time (26 women), 118 part-time (109 women); includes 10 minority (6 African Americans, 1 American Indian/Alaska Native, 1 Asian American or Pacific Islander, 2 Hispanic Americans), 2 international. Average age 38. *Entrance requirements:* For master's, minimum GPA of 3.0, interview, letters of recommendation, resume, IN nursing license, 1 year professional practice. Additional exam requirements/recommendations for international students: Required—TOEFL (minimum score 550 paper-based; 213 computer-based). *Application deadline:* For fall admission, 8/1 for domestic students; for winter admission, 12/15 for domestic students; for spring admission, 4/15 for domestic students. Applications are processed on a rolling basis. Application fee: $50. *Financial support:* Federal Work-Study available. *Unit head:* Dr. Anne Thomas, Dean, 317-788-3206, E-mail: athomas@uindy.edu. *Application contact:* T. C. Crum, Information Contact, 317-788-2128, Fax: 317-788-3542, E-mail: tcrum@uindy.edu.

The University of Kansas, University of Kansas Medical Center, School of Nursing, Kansas City, KS 66160. Offers clinical research management (PMC); family nurse practitioner (PMC); health care informatics (PMC); health professions educator (PMC); nurse midwife (PMC); nursing (MS, DNP, PhD); organizational leadership (PMC); psychiatric/mental health nurse practitioner (PMC); public health nursing (PMC). *Accreditation:* AACN; ACNM/DOA. Part-time programs available. Postbaccalaureate distance learning degree programs offered (minimal on-campus study). *Faculty:* 65. *Students:* 59 full-time (56 women), 309 part-time (285 women); includes 37 minority (17 African Americans, 4 American Indian/Alaska Native, 7 Asian Americans or Pacific Islanders, 9 Hispanic Americans), 10 international. Average age 38. 138 applicants, 59% accepted, 82 enrolled. In 2009, 78 master's, 3 doctorates awarded. Terminal master's awarded for partial completion of doctoral program. *Degree requirements:* For master's, thesis optional, general oral exam; for doctorate, one foreign language, thesis/dissertation, comprehensive oral and written exam. *Entrance requirements:* For master's, bachelor's degree in nursing, minimum GPA of 3.0, RN license, 1 year of clinical experience; for doctorate, GRE General Test, master's degree in nursing, minimum GPA of 3.5. Additional exam requirements/recommendations for international students: Required—TOEFL. *Application deadline:* For fall admission, 4/1 for domestic students; for spring admission, 9/1 for domestic students. Application fee: $60. Electronic applications accepted. *Expenses:* Tuition, state resident: full-time $6492; part-time $270.50 per credit hour. Tuition, nonresident: full-time $15,510; part-time $646.25 per credit hour. Required fees: $847; $70.56 per credit hour. Tuition and fees vary according to course load and program. *Financial support:* In 2009–10, 93 students received support, including 7 research assistantships (averaging $24,000 per year), 23 teaching assistantships with full and partial tuition reimbursements available (averaging $24,000 per year); traineeships also available. Financial award application deadline: 2/14; financial award applicants required to submit FAFSA. *Faculty research:* Breastfeeding practices of teen mothers, national database of nursing quality indicators, caregiving of families of patients using technology in the home, self care talk intervention partnership between caregivers of stroke survivors and nurses, smoking cessation. Total annual research expenditures: $5 million. *Unit head:* Dr. Karen L. Miller, Dean, 913-588-1601, Fax: 913-588-1660, E-mail: kmiller@kumc.edu. *Application contact:* Dr. Rita K. Clifford, Associate Dean, Student Affairs, 913-588-1619, Fax: 913-588-1615, E-mail: rcliffor@kumc.edu.

University of Maryland, Baltimore, Graduate School, School of Nursing, Master's Program in Nursing, Baltimore, MD 21201. Offers community health nursing (MS); gerontological nursing (MS); maternal-child nursing (MS); medical-surgical nursing (MS); nurse-midwifery education (MS); nursing administration (MS); nursing education (MS); nursing health policy (MS); primary care nursing (MS); psychiatric nursing (MS); MS/MBA. *Accreditation:* AACN; AANA/CANAEP; ACNM/DOA; NLN (one or more programs are accredited). Part-time programs available. *Students:* 387 full-time (338 women), 528 part-time (491 women); includes 330 minority (230 African Americans, 3 American Indian/Alaska Native, 81 Asian Americans or Pacific Islanders, 16 Hispanic Americans), 10 international. Average age 36. 849 applicants, 40% accepted, 255 enrolled. In 2009, 264 master's awarded. *Degree requirements:* For master's, comprehensive exam (for some programs), thesis or alternative. *Entrance requirements:* For master's, GRE General Test, minimum GPA of 2.75, course work in statistics, BS in nursing. Additional exam requirements/recommendations for international students: Required—TOEFL (minimum score 550 paper-based; 80 iBT), or IELTS (minimum score 7). *Application deadline:* For fall admission, 1/15 for international students. Application fee: $50. Electronic applications accepted. *Expenses:* Tuition, state resident: full-time $7290; part-time $405 per credit hour. Tuition, nonresident: full-time $12,780; part-time $710 per credit hour. Required fees: $774; $10 per credit hour. $297 per semester. Tuition and fees vary according to course load, degree level and program. *Financial support:* Fellowships, research assistantships, teaching assistantships, career-related internships or fieldwork and traineeships available. Support available to part-time students. Financial award application deadline: 2/15; financial award applicants required to submit FAFSA. *Unit head:* Dr. Jane Kapustin, Assistant Dean, 410-706-6741, Fax: 410-706-4231. *Application contact:* Marjorie Fass, Admissions Director, 410-706-0501, Fax: 410-706-7238.

University of Medicine and Dentistry of New Jersey, School of Health Related Professions, Department of Primary Care, Newark, NJ 07107-1709. Offers nurse midwifery (Certificate); physician assistant (MS). *Entrance requirements:* Additional exam requirements/recommendations for international students: Required—TOEFL. Electronic applications accepted.

University of Miami, Graduate School, School of Nursing and Health Studies, Coral Gables, FL 33124. Offers acute care (MSN), including acute care nurse practitioner, nurse anesthesia; nursing (PhD); primary care (MSN), including adult nurse practitioner, family nurse practitioner, nurse midwifery, women's health practitioner. *Accreditation:* AACN; AANA/CANAEP; ACNM/DOA (one or more programs are accredited). Part-time programs available. *Degree requirements:* For master's, thesis optional; for doctorate, thesis/dissertation. *Entrance requirements:* For master's, GRE General Test, BSN, minimum GPA of 3.0, Florida RN license; for doctorate, GRE General Test, BSN or MSN, minimum GPA of 3.0. Additional exam requirements/recommendations for international students: Required—TOEFL (minimum score 550 paper-based; 213 computer-based). Electronic applications accepted. *Faculty research:* Transcultural nursing, exercise and depression in Alzheimer's disease, infectious diseases/HIV–AIDS, postpartum depression, outcomes assessment.

University of Michigan, Horace H. Rackham School of Graduate Studies, School of Nursing, Division of Health Promotion and Risk Reduction, Program in Parent-Child Nursing, Ann Arbor, MI 48109. Offers infant, child, adolescent health nurse practitioner (MS); nurse midwifery (MS, Post Master's Certificate). *Accreditation:* AACN. Part-time programs available. Postbaccalaureate distance learning degree programs offered (minimal on-campus study). *Degree requirements:* For master's, thesis. *Entrance requirements:* For master's, GRE General Test (if cumulative BSN GPA less than 3.25), licensure, minimum GPA of 3.0 in BSN program. Additional exam requirements/recommendations for international students: Required—TOEFL (minimum score 560 paper-based; 220 computer-based). *Expenses:* Tuition, state resident: full-time $17,286; part-time $1099 per credit hour. Tuition, nonresident: full-time $34,944; part-time $2080 per credit hour. Required fees: $95 per semester. Tuition and fees vary according to course load, degree level and program.

University of Minnesota, Twin Cities Campus, Graduate School, School of Nursing, Nurse Midwifery Program, Minneapolis, MN 55455-0213. Offers MS. *Accreditation:* ACNM/DOA. Postbaccalaureate distance learning degree programs offered (minimal on-campus study). *Degree requirements:* For master's, final oral exam, project or thesis. *Entrance requirements:* Additional exam requirements/recommendations for international students: Required—TOEFL (minimum score 586 paper-based; 240 computer-based).

University of Pennsylvania, School of Nursing, Program in Nurse Midwifery, Philadelphia, PA 19104. Offers MSN. *Accreditation:* AACN; ACNM/DOA. Part-time programs available. *Students:* 25 full-time (all women), 11 part-time (all women); includes 5 minority (2 African Americans, 1 Asian American or Pacific Islander, 2 Hispanic Americans). In 2009, 15 master's awarded. *Entrance requirements:* For master's, GRE General Test, BSN, minimum GPA of 3.0, previous course work in statistics, physical assessment. Additional exam requirements/recommendations for international students: Required—TOEFL. *Application deadline:* For fall admission, 2/15 priority date for domestic students. Applications are processed on a rolling basis. Application fee: $70. *Expenses:* Contact institution. *Financial support:* Fellowships, research assistantships, teaching assistantships, career-related internships or fieldwork, Federal Work-Study, and institutionally sponsored loans available. Support available to part-time students. Financial award application deadline: 4/1. *Faculty research:* Breast-feeding protocols, history of midwifery, hydrotherapy in labor, cocaine abuse during pregnancy, stress in pregnancy.

University of Puerto Rico, Medical Sciences Campus, Graduate School of Public Health, Program in Nurse Midwifery, San Juan, PR 00936-5067. Offers MPH, Certificate. *Accreditation:* ACNM/DOA. Part-time programs available. *Entrance requirements:* For master's, GRE, previous course work in algebra.

University of South Africa, College of Human Sciences, Pretoria, South Africa. Offers adult education (M Ed); African languages (MA, PhD); African politics (MA, PhD); Afrikaans (MA, PhD); ancient history (MA, PhD); ancient Near Eastern studies (MA, PhD); anthropology (MA, PhD); applied linguistics (MA); Arabic (MA, PhD); archaeology (MA); art history (MA); Biblical archaeology (MA); Biblical studies (M Th, D Th, PhD); Christian spirituality (M Th, D Th); church history (M Th, D Th); classical studies (MA, PhD); clinical psychology (MA); communication (MA, PhD); comparative education (M Ed, Ed D); consulting psychology (D Admin, D Com, PhD); curriculum studies (M Ed, Ed D); development studies (M Admin, MA, D Admin, PhD); didactics (M Ed, Ed D); education (M Tech); education management (M Ed, Ed D); educational psychology (M Ed); English (MA); environmental education (M Ed); French (MA, PhD); German (MA, PhD); Greek (MA); guidance and counseling (M Ed); health studies (MA, PhD), including health sciences education (MA), health services management (MA), medical and surgical nursing science (critical care general) (MA), midwifery and neonatal nursing science (MA), trauma and emergency care (MA); history (MA, PhD); history of education (Ed D); inclusive education (M Ed, Ed D); information and communications technology policy and regulation (MA); information science (MA, MIS, PhD); international politics (MA, PhD); Islamic studies (MA, PhD); Italian (MA, PhD); Judaica (MA, PhD); linguistics (MA, PhD); mathematical education (M Ed); mathematics education (MA); missiology (M Th, D Th); modern Hebrew (MA, PhD); musicology (MA, MMus, D Mus, PhD); natural science education (M Ed); New Testament (M Th, D Th); Old Testament (D Th); pastoral therapy (M Th, D Th); philosophy (MA); philosophy of education (M Ed, Ed D); politics (MA, PhD); Portuguese (MA, PhD); practical theology (M Th, D Th); psychology (MA, MS, PhD); psychology of education (M Ed, Ed D); public health (MA); religious studies (MA, D Th, PhD); Romance languages (MA); Russian (MA, PhD); Semitic languages (MA, PhD); social behavior studies in HIV/AIDS (MA); social science (mental health) (MA); social science in development studies (MA); social science in psychology (MA); social science in social work (MA); social science in sociology (MA); social work (MSW, DSW, PhD); socio-education (M Ed, Ed D); sociolinguistics (MA); sociology (MA, PhD); Spanish (MA, PhD); systematic theology (M Th, D Th); TESOL (teaching English to speakers of other languages) (MA); theological ethics (M Th, D Th); theory of literature (MA, PhD); urban ministries (D Th); urban ministry (M Th).

Vanderbilt University, School of Nursing, Nashville, TN 37240. Offers adult acute care nurse practitioner (MSN); adult nurse practitioner/cardiovascular disease management and prevention (MSN); adult nurse practitioner/palliative care (MSN); clinical management (clinical nurse leader/specialist) (MSN); emergency nurse practitioner (MSN); family nurse practitioner (MSN); gerontology nurse practitioner (MSN); health systems management (MSN); neonatal nurse practitioner (MSN); nurse midwifery (MSN); nurse midwifery/family nurse practitioner (MSN); nursing informatics (MSN); nursing practice (DNP); nursing science (PhD); nutrition (MS); pediatric acute care nurse practitioner (MSN); pediatric primary care nurse practitioner (MSN); psychiatric-mental health nurse practitioner (MSN); women's health nurse practitioner (MSN), including urogynecology; women's health nurse practitioner/adult nurse practitioner (MSN); MSN/M Div; MSN/MTS. *Accreditation:* ACNM/DOA; NLN (one or more programs are accredited). Part-time programs available. Postbaccalaureate distance learning degree programs offered (minimal on-campus study). *Faculty:* 118 full-time (102 women), 429 part-time/adjunct (309 women). *Students:* 484 full-time (435 women), 319 part-time (284 women); includes 84 minority (55 African Americans, 4 American Indian/Alaska Native, 10 Asian Americans or Pacific Islanders, 15 Hispanic Americans), 16 international. Average age 32. 900 applicants, 65% accepted, 433 enrolled. In 2009, 303 master's, 1 doctorate awarded. *Degree requirements:* For doctorate, comprehensive exam, thesis/dissertation. *Entrance requirements:* For master's, GRE General Test, minimum B average in undergraduate course work, 3 letters of recommendation; for doctorate, GRE General Test, interview, 3 letters of recommendation from doctorally-prepared faculty, MSN, essay. Additional exam requirements/recommendations for international students: Required—TOEFL. *Application deadline:* For fall admission, 12/1 priority

Nurse Midwifery

Vanderbilt University (continued)
date for domestic and international students. Applications are processed on a rolling basis. Application fee: $50. *Expenses:* Contact institution. *Financial support:* In 2009–10, 389 students received support, including 1 research assistantship (averaging $5,000 per year); teaching assistantships, scholarships/grants, health care benefits, and tuition waivers also available. Support available to part-time students. Financial award application deadline: 3/15; financial award applicants required to submit FAFSA. *Faculty research:* Lymphedema, palliative care and bereavement, health services research including workforce, safety and quality of care, gerontology, better birth outcomes including nutrition. Total annual research expenditures: $1.4 million. *Unit head:* Dr. Colleen Conway-Welch, Dean, 615-343-8776, Fax: 615-343-7711, E-mail: colleen.conway-welch@vanderbilt.edu. *Application contact:* Cheryl Feldner, Assistant Director of Admissions, 615-322-3800, Fax: 615-343-0333, E-mail: cheryl.feldner@vanderbilt.edu.

Wichita State University, Graduate School, College of Health Professions, School of Nursing, Wichita, KS 67260. Offers clinical nurse specialist (MSN); nurse midwifery (MSN); nurse practitioner (MSN); nursing and healthcare systems administration (MSN); nursing practice (DNP); MSN/MBA. *Accreditation:* AACN. Part-time programs available. *Expenses:* Tuition, state resident: full-time $4247; part-time $235.95 per credit hour. Tuition, nonresident: full-time $11,171; part-time $620.60 per credit hour. Required fees: $34; $3.60 per credit hour. $17 per term. Tuition and fees vary according to campus/location and program. *Faculty research:* Adolescent pregnancy, alcoholism, arthritis and chronic disease, health practices of elderly, diabetes. *Unit head:* Dr. Mary Koehn, Chairperson, 316-978-3610, Fax: 316-978-3025, E-mail: mary.koehn@wichita.edu. *Application contact:* Dr. Mary Koehn, Chairperson, 316-978-3610, Fax: 316-978-3025, E-mail: mary.koehn@wichita.edu.

Nursing and Healthcare Administration

Abilene Christian University, Graduate School, School of Nursing, Abilene, TX 79699-9100. Offers education and administration (MSN); family nurse practitioner (MSN). *Accreditation:* AACN. Part-time programs available. *Faculty:* 6 part-time/adjunct (all women). *Students:* 3 full-time (all women), 4 part-time (2 women); includes 4 minority (1 American Indian/Alaska Native, 2 Asian Americans or Pacific Islanders, 1 Hispanic American). 11 applicants, 36% accepted, 4 enrolled. In 2009, 5 master's, 1 other advanced degree awarded. *Entrance requirements:* For master's, GRE General Test. *Application deadline:* For fall admission, 4/1 priority date for domestic students; for spring admission, 11/1 for domestic students. Applications are processed on a rolling basis. Application fee: $40. Electronic applications accepted. *Expenses:* Tuition: Full-time $11,520; part-time $640 per hour. Required fees: $1090; $53.50 per hour. $10 per term. Tuition and fees vary according to program. *Financial support:* In 2009–10, 6 students received support. Application deadline: 4/1. *Unit head:* Dr. Amy Toone, Graduate Director, 325-671-2361, Fax: 325-671-2386, E-mail: atoone@phssn.edu. *Application contact:* William Horn, Graduate Admissions Counselor, 325-674-2656, Fax: 325-674-6717, E-mail: gradinfo@acu.edu.

Allen College, Program in Nursing, Waterloo, IA 50703. Offers acute care nurse practitioner (MSN); adult nurse practitioner (MSN); adult psychiatric-mental health nurse practitioner (MSN); family nurse practitioner (MSN); gerontological nurse practitioner (MSN); health education (MSN); leadership in health care delivery (MSN). *Accreditation:* AACN; NLN. Part-time programs available. *Faculty:* 2 full-time (both women), 8 part-time/adjunct (all women). *Students:* 37 full-time (35 women), 103 part-time (99 women); includes 1 minority (Asian American or Pacific Islander). Average age 38. *Degree requirements:* For master's, thesis optional. *Entrance requirements:* For master's, minimum GPA of 3.0. Additional exam requirements/recommendations for international students: Required—TOEFL (minimum score 550 paper-based). *Application deadline:* For fall admission, 7/15 priority date for domestic students; for spring admission, 12/1 priority date for domestic students. Applications are processed on a rolling basis. Application fee: $50. Electronic applications accepted. *Expenses:* Tuition: Full-time $12,550; part-time $651 per credit hour. Required fees: $826; $65 per credit hour. One-time fee: $425. Tuition and fees vary according to course load. *Financial support:* Teaching assistantships, institutionally sponsored loans, scholarships/grants, and traineeships available. Support available to part-time students. Financial award application deadline: 8/15; financial award applicants required to submit FAFSA. *Faculty research:* Pain and aged, congestive heart failure. *Unit head:* Nancy Kramer, Dean, School of Nursing, 319-226-2040, Fax: 319-226-2070, E-mail: kramerna@ihs.org. *Application contact:* Michelle Koehn, Admissions Counselor, 319-226-2002, Fax: 319-226-2051, E-mail: koehnml@ihs.org.

American International College, School of Health Sciences, Department of Nursing, Springfield, MA 01109-3189. Offers nursing administration (MSN); nursing education (MSN). *Accreditation:* AACN. *Entrance requirements:* For master's, BSN. Additional exam requirements/recommendations for international students: Required—TOEFL. Electronic applications accepted. *Expenses:* Tuition: Full-time $12,510; part-time $695 per credit hour. Required fees: $35 per term.

Athabasca University, Centre for Nursing and Health Studies, Athabasca, AB T9S 3A3, Canada. Offers advanced nursing practice (MN, Advanced Diploma); generalist (MN); health studies-leadership (MHS). Part-time programs available. Postbaccalaureate distance learning degree programs offered. *Faculty:* 11 full-time (all women), 1 (woman) part-time/adjunct. *Students:* 542 part-time. Average age 38. 428 applicants, 51 enrolled. In 2009, 181 master's, 6 other advanced degrees awarded. *Degree requirements:* For master's, comprehensive exam (for some programs). *Entrance requirements:* For master's, bachelor's degree in health-related field, 2 years professional health service experience (MHS), bachelor's degree in nursing, 2 years nursing experience (MN), minimum GPA of 3.0 in final 30 credits; for Advanced Diploma, RN license, 2 years health care experience. *Application deadline:* For fall admission, 3/1 for domestic and international students. Application fee: $80. Electronic applications accepted. *Expenses:* Contact institution. *Unit head:* Dr. Donna Romyn, Dean, 800-788-9041 Ext. 6794, Fax: 780-675-6468, E-mail: dromyn@athabascau.ca. *Application contact:* Donna Dunn Hart, Academic Student Advisor—Graduate Programs, 800-788-9041 Ext. 6300, Fax: 780-675-6468, E-mail: donnad@athabascau.ca.

Austin Peay State University, College of Graduate Studies, College of Behavioral and Health Sciences, School of Nursing, Clarksville, TN 37044. Offers advanced practice (MSN); nursing administration (MSN); nursing education (MSN); nursing informatics (MSN). Part-time programs available. Postbaccalaureate distance learning degree programs offered. *Faculty:* 7 full-time (all women). *Students:* 15 full-time (14 women), 62 part-time (57 women); includes 6 minority (3 African Americans, 1 American Indian/Alaska Native, 2 Asian Americans or Pacific Islanders). Average age 39. 31 applicants, 100% accepted, 22 enrolled. In 2009, 9 master's awarded. *Degree requirements:* For master's, comprehensive exam. *Entrance requirements:* For master's, GRE General Test, minimum GPA of 3.0, RN license eligibility, 3 letters of recommendation. Additional exam requirements/recommendations for international students: Required—TOEFL (minimum score 600 paper-based). *Application deadline:* For fall admission, 7/27 priority date for domestic students; for spring admission, 12/17 priority date for domestic students. Applications are processed on a rolling basis. Application fee: $25. Electronic applications accepted. *Expenses:* Tuition, state resident: full-time $6160; part-time $608 per credit hour. Tuition, nonresident: full-time $17,080; part-time $854 per credit hour. Required fees: $1224; $61.20 per credit hour. *Financial support:* In 2009–10, 1 student received support, including 1 research assistantship with full tuition reimbursement available (averaging $5,184 per year); career-related internships or fieldwork, Federal Work-Study, institutionally sponsored loans, scholarships/grants, and unspecified assistantships also available. Support available to part-time students. *Unit head:* Dr. Francisca Ann Farrar, Director, 931-221-7737, Fax: 931-221-6490, E-mail: farrarf@apsu.edu. *Application contact:* Dr. Doris Davenport, Associate Professor, 931-221-7467, Fax: 931-221-7595, E-mail: davenportd@apsu.edu.

Barry University, School of Nursing, Program in Nursing Administration, Miami Shores, FL 33161-6695. Offers MSN, PhD, Certificate. *Accreditation:* AACN. Part-time and evening/weekend programs available. *Degree requirements:* For master's, research project or thesis. *Entrance requirements:* For master's, GRE General Test or MAT, BSN, minimum GPA of 3.0, course work in statistics. Electronic applications accepted. *Faculty research:* Power/empowerment, health delivery systems, managed care, employee health and well being.

Barry University, School of Nursing and Andreas School of Business, Program in Nursing Administration and Business Administration, Miami Shores, FL 33161-6695. Offers MSN/MBA. *Accreditation:* AACN. Part-time and evening/weekend programs available. Electronic applications accepted. *Faculty research:* Power/empowerment, health delivery systems, managed care, employee health well-being.

Baylor University, Graduate School, Louise Herrington School of Nursing, Dallas, TX 75246. Offers family nurse practitioner (MSN); neonatal nurse practitioner (MSN); nursing administration and management (MSN). *Accreditation:* AACN. *Students:* 32 full-time (31 women), 26 part-time (25 women); includes 12 minority (4 African Americans, 1 American Indian/Alaska Native, 3 Asian Americans or Pacific Islanders, 4 Hispanic Americans), 1 international. In 2009, 17 master's awarded. *Entrance requirements:* For master's, GRE General Test. *Application deadline:* For fall admission, 8/1 for domestic students; for spring admission, 12/1 for domestic students. Applications are processed on a rolling basis. Application fee: $25. *Unit head:* Dr. Mary Brucker, Graduate Program Director, 214-820-4111, Fax: 214-818-8692, E-mail: mary_brucker@baylor.edu. *Application contact:* Beverly Kurfees, Administrative Assistant, 214-820-4111, Fax: 254-710-3870, E-mail: beverly_kurfees@baylor.edu.

Bellarmine University, Donna and Allan Lansing School of Nursing and Health Sciences, Louisville, KY 40205-0671. Offers family nurse practitioner (MSN); nursing administration (MSN); nursing education (MSN); nursing practice (DNP); physical therapy (DPT). *Accreditation:* AACN; APTA. Part-time and evening/weekend programs available. *Faculty:* 16 full-time (11 women), 7 part-time/adjunct (6 women). *Students:* 126 full-time (94 women), 50 part-time (48 women); includes 4 minority (1 African American, 3 Asian Americans or Pacific Islanders). Average age 30. 350 applicants, 48 enrolled. In 2009, 9 master's, 41 doctorates awarded. *Degree requirements:* For doctorate, comprehensive exam, thesis/dissertation. *Entrance requirements:* For master's, GRE General Test, RN license; for doctorate, GRE General Test, Physical Therapist Centralized Application Service (for DPT). Additional exam requirements/recommendations for international students: Required—TOEFL (minimum score 550 paper-based; 213 computer-based; 80 iBT). Application fee: $25. Electronic applications accepted. *Expenses:* Contact institution. *Financial support:* Career-related internships or fieldwork and scholarships/grants available. *Faculty research:* Nursing: pain, empathy, leadership styles, control; physical therapy: service learning; exercise in chronic and pre-operative conditions, and athletes; women's health; aging. *Unit head:* Dr. Susan H. Davis, Dean, 800-274-4723 Ext. 8217, E-mail: sdavis@bellarmine.edu. *Application contact:* Julie Armstrong-Binnix, Health Science Recruiter, 800-274-4723 Ext. 8364, E-mail: julieab@bellarmine.edu.

Bellin College, Program in Nursing, Green Bay, WI 54305. Offers administrator (MSN); educator (MSN). *Accreditation:* AACN.

Bloomsburg University of Pennsylvania, School of Graduate Studies, College of Professional Studies, School of Health Sciences, Department of Nursing, Bloomsburg, PA 17815-1301. Offers adult and family nurse practitioner (MSN); adult health and illness (MSN); community health (MSN); nursing (MSN); nursing administration (MSN). *Accreditation:* AACN; AANA/CANAEP. *Degree requirements:* For master's, thesis. *Entrance requirements:* For master's, minimum QPA of 3.0. Additional exam requirements/recommendations for international students: Required—TOEFL. Electronic applications accepted. *Faculty research:* Cardiopulmonary nursing, cancer topics, women's health.

Bowie State University, Graduate Programs, Department of Nursing, Bowie, MD 20715-9465. Offers administration of nursing services (MS); family nurse practitioner (MS); nursing education (MS). *Accreditation:* NLN. Part-time programs available. *Degree requirements:* For master's, comprehensive exam, thesis, research paper. *Entrance requirements:* For master's, minimum GPA of 2.5. Electronic applications accepted. *Faculty research:* Minority health, women's health, gerontology, leadership management.

Bradley University, Graduate School, College of Education and Health Sciences, Department of Nursing, Peoria, IL 61625-0002. Offers nurse administered anesthesia (MSN); nursing administration (MSN). *Accreditation:* AANA/CANAEP; NLN. Part-time and evening/weekend programs available. *Degree requirements:* For master's, comprehensive exam, thesis optional. *Entrance requirements:* For master's, GRE General Test or MAT, interview, Illinois RN license, advanced cardiac life support certification, pediatric advanced life support certification, 3 letters of recommendation. Additional exam requirements/recommendations for international students: Required—TOEFL (minimum score 550 paper-based; 213 computer-based; 79 iBT).

Brenau University, Graduate Programs, School of Health and Science, Gainesville, GA 30501. Offers family nurse practitioner (MSN); nurse educator (MSN); nursing management (MSN); occupational therapy (MS); psychology (MS). *Accreditation:* AOTA; NLN. Part-time and evening/weekend programs available. *Faculty:* 14 full-time (12 women), 6 part-time/adjunct (5 women). *Students:* 97 full-time (92 women), 92 part-time (84 women); includes 46 minority (37 African Americans, 2 American Indian/Alaska Native, 2 Asian Americans or Pacific Islanders, 5 Hispanic Americans), 2 international. Average age 34. 168 applicants, 50% accepted, 68 enrolled. In 2009, 35 master's awarded. *Degree requirements:* For master's, comprehensive exam (for some programs), thesis (for some programs), clinical practicum hours. *Entrance requirements:* For master's, GRE General Test or MAT (for some programs), interview, writing sample, references (for some programs). Additional exam requirements/recommendations for international students: Required—TOEFL (minimum score 500 paper-based). *Application deadline:* Applications are processed on a rolling basis. Application fee: $35. Electronic applications accepted. *Expenses:* Contact institution. *Financial support:* In 2009–10, 32 students received support. Scholarships/grants and traineeships available. Support available to part-time students. Financial award application deadline: 7/15; financial award applicants required to submit FAFSA. *Unit head:* Dr. Gale Starich, Dean, 777-718-5305, Fax: 770-297-5929, E-mail: gstarich@brenau.edu. *Application contact:* Christina White, Admissions Coordinator, 770-718-5320, Fax: 770-770-5338, E-mail: cwhite@brenau.edu.

Capital University, School of Nursing, Columbus, OH 43209-2394. Offers administration (MSN); legal studies (MSN); theological studies (MSN); JD/MSN; MBA/MSN; MSN/MTS. *Accreditation:* AACN. Part-time and evening/weekend programs available. *Degree requirements:* For master's, thesis or alternative. *Entrance requirements:* For master's, BSN, current RN license, minimum GPA of 3.0, undergraduate courses in statistics and research. Additional exam requirements/recommendations for international students: Required—TOEFL (minimum

score 550 paper-based). *Expenses:* Contact institution. *Faculty research:* Bereavement, wellness/health promotion, emergency cardiac care, critical thinking, complementary and alternative healthcare.

Carlow University, School of Nursing, Pittsburgh, PA 15213-3165. Offers family nurse practitioner (MSN); home health advanced practice nursing (MSN); nursing (DNP); nursing case management/leadership (MSN); nursing leadership (MSN). *Accreditation:* AACN. Part-time and evening/weekend programs available. Postbaccalaureate distance learning degree programs offered (minimal on-campus study). *Degree requirements:* For master's, thesis or alternative. *Entrance requirements:* Additional exam requirements/recommendations for international students: Required—TOEFL (minimum score 550 paper-based; 213 computer-based). Electronic applications accepted. *Expenses:* Tuition: Full-time $11,250; part-time $625 per credit. Tuition and fees vary according to course load, degree level and program. *Faculty research:* Research utilization, community and home health, medically underserved.

Central Methodist University, College of Graduate and Extended Studies, Fayette, MO 65248-1198. Offers clinical counseling (MS); clinical nurse leader (MSN); education (M Ed). Part-time and evening/weekend programs available. Postbaccalaureate distance learning degree programs offered (no on-campus study). *Degree requirements:* For master's, thesis. *Entrance requirements:* For master's, GRE General Test, minimum GPA of 2.75. Electronic applications accepted.

Chatham University, Program in Nursing, Pittsburgh, PA 15232-2826. Offers education/leadership (MSN); nursing (DNP). *Accreditation:* AACN. *Students:* 48 full-time (41 women), 79 part-time (70 women). Average age 45. 139 applicants, 90% accepted, 69 enrolled. *Entrance requirements:* For master's and doctorate, RN license. Additional exam requirements/recommendations for international students: Required—TOEFL (minimum score 600 paper-based; 250 computer-based; 100 iBT), IELTS (minimum score 6.5), TWE. *Application deadline:* For fall admission, 5/1 priority date for domestic and international students. Applications are processed on a rolling basis. Application fee: $45. Electronic applications accepted. *Financial support:* Applicants required to submit FAFSA. *Unit head:* Dr. Elizabeth Gazza, Director, 412-365-2746, E-mail: egazza@chatham.edu. *Application contact:* David Vey, Admissions Support Specialist, 412-365-1498, Fax: 412-365-1720, E-mail: dvey@chatham.edu.

Clarke College, Department of Nursing and Health, Dubuque, IA 52001-3198. Offers administration of nursing systems (MSN); advanced practice nursing (MSN); education (MSN); family nurse practitioner (MSN, PMC). *Accreditation:* AACN. Part-time programs available. *Faculty:* 4 full-time (all women), 2 part-time/adjunct (1 woman). *Students:* 35 full-time (34 women), 19 part-time (all women). Average age 35. 48 applicants, 83% accepted, 25 enrolled. In 2009, 13 master's awarded. *Entrance requirements:* For master's, GRE General Test or MAT, BSN, minimum GPA of 3.0. *Application deadline:* For fall admission, 2/15 priority date for domestic students; for spring admission, 12/15 priority date for domestic students. Applications are processed on a rolling basis. Application fee: $25. Electronic applications accepted. *Expenses:* Tuition: Full-time $10,836; part-time $602 per credit hour. Required fees: $30 per credit hour. *Financial support:* In 2009–10, 6 students received support. Career-related internships or fieldwork available. Support available to part-time students. Financial award applicants required to submit FAFSA. *Faculty research:* Narrative pedagogy, ethics, end-of-life care, pedagogy, family systems. *Unit head:* Dr. Susan DeCrane, Chair, 800-224-2736, Fax: 319-584-8684. *Application contact:* Carrie Kirk, Information Contact, 563-588-6635, Fax: 563-588-6789, E-mail: graduate@clarke.edu.

Clarkson College, Master of Science in Nursing Program, Omaha, NE 68131. Offers adult nurse practitioner (MSN, Post-Master's Certificate); family nurse practitioner (MSN, Post-Master's Certificate); nursing education (MSN, Post-Master's Certificate); nursing health care leadership (MSN, Post-Master's Certificate). *Accreditation:* NLN. Part-time and evening/weekend programs available. Postbaccalaureate distance learning degree programs offered (minimal on-campus study). *Degree requirements:* For master's, on-campus skills assessment (family nurse practitioner, adult nurse practitioner), comprehensive exam or thesis. *Entrance requirements:* For master's, minimum GPA of 3.0, 2 references, resume. Additional exam requirements/recommendations for international students: Required—TOEFL (minimum score 600 paper-based; 250 computer-based; 100 iBT). Electronic applications accepted.

Clarkson College, Program in Health Care Administration, Omaha, NE 68131-2739. Offers MHCA. Part-time and evening/weekend programs available. Postbaccalaureate distance learning degree programs offered (no on-campus study). *Entrance requirements:* For master's, minimum GPA of 3.0, resume, references. Additional exam requirements/recommendations for international students: Required—TOEFL (minimum score 600 paper-based; 250 computer-based; 100 iBT). Electronic applications accepted.

College of Mount Saint Vincent, School of Professional and Continuing Studies, Department of Nursing, Riverdale, NY 10471-1093. Offers adult nurse practitioner (MSN, PMC); family nurse practitioner (MSN, PMC); nurse educator (PMC); nursing administration (MSN); nursing for the adult and aged (MSN). *Accreditation:* AACN. Part-time programs available. *Entrance requirements:* For master's, BSN, interview, RN license, minimum GPA of 3.0, letters of reference. Additional exam requirements/recommendations for international students: Required—TOEFL. *Expenses:* Contact institution.

The College of New Rochelle, Graduate School, Program in Nursing, New Rochelle, NY 10805-2308. Offers acute care nurse practitioner (MS, Certificate); clinical specialist in holistic nursing (MS, Certificate); family nurse practitioner (MS, Certificate); nursing and health care management (MS); nursing education (Certificate). *Accreditation:* AACN. Part-time programs available. *Entrance requirements:* For master's, GRE General Test or MAT, BSN, malpractice insurance, minimum GPA of 3.0, RN license. *Expenses:* Contact institution. *Faculty research:* Holistic modalities, academic success variables.

Daemen College, Department of Nursing, Amherst, NY 14226-3592. Offers adult nurse practitioner (MS); nursing education (MS, Post Master's Certificate); nursing executive leadership (MS); nursing practice (DNP); palliative care nursing (MS, Post Master's Certificate). *Accreditation:* NLN. Part-time programs available. *Faculty:* 3 full-time (all women), 6 part-time/adjunct (all women). *Students:* 8 full-time (all women), 105 part-time (98 women); includes 17 minority (10 African Americans, 1 American Indian/Alaska Native, 3 Asian Americans or Pacific Islanders, 3 Hispanic Americans), 1 international. Average age 42. 66 applicants, 79% accepted, 37 enrolled. In 2009, 24 master's, 4 other advanced degrees awarded. *Degree requirements:* For master's, thesis or alternative. *Entrance requirements:* For master's, BN, 1 year medical/surgical experience, RN license and state registration, 1 course in statistics with minimum grade of 'C', 3 letters of recommendation, minimum GPA of 3.25, interview; for doctorate, MS in advance nursing practice; New York state RN license; personal goal statement; resume; interview; statistics course with minimum grade of 'C'; for Post Master's Certificate, master's degree in clinical area; RN license and current registration; one year of clinical experience; statistics course with minimum grade of 'C'. Additional exam requirements/recommendations for international students: Required—TOEFL (minimum score 500 paper-based; 173 computer-based; 61 iBT). *Application deadline:* For fall admission, 3/1 priority date for domestic and international students; for spring admission, 10/1 priority date for domestic and international students. Applications are processed on a rolling basis. Application fee: $25. Electronic applications accepted. *Expenses:* Tuition: Part-time $770 per credit hour. Tuition and fees vary according to course load, program and reciprocity agreements. *Financial support:* In 2009–10, 1 student received support. Institutionally sponsored loans and scholarships/grants available. Financial award application deadline: 2/15; financial award applicants required to submit FAFSA. *Faculty research:* Professional stress, client behavior, drug therapy, treatment modalities and pulmonary cancers, chemical dependency. *Unit head:* Dr. Mary Lou Rusin, Chair, 716-839-8387, Fax: 716-839-8403, E-mail: mrusin@daemen.edu. *Application contact:* Scott Rowe, Associate Director of Graduate Programs, 716-839-8225, Fax: 716-839-8229, E-mail: srowe@daemen.edu.

Duke University, School of Nursing, Durham, NC 27708-0586. Offers adult acute care (Certificate); adult cardiovascular (Certificate); adult oncology (Certificate); adult primary care (Certificate); clinical nurse specialist (MSN), including adult oncology, gerontology, neonatal, pediatric; clinical research management (MSN, Certificate); family (Certificate); gerontology (Certificate); health and nursing ministries (MSN, Certificate); health systems leadership and outcomes (Certificate); neonatal (Certificate); neonatal/pediatric in rural health (MSN, Certificate); nurse anesthetist (MSN, Certificate); nurse practitioner (MSN), including adult acute care, adult cardiovascular, adult oncology, adult primary care, family, gerontology, neonatal, pediatric, pediatric acute care; nursing (DNP, PhD); nursing and healthcare leadership (MSN); nursing education (MSN); nursing informatics (MSN, Certificate); pediatric (Certificate); pediatric acute care (Certificate); MBA/MSN; MSN/MCM. *Accreditation:* AACN; AANA/CANAEP. Part-time programs available. Postbaccalaureate distance learning degree programs offered (minimal on-campus study). *Faculty:* 45 full-time (41 women), 169 part-time/adjunct (150 women). *Students:* 213 full-time (179 women), 116 part-time (105 women); includes 37 minority (17 African Americans, 13 Asian Americans or Pacific Islanders, 7 Hispanic Americans), 9 international. Average age 36. 234 applicants, 53% accepted, 97 enrolled. In 2009, 142 master's, 24 other advanced degrees awarded. Terminal master's awarded for partial completion of doctoral program. *Degree requirements:* For master's, thesis optional; for doctorate, Capstone Project. *Entrance requirements:* For master's, GRE General Test, 1 year of nursing experience, BSN, minimum GPA of 3.0, previous course work in statistics; for doctorate, GRE for BSN prepared, BSN or MSN, minimum GPA of 3.0. Portfolio; for Certificate, MSN. Additional exam requirements/recommendations for international students: Required—TOEFL (minimum score 550 paper-based; 213 computer-based), Commission on Graduates of Foreign Nursing Schools exam. *Application deadline:* For fall admission, 7/2 priority date for domestic and international students; for spring admission, 11/15 priority date for domestic and international students. Applications are processed on a rolling basis. Application fee: $50. Electronic applications accepted. *Expenses:* Contact institution. *Financial support:* Career-related internships or fieldwork, institutionally sponsored loans, scholarships/grants, traineeships, and tuition waivers (partial) available. Support available to part-time students. Financial award application deadline: 4/1; financial award applicants required to submit FAFSA. *Faculty research:* Cardiovascular disease, caregiver skill training, data mining, prostate cancer, neonatal immune system. Total annual research expenditures: $3.5 million. *Unit head:* Dr. Catherine L. Gilliss, Dean/Vice Chancellor for Nursing Affairs, 919-684-9444, Fax: 919-684-9414, E-mail: gilli025@mc.duke.edu. *Application contact:* Bebe T. Mills, Director of Admissions, 919-684-9151, Fax: 919-668-4693, E-mail: mills031@mc.duke.edu.

D'Youville College, Department of Nursing, Buffalo, NY 14201-1084. Offers community health nursing/education (MSN); community health nursing/high risk parents and children (MSN); community health nursing/management (MSN); family nurse practitioner (MS, Post-Master's Certificate); nursing and health-related professions (Certificate); nursing with clinical focus choice (MSN). *Accreditation:* AACN. Part-time and evening/weekend programs available. *Degree requirements:* For master's, thesis optional, membership on board of community agency, publishable paper. *Entrance requirements:* For master's, BS in nursing, minimum GPA of 3.0, course work in statistics and computers. Additional exam requirements/recommendations for international students: Required—TOEFL (minimum score 500 paper-based; 173 computer-based). Electronic applications accepted. *Faculty research:* Nursing curriculum, nursing theory-testing, wellness research, communication and socialization patterns.

See Close-Up on page 1611.

Eastern Michigan University, Graduate School, College of Health and Human Services, School of Health Sciences, Program in Clinical Research Administration, Ypsilanti, MI 48197. Offers MS, Graduate Certificate. Part-time and evening/weekend programs available. Postbaccalaureate distance learning degree programs offered (minimal on-campus study). *Students:* 21 full-time (15 women), 67 part-time (45 women); includes 16 minority (9 African Americans, 6 Asian Americans or Pacific Islanders, 1 Hispanic American), 42 international. Average age 31. In 2009, 7 master's, 8 other advanced degrees awarded. *Entrance requirements:* Additional exam requirements/recommendations for international students: Required—TOEFL. *Application deadline:* Applications are processed on a rolling basis. Application fee: $35. Tuition and fees vary according to course level. *Financial support:* Fellowships, research assistantships with full tuition reimbursements, teaching assistantships with full tuition reimbursements, career-related internships or fieldwork, Federal Work-Study, institutionally sponsored loans, scholarships/grants, tuition waivers (partial), and unspecified assistantships available. Support available to part-time students. Financial award applicants required to submit FAFSA. *Unit head:* Dr. Stephen Sonstein, Program Coordinator, 734-487-1238, Fax: 734-487-4095, E-mail: stephen.sonstein@emich.edu. *Application contact:* Dr. Stephen Sonstein, Program Coordinator, 734-487-1238, Fax: 734-487-4095, E-mail: stephen.sonstein@emich.edu.

Elms College, Division of Nursing, Chicopee, MA 01013-2839. Offers nursing and health services management (MSN); nursing education (MSN). *Accreditation:* AACN. Part-time and evening/weekend programs available. *Faculty:* 5 full-time (4 women), 3 part-time/adjunct (all women). *Students:* 8 full-time (all women), 27 part-time (26 women); includes 1 minority (African American). 11 applicants, 82% accepted, 8 enrolled. *Entrance requirements:* Additional exam requirements/recommendations for international students: Required—TOEFL. *Application deadline:* For fall admission, 7/1 priority date for domestic students; for spring admission, 11/1 priority date for domestic students. Applications are processed on a rolling basis. Application fee: $30. *Financial support:* Applicants required to submit FAFSA. *Unit head:* Dr. Kathleen Scoble, Director, 413-265-2204, E-mail: scoblek@elms.edu. *Application contact:* Dr. Cynthia L. Dakin, Assistant Director of Graduate Studies, 413-265-2455, Fax: 413-265-2335, E-mail: dakinc@elms.edu.

Emory University, Nell Hodgson Woodruff School of Nursing, Atlanta, GA 30322-1100. Offers adult and elder health advanced practice nursing (MSN), including acute care, adult nurse practitioner, gerontological nurse practitioner; emergency nurse practitioner (MSN); family nurse practitioner (MSN); family nurse-midwife (MSN); nurse midwifery (MSN); pediatric nurse practitioner acute and primary care (MSN); public health nursing leadership (MSN); women's health nurse practitioner (MSN); women's health title x (MSN); women's health/adult health nurse practitioner (MSN); MSN/MPH. *Accreditation:* AACN; ACNM/DOA (one or more programs are accredited). Part-time programs available. *Faculty:* 30 full-time (29 women), 11 part-time/adjunct (10 women). *Students:* 110 full-time (106 women), 53 part-time (51 women); includes 49 minority (35 African Americans, 2 American Indian/Alaska Native, 10 Asian Americans or Pacific Islanders, 2 Hispanic Americans), 4 international. Average age 32. 182 applicants, 63% accepted, 86 enrolled. In 2009, 81 master's awarded. *Entrance requirements:* For master's, GRE General Test or MAT, minimum GPA of 3.0, BS in nursing from an accredited institution, RN license and additional course work, 3 letters of recommendation. Additional exam requirements/recommendations for international students: Required—TOEFL (minimum score 600 paper-based; 100 iBT). *Application deadline:* For fall admission, 1/15 priority date for domestic and international students; for spring admission, 10/1 priority date for domestic and international students. Applications are processed on a rolling basis. Application fee: $50. Electronic applications accepted. *Expenses:* Contact institution. *Financial support:* In 2009–10, 14 fellowships (averaging $28,000 per year) were awarded; career-related internships or fieldwork, Federal Work-Study, institutionally sponsored loans, and scholarships/grants also available. Support available to part-time students. Financial award application deadline: 3/1; financial award applicants required to submit CSS PROFILE or FAFSA. *Faculty research:* Older adult falls and injuries, minority health issues, cardiac symptoms and quality of life, bio-ethics and decision making, menopausal issues. *Unit head:* Dr. Linda McCauley, Dean, 404-727-7976, Fax: 404-727-9800, E-mail: linda.mccauley@emory.edu. *Application contact:* Katie Kennedy, Associate Director for Admission and Financial Aid, 404-727-7980, Fax: 404-727-8509, E-mail: admit@nursing.emory.edu.

See Close-Up on page 1613.

Excelsior College, School of Health Sciences, Albany, NY 12203-5159. Offers healthcare informatics (Certificate); hospice and palliative care (Certificate); nursing management (Certificate). Part-time and evening/weekend programs available. Postbaccalaureate distance learning degree programs offered (no on-campus study). *Entrance requirements:* For degree,

Nursing and Healthcare Administration

Excelsior College (continued)
bachelor's degree in applicable field. Electronic applications accepted. *Faculty research:* Use of technology in online learning.

Fairfield University, School of Nursing, Fairfield, CT 06824-5195. Offers clinical nurse leader (MSN); family nurse practitioner (MSN, PMC); healthcare management (MSN); nurse anesthesia (MSN); psychiatric nurse practitioner (MSN, PMC). *Accreditation:* AACN; AANA/CANAEP. Part-time programs available. *Degree requirements:* For master's, capstone project. *Entrance requirements:* For master's, GRE (nurse anesthesia applicants only), minimum QPA of 3.0, RN license, resume, 2 recommendations; for PMC, 1 year of work experience as a registered nurse. Additional exam requirements/recommendations for international students: Required—TOEFL (minimum score 550 paper-based; 213 computer-based; 80 iBT). Electronic applications accepted. *Expenses:* Contact institution. *Faculty research:* Care of older adults, palliative care, spirituality and innovative partnerships, diabetes.

Fairmont State University, Graduate Studies, Program in Nursing, Fairmont, WV 26554. Offers nursing administration (MS); nursing education (MS).

Ferris State University, College of Allied Health Sciences, School of Nursing, Big Rapids, MI 49307. Offers nursing (MS); nursing administration (MS); nursing education (MS); nursing informatics (MS). *Accreditation:* NLN. Part-time and evening/weekend programs available. Postbaccalaureate distance learning degree programs offered (minimal on-campus study). *Faculty:* 1 (woman) full-time, 69 part-time/adjunct (63 women). *Students:* 1 (woman) full-time, 64 part-time (58 women). Average age 42. 30 applicants, 53% accepted, 11 enrolled. In 2009, 9 master's awarded. *Degree requirements:* For master's, comprehensive exam, practicum, scholarly project. *Entrance requirements:* For master's, BS in nursing, writing sample, letters of reference, 2 years clinical experience. Additional exam requirements/recommendations for international students: Required—TOEFL (minimum score 550 paper-based). *Application deadline:* For fall admission, 7/15 priority date for domestic students. Applications are processed on a rolling basis. Application fee: $30. Electronic applications accepted. *Financial support:* In 2009–10, 4 students received support; fellowships, research assistantships, teaching assistantships, scholarships/grants available. Financial award application deadline: 4/15. *Faculty research:* Nursing education-minority student focus, student attitudes toward aging. *Unit head:* Dr. Julie A. Coon, Director, 231-591-2267, Fax: 231-591-2325, E-mail: coonj@ferris.edu. *Application contact:* Debby Buck, Off Campus Program Secretary, 231-591-2270, Fax: 231-591-3788, E-mail: buckd@ferris.edu.

Florida Agricultural and Mechanical University, Division of Graduate Studies, Research, and Continuing Education, School of Allied Health Sciences, Tallahassee, FL 32307-3200. Offers health administration (MS); physical therapy (MPT). *Faculty:* 19 full-time (5 women). *Students:* 133 full-time (100 women), 13 part-time (10 women); includes 134 minority (133 African Americans, 1 Asian American or Pacific Islander), 3 international. In 2009, 27 master's awarded. *Degree requirements:* For master's, thesis (for some programs). *Entrance requirements:* For master's, GRE General Test or GMAT, minimum GPA of 3.0. Additional exam requirements/recommendations for international students: Required—TOEFL (minimum score 550 paper-based). *Application deadline:* For fall admission, 5/18 for domestic students, 12/18 for international students; for spring admission, 11/12 for domestic students, 5/12 for international students. Application fee: $30. *Unit head:* Dr. Cynthia Hughes-Harris, Dean, 850-599-3818, Fax: 850-561-2502. *Application contact:* Dr. Chanta M. Haywood, Dean of Graduate Studies, Research, and Continuing Education, 850-599-3315, Fax: 850-599-3727.

Framingham State University, Division of Graduate and Continuing Education, Program in Nursing, Framingham, MA 01701-9101. Offers nursing education (MSN); nursing leadership (MSN). *Accreditation:* AACN. *Entrance requirements:* For master's, BSN; minimum cumulative undergraduate GPA of 3.0, 3.25 in nursing courses; coursework in statistics; 2 letters of recommendation; interview. Electronic applications accepted.

Gannon University, School of Graduate Studies, Morosky College of Health Professions and Sciences, School of Health Professions, Villa Maria School of Nursing, Erie, PA 16541-0001. Offers anesthesia (MSN); business administration (MSN); family nurse practitioner (Certificate); medical-surgical nursing (MSN); nurse anesthesia (Certificate); nursing rural practitioner (MSN). *Accreditation:* AACN; AANA/CANAEP (one or more programs are accredited). Part-time and evening/weekend programs available. *Students:* 19 full-time (11 women), 59 part-time (45 women); includes 2 minority (both African Americans). Average age 36. 16 applicants, 81% accepted, 0 enrolled. In 2009, 19 master's awarded. *Degree requirements:* For master's, thesis. *Entrance requirements:* For master's, GRE General Test, degree in nursing. Additional exam requirements/recommendations for international students: Required—TOEFL (minimum score 79 iBT). *Application deadline:* For spring admission, 8/1 for domestic students. Application fee: $25. Electronic applications accepted. *Expenses:* Tuition: Full-time $13,590; part-time $755 per credit. Required fees: $524; $17 per credit. Tuition and fees vary according to course load, degree level, campus/location and program. *Financial support:* Scholarships/grants available. Financial award application deadline: 7/1; financial award applicants required to submit FAFSA. *Unit head:* Dr. Sharon Thompson, Director, 814-871-5345, E-mail: thompson001@gannon.edu. *Application contact:* Kara Morgan, Assistant Director of Graduate Admissions, 814-871-5831, Fax: 814-871-5827, E-mail: graduate@gannon.edu.

George Mason University, College of Health and Human Services, School of Nursing, Fairfax, VA 22030. Offers forensic nursing (Certificate); nursing (MSN, PhD); nursing administration (Certificate); nursing education (Certificate); nursing practice (DNP). *Faculty:* 36 full-time (all women), 52 part-time/adjunct (49 women). *Students:* 47 full-time (46 women), 275 part-time (259 women); includes 90 minority (43 African Americans, 3 American Indian/Alaska Native, 33 Asian Americans or Pacific Islanders, 11 Hispanic Americans), 10 international. Average age 42. 176 applicants, 66% accepted, 77 enrolled. In 2009, 72 master's, 8 doctorates, 3 other advanced degrees awarded. *Degree requirements:* For master's, comprehensive exam (for some programs), thesis in clinical classes; for doctorate, comprehensive exam (for some programs), thesis/dissertation (for some programs). *Entrance requirements:* For master's, resume, 2 recommendation letters, transcripts, nursing license, goal statement, at least 1 year working in the nursing field; for doctorate, resume, 3 recommendation letters, nursing license, at least 1 year of work in the nursing field. Additional exam requirements/recommendations for international students: Required—TOEFL. *Application deadline:* For fall admission, 4/1 priority date for domestic students; for spring admission, 11/1 priority date for domestic students. Applications are processed on a rolling basis. Application fee: $75. Electronic applications accepted. *Expenses:* Tuition, state resident: full-time $7568; part-time $315.33 per credit hour. Tuition, nonresident: full-time $21,704; part-time $904.33 per credit hour. Required fees: $2184; $91 per credit hour. *Financial support:* In 2009–10, 2 students received support, including 2 research assistantships with full and partial tuition reimbursements available (averaging $4,186 per year); Federal Work-Study, scholarships/grants, unspecified assistantships, and nurse faculty loan, health care benefits (full-time research or teaching assistantship recipients) also available. Support available to part-time students. Financial award application deadline: 3/1; financial award applicants required to submit FAFSA. Total annual research expenditures: $270,863. *Unit head:* Dr. Shirley S. Travis, Dean, 703-993-1918. *Application contact:* Janice Lee-Beverly, Program Support, 703-993-1947, E-mail: jleebev1@gmu.edu.

The George Washington University, School of Medicine and Health Sciences, Health Sciences Programs, Washington, DC 20052. Offers adult nurse practitioner (MSN, Post Master's Certificate); clinical practice management (MSHS); clinical research administration (MSHS); clinical research administration for nurses (MSN); emergency services management (MSHS); end-of-life care (MSHS, MSN); family nurse practitioner (MSN, Post Master's Certificate); immunohematology (MSHS); nursing (DNP); nursing leadership and management (MSN); physical therapy (DPT); physician assistant (MSHS); MSHS/MPH. Postbaccalaureate distance learning degree programs offered (no on-campus study). *Students:* 270 full-time (220 women), 491 part-time (406 women); includes 176 minority (83 African Americans, 5 American Indian/Alaska Native, 62 Asian Americans or Pacific Islanders, 26 Hispanic Americans), 26 international. Average age 35. 1,059 applicants, 47% accepted, 292 enrolled. In 2009, 155 master's, 22 doctorates, 75 other advanced degrees awarded. *Entrance requirements:* Additional exam requirements/recommendations for international students: Required—TOEFL (minimum score 550 paper-based; 213 computer-based). *Application deadline:* Applications are processed on a rolling basis. Application fee: $60. *Expenses:* Contact institution. *Unit head:* Jean E. Johnson, Senior Associate Dean, 202-994-3725, E-mail: jejohns@gwu.edu. *Application contact:* Joke Ogundiran, Director of Admission, 202-994-1668, Fax: 202-994-0870, E-mail: jokeogun@gwu.edu.

Georgia College & State University, Graduate School, College of Health Sciences, Graduate Nursing Program, Milledgeville, GA 31061. Offers adult health (MSN); family nurse practitioner (MSN); nursing administration (MSN); MSN/MBA. *Accreditation:* NLN. Part-time and evening/weekend programs available. *Faculty:* 22 full-time (21 women). *Students:* 13 full-time (all women), 44 part-time (42 women); includes 8 minority (all African Americans), 1 international. Average age 35. 22 applicants, 91% accepted, 18 enrolled. In 2009, 18 master's awarded. *Degree requirements:* For master's, comprehensive exam, thesis optional. *Entrance requirements:* For master's, GMAT, GRE General Test, or MAT, bachelor's degree in nursing, RN license. Additional exam requirements/recommendations for international students: Recommended—TOEFL (minimum score 550 paper-based; 213 computer-based; 79 iBT). *Application deadline:* For fall admission, 7/1 priority date for domestic students. Applications are processed on a rolling basis. Application fee: $40. Electronic applications accepted. *Expenses:* Tuition, area resident: Part-time $241 per credit hour. Tuition, state resident: full-time $4338. Tuition, nonresident: full-time $17,352; part-time $964 per credit hour. Required fees: $609 per semester. Tuition and fees vary according to course load and campus/location. *Financial support:* In 2009–10, 1 research assistantship with full tuition reimbursement was awarded; unspecified assistantships also available. Financial award applicants required to submit FAFSA. *Unit head:* Dr. Judith Malachowski, Director, School of Nursing, 478-445-5122, E-mail: judith.malachowski@gcsu.edu. *Application contact:* Lora Crowe, Coordinator, 478-445-5122, E-mail: lora.crowe@gcsu.edu.

Goshen College, Program in Nursing, Goshen, IN 46526-4794. Offers clinical nurse leader (MSN); family nurse practitioner (MSN). *Accreditation:* AACN. Part-time and evening/weekend programs available. *Faculty:* 1 (woman) full-time, 7 part-time/adjunct (all women). *Students:* 35 part-time (32 women), 2 international. Average age 39. 17 applicants, 88% accepted, 14 enrolled. *Degree requirements:* For master's, comprehensive exam (for some programs). *Entrance requirements:* Additional exam requirements/recommendations for international students: Required—TOEFL (minimum score 213 paper-based; 79 computer-based; 6 iBT). *Application deadline:* Applications are processed on a rolling basis. Application fee: $50. *Expenses:* Contact institution. *Financial support:* In 2009–10, 10 students received support. Scholarships/grants available. Financial award applicants required to submit FAFSA. *Unit head:* Dr. Brenda Srof, Director, 574-535-7375, E-mail: brendajs@goshen.edu. *Application contact:* Dr. Brenda Srof, 574-535-7375, E-mail: brendajs@goshen.edu.

Grand Canyon University, College of Nursing and Health Sciences, Phoenix, AZ 85017-1097. Offers addiction counseling (MS); nursing (MS), including adult clinical nurse specialist, family nurse practitioner, nursing education, nursing leadership in health care system; professional counseling (MS). Part-time and evening/weekend programs available. Postbaccalaureate distance learning degree programs offered (no on-campus study). *Entrance requirements:* Additional exam requirements/recommendations for international students: Required—TOEFL (minimum score 575 paper-based; 233 computer-based; 90 iBT), IELTS (minimum score 7).

Grand Valley State University, Kirkhof College of Nursing, Allendale, MI 49401-9403. Offers advanced practice (MSN); case management (MSN); nursing administration (MSN); nursing education (MSN); nursing practice (DNP); MSN/MBA. *Accreditation:* AACN. Part-time programs available. *Faculty:* 17 full-time (all women), 3 part-time/adjunct (all women). *Students:* 6 full-time (5 women), 69 part-time (61 women); includes 3 minority (all African Americans). Average age 39. 18 applicants, 100% accepted, 18 enrolled. In 2009, 23 master's awarded. *Degree requirements:* For master's, thesis optional. *Entrance requirements:* For master's, GRE, minimum GPA of 3.0 in upper-division course work, course work in statistics, Michigan RN license. Additional exam requirements/recommendations for international students: Required—TOEFL. *Application deadline:* For fall admission, 3/15 priority date for domestic students. Applications are processed on a rolling basis. Application fee: $30. Electronic applications accepted. *Expenses:* Tuition, state resident: part-time $471 per credit hour. Tuition, nonresident: part-time $646 per credit hour. Tuition and fees vary according to course level. *Financial support:* In 2009–10, 23 students received support, including 14 fellowships (averaging $3,207 per year), 9 research assistantships with full and partial tuition reimbursements available (averaging $8,053 per year); career-related internships or fieldwork, Federal Work-Study, institutionally sponsored loans, and traineeships also available. Financial award application deadline: 2/15. *Faculty research:* Multigenerational health promotion, chronic disease prevention, end-of-life issues, nursing workload, family caregiver health. Total annual research expenditures: $36,000. *Unit head:* Dr. Cynthia McCurren, Dean, 616-331-7161, Fax: 616-331-7362. *Application contact:* Dr. Jean Martin, Director of Graduate Programs, 616-331-7167, Fax: 616-331-7362, E-mail: martinj@gvsu.edu.

Grantham University, College of Arts and Sciences, Kansas City, MO 64153. Offers case management (MSN); health systems management (MS); healthcare administration (MHA); nursing (MSN); nursing education (MSN); nursing informatics (MSN); nursing management and organizational leadership (MSN). Part-time and evening/weekend programs available. Postbaccalaureate distance learning degree programs offered (no on-campus study). In 2009, 48 master's awarded. *Degree requirements:* For master's, thesis (for some programs), capstone project. *Entrance requirements:* For master's, bachelor's degree from accredited degree-granting institution. Additional exam requirements/recommendations for international students: Required—TOEFL (minimum score 500 paper-based; 213 computer-based; 61 iBT). *Application deadline:* Applications are processed on a rolling basis. Electronic applications accepted. *Expenses:* Tuition: Part-time $265 per credit hour. One-time fee: $30 part-time. *Financial support:* Institutionally sponsored loans and scholarships/grants available. *Unit head:* Dr. Kim Humerickhouse, Dean, 800-955-2527, Fax: 816-595-5757, E-mail: admissions@grantham.edu. *Application contact:* Matthew Hawes, Vice President of Enrollment Management, 800-955-2527, Fax: 816-595-5757, E-mail: admissions@grantham.edu.

Holy Family University, Graduate School, School of Nursing, Philadelphia, PA 19114. Offers community health nursing (MSN); nursing administration (MSN); nursing education (MSN). *Accreditation:* AACN. Part-time and evening/weekend programs available. *Faculty:* 1 (woman) full-time, 1 (woman) part-time/adjunct. *Students:* 1 (woman) full-time, 46 part-time (all women); includes 7 minority (5 African Americans, 2 Asian Americans or Pacific Islanders). Average age 41. 17 applicants, 76% accepted, 11 enrolled. In 2009, 3 master's awarded. *Degree requirements:* For master's, thesis or alternative. *Entrance requirements:* For master's, bachelor's degree in nursing, RN license, minimum GPA of 3.0, 2 letters of reference. *Application deadline:* For fall admission, 7/1 priority date for domestic students; for winter admission, 11/1 priority date for domestic students. Applications are processed on a rolling basis. Application fee: $25. *Expenses:* Tuition: Part-time $600 per credit. Required fees: $58 per semester. *Financial support:* Federal Work-Study available. Support available to part-time students. Financial award application deadline: 2/15; financial award applicants required to submit FAFSA. *Unit head:* Dr. Christine Rosner, Dean, 267-341-3292, Fax: 215-637-6598, E-mail: crosner@holyfamily.edu. *Application contact:* Gidget Matie Montelibano, Graduate Admissions Counselor, 267-341-3558, Fax: 215-637-1478, E-mail: gmontelibano@holyfamily.edu.

Holy Names University, Graduate Division, Department of Nursing, Oakland, CA 94619-1699. Offers administration/management (MS, Certificate); clinical faculty (MS, Certificate); community health nursing/case manager (MS); family nurse practitioner (MS, Certificate); MSN/Certificate; MSN/MBA. *Accreditation:* AACN. Part-time and evening/weekend programs available. *Entrance requirements:* For master's, bachelor's degree in nursing or related field, California RN license or eligibility, minimum GPA of 3.0, previous course work in research or statistics. Additional exam requirements/recommendations for international students: Required—

TOEFL (minimum score 500 paper-based). *Faculty research:* Women's reproductive health, gerontology, attitudes about aging, schizophrenic families, international health issues.

Independence University, Program in Nursing, Salt Lake City, UT 84107. Offers community health (MSN); gerontology (MSN); nursing administration (MSN); wellness promotion (MSN). *Expenses:* Required fees: $475 per credit. One-time fee: $100 part-time.

Indiana University–Purdue University Fort Wayne, College of Health and Human Services, Department of Nursing, Fort Wayne, IN 46805-1499. Offers adult nursing practice (MS); nursing administration (MS, Certificate); nursing education (MS); women's health nursing practice (MS). Part-time programs available. *Faculty:* 7 full-time (all women), 1 (woman) part-time/adjunct. *Students:* 5 full-time (all women), 34 part-time (32 women); includes 4 minority (3 African Americans, 1 American Indian/Alaska Native). Average age 37. 15 applicants, 93% accepted, 11 enrolled. *Entrance requirements:* For master's, GRE Writing Test (if GPA below 3.0), BS in nursing, eligibility for Indiana RN license, minimum GPA of 3.0, essay, copy of resume, three references, undergraduate course work in research and statistics within last 5 years. Additional exam requirements/recommendations for international students: Required—TOEFL (minimum score 550 paper-based; 213 computer-based; 77 iBT); Recommended—TWE. *Application deadline:* For fall admission, 5/1 priority date for domestic and international students. Applications are processed on a rolling basis. Application fee: $55 ($60 for international students). Electronic applications accepted. *Expenses:* Tuition, state resident: full-time $4595; part-time $255 per credit. Tuition, nonresident: full-time $10,963; part-time $609 per credit. Required fees: $528; $29.35 per credit. Tuition and fees vary according to course load. *Financial support:* In 2009–10, 11 teaching assistantships with partial tuition reimbursements (averaging $12,740 per year) were awarded; scholarships/grants also available. Support available to part-time students. Financial award application deadline: 3/1; financial award applicants required to submit FAFSA. *Unit head:* Dr. Carol Sternberger, Chair, 260-481-6816, Fax: 260-481-5767, E-mail: sternber@ipfw.edu. *Application contact:* Dr. Susan Ahrens, Graduate Program Director, 260-481-6816, Fax: 260-481-5767, E-mail: ahrenss@ipfw.edu.

Indiana Wesleyan University, College of Adult and Professional Studies, Department of Graduate Studies in Business, Marion, IN 46953. Offers accounting (MBA); applied management (MBA); business administration (MBA); health care (MBA); human resources (MBA); management (MS). Part-time and evening/weekend programs available. Postbaccalaureate distance learning degree programs offered (no on-campus study). *Degree requirements:* For master's, applied business or management project. *Entrance requirements:* For master's, minimum GPA of 2.5, 2 years of related work experience. Additional exam requirements/recommendations for international students: Required—TOEFL (minimum score 550 paper-based; 213 computer-based). Electronic applications accepted. *Expenses:* Tuition: Full-time $7380; part-time $410 per credit. One-time fee: $85. Tuition and fees vary according to campus/location.

Indiana Wesleyan University, College of Graduate Studies, School of Nursing, Marion, IN 46953-4974. Offers community health nursing (MS); nursing (Post Master's Certificate); nursing administration (MS); nursing education (MS); primary care nursing (MS). *Accreditation:* AACN. Part-time programs available. Postbaccalaureate distance learning degree programs offered (minimal on-campus study). *Degree requirements:* For master's, capstone project or thesis. *Entrance requirements:* For master's, writing sample, RN license, 1 year of related experience, graduate statistics course. Additional exam requirements/recommendations for international students: Required—TOEFL. *Expenses:* Contact institution. *Faculty research:* Primary health care with international emphasis, international nursing.

Jefferson College of Health Sciences, Program in Nursing, Roanoke, VA 24031-3186. Offers nursing education (MSN); nursing management (MSN). *Accreditation:* AACN. Part-time programs available. *Faculty:* 16 full-time (9 women), 1 part-time/adjunct (0 women). *Students:* 31 full-time (28 women), 10 part-time (9 women); includes 6 minority (3 African Americans, 2 Asian Americans or Pacific Islanders, 1 Hispanic American). Average age 43. 63 applicants, 59% accepted, 21 enrolled. In 2009, 13 master's awarded. *Degree requirements:* For master's, project. *Entrance requirements:* For master's, MAT. Additional exam requirements/recommendations for international students: Required—TOEFL (minimum score 550 paper-based; 213 computer-based; 80 iBT). *Application deadline:* Applications are processed on a rolling basis. Application fee: $35. Electronic applications accepted. *Financial support:* Career-related internships or fieldwork, Federal Work-Study, scholarships/grants, traineeships, health care benefits, and tuition waivers (full) available. Support available to part-time students. Financial award applicants required to submit FAFSA. *Faculty research:* Nursing, teaching and learning techniques, cultural competence, spirituality and nursing. *Unit head:* Dr. Ava Porter, Department Chair, 540-985-8531, E-mail: agporter@jchs.edu. *Application contact:* Judith McKeon, Director of Admissions, 540-985-9083, Fax: 540-985-9773, E-mail: jomckeon@jchs.edu.

The Johns Hopkins University, School of Nursing, Dual Major in Clinical Nurse Specialist and Health Systems Management, Baltimore, MD 21218-2699. Offers MSN. *Accreditation:* AACN. Part-time programs available. *Faculty:* 2 full-time (both women). *Students:* 1 (woman) full-time, 3 part-time (all women); includes 1 minority (Asian American or Pacific Islander), 1 international. Average age 38. 5 applicants, 60% accepted, 1 enrolled. In 2009, 1 master's awarded. *Degree requirements:* For master's, thesis optional, scholarly project or portfolio. *Entrance requirements:* For master's, interview, minimum GPA of 3.0, BSN, Maryland RN license. Additional exam requirements/recommendations for international students: Required—TOEFL (minimum score 550 paper-based; 213 computer-based). *Application deadline:* For fall admission, 3/1 priority date for domestic and international students; for spring admission, 7/1 priority date for domestic and international students. Applications are processed on a rolling basis. Application fee: $75. Electronic applications accepted. *Financial support:* Federal Work-Study, scholarships/grants, traineeships, and tuition waivers (partial) available. Support available to part-time students. Financial award application deadline: 3/1; financial award applicants required to submit FAFSA. *Faculty research:* Maternal/child health, outcomes measurement, symptom management, oncology, HIV/AIDS. *Unit head:* Dr. Julie A. Stanik-Hutt, Director, Master's Programs, 410-502-0184, Fax: 410-955-7463, E-mail: jstanik1@son.jhmi.edu. *Application contact:* Mary O'Rourke, Director of Admissions and Student Services, 410-955-7548, Fax: 410-614-7086, E-mail: orourke@son.jhmi.edu.

The Johns Hopkins University, School of Nursing, Program in Clinical Nurse Specialist, Baltimore, MD 21218-2699. Offers MSN. *Accreditation:* AACN. Part-time programs available. *Faculty:* 3 full-time (2 women). *Students:* 4 full-time (all women), 25 part-time (23 women); includes 6 minority (3 African Americans, 1 Asian American or Pacific Islander, 2 Hispanic Americans). Average age 35. 38 applicants, 82% accepted, 9 enrolled. In 2009, 5 master's awarded. *Degree requirements:* For master's, thesis optional, scholarly project or portfolio. *Entrance requirements:* For master's, interview, minimum GPA of 3.0, BSN, Maryland RN license. Additional exam requirements/recommendations for international students: Required—TOEFL (minimum score 550 paper-based; 213 computer-based). *Application deadline:* For fall admission, 3/1 priority date for domestic and international students; for spring admission, 7/1 priority date for domestic and international students. Applications are processed on a rolling basis. Application fee: $75. Electronic applications accepted. *Expenses:* Contact institution. *Financial support:* In 2009–10, 7 students received support. Federal Work-Study, scholarships/grants, traineeships, and tuition waivers (partial) available. Support available to part-time students. Financial award application deadline: 3/1; financial award applicants required to submit FAFSA. *Faculty research:* Maternal child health, symptom management, cardiovascular risk reduction, asthma, hypertension. *Unit head:* Dr. Julie A. Stanik-Hutt, Director, Master's Programs, 410-502-0184, Fax: 410-955-7463, E-mail: jstanik1@son.jhmi.edu. *Application contact:* Mary O'Rourke, Director of Admissions and Student Services, 410-955-7548, Fax: 410-614-7086, E-mail: orourke@son.jhmi.edu.

The Johns Hopkins University, School of Nursing, Program in Health Systems Management, Baltimore, MD 21218-2699. Offers MSN. *Accreditation:* AACN. Part-time programs available. *Faculty:* 2 full-time (both women), 2 part-time/adjunct (1 woman). *Students:* 1 (woman) full-time, 21 part-time (19 women); includes 3 minority (2 African Americans, 1 Asian American or Pacific Islander). Average age 43. 10 applicants, 100% accepted, 5 enrolled. In 2009, 16 master's awarded. *Degree requirements:* For master's, thesis optional, scholarly project or portfolio. *Entrance requirements:* For master's, interview, minimum GPA of 3.0, BSN, Maryland RN license. Additional exam requirements/recommendations for international students: Required—TOEFL (minimum score 550 paper-based; 213 computer-based). *Application deadline:* For fall admission, 3/1 priority date for domestic and international students; for spring admission, 7/1 priority date for domestic and international students. Applications are processed on a rolling basis. Application fee: $75. Electronic applications accepted. *Expenses:* Contact institution. *Financial support:* In 2009–10, 2 students received support. Federal Work-Study, scholarships/grants, traineeships, and tuition waivers (partial) available. Support available to part-time students. Financial award application deadline: 3/1; financial award applicants required to submit FAFSA. *Faculty research:* Program evaluation, program development, staff satisfaction, quality and safety. *Unit head:* Dr. Julie A. Stanik-Hutt, Director, Master's Programs, 410-502-0184, Fax: 410-955-7463, E-mail: jstanik1@son.jhmi.edu. *Application contact:* Mary O'Rourke, Director of Admissions and Student Services, 410-955-7548, Fax: 410-614-7086, E-mail: orourke@son.jhmi.edu.

Kaplan University, Davenport Campus, School of Nursing, Davenport, IA 52807-2095. Offers nurse administrator (MS); nurse educator (MS). Part-time and evening/weekend programs available. Postbaccalaureate distance learning degree programs offered (no on-campus study). *Entrance requirements:* For master's, RN. Additional exam requirements/recommendations for international students: Required—TOEFL (minimum score 550 paper-based; 80 computer-based).

Kean University, College of Natural, Applied and Health Sciences, Program in Nursing, Union, NJ 07083. Offers clinical management (MSN), including transcultural focus; community health nursing (MSN); school nursing (MSN). *Accreditation:* NLN. Part-time and evening/weekend programs available. *Faculty:* 7 full-time (all women). *Students:* 12 full-time (all women), 78 part-time (74 women); includes 46 minority (31 African Americans, 10 Asian Americans or Pacific Islanders, 5 Hispanic Americans). Average age 44. 44 applicants, 98% accepted, 26 enrolled. In 2009, 36 master's awarded. *Degree requirements:* For master's, thesis or alternative, clinical field experience. *Entrance requirements:* For master's, minimum GPA of 3.0; BS in nursing; RN license; 2 letters of recommendation; interview; 1 completed course of the following: Basic Health Assessment and Human Growth and Development across the life span. *Application deadline:* For fall admission, 5/1 for domestic students; for spring admission, 11/1 for domestic students. Application fee: $60 ($150 for international students). Electronic applications accepted. *Expenses:* Tuition, state resident: full-time $10,440; part-time $435 per credit. Tuition, nonresident: full-time $14,160; part-time $590 per credit. Required fees: $2642; $110 per credit. Part-time tuition and fees vary according to course load and degree level. *Financial support:* In 2009–10, 1 research assistantship with full tuition reimbursement (averaging $3,263 per year) was awarded; unspecified assistantships also available. *Unit head:* Dr. Cheryl Krause-Parello, Program Coordinator, 908-737-3390, E-mail: ckrausep@kean.edu. *Application contact:* Dorothy Rowe, Pre-Admissions Coordinator, 908-737-5928, Fax: 908-737-5965, E-mail: drowe@kean.edu.

Kent State University, College of Nursing, Kent, OH 44242-0001. Offers adult nurse practitioner (MSN); family nurse practitioner (MSN); geriatric nurse practitioner (MSN); nursing (PhD); nursing and health care management (MSN); nursing of adults (clinical nurse specialist) (MSN); pediatric nurse practitioner (MSN); psychiatric/mental health nursing (MSN); women's health nursing (MSN). *Accreditation:* AACN. Part-time programs available. *Degree requirements:* For master's, thesis optional; for doctorate, comprehensive exam, thesis/dissertation. *Entrance requirements:* For master's, GRE (if undergraduate GPA less than 3.0), minimum GPA of 2.75; for doctorate, GRE, MSN. Additional exam requirements/recommendations for international students: Required—TOEFL. Electronic applications accepted. *Expenses:* Contact institution. *Faculty research:* Women and violence, methodological specialties, osteoporosis in women, new caregivers and the elderly.

Lamar University, College of Graduate Studies, College of Arts and Sciences, Department of Nursing, Beaumont, TX 77710. Offers nursing administration (MSN); nursing education (MSN); MSN/MBA. *Accreditation:* NLN. Part-time and evening/weekend programs available. Postbaccalaureate distance learning degree programs offered. *Faculty:* 4 full-time (all women). *Students:* 3 full-time (2 women), 8 part-time (7 women); includes 2 minority (1 African American, 1 Hispanic American). Average age 41. 15 applicants. In 2009, 3 master's awarded. *Degree requirements:* For master's, comprehensive exam, practicum project presentation, evidence-based project. *Entrance requirements:* For master's, GRE General Test, MAT, criminal background check, RN license, NLN-accredited BSN, college course work in graduate statistics in past 5 years, letters of recommendation, minimum undergraduate GPA of 3.0. Additional exam requirements/recommendations for international students: Required—TOEFL. *Application deadline:* For fall admission, 8/1 priority date for domestic students; for spring admission, 12/1 priority date for domestic students. Applications are processed on a rolling basis. Application fee: $25 ($50 for international students). *Financial support:* In 2009–10, 3 students received support, including 2 teaching assistantships (averaging $24,000 per year); scholarships/grants and traineeships also available. Financial award application deadline: 4/1. *Faculty research:* Student retention, theory, caregiving, online course and research. *Unit head:* Dr. Nancy Blume, Director of Graduate Nursing Studies, 409-880-8820, Fax: 409-880-8698, E-mail: nancy.blume@lamar.edu. *Application contact:* Shelly R. Belk, Administrative Associate, 409-880-7720.

La Roche College, School of Graduate Studies and Adult Education, Program in Nursing, Pittsburgh, PA 15237-5898. Offers nursing education (MSN); nursing management (MSN). *Accreditation:* AANA/CANAEP; NLN. Part-time and evening/weekend programs available. Postbaccalaureate distance learning degree programs offered (minimal on-campus study). *Faculty:* 2 full-time (both women), 1 part-time/adjunct (0 women). *Students:* 8 full-time (all women), 3 part-time (all women), 6 international. Average age 36. 5 applicants, 80% accepted, 4 enrolled. In 2009, 3 master's awarded. *Degree requirements:* For master's, thesis optional, internship, practicum. *Entrance requirements:* For master's, GRE General Test, BSN, nursing license, work experience. Additional exam requirements/recommendations for international students: Recommended—TOEFL (minimum score 550 paper-based; 220 computer-based). *Application deadline:* For fall admission, 8/15 priority date for domestic students, 8/15 for international students; for spring admission, 12/15 priority date for domestic students, 12/15 for international students. Applications are processed on a rolling basis. Application fee: $50. Electronic applications accepted. *Expenses:* Contact institution. *Financial support:* Application deadline: 3/31. *Faculty research:* Patient education, perception. *Unit head:* Dr. Kathleen Sullivan, Division Chair, 412-536-1173, Fax: 412-536-1175, E-mail: sullivk1@laroche.edu. *Application contact:* Hope Schiffgens, Director of Graduate Studies and Adult Education, 412-536-1266, Fax: 412-536-1283, E-mail: schombh1@laroche.edu.

Le Moyne College, Department of Nursing, Syracuse, NY 13214. Offers nursing administration (MS, CAS); nursing education (MS, CAS). *Accreditation:* AACN. Part-time and evening/weekend programs available. *Faculty:* 2 full-time (both women), 6 part-time/adjunct (5 women). *Students:* 25 part-time (24 women); includes 2 minority (both African Americans). Average age 43. 14 applicants, 100% accepted, 14 enrolled. In 2009, 2 master's awarded. *Degree requirements:* For master's, scholarly project. *Entrance requirements:* For master's, interview, minimum GPA of 3.0, New York RN license, 2 letters of recommendation, writing sample. Additional exam requirements/recommendations for international students: Required—TOEFL (minimum score 550 paper-based; 213 computer-based; 79 iBT). *Application deadline:* For fall admission, 6/1 priority date for domestic and international students; for spring admission, 11/1 priority date for domestic and international students. Applications are processed on a rolling basis. Application fee: $50. *Expenses:* Contact institution. *Financial support:* In 2009–10, 7 students received support. Career-related internships or fieldwork, scholarships/grants, health care benefits, and unspecified assistantships available. Support available to part-time students. Financial award applicants required to submit FAFSA. *Faculty research:* Patient and staff education, inter-profession education, eldercare, utilization of free healthcare services by the insured, faculty perceptions of transgender nursing students. *Unit head:* Dr. Susan B. Bastable, Chair/Professor, 315-445-5436, Fax: 315-445-6024, E-mail: bastabsb@lemoyne.edu. *Application*

Nursing and Healthcare Administration

Le Moyne College (continued)

contact: Kristen P. Trapasso, Director of Graduate Admission, 315-445-4265, Fax: 315-445-6027, E-mail: trapaskp@lemoyne.edu.

Lewis University, College of Nursing and Health Professions, Program in Nursing, Romeoville, IL 60446. Offers adult nurse practitioner (MSN); nursing administration (MSN); nursing education (MSN). *Accreditation:* AACN. Part-time and evening/weekend programs available. Postbaccalaureate distance learning degree programs offered (no on-campus study). *Students:* 20 full-time (19 women), 172 part-time (169 women); includes 53 minority (32 African Americans, 11 Asian Americans or Pacific Islanders, 10 Hispanic Americans), 3 international. Average age 41. In 2009, 46 master's awarded. *Degree requirements:* For master's, clinical practicum. *Entrance requirements:* For master's, minimum undergraduate GPA of 2.75, degree in nursing, RN license, letter of recommendation, interview, resume or curriculum vitae. Additional exam requirements/recommendations for international students: Required—TOEFL (minimum score 550 paper-based; 213 computer-based). *Application deadline:* For fall admission, 5/1 priority date for international students; for spring admission, 11/15 priority date for international students. Applications are processed on a rolling basis. Application fee: $40. Electronic applications accepted. *Expenses:* Tuition: Full-time $6480; part-time $720 per credit. One-time fee: $40. Tuition and fees vary according to course load, degree level and program. *Financial support:* Federal Work-Study, scholarships/grants, tuition waivers (full and partial), and unspecified assistantships available. Financial award application deadline: 5/1; financial award applicants required to submit FAFSA. *Faculty research:* Cancer prevention, phenomenological methods, public policy analysis. Total annual research expenditures: $1,000. *Unit head:* Dr. Nan Yancey, Director, 815-838-0500 Ext. 5878, E-mail: yanceyna@lewisu.edu. *Application contact:* Kathy Lisak, Information Contact, 815-838-0500 Ext. 5355, E-mail: lisakka@lewisu.edu.

Loma Linda University, Department of Graduate Nursing, Program in Nursing Administration, Loma Linda, CA 92350. Offers MS. *Accreditation:* AACN. Part-time programs available. *Degree requirements:* For master's, thesis or alternative. *Entrance requirements:* For master's, GRE General Test, BSN, minimum GPA of 3.0, RN license. Additional exam requirements/recommendations for international students: Required—TOEFL. Electronic applications accepted. *Faculty research:* Job aspects contributing to satisfaction among leaders in health care institutions, leadership content significant to RN graduates.

Long Island University, Brooklyn Campus, School of Nursing, Department of Nurse Executive, Brooklyn, NY 11201-8423. Offers MS. *Accreditation:* AACN. *Entrance requirements:* For master's, New York RN license, 2 letters of recommendation. Additional exam requirements/recommendations for international students: Required—TOEFL (minimum score 500 paper-based; 173 computer-based).

Loyola University Chicago, Graduate School, Marcella Niehoff School of Nursing, Health Systems Management Program, Chicago, IL 60660. Offers MSN, Certificate. Part-time and evening/weekend programs available. Postbaccalaureate distance learning degree programs offered (minimal on-campus study). *Students:* 4 full-time (all women), 35 part-time (32 women); includes 6 minority (2 African Americans, 3 Asian Americans or Pacific Islanders, 1 Hispanic American). Average age 37. 8 applicants, 63% accepted, 4 enrolled. In 2009, 10 master's awarded. *Degree requirements:* For master's, comprehensive exam or oral thesis defense. *Entrance requirements:* For master's, BSN, minimum nursing GPA of 3.0, IL nursing license, 1000 hours experience before starting clincial. *Application deadline:* Applications are processed on a rolling basis. Application fee: $50. Electronic applications accepted. *Expenses:* Tuition: Full-time $14,220; part-time $790 per credit hour. Required fees: $60 per semester hour. Tuition and fees vary according to program. *Financial support:* Traineeships available. Financial award application deadline: 3/1. *Faculty research:* Patient classification systems, career/job mobility. *Unit head:* Dr. Ida Androwich, Professor, 708-216-9276, Fax: 708-216-9555, E-mail: iandrow@luc.edu. *Application contact:* Dr. Vicki A. Keough, Associate Professor/Master's Program Director, 708-216-3582, Fax: 708-216-9555, E-mail: vkeough@luc.edu.

Lynchburg College, Graduate Studies, School of Health Sciences and Human Performance, Lynchburg, VA 24501-3199. Offers clinical nurse leader (MSN); nursing education (MSN); physical therapy (DPT). *Expenses:* Tuition: Full-time $7020; part-time $390 per credit hour.

Madonna University, Program in Nursing, Livonia, MI 48150-1173. Offers adult health: chronic health conditions (MSN); adult nurse practitioner (MSN); nursing administration (MSN); MSN/MSBA. *Accreditation:* AACN. Part-time programs available. *Degree requirements:* For master's, thesis or alternative. *Entrance requirements:* For master's, GRE General Test, Michigan nursing license. Electronic applications accepted. *Faculty research:* Coping, caring.

Marywood University, Academic Affairs, College of Health and Human Services, Department of Nursing and Public Administration, Program in Nursing Administration, Scranton, PA 18509-1598. Offers MS. *Accreditation:* NLN. *Students:* 4 full-time (all women), 3 part-time (all women). Average age 43. In 2009, 6 master's awarded. *Entrance requirements:* Additional exam requirements/recommendations for international students: Required—TOEFL (minimum score 550 paper-based; 213 computer-based; 79 iBT). *Application deadline:* For fall admission, 4/1 for domestic students, 3/31 for international students; for spring admission, 11/1 for domestic students, 8/31 for international students. Applications are processed on a rolling basis. Application fee: $35. Electronic applications accepted. *Expenses:* Tuition: Part-time $715 per credit. Required fees: $270 per semester. Tuition and fees vary according to degree level, campus/location and program. *Financial support:* Career-related internships or fieldwork, scholarships/grants, and unspecified assistantships available. Support available to part-time students. Financial award application deadline: 6/30; financial award applicants required to submit FAFSA. *Application contact:* Tammy Manka, Assistant Director of Graduate Admissions, 866-279-9663, E-mail: tmanka@marywood.edu.

McKendree University, Graduate Programs, Master of Science in Nursing Program, Lebanon, IL 62254-1299. Offers nursing education (MSN); nursing management/administration (MSN). *Accreditation:* AACN. Part-time and evening/weekend programs available. Postbaccalaureate distance learning degree programs offered (no on-campus study). *Faculty:* 5 full-time (all women), 3 part-time/adjunct (2 women). *Students:* 1 full-time (0 women), 86 part-time (82 women); includes 6 minority (5 African Americans, 1 Hispanic American), 1 international. Average age 44. 80 applicants, 84% accepted, 52 enrolled. In 2009, 47 master's awarded. *Degree requirements:* For master's, research project or thesis. *Entrance requirements:* For master's, resume, references, valid Professional Registered Nurse license. Additional exam requirements/recommendations for international students: Required—TOEFL. *Application deadline:* Applications are processed on a rolling basis. Application fee: $0. Electronic applications accepted. *Expenses:* Tuition: Full-time $6300; part-time $350 per credit hour. One-time fee: $125. *Financial support:* Applicants required to submit FAFSA. *Unit head:* Dr. Richelle Rennegarbe, Division Chair, 618-537-2148, E-mail: rarennegarbe@mckendree.edu. *Application contact:* Kim Eichelberger, Director of Nursing Admission, 618-537-6411, Fax: 618-537-6410, E-mail: kaeichelberger@mckendree.edu.

McNeese State University, Doré School of Graduate Studies, College of Nursing, Lake Charles, LA 70609. Offers clinical nurse specialist (MSN); nurse educator (MSN); nurse practitioner (MSN); nursing leadership and administration (MSN). *Accreditation:* AACN. *Faculty:* 4 full-time (all women), 1 part-time/adjunct (0 women). *Students:* 17 full-time (9 women), 72 part-time (56 women); includes 14 minority (12 African Americans, 2 Asian Americans or Pacific Islanders). In 2009, 21 master's awarded. *Degree requirements:* For master's, comprehensive exam. *Entrance requirements:* For master's, GRE, eligibility for unencumbered licensure as RN in Louisiana. *Application deadline:* For fall admission, 5/15 priority date for domestic and international students; for spring admission, 10/15 priority date for domestic and international students. Applications are processed on a rolling basis. Application fee: $20 ($30 for international students). *Expenses:* Tuition, area resident: Full-time $2556. Tuition, state resident: full-time $2556. Required fees: $1031. Tuition and fees vary according to course load. *Financial support:* Application deadline: 5/1. *Unit head:* Dr. Peggy L. Wolfe, Dean, 337-475-5820, Fax: 337-475-5924, E-mail: pwolfe@mcneese.edu. *Application contact:* Valarie Waldmeier, Coordinator of Graduate Nursing, 337-475-5285, Fax: 337-475-5707, E-mail: vwaldmeier@mcneese.edu.

Medical College of Georgia, School of Graduate Studies, Clinical Nurse Leader Program, Augusta, GA 30912. Offers MSN. *Entrance requirements:* For master's, GRE General Test or MAT, bachelor's degree or higher in a non-nursing discipline. Additional exam requirements/recommendations for international students: Required—TOEFL (minimum score 550 paper-based; 213 computer-based; 79 iBT). Electronic applications accepted. Full-time tuition and fees vary according to campus/location, program and student level.

Medical University of South Carolina, College of Nursing, Nurse Administrator Program, Charleston, SC 29425. Offers MSN. *Accreditation:* AACN. Part-time programs available. Postbaccalaureate distance learning degree programs offered (no on-campus study). *Faculty:* 6 full-time (5 women), 2 part-time/adjunct (1 woman). *Students:* 1 (woman) full-time, 10 part-time (9 women). Average age 37. 10 applicants, 60% accepted, 6 enrolled. In 2009, 4 master's awarded. *Degree requirements:* For master's, thesis optional. *Entrance requirements:* For master's, BSN, nursing license, minimum GPA of 3.0. Additional exam requirements/recommendations for international students: Required—TOEFL (minimum score 600 paper-based; 250 computer-based). *Application deadline:* For fall admission, 2/1 priority date for domestic and international students. Application fee: $85. Electronic applications accepted. *Financial support:* Federal Work-Study, scholarships/grants, and traineeships available. Support available to part-time students. Financial award application deadline: 3/10; financial award applicants required to submit FAFSA. *Faculty research:* Hospital billing for nursing intensity. *Unit head:* Dr. Mary M. Martin, Lead Faculty, 843-792-3084, Fax: 843-792-1741, E-mail: martinmm@musc.edu. *Application contact:* Carolyn F. Page, Director, Student Services, 843-792-3844, Fax: 843-792-5395, E-mail: pagecf@musc.edu.

Mercy College, School of Health and Natural Sciences, Program in Nursing, Dobbs Ferry, NY 10522-1189. Offers nursing administration (MS); nursing education (MS). *Accreditation:* AACN. Part-time and evening/weekend programs available. Postbaccalaureate distance learning degree programs offered (no on-campus study). *Students:* 28 full-time (20 women), 113 part-time (108 women); includes 45 African Americans, 14 Asian Americans or Pacific Islanders, 8 Hispanic Americans, 16 international. Average age 42. 97 applicants, 48% accepted, 38 enrolled. In 2009, 33 master's awarded. *Degree requirements:* For master's, written comprehensive exam or the production of a comprehensive project. *Entrance requirements:* For master's, bachelor's degree, two letters of reference, interview/assessment, RN registration in the U.S. Additional exam requirements/recommendations for international students: Required—TOEFL (minimum score 600 paper-based; 250 computer-based; 100 iBT). *Application deadline:* For fall admission, 8/1 for international students. Applications are processed on a rolling basis. Application fee: $40. Electronic applications accepted. *Expenses:* Tuition: Full-time $13,158; part-time $731 per credit. Required fees: $500. Tuition and fees vary according to degree level and program. *Financial support:* Career-related internships or fieldwork, Federal Work-Study, scholarships/grants, and unspecified assistantships available. Support available to part-time students. Financial award applicants required to submit FAFSA. *Unit head:* Ellen Beatty, Director, 914-674-7548, E-mail: ebeatty@mercy.edu. *Application contact:* Mildred Burns, Administrative Assistant, 914-674-7865, Fax: 914-674-7623, E-mail: mburns@mercy.edu.

Metropolitan State University, College of Nursing and Health Sciences, St. Paul, MN 55106-5000. Offers adult/geriatric nurse practitioner (MSN); family nurse practitioner (MSN); leadership and management (MSN); nursing (MSN, DNP); oral health care practitioner (MS); public health nursing leadership (MSN); women's health care nurse practitioner (MSN). *Accreditation:* AACN. Part-time programs available. *Degree requirements:* For master's, thesis or alternative; for doctorate, thesis/dissertation or alternative. *Entrance requirements:* For master's, GRE General Test, minimum GPA of 3.0, RN license, B.S./BAN degree; for doctorate, minimum GPA of 3.0; RN licensure, MSN degree. Additional exam requirements/recommendations for international students: Required—TOEFL (minimum score 550 paper-based; 213 computer-based). *Expenses:* Tuition, state resident: full-time $5520; part-time $276 per credit hour. Tuition, nonresident: full-time $11,040; part-time $552 per credit hour. Required fees: $209; $10 per credit hour. Tuition and fees vary according to degree level. *Faculty research:* Women's health, gerontology.

Millikin University, School of Nursing, Decatur, IL 62522-2084. Offers clinical nurse leader (MSN); entry into nursing practice: pre-licensure (MSN); nurse educator (MSN). *Accreditation:* AACN. Part-time programs available. *Faculty:* 9 full-time (8 women). *Students:* 4 full-time (all women), 11 part-time (10 women); includes 1 minority (African American). Average age 41. 9 applicants, 100% accepted, 6 enrolled. In 2009, 3 master's awarded. *Degree requirements:* For master's, thesis or alternative, research project. *Entrance requirements:* For master's, GRE, official academic transcript(s), written essay, immunizations, statistics course, 2 letters of recommendation, CPR certification, professional liability insurance/malpractice insurance. Additional exam requirements/recommendations for international students: Required—TOEFL (minimum score 550 paper-based; 79 iBT). *Application deadline:* For spring admission, 11/1 priority date for domestic students. Applications are processed on a rolling basis. Application fee: $0. Electronic applications accepted. *Expenses:* Tuition: Full-time $24,890; part-time $655 per credit hour. *Financial support:* In 2009–10, 1 student received support. Institutionally sponsored loans available. Financial award applicants required to submit FAFSA. *Faculty research:* Congestive heart failure, quality of life, transcultural nursing issues, teaching/learning strategies, maternal—newborn. *Unit head:* Dr. Deborah Slayton, Director, 217-424-6348, Fax: 217-420-6731, E-mail: dslayton@millikin.edu. *Application contact:* Michelle Whitehead, Administrative Assistant, Master of Science in Nursing Program, 800-373-7733 Ext. 5034, Fax: 217-420-6677, E-mail: mwhitehead@millikin.edu.

Molloy College, Graduate Nursing Program, Rockville Centre, NY 11571-5002. Offers adult nurse practitioner (Advanced Certificate); clinical nurse specialist: adult health (Advanced Certificate); family nurse practitioner (Advanced Certificate); nurse practitioner psychiatry (Advanced Certificate); nursing (MS); nursing administration (Advanced Certificate); nursing administration with informatics (Advanced Certificate); nursing education (Advanced Certificate); nursing informatics (Advanced Certificate); pediatric nurse practitioner (Advanced Certificate). *Accreditation:* AACN. Part-time and evening/weekend programs available. *Faculty:* 23 full-time (22 women), 5 part-time/adjunct (4 women). *Students:* 11 full-time (10 women), 405 part-time (377 women); includes 206 minority (124 African Americans, 52 Asian Americans or Pacific Islanders, 30 Hispanic Americans), 2 international. Average age 39. In 2009, 64 master's awarded. *Degree requirements:* For master's, thesis optional. *Entrance requirements:* For master's, 3 letters of reference, BS in nursing, minimum undergraduate GPA of 3.0; for Advanced Certificate, 3 letters of reference, master's degree in nursing. *Application deadline:* For fall admission, 9/2 priority date for domestic students; for spring admission, 1/20 priority date for domestic students. Applications are processed on a rolling basis. Application fee: $60. *Expenses:* Tuition: Part-time $765 per credit. Required fees: $340 per semester. *Financial support:* Research assistantships with partial tuition reimbursements, teaching assistantships with partial tuition reimbursements, institutionally sponsored loans, scholarships/grants, and unspecified assistantships available. Support available to part-time students. Financial award application deadline: 4/1; financial award applicants required to submit FAFSA. *Unit head:* Dr. Mary T. O'Shaughnessy, Acting Director, 516-678-5000, Fax: 516-678-9718, E-mail: moshaughnessy@molloy.edu. *Application contact:* Alina Haitz, Assistant Director of Graduate Admissions, 516-678-5000 Ext. 6399, Fax: 516-256-2247, E-mail: ahaitz@molloy.edu.

Monmouth University, Graduate School, The Marjorie K. Unterberg School of Nursing and Health Studies, West Long Branch, NJ 07764-1898. Offers adult nurse practitioner (MSN); adult psychiatric and mental health advanced practice nursing (MSN, Post-Master's Certificate); advanced practice nursing (Post-Master's Certificate); family nurse practitioner (MSN, Post-Master's Certificate); forensic nursing (MSN, Certificate); nursing (MSN); nursing administration (MSN, Post-Master's Certificate); nursing education (MSN, Post-Master's Certificate); school nursing (MSN, Certificate). *Accreditation:* AACN. Part-time and evening/weekend programs available. *Faculty:* 11 full-time (all women), 2 part-time/adjunct (both women). *Students:* 15 full-time (14 women), 183 part-time (178 women); includes 51 minority (14 African Americans,

3 American Indian/Alaska Native, 26 Asian Americans or Pacific Islanders, 8 Hispanic Americans), 1 international. Average age 41. 95 applicants, 99% accepted, 44 enrolled. In 2009, 36 master's awarded. *Degree requirements:* For master's, practicum (for some tracks). *Entrance requirements:* For master's, GRE General Test, RN license, 1 year of work experience, minimum undergraduate GPA of 2.75. Additional exam requirements/recommendations for international students: Required—TOEFL (minimum score 550 paper-based; 213 computer-based; 79 iBT), IELTS (minimum score 5), Michigan English Language Assessment Battery (minimum score 77), Cambridge A, B, C. *Application deadline:* For fall admission, 7/15 priority date for domestic students, 6/1 for international students; for spring admission, 11/15 priority date for domestic students, 11/1 for international students. Applications are processed on a rolling basis. Application fee: $50. Electronic applications accepted. *Expenses:* Tuition: Part-time $773 per credit. Required fees: $157 per semester. *Financial support:* In 2009–10, 118 students received support, including 96 fellowships (averaging $1,308 per year), 4 research assistantships (averaging $3,610 per year); career-related internships or fieldwork, scholarships/grants, and unspecified assistantships also available. Support available to part-time students. Financial award applicants required to submit FAFSA. *Faculty research:* Relationship of undergraduate GPA and GRE to succeed in a graduate nursing program. *Unit head:* Dr. Janet Mahoney, Dean, 732-571-3443, Fax: 732-263-5131, E-mail: jmahoney@monmouth.edu. *Application contact:* Kevin Roane, Director, Office of Graduate Admission, 732-571-3452, Fax: 732-263-5123, E-mail: gradadm@monmouth.edu.

Moravian College, Moravian College Comenius Center, St. Luke's School of Nursing, Bethlehem, PA 18018-6650. Offers nurse administrator (MS); nurse educator (MS); nurse leadership (MS). Part-time and evening/weekend programs available. *Faculty:* 2 full-time (both women). *Students:* 31 part-time (all women); includes 2 minority (1 African American, 1 Asian American or Pacific Islander). 34 applicants, 94% accepted, 31 enrolled. *Degree requirements:* For master's, comprehensive exam (for some programs), evidence-based practice project. *Entrance requirements:* For master's, GRE or MAT. Additional exam requirements/recommendations for international students: Required—TOEFL (minimum score 550 paper-based; 260 computer-based; 90 iBT). *Application deadline:* Applications are processed on a rolling basis. Application fee: $40. *Expenses:* Tuition: Part-time $1132 per course. Required fees: $40 per term. One-time fee: $30 part-time. *Unit head:* Dr. Lori Hoffman, Director, Master of Science Program in Nursing, 610-861-1400, Fax: 610-861-1466, E-mail: comenius@moravian.edu. *Application contact:* Dr. Lori Hoffman, Director, Master of Science Program in Nursing, 610-861-1400, Fax: 610-861-1466, E-mail: comenius@moravian.edu.

Mountain State University, Graduate Studies, Program in Nursing, Beckley, WV 25802-9003. Offers administration/education (MSN); family nurse practitioner (MSN); nurse anesthesia (MSN); registered nurse anesthetist (Certificate). *Accreditation:* AANA/CANAEP; NLN. Part-time programs available. Postbaccalaureate distance learning degree programs offered (minimal on-campus study). *Faculty:* 4 full-time (all women), 10 part-time/adjunct (9 women). *Students:* 117 full-time (102 women); includes 10 minority (6 African Americans, 1 American Indian/Alaska Native, 3 Asian Americans or Pacific Islanders), 1 international. Average age 37. 46 applicants, 80% accepted, 37 enrolled. In 2009, 35 master's awarded. *Degree requirements:* For master's, comprehensive exam, thesis or alternative. *Entrance requirements:* For master's, GRE. Additional exam requirements/recommendations for international students: Required—TOEFL (minimum score 550 paper-based; 213 computer-based); Recommended—IELTS (minimum score 6.5). *Application deadline:* For spring admission, 6/30 for domestic and international students. Applications are processed on a rolling basis. Application fee: $25 ($50 for international students). Electronic applications accepted. *Expenses:* Contact institution. *Financial support:* Federal Work-Study, scholarships/grants, and unspecified assistantships available. Support available to part-time students. Financial award applicants required to submit FAFSA. *Unit head:* Dr. Judith Halle, Dean, School of Health Sciences, 304-929-1327, Fax: 304-929-1601, E-mail: jhalle@mountainstate.edu. *Application contact:* Melody Tilley, Program Specialist, 304-929-1576, Fax: 304-929-1601, E-mail: mtilley@mountainstate.edu.

Mount Carmel College of Nursing, Nursing Program, Columbus, OH 43222. Offers adult health CNS (clinical nurse specialist) (MS); nursing administration (MS); nursing education (MS). *Accreditation:* AACN. Part-time programs available. *Degree requirements:* For master's, professional manuscript. *Entrance requirements:* For master's, letters of recommendation, current resume, baccalaureate degree in nursing, current Ohio RN license, minimum cumulative GPA of 3.0. Additional exam requirements/recommendations for international students: Required—TOEFL (minimum score 550 paper-based; 213 computer-based; 80 iBT).

Mount Saint Mary College, Division of Nursing, Newburgh, NY 12550-3494. Offers adult nurse practitioner (MS), including nursing education, nursing management; clinical nurse specialist-adult health (MS), including nursing education, nursing management; family nurse practitioner (Advanced Certificate). *Accreditation:* AACN. Part-time and evening/weekend programs available. *Faculty:* 3 full-time (all women), 2 part-time/adjunct (both women). *Students:* 1 full-time (0 women), 53 part-time (50 women); includes 17 minority (8 African Americans, 4 Asian Americans or Pacific Islanders, 5 Hispanic Americans). Average age 39. 16 applicants, 100% accepted, 6 enrolled. In 2009, 5 master's awarded. *Degree requirements:* For master's, research utilization project. *Entrance requirements:* For master's, BSN, minimum GPA of 3.0, RN license. *Application deadline:* For fall admission, 6/3 priority date for domestic students; for spring admission, 10/31 priority date for domestic students. Applications are processed on a rolling basis. Application fee: $45. *Expenses:* Tuition: Full-time $13,356; part-time $742 per credit. Required fees: $50 per semester. *Financial support:* In 2009–10, 2 students received support. Unspecified assistantships available. Financial award application deadline: 4/15; financial award applicants required to submit FAFSA. *Unit head:* Dr. Karen Baldwin, Coordinator, 845-569-3512, Fax: 845-562-6762, E-mail: baldwin@msmc.edu. *Application contact:* Graduate Coordinator, 845-561-0800, Fax: 845-562-6762.

Mount St. Mary's College, Graduate Division, Program in Nursing, Los Angeles, CA 90049-1599. Offers clinical nurse specialist/adult health (MS); community health (MS); educator (MS); leadership and administration (MS); nursing (MS). *Accreditation:* AACN. *Faculty:* 2 full-time (both women), 11 part-time/adjunct (9 women). *Students:* 31 full-time (29 women), 8 part-time (6 women); includes 24 minority (5 African Americans, 12 Asian Americans or Pacific Islanders, 7 Hispanic Americans), 1 international. Average age 41. In 2009, 22 master's awarded. *Entrance requirements:* Additional exam requirements/recommendations for international students: Required—TOEFL (minimum score 550 iBT). *Application deadline:* For fall admission, 7/15 priority date for domestic students; for spring admission, 11/15 priority date for domestic students. *Expenses:* Tuition: Part-time $730 per unit. Part-time tuition and fees vary according to degree level and program. *Unit head:* Dr. Marsha Sato, Chair, 213-477-2980, E-mail: msato@msmc.la.edu. *Application contact:* Director of Graduate Admission.

New Mexico State University, Graduate School, College of Health and Social Services, School of Nursing, Las Cruces, NM 88003-8001. Offers community/public health (MSN); medical-surgical (adult health) (MSN); nursing (PhD); nursing administration (MSN); psychiatric/mental health (MSN). *Accreditation:* AACN. Part-time programs available. Postbaccalaureate distance learning degree programs offered (minimal on-campus study). *Faculty:* 10 full-time (all women), 5 part-time/adjunct (all women). *Students:* 59 full-time (48 women), 70 part-time (61 women); includes 47 minority (9 African Americans, 3 American Indian/Alaska Native, 5 Asian Americans or Pacific Islanders, 30 Hispanic Americans). Average age 43. 82 applicants, 96% accepted, 63 enrolled. In 2009, 32 master's, 1 doctorate awarded. *Degree requirements:* For master's, comprehensive exam, thesis optional, clinical practice; for doctorate, comprehensive exam, thesis/dissertation, clinical practice. *Entrance requirements:* For master's, NCLEX exam, BSN, minimum GPA of 3.0, course work in statistics, 3 letters of reference, writing sample, RN license, CPR certification, proof of liability, immunizations, criminal background check; for doctorate, NCLEX exam, MSN, minimum GPA of 3.0, 3 letters of reference, writing sample, RN license, CPR certification, proof of liability, immunizations, criminal background check. Additional exam requirements/recommendations for international students: Required—TOEFL (minimum score 550 paper-based). *Application deadline:* For fall admission, 3/1 priority date for domestic students; for spring admission, 10/1 priority date for domestic students. Applications are processed on a rolling basis. Application fee: $30 ($50 for international students). Electronic applications accepted. *Expenses:* Tuition, state resident: full-time $4080; part-time $223 per credit. Tuition, nonresident: full-time $14,256; part-time $647 per credit. Required fees: $1278; $639 per semester. *Financial support:* In 2009–10, 14 students received support, including 2 teaching assistantships (averaging $18,380 per year); fellowships, research assistantships, career-related internships or fieldwork, Federal Work-Study, scholarships/grants, traineeships, and health care benefits also available. Financial award application deadline: 3/1. *Faculty research:* Public policy, community health, health disparities, self efficacy and self management, psychiatric mental health. *Unit head:* Dr. Pamela Schultz, Director, 575-646-3812, Fax: 575-646-2167, E-mail: pschultz@nmsu.edu. *Application contact:* Dr. Kathleen Huttlinger, Associate Director for Graduate Studies, 575-646-4386, Fax: 575-646-2167.

Northeastern University, Bouvé College of Health Sciences Graduate School, School of Nursing, Program in Nursing Administration, Boston, MA 02115-5096. Offers MS, MS/MBA. *Accreditation:* AACN. *Students:* 7 full-time (6 women), 11 part-time (9 women); includes 1 African American, 1 Asian American or Pacific Islander, 3 international. Average age 42. 6 applicants, 100% accepted, 4 enrolled. In 2009, 6 master's awarded. *Degree requirements:* For master's, thesis or alternative. *Entrance requirements:* For master's, GRE General Test. Additional exam requirements/recommendations for international students: Required—TOEFL (minimum score 100 iBT). *Application deadline:* For fall admission, 8/1 priority date for domestic students; for spring admission, 12/1 for domestic students. Applications are processed on a rolling basis. Application fee: $50. *Financial support:* Research assistantships, teaching assistantships, tuition waivers (partial) available. Financial award application deadline: 7/1; financial award applicants required to submit FAFSA. *Faculty research:* Nursing informatics. *Unit head:* Dr. Jane Aroian, Director, 617-373-3128, E-mail: j.aroian@neu.edu. *Application contact:* Margaret Schnabel, Director of Graduate Admissions, 617-373-2708, E-mail: bouvegrad@neu.edu.

North Park University, School of Nursing, Chicago, IL 60625-4895. Offers advanced practice nursing (MS); leadership and management (MS); MBA/MS; MM/MSN; MS/MHR; MS/MNA. *Accreditation:* AACN. Part-time and evening/weekend programs available. *Degree requirements:* For master's, thesis. *Entrance requirements:* For master's, GMAT, MAT. *Faculty research:* Aging, consultation roles, critical thinking skills, family breakdown, science of caring.

Norwich University, School of Graduate and Continuing Studies, Program in Nursing Administration, Northfield, VT 05663. Offers nursing administration (MSN); nursing education (MSN). *Accreditation:* AACN. Evening/weekend programs available. *Faculty:* 5 part-time/adjunct (2 women). *Students:* 70 full-time (64 women); includes 9 minority (4 African Americans, 4 American Indian/Alaska Native, 1 Hispanic American). Average age 43. 79 applicants, 90% accepted, 70 enrolled. In 2009, 70 master's awarded. *Entrance requirements:* For master's, minimum undergraduate GPA of 2.75. Additional exam requirements/recommendations for international students: Required—TOEFL (minimum score 550 paper-based; 212 computer-based; 83 iBT). *Application deadline:* For fall admission, 8/10 for domestic and international students; for winter admission, 11/7 for domestic and international students; for spring admission, 2/6 for domestic and international students. Application fee: $50. Electronic applications accepted. Full-time tuition and fees vary according to course level and course load. *Financial support:* Scholarships/grants available. Financial award applicants required to submit FAFSA. *Unit head:* Anne Moore-Cox, Program Director, 802-485-2567, E-mail: amorreco@norwich.edu. *Application contact:* Rija Ramahatra, Administrative Director, 802-485-2892, Fax: 802-485-2533, E-mail: rramahatr@norwich.edu.

Ohio University, Graduate College, College of Health and Human Services, School of Nursing, Athens, OH 45701-2979. Offers family nurse practitioner (MSN); nurse administrator (MSN); nurse educator (MSN). *Accreditation:* AACN. *Faculty:* 8 full-time (all women). *Students:* 24 full-time (23 women), 31 part-time (25 women); includes 1 African American, 2 American Indian/Alaska Native. 36 applicants, 92% accepted, 25 enrolled. In 2009, 12 master's awarded. *Degree requirements:* For master's, capstone project. *Entrance requirements:* For master's, GRE, bachelor's degree in nursing from an accredited college or university, minimum overall undergraduate GPA of 3.0, official transcripts, statement of goals and objectives, resume, 3 letters of recommendation. Additional exam requirements/recommendations for international students: Required—TOEFL (minimum score 550 paper-based; 80 iBT) or IELTS Academic (minimum score 6.5). *Application deadline:* For fall admission, 3/1 priority date for domestic students, 2/1 priority date for international students. Applications are processed on a rolling basis. Application fee: $50 ($55 for international students). Electronic applications accepted. *Expenses:* Tuition, state resident: full-time $7839; part-time $323 per quarter hour. Tuition, nonresident: full-time $15,831; part-time $654 per quarter hour. Required fees: $2931. *Financial support:* Research assistantships, Federal Work-Study, institutionally sponsored loans, and unspecified assistantships available. Financial award application deadline: 3/1. *Unit head:* Mary Bowen, Director, 740-593-9134, E-mail: bowenm2@ohio.edu. *Application contact:* Cheryl Branham, Administrative Associate, 740-593-4494, E-mail: branhamc@ohio.edu.

Otterbein University, Department of Nursing, Westerville, OH 43081. Offers adult nurse practitioner (MSN, Certificate); clinical nurse leader (MSN); family nurse practitioner (MSN, Certificate); nurse service administration (MSN). *Accreditation:* AACN; NLN. Part-time and evening/weekend programs available. Postbaccalaureate distance learning degree programs offered (minimal on-campus study). *Degree requirements:* For master's, comprehensive exam (for some programs), thesis (for some programs). *Entrance requirements:* For master's, 2 reference forms, resume; for Certificate, official transcripts, 2 reference forms, essay, resumé. Additional exam requirements/recommendations for international students: Required—TOEFL (minimum score 550 paper-based; 213 computer-based; 79 iBT). *Faculty research:* Patient education, women's health, trauma curriculum development, administration.

Our Lady of the Lake College, School of Nursing, Program in Nursing, Baton Rouge, LA 70808. Offers administration (MS); education (MS). Part-time programs available. *Degree requirements:* For master's, capstone project. *Entrance requirements:* For master's, BSN with minimum GPA of 3.0 during the last 60 hours of undergraduate work, 1 year of clinical nursing experience as a registered nurse, current licensure or eligibility to practice as registered nurse in Louisiana, 3 professional references, 3 credit hours of undergraduate statistics with minimum C average.

Pace University, Lienhard School of Nursing, New York, NY 10038. Offers family nurse practitioner (MS); nursing education (MA); nursing leadership (Advanced Certificate); nursing practice (DNP). *Accreditation:* AACN. Part-time and evening/weekend programs available. *Faculty:* 9 full-time (all women), 18 part-time/adjunct (14 women). *Students:* 41 full-time (37 women), 333 part-time (303 women); includes 140 minority (63 African Americans, 41 Asian Americans or Pacific Islanders, 36 Hispanic Americans), 12 international. Average age 36. 459 applicants, 66% accepted, 125 enrolled. In 2009, 79 master's, 3 other advanced degrees awarded. *Degree requirements:* For master's, thesis. *Entrance requirements:* For master's, GRE General Test or MAT, RN license, resume, personal statement, 2 letters of recommendation, official transcripts; for doctorate, RN license, resume, personal statement, 2 letters of recommendation, official transcripts, accredited master's degree in nursing, minimum GPA of 3.3, advanced experience, state certification; for Advanced Certificate, RN license, completion of 2nd degree in nursing. Additional exam requirements/recommendations for international students: Required—TOEFL. *Application deadline:* For fall admission, 7/31 priority date for domestic students, 4/30 priority date for international students; for spring admission, 10/14 for domestic students, 9/14 for international students. Applications are processed on a rolling basis. Application fee: $70. Electronic applications accepted. *Expenses:* Contact institution. *Financial support:* Research assistantships, career-related internships or fieldwork, Federal Work-Study, and tuition waivers (partial) available. Support available to part-time students. Financial award applicants required to submit FAFSA. *Unit head:* Dr. Harriet Feldman, Dean, 914-773-3341. *Application contact:* Joanna Broda, Director of Graduate Admissions, 914-422-4283, Fax: 914-422-4287, E-mail: gradwp@pace.edu.

Pacific Lutheran University, Division of Graduate Studies, School of Nursing, Program in Care and Outcomes Manager, Tacoma, WA 98447. Offers client systems management (MSN); health care systems management (MSN). *Accreditation:* AACN. Part-time and evening/weekend programs available. *Degree requirements:* For master's, thesis or alternative. *Entrance*

Nursing and Healthcare Administration

Pacific Lutheran University (continued)

requirements: For master's, GRE General Test, minimum undergraduate GPA of 3.0. Additional exam requirements/recommendations for international students: Required—TOEFL (minimum score 550 paper-based; 213 computer-based). *Expenses:* Contact institution.

Prairie View A&M University, College of Nursing, Houston, TX 77030. Offers family nurse practitioner (MSN); nursing administration (MSN); nursing education (MSN). *Accreditation:* AACN; NLN. Part-time programs available. *Faculty:* 6 full-time (all women), 6 part-time/adjunct (all women). *Students:* 100 part-time (93 women); includes 82 minority (74 African Americans, 1 American Indian/Alaska Native, 4 Asian Americans or Pacific Islanders, 3 Hispanic Americans), 7 international. Average age 37. 37 applicants, 100% accepted, 32 enrolled. In 2009, 7 master's awarded. *Degree requirements:* For master's, comprehensive exam, thesis. *Entrance requirements:* For master's, MAT or GRE, BS in nursing; 2 years of experience as a registered nurse; 1 course each in statistics, basic health and assessment. *Application deadline:* For fall admission, 6/1 priority date for domestic students; for spring admission, 11/1 priority date for domestic students. Applications are processed on a rolling basis. Application fee: $50. *Expenses:* Tuition, state resident: full-time $2200. Tuition, nonresident: full-time $5600. Required fees: $1720. Tuition and fees vary according to course load. *Financial support:* In 2009–10, 17 students received support. Career-related internships or fieldwork, Federal Work-Study, institutionally sponsored loans, scholarships/grants, and traineeships available. Support available to part-time students. Financial award application deadline: 4/1; financial award applicants required to submit FAFSA. *Faculty research:* Software development and violence prevention, health promotion and disease prevention. Total annual research expenditures: $350,000. *Unit head:* Dr. Betty N. Adams, Dean, 713-797-7009, Fax: 713-797-7013, E-mail: bnadams@pvamu.edu. *Application contact:* Dr. Forest Smith, Director of Student Services and Admissions, 713-797-7031, Fax: 713-797-7012, E-mail: pcwillson@pvamu.edu.

Queens University of Charlotte, Presbyterian School of Nursing, Charlotte, NC 28274-0002. Offers nursing management (MSN). *Accreditation:* AACN. *Degree requirements:* For master's, research project. *Entrance requirements:* For master's, minimum GPA of 3.0. Additional exam requirements/recommendations for international students: Required—TOEFL. Electronic applications accepted. *Expenses:* Contact institution.

Regis University, Rueckert-Hartman School for Health Professions, Denver, CO 80221-1099. Offers clinical leadership for physician assistants (MS); family nurse practitioner (MSN); health informatics (Postbaccalaureate Certificate); health services administration (MS); healthcare education (Certificate); leadership in healthcare systems (MSN); neonatal nurse practitioner (MSN); nursing (MSN); pharmacy (Pharm D); physical therapy (DPT, TDPT). *Entrance requirements:* Additional exam requirements/recommendations for international students: Required—TOEFL (minimum score 550 paper-based; 213 computer-based; 82 iBT). Electronic applications accepted. *Expenses:* Contact institution. *Faculty research:* Normal and pathological balance and gait research, normal/pathological upper limb motor control/biomechanics, exercise energy/metabolism research, optical treatment protocols for therapeutic modalities.

Roberts Wesleyan College, Division of Nursing, Rochester, NY 14624-1997. Offers nursing administration (MSN); nursing education (MSN). *Accreditation:* AACN. *Entrance requirements:* For master's, minimum GPA of 3.0; BS in nursing; interview; RN license; resume; course work in statistics and health assessment. Additional exam requirements/recommendations for international students: Required—TOEFL.

Sacred Heart University, Graduate Programs, College of Education and Health Professions, Department of Nursing, Fairfield, CT 06825-1000. Offers clinical nurse leader (MSN); clinical practice in health care (DNP); family nurse practitioner (MSN); leadership in health care (DNP); nursing (DN Sc); patient care services administration (MSN). *Accreditation:* AACN. Part-time and evening/weekend programs available. Postbaccalaureate distance learning degree programs offered (minimal on-campus study). *Faculty:* 12 full-time (all women). *Students:* 7 full-time (6 women), 155 part-time (146 women); includes 27 minority (9 African Americans, 11 Asian Americans or Pacific Islanders, 7 Hispanic Americans), 1 international. Average age 39. 72 applicants, 93% accepted, 28 enrolled. In 2009, 13 master's awarded. *Entrance requirements:* For master's, BSN, minimum GPA of 3.0. Additional exam requirements/recommendations for international students: Required—TOEFL (minimum score 550 paper-based; 213 computer-based). *Application deadline:* Applications are processed on a rolling basis. Application fee: $50 ($100 for international students). Electronic applications accepted. *Expenses:* Contact institution. *Financial support:* Career-related internships or fieldwork, institutionally sponsored loans, and unspecified assistantships available. Support available to part-time students. Financial award applicants required to submit FAFSA. *Unit head:* Dr. Dori Sullivan, Chair, 203-371-7715. *Application contact:* Kathy Dilks, Assistant Dean of Graduate Admissions, Health Professions, 203-396-8259, Fax: 203-365-4732, E-mail: gradstudies@sacredheart.edu.

Sage Graduate School, Graduate School, School of Health Sciences, Department of Nursing, Troy, NY 12180-4115. Offers adult health (MS); adult nurse practitioner (MS, Post Master's Certificate); clinical nurse leader/specialist (Post Master's Certificate); community health (MS); education and leadership (DNS); family nurse practitioner (MS, Post Master's Certificate); gerontological nurse practitioner (Post Master's Certificate); nurse administrator/executive (Post Master's Certificate); nursing (Post Master's Certificate); psychiatric mental health nurse practitioner (MS, Post Master's Certificate), including psychiatric mental health. *Accreditation:* AACN. Part-time and evening/weekend programs available. *Faculty:* 5 full-time (all women), 8 part-time/adjunct (all women). *Students:* 23 full-time (22 women), 134 part-time (129 women); includes 16 minority (6 African Americans, 1 American Indian/Alaska Native, 8 Asian Americans or Pacific Islanders, 1 Hispanic American), 1 international. Average age 42. 97 applicants, 64% accepted, 49 enrolled. In 2009, 25 master's, 3 other advanced degrees awarded. *Degree requirements:* For master's, thesis or alternative. *Entrance requirements:* For master's, BS in nursing, minimum GPA of 2.75, resume, 2 letters of recommendation. Additional exam requirements/recommendations for international students: Required—TOEFL (minimum score 550 paper-based; 213 computer-based). *Application deadline:* Applications are processed on a rolling basis. Application fee: $40. *Expenses:* Tuition: Full-time $10,620; part-time $590 per credit hour. *Financial support:* Fellowships, research assistantships, Federal Work-Study, scholarships/grants, and unspecified assistantships available. Support available to part-time students. Financial award application deadline: 3/1; financial award applicants required to submit FAFSA. *Unit head:* Dr. Glenda Kelman, Chair, 518-244-2001, E-mail: kelmag@sage.edu. *Application contact:* Wendy D. Diefendorf, Director of Graduate and Adult Admission, 518-244-2443, Fax: 518-244-6880, E-mail: diefew@sage.edu.

Saginaw Valley State University, Crystal M. Lange College of Nursing and Health Sciences, Program in Health System Nurse Specialist, University Center, MI 48710. Offers MSN. *Accreditation:* AACN. Part-time and evening/weekend programs available. *Students:* 26 full-time (all women), 3 part-time (all women). Average age 39. 10 applicants, 80% accepted, 6 enrolled. In 2009, 6 master's awarded. *Degree requirements:* For master's, thesis optional. *Entrance requirements:* For master's, GRE. Additional exam requirements/recommendations for international students: Required—TOEFL (minimum score 525 paper-based; 237 computer-based; 92 iBT). *Application deadline:* Applications are processed on a rolling basis. Application fee: $25. Electronic applications accepted. *Financial support:* Federal Work-Study and scholarships/grants available. Support available to part-time students. Financial award application deadline: 4/1; financial award applicants required to submit FAFSA. *Unit head:* Dr. Sally Decker, Professor of Nursing, 989-964-4098, E-mail: decker@svsu.edu. *Application contact:* Dr. Sally Decker, Professor of Nursing, 989-964-4098, E-mail: decker@svsu.edu.

Saint Joseph's College of Maine, Department of Nursing, Standish, ME 04084. Offers nursing (MS); nursing administration and leadership (Certificate); nursing and health care education (Certificate). MS degree offered only through faculty-directed independent study. *Accreditation:* AACN. Part-time programs available. Postbaccalaureate distance learning degree programs offered (minimal on-campus study). *Degree requirements:* For master's, summer residency. *Entrance requirements:* For master's, MAT. Electronic applications accepted.

Saint Peter's College, School of Nursing, Nursing Program, Jersey City, NJ 07306-5997. Offers adult nurse practitioner (MSN); case management (MSN); nursing (DNP); RN to MSN bridge (MSN). *Accreditation:* AACN. Part-time and evening/weekend programs available. *Entrance requirements:* Additional exam requirements/recommendations for international students: Required—TOEFL. *Application deadline:* Applications are processed on a rolling basis. Electronic applications accepted. *Expenses:* Tuition: Part-time $971 per credit. *Financial support:* Federal Work-Study and institutionally sponsored loans available. *Unit head:* Dr. Ann Tritak, Director, 201-761-6270. *Application contact:* Dr. Ann Tritak, Director, 201-761-6270.

Saint Vincent College, Program in Health Services Leadership, Latrobe, PA 15650-2690. Offers MS.

Saint Xavier University, Graduate Studies, School of Nursing, Chicago, IL 60655-3105. Offers adult health clinical nurse specialist (MS); family nurse practitioner (MS, PMC); leadership in community health nursing (MS); psychiatric-mental health clinical nurse specialist (MS); psychiatric-mental health clinical specialist (PMC); MBA/MS. *Accreditation:* AACN. Part-time and evening/weekend programs available. *Entrance requirements:* For master's, GRE General Test or MAT, minimum GPA of 3.0, RN license. *Expenses:* Tuition: Part-time $743 per credit hour. Required fees: $135 per semester.

Samford University, Ida V. Moffett School of Nursing, Birmingham, AL 35229. Offers advance practice (DNP); anesthesia (MSN); family nurse practitioner (MSN); nurse educator (MSN); nurse executive (DNP); nurse manager (MSN); MBA/MSN. *Accreditation:* AACN; AANA/CANAEP (one or more programs are accredited). Part-time programs available. Postbaccalaureate distance learning degree programs offered (minimal on-campus study). *Faculty:* 10 full-time (all women), 1 part-time/adjunct (0 women). *Students:* 149 full-time (102 women), 31 part-time (24 women); includes 21 minority (14 African Americans, 4 Asian Americans or Pacific Islanders, 3 Hispanic Americans), 1 international. Average age 31. 56 applicants, 98% accepted, 52 enrolled. In 2009, 58 master's awarded. *Degree requirements:* For master's and doctorate, capstone project with oral presentation. *Entrance requirements:* For master's, GRE General Test or MAT. Additional exam requirements/recommendations for international students: Required—TOEFL (minimum score 550 paper-based; 213 computer-based; 80 iBT). *Application deadline:* For fall admission, 7/1 priority date for domestic and international students; for spring admission, 11/1 priority date for domestic and international students. Applications are processed on a rolling basis. Application fee: $35. *Expenses:* Contact institution. *Financial support:* Institutionally sponsored loans, scholarships/grants, and traineeships available. Financial award application deadline: 3/1; financial award applicants required to submit FAFSA. *Faculty research:* Issues in rural health care, vulnerable populations, genetics and disabilities in pediatrics, geriatrics, Parrish nursing research. *Unit head:* Dr. Nena F. Sanders, Dean, 205-726-2629, E-mail: nfsander@samford.edu. *Application contact:* Marian Carter, Director of Graduate Student Services, 205-726-2047, Fax: 205-726-4269, E-mail: mwcarter@samford.edu.

Samuel Merritt University, School of Nursing, Oakland, CA 94609-3108. Offers case management (MSN); family nurse practitioner (MSN, Certificate); nurse anesthetist (MSN, Certificate); nursing (MSN). *Accreditation:* AACN; AANA/CANAEP (one or more programs are accredited). Part-time and evening/weekend programs available. *Degree requirements:* For master's, thesis or alternative. *Entrance requirements:* For master's, minimum GPA of 2.5 in science, 3.0 overall; previous course work in statistics; current RN license. Additional exam requirements/recommendations for international students: Required—TOEFL. *Faculty research:* Gerontology, community health, maternal-child health, sexually transmitted diseases, substance abuse, oncology.

San Francisco State University, Division of Graduate Studies, College of Health and Human Services, School of Nursing, San Francisco, CA 94132-1722. Offers case management (MS), including long-term care, primary care/family nurse practitioner; nursing administration (MS); nursing education (MS). *Accreditation:* AACN. Part-time programs available.

San Jose State University, Graduate Studies and Research, College of Applied Sciences and Arts, School of Nursing, San Jose, CA 95192-0001. Offers gerontology nurse practitioner (MS); nursing (Certificate); nursing administration (MS); nursing education (MS). *Accreditation:* AACN. Part-time and evening/weekend programs available. *Students:* 8 full-time (7 women), 45 part-time (42 women); includes 20 minority (3 African Americans, 2 American Indian/Alaska Native, 12 Asian Americans or Pacific Islanders, 3 Hispanic Americans), 2 international. Average age 43. 35 applicants, 40% accepted, 8 enrolled. In 2009, 24 master's awarded. *Degree requirements:* For master's, thesis. *Entrance requirements:* For master's, BS in nursing, RN license. *Application deadline:* For fall admission, 6/29 for domestic students; for spring admission, 11/30 for domestic students. Applications are processed on a rolling basis. Application fee: $59. Electronic applications accepted. *Financial support:* Career-related internships or fieldwork, institutionally sponsored loans, and scholarships/grants available. Support available to part-time students. Financial award applicants required to submit FAFSA. *Faculty research:* Nurse-managed clinics, computers in nursing. *Unit head:* Jayne Cohen, Director, 408-924-3132, Fax: 408-924-3135. *Application contact:* Dr. Phyllis Connolly, Graduate Coordinator, 408-924-3144.

Seattle Pacific University, MS in Nursing Program, Seattle, WA 98119-1997. Offers administration (MSN); adult/gerontology nurse practitioner (MSN); clinical nurse specialist (MSN); family nurse practitioner (MSN, Certificate); informatics (MSN); nurse educator (MSN). *Accreditation:* AACN. Part-time programs available. *Faculty:* 3 full-time (all women), 7 part-time/adjunct (6 women). *Students:* 9 full-time (8 women), 63 part-time (57 women); includes 9 minority (1 American Indian/Alaska Native, 7 Asian Americans or Pacific Islanders, 1 Hispanic American), 1 international. Average age 46. 60 applicants, 45% accepted, 27 enrolled. In 2009, 12 master's awarded. *Degree requirements:* For master's, thesis. *Application deadline:* For fall admission, 2/1 priority date for domestic students. Applications are processed on a rolling basis. Application fee: $50. Electronic applications accepted. *Expenses:* Contact institution. *Financial support:* In 2009–10, 41 students received support; fellowships, scholarships/grants available. Financial award applicants required to submit FAFSA. *Unit head:* Dr. Susan Casey, Director, 206-281-2769, Fax: 206-281-2767, E-mail: caseys@spu.edu. *Application contact:* The Grad Center, 206-281-2091.

Seattle University, College of Nursing, Program in Nursing, Seattle, WA 98122-1090. Offers leadership in community nursing (MSN), including program development, spirituality and health; primary care nurse practitioner (MSN), including family nurse practitioner, psychiatric mental health nurse practitioner.

Seton Hall University, College of Nursing, South Orange, NJ 07079-2697. Offers advanced practice in primary health care (MSN), including adult nurse practitioner, gerontological nurse practitioner, pediatric nurse practitioner; entry into practice (MSN); health systems administration (MSN, DNP); nursing (PhD); nursing case management (MSN); nursing education (MA); school nurse (MSN); MSN/MA. *Accreditation:* AACN. Part-time programs available. Postbaccalaureate distance learning degree programs offered (minimal on-campus study). *Faculty:* 10 full-time (all women), 3 part-time/adjunct (1 woman). *Students:* 46 full-time (35 women), 94 part-time (90 women); includes 22 minority (8 African Americans, 5 Asian Americans or Pacific Islanders, 9 Hispanic Americans). 92 applicants, 88% accepted, 55 enrolled. *Degree requirements:* For master's, research project; for doctorate, dissertation or scholarly project. *Entrance requirements:* For doctorate, GRE. Additional exam requirements/recommendations for international students: Required—TOEFL. *Application deadline:* For fall admission, 6/15 priority date for domestic students. Applications are processed on a rolling basis. Electronic applications accepted. *Financial support:* Institutionally sponsored loans, scholarships/grants, traineeships, tuition waivers (partial), and unspecified assistantships available. Support available to part-time students. Financial award applicants required to submit FAFSA. *Faculty research:* Parent/child, adult, and gerontological nursing; breast cancer; families of children with HIV; parish nursing. *Unit head:* Dr. Phyllis Shanley Hansell, Dean. *Application contact:* Kristyn Kent Wuillermin, Director of Strategic Alliances, Marketing and Enrollment, 973-761-9291, Fax: 973-761-9607, E-mail: kristyn.kent@shu.edu.

Southern Adventist University, School of Nursing, Collegedale, TN 37315-0370. Offers acute care nurse practitioner (MSN); adult nurse practitioner (MSN); family nurse practitioner (MSN); nurse educator (MSN); MSN/MSBA. *Accreditation:* NLN. Part-time programs available. *Faculty:* 6 full-time (5 women). *Students:* 69 full-time (50 women), 28 part-time (25 women); includes 9 minority (6 African Americans, 1 American Indian/Alaska Native, 1 Asian American or Pacific Islander, 1 Hispanic American). Average age 35. 40 applicants, 95% accepted, 31 enrolled. In 2009, 21 master's awarded. *Degree requirements:* For master's, thesis or project. *Entrance requirements:* For master's, RN license. Additional exam requirements/recommendations for international students: Required—TOEFL (minimum score 600 paper-based; 250 computer-based). *Application deadline:* For fall admission, 7/1 for domestic and international students; for winter admission, 12/1 for domestic and international students. Applications are processed on a rolling basis. Application fee: $25. Electronic applications accepted. *Expenses:* Tuition: Full-time $13,149; part-time $487 per credit hour. *Financial support:* In 2009–10, 1 teaching assistantship with partial tuition reimbursement (averaging $5,000 per year) was awarded. *Faculty research:* Pain management, ethics, corporate wellness, caring spirituality, stress. *Unit head:* Dr. Barbara James, Dean, 423-236-2940, Fax: 423-236-1940, E-mail: bjames@southern.edu. *Application contact:* Diane Proffitt, Enrollment Counselor, 423-236-2941, Fax: 423-236-1940, E-mail: dproffitt@southern.edu.

Southern Connecticut State University, School of Graduate Studies, School of Health and Human Services, Department of Nursing, New Haven, CT 06515-1355. Offers nursing administration (MSN); nursing education (MSN). *Accreditation:* AACN; AANA/CANAEP. Part-time and evening/weekend programs available. *Faculty:* 6 full-time, 1 part-time/adjunct. *Students:* 2 full-time (both women), 29 part-time (27 women); includes 4 minority (3 African Americans, 1 Hispanic American). 33 applicants, 21% accepted, 7 enrolled. In 2009, 14 master's awarded. *Degree requirements:* For master's, thesis. *Entrance requirements:* For master's, GRE, MAT, interview, minimum QPA of 2.8, RN license, minimum 1 year of professional nursing experience. *Application deadline:* For fall admission, 7/15 priority date for domestic students. Applications are processed on a rolling basis. Application fee: $50. Electronic applications accepted. Tuition and fees vary according to program. *Financial support:* Application deadline: 4/15. *Unit head:* Dr. Lisa Rebeschi, Chairperson, 203-392-6485. *Application contact:* Dr. Antonia Nelson, Graduate Coordinator, 203-392-6480, Fax: 203-392-6493, E-mail: nelsona13@southernct.edu.

Southern Illinois University Edwardsville, Graduate Studies and Research, School of Nursing, Program in Health Care and Nursing Administration, Edwardsville, IL 62026-0001. Offers MS, Post-Master's Certificate. Part-time programs available. *Students:* 25 part-time (23 women); includes 3 minority (all African Americans). Average age 26. 11 applicants, 0% accepted. In 2009, 11 master's awarded. *Degree requirements:* For master's, comprehensive exam. *Entrance requirements:* Additional exam requirements/recommendations for international students: Required—TOEFL (minimum score 550 paper-based; 213 computer-based; 79 iBT), IELTS (minimum score 6.5). *Application deadline:* For fall admission, 3/1 for domestic and international students. Application fee: $30. Electronic applications accepted. *Expenses:* Tuition, state resident: part-time $1252.50 per semester. Tuition, nonresident: part-time $3131.25 per semester. Required fees: $586.85 per semester. Tuition and fees vary according to course load. *Financial support:* Career-related internships or fieldwork, Federal Work-Study, institutionally sponsored loans, scholarships/grants, traineeships, and unspecified assistantships available. Support available to part-time students. Financial award application deadline: 3/1; financial award applicants required to submit FAFSA. *Unit head:* Dr. Jacquelyn Clement, Director, 618-650-3923, E-mail: jclemen@siue.edu. *Application contact:* Dr. Jacquelyn Clement, Director, 618-650-3923, E-mail: jclemen@siue.edu.

Southern Nazarene University, Graduate College, School of Nursing, Bethany, OK 73008. Offers nursing education (MS); nursing leadership (MS). *Accreditation:* AACN. Part-time and evening/weekend programs available.

Southern University and Agricultural and Mechanical College, School of Nursing, Baton Rouge, LA 70813. Offers educator/administrator (PhD); family health nursing (MSN); family nurse practitioner (Post Master's Certificate); geriatric nurse practitioner/gerontology (PhD). *Accreditation:* AACN. Part-time programs available. *Degree requirements:* For master's, comprehensive exam, thesis; for doctorate, comprehensive exam, thesis/dissertation. *Entrance requirements:* For master's, GRE General Test, BSN, minimum GPA of 2.7; for doctorate, GRE General Test; for Post Master's Certificate, MSN. Additional exam requirements/recommendations for international students: Required—TOEFL (minimum score 525 paper-based; 193 computer-based). *Faculty research:* Health promotions, vulnerable populations, (community-based) cardiovascular participating research, health disparities chronic diseases, care of the elderly.

Spalding University, Graduate Studies, College of Health and Natural Sciences, School of Nursing, Louisville, KY 40203-2188. Offers adult nurse practitioner (MSN); family nurse practitioner (MSN); leadership in nursing and healthcare (MSN); pediatric nurse practitioner (MSN). *Accreditation:* AACN. Part-time and evening/weekend programs available. *Faculty:* 6 full-time (all women), 7 part-time/adjunct (all women). *Students:* 41 full-time (38 women), 36 part-time (34 women); includes 12 minority (9 African Americans, 3 Hispanic Americans), 2 international. Average age 38. 27 applicants, 70% accepted, 18 enrolled. In 2009, 25 master's awarded. *Degree requirements:* For master's, comprehensive exam (for some programs), thesis. *Entrance requirements:* For master's, GRE General Test, BSN or bachelor's degree and RN licensure. Additional exam requirements/recommendations for international students: Required—TOEFL (minimum score 535 paper-based; 203 computer-based). *Application deadline:* Applications are processed on a rolling basis. Application fee: $30. *Expenses:* Tuition: Full-time $11,340; part-time $630 per credit hour. Tuition and fees vary according to program. *Financial support:* In 2009–10, 53 students received support, including 2 research assistantships with partial tuition reimbursements available (averaging $4,020 per year); career-related internships or fieldwork, scholarships/grants, and traineeships also available. Support available to part-time students. Financial award application deadline: 3/15; financial award applicants required to submit FAFSA. *Faculty research:* Nurse educational administration, gerontology, bioterrorism, healthcare ethics, leadership. *Unit head:* Dr. Carolyn Lewis, Interim Chair, 502-585-9911 Ext. 2331, E-mail: clewis@spalding.edu. *Application contact:* Dr. Carolyn Lewis, Interim Chair, 502-585-9911 Ext. 2331, E-mail: clewis@spalding.edu.

State University of New York Institute of Technology, School of Nursing and Health Systems, Program in Nursing Administration, Utica, NY 13504-3050. Offers MS, CAS. *Accreditation:* AACN. Part-time programs available. *Degree requirements:* For master's, thesis or project. *Entrance requirements:* For master's, GRE General Test (if undergraduate GPA less than 3.3), minimum GPA of 3.0, 2 letters of recommendation. Additional exam requirements/recommendations for international students: Required—TOEFL (minimum score 550 paper-based; 213 computer-based). *Faculty research:* Community health, critical thinking, leadership, nursing informatics, child obesity, evidence-based practice.

Teachers College, Columbia University, Graduate Faculty of Education, Department of Organization and Leadership, Program in Nurse Executive, New York, NY 10027-6696. Offers Ed M, MA, Ed D. *Faculty:* 1 (woman) full-time. *Students:* 30 full-time (28 women), 20 part-time (18 women); includes 21 minority (13 African Americans, 7 Asian Americans or Pacific Islanders, 1 Hispanic American). Average age 46. In 2009, 4 doctorates awarded. *Degree requirements:* For master's, capstone project; for doctorate, thesis/dissertation. *Entrance requirements:* For master's, BSN; for doctorate, GRE General Test or MAT, BSN, nursing license. *Application deadline:* For fall admission, 5/15 for domestic students; for spring admission, 12/1 for domestic students. Application fee: $65. *Financial support:* Career-related internships or fieldwork, Federal Work-Study, institutionally sponsored loans, traineeships, and tuition waivers (full and partial) available. Support available to part-time students. Financial award application deadline: 2/1. *Faculty research:* Health care administration, health care law, nursing administration and education, consumer satisfaction with health care. *Unit head:* Warner Burke, Chair, 212-678-3258. *Application contact:* Debbie Lesperance, Assistant Director of Admission, 212-678-3710, Fax: 212-678-4171.

Tennessee Technological University, School of Nursing, Cookeville, TN 38505. Offers family nurse practitioner (MSN); informatics (MSN); nursing administration (MSN); nursing education (MSN). *Students:* 11 full-time (10 women), 30 part-time (27 women); includes 2 minority (1 African American, 1 Hispanic American). 40 applicants, 35% accepted, 10 enrolled. In 2009, 14 master's awarded. *Degree requirements:* For master's, comprehensive exam, thesis or alternative. *Entrance requirements:* Additional exam requirements/recommendations for international students: Required—TOEFL (minimum score 550 paper-based; 79 iBT), IELTS (minimum score 5.5). *Application deadline:* For fall admission, 8/1 for domestic students, 5/1 for international students; for spring admission, 12/1 for domestic students, 10/1 for international students. Application fee: $25 ($30 for international students). Electronic applications accepted. *Expenses:* Tuition, state resident: full-time $7034; part-time $368 per credit hour. *Financial support:* Application deadline: 4/1. *Unit head:* Dr. Sheila Green, Interim Dean, 931-372-3203, Fax: 931-372-6244, E-mail: sgreen@tntech.edu. *Application contact:* Shelia K. Kendrick, Coordinator of Graduate Studies, 931-372-3808, Fax: 931-372-3497, E-mail: skendrick@tntech.edu.

Texas A&M University–Corpus Christi, Graduate Studies and Research, College of Nursing and Health Sciences, Corpus Christi, TX 78412-5503. Offers clinical nurse specialist (MSN); family nurse practitioner (MSN); health care administration (MSN); leadership in nursing systems (MSN). *Accreditation:* AACN. Part-time and evening/weekend programs available. *Degree requirements:* For master's, comprehensive exam, thesis (for some programs). *Entrance requirements:* For master's, GRE General Test. Additional exam requirements/recommendations for international students: Required—TOEFL. Electronic applications accepted.

Texas Tech University Health Sciences Center, School of Nursing, Lubbock, TX 79430. Offers acute care nurse practitioner (MSN, Certificate); administration (MSN); advanced practice (DNP); education (MSN); executive leadership (DNP); family nurse practitioner (MSN, Certificate); geriatric nurse practitioner (MSN, Certificate); pediatric nurse practitioner (MSN, Certificate). *Accreditation:* AACN. Part-time programs available. Postbaccalaureate distance learning degree programs offered (minimal on-campus study). *Degree requirements:* For master's, thesis optional. *Entrance requirements:* For master's, minimum GPA of 3.0, 3 letters of reference, BSN, RN license; for Certificate, minimum GPA of 3.0, 3 letters of reference, RN license. Additional exam requirements/recommendations for international students: Required—TOEFL (minimum score 550 paper-based; 213 computer-based). *Faculty research:* Diabetes/obesity, nurse competency, disease management, intervention and measurements, health disparities.

Texas Woman's University, Graduate School, College of Nursing, Denton, TX 76201. Offers acute care nurse practitioner (MS); adult health clinical nurse specialist (MS); adult health nurse practitioner (MS); child health clinical nurse specialist (MS); clinical nurse leader (MS); community health (MS); family nurse practitioner (MS); health systems management (MS); nursing education (MS); nursing practice (DNP); nursing science (PhD); pediatric nurse practitioner (MS); women's health clinical nurse specialist (MS); women's health nurse practitioner (MS). *Accreditation:* AACN. Part-time programs available. Postbaccalaureate distance learning degree programs offered. *Faculty:* 85 full-time (80 women), 6 part-time/adjunct (all women). *Students:* 81 full-time (76 women), 602 part-time (571 women); includes 293 minority (154 African Americans, 3 American Indian/Alaska Native, 90 Asian Americans or Pacific Islanders, 46 Hispanic Americans), 19 international. Average age 39. 259 applicants, 81% accepted, 166 enrolled. In 2009, 100 master's, 22 doctorates awarded. *Degree requirements:* For master's, thesis or alternative; for doctorate, comprehensive exam, thesis/dissertation. *Entrance requirements:* For master's, GRE or MAT, minimum GPA of 3.0, RN license, BS in nursing, basic statistics course; for doctorate, GRE (Verbal 460, Quantitative 500) or MAT (50), MS in nursing, minimum GPA of 3.5, RN license, coursework in statistics, 2 letters of reference, curriculum vitae, nursing-theory course, graduate research course, letter stating professional and research goals. Additional exam requirements/recommendations for international students: Required—TOEFL (minimum score 550 paper-based; 213 computer-based; 79 iBT). *Application deadline:* For fall admission, 5/1 priority date for domestic students, 3/1 for international students; for spring admission, 9/15 priority date for domestic students, 7/1 for international students. Applications are processed on a rolling basis. Application fee: $50. Electronic applications accepted. *Expenses:* Tuition, state resident: full-time $3564; part-time $198 per credit hour. Tuition, nonresident: full-time $8550; part-time $475 per credit hour. Required fees: $69.26 per credit hour. Tuition and fees vary according to course load. *Financial support:* In 2009–10, 99 students received support, including 16 fellowships (averaging $17,325 per year), 5 research assistantships (averaging $11,484 per year), 5 teaching assistantships (averaging $11,484 per year); career-related internships or fieldwork, Federal Work-Study, institutionally sponsored loans, scholarships/grants, traineeships, health care benefits, and unspecified assistantships also available. Support available to part-time students. Financial award application deadline: 3/1; financial award applicants required to submit FAFSA. *Faculty research:* Evaluation of pre-natal care, screening for intimate partner violence, stressors and nursing success, breast surgery, breast feeding, adolescent needs during childbirth. *Unit head:* Dr. Patricia Holden-Huchton, Interim Dean, 940-898-2401, Fax: 940-898-2437, E-mail: pholdenhuchton@twu.edu. *Application contact:* Samuel Wheeler, Assistant Director of Admissions, 940-898-3188, Fax: 940-898-3081, E-mail: wheelersr@twu.edu.

TUI University, College of Health Sciences, Program in Health Sciences, Cypress, CA 90630. Offers clinical research administration (MS, Certificate); emergency and disaster management (MS, Certificate); environmental health science (Certificate); health care administration (PhD); health care management (MS), including health informatics; health education (MS, Certificate); health informatics (Certificate); health sciences (PhD); international health (MS); international health: educator or researcher option (PhD); international health: practitioner option (PhD); law and expert witness studies (MS, Certificate); public health (MS); quality assurance (Certificate). Part-time and evening/weekend programs available. Postbaccalaureate distance learning degree programs offered (no on-campus study). *Degree requirements:* For doctorate, comprehensive exam, thesis/dissertation, defense of dissertation. *Entrance requirements:* For master's, minimum GPA of 2.5 (students with GPA 3.0 or greater may transfer up to 30% of graduate level credits); for doctorate, minimum GPA of 3.4, curriculum vitae, course work in research methods or statistics. Additional exam requirements/recommendations for international students: Required—TOEFL. Electronic applications accepted.

Union University, School of Nursing, Jackson, TN 38305-3697. Offers executive leadership (DNP); nurse anesthesia (DNP); nurse anesthetist (PMC); nurse practitioner (DNP); nursing education (MSN, PMC). *Accreditation:* AACN; AANA/CANAEP. *Degree requirements:* For master's, thesis or alternative. *Entrance requirements:* For master's, GRE, 3 letters of reference, bachelor's degree in nursing, minimum GPA of 3.0. Additional exam requirements/recommendations for international students: Required—TOEFL (minimum score 560 paper-based; 220 computer-based). Electronic applications accepted. *Faculty research:* Children's health, occupational rehabilitation, informatics, health promotion.

University of Central Florida, College of Nursing, Orlando, FL 32816. Offers adult nurse practitioner (MSN, Post-Master's Certificate); clinical nurse leader (MSN, Post-Master's Certificate); clinical nurse specialist (MSN, Post-Master's Certificate); family nurse practitioner (MSN, Post-Master's Certificate); leadership and management (MSN); nurse educator (MSN); nursing (PhD); nursing education (Post-Master's Certificate); nursing practice (DNP); pediatric nurse practitioner (MSN, Post-Master's Certificate). *Accreditation:* AACN. Part-time and evening/weekend programs available. *Faculty:* 38 full-time (34 women), 49 part-time/adjunct (47 women). *Students:* 98 full-time (93 women), 371 part-time (350 women); includes 132 minority (63 African Americans, 2 American Indian/Alaska Native, 29 Asian Americans or Pacific Islanders, 38 Hispanic Americans), 9 international. Average age 39. 363 applicants, 49% accepted, 139 enrolled. In 2009, 72 master's, 3 doctorates, 8 other advanced degrees awarded. *Degree requirements:* For master's, thesis or alternative. *Entrance requirements:* For master's, GRE General Test, minimum GPA of 3.0 in last 60 hours. Additional exam requirements/recommendations for international students: Required—TOEFL. *Application deadline:* For fall admission, 2/15 for domestic students; for spring admission, 9/15 for domestic students. Application fee: $30. Electronic applications accepted. *Expenses:* Tuition, state resident: part-time $306.31 per credit hour. Tuition, nonresident: part-time $1099.01 per credit hour.

Nursing and Healthcare Administration

University of Central Florida (continued)

Part-time tuition and fees vary according to degree level and program. *Financial support:* In 2009–10, 30 students received support, including 30 fellowships with partial tuition reimbursements available (averaging $3,200 per year), 1 teaching assistantship with partial tuition reimbursement available (averaging $13,440 per year); research assistantships with partial tuition reimbursements available, career-related internships or fieldwork, Federal Work-Study, institutionally sponsored loans, traineeships, and unspecified assistantships also available. Financial award application deadline: 3/1; financial award applicants required to submit FAFSA. *Unit head:* Dr. Jean D. Leuner, Dean, 407-823-5496, Fax: 407-823-5675, E-mail: jleuner@mail.ucf.edu. *Application contact:* Dr. Jean D. Leuner, Dean, 407-823-5496, Fax: 407-823-5675, E-mail: jleuner@mail.ucf.edu.

University of Cincinnati, Graduate School, College of Nursing, Cincinnati, OH 45221-0038. Offers clinical nurse specialist (MSN), including adult health, community health, neonatal, nursing administration, occupational health, pediatric health, psychiatric nursing, women's health; nurse anesthesia (MSN); nurse midwifery (MSN); nurse practitioner (MSN), including acute care, ambulatory care, family, family/psychiatric, women's health; nursing (PhD); MBA/MSN. *Accreditation:* AACN; AANA/CANAEP (one or more programs are accredited); ACNM/DOA. Part-time programs available. Postbaccalaureate distance learning degree programs offered (no on-campus study). Terminal master's awarded for partial completion of doctoral program. *Degree requirements:* For master's, thesis or alternative; for doctorate, comprehensive exam, thesis/dissertation. *Entrance requirements:* For master's and doctorate, GRE General Test. Additional exam requirements/recommendations for international students: Required—TOEFL (minimum score 520 paper-based; 190 computer-based). Electronic applications accepted. *Faculty research:* Substance abuse, injury and violence, symptom management.

University of Colorado at Colorado Springs, Graduate School, Beth-El College of Nursing and Health Sciences, Colorado Springs, CO 80933-7150. Offers adult health nurse practitioner and clinical specialist (MSN); family practitioner (MSN), including community clinical specialist, forensic clinical specialist, holistic clinical specialist; neonatal nurse practitioner and clinical specialist (MSN); nursing administration (MSN); nursing practice (DNP); women nurse practitioner (MSN). *Accreditation:* AACN. Part-time programs available. Postbaccalaureate distance learning degree programs offered (minimal on-campus study). *Faculty:* 26 full-time (21 women), 3 part-time/adjunct (all women). *Students:* 132 full-time (112 women), 81 part-time (71 women); includes 35 minority (6 African Americans, 2 American Indian/Alaska Native, 6 Asian Americans or Pacific Islanders, 21 Hispanic Americans), 3 international. Average age 36. 245 applicants, 47% accepted, 58 enrolled. In 2009, 33 master's awarded. *Degree requirements:* For master's, comprehensive exam, thesis optional; for doctorate, capstone project. *Entrance requirements:* For master's, GRE General Test or MAT, BSN, minimum GPA of 3.0, unrestricted RN license; for doctorate, interview; active RN license; MA; minimum GPA of 3.3; National Certification as NP or CNS; portfolio. Additional exam requirements/recommendations for international students: Required—TOEFL. *Application deadline:* For fall admission, 6/1 priority date for domestic students; for spring admission, 11/15 for domestic students. Application fee: $60 ($75 for international students). Electronic applications accepted. *Expenses:* Contact institution. *Financial support:* Fellowships, career-related internships or fieldwork, Federal Work-Study, and scholarships/grants available. Support available to part-time students. Financial award application deadline: 3/1; financial award applicants required to submit FAFSA. *Faculty research:* Women's health, uncertainty, empowerment, family experience in chronic illness. Total annual research expenditures: $703,545. *Unit head:* Dr. Nancy Smith, Dean, 719-255-4411, Fax: 719-255-4416, E-mail: nsmith2@uccs.edu. *Application contact:* Jackie Crouch, Graduate Recruitment Coordinator, 719-255-4493, Fax: 719-255-4416, E-mail: jcrouch@uccs.edu.

University of Delaware, College of Health Sciences, School of Nursing, Newark, DE 19716. Offers adult nurse practitioner (MSN, PMC); cardiopulmonary clinical nurse specialist (MSN, PMC); cardiopulmonary clinical nurse specialist/adult nurse practitioner (MSN, PMC); family nurse practitioner (MSN, PMC); gerontology clinical nurse specialist (MSN, PMC); gerontology clinical nurse specialist geriatric nurse practitioner (PMC); gerontology clinical nurse specialist/geriatric nurse practitioner (MSN); health services administration (MSN, PMC); nursing of children clinical nurse specialist (MSN, PMC); nursing of children clinical nurse specialist/pediatric nurse practitioner (MSN, PMC); oncology/immune deficiency clinical nurse specialist (MSN, PMC); oncology/immune deficiency clinical nurse specialist/adult nurse practitioner (MSN, PMC); perinatal/women's health clinical nurse specialist (MSN, PMC); perinatal/women's health clinical nurse specialist/women's health nurse practitioner (MSN, PMC); psychiatric nursing clinical nurse specialist (MSN, PMC). *Accreditation:* AACN; NLN (one or more programs are accredited). Part-time and evening/weekend programs available. Postbaccalaureate distance learning degree programs offered (minimal on-campus study). *Degree requirements:* For master's, thesis optional. *Entrance requirements:* For master's, BSN, interview, RN license. Electronic applications accepted. *Faculty research:* Marriage and chronic illness, health promotion, congestive heart failure patient outcomes, school nursing, diabetes in children, culture, health disparities, cardiovascular, prison nursing, oncology, public policy, child obesity, smoking and teen pregnancy, blood pressure measurements, men's health.

University of Hawaii at Manoa, Graduate Division, School of Nursing and Dental Hygiene, Honolulu, HI 96822. Offers clinical nurse specialist (MS), including adult health, community mental health; nurse practitioner (MS), including adult health, community mental health, family nurse practitioner; nursing (PhD, Graduate Certificate); nursing administration (MS). *Accreditation:* AACN; NLN (one or more programs are accredited). Part-time programs available. Postbaccalaureate distance learning degree programs offered (minimal on-campus study). *Faculty:* 20 full-time (18 women), 16 part-time/adjunct (15 women). *Students:* 81 full-time (69 women), 135 part-time (121 women); includes 115 minority (4 African Americans, 2 American Indian/Alaska Native, 105 Asian Americans or Pacific Islanders, 4 Hispanic Americans), 2 international. Average age 38. 189 applicants, 52% accepted, 79 enrolled. In 2009, 25 master's, 4 doctorates awarded. *Degree requirements:* For master's, thesis optional; for doctorate, comprehensive exam, thesis/dissertation. *Entrance requirements:* For master's, Hawaii RN license. Additional exam requirements/recommendations for international students: Required—TOEFL (minimum score 580 paper-based; 237 computer-based; 92 iBT), IELTS (minimum score 5). *Application deadline:* For fall admission, 2/1 for domestic and international students. Application fee: $60. *Expenses:* Contact institution. *Financial support:* In 2009–10, 6 students received support, including 28 fellowships (averaging $960 per year), 7 research assistantships (averaging $18,080 per year). Total annual research expenditures: $1.8 million. *Unit head:* Mary Boland, Dean, 808-956-8522, Fax: 808-956-3257, E-mail: mgboland@hawaii.edu. *Application contact:* Kristine Qureshi, Graduate Chair, 808-956-8744, Fax: 808-956-3257, E-mail: kqureshi@hawaii.edu.

University of Illinois at Chicago, Graduate College, College of Nursing, Program in Nursing, Chicago, IL 60607-7128. Offers acute care clinical nurse specialist (MS); acute care nurse practitioner (MS); administrative studies in nursing (MS); adult nurse practitioner (MS); adult/geriatric nurse practitioner (MS); advanced community health nurse specialist (MS); family nurse practitioner (MS); geriatric clinical nurse specialist (MS); geriatric nurse practitioner (MS); mental health clinical nurse specialist (MS); mental health nurse practitioner (MS); nurse midwifery (MS); occupational health/advanced community health nurse specialist (MS); occupational health/family nurse practitioner (MS); pediatric clinical nurse specialist (MS); pediatric nurse practitioner (MS); perinatal clinical nurse specialist (MS); school/advanced community health nurse specialist (MS); school/family nurse practitioner (MS); women's health nurse practitioner (MS). *Accreditation:* AACN. Part-time programs available. *Degree requirements:* For master's, thesis or alternative. *Entrance requirements:* For master's, GRE General Test, minimum GPA of 2.75. Additional exam requirements/recommendations for international students: Required—TOEFL. Electronic applications accepted.

University of Indianapolis, Graduate Programs, School of Nursing, Indianapolis, IN 46227-3697. Offers family practice (post-RN) (MSN); gerontological nurse practitioner (MSN); nurse-midwifery (MSN); nursing (MSN); nursing administration (MSN); nursing education (MSN); MBA/MSN. *Accreditation:* AACN; ACNM. *Faculty:* 4 full-time (3 women), 2 part-time/adjunct (both women). *Students:* 27 full-time (26 women), 118 part-time (109 women); includes 10 minority (6 African Americans, 1 American Indian/Alaska Native, 1 Asian American or Pacific Islander, 2 Hispanic Americans), 2 international. Average age 38. *Entrance requirements:* For master's, minimum GPA of 3.0, interview, letters of recommendation, resume, IN nursing license, 1 year professional practice. Additional exam requirements/recommendations for international students: Required—TOEFL (minimum score 550 paper-based; 213 computer-based). *Application deadline:* For fall admission, 8/1 for domestic students; for winter admission, 12/15 for domestic students; for spring admission, 4/15 for domestic students. Applications are processed on a rolling basis. Application fee: $50. *Financial support:* Federal Work-Study available. *Unit head:* Dr. Anne Thomas, Dean, 317-788-3206, E-mail: athomas@uindy.edu. *Application contact:* T. C. Crum, Information Contact, 317-788-2128, Fax: 317-788-3542, E-mail: tcrum@uindy.edu.

The University of Kansas, University of Kansas Medical Center, School of Nursing, Kansas City, KS 66160. Offers clinical research management (PMC); family nurse practitioner (PMC); health care informatics (PMC); health professions educator (PMC); nurse midwife (PMC); nursing (MS, DNP, PhD); organizational leadership (PMC); psychiatric/mental health nurse practitioner (PMC); public health nursing (PMC). *Accreditation:* AACN; ACNM/DOA. Part-time programs available. Postbaccalaureate distance learning degree programs offered (minimal on-campus study). *Faculty:* 65. *Students:* 59 full-time (56 women), 309 part-time (285 women); includes 37 minority (17 African Americans, 4 American Indian/Alaska Native, 7 Asian Americans or Pacific Islanders, 9 Hispanic Americans), 10 international. Average age 38. 138 applicants, 59% accepted, 82 enrolled. In 2009, 78 master's, 3 doctorates awarded. Terminal master's awarded for partial completion of doctoral program. *Degree requirements:* For master's, thesis optional, general oral exam; for doctorate, one foreign language, thesis/dissertation, comprehensive oral and written exam. *Entrance requirements:* For master's, bachelor's degree in nursing, minimum GPA of 3.0, RN license, 1 year of clinical experience; for doctorate, GRE General Test, master's degree in nursing, minimum GPA of 3.5. Additional exam requirements/recommendations for international students: Required—TOEFL. *Application deadline:* For fall admission, 4/1 for domestic students; for spring admission, 9/1 for domestic students. Application fee: $60. Electronic applications accepted. *Expenses:* Tuition, state resident: full-time $6492; part-time $270.50 per credit hour. Tuition, nonresident: full-time $15,510; part-time $646.25 per credit hour. Required fees: $847; $70.56 per credit hour. Tuition and fees vary according to course load and program. *Financial support:* In 2009–10, 93 students received support, including 7 research assistantships (averaging $24,000 per year), 23 teaching assistantships with full and partial tuition reimbursements available (averaging $24,000 per year); traineeships also available. Financial award application deadline: 2/14; financial award applicants required to submit FAFSA. *Faculty research:* Breastfeeding practices of teen mothers, national database of nursing quality indicators, caregiving of families of patients using technology in the home, self care talk intervention partnership between caregivers of stroke survivors and nurses, smoking cessation. Total annual research expenditures: $5 million. *Unit head:* Dr. Karen L. Miller, Dean, 913-588-1601, Fax: 913-588-1660, E-mail: kmiller@kumc.edu. *Application contact:* Dr. Rita K. Clifford, Associate Dean, Student Affairs, 913-588-1619, Fax: 913-588-1615, E-mail: rcliffor@kumc.edu.

University of Mary, Division of Nursing, Bismarck, ND 58504-9652. Offers family nurse practitioner (MSN); nurse administrator (MSN); nursing educator (MSN). *Accreditation:* AACN. Part-time and evening/weekend programs available. Postbaccalaureate distance learning degree programs offered (minimal on-campus study). *Degree requirements:* For master's, comprehensive exam, thesis (for some programs), internship (family nurse practitioner), teaching practice. *Entrance requirements:* For master's, minimum GPA of 3.0 in nursing, interview, letters of recommendation. Additional exam requirements/recommendations for international students: Required—TOEFL. Electronic applications accepted. *Expenses:* Tuition: Full-time $10,062; part-time $430 per credit. Tuition and fees vary according to course load, degree level, program and student level. *Faculty research:* Gerontology issues, rural nursing, health policy, primary care, women's health.

University of Maryland, Baltimore, Graduate School, School of Nursing, Master's Program in Nursing, Baltimore, MD 21201. Offers community health nursing (MS); gerontological nursing (MS); maternal-child nursing (MS); medical-surgical nursing (MS); nurse-midwifery education (MS); nursing administration (MS); nursing education (MS); nursing health policy (MS); primary care nursing (MS); psychiatric nursing (MS); MS/MBA. *Accreditation:* AACN; AANA/CANAEP; ACNM/DOA; NLN (one or more programs are accredited). Part-time programs available. *Students:* 387 full-time (338 women), 528 part-time (491 women); includes 330 minority (230 African Americans, 3 American Indian/Alaska Native, 81 Asian Americans or Pacific Islanders, 16 Hispanic Americans), 10 international. Average age 36. 849 applicants, 40% accepted, 255 enrolled. In 2009, 264 master's awarded. *Degree requirements:* For master's, comprehensive exam (for some programs), thesis or alternative. *Entrance requirements:* For master's, GRE General Test, minimum GPA of 2.75, course work in statistics, BS in nursing. Additional exam requirements/recommendations for international students: Required—TOEFL (minimum score 550 paper-based; 80 iBT), or IELTS (minimum score 7). *Application deadline:* For fall admission, 1/15 for international students. Application fee: $50. Electronic applications accepted. *Expenses:* Tuition, state resident: full-time $7290; part-time $405 per credit hour. Tuition, nonresident: full-time $12,780; part-time $710 per credit hour. Required fees: $774; $10 per credit hour. $297 per semester. Tuition and fees vary according to course load, degree level and program. *Financial support:* Fellowships, research assistantships, teaching assistantships, career-related internships or fieldwork and traineeships available. Support available to part-time students. Financial award application deadline: 2/15; financial award applicants required to submit FAFSA. *Unit head:* Dr. Jane Kapustin, Assistant Dean, 410-706-6741, Fax: 410-706-4231. *Application contact:* Marjorie Fass, Admissions Director, 410-706-0501, Fax: 410-706-7238.

University of Massachusetts Lowell, School of Health and Environment, Department of Nursing, Program in Nursing, Lowell, MA 01854-2881. Offers PhD. *Accreditation:* AACN. *Degree requirements:* For doctorate, thesis/dissertation, qualifying examination. *Entrance requirements:* For doctorate, GRE General Test, master's degree in nursing with minimum GPA of 3.3, current MA RN license, 2 years of professional nursing experience, 3 letters of recommendation.

University of Michigan, Horace H. Rackham School of Graduate Studies, School of Nursing, Division of Nursing Business and Health Systems, Ann Arbor, MI 48109. Offers MS, MBA/MS, MHSA/MS, MS/MSI. MS/MSI offered with School of Information. *Accreditation:* AACN. Part-time and evening/weekend programs available. Postbaccalaureate distance learning degree programs offered (minimal on-campus study). *Degree requirements:* For master's, thesis. *Entrance requirements:* For master's, GRE General Test (if GPA less than 3.23), minimum GPA of 3.0. Electronic applications accepted. *Expenses:* Tuition, state resident: full-time $17,286; part-time $1099 per credit hour. Tuition, nonresident: full-time $34,944; part-time $2080 per credit hour. Required fees: $95 per semester. Tuition and fees vary according to course load, degree level and program. *Faculty research:* Outcomes research, nursing language, change management and innovation, nurse staffing, and informatics.

University of Minnesota, Twin Cities Campus, Graduate School, School of Nursing, Program in Nursing and Health Care Systems Administration, Minneapolis, MN 55455-0213. Offers MS. *Accreditation:* AACN. Part-time programs available. *Degree requirements:* For master's, final oral exam, project or thesis. *Entrance requirements:* Additional exam requirements/recommendations for international students: Required—TOEFL (minimum score 586 paper-based; 240 computer-based).

University of Missouri–Kansas City, School of Nursing, Kansas City, MO 64110-2499. Offers adult clinical nurse specialist (MSN), including adult nurse practitioner, women's health nurse practitioner; family nurse practitioner (MSN); neonatal nurse practitioner (MSN); nurse educator (MSN); nurse executive (MSN); nursing (PhD); nursing practice (DNP); pediatric nurse practitioner (MSN). *Accreditation:* AACN. Part-time programs available. Postbaccalaureate

distance learning degree programs offered (minimal on-campus study). *Faculty:* 36 full-time (30 women), 40 part-time/adjunct (all women). *Students:* 31 full-time (26 women), 310 part-time (287 women); includes 38 minority (17 African Americans, 2 American Indian/Alaska Native, 10 Asian Americans or Pacific Islanders, 9 Hispanic Americans). Average age 36. 151 applicants, 72% accepted, 109 enrolled. In 2009, 57 master's, 10 doctorates awarded. *Degree requirements:* For master's, thesis or alternative. *Entrance requirements:* For master's, minimum undergraduate GPA of 3.2; for doctorate, GRE, 3 letters of reference, interview by invitation. Additional exam requirements/recommendations for international students: Required—TOEFL (minimum score 550 paper-based; 213 computer-based; 80 iBT). *Application deadline:* For fall admission, 2/1 priority date for domestic and international students; for spring admission, 9/1 priority date for domestic and international students. Application fee: $45 ($50 for international students). *Expenses:* Tuition, state resident: full-time $5378; part-time $299 per credit hour. Tuition, nonresident: full-time $13,881; part-time $771 per credit hour. Required fees: $641; $71 per credit hour. Tuition and fees vary according to course load and program. *Financial support:* In 2009–10, 6 teaching assistantships with partial tuition reimbursements (averaging $4,402 per year) were awarded; fellowships, research assistantships, career-related internships or fieldwork, Federal Work-Study, institutionally sponsored loans, and tuition waivers (full and partial) also available. Support available to part-time students. Financial award application deadline: 3/1; financial award applicants required to submit FAFSA. *Faculty research:* Geriatrics/gerontology, children's pain, neonatology, Alzheimer's care, cancer caregivers. Total annual research expenditures: $2.1 million. *Unit head:* Dr. Lora Lacey-Haun, Dean, 816-235-1700, Fax: 816-235-1701, E-mail: lacey-haunc@umkc.edu. *Application contact:* Leah Wilder, Coordinator for Admissions and Recruitment, 816-235-5768, Fax: 816-235-1701, E-mail: wilderl@umkc.edu.

The University of North Carolina at Chapel Hill, School of Nursing, Chapel Hill, NC 27599-7460. Offers nursing (MSN, PhD, PMC), including adult nurse practitioner (MSN, PMC), children's health advanced practice (MSN, PMC), family nurse practitioner (MSN, PMC), health care systems (MSN, PMC), psychiatric/mental health nursing (MSN, PMC), women's health nursing (MSN, PMC). *Accreditation:* AACN; NLN (one or more programs are accredited). Part-time programs available. *Degree requirements:* For master's, comprehensive exam, thesis; for doctorate, thesis/dissertation, 3 exams. *Entrance requirements:* For master's and doctorate, GRE General Test. *Faculty research:* Chronic illness, parenting, cardiovascular health in children, elderly, HIV-AIDS.

The University of North Carolina at Greensboro, Graduate School, School of Nursing, Greensboro, NC 27412-5001. Offers adult clinical nurse specialist (MSN, PMC); adult/gerontological nurse practitioner (MSN, PMC); nurse anesthesia (MSN, PMC); nursing (PhD); nursing administration (MSN); nursing education (MSN); MSN/MBA. *Accreditation:* AACN; AANA/CANAEP; NLN. *Degree requirements:* For master's, thesis or alternative. *Entrance requirements:* For master's, GRE General Test or MAT, BSN, clinical experience, liability insurance, RN license; for PMC, liability insurance, MSN, RN license. Additional exam requirements/recommendations for international students: Required—TOEFL. Electronic applications accepted.

University of Pennsylvania, School of Nursing, Health Leadership Program, Philadelphia, PA 19104. Offers MSN. *Accreditation:* AACN. Part-time programs available. *Students:* 9 full-time (all women), 20 part-time (19 women); includes 4 minority (3 African Americans, 1 Hispanic American). In 2009, 7 master's awarded. *Entrance requirements:* For master's, GRE General Test, BSN, minimum GPA of 3.0, previous course work in statistics, 1 year of clinical experience in area of interest. Additional exam requirements/recommendations for international students: Required—TOEFL. *Application deadline:* For fall admission, 2/15 priority date for domestic students. Applications are processed on a rolling basis. Application fee: $70. *Expenses:* Contact institution. *Financial support:* Teaching assistantships, career-related internships or fieldwork, Federal Work-Study, and institutionally sponsored loans available. Support available to part-time students. Financial award application deadline: 4/1. *Faculty research:* Payment structures for nurse practitioners, delirium in older adults.

University of Pennsylvania, School of Nursing, Program in Nursing and Health Care Administration, Philadelphia, PA 19104. Offers MSN, PhD, MBA/MSN. *Accreditation:* AACN. Part-time programs available. *Students:* 3 full-time (all women), 19 part-time (15 women); includes 3 minority (1 African American, 1 Asian American or Pacific Islander, 1 Hispanic American). In 2009, 8 master's awarded. Terminal master's awarded for partial completion of doctoral program. *Degree requirements:* For doctorate, thesis/dissertation. *Entrance requirements:* For master's, GRE General Test, BSN, minimum GPA of 3.0, previous course work in statistics; for doctorate, GRE General Test, BSN or MSN, minimum GPA of 3.0. Additional exam requirements/recommendations for international students: Required—TOEFL. *Application deadline:* For fall admission, 2/15 priority date for domestic students. Applications are processed on a rolling basis. Application fee: $70. *Expenses:* Contact institution. *Financial support:* Research assistantships, teaching assistantships, career-related internships or fieldwork, Federal Work-Study, and institutionally sponsored loans available. Support available to part-time students. Financial award application deadline: 12/15. *Faculty research:* Nursing services and policy, home health services utilization.

University of Pittsburgh, School of Nursing, Nurse Specialty Role Program, Pittsburgh, PA 15260. Offers clinical nurse leader (MSN); nursing administration (MSN, DNP); nursing education (MSN); nursing informatics (MSN); nursing research (MSN). *Accreditation:* AACN. Part-time programs available. *Students:* 8 full-time (all women), 47 part-time (46 women); includes 5 minority (1 African American, 4 Asian Americans or Pacific Islanders). Average age 42. 16 applicants, 94% accepted, 13 enrolled. In 2009, 12 master's awarded. *Degree requirements:* For master's, comprehensive exam, thesis optional. *Entrance requirements:* For master's, GRE or MAT, BSN, RN license, letters of recommendation, resume, course work in statistics, 1-3 years of nursing experience. Additional exam requirements/recommendations for international students: Required—TOEFL (minimum score 550 paper-based; 213 computer-based; 80 iBT). *Application deadline:* For fall admission, 8/1 priority date for domestic students; for spring admission, 12/1 priority date for domestic students. Applications are processed on a rolling basis. Application fee: $50. Electronic applications accepted. *Expenses:* Tuition, state resident: full-time $16,402; part-time $665 per credit. Tuition, nonresident: full-time $28,694; part-time $1175 per credit. Required fees: $690; $175 per term. Tuition and fees vary according to program. *Unit head:* Dr. Helen Burns, Associate Dean for Clinical Education, 412-624-6616, Fax: 412-624-2401, E-mail: burnsh@pitt.edu. *Application contact:* Laurie Lapsley, Administrator of Graduate Student Services, 412-624-9670, Fax: 412-624-2409, E-mail: lapsleyl@pitt.edu.

University of Rhode Island, Graduate School, College of Nursing, Kingston, RI 02881. Offers administration (MS); clinical nurse leader (MS); clinical specialist in gerontology (MS); clinical specialist in psychiatric/mental health (MS); family nurse practitioner (MS); gerontological nurse practitioner (MS); nursing (DNP, PhD); nursing education (MS). *Accreditation:* AACN; ACNM/DOA (one or more programs are accredited). Part-time programs available. *Faculty:* 28 full-time (27 women), 3 part-time/adjunct (all women). *Students:* 21 full-time (20 women), 74 part-time (71 women); includes 3 minority (1 African American, 2 Asian Americans or Pacific Islanders), 5 international. In 2009, 29 master's, 2 doctorates awarded. *Degree requirements:* For master's, comprehensive exam; for doctorate, comprehensive exam, thesis/dissertation. *Entrance requirements:* For master's, GRE or MAT, 2 letters of recommendation, scholarly papers; for doctorate, GRE, 3 letters of recommendation, scholarly papers. Additional exam requirements/recommendations for international students: Required—TOEFL (minimum score 550 paper-based; 213 computer-based). *Application deadline:* For fall admission, 4/15 for domestic students, 2/1 for international students; for spring admission, 11/15 for domestic students, 7/15 for international students. Application fee: $65. Electronic applications accepted. *Expenses:* Tuition, state resident: full-time $8828; part-time $490 per credit hour. Tuition, nonresident: full-time $22,100; part-time $1228 per credit hour. Required fees: $1118; $57 per semester. Tuition and fees vary according to program. *Financial support:* In 2009–10, 3 teaching assistantships with full and partial tuition reimbursements (averaging $8,428 per year) were awarded. Financial award application deadline: 4/15; financial award applicants required to submit FAFSA. *Faculty research:* Group intervention for grieving women in prison, translating Best Practice in non-drug interventions for postoperative pain management, further development and testing of the pain assessment inventory, preschool motor and functional performance of two cohorts, neuroactivation of brain motor areas in preterm children. Total annual research expenditures: $926,949. *Unit head:* Dr. Dayle Joseph, Dean, 401-874-2766, Fax: 401-874-2061, E-mail: dayle@uri.edu. *Application contact:* Dr. Mary C. Sullivan, Director of Graduate Studies, 401-874-5339, Fax: 401-874-2061, E-mail: mcsullivan@uri.edu.

University of Rochester, School of Nursing, Rochester, NY 14642. Offers acute care nurse practitioner (MS); adult nurse practitioner (MS); adult psychiatric mental health nurse practitioner (MS); adult/geriatric nurse practitioner (MS); care of children and families/pediatric nurse practitioner (MS); care of children and families/pediatric nurse practitioner with pediatric behavioral health (MS); care of children and families/pediatric nurse practitioner/neonatal nurse practitioner (MS); child and adolescent psychiatric mental health nurse practitioner (MS); clinical nurse leader (MS); disaster response and emergency preparedness (MS); family nurse practitioner (MS); health care organization management and leadership (MS); health practice research (PhD); health promotion, education and technology (MS); nursing (Certificate). *Accreditation:* AACN; NLN (one or more programs are accredited). Part-time programs available. Postbaccalaureate distance learning degree programs offered (minimal on-campus study). *Faculty:* 26 full-time (24 women), 20 part-time/adjunct (15 women). *Students:* 50 full-time (45 women), 178 part-time (165 women); includes 33 minority (17 African Americans, 2 American Indian/Alaska Native, 10 Asian Americans or Pacific Islanders, 4 Hispanic Americans), 11 international. Average age 35. 56 applicants, 80% accepted, 35 enrolled. In 2009, 53 master's, 5 doctorates awarded. Terminal master's awarded for partial completion of doctoral program. *Degree requirements:* For master's, comprehensive exam or thesis; for doctorate, thesis/dissertation. *Entrance requirements:* For master's, BS in nursing, minimum GPA of 3.0, course work in statistics; for doctorate, GRE General Test, MS in nursing, minimum GPA of 3.5; for Certificate, MS in nursing. Additional exam requirements/recommendations for international students: Recommended—TOEFL (minimum score 560 paper-based; 230 computer-based; 88 iBT). *Application deadline:* For fall admission, 11/1 priority date for domestic and international students. Application fee: $50. *Financial support:* In 2009–10, 53 students received support, including 14 fellowships with full and partial tuition reimbursements available (averaging $17,497 per year); scholarships/grants, traineeships, health care benefits, tuition waivers (partial), and unspecified assistantships also available. Support available to part-time students. Financial award application deadline: 6/30. *Faculty research:* Clinical research in aging, managing asthma in children, interventions to improve outcomes in critically ill children and their mothers, nurse home visitation studies, medical device evaluation, critical care clinical studies, high risk behavior and prevention, palliative care, pregnancy-related weight gain. Total annual research expenditures: $4.8 million. *Unit head:* Dr. Kathy P. Parker, Dean, 585-273-5639, Fax: 585-273-1268, E-mail: kathy_parker@urmc.rochester.edu. *Application contact:* Elaine Andolina, Director of Admissions, 585-275-2375, Fax: 585-756-8299, E-mail: elaine_andolina@urmc.rochester.edu.

University of San Diego, Hahn School of Nursing and Health Science, San Diego, CA 92110-2492. Offers adult nurse practitioner/family nurse practitioner (MSN); adult-gerontology clinical nurse specialist (MSN); clinical nursing (MSN); entry-level nursing (for non-RNs) (MSN); executive nurse leader (MSN); family nurse practitioner (MSN); nursing (PhD); nursing practice (DNP); pediatric nurse practitioner/family nurse practitioner (MSN); psychiatric-mental health nurse practitioner (MSN). *Accreditation:* AACN. Part-time and evening/weekend programs available. *Faculty:* 18 full-time (17 women), 25 part-time/adjunct (22 women). *Students:* 141 full-time (117 women), 173 part-time (152 women); includes 95 minority (20 African Americans, 9 American Indian/Alaska Native, 45 Asian Americans or Pacific Islanders, 21 Hispanic Americans), 7 international. Average age 38. 404 applicants, 50% accepted, 132 enrolled. In 2009, 103 master's, 10 doctorates awarded. *Degree requirements:* For doctorate, thesis/dissertation (for some programs), residency (DNP). *Entrance requirements:* For master's, GRE General Test (entry-level nursing), BSN, current California RN licensure (except for entry-level nursing); minimum GPA of 3.0; for doctorate, minimum GPA of 3.5, MSN, current California RN licensure. Additional exam requirements/recommendations for international students: Required—TOEFL (minimum score 580 paper-based; 237 computer-based; 83 iBT), TWE. *Application deadline:* For fall admission, 3/1 priority date for domestic students, 3/1 for international students; for spring admission, 11/1 priority date for domestic students, 11/1 for international students. Applications are processed on a rolling basis. Application fee: $45. Electronic applications accepted. *Expenses:* Tuition: Full-time $21,042; part-time $1169 per unit. Required fees: $224. Full-time tuition and fees vary according to course load and degree level. *Financial support:* In 2009–10, 270 students received support. Scholarships/grants and traineeships available. Support available to part-time students. Financial award application deadline: 4/1; financial award applicants required to submit FAFSA. *Faculty research:* Health promotion, decision making, psychogeriatric nursing, historical nursing, leadership behavior. *Unit head:* Dr. Sally Hardin, Dean, 619-260-4550, Fax: 619-260-6814. *Application contact:* Dr. John Mosby, Associate Director of Graduate Admissions, 619-260-4524, Fax: 619-260-4158, E-mail: grads@sandiego.edu.

University of San Francisco, School of Nursing, Program in Nursing Practice, San Francisco, CA 94117-1080. Offers family nurse practitioner (DNP); healthcare systems leadership (DNP). *Faculty:* 2 full-time (both women), 5 part-time/adjunct (4 women). *Students:* 29 full-time (25 women), 24 part-time (22 women); includes 22 minority (7 African Americans, 12 Asian Americans or Pacific Islanders, 3 Hispanic Americans). Average age 47. 41 applicants, 59% accepted, 18 enrolled. In 2009, 9 doctorates awarded. *Entrance requirements:* For doctorate, nursing bachelor's degree, valid RN license in California. *Expenses:* Tuition: Full-time $19,710; part-time $1095 per unit. Part-time tuition and fees vary according to degree level, campus/location and program. *Financial support:* In 2009–10, 32 students received support. *Unit head:* Dr. Judith Karshmer, Dean, 415-422-6681, Fax: 415-422-6877, E-mail: nursing@usfca.edu. *Application contact:* Information Contact, 415-422-4723, Fax: 415-422-2217.

University of South Carolina, The Graduate School, College of Nursing, Program in Nursing Administration, Columbia, SC 29208. Offers MSN. *Accreditation:* AACN. Part-time programs available. *Degree requirements:* For master's, thesis or alternative. *Entrance requirements:* For master's, GRE General Test or MAT, BS in nursing, nursing license. Additional exam requirements/recommendations for international students: Required—TOEFL (minimum score 570 paper-based; 230 computer-based). Electronic applications accepted. *Faculty research:* System research, evidence based practice, breast cancer, violence.

University of Southern Mississippi, Graduate School, College of Health, School of Nursing, Hattiesburg, MS 39406-0001. Offers adult health nursing (MSN); community health nursing (MSN); ethics (PhD); family nurse practitioner (MSN); leadership (PhD); nursing service administration (MSN); policy analysis (PhD); psychiatric nursing (MSN). *Accreditation:* AACN. Part-time and evening/weekend programs available. *Faculty:* 17 full-time (16 women), 1 part-time/adjunct (0 women). *Students:* 63 full-time (57 women), 40 part-time (36 women); includes 23 minority (all African Americans). Average age 40. 69 applicants, 59% accepted, 37 enrolled. In 2009, 28 master's, 2 doctorates awarded. *Degree requirements:* For master's, comprehensive exam, thesis optional; for doctorate, comprehensive exam, thesis/dissertation. *Entrance requirements:* For master's, GRE General Test, minimum GPA of 2.75, nursing license, BS in nursing; for doctorate, GRE General Test, master's degree in nursing, minimum GPA of 3.5. Additional exam requirements/recommendations for international students: Required—TOEFL. *Application deadline:* For fall admission, 3/15 priority date for domestic students, 5/1 for international students. Applications are processed on a rolling basis. Application fee: $35. Electronic applications accepted. *Expenses:* Tuition, state resident: full-time $5096; part-time $284 per hour. Tuition, nonresident: full-time $13,052; part-time $726 per hour. Required fees: $402. Tuition and fees vary according to course level and course load. *Financial support:* In 2009–10, 14 research assistantships with full tuition reimbursements (averaging $12,577 per year) were awarded; teaching assistantships, Federal Work-Study and traineeships also available. Financial award application deadline: 3/15; financial award applicants required to submit FAFSA. *Faculty research:* Gerontology, caregivers, HIV, bereavement, pain, nursing leadership. *Unit head:* Dr. Katherine Nugent, Director and Associate Dean, 601-266-5500, Fax: 601-266-5927. *Application contact:* Dr. Anne Brock, Graduate Coordinator, 601-266-5500, Fax: 601-266-5927.

Nursing and Healthcare Administration

The University of Tennessee at Chattanooga, Graduate School, College of Health, Education and Professional Studies, School of Nursing, Chattanooga, TN 37403. Offers administration (MSN); certified nurse anesthetist (Post-Master's Certificate); education (MSN); family nurse practitioner (MSN, Post-Master's Certificate); health care informatics (Post-Master's Certificate); nurse anesthesia (MSN); nurse education (Post-Master's Certificate). *Accreditation:* AACN; AANA/CANAEP (one or more programs are accredited). *Faculty:* 4 full-time (all women). *Students:* 42 full-time (33 women), 53 part-time (38 women); includes 10 minority (5 African Americans, 1 American Indian/Alaska Native, 2 Asian Americans or Pacific Islanders, 2 Hispanic Americans). Average age 35. 13 applicants, 31% accepted, 3 enrolled. In 2009, 36 master's, 5 other advanced degrees awarded. *Degree requirements:* For master's, thesis optional, qualifying exams, professional project; for Post-Master's Certificate, thesis or alternative, practicum, seminar. *Entrance requirements:* For master's, GRE General Test, MAT, BSN, minimum GPA of 3.0, eligibility for Tennessee RN license, 1 year direct patient care experience; for Post-Master's Certificate, GRE General Test, MAT, MSN, minimum GPA of 3.0, eligibility for Tennessee RN license, one year of direct patient care experience. Additional exam requirements/recommendations for international students: Required—TOEFL (minimum score 550 paper-based; 213 computer-based; 79 iBT), IELTS (minimum score 6). *Application deadline:* For fall admission, 8/1 priority date for domestic students, 6/1 for international students; for spring admission, 12/1 priority date for domestic students, 10/1 for international students. Applications are processed on a rolling basis. Application fee: $35. Electronic applications accepted. *Expenses:* Tuition, state resident: full-time $5404; part-time $300 per credit hour. Tuition, nonresident: full-time $16,702; part-time $928 per credit hour. Required fees: $1150; $130 per credit hour. *Financial support:* Career-related internships or fieldwork and scholarships/grants available. Support available to part-time students. *Faculty research:* Diabetes in women, health care for elderly, alternative medicine, hypertension, nurse anesthesia. Total annual research expenditures: $1.5 million. *Unit head:* Dr. Kay R. Lindgren, Head, 423-425-4646, Fax: 423-425-4668, E-mail: kay-lindgren@utc.edu. *Application contact:* Dr. Stephanie Bellar, Dean of Graduate Studies, 423-425-4666, Fax: 423-425-5223, E-mail: stephanie-bellar@utc.edu.

The University of Texas at Arlington, Graduate School, School of Nursing, Arlington, TX 76019. Offers administration/supervision of nursing (MSN); nurse practitioner (MSN); nursing science (PhD); teaching of nursing (MSN). *Accreditation:* AACN. Part-time and evening/weekend programs available. *Faculty:* 12 full-time (all women), 8 part-time/adjunct (all women). *Students:* 59 full-time (52 women), 483 part-time (441 women); includes 151 minority (75 African Americans, 3 American Indian/Alaska Native, 32 Asian Americans or Pacific Islanders, 41 Hispanic Americans), 9 international. Average age 37. 227 applicants, 97% accepted, 130 enrolled. In 2009, 72 master's, 3 doctorates awarded. *Degree requirements:* For master's, comprehensive exam, thesis or project; for doctorate, comprehensive exam, thesis/dissertation, successful proposal defense. *Entrance requirements:* For master's, GRE General Test, minimum GPA of 3.0, Texas nursing license, minimum C in undergraduate statistics course, physical assessment course within last 3 years; for doctorate, GRE General Test, minimum undergraduate, graduate and statistics GPA of 3.0; Texas RN license; interview; 3 letters of reference, written statement of goals. Additional exam requirements/recommendations for international students: Required—TOEFL (minimum score 550 paper-based; 213 computer-based), IELTS (minimum score 7). *Application deadline:* For fall admission, 6/5 for domestic students, 4/3 for international students; for spring admission, 10/7 for domestic students, 9/5 for international students. Applications are processed on a rolling basis. Application fee: $40 ($70 for international students). *Financial support:* In 2009–10, 27 students received support, including 24 fellowships with partial tuition reimbursements available (averaging $3,000 per year), 6 research assistantships (averaging $7,992 per year), 7 teaching assistantships (averaging $10,080 per year); career-related internships or fieldwork and traineeships also available. Financial award application deadline: 6/1; financial award applicants required to submit FAFSA. *Faculty research:* Simulation in clinical education and practice, cultural diversity, vulnerable populations, substance abuse. *Unit head:* Dr. Elizabeth C. Poster, Dean, 817-272-2776, Fax: 817-272-5006, E-mail: poster@uta.edu. *Application contact:* Dr. Mary Schira, Graduate Advisor & Associate Dean, 817-272-2329, Fax: 817-272-2065, E-mail: schira@uta.edu.

The University of Texas at El Paso, Graduate School, School of Nursing, El Paso, TX 79968-0001. Offers evidence-based practice (Certificate); family nurse practitioner (MSN); health care leadership and management (Certificate); interdisciplinary health sciences (PhD); nurse clinical specialist (MSN); nursing (Post-Master's Certificate); nursing systems management (MSN). *Accreditation:* AACN. *Students:* 153 (124 women); includes 100 minority (11 African Americans, 1 American Indian/Alaska Native, 6 Asian Americans or Pacific Islanders, 82 Hispanic Americans), 5 international. Average age 34. 91 applicants, 49% accepted. In 2009, 33 master's awarded. *Degree requirements:* For master's, thesis optional; for doctorate, thesis/dissertation. *Entrance requirements:* For master's, GRE, minimum GPA of 3.0, course work in statistics, resume; for doctorate, GRE, letters of reference, relevant personal/professional experience, master's degree in health. Additional exam requirements/recommendations for international students: Required—TOEFL; Recommended—IELTS. *Application deadline:* For fall admission, 8/1 for domestic students, 3/1 for international students; for spring admission, 11/1 for domestic students, 9/1 for international students. Applications are processed on a rolling basis. Application fee: $45 ($80 for international students). Electronic applications accepted. *Financial support:* In 2009–10, research assistantships with partial tuition reimbursements (averaging $18,825 per year), teaching assistantships with partial tuition reimbursements (averaging $18,000 per year) were awarded; fellowships with partial tuition reimbursements, institutionally sponsored loans, scholarships/grants, health care benefits, tuition waivers (partial), and unspecified assistantships also available. Support available to part-time students. Financial award application deadline: 3/15; financial award applicants required to submit FAFSA. *Unit head:* Dr. Elias Provencio-Vasquez, Dean, 915-747-7273, Fax: 915-747-8266, E-mail: eprovenciovasquez@utep.edu. *Application contact:* Dr. Patricia D. Witherspoon, Dean of the Graduate School, 915-747-5491, Fax: 915-747-5788, E-mail: withersp@utep.edu.

The University of Texas at Tyler, College of Nursing and Health Sciences, Program in Nursing, Tyler, TX 75799-0001. Offers nurse practitioner (MSN); nursing (PhD); nursing administration (MSN); nursing education (MSN); MSN/MBA. *Accreditation:* AACN. Part-time and evening/weekend programs available. Postbaccalaureate distance learning degree programs offered (no on-campus study). *Faculty:* 15 full-time (all women). *Students:* 26 full-time (24 women), 158 part-time (139 women); includes 36 minority (17 African Americans, 3 American Indian/Alaska Native, 7 Asian Americans or Pacific Islanders, 9 Hispanic Americans). Average age 40. 51 applicants, 57% accepted, 15 enrolled. In 2009, 32 master's awarded. *Degree requirements:* For master's, comprehensive exam (for some programs), thesis (for some programs); for doctorate, thesis/dissertation. *Entrance requirements:* For master's, GRE General Test or MAT, GMAT, minimum undergraduate GPA of 3.0, course work in statistics, RN license, BSN. Additional exam requirements/recommendations for international students: Required—TOEFL (minimum score 79 computer-based). *Application deadline:* For fall admission, 8/17 priority date for domestic students, 7/1 priority date for international students; for spring admission, 12/21 priority date for domestic students, 11/1 priority date for international students. Applications are processed on a rolling basis. Application fee: $25 ($50 for international students). Electronic applications accepted. *Expenses:* Tuition, state resident: part-time $665 per semester hour. Tuition, nonresident: part-time $942 per semester hour. Part-time tuition and fees vary according to degree level and program. *Financial support:* In 2009–10, 15 students received support, including 1 fellowship (averaging $10,000 per year), 3 research assistantships (averaging $2,200 per year); institutionally sponsored loans and scholarships/grants also available. Financial award application deadline: 7/1; financial award applicants required to submit FAFSA. *Faculty research:* Psychosocial adjustment, aging, support/commitment of caregivers, psychological abuse and violence, hope/hopelessness, professional values, end of life care, suicidology, clinical supervision, workforce retention and issues, global health issues, health promotion. Total annual research expenditures: $258,200. *Unit head:* Dr. Susan Yarbrough, Assistant Dean, 903-566-1220, E-mail: syarbrou@mail.uttyl.edu. *Application contact:* Dr. Susan Yarbrough.

University of Victoria, Faculty of Graduate Studies, Faculty of Human and Social Development, School of Nursing, Victoria, BC V8W 2Y2, Canada. Offers advanced nursing practice (advanced practice leadership option) (MN); advanced nursing practice (nurse educator option) (MN); advanced nursing practice (nurse practitioner option) (MN); nursing (PhD). Part-time programs available. Postbaccalaureate distance learning degree programs offered (no on-campus study). *Entrance requirements:* Additional exam requirements/recommendations for international students: Required—TOEFL (minimum score 575 paper-based; 233 computer-based), IELTS (minimum score 7). Electronic applications accepted.

University of Virginia, School of Nursing, Charlottesville, VA 22903. Offers acute and specialty care (MSN); acute care nurse practitioner (MSN); clinical nurse leadership (MSN); community-public health leadership (MSN); nursing (DNP, PhD); psychiatric mental health counseling (MSN); MSN/MBA. *Accreditation:* AACN. Part-time programs available. *Faculty:* 50 full-time (47 women), 4 part-time/adjunct (3 women). *Students:* 158 full-time (135 women), 118 part-time (117 women); includes 41 minority (30 African Americans, 1 American Indian/Alaska Native, 4 Asian Americans or Pacific Islanders, 6 Hispanic Americans), 4 international. Average age 36. 302 applicants, 48% accepted, 106 enrolled. In 2009, 84 master's, 12 doctorates awarded. *Degree requirements:* For doctorate, comprehensive exam (for some programs), capstone project (DNP), dissertation (PhD). *Entrance requirements:* For master's, GRE General Test, MAT; for doctorate, GRE General Test. Additional exam requirements/recommendations for international students: Required—TOEFL, IELTS. *Application deadline:* Applications are processed on a rolling basis. Application fee: $60. Electronic applications accepted. *Expenses:* Contact institution. *Financial support:* Fellowships, research assistantships, teaching assistantships, Federal Work-Study and scholarships/grants available. Financial award applicants required to submit FAFSA. *Unit head:* Dorrie K. Fontaine, Dean, 434-924-0141, Fax: 434-982-1809. *Application contact:* Clay Hysell, Assistant Dean for Graduate Student Services, 434-924-0141, Fax: 434-982-1809, E-mail: nur-osa@virginia.edu.

University of West Florida, College of Professional Studies, Department of Professional and Community Leadership, Program in Administration, Pensacola, FL 32514-5750. Offers acquisition and contract administration (MSA); biomedical/pharmaceutical (MSA); criminal justice administration (MSA); database administration (MSA); education leadership (MSA); healthcare administration (MSA); human performance technology (MSA); leadership (MSA); nursing administration (MSA); public administration (MSA); software engineering administration (MSA). Part-time and evening/weekend programs available. Postbaccalaureate distance learning degree programs offered (no on-campus study). *Students:* 33 full-time (21 women), 168 part-time (97 women); includes 53 minority (32 African Americans, 2 American Indian/Alaska Native, 5 Asian Americans or Pacific Islanders, 14 Hispanic Americans), 1 international. Average age 34. 103 applicants, 74% accepted, 64 enrolled. In 2009, 47 master's awarded. *Entrance requirements:* For master's, GRE General Test, letter of intent, names of references. Additional exam requirements/recommendations for international students: Required—TOEFL (minimum score 550 paper-based; 213 computer-based). *Application deadline:* For fall admission, 6/1 for domestic students, 5/15 for international students; for spring admission, 11/1 for domestic students, 10/1 for international students. Applications are processed on a rolling basis. Application fee: $30. *Expenses:* Tuition, state resident: full-time $4982; part-time $260 per credit hour. Tuition, nonresident: full-time $20,059; part-time $919 per credit hour. Required fees: $1247; $52 per credit hour. *Financial support:* Unspecified assistantships available. Financial award application deadline: 4/15; financial award applicants required to submit FAFSA. *Unit head:* Dr. Karen Rasmussen, Chairperson, 850-474-2301, Fax: 850-474-2804. *Application contact:* Terry McCray, Assistant Director of Graduate Admissions, 850-473-7718, Fax: 850-473-7714, E-mail: gradadmissions@uwf.edu.

University of Wisconsin–Eau Claire, College of Nursing and Health Sciences, Program in Nursing, Eau Claire, WI 54702-4004. Offers adult health clinical nurse specialist (MSN); adult health in administration (MSN); adult health in education (MSN); adult health nurse practitioner (MSN); family health in administration (MSN); family health in education (MSN); family health nurse practitioner (MSN). Part-time programs available. *Faculty:* 15 full-time (14 women). *Students:* 34 full-time (32 women), 55 part-time (51 women); includes 1 minority (Asian American or Pacific Islander). Average age 35. 58 applicants, 59% accepted, 2 enrolled. In 2009, 32 master's awarded. Terminal master's awarded for partial completion of doctoral program. *Degree requirements:* For master's, thesis optional, 500-600 hours clinical practicum, oral and written exams. *Entrance requirements:* For master's, Wisconsin RN license, minimum GPA of 3.0, undergraduate statistics, course work in health assessment. Additional exam requirements/recommendations for international students: Required—TOEFL (minimum score 550 paper-based; 213 computer-based; 79 iBT). *Application deadline:* For fall admission, 1/15 priority date for domestic students, 6/1 priority date for international students; for spring admission, 11/1 priority date for international students. Applications are processed on a rolling basis. Application fee: $56. Electronic applications accepted. *Expenses:* Tuition, state resident: full-time $6705.90; part-time $372.55 per credit. Tuition, nonresident: full-time $16,771; part-time $931.74 per credit. Required fees: $925.50; $51.19 per credit. One-time fee: $56. *Financial support:* In 2009–10, 50 students received support, including 2 fellowships (averaging $500 per year); Federal Work-Study and unspecified assistantships also available. Financial award application deadline: 3/1; financial award applicants required to submit FAFSA. *Unit head:* Dr. Mary Zwygart-Stauffacher, Interim Dean, 715-836-5287, Fax: 715-836-5925, E-mail: zwygarmc@uwec.edu. *Application contact:* Kristina Anderson, Director of Admissions, 715-836-5415, Fax: 715-836-2409, E-mail: admissions@uwec.edu.

Ursuline College, School of Graduate Studies, Programs in Nursing, Pepper Pike, OH 44124-4398. Offers care management (MSN); nurse practitioner (MSN); nursing (DNP); nursing education (MSN); palliative care (MSN). *Accreditation:* AACN. Part-time programs available. *Faculty:* 2 full-time (both women), 2 part-time/adjunct (both women). *Students:* 1 (woman) full-time, 94 part-time (88 women); includes 12 minority (11 African Americans, 1 Asian American or Pacific Islander). Average age 39. 68 applicants, 78% accepted, 40 enrolled. In 2009, 22 master's awarded. *Degree requirements:* For master's, comprehensive exam. *Entrance requirements:* For master's, minimum undergraduate GPA of 3.0, bachelor's degree in nursing, eligibility for or current Ohio RN license. Additional exam requirements/recommendations for international students: Required—TOEFL (minimum score 500 paper-based; 173 computer-based). *Application deadline:* For fall admission, 8/1 priority date for domestic students. Applications are processed on a rolling basis. Application fee: $25. *Expenses:* Tuition: Full-time $14,544; part-time $808 per credit hour. Required fees: $230; $75 per semester. *Financial support:* In 2009–10, 11 students received support. Federal Work-Study available. Financial award application deadline: 3/1. *Unit head:* Dr. Janet Baker, Director, 440-864-8172, Fax: 440-684-6053. *Application contact:* Melanie Steele, Secretary, 440-646-8199, Fax: 440-684-6138, E-mail: gradsch@ursuline.edu.

Vanderbilt University, School of Nursing, Nashville, TN 37240. Offers adult acute care nurse practitioner (MSN); adult nurse practitioner/cardiovascular disease management and prevention (MSN); adult nurse practitioner/palliative care (MSN); clinical management (clinical nurse leader/specialist) (MSN); emergency nurse practitioner (MSN); family nurse practitioner (MSN); gerontology nurse practitioner (MSN); health systems management (MSN); neonatal nurse practitioner (MSN); nurse midwifery (MSN); nurse midwifery/family nurse practitioner (MSN); nursing informatics (MSN); nursing practice (DNP); nursing science (PhD); nutrition (MS); pediatric acute care nurse practitioner (MSN); pediatric primary care nurse practitioner (MSN); psychiatric-mental health nurse practitioner (MSN); women's health nurse practitioner (MSN), including urogynecology; women's health nurse practitioner/adult nurse practitioner (MSN); MSN/M Div; MSN/MTS. *Accreditation:* ACNM/DOA; NLN (one or more programs are accredited). Part-time programs available. Postbaccalaureate distance learning degree programs offered (minimal on-campus study). *Faculty:* 118 full-time (102 women), 429 part-time/adjunct (309 women). *Students:* 484 full-time (435 women), 319 part-time (284 women); includes 84 minority (55 African Americans, 4 American Indian/Alaska Native, 10 Asian Americans or Pacific Islanders, 15 Hispanic Americans), 16 international. Average age 32. 900 applicants, 65% accepted, 433 enrolled. In 2009, 303 master's, 1 doctorate awarded. *Degree requirements:* For doctorate, comprehensive exam, thesis/dissertation. *Entrance requirements:* For master's,

GRE General Test, minimum B average in undergraduate course work, 3 letters of recommendation; for doctorate, GRE General Test, interview, 3 letters of recommendation from doctorally-prepared faculty, MSN, essay. Additional exam requirements/recommendations for international students: Required—TOEFL. *Application deadline:* For fall admission, 12/1 priority date for domestic and international students. Applications are processed on a rolling basis. Application fee: $50. *Expenses:* Contact institution. *Financial support:* In 2009–10, 389 students received support, including 1 research assistantship (averaging $5,000 per year); teaching assistantships, scholarships/grants, health care benefits, and tuition waivers also available. Support available to part-time students. Financial award application deadline: 3/15; financial award applicants required to submit FAFSA. *Faculty research:* Lymphedema, palliative care and bereavement, health services research including workforce, safety and quality of care, gerontology, better birth outcomes including nutrition. Total annual research expenditures: $1.4 million. *Unit head:* Dr. Colleen Conway-Welch, Dean, 615-343-8776, Fax: 615-343-7711, E-mail: colleen.conway-welch@vanderbilt.edu. *Application contact:* Cheryl Feldner, Assistant Director of Admissions, 615-322-3800, Fax: 615-343-0333, E-mail: cheryl.feldner@vanderbilt.edu.

Villanova University, College of Nursing, Villanova, PA 19085-1699. Offers adult nurse practitioner (MSN, Post Master's Certificate); family nurse practitioner (MSN, Post Master's Certificate); health care administration (MSN); nurse anesthetist (MSN, Post Master's Certificate); nursing (PhD); nursing education (MSN, Post Master's Certificate); pediatric nurse practitioner (MSN, Post Master's Certificate). *Accreditation:* AACN; AANA/CANAEP. Part-time programs available. Postbaccalaureate distance learning degree programs offered (minimal on-campus study). *Faculty:* 15 full-time (all women), 3 part-time/adjunct (2 women). *Students:* 58 full-time (53 women), 188 part-time (164 women); includes 29 minority (13 African Americans, 1 American Indian/Alaska Native, 13 Asian Americans or Pacific Islanders, 2 Hispanic Americans), 3 international. Average age 33. 171 applicants, 70% accepted, 89 enrolled. In 2009, 32 master's, 1 doctorate awarded. *Degree requirements:* For master's, independent study project; for doctorate, comprehensive exam, thesis/dissertation. *Entrance requirements:* For master's, GRE or MAT, BSN, 1 year of recent nursing experience, physical assessment, course work in statistics; for doctorate, GRE, MSN. Additional exam requirements/recommendations for international students: Required—TOEFL. *Application deadline:* For fall admission, 7/1 priority date for domestic students, 7/1 for international students; for spring admission, 11/1 priority date for domestic students, 11/1 for international students. Applications are processed on a rolling basis. Application fee: $50. *Expenses:* Contact institution. *Financial support:* In 2009–10, 53 students received support, including 5 teaching assistantships with full tuition reimbursements available (averaging $13,100 per year); institutionally sponsored loans, scholarships/grants, traineeships, tuition waivers (full), and unspecified assistantships also available. Financial award application deadline: 3/1; financial award applicants required to submit FAFSA. *Faculty research:* Genetics, ethics, cognitive development of students, women with disabilities, nursing leadership. *Unit head:* Dr. Marguerite K. Schlag, Assistant Dean and Director, Graduate Program, 610-519-4907, Fax: 610-519-7650, E-mail: marguerite.schlag@villanova.edu. *Application contact:* Dean, Graduate School of Liberal Arts and Sciences.

Virginia Commonwealth University, Graduate School, School of Nursing, Richmond, VA 23284-9005. Offers adult health nursing (MS); child health nursing (MS); family health nursing (MS); health system (PhD); immunocompetence (PhD); nurse practitioner (MS, Certificate); nursing administration (MS), including clinical nurse manager, nurse executive; psychiatric-mental health nursing (MS); risk and resilience (PhD); women's health nursing (MS). *Accreditation:* NLN (one or more programs are accredited). Part-time and evening/weekend programs available. *Degree requirements:* For master's, thesis optional; for doctorate, thesis/dissertation. *Entrance requirements:* For master's, GRE General Test, BSN, minimum GPA of 2.8; for doctorate, GRE General Test.

Walden University, Graduate Programs, School of Nursing, Minneapolis, MN 55401. Offers education (MSN); informatics (MSN); leadership and management (MSN); nursing (Post-Master's Certificate), including nursing education, nursing informatics, nursing leadership and management. *Accreditation:* AACN. Part-time and evening/weekend programs available. Postbaccalaureate distance learning degree programs offered (no on-campus study). *Faculty:* 5 full-time, 105 part-time/adjunct. *Students:* 2,644 full-time (2,468 women), 805 part-time (755 women); includes 660 minority (430 African Americans, 23 American Indian/Alaska Native, 122 Asian Americans or Pacific Islanders, 85 Hispanic Americans), 34 international. Average age 44. In 2009, 624 master's, 1 other advanced degree awarded. *Entrance requirements:* For master's, bachelor's degree or equivalent in related field or RN; minimum GPA of 2.5. Additional exam requirements/recommendations for international students: Required—TOEFL (minimum score 550 paper-based; 213 computer-based), IELTS (minimum score 6.5), or Michigan English Language Assessment Battery (minimum score 82). *Application deadline:* Applications are processed on a rolling basis. Application fee: $50. Electronic applications accepted. *Expenses:* Tuition: Full-time $13,665; part-time $560 per credit. Required fees: $1375. Tuition and fees vary according to course load, degree level and program. *Financial support:* In 2009–10, 273 students received support; fellowships, Federal Work-Study, scholarships/grants, unspecified assistantships, and family tuition reduction, active duty/veteran tuition reduction, group tuition reduction, interest-free payment plans available. Support available to part-time students. Financial award applicants required to submit FAFSA. *Unit head:* Dr. Sara Torres, Associate Dean, 800-925-3368. *Application contact:* Jennifer Hall, Director of Enrollment, 866-4-WALDEN, E-mail: info@walden.edu.

Washington Adventist University, Program in Nursing—Business Leadership, Takoma Park, MD 20912. Offers MSN. Part-time programs available. *Students:* 1 (woman) full-time, 9 part-time (8 women); includes 8 minority (6 African Americans, 2 Asian Americans or Pacific Islanders). Average age 38. *Application deadline:* Applications are processed on a rolling basis. *Financial support:* Applicants required to submit FAFSA. *Unit head:* Dr. Davenia Lea, Dean of School of Graduate and Professional Studies, E-mail: dlea@wau.edu. *Application contact:* Rahneeka Hazelton, Director, 301-891-4092, E-mail: rhazelto@wau.edu.

Waynesburg University, Graduate and Professional Studies, Waynesburg, PA 15370-1222. Offers business (MBA), including finance, health systems, human resources, leadership, market development; counseling (MA), including addictions counseling, clinical mental health; education (MAT); nursing (MSN), including administration, education, informatics, palliative care; nursing practice (DNP); special education (M Ed); technology (M Ed); MSN/MBA. *Accreditation:* AACN. Part-time and evening/weekend programs available. *Faculty:* 11 full-time (5 women), 136 part-time/adjunct (80 women). *Students:* 116 full-time (85 women), 984 part-time (682 women). 711 applicants, 80% accepted, 485 enrolled. In 2009, 320 master's, 41 doctorates awarded. *Degree requirements:* For doctorate, thesis/dissertation. *Entrance requirements:* Additional exam requirements/recommendations for international students: Required—TOEFL. *Application deadline:* For fall admission, 8/1 priority date for domestic students. Applications are processed on a rolling basis. Electronic applications accepted. *Expenses:* Tuition: Part-time $520 per credit. Financial support: Available to part-time students. Application deadline: 5/1. *Unit head:* David Mariner, Dean, 724-743-4420, Fax: 724-743-4425, E-mail: dmariner@waynesburg.edu. *Application contact:* Michael Bednarski, Director of Admissions, 724-743-4420, Fax: 724-743-4425, E-mail: mbednars@waynesburg.edu.

West Chester University of Pennsylvania, Office of Graduate Studies, College of Health Sciences, Department of Nursing, West Chester, PA 19383. Offers administration (MSN); integrative health (MSN); nursing education (MSN, Certificate); school nursing (Teaching Certificate). *Accreditation:* AACN. Part-time and evening/weekend programs available. *Students:* 3 full-time (all women), 34 part-time (33 women); includes 2 minority (1 African American, 1 Asian American or Pacific Islander). Average age 42. 15 applicants, 100% accepted, 10 enrolled. In 2009, 10 master's awarded. *Entrance requirements:* For master's, RN license, BSN, minimum GPA of 2.8, two years' full-time experience as a clinical care nurse, three letters of recommendation; for other advanced degree, BSN, RN license, minimum GPA of 3.0 in last 48 nursing credits. Additional exam requirements/recommendations for international students: Required—TOEFL (minimum score 550 paper-based; 213 computer-based; 80 iBT). *Application deadline:* For fall admission, 4/15 priority date for domestic students, 3/15 for international students; for spring admission, 10/15 for domestic students, 9/1 for international students. Applications are processed on a rolling basis. Application fee: $35. Electronic applications accepted. *Expenses:* Tuition, state resident: full-time $6666; part-time $370 per credit. Tuition, nonresident: full-time $10,666; part-time $593 per credit. Required fees: $122.56 per credit. *Financial support:* In 2009–10, 1 research assistantship with full and partial tuition reimbursement (averaging $5,000 per year) was awarded; unspecified assistantships also available. Support available to part-time students. Financial award application deadline: 2/15; financial award applicants required to submit FAFSA. *Faculty research:* Violence against women. *Unit head:* Dr. Charlotte Mackey, Chair, 610-436-3474, E-mail: cmackey@wcupa.edu. *Application contact:* Ann Coghlan Stowe, Graduate Coordinator, 610-436-2331, E-mail: astowe@wcupa.edu.

Wichita State University, Graduate School, College of Health Professions, School of Nursing, Wichita, KS 67260. Offers clinical nurse specialist (MSN); nurse midwifery (MSN); nurse practitioner (MSN); nursing and healthcare systems administration (MSN); nursing practice (DNP); MSN/MBA. *Accreditation:* AACN. Part-time programs available. *Expenses:* Tuition, state resident: full-time $4247; part-time $235.95 per credit hour. Tuition, nonresident: full-time $11,171; part-time $620.60 per credit hour. Required fees: $34; $3.60 per credit hour. $17 per term. Tuition and fees vary according to campus/location and program. *Faculty research:* Adolescent pregnancy, alcoholism, arthritis and chronic disease, health practices of elderly, diabetes. *Unit head:* Dr. Mary Koehn, Chairperson, 316-978-3610, Fax: 316-978-3025, E-mail: mary.koehn@wichita.edu. *Application contact:* Dr. Mary Koehn, Chairperson, 316-978-3610, Fax: 316-978-3025, E-mail: mary.koehn@wichita.edu.

Winona State University, College of Nursing and Health Sciences, Winona, MN 55987-5838. Offers adult nurse practitioner (MS, Post Master's Certificate); clinical nurse specialist (MS, Post Master's Certificate); family nurse practitioner (MS, Post Master's Certificate); nurse administrator (MS); nurse educator (MS, Post Master's Certificate); nursing (DNP). *Accreditation:* AACN. Part-time programs available. Postbaccalaureate distance learning degree programs offered (no on-campus study). *Degree requirements:* For master's, thesis; for doctorate, capstone. *Entrance requirements:* For master's, GRE (if GPA less than 3.0). Additional exam requirements/recommendations for international students: Required—TOEFL (minimum score 550 paper-based). *Faculty research:* Job satisfaction; nursing diagnoses; dehydration among elderly; correlates to functional status in elderly.

Wright State University, School of Graduate Studies, College of Nursing and Health, Program in Nursing, Dayton, OH 45435. Offers acute care nurse practitioner (MS); administration of nursing and health care systems (MS); adult health (MS); child and adolescent health (MS); community health (MS); family nurse practitioner (MS); nurse practitioner (MS); school nurse (MS); MBA/MS. *Accreditation:* AACN. Part-time and evening/weekend programs available. *Degree requirements:* For master's, thesis or alternative. *Entrance requirements:* For master's, GRE General Test, BSN from NLN-accredited college, Ohio RN license. Additional exam requirements/recommendations for international students: Required—TOEFL. *Faculty research:* Clinical nursing and health, teaching, caring, pain administration, informatics and technology.

Xavier University, College of Social Sciences, Health and Education, School of Nursing, Cincinnati, OH 45207. Offers clinical nurse leader (MSN); education (MSN); forensic nursing (MSN); healthcare law (MSN); informatics (MSN); nursing administration (MSN); school nursing (MSN); MSN/M Ed; MSN/MBA; MSN/MS. *Accreditation:* AACN. Part-time and evening/weekend programs available. Postbaccalaureate distance learning degree programs offered (no on-campus study). *Faculty:* 10 full-time (all women), 10 part-time/adjunct (9 women). *Students:* 64 full-time (55 women), 148 part-time (146 women); includes 19 minority (17 African Americans, 1 Asian American or Pacific Islander, 1 Hispanic American), 2 international. Average age 38. 141 applicants, 88% accepted, 110 enrolled. In 2009, 48 master's awarded. *Degree requirements:* For master's, thesis, scholarly project. *Entrance requirements:* For master's, GRE. Additional exam requirements/recommendations for international students: Required—TOEFL. *Application deadline:* Applications are processed on a rolling basis. Application fee: $35. Electronic applications accepted. *Expenses:* Tuition: Part-time $697 per credit hour. One-time fee: $35 part-time. *Financial support:* In 2009–10, 68 students received support. Applicants required to submit FAFSA. *Faculty research:* Clinical nurse leader, simulation, employment satisfaction, nontraditional students, holistic nursing. *Unit head:* Dr. Susan M. Schmidt, Director, 513-745-3815, Fax: 513-745-1087, E-mail: schmidt@xavier.edu. *Application contact:* Marilyn Volk Gomez, Director of Nursing Student Services, 513-745-4392, Fax: 513-745-1087, E-mail: gomez@xavier.edu.

Nursing Education

Abilene Christian University, Graduate School, School of Nursing, Abilene, TX 79699-9100. Offers education and administration (MSN); family nurse practitioner (MSN). *Accreditation:* AACN. Part-time programs available. *Faculty:* 6 part-time/adjunct (all women). *Students:* 3 full-time (all women), 4 part-time (2 women); includes 4 minority (1 American Indian/Alaska Native, 2 Asian Americans or Pacific Islanders, 1 Hispanic American). 11 applicants, 36% accepted, 4 enrolled. In 2009, 5 master's, 1 other advanced degree awarded. *Entrance requirements:* For master's, GRE General Test. *Application deadline:* For fall admission, 4/1 priority date for domestic students; for spring admission, 11/1 for domestic students. Applications are processed on a rolling basis. Application fee: $40. Electronic applications accepted. *Expenses:* Tuition: Full-time $11,520; part-time $640 per hour. Required fees: $1090; $53.50 per hour. $10 per term. Tuition and fees vary according to program. *Financial support:* In 2009–10, 6 students received support. Application deadline: 4/1. *Unit head:* Dr. Amy Toone, Graduate Director, 325-671-2361, Fax: 325-671-2386, E-mail: atoone@phssn.edu. *Application

contact:* William Horn, Graduate Admissions Counselor, 325-674-2656, Fax: 325-674-6717, E-mail: gradinfo@acu.edu.

Albany State University, College of Sciences and Health Professions, Department of Nursing, Albany, GA 31705-2717. Offers RN to MSN family nurse practitioner (MSN); RN to MSN nurse educator (MSN). Part-time and evening/weekend programs available. Postbaccalaureate distance learning degree programs offered. *Students:* 12 full-time (11 women), 49 part-time (45 women); includes 32 minority (30 African Americans, 2 Asian Americans or Pacific Islanders). Average age 39. 20 applicants, 95% accepted, 16 enrolled. In 2009, 21 master's awarded. *Degree requirements:* For master's, comprehensive exam, thesis or major research project. *Entrance requirements:* For master's, GRE or MAT, baccalaureate degree in nursing, minimum GPA of 3.0, current Georgia RN practicing license, personal interview with the Coordinator of the Graduate Nursing Program, two letters of reference regarding professional accomplishments and academic potential, ASU medical and immunization forms. Additional exam

Nursing Education

Albany State University (continued)
requirements/recommendations for international students: Required—TOEFL. *Application deadline:* For fall admission, 11/16 for domestic students, 9/16 for international students; for spring admission, 4/19 for domestic students, 2/19 for international students. Applications are processed on a rolling basis. Application fee: $20. Electronic applications accepted. *Expenses:* Tuition, state resident: full-time $2970; part-time $162 per credit hour. Tuition, nonresident: full-time $12,168; part-time $676 per credit hour. Required fees: $962; $75 per credit hour. *Financial support:* Application deadline: 6/30. *Faculty research:* HIV issues, cancer-specifically breast, prostate, and lung, cultural diversity, health promotion, smoking cessation. *Unit head:* Linda Grimsley, Chairperson, 229-430-4724, Fax: 229-430-3937, E-mail: lgrimsl@asurams.edu. *Application contact:* Linda Grimsley, Chairperson, 229-430-4724, Fax: 229-430-3937, E-mail: linda.grimsley@asurams.edu.

American International College, School of Health Sciences, Department of Nursing, Springfield, MA 01109-3189. Offers nursing administration (MSN); nursing education (MSN). *Accreditation:* AACN. *Entrance requirements:* For master's, BSN. Additional exam requirements/recommendations for international students: Required—TOEFL. Electronic applications accepted. *Expenses:* Tuition: Full-time $12,510; part-time $695 per credit hour. Required fees: $35 per term.

Angelo State University, College of Graduate Studies, College of Nursing and Allied Health, Department of Nursing, San Angelo, TX 76909. Offers advanced practice registered nurse (MSN); nurse educator (MSN); nursing—RN to MSN (MSN). *Accreditation:* NLN. Part-time and evening/weekend programs available. *Faculty:* 7 full-time (all women). *Students:* 11 full-time (9 women), 41 part-time (38 women); includes 13 minority (3 African Americans, 4 Asian Americans or Pacific Islanders, 6 Hispanic Americans). Average age 41. 29 applicants, 93% accepted, 21 enrolled. In 2009, 13 master's awarded. *Degree requirements:* For master's, comprehensive exam. *Entrance requirements:* For master's, GRE General Test. Additional exam requirements/recommendations for international students: Required—TOEFL or IELTS. *Application deadline:* For fall admission, 7/15 priority date for domestic students, 6/10 for international students; for spring admission, 12/1 priority date for domestic students, 11/1 for international students. Applications are processed on a rolling basis. Application fee: $40 ($50 for international students). Electronic applications accepted. *Expenses:* Tuition, state resident: full-time $3396; part-time $142 per credit hour. Tuition, nonresident: full-time $10,152; part-time $423 per credit hour. Required fees: $1786; $36.25 per credit hour. $494 per semester. Full-time tuition and fees vary according to course load, degree level and program. *Financial support:* In 2009–10, 24 students received support. Career-related internships or fieldwork, Federal Work-Study, and scholarships/grants available. Support available to part-time students. Financial award application deadline: 3/1. *Unit head:* Dr. Susan S. Wilkinson, Department Head, 325-942-2060 Ext. 290, Fax: 325-942-2236, E-mail: susan.wilkinson@angelo.edu. *Application contact:* Dr. Molly J. Walker, Graduate Advisor, 325-942-2060 Ext. 246, Fax: 325-942-2236, E-mail: molly.walker@angelo.edu.

Arizona State University, Graduate College, College of Nursing and Healthcare Innovation, Tempe, AZ 85287. Offers child and adolescent mental health intervention specialist (Graduate Certificate); community and public health practice (Graduate Certificate); community health (MS); evidence-based practice in nursing (Graduate Certificate); exercise and wellness (MS, PhD), including exercise and wellness (MS), physical activity, nutrition and wellness (PhD); healthcare innovation (MHI); nurse education in academic and practice settings (Graduate Certificate); nurse educator (MS); nursing (MS); nursing and healthcare innovation (PhD); nursing practice (DNP); nutrition (MS). *Accreditation:* AACN. Postbaccalaureate distance learning degree programs offered.

Austin Peay State University, College of Graduate Studies, College of Behavioral and Health Sciences, School of Nursing, Clarksville, TN 37044. Offers advanced practice (MSN); nursing administration (MSN); nursing education (MSN); nursing informatics (MSN). Part-time programs available. Postbaccalaureate distance learning degree programs offered. *Faculty:* 7 full-time (all women). *Students:* 15 full-time (14 women), 62 part-time (57 women); includes 6 minority (3 African Americans, 1 American Indian/Alaska Native, 2 Asian Americans or Pacific Islanders). Average age 39. 31 applicants, 100% accepted, 22 enrolled. In 2009, 9 master's awarded. *Degree requirements:* For master's, comprehensive exam. *Entrance requirements:* For master's, GRE General Test, minimum GPA of 3.0, RN license eligibility, 3 letters of recommendation. Additional exam requirements/recommendations for international students: Required—TOEFL (minimum score 600 paper-based). *Application deadline:* For fall admission, 7/27 priority date for domestic students; for spring admission, 12/17 priority date for domestic students. Applications are processed on a rolling basis. Application fee: $25. Electronic applications accepted. *Expenses:* Tuition, state resident: full-time $6160; part-time $608 per credit hour. Tuition, nonresident: full-time $17,080; part-time $854 per credit hour. Required fees: $1224; $61.20 per credit hour. *Financial support:* In 2009–10, 1 student received support, including 1 research assistantship with full tuition reimbursement available (averaging $5,184 per year); career-related internships or fieldwork, Federal Work-Study, institutionally sponsored loans, scholarships/grants, and unspecified assistantships also available. Support available to part-time students. *Unit head:* Dr. Francisca Ann Farrar, Director, 931-221-7737, Fax: 931-221-6490, E-mail: farrarf@apsu.edu. *Application contact:* Dr. Doris Davenport, Associate Professor, 931-221-7467, Fax: 931-221-7595, E-mail: davenportd@apsu.edu.

Azusa Pacific University, School of Nursing, Azusa, CA 91702-7000. Offers nursing (MSN); nursing education (PhD). *Accreditation:* AACN. Part-time and evening/weekend programs available. *Degree requirements:* For master's, thesis optional. *Entrance requirements:* For master's, BSN. *Faculty research:* Family adaptation to illness and crisis, bioethical issues in nursing, self-care activities, quality of life issues, home health.

Barry University, School of Nursing, Program in Nursing Education, Miami Shores, FL 33161-6695. Offers MSN, Certificate. *Accreditation:* AACN. Part-time and evening/weekend programs available. *Degree requirements:* For master's, research project or thesis. *Entrance requirements:* For master's, GRE General Test or MAT, BSN, minimum GPA of 3.0, course work in statistics. Electronic applications accepted. *Faculty research:* HIV/AIDS, gerontology.

Bellarmine University, Donna and Allan Lansing School of Nursing and Health Sciences, Louisville, KY 40205-0671. Offers family nurse practitioner (MSN); nursing administration (MSN); nursing education (MSN); nursing practice (DNP); physical therapy (DPT). *Accreditation:* AACN; APTA. Part-time and evening/weekend programs available. *Faculty:* 16 full-time (11 women), 7 part-time/adjunct (6 women). *Students:* 126 full-time (94 women), 50 part-time (48 women); includes 4 minority (1 African American, 3 Asian Americans or Pacific Islanders). Average age 30. 350 applicants, 48 enrolled. In 2009, 9 master's, 41 doctorates awarded. *Degree requirements:* For doctorate, comprehensive exam, thesis/dissertation. *Entrance requirements:* For master's, GRE General Test, RN license; for doctorate, GRE General Test, Physical Therapist Centralized Application Service (for DPT). Additional exam requirements/recommendations for international students: Required—TOEFL (minimum score 550 paper-based; 213 computer-based; 80 iBT). Application fee: $25. Electronic applications accepted. *Expenses:* Contact institution. *Financial support:* Career-related internships or fieldwork and scholarships/grants available. *Faculty research:* Nursing: pain, empathy, leadership styles, control; physical therapy: service learning; exercise in chronic and pre-operative conditions, and athletes; women's health; aging. *Unit head:* Dr. Susan H. Davis, Dean, 800-274-4723 Ext. 8217, E-mail: sdavis@bellarmine.edu. *Application contact:* Julie Armstrong-Binnix, Health Science Recruiter, 800-274-4723 Ext. 8364, E-mail: julieab@bellarmine.edu.

Bellin College, Program in Nursing, Green Bay, WI 54305. Offers administrator (MSN); educator (MSN). *Accreditation:* AACN.

Bethel University, Graduate School, Department of Nursing, St. Paul, MN 55112-6999. Offers healthcare leadership (MA); nursing education (MA, Certificate). *Accreditation:* AACN. Evening/weekend programs available. *Faculty:* 12 full-time (10 women), 2 part-time/adjunct (both women). *Students:* 60 full-time (58 women), 11 part-time (9 women); includes 7 minority (4 African Americans, 3 Hispanic Americans), 3 international. Average age 42. 31 applicants, 84% accepted, 23 enrolled. In 2009, 13 master's awarded. *Degree requirements:* For master's, comprehensive exam, thesis, internship. *Entrance requirements:* For master's, MAT, interview, minimum GPA of 3.0, RN experience, bachelor's degree in nursing, letters of reference, course in statistics, current RN license. Additional exam requirements/recommendations for international students: Required—TOEFL (minimum score 550 paper-based; 213 computer-based; 80 iBT). *Application deadline:* For spring admission, 1/31 priority date for domestic students. Applications are processed on a rolling basis. Application fee: $25. Electronic applications accepted. *Expenses:* Contact institution. *Financial support:* Applicants required to submit FAFSA. *Unit head:* Dr. Diane Dahl, Assistant Dean, 651-635-8000, Fax: 651-635-8004, E-mail: diane-dahl@bethel.edu. *Application contact:* Michael Price, Director of Admissions, 651-635-8000, Fax: 651-635-8004, E-mail: m-price@bethel.edu.

Bowie State University, Graduate Programs, Department of Nursing, Bowie, MD 20715-9465. Offers administration of nursing services (MS); family nurse practitioner (MS); nursing education (MS). *Accreditation:* NLN. Part-time programs available. *Degree requirements:* For master's, comprehensive exam, thesis, research paper. *Entrance requirements:* For master's, minimum GPA of 2.5. Electronic applications accepted. *Faculty research:* Minority health, women's health, gerontology, leadership management.

Brenau University, Graduate Programs, School of Health and Science, Gainesville, GA 30501. Offers family nurse practitioner (MSN); nurse educator (MSN); nursing management (MSN); occupational therapy (MS); psychology (MS). *Accreditation:* AOTA; NLN. Part-time and evening/weekend programs available. *Faculty:* 14 full-time (12 women), 6 part-time/adjunct (5 women). *Students:* 97 full-time (92 women), 92 part-time (84 women); includes 46 minority (37 African Americans, 2 American Indian/Alaska Native, 2 Asian Americans or Pacific Islanders, 5 Hispanic Americans), 2 international. Average age 34. 168 applicants, 50% accepted, 68 enrolled. In 2009, 35 master's awarded. *Degree requirements:* For master's, comprehensive exam (for some programs), thesis (for some programs), clinical practicum hours. *Entrance requirements:* For master's, GRE General Test or MAT (for some programs), interview, writing sample, references (for some programs). Additional exam requirements/recommendations for international students: Required—TOEFL (minimum score 500 paper-based). *Application deadline:* Applications are processed on a rolling basis. Application fee: $35. Electronic applications accepted. *Expenses:* Contact institution. *Financial support:* In 2009–10, 32 students received support. Scholarships/grants and traineeships available. Support available to part-time students. Financial award application deadline: 7/15; financial award applicants required to submit FAFSA. *Unit head:* Dr. Gale Starich, Dean, 777-718-5305, Fax: 770-297-5929, E-mail: gstarich@brenau.edu. *Application contact:* Christina White, Admissions Coordinator, 770-718-5320, Fax: 770-770-5338, E-mail: cwhite@brenau.edu.

California State University, Fresno, Division of Graduate Studies, College of Health and Human Services, Department of Nursing, Fresno, CA 93740-8027. Offers nursing (MS), including clinical nurse, primary care nurse practitioner, specialist/nurse educator. *Accreditation:* AACN. Part-time and evening/weekend programs available. *Degree requirements:* For master's, thesis or alternative. *Entrance requirements:* For master's, GRE General Test, 1 year of clinical practice, previous course work in statistics, BSN, minimum GPA of 3.0 in nursing. Additional exam requirements/recommendations for international students: Required—TOEFL. Electronic applications accepted. *Faculty research:* Training grant, HIV assessment.

Capella University, School of Public Service Leadership, Minneapolis, MN 55402. Offers criminal justice (MS, PhD); emergency management (MS, PhD); general human services (MS, PhD); general public administration (MPA, DPA); gerontology (MS); health care administration (MS, PhD); health management and policy (MSPH); management of nonprofit agencies (MS, PhD); nurse educator (MS); public safety leadership (MS, PhD); social and community services (MS, PhD); social behavioral sciences (MSPH).

Carson-Newman College, Department of Nursing, Jefferson City, TN 37760. Offers family nurse practitioner (MSN); nurse educator (MSN). *Accreditation:* AACN. *Faculty:* 2 full-time (both women), 10 part-time/adjunct (9 women). *Students:* 21 full-time (19 women), 27 part-time (23 women); includes 3 minority (2 Asian Americans or Pacific Islanders, 1 Hispanic American). Average age 32. In 2009, 11 master's awarded. *Application deadline:* For fall admission, 7/15 priority date for domestic students. Applications are processed on a rolling basis. Application fee: $50. *Expenses:* Tuition: Full-time $5490; part-time $305 per semester hour. Required fees: $200. *Unit head:* Dr. Patricia Kraft, Dean and Chair, 865-471-3426. *Application contact:* Graduate Admissions and Services Adviser, 865-473-3468, Fax: 865-472-3475.

The Catholic University of America, School of Nursing, Washington, DC 20064. Offers adult health specialist with functional role as nurse educator (MSN); adult nurse practitioner (MSN); community/public health nurse specialist educator (MSN); family nurse practitioner (MSN); geriatric nurse practitioner (MSN); immigrant, refugee, and global health clinical nurse specialist (MSN); nursing (DNP, PhD, Certificate); pediatric nurse practitioner (MSN); promoting healthy families in vulnerable communities (MSN); psychiatric-mental health nursing (MSN). *Accreditation:* AACN. Part-time programs available. *Faculty:* 15 full-time (all women), 43 part-time/adjunct (41 women). *Students:* 28 full-time (26 women), 75 part-time (73 women); includes 37 minority (27 African Americans, 6 Asian Americans or Pacific Islanders, 4 Hispanic Americans), 4 international. Average age 42. 84 applicants, 64% accepted, 30 enrolled. In 2009, 23 master's, 7 doctorates, 3 other advanced degrees awarded. *Degree requirements:* For master's, comprehensive exam, thesis optional; for doctorate, comprehensive exam, thesis/dissertation, minimum GPA of 3.0, oral proposal defense. *Entrance requirements:* For master's, 3 letters of recommendation, BA in nursing, RN registration, official copies of academic transcripts, some post-baccalaureate nursing experience; for doctorate, GRE General Test, BA in nursing, professional portfolio (including statements, resume, copy of RN license, 3 letters of recommendation, narrative description of clinical practice, proposal), copy of research/scholarly paper related to clinical nursing. Additional exam requirements/recommendations for international students: Required—TOEFL (minimum score 580 paper-based; 237 computer-based). *Application deadline:* For fall admission, 8/1 priority date for domestic students, 7/15 for international students; for spring admission, 12/1 priority date for domestic students, 10/15 for international students. Applications are processed on a rolling basis. Application fee: $55. Electronic applications accepted. *Expenses:* Tuition: Full-time $31,740; part-time $1245 per credit hour. Required fees: $50; $25 per semester hour. One-time fee: $425. *Financial support:* Fellowships, research assistantships, teaching assistantships, Federal Work-Study, scholarships/grants, tuition waivers (full and partial), and unspecified assistantships available. Financial award application deadline: 2/1; financial award applicants required to submit FAFSA. *Faculty research:* Community involvement in health care services, primary health care services, pediatrics, chronic illness, cardiovascular disease. Total annual research expenditures: $311,172. *Unit head:* Dr. Nalini N. Jairath, Dean, 202-319-5403, Fax: 202-319-6485, E-mail: cua-deanschoolofnursing@cua.edu. *Application contact:* Julie Schwing, Director of Graduate Admissions, 202-319-5057, Fax: 202-319-6533, E-mail: cua-admissions@cua.edu.

Chatham University, Program in Nursing, Pittsburgh, PA 15232-2826. Offers education/leadership (MSN); nursing (DNP). *Accreditation:* AACN. *Students:* 48 full-time (41 women), 79 part-time (70 women). Average age 45. 139 applicants, 90% accepted, 69 enrolled. *Entrance requirements:* For master's and doctorate, RN license. Additional exam requirements/recommendations for international students: Required—TOEFL (minimum score 600 paper-based; 250 computer-based; 100 iBT), IELTS (minimum score 6.5), TWE. *Application deadline:* For fall admission, 5/1 priority date for domestic and international students. Applications are processed on a rolling basis. Application fee: $45. Electronic applications accepted. *Financial support:* Applicants required to submit FAFSA. *Unit head:* Dr. Elizabeth Gazza, Director, 412-365-2746, E-mail: egazza@chatham.edu. *Application contact:* David Vey, Admissions Support Specialist, 412-365-1498, Fax: 412-365-1720, E-mail: dvey@chatham.edu.

Clarke College, Department of Nursing and Health, Dubuque, IA 52001-3198. Offers administration of nursing systems (MSN); advanced practice nursing (MSN); education (MSN); family nurse practitioner (MSN, PMC). *Accreditation:* AACN. Part-time programs available. *Faculty:* 4 full-time (all women), 2 part-time/adjunct (1 woman). *Students:* 35 full-time (34 women), 19 part-time (all women). Average age 35. 48 applicants, 83% accepted, 25 enrolled.

In 2009, 13 master's awarded. *Entrance requirements:* For master's, GRE General Test or MAT, BSN, minimum GPA of 3.0. *Application deadline:* For fall admission, 2/15 priority date for domestic students; for spring admission, 12/15 priority date for domestic students. Applications are processed on a rolling basis. Application fee: $25. Electronic applications accepted. *Expenses:* Tuition: Full-time $10,836; part-time $602 per credit hour. Required fees: $30 per credit hour. *Financial support:* In 2009–10, 6 students received support. Career-related internships or fieldwork available. Support available to part-time students. Financial award applicants required to submit FAFSA. *Faculty research:* Narrative pedagogy, ethics, end-of-life care, pedagogy, family systems. *Unit head:* Dr. Susan DeCrane, Chair, 800-224-2736, Fax: 319-584-8684. *Application contact:* Carrie Kirk, Information Contact, 563-588-6635, Fax: 563-588-6789, E-mail: graduate@clarke.edu.

Clarkson College, Master of Science in Nursing Program, Omaha, NE 68131. Offers adult nurse practitioner (MSN, Post-Master's Certificate); family nurse practitioner (MSN, Post-Master's Certificate); nursing education (MSN, Post-Master's Certificate); nursing health care leadership (MSN, Post-Master's Certificate). *Accreditation:* NLN. Part-time and evening/weekend programs available. Postbaccalaureate distance learning degree programs offered (minimal on-campus study). *Degree requirements:* For master's, on-campus skills assessment (family nurse practitioner, adult nurse practitioner), comprehensive exam or thesis. *Entrance requirements:* For master's, minimum GPA of 3.0, 2 references, resume. Additional exam requirements/recommendations for international students: Required—TOEFL (minimum score 600 paper-based; 250 computer-based; 100 iBT). Electronic applications accepted.

Cleveland State University, College of Graduate Studies, College of Education and Human Services, School of Nursing, Cleveland, OH 44115. Offers clinical nursing leader (MSN); executive track (MSN); forensic nursing (MSN); nursing education (MSN); population health nursing (MSN); MSN/MBA. *Accreditation:* AACN. Part-time programs available. *Degree requirements:* For master's, thesis of alternative, portfolio, population health project. *Entrance requirements:* For master's, RN license, BSN, course work in statistics. Additional exam requirements/recommendations for international students: Required—TOEFL (minimum score 525 paper-based; 197 computer-based), IELTS (minimum score 6). Electronic applications accepted. *Faculty research:* Diabetes management, African-American elders medication compliance, risk in home visiting, suffering, COPD and stress.

College of Mount Saint Vincent, School of Professional and Continuing Studies, Department of Nursing, Riverdale, NY 10471-1093. Offers adult nurse practitioner (MSN, PMC); family nurse practitioner (MSN, PMC); nurse educator (PMC); nursing administration (MSN); nursing for the adult and aged (MSN). *Accreditation:* AACN. Part-time programs available. *Entrance requirements:* For master's, BSN, interview, RN license, minimum GPA of 3.0, letters of reference. Additional exam requirements/recommendations for international students: Required—TOEFL. *Expenses:* Contact institution.

The College of New Rochelle, Graduate School, Program in Nursing, New Rochelle, NY 10805-2308. Offers acute care nurse practitioner (MS, Certificate); clinical specialist in holistic nursing (MS, Certificate); family nurse practitioner (MS, Certificate); nursing and health care management (MS); nursing education (Certificate). *Accreditation:* AACN. Part-time programs available. *Entrance requirements:* For master's, GRE General Test or MAT, BSN, malpractice insurance, minimum GPA of 3.0, RN license. *Expenses:* Contact institution. *Faculty research:* Holistic modalities, academic success variables.

College of Staten Island of the City University of New York, Graduate Programs, Department of Nursing, Program in Nursing Education, Staten Island, NY 10314-6600. Offers 6th Year Certificate. *Faculty:* 4 full-time (all women), 4 part-time/adjunct (3 women). *Application deadline:* Applications are processed on a rolling basis. Electronic applications accepted. *Expenses:* Tuition, state resident: full-time $7360; part-time $310 per credit. Tuition, nonresident: part-time $575 per credit. Required fees: $378; $113 per semester. *Financial support:* Federal Work-Study available. Support available to part-time students. *Unit head:* Dr. Mary Ellen McMorrow, Coordinator, 718-982-3838, Fax: 718-982-3813, E-mail: maryellen.mcmorrow@csi.cuny.edu. *Application contact:* Sasha Spence, Assistant Director of Graduate Recruitment and Admissions, 718-982-2699, Fax: 718-982-2500, E-mail: sasha.spence@csi.cuny.edu.

Concordia University Wisconsin, Graduate Programs, School of Health and Human Services, Program in Nursing, Mequon, WI 53097-2402. Offers family nurse practitioner (MSN); geriatric nurse practitioner (MSN); nurse educator (MSN). *Accreditation:* AACN. Postbaccalaureate distance learning degree programs offered (minimal on-campus study). *Degree requirements:* For master's, comprehensive exam, thesis or alternative. *Entrance requirements:* Additional exam requirements/recommendations for international students: Required—TOEFL. *Expenses:* Contact institution.

Daemen College, Department of Nursing, Amherst, NY 14226-3592. Offers adult nurse practitioner (MS); nursing education (MS, Post Master's Certificate); nursing executive leadership (MS); nursing practice (DNP); palliative care nursing (MS, Post Master's Certificate). *Accreditation:* NLN. Part-time programs available. *Faculty:* 3 full-time (all women), 6 part-time/adjunct (all women). *Students:* 8 full-time (all women), 105 part-time (98 women); includes 17 minority (10 African Americans, 1 American Indian/Alaska Native, 3 Asian Americans or Pacific Islanders, 3 Hispanic Americans), 1 international. Average age 42. 66 applicants, 79% accepted, 37 enrolled. In 2009, 24 master's, 4 other advanced degrees awarded. *Degree requirements:* For master's, thesis or alternative. *Entrance requirements:* For master's, BN, 1 year medical/surgical experience, RN license and state registration, 1 course in statistics with minimum grade of 'C', 3 letters of recommendation, minimum GPA of 3.25, interview; for doctorate, MS in advance nursing practice; New York state RN license; personal goal statement; resume; interview; statistics course with minimum grade of 'C'; for Post Master's Certificate, master's degree in clinical area; RN license and current registration; one year of clinical experience; statistics course with minimum grade of 'C'. Additional exam requirements/recommendations for international students: Required—TOEFL (minimum score 500 paper-based; 173 computer-based; 61 iBT). *Application deadline:* For fall admission, 3/1 priority date for domestic and international students; for spring admission, 10/1 priority date for domestic and international students. Applications are processed on a rolling basis. Application fee: $25. Electronic applications accepted. *Expenses:* Tuition: Part-time $770 per credit hour. Tuition and fees vary according to course load, program and reciprocity agreements. *Financial support:* In 2009–10, 1 student received support. Institutionally sponsored loans and scholarships/grants available. Financial award application deadline: 2/15; financial award applicants required to submit FAFSA. *Faculty research:* Professional stress, client behavior, drug therapy, treatment modalities and pulmonary cancers, chemical dependency. *Unit head:* Dr. Mary Lou Rusin, Chair, 716-839-8387, Fax: 716-839-8403, E-mail: mrusin@daemen.edu. *Application contact:* Scott Rowe, Associate Director of Graduate Programs, 716-839-8225, Fax: 716-839-8229, E-mail: srowe@daemen.edu.

Delta State University, Graduate Programs, School of Nursing, Cleveland, MS 38733-0001. Offers family nurse practitioner (MSN); nurse administrator (MSN); nurse educator (MSN). *Accreditation:* AACN. Part-time programs available. *Degree requirements:* For master's, thesis optional. *Entrance requirements:* For master's, GRE General Test. Electronic applications accepted. *Expenses:* Tuition, state resident: full-time $4450; part-time $247 per credit hour. Tuition, nonresident: full-time $11,520; part-time $640 per credit hour.

DeSales University, Graduate Division, Programs in Nursing, Center Valley, PA 18034-9568. Offers adult advanced practice nurse specialist (MSN); certified nurse midwives (MSN); certified nurse practitioners (MSN); family nurse practitioner (MSN); nurse educator (MSN); MSN/MBA. *Accreditation:* NLN. Part-time programs available. *Students:* 67 part-time. In 2009, 218 master's awarded. *Degree requirements:* For master's, thesis optional. *Entrance requirements:* For master's, GRE General Test, MAT, minimum B average in undergraduate course work, health assessment course or equivalent, course work in statistics. Additional exam requirements/recommendations for international students: Required—TOEFL. *Application deadline:* Applications are processed on a rolling basis. Application fee: $35. Electronic applications accepted. *Expenses:* Tuition: Full-time $17,500; part-time $665 per credit. Full-time tuition and fees vary according to program. Part-time tuition and fees vary according to course load. *Financial support:* Applicants required to submit FAFSA. *Faculty research:* Women's health, theory validation, needs of homeless, behavior risk evaluation, wound healing. *Unit head:* Dr. Carol Gullo Mest, Director, 610-282-1100 Ext. 1394, Fax: 610-282-2091, E-mail: carol.mest@desales.edu. *Application contact:* Caryn Stopper, Director of Graduate Admissions, 610-282-1100 Ext. 1768, Fax: 610-282-2254, E-mail: caryn.stopper@desales.edu.

Dominican University of California, Graduate Programs, School of Health and Natural Sciences, Program in Nursing, San Rafael, CA 94901-2298. Offers geriatric and nurse educator (MS); integrated health practices (clinical nursing specialist) (MS). *Accreditation:* AACN. Part-time and evening/weekend programs available. *Degree requirements:* For master's, thesis. *Entrance requirements:* For master's, minimum GPA of 3.0; clinical experience; course work in nursing research and statistics; CPR certification; professional liability and malpractice insurance; interview. Additional exam requirements/recommendations for international students: Required—TOEFL (minimum score 550 paper-based; 213 computer-based). Electronic applications accepted.

Duke University, School of Nursing, Durham, NC 27708-0586. Offers adult acute care (Certificate); adult cardiovascular (Certificate); adult oncology (Certificate); adult primary care (Certificate); clinical nurse specialist (MSN), including adult oncology, gerontology, neonatal, pediatric; clinical research management (MSN, Certificate); family (Certificate); gerontology (Certificate); health and nursing ministries (MSN, Certificate); health systems leadership and outcomes (Certificate); neonatal (Certificate); neonatal/pediatric in rural health (MSN, Certificate); nurse anesthetist (MSN, Certificate); nurse practitioner (MSN), including adult acute care, adult cardiovascular, adult oncology, adult primary care, family, gerontology, neonatal, pediatric, pediatric acute care; nursing (DNP, PhD); nursing and healthcare leadership (MSN); nursing education (MSN); nursing informatics (MSN, Certificate); pediatric (Certificate); pediatric acute care (Certificate); MBA/MSN; MSN/MCM. *Accreditation:* AACN; AANA/CANAEP. Part-time programs available. Postbaccalaureate distance learning degree programs offered (minimal on-campus study). *Faculty:* 45 full-time (41 women), 169 part-time/adjunct (150 women). *Students:* 213 full-time (179 women), 116 part-time (105 women); includes 37 minority (17 African Americans, 13 Asian Americans or Pacific Islanders, 7 Hispanic Americans), 9 international. Average age 36. 234 applicants, 53% accepted, 97 enrolled. In 2009, 142 master's, 24 other advanced degrees awarded. Terminal master's awarded for partial completion of doctoral program. *Degree requirements:* For master's, thesis optional; for doctorate, Capstone Project. *Entrance requirements:* For master's, GRE General Test, 1 year of nursing experience, BSN, minimum GPA of 3.0, previous course work in statistics; for doctorate, GRE for BSN prepared, BSN or MSN, minimum GPA of 3.0. Portfolio; for Certificate, MSN. Additional exam requirements/recommendations for international students: Required—TOEFL (minimum score 550 paper-based; 213 computer-based), Commission on Graduates of Foreign Nursing Schools exam. *Application deadline:* For fall admission, 7/2 priority date for domestic and international students; for spring admission, 11/15 priority date for domestic and international students. Applications are processed on a rolling basis. Application fee: $50. Electronic applications accepted. *Expenses:* Contact institution. *Financial support:* Career-related internships or fieldwork, institutionally sponsored loans, scholarships/grants, traineeships, and tuition waivers (partial) available. Support available to part-time students. Financial award application deadline: 4/1; financial award applicants required to submit FAFSA. *Faculty research:* Cardiovascular disease, caregiver skill training, data mining, prostate cancer, neonatal immune system. Total annual research expenditures: $3.5 million. *Unit head:* Dr. Catherine L. Gilliss, Dean/Vice Chancellor for Nursing Affairs, 919-684-9444, Fax: 919-684-9414, E-mail: gilli025@mc.duke.edu. *Application contact:* Bebe T. Mills, Director of Admissions, 919-684-9151, Fax: 919-668-4693, E-mail: mills031@mc.duke.edu.

Duquesne University, School of Nursing, Master of Science in Nursing Program, Pittsburgh, PA 15282-0001. Offers family nurse practitioner (MSN); forensic nursing (MSN); nursing education (MSN). *Accreditation:* AACN. Part-time and evening/weekend programs available. Postbaccalaureate distance learning degree programs offered (minimal on-campus study). *Faculty:* 15 full-time (13 women), 4 part-time/adjunct (all women). *Students:* 73 full-time (69 women), 43 part-time (42 women); includes 8 minority (6 African Americans, 2 Asian Americans or Pacific Islanders). 131 applicants, 32% accepted, 36 enrolled. In 2009, 39 master's awarded. *Degree requirements:* For master's, culminating paper. *Entrance requirements:* For master's, current RN license; BSN with minimum GPA of 3.0; minimum of 1 year full-time work experience as RN prior to registration in clinical or specialty course. Additional exam requirements/recommendations for international students: Required—TOEFL (minimum score 600 paper-based; 80 iBT). *Application deadline:* For fall admission, 4/1 for domestic and international students. *Expenses:* Tuition: Part-time $851 per credit. Required fees: $81 per credit. *Financial support:* In 2009–10, 38 students received support, including 4 research assistantships with partial tuition reimbursements available (averaging $2,250 per year), 4 teaching assistantships with partial tuition reimbursements available (averaging $1,075 per year); institutionally sponsored loans, scholarships/grants, traineeships, and tuition waivers (partial) also available. Support available to part-time students. Financial award application deadline: 7/1. *Faculty research:* Vulnerable populations, social justice, cultural competence, health disparities, wellness within chronic illness. Total annual research expenditures: $457,857. *Unit head:* Dr. Joan Such Lockhart, Professor and Associate Dean of Academic Affairs, 412-396-6540, Fax: 412-396-1821, E-mail: lockhart@duq.edu. *Application contact:* Susan Hardner, Nurse Recruiter, 412-396-4945, Fax: 412-396-6346, E-mail: nursing@duq.edu.

D'Youville College, Department of Nursing, Buffalo, NY 14201-1084. Offers community health nursing/education (MSN); community health nursing/high risk parents and children (MSN); community health nursing/management (MSN); family nurse practitioner (MS, Post-Master's Certificate); nursing and health-related professions (Certificate); nursing with clinical focus choice (MSN). *Accreditation:* AACN. Part-time and evening/weekend programs available. *Degree requirements:* For master's, thesis optional, membership on board of community agency, publishable paper. *Entrance requirements:* For master's, BS in nursing, minimum GPA of 3.0, course work in statistics and computers. Additional exam requirements/recommendations for international students: Required—TOEFL (minimum score 500 paper-based; 173 computer-based). Electronic applications accepted. *Faculty research:* Nursing curriculum, nursing theory-testing, wellness research, communication and socialization patterns.

See Display on page 1487 and Close-Up on page 1611.

Eastern Michigan University, Graduate School, College of Health and Human Services, School of Nursing, Ypsilanti, MI 48197. Offers nursing (MSN); quality improvement in health care systems (Graduate Certificate); teaching in health care systems (MSN, Graduate Certificate). *Accreditation:* AACN. Part-time and evening/weekend programs available. Postbaccalaureate distance learning degree programs offered (minimal on-campus study). *Faculty:* 21 full-time (19 women). *Students:* 14 full-time (all women), 45 part-time (38 women); includes 17 minority (14 African Americans, 3 Asian Americans or Pacific Islanders), 3 international. Average age 42. 23 applicants, 65% accepted, 11 enrolled. In 2009, 15 master's, 19 other advanced degrees awarded. *Degree requirements:* For master's, thesis optional. *Entrance requirements:* For master's, GRE General Test, Michigan RN license. Additional exam requirements/recommendations for international students: Required—TOEFL. *Application deadline:* Applications are processed on a rolling basis. Application fee: $35. Tuition and fees vary according to course level. *Financial support:* In 2009–10, 2 research assistantships with full tuition reimbursements (averaging $8,400 per year) were awarded; fellowships, teaching assistantships with full tuition reimbursements, career-related internships or fieldwork, Federal Work-Study, institutionally sponsored loans, scholarships/grants, tuition waivers (partial), and unspecified assistantships also available. Support available to part-time students. Financial award applicants required to submit FAFSA. *Unit head:* Dr. Betty Beard, Director, 734-487-2310, Fax: 734-487-9646, E-mail: bbeard@emich.edu. *Application contact:* Dr. Barbara Scheffer, MSN Coordinator, 734-487-2310, Fax: 734-487-9646, E-mail: bscheffer@emich.edu.

Eastern Washington University, Graduate Studies, Intercollegiate College of Nursing, Cheney, WA 99004-2431. Offers MN. *Degree requirements:* For master's, comprehensive exam, thesis. *Entrance requirements:* For master's, GRE General Test, minimum GPA of 3.0. *Expenses:*

Nursing Education

Eastern Washington University (continued)
Tuition, state resident: full-time $7476; part-time $249 per quarter hour. Tuition, nonresident: full-time $18,030; part-time $601 per quarter hour. Required fees: $3.50 per quarter hour. $142 per quarter.

Edinboro University of Pennsylvania, School of Graduate Studies and Research, School of Science, Management and Technology, Department of Nursing, Edinboro, PA 16444. Offers family nurse practitioner (MSN); nurse educator (Certificate); nursing (MSN); palliative and end-of-life care (Certificate). *Accreditation:* NLN. Part-time and evening/weekend programs available. *Faculty:* 5 full-time (all women). *Students:* 47 part-time (42 women); includes 4 minority (3 African Americans, 1 Hispanic American). Average age 40. In 2009, 26 master's, 3 other advanced degrees awarded. *Degree requirements:* For master's, thesis, competency exam. *Entrance requirements:* For master's, GRE or MAT, minimum QPA of 2.5. *Application deadline:* Applications are processed on a rolling basis. Application fee: $30. Electronic applications accepted. *Expenses:* Tuition, state resident: full-time $6666; part-time $370 per credit. Tuition, nonresident: full-time $10,666; part-time $593 per credit. Required fees: $2206.28. One-time fee: $204 part-time. *Financial support:* In 2009–10, 2 research assistantships with full and partial tuition reimbursements (averaging $4,050 per year) were awarded; career-related internships or fieldwork, Federal Work-Study, scholarships/grants, and unspecified assistantships also available. Support available to part-time students. Financial award application deadline: 2/15; financial award applicants required to submit FAFSA. *Unit head:* Dr. Alice Conway, Program Head, 814-732-2285, E-mail: aconwayt@edinboro.edu. *Application contact:* Dr. Alice Conway, Program Head, 814-732-2285, E-mail: aconwayt@edinboro.edu.

Elms College, Division of Nursing, Chicopee, MA 01013-2839. Offers nursing and health services management (MSN); nursing education (MSN). *Accreditation:* AACN. Part-time and evening/weekend programs available. *Faculty:* 5 full-time (4 women), 3 part-time/adjunct (all women). *Students:* 8 full-time (all women), 27 part-time (26 women); includes 1 minority (African American). 11 applicants, 82% accepted, 8 enrolled. *Entrance requirements:* Additional exam requirements/recommendations for international students: Required—TOEFL. *Application deadline:* For fall admission, 7/1 priority date for domestic students; for spring admission, 11/1 priority date for domestic students. Applications are processed on a rolling basis. Application fee: $30. *Financial support:* Applicants required to submit FAFSA. *Unit head:* Dr. Kathleen Scoble, Director, 413-265-2204, E-mail: scoblek@elms.edu. *Application contact:* Dr. Cynthia L. Dakin, Assistant Director of Graduate Studies, 413-265-2455, Fax: 413-265-2335, E-mail: dakinc@elms.edu.

Fairmont State University, Graduate Studies, Program in Nursing, Fairmont, WV 26554. Offers nursing administration (MS); nursing education (MS).

Felician College, Program in Nursing, Lodi, NJ 07644-2117. Offers adult health nurse (MSN, PMC); family practice nurse (MSN, PMC); nursing (MSN); nursing education (MSN). *Accreditation:* AACN. Part-time and evening/weekend programs available. Postbaccalaureate distance learning degree programs offered (no on-campus study). *Students:* 4 full-time (all women), 74 part-time (64 women); includes 18 minority (10 African Americans, 5 Asian Americans or Pacific Islanders, 3 Hispanic Americans). Average age 42. 29 applicants, 90% accepted, 24 enrolled. *Degree requirements:* For master's, scholarly project. *Entrance requirements:* For master's, BS in nursing or equivalent, minimum GPA of 3.0, 2 letters of recommendation, RN license; for PMC, RN license, minimum GPA of 2.75. Additional exam requirements/recommendations for international students: Recommended—TOEFL (minimum score 550 paper-based; 213 computer-based). *Application deadline:* Applications are processed on a rolling basis. Application fee: $40. *Financial support:* In 2009–10, 10 students received support. Traineeships available. Financial award applicants required to submit FAFSA. *Faculty research:* Anxiety and fear, curriculum innovation, health promotion. *Unit head:* Dr. Muriel Shore, Dean, Division of Health Sciences, 201-559-6030, E-mail: shorem@felician.edu. *Application contact:* Dr. Wendy Lin-Cook, Director of Adult and Graduate Admission, 201-559-6077, Fax: 201-559-6138, E-mail: adultandgraduate@felician.edu.

See Close-Up on page 1615.

Ferris State University, College of Allied Health Sciences, School of Nursing, Big Rapids, MI 49307. Offers nursing (MS); nursing administration (MS); nursing education (MS); nursing informatics (MS). *Accreditation:* NLN. Part-time and evening/weekend programs available. Postbaccalaureate distance learning degree programs offered (minimal on-campus study). *Faculty:* 1 (woman) full-time, 69 part-time/adjunct (63 women). *Students:* 1 (woman) full-time, 64 part-time (58 women). Average age 42. 30 applicants, 53% accepted, 11 enrolled. In 2009, 9 master's awarded. *Degree requirements:* For master's, comprehensive exam, practicum, scholarly project. *Entrance requirements:* For master's, BS in nursing, writing sample, letters of reference, 2 years clinical experience. Additional exam requirements/recommendations for international students: Required—TOEFL (minimum score 550 paper-based). *Application deadline:* For fall admission, 7/15 priority date for domestic students. Applications are processed on a rolling basis. Application fee: $30. Electronic applications accepted. *Financial support:* In 2009–10, 4 students received support; fellowships, research assistantships, teaching assistantships, scholarships/grants available. Financial award application deadline: 4/15. *Faculty research:* Nursing education-minority student focus, student attitudes toward aging. *Unit head:* Dr. Julie A. Coon, Director, 231-591-2267, Fax: 231-591-2325, E-mail: coonj@ferris.edu. *Application contact:* Debby Buck, Off Campus Program Secretary, 231-591-2270, Fax: 231-591-3788, E-mail: buckd@ferris.edu.

Florida State University, The Graduate School, College of Nursing, Tallahassee, FL 32312. Offers family nurse practitioner (MSN, DNP); health systems leadership (DNP); nurse educator (MSN, Certificate). *Accreditation:* AACN. Part-time programs available. Postbaccalaureate distance learning degree programs offered (no on-campus study). *Faculty:* 13 full-time (12 women). *Students:* 13 full-time (4 women), 102 part-time (100 women); includes 13 minority (7 African Americans, 3 Asian Americans or Pacific Islanders, 3 Hispanic Americans). Average age 35. 42 applicants, 71% accepted, 29 enrolled. In 2009, 25 master's, 3 other advanced degrees awarded. *Degree requirements:* For master's, thesis optional. *Entrance requirements:* For master's, GRE General Test, MAT, minimum GPA of 3.0, BSN, Florida RN license; for doctorate, GRE General Test, MAT, minimum GPA of 3.0, BSN or MSN, Florida RN license. Additional exam requirements/recommendations for international students: Required—TOEFL (minimum score 550 paper-based). *Application deadline:* For fall admission, 7/1 for domestic and international students. Application fee: $30. Electronic applications accepted. *Expenses:* Tuition, state resident: full-time $7413. Tuition, nonresident: full-time $22,567. *Financial support:* In 2009–10, 101 students received support, including fellowships with partial tuition reimbursements available (averaging $6,300 per year), research assistantships with partial tuition reimbursements available (averaging $3,000 per year), 3 teaching assistantships with partial tuition reimbursements available (averaging $3,000 per year); career-related internships or fieldwork, Federal Work-Study, institutionally sponsored loans, scholarships/grants, traineeships, and tuition waivers (partial) also available. Financial award application deadline: 4/15; financial award applicants required to submit FAFSA. *Faculty research:* Distance learning, gerontology, health promotion, educational strategies, rehabilitation of brain injured patients. *Unit head:* Dr. Lisa Ann Plowfield, Dean, 850-644-3297, Fax: 850-644-7660, E-mail: lplowfield@nursing.fsu.edu. *Application contact:* Brenda Pereira, Graduate Program Coordinator, 850-644-5638, Fax: 850-645-7249, E-mail: bpereira@fsu.edu.

Framingham State University, Division of Graduate and Continuing Education, Program in Nursing, Framingham, MA 01701-9101. Offers nursing education (MSN); nursing leadership (MSN). *Accreditation:* AACN. *Entrance requirements:* For master's, BSN; minimum cumulative undergraduate GPA of 3.0, 3.25 in nursing courses; coursework in statistics; 2 letters of recommendation; interview. Electronic applications accepted.

George Mason University, College of Health and Human Services, School of Nursing, Fairfax, VA 22030. Offers forensic nursing (Certificate); nursing (MSN, PhD); nursing administration (Certificate); nursing education (Certificate); nursing practice (DNP). *Faculty:* 36 full-time (all women), 52 part-time/adjunct (49 women). *Students:* 47 full-time (46 women), 275 part-time (259 women); includes 90 minority (43 African Americans, 3 American Indian/Alaska Native, 33 Asian Americans or Pacific Islanders, 11 Hispanic Americans), 10 international. Average age 42. 176 applicants, 66% accepted, 77 enrolled. In 2009, 72 master's, 8 doctorates, 3 other advanced degrees awarded. *Degree requirements:* For master's, comprehensive exam (for some programs), thesis in clinical classes; for doctorate, comprehensive exam (for some programs), thesis/dissertation (for some programs). *Entrance requirements:* For master's, resume, 2 recommendation letters, transcripts, nursing license, goal statement, at least 1 year working in the nursing field; for doctorate, resume, 3 recommendation letters, nursing license, at least 1 year of work in the nursing field. Additional exam requirements/recommendations for international students: Required—TOEFL. *Application deadline:* For fall admission, 4/1 priority date for domestic students; for spring admission, 11/1 priority date for domestic students. Applications are processed on a rolling basis. Application fee: $75. Electronic applications accepted. *Expenses:* Tuition, state resident: full-time $7568; part-time $315.33 per credit hour. Tuition, nonresident: full-time $21,704; part-time $904.33 per credit hour. Required fees: $2184; $91 per credit hour. *Financial support:* In 2009–10, 2 students received support, including 2 research assistantships with full and partial tuition reimbursements available (averaging $4,186 per year); Federal Work-Study, scholarships/grants, unspecified assistantships, and nurse faculty loan, health care benefits (full-time research or teaching assistantship recipients) also available. Support available to part-time students. Financial award application deadline: 3/1; financial award applicants required to submit FAFSA. Total annual research expenditures: $270,863. *Unit head:* Dr. Shirley S. Travis, Dean, 703-993-1918. *Application contact:* Janice Lee-Beverly, Program Support, 703-993-1947, E-mail: jleebev1@gmu.edu.

Georgetown University, Graduate School of Arts and Sciences, School of Nursing and Health Studies, Washington, DC 20057. Offers acute care nurse practitioner (MS); clinical nurse specialist (MS); family nurse practitioner (MS); nurse anesthesia (MS); nurse-midwifery (MS); nursing education (MS). *Accreditation:* AACN; AANA/CANAEP; ACNM/DOA. *Degree requirements:* For master's, thesis optional. *Entrance requirements:* For master's, GRE General Test or MAT, bachelor's degree in nursing from NLN-accredited school, minimum undergraduate GPA of 3.0. Additional exam requirements/recommendations for international students: Required—TOEFL.

Goldfarb School of Nursing at Barnes-Jewish College, Goldfarb School of Nursing at Barnes-Jewish College, St Louis, MO 63110. Offers adult acute care nurse practitioner (MSN); adult nurse practitioner (MSN); neonatal nurse practitioner (MSN); nurse anesthesia (MSN); nurse educator (MSN); nurse executive (MSN). *Accreditation:* AACN; AANA/CANAEP. Part-time and evening/weekend programs available. Postbaccalaureate distance learning degree programs offered (minimal on-campus study). *Faculty:* 18 full-time (16 women), 3 part-time/adjunct (2 women). *Students:* 28 full-time (25 women), 81 part-time (73 women); includes 34 minority (27 African Americans, 6 Asian Americans or Pacific Islanders, 1 Hispanic American), 3 international. Average age 38. 60 applicants, 75% accepted, 40 enrolled. In 2009, 26 master's awarded. *Degree requirements:* For master's, thesis or alternative. *Entrance requirements:* For master's, minimum GPA of 3.0, 2 references, statistics course. Additional exam requirements/recommendations for international students: Required—TOEFL (minimum score 550 paper-based; 213 computer-based). *Application deadline:* For fall admission, 2/1 priority date for international students; for spring admission, 10/1 priority date for international students. Applications are processed on a rolling basis. Application fee: $150. *Financial support:* In 2009–10, 60 students received support, including 20 fellowships (averaging $4,000 per year), 4 research assistantships (averaging $5,000 per year); Federal Work-Study, institutionally sponsored loans, and scholarships/grants also available. Support available to part-time students. Financial award applicants required to submit FAFSA. *Faculty research:* HIV Stigma, HIV symptom management, palliative care with children and their families, heart disease prevention in Hispanic women, depression in the well elderly, alternative therapies in pre-term infants. *Unit head:* Dr. Michael L. Evans, Dean, 314-362-6289, Fax: 314-362-0984, E-mail: mevans@bjc.org. *Application contact:* Dr. Michael Ward, Associate Dean for Student Programs, 314-362-9155, Fax: 314-362-9250, E-mail: mward@bjc.org.

Graceland University, School of Nursing, Independence, MO 64050-3434. Offers family nurse practitioner (MSN, PMC); nurse educator (MSN, PMC). Part-time programs available. Postbaccalaureate distance learning degree programs offered (minimal on-campus study). *Faculty:* 9 full-time (all women), 9 part-time/adjunct (7 women). *Students:* 138 full-time (128 women), 146 part-time (126 women); includes 14 minority (8 African Americans, 1 American Indian/Alaska Native, 4 Asian Americans or Pacific Islanders, 1 Hispanic American). Average age 40. 251 applicants, 51% accepted, 90 enrolled. In 2009, 44 master's, 2 other advanced degrees awarded. *Degree requirements:* For master's, comprehensive exam (for some programs), thesis optional. *Entrance requirements:* For master's, BSN from nationally accredited program, portfolio, RN license, minimum GPA of 3.0. *Application deadline:* For fall admission, 6/1 priority date for domestic students; for winter admission, 10/1 priority date for domestic students; for spring admission, 3/1 priority date for domestic students. Application fee: $50. Electronic applications accepted. *Expenses:* Contact institution. *Financial support:* In 2009–10, 117 students received support. Institutionally sponsored loans and traineeships available. Support available to part-time students. Financial award applicants required to submit FAFSA. *Faculty research:* International nursing, family care-giving, health promotion. *Unit head:* Dr. Claudia D. Horton, Dean, 816-833-0524 Ext. 4214, Fax: 816-833-2990, E-mail: horton@graceland.edu. *Application contact:* Abbey Riley, Program Consultant, 816-833-0524 Ext. 4803, Fax: 816-833-2990, E-mail: ajriley@graceland.edu.

Grambling State University, School of Graduate Studies and Research, College of Professional Studies, School of Nursing, Grambling, LA 71245. Offers family nurse practitioner (MSN, PMC); nurse educator (MSN). *Accreditation:* NLN. Part-time programs available. *Faculty:* 8 full-time (all women). *Students:* 40 full-time (37 women), 15 part-time (13 women); includes 20 minority (19 African Americans, 1 Asian American or Pacific Islander), 1 international. Average age 38. 9 applicants, 67% accepted, 5 enrolled. In 2009, 17 master's awarded. *Degree requirements:* For master's, comprehensive exam (for some programs), thesis (for some programs). *Entrance requirements:* For master's, GRE, minimum GPA of 3.0 on last degree, interview, 2 years experience as RN. Additional exam requirements/recommendations for international students: Required—TOEFL (minimum score 500 paper-based; 173 computer-based; 61 iBT). *Application deadline:* For fall admission, 7/1 for domestic and international students; for spring admission, 12/1 for domestic and international students. Applications are processed on a rolling basis. Application fee: $20 ($30 for international students). Electronic applications accepted. *Expenses:* Tuition, state resident: full-time $2610. Tuition, nonresident: full-time $2610. *Financial support:* Health care benefits and tuition waivers (full and partial) available. Financial award application deadline: 5/31; financial award applicants required to submit FAFSA. *Unit head:* Dr. Rhonda Hensley, MSN Program Director, 318-274-2897, Fax: 318-274-3491, E-mail: hensleyr@gram.edu. *Application contact:* Katina Crowe, Special Assistant to Associate Vice President/Dean, 318-274-2158, Fax: 318-274-7373, E-mail: croweks@gram.edu.

Grand Canyon University, College of Nursing and Health Sciences, Phoenix, AZ 85017-1097. Offers addiction counseling (MS); nursing (MS), including adult clinical nurse specialist, family nurse practitioner, nursing education, nursing leadership in health care system; professional counseling (MS). Part-time and evening/weekend programs available. Postbaccalaureate distance learning degree programs offered (no on-campus study). *Entrance requirements:* Additional exam requirements/recommendations for international students: Required—TOEFL (minimum score 575 paper-based; 233 computer-based; 90 iBT), IELTS (minimum score 7).

Grand Valley State University, Kirkhof College of Nursing, Allendale, MI 49401-9403. Offers advanced practice (MSN); case management (MSN); nursing administration (MSN); nursing education (MSN); nursing practice (DNP); MSN/MBA. *Accreditation:* AACN. Part-time programs available. *Faculty:* 17 full-time (all women), 3 part-time/adjunct (all women). *Students:* 6 full-time (5 women), 69 part-time (61 women); includes 3 minority (all African Americans). Average age 39. 18 applicants, 100% accepted, 18 enrolled. In 2009, 23 master's awarded. *Degree requirements:* For master's, thesis optional. *Entrance requirements:* For master's, GRE, minimum GPA of 3.0 in upper-division course work, course work in statistics, Michigan

RN license. Additional exam requirements/recommendations for international students: Required—TOEFL. *Application deadline:* For fall admission, 3/15 priority date for domestic students. Applications are processed on a rolling basis. Application fee: $30. Electronic applications accepted. *Expenses:* Tuition, state resident: part-time $471 per credit hour. Tuition, nonresident: part-time $646 per credit hour. Tuition and fees vary according to course level. *Financial support:* In 2009–10, 23 students received support, including 14 fellowships (averaging $3,207 per year), 9 research assistantships with full and partial tuition reimbursements available (averaging $8,053 per year); career-related internships or fieldwork, Federal Work-Study, institutionally sponsored loans, and traineeships also available. Financial award application deadline: 2/15. *Faculty research:* Multigenerational health promotion, chronic disease prevention, end-of-life issues, nursing workload, family caregiver health. Total annual research expenditures: $36,000. *Unit head:* Dr. Cynthia McCurren, Dean, 616-331-7161, Fax: 616-331-7362. *Application contact:* Dr. Jean Martin, Director of Graduate Programs, 616-331-7167, Fax: 616-331-7362, E-mail: martinj@gvsu.edu.

Grantham University, College of Arts and Sciences, Kansas City, MO 64153. Offers case management (MSN); health systems management (MS); healthcare administration (MHA); nursing (MSN); nursing education (MSN); nursing informatics (MSN); nursing management and organizational leadership (MSN). Part-time and evening/weekend programs available. Postbaccalaureate distance learning degree programs offered (no on-campus study). In 2009, 48 master's awarded. *Degree requirements:* For master's, thesis (for some programs), capstone project. *Entrance requirements:* For master's, bachelor's degree from accredited degree-granting institution. Additional exam requirements/recommendations for international students: Required—TOEFL (minimum score 500 paper-based; 213 computer-based; 61 iBT). *Application deadline:* Applications are processed on a rolling basis. Electronic applications accepted. *Expenses:* Tuition: Part-time $265 per credit hour. One-time fee: $30 part-time. *Financial support:* Institutionally sponsored loans and scholarships/grants available. *Unit head:* Dr. Kim Humerickhouse, Dean, 800-955-2527, Fax: 816-595-5757, E-mail: admissions@grantham.edu. *Application contact:* Matthew Hawes, Vice President of Enrollment Management, 800-955-2527, Fax: 816-595-5757, E-mail: admissions@grantham.edu.

Holy Family University, Graduate School, School of Nursing, Philadelphia, PA 19114. Offers community health nursing (MSN); nursing administration (MSN); nursing education (MSN). *Accreditation:* AACN. Part-time and evening/weekend programs available. *Faculty:* 1 (woman) full-time, 1 (woman) part-time/adjunct. *Students:* 1 (woman) full-time, 46 part-time (all women); includes 7 minority (5 African Americans, 2 Asian Americans or Pacific Islanders). Average age 41. 17 applicants, 76% accepted, 11 enrolled. In 2009, 3 master's awarded. *Degree requirements:* For master's, thesis or alternative. *Entrance requirements:* For master's, bachelor's degree in nursing, RN license, minimum GPA of 3.0, 2 letters of reference. *Application deadline:* For fall admission, 7/1 priority date for domestic students; for winter admission, 11/1 priority date for domestic students. Applications are processed on a rolling basis. Application fee: $25. *Expenses:* Tuition: Part-time $600 per credit. Required fees: $58 per semester. *Financial support:* Federal Work-Study available. Support available to part-time students. Financial award application deadline: 2/15; financial award applicants required to submit FAFSA. *Unit head:* Dr. Christine Rosner, Dean, 267-341-3292, Fax: 215-637-6598, E-mail: crosner@holyfamily.edu. *Application contact:* Gidget Matie Montelibano, Graduate Admissions Counselor, 267-341-3558, Fax: 215-637-1478, E-mail: gmontelibano@holyfamily.edu.

Holy Names University, Graduate Division, Department of Nursing, Oakland, CA 94619-1699. Offers administration/management (MS, Certificate); clinical faculty (MS, Certificate); community health nursing/case manager (MS); family nurse practitioner (MS, Certificate); MSN/Certificate; MSN/MBA. *Accreditation:* AACN. Part-time and evening/weekend programs available. *Entrance requirements:* For master's, bachelor's degree in nursing or related field, California RN license or eligibility, minimum GPA of 3.0, previous course work in research or statistics. Additional exam requirements/recommendations for international students: Required—TOEFL (minimum score 500 paper-based). *Faculty research:* Women's reproductive health, gerontology, attitudes about aging, schizophrenic families, international health issues.

Indiana University–Purdue University Fort Wayne, College of Health and Human Services, Department of Nursing, Fort Wayne, IN 46805-1499. Offers adult nursing practice (MS); nursing administration (MS, Certificate); nursing education (MS); women's health nursing practice (MS). Part-time programs available. *Faculty:* 7 full-time (all women), 1 (woman) part-time/adjunct. *Students:* 5 full-time (all women), 34 part-time (32 women); includes 4 minority (3 African Americans, 1 American Indian/Alaska Native). Average age 37. 15 applicants, 93% accepted, 11 enrolled. *Entrance requirements:* For master's, GRE Writing Test (if GPA below 3.0), BS in nursing, eligibility for Indiana RN license, minimum GPA of 3.0, essay, copy of resume, three references, undergraduate course work in research and statistics within last 5 years. Additional exam requirements/recommendations for international students: Required—TOEFL (minimum score 550 paper-based; 213 computer-based; 77 iBT); Recommended—TWE. *Application deadline:* For fall admission, 5/1 priority date for domestic and international students. Applications are processed on a rolling basis. Application fee: $55 ($60 for international students). Electronic applications accepted. *Expenses:* Tuition, state resident: full-time $4595; part-time $255 per credit. Tuition, nonresident: full-time $10,963; part-time $609 per credit. Required fees: $528; $29.35 per credit. Tuition and fees vary according to course load. *Financial support:* In 2009–10, 11 teaching assistantships with partial tuition reimbursements (averaging $12,740 per year) were awarded; scholarships/grants also available. Support available to part-time students. Financial award application deadline: 3/1; financial award applicants required to submit FAFSA. *Unit head:* Dr. Carol Sternberger, Chair, 260-481-6816, Fax: 260-481-5767, E-mail: sternber@ipfw.edu. *Application contact:* Dr. Susan Ahrens, Graduate Program Director, 260-481-6816, Fax: 260-481-5767, E-mail: ahrenss@ipfw.edu.

Indiana Wesleyan University, College of Graduate Studies, School of Nursing, Marion, IN 46953-4974. Offers community health nursing (MS); nursing (Post Master's Certificate); nursing administration (MS); nursing education (MS); primary care nursing (MS). *Accreditation:* AACN. Part-time programs available. Postbaccalaureate distance learning degree programs offered (minimal on-campus study). *Degree requirements:* For master's, capstone project or thesis. *Entrance requirements:* For master's, writing sample, RN license, 1 year of related experience, graduate statistics course. Additional exam requirements/recommendations for international students: Required—TOEFL. *Expenses:* Contact institution. *Faculty research:* Primary health care with international emphasis, international nursing.

Jefferson College of Health Sciences, Program in Nursing, Roanoke, VA 24031-3186. Offers nursing education (MSN); nursing management (MSN). *Accreditation:* AACN. Part-time programs available. *Faculty:* 16 full-time (9 women), 1 part-time/adjunct (0 women). *Students:* 31 full-time (28 women), 10 part-time (9 women); includes 6 minority (3 African Americans, 2 Asian Americans or Pacific Islanders, 1 Hispanic American). Average age 43. 63 applicants, 59% accepted, 21 enrolled. In 2009, 13 master's awarded. *Degree requirements:* For master's, project. *Entrance requirements:* For master's, MAT. Additional exam requirements/recommendations for international students: Required—TOEFL (minimum score 550 paper-based; 213 computer-based; 80 iBT). *Application deadline:* Applications are processed on a rolling basis. Application fee: $35. Electronic applications accepted. *Financial support:* Career-related internships or fieldwork, Federal Work-Study, scholarships/grants, traineeships, health care benefits, and tuition waivers (full) available. Support available to part-time students. Financial award applicants required to submit FAFSA. *Faculty research:* Nursing, teaching and learning techniques, cultural competence, spirituality and nursing. *Unit head:* Dr. Ava Porter, Department Chair, 540-985-8531, E-mail: agporter@jchs.edu. *Application contact:* Judith McKeon, Director of Admissions, 540-985-9083, Fax: 540-985-9773, E-mail: jomckeon@jchs.edu.

Kaplan University, Davenport Campus, School of Nursing, Davenport, IA 52807-2095. Offers nurse administrator (MS); nurse educator (MS). Part-time and evening/weekend programs available. Postbaccalaureate distance learning degree programs offered (no on-campus study). *Entrance requirements:* For master's, RN. Additional exam requirements/recommendations for international students: Required—TOEFL (minimum score 550 paper-based; 80 computer-based).

Lamar University, College of Graduate Studies, College of Arts and Sciences, Department of Nursing, Beaumont, TX 77710. Offers nursing administration (MSN); nursing education (MSN); MSN/MBA. *Accreditation:* NLN. Part-time and evening/weekend programs available. Postbaccalaureate distance learning degree programs offered. *Faculty:* 4 full-time (all women). *Students:* 3 full-time (2 women), 8 part-time (7 women); includes 2 minority (1 African American, 1 Hispanic American). Average age 41. 15 applicants. In 2009, 3 master's awarded. *Degree requirements:* For master's, comprehensive exam, practicum project presentation, evidence-based project. *Entrance requirements:* For master's, GRE General Test, MAT, criminal background check, RN license, NLN-accredited BSN, college course work in graduate statistics in past 5 years, letters of recommendation, minimum undergraduate GPA of 3.0. Additional exam requirements/recommendations for international students: Required—TOEFL. *Application deadline:* For fall admission, 8/1 priority date for domestic students; for spring admission, 12/1 priority date for domestic students. Applications are processed on a rolling basis. Application fee: $25 ($50 for international students). *Financial support:* In 2009–10, 3 students received support, including 2 teaching assistantships (averaging $24,000 per year); scholarships/grants and traineeships also available. Financial award application deadline: 4/1. *Faculty research:* Student retention, theory, caregiving, online course and research. *Unit head:* Dr. Nancy Blume, Director of Graduate Nursing Studies, 409-880-8820, Fax: 409-880-8698, E-mail: nancy.blume@lamar.edu. *Application contact:* Shelly R. Belk, Administrative Associate, 409-880-7720.

La Roche College, School of Graduate Studies and Adult Education, Program in Nursing, Pittsburgh, PA 15237-5898. Offers nursing education (MSN); nursing management (MSN). *Accreditation:* AANA/CANAEP; NLN. Part-time and evening/weekend programs available. Postbaccalaureate distance learning degree programs offered (minimal on-campus study). *Faculty:* 2 full-time (both women), 1 part-time/adjunct (0 women). *Students:* 8 full-time (all women), 3 part-time (all women), 6 international. Average age 36. 5 applicants, 80% accepted, 4 enrolled. In 2009, 3 master's awarded. *Degree requirements:* For master's, thesis optional, internship, practicum. *Entrance requirements:* For master's, GRE General Test, BSN, nursing license, work experience. Additional exam requirements/recommendations for international students: Recommended—TOEFL (minimum score 550 paper-based; 220 computer-based). *Application deadline:* For fall admission, 8/15 priority date for domestic students, 8/15 for international students; for spring admission, 12/15 priority date for domestic students, 12/15 for international students. Applications are processed on a rolling basis. Application fee: $50. Electronic applications accepted. *Expenses:* Contact institution. *Financial support:* Application deadline: 3/31. *Faculty research:* Patient education, perception. *Unit head:* Dr. Kathleen Sullivan, Division Chair, 412-536-1173, Fax: 412-536-1175, E-mail: sullivk1@laroche.edu. *Application contact:* Hope Schiffgens, Director of Graduate Studies and Adult Education, 412-536-1266, Fax: 412-536-1283, E-mail: schombh1@laroche.edu.

Le Moyne College, Department of Nursing, Syracuse, NY 13214. Offers nursing administration (MS, CAS); nursing education (MS, CAS). *Accreditation:* AACN. Part-time and evening/weekend programs available. *Faculty:* 2 full-time (both women), 6 part-time/adjunct (5 women). *Students:* 25 part-time (24 women); includes 2 minority (both African Americans). Average age 43. 14 applicants, 100% accepted, 14 enrolled. In 2009, 2 master's awarded. *Degree requirements:* For master's, scholarly project. *Entrance requirements:* For master's, interview, minimum GPA of 3.0, New York RN license, 2 letters of recommendation, writing sample. Additional exam requirements/recommendations for international students: Required—TOEFL (minimum score 550 paper-based; 213 computer-based; 79 iBT). *Application deadline:* For fall admission, 6/1 priority date for domestic and international students; for spring admission, 11/1 priority date for domestic and international students. Applications are processed on a rolling basis. Application fee: $50. *Expenses:* Contact institution. *Financial support:* In 2009–10, 7 students received support. Career-related internships or fieldwork, scholarships/grants, health care benefits, and unspecified assistantships available. Support available to part-time students. Financial award applicants required to submit FAFSA. *Faculty research:* Patient and staff education, inter-profession education, eldercare, utilization of free healthcare services by the insured, faculty perceptions of transgender nursing students. *Unit head:* Dr. Susan B. Bastable, Chair/Professor, 315-445-5436, Fax: 315-445-6024, E-mail: bastabsb@lemoyne.edu. *Application contact:* Kristen P. Trapasso, Director of Graduate Admission, 315-445-4265, Fax: 315-445-6027, E-mail: trapaskp@lemoyne.edu.

Lewis University, College of Nursing and Health Professions, Program in Nursing, Romeoville, IL 60446. Offers adult nurse practitioner (MSN); nursing administration (MSN); nursing education (MSN). *Accreditation:* AACN. Part-time and evening/weekend programs available. Postbaccalaureate distance learning degree programs offered (no on-campus study). *Students:* 20 full-time (19 women), 172 part-time (169 women); includes 53 minority (32 African Americans, 11 Asian Americans or Pacific Islanders, 10 Hispanic Americans), 3 international. Average age 41. In 2009, 46 master's awarded. *Degree requirements:* For master's, clinical practicum. *Entrance requirements:* For master's, minimum undergraduate GPA of 2.75, degree in nursing, RN license, letter of recommendation, interview, resume or curriculum vitae. Additional exam requirements/recommendations for international students: Required—TOEFL (minimum score 550 paper-based; 213 computer-based). *Application deadline:* For fall admission, 5/1 priority date for international students; for spring admission, 11/15 priority date for international students. Applications are processed on a rolling basis. Application fee: $40. Electronic applications accepted. *Expenses:* Tuition: Full-time $6480; part-time $720 per credit. One-time fee: $40. Tuition and fees vary according to course load, degree level and program. *Financial support:* Federal Work-Study, scholarships/grants, tuition waivers (full and partial), and unspecified assistantships available. Financial award application deadline: 5/1; financial award applicants required to submit FAFSA. *Faculty research:* Cancer prevention, phenomenological methods, public policy analysis. Total annual research expenditures: $1,000. *Unit head:* Dr. Nan Yancey, Director, 815-838-0500 Ext. 5878, E-mail: yanceyna@lewisu.edu. *Application contact:* Kathy Lisak, Information Contact, 815-838-0500 Ext. 5355, E-mail: lisakka@lewisu.edu.

Lynchburg College, Graduate Studies, School of Health Sciences and Human Performance, Lynchburg, VA 24501-3199. Offers clinical nurse leader (MSN); nursing education (MSN); physical therapy (DPT). *Expenses:* Tuition: Full-time $7020; part-time $390 per credit hour.

Marian University, School of Nursing, Fond du Lac, WI 54935-4699. Offers adult nurse practitioner (MSN); nurse educator (MSN). *Accreditation:* AACN. Part-time and evening/weekend programs available. *Faculty:* 6 full-time (5 women), 5 part-time/adjunct (4 women). *Students:* 40 full-time (37 women), 25 part-time (all women); includes 4 minority (3 Asian Americans or Pacific Islanders, 1 Hispanic American). Average age 39. 28 applicants, 89% accepted, 25 enrolled. In 2009, 21 master's awarded. *Degree requirements:* For master's, thesis, 675 clinical practicum hours. *Entrance requirements:* For master's, 3 letters of professional recommendation; undergraduate work in nursing research, statistics, health assessment. Additional exam requirements/recommendations for international students: Required—TOEFL (minimum score 525 paper-based). *Application deadline:* Applications are processed on a rolling basis. Application fee: $50. Electronic applications accepted. *Expenses:* Contact institution. *Financial support:* In 2009–10, 25 students received support. Institutionally sponsored loans and scholarships/grants available. Support available to part-time students. Financial award application deadline: 3/1; financial award applicants required to submit FAFSA. *Unit head:* Greta Kostac, Interim Assistant Dean, 920-923-8094, Fax: 920-923-8770, E-mail: gmkostac@marianuniversity.edu. *Application contact:* Dr. Greta Kostac, Director, 920-923-7603, Fax: 920-923-8770, E-mail: gmkostac@marianuniversity.edu.

Marymount University, School of Health Professions, Program in Nursing, Arlington, VA 22207-4299. Offers family nurse practitioner (MSN, Certificate); nursing (DNP); nursing education (MSN, Certificate); RN to MSN (MSN). *Accreditation:* AACN. Part-time and evening/weekend programs available. *Faculty:* 5 full-time (all women), 2 part-time/adjunct (both women). *Students:* 13 full-time (12 women), 66 part-time (60 women); includes 38 minority (26 African Americans, 9 Asian Americans or Pacific Islanders, 3 Hispanic Americans), 4 international. Average age 38. 56 applicants, 79% accepted, 30 enrolled. In 2009, 17 master's awarded. *Degree requirements:* For master's, comprehensive exam; for doctorate, thesis/dissertation or alternative. *Entrance requirements:* For master's, 2 letters of recommendation, interview, resume, RN license; for doctorate, 2 letters of recommendation, interview, resume, RN license, minimum

Nursing Education

Marymount University (continued)

MSN GPA of 3.5 or BSN GPA of 3.3; for Certificate, interview, master's degree in nursing. Additional exam requirements/recommendations for international students: Required—TOEFL (minimum score 600 paper-based; 250 computer-based; 96 iBT), IELTS (minimum score 6.5). *Application deadline:* For fall admission, 7/1 for international students; for spring admission, 10/15 for international students. Applications are processed on a rolling basis. Application fee: $40. Electronic applications accepted. *Expenses:* Tuition: Full-time $13,050; part-time $725 per credit hour. Required fees: $135; $7.50 per credit hour. *Financial support:* In 2009–10, 8 students received support; research assistantships with partial tuition reimbursements available, career-related internships or fieldwork, Federal Work-Study, scholarships/grants, and unspecified assistantships available. Support available to part-time students. Financial award applicants required to submit FAFSA. *Unit head:* Dr. Susan Bidwell, Chair, 703-284-1593, Fax: 703-284-3819, E-mail: susan.bidwell@marymount.edu. *Application contact:* Francesca Reed, Director, Graduate Admissions, 703-284-5901, Fax: 703-527-3815, E-mail: grad.admissions@marymount.edu.

Maryville University of Saint Louis, School of Health Professions, Nursing Program, St. Louis, MO 63141-7299. Offers accelerated RN to MSN (MSN); adult nurse practitioner (MSN); advanced practice nursing (DNP); family nurse practitioner (MSN); nursing education (MSN). *Accreditation:* AACN. Postbaccalaureate distance learning degree programs offered. *Students:* 23 full-time (22 women), 96 part-time (92 women); includes 6 African Americans, 6 Asian Americans or Pacific Islanders, 2 Hispanic Americans. Average age 36. In 2009, 23 master's awarded. *Degree requirements:* For master's, practicum. *Entrance requirements:* For master's, BSN, current licensure, minimum GPA of 3.0, 3 letters of recommendation, curriculum vitae. Additional exam requirements/recommendations for international students: Required—TOEFL (minimum score 550 paper-based). *Application deadline:* Applications are processed on a rolling basis. Application fee: $40 ($60 for international students). Electronic applications accepted. *Expenses:* Tuition: Full-time $20,384; part-time $627.50 per credit hour. Required fees: $100 per semester. *Financial support:* Federal Work-Study and campus employment available. Support available to part-time students. Financial award application deadline: 3/1; financial award applicants required to submit FAFSA. *Unit head:* Dr. Mary Curtis, Director, 314-529-9478, Fax: 314-529-9139, E-mail: mcurtis@maryville.edu. *Application contact:* Dr. Mary Curtis, Director, 314-529-9478, Fax: 314-529-9139, E-mail: mcurtis@maryville.edu.

McKendree University, Graduate Programs, Master of Science in Nursing Program, Lebanon, IL 62254-1299. Offers nursing education (MSN); nursing management/administration (MSN). *Accreditation:* AACN. Part-time and evening/weekend programs available. Postbaccalaureate distance learning degree programs offered (no on-campus study). *Faculty:* 5 full-time (all women), 3 part-time/adjunct (2 women). *Students:* 1 full-time (0 women), 86 part-time (82 women); includes 6 minority (5 African Americans, 1 Hispanic American), 1 international. Average age 44. 80 applicants, 84% accepted, 52 enrolled. In 2009, 47 master's awarded. *Degree requirements:* For master's, research project or thesis. *Entrance requirements:* For master's, resume, references, valid Professional Registered Nurse license. Additional exam requirements/recommendations for international students: Required—TOEFL. *Application deadline:* Applications are processed on a rolling basis. Application fee: $0. Electronic applications accepted. *Expenses:* Tuition: Full-time $6300; part-time $350 per credit hour. One-time fee: $125. *Financial support:* Applicants required to submit FAFSA. *Unit head:* Dr. Richelle Rennegarbe, Division Chair, 618-537-2148, E-mail: rarennegarbe@mckendree.edu. *Application contact:* Kim Eichelberger, Director of Nursing Admission, 618-537-6411, Fax: 618-537-6410, E-mail: kaeichelberger@mckendree.edu.

McNeese State University, Doré School of Graduate Studies, College of Nursing, Lake Charles, LA 70609. Offers clinical nurse specialist (MSN); nurse educator (MSN); nurse practitioner (MSN); nursing leadership and administration (MSN). *Accreditation:* AACN. *Faculty:* 4 full-time (all women), 1 part-time/adjunct (0 women). *Students:* 17 full-time (9 women), 72 part-time (56 women); includes 14 minority (12 African Americans, 2 Asian Americans or Pacific Islanders). In 2009, 21 master's awarded. *Degree requirements:* For master's, comprehensive exam. *Entrance requirements:* For master's, GRE, eligibility for unencumbered licensure as RN in Louisiana. *Application deadline:* For fall admission, 5/15 priority date for domestic and international students; for spring admission, 10/15 priority date for domestic and international students. Applications are processed on a rolling basis. Application fee: $20 ($30 for international students). *Expenses:* Tuition, area resident: Full-time $2556. Tuition, state resident: full-time $2556. Required fees: $1031. Tuition and fees vary according to course load. *Financial support:* Application deadline: 5/1. *Unit head:* Dr. Peggy L. Wolfe, Dean, 337-475-5820, Fax: 337-475-5924, E-mail: pwolfe@mcneese.edu. *Application contact:* Valarie Waldmeier, Coordinator of Graduate Nursing, 337-475-5285, Fax: 337-475-5707, E-mail: vwaldmeier@mcneese.edu.

Medical University of South Carolina, College of Nursing, Nurse Educator Program, Charleston, SC 29425. Offers MSN. Part-time and evening/weekend programs available. Postbaccalaureate distance learning degree programs offered (no on-campus study). *Faculty:* 6 full-time (all women), 3 part-time/adjunct (2 women). *Students:* 3 full-time (all women), 12 part-time (all women); includes 3 minority (all African Americans). Average age 37. 14 applicants, 64% accepted, 7 enrolled. In 2009, 10 master's awarded. *Degree requirements:* For master's, thesis optional. *Entrance requirements:* For master's, BSN, course work in statistics, nursing license, minimum GPA of 3.0. Additional exam requirements/recommendations for international students: Required—TOEFL (minimum score 600 paper-based; 250 computer-based). *Application deadline:* For fall admission, 2/1 priority date for domestic and international students. Application fee: $85. Electronic applications accepted. *Financial support:* Federal Work-Study, scholarships/grants, and traineeships available. Support available to part-time students. Financial award application deadline: 3/10; financial award applicants required to submit FAFSA. *Faculty research:* Prenatal care outcomes, perinatal wellness in Hispanic women, use of PDAs. *Unit head:* Carol J. McDougall, Lead Faculty, 843-792-3682, Fax: 843-792-5395, E-mail: mcdougac@musc.edu. *Application contact:* Carolyn G. Page, Director, Student Services, 843-792-3844, Fax: 843-792-5395, E-mail: pagecf@musc.edu.

Mercy College, School of Health and Natural Sciences, Program in Nursing, Dobbs Ferry, NY 10522-1189. Offers nursing administration (MS); nursing education (MS). *Accreditation:* AACN. Part-time and evening/weekend programs available. Postbaccalaureate distance learning degree programs offered (no on-campus study). *Students:* 28 full-time (20 women), 113 part-time (108 women); includes 45 African Americans, 14 Asian Americans or Pacific Islanders, 8 Hispanic Americans, 16 international. Average age 42. 97 applicants, 48% accepted, 38 enrolled. In 2009, 33 master's awarded. *Degree requirements:* For master's, written comprehensive exam or the production of a comprehensive project. *Entrance requirements:* For master's, bachelor's degree, two letters of reference, interview/assessment, RN registration in the U.S. Additional exam requirements/recommendations for international students: Required—TOEFL (minimum score 600 paper-based; 250 computer-based; 100 iBT). *Application deadline:* For fall admission, 8/1 for international students. Applications are processed on a rolling basis. Application fee: $40. Electronic applications accepted. *Expenses:* Tuition: Full-time $13,158; part-time $731 per credit. Required fees: $500. Tuition and fees vary according to degree level and program. *Financial support:* Career-related internships or fieldwork, Federal Work-Study, scholarships/grants, and unspecified assistantships available. Support available to part-time students. Financial award applicants required to submit FAFSA. *Unit head:* Ellen Beatty, Director, 914-674-7548, E-mail: ebeatty@mercy.edu. *Application contact:* Mildred Burns, Administrative Assistant, 914-674-7865, Fax: 914-674-7623, E-mail: mburns@mercy.edu.

MGH Institute of Health Professions, Graduate Programs, School of Nursing, Boston, MA 02129. Offers advanced practice nursing (MSN); gerontological nursing (MSN); nursing (DNP); pediatric nursing (MSN); psychiatric nursing (MSN); teaching and learning for health care education (Certificate); women's health nursing (MSN). *Accreditation:* AACN; NLN (one or more programs are accredited). *Faculty:* 37 full-time (33 women), 11 part-time/adjunct (10 women). *Students:* 325 full-time (275 women), 72 part-time (59 women); includes 48 minority (22 African Americans, 1 American Indian/Alaska Native, 18 Asian Americans or Pacific Islanders, 7 Hispanic Americans). Average age 31. 840 applicants, 53% accepted, 221 enrolled. In 2009, 78 master's, 12 doctorates, 45 other advanced degrees awarded. *Degree requirements:* For master's, thesis or alternative. *Entrance requirements:* For master's, GRE General Test. Additional exam requirements/recommendations for international students: Required—TOEFL (minimum score 550 paper-based; 213 computer-based; 80 iBT). *Application deadline:* For fall admission, 1/10 for domestic and international students. Application fee: $50. Electronic applications accepted. *Expenses:* Tuition: Part-time $943 per credit. Required fees: $943 per credit. Tuition and fees vary according to course load. *Financial support:* In 2009–10, 292 students received support, including 1 research assistantship (averaging $1,200 per year), 2 teaching assistantships (averaging $1,200 per year); career-related internships or fieldwork, scholarships/grants, traineeships, tuition waivers (full and partial), and unspecified assistantships also available. Support available to part-time students. Financial award application deadline: 3/1; financial award applicants required to submit FAFSA. *Faculty research:* Biobehavioral nursing, HIV/AIDS, gerontological nursing, women's health, vulnerable populations, health systems. *Unit head:* Margery Chisholm, Dean, 617-724-0480, Fax: 617-726-8022, E-mail: mchisholm@mghihp.edu. *Application contact:* Maureen Rika Judd, Manager of Admissions, 617-726-6069, Fax: 617-726-8010, E-mail: admissions@mghihp.edu.

Midwestern State University, Graduate Studies, College of Health Sciences and Human Services, Nursing Program, Wichita Falls, TX 76308. Offers family nurse practitioner (MSN); health services administration (MSN); nurse educator (MSN). *Accreditation:* AACN. Part-time and evening/weekend programs available. *Degree requirements:* For master's, comprehensive exam, thesis optional. *Entrance requirements:* For master's, GRE General Test or MAT. Additional exam requirements/recommendations for international students: Required—TOEFL (minimum score 550 paper-based; 213 computer-based). Electronic applications accepted. *Expenses:* Tuition, state resident: full-time $1620; part-time $90 per credit hour. Tuition, nonresident: full-time $2160; part-time $120 per credit hour. International tuition: $7506 full-time. Required fees: $3068.80; $145.60 per credit hour. $179 per semester.

Millikin University, School of Nursing, Decatur, IL 62522-2084. Offers clinical nurse leader (MSN); entry into nursing practice: pre-licensure (MSN); nurse educator (MSN). *Accreditation:* AACN. Part-time programs available. *Faculty:* 9 full-time (8 women). *Students:* 4 full-time (all women), 11 part-time (10 women); includes 1 minority (African American). Average age 41. 9 applicants, 100% accepted, 6 enrolled. In 2009, 3 master's awarded. *Degree requirements:* For master's, thesis or alternative, research project. *Entrance requirements:* For master's, GRE, official academic transcript(s), written essay, immunizations, statistics course, 2 letters of recommendation, CPR certification, professional liability insurance/malpractice insurance. Additional exam requirements/recommendations for international students: Required—TOEFL (minimum score 550 paper-based; 79 iBT). *Application deadline:* For spring admission, 11/1 priority date for domestic students. Applications are processed on a rolling basis. Application fee: $0. Electronic applications accepted. *Expenses:* Tuition: Full-time $24,890; part-time $655 per credit hour. *Financial support:* In 2009–10, 1 student received support. Institutionally sponsored loans available. Financial award applicants required to submit FAFSA. *Faculty research:* Congestive heart failure, quality of life, transcultural nursing issues, teaching/learning strategies, maternal—newborn. *Unit head:* Dr. Deborah Slayton, Director, 217-424-6348, Fax: 217-420-6731, E-mail: dslayton@millikin.edu. *Application contact:* Michelle Whitehead, Administrative Assistant, Master of Science in Nursing Program, 800-373-7733 Ext. 5034, Fax: 217-420-6677, E-mail: mwhitehead@millikin.edu.

Minnesota State University Moorhead, Graduate Studies, College of Education and Human Services, Tri-College University Nursing Consortium, Moorhead, MN 56563-0002. Offers MS. Program offered jointly with North Dakota State University and Concordia College. *Accreditation:* AACN. *Degree requirements:* For master's, thesis or alternative, final oral exam. *Entrance requirements:* For master's, 3 letters of recommendation, minimum GPA of 3.0, RN licensure, bachelor's degree with nursing major. Additional exam requirements/recommendations for international students: Required—TOEFL (minimum score 550 paper-based; 213 computer-based). Electronic applications accepted. *Expenses:* Contact institution.

Missouri State University, Graduate College, College of Health and Human Services, Department of Nursing, Springfield, MO 65897. Offers nursing (MSN), including family nurse practitioner, nurse educator. *Accreditation:* AACN. *Faculty:* 7 full-time (all women), 3 part-time/adjunct (all women). *Students:* 20 full-time (19 women), 22 part-time (19 women); includes 1 minority (Asian American or Pacific Islander), 1 international. Average age 37. 2 applicants, 50% accepted, 1 enrolled. In 2009, 6 master's awarded. *Degree requirements:* For master's, comprehensive exam, thesis or alternative. *Entrance requirements:* For master's, GRE General Test, minimum GPA of 3.0, RN license (MSN), 1 year work experience (MPH). Additional exam requirements/recommendations for international students: Required—TOEFL (minimum score 550 paper-based; 213 computer-based; 79 iBT). *Application deadline:* For fall admission, 7/20 priority date for domestic students, 5/1 for international students; for spring admission, 12/20 priority date for domestic students, 9/1 for international students. Applications are processed on a rolling basis. Application fee: $35 ($50 for international students). Electronic applications accepted. *Expenses:* Tuition, state resident: full-time $3852; part-time $214 per credit hour. Tuition, nonresident: full-time $7524; part-time $418 per credit hour. Required fees: $696; $172 per semester. Tuition and fees vary according to course level, course load, degree level and program. *Financial support:* Federal Work-Study, institutionally sponsored loans, scholarships/grants, and unspecified assistantships available. Financial award application deadline: 3/31; financial award applicants required to submit FAFSA. *Faculty research:* Preconceptual health, women's health, nursing satisfaction, nursing education. *Unit head:* Dr. Kathryn Hope, Head, 417-836-5310, Fax: 417-836-5484, E-mail: nursing@missouristate.edu. *Application contact:* Eric Eckert, Coordinator of Admissions and Recruitment, 417-836-5331, Fax: 417-836-6200, E-mail: tobinbushman@missouristate.edu.

Molloy College, Graduate Nursing Program, Rockville Centre, NY 11571-5002. Offers adult nurse practitioner (Advanced Certificate); clinical nurse specialist: adult health (Advanced Certificate); family nurse practitioner (Advanced Certificate); nurse practitioner psychiatry (Advanced Certificate); nursing (MS); nursing administration (Advanced Certificate); nursing administration with informatics (Advanced Certificate); nursing education (Advanced Certificate); nursing informatics (Advanced Certificate); pediatric nurse practitioner (Advanced Certificate). *Accreditation:* AACN. Part-time and evening/weekend programs available. *Faculty:* 23 full-time (22 women), 5 part-time/adjunct (4 women). *Students:* 11 full-time (10 women), 405 part-time (377 women); includes 206 minority (124 African Americans, 52 Asian Americans or Pacific Islanders, 30 Hispanic Americans), 2 international. Average age 39. In 2009, 64 master's awarded. *Degree requirements:* For master's, thesis optional. *Entrance requirements:* For master's, 3 letters of reference, BS in nursing, minimum undergraduate GPA of 3.0; for Advanced Certificate, 3 letters of reference, master's degree in nursing. *Application deadline:* For fall admission, 9/2 priority date for domestic students; for spring admission, 1/20 priority date for domestic students. Applications are processed on a rolling basis. Application fee: $60. *Expenses:* Tuition: Part-time $765 per credit. Required fees: $340 per semester. *Financial support:* Research assistantships with partial tuition reimbursements, teaching assistantships with partial tuition reimbursements, institutionally sponsored loans, scholarships/grants, and unspecified assistantships available. Support available to part-time students. Financial award application deadline: 4/1; financial award applicants required to submit FAFSA. *Unit head:* Dr. Mary T. O'Shaughnessy, Acting Director, 516-678-5000, Fax: 516-678-9718, E-mail: moshaughnessy@molloy.edu. *Application contact:* Alina Haitz, Assistant Director of Graduate Admissions, 516-678-5000 Ext. 6399, Fax: 516-256-2247, E-mail: ahaitz@molloy.edu.

Monmouth University, Graduate School, The Marjorie K. Unterberg School of Nursing and Health Studies, West Long Branch, NJ 07764-1898. Offers adult nurse practitioner (MSN); adult psychiatric and mental health advanced practice nursing (MSN, Post-Master's Certificate); advanced practice nursing (Post-Master's Certificate); family nurse practitioner (MSN, Post-Master's Certificate); forensic nursing (MSN, Certificate); nursing (MSN); nursing administration (MSN, Post-Master's Certificate); nursing education (MSN, Post-Master's Certificate); school nursing (MSN, Certificate). *Accreditation:* AACN. Part-time and evening/weekend programs available. *Faculty:* 11 full-time (all women), 2 part-time/adjunct (both women). *Students:* 15

full-time (14 women), 183 part-time (178 women); includes 51 minority (14 African Americans, 3 American Indian/Alaska Native, 26 Asian Americans or Pacific Islanders, 8 Hispanic Americans), 1 international. Average age 41. 95 applicants, 99% accepted, 44 enrolled. In 2009, 36 master's awarded. *Degree requirements:* For master's, practicum (for some tracks). *Entrance requirements:* For master's, GRE General Test, RN license, 1 year of work experience, minimum undergraduate GPA of 2.75. Additional exam requirements/recommendations for international students: Required—TOEFL (minimum score 550 paper-based; 213 computer-based; 79 iBT), IELTS (minimum score 5), Michigan English Language Assessment Battery (minimum score 77), Cambridge A, B, C. *Application deadline:* For fall admission, 7/15 priority date for domestic students, 6/1 for international students; for spring admission, 11/15 priority date for domestic students, 11/1 for international students. Applications are processed on a rolling basis. Application fee: $50. Electronic applications accepted. *Expenses:* Tuition: Part-time $773 per credit. Required fees: $157 per semester. *Financial support:* In 2009–10, 118 students received support, including 96 fellowships (averaging $1,308 per year), 4 research assistantships (averaging $3,610 per year); career-related internships or fieldwork, scholarships/grants, and unspecified assistantships also available. Support available to part-time students. Financial award applicants required to submit FAFSA. *Faculty research:* Relationship of undergraduate GPA and GRE to succeed in a graduate nursing program. *Unit head:* Dr. Janet Mahoney, Dean, 732-571-3443, Fax: 732-263-5131, E-mail: jmahoney@monmouth.edu. *Application contact:* Kevin Roane, Director, Office of Graduate Admission, 732-571-3452, Fax: 732-263-5123, E-mail: gradadm@monmouth.edu.

Montana State University, College of Graduate Studies, College of Nursing, Bozeman, MT 59717. Offers clinical nurse specialist (CNS) (MN, Post-Master's Certificate); family nurse practitioner (MN, Post-Master's Certificate); nursing education (Certificate); psychiatric mental health nurse practitioner (MN). *Accreditation:* AACN. Part-time programs available. Postbaccalaureate distance learning degree programs offered (no on-campus study). *Faculty:* 49 full-time (46 women), 25 part-time/adjunct (all women). *Students:* 41 full-time (39 women), 24 part-time (23 women); includes 8 minority (7 American Indian/Alaska Native, 1 Hispanic American). Average age 38. 54 applicants, 33% accepted, 16 enrolled. In 2009, 13 master's awarded. *Degree requirements:* For master's, comprehensive exam, thesis (for some programs). *Entrance requirements:* For master's, GRE General Test. Additional exam requirements/recommendations for international students: Required—TOEFL (minimum score 580 paper-based; 213 computer-based). *Application deadline:* For fall admission, 7/15 priority date for domestic students, 5/15 priority date for international students; for spring admission, 12/1 priority date for domestic students, 10/1 priority date for international students. Applications are processed on a rolling basis. Application fee: $30. Electronic applications accepted. *Expenses:* Tuition, state resident: full-time $5635; part-time $3492 per year. Tuition, nonresident: full-time $17,212; part-time $7865.10 per year. Required fees: $1441; $153.15 per credit. Tuition and fees vary according to course load and program. *Financial support:* In 2009–10, 16 students received support, including 3 fellowships with full tuition reimbursements available (averaging $15,000 per year), 1 research assistantship (averaging $7,000 per year), 8 teaching assistantships with partial tuition reimbursements available (averaging $7,050 per year); traineeships and tuition waivers (partial) also available. Financial award application deadline: 3/1; financial award applicants required to submit FAFSA. *Faculty research:* Environmental exposures, chronic illness, sleep habits, oral health, pressure ulcers. Total annual research expenditures: $2.3 million. *Unit head:* Dr. Elizabeth Kinion, Dean, 406-994-2725, Fax: 406-994-6020, E-mail: ekinion@montana.edu. *Application contact:* Dr. Carl A. Fox, Vice Provost for Graduate Education, 406-994-4145, Fax: 406-994-7433, E-mail: gradstudy@montana.edu.

Moravian College, Moravian College Comenius Center, St. Luke's School of Nursing, Bethlehem, PA 18018-6650. Offers nurse administrator (MS); nurse educator (MS); nurse leadership (MS). Part-time and evening/weekend programs available. *Faculty:* 2 full-time (both women). *Students:* 31 part-time (all women); includes 2 minority (1 African American, 1 Asian American or Pacific Islander). 34 applicants, 94% accepted, 31 enrolled. *Degree requirements:* For master's, comprehensive exam (for some programs), evidence-based practice project. *Entrance requirements:* For master's, GRE or MAT. Additional exam requirements/recommendations for international students: Required—TOEFL (minimum score 550 paper-based; 260 computer-based; 90 iBT). *Application deadline:* Applications are processed on a rolling basis. Application fee: $40. *Expenses:* Tuition: Part-time $1132 per course. Required fees: $40 per term. One-time fee: $30 part-time. *Unit head:* Dr. Lori Hoffman, Director, Master of Science Program in Nursing, 610-861-1400, Fax: 610-861-1466, E-mail: comenius@moravian.edu. *Application contact:* Dr. Lori Hoffman, Director, Master of Science Program in Nursing, 610-861-1400, Fax: 610-861-1466, E-mail: comenius@moravian.edu.

Mountain State University, Graduate Studies, Program in Nursing, Beckley, WV 25802-9003. Offers administration/education (MSN); family nurse practitioner (MSN); nurse anesthesia (MSN); registered nurse anesthetist (Certificate). *Accreditation:* AANA/CANAEP; NLN. Part-time programs available. Postbaccalaureate distance learning degree programs offered (minimal on-campus study). *Faculty:* 4 full-time (all women), 10 part-time/adjunct (9 women). *Students:* 117 full-time (102 women); includes 10 minority (6 African Americans, 1 American Indian/Alaska Native, 3 Asian Americans or Pacific Islanders), 1 international. Average age 37. 46 applicants, 80% accepted, 37 enrolled. In 2009, 35 master's awarded. *Degree requirements:* For master's, comprehensive exam, thesis or alternative. *Entrance requirements:* For master's, GRE. Additional exam requirements/recommendations for international students: Required—TOEFL (minimum score 550 paper-based; 213 computer-based); Recommended—IELTS (minimum score 6.5). *Application deadline:* For spring admission, 6/30 for domestic and international students. Applications are processed on a rolling basis. Application fee: $25 ($50 for international students). Electronic applications accepted. *Expenses:* Contact institution. *Financial support:* Federal Work-Study, scholarships/grants, and unspecified assistantships available. Support available to part-time students. Financial award applicants required to submit FAFSA. *Unit head:* Dr. Judith Halle, Dean, School of Health Sciences, 304-929-1327, Fax: 304-929-1601, E-mail: jhalle@mountainstate.edu. *Application contact:* Melody Tilley, Program Specialist, 304-929-1576, Fax: 304-929-1601, E-mail: mtilley@mountainstate.edu.

Mount Carmel College of Nursing, Nursing Program, Columbus, OH 43222. Offers adult health CNS (clinical nurse specialist) (MS); nursing administration (MS); nursing education (MS). *Accreditation:* AACN. Part-time programs available. *Degree requirements:* For master's, professional manuscript. *Entrance requirements:* For master's, letters of recommendation, current resume, baccalaureate degree in nursing, current Ohio RN license, minimum cumulative GPA of 3.0. Additional exam requirements/recommendations for international students: Required—TOEFL (minimum score 550 paper-based; 213 computer-based; 80 iBT).

Mount Saint Mary College, Division of Nursing, Newburgh, NY 12550-3494. Offers adult nurse practitioner (MS), including nursing education, nursing management; clinical nurse specialist-adult health (MS), including nursing education, nursing management; family nurse practitioner (Advanced Certificate). *Accreditation:* AACN. Part-time and evening/weekend programs available. *Faculty:* 3 full-time (all women), 2 part-time/adjunct (both women). *Students:* 1 full-time (0 women), 53 part-time (50 women); includes 17 minority (8 African Americans, 4 Asian Americans or Pacific Islanders, 5 Hispanic Americans). Average age 39. 16 applicants, 100% accepted, 6 enrolled. In 2009, 5 master's awarded. *Degree requirements:* For master's, research utilization project. *Entrance requirements:* For master's, BSN, minimum GPA of 3.0, RN license. *Application deadline:* For fall admission, 6/3 priority date for domestic students; for spring admission, 10/31 priority date for domestic students. Applications are processed on a rolling basis. Application fee: $45. *Expenses:* Tuition: Full-time $13,356; part-time $742 per credit. Required fees: $50 per semester. *Financial support:* In 2009–10, 2 students received support. Unspecified assistantships available. Financial award application deadline: 4/15; financial award applicants required to submit FAFSA. *Unit head:* Dr. Karen Baldwin, Coordinator, 845-569-3512, Fax: 845-562-6762, E-mail: baldwin@msmc.edu. *Application contact:* Graduate Coordinator, 845-561-0800, Fax: 845-562-6762.

Mount St. Mary's College, Graduate Division, Program in Nursing, Los Angeles, CA 90049-1599. Offers clinical nurse specialist/adult health (MS); community health (MS); educator (MS); leadership and administration (MS); nursing (MS). *Accreditation:* AACN. *Faculty:* 2 full-time (both women), 11 part-time/adjunct (9 women). *Students:* 31 full-time (29 women), 8 part-time (6 women); includes 24 minority (5 African Americans, 12 Asian Americans or Pacific Islanders, 7 Hispanic Americans), 1 international. Average age 41. In 2009, 22 master's awarded. *Entrance requirements:* Additional exam requirements/recommendations for international students: Required—TOEFL (minimum score 550 iBT). *Application deadline:* For fall admission, 7/15 priority date for domestic students; for spring admission, 11/15 priority date for domestic students. *Expenses:* Tuition: Part-time $730 per unit. Part-time tuition and fees vary according to degree level and program. *Unit head:* Dr. Marsha Sato, Chair, 213-477-2980, E-mail: msato@msmc.la.edu. *Application contact:* Director of Graduate Admission.

New York University, College of Nursing, Programs in Advanced Practice Nursing, New York, NY 10012-1019. Offers advanced practice nursing: adult acute care (MS, Advanced Certificate); advanced practice nursing: adult nurse practitioner/palliative care nursing (MS); advanced practice nursing: adult nurse practitioner/holistic nurse practitioner (Advanced Certificate); advanced practice nursing: adult nurse practitioner/holistic nursing (MS); advanced practice nursing: adult nurse practitioner/palliative care nurse practitioner (Advanced Certificate); advanced practice nursing: adult primary care (MS, Advanced Certificate); advanced practice nursing: adult primary care/geriatrics (MS); advanced practice nursing: geriatrics (MS, Advanced Certificate); advanced practice nursing: mental health (MS); advanced practice nursing: mental health nursing (Advanced Certificate); advanced practice nursing: pediatrics (MS, Advanced Certificate); advanced practice nursing:adult primary care and geriatrics (Advanced Certificate); nurse midwifery (MS, Advanced Certificate); nursing administration (MS, Advanced Certificate); nursing education (MS, Advanced Certificate); nursing informatics (MS, Advanced Certificate); MS/MPH; MS/MS. *Accreditation:* AACN; ACNM/DOA. Part-time and evening/weekend programs available. *Faculty:* 17 full-time (all women), 22 part-time/adjunct (19 women). *Students:* 18 full-time (17 women), 524 part-time (485 women); includes 238 minority (90 African Americans, 119 Asian Americans or Pacific Islanders, 29 Hispanic Americans). Average age 33. 191 applicants, 89% accepted, 120 enrolled. In 2009, 117 master's, 2 other advanced degrees awarded. *Degree requirements:* For master's, thesis (for some programs). *Entrance requirements:* For master's, BS in nursing, AS in nursing with another BS/BA, interview; for Advanced Certificate, master's degree. Additional exam requirements/recommendations for international students: Required—TOEFL. *Application deadline:* For fall admission, 7/1 priority date for domestic students, 7/1 for international students; for spring admission, 12/1 for domestic and international students. Applications are processed on a rolling basis. Application fee: $75. *Expenses:* Tuition: Full-time $30,528; part-time $1272 per credit. Required fees: $2177. *Financial support:* Career-related internships or fieldwork, institutionally sponsored loans, scholarships/grants, traineeships, and tuition waivers (partial) available. Support available to part-time students. Financial award application deadline: 2/1; financial award applicants required to submit FAFSA. *Faculty research:* Elderly black diabetics, families and illness, public health nursing, parent-child nursing, health policy costs. *Unit head:* Dr. Judith Haber, Associate Dean for Graduate Programs, 212-998-9020, Fax: 212-995-3143. *Application contact:* Amy Knowles, Assistant Dean for Student Affairs and Admissions, 212-998-5333, Fax: 212-995-4302, E-mail: ak96@nyu.edu.

Northern Arizona University, Graduate College, College of Health and Human Services, School of Nursing, Flagstaff, AZ 86011. Offers family nurse practitioner (MSN, Certificate); nurse educator (MSN); nurse generalist (MSN); nursing (MSN). *Accreditation:* AACN. *Faculty:* 19 full-time (all women). *Students:* 17 full-time (14 women), 32 part-time (29 women); includes 4 minority (1 American Indian/Alaska Native, 3 Hispanic Americans). Average age 30. 43 applicants, 19% accepted, 4 enrolled. In 2009, 7 master's awarded. *Degree requirements:* For master's, project or thesis. *Entrance requirements:* For master's, GRE General Test or minimum GPA of 3.0, undergraduate statistics or health assessment with minimum grade of B in last 5 years or 3 years of RN experience (nursing education). Additional exam requirements/recommendations for international students: Required—TOEFL (minimum score 550 paper-based; 213 computer-based; 80 iBT), IELTS (minimum score 7), or a bachelor's degree from an English-speaking university and demonstrated proficiency. *Application deadline:* For fall admission, 1/15 priority date for domestic students, 9/1 priority date for international students. Application fee: $65. Electronic applications accepted. *Financial support:* In 2009–10, 4 teaching assistantships with partial tuition reimbursements were awarded; career-related internships or fieldwork, Federal Work-Study, traineeships, health care benefits, tuition waivers, and unspecified assistantships also available. Support available to part-time students. Financial award application deadline: 3/30; financial award applicants required to submit FAFSA. *Unit head:* Debera Thomas, Chair, 928-523-2656, Fax: 928-523-7171, E-mail: debera.thomas@nau.edu. *Application contact:* Penny Susan Walior, Student Academic Specialist, 928-523-6717, Fax: 928-523-9155, E-mail: penny.walior@nau.edu.

North Georgia College & State University, Graduate Studies, Department of Nursing, Dahlonega, GA 30597. Offers family nurse practitioner (MSN); nursing education (MSN). *Accreditation:* NLN. Part-time programs available. *Degree requirements:* For master's, one foreign language, comprehensive exam, thesis. *Entrance requirements:* For master's, GRE General Test or MAT, minimum GPA of 2.75, 3 letters of recommendation, current Georgia RN license, 1 year of post-licensure work, BSN. Electronic applications accepted.

Norwich University, School of Graduate and Continuing Studies, Program in Nursing Administration, Northfield, VT 05663. Offers nursing administration (MSN); nursing education (MSN). *Accreditation:* AACN. Evening/weekend programs available. *Faculty:* 5 part-time/adjunct (2 women). *Students:* 70 full-time (64 women); includes 9 minority (4 African Americans, 4 American Indian/Alaska Native, 1 Hispanic American). Average age 43. 79 applicants, 90% accepted, 70 enrolled. In 2009, 70 master's awarded. *Entrance requirements:* For master's, minimum undergraduate GPA of 2.75. Additional exam requirements/recommendations for international students: Required—TOEFL (minimum score 550 paper-based; 212 computer-based; 83 iBT). *Application deadline:* For fall admission, 8/10 for domestic and international students; for winter admission, 11/7 for domestic and international students; for spring admission, 2/6 for domestic and international students. Application fee: $50. Electronic applications accepted. Full-time tuition and fees vary according to course level and course load. *Financial support:* Scholarships/grants available. Financial award applicants required to submit FAFSA. *Unit head:* Anne Moore-Cox, Program Director, 802-485-2567, E-mail: amorreco@norwich.edu. *Application contact:* Rija Ramahatra, Administrative Director, 802-485-2892, Fax: 802-485-2533, E-mail: rramahatr@norwich.edu.

Oakland University, Graduate Study and Lifelong Learning, School of Nursing, Program in Nursing Education, Rochester, MI 48309-4401. Offers MSN, Certificate.

Ohio University, Graduate College, College of Health and Human Services, School of Nursing, Athens, OH 45701-2979. Offers family nurse practitioner (MSN); nurse administrator (MSN); nurse educator (MSN). *Accreditation:* AACN. *Faculty:* 8 full-time (all women). *Students:* 24 full-time (23 women), 31 part-time (25 women); includes 1 African American, 2 American Indian/Alaska Native. 36 applicants, 92% accepted, 25 enrolled. In 2009, 12 master's awarded. *Degree requirements:* For master's, capstone project. *Entrance requirements:* For master's, GRE, bachelor's degree in nursing from an accredited college or university, minimum overall undergraduate GPA of 3.0, official transcripts, statement of goals and objectives, resume, 3 letters of recommendation. Additional exam requirements/recommendations for international students: Required—TOEFL (minimum score 550 paper-based; 80 iBT) or IELTS Academic (minimum score 6.5). *Application deadline:* For fall admission, 3/1 priority date for domestic students, 2/1 priority date for international students. Applications are processed on a rolling basis. Application fee: $50 ($55 for international students). Electronic applications accepted. *Expenses:* Tuition, state resident: full-time $7839; part-time $323 per quarter hour. Tuition, nonresident: full-time $15,831; part-time $654 per quarter hour. Required fees: $2931. *Financial support:* Research assistantships, Federal Work-Study, institutionally sponsored loans, and unspecified assistantships available. Financial award application deadline: 3/1. *Unit head:* Mary Bowen, Director, 740-593-9134, E-mail: bowenm2@ohio.edu. *Application contact:* Cheryl Branham, Administrative Associate, 740-593-4494, E-mail: branhamc@ohio.edu.

Old Dominion University, College of Health Sciences, School of Nursing, Norfolk, VA 23529. Offers family nurse practitioner (MSN); nurse anesthesia (MSN); nurse educator (MSN); nurse

Nursing Education

Old Dominion University (continued)

midwifery (MSN); women's health nurse practitioner (MSN). *Accreditation:* AACN; AANA/CANAEP. Part-time programs available. Postbaccalaureate distance learning degree programs offered (no on-campus study). *Faculty:* 11 full-time (10 women), 15 part-time/adjunct (14 women). *Students:* 122 full-time (113 women), 101 part-time (97 women); includes 49 minority (23 African Americans, 2 American Indian/Alaska Native, 19 Asian Americans or Pacific Islanders, 5 Hispanic Americans). Average age 37. 169 applicants, 81% accepted, 122 enrolled. In 2009, 77 master's awarded. *Degree requirements:* For master's, comprehensive exam. *Entrance requirements:* For master's, GRE or MAT, BSN, minimum GPA of 3.0 in nursing and overall. Additional exam requirements/recommendations for international students: Required—TOEFL. *Application deadline:* For fall admission, 5/1 for domestic students. Applications are processed on a rolling basis. Application fee: $40. Electronic applications accepted. *Expenses:* Tuition, state resident: full-time $8112; part-time $338 per credit. Tuition, nonresident: full-time $20,256; part-time $844 per credit. Required fees: $119 per semester. One-time fee: $50. *Financial support:* In 2009–10, 18 students received support, including 2 research assistantships with tuition reimbursements available (averaging $10,000 per year); teaching assistantships, career-related internships or fieldwork, scholarships/grants, traineeships, and tuition waivers (partial) also available. Support available to part-time students. Financial award application deadline: 2/15; financial award applicants required to submit FAFSA. *Faculty research:* Health and culture, cardiovascular health, transition of military families, genetics, cultural diversity. Total annual research expenditures: $231,117. *Unit head:* Dr. Karen Karlowicz, Chair, 757-683-5262, Fax: 757-683-5253, E-mail: nursgpd@odu.edu. *Application contact:* Sue Parker, Coordinator, Graduate Student Services, 757-683-4298, Fax: 757-683-5253, E-mail: sparker@odu.edu.

Oregon Health & Science University, School of Nursing, Program in Nursing Education, Portland, OR 97239-3098. Offers MN, MS, Post Master's Certificate. Tuition and fees vary according to course level, course load, degree level, program and reciprocity agreements.

Our Lady of the Lake College, School of Nursing, Program in Nursing, Baton Rouge, LA 70808. Offers administration (MS); education (MS). Part-time programs available. *Degree requirements:* For master's, capstone project. *Entrance requirements:* For master's, BSN with minimum GPA of 3.0 during the last 60 hours of undergraduate work, 1 year of clinical nursing experience as a registered nurse, current licensure or eligibility to practice as registered nurse in Louisiana, 3 professional references, 3 credit hours of undergraduate statistics with minimum C average.

Pace University, Lienhard School of Nursing, New York, NY 10038. Offers family nurse practitioner (MS); nursing education (MA); nursing leadership (Advanced Certificate); nursing practice (DNP). *Accreditation:* AACN. Part-time and evening/weekend programs available. *Faculty:* 9 full-time (all women), 18 part-time/adjunct (14 women). *Students:* 41 full-time (37 women), 333 part-time (303 women); includes 140 minority (63 African Americans, 41 Asian Americans or Pacific Islanders, 36 Hispanic Americans), 12 international. Average age 36. 459 applicants, 66% accepted, 125 enrolled. In 2009, 79 master's, 3 other advanced degrees awarded. *Degree requirements:* For master's, thesis. *Entrance requirements:* For master's, GRE General Test or MAT, RN license, resume, personal statement, 2 letters of recommendation, official transcripts; for doctorate, RN license, resume, personal statement, 2 letters of recommendation, official transcripts, accredited master's degree in nursing, minimum GPA of 3.3, advanced experience, state certification; for Advanced Certificate, RN license, completion of 2nd degree in nursing. Additional exam requirements/recommendations for international students: Required—TOEFL. *Application deadline:* For fall admission, 7/31 priority date for domestic students, 4/30 priority date for international students; for spring admission, 10/14 for domestic students, 9/14 for international students. Applications are processed on a rolling basis. Application fee: $70. Electronic applications accepted. *Expenses:* Contact institution. *Financial support:* Research assistantships, career-related internships or fieldwork, Federal Work-Study, and tuition waivers (partial) available. Support available to part-time students. Financial award applicants required to submit FAFSA. *Unit head:* Dr. Harriet Feldman, Dean, 914-773-3341. *Application contact:* Joanna Broda, Director of Graduate Admissions, 914-422-4283, Fax: 914-422-4287, E-mail: gradwp@pace.edu.

Prairie View A&M University, College of Nursing, Houston, TX 77030. Offers family nurse practitioner (MSN); nursing administration (MSN); nursing education (MSN). *Accreditation:* AACN; NLN. Part-time programs available. *Faculty:* 6 full-time (all women), 6 part-time/adjunct (all women). *Students:* 100 part-time (93 women); includes 82 minority (74 African Americans, 1 American Indian/Alaska Native, 4 Asian Americans or Pacific Islanders, 3 Hispanic Americans), 7 international. Average age 37. 37 applicants, 100% accepted, 32 enrolled. In 2009, 7 master's awarded. *Degree requirements:* For master's, comprehensive exam, thesis. *Entrance requirements:* For master's, MAT or GRE, BS in nursing; 2 years of experience as a registered nurse; 1 course each in statistics, basic health and assessment. *Application deadline:* For fall admission, 6/1 priority date for domestic students; for spring admission, 11/1 priority date for domestic students. Applications are processed on a rolling basis. Application fee: $50. *Expenses:* Tuition, state resident: full-time $2200. Tuition, nonresident: full-time $5600. Required fees: $1720. Tuition and fees vary according to course load. *Financial support:* In 2009–10, 17 students received support. Career-related internships or fieldwork, Federal Work-Study, institutionally sponsored loans, scholarships/grants, and traineeships available. Support available to part-time students. Financial award application deadline: 4/1; financial award applicants required to submit FAFSA. *Faculty research:* Software development and violence prevention, health promotion and disease prevention. Total annual research expenditures: $350,000. *Unit head:* Dr. Betty N. Adams, Dean, 713-797-7009, Fax: 713-797-7013, E-mail: bnadams@pvamu.edu. *Application contact:* Dr. Forest Smith, Director of Student Services and Admissions, 713-797-7031, Fax: 713-797-7012, E-mail: pcwillson@pvamu.edu.

Ramapo College of New Jersey, Master of Science in Nursing Program, Mahwah, NJ 07430. Offers nursing education (MSN). *Accreditation:* NLN. Part-time programs available. Postbaccalaureate distance learning degree programs offered (minimal on-campus study). *Faculty:* 7 part-time/adjunct (5 women). *Students:* 34 full-time (32 women), 4 part-time (all women); includes 6 minority (4 African Americans, 2 Asian Americans or Pacific Islanders). Average age 42. 30 applicants, 100% accepted, 12 enrolled. In 2009, 16 master's awarded. *Degree requirements:* For master's, capstone project. *Entrance requirements:* For master's, minimum GPA of 3.0, current RN licensure, 2 letters of recommendation. Additional exam requirements/recommendations for international students: Required—TOEFL (minimum score 550 paper-based; 213 computer-based; 95 iBT). *Application deadline:* Applications are processed on a rolling basis. Application fee: $60. *Expenses:* Tuition, state resident: part-time $525.30 per credit. Tuition, nonresident: part-time $675.20 per credit. Required fees: $53.55 per credit. *Financial support:* In 2009–10, 10 students received support, including 10 fellowships with partial tuition reimbursements available (averaging $1,992 per year); traineeships also available. Financial award applicants required to submit FAFSA. *Unit head:* Dr. Kathleen M. Burke, Assistant Dean, 201-684-7737, E-mail: kmburke@ramapo.edu. *Application contact:* Ulysses Simpkins, Program Assistant, 201-684-7749, E-mail: usimpkin@ramapo.edu.

Regis College, School of Nursing and Health Professions, Weston, MA 02493. Offers health administration (MS); nurse educator (Certificate); nurse practitioner (Certificate); nursing (MS, DNP). *Accreditation:* NLN. Part-time and evening/weekend programs available. *Faculty:* 18 full-time (all women), 12 part-time/adjunct (all women). *Students:* 158 full-time (147 women), 324 part-time (299 women); includes 50 minority (29 African Americans, 1 American Indian/Alaska Native, 15 Asian Americans or Pacific Islanders, 5 Hispanic Americans). Average age 38. 320 applicants, 63% accepted, 155 enrolled. In 2009, 47 master's, 7 other advanced degrees awarded. *Degree requirements:* For master's, thesis. *Entrance requirements:* For master's, GRE General Test or MAT, minimum GPA of 3.0; for doctorate, MAT or GRE if GPA from master's lower than 3.5. Additional exam requirements/recommendations for international students: Required—TOEFL (minimum score 550 paper-based; 213 computer-based). *Application deadline:* Applications are processed on a rolling basis. Application fee: $50. Electronic applications accepted. *Expenses:* Tuition: Full-time $29,000; part-time $800 per credit. Tuition and fees vary according to course load, degree level and program. *Financial support:* In 2009–10, 28 students received support, including 13 research assistantships; Federal Work-Study, scholarships/grants, traineeships, and unspecified assistantships also available. Support available to part-time students. Financial award applicants required to submit FAFSA. *Faculty research:* Health policy, education, aging, job satisfaction, psychiatric nursing, critical thinking. *Unit head:* Dr. Antoinette Hays, Dean, 781-768-7091, Fax: 781-768-8339, E-mail: antoinette.hays@regiscollege.edu. *Application contact:* Christine Petherick, Administrative Coordinator, Graduate Admission, 866-438-7344, Fax: 781-768-7071, E-mail: christine.petherick@regiscollege.edu.

Research College of Nursing, Nursing Program, Kansas City, MO 64132. Offers executive nurse practitioner (MSN); family nurse practitioner (MSN); nursing education (MSN). *Accreditation:* AACN. Part-time programs available. Postbaccalaureate distance learning degree programs offered (no on-campus study). *Degree requirements:* For master's, research project. *Entrance requirements:* For master's, minimum GPA of 3.0, interview, 3 letters of recommendation. Additional exam requirements/recommendations for international students: Required—TOEFL (minimum score 550 paper-based; 213 computer-based), TWE. *Expenses:* Tuition: Part-time $400 per credit hour. Required fees: $25 per credit hour. $50 per semester.

Rivier College, School of Graduate Studies, Division of Nursing, Nashua, NH 03060. Offers family nurse practitioner (MS); nursing education (MS). *Accreditation:* NLN. Part-time and evening/weekend programs available. *Faculty:* 4 full-time (3 women). *Students:* 4 full-time (3 women), 37 part-time (36 women); includes 4 minority (1 African American, 2 Asian Americans or Pacific Islanders, 1 Hispanic American). Average age 36. 29 applicants, 52% accepted, 4 enrolled. In 2009, 12 master's awarded. *Entrance requirements:* For master's, GRE, MAT. *Application deadline:* Applications are processed on a rolling basis. Application fee: $25. Electronic applications accepted. *Expenses:* Tuition: Part-time $447 per credit. *Financial support:* Available to part-time students. Application deadline: 2/1. *Unit head:* Dr. Paula Williams, Head, 603-897-8529. *Application contact:* Mathew Kittredge, Director of Graduate Admissions, 603-897-8129, Fax: 603-897-8810, E-mail: mkittredge@rivier.edu.

Roberts Wesleyan College, Division of Nursing, Rochester, NY 14624-1997. Offers nursing administration (MSN); nursing education (MSN). *Accreditation:* AACN. *Entrance requirements:* For master's, minimum GPA of 3.0; BS in nursing; interview; RN license; resume; course work in statistics and health assessment. Additional exam requirements/recommendations for international students: Required—TOEFL.

Sage Graduate School, Graduate School, School of Health Sciences, Department of Nursing, Program in Education and Leadership, Troy, NY 12180-4115. Offers DNS. *Faculty:* 5 full-time (all women), 8 part-time/adjunct (all women). *Students:* 32 part-time (all women). Average age 49. 24 applicants, 63% accepted, 13 enrolled. *Degree requirements:* For doctorate, thesis/dissertation. *Entrance requirements:* For doctorate, master's degree in nursing from accredited institution; minimum GPA of 3.5; official transcripts; academic curriculum vitae; 3 letters of recommendation; 1-2 page personal essay; interview; current registered nurse license. Additional exam requirements/recommendations for international students: Required—TOEFL (minimum score 550 paper-based; 213 computer-based). Application fee: $40. *Expenses:* Tuition: Full-time $10,620; part-time $590 per credit hour. *Financial support:* Fellowships, research assistantships, Federal Work-Study, scholarships/grants, and unspecified assistantships available. Support available to part-time students. *Unit head:* Dr. Joan Dacher, Associate Professor, Nursing, 518-244-2042, E-mail: dachej@sage.edu. *Application contact:* Wendy D. Diefendorf, Director of Graduate and Adult Admission, 518-244-2443, Fax: 518-244-6880, E-mail: diefew@sage.edu.

Saint Francis Medical Center College of Nursing, Graduate Program, Peoria, IL 61603-3783. Offers child and family nursing (MSN); clinical nurse leader (MSN); medical-surgical nursing (MSN); neonatal nurse practitioner (MSN); nurse clinician (Post-Graduate Certificate); nurse educator (Post-Graduate Certificate); nursing (DNP). *Accreditation:* NLN. Part-time programs available. Postbaccalaureate distance learning degree programs offered (minimal on-campus study). *Faculty:* 3 full-time (all women), 9 part-time/adjunct (all women). *Students:* 8 full-time (all women), 135 part-time (122 women); includes 6 minority (1 African American, 4 Asian Americans or Pacific Islanders, 1 Hispanic American). Average age 28. 19 applicants, 100% accepted, 19 enrolled. In 2009, 24 master's awarded. *Degree requirements:* For master's, research experience, portfolio, practicum. *Entrance requirements:* For master's, nursing research, health assessment, graduate course work in statistics, RN license. Additional exam requirements/recommendations for international students: Required—TOEFL. *Application deadline:* For fall admission, 6/1 priority date for domestic and international students; for spring admission, 11/15 priority date for domestic and international students. Applications are processed on a rolling basis. Application fee: $50. Electronic applications accepted. *Expenses:* Tuition: Part-time $472 per semester hour. Required fees: $130 per semester. *Financial support:* In 2009–10, 6 students received support. Scholarships/grants and tuition waivers (partial) available. Support available to part-time students. Financial award application deadline: 6/15; financial award applicants required to submit FAFSA. *Faculty research:* Outcome and curriculum planning, health promotion, NCLEX-RN results, decision making program evaluation. *Unit head:* Dr. Lois J. Hamilton, Dean, 309-655-2201, Fax: 309-624-8973, E-mail: lois.j.hamilton@osfhealthcare.org. *Application contact:* Dr. Janice F. Boundy, Associate Dean, 309-655-2230, Fax: 309-624-8973, E-mail: jan.f.boundy@osfhealthcare.org.

St. John Fisher College, Wegmans School of Nursing, Advanced Practice Nursing Program, Rochester, NY 14618-3597. Offers advanced practice nursing (MS); clinical nurse specialist (Certificate); family nurse practitioner (Certificate); nurse educator (Certificate). *Accreditation:* AACN. Part-time and evening/weekend programs available. *Faculty:* 9 full-time (all women). *Students:* 5 full-time (4 women), 88 part-time (83 women); includes 7 minority (all African Americans), 1 international. Average age 38. 60 applicants, 87% accepted, 30 enrolled. In 2009, 9 master's awarded. *Degree requirements:* For master's, clinical practice, project; for Certificate, clinical practice. *Entrance requirements:* For master's, BSN; undergraduate course work in statistics, health assessment, and nursing research; current New York State RN License; 2 letters of recommendation; current resume. Additional exam requirements/recommendations for international students: Required—TOEFL (minimum score 575 paper-based; 233 computer-based; 80 iBT). *Application deadline:* Applications are processed on a rolling basis. Application fee: $30. Electronic applications accepted. *Expenses:* Tuition: Part-time $680 per credit hour. Required fees: $25 per semester. Tuition and fees vary according to degree level and program. *Financial support:* In 2009–10, 64 students received support. Federal Work-Study, scholarships/grants, and traineeships available. Financial award applicants required to submit FAFSA. *Faculty research:* Chronic illness, pediatric injury, women's health, public health policy, health care teams. *Unit head:* Dr. Cynthia McCloskey, Graduate Director, 585-385-8471, Fax: 585-385-8466, E-mail: cmccloskey@sjfc.edu. *Application contact:* Jose Perales, Director of Graduate Admissions, 585-385-8067, E-mail: jperales@sjfc.edu.

Saint Joseph's College of Maine, Department of Nursing, Standish, ME 04084. Offers nursing (MS); nursing administration and leadership (Certificate); nursing and health care education (Certificate). MS degree offered only through faculty-directed independent study. *Accreditation:* AACN. Part-time programs available. Postbaccalaureate distance learning degree programs offered (minimal on-campus study). *Degree requirements:* For master's, summer residency. *Entrance requirements:* For master's, MAT. Electronic applications accepted.

Samford University, Ida V. Moffett School of Nursing, Birmingham, AL 35229. Offers advance practice (DNP); anesthesia (MSN); family nurse practitioner (MSN); nurse educator (MSN); nurse executive (DNP); nurse manager (MSN); MBA/MSN. *Accreditation:* AACN; AANA/CANAEP (one or more programs are accredited). Part-time programs available. Postbaccalaureate distance learning degree programs offered (minimal on-campus study). *Faculty:* 10 full-time (all women), 1 part-time/adjunct (0 women). *Students:* 149 full-time (102 women), 31 part-time (24 women); includes 21 minority (14 African Americans, 4 Asian Americans or Pacific Islanders, 3 Hispanic Americans), 1 international. Average age 31. 56 applicants, 98% accepted, 52 enrolled. In 2009, 58 master's awarded. *Degree requirements:* For master's and doctorate, capstone project with oral presentation. *Entrance requirements:* For master's, GRE

General Test or MAT. Additional exam requirements/recommendations for international students: Required—TOEFL (minimum score 550 paper-based; 213 computer-based; 80 iBT). *Application deadline:* For fall admission, 7/1 priority date for domestic and international students; for spring admission, 11/1 priority date for domestic and international students. Applications are processed on a rolling basis. Application fee: $35. *Expenses:* Contact institution. *Financial support:* Institutionally sponsored loans, scholarships/grants, and traineeships available. Financial award application deadline: 3/1; financial award applicants required to submit FAFSA. *Faculty research:* Issues in rural health care, vulnerable populations, genetics and disabilities in pediatrics, geriatrics, Parrish nursing research. *Unit head:* Dr. Nena F. Sanders, Dean, 205-726-2629, E-mail: nfsander@samford.edu. *Application contact:* Marian Carter, Director of Graduate Student Services, 205-726-2047, Fax: 205-726-4269, E-mail: mwcarter@samford.edu.

San Francisco State University, Division of Graduate Studies, College of Health and Human Services, School of Nursing, San Francisco, CA 94132-1722. Offers case management (MS), including long-term care, primary care/family nurse practitioner; nursing administration (MS); nursing education (MS). *Accreditation:* AACN. Part-time programs available.

San Jose State University, Graduate Studies and Research, College of Applied Sciences and Arts, School of Nursing, San Jose, CA 95192-0001. Offers gerontology nurse practitioner (MS); nursing (Certificate); nursing administration (MS); nursing education (MS). *Accreditation:* AACN. Part-time and evening/weekend programs available. *Students:* 8 full-time (7 women), 45 part-time (42 women); includes 20 minority (3 African Americans, 2 American Indian/Alaska Native, 12 Asian Americans or Pacific Islanders, 3 Hispanic Americans), 2 international. Average age 43. 35 applicants, 40% accepted, 8 enrolled. In 2009, 24 master's awarded. *Degree requirements:* For master's, thesis. *Entrance requirements:* For master's, BS in nursing, RN license. *Application deadline:* For fall admission, 6/29 for domestic students; for spring admission, 11/30 for domestic students. Applications are processed on a rolling basis. Application fee: $59. Electronic applications accepted. *Financial support:* Career-related internships or fieldwork, institutionally sponsored loans, and scholarships/grants available. Support available to part-time students. Financial award applicants required to submit FAFSA. *Faculty research:* Nurse-managed clinics, computers in nursing. *Unit head:* Jayne Cohen, Director, 408-924-3132, Fax: 408-924-3135. *Application contact:* Dr. Phyllis Connolly, Graduate Coordinator, 408-924-3144.

Seattle Pacific University, MS in Nursing Program, Seattle, WA 98119-1997. Offers administration (MSN); adult/gerontology nurse practitioner (MSN); clinical nurse specialist (MSN); family nurse practitioner (MSN, Certificate); informatics (MSN); nurse educator (MSN). *Accreditation:* AACN. Part-time programs available. *Faculty:* 3 full-time (all women), 7 part-time/adjunct (6 women). *Students:* 9 full-time (8 women), 63 part-time (57 women); includes 9 minority (1 American Indian/Alaska Native, 7 Asian Americans or Pacific Islanders, 1 Hispanic American), 1 international. Average age 46. 60 applicants, 45% accepted, 27 enrolled. In 2009, 12 master's awarded. *Degree requirements:* For master's, thesis. *Application deadline:* For fall admission, 2/1 priority date for domestic students. Applications are processed on a rolling basis. Application fee: $50. Electronic applications accepted. *Expenses:* Contact institution. *Financial support:* In 2009–10, 41 students received support; fellowships, scholarships/grants available. Financial award applicants required to submit FAFSA. *Unit head:* Dr. Susan Casey, Director, 206-281-2769, Fax: 206-281-2767, E-mail: caseys@spu.edu. *Application contact:* The Grad Center, 206-281-2091.

Seton Hall University, College of Nursing, South Orange, NJ 07079-2697. Offers advanced practice in primary health care (MSN), including adult nurse practitioner, gerontological nurse practitioner, pediatric nurse practitioner; entry into practice (MSN); health systems administration (MSN, DNP); nursing (PhD); nursing case management (MSN); nursing education (MA); school nurse (MSN); MSN/MA. *Accreditation:* AACN. Part-time programs available. Postbaccalaureate distance learning degree programs offered (minimal on-campus study). *Faculty:* 10 full-time (all women), 3 part-time/adjunct (1 woman). *Students:* 46 full-time (35 women), 94 part-time (90 women); includes 22 minority (8 African Americans, 5 Asian Americans or Pacific Islanders, 9 Hispanic Americans). 92 applicants, 88% accepted, 55 enrolled. *Degree requirements:* For master's, research project; for doctorate, dissertation or scholarly project. *Entrance requirements:* For doctorate, GRE. Additional exam requirements/recommendations for international students: Required—TOEFL. *Application deadline:* For fall admission, 6/15 priority date for domestic students. Applications are processed on a rolling basis. Electronic applications accepted. *Financial support:* Institutionally sponsored loans, scholarships/grants, traineeships, tuition waivers (partial), and unspecified assistantships available. Support available to part-time students. Financial award applicants required to submit FAFSA. *Faculty research:* Parent/child, adult, and gerontological nursing; breast cancer; families of children with HIV; parish nursing. *Unit head:* Dr. Phyllis Shanley Hansell, Dean. *Application contact:* Kristyn Kent Wuillermin, Director of Strategic Alliances, Marketing and Enrollment, 973-761-9291, Fax: 973-761-9607, E-mail: kristyn.kent@shu.edu.

Shenandoah University, School of Health Professions, Division of Nursing, Winchester, VA 22601-5195. Offers family nurse practitioner (Certificate); nurse-midwifery (Certificate); nurse-midwifery endorsement (Certificate); nursing (MSN, DNP); post-master's in nursing education (Certificate); psychiatric mental health nurse practitioner (Certificate). *Accreditation:* AACN; ACNM/DOA. Part-time programs available. *Faculty:* 11 full-time (all women), 4 part-time/adjunct (all women). *Students:* 21 full-time (20 women), 67 part-time (64 women); includes 11 minority (7 African Americans, 2 Asian Americans or Pacific Islanders, 2 Hispanic Americans). Average age 39. 71 applicants, 97% accepted, 53 enrolled. In 2009, 8 master's, 6 other advanced degrees awarded. *Degree requirements:* For master's, research project, clinical hours; for doctorate and Certificate, clinical hours. *Entrance requirements:* For master's, GRE General Test, previous course work in statistics, community nursing, and physical assessment; RN license; BSN; minimum undergraduate GPA of 3.0; appropriate clinical experience; curriculum vitae; 3 letters of recommendation; for Certificate, MSN, minimum GPA of 3.0, 3 letters of recommendation. Additional exam requirements/recommendations for international students: Required—TOEFL (minimum score 550 paper-based; 213 computer-based; 79 iBT), IELTS (minimum score 6.5). *Application deadline:* For fall admission, 6/15 priority date for domestic and international students. Applications are processed on a rolling basis. Application fee: $30. Electronic applications accepted. *Expenses:* Tuition: Full-time $11,925; part-time $695 per credit. Required fees: $400 per semester. *Financial support:* Application deadline: 3/15. *Unit head:* Dr. Kathryn Ganske, Director, 540-678-4381, Fax: 540-665-5519. *Application contact:* David Anthony, Dean of Admissions, 540-665-4581, Fax: 540-665-4627, E-mail: admit@su.edu.

Southern Connecticut State University, School of Graduate Studies, School of Health and Human Services, Department of Nursing, New Haven, CT 06515-1355. Offers nursing administration (MSN); nursing education (MSN). *Accreditation:* AACN; AANA/CANAEP. Part-time and evening/weekend programs available. *Faculty:* 6 full-time, 1 part-time/adjunct. *Students:* 2 full-time (both women), 29 part-time (27 women); includes 4 minority (3 African Americans, 1 Hispanic American). 33 applicants, 21% accepted, 7 enrolled. In 2009, 14 master's awarded. *Degree requirements:* For master's, thesis. *Entrance requirements:* For master's, GRE, MAT, interview, minimum QPA of 2.8, RN license, minimum 1 year of professional nursing experience. *Application deadline:* For fall admission, 7/15 priority date for domestic students. Applications are processed on a rolling basis. Application fee: $50. Electronic applications accepted. Tuition and fees vary according to program. *Financial support:* Application deadline: 4/15. *Unit head:* Dr. Lisa Rebeschi, Chairperson, 203-392-6485. *Application contact:* Dr. Antonia Nelson, Graduate Coordinator, 203-392-6480, Fax: 203-392-6493, E-mail: nelsona13@southernct.edu.

Southern Illinois University Edwardsville, Graduate Studies and Research, School of Nursing, Program in Nurse Educator, Edwardsville, IL 62026-0001. Offers MS, Post-Master's Certificate. Part-time programs available. *Students:* 32 part-time (all women); includes 6 minority (5 African Americans, 1 Asian American or Pacific Islander). Average age 26. 25 applicants, 48% accepted. In 2009, 3 master's awarded. *Degree requirements:* For master's, comprehensive exam. *Entrance requirements:* Additional exam requirements/recommendations for international students: Required—TOEFL (minimum score 550 paper-based; 213 computer-based; 79 iBT), IELTS (minimum score 6.5). *Application deadline:* For fall admission, 3/1 for domestic and international students. Application fee: $30. Electronic applications accepted. *Expenses:* Tuition, state resident: part-time $1252.50 per semester. Tuition, nonresident: part-time $3131.25 per semester. Required fees: $586.85 per semester. Tuition and fees vary according to course load. *Financial support:* Career-related internships or fieldwork, Federal Work-Study, institutionally sponsored loans, scholarships/grants, traineeships, and unspecified assistantships available. Support available to part-time students. Financial award application deadline: 3/1; financial award applicants required to submit FAFSA. *Unit head:* Dr. Jacquelyn Clement, Director, 618-650-3923, E-mail: jclemen@siue.edu. *Application contact:* Dr. Jacquelyn Clement, Director, 618-650-3923, E-mail: jclemen@siue.edu.

Southern Nazarene University, Graduate College, School of Nursing, Bethany, OK 73008. Offers nursing education (MS); nursing leadership (MS). *Accreditation:* AACN. Part-time and evening/weekend programs available.

Southern University and Agricultural and Mechanical College, School of Nursing, Baton Rouge, LA 70813. Offers educator/administrator (PhD); family health nursing (MSN); family nurse practitioner (Post Master's Certificate); geriatric nurse practitioner/gerontology (PhD). *Accreditation:* AACN. Part-time programs available. *Degree requirements:* For master's, comprehensive exam, thesis; for doctorate, comprehensive exam, thesis/dissertation. *Entrance requirements:* For master's, GRE General Test, BSN, minimum GPA of 2.7; for doctorate, GRE General Test; for Post Master's Certificate, MSN. Additional exam requirements/recommendations for international students: Required—TOEFL (minimum score 525 paper-based; 193 computer-based). *Faculty research:* Health promotions, vulnerable populations, (community-based) cardiovascular participating research, health disparities chronic diseases, care of the elderly.

State University of New York Institute of Technology, School of Nursing and Health Systems, Program in Nursing Education, Utica, NY 13504-3050. Offers MS, CAS. *Entrance requirements:* For master's, GRE General Test (if undergraduate GPA less than 3.3), minimum GPA of 3.0 in last 30 hours of undergraduate work, bachelor's in nursing, 1 year RN experience, RN license, 2 letters of recommendation, interview. Additional exam requirements/recommendations for international students: Required—TOEFL (minimum score 550 paper-based; 213 computer-based). *Faculty research:* Nursing faculty shortages, curriculum enhancements, measurement and assessment, evidence-based practice.

Teachers College, Columbia University, Graduate Faculty of Education, Department of Health and Behavioral Studies, Program in Nursing, Professional Role, New York, NY 10027-6696. Offers Ed M, MA, Ed D. *Faculty:* 1 (woman) full-time. *Students:* 5 full-time (all women), 9 part-time (8 women); includes 3 minority (all African Americans). Average age 49. 3 applicants, 0% accepted. *Degree requirements:* For master's, capstone project; for doctorate, thesis/dissertation. *Entrance requirements:* For master's, BSN, nursing license; for doctorate, GRE General Test or MAT, BSN, nursing license. *Application deadline:* For fall admission, 5/15 for domestic students; for spring admission, 12/1 for domestic students. Application fee: $65. *Financial support:* Career-related internships or fieldwork, Federal Work-Study, institutionally sponsored loans, traineeships, and tuition waivers (full and partial) available. Support available to part-time students. Financial award application deadline: 2/1. *Faculty research:* Empathy in nurses, clinical teaching for basic nursing students, interdisciplinary health care team. *Unit head:* Dr. Chuck Basch, Chair, 212-678-3964, E-mail: ceb35@columbia.edu. *Application contact:* Peter Shon, Assistant Director of Admission, 212-678-3305, Fax: 212-678-4171, E-mail: shon@exchange.tc.columbia.edu.

Teachers College, Columbia University, Graduate Faculty of Education, Department of Organization and Leadership, New York, NY 10027-6696. Offers adult education (MA, Ed D); education leadership (Ed M, MA, Ed D, PhD), including education leadership (PhD), education leadership studies (Ed M, MA, Ed D), leadership, policy and politics, private school leadership (Ed M, MA, Ed D), public school and school district leadership (Ed M, MA, Ed D); educational administration (Ed M, MA, Ed D, PhD); higher education (Ed M, MA, Ed D, PhD); inquiry in education leadership (Ed D); nurse executive (Ed M, MA, Ed D); politics and education (Ed M, MA, Ed D, PhD); social and organizational psychology (MA, Ed D, PhD), including organizational psychology, social psychology (Ed D, PhD); student personnel administration (Ed M, MA, Ed D); MBA/Ed D. Part-time and evening/weekend programs available. *Faculty:* 23 full-time (12 women). *Students:* 347 full-time (235 women), 549 part-time (362 women); includes 297 minority (144 African Americans, 85 Asian Americans or Pacific Islanders, 68 Hispanic Americans), 49 international. Average age 34. 657 applicants, 60% accepted, 188 enrolled. In 2009, 371 master's, 34 doctorates awarded. *Degree requirements:* For doctorate, thesis/dissertation. *Application deadline:* For fall admission, 5/15 for domestic students. Application fee: $65. *Financial support:* Fellowships, research assistantships, career-related internships or fieldwork, Federal Work-Study, institutionally sponsored loans, and tuition waivers (full and partial) available. Support available to part-time students. Financial award application deadline: 2/1. *Unit head:* Warner Burke, Chair, 212-678-3258. *Application contact:* Debbie Lesperance, Assistant Director of Admission, 212-678-3710, Fax: 212-678-4171.

Tennessee Technological University, School of Nursing, Cookeville, TN 38505. Offers family nurse practitioner (MSN); informatics (MSN); nursing administration (MSN); nursing education (MSN). *Students:* 11 full-time (10 women), 30 part-time (27 women); includes 2 minority (1 African American, 1 Hispanic American). 40 applicants, 35% accepted, 10 enrolled. In 2009, 14 master's awarded. *Degree requirements:* For master's, comprehensive exam, thesis or alternative. *Entrance requirements:* Additional exam requirements/recommendations for international students: Required—TOEFL (minimum score 550 paper-based; 79 iBT), IELTS (minimum score 5.5). *Application deadline:* For fall admission, 8/1 for domestic students, 5/1 for international students; for spring admission, 12/1 for domestic students, 10/1 for international students. Application fee: $25 ($30 for international students). Electronic applications accepted. *Expenses:* Tuition, state resident: full-time $7034; part-time $368 per credit hour. *Financial support:* Application deadline: 4/1. *Unit head:* Dr. Sheila Green, Interim Dean, 931-372-3203, Fax: 931-372-6244, E-mail: sgreen@tntech.edu. *Application contact:* Shelia K. Kendrick, Coordinator of Graduate Studies, 931-372-3808, Fax: 931-372-3497, E-mail: skendrick@tntech.edu.

Texas Tech University Health Sciences Center, School of Nursing, Lubbock, TX 79430. Offers acute care nurse practitioner (MSN, Certificate); administration (MSN); advanced practice (DNP); education (MSN); executive leadership (DNP); family nurse practitioner (MSN, Certificate); geriatric nurse practitioner (MSN, Certificate); pediatric nurse practitioner (MSN, Certificate). *Accreditation:* AACN. Part-time programs available. Postbaccalaureate distance learning degree programs offered (minimal on-campus study). *Degree requirements:* For master's, thesis optional. *Entrance requirements:* For master's, minimum GPA of 3.0, 3 letters of reference, BSN, RN license; for Certificate, minimum GPA of 3.0, 3 letters of reference, RN license. Additional exam requirements/recommendations for international students: Required—TOEFL (minimum score 550 paper-based; 213 computer-based). *Faculty research:* Diabetes/obesity, nurse competency, disease management, intervention and measurements, health disparities.

Texas Woman's University, Graduate School, College of Nursing, Denton, TX 76201. Offers acute care nurse practitioner (MS); adult health clinical nurse specialist (MS); adult health nurse practitioner (MS); child health clinical nurse specialist (MS); clinical nurse leader (MS); community health (MS); family nurse practitioner (MS); health systems management (MS); nursing education (MS); nursing practice (DNP); nursing science (PhD); pediatric nurse practitioner (MS); women's health clinical nurse specialist (MS); women's health nurse practitioner (MS). *Accreditation:* AACN. Part-time programs available. Postbaccalaureate distance learning degree programs offered. *Faculty:* 85 full-time (80 women), 6 part-time/adjunct (all women). *Students:* 81 full-time (76 women), 602 part-time (571 women); includes 293 minority (154 African Americans, 3 American Indian/Alaska Native, 90 Asian Americans or Pacific Islanders, 46 Hispanic Americans), 19 international. Average age 39. 259 applicants, 81% accepted, 166 enrolled. In 2009, 100 master's, 22 doctorates awarded. *Degree requirements:* For master's, thesis or alternative; for doctorate, comprehensive exam, thesis/dissertation. *Entrance requirements:* For master's, GRE or MAT, minimum GPA of 3.0, RN license, BS in nursing,

Nursing Education

Texas Woman's University (continued)

basic statistics course; for doctorate, GRE (Verbal 460, Quantitative 500) or MAT (50), MS in nursing, minimum GPA of 3.5, RN license, coursework in statistics, 2 letters of reference, curriculum vitae, nursing-theory course, graduate research course, letter stating professional and research goals. Additional exam requirements/recommendations for international students: Required—TOEFL (minimum score 550 paper-based; 213 computer-based; 79 iBT). *Application deadline:* For fall admission, 5/1 priority date for domestic students, 3/1 for international students; for spring admission, 9/15 priority date for domestic students, 7/1 for international students. Applications are processed on a rolling basis. Application fee: $50. Electronic applications accepted. *Expenses:* Tuition, state resident: full-time $3564; part-time $198 per credit hour. Tuition, nonresident: full-time $8550; part-time $475 per credit hour. Required fees: $69.26 per credit hour. Tuition and fees vary according to course load. *Financial support:* In 2009–10, 99 students received support, including 16 fellowships (averaging $17,325 per year), 5 research assistantships (averaging $11,484 per year), 5 teaching assistantships (averaging $11,484 per year); career-related internships or fieldwork, Federal Work-Study, institutionally sponsored loans, scholarships/grants, traineeships, health care benefits, and unspecified assistantships also available. Support available to part-time students. Financial award application deadline: 3/1; financial award applicants required to submit FAFSA. *Faculty research:* Evaluation of pre-natal care, screening for intimate partner violence, stressors and nursing success, breast surgery, breast feeding, adolescent needs during childbirth. *Unit head:* Dr. Patricia Holden-Huchton, Interim Dean, 940-898-2401, Fax: 940-898-2437, E-mail: pholdenhuchton@twu.edu. *Application contact:* Samuel Wheeler, Assistant Director of Admissions, 940-898-3188, Fax: 940-898-3081, E-mail: wheelersr@twu.edu.

Thomas Edison State College, School of Nursing, Program in Nurse Educator, Trenton, NJ 08608-1176. Offers Post-Master's Certificate. *Accreditation:* AACN. Part-time programs available. Postbaccalaureate distance learning degree programs offered (no on-campus study). *Degree requirements:* For Post-Master's Certificate, nursing education seminar and online practicum. *Entrance requirements:* For degree, master's degree in nursing, RN. Additional exam requirements/recommendations for international students: Required—TOEFL (minimum score 550 paper-based; 213 computer-based; 79 iBT). *Application deadline:* For fall admission, 8/15 for domestic and international students; for winter admission, 11/15 for domestic and international students; for spring admission, 2/15 for domestic and international students. Application fee: $75. Electronic applications accepted. *Expenses:* Tuition, area resident: Part-time $479 per credit. Tuition, state resident: part-time $479 per credit. Tuition, nonresident: part-time $479 per credit. *Financial support:* Applicants required to submit FAFSA. *Unit head:* Dr. Susan O'Brien, Dean, School of Nursing, 609-633-6460, Fax: 609-292-8279, E-mail: nursing@tesc.edu. *Application contact:* David Hoftiezer, Director of Admissions, 888-442-8372, Fax: 609-984-8447, E-mail: admissions@tesc.edu.

Towson University, College of Graduate Studies and Research, Program in Nursing, Towson, MD 21252-0001. Offers nursing (MS); nursing education (Certificate). *Accreditation:* AACN. Part-time programs available. *Degree requirements:* For master's, thesis optional. *Entrance requirements:* For master's, minimum GPA of 3.0, copy of current nursing license, bachelor's degree in nursing, curriculum vitae; for Certificate, minimum GPA of 3.0, copy of current nursing license, curriculum vitae, bachelor's degree in nursing. Electronic applications accepted. *Faculty research:* End of life care, caring, health policy, parish nursing.

Union University, School of Nursing, Jackson, TN 38305-3697. Offers executive leadership (DNP); nurse anesthesia (DNP); nurse anesthetist (PMC); nurse practitioner (DNP); nursing education (MSN, PMC). *Accreditation:* AACN; AANA/CANAEP. *Degree requirements:* For master's, thesis or alternative. *Entrance requirements:* For master's, GRE, 3 letters of reference, bachelor's degree in nursing, minimum GPA of 3.0. Additional exam requirements/recommendations for international students: Required—TOEFL (minimum score 560 paper-based; 220 computer-based). Electronic applications accepted. *Faculty research:* Children's health, occupational rehabilitation, informatics, health promotion.

The University of Alabama in Huntsville, School of Graduate Studies, College of Nursing, Huntsville, AL 35899. Offers family nurse practitioner (Certificate); nursing (MSN, DNP), including acute care nurse practitioner (MSN), adult clinical nursing specialist (MSN), clinical nurse leader (MSN), family nurse practitioner (MSN), leadership in health care systems (MSN); nursing education (Certificate). *Accreditation:* AACN. Part-time and evening/weekend programs available. Postbaccalaureate distance learning degree programs offered (minimal on-campus study). *Faculty:* 13 full-time (11 women), 3 part-time/adjunct (2 women). *Students:* 45 full-time (43 women), 121 part-time (111 women); includes 25 minority (17 African Americans, 5 American Indian/Alaska Native, 3 Asian Americans or Pacific Islanders), 3 international. Average age 39. 151 applicants, 68% accepted, 74 enrolled. In 2009, 52 master's, 5 other advanced degrees awarded. *Degree requirements:* For master's, comprehensive exam, thesis or alternative, oral and written exams; for doctorate, comprehensive exam, thesis/dissertation or alternative, oral and written exams. *Entrance requirements:* For master's, MAT or GRE, Alabama RN license, BSN, minimum GPA of 3.0; for doctorate, master's degree in nursing in an advanced practice area; for Certificate, MAT or GRE, minimum GPA of 3.0. Additional exam requirements/recommendations for international students: Required—TOEFL (minimum score 500 paper-based; 173 computer-based; 62 iBT). *Application deadline:* For fall admission, 7/15 for domestic students, 4/1 for international students; for spring admission, 11/30 for domestic students, 9/1 for international students. Applications are processed on a rolling basis. Application fee: $40 ($50 for international students). Electronic applications accepted. *Expenses:* Tuition, state resident: part-time $355.75 per credit hour. Tuition, nonresident: part-time $847.10 per credit hour. Required fees: $210.80 per semester. Tuition and fees vary according to course load and program. *Financial support:* In 2009–10, 11 students received support, including 11 teaching assistantships with full and partial tuition reimbursements available (averaging $9,996 per year); career-related internships or fieldwork, Federal Work-Study, institutionally sponsored loans, scholarships/grants, traineeships, health care benefits, and unspecified assistantships also available. Support available to part-time students. Financial award application deadline: 4/1; financial award applicants required to submit FAFSA. *Faculty research:* Home health care, gerontology, pediatric nursing, family nurse practitioner, adult acute care administration. *Unit head:* Dr. Fay Raines, Dean, 256-824-6345, Fax: 256-824-6026, E-mail: rainesc@uah.edu. *Application contact:* Charles Davis, Associate Director of Nursing Student Affairs Graduate Programs, 256-824-6669, Fax: 256-824-6026, E-mail: charles.davis@uah.edu.

University of Alaska Anchorage, College of Health and Social Welfare, School of Nursing, Anchorage, AK 99508. Offers family nurse practitioner (Certificate); nursing (MS); nursing education (Certificate); psychiatric nurse practitioner (Certificate). *Accreditation:* NLN. Part-time and evening/weekend programs available. *Degree requirements:* For master's, comprehensive exam, individual project. *Entrance requirements:* For master's, GRE or MAT, BS in nursing, interview, minimum GPA of 3.0, RN license, 1 year of part-time or 6 months of full-time clinical experience. Additional exam requirements/recommendations for international students: Required—TOEFL (minimum score 550 paper-based; 213 computer-based).

University of Central Florida, College of Nursing, Orlando, FL 32816. Offers adult nurse practitioner (MSN, Post-Master's Certificate); clinical nurse leader (MSN, Post-Master's Certificate); clinical nurse specialist (MSN, Post-Master's Certificate); family nurse practitioner (MSN, Post-Master's Certificate); leadership and management (MSN); nurse educator (MSN); nursing (PhD); nursing education (Post-Master's Certificate); nursing practice (DNP); pediatric nurse practitioner (MSN, Post-Master's Certificate). *Accreditation:* AACN. Part-time and evening/weekend programs available. *Faculty:* 38 full-time (34 women), 49 part-time/adjunct (47 women). *Students:* 98 full-time (93 women), 371 part-time (350 women); includes 132 minority (63 African Americans, 2 American Indian/Alaska Native, 29 Asian Americans or Pacific Islanders, 38 Hispanic Americans), 9 international. Average age 39. 363 applicants, 49% accepted, 139 enrolled. In 2009, 72 master's, 3 doctorates, 8 other advanced degrees awarded. *Degree requirements:* For master's, thesis or alternative. *Entrance requirements:* For master's, GRE General Test, minimum GPA of 3.0 in last 60 hours. Additional exam requirements/recommendations for international students: Required—TOEFL. *Application deadline:* For fall admission, 2/15 for domestic students; for spring admission, 9/15 for domestic students. Application fee: $30. Electronic applications accepted. *Expenses:* Tuition, state resident: part-time $306.31 per credit hour. Tuition, nonresident: part-time $1099.01 per credit hour. Part-time tuition and fees vary according to degree level and program. *Financial support:* In 2009–10, 30 students received support, including 30 fellowships with partial tuition reimbursements available (averaging $3,200 per year), 1 teaching assistantship with partial tuition reimbursement available (averaging $13,440 per year); research assistantships with partial tuition reimbursements available, career-related internships or fieldwork, Federal Work-Study, institutionally sponsored loans, traineeships, and unspecified assistantships also available. Financial award application deadline: 3/1; financial award applicants required to submit FAFSA. *Unit head:* Dr. Jean D. Leuner, Dean, 407-823-5496, Fax: 407-823-5675, E-mail: jleuner@mail.ucf.edu. *Application contact:* Dr. Jean D. Leuner, Dean, 407-823-5496, Fax: 407-823-5675, E-mail: jleuner@mail.ucf.edu.

University of Hartford, College of Education, Nursing, and Health Professions, Program in Nursing, West Hartford, CT 06117-1599. Offers community/public health nursing (MSN); nursing education (MSN); nursing management (MSN). *Accreditation:* AACN. Part-time and evening/weekend programs available. *Degree requirements:* For master's, research project. *Entrance requirements:* For master's, BSN, Connecticut RN license. Additional exam requirements/recommendations for international students: Required—TOEFL (minimum score 550 paper-based; 213 computer-based). Electronic applications accepted. *Expenses:* Contact institution. *Faculty research:* Child development, women in doctoral study, applying feminist theory in teaching methods, near death experience, grandmothers as primary care providers.

University of Indianapolis, Graduate Programs, School of Nursing, Indianapolis, IN 46227-3697. Offers family practice (post-RN) (MSN); gerontological nurse practitioner (MSN); nurse-midwifery (MSN); nursing (MSN); nursing administration (MSN); nursing education (MSN); MBA/MSN. *Accreditation:* AACN; ACNM. *Faculty:* 4 full-time (3 women), 2 part-time/adjunct (both women). *Students:* 27 full-time (26 women), 118 part-time (109 women); includes 10 minority (6 African Americans, 1 American Indian/Alaska Native, 1 Asian American or Pacific Islander, 2 Hispanic Americans), 2 international. Average age 38. *Entrance requirements:* For master's, minimum GPA of 3.0, interview, letters of recommendation, resume, IN nursing license, 1 year professional practice. Additional exam requirements/recommendations for international students: Required—TOEFL (minimum score 550 paper-based; 213 computer-based). *Application deadline:* For fall admission, 8/1 for domestic students; for winter admission, 12/15 for domestic students; for spring admission, 4/15 for domestic students. Applications are processed on a rolling basis. Application fee: $50. *Financial support:* Federal Work-Study available. *Unit head:* Dr. Anne Thomas, Dean, 317-788-3206, E-mail: athomas@uindy.edu. *Application contact:* T. C. Crum, Information Contact, 317-788-2128, Fax: 317-788-3542, E-mail: tcrum@uindy.edu.

University of Mary, Division of Nursing, Bismarck, ND 58504-9652. Offers family nurse practitioner (MSN); nurse administrator (MSN); nursing educator (MSN). *Accreditation:* AACN. Part-time and evening/weekend programs available. Postbaccalaureate distance learning degree programs offered (minimal on-campus study). *Degree requirements:* For master's, comprehensive exam, thesis (for some programs), internship (family nurse practitioner), teaching practice. *Entrance requirements:* For master's, minimum GPA of 3.0 in nursing, interview, letters of recommendation. Additional exam requirements/recommendations for international students: Required—TOEFL. Electronic applications accepted. *Expenses:* Tuition: Full-time $10,062; part-time $430 per credit. Tuition and fees vary according to course load, degree level, program and student level. *Faculty research:* Gerontology issues, rural nursing, health policy, primary care, women's health.

University of Maryland, Baltimore, Graduate School, School of Nursing, Master's Program in Nursing, Baltimore, MD 21201. Offers community health nursing (MS); gerontological nursing (MS); maternal-child nursing (MS); medical-surgical nursing (MS); nurse-midwifery education (MS); nursing administration (MS); nursing education (MS); nursing health policy (MS); primary care nursing (MS); psychiatric nursing (MS); MS/MBA. *Accreditation:* AACN; AANA/CANAEP; ACNM/DOA; NLN (one or more programs are accredited). Part-time programs available. *Students:* 387 full-time (338 women), 528 part-time (491 women); includes 330 minority (230 African Americans, 3 American Indian/Alaska Native, 81 Asian Americans or Pacific Islanders, 16 Hispanic Americans), 10 international. Average age 36. 849 applicants, 40% accepted, 255 enrolled. In 2009, 264 master's awarded. *Degree requirements:* For master's, comprehensive exam (for some programs), thesis or alternative. *Entrance requirements:* For master's, GRE General Test, minimum GPA of 2.75, course work in statistics, BS in nursing. Additional exam requirements/recommendations for international students: Required—TOEFL (minimum score 550 paper-based; 80 iBT), or IELTS (minimum score 7). *Application deadline:* For fall admission, 1/15 for international students. Application fee: $50. Electronic applications accepted. *Expenses:* Tuition, state resident: full-time $7290; part-time $405 per credit hour. Tuition, nonresident: full-time $12,780; part-time $710 per credit hour. Required fees: $774; $10 per credit hour. $297 per semester. Tuition and fees vary according to course load, degree level and program. *Financial support:* Fellowships, research assistantships, teaching assistantships, career-related internships or fieldwork and traineeships available. Support available to part-time students. Financial award application deadline: 2/15; financial award applicants required to submit FAFSA. *Unit head:* Dr. Jane Kapustin, Assistant Dean, 410-706-6741, Fax: 410-706-4231. *Application contact:* Marjorie Fass, Admissions Director, 410-706-0501, Fax: 410-706-7238.

University of Massachusetts Lowell, School of Health and Environment, Department of Nursing, Lowell, MA 01854-2881. Offers adult psychiatric and mental health nursing (MS, Graduate Certificate); family health nursing (MS); gerontological nursing (MS, Graduate Certificate); geropsychiatric nursing (Graduate Certificate); nursing (PhD); nursing education (Graduate Certificate); palliative and end-of-life nursing care (Graduate Certificate). *Accreditation:* AACN. *Degree requirements:* For master's, thesis optional; for doctorate, thesis/dissertation. *Entrance requirements:* For master's and doctorate, GRE General Test. *Faculty research:* Gerontology, women's health issues, long-term care, alcoholism, health promotion.

University of Massachusetts Worcester, Graduate School of Nursing, Worcester, MA 01655-0115. Offers adult acute/critical care nurse practitioner (MS, Post Master's Certificate); adult acute/critical care nurse practitioner and gerontological nurse practitioner (MS, Post Master's Certificate); adult primary care nurse practitioner (MS, Post Master's Certificate); adult primary care nurse practitioner and gerontological nurse practitioner (MS, Post Master's Certificate); family nurse practitioner (MS); gerontological nurse practitioner (Post Master's Certificate); nurse educator (MS); nursing (PhD). *Accreditation:* AACN. *Faculty:* 15 full-time (13 women), 31 part-time/adjunct (29 women). *Students:* 151 full-time (131 women), 6 part-time (all women); includes 14 minority (5 African Americans, 1 American Indian/Alaska Native, 5 Asian Americans or Pacific Islanders, 3 Hispanic Americans). Average age 37. 206 applicants, 34% accepted, 61 enrolled. In 2009, 62 master's, 3 doctorates awarded. *Degree requirements:* For doctorate, comprehensive exam, thesis/dissertation. *Entrance requirements:* For master's, GRE General Test, bachelor's degree, course work in statistics; for doctorate, GRE General Test, bachelor's or master's degree, RN licensure; for Post Master's Certificate, MS in nursing. Additional exam requirements/recommendations for international students: Required—TOEFL. *Application deadline:* For fall admission, 3/15 for domestic students. Applications are processed on a rolling basis. Application fee: $40 ($60 for international students). *Expenses:* Contact institution. *Financial support:* In 2009–10, 130 students received support. Scholarships/grants and traineeships available. Support available to part-time students. Financial award application deadline: 5/18; financial award applicants required to submit FAFSA. *Faculty research:* Symptom management, interventions, individual and family adjustment to chronic illness, women's health. *Unit head:* Dr. Paulette Seymour-Route, Dean, 508-856-5801, Fax: 508-856-6552, E-mail: paulette.seymour-route@umassmed.edu. *Application contact:* Diane Brescia, Admissions Coordinator, 508-856-3488, Fax: 508-856-5851, E-mail: diane.brescia@umassmed.edu.

University of Missouri–Kansas City, School of Nursing, Kansas City, MO 64110-2499. Offers adult clinical nurse specialist (MSN), including adult nurse practitioner, women's health

nurse practitioner; family nurse practitioner (MSN); neonatal nurse practitioner (MSN); nurse educator (MSN); nurse executive (MSN); nursing (PhD); nursing practice (DNP); pediatric nurse practitioner (MSN). *Accreditation:* AACN. Part-time programs available. Postbaccalaureate distance learning degree programs offered (minimal on-campus study). *Faculty:* 36 full-time (30 women), 40 part-time/adjunct (all women). *Students:* 31 full-time (26 women), 310 part-time (287 women); includes 38 minority (17 African Americans, 2 American Indian/Alaska Native, 10 Asian Americans or Pacific Islanders, 9 Hispanic Americans). Average age 36. 151 applicants, 72% accepted, 109 enrolled. In 2009, 57 master's, 10 doctorates awarded. *Degree requirements:* For master's, thesis or alternative. *Entrance requirements:* For master's, minimum undergraduate GPA of 3.2; for doctorate, GRE, 3 letters of reference, interview by invitation. Additional exam requirements/recommendations for international students: Required—TOEFL (minimum score 550 paper-based; 213 computer-based; 80 iBT). *Application deadline:* For fall admission, 2/1 priority date for domestic and international students; for spring admission, 9/1 priority date for domestic and international students. Application fee: $45 ($50 for international students). *Expenses:* Tuition, state resident: full-time $5378; part-time $299 per credit hour. Tuition, nonresident: full-time $13,881; part-time $771 per credit hour. Required fees: $641; $71 per credit hour. Tuition and fees vary according to course load and program. *Financial support:* In 2009–10, 6 teaching assistantships with partial tuition reimbursements (averaging $4,402 per year) were awarded; fellowships, research assistantships, career-related internships or fieldwork, Federal Work-Study, institutionally sponsored loans, and tuition waivers (full and partial) also available. Support available to part-time students. Financial award application deadline: 3/1; financial award applicants required to submit FAFSA. *Faculty research:* Geriatrics/gerontology, children's pain, neonatology, Alzheimer's care, cancer caregivers. Total annual research expenditures: $2.1 million. *Unit head:* Dr. Lora Lacey-Haun, Dean, 816-235-1700, Fax: 816-235-1701, E-mail: lacey-haunc@umkc.edu. *Application contact:* Leah Wilder, Coordinator for Admissions and Recruitment, 816-235-5768, Fax: 816-235-1701, E-mail: wilderl@umkc.edu.

University of Missouri–St. Louis, College of Nursing, St. Louis, MO 63121. Offers nurse educator (MSN); nurse practitioner (MSN, Post Master's Certificate); nursing (DNP, PhD). *Accreditation:* AACN. Part-time programs available. *Faculty:* 14 full-time (13 women), 19 part-time/adjunct (18 women). *Students:* 9 full-time (all women), 216 part-time (203 women); includes 31 minority (29 African Americans, 1 American Indian/Alaska Native, 1 Asian American or Pacific Islander). Average age 37. In 2009, 47 master's, 3 doctorates, 1 other advanced degree awarded. *Degree requirements:* For doctorate, comprehensive exam, thesis/dissertation; for Post Master's Certificate, thesis. *Entrance requirements:* For master's, GRE, 2 recommendation letters; minimum GPA of 3.0; BSN; nursing licensure; statement of purpose; for doctorate, GRE, 2 letters of recommendation, MSN, minimum GPA of 3.2; for Post Master's Certificate, 2 recommendation letters; MSN; advanced practice certificate; minimum GPA of 3.0; essay. Additional exam requirements/recommendations for international students: Required—TOEFL (minimum score 550 paper-based; 213 computer-based). *Application deadline:* For fall admission, 4/1 for domestic and international students; for spring admission, 10/1 for domestic and international students. Application fee: $35 ($40 for international students). Electronic applications accepted. *Expenses:* Tuition, state resident: full-time $5377; part-time $297.70 per credit hour. Tuition, nonresident: full-time $13,882; part-time $771.20 per credit hour. Required fees: $220; $12.20 per credit hour. One-time fee: $12. Tuition and fees vary according to course level, campus/location and program. *Financial support:* In 2009–10, 1 research assistantship with full and partial tuition reimbursement (averaging $12,339 per year), 4 teaching assistantships with full and partial tuition reimbursements (averaging $12,339 per year) were awarded. Financial award application deadline: 4/1; financial award applicants required to submit FAFSA. *Faculty research:* Health promotion and restoration, family disruption, violence, abuse, battered women, health survey methods. *Unit head:* Dean Juliann Sebastian, Dean, 314-516-6066. *Application contact:* 314-516-5458, Fax: 314-516-6996, E-mail: gradadm@umsl.edu.

University of Nevada, Las Vegas, Graduate College, School of Nursing, Las Vegas, NV 89154-3018. Offers family nurse practitioner (Advanced Certificate); nursing (MS, PhD); nursing education (Advanced Certificate). *Accreditation:* AACN; NLN. Part-time programs available. Postbaccalaureate distance learning degree programs offered (minimal on-campus study). *Faculty:* 35 full-time (30 women), 5 part-time/adjunct (all women). *Students:* 68 full-time (56 women), 94 part-time (83 women); includes 30 minority (3 African Americans, 1 American Indian/Alaska Native, 18 Asian Americans or Pacific Islanders, 8 Hispanic Americans), 19 international. Average age 41. 147 applicants, 46% accepted, 51 enrolled. In 2009, 50 master's, 4 doctorates, 1 other advanced degree awarded. *Entrance requirements:* For doctorate, GRE General Test. Additional exam requirements/recommendations for international students: Recommended—TOEFL (minimum score 550 paper-based; 213 computer-based; 80 iBT), IELTS (minimum score 7). *Application deadline:* For fall admission, 3/1 priority date for domestic and international students. Applications are processed on a rolling basis. Application fee: $60 ($95 for international students). Electronic applications accepted. *Financial support:* In 2009–10, 9 students received support, including 8 research assistantships with partial tuition reimbursements available (averaging $14,275 per year), 1 teaching assistantship (averaging $12,000 per year); institutionally sponsored loans, scholarships/grants, health care benefits, and unspecified assistantships also available. Financial award application deadline: 3/1. *Faculty research:* Obesity, weight loss maintenance; eukocyte response to exercise-related skeletal muscle injury; smoke-free policy, smoking cessation; exercise, health promotion; community-based participatory research, occupational health/injury, low-back pain. *Unit head:* Dr. Carolyn Yucha, Interim Dean, 702-895-3906, Fax: 702-895-5050, E-mail: carolyn.yucha@unlv.edu. *Application contact:* Graduate College Admissions Evaluator, 702-895-3320, Fax: 702-895-4180, E-mail: gradcollege@unlv.edu.

University of New Brunswick Fredericton, School of Graduate Studies, Faculty of Nursing, Fredericton, NB E3B 5A3, Canada. Offers nurse educator (MN); nurse practitioner (MN); nursing (MN). Part-time programs available. Postbaccalaureate distance learning degree programs offered. *Faculty:* 27 full-time (all women), 5 part-time/adjunct (4 women). *Students:* 15 full-time (13 women), 32 part-time (all women). In 2009, 13 master's awarded. *Degree requirements:* For master's, comprehensive exam (for some programs), thesis (for some programs). *Entrance requirements:* For master's, undergraduate coursework in statistics and nursing research, minimum GPA of 3.3, registration as a nurse in New Brunswick (or eligibility). Additional exam requirements/recommendations for international students: Required—TOEFL (minimum score 600 paper-based; 250 computer-based). *Application deadline:* For winter admission, 2/5 for domestic students. Application fee: $50 Canadian dollars. Electronic applications accepted. Tuition and fees charges are reported in Canadian dollars. *Expenses:* Tuition, area resident: Full-time $5562 Canadian dollars; part-time $2781 Canadian dollars per year. Required fees: $49.75 Canadian dollars per term. *Faculty research:* Violence and abuse; healthy child development, chronic illness and addiction; rural populations access to health care and primary healthcare; teaching and learning in classroom, clinical lab, and by distance. *Unit head:* Gail Storr, Director of Graduate Studies, 506-458-7643, Fax: 506-447-3057, E-mail: storr@unb.ca. *Application contact:* Francis Perry, Graduate Secretary, 506-451-6844, Fax: 506-447-3057, E-mail: fperry@unb.ca.

The University of North Carolina at Greensboro, Graduate School, School of Nursing, Greensboro, NC 27412-5001. Offers adult clinical nurse specialist (MSN, PMC); adult/gerontological nurse practitioner (MSN, PMC); nurse anesthesia (MSN, PMC); nursing (PhD); nursing administration (MSN); nursing education (MSN); MSN/MBA. *Accreditation:* AACN; AANA/CANAEP; NLN. *Degree requirements:* For master's, thesis or alternative. *Entrance requirements:* For master's, GRE General Test or MAT, BSN, clinical experience, liability insurance, RN license; for PMC, liability insurance, MSN, RN license. Additional exam requirements/recommendations for international students: Required—TOEFL. Electronic applications accepted.

The University of North Carolina Wilmington, School of Nursing, Wilmington, NC 28403-3297. Offers family nurse practitioner (MSN); nurse educator (MSN). *Accreditation:* AACN; NLN. *Degree requirements:* For master's, comprehensive exam, thesis or project. *Entrance requirements:* For master's, GRE General Test, bachelor's degree in nursing. Additional exam requirements/recommendations for international students: Required—TOEFL (minimum score 550 paper-based; 217 computer-based; 79 iBT), IELTS (minimum score 6.5). Electronic applications accepted.

University of Northern Colorado, Graduate School, College of Natural and Health Sciences, School of Nursing, Greeley, CO 80639. Offers clinical nurse specialist in chronic illness (MS); family nurse practitioner (MS); nursing education (MS, PhD). *Accreditation:* AACN. Postbaccalaureate distance learning degree programs offered. *Faculty:* 9 full-time (all women). *Students:* 35 part-time (34 women); includes 2 minority (both Hispanic Americans). Average age 35. 84 applicants, 64% accepted, 13 enrolled. In 2009, 27 master's, 2 doctorates awarded. *Degree requirements:* For master's, comprehensive exam, thesis or alternative; for doctorate, comprehensive exam, thesis/dissertation. *Entrance requirements:* For master's and doctorate, GRE General Test, minimum GPA of 3.0 in last 60 hours, BS in nursing, 2 letters of recommendation. *Application deadline:* Applications are processed on a rolling basis. Application fee: $50 ($60 for international students). Electronic applications accepted. *Expenses:* Tuition, state resident: full-time $5770; part-time $320.55 per credit hour. Tuition, nonresident: full-time $13,847; part-time $769.27 per credit hour. Required fees: $948.78; $52.72 per credit. *Financial support:* In 2009–10, 7 research assistantships (averaging $6,183 per year), 1 teaching assistantship (averaging $2,849 per year) were awarded; fellowships, unspecified assistantships also available. Financial award application deadline: 3/1; financial award applicants required to submit FAFSA. *Unit head:* Dr. Kathleen Bradshaw-LaSala, Director, 970-351-2293, Fax: 970-351-1707. *Application contact:* Linda Sisson, Graduate Student Admission Coordinator, 970-351-1807, Fax: 970-351-2371, E-mail: linda.sisson@unco.edu.

University of Phoenix–Atlanta Campus, The Artemis School, College of Health and Human Services, Sandy Springs, GA 30350-4153. Offers administration of justice and security (MS); health administration (MHA); health care management (MBA); nursing (MSN); nursing/health care education (MSN); MSN/MBA; MSN/MHA. Evening/weekend programs available. Postbaccalaureate distance learning degree programs offered. *Degree requirements:* For master's, thesis (for some programs). *Entrance requirements:* For master's, minimum undergraduate GPA of 2.5, 3 years of work experience. Additional exam requirements/recommendations for international students: Required—TOEFL (minimum score 550 paper-based; 213 computer-based; 79 iBT). Electronic applications accepted.

University of Phoenix–Augusta Campus, College of Health and Human Services, Augusta, GA 30909-4583. Offers health administration (MHA); health care management (MBA); nursing (MSN); nursing/health care education (MSN); MSN/MBA; MSN/MHA. Postbaccalaureate distance learning degree programs offered.

University of Phoenix–Bay Area Campus, The Artemis School, College of Health and Human Services, Pleasanton, CA 94588-3677. Offers administration of justice and security (MS); family nurse practitioner (MSN); health care management (MBA); marriage, family and child therapy (MSC); nursing (MSN); nursing/health care education (MSN); MSN/MBA. Evening/weekend programs available. Postbaccalaureate distance learning degree programs offered (no on-campus study). *Degree requirements:* For master's, thesis (for some programs). *Entrance requirements:* For master's, minimum undergraduate GPA of 2.5, 3 years of work experience, RN license. Additional exam requirements/recommendations for international students: Required—TOEFL (minimum score 550 paper-based; 213 computer-based; 79 iBT). Electronic applications accepted.

University of Phoenix–Birmingham Campus, College of Health and Human Services, Birmingham, AL 35244. Offers education (MHA); gerontology (MHA); health administration (MHA); health care management (MBA); informatics (MHA); nursing (MSN); nursing/health care education (MSN); MSN/MBA; MSN/MHA.

University of Phoenix–Central Florida Campus, The Artemis School, College of Health and Human Services, Maitland, FL 32751-7057. Offers health administration (MHA); health and human services (MSN); health care management (MBA); nursing (MSN); nursing/health care education (MSN); MSN/MBA; MSN/MHA. Evening/weekend programs available. *Degree requirements:* For master's, thesis (for some programs). *Entrance requirements:* For master's, minimum undergraduate GPA of 2.5, 3 years work experience, RN license. Additional exam requirements/recommendations for international students: Required—TOEFL (minimum score 550 paper-based; 213 computer-based; 79 iBT). Electronic applications accepted.

University of Phoenix–Cheyenne Campus, College of Health and Human Services, Cheyenne, WY 82009. Offers health administration (MHA); health care management (MBA); nursing (MSN); nursing/health care education (MSN); MSN/MBA; MSN/MHA. Postbaccalaureate distance learning degree programs offered.

University of Phoenix–Harrisburg Campus, College of Health and Human Services, Harrisburg, PA 17112. Offers health administration (MHA); health care management (MBA); nursing (MSN); nursing/health care education (MSN); MSN/MBA; MSN/MHA. Postbaccalaureate distance learning degree programs offered.

University of Phoenix–Hawaii Campus, The Artemis School, College of Health and Human Services, Honolulu, HI 96813-4317. Offers administration of justice and security (MS); community counseling (MSC); education (MHA); family nurse practitioner (MSN); gerontology (MHA); health administration (MHA); health care management (MBA); marriage, family and child therapy (MSC); nursing (MSN); nursing/health care education (MSN); psychology (MS); MSN/MBA. Evening/weekend programs available. *Degree requirements:* For master's, thesis (for some programs). *Entrance requirements:* For master's, minimum undergraduate GPA of 2.5, 3 years of work experience, RN license. Additional exam requirements/recommendations for international students: Required—TOEFL (minimum score 550 paper-based; 213 computer-based; 79 iBT). Electronic applications accepted.

University of Phoenix–Idaho Campus, The Artemis School, College of Health and Human Services, Meridian, ID 83642-3014. Offers administration of justice and security (MS); health administration (MHA); health care management (MBA); nursing (MSN); nursing/health care education (MSN); psychology (MS); MSN/MBA. Evening/weekend programs available. Postbaccalaureate distance learning degree programs offered. *Degree requirements:* For master's, thesis (for some programs). *Entrance requirements:* For master's, minimum undergraduate GPA of 2.5, 3 years of work experience. Additional exam requirements/recommendations for international students: Required—TOEFL (minimum score 550 paper-based; 213 computer-based). Electronic applications accepted.

University of Phoenix–Indianapolis Campus, The Artemis School, College of Health and Human Services, Indianapolis, IN 46250-932. Offers administration of justice and security (MS); health administration (MHA); health care management (MBA); nursing (MSN); nursing/health care education (MSN); psychology (MS); MSN/MBA; MSN/MHA. Evening/weekend programs available. Postbaccalaureate distance learning degree programs offered. *Degree requirements:* For master's, thesis. *Entrance requirements:* For master's, 3 years work experience, minimum undergraduate GPA of 2.5. Additional exam requirements/recommendations for international students: Required—TOEFL (minimum score 500 paper-based; 213 computer-based). Electronic applications accepted.

University of Phoenix–Las Vegas Campus, The Artemis School, College of Health and Human Services, Las Vegas, NV 89128. Offers administration of justice and security (MS); health administration (MHA); health care management (MBA); marriage, family, and child therapy (MSC); mental health counseling (MSC); nursing (MSN); nursing/health care education (MSN); psychology (MS); MSN/MBA; MSN/MHA. Postbaccalaureate distance learning degree programs offered. *Entrance requirements:* For master's, minimum undergraduate GPA of 2.5, 3 years of work experience. Additional exam requirements/recommendations for international students: Required—TOEFL (minimum score 550 paper-based; 213 computer-based; 79 iBT). Electronic applications accepted.

University of Phoenix–Maryland Campus, The Artemis School, College of Health and Human Services, Columbia, MD 21045-5424. Offers administration of justice and security

Nursing Education

University of Phoenix–Maryland Campus (continued)
(MS); health administration (MHA); health care education (MSN); health care management (MBA); nursing (MSN); psychology (MS); MSN/MBA; MSN/MHA. Evening/weekend programs available. *Degree requirements:* For master's, thesis (for some programs). *Entrance requirements:* For master's, minimum undergraduate GPA of 2.5, 3 years work experience. Additional exam requirements/recommendations for international students: Required—TOEFL (minimum score 550 paper-based; 213 computer-based; 79 iBT). Electronic applications accepted.

University of Phoenix–Metro Detroit Campus, College of Nursing, Southfield, MI 48076. Offers health care education (MSN); nursing (MSN). Evening/weekend programs available. *Faculty:* 1 (woman) full-time, 3 part-time/adjunct (all women). *Students:* 4 full-time (all women), 1 international. Average age 49. In 2009, 8 master's awarded. *Degree requirements:* For master's, thesis (for some programs). *Entrance requirements:* For master's, minimum undergraduate GPA of 2.5, 3 years of work experience, RN license. Additional exam requirements/recommendations for international students: Required—TOEFL (minimum score 550 paper-based; 213 computer-based; 79 iBT). *Application deadline:* Applications are processed on a rolling basis. Application fee: $45. Electronic applications accepted. *Expenses:* Tuition: Full-time $14,136. Required fees: $660. *Financial support:* Institutionally sponsored loans and scholarships/grants available. Financial award applicants required to submit FAFSA. *Unit head:* Dr. Pam Fuller, Dean/Executive Director, 480-557-1140, E-mail: pam.fuller@phoenix.edu. *Application contact:* Chair, 800-834-2438, Fax: 248-267-0147.

University of Phoenix–Minneapolis/St. Louis Park Campus, College of Health and Human Services, St. Louis Park, MN 55426. Offers community counseling (MSC); family nurse practitioner (MSN); health care education (MSN); health care management (MBA); nursing (MSN).

University of Phoenix–New Mexico Campus, The Artemis School, College of Health and Human Services, Albuquerque, NM 87113-1570. Offers administration of justice and security (MS); health administration (MHA); health care education (MSN); health care management (MBA); marriage and family therapy (MSC); nursing (MSN); psychology (MS); MSN/MBA. Evening/weekend programs available. *Degree requirements:* For master's, thesis (for some programs). *Entrance requirements:* For master's, minimum undergraduate GPA of 2.5, 3 years of work experience, RN license. Additional exam requirements/recommendations for international students: Required—TOEFL (minimum score 550 paper-based; 213 computer-based; 79 iBT). Electronic applications accepted.

University of Phoenix–Northern Nevada Campus, College of Health and Human Services, Reno, NV 89521-5862. Offers health administration (MHA); health care education (MSN); health care management (MBA); nursing (MSN); MSN/MBA; MSN/MHA.

University of Phoenix–North Florida Campus, The Artemis School, College of Health and Human Services, Jacksonville, FL 32216-0959. Offers health administration (MHA); health care education (MSN); health care management (MBA); nursing (MSN); MSN/MBA; MSN/MHA. Evening/weekend programs available. *Degree requirements:* For master's, thesis (for some programs). *Entrance requirements:* For master's, minimum undergraduate GPA of 2.5, 3 years work experience, RN license. Additional exam requirements/recommendations for international students: Required—TOEFL (minimum score 550 paper-based; 213 computer-based; 79 iBT). Electronic applications accepted.

University of Phoenix–Northwest Arkansas Campus, College of Health and Human Services, Rogers, AR 72756-9615. Offers health administration (MHA); health care education (MSN); health care management (MBA); nursing (MSN); MSN/MBA.

University of Phoenix–Philadelphia Campus, The Artemis School, College of Health and Human Services, Wayne, PA 19087-2121. Offers administration of justice and security (MS); health administration (MHA); health care education (MSN); health care management (MBA); nursing (MSN); psychology (MS); MSN/MBA. Evening/weekend programs available. *Degree requirements:* For master's, thesis (for some programs). *Entrance requirements:* For master's, minimum undergraduate GPA of 2.5, 3 years work experience. Additional exam requirements/recommendations for international students: Required—TOEFL (minimum score 550 paper-based; 213 computer-based; 79 iBT). Electronic applications accepted.

University of Phoenix–Phoenix Campus, College of Social Sciences, College of Nursing, Phoenix, AZ 85040-1958. Offers health care education (MSN); nursing (MSN). Evening/weekend programs available. *Faculty:* 45 full-time (20 women), 510 part-time/adjunct (308 women). *Students:* 148 full-time (136 women); includes 22 minority (8 African Americans, 1 American Indian/Alaska Native, 8 Asian Americans or Pacific Islanders, 5 Hispanic Americans), 5 international. Average age 38. In 2009, 54 master's awarded. *Degree requirements:* For master's, thesis (for some programs). *Entrance requirements:* For master's, 3 years of work experience in field, minimum undergraduate GPA of 2.5, RN license. Additional exam requirements/recommendations for international students: Required—TOEFL (minimum score 550 paper-based; 213 computer-based; 79 iBT). *Application deadline:* Applications are processed on a rolling basis. Application fee: $45. Electronic applications accepted. *Expenses:* Tuition: Full-time $10,272. Required fees: $760. *Financial support:* Institutionally sponsored loans and scholarships/grants available. Financial award applicants required to submit FAFSA. *Unit head:* Dr. Pam Fuller, Dean/Executive Director, 480-557-1140, Fax: 480-929-7164, E-mail: pam.fuller@phoenix.edu. *Application contact:* Chair, 800-866-0766.

University of Phoenix–Pittsburgh Campus, The Artemis School, College of Health and Human Services, Pittsburgh, PA 15276. Offers administration of justice and security (MS); health administration (MHA); health care education (MSN); health care management (MBA); nursing (MSN); psychology (MS); MSN/MBA; MSN/MHA. Evening/weekend programs available. *Degree requirements:* For master's, thesis (for some programs). *Entrance requirements:* For master's, minimum undergraduate GPA of 2.5, 3 years work experience, current RN license (nursing). Additional exam requirements/recommendations for international students: Required—TOEFL (minimum score 550 paper-based; 213 computer-based; 79 iBT). Electronic applications accepted.

University of Phoenix–Richmond Campus, The Artemis School, College of Health and Human Services, Richmond, VA 23230. Offers administration of justice and security (MS); health administration (MHA); health care education (MSN); health care management (MBA); nursing (MSN); psychology (MS); MSN/MBA; MSN/MHA. Evening/weekend programs available. *Degree requirements:* For master's, thesis (for some programs). *Entrance requirements:* For master's, minimum undergraduate GPA of 2.5, 3 years work experience, current RN license for nursing programs. Additional exam requirements/recommendations for international students: Required—TOEFL (minimum score 500 paper-based; 213 computer-based; 79 iBT). Electronic applications accepted.

University of Phoenix–Sacramento Valley Campus, The Artemis School, College of Health and Human Services, Sacramento, CA 95833-3632. Offers administration of justice and security (MS); community counseling (MSC); family nurse practitioner (MSN); health administration (MHA); health care education (MSN); health care management (MBA); marriage, family and child counseling (MSC); nursing (MSN); psychology (MS); MSN/MBA. Evening/weekend programs available. *Degree requirements:* For master's, thesis (for some programs). *Entrance requirements:* For master's, RN license, minimum undergraduate GPA of 2.5, 3 years work experience. Additional exam requirements/recommendations for international students: Required—TOEFL (minimum score 550 paper-based; 213 computer-based; 79 iBT). Electronic applications accepted.

University of Phoenix–San Diego Campus, The Artemis School, College of Health and Human Services, San Diego, CA 92123. Offers administration of justice and security (MS); health care education (MSN); health care management (MBA); marriage, family and child counseling (MSC); marriage, family and child therapy (MSC); nursing (MSN); MSN/MBA. Evening/weekend programs available. *Degree requirements:* For master's, thesis (for some programs). *Entrance requirements:* For master's, minimum undergraduate GPA of 2.5, 3 years work experience, RN license. Additional exam requirements/recommendations for international students: Required—TOEFL (minimum score 550 paper-based; 213 computer-based; 79 iBT). Electronic applications accepted.

University of Phoenix–Savannah Campus, College of Health and Human Services, Savannah, GA 31405-7400. Offers health administration (MHA); health care management (MBA); nursing (MSN); nursing/health care education (MSN); MSN/MBA; MSN/MHA.

University of Phoenix–Southern California Campus, College of Nursing, Costa Mesa, CA 92626. Offers family nurse practitioner (MSN); health care education (MSN); nursing (MSN); MSN/MBA; MSN/MHA. Evening/weekend programs available. *Faculty:* 3 full-time (all women), 41 part-time/adjunct (32 women). *Students:* 79 full-time (42 women); includes 155 minority (48 African Americans, 1 American Indian/Alaska Native, 76 Asian Americans or Pacific Islanders, 30 Hispanic Americans), 27 international. Average age 44. In 2009, 154 master's awarded. *Degree requirements:* For master's, thesis (for some programs). *Entrance requirements:* For master's, minimum undergraduate GPA of 2.5, 3 years work experience, RN license. Additional exam requirements/recommendations for international students: Required—TOEFL (minimum score 550 paper-based; 213 computer-based; 79 iBT). *Application deadline:* Applications are processed on a rolling basis. Application fee: $45. Electronic applications accepted. *Expenses:* Tuition: Full-time $15,120. Required fees: $660. *Financial support:* Institutionally sponsored loans and scholarships/grants available. Financial award applicants required to submit FAFSA. *Unit head:* Dr. Pam Fuller, Dean/Executive Director, 480-557-1140, E-mail: pam.fuller@phoenix.edu. *Application contact:* Campus College Chair, 714-398-1878, Fax: 714-378-5856.

University of Phoenix–South Florida Campus, The Artemis School, College of Health and Human Services, Fort Lauderdale, FL 33309. Offers health administration (MHA); health care education (MSN); health care management (MBA); nursing (MSN); MSN/MBA; MSN/MHA. Evening/weekend programs available. *Degree requirements:* For master's, thesis (for some programs). *Entrance requirements:* For master's, minimum undergraduate GPA of 2.5, 3 years work experience, RN license. Additional exam requirements/recommendations for international students: Required—TOEFL (minimum score 550 paper-based; 213 computer-based; 79 iBT). Electronic applications accepted.

University of Phoenix–Utah Campus, The Artemis School, College of Health and Human Services, Salt Lake City, UT 84123-4617. Offers health care management (MBA); healthcare education (MSN); mental health counseling (MSC); nursing (MSN); MSN/MBA. Evening/weekend programs available. *Degree requirements:* For master's, thesis (for some programs). *Entrance requirements:* For master's, minimum undergraduate GPA of 2.5, 3 years work experience, RN license. Additional exam requirements/recommendations for international students: Required—TOEFL (minimum score 550 paper-based; 213 computer-based; 79 iBT). Electronic applications accepted.

University of Phoenix–Western Washington Campus, College of Health and Human Services, Tukwila, WA 98188. Offers health administration (MHA); health care education (MSN); health care management (MBA); nursing (MSN); MSN/MBA; MSN/MHA. Evening/weekend programs available. *Degree requirements:* For master's, thesis (for some programs). *Entrance requirements:* For master's, minimum undergraduate GPA of 2.5, 3 years of work experience. Additional exam requirements/recommendations for international students: Required—TOEFL (minimum score 550 paper-based; 213 computer-based; 79 iBT). Electronic applications accepted.

University of Phoenix–West Florida Campus, The Artemis School, College of Health and Human Services, Temple Terrace, FL 33637. Offers health administration (MHA); health care education (MSN); health care management (MBA); nursing (MSN); MSN/MBA; MSN/MHA. Evening/weekend programs available. Postbaccalaureate distance learning degree programs offered. *Degree requirements:* For master's, thesis (for some programs). *Entrance requirements:* For master's, minimum undergraduate GPA of 2.5, RN license, 3 years work experience. Additional exam requirements/recommendations for international students: Required—TOEFL (minimum score 550 paper-based; 213 computer-based; 79 iBT). Electronic applications accepted.

University of Pittsburgh, School of Nursing, Nurse Specialty Role Program, Pittsburgh, PA 15260. Offers clinical nurse leader (MSN); nursing administration (MSN, DNP); nursing education (MSN); nursing informatics (MSN); nursing research (MSN). *Accreditation:* AACN. Part-time programs available. *Students:* 8 full-time (all women), 47 part-time (46 women); includes 5 minority (1 African American, 4 Asian Americans or Pacific Islanders). Average age 42. 16 applicants, 94% accepted, 13 enrolled. In 2009, 12 master's awarded. *Degree requirements:* For master's, comprehensive exam, thesis optional. *Entrance requirements:* For master's, GRE or MAT, BSN, RN license, letters of recommendation, resume, course work in statistics, 1-3 years of nursing experience. Additional exam requirements/recommendations for international students: Required—TOEFL (minimum score 550 paper-based; 213 computer-based; 80 iBT). *Application deadline:* For fall admission, 8/1 priority date for domestic students; for spring admission, 12/1 priority date for domestic students. Applications are processed on a rolling basis. Application fee: $50. Electronic applications accepted. *Expenses:* Tuition, state resident: full-time $16,402; part-time $665 per credit. Tuition, nonresident: full-time $28,694; part-time $1175 per credit. Required fees: $690; $175 per term. Tuition and fees vary according to program. *Unit head:* Dr. Helen Burns, Associate Dean for Clinical Education, 412-624-6616, Fax: 412-624-2401, E-mail: burnsh@pitt.edu. *Application contact:* Laurie Lapsley, Administrator of Graduate Student Services, 412-624-9670, Fax: 412-624-2409, E-mail: lapsleyl@pitt.edu.

University of Rhode Island, Graduate School, College of Nursing, Kingston, RI 02881. Offers administration (MS); clinical nurse leader (MS); clinical specialist in gerontology (MS); clinical specialist in psychiatric/mental health (MS); family nurse practitioner (MS); gerontological nurse practitioner (MS); nursing (DNP, PhD); nursing education (MS). *Accreditation:* AACN; ACNM/DOA (one or more programs are accredited). Part-time programs available. *Faculty:* 28 full-time (27 women), 3 part-time/adjunct (all women). *Students:* 21 full-time (20 women), 74 part-time (71 women); includes 3 minority (1 African American, 2 Asian Americans or Pacific Islanders), 5 international. In 2009, 29 master's, 2 doctorates awarded. *Degree requirements:* For master's, comprehensive exam; for doctorate, comprehensive exam, thesis/dissertation. *Entrance requirements:* For master's, GRE or MAT, 2 letters of recommendation, scholarly papers; for doctorate, GRE, 3 letters of recommendation, scholarly papers. Additional exam requirements/recommendations for international students: Required—TOEFL (minimum score 550 paper-based; 213 computer-based). *Application deadline:* For fall admission, 4/15 for domestic students, 2/1 for international students; for spring admission, 11/15 for domestic students, 7/15 for international students. Application fee: $65. Electronic applications accepted. *Expenses:* Tuition, state resident: full-time $8828; part-time $490 per credit hour. Tuition, nonresident: full-time $22,100; part-time $1228 per credit hour. Required fees: $1118; $57 per semester. Tuition and fees vary according to program. *Financial support:* In 2009–10, 3 teaching assistantships with full and partial tuition reimbursements (averaging $8,428 per year) were awarded. Financial award application deadline: 4/15; financial award applicants required to submit FAFSA. *Faculty research:* Group intervention for grieving women in prison, translating Best Practice in non-drug interventions for postoperative pain management, further development and testing of the pain assessment inventory, preschool motor and functional performance of two cohorts, neuroactivation of brain motor areas in preterm children. Total annual research expenditures: $926,949. *Unit head:* Dr. Dayle Joseph, Dean, 401-874-2766, Fax: 401-874-2061, E-mail: dayle@uri.edu. *Application contact:* Dr. Mary C. Sullivan, Director of Graduate Studies, 401-874-5339, Fax: 401-874-2061, E-mail: mcsullivan@uri.edu.

The University of Tennessee at Chattanooga, Graduate School, College of Health, Education and Professional Studies, School of Nursing, Chattanooga, TN 37403. Offers administration (MSN); certified nurse anesthetist (Post-Master's Certificate); education (MSN); family nurse practitioner (MSN, Post-Master's Certificate); health care informatics (Post-Master's Certificate); nurse anesthesia (MSN); nurse education (Post-Master's Certificate). *Accreditation:* AACN; AANA/CANAEP (one or more programs are accredited). *Faculty:* 4 full-time (all women). *Students:* 42 full-time (33 women), 53 part-time (38 women); includes 10 minority (5 African

Americans, 1 American Indian/Alaska Native, 2 Asian Americans or Pacific Islanders, 2 Hispanic Americans). Average age 35. 13 applicants, 31% accepted, 3 enrolled. In 2009, 36 master's, 5 other advanced degrees awarded. *Degree requirements:* For master's, thesis optional, qualifying exams, professional project; for Post-Master's Certificate, thesis or alternative, practicum, seminar. *Entrance requirements:* For master's, GRE General Test, MAT, BSN, minimum GPA of 3.0, eligibility for Tennessee RN license, 1 year direct patient care experience; for Post-Master's Certificate, GRE General Test, MAT, MSN, minimum GPA of 3.0, eligibility for Tennessee RN license, one year of direct patient care experience. Additional exam requirements/recommendations for international students: Required—TOEFL (minimum score 550 paper-based; 213 computer-based; 79 iBT), IELTS (minimum score 6). *Application deadline:* For fall admission, 8/1 priority date for domestic students, 6/1 for international students; for spring admission, 12/1 priority date for domestic students, 10/1 for international students. Applications are processed on a rolling basis. Application fee: $35. Electronic applications accepted. *Expenses:* Tuition, state resident: full-time $5404; part-time $300 per credit hour. Tuition, nonresident: full-time $16,702; part-time $928 per credit hour. Required fees: $1150; $130 per credit hour. *Financial support:* Career-related internships or fieldwork and scholarships/grants available. Support available to part-time students. *Faculty research:* Diabetes in women, health care for elderly, alternative medicine, hypertension, nurse anesthesia. Total annual research expenditures: $1.5 million. *Unit head:* Dr. Kay R. Lindgren, Head, 423-425-4646, Fax: 423-425-4668, E-mail: kay-lindgren@utc.edu. *Application contact:* Dr. Stephanie Bellar, Dean of Graduate Studies, 423-425-4666, Fax: 423-425-5223, E-mail: stephanie-bellar@utc.edu.

The University of Texas at Arlington, Graduate School, School of Nursing, Arlington, TX 76019. Offers administration/supervision of nursing (MSN); nurse practitioner (MSN); nursing science (PhD); teaching of nursing (MSN). *Accreditation:* AACN. Part-time and evening/weekend programs available. *Faculty:* 12 full-time (all women), 8 part-time/adjunct (all women). *Students:* 59 full-time (52 women), 483 part-time (441 women); includes 151 minority (75 African Americans, 3 American Indian/Alaska Native, 32 Asian Americans or Pacific Islanders, 41 Hispanic Americans), 9 international. Average age 37. 227 applicants, 97% accepted, 130 enrolled. In 2009, 72 master's, 3 doctorates awarded. *Degree requirements:* For master's, comprehensive exam, thesis or project; for doctorate, comprehensive exam, thesis/dissertation, successful proposal defense. *Entrance requirements:* For master's, GRE General Test, minimum GPA of 3.0, Texas nursing license, minimum C in undergraduate statistics course, physical assessment course within last 3 years; for doctorate, GRE General Test, minimum undergraduate, graduate and statistics GPA of 3.0; Texas RN license; interview; 3 letters of reference, written statement of goals. Additional exam requirements/recommendations for international students: Required—TOEFL (minimum score 550 paper-based; 213 computer-based), IELTS (minimum score 7). *Application deadline:* For fall admission, 6/5 for domestic students, 4/3 for international students; for spring admission, 10/7 for domestic students, 9/5 for international students. Applications are processed on a rolling basis. Application fee: $40 ($70 for international students). *Financial support:* In 2009–10, 27 students received support, including 24 fellowships with partial tuition reimbursements available (averaging $3,000 per year), 6 research assistantships (averaging $7,992 per year), 7 teaching assistantships (averaging $10,080 per year); career-related internships or fieldwork and traineeships also available. Financial award application deadline: 6/1; financial award applicants required to submit FAFSA. *Faculty research:* Simulation in clinical education and practice, cultural diversity, vulnerable populations, substance abuse. *Unit head:* Dr. Elizabeth C. Poster, Dean, 817-272-2776, Fax: 817-272-5006, E-mail: poster@uta.edu. *Application contact:* Dr. Mary Schira, Graduate Advisor & Associate Dean, 817-272-2329, Fax: 817-272-2065, E-mail: schira@uta.edu.

The University of Texas at Tyler, College of Nursing and Health Sciences, Program in Nursing, Tyler, TX 75799-0001. Offers nurse practitioner (MSN); nursing (PhD); nursing administration (MSN); nursing education (MSN); MSN/MBA. *Accreditation:* AACN. Part-time and evening/weekend programs available. Postbaccalaureate distance learning degree programs offered (no on-campus study). *Faculty:* 15 full-time (all women). *Students:* 26 full-time (24 women), 158 part-time (139 women); includes 36 minority (17 African Americans, 3 American Indian/Alaska Native, 7 Asian Americans or Pacific Islanders, 9 Hispanic Americans). Average age 40. 51 applicants, 57% accepted, 15 enrolled. In 2009, 32 master's awarded. *Degree requirements:* For master's, comprehensive exam (for some programs), thesis (for some programs); for doctorate, thesis/dissertation. *Entrance requirements:* For master's, GRE General Test or MAT, GMAT, minimum undergraduate GPA of 3.0, course work in statistics, RN license, BSN. Additional exam requirements/recommendations for international students: Required—TOEFL (minimum score 79 computer-based). *Application deadline:* For fall admission, 8/17 priority date for domestic students, 7/1 priority date for international students; for spring admission, 12/21 priority date for domestic students, 11/1 priority date for international students. Applications are processed on a rolling basis. Application fee: $25 ($50 for international students). Electronic applications accepted. *Expenses:* Tuition, state resident: part-time $665 per semester hour. Tuition, nonresident: part-time $942 per semester hour. Part-time tuition and fees vary according to degree level and program. *Financial support:* In 2009–10, 15 students received support, including 1 fellowship (averaging $10,000 per year), 3 research assistantships (averaging $2,200 per year); institutionally sponsored loans and scholarships/grants also available. Financial award application deadline: 7/1; financial award applicants required to submit FAFSA. *Faculty research:* Psychosocial adjustment, aging, support/commitment of caregivers, psychological abuse and violence, hope/hopelessness, professional values, end of life care, suicidology, clinical supervision, workforce retention and issues, global health issues, health promotion. Total annual research expenditures: $258,200. *Unit head:* Dr. Susan Yarbrough, Assistant Dean, 903-566-1220, E-mail: syarbrou@mail.uttyl.edu. *Application contact:* Dr. Susan Yarbrough.

The University of Toledo, College of Graduate Studies, College of Nursing, Toledo, OH 43606-3390. Offers adult health practitioner/clinical nurse specialist (MSN); adult nurse practitioner (Certificate); entry-level nursing initiative (GEMINI) (MSN); family nurse practitioner (MSN, Certificate); nursing education (Certificate); pediatric nurse practitioner (Certificate); pediatric nurse practitioner/clinical nurse specialist (MSN); RN to MSN (MSN). *Accreditation:* AACN. Part-time programs available. *Degree requirements:* For master's, thesis or scholarly project. *Entrance requirements:* For master's, GRE General Test, BS in nursing, minimum undergraduate GPA of 3.0. *Expenses:* Contact institution. *Faculty research:* Sexuality issues, prenatal testing, health care of homeless, nursing education, chronic/acute pain, eating disorders, low birth weight infants.

University of Victoria, Faculty of Graduate Studies, Faculty of Human and Social Development, School of Nursing, Victoria, BC V8W 2Y2, Canada. Offers advanced nursing practice (advanced practice leadership option) (MN); advanced nursing practice (nurse educator option) (MN); advanced nursing practice (nurse practitioner option) (MN); nursing (PhD). Part-time programs available. Postbaccalaureate distance learning degree programs offered (no on-campus study). *Entrance requirements:* Additional exam requirements/recommendations for international students: Required—TOEFL (minimum score 575 paper-based; 233 computer-based), IELTS (minimum score 7). Electronic applications accepted.

University of West Georgia, Graduate School, School of Nursing, Carrollton, GA 30118. Offers health systems leadership (Post-Master's Certificate); nursing (MSN); nursing education (Post-Master's Certificate). *Accreditation:* AACN. Part-time programs available. *Faculty:* 23 full-time (all women), 8 part-time/adjunct (all women). *Students:* 17 full-time (all women), 12 part-time (all women); includes 4 minority (all African Americans), 5 international. Average age 36. 30 applicants, 70% accepted, 10 enrolled. In 2009, 11 master's awarded. *Degree requirements:* For master's, comprehensive exam, thesis or alternative. *Entrance requirements:* For master's, GRE or MAT, BSN, Georgia RN license, minimum GPA of 3.0 for upper-division nursing courses, completion of basic undergraduate statistics course. *Application deadline:* For fall admission, 7/17 for domestic students; for spring admission, 11/20 for domestic students. Applications are processed on a rolling basis. Application fee: $30. Electronic applications accepted. *Expenses:* Tuition, state resident: full-time $2952; part-time $164 per semester hour. Tuition, nonresident: full-time $11,808; part-time $656 per semester hour. Required fees:

$42.90 per semester hour. $307 per semester. Tuition and fees vary according to course load. *Financial support:* In 2009–10, 1 research assistantship with full tuition reimbursement (averaging $6,000 per year) was awarded. Financial award application deadline: 7/1; financial award applicants required to submit FAFSA. *Faculty research:* Caring in nursing education, pain assessment in older adults, pain outcomes. *Unit head:* Dr. Kathryn Mary Grams, Dean, 678-839-6552, Fax: 678-839-6553, E-mail: kgrams@westga.edu. *Application contact:* Dr. Charles W. Clark, Dean, 678-839-6508, E-mail: cclark@westga.edu.

University of Wisconsin–Eau Claire, College of Nursing and Health Sciences, Program in Nursing, Eau Claire, WI 54702-4004. Offers adult health clinical nurse specialist (MSN); adult health in administration (MSN); adult health in education (MSN); adult health nurse practitioner (MSN); family health in administration (MSN); family health in education (MSN); family health nurse practitioner (MSN). Part-time programs available. *Faculty:* 15 full-time (14 women). *Students:* 34 full-time (32 women), 55 part-time (51 women); includes 1 minority (Asian American or Pacific Islander). Average age 35. 58 applicants, 59% accepted, 2 enrolled. In 2009, 32 master's awarded. Terminal master's awarded for partial completion of doctoral program. *Degree requirements:* For master's, thesis optional, 500-600 hours clinical practicum, oral and written exams. *Entrance requirements:* For master's, Wisconsin RN license, minimum GPA of 3.0, undergraduate statistics, course work in health assessment. Additional exam requirements/recommendations for international students: Required—TOEFL (minimum score 550 paper-based; 213 computer-based; 79 iBT). *Application deadline:* For fall admission, 1/15 priority date for domestic students, 6/1 priority date for international students; for spring admission, 11/1 priority date for international students. Applications are processed on a rolling basis. Application fee: $56. Electronic applications accepted. *Expenses:* Tuition, state resident: full-time $6705.90; part-time $372.55 per credit. Tuition, nonresident: full-time $16,771; part-time $931.74 per credit. Required fees: $925.50; $51.19 per credit. One-time fee: $56. *Financial support:* In 2009–10, 50 students received support, including 2 fellowships (averaging $500 per year); Federal Work-Study and unspecified assistantships also available. Financial award application deadline: 3/1; financial award applicants required to submit FAFSA. *Unit head:* Dr. Mary Zwygart-Stauffacher, Interim Dean, 715-836-5287, Fax: 715-836-5925, E-mail: zwygarmc@uwec.edu. *Application contact:* Kristina Anderson, Director of Admissions, 715-836-5415, Fax: 715-836-2409, E-mail: admissions@uwec.edu.

Ursuline College, School of Graduate Studies, Programs in Nursing, Pepper Pike, OH 44124-4398. Offers care management (MSN); nurse practitioner (MSN); nursing (DNP); nursing education (MSN); palliative care (MSN). *Accreditation:* AACN. Part-time programs available. *Faculty:* 2 full-time (both women), 2 part-time/adjunct (both women). *Students:* 1 (woman) full-time, 94 part-time (88 women); includes 12 minority (11 African Americans, 1 Asian American or Pacific Islander). Average age 39. 68 applicants, 78% accepted, 40 enrolled. In 2009, 22 master's awarded. *Degree requirements:* For master's, comprehensive exam. *Entrance requirements:* For master's, minimum undergraduate GPA of 3.0, bachelor's degree in nursing, eligibility for or current Ohio RN license. Additional exam requirements/recommendations for international students: Required—TOEFL (minimum score 500 paper-based; 173 computer-based). *Application deadline:* For fall admission, 8/1 priority date for domestic students. Applications are processed on a rolling basis. Application fee: $25. *Expenses:* Tuition: Full-time $14,544; part-time $808 per credit hour. Required fees: $230; $75 per semester. *Financial support:* In 2009–10, 11 students received support. Federal Work-Study available. Financial award application deadline: 3/1. *Unit head:* Dr. Janet Baker, Director, 440-864-8172, Fax: 440-684-6053. *Application contact:* Melanie Steele, Secretary, 440-646-8199, Fax: 440-684-6138, E-mail: gradsch@ursuline.edu.

Valparaiso University, Graduate School, College of Nursing, Valparaiso, IN 46383. Offers management (Certificate); nursing education (MSN, Certificate); MSN/MBA. *Accreditation:* AACN. Part-time and evening/weekend programs available. *Faculty:* 7 part-time/adjunct (all women). *Students:* 26 full-time (23 women), 46 part-time (all women); includes 7 minority (4 African Americans, 1 Asian American or Pacific Islander, 2 Hispanic Americans), 1 international. Average age 42. In 2009, 16 master's, 12 other advanced degrees awarded. *Entrance requirements:* For master's, minimum GPA of 3.0, undergraduate major in nursing, Indiana registered nursing license, undergraduate courses in research and statistics. Additional exam requirements/recommendations for international students: Required—TOEFL (minimum score 550 paper-based; 213 computer-based; 80 iBT). *Application deadline:* Applications are processed on a rolling basis. Application fee: $30 ($50 for international students). Electronic applications accepted. *Expenses:* Contact institution. *Financial support:* Scholarships/grants available. Support available to part-time students. Financial award applicants required to submit FAFSA. *Unit head:* Dr. Janet Brown, Dean, 219-464-5289, Fax: 219-464-5425, E-mail: janet.brown@valpo.edu. *Application contact:* Jamie Haney, Coordinator of Graduate Admission, 219-464-5313, Fax: 219-464-5381, E-mail: jamie.haney@valpo.edu.

Villanova University, College of Nursing, Villanova, PA 19085-1699. Offers adult nurse practitioner (MSN, Post Master's Certificate); family nurse practitioner (MSN, Post Master's Certificate); health care administration (MSN); nurse anesthetist (MSN, Post Master's Certificate); nursing (PhD); nursing education (MSN, Post Master's Certificate); pediatric nurse practitioner (MSN, Post Master's Certificate). *Accreditation:* AACN; AANA/CANAEP. Part-time programs available. Postbaccalaureate distance learning degree programs offered (minimal on-campus study). *Faculty:* 15 full-time (all women), 3 part-time/adjunct (2 women). *Students:* 58 full-time (53 women), 188 part-time (164 women); includes 29 minority (13 African Americans, 1 American Indian/Alaska Native, 13 Asian Americans or Pacific Islanders, 2 Hispanic Americans), 3 international. Average age 33. 171 applicants, 70% accepted, 89 enrolled. In 2009, 32 master's, 1 doctorate awarded. *Degree requirements:* For master's, independent study project; for doctorate, comprehensive exam, thesis/dissertation. *Entrance requirements:* For master's, GRE or MAT, BSN, 1 year of recent nursing experience, physical assessment, course work in statistics; for doctorate, GRE, MSN. Additional exam requirements/recommendations for international students: Required—TOEFL. *Application deadline:* For fall admission, 7/1 priority date for domestic students, 7/1 for international students; for spring admission, 11/1 priority date for domestic students, 11/1 for international students. Applications are processed on a rolling basis. Application fee: $50. *Expenses:* Contact institution. *Financial support:* In 2009–10, 53 students received support, including 5 teaching assistantships with full tuition reimbursements available (averaging $13,100 per year); institutionally sponsored loans, scholarships/grants, traineeships, tuition waivers (full), and unspecified assistantships also available. Financial award application deadline: 3/1; financial award applicants required to submit FAFSA. *Faculty research:* Genetics, ethics, cognitive development of students, women with disabilities, nursing leadership. *Unit head:* Dr. Marguerite K. Schlag, Assistant Dean and Director, Graduate Program, 610-519-4907, Fax: 610-519-7650, E-mail: marguerite.schlag@villanova.edu. *Application contact:* Dean, Graduate School of Liberal Arts and Sciences.

Walden University, Graduate Programs, School of Nursing, Minneapolis, MN 55401. Offers education (MSN); informatics (MSN); leadership and management (MSN); nursing (Post-Master's Certificate), including nursing education, nursing informatics, nursing leadership and management. *Accreditation:* AACN. Part-time and evening/weekend programs available. Postbaccalaureate distance learning degree programs offered (no on-campus study). *Faculty:* 5 full-time, 105 part-time/adjunct. *Students:* 2,644 full-time (2,468 women), 805 part-time (755 women); includes 660 minority (430 African Americans, 23 American Indian/Alaska Native, 122 Asian Americans or Pacific Islanders, 85 Hispanic Americans), 34 international. Average age 44. In 2009, 624 master's, 1 other advanced degree awarded. *Entrance requirements:* For master's, bachelor's degree or equivalent in related field or RN; minimum GPA of 2.5. Additional exam requirements/recommendations for international students: Required—TOEFL (minimum score 550 paper-based; 213 computer-based), IELTS (minimum score 6.5), or Michigan English Language Assessment Battery (minimum score 82). *Application deadline:* Applications are processed on a rolling basis. Application fee: $50. Electronic applications accepted. *Expenses:* Tuition: Full-time $13,665; part-time $560 per credit. Required fees: $1375. Tuition and fees vary according to course load, degree level and program. *Financial support:* In 2009–10, 273 students received support; fellowships, Federal Work-Study, scholarships/grants, unspecified assistantships, and family tuition reduction, active duty/veteran tuition

Walden University (continued)
reduction, group tuition reduction, interest-free payment plans available. Support available to part-time students. Financial award applicants required to submit FAFSA. *Unit head:* Dr. Sara Torres, Associate Dean, 800-925-3368. *Application contact:* Jennifer Hall, Director of Enrollment, 866-4-WALDEN, E-mail: info@walden.edu.

Waynesburg University, Graduate and Professional Studies, Waynesburg, PA 15370-1222. Offers business (MBA), including finance, health systems, human resources, leadership, market development; counseling (MA), including addictions counseling, clinical mental health; education (MAT); nursing (MSN), including administration, education, informatics, palliative care; nursing practice (DNP); special education (M Ed); technology (M Ed); MSN/MBA. *Accreditation:* AACN. Part-time and evening/weekend programs available. *Faculty:* 11 full-time (5 women), 136 part-time/adjunct (80 women). *Students:* 116 full-time (85 women), 984 part-time (682 women). 711 applicants, 80% accepted, 485 enrolled. In 2009, 320 master's, 41 doctorates awarded. *Degree requirements:* For doctorate, thesis/dissertation. *Entrance requirements:* Additional exam requirements/recommendations for international students: Required—TOEFL. *Application deadline:* For fall admission, 8/1 priority date for domestic students. Applications are processed on a rolling basis. Electronic applications accepted. *Expenses:* Tuition: Part-time $520 per credit. *Financial support:* Available to part-time students. Application deadline: 5/1. *Unit head:* David Mariner, Dean, 724-743-4420, Fax: 724-743-4425, E-mail: dmariner@waynesburg.edu. *Application contact:* Michael Bednarski, Director of Admissions, 724-743-4420, Fax: 724-743-4425, E-mail: mbednars@waynesburg.edu.

Wayne State University, College of Nursing, Program in Nursing Education, Detroit, MI 48202. Offers nursing education (Certificate); transcultural nursing (MSN, Certificate). *Entrance requirements:* For degree, GRE General Test, minimum GPA of 2.8. Additional exam requirements/recommendations for international students: Required—TOEFL (minimum score 550 paper-based; 213 computer-based); Recommended—TWE (minimum score 6). Electronic applications accepted. *Faculty research:* Clinical teaching, curriculum development and evaluation, teaching methodology.

West Chester University of Pennsylvania, Office of Graduate Studies, College of Health Sciences, Department of Nursing, West Chester, PA 19383. Offers administration (MSN); integrative health (MSN); nursing education (MSN, Certificate); school nursing (Teaching Certificate). *Accreditation:* AACN. Part-time and evening/weekend programs available. *Students:* 3 full-time (all women), 34 part-time (33 women); includes 2 minority (1 African American, 1 Asian American or Pacific Islander). Average age 42. 15 applicants, 100% accepted, 10 enrolled. In 2009, 10 master's awarded. *Entrance requirements:* For master's, RN license, BSN, minimum GPA of 2.8, two years' full-time experience as a clinical care nurse, three letters of recommendation; for other advanced degree, BSN, RN license, minimum GPA of 3.0 in last 48 nursing credits. Additional exam requirements/recommendations for international students: Required—TOEFL (minimum score 550 paper-based; 213 computer-based; 80 iBT). *Application deadline:* For fall admission, 4/15 priority date for domestic students, 3/15 for international students; for spring admission, 10/15 for domestic students, 9/1 for international students. Applications are processed on a rolling basis. Application fee: $35. Electronic applications accepted. *Expenses:* Tuition, state resident: full-time $6666; part-time $370 per credit. Tuition, nonresident: full-time $10,666; part-time $593 per credit. Required fees: $122.56 per credit. *Financial support:* In 2009–10, 1 research assistantship with full and partial tuition reimbursement (averaging $5,000 per year) was awarded; unspecified assistantships also available. Support available to part-time students. Financial award application deadline: 2/15; financial award applicants required to submit FAFSA. *Faculty research:* Violence against women. *Unit head:* Dr. Charlotte Mackey, Chair, 610-436-3474, E-mail: cmackey@wcupa.edu. *Application contact:* Ann Coghlan Stowe, Graduate Coordinator, 610-436-2331, E-mail: astowe@wcupa.edu.

Western Carolina University, Graduate School, College of Health and Human Sciences, School of Nursing, Cullowhee, NC 28723. Offers nurse educator (PMC); nursing (MSN). *Accreditation:* AACN; AANA/CANAEP. Part-time and evening/weekend programs available. *Students:* 31 full-time (20 women), 61 part-time (51 women). Average age 38. 51 applicants, 76% accepted, 26 enrolled. In 2009, 13 master's awarded. *Degree requirements:* For master's, comprehensive exam, thesis or alternative. *Entrance requirements:* For master's, GRE General Test, BSN with minimum GPA of 3.0, 3 references, 1 year of clinical experience. Additional exam requirements/recommendations for international students: Required—TOEFL (minimum score 550 paper-based; 270 computer-based; 79 iBT). *Application deadline:* For fall admission, 2/15 for domestic students; for spring admission, 6/15 for domestic students. Applications are processed on a rolling basis. Application fee: $45. *Financial support:* In 2009–10, 1 student received support; fellowships, research assistantships with full and partial tuition reimbursements available, teaching assistantships with full and partial tuition reimbursements available, career-related internships or fieldwork, institutionally sponsored loans, scholarships/grants, and unspecified assistantships available. Financial award application deadline: 3/31; financial award applicants required to submit FAFSA. *Unit head:* Dr. Vincent Hall, Head, 828-227-3511, Fax: 828-227-7052, E-mail: hallv@email.wcu.edu. *Application contact:* Admissions Specialist for Nursing, 828-227-7398, Fax: 828-227-7480, E-mail: gradsch@email.wcu.edu.

Westminster College, School of Nursing and Health Sciences, Salt Lake City, UT 84105-3697. Offers family nurse practitioner (MSN); nurse anesthesia (MSNA); nurse education (MSNED); nursing (MSN); public health (MPH). *Accreditation:* AACN; AANA/CANAEP. *Faculty:* 11 full-time (6 women), 12 part-time/adjunct (6 women). *Students:* 77 full-time (54 women), 49 part-time (16 women); includes 11 minority (3 African Americans, 6 Asian Americans or Pacific Islanders, 2 Hispanic Americans), 2 international. Average age 34. 152 applicants, 57% accepted, 48 enrolled. In 2009, 23 master's awarded. *Degree requirements:* For master's, clinical practicum, 504 clinical practice hours. *Entrance requirements:* For master's, GRE, resume, Utah RN license in good standing, minimum GPA of 3.0, 3 letters of reference, BSN from accredited nursing program, proof of clear state and federal background check, drug test results, personal interview, current PALS certification, current ACLS certification. Additional exam requirements/recommendations for international students: Required—TOEFL (minimum score 600 paper-based; 250 computer-based; 100 iBT). *Application deadline:* Applications are processed on a rolling basis. Application fee: $40. Electronic applications accepted. *Expenses:* Contact institution. *Financial support:* In 2009–10, 60 students received support. Career-related internships or fieldwork and tuition reimbursement, tuition remission available. Support available to part-time students. Financial award applicants required to submit FAFSA. *Faculty research:* Emotional intelligence, graduate faculty mentorship, parish nursing roles in women's disease prevention, psychiatric nursing students' self-assessment of therapeutic relationships, psychosocial nurse practitioner's self-assessment of therapeutic relationships, curriculum simulation. *Unit head:* Dr. Sheryl Steadman, Dean, 801-832-2164, Fax: 801-832-3110, E-mail: ssteadman@westminstercollege.edu. *Application contact:* Joel Bauman, Vice President of Enrollment Services, 801-832-2200, Fax: 801-832-3101, E-mail: admission@westminstercollege.edu.

Winona State University, College of Nursing and Health Sciences, Winona, MN 55987-5838. Offers adult nurse practitioner (MS, Post Master's Certificate); clinical nurse specialist (MS, Post Master's Certificate); family nurse practitioner (MS, Post Master's Certificate); nurse administrator (MS); nurse educator (MS, Post Master's Certificate); nursing (DNP). *Accreditation:* AACN. Part-time programs available. Postbaccalaureate distance learning degree programs offered (no on-campus study). *Degree requirements:* For master's, thesis; for doctorate, capstone. *Entrance requirements:* For master's, GRE (if GPA less than 3.0). Additional exam requirements/recommendations for international students: Required—TOEFL (minimum score 550 paper-based). *Faculty research:* Job satisfaction; nursing diagnoses; dehydration among elderly; correlates to functional status in elderly.

Xavier University, College of Social Sciences, Health and Education, School of Nursing, Cincinnati, OH 45207. Offers clinical nurse leader (MSN); education (MSN); forensic nursing (MSN); healthcare law (MSN); informatics (MSN); nursing administration (MSN); school nursing (MSN); MSN/M Ed; MSN/MBA; MSN/MS. *Accreditation:* AACN. Part-time and evening/weekend programs available. Postbaccalaureate distance learning degree programs offered (no on-campus study). *Faculty:* 10 full-time (all women), 10 part-time/adjunct (9 women). *Students:* 64 full-time (55 women), 148 part-time (146 women); includes 19 minority (17 African Americans, 1 Asian American or Pacific Islander, 1 Hispanic American), 2 international. Average age 38. 141 applicants, 88% accepted, 110 enrolled. In 2009, 48 master's awarded. *Degree requirements:* For master's, thesis, scholarly project. *Entrance requirements:* For master's, GRE. Additional exam requirements/recommendations for international students: Required—TOEFL. *Application deadline:* Applications are processed on a rolling basis. Application fee: $35. Electronic applications accepted. *Expenses:* Tuition: Part-time $697 per credit hour. One-time fee: $35 part-time. *Financial support:* In 2009–10, 68 students received support. Applicants required to submit FAFSA. *Faculty research:* Clinical nurse leader, simulation, employment satisfaction, nontraditional students, holistic nursing. *Unit head:* Dr. Susan M. Schmidt, Director, 513-745-3815, Fax: 513-745-1087, E-mail: schmidt@xavier.edu. *Application contact:* Marilyn Volk Gomez, Director of Nursing Student Services, 513-745-4392, Fax: 513-745-1087, E-mail: gomez@xavier.edu.

Nursing Informatics

Austin Peay State University, College of Graduate Studies, College of Behavioral and Health Sciences, School of Nursing, Clarksville, TN 37044. Offers advanced practice (MSN); nursing administration (MSN); nursing education (MSN); nursing informatics (MSN). Part-time programs available. Postbaccalaureate distance learning degree programs offered. *Faculty:* 7 full-time (all women). *Students:* 15 full-time (14 women), 62 part-time (57 women); includes 6 minority (3 African Americans, 1 American Indian/Alaska Native, 2 Asian Americans or Pacific Islanders). Average age 39. 31 applicants, 100% accepted, 22 enrolled. In 2009, 9 master's awarded. *Degree requirements:* For master's, comprehensive exam. *Entrance requirements:* For master's, GRE General Test, minimum GPA of 3.0, RN license eligibility, 3 letters of recommendation. Additional exam requirements/recommendations for international students: Required—TOEFL (minimum score 600 paper-based). *Application deadline:* For fall admission, 7/27 priority date for domestic students; for spring admission, 12/17 priority date for domestic students. Applications are processed on a rolling basis. Application fee: $25. Electronic applications accepted. *Expenses:* Tuition, state resident: full-time $6160; part-time $608 per credit hour. Tuition, nonresident: full-time $17,080; part-time $854 per credit hour. Required fees: $1224; $61.20 per credit hour. *Financial support:* In 2009–10, 1 student received support, including 1 research assistantship with full tuition reimbursement available (averaging $5,184 per year); career-related internships or fieldwork, Federal Work-Study, institutionally sponsored loans, scholarships/grants, and unspecified assistantships also available. Support available to part-time students. *Unit head:* Dr. Francisca Ann Farrar, Director, 931-221-7737, Fax: 931-221-6490, E-mail: farrarf@apsu.edu. *Application contact:* Dr. Doris Davenport, Associate Professor, 931-221-7467, Fax: 931-221-7595, E-mail: davenportd@apsu.edu.

Case Western Reserve University, Frances Payne Bolton School of Nursing, Master's Programs in Nursing, Program in Nursing Informatics, Cleveland, OH 44106. Offers MSN. Part-time programs available. *Entrance requirements:* For master's, GRE General Test or MAT. Additional exam requirements/recommendations for international students: Required—TOEFL.

Duke University, School of Nursing, Durham, NC 27708-0586. Offers adult acute care (Certificate); adult cardiovascular (Certificate); adult oncology (Certificate); adult primary care (Certificate); clinical nurse specialist (MSN), including adult oncology, gerontology, neonatal, pediatric; clinical research management (MSN, Certificate); family (Certificate); gerontology (Certificate); health and nursing ministries (MSN, Certificate); health systems leadership and outcomes (Certificate); neonatal (Certificate); neonatal/pediatric in rural health (MSN, Certificate); nurse anesthetist (MSN, Certificate); nurse practitioner (MSN), including adult acute care, adult cardiovascular, adult oncology, adult primary care, family, gerontology, neonatal, pediatric, pediatric acute care; nursing (DNP, PhD); nursing and healthcare leadership (MSN); nursing education (MSN); nursing informatics (MSN, Certificate); pediatric (Certificate); pediatric acute care (Certificate); MBA/MSN; MSN/MCM. *Accreditation:* AACN; AANA/CANAEP. Part-time programs available. Postbaccalaureate distance learning degree programs offered (minimal on-campus study). *Faculty:* 45 full-time (41 women), 169 part-time/adjunct (150 women). *Students:* 213 full-time (179 women), 116 part-time (105 women); includes 37 minority (17 African Americans, 13 Asian Americans or Pacific Islanders, 7 Hispanic Americans), 9 international. Average age 36. 234 applicants, 53% accepted, 97 enrolled. In 2009, 142 master's, 24 other advanced degrees awarded. Terminal master's awarded for partial completion of doctoral program. *Degree requirements:* For master's, thesis optional; for doctorate, Capstone Project. *Entrance requirements:* For master's, GRE General Test, 1 year of nursing experience, BSN, minimum GPA of 3.0, previous course work in statistics; for doctorate, GRE for BSN prepared, BSN or MSN, minimum GPA of 3.0. Portfolio; for Certificate, MSN. Additional exam requirements/recommendations for international students: Required—TOEFL (minimum score 550 paper-based; 213 computer-based), Commission on Graduates of Foreign Nursing Schools exam. *Application deadline:* For fall admission, 7/2 priority date for domestic and international students; for spring admission, 11/15 priority date for domestic and international students. Applications are processed on a rolling basis. Application fee: $50. Electronic applications accepted. *Expenses:* Contact institution. *Financial support:* Career-related internships or fieldwork, institutionally sponsored loans, scholarships/grants, traineeships, and tuition waivers (partial) available. Support available to part-time students. Financial award application deadline: 4/1; financial award applicants required to submit FAFSA. *Faculty research:* Cardiovascular disease, caregiver skill training, data mining, prostate cancer, neonatal immune system. Total annual research expenditures: $3.5 million. *Unit head:* Dr. Catherine L. Gilliss, Dean/Vice Chancellor for Nursing Affairs, 919-684-9444, Fax: 919-684-9414, E-mail: gilli025@mc.duke.edu. *Application contact:* Bebe T. Mills, Director of Admissions, 919-684-9151, Fax: 919-668-4693, E-mail: mills031@mc.duke.edu.

Ferris State University, College of Allied Health Sciences, School of Nursing, Big Rapids, MI 49307. Offers nursing (MS); nursing administration (MS); nursing education (MS); nursing informatics (MS). *Accreditation:* NLN. Part-time and evening/weekend programs available. Postbaccalaureate distance learning degree programs offered (minimal on-campus study). *Faculty:* 1 (woman) full-time, 69 part-time/adjunct (63 women). *Students:* 1 (woman) full-time, 64 part-time (58 women). Average age 42. 30 applicants, 53% accepted, 11 enrolled. In 2009, 9 master's awarded. *Degree requirements:* For master's, comprehensive exam, practicum, scholarly project. *Entrance requirements:* For master's, BS in nursing, writing sample, letters of reference, 2 years clinical experience. Additional exam requirements/recommendations for international students: Required—TOEFL (minimum score 550 paper-based). *Application deadline:* For fall admission, 7/15 priority date for domestic students. Applications are processed

on a rolling basis. Application fee: $30. Electronic applications accepted. *Financial support:* In 2009–10, 4 students received support; fellowships, research assistantships, teaching assistantships, scholarships/grants available. Financial award application deadline: 4/15. *Faculty research:* Nursing education-minority student focus, student attitudes toward aging. *Unit head:* Dr. Julie A. Coon, Director, 231-591-2267, Fax: 231-591-2325, E-mail: coonj@ferris.edu. *Application contact:* Debby Buck, Off Campus Program Secretary, 231-591-2270, Fax: 231-591-3788, E-mail: buckd@ferris.edu.

Grantham University, College of Arts and Sciences, Kansas City, MO 64153. Offers case management (MSN); health systems management (MS); healthcare administration (MHA); nursing (MSN); nursing education (MSN); nursing informatics (MSN); nursing management and organizational leadership (MSN). Part-time and evening/weekend programs available. Postbaccalaureate distance learning degree programs offered (no on-campus study). In 2009, 48 master's awarded. *Degree requirements:* For master's, thesis (for some programs), capstone project. *Entrance requirements:* For master's, bachelor's degree from accredited degree-granting institution. Additional exam requirements/recommendations for international students: Required—TOEFL (minimum score 500 paper-based; 213 computer-based; 61 iBT). *Application deadline:* Applications are processed on a rolling basis. Electronic applications accepted. *Expenses:* Tuition: Part-time $265 per credit hour. One-time fee: $30 part-time. *Financial support:* Institutionally sponsored loans and scholarships/grants available. *Unit head:* Dr. Kim Humerickhouse, Dean, 800-955-2527, Fax: 816-595-5757, E-mail: admissions@grantham.edu. *Application contact:* Matthew Hawes, Vice President of Enrollment Management, 800-955-2527, Fax: 816-595-5757, E-mail: admissions@grantham.edu.

Loyola University Chicago, Graduate School, Marcella Niehoff School of Nursing, Family Nurse Practitioner Program, Chicago, IL 60660. Offers family nurse practitioner (MSN); family practice nurse practitioner (Certificate); informatics (Certificate); manager care (Certificate). Part-time and evening/weekend programs available. *Students:* 7 full-time (all women), 67 part-time (66 women); includes 18 minority (5 African Americans, 12 Asian Americans or Pacific Islanders, 1 Hispanic American). Average age 33. 38 applicants, 55% accepted, 15 enrolled. In 2009, 4 master's awarded. *Entrance requirements:* For master's, BSN, Illinois nursing license, minimum nursing GPA of 3.0, 1000 hours experience before starting clinical. *Application deadline:* Applications are processed on a rolling basis. Application fee: $50. Electronic applications accepted. *Expenses:* Tuition: Full-time $14,220; part-time $790 per credit hour. Required fees: $60 per semester hour. Tuition and fees vary according to program. *Financial support:* Traineeships available. Financial award applicants required to submit FAFSA. *Unit head:* Dr. Marijo Letizia, Associate Professor, 708-216-9325, Fax: 708-216-9555, E-mail: mletizi@luc.edu. *Application contact:* Dr. Vicki A. Keough, Associate Professor/Master's Program Director, 708-216-3582, Fax: 708-216-9555, E-mail: vkeough@luc.edu.

Molloy College, Graduate Nursing Program, Rockville Centre, NY 11571-5002. Offers adult nurse practitioner (Advanced Certificate); clinical nurse specialist: adult health (Advanced Certificate); family nurse practitioner (Advanced Certificate); nurse practitioner psychiatry (Advanced Certificate); nursing (MS); nursing administration (Advanced Certificate); nursing administration with informatics (Advanced Certificate); nursing education (Advanced Certificate); nursing informatics (Advanced Certificate); pediatric nurse practitioner (Advanced Certificate). *Accreditation:* AACN. Part-time and evening/weekend programs available. *Faculty:* 23 full-time (22 women), 5 part-time/adjunct (4 women). *Students:* 11 full-time (10 women), 405 part-time (377 women); includes 206 minority (124 African Americans, 52 Asian Americans or Pacific Islanders, 30 Hispanic Americans), 2 international. Average age 39. In 2009, 64 master's awarded. *Degree requirements:* For master's, thesis optional. *Entrance requirements:* For master's, 3 letters of reference, BS in nursing, minimum undergraduate GPA of 3.0; for Advanced Certificate, 3 letters of reference, master's degree in nursing. *Application deadline:* For fall admission, 9/2 priority date for domestic students; for spring admission, 1/20 priority date for domestic students. Applications are processed on a rolling basis. Application fee: $60. *Expenses:* Tuition: Part-time $765 per credit. Required fees: $340 per semester. *Financial support:* Research assistantships with partial tuition reimbursements, teaching assistantships with partial tuition reimbursements, institutionally sponsored loans, scholarships/grants, and unspecified assistantships available. Support available to part-time students. Financial award application deadline: 4/1; financial award applicants required to submit FAFSA. *Unit head:* Dr. Mary T. O'Shaughnessy, Acting Director, 516-678-5000, Fax: 516-678-9718, E-mail: moshaughnessy@molloy.edu. *Application contact:* Alina Haitz, Assistant Director of Graduate Admissions, 516-678-5000 Ext. 6399, Fax: 516-256-2247, E-mail: ahaitz@molloy.edu.

New York University, College of Nursing, Programs in Advanced Practice Nursing, New York, NY 10012-1019. Offers advanced practice nursing: adult acute care (MS, Advanced Certificate); advanced practice nursing: adult nurse practictioner/palliative care nursing (MS); advanced practice nursing: adult nurse practitioner/holistic nurse practitioner (Advanced Certificate); advanced practice nursing: adult nurse practitioner/holistic nursing (MS); advanced practice nursing: adult nurse practitioner/palliative care nurse practitioner (Advanced Certificate); advanced practice nursing: adult primary care (MS, Advanced Certificate); advanced practice nursing: adult primary care/geriatrics (MS); advanced practice nursing: geriatrics (MS, Advanced Certificate); advanced practice nursing: mental health (MS); advanced practice nursing: mental health nursing (Advanced Certificate); advanced practice nursing: pediatrics (MS, Advanced Certificate); advanced practice nursing:adult primary care and geriatrics (Advanced Certificate); nurse midwifery (MS, Advanced Certificate); nursing administration (MS, Advanced Certificate); nursing education (MS, Advanced Certificate); nursing informatics (MS, Advanced Certificate); MS/MPH; MS/MS. *Accreditation:* AACN; ACNM/DOA. Part-time and evening/weekend programs available. *Faculty:* 17 full-time (all women), 22 part-time/adjunct (19 women). *Students:* 18 full-time (17 women), 524 part-time (485 women); includes 238 minority (90 African Americans, 119 Asian Americans or Pacific Islanders, 29 Hispanic Americans). Average age 33. 191 applicants, 89% accepted, 120 enrolled. In 2009, 117 master's, 2 other advanced degrees awarded. *Degree requirements:* For master's, thesis (for some programs). *Entrance requirements:* For master's, BS in nursing, AS in nursing with another BS/BA, interview; for Advanced Certificate, master's degree. Additional exam requirements/recommendations for international students: Required—TOEFL. *Application deadline:* For fall admission, 7/1 priority date for domestic students, 7/1 for international students; for spring admission, 12/1 for domestic and international students. Applications are processed on a rolling basis. Application fee: $75. *Expenses:* Tuition: Full-time $30,528; part-time $1272 per credit. Required fees: $2177. *Financial support:* Career-related internships or fieldwork, institutionally sponsored loans, scholarships/grants, traineeships, and tuition waivers (partial) available. Support available to part-time students. Financial award application deadline: 2/1; financial award applicants required to submit FAFSA. *Faculty research:* Elderly black diabetics, families and illness, public health nursing, parent-child nursing, health policy costs. *Unit head:* Dr. Judith Haber, Associate Dean for Graduate Programs, 212-998-9020, Fax: 212-995-3143. *Application contact:* Amy Knowles, Assistant Dean for Student Affairs and Admissions, 212-998-5333, Fax: 212-995-4302, E-mail: ak96@nyu.edu.

Seattle Pacific University, MS in Nursing Program, Seattle, WA 98119-1997. Offers administration (MSN); adult/gerontology nurse practitioner (MSN); clinical nurse specialist (MSN); family nurse practitioner (MSN, Certificate); informatics (MSN); nurse educator (MSN). *Accreditation:* AACN. Part-time programs available. *Faculty:* 3 full-time (all women), 7 part-time/adjunct (6 women). *Students:* 9 full-time (8 women), 63 part-time (57 women); includes 9 minority (1 American Indian/Alaska Native, 7 Asian Americans or Pacific Islanders, 1 Hispanic American), 1 international. Average age 46. 60 applicants, 45% accepted, 27 enrolled. In 2009, 12 master's awarded. *Degree requirements:* For master's, thesis. *Application deadline:* For fall admission, 2/1 priority date for domestic students. Applications are processed on a rolling basis. Application fee: $50. Electronic applications accepted. *Expenses:* Contact institution. *Financial support:* In 2009–10, 41 students received support; fellowships, scholarships/grants available. Financial award applicants required to submit FAFSA. *Unit head:* Dr. Susan Casey, Director, 206-281-2769, Fax: 206-281-2767, E-mail: caseys@spu.edu. *Application contact:* The Grad Center, 206-281-2091.

Tennessee State University, The School of Graduate Studies and Research, School of Nursing, Nashville, TN 37209-1561. Offers family nurse practitioner (MSN); holistic nursing (MSN); nursing administration (MSN); nursing education (MSN); nursing informatics (MSN). *Accreditation:* NLN. *Entrance requirements:* For master's, GRE General Test or MAT, BSN, current RN license, minimum GPA of 3.0.

Tennessee Technological University, School of Nursing, Cookeville, TN 38505. Offers family nurse practitioner (MSN); informatics (MSN); nursing administration (MSN); nursing education (MSN). *Students:* 11 full-time (10 women), 30 part-time (27 women); includes 2 minority (1 African American, 1 Hispanic American). 40 applicants, 35% accepted, 10 enrolled. In 2009, 14 master's awarded. *Degree requirements:* For master's, comprehensive exam, thesis or alternative. *Entrance requirements:* Additional exam requirements/recommendations for international students: Required—TOEFL (minimum score 550 paper-based; 79 iBT), IELTS (minimum score 5.5). *Application deadline:* For fall admission, 8/1 for domestic students, 5/1 for international students; for spring admission, 12/1 for domestic students, 10/1 for international students. Application fee: $25 ($30 for international students). Electronic applications accepted. *Expenses:* Tuition, state resident: full-time $7034; part-time $368 per credit hour. *Financial support:* Application deadline: 4/1. *Unit head:* Dr. Sheila Green, Interim Dean, 931-372-3203, Fax: 931-372-6244, E-mail: sgreen@tntech.edu. *Application contact:* Shelia K. Kendrick, Coordinator of Graduate Studies, 931-372-3808, Fax: 931-372-3497, E-mail: skendrick@tntech.edu.

Troy University, Graduate School, College of Health and Human Services, Program in Nursing, Troy, AL 36082. Offers adult health (MSN); clinical nurse specialist adult health (DNP); clinical nurse specialist nurse practitioner (DNP); family nurse practitioner (MSN); informatics specialist (MSN); maternal infant (MSN). *Accreditation:* NLN. Part-time and evening/weekend programs available. *Students:* 28 full-time (all women), 102 part-time (93 women); includes 49 minority (48 African Americans, 1 American Indian/Alaska Native). Average age 37. 76 applicants, 86% accepted. In 2009, 25 master's awarded. *Degree requirements:* For master's, comprehensive exam, thesis optional. *Entrance requirements:* For master's, MAT (minimum score 396) or GRE (minimum score 850), minimum GPA of 2.5, BSN. Additional exam requirements/recommendations for international students: Required—TOEFL (minimum score 523 paper-based; 193 computer-based; 70 iBT), IELTS (minimum score 6), TOEFL or IELTS or ACT Compass ESL (minimum score 270 on Listening, Reading, and Grammar with no individual score below 85 and minimum score of 8 out of 12 on writing test). *Application deadline:* Applications are processed on a rolling basis. Application fee: $50. Electronic applications accepted. *Financial support:* Available to part-time students. Applicants required to submit FAFSA. *Application contact:* Brenda K. Campbell, Director of Graduate Admissions, 334-670-3178, Fax: 334-670-3733, E-mail: bcamp@troy.edu.

University of Medicine and Dentistry of New Jersey, School of Nursing, Program in Nursing Informatics—Newark, Newark, NJ 07107-1709. Offers MSN. *Entrance requirements:* Additional exam requirements/recommendations for international students: Required—TOEFL. Electronic applications accepted.

University of Medicine and Dentistry of New Jersey, School of Nursing, Program in Nursing Informatics—Stratford, Newark, NJ 07107-1709. Offers MSN. *Entrance requirements:* Additional exam requirements/recommendations for international students: Required—TOEFL. Electronic applications accepted.

Vanderbilt University, School of Nursing, Nashville, TN 37240. Offers adult acute care nurse practitioner (MSN); adult nurse practitioner/cardiovascular disease management and prevention (MSN); adult nurse practitioner/palliative care (MSN); clinical management (clinical nurse leader/specialist) (MSN); emergency nurse practitioner (MSN); family nurse practitioner (MSN); gerontology nurse practitioner (MSN); health systems management (MSN); neonatal nurse practitioner (MSN); nurse midwifery (MSN); nurse midwifery/family nurse practitioner (MSN); nursing informatics (MSN); nursing practice (DNP); nursing science (PhD); nutrition (MS); pediatric acute care nurse practitioner (MSN); pediatric primary care nurse practitioner (MSN); psychiatric-mental health nurse practitioner (MSN); women's health nurse practitioner (MSN), including urogynecology; women's health nurse practitioner/adult nurse practitioner (MSN); MSN/M Div; MSN/MTS. *Accreditation:* ACNM/DOA; NLN (one or more programs are accredited). Part-time programs available. Postbaccalaureate distance learning degree programs offered (minimal on-campus study). *Faculty:* 118 full-time (102 women), 429 part-time/adjunct (309 women). *Students:* 484 full-time (435 women), 319 part-time (284 women); includes 84 minority (55 African Americans, 4 American Indian/Alaska Native, 10 Asian Americans or Pacific Islanders, 15 Hispanic Americans), 16 international. Average age 32. 900 applicants, 65% accepted, 433 enrolled. In 2009, 303 master's, 1 doctorate awarded. *Degree requirements:* For doctorate, comprehensive exam, thesis/dissertation. *Entrance requirements:* For master's, GRE General Test, minimum B average in undergraduate course work, 3 letters of recommendation; for doctorate, GRE General Test, interview, 3 letters of recommendation from doctorally-prepared faculty, MSN, essay. Additional exam requirements/recommendations for international students: Required—TOEFL. *Application deadline:* For fall admission, 12/1 priority date for domestic and international students. Applications are processed on a rolling basis. Application fee: $50. *Expenses:* Contact institution. *Financial support:* In 2009–10, 389 students received support, including 1 research assistantship (averaging $5,000 per year); teaching assistantships, scholarships/grants, health care benefits, and tuition waivers also available. Support available to part-time students. Financial award application deadline: 3/15; financial award applicants required to submit FAFSA. *Faculty research:* Lymphedema, palliative care and bereavement, health services research including workforce, safety and quality of care, gerontology, better birth outcomes including nutrition. Total annual research expenditures: $1.4 million. *Unit head:* Dr. Colleen Conway-Welch, Dean, 615-343-8776, Fax: 615-343-7711, E-mail: colleen.conway-welch@vanderbilt.edu. *Application contact:* Cheryl Feldner, Assistant Director of Admissions, 615-322-3800, Fax: 615-343-0333, E-mail: cheryl.feldner@vanderbilt.edu.

Walden University, Graduate Programs, School of Nursing, Minneapolis, MN 55401. Offers education (MSN); informatics (MSN); leadership and management (MSN); nursing (Post-Master's Certificate), including nursing education, nursing informatics, nursing leadership and management. *Accreditation:* AACN. Part-time and evening/weekend programs available. Postbaccalaureate distance learning degree programs offered (no on-campus study). *Faculty:* 5 full-time, 105 part-time/adjunct. *Students:* 2,644 full-time (2,468 women), 805 part-time (755 women); includes 660 minority (430 African Americans, 23 American Indian/Alaska Native, 122 Asian Americans or Pacific Islanders, 85 Hispanic Americans), 34 international. Average age 44. In 2009, 624 master's, 1 other advanced degree awarded. *Entrance requirements:* For master's, bachelor's degree or equivalent in related field or RN; minimum GPA of 2.5. Additional exam requirements/recommendations for international students: Required—TOEFL (minimum score 550 paper-based; 213 computer-based), IELTS (minimum score 6.5), or Michigan English Language Assessment Battery (minimum score 82). *Application deadline:* Applications are processed on a rolling basis. Application fee: $50. Electronic applications accepted. *Expenses:* Tuition: Full-time $13,665; part-time $560 per credit. Required fees: $1375. Tuition and fees vary according to course load, degree level and program. *Financial support:* In 2009–10, 273 students received support; fellowships, Federal Work-Study, scholarships/grants, unspecified assistantships, and family tuition reduction, active duty/veteran tuition reduction, group tuition reduction, interest-free payment plans available. Support available to part-time students. Financial award applicants required to submit FAFSA. *Unit head:* Dr. Sara Torres, Associate Dean, 800-925-3368. *Application contact:* Jennifer Hall, Director of Enrollment, 866-4-WALDEN, E-mail: info@walden.edu.

Waynesburg University, Graduate and Professional Studies, Waynesburg, PA 15370-1222. Offers business (MBA), including finance, health systems, human resources, leadership, market development; counseling (MA), including addictions counseling, clinical mental health; education (MAT); nursing (MSN), including administration, education, informatics, palliative care; nursing practice (DNP); special education (M Ed); technology (M Ed); MSN/MBA. *Accreditation:* AACN. Part-time and evening/weekend programs available. *Faculty:* 11 full-time (5 women), 136 part-time/adjunct (80 women). *Students:* 116 full-time (85 women), 984 part-time (682 women). 711 applicants, 80% accepted, 485 enrolled. In 2009, 320 master's, 41

Nursing Informatics

Waynesburg University (continued)

doctorates awarded. *Degree requirements:* For doctorate, thesis/dissertation. *Entrance requirements:* Additional exam requirements/recommendations for international students: Required—TOEFL. *Application deadline:* For fall admission, 8/1 priority date for domestic students. Applications are processed on a rolling basis. Electronic applications accepted. *Expenses:* Tuition: Part-time $520 per credit. *Financial support:* Available to part-time students. Application deadline: 5/1. *Unit head:* David Mariner, Dean, 724-743-4420, Fax: 724-743-4425, E-mail: dmariner@waynesburg.edu. *Application contact:* Michael Bednarski, Director of Admissions, 724-743-4420, Fax: 724-743-4425, E-mail: mbednars@waynesburg.edu.

Xavier University, College of Social Sciences, Health and Education, School of Nursing, Cincinnati, OH 45207. Offers clinical nurse leader (MSN); education (MSN); forensic nursing (MSN); healthcare law (MSN); informatics (MSN); nursing administration (MSN); school nursing (MSN); MSN/M Ed; MSN/MBA; MSN/MS. *Accreditation:* AACN. Part-time and evening/weekend programs available. Postbaccalaureate distance learning degree programs offered (no on-campus study). *Faculty:* 10 full-time (all women), 10 part-time/adjunct (9 women). *Students:* 64 full-time (55 women), 148 part-time (146 women); includes 19 minority (17 African Americans, 1 Asian American or Pacific Islander, 1 Hispanic American), 2 international. Average age 38. 141 applicants, 88% accepted, 110 enrolled. In 2009, 48 master's awarded. *Degree requirements:* For master's, thesis, scholarly project. *Entrance requirements:* For master's, GRE. Additional exam requirements/recommendations for international students: Required—TOEFL. *Application deadline:* Applications are processed on a rolling basis. Application fee: $35. Electronic applications accepted. *Expenses:* Tuition: Part-time $697 per credit hour. One-time fee: $35 part-time. *Financial support:* In 2009–10, 68 students received support. Applicants required to submit FAFSA. *Faculty research:* Clinical nurse leader, simulation, employment satisfaction, nontraditional students, holistic nursing. *Unit head:* Dr. Susan M. Schmidt, Director, 513-745-3815, Fax: 513-745-1087, E-mail: schmidt@xavier.edu. *Application contact:* Marilyn Volk Gomez, Director of Nursing Student Services, 513-745-4392, Fax: 513-745-1087, E-mail: gomez@xavier.edu.

Occupational Health Nursing

University of Cincinnati, Graduate School, College of Nursing, Cincinnati, OH 45221-0038. Offers clinical nurse specialist (MSN), including adult health, community health, neonatal, nursing administration, occupational health, pediatric health, psychiatric nursing, women's health; nurse anesthesia (MSN); nurse midwifery (MSN); nurse practitioner (MSN), including acute care, ambulatory care, family, family/psychiatric, women's health; nursing (PhD); MBA/MSN. *Accreditation:* AACN; AANA/CANAEP (one or more programs are accredited); ACNM/DOA. Part-time programs available. Postbaccalaureate distance learning degree programs offered (no on-campus study). Terminal master's awarded for partial completion of doctoral program. *Degree requirements:* For master's, thesis or alternative; for doctorate, comprehensive exam, thesis/dissertation. *Entrance requirements:* For master's and doctorate, GRE General Test. Additional exam requirements/recommendations for international students: Required—TOEFL (minimum score 520 paper-based; 190 computer-based). Electronic applications accepted. *Faculty research:* Substance abuse, injury and violence, symptom management.

University of Illinois at Chicago, Graduate College, College of Nursing, Program in Nursing, Chicago, IL 60607-7128. Offers acute care clinical nurse specialist (MS); acute care nurse practitioner (MS); administrative studies in nursing (MS); adult nurse practitioner (MS); adult/geriatric nurse practitioner (MS); advanced community health nurse specialist (MS); family nurse practitioner (MS); geriatric clinical nurse specialist (MS); geriatric nurse practitioner (MS); mental health clinical nurse specialist (MS); mental health nurse practitioner (MS); nurse midwifery (MS); occupational health/advanced community health nurse specialist (MS); occupational health/family nurse practitioner (MS); pediatric clinical nurse specialist (MS); pediatric nurse practitioner (MS); perinatal clinical nurse specialist (MS); school/advanced community health nurse specialist (MS); school/family nurse practitioner (MS); women's health nurse practitioner (MS). *Accreditation:* AACN. Part-time programs available. *Degree requirements:* For master's, thesis or alternative. *Entrance requirements:* For master's, GRE General Test, minimum GPA of 2.75. Additional exam requirements/recommendations for international students: Required—TOEFL. Electronic applications accepted.

University of Medicine and Dentistry of New Jersey, School of Nursing, Newark, NJ 07107-3001. Offers adult health (MSN); adult occupational health (MSN); advanced practice nursing (MSN, Post Master's Certificate); family nurse practitioner (MSN); nurse anesthesia (MSN); nursing (MSN); nursing informatics (MSN); urban health (PhD); women's health practitioner (MSN). *Accreditation:* AANA/CANAEP; NLN (one or more programs are accredited). Part-time programs available. *Entrance requirements:* For master's, GRE, RN license; basic life support, statistics, and health assessment experience. Additional exam requirements/recommendations for international students: Required—TOEFL. Electronic applications accepted. *Expenses:* Contact institution. *Faculty research:* HIV/AIDS, diabetes education, learned helplessness, nursing science, psychoeducation.

University of Michigan, Horace H. Rackham School of Graduate Studies, School of Nursing, Division of Health Promotion and Risk Reduction, Program in Community Health Nursing, Ann Arbor, MI 48109. Offers adult nurse practitioner (Post Master's Certificate); adult primary care/adult nurse practitioner (MS); community care (Post Master's Certificate); community care/home care (MS); family nurse practitioner (MS, Post Master's Certificate); occupational health nursing (MS). *Accreditation:* AACN. Part-time and evening/weekend programs available. *Degree requirements:* For master's, thesis. *Entrance requirements:* For master's, GRE General Test (if cumulative BSN GPA less than 3.25), licensure, minimum GPA of 3.0 in BSN program. Additional exam requirements/recommendations for international students: Required—TOEFL (minimum score 560 paper-based; 220 computer-based). *Expenses:* Tuition, state resident: full-time $17,286; part-time $1099 per credit hour. Tuition, nonresident: full-time $34,944; part-time $2080 per credit hour. Required fees: $95 per semester. Tuition and fees vary according to course load, degree level and program.

University of Minnesota, Twin Cities Campus, School of Public Health, Division of Environmental Health Sciences, Area in Occupational Health Nursing, Minneapolis, MN 55455-0213. Offers MPH, MS, PhD, MPH/MS. *Accreditation:* AACN. *Degree requirements:* For doctorate, thesis/dissertation. *Entrance requirements:* For master's and doctorate, GRE General Test. Electronic applications accepted.

The University of North Carolina at Chapel Hill, Graduate School, School of Public Health, Public Health Leadership Program, Chapel Hill, NC 27599. Offers health care and prevention (MPH); leadership (MPH); occupational health nursing (MPH); public health nursing (MS). Part-time programs available. Postbaccalaureate distance learning degree programs offered (minimal on-campus study). *Degree requirements:* For master's, comprehensive exam, thesis (MS), paper (MPH). *Entrance requirements:* For master's, GRE General Test, minimum GPA of 3.0, public health experience. Additional exam requirements/recommendations for international students: Required—TOEFL. Electronic applications accepted. *Faculty research:* Occupational health issues, clinical outcomes, prenatal and early childcare, adolescent health, effectiveness of home visiting, issues in occupational health nursing, community-based interventions.

University of Pennsylvania, School of Nursing, Occupational Health Nurse Practitioner Program, Philadelphia, PA 19104. Offers administration/consulting (MSN); primary care (MSN). *Accreditation:* AACN. Part-time programs available. *Entrance requirements:* For master's, GRE General Test, BSN, minimum GPA of 3.0, previous course work in statistics. Additional exam requirements/recommendations for international students: Required—TOEFL. *Expenses:* Contact institution. *Faculty research:* Injury prevention.

University of the Sacred Heart, Graduate Programs, Department of Natural Sciences, San Juan, PR 00914-0383. Offers occupational health and safety (MS); occupational nursing (MSN). Part-time and evening/weekend programs available.

Oncology Nursing

Columbia University, School of Nursing, Program in Oncology Nursing, New York, NY 10032. Offers MS, Adv C. *Accreditation:* AACN. Part-time programs available. *Entrance requirements:* For master's, GRE General Test, BSN, 1 year of clinical experience (preferred); for Adv C, MSN. Electronic applications accepted.

Duke University, School of Nursing, Durham, NC 27708-0586. Offers adult acute care (Certificate); adult cardiovascular (Certificate); adult oncology (Certificate); adult primary care (Certificate); clinical nurse specialist (MSN), including adult oncology, gerontology, neonatal, pediatric; clinical research management (MSN, Certificate); family (Certificate); gerontology (Certificate); health and nursing ministries (MSN, Certificate); health systems leadership and outcomes (Certificate); neonatal (Certificate); neonatal/pediatric in rural health (MSN, Certificate); nurse anesthetist (MSN, Certificate); nurse practitioner (MSN), including adult acute care, adult cardiovascular, adult oncology, adult primary care, family, gerontology, neonatal, pediatric, pediatric acute care; nursing (DNP, PhD); nursing and healthcare leadership (MSN); nursing education (MSN); nursing informatics (MSN, Certificate); pediatric (Certificate); pediatric acute care (Certificate); MBA/MSN; MSN/MCM. *Accreditation:* AACN; AANA/CANAEP. Part-time programs available. Postbaccalaureate distance learning degree programs offered (minimal on-campus study). *Faculty:* 45 full-time (41 women), 169 part-time/adjunct (150 women). *Students:* 213 full-time (179 women), 116 part-time (105 women); includes 37 minority (17 African Americans, 13 Asian Americans or Pacific Islanders, 7 Hispanic Americans), 9 international. Average age 36. 234 applicants, 53% accepted, 97 enrolled. In 2009, 142 master's, 24 other advanced degrees awarded. Terminal master's awarded for partial completion of doctoral program. *Degree requirements:* For master's, thesis optional; for doctorate, Capstone Project. *Entrance requirements:* For master's, GRE General Test, 1 year of nursing experience, BSN, minimum GPA of 3.0, previous course work in statistics; for doctorate, GRE for BSN prepared, BSN or MSN, minimum GPA of 3.0. Portfolio; for Certificate, MSN. Additional exam requirements/recommendations for international students: Required—TOEFL (minimum score 550 paper-based; 213 computer-based), Commission on Graduates of Foreign Nursing Schools exam. *Application deadline:* For fall admission, 7/2 priority date for domestic and international students; for spring admission, 11/15 priority date for domestic and international students. Applications are processed on a rolling basis. Application fee: $50. Electronic applications accepted. *Expenses:* Contact institution. *Financial support:* Career-related internships or fieldwork, institutionally sponsored loans, scholarships/grants, traineeships, and tuition waivers (partial) available. Support available to part-time students. Financial award application deadline: 4/1; financial award applicants required to submit FAFSA. *Faculty research:* Cardiovascular disease, caregiver skill training, data mining, prostate cancer, neonatal immune system. Total annual research expenditures: $3.5 million. *Unit head:* Dr. Catherine L. Gilliss, Dean/Vice Chancellor for Nursing Affairs, 919-684-9444, Fax: 919-684-9414, E-mail: gilli025@mc.duke.edu. *Application contact:* Bebe T. Mills, Director of Admissions, 919-684-9151, Fax: 919-668-4693, E-mail: mills031@mc.duke.edu.

Goldfarb School of Nursing at Barnes-Jewish College, Goldfarb School of Nursing at Barnes-Jewish College, St Louis, MO 63110. Offers adult acute care nurse practitioner (MSN); adult nurse practitioner (MSN); neonatal nurse practitioner (MSN); nurse anesthesia (MSN); nurse educator (MSN); nurse executive (MSN). *Accreditation:* AACN; AANA/CANAEP. Part-time and evening/weekend programs available. Postbaccalaureate distance learning degree programs offered (minimal on-campus study). *Faculty:* 18 full-time (16 women), 3 part-time/adjunct (2 women). *Students:* 28 full-time (25 women), 81 part-time (73 women); includes 34 minority (27 African Americans, 6 Asian Americans or Pacific Islanders, 1 Hispanic American), 3 international. Average age 38. 60 applicants, 75% accepted, 40 enrolled. In 2009, 26 master's awarded. *Degree requirements:* For master's, thesis or alternative. *Entrance requirements:* For master's, minimum GPA of 3.0, 2 references, statistics course. Additional exam requirements/recommendations for international students: Required—TOEFL (minimum score 550 paper-based; 213 computer-based). *Application deadline:* For fall admission, 2/1 priority date for international students; for spring admission, 10/1 priority date for international students. Applications are processed on a rolling basis. Application fee: $150. *Financial support:* In 2009–10, 60 students received support, including 20 fellowships (averaging $4,000 per year), 4 research assistantships (averaging $5,000 per year); Federal Work-Study, institutionally sponsored loans, and scholarships/grants also available. Support available to part-time students. Financial award applicants required to submit FAFSA. *Faculty research:* HIV Stigma, HIV symptom management, palliative care with children and their families, heart disease prevention in Hispanic women, depression in the well elderly, alternative therapies in pre-term infants. *Unit head:* Dr. Michael L. Evans, Dean, 314-362-6289, Fax: 314-362-0984, E-mail: mevans@bjc.org. *Application contact:* Dr. Michael Ward, Associate Dean for Student Programs, 314-362-9155, Fax: 314-362-9250, E-mail: mward@bjc.org.

Gwynedd-Mercy College, School of Nursing, Gwynedd Valley, PA 19437-0901. Offers clinical nurse specialist (MSN), including gerontology, oncology, pediatrics; nurse practitioner (MSN), including adult health, pediatric health. *Accreditation:* NLN. *Degree requirements:* For master's, thesis optional. *Entrance requirements:* For master's, GRE General Test or MAT, current nursing experience, physical assessment, course work in statistics, BSN from an NLNAC

accredited program, 2 letters of recommendation, personal interview. Additional exam requirements/recommendations for international students: Required—TOEFL (minimum score 575 paper-based). Electronic applications accepted. *Expenses:* Contact institution. *Faculty research:* Critical thinking, primary care, domestic violence, multiculturalism, nursing centers.

Loyola University Chicago, Graduate School, Marcella Niehoff School of Nursing, Adult Clinical Nurse Specialist Program, Chicago, IL 60660. Offers adult clinical nurse specialist (MSN, Certificate); cardiovascular health (Certificate); oncology nursing (Certificate). Part-time and evening/weekend programs available. Postbaccalaureate distance learning degree programs offered (minimal on-campus study). In 2009, 1 master's awarded. *Entrance requirements:* For master's, Illinois nursing license, BSN, minimum nursing GPA of 3.0, 3 letters of recommendation, 1,000 hours experience in area of specialty. *Expenses:* Tuition: Full-time $14,220; part-time $790 per credit hour. Required fees: $60 per semester hour. Tuition and fees vary according to program. *Unit head:* Dr. Meg Gulanick, Professor, 708-216-9687, Fax: 708-216-9555, E-mail: mgulani@luc.edu. *Application contact:* Dr. Vicki A. Keough, Associate Professor/Master's Program Director, 708-216-3582, Fax: 708-216-9555, E-mail: vkeough@luc.edu.

Loyola University Chicago, Graduate School, Marcella Niehoff School of Nursing, Oncology Clinical Nurse Specialist Program, Chicago, IL 60660. Offers nursing oncology (Certificate); oncology clinical nurse specialist (MSN). *Accreditation:* AACN. Part-time and evening/weekend programs available. Postbaccalaureate distance learning degree programs offered (minimal on-campus study). *Students:* 3 full-time (all women), 14 part-time (all women). Average age 34. 10 applicants, 30% accepted, 2 enrolled. In 2009, 2 master's awarded. *Degree requirements:* For master's, comprehensive exam or oral thesis defense. *Entrance requirements:* For master's, Illinois nursing license, BSN, minimum nursing GPA of 3.0, 3 letters of recommendation, 1000 hours experience before starting clinical. *Application deadline:* Applications are processed on a rolling basis. Application fee: $50. Electronic applications accepted. *Expenses:* Tuition: Full-time $14,220; part-time $790 per credit hour. Required fees: $60 per semester hour. Tuition and fees vary according to program. *Financial support:* Teaching assistantships, traineeships and unspecified assistantships available. Financial award application deadline: 3/1. *Faculty research:* Breast cancer, coping with cancer, pain. *Unit head:* Dr. Patricia Friend, Assistant Professor, 708-216-9553, Fax: 708-216-9555, E-mail: pfriend@luc.edu. *Application contact:* Dr. Vicki A. Keough, Associate Professor/Master's Program Director, 708-216-3582, Fax: 708-216-9555, E-mail: vkeough@luc.edu.

University of Delaware, College of Health Sciences, School of Nursing, Newark, DE 19716. Offers adult nurse practitioner (MSN, PMC); cardiopulmonary clinical nurse specialist (MSN, PMC); cardiopulmonary clinical nurse specialist/adult nurse practitioner (MSN, PMC); family nurse practitioner (MSN, PMC); gerontology clinical nurse specialist (MSN, PMC); gerontology clinical nurse specialist geriatric nurse practitioner (PMC); gerontology clinical nurse specialist/geriatric nurse practitioner (MSN); health services administration (MSN, PMC); nursing of children clinical nurse specialist (MSN, PMC); nursing of children clinical nurse specialist/pediatric nurse practitioner (MSN, PMC); oncology/immune deficiency clinical nurse specialist (MSN, PMC); oncology/immune deficiency clinical nurse specialist/adult nurse practitioner (MSN, PMC); perinatal/women's health clinical nurse specialist (MSN, PMC); perinatal/women's health clinical nurse specialist/women's health nurse practitioner (MSN, PMC); psychiatric nursing clinical nurse specialist (MSN, PMC). *Accreditation:* AACN; NLN (one or more programs are accredited). Part-time and evening/weekend programs available. Postbaccalaureate distance learning degree programs offered (minimal on-campus study). *Degree requirements:* For master's, thesis optional. *Entrance requirements:* For master's, BSN, interview, RN license. Electronic applications accepted. *Faculty research:* Marriage and chronic illness, health promotion, congestive heart failure patient outcomes, school nursing, diabetes in children, culture, health disparities, cardiovascular, prison nursing, oncology, public policy, child obesity, smoking and teen pregnancy, blood pressure measurements, men's health.

University of Pennsylvania, School of Nursing, Adult Oncology Nurse Practitioner Program, Philadelphia, PA 19104. Offers MSN. *Accreditation:* AACN. Part-time programs available. *Students:* 2 full-time (both women), 15 part-time (all women), 1 international. In 2009, 4 master's awarded. *Entrance requirements:* For master's, GRE General Test, BSN, minimum GPA of 3.0, previous course work in statistics. Additional exam requirements/recommendations for international students: Required—TOEFL. *Application deadline:* For fall admission, 2/15 priority date for domestic students. Applications are processed on a rolling basis. Application fee: $70. *Expenses:* Contact institution. *Financial support:* Fellowships, research assistantships, teaching assistantships, career-related internships or fieldwork, Federal Work-Study, and institutionally sponsored loans available. Support available to part-time students. Financial award application deadline: 4/1. *Faculty research:* Randomized clinical trials to evaluate advanced nursing practice in oncology patients and their caregivers, symptoms management.

University of Pennsylvania, School of Nursing, Pediatric Oncology Nurse Practitioner Program, Philadelphia, PA 19104. Offers MSN. *Accreditation:* AACN. *Entrance requirements:* For master's, GRE General Test, BSN, minimum GPA of 3.0, previous course work in statistics. Additional exam requirements/recommendations for international students: Required—TOEFL. *Expenses:* Contact institution.

Pediatric Nursing

Boston College, William F. Connell School of Nursing, Chestnut Hill, MA 02467-3800. Offers adult health nursing (MS); community health nursing (MS); family health (MS); forensic nursing (MS); gerontology (MS); maternal/child health nursing (MS), including pediatric and women's health; nurse anesthesia (MS); nursing (PhD); palliative care (MS), including adult and pediatric; psychiatric-mental health nursing (MS); MBA/MS; MS/MA; MS/PhD. *Accreditation:* AACN; AANA/CANAEP (one or more programs are accredited). Part-time programs available. *Faculty:* 48 full-time (46 women), 31 part-time/adjunct (29 women). *Students:* 183 full-time (169 women), 147 part-time (140 women); includes 36 minority (15 African Americans, 2 American Indian/Alaska Native, 17 Asian Americans or Pacific Islanders, 2 Hispanic Americans), 7 international. Average age 29. 347 applicants, 53% accepted, 103 enrolled. In 2009, 79 master's, 7 doctorates awarded. *Degree requirements:* For master's, comprehensive exam, research project; for doctorate, comprehensive exam, thesis/dissertation, computer literacy exam or foreign language. *Entrance requirements:* For master's, bachelor's degree in nursing; for doctorate, GRE General Test, master's degree in nursing. Additional exam requirements/recommendations for international students: Required—TOEFL (minimum score 550 paper-based; 213 computer-based). *Application deadline:* For fall admission, 11/1 for domestic and international students; for winter admission, 12/31 for domestic and international students; for spring admission, 9/15 for domestic and international students. Applications are processed on a rolling basis. Application fee: $40. Electronic applications accepted. *Financial support:* In 2009–10, 83 students received support, including 12 fellowships with partial tuition reimbursements available (averaging $15,000 per year), 5 teaching assistantships (averaging $13,746 per year); research assistantships, Federal Work-Study, institutionally sponsored loans, scholarships/grants, traineeships, health care benefits, and tuition waivers (partial) also available. Support available to part-time students. Financial award application deadline: 3/1; financial award applicants required to submit FAFSA. *Faculty research:* Ethics, reduction of risk behaviors, support during chronic illness, violence, gerontology. Total annual research expenditures: $1.4 million. *Unit head:* Dr. Susan Gennaro, Dean, 617-552-4251, Fax: 617-552-0931, E-mail: susan.gennaro@bc.edu. *Application contact:* MaryBeth Crowley, Graduate Programs Assistant, 617-552-4928, Fax: 617-552-2121, E-mail: csongrad@bc.edu.

Caribbean University, Graduate School, Bayamón, PR 00960-0493. Offers administration and supervision (MA Ed); criminal justice (MA); curriculum and instruction (MA Ed), including elementary education, English education, history education, mathematics education, primary education, science education, Spanish education; education (PhD); gerontology (MSN); human resources (MBA); museology, archiving and art history (MA Ed); neonatal pediatrics (MSN); physical education (MA Ed); special education (MA Ed). *Entrance requirements:* For master's, interview, minimum GPA of 2.5.

Case Western Reserve University, Frances Payne Bolton School of Nursing, Doctor of Nursing Practice Program, Cleveland, OH 44106. Offers acute care nurse practitioner (DNP); adult nurse practitioner (DNP); family nurse practitioner (DNP); gerontological nurse practitioner (DNP); graduate entry/pre-licensure option (DNP); medical-surgical nursing (DNP); midwifery/family nursing (DNP); neonatal nurse practitioner (DNP); pediatric nurse practitioner (DNP); post-licensure option (DNP); psychiatric-mental health nurse practitioner (DNP); women's health nurse practitioner (DNP). Graduate entry option allows baccalaureate-prepared college graduates from non-nursing backgrounds to earn certificate and MSN in addition to ND. Terminal master's awarded for partial completion of doctoral program. *Degree requirements:* For doctorate, thesis/dissertation. *Entrance requirements:* For doctorate, GRE General Test or MAT. *Faculty research:* Clinical nursing, acute care, gerontology, mental health, critical care.

Case Western Reserve University, Frances Payne Bolton School of Nursing, Master's Programs in Nursing, Nurse Practitioner Program, Cleveland, OH 44106. Offers acute care cardiovascular nursing (MSN); acute care nurse practitioner (MSN); acute care/flight nurse (MSN); adult nurse practitioner (MSN); family nurse practitioner (MSN); gerontological nurse practitioner (MSN); neonatal nurse practitioner (MSN); pediatric nurse practitioner (MSN); psychiatric-mental health nurse practitioner (MSN); women's health nurse practitioner (MSN). *Accreditation:* NLN. Part-time programs available. Postbaccalaureate distance learning degree programs offered (minimal on-campus study). *Degree requirements:* For master's, thesis optional. *Entrance requirements:* For master's, GRE General Test or MAT. Additional exam requirements/recommendations for international students: Required—TOEFL. *Faculty research:* Positive and negative mood states in parents of twins, effect of a carepath on chronic obstructive pulmonary disease home care.

The Catholic University of America, School of Nursing, Washington, DC 20064. Offers adult health specialist with functional role as nurse educator (MSN); adult nurse practitioner (MSN); community/public health nurse specialist educator (MSN); family nurse practitioner (MSN); geriatric nurse practitioner (MSN); immigrant, refugee, and global health clinical nurse specialist (MSN); nursing (DNP, PhD, Certificate); pediatric nurse practitioner (MSN); promoting healthy families in vulnerable communities (MSN); psychiatric-mental health nursing (MSN). *Accreditation:* AACN. Part-time programs available. *Faculty:* 15 full-time (all women), 43 part-time/adjunct (41 women). *Students:* 28 full-time (26 women), 75 part-time (73 women); includes 37 minority (27 African Americans, 6 Asian Americans or Pacific Islanders, 4 Hispanic Americans), 4 international. Average age 42. 84 applicants, 64% accepted, 30 enrolled. In 2009, 23 master's, 7 doctorates, 3 other advanced degrees awarded. *Degree requirements:* For master's, comprehensive exam, thesis optional; for doctorate, comprehensive exam, thesis/dissertation, minimum GPA of 3.0, oral proposal defense. *Entrance requirements:* For master's, 3 letters of recommendation, BA in nursing, RN registration, official copies of academic transcripts, some post-baccalaureate nursing experience; for doctorate, GRE General Test, BA in nursing, professional portfolio (including statements, resume, copy of RN license, 3 letters of recommendation, narrative description of clinical practice, proposal), copy of research/scholarly paper related to clinical nursing. Additional exam requirements/recommendations for international students: Required—TOEFL (minimum score 580 paper-based; 237 computer-based). *Application deadline:* For fall admission, 8/1 priority date for domestic students, 7/15 for international students; for spring admission, 12/1 priority date for domestic students, 10/15 for international students. Applications are processed on a rolling basis. Application fee: $55. Electronic applications accepted. *Expenses:* Tuition: Full-time $31,740; part-time $1245 per credit hour. Required fees: $50; $25 per semester hour. One-time fee: $425. *Financial support:* Fellowships, research assistantships, teaching assistantships, Federal Work-Study, scholarships/grants, tuition waivers (full and partial), and unspecified assistantships available. Financial award application deadline: 2/1; financial award applicants required to submit FAFSA. *Faculty research:* Community involvement in health care services, primary health care services, pediatrics, chronic illness, cardiovascular disease. Total annual research expenditures: $311,172. *Unit head:* Dr. Nalini N. Jairath, Dean, 202-319-5403, Fax: 202-319-6485, E-mail: cua-deanschoolofnursing@cua.edu. *Application contact:* Julie Schwing, Director of Graduate Admissions, 202-319-5057, Fax: 202-319-6533, E-mail: cua-admissions@cua.edu.

Columbia University, School of Nursing, Program in Pediatric Nurse Practitioner, New York, NY 10032. Offers MS, Adv C. *Accreditation:* AACN. Part-time programs available. *Entrance requirements:* For master's, GRE General Test, BSN, 1 year of clinical experience (preferred); for Adv C, MSN. Electronic applications accepted.

Duke University, School of Nursing, Durham, NC 27708-0586. Offers adult acute care (Certificate); adult cardiovascular (Certificate); adult oncology (Certificate); adult primary care (Certificate); clinical nurse specialist (MSN), including adult oncology, gerontology, neonatal, pediatric; clinical research management (MSN, Certificate); family (Certificate); gerontology (Certificate); health and nursing ministries (MSN, Certificate); health systems leadership and outcomes (Certificate); neonatal (Certificate); neonatal/pediatric in rural health (MSN, Certificate); nurse anesthetist (MSN, Certificate); nurse practitioner (MSN), including adult acute care, adult cardiovascular, adult oncology, adult primary care, family, gerontology, neonatal, pediatric, pediatric acute care; nursing (DNP, PhD); nursing and healthcare leadership (MSN); nursing education (MSN); nursing informatics (MSN, Certificate); pediatric (Certificate); pediatric acute care (Certificate); MBA/MSN; MSN/MCM. *Accreditation:* AACN; AANA/CANAEP. Part-time programs available. Postbaccalaureate distance learning degree programs offered (minimal on-campus study). *Faculty:* 45 full-time (41 women), 169 part-time/adjunct (150 women). *Students:* 213 full-time (179 women), 116 part-time (105 women); includes 37 minority (17 African Americans, 13 Asian Americans or Pacific Islanders, 7 Hispanic Americans), 9 international. Average age 36. 234 applicants, 53% accepted, 97 enrolled. In 2009, 142 master's, 24 other advanced degrees awarded. Terminal master's awarded for partial completion of doctoral program. *Degree requirements:* For master's, thesis optional; for doctorate, Capstone Project. *Entrance requirements:* For master's, GRE General Test, 1 year of nursing experience, BSN, minimum GPA of 3.0, previous course work in statistics; for doctorate, GRE for BSN prepared, BSN or MSN, minimum GPA of 3.0. Portfolio; for Certificate, MSN. Additional exam requirements/recommendations for international students: Required—TOEFL (minimum score 550 paper-based; 213 computer-based), Commission on Graduates of Foreign Nursing Schools exam. *Application deadline:* For fall admission, 7/2 priority date for domestic and international students; for spring admission, 11/15 priority date for domestic and international students. Applications are processed on a rolling basis. Application fee: $50. Electronic applications accepted. *Expenses:* Contact institution. *Financial support:* Career-related internships or fieldwork, institutionally sponsored loans, scholarships/grants, traineeships, and tuition waivers (partial) available. Support available to part-time students. Financial award application deadline: 4/1; financial award applicants required to submit FAFSA. *Faculty research:* Cardiovascular disease, caregiver skill training, data mining, prostate cancer, neonatal immune system. Total

Pediatric Nursing

Duke University (continued)

annual research expenditures: $3.5 million. *Unit head:* Dr. Catherine L. Gilliss, Dean/Vice Chancellor for Nursing Affairs, 919-684-9444, Fax: 919-684-9414, E-mail: gilli025@mc.duke.edu. *Application contact:* Bebe T. Mills, Director of Admissions, 919-684-9151, Fax: 919-668-4693, E-mail: mills031@mc.duke.edu.

Emory University, Nell Hodgson Woodruff School of Nursing, Atlanta, GA 30322-1100. Offers adult and elder health advanced practice nursing (MSN), including acute care, adult nurse practitioner, gerontological nurse practitioner; emergency nurse practitioner (MSN); family nurse practitioner (MSN); family nurse-midwife (MSN); nurse midwifery (MSN); pediatric nurse practitioner acute and primary care (MSN); public health nursing leadership (MSN); women's health nurse practitioner (MSN); women's health title x (MSN); women's health/adult health nurse practitioner (MSN); MSN/MPH. *Accreditation:* AACN; ACNM/DOA (one or more programs are accredited). Part-time programs available. *Faculty:* 30 full-time (29 women), 11 part-time/adjunct (10 women). *Students:* 110 full-time (106 women), 53 part-time (51 women); includes 49 minority (35 African Americans, 2 American Indian/Alaska Native, 10 Asian Americans or Pacific Islanders, 2 Hispanic Americans), 4 international. Average age 32. 182 applicants, 63% accepted, 86 enrolled. In 2009, 81 master's awarded. *Entrance requirements:* For master's, GRE General Test or MAT, minimum GPA of 3.0, BS in nursing from an accredited institution, RN license and additional course work, 3 letters of recommendation. Additional exam requirements/recommendations for international students: Required—TOEFL (minimum score 600 paper-based; 100 iBT). *Application deadline:* For fall admission, 1/15 priority date for domestic and international students; for spring admission, 10/1 priority date for domestic and international students. Applications are processed on a rolling basis. Application fee: $50. Electronic applications accepted. *Expenses:* Contact institution. *Financial support:* In 2009–10, 14 fellowships (averaging $28,000 per year) were awarded; career-related internships or fieldwork, Federal Work-Study, institutionally sponsored loans, and scholarships/grants also available. Support available to part-time students. Financial award application deadline: 3/1; financial award applicants required to submit CSS PROFILE or FAFSA. *Faculty research:* Older adult falls and injuries, minority health issues, cardiac symptoms and quality of life, bio-ethics and decision making, menopausal issues. *Unit head:* Dr. Linda McCauley, Dean, 404-727-7976, Fax: 404-727-9800, E-mail: linda.mccauley@emory.edu. *Application contact:* Katie Kennedy, Associate Director for Admission and Financial Aid, 404-727-7980, Fax: 404-727-8509, E-mail: admit@nursing.emory.edu.

See Close-Up on page 1613.

Georgia State University, College of Health and Human Sciences, Byrdine F. Lewis School of Nursing, Atlanta, GA 30302-3083. Offers adult health (MS); adult health nursing (Certificate); child health (MS); family nurse practitioner (MS, Certificate); health promotion, protection and restoration (PhD); perinatal/women's health (MS); psychiatric mental health nursing (Certificate); psychiatric/mental health (MS); women's health nursing (Certificate). *Accreditation:* AACN. Part-time and evening/weekend programs available. Postbaccalaureate distance learning degree programs offered (minimal on-campus study). *Degree requirements:* For master's, research activity; for doctorate, comprehensive exam, thesis/dissertation. *Entrance requirements:* For master's, MAT (preferred) or GRE, interview, RN license; for doctorate, GRE General Test. Additional exam requirements/recommendations for international students: Required—TOEFL (minimum score 550 paper-based; 213 computer-based). Electronic applications accepted. *Expenses:* Contact institution. *Faculty research:* Breast cancer prevention, sexually compulsive behaviors, health risks in minority youth, asthma treatment strategies, adolescent alcohol-related issues.

Gwynedd-Mercy College, School of Nursing, Gwynedd Valley, PA 19437-0901. Offers clinical nurse specialist (MSN), including gerontology, oncology, pediatrics; nurse practitioner (MSN), including adult health, pediatric health. *Accreditation:* NLN. *Degree requirements:* For master's, thesis optional. *Entrance requirements:* For master's, GRE General Test or MAT, current nursing experience, physical assessment, course work in statistics, BSN from an NLNAC accredited program, 2 letters of recommendation, personal interview. Additional exam requirements/recommendations for international students: Required—TOEFL (minimum score 575 paper-based). Electronic applications accepted. *Expenses:* Contact institution. *Faculty research:* Critical thinking, primary care, domestic violence, multiculturalism, nursing centers.

Hampton University, Graduate College, School of Nursing, Hampton, VA 23668. Offers advanced adult nursing (MS); community health nursing (MS); community mental health/psychiatric nursing (MS); family nursing (MS); gerontological nursing for the nurse practitioner (MS); pediatric nursing (MS); women's health nursing (MS). *Accreditation:* AACN; NLN. Part-time and evening/weekend programs available. *Degree requirements:* For master's, thesis optional. *Entrance requirements:* For master's, GRE General Test. *Faculty research:* Curriculum development, physical and mental assessment.

Indiana University–Purdue University Indianapolis, School of Nursing, Indianapolis, IN 46202-2896. Offers acute care nurse practitioner (MSN); adult health clinical nurse specialist (MSN); adult health nursing (MSN), including adult clinical nurse specialist; adult nurse practitioner (MSN); adult psychiatric/mental health nursing (MSN); child psychiatric/mental health nursing (MSN); community health nursing (MSN); family nurse practitioner (MSN); neonatal nurse practitioner (MSN); nursing science (PhD); pediatric clinical nurse specialist (MSN); women's health nurse practitioner (MSN); MSN/MPA; MSN/MPH. *Accreditation:* AACN; NLN (one or more programs are accredited). Part-time programs available. *Faculty:* 85 full-time (82 women), 60 part-time/adjunct (all women). *Students:* 46 full-time (43 women), 369 part-time (354 women); includes 30 minority (21 African Americans, 6 Asian Americans or Pacific Islanders, 3 Hispanic Americans), 5 international. Average age 39. 121 applicants, 82% accepted, 67 enrolled. In 2009, 106 master's, 3 doctorates awarded. Terminal master's awarded for partial completion of doctoral program. *Degree requirements:* For master's, thesis; for doctorate, thesis/dissertation. *Entrance requirements:* For master's, minimum GPA of 3.0, RN license; for doctorate, GRE General Test, minimum GPA of 3.0, MSN, RN license, graduate statistics course with B grade or better (not older than 3 years). Additional exam requirements/recommendations for international students: Required—TOEFL. *Application deadline:* For fall admission, 2/15 for domestic students; for spring admission, 9/15 for domestic students. Application fee: $55 ($65 for international students). *Financial support:* In 2009–10, 93 students received support, including 9 fellowships with full tuition reimbursements available (averaging $7,039 per year), 7 teaching assistantships with full tuition reimbursements available (averaging $5,300 per year); research assistantships with full tuition reimbursements available, Federal Work-Study, institutionally sponsored loans, scholarships/grants, and tuition waivers (full) also available. Support available to part-time students. Financial award application deadline: 5/1. *Faculty research:* Clinical science, health systems. Total annual research expenditures: $3 million. *Unit head:* Associate Dean for Graduate Programs, 317-274-2806, E-mail: nursing@iupui.edu. *Application contact:* Information Contact, 317-274-2806.

The Johns Hopkins University, School of Nursing, Nurse Practitioner Program, Baltimore, MD 21218-2699. Offers adult acute/critical care (MSN, Certificate); adult and pediatric primary care (MSN); adult or pediatric primary care (Certificate); emergency preparedness/disaster response (Certificate); family primary care (MSN, Certificate); women's health (Certificate). *Accreditation:* AACN; NLN (one or more programs are accredited). Part-time programs available. *Faculty:* 9 full-time (all women), 10 part-time/adjunct (all women). *Students:* 28 full-time (27 women), 75 part-time (73 women); includes 33 minority (14 African Americans, 16 Asian Americans or Pacific Islanders, 3 Hispanic Americans), 3 international. Average age 31. 223 applicants, 80% accepted, 29 enrolled. In 2009, 37 master's awarded. *Degree requirements:* For master's, thesis optional, scholarly project or portfolio. *Entrance requirements:* For master's, GRE, interview, minimum GPA of 3.0, BSN, Maryland RN license. Additional exam requirements/recommendations for international students: Required—TOEFL (minimum score 550 paper-based; 213 computer-based). *Application deadline:* For fall admission, 3/1 priority date for domestic and international students; for spring admission, 7/1 priority date for domestic and international students. Application fee: $75. Electronic applications accepted. *Expenses:* Contact institution. *Financial support:* In 2009–10, 25 students received support. Federal Work-Study,

scholarships/grants, traineeships, and tuition waivers (partial) available. Support available to part-time students. Financial award application deadline: 3/1; financial award applicants required to submit FAFSA. *Faculty research:* Community outreach, primary care of underserved populations, substance abusing individuals, childhood violence, women's health. *Unit head:* Dr. Julie A. Stanik-Hutt, Director, Master's Programs, 410-502-0184, Fax: 410-955-7463, E-mail: jstanik1@son.jhmi.edu. *Application contact:* Mary O'Rourke, Director of Admissions and Student Services, 410-955-7548, Fax: 410-614-7086, E-mail: orourke@son.jhmi.edu.

Kent State University, College of Nursing, Kent, OH 44242-0001. Offers adult nurse practitioner (MSN); family nurse practitioner (MSN); geriatric nurse practitioner (MSN); nursing (PhD); nursing and health care management (MSN); nursing of adults (clinical nurse specialist) (MSN); pediatric nurse practitioner (MSN); psychiatric/mental health nursing (MSN); women's health nursing (MSN). *Accreditation:* AACN. Part-time programs available. *Degree requirements:* For master's, thesis optional; for doctorate, comprehensive exam, thesis/dissertation. *Entrance requirements:* For master's, GRE (if undergraduate GPA less than 3.0), minimum GPA of 2.75; for doctorate, GRE, MSN. Additional exam requirements/recommendations for international students: Required—TOEFL. Electronic applications accepted. *Expenses:* Contact institution. *Faculty research:* Women and violence, methodological specialties, osteoporosis in women, new caregivers and the elderly.

Lehman College of the City University of New York, Division of Natural and Social Sciences, Department of Nursing, Bronx, NY 10468-1589. Offers adult health nursing (MS); nursing of older adults (MS); parent-child nursing (MS); pediatric nurse practitioner (MS). *Accreditation:* AACN. Part-time and evening/weekend programs available. *Entrance requirements:* For master's, bachelor's degree in nursing, New York RN license.

Loma Linda University, Department of Graduate Nursing, Program in Growing Family Nursing, Loma Linda, CA 92350. Offers MS. *Accreditation:* AACN. Part-time programs available. *Degree requirements:* For master's, thesis or alternative. *Entrance requirements:* For master's, GRE General Test, BSN, minimum GPA of 3.0, RN license. Additional exam requirements/recommendations for international students: Required—TOEFL. Electronic applications accepted. *Faculty research:* Family coping in chronic illness; women, identity, and career/family issues.

Marquette University, Graduate School, College of Nursing, Milwaukee, WI 53201-1881. Offers adult nurse practitioner (Certificate); advanced practice nursing (MSN), including adult, children, neonatal nurse practitioner, nurse-midwifery, older adult; gerontological nurse practitioner (Certificate); neonatal nurse practitioner (Certificate); nurse-midwifery (Certificate); nursing (PhD); pediatric nurse practitioner (Certificate). *Accreditation:* AACN. Part-time and evening/weekend programs available. *Faculty:* 29 full-time (27 women), 43 part-time/adjunct (all women). *Students:* 115 full-time (105 women), 209 part-time (197 women); includes 28 minority (13 African Americans, 2 American Indian/Alaska Native, 8 Asian Americans or Pacific Islanders, 5 Hispanic Americans), 1 international. Average age 32. 143 applicants, 91% accepted, 86 enrolled. In 2009, 64 master's, 10 doctorates awarded. *Degree requirements:* For master's, comprehensive exam, thesis or alternative. *Entrance requirements:* For master's, GRE General Test, BSN, Wisconsin RN license. Additional exam requirements/recommendations for international students: Required—TOEFL. Application fee: $40. *Financial support:* In 2009–10, 6 research assistantships, 1 teaching assistantship were awarded; career-related internships or fieldwork, Federal Work-Study, institutionally sponsored loans, scholarships/grants, and tuition waivers (full and partial) also available. Support available to part-time students. Financial award application deadline: 2/15. *Faculty research:* Psychosocial adjustment to chronic illness, gerontology, reminiscence, health policy: uninsured and access, hospital care delivery systems. *Unit head:* Dr. Lea Acord, Dean, 414-288-3812, Fax: 414-288-1578. *Application contact:* Dr. Judy Miller, Director of Graduate Studies, 414-288-3810, Fax: 414-288-1578.

Medical College of Georgia, School of Graduate Studies, Pediatric Nurse Practitioner Program, Augusta, GA 30912. Offers MSN. *Entrance requirements:* For master's, GRE General Test or MAT, Georgia license as a registered professional nurse. Additional exam requirements/recommendations for international students: Required—TOEFL (minimum score 550 paper-based; 213 computer-based; 79 iBT). Electronic applications accepted. Full-time tuition and fees vary according to campus/location, program and student level.

Medical University of South Carolina, College of Nursing, Doctor of Nursing Practice Program, Charleston, SC 29425. Offers adult nurse practitioner (DNP); family nurse practitioner (DNP); pediatric nurse practitioner (DNP); post-master's for advanced practice nurses (DNP). Part-time programs available. Postbaccalaureate distance learning degree programs offered (minimal on-campus study). *Faculty:* 20 full-time (19 women), 2 part-time/adjunct (1 woman). *Students:* 28 full-time (all women), 17 part-time (16 women); includes 7 minority (5 African Americans, 1 American Indian/Alaska Native, 1 Hispanic American). Average age 32. 99 applicants, 54% accepted, 45 enrolled. *Degree requirements:* For doctorate, thesis/dissertation (for some programs), practice inquiry project. *Entrance requirements:* For doctorate, BSN or MSN, minimum GPA of 3.0, course work in statistics, RN license, 3 references, interview (if requested). Additional exam requirements/recommendations for international students: Required—TOEFL (minimum score 600 paper-based; 250 computer-based). *Application deadline:* For fall admission, 2/1 priority date for domestic and international students. Application fee: $85. Electronic applications accepted. *Financial support:* Federal Work-Study and scholarships/grants available. Support available to part-time students. Financial award applicants required to submit FAFSA. *Faculty research:* Community partnerships, smoking cessation, gerontology, lateral violence in the workplace. *Unit head:* Dr. Robin L. Bissinger, Director of Graduate Programs, 843-792-0531, Fax: 843-792-9258, E-mail: bissinrl@musc.edu. *Application contact:* Carolyn F. Page, Director, Student Services, 843-792-3844, Fax: 843-792-5395, E-mail: pagecf@musc.edu.

MGH Institute of Health Professions, Graduate Programs, School of Nursing, Boston, MA 02129. Offers advanced practice nursing (MSN); gerontological nursing (MSN); nursing (DNP); pediatric nursing (MSN); psychiatric nursing (MSN); teaching and learning for health care education (Certificate); women's health nursing (MSN). *Accreditation:* AACN; NLN (one or more programs are accredited). *Faculty:* 37 full-time (33 women), 11 part-time/adjunct (10 women). *Students:* 325 full-time (275 women), 72 part-time (59 women); includes 48 minority (22 African Americans, 1 American Indian/Alaska Native, 18 Asian Americans or Pacific Islanders, 7 Hispanic Americans). Average age 31. 840 applicants, 53% accepted, 221 enrolled. In 2009, 78 master's, 12 doctorates, 45 other advanced degrees awarded. *Degree requirements:* For master's, thesis or alternative. *Entrance requirements:* For master's, GRE General Test. Additional exam requirements/recommendations for international students: Required—TOEFL (minimum score 550 paper-based; 213 computer-based; 80 iBT). *Application deadline:* For fall admission, 1/10 for domestic and international students. Application fee: $50. Electronic applications accepted. *Expenses:* Tuition: Part-time $943 per credit. Required fees: $943 per credit. Tuition and fees vary according to course load. *Financial support:* In 2009–10, 292 students received support, including 1 research assistantship (averaging $1,200 per year), 2 teaching assistantships (averaging $1,200 per year); career-related internships or fieldwork, scholarships/grants, traineeships, tuition waivers (full and partial), and unspecified assistantships also available. Support available to part-time students. Financial award application deadline: 3/1; financial award applicants required to submit FAFSA. *Faculty research:* Biobehavioral nursing, HIV/AIDS, gerontological nursing, women's health, vulnerable populations, health systems. *Unit head:* Margery Chisholm, Dean, 617-724-0480, Fax: 617-726-8022, E-mail: mchisholm@mghihp.edu. *Application contact:* Maureen Rika Judd, Manager of Admissions, 617-726-6069, Fax: 617-726-8010, E-mail: admissions@mghihp.edu.

Molloy College, Graduate Nursing Program, Rockville Centre, NY 11571-5002. Offers adult nurse practitioner (Advanced Certificate); clinical nurse specialist: adult health (Advanced Certificate); family nurse practitioner (Advanced Certificate); nurse practitioner psychiatry (Advanced Certificate); nursing (MS); nursing administration (Advanced Certificate); nursing administration with informatics (Advanced Certificate); nursing education (Advanced Certificate); nursing informatics (Advanced Certificate); pediatric nurse practitioner (Advanced Certificate). *Accreditation:* AACN. Part-time and evening/weekend programs available. *Faculty:* 23 full-time (22 women), 5 part-time/adjunct (4 women). *Students:* 11 full-time (10 women), 405 part-time

(377 women); includes 206 minority (124 African Americans, 52 Asian Americans or Pacific Islanders, 30 Hispanic Americans), 2 international. Average age 39. In 2009, 64 master's awarded. *Degree requirements:* For master's, thesis optional. *Entrance requirements:* For master's, 3 letters of reference, BS in nursing, minimum undergraduate GPA of 3.0; for Advanced Certificate, 3 letters of reference, master's degree in nursing. *Application deadline:* For fall admission, 9/2 priority date for domestic students; for spring admission, 1/20 priority date for domestic students. Applications are processed on a rolling basis. Application fee: $60. *Expenses:* Tuition: Part-time $765 per credit. Required fees: $340 per semester. *Financial support:* Research assistantships with partial tuition reimbursements, teaching assistantships with partial tuition reimbursements, institutionally sponsored loans, scholarships/grants, and unspecified assistantships available. Support available to part-time students. Financial award application deadline: 4/1; financial award applicants required to submit FAFSA. *Unit head:* Dr. Mary T. O'Shaughnessy, Acting Director, 516-678-5000, Fax: 516-678-9718, E-mail: moshaughnessy@molloy.edu. *Application contact:* Alina Haitz, Assistant Director of Graduate Admissions, 516-678-5000 Ext. 6399, Fax: 516-256-2247, E-mail: ahaitz@molloy.edu.

New York University, College of Nursing, Programs in Advanced Practice Nursing, New York, NY 10012-1019. Offers advanced practice nursing: adult acute care (MS, Advanced Certificate); advanced practice nursing: adult nurse practictioner/palliative care nursing (MS); advanced practice nursing: adult nurse practitioner/holistic nurse practitioner (Advanced Certificate); advanced practice nursing: adult nurse practitioner/holistic nursing (MS); advanced practice nursing: adult nurse practitioner/palliative care nurse practitioner (Advanced Certificate); advanced practice nursing: adult primary care (MS, Advanced Certificate); advanced practice nursing: adult primary care/geriatrics (MS); advanced practice nursing: geriatrics (MS, Advanced Certificate); advanced practice nursing: mental health (MS); advanced practice nursing: mental health nursing (Advanced Certificate); advanced practice nursing: pediatrics (MS, Advanced Certificate); advanced practice nursing:adult primary care and geriatrics (Advanced Certificate); nurse midwifery (MS, Advanced Certificate); nursing administration (MS, Advanced Certificate); nursing education (MS, Advanced Certificate); nursing informatics (MS, Advanced Certificate); MS/MPH; MS/MS. *Accreditation:* AACN; ACNM/DOA. Part-time and evening/weekend programs available. *Faculty:* 17 full-time (all women), 22 part-time/adjunct (19 women). *Students:* 18 full-time (17 women), 524 part-time (485 women); includes 238 minority (90 African Americans, 119 Asian Americans or Pacific Islanders, 29 Hispanic Americans). Average age 33. 191 applicants, 89% accepted, 120 enrolled. In 2009, 117 master's, 2 other advanced degrees awarded. *Degree requirements:* For master's, thesis (for some programs). *Entrance requirements:* For master's, BS in nursing, AS in nursing with another BS/BA, interview; for Advanced Certificate, master's degree. Additional exam requirements/recommendations for international students: Required—TOEFL. *Application deadline:* For fall admission, 7/1 priority date for domestic students, 7/1 for international students; for spring admission, 12/1 for domestic and international students. Applications are processed on a rolling basis. Application fee: $75. *Expenses:* Tuition: Full-time $30,528; part-time $1272 per credit. Required fees: $2177. *Financial support:* Career-related internships or fieldwork, institutionally sponsored loans, scholarships/grants, traineeships, and tuition waivers (partial) available. Support available to part-time students. Financial award application deadline: 2/1; financial award applicants required to submit FAFSA. *Faculty research:* Elderly black diabetics, families and illness, public health nursing, parent-child nursing, health policy costs. *Unit head:* Dr. Judith Haber, Associate Dean for Graduate Programs, 212-998-9020, Fax: 212-995-3143. *Application contact:* Amy Knowles, Assistant Dean for Student Affairs and Admissions, 212-998-5333, Fax: 212-995-4302, E-mail: ak96@nyu.edu.

Northeastern University, Bouvé College of Health Sciences Graduate School, School of Nursing, Program in Pediatric Nurse Practitioner, Boston, MA 02115-5096. Offers MS, CAGS. Part-time programs available. *Students:* 17 full-time (15 women), 19 part-time (18 women); includes 1 African American, 1 Asian American or Pacific Islander, 1 Hispanic American. 2 applicants, 100% accepted, 1 enrolled. In 2009, 8 master's awarded. *Entrance requirements:* For master's, GRE General Test. Additional exam requirements/recommendations for international students: Required—TOEFL (minimum score 100 iBT). *Application deadline:* For fall admission, 7/1 for domestic students. Applications are processed on a rolling basis. Application fee: $50. Electronic applications accepted. *Financial support:* Research assistantships, teaching assistantships, scholarships/grants, traineeships, and unspecified assistantships available. *Unit head:* Prof. Michelle Beauchesne, Coordinator, 617-373-3621, E-mail: m.beauchesne@neu.edu. *Application contact:* Margaret Schnabel, Director of Graduate Admissions, 617-373-2708, E-mail: bouvegrad@neu.edu.

Queen's University at Kingston, School of Graduate Studies and Research, Faculty of Health Sciences, School of Nursing, Kingston, ON K7L 3N6, Canada. Offers health and chronic illness (M Sc); nurse scientist (PhD); primary health care nurse practitioner (Certificate); women's and children's health (M Sc). *Degree requirements:* For master's, thesis. *Entrance requirements:* For master's, RN license. Additional exam requirements/recommendations for international students: Required—TOEFL. *Faculty research:* Women and children's health, health and chronic illness.

Rush University, College of Nursing, Department of Women's and Children's Health Nursing, Chicago, IL 60612-3832. Offers neonatal nurse practitioner (MSN, Post-Master's Certificate); pediatric acute/chronic care nurse practitioner (MSN); pediatric clinical nurse specialist (MSN); pediatric nurse practitioner (MSN, Post-Master's Certificate); women's and children's health nursing (DNP, PhD). *Accreditation:* AACN. Part-time programs available. Postbaccalaureate distance learning degree programs offered (minimal on-campus study). Terminal master's awarded for partial completion of doctoral program. *Degree requirements:* For master's, capstone project; for doctorate, thesis/dissertation, DNP leadership project. *Entrance requirements:* For master's, GRE General Test (waived if nursing GPA is above 3.0 or cumulative GPA is above 3.25), interview; for doctorate, GRE General Test, interview, course work in statistics (PhD). Additional exam requirements/recommendations for international students: Required—TOEFL, TWE. Electronic applications accepted. *Faculty research:* Family-centered care, women's health, health outcomes of human milk feeding for VhBW infants.

Seton Hall University, College of Nursing, South Orange, NJ 07079-2697. Offers advanced practice in primary health care (MSN), including adult nurse practitioner, gerontological nurse practitioner, pediatric nurse practitioner; entry into practice (MSN); health systems administration (MSN, DNP); nursing (PhD); nursing case management (MSN); nursing education (MA); school nurse (MSN); MSN/MA. *Accreditation:* AACN. Part-time programs available. Postbaccalaureate distance learning degree programs offered (minimal on-campus study). *Faculty:* 10 full-time (all women), 3 part-time/adjunct (1 woman). *Students:* 46 full-time (35 women), 94 part-time (90 women); includes 22 minority (8 African Americans, 5 Asian Americans or Pacific Islanders, 9 Hispanic Americans). 92 applicants, 88% accepted, 55 enrolled. *Degree requirements:* For master's, research project; for doctorate, dissertation or scholarly project. *Entrance requirements:* For doctorate, GRE. Additional exam requirements/recommendations for international students: Required—TOEFL. *Application deadline:* For fall admission, 6/15 priority date for domestic students. Applications are processed on a rolling basis. Electronic applications accepted. *Financial support:* Institutionally sponsored loans, scholarships/grants, traineeships, tuition waivers (partial), and unspecified assistantships available. Support available to part-time students. Financial award applicants required to submit FAFSA. *Faculty research:* Parent/child, adult, and gerontological nursing; breast cancer; families of children with HIV; parish nursing. *Unit head:* Dr. Phyllis Shanley Hansell, Dean. *Application contact:* Kristyn Kent Wuillermin, Director of Strategic Alliances, Marketing and Enrollment, 973-761-9291, Fax: 973-761-9607, E-mail: kristyn.kent@shu.edu.

Spalding University, Graduate Studies, College of Health and Natural Sciences, School of Nursing, Louisville, KY 40203-2188. Offers adult nurse practitioner (MSN); family nurse practitioner (MSN); leadership in nursing and healthcare (MSN); pediatric nurse practitioner (MSN). *Accreditation:* AACN. Part-time and evening/weekend programs available. *Faculty:* 6 full-time (all women), 7 part-time/adjunct (all women). *Students:* 41 full-time (38 women), 36 part-time (34 women); includes 12 minority (9 African Americans, 3 Hispanic Americans), 2 international. Average age 38. 27 applicants, 70% accepted, 18 enrolled. In 2009, 25 master's awarded. *Degree requirements:* For master's, comprehensive exam (for some programs), thesis. *Entrance requirements:* For master's, GRE General Test, BSN or bachelor's degree and RN licensure. Additional exam requirements/recommendations for international students: Required—TOEFL (minimum score 535 paper-based; 203 computer-based). *Application deadline:* Applications are processed on a rolling basis. Application fee: $30. *Expenses:* Tuition: Full-time $11,340; part-time $630 per credit hour. Tuition and fees vary according to program. *Financial support:* In 2009–10, 53 students received support, including 2 research assistantships with partial tuition reimbursements available (averaging $4,020 per year); career-related internships or fieldwork, scholarships/grants, and traineeships also available. Support available to part-time students. Financial award application deadline: 3/15; financial award applicants required to submit FAFSA. *Faculty research:* Nurse educational administration, gerontology, bioterrorism, healthcare ethics, leadership. *Unit head:* Dr. Carolyn Lewis, Interim Chair, 502-585-9911 Ext. 2331, E-mail: clewis@spalding.edu. *Application contact:* Dr. Carolyn Lewis, Interim Chair, 502-585-9911 Ext. 2331, E-mail: clewis@spalding.edu.

Stony Brook University, State University of New York, Stony Brook University Medical Center, Health Sciences Center, School of Nursing, Program in Child Health Nursing, Stony Brook, NY 11794. Offers child health nurse practitioner (Certificate); child health nursing (MS). *Accreditation:* AACN. Postbaccalaureate distance learning degree programs offered. *Students:* 12 full-time (all women), 28 part-time (24 women); includes 4 minority (2 African Americans, 1 Asian American or Pacific Islander, 1 Hispanic American). In 2009, 14 master's awarded. *Degree requirements:* For master's, thesis. *Entrance requirements:* For master's, BSN, minimum GPA of 3.0, course work in statistics. *Application deadline:* For fall admission, 1/15 for domestic students. Application fee: $60. *Expenses:* Tuition, state resident: full-time $8370; part-time $349 per credit. Tuition, nonresident: full-time $13,250; part-time $552 per credit. Required fees: $933. *Financial support:* Application deadline: 3/15. *Unit head:* Prof. Arleen Steckel, Chair, 631-444-3264, Fax: 631-444-3136, E-mail: arleen.steckel@stonybrook.edu. *Application contact:* Dr. Kent Marks, Assistant Dean, Admissions and Records, 631-632-4723, Fax: 631-632-7243, E-mail: kmarks@notes.cc.sunysb.edu.

Texas Christian University, Harris College of Nursing and Health Sciences, Program in Nursing, Fort Worth, TX 76129-0002. Offers adult nursing (CNS) (MSN); nursing (DNP); pediatric nursing (CNS) (MSN). *Accreditation:* AACN; AANA/CANAEP (one or more programs are accredited). Part-time programs available. Postbaccalaureate distance learning degree programs offered (minimal on-campus study). *Degree requirements:* For master's and doctorate, professional project. *Entrance requirements:* For master's, GRE General Test or MAT, 3 letters of reference, 2 years full-time experience in nursing, current nursing licensure. Additional exam requirements/recommendations for international students: Required—TOEFL. *Application deadline:* For fall admission, 2/1 for domestic students. Application fee: $0. *Expenses:* Tuition: Full-time $17,640; part-time $980 per credit hour. Tuition and fees vary according to program. *Financial support:* Application deadline: 2/1. *Unit head:* Dr. Pamela Frable, Director, 817-257-5840, E-mail: p.frable@tcu.edu. *Application contact:* Dr. Kathleen Baldwin, Director of Graduate Studies, 817-257-6756, E-mail: k.baldwin@tcu.edu.

Texas Tech University Health Sciences Center, School of Nursing, Lubbock, TX 79430. Offers acute care nurse practitioner (MSN, Certificate); administration (MSN); advanced practice (DNP); education (MSN); executive leadership (DNP); family nurse practitioner (MSN, Certificate); geriatric nurse practitioner (MSN, Certificate); pediatric nurse practitioner (MSN, Certificate). *Accreditation:* AACN. Part-time programs available. Postbaccalaureate distance learning degree programs offered (minimal on-campus study). *Degree requirements:* For master's, thesis optional. *Entrance requirements:* For master's, minimum GPA of 3.0, 3 letters of reference, BSN, RN license; for Certificate, minimum GPA of 3.0, 3 letters of reference, RN license. Additional exam requirements/recommendations for international students: Required—TOEFL (minimum score 550 paper-based; 213 computer-based). *Faculty research:* Diabetes/obesity, nurse competency, disease management, intervention and measurements, health disparities.

Texas Woman's University, Graduate School, College of Nursing, Denton, TX 76201. Offers acute care nurse practitioner (MS); adult health clinical nurse specialist (MS); adult health nurse practitioner (MS); child health clinical nurse specialist (MS); clinical nurse leader (MS); community health (MS); family nurse practitioner (MS); health systems management (MS); nursing education (MS); nursing practice (DNP); nursing science (PhD); pediatric nurse practitioner (MS); women's health clinical nurse specialist (MS); women's health nurse practitioner (MS). *Accreditation:* AACN. Part-time programs available. Postbaccalaureate distance learning degree programs offered. *Faculty:* 85 full-time (80 women), 6 part-time/adjunct (all women). *Students:* 81 full-time (76 women), 602 part-time (571 women); includes 293 minority (154 African Americans, 3 American Indian/Alaska Native, 90 Asian Americans or Pacific Islanders, 46 Hispanic Americans), 19 international. Average age 39. 259 applicants, 81% accepted, 166 enrolled. In 2009, 100 master's, 22 doctorates awarded. *Degree requirements:* For master's, thesis or alternative; for doctorate, comprehensive exam, thesis/dissertation. *Entrance requirements:* For master's, GRE or MAT, minimum GPA of 3.0, RN license, BS in nursing, basic statistics course; for doctorate, GRE (Verbal 460, Quantitative 500) or MAT (50), MS in nursing, minimum GPA of 3.5, RN license, coursework in statistics, 2 letters of reference, curriculum vitae, nursing-theory course, graduate research course, letter stating professional and research goals. Additional exam requirements/recommendations for international students: Required—TOEFL (minimum score 550 paper-based; 213 computer-based; 79 iBT). *Application deadline:* For fall admission, 5/1 priority date for domestic students, 3/1 for international students; for spring admission, 9/15 priority date for domestic students, 7/1 for international students. Applications are processed on a rolling basis. Application fee: $50. Electronic applications accepted. *Expenses:* Tuition, state resident: full-time $3564; part-time $198 per credit hour. Tuition, nonresident: full-time $8550; part-time $475 per credit hour. Required fees: $69.26 per credit hour. Tuition and fees vary according to course load. *Financial support:* In 2009–10, 99 students received support, including 16 fellowships (averaging $17,325 per year), 5 research assistantships (averaging $11,484 per year), 5 teaching assistantships (averaging $11,484 per year); career-related internships or fieldwork, Federal Work-Study, institutionally sponsored loans, scholarships/grants, traineeships, health care benefits, and unspecified assistantships also available. Support available to part-time students. Financial award application deadline: 3/1; financial award applicants required to submit FAFSA. *Faculty research:* Evaluation of pre-natal care, screening for intimate partner violence, stressors and nursing success, breast surgery, breast feeding, adolescent needs during childbirth. *Unit head:* Dr. Patricia Holden-Huchton, Interim Dean, 940-898-2401, Fax: 940-898-2437, E-mail: pholdenhuchton@twu.edu. *Application contact:* Samuel Wheeler, Assistant Director of Admissions, 940-898-3188, Fax: 940-898-3081, E-mail: wheelersr@twu.edu.

University of Central Florida, College of Nursing, Orlando, FL 32816. Offers adult nurse practitioner (MSN, Post-Master's Certificate); clinical nurse leader (MSN, Post-Master's Certificate); clinical nurse specialist (MSN, Post-Master's Certificate); family nurse practitioner (MSN, Post-Master's Certificate); leadership and management (MSN); nurse educator (MSN); nursing (PhD); nursing education (Post-Master's Certificate); nursing practice (DNP); pediatric nurse practitioner (MSN, Post-Master's Certificate). *Accreditation:* AACN. Part-time and evening/weekend programs available. *Faculty:* 38 full-time (34 women), 49 part-time/adjunct (47 women). *Students:* 98 full-time (93 women), 371 part-time (350 women); includes 132 minority (63 African Americans, 2 American Indian/Alaska Native, 29 Asian Americans or Pacific Islanders, 38 Hispanic Americans), 9 international. Average age 39. 363 applicants, 49% accepted, 139 enrolled. In 2009, 72 master's, 3 doctorates, 8 other advanced degrees awarded. *Degree requirements:* For master's, thesis or alternative. *Entrance requirements:* For master's, GRE General Test, minimum GPA of 3.0 in last 60 hours. Additional exam requirements/recommendations for international students: Required—TOEFL. *Application deadline:* For fall admission, 2/15 for domestic students; for spring admission, 9/15 for domestic students. Application fee: $30. Electronic applications accepted. *Expenses:* Tuition, state resident: part-time $306.31 per credit hour. Tuition, nonresident: part-time $1099.01 per credit hour. Part-time tuition and fees vary according to degree level and program. *Financial support:* In 2009–10, 30 students received support, including 30 fellowships with partial tuition reimbursements available (averaging $3,200 per year), 1 teaching assistantship with partial tuition

Pediatric Nursing

University of Central Florida (continued)
reimbursement available (averaging $13,440 per year); research assistantships with partial tuition reimbursements available, career-related internships or fieldwork, Federal Work-Study, institutionally sponsored loans, traineeships, and unspecified assistantships also available. Financial award application deadline: 3/1; financial award applicants required to submit FAFSA. *Unit head:* Dr. Jean D. Leuner, Dean, 407-823-5496, Fax: 407-823-5675, E-mail: jleuner@mail.ucf.edu. *Application contact:* Dr. Jean D. Leuner, Dean, 407-823-5496, Fax: 407-823-5675, E-mail: jleuner@mail.ucf.edu.

University of Cincinnati, Graduate School, College of Nursing, Cincinnati, OH 45221-0038. Offers clinical nurse specialist (MSN), including adult health, community health, neonatal, nursing administration, occupational health, pediatric health, psychiatric nursing, women's health; nurse anesthesia (MSN); nurse midwifery (MSN); nurse practitioner (MSN), including acute care, ambulatory care, family, family/psychiatric, women's health; nursing (PhD); MBA/MSN. *Accreditation:* AACN; AANA/CANAEP (one or more programs are accredited); ACNM/DOA. Part-time programs available. Postbaccalaureate distance learning degree programs offered (no on-campus study). Terminal master's awarded for partial completion of doctoral program. *Degree requirements:* For master's, thesis or alternative; for doctorate, comprehensive exam, thesis/dissertation. *Entrance requirements:* For master's and doctorate, GRE General Test. Additional exam requirements/recommendations for international students: Required—TOEFL (minimum score 520 paper-based; 190 computer-based). Electronic applications accepted. *Faculty research:* Substance abuse, injury and violence, symptom management.

University of Colorado Denver, School of Medicine, Physician Assistant Program, Denver, CO 80217-3364. Offers MPAS. *Accreditation:* ARC-PA. *Students:* 120 full-time (103 women), 10 part-time (8 women); includes 6 minority (1 African American, 2 American Indian/Alaska Native, 2 Asian Americans or Pacific Islanders, 1 Hispanic American). In 2009, 11 master's awarded. *Entrance requirements:* For master's, GRE General Test, minimum GPA of 2.8, 3 letters of recommendation. Additional exam requirements/recommendations for international students: Required—TOEFL (minimum score 550 paper-based; 213 computer-based). *Application deadline:* For fall admission, 10/15 for domestic students. Application fee: $85. *Expenses:* Contact institution. *Financial support:* Career-related internships or fieldwork, Federal Work-Study, and institutionally sponsored loans available. Support available to part-time students. Financial award application deadline: 3/15; financial award applicants required to submit FAFSA. *Unit head:* Dr. Anita Glicken, Director, 303-724-1338, E-mail: anita.glicken@ucdenver.edu. *Application contact:* Melinda Sogo, Admissions and Course Support, 303-724-1340, E-mail: melinda.sogo@ucdenver.edu.

University of Delaware, College of Health Sciences, School of Nursing, Newark, DE 19716. Offers adult nurse practitioner (MSN, PMC); cardiopulmonary clinical nurse specialist (MSN, PMC); cardiopulmonary clinical nurse specialist/adult nurse practitioner (MSN, PMC); family nurse practitioner (MSN, PMC); gerontology clinical nurse specialist (MSN, PMC); gerontology clinical nurse specialist geriatric nurse practitioner (PMC); gerontology clinical nurse specialist/geriatric nurse practitioner (MSN); health services administration (MSN, PMC); nursing of children clinical nurse specialist (MSN, PMC); nursing of children clinical nurse specialist/pediatric nurse practitioner (MSN, PMC); oncology/immune deficiency clinical nurse specialist (MSN, PMC); oncology/immune deficiency clinical nurse specialist/adult nurse practitioner (MSN, PMC); perinatal/women's health clinical nurse specialist (MSN, PMC); perinatal/women's health clinical nurse specialist/women's health nurse practitioner (MSN, PMC); psychiatric nursing clinical nurse specialist (MSN, PMC). *Accreditation:* AACN; NLN (one or more programs are accredited). Part-time and evening/weekend programs available. Postbaccalaureate distance learning degree programs offered (minimal on-campus study). *Degree requirements:* For master's, thesis optional. *Entrance requirements:* For master's, BSN, interview, RN license. Electronic applications accepted. *Faculty research:* Marriage and chronic illness, health promotion, congestive heart failure patient outcomes, school nursing, diabetes in children, culture, health disparities, cardiovascular, prison nursing, oncology, public policy, child obesity, smoking and teen pregnancy, blood pressure measurements, men's health.

University of Illinois at Chicago, Graduate College, College of Nursing, Program in Nursing, Chicago, IL 60607-7128. Offers acute care clinical nurse specialist (MS); acute care nurse practitioner (MS); administrative studies in nursing (MS); adult nurse practitioner (MS); adult/geriatric nurse practitioner (MS); advanced community health nurse specialist (MS); family nurse practitioner (MS); geriatric clinical nurse specialist (MS); geriatric nurse practitioner (MS); mental health clinical nurse specialist (MS); mental health nurse practitioner (MS); nurse midwifery (MS); occupational health/advanced community health nurse specialist (MS); occupational health/family nurse practitioner (MS); pediatric clinical nurse specialist (MS); pediatric nurse practitioner (MS); perinatal clinical nurse specialist (MS); school/advanced community health nurse specialist (MS); school/family nurse practitioner (MS); women's health nurse practitioner (MS). *Accreditation:* AACN. Part-time programs available. *Degree requirements:* For master's, thesis or alternative. *Entrance requirements:* For master's, GRE General Test, minimum GPA of 2.75. Additional exam requirements/recommendations for international students: Required—TOEFL. Electronic applications accepted.

University of Maryland, Baltimore, Graduate School, School of Nursing, Master's Program in Nursing, Baltimore, MD 21201. Offers community health nursing (MS); gerontological nursing (MS); maternal-child nursing (MS); medical-surgical nursing (MS); nurse-midwifery education (MS); nursing administration (MS); nursing education (MS); nursing health policy (MS); primary care nursing (MS); psychiatric nursing (MS); MS/MBA. *Accreditation:* AACN; AANA/CANAEP; ACNM/DOA; NLN (one or more programs are accredited). Part-time programs available. *Students:* 387 full-time (338 women), 528 part-time (491 women); includes 330 minority (230 African Americans, 3 American Indian/Alaska Native, 81 Asian Americans or Pacific Islanders, 16 Hispanic Americans), 10 international. Average age 36. 849 applicants, 40% accepted, 255 enrolled. In 2009, 264 master's awarded. *Degree requirements:* For master's, comprehensive exam (for some programs), thesis or alternative. *Entrance requirements:* For master's, GRE General Test, minimum GPA of 2.75, course work in statistics, BS in nursing. Additional exam requirements/recommendations for international students: Required—TOEFL (minimum score 550 paper-based; 80 iBT), or IELTS (minimum score 7). *Application deadline:* For fall admission, 1/15 for international students. Application fee: $50. Electronic applications accepted. *Expenses:* Tuition, state resident: full-time $7290; part-time $405 per credit hour. Tuition, nonresident: full-time $12,780; part-time $710 per credit hour. Required fees: $774; $10 per credit hour. $297 per semester. Tuition and fees vary according to course load, degree level and program. *Financial support:* Fellowships, research assistantships, teaching assistantships, career-related internships or fieldwork and traineeships available. Support available to part-time students. Financial award application deadline: 2/15; financial award applicants required to submit FAFSA. *Unit head:* Dr. Jane Kapustin, Assistant Dean, 410-706-6741, Fax: 410-706-4231. *Application contact:* Marjorie Fass, Admissions Director, 410-706-0501, Fax: 410-706-7238.

University of Michigan, Horace H. Rackham School of Graduate Studies, School of Nursing, Division of Health Promotion and Risk Reduction, Program in Parent-Child Nursing, Ann Arbor, MI 48109. Offers infant, child, adolescent health nurse practitioner (MS); nurse midwifery (MS, Post Master's Certificate). *Accreditation:* AACN. Part-time programs available. Postbaccalaureate distance learning degree programs offered (minimal on-campus study). *Degree requirements:* For master's, thesis. *Entrance requirements:* For master's, GRE General Test (if cumulative BSN GPA less than 3.25), licensure, minimum GPA of 3.0 in BSN program. Additional exam requirements/recommendations for international students: Required—TOEFL (minimum score 560 paper-based; 220 computer-based). *Expenses:* Tuition, state resident: full-time $17,286; part-time $1099 per credit hour. Tuition, nonresident: full-time $34,944; part-time $2080 per credit hour. Required fees: $95 per semester. Tuition and fees vary according to course load, degree level and program.

University of Minnesota, Twin Cities Campus, Graduate School, School of Nursing, Children with Special Health Care Needs Program, Minneapolis, MN 55455-0213. Offers MS. *Entrance requirements:* Additional exam requirements/recommendations for international students: Required—TOEFL (minimum score 586 paper-based; 240 computer-based).

University of Minnesota, Twin Cities Campus, Graduate School, School of Nursing, Pediatric Clinical Nurse Specialist Program, Minneapolis, MN 55455-0213. Offers MS. *Accreditation:* AACN. Part-time programs available. *Degree requirements:* For master's, final oral exam, project or thesis.

University of Minnesota, Twin Cities Campus, Graduate School, School of Nursing, Pediatric Nurse Practitioner Program, Minneapolis, MN 55455-0213. Offers MS. *Accreditation:* AACN. *Degree requirements:* For master's, final oral exam, project or thesis.

University of Minnesota, Twin Cities Campus, Graduate School, School of Nursing, Program in Adolescent Nursing, Minneapolis, MN 55455-0213. Offers MS. *Accreditation:* AACN. Part-time programs available. *Degree requirements:* For master's, final oral exam, project or thesis. *Entrance requirements:* Additional exam requirements/recommendations for international students: Required—TOEFL (minimum score 586 paper-based; 240 computer-based).

University of Missouri–Kansas City, School of Nursing, Kansas City, MO 64110-2499. Offers adult clinical nurse specialist (MSN), including adult nurse practitioner, women's health nurse practitioner; family nurse practitioner (MSN); neonatal nurse practitioner (MSN); nurse educator (MSN); nurse executive (MSN); nursing (PhD); nursing practice (DNP); pediatric nurse practitioner (MSN). *Accreditation:* AACN. Part-time programs available. Postbaccalaureate distance learning degree programs offered (minimal on-campus study). *Faculty:* 36 full-time (30 women), 40 part-time/adjunct (all women). *Students:* 31 full-time (26 women), 310 part-time (287 women); includes 38 minority (17 African Americans, 2 American Indian/Alaska Native, 10 Asian Americans or Pacific Islanders, 9 Hispanic Americans). Average age 36. 151 applicants, 72% accepted, 109 enrolled. In 2009, 57 master's, 10 doctorates awarded. *Degree requirements:* For master's, thesis or alternative. *Entrance requirements:* For master's, minimum undergraduate GPA of 3.2; for doctorate, GRE, 3 letters of reference, interview by invitation. Additional exam requirements/recommendations for international students: Required—TOEFL (minimum score 550 paper-based; 213 computer-based; 80 iBT). *Application deadline:* For fall admission, 2/1 priority date for domestic and international students; for spring admission, 9/1 priority date for domestic and international students. Application fee: $45 ($50 for international students). *Expenses:* Tuition, state resident: full-time $5378; part-time $299 per credit hour. Tuition, nonresident: full-time $13,881; part-time $771 per credit hour. Required fees: $641; $71 per credit hour. Tuition and fees vary according to course load and program. *Financial support:* In 2009–10, 6 teaching assistantships with partial tuition reimbursements (averaging $4,402 per year) were awarded; fellowships, research assistantships, career-related internships or fieldwork, Federal Work-Study, institutionally sponsored loans, and tuition waivers (full and partial) also available. Support available to part-time students. Financial award application deadline: 3/1; financial award applicants required to submit FAFSA. *Faculty research:* Geriatrics/gerontology, children's pain, neonatology, Alzheimer's care, cancer caregivers. Total annual research expenditures: $2.1 million. *Unit head:* Dr. Lora Lacey-Haun, Dean, 816-235-1700, Fax: 816-235-1701, E-mail: lacey-haunc@umkc.edu. *Application contact:* Leah Wilder, Coordinator for Admissions and Recruitment, 816-235-5768, Fax: 816-235-1701, E-mail: wilderl@umkc.edu.

The University of North Carolina at Chapel Hill, School of Nursing, Chapel Hill, NC 27599-7460. Offers nursing (MSN, PhD, PMC), including adult nurse practitioner (MSN, PMC), children's health advanced practice (MSN, PMC), family nurse practitioner (MSN, PMC), health care systems (MSN, PMC), psychiatric/mental health nursing (MSN, PMC), women's health nursing (MSN, PMC). *Accreditation:* AACN; NLN (one or more programs are accredited). Part-time programs available. *Degree requirements:* For master's, comprehensive exam, thesis; for doctorate, thesis/dissertation, 3 exams. *Entrance requirements:* For master's and doctorate, GRE General Test. *Faculty research:* Chronic illness, parenting, cardiovascular health in children, elderly, HIV-AIDS.

University of Pennsylvania, School of Nursing, Pediatric Acute/Chronic Care Nurse Practitioner Program, Philadelphia, PA 19104. Offers MSN. *Accreditation:* AACN. Part-time programs available. Postbaccalaureate distance learning degree programs offered. *Students:* 12 full-time (all women), 13 part-time (all women); includes 1 minority (Hispanic American). In 2009, 11 master's awarded. *Entrance requirements:* For master's, GRE General Test, 1 year of clinical course work, BSN, minimum GPA of 3.0, previous course work in statistics. Additional exam requirements/recommendations for international students: Required—TOEFL. *Application deadline:* For fall admission, 2/15 priority date for domestic students. Applications are processed on a rolling basis. Application fee: $70. *Expenses:* Contact institution. *Financial support:* Research assistantships, teaching assistantships, career-related internships or fieldwork and institutionally sponsored loans available. Support available to part-time students. Financial award application deadline: 4/1. *Faculty research:* Hispanic health, bereavement, pediatric AIDS, chronically ill children and their families.

University of Pennsylvania, School of Nursing, Pediatric Critical Care Nurse Practitioner Program, Philadelphia, PA 19104. Offers MSN. *Accreditation:* AACN. *Students:* 7 full-time (all women), 8 part-time (7 women); includes 3 minority (all Asian Americans or Pacific Islanders). In 2009, 7 master's awarded. *Entrance requirements:* For master's, GRE General Test, BSN, minimum GPA of 3.0, previous course work in statistics, 1 year of clinical course work. Additional exam requirements/recommendations for international students: Required—TOEFL. *Application deadline:* For fall admission, 2/15 priority date for domestic students. Applications are processed on a rolling basis. Application fee: $70. *Expenses:* Contact institution. *Financial support:* Application deadline: 4/1.

University of Pennsylvania, School of Nursing, Pediatric Nurse Practitioner Program, Philadelphia, PA 19104. Offers MSN. *Accreditation:* AACN. Part-time programs available. *Students:* 5 full-time (all women), 10 part-time (all women); includes 1 minority (African American). In 2009, 16 master's awarded. *Entrance requirements:* For master's, GRE General Test, 1 year of clinical experience in area of interest, BSN, minimum GPA of 3.0, previous course work in statistics. Additional exam requirements/recommendations for international students: Required—TOEFL. *Application deadline:* For fall admission, 2/15 priority date for domestic students. Applications are processed on a rolling basis. Application fee: $70. *Expenses:* Contact institution. *Financial support:* Research assistantships, teaching assistantships, career-related internships or fieldwork, Federal Work-Study, and institutionally sponsored loans available. Support available to part-time students. Financial award application deadline: 4/1. *Faculty research:* Adolescent behavior change, prevention of teenage pregnancy, community schools. Total annual research expenditures: $500,000.

University of Pittsburgh, School of Nursing, Nurse Practitioner Program, Pittsburgh, PA 15260. Offers acute care nurse practitioner (MSN, DNP); adult nurse practitioner (MSN, DNP); family nurse practitioner (MSN, DNP); neonatal (MSN, DNP); nursing practice (DNP); pediatric nurse practitioner (MSN, DNP); psychiatric primary care nurse practitioner (MSN, DNP). *Accreditation:* AACN. Part-time programs available. *Students:* 27 full-time (26 women), 89 part-time (84 women); includes 6 minority (5 African Americans, 1 Asian American or Pacific Islander). Average age 34. 44 applicants, 64% accepted, 25 enrolled. In 2009, 28 master's awarded. *Degree requirements:* For master's, comprehensive exam, thesis optional. *Entrance requirements:* For master's, GRE General Test or MAT, BSN, RN license, letters of recommendation, resume, course work in statistics, 1-3 years of nursing experience; for doctorate, GRE General Test, BSN, RN license, minimum GPA of 3.5, 3 letters of recommendation. Additional exam requirements/recommendations for international students: Required—TOEFL (minimum score 550 paper-based; 213 computer-based; 80 iBT). *Application deadline:* For fall admission, 8/1 priority date for domestic students, 8/1 for international students; for spring admission, 12/1 priority date for domestic students, 12/1 for international students. Applications are processed on a rolling basis. Application fee: $50. Electronic applications accepted. *Expenses:* Tuition, state resident: full-time $16,402; part-time $665 per credit. Tuition, nonresident: full-time $28,694; part-time $1175 per credit. Required fees: $690; $175 per term. Tuition and fees vary according to program. *Unit head:* Dr. Helen Burns, Associate Dean for Clinical Education, 412-624-6616, Fax: 412-624-2401, E-mail: burnsh@pitt.edu. *Application*

contact: Laurie Lapsley, Administrator of Graduate Student Services, 412-624-9670, Fax: 412-624-2409, E-mail: lapsleyl@pitt.edu.

University of Rochester, School of Nursing, Rochester, NY 14642. Offers acute care nurse practitioner (MS); adult nurse practitioner (MS); adult psychiatric mental health nurse practitioner (MS); adult/geriatric nurse practitioner (MS); care of children and families/pediatric nurse practitioner (MS); care of children and families/pediatric nurse practitioner with pediatric behavioral health (MS); care of children and families/pediatric nurse practitioner/neonatal nurse practitioner (MS); child and adolescent psychiatric mental health nurse practitioner (MS); clinical nurse leader (MS); disaster response and emergency preparedness (MS); family nurse practitioner (MS); health care organization management and leadership (MS); health practice research (PhD); health promotion, education and technology (MS); nursing (Certificate). *Accreditation:* AACN; NLN (one or more programs are accredited). Part-time programs available. Postbaccalaureate distance learning degree programs offered (minimal on-campus study). *Faculty:* 26 full-time (24 women), 20 part-time/adjunct (15 women). *Students:* 50 full-time (45 women), 178 part-time (165 women); includes 33 minority (17 African Americans, 2 American Indian/Alaska Native, 10 Asian Americans or Pacific Islanders, 4 Hispanic Americans), 11 international. Average age 35. 56 applicants, 80% accepted, 35 enrolled. In 2009, 53 master's, 5 doctorates awarded. Terminal master's awarded for partial completion of doctoral program. *Degree requirements:* For master's, comprehensive exam or thesis; for doctorate, thesis/dissertation. *Entrance requirements:* For master's, BS in nursing, minimum GPA of 3.0, course work in statistics; for doctorate, GRE General Test, MS in nursing, minimum GPA of 3.5; for Certificate, MS in nursing. Additional exam requirements/recommendations for international students: Recommended—TOEFL (minimum score 560 paper-based; 230 computer-based; 88 iBT). *Application deadline:* For fall admission, 11/1 priority date for domestic and international students. Application fee: $50. *Financial support:* In 2009–10, 53 students received support, including 14 fellowships with full and partial tuition reimbursements available (averaging $17,497 per year); scholarships/grants, traineeships, health care benefits, tuition waivers (partial), and unspecified assistantships also available. Support available to part-time students. Financial award application deadline: 6/30. *Faculty research:* Clinical research in aging, managing asthma in children, interventions to improve outcomes in critically ill children and their mothers, nurse home visitation studies, medical device evaluation, critical care clinical studies, high risk behavior and prevention, palliative care, pregnancy-related weight gain. Total annual research expenditures: $4.8 million. *Unit head:* Dr. Kathy P. Parker, Dean, 585-273-5639, Fax: 585-273-1268, E-mail: kathy_parker@urmc.rochester.edu. *Application contact:* Elaine Andolina, Director of Admissions, 585-275-2375, Fax: 585-756-8299, E-mail: elaine_andolina@urmc.rochester.edu.

University of San Diego, Hahn School of Nursing and Health Science, San Diego, CA 92110-2492. Offers adult nurse practitioner/family nurse practitioner (MSN); adult-gerontology clinical nurse specialist (MSN); clinical nursing (MSN); entry-level nursing (for non-RNs) (MSN); executive nurse leader (MSN); family nurse practitioner (MSN); nursing (PhD); nursing practice (DNP); pediatric nurse practitioner/family nurse practitioner (MSN); psychiatric-mental health nurse practitioner (MSN). *Accreditation:* AACN. Part-time and evening/weekend programs available. *Faculty:* 18 full-time (17 women), 25 part-time/adjunct (22 women). *Students:* 141 full-time (117 women), 173 part-time (152 women); includes 95 minority (20 African Americans, 9 American Indian/Alaska Native, 45 Asian Americans or Pacific Islanders, 21 Hispanic Americans), 7 international. Average age 38. 404 applicants, 50% accepted, 132 enrolled. In 2009, 103 master's, 10 doctorates awarded. *Degree requirements:* For doctorate, thesis/dissertation (for some programs), residency (DNP). *Entrance requirements:* For master's, GRE General Test (entry-level nursing), BSN, current California RN licensure (except for entry-level nursing); minimum GPA of 3.0; for doctorate, minimum GPA of 3.5, MSN, current California RN licensure. Additional exam requirements/recommendations for international students: Required—TOEFL (minimum score 580 paper-based; 237 computer-based; 83 iBT), TWE. *Application deadline:* For fall admission, 3/1 priority date for domestic students, 3/1 for international students; for spring admission, 11/1 priority date for domestic students, 11/1 for international students. Applications are processed on a rolling basis. Application fee: $45. Electronic applications accepted. *Expenses:* Tuition: Full-time $21,042; part-time $1169 per unit. Required fees: $224. Full-time tuition and fees vary according to course load and degree level. *Financial support:* In 2009–10, 270 students received support. Scholarships/grants and traineeships available. Support available to part-time students. Financial award application deadline: 4/1; financial award applicants required to submit FAFSA. *Faculty research:* Health promotion, decision making, psychogeriatric nursing, historical nursing, leadership behavior. *Unit head:* Dr. Sally Hardin, Dean, 619-260-4550, Fax: 619-260-6814. *Application contact:* Dr. John Mosby, Associate Director of Graduate Admissions, 619-260-4524, Fax: 619-260-4158, E-mail: grads@sandiego.edu.

University of South Carolina, The Graduate School, College of Nursing, Program in Health Nursing, Columbia, SC 29208. Offers adult nurse practitioner (MSN); community/public health clinical nurse specialist (MSN); family nurse practitioner (MSN); pediatric nurse practitioner (MSN). *Accreditation:* AACN. Part-time programs available. *Degree requirements:* For master's, thesis or alternative. *Entrance requirements:* For master's, GRE General Test or MAT, BS in nursing, nursing license. Additional exam requirements/recommendations for international students: Required—TOEFL (minimum score 570 paper-based; 230 computer-based). Electronic applications accepted. *Faculty research:* System research, evidence based practice, breast cancer, violence.

The University of Texas–Pan American, College of Health Sciences and Human Services, Department of Nursing, Edinburg, TX 78539. Offers adult health nursing (MSN); family nurse practitioner (MSN); pediatric nurse practitioner (MSN). *Accreditation:* AACN. Part-time and evening/weekend programs available. *Degree requirements:* For master's, thesis optional. *Entrance requirements:* For master's, Texas RN licensure, undergraduate physical statistic course. Additional exam requirements/recommendations for international students: Required—TOEFL (minimum score 550 paper-based). Electronic applications accepted. *Expenses:* Contact institution. *Faculty research:* Health promotion, adolescent pregnancy, herbal and nontraditional approaches, healing touch stress.

The University of Toledo, College of Graduate Studies, College of Nursing, Toledo, OH 43606-3390. Offers adult health practitioner/clinical nurse specialist (MSN); adult nurse practitioner (Certificate); entry-level nursing initiative (GEMINI) (MSN); family nurse practitioner (MSN, Certificate); nursing education (Certificate); pediatric nurse practitioner (Certificate); pediatric nurse practitioner/clinical nurse specialist (MSN); RN to MSN (MSN). *Accreditation:* AACN. Part-time programs available. *Degree requirements:* For master's, thesis or scholarly project. *Entrance requirements:* For master's, GRE General Test, BS in nursing, minimum undergraduate GPA of 3.0. *Expenses:* Contact institution. *Faculty research:* Sexuality issues, prenatal testing, health care of homeless, nursing education, chronic/acute pain, eating disorders, low birth weight infants.

Vanderbilt University, School of Nursing, Nashville, TN 37240. Offers adult acute care nurse practitioner (MSN); adult nurse practitioner/cardiovascular disease management and prevention (MSN); adult nurse practitioner/palliative care (MSN); clinical management (clinical nurse leader/specialist) (MSN); emergency nurse practitioner (MSN); family nurse practitioner (MSN); gerontology nurse practitioner (MSN); health systems management (MSN); neonatal nurse practitioner (MSN); nurse midwifery (MSN); nurse midwifery/family nurse practitioner (MSN); nursing informatics (MSN); nursing practice (DNP); nursing science (PhD); nutrition (MS); pediatric acute care nurse practitioner (MSN); pediatric primary care nurse practitioner (MSN); psychiatric-mental health nurse practitioner (MSN); women's health nurse practitioner (MSN), including urogynecology; women's health nurse practitioner/adult nurse practitioner (MSN); MSN/M Div; MSN/MTS. *Accreditation:* ACNM/DOA; NLN (one or more programs are accredited). Part-time programs available. Postbaccalaureate distance learning degree programs offered (minimal on-campus study). *Faculty:* 118 full-time (102 women), 429 part-time/adjunct (309 women). *Students:* 484 full-time (435 women), 319 part-time (284 women); includes 84 minority (55 African Americans, 4 American Indian/Alaska Native, 10 Asian Americans or Pacific Islanders, 15 Hispanic Americans), 16 international. Average age 32. 900 applicants, 65% accepted, 433 enrolled. In 2009, 303 master's, 1 doctorate awarded. *Degree requirements:* For doctorate, comprehensive exam, thesis/dissertation. *Entrance requirements:* For master's, GRE General Test, minimum B average in undergraduate course work, 3 letters of recommendation; for doctorate, GRE General Test, interview, 3 letters of recommendation from doctorally-prepared faculty, MSN, essay. Additional exam requirements/recommendations for international students: Required—TOEFL. *Application deadline:* For fall admission, 12/1 priority date for domestic and international students. Applications are processed on a rolling basis. Application fee: $50. *Expenses:* Contact institution. *Financial support:* In 2009–10, 389 students received support, including 1 research assistantship (averaging $5,000 per year); teaching assistantships, scholarships/grants, health care benefits, and tuition waivers also available. Support available to part-time students. Financial award application deadline: 3/15; financial award applicants required to submit FAFSA. *Faculty research:* Lymphedema, palliative care and bereavement, health services research including workforce, safety and quality of care, gerontology, better birth outcomes including nutrition. Total annual research expenditures: $1.4 million. *Unit head:* Dr. Colleen Conway-Welch, Dean, 615-343-8776, Fax: 615-343-7711, E-mail: colleen.conway-welch@vanderbilt.edu. *Application contact:* Cheryl Feldner, Assistant Director of Admissions, 615-322-3800, Fax: 615-343-0333, E-mail: cheryl.feldner@vanderbilt.edu.

Villanova University, College of Nursing, Villanova, PA 19085-1699. Offers adult nurse practitioner (MSN, Post Master's Certificate); family nurse practitioner (MSN, Post Master's Certificate); health care administration (MSN); nurse anesthetist (MSN, Post Master's Certificate); nursing (PhD); nursing education (MSN, Post Master's Certificate); pediatric nurse practitioner (MSN, Post Master's Certificate). *Accreditation:* AACN; AANA/CANAEP. Part-time programs available. Postbaccalaureate distance learning degree programs offered (minimal on-campus study). *Faculty:* 15 full-time (all women), 3 part-time/adjunct (2 women). *Students:* 58 full-time (53 women), 188 part-time (164 women); includes 29 minority (13 African Americans, 1 American Indian/Alaska Native, 13 Asian Americans or Pacific Islanders, 2 Hispanic Americans), 3 international. Average age 33. 171 applicants, 70% accepted, 89 enrolled. In 2009, 32 master's, 1 doctorate awarded. *Degree requirements:* For master's, independent study project; for doctorate, comprehensive exam, thesis/dissertation. *Entrance requirements:* For master's, GRE or MAT, BSN, 1 year of recent nursing experience, physical assessment, course work in statistics; for doctorate, GRE, MSN. Additional exam requirements/recommendations for international students: Required—TOEFL. *Application deadline:* For fall admission, 7/1 priority date for domestic students, 7/1 for international students; for spring admission, 11/1 priority date for domestic students, 11/1 for international students. Applications are processed on a rolling basis. Application fee: $50. *Expenses:* Contact institution. *Financial support:* In 2009–10, 53 students received support, including 5 teaching assistantships with full tuition reimbursements available (averaging $13,100 per year); institutionally sponsored loans, scholarships/grants, traineeships, tuition waivers (full), and unspecified assistantships also available. Financial award application deadline: 3/1; financial award applicants required to submit FAFSA. *Faculty research:* Genetics, ethics, cognitive development of students, women with disabilities, nursing leadership. *Unit head:* Dr. Marguerite K. Schlag, Assistant Dean and Director, Graduate Program, 610-519-4907, Fax: 610-519-7650, E-mail: marguerite.schlag@villanova.edu. *Application contact:* Dean, Graduate School of Liberal Arts and Sciences.

Virginia Commonwealth University, Graduate School, School of Nursing, Richmond, VA 23284-9005. Offers adult health nursing (MS); child health nursing (MS); family health nursing (MS); health system (PhD); immunocompetence (PhD); nurse practitioner (MS, Certificate); nursing administration (MS), including clinical nurse manager, nurse executive; psychiatric-mental health nursing (MS); risk and resilience (PhD); women's health nursing (MS). *Accreditation:* NLN (one or more programs are accredited). Part-time and evening/weekend programs available. *Degree requirements:* For master's, thesis optional; for doctorate, thesis/dissertation. *Entrance requirements:* For master's, GRE General Test, BSN, minimum GPA of 2.8; for doctorate, GRE General Test.

Wayne State University, College of Nursing, Program in Advanced Practice Nursing with Women, Neonates and Children, Detroit, MI 48202. Offers advanced practice nursing with women, neonates and children (MSN); neonatal nurse practitioner (Certificate). *Accreditation:* AACN. Part-time programs available. *Degree requirements:* For master's, thesis or alternative. *Entrance requirements:* For master's, minimum GPA of 2.8. Additional exam requirements/recommendations for international students: Required—TOEFL (minimum score 550 paper-based; 213 computer-based); Recommended—TWE (minimum score 6). Electronic applications accepted. *Faculty research:* Acculturation and parenting, domestic violence, evidence-based midwifery practice, pain in children, trauma and community violence.

Wright State University, School of Graduate Studies, College of Nursing and Health, Program in Nursing, Dayton, OH 45435. Offers acute care nurse practitioner (MS); administration of nursing and health care systems (MS); adult health (MS); child and adolescent health (MS); community health (MS); family nurse practitioner (MS); nurse practitioner (MS); school nurse (MS); MBA/MS. *Accreditation:* AACN. Part-time and evening/weekend programs available. *Degree requirements:* For master's, thesis or alternative. *Entrance requirements:* For master's, GRE General Test, BSN from NLN-accredited college, Ohio RN license. Additional exam requirements/recommendations for international students: Required—TOEFL. *Faculty research:* Clinical nursing and health, teaching, caring, pain administration, informatics and technology.

Psychiatric Nursing

Allen College, Program in Nursing, Waterloo, IA 50703. Offers acute care nurse practitioner (MSN); adult nurse practitioner (MSN); adult psychiatric-mental health nurse practitioner (MSN); family nurse practitioner (MSN); gerontological nurse practitioner (MSN); health education (MSN); leadership in health care delivery (MSN). *Accreditation:* AACN; NLN. Part-time programs available. *Faculty:* 2 full-time (both women), 8 part-time/adjunct (all women). *Students:* 37 full-time (35 women), 103 part-time (99 women); includes 1 minority (Asian American or Pacific Islander). Average age 38. *Degree requirements:* For master's, thesis optional. *Entrance requirements:* For master's, minimum GPA of 3.0. Additional exam requirements/recommendations for international students: Required—TOEFL (minimum score 550 paper-based). *Application deadline:* For fall admission, 7/15 priority date for domestic students; for spring admission, 12/1 priority date for domestic students. Applications are processed on a rolling basis. Application fee: $50. Electronic applications accepted. *Expenses:* Tuition: Full-time $12,550; part-time $651 per credit hour. Required fees: $826; $65 per credit hour. One-time fee: $425. Tuition and fees vary according to course load. *Financial support:* Teaching assistantships, institutionally sponsored loans, scholarships/grants, and traineeships available. Support available to part-time students. Financial award application deadline: 8/15; financial award

Psychiatric Nursing

Allen College (continued)
applicants required to submit FAFSA. *Faculty research:* Pain and aged, congestive heart failure. *Unit head:* Nancy Kramer, Dean, School of Nursing, 319-226-2040, Fax: 319-226-2070, E-mail: kramerna@ihs.org. *Application contact:* Michelle Koehn, Admissions Counselor, 319-226-2002, Fax: 319-226-2051, E-mail: koehnml@ihs.org.

Arizona State University, Graduate College, College of Nursing and Healthcare Innovation, Tempe, AZ 85287. Offers child and adolescent mental health intervention specialist (Graduate Certificate); community and public health practice (Graduate Certificate); community health (MS); evidence-based practice in nursing (Graduate Certificate); exercise and wellness (MS, PhD), including exercise and wellness (MS), physical activity, nutrition and wellness (PhD); healthcare innovation (MHI); nurse education in academic and practice settings (Graduate Certificate); nurse educator (MS); nursing (MS); nursing and healthcare innovation (PhD); nursing practice (DNP); nutrition (MS). *Accreditation:* AACN. Postbaccalaureate distance learning degree programs offered.

Boston College, William F. Connell School of Nursing, Chestnut Hill, MA 02467-3800. Offers adult health nursing (MS); community health nursing (MS); family health (MS); forensic nursing (MS); gerontology (MS); maternal/child health nursing (MS), including pediatric and women's health; nurse anesthesia (MS); nursing (PhD); palliative care (MS), including adult and pediatric; psychiatric-mental health nursing (MS); MBA/MS; MS/MA; MS/PhD. *Accreditation:* AACN; AANA/CANAEP (one or more programs are accredited). Part-time programs available. *Faculty:* 48 full-time (46 women), 31 part-time/adjunct (29 women). *Students:* 183 full-time (169 women), 147 part-time (140 women); includes 36 minority (15 African Americans, 2 American Indian/Alaska Native, 17 Asian Americans or Pacific Islanders, 2 Hispanic Americans), 7 international. Average age 29. 347 applicants, 53% accepted, 103 enrolled. In 2009, 79 master's, 7 doctorates awarded. *Degree requirements:* For master's, comprehensive exam, research project; for doctorate, comprehensive exam, thesis/dissertation, computer literacy exam or foreign language. *Entrance requirements:* For master's, bachelor's degree in nursing; for doctorate, GRE General Test, master's degree in nursing. Additional exam requirements/recommendations for international students: Required—TOEFL (minimum score 550 paper-based; 213 computer-based). *Application deadline:* For fall admission, 11/1 for domestic and international students; for winter admission, 12/31 for domestic and international students; for spring admission, 9/15 for domestic and international students. Applications are processed on a rolling basis. Application fee: $40. Electronic applications accepted. *Financial support:* In 2009–10, 83 students received support, including 12 fellowships with partial tuition reimbursements available (averaging $15,000 per year), 5 teaching assistantships (averaging $13,746 per year); research assistantships, Federal Work-Study, institutionally sponsored loans, scholarships/grants, traineeships, health care benefits, and tuition waivers (partial) also available. Support available to part-time students. Financial award application deadline: 3/1; financial award applicants required to submit FAFSA. *Faculty research:* Ethics, reduction of risk behaviors, support during chronic illness, violence, gerontology. Total annual research expenditures: $1.4 million. *Unit head:* Dr. Susan Gennaro, Dean, 617-552-4251, Fax: 617-552-0931, E-mail: susan.gennaro@bc.edu. *Application contact:* MaryBeth Crowley, Graduate Programs Assistant, 617-552-4928, Fax: 617-552-2121, E-mail: csongrad@bc.edu.

Case Western Reserve University, Frances Payne Bolton School of Nursing, Doctor of Nursing Practice Program, Cleveland, OH 44106. Offers acute care nurse practitioner (DNP); adult nurse practitioner (DNP); family nurse practitioner (DNP); gerontological nurse practitioner (DNP); graduate entry/pre-licensure option (DNP); medical-surgical nursing (DNP); midwifery/family nursing (DNP); neonatal nurse practitioner (DNP); pediatric nurse practitioner (DNP); post-licensure option (DNP); psychiatric-mental health nurse practitioner (DNP); women's health nurse practitioner (DNP). Graduate entry option allows baccalaureate-prepared college graduates from non-nursing backgrounds to earn certificate and MSN in addition to ND. Terminal master's awarded for partial completion of doctoral program. *Degree requirements:* For doctorate, thesis/dissertation. *Entrance requirements:* For doctorate, GRE General Test or MAT. *Faculty research:* Clinical nursing, acute care, gerontology, mental health, critical care.

Case Western Reserve University, Frances Payne Bolton School of Nursing, Master's Programs in Nursing, Nurse Practitioner Program, Cleveland, OH 44106. Offers acute care cardiovascular nursing (MSN); acute care nurse practitioner (MSN); acute care/flight nurse (MSN); adult nurse practitioner (MSN); family nurse practitioner (MSN); gerontological nurse practitioner (MSN); neonatal nurse practitioner (MSN); pediatric nurse practitioner (MSN); psychiatric-mental health nurse practitioner (MSN); women's health nurse practitioner (MSN). *Accreditation:* NLN. Part-time programs available. Postbaccalaureate distance learning degree programs offered (minimal on-campus study). *Degree requirements:* For master's, thesis optional. *Entrance requirements:* For master's, GRE General Test or MAT. Additional exam requirements/recommendations for international students: Required—TOEFL. *Faculty research:* Positive and negative mood states in parents of twins, effect of a carepath on chronic obstructive pulmonary disease home care.

The Catholic University of America, School of Nursing, Washington, DC 20064. Offers adult health specialist with functional role as nurse educator (MSN); adult nurse practitioner (MSN); community/public health nurse specialist educator (MSN); family nurse practitioner (MSN); geriatric nurse practitioner (MSN); immigrant, refugee, and global health clinical nurse specialist (MSN); nursing (DNP, PhD, Certificate); pediatric nurse practitioner (MSN); promoting healthy families in vulnerable communities (MSN); psychiatric-mental health nursing (MSN). *Accreditation:* AACN. Part-time programs available. *Faculty:* 15 full-time (all women), 43 part-time/adjunct (41 women). *Students:* 28 full-time (26 women), 75 part-time (73 women); includes 37 minority (27 African Americans, 6 Asian Americans or Pacific Islanders, 4 Hispanic Americans), 4 international. Average age 42. 84 applicants, 64% accepted, 30 enrolled. In 2009, 23 master's, 7 doctorates, 3 other advanced degrees awarded. *Degree requirements:* For master's, comprehensive exam, thesis optional; for doctorate, comprehensive exam, thesis/dissertation, minimum GPA of 3.0, oral proposal defense. *Entrance requirements:* For master's, 3 letters of recommendation, BA in nursing, RN registration, official copies of academic transcripts, some post-baccalaureate nursing experience; for doctorate, GRE General Test, BA in nursing, professional portfolio (including statements, resume, copy of RN license, 3 letters of recommendation, narrative description of clinical practice, proposal), copy of research/scholarly paper related to clinical nursing. Additional exam requirements/recommendations for international students: Required—TOEFL (minimum score 580 paper-based; 237 computer-based). *Application deadline:* For fall admission, 8/1 priority date for domestic students, 7/15 for international students; for spring admission, 12/1 priority date for domestic students, 10/15 for international students. Applications are processed on a rolling basis. Application fee: $55. Electronic applications accepted. *Expenses:* Tuition: Full-time $31,740; part-time $1245 per credit hour. Required fees: $50; $25 per semester hour. One-time fee: $425. *Financial support:* Fellowships, research assistantships, teaching assistantships, Federal Work-Study, scholarships/grants, tuition waivers (full and partial), and unspecified assistantships available. Financial award application deadline: 2/1; financial award applicants required to submit FAFSA. *Faculty research:* Community involvement in health care services, primary health care services, pediatrics, chronic illness, cardiovascular disease. Total annual research expenditures: $311,172. *Unit head:* Dr. Nalini N. Jairath, Dean, 202-319-5403, Fax: 202-319-6485, E-mail: cua-deanschoolofnursing@cua.edu. *Application contact:* Julie Schwing, Director of Graduate Admissions, 202-319-5057, Fax: 202-319-6533, E-mail: cua-admissions@cua.edu.

Columbia University, School of Nursing, Program in Psychiatric Mental Health Nursing, New York, NY 10032. Offers MS, Adv C. *Accreditation:* AACN. Part-time programs available. *Entrance requirements:* For master's, GRE General Test, BSN, 1 year of clinical experience (preferred); for Adv C, MSN. Electronic applications accepted.

Fairfield University, School of Nursing, Fairfield, CT 06824-5195. Offers clinical nurse leader (MSN); family nurse practitioner (MSN, PMC); healthcare management (MSN); nurse anesthesia (MSN); psychiatric nurse practitioner (MSN, PMC). *Accreditation:* AACN; AANA/CANAEP. Part-time programs available. *Degree requirements:* For master's, capstone project. *Entrance requirements:* For master's, GRE (nurse anesthesia applicants only), minimum QPA of 3.0, RN license, resume, 2 recommendations; for PMC, 1 year of work experience as a registered nurse. Additional exam requirements/recommendations for international students: Required—TOEFL (minimum score 550 paper-based; 213 computer-based; 80 iBT). Electronic applications accepted. *Expenses:* Contact institution. *Faculty research:* Care of older adults, palliative care, spirituality and innovative partnerships, diabetes.

Georgia State University, College of Health and Human Sciences, Byrdine F. Lewis School of Nursing, Atlanta, GA 30302-3083. Offers adult health (MS); adult health nursing (Certificate); child health (MS); family nurse practitioner (MS, Certificate); health promotion, protection and restoration (PhD); perinatal/women's health (MS); psychiatric mental health nursing (Certificate); psychiatric/mental health (MS); women's health nursing (Certificate). *Accreditation:* AACN. Part-time and evening/weekend programs available. Postbaccalaureate distance learning degree programs offered (minimal on-campus study). *Degree requirements:* For master's, research activity; for doctorate, comprehensive exam, thesis/dissertation. *Entrance requirements:* For master's, MAT (preferred) or GRE, interview, RN license; for doctorate, GRE General Test. Additional exam requirements/recommendations for international students: Required—TOEFL (minimum score 550 paper-based; 213 computer-based). Electronic applications accepted. *Expenses:* Contact institution. *Faculty research:* Breast cancer prevention, sexually compulsive behaviors, health risks in minority youth, asthma treatment strategies, adolescent alcohol-related issues.

Hampton University, Graduate College, School of Nursing, Hampton, VA 23668. Offers advanced adult nursing (MS); community health nursing (MS); community mental health/psychiatric nursing (MS); family nursing (MS); gerontological nursing for the nurse practitioner (MS); pediatric nursing (MS); women's health nursing (MS). *Accreditation:* AACN; NLN. Part-time and evening/weekend programs available. *Degree requirements:* For master's, thesis optional. *Entrance requirements:* For master's, GRE General Test. *Faculty research:* Curriculum development, physical and mental assessment.

Hunter College of the City University of New York, Graduate School, Schools of the Health Professions, Hunter-Bellevue School of Nursing, Program in Psychiatric Nursing, New York, NY 10021-5085. Offers MS, AC. *Accreditation:* AACN. Part-time programs available. *Faculty:* 15 full-time (11 women). *Students:* 1 (woman) full-time, 29 part-time (22 women); includes 12 minority (3 African Americans, 6 Asian Americans or Pacific Islanders, 3 Hispanic Americans). Average age 53. 20 applicants, 70% accepted, 11 enrolled. In 2009, 2 master's, 9 other advanced degrees awarded. *Degree requirements:* For master's, practicum. *Entrance requirements:* For master's; minimum GPA of 3.0, New York RN license, BSN. Additional exam requirements/recommendations for international students: Required—TOEFL. *Application deadline:* For fall admission, 4/1 for domestic students, 2/1 for international students; for spring admission, 11/1 for domestic students, 9/1 for international students. Applications are processed on a rolling basis. Application fee: $125. *Expenses:* Tuition, state resident: full-time $7360; part-time $310 per credit. Required fees: $250 per semester. *Financial support:* Federal Work-Study, scholarships/grants, traineeships, and tuition waivers (partial) available. Support available to part-time students. Financial award application deadline: 5/1; financial award applicants required to submit FAFSA. *Faculty research:* Nursing approaches with the homeless, chronic mentally ill, and depressed; power and empathy. *Unit head:* Dr. Kunsook Bernstein, Coordinator, 212-481-4346, Fax: 212-481-5078, E-mail: kbernst@hunter.cuny.edu. *Application contact:* William Zlata, Director for Graduate Admissions, 212-772-4482, Fax: 212-650-3336, E-mail: admissions@hunter.cuny.edu.

Husson University, School of Graduate and Professional Studies, Program in Nursing, Bangor, ME 04401-2999. Offers advanced practice psychiatric nursing (MSN, PMC); family and community nurse practitioner (MSN, PMC). *Accreditation:* AACN. *Entrance requirements:* For master's, MAT, BSN. *Expenses:* Contact institution.

Indiana University–Purdue University Indianapolis, School of Nursing, Indianapolis, IN 46202-2896. Offers acute care nurse practitioner (MSN); adult health clinical nurse specialist (MSN); adult health nursing (MSN), including adult clinical nurse specialist; adult nurse practitioner (MSN); adult psychiatric/mental health nursing (MSN); child psychiatric/mental health nursing (MSN); community health nursing (MSN); family nurse practitioner (MSN); neonatal nurse practitioner (MSN); nursing science (PhD); pediatric clinical nurse specialist (MSN); women's health nurse practitioner (MSN); MSN/MPA; MSN/MPH. *Accreditation:* AACN; NLN (one or more programs are accredited). Part-time programs available. *Faculty:* 85 full-time (82 women), 60 part-time/adjunct (all women). *Students:* 46 full-time (43 women), 369 part-time (354 women); includes 30 minority (21 African Americans, 6 Asian Americans or Pacific Islanders, 3 Hispanic Americans), 5 international. Average age 39. 121 applicants, 82% accepted, 67 enrolled. In 2009, 106 master's, 3 doctorates awarded. Terminal master's awarded for partial completion of doctoral program. *Degree requirements:* For master's, thesis; for doctorate, thesis/dissertation. *Entrance requirements:* For master's, minimum GPA of 3.0, RN license; for doctorate, GRE General Test, minimum GPA of 3.0, MSN, RN license, graduate statistics course with B grade or better (not older than 3 years). Additional exam requirements/recommendations for international students: Required—TOEFL. *Application deadline:* For fall admission, 2/15 for domestic students; for spring admission, 9/15 for domestic students. Application fee: $55 ($65 for international students). *Financial support:* In 2009–10, 93 students received support, including 9 fellowships with full tuition reimbursements available (averaging $7,039 per year), 7 teaching assistantships with full tuition reimbursements available (averaging $5,300 per year); research assistantships with full tuition reimbursements available, Federal Work-Study, institutionally sponsored loans, scholarships/grants, and tuition waivers (full) also available. Support available to part-time students. Financial award application deadline: 5/1. *Faculty research:* Clinical science, health systems. Total annual research expenditures: $3 million. *Unit head:* Associate Dean for Graduate Programs, 317-274-2806, E-mail: nursing@iupui.edu. *Application contact:* Information Contact, 317-274-2806.

Kent State University, College of Nursing, Kent, OH 44242-0001. Offers adult nurse practitioner (MSN); family nurse practitioner (MSN); geriatric nurse practitioner (MSN); nursing (PhD); nursing and health care management (MSN); nursing of adults (clinical nurse specialist) (MSN); pediatric nurse practitioner (MSN); psychiatric/mental health nursing (MSN); women's health nursing (MSN). *Accreditation:* AACN. Part-time programs available. *Degree requirements:* For master's, thesis optional; for doctorate, comprehensive exam, thesis/dissertation. *Entrance requirements:* For master's, GRE (if undergraduate GPA less than 3.0), minimum GPA of 2.75; for doctorate, GRE, MSN. Additional exam requirements/recommendations for international students: Required—TOEFL. Electronic applications accepted. *Expenses:* Contact institution. *Faculty research:* Women and violence, methodological specialties, osteoporosis in women, new caregivers and the elderly.

MGH Institute of Health Professions, Graduate Programs, School of Nursing, Boston, MA 02129. Offers advanced practice nursing (MSN); gerontological nursing (MSN); nursing (DNP); pediatric nursing (MSN); psychiatric nursing (MSN); teaching and learning for health care education (Certificate); women's health nursing (MSN). *Accreditation:* AACN; NLN (one or more programs are accredited). *Faculty:* 37 full-time (33 women), 11 part-time/adjunct (10 women). *Students:* 325 full-time (275 women), 72 part-time (59 women); includes 48 minority (22 African Americans, 1 American Indian/Alaska Native, 18 Asian Americans or Pacific Islanders, 7 Hispanic Americans). Average age 31. 840 applicants, 53% accepted, 221 enrolled. In 2009, 78 master's, 12 doctorates, 45 other advanced degrees awarded. *Degree requirements:* For master's, thesis or alternative. *Entrance requirements:* For master's, GRE General Test. Additional exam requirements/recommendations for international students: Required—TOEFL (minimum score 550 paper-based; 213 computer-based; 80 iBT). *Application deadline:* For fall admission, 1/10 for domestic and international students. Application fee: $50. Electronic applications accepted. *Expenses:* Tuition: Part-time $943 per credit. Required fees: $943 per credit. Tuition and fees vary according to course load. *Financial support:* In 2009–10, 292 students received support, including 1 research assistantship (averaging $1,200 per year), 2 teaching assistantships (averaging $1,200 per year); career-related internships or fieldwork, scholarships/grants, traineeships, tuition waivers (full and partial), and unspecified assistantships also available. Support available to part-time students. Financial award application

deadline: 3/1; financial award applicants required to submit FAFSA. *Faculty research:* Biobehavioral nursing, HIV/AIDS, gerontological nursing, women's health, vulnerable populations, health systems. *Unit head:* Margery Chisholm, Dean, 617-724-0480, Fax: 617-726-8022, E-mail: mchisholm@mghihp.edu. *Application contact:* Maureen Rika Judd, Manager of Admissions, 617-726-6069, Fax: 617-726-8010, E-mail: admissions@mghihp.edu.

Molloy College, Graduate Nursing Program, Rockville Centre, NY 11571-5002. Offers adult nurse practitioner (Advanced Certificate); clinical nurse specialist: adult health (Advanced Certificate); family nurse practitioner (Advanced Certificate); nurse practitioner psychiatry (Advanced Certificate); nursing (MS); nursing administration (Advanced Certificate); nursing administration with informatics (Advanced Certificate); nursing education (Advanced Certificate); nursing informatics (Advanced Certificate); pediatric nurse practitioner (Advanced Certificate). *Accreditation:* AACN. Part-time and evening/weekend programs available. *Faculty:* 23 full-time (22 women), 5 part-time/adjunct (4 women). *Students:* 11 full-time (10 women), 405 part-time (377 women); includes 206 minority (124 African Americans, 52 Asian Americans or Pacific Islanders, 30 Hispanic Americans), 2 international. Average age 39. In 2009, 64 master's awarded. *Degree requirements:* For master's, thesis optional. *Entrance requirements:* For master's, 3 letters of reference, BS in nursing, minimum undergraduate GPA of 3.0; for Advanced Certificate, 3 letters of reference, master's degree in nursing. *Application deadline:* For fall admission, 9/2 priority date for domestic students; for spring admission, 1/20 priority date for domestic students. Applications are processed on a rolling basis. Application fee: $60. *Expenses:* Tuition: Part-time $765 per credit. Required fees: $340 per semester. *Financial support:* Research assistantships with partial tuition reimbursements, teaching assistantships with partial tuition reimbursements, institutionally sponsored loans, scholarships/grants, and unspecified assistantships available. Support available to part-time students. Financial award application deadline: 4/1; financial award applicants required to submit FAFSA. *Unit head:* Dr. Mary T. O'Shaughnessy, Acting Director, 516-678-5000, Fax: 516-678-9718, E-mail: moshaughnessy@molloy.edu. *Application contact:* Alina Haitz, Assistant Director of Graduate Admissions, 516-678-5000 Ext. 6399, Fax: 516-256-2247, E-mail: ahaitz@molloy.edu.

Monmouth University, Graduate School, The Marjorie K. Unterberg School of Nursing and Health Studies, West Long Branch, NJ 07764-1898. Offers adult nurse practitioner (MSN); adult psychiatric and mental health advanced practice nursing (MSN, Post-Master's Certificate); advanced practice nursing (Post-Master's Certificate); family nurse practitioner (MSN, Post-Master's Certificate); forensic nursing (MSN, Certificate); nursing (MSN); nursing administration (MSN, Post-Master's Certificate); nursing education (MSN, Post-Master's Certificate); school nursing (MSN, Certificate). *Accreditation:* AACN. Part-time and evening/weekend programs available. *Faculty:* 11 full-time (all women), 2 part-time/adjunct (both women). *Students:* 15 full-time (14 women), 183 part-time (178 women); includes 51 minority (14 African Americans, 3 American Indian/Alaska Native, 26 Asian Americans or Pacific Islanders, 8 Hispanic Americans), 1 international. Average age 41. 95 applicants, 99% accepted, 44 enrolled. In 2009, 36 master's awarded. *Degree requirements:* For master's, practicum (for some tracks). *Entrance requirements:* For master's, GRE General Test, RN license, 1 year of work experience, minimum undergraduate GPA of 2.75. Additional exam requirements/recommendations for international students: Required—TOEFL (minimum score 550 paper-based; 213 computer-based; 79 iBT), IELTS (minimum score 5), Michigan English Language Assessment Battery (minimum score 77), Cambridge A, B, C. *Application deadline:* For fall admission, 7/15 priority date for domestic students, 6/1 for international students; for spring admission, 11/15 priority date for domestic students, 11/1 for international students. Applications are processed on a rolling basis. Application fee: $50. Electronic applications accepted. *Expenses:* Tuition: Part-time $773 per credit. Required fees: $157 per semester. *Financial support:* In 2009–10, 118 students received support, including 96 fellowships (averaging $1,308 per year), 4 research assistantships (averaging $3,610 per year); career-related internships or fieldwork, scholarships/grants, and unspecified assistantships also available. Support available to part-time students. Financial award applicants required to submit FAFSA. *Faculty research:* Relationship of undergraduate GPA and GRE to succeed in a graduate nursing program. *Unit head:* Dr. Janet Mahoney, Dean, 732-571-3443, Fax: 732-263-5131, E-mail: jmahoney@monmouth.edu. *Application contact:* Kevin Roane, Director, Office of Graduate Admission, 732-571-3452, Fax: 732-263-5123, E-mail: gradadm@monmouth.edu.

Montana State University, College of Graduate Studies, College of Nursing, Bozeman, MT 59717. Offers clinical nurse specialist (CNS) (MN, Post-Master's Certificate); family nurse practitioner (MN, Post-Master's Certificate); nursing education (Certificate); psychiatric mental health nurse practitioner (MN). *Accreditation:* AACN. Part-time programs available. Postbaccalaureate distance learning degree programs offered (no on-campus study). *Faculty:* 49 full-time (46 women), 25 part-time/adjunct (all women). *Students:* 41 full-time (39 women), 24 part-time (23 women); includes 8 minority (7 American Indian/Alaska Native, 1 Hispanic American). Average age 38. 54 applicants, 33% accepted, 16 enrolled. In 2009, 13 master's awarded. *Degree requirements:* For master's, comprehensive exam, thesis (for some programs). *Entrance requirements:* For master's, GRE General Test. Additional exam requirements/recommendations for international students: Required—TOEFL (minimum score 580 paper-based; 213 computer-based). *Application deadline:* For fall admission, 7/15 priority date for domestic students, 5/15 priority date for international students; for spring admission, 12/1 priority date for domestic students, 10/1 priority date for international students. Applications are processed on a rolling basis. Application fee: $30. Electronic applications accepted. *Expenses:* Tuition, state resident: full-time $5635; part-time $3492 per year. Tuition, nonresident: full-time $17,212; part-time $7865.10 per year. Required fees: $1441; $153.15 per credit. Tuition and fees vary according to course load and program. *Financial support:* In 2009–10, 16 students received support, including 3 fellowships with full tuition reimbursements available (averaging $15,000 per year), 1 research assistantship (averaging $7,000 per year), 8 teaching assistantships with partial tuition reimbursements available (averaging $7,050 per year); traineeships and tuition waivers (partial) also available. Financial award application deadline: 3/1; financial award applicants required to submit FAFSA. *Faculty research:* Environmental exposures, chronic illness, sleep habits, oral health, pressure ulcers. Total annual research expenditures: $2.3 million. *Unit head:* Dr. Elizabeth Kinion, Dean, 406-994-2725, Fax: 406-994-6020, E-mail: ekinion@montana.edu. *Application contact:* Dr. Carl A. Fox, Vice Provost for Graduate Education, 406-994-4145, Fax: 406-994-7433, E-mail: gradstudy@montana.edu.

New Mexico State University, Graduate School, College of Health and Social Services, School of Nursing, Las Cruces, NM 88003-8001. Offers community/public health (MSN); medical-surgical (adult health) (MSN); nursing (PhD); nursing administration (MSN); psychiatric/mental health (MSN). *Accreditation:* AACN. Part-time programs available. Postbaccalaureate distance learning degree programs offered (minimal on-campus study). *Faculty:* 10 full-time (all women), 5 part-time/adjunct (all women). *Students:* 59 full-time (48 women), 70 part-time (61 women); includes 47 minority (9 African Americans, 3 American Indian/Alaska Native, 5 Asian Americans or Pacific Islanders, 30 Hispanic Americans). Average age 43. 82 applicants, 96% accepted, 63 enrolled. In 2009, 32 master's, 1 doctorate awarded. *Degree requirements:* For master's, comprehensive exam, thesis optional, clinical practice; for doctorate, comprehensive exam, thesis/dissertation, clinical practice. *Entrance requirements:* For master's, NCLEX exam, BSN, minimum GPA of 3.0, course work in statistics, 3 letters of reference, writing sample, RN license, CPR certification, proof of liability, immunizations, criminal background check; for doctorate, NCLEX exam, MSN, minimum GPA of 3.0, 3 letters of reference, writing sample, RN license, CPR certification, proof of liability, immunizations, criminal background check. Additional exam requirements/recommendations for international students: Required—TOEFL (minimum score 550 paper-based). *Application deadline:* For fall admission, 3/1 priority date for domestic students; for spring admission, 10/1 priority date for domestic students. Applications are processed on a rolling basis. Application fee: $30 ($50 for international students). Electronic applications accepted. *Expenses:* Tuition, state resident: full-time $4080; part-time $223 per credit. Tuition, nonresident: full-time $14,256; part-time $647 per credit. Required fees: $1278; $639 per semester. *Financial support:* In 2009–10, 14 students received support, including 2 teaching assistantships (averaging $18,380 per year); fellowships, research assistantships, career-related internships or fieldwork, Federal Work-Study, scholarships/grants, traineeships, and health care benefits also available. Financial award application deadline: 3/1. *Faculty research:* Public policy, community health, health disparities, self efficacy and self management, psychiatric mental health. *Unit head:* Dr. Pamela Schultz, Director, 575-646-3812, Fax: 575-646-2167, E-mail: pschultz@nmsu.edu. *Application contact:* Dr. Kathleen Huttlinger, Associate Director for Graduate Studies, 575-646-4386, Fax: 575-646-2167.

New York University, College of Nursing, Programs in Advanced Practice Nursing, New York, NY 10012-1019. Offers advanced practice nursing: adult acute care (MS, Advanced Certificate); advanced practice nursing: adult nurse practitioner/palliative care nursing (MS); advanced practice nursing: adult nurse practitioner/holistic nurse practitioner (Advanced Certificate); advanced practice nursing: adult nurse practitioner/holistic nursing (MS); advanced practice nursing: adult nurse practitioner/palliative care nurse practitioner (Advanced Certificate); advanced practice nursing: adult primary care (MS, Advanced Certificate); advanced practice nursing: adult primary care/geriatrics (MS); advanced practice nursing: geriatrics (MS, Advanced Certificate); advanced practice nursing: mental health (MS); advanced practice nursing: mental health nursing (Advanced Certificate); advanced practice nursing: pediatrics (MS, Advanced Certificate); advanced practice nursing:adult primary care and geriatrics (Advanced Certificate); nurse midwifery (MS, Advanced Certificate); nursing administration (MS, Advanced Certificate); nursing education (MS, Advanced Certificate); nursing informatics (MS, Advanced Certificate); MS/MPH; MS/MS. *Accreditation:* AACN; ACNM/DOA. Part-time and evening/weekend programs available. *Faculty:* 17 full-time (all women), 22 part-time/adjunct (19 women). *Students:* 18 full-time (17 women), 524 part-time (485 women); includes 238 minority (90 African Americans, 119 Asian Americans or Pacific Islanders, 29 Hispanic Americans). Average age 33. 191 applicants, 89% accepted, 120 enrolled. In 2009, 117 master's, 2 other advanced degrees awarded. *Degree requirements:* For master's, thesis (for some programs). *Entrance requirements:* For master's, BS in nursing, AS in nursing with another BS/BA, interview; for Advanced Certificate, master's degree. Additional exam requirements/recommendations for international students: Required—TOEFL. *Application deadline:* For fall admission, 7/1 priority date for domestic students, 7/1 for international students; for spring admission, 12/1 for domestic and international students. Applications are processed on a rolling basis. Application fee: $75. *Expenses:* Tuition: Full-time $30,528; part-time $1272 per credit. Required fees: $2177. *Financial support:* Career-related internships or fieldwork, institutionally sponsored loans, scholarships/grants, traineeships, and tuition waivers (partial) available. Support available to part-time students. Financial award application deadline: 2/1; financial award applicants required to submit FAFSA. *Faculty research:* Elderly black diabetics, families and illness, public health nursing, parent-child nursing, health policy costs. *Unit head:* Dr. Judith Haber, Associate Dean for Graduate Programs, 212-998-9020, Fax: 212-995-3143. *Application contact:* Amy Knowles, Assistant Dean for Student Affairs and Admissions, 212-998-5333, Fax: 212-995-4302, E-mail: ak96@nyu.edu.

Northeastern University, Bouvé College of Health Sciences Graduate School, School of Nursing, Program in Psychiatric-Mental Health Nursing, Boston, MA 02115-5096. Offers MS, CAGS, CAS. *Accreditation:* AACN. *Students:* 9 full-time (8 women), 4 part-time (all women). Average age 45. 12 applicants, 92% accepted, 7 enrolled. In 2009, 4 master's, 2 other advanced degrees awarded. *Degree requirements:* For master's, thesis or alternative. *Entrance requirements:* For master's, GRE General Test; for other advanced degree, MS in nursing. Additional exam requirements/recommendations for international students: Required—TOEFL (minimum score 100 iBT). *Application deadline:* For fall admission, 7/1 for domestic students. Application fee: $50. Electronic applications accepted. *Financial support:* Research assistantships, teaching assistantships, scholarships/grants, traineeships, and tuition waivers (partial) available. Financial award application deadline: 7/1; financial award applicants required to submit FAFSA. *Faculty research:* Clinical psychopharmacology, access to mental health care, child abuse, seasonal affective disorder (SAD), chronic and persistent mental illness. *Unit head:* Ann Polcari, Psychiatric Graduate Program Coordinator, 617-373-7571, E-mail: a.polcari@neu.edu. *Application contact:* Margaret Schnabel, Director of Graduate Admissions, 617-373-2708, E-mail: bouvegrad@neu.edu.

Oregon Health & Science University, School of Nursing, Program in Mental Health Nursing, Portland, OR 97239-3098. Offers MN, MS, Post Master's Certificate. *Accreditation:* AACN. *Degree requirements:* For master's, thesis optional. *Entrance requirements:* For master's, GRE General Test, bachelor's degree in nursing, minimum undergraduate GPA of 3.0, previous course work in statistics; for Post Master's Certificate, master's degree in nursing. Tuition and fees vary according to course level, course load, degree level, program and reciprocity agreements.

Pontifical Catholic University of Puerto Rico, College of Sciences, Department of Nursing, Program in Mental Health and Psychiatric Nursing, Ponce, PR 00717-0777. Offers MS. Part-time and evening/weekend programs available. *Degree requirements:* For master's, comprehensive exam (for some programs), thesis, clinical research paper. *Entrance requirements:* For master's, GRE General Test, 2 letters of recommendation, interview, minimum GPA of 2.75. Electronic applications accepted.

Rush University, College of Nursing, Department of Community Systems and Mental Health Nursing, Chicago, IL 60612-3832. Offers community and mental health nursing (DNP, PhD); family nurse practitioner (MSN, Post-Master's Certificate); psychiatric clinical specialist (MSN); psychiatric nurse practitioner—adult (MSN); psychiatric nurse practitioner—family (MSN); psychiatric-mental health clinical specialist (Post-Master's Certificate); psychiatric-mental health nurse practitioner (Post-Master's Certificate); public health nursing (MSN). *Accreditation:* AACN. Part-time programs available. Postbaccalaureate distance learning degree programs offered (minimal on-campus study). Terminal master's awarded for partial completion of doctoral program. *Degree requirements:* For master's, capstone project; for doctorate, thesis/dissertation, DNP leadership project. *Entrance requirements:* For master's, GRE General Test (waived if nursing GPA is above 3.0 or cumulative GPA is above 3.25), interview; for doctorate, GRE General Test, interview, course work in statistics (DN Sc). Electronic applications accepted. *Faculty research:* Immigrant mental health, de-escalation strategies, caregiver interventions, parent-teacher training, restraint use.

Rutgers, The State University of New Jersey, Newark, Graduate School, Program in Nursing, Newark, NJ 07102. Offers nursing (MS), including acute care of adults and aged, advanced practice in pediatric nursing, advanced practice with childbearing families, community health nursing, family nurse practitioner, primary care of adults and aged, psychiatric/mental health nursing. *Accreditation:* AACN. Part-time programs available. *Degree requirements:* For master's, comprehensive exam. *Entrance requirements:* For master's, GRE General Test, RN license, minimum B average, BS in nursing. Additional exam requirements/recommendations for international students: Required—TOEFL. Electronic applications accepted. *Faculty research:* HIV/AIDS, quality of life—MS and breast cancer, sleep patterns of cardiac patients.

Sage Graduate School, Graduate School, School of Health Sciences, Department of Nursing, Program in Psychiatric Mental Health Nurse Practitioner, Troy, NY 12180-4115. Offers psychiatric mental health (MS, Post Master's Certificate). *Accreditation:* AACN. Part-time and evening/weekend programs available. *Faculty:* 5 full-time (all women), 8 part-time/adjunct (all women). *Students:* 7 full-time (all women), 18 part-time (16 women); includes 6 minority (3 African Americans, 1 American Indian/Alaska Native, 2 Asian Americans or Pacific Islanders). Average age 46. 13 applicants, 54% accepted, 6 enrolled. In 2009, 2 master's, 1 other advanced degree awarded. *Degree requirements:* For master's, thesis or alternative. *Entrance requirements:* For master's, BS in nursing, minimum GPA of 2.75, resume, 2 letters of recommendation. Additional exam requirements/recommendations for international students: Required—TOEFL (minimum score 550 paper-based; 213 computer-based). *Application deadline:* Applications are processed on a rolling basis. Application fee: $40. *Expenses:* Tuition: Full-time $10,620; part-time $590 per credit hour. *Financial support:* Fellowships, research assistantships, teaching assistantships, Federal Work-Study, scholarships/grants, and unspecified assistantships available. Support available to part-time students. Financial award application deadline: 3/1; financial award applicants required to submit FAFSA. *Unit head:* Arlene Pericak, Director, 518-244-2012, E-mail: perica@sage.edu. *Application contact:*

Psychiatric Nursing

Sage Graduate School (continued)
Wendy D. Diefendorf, Director of Graduate and Adult Admission, 518-244-2443, Fax: 518-244-6880, E-mail: diefew@sage.edu.

Saint Xavier University, Graduate Studies, School of Nursing, Chicago, IL 60655-3105. Offers adult health clinical nurse specialist (MS); family nurse practitioner (MS, PMC); leadership in community health nursing (MS); psychiatric-mental health clinical nurse specialist (MS); psychiatric-mental health clinical specialist (PMC); MBA/MS. *Accreditation:* AACN. Part-time and evening/weekend programs available. *Entrance requirements:* For master's, GRE General Test or MAT, minimum GPA of 3.0, RN license. *Expenses:* Tuition: Part-time $743 per credit hour. Required fees: $135 per semester.

Seattle University, College of Nursing, Program in Nursing, Seattle, WA 98122-1090. Offers leadership in community nursing (MSN), including program development, spirituality and health; primary care nurse practitioner (MSN), including family nurse practitioner, psychiatric mental health nurse practitioner.

Shenandoah University, School of Health Professions, Division of Nursing, Winchester, VA 22601-5195. Offers family nurse practitioner (Certificate); nurse-midwifery (Certificate); nurse-midwifery endorsement (Certificate); nursing (MSN, DNP); post-master's in nursing education (Certificate); psychiatric mental health nurse practitioner (Certificate). *Accreditation:* AACN; ACNM/DOA. Part-time programs available. *Faculty:* 11 full-time (all women), 4 part-time/adjunct (all women). *Students:* 21 full-time (20 women), 67 part-time (64 women); includes 11 minority (7 African Americans, 2 Asian Americans or Pacific Islanders, 2 Hispanic Americans). Average age 39. 71 applicants, 97% accepted, 53 enrolled. In 2009, 8 master's, 6 other advanced degrees awarded. *Degree requirements:* For master's, research project, clinical hours; for doctorate and Certificate, clinical hours. *Entrance requirements:* For master's, GRE General Test, previous course work in statistics, community nursing, and physical assessment; RN license; BSN; minimum undergraduate GPA of 3.0; appropriate clinical experience; curriculum vitae; 3 letters of recommendation; for Certificate, MSN, minimum GPA of 3.0, 3 letters of recommendation. Additional exam requirements/recommendations for international students: Required—TOEFL (minimum score 550 paper-based; 213 computer-based; 79 iBT), IELTS (minimum score 6.5). *Application deadline:* For fall admission, 6/15 priority date for domestic and international students. Applications are processed on a rolling basis. Application fee: $30. Electronic applications accepted. *Expenses:* Tuition: Full-time $11,925; part-time $695 per credit. Required fees: $400 per semester. *Financial support:* Application deadline: 3/15. *Unit head:* Dr. Kathryn Ganske, Director, 540-678-4381, Fax: 540-665-5519. *Application contact:* David Anthony, Dean of Admissions, 540-665-4581, Fax: 540-665-4627, E-mail: admit@su.edu.

Southern Arkansas University–Magnolia, Graduate Programs, Magnolia, AR 71753. Offers agriculture (MS); business administration (MBA); computer and information sciences (MS); counseling (MS); education (M Ed), including counseling and development, curriculum and instruction emphasis, educational administration and supervision, elementary education, middle level emphasis, reading emphasis, secondary education, TESOL emphasis; kinesiology (MS); library media and information specialist (M Ed); mental health and clinical counseling (MS); public administration (EMPA); school counseling (M Ed); teaching (MAT). *Accreditation:* NCATE. Part-time and evening/weekend programs available. *Faculty:* 43 full-time (24 women), 12 part-time/adjunct (7 women). *Students:* 116 full-time (78 women), 333 part-time (255 women); includes 105 minority (98 African Americans, 3 American Indian/Alaska Native, 3 Asian Americans or Pacific Islanders, 1 Hispanic American), 11 international. Average age 33. In 2009, 88 master's awarded. *Degree requirements:* For master's, comprehensive exam, thesis optional. *Entrance requirements:* For master's, GRE, MAT or GMAT, minimum GPA of 2.75. *Application deadline:* For fall admission, 8/15 for domestic students; for winter admission, 1/8 for domestic students; for spring admission, 1/8 for domestic students. Applications are processed on a rolling basis. Application fee: $0. *Expenses:* Tuition, state resident: full-time $3798; part-time $211 per hour. Tuition, nonresident: full-time $5580; part-time $310 per hour. Required fees: $584. *Financial support:* Career-related internships or fieldwork, Federal Work-Study, scholarships/grants, tuition waivers (full), and unspecified assistantships available. Financial award applicants required to submit FAFSA. *Faculty research:* Alternative certification for teachers, supervision of instruction, instructional leadership, counseling. *Unit head:* Dr. Kim Bloss, Dean, Graduate Studies, 870-235-4150, Fax: 870-235-5227, E-mail: kkbloss@saumag.edu. *Application contact:* Dr. Kim Bloss, Dean, Graduate Studies, 870-235-4150, Fax: 870-235-5227, E-mail: kkbloss@saumag.edu.

Stony Brook University, State University of New York, Stony Brook University Medical Center, Health Sciences Center, School of Nursing, Program in Mental Health/Psychiatric Nursing, Stony Brook, NY 11794. Offers MS, Certificate. *Accreditation:* AACN. *Students:* 19 full-time (17 women), 51 part-time (45 women); includes 20 minority (14 African Americans, 6 Asian Americans or Pacific Islanders). In 2009, 18 master's, 5 other advanced degrees awarded. *Degree requirements:* For master's, thesis. *Entrance requirements:* For master's, BSN, minimum GPA of 3.0, course work in statistics. *Application deadline:* For fall admission, 1/15 for domestic students. Application fee: $60. *Expenses:* Tuition, state resident: full-time $8370; part-time $349 per credit. Tuition, nonresident: full-time $13,250; part-time $552 per credit. Required fees: $933. *Financial support:* Application deadline: 3/15. *Unit head:* Dr. Michael Chiarello, Chair, 631-444-3299, Fax: 631-444-3136, E-mail: michael.chiarello@stonybrook.edu. *Application contact:* Dr. Kent Marks, Assistant Dean, Admissions and Records, 631-632-4723, Fax: 631-632-7243, E-mail: kmarks@notes.cc.sunysb.edu.

Uniformed Services University of the Health Sciences, Graduate School of Nursing, Bethesda, MD 20814-4799. Offers family nurse practitioner (MSN); nurse anesthesia (MSN); perioperative clinical nurse specialty (MSN); psychiatric mental health nurse practitioner (MSN). Available to military officers only. *Accreditation:* AACN; NLN. Postbaccalaureate distance learning degree programs offered (no on-campus study). *Faculty:* 27 full-time (18 women), 2 part-time/adjunct (both women). *Students:* 75 full-time (32 women), 3 part-time (all women); includes 20 minority (8 African Americans, 5 Asian Americans or Pacific Islanders, 7 Hispanic Americans). Average age 36. 108 applicants, 72% accepted, 78 enrolled. In 2009, 54 master's awarded. *Degree requirements:* For master's, thesis or alternative. *Entrance requirements:* For master's, GRE, BSN, clinical experience, minimum GPA of 3.0, previous course work in science. *Application deadline:* For fall admission, 7/1 for domestic students; for winter admission, 2/15 for domestic students. Application fee: $0. Electronic applications accepted. *Faculty research:* Prenatal care, military health care, military readiness, distance learning. *Unit head:* Col. Bruce A. Schoneboom, Associate Dean for Academic Affairs, 301-295-1180, Fax: 301-295-1707, E-mail: bschoneboom@usuhs.mil. *Application contact:* Terry Lynn Malavakis, Recording Secretary for Admissions Committee, 301-295-1055, Fax: 301-295-1707, E-mail: tmalavakis@usuhs.mil.

University at Buffalo, the State University of New York, Graduate School, School of Nursing, Buffalo, NY 14260. Offers adult health nursing (MS); family nursing (MS); nurse anesthetist (MS); nursing (PhD); nursing education (Certificate); psychiatric/mental health nursing (MS). *Accreditation:* AACN; AANA/CANAEP (one or more programs are accredited). Part-time programs available. Postbaccalaureate distance learning degree programs offered (minimal on-campus study). *Faculty:* 42 full-time (38 women), 16 part-time/adjunct (all women). *Students:* 128 full-time (102 women), 69 part-time (58 women); includes 27 minority (7 African Americans, 1 American Indian/Alaska Native, 12 Asian Americans or Pacific Islanders, 7 Hispanic Americans), 15 international. Average age 34. 375 applicants, 25% accepted, 65 enrolled. In 2009, 58 master's, 3 doctorates, 4 other advanced degrees awarded. Terminal master's awarded for partial completion of doctoral program. *Degree requirements:* For master's, thesis optional, comprehensive exams or project; for doctorate, comprehensive exam, thesis/dissertation. *Entrance requirements:* For master's, GRE General Test (if overall GPA less than 3.0), interview, minimum GPA of 3.0, RN license, 3 references; for doctorate, GRE General Test, MAT, minimum GPA of 3.25, RN license, BS or MS in nursing, 3 references, writing sample; for Certificate, interview, minimum GPA of 3.0 or GRE General Test, RN license, MS in nursing. Additional exam requirements/recommendations for international students: Required—TOEFL (minimum score 550 paper-based; 213 computer-based; 79 iBT), IELTS (minimum score 6.5). *Application deadline:* For fall admission, 6/1 priority date for domestic students, 4/1 priority date for international students; for spring admission, 11/1 for domestic students, 10/1 priority date for international students. Applications are processed on a rolling basis. Application fee: $75. Electronic applications accepted. *Financial support:* In 2009–10, 78 students received support, including 14 fellowships with full tuition reimbursements available (averaging $8,200 per year), 5 research assistantships with full tuition reimbursements available (averaging $16,794 per year), 13 teaching assistantships with full tuition reimbursements available (averaging $10,636 per year); scholarships/grants, traineeships, health care benefits, and unspecified assistantships also available. Financial award application deadline: 3/15; financial award applicants required to submit FAFSA. *Faculty research:* Oncology symptom management, end of life decision making, changing behaviors using the transtheoretical model, addictions, nursing workforce. Total annual research expenditures: $1.3 million. *Unit head:* Dr. Jean K. Brown, Dean and Professor, 716-829-2533, Fax: 716-829-2566, E-mail: ubnursingdean@buffalo.edu. *Application contact:* Dr. David J. Lang, Director of Student Affairs, 716-829-2537, Fax: 716-829-2021, E-mail: langdj@buffalo.edu.

University of Alaska Anchorage, College of Health and Social Welfare, School of Nursing, Anchorage, AK 99508. Offers family nurse practitioner (Certificate); nursing (MS); nursing education (Certificate); psychiatric nurse practitioner (Certificate). *Accreditation:* NLN. Part-time and evening/weekend programs available. *Degree requirements:* For master's, comprehensive exam, individual project. *Entrance requirements:* For master's, GRE or MAT, BS in nursing, interview, minimum GPA of 3.0, RN license, 1 year of part-time or 6 months of full-time clinical experience. Additional exam requirements/recommendations for international students: Required—TOEFL (minimum score 550 paper-based; 213 computer-based).

University of Cincinnati, Graduate School, College of Nursing, Cincinnati, OH 45221-0038. Offers clinical nurse specialist (MSN), including adult health, community health, neonatal, nursing administration, occupational health, pediatric health, psychiatric nursing, women's health; nurse anesthesia (MSN); nurse midwifery (MSN); nurse practitioner (MSN), including acute care, ambulatory care, family, family/psychiatric, women's health; nursing (PhD); MBA/MSN. *Accreditation:* AACN; AANA/CANAEP (one or more programs are accredited); ACNM/DOA. Part-time programs available. Postbaccalaureate distance learning degree programs offered (no on-campus study). Terminal master's awarded for partial completion of doctoral program. *Degree requirements:* For master's, thesis or alternative; for doctorate, comprehensive exam, thesis/dissertation. *Entrance requirements:* For master's and doctorate, GRE General Test. Additional exam requirements/recommendations for international students: Required—TOEFL (minimum score 520 paper-based; 190 computer-based). Electronic applications accepted. *Faculty research:* Substance abuse, injury and violence, symptom management.

University of Delaware, College of Health Sciences, School of Nursing, Newark, DE 19716. Offers adult nurse practitioner (MSN, PMC); cardiopulmonary clinical nurse specialist (MSN, PMC); cardiopulmonary clinical nurse specialist/adult nurse practitioner (MSN, PMC); family nurse practitioner (MSN, PMC); gerontology clinical nurse specialist (MSN, PMC); gerontology clinical nurse specialist geriatric nurse practitioner (PMC); gerontology clinical nurse specialist/geriatric nurse practitioner (MSN); health services administration (MSN, PMC); nursing of children clinical nurse specialist (MSN, PMC); nursing of children clinical nurse specialist/pediatric nurse practitioner (MSN, PMC); oncology/immune deficiency clinical nurse specialist (MSN, PMC); oncology/immune deficiency clinical nurse specialist/adult nurse practitioner (MSN, PMC); perinatal/women's health clinical nurse specialist (MSN, PMC); perinatal/women's health clinical nurse specialist/women's health nurse practitioner (MSN, PMC); psychiatric nursing clinical nurse specialist (MSN, PMC). *Accreditation:* AACN; NLN (one or more programs are accredited). Part-time and evening/weekend programs available. Postbaccalaureate distance learning degree programs offered (minimal on-campus study). *Degree requirements:* For master's, thesis optional. *Entrance requirements:* For master's, BSN, interview, RN license. Electronic applications accepted. *Faculty research:* Marriage and chronic illness, health promotion, congestive heart failure patient outcomes, school nursing, diabetes in children, culture, health disparities, cardiovascular, prison nursing, oncology, public policy, child obesity, smoking and teen pregnancy, blood pressure measurements, men's health.

University of Illinois at Chicago, Graduate College, College of Nursing, Program in Nursing, Chicago, IL 60607-7128. Offers acute care clinical nurse specialist (MS); acute care nurse practitioner (MS); administrative studies in nursing (MS); adult nurse practitioner (MS); adult/geriatric nurse practitioner (MS); advanced community health nurse specialist (MS); family nurse practitioner (MS); geriatric clinical nurse specialist (MS); geriatric nurse practitioner (MS); mental health clinical nurse specialist (MS); mental health nurse practitioner (MS); nurse midwifery (MS); occupational health/advanced community health nurse specialist (MS); occupational health/family nurse practitioner (MS); pediatric clinical nurse specialist (MS); pediatric nurse practitioner (MS); perinatal clinical nurse specialist (MS); school/advanced community health nurse specialist (MS); school/family nurse practitioner (MS); women's health nurse practitioner (MS). *Accreditation:* AACN. Part-time programs available. *Degree requirements:* For master's, thesis or alternative. *Entrance requirements:* For master's, GRE General Test, minimum GPA of 2.75. Additional exam requirements/recommendations for international students: Required—TOEFL. Electronic applications accepted.

The University of Kansas, University of Kansas Medical Center, School of Nursing, Kansas City, KS 66160. Offers clinical research management (PMC); family nurse practitioner (PMC); health care informatics (PMC); health professions educator (PMC); nurse midwife (PMC); nursing (MS, DNP, PhD); organizational leadership (PMC); psychiatric/mental health nurse practitioner (PMC); public health nursing (PMC). *Accreditation:* AACN; ACNM/DOA. Part-time programs available. Postbaccalaureate distance learning degree programs offered (minimal on-campus study). *Faculty:* 65. *Students:* 59 full-time (56 women), 309 part-time (285 women); includes 37 minority (17 African Americans, 4 American Indian/Alaska Native, 7 Asian Americans or Pacific Islanders, 9 Hispanic Americans), 10 international. Average age 38. 138 applicants, 59% accepted, 82 enrolled. In 2009, 78 master's, 3 doctorates awarded. Terminal master's awarded for partial completion of doctoral program. *Degree requirements:* For master's, thesis optional, general oral exam; for doctorate, one foreign language, thesis/dissertation, comprehensive oral and written exam. *Entrance requirements:* For master's, bachelor's degree in nursing, minimum GPA of 3.0, RN license, 1 year of clinical experience; for doctorate, GRE General Test, master's degree in nursing, minimum GPA of 3.5. Additional exam requirements/recommendations for international students: Required—TOEFL. *Application deadline:* For fall admission, 4/1 for domestic students; for spring admission, 9/1 for domestic students. Application fee: $60. Electronic applications accepted. *Expenses:* Tuition, state resident: full-time $6492; part-time $270.50 per credit hour. Tuition, nonresident: full-time $15,510; part-time $646.25 per credit hour. Required fees: $847; $70.56 per credit hour. Tuition and fees vary according to course load and program. *Financial support:* In 2009–10, 93 students received support, including 7 research assistantships (averaging $24,000 per year), 23 teaching assistantships with full and partial tuition reimbursements available (averaging $24,000 per year); traineeships also available. Financial award application deadline: 2/14; financial award applicants required to submit FAFSA. *Faculty research:* Breastfeeding practices of teen mothers, national database of nursing quality indicators, caregiving of families of patients using technology in the home, self care talk intervention partnership between caregivers of stroke survivors and nurses, smoking cessation. Total annual research expenditures: $5 million. *Unit head:* Dr. Karen L. Miller, Dean, 913-588-1601, Fax: 913-588-1660, E-mail: kmiller@kumc.edu. *Application contact:* Dr. Rita K. Clifford, Associate Dean, Student Affairs, 913-588-1619, Fax: 913-588-1615, E-mail: rcliffor@kumc.edu.

University of Louisville, Graduate School, School of Nursing, Louisville, KY 40202. Offers adult nurse practitioner (MSN); family nurse practitioner (MSN); health professions education (MSN); neonatal nurse practitioner (MSN); nursing research (PhD); psychiatric mental health nurse practitioner (MSN). *Accreditation:* AACN. Part-time programs available. *Faculty:* 28 full-time (25 women), 4 part-time/adjunct (3 women). *Students:* 72 full-time (66 women), 57 part-time (52 women); includes 15 minority (11 African Americans, 3 Asian Americans or Pacific Islanders, 1 Hispanic American), 4 international. Average age 35. 45 applicants, 82%

accepted, 31 enrolled. In 2009, 28 master's, 3 doctorates awarded. Terminal master's awarded for partial completion of doctoral program. *Degree requirements:* For master's, thesis optional; for doctorate, comprehensive exam, thesis/dissertation. *Entrance requirements:* For master's, GRE General Test, bachelor's degree in nursing, minimum GPA of 3.0, RN license; for doctorate, GRE General Test, BSN and MSN with recommended minimum GPA of 3.0. Additional exam requirements/recommendations for international students: Required—TOEFL. *Application deadline:* For fall admission, 4/1 priority date for domestic students, 4/1 for international students; for spring admission, 10/1 priority date for domestic students, 10/1 for international students. Applications are processed on a rolling basis. Application fee: $50. Electronic applications accepted. *Financial support:* In 2009–10, 45 students received support, including 2 fellowships with full tuition reimbursements available (averaging $20,000 per year), 5 research assistantships with full tuition reimbursements available (averaging $18,000 per year), 5 teaching assistantships with full tuition reimbursements available (averaging $18,000 per year); institutionally sponsored loans, scholarships/grants, traineeships, health care benefits, and unspecified assistantships also available. Support available to part-time students. Financial award application deadline: 4/15; financial award applicants required to submit FAFSA. *Faculty research:* Maternal-child/family stress after pregnancy loss, postpartum depression, access to healthcare (underserved populations), quality of life issues, physical activity (impact on chronic/acute conditions). Total annual research expenditures: $363,876. *Unit head:* Dr. Marcia J. Hern, Dean, 502-852-8300, Fax: 502-852-5044, E-mail: m.hern@gwise.louisville.edu. *Application contact:* Dr. Rosalie O'Dell Mainous, Associate Dean for Graduate Academic Affairs, 502-852-8387, Fax: 502-852-8783, E-mail: romain01@louisville.edu.

University of Maryland, Baltimore, Graduate School, School of Nursing, Master's Program in Nursing, Baltimore, MD 21201. Offers community health nursing (MS); gerontological nursing (MS); maternal-child nursing (MS); medical-surgical nursing (MS); nurse-midwifery education (MS); nursing administration (MS); nursing education (MS); nursing health policy (MS); primary care nursing (MS); psychiatric nursing (MS); MS/MBA. *Accreditation:* AACN; AANA/CANAEP; ACNM/DOA; NLN (one or more programs are accredited). Part-time programs available. *Students:* 387 full-time (338 women), 528 part-time (491 women); includes 330 minority (230 African Americans, 3 American Indian/Alaska Native, 81 Asian Americans or Pacific Islanders, 16 Hispanic Americans), 10 international. Average age 36. 849 applicants, 40% accepted, 255 enrolled. In 2009, 264 master's awarded. *Degree requirements:* For master's, comprehensive exam (for some programs), thesis or alternative. *Entrance requirements:* For master's, GRE General Test, minimum GPA of 2.75, course work in statistics, BS in nursing. Additional exam requirements/recommendations for international students: Required—TOEFL (minimum score 550 paper-based; 80 iBT), or IELTS (minimum score 7). *Application deadline:* For fall admission, 1/15 for international students. Application fee: $50. Electronic applications accepted. *Expenses:* Tuition, state resident: full-time $7290; part-time $405 per credit hour. Tuition, nonresident: full-time $12,780; part-time $710 per credit hour. Required fees: $774; $10 per credit hour. $297 per semester. Tuition and fees vary according to course load, degree level and program. *Financial support:* Fellowships, research assistantships, teaching assistantships, career-related internships or fieldwork and traineeships available. Support available to part-time students. Financial award application deadline: 2/15; financial award applicants required to submit FAFSA. *Unit head:* Dr. Jane Kapustin, Assistant Dean, 410-706-6741, Fax: 410-706-4231. *Application contact:* Marjorie Fass, Admissions Director, 410-706-0501, Fax: 410-706-7238.

University of Massachusetts Lowell, School of Health and Environment, Department of Nursing, Program in Adult Psychiatric and Mental Health Nursing, Lowell, MA 01854-2881. Offers MS, Graduate Certificate. *Accreditation:* AACN. Part-time programs available. *Degree requirements:* For master's, thesis optional. *Entrance requirements:* For master's, GRE General Test, minimum GPA of 3.0, MA nursing license, interview, 3 letters of recommendation.

University of Michigan, Horace H. Rackham School of Graduate Studies, School of Nursing, Division of Acute, Critical and Long-term Care, Program in Psychiatric Mental Health Nursing, Ann Arbor, MI 48109. Offers psychiatric mental health nurse practitioner (MS); psychiatric mental health nursing- clinical nurse specialist (MS). *Accreditation:* AACN. Part-time programs available. *Degree requirements:* For master's, thesis. *Entrance requirements:* For master's, GRE General Test (if BSN GPA less than 3.25), Michigan licensure, minimum of B average in BSN program. Additional exam requirements/recommendations for international students: Required—TOEFL (minimum score 560 paper-based; 220 computer-based). Electronic applications accepted. *Expenses:* Tuition, state resident: full-time $17,286; part-time $1099 per credit hour. Tuition, nonresident: full-time $34,944; part-time $2080 per credit hour. Required fees: $95 per semester. Tuition and fees vary according to course load, degree level and program. *Faculty research:* Clinical specialist roles, depression, eating disorders, care of chronically mentally ill.

University of Minnesota, Twin Cities Campus, Graduate School, School of Nursing, Program in Psychiatric Mental Health Clinical Nurse Specialist, Minneapolis, MN 55455-0213. Offers MS. *Accreditation:* AACN. Part-time programs available. *Entrance requirements:* Additional exam requirements/recommendations for international students: Required—TOEFL (minimum score 586 paper-based; 240 computer-based).

The University of North Carolina at Chapel Hill, School of Nursing, Chapel Hill, NC 27599-7460. Offers nursing (MSN, PhD, PMC), including adult nurse practitioner (MSN, PMC), children's health advanced practice (MSN, PMC), family nurse practitioner (MSN, PMC), health care systems (MSN, PMC), psychiatric/mental health nursing (MSN, PMC), women's health nursing (MSN, PMC). *Accreditation:* AACN; NLN (one or more programs are accredited). Part-time programs available. *Degree requirements:* For master's, comprehensive exam, thesis; for doctorate, thesis/dissertation, 3 exams. *Entrance requirements:* For master's and doctorate, GRE General Test. *Faculty research:* Chronic illness, parenting, cardiovascular health in children, elderly, HIV-AIDS.

University of Pennsylvania, School of Nursing, Psychiatric Mental Health Advanced Practice Nurse Program, Philadelphia, PA 19104. Offers adult and special populations (MSN); child and family (MSN); geropsychiatrics (MSN). *Accreditation:* AACN. Part-time programs available. *Students:* 5 full-time (all women), 17 part-time (14 women); includes 3 minority (2 African Americans, 1 Asian American or Pacific Islander). In 2009, 2 master's awarded. *Entrance requirements:* For master's, GRE General Test, BSN, minimum GPA of 3.0, previous course work in statistics. Additional exam requirements/recommendations for international students: Required—TOEFL. *Application deadline:* For fall admission, 2/15 priority date for domestic students. Applications are processed on a rolling basis. Application fee: $70. *Expenses:* Contact institution. *Financial support:* Fellowships, research assistantships, teaching assistantships, career-related internships or fieldwork, Federal Work-Study, and institutionally sponsored loans available. Support available to part-time students. Financial award application deadline: 4/1. *Faculty research:* Use of restraints in psychiatry, victims of trauma, spiritual use of prayer by cancer patients, coping strategies of African-Americans, urban health care.

University of Pittsburgh, School of Nursing, Clinical Nurse Specialist Program, Pittsburgh, PA 15260. Offers medical/surgical clinical nurse specialist (MSN, DNP); psychiatric and mental health clinical nurse specialist (MSN, DNP). *Accreditation:* AACN. Part-time programs available. *Students:* 3 full-time (2 women), 17 part-time (16 women); includes 1 minority (Asian American or Pacific Islander). Average age 39. 8 applicants, 75% accepted, 6 enrolled. In 2009, 9 master's awarded. *Degree requirements:* For master's, comprehensive exam, thesis optional. *Entrance requirements:* For master's, GRE or MAT, BSN, RN license, letters of recommendation, resume, course work in statistics, 1-3 years of nursing experience. Additional exam requirements/recommendations for international students: Required—TOEFL (minimum score 550 paper-based; 213 computer-based; 80 iBT). *Application deadline:* For fall admission, 8/1 priority date for domestic students; for spring admission, 12/1 priority date for domestic students. Applications are processed on a rolling basis. Application fee: $50. Electronic applications accepted. *Expenses:* Tuition, state resident: full-time $16,402; part-time $665 per credit. Tuition, nonresident: full-time $28,694; part-time $1175 per credit. Required fees: $690; $175 per term. Tuition and fees vary according to program. *Unit head:* Dr. Helen Burns, Associate Dean for Clinical Education, 412-624-6616, Fax: 412-624-2401, E-mail: burnsh@pitt.edu. *Application contact:* Laurie Lapsley, Administrator of Graduate Student Services, 412-624-9670, Fax: 412-624-2409, E-mail: lapsleyl@pitt.edu.

University of Pittsburgh, School of Nursing, Nurse Practitioner Program, Pittsburgh, PA 15260. Offers acute care nurse practitioner (MSN, DNP); adult nurse practitioner (MSN, DNP); family nurse practitioner (MSN, DNP); neonatal (MSN, DNP); nursing practice (DNP); pediatric nurse practitioner (MSN, DNP); psychiatric primary care nurse practitioner (MSN, DNP). *Accreditation:* AACN. Part-time programs available. *Students:* 27 full-time (26 women), 89 part-time (84 women); includes 6 minority (5 African Americans, 1 Asian American or Pacific Islander). Average age 34. 44 applicants, 64% accepted, 25 enrolled. In 2009, 28 master's awarded. *Degree requirements:* For master's, comprehensive exam, thesis optional. *Entrance requirements:* For master's, GRE General Test or MAT, BSN, RN license, letters of recommendation, resume, course work in statistics, 1-3 years of nursing experience; for doctorate, GRE General Test, BSN, RN license, minimum GPA of 3.5, 3 letters of recommendation. Additional exam requirements/recommendations for international students: Required—TOEFL (minimum score 550 paper-based; 213 computer-based; 80 iBT). *Application deadline:* For fall admission, 8/1 priority date for domestic students, 8/1 for international students; for spring admission, 12/1 priority date for domestic students, 12/1 for international students. Applications are processed on a rolling basis. Application fee: $50. Electronic applications accepted. *Expenses:* Tuition, state resident: full-time $16,402; part-time $665 per credit. Tuition, nonresident: full-time $28,694; part-time $1175 per credit. Required fees: $690; $175 per term. Tuition and fees vary according to program. *Unit head:* Dr. Helen Burns, Associate Dean for Clinical Education, 412-624-6616, Fax: 412-624-2401, E-mail: burnsh@pitt.edu. *Application contact:* Laurie Lapsley, Administrator of Graduate Student Services, 412-624-9670, Fax: 412-624-2409, E-mail: lapsleyl@pitt.edu.

University of Puerto Rico, Medical Sciences Campus, School of Nursing, San Juan, PR 00936-5067. Offers anesthesia (MSN); critical care nursing (MSN); family and community nursing (MSN); family nurse practitioner (MSN); mental health and psychiatric nursing (MSN); nursing (MSN). *Accreditation:* AACN; AANA/CANAEP. *Entrance requirements:* For master's, GRE or EXADEP, interview, Puerto Rico RN license or professional license for international students, general and specific point average, article analysis. Electronic applications accepted. *Faculty research:* HIV, health disparities, teen violence, women and violence, neurological disorders.

University of Rhode Island, Graduate School, College of Nursing, Kingston, RI 02881. Offers administration (MS); clinical nurse leader (MS); clinical specialist in gerontology (MS); clinical specialist in psychiatric/mental health (MS); family nurse practitioner (MS); gerontological nurse practitioner (MS); nursing (DNP, PhD); nursing education (MS). *Accreditation:* AACN; ACNM/DOA (one or more programs are accredited). Part-time programs available. *Faculty:* 28 full-time (27 women), 3 part-time/adjunct (all women). *Students:* 21 full-time (20 women), 74 part-time (71 women); includes 3 minority (1 African American, 2 Asian Americans or Pacific Islanders), 5 international. In 2009, 29 master's, 2 doctorates awarded. *Degree requirements:* For master's, comprehensive exam; for doctorate, comprehensive exam, thesis/dissertation. *Entrance requirements:* For master's, GRE or MAT, 2 letters of recommendation, scholarly papers; for doctorate, GRE, 3 letters of recommendation, scholarly papers. Additional exam requirements/recommendations for international students: Required—TOEFL (minimum score 550 paper-based; 213 computer-based). *Application deadline:* For fall admission, 4/15 for domestic students, 2/1 for international students; for spring admission, 11/15 for domestic students, 7/15 for international students. Application fee: $65. Electronic applications accepted. *Expenses:* Tuition, state resident: full-time $8828; part-time $490 per credit hour. Tuition, nonresident: full-time $22,100; part-time $1228 per credit hour. Required fees: $1118; $57 per semester. Tuition and fees vary according to program. *Financial support:* In 2009–10, 3 teaching assistantships with full and partial tuition reimbursements (averaging $8,428 per year) were awarded. Financial award application deadline: 4/15; financial award applicants required to submit FAFSA. *Faculty research:* Group intervention for grieving women in prison, translating Best Practice in non-drug interventions for postoperative pain management, further development and testing of the pain assessment inventory, preschool motor and functional performance of two cohorts, neuroactivation of brain motor areas in preterm children. Total annual research expenditures: $926,949. *Unit head:* Dr. Dayle Joseph, Dean, 401-874-2766, Fax: 401-874-2061, E-mail: dayle@uri.edu. *Application contact:* Dr. Mary C. Sullivan, Director of Graduate Studies, 401-874-5339, Fax: 401-874-2061, E-mail: mcsullivan@uri.edu.

University of Rochester, School of Nursing, Rochester, NY 14642. Offers acute care nurse practitioner (MS); adult nurse practitioner (MS); adult psychiatric mental health nurse practitioner (MS); adult/geriatric nurse practitioner (MS); care of children and families/pediatric nurse practitioner (MS); care of children and families/pediatric nurse practitioner with pediatric behavioral health (MS); care of children and families/pediatric nurse practitioner/neonatal nurse practitioner (MS); child and adolescent psychiatric mental health nurse practitioner (MS); clinical nurse leader (MS); disaster response and emergency preparedness (MS); family nurse practitioner (MS); health care organization management and leadership (MS); health practice research (PhD); health promotion, education and technology (MS); nursing (Certificate). *Accreditation:* AACN; NLN (one or more programs are accredited). Part-time programs available. Postbaccalaureate distance learning degree programs offered (minimal on-campus study). *Faculty:* 26 full-time (24 women), 20 part-time/adjunct (15 women). *Students:* 50 full-time (45 women), 178 part-time (165 women); includes 33 minority (17 African Americans, 2 American Indian/Alaska Native, 10 Asian Americans or Pacific Islanders, 4 Hispanic Americans), 11 international. Average age 35. 56 applicants, 80% accepted, 35 enrolled. In 2009, 53 master's, 5 doctorates awarded. Terminal master's awarded for partial completion of doctoral program. *Degree requirements:* For master's, comprehensive exam or thesis; for doctorate, thesis/dissertation. *Entrance requirements:* For master's, BS in nursing, minimum GPA of 3.0, course work in statistics; for doctorate, GRE General Test, MS in nursing, minimum GPA of 3.5; for Certificate, MS in nursing. Additional exam requirements/recommendations for international students: Recommended—TOEFL (minimum score 560 paper-based; 230 computer-based; 88 iBT). *Application deadline:* For fall admission, 11/1 priority date for domestic and international students. Application fee: $50. *Financial support:* In 2009–10, 53 students received support, including 14 fellowships with full and partial tuition reimbursements available (averaging $17,497 per year); scholarships/grants, traineeships, health care benefits, tuition waivers (partial), and unspecified assistantships also available. Support available to part-time students. Financial award application deadline: 6/30. *Faculty research:* Clinical research in aging, managing asthma in children, interventions to improve outcomes in critically ill children and their mothers, nurse home visitation studies, medical device evaluation, critical care clinical studies, high risk behavior and prevention, palliative care, pregnancy-related weight gain. Total annual research expenditures: $4.8 million. *Unit head:* Dr. Kathy P. Parker, Dean, 585-273-5639, Fax: 585-273-1268, E-mail: kathy_parker@urmc.rochester.edu. *Application contact:* Elaine Andolina, Director of Admissions, 585-275-2375, Fax: 585-756-8299, E-mail: elaine_andolina@urmc.rochester.edu.

University of San Diego, Hahn School of Nursing and Health Science, San Diego, CA 92110-2492. Offers adult nurse practitioner/family nurse practitioner (MSN); adult-gerontology clinical nurse specialist (MSN); clinical nursing (MSN); entry-level nursing (for non-RNs) (MSN); executive nurse leader (MSN); family nurse practitioner (MSN); nursing (PhD); nursing practice (DNP); pediatric nurse practitioner/family nurse practitioner (MSN); psychiatric-mental health nurse practitioner (MSN). *Accreditation:* AACN. Part-time and evening/weekend programs available. *Faculty:* 18 full-time (17 women), 25 part-time/adjunct (22 women). *Students:* 141 full-time (117 women), 173 part-time (152 women); includes 95 minority (20 African Americans, 9 American Indian/Alaska Native, 45 Asian Americans or Pacific Islanders, 21 Hispanic Americans), 7 international. Average age 38. 404 applicants, 50% accepted, 132 enrolled. In 2009, 103 master's, 10 doctorates awarded. *Degree requirements:* For doctorate, thesis/dissertation (for some programs), residency (DNP). *Entrance requirements:* For master's, GRE General Test (entry-level nursing), BSN, current California RN licensure (except for entry-level nursing); minimum GPA of 3.0; for doctorate, minimum GPA of 3.5, MSN, current California RN licensure. Additional exam requirements/recommendations for international

Psychiatric Nursing

University of San Diego *(continued)*
students: Required—TOEFL (minimum score 580 paper-based; 237 computer-based; 83 iBT), TWE. *Application deadline:* For fall admission, 3/1 priority date for domestic students, 3/1 for international students; for spring admission, 11/1 priority date for domestic students, 11/1 for international students. Applications are processed on a rolling basis. Application fee: $45. Electronic applications accepted. *Expenses:* Tuition: Full-time $21,042; part-time $1169 per unit. Required fees: $224. Full-time tuition and fees vary according to course load and degree level. *Financial support:* In 2009–10, 270 students received support. Scholarships/grants and traineeships available. Support available to part-time students. Financial award application deadline: 4/1; financial award applicants required to submit FAFSA. *Faculty research:* Health promotion, decision making, psychogeriatric nursing, historical nursing, leadership behavior. *Unit head:* Dr. Sally Hardin, Dean, 619-260-4550, Fax: 619-260-6814. *Application contact:* Dr. John Mosby, Associate Director of Graduate Admissions, 619-260-4524, Fax: 619-260-4158, E-mail: grads@sandiego.edu.

University of South Carolina, The Graduate School, College of Nursing, Program in Advanced Practice Nursing in Psychiatric Mental Health, Columbia, SC 29208. Offers MSN, Certificate. Part-time programs available. Postbaccalaureate distance learning degree programs offered (minimal on-campus study). *Entrance requirements:* For master's, master's degree in nursing, RN license; for Certificate, MSN. Additional exam requirements/recommendations for international students: Required—TOEFL (minimum score 570 paper-based; 213 computer-based). Electronic applications accepted. *Faculty research:* Systems research, evidence based practice, breast cancer, violence.

University of South Carolina, The Graduate School, College of Nursing, Program in Community Mental Health and Psychiatric Health Nursing, Columbia, SC 29208. Offers psychiatric/mental health nurse practitioner (MSN); psychiatric/mental health specialist (MSN). *Accreditation:* AACN. Part-time programs available. *Degree requirements:* For master's, thesis or alternative. *Entrance requirements:* For master's, GRE General Test, MAT, BS in nursing, nursing license. Additional exam requirements/recommendations for international students: Required—TOEFL (minimum score 570 paper-based; 230 computer-based). Electronic applications accepted. *Faculty research:* Systems research, evidence based practice, breast cancer, violence.

University of Southern Maine, College of Nursing and Health Professions, Portland, ME 04104-9300. Offers adult health nursing (PMC); clinical nurse leader (MS); clinical nurse specialist psychiatric-mental health nursing (MS); family nursing (PMC); medical/surgical nursing (MS); nurse practitioner adult health nursing (MS); nurse practitioner family nursing (MS); nurse practitioner psychiatric/mental health nursing (MS); psychiatric-mental health nursing (PMC); MBA/MSN. *Accreditation:* AACN. Part-time programs available. *Faculty:* 15 full-time (13 women), 4 part-time/adjunct (2 women). *Students:* 51 full-time (40 women), 54 part-time (49 women); includes 4 minority (1 American Indian/Alaska Native, 2 Asian Americans or Pacific Islanders, 1 Hispanic American). Average age 36. 95 applicants, 52% accepted, 27 enrolled. In 2009, 34 master's awarded. *Degree requirements:* For master's, thesis optional. *Entrance requirements:* For master's, GRE General Test or MAT, minimum GPA of 3.0. Additional exam requirements/recommendations for international students: Required—TOEFL (minimum score 550 paper-based; 213 computer-based). *Application deadline:* For fall admission, 4/1 for domestic and international students; for spring admission, 10/1 for domestic and international students. Application fee: $50. Electronic applications accepted. *Financial support:* In 2009–10, 10 students received support, including 5 research assistantships with tuition reimbursements available (averaging $3,375 per year), 3 teaching assistantships with tuition reimbursements available (averaging $3,375 per year); career-related internships or fieldwork, Federal Work-Study, scholarships/grants, traineeships, tuition waivers (full and partial), and unspecified assistantships also available. Support available to part-time students. Financial award application deadline: 2/15; financial award applicants required to submit FAFSA. *Faculty research:* Women's health, nursing history, weight control, community services, substance abuse. *Unit head:* Krista M. Meinersmann, Director of Nursing Program, 207-780-4505, Fax: 207-228-8177, E-mail: kmeinersmann@usm.maine.edu. *Application contact:* Mary Sloan, Assistant Director, Office of Graduate Studies, 207-780-4386, Fax: 207-780-4969, E-mail: gradstudies@usm.maine.edu.

University of Southern Mississippi, Graduate School, College of Health, School of Nursing, Hattiesburg, MS 39406-0001. Offers adult health nursing (MSN); community health nursing (MSN); ethics (PhD); family nurse practitioner (MSN); leadership (PhD); nursing service administration (MSN); policy analysis (PhD); psychiatric nursing (MSN). *Accreditation:* AACN. Part-time and evening/weekend programs available. *Faculty:* 17 full-time (16 women), 1 part-time/adjunct (0 women). *Students:* 63 full-time (57 women), 40 part-time (36 women); includes 23 minority (all African Americans). Average age 40. 69 applicants, 59% accepted, 37 enrolled. In 2009, 28 master's, 2 doctorates awarded. *Degree requirements:* For master's, comprehensive exam, thesis optional; for doctorate, comprehensive exam, thesis/dissertation. *Entrance requirements:* For master's, GRE General Test, minimum GPA of 2.75, nursing license, BS in nursing; for doctorate, GRE General Test, master's degree in nursing, minimum GPA of 3.5. Additional exam requirements/recommendations for international students: Required—TOEFL. *Application deadline:* For fall admission, 3/15 priority date for domestic students, 5/1 for international students. Applications are processed on a rolling basis. Application fee: $35. Electronic applications accepted. *Expenses:* Tuition, state resident: full-time $5096; part-time $284 per hour. Tuition, nonresident: full-time $13,052; part-time $726 per hour. Required fees: $402. Tuition and fees vary according to course level and course load. *Financial support:* In 2009–10, 14 research assistantships with full tuition reimbursements

(averaging $12,577 per year) were awarded; teaching assistantships, Federal Work-Study and traineeships also available. Financial award application deadline: 3/15; financial award applicants required to submit FAFSA. *Faculty research:* Gerontology, caregivers, HIV, bereavement, pain, nursing leadership. *Unit head:* Dr. Katherine Nugent, Director and Associate Dean, 601-266-5500, Fax: 601-266-5927. *Application contact:* Dr. Anne Brock, Graduate Coordinator, 601-266-5500, Fax: 601-266-5927.

University of Virginia, School of Nursing, Charlottesville, VA 22903. Offers acute and specialty care (MSN); acute care nurse practitioner (MSN); clinical nurse leadership (MSN); community-public health leadership (MSN); nursing (DNP, PhD); psychiatric mental health counseling (MSN); MSN/MBA. *Accreditation:* AACN. Part-time programs available. *Faculty:* 50 full-time (47 women), 4 part-time/adjunct (3 women). *Students:* 158 full-time (135 women), 118 part-time (117 women); includes 41 minority (30 African Americans, 1 American Indian/Alaska Native, 4 Asian Americans or Pacific Islanders, 6 Hispanic Americans), 4 international. Average age 36. 302 applicants, 48% accepted, 106 enrolled. In 2009, 84 master's, 12 doctorates awarded. *Degree requirements:* For doctorate, comprehensive exam (for some programs), capstone project (DNP), dissertation (PhD). *Entrance requirements:* For master's, GRE General Test, MAT; for doctorate, GRE General Test. Additional exam requirements/recommendations for international students: Required—TOEFL, IELTS. *Application deadline:* Applications are processed on a rolling basis. Application fee: $60. Electronic applications accepted. *Expenses:* Contact institution. *Financial support:* Fellowships, research assistantships, teaching assistantships, Federal Work-Study and scholarships/grants available. Financial award applicants required to submit FAFSA. *Unit head:* Dorrie K. Fontaine, Dean, 434-924-0141, Fax: 434-982-1809. *Application contact:* Clay Hysell, Assistant Dean for Graduate Student Services, 434-924-0141, Fax: 434-982-1809, E-mail: nur-osa@virginia.edu.

Vanderbilt University, School of Nursing, Nashville, TN 37240. Offers adult acute care nurse practitioner (MSN); adult nurse practitioner/cardiovascular disease management and prevention (MSN); adult nurse practitioner/palliative care (MSN); clinical management (clinical nurse leader/specialist) (MSN); emergency nurse practitioner (MSN); family nurse practitioner (MSN); gerontology nurse practitioner (MSN); health systems management (MSN); neonatal nurse practitioner (MSN); nurse midwifery (MSN); nurse midwifery/family nurse practitioner (MSN); nursing informatics (MSN); nursing practice (DNP); nursing science (PhD); nutrition (MS); pediatric acute care nurse practitioner (MSN); pediatric primary care nurse practitioner (MSN); psychiatric-mental health nurse practitioner (MSN); women's health nurse practitioner (MSN), including urogynecology; women's health nurse practitioner/adult nurse practitioner (MSN); MSN/M Div; MSN/MTS. *Accreditation:* ACNM/DOA; NLN (one or more programs are accredited). Part-time programs available. Postbaccalaureate distance learning degree programs offered (minimal on-campus study). *Faculty:* 118 full-time (102 women), 429 part-time/adjunct (309 women). *Students:* 484 full-time (435 women), 319 part-time (284 women); includes 84 minority (55 African Americans, 4 American Indian/Alaska Native, 10 Asian Americans or Pacific Islanders, 15 Hispanic Americans), 16 international. Average age 32. 900 applicants, 65% accepted, 433 enrolled. In 2009, 303 master's, 1 doctorate awarded. *Degree requirements:* For doctorate, comprehensive exam, thesis/dissertation. *Entrance requirements:* For master's, GRE General Test, minimum B average in undergraduate course work, 3 letters of recommendation; for doctorate, GRE General Test, interview, 3 letters of recommendation from doctorally-prepared faculty, MSN, essay. Additional exam requirements/recommendations for international students: Required—TOEFL. *Application deadline:* For fall admission, 12/1 priority date for domestic and international students. Applications are processed on a rolling basis. Application fee: $50. *Expenses:* Contact institution. *Financial support:* In 2009–10, 389 students received support, including 1 research assistantship (averaging $5,000 per year); teaching assistantships, scholarships/grants, health care benefits, and tuition waivers also available. Support available to part-time students. Financial award application deadline: 3/15; financial award applicants required to submit FAFSA. *Faculty research:* Lymphedema, palliative care and bereavement, health services research including workforce, safety and quality of care, gerontology, better birth outcomes including nutrition. Total annual research expenditures: $1.4 million. *Unit head:* Dr. Colleen Conway-Welch, Dean, 615-343-8776, Fax: 615-343-7711, E-mail: colleen.conway-welch@vanderbilt.edu. *Application contact:* Cheryl Feldner, Assistant Director of Admissions, 615-322-3800, Fax: 615-343-0333, E-mail: cheryl.feldner@vanderbilt.edu.

Virginia Commonwealth University, Graduate School, School of Nursing, Richmond, VA 23284-9005. Offers adult health nursing (MS); child health nursing (MS); family health nursing (MS); health system (PhD); immunocompetence (PhD); nurse practitioner (MS, Certificate); nursing administration (MS), including clinical nurse manager, nurse executive; psychiatric-mental health nursing (MS); risk and resilience (PhD); women's health nursing (MS). *Accreditation:* NLN (one or more programs are accredited). Part-time and evening/weekend programs available. *Degree requirements:* For master's, thesis optional; for doctorate, thesis/dissertation. *Entrance requirements:* For master's, GRE General Test, BSN, minimum GPA of 2.8; for doctorate, GRE General Test.

Wayne State University, College of Nursing, Program in Psychiatric Mental Health Nurse Practitioner, Detroit, MI 48202. Offers MSN, Certificate. *Accreditation:* AACN. Part-time programs available. *Degree requirements:* For master's, thesis or alternative. *Entrance requirements:* For master's, minimum GPA of 2.8. Additional exam requirements/recommendations for international students: Required—TOEFL (minimum score 550 paper-based; 213 computer-based); Recommended—TWE (minimum score 6). Electronic applications accepted. *Faculty research:* Immigrant and minority health, homelessness, HIV/AIDS, promotion of sleep, substance abuse.

School Nursing

Cambridge College, School of Education, Cambridge, MA 02138-5304. Offers autism specialist (M Ed); autism/behavior analyst (M Ed); behavior analyst (Post-Master's Certificate); behavioral management (M Ed); early childhood teacher (M Ed); education specialist in curriculum and instruction (CAGS); educational leadership (Ed D); elementary teacher (M Ed); English as a second language (M Ed, Certificate); general science (M Ed); health education, health promotion (Post-Master's Certificate); health/family and consumer sciences (M Ed); history (M Ed); individualized degree (M Ed); information technology literacy (M Ed); instructional technology (M Ed); interdisciplinary studies (M Ed); library teacher (M Ed); literacy education (M Ed); mathematics (M Ed); mathematics specialist (Certificate); middle school mathematics and science (M Ed); school administration (M Ed, CAGS); school guidance counselor (M Ed); school nurse education (M Ed); school social worker/school adjustment counselor (M Ed); special education administrator (CAGS); special education/moderate disabilities (M Ed); teaching skills and methodologies (M Ed). Part-time and evening/weekend programs available. Postbaccalaureate distance learning degree programs offered (minimal on-campus study). *Faculty:* 10 full-time (3 women), 283 part-time/adjunct (187 women). *Students:* 974 full-time (755 women), 1,071 part-time (835 women); includes 940 minority (762 African Americans, 4 American Indian/Alaska Native, 22 Asian Americans or Pacific Islanders, 152 Hispanic Americans), 28 international. Average age 39. In 2009, 866 master's, 4 doctorates, 209 CAGSs awarded. *Degree requirements:* For master's, thesis, internship/practicum (licensure program only); for doctorate, thesis/dissertation; for other advanced degree, thesis. *Entrance requirements:* For master's, interview, resume, documentation of licensure, 2 professional references; for doctorate, official transcripts, interview, resume, documentation of licensure (if any), written personal statement/essay, portfolio of scholarly and professional work, qualifying assessment, 2 professional references, health insurance, immunizations form; for other advanced degree, official transcripts, interview, resume, documentation of licensure (if any), written personal statement/essay, 2 professional references, health insurance, immunizations form. Additional exam requirements/recommendations for international students: Required—TOEFL (minimum score 550 paper-based; 213 computer-based; 79 iBT); Recommended—IELTS (minimum score 6). *Application deadline:* Applications are processed on a rolling basis. Application fee: $30. Electronic applications accepted. *Expenses:* Contact institution. *Financial support:* In 2009–10, 1,373 students received support. Career-related internships or fieldwork, Federal Work-Study, and scholarships/grants available. Financial award applicants required to submit FAFSA. *Faculty research:* Adult education, accelerated learning, mathematics education, brain compatible learning, special education and law. *Unit head:* Dr. N. Alan Sheppard, Interim Associate Dean, 617-873-0619, E-mail: alan.sheppard@cambridgecollege.edu. *Application contact:* Stephen Lyons, Director of Enrollment, Graduate and N.I.T.E. Programs, 617-868-1000, Fax: 617-349-3561, E-mail: stephen.lyons@cambridgecollege.edu.

Eastern University, Graduate Education Programs, St. Davids, PA 19087-3696. Offers multi-cultural education (M Ed); school health services (M Ed); school nurse (Certificate). Part-time programs available. *Entrance requirements:* For master's, minimum GPA of 2.5. Additional exam requirements/recommendations for international students: Required—TOEFL.

Felician College, Program in Education, Lodi, NJ 07644-2117. Offers education (MA); educational supervision (MA, PMC); elementary education (MA); principal (PMC); principal/supervision dual certification (MA); school nurse/health (MA); school nurse/health educator (Certificate); special education (MA). *Accreditation:* Teacher Education Accreditation Council.

Part-time and evening/weekend programs available. *Students:* 12 full-time (9 women), 93 part-time (83 women); includes 5 African Americans, 1 Asian American or Pacific Islander, 9 Hispanic Americans, 3 international. Average age 37. 18 applicants, 50% accepted, 9 enrolled. *Degree requirements:* For master's, project. *Entrance requirements:* For master's, MAT, minimum GPA of 3.0, 3 letters of recommendation. Additional exam requirements/recommendations for international students: Recommended—TOEFL (minimum score 550 paper-based; 213 computer-based). *Application deadline:* Applications are processed on a rolling basis. Application fee: $40. *Financial support:* Federal Work-Study available. *Unit head:* Dr. Rosemarie Liebmann, Associate Dean, 201-559-3537, E-mail: liebmannr@felician.edu. *Application contact:* Dr. Wendy Lin-Cook, Director of Adult and Graduate Admission, 201-559-6077, Fax: 201-559-6138, E-mail: adultandgraduate@felician.edu.

See Close-Up on page 709.

Kean University, College of Natural, Applied and Health Sciences, Program in Nursing, Union, NJ 07083. Offers clinical management (MSN), including transcultural focus; community health nursing (MSN); school nursing (MSN). *Accreditation:* NLN. Part-time and evening/weekend programs available. *Faculty:* 7 full-time (all women). *Students:* 12 full-time (all women), 78 part-time (74 women); includes 46 minority (31 African Americans, 10 Asian Americans or Pacific Islanders, 5 Hispanic Americans). Average age 44. 44 applicants, 98% accepted, 26 enrolled. In 2009, 36 master's awarded. *Degree requirements:* For master's, thesis or alternative, clinical field experience. *Entrance requirements:* For master's, minimum GPA of 3.0; BS in nursing; RN license; 2 letters of recommendation; interview; 1 completed course of the following: Basic Health Assessment and Human Growth and Development across the life span. *Application deadline:* For fall admission, 5/1 for domestic students; for spring admission, 11/1 for domestic students. Application fee: $60 ($150 for international students). Electronic applications accepted. *Expenses:* Tuition, state resident: full-time $10,440; part-time $435 per credit. Tuition, nonresident: full-time $14,160; part-time $590 per credit. Required fees: $2642; $110 per credit. Part-time tuition and fees vary according to course load and degree level. *Financial support:* In 2009–10, 1 research assistantship with full tuition reimbursement (averaging $3,263 per year) was awarded; unspecified assistantships also available. *Unit head:* Dr. Cheryl Krause-Parello, Program Coordinator, 908-737-3390, E-mail: ckrausep@kean.edu. *Application contact:* Dorothy Rowe, Pre-Admissions Coordinator, 908-737-5928, Fax: 908-737-5965, E-mail: drowe@kean.edu.

Kutztown University of Pennsylvania, College of Liberal Arts and Sciences, Program in School Nursing, Kutztown, PA 19530-0730. Offers MSN, Certificate. Part-time and evening/weekend programs available. *Faculty:* 2 full-time (both women). *Students:* 26 part-time (all women), 1 international. Average age 42. 17 applicants, 76% accepted, 4 enrolled. In 2009, 2 master's awarded. *Entrance requirements:* Additional exam requirements/recommendations for international students: Required—TOEFL. *Application deadline:* For fall admission, 8/15 priority date for domestic and international students; for spring admission, 12/15 priority date for domestic and international students. Applications are processed on a rolling basis. Application fee: $35. Electronic applications accepted. *Expenses:* Tuition, state resident: full-time $6666; part-time $370 per credit. Tuition, nonresident: full-time $10,666; part-time $593 per credit. Required fees: $62 per credit. $60 per semester. *Financial support:* Career-related internships or fieldwork, Federal Work-Study, scholarships/grants, and unspecified assistantships available. Financial award application deadline: 3/1. *Unit head:* Dr. Mary Ann Dailey, Chairperson, 610-683-4329, Fax: 610-683-4708, E-mail: mdailey@kutztown.edu. *Application contact:* Kelly D. Burr, Associate Director, Graduate Admissions, 610-683-4200, Fax: 610-683-1393, E-mail: graduate@kutztown.edu.

Monmouth University, Graduate School, The Marjorie K. Unterberg School of Nursing and Health Studies, West Long Branch, NJ 07764-1898. Offers adult nurse practitioner (MSN); adult psychiatric and mental health advanced practice nursing (MSN, Post-Master's Certificate); advanced practice nursing (Post-Master's Certificate); family nurse practitioner (MSN, Post-Master's Certificate); forensic nursing (MSN, Certificate); nursing (MSN); nursing administration (MSN, Post-Master's Certificate); nursing education (MSN, Post-Master's Certificate); school nursing (MSN, Certificate). *Accreditation:* AACN. Part-time and evening/weekend programs available. *Faculty:* 11 full-time (all women), 2 part-time/adjunct (both women). *Students:* 15 full-time (14 women), 183 part-time (178 women); includes 51 minority (14 African Americans, 3 American Indian/Alaska Native, 26 Asian Americans or Pacific Islanders, 8 Hispanic Americans), 1 international. Average age 41. 95 applicants, 99% accepted, 44 enrolled. In 2009, 36 master's awarded. *Degree requirements:* For master's, practicum (for some tracks). *Entrance requirements:* For master's, GRE General Test, RN license, 1 year of work experience, minimum undergraduate GPA of 2.75. Additional exam requirements/recommendations for international students: Required—TOEFL (minimum score 550 paper-based; 213 computer-based; 79 iBT), IELTS (minimum score 5), Michigan English Language Assessment Battery (minimum score 77), Cambridge A, B, C. *Application deadline:* For fall admission, 7/15 priority date for domestic students, 6/1 for international students; for spring admission, 11/15 priority date for domestic students, 11/1 for international students. Applications are processed on a rolling basis. Application fee: $50. Electronic applications accepted. *Expenses:* Tuition: Part-time $773 per credit. Required fees: $157 per semester. *Financial support:* In 2009–10, 118 students received support, including 96 fellowships (averaging $1,308 per year), 4 research assistantships (averaging $3,610 per year); career-related internships or fieldwork, scholarships/grants, and unspecified assistantships also available. Support available to part-time students. Financial award applicants required to submit FAFSA. *Faculty research:* Relationship of undergraduate GPA and GRE to succeed in a graduate nursing program. *Unit head:* Dr. Janet Mahoney, Dean, 732-571-3443, Fax: 732-263-5131, E-mail: jmahoney@monmouth.edu. *Application contact:* Kevin Roane, Director, Office of Graduate Admission, 732-571-3452, Fax: 732-263-5123, E-mail: gradadm@monmouth.edu.

Saint Joseph's University, College of Arts and Sciences, Department of Health Services, Philadelphia, PA 19131-1395. Offers health administration (MS, Post-Master's Certificate); health care ethics (Post-Master's Certificate); health education (MS, Post-Master's Certificate); health informatics (Post-Master's Certificate); healthcare ethics (MS); nurse anesthesia (MS); school nurse certification (MS). Part-time and evening/weekend programs available. *Students:* 10 full-time (5 women), 180 part-time (135 women); includes 67 minority (50 African Americans, 11 Asian Americans or Pacific Islanders, 6 Hispanic Americans), 8 international. Average age 36. In 2009, 72 master's awarded. *Entrance requirements:* For master's, GRE (if GPA less than 2.75), 2 letters of recommendation, minimum GPA of 2.75, resume. Additional exam requirements/recommendations for international students: Required—TOEFL (minimum score 550 paper-based; 213 computer-based; 79 iBT). *Application deadline:* For fall admission, 7/15 priority date for domestic students, 4/15 for international students; for winter admission, 1/15 for international students; for spring admission, 11/15 priority date for domestic students, 10/15 for international students. Applications are processed on a rolling basis. Application fee: $35. Electronic applications accepted. *Expenses:* Tuition: Part-time $729 per credit hour. Tuition and fees vary according to degree level and program. *Financial support:* Career-related internships or fieldwork and unspecified assistantships available. Financial award applicants required to submit FAFSA. *Unit head:* Nakia Henderson, Director, 610-660-2952, E-mail: nakia.henderson@sju.edu. *Application contact:* Kate McConnell, Director, Graduate College of Arts and Sciences Admissions and Retention, 610-660-3184, Fax: 610-660-3230, E-mail: kate.mcconnell@sju.edu.

Seton Hall University, College of Nursing, South Orange, NJ 07079-2697. Offers advanced practice in primary health care (MSN), including adult nurse practitioner, gerontological nurse practitioner, pediatric nurse practitioner; entry into practice (MSN); health systems administration (MSN, DNP); nursing (PhD); nursing case management (MSN); nursing education (MA); school nurse (MSN); MSN/MA. *Accreditation:* AACN. Part-time programs available. Post-baccalaureate distance learning degree programs offered (minimal on-campus study). *Faculty:* 10 full-time (all women), 3 part-time/adjunct (1 woman). *Students:* 46 full-time (35 women), 94 part-time (90 women); includes 22 minority (8 African Americans, 5 Asian Americans or Pacific Islanders, 9 Hispanic Americans). 92 applicants, 88% accepted, 55 enrolled. *Degree requirements:* For master's, research project; for doctorate, dissertation or scholarly project. *Entrance requirements:* For doctorate, GRE. Additional exam requirements/recommendations for international students: Required—TOEFL. *Application deadline:* For fall admission, 6/15 priority date for domestic students. Applications are processed on a rolling basis. Electronic applications accepted. *Financial support:* Institutionally sponsored loans, scholarships/grants, traineeships, tuition waivers (partial), and unspecified assistantships available. Support available to part-time students. Financial award applicants required to submit FAFSA. *Faculty research:* Parent/child, adult, and gerontological nursing; breast cancer; families of children with HIV; parish nursing. *Unit head:* Dr. Phyllis Shanley Hansell, Dean. *Application contact:* Kristyn Kent Wuillermin, Director of Strategic Alliances, Marketing and Enrollment, 973-761-9291, Fax: 973-761-9607, E-mail: kristyn.kent@shu.edu.

University of Illinois at Chicago, Graduate College, College of Nursing, Program in Nursing, Chicago, IL 60607-7128. Offers acute care clinical nurse specialist (MS); acute care nurse practitioner (MS); administrative studies in nursing (MS); adult nurse practitioner (MS); adult/geriatric nurse practitioner (MS); advanced community health nurse specialist (MS); family nurse practitioner (MS); geriatric clinical nurse specialist (MS); geriatric nurse practitioner (MS); mental health clinical nurse specialist (MS); mental health nurse practitioner (MS); nurse midwifery (MS); occupational health/advanced community health nurse specialist (MS); occupational health/family nurse practitioner (MS); pediatric clinical nurse specialist (MS); pediatric nurse practitioner (MS); perinatal clinical nurse specialist (MS); school/advanced community health nurse specialist (MS); school/family nurse practitioner (MS); women's health nurse practitioner (MS). *Accreditation:* AACN. Part-time programs available. *Degree requirements:* For master's, thesis or alternative. *Entrance requirements:* For master's, GRE General Test, minimum GPA of 2.75. Additional exam requirements/recommendations for international students: Required—TOEFL. Electronic applications accepted.

West Chester University of Pennsylvania, Office of Graduate Studies, College of Health Sciences, Department of Nursing, West Chester, PA 19383. Offers administration (MSN); integrative health (MSN); nursing education (MSN, Certificate); school nursing (Teaching Certificate). *Accreditation:* AACN. Part-time and evening/weekend programs available. *Students:* 3 full-time (all women), 34 part-time (33 women); includes 2 minority (1 African American, 1 Asian American or Pacific Islander). Average age 42. 15 applicants, 100% accepted, 10 enrolled. In 2009, 10 master's awarded. *Entrance requirements:* For master's, RN license, BSN, minimum GPA of 2.8, two years' full-time experience as a clinical care nurse, three letters of recommendation; for other advanced degree, BSN, RN license, minimum GPA of 3.0 in last 48 nursing credits. Additional exam requirements/recommendations for international students: Required—TOEFL (minimum score 550 paper-based; 213 computer-based; 80 iBT). *Application deadline:* For fall admission, 4/15 priority date for domestic students, 3/15 for international students; for spring admission, 10/15 for domestic students, 9/1 for international students. Applications are processed on a rolling basis. Application fee: $35. Electronic applications accepted. *Expenses:* Tuition, state resident: full-time $6666; part-time $370 per credit. Tuition, nonresident: full-time $10,666; part-time $593 per credit. Required fees: $122.56 per credit. *Financial support:* In 2009–10, 1 research assistantship with full and partial tuition reimbursement (averaging $5,000 per year) was awarded; unspecified assistantships also available. Support available to part-time students. Financial award application deadline: 2/15; financial award applicants required to submit FAFSA. *Faculty research:* Violence against women. *Unit head:* Dr. Charlotte Mackey, Chair, 610-436-3474, E-mail: cmackey@wcupa.edu. *Application contact:* Ann Coghlan Stowe, Graduate Coordinator, 610-436-2331, E-mail: astowe@wcupa.edu.

Wright State University, School of Graduate Studies, College of Nursing and Health, Program in Nursing, Dayton, OH 45435. Offers acute care nurse practitioner (MS); administration of nursing and health care systems (MS); adult health (MS); child and adolescent health (MS); community health (MS); family nurse practitioner (MS); nurse practitioner (MS); school nurse (MS); MBA/MS. *Accreditation:* AACN. Part-time and evening/weekend programs available. *Degree requirements:* For master's, thesis or alternative. *Entrance requirements:* For master's, GRE General Test, BSN from NLN-accredited college, Ohio RN license. Additional exam requirements/recommendations for international students: Required—TOEFL. *Faculty research:* Clinical nursing and health, teaching, caring, pain administration, informatics and technology.

Transcultural Nursing

Augsburg College, Program in Transcultural Community Health Nursing, Minneapolis, MN 55454-1351. Offers MA. *Accreditation:* AACN. *Degree requirements:* For master's, thesis or alternative. *Expenses:* Tuition: Full-time $16,713; part-time $1857 per course. Required fees: $450; $50 per course. Tuition and fees vary according to course load and program.

University of Medicine and Dentistry of New Jersey, School of Nursing, Program in Urban Health, Newark, NJ 07107-1709. Offers PhD. Part-time and evening/weekend programs available. *Entrance requirements:* Additional exam requirements/recommendations for international students: Required—TOEFL. Electronic applications accepted.

Women's Health Nursing

Case Western Reserve University, Frances Payne Bolton School of Nursing, Doctor of Nursing Practice Program, Cleveland, OH 44106. Offers acute care nurse practitioner (DNP); adult nurse practitioner (DNP); family nurse practitioner (DNP); gerontological nurse practitioner (DNP); graduate entry/pre-licensure option (DNP); medical-surgical nursing (DNP); midwifery/family nursing (DNP); neonatal nurse practitioner (DNP); pediatric nurse practitioner (DNP); post-licensure option (DNP); psychiatric-mental health nurse practitioner (DNP); women's health nurse practitioner (DNP). Graduate entry option allows baccalaureate-prepared college graduates from non-nursing backgrounds to earn certificate and MSN in addition to ND. Terminal master's awarded for partial completion of doctoral program. *Degree requirements:* For doctorate, thesis/dissertation. *Entrance requirements:* For doctorate, GRE General Test or MAT. *Faculty research:* Clinical nursing, acute care, gerontology, mental health, critical care.

Case Western Reserve University, Frances Payne Bolton School of Nursing, Master's Programs in Nursing, Nurse Practitioner Program, Cleveland, OH 44106. Offers acute care cardiovascular nursing (MSN); acute care nurse practitioner (MSN); acute care/flight nurse (MSN); adult nurse practitioner (MSN); family nurse practitioner (MSN); gerontological nurse practitioner (MSN); neonatal nurse practitioner (MSN); pediatric nurse practitioner (MSN); psychiatric-mental health nurse practitioner (MSN); women's health nurse practitioner (MSN). *Accreditation:* NLN. Part-time programs available. Postbaccalaureate distance learning degree programs offered (minimal on-campus study). *Degree requirements:* For master's, thesis optional. *Entrance requirements:* For master's, GRE General Test or MAT. Additional exam requirements/recommendations for international students: Required—TOEFL. *Faculty research:* Positive and negative mood states in parents of twins, effect of a carepath on chronic obstructive pulmonary disease home care.

Columbia University, School of Nursing, Program in Women's Health Nurse Practitioner, New York, NY 10032. Offers Adv C. *Accreditation:* AACN. Part-time programs available. *Entrance requirements:* For degree, MSN. Electronic applications accepted.

Emory University, Nell Hodgson Woodruff School of Nursing, Atlanta, GA 30322-1100. Offers adult and elder health advanced practice nursing (MSN), including acute care, adult nurse practitioner, gerontological nurse practitioner; emergency nurse practitioner (MSN); family nurse practitioner (MSN); family nurse-midwife (MSN); nurse midwifery (MSN); pediatric nurse practitioner acute and primary care (MSN); public health nursing leadership (MSN); women's health nurse practitioner (MSN); women's health title x (MSN); women's health/adult health nurse practitioner (MSN); MSN/MPH. *Accreditation:* AACN; ACNM/DOA (one or more programs are accredited). Part-time programs available. *Faculty:* 30 full-time (29 women), 11 part-time/adjunct (10 women). *Students:* 110 full-time (106 women), 53 part-time (51 women); includes 49 minority (35 African Americans, 2 American Indian/Alaska Native, 10 Asian Americans or Pacific Islanders, 2 Hispanic Americans), 4 international. Average age 32. 182 applicants, 63% accepted, 86 enrolled. In 2009, 81 master's awarded. *Entrance requirements:* For master's, GRE General Test or MAT, minimum GPA of 3.0, BS in nursing from an accredited institution, RN license and additional course work, 3 letters of recommendation. Additional exam requirements/recommendations for international students: Required—TOEFL (minimum score 600 paper-based; 100 iBT). *Application deadline:* For fall admission, 1/15 priority date for domestic and international students; for spring admission, 10/1 priority date for domestic and international students. Applications are processed on a rolling basis. Application fee: $50. Electronic applications accepted. *Expenses:* Contact institution. *Financial support:* In 2009–10, 14 fellowships (averaging $28,000 per year) were awarded; career-related internships or fieldwork, Federal Work-Study, institutionally sponsored loans, and scholarships/grants also available. Support available to part-time students. Financial award application deadline: 3/1; financial award applicants required to submit CSS PROFILE or FAFSA. *Faculty research:* Older adult falls and injuries, minority health issues, cardiac symptoms and quality of life, bio-ethics and decision making, menopausal issues. *Unit head:* Dr. Linda McCauley, Dean, 404-727-7976, Fax: 404-727-9800, E-mail: linda.mccauley@emory.edu. *Application contact:* Katie Kennedy, Associate Director for Admission and Financial Aid, 404-727-7980, Fax: 404-727-8509, E-mail: admit@nursing.emory.edu.

See Close-Up on page 1613.

Frontier School of Midwifery and Family Nursing, Graduate Programs, Hyden, KY 41749. Offers community-based family nurse practitioner (MSN, Post Master's Certificate); community-based nurse-midwifery education (MSN, Post Master's Certificate); community-based women[0092]s health care nurse practitioner (MSN, Post Master's Certificate). *Accreditation:* ACNM; NLN.

Georgia Southern University, Jack N. Averitt College of Graduate Studies, College of Health and Human Sciences, School of Nursing, Statesboro, GA 30460. Offers clinical nurse specialist (MSN, Certificate); nurse practitioner (MSN, Certificate); nursing science (DNP); rural community health nurse practitioner (MSN); rural community health nurse specialist (Certificate); rural family nurse practitioner (MSN, Certificate); women's health nurse practitioner (MSN, Certificate). *Accreditation:* AACN. Part-time programs available. Postbaccalaureate distance learning degree programs offered. *Students:* 12 full-time (all women), 89 part-time (80 women); includes 17 minority (11 African Americans, 1 American Indian/Alaska Native, 3 Asian Americans or Pacific Islanders, 2 Hispanic Americans). Average age 39. 34 applicants, 85% accepted, 24 enrolled. In 2009, 7 master's awarded. *Degree requirements:* For master's, comprehensive exam, thesis optional; for doctorate, clinical immersion project, capstone practicum. *Entrance requirements:* For master's, GRE General Test or MAT, minimum GPA of 3.0, Georgia nursing license, 2 years of clinical experience, CPR certification; for doctorate, GRE, MAT, portfolio, certification, RN licensure, clinical hours; for Certificate, MSN. Additional exam requirements/recommendations for international students: Required—TOEFL (minimum score 550 paper-based; 213 computer-based; 80 iBT). *Application deadline:* For fall admission, 3/1 priority date for domestic and international students; for spring admission, 10/1 priority date for domestic students, 10/1 for international students. Applications are processed on a rolling basis. Application fee: $50. Electronic applications accepted. *Expenses:* Tuition, state resident: full-time $5040; part-time $210 per credit hour. Tuition, nonresident: full-time $20,136; part-time $839 per credit hour. Required fees: $1644. *Financial support:* In 2009–10, 101 students received support, including research assistantships with partial tuition reimbursements available (averaging $7,200 per year), teaching assistantships with partial tuition reimbursements available (averaging $7,200 per year); career-related internships or fieldwork, Federal Work-Study, scholarships/grants, traineeships, tuition waivers (partial), and unspecified assistantships also available. Support available to part-time students. Financial award application deadline: 4/15; financial award applicants required to submit FAFSA. *Faculty research:* Obesity, cardiac disease, rural healthcare, nursing education, health literacy. Total annual research expenditures: $189,915. *Unit head:* Dr. Donna Hodnicki, Chair, 912-478-5056, Fax: 912-478-0536, E-mail: dhodnick@georgiasouthern.edu. *Application contact:* Dr. Charles Ziglar, Coordinator for Graduate Student Recruitment, 912-478-5635, Fax: 912-478-0740, E-mail: gradadmissionss@georgiasouthern.edu.

Georgia State University, College of Health and Human Sciences, Byrdine F. Lewis School of Nursing, Atlanta, GA 30302-3083. Offers adult health (MS); adult health nursing (Certificate); child health (MS); family nurse practitioner (MS, Certificate); health promotion, protection and restoration (PhD); perinatal/women's health (MS); psychiatric mental health nursing (Certificate); psychiatric/mental health (MS); women's health nursing (Certificate). *Accreditation:* AACN. Part-time and evening/weekend programs available. Postbaccalaureate distance learning degree programs offered (minimal on-campus study). *Degree requirements:* For master's, research activity; for doctorate, comprehensive exam, thesis/dissertation. *Entrance requirements:* For master's, MAT (preferred) or GRE, interview, RN license; for doctorate, GRE General Test. Additional exam requirements/recommendations for international students: Required—TOEFL (minimum score 550 paper-based; 213 computer-based). Electronic applications accepted. *Expenses:* Contact institution. *Faculty research:* Breast cancer prevention, sexually compulsive behaviors, health risks in minority youth, asthma treatment strategies, adolescent alcohol-related issues.

Hampton University, Graduate College, School of Nursing, Hampton, VA 23668. Offers advanced adult nursing (MS); community health nursing (MS); community mental health/psychiatric nursing (MS); family nursing (MS); gerontological nursing for the nurse practitioner (MS); pediatric nursing (MS); women's health nursing (MS). *Accreditation:* AACN; NLN. Part-time and evening/weekend programs available. *Degree requirements:* For master's, thesis optional. *Entrance requirements:* For master's, GRE General Test. *Faculty research:* Curriculum development, physical and mental assessment.

Indiana University–Purdue University Fort Wayne, College of Health and Human Services, Department of Nursing, Fort Wayne, IN 46805-1499. Offers adult nursing practice (MS); nursing administration (MS, Certificate); nursing education (MS); women's health nursing practice (MS). Part-time programs available. *Faculty:* 7 full-time (all women), 1 (woman) part-time/adjunct. *Students:* 5 full-time (all women), 34 part-time (32 women); includes 4 minority (3 African Americans, 1 American Indian/Alaska Native). Average age 37. 15 applicants, 93% accepted, 11 enrolled. *Entrance requirements:* For master's, GRE Writing Test (if GPA below 3.0), BS in nursing, eligibility for Indiana RN license, minimum GPA of 3.0, essay, copy of resume, three references, undergraduate course work in research and statistics within last 5 years. Additional exam requirements/recommendations for international students: Required—TOEFL (minimum score 550 paper-based; 213 computer-based; 77 iBT); Recommended—TWE. *Application deadline:* For fall admission, 5/1 priority date for domestic and international students. Applications are processed on a rolling basis. Application fee: $55 ($60 for international students). Electronic applications accepted. *Expenses:* Tuition, state resident: full-time $4595; part-time $255 per credit. Tuition, nonresident: full-time $10,963; part-time $609 per credit. Required fees: $528; $29.35 per credit. Tuition and fees vary according to course load. *Financial support:* In 2009–10, 11 teaching assistantships with partial tuition reimbursements (averaging $12,740 per year) were awarded; scholarships/grants also available. Support available to part-time students. Financial award application deadline: 3/1; financial award applicants required to submit FAFSA. *Unit head:* Dr. Carol Sternberger, Chair, 260-481-6816, Fax: 260-481-5767, E-mail: sternber@ipfw.edu. *Application contact:* Dr. Susan Ahrens, Graduate Program Director, 260-481-6816, Fax: 260-481-5767, E-mail: ahrenss@ipfw.edu.

Indiana University–Purdue University Indianapolis, School of Nursing, Indianapolis, IN 46202-2896. Offers acute care nurse practitioner (MSN); adult health clinical nurse specialist (MSN); adult health nursing (MSN), including adult clinical nurse specialist; adult nurse practitioner (MSN); adult psychiatric/mental health nursing (MSN); child psychiatric/mental health nursing (MSN); community health nursing (MSN); family nurse practitioner (MSN); neonatal nurse practitioner (MSN); nursing science (PhD); pediatric clinical nurse specialist (MSN); women's health nurse practitioner (MSN); MSN/MPA; MSN/MPH. *Accreditation:* AACN; NLN (one or more programs are accredited). Part-time programs available. *Faculty:* 85 full-time (82 women), 60 part-time/adjunct (all women). *Students:* 46 full-time (43 women), 369 part-time (354 women); includes 30 minority (21 African Americans, 6 Asian Americans or Pacific Islanders, 3 Hispanic Americans), 5 international. Average age 39. 121 applicants, 82% accepted, 67 enrolled. In 2009, 106 master's, 3 doctorates awarded. Terminal master's awarded for partial completion of doctoral program. *Degree requirements:* For master's, thesis; for doctorate, thesis/dissertation. *Entrance requirements:* For master's, minimum GPA of 3.0, RN license; for doctorate, GRE General Test, minimum GPA of 3.0, MSN, RN license, graduate statistics course with B grade or better (not older than 3 years). Additional exam requirements/recommendations for international students: Required—TOEFL. *Application deadline:* For fall admission, 2/15 for domestic students; for spring admission, 9/15 for domestic students. Application fee: $55 ($65 for international students). *Financial support:* In 2009–10, 93 students received support, including 9 fellowships with full tuition reimbursements available (averaging $7,039 per year), 7 teaching assistantships with full tuition reimbursements available (averaging $5,300 per year); research assistantships with full tuition reimbursements available, Federal Work-Study, institutionally sponsored loans, scholarships/grants, and tuition waivers (full) also available. Support available to part-time students. Financial award application deadline: 5/1. *Faculty research:* Clinical science, health systems. Total annual research expenditures: $3 million. *Unit head:* Associate Dean for Graduate Programs, 317-274-2806, E-mail: nursing@iupui.edu. *Application contact:* Information Contact, 317-274-2806.

The Johns Hopkins University, School of Nursing, Nurse Practitioner Program, Baltimore, MD 21218-2699. Offers adult acute/critical care (MSN, Certificate); adult and pediatric primary care (MSN); adult or pediatric primary care (Certificate); emergency preparedness/disaster response (Certificate); family primary care (MSN, Certificate); women's health (Certificate). *Accreditation:* AACN; NLN (one or more programs are accredited). Part-time programs available. *Faculty:* 9 full-time (all women), 10 part-time/adjunct (all women). *Students:* 28 full-time (27 women), 75 part-time (73 women); includes 33 minority (14 African Americans, 16 Asian Americans or Pacific Islanders, 3 Hispanic Americans), 3 international. Average age 31. 223 applicants, 80% accepted, 29 enrolled. In 2009, 37 master's awarded. *Degree requirements:* For master's, thesis optional, scholarly project or portfolio. *Entrance requirements:* For master's, GRE, interview, minimum GPA of 3.0, BSN, Maryland RN license. Additional exam requirements/recommendations for international students: Required—TOEFL (minimum score 550 paper-based; 213 computer-based). *Application deadline:* For fall admission, 3/1 priority date for domestic and international students; for spring admission, 7/1 priority date for domestic and international students. Application fee: $75. Electronic applications accepted. *Expenses:* Contact institution. *Financial support:* In 2009–10, 25 students received support. Federal Work-Study, scholarships/grants, traineeships, and tuition waivers (partial) available. Support available to part-time students. Financial award application deadline: 3/1; financial award applicants required to submit FAFSA. *Faculty research:* Community outreach, primary care of underserved populations, substance abusing individuals, childhood violence, women's health. *Unit head:* Dr. Julie A. Stanik-Hutt, Director, Master's Programs, 410-502-0184, Fax: 410-955-7463, E-mail: jstanik1@son.jhmi.edu. *Application contact:* Mary O'Rourke, Director of Admissions and Student Services, 410-955-7548, Fax: 410-614-7086, E-mail: orourke@son.jhmi.edu.

Kent State University, College of Nursing, Kent, OH 44242-0001. Offers adult nurse practitioner (MSN); family nurse practitioner (MSN); geriatric nurse practitioner (MSN); nursing (PhD); nursing and health care management (MSN); nursing of adults (clinical nurse specialist) (MSN); pediatric nurse practitioner (MSN); psychiatric/mental health nursing (MSN); women's health nursing (MSN). *Accreditation:* AACN. Part-time programs available. *Degree requirements:* For master's, thesis optional; for doctorate, comprehensive exam, thesis/dissertation. *Entrance requirements:* For master's, GRE (if undergraduate GPA less than 3.0), minimum GPA of 2.75; for doctorate, GRE, MSN. Additional exam requirements/recommendations for international students: Required—TOEFL. Electronic applications accepted. *Expenses:* Contact institution. *Faculty research:* Women and violence, methodological specialties, osteoporosis in women, new caregivers and the elderly.

Loyola University Chicago, Graduate School, Marcella Niehoff School of Nursing, Women's Health Nurse Practitioner Program, Chicago, IL 60660. Offers MSN. *Accreditation:* AACN. Part-time and evening/weekend programs available. *Students:* 16 part-time (all women); includes 5 minority (4 African Americans, 1 Asian American or Pacific Islander). Average age 32. 9 applicants, 44% accepted, 4 enrolled. In 2009, 1 master's awarded. *Degree requirements:* For master's, comprehensive exam or oral thesis defense. *Entrance requirements:* For master's, BSN, minimum nursing GPA of 3.0, 1000 hours experience before starting clinical, Illinois nursing license, 3 letters of reference. *Application deadline:* Applications are processed on a rolling basis. Application fee: $50. Electronic applications accepted. *Expenses:* Tuition: Full-time $14,220; part-time $790 per credit hour. Required fees: $60 per semester hour. Tuition and fees vary according to program. *Financial support:* Teaching assistantships, traineeships available. Financial award application deadline: 3/1. *Faculty research:* Breast feeding, postpartum depression, pre-term labor toxicity. *Unit head:* Dr. Penny Marzalik, Associate Professor, 708-216-9101, Fax: 708-216-9555, E-mail: pmarzal@luc.edu. *Application contact:* Dr. Vicki A. Keough, Associate Dean, 773-216-3582, Fax: 708-216-9555, E-mail: vkeough@luc.edu.

Metropolitan State University, College of Nursing and Health Sciences, St. Paul, MN 55106-5000. Offers adult/geriatric nurse practitioner (MSN); family nurse practitioner (MSN); leadership and management (MSN); nursing (MSN, DNP); oral health care practitioner (MS); public health nursing leadership (MSN); women's health care nurse practitioner (MSN). *Accreditation:* AACN. Part-time programs available. *Degree requirements:* For master's, thesis or alternative; for doctorate, thesis/dissertation or alternative. *Entrance requirements:* For master's, GRE General Test, minimum GPA of 3.0, RN license, B.S./BAN degree; for doctorate, minimum GPA of 3.0; RN licensure, MSN degree. Additional exam requirements/recommendations for international students: Required—TOEFL (minimum score 550 paper-based; 213 computer-based). *Expenses:* Tuition, state resident: full-time $5520; part-time $276 per credit hour. Tuition, nonresident: full-time $11,040; part-time $552 per credit hour. Required fees: $209; $10 per credit hour. Tuition and fees vary according to degree level. *Faculty research:* Women's health, gerontology.

MGH Institute of Health Professions, Graduate Programs, School of Nursing, Boston, MA 02129. Offers advanced practice nursing (MSN); gerontological nursing (MSN); nursing (DNP); pediatric nursing (MSN); psychiatric nursing (MSN); teaching and learning for health care education (Certificate); women's health nursing (MSN). *Accreditation:* AACN; NLN (one or more programs are accredited). *Faculty:* 37 full-time (33 women), 11 part-time/adjunct (10 women). *Students:* 325 full-time (275 women), 72 part-time (59 women); includes 48 minority (22 African Americans, 1 American Indian/Alaska Native, 18 Asian Americans or Pacific Islanders, 7 Hispanic Americans). Average age 31. 840 applicants, 53% accepted, 221 enrolled. In 2009, 78 master's, 12 doctorates, 45 other advanced degrees awarded. *Degree requirements:* For master's, thesis or alternative. *Entrance requirements:* For master's, GRE General Test. Additional exam requirements/recommendations for international students: Required—TOEFL (minimum score 550 paper-based; 213 computer-based; 80 iBT). *Application deadline:* For fall admission, 1/10 for domestic and international students. Application fee: $50. Electronic applications accepted. *Expenses:* Tuition: Part-time $943 per credit. Required fees: $943 per credit. Tuition and fees vary according to course load. *Financial support:* In 2009–10, 292 students received support, including 1 research assistantship (averaging $1,200 per year), 2 teaching assistantships (averaging $1,200 per year); career-related internships or fieldwork, scholarships/grants, traineeships, tuition waivers (full and partial), and unspecified assistantships also available. Support available to part-time students. Financial award application deadline: 3/1; financial award applicants required to submit FAFSA. *Faculty research:* Biobehavioral nursing, HIV/AIDS, gerontological nursing, women's health, vulnerable populations, health systems. *Unit head:* Margery Chisholm, Dean, 617-724-0480, Fax: 617-726-8022, E-mail: mchisholm@mghihp.edu. *Application contact:* Maureen Rika Judd, Manager of Admissions, 617-726-6069, Fax: 617-726-8010, E-mail: admissions@mghihp.edu.

Old Dominion University, College of Health Sciences, School of Nursing, Norfolk, VA 23529. Offers family nurse practitioner (MSN); nurse anesthesia (MSN); nurse educator (MSN); nurse midwifery (MSN); women's health nurse practitioner (MSN). *Accreditation:* AACN; AANA/CANAEP. Part-time programs available. Postbaccalaureate distance learning degree programs offered (no on-campus study). *Faculty:* 11 full-time (10 women), 15 part-time/adjunct (14 women). *Students:* 122 full-time (113 women), 101 part-time (97 women); includes 49 minority (23 African Americans, 2 American Indian/Alaska Native, 19 Asian Americans or Pacific Islanders, 5 Hispanic Americans). Average age 37. 169 applicants, 81% accepted, 122 enrolled. In 2009, 77 master's awarded. *Degree requirements:* For master's, comprehensive exam. *Entrance requirements:* For master's, GRE or MAT, BSN, minimum GPA of 3.0 in nursing and overall. Additional exam requirements/recommendations for international students: Required—TOEFL. *Application deadline:* For fall admission, 5/1 for domestic students. Applications are processed on a rolling basis. Application fee: $40. Electronic applications accepted. *Expenses:* Tuition, state resident: full-time $8112; part-time $338 per credit. Tuition, nonresident: full-time $20,256; part-time $844 per credit. Required fees: $119 per semester. One-time fee: $50. *Financial support:* In 2009–10, 18 students received support, including 2 research assistantships with tuition reimbursements available (averaging $10,000 per year); teaching assistantships, career-related internships or fieldwork, scholarships/grants, traineeships, and tuition waivers (partial) also available. Support available to part-time students. Financial award application deadline: 2/15; financial award applicants required to submit FAFSA. *Faculty research:* Health and culture, cardiovascular health, transition of military families, genetics, cultural diversity. Total annual research expenditures: $231,117. *Unit head:* Dr. Karen Karlowicz, Chair, 757-683-5262, Fax: 757-683-5253, E-mail: nursgpd@odu.edu. *Application contact:* Sue Parker, Coordinator, Graduate Student Services, 757-683-4298, Fax: 757-683-5253, E-mail: sparker@odu.edu.

Queen's University at Kingston, School of Graduate Studies and Research, Faculty of Health Sciences, School of Nursing, Kingston, ON K7L 3N6, Canada. Offers health and chronic illness (M Sc); nurse scientist (PhD); primary health care nurse practitioner (Certificate); women's and children's health (M Sc). *Degree requirements:* For master's, thesis. *Entrance requirements:* For master's, RN license. Additional exam requirements/recommendations for international students: Required—TOEFL. *Faculty research:* Women and children's health, health and chronic illness.

Rosalind Franklin University of Medicine and Science, College of Health Professions, Department of Interprofessional Healthcare Studies, Women's Healthcare Studies Program, North Chicago, IL 60064-3095. Offers MS, Certificate. Part-time and evening/weekend programs available. Postbaccalaureate distance learning degree programs offered (minimal on-campus study). *Faculty:* 2 full-time (both women), 5 part-time/adjunct (3 women). *Students:* 3 part-time (all women); includes 1 minority (Hispanic American). Average age 39. 1 applicant, 100% accepted, 1 enrolled. *Degree requirements:* For master's, thesis optional, project. *Entrance requirements:* For master's, licensure/registration/certification in clinical health field, minimum GPA of 3.0, BS or BA. Additional exam requirements/recommendations for international students: Required—TOEFL. *Application deadline:* For fall admission, 8/5 for domestic students; for winter admission, 10/29 for domestic students; for spring admission, 2/5 for domestic students. Applications are processed on a rolling basis. Application fee: $50. *Financial support:* Institutionally sponsored loans available. Support available to part-time students. Financial award application deadline: 6/9; financial award applicants required to submit FAFSA. *Unit head:* Dr. Susan K. Tappert, Chair, 847-578-8693, Fax: 847-578-8623, E-mail: susan.tappert@rosalindfranklin.edu. *Application contact:* Melissa Knox, Admissions Officer, 847-578-8772, Fax: 847-775-6559, E-mail: melissa.knox@rosalindfranklin.edu.

Stony Brook University, State University of New York, Stony Brook University Medical Center, Health Sciences Center, School of Nursing, Program in Perinatal Women's Health Nursing, Stony Brook, NY 11794. Offers MS, Certificate. *Accreditation:* AACN. Postbaccalaureate distance learning degree programs offered. *Students:* 2 full-time (both women), 25 part-time (all women); includes 6 minority (4 African Americans, 2 Hispanic Americans). In 2009, 2 master's awarded. *Degree requirements:* For master's, thesis. *Entrance requirements:* For master's, BSN, minimum GPA of 3.0, course work in statistics. *Application deadline:* For fall admission, 1/15 for domestic students. Application fee: $60. *Expenses:* Tuition, state resident: full-time $8370; part-time $349 per credit. Tuition, nonresident: full-time $13,250; part-time $552 per credit. Required fees: $933. *Financial support:* Application deadline: 3/15. *Unit head:* Prof. Arleen Steckel, Chair, 631-444-3298, Fax: 631-444-3136. *Application contact:* Dr. Kent Marks, Assistant Dean, Admissions and Records, 631-632-4723, Fax: 631-632-7243, E-mail: kmarks@notes.cc.sunysb.edu.

Texas Woman's University, Graduate School, College of Nursing, Denton, TX 76201. Offers acute care nurse practitioner (MS); adult health clinical nurse specialist (MS); adult health nurse practitioner (MS); child health clinical nurse specialist (MS); clinical nurse leader (MS); community health (MS); family nurse practitioner (MS); health systems management (MS); nursing education (MS); nursing practice (DNP); nursing science (PhD); pediatric nurse practitioner (MS); women's health clinical nurse specialist (MS); women's health nurse practitioner (MS). *Accreditation:* AACN. Part-time programs available. Postbaccalaureate distance learning degree programs offered. *Faculty:* 85 full-time (80 women), 6 part-time/adjunct (all women). *Students:* 81 full-time (76 women), 602 part-time (571 women); includes 293 minority (154 African Americans, 3 American Indian/Alaska Native, 90 Asian Americans or Pacific Islanders, 46 Hispanic Americans), 19 international. Average age 39. 259 applicants, 81% accepted, 166 enrolled. In 2009, 100 master's, 22 doctorates awarded. *Degree requirements:* For master's, thesis or alternative; for doctorate, comprehensive exam, thesis/dissertation. *Entrance requirements:* For master's, GRE or MAT, minimum GPA of 3.0, RN license, BS in nursing, basic statistics course; for doctorate, GRE (Verbal 460, Quantitative 500) or MAT (50), MS in nursing, minimum GPA of 3.5, RN license, coursework in statistics, 2 letters of reference, curriculum vitae, nursing-theory course, graduate research course, letter stating professional and research goals. Additional exam requirements/recommendations for international students: Required—TOEFL (minimum score 550 paper-based; 213 computer-based; 79 iBT). *Application deadline:* For fall admission, 5/1 priority date for domestic students, 3/1 for international students; for spring admission, 9/15 priority date for domestic students, 7/1 for international students. Applications are processed on a rolling basis. Application fee: $50. Electronic applications accepted. *Expenses:* Tuition, state resident: full-time $3564; part-time $198 per credit hour. Tuition, nonresident: full-time $8550; part-time $475 per credit hour. Required fees: $69.26 per credit hour. Tuition and fees vary according to course load. *Financial support:* In 2009–10, 99 students received support, including 16 fellowships (averaging $17,325 per year), 5 research assistantships (averaging $11,484 per year), 5 teaching assistantships (averaging $11,484 per year); career-related internships or fieldwork, Federal Work-Study, institutionally sponsored loans, scholarships/grants, traineeships, health care benefits, and unspecified assistantships also available. Support available to part-time students. Financial award application deadline: 3/1; financial award applicants required to submit FAFSA. *Faculty research:* Evaluation of pre-natal care, screening for intimate partner violence, stressors and nursing success, breast surgery, breast feeding, adolescent needs during childbirth. *Unit head:* Dr. Patricia Holden-Huchton, Interim Dean, 940-898-2401, Fax: 940-898-2437, E-mail: pholdenhuchton@twu.edu. *Application contact:* Samuel Wheeler, Assistant Director of Admissions, 940-898-3188, Fax: 940-898-3081, E-mail: wheelersr@twu.edu.

University of Cincinnati, Graduate School, College of Nursing, Cincinnati, OH 45221-0038. Offers clinical nurse specialist (MSN), including adult health, community health, neonatal, nursing administration, occupational health, pediatric health, psychiatric nursing, women's health; nurse anesthesia (MSN); nurse midwifery (MSN); nurse practitioner (MSN), including acute care, ambulatory care, family, family/psychiatric, women's health; nursing (PhD); MBA/MSN. *Accreditation:* AACN; AANA/CANAEP (one or more programs are accredited); ACNM/DOA. Part-time programs available. Postbaccalaureate distance learning degree programs offered (no on-campus study). Terminal master's awarded for partial completion of doctoral program. *Degree requirements:* For master's, thesis or alternative; for doctorate, comprehensive exam, thesis/dissertation. *Entrance requirements:* For master's and doctorate, GRE General Test. Additional exam requirements/recommendations for international students: Required—TOEFL (minimum score 520 paper-based; 190 computer-based). Electronic applications accepted. *Faculty research:* Substance abuse, injury and violence, symptom management.

University of Colorado at Colorado Springs, Graduate School, Beth-El College of Nursing and Health Sciences, Colorado Springs, CO 80933-7150. Offers adult health nurse practitioner and clinical specialist (MSN); family practitioner (MSN), including community clinical specialist, forensic clinical specialist, holistic clinical specialist; neonatal nurse practitioner and clinical specialist (MSN); nursing administration (MSN); nursing practice (DNP); women nurse practitioner (MSN). *Accreditation:* AACN. Part-time programs available. Postbaccalaureate distance learning degree programs offered (minimal on-campus study). *Faculty:* 26 full-time (21 women), 3 part-time/adjunct (all women). *Students:* 132 full-time (112 women), 81 part-time (71 women); includes 35 minority (6 African Americans, 2 American Indian/Alaska Native, 6 Asian Americans or Pacific Islanders, 21 Hispanic Americans), 3 international. Average age 36. 245 applicants, 47% accepted, 58 enrolled. In 2009, 33 master's awarded. *Degree requirements:* For master's, comprehensive exam, thesis optional; for doctorate, capstone project. *Entrance requirements:* For master's, GRE General Test or MAT, BSN, minimum GPA of 3.0, unrestricted RN license; for doctorate, interview; active RN license; MA; minimum GPA of 3.3; National Certification as NP or CNS; portfolio. Additional exam requirements/recommendations for international students: Required—TOEFL. *Application deadline:* For fall admission, 6/1 priority date for domestic students; for spring admission, 11/15 for domestic students. Application fee: $60 ($75 for international students). Electronic applications accepted. *Expenses:* Contact institution. *Financial support:* Fellowships, career-related internships or fieldwork, Federal Work-Study, and scholarships/grants available. Support available to part-time students. Financial award application deadline: 3/1; financial award applicants required to submit FAFSA. *Faculty research:* Women's health, uncertainty, empowerment, family experience in chronic illness. Total annual research expenditures: $703,545. *Unit head:* Dr. Nancy Smith, Dean, 719-255-4411, Fax: 719-255-4416, E-mail: nsmith2@uccs.edu. *Application contact:* Jackie Crouch, Graduate Recruitment Coordinator, 719-255-4493, Fax: 719-255-4416, E-mail: jcrouch@uccs.edu.

University of Delaware, College of Health Sciences, School of Nursing, Newark, DE 19716. Offers adult nurse practitioner (MSN, PMC); cardiopulmonary clinical nurse specialist (MSN, PMC); cardiopulmonary clinical nurse specialist/adult nurse practitioner (MSN, PMC); family nurse practitioner (MSN, PMC); gerontology clinical nurse specialist (MSN, PMC); gerontology clinical nurse specialist geriatric nurse practitioner (PMC); gerontology clinical nurse specialist/geriatric nurse practitioner (MSN); health services administration (MSN, PMC); nursing of children clinical nurse specialist (MSN, PMC); nursing of children clinical nurse specialist/pediatric nurse practitioner (MSN, PMC); oncology/immune deficiency clinical nurse specialist (MSN, PMC); oncology/immune deficiency clinical nurse specialist/adult nurse practitioner (MSN, PMC); perinatal/women's health clinical nurse specialist (MSN, PMC); perinatal/women's health clinical nurse specialist/women's health nurse practitioner (MSN, PMC); psychiatric nursing clinical nurse specialist (MSN, PMC). *Accreditation:* AACN; NLN (one or more programs are accredited). Part-time and evening/weekend programs available. Postbaccalaureate distance learning degree programs offered (minimal on-campus study). *Degree requirements:* For master's, thesis optional. *Entrance requirements:* For master's, BSN, interview, RN license. Electronic applications accepted. *Faculty research:* Marriage and chronic illness, health promotion, congestive heart failure patient outcomes, school nursing, diabetes in children, culture, health disparities, cardiovascular, prison nursing, oncology, public policy, child obesity, smoking and teen pregnancy, blood pressure measurements, men's health.

University of Illinois at Chicago, Graduate College, College of Nursing, Program in Nursing, Chicago, IL 60607-7128. Offers acute care clinical nurse specialist (MS); acute care nurse practitioner (MS); administrative studies in nursing (MS); adult nurse practitioner (MS); adult/geriatric nurse practitioner (MS); advanced community health nurse specialist (MS); family nurse practitioner (MS); geriatric clinical nurse specialist (MS); geriatric nurse practitioner (MS); mental health clinical nurse specialist (MS); mental health nurse practitioner (MS); nurse midwifery (MS); occupational health/advanced community health nurse specialist (MS); occupational health/family nurse practitioner (MS); pediatric clinical nurse specialist (MS); pediatric nurse practitioner (MS); perinatal clinical nurse specialist (MS); school/advanced community health nurse specialist (MS); school/family nurse practitioner (MS); women's health nurse practitioner (MS). *Accreditation:* AACN. Part-time programs available. *Degree requirements:* For master's, thesis or alternative. *Entrance requirements:* For master's, GRE General Test, minimum GPA of 2.75. Additional exam requirements/recommendations for international students: Required—TOEFL. Electronic applications accepted.

University of Medicine and Dentistry of New Jersey, School of Nursing, Newark, NJ 07107-3001. Offers adult health (MSN); adult occupational health (MSN); advanced practice nursing (MSN, Post Master's Certificate); family nurse practitioner (MSN); nurse anesthesia (MSN); nursing (MSN); nursing informatics (MSN); urban health (PhD); women's health practitioner (MSN). *Accreditation:* AANA/CANAEP; NLN (one or more programs are accredited). Part-time programs available. *Entrance requirements:* For master's, GRE, RN license; basic life support, statistics, and health assessment experience. Additional exam requirements/recommendations for international students: Required—TOEFL. Electronic applications accepted. *Expenses:* Contact institution. *Faculty research:* HIV/AIDS, diabetes education, learned helplessness, nursing science, psychoeducation.

Women's Health Nursing

University of Minnesota, Twin Cities Campus, Graduate School, School of Nursing, Program in Women's Health Nurse Practitioner, Minneapolis, MN 55455-0213. Offers MS. *Accreditation:* AACN. Postbaccalaureate distance learning degree programs offered (minimal on-campus study). *Entrance requirements:* Additional exam requirements/recommendations for international students: Required—TOEFL (minimum score 586 paper-based; 240 computer-based).

University of Missouri–Kansas City, School of Nursing, Kansas City, MO 64110-2499. Offers adult clinical nurse specialist (MSN), including adult nurse practitioner, women's health nurse practitioner; family nurse practitioner (MSN); neonatal nurse practitioner (MSN); nurse educator (MSN); nurse executive (MSN); nursing (PhD); nursing practice (DNP); pediatric nurse practitioner (MSN). *Accreditation:* AACN. Part-time programs available. Postbaccalaureate distance learning degree programs offered (minimal on-campus study). *Faculty:* 36 full-time (30 women), 40 part-time/adjunct (all women). *Students:* 31 full-time (26 women), 310 part-time (287 women); includes 38 minority (17 African Americans, 2 American Indian/Alaska Native, 10 Asian Americans or Pacific Islanders, 9 Hispanic Americans). Average age 36. 151 applicants, 72% accepted, 109 enrolled. In 2009, 57 master's, 10 doctorates awarded. *Degree requirements:* For master's, thesis or alternative. *Entrance requirements:* For master's, minimum undergraduate GPA of 3.2; for doctorate, GRE, 3 letters of reference, interview by invitation. Additional exam requirements/recommendations for international students: Required—TOEFL (minimum score 550 paper-based; 213 computer-based; 80 iBT). *Application deadline:* For fall admission, 2/1 priority date for domestic and international students; for spring admission, 9/1 priority date for domestic and international students. Application fee: $45 ($50 for international students). *Expenses:* Tuition, state resident: full-time $5378; part-time $299 per credit hour. Tuition, nonresident: full-time $13,881; part-time $771 per credit hour. Required fees: $641; $71 per credit hour. Tuition and fees vary according to course load and program. *Financial support:* In 2009–10, 6 teaching assistantships with partial tuition reimbursements (averaging $4,402 per year) were awarded; fellowships, research assistantships, career-related internships or fieldwork, Federal Work-Study, institutionally sponsored loans, and tuition waivers (full and partial) also available. Support available to part-time students. Financial award application deadline: 3/1; financial award applicants required to submit FAFSA. *Faculty research:* Geriatrics/gerontology, children's pain, neonatology, Alzheimer's care, cancer caregivers. Total annual research expenditures: $2.1 million. *Unit head:* Dr. Lora Lacey-Haun, Dean, 816-235-1700, Fax: 816-235-1701, E-mail: lacey-haunc@umkc.edu. *Application contact:* Leah Wilder, Coordinator for Admissions and Recruitment, 816-235-5768, Fax: 816-235-1701, E-mail: wilderl@umkc.edu.

The University of North Carolina at Chapel Hill, School of Nursing, Chapel Hill, NC 27599-7460. Offers nursing (MSN, PhD, PMC), including adult nurse practitioner (MSN, PMC), children's health advanced practice (MSN, PMC), family nurse practitioner (MSN, PMC), health care systems (MSN, PMC), psychiatric/mental health nursing (MSN, PMC), women's health nursing (MSN, PMC). *Accreditation:* AACN; NLN (one or more programs are accredited). Part-time programs available. *Degree requirements:* For master's, comprehensive exam, thesis; for doctorate, thesis/dissertation, 3 exams. *Entrance requirements:* For master's and doctorate, GRE General Test. *Faculty research:* Chronic illness, parenting, cardiovascular health in children, elderly, HIV-AIDS.

University of Pennsylvania, School of Nursing, Women's Healthcare Nurse Practitioner Program, Philadelphia, PA 19104. Offers MSN. *Accreditation:* AACN. Part-time programs available. Postbaccalaureate distance learning degree programs offered (minimal on-campus study). *Entrance requirements:* For master's, GRE General Test, BSN, minimum GPA of 3.0, previous course work in statistics, physical assessment experience. Additional exam requirements/recommendations for international students: Required—TOEFL. *Expenses:* Contact institution. *Faculty research:* New mother and infant healthcare follow-up, adequacy of antepartum care, models of healthcare.

University of South Carolina, The Graduate School, College of Nursing, Program in Clinical Nursing, Columbia, SC 29208. Offers acute care clinical specialist (MSN); acute care nurse practitioner (MSN); women's health nurse practitioner (MSN). *Accreditation:* AACN. Part-time programs available. *Degree requirements:* For master's, thesis or alternative. *Entrance requirements:* For master's, GRE General Test or MAT, BS in nursing, RN licensure. Additional exam requirements/recommendations for international students: Required—TOEFL (minimum score 570 paper-based; 230 computer-based). Electronic applications accepted. *Faculty research:* Systems research, evidence based practice, breast cancer, violence.

Vanderbilt University, School of Nursing, Nashville, TN 37240. Offers adult acute care nurse practitioner (MSN); adult nurse practitioner/cardiovascular disease management and prevention (MSN); adult nurse practitioner/palliative care (MSN); clinical management (clinical nurse leader/specialist) (MSN); emergency nurse practitioner (MSN); family nurse practitioner (MSN); gerontology nurse practitioner (MSN); health systems management (MSN); neonatal nurse practitioner (MSN); nurse midwifery (MSN); nurse midwifery/family nurse practitioner (MSN); nursing informatics (MSN); nursing practice (DNP); nursing science (PhD); nutrition (MS); pediatric acute care nurse practitioner (MSN); pediatric primary care nurse practitioner (MSN); psychiatric-mental health nurse practitioner (MSN); women's health nurse practitioner (MSN), including urogynecology; women's health nurse practitioner/adult nurse practitioner (MSN); MSN/M Div; MSN/MTS. *Accreditation:* ACNM/DOA; NLN (one or more programs are accredited). Part-time programs available. Postbaccalaureate distance learning degree programs offered (minimal on-campus study). *Faculty:* 118 full-time (102 women), 429 part-time/adjunct (309 women). *Students:* 484 full-time (435 women), 319 part-time (284 women); includes 84 minority (55 African Americans, 4 American Indian/Alaska Native, 10 Asian Americans or Pacific Islanders, 15 Hispanic Americans), 16 international. Average age 32. 900 applicants, 65% accepted, 433 enrolled. In 2009, 303 master's, 1 doctorate awarded. *Degree requirements:* For doctorate, comprehensive exam, thesis/dissertation. *Entrance requirements:* For master's, GRE General Test, minimum B average in undergraduate course work, 3 letters of recommendation; for doctorate, GRE General Test, interview, 3 letters of recommendation from doctorally-prepared faculty, MSN, essay. Additional exam requirements/recommendations for international students: Required—TOEFL. *Application deadline:* For fall admission, 12/1 priority date for domestic and international students. Applications are processed on a rolling basis. Application fee: $50. *Expenses:* Contact institution. *Financial support:* In 2009–10, 389 students received support, including 1 research assistantship (averaging $5,000 per year); teaching assistantships, scholarships/grants, health care benefits, and tuition waivers also available. Support available to part-time students. Financial award application deadline: 3/15; financial award applicants required to submit FAFSA. *Faculty research:* Lymphedema, palliative care and bereavement, health services research including workforce, safety and quality of care, gerontology, better birth outcomes including nutrition. Total annual research expenditures: $1.4 million. *Unit head:* Dr. Colleen Conway-Welch, Dean, 615-343-8776, Fax: 615-343-7711, E-mail: colleen.conway-welch@vanderbilt.edu. *Application contact:* Cheryl Feldner, Assistant Director of Admissions, 615-322-3800, Fax: 615-343-0333, E-mail: cheryl.feldner@vanderbilt.edu.

Virginia Commonwealth University, Graduate School, School of Nursing, Richmond, VA 23284-9005. Offers adult health nursing (MS); child health nursing (MS); family health nursing (MS); health system (PhD); immunocompetence (PhD); nurse practitioner (MS, Certificate); nursing administration (MS), including clinical nurse manager, nurse executive; psychiatric-mental health nursing (MS); risk and resilience (PhD); women's health nursing (MS). *Accreditation:* NLN (one or more programs are accredited). Part-time and evening/weekend programs available. *Degree requirements:* For master's, thesis optional; for doctorate, thesis/dissertation. *Entrance requirements:* For master's, GRE General Test, BSN, minimum GPA of 2.8; for doctorate, GRE General Test.

Wilmington University, College of Health Professions, New Castle, DE 19720-6491. Offers adult nurse practitioner (MSN); family nurse practitioner (MSN); gerontology (MSN); leadership (MSN); nursing (MSN); women's nurse practitioner (MSN). *Accreditation:* AACN. Part-time programs available. *Degree requirements:* For master's, thesis. *Entrance requirements:* For master's, BSN, RN license, interview, 3 letters of recommendation. Additional exam requirements/recommendations for international students: Required—TOEFL (minimum score 500 paper-based; 173 computer-based). Electronic applications accepted. *Faculty research:* Outcomes assessment, student writing ability.

BRIGHAM YOUNG UNIVERSITY

College of Nursing

Programs of Study

The Brigham Young University (BYU) College of Nursing offers a Master of Science (M.S.) degree that prepares students as family nurse practitioners (FNP). A post-master's family nurse practitioner degree is available for those who have already received a master's degree in nursing. Graduates are eligible to apply for certification examinations. The program can be completed in six semesters of full-time study.

Research Facilities

The research center offers work space for faculty members and students, research resources, research journals, and eight computer work stations. Current software includes several programs for quantitative and qualitative data analysis, media presentation preparation, scanning, and word processing. Statistical consultation services are available to students with data analysis during the thesis/project process.

Financial Aid

Tuition scholarships are available, along with research and teaching assistantships. Federal monies specific to nurses are available. University loans and Federal Stafford Student Loans are also available.

Cost of Study

Tuition at BYU is charged on the basis of the student's membership or nonmembership in the Church of Jesus Christ of Latter-Day Saints (LDS). Full-time graduate nursing students enrolled in the fall or winter semester pay $2790 if they are LDS members or $5580 if they are nonmembers. Those enrolled in the spring or summer term pay $1395 if they are LDS members or $2790 if they are nonmembers. Part-time tuition per credit hour is $310 for LDS students and $620 for non-LDS students. During fall and winter semesters, full-time study consists of 8.5 or more hours, and for spring and summer terms it consists of at least 4.5 credit hours.

Living and Housing Costs

A variety of on-campus and off-campus housing is available. A large number of off-campus apartments are also available.

Student Groups

There are approximately 30 students in the graduate program. Students gain knowledge and are provided opportunities to develop the commitment to service and lifelong learning. BYU students have a long tradition of a high pass rate on the certification examination, and are highly recruited.

Location

The University is nestled at the foot of the beautifully rugged Wasatch Range of the Rocky Mountains. The campus is the focal point of the Provo/Orem community of 163,000 people. The valley lies 45 miles south of Salt Lake City; it is bounded on the west by Utah Lake and on the east by the Wasatch Mountains. The setting offers a variety of recreational opportunities, including numerous ski resorts, mountain climbing, and spectacular national parks.

The University and The College

Brigham Young University is sponsored and operated by the Church of Jesus Christ of Latter-Day Saints. Founded in 1875, BYU is one of the largest privately owned, church-sponsored universities in the United States, with 1,283 faculty members and 32,955 students. Students represent all fifty states and more than 120 other countries. In keeping with an inscription at the campus entrance—"The world is our campus"—the University offers students many local and international learning experiences. Facilities and programs include a 793-acre research farm, a PBS television station, a 3-million-volume library, and study centers in Washington, D.C.; London; Vienna; and Jerusalem. Programs also extend into South America, the Middle East, Africa, Eastern Europe, and other parts of the world.

The College of Nursing was established in 1952. Following in the footsteps of pioneer nurses and midwives, College alumni have established a legacy of service as clinicians, nurse practitioners, administrators, educators, health and welfare missionaries, and scholars. The University and the College of Nursing endeavor to provide students with the broad-based education and skills necessary for becoming professionals and informed citizens.

Applying

Applicants can obtain application forms from the University Web site or the Office of Graduate Studies, B-356 ASB, Provo, Utah 84602-1339 (telephone: 801-422-4091). Application packages should include a statement of intent for graduate education, official transcripts of previous academic work, standardized test scores, and three letters of recommendation from former instructors or employers. Application may be made online or by regular mail. The deadline for submission of the form and supporting documents is December 1. Entry to both the M.S. program and the post-master's program is restricted to spring semester. A personal interview with faculty members and completion of a short writing exercise are necessary. The application fee is $50.

Correspondence and Information

Stephanie Wilson
Graduate Program
400 Spencer W. Kimball Tower (SWKT)
Brigham Young University
Provo, Utah 84602

Phone: 801-422-4142
Fax: 801-422-0538
E-mail: stephanie_wilson@byu.edu
Web site: http://nursing.byu.edu

Brigham Young University

THE FACULTY AND THEIR RESEARCH

Renea Beckstrand, Associate Professor; Ph.D., Utah, 2001. End of life and critical care.
Ana C. Birkhead, Assistant Professor, Ph.D., California, San Francisco, 2007. Hispanic women's health.
Kent Blad, Associate Teaching Professor; D.N.P., Utah, 2010. Acute care.
Beth Cole, Professor; Ph.D., BYU, 1978. Caring connections: A hope and comfort in grief.
Catherine R. Coverston, Associate Professor; Ph.D., Utah, 2001. Maternal and child care.
Karen Dearing, Assistant Professor; Ph.D., Utah, 2003. Schizophrenia recovery, nurse-patient relations.
Donna Freeborn, Assistant Professor; Ph.D., Oregon Health Sciences, 2008. Women's issues.
Barbara Heise, Assistant Professor; Ph.D., Virginia, 2006. Adult and gerontological mental health, alcohol and drug abuse.
Jane Lassetter, Associate Professor; Ph.D., Oregon Health & Science, 2008. Culture and health.
Beth Luthy, Assistant Professor; D.N.P., Rush, 2008. Childhood immunizations.
Barbara L. Mandleco, Professor; Ph.D., Brigham Young, 1991. Growth and development, resilience in children.
Erin Maughan, Assistant Professor; Ph.D., Utah, 2006. Community nursing, specializing in school nursing.
Sabrina Jarvis, Assistant Professor; D.N.P., Utah, 2010. Acute care.
Patty Ravert, Associate Professor and Director, Nursing Learning Center; Ph.D., Utah, 2004. Outcomes of simulated learning experiences.
Mary Williams, Associate Professor; Ph.D., Arizona, 1991. Transplant anxiety, instrumentation, qualitative methodology.

COLUMBIA UNIVERSITY

School of Nursing

Programs of Study

Columbia University School of Nursing is distinguished by the clinical excellence of its programs and graduates. The School strives to accommodate the widely varying pool of applicants with multiple pathways to reach the master's degree, including the Entry to Practice (ETP) Program, an accelerated B.S./M.S. combined-degree program for college graduates with non-nursing degrees. The School offers specialization in several different specialties, including adult, pediatric, family, and neonatal primary care; acute care; psychiatric–mental health; nurse anesthesia; nurse midwifery; and women's health. In addition, subspecialization is available in oncology, HIV/AIDS, addictive behaviors, genetics in advance practice, and palliative/end-of-life care. The Ph.D. program is a research-intensive curriculum preparing nurse scholars who are ready to conduct research in outcomes and health policy independently and as part of interdisciplinary teams. The Doctor of Nursing Practice (D.N.P.) prepares nurse clinicians with the knowledge and skills necessary for fully accountable practice with patients across sites and over time.

Research Facilities

The School of Nursing is part of the Columbia University Medical Center, along with the School of Public Health, the School of Dental Medicine, and the College of Physicians and Surgeons, which, together with New York-Presbyterian Hospital, create one of the world's greatest academic health centers. Other facilities include the Neurological Institute, New York State Psychiatric Institute, Morgan Stanley Children's Hospital of New York Presbyterian, the Organ Transplant Center, and the Center for Health Promotion and Disease Prevention. In addition, approximately 200 other sites in the tristate area are available for clinical education. The Augustus C. Long Library is the fourth-largest academic medical library in the country and is part of the Columbia University Library system, which encompasses approximately forty libraries and more than 4 million volumes. The Long Library houses more than 400,000 volumes and receives more than 4,500 journals, most of which can be accessed through online computer search programs. The Media and Computer Center contains more than 3,000 audiovisual and computer-assisted instruction programs, including slides, videodiscs, tapes, and a wide variety of personal computer applications. The Special Collections section houses several thousand rare and unique works, including the Florence Nightingale Collection, which is featured at exhibitions along with rare holdings of Freud and Webster. The School of Nursing's Technology Learning Center contains two patient units, which provide a hands-on environment for developing psychomotor skills, as well as state-of-the-art, computer-assisted monitoring equipment that simulates a real clinical environment.

Financial Aid

The goal of the School of Nursing financial aid program is to provide as many students as possible with sufficient resources to meet their needs by distributing funds to eligible students in a fair and equitable manner. Financial aid is met through a combination of scholarships, grants, teaching assistantships, and loans. Students should be able to meet all expenses for the academic year through a combination of these resources. Over 90 percent of students receive some financial assistance or scholarship from the School of Nursing.

Cost of Study

During the 2010–11 academic year, graduate tuition is estimated to be $1212 per credit for undergraduate and graduate credits and $1568 for doctoral credits.

Living and Housing Costs

Housing costs on the Health Sciences Campus range from $4000 to $6000 per term. Other expenses, including health fees, books, personal expenses, transportation, and uniforms, are estimated at $5000.

Student Outcomes

Columbia University School of Nursing's faculty members are outstanding educators who are committed to providing the best educational experience possible. They are responsive to student needs and to changes in the health-care market. As a result, Columbia graduates are sought after by employers, and more than 90 percent of recent graduates have secured employment in positions that are consistent with their education.

Location

The School of Nursing is part of the Columbia University Medical Center, a 20-acre campus overlooking the Hudson River on Manhattan's Upper West Side. Students can take advantage of the world-renowned recreational, cultural, educational, and entertainment events and sites that have made New York City famous.

The University and The School

By royal charter of King George II of England, Columbia University was founded in 1754 as King's College. It is the oldest institution of higher learning in New York State and the fifth oldest in the nation. A private, nonsectarian institution, Columbia University is organized into fifteen schools and is associated with more than seventy research and public service institutions and twenty-two scholarly journals. Founded in 1892 as the Presbyterian Hospital School of Nursing, the School began offering baccalaureate degrees when it joined Columbia University's Faculty of Medicine in 1937. In 1956, it became the first nursing program in the country to award a master's degree in a clinical nursing specialty.

Applying

Columbia University School of Nursing only accepts applications for summer and fall semesters; certain programs have specific entry times. All clinical sequences begin in the fall semester. Applicants interested in full-time status must apply for the summer semester. Students may apply for part-time status for either semester.

The Nurse Anesthesia program application deadline is November 1. This deadline is for both the M.S. and Post-Master's Certificate programs in anesthesia.

The Entry To Practice (ETP) is a full-time combined B.S./M.S. program. It enrolls just once per year at the end of May. Applications are due by November 15.

The Ph.D. program enrolls once per year in September. Applications are due by February 1.

The Doctor of Nursing Practice program enrolls once per year in September. Applications are due by March 1.

Applicants applying for all other programs must apply by December 15 for summer entry or April 15 for fall entry.

Admission is based on past academic and professional performance. Admission requirements include an online application and fee; a typed, double-spaced, twelve-point font, two-page personal statement describing professional goals and aspirations; three completed recommendation forms; official transcripts from all postsecondary schools; official GRE scores; resume or CV; a copy of an RN license and current registration (if applicable); and an undergraduate course in statistics and in physical assessment. Students should consult the School of Nursing Web site for specific admission criteria as certain programs have additional admissions requirements.

Correspondence and Information

Office of Admissions
Columbia University School of Nursing
630 West 168th Street, Box 6
New York, New York 10032
Phone: 212-305-5756
        800-899-8895 (toll-free)
E-mail: nursing@columbia.edu
Web site: http://www.nursing.columbia.edu

Columbia University

THE FACULTY

The faculty at Columbia University School of Nursing is comprised of a multitalented group of researchers, practitioners, and educators.

Research faculty members are all doctorally prepared and engaged in a variety of funded research projects, such as symptom management of HIV/AIDS using alternative and complementary medicine, evaluation of advanced practice nursing, domestic violence, health-care needs of perimenopausal women, health policy, and infection control. They have received national and international recognition for their work.

Practice faculty members are all nationally certified in their clinical specialties and maintain a faculty practice that is consistent with their certification. The practice faculty members are on the leading edge of advanced practice nursing and have received national and international recognition for innovative practice endeavors.

Dean: Bobbie Berkowitz, Mary O. Mundinger Professor and Senior Vice President, Columbia University Medical Center; Ph.D., RN, FAAN.

D'YOUVILLE COLLEGE

Department of Nursing

Programs of Study

At the graduate level, nursing programs include Master of Science (M.S.) in community health nursing with concentrations in advanced clinical nursing, nursing management, and nursing education; Master of Science in nursing with choice of clinical focus; and Master of Science in family nurse practitioner studies as well as a post-master's certificate in family nurse practitioner studies. A five-year Bachelor of Science in Nursing/Master of Science in nursing (B.S.N./M.S.) degree program, degree-completion programs for nurses who have already received their associate degrees, RN to B.S.N./M.S. program, and an RN to B.S.N./M.S. in community health nursing program are also available.

Innovative class scheduling provides working nursing professionals the opportunity to study full-time by attending only one day per week. This alternative scheduling allows students to continue working in their professions while earning their degrees.

Research Facilities

D'Youville's modern Library Resource Center contains 154,000 volumes, including microtext and software, and subscriptions to 870 periodicals and newspapers. The multimillion-dollar Health Science Building houses laboratories, including those for anatomy, organic chemistry, quantitative analysis, and computer science. It also houses classrooms, faculty member offices, and development centers, including one for career development.

Financial Aid

D'Youville attempts to provide financial aid for students who would not otherwise be able to attend. Determination of aid is based on the Free Application for Federal Student Aid. Aid is available in the form of grants, loans, and employment on campus. In addition, D'Youville offers scholarships for academic achievement to incoming students.

Graduate students must be matriculated for 6 or more credits in a degree program. Nurse traineeship assistance is available to students enrolled for a minimum of 9 credit hours per semester in the graduate nursing program. Canadian students (citizens and landed immigrants), except those enrolled in the RN degree-completion program, are offered a 20 percent tuition reduction and may also apply for the Ontario Student Assistance Program (OSAP). All students enrolled in the RN degree-completion program are offered a 50 percent tuition reduction.

Cost of Study

Graduate tuition for 2010–11 is $760 per credit hour for master's and advanced certificate programs and $825 per credit hour for doctoral programs. A general College fee of between $50 and $155 is required, based on credit hours taken.

Living and Housing Costs

Marguerite Hall, the residence facility, houses men and women on separate floors and includes a coed floor for graduate and adult students. For 2010–11, room and board cost $4900 per semester. Overnight accommodations are available at a rate of $28 per night (space permitting). A residence-apartment complex houses 175 junior, senior, and graduate students in one- and four-bedroom apartments. The resident apartment complex rates are around $4000 per semester, based on the type of apartment reserved.

Student Group

Graduate degree programs are enhanced by a 13:1 student-faculty ratio. The current enrollment is 808 full-time and 556 part-time graduate students. Seventy-three percent of the students are women, 14 percent are members of minority groups, and 62 percent are internationals students. D'Youville's proximity to the Canadian border accounts for the majority of the international student population.

Location

D'Youville is situated on Buffalo's residential west side. The College is within minutes of many social attractions, including the downtown shopping center, the Kleinhans Music hall, the Albright-Knox Art Gallery, two museums, and several theaters that offer stage productions. Seasonal changes in the area offer a variety of recreational opportunities. Buffalo is only 90 miles from Toronto and 25 minutes from Niagara Falls, making it a gateway to recreation areas in western New York and Ontario. Holiday Valley, a skier's paradise, is an hour's drive away. The city is serviced by the New York State Thruway, Amtrak, Greyhound and Trailways bus lines, and most major airlines.

D'Youville enjoys a diversified interchange with the community due to its affiliations with schools, hospitals, and social agencies in the area. College students in the Buffalo area number more than 60,000.

The College

Commencing in 1942, D'Youville College was the first private college in New York State to offer a four-year Bachelor of Science in Nursing degree program. The College offers four doctoral, eight master's-level, and five postbaccalaureate programs as well as baccalaureate and advanced certificate programs. Graduate programs in addition to nursing include childhood, adolescence, and special education; health services administration; international business; and occupational therapy. Doctoral programs include chiropractic, educational leadership, health policy and health education, and physical therapy. D'Youville offers the undergraduate degrees of Bachelor of Arts (B.A.), Bachelor of Science (B.S.), and Bachelor of Science in Nursing (B.S.N.). Majors include accounting, biology, business management, chiropractic (seven-year B.S./D.C.), dietetics, education (early childhood, childhood, adolescence, and special), English, exercise and sports studies, global studies, health services, history, information technology, nursing, occupational therapy, philosophy, physical therapy, physician assistant, preprofessional studies (dental, law, medicine, and veterinary studies), psychology, and sociology. Five-year combined bachelor's/master's (B.S./M.S.) programs are offered in dietetics, education, information technology (B.S.)/international business (M.S.), nursing, and occupational therapy. A six-year B.S./D.P.T. program is offered in physical therapy.

Applying

A baccalaureate degree in nursing from an approved or accredited college or university and RN licensure are required for admission to the graduate nursing programs. Licensure as a registered nurse in New York State and a minimum of one year of experience as a registered nurse are required of candidates applying to the nurse practitioner programs. Admissions to graduate programs is based on an overall evaluation of credentials, including the applicant's undergraduate record, with a minimum 3.0 GPA average in the major field. Applicants who do not fulfill admission requirements may be admitted provisionally. Applicants whose native language is not English must submit a minimum TOEFL score of 500. Graduate application files are reviewed on a rolling basis.

Correspondence and Information

Linda E. Fisher
Director of Graduate Admission
D'Youville College
One D'Youville Square
320 Porter Avenue
Buffalo, New York 14201
Phone: 716-829-8400
　　　　800-777-3921 (toll-free)
E-mail: graduateadmissions@dyc.edu
Web site: http://www.dyc.edu

D'Youville College

THE FACULTY

Denise Dunford, Assistant Professor and Director of Family Nurse Practitioner Program; D.N.S., SUNY at Buffalo.

Carol A. Gutt, Associate Professor; Ed.D., SUNY at Buffalo.

Judith Lewis, Dean, School of Nursing; Ed.D., Cincinnati.

Kathleen Mariano, Assistant Professor; D.N.S., SUNY at Buffalo.

Abigail Mitchell; D.H.Ed., A. T. Still.

Eileen Nahigian, Assistant Professor; D.N.S., SUNY at Buffalo.

Judith Stanley, Assistant Professor; D.H.Sc., Nova Southeastern.

EMORY
NELL HODGSON
WOODRUFF
SCHOOL OF
NURSING

EMORY UNIVERSITY

Nell Hodgson Woodruff School of Nursing

Programs of Study

Emory University School of Nursing graduate programs prepare students with advanced nursing knowledge, produce nurse leaders in practice and research, and create forerunners in the design of new models of care. The graduate curriculum combines comprehensive nursing theory and research with a rich clinical core and extensive specialty courses. A wealth of clinical venues is available in the Atlanta metropolitan area, and clinical experiences are precisely geared to students' career focus.

Programs of study leading to the Master of Science in Nursing (M.S.N.) include the following specialties: acute care nurse practitioner, adult nurse practitioner, emergency nurse practitioner, family nurse midwife, family nurse practitioner, gerontological nurse practitioner, nurse midwifery, pediatric nurse practitioner-acute care, pediatric nurse practitioner-primary care, public health nursing leadership, women's health (Title X), women's health nurse practitioner, and women's health/adult health nurse practitioner. The length of the specialty programs ranges from three to five consecutive semesters of full-time study; part-time study is available. Upon completion of the M.S.N. degree students are eligible to sit for certification as a certified nurse midwife or nurse practitioner. An RN-M.S.N. bridge program is available for associate degree or diploma prepared nurses. Applicants must be graduates of a regionally accredited, state board–accredited, National League for Nursing–accredited, or Commission on Collegiate Nursing Education–accredited associate degree or diploma nursing program. Students in the RN-M.S.N. program complete 17 semester hours of bridge course work prior to beginning the specialty curriculum of choice. A dual Master of Science in Nursing/Master of Public Health (M.S.N./M.P.H.) is available in conjunction with Emory's Rollins School of Public Health. Post-master's options are available in all graduate specialty areas, except the emergency nurse practitioner.

The Ph.D. in nursing offers flexible specialization options and is a four-year, full-time program.

Research Facilities

The School of Nursing is a state-of-the-art facility for nursing study and research. The building unites scholarship and teaching under one roof and enhances the School's mission of scholarship, leadership, and social responsibility. Designed with tomorrow's technology in mind, the building offers ample space for research and clinical training. In 2000, the School of Nursing opened the Lillian Carter Center for International Nursing. The center focuses on improving the health of vulnerable people worldwide through nursing practice, education, and research. The School of Nursing is part of the Robert W. Woodruff Health Sciences Center, a major provider of patient care and a national leader in clinical and research programs. The other components are Emory University School of Medicine, Rollins School of Public Health, Yerkes Regional Primate Research Center, Emory HealthCare, the Emory Clinic, and the Wesley Woods Center of Emory University. Emory University is a close collaborator with the Carter Center, a nonprofit, nonpartisan public policy institute founded by former President Jimmy Carter and his wife, Rosalynn. The center is dedicated to fighting disease, hunger, poverty, conflict, and oppression on a worldwide basis. Holdings of the five Emory libraries total approximately 2.5 million volumes. The libraries also offer access to thousands of electronic information resources. The primary research resources for nursing students are the Asa Griggs Candler Library, the Health Sciences Library, and the Robert W. Woodruff Library for Advanced Studies. EUCLID, the library's integrated library computer system, can be searched at all Emory libraries and through the campus network.

Financial Aid

Ninety-six percent of currently enrolled School of Nursing graduate students receive some form of financial assistance. A variety of need-based and merit-based awards are available. Dean's Scholarships are awarded to students based on academic achievement. Five full-tuition Woodruff Fellowships are awarded to incoming graduate students each year based on academic achievement, leadership, and service. Need-based grants and loans are also available.

For the 2010–11 academic year all admitted full-time Ph.D. students receive a full-tuition waiver and a $17,000 annual stipend in exchange for teaching and research services.

Cost of Study

Tuition for full-time study is $17,400 per semester and $1450 per credit hour for the 2010–11 academic year. This cost does not include books and fees.

Living and Housing Costs

On-campus housing is available to full-time graduate students and is offered on a first-come, first-served basis because it is limited. Emory's location in the middle of a residential area offers ample opportunities for off-campus housing. More information may be obtained by contacting the Office of Residence Life of Emory University (http://www.emory.edu/HOUSING/).

Student Group

During the 2009–10 academic year, the School of Nursing enrolled 218 undergraduate and 160 graduate students. Ninety-three percent of graduate students were women, 7 percent were men, and 54 percent pursued the graduate degree full-time. The students represented seventeen states and two countries. Faculty members look for high academic achievement, solid verbal and written communication skills, and a strong commitment to advanced practice nursing.

Location

The School of Nursing is located on the 631-acre Emory campus in Atlanta, Georgia. It is situated 15 minutes from downtown Atlanta and is positioned along the Clifton Corridor, which also includes the U.S. Centers for Disease Control and Prevention. Atlanta is the fastest-growing city in the South, with premier athletic teams, museums, and various other local attractions.

The University

Emory University has approximately 12,000 students and 2,500 faculty members who represent all regions of the U.S. and ninety countries. Emory was founded by the Methodist Church in 1836. Emory has nine major academic divisions, numerous centers for advanced study, and a host of prestigious affiliated institutions. The academic units include an undergraduate college; a graduate school of arts and sciences; professional schools of medicine, theology, law, nursing, public health, and business; and a two-year undergraduate division.

Applying

Admission requirements include graduation from a National League for Nursing–accredited or Commission on Collegiate Nursing Education–accredited Bachelor of Science in nursing program with a preferred minimum grade point average of 3.0 in nursing and supportive course work, a current license to practice nursing, a recommended minimum of one year of work experience, an application, statement of purpose, satisfactory scores on the Graduate Record Examinations (GRE) or Miller Analogies Test (MAT), three recommendations, a resume or curriculum vitae, transcripts from all institutions attended, and a faculty interview. Admission decisions are on a rolling basis. The priority deadline for admission and scholarships for fall and summer term is January 15 and for spring is October 1; however, applications will continue to be reviewed on a space available basis.

Correspondence and Information

Office of Admission and Student Services
School of Nursing
Emory University
1520 Clifton Road
Atlanta, Georgia 30322
Phone: 404-727-7980
        800-222-3879 (toll-free)
Fax: 404-727-8509
E-mail: admit@nursing.emory.edu
Web site: http://www.nursing.emory.edu

Emory University

THE FACULTY

Corrine Abraham, Associate; M.N., Emory, 1985. Adult and elder health.
Susan Bauer-Wu, Associate Professor; D.N.Sc., Rush, 1997. Adult and elder health.
Kelly Brewer, Associate; M.S.N., Arkansas, 1992. Adult and elder health.
EunSeok (Julie) Cha, Assistant Professor; Ph.D., Pittsburgh, 2009. Family and community nursing.
Carolyn Clevenger, Clinical Assistant Professor; D.N.P., Medical College of Georgia, 2007. Adult and elder health.
Caroline Coburn, Instructor; M.S., Emory, 1981. Adult and elder health.
Ann Connor, Clinical Assistant Professor; M.S.N., Alabama, 1980. Family and community nursing.
Safiya Dalmida, Assistant Professor; Ph.D., Emory, 2006. Family and community nursing.
Julie Davey, Instructor; M.S.N., Emory, 2001. Adult and elder health.
Madge M. Donnellan, Clinical Associate Professor; Ph.D., Tennessee, 1988. Family and community nursing.
Monica Donohue, Instructor; M.N., South Carolina, 1980. Family and community nursing.
Elizabeth Downes, Clinical Assistant Professor; M.S.N., Tennessee, 1986. Family and community nursing.
Sandra B. Dunbar, Charles Howard Candler Professor of Cardiovascular Nursing; D.S.N., Alabama at Birmingham, 1982. Adaptation to the stresses of acute and chronic cardiovascular illness.
Sara Edwards, Instructor; M.S.N./M.P.H., Emory, 1994. Family and community nursing.
Jennifer Foster, Assistant Professor; Ph.D., Massachusetts, 2003. Family and community nursing.
Sarah B. Freeman, Clinical Professor; Ph.D., Georgia State, 1989. Family and community nursing.
Rebecca Gary, Assistant Professor; Ph.D., North Carolina, 1979. Adult and elder health.
Maggie P. Gilead, Associate Professor; Ph.D., Emory, 1981. Adult and elder health.
Linda Grabbe, Instructor; Ph.D., Georgia State, 1992. Family and community nursing.
Susan M. Grant, Associate Dean of Clinical Leadership; M.N., South Carolina, 1991.
Kenneth Hepburn, Associate Dean for Research and Professor; Ph.D., Washington (Seattle), 1968.
Erin Hernadez, Instructor; M.S., Georgia State, 1995. Family and community nursing.
Leslie Holmes, Instructor; M.S.N., Medical University of South Carolina, 1993. Family and community nursing.
Ursula A. Kelly, Visiting Scholar; Ph.D., Boston College, 2004; Family and community nursing.
Marcia McDonnell Holstad, Assistant Professor; D.S.N., Alabama, 1996. Family and community nursing.
Maeve Howett, Clinical Assistant Professor; Ph.D., Emory, 2006. Family and community nursing.
Barbara Kaplan, Instructor; M.S.N., Emory, 1992. Family and community nursing.
Maureen A. Kelley, Clinical Associate Professor and Chair, Family and Community Nursing; Ph.D., Medical College of Georgia, 1993. Midwifery.
Joyce L. King, Clinical Assistant Professor; Ph.D., Emory, 1995. Family and community nursing.
Sally T. Lehr, Clinical Assistant Professor; Ph.D., Georgia State, 2001. Adult and elder health.
Marsha Lewis, Associate Dean for Education and Associate Professor; Ph.D., Minnesota, 1992.
Kathy Markowski, Associate; M.S.N., DePaul, 1980. Adult and elder health.
Jane E. Mashburn, Clinical Associate Professor and Interim Assistant Dean for the M.S.N. Program; M.N., Emory, 1978. Midwifery, family and community nursing.
Kathryn Matthews, Clinical Assistant Professor; D.N.P., Medical College of Georgia, 2007. Family and community nursing.
Joyce P. Murray, Professor; Ed.D., Georgia, 1989. Adult and elder health.
Helen S. O'Shea, Professor Emerita; Ph.D., Georgia State, 1980. Adult health.
Quyen Phan, Instructor; M.S.N., Emory, 2003. Adult and elder health.
William J. Puentes, Clinical Associate Professor; Ph.D., Widener, 1995. Adult and elder health.
Marcene L. Powell, Professor; D.S.W., Utah, 1981. Family and community nursing.
Barbara D. Reeves, Clinical Assistant Professor; M.S.N., Vanderbilt, 1979. Family and community nursing.
Carolyn Miller Reilly, Assistant Professor; Ph.D., Nebraska, 2006. Adult and elder health.
Bethany D. Robertson, Clinical Assistant Professor and Interim Director, Educational Technology; D.N.P., Medical College of Georgia, 2007. Family and community nursing.
Ann E. Rogers, Professor; Ph.D., Northwestern, 1986. Adult and elder health.
Martha F. Rogers, Clinical Professor; M.D., Medical College of Georgia, 1976. Family and community nursing.
Deborah A. Ryan, Clinical Associate Professor and Interim Assistant Dean, B.S.N. Program; M.S.N., Marquette, 1981. Family and community nursing.
Susan E. Shapiro, Associate Clinical Professor; Ph.D., Oregon Health & Science, 2003; Adult and elder health.
Lynn Sibley, Associate Professor; Ph.D., Colorado, 1993. Family and community nursing.
Linda Spencer, Clinical Associate Professor; Ph.D., Georgia State, 1988. Family and community nursing.
Ora Strickland, Professor; Ph.D., North Carolina at Greensboro, 1977. Family and community nursing.
Darla R. Ura, Clinical Associate Professor; M.A., Ball State, 1974. Adult and elder health.
Marylee Van Keuren, Instructor; M.S.N., Wayne State, 1987. Adult and elder health.
Catherine Vena, Assistant Professor; Ph.D., Emory, 2004. Adult and elder health.
Jeannie Weston, Instructor; M.S., Maryland, 1982. Family and community nursing.
Sandra White, Instructor; M.S.N., Emory, 2004. Adult and elder health.
Kathryn Woeber, Instructor; M.S.N./M.P.H., Emory, 1999. Family and community nursing.
Weihua Zhang, Clinical Assistant Professor; Ph.D., Georgia State, 2004. Adult and elder health.

FELICIAN COLLEGE

Master of Science in Nursing
Advanced Practice Track and Education Track

Programs of Study

The Master of Science in Nursing (M.S.N.) Program at Felician College is designed to prepare the registered nurse with a Bachelor of Science in Nursing (B.S.N.) degree for advanced practice as nurse practitioners in primary-care settings or as nurse educators in higher education, staff development and continuing education, and patient and community education settings. The advanced practice track emphasizes nursing care of families or adults, with a specific focus on vulnerable and underserved populations. The education track emphasizes the preparation of leaders in education to support nurses' professional development as well as to coordinate, develop, implement, and evaluate patient, family, and community education programs that promote and restore health and prevent disease. The advanced practice student is offered a choice of either a completely online format or a cohort-based, on-campus model with a hybrid delivery method, blending classroom and e-learning. The nurse educator track, also cohort based, is offered on campus, with the majority of classes presented as hybrids.

The adult nurse practitioner track requires 43 credits and 600 clinical hours, while the family nurse practitioner track requires 46 credits and 780 clinical hours. Courses are taught on a trimester schedule, with 12-week sessions and terms that start in September, January, and April. Students choosing the on-campus cohort model meet one day per week for each session. Students generally take at least two courses per term and can complete the degree in as little as two years. All students are required to take 28 credits of professional core courses before they complete the course work required for their track of choice. Graduates are eligible to take the advanced practice national certification examination in family or adult health. Graduates are also eligible to apply for admission to doctoral programs.

The education track requires 42 credits as well as clinical and practicum hours, based on individual course requirements. Courses are taught in a trimester schedule, cohort model, meeting one day per week for twelve-week sessions. Students take two courses per session and can complete the degree in just over two years. Students take 22 credits of professional core courses before beginning the 20 credits of specialty courses in education. Graduates of the education track are eligible to take the ANCC Nursing Professional Development Certification Examination and the National League for Nursing Certification in Nurse Educator Examination. Graduates of the program are eligible to apply for admission to doctoral study.

The Post-Master's Certificate Program in advanced practice prepares a nurse with a master's degree in nursing for primary-care practice in family or adult advanced practice. The credits required for the certificate range from 10 to 31, based on the student's educational background and prerequisite course work. The program consists of four foundation courses, with more courses in the chosen area of specialization, as well as clinical experience. A post-master's certificate in nursing education is also offered.

Research Facilities

The Nursing Resource and Simulation Center, a multifaceted center of learning for all nursing students, is located on the Lodi campus. The center has a state-of-the-art computer room, where CD-ROM and interactive video programs are used to intensify the learning experience. The Nursing Resource and Simulation Center staff members assist students with clinical competencies through the use of mannequins and other equipment that simulates clinical procedures. Individual tutoring and workshops are offered to enhance theory comprehension.

A center for child care and simulated nursing practice is also available on the Lodi campus. The first floor is devoted to a well-equipped Child Care Center for the convenience of students and faculty members. The upper floor houses the Nursing Resource and Simulation Laboratory, which provides a simulated hospital setting for the clinical training of students in the nursing programs.

The College Library is a two-story building that serves the needs of students, faculty and staff members, and alumni with more than 110,000 books and over 800 periodical subscriptions. This collection is enhanced by large holdings of materials in microform, which can be used on the library's reader/printer equipment. With its computers linked to information services such as DIALOG and OCLC, and as a member of the New Jersey Library Network and VALE, the library locates and obtains information, journal articles, and books not available in its collection from sources all over the country. Computerized databases can also be accessed directly by users through the online First Search workstation, where up-to-date information on 40 million books and an index of 15,000 periodicals is available. The library is also connected to the Internet and has several CD-ROM workstations. Through EBSCOhost, Bell & Howell's Proquest, CINAHL, and other services, students and faculty and staff members have access to numerous online journal indexes—as well as articles from thousands of periodicals—from anywhere on the campus computer network or from their home computers. An experienced staff of professional librarians is available to assist users.

The College's computer facilities include an academic and administrative network, four computerized labs, a computerized learning center, and two computer centers that are available for students, with a total of about 200 computers available for student/faculty member use. All classrooms, offices, and facilities are wired for Internet and e-mail.

Financial Aid

Fellowships and loans are available. To qualify for financial aid, a student must complete the Free Application for Federal Student Aid (FAFSA).

Cost of Study

In 2010–11, graduate tuition is $825 per credit. Fees are additional.

Living and Housing Costs

Students are housed in two dormitories on the Rutherford campus, Milton and Elliott Halls. Both buildings have housing organized around student suites containing semiprivate baths. On-campus room and board is approximately $10,150 per year. On-campus housing is not available to married students.

Student Group

Felician College enrolls approximately 2,300 students. In fall 2009 there were approximately 350 students enrolled in graduate programs.

Location

Felician College's Lodi campus is located on the banks of the Saddle River on a beautifully landscaped campus of 27 acres and offers a collegiate setting in suburban Bergen County, within easy driving distance of New York City. The Felician College Rutherford Campus is set on 10.5 beautifully landscaped acres in the heart of the historic community of Rutherford, New Jersey. Only 15 minutes from the Lodi campus, the Rutherford complex contains student residences, classroom buildings, a student center, and a gymnasium. The campus is a short distance from downtown Rutherford, where there are many shops and businesses of interest to students.

The College

Felician College, a coeducational liberal arts college, is a Catholic, private, independent institution for students representing diverse religious, racial, and ethnic backgrounds. The College operates on two campuses in Lodi and Rutherford, New Jersey. The College is one of the institutions of higher learning conducted by the Felician Sisters in the United States. Its mission is to provide a values-oriented education based in the liberal arts while it prepares students for meaningful lives and careers in contemporary society. To meet the needs of students and to provide personal enrichment courses to matriculated and nonmatriculated students, Felician College offers day, evening, and weekend programs. The College is accredited by the Middle States Association of Colleges and Schools and carries program accreditation from the National Accrediting Agency for Clinical Laboratory Sciences and the International Assembly for Collegiate Business Education.

Applying

In addition to being licensed as a registered nurse, applicants must have a Bachelor of Science in Nursing degree from a program accredited by a national accrediting agency and approved by the Board of Nursing, with a minimum cumulative GPA of 3.0. Successful completion of undergraduate courses in nursing research, statistics, pathophysiology, and health assessment is required. Applicants must submit the completed application, the $40 nonrefundable application fee, all official academic transcripts, and two professional or academic references from persons qualified to judge the applicant's ability to succeed in graduate study. Applicants must also submit copies of all licensure held as a registered professional nurse, including New Jersey, and/or the state of the clinical practicum. The licensee cannot have any pending disciplinary action against their nursing license from any Board of Nursing. International credential requirements are reviewed on an individual basis. Applications are processed on a rolling basis. Applicants for the advanced practice curriculum must have at least one year of clinical practice and must be currently employed in professional practice.

Correspondence and Information

Programs in Advanced Practice Nursing and Nursing Education
Felician College
262 South Main Street
Lodi, New Jersey 07644-2117
Phone: 201-559-6077
Fax: 201-559-6138
E-mail: adultandgraduate@felician.edu
Web site: http://www.felician.edu/

Felician College

THE FACULTY

Karen Breitkreuz, Instructor; Ed.D., Columbia Teachers College; RN.
Rachel Baird Carlton, Instructor, D.N.P., Arizona State; RN, FNP-C.
Jean Conlon-Yoo, Instructor; M.S.N., Pace; RN.
Marie A. Cueman, Assistant Professor; Ph.D., Seton Hall; RN.
Margaret A. Farrell Daingerfield, Associate Professor and Associate Dean of Graduate Nursing; Ed.D., Rutgers; RN.
Janet Daly, Instructor; M.A., NYU; RN.
Kathleen Diciedue, Associate Professor; M.S.N., Seton Hall; RN.
Arlene Farmer, off-campus faculty; Ed.D., Nova Southeastern, RN.
Susan Gentile, Instructor; M.S.N., University of Medicine and Dentistry of New Jersey; M.A., Pennsylvania; RN, APN.
Rochelle Greenfield, Assistant Professor; M.A. NYU, RN, APN.
Catherine Jennings, Instructor and Chair, Advanced Practice; M.S.N., SUNY at Stony Brook; RN, APN.
Kathleen Kavanagh, Instructor; M.S.N., Ramapo College of New Jersey/University of Medicine and Dentistry of New Jersey; RN.
Sr. Patricia Kennedy, Assistant Nursing Resource and Simulation Center Coordinator; RN.
Debra Masterson, Instructor; M.S.N, RN.
Christine Mihal, Associate Professor and Associate Dean, RN-B.S.N. Programs; M.S.N., Ed.D., Seton Hall; RN.
Patricia O'Brien-Barry, Associate Professor; Ph.D., NYU; RN.
Lisa Perrota, Assistant Director Nursing Resource and Simulation Center; RN.
Albert Rundio, Jr., Associate Professor; Ph.D., Pennsylvania; D.N.P., Chatham; APRN, NEA, CARN-AP, BC.
Susan Schwade, Assistant Professor; M.S.N., Wayne State; RN.
Muriel M. Shore, Professor and Dean; Ed.D., Seton Hall; RN.
Elizabeth Stallings, Instructor; M.A., NYU; RN.
Teresa Brennan Turi, Instructor; M.S.N., Stony Brook, SUNY; RN.
Salimah Walani, Assistant Professor; Ph.D., NYU; M.S.N., Simmons; M.P.H., Harvard; RN.
Elizabeth Zweighaft, Assistant Professor and Associate Dean of Undergraduate Nursing; Ed.M., Columbia Teachers College; RN.

ST. JOSEPH'S COLLEGE, NEW YORK

Department of Nursing
Master of Science with a Major in Nursing

Programs of Study

St. Joseph's College (SJC) offers the Master of Science degree with a major in nursing. The program, registered with the New York State Education Department, enrolled its first class in 2005. Students pick one of two concentrations—clinical nurse specialist in adult health or nursing education.

The graduate curriculum, consisting of a core and specialty concentrations, builds on the knowledge base and practice competencies of the baccalaureate-prepared nurse and prepares the graduate for advanced professional practice. Graduates of the clinical nurse specialist (CNS) in adult health concentration (38 credits) are prepared to actualize the multifaceted role of the CNS in a variety of health-care settings, reflecting three spheres of relationships—patient and client, nurses and nursing practice, and organizations and systems. Graduates of the nursing education concentration (37 credits) are ready to assume nurse educator positions in either academic or service settings or in patient education.

The program meets the needs of the working professional. Designed for part-time study, the program can be completed in seven semesters. Each class enters as a cohort group, attending classes one day per week during the fall and spring semesters and one summer. Additional hours are required for clinical/practicum courses.

Research Facilities

The Callahan Library at the Long Island Campus is a modern, 25,000-square-foot freestanding facility with seating for more than 300 readers. A curriculum library, seminar rooms, administrative offices, and two classrooms are housed in this building. Holdings include more than 105,000 volumes and 307 periodical titles, and they are supplemented by videos and other instructional aids. Patrons have access to the Internet and to several online academic databases. A fully automated library system, Endeavor, ensures the efficient retrieval and management of all library resources. Other resources include the library at St. Joseph's Brooklyn Campus, with more than 109,000 volumes and membership in the Long Island Library Resources Council. This facilitates cooperative associations with the academic and special libraries on Long Island. Internet access, subscriptions to several online full-text databases, and membership in the international bibliographic utility OCLC allow almost limitless access to available information.

McEntegart Hall is a fully air-conditioned five-level structure. Three spacious reading areas with a capacity for 300 readers, including individual study carrels and shelf space for 200,000 volumes, provide an excellent environment for research. In addition, McEntegart Hall houses the College archives, a curriculum library, three computer laboratories, a nursing education laboratory, and a videoconference room. There are eight classrooms, a chapel, a cafeteria, and faculty and student lounges.

A high-speed fiber-optic intracampus network connects all offices, instructional facilities, computer laboratories, and libraries on both the Brooklyn and Long Island Campuses. The network provides Internet access to all students and faculty and staff members. An integrated online library system enables students to search for and check out books at either campus. Online databases and other electronic resources are available to students from either campus or from their home computers. Two wireless laptop classrooms with smart-classroom features provide flexible instruction spaces with the latest technologies. Videoconferencing facilities connect the two campuses, allowing for real-time distance learning in a small-group setting.

Financial Aid

Financial aid is available in the form of federal and private loans, scholarships, and work-study programs. Students should contact the Financial Aid Office for more information (Brooklyn Campus, telephone: 718-940-5700; Long Island Campus, telephone: 631-687-2600).

Cost of Study

In 2010–11, tuition is $650 per credit. The College and technology fees per semester for 12 or more credits totaled $200, and the nursing lab fee was $100.

Student Group

The total enrollment for all graduate programs on both campuses is 678.

Location

St. Joseph's College has two campuses—the main campus in the residential Clinton Hill section of Brooklyn and the Long Island branch campus in Patchogue, New York. The main campus offers easy access to all transit lines; to the Long Island Expressway; to all bridges in Brooklyn, Manhattan, and Queens; and to the Verrazano-Narrows Bridge to Staten Island. Within 30 minutes, students leaving St. Joseph's College can find themselves at the Metropolitan Museum of Art, the 42nd Street Library, Carnegie Hall and Lincoln Center, the Broadway theater district, Madison Square Garden, or Shea Stadium. The College itself stands in the center of one of the nation's most diversified academic communities, consisting of six colleges and universities within a 2-mile radius of each other. The 27-acre Long Island Campus, adjacent to Great Patchogue Lake, is an ideal setting for studying, socializing, and partaking in extracurricular activities. Located just off Sunrise Highway, the Long Island Campus is easily accessible from all parts of Long Island.

The College and The Department

St. Joseph's College is a fully accredited institution that has been dedicated to providing a diverse population of students in the New York metropolitan area with an affordable education rooted in the liberal arts tradition since 1916. Independent and coeducational, the College provides a strong academic and value-oriented education at the undergraduate and graduate levels. For the eighth year in a row, the 2010 ranking of "America's Best Colleges" by *U.S. News & World Report* placed St. Joseph's College in the top tier of the Northern Comprehensive Colleges–Bachelor's category.

The mission of the Department of Nursing is to provide professional nursing education that prepares the student to think critically and to utilize nursing theory, related sciences, and humanities to improve their practice; assists the student to internalize professional values and standards of practice; provides learning experiences that acknowledge the needs of a diversified student population with varied nursing practice experience; encourages students to actively participate in all aspects of their educational experiences; and facilitates student development of a spirit of inquiry and an appreciation of learning as a lifelong process.

Applying

Students must possess a B.S. degree with a major in nursing from a nationally accredited nursing program (NLNAC or CCNE). Prerequisite courses include an undergraduate health assessment course and an undergraduate statistics course. Students should have a minimum GPA of 3.0; preference is given to applicants with a GPA of 3.3 or above. One year of professional clinical practice should be completed prior to admission. Applicants must submit the completed application, the application fee, official transcripts, a current curriculum vitae, a personal statement, and two letters of recommendation. In addition, applicants must provide proof of New York State RN licensure, current professional registration, and professional malpractice insurance. An interview is required.

Correspondence and Information

Brooklyn Campus
St. Joseph's College
245 Clinton Avenue
Brooklyn, New York 11205
Phone: 718-940-5800
E-mail: brooklynap@sjcny.edu
Web site: http://www.sjcny.edu/Academics/MS-degree-with-a-
 Major-in-Nursing/250

Long Island Campus
St. Joseph's College
155 West Roe Boulevard
Patchogue, New York 11772
Phone: 631-687-4501
E-mail: suffolkap@sjcny.edu

St. Joseph's College, New York

THE FACULTY

Lorraine Brown, Assistant Professor; M.S.N., Boston University; RN.
Barbara Carlstrom, Assistant Professor; M.S.N., Stony Brook, SUNY; RN.
Maria Fletcher, Associate Professor; Ph.D., Adelphi; RN.
Laurel Janssen-Breen, Assistant Professor; M.A., NYU; RN.
Florence Jerdan, Associate Professor; Ph.D., Adelphi; RN.
Tae Sook Kim, Associate Professor; Ph.D., NYU; RN.
Linda Morgante, Assistant Professor; M.S.N., CUNY, Hunter; RN.
Catherine Pearsall, Assistant Professor; Ph.D., Duquesne; CNE, FNP, ANPC, RN.
Barbara Sands, Professor and Director; Ph.D., Adelphi; RN.
Boas Yu, Assistant Professor; Ed.D., Columbia Teachers College; RN.

Section 31
Public Health

This section contains a directory of institutions offering graduate work in public health, followed by in-depth entries submitted by institutions that chose to prepare detailed program descriptions. Additional information about programs listed in the directory but not augmented by an in-depth entry may be obtained by writing directly to the dean of a graduate school or chair of a department at the address given in the directory.

For programs offering related work, see also in this book *Allied Health, Education, Health Services,* and *Nursing.* In the other guides in this series:

Graduate Programs in the Humanities, Arts & Social Sciences
See *Family and Consumer Sciences (Gerontology)* and *Sociology, Anthropology, and Archaeology (Demography and Population Studies)*

Graduate Programs in the Biological Sciences
See *Biological and Biomedical Sciences; Ecology, Environmental Biology, and Evolutionary Biology; Microbiological Sciences;* and *Nutrition*

Graduate Programs in the Physical Sciences, Mathematics, Agricultural Sciences, the Environment & Natural Resources
See *Mathematical Sciences* and *Environmental Sciences and Management*

Graduate Programs in Engineering & Applied Sciences
See *Biomedical Engineering and Biotechnology, Civil and Environmental Engineering, Industrial Engineering, Energy and Power Engineering (Nuclear Engineering),* and *Management of Engineering and Technology*

CONTENTS

Public Health—General

Adelphi University, University College, Graduate Certificate in Emergency Management Program, Garden City, NY 11530-0701. Offers Certificate. Part-time and evening/weekend programs available. *Students:* 3 part-time (1 woman). Average age 27. 11 applicants, 55% accepted. *Application deadline:* For fall admission, 5/1 for international students; for spring admission, 12/1 for international students. Applications are processed on a rolling basis. Application fee: $50. Electronic applications accepted. *Expenses:* Tuition: Full-time $28,340; part-time $830 per credit. Required fees: $600; $250 per credit. Full-time tuition and fees vary according to course load and program. *Financial support:* Research assistantships with partial tuition reimbursements, Federal Work-Study and institutionally sponsored loans available. *Faculty research:* Emergency nursing, disaster management, disaster preparedness. *Unit head:* Shawn O'Riley, Executive Director, 516-877-3412, E-mail: ucinfo@adelphi.edu. *Application contact:* Christine Murphy, Director of Admissions, 516-877-3050, Fax: 516-877-3039, E-mail: graduateadmissions@adelphi.edu.

American Public University System, AMU/APU Graduate Programs, Charles Town, WV 25414. Offers air warfare (MA Military Studies); American Revolution (MA Military Studies); business administration (MBA); Civil War (MA Military Studies); criminal justice (MA); defense management (MA Military Studies); emergency and disaster management (MA); environmental policy and management (MS); fire science management (MA); global engagement (MA); history (MA); homeland security (MA); humanities (MA); intelligence (MA Military Studies, MA Strategic Intelligence); international peace and conflict resolution (MA); international relations and conflict resolution (MA); joint warfare (MA Military Studies); land warfare international perspective (MA Military Studies); management (MA); military history (MA); military leadership (MA Military Studies); national security studies (MA); naval warfare international (MA Military Studies); naval warfare US (MA Military Studies); political science (MA); public administration (MA); public health (MA); security management (MA); space studies (MS); special ops/LIC (MA Military Studies); sports management (MA); transportation and logistics management (MA); transportation management (MA); unconventional warfare (MA Military Studies); World War II (MA Military Studies). Programs offered via distance learning only. Part-time and evening/weekend programs available. Postbaccalaureate distance learning degree programs offered (no on-campus study). *Students:* 788 full-time (330 women), 6,916 part-time (2,050 women); includes 1,767 minority (908 African Americans, 70 American Indian/Alaska Native, 223 Asian Americans or Pacific Islanders, 566 Hispanic Americans), 77 international. Average age 35. *Degree requirements:* For master's, comprehensive exam or practicum. *Entrance requirements:* For master's, bachelor's degree or equivalent, minimum GPA of 2.7 in last 60 hours of course work. *Application deadline:* Applications are processed on a rolling basis. Application fee: $0. Electronic applications accepted. *Financial support:* Applicants required to submit FAFSA. *Faculty research:* Military history, criminal justice, management performance, national security. *Unit head:* Dr. Frank McCluskey, Provost, 877-468-6268, Fax: 304-724-3780. *Application contact:* Terry Grant, Director of Enrollment Management, 877-468-6268, Fax: 304-724-3780, E-mail: info@apus.edu.

American University of Beirut, Graduate Programs, Faculty of Health Sciences, Beirut, Lebanon. Offers environmental sciences (MSES), including environmental health; epidemiology (MS); epidemiology and biostatistics (MPH); health behavior and education (MPH); population health (MS); public health (MPH). Part-time programs available. *Degree requirements:* For master's, one foreign language, comprehensive exam, thesis (for some programs). *Entrance requirements:* For master's, 2 letters of recommendation. Additional exam requirements/recommendations for international students: Required—TOEFL (minimum score 573 paper-based; 230 computer-based; 98 iBT), IELTS (minimum score 7.5). Electronic applications accepted. *Faculty research:* Urban health, childbirth, tobacco control, HIV/AIDS surveillance, health finance and policies.

Arizona State University, Graduate College, College of Nursing and Healthcare Innovation, Tempe, AZ 85287. Offers child and adolescent mental health intervention specialist (Graduate Certificate); community and public health practice (Graduate Certificate); community health (MS); evidence-based practice in nursing (Graduate Certificate); exercise and wellness (MS, PhD), including exercise and wellness (MS), physical activity, nutrition and wellness (PhD); healthcare innovation (MHI); nurse education in academic and practice settings (Graduate Certificate); nurse educator (MS); nursing (MS); nursing and healthcare innovation (PhD); nursing practice (DNP); nutrition (MS). *Accreditation:* AACN. Postbaccalaureate distance learning degree programs offered.

Arizona State University, Graduate College, W.P. Carey School of Business, School of Health Management and Policy, Tempe, AZ 85287. Offers health sector management (MHSM); urban health (MPH); MBA/MHSM. *Accreditation:* CAHME. *Entrance requirements:* For master's, GMAT.

Armstrong Atlantic State University, School of Graduate Studies, Program in Health Science, Savannah, GA 31419-1997. Offers health services administration (MHSA); public health (MPH). *Accreditation:* CAHME; CEPH. Part-time and evening/weekend programs available. Postbaccalaureate distance learning degree programs offered (no on-campus study). *Degree requirements:* For master's, comprehensive exam, thesis optional, internship. *Entrance requirements:* For master's, GMAT or GRE General Test, MAT, minimum GPA of 2.6. Additional exam requirements/recommendations for international students: Required—TOEFL (minimum score 523 paper-based; 193 computer-based). Electronic applications accepted. *Faculty research:* Health administration, community health, health education.

A.T. Still University of Health Sciences, School of Health Management, Kirksville, MO 63501. Offers geriatric healthcare (MGH); health administration (MHA); health education (MH Ed, DH Ed); public health (MPH). Part-time and evening/weekend programs available. Postbaccalaureate distance learning degree programs offered (minimal on-campus study). *Faculty:* 12 full-time (6 women), 31 part-time/adjunct (12 women). *Students:* 84 full-time (59 women), 503 part-time (340 women); includes 179 minority (103 African Americans, 11 American Indian/Alaska Native, 37 Asian Americans or Pacific Islanders, 28 Hispanic Americans). Average age 32. 179 applicants, 100% accepted, 98 enrolled. In 2009, 98 master's, 22 doctorates awarded. *Degree requirements:* For master's, thesis (for some programs), integrated terminal project; for doctorate, thesis/dissertation. *Entrance requirements:* For master's, minimum GPA of 2.5, bachelor's degree or equivalent from U.S. institution; for doctorate, minimum GPA of 2.5, master's or terminal degree, employment. Additional exam requirements/recommendations for international students: Required—TOEFL (minimum score 550 paper-based; 213 computer-based; 80 iBT). *Application deadline:* For fall admission, 8/7 for domestic and international students; for winter admission, 10/23 for domestic and international students; for spring admission, 2/5 for domestic and international students. Applications are processed on a rolling basis. Application fee: $60. Electronic applications accepted. *Expenses:* Contact institution. *Financial support:* In 2009–10, 408 students received support. Application deadline: 5/1. *Unit head:* Dr. Kimberly O'Reilly, Interim Dean, 660-626-2820, Fax: 660-626-2826, E-mail: koreilley@atsu.edu. *Application contact:* Sarah Spencer, Director of Recruitment, 660-626-2820 Ext. 2669, Fax: 660-626-2826, E-mail: sbartlett@atsu.edu.

Austin Peay State University, College of Graduate Studies, College of Behavioral and Health Sciences, Department of Health and Human Performance, Clarksville, TN 37044. Offers health leadership (MS). Part-time and evening/weekend programs available. Postbaccalaureate distance learning degree programs offered (no on-campus study). *Faculty:* 5 full-time (3 women). *Students:* 28 full-time (19 women), 45 part-time (35 women); includes 33 minority (28 African Americans, 1 Asian American or Pacific Islander, 4 Hispanic Americans). Average age 32. 72 applicants, 96% accepted, 39 enrolled. In 2009, 23 master's awarded. *Degree requirements:* For master's, comprehensive exam, thesis optional. *Entrance requirements:* For master's, GRE General Test, 3 letters of recommendation, minimum undergraduate GPA of 2.5. Additional exam requirements/recommendations for international students: Required—TOEFL (minimum score 500 paper-based; 173 computer-based). *Application deadline:* For fall

admission, 7/27 priority date for domestic students; for spring admission, 12/17 priority date for domestic students. Applications are processed on a rolling basis. Application fee: $25. Electronic applications accepted. *Expenses:* Tuition, state resident: full-time $6160; part-time $608 per credit hour. Tuition, nonresident: full-time $17,080; part-time $854 per credit hour. Required fees: $1224; $61.20 per credit hour. *Financial support:* In 2009–10, 9 students received support, including 9 research assistantships with full tuition reimbursements available (averaging $5,184 per year); career-related internships or fieldwork, Federal Work-Study, institutionally sponsored loans, scholarships/grants, and unspecified assistantships also available. Support available to part-time students. Financial award application deadline: 3/1; financial award applicants required to submit FAFSA. *Faculty research:* Aging and physical activity. *Unit head:* Dr. Marcy Maurer, Interim Chair, 931-221-6105, Fax: 931-221-7040, E-mail: maurerm@apsu.edu. *Application contact:* Dr. Dixie Dennis, Dean, College of Graduate Studies, 931-221-7662, Fax: 931-221-7641, E-mail: dennisdi@apsu.edu.

Barry University, School of Graduate Medical Sciences, Podiatric Medicine and Surgery Program, Podiatric Medicine/Public Health Option, Miami Shores, FL 33161-6695. Offers DPM/MPH.

Barry University, School of Graduate Medical Sciences and College of Health Sciences, Program in Public Health, Miami Shores, FL 33161-6695. Offers MPH. *Entrance requirements:* For master's, GRE.

Bellevue University, Graduate School, Bellevue, NE 68005-3098. Offers acquisition and contract management (MS); business administration (MBA); clinical counseling (MS); computer information systems (MS); healthcare administration (MA, MHA, MS), including healthcare administration (MHA), human services (MA, MS); human capital management (MS, PhD); instructional design and development (MS); leadership (MA); management (MA); management information systems (MS); organizational performance (MS); public administration (MPA); public health (MPH); security management (MS). Part-time and evening/weekend programs available. Postbaccalaureate distance learning degree programs offered (no on-campus study). *Degree requirements:* For master's, thesis or project. *Entrance requirements:* For master's, minimum GPA of 2.5 in last 60 hours. Additional exam requirements/recommendations for international students: Required—TOEFL (minimum score 538 paper-based; 200 computer-based).

Benedictine University, Graduate Programs, Program in Public Health, Lisle, IL 60532-0900. Offers administration of health care institutions (MPH); dietetics (MPH); disaster management (MPH); health education (MPH); health information systems (MPH); MBA/MPH; MPH/MS. Part-time and evening/weekend programs available. Postbaccalaureate distance learning degree programs offered. *Faculty:* 2 full-time (0 women), 8 part-time/adjunct (3 women). *Students:* 132 full-time (92 women), 354 part-time (286 women); includes 171 minority (112 African Americans, 1 American Indian/Alaska Native, 35 Asian Americans or Pacific Islanders, 23 Hispanic Americans), 14 international. Average age 33. 247 applicants, 94% accepted, 180 enrolled. In 2009, 77 master's awarded. *Entrance requirements:* For master's, MAT, GRE, or GMAT. Additional exam requirements/recommendations for international students: Required—TOEFL (minimum score 550 paper-based; 213 computer-based). *Application deadline:* For fall admission, 9/1 for domestic students; for winter admission, 12/1 for domestic students; for spring admission, 2/15 for domestic students. Application fee: $40. *Expenses:* Tuition: Part-time $750 per credit hour. Tuition and fees vary according to campus/location and program. *Financial support:* Career-related internships or fieldwork and health care benefits available. Support available to part-time students. *Unit head:* Dr. Alan Gorr, Director, 630-829-6566, Fax: 630-960-1126, E-mail: agorr@ben.edu. *Application contact:* Kari Gibbons, Director, Admissions, 630-829-6200, Fax: 630-829-6584, E-mail: kgibbons@ben.edu.

Boise State University, Graduate College, College of Health Science, Boise, ID 83725-0399. Offers MHS. Part-time programs available. *Degree requirements:* For master's, thesis. *Entrance requirements:* For master's, GRE General Test, GMAT or MAT, minimum GPA of 3.0. Electronic applications accepted. *Expenses:* Tuition, state resident: full-time $3106; part-time $209 per credit. Tuition, nonresident: part-time $284 per credit.

Boston University, Goldman School of Dental Medicine, Graduate Programs in Dentistry, Boston, MA 02215. Offers advanced general dentistry (CAGS); dental public health (MS, MSD, D Sc D, CAGS); dentistry (DMD); endodontics (MSD, D Sc D, CAGS); implantology (CAGS); operative dentistry (MSD, D Sc D, CAGS); oral and maxillofacial surgery (MSD, D Sc D, CAGS); oral biology (MSD, D Sc, D Sc D, PhD); orthodontics (MSD, D Sc D, CAGS); pediatric dentistry (MSD, D Sc D, CAGS); periodontology (MSD, D Sc D, CAGS); prosthodontics (MSD, D Sc D, CAGS). *Students:* 606 full-time (295 women); includes 149 minority (7 African Americans, 3 American Indian/Alaska Native, 113 Asian Americans or Pacific Islanders, 26 Hispanic Americans), 209 international. Average age 26. In 2009, 175 first professional degrees awarded. *Degree requirements:* For master's, thesis; for doctorate, thesis/dissertation; for CAGS, thesis (for some programs). *Entrance requirements:* For DMD, DAT, minimum GPA of 3.0; for CAGS, dental degree. *Application deadline:* For fall admission, 5/1 for domestic students. Applications are processed on a rolling basis. Application fee: $60. *Expenses:* Contact institution. *Financial support:* Career-related internships or fieldwork and institutionally sponsored loans available. Financial award application deadline: 4/15; financial award applicants required to submit CSS PROFILE or FAFSA. *Faculty research:* Defensive mechanisms, bone-cell regulation, protein biochemistry, molecular biology, biomaterials. *Unit head:* Dr. Jeffrey W. Hutter, Interim Dean, 617-638-4780. *Application contact:* 617-638-4787, Fax: 617-638-4798.

Boston University, School of Public Health, Boston, MA 02118. Offers M Sc, MA, MPH, Dr PH, PhD, Certificate, JD/MPH, MBA/MPH, MD/MPH, MPH/MA, MSW/MPH. *Accreditation:* CEPH. Part-time and evening/weekend programs available. *Faculty:* 153 full-time, 271 part-time/adjunct. *Students:* 419 full-time (332 women), 303 part-time (253 women); includes 132 minority (35 African Americans, 2 American Indian/Alaska Native, 64 Asian Americans or Pacific Islanders, 31 Hispanic Americans), 66 international. Average age 28. 1,829 applicants, 70% accepted, 272 enrolled. In 2009, 318 master's, 14 doctorates awarded. *Degree requirements:* For master's, comprehensive exam (for some programs), thesis optional, culminating experience and practicum; for doctorate, comprehensive exam, thesis/dissertation, comprehensive written and oral exams. *Entrance requirements:* For master's, GRE, MCAT, GMAT, LSAT, DAT, U.S. bachelor's degree or international equivalent; for doctorate, GRE, MCAT, GMAT, LSAT, MPH or equivalent. Additional exam requirements/recommendations for international students: Required—TOEFL (minimum score 600 paper-based; 250 computer-based; 100 iBT), IELTS (minimum score 6). *Application deadline:* For fall admission, 2/1 priority date for domestic and international students; for spring admission, 10/15 priority date for domestic and international students. Applications are processed on a rolling basis. Application fee: $95. Electronic applications accepted. *Expenses:* Contact institution. *Financial support:* Fellowships, career-related internships or fieldwork, Federal Work-Study, institutionally sponsored loans, scholarships/grants, and traineeships available. Support available to part-time students. Financial award application deadline: 3/1; financial award applicants required to submit FAFSA. *Faculty research:* Clinical trials, observational studies, environmental epidemiology, global ecology, environmental sustainability, community health, environmental justice, infectious disease, non-infectious disease, research methods, genetic epi, pharmaceutical assessment, bioethics, health law, human rights, health policy, management, finance and management, family health, disease control in developing countries, child and adolescent health, women's health, health disparities, communication and intervention. *Unit head:* Dr. Robert F. Meenan, Dean, 617-638-4640, Fax: 617-638-5299. *Application contact:* LePhan Quan, Associate Director of Admissions, 617-638-4640, Fax: 617-638-5299, E-mail: asksph@bu.edu.

Bowling Green State University, Graduate College, College of Health and Human Services, Program in Public Health, Bowling Green, OH 43403. Offers MPH. *Accreditation:* CEPH. Part-time programs available. *Degree requirements:* For master's, thesis or alternative. *Entrance*

requirements: For master's, GRE General Test, minimum GPA of 3.0. Additional exam requirements/recommendations for international students: Required—TOEFL. Electronic applications accepted.

Brooklyn College of the City University of New York, Division of Graduate Studies, Department of Health and Nutrition Science, Program in Public Health, Brooklyn, NY 11210-2889. Offers community-public health (MPH). *Accreditation:* CEPH. *Students:* 8 full-time (4 women), 44 part-time (37 women); includes 22 minority (12 African Americans, 3 Asian Americans or Pacific Islanders, 7 Hispanic Americans), 4 international. Average age 32. 48 applicants, 85% accepted, 7 enrolled. In 2009, 19 master's awarded. *Degree requirements:* For master's, thesis or alternative, 46 credits. *Entrance requirements:* For master's, GRE, 2 letters of recommendation, essay, interview. *Application deadline:* For fall admission, 3/1 priority date for domestic students, 2/1 priority date for international students; for spring admission, 11/1 priority date for domestic students, 10/1 priority date for international students. Applications are processed on a rolling basis. Application fee: $125. Electronic applications accepted. *Expenses:* Tuition, state resident: full-time $7360; part-time $310 per credit hour. Tuition, nonresident: full-time $13,800; part-time $575 per credit hour. Required fees: $140.10 per semester. *Financial support:* Application deadline: 5/1. *Unit head:* Dr. Elizabeth Eastwood, Graduate Deputy Chairperson, 718-951-5026, Fax: 718-951-4670, E-mail: eastwood@brooklyn.cuny.edu. *Application contact:* Hernan Sierra, Graduate Admissions Coordinator, 718-951-4536, Fax: 718-951-4506, E-mail: grads@brooklyn.cuny.edu.

Brown University, Graduate School, Division of Biology and Medicine, Department of Community Health, Program in Public Health, Providence, RI 02912. Offers MPH. *Accreditation:* CEPH. *Entrance requirements:* For master's, GRE General Test or MCAT. Additional exam requirements/recommendations for international students: Required—TOEFL.

California State University, Fresno, Division of Graduate Studies, College of Health and Human Services, Department of Public Health, Fresno, CA 93740-8027. Offers health policy and management (MPH); health promotion (MPH). *Accreditation:* CEPH. Part-time and evening/weekend programs available. *Degree requirements:* For master's, thesis or alternative. *Entrance requirements:* For master's, GRE General Test, minimum GPA of 2.5. Additional exam requirements/recommendations for international students: Required—TOEFL. Electronic applications accepted. *Faculty research:* Foster parent training, geriatrics, tobacco control.

California State University, Fullerton, Graduate Studies, College of Health and Human Development, Department of Health Science, Fullerton, CA 92834-9480. Offers public health (MPH). *Accreditation:* CEPH. Part-time programs available. *Students:* 33 full-time (26 women), 36 part-time (27 women); includes 38 minority (5 African Americans, 17 Asian Americans or Pacific Islanders, 16 Hispanic Americans), 5 international. Average age 32. 157 applicants, 30% accepted, 33 enrolled. In 2009, 28 master's awarded. *Entrance requirements:* For master's, minimum GPA of 3.0 in last 60 units attempted. Application fee: $55. *Expenses:* Tuition, nonresident: full-time $11,160; part-time $373 per credit. Required fees: $1440 per term. Tuition and fees vary according to course load, degree level and program. *Financial support:* Career-related internships or fieldwork, Federal Work-Study, institutionally sponsored loans, and scholarships/grants available. Support available to part-time students. Financial award application deadline: 3/1; financial award applicants required to submit FAFSA. *Unit head:* Dr. Shari McMahan, Department Head, 657-278-7000. *Application contact:* Admissions/Applications, 657-278-2371.

California State University, Northridge, Graduate Studies, College of Health and Human Development, Department of Health Sciences, Northridge, CA 91330. Offers health administration (MS); public health (MPH). *Accreditation:* CEPH. *Faculty:* 14 full-time (7 women), 54 part-time/adjunct (34 women). *Students:* 89 full-time (65 women), 65 part-time (49 women); includes 73 minority (16 African Americans, 32 Asian Americans or Pacific Islanders, 25 Hispanic Americans), 18 international. Average age 30. 659 applicants, 61% accepted, 99 enrolled. In 2009, 36 master's awarded. *Entrance requirements:* For master's, GRE General Test or minimum GPA of 3.0. Additional exam requirements/recommendations for international students: Required—TOEFL. *Application deadline:* For fall admission, 11/30 for domestic students. Application fee: $55. *Financial support:* Teaching assistantships available. Financial award application deadline: 3/1. *Faculty research:* Labor market needs assessment, health education products, dental hygiene, independent practice prototype. *Unit head:* Dr. Brian Malec, Chair, 818-677-3101. *Application contact:* Dr. Janet T. Reagan, Graduate Coordinator, 818-677-2298, E-mail: janet.reagan@csun.edu.

California State University, San Bernardino, Graduate Studies, College of Natural Sciences, Program in Health Science, San Bernardino, CA 92407-2397. Offers health science (MS); public health (MPH). *Faculty:* 5 full-time (1 woman), 2 part-time/adjunct (1 woman). *Students:* 10 full-time (9 women), 17 part-time (15 women); includes 14 minority (5 African Americans, 1 Asian American or Pacific Islander, 8 Hispanic Americans), 1 international. Average age 35. 12 applicants, 92% accepted, 3 enrolled. In 2009, 1 master's awarded. *Unit head:* Dr. Cynthia Paxton, Assistant Dean, 909-537-5343, Fax: 909-537-7037, E-mail: cpaxton@csusb.edu. *Application contact:* Olivia Rosas, Director of Admissions, 909-537-7577, Fax: 909-537-7034, E-mail: orosas@csusb.edu.

Case Western Reserve University, Frances Payne Bolton School of Nursing, Nursing/Public Health Program, Cleveland, OH 44106. Offers MSN/MPH.

Case Western Reserve University, School of Medicine and School of Graduate Studies, Graduate Programs in Medicine, Department of Epidemiology and Biostatistics, Program in Public Health, Cleveland, OH 44106. Offers MPH. *Accreditation:* CEPH. Part-time programs available. *Degree requirements:* For master's, essay, field experience, presentation. *Entrance requirements:* For master's, GRE General Test or MCAT, 3 letters of recommendation. Additional exam requirements/recommendations for international students: Required—TOEFL. Electronic applications accepted. *Faculty research:* Public policy and aging, statistical modeling, behavioral medicine and evaluation, continuous quality improvement, tobacco cessation and prevention.

Charles Drew University of Medicine and Science, College of Science and Health, Los Angeles, CA 90059. Offers urban public health (MPH).

Claremont Graduate University, Graduate Programs, School of Community and Global Health, San Dimas, CA 91773. Offers health promotion science (PhD); public health (MPH). *Faculty:* 9 full-time (4 women). *Students:* 10 full-time (7 women), 4 part-time (all women); includes 7 minority (2 African Americans, 1 American Indian/Alaska Native, 1 Asian American or Pacific Islander, 3 Hispanic Americans). Average age 30. *Entrance requirements:* For master's and doctorate, GRE. Additional exam requirements/recommendations for international students: Required—TOEFL (minimum score 550 paper-based; 213 computer-based; 80 iBT). *Application deadline:* For fall admission, 2/1 priority date for domestic students; for spring admission, 11/1 priority date for domestic students. Applications are processed on a rolling basis. Application fee: $60. Electronic applications accepted. *Expenses:* Tuition: Full-time $35,046; part-time $1524 per credit. Required fees: $161 per semester. *Financial support:* Fellowships, research assistantships, teaching assistantships, Federal Work-Study, institutionally sponsored loans, and scholarships/grants available. Support available to part-time students. Financial award application deadline: 2/15; financial award applicants required to submit FAFSA. *Unit head:* C. Anderson Johnson, Dean, 909-607-8235, E-mail: andy.johnson@cgu.edu. *Application contact:* C. Anderson Johnson, Dean, 909-607-8235, E-mail: andy.johnson@cgu.edu.

Cleveland State University, College of Graduate Studies, College of Education and Human Services, Department of Health, Physical Education, Recreation and Dance, Cleveland, OH 44115. Offers community health education (M Ed); exercise science (M Ed); human performance (M Ed); physical education pedagogy (M Ed); public health (MPH); school health education (M Ed); sport and exercise psychology (M Ed); sports management (M Ed). Part-time programs available. *Degree requirements:* For master's, comprehensive exam, thesis optional. *Entrance requirements:* For master's, GRE General Test or MAT (if undergraduate GPA less than 2.75), minimum undergraduate GPA of 2.75. Additional exam requirements/recommendations for

international students: Required—TOEFL (minimum score 525 paper-based; 197 computer-based), IELTS (minimum score 6). Electronic applications accepted. *Faculty research:* Bone density, marketing fitness centers, motor development of disabled, online learning and survey research.

Columbia University, Columbia University Mailman School of Public Health, New York, NY 10032. Offers Exec MPH, MPH, MS, Dr PH, PhD, DDS/MPH, MBA/MPH, MD/MPH, MPA/MPH, MPH/MIA, MPH/MOT, MPH/MS, MPH/MSN, MPH/MSSW. PhD offered in cooperation with the Graduate School of Arts and Sciences. *Accreditation:* CEPH (one or more programs are accredited). Part-time and evening/weekend programs available. *Faculty:* 312 full-time (155 women), 284 part-time/adjunct (128 women). *Students:* 539 full-time (442 women), 542 part-time (390 women); includes 322 minority (92 African Americans, 5 American Indian/Alaska Native, 162 Asian Americans or Pacific Islanders, 63 Hispanic Americans), 146 international. Average age 30. 1,889 applicants, 61% accepted, 430 enrolled. In 2009, 431 master's, 20 doctorates awarded. *Degree requirements:* For master's, thesis (for some programs); for doctorate, comprehensive exam, thesis/dissertation. *Entrance requirements:* For master's, GRE General Test; for doctorate, GRE General Test, MPH or equivalent (Dr PH). Additional exam requirements/recommendations for international students: Required—TOEFL (minimum score 600 paper-based; 250 computer-based; 100 iBT). *Application deadline:* For fall admission, 1/5 for domestic and international students. Application fee: $60. Electronic applications accepted. *Expenses:* Contact institution. *Financial support:* In 2009–10, 600 students received support; fellowships, research assistantships, teaching assistantships, career-related internships or fieldwork, Federal Work-Study, and traineeships available. Support available to part-time students. Financial award application deadline: 2/1; financial award applicants required to submit FAFSA. *Unit head:* Dr. Linda P. Fried, Dean/Professor, 212-305-9300, Fax: 212-305-9342, E-mail: lpfried@columbia.edu. *Application contact:* Dr. Joseph Korevec, Director of Admissions and Financial Aid, 212-305-8698, Fax: 212-342-1861, E-mail: ph-admit@columbia.edu.

Dartmouth College, The Dartmouth Institute, Program in Public Health, Hanover, NH 03755. Offers MPH. Degree awarded through Medical School. *Accreditation:* CEPH. Part-time programs available. *Faculty:* 32 full-time (17 women), 10 part-time/adjunct (7 women). *Students:* 26 full-time (7 women), 42 part-time (41 women); includes 17 minority (2 African Americans, 12 Asian Americans or Pacific Islanders, 3 Hispanic Americans), 4 international. Average age 31. 173 applicants, 83% accepted, 60 enrolled. In 2009, 47 master's awarded. *Degree requirements:* For master's, research project or practicum. *Entrance requirements:* For master's, GRE or MCAT, 3 letters of recommendation. Additional exam requirements/recommendations for international students: Required—TOEFL. *Application deadline:* For fall admission, 1/15 for domestic students. Applications are processed on a rolling basis. Application fee: $50. *Application contact:* Susan M. Benson, Academic Programs Director, 603-650-1782, Fax: 603-650-1900, E-mail: susan.benson@dartmouth.edu.

Davenport University, Sneden Graduate School, Grand Rapids, MI 49503. Offers accounting (MBA); business administration (EMBA); finance (MBA); health care management (MBA); human resources (MBA); information assurance (MS); public health (MPH); strategic management (MBA). Evening/weekend programs available. *Entrance requirements:* For master's, GMAT, minimum undergraduate GPA of 2.75. Additional exam requirements/recommendations for international students: Required—TOEFL. Electronic applications accepted. *Faculty research:* Leadership, management, marketing, organizational culture.

Davenport University, Sneden Graduate School, Warren, MI 48092-5209. Offers accounting (MBA); business administration (EMBA); finance (MBA); health care management (MBA); human resources management (MBA); information assurance (MS); public health (MPH); strategic management (MBA). *Entrance requirements:* For master's, minimum undergraduate GPA of 2.7.

Davenport University, Sneden Graduate School, Dearborn, MI 48126-3799. Offers accounting (MBA); business administration (EMBA); finance (MBA); health care management (MBA); human resources management (MBA); information assurance (MS); marketing (MBA); public health (MPH); strategic management (MBA). Part-time and evening/weekend programs available. Postbaccalaureate distance learning degree programs offered (no on-campus study). *Entrance requirements:* For master's, minimum GPA of 2.7, previous course work in accounting and statistics. *Faculty research:* Accounting, international accounting, social and environmental accounting, finance.

Des Moines University, College of Health Sciences, Program in Public Health, Des Moines, IA 50312-4104. Offers MPH. *Accreditation:* CEPH. Part-time and evening/weekend programs available. *Faculty:* 1 (woman) full-time, 1 (woman) part-time/adjunct. *Students:* 167 part-time (92 women); includes 38 minority (21 African Americans, 1 American Indian/Alaska Native, 14 Asian Americans or Pacific Islanders, 2 Hispanic Americans), 2 international. 324 applicants, 26% accepted, 84 enrolled. In 2009, 35 master's awarded. *Entrance requirements:* For master's, minimum GPA of 3.0. Additional exam requirements/recommendations for international students: Required—TOEFL (minimum score 600 paper-based). *Application deadline:* For fall admission, 7/1 for domestic and international students; for winter admission, 11/1 for domestic and international students; for spring admission, 3/1 for domestic and international students. Electronic applications accepted. *Expenses:* Contact institution. *Financial support:* In 2009–10, 1 student received support. Career-related internships or fieldwork, institutionally sponsored loans, scholarships/grants, and university employment available. Financial award applicants required to submit FAFSA. *Faculty research:* Quality improvement, women's health, health promotion, patient education. *Unit head:* Dr. Wendy Ringgenberg, Director, 515-271-1367, E-mail: wendy.ringgenberg@dmu.edu. *Application contact:* Lisa Vroegh, Admissions Coordinator, 515-271-1364, Fax: 515-271-7162, E-mail: hmadmit@dmu.edu.

Dominican University of California, Graduate Programs, School of Health and Natural Sciences, Program in Nursing, San Rafael, CA 94901-2298. Offers geriatric and nurse educator (MS); integrated health practices (clinical nursing specialist) (MS). *Accreditation:* AACN. Part-time and evening/weekend programs available. *Degree requirements:* For master's, thesis. *Entrance requirements:* For master's, minimum GPA of 3.0; clinical experience; course work in nursing research and statistics; CPR certification; professional liability and malpractice insurance; interview. Additional exam requirements/recommendations for international students: Required—TOEFL (minimum score 550 paper-based; 213 computer-based). Electronic applications accepted.

Drexel University, School of Public Health, Philadelphia, PA 19104-2875. Offers MPH, MS, PhD, Certificate. *Accreditation:* CEPH. *Entrance requirements:* For master's, GMAT, GRE, LSAT, or MCAT, previous course work in statistics and word processing. Additional exam requirements/recommendations for international students: Required—TOEFL. Electronic applications accepted. *Expenses:* Contact institution. *Faculty research:* Epidemiology, behavioral and social sciences, problem-based learning.

East Carolina University, Brody School of Medicine, Program in Public Health, Greenville, NC 27858-4353. Offers MPH. *Accreditation:* CEPH. Part-time programs available. *Degree requirements:* For master's, field placement professional paper. *Entrance requirements:* For master's, GRE or MCAT. Additional exam requirements/recommendations for international students: Required—TOEFL (minimum score 550 paper-based; 213 computer-based). Electronic applications accepted. *Faculty research:* Public health, disparities in public health.

East Carolina University, Graduate School, College of Fine Arts and Communication, School of Communication, Greenville, NC 27858-4353. Offers health communication (MA). *Entrance requirements:* For master's, GRE.

Eastern Virginia Medical School, Master of Public Health Program, Norfolk, VA 23501-1980. Offers MPH. *Accreditation:* CEPH. Evening/weekend programs available. *Faculty:* 5 full-time (3 women), 31 part-time/adjunct (17 women). *Students:* 64 full-time (46 women); includes 21 African Americans, 8 Asian Americans or Pacific Islanders, 3 Hispanic Americans. 70 applicants, 57% accepted, 37 enrolled. In 2009, 29 master's awarded. *Degree requirements:* For master's, field practicum. *Entrance requirements:* For master's, GRE General Test. Additional exam

Public Health—General

Eastern Virginia Medical School (continued)
requirements/recommendations for international students: Required—TOEFL (minimum score 650 paper-based; 278 computer-based). *Application deadline:* For fall admission, 4/30 for domestic and international students. Applications are processed on a rolling basis. Application fee: $60. Electronic applications accepted. *Expenses:* Contact institution. *Financial support:* Applicants required to submit FAFSA. *Faculty research:* Community-based health research. *Unit head:* Dr. David O. Matson, Director, 757-466-6120, Fax: 757-446-6121, E-mail: matsondo@evms.edu. *Application contact:* Paula M. Swartz, Administrative Support Coordinator, 757-446-6120, Fax: 757-446-6121, E-mail: swartzpm@evms.edu.

East Stroudsburg University of Pennsylvania, Graduate School, College of Health Sciences, Program in Public Health, East Stroudsburg, PA 18301-2999. Offers community health education (MPH). Part-time and evening/weekend programs available. Postbaccalaureate distance learning degree programs offered (minimal on-campus study). *Faculty:* 6 full-time (4 women), 2 part-time/adjunct (both women). *Students:* 29 full-time (25 women), 12 part-time (8 women); includes 8 minority (2 African Americans, 2 Asian Americans or Pacific Islanders, 4 Hispanic Americans), 6 international. Average age 30. In 2009, 8 master's awarded. *Degree requirements:* For master's, comprehensive exam, publishable paper, oral comprehensive exam. *Entrance requirements:* For master's, GRE, 3 letters of recommendation. Additional exam requirements/recommendations for international students: Required—TOEFL (minimum score 560 paper-based; 220 computer-based; 83 iBT). *Application deadline:* For fall admission, 7/31 priority date for domestic students, 3/1 for international students; for spring admission, 11/30 for domestic students, 10/1 for international students. Applications are processed on a rolling basis. Application fee: $50. Electronic applications accepted. *Expenses:* Tuition, state resident: full-time $9942; part-time $387 per credit. Tuition, nonresident: full-time $14,240; part-time $619 per credit. *Financial support:* In 2009–10, 40 research assistantships with partial tuition reimbursements (averaging $2,270 per year) were awarded; career-related internships or fieldwork and unspecified assistantships also available. *Faculty research:* Public health infrastructure. Total annual research expenditures: $500,000. *Unit head:* Dr. Steve Godin, MPH Program Director, 570-422-3562, E-mail: sgodin@po-box.esu.edu. *Application contact:* Kevin Quintero, Graduate Admissions Coordinator, 570-422-3890, Fax: 570-422-2711, E-mail: kquintero@po-box.esu.edu.

East Tennessee State University, School of Graduate Studies, College of Public and Allied Health, Department of Public Health, Johnson City, TN 37614. Offers community health (MPH); epidemiology (Certificate); gerontology (Certificate); health care management (Certificate); public health (MPH); public health administration (MPH). *Accreditation:* CEPH. Part-time programs available. *Degree requirements:* For master's, comprehensive exam, thesis optional. *Entrance requirements:* For master's, GRE General Test, 2 years of community health experience. Additional exam requirements/recommendations for international students: Required—TOEFL (minimum score 550 paper-based; 213 computer-based). *Faculty research:* Rural health issues, youth and adolescent health, health of the elderly, environmental epidemiology, spatial analysis of data.

Emory University, Rollins School of Public Health, Atlanta, GA 30322. Offers MPH, MSPH, PhD, MM Sc/MPH, JD/MPH, MBA/MPH, MD/MPH, MSN/MPH. *Accreditation:* CEPH (one or more programs are accredited). Part-time and evening/weekend programs available. Postbaccalaureate distance learning degree programs offered (minimal on-campus study). *Degree requirements:* For master's, variable foreign language requirement, comprehensive exam (for some programs), thesis (for some programs), practicum. *Entrance requirements:* For master's, GRE General Test. Additional exam requirements/recommendations for international students: Required—TOEFL (minimum score 550 paper-based; 213 computer-based; 80 iBT), IELTS can be submitted in place of TOEFL. Electronic applications accepted. *Expenses:* Contact institution. *Faculty research:* HIV/AIDS prevention, infectious disease, minority health, health disparities, bioterrorism.

Florida Agricultural and Mechanical University, Division of Graduate Studies, Research, and Continuing Education, College of Pharmacy and Pharmaceutical Sciences, Institute of Public Health, Tallahassee, FL 32307-3200. Offers MPH. *Accreditation:* CEPH. *Faculty:* 8 full-time (5 women). *Students:* 54 full-time (43 women), 8 part-time (6 women); includes 58 minority (all African Americans). In 2009, 16 master's awarded. *Entrance requirements:* Additional exam requirements/recommendations for international students: Required—TOEFL. *Application deadline:* For fall admission, 4/1 for domestic students. *Unit head:* Dr. Cynthia Harris, Director, 850-599-3345, Fax: 850-599-8830. *Application contact:* Gloria James, Graduate Coordinator, 850-599-3144.

Florida International University, Stempel College of Public Health and Social Work, Programs in Public Health, Miami, FL 33199. Offers biostatistics (MPH); environmental and occupational health (MPH, PhD); epidemiology (MPH, PhD); health policy and management (MPH); health promotion and disease prevention (PhD); health promotion and diseases prevention (MPH). PhD only admits in Fall. *Accreditation:* CEPH. Part-time and evening/weekend programs available. Postbaccalaureate distance learning degree programs offered (no on-campus study). *Faculty:* 18 full-time (6 women). *Students:* 249 full-time (186 women), 185 part-time (144 women); includes 309 minority (154 African Americans, 2 American Indian/Alaska Native, 26 Asian Americans or Pacific Islanders, 127 Hispanic Americans), 48 international. Average age 35. 484 applicants, 29% accepted, 123 enrolled. In 2009, 79 master's, 1 doctorate awarded. *Degree requirements:* For master's, thesis optional; for doctorate, comprehensive exam, thesis/dissertation. *Entrance requirements:* For master's, minimum GPA of 3.0, letters of recommendation; for doctorate, GRE, resume, minimum GPA of 3.0, letters of recommendation, letter of intent. Additional exam requirements/recommendations for international students: Required—TOEFL (minimum score 550 paper-based; 80 iBT). *Application deadline:* For fall admission, 6/1 for domestic students, 4/1 for international students; for spring admission, 10/1 for domestic students, 9/1 for international students. Applications are processed on a rolling basis. Application fee: $30. Electronic applications accepted. *Expenses:* Contact institution. *Financial support:* Institutionally sponsored loans, scholarships/grants, and tuition waivers (full) available. Financial award application deadline: 3/1; financial award applicants required to submit FAFSA. *Faculty research:* Drugs/AIDS intervention among migrant workers, provision of services for active/recovering drug users with HIV. *Unit head:* Dr. Gilbert Ramirez, Associate Dean for Academic and Student Affairs, 305-348-7442, E-mail: ph@fiu.edu. *Application contact:* Nanett Rojas, Assistant Director of Graduate Admissions, 305-348-7442, Fax: 305-348-7441, E-mail: gradadm@fiu.edu.

Florida State University, The Graduate School, College of Social Sciences and Public Policy, Public Health Program, Tallahassee, FL 32306. Offers MPH. Part-time programs available. *Faculty:* 6 full-time (1 woman), 2 part-time/adjunct (0 women). *Students:* 16 full-time (9 women), 24 part-time (16 women); includes 20 minority (10 African Americans, 1 American Indian/Alaska Native, 1 Asian American or Pacific Islander, 8 Hispanic Americans), 4 international. Average age 26. 52 applicants, 85% accepted, 16 enrolled. In 2009, 17 master's awarded. *Degree requirements:* For master's, internship, research paper. *Entrance requirements:* For master's, GRE General Test, minimum GPA of 3.0. Additional exam requirements/recommendations for international students: Required—TOEFL (minimum score 550 paper-based; 213 computer-based; 80 iBT). *Application deadline:* For fall admission, 7/1 priority date for domestic students, 7/1 for international students; for spring admission, 11/1 for domestic and international students. Applications are processed on a rolling basis. Application fee: $30. Electronic applications accepted. *Expenses:* Tuition, state resident: full-time $7413. Tuition, nonresident: full-time $22,567. *Financial support:* In 2009–10, 3 students received support, including 3 research assistantships with full tuition reimbursements available (averaging $5,000 per year); fellowships with tuition reimbursements available, career-related internships or fieldwork, Federal Work-Study, institutionally sponsored loans, and unspecified assistantships also available. Financial award application deadline: 2/15. *Faculty research:* Health behavior surveillance, long term care policy, long term care evaluation, HMO's, Medicaid. Total annual research expenditures: $1 million. *Unit head:* Dr. William G. Weissert, Director, 850-644-4418, Fax: 850-644-1367, E-mail: william.weissert@fsu.edu. *Application contact:* Patty Lollis, Academic Program Specialist, 850-644-4418, E-mail: plollis@fsu.edu.

Fort Valley State University, College of Graduate Studies and Extended Education, Program in Public Health, Fort Valley, GA 31030. Offers environmental health (MPH). *Degree requirements:* For master's, thesis. *Entrance requirements:* For master's, GRE General Test.

George Mason University, College of Health and Human Services, Department of Global and Community Health, Fairfax, VA 22030. Offers biostatistics (Certificate); epidemiology (Certificate); epidemiology and biostatistics (MS); gerontology (Certificate); global health (MS, Certificate); nutrition (Certificate); public health (MPH, Certificate); rehabilitation science (Certificate). *Faculty:* 14 full-time (8 women), 12 part-time/adjunct (8 women). *Students:* 93 full-time (75 women), 106 part-time (92 women); includes 87 minority (46 African Americans, 1 American Indian/Alaska Native, 31 Asian Americans or Pacific Islanders, 9 Hispanic Americans), 22 international. Average age 31. 269 applicants, 69% accepted, 146 enrolled. In 2009, 17 master's, 2 other advanced degrees awarded. *Degree requirements:* For master's, comprehensive exam (for some programs), thesis or practicum. *Entrance requirements:* For master's, GRE, BA with minimum GPA of 3.0, 2 letters of recommendation. Additional exam requirements/recommendations for international students: Required—TOEFL. *Application deadline:* For fall admission, 4/1 priority date for domestic students, 4/1 for international students; for spring admission, 11/1 for domestic and international students. Applications are processed on a rolling basis. Application fee: $75. Electronic applications accepted. *Expenses:* Tuition, state resident: full-time $7568; part-time $315.33 per credit hour. Tuition, nonresident: full-time $21,704; part-time $904.33 per credit hour. Required fees: $2184; $91 per credit hour. *Financial support:* In 2009–10, 4 students received support, including 2 research assistantships with full and partial tuition reimbursements available (averaging $3,500 per year), 2 teaching assistantships with full and partial tuition reimbursements available (averaging $2,790 per year); Federal Work-Study, scholarships/grants, unspecified assistantships, and research awards, health care benefits health care benefits (full-time research or teaching assistantship recipients) also available. Support available to part-time students. Financial award application deadline: 3/1. *Faculty research:* Providing introductory and advanced degrees in health-related disciplines centered in global and community issues, health issues and the needs of affected populations at the regional and global level. *Unit head:* Dr. Shirley S. Travis, Dean, 703-993-1918. *Application contact:* Allan Weiss, Office Manager, 703-993-3126, E-mail: aweiss2@gmu.edu.

Georgetown University, Graduate School of Arts and Sciences, Programs in Biomedical Sciences, Department of Microbiology and Immunology, Washington, DC 20057. Offers biohazardous threat agents and emerging infectious diseases (MS); general microbiology and immunology (MS); global infectious diseases (PhD); microbiology and immunology research (PhD); science policy and advocacy (MS). Part-time programs available. *Degree requirements:* For master's, 30 credit hours of coursework; for doctorate, comprehensive exam, thesis/dissertation. *Entrance requirements:* For master's, GRE General Test, 3 letters of reference, bachelor's degree in related field; for doctorate, GRE General Test, 3 letters of reference, MS/BS in related field. Additional exam requirements/recommendations for international students: Required—TOEFL (minimum score 505 paper-based; 213 computer-based). Electronic applications accepted. *Faculty research:* Pathogenesis and basic biology of the fungus Candida albicans, molecular biology of viral immunopathological mechanisms in Multiple Sclerosis.

The George Washington University, School of Public Health and Health Services, Department of Global Health, Washington, DC 20052. Offers MPH, JD/MPH, LL M/MPH, MD/MPH. *Accreditation:* CEPH. *Students:* 121 full-time (106 women), 85 part-time (72 women); includes 60 minority (17 African Americans, 2 American Indian/Alaska Native, 28 Asian Americans or Pacific Islanders, 13 Hispanic Americans), 10 international. Average age 27. 341 applicants, 87% accepted, 85 enrolled. In 2009, 52 master's awarded. *Degree requirements:* For master's, case study or special project. *Entrance requirements:* For master's, GMAT, GRE General Test, or MCAT. Additional exam requirements/recommendations for international students: Required—TOEFL. *Application deadline:* For fall admission, 4/15 priority date for domestic students, 4/15 for international students; for spring admission, 11/1 for domestic and international students. Applications are processed on a rolling basis. Application fee: $60. *Financial support:* In 2009–10, 24 students received support. Tuition waivers available. Financial award application deadline: 2/15. *Unit head:* Dr. James Sherry, Chair, 202-994-0270, Fax: 202-994-1955, E-mail: sherry@gwu.edu. *Application contact:* Jane Smith, Director of Admissions, 202-994-0248, Fax: 202-994-1860, E-mail: sphhsinfo@gwumc.edu.

The George Washington University, School of Public Health and Health Services, Department of Health Services Management and Leadership, Washington, DC 20052. Offers health management and leadership (MHSA); health policy (MHSA); health services administration (Specialist); public health management (MPH). *Accreditation:* CAHME (one or more programs are accredited). *Degree requirements:* For master's, internship or residency. *Entrance requirements:* For master's, GMAT or GRE; for Specialist, GMAT or GRE, master's degree in related field. Additional exam requirements/recommendations for international students: Required—TOEFL. *Faculty research:* Hospital administration, ambulatory health care, social gerontology, health care financing, health care ethics.

Georgia Southern University, Jack N. Averitt College of Graduate Studies, Jiann-Ping Hsu College of Public Health, Program in Public Health, Statesboro, GA 30460. Offers biostatistics (MPH, Dr PH); community health behavior and education (Dr PH); community health education (MPH); environmental health sciences (MPH); epidemiology (MPH); health services policy management (MPH); public health leadership (Dr PH). Part-time programs available. *Students:* 75 full-time (47 women), 23 part-time (15 women); includes 39 minority (36 African Americans, 3 Asian Americans or Pacific Islanders), 24 international. Average age 30. 50 applicants, 80% accepted, 20 enrolled. In 2009, 20 master's awarded. *Degree requirements:* For master's, thesis optional, practicum; for doctorate, comprehensive exam, thesis/dissertation, practicum. *Entrance requirements:* For master's, GRE General Test, minimum GPA of 2.75, resume, 3 letters of reference; for doctorate, GRE, GMAT, MCAT, LSAT, 3 letters of reference, statement of purpose, resume or curriculum vitae. Additional exam requirements/recommendations for international students: Required—TOEFL (minimum score 550 paper-based; 213 computer-based; 80 iBT). *Application deadline:* For fall admission, 3/1 priority date for domestic and international students; for spring admission, 10/1 priority date for domestic students, 10/1 for international students. Applications are processed on a rolling basis. Application fee: $50. Electronic applications accepted. *Expenses:* Contact institution. *Financial support:* In 2009–10, 83 students received support, including research assistantships with partial tuition reimbursements available (averaging $7,200 per year), teaching assistantships with partial tuition reimbursements available (averaging $7,200 per year); career-related internships or fieldwork, Federal Work-Study, scholarships/grants, tuition waivers (partial), and unspecified assistantships also available. Support available to part-time students. Financial award application deadline: 4/15; financial award applicants required to submit FAFSA. *Faculty research:* Biostatistics, community health, environmental health sciences, epidemiology, health policy and management, community health behavior and education, public health leadership. *Unit head:* Dr. Charles Hardy, Dean, 912-478-2674, Fax: 912-478-5811, E-mail: chardy@georgiasouthern.edu. *Application contact:* Dr. Charles Ziglar, Coordinator for Graduate Student Recruitment, 912-478-5635, Fax: 912-478-0740, E-mail: gradadmissions@georgiasouthern.edu.

Georgia State University, Andrew Young School of Policy Studies, Department of Public Management and Policy, Atlanta, GA 30303. Offers disaster management (Certificate); nonprofit management (Certificate); planning and economic development (Certificate); public administration (MPA), including criminal justice, management and finance, nonprofit management, planning and economic development, policy analysis and evaluation, public health; public policy (MPP, PhD), including disaster policy (MPP), nonprofit policy (MPP), planning and economic development policy (MPP), public finance policy (MPP), social policy (MPP); JD/MPA. *Accreditation:* NASPAA (one or more programs are accredited). Part-time and evening/weekend programs available. Terminal master's awarded for partial completion of doctoral program. *Degree requirements:* For master's, thesis optional; for doctorate, comprehensive exam, thesis/dissertation. *Entrance requirements:* For master's and doctorate, GRE General

Test. Additional exam requirements/recommendations for international students: Required—TOEFL. Electronic applications accepted. *Faculty research:* Public management, policy analysis, public finance, planning and economic development, nonprofit leadership and policy.

Georgia State University, College of Health and Human Sciences, Institute of Public Health, Atlanta, GA 30302-3995. Offers MPH, Certificate. *Accreditation:* CEPH. Part-time and evening/weekend programs available. *Degree requirements:* For master's, thesis, practicum. *Entrance requirements:* For master's and Certificate, GRE, GMAT. Additional exam requirements/recommendations for international students: Required—TOEFL (minimum score 550 paper-based; 213 computer-based; 80 iBT). Electronic applications accepted. *Faculty research:* Health promotion and behavior, prevention sciences, health policy and management.

Graduate School and University Center of the City University of New York, Graduate Studies, Program in Public Health, New York, NY 10016-4039. Offers DPH. Part-time programs available. *Faculty:* 5 full-time (4 women). *Students:* 17 full-time (13 women), 27 part-time (22 women); includes 19 minority (7 African Americans, 3 Asian Americans or Pacific Islanders, 9 Hispanic Americans), 1 international. Average age 39. 40 applicants, 43% accepted, 14 enrolled. *Degree requirements:* For doctorate, thesis/dissertation, exams, research seminars. *Entrance requirements:* For doctorate, GRE General Test, MPH, 2 letters of recommendation, curriculum vitae or resume. *Application deadline:* For fall admission, 3/1 for domestic students. Application fee: $125. *Financial support:* In 2009–10, 11 students received support, including 6 fellowships. *Unit head:* Prof. Nicholas Freudenberg, Director, 212-817-7980, E-mail: nfreuden@hunter.cuny.edu. *Application contact:* Les Gribben, Director of Admissions, 212-817-7470, Fax: 212-817-1624, E-mail: lgribben@gc.cuny.edu.

Harvard University, Cyprus International Institute for the Environment and Public Health in Association with Harvard School of Public Health, Cambridge, MA 02138. Offers environmental health (MS). *Entrance requirements:* For master's, GRE, resume, 3 letters of recommendation, BA or BS. Additional exam requirements/recommendations for international students: Required—TOEFL (minimum score 220 computer-based), IELTS (minimum score 7). Electronic applications accepted. *Expenses:* Tuition: Full-time $33,696. Required fees: $1126. Full-time tuition and fees vary according to program. *Faculty research:* Air pollution, climate change, biostatistics, sustainable development, environmental management.

Harvard University, School of Public Health, Boston, MA 02115-6096. Offers MOH, MPH, SM, DPH, PhD, SD, JD/MPH, MD/MPH. *Accreditation:* CEPH (one or more programs are accredited). Part-time programs available. *Faculty:* 306 full-time (205 women), 125 part-time/adjunct (84 women). *Students:* 827 full-time, 240 part-time; includes 196 minority (56 African Americans, 5 American Indian/Alaska Native, 105 Asian Americans or Pacific Islanders, 30 Hispanic Americans), 350 international. Average age 31. 1,814 applicants, 42% accepted, 500 enrolled. In 2009, 388 master's, 67 doctorates awarded. Terminal master's awarded for partial completion of doctoral program. *Degree requirements:* For master's, comprehensive exam (for some programs), thesis (for some programs); for doctorate, thesis/dissertation, qualifying exam. *Entrance requirements:* For master's and doctorate, GRE. Additional exam requirements/recommendations for international students: Required—TOEFL (minimum score 590 paper-based; 240 computer-based; 95 iBT); Recommended—IELTS (minimum score 7). *Application deadline:* For fall admission, 12/15 for domestic and international students. Application fee: $115. Electronic applications accepted. *Expenses:* Contact institution. *Financial support:* Fellowships, research assistantships, teaching assistantships, career-related internships or fieldwork, Federal Work-Study, scholarships/grants, traineeships, and unspecified assistantships available. Support available to part-time students. Financial award application deadline: 2/8; financial award applicants required to submit FAFSA. *Unit head:* Dr. Julio Frenk, Dean of the Faculty, 617-432-1025, Fax: 617-277-5320, E-mail: deansoff@hsph.harvard.edu. *Application contact:* Vincent W. James, Director of Admissions, 617-432-1031, Fax: 617-432-7080, E-mail: admisofc@hsph.harvard.edu.

See Close-Up on page 1667.

Howard University, College of Medicine, Program in Public Health, Washington, DC 20059-0002. Offers MPH.

Hunter College of the City University of New York, Graduate School, Schools of the Health Professions, School of Health Sciences, Programs in Urban Public Health, New York, NY 10021-5085. Offers community health education (MPH); environmental and occupational health education (MS); epidemiology and biostatistics (MPH); health policy management (MPH); nutrition and public health (MPH); MS/MPH. Part-time programs available. *Faculty:* 27 full-time (17 women), 3 part-time/adjunct (2 women). *Students:* 55 full-time (46 women), 223 part-time (168 women); includes 114 minority (40 African Americans, 1 American Indian/Alaska Native, 54 Asian Americans or Pacific Islanders, 19 Hispanic Americans). Average age 36. 662 applicants, 37% accepted, 147 enrolled. In 2009, 32 master's awarded. *Degree requirements:* For master's, comprehensive exam. *Entrance requirements:* For master's, GRE General Test, undergraduate major in natural or social sciences, health studies, nutrition or related field; 1 year of work or volunteer experience related to public health, nutrition, environmental health, social services, or community organization. Additional exam requirements/recommendations for international students: Required—TOEFL. *Application deadline:* For fall admission, 4/1 for domestic students, 2/1 for international students; for spring admission, 11/1 for domestic students, 9/1 for international students. Application fee: $125. *Expenses:* Tuition, state resident: full-time $7360; part-time $310 per credit. Required fees: $250 per semester. *Financial support:* Application deadline: 3/1. *Unit head:* Bernice Rumala, Director of Recruitment and Student Support Services, 212-481-3478, Fax: 212-481-5260, E-mail: brumala@hunter.cuny.edu. *Application contact:* Michael Goldstein, Assistant Director for Graduate Admissions, 212-772-4288, Fax: 212-650-3336, E-mail: admissions@hunter.cuny.edu.

Idaho State University, Office of Graduate Studies, College of Education, Department of Educational Foundations, Pocatello, ID 83209-8059. Offers child and family studies (M Ed); curriculum leadership (M Ed); education (M Ed); educational administration (M Ed); educational foundations (5th Year Certificate); elementary education (M Ed), including K-12 education, literacy, secondary education. Part-time programs available. *Faculty:* 13 full-time (8 women). *Students:* 15 full-time (9 women), 100 part-time (64 women); includes 2 minority (1 African American, 1 Hispanic American), 3 international. Average age 39. In 2009, 25 master's awarded. *Degree requirements:* For master's, comprehensive exam, thesis optional, oral exam, written exam; for 5th Year Certificate, comprehensive exam, thesis (for some programs), oral exam, written exam. *Entrance requirements:* For master's, GRE General Test or MAT, minimum undergraduate GPA of 3.0; for 5th Year Certificate, GRE General Test, minimum undergraduate GPA of 3.0, master's degree. Additional exam requirements/recommendations for international students: Required—TOEFL (minimum score 550 paper-based; 213 computer-based; 80 iBT). *Application deadline:* For fall admission, 7/1 for domestic students, 6/1 for international students; for spring admission, 12/1 for domestic students, 11/1 for international students. Applications are processed on a rolling basis. Application fee: $55. Electronic applications accepted. *Expenses:* Tuition, state resident: full-time $3318; part-time $297 per credit hour. Tuition, nonresident: full-time $13,120; part-time $437 per credit hour. Required fees: $2530. Tuition and fees vary according to program. *Financial support:* Research assistantships with full and partial tuition reimbursements, teaching assistantships with full and partial tuition reimbursements, career-related internships or fieldwork, Federal Work-Study, institutionally sponsored loans, scholarships/grants, traineeships, health care benefits, tuition waivers (full and partial), and unspecified assistantships available. Support available to part-time students. Financial award application deadline: 1/1; financial award applicants required to submit FAFSA. *Faculty research:* Child and families studies; business education; special education; math, science, and technology education. *Unit head:* Dr. Beverly Ray, Chair, 208-282-4516, Fax: 208-282-3791, E-mail: raybeve@isu.edu. *Application contact:* Dr. Peter Denner, Assistant Dean, 208-282-3807, Fax: 208-282-4697, E-mail: dennpete@isu.edu.

Idaho State University, Office of Graduate Studies, Kasiska College of Health Professions, Department of Health and Nutrition Sciences, Program in Public Health, Pocatello, ID 83209-8109. Offers MPH. *Accreditation:* CEPH. Part-time programs available. *Faculty:* 2 full-time (1 woman). *Students:* 22 full-time (13 women), 23 part-time (14 women); includes 6 minority (1 African American, 1 American Indian/Alaska Native, 2 Asian Americans or Pacific Islanders, 2 Hispanic Americans), 6 international. Average age 30. In 2009, 6 master's awarded. *Degree requirements:* For master's, comprehensive exam, thesis. *Entrance requirements:* For master's, GRE General Test, minimum GPA of 3.0 for upper division classes, 2 letters of recommendation. Additional exam requirements/recommendations for international students: Required—TOEFL (minimum score 600 paper-based; 213 computer-based). *Application deadline:* For fall admission, 7/1 for domestic students, 6/1 for international students; for spring admission, 12/1 for domestic students, 11/1 for international students. Applications are processed on a rolling basis. Application fee: $55. Electronic applications accepted. *Expenses:* Tuition, state resident: full-time $3318; part-time $297 per credit hour. Tuition, nonresident: full-time $13,120; part-time $437 per credit hour. Required fees: $2530. Tuition and fees vary according to program. *Financial support:* In 2009–10, research assistantships with full and partial tuition reimbursements (averaging $10,841 per year); teaching assistantships with full and partial tuition reimbursements, career-related internships or fieldwork, Federal Work-Study, institutionally sponsored loans, scholarships/grants, traineeships, health care benefits, tuition waivers (full and partial), and unspecified assistantships also available. Support available to part-time students. Financial award application deadline: 1/1; financial award applicants required to submit FAFSA. *Unit head:* Dr. Willis McAleese, Chairman, 208-282-2729, Fax: 208-282-4000, E-mail: mcalwill@isu.edu. *Application contact:* Tami Carson, Graduate School Technical Records Specialist, 208-282-2150, Fax: 208-282-4847, E-mail: carstami@isu.edu.

Independence University, Program in Public Health, Salt Lake City, UT 84107. Offers MPH. Part-time and evening/weekend programs available. Postbaccalaureate distance learning degree programs offered (no on-campus study). *Degree requirements:* For master's, final project or thesis. *Expenses:* Required fees: $475 per credit. One-time fee: $100 part-time.

Indiana University Bloomington, School of Health, Physical Education and Recreation, Department of Applied Health Science, Bloomington, IN 47405-7000. Offers health behavior (PhD); health promotion (MS); human development/family studies (MS); nutrition science (MS); public health (MPH); safety management (MS); school and college health programs (MS). *Accreditation:* CEPH (one or more programs are accredited). *Faculty:* 24 full-time (12 women). *Students:* 131 full-time (92 women), 22 part-time (20 women); includes 35 minority (22 African Americans, 1 American Indian/Alaska Native, 5 Asian Americans or Pacific Islanders, 7 Hispanic Americans), 29 international. Average age 31. 118 applicants, 71% accepted, 52 enrolled. In 2009, 43 master's, 6 doctorates awarded. *Degree requirements:* For master's, thesis optional; for doctorate, thesis/dissertation. *Entrance requirements:* For master's, GRE (MS in nutrition science), 3 recommendations; for doctorate, GRE, 3 recommendations. Additional exam requirements/recommendations for international students: Required—TOEFL (minimum score 550 paper-based; 213 computer-based; 79 iBT). *Application deadline:* For fall admission, 4/30 priority date for domestic students, 12/1 priority date for international students; for spring admission, 11/15 priority date for domestic students, 9/1 priority date for international students. Application fee: $55 ($65 for international students). *Financial support:* In 2009–10, 80 students received support, including 12 fellowships (averaging $2,316 per year), 50 research assistantships with full and partial tuition reimbursements available (averaging $6,973 per year), 27 teaching assistantships with full and partial tuition reimbursements available (averaging $11,067 per year); career-related internships or fieldwork, Federal Work-Study, institutionally sponsored loans, scholarships/grants, tuition waivers (partial), and fee remissions also available. Financial award application deadline: 3/1. *Faculty research:* Cancer education, HIV/AIDS and drug education, public health, parent-child interactions, safety education. Total annual research expenditures: $2.8 million. *Unit head:* Dr. Mohammad R. Torabi, Chair, 812-855-4808, Fax: 812-855-3936, E-mail: torabi@indiana.edu. *Application contact:* Dr. Mohammad R. Torabi, Chair, 812-855-4808, Fax: 812-855-3936, E-mail: torabi@indiana.edu.

Indiana University–Purdue University Indianapolis, Indiana University School of Medicine, Department of Public Health, Indianapolis, IN 46202-2896. Offers behavioral health science (MPH); epidemiology (MPH); health policy and management (MPH). *Students:* 62 full-time (47 women), 71 part-time (54 women); includes 37 minority (24 African Americans, 12 Asian Americans or Pacific Islanders, 1 Hispanic American), 15 international. Average age 31. 17 applicants, 65% accepted, 6 enrolled.Application fee: $55 ($65 for international students). *Expenses:* Contact institution. *Financial support:* In 2009–10, 1 teaching assistantship (averaging $14,058 per year) was awarded. *Unit head:* Dr. Carole Kacius, Director, 317-274-3126. *Application contact:* Robert M. Stump, Director of Admissions, 317-274-3772, E-mail: inmedadm@iupui.edu.

The Johns Hopkins University, Bloomberg School of Public Health, Baltimore, MD 21205. Offers MHA, MHS, MPH, Sc M, Dr PH, PhD, Sc D, JD/MPH, MBA/MPH, MHS/MA, MSN/MPH, MSW/MPH. *Accreditation:* CEPH (one or more programs are accredited). Part-time and evening/weekend programs available. Postbaccalaureate distance learning degree programs offered (minimal on-campus study). *Faculty:* 546 full-time (277 women), 680 part-time/adjunct (282 women). *Students:* 1,273 full-time (919 women), 444 part-time (275 women); includes 433 minority (117 African Americans, 6 American Indian/Alaska Native, 255 Asian Americans or Pacific Islanders, 55 Hispanic Americans), 413 international. Average age 29. 3,274 applicants, 51% accepted, 716 enrolled. In 2009, 634 master's, 129 doctorates awarded. *Degree requirements:* For master's, comprehensive exam (for some programs), thesis (for some programs); for doctorate, comprehensive exam, thesis/dissertation. *Entrance requirements:* For master's and doctorate, GRE General Test, 3 letters of recommendation, resume. Additional exam requirements/recommendations for international students: Required—TOEFL (minimum score 600 paper-based; 250 computer-based). *Application deadline:* Applications are processed on a rolling basis. Application fee: $45. Electronic applications accepted. *Financial support:* In 2009–10, 1,256 students received support, including 38 fellowships (averaging $34,333 per year), 59 research assistantships (averaging $23,525 per year), 11 teaching assistantships (averaging $3,126 per year); career-related internships or fieldwork, Federal Work-Study, institutionally sponsored loans, scholarships/grants, traineeships, health care benefits, and stipends also available. Support available to part-time students. Financial award application deadline: 3/15; financial award applicants required to submit FAFSA. *Faculty research:* Biodefense studies, infectious/chronic disease, human nutrition, environmental hazards, genetics. Total annual research expenditures: $323.6 million. *Unit head:* Dr. Michael J. Klag, Dean, 410-955-3540, Fax: 410-955-0121, E-mail: mklag@jhsph.edu. *Application contact:* Leslie K. Vink, Director of Recruitment, Communications and Special Projects, 410-955-3543, Fax: 410-955-0464, E-mail: lvink@jhsph.edu.

Laurentian University, School of Graduate Studies and Research, Interdisciplinary Program in Rural and Northern Health, Sudbury, ON P3E 2C6, Canada. Offers PhD.

Loma Linda University, School of Public Health, Loma Linda, CA 92350. Offers MBA, MHA, MPH, MSPH, Dr PH, Postbaccalaureate Certificate. *Accreditation:* CEPH (one or more programs are accredited). Part-time programs available. *Degree requirements:* For doctorate, thesis/dissertation. *Entrance requirements:* For master's, GRE General Test, baccalaureate degree, minimum 3.0 GPA; for doctorate, GRE General Test, minimum GPA of 3.2. Additional exam requirements/recommendations for international students: Required—TOEFL (minimum score 550 paper-based; 213 computer-based), Michigan English Language Assessment Battery or TOEFL. Electronic applications accepted. *Faculty research:* Lifestyle and health, nutrition and cancer, nutrition and cardiovascular disease, smoking and health, aging and longevity.

Louisiana State University in Shreveport, College of Education and Human Development, Program in Public Health, Shreveport, LA 71115-2399. Offers MPH. Part-time and evening/weekend programs available. *Students:* 11 full-time (7 women), 3 part-time (2 women); includes 6 minority (all African Americans), 1 international. Average age 28. 9 applicants, 100% accepted, 6 enrolled. *Entrance requirements:* For master's, GRE or MCAT, 3 letters of recommendation, professional statement, personal interview. Additional exam requirements/recommendations for international students: Required—TOEFL (minimum score 550 paper-based; 213 computer-based). *Application deadline:* For fall admission, 6/30 for domestic and international students; for spring admission, 11/30 for domestic and international students. Application fee: $10 ($20

Public Health—General

Louisiana State University in Shreveport (continued)

for international students). *Unit head:* Dr. Rosevelt Jacobs, Program Director, E-mail: rosevelt.jacobs@lsus.edu. *Application contact:* Dr. Rosevelt Jacobs, Program Director, E-mail: rosevelt.jacobs@lsus.edu.

Loyola University Chicago, Graduate School, Marcella Niehoff School of Nursing, Public Health Program, Chicago, IL 60660. Offers MPH. *Students:* 4 full-time (3 women), 6 part-time (4 women); includes 4 minority (1 African American, 3 Asian Americans or Pacific Islanders). Average age 30. 18 applicants, 67% accepted, 9 enrolled. *Expenses:* Tuition: Full-time $14,220; part-time $790 per credit hour. Required fees: $60 per semester hour. Tuition and fees vary according to program. *Unit head:* Dr. Mary K. Walker, Dean, 708-216-5448, Fax: 708-216-9555, E-mail: mwalker1@luc.edu. *Application contact:* Dr. Vicki A. Keough, Associate Professor/Master's Program Director, 708-216-3582, Fax: 708-216-9555, E-mail: vkeough@luc.edu.

Medical College of Wisconsin, Graduate School of Biomedical Sciences, Department of Population Health, Program in Public Health, Milwaukee, WI 53226-0509. Offers public and community health (PhD); public health (MPH, Graduate Certificate).

Medical College of Wisconsin, Graduate School of Biomedical Sciences, Program in Public and Community Health, Milwaukee, WI 53226-0509. Offers PhD, MD/PhD. *Degree requirements:* For doctorate, comprehensive exam, thesis/dissertation. *Entrance requirements:* For doctorate, GRE. Additional exam requirements/recommendations for international students: Required—TOEFL (minimum score 580 paper-based; 273 computer-based; 100 iBT). Electronic applications accepted. *Expenses:* Contact institution. *Faculty research:* Community-academic partnerships, community-based participatory research, injury prevention, health policy, women's health, emergency medical services.

Medical College of Wisconsin, Medical School, Department of Preventive Medicine, Milwaukee, WI 53226-0509. Offers occupational health and medicine (MPH); public and community health (MPH). *Accreditation:* CEPH. Part-time programs available. Postbaccalaureate distance learning degree programs offered (no on-campus study). *Degree requirements:* For master's, project. *Entrance requirements:* For master's, MD/DO license to practice medicine in U.S. or Canada. Additional exam requirements/recommendations for international students: Required—TOEFL. *Faculty research:* Environmental medicine, ergonomics, epidemiology, surveillance, distance education.

Michigan State University, College of Human Medicine and The Graduate School, Graduate Programs in Human Medicine, Program in Public Health, East Lansing, MI 48824. Offers MPH. *Students:* 23 full-time (14 women), 19 part-time (16 women); includes 9 minority (6 African Americans, 1 American Indian/Alaska Native, 1 Asian American or Pacific Islander, 1 Hispanic American), 4 international. Average age 30. 74 applicants, 53% accepted. *Expenses:* Tuition, state resident: part-time $478.25 per credit hour. Tuition, nonresident: part-time $966.50 per credit hour. Part-time tuition and fees vary according to program. *Financial support:* In 2009–10, 1 research assistantship with tuition reimbursement (averaging $5,904 per year), 2 teaching assistantships with tuition reimbursements (averaging $5,797 per year) were awarded. *Unit head:* Dr. Michael R. Rip, Dean, 517-432-4840, E-mail: rip@msu.edu. *Application contact:* Leslie A. Johnson, Information Contact, 517-353-4883, E-mail: leslie.johnson@hc.msu.edu.

Missouri State University, Graduate College, College of Health and Human Services, Program in Public Health, Springfield, MO 65897. Offers MPH. *Faculty:* 3 full-time (1 woman). *Students:* 19 full-time (7 women), 34 part-time (8 women); includes 3 minority (all African Americans), 38 international. Average age 31. 18 applicants, 83% accepted, 3 enrolled. In 2009, 25 master's awarded. *Degree requirements:* For master's, comprehensive exam, thesis or alternative. *Entrance requirements:* For master's, GRE, minimum GPA of 3.0, 1 year work experience. Additional exam requirements/recommendations for international students: Required—TOEFL (minimum score 550 paper-based; 213 computer-based; 79 iBT). *Application deadline:* For fall admission, 7/20 priority date for domestic students, 5/1 for international students; for spring admission, 12/20 priority date for domestic students, 9/1 for international students. Applications are processed on a rolling basis. Application fee: $35 ($50 for international students). Electronic applications accepted. *Expenses:* Tuition, state resident: full-time $3852; part-time $214 per credit hour. Tuition, nonresident: full-time $7524; part-time $418 per credit hour. Required fees: $696; $172 per semester. Tuition and fees vary according to course level, course load, degree level and program. *Financial support:* Federal Work-Study, institutionally sponsored loans, scholarships/grants, and unspecified assistantships available. Financial award application deadline: 3/31; financial award applicants required to submit FAFSA. *Unit head:* Dr. Vickie Sanchez, Program Director, 417-836-6304, E-mail: vickiesanchez@missouristate.edu. *Application contact:* Eric Eckert, Coordinator of Graduate Admissions and Recruitment, 417-836-5331, Fax: 417-836-6200, E-mail: ericeckert@missouristate.edu.

Morehouse School of Medicine, Master of Public Health Program, Atlanta, GA 30310-1495. Offers epidemiology (MPH); health administration, management and policy (MPH); health education/health promotion (MPH); international health (MPH). *Accreditation:* CEPH. Part-time programs available. *Faculty:* 4 full-time (1 woman), 36 part-time/adjunct (21 women). *Students:* 54 full-time (37 women), 3 part-time (2 women); includes 34 minority (33 African Americans, 1 American Indian/Alaska Native). Average age 28. 62 applicants, 48% accepted, 29 enrolled. In 2009, 13 master's awarded. *Degree requirements:* For master's, thesis, practicum, public health leadership seminar. *Entrance requirements:* For master's, GRE General Test, writing test, public health or human service experience. Additional exam requirements/recommendations for international students: Required—TOEFL (minimum score 550 paper-based; 200 computer-based). *Application deadline:* For fall admission, 3/1 for domestic and international students. Application fee: $50. Electronic applications accepted. *Expenses:* Contact institution. *Financial support:* In 2009–10, 32 students received support, including 6 research assistantships with partial tuition reimbursements available (averaging $10,000 per year); fellowships, teaching assistantships, career-related internships or fieldwork, Federal Work-Study, institutionally sponsored loans, scholarships/grants, and unspecified assistantships also available. Support available to part-time students. Financial award application deadline: 5/1; financial award applicants required to submit FAFSA. *Faculty research:* Women's and adolescent health, violence prevention, cancer epidemiology/disparities, substance abuse prevention. Total annual research expenditures: $640,176. *Unit head:* Dr. Patricia Rodney, Director/Assistant Dean for Public Health Education, 404-752-1944, Fax: 404-752-1051, E-mail: prodney@msm.edu. *Application contact:* Dr. Sterling Roaf, Director of Admissions, 404-752-1650, Fax: 404-752-1512, E-mail: mphadmissions@msm.edu.

Morgan State University, School of Graduate Studies, School of Community Health and Policy, Baltimore, MD 21251. Offers nursing (MS, PhD); public health (MPH, Dr PH). *Accreditation:* CEPH. *Degree requirements:* For doctorate, thesis/dissertation. *Entrance requirements:* For doctorate, GRE, minimum GPA of 3.0. Additional exam requirements/recommendations for international students: Required—TOEFL (minimum score 550 paper-based; 213 computer-based).

New Mexico State University, Graduate School, College of Health and Social Services, Department of Health Science, Las Cruces, NM 88003-8001. Offers community health education (MPH). Part-time programs available. Postbaccalaureate distance learning degree programs offered (minimal on-campus study). *Faculty:* 9 full-time (5 women), 1 (woman) part-time/adjunct. *Students:* 51 full-time (40 women), 38 part-time (28 women); includes 41 minority (6 African Americans, 13 American Indian/Alaska Native, 2 Asian Americans or Pacific Islanders, 20 Hispanic Americans), 11 international. Average age 34. 64 applicants, 81% accepted, 29 enrolled. In 2009, 18 master's awarded. *Degree requirements:* For master's, thesis optional. *Entrance requirements:* For master's, GRE, 6 hours in psychosocial course work, 4 hours in biology, 3 hours in statistics. Additional exam requirements/recommendations for international students: Required—TOEFL. *Application deadline:* For fall admission, 4/1 for domestic students. Application fee: $30 ($50 for international students). *Expenses:* Tuition, state resident: full-time $4080; part-time $223 per credit. Tuition, nonresident: full-time $14,256; part-time $647 per credit. Required fees: $1278; $639 per semester. *Financial support:* In 2009–10, 2 research assistantships (averaging $3,950 per year), 21 teaching assistantships (averaging $5,047 per

year) were awarded; fellowships, career-related internships or fieldwork and health care benefits also available. Financial award application deadline: 4/1. *Faculty research:* Community health education, health issues of U.S.-Mexico border, health policy and management, victims of violence, environmental and occupational health issues. *Unit head:* Dr. Stephen Arnold, Interim Head, 575-646-4300, Fax: 575-646-4343, E-mail: sarnold@nmsu.edu. *Application contact:* Dr. Stephen Arnold, Interim Head, 575-646-4300, Fax: 575-646-4343, E-mail: sarnold@nmsu.edu.

New York Medical College, School of Health Sciences and Practice, Valhalla, NY 10595-1691. Offers MPH, MS, DPT, Dr PH, Graduate Certificate. *Accreditation:* CEPH. Part-time and evening/weekend programs available. Postbaccalaureate distance learning degree programs offered (no on-campus study). *Faculty:* 47 full-time (28 women), 195 part-time/adjunct (109 women). *Students:* 153 full-time (119 women), 278 part-time (188 women); includes 170 minority (69 African Americans, 1 American Indian/Alaska Native, 70 Asian Americans or Pacific Islanders, 30 Hispanic Americans). Average age 32. 342 applicants, 67% accepted, 119 enrolled. In 2009, 108 master's, 16 doctorates awarded. *Degree requirements:* For master's, thesis; for doctorate, comprehensive exam, thesis/dissertation, project (DPT only). *Entrance requirements:* For master's, minimum undergraduate GPA of 3.0; for doctorate, GRE, minimum graduate GPA of 3.2. Additional exam requirements/recommendations for international students: Required—TOEFL (minimum score 637 paper-based; 250 computer-based; 110 iBT), IELTS (minimum score 7). *Application deadline:* For fall admission, 8/1 priority date for domestic students, 5/15 for international students; for spring admission, 12/1 priority date for domestic students, 10/15 for international students. Applications are processed on a rolling basis. Application fee: $50 ($100 for international students). Electronic applications accepted. *Expenses:* Contact institution. *Financial support:* In 2009–10, 139 students received support; research assistantships with full and partial tuition reimbursements available, teaching assistantships with full and partial tuition reimbursements available, career-related internships or fieldwork, Federal Work-Study, institutionally sponsored loans, health care benefits, tuition waivers (partial), and tuition reimbursements available. Support available to part-time students. Financial award applicants required to submit FAFSA. *Faculty research:* Disaster preparedness, autism, health literacy, adolescent HIV, health disparities, women's health issues, tobacco control, sexual trauma, homelessness, workplace health promotion and stress management. Total annual research expenditures: $932,000. *Unit head:* Dr. Robert W. Amler, Dean, 914-594-4843, Fax: 914-594-4292. *Application contact:* Pamela Suett, Director of Recruitment, 914-594-4510, Fax: 914-594-4292, E-mail: shsp_admissions@nymc.edu.

New York University, Steinhardt School of Culture, Education, and Human Development, Department of Nutrition, Food Studies, and Public Health, Program in Community Public Health, New York, NY 10012-1019. Offers community public health (MPH), including community health, international community health, public health nutrition; public health (PhD). *Accreditation:* CEPH. Part-time programs available. *Students:* 90 full-time (77 women), 45 part-time (41 women); includes 34 minority (11 African Americans, 17 Asian Americans or Pacific Islanders, 6 Hispanic Americans), 10 international. Average age 28. 257 applicants, 81% accepted, 52 enrolled. In 2009, 36 master's awarded. *Degree requirements:* For master's, thesis (for some programs). *Entrance requirements:* For master's, GRE General Test; for doctorate, GRE General Test, interview. Additional exam requirements/recommendations for international students: Required—TOEFL. *Application deadline:* For fall admission, 12/15 priority date for domestic and international students; for spring admission, 11/1 for domestic and international students. Applications are processed on a rolling basis. Application fee: $75. Electronic applications accepted. *Expenses:* Tuition: Full-time $30,528; part-time $1272 per credit. Required fees: $2177. *Financial support:* Fellowships with full and partial tuition reimbursements, career-related internships or fieldwork, Federal Work-Study, institutionally sponsored loans, scholarships/grants, and tuition waivers (partial) available. Support available to part-time students. Financial award application deadline: 2/1; financial award applicants required to submit FAFSA. *Faculty research:* Social epidemiology, primary health care, global health, immigrants and health, infectious disease prevention, HIV/AIDS. *Unit head:* Director, 212-998-5580, Fax: 212-995-4192. *Application contact:* 212-998-5030, Fax: 212-995-4328, E-mail: steinhardt.gradadmissions@nyu.edu.

Northeastern University, Bouvé College of Health Sciences Graduate School, Master of Public Health Program, Boston, MA 02115-5096. Offers urban health (MPH). Part-time programs available. *Students:* 20 full-time (17 women), 3 part-time (all women). 49 applicants, 24% accepted, 3 enrolled. *Degree requirements:* For master's, capstone project. *Entrance requirements:* For master's, GRE, minimum undergraduate GPA of 3.0, 3 letters of recommendation. Additional exam requirements/recommendations for international students: Required—TOEFL (minimum score 100 iBT). *Application deadline:* For fall admission, 5/1 for domestic students; for spring admission, 10/1 for domestic students. Applications are processed on a rolling basis. Application fee: $50. Electronic applications accepted. *Financial support:* Scholarships/grants available. *Unit head:* Dr. Shan Mohammed, Program Director, 617-373-7729, E-mail: s.mohammed@neu.edu. *Application contact:* Margaret Schnabel, Director of Graduate Admissions, 617-373-2708, E-mail: bouvegrad@neu.edu.

Northern Arizona University, Graduate College, College of Health and Human Services, Program in Clinical and Translational Sciences, Flagstaff, AZ 86011. Offers Certificate. *Students:* 3 full-time (all women); includes 1 minority (American Indian/Alaska Native). 1 applicant, 100% accepted. Application fee: $50.

Northern Illinois University, Graduate School, College of Health and Human Sciences, School of Nursing and Health Studies, De Kalb, IL 60115-2854. Offers nursing (MS); public health (MPH). *Accreditation:* AACN. Part-time programs available. *Faculty:* 12 full-time (11 women), 1 (woman) part-time/adjunct. *Students:* 28 full-time (22 women), 184 part-time (170 women); includes 38 minority (11 African Americans, 18 Asian Americans or Pacific Islanders, 9 Hispanic Americans), 14 international. Average age 36. 77 applicants, 68% accepted, 35 enrolled. In 2009, 46 master's awarded. *Degree requirements:* For master's, thesis optional, internship. *Entrance requirements:* For master's, minimum GPA of 3.0 in last 60 hours, BA in nursing, nursing license. Additional exam requirements/recommendations for international students: Required—TOEFL (minimum score 550 paper-based; 213 computer-based). *Application deadline:* For fall admission, 6/1 for domestic students, 5/1 for international students; for spring admission, 11/1 for domestic students, 10/1 for international students. Applications are processed on a rolling basis. Application fee: $30. Electronic applications accepted. *Expenses:* Tuition, state resident: full-time $6576; part-time $274 per credit hour. Tuition, nonresident: full-time $13,152; part-time $548 per credit hour. Required fees: $1813; $75.53 per credit hour. Part-time tuition and fees vary according to course load. *Financial support:* In 2009–10, 13 research assistantships with full tuition reimbursements, 7 teaching assistantships with full tuition reimbursements were awarded; fellowships with full tuition reimbursements, career-related internships or fieldwork, Federal Work-Study, scholarships/grants, tuition waivers (full), and unspecified assistantships also available. Support available to part-time students. Financial award applicants required to submit FAFSA. *Faculty research:* Neonatal intensive care, stress and coping, refugee and immigrant issues, older adults, autoimmune disorders. *Unit head:* Dr. Brigid Lusk, Chair, 815-753-0663, Fax: 815-753-0814, E-mail: blusk@niu.edu. *Application contact:* Graduate School Office, 815-753-0395, E-mail: gradsch@niu.edu.

Northwestern University, The Graduate School, Program in Public Health, Evanston, IL 60208. Offers MPH. Part-time and evening/weekend programs available. *Entrance requirements:* For master's, GRE General Test. Additional exam requirements/recommendations for international students: Required—TOEFL. *Faculty research:* Cardiovascular epidemiology, cancer epidemiology, nutritional interventions for the prevention of cardiovascular disease and cancer, women's health, outcomes research.

Nova Southeastern University, Health Professions Division, College of Osteopathic Medicine, Master of Public Health Program, Ft. Lauderdale, FL 33328. Offers MPH. Program offered online and on-site in English, online in Spanish. *Accreditation:* CEPH. Part-time programs available. Postbaccalaureate distance learning degree programs offered (minimal on-campus

study). *Faculty:* 5 full-time (1 woman), 40 part-time/adjunct (16 women). *Students:* 47 full-time (33 women), 38 part-time (28 women); includes 42 minority (16 African Americans, 11 Asian Americans or Pacific Islanders, 15 Hispanic Americans), 4 international. Average age 31. 63 applicants, 68% accepted, 36 enrolled. In 2009, 30 degrees awarded. *Degree requirements:* For master's, 2 foreign languages, comprehensive exam, field experience. *Entrance requirements:* For master's, GRE, MCAT, DAT, GMAT, LSAT, AHPAT, PCAT, OAT (for non-health professionals). Additional exam requirements/recommendations for international students: Required—TOEFL. *Application deadline:* For fall admission, 7/1 for domestic and international students; for winter admission, 12/1 for domestic and international students; for spring admission, 5/1 for domestic and international students. Applications are processed on a rolling basis. Application fee: $50. Electronic applications accepted. *Expenses:* Contact institution. *Financial support:* In 2009–10, 64 students received support; research assistantships, Federal Work-Study, institutionally sponsored loans, scholarships/grants, and tuition waivers (partial) available. Financial award application deadline: 6/30; financial award applicants required to submit FAFSA. *Unit head:* Dr. Cyril Blavo, Director, 954-262-1614, Fax: 954-262-3257, E-mail: cblavo@nova.edu. *Application contact:* Ellen Rondino, Associate Director of Admissions, 954-262-1113, E-mail: er499@nova.edu.

The Ohio State University, College of Public Health, Columbus, OH 43210. Offers MHA, MPH, MS, PhD, JD/MHA, MHA/MBA, MHA/MD, MHA/MPA, MHA/MS, MPH/JD, MPH/MD, OD/MPH. *Accreditation:* CAHME; CEPH. *Students:* 434 full-time (260 women), 97 part-time (55 women); includes 79 minority (25 African Americans, 1 American Indian/Alaska Native, 44 Asian Americans or Pacific Islanders, 9 Hispanic Americans), 22 international. Average age 28. In 2009, 116 master's, 6 doctorates awarded. *Degree requirements:* For master's, thesis optional, practicum. *Entrance requirements:* For master's, GRE. Additional exam requirements/recommendations for international students: Required—TOEFL. *Application deadline:* Applications are processed on a rolling basis. Application fee: $40 ($50 for international students). Electronic applications accepted. *Expenses:* Tuition, state resident: full-time $10,683. Tuition, nonresident: full-time $25,923. Tuition and fees vary according to course load and program. *Financial support:* Fellowships, research assistantships available. *Unit head:* Stanley Lemeshow, Dean, 614-293-3913, Fax: 614-293-3937, E-mail: lemeshow.1@osu.edu. *Application contact:* Graduate Admissions, 614-292-9444, Fax: 614-292-3895, E-mail: domestic.grad@osu.edu.

Old Dominion University, College of Health Sciences, Program in Community Health and Environmental Health, Norfolk, VA 23529. Offers environmental health (MS). Part-time and evening/weekend programs available. Postbaccalaureate distance learning degree programs offered (no on-campus study). *Faculty:* 7 full-time (4 women), 6 part-time/adjunct (3 women). *Students:* 3 full-time (1 woman), 13 part-time (8 women); includes 6 minority (5 African Americans, 1 Asian American or Pacific Islander), 1 international. Average age 29. 32 applicants, 47% accepted, 9 enrolled. In 2009, 10 master's awarded. *Degree requirements:* For master's, comprehensive exam, oral exam, written exam, practicum or thesis. *Entrance requirements:* For master's, GRE General Test, minimum GPA of 2.75. Additional exam requirements/recommendations for international students: Required—TOEFL (minimum score 650 paper-based; 278 computer-based). *Application deadline:* For fall admission, 8/1 priority date for domestic students, 7/1 priority date for international students; for winter admission, 11/1 priority date for domestic students, 10/1 priority date for international students; for spring admission, 4/1 priority date for domestic students, 3/1 priority date for international students. Applications are processed on a rolling basis. Application fee: $50. Electronic applications accepted. *Expenses:* Tuition, state resident: full-time $8112; part-time $338 per credit. Tuition, nonresident: full-time $20,256; part-time $844 per credit. Required fees: $119 per semester. One-time fee: $50. *Financial support:* In 2009–10, 5 research assistantships with tuition reimbursements (averaging $14,000 per year) were awarded; career-related internships or fieldwork, institutionally sponsored loans, scholarships/grants, and tuition waivers (partial) also available. Financial award applicants required to submit FAFSA. *Faculty research:* Toxicology, domestic violence, health policy and planning, environmental hazards, obesity, substance abuse, minority health spirituality, women's health. Total annual research expenditures: $150,133. *Unit head:* A. James English, Graduate Program Director, 757-683-6010, Fax: 757-683-4410, E-mail: chpgpd@odu.edu. *Application contact:* A. James English, Graduate Program Director, 757-683-6010, Fax: 757-683-4410, E-mail: chpgpd@odu.edu.

Old Dominion University, College of Health Sciences, Program in Public Health, Norfolk, VA 23529. Offers environmental health (MPH); health promotion (MPH). *Accreditation:* CEPH. Part-time and evening/weekend programs available. *Faculty:* 7 full-time (4 women), 6 part-time/adjunct (3 women). *Students:* 26 full-time (21 women), 20 part-time (15 women); includes 24 minority (18 African Americans, 4 Asian Americans or Pacific Islanders, 2 Hispanic Americans), 1 international. Average age 29. 67 applicants, 60% accepted, 30 enrolled. In 2009, 16 master's awarded. *Degree requirements:* For master's, field practicum, capstone project. *Entrance requirements:* For master's, GRE, MCAT, minimum GPA of 2.75. Additional exam requirements/recommendations for international students: Required—TOEFL (minimum score 650 paper-based; 278 computer-based). *Application deadline:* For fall admission, 5/31 priority date for domestic students, 4/30 for international students. Application fee: $50 ($100 for international students). Electronic applications accepted. *Expenses:* Tuition, state resident: full-time $8112; part-time $338 per credit. Tuition, nonresident: full-time $20,256; part-time $844 per credit. Required fees: $119 per semester. One-time fee: $50. *Financial support:* Career-related internships or fieldwork, institutionally sponsored loans, and scholarships/grants available. Financial award application deadline: 5/1; financial award applicants required to submit FAFSA. *Faculty research:* Community-based health research, public health research in environmental health and health promotion. Total annual research expenditures: $150,133. *Unit head:* A. James English, Associate Director, 757-683-6010, Fax: 757-446-6121, E-mail: jenglish@odu.edu. *Application contact:* A. James English, Associate Director, 757-683-6010, Fax: 757-446-6121, E-mail: jenglish@odu.edu.

Oregon State University, Graduate School, College of Health and Human Sciences, Department of Public Health, Corvallis, OR 97331. Offers environmental health and occupational safety management (MAIS, MS); health management and policy (MS, PhD); health promotion and health behavior (MS, PhD); public health (MPH, PhD). *Accreditation:* CEPH. *Faculty:* 13 full-time (8 women), 3 part-time/adjunct (1 woman). *Students:* 84 full-time (66 women), 19 part-time (15 women); includes 10 minority (4 African Americans, 2 American Indian/Alaska Native, 2 Asian Americans or Pacific Islanders, 2 Hispanic Americans), 9 international. Average age 32. In 2009, 30 master's, 1 doctorate awarded. Terminal master's awarded for partial completion of doctoral program. *Degree requirements:* For doctorate, one foreign language, thesis/dissertation. *Entrance requirements:* For master's and doctorate, minimum GPA of 3.0 in last 90 hours. Additional exam requirements/recommendations for international students: Required—TOEFL. *Application deadline:* For fall admission, 3/1 for domestic students. Applications are processed on a rolling basis. Application fee: $50. *Expenses:* Tuition, state resident: full-time $9774; part-time $362 per credit. Tuition, nonresident: full-time $15,849; part-time $587 per credit. Required fees: $1639. Full-time tuition and fees vary according to course load and program. *Financial support:* Fellowships, research assistantships, teaching assistantships, career-related internships or fieldwork, Federal Work-Study, and institutionally sponsored loans available. Support available to part-time students. Financial award application deadline: 2/1. *Faculty research:* Traffic safety, health safety, injury control, health promotion. *Unit head:* Dr. S. Marie Harvey, Chair, 541-737-3825, Fax: 541-737-4001, E-mail: marie.harvey@oregonstate.edu. *Application contact:* Dr. S. Marie Harvey, Chair, 541-737-3825, Fax: 541-737-4001, E-mail: marie.harvey@oregonstate.edu.

Penn State Hershey Medical Center, College of Medicine, Graduate School Programs in the Biomedical Sciences, Graduate Program in Public Health Sciences, Hershey, PA 17033. Offers MS. Part-time programs available. *Students:* 9 applicants, 67% accepted, 6 enrolled. *Degree requirements:* For master's, thesis or alternative. *Entrance requirements:* Additional exam requirements/recommendations for international students: Required—TOEFL (minimum score 550 paper-based). *Application deadline:* For fall admission, 1/31 priority date for domestic students, 2/1 priority date for international students. Applications are processed on a rolling basis. Application fee: $65. Electronic applications accepted. *Expenses:* Tuition, state resident:

part-time $644 per credit. Tuition, nonresident: part-time $1142 per credit. Required fees: $22 per semester. *Financial support:* Fellowships available. Financial award applicants required to submit FAFSA. *Faculty research:* Clinical trials, statistical methods in genetic epidemiology, genetic factors in nicotine dependence and dementia syndromes, health economics, cancer. *Unit head:* Dr. Christopher Hollenbeak, Chair, 717-531-5890, Fax: 717-531-5779, E-mail: hes-grad-hmc@psu.edu. *Application contact:* Mardi Sawyer, Program Administrator, 717-531-7178, Fax: 717-531-5779, E-mail: hes-grad-hmc@psu.edu.

Ponce School of Medicine, Program in Public Health, Ponce, PR 00732-7004. Offers epidemiology (Dr PH); public health (MPH). *Faculty:* 9 full-time (5 women), 15 part-time/adjunct (5 women). *Students:* 49 full-time (35 women); includes 48 minority (all Hispanic Americans). Average age 30. 72 applicants, 75% accepted. In 2009, 26 degrees awarded. *Degree requirements:* For master's, one foreign language, comprehensive exam, thesis. *Entrance requirements:* For master's, GRE General Test or EXADEP, proficiency in Spanish and English, minimum GPA of 2.7, 3 letters of recommendation. *Application deadline:* For fall admission, 3/15 for domestic and international students. Application fee: $100. *Expenses:* Tuition: Part-time $225 per credit hour. Part-time tuition and fees vary according to program. *Financial support:* In 2009–10, 46 students received support. Scholarships/grants available. Financial award application deadline: 5/30; financial award applicants required to submit FAFSA. *Unit head:* Dr. Manuel Bayona, Head, 787-840-2575 Ext. 2232, E-mail: mbayona@psm.edu. *Application contact:* Maria Colon, Admissions Officer, 787-840-2575 Ext. 2143, E-mail: mcolon@psm.edu.

Portland State University, Graduate Studies, College of Urban and Public Affairs, School of Community Health, Portland, OR 97207-0751. Offers aging (Certificate); health education (MA, MS); health education and health promotion (MPH); health studies (MPA, MPH), including health administration. *Accreditation:* CEPH. Part-time programs available. *Degree requirements:* For master's, oral and written exams. *Entrance requirements:* For master's, GRE General Test, 3 letters of recommendation, minimum GPA of 3.0. Additional exam requirements/recommendations for international students: Required—TOEFL (minimum score 550 paper-based; 213 computer-based).

Purdue University, School of Veterinary Medicine and Graduate School, Graduate Programs in Veterinary Medicine, Department of Comparative Pathobiology, West Lafayette, IN 47907-2027. Offers comparative epidemiology and public health (MS); comparative epidemiology and public heath (PhD); comparative microbiology and immunology (MS, PhD); comparative pathobiology (MS, PhD); interdisciplinary studies (PhD), including microbial pathogenesis, molecular signaling and cancer biology, molecular virology; lab animal medicine (MS); veterinary anatomic pathology (MS); veterinary clinical pathology (MS). *Faculty:* 37 full-time (10 women), 4 part-time/adjunct (2 women). *Students:* 53 full-time (31 women), 2 part-time (1 woman); includes 3 minority (2 African Americans, 1 Hispanic American), 32 international. Average age 35. In 2009, 6 master's, 2 doctorates awarded. Terminal master's awarded for partial completion of doctoral program. *Degree requirements:* For master's, thesis (for some programs); for doctorate, thesis/dissertation. *Entrance requirements:* For master's and doctorate, GRE General Test. Additional exam requirements/recommendations for international students: Required—TOEFL (minimum score 575 paper-based; 232 computer-based), IELTS (minimum score 6.5), TWE (minimum score 4). *Application deadline:* For fall admission, 8/12 for domestic students, 6/15 for international students; for spring admission, 1/12 for domestic students, 10/15 for international students. Application fee: $55. Electronic applications accepted. *Financial support:* Fellowships, research assistantships, teaching assistantships available. Financial award application deadline: 3/1; financial award applicants required to submit FAFSA. *Unit head:* Dr. Suresh Mittal, Interim Head, 765-494-7543. *Application contact:* Denise A. Ottinger, Director, Student Services and Admissions, 765-494-7893, Fax: 765-496-2891, E-mail: vetadmissions@purdue.edu.

Queen's University at Kingston, School of Graduate Studies and Research, Faculty of Health Sciences, Department of Community Health and Epidemiology, Kingston, ON K7L 3N6, Canada. Offers epidemiology (PhD); epidemiology and population health (M Sc); health services (M Sc); policy research and clinical epidemiology (M Sc); public health (MPH). Part-time programs available. *Degree requirements:* For master's, thesis. *Entrance requirements:* For master's, GRE General Test (strongly recommended). Additional exam requirements/recommendations for international students: Required—TOEFL (minimum score 600 paper-based; 250 computer-based). *Faculty research:* Cancer epidemiology, clinical trials, biostatistics health services research, health policy.

Rutgers, The State University of New Jersey, New Brunswick, Edward J. Bloustein School of Planning and Public Policy, Program in Public Health, Piscataway, NJ 08854-8097. Offers MPH, Dr PH, PhD, MBA/MPH, MD/MPH. *Accreditation:* CEPH. Part-time and evening/weekend programs available. *Degree requirements:* For master's, internship; for doctorate, thesis/dissertation. *Entrance requirements:* For master's, GMAT, GRE General Test; for doctorate, GRE General Test, MPH (Dr PH). Additional exam requirements/recommendations for international students: Required—TOEFL. *Faculty research:* Epidemiology, risk perception, statistical research design, health care utilization, health promotion.

St. Catherine University, Graduate Programs, Program in Holistic Health Studies, St. Paul, MN 55105. Offers MA. Part-time programs available. *Faculty:* 6. *Students:* 43 full-time (41 women), 66 part-time (65 women); includes 6 minority (3 African Americans, 2 Asian Americans or Pacific Islanders, 1 Hispanic American). Average age 43. 61 applicants, 77% accepted, 42 enrolled. In 2009, 13 master's awarded. *Degree requirements:* For master's, thesis optional. *Entrance requirements:* For master's, 1 course in anatomy, physiology and psychology. Additional exam requirements/recommendations for international students: Required—TOEFL (minimum score 600 paper-based; 250 computer-based; 100 iBT). *Application deadline:* For fall admission, 7/1 priority date for domestic students. Application fee: $35. *Expenses:* Contact institution. *Financial support:* In 2009–10, 52 students received support. *Unit head:* Janet L. Dahllem, Director, 651-690-7836, Fax: 651-690-7849. *Application contact:* Office of Admission, 651-690-6933, Fax: 651-690-6064.

Saint Louis University, Graduate School, School of Public Health and Graduate School, Department of Health Management and Policy, St. Louis, MO 63103-2097. Offers health administration (MHA); health policy (MPH); public health studies (PhD). *Accreditation:* CAHME. Part-time programs available. *Degree requirements:* For master's, comprehensive exam, internship. *Entrance requirements:* For master's, GMAT or GRE General Test, LSAT, MCAT, letters of recommendation, resume. Additional exam requirements/recommendations for international students: Required—TOEFL (minimum score 525 paper-based; 194 computer-based). *Faculty research:* Management of HIV/AIDS, rural health services, prevention of asthma, genetics and health services use, health insurance and access to care.

Saint Xavier University, Graduate Studies, Graham School of Management, Chicago, IL 60655-3105. Offers e-commerce (MBA); employee health benefits (Certificate); finance (MBA, MS); financial analysis and investments (MBA); financial planning (MBA, Certificate); financial trading and practice (MBA, Certificate); generalist/administration (MBA); health administration (MBA, MS); managed care (Certificate); management (MBA, MS); marketing (MBA); public and non-profit management (MBA); public health (MPH); service management (MBA); training and performance management (MBA); MBA/MS. *Accreditation:* ACBSP. Part-time and evening/weekend programs available. *Entrance requirements:* For master's, GMAT, minimum GPA of 3.0, 2 years of work experience. Electronic applications accepted. *Expenses:* Contact institution.

San Diego State University, Graduate and Research Affairs, College of Health and Human Services, Graduate School of Public Health, San Diego, CA 92182. Offers environmental health (MPH); epidemiology (MPH, PhD), including biostatistics (MPH); global emergency preparedness and response (MS); global health (PhD); health behavior (PhD); health promotion (MPH); health services administration (MPH); toxicology (MS); MPH/MA; MSW/MPH. *Accreditation:* ABET (one or more programs are accredited); CAHME (one or more programs are accredited); CEPH (one or more programs are accredited). Part-time programs available. *Degree requirements:* For master's, comprehensive exam (for some programs), thesis (for

Public Health—General

San Diego State University (continued)
some programs); for doctorate, thesis/dissertation. *Entrance requirements:* For master's, GMAT (MPH in health services administration), GRE General Test; for doctorate, GRE General Test. Additional exam requirements/recommendations for international students: Required—TOEFL. *Faculty research:* Evaluation of tobacco, AIDS prevalence and prevention, mammography, infant death project, Alzheimer's in elderly Chinese.

San Francisco State University, Division of Graduate Studies, College of Health and Human Services, Department of Health Education, San Francisco, CA 94132-1722. Offers MPH. *Accreditation:* CEPH. Part-time programs available.

San Jose State University, Graduate Studies and Research, College of Applied Sciences and Arts, Department of Health Science, San Jose, CA 95192-0001. Offers applied social gerontology (Certificate); community health education (MPH). *Accreditation:* CEPH (one or more programs are accredited). Postbaccalaureate distance learning degree programs offered. *Students:* 26 full-time (21 women), 51 part-time (45 women); includes 42 minority (6 African Americans, 1 American Indian/Alaska Native, 16 Asian Americans or Pacific Islanders, 19 Hispanic Americans), 3 international. Average age 33. 121 applicants, 24% accepted, 25 enrolled. In 2009, 11 master's awarded. *Entrance requirements:* For master's, GRE General Test. *Application deadline:* For fall admission, 6/29 for domestic students; for spring admission, 11/30 for domestic students. Applications are processed on a rolling basis. Application fee: $59. Electronic applications accepted. *Financial support:* Career-related internships or fieldwork, Federal Work-Study, and institutionally sponsored loans available. Support available to part-time students. Financial award applicants required to submit FAFSA. *Faculty research:* Behavioral science in occupational and health care settings, epidemiology in health care settings. *Unit head:* Dr. Kathleen Roe, Chair, 408-924-2976, Fax: 408-924-2979. *Application contact:* Dr. Kathleen Roe, Chair, 408-924-2976, Fax: 408-924-2979.

Sarah Lawrence College, Graduate Studies, Program in Health Advocacy, Bronxville, NY 10708-5999. Offers MA. Part-time programs available. *Faculty:* 11 part-time/adjunct (8 women). *Students:* 20 full-time (19 women), 13 part-time (all women); includes 6 minority (3 African Americans, 3 Asian Americans or Pacific Islanders). Average age 40. 29 applicants, 72% accepted, 14 enrolled. In 2009, 5 master's awarded. *Degree requirements:* For master's, fieldwork. *Entrance requirements:* For master's, previous course work in biology and microeconomics, minimum B average in undergraduate course work. Additional exam requirements/recommendations for international students: Required—TOEFL (minimum score 600 paper-based). *Application deadline:* For fall admission, 3/1 priority date for domestic students. Applications are processed on a rolling basis. Application fee: $60. *Expenses:* Contact institution. *Financial support:* In 2009–10, 11 fellowships (averaging $5,308 per year) were awarded; career-related internships or fieldwork and scholarships/grants also available. Support available to part-time students. Financial award application deadline: 3/1; financial award applicants required to submit CSS PROFILE or FAFSA. *Unit head:* Laura Weil, Director, 914-395-2371. *Application contact:* Emanual Lomax, Director of Graduate Admission, 914-395-2371, E-mail: elomax@sarahlawrence.edu.

Simon Fraser University, Graduate Studies, Faculty of Health Sciences, Burnaby, BC V5A 1S6, Canada. Offers population and public health (M Sc). *Degree requirements:* For master's, thesis, practicum or project.

Southern Connecticut State University, School of Graduate Studies, School of Health and Human Services, Department of Public Health, New Haven, CT 06515-1355. Offers MPH. *Accreditation:* CEPH. Part-time and evening/weekend programs available. *Faculty:* 9 full-time. *Students:* 34 full-time (29 women), 51 part-time (39 women); includes 19 minority (13 African Americans, 6 Asian Americans or Pacific Islanders), 2 international. 83 applicants, 48% accepted, 29 enrolled. In 2009, 25 master's awarded. *Degree requirements:* For master's, thesis or alternative. *Entrance requirements:* For master's, minimum undergraduate QPA of 3.0 in graduate major field or 2.5 overall, interview. *Application deadline:* For fall admission, 3/15 for domestic students. Application fee: $50. Electronic applications accepted. Tuition and fees vary according to program. *Financial support:* In 2009–10, 1 teaching assistantship was awarded; career-related internships or fieldwork also available. Financial award application deadline: 4/15; financial award applicants required to submit FAFSA. *Unit head:* Dr. William Faraclas, Chairperson, 203-392-6950, Fax: 203-392-6965, E-mail: faraclas@southernct.edu. *Application contact:* Dr. Deborah Flynn, Graduate Coordinator, 203-392-6969, Fax: 203-392-6965, E-mail: flynnd1@southernct.edu.

State University of New York Downstate Medical Center, College of Medicine, Program in Public Health, Brooklyn, NY 11203-2098. Offers urban and immigrant health (MPH); MD/MPH. Part-time programs available. *Degree requirements:* For master's, practicum. *Entrance requirements:* For master's, GRE, MCAT or OAT, 2 letters of recommendation, minimum undergraduate GPA of 3.0. Additional exam requirements/recommendations for international students: Required—TOEFL (minimum score 550 paper-based).

See Close-Up on page 1669.

Stony Brook University, State University of New York, Stony Brook University Medical Center, School of Medicine, Program in Public Health, Stony Brook, NY 11794. Offers community health (MPH); evaluation sciences (MPH); family violence (MPH); health economics (MPH); population health (MPH); substance abuse (MPH). *Accreditation:* CEPH. *Students:* 16 full-time (8 women), 29 part-time (24 women); includes 14 minority (6 African Americans, 6 Asian Americans or Pacific Islanders, 2 Hispanic Americans), 5 international. Average age 39. 77 applicants, 64% accepted. In 2009, 10 master's awarded. *Entrance requirements:* For master's, GRE, 3 references. Additional exam requirements/recommendations for international students: Required—TOEFL. *Application deadline:* For fall admission, 1/15 for domestic and international students. Application fee: $60. Electronic applications accepted. *Expenses:* Tuition, state resident: full-time $8370; part-time $349 per credit. Tuition, nonresident: full-time $13,250; part-time $552 per credit. Required fees: $933. *Faculty research:* Population health, health service research, health economics. *Unit head:* Dr. Raymond L. Goldsteen, Director, 631-444-2074, Fax: 631-444-3480, E-mail: raymond.goldsteen@stonybrook.edu. *Application contact:* Dr. Raymond L. Goldsteen, Director, 631-444-2074, Fax: 631-444-3480, E-mail: raymond.goldsteen@stonybrook.edu.

Teachers College, Columbia University, Graduate Faculty of Education, Department of Health and Behavioral Studies, Program in Nutrition and Public Health, New York, NY 10027-6696. Offers MS, Ed D.

Temple University, Health Sciences Center and Graduate School, College of Health Professions, Department of Public Health, Philadelphia, PA 19122-6096. Offers Ed M, MPH, MS, PhD. *Accreditation:* CEPH (one or more programs are accredited). Part-time and evening/weekend programs available. Terminal master's awarded for partial completion of doctoral program. *Degree requirements:* For doctorate, thesis/dissertation. *Entrance requirements:* For master's and doctorate, minimum undergraduate GPA of 3.0. Additional exam requirements/recommendations for international students: Required—TOEFL (minimum score 550 paper-based; 213 computer-based; 79 iBT). Electronic applications accepted. *Faculty research:* Program development and evaluation in HIV prevention, violence prevention, women's health policy, psychosocial aspects of disability.

Texas A&M Health Science Center, School of Rural Public Health, College Station, TX 77840. Offers environmental/occupational health (MPH); epidemiology/biostatistics (MPH); health policy/management (MPH); social and behavioral health (MPH). *Accreditation:* CEPH. Part-time programs available. Postbaccalaureate distance learning degree programs offered (no on-campus study). *Degree requirements:* For master's, thesis optional. *Entrance requirements:* For master's, GRE General Test, minimum undergraduate GPA of 3.0. Electronic applications accepted. *Faculty research:* Tobacco cessation, youth health risk.

Texas A&M University, College of Veterinary Medicine, Department of Veterinary Integrative Biosciences, College Station, TX 77843. Offers epidemiology (MS); food safety/toxicology (MS); veterinary anatomy (MS, PhD); veterinary public health (MS). *Faculty:* 25. *Students:* 34 full-time (22 women), 8 part-time (5 women); includes 2 minority (1 African American, 1 Asian American or Pacific Islander), 20 international. Average age 30. In 2009, 1 master's, 1 doctorate awarded. Terminal master's awarded for partial completion of doctoral program. *Degree requirements:* For master's, comprehensive exam, thesis; for doctorate, comprehensive exam, thesis/dissertation. *Entrance requirements:* For master's and doctorate, GRE General Test, minimum undergraduate GPA of 3.0. Additional exam requirements/recommendations for international students: Required—TOEFL. *Application deadline:* For fall admission, 7/15 priority date for domestic students, 4/1 priority date for international students; for spring admission, 10/1 priority date for domestic students, 9/15 priority date for international students. Applications are processed on a rolling basis. Application fee: $50 ($75 for international students). Electronic applications accepted. *Expenses:* Tuition, state resident: full-time $3991; part-time $221.74 per credit hour. Tuition, nonresident: full-time $9049; part-time $502.74 per credit hour. *Financial support:* In 2009–10, fellowships (averaging $18,000 per year), research assistantships (averaging $15,600 per year), teaching assistantships (averaging $15,600 per year) were awarded; institutionally sponsored loans, unspecified assistantships, and clinical associateships also available. Financial award application deadline: 7/15; financial award applicants required to submit FAFSA. *Faculty research:* Metal toxicology, reproductive biology, genetics of neural development, developmental biology, environmental toxicology. *Unit head:* Dr. E. Tiffany-Castiglioni, Head, 979-862-6559, E-mail: ecastiglioni@cvm.tamu.edu. *Application contact:* Dr. Jane Welsh, Chair, Fax: 979-847-8981, E-mail: jwelsh@cum.tamu.edu.

Thomas Jefferson University, Jefferson School of Population Health, Program in Public Health, Philadelphia, PA 19107. Offers MPH. *Accreditation:* CEPH. Part-time programs available. Postbaccalaureate distance learning degree programs offered (minimal on-campus study). *Degree requirements:* For master's, capstone project or thesis. *Entrance requirements:* For master's, GRE General Test or MCAT, minimum GPA of 3.0. Additional exam requirements/recommendations for international students: Required—TOEFL (minimum score 250 computer-based; 100 iBT). *Application deadline:* For fall admission, 8/2 priority date for domestic and international students; for spring admission, 12/1 priority date for domestic and international students. Applications are processed on a rolling basis. Application fee: $25. Electronic applications accepted. *Expenses:* Tuition: Full-time $26,858; part-time $879 per credit. Required fees: $525. *Unit head:* Dr. Caroline Golab, Associate Dean, Academic and Student Affairs, 215-503-8468, Fax: 215-923-6939, E-mail: caroline.golab@jefferson.edu. *Application contact:* April L. Smith, Program/Admissions Coordinator, Jefferson School of Population Health, 215-503-5305, Fax: 215-503-5305, E-mail: april.smith@jefferson.edu.

Touro College, School of Health Sciences, Bay Shore, NY 11706. Offers acupuncture (MS); occupational therapy (MS); oriental medicine (MSOM); physical therapy (DPT); public health (MPH); speech-language pathology (MS). *Expenses:* Contact institution.

Touro University, Graduate Programs, Vallejo, CA 94592. Offers education (MA); osteopathic medicine (DO); pharmacy (Pharm D); physical therapy (DPT); physician assistant studies (MS); public health (MPH). *Accreditation:* AOsA; ARC-PA. Part-time and evening/weekend programs available. *Faculty:* 91 full-time (52 women), 51 part-time/adjunct (28 women). *Students:* 1,439 full-time (891 women). 6,914 applicants, 12% accepted, 503 enrolled. In 2009, 229 first professional degrees, 103 master's awarded. *Degree requirements:* For master's, comprehensive exam, thesis; for first professional degree, comprehensive exam. *Entrance requirements:* BS/BA. *Application deadline:* For fall admission, 3/15 for domestic students; for winter admission, 12/1 for domestic students. Applications are processed on a rolling basis. Application fee: $100. Electronic applications accepted. *Financial support:* In 2009–10, 1,236 students received support, including 119 fellowships (averaging $1,535 per year), 24 research assistantships (averaging $3,686 per year), 13 teaching assistantships (averaging $4,058 per year); Federal Work-Study and scholarships/grants also available. Support available to part-time students. Financial award applicants required to submit FAFSA. *Faculty research:* Cancer, heart disease. *Application contact:* Steve Davis, Associate Director of Admissions, 707-638-5270, Fax: 707-638-5250, E-mail: steven.davis@tu.edu.

Trinity (Washington) University, School of Professional Studies, Washington, DC 20017-1094. Offers business administration (MBA); communication (MA); international security studies (MA); organizational management (MSA), including federal program management, human resource management, nonprofit management, organizational development, public and community health. Part-time and evening/weekend programs available. *Degree requirements:* For master's, thesis (for some programs), capstone project (MSA). *Entrance requirements:* For master's, minimum GPA of 2.5. Additional exam requirements/recommendations for international students: Required—TOEFL (minimum score 550 paper-based; 213 computer-based).

Tufts University, School of Medicine, Public Health and Professional Degree Programs, Boston, MA 02111. Offers biomedical sciences (MS); health communication (MS); pain research, education and policy (MS); public health (MPH). *Accreditation:* CEPH (one or more programs are accredited). Part-time and evening/weekend programs available. *Faculty:* 57 full-time (25 women), 44 part-time/adjunct (17 women). *Students:* 210 full-time (123 women), 68 part-time (54 women); includes 94 minority (19 African Americans, 1 American Indian/Alaska Native, 58 Asian Americans or Pacific Islanders, 16 Hispanic Americans), 13 international. Average age 27. 857 applicants, 55% accepted, 173 enrolled. In 2009, 97 master's awarded. *Degree requirements:* For master's, thesis (for some programs). *Entrance requirements:* For master's, GRE General Test. Additional exam requirements/recommendations for international students: Required—TOEFL. *Application deadline:* For fall admission, 3/15 priority date for domestic students, 3/15 for international students; for spring admission, 10/25 priority date for domestic students, 10/25 for international students. Applications are processed on a rolling basis. Application fee: $70. Electronic applications accepted. *Expenses:* Contact institution. *Financial support:* Federal Work-Study and scholarships/grants available. Support available to part-time students. Financial award application deadline: 2/27; financial award applicants required to submit FAFSA. *Faculty research:* Environmental and occupational health, nutrition, epidemiology, health communication, health services management and policy, biostatistics, protein interaction, mRNA processing, vascular pathology. *Unit head:* Dr. Aviva Must, Dean, 617-636-0935, Fax: 617-636-0898, E-mail: aviva.must@tufts.edu. *Application contact:* Emily Keily, Director of Admissions, 617-636-6645, Fax: 617-636-0898, E-mail: med-phpd@tufts.edu.

TUI University, College of Health Sciences, Cypress, CA 90630. Offers MS, PhD, Certificate. Part-time and evening/weekend programs available. Postbaccalaureate distance learning degree programs offered (no on-campus study). *Degree requirements:* For doctorate, comprehensive exam, thesis/dissertation. *Entrance requirements:* For master's, minimum GPA of 2.5 (students with GPA 3.0 or greater may transfer up to 30% of graduate level credits); for doctorate, minimum GPA of 3.4. Additional exam requirements/recommendations for international students: Required—TOEFL. Electronic applications accepted.

Tulane University, School of Public Health and Tropical Medicine, New Orleans, LA 70118-5669. Offers MHA, MMM, MPH, MPHTM, MS, MSPH, Dr PH, PhD, Sc D, Diploma, JD/MHA, JD/MPH, MD/MPH, MD/MPHTM, MD/MSPH, MD/PhD, MSW/MPH. MS, PhD offered through the Graduate School. *Accreditation:* CAHME (one or more programs are accredited); CEPH (one or more programs are accredited). Part-time and evening/weekend programs available. Postbaccalaureate distance learning degree programs offered (no on-campus study). Terminal master's awarded for partial completion of doctoral program. *Degree requirements:* For master's, comprehensive exam (for some programs); for doctorate, comprehensive exam, thesis/dissertation. *Entrance requirements:* For master's and doctorate, GRE General Test. Additional exam requirements/recommendations for international students: Required—TOEFL. Electronic applications accepted. *Expenses:* Contact institution.

Uniformed Services University of the Health Sciences, School of Medicine, Graduate Programs in the Biomedical Sciences and Public Health, Bethesda, MD 20814. Offers emerging infectious diseases (PhD); medical and clinical psychology (PhD), including clinical psychology, medical and clinical psychology (clinical/dual track), medical and clinical psychology (research track); molecular and cell biology (PhD); neuroscience (PhD); preventive medicine and biometrics (MPH, MSPH, MTMH, Dr PH, PhD), including environmental health science (PhD),

medical zoology (PhD), public health (MPH, MSPH, Dr PH), tropical medicine and hygiene (MTMH). *Faculty:* 372 full-time (119 women), 4,044 part-time/adjunct (908 women). *Students:* 176 full-time (96 women); includes 31 minority (6 African Americans, 4 American Indian/Alaska Native, 14 Asian Americans or Pacific Islanders, 7 Hispanic Americans), 11 international. Average age 28. 278 applicants, 20% accepted, 47 enrolled. In 2009, 36 master's, 17 doctorates awarded. Terminal master's awarded for partial completion of doctoral program. *Degree requirements:* For master's, comprehensive exam, thesis or alternative; for doctorate, comprehensive exam, thesis/dissertation, qualifying exam. *Entrance requirements:* For master's, GRE General Test; for doctorate, GRE General Test, minimum GPA of 3.0. Additional exam requirements/recommendations for international students: Required—TOEFL. *Application deadline:* For fall admission, 1/15 priority date for domestic and international students. Applications are processed on a rolling basis. Application fee: $0. Electronic applications accepted. *Financial support:* In 2009–10, fellowships with full tuition reimbursements (averaging $26,000 per year), research assistantships with full tuition reimbursements (averaging $26,000 per year) were awarded; career-related internships or fieldwork, scholarships/grants, health care benefits, and tuition waivers (full) also available. *Unit head:* Dr. Eleanor S. Metcalf, Associate Dean, 301-295-1104, E-mail: emetcalf@usuhs.mil. *Application contact:* Elena Marina Sherman, Graduate Program Coordinator, 301-295-3913, Fax: 301-295-6772, E-mail: elena.sherman@usuhs.mil.

Uniformed Services University of the Health Sciences, School of Medicine, Graduate Programs in the Biomedical Sciences and Public Health, Department of Preventive Medicine and Biometrics, Program in Public Health, Bethesda, MD 20814-4799. Offers MPH, MSPH, Dr PH. *Accreditation:* CEPH (one or more programs are accredited). *Faculty:* 43 full-time (14 women), 143 part-time/adjunct (25 women). *Students:* 52 full-time (17 women); includes 12 minority (1 African American, 3 American Indian/Alaska Native, 6 Asian Americans or Pacific Islanders, 2 Hispanic Americans), 9 international. Average age 30. 71 applicants, 63% accepted, 32 enrolled. In 2009, 37 master's, 2 doctorates awarded. *Degree requirements:* For master's, comprehensive exam; for doctorate, thesis/dissertation, qualifying exam. *Entrance requirements:* For master's, GRE General Test; for doctorate, GRE General Test, minimum GPA of 3.0. Additional exam requirements/recommendations for international students: Required—TOEFL. *Application deadline:* For fall admission, 1/15 priority date for domestic students. Applications are processed on a rolling basis. Application fee: $0. *Financial support:* In 2009–10, fellowships with full tuition reimbursements (averaging $26,000 per year); scholarships/grants, health care benefits, and tuition waivers (full) also available. *Faculty research:* Epidemiology, biostatistics, health services administration, environmental and occupational health, tropical public health. *Unit head:* Dr. David Cruess, Graduate Program Director, 301-295-3465, Fax: 301-295-1933, E-mail: dcruess@usuhs.mil. *Application contact:* Elena Marina Sherman, Graduate Program Coordinator, 301-295-3913, Fax: 301-295-6772, E-mail: elena.sherman@usuhs.mil.

Universidad Central del Este, Graduate School, San Pedro de Macoris, Dominican Republic. Offers administration (M Ad); dentistry (DMD); development of educational and social policies (PhD); environmental engineering (ME); financial management (M Ad); higher education (M Ed); human resources (M Ad); public health (MPH). *Entrance requirements:* For master's, letters of recommendation.

Université de Montréal, Faculty of Arts and Sciences, Programs in Societies, Public Policies and Health, Montréal, QC H3C 3J7, Canada.

Université de Montréal, Faculty of Medicine, Program in Communal and Public Health, Montréal, QC H3C 3J7, Canada. Offers community health (M Sc, DESS); public health (PhD). *Accreditation:* CEPH. Part-time programs available. *Students:* 91 full-time (59 women), 174 part-time (130 women). 219 applicants, 41% accepted, 77 enrolled. In 2009, 26 master's, 12 doctorates, 5 other advanced degrees awarded. Terminal master's awarded for partial completion of doctoral program. *Degree requirements:* For master's, thesis; for doctorate, thesis/dissertation, general exam. *Entrance requirements:* For master's and doctorate, proficiency in French, knowledge of English; for DESS, proficiency in French. *Application deadline:* For fall admission, 2/1 priority date for domestic students; for winter admission, 11/1 priority date for domestic students; for spring admission, 2/1 priority date for domestic students. Application fee: $100. Electronic applications accepted. *Financial support:* Fellowships with partial tuition reimbursements, scholarships/grants and tuition waivers (partial) available. *Faculty research:* Epidemiology, health services utilization, health promotion and education, health behaviors, poverty and child health. *Unit head:* Marie-France Raynault, Head, 514-343-6140, Fax: 514-343-5645, E-mail: marie-france.raynault@umontreal.ca. *Application contact:* Marie Hatem, Information Contact/ Community Health Programs, 514-343-5652, Fax: 514-343-5645, E-mail: marie.hatem@umontreal.ca.

University at Albany, State University of New York, School of Public Health, Program in Public Health, Rensselaer, NY 12144. Offers MPH, Dr PH. *Degree requirements:* For master's, thesis; for doctorate, thesis/dissertation. *Entrance requirements:* For master's and doctorate, GRE General Test. Additional exam requirements/recommendations for international students: Required—TOEFL (minimum score 550 paper-based; 213 computer-based). Electronic applications accepted.

University at Buffalo, the State University of New York, Graduate School, School of Public Health and Health Professions, Department of Social and Preventive Medicine, Buffalo, NY 14260. Offers community health (PhD); epidemiology (MS, PhD); public health (MPH). Part-time programs available. *Faculty:* 11 full-time (7 women), 11 part-time/adjunct (5 women). *Students:* 19 full-time (11 women), 15 part-time (8 women); includes 4 minority (all Asian Americans or Pacific Islanders), 3 international. Average age 30. 127 applicants, 41% accepted. In 2009, 4 master's, 4 doctorates awarded. Terminal master's awarded for partial completion of doctoral program. *Degree requirements:* For master's, comprehensive exam, thesis; for doctorate, comprehensive exam, thesis/dissertation. *Entrance requirements:* For master's and doctorate, GRE General Test. Additional exam requirements/recommendations for international students: Required—TOEFL (minimum score 600 paper-based; 250 computer-based; 100 iBT). *Application deadline:* For fall admission, 1/15 priority date for domestic and international students. Applications are processed on a rolling basis. Application fee: $50. Electronic applications accepted. *Financial support:* In 2009–10, 10 students received support, including 1 fellowship with full tuition reimbursement available (averaging $15,000 per year), 8 research assistantships with full tuition reimbursements available (averaging $15,000 per year); teaching assistantships with full tuition reimbursements available, career-related internships or fieldwork, Federal Work-Study, institutionally sponsored loans, health care benefits, and unspecified assistantships also available. Financial award application deadline: 2/1; financial award applicants required to submit FAFSA. *Faculty research:* Epidemiology of community health services including cancer and nutrition, cardiovascular disease, epidemiology of cancer, cardiovascular diseases, health services research. Total annual research expenditures: $5.5 million. *Unit head:* Dr. Jo Freudenheim, Chair, 716-829-2975 Ext. 612, Fax: 716-829-2979, E-mail: jfreuden@buffalo.edu. *Application contact:* Dr. Carl Li, Director of Graduate Studies, 716-829-2975 Ext. 618, Fax: 716-829-2979, E-mail: carlli@buffalo.edu.

The University of Akron, Graduate School, College of Nursing, Akron, OH 44325. Offers nursing (MSN, PhD); public health (MPH). *Accreditation:* AACN; AANA/CANAEP (one or more programs are accredited). Part-time programs available. *Faculty:* 48 full-time (46 women), 55 part-time/adjunct (54 women). *Students:* 75 full-time (68 women), 265 part-time (225 women); includes 32 minority (23 African Americans, 1 American Indian/Alaska Native, 5 Asian Americans or Pacific Islanders, 3 Hispanic Americans), 8 international. Average age 35. 101 applicants, 88% accepted, 54 enrolled. In 2009, 76 master's, 1 doctorate awarded. *Degree requirements:* For doctorate, one foreign language, thesis/dissertation, qualifying exam. *Entrance requirements:* For master's, GRE, interview, letters of recommendation, minimum GPA of 3.0, current license to practice nursing; for doctorate, GRE, minimum GPA of 3.0, MSN, nursing license or eligibility for licensure, writing sample, letters of recommendation, interview, resume, personal statement. Additional exam requirements/recommendations for international students: Required—TOEFL (minimum score 550 paper-based; 213 computer-based; 79 iBT). *Application deadline:* Applications are processed on a rolling basis. Application fee: $30 ($40 for international students). Electronic applications accepted. *Expenses:* Tuition, state resident: full-time $6570; part-time $365 per credit hour. Tuition, nonresident: full-time $11,250; part-time $625 per credit hour. *Financial support:* In 2009–10, 7 research assistantships with full tuition reimbursements, 8 teaching assistantships with full tuition reimbursements were awarded; career-related internships or fieldwork and Federal Work-Study also available. *Faculty research:* Health promotion and chronic disease prevention; mental health and psychosocial resilience; gerontological health, trauma and violence; gut oxygenation during shock and trauma, simulation and the pedagogy of teaching and learning. Total annual research expenditures: $728,561. *Unit head:* Dr. Margaret Wineman, Dean, 330-972-7551, E-mail: wineman@uakron.edu. *Application contact:* Dr. Marlene Huff, Graduate Director, 330-972-7555, E-mail: mhuff@uakron.edu.

The University of Alabama at Birmingham, School of Public Health, Program in Public Health, Birmingham, AL 35294. Offers MPH, MSPH, DPH. *Accreditation:* CEPH.

University of Alaska Anchorage, College of Health and Social Welfare, Division of Health Sciences, Anchorage, AK 99508. Offers public health practice (MPH). Part-time programs available. *Degree requirements:* For master's, comprehensive exam, thesis. *Entrance requirements:* For master's, writing sample. Additional exam requirements/recommendations for international students: Required—TOEFL (minimum score 550 paper-based; 213 computer-based).

University of Alberta, School of Public Health, Department of Public Health Sciences, Edmonton, AB T6G 2E1, Canada. Offers clinical epidemiology (M Sc, MPH); environmental and occupational health (MPH); environmental health sciences (M Sc); epidemiology (M Sc); global health (M Sc, MPH); health policy and management (MPH); health policy research (M Sc); health technology assessment (MPH); occupational health (M Sc); population health (M Sc); public health leadership (MPH); public health sciences (PhD); quantitative methods (MPH). *Accreditation:* CEPH (one or more programs are accredited). *Faculty:* 24 full-time (5 women), 59 part-time/adjunct (13 women). *Students:* 49 full-time, 49 part-time. 81 applicants, 31% accepted. In 2009, 28 master's awarded. Terminal master's awarded for partial completion of doctoral program. *Degree requirements:* For master's, thesis (for some programs); for doctorate, thesis/dissertation. *Entrance requirements:* For master's, GMAT or GRE General Test. Additional exam requirements/recommendations for international students: Required—TOEFL (minimum score 550 paper-based; 213 computer-based) or IELTS (minimum score 6). *Application deadline:* For fall admission, 3/15 for domestic students, 7/1 for international students; for winter admission, 11/1 for international students; for spring admission, 3/1 for international students. Applications are processed on a rolling basis. Application fee: $0. Electronic applications accepted. Tuition and fees charges are reported in Canadian dollars. *Expenses:* Tuition, area resident: Full-time $4626 Canadian dollars; part-time $99.72 Canadian dollars per unit. International tuition: $8216 Canadian dollars full-time. Required fees: $3590 Canadian dollars; $99.72 Canadian dollars per unit. $215 Canadian dollars per term. *Financial support:* In 2009–10, 11 students received support, including 6 research assistantships with tuition reimbursements available (averaging $2,200 per year); fellowships, teaching assistantships, career-related internships or fieldwork and tuition waivers (partial) also available. Financial award application deadline: 2/1. *Faculty research:* Biostatistics, health promotion and socio-behavioral health science. Total annual research expenditures: $5.7 million. *Unit head:* L. Duncan Saunders, Acting Chair, 780-492-6814, Fax: 780-492-0364. *Application contact:* Felicity R. Hey, Graduate Programs Administrator, 780-492-6407, Fax: 780-492-0364, E-mail: felicity.hey@ualberta.ca.

The University of Arizona, Mel and Enid Zuckerman College of Public Health, Tucson, AZ 85724. Offers MPH, MS, Dr PH, PhD. *Accreditation:* CEPH. *Faculty:* 31. *Students:* 112 full-time (86 women), 112 part-time (84 women); includes 47 minority (8 African Americans, 7 American Indian/Alaska Native, 8 Asian Americans or Pacific Islanders, 24 Hispanic Americans), 18 international. Average age 34. 363 applicants, 39% accepted, 79 enrolled. In 2009, 74 master's, 6 doctorates awarded. *Entrance requirements:* Additional exam requirements/recommendations for international students: Required—TOEFL (minimum score 550 paper-based; 213 computer-based; 79 iBT). *Application deadline:* For fall admission, 1/1 for domestic and international students. Applications are processed on a rolling basis. Application fee: $75. Electronic applications accepted. *Expenses:* Tuition, state resident: full-time $9028. Tuition, nonresident: full-time $24,890. *Financial support:* In 2009–10, 28 research assistantships with full tuition reimbursements (averaging $14,037 per year), 22 teaching assistantships with full tuition reimbursements (averaging $14,326 per year) were awarded; health care benefits and unspecified assistantships also available. Total annual research expenditures: $9.9 million. *Unit head:* Dr. Iman Hakim, Interim Dean, 520-626-7083, E-mail: ihakim@email.arizona.edu. *Application contact:* Lorraine Varela, Special Assistant to the Dean, 520-626-3201, E-mail: varelal@coph.arizona.edu.

The University of British Columbia, Faculty of Medicine, School of Population and Public Health, Vancouver, BC V6T 1Z3, Canada. Offers health administration (MHA); health care and epidemiology (MH Sc, PhD); public health (MPH). *Accreditation:* CEPH (one or more programs are accredited). Postbaccalaureate distance learning degree programs offered (minimal on-campus study). *Degree requirements:* For master's, thesis (for some programs), major paper (MH Sc), research project (MHA); for doctorate, thesis/dissertation. *Entrance requirements:* For master's, GRE General Test or GMAT, PCAT, MCAT (MHA), MD or equivalent (for MH Sc); 4-year undergraduate degree from accredited university with minimum B+ overall academic average and in math or statistics course at undergraduate level (for MPH); 4-year undergraduate degree from accredited university with minimum B+ overall academic average plus work experience (for MHA); for doctorate, master's degree from accredited university with minimum B+ overall academic average and in math or statistics course at undergraduate level. Additional exam requirements/recommendations for international students: Required—TOEFL. Electronic applications accepted. *Faculty research:* Population and public health, clinical epidemiology, epidemiology and biostatistics, global health and vulnerable populations, health care services and systems, occupational and environmental health, public health emerging threats and rapid response, social and life course determinants of health, health administration.

University of California, Berkeley, Graduate Division, Haas School of Business and School of Public Health, Concurrent MBA/MPH Program, Berkeley, CA 94720-1500. Offers MBA/MPH. *Accreditation:* AACSB; CEPH. *Students:* 39 full-time (23 women); includes 9 minority (all Asian Americans or Pacific Islanders), 6 international. Average age 28. *Entrance requirements:* Additional exam requirements/recommendations for international students: Required—TOEFL. Application fee: $200. Electronic applications accepted. *Financial support:* Fellowships with tuition reimbursements, teaching assistantships with tuition reimbursements, career-related internships or fieldwork, scholarships/grants, and unspecified assistantships available. Financial award applicants required to submit FAFSA. *Unit head:* Prof. Kristi Raube, Director, Health Services Management Program, 510-642-5023, Fax: 510-643-6659, E-mail: raube@haas.berkeley.edu. *Application contact:* Lee Forgue, Student Affairs Officer, 510-642-5023, Fax: 510-643-6659, E-mail: eilis@haas.berkeley.edu.

University of California, Berkeley, Graduate Division, School of Public Health, Group in Environmental Health Sciences, Berkeley, CA 94720-1500. Offers MPH, MS, Dr PH, PhD. *Students:* 35 full-time (22 women). Average age 31. 29 applicants, 7 enrolled. In 2009, 6 master's, 2 doctorates awarded. *Degree requirements:* For master's, comprehensive exam (MPH), project or thesis (MS); for doctorate, thesis/dissertation, departmental and qualifying exams. *Entrance requirements:* For master's, GRE General Test, minimum GPA of 3.0; previous course work in biology, calculus, and chemistry; 3 letters of recommendation; for doctorate, GRE General Test, master's degree in relevant scientific discipline or engineering; minimum GPA of 3.0; previous course work in biology, calculus, and chemistry; 3 letters of recommendation. Additional exam requirements/recommendations for international students: Required—TOEFL. *Application deadline:* For fall admission, 12/1 for domestic students. Applications are processed on a rolling basis. Application fee: $70 ($90 for international students). *Financial support:* Fellowships, research assistantships, teaching assistantships, unspecified assistantships available. *Faculty research:* Toxicology, industrial hygiene, exposure assessment,

Public Health—General

University of California, Berkeley (continued)
risk assessment, ergonomics. *Unit head:* Prof. Katharine Hammond, Chair, 510-643-5160, E-mail: ehs_div@berkeley.edu. *Application contact:* Norma Firestone, Graduate Assistant for Admission, 510-643-0881, Fax: 510-642-5815, E-mail: sphinfo@berkeley.edu.

University of California, Berkeley, Graduate Division, School of Public Health, Group in Epidemiology, Berkeley, CA 94720-1500. Offers epidemiology (MS, PhD); infectious diseases (MPH, PhD). *Accreditation:* CEPH (one or more programs are accredited). *Students:* 48 full-time (34 women). Average age 33. 85 applicants, 8 enrolled. In 2009, 2 master's, 17 doctorates awarded. *Degree requirements:* For master's, comprehensive exam; for doctorate, thesis/dissertation, oral and written exam. *Entrance requirements:* For master's, GRE General Test, minimum GPA of 3.0; MD, DDS, DVM, or PhD in biomedical science (MPH); for doctorate, GRE General Test, minimum GPA of 3.0. *Application deadline:* For fall admission, 12/1 for domestic students. Applications are processed on a rolling basis. Application fee: $70 ($90 for international students). *Financial support:* Fellowships, research assistantships, teaching assistantships, Federal Work-Study and unspecified assistantships available. *Unit head:* Prof. Arthur L. Reingold, Head, 510-642-3997, E-mail: robertamyers@berkeley.edu. *Application contact:* Roberta Meyers, Graduate Assistant, 510-643-2731, E-mail: robertamyers@berkeley.edu.

University of California, Berkeley, Graduate Division, School of Public Health, Programs in Public Health, Berkeley, CA 94720-1500. Offers MPH, Dr PH. *Accreditation:* CEPH. *Students:* 302 full-time (242 women). Average age 30. 855 applicants, 158 enrolled. In 2009, 131 master's, 8 doctorates awarded. *Degree requirements:* For doctorate, thesis/dissertation, exam. *Entrance requirements:* For doctorate, GRE General Test, minimum GPA of 3.0. *Application deadline:* For fall admission, 12/1 for domestic students. Applications are processed on a rolling basis. Application fee: $70 ($90 for international students). *Financial support:* Unspecified assistantships available. *Unit head:* Prof. Stephen M. Shortell, Dean, School of Public Health, 510-643-8451, E-mail: candido@berkeley.edu. *Application contact:* Rick Love, Student Affairs Officer, 510-643-8452, E-mail: sphdocs@uclink.berkeley.edu.

University of California, Los Angeles, Graduate Division, School of Public Health, Los Angeles, CA 90095. Offers MPH, MS, D Env, Dr PH, PhD, JD/MPH, MA/MPH, MBA/MPH, MD/MPH, MD/PhD, MSW/MPH. *Accreditation:* CAHME (one or more programs are accredited); CEPH (one or more programs are accredited). *Degree requirements:* For doctorate, thesis/dissertation, oral and written qualifying exams. *Entrance requirements:* For master's, GRE General Test, minimum GPA of 3.0; for doctorate, GRE General Test, minimum undergraduate GPA of 3.0. Electronic applications accepted.

University of California, San Diego, Office of Graduate Studies, Program in Public Health and Epidemiology, La Jolla, CA 92093. Offers PhD. Electronic applications accepted.

University of Colorado Denver, Colorado School of Public Health, Program in Public Health, Denver, CO 80217-3364. Offers MPH, MS. *Accreditation:* CEPH. *Students:* 154 full-time (115 women), 17 part-time (14 women); includes 23 minority (6 African Americans, 1 American Indian/Alaska Native, 4 Asian Americans or Pacific Islanders, 12 Hispanic Americans), 5 international. In 2009, 39 master's awarded. *Entrance requirements:* Additional exam requirements/recommendations for international students: Required—TOEFL (minimum score 550 paper-based; 213 computer-based). *Application deadline:* For fall admission, 2/1 for domestic students. Application fee: $50. *Financial support:* Application deadline: 3/15. *Faculty research:* Cancer prevention by nutrition, cancer survivorship outcomes, social and cultural factors related to health. *Unit head:* Dr. Jack Barnette, Program Director, 303-724-4472, E-mail: jack.barnette@ucdenver.edu. *Application contact:* Information Contact, 303-724-4613, E-mail: colorado.sph@ucdenver.edu.

University of Connecticut, Graduate School, University of Connecticut Health Center, Field of Public Health, Storrs, CT 06269. Offers MPH, JD/MPH. *Faculty:* 57 full-time (25 women). *Students:* 41 full-time (27 women), 86 part-time (60 women); includes 25 minority (13 African Americans, 6 Asian Americans or Pacific Islanders, 6 Hispanic Americans), 8 international. Average age 36. 117 applicants, 30% accepted, 33 enrolled. In 2009, 35 master's awarded. *Degree requirements:* For master's, comprehensive exam. *Entrance requirements:* Additional exam requirements/recommendations for international students: Required—TOEFL (minimum score 550 paper-based; 213 computer-based). *Application deadline:* For fall admission, 2/1 priority date for domestic and international students; for spring admission, 11/1 for domestic students, 10/1 for international students. Applications are processed on a rolling basis. Application fee: $55. Electronic applications accepted. *Expenses:* Tuition, state resident: full-time $4725; part-time $525 per credit. Tuition, nonresident: full-time $12,267; part-time $1363 per credit. Required fees: $346 per semester. Tuition and fees vary according to course load. *Financial support:* In 2009–10, 16 research assistantships with full tuition reimbursements, 1 teaching assistantship with full tuition reimbursement were awarded; Federal Work-Study, scholarships/grants, health care benefits, and unspecified assistantships also available. Financial award application deadline: 2/1; financial award applicants required to submit FAFSA. *Unit head:* David Gregorio, Director, 860-679-1510, E-mail: gregorio@nso.uchc.edu. *Application contact:* Barbara Case, Administrative Assistant, 860-679-1503, E-mail: bcase@nso.uchc.edu.

University of Connecticut Health Center, Graduate School, Program in Public Health, Farmington, CT 06030. Offers MPH, DMD/MPH, MD/MPH. *Accreditation:* CEPH. Part-time and evening/weekend programs available. *Faculty:* 23 full-time (9 women), 8 part-time/adjunct (3 women). *Students:* 39 full-time (26 women), 84 part-time (59 women); includes 24 minority (12 African Americans, 6 Asian Americans or Pacific Islanders, 6 Hispanic Americans), 8 international. 87 applicants, 37% accepted, 26 enrolled. In 2009, 34 master's awarded. *Degree requirements:* For master's, thesis optional. *Entrance requirements:* For master's, GRE. Additional exam requirements/recommendations for international students: Required—TOEFL (minimum score 600 paper-based; 250 computer-based). *Application deadline:* For fall admission, 2/1 priority date for domestic students, 1/1 priority date for international students; for spring admission, 11/1 for domestic students, 10/1 for international students. Applications are processed on a rolling basis. Application fee: $55. Electronic applications accepted. *Financial support:* In 2009–10, 8 research assistantships with full tuition reimbursements were awarded; teaching assistantships with full tuition reimbursements. Financial award application deadline: 2/1; financial award applicants required to submit FAFSA. *Faculty research:* Cancer epidemiology, birth defects, gerontology, health manpower, health services. *Unit head:* Dr. David Gregorio, Director, 860-679-5480, Fax: 860-679-5463, E-mail: gregorio@nso.uchc.edu. *Application contact:* Prof. Joan Segal, Associate Director, 860-679-3351, Fax: 860-679-8823, E-mail: segal@nso.uchc.edu.

University of Florida, College of Medicine, Program in Clinical Investigation, Gainesville, FL 32611. Offers clinical investigation (MS); epidemiology (MS); public health (MPH). Part-time programs available. *Entrance requirements:* For master's, GRE, MD, PhD, DMD/DDS or Pharm D.

University of Florida, Graduate School, College of Public Health and Health Professions and College of Medicine, Programs in Public Health, Gainesville, FL 32611. Offers biostatistics (MPH); environmental health (MPH); epidemiology (MPH); public health management and policy (MPH); public health practice (MPH); social and behavioral sciences (MPH). *Entrance requirements:* For master's, GRE General Test, minimum GPA of 3.0. Additional exam requirements/recommendations for international students: Required—TOEFL (minimum score 550 paper-based; 213 computer-based).

University of Hawaii at Manoa, John A. Burns School of Medicine, Department of Public Health Sciences and Epidemiology, Honolulu, HI 96822. Offers epidemiology (PhD); global health and population studies (Graduate Certificate); public health (MPH, MS, Dr PH). *Accreditation:* CEPH. Part-time programs available. *Faculty:* 27 full-time (10 women), 9 part-time/adjunct (7 women). *Students:* 62 full-time (47 women), 16 part-time (12 women); includes 31 minority (2 American Indian/Alaska Native, 26 Asian Americans or Pacific Islanders, 3 Hispanic Americans), 14 international. Average age 31. 98 applicants, 58% accepted, 40

enrolled. In 2009, 18 master's awarded. *Entrance requirements:* Additional exam requirements/recommendations for international students: Required—TOEFL (minimum score 550 paper-based; 213 computer-based; 79 iBT), IELTS (minimum score 5). *Application deadline:* For fall admission, 3/1 for domestic and international students; for spring admission, 9/1 for domestic and international students. Application fee: $60. *Expenses:* Tuition, state resident: full-time $8900; part-time $372 per credit. Tuition, nonresident: full-time $21,400; part-time $898 per credit. Required fees: $207 per semester. *Financial support:* In 2009–10, 6 students received support, including 19 fellowships (averaging $1,203 per year), 17 research assistantships (averaging $17,361 per year), 1 teaching assistantship (averaging $14,382 per year). Total annual research expenditures: $242,000. *Application contact:* Alan Katz, Graduate Chair, 808-956-8577, Fax: 808-956-5818, E-mail: katz@hawaii.edu.

University of Illinois at Chicago, Graduate College, School of Public Health, Chicago, IL 60607-7128. Offers MHA, MPH, MS, Dr PH, PhD, DDS/MPH, MBA/MPH, MD/PhD, MPH/MS. *Accreditation:* CEPH (one or more programs are accredited). Part-time programs available. Terminal master's awarded for partial completion of doctoral program. *Degree requirements:* For master's, thesis, field practicum; for doctorate, thesis/dissertation, independent research, internship. *Entrance requirements:* For master's and doctorate, GRE General Test, minimum GPA of 2.75. Additional exam requirements/recommendations for international students: Required—TOEFL. Electronic applications accepted.

University of Illinois at Springfield, Graduate Programs, College of Public Affairs and Administration, Program in Public Health, Springfield, IL 62703-5407. Offers MPH. Part-time and evening/weekend programs available. Postbaccalaureate distance learning degree programs offered (no on-campus study). *Faculty:* 5 full-time (2 women), 4 part-time/adjunct (2 women). *Students:* 24 full-time (12 women), 46 part-time (27 women); includes 12 minority (10 African Americans, 1 Asian American or Pacific Islander, 1 Hispanic American), 7 international. Average age 31. 63 applicants, 59% accepted, 21 enrolled. In 2009, 12 master's awarded. *Degree requirements:* For master's, comprehensive exam, internship. *Entrance requirements:* For master's, GRE, minimum undergraduate GPA of 3.0, 3 letters of recommendation. Additional exam requirements/recommendations for international students: Required—TOEFL (minimum score 500 paper-based; 176 computer-based; 61 iBT). *Application deadline:* Applications are processed on a rolling basis. Application fee: $50 ($60 for international students). Electronic applications accepted. *Expenses:* Tuition, state resident: full-time $6390; part-time $266.25 per credit hour. Tuition, nonresident: full-time $14,226; part-time $592.75 per credit hour. Required fees: $2044; $14.36 per credit hour. $722.50 per term. *Financial support:* In 2009–10, research assistantships with full tuition reimbursements (averaging $8,109 per year), teaching assistantships with full tuition reimbursements (averaging $8,109 per year) were awarded; career-related internships or fieldwork, Federal Work-Study, scholarships/grants, health care benefits, and unspecified assistantships also available. Support available to part-time students. Financial award application deadline: 11/15; financial award applicants required to submit FAFSA. *Unit head:* Dr. Sharron Lafollette, Program Administrator, 217-206-7894, Fax: 217-206-7279, E-mail: lafollette.sharron@uis.edu. *Application contact:* Dr. Lynn Pardie, Office of Graduate Studies, 800-252-8533, Fax: 217-206-7623, E-mail: pardie.lynn@uis.edu.

University of Illinois at Urbana–Champaign, Graduate College, College of Applied Health Sciences, Department of Kinesiology and Community Health, Champaign, IL 61820. Offers community health (MS, MSPH, PhD); kinesiology (MS, PhD); public health (MPH); rehabilitation (MS). *Faculty:* 31 full-time (16 women). *Students:* 110 full-time (62 women), 17 part-time (9 women); includes 26 minority (15 African Americans, 1 American Indian/Alaska Native, 8 Asian Americans or Pacific Islanders, 2 Hispanic Americans), 23 international. 139 applicants, 28% accepted, 26 enrolled. In 2009, 26 master's, 9 doctorates awarded. *Entrance requirements:* For master's, GRE, minimum GPA of 3.0; for doctorate, GRE, minimum graduate GPA of 3.5. Additional exam requirements/recommendations for international students: Required—TOEFL. *Application deadline:* Applications are processed on a rolling basis. Application fee: $60 ($75 for international students). Electronic applications accepted. *Financial support:* In 2009–10, 13 fellowships, 55 research assistantships, 71 teaching assistantships were awarded; tuition waivers (full and partial) also available. *Unit head:* Wojciech Chodzko-Zajko, Head, 217-244-0823, Fax: 217-244-7322, E-mail: wojtek@illinois.edu. *Application contact:* Tina M. Candler, Office Manager, 217-333-1083, Fax: 217-244-7322, E-mail: tcandler@illinois.edu.

The University of Iowa, College of Dentistry and Graduate College, Graduate Programs in Dentistry, Department of Preventive and Community Dentistry, Iowa City, IA 52242-1316. Offers dental public health (MS). *Degree requirements:* For master's, thesis. *Entrance requirements:* For master's, GRE, DDS. Additional exam requirements/recommendations for international students: Required—TOEFL.

The University of Iowa, Graduate College, College of Public Health, Iowa City, IA 52242-1316. Offers MHA, MPH, MS, PhD, Certificate, DVM/MPH, JD/MHA, JD/MPH, MBA/MHA, MD/MPH, MHA/MA, MHA/MS, MS/MA, MS/MS, MSN/MPH, Pharm D/MPH. *Degree requirements:* For master's, exam; for doctorate, comprehensive exam, thesis/dissertation. *Entrance requirements:* For master's and doctorate, GRE General Test, minimum GPA of 3.0. Additional exam requirements/recommendations for international students: Required—TOEFL. Electronic applications accepted. *Expenses:* Contact institution.

The University of Kansas, University of Kansas Medical Center, School of Medicine, Department of Preventive Medicine, Kansas City, KS 66160. Offers clinical research (MS); public health (MPH); MD/MPH. Part-time programs available. *Faculty:* 31 full-time, 9 part-time/adjunct. *Students:* 37 full-time (32 women), 55 part-time (36 women); includes 22 minority (8 African Americans, 3 American Indian/Alaska Native, 4 Asian Americans or Pacific Islanders, 7 Hispanic Americans), 15 international. Average age 32. 57 applicants, 56% accepted, 24 enrolled. In 2009, 32 master's awarded. *Degree requirements:* For master's, thesis. *Entrance requirements:* For master's, GRE, MCAT, LSAT, GMAT or other equivalent graduate professional exam, minimum GPA of 3.0. Additional exam requirements/recommendations for international students: Required—TOEFL. *Application deadline:* For fall admission, 3/31 for domestic and international students. Applications are processed on a rolling basis. Application fee: $35. *Expenses:* Tuition, state resident: full-time $6492; part-time $270.50 per credit hour. Tuition, nonresident: full-time $15,510; part-time $646.25 per credit hour. Required fees: $847; $70.56 per credit hour. Tuition and fees vary according to course load and program. *Financial support:* In 2009–10, 25 research assistantships (averaging $6,400 per year) were awarded; career-related internships or fieldwork, Federal Work-Study, scholarships/grants, and unspecified assistantships also available. Financial award application deadline: 3/30; financial award applicants required to submit FAFSA. *Faculty research:* Cancer screening and prevention, smoking cessation, obesity and physical activity, health services/outcomes research. Total annual research expenditures: $6.6 million. *Unit head:* Dr. Edward F. Ellerbeck, Chairman, 913-588-2774, Fax: 913-588-2780, E-mail: eellerbe@kumc.edu. *Application contact:* Tanya Honderick, Assistant Director, KU-MPH, 913-588-2720, Fax: 913-588-8505, E-mail: mwoirhaye@kumc.edu.

University of Kentucky, Graduate School, College of Public Health, Program in Public Health, Lexington, KY 40506-0032. Offers MPH. *Entrance requirements:* For master's, GRE General Test, minimum undergraduate GPA of 2.75. Additional exam requirements/recommendations for international students: Required—TOEFL (minimum score 550 paper-based; 213 computer-based). Electronic applications accepted.

University of Louisville, Graduate School, School of Public Health and Information Sciences, Department of Epidemiology and Population Health, Louisville, KY 40292-0001. Offers epidemiology (MS); public health sciences (PhD), including epidemiology. *Faculty:* 10 full-time (5 women). *Students:* 1 (woman) full-time. Average age 44. 8 applicants, 25% accepted, 0 enrolled. *Entrance requirements:* For master's and doctorate, GRE (greater than 50th percentile in both sections), 2 letters of recommendation on letterhead. Additional exam requirements/recommendations for international students: Required—TOEFL (minimum score 547 paper-based; 210 computer-based; 78 iBT). *Application deadline:* For fall admission, 4/30 for domestic and international students. Application fee: $50. Electronic applications accepted. *Financial support:* In 2009–10, 6 research assistantships with full tuition reimbursements (averaging

$20,000 per year) were awarded; unspecified assistantships also available. Financial award application deadline: 5/1. *Faculty research:* Cancer, cardiovascular disease, aging, infectious disease (specifically tuberculosis and AIDS), diabetes and occupational safety among adolescents. Total annual research expenditures: $484,000. *Unit head:* Dr. Richard Baumgartner, Department Chair, 502-852-2038, Fax: 502-852-3291, E-mail: rnbaum01@gwise.louisville.edu. *Application contact:* Vicki Lewis, Administrative Assistant, 502-852-1798, Fax: 502-852-3294, E-mail: vicki.lewis@louisville.edu.

University of Maryland, College Park, Academic Affairs, School of Public Health, College Park, MD 20742. Offers MA, MHA, MPH, MS, PhD. Part-time and evening/weekend programs available. *Faculty:* 88 full-time (52 women), 42 part-time/adjunct (29 women). *Students:* 177 full-time (134 women), 43 part-time (35 women); includes 52 minority (34 African Americans, 1 American Indian/Alaska Native, 11 Asian Americans or Pacific Islanders, 6 Hispanic Americans), 33 international. 506 applicants, 20% accepted, 56 enrolled. In 2009, 33 master's, 18 doctorates awarded. *Degree requirements:* For doctorate, thesis/dissertation. *Entrance requirements:* For master's and doctorate, GRE General Test, minimum GPA of 3.0, 3 letters of recommendation. Additional exam requirements/recommendations for international students: Required—TOEFL. *Application deadline:* For fall admission, 5/1 for domestic students, 2/1 for international students; for spring admission, 10/1 for domestic students, 6/1 for international students. Applications are processed on a rolling basis. Application fee: $60. Electronic applications accepted. *Expenses:* Tuition, area resident: Part-time $471 per credit hour. Tuition, state resident: part-time $471 per credit hour. Tuition, nonresident: part-time $1016 per credit hour. Required fees: $337.04 per term. *Financial support:* In 2009–10, 17 fellowships with full and partial tuition reimbursements (averaging $14,992 per year), 23 research assistantships with tuition reimbursements (averaging $15,907 per year), 85 teaching assistantships with tuition reimbursements (averaging $16,108 per year) were awarded; career-related internships or fieldwork, Federal Work-Study, and scholarships/grants also available. Support available to part-time students. Financial award applicants required to submit FAFSA. Total annual research expenditures: $7.8 million. *Unit head:* Dr. Robert Gold, Dean, 301-405-2437, Fax: 301-314-9167, E-mail: rsgold@umd.edu. *Application contact:* Dean of Graduate School, 301-405-0358.

University of Massachusetts Amherst, Graduate School, School of Public Health and Health Sciences, Department of Nutrition, Amherst, MA 01003. Offers nutrition (MPH, MS); public health (PhD). Part-time and evening/weekend programs available. Postbaccalaureate distance learning degree programs offered (no on-campus study). *Faculty:* 11 full-time (7 women). *Students:* 7 full-time (all women), 2 part-time (both women); includes 1 minority (Hispanic American), 2 international. Average age 25. 38 applicants, 39% accepted, 5 enrolled. In 2009, 4 master's awarded. Terminal master's awarded for partial completion of doctoral program. *Degree requirements:* For master's, thesis or alternative; for doctorate, comprehensive exam, thesis/dissertation. *Entrance requirements:* For master's, GRE General Test. Additional exam requirements/recommendations for international students: Required—TOEFL (minimum score 550 paper-based; 213 computer-based; 80 iBT), IELTS (minimum score 6.5). *Application deadline:* For fall admission, 2/1 for domestic and international students; for spring admission, 10/1 for domestic and international students. Applications are processed on a rolling basis. Application fee: $50 ($65 for international students). Electronic applications accepted. *Expenses:* Tuition, state resident: full-time $2640; part-time $110 per credit. Tuition, nonresident: full-time $9936; part-time $414 per credit. Tuition and fees vary according to course load. *Financial support:* In 2009–10, 3 research assistantships with full tuition reimbursements (averaging $10,963 per year), 9 teaching assistantships with full tuition reimbursements (averaging $10,887 per year) were awarded; fellowships, career-related internships or fieldwork, Federal Work-Study, scholarships/grants, traineeships, health care benefits, tuition waivers (full), and unspecified assistantships also available. Support available to part-time students. Financial award application deadline: 2/1. *Unit head:* Dr. Elena T. Carbone, Graduate Program Director, 413-545-0740, Fax: 413-545-1074. *Application contact:* Jean M. Ames, Supervisor of Admissions, 413-545-0722, Fax: 413-577-0010, E-mail: gradadm@grad.umass.edu.

University of Massachusetts Amherst, Graduate School, School of Public Health and Health Sciences, Department of Public Health, Amherst, MA 01003. Offers biostatistics (MS, PhD); community health education (MS); environmental health sciences (MPH, MS); epidemiology (MPH, MS); health policy and management (MPH, MS); nutrition (PhD); public health practice (MPH). *Accreditation:* CEPH (one or more programs are accredited). Part-time and evening/weekend programs available. Postbaccalaureate distance learning degree programs offered (no on-campus study). *Faculty:* 38 full-time (23 women). *Students:* 96 full-time (71 women), 232 part-time (153 women); includes 41 minority (14 African Americans, 17 Asian Americans or Pacific Islanders, 10 Hispanic Americans), 65 international. Average age 36. 316 applicants, 61% accepted, 79 enrolled. In 2009, 91 master's, 5 doctorates awarded. Terminal master's awarded for partial completion of doctoral program. *Degree requirements:* For master's, thesis (for some programs); for doctorate, comprehensive exam, thesis/dissertation. *Entrance requirements:* For master's and doctorate, GRE General Test. Additional exam requirements/recommendations for international students: Required—TOEFL (minimum score 550 paper-based; 213 computer-based; 80 iBT), IELTS (minimum score 6.5). *Application deadline:* For fall admission, 2/1 for domestic and international students. Applications are processed on a rolling basis. Application fee: $40 ($65 for international students). Electronic applications accepted. *Expenses:* Tuition, state resident: full-time $2640; part-time $110 per credit. Tuition, nonresident: full-time $9936; part-time $414 per credit. Tuition and fees vary according to course load. *Financial support:* In 2009–10, 3 fellowships with full tuition reimbursements (averaging $2,791 per year), 32 research assistantships with full tuition reimbursements (averaging $9,196 per year), 24 teaching assistantships with full tuition reimbursements (averaging $5,789 per year) were awarded; career-related internships or fieldwork, Federal Work-Study, scholarships/grants, traineeships, health care benefits, tuition waivers (full), and unspecified assistantships also available. Support available to part-time students. Financial award application deadline: 2/1. *Unit head:* Dr. Paula Stamps, Graduate Program Director, 413-545-2861, Fax: 413-545-0964. *Application contact:* Jean M. Ames, Supervisor of Admissions, 413-545-0722, Fax: 413-577-0010, E-mail: gradadm@grad.umass.edu.

University of Massachusetts Lowell, School of Health and Environment, Department of Clinical Laboratory and Nutritional Sciences, Lowell, MA 01854-2881. Offers clinical laboratory sciences (MS); clinical pathology (Graduate Certificate); nutritional sciences (Graduate Certificate); public health laboratory sciences (Graduate Certificate). *Accreditation:* NAACLS. Part-time programs available. Postbaccalaureate distance learning degree programs offered. *Degree requirements:* For master's, thesis optional. *Entrance requirements:* For master's, GRE General Test, minimum GPA of 3.0, letters of recommendation. *Faculty research:* Cardiovascular disease, lipoprotein metabolism, micronutrient evaluation, alcohol metabolism, mycobacterial drug resistance.

University of Medicine and Dentistry of New Jersey, UMDNJ–School of Public Health (UMDNJ, Rutgers, NJIT) Newark Campus, Newark, NJ 07107-1709. Offers MPH, Dr PH, PhD, Certificate, DMD/MPH, MD/MPH, MS/MPH. *Degree requirements:* For master's, internship. *Entrance requirements:* For master's, GRE General Test. Additional exam requirements/recommendations for international students: Required—TOEFL. Electronic applications accepted.

University of Medicine and Dentistry of New Jersey, UMDNJ–School of Public Health (UMDNJ, Rutgers, NJIT) Piscataway/New Brunswick Campus, Piscataway, NJ 08854. Offers biostatistics (MS); epidemiology (Certificate); general public health (Certificate); public health (MPH, Dr PH, PhD); DO/MPH; MD/MPH; MPH/MBA; MPH/MSPA; Psy D/MPH. *Degree requirements:* For master's, internship; for doctorate, thesis/dissertation. *Entrance requirements:* For master's, GRE General Test; for doctorate, GRE General Test, MPH (Dr PH); MA, MPH, or MS (PhD). Additional exam requirements/recommendations for international students: Required—TOEFL. Electronic applications accepted.

University of Medicine and Dentistry of New Jersey, UMDNJ–School of Public Health (UMDNJ, Rutgers, NJIT) Stratford/Camden Campus, Stratford, NJ 08084. Offers general public health (Certificate); public health (MPH); DO/MPH. *Degree requirements:* For master's,

internship. *Entrance requirements:* For master's, GRE General Test. Additional exam requirements/recommendations for international students: Required—TOEFL. Electronic applications accepted.

University of Memphis, Graduate School, School of Public Health, Memphis, TN 38152. Offers biostatistics (MPH); environmental health (MPH); epidemiology (MPH); health systems management (MPH); public health (MHA); social and behavioral sciences (MPH). Part-time and evening/weekend programs available. Postbaccalaureate distance learning degree programs offered. *Faculty:* 5 full-time (2 women), 4 part-time/adjunct (2 women). *Students:* 45 full-time (23 women), 29 part-time (14 women); includes 19 African Americans, 6 Asian Americans or Pacific Islanders, 2 Hispanic Americans, 7 international. Average age 32. 57 applicants, 70% accepted, 22 enrolled. In 2009, 17 master's awarded. *Degree requirements:* For master's, comprehensive exam, thesis. *Entrance requirements:* For master's, GRE, MAT, DAT, GMAT or LSAT, letters of recommendation. Additional exam requirements/recommendations for international students: Required—TOEFL. *Application deadline:* For fall admission, 11/1 for domestic students; for spring admission, 4/1 for domestic students. Application fee: $35 ($60 for international students). Electronic applications accepted. *Expenses:* Tuition, state resident: full-time $6246; part-time $347 per credit hour. Tuition, nonresident: full-time $15,894; part-time $883 per credit hour. Required fees: $1160. Full-time tuition and fees vary according to course load, degree level and program. *Financial support:* In 2009–10, 46 students received support; research assistantships with full tuition reimbursements available, Federal Work-Study, scholarships/grants, and unspecified assistantships available. Financial award application deadline: 2/15; financial award applicants required to submit FAFSA. *Faculty research:* Health and medical savings accounts, adoption rates, health informatics, Telehealth technologies, biostatistics, environmental health, epidemiology, health systems management, social and behavioral sciences. *Unit head:* Dr. Lisa M. Klesges, Director, 901-678-4637, E-mail: lmklsges@memphis.edu. *Application contact:* Dr. Lisa M. Klesges, Director, 901-678-4637, E-mail: lmklsges@memphis.edu.

University of Miami, Graduate School, Miller School of Medicine, Graduate Programs in Medicine, Department of Epidemiology and Public Health, Teaching Programs in Public Health, Coral Gables, FL 33124. Offers MPH, MSPH, JD/MPH, MD/MPH, MPA/MPH, MPH/MAIA. *Accreditation:* CEPH. Part-time programs available. *Degree requirements:* For master's, thesis (for some programs), project, practicum. *Entrance requirements:* For master's, GRE General Test, minimum GPA of 3.0, 3 letters of recommendation. Additional exam requirements/recommendations for international students: Required—TOEFL (minimum score 550 paper-based; 213 computer-based; 59 iBT). Electronic applications accepted. *Faculty research:* Behavioral epidemiology, AIDS, cardiovascular diseases, cancer prevention, substance abuse epidemiology, women's health.

University of Michigan, School of Public Health, Ann Arbor, MI 48109. Offers MHSA, MPH, MS, PhD, JD/MHSA, MD/MPH, MHSA/MBA, MHSA/MNA, MHSA/MPP, MHSA/MSIOE, MPH/JD, MPH/MA, MPH/MBA, MPH/MPP, MPH/MS, MPH/MSW. MS and PhD offered through the Horace H. Rackham School of Graduate Studies. *Accreditation:* CAHME (one or more programs are accredited); CEPH (one or more programs are accredited). Part-time and evening/weekend programs available. Terminal master's awarded for partial completion of doctoral program. *Degree requirements:* For doctorate, oral defense of dissertation, preliminary exam. *Entrance requirements:* For master's and doctorate, GRE General Test. Additional exam requirements/recommendations for international students: Required—TOEFL (minimum score 560 paper-based; 220 computer-based; 100 iBT). Electronic applications accepted. *Expenses:* Tuition, state resident: full-time $17,286; part-time $1099 per credit hour. Tuition, nonresident: full-time $34,944; part-time $2080 per credit hour. Required fees: $95 per semester. Tuition and fees vary according to course load, degree level and program.

University of Minnesota, Twin Cities Campus, School of Public Health, Minneapolis, MN 55455. Offers MHA, MPH, MS, PhD, Certificate, DVM/MPH, JD/MS, JD/PhD, MD/MPH, MD/PhD, MPH/JD, MPH/MS, MPH/MSN, MPP/MS. *Accreditation:* CEPH (one or more programs are accredited). Part-time programs available. Postbaccalaureate distance learning degree programs offered (minimal on-campus study). Terminal master's awarded for partial completion of doctoral program. *Degree requirements:* For doctorate, thesis/dissertation. *Entrance requirements:* For master's and doctorate, GRE General Test. Additional exam requirements/recommendations for international students: Required—TOEFL. Electronic applications accepted. *Expenses:* Contact institution.

University of Missouri, Graduate School, Masters of Public Health Program, Columbia, MO 65211. Offers MPH. *Entrance requirements:* Additional exam requirements/recommendations for international students: Required—TOEFL (minimum score 550 paper-based; 215 computer-based; 80 iBT).

University of Missouri, School of Medicine, Program in Public Health, Columbia, MO 65211. Offers MS.

The University of Montana, Graduate School, College of Health Professions and Biomedical Sciences, School of Public and Community Health Sciences, Missoula, MT 59812-0002. Offers public health (MPH, CPH). Part-time programs available. Postbaccalaureate distance learning degree programs offered.

University of Nebraska Medical Center, Graduate Studies, Program in Public Health, Omaha, NE 68198. Offers MPH. *Accreditation:* CEPH. Part-time programs available. Postbaccalaureate distance learning degree programs offered (minimal on-campus study). *Degree requirements:* For master's, service-learning capstone course. *Entrance requirements:* Additional exam requirements/recommendations for international students: Required—TOEFL (minimum score 550 paper-based; 213 computer-based), GRE. Electronic applications accepted. *Faculty research:* Ethics, environmental health, cultural influence on health, rural health policy, cancer prevention.

University of Nevada, Reno, Graduate School, Division of Health Sciences, Department of Public Health, Reno, NV 89557. Offers MPH, PhD, MPH/MSN. Terminal master's awarded for partial completion of doctoral program. *Degree requirements:* For master's, thesis optional, culminating experience; for doctorate, thesis/dissertation. *Entrance requirements:* For master's, GRE General Test, GMAT, LSAT, MCAT or DAT, minimum GPA of 2.75; for doctorate, GRE General Test, GMAT, LSAT, MCAT or DAT, minimum GPA of 3.0. Additional exam requirements/recommendations for international students: Required—TOEFL (minimum score 500 paper-based; 173 computer-based; 61 iBT), IELTS (minimum score 6). Electronic applications accepted. *Faculty research:* Biomechanics and basic fundamentals of skiing, social psychology in sports and recreation, fitness and aging, elementary physical education, body fat evaluation.

University of New England, College of Graduate Studies, Program in Public Health, Biddeford, ME 04005-9526. Offers MPH, Certificate. Part-time programs available. Postbaccalaureate distance learning degree programs offered. *Faculty:* 1 (woman) full-time, 2 part-time/adjunct (1 woman). *Students:* 27 full-time (20 women), 17 part-time (13 women); includes 3 minority (1 African American, 1 Asian American or Pacific Islander, 1 Hispanic American). In 2009, 1 other advanced degree awarded. *Degree requirements:* For Certificate, practicum. *Entrance requirements:* For degree, undergraduate course work in math and science. Additional exam requirements/recommendations for international students: Required—TOEFL (minimum score 550 paper-based; 213 computer-based). *Application deadline:* Applications are processed on a rolling basis. Electronic applications accepted. *Expenses:* Contact institution. *Financial support:* Available to part-time students. Application deadline: 5/1. *Unit head:* Timothy Ford, Director, 207-602-2886, E-mail: bwhittenmore@une.edu. *Application contact:* Stacy Gato, Director of Graduate Admissions, 207-221-4225, Fax: 207-221-4898, E-mail: gradadmissions@une.edu.

University of New Hampshire, Center for Graduate and Professional Studies, Manchester, NH 03101. Offers business administration (MBA); counseling (M Ed); education (M Ed, MAT); educational administration and supervision (M Ed, CAGS); industrial statistics (Certificate); public administration (MPA); public health (MPH, Certificate); social work (MSW). Part-time

Public Health—General

University of New Hampshire (continued)
and evening/weekend programs available. *Students:* 86 full-time (57 women), 150 part-time (87 women); includes 13 minority (3 African Americans, 6 Asian Americans or Pacific Islanders, 4 Hispanic Americans), 7 international. 127 applicants, 73% accepted, 60 enrolled. In 2009, 81 master's, 5 other advanced degrees awarded. *Degree requirements:* For master's, thesis or alternative. *Entrance requirements:* Additional exam requirements/recommendations for international students: Required—TOEFL (minimum score 550 paper-based; 213 computer-based; 80 iBT), TOEIC, TSE. *Application deadline:* For fall admission, 6/1 for domestic students, 4/1 for international students; for spring admission, 12/1 for domestic students. Applications are processed on a rolling basis. Application fee: $65. Electronic applications accepted. *Expenses:* Tuition, state resident: full-time $10,380; part-time $577 per credit hour. Tuition, nonresident: full-time $24,350; part-time $1002 per credit hour. Required fees: $1550; $387.50 per semester. Tuition and fees vary according to course load and program. *Financial support:* In 2009–10, 20 students received support, including 1 fellowship, 1 teaching assistantship; research assistantships, Federal Work-Study, scholarships/grants, health care benefits, and unspecified assistantships also available. Support available to part-time students. Financial award application deadline: 3/1; financial award applicants required to submit FAFSA. *Unit head:* Kate Ferreira, Director, 603-641-4313, E-mail: unhm.gradcenter@unh.edu. *Application contact:* Graduate Admissions Office, 603-862-3000, Fax: 603-862-0275, E-mail: grad.school@unh.edu.

University of New Hampshire, Graduate School, School of Health and Human Services, Department of Health Management and Policy, Durham, NH 03824. Offers public health (MPH, Postbaccalaureate Certificate). Part-time and evening/weekend programs available. *Faculty:* 15 full-time (3 women). *Students:* 16 full-time (14 women), 38 part-time (30 women); includes 3 minority (2 African Americans, 1 Asian American or Pacific Islander), 1 international. Average age 41. 41 applicants, 63% accepted, 11 enrolled. In 2009, 8 master's, 1 other advanced degree awarded. *Entrance requirements:* For master's, GMAT or GRE General Test. Additional exam requirements/recommendations for international students: Required—TOEFL (minimum score 550 paper-based; 213 computer-based; 80 iBT). *Application deadline:* For fall admission, 6/1 priority date for domestic students, 4/1 for international students; for spring admission, 12/1 for domestic students. Applications are processed on a rolling basis. Application fee: $65. Electronic applications accepted. *Expenses:* Contact institution. *Financial support:* In 2009–10, 3 students received support, including 1 fellowship; research assistantships, teaching assistantships, scholarships/grants also available. Financial award application deadline: 2/15. *Unit head:* Dr. Jim Lewis, Chairperson, 603-862-3413. *Application contact:* Ann-Marie Matteucci, Administrative Assistant, 603-862-2733, E-mail: masterof.publichealth@unh.edu.

University of New Mexico, School of Medicine, Program in Public Health, Albuquerque, NM 87131-5196. Offers MPH. *Accreditation:* CEPH. Part-time programs available. Postbaccalaureate distance learning degree programs offered. *Degree requirements:* For master's, thesis. *Entrance requirements:* For master's, GRE, MCAT, 2 years of experience in health field. Additional exam requirements/recommendations for international students: Required—TOEFL. *Expenses:* Tuition, state resident: full-time $2099; part-time $233.20 per credit hour. Tuition, nonresident: full-time $6650. Required fees: $25 per semester. Tuition and fees vary according to course load, program and reciprocity agreements. *Faculty research:* Epidemiology, rural health, environmental health, Native American health issues.

The University of North Carolina at Chapel Hill, Graduate School, School of Public Health, Chapel Hill, NC 27599. Offers MHA, MPH, MS, MSEE, MSPH, Dr PH, PhD, DDS/MPH, JD/MPH, MBA/MHA, MD/MPH, MHA/MBA, MHA/MSIS, MHA/MSLS, MPH/MRP, MPH/MSW, MSPH/MSW. *Accreditation:* CAHME (one or more programs are accredited); CEPH (one or more programs are accredited). Part-time programs available. Postbaccalaureate distance learning degree programs offered (minimal on-campus study). Terminal master's awarded for partial completion of doctoral program. *Degree requirements:* For master's, comprehensive exam, thesis, paper, capstone; for doctorate, comprehensive exam, thesis/dissertation. *Entrance requirements:* For master's and doctorate, GRE General Test, minimum GPA of 3.0. Additional exam requirements/recommendations for international students: Required—TOEFL. Electronic applications accepted. *Faculty research:* Health promotion and disease prevention, injury prevention, international health, environmental studies, occupational health studies.

The University of North Carolina at Charlotte, Graduate School, College of Health and Human Services, Department of Health Behavior and Administration, Charlotte, NC 28223-0001. Offers health care administration (MHA); public health (MSPH). *Accreditation:* CAHME. *Faculty:* 15 full-time (9 women), 18 part-time/adjunct (10 women). *Students:* 23 full-time (19 women), 8 part-time (6 women); includes 8 minority (6 African Americans, 1 Asian American or Pacific Islander, 1 Hispanic American), 4 international. Average age 28. 42 applicants, 71% accepted, 13 enrolled. In 2009, 8 master's awarded. *Degree requirements:* For master's, thesis or comprehensive exam. *Entrance requirements:* For master's, GRE or MAT (public health), GRE or GMAT (health administration), minimum GPA of 3.0 during previous 2 years, 2.75 overall. Additional exam requirements/recommendations for international students: Required—TOEFL (minimum score 557 paper-based; 220 computer-based; 83 iBT). *Application deadline:* For fall admission, 7/1 for domestic students, 5/1 for international students; for spring admission, 11/1 for domestic students, 10/1 for international students. Applications are processed on a rolling basis. Application fee: $55. Electronic applications accepted. *Financial support:* Career-related internships or fieldwork, Federal Work-Study, institutionally sponsored loans, scholarships/grants, and unspecified assistantships available. Support available to part-time students. Financial award application deadline: 4/1; financial award applicants required to submit FAFSA. *Faculty research:* Pediatric asthma self-management, reproductive epidemiology, social aspects of injury prevention, chronic illness self-care, competency-based professional education. Total annual research expenditures: $649,694. *Unit head:* Dr. Andrew R. Harver, Chair, 704-687-8680, Fax: 704-687-6122, E-mail: arharver@uncc.edu. *Application contact:* Kathy B. Giddings, Director of Graduate Admissions, 704-687-5503, Fax: 704-687-3279, E-mail: gradadm@uncc.edu.

University of Northern Colorado, Graduate School, College of Natural and Health Sciences, School of Human Sciences, Program in Public Health, Greeley, CO 80639. Offers public health education (MPH). *Faculty:* 1 (woman) full-time. *Students:* 5 full-time (all women), 11 part-time (9 women); includes 2 minority (1 African American, 1 Hispanic American), 1 international. Average age 26. 1 applicant, 100% accepted, 1 enrolled. In 2009, 7 master's awarded. *Degree requirements:* For master's, comprehensive exam, thesis or alternative. *Entrance requirements:* For master's, GRE General Test, 2 letters of recommendation. *Application deadline:* Applications are processed on a rolling basis. Application fee: $50 ($60 for international students). Electronic applications accepted. *Expenses:* Tuition, state resident: full-time $5770; part-time $320.55 per credit hour. Tuition, nonresident: full-time $13,847; part-time $769.27 per credit hour. Required fees: $948.78; $52.72 per credit. *Financial support:* Fellowships, research assistantships, teaching assistantships, unspecified assistantships available. Financial award application deadline: 3/1; financial award applicants required to submit FAFSA. *Unit head:* Dr. Deborah Givray, Program Coordinator, 970-351-2403. *Application contact:* Linda Sisson, Graduate Student Admission Coordinator, 970-351-1807, Fax: 970-351-2371, E-mail: linda.sisson@unco.edu.

University of North Florida, Brooks College of Health, Department of Public Health, Jacksonville, FL 32224. Offers community health (MPH); geriatric management (MSH); health administration (MHA); health behavior research and evaluation (Certificate); nutrition (MSH); rehabilitation counseling (MS). *Accreditation:* CEPH. Part-time and evening/weekend programs available. *Faculty:* 23 full-time (17 women). *Students:* 118 full-time (91 women), 82 part-time (61 women); includes 42 minority (23 African Americans, 8 Asian Americans or Pacific Islanders, 11 Hispanic Americans), 9 international. Average age 31. 192 applicants, 26% accepted, 23 enrolled. In 2009, 69 master's awarded. *Degree requirements:* For master's, thesis optional. *Entrance requirements:* For master's, GRE General Test (MSH, MS, MPH); GMAT or GRE General Test (MHA), minimum GPA of 3.0 in last 60 hours. Additional exam requirements/recommendations for international students: Required—TOEFL (minimum score 500 paper-based; 173 computer-based). *Application deadline:* For fall admission, 7/1 priority date for domestic students, 5/1 for international students; for spring admission, 11/1 priority date for domestic students, 10/1 for international students. Applications are processed on a rolling basis. Application fee: $30. Electronic applications accepted. *Expenses:* Tuition, state resident: full-time $6649.20; part-time $277.05 per credit hour. Tuition, nonresident: full-time $22,970; part-time $957.08 per credit hour. Required fees: $985; $41.03 per credit hour. *Financial support:* In 2009–10, 99 students received support, including 1 teaching assistantship (averaging $1,004 per year); research assistantships, career-related internships or fieldwork, Federal Work-Study, scholarships/grants, and tuition waivers (partial) also available. Support available to part-time students. Financial award application deadline: 4/1; financial award applicants required to submit FAFSA. *Faculty research:* Dietary supplements; alcohol, tobacco, and other drug use prevention; turnover among health professionals; aging; psychosocial aspects of disabilities. Total annual research expenditures: $335,106. *Unit head:* Dr. JoAnn Nolin, Chair, 904-620-2840, Fax: 904-620-2848, E-mail: jnolin@unf.edu. *Application contact:* Heather Kenney, Director of Advising, 904-620-2810, Fax: 904-620-1030, E-mail: heather.kenney@unf.edu.

University of North Texas Health Science Center at Fort Worth, School of Public Health, Fort Worth, TX 76107-2699. Offers biostatistics (MPH); community health (MPH); disease control and prevention (Dr PH); environmental and occupational health sciences (MPH); epidemiology (MPH); health administration (MHA); health policy and management (MPH, Dr PH); DO/MPH; MS/MPH; MSN/MPH. *Accreditation:* CEPH. Part-time and evening/weekend programs available. *Degree requirements:* For master's, thesis or alternative, supervised internship; for doctorate, thesis/dissertation, supervised internship. *Entrance requirements:* For master's, GRE General Test. Additional exam requirements/recommendations for international students: Required—TOEFL. Electronic applications accepted.

University of Oklahoma Health Sciences Center, Graduate College, College of Public Health, Program in General Public Health, Oklahoma City, OK 73190. Offers MPH, Dr PH. *Faculty:* 4 full-time (2 women), 1 part-time/adjunct. *Students:* 47 full-time (34 women), 57 part-time (40 women); includes 35 minority (8 African Americans, 17 American Indian/Alaska Native, 8 Asian Americans or Pacific Islanders, 2 Hispanic Americans), 9 international. Average age 31. 144 applicants, 58% accepted, 32 enrolled. In 2009, 16 master's, 1 doctorate awarded. *Expenses:* Tuition, state resident: full-time $3120; part-time $156 per credit hour. Tuition, nonresident: full-time $11,314; part-time $409.70 per credit hour. Required fees: $1471; $51.20 per credit hour. $223.25 per term. *Unit head:* Dr. Gary Raskob, Dean, 405-271-2232. *Application contact:* Robin Howell, Information Contact, 405-271-2308, E-mail: robin_howell@ouhsc.edu.

University of Oklahoma Health Sciences Center, Graduate College, College of Public Health, Program in Preparedness and Terrorism, Oklahoma City, OK 73190. Offers MPH. *Faculty:* 13 full-time (7 women). *Students:* 4 full-time (2 women), 3 part-time (1 woman); includes 1 minority (American Indian/Alaska Native). Average age 40. 1 applicant, 0% accepted, 0 enrolled. In 2009, 3 master's awarded. *Expenses:* Tuition, state resident: full-time $3120; part-time $156 per credit hour. Tuition, nonresident: full-time $11,314; part-time $409.70 per credit hour. Required fees: $1471; $51.20 per credit hour. $223.25 per term. *Unit head:* Dr. Gary Raskob, Dean, 405-271-2232. *Application contact:* Robin Howell, Information Contact, 405-271-2308, E-mail: robin_howell@ouhsc.edu.

University of Oklahoma—Tulsa, College of Public Health, Tulsa, OK 74135-2512. Offers general public health (MPH); health administration and policy (MPH); public health preparedness and terrorism (MPH).

University of Ottawa, Faculty of Graduate and Postdoctoral Studies, Interdisciplinary Programs, Program in Population Health, Ottawa, ON K1N 6N5, Canada. Offers PhD. *Degree requirements:* For doctorate, comprehensive exam, thesis/dissertation. Electronic applications accepted. *Faculty research:* Population health.

University of Pittsburgh, Graduate School of Public Health, Pittsburgh, PA 15260. Offers MHA, MPH, MS, Dr PH, PhD, Certificate, JD/MPH, MD/MPH, MD/PhD, MID/MPH, MPH/MPA, MPH/MSW, MPH/PhD. *Accreditation:* CEPH (one or more programs are accredited). Part-time programs available. *Faculty:* 158 full-time (74 women), 108 part-time/adjunct (36 women). *Students:* 433 full-time (306 women), 196 part-time (131 women); includes 105 minority (51 African Americans, 1 American Indian/Alaska Native, 42 Asian Americans or Pacific Islanders, 11 Hispanic Americans), 145 international. Average age 31. 1,378 applicants, 57% accepted, 202 enrolled. In 2009, 63 master's, 26 doctorates awarded. Terminal master's awarded for partial completion of doctoral program. *Degree requirements:* For master's, comprehensive exam (for some programs), thesis; for doctorate, comprehensive exam, thesis/dissertation. *Entrance requirements:* For master's, GRE, recommendations; for doctorate and Certificate, GRE, bachelor's degree, recommendations, professional statement, transcripts. Additional exam requirements/recommendations for international students: Required—TOEFL (minimum score 550 paper-based; 213 computer-based; 80 iBT). *Application deadline:* For fall admission, 1/4 priority date for domestic and international students; for winter admission, 11/1 priority date for domestic students, 8/1 priority date for international students; for spring admission, 3/1 priority date for domestic students, 2/1 priority date for international students. Applications are processed on a rolling basis. Application fee: $95. Electronic applications accepted. *Expenses:* Tuition, state resident: full-time $16,402; part-time $665 per credit. Tuition, nonresident: full-time $28,694; part-time $1175 per credit. Required fees: $690; $175 per term. Tuition and fees vary according to program. *Financial support:* In 2009–10, 153 students received support, including 8 fellowships with full and partial tuition reimbursements available (averaging $49,194 per year), 138 research assistantships with full and partial tuition reimbursements available, 7 teaching assistantships with full tuition reimbursements available (averaging $60,261 per year); career-related internships or fieldwork, scholarships/grants, traineeships, health care benefits, tuition waivers (full and partial), and unspecified assistantships also available. Support available to part-time students. *Faculty research:* Clampsia and fetal maternal factors, cardiovascular disease and sexual identity, health disparities, protein families and genomes, cell immunity to human immunodeficiency virus. Total annual research expenditures: $65.8 million. *Unit head:* Dr. Donald S. Burke, Dean, 412-624-3001, Fax: 412-624-3309, E-mail: donburke@pitt.edu. *Application contact:* 412-624-5200, Fax: 412-624-3755, E-mail: stuaff@pitt.edu.

University of Puerto Rico, Medical Sciences Campus, Graduate School of Public Health, Program in Public Health, San Juan, PR 00936-5067. Offers MPH. *Accreditation:* CEPH. Part-time programs available. *Entrance requirements:* For master's, GRE, previous course work in algebra.

University of Rochester, School of Medicine and Dentistry, Graduate Programs in Medicine and Dentistry, Department of Community and Preventive Medicine, Program in Public Health, Rochester, NY 14627. Offers MPH, MBA/MPH, MD/MPH, MPH/MS, MPH/PhD. *Accreditation:* CEPH. *Entrance requirements:* For master's, GRE General Test.

University of South Africa, College of Human Sciences, Pretoria, South Africa. Offers adult education (M Ed); African languages (MA, PhD); African politics (MA, PhD); Afrikaans (MA, PhD); ancient history (MA, PhD); ancient Near Eastern studies (MA, PhD); anthropology (MA, PhD); applied linguistics (MA); Arabic (MA, PhD); archaeology (MA); art history (MA); Biblical archaeology (MA); Biblical studies (M Th, D Th, PhD); Christian spirituality (M Th, D Th); church history (M Th, D Th); classical studies (MA, PhD); clinical psychology (MA); communication (MA, PhD); comparative education (M Ed, Ed D); consulting psychology (D Admin, D Com, PhD); curriculum studies (M Ed, Ed D); development studies (M Admin, MA, D Admin, PhD); didactics (M Ed, Ed D); education (M Tech); education management (M Ed, Ed D); educational psychology (M Ed); English (MA); environmental education (M Ed); French (MA, PhD); German (MA, PhD); Greek (MA); guidance and counseling (M Ed); health studies (MA, PhD), including health sciences education (MA), health services management (MA), medical and surgical nursing science (critical care general) (MA), midwifery and neonatal nursing science (MA), trauma and emergency care (MA); history (MA, PhD); history of education (Ed D); inclusive education (M Ed, Ed D); information and communications technology policy and regulation (MA); information science (MA, MIS, PhD); international politics (MA, PhD); Islamic studies (MA, PhD); Italian (MA, PhD); Judaica (MA, PhD); linguistics (MA, PhD);

mathematical education (M Ed); mathematics education (MA); missiology (M Th, D Th); modern Hebrew (MA, PhD); musicology (MA, MMus, D Mus, PhD); natural science education (M Ed); New Testament (M Th, D Th); Old Testament (D Th); pastoral therapy (M Th, D Th); philosophy (MA); philosophy of education (M Ed, Ed D); politics (MA, PhD); Portuguese (MA, PhD); practical theology (M Th, D Th); psychology (MA, MS, PhD); psychology of education (M Ed, Ed D); public health (MA); religious studies (MA, D Th, PhD); Romance languages (MA); Russian (MA, PhD); Semitic languages (MA, PhD); social behavior studies in HIV/AIDS (MA); social science (mental health) (MA); social science in development studies (MA); social science in psychology (MA); social science in social work (MA); social science in sociology (MA); social work (MSW, DSW, PhD); socio-education (M Ed, Ed D); sociolinguistics (MA); sociology (MA, PhD); Spanish (MA, PhD); systematic theology (M Th, D Th); TESOL (teaching English to speakers of other languages) (MA); theological ethics (M Th, D Th); theory of literature (MA, PhD); urban ministries (D Th); urban ministry (M Th).

University of South Carolina, The Graduate School, Arnold School of Public Health, Program in General Public Health, Columbia, SC 29208. Offers MPH. *Accreditation:* CEPH. Part-time programs available. *Degree requirements:* For master's, comprehensive exam, practicum. *Entrance requirements:* For master's, DAT or MCAT, GRE General Test, previously earned MD or doctoral degree. Additional exam requirements/recommendations for international students: Required—TOEFL (minimum score 570 paper-based; 230 computer-based). Electronic applications accepted.

University of South Carolina, The Graduate School, Arnold School of Public Health, Program in Physical Activity and Public Health, Columbia, SC 29208. Offers MPH. *Accreditation:* CEPH. Part-time programs available. *Degree requirements:* For master's, comprehensive exam, practicum. *Entrance requirements:* For master's, GRE. Additional exam requirements/recommendations for international students: Required—TOEFL (minimum score 570 paper-based; 230 computer-based). Electronic applications accepted.

University of South Carolina, The Graduate School, College of Nursing, Program in Nursing and Public Health, Columbia, SC 29208. Offers MPH/MSN. *Accreditation:* AACN; CEPH. Part-time programs available. *Entrance requirements:* Additional exam requirements/recommendations for international students: Required—TOEFL (minimum score 570 paper-based; 230 computer-based). Electronic applications accepted. *Faculty research:* System research, evidence based practice, breast cancer, violence.

University of Southern California, Keck School of Medicine and Graduate School, Graduate Programs in Medicine, Department of Preventive Medicine, Master of Public Health Program, Alhambra, CA 91803. Offers biostatistics/epidemiology (MPH); child and family health (MPH); global health leadership (MPH); health communication (MPH); health promotion (MPH). *Accreditation:* CEPH. Part-time programs available. *Faculty:* 22 full-time (12 women), 3 part-time/adjunct (0 women). *Students:* 215 full-time (158 women), 3 part-time (2 women); includes 148 minority (13 African Americans, 3 American Indian/Alaska Native, 114 Asian Americans or Pacific Islanders, 18 Hispanic Americans), 25 international. Average age 26. 208 applicants, 74% accepted, 76 enrolled. In 2009, 60 master's awarded. *Degree requirements:* For master's, practicum, final report, oral presentation. *Entrance requirements:* For master's, GRE General Test, MCAT, GMAT, minimum GPA of 3.0. Additional exam requirements/recommendations for international students: Required—TOEFL (minimum score 600 paper-based; 250 computer-based; 100 iBT). *Application deadline:* For fall admission, 6/1 priority date for domestic and international students; for spring admission, 11/1 priority date for domestic students, 10/1 priority date for international students. Applications are processed on a rolling basis. Application fee: $85. Electronic applications accepted. *Expenses:* Tuition: Full-time $25,980; part-time $1315 per unit. Required fees: $554. One-time fee: $35 full-time. Full-time tuition and fees vary according to degree level and program. *Financial support:* In 2009–10, 175 students received support, including 20 fellowships (averaging $3,200 per year); career-related internships or fieldwork, Federal Work-Study, institutionally sponsored loans, and scholarships/grants also available. Support available to part-time students. Financial award application deadline: 5/1; financial award applicants required to submit CSS PROFILE or FAFSA. *Faculty research:*

Substance abuse prevention, cancer and heart disease prevention, mass media and health communication research, health promotion, treatment compliance. *Unit head:* Dr. Thomas W. Valente, Director, 626-457-4139, Fax: 626-457-6699, E-mail: tvalente@usc.edu. *Application contact:* Chrystal Romero, Admissions Counselor, 626-457-6676, Fax: 626-457-6699, E-mail: ccromero@usc.edu.

See Display below and Close-Up on page 1671.

University of Southern Mississippi, Graduate School, College of Health, Department of Community Health Sciences, Hattiesburg, MS 39406-0001. Offers epidemiology and biostatistics (MPH); health education (MPH); health policy/administration (MPH); occupational/environmental health (MPH); public health nutrition (MPH). *Accreditation:* CEPH. Part-time and evening/weekend programs available. *Faculty:* 8 full-time (4 women), 1 part-time/adjunct (0 women). *Students:* 92 full-time (59 women), 20 part-time (14 women); includes 40 minority (36 African Americans, 1 Asian American or Pacific Islander, 3 Hispanic Americans), 13 international. Average age 32. 90 applicants, 73% accepted, 47 enrolled. In 2009, 4 master's awarded. *Degree requirements:* For master's, comprehensive exam, thesis (for some programs). *Entrance requirements:* For master's, GRE General Test, minimum GPA of 2.75 in last 60 hours. Additional exam requirements/recommendations for international students: Required—TOEFL. *Application deadline:* For fall admission, 3/1 for domestic and international students. Applications are processed on a rolling basis. Application fee: $35. *Expenses:* Tuition, state resident: full-time $5096; part-time $284 per hour. Tuition, nonresident: full-time $13,052; part-time $726 per hour. Required fees: $402. Tuition and fees vary according to course level and course load. *Financial support:* In 2009–10, 5 research assistantships with full tuition reimbursements (averaging $7,000 per year), 1 teaching assistantship with full tuition reimbursement (averaging $8,263 per year) were awarded; career-related internships or fieldwork and Federal Work-Study also available. Financial award application deadline: 3/15; financial award applicants required to submit FAFSA. *Faculty research:* Rural health care delivery, school health, nutrition of pregnant teens, risk factor reduction, sexually transmitted diseases. *Unit head:* Dr. James McGuire, Chair, 601-266-5437, Fax: 601-266-5043. *Application contact:* Shonna Breland, Manager of Graduate Admissions, 601-266-6563, Fax: 601-266-5138.

University of South Florida, Graduate School, College of Public Health, Tampa, FL 33612. Offers MHA, MPH, MSPH, Dr PH, PhD. *Accreditation:* CEPH (one or more programs are accredited). Part-time and evening/weekend programs available. Postbaccalaureate distance learning degree programs offered (minimal on-campus study). *Faculty:* 60 full-time (27 women), 34 part-time/adjunct (13 women). *Students:* 399 full-time (278 women), 399 part-time (298 women); includes 237 minority (122 African Americans, 3 American Indian/Alaska Native, 48 Asian Americans or Pacific Islanders, 64 Hispanic Americans), 94 international. Average age 33. 659 applicants, 69% accepted, 200 enrolled. In 2009, 136 master's, 6 doctorates awarded. *Degree requirements:* For master's, comprehensive exam, thesis (for some programs); for doctorate, comprehensive exam, thesis/dissertation. *Entrance requirements:* For master's, GRE General Test, minimum GPA of 3.0 in upper-level course work, 3 professional letters of recommendation, resume/curriculum vitae; for doctorate, GRE General Test, minimum GPA of 3.0 in upper-level course work, goal statement letter, three professional letters of recommendation, resume/curriculum vitae, writing sample. Additional exam requirements/recommendations for international students: Required—TOEFL (minimum score 550 paper-based; 213 computer-based; 79 iBT). *Application deadline:* For fall admission, 6/1 for domestic students, 1/2 for international students; for spring admission, 10/15 for domestic students, 7/1 for international students. Applications are processed on a rolling basis. Application fee: $30. Electronic applications accepted. *Financial support:* In 2009–10, 46 students received support, including 18 fellowships with full tuition reimbursements available (averaging $32,033 per year), 135 research assistantships with full and partial tuition reimbursements available (averaging $19,597 per year), 66 teaching assistantships (averaging $19,296 per year); career-related internships or fieldwork, Federal Work-Study, institutionally sponsored loans, scholarships/grants, traineeships, and unspecified assistantships also available. Support available to part-time students. Financial award applicants required to submit FAFSA. Total annual research expenditures: $17.3 million. *Unit head:* Dr. Donna J. Petersen, Dean, 813-974-3623, Fax:

Public Health—General

University of South Florida (continued)
813-974-7390. *Application contact:* Michelle Hodge, Academic Advisor, 813-974-6665, Fax: 813-974-8121, E-mail: mhodge1@health.usf.edu.

The University of Tennessee, Graduate School, College of Education, Health and Human Sciences, Program in Public Health, Knoxville, TN 37996. Offers community health education (MPH); gerontology (MPH); health planning/administration (MPH); MS/MPH. *Accreditation:* CEPH. *Degree requirements:* For master's, thesis optional. *Entrance requirements:* For master's, minimum GPA of 2.7. Additional exam requirements/recommendations for international students: Required—TOEFL. Electronic applications accepted. *Expenses:* Tuition, state resident: full-time $6826; part-time $380 per semester hour. Tuition, nonresident: full-time $21,844; part-time $1147 per semester hour. Tuition and fees vary according to program.

The University of Texas at El Paso, Graduate School, College of Health Sciences, Department of Health Promotion, El Paso, TX 79968-0001. Offers public health (MPH). Part-time and evening/weekend programs available. *Students:* 26 (21 women); includes 20 minority (all Hispanic Americans), 4 international. Average age 34. In 2009, 6 master's awarded. *Degree requirements:* For master's, thesis optional. *Entrance requirements:* For master's, GRE, minimum GPA of 3.0, resume, letters of recommendation. Additional exam requirements/recommendations for international students: Required—TOEFL; Recommended—IELTS. *Application deadline:* For fall admission, 8/1 priority date for domestic students, 3/1 for international students; for spring admission, 11/1 priority date for domestic students, 9/1 for international students. Applications are processed on a rolling basis. Application fee: $45 ($80 for international students). Electronic applications accepted. *Financial support:* In 2009–10, research assistantships (averaging $18,825 per year), teaching assistantships with partial tuition reimbursements (averaging $18,000 per year) were awarded; fellowships with partial tuition reimbursements, institutionally sponsored loans, scholarships/grants, health care benefits, tuition waivers (partial), and unspecified assistantships also available. Support available to part-time students. Financial award application deadline: 3/15; financial award applicants required to submit FAFSA. *Unit head:* Dr. Maria O. Duarte-Gardea, Chair, 915-747-8214 Ext. 7252, E-mail: moduarte@utep.edu. *Application contact:* Dr. Patricia D. Witherspoon, Dean of the Graduate School, 915-747-5491, Fax: 915-747-5788, E-mail: withersp@utep.edu.

The University of Texas Health Science Center at Houston, The University of Texas School of Public Health, Houston, TN 77030. Offers MPH, MS, Dr PH, PhD, Certificate, JD/MPH, MD/MPH, MS/MPH, MSN/MPH, MSW/MPH, PhD/MPH. *Accreditation:* CEPH. Part-time programs available. *Faculty:* 142 full-time (68 women), 13 part-time/adjunct (4 women). *Students:* 415 full-time (290 women), 435 part-time (319 women); includes 318 minority (82 African Americans, 5 American Indian/Alaska Native, 118 Asian Americans or Pacific Islanders, 113 Hispanic Americans), 200 international. Average age 33. 1,052 applicants, 53% accepted, 250 enrolled. In 2009, 134 master's, 39 doctorates awarded. *Degree requirements:* For master's, thesis; for doctorate, comprehensive exam, thesis/dissertation. *Entrance requirements:* For master's and doctorate, GRE General Test. Additional exam requirements/recommendations for international students: Required—TOEFL (minimum score 565 paper-based; 225 computer-based; 86 iBT). *Application deadline:* For fall admission, 2/1 for domestic and international students; for spring admission, 8/1 for domestic and international students. Applications are processed on a rolling basis. Application fee: $94. Electronic applications accepted. *Financial support:* Career-related internships or fieldwork, institutionally sponsored loans, scholarships/grants, traineeships, health care benefits, and unspecified assistantships available. Support available to part-time students. Financial award application deadline: 5/5; financial award applicants required to submit FAFSA. *Faculty research:* Big-security and public health preparedness, health promotion and prevention research, health services research, infectious diseases, environmental and occupational health. Total annual research expenditures: $42.3 million. *Unit head:* Dr. Mary Ann Smith, Associate Dean for Student Affairs, 713-500-9236, Fax: 713-500-9068, E-mail: mary.a.smith@uth.tmc.edu. *Application contact:* Tiaresa E. Carter, Admissions Coordinator, 713-500-9035, Fax: 713-500-9068, E-mail: tiaresa.e.carter@uth.tmc.edu.

The University of Texas Medical Branch, Graduate School of Biomedical Sciences, Program in Preventive Medicine and Community Health, Program in Public Health, Galveston, TX 77555. Offers MPH. *Accreditation:* CEPH. *Students:* 9 full-time (3 women); includes 1 minority (Asian American or Pacific Islander). Average age 37. In 2009, 8 master's awarded. *Degree requirements:* For master's, thesis. *Entrance requirements:* For master's, GRE, United States Medical Licensing Exam (USMLE) or NBE, preventive medicine residency. Additional exam requirements/recommendations for international students: Required—TOEFL (minimum score 550 paper-based; 213 computer-based). *Application deadline:* For fall admission, 7/1 priority date for domestic and international students; for winter admission, 11/1 priority date for domestic and international students; for spring admission, 3/1 priority date for domestic and international students. Applications are processed on a rolling basis. Application fee: $30 ($75 for international students). Electronic applications accepted. *Financial support:* Applicants required to submit FAFSA. *Unit head:* Dr. Laura Rudkin, Vice-Chairman of Education and Director, 409-772-9141, Fax: 409-772-5272, E-mail: lrudkin@utmb.edu. *Application contact:* Tonya R. Groh, Coordinator for Special Programs, 409-772-1123, Fax: 409-772-5272, E-mail: trgroh@utmb.edu.

University of the Sciences in Philadelphia, College of Graduate Studies, Mayes College of Healthcare Business and Policy, Program in Public Health, Philadelphia, PA 19104-4495. Offers MPH. *Expenses:* Tuition: Full-time $22,230; part-time $1235 per credit. Tuition and fees vary according to program.

University of the Sciences in Philadelphia, College of Graduate Studies, Program in Health Policy and Public Health, Philadelphia, PA 19104-4495. Offers health policy (MPH, MS); public health (MPH). Part-time and evening/weekend programs available. *Degree requirements:* For doctorate, comprehensive exam, thesis/dissertation. *Entrance requirements:* For master's and doctorate, GRE General Test. Additional exam requirements/recommendations for international students: Required—TOEFL, TWE. *Expenses:* Contact institution. *Faculty research:* Managed care, pharmacoeconomics, health law and regulation, rehabilitation, genetic technologies.

The University of Toledo, College of Graduate Studies, College of Medicine, Department of Public Health and Homeland Security, Program in Public Health, Toledo, OH 43606-3390. Offers biostatistics and epidemiology (Certificate); emergency response (Certificate); global health (Certificate); public health (MPH); MD/MPH.

University of Toronto, School of Graduate Studies, Life Sciences Division, Department of Public Health Sciences, Toronto, ON M5S 1A1, Canada. Offers M Sc, MH Sc, PhD. *Accreditation:* CAHME (one or more programs are accredited); CEPH (one or more programs are accredited). Part-time programs available. *Degree requirements:* For master's, thesis (for some programs); practicum; for doctorate, comprehensive exam, thesis/dissertation, oral thesis defense. *Entrance requirements:* For master's, 2 letters of reference, relevant professional/research experience, minimum B average in final year; for doctorate, 2 letters of reference, relevant professional/research experience, minimum B+ average. Additional exam requirements/recommendations for international students: Required—TOEFL (minimum score 580 paper-based; 237 computer-based), TWE (minimum score 5). *Expenses:* Contact institution.

University of Utah, School of Medicine and Graduate School, Graduate Programs in Medicine, Programs in Public Health, Salt Lake City, UT 84112-1107. Offers biostatistics (M Stat); public health (MPH, MSPH, PhD). *Accreditation:* CEPH (one or more programs are accredited). Part-time programs available. *Degree requirements:* For master's, comprehensive exam, thesis or project (MSPH); for doctorate, comprehensive exam, thesis/dissertation. *Entrance requirements:* For master's and doctorate, GRE General Test, 3 letters of reference, in-person interviews, minimum GPA of 3.0. Additional exam requirements/recommendations for international students: Required—TOEFL (minimum score 550 paper-based; 175 computer-based). Electronic applications accepted. *Expenses:* Tuition, state resident: full-time $4004; part-time $1674 per semester. Tuition, nonresident: full-time $14,134; part-time $5915 per semester. Required fees: $324 per semester. Tuition and fees vary according to course load,

degree level and program. *Faculty research:* Health services, health policy, epidemiology of chronic disease, infectious disease epidemiology, cancer epidemiology.

University of Virginia, School of Medicine, Department of Public Health Sciences, Program in Public Health, Charlottesville, VA 22903. Offers MPH. *Accreditation:* CEPH. *Students:* 18 full-time (11 women), 6 part-time (all women); includes 7 minority (3 African Americans, 2 Asian Americans or Pacific Islanders, 2 Hispanic Americans). Average age 29. 85 applicants, 46% accepted, 23 enrolled. In 2009, 14 master's awarded. *Degree requirements:* For master's, written or oral comprehensive exam or thesis. *Entrance requirements:* For master's, GRE, MCAT, LSAT or GMAT, 2 letters of recommendation. Additional exam requirements/recommendations for international students: Required—TOEFL. *Application deadline:* For fall admission, 3/30 for domestic and international students. Applications are processed on a rolling basis. Application fee: $60. Electronic applications accepted. *Financial support:* Applicants required to submit FAFSA. *Unit head:* Dr. William A. Knaus, Chair, 434-924-8430, Fax: 434-924-8437. *Application contact:* Tracey L. Brookman, Academic Programs Administrator, 434-924-8430, Fax: 434-924-8437, E-mail: ms-hes@virginia.edu.

University of Virginia, School of Nursing, Charlottesville, VA 22903. Offers acute and specialty care (MSN); acute care nurse practitioner (MSN); clinical nurse leadership (MSN); community-public health leadership (MSN); nursing (DNP, PhD); psychiatric mental health counseling (MSN); MSN/MBA. *Accreditation:* AACN. Part-time programs available. *Faculty:* 50 full-time (47 women), 4 part-time/adjunct (3 women). *Students:* 158 full-time (135 women), 118 part-time (117 women); includes 41 minority (30 African Americans, 1 American Indian/Alaska Native, 4 Asian Americans or Pacific Islanders, 6 Hispanic Americans), 4 international. Average age 36. 302 applicants, 48% accepted, 106 enrolled. In 2009, 84 master's, 12 doctorates awarded. *Degree requirements:* For doctorate, comprehensive exam (for some programs), capstone project (DNP), dissertation (PhD). *Entrance requirements:* For master's, GRE General Test, MAT; for doctorate, GRE General Test. Additional exam requirements/recommendations for international students: Required—TOEFL, IELTS. *Application deadline:* Applications are processed on a rolling basis. Application fee: $60. Electronic applications accepted. *Expenses:* Contact institution. *Financial support:* Fellowships, research assistantships, teaching assistantships, Federal Work-Study and scholarships/grants available. Financial award applicants required to submit FAFSA. *Unit head:* Dorrie K. Fontaine, Dean, 434-924-0141, Fax: 434-982-1809. *Application contact:* Clay Hysell, Assistant Dean for Graduate Student Services, 434-924-0141, Fax: 434-982-1809, E-mail: nur-osa@virginia.edu.

University of Waterloo, Graduate Studies, Faculty of Applied Health Sciences, Department of Health Studies and Gerontology, Program in Public Health, Waterloo, ON N2L 3G1, Canada. Offers MPH. Part-time programs available. Postbaccalaureate distance learning degree programs offered (minimal on-campus study). *Degree requirements:* For master's, practicum. *Entrance requirements:* For master's, honour's degree, minimum B average, resume, 1 year work experience. Additional exam requirements/recommendations for international students: Required—TOEFL, TWE. Electronic applications accepted. *Faculty research:* Public health, population health, health communication, health promotion and disease prevention, environmental health.

University of West Florida, College of Arts and Sciences: Sciences, School of Allied Health and Life Sciences, Program in Public Health, Pensacola, FL 32514-5750. Offers MPH. *Accreditation:* CEPH. Part-time and evening/weekend programs available. *Faculty:* 1 full-time (0 women), 4 part-time/adjunct (2 women). *Students:* 10 full-time (6 women), 24 part-time (19 women); includes 12 minority (8 African Americans, 1 American Indian/Alaska Native, 2 Asian Americans or Pacific Islanders, 1 Hispanic American). Average age 34. 21 applicants, 52% accepted, 10 enrolled. In 2009, 4 master's awarded. *Entrance requirements:* Additional exam requirements/recommendations for international students: Required—TOEFL (minimum score 550 paper-based; 213 computer-based). *Application deadline:* For fall admission, 6/1 for domestic students, 5/15 for international students; for spring admission, 11/1 for domestic students, 10/1 for international students. Applications are processed on a rolling basis. Application fee: $30. *Expenses:* Tuition, state resident: full-time $4982; part-time $260 per credit hour. Tuition, nonresident: full-time $20,059; part-time $919 per credit hour. Required fees: $1247; $52 per credit hour. *Financial support:* Application deadline: 4/15. *Unit head:* Dr. George L. Stewart, Chairperson, 850-474-2748. *Application contact:* Terry McCray, Assistant Director of Graduate Studies, 850-473-7718, Fax: 850-474-7714, E-mail: gradadmissions@uwf.edu.

University of Wisconsin–La Crosse, Office of University Graduate Studies, College of Science and Health, Department of Health Education and Health Promotion, La Crosse, WI 54601-3742. Offers community health education (MPH, MS); school health education (MS). *Accreditation:* CEPH (one or more programs are accredited). Part-time and evening/weekend programs available. *Faculty:* 8 full-time (5 women). *Students:* 14 full-time (12 women), 23 part-time (21 women); includes 1 minority (Asian American or Pacific Islander), 5 international. Average age 31. 14 applicants, 71% accepted, 7 enrolled. In 2009, 21 master's awarded. *Degree requirements:* For master's, thesis (for some programs), community health education preceptorship. *Entrance requirements:* For master's, GRE General Test, GRE Subject Test (MPH), minimum GPA of 3.0 (MPH), 2.85 (MS). Additional exam requirements/recommendations for international students: Required—TOEFL (minimum score 550 paper-based; 213 computer-based). *Application deadline:* For spring admission, 2/15 for domestic students. Applications are processed on a rolling basis. Application fee: $56. Electronic applications accepted. *Financial support:* Research assistantships with partial tuition reimbursements, career-related internships or fieldwork, traineeships, health care benefits, unspecified assistantships, and grant-funded positions available. Support available to part-time students. Financial award application deadline: 2/15; financial award applicants required to submit FAFSA. *Faculty research:* Stress management, wellness inventories, needs assessment, health promotion, drug and alcohol use, education, school curriculum. *Unit head:* Dr. Dan Duquette, Chair, 608-785-8161, Fax: 608-785-6792, E-mail: duquette.rode@uwlax.edu. *Application contact:* Kathryn Kiefer, Associate Director of Admissions, 608-785-8939, E-mail: admissions@uwlax.edu.

University of Wisconsin–Milwaukee, Graduate School, College of Nursing, Milwaukee, WI 53201-0413. Offers family nursing practitioner (Post Master's Certificate); health professional education (Certificate); nursing (MS, PhD); public health (Certificate). *Accreditation:* AACN. Part-time programs available. *Faculty:* 34 full-time (33 women). *Students:* 159 full-time (148 women), 118 part-time (100 women); includes 32 minority (15 African Americans, 1 American Indian/Alaska Native, 11 Asian Americans or Pacific Islanders, 5 Hispanic Americans), 6 international. Average age 40. 123 applicants, 54% accepted, 37 enrolled. In 2009, 53 master's, 13 doctorates awarded. *Degree requirements:* For master's, thesis; for doctorate, thesis/dissertation. *Entrance requirements:* For master's, GRE General Test or MAT, autobiographical sketch; for doctorate, GRE, minimum GPA of 3.2. Additional exam requirements/recommendations for international students: Required—TOEFL (minimum score 550 paper-based; 79 iBT), IELTS (minimum score 6.5). *Application deadline:* For fall admission, 1/1 priority date for domestic students; for spring admission, 9/1 for domestic students. Applications are processed on a rolling basis. Application fee: $45 ($75 for international students). *Expenses:* Tuition, state resident: full-time $8800. Tuition, nonresident: full-time $20,760. Tuition and fees vary according to program and reciprocity agreements. *Financial support:* In 2009–10, 8 teaching assistantships were awarded; career-related internships or fieldwork, Federal Work-Study, and unspecified assistantships also available. Support available to part-time students. Financial award application deadline: 4/15. Total annual research expenditures: $3.4 million. *Unit head:* Dr. Sally Lundeen, Dean, 414-229-4189, E-mail: slundeen@uwm.edu. *Application contact:* Ellen K. Murphy, Representative, 414-229-5468.

Vanderbilt University, Graduate School, Center for Medicine, Health, and Society, Nashville, TN 37240-1001. Offers MA, MD/MA. *Students:* 1 full-time (0 women), 1 (woman) part-time. Average age 29. 7 applicants, 57% accepted, 0 enrolled. *Degree requirements:* For master's, comprehensive exam (for some programs), thesis (for some programs). *Entrance requirements:* Additional exam requirements/recommendations for international students: Required—TOEFL (minimum score 570 paper-based; 230 computer-based; 88 iBT). *Application deadline:* For fall

admission, 1/15 for domestic and international students. Application fee: $0. Electronic applications accepted. *Financial support:* Federal Work-Study, scholarships/grants, and health care benefits available. Financial award application deadline: 1/15; financial award applicants required to submit CSS PROFILE or FAFSA. *Faculty research:* Cultural history of health and disease, the rise of scientific medicine, scientific and medical constructions of gender and sexuality, integrative medicine, domestic and international public health, healthcare administration. *Unit head:* Dr. Arlene Tuchman, Director, E-mail: arleen.m.tuchman@vanderbilt.edu. *Application contact:* Walter B. Bieschke, Program Coordinator for Graduate Admissions, 615-343-6321, Fax: 615-343-6687, E-mail: vandygrad@vanderbilt.edu.

Vanderbilt University, School of Medicine, Program in Public Health, Nashville, TN 37240-1001. Offers MPH. *Degree requirements:* For master's, thesis, project. *Entrance requirements:* For master's, curriculum vitae.

Walden University, Graduate Programs, School of Health Sciences, Minneapolis, MN 55401. Offers clinical research administration (MS); health informatics (MS); health services (PhD), including community health promotion and education, general program, health management and policy; healthcare administration (MHA); public health (MPH, PhD), including community health promotion and education (PhD), epidemiology (PhD). Part-time and evening/weekend programs available. Postbaccalaureate distance learning degree programs offered (minimal on-campus study). *Faculty:* 14 full-time, 136 part-time/adjunct. *Students:* 2,121 full-time (1,670 women), 724 part-time (568 women); includes 1,370 minority (1,149 African Americans, 20 American Indian/Alaska Native, 95 Asian Americans or Pacific Islanders, 106 Hispanic Americans), 134 international. Average age 40. In 2009, 232 master's, 24 doctorates awarded. *Degree requirements:* For doctorate, thesis/dissertation, residency. *Entrance requirements:* For master's, bachelor's degree or equivalent in related field, minimum GPA of 2.5; for doctorate, master's degree or equivalent in related field; minimum GPA of 3.0; official transcripts; three years of related professional/academic experience (preferred); access to computer and Internet. Additional exam requirements/recommendations for international students: Required—TOEFL (minimum score 550 paper-based; 213 computer-based), IELTS (minimum score 6.5), or Michigan English Language Assessment Battery (minimum score 82). *Application deadline:* Applications are processed on a rolling basis. Application fee: $50. Electronic applications accepted. *Expenses:* Tuition: Full-time $13,665; part-time $560 per credit. Required fees: $1375. Tuition and fees vary according to course load, degree level and program. *Financial support:* In 2009–10, 152 students received support; fellowships, Federal Work-Study, scholarships/grants, unspecified assistantships, and family tuition reduction, active duty/veteran tuition reduction, group tuition reduction, interest-free payment plans available. Support available to part-time students. Financial award applicants required to submit FAFSA. *Unit head:* Dr. Jorg Westermann, Interim Associate Dean, 800-925-3368. *Application contact:* Jennifer Hall, Director of Enrollment, 866-4-WALDEN, E-mail: info@waldenu.edu.

Washington University in St. Louis, George Warren Brown School of Social Work, St. Louis, MO 63130-4899. Offers public health (MPH); social work (MSW, PhD); JD/MSW; M Arch/MSW; MBA/MSW; MSW/M Div; MSW/MAJCS; MSW/MAPS; MSW/MPH. *Accreditation:* CSWE (one or more programs are accredited). *Faculty:* 44 full-time, 48 part-time/adjunct. *Students:* 504 full-time (428 women); includes 89 minority (48 African Americans, 10 American Indian/Alaska Native, 20 Asian Americans or Pacific Islanders, 11 Hispanic Americans), 98 international. Average age 27. 716 applicants, 63% accepted, 225 enrolled. In 2009, 212 master's, 13 doctorates awarded. *Degree requirements:* For master's, 60 credit hours, including practicum (MSW); 45 credit hours, including practicum (MPH); for doctorate, comprehensive exam, thesis/dissertation. *Entrance requirements:* For master's, GRE, GMAT, LSAT, or MCAT (public health program), minimum GPA of 3.0; for doctorate, GRE, MA or MSW. Additional exam requirements/recommendations for international students: Required—TOEFL (minimum score 575 paper-based; 233 computer-based; 90 iBT). *Application deadline:* For fall admission, 12/15 priority date for domestic and international students. Applications are processed on a rolling basis. Application fee: $40. Electronic applications accepted. *Expenses:* Contact institution. *Financial support:* In 2009–10, 486 students received support. Federal Work-Study, institutionally sponsored loans, scholarships/grants, health care benefits, tuition waivers (partial), and research assistantships, partial tuition waivers available. Support available to part-time students. Financial award applicants required to submit FAFSA. *Faculty research:* Mental health services, social development, child welfare, at-risk teens, autism, environmental health, health policy, health communications, obesity, violence and injury prevention, chronic disease prevention, poverty, public health, productive aging/gerontology, social work, civic engagement, school social work, program evaluation, health disparities. Total annual research expenditures: $14.7 million. *Unit head:* Dr. Edward F. Lawlor, Dean and William E. Gordon Professor, 314-935-6693, Fax: 314-935-8511, E-mail: elawlor@wustl.edu. *Application contact:* Richard Sigg, Director of Admissions and Recruiting, 314-935-6676, Fax: 314-935-4859, E-mail: rsigg@wustl.edu.

See Close-Up on page 1899.

Wayne State University, School of Medicine, Graduate Programs in Medicine, Department of Family Medicine and Public Health Sciences, Detroit, MI 48202. Offers community health (MS); community health services (Certificate); public health (MPH); public health practice (Certificate). *Degree requirements:* For master's, thesis (for some programs). *Entrance requirements:* For master's, GRE, minimum GPA of 2.6. Additional exam requirements/recommendations for international students: Required—TOEFL (minimum score 550 paper-based; 213 computer-based); Recommended—TWE (minimum score 6). Electronic applications accepted. *Faculty research:* Urban health disparities, community health promotion, substance abuse etiology and prevention, HIV/AIDS, interpersonal violence.

West Chester University of Pennsylvania, Office of Graduate Studies, College of Health Sciences, Department of Health, West Chester, PA 19383. Offers emergency preparedness (Certificate); health care administration (Certificate); integrative health (Certificate); public health (MPH), including administration, community, environment, integrative, nutrition; school

health (M Ed). *Accreditation:* CEPH. Part-time and evening/weekend programs available. *Students:* 15 full-time (9 women), 128 part-time (91 women); includes 41 minority (34 African Americans, 2 American Indian/Alaska Native, 5 Asian Americans or Pacific Islanders), 22 international. Average age 30. 83 applicants, 88% accepted, 41 enrolled. In 2009, 45 master's, 8 other advanced degrees awarded. *Degree requirements:* For master's, thesis (for some programs). *Entrance requirements:* For master's, one-page statement of career objectives, two letters of reference. Additional exam requirements/recommendations for international students: Required—TOEFL (minimum score 550 paper-based; 213 computer-based; 80 iBT). *Application deadline:* For fall admission, 4/15 priority date for domestic students, 3/15 for international students; for spring admission, 10/15 for domestic students, 9/1 for international students. Applications are processed on a rolling basis. Application fee: $35. Electronic applications accepted. *Expenses:* Tuition, state resident: full-time $6666; part-time $370 per credit. Tuition, nonresident: full-time $10,666; part-time $593 per credit. Required fees: $122.56 per credit. *Financial support:* In 2009–10, 11 research assistantships with full and partial tuition reimbursements (averaging $5,000 per year) were awarded; unspecified assistantships also available. Support available to part-time students. Financial award application deadline: 2/15; financial award applicants required to submit FAFSA. *Faculty research:* HIV/AIDS education, teacher preparation, water quality. *Unit head:* Dr. Roger Mustalish, Chair, 610-436-2931, E-mail: rmustalish@wcupa.edu. *Application contact:* Dr. Bethann Cinelli, Graduate Coordinator, 610-436-2267, E-mail: bcinelli@wcupa.edu.

Western Kentucky University, Graduate Studies, College of Health and Human Services, Department of Public Health, Bowling Green, KY 42101. Offers healthcare administration (MHA); public health (MPH). *Accreditation:* CEPH. Part-time and evening/weekend programs available. *Degree requirements:* For master's, comprehensive exam, thesis or alternative. *Entrance requirements:* For master's, GRE General Test, minimum GPA of 2.75. Additional exam requirements/recommendations for international students: Required—TOEFL (minimum score 555 paper-based; 213 computer-based; 79 iBT). *Expenses:* Tuition, state resident: full-time $4160; part-time $416 per credit hour. Tuition, nonresident: full-time $9550; part-time $506 per credit hour. Tuition and fees vary according to campus/location and reciprocity agreements. *Faculty research:* Health education training, driver traffic safety, community readiness, occupational injuries, local health departments.

Westminster College, School of Nursing and Health Sciences, Salt Lake City, UT 84105-3697. Offers family nurse practitioner (MSN); nurse anesthesia (MSNA); nurse education (MSNED); nursing (MSN); public health (MPH). *Accreditation:* AACN; AANA/CANAEP. *Faculty:* 11 full-time (6 women), 12 part-time/adjunct (6 women). *Students:* 77 full-time (54 women), 49 part-time (16 women); includes 11 minority (3 African Americans, 6 Asian Americans or Pacific Islanders, 2 Hispanic Americans), 2 international. Average age 34. 152 applicants, 57% accepted, 48 enrolled. In 2009, 23 master's awarded. *Degree requirements:* For master's, clinical practicum, 504 clinical practice hours. *Entrance requirements:* For master's, GRE, resume, Utah RN license in good standing, minimum GPA of 3.0, 3 letters of reference, BSN from accredited nursing program, proof of clear state and federal background check, drug test results, personal interview, current PALS certification, current ACLS certification. Additional exam requirements/recommendations for international students: Required—TOEFL (minimum score 600 paper-based; 250 computer-based; 100 iBT). *Application deadline:* Applications are processed on a rolling basis. Application fee: $40. Electronic applications accepted. *Expenses:* Contact institution. *Financial support:* In 2009–10, 60 students received support. Career-related internships or fieldwork and tuition reimbursement, tuition remission available. Support available to part-time students. Financial award applicants required to submit FAFSA. *Faculty research:* Emotional intelligence, graduate faculty mentorship, parish nursing roles in women's disease prevention, psychiatric nursing students' self-assessment of therapeutic relationships, psychosocial nurse practitioner's self-assessment of therapeutic relationships, curriculum simulation. *Unit head:* Dr. Sheryl Steadman, Dean, 801-832-2164, Fax: 801-832-3110, E-mail: ssteadman@westminstercollege.edu. *Application contact:* Joel Bauman, Vice President of Enrollment Services, 801-832-2200, Fax: 801-832-3101, E-mail: admission@westminstercollege.edu.

West Virginia University, School of Medicine, Department of Community Medicine, Program in Public Health, Morgantown, WV 26506. Offers community health/preventative medicine (MPH). *Accreditation:* CEPH. Part-time programs available. Postbaccalaureate distance learning degree programs offered (minimal on-campus study). *Degree requirements:* For master's, practicum, project. *Entrance requirements:* For master's, GRE General Test, MCAT, medical degree, medical internship. *Expenses:* Contact institution. *Faculty research:* Occupational health, environmental health, clinical epidemiology, health care management, prevention.

Wright State University, School of Medicine, Program in Public Health, Dayton, OH 45435. Offers health promotion and education (MPH); public health management (MPH); public health nursing (MPH). *Accreditation:* CEPH.

Yale University, School of Medicine, School of Public Health, New Haven, CT 06520. Offers biostatistics (MPH, MS, PhD); chronic disease epidemiology (MPH, PhD); environmental health sciences (MPH, PhD); epidemiology of microbial diseases (MPH, PhD); health management (MPH); health policy and administration (MPH, PhD); social and behavioral sciences (MPH); MBA/MPH; MD/MPH; MPH/MA; MSN/MPH. MS and PhD offered through the Graduate School. Part-time programs available. Terminal master's awarded for partial completion of doctoral program. *Degree requirements:* For master's, thesis, internship; for doctorate, comprehensive exam, thesis/dissertation, residency. *Entrance requirements:* For master's, GMAT, GRE, or MCAT, previous undergraduate course work in mathematics and science; for doctorate, GRE General Test. Additional exam requirements/recommendations for international students: Required—TOEFL. Electronic applications accepted. *Expenses:* Contact institution. *Faculty research:* Genetic and emerging infections epidemiology, virology, cost/quality, vector biology, quantitative methods.

Community Health

Adelphi University, School of Education, Program in Health Studies, Garden City, NY 11530-0701. Offers community health education (MA, Certificate); school health education (MA). Part-time and evening/weekend programs available. *Students:* 7 full-time (4 women), 73 part-time (41 women); includes 2 minority (1 Asian American or Pacific Islander, 1 Hispanic American). Average age 27. In 2009, 27 master's awarded. *Degree requirements:* For master's, internship. *Entrance requirements:* For master's, 3 letters of recommendation, resume, minimum cumulative GPA of 2.75. Additional exam requirements/recommendations for international students: Required—TOEFL (minimum score 550 paper-based; 213 computer-based; 80 iBT). *Application deadline:* For fall admission, 4/1 for international students; for spring admission, 11/1 for international students. Applications are processed on a rolling basis. Application fee: $50. Electronic applications accepted. *Expenses:* Tuition: Full-time $28,340; part-time $880 per credit. Required fees: $600; $250 per credit. Full-time tuition and fees vary according to course load and program. *Financial support:* Fellowships, research assistantships with partial tuition reimbursements, teaching assistantships, career-related internships or fieldwork, Federal Work-Study, institutionally sponsored loans, and tuition waivers (full) available. Support available to part-time students. Financial award application deadline: 2/15; financial award applicants required to submit FAFSA. *Faculty research:* Alcohol abuse, tobacco cessation, drug abuse, healthy family lives, healthy personal living. *Unit head:* Dr. Stanley Snegroff, Director, 516-877-

4283, E-mail: snegroff@adelphi.edu. *Application contact:* Christine Murphy, Director of Admissions, 516-877-3050, Fax: 516-877-3039, E-mail: graduateadmissions@adelphi.edu.

Arcadia University, Graduate Studies, Department of Medical Science and Community Health, Glenside, PA 19038-3295. Offers MM Sc, MPH, MSHE, MSPH, MM Sc/MAHE, MM Sc/MSPH. *Students:* 215 full-time (186 women), 13 part-time (12 women); includes 11 minority (7 African Americans, 4 Asian Americans or Pacific Islanders), 1 international. Average age 25. In 2009, 94 master's awarded. *Entrance requirements:* For master's, GRE General Test or MCAT. Additional exam requirements/recommendations for international students: Required—TOEFL. *Application deadline:* For fall admission, 1/5 priority date for domestic students. Application fee: $50. *Expenses:* Contact institution. *Financial support:* Tuition waivers (partial) available. *Unit head:* Michael Dryer, Chair and Program Director, 215-572-2083. *Application contact:* 215-572-2910, Fax: 215-572-4041, E-mail: admiss@arcadia.edu.

Arizona State University, Graduate College, College of Nursing and Healthcare Innovation, Tempe, AZ 85287. Offers child and adolescent mental health intervention specialist (Graduate Certificate); community and public health practice (Graduate Certificate); community health (MS); evidence-based practice in nursing (Graduate Certificate); exercise and wellness (MS, PhD), including exercise and wellness (MS), physical activity, nutrition and wellness (PhD); healthcare innovation (MHI); nurse education in academic and practice settings (Graduate

Community Health

Arizona State University (continued)
Certificate); nurse educator (MS); nursing (MS); nursing and healthcare innovation (PhD); nursing practice (DNP); nutrition (MS). *Accreditation:* AACN. Postbaccalaureate distance learning degree programs offered.

Austin Peay State University, College of Graduate Studies, College of Behavioral and Health Sciences, Department of Health and Human Performance, Clarksville, TN 37044. Offers health leadership (MS). Part-time and evening/weekend programs available. Postbaccalaureate distance learning degree programs offered (no on-campus study). *Faculty:* 5 full-time (3 women). *Students:* 28 full-time (19 women), 45 part-time (35 women); includes 33 minority (28 African Americans, 1 Asian American or Pacific Islander, 4 Hispanic Americans). Average age 32. 72 applicants, 96% accepted, 39 enrolled. In 2009, 23 master's awarded. *Degree requirements:* For master's, comprehensive exam, thesis optional. *Entrance requirements:* For master's, GRE General Test, 3 letters of recommendation, minimum undergraduate GPA of 2.5. Additional exam requirements/recommendations for international students: Required—TOEFL (minimum score 500 paper-based; 173 computer-based). *Application deadline:* For fall admission, 7/27 priority date for domestic students; for spring admission, 12/17 priority date for domestic students. Applications are processed on a rolling basis. Application fee: $25. Electronic applications accepted. *Expenses:* Tuition, state resident: full-time $6160; part-time $608 per credit hour. Tuition, nonresident: full-time $17,080; part-time $854 per credit hour. Required fees: $1224; $61.20 per credit hour. *Financial support:* In 2009–10, 9 students received support, including 9 research assistantships with full tuition reimbursements available (averaging $5,184 per year); career-related internships or fieldwork, Federal Work-Study, institutionally sponsored loans, scholarships/grants, and unspecified assistantships also available. Support available to part-time students. Financial award application deadline: 3/1; financial award applicants required to submit FAFSA. *Faculty research:* Aging and physical activity. *Unit head:* Dr. Marcy Maurer, Interim Chair, 931-221-6105, Fax: 931-221-7040, E-mail: maurerm@apsu.edu. *Application contact:* Dr. Dixie Dennis, Dean, College of Graduate Studies, 931-221-7662, Fax: 931-221-7641, E-mail: dennisdi@apsu.edu.

Bloomsburg University of Pennsylvania, School of Graduate Studies, College of Professional Studies, School of Health Sciences, Department of Nursing, Bloomsburg, PA 17815-1301. Offers adult and family nurse practitioner (MSN); adult health and illness (MSN); community health (MSN); nursing (MSN); nursing administration (MSN). *Accreditation:* AACN; AANA/CANAEP. *Degree requirements:* For master's, thesis. *Entrance requirements:* For master's, minimum QPA of 3.0. Additional exam requirements/recommendations for international students: Required—TOEFL. Electronic applications accepted. *Faculty research:* Cardiopulmonary nursing, cancer topics, women's health.

Brooklyn College of the City University of New York, Division of Graduate Studies, Department of Health and Nutrition Science, Program in Community Health, Brooklyn, NY 11210-2889. Offers community health education (MA); computer science and health science (MS); health care management (MPH); health care policy and administration (MPH); thanatology (MA). *Accreditation:* CEPH. *Students:* 5 full-time (3 women), 46 part-time (38 women); includes 39 minority (32 African Americans, 5 Asian Americans or Pacific Islanders, 2 Hispanic Americans), 2 international. Average age 36. 22 applicants, 95% accepted, 15 enrolled. In 2009, 9 master's awarded. *Degree requirements:* For master's, thesis or alternative. *Entrance requirements:* For master's, 18 credits, 2 letters of recommendation, essay. Additional exam requirements/recommendations for international students: Required—TOEFL. *Application deadline:* For fall admission, 3/1 priority date for domestic students, 2/1 priority date for international students; for spring admission, 11/1 priority date for domestic students, 10/1 priority date for international students. Applications are processed on a rolling basis. Application fee: $125. Electronic applications accepted. *Expenses:* Tuition, state resident: full-time $7360; part-time $310 per credit hour. Tuition, nonresident: full-time $13,800; part-time $575 per credit hour. Required fees: $140.10 per semester. *Financial support:* Federal Work-Study, institutionally sponsored loans, and scholarships/grants available. Support available to part-time students. Financial award application deadline: 5/1; financial award applicants required to submit FAFSA. *Faculty research:* Diet restriction, religious practices in bereavement, diabetes, stress management, palliative care. *Unit head:* Dr. Elizabeth Eastwood, Graduate Deputy Chairperson, 718-951-5026, Fax: 718-951-4670, E-mail: eastwood@brooklyn.cuny.edu. *Application contact:* Hernan Sierra, Graduate Admissions Coordinator, 718-951-4536, Fax: 718-951-4506, E-mail: grads@brooklyn.cuny.edu.

Brooklyn College of the City University of New York, Division of Graduate Studies, Department of Health and Nutrition Science, Program in Public Health, Brooklyn, NY 11210-2889. Offers community-public health (MPH). *Accreditation:* CEPH. *Students:* 8 full-time (4 women), 44 part-time (37 women); includes 22 minority (12 African Americans, 3 Asian Americans or Pacific Islanders, 7 Hispanic Americans), 4 international. Average age 32. 48 applicants, 85% accepted, 7 enrolled. In 2009, 19 master's awarded. *Degree requirements:* For master's, thesis or alternative, 46 credits. *Entrance requirements:* For master's, GRE, 2 letters of recommendation, essay, interview. *Application deadline:* For fall admission, 3/1 priority date for domestic students, 2/1 priority date for international students; for spring admission, 11/1 priority date for domestic students, 10/1 priority date for international students. Applications are processed on a rolling basis. Application fee: $125. Electronic applications accepted. *Expenses:* Tuition, state resident: full-time $7360; part-time $310 per credit hour. Tuition, nonresident: full-time $13,800; part-time $575 per credit hour. Required fees: $140.10 per semester. *Financial support:* Application deadline: 5/1. *Unit head:* Dr. Elizabeth Eastwood, Graduate Deputy Chairperson, 718-951-5026, Fax: 718-951-4670, E-mail: eastwood@brooklyn.cuny.edu. *Application contact:* Hernan Sierra, Graduate Admissions Coordinator, 718-951-4536, Fax: 718-951-4506, E-mail: grads@brooklyn.cuny.edu.

Brown University, Graduate School, Division of Biology and Medicine, Department of Community Health, Providence, RI 02912. Offers health services research (MS, PhD); public health (MPH); statistical science (MS, PhD), including biostatistics, epidemiology; MD/PhD. *Accreditation:* CEPH. *Degree requirements:* For doctorate, thesis/dissertation, preliminary exam. *Entrance requirements:* For master's and doctorate, GRE General Test. Additional exam requirements/recommendations for international students: Required—TOEFL.

The Catholic University of America, School of Nursing, Washington, DC 20064. Offers adult health specialist with functional role as nurse educator (MSN); adult nurse practitioner (MSN); community/public health nurse specialist educator (MSN); family nurse practitioner (MSN); geriatric nurse practitioner (MSN); immigrant, refugee, and global health clinical nurse specialist (MSN); nursing (DNP, PhD, Certificate); pediatric nurse practitioner (MSN); promoting healthy families in vulnerable communities (MSN); psychiatric-mental health nursing (MSN). *Accreditation:* AACN. Part-time programs available. *Faculty:* 15 full-time (all women), 43 part-time/adjunct (41 women). *Students:* 28 full-time (26 women), 75 part-time (73 women); includes 37 minority (27 African Americans, 6 Asian Americans or Pacific Islanders, 4 Hispanic Americans), 4 international. Average age 42. 84 applicants, 64% accepted, 30 enrolled. In 2009, 23 master's, 7 doctorates, 3 other advanced degrees awarded. *Degree requirements:* For master's, comprehensive exam, thesis optional; for doctorate, comprehensive exam, thesis/dissertation, minimum GPA of 3.0, oral proposal defense. *Entrance requirements:* For master's, 3 letters of recommendation, BA in nursing, RN registration, official copies of academic transcripts, some post-baccalaureate nursing experience; for doctorate, GRE General Test, BA in nursing, professional portfolio (including statements, resume, copy of RN license, 3 letters of recommendation, narrative description of clinical practice, proposal), copy of research/scholarly paper related to clinical nursing. Additional exam requirements/recommendations for international students: Required—TOEFL (minimum score 580 paper-based; 237 computer-based). *Application deadline:* For fall admission, 8/1 priority date for domestic students, 7/15 for international students; for spring admission, 12/1 priority date for domestic students, 10/15 for international students. Applications are processed on a rolling basis. Application fee: $55. Electronic applications accepted. *Expenses:* Tuition: Full-time $31,740; part-time $1245 per credit hour. Required fees: $50; $25 per semester hour. One-time fee: $425. *Financial support:* Fellowships, research assistantships, teaching assistantships, Federal Work-Study, scholarships/grants, tuition waivers (full and partial), and unspecified assistantships available. Financial award application deadline: 2/1; financial award applicants required to submit FAFSA. *Faculty research:* Community involvement in health care services, primary health care services, pediatrics, chronic illness, cardiovascular disease. Total annual research expenditures: $311,172. *Unit head:* Dr. Nalini N. Jairath, Dean, 202-319-5403, Fax: 202-319-6485, E-mail: cua-deanschoolofnursing@cua.edu. *Application contact:* Julie Schwing, Director of Graduate Admissions, 202-319-5057, Fax: 202-319-6533, E-mail: cua-admissions@cua.edu.

The College at Brockport, State University of New York, School of Health and Human Performance, Department of Health Science, Brockport, NY 14420-2997. Offers health education (MS Ed), including community health education, health education K-12. *Students:* 3 full-time (1 woman), 6 part-time (5 women). 8 applicants, 38% accepted, 3 enrolled. In 2009, 10 master's awarded. *Degree requirements:* For master's, thesis or alternative. *Entrance requirements:* For master's, GRE General Test, minimum GPA of 3.0, letters of recommendation. Additional exam requirements/recommendations for international students: Required—TOEFL (minimum score 550 paper-based; 213 computer-based; 79 iBT). *Application deadline:* For fall admission, 4/1 priority date for domestic and international students; for spring admission, 11/1 priority date for domestic and international students. Application fee: $80. Electronic applications accepted. *Expenses:* Tuition, state resident: full-time $8370; part-time $349 per credit. Tuition, nonresident: full-time $13,250; part-time $522 per credit. *Financial support:* In 2009–10, 1 teaching assistantship with full tuition reimbursement (averaging $6,000 per year) was awarded; Federal Work-Study, scholarships/grants, and unspecified assistantships also available. Support available to part-time students. Financial award application deadline: 3/15; financial award applicants required to submit FAFSA. *Faculty research:* Nutrition, substance use, HIV/AIDS, bioethics, worksite health. *Unit head:* Dr. Patti Follensbee, Chairperson, 585-395-5483, Fax: 585-395-5246, E-mail: pfallons@brockport.edu. *Application contact:* Dr. Patti Follansbee, Admissions Coordinator, 585-395-5483, Fax: 585-395-5246, E-mail: pfollans@brockport.edu.

Columbia University, Columbia University Mailman School of Public Health, Division of Sociomedical Sciences, New York, NY 10032. Offers MPH, Dr PH, PhD. PhD offered in cooperation with the Graduate School of Arts and Sciences. *Accreditation:* CEPH (one or more programs are accredited). Part-time programs available. *Students:* 141 full-time (129 women), 134 part-time (113 women); includes 96 minority (42 African Americans, 34 Asian Americans or Pacific Islanders, 20 Hispanic Americans), 19 international. Average age 30. 506 applicants, 51% accepted, 95 enrolled. In 2009, 83 master's, 6 doctorates awarded. *Degree requirements:* For master's, thesis; for doctorate, thesis/dissertation. *Entrance requirements:* For master's, GRE General Test; for doctorate, GRE General Test, MPH or equivalent (Dr PH). Additional exam requirements/recommendations for international students: Required—TOEFL (minimum score 600 paper-based; 250 computer-based; 100 iBT). *Application deadline:* For fall admission, 1/5 for domestic students. Application fee: $60. Electronic applications accepted. *Financial support:* Research assistantships, teaching assistantships, career-related internships or fieldwork and Federal Work-Study available. Support available to part-time students. Financial award application deadline: 2/1; financial award applicants required to submit FAFSA. *Faculty research:* Social and cultural factors in health and health care, health services delivery and utilization, health promotion and disease prevention, AIDS. *Unit head:* Dr. Amy Fairchild, Chair, 212-305-1724. *Application contact:* Dr. Amy Fairchild, Chair, 212-305-1724.

Dalhousie University, Faculty of Medicine, Department of Community Health and Epidemiology, Halifax, NS B3H 4R2, Canada. Offers M Sc. *Degree requirements:* For master's, thesis. *Entrance requirements:* Additional exam requirements/recommendations for international students: Required—TOEFL, IELTS, 1 of the following 5 approved tests: TOEFL, IELTS, CANTEST, CAEL, Michigan English Language Assessment Battery. Electronic applications accepted. *Expenses:* Contact institution. *Faculty research:* Population health, health promotion and disease prevention, health services utilization, chronic disease epidemiology.

Duquesne University, School of Education, Department of Counseling, Psychology, and Special Education, Program in Special Education, Pittsburgh, PA 15282-0001. Offers community mental health (MS Ed); special education (MS Ed), including special education. Part-time and evening/weekend programs available. *Faculty:* 6 full-time (all women). *Students:* 42 full-time (38 women), 7 part-time (6 women); includes 1 minority (African American). Average age 27. 20 applicants, 85% accepted, 12 enrolled. In 2009, 12 master's awarded. *Degree requirements:* For master's, thesis optional. *Entrance requirements:* For master's, MAT, minimum GPA of 3.0. Additional exam requirements/recommendations for international students: Required—TOEFL (minimum score 550 paper-based; 80 computer-based). *Application deadline:* For fall admission, 5/1 priority date for domestic students; for spring admission, 1/1 for domestic students. Applications are processed on a rolling basis. Application fee: $0. Electronic applications accepted. *Expenses:* Tuition: Part-time $851 per credit. Required fees: $81 per credit. *Financial support:* In 2009–10, 1 research assistantship was awarded. Support available to part-time students. *Unit head:* Dr. Lisa Vernon-Dotson, Assistant Professor, 412-396-1103, Fax: 412-396-1340, E-mail: vernonl@duq.edu. *Application contact:* Michael Dolinger, Director of Student and Academic Services, 412-396-6647, Fax: 412-396-5585, E-mail: dolingerm@duq.edu.

Eastern Kentucky University, The Graduate School, College of Health Sciences, Department of Health Promotion and Administration, Richmond, KY 40475-3102. Offers community health (MPH). *Degree requirements:* For master's, comprehensive exam, thesis optional. *Entrance requirements:* For master's, GRE or MAT, letters of recommendation. *Faculty research:* Risk behavior, health systems, injury control, nutrition.

East Stroudsburg University of Pennsylvania, Graduate School, College of Health Sciences, Program in Public Health, East Stroudsburg, PA 18301-2999. Offers community health education (MPH). Part-time and evening/weekend programs available. Postbaccalaureate distance learning degree programs offered (minimal on-campus study). *Faculty:* 6 full-time (4 women), 2 part-time/adjunct (both women). *Students:* 29 full-time (25 women), 12 part-time (8 women); includes 8 minority (2 African Americans, 2 Asian Americans or Pacific Islanders, 4 Hispanic Americans), 6 international. Average age 30. In 2009, 8 master's awarded. *Degree requirements:* For master's, comprehensive exam, publishable paper, oral comprehensive exam. *Entrance requirements:* For master's, GRE, 3 letters of recommendation. Additional exam requirements/recommendations for international students: Required—TOEFL (minimum score 560 paper-based; 220 computer-based; 83 iBT). *Application deadline:* For fall admission, 7/31 priority date for domestic students, 3/1 for international students; for spring admission, 11/30 for domestic students, 10/1 for international students. Applications are processed on a rolling basis. Application fee: $50. Electronic applications accepted. *Expenses:* Tuition, state resident: full-time $9942; part-time $387 per credit. Tuition, nonresident: full-time $14,240; part-time $619 per credit. *Financial support:* In 2009–10, 40 research assistantships with partial tuition reimbursements (averaging $2,270 per year) were awarded; career-related internships or fieldwork and unspecified assistantships also available. *Faculty research:* Public health infrastructure. Total annual research expenditures: $500,000. *Unit head:* Dr. Steve Godin, MPH Program Director, 570-422-3562, E-mail: sgodin@po-box.esu.edu. *Application contact:* Kevin Quintero, Graduate Admissions Coordinator, 570-422-3890, Fax: 570-422-2711, E-mail: kquintero@po-box.esu.edu.

East Tennessee State University, School of Graduate Studies, College of Public and Allied Health, Department of Public Health, Johnson City, TN 37614. Offers community health (MPH); epidemiology (Certificate); gerontology (Certificate); health care management (Certificate); public health (MPH); public health administration (MPH). *Accreditation:* CEPH. Part-time programs available. *Degree requirements:* For master's, comprehensive exam, thesis optional. *Entrance requirements:* For master's, GRE General Test, 2 years of community health experience. Additional exam requirements/recommendations for international students: Required—TOEFL (minimum score 550 paper-based; 213 computer-based). *Faculty research:* Rural health issues, youth and adolescent health, health of the elderly, environmental epidemiology, spatial analysis of data.

George Mason University, College of Health and Human Services, Department of Global and Community Health, Fairfax, VA 22030. Offers biostatistics (Certificate); epidemiology (Certificate);

epidemiology and biostatistics (MS); gerontology (Certificate); global health (MS, Certificate); nutrition (Certificate); public health (MPH, Certificate); rehabilitation science (Certificate). *Faculty:* 14 full-time (8 women), 12 part-time/adjunct (8 women). *Students:* 93 full-time (75 women), 106 part-time (92 women); includes 87 minority (46 African Americans, 1 American Indian/Alaska Native, 31 Asian Americans or Pacific Islanders, 9 Hispanic Americans), 22 international. Average age 31. 269 applicants, 69% accepted, 146 enrolled. In 2009, 17 master's, 2 other advanced degrees awarded. *Degree requirements:* For master's, comprehensive exam (for some programs), thesis or practicum. *Entrance requirements:* For master's, GRE, BA with minimum GPA of 3.0, 2 letters of recommendation. Additional exam requirements/recommendations for international students: Required—TOEFL. *Application deadline:* For fall admission, 4/1 priority date for domestic students, 4/1 for international students; for spring admission, 11/1 for domestic and international students. Applications are processed on a rolling basis. Application fee: $75. Electronic applications accepted. *Expenses:* Tuition, state resident: full-time $7568; part-time $315.33 per credit hour. Tuition, nonresident: full-time $21,704; part-time $904.33 per credit hour. Required fees: $2184; $91 per credit hour. *Financial support:* In 2009–10, 4 students received support, including 2 research assistantships with full and partial tuition reimbursements available (averaging $3,500 per year), 2 teaching assistantships with full and partial tuition reimbursements available (averaging $2,790 per year); Federal Work-Study, scholarships/grants, unspecified assistantships, and research awards, health care benefits health care benefits (full-time research or teaching assistantship recipients) also available. Support available to part-time students. Financial award application deadline: 3/1. *Faculty research:* Providing introductory and advanced degrees in health-related disciplines centered in global and community issues, health issues and the needs of affected populations at the regional and global level. *Unit head:* Dr. Shirley S. Travis, Dean, 703-993-1918. *Application contact:* Allan Weiss, Office Manager, 703-993-3126, E-mail: aweiss2@gmu.edu.

Georgia Southern University, Jack N. Averitt College of Graduate Studies, Jiann-Ping Hsu College of Public Health, Program in Public Health, Statesboro, GA 30460. Offers biostatistics (MPH, Dr PH); community health behavior and education (Dr PH); community health education (MPH); environmental health sciences (MPH); epidemiology (MPH); health services policy management (MPH); public health leadership (Dr PH). Part-time programs available. *Students:* 75 full-time (47 women), 23 part-time (15 women); includes 39 minority (36 African Americans, 3 Asian Americans or Pacific Islanders), 24 international. Average age 30. 50 applicants, 80% accepted, 20 enrolled. In 2009, 20 master's awarded. *Degree requirements:* For master's, thesis optional, practicum; for doctorate, comprehensive exam, thesis/dissertation, practicum. *Entrance requirements:* For master's, GRE General Test, minimum GPA of 2.75, resume, 3 letters of reference; for doctorate, GRE, GMAT, MCAT, LSAT, 3 letters of reference, statement of purpose, resume or curriculum vitae. Additional exam requirements/recommendations for international students: Required—TOEFL (minimum score 550 paper-based; 213 computer-based; 80 iBT). *Application deadline:* For fall admission, 3/1 priority date for domestic and international students; for spring admission, 10/1 priority date for domestic students, 10/1 for international students. Applications are processed on a rolling basis. Application fee: $50. Electronic applications accepted. *Expenses:* Contact institution. *Financial support:* In 2009–10, 83 students received support, including research assistantships with partial tuition reimbursements available (averaging $7,200 per year), teaching assistantships with partial tuition reimbursements available (averaging $7,200 per year); career-related internships or fieldwork, Federal Work-Study, scholarships/grants, tuition waivers (partial), and unspecified assistantships also available. Support available to part-time students. Financial award application deadline: 4/15; financial award applicants required to submit FAFSA. *Faculty research:* Biostatistics, community health, environmental health sciences, epidemiology, health policy and management, community health behavior and education, public health leadership. *Unit head:* Dr. Charles Hardy, Dean, 912-478-2674, Fax: 912-478-5811, E-mail: chardy@georgiasouthern.edu. *Application contact:* Dr. Charles Ziglar, Coordinator for Graduate Student Recruitment, 912-478-5635, Fax: 912-478-0740, E-mail: gradadmissions@georgiasouthern.edu.

Hofstra University, School of Education, Health, and Human Services, Department of Health Professions and Family Studies, Program in Community Health, Hempstead, NY 11549. Offers MS. Part-time and evening/weekend programs available. *Students:* 13 full-time (9 women), 9 part-time (8 women); includes 6 minority (5 African Americans, 1 Hispanic American), 2 international. Average age 31. 21 applicants, 90% accepted, 12 enrolled. In 2009, 1 master's awarded. *Degree requirements:* For master's, internship. *Entrance requirements:* For master's, interview, 2 reference letters. Additional exam requirements/recommendations for international students: Required—TOEFL (minimum score 550 paper-based; 213 computer-based; 80 iBT). *Application deadline:* Applications are processed on a rolling basis. Application fee: $60. Electronic applications accepted. *Expenses:* Tuition: Full-time $16,200; part-time $900 per credit hour. Required fees: $970; $145 per term. Tuition and fees vary according to program. *Financial support:* In 2009–10, 10 students received support, including 1 fellowship (averaging $3,000 per year), 1 research assistantship (averaging $21,300 per year); Federal Work-Study, institutionally sponsored loans, scholarships/grants, and tuition waivers (full and partial) also available. Support available to part-time students. *Faculty research:* Integrated long term care, long term care policy reform, health equity, chronic illness and disability, building capacity of community based health organizations. *Unit head:* Prof. Andrew Herman, Program Director, 516-463-6673, Fax: 516-463-4810, E-mail: hprazh@hofstra.edu. *Application contact:* Carol Drummer, Dean of Graduate Admissions, 516-463-4876, Fax: 516-463-4664, E-mail: gradstudent@hofstra.edu.

Hunter College of the City University of New York, Graduate School, Schools of the Health Professions, School of Health Sciences, Programs in Urban Public Health, Program in Community Health Education, New York, NY 10021-5085. Offers MPH. Part-time and evening/weekend programs available. *Faculty:* 27 full-time (17 women), 3 part-time/adjunct (2 women). *Students:* 4 full-time (3 women), 83 part-time (76 women); includes 20 minority (8 African Americans, 1 American Indian/Alaska Native, 4 Asian Americans or Pacific Islanders, 7 Hispanic Americans). Average age 32. 63 applicants, 60% accepted, 21 enrolled. *Degree requirements:* For master's, comprehensive exam, thesis optional, internship. *Entrance requirements:* For master's, GRE General Test, previous course work in calculus and statistics. Additional exam requirements/recommendations for international students: Required—TOEFL. *Application deadline:* For fall admission, 4/1 for domestic students; for spring admission, 11/1 for domestic students. Application fee: $125. *Expenses:* Tuition, state resident: full-time $7360; part-time $310 per credit. Required fees: $250 per semester. *Financial support:* In 2009–10, 6 fellowships were awarded; career-related internships or fieldwork, Federal Work-Study, institutionally sponsored loans, and tuition waivers (partial) also available. Support available to part-time students. Financial award application deadline: 3/1. *Unit head:* Beatrice Krauss, Director, Center of Community and Urban Health, 212-481-4283, Fax: 212-481-5260, E-mail: bkrauss@hunter.cuny.edu. *Application contact:* William Zlata, Director of Graduate Admissions, 212-772-4482, Fax: 212-650-3336, E-mail: admissions@hunter.cuny.edu.

Idaho State University, Office of Graduate Studies, Kasiska College of Health Professions, Department of Family Medicine, Pocatello, ID 83209-8357. Offers Post-Master's Certificate. *Faculty:* 1 part-time/adjunct (0 women). *Students:* 18 full-time (3 women); includes 1 minority (Asian American or Pacific Islander). Average age 32. *Degree requirements:* For Post-Master's Certificate, comprehensive exam, thesis optional, 3 year residency program. *Entrance requirements:* For degree, GRE General Test, MD or DO. Additional exam requirements/recommendations for international students: Required—TOEFL (minimum score 600 paper-based; 213 computer-based). *Application deadline:* For fall admission, 7/1 for domestic students, 6/1 for international students; for spring admission, 12/1 for domestic students, 11/1 for international students. Applications are processed on a rolling basis. Application fee: $55. Electronic applications accepted. *Expenses:* Tuition, state resident: full-time $3318; part-time $297 per credit hour. Tuition, nonresident: full-time $13,120; part-time $437 per credit hour. Required fees: $2530. Tuition and fees vary according to program. *Financial support:* Career-related internships or fieldwork and traineeships available. Financial award application deadline: 1/1; financial award applicants required to submit FAFSA. *Faculty research:* Health disparities in primary care, cardiovascular risk reduction (particularly in dyslipidemia, diabetes, hypertension), health application of geographic information systems, mechanisms for increasing

quality in primary care, collaborative care models for improving health. *Unit head:* Dr. Jonathan Cree, Director, 208-282-4704, Fax: 208-282-4818, E-mail: joncree@otc.isu.edu. *Application contact:* Tami Carson, Graduate School Technical Records Specialist, 208-282-2150, Fax: 208-282-4847, E-mail: carstami@isu.edu.

Independence University, Program in Health Services, Salt Lake City, UT 84107. Offers community health (MSHS); wellness promotion (MSHS). Part-time and evening/weekend programs available. Postbaccalaureate distance learning degree programs offered (no on-campus study). *Degree requirements:* For master's, fieldwork, internship, final project (wellness promotion). *Entrance requirements:* For master's, previous course work in psychology. *Expenses:* Required fees: $475 per credit. One-time fee: $100 part-time.

Indiana State University, School of Graduate Studies, College of Nursing, Health and Human Services, Department of Health, Safety, and Environmental Health Sciences, Terre Haute, IN 47809. Offers community health promotion (MA, MS); health and safety education (MA, MS); occupational safety management (MA, MS). *Accreditation:* NCATE (one or more programs are accredited). *Degree requirements:* For master's, thesis or alternative. *Entrance requirements:* For master's, GRE General Test. Electronic applications accepted.

The Johns Hopkins University, Bloomberg School of Public Health, Department of Health, Behavior and Society, Baltimore, MD 21218-2699. Offers genetic counseling (Sc M); health education and health communication (MHS); social and behavioral sciences (Dr PH, PhD, Sc D); social factors in health (MHS). *Faculty:* 43 full-time (30 women), 59 part-time/adjunct (40 women). *Students:* 100 full-time (89 women), 4 part-time (3 women); includes 28 minority (13 African Americans, 12 Asian Americans or Pacific Islanders, 3 Hispanic Americans), 13 international. Average age 29. 227 applicants, 31% accepted, 26 enrolled. In 2009, 25 master's, 8 doctorates awarded. *Degree requirements:* For master's, comprehensive exam (for some programs), thesis (for some programs); for doctorate, comprehensive exam, thesis/dissertation. *Entrance requirements:* For master's, GRE, curriculum vitae, 3 letters of recommendation; for doctorate, GRE, transcripts, curriculum vitae, 3 recommendation letters. Additional exam requirements/recommendations for international students: Required—TOEFL (minimum score 600 paper-based; 250 computer-based; 100 iBT). *Application deadline:* For fall admission, 12/1 for domestic and international students. Applications are processed on a rolling basis. Application fee: $45. Electronic applications accepted. *Financial support:* In 2009–10, 96 students received support, including 17 fellowships with tuition reimbursements available (averaging $23,634 per year), 30 research assistantships (averaging $7,800 per year), 25 teaching assistantships (averaging $2,759 per year); career-related internships or fieldwork, Federal Work-Study, scholarships/grants, traineeships, health care benefits, unspecified assistantships, and stipends also available. Financial award application deadline: 3/15. *Faculty research:* Social determinants of health, and structural- and community-level inventions to improve health; communication and health education; behavioral and social aspects of genetic counseling. Total annual research expenditures: $6.3 million. *Unit head:* Georgean Smith, Administrator, 410-502-3715, Fax: 410-502-4333, E-mail: gcsmith@jhsph.edu. *Application contact:* Barbara W. Diehl, Senior Academic Program Coordinator, 410-502-4415, Fax: 410-502-4333, E-mail: bdiehl@jhsph.edu.

Kean University, College of Natural, Applied and Health Sciences, Program in Nursing and Public Administration, Union, NJ 07083. Offers MSN/MPA. *Accreditation:* NLN. Part-time and evening/weekend programs available. *Faculty:* 7 full-time (all women). *Students:* 6 part-time (5 women); includes 5 minority (all African Americans). Average age 40. 8 applicants, 88% accepted, 3 enrolled. *Application deadline:* For fall admission, 5/1 for domestic students; for spring admission, 11/1 for domestic students. Application fee: $60 ($150 for international students). Electronic applications accepted. *Expenses:* Tuition, state resident: full-time $10,440; part-time $435 per credit. Tuition, nonresident: full-time $14,160; part-time $590 per credit. Required fees: $2642; $110 per credit. Part-time tuition and fees vary according to course load and degree level. *Financial support:* Research assistantships with full tuition reimbursements, unspecified assistantships available. *Unit head:* Dr. Estelle Pisani, Program Coordinator, 908-737-3390, E-mail: episani@kean.edu. *Application contact:* Dorothy Rowe, Pre-Admissions Coordinator, 908-737-5928, Fax: 908-737-5965, E-mail: drowe@kean.edu.

Long Island University, Brooklyn Campus, School of Health Professions, Department of Community Health, Brooklyn, NY 11201-8423. Offers community mental health (MS); family health (MS); health management (MS). Part-time and evening/weekend programs available. *Entrance requirements:* For master's, 2 letters of recommendation. Additional exam requirements/recommendations for international students: Required—TOEFL (minimum score 500 paper-based; 173 computer-based). Electronic applications accepted.

Massachusetts College of Pharmacy and Health Sciences, Graduate Studies, Program in Community Oral Health, Boston, MA 02115-5896. Offers MS. Part-time programs available. Postbaccalaureate distance learning degree programs offered (minimal on-campus study). *Students:* 9 part-time (all women); includes 1 African American. Average age 37. 12 applicants, 100% accepted, 9 enrolled. *Entrance requirements:* For master's, 2 years of work experience in health care. Additional exam requirements/recommendations for international students: Required—TOEFL (minimum score 550 paper-based; 213 computer-based; 79 iBT). *Application deadline:* For fall admission, 7/1 priority date for domestic students. Application fee: $70. *Expenses:* Tuition: Full-time $28,000; part-time $875 per credit hour. Required fees: $750; $190 per semester. Part-time tuition and fees vary according to course load, campus/location, program and student level. *Unit head:* Becky DeSpain Eden, Assistant Dean of Graduate Studies, 617-735-1594, E-mail: becky.eden@mcphs.edu. *Application contact:* Tara Hennesey, Coordinator of Graduate Admission, 617-732-2850, E-mail: admissions@mcphs.edu.

McGill University, Faculty of Graduate and Postdoctoral Studies, Faculty of Medicine, Department of Epidemiology and Biostatistics, Montréal, QC H3A 2T5, Canada. Offers community health (M Sc); environmental health (M Sc); epidemiology and biostatistics (M Sc, PhD, Diploma); health care evaluation (M Sc); medical statistics (M Sc). *Accreditation:* CEPH (one or more programs are accredited).

Medical College of Wisconsin, Graduate School of Biomedical Sciences, Department of Population Health, Program in Public Health, Milwaukee, WI 53226-0509. Offers public and community health (PhD); public health (MPH, Graduate Certificate).

Medical College of Wisconsin, Graduate School of Biomedical Sciences, Program in Public and Community Health, Milwaukee, WI 53226-0509. Offers PhD, MD/PhD. *Degree requirements:* For doctorate, comprehensive exam, thesis/dissertation. *Entrance requirements:* For doctorate, GRE. Additional exam requirements/recommendations for international students: Required—TOEFL (minimum score 580 paper-based; 273 computer-based; 100 iBT). Electronic applications accepted. *Expenses:* Contact institution. *Faculty research:* Community-academic partnerships, community-based participatory research, injury prevention, health policy, women's health, emergency medical services.

Meharry Medical College, School of Graduate Studies, Division of Community Health Sciences, Nashville, TN 37208-9989. Offers occupational medicine (MSPH); public health administration (MSPH). *Accreditation:* CEPH. Part-time and evening/weekend programs available. *Degree requirements:* For master's, thesis, externship. *Entrance requirements:* For master's, GRE General Test, GMAT. *Expenses:* Contact institution. *Faculty research:* Policy and management, health care financing, health education and promotion.

Memorial University of Newfoundland, Faculty of Medicine and School of Graduate Studies, Graduate Programs in Medicine, Division of Community Health and Humanities, St. John's, NL A1C 5S7, Canada. Offers community health (M Sc, PhD, Diploma). Part-time programs available. *Degree requirements:* For master's, thesis; for doctorate, comprehensive exam, thesis/dissertation, oral defense of thesis. *Entrance requirements:* For master's, MD or B Sc; for doctorate, MD or M Sc; for Diploma, bachelor's degree in health-related field. Additional exam requirements/recommendations for international students: Required—TOEFL. *Faculty research:* Health care delivery and administration, health services, psychosocial, aging.

Community Health

Minnesota State University Mankato, College of Graduate Studies, College of Allied Health and Nursing, Department of Health Science, Mankato, MN 56001. Offers community health (MS); health science (MS, MT); school health (MS). Part-time programs available. *Students:* 14 full-time (9 women), 39 part-time (20 women). *Degree requirements:* For master's, comprehensive exam, thesis or alternative. *Entrance requirements:* For master's, minimum GPA of 3.0 during previous 2 years. Additional exam requirements/recommendations for international students: Required—TOEFL (minimum score 500 paper-based; 173 computer-based; 61 iBT). *Application deadline:* For fall admission, 7/1 for domestic students, 5/1 for international students; for spring admission, 11/1 for domestic students, 10/1 for international students. Applications are processed on a rolling basis. Application fee: $40. Electronic applications accepted. *Expenses:* Tuition, state resident: full-time $5364. Tuition, nonresident: full-time $8314. *Financial support:* Research assistantships with full tuition reimbursements, teaching assistantships with full tuition reimbursements, career-related internships or fieldwork and Federal Work-Study available. Support available to part-time students. Financial award application deadline: 3/15; financial award applicants required to submit FAFSA. *Faculty research:* Teaching methods, stress prophylaxis and management, effects of alcohol. *Unit head:* Dr. Dawn Larsen, Graduate Coordinator, 507-389-2113. *Application contact:* 507-389-2321, E-mail: grad@mnsu.edu.

Montclair State University, The Graduate School, College of Education and Human Services, Department of Health and Nutrition Sciences, Montclair, NJ 07043-1624. Offers American Dietetic Association (Certificate); community health education (MPH); food safety instructor (Certificate); health education (MA); nutrition and exercise science (MS); nutrition and food science (MS). Part-time and evening/weekend programs available. *Faculty:* 15 full-time (10 women), 55 part-time/adjunct (40 women). *Students:* 38 full-time (32 women), 78 part-time (68 women). Average age 32. 53 applicants, 64% accepted, 23 enrolled. In 2009, 19 master's, 2 other advanced degrees awarded. *Degree requirements:* For master's, comprehensive exam, thesis optional. *Entrance requirements:* For master's, GRE, 2 letters of recommendation. Additional exam requirements/recommendations for international students: Required—TOEFL (minimum score 83 computer-based), or IELTS. *Application deadline:* For fall admission, 6/1 for international students; for spring admission, 10/1 for international students. Application fee: $60. *Expenses:* Tuition, area resident: Part-time $486.74 per credit. Tuition, state resident: part-time $486.74 per credit. Tuition, nonresident: part-time $751.34 per credit. Tuition and fees vary according to degree level and program. *Financial support:* In 2009–10, 8 research assistantships with full tuition reimbursements (averaging $7,000 per year) were awarded; Federal Work-Study, scholarships/grants, and unspecified assistantships also available. Support available to part-time students. Financial award application deadline: 3/1; financial award applicants required to submit FAFSA. *Faculty research:* Adolescent physical activity. *Unit head:* Dr. Eva Goldfarb, Chairperson, 973-655-4154. *Application contact:* Amy Aiello, Director of Graduate Admissions and Operations, 973-655-5147, Fax: 973-655-7869, E-mail: graduate.school@montclair.edu.

Mount St. Mary's College, Graduate Division, Program in Nursing, Los Angeles, CA 90049-1599. Offers clinical nurse specialist/adult health (MS); community health (MS); educator (MS); leadership and administration (MS); nursing (MS). *Accreditation:* AACN. *Faculty:* 2 full-time (both women), 11 part-time/adjunct (9 women). *Students:* 31 full-time (29 women), 8 part-time (6 women); includes 24 minority (5 African Americans, 12 Asian Americans or Pacific Islanders, 7 Hispanic Americans), 1 international. Average age 41. In 2009, 22 master's awarded. *Entrance requirements:* Additional exam requirements/recommendations for international students: Required—TOEFL (minimum score 550 iBT). *Application deadline:* For fall admission, 7/15 priority date for domestic students; for spring admission, 11/15 priority date for domestic students. *Expenses:* Tuition: Part-time $730 per unit. Part-time tuition and fees vary according to degree level and program. *Unit head:* Dr. Marsha Sato, Chair, 213-477-2980, E-mail: msato@msmc.la.edu. *Application contact:* Director of Graduate Admission.

Mount Sinai School of Medicine of New York University, Graduate School of Biological Sciences, New York, NY 10029-6504. Offers bioethics (MS); biological sciences (PhD); clinical research (MS); community medicine (MPH); genetic counseling (MS); neurosciences (PhD); MD/PhD. Terminal master's awarded for partial completion of doctoral program. *Degree requirements:* For master's, thesis; for doctorate, comprehensive exam, thesis/dissertation. *Entrance requirements:* For master's, GRE General Test; for doctorate, GRE General Test, GRE Subject Test, 3 years of college pre-med course work. Additional exam requirements/recommendations for international students: Required—TOEFL. Electronic applications accepted. *Faculty research:* Cancer, genetics and genomics, immunology, neuroscience, developmental and stem cell biology, translational research.

New Jersey City University, Graduate Studies and Continuing Education, College of Professional Studies, Department of Health Sciences, Jersey City, NJ 07305-1597. Offers community health education (MS); health administration (MS); school health education (MS). Part-time and evening/weekend programs available. *Faculty:* 3. *Students:* 8 full-time (6 women), 42 part-time (32 women); includes 18 minority (10 African Americans, 1 American Indian/Alaska Native, 3 Asian Americans or Pacific Islanders, 4 Hispanic Americans), 3 international. Average age 41. In 2009, 21 master's awarded. *Degree requirements:* For master's, thesis or alternative, internship. *Entrance requirements:* For master's, GRE General Test or MAT. Additional exam requirements/recommendations for international students: Required—TOEFL. *Application deadline:* For fall admission, 8/1 priority date for domestic students; for spring admission, 12/1 for domestic students. Applications are processed on a rolling basis. Application fee: $0. *Expenses:* Tuition, area resident: Part-time $456.75 per credit. Tuition, nonresident: part-time $842.55 per credit. Required fees: $65 per term. *Financial support:* Career-related internships or fieldwork and unspecified assistantships available. *Unit head:* Dr. Gail Gordon, Chairperson, 201-200-3431, E-mail: ggordon@njcu.edu. *Application contact:* Dr. Gail Gordon, Chairperson, 201-200-3431, E-mail: ggordon@njcu.edu.

New Mexico State University, Graduate School, College of Health and Social Services, Department of Health Science, Las Cruces, NM 88003-8001. Offers community health education (MPH). Part-time programs available. Postbaccalaureate distance learning degree programs offered (minimal on-campus study). *Faculty:* 9 full-time (5 women), 1 (woman) part-time/adjunct. *Students:* 51 full-time (40 women), 38 part-time (28 women); includes 41 minority (6 African Americans, 13 American Indian/Alaska Native, 2 Asian Americans or Pacific Islanders, 20 Hispanic Americans), 11 international. Average age 34. 64 applicants, 81% accepted, 29 enrolled. In 2009, 18 master's awarded. *Degree requirements:* For master's, thesis optional. *Entrance requirements:* For master's, GRE, 6 hours in psychosocial course work, 4 hours in biology, 3 hours in statistics. Additional exam requirements/recommendations for international students: Required—TOEFL. *Application deadline:* For fall admission, 4/1 for domestic students. Application fee: $30 ($50 for international students). *Expenses:* Tuition, state resident: full-time $4080; part-time $223 per credit. Tuition, nonresident: full-time $14,256; part-time $647 per credit. Required fees: $1278; $639 per semester. *Financial support:* In 2009–10, 2 research assistantships (averaging $3,950 per year), 21 teaching assistantships (averaging $5,047 per year) were awarded; fellowships, career-related internships or fieldwork and health care benefits also available. Financial award application deadline: 4/1. *Faculty research:* Community health education, health issues of U.S.-Mexico border, health policy and management, victims of violence, environmental and occupational health issues. *Unit head:* Dr. Stephen Arnold, Interim Head, 575-646-4300, Fax: 575-646-4343, E-mail: sarnold@nmsu.edu. *Application contact:* Dr. Stephen Arnold, Interim Head, 575-646-4300, Fax: 575-646-4343, E-mail: sarnold@nmsu.edu.

New York University, Steinhardt School of Culture, Education, and Human Development, Department of Nutrition, Food Studies, and Public Health, Program in Community Public Health, New York, NY 10012-1019. Offers community public health (MPH), including community health, international community health, public health nutrition; public health (PhD). *Accreditation:* CEPH. Part-time programs available. *Students:* 90 full-time (77 women), 45 part-time (41 women); includes 34 minority (11 African Americans, 17 Asian Americans or Pacific Islanders, 6 Hispanic Americans), 10 international. Average age 28. 257 applicants, 81% accepted, 52 enrolled. In 2009, 36 master's awarded. *Degree requirements:* For master's,

thesis (for some programs). *Entrance requirements:* For master's, GRE General Test; for doctorate, GRE General Test, interview. Additional exam requirements/recommendations for international students: Required—TOEFL. *Application deadline:* For fall admission, 12/15 priority date for domestic and international students; for spring admission, 11/1 for domestic and international students. Applications are processed on a rolling basis. Application fee: $75. Electronic applications accepted. *Expenses:* Tuition: Full-time $30,528; part-time $1272 per credit. Required fees: $2177. *Financial support:* Fellowships with full and partial tuition reimbursements, career-related internships or fieldwork, Federal Work-Study, institutionally sponsored loans, scholarships/grants, and tuition waivers (partial) available. Support available to part-time students. Financial award application deadline: 2/1; financial award applicants required to submit FAFSA. *Faculty research:* Social epidemiology, primary health care, global health, immigrants and health, infectious disease prevention, HIV/AIDS. *Unit head:* Director, 212-998-5580, Fax: 212-995-4192. *Application contact:* 212-998-5030, Fax: 212-995-4328, E-mail: steinhardt.gradadmissions@nyu.edu.

Sage Graduate School, Graduate School, School of Health Sciences, Department of Psychology, Troy, NY 12180-4115. Offers community psychology (MA), including child care and children's services, community counseling, community health education, community psychology, general psychology; counseling and community psychology (MA). Part-time and evening/weekend programs available. *Faculty:* 3 full-time (all women), 5 part-time/adjunct (3 women). *Students:* 35 full-time (33 women), 55 part-time (51 women); includes 14 minority (8 African Americans, 1 American Indian/Alaska Native, 1 Asian American or Pacific Islander, 4 Hispanic Americans). Average age 28. 78 applicants, 46% accepted, 21 enrolled. In 2009, 29 master's awarded. *Degree requirements:* For master's, thesis or alternative. *Entrance requirements:* For master's, GRE General Test. Additional exam requirements/recommendations for international students: Required—TOEFL (minimum score 550 paper-based; 213 computer-based). *Application deadline:* Applications are processed on a rolling basis. Application fee: $40. *Expenses:* Tuition: Full-time $10,620; part-time $590 per credit hour. *Financial support:* Fellowships, research assistantships, Federal Work-Study, scholarships/grants, and unspecified assistantships available. Support available to part-time students. Financial award application deadline: 3/1; financial award applicants required to submit FAFSA. *Faculty research:* Effectiveness of arts integration programs in elementary/secondary schools, literacy-based substance abuse program, outcome evaluation of program to increase college entry among urban youth. *Unit head:* Dr. Jean Poppei, Chair, 518-244-2076, Fax: 518-244-4545, E-mail: poppei@sage.edu. *Application contact:* Wendy D. Diefendorf, Director of Graduate and Adult Admission, 518-244-2443, Fax: 518-244-6880, E-mail: diefew@sage.edu.

Saint Louis University, Graduate School, School of Public Health and Graduate School, Department of Community Health, St. Louis, MO 63103-2097. Offers MPH, MS, MSPH. *Accreditation:* CEPH. Part-time programs available. Postbaccalaureate distance learning degree programs offered (no on-campus study). *Degree requirements:* For master's, comprehensive exam. *Entrance requirements:* For master's, GRE General Test, LSAT, GMAT or MCAT, letters of recommendation, resume. Additional exam requirements/recommendations for international students: Required—TOEFL (minimum score 525 paper-based; 194 computer-based). Electronic applications accepted. *Faculty research:* Obesity prevention, health disparities, health policy, child health.

Simon Fraser University, Graduate Studies, Faculty of Health Sciences, Burnaby, BC V5A 1S6, Canada. Offers population and public health (M Sc). *Degree requirements:* For master's, thesis, practicum or project.

Southern Illinois University Carbondale, Graduate School, College of Education, Department of Health Education and Recreation, Program in Community Health Education, Carbondale, IL 62901-4701. Offers MPH.

Southern New Hampshire University, School of Liberal Arts, Manchester, NH 03106-1045. Offers clinical services for adults psychiatric disabilities (Certificate); clinical services for children and adolescents with psychiatric disabilities (Certificate); clinical services for persons with co-occurring substance abuse and psychiatric disabilities (Certificate); community mental health (MS); fiction writing (MFA); non-fiction writing (MFA); teaching English as a foreign language (MS). Part-time and evening/weekend programs available. *Degree requirements:* For master's, one foreign language, thesis. *Entrance requirements:* For master's, minimum GPA of 2.75: MS-TEFL, 3.0: MFA. Additional exam requirements/recommendations for international students: Required—TOEFL (minimum score 550 paper-based; 213 computer-based; 79 iBT), IELTS (minimum score 6.5), TWE (minimum score 5). Electronic applications accepted. *Expenses:* Contact institution. *Faculty research:* Action research, state of the art practice in behavioral health services, wraparound approaches to working with youth, learning styles.

State University of New York Downstate Medical Center, College of Medicine, Program in Public Health, Brooklyn, NY 11203-2098. Offers urban and immigrant health (MPH); MD/MPH. Part-time programs available. *Degree requirements:* For master's, practicum. *Entrance requirements:* For master's, GRE, MCAT or OAT, 2 letters of recommendation, minimum undergraduate GPA of 3.0. Additional exam requirements/recommendations for international students: Required—TOEFL (minimum score 550 paper-based).

See Close-Up on page 1669.

Stony Brook University, State University of New York, Stony Brook University Medical Center, School of Medicine, Program in Population Health and Clinical Outcomes Research, Stony Brook, NY 11794. Offers PhD. *Expenses:* Tuition, state resident: full-time $8370; part-time $349 per credit. Tuition, nonresident: full-time $13,250; part-time $552 per credit. Required fees: $933. *Unit head:* Dr. A. Laurie Shroyer, Director, E-mail: annielaurie.shroyer@stonybrook.edu. *Application contact:* Jamie Romeiser, Coordinator, E-mail: jamie.romeiser@stonybrook.edu.

Stony Brook University, State University of New York, Stony Brook University Medical Center, School of Medicine, Program in Public Health, Stony Brook, NY 11794. Offers community health (MPH); evaluation sciences (MPH); family violence (MPH); health economics (MPH); population health (MPH); substance abuse (MPH). *Accreditation:* CEPH. *Students:* 16 full-time (8 women), 29 part-time (24 women); includes 14 minority (6 African Americans, 6 Asian Americans or Pacific Islanders, 2 Hispanic Americans), 5 international. Average age 39. 77 applicants, 64% accepted. In 2009, 10 master's awarded. *Entrance requirements:* For master's, GRE, 3 references. Additional exam requirements/recommendations for international students: Required—TOEFL. *Application deadline:* For fall admission, 1/15 for domestic and international students. Application fee: $60. Electronic applications accepted. *Expenses:* Tuition, state resident: full-time $8370; part-time $349 per credit. Tuition, nonresident: full-time $13,250; part-time $552 per credit. Required fees: $933. *Faculty research:* Population health, health service research, health economics. *Unit head:* Dr. Raymond L. Goldsteen, Director, 631-444-2074, Fax: 631-444-3480, E-mail: raymond.goldsteen@stonybrook.edu. *Application contact:* Dr. Raymond L. Goldsteen, Director, 631-444-2074, Fax: 631-444-3480, E-mail: raymond.goldsteen@stonybrook.edu.

Temple University, Health Sciences Center and Graduate School, College of Health Professions, Department of Public Health, Program in Community Health Education, Philadelphia, PA 19122-6096. Offers MPH. *Accreditation:* CEPH. Part-time programs available. *Entrance requirements:* For master's, GRE General Test. Additional exam requirements/recommendations for international students: Required—TOEFL (minimum score 550 paper-based; 213 computer-based; 79 iBT). Electronic applications accepted.

Texas Woman's University, Graduate School, College of Nursing, Denton, TX 76201. Offers acute care nurse practitioner (MS); adult health clinical nurse specialist (MS); adult health nurse practitioner (MS); child health clinical nurse specialist (MS); clinical nurse leader (MS); community health (MS); family nurse practitioner (MS); health systems management (MS); nursing education (MS); nursing practice (DNP); nursing science (PhD); pediatric nurse practitioner (MS); women's health clinical nurse specialist (MS); women's health nurse practitioner (MS). *Accreditation:* AACN. Part-time programs available. Postbaccalaureate distance learning degree programs offered. *Faculty:* 85 full-time (80 women), 6 part-time/adjunct (all women).

Students: 81 full-time (76 women), 602 part-time (571 women); includes 293 minority (154 African Americans, 3 American Indian/Alaska Native, 90 Asian Americans or Pacific Islanders, 46 Hispanic Americans), 19 international. Average age 39. 259 applicants, 81% accepted, 166 enrolled. In 2009, 100 master's, 22 doctorates awarded. *Degree requirements:* For master's, thesis or alternative; for doctorate, comprehensive exam, thesis/dissertation. *Entrance requirements:* For master's, GRE or MAT, minimum GPA of 3.0, RN license, BS in nursing, basic statistics course; for doctorate, GRE (Verbal 460, Quantitative 500) or MAT (50), MS in nursing, minimum GPA of 3.5, RN license, coursework in statistics, 2 letters of reference, curriculum vitae, nursing-theory course, graduate research course, letter stating professional and research goals. Additional exam requirements/recommendations for international students: Required—TOEFL (minimum score 550 paper-based; 213 computer-based; 79 iBT). *Application deadline:* For fall admission, 5/1 priority date for domestic students, 3/1 for international students; for spring admission, 9/15 priority date for domestic students, 7/1 for international students. Applications are processed on a rolling basis. Application fee: $50. Electronic applications accepted. *Expenses:* Tuition, state resident: full-time $3564; part-time $198 per credit hour. Tuition, nonresident: full-time $8550; part-time $475 per credit hour. Required fees: $69.26 per credit hour. Tuition and fees vary according to course load. *Financial support:* In 2009–10, 99 students received support, including 16 fellowships (averaging $17,325 per year), 5 research assistantships (averaging $11,484 per year), 5 teaching assistantships (averaging $11,484 per year); career-related internships or fieldwork, Federal Work-Study, institutionally sponsored loans, scholarships/grants, traineeships, health care benefits, and unspecified assistantships also available. Support available to part-time students. Financial award application deadline: 3/1; financial award applicants required to submit FAFSA. *Faculty research:* Evaluation of pre-natal care, screening for intimate partner violence, stressors and nursing success, breast surgery, breast feeding, adolescent needs during childbirth. *Unit head:* Dr. Patricia Holden-Huchton, Interim Dean, 940-898-2401, Fax: 940-898-2437, E-mail: pholdenhuchton@twu.edu. *Application contact:* Samuel Wheeler, Assistant Director of Admissions, 940-898-3188, Fax: 940-898-3081, E-mail: wheelersr@twu.edu.

Universidad de Ciencias Medicas, Graduate Programs, San Jose, Costa Rica. Offers dermatology (SP); family health (MS); health service center administration (MHA); human anatomy (MS); medical and surgery (MD); occupational medicine (MS); pharmacy (Pharm D). Part-time programs available. *Degree requirements:* For master's, thesis; for first professional degree and SP, comprehensive exam. *Entrance requirements:* For first professional degree, admissions test; for master's, MD or bachelors degree; for SP, admissions test, MD degree.

Université de Montréal, Faculty of Medicine, Program in Communal and Public Health, Montréal, QC H3C 3J7, Canada. Offers community health (M Sc, DESS); public health (PhD). *Accreditation:* CEPH. Part-time programs available. *Students:* 91 full-time (59 women), 174 part-time (130 women). 219 applicants, 41% accepted, 77 enrolled. In 2009, 26 master's, 12 doctorates, 5 other advanced degrees awarded. Terminal master's awarded for partial completion of doctoral program. *Degree requirements:* For master's, thesis; for doctorate, thesis/dissertation, general exam. *Entrance requirements:* For master's and doctorate, proficiency in French, knowledge of English; for DESS, proficiency in French. *Application deadline:* For fall admission, 2/1 priority date for domestic students; for winter admission, 11/1 priority date for domestic students; for spring admission, 2/1 priority date for domestic students. Application fee: $100. Electronic applications accepted. *Financial support:* Fellowships with partial tuition reimbursements, scholarships/grants and tuition waivers (partial) available. *Faculty research:* Epidemiology, health services utilization, health promotion and education, health behaviors, poverty and child health. *Unit head:* Marie-France Raynault, Head, 514-343-6140, Fax: 514-343-5645, E-mail: marie-france.raynault@umontreal.ca. *Application contact:* Marie Hatem, Information Contact/ Community Health Programs, 514-343-5652, Fax: 514-343-5645, E-mail: marie.hatem@umontreal.ca.

Université Laval, Faculty of Medicine, Graduate Programs in Medicine, Department of Social and Preventive Medicine, Program in Community Health, Québec, QC G1K 7P4, Canada. Offers M Sc, PhD. Part-time programs available. Terminal master's awarded for partial completion of doctoral program. *Degree requirements:* For master's, thesis (for some programs); for doctorate, comprehensive exam, thesis/dissertation. *Entrance requirements:* For master's, knowledge of French, comprehension of written English; for doctorate, French exam, comprehension of French, written comprehension of English. Electronic applications accepted.

Université Laval, Faculty of Medicine, Post-Professional Programs in Medical Studies, Québec, QC G1K 7P4, Canada. Offers anatomy–pathology (DESS); anesthesiology (DESS); cardiology (DESS); care of older people (Diploma); clinical research (DESS); community health (DESS); dermatology (DESS); diagnostic radiology (DESS); emergency medicine (Diploma); family medicine (DESS); general surgery (DESS); geriatrics (DESS); hematology (DESS); internal medicine (DESS); maternal and fetal medicine (Diploma); medical biochemistry (DESS); medical microbiology and infectious diseases (DESS); medical oncology (DESS); nephrology (DESS); neurology (DESS); neurosurgery (DESS); obstetrics and gynecology (DESS); ophthalmology (DESS); orthopedic surgery (DESS); oto-rhino-laryngology (DESS); palliative medicine (Diploma); pediatrics (DESS); plastic surgery (DESS); psychiatry (DESS); pulmonary medicine (DESS); radiology–oncology (DESS); thoracic surgery (DESS); urology (DESS). *Degree requirements:* For other advanced degree, comprehensive exam. *Entrance requirements:* For degree, knowledge of French. Electronic applications accepted.

University at Buffalo, the State University of New York, Graduate School, School of Public Health and Health Professions, Department of Social and Preventive Medicine, Buffalo, NY 14260. Offers community health (PhD); epidemiology (MS, PhD); public health (MPH). Part-time programs available. *Faculty:* 11 full-time (7 women), 11 part-time/adjunct (5 women). *Students:* 19 full-time (11 women), 15 part-time (8 women); includes 4 minority (all Asian Americans or Pacific Islanders), 3 international. Average age 30. 127 applicants, 41% accepted. In 2009, 4 master's, 4 doctorates awarded. Terminal master's awarded for partial completion of doctoral program. *Degree requirements:* For master's, comprehensive exam, thesis; for doctorate, comprehensive exam, thesis/dissertation. *Entrance requirements:* For master's and doctorate, GRE General Test. Additional exam requirements/recommendations for international students: Required—TOEFL (minimum score 600 paper-based; 250 computer-based; 100 iBT). *Application deadline:* For fall admission, 1/15 priority date for domestic and international students. Applications are processed on a rolling basis. Application fee: $50. Electronic applications accepted. *Financial support:* In 2009–10, 10 students received support, including 1 fellowship with full tuition reimbursement available (averaging $15,000 per year), 8 research assistantships with full tuition reimbursements available (averaging $15,000 per year); teaching assistantships with full tuition reimbursements available, career-related internships or fieldwork, Federal Work-Study, institutionally sponsored loans, health care benefits, and unspecified assistantships also available. Financial award application deadline: 2/1; financial award applicants required to submit FAFSA. *Faculty research:* Epidemiology of community health services including cancer and nutrition, cardiovascular disease, epidemiology of cancer, cardiovascular diseases, health services research. Total annual research expenditures: $5.5 million. *Unit head:* Dr. Jo Freudenheim, Chair, 716-829-2975 Ext. 612, Fax: 716-829-2979, E-mail: jfreuden@buffalo.edu. *Application contact:* Dr. Carl Li, Director of Graduate Studies, 716-829-2975 Ext. 618, Fax: 716-829-2979, E-mail: carlli@buffalo.edu.

The University of Alabama, Graduate School, College of Human Environmental Sciences, Program in Human Environmental Science, Tuscaloosa, AL 35487. Offers family financial planning and counseling (MS); interactive technology (MS); quality management (MS); restaurant and meeting management (MS); rural community health (MS); sport management (MS). *Students:* 70 full-time (40 women), 99 part-time (45 women); includes 44 minority (42 African Americans, 2 Hispanic Americans), 1 international. Average age 33. 124 applicants, 71% accepted, 71 enrolled. In 2009, 70 degrees awarded. *Degree requirements:* For master's, comprehensive exam. *Entrance requirements:* For master's, GRE (for some specializations), minimum GPA of 3.0. Additional exam requirements/recommendations for international students: Required—TOEFL. *Application deadline:* Applications are processed on a rolling basis. Application fee: $50 ($60 for international students). Electronic applications accepted. *Expenses:* Tuition, state resident: full-time $7000. Tuition, nonresident: full-time $19,200. *Faculty research:* Hospitality management, sports medicine education, technology and education. *Unit head:* Dr. Milla D. Boschung, Dean, 205-348-6250, Fax: 205-348-1786, E-mail: mboschun@ches.ua.edu. *Application contact:* Dr. Stuart Usdan, Associate Dean, 205-348-6150, Fax: 205-348-3789, E-mail: susdan@ches.ua.edu.

University of Alberta, School of Public Health, Department of Public Health Sciences, Edmonton, AB T6G 2E1, Canada. Offers clinical epidemiology (M Sc, MPH); environmental and occupational health (MPH); environmental health sciences (M Sc); epidemiology (M Sc); global health (M Sc, MPH); health policy and management (MPH); health policy research (M Sc); health technology assessment (MPH); occupational health (M Sc); population health (M Sc); public health leadership (MPH); public health sciences (PhD); quantitative methods (MPH). *Accreditation:* CEPH (one or more programs are accredited). *Faculty:* 24 full-time (5 women), 59 part-time/adjunct (13 women). *Students:* 49 full-time, 49 part-time. 81 applicants, 31% accepted. In 2009, 28 master's awarded. Terminal master's awarded for partial completion of doctoral program. *Degree requirements:* For master's, thesis (for some programs); for doctorate, thesis/dissertation. *Entrance requirements:* For master's, GMAT or GRE General Test. Additional exam requirements/recommendations for international students: Required—TOEFL (minimum score 550 paper-based; 213 computer-based) or IELTS (minimum score 6). *Application deadline:* For fall admission, 3/15 for domestic students, 7/1 for international students; for winter admission, 11/1 for international students; for spring admission, 3/1 for international students. Applications are processed on a rolling basis. Application fee: $0. Electronic applications accepted. Tuition and fees charges are reported in Canadian dollars. *Expenses:* Tuition, area resident: Full-time $4626 Canadian dollars; part-time $99.72 Canadian dollars per unit. International tuition: $8216 Canadian dollars full-time. Required fees: $3590 Canadian dollars; $99.72 Canadian dollars per unit. $215 Canadian dollars per term. *Financial support:* In 2009–10, 11 students received support, including 6 research assistantships with tuition reimbursements available (averaging $2,200 per year); fellowships, teaching assistantships, career-related internships or fieldwork and tuition waivers (partial) also available. Financial award application deadline: 2/1. *Faculty research:* Biostatistics, health promotion and sociobehavioral health science. Total annual research expenditures: $5.7 million. *Unit head:* L. Duncan Saunders, Acting Chair, 780-492-6814, Fax: 780-492-0364. *Application contact:* Felicity R. Hey, Graduate Programs Administrator, 780-492-6407, Fax: 780-492-0364, E-mail: felicity.hey@ualberta.ca.

University of Calgary, Faculty of Graduate Studies, Faculty of Education, Graduate Division of Educational Research, Calgary, AB T2N 1N4, Canada. Offers community rehabilitation and disability studies (M Ed, M Sc, Ed D, PhD, Graduate Certificate, Graduate Diploma); curriculum, teaching and learning (M Ed, M Sc, MA, Ed D, PhD, Graduate Certificate, Graduate Diploma); educational contexts (M Ed, MA, Ed D, PhD, Graduate Certificate, Graduate Diploma); educational leadership (M Ed, MA, Ed D, PhD, Graduate Certificate, Graduate Diploma); educational technology (M Ed, M Sc, MA, Ed D, PhD, Graduate Certificate, Graduate Diploma); gifted education (M Sc, MA, Ed D, PhD, Graduate Certificate, Graduate Diploma); higher education administration (Ed D); interpretive studies in education (M Ed, M Sc, MA, Ed D, PhD, Graduate Certificate, Graduate Diploma); second language teaching (M Ed, Ed D, PhD, Graduate Certificate, Graduate Diploma); teaching English as a second language (M Ed, M Sc, MA, Ed D, PhD, Graduate Certificate, Graduate Diploma); workplace and adult learning (M Ed, MA, Ed D, PhD, Graduate Certificate, Graduate Diploma). Ed D in both higher education administration and educational leadership offered via distance delivery. Part-time and evening/weekend programs available. Postbaccalaureate distance learning degree programs offered (minimal on-campus study). *Degree requirements:* For master's, thesis (for some programs); for doctorate, thesis/dissertation, candidacy exam. *Entrance requirements:* For master's, minimum GPA of 3.0, 3 letters of reference; for doctorate, minimum GPA of 3.5, 3 letters of reference; for other advanced degree, minimum GPA of 3.0. Additional exam requirements/recommendations for international students: Required—TOEFL, IELTS. Electronic applications accepted. *Faculty research:* Curriculum, leadership, technology, contexts, gifted, second language teaching, work place and adult learning.

University of Calgary, Faculty of Medicine and Faculty of Graduate Studies, Department of Community Health Sciences, Calgary, AB T2N 1N4, Canada. Offers M Sc, MCM, PhD. *Degree requirements:* For master's, thesis; for doctorate, thesis/dissertation, candidacy exam. *Entrance requirements:* For master's and doctorate, minimum GPA of 3.2. Additional exam requirements/recommendations for international students: Required—TOEFL (minimum score 600 paper-based; 250 computer-based). Electronic applications accepted. *Faculty research:* Epidemiology, health research, biostatistics, health economics, health policy.

University of California, Los Angeles, Graduate Division, School of Public Health, Department of Community Health Sciences, Los Angeles, CA 90095. Offers public health (MPH, MS, Dr PH, PhD); JD/MPH; MA/MPH; MD/MPH; MSW/MPH. *Degree requirements:* For master's, comprehensive exam or thesis; for doctorate, thesis/dissertation, oral and written qualifying exams. *Entrance requirements:* For master's, GRE General Test, minimum GPA of 3.0; for doctorate, GRE General Test, minimum undergraduate GPA of 3.0. Electronic applications accepted.

University of Illinois at Chicago, Graduate College, School of Public Health, Division of Community Health Sciences, Chicago, IL 60607-7128. Offers MPH, MS, Dr PH, PhD. *Accreditation:* CEPH (one or more programs are accredited). Part-time programs available. Terminal master's awarded for partial completion of doctoral program. *Degree requirements:* For master's, thesis, field practicum; for doctorate, thesis/dissertation, independent research, internship. *Entrance requirements:* For master's and doctorate, GRE General Test, minimum GPA of 2.75. Additional exam requirements/recommendations for international students: Required—TOEFL. Electronic applications accepted.

University of Illinois at Urbana–Champaign, Graduate College, College of Applied Health Sciences, Department of Kinesiology and Community Health, Champaign, IL 61820. Offers community health (MS, MSPH, PhD); kinesiology (MS, PhD); public health (MPH); rehabilitation (MS). *Faculty:* 31 full-time (16 women). *Students:* 110 full-time (62 women), 17 part-time (9 women); includes 26 minority (15 African Americans, 1 American Indian/Alaska Native, 8 Asian Americans or Pacific Islanders, 2 Hispanic Americans), 23 international. 139 applicants, 28% accepted, 26 enrolled. In 2009, 26 master's, 9 doctorates awarded. *Entrance requirements:* For master's, GRE, minimum GPA of 3.0; for doctorate, GRE, minimum graduate GPA of 3.5. Additional exam requirements/recommendations for international students: Required—TOEFL. *Application deadline:* Applications are processed on a rolling basis. Application fee: $60 ($75 for international students). Electronic applications accepted. *Financial support:* In 2009–10, 13 fellowships, 55 research assistantships, 71 teaching assistantships were awarded; tuition waivers (full and partial) also available. *Unit head:* Wojciech Chodzko-Zajko, Head, 217-244-0823, Fax: 217-244-7322, E-mail: wojtek@illinois.edu. *Application contact:* Tina M. Candler, Office Manager, 217-333-1083, Fax: 217-244-7322, E-mail: tcandler@illinois.edu.

The University of Iowa, Graduate College, College of Public Health, Department of Community and Behavioral Health, Iowa City, IA 52242-1316. Offers MS, PhD. *Degree requirements:* For master's, thesis; for doctorate, comprehensive exam, thesis/dissertation. *Entrance requirements:* For master's and doctorate, GRE General Test, minimum GPA of 3.0. Additional exam requirements/recommendations for international students: Required—TOEFL (minimum score 600 paper-based; 250 computer-based; 100 iBT). Electronic applications accepted.

University of Louisville, Graduate School, College of Education and Human Development, Department of Health and Sport Sciences, Louisville, KY 40292-0001. Offers community health education (M Ed); exercise physiology (MS); health and physical education (MAT); sport administration (MS). Part-time and evening/weekend programs available. *Faculty:* 17 full-time (8 women), 1 part-time/adjunct (0 women). *Students:* 73 full-time (28 women), 28 part-time (17 women); includes 13 minority (11 African Americans, 2 Asian Americans or Pacific Islanders), 8 international. Average age 26. 154 applicants, 67% accepted, 59 enrolled. In 2009, 42 master's awarded. *Entrance requirements:* For master's, GRE General Test. Additional exam requirements/recommendations for international students: Required—TOEFL (minimum score 560 paper-based; 210 computer-based; 83 iBT). Application fee: $50. Electronic

Community Health

University of Louisville (continued)
applications accepted. *Financial support:* In 2009–10, 21 students received support; fellowships, research assistantships, teaching assistantships, career-related internships or fieldwork, Federal Work-Study, scholarships/grants, and unspecified assistantships available. Financial award application deadline: 6/1; financial award applicants required to submit FAFSA. *Faculty research:* Impact of sports and sport marketing on society, factors associated with school and community health, cardiac and pulmonary rehabilitation, impact of participation in activities on student retention and graduation, strength and conditioning. Total annual research expenditures: $58,888. *Unit head:* Dr. David W. Britt, Chair, 502-852-6645, Fax: 502-852-4534, E-mail: david.britt@louisville.edu. *Application contact:* Libby Leggett, Director, Graduate Admissions, 502-852-3101, Fax: 502-852-6536, E-mail: gradadm@louisville.edu.

University of Manitoba, Faculty of Medicine and Faculty of Graduate Studies, Graduate Programs in Medicine, Department of Community Health Sciences, Winnipeg, MB R3T 2N2, Canada. Offers M Sc, MPH, PhD, G Dip. Part-time programs available. *Degree requirements:* For master's, thesis; for doctorate, thesis/dissertation. *Entrance requirements:* For master's and doctorate, minimum GPA of 3.0. *Faculty research:* Health services, aboriginal health, health policy, epidemiology, international health.

University of Massachusetts Amherst, Graduate School, School of Public Health and Health Sciences, Department of Public Health, Amherst, MA 01003. Offers biostatistics (MS, PhD); community health education (MS); environmental health sciences (MPH, MS); epidemiology (MPH, MS); health policy and management (MPH, MS); nutrition (PhD); public health practice (MPH). *Accreditation:* CEPH (one or more programs are accredited). Part-time and evening/weekend programs available. Postbaccalaureate distance learning degree programs offered (no on-campus study). *Faculty:* 38 full-time (23 women). *Students:* 96 full-time (71 women), 232 part-time (153 women); includes 41 minority (14 African Americans, 17 Asian Americans or Pacific Islanders, 10 Hispanic Americans), 65 international. Average age 36. 316 applicants, 61% accepted, 79 enrolled. In 2009, 91 master's, 5 doctorates awarded. Terminal master's awarded for partial completion of doctoral program. *Degree requirements:* For master's, thesis (for some programs); for doctorate, comprehensive exam, thesis/dissertation. *Entrance requirements:* For master's and doctorate, GRE General Test. Additional exam requirements/recommendations for international students: Required—TOEFL (minimum score 550 paper-based; 213 computer-based; 80 iBT), IELTS (minimum score 6.5). *Application deadline:* For fall admission, 2/1 for domestic and international students. Applications are processed on a rolling basis. Application fee: $40 ($65 for international students). Electronic applications accepted. *Expenses:* Tuition, state resident: full-time $2640; part-time $110 per credit. Tuition, nonresident: full-time $9936; part-time $414 per credit. Tuition and fees vary according to course load. *Financial support:* In 2009–10, 3 fellowships with full tuition reimbursements (averaging $2,791 per year), 32 research assistantships with full tuition reimbursements (averaging $9,196 per year), 24 teaching assistantships with full tuition reimbursements (averaging $5,789 per year) were awarded; career-related internships or fieldwork, Federal Work-Study, scholarships/grants, traineeships, health care benefits, tuition waivers (full), and unspecified assistantships also available. Support available to part-time students. Financial award application deadline: 2/1. *Unit head:* Dr. Paula Stamps, Graduate Program Director, 413-545-2861, Fax: 413-545-0964. *Application contact:* Jean M. Ames, Supervisor of Admissions, 413-545-0722, Fax: 413-577-0010, E-mail: gradadm@grad.umass.edu.

University of Minnesota, Twin Cities Campus, School of Public Health, Major in Community Health Education, Minneapolis, MN 55455-0213. Offers MPH. *Accreditation:* CEPH. Part-time programs available. *Degree requirements:* For master's, fieldwork, project. *Entrance requirements:* For master's, GRE General Test. Additional exam requirements/recommendations for international students: Required—TOEFL. Electronic applications accepted. *Faculty research:* Assessing population behavior, designing community-wide prevention and treatment, preventing alcohol and drug abuse, influencing health policies.

University of Nevada, Las Vegas, Graduate College, College of Education, Department of Counselor Education, Las Vegas, NV 89154-3066. Offers addiction studies (Advanced Certificate); community mental health (MS); rehabilitation counseling (Advanced Certificate); school counseling (M Ed). *Faculty:* 7 full-time (2 women), 10 part-time/adjunct (7 women). *Students:* 47 full-time (39 women), 37 part-time (31 women); includes 14 minority (3 African Americans, 1 Asian American or Pacific Islander, 10 Hispanic Americans). Average age 32. 97 applicants, 95% accepted, 57 enrolled. In 2009, 19 master's awarded. *Degree requirements:* For master's, comprehensive exam (for some programs), thesis (for some programs); for Advanced Certificate, thesis (for some programs). *Entrance requirements:* Additional exam requirements/recommendations for international students: Required—TOEFL (minimum score 550 paper-based; 213 computer-based; 80 iBT), IELTS (minimum score 7). *Application deadline:* For fall admission, 2/1 priority date for domestic and international students. Applications are processed on a rolling basis. Application fee: $60 ($95 for international students). Electronic applications accepted. *Financial support:* In 2009–10, 10 students received support, including 6 research assistantships with partial tuition reimbursements available (averaging $10,000 per year), 4 teaching assistantships with partial tuition reimbursements available (averaging $10,000 per year); institutionally sponsored loans, scholarships/grants, health care benefits, and unspecified assistantships also available. Financial award application deadline: 3/1. *Faculty research:* Social justice and multicultural competencies for counselors, therapeutic storytelling and bibliotherapy, school counselor education pedagogy, counseling program evaluation, addictions prevention and related trauma. *Unit head:* Dr. Dale Pehrsson, Chair/ Associate Professor, 702-895-5994, Fax: 702-895-5550, E-mail: dale.pehrsson@unlv.edu. *Application contact:* Graduate College Admissions Evaluator, 702-895-3320, Fax: 702-895-4180, E-mail: gradcollege@unlv.edu.

University of Nevada, Las Vegas, Graduate College, School of Community Health Sciences, Las Vegas, NV 89154-3063. Offers M Ed, MHA, MPH. *Faculty:* 15 full-time (5 women). *Students:* 70 full-time (50 women), 95 part-time (73 women); includes 38 minority (18 African Americans, 1 American Indian/Alaska Native, 12 Asian Americans or Pacific Islanders, 7 Hispanic Americans), 12 international. Average age 34. 126 applicants, 66% accepted, 58 enrolled. In 2009, 47 master's awarded. *Entrance requirements:* Additional exam requirements/recommendations for international students: Required—TOEFL, IELTS (minimum score 7). *Application deadline:* For fall admission, 6/1 priority date for domestic students, 5/1 for international students; for spring admission, 11/1 priority date for domestic students, 10/1 for international students. Applications are processed on a rolling basis. Application fee: $60 ($95 for international students). Electronic applications accepted. *Financial support:* In 2009–10, 18 students received support, including 18 research assistantships with partial tuition reimbursements available (averaging $11,109 per year); institutionally sponsored loans, scholarships/grants, health care benefits, and unspecified assistantships also available. Financial award application deadline: 3/1. *Unit head:* Dr. Mary Guinan, Dean, 702-895-5090, Fax: 702-895-5184, E-mail: mary.guinan@unlv.edu. *Application contact:* Dr. Mary Guinan, Dean, 702-895-5090, Fax: 702-895-5184, E-mail: mary.guinan@unlv.edu.

The University of North Carolina at Greensboro, Graduate School, School of Health and Human Performance, Department of Public Health Education, Greensboro, NC 27412-5001. Offers community health education (MPH, Dr PH). *Accreditation:* CEPH; NCATE. *Degree requirements:* For master's, comprehensive exam, thesis or alternative. *Entrance requirements:* For master's, GRE General Test or MAT. Additional exam requirements/recommendations for international students: Required—TOEFL. Electronic applications accepted. *Faculty research:* Peer facilitator training, innovative health education approaches.

University of Northern British Columbia, Office of Graduate Studies, Prince George, BC V2N 4Z9, Canada. Offers business administration (Diploma); community health science (M Sc); disability management (MA); education (M Ed); first nations studies (MA); gender studies (MA); history (MA); interdisciplinary studies (MA); international studies (MA); mathematical, computer and physical sciences (M Sc); natural resources and environmental studies (M Sc, MA, MNRES, PhD); political science (MA); psychology (M Sc, PhD); social work (MSW). Part-time and evening/weekend programs available. Postbaccalaureate distance learning degree programs offered (no on-campus study). *Degree requirements:* For master's, thesis; for doctorate, thesis/dissertation. *Entrance requirements:* For master's, GRE, minimum B average in undergraduate course work; for doctorate, candidacy exam, minimum A average in graduate course work.

University of Northern Iowa, Graduate College, College of Education, School of Health, Physical Education, and Leisure Services, Cedar Falls, IA 50614. Offers community health education (Ed D); health education (MA, Ed D); leisure services (MA, Ed D), including leisure services (Ed D), program administration (MA), youth/human services administration (MA); physical education (MA), including physical education, scientific basis of physical education, teaching/coaching; rehabilitation studies (Ed D). Part-time and evening/weekend programs available. *Students:* 79 full-time (43 women), 39 part-time (16 women); includes 23 minority (18 African Americans, 2 Asian Americans or Pacific Islanders, 3 Hispanic Americans), 13 international. 89 applicants, 71% accepted, 43 enrolled. In 2009, 29 master's, 1 doctorate awarded. *Degree requirements:* For master's, comprehensive exam, thesis or alternative; for doctorate, thesis/dissertation. *Entrance requirements:* For master's, minimum GPA of 3.0; for doctorate, GRE, minimum GPA of 3.5. Additional exam requirements/recommendations for international students: Required—TOEFL (minimum score 500 paper-based; 180 computer-based; 61 iBT). *Application deadline:* Applications are processed on a rolling basis. Application fee: $30 ($50 for international students). *Financial support:* Career-related internships or fieldwork, Federal Work-Study, institutionally sponsored loans, scholarships/grants, tuition waivers (full and partial), and unspecified assistantships available. Support available to part-time students. Financial award application deadline: 2/1. *Unit head:* Dr. Christopher R. Edginton, Director, 319-273-2840, Fax: 319-273-5958, E-mail: christopher.edginton@uni.edu. *Application contact:* Laurie S. Russell, Record Analyst, 319-273-2623, Fax: 319-273-6792, E-mail: laurie.russell@uni.edu.

University of North Florida, Brooks College of Health, Department of Public Health, Jacksonville, FL 32224. Offers community health (MPH); geriatric management (MSH); health administration (MHA); health behavior research and evaluation (Certificate); nutrition (MSH); rehabilitation counseling (MS). *Accreditation:* CEPH. Part-time and evening/weekend programs available. *Faculty:* 23 full-time (17 women). *Students:* 118 full-time (91 women), 82 part-time (61 women); includes 42 minority (23 African Americans, 8 Asian Americans or Pacific Islanders, 11 Hispanic Americans), 9 international. Average age 31. 192 applicants, 26% accepted, 23 enrolled. In 2009, 69 master's awarded. *Degree requirements:* For master's, thesis optional. *Entrance requirements:* For master's, GRE General Test (MSH, MS, MPH); GMAT or GRE General Test (MHA), minimum GPA of 3.0 in last 60 hours. Additional exam requirements/recommendations for international students: Required—TOEFL (minimum score 500 paper-based; 173 computer-based). *Application deadline:* For fall admission, 7/1 priority date for domestic students, 5/1 for international students; for spring admission, 11/1 priority date for domestic students, 10/1 for international students. Applications are processed on a rolling basis. Application fee: $30. Electronic applications accepted. *Expenses:* Tuition, state resident: full-time $6649.20; part-time $277.05 per credit hour. Tuition, nonresident: full-time $22,970; part-time $957.08 per credit hour. Required fees: $985; $41.03 per credit hour. *Financial support:* In 2009–10, 99 students received support, including 1 teaching assistantship (averaging $1,004 per year); research assistantships, career-related internships or fieldwork, Federal Work-Study, scholarships/grants, and tuition waivers (partial) also available. Support available to part-time students. Financial award application deadline: 4/1; financial award applicants required to submit FAFSA. *Faculty research:* Dietary supplements; alcohol, tobacco, and other drug use prevention; turnover among health professionals; aging; psychosocial aspects of disabilities. Total annual research expenditures: $335,106. *Unit head:* Dr. JoAnn Nolin, Chair, 904-620-2840, Fax: 904-620-2848, E-mail: jnolin@unf.edu. *Application contact:* Heather Kenney, Director of Advising, 904-620-2810, Fax: 904-620-1030, E-mail: heather.kenney@unf.edu.

University of North Texas, Robert B. Toulouse School of Graduate Studies, College of Public Affairs and Community Service, Department of Sociology, Denton, TX 76203-5017. Offers global and comparative (PhD); health and illness (PhD); social stratification and inequality (PhD); sociology (MA, MS). Terminal master's awarded for partial completion of doctoral program. *Degree requirements:* For master's, variable foreign language requirement, comprehensive exam, thesis (for some programs); for doctorate, variable foreign language requirement, comprehensive exam, thesis/dissertation. *Entrance requirements:* For master's, GRE General Test, 4 letters of recommendation; for doctorate, GRE General Test, master's degree, 4 letters of recommendation. Additional exam requirements/recommendations for international students: Required—TOEFL (minimum score 550 paper-based; 213 computer-based; 79 iBT), proof of English language proficiency required for non-native English speakers. *Application deadline:* Applications are processed on a rolling basis. Application fee: $50 ($75 for international students). Electronic applications accepted. *Expenses:* Tuition, state resident: full-time $4298; part-time $239 per contact hour. Tuition, nonresident: full-time $9878; part-time $549 per contact hour. Required fees: $265 per contact hour. *Financial support:* Fellowships, research assistantships, teaching assistantships, career-related internships or fieldwork, Federal Work-Study, institutionally sponsored loans, scholarships/grants, health care benefits, tuition waivers (partial), and unspecified assistantships available. Support available to part-time students. Financial award applicants required to submit FAFSA. *Faculty research:* Health and illness, social inequality, globalization and development, family. *Application contact:* Graduate Adviser, 940-565-2296, Fax: 940-369-7035, E-mail: seward@unt.edu.

University of North Texas Health Science Center at Fort Worth, School of Public Health, Fort Worth, TX 76107-2699. Offers biostatistics (MPH); community health (MPH); disease control and prevention (Dr PH); environmental and occupational health sciences (MPH); epidemiology (MPH); health administration (MHA); health policy and management (MPH, Dr PH); DO/MPH; MS/MPH; MSN/MPH. *Accreditation:* CEPH. Part-time and evening/weekend programs available. *Degree requirements:* For master's, thesis or alternative, supervised internship; for doctorate, thesis/dissertation, supervised internship. *Entrance requirements:* For master's, GRE General Test. Additional exam requirements/recommendations for international students: Required—TOEFL. Electronic applications accepted.

University of Oklahoma—Tulsa, School of Community Medicine, Tulsa, OK 74135-2512. Offers MD.

University of Ottawa, Faculty of Graduate and Postdoctoral Studies, Faculty of Medicine, Department of Epidemiology and Community Medicine, Ottawa, ON K1N 6N5, Canada. Offers epidemiology (M Sc), including health technology assessment. *Degree requirements:* For master's, thesis. *Entrance requirements:* For master's, honors degree or equivalent, minimum B average. Electronic applications accepted. *Faculty research:* Epidemiologic concepts and methods, health technology assessment.

University of Ottawa, Faculty of Graduate and Postdoctoral Studies, Interdisciplinary Programs, Ottawa, ON K1N 6N5, Canada. Offers e-business (Certificate); e-commerce (Certificate); finance (Certificate); health services and policies research (Diploma); population health (PhD); population health risk assessment and management (Certificate); public management and governance (Certificate); systems science (Certificate).

University of Phoenix, College of Natural Sciences, College of Nursing, Phoenix, AZ 85034-7209. Offers education (MHA); gerontology (MHA); informatics (MHA, MSN); nursing (MSN); MSN/MBA; MSN/MHA. *Accreditation:* AACN. Evening/weekend programs available. Postbaccalaureate distance learning degree programs offered. *Faculty:* 13 full-time (11 women), 327 part-time/adjunct (252 women). *Students:* 5,797 full-time (5,365 women); includes 1,337 minority (831 African Americans, 46 American Indian/Alaska Native, 292 Asian Americans or Pacific Islanders, 168 Hispanic Americans), 302 international. Average age 40. In 2009, 1,646 master's awarded. *Degree requirements:* For master's, thesis (for some programs). *Entrance requirements:* For master's, 3 years of work experience, minimum undergraduate GPA of 2.5, RN license. Additional exam requirements/recommendations for international students: Required—TOEFL (minimum score 550 paper-based; 213 computer-based; 79 iBT). *Application deadline:* Applications are processed on a rolling basis. Application fee: $45. Electronic applications accepted. *Expenses:* Tuition: Full-time $13,272. Required fees: $660. Full-time

tuition and fees vary according to course level, degree level and program. *Financial support:* Institutionally sponsored loans and scholarships/grants available. Financial award applicants required to submit FAFSA. *Unit head:* Dr. Pam Fuller, Dean/Executive Director, 480-557-1140, Fax: 480-929-7164, E-mail: pam.fuller@phoenix.edu. *Application contact:* Chair, 866-766-0766, Fax: 602-387-6020.

University of Phoenix–Birmingham Campus, College of Health and Human Services, Birmingham, AL 35244. Offers education (MHA); gerontology (MHA); health administration (MHA); health care management (MBA); informatics (MHA); nursing (MSN); nursing/health care education (MSN); MSN/MBA; MSN/MHA.

University of Phoenix–Central Valley Campus, College of Health and Human Services, Fresno, CA 93720-1562. Offers education (MHA); gerontology (MHA); health administration (MHA); health care management (MBA); nursing (MSN); MSN/MBA.

University of Phoenix–Chattanooga Campus, College of Health and Human Services, Chattanooga, TN 37421-3707. Offers education (MHA); gerontology (MHA); health administration (MHA); health care management (MBA).

University of Phoenix–Hawaii Campus, The Artemis School, College of Health and Human Services, Honolulu, HI 96813-4317. Offers administration of justice and security (MS); community counseling (MSC); education (MHA); family nurse practitioner (MSN); gerontology (MHA); health administration (MHA); health care management (MBA); marriage, family and child therapy (MSC); nursing (MSN); nursing/health care education (MSN); psychology (MS); MSN/MBA. Evening/weekend programs available. *Degree requirements:* For master's, thesis (for some programs). *Entrance requirements:* For master's, minimum undergraduate GPA of 2.5, 3 years of work experience, RN license. Additional exam requirements/recommendations for international students: Required—TOEFL (minimum score 550 paper-based; 213 computer-based; 79 iBT). Electronic applications accepted.

University of Pittsburgh, Graduate School of Public Health, Department of Behavioral and Community Health Science, Pittsburgh, PA 15260. Offers behavioral and community health sciences (MPH, Dr PH); lesbian, gay, bisexual and transgender health and wellness (Certificate); minority health and health disparities (Certificate); program evaluation (Certificate); public health and aging (Certificate); public health preparedness (Certificate); MID/MPH; MPH/MPA; MPH/MSW; MPH/PhD. *Accreditation:* CAHME (one or more programs are accredited). Part-time programs available. *Faculty:* 17 full-time (8 women), 13 part-time/adjunct (3 women). *Students:* 86 full-time (66 women), 46 part-time (37 women); includes 27 minority (20 African Americans, 1 American Indian/Alaska Native, 4 Asian Americans or Pacific Islanders, 2 Hispanic Americans), 7 international. Average age 30. 235 applicants, 74% accepted, 46 enrolled. In 2009, 30 master's, 5 doctorates awarded. *Degree requirements:* For master's, thesis; for doctorate, comprehensive exam, thesis/dissertation, preliminary exams. *Entrance requirements:* For master's and Certificate, GRE; for doctorate, GRE, master's degree in public health or related field. Additional exam requirements/recommendations for international students: Required—TOEFL (minimum score 550 paper-based; 213 computer-based; 80 iBT). *Application deadline:* For fall admission, 5/1 priority date for domestic students, 4/1 for international students; for winter admission, 9/1 for international students; for spring admission, 10/1 priority date for domestic students, 2/1 for international students. Applications are processed on a rolling basis. Application fee: $95. Electronic applications accepted. *Expenses:* Tuition, state resident: full-time $16,402; part-time $665 per credit. Tuition, nonresident: full-time $28,694; part-time $1175 per credit. Required fees: $690; $175 per term. Tuition and fees vary according to program. *Financial support:* In 2009–10, 21 students received support, including 1 fellowship with full tuition reimbursement available (averaging $20,976 per year), 19 research assistantships with full and partial tuition reimbursements available (averaging $12,300 per year), 2 teaching assistantships with full tuition reimbursements available (averaging $15,065 per year); unspecified assistantships also available. *Faculty research:* Maternal and child health, program evaluation, community-based participatory research, minority health and health disparities, aging. Total annual research expenditures: $1.7 million. *Unit head:* Dr. Ronald D. Stall, Chairman, 412-624-7933, Fax: 412-648-5975, E-mail: rstall@pitt.edu. *Application contact:* Natalie C. Arnold, Recruitment and Academic Affairs Administrator, 412-624-3107, Fax: 412-624-5510, E-mail: narnold@pitt.edu.

University of Pittsburgh, Graduate School of Public Health, Department of Infectious Diseases and Microbiology, Pittsburgh, PA 15260. Offers bioscience of infectious diseases (MPH); community and behavioral intervention of infectious diseases (MPH); infectious diseases and microbiology (MS, Dr PH, PhD); LGBT health and wellness (Certificate). Part-time programs available. *Faculty:* 20 full-time (7 women), 2 part-time/adjunct (1 woman). *Students:* 46 full-time (33 women), 8 part-time (6 women); includes 7 minority (2 African Americans, 4 Asian Americans or Pacific Islanders, 1 Hispanic American), 6 international. Average age 28. 176 applicants, 43% accepted, 18 enrolled. In 2009, 11 master's, 9 doctorates awarded. Terminal master's awarded for partial completion of doctoral program. *Degree requirements:* For master's, one foreign language, comprehensive exam (for some programs), thesis; for doctorate, one foreign language, comprehensive exam, thesis/dissertation. *Entrance requirements:* For master's and doctorate, GRE General Test, MCAT, or DAT. Additional exam requirements/recommendations for international students: Required—TOEFL (minimum score 550 paper-based; 213 computer-based; 80 iBT). *Application deadline:* For fall admission, 1/4 for domestic students. Applications are processed on a rolling basis. Application fee: $95. Electronic applications accepted. *Expenses:* Tuition, state resident: full-time $16,402; part-time $665 per credit. Tuition, nonresident: full-time $28,694; part-time $1175 per credit. Required fees: $690; $175 per term. Tuition and fees vary according to program. *Financial support:* In 2009–10, 16 students received support, including 16 research assistantships with full tuition reimbursements available (averaging $23,500 per year). Financial award applicants required to submit FAFSA. *Faculty research:* HIV, Epstein-Barr virus, virology, immunology, malaria. Total annual research expenditures: $13.6 million. *Unit head:* Dr. Charles R. Rinaldo, Chairman, 412-624-3928, Fax: 412-624-4953, E-mail: rinaldo@pitt.edu. *Application contact:* Dr. Jeremy Martinson, Assistant Professor, 412-624-5646, Fax: 412-383-8926, E-mail: jmartins@pitt.edu.

University of Saskatchewan, College of Medicine, Department of Community Health and Epidemiology, Saskatoon, SK S7N 5A2, Canada. Offers M Sc, PhD. *Degree requirements:* For master's, thesis; for doctorate, thesis/dissertation. *Entrance requirements:* Additional exam requirements/recommendations for international students: Required—TOEFL. Tuition and fees charges are reported in Canadian dollars. *Expenses:* Tuition, area resident: Full-time $3000 Canadian dollars; part-time $500 Canadian dollars per term. Required fees: $700 Canadian dollars; $100 Canadian dollars per term.

University of South Florida, Graduate School, College of Public Health, Department of Community and Family Health, Tampa, FL 33620-9951. Offers MPH, MSPH, Dr PH, PhD. *Accreditation:* CEPH (one or more programs are accredited). Part-time and evening/weekend programs available. *Faculty:* 15 full-time (11 women), 7 part-time/adjunct (2 women). *Students:* 94 full-time (78 women), 60 part-time (56 women); includes 46 minority (30 African Americans, 1 American Indian/Alaska Native, 3 Asian Americans or Pacific Islanders, 12 Hispanic Americans), 11 international. Average age 31. 138 applicants, 72% accepted, 45 enrolled. In 2009, 27 master's, 3 doctorates awarded. *Degree requirements:* For master's, comprehensive exam, thesis (for some programs); for doctorate, comprehensive exam, thesis/dissertation. *Entrance requirements:* For master's, GRE General Test, minimum GPA of 3.0 in upper-level course work, goal statement letter, two professional letters of recommendation, resume/curriculum vitae; for doctorate, GRE General Test, minimum GPA of 3.0 in upper-level course work, goal statement letter, three professional letters of recommendation, resume/curriculum vitae, writing sample. Additional exam requirements/recommendations for international students: Required—TOEFL (minimum score 550 paper-based; 213 computer-based; 79 iBT). *Application deadline:* For fall admission, 6/1 for domestic students, 1/2 for international students; for spring admission, 10/15 for domestic students, 7/1 for international students. Applications are processed on a rolling basis. Application fee: $30. Electronic applications accepted. *Financial support:* In 2009–10, 7 fellowships with full tuition reimbursements (averaging $6,904 per year), 70 research assistantships with full and partial tuition reimbursements (averaging $4,771 per

year), 22 teaching assistantships (averaging $3,508 per year) were awarded; career-related internships or fieldwork, Federal Work-Study, institutionally sponsored loans, scholarships/grants, traineeships, and unspecified assistantships also available. Support available to part-time students. Financial award applicants required to submit FAFSA. *Faculty research:* Family violence, high-risk infants, medical material and child health, healthy start, social marketing, adolescent health, high-risk behaviors. Total annual research expenditures: $5.1 million. *Unit head:* Dr. Julie Baldwin, Chairperson, 813-974-4867, Fax: 813-974-5172. *Application contact:* Michelle Hodge, Academic Advisor, 813-974-6665, Fax: 813-974-8121, E-mail: mhodge1@health.usf.edu.

The University of Tennessee, Graduate School, College of Education, Health and Human Sciences, Program in Human Ecology, Knoxville, TN 37996. Offers child and family studies (PhD); community health (PhD); nutrition science (PhD); retailing and consumer sciences (PhD); textile science (PhD). *Degree requirements:* For doctorate, thesis/dissertation. *Entrance requirements:* For doctorate, GRE General Test, minimum GPA of 2.7. Additional exam requirements/recommendations for international students: Required—TOEFL. Electronic applications accepted. *Expenses:* Tuition, state resident: full-time $6826; part-time $380 per semester hour. Tuition, nonresident: full-time $21,844; part-time $1147 per semester hour. Tuition and fees vary according to program.

The University of Tennessee, Graduate School, College of Education, Health and Human Sciences, Program in Public Health, Knoxville, TN 37996. Offers community health education (MPH); gerontology (MPH); health planning/administration (MPH); MS/MPH. *Accreditation:* CEPH. *Degree requirements:* For master's, thesis optional. *Entrance requirements:* For master's, minimum GPA of 2.7. Additional exam requirements/recommendations for international students: Required—TOEFL. Electronic applications accepted. *Expenses:* Tuition, state resident: full-time $6826; part-time $380 per semester hour. Tuition, nonresident: full-time $21,844; part-time $1147 per semester hour. Tuition and fees vary according to program.

The University of Texas Medical Branch, Graduate School of Biomedical Sciences, Program in Preventive Medicine and Community Health, Galveston, TX 77555. Offers MPH, MS, PhD. *Accreditation:* CEPH. *Students:* 31 full-time (20 women), 7 part-time (4 women); includes 8 minority (1 African American, 2 Asian Americans or Pacific Islanders, 5 Hispanic Americans), 5 international. Average age 37. In 2009, 5 master's, 11 doctorates awarded. *Degree requirements:* For master's, thesis; for doctorate, thesis/dissertation. *Entrance requirements:* For master's, GRE General Test or MAT; for doctorate, GRE General Test. Additional exam requirements/recommendations for international students: Required—TOEFL (minimum score 550 paper-based; 213 computer-based). *Application deadline:* Applications are processed on a rolling basis. Application fee: $30 ($75 for international students). Electronic applications accepted. *Financial support:* In 2009–10, fellowships (averaging $25,000 per year), research assistantships with full tuition reimbursements (averaging $25,000 per year) were awarded. Financial award applicants required to submit FAFSA. *Unit head:* Dr. Laura Rudkin, Vice Chair for Education/Director, 409-772-9141, Fax: 409-772-5272, E-mail: lrudkin@utmb.edu. *Application contact:* Tonya R. Groh, Coordinator for Special Programs, 409-772-1123, Fax: 409-772-5272, E-mail: trgroh@utmb.edu.

University of Virginia, School of Nursing, Charlottesville, VA 22903. Offers acute and specialty care (MSN); acute care nurse practitioner (MSN); clinical nurse leadership (MSN); community-public health leadership (MSN); nursing (DNP, PhD); psychiatric mental health counseling (MSN); MSN/MBA. *Accreditation:* AACN. Part-time programs available. *Faculty:* 50 full-time (47 women), 4 part-time/adjunct (3 women). *Students:* 158 full-time (135 women), 118 part-time (117 women); includes 41 minority (30 African Americans, 1 American Indian/Alaska Native, 4 Asian Americans or Pacific Islanders, 6 Hispanic Americans), 4 international. Average age 36. 302 applicants, 48% accepted, 106 enrolled. In 2009, 84 master's, 12 doctorates awarded. *Degree requirements:* For doctorate, comprehensive exam (for some programs), capstone project (DNP), dissertation (PhD). *Entrance requirements:* For master's, GRE General Test, MAT; for doctorate, GRE General Test. Additional exam requirements/recommendations for international students: Required—TOEFL, IELTS. *Application deadline:* Applications are processed on a rolling basis. Application fee: $60. Electronic applications accepted. *Expenses:* Contact institution. *Financial support:* Fellowships, research assistantships, teaching assistantships, Federal Work-Study and scholarships/grants available. Financial award applicants required to submit FAFSA. *Unit head:* Dorrie K. Fontaine, Dean, 434-924-0141, Fax: 434-982-1809. *Application contact:* Clay Hysell, Assistant Dean for Graduate Student Services, 434-924-0141, Fax: 434-982-1809, E-mail: nur-osa@virginia.edu.

University of Washington, Graduate School, School of Public Health, Department of Health Services, Seattle, WA 98195. Offers bioinformatics (PhD); cancer prevention and control (PhD); clinical research (MS); community oriented public health practice (MPH); economics or finance (PhD); evaluation sciences (PhD); executive program (MHA); health behavior and health promotion (PhD); health care and population health research (MPH); health policy analysis and process (PhD); health policy and analysis and process (MPH); health services (MS, PhD); health services administration (EMHA, MHA); in residence program (MHA); occupational health (PhD); population health and social determinants (PhD); social and behavioral sciences (MPH); sociology and demography (PhD); JD/MHA; MHA/MBA; MHA/MD; MHA/MPA; MPH/JD; MPH/MD; MPH/MN; MPH/MPA; MPH/MSD; MPH/MSW; MPH/PhD. Part-time and evening/weekend programs available. Postbaccalaureate distance learning degree programs offered (minimal on-campus study). *Faculty:* 52 full-time (24 women), 60 part-time/adjunct (28 women). *Students:* 104 full-time (83 women), 100 part-time (76 women); includes 21 minority (6 African Americans, 1 American Indian/Alaska Native, 11 Asian Americans or Pacific Islanders, 3 Hispanic Americans), 6 international. Average age 34. 375 applicants, 17% accepted, 24 enrolled. In 2009, 33 master's awarded. Terminal master's awarded for partial completion of doctoral program. *Degree requirements:* For master's, thesis (for some programs), practicum (MPH); for doctorate, comprehensive exam, thesis/dissertation. *Entrance requirements:* For master's and doctorate, GRE General Test, minimum GPA of 3.0. Additional exam requirements/recommendations for international students: Required—TOEFL. *Application deadline:* For fall admission, 1/15 for domestic students, 11/1 for international students. Application fee: 50 Albanian leks. Electronic applications accepted. *Financial support:* In 2009–10, 64 students received support, including 10 fellowships with full and partial tuition reimbursements available (averaging $21,000 per year), 10 research assistantships with full and partial tuition reimbursements available (averaging $18,000 per year), 3 teaching assistantships with full and partial tuition reimbursements available (averaging $18,000 per year); career-related internships or fieldwork, Federal Work-Study, institutionally sponsored loans, and traineeships also available. Financial award application deadline: 2/28; financial award applicants required to submit FAFSA. *Faculty research:* Health promotion and disease prevention, maternal and child health, health services research design, program evaluation, health policy. Total annual research expenditures: $10.5 million. *Unit head:* Dr. Larry Kessler, Chair, 206-543-616-2930. *Application contact:* Kitty A. Andert, Program Manager, 206-616-2926, Fax: 206-543-3964, E-mail: kitander@u.washington.edu.

University of West Florida, College of Professional Studies, Division of Health, Leisure, and Exercise Science, Community Health Education, Pensacola, FL 32514-5750. Offers aging studies (MS); promotion and worksite wellness (MS); psycho-social (MS). Part-time and evening/weekend programs available. *Faculty:* 2 full-time (1 woman), 1 (woman) part-time/adjunct. *Students:* 7 full-time (6 women), 7 part-time (all women); includes 4 minority (1 African American, 1 American Indian/Alaska Native, 1 Asian American or Pacific Islander, 1 Hispanic American), 1 international. Average age 34. 7 applicants, 86% accepted, 5 enrolled. In 2009, 13 master's awarded. *Degree requirements:* For master's, thesis or alternative. *Entrance requirements:* For master's, GRE General Test, minimum GPA of 3.0. Additional exam requirements/recommendations for international students: Required—TOEFL (minimum score 550 paper-based; 213 computer-based). *Application deadline:* For fall admission, 6/1 for domestic students, 5/15 for international students; for spring admission, 11/1 for domestic students, 10/1 for international students. Applications are processed on a rolling basis. Application fee: $30. *Expenses:* Tuition, state resident: full-time $4982; part-time $260 per credit hour. Tuition, nonresident: full-time $20,059; part-time $919 per credit hour. Required fees: $1247;

Community Health

University of West Florida (continued)

$52 per credit hour. *Financial support:* Research assistantships, teaching assistantships, unspecified assistantships available. *Unit head:* Dr. John Todorovich, Chairperson, 850-473-7248, Fax: 850-474-2106. *Application contact:* Terry McCray, Assistant Director of Graduate Admissions, 850-473-7718, Fax: 850-473-7714, E-mail: gradadmissions@uwf.edu.

University of Wisconsin–La Crosse, Office of University Graduate Studies, College of Science and Health, Department of Health Education and Health Promotion, Program in Community Health Education, La Crosse, WI 54601-3742. Offers MPH, MS. *Accreditation:* CEPH. *Students:* 13 full-time (11 women), 19 part-time (18 women); includes 1 minority (Asian American or Pacific Islander), 5 international. Average age 30. 10 applicants, 80% accepted, 7 enrolled. In 2009, 18 master's awarded. *Degree requirements:* For master's, thesis. *Entrance requirements:* For master's, GRE General Test, GRE Subject Test (MPH), 3 letters of recommendation. Additional exam requirements/recommendations for international students: Required—TOEFL (minimum score 550 paper-based; 213 computer-based; 79 iBT). Application fee: $56. Electronic applications accepted. *Financial support:* Research assistantships available. *Unit head:* Dr. Gary Gilmore, Director, 608-785-8163, E-mail: gilmore.gary@uwlax.edu. *Application contact:* Kathryn Kiefer, Director of Admissions, 608-785-8939, E-mail: admissions@uwlax.edu.

University of Wisconsin–Madison, School of Medicine and Public Health and Graduate School, Graduate Programs in Medicine, Department of Population Health Sciences, Madison, WI 53726. Offers clinical research (MS, PhD); epidemiology (MS, PhD); health services research (MS, PhD); population health sciences (MPH); social and behavioral health sciences (MS, PhD); DPT/MPH; DVM/MPH; MD/MPH; MPA/MPH; MS/MPH; Pharm D/MPH. *Accreditation:* CEPH. Part-time programs available. *Faculty:* 104 full-time (54 women), 2 part-time/adjunct (0 women). *Students:* 105 full-time (76 women), 38 part-time (31 women); includes 19 minority (8 African Americans, 8 Asian Americans or Pacific Islanders, 3 Hispanic Americans), 15 international. Average age 30. 126 applicants, 75% accepted, 58 enrolled. In 2009, 13 master's, 8 doctorates awarded. Terminal master's awarded for partial completion of doctoral program. *Degree requirements:* For master's, thesis, defense; for doctorate, comprehensive exam, thesis/dissertation, qualifying exam, preliminary exam, dissertation defense. *Entrance requirements:* For master's and doctorate, GRE (separate guidelines for those with doctoral degrees), minimum GPA of 3.0, quantitative preparation (calculus, statistics, or other) with minimum B average. Additional exam requirements/recommendations for international students: Required—TOEFL (minimum score 600 paper-based; 250 computer-based; 100 iBT). *Application deadline:* For fall admission, 1/15 for domestic and international students. Application fee: $56. Electronic applications accepted. *Expenses:* Tuition, state resident: part-time $594 per credit. Tuition, nonresident: part-time $1504 per credit. Required fees: $65 per credit. Tuition and fees vary according to course load, program and reciprocity agreements. *Financial support:* In 2009–10, 73 students received support, including 16 fellowships with full tuition reimbursements available (averaging $21,000 per year), 38 research assistantships with full tuition reimbursements available (averaging $17,300 per year), 7 teaching assistantships with full tuition reimbursements available (averaging $17,300 per year); scholarships/grants, traineeships, health care benefits, and unspecified assistantships also available. Support available to part-time students. *Faculty research:* Epidemiology (cancer, environmental, aging, infectious disease and genetic), determinants of population health, health services research, social and behavioral health sciences, biostatistics. Total annual research expenditures: $11.4 million. *Unit head:* Dr. F. Javier Nieto, Chair, 608-265-5242, Fax: 608-263-2820, E-mail: fjnieto@wisc.edu. *Application contact:* Kelly Haslam, Graduate Program Coordinator, 608-265-8108, Fax: 608-263-2820, E-mail: haslam@wisc.edu.

University of Wyoming, College of Education, Department of Counselor Education, Laramie, WY 82070. Offers community mental health (MS); counselor education and supervision (PhD); school counseling (MS); student affairs (MS). *Accreditation:* ACA (one or more programs are accredited). *Degree requirements:* For master's, comprehensive exam (for some programs), thesis optional; for doctorate, thesis/dissertation, video demonstration. *Entrance requirements:* For master's, interview, background check; for doctorate, video tape session, interview, writing sample, master's degree, background check. Additional exam requirements/recommendations for international students: Required—TOEFL. *Faculty research:* Wyoming SAGE photovoice project; accountable school counseling programs; GLBT issues; addictions; play therapy-early childhood mental health.

Virginia Commonwealth University, Medical College of Virginia-Professional Programs, School of Medicine, School of Medicine Graduate Programs, Program in Epidemiology and Community Health, Richmond, VA 23284-9005. Offers PhD. *Accreditation:* CEPH. Part-time programs available. *Degree requirements:* For doctorate, comprehensive exam, thesis/dissertation. *Entrance requirements:* For doctorate, GRE General Test, interview, 3 letters of recommendation, minimum graduate GPA of 3.0, master's degree in public health or related field including epidemiology and biostatistics. Additional exam requirements/recommendations for international students: Required—TOEFL (minimum score 600 paper-based). Electronic applications accepted. *Faculty research:* Sickle cell anemia, breast cancer, HIV/AIDS, hospital epidemiology, infectious diseases.

Virginia State University, School of Graduate Studies, Research, and Outreach, School of Engineering, Science and Technology, Department of Psychology, Petersburg, VA 23806-0001. Offers behavioral and community health sciences (PhD); clinical health psychology (PhD); clinical psychology (MS); general psychology (MS). *Degree requirements:* For master's, one foreign language, thesis. *Entrance requirements:* For master's, GRE General Test.

Walden University, Graduate Programs, School of Health Sciences, Minneapolis, MN 55401. Offers clinical research administration (MS); health informatics (MS); health services (PhD), including community health promotion and education, general program, health management and policy; healthcare administration (MHA); public health (MPH, PhD), including community health promotion and education (PhD), epidemiology (PhD). Part-time and evening/weekend programs available. Postbaccalaureate distance learning degree programs offered (minimal on-campus study). *Faculty:* 14 full-time, 136 part-time/adjunct. *Students:* 2,121 full-time (1,670 women), 724 part-time (568 women); includes 1,370 minority (1,149 African Americans, 20 American Indian/Alaska Native, 95 Asian Americans or Pacific Islanders, 106 Hispanic Americans), 134 international. Average age 40. In 2009, 232 master's, 24 doctorates awarded. *Degree requirements:* For doctorate, thesis/dissertation, residency. *Entrance requirements:* For master's, bachelor's degree or equivalent in related field, minimum GPA of 2.5; for doctorate, master's degree or equivalent in related field; minimum GPA of 3.0; official transcripts; three years of related professional/academic experience (preferred); access to computer and Internet. Additional exam requirements/recommendations for international students: Required—TOEFL (minimum score 550 paper-based; 213 computer-based), IELTS (minimum score 6.5), or Michigan English Language Assessment Battery (minimum score 82). *Application deadline:* Applications are processed on a rolling basis. Application fee: $50. Electronic applications accepted. *Expenses:* Tuition: Full-time $13,665; part-time $560 per credit. Required fees: $1375. Tuition and fees vary according to course load, degree level and program. *Financial support:* In 2009–10, 152 students received support; fellowships, Federal Work-Study, scholarships/grants, unspecified assistantships, and family tuition reduction, active duty/veteran tuition reduction, group tuition reduction, interest-free payment plans available. Support available to part-time students. Financial award applicants required to submit FAFSA. *Unit head:* Dr. Jorg Westermann, Interim Associate Dean, 800-925-3368. *Application contact:* Jennifer Hall, Director of Enrollment, 866-4-WALDEN, E-mail: info@waldenu.edu.

Wayne State University, School of Medicine, Graduate Programs in Medicine, Department of Family Medicine and Public Health Sciences, Detroit, MI 48202. Offers community health (MS); community health services (Certificate); public health (MPH); public health practice (Certificate). *Degree requirements:* For master's, thesis (for some programs). *Entrance requirements:* For master's, GRE, minimum GPA of 2.6. Additional exam requirements/recommendations for international students: Required—TOEFL (minimum score 550 paper-based; 213 computer-based); Recommended—TWE (minimum score 6). Electronic applications accepted. *Faculty research:* Urban health disparities, community health promotion, substance abuse etiology and prevention, HIV/AIDS, interpersonal violence.

West Chester University of Pennsylvania, Office of Graduate Studies, College of Health Sciences, Department of Health, West Chester, PA 19383. Offers emergency preparedness (Certificate); health care administration (Certificate); integrative health (Certificate); public health (MPH), including administration, community, environment, integrative, nutrition; school health (M Ed). *Accreditation:* CEPH. Part-time and evening/weekend programs available. *Students:* 15 full-time (9 women), 128 part-time (91 women); includes 41 minority (34 African Americans, 2 American Indian/Alaska Native, 5 Asian Americans or Pacific Islanders), 22 international. Average age 30. 83 applicants, 88% accepted, 41 enrolled. In 2009, 45 master's, 8 other advanced degrees awarded. *Degree requirements:* For master's, thesis (for some programs). *Entrance requirements:* For master's, one-page statement of career objectives, two letters of reference. Additional exam requirements/recommendations for international students: Required—TOEFL (minimum score 550 paper-based; 213 computer-based; 80 iBT). *Application deadline:* For fall admission, 4/15 priority date for domestic students, 3/15 for international students; for spring admission, 10/15 for domestic students, 9/1 for international students. Applications are processed on a rolling basis. Application fee: $35. Electronic applications accepted. *Expenses:* Tuition, state resident: full-time $6666; part-time $370 per credit. Tuition, nonresident: full-time $10,666; part-time $593 per credit. Required fees: $122.56 per credit. *Financial support:* In 2009–10, 11 research assistantships with full and partial tuition reimbursements (averaging $5,000 per year) were awarded; unspecified assistantships also available. Support available to part-time students. Financial award application deadline: 2/15; financial award applicants required to submit FAFSA. *Faculty research:* HIV/AIDS education, teacher preparation, water quality. *Unit head:* Dr. Roger Mustalish, Chair, 610-436-2931, E-mail: rmustalish@wcupa.edu. *Application contact:* Dr. Bethann Cinelli, Graduate Coordinator, 610-436-2267, E-mail: bcinelli@wcupa.edu.

West Virginia University, School of Medicine, Department of Community Medicine, Program in Public Health, Morgantown, WV 26506. Offers community health/preventative medicine (MPH). *Accreditation:* CEPH. Part-time programs available. Postbaccalaureate distance learning degree programs offered (minimal on-campus study). *Degree requirements:* For master's, practicum, project. *Entrance requirements:* For master's, GRE General Test, MCAT, medical degree, medical internship. *Expenses:* Contact institution. *Faculty research:* Occupational health, environmental health, clinical epidemiology, health care management, prevention.

Environmental and Occupational Health

American University of Beirut, Graduate Programs, Faculty of Health Sciences, Beirut, Lebanon. Offers environmental sciences (MSES), including environmental health; epidemiology (MS); epidemiology and biostatistics (MPH); health behavior and education (MPH); population health (MS); public health (MPH). Part-time programs available. *Degree requirements:* For master's, one foreign language, comprehensive exam, thesis (for some programs). *Entrance requirements:* For master's, 2 letters of recommendation. Additional exam requirements/recommendations for international students: Required—TOEFL (minimum score 573 paper-based; 230 computer-based; 98 iBT), IELTS (minimum score 7.5). Electronic applications accepted. *Faculty research:* Urban health, childbirth, tobacco control, HIV/AIDS surveillance, health finance and policies.

Anna Maria College, Graduate Division, Program in Occupational and Environmental Health and Safety, Paxton, MA 01612. Offers MS. Part-time and evening/weekend programs available. *Degree requirements:* For master's, thesis. *Entrance requirements:* For master's, minimum GPA of 2.7. Additional exam requirements/recommendations for international students: Required—TOEFL (minimum score 500 paper-based). Electronic applications accepted.

Boston University, School of Public Health, Environmental Health Department, Boston, MA 02215. Offers MPH, PhD. *Accreditation:* CEPH (one or more programs are accredited). Part-time and evening/weekend programs available. *Students:* 24 full-time (20 women), 19 part-time (14 women); includes 8 minority (2 African Americans, 1 American Indian/Alaska Native, 5 Asian Americans or Pacific Islanders), 2 international. Average age 29. In 2009, 7 master's, 2 doctorates awarded. *Degree requirements:* For doctorate, one foreign language, thesis/dissertation, comprehensive written and oral exams. *Entrance requirements:* For master's, GRE, LSAT, GMAT, DAT, or MCAT, U.S. bachelor's degree or foreign equivalent; for doctorate, GRE, MCAT, MPH or equivalent. Additional exam requirements/recommendations for international students: Required—TOEFL (minimum score 600 paper-based; 250 computer-based; 100 iBT) or IELTS (minimum score 6). *Application deadline:* For fall admission, 2/1 priority date for domestic and international students; for spring admission, 10/15 priority date for domestic and international students. Applications are processed on a rolling basis. Application fee: $95. Electronic applications accepted. *Expenses:* Tuition: Full-time $37,910; part-time $1184 per credit hour. Required fees: $386; $40 per semester. Part-time tuition and fees vary according to class time, course level, degree level and program. *Financial support:* Career-related internships or fieldwork, Federal Work-Study, institutionally sponsored loans, scholarships/grants, and tuition waivers (partial) available. Support available to part-time students. Financial award application deadline: 3/1; financial award applicants required to submit FAFSA. *Unit head:* Dr. Roberta White, Chair, 617-638-4620, E-mail: envhlth@bu.edu. *Application contact:* LePhan Quan, Assistant Director of Admissions, 617-638-4640, Fax: 617-638-5299, E-mail: asksph@bu.edu.

California State University, Northridge, Graduate Studies, College of Health and Human Development, Department of Environmental and Occupational Health, Northridge, CA 91330. Offers environmental and occupational health (MS); industrial hygiene (MS). *Faculty:* 6 full-time (0 women), 9 part-time/adjunct (3 women). *Students:* 29 full-time (16 women), 32 part-time (21 women); includes 29 minority (5 African Americans, 1 American Indian/Alaska Native, 14 Asian Americans or Pacific Islanders, 9 Hispanic Americans), 3 international. Average age 30. 48 applicants, 67% accepted, 23 enrolled. In 2009, 21 master's awarded. *Degree requirements:* For master's, seminar, field experience, comprehensive exam or thesis. *Entrance requirements:* For master's, GRE General Test or minimum GPA of 3.0. Additional exam requirements/recommendations for international students: Required—TOEFL. *Application deadline:* For fall admission, 11/30 for domestic students. Application fee: $55. *Financial support:* Application deadline: 3/1. *Unit head:* Dr. Thomas Hatfield, Chair, 818-677-7476. *Application contact:* Dr. Thomas Hatfield, Chair, 818-677-7476.

Capella University, School of Public Service Leadership, Minneapolis, MN 55402. Offers criminal justice (MS, PhD); emergency management (MS, PhD); general human services (MS, PhD); general public administration (MPA, DPA); gerontology (MS); health care administration (MS, PhD); health management and policy (MSPH); management of nonprofit agencies (MS,

PhD); nurse educator (MS); public safety leadership (MS, PhD); social and community services (MS, PhD); social behavioral sciences (MSPH).

Colorado State University, College of Veterinary Medicine and Biomedical Sciences, Department of Environmental and Radiological Health Sciences, Fort Collins, CO 80523-1681. Offers environmental health (MS, PhD); radiological health sciences (MS, PhD). *Faculty:* 22 full-time (8 women), 3 part-time/adjunct (0 women). *Students:* 66 full-time (39 women), 37 part-time (22 women); includes 12 minority (4 African Americans, 2 American Indian/Alaska Native, 4 Asian Americans or Pacific Islanders, 2 Hispanic Americans), 8 international. Average age 29. 88 applicants, 76% accepted, 49 enrolled. In 2009, 25 master's, 4 doctorates awarded. Terminal master's awarded for partial completion of doctoral program. *Degree requirements:* For master's, thesis (for some programs), publishable paper; for doctorate, comprehensive exam, thesis/dissertation, publishable paper. *Entrance requirements:* For master's, GRE General Test, 1 year of course work in biology lab and chemistry lab, 1 semester of course work in organic chemistry, course work in calculus, resume, letters of recommendation; for doctorate, GRE General Test, 1 year of course work in biology lab and chemistry lab, 1 semester of course work in organic chemistry, course work in calculus, resume, letters of recommendation, evidence of research capability. Additional exam requirements/recommendations for international students: Required—TOEFL (minimum score 550 paper-based; 213 computer-based). *Application deadline:* For fall admission, 3/1 for domestic students, 2/1 priority date for international students; for spring admission, 10/1 for domestic students. Application fee: $50. Electronic applications accepted. *Expenses:* Tuition, state resident: full-time $6434; part-time $359.10 per credit. Tuition, nonresident: full-time $18,116; part-time $1006.45 per credit. Required fees: $1496; $83 per credit. *Financial support:* In 2009–10, 23 students received support, including 5 fellowships with partial tuition reimbursements available (averaging $38,888 per year), 14 research assistantships (averaging $16,063 per year), 4 teaching assistantships with full tuition reimbursements available (averaging $10,688 per year); career-related internships or fieldwork, Federal Work-Study, institutionally sponsored loans, traineeships, and unspecified assistantships also available. Support available to part-time students. Financial award application deadline: 2/1. *Faculty research:* Epidemiology, toxicology, industrial hygiene, occupational health, radiation therapy. Total annual research expenditures: $9 million. *Unit head:* Dr. Jac A. Nickoloff, Head, 970-491-6674, Fax: 970-491-0623, E-mail: j.nickoloff@colostate.edu. *Application contact:* Jeanne A. Brockway, Graduate Program Coordinator, 970-491-5003, Fax: 970-491-0623, E-mail: jeanne.brockway@colostate.edu.

Columbia Southern University, College of Safety and Emergency Services, Orange Beach, AL 36561. Offers criminal justice (MS); environmental management (MS); occupational safety and health (MS); occupational safety and health/environmental management (MS). Part-time and evening/weekend programs available. Postbaccalaureate distance learning degree programs offered (no on-campus study). *Entrance requirements:* For master's, bachelor's degree from accredited/approved institution. Additional exam requirements/recommendations for international students: Required—TOEFL. Electronic applications accepted.

Columbia University, Columbia University Mailman School of Public Health, Division of Environmental Health Sciences, New York, NY 10032. Offers MPH, Dr PH, PhD. PhD offered in cooperation with the Graduate School of Arts and Sciences. *Accreditation:* CEPH (one or more programs are accredited). Part-time programs available. *Students:* 42 full-time (31 women), 40 part-time (24 women); includes 25 minority (2 African Americans, 22 Asian Americans or Pacific Islanders, 1 Hispanic American), 12 international. Average age 30. 114 applicants, 63% accepted, 23 enrolled. In 2009, 20 master's, 3 doctorates awarded. *Degree requirements:* For master's, thesis optional; for doctorate, thesis/dissertation. *Entrance requirements:* For master's, GRE General Test, 1 year of course work in biology, general chemistry, organic chemistry, and mathematics; for doctorate, GRE General Test, MPH or equivalent (Dr PH). Additional exam requirements/recommendations for international students: Required—TOEFL (minimum score 600 paper-based; 250 computer-based; 100 iBT). *Application deadline:* For fall admission, 1/5 for domestic students. Applications are processed on a rolling basis. Application fee: $60. Electronic applications accepted. *Financial support:* Research assistantships, teaching assistantships, career-related internships or fieldwork and Federal Work-Study available. Support available to part-time students. Financial award application deadline: 2/1; financial award applicants required to submit FAFSA. *Faculty research:* Health effects of environmental and occupational exposure to chemicals and radiation, molecular epidemiology, risk assessment, molecular toxicology, and environmental policy. *Unit head:* Dr. Joseph Graziano, Interim Department Chair, 212-305-3464, Fax: 212-305-4012, E-mail: jg24@columbia.edu. *Application contact:* Dr. Joseph Graziano, Interim Department Chair, 212-305-3464, Fax: 212-305-4012, E-mail: jg24@columbia.edu.

Duke University, Graduate School, Integrated Toxicology and Environmental Health Program, Durham, NC 27708. Offers PhD, Certificate. *Faculty:* 36 full-time. *Students:* 5 full-time (4 women). 22 applicants, 27% accepted, 4 enrolled. *Entrance requirements:* For doctorate, GRE General Test, GRE Subject Test (recommended). Additional exam requirements/recommendations for international students: Required—TOEFL (minimum score 550 paper-based; 213 computer-based; 83 iBT), IELTS (minimum score 7). *Application deadline:* For fall admission, 12/8 priority date for domestic and international students. Application fee: $75. Electronic applications accepted. *Financial support:* Fellowships available. Financial award application deadline: 12/31. *Unit head:* Tim Lenoir, Director, 919-668-1952, Fax: 919-668-1799, E-mail: emarion@duke.edu. *Application contact:* Cynthia Robertson, Associate Dean for Enrollment Services, 919-684-3913, E-mail: grad-admissions@duke.edu.

Duke University, Nicholas School of the Environment, Durham, NC 27708-0328. Offers coastal environmental management (MEM); DEL-environmental leadership (MEM); energy and environment (MEM); environmental economics and policy (MEM); environmental health and security (MEM); forest resource management (MF); global environmental change (MEM); resource ecology (MEM); water and air resources (MEM); JD/AM; JD/MEM; JD/MF; MAT/MEM; MBA/MEM; MBA/MF; MEM/MPP; MF/MPP. *Accreditation:* SAF (one or more programs are accredited). Part-time programs available. *Degree requirements:* For master's, thesis. *Entrance requirements:* For master's, GRE General Test, previous course work in biology or ecology, calculus, statistics, and microeconomics; computer familiarity with word processing and data analysis. Additional exam requirements/recommendations for international students: Required—TOEFL (minimum score 550 paper-based; 213 computer-based). Electronic applications accepted. *Expenses:* Contact institution. *Faculty research:* Ecosystem management, conservation ecology, earth systems, risk assessment.

East Carolina University, Graduate School, College of Health and Human Performance, Department of Health Education and Promotion, Greenville, NC 27858-4353. Offers environmental health (MS); health education (MA, MA Ed). *Accreditation:* NCATE. *Degree requirements:* For master's, comprehensive exam, thesis optional. *Entrance requirements:* For master's, GRE General Test or MAT. Additional exam requirements/recommendations for international students: Required—TOEFL. *Faculty research:* Community health education, worksite health promotion, school health education, environmental health.

Eastern Kentucky University, The Graduate School, College of Health Sciences, Department of Clinical Laboratory Science/Environmental Health Science, Richmond, KY 40475-3102. Offers environmental health science (MPH). *Accreditation:* CEPH. *Degree requirements:* For master's, comprehensive exam, thesis optional, practicum, capstone course. *Entrance requirements:* For master's, GRE. *Faculty research:* Water quality, food safety, occupational health, air quality.

East Tennessee State University, School of Graduate Studies, College of Public and Allied Health, Department of Environmental Health, Johnson City, TN 37614. Offers environmental health (MSEH), including administrative option, specialist option. Part-time programs available. *Degree requirements:* For master's, comprehensive exam, thesis optional. *Entrance requirements:* For master's, GRE, 30 hours of course work in natural and physical sciences, minimum GPA of 2.5. Additional exam requirements/recommendations for international students: Required—TOEFL (minimum score 550 paper-based; 213 computer-based). *Faculty research:* Water quality, ecotoxicology, occupational health.

Emory University, Rollins School of Public Health, Department of Environmental and Occupational Health, Atlanta, GA 30322-1100. Offers MPH, MSPH. *Accreditation:* CEPH. Part-time programs available. *Degree requirements:* For master's, thesis, practicum. *Entrance requirements:* For master's, GRE General Test. Additional exam requirements/recommendations for international students: Required—TOEFL. Electronic applications accepted.

Florida International University, Stempel College of Public Health and Social Work, Programs in Public Health, Miami, FL 33199. Offers biostatistics (MPH); environmental and occupational health (MPH, PhD); epidemiology (MPH, PhD); health policy and management (MPH); health promotion and disease prevention (PhD); health promotion and diseases prevention (MPH). PhD only admits in Fall. *Accreditation:* CEPH. Part-time and evening/weekend programs available. Postbaccalaureate distance learning degree programs offered (no on-campus study). *Faculty:* 18 full-time (6 women). *Students:* 249 full-time (186 women), 185 part-time (144 women); includes 309 minority (154 African Americans, 2 American Indian/Alaska Native, 26 Asian Americans or Pacific Islanders, 127 Hispanic Americans), 48 international. Average age 35. 484 applicants, 29% accepted, 123 enrolled. In 2009, 79 master's, 1 doctorate awarded. *Degree requirements:* For master's, thesis optional; for doctorate, comprehensive exam, thesis/dissertation. *Entrance requirements:* For master's, minimum GPA of 3.0, letters of recommendation; for doctorate, GRE, resume, minimum GPA of 3.0, letters of recommendation, letter of intent. Additional exam requirements/recommendations for international students: Required—TOEFL (minimum score 550 paper-based; 80 iBT). *Application deadline:* For fall admission, 6/1 for domestic students, 4/1 for international students; for spring admission, 10/1 for domestic students, 9/1 for international students. Applications are processed on a rolling basis. Application fee: $30. Electronic applications accepted. *Expenses:* Contact institution. *Financial support:* Institutionally sponsored loans, scholarships/grants, and tuition waivers (full) available. Financial award application deadline: 3/1; financial award applicants required to submit FAFSA. *Faculty research:* Drugs/AIDS intervention among migrant workers, provision of services for active/recovering drug users with HIV. *Unit head:* Dr. Gilbert Ramirez, Associate Dean for Academic and Student Affairs, 305-348-7442, E-mail: ph@fiu.edu. *Application contact:* Nanett Rojas, Assistant Director of Graduate Admissions, 305-348-7442, Fax: 305-348-7441, E-mail: gradadm@fiu.edu.

Fort Valley State University, College of Graduate Studies and Extended Education, Program in Public Health, Fort Valley, GA 31030. Offers environmental health (MPH). *Degree requirements:* For master's, thesis. *Entrance requirements:* For master's, GRE General Test.

Gannon University, School of Graduate Studies, College of Engineering and Business, School of Engineering and Computer Science, Program in Environmental and Occupational Science and Health, Erie, PA 16541-0001. Offers Certificate. Part-time and evening/weekend programs available. *Entrance requirements:* Additional exam requirements/recommendations for international students: Required—TOEFL (minimum score 79 iBT). *Application deadline:* Applications are processed on a rolling basis. Application fee: $25. Electronic applications accepted. *Expenses:* Tuition: Full-time $13,590; part-time $755 per credit. Required fees: $524; $17 per credit. Tuition and fees vary according to course load, degree level, campus/location and program. *Financial support:* Scholarships/grants available. Financial award application deadline: 7/1; financial award applicants required to submit FAFSA. *Unit head:* Dr. Harry Diz, Chair, 814-871-7633, E-mail: diz001@gannon.edu. *Application contact:* Kara Morgan, Assistant Director of Graduate Admissions, 814-871-5831, Fax: 814-871-5827, E-mail: graduate@gannon.edu.

The George Washington University, School of Public Health and Health Services, Department of Environmental and Occupational Health, Washington, DC 20052. Offers environmental health science and policy (MPH); public health (MPH). *Accreditation:* CEPH. *Faculty:* 4 full-time (3 women), 34 part-time/adjunct (11 women). *Students:* 6 full-time (4 women), 26 part-time (24 women); includes 7 minority (3 African Americans, 2 Asian Americans or Pacific Islanders, 2 Hispanic Americans). Average age 33. 1 applicant, 100% accepted, 0 enrolled. In 2009, 6 master's awarded. *Degree requirements:* For master's, case study or special project. *Entrance requirements:* For master's, GMAT, GRE General Test, or MCAT. Additional exam requirements/recommendations for international students: Required—TOEFL. *Application deadline:* For fall admission, 4/15 priority date for domestic students, 4/15 for international students; for spring admission, 11/1 for domestic and international students. Applications are processed on a rolling basis. Application fee: $60. *Financial support:* In 2009–10, 7 students received support. Tuition waivers available. Financial award application deadline: 2/15. *Unit head:* Dr. David Michaels, Director, 202-994-2461, E-mail: eohdmm@gwumc.edu. *Application contact:* Jane Smith, Director of Admissions, 202-994-0248, Fax: 202-994-1860, E-mail: sphhsinfo@gwumc.edu.

Georgia Southern University, Jack N. Averitt College of Graduate Studies, Jiann-Ping Hsu College of Public Health, Program in Public Health, Statesboro, GA 30460. Offers biostatistics (MPH, Dr PH); community health behavior and education (Dr PH); community health education (MPH); environmental health sciences (MPH); epidemiology (MPH); health services policy management (MPH); public health leadership (Dr PH). Part-time programs available. *Students:* 75 full-time (47 women), 23 part-time (15 women); includes 39 minority (36 African Americans, 3 Asian Americans or Pacific Islanders), 24 international. Average age 30. 50 applicants, 80% accepted, 20 enrolled. In 2009, 20 master's awarded. *Degree requirements:* For master's, thesis optional, practicum; for doctorate, comprehensive exam, thesis/dissertation, practicum. *Entrance requirements:* For master's, GRE General Test, minimum GPA of 2.75, resume, 3 letters of reference; for doctorate, GRE, GMAT, MCAT, LSAT, 3 letters of reference, statement of purpose, resume or curriculum vitae. Additional exam requirements/recommendations for international students: Required—TOEFL (minimum score 550 paper-based; 213 computer-based; 80 iBT). *Application deadline:* For fall admission, 3/1 priority date for domestic and international students; for spring admission, 10/1 priority date for domestic students, 10/1 for international students. Applications are processed on a rolling basis. Application fee: $50. Electronic applications accepted. *Expenses:* Contact institution. *Financial support:* In 2009–10, 83 students received support, including research assistantships with partial tuition reimbursements available (averaging $7,200 per year), teaching assistantships with partial tuition reimbursements available (averaging $7,200 per year); career-related internships or fieldwork, Federal Work-Study, scholarships/grants, tuition waivers (partial), and unspecified assistantships also available. Support available to part-time students. Financial award application deadline: 4/15; financial award applicants required to submit FAFSA. *Faculty research:* Biostatistics, community health, environmental health sciences, epidemiology, health policy and management, community health behavior and education, public health leadership. *Unit head:* Dr. Charles Hardy, Dean, 912-478-2674, Fax: 912-478-5811, E-mail: chardy@georgiasouthern.edu. *Application contact:* Dr. Charles Ziglar, Coordinator for Graduate Student Recruitment, 912-478-5635, Fax: 912-478-0740, E-mail: gradadmissions@georgiasouthern.edu.

Harvard University, Cyprus International Institute for the Environment and Public Health in Association with Harvard School of Public Health, Cambridge, MA 02138. Offers environmental health (MS). *Entrance requirements:* For master's, GRE, resume, 3 letters of recommendation, BA or BS. Additional exam requirements/recommendations for international students: Required—TOEFL (minimum score 220 computer-based), IELTS (minimum score 7). Electronic applications accepted. *Expenses:* Tuition: Full-time $33,696. Required fees: $1126. Full-time tuition and fees vary according to program. *Faculty research:* Air pollution, climate change, biostatistics, sustainable development, environmental management.

Harvard University, School of Public Health, Department of Environmental Health, Boston, MA 02115-6096. Offers environmental health (MOH, SM, DPH, PhD, SD); occupational health (MOH, SM, DPH, SD); physiology (PhD, SD). Part-time programs available. *Faculty:* 44 full-time (9 women), 22 part-time/adjunct (5 women). *Students:* 85 full-time, 4 part-time; includes 6 minority (all Asian Americans or Pacific Islanders), 42 international. Average age 32. 80 applicants, 48% accepted, 32 enrolled. In 2009, 15 master's, 10 doctorates awarded. *Degree requirements:* For doctorate, thesis/dissertation, qualifying exam. *Entrance requirements:* For master's and doctorate, GRE. Additional exam requirements/recommendations for international students: Required—TOEFL (minimum score 595 paper-based; 240 computer-based;

Environmental and Occupational Health

Harvard University (continued)

95 iBT); Recommended—IELTS (minimum score 7). *Application deadline:* For fall admission, 12/15 for domestic and international students. Application fee: $115. Electronic applications accepted. *Expenses:* Tuition: Full-time $33,696. Required fees: $1126. Full-time tuition and fees vary according to program. *Financial support:* Fellowships, research assistantships, teaching assistantships, career-related internships or fieldwork, Federal Work-Study, scholarships/grants, traineeships, tuition waivers (partial), and unspecified assistantships available. Support available to part-time students. Financial award application deadline: 2/8; financial award applicants required to submit FAFSA. *Faculty research:* Industrial hygiene and occupational safety, population genetics, indoor and outdoor air pollution, cell and molecular biology of the lungs, infectious diseases. *Unit head:* Dr. Douglas Dockery, Chairman, 617-432-1270, Fax: 617-432-6913. *Application contact:* Vincent W. James, Director of Admissions, 617-432-1031, Fax: 617-432-7080, E-mail: admisofc@hsph.harvard.edu.

See Close-Up on page 1667.

Hunter College of the City University of New York, Graduate School, Schools of the Health Professions, School of Health Sciences, Programs in Urban Public Health, Program in Environmental and Occupational Health Education, New York, NY 10021-5085. Offers MS. *Accreditation:* ABET. Part-time and evening/weekend programs available. *Faculty:* 27 full-time (17 women), 3 part-time/adjunct (2 women). *Students:* 1 (woman) full-time, 32 part-time (15 women); includes 15 minority (5 African Americans, 8 Asian Americans or Pacific Islanders, 2 Hispanic Americans). Average age 32. 10 applicants, 70% accepted, 5 enrolled. In 2009, 5 master's awarded. *Degree requirements:* For master's, comprehensive exam, thesis optional, internship. *Entrance requirements:* For master's, GRE General Test, previous course work in calculus and statistics. Additional exam requirements/recommendations for international students: Required—TOEFL. *Application deadline:* For fall admission, 4/1 for domestic students, 2/1 for international students; for spring admission, 11/1 for domestic students, 9/1 for international students. Application fee: $125. *Expenses:* Tuition, state resident: full-time $7360; part-time $310 per credit. Required fees: $250 per semester. *Financial support:* In 2009–10, 6 fellowships were awarded; career-related internships or fieldwork, Federal Work-Study, institutionally sponsored loans, and tuition waivers (partial) also available. Support available to part-time students. Financial award application deadline: 3/1. *Faculty research:* Hazardous waste, asbestos, lead exposures, worker training, public employees. *Unit head:* Jack Caravanos, Director, 212-481-7569. *Application contact:* William Zlata, Director for Graduate Admissions, 212-772-4482, Fax: 212-650-3336, E-mail: admissions@hunter.cuny.edu.

Illinois Institute of Technology, Graduate College, College of Science and Letters, Department of Social Sciences, Chicago, IL 60616-3793. Offers nonprofit management (MPA); public administration (MPA); public safety and crisis management (MPA); JD/MPA; MBA/MPA. Part-time and evening/weekend programs available. *Faculty:* 10 full-time (2 women), 14 part-time/adjunct (2 women). *Students:* 69 full-time (31 women), 43 part-time (26 women); includes 15 minority (12 African Americans, 3 Hispanic Americans), 71 international. Average age 33. 160 applicants, 84% accepted, 66 enrolled. In 2009, 71 master's awarded. *Degree requirements:* For master's, comprehensive exam, capstone course (practicum). *Entrance requirements:* For master's, minimum undergraduate GPA of 3.0, 2 letters of recommendation. Additional exam requirements/recommendations for international students: Required—TOEFL (minimum score 523 paper-based; 70 iBT). *Application deadline:* For fall admission, 5/1 for domestic and international students; for spring admission, 10/15 for domestic and international students. Applications are processed on a rolling basis. Application fee: $50. Electronic applications accepted. *Expenses:* Tuition: Full-time $17,550; part-time $888 per credit hour. Required fees: $850; $7.50 per credit hour. One-time fee: $50 full-time. Full-time tuition and fees vary according to program. *Financial support:* Federal Work-Study, institutionally sponsored loans, scholarships/grants, and health care benefits available. Support available to part-time students. Financial award applicants required to submit FAFSA. *Faculty research:* Comparative public administration and policy, migration and ethnic politics, social dimension and impact of science and technology, urban politics, urban ethnography. *Unit head:* Dr. Patrick R. Ireland, Professor and Chairman, 312-567-5128, Fax: 312-567-6821, E-mail: socscience@iit.edu. *Application contact:* Lawerence Ruffolo, Assistant Director, Graduate Program in Public Administration, 312-906-5197, Fax: 312-906-5199, E-mail: lruffolo@kentlaw.edu.

Indiana State University, School of Graduate Studies, College of Nursing, Health and Human Services, Department of Health, Safety, and Environmental Health Sciences, Terre Haute, IN 47809. Offers community health promotion (MA, MS); health and safety education (MA, MS); occupational safety management (MA, MS). *Accreditation:* NCATE (one or more programs are accredited). *Degree requirements:* For master's, thesis or alternative. *Entrance requirements:* For master's, GRE General Test. Electronic applications accepted.

Indiana University of Pennsylvania, School of Graduate Studies and Research, College of Health and Human Services, Department of Safety Sciences, Program in Safety Sciences, Indiana, PA 15705-1087. Offers MS. Part-time programs available. *Faculty:* 3 full-time (1 woman). *Students:* 15 full-time (4 women), 64 part-time (15 women); includes 7 minority (3 African Americans, 1 American Indian/Alaska Native, 1 Asian American or Pacific Islander, 2 Hispanic Americans), 5 international. Average age 35. 92 applicants, 51% accepted, 37 enrolled. In 2009, 28 master's awarded. *Degree requirements:* For master's, thesis optional. *Entrance requirements:* For master's, 2 letters of recommendation. Additional exam requirements/recommendations for international students: Required—TOEFL. *Application deadline:* For fall admission, 7/1 priority date for domestic students; for spring admission, 11/1 for domestic students. Applications are processed on a rolling basis. Application fee: $40. *Expenses:* Tuition, state resident: full-time $6666; part-time $370 per credit hour. Tuition, nonresident: full-time $10,666; part-time $593 per credit hour. Required fees: $813 per semester. *Financial support:* In 2009–10, 1 fellowship (averaging $500 per year), 4 research assistantships with full and partial tuition reimbursements (averaging $5,565 per year) were awarded. Financial award application deadline: 3/15; financial award applicants required to submit FAFSA. *Unit head:* Dr. Chris Janicak, Graduate Coordinator, 724-357-3270. *Application contact:* Dr. Robert Soule, Graduate Coordinator, 724-357-3270, E-mail: bobsoule@iup.edu.

The Johns Hopkins University, Bloomberg School of Public Health, Department of Environmental Health Sciences, Baltimore, MD 21218-2699. Offers environmental health engineering (PhD); environmental health sciences (MHS, Dr PH); occupational and environmental health (PhD); occupational and environmental hygiene (MHS, MHS); physiology (PhD); toxicology (PhD). Postbaccalaureate distance learning degree programs offered (minimal on-campus study). *Faculty:* 71 full-time (27 women), 58 part-time/adjunct (26 women). *Students:* 65 full-time (43 women), 17 part-time (12 women); includes 22 minority (4 African Americans, 1 American Indian/Alaska Native, 13 Asian Americans or Pacific Islanders, 4 Hispanic Americans), 11 international. Average age 31. 101 applicants, 49% accepted, 31 enrolled. In 2009, 22 master's, 13 doctorates awarded. *Degree requirements:* For master's, essay, presentation; for doctorate, comprehensive exam, thesis/dissertation, 1 year full-time residency, oral and written exams. *Entrance requirements:* For master's, GRE General Test or MCAT, 3 letters of recommendation, transcripts; for doctorate, GRE General Test or MCAT, 3 letters of recommendation. Additional exam requirements/recommendations for international students: Required—TOEFL (minimum score 600 paper-based; 250 computer-based). *Application deadline:* For fall admission, 12/15 priority date for domestic and international students. Applications are processed on a rolling basis. Application fee: $45. Electronic applications accepted. *Financial support:* In 2009–10, 5 fellowships with full tuition reimbursements (averaging $26,500 per year) were awarded; Federal Work-Study, institutionally sponsored loans, scholarships/grants, traineeships, health care benefits, and stipends also available. Support available to part-time students. Financial award application deadline: 3/15; financial award applicants required to submit FAFSA. *Faculty research:* Chemical carcinogenesis/toxicology, lung disease, occupational and environmental health, nuclear imaging, molecular epidemiology. Total annual research expenditures: $23.7 million. *Unit head:* Dr. John Davis Groopman, Chair, 410-955-3720, Fax: 410-955-0617, E-mail: jgroopma@jhsph.edu. *Application contact:* Nina J. Kulacki, Academic Program Manager, 410-955-2212, Fax: 410-955-0617, E-mail: nkulacki@jhsph.edu.

Lewis University, College of Arts and Sciences, Program in Public Safety Administration, Romeoville, IL 60446. Offers MS. Part-time and evening/weekend programs available. *Faculty:* 3 full-time (0 women), 8 part-time/adjunct (1 woman). *Students:* 3 full-time (0 women), 84 part-time (19 women); includes 22 minority (13 African Americans, 9 Hispanic Americans), 1 international. Average age 35. In 2009, 33 master's awarded. *Entrance requirements:* For master's, bachelor's degree, 2 letters of recommendation. Additional exam requirements/recommendations for international students: Required—TOEFL (minimum score 500 paper-based; 213 computer-based). *Application deadline:* For fall admission, 5/1 priority date for international students; for spring admission, 11/15 priority date for international students. Applications are processed on a rolling basis. Application fee: $40. Electronic applications accepted. *Expenses:* Tuition: Full-time $6480; part-time $720 per credit. One-time fee: $40. Tuition and fees vary according to course load, degree level and program. *Financial support:* Application deadline: 5/1. *Unit head:* Dr. Calvin Edwards, Chair of Justice, Law and Public Safety Studies, 815-838-0500, Fax: 815-836-5870, E-mail: koloshsa@lewisu.edu. *Application contact:* Sarah Wiegman, Coordinator, 815-838-0500 Ext. 5686, Fax: 815-836-5870, E-mail: wiegmasa@lewisu.edu.

Loma Linda University, School of Public Health, Programs in Environmental and Occupational Health, Loma Linda, CA 92350. Offers MPH, MSPH. *Accreditation:* CEPH. *Entrance requirements:* Additional exam requirements/recommendations for international students: Required—Michigan English Language Assessment Battery or TOEFL. *Faculty research:* Human exposure to toxins, smog.

Loyola University Chicago, Graduate School, Marcella Niehoff School of Nursing, Population-Based Infection Control and Environmental Safety Program, Chicago, IL 60660. Offers population based infection control (MSN, Certificate). Part-time and evening/weekend programs available. *Students:* 17 part-time (all women); includes 2 minority (1 African American, 1 Asian American or Pacific Islander). Average age 42. 6 applicants, 67% accepted, 2 enrolled. In 2009, 1 master's awarded. *Entrance requirements:* For master's, Illinois nursing license, 3 letters of recommendation, minimum nursing GPA of 3.0, 1000 hours experience before starting clinical. Application fee: $50. *Expenses:* Tuition: Full-time $14,220; part-time $790 per credit hour. Required fees: $60 per semester hour. Tuition and fees vary according to program. *Financial support:* Traineeships available. *Unit head:* Dr. Ida Androwich, Professor, 708-216-9276, Fax: 708-216-9555, E-mail: iandrow@luc.edu. *Application contact:* Dr. Vicki A. Keough, Associate Dean, 773-508-3263, Fax: 773-508-3241, E-mail: vkeough@luc.edu.

McGill University, Faculty of Graduate and Postdoctoral Studies, Faculty of Medicine, Department of Epidemiology and Biostatistics, Montréal, QC H3A 2T5, Canada. Offers community health (M Sc); environmental health (M Sc); epidemiology and biostatistics (M Sc, PhD, Diploma); health care evaluation (M Sc); medical statistics (M Sc). *Accreditation:* CEPH (one or more programs are accredited).

McGill University, Faculty of Graduate and Postdoctoral Studies, Faculty of Medicine and Department of Epidemiology and Biostatistics, Department of Occupational Health, Montréal, QC H3A 2T5, Canada. Offers M Sc, PhD.

Medical College of Wisconsin, Medical School, Department of Preventive Medicine, Milwaukee, WI 53226-0509. Offers occupational health and medicine (MPH); public and community health (MPH). *Accreditation:* CEPH. Part-time programs available. Postbaccalaureate distance learning degree programs offered (no on-campus study). *Degree requirements:* For master's, project. *Entrance requirements:* For master's, MD/DO license to practice medicine in U.S. or Canada. Additional exam requirements/recommendations for international students: Required—TOEFL. *Faculty research:* Environmental medicine, ergonomics, epidemiology, surveillance, distance education.

Meharry Medical College, School of Graduate Studies, Division of Community Health Sciences, Nashville, TN 37208-9989. Offers occupational medicine (MSPH); public health administration (MSPH). *Accreditation:* CEPH. Part-time and evening/weekend programs available. *Degree requirements:* For master's, thesis, externship. *Entrance requirements:* For master's, GRE General Test, GMAT. *Expenses:* Contact institution. *Faculty research:* Policy and management, health care financing, health education and promotion.

Mississippi Valley State University, Department of Natural Science and Environmental Health, Program in Environmental Health, Itta Bena, MS 38941-1400. Offers MS. Evening/weekend programs available.

Montclair State University, The Graduate School, College of Science and Mathematics, Department of Earth and Environmental Studies, Montclair, NJ 07043-1624. Offers earth science (Certificate); environmental management (MA, D Env M); environmental studies (MS), including environmental education, environmental health, environmental management, environmental science; geographic information science (Certificate); geoscience (MS, Certificate), including geoscience (MS), water resource management (Certificate). Part-time and evening/weekend programs available. *Faculty:* 16 full-time (2 women), 13 part-time/adjunct (4 women). *Students:* 36 full-time (17 women), 60 part-time (26 women). Average age 34. 42 applicants, 60% accepted, 17 enrolled. In 2009, 11 degrees awarded. *Degree requirements:* For master's, comprehensive exam, thesis or alternative; for doctorate, thesis/dissertation. *Entrance requirements:* For master's, GRE General Test, 2 letters of recommendation; for doctorate, GRE General Test, 3 letters of recommendation. Additional exam requirements/recommendations for international students: Required—TOEFL (minimum score 83 computer-based), or IELTS. *Application deadline:* For fall admission, 6/1 for international students; for spring admission, 10/1 for international students. Applications are processed on a rolling basis. Application fee: $60. Electronic applications accepted. *Expenses:* Tuition, area resident: Part-time $486.74 per credit. Tuition, state resident: part-time $486.74 per credit. Tuition, nonresident: part-time $751.34 per credit. Tuition and fees vary according to degree level and program. *Financial support:* In 2009–10, 3 fellowships (averaging $15,000 per year), 12 research assistantships with full tuition reimbursements (averaging $8,500 per year), 11 teaching assistantships with full tuition reimbursements (averaging $15,000 per year) were awarded; Federal Work-Study, scholarships/grants, and unspecified assistantships also available. Support available to part-time students. Financial award application deadline: 3/1; financial award applicants required to submit FAFSA. *Faculty research:* Antarctica, carbon pools, contaminated sediments, wetlands. *Unit head:* Dr. Duke Ophori, Chairperson, 973-655-7558. *Application contact:* Amy Aiello, Director of Graduate Admissions and Operations, 973-655-5147, Fax: 973-655-7869, E-mail: graduate.school@montclair.edu.

Murray State University, College of Health Sciences and Human Services, Program in Occupational Safety and Health, Murray, KY 42071. Offers environmental science (MS); industrial hygiene (MS); safety management (MS). *Accreditation:* ABET. Part-time programs available. *Degree requirements:* For master's, comprehensive exam, thesis optional, professional internship. Electronic applications accepted. *Faculty research:* Light effects on plant growth, ergonomics, toxic effects of pets' pesticides, traffic safety.

New York Medical College, School of Health Sciences and Practice, Department of Environmental Health Science, Valhalla, NY 10595-1691. Offers environmental health science (MPH); industrial hygiene (Graduate Certificate). *Accreditation:* CEPH. Part-time and evening/weekend programs available. *Faculty:* 4 full-time, 9 part-time/adjunct. *Students:* 21 full-time, 32 part-time. 31 applicants, 74% accepted, 19 enrolled. In 2009, 10 master's awarded. *Degree requirements:* For master's, thesis. *Entrance requirements:* For master's, minimum undergraduate GPA of 3.0. Additional exam requirements/recommendations for international students: Required—TOEFL (minimum score 637 paper-based; 250 computer-based; 110 iBT), IELTS (minimum score 7). *Application deadline:* For fall admission, 8/1 priority date for domestic students, 5/15 for international students; for spring admission, 12/1 priority date for domestic students, 10/15 for international students. Applications are processed on a rolling basis. Application fee: $50 ($100 for international students). Electronic applications accepted. *Expenses:* Tuition: Full-time $18,170; part-time $790 per credit. Required fees: $790 per credit. $20 per semester. One-time fee: $100. Tuition and fees vary according to class time, course level, course load, degree level, program, student level and student's religious affiliation. *Financial*

support: Career-related internships or fieldwork, Federal Work-Study, institutionally sponsored loans, health care benefits, tuition waivers (partial), and tuition reimbursement available. Support available to part-time students. Financial award applicants required to submit FAFSA. *Unit head:* Dr. Diane E. Heck, Chair, 914-594-4804, Fax: 914-594-4292, E-mail: diane_heck@nymc.edu. *Application contact:* Pamela Suett, Director of Recruitment, 914-594-4510, Fax: 914-594-4292, E-mail: shsp_admissions@nymc.edu.

New York University, Graduate School of Arts and Science, Department of Environmental Medicine, New York, NY 10012-1019. Offers environmental health sciences (MS, PhD), including biostatistics (PhD), environmental hygiene (MS), epidemiology (PhD), ergonomics and biomechanics (PhD), exposure assessment and health effects (PhD), molecular toxicology/carcinogenesis (PhD), toxicology. Part-time programs available. *Faculty:* 26 full-time (7 women). *Students:* 45 full-time (37 women), 15 part-time (8 women); includes 9 minority (3 African Americans, 3 Asian Americans or Pacific Islanders, 3 Hispanic Americans), 23 international. Average age 31. 60 applicants, 48% accepted, 14 enrolled. In 2009, 11 master's, 10 doctorates awarded. Terminal master's awarded for partial completion of doctoral program. *Degree requirements:* For master's, thesis or alternative; for doctorate, one foreign language, thesis/dissertation, oral and written exams. *Entrance requirements:* For master's and doctorate, GRE General Test, GRE Subject Test, minimum GPA of 3.0; bachelor's degree in biological, physical, or engineering science. Additional exam requirements/recommendations for international students: Required—TOEFL. *Application deadline:* For fall admission, 12/12 for domestic students. Application fee: $90. *Expenses:* Tuition: Full-time $30,528; part-time $1272 per credit. Required fees: $2177. *Financial support:* Fellowships with tuition reimbursements, teaching assistantships with tuition reimbursements, career-related internships or fieldwork, Federal Work-Study, institutionally sponsored loans, and health care benefits available. Financial award application deadline: 12/12; financial award applicants required to submit FAFSA. *Unit head:* Dr. Max Costa, Chair, 845-731-3661, Fax: 845-351-4510, E-mail: ehs@env.med.nyu.edu. *Application contact:* Dr. Jerome J. Solomon, Director of Graduate Studies, 845-731-3661, Fax: 845-351-4510, E-mail: ehs@env.med.nyu.edu.

North Carolina Agricultural and Technical State University, Graduate School, School of Technology, Department of Construction Management and Occupational Safety and Health, Greensboro, NC 27411. Offers construction management (MSIT); occupational safety and health (MSIT).

Oakland University, Graduate Study and Lifelong Learning, School of Health Sciences, Program in Safety Management, Rochester, MI 48309-4401. Offers MS.

OGI School of Science & Engineering at Oregon Health & Science University, Graduate Studies, Department of Environmental and Biomolecular Systems, Beaverton, OR 97006-8921. Offers biochemistry and molecular biology (MS, PhD); environmental health systems (MS); environmental information technology (MS, PhD); environmental science and engineering (MS, PhD). Part-time programs available. Terminal master's awarded for partial completion of doctoral program. *Degree requirements:* For master's, thesis optional; for doctorate, comprehensive exam, oral defense of dissertation. *Entrance requirements:* For master's and doctorate, GRE General Test. Additional exam requirements/recommendations for international students: Required—TOEFL. Electronic applications accepted. *Faculty research:* Air and water science, hydrogeology, estuarine and coastal modeling, environmental microbiology, contaminant transport, biochemistry, biomolecular systems.

Old Dominion University, College of Health Sciences, Program in Community Health and Environmental Health, Norfolk, VA 23529. Offers environmental health (MS). Part-time and evening/weekend programs available. Postbaccalaureate distance learning degree programs offered (no on-campus study). *Faculty:* 7 full-time (4 women), 6 part-time/adjunct (3 women). *Students:* 3 full-time (1 woman), 13 part-time (8 women); includes 6 minority (5 African Americans, 1 Asian American or Pacific Islander), 1 international. Average age 29. 32 applicants, 47% accepted, 9 enrolled. In 2009, 10 master's awarded. *Degree requirements:* For master's, comprehensive exam, oral exam, written exam, practicum or thesis. *Entrance requirements:* For master's, GRE General Test, minimum GPA of 2.75. Additional exam requirements/recommendations for international students: Required—TOEFL (minimum score 650 paper-based; 278 computer-based). *Application deadline:* For fall admission, 8/1 priority date for domestic students, 7/1 priority date for international students; for winter admission, 11/1 priority date for domestic students, 10/1 priority date for international students; for spring admission, 4/1 priority date for domestic students, 3/1 priority date for international students. Applications are processed on a rolling basis. Application fee: $50. Electronic applications accepted. *Expenses:* Tuition, state resident: full-time $8112; part-time $338 per credit. Tuition, nonresident: full-time $20,256; part-time $844 per credit. Required fees: $119 per semester. One-time fee: $50. *Financial support:* In 2009–10, 5 research assistantships with tuition reimbursements (averaging $14,000 per year) were awarded; career-related internships or fieldwork, institutionally sponsored loans, scholarships/grants, and tuition waivers (partial) also available. Financial award applicants required to submit FAFSA. *Faculty research:* Toxicology, domestic violence, health policy and planning, environmental hazards, obesity, substance abuse, minority health spirituality, women's health. Total annual research expenditures: $150,133. *Unit head:* A. James English, Graduate Program Director, 757-683-6010, Fax: 757-683-4410, E-mail: chpgpd@odu.edu. *Application contact:* A. James English, Graduate Program Director, 757-683-6010, Fax: 757-683-4410, E-mail: chpgpd@odu.edu.

Old Dominion University, College of Health Sciences, Program in Public Health, Norfolk, VA 23529. Offers environmental health (MPH); health promotion (MPH). *Accreditation:* CEPH. Part-time and evening/weekend programs available. *Faculty:* 7 full-time (4 women), 6 part-time/adjunct (3 women). *Students:* 26 full-time (21 women), 20 part-time (15 women); includes 24 minority (18 African Americans, 4 Asian Americans or Pacific Islanders, 2 Hispanic Americans), 1 international. Average age 29. 67 applicants, 60% accepted, 30 enrolled. In 2009, 16 master's awarded. *Degree requirements:* For master's, field practicum, capstone project. *Entrance requirements:* For master's, GRE, MCAT, minimum GPA of 2.75. Additional exam requirements/recommendations for international students: Required—TOEFL (minimum score 650 paper-based; 278 computer-based). *Application deadline:* For fall admission, 5/31 priority date for domestic students, 4/30 for international students. Application fee: $50 ($100 for international students). Electronic applications accepted. *Expenses:* Tuition, state resident: full-time $8112; part-time $338 per credit. Tuition, nonresident: full-time $20,256; part-time $844 per credit. Required fees: $119 per semester. One-time fee: $50. *Financial support:* Career-related internships or fieldwork, institutionally sponsored loans, and scholarships/grants available. Financial award application deadline: 5/1; financial award applicants required to submit FAFSA. *Faculty research:* Community-based health research, public health research in environmental health and health promotion. Total annual research expenditures: $150,133. *Unit head:* A. James English, Associate Director, 757-683-6010, Fax: 757-446-6121, E-mail: jenglish@odu.edu. *Application contact:* A. James English, Associate Director, 757-683-6010, Fax: 757-446-6121, E-mail: jenglish@odu.edu.

Oregon State University, Graduate School, College of Health and Human Sciences, Department of Public Health, Program in Environmental Health and Occupational Safety Management, Corvallis, OR 97331. Offers MAIS, MS. *Degree requirements:* For master's, thesis. *Entrance requirements:* For master's, GRE General Test, minimum GPA of 3.0 in last 90 hours. Additional exam requirements/recommendations for international students: Required—TOEFL. *Application deadline:* For fall admission, 3/1 for domestic students. Applications are processed on a rolling basis. Application fee: $50. *Expenses:* Tuition, state resident: full-time $9774; part-time $362 per credit. Tuition, nonresident: full-time $15,849; part-time $587 per credit. Required fees: $1639. Full-time tuition and fees vary according to course load and program. *Financial support:* Research assistantships, teaching assistantships, career-related internships or fieldwork, Federal Work-Study, and institutionally sponsored loans available. Support available to part-time students. Financial award application deadline: 2/1. *Unit head:* Dr. Cathy Neumann, Coordinator, 541-737-3833, Fax: 541-737-4001, E-mail: cathy.neumann@orst.edu. *Application contact:* Anna Harding, Graduate Coordinator, 541-737-3890, Fax: 541-737-4001, E-mail: anna.harding@oregonstate.edu.

Saint Joseph's University, College of Arts and Sciences, Programs in Environmental Protection and Safety Management, Philadelphia, PA 19131-1395. Offers environmental protection and safety management (MS, Post-Master's Certificate). Part-time and evening/weekend programs available. *Students:* 16 part-time (6 women). Average age 35. In 2009, 10 master's awarded. *Entrance requirements:* For master's, GRE (if GPA less than 2.75), minimum GPA of 2.75, 2 letters of recommendation, resume. Additional exam requirements/recommendations for international students: Required—TOEFL (minimum score 550 paper-based; 213 computer-based; 79 iBT). *Application deadline:* For fall admission, 7/15 priority date for domestic students; 4/15 for international students; for winter admission, 1/15 for international students; for spring admission, 11/15 priority date for domestic students, 10/15 for international students. Applications are processed on a rolling basis. Application fee: $35. Electronic applications accepted. *Expenses:* Tuition: Part-time $729 per credit hour. Tuition and fees vary according to degree level and program. *Financial support:* Applicants required to submit FAFSA. *Unit head:* Patricia Griffin, Director, 610-660-1294, E-mail: pgriffin@sju.edu. *Application contact:* Kate McConnell, Director, Graduate College of Arts and Sciences Admissions and Retention, 610-660-3184, Fax: 610-660-3230, E-mail: kate.mcconnell@sju.edu.

Saint Joseph's University, College of Arts and Sciences, Programs in Public Safety and Management, Philadelphia, PA 19131-1395. Offers homeland security (MS, Certificate); public safety management (MS, Certificate). Part-time and evening/weekend programs available. *Students:* 64 part-time (3 women); includes 14 minority (10 African Americans, 2 Asian Americans or Pacific Islanders, 2 Hispanic Americans). Average age 40. In 2009, 18 master's awarded. *Entrance requirements:* For master's, GRE (if GPA less than 2.75), minimum GPA of 2.75, 2 letters of recommendation, resume. Additional exam requirements/recommendations for international students: Required—TOEFL (minimum score 550 paper-based; 213 computer-based; 79 iBT). *Application deadline:* For fall admission, 7/15 priority date for domestic students, 4/15 for international students; for winter admission, 1/15 for international students; for spring admission, 11/15 priority date for domestic students, 10/15 for international students. Applications are processed on a rolling basis. Application fee: $35. Electronic applications accepted. *Expenses:* Tuition: Part-time $729 per credit hour. Tuition and fees vary according to degree level and program. *Financial support:* Applicants required to submit FAFSA. *Unit head:* Patricia Griffin, Director, 610-660-1294, E-mail: pgriffin@sju.edu. *Application contact:* Kate McConnell, Assistant Director of Graduate Admissions, 610-660-3184, Fax: 610-660-3230, E-mail: kate.mcconnell@sju.edu.

Saint Mary's University of Minnesota, Schools of Graduate and Professional Programs, Graduate School of Business and Technology, Public Safety Administration Program, Winona, MN 55987-1399. Offers MA. *Unit head:* Lora Setter, Director, 612-238-4547, E-mail: llsetter@smumn.edu. *Application contact:* Yasin Alsaidi, Director of Admissions for Graduate and Professional Programs, 612-728-5207, Fax: 612-728-5121, E-mail: yalsaidi@smumn.edu.

San Diego State University, Graduate and Research Affairs, College of Health and Human Services, Graduate School of Public Health, San Diego, CA 92182. Offers environmental health (MPH); epidemiology (MPH, PhD), including biostatistics (MPH); global emergency preparedness and response (MS); global health (PhD); health behavior (PhD); health promotion (MPH); health services administration (MPH); toxicology (MS); MPH/MA; MSW/MPH. *Accreditation:* ABET (one or more programs are accredited); CAHME (one or more programs are accredited); CEPH (one or more programs are accredited). Part-time programs available. *Degree requirements:* For master's, comprehensive exam (for some programs), thesis (for some programs); for doctorate, thesis/dissertation. *Entrance requirements:* For master's, GMAT (MPH in health services administration), GRE General Test; for doctorate, GRE General Test. Additional exam requirements/recommendations for international students: Required—TOEFL. *Faculty research:* Evaluation of tobacco, AIDS prevalence and prevention, mammography, infant death project, Alzheimer's in elderly Chinese.

Stony Brook University, State University of New York, School of Professional Development, Stony Brook, NY 11794. Offers biology-grade 7-12 (MAT); chemistry-grade 7-12 (MAT); coaching (Graduate Certificate); computer integrated engineering (Graduate Certificate); earth science-grade 7-12 (MAT); educational computing (Graduate Certificate); educational leadership (Advanced Certificate); English-grade 7-12 (MAT); environmental management (Graduate Certificate); environmental/occupational health and safety (Graduate Certificate); French-grade 7-12 (MAT); German-grade 7-12 (MAT); human resource management (Graduate Certificate); information systems management (Graduate Certificate); Italian-grade 7-12 (MAT); liberal studies (MA); mathematics-grade 7-12 (MAT); operation research (Graduate Certificate); physics-grade 7-12 (MAT); school administration and supervision (Graduate Certificate); school building leadership (Graduate Certificate); school district administration (Graduate Certificate); school district business leadership (Advanced Certificate); school district leadership (Graduate Certificate); social science and the professions (MPS), including environmental waste management, human resource management; social studies-grade 7-12 (MAT); Spanish-grade 7-12 (MAT); waste management (Graduate Certificate). Part-time and evening/weekend programs available. Postbaccalaureate distance learning degree programs offered. *Faculty:* 5 full-time (3 women), 131 part-time/adjunct (53 women). *Students:* 317 full-time (187 women), 1,200 part-time (773 women); includes 187 minority (77 African Americans, 2 American Indian/Alaska Native, 22 Asian Americans or Pacific Islanders, 86 Hispanic Americans), 11 international. Average age 28. In 2009, 597 master's, 234 other advanced degrees awarded. *Degree requirements:* For master's, one foreign language, thesis or alternative. *Application deadline:* Applications are processed on a rolling basis. Application fee: $62. *Expenses:* Tuition, state resident: full-time $8370; part-time $349 per credit. Tuition, nonresident: full-time $13,250; part-time $552 per credit. Required fees: $933. *Financial support:* Fellowships, research assistantships, teaching assistantships, career-related internships or fieldwork available. Support available to part-time students. *Unit head:* Dr. Paul J. Edelson, Dean, 631-632-7052, Fax: 631-632-9046, E-mail: paul.edelson@stonybrook.edu. *Application contact:* Dr. Paul J. Edelson, Dean, 631-632-7052, Fax: 631-632-9046, E-mail: paul.edelson@stonybrook.edu.

Temple University, Health Sciences Center and Graduate School, College of Health Professions, Department of Public Health, Program in Environmental Health, Philadelphia, PA 19122-6096. Offers MS. Part-time and evening/weekend programs available. *Entrance requirements:* For master's, GRE General Test. Additional exam requirements/recommendations for international students: Required—TOEFL (minimum score 550 paper-based; 213 computer-based; 79 iBT). Electronic applications accepted. *Faculty research:* Air pollution, industrial hygiene, exposure assessment, nonionizing radiation.

Texas A&M Health Science Center, School of Rural Public Health, College Station, TX 77840. Offers environmental/occupational health (MPH); epidemiology/biostatistics (MPH); health policy/management (MPH); social and behavioral health (MPH). *Accreditation:* CEPH. Part-time programs available. Postbaccalaureate distance learning degree programs offered (no on-campus study). *Degree requirements:* For master's, thesis optional. *Entrance requirements:* For master's, GRE General Test, minimum undergraduate GPA of 3.0. Electronic applications accepted. *Faculty research:* Tobacco cessation, youth health risk.

Towson University, College of Graduate Studies and Research, Program in Occupational Science, Towson, MD 21252-0001. Offers Sc D. Part-time and evening/weekend programs available. *Degree requirements:* For doctorate, thesis/dissertation, comprehensive assessment. *Entrance requirements:* For doctorate, GRE or MAT, NBCOT certification, minimum GPA of 3.25. Additional exam requirements/recommendations for international students: Required—TOEFL (minimum score 600 paper-based; 250 computer-based). Electronic applications accepted. *Faculty research:* Successful aging, family quality of life, community living and individuals with mental illness.

Tufts University, School of Engineering, Department of Civil and Environmental Engineering, Medford, MA 02155. Offers civil engineering (ME, MS, PhD), including geotechnical engineering, structural engineering; environmental engineering (ME, MS, PhD), including environmental engineering and environmental sciences, environmental geotechnology, environmental health, environmental science and management, hazardous materials management, water resources engineering. Part-time programs available. *Faculty:* 17 full-time, 7 part-time/adjunct. *Students:*

Environmental and Occupational Health

Tufts University (continued)
72 (33 women); includes 6 minority (2 African Americans, 4 Asian Americans or Pacific Islanders), 17 international. Average age 27. 170 applicants, 59% accepted, 20 enrolled. In 2009, 17 master's, 3 doctorates awarded. Terminal master's awarded for partial completion of doctoral program. *Degree requirements:* For master's, thesis or alternative; for doctorate, thesis/dissertation. *Entrance requirements:* For master's and doctorate, GRE General Test. Additional exam requirements/recommendations for international students: Required—TOEFL (minimum score 550 paper-based; 213 computer-based; 80 iBT). *Application deadline:* For fall admission, 1/15 priority date for domestic students, 12/15 for international students; for spring admission, 10/15 for domestic students, 9/15 for international students. Applications are processed on a rolling basis. Application fee: $75. Electronic applications accepted. *Expenses:* Tuition: Full-time $38,096; part-time $3962 per credit. Required fees: $686; $40 per year. Tuition and fees vary according to course level, course load, degree level, program and student level. *Financial support:* Fellowships with full tuition reimbursements, research assistantships with full and partial tuition reimbursements, teaching assistantships with full and partial tuition reimbursements, Federal Work-Study, scholarships/grants, tuition waivers (partial), and unspecified assistantships available. Financial award application deadline: 1/15; financial award applicants required to submit FAFSA. *Unit head:* Dr. Kurt Penell, Chair, 617-627-3211, Fax: 617-627-3994. *Application contact:* Laura Sacco, Information Contact, 617-627-3211.

TUI University, College of Health Sciences, Program in Health Sciences, Cypress, CA 90630. Offers clinical research administration (MS, Certificate); emergency and disaster management (MS, Certificate); environmental health science (Certificate); health care administration (PhD); health care management (MS), including health informatics; health education (MS, Certificate); health informatics (Certificate); health sciences (PhD); international health (MS); international health: educator or researcher option (PhD); international health: practitioner option (PhD); law and expert witness studies (MS, Certificate); public health (MS); quality assurance (Certificate). Part-time and evening/weekend programs available. Postbaccalaureate distance learning degree programs offered (no on-campus study). *Degree requirements:* For doctorate, comprehensive exam, thesis/dissertation, defense of dissertation. *Entrance requirements:* For master's, minimum GPA of 2.5 (students with GPA 3.0 or greater may transfer up to 30% of graduate level credits); for doctorate, minimum GPA of 3.4, curriculum vitae, course work in research methods or statistics. Additional exam requirements/recommendations for international students: Required—TOEFL. Electronic applications accepted.

Tulane University, School of Public Health and Tropical Medicine, Department of Environmental Health Sciences, New Orleans, LA 70118-5669. Offers MPH, MSPH, Dr PH, PhD, JD/MSPH. *Accreditation:* ABET (one or more programs are accredited); CEPH (one or more programs are accredited). *Degree requirements:* For doctorate, comprehensive exam, thesis/dissertation. *Entrance requirements:* For master's and doctorate, GRE General Test. Additional exam requirements/recommendations for international students: Required—TOEFL. Electronic applications accepted.

Uniformed Services University of the Health Sciences, School of Medicine, Graduate Programs in the Biomedical Sciences and Public Health, Bethesda, MD 20814. Offers emerging infectious diseases (PhD); medical and clinical psychology (PhD), including clinical psychology, medical and clinical psychology (clinical/dual track), medical and clinical psychology (research track); molecular and cell biology (PhD); neuroscience (PhD); preventive medicine and biometrics (MPH, MSPH, MTMH, Dr PH, PhD), including environmental health science (PhD), medical zoology (PhD), public health (MPH, MSPH, Dr PH), tropical medicine and hygiene (MTMH). *Faculty:* 372 full-time (119 women), 4,044 part-time/adjunct (908 women). *Students:* 176 full-time (96 women); includes 31 minority (6 African Americans, 4 American Indian/Alaska Native, 14 Asian Americans or Pacific Islanders, 7 Hispanic Americans), 11 international. Average age 28. 278 applicants, 20% accepted, 47 enrolled. In 2009, 36 master's, 17 doctorates awarded. Terminal master's awarded for partial completion of doctoral program. *Degree requirements:* For master's, comprehensive exam, thesis or alternative; for doctorate, comprehensive exam, thesis/dissertation, qualifying exam. *Entrance requirements:* For master's, GRE General Test; for doctorate, GRE General Test, minimum GPA of 3.0. Additional exam requirements/recommendations for international students: Required—TOEFL. *Application deadline:* For fall admission, 1/15 priority date for domestic and international students. Applications are processed on a rolling basis. Application fee: $0. Electronic applications accepted. *Financial support:* In 2009–10, fellowships with full tuition reimbursements (averaging $26,000 per year), research assistantships with full tuition reimbursements (averaging $26,000 per year) were awarded; career-related internships or fieldwork, scholarships/grants, health care benefits, and tuition waivers (full) also available. *Unit head:* Dr. Eleanor S. Metcalf, Associate Dean, 301-295-1104, E-mail: emetcalf@usuhs.mil. *Application contact:* Elena Marina Sherman, Graduate Program Coordinator, 301-295-3913, Fax: 301-295-6772, E-mail: elena.sherman@usuhs.mil.

Uniformed Services University of the Health Sciences, School of Medicine, Graduate Programs in the Biomedical Sciences and Public Health, Department of Preventive Medicine and Biometrics, Program in Environmental Health Science, Bethesda, MD 20814-4799. Offers PhD. *Accreditation:* CEPH. *Faculty:* 43 full-time (14 women), 143 part-time/adjunct (25 women). *Students:* 2 full-time (0 women); includes 1 minority (Hispanic American). Average age 30. 1 applicant, 0% accepted. In 2009, 2 doctorates awarded. *Degree requirements:* For doctorate, comprehensive exam, thesis/dissertation, qualifying exam. *Entrance requirements:* For doctorate, GRE, minimum GPA of 3.0. Additional exam requirements/recommendations for international students: Required—TOEFL. *Application deadline:* For fall admission, 1/15 priority date for domestic students. Applications are processed on a rolling basis. Application fee: $0. *Financial support:* In 2009–10, fellowships with full tuition reimbursements (averaging $26,000 per year); tuition waivers (full) also available. *Unit head:* Dr. David Cruess, Graduate Program Director, 301-295-3465, Fax: 301-295-1933, E-mail: dcruess@usuhs.mil. *Application contact:* Elena Marina Sherman, Graduate Program Coordinator, 301-295-3913, Fax: 301-295-6772, E-mail: elena.sherman@usuhs.mil.

Universidad Autonoma de Guadalajara, Graduate Programs, Guadalajara, Mexico. Offers administrative law and justice (LL M); advertising and corporate communications (MA); architecture (M Arch); business (MBA); computational science (MCC); education (Ed M, Ed D); English-Spanish translation (MA); fiscal law (MA); integrated management of digital animation (MA); international business (MIB); international corporate law (LL M); internet technologies (MS); labor health (MS); manufacturing systems (MMS); philosophy (MA, PhD); power electronics (MS); quality systems (MQS); renewable energy (MS); social evaluation of projects (MBA); strategic market research (MBA); teaching mathematics (MA).

Universidad de Ciencias Medicas, Graduate Programs, San Jose, Costa Rica. Offers dermatology (SP); family health (MS); health service center administration (MHA); human anatomy (MS); medical and surgery (MD); occupational medicine (MS); pharmacy (Pharm D). Part-time programs available. *Degree requirements:* For master's, thesis; for first professional degree and SP, comprehensive exam. *Entrance requirements:* For first professional degree, admissions test; for master's, MD or bachelors degree; for SP, admissions test, MD degree.

Université de Montréal, Faculty of Medicine, Department of Environmental and Occupational Health, Montréal, QC H3C 3J7, Canada. Offers M Sc. *Accreditation:* CEPH. *Faculty:* 14 full-time (5 women), 14 part-time/adjunct (5 women). *Students:* 41 full-time (21 women), 70 part-time (50 women). 55 applicants, 53% accepted, 28 enrolled. In 2009, 20 master's awarded. *Degree requirements:* For master's, thesis. *Entrance requirements:* For master's, proficiency in French, knowledge of English. *Application deadline:* For fall admission, 2/1 priority date for domestic students; for winter admission, 11/1 priority date for domestic students; for spring admission, 2/1 priority date for domestic students. Applications are processed on a rolling basis. Application fee: $100. Electronic applications accepted. *Faculty research:* Metabolism of chemical substances, toxicity, biological surveillance, risk analysis. Total annual research expenditures: $590,120. *Unit head:* Andre Dufresne, Director, 514-343-6134, Fax: 514-343-2200, E-mail: andre.dufesne@umontreal.ca. *Application contact:* Adolf Vyskocil, Program Director, 514-343-6146, Fax: 514-343-2200, E-mail: adolf.vyskocil@umontreal.ca.

Université du Québec à Montréal, Graduate Programs, Program in Ergonomics in Occupational Health and Safety, Montréal, QC H3C 3P8, Canada. Offers Diploma. Part-time programs available. *Entrance requirements:* For degree, appropriate bachelor's degree or equivalent, proficiency in French.

Université Laval, Faculty of Medicine, Graduate Programs in Medicine, Department of Social and Preventive Medicine, Program in Accident Prevention and Occupational Health and Safety Management, Québec, QC G1K 7P4, Canada. Offers Diploma. Part-time programs available. *Entrance requirements:* For degree, knowledge of French. Electronic applications accepted.

University at Albany, State University of New York, School of Public Health, Department of Environmental Health Sciences, Albany, NY 12222-0001. Offers environmental and analytical chemistry (MS, PhD); environmental and occupational health (MS, PhD); toxicology (MS, PhD). *Degree requirements:* For master's, thesis; for doctorate, comprehensive exam, thesis/dissertation. *Entrance requirements:* For master's and doctorate, GRE General Test, GRE Subject Test, 3 letters of reference. Additional exam requirements/recommendations for international students: Required—TOEFL (minimum score 600 paper-based; 213 computer-based). Electronic applications accepted. *Faculty research:* Xenobiotic metabolism, neurotoxicity of halogenated hydrocarbons, pharmac/toxicogenomics, environmental analytical chemistry.

The University of Alabama at Birmingham, School of Public Health, Program in Environmental Health Sciences, Birmingham, AL 35294. Offers PhD. *Degree requirements:* For doctorate, thesis/dissertation. *Entrance requirements:* For doctorate, GRE General Test. Additional exam requirements/recommendations for international students: Required—TOEFL. Electronic applications accepted. *Faculty research:* Aquatic toxicology, virology.

University of Alberta, School of Public Health, Department of Public Health Sciences, Edmonton, AB T6G 2E1, Canada. Offers clinical epidemiology (M Sc, MPH); environmental and occupational health (MPH); environmental health sciences (M Sc); epidemiology (M Sc); global health (M Sc, MPH); health policy and management (MPH); health policy research (M Sc); health technology assessment (MPH); occupational health (M Sc); population health (M Sc); public health leadership (MPH); public health sciences (PhD); quantitative methods (MPH). *Accreditation:* CEPH (one or more programs are accredited). *Faculty:* 24 full-time (5 women), 59 part-time/adjunct (13 women). *Students:* 49 full-time, 49 part-time. 81 applicants, 31% accepted. In 2009, 28 master's awarded. Terminal master's awarded for partial completion of doctoral program. *Degree requirements:* For master's, thesis (for some programs); for doctorate, thesis/dissertation. *Entrance requirements:* For master's, GMAT or GRE General Test. Additional exam requirements/recommendations for international students: Required—TOEFL (minimum score 550 paper-based; 213 computer-based) or IELTS (minimum score 6). *Application deadline:* For fall admission, 3/15 for domestic students, 7/1 for international students; for winter admission, 11/1 for international students; for spring admission, 3/1 for international students. Applications are processed on a rolling basis. Application fee: $0. Electronic applications accepted. Tuition and fees charges are reported in Canadian dollars. *Expenses:* Tuition, area resident: Full-time $4626 Canadian dollars; part-time $99.72 Canadian dollars per unit. International tuition: $8216 Canadian dollars full-time. Required fees: $3590 Canadian dollars; $99.72 Canadian dollars per unit. $215 Canadian dollars per term. *Financial support:* In 2009–10, 11 students received support, including 6 research assistantships with tuition reimbursements available (averaging $2,200 per year); fellowships, teaching assistantships, career-related internships or fieldwork and tuition waivers (partial) also available. Financial award application deadline: 2/1. *Faculty research:* Biostatistics, health promotion and sociobehavioral health science. Total annual research expenditures: $5.7 million. *Unit head:* L. Duncan Saunders, Acting Chair, 780-492-6814, Fax: 780-492-0364. *Application contact:* Felicity R. Hey, Graduate Programs Administrator, 780-492-6407, Fax: 780-492-0364, E-mail: felicity.hey@ualberta.ca.

University of Arkansas for Medical Sciences, Graduate School, Occupational and Environmental Health Program, Little Rock, AR 72205-7199. Offers MS, Certificate. Offered jointly with the University of Arkansas at Little Rock and the National Center for Toxicological Research. *Accreditation:* CEPH. *Faculty:* 6 full-time (1 woman), 13 part-time/adjunct (3 women). *Students:* 3 part-time. In 2009, 2 master's awarded. *Degree requirements:* For master's, thesis or alternative. *Entrance requirements:* For master's, GRE General Test. Additional exam requirements/recommendations for international students: Required—TOEFL. *Application deadline:* Applications are processed on a rolling basis. Application fee: $0. *Financial support:* Fellowships available. Support available to part-time students. *Unit head:* Dr. Jay Gandy, Chair and Program Director, 501-686-5239, E-mail: jgandy@uams.edu. *Application contact:* Dr. Jay Gandy, Chair and Program Director, 501-686-5239, E-mail: jgandy@uams.edu.

The University of British Columbia, School of Environmental Health, Vancouver, BC V6T 1Z1, Canada. Offers M Sc, PhD. Part-time programs available. *Degree requirements:* For master's, comprehensive exam (for some programs), thesis optional; for doctorate, comprehensive exam, thesis/dissertation. *Entrance requirements:* For master's and doctorate, GRE. Additional exam requirements/recommendations for international students: Required—TOEFL (minimum score 600 paper-based; 250 computer-based; 100 iBT); Recommended—TWE. Electronic applications accepted. *Faculty research:* Acoustics, exposure assessment and epidemiology, occupational and environmental respiratory disease, occupational and environmental policy.

University of California, Berkeley, Graduate Division, School of Public Health, Group in Environmental Health Sciences, Berkeley, CA 94720-1500. Offers MPH, MS, Dr PH, PhD. *Students:* 35 full-time (22 women). Average age 31. 29 applicants, 7 enrolled. In 2009, 6 master's, 2 doctorates awarded. *Degree requirements:* For master's, comprehensive exam (MPH), project or thesis (MS); for doctorate, thesis/dissertation, departmental and qualifying exams. *Entrance requirements:* For master's, GRE General Test, minimum GPA of 3.0; previous course work in biology, calculus, and chemistry; 3 letters of recommendation; for doctorate, GRE General Test, master's degree in relevant scientific discipline or engineering; minimum GPA of 3.0; previous course work in biology, calculus, and chemistry; 3 letters of recommendation. Additional exam requirements/recommendations for international students: Required—TOEFL. *Application deadline:* For fall admission, 12/1 for domestic students. Applications are processed on a rolling basis. Application fee: $70 ($90 for international students). *Financial support:* Fellowships, research assistantships, teaching assistantships, unspecified assistantships available. *Faculty research:* Toxicology, industrial hygiene, exposure assessment, risk assessment, ergonomics. *Unit head:* Prof. Katharine Hammond, Chair, 510-643-5160, E-mail: ehs_div@berkeley.edu. *Application contact:* Norma Firestone, Graduate Assistant for Admission, 510-643-0881, Fax: 510-642-5815, E-mail: sphinfo@berkeley.edu.

University of California, Los Angeles, Graduate Division, School of Public Health, Department of Environmental Health Sciences, Los Angeles, CA 90095. Offers environmental health sciences (MS, PhD); environmental science and engineering (D Env); molecular toxicology (PhD); JD/MPH. *Accreditation:* ABET (one or more programs are accredited). *Degree requirements:* For master's, comprehensive exam or thesis; for doctorate, thesis/dissertation, oral and written qualifying exams. *Entrance requirements:* For master's, GRE General Test, minimum GPA of 3.0; for doctorate, GRE General Test, minimum undergraduate GPA of 3.0. Electronic applications accepted.

University of Central Missouri, The Graduate School, College of Health and Human Services, Warrensburg, MO 64093. Offers criminal justice (MS); industrial hygiene (MS); occupational safety management (MS); physical education/exercise and sport science (MS); rural family nursing (MS); social gerontology (MS); sociology (MA); speech language pathology and audiology (MS). *Accreditation:* NCATE. Part-time programs available. Postbaccalaureate distance learning degree programs offered. *Faculty:* 53. *Students:* 169 full-time (107 women), 364 part-time (210 women); includes 65 minority (46 African Americans, 1 American Indian/Alaska Native, 5 Asian Americans or Pacific Islanders, 13 Hispanic Americans), 27 international. Average age 32. 236 applicants, 92% accepted, 211 enrolled. In 2009, 153 master's awarded. *Entrance requirements:* Additional exam requirements/recommendations for international students: Required—TOEFL (minimum score 550 paper-based; 79 computer-based). *Application deadline:* For fall admission, 6/1 priority date for domestic students, 5/1 for international

students; for spring admission, 10/1 priority date for domestic students, 10/1 for international students. Applications are processed on a rolling basis. Application fee: $30 ($75 for international students). Electronic applications accepted. *Expenses:* Tuition, area resident: Part-time $245.80 per credit hour. Tuition, nonresident: part-time $491.60 per credit hour. Required fees: $24.20 per credit hour. Full-time tuition and fees vary according to course load, degree level, campus/location and reciprocity agreements. *Financial support:* Research assistantships with full and partial tuition reimbursements, teaching assistantships with full and partial tuition reimbursements, career-related internships or fieldwork, Federal Work-Study, scholarships/grants, and administrative and laboratory assistantships available. Support available to part-time students. Financial award application deadline: 3/1; financial award applicants required to submit FAFSA. *Unit head:* Dr. Rick Sluder, Dean, 660-543-4245, Fax: 660-543-4167, E-mail: sluder@ucmo.edu. *Application contact:* Laurie Delap, Admissions Coordinator, 660-543-4621, Fax: 660-543-4778, E-mail: gradinfo@ucmo.edu.

University of Cincinnati, Graduate School, College of Medicine, Graduate Programs in Biomedical Sciences, Department of Environmental Health, Cincinnati, OH 45221. Offers environmental and industrial hygiene (MS, PhD); environmental and occupational medicine (MS); environmental genetics and molecular toxicology (MS, PhD); epidemiology and biostatistics (MS, PhD); occupational safety and ergonomics (MS, PhD). *Accreditation:* ABET (one or more programs are accredited). Terminal master's awarded for partial completion of doctoral program. *Degree requirements:* For master's, thesis; for doctorate, thesis/dissertation, qualifying exam. *Entrance requirements:* For master's, GRE General Test, bachelor's degree in science; for doctorate, GRE General Test. Additional exam requirements/recommendations for international students: Required—TOEFL (minimum score 600 paper-based; 250 computer-based; 100 iBT). Electronic applications accepted. *Faculty research:* Carcinogens and mutagenesis, pulmonary studies, reproduction and development.

University of Connecticut, Graduate School, Center for Continuing Studies, Program in Occupational Safety and Health Management, Storrs, CT 06269. Offers MPS. *Students:* 9 part-time (4 women); includes 1 minority (African American). Average age 41. *Expenses:* Tuition, state resident: full-time $4725; part-time $525 per credit. Tuition, nonresident: full-time $12,267; part-time $1363 per credit. Required fees: $346 per semester. Tuition and fees vary according to course load. *Unit head:* Susan W. Nesbitt, Director, 860-486-5941. *Application contact:* Peter Diplock, Information Contact, 860-486-2915, E-mail: peter.diplock@uconn.edu.

University of Florida, Graduate School, College of Public Health and Health Professions and College of Medicine, Programs in Public Health, Gainesville, FL 32611. Offers biostatistics (MPH); environmental health (MPH); epidemiology (MPH); public health management and policy (MPH); public health practice (MPH); social and behavioral sciences (MPH). *Entrance requirements:* For master's, GRE General Test, minimum GPA of 3.0. Additional exam requirements/recommendations for international students: Required—TOEFL (minimum score 550 paper-based; 213 computer-based).

University of Georgia, College of Public Health, Department of Environmental Health Science, Athens, GA 30602. Offers MS, PhD. *Accreditation:* CEPH. *Faculty:* 7 full-time (2 women), 1 (woman) part-time/adjunct. *Students:* 18 full-time (8 women), 1 (woman) part-time; includes 4 minority (3 African Americans, 1 Asian American or Pacific Islander), 9 international. Average age 25. 17 applicants, 35% accepted, 1 enrolled. In 2009, 5 master's, 2 doctorates awarded. Terminal master's awarded for partial completion of doctoral program. *Degree requirements:* For master's, thesis; for doctorate, comprehensive exam, thesis/dissertation. *Entrance requirements:* For master's and doctorate, GRE General Test. Additional exam requirements/recommendations for international students: Required—TOEFL. *Application deadline:* For fall admission, 3/1 priority date for domestic students; for spring admission, 11/15 for domestic students. Application fee: $50. Electronic applications accepted. *Expenses:* Tuition, state resident: full-time $6000; part-time $250 per credit hour. Tuition, nonresident: full-time $20,904; part-time $871 per credit hour. Required fees: $730 per semester. *Financial support:* Research assistantships with full tuition reimbursements available. *Faculty research:* Risk assessment, environmental toxicology, water quality, air quality. *Unit head:* Dr. Jia-Sheng Wang, Head, 706-542-2454, Fax: 706-542-7472, E-mail: jswang@uga.edu. *Application contact:* Dr. Marsha C. Black, Graduate Coordinator, 706-542-0998, Fax: 706-542-7472, E-mail: mblack@uga.edu.

University of Illinois at Chicago, Graduate College, School of Public Health, Division of Environmental and Occupational Health Sciences, Chicago, IL 60607-7128. Offers MPH, MS, Dr PH, PhD. *Accreditation:* ABET (one or more programs are accredited); CEPH (one or more programs are accredited). Part-time programs available. Terminal master's awarded for partial completion of doctoral program. *Degree requirements:* For master's, thesis, field practicum; for doctorate, thesis/dissertation, independent research, internship. *Entrance requirements:* For master's and doctorate, GRE General Test, minimum GPA of 2.75. Additional exam requirements/recommendations for international students: Required—TOEFL. Electronic applications accepted.

The University of Iowa, Graduate College, College of Public Health, Department of Occupational and Environmental Health, Iowa City, IA 52242-1316. Offers MS, PhD, Certificate, MS/MA, MS/MS. *Accreditation:* ABET (one or more programs are accredited). *Degree requirements:* For master's, thesis optional, exam; for doctorate, comprehensive exam, thesis/dissertation. *Entrance requirements:* For master's and doctorate, GRE General Test, minimum GPA of 3.0. Additional exam requirements/recommendations for international students: Required—TOEFL (minimum score 600 paper-based; 250 computer-based; 100 iBT). Electronic applications accepted.

University of Louisville, Graduate School, School of Public Health and Information Sciences, Louisville, KY 40292-0001. Offers bioinformatics and biostatistics (MS, PhD), including biostatistics (MPH, MS, PhD); decision science (MS); clinical investigation sciences (Certificate); population health and epidemiology (MS, PhD), including epidemiology (MPH, MS, PhD); public health sciences (PhD); public health (MPH), including biostatistics (MPH, MS, PhD), environmental and occupational health, epidemiology (MPH, MS, PhD), health management (MPH, PhD), health promotion and behavior; public health sciences (PhD), including environmental health, epidemiology (MPH, MS, PhD), health management (MPH, PhD), health promotion. Part-time and evening/weekend programs available. *Faculty:* 39 full-time (13 women), 1 part-time/adjunct (0 women). *Students:* 92 full-time (52 women), 72 part-time (47 women); includes 36 minority (15 African Americans, 19 Asian Americans or Pacific Islanders, 2 Hispanic Americans), 21 international. Average age 33. 194 applicants, 47% accepted, 65 enrolled. In 2009, 35 master's, 4 doctorates awarded. *Degree requirements:* For master's, thesis; for doctorate, thesis/dissertation. *Entrance requirements:* For master's, GRE General Test, GMAT, DAT, MCAT, minimum of 2 letters of recommendation; for doctorate, GRE General Test, minimum of 2 letters of recommendation. Additional exam requirements/recommendations for international students: Required—TOEFL (minimum score 600 paper-based; 250 computer-based; 100 iBT). *Application deadline:* For fall admission, 2/1 for domestic and international students. Applications are processed on a rolling basis. Application fee: $50. Electronic applications accepted. *Financial support:* In 2009–10, 30 students received support, including 11 research assistantships with full tuition reimbursements available (averaging $20,000 per year); unspecified assistantships also available. Financial award application deadline: 5/1; financial award applicants required to submit FAFSA. *Faculty research:* Clinical research training, cancer and environmental exposure, health effects of air pollution, occupational injuries and illness, network science applications in health. Total annual research expenditures: $3.2 million. *Unit head:* Dr. Pete Walton, Associate Dean for Academic Affairs, 502-852-4493, Fax: 502-852-3291, E-mail: pete.walton@gwise.louisville.edu. *Application contact:* Vicki Lewis, Administrative Assistant, 502-852-1798, Fax: 502-852-3294, E-mail: vicki.lewis@louisville.edu.

University of Maryland, College Park, Academic Affairs, School of Public Health, Department of Public and Community Health, College Park, MD 20742. Offers biostatistics (MPH); community health education (MPH); environmental health sciences (MPH); epidemiology (MPH); public/community health (PhD). *Accreditation:* CEPH. Part-time and evening/weekend programs available. *Faculty:* 26 full-time (16 women), 7 part-time/adjunct (6 women). *Students:* 56 full-time (47 women), 31 part-time (29 women); includes 25 minority (19 African Americans, 4 Asian Americans or Pacific Islanders, 2 Hispanic Americans), 12 international. 252 applicants,

25% accepted, 25 enrolled. In 2009, 14 master's, 4 doctorates awarded. *Degree requirements:* For master's, thesis optional; for doctorate, comprehensive exam, thesis/dissertation. *Entrance requirements:* For master's, GRE General Test, minimum GPA of 3.0, 3 letters of recommendation; for doctorate, GRE General Test, minimum GPA of 3.5, 3 letters of recommendation. Additional exam requirements/recommendations for international students: Required—TOEFL. *Application deadline:* For fall admission, 1/15 for domestic and international students; for spring admission, 6/1 for international students. Applications are processed on a rolling basis. Application fee: $60. Electronic applications accepted. *Expenses:* Tuition, area resident: Part-time $471 per credit hour. Tuition, state resident: part-time $471 per credit hour. Tuition, nonresident: part-time $1016 per credit hour. Required fees: $337.04 per term. *Financial support:* In 2009–10, 14 research assistantships with tuition reimbursements (averaging $15,827 per year), 21 teaching assistantships with tuition reimbursements (averaging $16,363 per year) were awarded; fellowships, career-related internships or fieldwork, Federal Work-Study, and scholarships/grants also available. Support available to part-time students. Financial award applicants required to submit FAFSA. *Faculty research:* Controlling stress and tension, women's health, aging and public policy, adolescent health, long-term care. Total annual research expenditures: $3.2 million. *Unit head:* Dr. Elbert Glover, Chair, 301-405-2467, Fax: 301-314-9167, E-mail: eglover1@umd.edu. *Application contact:* Dean of Graduate School, 301-405-0358.

University of Massachusetts Amherst, Graduate School, School of Public Health and Health Sciences, Department of Public Health, Amherst, MA 01003. Offers biostatistics (MS, PhD); community health education (MS); environmental health sciences (MPH, MS); epidemiology (MPH, MS); health policy and management (MPH, MS); nutrition (PhD); public health practice (MPH). *Accreditation:* CEPH (one or more programs are accredited). Part-time and evening/weekend programs available. Postbaccalaureate distance learning degree programs offered (no on-campus study). *Faculty:* 38 full-time (23 women). *Students:* 96 full-time (71 women), 232 part-time (153 women); includes 41 minority (14 African Americans, 17 Asian Americans or Pacific Islanders, 10 Hispanic Americans), 65 international. Average age 36. 316 applicants, 61% accepted, 79 enrolled. In 2009, 91 master's, 5 doctorates awarded. Terminal master's awarded for partial completion of doctoral program. *Degree requirements:* For master's, thesis (for some programs); for doctorate, comprehensive exam, thesis/dissertation. *Entrance requirements:* For master's and doctorate, GRE General Test. Additional exam requirements/recommendations for international students: Required—TOEFL (minimum score 550 paper-based; 213 computer-based; 80 iBT), IELTS (minimum score 6.5). *Application deadline:* For fall admission, 2/1 for domestic and international students. Applications are processed on a rolling basis. Application fee: $40 ($65 for international students). Electronic applications accepted. *Expenses:* Tuition, state resident: full-time $2640; part-time $110 per credit. Tuition, nonresident: full-time $9936; part-time $414 per credit. Tuition and fees vary according to course load. *Financial support:* In 2009–10, 3 fellowships with full tuition reimbursements (averaging $2,791 per year), 32 research assistantships with full tuition reimbursements (averaging $9,196 per year), 24 teaching assistantships with full tuition reimbursements (averaging $5,789 per year) were awarded; career-related internships or fieldwork, Federal Work-Study, scholarships/grants, traineeships, health care benefits, tuition waivers (full), and unspecified assistantships also available. Support available to part-time students. Financial award application deadline: 2/1. *Unit head:* Dr. Paula Stamps, Graduate Program Director, 413-545-2861, Fax: 413-545-0964. *Application contact:* Jean M. Ames, Supervisor of Admissions, 413-545-0722, Fax: 413-577-0010, E-mail: gradadm@grad.umass.edu.

University of Memphis, Graduate School, School of Public Health, Memphis, TN 38152. Offers biostatistics (MPH); environmental health (MPH); epidemiology (MPH); health systems management (MPH); public health (MHA); social and behavioral sciences (MPH). Part-time and evening/weekend programs available. Postbaccalaureate distance learning degree programs offered. *Faculty:* 5 full-time (2 women), 4 part-time/adjunct (2 women). *Students:* 45 full-time (23 women), 29 part-time (14 women); includes 19 African Americans, 6 Asian Americans or Pacific Islanders, 2 Hispanic Americans, 7 international. Average age 32. 57 applicants, 70% accepted, 22 enrolled. In 2009, 17 master's awarded. *Degree requirements:* For master's, comprehensive exam, thesis. *Entrance requirements:* For master's, GRE, MAT, DAT, GMAT or LSAT, letters of recommendation. Additional exam requirements/recommendations for international students: Required—TOEFL. *Application deadline:* For fall admission, 11/1 for domestic students; for spring admission, 4/1 for domestic students. Application fee: $35 ($60 for international students). Electronic applications accepted. *Expenses:* Tuition, state resident: full-time $6246; part-time $347 per credit hour. Tuition, nonresident: full-time $15,894; part-time $883 per credit hour. Required fees: $1160. Full-time tuition and fees vary according to course load, degree level and program. *Financial support:* In 2009–10, 46 students received support; research assistantships with full tuition reimbursements available, Federal Work-Study, scholarships/grants, and unspecified assistantships available. Financial award application deadline: 2/15; financial award applicants required to submit FAFSA. *Faculty research:* Health and medical savings accounts, adoption rates, health informatics, Telehealth technologies, biostatistics, environmental health, epidemiology, health systems management, social and behavioral sciences. *Unit head:* Dr. Lisa M. Klesges, Director, 901-678-4637, E-mail: lmklsges@memphis.edu. *Application contact:* Dr. Lisa M. Klesges, Director, 901-678-4637, E-mail: lmklsges@memphis.edu.

University of Miami, Graduate School, College of Engineering, Department of Industrial Engineering, Program in Occupational Ergonomics and Safety, Coral Gables, FL 33124. Offers environmental health and safety (MS); occupational ergonomics and safety (MSOES). Part-time programs available. *Degree requirements:* For master's, thesis optional. *Entrance requirements:* For master's, GRE General Test, minimum GPA of 3.0. Additional exam requirements/recommendations for international students: Required—TOEFL (minimum score 550 paper-based; 213 computer-based). Electronic applications accepted. *Faculty research:* Noise, heat stress, water pollution.

University of Michigan, School of Public Health, Department of Environmental Health Sciences, Ann Arbor, MI 48109. Offers environmental health sciences (MS, PhD); environmental quality and health (MPH); human nutrition (MPH); industrial hygiene (MPH, MS); nutritional sciences (MS); occupational and environmental epidemiology (MPH); toxicology (MPH, MS, PhD). *Accreditation:* CEPH (one or more programs are accredited). Part-time programs available. Terminal master's awarded for partial completion of doctoral program. *Degree requirements:* For master's, thesis (for some programs); for doctorate, thesis/dissertation, qualifying exam, oral defense of dissertation, preliminary exam. *Entrance requirements:* For master's and doctorate, GRE General Test and/or MCAT. Additional exam requirements/recommendations for international students: Required—TOEFL (minimum score 560 paper-based; 220 computer-based; 100 iBT). Electronic applications accepted. *Expenses:* Tuition, state resident: full-time $17,286; part-time $1099 per credit hour. Tuition, nonresident: full-time $34,944; part-time $2080 per credit hour. Required fees: $95 per semester. Tuition and fees vary according to course load, degree level and program. *Faculty research:* Toxicology; occupational hygiene; nutrition; environmental exposure sciences; environmental epidemiology.

University of Minnesota, Twin Cities Campus, School of Public Health, Division of Environmental Health Sciences, Area in Environmental Health Policy, Minneapolis, MN 55455-0213. Offers MPH, MS, PhD. *Accreditation:* CEPH (one or more programs are accredited). *Degree requirements:* For doctorate, thesis/dissertation. *Entrance requirements:* For master's and doctorate, GRE General Test. Electronic applications accepted.

University of Minnesota, Twin Cities Campus, School of Public Health, Division of Environmental Health Sciences, Area in Occupational Medicine, Minneapolis, MN 55455-0213. Offers MPH. *Accreditation:* CEPH. *Entrance requirements:* For master's, GRE General Test. Electronic applications accepted.

University of Minnesota, Twin Cities Campus, School of Public Health, Major in Public Health Practice, Minneapolis, MN 55455-0213. Offers core concepts (Certificate); food safety and biosecurity (Certificate); occupational health and safety (Certificate); preparedness, response and recovery (Certificate); public health practice (MPH); DVM/MPH; MD/MPH. Part-time

Environmental and Occupational Health

University of Minnesota, Twin Cities Campus (continued)
programs available. Postbaccalaureate distance learning degree programs offered (no on-campus study). *Degree requirements:* For master's, thesis. *Entrance requirements:* For master's, GRE, MCAT, United States Medical Licensing Exam. Additional exam requirements/recommendations for international students: Required—TOEFL (minimum score 600 paper-based; 250 computer-based). Electronic applications accepted.

University of Nevada, Las Vegas, Graduate College, School of Community Health Sciences, Department of Environmental and Occupational Health, Las Vegas, NV 89154-3064. Offers public health (MPH). *Faculty:* 9 full-time (5 women). *Students:* 39 full-time (26 women), 40 part-time (25 women); includes 20 minority (9 African Americans, 1 American Indian/Alaska Native, 6 Asian Americans or Pacific Islanders, 4 Hispanic Americans), 7 international. Average age 33. 66 applicants, 70% accepted, 33 enrolled. In 2009, 22 master's awarded. *Entrance requirements:* Additional exam requirements/recommendations for international students: Required—TOEFL (minimum score 550 paper-based; 213 computer-based; 80 iBT), IELTS (minimum score 7). *Application deadline:* For fall admission, 6/1 priority date for domestic students, 5/1 for international students; for spring admission, 11/1 priority date for domestic students, 10/1 for international students. Applications are processed on a rolling basis. Application fee: $60 ($95 for international students). Electronic applications accepted. *Financial support:* In 2009–10, 13 students received support, including 13 research assistantships with partial tuition reimbursements available (averaging $10,826 per year); institutionally sponsored loans, scholarships/grants, health care benefits, and unspecified assistantships also available. Financial award application deadline: 3/1. *Faculty research:* Elimination of health disparities, childhood lead poisoning prevention, prevention of HIV/AIDS quagga mussels in Lake Mead, childhood asthma. *Unit head:* Dr. Shawn Gerstenberger, Chair/ Associate Professor, 702-895-1565, Fax: 702-895-5573, E-mail: shawn.gerstenberger@unlv.edu. *Application contact:* Graduate College Admissions Evaluator, 702-895-3320, Fax: 702-895-4180, E-mail: gradcollege@unlv.edu.

University of Nevada, Reno, Graduate School, Interdisciplinary Program in Environmental Sciences and Health, Reno, NV 89557. Offers MS, PhD. Terminal master's awarded for partial completion of doctoral program. *Degree requirements:* For master's, thesis; for doctorate, thesis/dissertation. *Entrance requirements:* For master's, GRE General Test, minimum GPA of 2.75; for doctorate, GRE General Test, minimum GPA of 3.0. Additional exam requirements/recommendations for international students: Required—TOEFL (minimum score 500 paper-based; 173 computer-based; 61 iBT), IELTS (minimum score 6). Electronic applications accepted. *Faculty research:* Environmental chemistry, environmental toxicology, ecological toxicology.

University of New Haven, Graduate School, College of Arts and Sciences, Program in Environmental Sciences, West Haven, CT 06516-1916. Offers environmental ecology (Certificate); environmental geoscience (MS); environmental health and management (MS); environmental science (MS); geographical information systems (Certificate). Part-time and evening/weekend programs available. *Faculty:* 6 full-time (3 women), 8 part-time/adjunct (2 women). *Students:* 8 full-time (5 women), 21 part-time (9 women); includes 2 minority (both African Americans), 4 international. Average age 27. 28 applicants, 79% accepted, 4 enrolled. In 2009, 7 master's, 5 other advanced degrees awarded. *Degree requirements:* For master's, thesis or alternative. *Entrance requirements:* Additional exam requirements/recommendations for international students: Required—TOEFL (minimum score 520 paper-based; 190 computer-based; 70 iBT); Recommended—IELTS (minimum score 5.5). *Application deadline:* For fall admission, 5/31 for international students; for winter admission, 10/15 for international students; for spring admission, 1/15 for international students. Applications are processed on a rolling basis. Application fee: $50. Electronic applications accepted. *Expenses:* Tuition: Part-time $700 per credit. Required fees: $45 per term. One-time fee: $390 part-time. *Financial support:* Research assistantships with partial tuition reimbursements, teaching assistantships with partial tuition reimbursements, career-related internships or fieldwork, Federal Work-Study, scholarships/grants, tuition waivers, and unspecified assistantships available. Support available to part-time students. Financial award applicants required to submit FAFSA. *Faculty research:* Mapping and assessing geological and living resources in Long Island Sound, geology, San Salvador Island, Bahamas. *Unit head:* Dr. Roman Zajac, Coordinator, 203-932-7108. *Application contact:* Eloise Gormley, Director of Graduate Admissions, 203-932-7449, Fax: 203-932-7137, E-mail: gradinfo@newhaven.edu.

University of New Haven, Graduate School, Henry C. Lee College of Criminal Justice and Forensic Sciences, Program in Occupational Safety and Health Management, West Haven, CT 06516-1916. Offers occupational safety (Certificate); occupational safety and health management (MS). Part-time and evening/weekend programs available. *Students:* 2 part-time (0 women). Average age 42. In 2009, 5 master's awarded. *Degree requirements:* For master's, thesis or alternative. *Entrance requirements:* Additional exam requirements/recommendations for international students: Required—TOEFL (minimum score 520 paper-based; 190 computer-based; 70 iBT), IELTS (minimum score 5.5). *Application deadline:* For fall admission, 5/31 for international students; for winter admission, 10/15 for international students; for spring admission, 1/15 for international students. Applications are processed on a rolling basis. Application fee: $50. Electronic applications accepted. *Expenses:* Tuition: Part-time $700 per credit. Required fees: $45 per term. One-time fee: $390 part-time. *Financial support:* Career-related internships or fieldwork and Federal Work-Study available. Support available to part-time students. Financial award application deadline: 5/1; financial award applicants required to submit FAFSA. *Unit head:* Dr. William Tafoya, Director, 203-932-7175. *Application contact:* Eloise Gormley, Director of Graduate Admissions, 203-932-7449, Fax: 203-932-7137, E-mail: gradinfo@newhaven.edu.

The University of North Carolina at Chapel Hill, Graduate School, School of Public Health, Department of Environmental Sciences and Engineering, Chapel Hill, NC 27599. Offers air, radiation and industrial hygiene (MPH, MS, MSEE, MSPH, PhD); aquatic and atmospheric sciences (MPH, MS, MSPH, PhD); environmental engineering (MPH, MS, MSEE, MSPH, PhD); environmental health sciences (MPH, MS, MSPH, PhD); environmental management and policy (MPH, MS, MSPH, PhD). Terminal master's awarded for partial completion of doctoral program. *Degree requirements:* For master's, comprehensive exam, thesis (for some programs), research paper; for doctorate, comprehensive exam, thesis/dissertation. *Entrance requirements:* For master's and doctorate, GRE General Test, minimum GPA of 3.0. Additional exam requirements/recommendations for international students: Required—TOEFL. Electronic applications accepted. *Faculty research:* Air, radiation and industrial hygiene, aquatic and atmospheric sciences, environmental health sciences, environmental management and policy, water resources engineering.

University of North Texas Health Science Center at Fort Worth, School of Public Health, Fort Worth, TX 76107-2699. Offers biostatistics (MPH); community health (MPH); disease control and prevention (Dr PH); environmental and occupational health sciences (MPH); epidemiology (MPH); health administration (MHA); health policy and management (MPH, Dr PH); DO/MPH; MS/MPH; MSN/MPH. *Accreditation:* CEPH. Part-time and evening/weekend programs available. *Degree requirements:* For master's, thesis or alternative, supervised internship; for doctorate, thesis/dissertation, supervised internship. *Entrance requirements:* For master's, GRE General Test. Additional exam requirements/recommendations for international students: Required—TOEFL. Electronic applications accepted.

University of Oklahoma, Graduate College, College of Engineering, School of Civil Engineering and Environmental Science, Program in Environmental Science, Norman, OK 73019-0390. Offers air (M Env Sc); environmental science (PhD); groundwater management (M Env Sc); hazardous solid waste (M Env Sc); occupational safety and health (M Env Sc); process design (M Env Sc); water quality resources (M Env Sc). *Students:* 9 full-time (4 women), 8 part-time (6 women); includes 3 minority (1 African American, 2 American Indian/Alaska Native), 2 international. 9 applicants, 67% accepted, 4 enrolled. In 2009, 4 master's, 2 doctorates awarded. Terminal master's awarded for partial completion of doctoral program. *Degree requirements:* For master's, comprehensive exam, oral exams; for doctorate, comprehensive exam, thesis/dissertation, oral and qualifying exams. *Entrance requirements:* For master's, minimum GPA of 3.0; for doctorate, minimum graduate GPA of 3.5. Additional exam requirements/recommendations for international students: Required—TOEFL (minimum score 600 paper-based; 250 computer-based). *Application deadline:* For fall admission, 4/1 priority date for domestic students, 4/1 for international students; for spring admission, 11/1 for domestic students, 9/1 for international students. Applications are processed on a rolling basis. Application fee: $40 ($90 for international students). Electronic applications accepted. *Expenses:* Tuition, state resident: full-time $3744; part-time $156 per credit hour. Tuition, nonresident: full-time $13,577; part-time $565.70 per credit hour. Required fees: $2415; $90.10 per credit hour. *Financial support:* In 2009–10, 10 students received support. Scholarships/grants available. Financial award application deadline: 3/1; financial award applicants required to submit FAFSA. *Faculty research:* Treatment wetlands, soil remediation, biomediation. *Unit head:* Robert C. Knox, Director, 405-325-5911, Fax: 405-325-4217, E-mail: rknox@ou.edu. *Application contact:* Robert C. Knox, Director, 405-325-5911, Fax: 405-325-4217, E-mail: rknox@ou.edu.

University of Oklahoma Health Sciences Center, Graduate College, College of Public Health, Department of Occupational and Environmental Health, Oklahoma City, OK 73190. Offers MPH, MS, Dr PH, PhD, JD/MPH, JD/MS. *Accreditation:* ABET (one or more programs are accredited); CEPH (one or more programs are accredited). Part-time programs available. *Faculty:* 5 full-time (2 women). *Students:* 9 full-time (4 women), 16 part-time (6 women); includes 5 minority (2 African Americans, 1 American Indian/Alaska Native, 1 Asian American or Pacific Islander, 1 Hispanic American). Average age 33. 7 applicants, 29% accepted, 2 enrolled. In 2009, 3 master's awarded. *Degree requirements:* For master's, comprehensive exam, thesis (for some programs); for doctorate, comprehensive exam, thesis/dissertation. *Entrance requirements:* For master's, GRE General Test (for all except occupational medicine), 3 letters of recommendation, resume; for doctorate, GRE (for all except occupational medicine), 3 letters of recommendation, resume. Additional exam requirements/recommendations for international students: Required—TOEFL (minimum score 570 paper-based; 230 computer-based). *Application deadline:* For fall admission, 7/1 for domestic students; for winter admission, 4/1 for domestic students; for spring admission, 12/1 for domestic students. Applications are processed on a rolling basis. Application fee: $50. *Expenses:* Tuition, state resident: full-time $3120; part-time $156 per credit hour. Tuition, nonresident: full-time $11,314; part-time $409.70 per credit hour. Required fees: $1471; $51.20 per credit hour. $223.25 per term. *Financial support:* In 2009–10, 6 research assistantships (averaging $15,000 per year) were awarded; career-related internships or fieldwork, institutionally sponsored loans, traineeships, and tuition waivers (partial) also available. Support available to part-time students. Financial award application deadline: 5/1. *Faculty research:* Environmental safety, accident prevention and injury control. *Unit head:* Dr. Margaret Phillips, Interim Chair, 405-271-2070, E-mail: margaret.phillips@ouhsc.edu. *Application contact:* Robin Howell, Information Contact, 405-271-2308, E-mail: robin_howell@ouhsc.edu.

University of Pittsburgh, Graduate School of Public Health, Department of Environmental and Occupational Health, Pittsburgh, PA 15260. Offers environmental and occupational health (MPH, MS, PhD); environmental health risk assessment (Certificate); global health (Certificate); public health preparedness and disaster response (Certificate); MD/MPH. *Accreditation:* CEPH (one or more programs are accredited). Part-time programs available. *Faculty:* 28 full-time (8 women), 26 part-time/adjunct (6 women). *Students:* 23 full-time (11 women), 17 part-time (11 women); includes 3 minority (1 African American, 1 Asian American or Pacific Islander, 1 Hispanic American), 9 international. Average age 34. 69 applicants, 57% accepted, 16 enrolled. In 2009, 3 master's awarded. *Degree requirements:* For master's, comprehensive exam, thesis; for doctorate, comprehensive exam, thesis/dissertation, preliminary exams. *Entrance requirements:* For master's and Certificate, GRE General Test; for doctorate, GRE General Test, minimum GPA of 3.4; background in biology, physics, chemistry and calculus. Additional exam requirements/recommendations for international students: Required—TOEFL (minimum score 550 paper-based; 213 computer-based; 80 iBT). *Application deadline:* For fall admission, 2/15 priority date for domestic students, 2/15 for international students; for winter admission, 9/1 for international students; for spring admission, 2/1 for international students. Applications are processed on a rolling basis. Application fee: $95. Electronic applications accepted. *Expenses:* Tuition, state resident: full-time $16,402; part-time $665 per credit. Tuition, nonresident: full-time $28,694; part-time $1175 per credit. Required fees: $690; $175 per term. Tuition and fees vary according to program. *Financial support:* In 2009–10, 10 students received support, including 10 research assistantships with full tuition reimbursements available (averaging $24,000 per year); scholarships/grants and unspecified assistantships also available. *Faculty research:* Molecular toxicology, redox signaling, gene environment interaction, progenitor-progeny lineage, occupational and pulmonary medicine. Total annual research expenditures: $9.1 million. *Unit head:* Dr. Bruce R. Pitt, Chairman, 412-383-8400, Fax: 412-383-7658, E-mail: brucep@pitt.edu. *Application contact:* Eileen Penny Weiss, Student Affairs Administrator, 412-383-7297, Fax: 412-383-7658, E-mail: pweiss@pitt.edu.

University of Puerto Rico, Medical Sciences Campus, Graduate School of Public Health, Doctoral Program in Environmental Health, San Juan, PR 00936-5067. Offers Dr PH. Part-time programs available. *Expenses:* Contact institution.

University of Puerto Rico, Medical Sciences Campus, Graduate School of Public Health, Master's Program in Environmental Health, San Juan, PR 00936-5067. Offers MS. *Degree requirements:* For master's, thesis. *Entrance requirements:* For master's, GRE, course work in biology, chemistry, mathematics, and physics. *Expenses:* Contact institution.

University of South Alabama, Graduate School, Program in Environmental Toxicology, Mobile, AL 36688-0002. Offers MS. *Entrance requirements:* For master's, GRE. *Expenses:* Tuition, state resident: part-time $218 per contact hour. Required fees: $1102 per year.

University of South Carolina, The Graduate School, Arnold School of Public Health, Department of Environmental Health Sciences, Program in Environmental Quality, Columbia, SC 29208. Offers MPH, MS, MSPH, PhD. *Accreditation:* CEPH (one or more programs are accredited). Part-time programs available. *Degree requirements:* For master's, comprehensive exam, thesis (for some programs), practicum (MPH); for doctorate, one foreign language, comprehensive exam, thesis/dissertation. *Entrance requirements:* For master's and doctorate, GRE General Test. Additional exam requirements/recommendations for international students: Required—TOEFL (minimum score 570 paper-based; 230 computer-based). Electronic applications accepted. *Faculty research:* Environmental assessment and planning; environmental toxicology; ecosystems analysis; air quality monitoring and modeling.

University of Southern Mississippi, Graduate School, College of Health, Department of Community Health Sciences, Hattiesburg, MS 39406-0001. Offers epidemiology and biostatistics (MPH); health education (MPH); health policy/administration (MPH); occupational/environmental health (MPH); public health nutrition (MPH). *Accreditation:* CEPH. Part-time and evening/weekend programs available. *Faculty:* 8 full-time (4 women), 1 part-time/adjunct (0 women). *Students:* 92 full-time (59 women), 20 part-time (14 women); includes 40 minority (36 African Americans, 1 Asian American or Pacific Islander, 3 Hispanic Americans), 13 international. Average age 32. 90 applicants, 73% accepted, 47 enrolled. In 2009, 4 master's awarded. *Degree requirements:* For master's, comprehensive exam, thesis (for some programs). *Entrance requirements:* For master's, GRE General Test, minimum GPA of 2.75 in last 60 hours. Additional exam requirements/recommendations for international students: Required—TOEFL. *Application deadline:* For fall admission, 3/1 for domestic and international students. Applications are processed on a rolling basis. Application fee: $35. *Expenses:* Tuition, state resident: full-time $5096; part-time $284 per hour. Tuition, nonresident: full-time $13,052; part-time $726 per hour. Required fees: $402. Tuition and fees vary according to course level and course load. *Financial support:* In 2009–10, 5 research assistantships with full tuition reimbursements (averaging $7,000 per year), 1 teaching assistantship with full tuition reimbursement (averaging $8,263 per year) were awarded; career-related internships or fieldwork and Federal Work-Study also available. Financial award application deadline: 3/15; financial award applicants required to submit FAFSA. *Faculty research:* Rural health care delivery, school health, nutrition of pregnant teens, risk factor reduction, sexually transmitted diseases. *Unit head:* Dr. James McGuire, Chair, 601-266-5437, Fax: 601-266-5043. *Application contact:* Shonna Breland, Manager of Graduate Admissions, 601-266-6563, Fax: 601-266-5138.

University of South Florida, Graduate School, College of Public Health, Department of Environmental and Occupational Health, Tampa, FL 33620-9951. Offers MPH, MSPH, PhD. *Accreditation:* ABET (one or more programs are accredited); CEPH (one or more programs are accredited). Part-time and evening/weekend programs available. *Faculty:* 12 full-time (3 women), 11 part-time/adjunct (3 women). *Students:* 36 full-time (17 women), 34 part-time (18 women); includes 13 minority (7 African Americans, 2 Asian Americans or Pacific Islanders, 4 Hispanic Americans), 5 international. Average age 36. 38 applicants, 76% accepted, 15 enrolled. In 2009, 11 master's, 1 doctorate awarded. *Degree requirements:* For master's, comprehensive exam, thesis (for some programs); for doctorate, comprehensive exam, thesis/dissertation. *Entrance requirements:* For master's, GRE General Test, minimum GPA of 3.0 in upper-level course work, goal statement letter, two professional letters of recommendation, resume/curriculum vitae; for doctorate, GRE General Test, minimum GPA of 3.0 in upper-level course work, goal statement letter, three professional letters of recommendation, resume/curriculum vitae, writing sample. Additional exam requirements/recommendations for international students: Required—TOEFL (minimum score 550 paper-based; 213 computer-based; 79 iBT). *Application deadline:* For fall admission, 6/1 for domestic students, 1/2 for international students; for spring admission, 10/15 for domestic students, 7/1 for international students. Applications are processed on a rolling basis. Application fee: $30. Electronic applications accepted. *Financial support:* In 2009–10, 1 fellowship with full tuition reimbursement (averaging $6,272 per year), 19 research assistantships with full and partial tuition reimbursements (averaging $4,843 per year), 4 teaching assistantships with tuition reimbursements (averaging $4,901 per year) were awarded; Federal Work-Study, institutionally sponsored loans, scholarships/grants, traineeships, and unspecified assistantships also available. Support available to part-time students. Financial award applicants required to submit FAFSA. *Faculty research:* Biomedical assessment/stress test, risk impact, nitrobenzes on mammalism glutathion transferases, lysimeter research management, independent hygiene development. Total annual research expenditures: $5 million. *Unit head:* Dr. Thomas Bernard, Chairperson, 813-974-3144, Fax: 813-974-4986. *Application contact:* Michelle Hodge, Academic Advisor, 813-974-6665, Fax: 813-974-8121, E-mail: mhodge1@health.usf.edu.

The University of Texas at Tyler, College of Engineering and Computer Science, Department of Civil Engineering, Tyler, TX 75799-0001. Offers environmental engineering (MS); industrial safety (MS); structural engineering (MS); transportation engineering (MS); water resources engineering (MS). Part-time and evening/weekend programs available. *Faculty:* 6 full-time (0 women). *Students:* 5 full-time (1 woman), 7 part-time (1 woman); includes 1 African American, 1 Asian American or Pacific Islander, 1 Hispanic American, 1 international. Average age 26. 5 applicants, 80% accepted, 3 enrolled. *Degree requirements:* For master's, thesis optional. *Entrance requirements:* For master's, GRE General Test, bachelor's degree in engineering, associated science degree. Additional exam requirements/recommendations for international students: Required—TOEFL (minimum score 79 computer-based). *Application deadline:* For fall admission, 8/17 priority date for domestic students, 7/1 priority date for international students; for spring admission, 12/21 priority date for domestic students, 11/1 priority date for international students. Application fee: $25 ($50 for international students). *Expenses:* Tuition, state resident: part-time $665 per semester hour. Tuition, nonresident: part-time $942 per semester hour. Part-time tuition and fees vary according to degree level and program. *Financial support:* Application deadline: 7/1. *Faculty research:* Non-destructive strength testing, indoor air quality, transportation routing and signaling, pavement replacement criteria, flood water routing, construction and long-term behavior of innovative geotechnical foundation and embankment construction used in highway construction, engineering education. *Unit head:* Dr. Ron Welch, Chair, 903-566-7002, Fax: 903-566-7337, E-mail: rwelch@uttyler.edu. *Application contact:* Dr. Torey Nalbone, Program Chair, 903-565-5520, Fax: 903-566-7337, E-mail: tnalbone@uttyler.edu.

University of the Sacred Heart, Graduate Programs, Department of Natural Sciences, Program in Occupational Health and Safety, San Juan, PR 00914-0383. Offers MS.

The University of Toledo, College of Graduate Studies, College of Medicine, Department of Public Health and Homeland Security, Program in Occupational Health, Toledo, OH 43606-3390. Offers MSOH, Certificate.

University of Washington, Graduate School, School of Public Health, Department of Environmental and Occupational Health Sciences, Seattle, WA 98195. Offers environmental and occupational health (MPH); environmental and occupational hygiene (PhD); environmental health (MS); occupational and environmental exposure sciences (MS); occupational and environmental medicine (MPH); toxicology (MS, PhD). Part-time programs available. *Faculty:* 32 full-time (5 women), 10 part-time/adjunct (4 women). *Students:* 59 full-time (40 women), 11 part-time (4 women); includes 17 minority (2 African Americans, 1 American Indian/Alaska Native, 12 Asian Americans or Pacific Islanders, 2 Hispanic Americans), 5 international. Average age 29. 114 applicants, 31% accepted, 20 enrolled. In 2009, 23 master's, 6 doctorates awarded. Terminal master's awarded for partial completion of doctoral program. *Degree requirements:* For master's, thesis (for some programs), project or portfolio (for some tracks); for doctorate, comprehensive exam, thesis/dissertation. *Entrance requirements:* For master's and doctorate, GRE General Test, minimum GPA of 3.0, prerequisite course work in biology, chemistry, physics, calculus. Additional exam requirements/recommendations for international students: Required—TOEFL (minimum score 580 paper-based; 237 computer-based; 70 iBT). *Application deadline:* For fall admission, 1/1 for domestic students, 11/1 for international students. Application fee: $50. Electronic applications accepted. *Financial support:* In 2009–10, 53 students received support, including 19 fellowships with full tuition reimbursements available (averaging $21,048 per year), 33 research assistantships with full tuition reimbursements available (averaging $21,048 per year), 4 teaching assistantships with full tuition reimbursements available (averaging $21,048 per year); career-related internships or fieldwork, institutionally sponsored loans, traineeships, health care benefits, and unspecified assistantships also available. Financial award application deadline: 1/1. *Faculty research:* Developmental toxicology, biochemical toxicology, exposure assessment, hazardous waste, industrial chemistry. Total annual research expenditures: $14.5 million. *Unit head:* Dr. Rich Fenske, Acting Chair, 206-543-6991. *Application contact:* Rory A. Murphy, Manager, Student Services, 206-543-6991, Fax: 206-543-0477, E-mail: ehgrad@u.washington.edu.

University of Washington, Graduate School, School of Public Health, Department of Health Services, Seattle, WA 98195. Offers bioinformatics (PhD); cancer prevention and control (PhD); clinical research (MS); community oriented public health practice (MPH); economics or finance (PhD); evaluation sciences (PhD); executive program (MHA); health behavior and health promotion (PhD); health care and population health research (MPH); health policy analysis and process (PhD); health policy and analysis and process (MPH); health services (MS, PhD); health services administration (EMHA, MHA); in residence program (MHA); occupational health (PhD); population health and social determinants (PhD); social and behavioral sciences (MPH); sociology and demography (PhD); JD/MHA; MHA/MBA; MHA/MD; MHA/MPA; MPH/JD; MPH/MD; MPH/MN; MPH/MPA; MPH/MSD; MPH/MSW; MPH/PhD. Part-time and evening/weekend programs available. Postbaccalaureate distance learning degree programs offered (minimal on-campus study). *Faculty:* 52 full-time (24 women), 60 part-time/adjunct (28 women). *Students:* 104 full-time (83 women), 100 part-time (76 women); includes 21 minority (6 African Americans, 1 American Indian/Alaska Native, 11 Asian Americans or Pacific Islanders, 3 Hispanic Americans), 6 international. Average age 34. 375 applicants, 17% accepted, 24 enrolled. In 2009, 33 master's awarded. Terminal master's awarded for partial completion of doctoral program. *Degree requirements:* For master's, thesis (for some programs), practicum (MPH); for doctorate, comprehensive exam, thesis/dissertation. *Entrance requirements:* For master's and doctorate, GRE General Test, minimum GPA of 3.0. Additional exam requirements/recommendations for international students: Required—TOEFL. *Application deadline:* For fall admission, 1/15 for domestic students, 11/1 for international students. Application fee: 50 Albanian leks. Electronic applications accepted. *Financial support:* In 2009–10, 64 students received support, including 10 fellowships with full and partial tuition reimbursements available (averaging $21,000 per year), 10 research assistantships with full and partial tuition reimbursements available (averaging $18,000 per year), 3 teaching assistantships with full and partial tuition reimbursements available (averaging $18,000 per year); career-related internships or fieldwork, Federal Work-Study, institutionally sponsored loans, and traineeships also available. Financial award application deadline: 2/28; financial award applicants required to submit FAFSA. *Faculty research:* Health promotion and disease prevention, maternal and child health, health services research design, program evaluation, health policy. Total annual research expenditures: $10.5 million. *Unit head:* Dr. Larry Kessler, Chair, 206-543-616-2930. *Application contact:* Kitty A. Andert, Program Manager, 206-616-2926, Fax: 206-543-3964, E-mail: kitander@u.washington.edu.

University of West Florida, College of Professional Studies, Division of Health, Leisure, and Exercise Science, Community Health Education, Pensacola, FL 32514-5750. Offers aging studies (MS); promotion and worksite wellness (MS); psycho-social (MS). Part-time and evening/weekend programs available. *Faculty:* 2 full-time (1 woman), 1 (woman) part-time/adjunct. *Students:* 7 full-time (6 women), 7 part-time (all women); includes 4 minority (1 African American, 1 American Indian/Alaska Native, 1 Asian American or Pacific Islander, 1 Hispanic American), 1 international. Average age 34. 7 applicants, 86% accepted, 5 enrolled. In 2009, 13 master's awarded. *Degree requirements:* For master's, thesis or alternative. *Entrance requirements:* For master's, GRE General Test, minimum GPA of 3.0. Additional exam requirements/recommendations for international students: Required—TOEFL (minimum score 550 paper-based; 213 computer-based). *Application deadline:* For fall admission, 6/1 for domestic students, 5/15 for international students; for spring admission, 11/1 for domestic students, 10/1 for international students. Applications are processed on a rolling basis. Application fee: $30. *Expenses:* Tuition, state resident: full-time $4982; part-time $260 per credit hour. Tuition, nonresident: full-time $20,059; part-time $919 per credit hour. Required fees: $1247; $52 per credit hour. *Financial support:* Research assistantships, teaching assistantships, unspecified assistantships available. *Unit head:* Dr. John Todorovich, Chairperson, 850-473-7248, Fax: 850-474-2106. *Application contact:* Terry McCray, Assistant Director of Graduate Admissions, 850-473-7718, Fax: 850-473-7714, E-mail: gradadmissions@uwf.edu.

University of Wisconsin–Whitewater, School of Graduate Studies, College of Education, Department of Occupational and Environmental Safety, Whitewater, WI 53190-1790. Offers safety (MS). Part-time and evening/weekend programs available. Postbaccalaureate distance learning degree programs offered (no on-campus study). *Degree requirements:* For master's, thesis or alternative. *Entrance requirements:* For master's, 3 letters of recommendation, interview. Additional exam requirements/recommendations for international students: Required—TOEFL (minimum score 550 paper-based; 213 computer-based). Electronic applications accepted. *Faculty research:* Industrial ergonomics; work, measurement, and design; product design/evaluation.

Virginia Commonwealth University, Graduate School, School of Life Sciences, Center for Environmental Studies, Richmond, VA 23284-9005. Offers environmental communication (MIS); environmental health (MIS); environmental policy (MIS); environmental sciences (MIS). *Degree requirements:* For master's, thesis. *Entrance requirements:* For master's, GRE General Test.

Wayne State University, Eugene Applebaum College of Pharmacy and Health Sciences, Department of Fundamental and Applied Sciences, Program in Occupational and Environmental Health Sciences, Detroit, MI 48202. Offers MPH, MS, Certificate, Post-Master's Certificate. *Entrance requirements:* Additional exam requirements/recommendations for international students: Required—TOEFL.

West Chester University of Pennsylvania, Office of Graduate Studies, College of Health Sciences, Department of Health, West Chester, PA 19383. Offers emergency preparedness (Certificate); health care administration (Certificate); integrative health (Certificate); public health (MPH), including administration, community, environment, integrative, nutrition; school health (M Ed). *Accreditation:* CEPH. Part-time and evening/weekend programs available. *Students:* 15 full-time (9 women), 128 part-time (91 women); includes 41 minority (34 African Americans, 2 American Indian/Alaska Native, 5 Asian Americans or Pacific Islanders), 22 international. Average age 30. 83 applicants, 88% accepted, 41 enrolled. In 2009, 45 master's, 8 other advanced degrees awarded. *Degree requirements:* For master's, thesis (for some programs). *Entrance requirements:* For master's, one-page statement of career objectives, two letters of reference. Additional exam requirements/recommendations for international students: Required—TOEFL (minimum score 550 paper-based; 213 computer-based; 80 iBT). *Application deadline:* For fall admission, 4/15 priority date for domestic students, 3/15 for international students; for spring admission, 10/15 for domestic students, 9/1 for international students. Applications are processed on a rolling basis. Application fee: $35. Electronic applications accepted. *Expenses:* Tuition, state resident: full-time $6666; part-time $370 per credit. Tuition, nonresident: full-time $10,666; part-time $593 per credit. Required fees: $122.56 per credit. *Financial support:* In 2009–10, 11 research assistantships with full and partial tuition reimbursements (averaging $5,000 per year) were awarded; unspecified assistantships also available. Support available to part-time students. Financial award application deadline: 2/15; financial award applicants required to submit FAFSA. *Faculty research:* HIV/AIDS education, teacher preparation, water quality. *Unit head:* Dr. Roger Mustalish, Chair, 610-436-2931, E-mail: rmustalish@wcupa.edu. *Application contact:* Dr. Bethann Cinelli, Graduate Coordinator, 610-436-2267, E-mail: bcinelli@wcupa.edu.

West Virginia University, College of Engineering and Mineral Resources, Department of Industrial and Management Systems Engineering, Program in Occupational Safety and Health, Morgantown, WV 26506. Offers PhD. Part-time programs available. Postbaccalaureate distance learning degree programs offered (minimal on-campus study). *Degree requirements:* For doctorate, comprehensive exam, thesis/dissertation. *Entrance requirements:* For doctorate, GRE General Test, Minimum GPA of 3.5. Additional exam requirements/recommendations for international students: Required—TOEFL. *Faculty research:* Safety management, ergonomics and workplace design, safety and health training, construction safety.

Yale University, School of Medicine, School of Public Health, Division of Environmental Health Sciences, New Haven, CT 06520. Offers MPH, PhD. PhD offered through the Graduate School. *Accreditation:* CEPH (one or more programs are accredited). Part-time programs available. Terminal master's awarded for partial completion of doctoral program. *Degree requirements:* For master's, thesis, internship. *Entrance requirements:* For master's, GMAT, GRE, or MCAT, previous undergraduate course work in mathematics and science. Additional exam requirements/recommendations for international students: Required—TOEFL. Electronic applications accepted. *Expenses:* Contact institution. *Faculty research:* Asthma and environmental agents, environmental epidemiology, sensory perceptions, indoor/outdoor air quality, exercise physiology.

Epidemiology

American University of Beirut, Graduate Programs, Faculty of Health Sciences, Beirut, Lebanon. Offers environmental sciences (MSES), including environmental health; epidemiology (MS); epidemiology and biostatistics (MPH); health behavior and education (MPH); population health (MS); public health (MPH). Part-time programs available. *Degree requirements:* For master's, one foreign language, comprehensive exam, thesis (for some programs). *Entrance requirements:* For master's, 2 letters of recommendation. Additional exam requirements/ recommendations for international students: Required—TOEFL (minimum score 573 paper-based; 230 computer-based; 98 iBT), IELTS (minimum score 7.5). Electronic applications accepted. *Faculty research:* Urban health, childbirth, tobacco control, HIV/AIDS surveillance, health finance and policies.

Boston University, School of Public Health, Epidemiology Department, Boston, MA 02215. Offers M Sc, MPH, PhD. *Accreditation:* CEPH (one or more programs are accredited). Part-time and evening/weekend programs available. *Students:* 92 full-time (69 women), 75 part-time (59 women); includes 37 minority (10 African Americans, 19 Asian Americans or Pacific Islanders, 8 Hispanic Americans), 23 international. Average age 28. In 2009, 66 master's, 5 doctorates awarded. *Degree requirements:* For master's, comprehensive exam. *Entrance requirements:* For master's, GRE, LSAT, GMAT, DAT or MCAT, U.S. bachelor's degree or foreign equivalent; for doctorate, GRE, MCAT, GMAT, LSAT, MPH or equivalent. Additional exam requirements/ recommendations for international students: Required—TOEFL (minimum score 600 paper-based; 250 computer-based; 100 iBT), IELTS (minimum score 6). *Application deadline:* For fall admission, 2/1 priority date for domestic and international students; for spring admission, 10/15 priority date for domestic and international students. Applications are processed on a rolling basis. Application fee: $95. Electronic applications accepted. *Expenses:* Tuition: Full-time $37,910; part-time $1184 per credit hour. Required fees: $386; $40 per semester. Part-time tuition and fees vary according to class time, course level, degree level and program. *Financial support:* Career-related internships or fieldwork, Federal Work-Study, institutionally sponsored loans, and scholarships/grants available. Support available to part-time students. Financial award applicants required to submit FAFSA. *Unit head:* Dr. C. Robert Horsburgh, Chair, 617-638-7775, E-mail: epi@bu.edu. *Application contact:* LePhan Quan, Assistant Director of Admissions, 617-638-4640, Fax: 617-638-5299, E-mail: asksph@bu.edu.

Brown University, Graduate School, Division of Biology and Medicine, Department of Community Health, Providence, RI 02912. Offers health services research (MS, PhD); public health (MPH); statistical science (MS, PhD), including biostatistics, epidemiology; MD/PhD. *Accreditation:* CEPH. *Degree requirements:* For doctorate, thesis/dissertation, preliminary exam. *Entrance requirements:* For master's and doctorate, GRE General Test. Additional exam requirements/recommendations for international students: Required—TOEFL.

Brown University, Graduate School, Division of Biology and Medicine, Department of Community Health, Center for Statistical Science, Program in Epidemiology, Providence, RI 02912. Offers MS, PhD, MD/PhD. *Degree requirements:* For doctorate, thesis/dissertation, preliminary exam. *Entrance requirements:* For master's and doctorate, GRE General Test.

Case Western Reserve University, School of Medicine and School of Graduate Studies, Graduate Programs in Medicine, Department of Epidemiology and Biostatistics, Program in Epidemiology, Cleveland, OH 44106. Offers MS, PhD. *Accreditation:* CEPH. Part-time programs available. Terminal master's awarded for partial completion of doctoral program. *Degree requirements:* For master's, comprehensive exam, thesis; for doctorate, comprehensive exam, thesis/dissertation. *Entrance requirements:* For master's, GRE General Test or MCAT, 3 recommendations; for doctorate, GRE General Test, 3 recommendations. Additional exam requirements/recommendations for international students: Required—TOEFL (minimum score 550 paper-based; 213 computer-based). Electronic applications accepted. *Faculty research:* Cardiovascular epidemiology, cancer risk factors, HIV in underserved populations, effectiveness studies in Medicare patients.

Case Western Reserve University, School of Medicine and School of Graduate Studies, Graduate Programs in Medicine, Department of Epidemiology and Biostatistics, Program in Genetic and Molecular Epidemiology, Cleveland, OH 44106. Offers MS, PhD. *Degree requirements:* For master's, comprehensive exam, thesis; for doctorate, comprehensive exam, thesis/dissertation. *Entrance requirements:* For master's and doctorate, GRE. Additional exam requirements/recommendations for international students: Required—TOEFL (minimum score 550 paper-based; 213 computer-based).

Columbia University, Columbia University Mailman School of Public Health, Division of Epidemiology, New York, NY 10032. Offers MPH, MS, Dr PH, PhD. PhD offered in cooperation with the Graduate School of Arts and Sciences. *Accreditation:* CEPH (one or more programs are accredited). Part-time programs available. *Students:* 80 full-time (55 women), 111 part-time (89 women); includes 60 minority (14 African Americans, 3 American Indian/Alaska Native, 31 Asian Americans or Pacific Islanders, 12 Hispanic Americans), 24 international. Average age 31. 391 applicants, 57% accepted, 74 enrolled. In 2009, 68 master's, 3 doctorates awarded. *Degree requirements:* For master's, thesis; for doctorate, thesis/dissertation. *Entrance requirements:* For master's, GRE General Test; for doctorate, GRE General Test, MPH or equivalent (Dr PH). Additional exam requirements/recommendations for international students: Required—TOEFL (minimum score 600 paper-based; 250 computer-based; 100 iBT). *Application deadline:* For fall admission, 1/5 for domestic students. Application fee: $60. Electronic applications accepted. *Financial support:* Research assistantships, teaching assistantships, career-related internships or fieldwork and Federal Work-Study available. Support available to part-time students. Financial award application deadline: 2/1; financial award applicants required to submit FAFSA. *Faculty research:* Infectious disease epidemiology, chronic disease epidemiology, social epidemiology, psychiatric epidemiology, and neurological epidemiology. *Unit head:* Dr. William Friedewald, Interim Chair, 212-305-3017. *Application contact:* Dr. William Friedewald, Interim Chair, 212-305-3017.

Cornell University, Graduate School, Graduate Fields of Comparative Biomedical Sciences, Field of Comparative Biomedical Sciences, Ithaca, NY 14853-0001. Offers cellular and molecular medicine (MS, PhD); developmental and reproductive biology (MS, PhD); infectious diseases (MS, PhD); population medicine and epidemiology (MS, PhD); structural and functional biology (MS, PhD). *Faculty:* 106 full-time (29 women). *Students:* 41 full-time (28 women); includes 1 minority (African American), 17 international. Average age 32. 32 applicants, 31% accepted, 9 enrolled. In 2009, 1 master's, 10 doctorates awarded. *Degree requirements:* For master's, thesis; for doctorate, comprehensive exam, thesis/dissertation. *Entrance requirements:* For master's and doctorate, GRE General Test, 2 letters of recommendation. Additional exam requirements/recommendations for international students: Required—TOEFL (minimum score 550 paper-based; 213 computer-based; 77 iBT). *Application deadline:* For fall admission, 12/15 for domestic students. Application fee: $70. Electronic applications accepted. *Expenses:* Tuition: Full-time $29,500. Required fees: $70. Full-time tuition and fees vary according to degree level, program and student level. *Financial support:* In 2009–10, 4 fellowships with full tuition reimbursements, 2 research assistantships with full tuition reimbursements were awarded; teaching assistantships with full tuition reimbursements, institutionally sponsored loans, scholarships/grants, health care benefits, tuition waivers (full and partial), and unspecified assistantships also available. Financial award applicants required to submit FAFSA. *Faculty research:* Receptors and signal transduction, viral and bacterial infectious diseases, tumor metastasis, clinical sciences/nutritional disease, developmental/neurological disorders. *Unit head:* Director of Graduate Studies, 607-253-3276, Fax: 607-253-3756. *Application contact:* Graduate Field Assistant, 607-253-3276, Fax: 607-253-3756, E-mail: graduate_edcvm@cornell.edu.

Cornell University, Joan and Sanford I. Weill Medical College and Graduate School of Medical Sciences, Weill Cornell Graduate School of Medical Sciences, Program in Clinical Epidemiology and Health Services Research, New York, NY 10021. Offers MS. *Faculty:* 22 full-time (8 women). *Students:* 22 full-time (12 women); includes 6 minority (2 African Americans,

3 Asian Americans or Pacific Islanders, 1 Hispanic American), 3 international. Average age 35. 14 applicants, 50% accepted, 7 enrolled. In 2009, 3 master's awarded. *Degree requirements:* For master's, thesis. *Entrance requirements:* For master's, 3 years of work experience, MD or RN certificate. *Application deadline:* For fall admission, 12/15 for domestic students. Application fee: $60. *Expenses:* Tuition: Full-time $44,650. Required fees: $2805. *Financial support:* Scholarships/grants available. *Faculty research:* Research methodology, biostatistical techniques, data management, decision analysis, health economics. *Unit head:* Dr. Carol Mancuso, Director, 212-746-5454. *Application contact:* Alison Kenny, Administrator of Clinical and Educational Programs, 212-746-1608, Fax: 212-746-7443, E-mail: alh2006@med.cornell.edu.

Dalhousie University, Faculty of Medicine, Department of Community Health and Epidemiology, Halifax, NS B3H 4R2, Canada. Offers M Sc. *Degree requirements:* For master's, thesis. *Entrance requirements:* Additional exam requirements/recommendations for international students: Required—TOEFL, IELTS, 1 of the following 5 approved tests: TOEFL, IELTS, CANTEST, CAEL, Michigan English Language Assessment Battery. Electronic applications accepted. *Expenses:* Contact institution. *Faculty research:* Population health, health promotion and disease prevention, health services utilization, chronic disease epidemiology.

Drexel University, School of Public Health, Department of Epidemiology and Biostatistics, Philadelphia, PA 19104-2875. Offers biostatistics (MS); epidemiology (PhD); epidemiology and biostatistics (Certificate).

East Tennessee State University, School of Graduate Studies, College of Public and Allied Health, Department of Public Health, Johnson City, TN 37614. Offers community health (MPH); epidemiology (Certificate); gerontology (Certificate); health care management (Certificate); public health (MPH); public health administration (MPH). *Accreditation:* CEPH. Part-time programs available. *Degree requirements:* For master's, comprehensive exam, thesis optional. *Entrance requirements:* For master's, GRE General Test, 2 years of community health experience. Additional exam requirements/recommendations for international students: Required—TOEFL (minimum score 550 paper-based; 213 computer-based). *Faculty research:* Rural health issues, youth and adolescent health, health of the elderly, environmental epidemiology, spatial analysis of data.

Emory University, Rollins School of Public Health, Department of Epidemiology, Atlanta, GA 30322-1100. Offers MPH, MSPH, PhD. *Accreditation:* CEPH. Part-time programs available. *Degree requirements:* For master's, thesis, practicum. *Entrance requirements:* For master's, GRE General Test. Additional exam requirements/recommendations for international students: Required—TOEFL (minimum score 550 paper-based; 213 computer-based; 80 iBT). Electronic applications accepted. *Expenses:* Contact institution. *Faculty research:* Cancer, infectious diseases, epidemiological methods, environmental/occupational health, women's and children's health.

Emory University, Rollins School of Public Health, Online Program in Public Health, Atlanta, GA 30322-1100. Offers applied epidemiology (MPH); healthcare outcomes (MPH); prevention science (MPH). Part-time and evening/weekend programs available. Postbaccalaureate distance learning degree programs offered (minimal on-campus study). *Degree requirements:* For master's, thesis, practicum. *Entrance requirements:* For master's, GRE (may be waived). Additional exam requirements/recommendations for international students: Required—TOEFL (minimum score 550 paper-based; 213 computer-based; 80 iBT). Electronic applications accepted.

Florida International University, Stempel College of Public Health and Social Work, Programs in Public Health, Miami, FL 33199. Offers biostatistics (MPH); environmental and occupational health (MPH, PhD); epidemiology (MPH, PhD); health policy and management (MPH); health promotion and disease prevention (PhD); health promotion and diseases prevention (MPH). PhD only admits in Fall. *Accreditation:* CEPH. Part-time and evening/weekend programs available. Postbaccalaureate distance learning degree programs offered (no on-campus study). *Faculty:* 18 full-time (6 women). *Students:* 249 full-time (186 women), 185 part-time (144 women); includes 309 minority (154 African Americans, 2 American Indian/Alaska Native, 26 Asian Americans or Pacific Islanders, 127 Hispanic Americans), 48 international. Average age 35. 484 applicants, 29% accepted, 123 enrolled. In 2009, 79 master's, 1 doctorate awarded. *Degree requirements:* For master's, thesis optional; for doctorate, comprehensive exam, thesis/dissertation. *Entrance requirements:* For master's, minimum GPA of 3.0, letters of recommendation; for doctorate, GRE, resume, minimum GPA of 3.0, letters of recommendation, letter of intent. Additional exam requirements/recommendations for international students: Required—TOEFL (minimum score 550 paper-based; 80 iBT). *Application deadline:* For fall admission, 6/1 for domestic students, 4/1 for international students; for spring admission, 10/1 for domestic students, 9/1 for international students. Applications are processed on a rolling basis. Application fee: $30. Electronic applications accepted. *Expenses:* Contact institution. *Financial support:* Institutionally sponsored loans, scholarships/grants, and tuition waivers (full) available. Financial award application deadline: 3/1; financial award applicants required to submit FAFSA. *Faculty research:* Drugs/AIDS intervention among migrant workers, provision of services for active/recovering drug users with HIV. *Unit head:* Dr. Gilbert Ramirez, Associate Dean for Academic and Student Affairs, 305-348-7442, E-mail: ph@fiu.edu. *Application contact:* Nanett Rojas, Assistant Director of Graduate Admissions, 305-348-7442, Fax: 305-348-7441, E-mail: gradadm@fiu.edu.

George Mason University, College of Health and Human Services, Department of Global and Community Health, Fairfax, VA 22030. Offers biostatistics (Certificate); epidemiology (Certificate); epidemiology and biostatistics (MS); gerontology (Certificate); global health (MS, Certificate); nutrition (Certificate); public health (MPH, Certificate); rehabilitation science (Certificate). *Faculty:* 14 full-time (8 women), 12 part-time/adjunct (8 women). *Students:* 93 full-time (75 women), 106 part-time (92 women); includes 87 minority (46 African Americans, 1 American Indian/ Alaska Native, 31 Asian Americans or Pacific Islanders, 9 Hispanic Americans), 22 international. Average age 31. 269 applicants, 69% accepted, 146 enrolled. In 2009, 17 master's, 2 other advanced degrees awarded. *Degree requirements:* For master's, comprehensive exam (for some programs), thesis or practicum. *Entrance requirements:* For master's, GRE, BA with minimum GPA of 3.0, 2 letters of recommendation. Additional exam requirements/ recommendations for international students: Required—TOEFL. *Application deadline:* For fall admission, 4/1 priority date for domestic students, 4/1 for international students; for spring admission, 11/1 for domestic and international students. Applications are processed on a rolling basis. Application fee: $75. Electronic applications accepted. *Expenses:* Tuition, state resident: full-time $7568; part-time $315.33 per credit hour. Tuition, nonresident: full-time $21,704; part-time $904.33 per credit hour. Required fees: $2184; $91 per credit hour. *Financial support:* In 2009–10, 4 students received support, including 2 research assistantships with full and partial tuition reimbursements available (averaging $3,500 per year), 2 teaching assistantships with full and partial tuition reimbursements available (averaging $2,790 per year); Federal Work-Study, scholarships/grants, unspecified assistantships, and research awards, health care benefits health care benefits (full-time research or teaching assistantship recipients) also available. Support available to part-time students. Financial award application deadline: 3/1. *Faculty research:* Providing introductory and advanced degrees in health-related disciplines centered in global and community issues, health issues and the needs of affected populations at the regional and global level. *Unit head:* Dr. Shirley S. Travis, Dean, 703-993-1918. *Application contact:* Allan Weiss, Office Manager, 703-993-3126, E-mail: aweiss2@gmu.edu.

Georgetown University, Graduate School of Arts and Sciences, Programs in Biomedical Sciences, Department of Biostatistics, Bioinformatics and Biomathematics, Washington, DC 20057-1484. Offers biostatistics (MS), including bioinformatics, epidemiology. *Entrance requirements:* For master's, GRE General Test. Additional exam requirements/recommendations for international students: Required—TOEFL. *Faculty research:* Occupation epidemiology, cancer.

The George Washington University, Columbian College of Arts and Sciences, Program in Epidemiology, Washington, DC 20052. Offers MS, PhD. Part-time and evening/weekend programs available. *Students:* 4 full-time (all women), 16 part-time (9 women); includes 7 minority (3 Asian Americans or Pacific Islanders, 4 Hispanic Americans), 2 international. Average age 31. 24 applicants, 58% accepted, 3 enrolled. In 2009, 3 master's, 3 doctorates awarded. *Degree requirements:* For master's, comprehensive exam; for doctorate, thesis/dissertation, general exam. *Entrance requirements:* For master's and doctorate, GRE General Test, minimum GPA of 3.0. Additional exam requirements/recommendations for international students: Required—TOEFL (minimum score 550 paper-based; 213 computer-based; 80 iBT). *Application deadline:* For fall admission, 1/15 priority date for domestic and international students; for spring admission, 10/1 priority date for domestic students, 9/1 priority date for international students. Applications are processed on a rolling basis. Application fee: $60. Electronic applications accepted. *Financial support:* In 2009–10, 1 student received support; fellowships with tuition reimbursements available, teaching assistantships, tuition waivers available. *Unit head:* Dr. Sean D. Cleary, Director, 202-994-5757, Fax: 202-994-0082, E-mail: sphsdc@gwumc.edu. *Application contact:* Dr. Sean D. Cleary, Director, 202-994-5757, Fax: 202-994-0082, E-mail: sphsdc@gwumc.edu.

The George Washington University, School of Public Health and Health Services, Department of Epidemiology and Biostatistics, Washington, DC 20052. Offers biostatistics (MPH); epidemiology (MPH); microbiology and emerging infectious diseases (MSPH). *Faculty:* 16 full-time (7 women), 14 part-time/adjunct (8 women). *Students:* 52 full-time (40 women), 53 part-time (37 women); includes 44 minority (14 African Americans, 25 Asian Americans or Pacific Islanders, 5 Hispanic Americans), 5 international. Average age 28. 165 applicants, 85% accepted, 37 enrolled. In 2009, 28 master's awarded. *Degree requirements:* For master's, case study or special project. *Entrance requirements:* For master's, GMAT, GRE General Test, or MCAT. Additional exam requirements/recommendations for international students: Required—TOEFL. *Application deadline:* For fall admission, 4/15 priority date for domestic students, 4/15 for international students; for spring admission, 11/1 for domestic and international students. Applications are processed on a rolling basis. Application fee: $60. *Financial support:* In 2009–10, 6 students received support. Tuition waivers available. Financial award application deadline: 2/15. *Unit head:* Dr. Alan E. Greenberg, Chair, 202-994-0612, E-mail: aeg1@gwu.edu. *Application contact:* Jane Smith, Director of Admissions, 202-994-0248, Fax: 202-994-1860, E-mail: sphhsinfo@gwumc.edu.

Georgia Southern University, Jack N. Averitt College of Graduate Studies, Jiann-Ping Hsu College of Public Health, Program in Public Health, Statesboro, GA 30460. Offers biostatistics (MPH, Dr PH); community health behavior and education (Dr PH); community health education (MPH); environmental health sciences (MPH); epidemiology (MPH); health services policy management (MPH); public health leadership (Dr PH). Part-time programs available. *Students:* 75 full-time (47 women), 23 part-time (15 women); includes 39 minority (36 African Americans, 3 Asian Americans or Pacific Islanders), 24 international. Average age 30. 50 applicants, 80% accepted, 20 enrolled. In 2009, 20 master's awarded. *Degree requirements:* For master's, thesis optional, practicum; for doctorate, comprehensive exam, thesis/dissertation, practicum. *Entrance requirements:* For master's, GRE General Test, minimum GPA of 2.75, resume, 3 letters of reference; for doctorate, GRE, GMAT, MCAT, LSAT, 3 letters of reference, statement of purpose, resume or curriculum vitae. Additional exam requirements/recommendations for international students: Required—TOEFL (minimum score 550 paper-based; 213 computer-based; 80 iBT). *Application deadline:* For fall admission, 3/1 priority date for domestic and international students; for spring admission, 10/1 priority date for domestic students, 10/1 for international students. Applications are processed on a rolling basis. Application fee: $50. Electronic applications accepted. *Expenses:* Contact institution. *Financial support:* In 2009–10, 83 students received support, including research assistantships with partial tuition reimbursements available (averaging $7,200 per year), teaching assistantships with partial tuition reimbursements available (averaging $7,200 per year); career-related internships or fieldwork, Federal Work-Study, scholarships/grants, tuition waivers (partial), and unspecified assistantships also available. Support available to part-time students. Financial award application deadline: 4/15; financial award applicants required to submit FAFSA. *Faculty research:* Biostatistics, community health, environmental health sciences, epidemiology, health policy and management, community health behavior and education, public health leadership. *Unit head:* Dr. Charles Hardy, Dean, 912-478-2674, Fax: 912-478-5811, E-mail: chardy@georgiasouthern.edu. *Application contact:* Dr. Charles Ziglar, Coordinator for Graduate Student Recruitment, 912-478-5635, Fax: 912-478-0740, E-mail: gradadmissions@georgiasouthern.edu.

Harvard University, School of Public Health, Department of Epidemiology, Boston, MA 02115-6096. Offers cancer epidemiology (SM, DPH); cardiovascular epidemiology (SM, DPH, SD); clinical epidemiology (SM, DPH, SD); environmental/occupational epidemiology (SM, SD); epidemiologic methods (DPH, SD); epidemiology (SM, DPH, SD); epidemiology of aging (SM, DPH, SD); infectious diseases (SM, DPH, SD); molecular/genetic epidemiology (DPH, SD); neuroepidemiology (DPH, SD); nutritional epidemiology (DPH); oral and dental health epidemiology (SM, SD); pharmacoepidemiology (SM, DPH, SD); psychiatric epidemiology (SM, DPH); reproductive epidemiology (SM, SD). Part-time programs available. *Faculty:* 58 full-time (26 women), 21 part-time/adjunct (6 women). *Students:* 119 full-time, 37 part-time; includes 25 minority (4 African Americans, 1 American Indian/Alaska Native, 17 Asian Americans or Pacific Islanders, 3 Hispanic Americans), 61 international. Average age 30. 300 applicants, 31% accepted, 63 enrolled. In 2009, 36 master's, 10 doctorates awarded. *Degree requirements:* For doctorate, thesis/dissertation, qualifying exam. *Entrance requirements:* For master's and doctorate, GRE. Additional exam requirements/recommendations for international students: Required—TOEFL (minimum score 595 paper-based; 240 computer-based; 95 iBT); Recommended—IELTS (minimum score 7). *Application deadline:* For fall admission, 12/15 for domestic and international students. Application fee: $115. Electronic applications accepted. *Expenses:* Tuition: Full-time $33,696. Required fees: $1126. Full-time tuition and fees vary according to program. *Financial support:* Fellowships, research assistantships, teaching assistantships, Federal Work-Study, scholarships/grants, traineeships, tuition waivers (partial), and unspecified assistantships available. Support available to part-time students. Financial award application deadline: 2/8; financial award applicants required to submit FAFSA. *Faculty research:* Cancer prevention and epidemiology, cardiovascular epidemiology, environmental and occupational epidemiology, pharmacoepidemiology, psychiatric epidemiology. *Unit head:* Dr. Hans-Olov Adami, Chair, 617-432-1050, Fax: 617-432-7805, E-mail: hadami@hsph.harvard.edu. *Application contact:* Vincent W. James, Director of Admissions, 617-432-1031, Fax: 617-432-7080, E-mail: admisofc@hsph.harvard.edu.

Harvard University, School of Public Health, Department of Nutrition, Boston, MA 02115-6096. Offers nutrition (DPH, PhD, SD); nutritional epidemiology (DPH, SD); public health nutrition (DPH, SD). *Faculty:* 14 full-time (3 women), 7 part-time/adjunct (2 women). *Students:* 30 full-time, 1 part-time; includes 1 minority (Hispanic American), 22 international. Average age 33. 30 applicants, 30% accepted, 6 enrolled. In 2009, 11 doctorates awarded. *Degree requirements:* For doctorate, thesis/dissertation, qualifying exam. *Entrance requirements:* For doctorate, GRE. Additional exam requirements/recommendations for international students: Required—TOEFL (minimum score 595 paper-based; 240 computer-based; 95 iBT); Recommended—IELTS (minimum score 7). *Application deadline:* For fall admission, 12/15 for domestic and international students. Application fee: $115. Electronic applications accepted. *Expenses:* Tuition: Full-time $33,696. Required fees: $1126. Full-time tuition and fees vary according to program. *Financial support:* Fellowships, research assistantships, teaching assistantships, Federal Work-Study, scholarships/grants, traineeships, tuition waivers (partial), and unspecified assistantships available. Support available to part-time students. Financial award application deadline: 2/8; financial award applicants required to submit FAFSA. *Faculty research:* Dietary and genetic factors affecting heart diseases in humans; interactions among nutrition, immunity, and infection; role of diet and lifestyle in preventing macrovascular complications in diabetics. *Unit head:* Dr. Walter Willett, Chair, 617-432-1333, Fax: 617-432-2435, E-mail: walter.willett@channing.harvard.edu. *Application contact:* Vincent W. James, Director of Admissions, 617-432-1031, Fax: 617-432-7080, E-mail: admisofc@hsph.harvard.edu.

Hunter College of the City University of New York, Graduate School, Schools of the Health Professions, School of Health Sciences, Programs in Urban Public Health, Program in Epidemiology and Biostatistics, New York, NY 10021-5085. Offers MPH. Part-time and evening/weekend programs available. *Faculty:* 27 full-time (17 women), 3 part-time/adjunct (2 women). *Students:* 8 full-time (7 women), 16 part-time (10 women); includes 12 minority (6 African Americans, 5 Asian Americans or Pacific Islanders, 1 Hispanic American). Average age 32. 31 applicants, 61% accepted, 11 enrolled. *Degree requirements:* For master's, comprehensive exam, thesis optional, internship. *Entrance requirements:* For master's, GRE General Test, previous course work in calculus and statistics. Additional exam requirements/recommendations for international students: Required—TOEFL. *Application deadline:* For fall admission, 4/1 for domestic students; for spring admission, 11/1 for domestic students. Application fee: $125. *Expenses:* Tuition, state resident: full-time $7360; part-time $310 per credit. Required fees: $250 per semester. *Financial support:* In 2009–10, 6 fellowships were awarded; career-related internships or fieldwork, Federal Work-Study, institutionally sponsored loans, and tuition waivers (partial) also available. Support available to part-time students. Financial award application deadline: 3/1. *Unit head:* Victoria Frye, Coordinator, 212-481-7580, Fax: 212-481-5260, E-mail: vfrye@hunter.cuny.edu. *Application contact:* Milena Solo, Director for Graduate Admissions, 212-772-4288, Fax: 212-650-3336, E-mail: milena.solo@hunter.cuny.edu.

Indiana University–Purdue University Indianapolis, Indiana University School of Medicine, Department of Public Health, Indianapolis, IN 46202-2896. Offers behavioral health science (MPH); epidemiology (MPH); health policy and management (MPH). *Students:* 62 full-time (47 women), 71 part-time (54 women); includes 37 minority (24 African Americans, 12 Asian Americans or Pacific Islanders, 1 Hispanic American), 15 international. Average age 31. 17 applicants, 65% accepted, 6 enrolled.Application fee: $55 ($65 for international students). *Expenses:* Contact institution. *Financial support:* In 2009–10, 1 teaching assistantship (averaging $14,058 per year) was awarded. *Unit head:* Dr. Carole Kacius, Director, 317-274-3126. *Application contact:* Robert M. Stump, Director of Admissions, 317-274-3772, E-mail: inmedadm@iupui.edu.

The Johns Hopkins University, Bloomberg School of Public Health, Department of Epidemiology, Baltimore, MD 21205. Offers cancer epidemiology (MHS, Sc M, PhD, Sc D); cardiovascular disease epidemiology (MHS, Sc M, PhD, Sc D); clinical epidemiology (MHS, Sc M, PhD, Sc D); clinical trials (PhD, Sc D); epidemiology (Dr PH); epidemiology (general) (MHS, Sc M, PhD, Sc D); epidemiology of aging (MHS, Sc M, PhD, Sc D); human genetics/genetic epidemiology (MHS, Sc M, PhD, Sc D); infectious disease epidemiology (MHS, Sc M, PhD, Sc D); occupational/environmental epidemiology (MHS, Sc M, PhD, Sc D). Part-time programs available. *Faculty:* 80 full-time (44 women), 82 part-time/adjunct (36 women). *Students:* 142 full-time (102 women), 24 part-time (17 women); includes 44 minority (13 African Americans, 28 Asian Americans or Pacific Islanders, 3 Hispanic Americans), 41 international. Average age 30. 263 applicants, 41% accepted, 52 enrolled. In 2009, 61 master's, 25 doctorates awarded. *Degree requirements:* For master's, comprehensive exam, thesis, 1 year full-time residency; for doctorate, comprehensive exam, thesis/dissertation, 2 years full-time residency, oral and written exams, student teaching. *Entrance requirements:* For master's, GRE General Test or MCAT, 3 letters of recommendation, curriculum vitae; for doctorate, GRE General Test, minimum 1 year of work experience, 3 letters of recommendation, curriculum vitae, academic records from all schools. Additional exam requirements/recommendations for international students: Required—TOEFL (minimum score 600 paper-based; 250 computer-based; 100 iBT); Recommended—IELTS (minimum score 7.5), TWE. *Application deadline:* For fall admission, 12/1 priority date for domestic students. Applications are processed on a rolling basis. Application fee: $45. Electronic applications accepted. *Financial support:* In 2009–10, 2 fellowships (averaging $28,859 per year) were awarded; Federal Work-Study, institutionally sponsored loans, scholarships/grants, traineeships, tuition waivers (partial), and stipends also available. Support available to part-time students. Financial award application deadline: 3/15; financial award applicants required to submit FAFSA. *Faculty research:* Cancer and congenital malformations, nutritional epidemiology, AIDS, tuberculosis, cardiovascular disease, risk assessment. Total annual research expenditures: $70.1 million. *Unit head:* Dr. David D. Celentano, Chair, 410-955-3286, Fax: 410-955-0863, E-mail: dcelenta@jhsph.edu. *Application contact:* Frances S. Burman, Academic Program Manager, 410-955-3926, Fax: 410-955-0863, E-mail: fburman@jhsph.edu.

The Johns Hopkins University, Bloomberg School of Public Health, Department of International Health, Baltimore, MD 21205. Offers global disease epidemiology and control (MHS, PhD); health systems (MHS, PhD); human nutrition (MHS, PhD); international health (Dr PH); social and behavioral interventions (MHS, PhD). *Faculty:* 137 full-time (82 women), 185 part-time/adjunct (63 women). *Students:* 242 full-time (189 women), 1 (woman) part-time; includes 61 minority (9 African Americans, 41 Asian Americans or Pacific Islanders, 11 Hispanic Americans), 71 international. Average age 28. 494 applicants, 48% accepted, 100 enrolled. In 2009, 66 master's, 15 doctorates awarded. *Degree requirements:* For master's, comprehensive exam, thesis (for some programs), 1 year full-time residency, 4-9 month internship; for doctorate, comprehensive exam, thesis/dissertation or alternative, 1.5 years full-time residency, oral and written exams. *Entrance requirements:* For master's, GRE General Test or MCAT, 3 letters of recommendation, resume; for doctorate, GRE General Test or MCAT, 3 letters of recommendation, resume, transcripts. Additional exam requirements/recommendations for international students: Required—TOEFL (minimum score 600 paper-based; 250 computer-based; 100 iBT); Recommended—IELTS (minimum score 7). *Application deadline:* For fall admission, 1/2 priority date for domestic and international students. Applications are processed on a rolling basis. Application fee: $45. Electronic applications accepted. *Financial support:* In 2009–10, 188 students received support, including 15 fellowships (averaging $50,000 per year); Federal Work-Study, institutionally sponsored loans, scholarships/grants, traineeships, and stipends also available. Financial award application deadline: 1/2. *Faculty research:* Nutrition, infectious diseases, health systems, health economics, humanitarian emergencies. Total annual research expenditures: $72 million. *Unit head:* Dr. Robert E. Black, Chairman, 410-955-3934, Fax: 410-955-7159, E-mail: rblack@jhsph.edu. *Application contact:* Cristina G. Salazar, Academic Program Manager, 410-955-3734, Fax: 410-955-7159, E-mail: csalazar@jhsph.edu.

Loma Linda University, School of Public Health, Programs in Epidemiology and Biostatistics, Loma Linda, CA 92350. Offers MPH, MSPH, Dr PH, Postbaccalaureate Certificate. *Entrance requirements:* Additional exam requirements/recommendations for international students: Required—Michigan English Language Assessment Battery or TOEFL.

McGill University, Faculty of Graduate and Postdoctoral Studies, Faculty of Medicine, Department of Epidemiology and Biostatistics, Montréal, QC H3A 2T5, Canada. Offers community health (M Sc); environmental health (M Sc); epidemiology and biostatistics (M Sc, PhD, Diploma); health care evaluation (M Sc); medical statistics (M Sc). *Accreditation:* CEPH (one or more programs are accredited).

Medical College of Wisconsin, Graduate School of Biomedical Sciences, Department of Population Health, Program in Epidemiology, Milwaukee, WI 53226-0509. Offers MS. Part-time programs available. *Degree requirements:* For master's, thesis. *Entrance requirements:* For master's, GRE General Test, interview. Additional exam requirements/recommendations for international students: Required—TOEFL. *Faculty research:* Descriptive epidemiology of health care delivery using large databases.

Medical University of South Carolina, College of Graduate Studies, Division of Biostatistics and Epidemiology, Charleston, SC 29425. Offers biostatistics (MS, PhD); epidemiology (MS, PhD); DMD/PhD; MD/PhD. *Faculty:* 21 full-time (14 women), 1 part-time/adjunct (0 women). *Students:* 20 full-time (15 women), 1 (woman) part-time; includes 4 minority (3 African Americans, 1 Hispanic American), 4 international. Average age 29. 8 applicants, 63% accepted, 2 enrolled. In 2009, 6 master's, 9 doctorates awarded. Terminal master's awarded for partial completion of doctoral program. *Degree requirements:* For master's, thesis; for doctorate, thesis/dissertation, oral and written exams. *Entrance requirements:* For master's, GRE General Test; for doctorate, GRE General Test, interview, minimum GPA of 3.0. Additional exam requirements/

Epidemiology

Medical University of South Carolina (continued)
recommendations for international students: Required—TOEFL (minimum score 600 paper-based; 250 computer-based; 100 iBT). *Application deadline:* For fall admission, 1/15 priority date for domestic and international students. Applications are processed on a rolling basis. Application fee: $0 ($85 for international students). Electronic applications accepted. *Financial support:* In 2009–10, 18 research assistantships with partial tuition reimbursements (averaging $23,000 per year) were awarded; Federal Work-Study and scholarships/grants also available. Support available to part-time students. Financial award application deadline: 3/10; financial award applicants required to submit FAFSA. *Faculty research:* Health disparities, central nervous system injuries, radiation exposure, analysis of clinical trial data, biomedical information. *Unit head:* Dr. Yuko Y. Palesch, Professor/Director, 843-876-1917, Fax: 843-792-6590, E-mail: paleschy@musc.edu. *Application contact:* Dr. Anbesaw Selassie, Associate Professor, 843-876-1140, Fax: 843-792-6590, E-mail: selassie@musc.edu.

Memorial University of Newfoundland, Faculty of Medicine and School of Graduate Studies, Graduate Programs in Medicine, Division of Clinical Epidemiology, St. John's, NL A1C 5S7, Canada. Offers M Sc, PhD, Diploma.

Michigan State University, College of Human Medicine and The Graduate School, Graduate Programs in Human Medicine, Department of Epidemiology, East Lansing, MI 48824. Offers MS, PhD. *Faculty:* 12 full-time (4 women). *Students:* 18 full-time (9 women), 10 part-time (7 women); includes 6 minority (1 African American, 3 Asian Americans or Pacific Islanders, 2 Hispanic Americans), 8 international. Average age 32. 20 applicants, 40% accepted. In 2009, 5 master's, 6 doctorates awarded. *Degree requirements:* For master's, oral thesis defense. *Entrance requirements:* Additional exam requirements/recommendations for international students: Required—TOEFL. *Application deadline:* Applications are processed on a rolling basis. Electronic applications accepted. *Expenses:* Tuition, state resident: part-time $478.25 per credit hour. Tuition, nonresident: part-time $966.50 per credit hour. Part-time tuition and fees vary according to program. *Financial support:* In 2009–10, 7 research assistantships with tuition reimbursements (averaging $6,375 per year) were awarded. Total annual research expenditures: $3.1 million. *Unit head:* Dr. Joseph Gardiner, Interim Chairperson, 517-353-8623, Fax: 517-432-1130, E-mail: jgardiner@epi.msu.edu. *Application contact:* Angie Williams, Graduate Secretary, 517-432-3921, Fax: 517-432-1130, E-mail: epigrad@epi.msu.edu.

Morehouse School of Medicine, Master of Public Health Program, Atlanta, GA 30310-1495. Offers epidemiology (MPH); health administration, management and policy (MPH); health education/health promotion (MPH); international health (MPH). *Accreditation:* CEPH. Part-time programs available. *Faculty:* 4 full-time (1 woman), 36 part-time/adjunct (21 women). *Students:* 54 full-time (37 women), 3 part-time (2 women); includes 34 minority (33 African Americans, 1 American Indian/Alaska Native). Average age 28. 62 applicants, 48% accepted, 29 enrolled. In 2009, 13 master's awarded. *Degree requirements:* For master's, thesis, practicum, public health leadership seminar. *Entrance requirements:* For master's, GRE General Test, writing test, public health or human service experience. Additional exam requirements/recommendations for international students: Required—TOEFL (minimum score 550 paper-based; 200 computer-based). *Application deadline:* For fall admission, 3/1 for domestic and international students. Application fee: $50. Electronic applications accepted. *Expenses:* Contact institution. *Financial support:* In 2009–10, 32 students received support, including 6 research assistantships with partial tuition reimbursements available (averaging $10,000 per year); fellowships, teaching assistantships, career-related internships or fieldwork, Federal Work-Study, institutionally sponsored loans, scholarships/grants, and unspecified assistantships also available. Support available to part-time students. Financial award application deadline: 5/1; financial award applicants required to submit FAFSA. *Faculty research:* Women's and adolescent health, violence prevention, cancer epidemiology/disparities, substance abuse prevention. Total annual research expenditures: $640,176. *Unit head:* Dr. Patricia Rodney, Director/Assistant Dean for Public Health Education, 404-752-1944, Fax: 404-752-1051, E-mail: prodney@msm.edu. *Application contact:* Dr. Sterling Roaf, Director of Admissions, 404-752-1650, Fax: 404-752-1512, E-mail: mphadmissions@msm.edu.

New York Medical College, School of Health Sciences and Practice, Department of Epidemiology and Community Health, Program in Epidemiology, Valhalla, NY 10595-1691. Offers MPH. *Accreditation:* CEPH. Part-time and evening/weekend programs available. *Faculty:* 4 full-time, 14 part-time/adjunct. *Students:* 25 full-time, 40 part-time. Average age 32. 35 applicants, 80% accepted, 25 enrolled. *Degree requirements:* For master's, thesis. *Entrance requirements:* For master's, minimum undergraduate GPA of 3.0. Additional exam requirements/recommendations for international students: Required—TOEFL (minimum score 600 paper-based; 250 computer-based; 100 iBT), IELTS (minimum score 7). *Application deadline:* For fall admission, 8/1 priority date for domestic students, 5/15 for international students; for spring admission, 12/1 priority date for domestic students, 12/1 for international students. Applications are processed on a rolling basis. Application fee: $50 ($100 for international students). Electronic applications accepted. *Expenses:* Tuition: Full-time $18,170; part-time $790 per credit. Required fees: $790 per credit. $20 per semester. One-time fee: $100. Tuition and fees vary according to class time, course level, course load, degree level, program, student level and student's religious affiliation. *Financial support:* Career-related internships or fieldwork, Federal Work-Study, institutionally sponsored loans, health care benefits, tuition waivers (partial), and tuition reimbursements available. Support available to part-time students. Financial award applicants required to submit FAFSA. *Unit head:* Dr. Howell Sasser, Director of MPH Studies, 914-594-4804, Fax: 914-594-4292, E-mail: howell_sasser@nymc.edu. *Application contact:* Pamela Suett, Director of Recruitment, 914-594-4510, Fax: 914-594-4292, E-mail: shsp_admissions@nymc.edu.

New York University, Graduate School of Arts and Science, Department of Environmental Medicine, New York, NY 10012-1019. Offers environmental health sciences (MS, PhD), including biostatistics (PhD), environmental hygiene (MS), epidemiology (PhD), ergonomics and biomechanics (PhD), exposure assessment and health effects (PhD), molecular toxicology/carcinogenesis (PhD), toxicology. Part-time programs available. *Faculty:* 26 full-time (7 women). *Students:* 45 full-time (37 women), 15 part-time (8 women); includes 9 minority (3 African Americans, 3 Asian Americans or Pacific Islanders, 3 Hispanic Americans), 23 international. Average age 31. 60 applicants, 48% accepted, 14 enrolled. In 2009, 11 master's, 10 doctorates awarded. Terminal master's awarded for partial completion of doctoral program. *Degree requirements:* For master's, thesis or alternative; for doctorate, one foreign language, thesis/dissertation, oral and written exams. *Entrance requirements:* For master's and doctorate, GRE General Test, GRE Subject Test, minimum GPA of 3.0; bachelor's degree in biological, physical, or engineering science. Additional exam requirements/recommendations for international students: Required—TOEFL. *Application deadline:* For fall admission, 12/12 for domestic students. Application fee: $90. *Expenses:* Tuition: Full-time $30,528; part-time $1272 per credit. Required fees: $2177. *Financial support:* Fellowships with tuition reimbursements, teaching assistantships with tuition reimbursements, career-related internships or fieldwork, Federal Work-Study, institutionally sponsored loans, and health care benefits available. Financial award application deadline: 12/12; financial award applicants required to submit FAFSA. *Unit head:* Dr. Max Costa, Chair, 845-731-3661, Fax: 845-351-4510, E-mail: ehs@env.med.nyu.edu. *Application contact:* Dr. Jerome J. Solomon, Director of Graduate Studies, 845-731-3661, Fax: 845-351-4510, E-mail: ehs@env.med.nyu.edu.

North Carolina State University, College of Veterinary Medicine, Program in Comparative Biomedical Sciences, Raleigh, NC 27695. Offers cell biology (MS, PhD); infectious disease (MS, PhD); pathology (MS, PhD); pharmacology (MS, PhD); population medicine (MS, PhD). Part-time programs available. *Degree requirements:* For master's, thesis; for doctorate, thesis/dissertation. *Entrance requirements:* For master's and doctorate, GRE General Test. Additional exam requirements/recommendations for international students: Required—TOEFL (minimum score 550 paper-based; 213 computer-based). Electronic applications accepted. *Expenses:* Contact institution. *Faculty research:* Infectious diseases, cell biology, pharmacology and toxicology, genomics, pathology and population medicine.

Oregon Health & Science University, School of Medicine, Graduate Programs in Medicine, Department of Public Health and Preventive Medicine, Portland, OR 97239-3098. Offers epidemiology and biostatistics (MPH). *Accreditation:* CEPH. Part-time programs available. *Degree requirements:* For master's, thesis, fieldwork/internship. *Entrance requirements:* For master's, GRE General Test 500 Verbal, 600 Quantitative, 4.5 Analytical, previous undergraduate course work in statistics. Additional exam requirements/recommendations for international students: Required—TOEFL (minimum score 550 paper-based; 213 computer-based; 87 iBT). *Application deadline:* For fall admission, 2/1 for domestic students. Application fee: $65. Electronic applications accepted. Tuition and fees vary according to course level, course load, degree level, program and reciprocity agreements. *Faculty research:* Health services, health care access, health policy, environmental and occupational health. *Unit head:* Thomas M Becker, MD, Professor & Chair, 503-494-8257, Fax: 503-494-4981, E-mail: pmph@ohsu.edu. *Application contact:* Tree Triano, Education Manager, 503-494-2012, Fax: 503-494-4981, E-mail: pmph@ohsu.edu.

Ponce School of Medicine, Program in Public Health, Ponce, PR 00732-7004. Offers epidemiology (Dr PH); public health (MPH). *Faculty:* 9 full-time (5 women), 15 part-time/adjunct (5 women). *Students:* 49 full-time (35 women); includes 48 minority (all Hispanic Americans). Average age 30. 72 applicants, 75% accepted. In 2009, 26 degrees awarded. *Degree requirements:* For master's, one foreign language, comprehensive exam, thesis. *Entrance requirements:* For master's, GRE General Test or EXADEP, proficiency in Spanish and English, minimum GPA of 2.7, 3 letters of recommendation. *Application deadline:* For fall admission, 3/15 for domestic and international students. Application fee: $100. *Expenses:* Tuition: Part-time $225 per credit hour. Part-time tuition and fees vary according to program. *Financial support:* In 2009–10, 46 students received support. Scholarships/grants available. Financial award application deadline: 5/30; financial award applicants required to submit FAFSA. *Unit head:* Dr. Manuel Bayona, Head, 787-840-2575 Ext. 2232, E-mail: mbayona@psm.edu. *Application contact:* Maria Colon, Admissions Officer, 787-840-2575 Ext. 2143, E-mail: mcolon@psm.edu.

Purdue University, School of Veterinary Medicine and Graduate School, Graduate Programs in Veterinary Medicine, Department of Comparative Pathobiology, West Lafayette, IN 47907-2027. Offers comparative epidemiology and public health (MS); comparative epidemiology and public heath (PhD); comparative microbiology and immunology (MS, PhD); comparative pathobiology (MS, PhD); interdisciplinary studies (PhD), including microbial pathogenesis, molecular signaling and cancer biology, molecular virology; lab animal medicine (MS); veterinary anatomic pathology (MS); veterinary clinical pathology (MS). *Faculty:* 37 full-time (10 women), 4 part-time/adjunct (2 women). *Students:* 53 full-time (31 women), 2 part-time (1 woman); includes 3 minority (2 African Americans, 1 Hispanic American), 32 international. Average age 35. In 2009, 6 master's, 2 doctorates awarded. Terminal master's awarded for partial completion of doctoral program. *Degree requirements:* For master's, thesis (for some programs); for doctorate, thesis/dissertation. *Entrance requirements:* For master's and doctorate, GRE General Test. Additional exam requirements/recommendations for international students: Required—TOEFL (minimum score 575 paper-based; 232 computer-based), IELTS (minimum score 6.5), TWE (minimum score 4). *Application deadline:* For fall admission, 8/12 for domestic students, 6/15 for international students; for spring admission, 1/12 for domestic students, 10/15 for international students. Application fee: $55. Electronic applications accepted. *Financial support:* Fellowships, research assistantships, teaching assistantships available. Financial award application deadline: 3/1; financial award applicants required to submit FAFSA. *Unit head:* Dr. Suresh Mittal, Interim Head, 765-494-7543. *Application contact:* Denise A. Ottinger, Director, Student Services and Admissions, 765-494-7893, Fax: 765-496-2891, E-mail: vetadmissions@purdue.edu.

Queen's University at Kingston, School of Graduate Studies and Research, Faculty of Health Sciences, Department of Community Health and Epidemiology, Kingston, ON K7L 3N6, Canada. Offers epidemiology (PhD); epidemiology and population health (M Sc); health services (M Sc); policy research and clinical epidemiology (M Sc); public health (MPH). Part-time programs available. *Degree requirements:* For master's, thesis. *Entrance requirements:* For master's, GRE General Test (strongly recommended). Additional exam requirements/recommendations for international students: Required—TOEFL (minimum score 600 paper-based; 250 computer-based). *Faculty research:* Cancer epidemiology, clinical trials, biostatistics health services research, health policy.

San Diego State University, Graduate and Research Affairs, College of Health and Human Services, Graduate School of Public Health, San Diego, CA 92182. Offers environmental health (MPH); epidemiology (MPH, PhD), including biostatistics (MPH); global emergency preparedness and response (MS); global health (PhD); health behavior (PhD); health promotion (MPH); health services administration (MPH); toxicology (MS); MPH/MA; MSW/MPH. *Accreditation:* ABET (one or more programs are accredited); CAHME (one or more programs are accredited); CEPH (one or more programs are accredited). Part-time programs available. *Degree requirements:* For master's, comprehensive exam (for some programs), thesis (for some programs); for doctorate, thesis/dissertation. *Entrance requirements:* For master's, GMAT (MPH in health services administration), GRE General Test; for doctorate, GRE General Test. Additional exam requirements/recommendations for international students: Required—TOEFL. *Faculty research:* Evaluation of tobacco, AIDS prevalence and prevention, mammography, infant death project, Alzheimer's in elderly Chinese.

Stanford University, School of Medicine, Graduate Programs in Medicine, Department of Epidemiology, Stanford, CA 94305-9991. Offers MS, PhD. *Degree requirements:* For master's, thesis; for doctorate, thesis/dissertation, qualifying examinations. *Entrance requirements:* For doctorate, GRE General Test or MCAT. Additional exam requirements/recommendations for international students: Required—TOEFL. Electronic applications accepted. *Expenses:* Tuition: Full-time $37,380; part-time $2760 per quarter. Required fees: $501.

Temple University, Health Sciences Center and Graduate School, College of Health Professions, Department of Public Health, Program in Epidemiology, Philadelphia, PA 19122-6096. Offers MS. Part-time and evening/weekend programs available. *Entrance requirements:* For master's, GRE or MCAT. Additional exam requirements/recommendations for international students: Required—TOEFL (minimum score 550 paper-based; 213 computer-based; 79 iBT). Electronic applications accepted.

Texas A&M Health Science Center, School of Rural Public Health, College Station, TX 77840. Offers environmental/occupational health (MPH); epidemiology/biostatistics (MPH); health policy/management (MPH); social and behavioral health (MPH). *Accreditation:* CEPH. Part-time programs available. Postbaccalaureate distance learning degree programs offered (no on-campus study). *Degree requirements:* For master's, thesis optional. *Entrance requirements:* For master's, GRE General Test, minimum undergraduate GPA of 3.0. Electronic applications accepted. *Faculty research:* Tobacco cessation, youth health risk.

Texas A&M University, College of Veterinary Medicine, Department of Veterinary Integrative Biosciences, College Station, TX 77843. Offers epidemiology (MS); food safety/toxicology (MS); veterinary anatomy (MS, PhD); veterinary public health (MS). *Faculty:* 25. *Students:* 34 full-time (22 women), 8 part-time (5 women); includes 2 minority (1 African American, 1 Asian American or Pacific Islander), 20 international. Average age 30. In 2009, 1 master's, 1 doctorate awarded. Terminal master's awarded for partial completion of doctoral program. *Degree requirements:* For master's, comprehensive exam, thesis; for doctorate, comprehensive exam, thesis/dissertation. *Entrance requirements:* For master's and doctorate, GRE General Test, minimum undergraduate GPA of 3.0. Additional exam requirements/recommendations for international students: Required—TOEFL. *Application deadline:* For fall admission, 7/15 priority date for domestic students, 4/1 priority date for international students; for spring admission, 10/1 priority date for domestic students, 9/15 priority date for international students. Applications are processed on a rolling basis. Application fee: $50 ($75 for international students). Electronic applications accepted. *Expenses:* Tuition, state resident: full-time $3991; part-time $221.74 per credit hour. Tuition, nonresident: full-time $9049; part-time $502.74 per credit hour. *Financial support:* In 2009–10, fellowships (averaging $18,000 per year), research

assistantships (averaging $15,600 per year), teaching assistantships (averaging $15,600 per year) were awarded; institutionally sponsored loans, unspecified assistantships, and clinical associateships also available. Financial award application deadline: 7/15; financial award applicants required to submit FAFSA. *Faculty research:* Metal toxicology, reproductive biology, genetics of neural development, developmental biology, environmental toxicology. *Unit head:* Dr. E. Tiffany-Castiglioni, Head, 979-862-6559, E-mail: ecastiglioni@cvm.tamu.edu. *Application contact:* Dr. Jane Welsh, Chair, Fax: 979-847-8981, E-mail: jwelsh@cum.tamu.edu.

Thomas Edison State College, School of Applied Science and Technology, Program in Clinical Trials Management, Trenton, NJ 08608-1176. Offers Graduate Certificate. Part-time programs available. Postbaccalaureate distance learning degree programs offered (no on-campus study). *Students:* 25 part-time (17 women); includes 5 minority (3 African Americans, 1 Asian American or Pacific Islander, 1 Hispanic American). Average age 42. In 2009, 7 degrees awarded. *Entrance requirements:* Additional exam requirements/recommendations for international students: Required—TOEFL (minimum score 550 paper-based; 213 computer-based; 79 iBT). *Application deadline:* For fall admission, 8/15 priority date for domestic and international students; for winter admission, 11/15 priority date for domestic and international students; for spring admission, 2/15 priority date for domestic students, 2/18 priority date for international students. Applications are processed on a rolling basis. Application fee: $75. Electronic applications accepted. *Expenses:* Tuition, area resident: Part-time $479 per credit. Tuition, state resident: part-time $479 per credit. Tuition, nonresident: part-time $479 per credit. *Financial support:* Applicants required to submit FAFSA. *Unit head:* Dr. Marcus Tillery, Dean, School of Applied Science and Technology, 609-984-1130, Fax: 609-984-3898, E-mail: info@tesc.edu. *Application contact:* David Hoftiezer, Director of Admissions, 888-442-8372, Fax: 609-984-8447, E-mail: admissions@tesc.edu.

Thomas Jefferson University, Jefferson School of Population Health, Program in Chronic Care Management, Philadelphia, PA 19107. Offers MS. Postbaccalaureate distance learning degree programs offered. *Entrance requirements:* For master's, GRE or equivalent, 2 letters of recommendation, interview. Additional exam requirements/recommendations for international students: Required—TOEFL. Electronic applications accepted. *Expenses:* Tuition: Full-time $26,858; part-time $879 per credit. Required fees: $525.

Tufts University, Graduate School of Arts and Sciences, Graduate Certificate Programs, Program in Epidemiology, Medford, MA 02155. Offers Certificate. Electronic applications accepted. *Expenses:* Tuition: Full-time $38,096; part-time $3962 per credit. Required fees: $686; $40 per year. Tuition and fees vary according to course level, course load, degree level, program and student level.

Tufts University, Sackler School of Graduate Biomedical Sciences, Division of Clinical Care Research, Medford, MA 02155. Offers MS, PhD. *Faculty:* 37 full-time (11 women). *Students:* 23 full-time (15 women), 1 part-time (0 women); includes 5 minority (1 African American, 4 Asian Americans or Pacific Islanders), 10 international. Average age 33. 32 applicants, 41% accepted, 13 enrolled. In 2009, 7 master's awarded. Terminal master's awarded for partial completion of doctoral program. *Degree requirements:* For master's, thesis; for doctorate, thesis/dissertation. *Entrance requirements:* For master's and doctorate, MD or PhD, strong clinical research background. Additional exam requirements/recommendations for international students: Required—TOEFL. *Application deadline:* For fall admission, 12/15 for domestic and international students. Applications are processed on a rolling basis. Application fee: $70. Electronic applications accepted. *Expenses:* Tuition: Full-time $38,096; part-time $3962 per credit. Required fees: $686; $40 per year. Tuition and fees vary according to course level, course load, degree level, program and student level. *Financial support:* In 2009–10, 27 fellowships with full tuition reimbursements were awarded. Financial award application deadline: 12/15. *Faculty research:* Clinical study design, mathematical modeling, meta analysis, epidemiologic research, coronary heart disease. *Unit head:* Dr. Harry P. Selker, Program Director, 617-636-5009, Fax: 617-636-8023, E-mail: hselker@lifespan.org. *Application contact:* Kellie Johnston, Associate Director of Admissions, 617-636-6767, Fax: 617-636-0375, E-mail: sackler-school@tufts.edu.

Tulane University, School of Public Health and Tropical Medicine, Department of Epidemiology, New Orleans, LA 70118-5669. Offers MPH, MS, Dr PH, PhD. MS and PhD offered through the Graduate School. *Accreditation:* CEPH (one or more programs are accredited). Part-time programs available. *Degree requirements:* For doctorate, comprehensive exam, thesis/dissertation. *Entrance requirements:* For master's and doctorate, GRE General Test. Additional exam requirements/recommendations for international students: Required—TOEFL. Electronic applications accepted. *Faculty research:* Environment, cancer, cardiovascular epidemiology, women's health.

Université Laval, Faculty of Medicine, Graduate Programs in Medicine, Department of Medicine, Programs in Epidemiology, Québec, QC G1K 7P4, Canada. Offers M Sc, PhD. Terminal master's awarded for partial completion of doctoral program. *Degree requirements:* For master's, thesis; for doctorate, comprehensive exam, thesis/dissertation. *Entrance requirements:* For master's and doctorate, knowledge of French, comprehension of written English. Electronic applications accepted.

University at Albany, State University of New York, School of Public Health, Department of Epidemiology and Biostatistics, Albany, NY 12222-0001. Offers MS, PhD. *Degree requirements:* For master's, thesis; for doctorate, thesis/dissertation. *Entrance requirements:* For master's and doctorate, GRE General Test. Additional exam requirements/recommendations for international students: Required—TOEFL (minimum score 550 paper-based; 213 computer-based). Electronic applications accepted.

University at Buffalo, the State University of New York, Graduate School, School of Public Health and Health Professions, Department of Social and Preventive Medicine, Buffalo, NY 14260. Offers community health (PhD); epidemiology (MS, PhD); public health (MPH). Part-time programs available. *Faculty:* 11 full-time (7 women), 11 part-time/adjunct (5 women). *Students:* 19 full-time (11 women), 15 part-time (8 women); includes 4 minority (all Asian Americans or Pacific Islanders), 3 international. Average age 30. 127 applicants, 41% accepted. In 2009, 4 master's, 4 doctorates awarded. Terminal master's awarded for partial completion of doctoral program. *Degree requirements:* For master's, comprehensive exam, thesis; for doctorate, comprehensive exam, thesis/dissertation. *Entrance requirements:* For master's and doctorate, GRE General Test. Additional exam requirements/recommendations for international students: Required—TOEFL (minimum score 600 paper-based; 250 computer-based; 100 iBT). *Application deadline:* For fall admission, 1/15 priority date for domestic and international students. Applications are processed on a rolling basis. Application fee: $50. Electronic applications accepted. *Financial support:* In 2009–10, 10 students received support, including 1 fellowship with full tuition reimbursement available (averaging $15,000 per year), 8 research assistantships with full tuition reimbursements available (averaging $15,000 per year); teaching assistantships with full tuition reimbursements available, career-related internships or fieldwork, Federal Work-Study, institutionally sponsored loans, health care benefits, and unspecified assistantships also available. Financial award application deadline: 2/1; financial award applicants required to submit FAFSA. *Faculty research:* Epidemiology of community health services including cancer and nutrition, cardiovascular disease, epidemiology of cancer, cardiovascular diseases, health services research. Total annual research expenditures: $5.5 million. *Unit head:* Dr. Jo Freudenheim, Chair, 716-829-2975 Ext. 612, Fax: 716-829-2979, E-mail: jfreuden@buffalo.edu. *Application contact:* Dr. Carl Li, Director of Graduate Studies, 716-829-2975 Ext. 618, Fax: 716-829-2979, E-mail: carlli@buffalo.edu.

The University of Alabama at Birmingham, School of Public Health, Program in Epidemiology, Birmingham, AL 35294. Offers PhD. *Degree requirements:* For doctorate, thesis/dissertation. *Entrance requirements:* For doctorate, GRE General Test or MAT, MPH or MSPH. Electronic applications accepted. *Faculty research:* Biometry.

University of Alberta, School of Public Health, Department of Public Health Sciences, Edmonton, AB T6G 2E1, Canada. Offers clinical epidemiology (M Sc, MPH); environmental and occupational health (MPH); environmental health sciences (M Sc); epidemiology (M Sc); global health (M Sc, MPH); health policy and management (MPH); health policy research (M Sc); health technology assessment (MPH); occupational health (M Sc); population health (M Sc); public health leadership (MPH); public health sciences (PhD); quantitative methods (MPH). *Accreditation:* CEPH (one or more programs are accredited). *Faculty:* 24 full-time (5 women), 59 part-time/adjunct (13 women). *Students:* 49 full-time, 49 part-time. 81 applicants, 31% accepted. In 2009, 28 master's awarded. Terminal master's awarded for partial completion of doctoral program. *Degree requirements:* For master's, thesis (for some programs); for doctorate, thesis/dissertation. *Entrance requirements:* For master's, GMAT or GRE General Test. Additional exam requirements/recommendations for international students: Required—TOEFL (minimum score 550 paper-based; 213 computer-based) or IELTS (minimum score 6). *Application deadline:* For fall admission, 3/15 for domestic students, 7/1 for international students; for winter admission, 11/1 for international students; for spring admission, 3/1 for international students. Applications are processed on a rolling basis. Application fee: $0. Electronic applications accepted. Tuition and fees charges are reported in Canadian dollars. *Expenses:* Tuition, area resident: Full-time $4626 Canadian dollars; part-time $99.72 Canadian dollars per unit. International tuition: $8216 Canadian dollars full-time. Required fees: $3590 Canadian dollars; $99.72 Canadian dollars per unit. $215 Canadian dollars per term. *Financial support:* In 2009–10, 11 students received support, including 6 research assistantships with tuition reimbursements available (averaging $2,200 per year); fellowships, teaching assistantships, career-related internships or fieldwork and tuition waivers (partial) also available. Financial award application deadline: 2/1. *Faculty research:* Biostatistics, health promotion and socio-behavioral health science. Total annual research expenditures: $5.7 million. *Unit head:* L. Duncan Saunders, Acting Chair, 780-492-6814, Fax: 780-492-0364. *Application contact:* Felicity R. Hey, Graduate Programs Administrator, 780-492-6407, Fax: 780-492-0364, E-mail: felicity.hey@ualberta.ca.

The University of Arizona, Mel and Enid Zuckerman College of Public Health, Program in Epidemiology, Tucson, AZ 85721. Offers MS, PhD. *Faculty:* 8. *Students:* 7 full-time (5 women), 20 part-time (13 women); includes 6 minority (1 African American, 1 American Indian/Alaska Native, 4 Hispanic Americans), 3 international. Average age 37. 34 applicants, 29% accepted, 4 enrolled. In 2009, 1 master's, 6 doctorates awarded. *Entrance requirements:* Additional exam requirements/recommendations for international students: Required—TOEFL (minimum score 550 paper-based; 213 computer-based; 79 iBT). *Application deadline:* For fall admission, 1/1 for domestic and international students. Applications are processed on a rolling basis. Application fee: $75. Electronic applications accepted. *Expenses:* Tuition, state resident: full-time $9028. Tuition, nonresident: full-time $24,890. Total annual research expenditures: $1.2 million. *Unit head:* Dr. Iman Hakim, Interim Dean, 520-626-7083, E-mail: ihakim@email.arizona.edu. *Application contact:* Lorraine Varela, Special Assistant to the Dean, 520-626-3201, E-mail: varelal@coph.arizona.edu.

The University of British Columbia, Faculty of Medicine, School of Population and Public Health, Vancouver, BC V6T 1Z3, Canada. Offers health administration (MHA); health care and epidemiology (MH Sc, PhD); public health (MPH). *Accreditation:* CEPH (one or more programs are accredited). Postbaccalaureate distance learning degree programs offered (minimal on-campus study). *Degree requirements:* For master's, thesis (for some programs), major paper (MH Sc), research project (MHA); for doctorate, thesis/dissertation. *Entrance requirements:* For master's, GRE General Test or GMAT, PCAT, MCAT (MHA), MD or equivalent (for MH Sc); 4-year undergraduate degree from accredited university with minimum B+ overall academic average and in math or statistics course at undergraduate level (for MPH); 4-year undergraduate degree from accredited university with minimum B+ overall academic average plus work experience (for MHA); for doctorate, master's degree from accredited university with minimum B+ overall academic average and in math or statistics course at undergraduate level. Additional exam requirements/recommendations for international students: Required—TOEFL. Electronic applications accepted. *Faculty research:* Population and public health, clinical epidemiology, epidemiology and biostatistics, global health and vulnerable populations, health care services and systems, occupational and environmental health, public health emerging threats and rapid response, social and life course determinants of health, health administration.

University of Calgary, Faculty of Medicine and Faculty of Graduate Studies, Department of Microbiology and Infectious Diseases, Calgary, AB T2N 1N4, Canada. Offers M Sc, PhD. *Degree requirements:* For master's, thesis, oral thesis exam; for doctorate, thesis/dissertation, candidacy exam, oral thesis exam. *Entrance requirements:* For master's and doctorate, minimum GPA of 3.2. Additional exam requirements/recommendations for international students: Required—TOEFL (minimum score 580 paper-based; 237 computer-based). Electronic applications accepted. *Faculty research:* Bacteriology, virology, parasitology, immunology.

University of California, Berkeley, Graduate Division, School of Public Health, Group in Epidemiology, Berkeley, CA 94720-1500. Offers epidemiology (MS, PhD); infectious diseases (MPH, PhD). *Accreditation:* CEPH (one or more programs are accredited). *Students:* 48 full-time (34 women). Average age 33. 85 applicants, 8 enrolled. In 2009, 2 master's, 17 doctorates awarded. *Degree requirements:* For master's, comprehensive exam; for doctorate, thesis/dissertation, oral and written exam. *Entrance requirements:* For master's, GRE General Test, minimum GPA of 3.0; MD, DDS, DVM, or PhD in biomedical science (MPH); for doctorate, GRE General Test, minimum GPA of 3.0. *Application deadline:* For fall admission, 12/1 for domestic students. Applications are processed on a rolling basis. Application fee: $70 ($90 for international students). *Financial support:* Fellowships, research assistantships, teaching assistantships, Federal Work-Study and unspecified assistantships available. *Unit head:* Prof. Arthur L. Reingold, Head, 510-642-3997, E-mail: robertamyers@berkeley.edu. *Application contact:* Roberta Meyers, Graduate Assistant, 510-643-2731, E-mail: robertamyers@berkeley.edu.

University of California, Davis, Graduate Studies, Graduate Group in Epidemiology, Davis, CA 95616. Offers MS, PhD. Terminal master's awarded for partial completion of doctoral program. *Degree requirements:* For master's, comprehensive exam (for some programs), thesis (for some programs); for doctorate, thesis/dissertation. *Entrance requirements:* For master's and doctorate, GRE General Test, GRE Subject Test (biology), minimum GPA of 3.25. Additional exam requirements/recommendations for international students: Required—TOEFL (minimum score 550 paper-based; 213 computer-based). Electronic applications accepted. *Faculty research:* Environmental/occupational wildlife, reproductive and veterinary epidemiology, infectious/chronic disease epidemiology, public health.

University of California, Irvine, School of Medicine, Department of Epidemiology, Irvine, CA 92697. Offers MS, PhD. Terminal master's awarded for partial completion of doctoral program. *Degree requirements:* For master's, comprehensive exam, thesis; for doctorate, comprehensive exam, thesis/dissertation, 72 quarter units. *Entrance requirements:* For master's, GRE, minimum GPA of 3.0, letters of recommendation; for doctorate, GRE, minimum GPA of 3.0, personal statement, letters of recommendation. Additional exam requirements/recommendations for international students: Required—TOEFL (minimum score 550 paper-based; 213 computer-based; 80 iBT), IELTS (minimum score 7). Electronic applications accepted. *Faculty research:* Genetic/molecular epidemiology, cancer epidemiology, biostatistics, environmental health, occupational health.

University of California, Los Angeles, Graduate Division, School of Public Health, Department of Epidemiology, Los Angeles, CA 90095. Offers MPH, MS, Dr PH, PhD, MD/MPH. *Degree requirements:* For master's, comprehensive exam or thesis; for doctorate, thesis/dissertation, oral and written qualifying exams. *Entrance requirements:* For master's, GRE General Test, minimum GPA of 3.0; for doctorate, GRE General Test, minimum undergraduate GPA of 3.0. Electronic applications accepted.

University of California, San Diego, Office of Graduate Studies, Program in Public Health and Epidemiology, La Jolla, CA 92093. Offers PhD. Electronic applications accepted.

University of Cincinnati, Graduate School, College of Medicine, Graduate Programs in Biomedical Sciences, Department of Environmental Health, Cincinnati, OH 45221. Offers environmental and industrial hygiene (MS, PhD); environmental and occupational medicine

Epidemiology

University of Cincinnati (continued)
(MS); environmental genetics and molecular toxicology (MS, PhD); epidemiology and biostatistics (MS, PhD); occupational safety and ergonomics (MS, PhD). *Accreditation:* ABET (one or more programs are accredited). Terminal master's awarded for partial completion of doctoral program. *Degree requirements:* For master's, thesis; for doctorate, thesis/dissertation, qualifying exam. *Entrance requirements:* For master's, GRE General Test, bachelor's degree in science; for doctorate, GRE General Test. Additional exam requirements/recommendations for international students: Required—TOEFL (minimum score 600 paper-based; 250 computer-based; 100 iBT). Electronic applications accepted. *Faculty research:* Carcinogens and mutagenesis, pulmonary studies, reproduction and development.

University of Colorado Denver, Colorado School of Public Health, Health Services Research Program, Denver, CO 80217-3364. Offers computational bioscience (PhD); epidemiology (PhD); health services research (PhD). *Students:* 35 full-time (17 women), 3 part-time (all women); includes 3 minority (all Hispanic Americans), 3 international. In 2009, 3 doctorates awarded. *Degree requirements:* For doctorate, comprehensive exam, thesis/dissertation. *Entrance requirements:* For doctorate, GRE, interview, 3 letters of recommendation. Additional exam requirements/recommendations for international students: Required—TOEFL (minimum score 550 paper-based; 213 computer-based). *Application deadline:* For fall admission, 2/1 for domestic students. Application fee: $50. *Financial support:* Application deadline: 3/1. *Faculty research:* Biochemical functions of proteins, description and classification of enzymatic functions, optimization of genome-shuffling in gram negative bacteria. *Application contact:* Information Contact, 303-724-4613, Fax: 303-724-4620, E-mail: colorado.sph@ucdenver.edu.

University of Florida, College of Medicine, Program in Clinical Investigation, Gainesville, FL 32611. Offers clinical investigation (MS); epidemiology (MS); public health (MPH). Part-time programs available. *Entrance requirements:* For master's, GRE, MD, PhD, DMD/DDS or Pharm D.

University of Florida, Graduate School, College of Public Health and Health Professions and College of Medicine, Programs in Public Health, Gainesville, FL 32611. Offers biostatistics (MPH); environmental health (MPH); epidemiology (MPH); public health management and policy (MPH); public health practice (MPH); social and behavioral sciences (MPH). *Entrance requirements:* For master's, GRE General Test, minimum GPA of 3.0. Additional exam requirements/recommendations for international students: Required—TOEFL (minimum score 550 paper-based; 213 computer-based).

University of Guelph, Ontario Veterinary College and Graduate Program Services, Graduate Programs in Veterinary Sciences, Department of Population Medicine, Guelph, ON N1G 2W1, Canada. Offers epidemiology (M Sc, DV Sc, PhD); health management (DV Sc); population medicine and health management (M Sc); swine health management (M Sc); theriogenology (M Sc, DV Sc). *Degree requirements:* For master's, thesis; for doctorate, comprehensive exam, thesis/dissertation. *Entrance requirements:* Additional exam requirements/recommendations for international students: Required—TOEFL.

University of Hawaii at Manoa, John A. Burns School of Medicine, Department of Public Health Sciences and Epidemiology, Honolulu, HI 96822. Offers epidemiology (PhD); global health and population studies (Graduate Certificate); public health (MPH, MS, Dr PH). *Accreditation:* CEPH. Part-time programs available. *Faculty:* 27 full-time (10 women), 9 part-time/adjunct (7 women). *Students:* 62 full-time (47 women), 16 part-time (12 women); includes 31 minority (2 American Indian/Alaska Native, 26 Asian Americans or Pacific Islanders, 3 Hispanic Americans), 14 international. Average age 31. 98 applicants, 58% accepted, 40 enrolled. In 2009, 18 master's awarded. *Entrance requirements:* Additional exam requirements/recommendations for international students: Required—TOEFL (minimum score 550 paper-based; 213 computer-based; 79 iBT), IELTS (minimum score 5). *Application deadline:* For fall admission, 3/1 for domestic and international students; for spring admission, 9/1 for domestic and international students. Application fee: $60. *Expenses:* Tuition, state resident: full-time $8900; part-time $372 per credit. Tuition, nonresident: full-time $21,400; part-time $898 per credit. Required fees: $207 per semester. *Financial support:* In 2009–10, 6 students received support, including 19 fellowships (averaging $1,203 per year), 17 research assistantships (averaging $17,361 per year), 1 teaching assistantship (averaging $14,382 per year). Total annual research expenditures: $242,000. *Application contact:* Alan Katz, Graduate Chair, 808-956-8577, Fax: 808-956-5818, E-mail: katz@hawaii.edu.

University of Illinois at Chicago, Graduate College, School of Public Health, Program in Epidemiology, Chicago, IL 60607-7128. Offers cancer epidemiology (MS, PhD); epidemiology (MPH, MS, Dr PH, PhD). *Accreditation:* CEPH (one or more programs are accredited). Part-time programs available. Terminal master's awarded for partial completion of doctoral program. *Degree requirements:* For master's, thesis, field practicum; for doctorate, thesis/dissertation, independent research, internship. *Entrance requirements:* For master's and doctorate, GRE General Test, minimum GPA of 2.75. Additional exam requirements/recommendations for international students: Required—TOEFL. Electronic applications accepted.

The University of Iowa, Graduate College, College of Public Health, Department of Epidemiology, Iowa City, IA 52242-1316. Offers clinical investigation (MS); epidemiology (MS, PhD). *Degree requirements:* For master's, thesis optional, exam; for doctorate, comprehensive exam, thesis/dissertation. *Entrance requirements:* For master's and doctorate, GRE General Test, minimum GPA of 3.0. Additional exam requirements/recommendations for international students: Required—TOEFL (minimum score 600 paper-based; 250 computer-based; 100 iBT). Electronic applications accepted.

University of Louisville, Graduate School, School of Public Health and Information Sciences, Department of Epidemiology and Population Health, Louisville, KY 40292-0001. Offers epidemiology (MS); public health sciences (PhD), including epidemiology. *Faculty:* 10 full-time (5 women). *Students:* 1 (woman) full-time. Average age 44. 8 applicants, 25% accepted, 0 enrolled. *Entrance requirements:* For master's and doctorate, GRE (greater than 50th percentile in both sections), 2 letters of recommendation on letterhead. Additional exam requirements/recommendations for international students: Required—TOEFL (minimum score 547 paper-based; 210 computer-based; 78 iBT). *Application deadline:* For fall admission, 4/30 for domestic and international students. Application fee: $50. Electronic applications accepted. *Financial support:* In 2009–10, 6 research assistantships with full tuition reimbursements (averaging $20,000 per year) were awarded; unspecified assistantships also available. Financial award application deadline: 5/1. *Faculty research:* Cancer, cardiovascular disease, aging, infectious disease (specifically tuberculosis and AIDS), diabetes and occupational safety among adolescents. Total annual research expenditures: $484,000. *Unit head:* Dr. Richard Baumgartner, Department Chair, 502-852-2038, Fax: 502-852-3291, E-mail: rnbaum01@gwise.louisville.edu. *Application contact:* Vicki Lewis, Administrative Assistant, 502-852-1798, Fax: 502-852-3294, E-mail: vicki.lewis@louisville.edu.

University of Maryland, Baltimore, Graduate School, Graduate Program in Life Sciences, Baltimore, MD 21201. Offers biochemistry and molecular biology (MS, PhD), including biochemistry; epidemiology (PhD); gerontology (PhD); molecular medicine (MS, PhD), including cancer biology (PhD), cell and molecular physiology (PhD), human genetics and genomic medicine (PhD), molecular medicine (MS), molecular toxicology and pharmacology (PhD); molecular microbiology and immunology (PhD); neuroscience (PhD); physical rehabilitation science (PhD); toxicology (MS, PhD); MD/MS; MD/PhD. *Students:* 248 full-time (148 women), 72 part-time (40 women); includes 80 minority (25 African Americans, 1 American Indian/Alaska Native, 39 Asian Americans or Pacific Islanders, 15 Hispanic Americans), 47 international. Average age 29. 719 applicants, 22% accepted, 64 enrolled. In 2009, 29 master's, 39 doctorates awarded. *Degree requirements:* For master's, comprehensive exam (for some programs), thesis (for some programs); for doctorate, comprehensive exam, thesis/dissertation. *Entrance requirements:* For master's and doctorate, GRE. Additional exam requirements/recommendations for international students: Required—TOEFL (minimum score 550 paper-based; 80 iBT); Recommended—IELTS (minimum score 7). *Application deadline:* For fall admission, 1/15 for domestic and international students. Application fee: $50. Electronic applications accepted. *Expenses:* Tuition, state resident: full-time $7290; part-time $405 per credit hour. Tuition, nonresident: full-time $12,780; part-time $710 per credit hour. Required fees: $774; $10 per credit hour. $297 per semester. Tuition and fees vary according to course load, degree level and program. *Financial support:* In 2009–10, research assistantships with partial tuition reimbursements (averaging $25,000 per year); fellowships, scholarships/grants, health care benefits, and unspecified assistantships also available. Financial award application deadline: 3/1. *Faculty research:* Cancer, reproduction, cardiovascular, immunology. *Unit head:* Dr. Margaret Merryl McCarthy, Assistant Dean for Graduate Studies, 410-706-2655, Fax: 410-706-8341, E-mail: mmcarthy@umaryland.edu. *Application contact:* Dr. Margaret Merryl McCarthy, Assistant Dean for Graduate Studies, 410-706-2655, Fax: 410-706-8341, E-mail: mmcarthy@umaryland.edu.

University of Maryland, Baltimore, Graduate School, Graduate Programs in Pharmacy, Department of Pharmaceutical Health Service Research, Baltimore, MD 21201. Offers epidemiology (MS); pharmacy administration (PhD); Pharm D/PhD. *Degree requirements:* For doctorate, comprehensive exam, thesis/dissertation. *Entrance requirements:* For doctorate, GRE General Test. Additional exam requirements/recommendations for international students: Required—TOEFL, IELTS. Electronic applications accepted. *Expenses:* Tuition, state resident: full-time $7290; part-time $405 per credit hour. Tuition, nonresident: full-time $12,780; part-time $710 per credit hour. Required fees: $774; $10 per credit hour. $297 per semester. Tuition and fees vary according to course load, degree level and program. *Faculty research:* Pharmacoeconomics, outcomes research, public health policy, drug therapy and aging.

University of Maryland, Baltimore, School of Medicine, Department of Epidemiology and Preventive Medicine, Baltimore, MD 21201. Offers biostatistics (MS); clinical research (MS); epidemiology (PhD); epidemiology and preventive medicine (MPH, MS); gerontology (PhD); human genetics and genomic (MS, PhD); molecular epidemiology (PhD); toxicology (MS, PhD); JD/MS; MD/PhD; MS/PhD. *Accreditation:* CEPH. Part-time programs available. *Students:* 64 full-time (42 women), 60 part-time (40 women); includes 40 minority (17 African Americans, 19 Asian Americans or Pacific Islanders, 4 Hispanic Americans), 16 international. Average age 31. 207 applicants, 48% accepted, 50 enrolled. In 2009, 24 master's, 9 doctorates awarded. *Entrance requirements:* For master's and doctorate, GRE General Test, minimum GPA of 3.0. Additional exam requirements/recommendations for international students: Required—TOEFL; Recommended—IELTS. *Application deadline:* For fall admission, 1/15 for domestic and international students. Application fee: $50. Electronic applications accepted. *Expenses:* Tuition, state resident: full-time $7290; part-time $405 per credit hour. Tuition, nonresident: full-time $12,780; part-time $710 per credit hour. Required fees: $774; $10 per credit hour. $297 per semester. Tuition and fees vary according to course load, degree level and program. *Financial support:* In 2009–10, research assistantships with partial tuition reimbursements (averaging $25,000 per year); fellowships also available. Financial award application deadline: 3/1. *Unit head:* Dr. Patricia Langenberg, Program Director, 410-706-3251, Fax: 410-706-8013. *Application contact:* Rachael Holmes, Academic Coordinator, 410-706-8492, Fax: 410-706-4225, E-mail: rholmes@epi.umaryland.edu.

University of Maryland, Baltimore County, Graduate School, College of Arts, Humanities and Social Sciences, Department of Emergency Health Services, Baltimore, MD 21250. Offers administration, planning, and policy (MS); education (MS); emergency health services (MS); emergency management (Postbaccalaureate Certificate); preventive medicine and epidemiology (MS). Part-time and evening/weekend programs available. Postbaccalaureate distance learning degree programs offered (no on-campus study). *Faculty:* 4 full-time (0 women), 7 part-time/adjunct (1 woman). *Students:* 20 full-time (8 women), 21 part-time (10 women); includes 2 minority (both African Americans), 6 international. Average age 32. 13 applicants, 85% accepted, 10 enrolled. In 2009, 13 master's awarded. *Degree requirements:* For master's, comprehensive exam, thesis (for some programs). *Entrance requirements:* For master's, GRE General Test, minimum GPA of 3.0. Additional exam requirements/recommendations for international students: Required—TOEFL (minimum score 550 paper-based; 213 computer-based; 80 iBT). *Application deadline:* For fall admission, 7/1 for domestic students, 4/1 for international students. Applications are processed on a rolling basis. Application fee: $45. Electronic applications accepted. *Financial support:* In 2009–10, 2 students received support, including fellowships with tuition reimbursements available (averaging $70,000 per year), research assistantships with tuition reimbursements available (averaging $21,000 per year); career-related internships or fieldwork, Federal Work-Study, health care benefits, and unspecified assistantships also available. Financial award application deadline: 5/30; financial award applicants required to submit FAFSA. *Faculty research:* EMS management, disaster health services, emergency management. Total annual research expenditures: $50,000. *Unit head:* Dr. Bruce Walz, Chairman, 410-455-3223. *Application contact:* Dr. Rick Bissell, Program Director, 410-455-3776, Fax: 410-455-3045, E-mail: bissell@umbc.edu.

University of Maryland, College Park, Academic Affairs, School of Public Health, Department of Epidemiology and Biostatistics, College Park, MD 20742. Offers biostatistics (MPH); epidemiology (MPH, PhD). *Faculty:* 12 full-time (9 women), 2 part-time/adjunct (1 woman). *Students:* 5 full-time (3 women); includes 2 minority (1 Asian American or Pacific Islander, 1 Hispanic American). 37 applicants, 8% accepted, 3 enrolled. *Application deadline:* For fall admission, 1/15 for domestic and international students; for spring admission, 6/1 for international students. *Expenses:* Tuition, area resident: Part-time $471 per credit hour. Tuition, state resident: part-time $471 per credit hour. Tuition, nonresident: part-time $1016 per credit hour. Required fees: $337.04 per term. *Financial support:* In 2009–10, 3 fellowships with full tuition reimbursements (averaging $22,544 per year), 2 research assistantships (averaging $15,878 per year), 1 teaching assistantship (averaging $15,694 per year) were awarded. Total annual research expenditures: $988,635. *Unit head:* Dr. Deborah Young, Chair, 301-405-2496, E-mail: dryoung@umd.edu. *Application contact:* Dean of Graduate School, 301-405-0358.

University of Maryland, College Park, Academic Affairs, School of Public Health, Department of Public and Community Health, College Park, MD 20742. Offers biostatistics (MPH); community health education (MPH); environmental health sciences (MPH); epidemiology (MPH); public/community health (PhD). *Accreditation:* CEPH. Part-time and evening/weekend programs available. *Faculty:* 26 full-time (16 women), 7 part-time/adjunct (6 women). *Students:* 56 full-time (47 women), 31 part-time (29 women); includes 25 minority (19 African Americans, 4 Asian Americans or Pacific Islanders, 2 Hispanic Americans), 12 international. 252 applicants, 25% accepted, 25 enrolled. In 2009, 14 master's, 4 doctorates awarded. *Degree requirements:* For master's, thesis optional; for doctorate, comprehensive exam, thesis/dissertation. *Entrance requirements:* For master's, GRE General Test, minimum GPA of 3.0, 3 letters of recommendation; for doctorate, GRE General Test, minimum GPA of 3.5, 3 letters of recommendation. Additional exam requirements/recommendations for international students: Required—TOEFL. *Application deadline:* For fall admission, 1/15 for domestic and international students; for spring admission, 6/1 for international students. Applications are processed on a rolling basis. Application fee: $60. Electronic applications accepted. *Expenses:* Tuition, area resident: Part-time $471 per credit hour. Tuition, state resident: part-time $471 per credit hour. Tuition, nonresident: part-time $1016 per credit hour. Required fees: $337.04 per term. *Financial support:* In 2009–10, 14 research assistantships with tuition reimbursements (averaging $15,827 per year), 21 teaching assistantships with tuition reimbursements (averaging $16,363 per year) were awarded; fellowships, career-related internships or fieldwork, Federal Work-Study, and scholarships/grants also available. Support available to part-time students. Financial award applicants required to submit FAFSA. *Faculty research:* Controlling stress and tension, women's health, aging and public policy, adolescent health, long-term care. Total annual research expenditures: $3.2 million. *Unit head:* Dr. Elbert Glover, Chair, 301-405-2467, Fax: 301-314-9167, E-mail: eglover1@umd.edu. *Application contact:* Dean of Graduate School, 301-405-0358.

University of Massachusetts Amherst, Graduate School, School of Public Health and Health Sciences, Department of Public Health, Amherst, MA 01003. Offers biostatistics (MS, PhD); community health education (MS); environmental health sciences (MPH, MS); epidemiology (MPH, MS); health policy and management (MPH, MS); nutrition (PhD); public health practice (MPH). *Accreditation:* CEPH (one or more programs are accredited). Part-time

and evening/weekend programs available. Postbaccalaureate distance learning degree programs offered (no on-campus study). *Faculty:* 38 full-time (23 women). *Students:* 96 full-time (71 women), 232 part-time (153 women); includes 41 minority (14 African Americans, 17 Asian Americans or Pacific Islanders, 10 Hispanic Americans), 65 international. Average age 36. 316 applicants, 61% accepted, 79 enrolled. In 2009, 91 master's, 5 doctorates awarded. Terminal master's awarded for partial completion of doctoral program. *Degree requirements:* For master's, thesis (for some programs); for doctorate, comprehensive exam, thesis/dissertation. *Entrance requirements:* For master's and doctorate, GRE General Test. Additional exam requirements/recommendations for international students: Required—TOEFL (minimum score 550 paper-based; 213 computer-based; 80 iBT), IELTS (minimum score 6.5). *Application deadline:* For fall admission, 2/1 for domestic and international students. Applications are processed on a rolling basis. Application fee: $40 ($65 for international students). Electronic applications accepted. *Expenses:* Tuition, state resident: full-time $2640; part-time $110 per credit. Tuition, nonresident: full-time $9936; part-time $414 per credit. Tuition and fees vary according to course load. *Financial support:* In 2009–10, 3 fellowships with full tuition reimbursements (averaging $2,791 per year), 32 research assistantships with full tuition reimbursements (averaging $9,196 per year), 24 teaching assistantships with full tuition reimbursements (averaging $5,789 per year) were awarded; career-related internships or fieldwork, Federal Work-Study, scholarships/grants, traineeships, health care benefits, tuition waivers (full), and unspecified assistantships also available. Support available to part-time students. Financial award application deadline: 2/1. *Unit head:* Dr. Paula Stamps, Graduate Program Director, 413-545-2861, Fax: 413-545-0964. *Application contact:* Jean M. Ames, Supervisor of Admissions, 413-545-0722, Fax: 413-577-0010, E-mail: gradadm@grad.umass.edu.

University of Massachusetts Lowell, School of Health and Environment, Department of Work Environment, Lowell, MA 01854-2881. Offers cleaner production and pollution prevention (MS, Sc D); environmental risk assessment (Certificate); epidemiology (MS, Sc D); ergonomics and safety (MS, Sc D); identification and control of ergonomic hazards (Certificate); job stress and healthy job redesign (Certificate); occupational and environmental hygiene (MS, Sc D); radiological health physics and general work environment protection (Certificate); work environment policy (MS, Sc D). *Accreditation:* ABET (one or more programs are accredited). Part-time programs available. Terminal master's awarded for partial completion of doctoral program. *Degree requirements:* For master's, thesis optional; for doctorate, thesis/dissertation. *Entrance requirements:* For master's and doctorate, GRE General Test. Additional exam requirements/recommendations for international students: Required—TOEFL.

University of Massachusetts Worcester, Graduate School of Biomedical Sciences, Program in Clinical and Population Health Research, Worcester, MA 01655-0115. Offers PhD. *Degree requirements:* For doctorate, comprehensive exam, thesis/dissertation. *Entrance requirements:* For doctorate, GRE General Test, master's degree in public health, clinical research, or in one of the social, psychological, physical, or biological sciences, with adequate introductory course work in biostatistics and epidemiology; 3 letters of recommendation. Additional exam requirements/recommendations for international students: Required—TOEFL (minimum score 600 paper-based; 250 computer-based; 100 iBT). Electronic applications accepted.

University of Medicine and Dentistry of New Jersey, UMDNJ–School of Public Health (UMDNJ, Rutgers, NJIT) Piscataway/New Brunswick Campus, Piscataway, NJ 08854. Offers biostatistics (MS); epidemiology (Certificate); general public health (Certificate); public health (MPH, Dr PH, PhD); DO/MPH; MD/MPH; MPH/MBA; MPH/MSPA; Psy D/MPH. *Degree requirements:* For master's, internship; for doctorate, thesis/dissertation. *Entrance requirements:* For master's, GRE General Test; for doctorate, GRE General Test, MPH (Dr PH); MA, MPH, or MS (PhD). Additional exam requirements/recommendations for international students: Required—TOEFL. Electronic applications accepted.

University of Memphis, Graduate School, School of Public Health, Memphis, TN 38152. Offers biostatistics (MPH); environmental health (MPH); epidemiology (MPH); health systems management (MPH); public health (MHA); social and behavioral sciences (MPH). Part-time and evening/weekend programs available. Postbaccalaureate distance learning degree programs offered. *Faculty:* 5 full-time (2 women), 4 part-time/adjunct (2 women). *Students:* 45 full-time (23 women), 29 part-time (14 women); includes 19 African Americans, 6 Asian Americans or Pacific Islanders, 2 Hispanic Americans, 7 international. Average age 32. 57 applicants, 70% accepted, 22 enrolled. In 2009, 17 master's awarded. *Degree requirements:* For master's, comprehensive exam, thesis. *Entrance requirements:* For master's, GRE, MAT, DAT, GMAT or LSAT, letters of recommendation. Additional exam requirements/recommendations for international students: Required—TOEFL. *Application deadline:* For fall admission, 11/1 for domestic students; for spring admission, 4/1 for domestic students. Application fee: $35 ($60 for international students). Electronic applications accepted. *Expenses:* Tuition, state resident: full-time $6246; part-time $347 per credit hour. Tuition, nonresident: full-time $15,894; part-time $883 per credit hour. Required fees: $1160. Full-time tuition and fees vary according to course load, degree level and program. *Financial support:* In 2009–10, 46 students received support; research assistantships with full tuition reimbursements available, Federal Work-Study, scholarships/grants, and unspecified assistantships available. Financial award application deadline: 2/15; financial award applicants required to submit FAFSA. *Faculty research:* Health and medical savings accounts, adoption rates, health informatics, Telehealth technologies, biostatistics, environmental health, epidemiology, health systems management, social and behavioral sciences. *Unit head:* Dr. Lisa M. Klesges, Director, 901-678-4637, E-mail: lmklsges@memphis.edu. *Application contact:* Dr. Lisa M. Klesges, Director, 901-678-4637, E-mail: lmklsges@memphis.edu.

University of Miami, Graduate School, Miller School of Medicine, Graduate Programs in Medicine, Department of Epidemiology and Public Health, Teaching Programs in Epidemiology, Coral Gables, FL 33124. Offers PhD, MD/PhD. *Degree requirements:* For doctorate, comprehensive exam, thesis/dissertation. *Entrance requirements:* For doctorate, GRE General Test, minimum GPA of 3.0, course work in epidemiology and statistics, 3 letters of recommendation. Additional exam requirements/recommendations for international students: Required—TOEFL (minimum score 550 paper-based; 213 computer-based; 59 iBT). Electronic applications accepted. *Faculty research:* Behavioral epidemiology, substance abuse, AIDS, cardiovascular diseases, cancer epidemiology.

University of Michigan, School of Public Health, Department of Epidemiology, Ann Arbor, MI 48109-2029. Offers dental public health (MPH); epidemiological science (PhD); epidemiology (MS); general epidemiology (MPH); hospital and molecular epidemiology (MPH); international health (MPH). PhD and MS offered through the Horace H. Rackham School of Graduate Studies. *Accreditation:* CEPH (one or more programs are accredited). Part-time programs available. *Faculty:* 33 full-time (20 women), 25 part-time/adjunct (9 women). *Students:* 192 full-time (147 women), 7 part-time (5 women); includes 48 minority (17 African Americans, 1 American Indian/Alaska Native, 24 Asian Americans or Pacific Islanders, 6 Hispanic Americans), 13 international. 587 applicants, 61% accepted, 88 enrolled. In 2009, 80 master's, 13 doctorates awarded. Terminal master's awarded for partial completion of doctoral program. *Degree requirements:* For master's, thesis (for some programs); for doctorate, comprehensive exam, thesis/dissertation, oral defense of dissertation, preliminary exam. *Entrance requirements:* For master's and doctorate, GRE General Test, MCAT. Additional exam requirements/recommendations for international students: Required—TOEFL (minimum score 560 paper-based; 220 computer-based; 100 iBT). *Application deadline:* For fall admission, 12/1 priority date for domestic students, 1/15 priority date for international students. Applications are processed on a rolling basis. Application fee: $60 ($75 for international students). Electronic applications accepted. *Expenses:* Tuition, state resident: full-time $17,286; part-time $1099 per credit hour. Tuition, nonresident: full-time $34,944; part-time $2080 per credit hour. Required fees: $95 per semester. Tuition and fees vary according to course load, degree level and program. *Financial support:* In 2009–10, 112 students received support, including 112 fellowships with full and partial tuition reimbursements available, 20 research assistantships with full tuition reimbursements available (averaging $8,400 per year), 12 teaching assistantships with full tuition reimbursements available (averaging $16,000 per year); career-related internships or fieldwork, Federal Work-Study, and scholarships/grants also available. Financial award application deadline: 3/1. *Faculty research:* Molecular virology, infectious diseases, women's health, genetics, social epidemiology. *Unit head:* Dr. Sharon Kardia, Chair, 734-764-5435, Fax: 734-764-3192. *Application contact:* Sally Musselman, Student Services Coordinator, 734-764-5415, Fax: 734-763-3192, E-mail: musselms@umich.edu.

University of Minnesota, Twin Cities Campus, School of Public Health, Division of Environmental Health Sciences, Area in Environmental and Occupational Epidemiology, Minneapolis, MN 55455-0213. Offers MPH, MS, PhD. *Accreditation:* CEPH (one or more programs are accredited). *Degree requirements:* For doctorate, thesis/dissertation. *Entrance requirements:* For master's and doctorate, GRE General Test. Electronic applications accepted.

University of Minnesota, Twin Cities Campus, School of Public Health, Major in Epidemiology, Minneapolis, MN 55455-0213. Offers MPH, PhD. *Accreditation:* CEPH (one or more programs are accredited). Part-time programs available. Terminal master's awarded for partial completion of doctoral program. *Degree requirements:* For master's, fieldwork, project; for doctorate, comprehensive exam, thesis/dissertation. *Entrance requirements:* For master's, GRE General Test; for doctorate, GRE General Test, master's degree in related field. Additional exam requirements/recommendations for international students: Required—TOEFL. Electronic applications accepted. *Expenses:* Contact institution. *Faculty research:* Prevention of cardiovascular disease, nutrition, genetic epidemiology, behavioral interventions, research methods.

The University of North Carolina at Chapel Hill, Graduate School, School of Public Health, Department of Epidemiology, Chapel Hill, NC 27599. Offers MPH, PhD. *Accreditation:* CEPH (one or more programs are accredited). Terminal master's awarded for partial completion of doctoral program. *Degree requirements:* For master's, comprehensive exam, major paper; for doctorate, comprehensive exam, thesis/dissertation. *Entrance requirements:* For master's and doctorate, GRE General Test, minimum GPA of 3.0. Additional exam requirements/recommendations for international students: Required—TOEFL. Electronic applications accepted. *Faculty research:* Chronic disease: cancer, cardiovascular, nutritional; environmental/occupational injury; infectious diseases; reproductive diseases; healthcare.

The University of North Carolina at Chapel Hill, School of Dentistry and Graduate School, Graduate Programs in Dentistry, Chapel Hill, NC 27599. Offers dental hygiene (MS); endodontics (MS); epidemiology (PhD); operative dentistry (MS); oral and maxillofacial pathology (MS); oral and maxillofacial radiology (MS); oral biology (PhD); orthodontics (MS); pediatric dentistry (MS); periodontology (MS); prosthodontics (MS). *Degree requirements:* For master's, thesis; for doctorate, thesis/dissertation. *Entrance requirements:* For master's, dental degree; for doctorate, GRE General Test. Additional exam requirements/recommendations for international students: Required—TOEFL (minimum score 550 paper-based; 213 computer-based). Electronic applications accepted. *Expenses:* Contact institution. *Faculty research:* Inflammation, cell biology, immunology, microbiology, neuroscience, molecular biology.

University of North Texas Health Science Center at Fort Worth, School of Public Health, Fort Worth, TX 76107-2699. Offers biostatistics (MPH); community health (MPH); disease control and prevention (Dr PH); environmental and occupational health sciences (MPH); epidemiology (MPH); health administration (MHA); health policy and management (MPH, Dr PH); DO/MPH; MS/MPH; MSN/MPH. *Accreditation:* CEPH. Part-time and evening/weekend programs available. *Degree requirements:* For master's, thesis or alternative, supervised internship; for doctorate, thesis/dissertation, supervised internship. *Entrance requirements:* For master's, GRE General Test. Additional exam requirements/recommendations for international students: Required—TOEFL. Electronic applications accepted.

University of Oklahoma Health Sciences Center, Graduate College, College of Public Health, Program in Biostatistics and Epidemiology, Oklahoma City, OK 73190. Offers biostatistics (MPH, MS, Dr PH, PhD); epidemiology (MPH, MS, Dr PH, PhD). *Accreditation:* CEPH (one or more programs are accredited). Part-time programs available. *Faculty:* 9 full-time (8 women). *Students:* 23 full-time (13 women), 21 part-time (13 women); includes 7 minority (3 African Americans, 3 Asian Americans or Pacific Islanders, 1 Hispanic American), 10 international. Average age 31. 45 applicants, 24% accepted, 3 enrolled. In 2009, 16 master's, 3 doctorates awarded. *Degree requirements:* For master's, comprehensive exam, thesis (for some programs); for doctorate, comprehensive exam, thesis/dissertation. *Entrance requirements:* For master's, 3 letters of recommendation, resume; for doctorate, GRE General Test, letters of recommendation. Additional exam requirements/recommendations for international students: Required—TOEFL (minimum score 570 paper-based; 230 computer-based), TWE. *Application deadline:* For fall admission, 7/1 for domestic students; for winter admission, 4/1 for domestic students; for spring admission, 12/1 for domestic students. Applications are processed on a rolling basis. Application fee: $50. *Expenses:* Tuition, state resident: full-time $3120; part-time $156 per credit hour. Tuition, nonresident: full-time $11,314; part-time $409.70 per credit hour. Required fees: $1471; $51.20 per credit hour. $223.25 per term. *Financial support:* In 2009–10, 7 research assistantships (averaging $14,000 per year) were awarded; career-related internships or fieldwork, institutionally sponsored loans, and traineeships also available. Support available to part-time students. Financial award application deadline: 5/1. *Faculty research:* Statistical methodology, applied statistics, acute and chronic disease epidemiology. *Unit head:* Dr. Willis Owen, Interim Chair, 405-271-2229, E-mail: willis-owen@ouhsc.edu. *Application contact:* Robin Howell, Information Contact, 405-271-2308, E-mail: robin_howell@ouhsc.edu.

University of Ottawa, Faculty of Graduate and Postdoctoral Studies, Faculty of Medicine, Department of Epidemiology and Community Medicine, Ottawa, ON K1N 6N5, Canada. Offers epidemiology (M Sc), including health technology assessment. *Degree requirements:* For master's, thesis. *Entrance requirements:* For master's, honors degree or equivalent, minimum B average. Electronic applications accepted. *Faculty research:* Epidemiologic concepts and methods, health technology assessment.

University of Pennsylvania, School of Medicine, Center for Clinical Epidemiology and Biostatistics, Philadelphia, PA 19104. Offers clinical epidemiology (MSCE); epidemiology (PhD). PhD offered through the School of Arts and Sciences. *Accreditation:* CEPH. Part-time programs available. *Faculty:* 72 full-time (27 women), 119 part-time/adjunct (40 women). *Students:* 89 full-time (49 women), 15 part-time (10 women); includes 33 minority (7 African Americans, 23 Asian Americans or Pacific Islanders, 3 Hispanic Americans). Average age 30. 50 applicants, 70% accepted, 30 enrolled. In 2009, 32 master's awarded. *Degree requirements:* For master's, comprehensive exam, thesis; for doctorate, comprehensive exam, thesis/dissertation, qualifying exam, candidacy exam. *Entrance requirements:* For master's and doctorate, GRE General Test or MCAT, advanced degree, clinical experience. Additional exam requirements/recommendations for international students: Required—TOEFL. *Application deadline:* For fall admission, 1/15 priority date for domestic and international students. Applications are processed on a rolling basis. Application fee: $0. Electronic applications accepted. *Expenses:* Contact institution. *Financial support:* In 2009–10, 65 students received support, including 60 fellowships with full and partial tuition reimbursements available (averaging $42,000 per year); career-related internships or fieldwork, scholarships/grants, health care benefits, and unspecified assistantships also available. Financial award application deadline: 1/15. *Faculty research:* Health services research, pharmacoepidemiology, women's health, cancer epidemiology, genetic epidemiology. Total annual research expenditures: $38.6 million. *Unit head:* Dr. Harold I. Feldman, Director, 215-573-0901, Fax: 215-573-2265, E-mail: hfeldman@mail.med.upenn.edu. *Application contact:* Jennifer E. Kuklinski, Associate Director for Graduate Training in Epidemiology, 215-573-2382, Fax: 215-573-5315, E-mail: jkuklins@mail.med.upenn.edu.

University of Pittsburgh, Graduate School of Public Health, Department of Epidemiology, Pittsburgh, PA 15260. Offers MPH, MS, Dr PH, PhD, MD/PhD. *Accreditation:* CEPH (one or more programs are accredited). Part-time programs available. *Faculty:* 44 full-time (30 women), 44 part-time/adjunct (19 women). *Students:* 94 full-time (65 women), 41 part-time (29 women); includes 21 minority (15 African Americans, 4 Asian Americans or Pacific Islanders, 2 Hispanic Americans), 23 international. Average age 32. 340 applicants, 49% accepted, 28 enrolled. In 2009, 23 master's, 22 doctorates awarded. Terminal master's awarded for partial completion of doctoral program. *Degree requirements:* For master's, comprehensive exam (for some

Epidemiology

University of Pittsburgh (continued)

programs), thesis (for some programs), internship experience (MPH); for doctorate, comprehensive exam, thesis/dissertation, teaching practicum. *Entrance requirements:* For master's, GRE General Test, DAT, MCAT, 3 credits of course work in human biology, 3 credits of algebra or higher mathematics, 6 credits of course work in behavioral science (MPH), minimum GPA of 3.0; for doctorate, GRE General Test, DAT, MCAT, 3 credits of course work in biology and math, minimum GPA of 3.0. Additional exam requirements/recommendations for international students: Required—TOEFL (minimum score 550 paper-based; 213 computer-based; 80 iBT). *Application deadline:* For fall admission, 1/5 priority date for domestic and international students; for spring admission, 11/1 priority date for domestic students, 8/1 for international students. Applications are processed on a rolling basis. Application fee: $115. Electronic applications accepted. *Expenses:* Tuition, state resident: full-time $16,402; part-time $665 per credit. Tuition, nonresident: full-time $28,694; part-time $1175 per credit. Required fees: $690; $175 per term. Tuition and fees vary according to program. *Financial support:* In 2009–10, 28 students received support, including 1 fellowship with full tuition reimbursement available (averaging $23,513 per year), 26 research assistantships with full tuition reimbursements available (averaging $18,450 per year), 1 teaching assistantship with full tuition reimbursement available (averaging $22,598 per year); career-related internships or fieldwork, scholarships/grants, and traineeships also available. Support available to part-time students. Financial award applicants required to submit FAFSA. *Faculty research:* Aging, cardiovascular, clinical trials, diabetes, psychiatric, women's health, genetics, alcohol. Total annual research expenditures: $30.7 million. *Unit head:* Dr. Trevor J. Orchard, Interim Chair, 412-624-3056, Fax: 412-624-3737, E-mail: orchardt@edc.pitt.edu. *Application contact:* Lori S. Smith, Student Services Coordinator, 412-383-5269, E-mail: smithl@edc.pitt.edu.

University of Prince Edward Island, Atlantic Veterinary College, Graduate Program in Veterinary Medicine, Charlottetown, PE C1A 4P3, Canada. Offers anatomy (M Sc, PhD); bacteriology (M Sc, PhD); clinical pharmacology (M Sc, PhD); clinical sciences (M Sc, PhD); epidemiology (M Sc, PhD), including reproduction; fish health (M Sc, PhD); food animal nutrition (M Sc, PhD); immunology (M Sc, PhD); microanatomy (M Sc, PhD); parasitology (M Sc, PhD); pathology (M Sc, PhD); pharmacology (M Sc, PhD); physiology (M Sc, PhD); toxicology (M Sc, PhD); veterinary science (M Vet Sc); virology (M Sc, PhD). Part-time programs available. *Degree requirements:* For master's, thesis; for doctorate, thesis/dissertation. *Entrance requirements:* For master's, DVM, B Sc honors degree, or equivalent; for doctorate, M Sc. Additional exam requirements/recommendations for international students: Required—TOEFL (minimum score 550 paper-based; 213 computer-based; 80 iBT). *Expenses:* Contact institution. *Faculty research:* Animal health management, infectious diseases, fin fish and shellfish health, basic biomedical sciences, ecosystem health.

University of Puerto Rico, Medical Sciences Campus, Graduate School of Public Health, Program in Epidemiology, San Juan, PR 00936-5067. Offers MPH, MS. *Accreditation:* CEPH (one or more programs are accredited). Part-time programs available. *Entrance requirements:* For master's, GRE, previous course work in biology, chemistry, physics, mathematics, and social sciences. *Expenses:* Contact institution.

University of Rochester, School of Medicine and Dentistry, Graduate Programs in Medicine and Dentistry, Department of Community and Preventive Medicine, Program in Epidemiology, Rochester, NY 14627. Offers MS, PhD. *Degree requirements:* For doctorate, thesis/dissertation, qualifying exam. *Entrance requirements:* For doctorate, GRE General Test.

University of Saskatchewan, College of Medicine, Department of Community Health and Epidemiology, Saskatoon, SK S7N 5A2, Canada. Offers M Sc, PhD. *Degree requirements:* For master's, thesis; for doctorate, thesis/dissertation. *Entrance requirements:* Additional exam requirements/recommendations for international students: Required—TOEFL. Tuition and fees charges are reported in Canadian dollars. *Expenses:* Tuition, area resident: Full-time $3000 Canadian dollars; part-time $500 Canadian dollars per term. Required fees: $700 Canadian dollars; $100 Canadian dollars per term.

University of South Carolina, The Graduate School, Arnold School of Public Health, Department of Epidemiology and Biostatistics, Program in Epidemiology, Columbia, SC 29208. Offers MPH, MSPH, Dr PH, PhD. *Accreditation:* CEPH (one or more programs are accredited). Part-time programs available. *Degree requirements:* For master's, comprehensive exam, thesis (for some programs), practicum (MPH); for doctorate, comprehensive exam, thesis/dissertation (for some programs), practicum. *Entrance requirements:* For master's, GRE General Test; for doctorate, GRE General Test, master's degree. Additional exam requirements/recommendations for international students: Required—TOEFL (minimum score 570 paper-based; 230 computer-based; 88 iBT). Electronic applications accepted. *Faculty research:* Cancer epidemiology, mental health epidemiology, health effects of physical activity, environmental epidemiology, genetic epidemiology, asthma epidemiology.

University of Southern California, Keck School of Medicine and Graduate School, Graduate Programs in Medicine, Department of Preventive Medicine, Division of Biostatistics, Los Angeles, CA 90089. Offers applied biostatistics/epidemiology (MS); biostatistics (MS, PhD); epidemiology (PhD); genetic epidemiology and statistical genetics (PhD); molecular epidemiology (MS, PhD). *Faculty:* 71 full-time (30 women). *Students:* 108 full-time (63 women); includes 24 minority (18 Asian Americans or Pacific Islanders, 6 Hispanic Americans), 58 international. Average age 29. 79 applicants, 52% accepted, 18 enrolled. In 2009, 12 master's, 4 doctorates awarded. Terminal master's awarded for partial completion of doctoral program. *Degree requirements:* For master's, thesis; for doctorate, thesis/dissertation. *Entrance requirements:* For master's and doctorate, GRE General Test, GRE Subject Test, minimum GPA of 3.0. Additional exam requirements/recommendations for international students: Required—TOEFL (minimum score 600 paper-based; 250 computer-based; 100 iBT). *Application deadline:* For fall admission, 12/1 priority date for domestic students, 12/1 for international students. Application fee: $85. Electronic applications accepted. *Expenses:* Tuition: Full-time $25,980; part-time $1315 per unit. Required fees: $554. One-time fee: $35 full-time. Full-time tuition and fees vary according to degree level and program. *Financial support:* In 2009–10, 3 fellowships with full tuition reimbursements (averaging $27,060 per year), 55 research assistantships with full tuition reimbursements (averaging $27,060 per year), 19 teaching assistantships with full and partial tuition reimbursements (averaging $13,530 per year) were awarded; career-related internships or fieldwork, Federal Work-Study, institutionally sponsored loans, scholarships/grants, health care benefits, and unspecified assistantships also available. Financial award application deadline: 5/5. *Faculty research:* Clinical trials in ophthalmology and cancer research, methods of analysis for epidemiological studies, genetic epidemiology. Total annual research expenditures: $1.3 million. *Unit head:* Dr. Stanley P. Azen, Co-Director, 323-442-1810, Fax: 323-442-2993, E-mail: mtrujill@usc.edu. *Application contact:* Mary L. Trujillo, Student Adviser, 323-442-1810, Fax: 323-442-2993, E-mail: mtrujill@usc.edu.

University of Southern California, Keck School of Medicine and Graduate School, Graduate Programs in Medicine, Department of Preventive Medicine, Master of Public Health Program, Alhambra, CA 91803. Offers biostatistics/epidemiology (MPH); child and family health (MPH); global health leadership (MPH); health communication (MPH); health promotion (MPH). *Accreditation:* CEPH. Part-time programs available. *Faculty:* 22 full-time (12 women), 3 part-time/adjunct (0 women). *Students:* 215 full-time (158 women), 3 part-time (2 women); includes 148 minority (13 African Americans, 3 American Indian/Alaska Native, 114 Asian Americans or Pacific Islanders, 18 Hispanic Americans), 25 international. Average age 26. 208 applicants, 74% accepted, 76 enrolled. In 2009, 60 master's awarded. *Degree requirements:* For master's, practicum, final report, oral presentation. *Entrance requirements:* For master's, GRE General Test, MCAT, GMAT, minimum GPA of 3.0. Additional exam requirements/recommendations for international students: Required—TOEFL (minimum score 600 paper-based; 250 computer-based; 100 iBT). *Application deadline:* For fall admission, 6/1 priority date for domestic and international students; for spring admission, 11/1 priority date for domestic students, 10/1 priority date for international students. Applications are processed on a rolling basis. Application fee: $85. Electronic applications accepted. *Expenses:* Tuition: Full-time $25,980; part-time $1315 per unit. Required fees: $554. One-time fee: $35 full-time. Full-time tuition and fees vary according to degree level and program. *Financial support:* In 2009–10, 175 students received support, including 20 fellowships (averaging $3,200 per year); career-related internships or fieldwork, Federal Work-Study, institutionally sponsored loans, and scholarships/grants also available. Support available to part-time students. Financial award application deadline: 5/1; financial award applicants required to submit CSS PROFILE or FAFSA. *Faculty research:* Substance abuse prevention, cancer and heart disease prevention, mass media and health communication research, health promotion, treatment compliance. *Unit head:* Dr. Thomas W. Valente, Director, 626-457-4139, Fax: 626-457-6699, E-mail: tvalente@usc.edu. *Application contact:* Chrystal Romero, Admissions Counselor, 626-457-6676, Fax: 626-457-6699, E-mail: ccromero@usc.edu.

University of Southern Mississippi, Graduate School, College of Health, Department of Community Health Sciences, Hattiesburg, MS 39406-0001. Offers epidemiology and biostatistics (MPH); health education (MPH); health policy/administration (MPH); occupational/environmental health (MPH); public health nutrition (MPH). *Accreditation:* CEPH. Part-time and evening/weekend programs available. *Faculty:* 8 full-time (4 women), 1 part-time/adjunct (0 women). *Students:* 92 full-time (59 women), 20 part-time (14 women); includes 40 minority (36 African Americans, 1 Asian American or Pacific Islander, 3 Hispanic Americans), 13 international. Average age 32. 90 applicants, 73% accepted, 47 enrolled. In 2009, 4 master's awarded. *Degree requirements:* For master's, comprehensive exam, thesis (for some programs). *Entrance requirements:* For master's, GRE General Test, minimum GPA of 2.75 in last 60 hours. Additional exam requirements/recommendations for international students: Required—TOEFL. *Application deadline:* For fall admission, 3/1 for domestic and international students. Applications are processed on a rolling basis. Application fee: $35. *Expenses:* Tuition, state resident: full-time $5096; part-time $284 per hour. Tuition, nonresident: full-time $13,052; part-time $726 per hour. Required fees: $402. Tuition and fees vary according to course level and course load. *Financial support:* In 2009–10, 5 research assistantships with full tuition reimbursements (averaging $7,000 per year), 1 teaching assistantship with full tuition reimbursement (averaging $8,263 per year) were awarded; career-related internships or fieldwork and Federal Work-Study also available. Financial award application deadline: 3/15; financial award applicants required to submit FAFSA. *Faculty research:* Rural health care delivery, school health, nutrition of pregnant teens, risk factor reduction, sexually transmitted diseases. *Unit head:* Dr. James McGuire, Chair, 601-266-5437, Fax: 601-266-5043. *Application contact:* Shonna Breland, Manager of Graduate Admissions, 601-266-6563, Fax: 601-266-5138.

University of South Florida, Graduate School, College of Public Health, Department of Epidemiology and Biostatistics, Tampa, FL 33620-9951. Offers MPH, MSPH, PhD. *Accreditation:* CEPH (one or more programs are accredited). Part-time and evening/weekend programs available. *Faculty:* 12 full-time (5 women), 7 part-time/adjunct (5 women). *Students:* 71 full-time (43 women), 67 part-time (51 women); includes 35 minority (12 African Americans, 12 Asian Americans or Pacific Islanders, 11 Hispanic Americans), 26 international. Average age 31. 115 applicants, 68% accepted, 30 enrolled. In 2009, 24 master's awarded. *Degree requirements:* For master's, comprehensive exam, thesis (for some programs); for doctorate, comprehensive exam, thesis/dissertation. *Entrance requirements:* For master's, GRE General Test, minimum GPA of 3.0 in upper-level course work, goal statement letter, two professional letters of recommendation, resume/curriculum vitae; for doctorate, GRE General Test, minimum GPA of 3.0 in upper-level course work, 3 professional letters of recommendation, resume/curriculum vitae, writing sample. Additional exam requirements/recommendations for international students: Required—TOEFL (minimum score 550 paper-based; 213 computer-based; 79 iBT). *Application deadline:* For fall admission, 6/1 for domestic students, 1/2 for international students; for spring admission, 10/15 for domestic students, 7/1 for international students. Applications are processed on a rolling basis. Application fee: $30. Electronic applications accepted. *Financial support:* In 2009–10, 3 fellowships with full tuition reimbursements (averaging $3,800 per year), 11 research assistantships with full and partial tuition reimbursements (averaging $3,324 per year), 19 teaching assistantships (averaging $3,044 per year) were awarded; career-related internships or fieldwork, Federal Work-Study, institutionally sponsored loans, scholarships/grants, traineeships, and unspecified assistantships also available. Support available to part-time students. Financial award applicants required to submit FAFSA. *Faculty research:* Dementia, mental illness, mental health preventative trails, rural health outreach, clinical and administrative studies. Total annual research expenditures: $1.5 million. *Unit head:* Dr. Heather Stockwell, Chairperson, 813-974-4860, Fax: 813-974-4719, E-mail: stockwell@hsc.usf.edu. *Application contact:* Michelle Hodge, Academic Advisor, 813-974-6665, Fax: 813-974-8121, E-mail: mhodge1@health.usf.edu.

The University of Toledo, College of Graduate Studies, College of Medicine, Department of Public Health and Homeland Security, Program in Public Health, Toledo, OH 43606-3390. Offers biostatistics and epidemiology (Certificate); emergency response (Certificate); global health (Certificate); public health (MPH); MD/MPH.

University of Washington, Graduate School, School of Public Health, Department of Epidemiology, Seattle, WA 98195. Offers clinical research (MS); epidemiology (MPH, MS, PhD); global health (MPH); maternal/child health (MPH); nutritional sciences (MPH, MS, PhD); public health genetics (MPH, MS, PhD), including genetic epidemiology (MS), public health genetics (MPH, PhD). *Accreditation:* CEPH (one or more programs are accredited). Part-time programs available. *Faculty:* 66 full-time (40 women), 46 part-time/adjunct (20 women). *Students:* 145 full-time (101 women), 43 part-time (26 women); includes 33 minority (6 African Americans, 1 American Indian/Alaska Native, 18 Asian Americans or Pacific Islanders, 8 Hispanic Americans), 20 international. Average age 32. 236 applicants, 48% accepted, 60 enrolled. In 2009, 44 master's, 16 doctorates awarded. Terminal master's awarded for partial completion of doctoral program. *Degree requirements:* For master's, thesis; for doctorate, comprehensive exam, thesis/dissertation, preliminary exam, original data collection. *Entrance requirements:* For master's, GRE General Test (except applicants with U.S. doctorate); for doctorate, GRE General Test. Additional exam requirements/recommendations for international students: Required—TOEFL (minimum score 580 paper-based; 237 computer-based; 92 iBT) or IELTS (minimum score 7). *Application deadline:* For fall admission, 12/1 for domestic students, 11/1 for international students. Application fee: $50. Electronic applications accepted. *Expenses:* Contact institution. *Financial support:* In 2009–10, 90 fellowships with full tuition reimbursements (averaging $20,976 per year), 43 research assistantships with full tuition reimbursements (averaging $19,668 per year), 12 teaching assistantships with full tuition reimbursements (averaging $16,398 per year) were awarded; career-related internships or fieldwork, Federal Work-Study, institutionally sponsored loans, scholarships/grants, traineeships, health care benefits, unspecified assistantships, and tuition waiver also available. Financial award application deadline: 2/15; financial award applicants required to submit FAFSA. *Faculty research:* Chronic diseases, sexually transmitted diseases, injury, materials and child health, molecular and genetic epidemiology. *Unit head:* Dr. Scott Davis, Chair, 206-543-1065, Fax: 206-543-1065, E-mail: sdavis@fhcrc.org. *Application contact:* Kate O'Brien, Student Services Manager, 206-543-1065, Fax: 206-543-8525, E-mail: apply@u.washington.edu.

The University of Western Ontario, Faculty of Graduate Studies, Biosciences Division, Department of Epidemiology and Biostatistics, London, ON N6A 5B8, Canada. Offers M Sc, PhD. *Accreditation:* CEPH (one or more programs are accredited). Part-time programs available. *Degree requirements:* For master's, thesis; for doctorate, comprehensive exam, thesis proposal defense. *Entrance requirements:* For master's, BA or B Sc honors degree, minimum B+ average in last 10 courses; for doctorate, M Sc or equivalent, minimum B+ average in last 10 courses. *Faculty research:* Chronic disease epidemiology, clinical epidemiology.

University of Wisconsin–Madison, School of Medicine and Public Health and Graduate School, Graduate Programs in Medicine, Department of Population Health Sciences, Madison, WI 53726. Offers clinical research (MS, PhD); epidemiology (MS, PhD); health services research (MS, PhD); population health sciences (MPH); social and behavioral health sciences (MS, PhD); DPT/MPH; DVM/MPH; MD/MPH; MPA/MPH; MS/MPH; Pharm D/MPH. *Accreditation:* CEPH. Part-time programs available. *Faculty:* 104 full-time (54 women), 2 part-time/adjunct (0 women). *Students:* 105 full-time (76 women), 38 part-time (31 women); includes 19 minority (8 African Americans, 8 Asian Americans or Pacific Islanders, 3 Hispanic Americans), 15

international. Average age 30. 126 applicants, 75% accepted, 58 enrolled. In 2009, 13 master's, 8 doctorates awarded. Terminal master's awarded for partial completion of doctoral program. *Degree requirements:* For master's, thesis, defense; for doctorate, comprehensive exam, thesis/dissertation, qualifying exam, preliminary exam, dissertation defense. *Entrance requirements:* For master's and doctorate, GRE (separate guidelines for those with doctoral degrees), minimum GPA of 3.0, quantitative preparation (calculus, statistics, or other) with minimum B average. Additional exam requirements/recommendations for international students: Required—TOEFL (minimum score 600 paper-based; 250 computer-based; 100 iBT). *Application deadline:* For fall admission, 1/15 for domestic and international students. Application fee: $56. Electronic applications accepted. *Expenses:* Tuition, state resident: part-time $594 per credit. Tuition, nonresident: part-time $1504 per credit. Required fees: $65 per credit. Tuition and fees vary according to course load, program and reciprocity agreements. *Financial support:* In 2009–10, 73 students received support, including 16 fellowships with full tuition reimbursements available (averaging $21,000 per year), 38 research assistantships with full tuition reimbursements available (averaging $17,300 per year), 7 teaching assistantships with full tuition reimbursements available (averaging $17,300 per year); scholarships/grants, traineeships, health care benefits, and unspecified assistantships also available. Support available to part-time students. *Faculty research:* Epidemiology (cancer, environmental, aging, infectious disease and genetic), determinants of population health, health services research, social and behavioral health sciences, biostatistics. Total annual research expenditures: $11.4 million. *Unit head:* Dr. F. Javier Nieto, Chair, 608-265-5242, Fax: 608-263-2820, E-mail: fjnieto@wisc.edu. *Application contact:* Kelly Haslam, Graduate Program Coordinator, 608-265-8108, Fax: 608-263-2820, E-mail: haslam@wisc.edu.

Virginia Commonwealth University, Medical College of Virginia-Professional Programs, School of Medicine, School of Medicine Graduate Programs, Program in Epidemiology and Community Health, Richmond, VA 23284-9005. Offers PhD. *Accreditation:* CEPH. Part-time programs available. *Degree requirements:* For doctorate, comprehensive exam, thesis/dissertation. *Entrance requirements:* For doctorate, GRE General Test, interview, 3 letters of recommendation, minimum graduate GPA of 3.0, master's degree in public health or related field including epidemiology and biostatistics. Additional exam requirements/recommendations for international students: Required—TOEFL (minimum score 600 paper-based). Electronic applications accepted. *Faculty research:* Sickle cell anemia, breast cancer, HIV/AIDS, hospital epidemiology, infectious diseases.

Walden University, Graduate Programs, School of Health Sciences, Minneapolis, MN 55401. Offers clinical research administration (MS); health informatics (MS); health services (PhD); including community health promotion and education, general program, health management and policy; healthcare administration (MHA); public health (MPH, PhD), including community health promotion and education (PhD), epidemiology (PhD). Part-time and evening/weekend programs available. Postbaccalaureate distance learning degree programs offered (minimal

on-campus study). *Faculty:* 14 full-time, 136 part-time/adjunct. *Students:* 2,121 full-time (1,670 women), 724 part-time (568 women); includes 1,370 minority (1,149 African Americans, 20 American Indian/Alaska Native, 95 Asian Americans or Pacific Islanders, 106 Hispanic Americans), 134 international. Average age 40. In 2009, 232 master's, 24 doctorates awarded. *Degree requirements:* For doctorate, thesis/dissertation, residency. *Entrance requirements:* For master's, bachelor's degree or equivalent in related field, minimum GPA of 2.5; for doctorate, master's degree or equivalent in related field; minimum GPA of 3.0; official transcripts; three years of related professional/academic experience (preferred); access to computer and Internet. Additional exam requirements/recommendations for international students: Required—TOEFL (minimum score 550 paper-based; 213 computer-based), IELTS (minimum score 6.5), or Michigan English Language Assessment Battery (minimum score 82). *Application deadline:* Applications are processed on a rolling basis. Application fee: $50. Electronic applications accepted. *Expenses:* Tuition: Full-time $13,665; part-time $560 per credit. Required fees: $1375. Tuition and fees vary according to course load, degree level and program. *Financial support:* In 2009–10, 152 students received support; fellowships, Federal Work-Study, scholarships/grants, unspecified assistantships, and family tuition reduction, active duty/veteran tuition reduction, group tuition reduction, interest-free payment plans available. Support available to part-time students. Financial award applicants required to submit FAFSA. *Unit head:* Dr. Jorg Westermann, Interim Associate Dean, 800-925-3368. *Application contact:* Jennifer Hall, Director of Enrollment, 866-4-WALDEN, E-mail: info@waldenu.edu.

Yale University, School of Medicine, School of Public Health, Division of Chronic Disease Epidemiology, New Haven, CT 06520. Offers MPH, PhD. PhD offered through the Graduate School. *Accreditation:* CEPH (one or more programs are accredited). Part-time programs available. Terminal master's awarded for partial completion of doctoral program. *Degree requirements:* For master's, thesis, internship. *Entrance requirements:* For master's, GMAT, GRE, LSAT, or MCAT, previous undergraduate course work in mathematics and science. Additional exam requirements/recommendations for international students: Required—TOEFL. Electronic applications accepted. *Expenses:* Contact institution. *Faculty research:* Perinatal epidemiology, epidemiology of aging, psychiatric and social epidemiology, cancer and cardiovascular epidemiology, pharmacoepidemiology.

Yale University, School of Medicine, School of Public Health, Division of Epidemiology of Microbial Diseases, New Haven, CT 06520. Offers MPH, PhD. PhD offered through the Graduate School. *Accreditation:* CEPH (one or more programs are accredited). Part-time programs available. Terminal master's awarded for partial completion of doctoral program. *Degree requirements:* For master's, thesis, internship. *Entrance requirements:* For master's, GMAT, GRE, or MCAT, previous undergraduate course work in mathematics and science. Additional exam requirements/recommendations for international students: Required—TOEFL. Electronic applications accepted. *Expenses:* Contact institution. *Faculty research:* Insect vector competence, vector biology, emerging infections, parasitology, microbial diseases and defense.

Health Promotion

Auburn University, Graduate School, College of Education, Department of Kinesiology, Auburn University, AL 36849. Offers exercise science (M Ed, MS, PhD); health promotion (M Ed, MS); kinesiology (PhD); physical education/teacher education (M Ed, MS, Ed D, EdS). *Accreditation:* NCATE. Part-time programs available. *Faculty:* 16 full-time (7 women), 1 part-time/adjunct (0 women). *Students:* 70 full-time (46 women), 21 part-time (8 women); includes 10 minority (8 African Americans, 2 Asian Americans or Pacific Islanders), 10 international. Average age 26. 109 applicants, 68% accepted, 53 enrolled. In 2009, 26 master's, 7 doctorates awarded. *Degree requirements:* For master's, thesis (for some programs); for doctorate, thesis/dissertation; for Ed S, exam, field project. *Entrance requirements:* For master's, GRE General Test; for doctorate and Ed S, GRE General Test, interview, master's degree. *Application deadline:* For fall admission, 7/7 for domestic students; for spring admission, 11/24 for domestic students. Applications are processed on a rolling basis. Application fee: $50 ($60 for international students). Electronic applications accepted. *Expenses:* Tuition, state resident: full-time $6240. Tuition, nonresident: full-time $18,720. International tuition: $18,938 full-time. Required fees: $492. Tuition and fees vary according to course load, program and reciprocity agreements. *Financial support:* Research assistantships, teaching assistantships, Federal Work-Study available. Support available to part-time students. Financial award application deadline: 3/15; financial award applicants required to submit FAFSA. *Faculty research:* Biomechanics, exercise physiology, motor skill learning, school health, curriculum development. *Unit head:* Dr. Mary E. Rudisill, Head, 334-844-4483. *Application contact:* Dr. George Flowers, Dean of the Graduate School, 334-844-2125.

Ball State University, Graduate School, College of Applied Science and Technology, Fisher Institute for Wellness, Interdepartmental Program in Wellness Management, Muncie, IN 47306-1099. Offers MA, MS. *Entrance requirements:* For master's, GRE General Test, interview.

Benedictine University, Graduate Programs, Program in Nutrition and Wellness, Lisle, IL 60532-0900. Offers MS. *Students:* 21 full-time (20 women), 20 part-time (all women); includes 4 minority (1 African American, 2 Asian Americans or Pacific Islanders, 1 Hispanic American). 44 applicants, 82% accepted, 15 enrolled. In 2009, 7 master's awarded. *Entrance requirements:* Additional exam requirements/recommendations for international students: Required—TOEFL (minimum score 550 paper-based; 213 computer-based). *Application deadline:* For fall admission, 9/1 for domestic students; for winter admission, 12/1 for domestic students; for spring admission, 2/15 for domestic students. Applications are processed on a rolling basis. Application fee: $40. Electronic applications accepted. *Expenses:* Tuition: Part-time $750 per credit hour. Tuition and fees vary according to campus/location and program. *Financial support:* Career-related internships or fieldwork and health care benefits available. Support available to part-time students. *Faculty research:* Community and corporate wellness risk assessment, health behavior change, self-efficacy, evaluation of health program impact and effectiveness. Total annual research expenditures: $8,335. *Unit head:* Catherine Arnold, Director, 630-829-6534, E-mail: carnold@ben.edu. *Application contact:* Kari Gibbons, Director, Admissions, 630-829-6200, Fax: 630-829-6584, E-mail: kgibbons@ben.edu.

Boston University, School of Public Health, Social and Behavioral Sciences Department, Boston, MA 02215. Offers health behavior, health promotion, and disease prevention (MPH); social behavioral sciences (Dr PH). *Accreditation:* CEPH. Part-time and evening/weekend programs available. *Students:* 49 full-time (45 women), 38 part-time (all women); includes 12 minority (6 African Americans, 3 Asian Americans or Pacific Islanders, 3 Hispanic Americans), 2 international. Average age 28. *Entrance requirements:* For master's, GRE, DAT, GMAT, LSAT, MCAT; for doctorate, GRE, GMAT. Additional exam requirements/recommendations for international students: Required—TOEFL (minimum score 600 paper-based; 250 computer-based; 100 iBT) or IELTS (minimum score 6). *Application deadline:* For fall admission, 2/1 priority date for domestic and international students; for spring admission, 10/15 priority date for domestic and international students. Applications are processed on a rolling basis. Application fee: $95. Electronic applications accepted. *Expenses:* Tuition: Full-time $37,910; part-time $1184 per credit hour. Required fees: $386; $40 per semester. Part-time tuition and fees vary according to class time, course level, degree level and program. *Financial support:* Career-related internships or fieldwork, Federal Work-Study, institutionally sponsored loans, scholarships/grants, and tuition waivers (partial) available. Support available to part-time students. Financial award application deadline: 3/1; financial award applicants required to submit FAFSA. *Unit*

head: Dr. Deborah Bowen, Chair, 617-638-5160, E-mail: socbeh@bu.edu. *Application contact:* LePhan Quan, Assistant Director of Admissions, 617-638-4640, Fax: 617-638-5299, E-mail: asksph@bu.edu.

Bridgewater State University, School of Graduate Studies, School of Education and Allied Science, Department of Movement Arts, Health Promotion, and Leisure Studies, Program in Health Promotion, Bridgewater, MA 02325-0001. Offers M Ed. Part-time and evening/weekend programs available. *Entrance requirements:* For master's, GRE General Test.

Brigham Young University, Graduate Studies, College of Life Sciences, Department of Exercise Sciences, Provo, UT 84602. Offers athletic training (MS); exercise physiology (MS, PhD); exercise science (MS); health promotion (MS, PhD); physical medicine and rehabilitation (PhD). *Faculty:* 19 full-time (2 women). *Students:* 22 full-time (13 women), 41 part-time (19 women); includes 1 American Indian/Alaska Native, 3 Asian Americans or Pacific Islanders, 2 international. Average age 32. 30 applicants, 80% accepted, 22 enrolled. In 2009, 21 master's, 7 doctorates awarded. *Degree requirements:* For master's, thesis, oral defense; for doctorate, comprehensive exam, thesis/dissertation, oral defense, oral and written exams. *Entrance requirements:* For master's, GRE General Test, minimum GPA of 3.0 in last 60 hours of course work; for doctorate, GRE General Test, minimum GPA of 3.5 in last 60 hours of course work. Additional exam requirements/recommendations for international students: Required—TOEFL (minimum score 580 paper-based; 237 computer-based; 85 iBT), IELTS (minimum score 7). *Application deadline:* For fall admission, 2/1 for domestic and international students. Application fee: $50. Electronic applications accepted. *Expenses:* Tuition: Full-time $5580; part-time $301 per credit hour. Tuition and fees vary according to student's religious affiliation. *Financial support:* In 2009–10, 46 students received support, including 15 research assistantships with full and partial tuition reimbursements available (averaging $5,615 per year), 34 teaching assistantships with full and partial tuition reimbursements available (averaging $10,106 per year); fellowships, career-related internships or fieldwork, institutionally sponsored loans, tuition waivers (full and partial), and unspecified assistantships also available. Financial award application deadline: 3/1. *Faculty research:* Injury prevention and rehabilitation, human skeletal muscle adaptation, cardiovascular health and fitness, lifestyle modification and health promotion. Total annual research expenditures: $18,096. *Unit head:* Dr. Larry Hall, Chair, 801-422-7303, Fax: 801-422-0543, E-mail: larry_hall@byu.edu. *Application contact:* Dr. Jeffrey Brent Feland, Graduate Coordinator, 801-422-1182, Fax: 801-422-0543, E-mail: brent_feland@byu.edu.

California State University, Fresno, Division of Graduate Studies, College of Health and Human Services, Department of Public Health, Fresno, CA 93740-8027. Offers health policy and management (MPH); health promotion (MPH). *Accreditation:* CEPH. Part-time and evening/weekend programs available. *Degree requirements:* For master's, thesis or alternative. *Entrance requirements:* For master's, GRE General Test, minimum GPA of 2.5. Additional exam requirements/recommendations for international students: Required—TOEFL. Electronic applications accepted. *Faculty research:* Foster parent training, geriatrics, tobacco control.

Cambridge College, School of Education, Cambridge, MA 02138-5304. Offers autism specialist (M Ed); autism/behavior analyst (M Ed); behavior analyst (Post-Master's Certificate); behavioral management (M Ed); early childhood teacher (M Ed); education specialist in curriculum and instruction (CAGS); educational leadership (Ed D); elementary teacher (M Ed); English as a second language (M Ed, Certificate); general science (M Ed); health education, health promotion (Post-Master's Certificate); health/family and consumer sciences (M Ed); history (M Ed); individualized degree (M Ed); information technology literacy (M Ed); instructional technology (M Ed); interdisciplinary studies (M Ed); library teacher (M Ed); literacy education (M Ed); mathematics (M Ed); mathematics specialist (Certificate); middle school mathematics and science (M Ed); school administration (M Ed, CAGS); school guidance counselor (M Ed); school nurse education (M Ed); school social worker/school adjustment counselor (M Ed); special education administrator (CAGS); special education/moderate disabilities (M Ed); teaching skills and methodologies (M Ed). Part-time and evening/weekend programs available. Postbaccalaureate distance learning degree programs offered (minimal on-campus study). *Faculty:* 10 full-time (3 women), 283 part-time/adjunct (187 women). *Students:* 974 full-time (755 women), 1,071 part-time (835 women); includes 940 minority (762 African Americans, 4 American Indian/Alaska Native, 22 Asian Americans or Pacific Islanders, 152 Hispanic Americans), 28 international. Average age 39. In 2009, 866 master's, 4 doctorates, 209

Health Promotion

Cambridge College (continued)

CAGSs awarded. *Degree requirements:* For master's, thesis, internship/practicum (licensure program only); for doctorate, thesis/dissertation; for other advanced degree, thesis. *Entrance requirements:* For master's, interview, resume, documentation of licensure, 2 professional references; for doctorate, official transcripts, interview, resume, documentation of licensure (if any), written personal statement/essay, portfolio of scholarly and professional work, qualifying assessment, 2 professional references, health insurance, immunizations form; for other advanced degree, official transcripts, interview, resume, documentation of licensure (if any), written personal statement/essay, 2 professional references, health insurance, immunizations form. Additional exam requirements/recommendations for international students: Required—TOEFL (minimum score 550 paper-based; 213 computer-based; 79 iBT); Recommended—IELTS (minimum score 6). *Application deadline:* Applications are processed on a rolling basis. Application fee: $30. Electronic applications accepted. *Expenses:* Contact institution. *Financial support:* In 2009–10, 1,373 students received support. Career-related internships or fieldwork, Federal Work-Study, and scholarships/grants available. Financial award applicants required to submit FAFSA. *Faculty research:* Adult education, accelerated learning, mathematics education, brain compatible learning, special education and law. *Unit head:* Dr. N. Alan Sheppard, Interim Associate Dean, 617-873-0619, E-mail: alan.sheppard@cambridgecollege.edu. *Application contact:* Stephen Lyons, Director of Enrollment, Graduate and N.I.T.E. Programs, 617-868-1000, Fax: 617-349-3561, E-mail: stephen.lyons@cambridgecollege.edu.

Canisius College, Graduate Division, School of Education and Human Services, Department of Health and Human Performance, Buffalo, NY 14208-1098. Offers MS. Part-time and evening/weekend programs available. *Faculty:* 3 full-time (0 women), 3 part-time/adjunct (1 woman). *Students:* 13 full-time (10 women), 10 part-time (8 women); includes 1 minority (African American). Average age 24. 26 applicants, 81% accepted, 12 enrolled. In 2009, 9 master's awarded. *Degree requirements:* For master's, thesis, project internship. Application fee: $25. *Financial support:* In 2009–10, 9 students received support, including 1 research assistantship with tuition reimbursement available (averaging $6,000 per year); career-related internships or fieldwork, institutionally sponsored loans, health care benefits, and unspecified assistantships also available. *Faculty research:* Delayed onset of muscle soreness, exercising muscle blood flow, aging. Total annual research expenditures: $13,000. *Unit head:* Dr. Peter M. Koehneke, Chair, 716-888-2954, E-mail: koehneke@canisius.edu. *Application contact:* James D. Bagwell, Director of Graduate Recruitment and Admissions, 716-888-2544, Fax: 716-888-3290, E-mail: bagwellj@canisius.edu.

Claremont Graduate University, Graduate Programs, School of Community and Global Health, San Dimas, CA 91773. Offers health promotion science (PhD); public health (MPH). *Faculty:* 9 full-time (4 women). *Students:* 10 full-time (7 women), 4 part-time (all women); includes 7 minority (2 African Americans, 1 American Indian/Alaska Native, 1 Asian American or Pacific Islander, 3 Hispanic Americans). Average age 30. *Entrance requirements:* For master's and doctorate, GRE. Additional exam requirements/recommendations for international students: Required—TOEFL (minimum score 550 paper-based; 213 computer-based; 80 iBT). *Application deadline:* For fall admission, 2/1 priority date for domestic students; for spring admission, 11/1 priority date for domestic students. Applications are processed on a rolling basis. Application fee: $60. Electronic applications accepted. *Expenses:* Tuition: Full-time $35,046; part-time $1524 per credit. Required fees: $161 per semester. *Financial support:* Fellowships, research assistantships, teaching assistantships, Federal Work-Study, institutionally sponsored loans, and scholarships/grants available. Support available to part-time students. Financial award application deadline: 2/15; financial award applicants required to submit FAFSA. *Unit head:* C. Anderson Johnson, Dean, 909-607-8235, E-mail: andy.johnson@cgu.edu. *Application contact:* C. Anderson Johnson, Dean, 909-607-8235, E-mail: andy.johnson@cgu.edu.

Cleveland Chiropractic College–Kansas City Campus, Program in Health Promotion, Overland Park, KS 66210. Offers MSHP.

Cleveland Chiropractic College–Los Angeles Campus, Program in Health Promotion, Los Angeles, CA 90004-2196. Offers MSHP. *Expenses:* Tuition: Full-time $17,472; part-time $8736 per year. Required fees: $825 per year.

Concord University, Graduate Studies, Athens, WV 24712-1000. Offers behavioral science (M Ed); educational leadership and supervision (M Ed); geography (M Ed); health promotion (M Ed); reading specialist (M Ed); social studies (M Ed). Postbaccalaureate distance learning degree programs offered. *Entrance requirements:* For master's, GRE or MAT, baccalaureate degree with minimum GPA of 2.5 GPA from regionally accredited institution; teaching license; 2 letters of recommendation.

Eastern Kentucky University, The Graduate School, College of Health Sciences, Department of Exercise and Sport Science, Richmond, KY 40475-3102. Offers exercise and sport science (MS); exercise and wellness (MS); sports administration (MS). Part-time programs available. *Entrance requirements:* For master's, GRE General Test (minimum score 700 verbal and quantitative), minimum GPA of 2.5 (for most), minimum GPA of 3.0 (analytical writing). *Faculty research:* Nutrition and exercise.

Eastern Michigan University, Graduate School, College of Health and Human Services, School of Health Promotion and Human Performance, Ypsilanti, MI 48197. Offers MS, Graduate Certificate. Part-time and evening/weekend programs available. Postbaccalaureate distance learning degree programs offered (minimal on-campus study). *Faculty:* 21 full-time (8 women). *Students:* 55 full-time (24 women), 109 part-time (49 women); includes 25 minority (18 African Americans, 1 American Indian/Alaska Native, 1 Asian American or Pacific Islander, 5 Hispanic Americans), 2 international. Average age 29. 181 applicants, 62% accepted, 71 enrolled. In 2009, 44 master's, 3 other advanced degrees awarded. *Entrance requirements:* For master's, MAT (orthotics and prosthetics). Additional exam requirements/recommendations for international students: Required—TOEFL. *Application deadline:* For fall admission, 8/1 for domestic students, 5/1 for international students; for winter admission, 12/1 for domestic students, 10/1 for international students; for spring admission, 4/15 for domestic students, 3/1 for international students. Applications are processed on a rolling basis. Application fee: $35. Tuition and fees vary according to course level. *Financial support:* In 2009–10, 4 research assistantships with full tuition reimbursements (averaging $6,663 per year) were awarded; fellowships, teaching assistantships with full tuition reimbursements, career-related internships or fieldwork, Federal Work-Study, institutionally sponsored loans, scholarships/grants, tuition waivers (partial), and unspecified assistantships also available. Support available to part-time students. Financial award applicants required to submit FAFSA. *Unit head:* Dr. Christine Karshin, Interim Director, 734-487-0090, Fax: 734-487-2024, E-mail: christine.karshin@emich.edu. *Application contact:* Dr. Brenda Riemer, Chair, Graduate Programs, 734-487-0090 Ext. 2745, Fax: 734-487-2024, E-mail: briemer@emich.edu.

Emory University, Rollins School of Public Health, Online Program in Public Health, Atlanta, GA 30322-1100. Offers applied epidemiology (MPH); healthcare outcomes (MPH); prevention science (MPH). Part-time and evening/weekend programs available. Postbaccalaureate distance learning degree programs offered (minimal on-campus study). *Degree requirements:* For master's, thesis, practicum. *Entrance requirements:* For master's, GRE (may be waived). Additional exam requirements/recommendations for international students: Required—TOEFL (minimum score 550 paper-based; 213 computer-based; 80 iBT). Electronic applications accepted.

Florida Atlantic University, College of Education, Department of Exercise Science and Health Promotion, Boca Raton, FL 33431-0991. Offers MS. Part-time and evening/weekend programs available. *Faculty:* 8 full-time (3 women), 13 part-time/adjunct (7 women). *Students:* 31 full-time (13 women), 17 part-time (10 women); includes 13 minority (6 African Americans, 1 Asian American or Pacific Islander, 6 Hispanic Americans), 1 international. Average age 26. 56 applicants, 68% accepted, 5 enrolled. In 2009, 15 master's awarded. *Degree requirements:* For master's, comprehensive exam, thesis optional. *Entrance requirements:* For master's, GRE General Test, minimum GPA of 3.0 during last 60 hours of course work. Additional exam requirements/recommendations for international students: Required—TOEFL (minimum score 500 paper-based). *Application deadline:* For fall admission, 7/1 priority date for domestic students, 2/15 for international students; for spring admission, 11/1 priority date for domestic students, 7/15 for international students. Applications are processed on a rolling basis. Application fee: $30. *Expenses:* Tuition, state resident: full-time $7055; part-time $293.94 per credit hour. Tuition, nonresident: full-time $22,096; part-time $920.66 per credit hour. *Financial support:* Research assistantships with partial tuition reimbursements, teaching assistantships with partial tuition reimbursements, career-related internships or fieldwork available. *Faculty research:* Pulmonary limitations during exercise, metabolism regulation, determinants of performance, age related change in functional mobility and geriatric exercise, behavioral change aimed at promoting active lifestyles. *Unit head:* Dr. Sue Graves, Chair, 954-236-1261, Fax: 954-236-1259. *Application contact:* Dr. Joseph A. O'Kroy, Graduate Coordinator, 954-236-1266, Fax: 954-236-1259, E-mail: okroy@fau.edu.

Florida International University, Stempel College of Public Health and Social Work, Programs in Public Health, Miami, FL 33199. Offers biostatistics (MPH); environmental and occupational health (MPH, PhD); epidemiology (MPH, PhD); health policy and management (MPH); health promotion and disease prevention (PhD); health promotion and diseases prevention (MPH). PhD only admits in Fall. *Accreditation:* CEPH. Part-time and evening/weekend programs available. Postbaccalaureate distance learning degree programs offered (no on-campus study). *Faculty:* 18 full-time (6 women). *Students:* 249 full-time (186 women), 185 part-time (144 women); includes 309 minority (154 African Americans, 2 American Indian/Alaska Native, 26 Asian Americans or Pacific Islanders, 127 Hispanic Americans), 48 international. Average age 35. 484 applicants, 29% accepted, 123 enrolled. In 2009, 79 master's, 1 doctorate awarded. *Degree requirements:* For master's, thesis optional; for doctorate, comprehensive exam, thesis/dissertation. *Entrance requirements:* For master's, minimum GPA of 3.0, letters of recommendation; for doctorate, GRE, resume, minimum GPA of 3.0, letters of recommendation, letter of intent. Additional exam requirements/recommendations for international students: Required—TOEFL (minimum score 550 paper-based; 80 iBT). *Application deadline:* For fall admission, 6/1 for domestic students, 4/1 for international students; for spring admission, 10/1 for domestic students, 9/1 for international students. Applications are processed on a rolling basis. Application fee: $30. Electronic applications accepted. *Expenses:* Contact institution. *Financial support:* Institutionally sponsored loans, scholarships/grants, and tuition waivers (full) available. Financial award application deadline: 3/1; financial award applicants required to submit FAFSA. *Faculty research:* Drugs/AIDS intervention among migrant workers, provision of services for active/recovering drug users with HIV. *Unit head:* Dr. Gilbert Ramirez, Associate Dean for Academic and Student Affairs, 305-348-7442, E-mail: ph@fiu.edu. *Application contact:* Nanett Rojas, Assistant Director of Graduate Admissions, 305-348-7442, Fax: 305-348-7441, E-mail: gradadm@fiu.edu.

George Mason University, College of Education and Human Development, School of Recreation, Health and Tourism, Manassas, VA 20110. Offers exercise, fitness, and health promotion (MS). *Faculty:* 26 full-time (10 women), 50 part-time/adjunct (29 women). *Students:* 3 full-time (1 woman), 13 part-time (7 women); includes 1 minority (Asian American or Pacific Islander). Average age 32. 16 applicants, 56% accepted, 5 enrolled. In 2009, 7 master's awarded. *Degree requirements:* For master's, thesis (for some programs). *Entrance requirements:* For master's, GRE or MAT, 3 letters of recommendation. Additional exam requirements/recommendations for international students: Required—TOEFL. *Application deadline:* For fall admission, 11/1 priority date for domestic students, 11/1 for international students; for spring admission, 4/1 for domestic and international students. Application fee: $75. Electronic applications accepted. *Expenses:* Tuition, state resident: full-time $7568; part-time $315.33 per credit hour. Tuition, nonresident: full-time $21,704; part-time $904.33 per credit hour. Required fees: $2184; $91 per credit hour. *Financial support:* In 2009–10, 2 students received support, including 2 research assistantships with full and partial tuition reimbursements available (averaging $5,374 per year); Federal Work-Study, scholarships/grants, unspecified assistantships, and health care benefits (full-time research or teaching assistantship recipients) also available. Support available to part-time students. Financial award application deadline: 3/1; financial award applicants required to submit FAFSA. *Faculty research:* Informing policy; promoting economic development; advocating stewardship of natural resources; improving the quality of life of individuals, families, and communities at the local, national and international levels. Total annual research expenditures: $77,515. *Unit head:* David Wiggins, Director, 703-993-2057, E-mail: dwiggin1@gmu.edu. *Application contact:* Dr. Pierre Rodgers, Associate Professor/Co-Coordinator of the Graduate Program, 703-993-8317, E-mail: prodgers@gmu.edu.

Georgetown University, Graduate School of Arts and Sciences, Programs in Biomedical Sciences, Department of Microbiology and Immunology, Washington, DC 20057. Offers biohazardous threat agents and emerging infectious diseases (MS); general microbiology and immunology (MS); global infectious diseases (PhD); microbiology and immunology research (PhD); science policy and advocacy (MS). Part-time programs available. *Degree requirements:* For master's, 30 credit hours of coursework; for doctorate, comprehensive exam, thesis/dissertation. *Entrance requirements:* For master's, GRE General Test, 3 letters of reference, bachelor's degree in related field; for doctorate, GRE General Test, 3 letters of reference, MS/BS in related field. Additional exam requirements/recommendations for international students: Required—TOEFL (minimum score 505 paper-based; 213 computer-based). Electronic applications accepted. *Faculty research:* Pathogenesis and basic biology of the fungus Candida albicans, molecular biology of viral immunopathological mechanisms in Multiple Sclerosis.

Georgia College & State University, Graduate School, College of Health Sciences, Department of Kinesiology, Milledgeville, GA 31061. Offers health promotion (M Ed); human performance (M Ed); kinesiology (MAT); outdoor education (M Ed). *Accreditation:* NCATE (one or more programs are accredited). Part-time and evening/weekend programs available. *Faculty:* 12 full-time (5 women). *Students:* 25 full-time (13 women), 7 part-time (5 women); includes 4 minority (2 African Americans, 2 Hispanic Americans), 3 international. Average age 26. 23 applicants, 87% accepted, 19 enrolled. In 2009, 7 master's awarded. *Degree requirements:* For master's, thesis optional. *Entrance requirements:* For master's, GRE General Test or MAT, minimum GPA of 2.75 in upper-level undergraduate courses, 2 letters of reference. Additional exam requirements/recommendations for international students: Recommended—TOEFL (minimum score 550 paper-based; 213 computer-based; 79 iBT). *Application deadline:* For fall admission, 7/15 priority date for domestic students; for spring admission, 11/15 for domestic students. Applications are processed on a rolling basis. Application fee: $40. Electronic applications accepted. *Expenses:* Tuition, area resident: Part-time $241 per credit hour. Tuition, state resident: full-time $4338. Tuition, nonresident: full-time $17,352; part-time $964 per credit hour. Required fees: $609 per semester. Tuition and fees vary according to course load and campus/location. *Financial support:* In 2009–10, 20 research assistantships with full tuition reimbursements were awarded; career-related internships or fieldwork and unspecified assistantships also available. Support available to part-time students. Financial award applicants required to submit FAFSA. *Unit head:* Dr. Jude Hirsch, Chair, 478-445-4072, Fax: 478-445-1790, E-mail: jude.hirsch@gcsu.edu. *Application contact:* Dr. Jude Hirsch, Chair, 478-445-4072, Fax: 478-445-1790, E-mail: jude.hirsch@gcsu.edu.

Georgia State University, College of Health and Human Sciences, Byrdine F. Lewis School of Nursing, Atlanta, GA 30302-3083. Offers adult health (MS); adult health nursing (Certificate); child health (MS); family nurse practitioner (MS, Certificate); health promotion, protection and restoration (PhD); perinatal/women's health (MS); psychiatric mental health nursing (Certificate); psychiatric/mental health (MS); women's health nursing (Certificate). *Accreditation:* AACN. Part-time and evening/weekend programs available. Postbaccalaureate distance learning degree programs offered (minimal on-campus study). *Degree requirements:* For master's, research activity; for doctorate, comprehensive exam, thesis/dissertation. *Entrance requirements:* For

master's, MAT (preferred) or GRE, interview, RN license; for doctorate, GRE General Test. Additional exam requirements/recommendations for international students: Required—TOEFL (minimum score 550 paper-based; 213 computer-based). Electronic applications accepted. *Expenses:* Contact institution. *Faculty research:* Breast cancer prevention, sexually compulsive behaviors, health risks in minority youth, asthma treatment strategies, adolescent alcohol-related issues.

Goddard College, Graduate Division, Master of Arts in Health Arts and Sciences Program, Plainfield, VT 05667-9432. Offers MA. *Faculty:* 9 part-time/adjunct (8 women). *Students:* 20 full-time. Average age 38. 14 applicants, 79% accepted, 9 enrolled. *Degree requirements:* For master's, thesis. *Entrance requirements:* For master's, 3 letters of recommendation, study plan and resource list, interview. *Application deadline:* Applications are processed on a rolling basis. Application fee: $40. Electronic applications accepted. *Expenses:* Tuition: Part-time $7223 per semester. Part-time tuition and fees vary according to program. *Financial support:* In 2009–10, 20 students received support. Applicants required to submit FAFSA. *Unit head:* S. B. Sowbel, Interim Program Director, 802-454-8311, Fax: 802-454-1029, E-mail: sowbel@goddard.edu. *Application contact:* Jamie Kline, 800-906-8312 Ext. 311, Fax: 802-454-1029, E-mail: jamie.kline@goddard.edu.

Harvard University, School of Public Health, Department of Society, Human Development and Health, Boston, MA 02115-6096. Offers SM, DPH, SD. Part-time programs available. *Faculty:* 32 full-time (17 women), 16 part-time/adjunct (9 women). *Students:* 85 full-time, 7 part-time; includes 26 minority (13 African Americans, 6 Asian Americans or Pacific Islanders, 7 Hispanic Americans), 14 international. Average age 29. 200 applicants, 34% accepted, 39 enrolled. In 2009, 17 master's, 17 doctorates awarded. *Degree requirements:* For doctorate, thesis/dissertation, qualifying exam. *Entrance requirements:* For master's and doctorate, GRE. Additional exam requirements/recommendations for international students: Required—TOEFL (minimum score 590 paper-based; 240 computer-based; 95 iBT); Recommended—IELTS (minimum score 7). *Application deadline:* For fall admission, 12/15 for domestic and international students. Application fee: $115. Electronic applications accepted. *Expenses:* Tuition: Full-time $33,696. Required fees: $1126. Full-time tuition and fees vary according to program. *Financial support:* Fellowships, research assistantships, teaching assistantships, Federal Work-Study, scholarships/grants, traineeships, tuition waivers (partial), and unspecified assistantships available. Support available to part-time students. Financial award application deadline: 2/8; financial award applicants required to submit FAFSA. *Faculty research:* Social determinants of health, program design and planned social change, health and social policy, heath care and community-based interventions, health effects and prevention of gender-based violence. *Unit head:* Dr. Ichiro Kawachi, Chair, 617-432-1135, Fax: 617-432-3123, E-mail: ikawachi@hsph.harvard.edu. *Application contact:* Vincent W. James, Director of Admissions, 617-432-1031, Fax: 617-432-7080, E-mail: admisofc@hsph.harvard.edu.

Independence University, Program in Health Services, Salt Lake City, UT 84107. Offers community health (MSHS); wellness promotion (MSHS). Part-time and evening/weekend programs available. Postbaccalaureate distance learning degree programs offered (no on-campus study). *Degree requirements:* For master's, fieldwork, internship, final project (wellness promotion). *Entrance requirements:* For master's, previous course work in psychology. *Expenses:* Required fees: $475 per credit. One-time fee: $100 part-time.

Independence University, Program in Nursing, Salt Lake City, UT 84107. Offers community health (MSN); gerontology (MSN); nursing administration (MSN); wellness promotion (MSN). *Expenses:* Required fees: $475 per credit. One-time fee: $100 part-time.

Indiana State University, School of Graduate Studies, College of Nursing, Health and Human Services, Department of Health, Safety, and Environmental Health Sciences, Terre Haute, IN 47809. Offers community health promotion (MA, MS); health and safety education (MA, MS); occupational safety management (MA, MS). *Accreditation:* NCATE (one or more programs are accredited). *Degree requirements:* For master's, thesis or alternative. *Entrance requirements:* For master's, GRE General Test. Electronic applications accepted.

Indiana University Bloomington, School of Health, Physical Education and Recreation, Department of Applied Health Science, Bloomington, IN 47405-7000. Offers health behavior (PhD); health promotion (MS); human development/family studies (MS); nutrition science (MS); public health (MPH); safety management (MS); school and college health programs (MS). *Accreditation:* CEPH (one or more programs are accredited). *Faculty:* 24 full-time (12 women). *Students:* 131 full-time (92 women), 22 part-time (20 women); includes 35 minority (22 African Americans, 1 American Indian/Alaska Native, 5 Asian Americans or Pacific Islanders, 7 Hispanic Americans), 29 international. Average age 31. 118 applicants, 71% accepted, 52 enrolled. In 2009, 43 master's, 6 doctorates awarded. *Degree requirements:* For master's, thesis optional; for doctorate, thesis/dissertation. *Entrance requirements:* For master's, GRE (MS in nutrition science), 3 recommendations; for doctorate, GRE, 3 recommendations. Additional exam requirements/recommendations for international students: Required—TOEFL (minimum score 550 paper-based; 213 computer-based; 79 iBT). *Application deadline:* For fall admission, 4/30 priority date for domestic students, 12/1 priority date for international students; for spring admission, 11/15 priority date for domestic students, 9/1 priority date for international students. Application fee: $55 ($65 for international students). *Financial support:* In 2009–10, 80 students received support, including 12 fellowships (averaging $2,316 per year), 50 research assistantships with full and partial tuition reimbursements available (averaging $6,973 per year), 27 teaching assistantships with full and partial tuition reimbursements available (averaging $11,067 per year); career-related internships or fieldwork, Federal Work-Study, institutionally sponsored loans, scholarships/grants, tuition waivers (partial), and fee remissions also available. Financial award application deadline: 3/1. *Faculty research:* Cancer education, HIV/AIDS and drug education, public health, parent-child interactions, safety education. Total annual research expenditures: $2.8 million. *Unit head:* Dr. Mohammad R. Torabi, Chair, 812-855-4808, Fax: 812-855-3936, E-mail: torabi@indiana.edu. *Application contact:* Dr. Mohammad R. Torabi, Chair, 812-855-4808, Fax: 812-855-3936, E-mail: torabi@indiana.edu.

Lehman College of the City University of New York, Division of Natural and Social Sciences, Department of Health Sciences, Program in Health Education and Promotion, Bronx, NY 10468-1589. Offers MA. *Accreditation:* NCATE. Part-time and evening/weekend programs available. *Degree requirements:* For master's, thesis or alternative. *Entrance requirements:* For master's, minimum GPA of 2.7.

Loma Linda University, School of Public Health, Programs in Health Promotion and Education, Loma Linda, CA 92350. Offers MPH, Dr PH. *Accreditation:* CEPH (one or more programs are accredited). *Degree requirements:* For doctorate, thesis/dissertation. *Entrance requirements:* For doctorate, GRE General Test. Additional exam requirements/recommendations for international students: Required—Michigan English Language Assessment Battery or TOEFL.

Louisiana State University in Shreveport, College of Education and Human Development, Program in Kinesiology and Wellness, Shreveport, LA 71115-2399. Offers MS. Part-time and evening/weekend programs available. *Students:* 6 full-time (3 women), 6 part-time (3 women); includes 3 minority (all African Americans). 11 applicants, 82% accepted, 6 enrolled. In 2009, 1 master's awarded. *Entrance requirements:* For master's, GRE, baccalaureate degree with minimum GPA of 2.5 or 2.75 on last 60 credit hours attempted in degree program. Additional exam requirements/recommendations for international students: Required—TOEFL (minimum score 500 paper-based; 173 computer-based; 61 iBT). *Application deadline:* For fall admission, 6/30 for domestic and international students; for spring admission, 11/30 for domestic and international students. Application fee: $10 ($20 for international students). *Financial support:* Unspecified assistantships available. *Unit head:* Dr. Timothy P. Winter, Program Director, 318-797-5264, Fax: 318-797-5386, E-mail: timothy.winter@lsus.edu. *Application contact:* Dr. Timothy P. Winter, Program Director, 318-797-5264, Fax: 318-797-5386, E-mail: timothy.winter@lsus.edu.

Marymount University, School of Health Professions, Program in Health Promotion Management, Arlington, VA 22207-4299. Offers MS. Part-time and evening/weekend programs available. *Faculty:* 2 full-time (1 woman), 1 part-time/adjunct (0 women). *Students:* 15 full-time (12 women), 16 part-time (12 women); includes 9 minority (7 African Americans, 1 Asian American or Pacific Islander, 1 Hispanic American), 3 international. Average age 28. 20 applicants, 85% accepted, 11 enrolled. In 2009, 15 master's awarded. *Entrance requirements:* For master's, GRE or MAT, 2 letters of recommendation, interview, resume. Additional exam requirements/recommendations for international students: Required—TOEFL (minimum score 600 paper-based; 250 computer-based; 96 iBT), IELTS (minimum score 6.5). *Application deadline:* For fall admission, 7/1 for international students; for spring admission, 10/15 for international students. Applications are processed on a rolling basis. Application fee: $40. Electronic applications accepted. *Expenses:* Tuition: Full-time $13,050; part-time $725 per credit hour. Required fees: $135; $7.50 per credit hour. *Financial support:* In 2009–10, 3 students received support; research assistantships with full tuition reimbursements available, career-related internships or fieldwork, Federal Work-Study, scholarships/grants, and unspecified assistantships available. Support available to part-time students. Financial award applicants required to submit FAFSA. *Unit head:* Dr. Michael Nordvall, Chair, 703-526-6876, Fax: 703-284-3819, E-mail: michael.nordvall@marymount.edu. *Application contact:* Francesca Reed, Director, Graduate Admissions, 703-284-5901, Fax: 703-527-3815, E-mail: grad.admissions@marymount.edu.

McNeese State University, Doré School of Graduate Studies, Burton College of Education, Department of Health and Human Performance, Lake Charles, LA 70609. Offers exercise physiology (MS); health promotion (MS); nutrition and wellness (MS). *Accreditation:* NCATE. Evening/weekend programs available. *Faculty:* 5 full-time (2 women). *Students:* 40 full-time (32 women), 6 part-time (4 women); includes 6 minority (all African Americans), 4 international. In 2009, 22 master's awarded. *Entrance requirements:* For master's, GRE, undergraduate major or minor in health and human performance or related field of study. *Application deadline:* For fall admission, 5/15 priority date for domestic and international students; for spring admission, 10/15 priority date for domestic and international students. Applications are processed on a rolling basis. Application fee: $20 ($30 for international students). *Expenses:* Tuition, area resident: Full-time $2556. Tuition, state resident: full-time $2556. Required fees: $1031. Tuition and fees vary according to course load. *Financial support:* Application deadline: 5/1. *Unit head:* Dr. Michael Soileau, Head, 337-475-5374, Fax: 337-475-5947, E-mail: msoileau@mcneese.edu. *Application contact:* Dr. George F. Mead, Interim Dean of Dore' School of Graduate Studies, 337-475-5396, Fax: 337-475-5397, E-mail: admissions@mcneese.edu.

Missouri State University, Graduate College, College of Health and Human Services, Department of Health, Physical Education, and Recreation, Springfield, MO 65897. Offers health promotion and wellness management (MS); secondary education (MS Ed), including physical education. Part-time programs available. *Faculty:* 13 full-time (5 women). *Students:* 20 full-time (10 women), 10 part-time (6 women), 1 international. Average age 27. 17 applicants, 94% accepted, 12 enrolled. In 2009, 10 master's awarded. *Degree requirements:* For master's, comprehensive exam, thesis or alternative. *Entrance requirements:* For master's, GRE (MS), minimum GPA of 2.8 (MS); 9-12 teaching certification (MS Ed). Additional exam requirements/recommendations for international students: Required—TOEFL (minimum score 550 paper-based; 213 computer-based; 79 iBT). *Application deadline:* For fall admission, 7/20 priority date for domestic students, 5/1 for international students; for spring admission, 12/20 priority date for domestic students, 9/1 for international students. Applications are processed on a rolling basis. Application fee: $35 ($50 for international students). Electronic applications accepted. *Expenses:* Tuition, state resident: full-time $3852; part-time $214 per credit hour. Tuition, nonresident: full-time $7524; part-time $418 per credit hour. Required fees: $696; $172 per semester. Tuition and fees vary according to course level, course load, degree level and program. *Financial support:* In 2009–10, 5 teaching assistantships with full tuition reimbursements (averaging $7,340 per year) were awarded; Federal Work-Study, institutionally sponsored loans, scholarships/grants, and unspecified assistantships also available. Financial award application deadline: 3/31; financial award applicants required to submit FAFSA. *Unit head:* Dr. Sarah McCallister, Acting Head, 417-836-6582, Fax: 417-836-5371, E-mail: sarahmccallister@missouristate.edu. *Application contact:* Eric Eckert, Coordinator of Graduate Admissions and Recruitment, 417-836-5331, Fax: 417-836-6200, E-mail: ericeckert@missouristate.edu.

Montana State University, College of Graduate Studies, College of Education, Health, and Human Development, Department of Health and Human Development, Bozeman, MT 59717. Offers health and human development (MS), including counseling, exercise and nutrition sciences, family and consumer sciences, family financial planning, health promotion and education. *Accreditation:* ACA. Part-time programs available. Postbaccalaureate distance learning degree programs offered (no on-campus study). *Faculty:* 27 full-time (18 women), 7 part-time/adjunct (6 women). *Students:* 54 full-time (47 women), 18 part-time (15 women); includes 1 minority (Hispanic American). Average age 30. 32 applicants, 34% accepted, 10 enrolled. In 2009, 26 master's awarded. *Degree requirements:* For master's, comprehensive exam. *Entrance requirements:* For master's, GRE General Test. Additional exam requirements/recommendations for international students: Required—TOEFL (minimum score 550 paper-based; 213 computer-based). *Application deadline:* For fall admission, 7/15 priority date for domestic students, 5/15 priority date for international students; for spring admission, 12/1 priority date for domestic students, 10/1 priority date for international students. Applications are processed on a rolling basis. Application fee: $30. Electronic applications accepted. *Expenses:* Tuition, state resident: full-time $5635; part-time $3492 per year. Tuition, nonresident: full-time $17,212; part-time $7865.10 per year. Required fees: $1441; $153.15 per credit. Tuition and fees vary according to course load and program. *Financial support:* In 2009–10, 24 students received support, including 7 research assistantships (averaging $1,000 per year), 17 teaching assistantships with full tuition reimbursements available (averaging $8,000 per year). Financial award application deadline: 3/1; financial award applicants required to submit FAFSA. *Faculty research:* Gait analysis, cancer prevention, obesity prevention, energy expenditure, decision making. Total annual research expenditures: $2.8 million. *Unit head:* Dr. Tim Dunnagan, Head, 404-994-3242, Fax: 404-994-2013, E-mail: dunnagan@montana.edu. *Application contact:* Dr. Carl Fox.

Morehouse School of Medicine, Master of Public Health Program, Atlanta, GA 30310-1495. Offers epidemiology (MPH); health administration, management and policy (MPH); health education/health promotion (MPH); international health (MPH). *Accreditation:* CEPH. Part-time programs available. *Faculty:* 4 full-time (1 woman), 36 part-time/adjunct (21 women). *Students:* 54 full-time (37 women), 3 part-time (2 women); includes 34 minority (33 African Americans, 1 American Indian/Alaska Native). Average age 28. 62 applicants, 48% accepted, 29 enrolled. In 2009, 13 master's awarded. *Degree requirements:* For master's, thesis, practicum, public health leadership seminar. *Entrance requirements:* For master's, GRE General Test, writing test, public health or human service experience. Additional exam requirements/recommendations for international students: Required—TOEFL (minimum score 550 paper-based; 200 computer-based). *Application deadline:* For fall admission, 3/1 for domestic and international students. Application fee: $50. Electronic applications accepted. *Expenses:* Contact institution. *Financial support:* In 2009–10, 32 students received support, including 6 research assistantships with partial tuition reimbursements available (averaging $10,000 per year); fellowships, teaching assistantships, career-related internships or fieldwork, Federal Work-Study, institutionally sponsored loans, scholarships/grants, and unspecified assistantships also available. Support available to part-time students. Financial award application deadline: 5/1; financial award applicants required to submit FAFSA. *Faculty research:* Women's and adolescent health, violence prevention, cancer epidemiology/disparities, substance abuse prevention. Total annual research expenditures: $640,176. *Unit head:* Dr. Patricia Rodney, Director/Assistant Dean for Public Health Education, 404-752-1944, Fax: 404-752-1051, E-mail: prodney@msm.edu. *Application contact:* Dr. Sterling Roaf, Director of Admissions, 404-752-1650, Fax: 404-752-1512, E-mail: mphadmissions@msm.edu.

Nebraska Methodist College, Program in Health Promotion Management, Omaha, ND 68114. Offers MS. Evening/weekend programs available. Postbaccalaureate distance learning degree

Health Promotion

Nebraska Methodist College (continued)
programs offered (no on-campus study). *Faculty:* 7 part-time/adjunct (6 women). *Students:* 21 full-time; includes 2 minority (both American Indian/Alaska Native). Average age 24. 11 applicants, 82% accepted, 6 enrolled. In 2009, 10 master's awarded. *Degree requirements:* For master's, thesis or alternative, capstone project. *Entrance requirements:* For master's, interview. Additional exam requirements/recommendations for international students: Required—TOEFL (minimum score 550 paper-based; 213 computer-based; 80 iBT). *Application deadline:* Applications are processed on a rolling basis. Application fee: $25. *Expenses:* Tuition: Full-time $6552; part-time $546 per credit hour. Required fees: $300; $25 per credit hour. *Financial support:* In 2009–10, 8 students received support; research assistantships with full and partial tuition reimbursements available, scholarships/grants available. Support available to part-time students. Financial award applicants required to submit FAFSA. *Faculty research:* Congregational health promotion, fitness testing with elderly, educational assessment, statistics instruction. *Unit head:* Beth Pernie, Program Development Officer, 402-354-7138, Fax: 402-354-7020, E-mail: beth.pirnie@methodistcollege.edu. *Application contact:* Sara Bonney, Director of Admissions, 402-354-7111, Fax: 402-354-7020, E-mail: admissions@methodistcollege.edu.

New York Medical College, School of Health Sciences and Practice, Department of Epidemiology and Community Health, Program in Behavioral Sciences and Health Promotion, Valhalla, NY 10595-1691. Offers MPH. Part-time and evening/weekend programs available. *Faculty:* 4 full-time, 16 part-time/adjunct. *Students:* 31 full-time, 46 part-time. Average age 32. 35 applicants, 69% accepted, 21 enrolled. In 2009, 25 master's awarded. *Degree requirements:* For master's, thesis. *Entrance requirements:* For master's, minimum undergraduate GPA of 3.0. Additional exam requirements/recommendations for international students: Required—TOEFL (minimum score 637 paper-based; 250 computer-based; 110 iBT), IELTS (minimum score 7). *Application deadline:* For fall admission, 8/1 priority date for domestic students, 5/15 for international students; for spring admission, 12/1 priority date for domestic students, 10/15 for international students. Applications are processed on a rolling basis. Application fee: $50 ($100 for international students). Electronic applications accepted. *Expenses:* Tuition: Full-time $18,170; part-time $790 per credit. Required fees: $790 per credit. $20 per semester. One-time fee: $100. Tuition and fees vary according to class time, course level, course load, degree level, program, student level and student's religious affiliation. *Financial support:* Career-related internships or fieldwork, Federal Work-Study, institutionally sponsored loans, health care benefits, and tuition reimbursements available. Support available to part-time students. Financial award applicants required to submit FAFSA. *Unit head:* Dr. Martin K. Diner, Assistant Professor, 914-594-4804, Fax: 914-594-3481, E-mail: martin_diner@nymc.edu. *Application contact:* Pamela Suett, Director of Recruitment, 914-594-4510, Fax: 914-594-4292, E-mail: shsp_admissions@nymc.edu.

New York University, Steinhardt School of Culture, Education, and Human Development, Department of Applied Psychology, Program in Counselor Education, New York, NY 10012-1019. Offers counseling and guidance (MA, Advanced Certificate), including bilingual school counseling (MA), school counseling (MA); counseling for mental health and wellness (MA); counseling psychology (PhD). *Accreditation:* APA (one or more programs are accredited). Part-time programs available. *Students:* 123 full-time (89 women), 77 part-time (60 women); includes 72 minority (24 African Americans, 1 American Indian/Alaska Native, 24 Asian Americans or Pacific Islanders, 23 Hispanic Americans), 20 international. Average age 30. 769 applicants, 27% accepted, 80 enrolled. In 2009, 80 master's, 6 doctorates awarded. *Degree requirements:* For master's, thesis (for some programs); for doctorate, thesis/dissertation. *Entrance requirements:* For doctorate, GRE General Test, interview. Additional exam requirements/recommendations for international students: Required—TOEFL. *Application deadline:* For fall admission, 12/15 priority date for domestic and international students. Applications are processed on a rolling basis. Application fee: $75. Electronic applications accepted. *Expenses:* Tuition: Full-time $30,528; part-time $1272 per credit. Required fees: $2177. *Financial support:* Fellowships with full and partial tuition reimbursements, research assistantships, teaching assistantships with partial tuition reimbursements, career-related internships or fieldwork, Federal Work-Study, institutionally sponsored loans, scholarships/grants, tuition waivers (partial), and unspecified assistantships available. Support available to part-time students. Financial award application deadline: 2/1; financial award applicants required to submit FAFSA. *Faculty research:* Cross-cultural counseling; group dynamics; culture, race and ethnicity; religiosity and psychological development; well-being and mental health. *Application contact:* 212-998-5030, Fax: 212-995-4328, E-mail: steinhardt.gradadmissions@nyu.edu.

Oakland University, Graduate Study and Lifelong Learning, School of Health Sciences, Program in Complimentary Medicine and Wellness, Rochester, MI 48309-4401. Offers Certificate.

Old Dominion University, College of Health Sciences, Program in Public Health, Norfolk, VA 23529. Offers environmental health (MPH); health promotion (MPH). *Accreditation:* CEPH. Part-time and evening/weekend programs available. *Faculty:* 7 full-time (4 women), 6 part-time/adjunct (3 women). *Students:* 26 full-time (21 women), 20 part-time (15 women); includes 24 minority (18 African Americans, 4 Asian Americans or Pacific Islanders, 2 Hispanic Americans), 1 international. Average age 29. 67 applicants, 60% accepted, 30 enrolled. In 2009, 16 master's awarded. *Degree requirements:* For master's, field practicum, capstone project. *Entrance requirements:* For master's, GRE, MCAT, minimum GPA of 2.75. Additional exam requirements/recommendations for international students: Required—TOEFL (minimum score 650 paper-based; 278 computer-based). *Application deadline:* For fall admission, 5/31 priority date for domestic students, 4/30 for international students. Application fee: $50 ($100 for international students). Electronic applications accepted. *Expenses:* Tuition, state resident: full-time $8112; part-time $338 per credit. Tuition, nonresident: full-time $20,256; part-time $844 per credit. Required fees: $119 per semester. One-time fee: $50. *Financial support:* Career-related internships or fieldwork, institutionally sponsored loans, and scholarships/grants available. Financial award application deadline: 5/1; financial award applicants required to submit FAFSA. *Faculty research:* Community-based health research, public health research in environmental health and health promotion. Total annual research expenditures: $150,133. *Unit head:* A. James English, Associate Director, 757-683-6010, Fax: 757-446-6121, E-mail: jenglish@odu.edu. *Application contact:* A. James English, Associate Director, 757-683-6010, Fax: 757-446-6121, E-mail: jenglish@odu.edu.

Old Dominion University, Darden College of Education, Program in Physical Education, Exercise and Wellness Emphasis, Norfolk, VA 23529. Offers MS Ed. Part-time and evening/weekend programs available. *Faculty:* 7 full-time (4 women). *Students:* 19 full-time (13 women), 7 part-time (5 women); includes 4 minority (3 African Americans, 1 Hispanic American), 3 international. Average age 27. 12 applicants, 100% accepted, 10 enrolled. In 2009, 11 master's awarded. *Degree requirements:* For master's, comprehensive exam, thesis or alternative, internship, research project. *Entrance requirements:* For master's, GRE, minimum GPA of 2.8 overall, 3.0 in major. Additional exam requirements/recommendations for international students: Required—TOEFL (minimum score 500 paper-based; 200 computer-based). *Application deadline:* For fall admission, 7/1 for domestic students; for spring admission, 11/1 for domestic students. Applications are processed on a rolling basis. Application fee: $40. *Expenses:* Tuition, state resident: full-time $8112; part-time $338 per credit. Tuition, nonresident: full-time $20,256; part-time $844 per credit. Required fees: $119 per semester. One-time fee: $50. *Financial support:* In 2009–10, 1 teaching assistantship (averaging $9,000 per year) was awarded; career-related internships or fieldwork and scholarships/grants also available. Financial award application deadline: 4/15. *Faculty research:* Diabetes, exercise, prescription, gait and balance. Total annual research expenditures: $105,000. *Unit head:* Liz Dowling, Graduate Program Director, 757-683-4995, E-mail: ldowling@odu.edu. *Application contact:* Liz Dowling, Graduate Program Director, 757-683-4995, E-mail: ldowling@odu.edu.

Oregon State University, Graduate School, College of Health and Human Sciences, Department of Public Health, Corvallis, OR 97331. Offers environmental health and occupational safety management (MAIS, MS); health management and policy (MS, PhD); health promotion and health behavior (MS, PhD); public health (MPH, PhD). *Accreditation:* CEPH. *Faculty:* 13 full-time (8 women), 3 part-time/adjunct (1 woman). *Students:* 84 full-time (66 women), 19 part-time (15 women); includes 10 minority (4 African Americans, 2 American Indian/Alaska Native, 2 Asian Americans or Pacific Islanders, 2 Hispanic Americans), 9 international. Average age 32. In 2009, 30 master's, 1 doctorate awarded. Terminal master's awarded for partial completion of doctoral program. *Degree requirements:* For doctorate, one foreign language, thesis/dissertation. *Entrance requirements:* For master's and doctorate, minimum GPA of 3.0 in last 90 hours. Additional exam requirements/recommendations for international students: Required—TOEFL. *Application deadline:* For fall admission, 3/1 for domestic students. Applications are processed on a rolling basis. Application fee: $50. *Expenses:* Tuition, state resident: full-time $9774; part-time $362 per credit. Tuition, nonresident: full-time $15,849; part-time $587 per credit. Required fees: $1639. Full-time tuition and fees vary according to course load and program. *Financial support:* Fellowships, research assistantships, teaching assistantships, career-related internships or fieldwork, Federal Work-Study, and institutionally sponsored loans available. Support available to part-time students. Financial award application deadline: 2/1. *Faculty research:* Traffic safety, health safety, injury control, health promotion. *Unit head:* Dr. S. Marie Harvey, Chair, 541-737-3825, Fax: 541-737-4001, E-mail: marie.harvey@oregonstate.edu. *Application contact:* Dr. S. Marie Harvey, Chair, 541-737-3825, Fax: 541-737-4001, E-mail: marie.harvey@oregonstate.edu.

Portland State University, Graduate Studies, College of Urban and Public Affairs, School of Community Health, Portland, OR 97207-0751. Offers aging (Certificate); health education (MA, MS); health education and health promotion (MPH); health studies (MPA, MPH), including health administration. *Accreditation:* CEPH. Part-time programs available. *Degree requirements:* For master's, oral and written exams. *Entrance requirements:* For master's, GRE General Test, 3 letters of recommendation, minimum GPA of 3.0. Additional exam requirements/recommendations for international students: Required—TOEFL (minimum score 550 paper-based; 213 computer-based).

Purdue University, Graduate School, College of Liberal Arts, Department of Health and Kinesiology, West Lafayette, IN 47907. Offers exercise, human physiology of movement and sport (PhD); health and fitness (MS); health promotion (MS); health promotion and disease prevention (PhD); movement and sport science (MS); pedagogy and administration (MS); pedagogy of physical activity and health (PhD); psychology of sport and exercise, and motor behavior (PhD). Part-time programs available. *Degree requirements:* For master's, thesis (for some programs); for doctorate, thesis/dissertation. *Entrance requirements:* For master's and doctorate, GRE General Test. Additional exam requirements/recommendations for international students: Required—TOEFL. Electronic applications accepted. *Faculty research:* Wellness, motivation, teaching effectiveness, learning and development.

Rowan University, Graduate School, College of Education, Department of Health and Exercise Science, Glassboro, NJ 08028-1701. Offers health promotion management (MA). *Faculty:* 2 full-time (1 woman), 1 (woman) part-time/adjunct. *Students:* 8 part-time (6 women). Average age 31. 15 applicants, 100% accepted, 8 enrolled. *Degree requirements:* For master's, comprehensive exam, thesis. *Entrance requirements:* For master's, GRE General Test, GRE Subject Test, interview, minimum GPA of 2.8. Additional exam requirements/recommendations for international students: Required—TOEFL. *Application deadline:* Applications are processed on a rolling basis. Application fee: $50. Electronic applications accepted. *Expenses:* Tuition, state resident: full-time $10,624; part-time $590 per semester hour. Tuition, nonresident: full-time $10,624; part-time $590 per semester hour. Required fees: $2320; $125 per semester hour. *Financial support:* Career-related internships or fieldwork, Federal Work-Study, and unspecified assistantships available. Support available to part-time students. *Unit head:* Richard Fopeano, Chair, 856-256-4500 Ext. 3740, E-mail: fopeano@rowan.edu. *Application contact:* Karen Haynes, Graduate Coordinator, 856-256-4052, Fax: 856-256-4436, E-mail: haynes@rowan.edu.

San Diego State University, Graduate and Research Affairs, College of Health and Human Services, Graduate School of Public Health, San Diego, CA 92182. Offers environmental health (MPH); epidemiology (MPH, PhD), including biostatistics (MPH); global emergency preparedness and response (MS); global health (PhD); health behavior (PhD); health promotion (MPH); health services administration (MPH); toxicology (MS); MPH/MA; MSW/MPH. *Accreditation:* ABET (one or more programs are accredited); CAHME (one or more programs are accredited); CEPH (one or more programs are accredited). Part-time programs available. *Degree requirements:* For master's, comprehensive exam (for some programs), thesis (for some programs); for doctorate, thesis/dissertation. *Entrance requirements:* For master's, GMAT (MPH in health services administration), GRE General Test; for doctorate, GRE General Test. Additional exam requirements/recommendations for international students: Required—TOEFL. *Faculty research:* Evaluation of tobacco, AIDS prevalence and prevention, mammography, infant death project, Alzheimer's in elderly Chinese.

Simmons College, School of Health Sciences, Program in Nutrition and Health Promotion, Boston, MA 02115. Offers didactic program in dietetics (Certificate); nutrition (dietetic internship) (Certificate); nutrition and health promotion (MS); sports nutrition (Certificate). Part-time programs available. Postbaccalaureate distance learning degree programs offered (no on-campus study). *Faculty:* 5 full-time (all women), 4 part-time/adjunct (all women). *Students:* 17 full-time (all women), 40 part-time (37 women); includes 7 minority (1 African American, 1 American Indian/Alaska Native, 3 Asian Americans or Pacific Islanders, 2 Hispanic Americans). Average age 31. 45 applicants, 84% accepted, 35 enrolled. In 2009, 13 master's, 28 other advanced degrees awarded. *Degree requirements:* For master's, research project. *Entrance requirements:* For master's, GRE, courses in community nutrition, nutritional metabolism, introduction to nutrition, organic and inorganic chemistry, statistics, anatomy and physiology; for Certificate, 1 year of anatomy and physiology with lab, half-year of introductory nutrition, bachelor's degree. Additional exam requirements/recommendations for international students: Required—TOEFL (minimum score 570 paper-based; 230 computer-based; 88 iBT). *Application deadline:* For fall admission, 3/1 for domestic and international students; for spring admission, 11/1 for domestic students. Application fee: $50. *Expenses:* Contact institution. *Financial support:* Application deadline: 3/1. *Faculty research:* Good insecurity, chronic disease and nutrition, childhood obesity, dietary assessment, food safety. Total annual research expenditures: $60,000. *Unit head:* Dr. Nancie Herbold, Director, 617-521-2711, Fax: 617-521-3137, E-mail: herbold@simmons.edu. *Application contact:* Carmen Fortin, Assistant Dean/Director of Admission, 617-521-2605, Fax: 617-521-3137, E-mail: shs@simmons.edu.

Springfield College, Graduate Programs, Programs in Exercise Science and Sport Studies, Springfield, MA 01109-3797. Offers athletic training (MS); exercise physiology (MS), including clinical exercise physiology, science and research; exercise science and sport studies (PhD); health promotion and disease prevention (MS); sport psychology (MS). Part-time programs available. Terminal master's awarded for partial completion of doctoral program. *Degree requirements:* For master's, comprehensive exam, research project or thesis; for doctorate, comprehensive exam, thesis/dissertation. *Entrance requirements:* For master's and doctorate, GRE General Test. Additional exam requirements/recommendations for international students: Required—TOEFL (minimum score 550 paper-based; 213 computer-based). Electronic applications accepted. *Expenses:* Tuition: Full-time $19,800; part-time $825 per credit hour. Required fees: $150.

Texas A&M University–Commerce, Graduate School, College of Education and Human Services, Department of Health and Human Performance, Commerce, TX 75429-3011. Offers exercise physiology (MS); health and human performance (M Ed); health promotion (MS); health, kinesiology and sports studies (Ed D); motor performance (MS); sport studies (MS). Part-time programs available. *Degree requirements:* For master's, comprehensive exam, thesis (for some programs). *Entrance requirements:* For master's, GRE General Test. Electronic applications accepted. *Faculty research:* Teaching, physical fitness.

Union Institute & University, Master of Arts Program–Online, Montpelier, VT 05602. Offers creativity studies (MA); education (MA); health and wellness (MA); history and culture (MA); leadership, public policy, and social issues (MA); literature and writing (MA); psychology (MA). Part-time programs available. Postbaccalaureate distance learning degree programs offered (no on-campus study). *Faculty:* 3 full-time (1 woman), 16 part-time/adjunct (11 women). *Students:* 27 full-time (23 women), 113 part-time (84 women); includes 30 minority (22 African Americans, 2 American Indian/Alaska Native, 1 Asian American or Pacific Islander, 5 Hispanic Americans). Average age 40. In 2009, 26 master's awarded. *Degree requirements:* For master's, thesis. *Application deadline:* Applications are processed on a rolling basis. Application fee: $50. Electronic applications accepted. *Expenses:* Contact institution. *Financial support:* Career-related internships or fieldwork and tuition waivers available. Financial award applicants required to submit FAFSA. *Unit head:* Dr. Brian Webb, Program Director, 802-828-8777, E-mail: brian.webb@tui.edu. *Application contact:* Kathleen Murphy, Interim Director of Admissions—Montpelier, 888-828-8575, E-mail: admissions@myunion.edu.

Universidad del Turabo, Graduate Programs, Programs in Education, Program in Wellness, Gurabo, PR 00778-3030. Offers MPHE. *Students:* 11 full-time (2 women), 5 part-time (3 women); includes 15 Hispanic Americans. Average age 28. 6 applicants, 100% accepted, 4 enrolled. *Unit head:* Angela Candelario, Dean, 787-743-7979 Ext. 4126. *Application contact:* Virginia Gonzalez, Admissions Officer, 787-746-3009.

The University of Alabama, Graduate School, College of Human Environmental Sciences, Department of Health Science, Tuscaloosa, AL 35487-0311. Offers health education and promotion (PhD); health studies (MA). Part-time programs available. Postbaccalaureate distance learning degree programs offered (no on-campus study). *Faculty:* 6 full-time (4 women), 1 part-time/adjunct (0 women). *Students:* 40 full-time (31 women), 77 part-time (48 women); includes 38 minority (29 African Americans, 3 American Indian/Alaska Native, 4 Asian Americans or Pacific Islanders, 2 Hispanic Americans), 2 international. Average age 34. 112 applicants, 54% accepted, 37 enrolled. In 2009, 58 master's, 3 doctorates awarded. *Median time to degree:* Of those who began their doctoral program in fall 2001, 100% received their degree in 8 years or less. *Degree requirements:* For master's, comprehensive exam, thesis optional; for doctorate, one foreign language, comprehensive exam, thesis/dissertation. *Entrance requirements:* For master's, minimum GPA of 3.0; for doctorate, GRE General Test, minimum GPA of 3.0, prerequisites in health education. Additional exam requirements/recommendations for international students: Required—TOEFL. *Application deadline:* For fall admission, 3/15 priority date for domestic students, 3/15 for international students. Applications are processed on a rolling basis. Application fee: $50 ($60 for international students). Electronic applications accepted. *Expenses:* Tuition, state resident: full-time $7000. Tuition, nonresident: full-time $19,200. *Financial support:* In 2009–10, 2 research assistantships with full tuition reimbursements (averaging $10,500 per year), 6 teaching assistantships with full tuition reimbursements (averaging $10,500 per year) were awarded; career-related internships or fieldwork, Federal Work-Study, institutionally sponsored loans, health care benefits, and unspecified assistantships also available. Financial award application deadline: 4/14. *Faculty research:* Program planning, substance abuse prevention, obesity prevention, nutrition, physical activity, athletic training, osteoporosis, health behavior. Total annual research expenditures: $66,836. *Unit head:* Dr. Lori W. Turner, Department Head and Professor, 205-348-2956, Fax: 205-348-7568, E-mail: lwturner@ches.ua.edu. *Application contact:* Dr. Stuart Usdan, Associate Professor and Doctoral Program Coordinator, 205-348-8373, Fax: 205-348-7568, E-mail: susdan@ches.ua.edu.

The University of Alabama at Birmingham, College of Arts and Sciences, School of Education, Program in Health Education and Promotion, Birmingham, AL 35294. Offers PhD. *Accreditation:* NCATE. *Degree requirements:* For doctorate, thesis/dissertation. *Entrance requirements:* For doctorate, GRE General Test, MAT, minimum GPA of 3.25. Electronic applications accepted.

University of Alberta, School of Public Health, Centre for Health Promotion Studies, Edmonton, AB T6G 2E1, Canada. Offers health promotion (M Sc, Postgraduate Diploma). Part-time programs available. Postbaccalaureate distance learning degree programs offered. Tuition and fees charges are reported in Canadian dollars. *Expenses:* Tuition, area resident: Full-time $4626 Canadian dollars; part-time $99.72 Canadian dollars per unit. International tuition: $8216 Canadian dollars full-time. Required fees: $3590 Canadian dollars; $99.72 Canadian dollars per unit. $215 Canadian dollars per term. *Unit head:* Kim Raine, Director, 780-492-9415, E-mail: kim.raine@ualberta.ca. *Application contact:* Dr. Helen M. Madill, Graduate Coordinator, 780-492-8661, Fax: 780-492-9347, E-mail: helen.madill@ualberta.ca.

University of Arkansas for Medical Sciences, Graduate School, Program in Health Promotion and Prevention Research, Little Rock, AR 72205-7199. Offers PhD. *Application deadline:* For fall admission, 1/15 for domestic students. *Unit head:* Dr. Paul Greene, Coordinator, 501-526-6707, E-mail: pggreene@uams.edu. *Application contact:* Dr. Kristen Sterba, Assistant Dean, Office of Graduate Student Recruiting and Retention, 501-526-7396, E-mail: kmsterba@uams.edu.

University of Chicago, Division of the Biological Sciences, Program in Health Studies, Chicago, IL 60637-1513. Offers MS, PhD. Part-time programs available. *Faculty:* 14 full-time (4 women), 4 part-time/adjunct (3 women). *Students:* 13 full-time (9 women); includes 4 minority (all Asian Americans or Pacific Islanders), 2 international. Average age 35. 31 applicants, 35% accepted, 8 enrolled. In 2009, 4 master's awarded. *Degree requirements:* For master's, thesis; for doctorate, comprehensive exam, thesis/dissertation, ethics class, 2 teaching assistantships. *Entrance requirements:* For doctorate, GRE General Test. Additional exam requirements/recommendations for international students: Required—TOEFL (minimum score 600 paper-based; 250 computer-based; 104 iBT), IELTS (minimum score 7). *Application deadline:* For fall admission, 12/1 priority date for domestic and international students. Application fee: $55. Electronic applications accepted. *Financial support:* In 2009–10, 13 students received support. Applicants required to submit FAFSA. *Unit head:* Dr. Ronald Thisted, Chair, 773-834-1242, Fax: 773-702-1979, E-mail: thisted@health.bsd.uchicago.edu. *Application contact:* Michele Thompson, Education Program Manager, 773-834-1836, E-mail: mthompso@health.bsd.uchicago.edu.

University of Delaware, College of Health Sciences, Department of Health, Nutrition, and Exercise Sciences, Newark, DE 19716. Offers exercise science (MS), including biomechanics, exercise physiology, motor control; health promotion (MS); human nutrition (MS). Part-time programs available. *Degree requirements:* For master's, thesis. *Entrance requirements:* For master's, GRE General Test, interview, minimum GPA of 3.0. Additional exam requirements/recommendations for international students: Required—TOEFL (minimum score 550 paper-based; 213 computer-based). Electronic applications accepted. *Faculty research:* Sport biomechanics, rehabilitation biomechanics, vascular dynamics.

University of Georgia, College of Public Health, Department of Health Promotion and Behavior, Athens, GA 30602. Offers MA, MPH, PhD. *Accreditation:* CEPH; NCATE (one or more programs are accredited). *Faculty:* 7 full-time (5 women). *Students:* 12 full-time (9 women), 7 part-time (6 women); includes 8 minority (4 African Americans, 2 Asian Americans or Pacific Islanders, 2 Hispanic Americans), 1 international. 31 applicants, 26% accepted, 7 enrolled. In 2009, 3 doctorates awarded. *Degree requirements:* For master's, thesis (MA); for doctorate, thesis/dissertation. *Entrance requirements:* For master's, GRE General Test or MAT; for doctorate, GRE General Test. *Application deadline:* For fall admission, 7/1 priority date for domestic students; for spring admission, 11/15 for domestic students. Application fee: $50. Electronic applications accepted. *Expenses:* Tuition, state resident: full-time $6000; part-time $250 per credit hour. Tuition, nonresident: full-time $20,904; part-time $871 per credit hour. Required fees: $730 per semester. *Financial support:* Fellowships, research assistantships, teaching assistantships, unspecified assistantships available. *Unit head:* Dr. Mark G. Wilson, Head, 706-542-4364, Fax: 706-542-4956, E-mail: mwilson@coe.uga.edu. *Application contact:* Dr. Marsha Davis, Graduate Coordinator, 706-542-4364, Fax: 706-542-4956, E-mail: davism@uga.edu.

University of Kentucky, Graduate School, College of Education, Program in Kinesiology and Health Promotion, Lexington, KY 40506-0032. Offers exercise science (PhD); kinesiology (MS, Ed D). Terminal master's awarded for partial completion of doctoral program. *Degree requirements:* For master's, comprehensive exam, thesis optional; for doctorate, comprehensive exam, thesis/dissertation. *Entrance requirements:* For master's, GRE General Test, minimum undergraduate GPA of 2.75; for doctorate, GRE General Test, minimum graduate GPA of 3.0. Additional exam requirements/recommendations for international students: Required—TOEFL (minimum score 550 paper-based; 213 computer-based). Electronic applications accepted.

University of Louisville, Graduate School, School of Public Health and Information Sciences, Louisville, KY 40292-0001. Offers bioinformatics and biostatistics (MS, PhD), including biostatistics (MPH, MS, PhD), decision science (MS); clinical investigation sciences (Certificate); population health and epidemiology (MS, PhD), including epidemiology (MPH, MS, PhD), public health sciences (PhD); public health (MPH), including biostatistics (MPH, MS, PhD), environmental and occupational health, epidemiology (MPH, MS, PhD), health management (MPH, PhD), health promotion and behavior; public health sciences (PhD), including environmental health, epidemiology (MPH, MS, PhD), health management (MPH, PhD), health promotion. Part-time and evening/weekend programs available. *Faculty:* 39 full-time (13 women), 1 part-time/adjunct (0 women). *Students:* 92 full-time (52 women), 72 part-time (47 women); includes 36 minority (15 African Americans, 19 Asian Americans or Pacific Islanders, 2 Hispanic Americans), 21 international. Average age 33. 194 applicants, 47% accepted, 65 enrolled. In 2009, 35 master's, 4 doctorates awarded. *Degree requirements:* For master's, thesis; for doctorate, thesis/dissertation. *Entrance requirements:* For master's, GRE General Test, GMAT, DAT, MCAT, minimum of 2 letters of recommendation; for doctorate, GRE General Test, minimum of 2 letters of recommendation. Additional exam requirements/recommendations for international students: Required—TOEFL (minimum score 600 paper-based; 250 computer-based; 100 iBT). *Application deadline:* For fall admission, 2/1 for domestic and international students. Applications are processed on a rolling basis. Application fee: $50. Electronic applications accepted. *Financial support:* In 2009–10, 30 students received support, including 11 research assistantships with full tuition reimbursements available (averaging $20,000 per year); unspecified assistantships also available. Financial award application deadline: 5/1; financial award applicants required to submit FAFSA. *Faculty research:* Clinical research training, cancer and environmental exposure, health effects of air pollution, occupational injuries and illness, network science applications in health. Total annual research expenditures: $3.2 million. *Unit head:* Dr. Pete Walton, Associate Dean for Academic Affairs, 502-852-4493, Fax: 502-852-3291, E-mail: pete.walton@gwise.louisville.edu. *Application contact:* Vicki Lewis, Administrative Assistant, 502-852-1798, Fax: 502-852-3294, E-mail: vicki.lewis@louisville.edu.

University of Massachusetts Lowell, School of Health and Environment, Department of Nursing, Program in Nursing, Lowell, MA 01854-2881. Offers PhD. *Accreditation:* AACN. *Degree requirements:* For doctorate, thesis/dissertation, qualifying examination. *Entrance requirements:* For doctorate, GRE General Test, master's degree in nursing with minimum GPA of 3.3, current MA RN license, 2 years of professional nursing experience, 3 letters of recommendation.

University of Memphis, Graduate School, College of Education, Department of Health and Sport Sciences, Memphis, TN 38152. Offers clinical nutrition (MS); exercise and sport science (MS); health promotion (MS); physical education teacher education (MS), including teacher education; sport and leisure commerce (MS). Part-time and evening/weekend programs available. *Faculty:* 18 full-time (9 women), 3 part-time/adjunct (1 woman). *Students:* 64 full-time (35 women), 36 part-time (23 women); includes 17 African Americans, 1 Asian American or Pacific Islander, 1 Hispanic American, 4 international. Average age 27. 99 applicants, 72% accepted, 50 enrolled. In 2009, 35 master's awarded. *Degree requirements:* For master's, comprehensive exam, thesis. *Entrance requirements:* For master's, GRE General Test or GMAT (sport and leisure commerce). *Application deadline:* For fall admission, 5/1 priority date for domestic students; for spring admission, 11/1 for domestic students. Applications are processed on a rolling basis. Application fee: $35 ($60 for international students). *Expenses:* Tuition, state resident: full-time $6246; part-time $347 per credit hour. Tuition, nonresident: full-time $15,894; part-time $883 per credit hour. Required fees: $1160. Full-time tuition and fees vary according to course load, degree level and program. *Financial support:* In 2009–10, 59 students received support; research assistantships with full tuition reimbursements available, teaching assistantships with full tuition reimbursements available, career-related internships or fieldwork, Federal Work-Study, scholarships/grants, tuition waivers (partial), and unspecified assistantships available. Financial award application deadline: 2/15; financial award applicants required to submit FAFSA. *Faculty research:* Sport marketing and consumer analysis, health psychology, smoking cessation, psychosocial aspects of cardiovascular disease, global health promotion. *Unit head:* Linda H. Clemens, Interim Chair, 901-678-2324, Fax: 901-678-3591, E-mail: lhclemns@memphis.edu. *Application contact:* Dr. Kenneth Ward, Graduate Studies Coordinator, 901-678-1714, E-mail: kdward@memphis.edu.

University of Michigan, School of Public Health, Department of Health Behavior and Health Education, Ann Arbor, MI 48109. Offers MPH, PhD, MPH/MSW. PhD offered through the Horace H. Rackham School of Graduate Studies. *Accreditation:* CEPH (one or more programs are accredited). Terminal master's awarded for partial completion of doctoral program. *Degree requirements:* For doctorate, oral defense of dissertation, preliminary exam. *Entrance requirements:* For master's and doctorate, GRE General Test. Additional exam requirements/recommendations for international students: Required—TOEFL (minimum score 560 paper-based; 220 computer-based). Electronic applications accepted. *Expenses:* Tuition, state resident: full-time $17,286; part-time $1099 per credit hour. Tuition, nonresident: full-time $34,944; part-time $2080 per credit hour. Required fees: $95 per semester. Tuition and fees vary according to course load, degree level and program. *Faculty research:* Empowerment theory; structure, culture, and health; health disparities; community-based participatory research; health and medical decision-making.

The University of Montana, Graduate School, School of Education, Department of Health and Human Performance, Missoula, MT 59812-0002. Offers exercise science (MS); health and human performance (MS); health promotion (MS). Part-time programs available. *Entrance requirements:* For master's, GRE General Test. Additional exam requirements/recommendations for international students: Required—TOEFL. *Faculty research:* Exercise physiology, performance psychology, nutrition, pre-employment physical screening, program evaluation.

University of Nebraska–Lincoln, Graduate College, College of Education and Human Sciences, Department of Nutrition and Health Sciences, Lincoln, NE 68588. Offers community nutrition and health promotion (MS); nutrition (MS, PhD); nutrition and exercise (MS); nutrition and health sciences (MS, PhD). *Degree requirements:* For master's, thesis optional. *Entrance requirements:* For master's, GRE General Test. Additional exam requirements/recommendations for international students: Required—TOEFL (minimum score 550 paper-based; 213 computer-based). Electronic applications accepted. *Faculty research:* Foods/food service administration, community nutrition science, diet-health relationships.

University of Nevada, Las Vegas, Graduate College, School of Community Health Sciences, Department of Health Promotion, Las Vegas, NV 89154-3050. Offers health care promotion (M Ed). Part-time and evening/weekend programs available. *Faculty:* 2 full-time (0 women). *Students:* 16 full-time (14 women), 35 part-time (31 women); includes 14 minority (8 African Americans, 4 Asian Americans or Pacific Islanders, 2 Hispanic Americans), 3 international. Average age 35. 13 applicants, 69% accepted, 6 enrolled. In 2009, 22 master's awarded. *Degree requirements:* For master's, comprehensive exam (for some programs), project. *Entrance requirements:* Additional exam requirements/recommendations for international students:

Health Promotion

University of Nevada, Las Vegas *(continued)*
Required—TOEFL (minimum score 550 paper-based; 213 computer-based; 80 iBT), IELTS (minimum score 7). *Application deadline:* For fall admission, 6/1 priority date for domestic students, 5/1 for international students; for spring admission, 11/1 priority date for domestic students, 10/1 for international students. Applications are processed on a rolling basis. Application fee: $60 ($95 for international students). Electronic applications accepted. *Financial support:* In 2009–10, 2 students received support, including 2 research assistantships with partial tuition reimbursements available (averaging $12,500 per year); institutionally sponsored loans, scholarships/grants, health care benefits, and unspecified assistantships also available. Financial award application deadline: 3/1. *Unit head:* Dr. Shawn Gerstenberger, Chair/Associate Professor, 702-895-1565, Fax: 702-895-3979, E-mail: shawn.gerstenberger@unlv.edu. *Application contact:* Graduate College Admissions Evaluator, 702-895-3320, Fax: 702-895-4180, E-mail: gradcollege@unlv.edu.

The University of North Carolina at Chapel Hill, Graduate School, School of Public Health, Public Health Leadership Program, Chapel Hill, NC 27599. Offers health care and prevention (MPH); leadership (MPH); occupational health nursing (MPH); public health nursing (MS). Part-time programs available. Postbaccalaureate distance learning degree programs offered (minimal on-campus study). *Degree requirements:* For master's, comprehensive exam, thesis (MS), paper (MPH). *Entrance requirements:* For master's, GRE General Test, minimum GPA of 3.0, public health experience. Additional exam requirements/recommendations for international students: Required—TOEFL. Electronic applications accepted. *Faculty research:* Occupational health issues, clinical outcomes, prenatal and early childcare, adolescent health, effectiveness of home visiting, issues in occupational health nursing, community-based interventions.

University of Oklahoma Health Sciences Center, Graduate College, College of Public Health, Department of Health Promotion Sciences, Oklahoma City, OK 73190. Offers MPH, MS, Dr PH, PhD. *Accreditation:* CEPH (one or more programs are accredited). Part-time programs available. *Faculty:* 6 full-time (4 women). *Students:* 4 full-time (all women), 11 part-time (all women); includes 1 minority (Asian American or Pacific Islander), 2 international. Average age 35. 9 applicants, 44% accepted, 3 enrolled. In 2009, 8 master's awarded. *Degree requirements:* For master's, comprehensive exam, thesis (for some programs); for doctorate, 2 foreign languages, comprehensive exam, thesis/dissertation. *Entrance requirements:* For master's, letters of recommendation, resume; for doctorate, GRE, letters of recommendation. Additional exam requirements/recommendations for international students: Required—TOEFL (minimum score 570 paper-based; 230 computer-based). *Application deadline:* For fall admission, 7/1 for domestic students; for winter admission, 4/1 for domestic students; for spring admission, 12/1 for domestic students. Applications are processed on a rolling basis. Application fee: $50. *Expenses:* Tuition, state resident: full-time $3120; part-time $156 per credit hour. Tuition, nonresident: full-time $11,314; part-time $409.70 per credit hour. Required fees: $1471; $51.20 per credit hour. $223.25 per term. *Financial support:* In 2009–10, 10 research assistantships (averaging $10,000 per year) were awarded; career-related internships or fieldwork, institutionally sponsored loans, traineeships, and tuition waivers (partial) also available. Support available to part-time students. Financial award application deadline: 5/1. *Faculty research:* Health education, school health, health behavior, American Indian health. *Unit head:* Dr. Robert John, Chair, 405-271-2017, E-mail: robert-john@ouhsc.edu. *Application contact:* Robin Howell, Information Contact, 405-271-2308, E-mail: robin_howell@ouhsc.edu.

University of Pittsburgh, Graduate School of Public Health, Department of Infectious Diseases and Microbiology, Pittsburgh, PA 15260. Offers bioscience of infectious diseases (MPH); community and behavioral intervention of infectious diseases (MPH); infectious diseases and microbiology (MS, Dr PH, PhD); LGBT health and wellness (Certificate). Part-time programs available. *Faculty:* 20 full-time (7 women), 2 part-time/adjunct (1 woman). *Students:* 46 full-time (33 women), 8 part-time (6 women); includes 7 minority (2 African Americans, 4 Asian Americans or Pacific Islanders, 1 Hispanic American), 6 international. Average age 28. 176 applicants, 43% accepted, 18 enrolled. In 2009, 11 master's, 9 doctorates awarded. Terminal master's awarded for partial completion of doctoral program. *Degree requirements:* For master's, one foreign language, comprehensive exam (for some programs), thesis; for doctorate, one foreign language, comprehensive exam, thesis/dissertation. *Entrance requirements:* For master's and doctorate, GRE General Test, MCAT, or DAT. Additional exam requirements/recommendations for international students: Required—TOEFL (minimum score 550 paper-based; 213 computer-based; 80 iBT). *Application deadline:* For fall admission, 1/4 for domestic students. Applications are processed on a rolling basis. Application fee: $95. Electronic applications accepted. *Expenses:* Tuition, state resident: full-time $16,402; part-time $665 per credit. Tuition, nonresident: full-time $28,694; part-time $1175 per credit. Required fees: $690; $175 per term. Tuition and fees vary according to program. *Financial support:* In 2009–10, 16 students received support, including 16 research assistantships with full tuition reimbursements available (averaging $23,500 per year). Financial award applicants required to submit FAFSA. *Faculty research:* HIV, Epstein-Barr virus, virology, immunology, malaria. Total annual research expenditures: $13.6 million. *Unit head:* Dr. Charles R. Rinaldo, Chairman, 412-624-3928, Fax: 412-624-4953, E-mail: rinaldo@pitt.edu. *Application contact:* Dr. Jeremy Martinson, Assistant Professor, 412-624-5646, Fax: 412-383-8926, E-mail: jmartins@pitt.edu.

University of Pittsburgh, School of Health and Rehabilitation Sciences, Master's Programs in Health and Rehabilitation Sciences, Pittsburgh, PA 15260. Offers health and rehabilitation sciences (MS), including clinical dietetics and nutrition, health care supervision and management, health information systems, occupational therapy, physical therapy, rehabilitation counseling, rehabilitation science and technology, sports medicine, wellness and human performance. *Accreditation:* APTA. Part-time and evening/weekend programs available. *Faculty:* 30 full-time (14 women), 4 part-time/adjunct (3 women). *Students:* 81 full-time (47 women), 54 part-time (27 women); includes 10 minority (6 African Americans, 4 Asian Americans or Pacific Islanders), 44 international. Average age 29. 326 applicants, 65% accepted, 130 enrolled. In 2009, 93 master's awarded. *Degree requirements:* For master's, comprehensive exam (for some programs), thesis optional. *Entrance requirements:* For master's, minimum GPA of 3.0. Additional exam requirements/recommendations for international students: Required—TOEFL, IELTS. *Application deadline:* For fall admission, 1/31 for international students; for spring admission, 7/31 for international students. Applications are processed on a rolling basis. Application fee: $50. Electronic applications accepted. *Expenses:* Contact institution. *Financial support:* In 2009–10, 3 research assistantships with full tuition reimbursements (averaging $18,450 per year) were awarded; teaching assistantships, Federal Work-Study, institutionally sponsored loans, traineeships, and unspecified assistantships also available. Financial award applicants required to submit FAFSA. *Faculty research:* Assistive technology, seating and wheeled mobility, cellular neurophysiology, low back syndrome, augmentative communication. Total annual research expenditures: $6.5 million. *Unit head:* Dr. Clifford E. Brubaker, Dean, 412-383-6560, Fax: 412-383-6535, E-mail: cliffb@pitt.edu. *Application contact:* Shameem Gangjee, Director of Admissions, 412-383-6558, Fax: 412-383-6535, E-mail: admissions@shrs.pitt.edu.

University of Puerto Rico, Medical Sciences Campus, Graduate School of Public Health, Program in School Health Promotion, San Juan, PR 00936-5067. Offers Certificate.

University of Rochester, School of Nursing, Rochester, NY 14642. Offers acute care nurse practitioner (MS); adult nurse practitioner (MS); adult psychiatric mental health nurse practitioner (MS); adult/geriatric nurse practitioner (MS); care of children and families/pediatric nurse practitioner (MS); care of children and families/pediatric nurse practitioner with pediatric behavioral health (MS); care of children and families/pediatric nurse practitioner/neonatal nurse practitioner (MS); child and adolescent psychiatric mental health nurse practitioner (MS); clinical nurse leader (MS); disaster response and emergency preparedness (MS); family nurse practitioner (MS); health care organization management and leadership (MS); health practice research (PhD); health promotion, education and technology (MS); nursing (Certificate). *Accreditation:* AACN; NLN (one or more programs are accredited). Part-time programs available.

Postbaccalaureate distance learning degree programs offered (minimal on-campus study). *Faculty:* 26 full-time (24 women), 20 part-time/adjunct (15 women). *Students:* 50 full-time (45 women), 178 part-time (165 women); includes 33 minority (17 African Americans, 2 American Indian/Alaska Native, 10 Asian Americans or Pacific Islanders, 4 Hispanic Americans), 11 international. Average age 35. 56 applicants, 80% accepted, 35 enrolled. In 2009, 53 master's, 5 doctorates awarded. Terminal master's awarded for partial completion of doctoral program. *Degree requirements:* For master's, comprehensive exam or thesis; for doctorate, thesis/dissertation. *Entrance requirements:* For master's, BS in nursing, minimum GPA of 3.0, course work in statistics; for doctorate, GRE General Test, MS in nursing, minimum GPA of 3.5; for Certificate, MS in nursing. Additional exam requirements/recommendations for international students: Recommended—TOEFL (minimum score 560 paper-based; 230 computer-based; 88 iBT). *Application deadline:* For fall admission, 11/1 priority date for domestic and international students. Application fee: $50. *Financial support:* In 2009–10, 53 students received support, including 14 fellowships with full and partial tuition reimbursements available (averaging $17,497 per year); scholarships/grants, traineeships, health care benefits, tuition waivers (partial), and unspecified assistantships also available. Support available to part-time students. Financial award application deadline: 6/30. *Faculty research:* Clinical research in aging, managing asthma in children, interventions to improve outcomes in critically ill children and their mothers, nurse home visitation studies, medical device evaluation, critical care clinical studies, high risk behavior and prevention, palliative care, pregnancy-related weight gain. Total annual research expenditures: $4.8 million. *Unit head:* Dr. Kathy P. Parker, Dean, 585-273-5639, Fax: 585-273-1268, E-mail: kathy_parker@urmc.rochester.edu. *Application contact:* Elaine Andolina, Director of Admissions, 585-275-2375, Fax: 585-756-8299, E-mail: elaine_andolina@urmc.rochester.edu.

University of South Carolina, The Graduate School, Arnold School of Public Health, Department of Health Promotion, Education, and Behavior, Columbia, SC 29208. Offers health education (MAT); health promotion, education, and behavior (MPH, MS, MSPH, Dr PH, PhD); school health education (Certificate); MSW/MPH. MAT offered in cooperation with the College of Education. *Accreditation:* CEPH (one or more programs are accredited); NCATE (one or more programs are accredited). Part-time programs available. *Degree requirements:* For master's, comprehensive exam, thesis or alternative, practicum (MPH), project (MS); for doctorate, comprehensive exam, thesis/dissertation. *Entrance requirements:* For master's and doctorate, GRE General Test. Additional exam requirements/recommendations for international students: Required—TOEFL (minimum score 570 paper-based; 230 computer-based; 75 iBT). Electronic applications accepted. *Faculty research:* Health disparities and inequalities in communities, global health and nutrition, cancer and HIV/AIDS prevention, health communication, policy and program design.

University of South Carolina, The Graduate School, Arnold School of Public Health, Program in Physical Activity and Public Health, Columbia, SC 29208. Offers MPH. *Accreditation:* CEPH. Part-time programs available. *Degree requirements:* For master's, comprehensive exam, practicum. *Entrance requirements:* For master's, GRE. Additional exam requirements/recommendations for international students: Required—TOEFL (minimum score 570 paper-based; 230 computer-based). Electronic applications accepted.

University of Southern California, Keck School of Medicine and Graduate School, Graduate Programs in Medicine, Department of Preventive Medicine, Master of Public Health Program, Alhambra, CA 91803. Offers biostatistics/epidemiology (MPH); child and family health (MPH); global health leadership (MPH); health communication (MPH); health promotion (MPH). *Accreditation:* CEPH. Part-time programs available. *Faculty:* 22 full-time (12 women), 3 part-time/adjunct (0 women). *Students:* 215 full-time (158 women), 3 part-time (2 women); includes 148 minority (13 African Americans, 3 American Indian/Alaska Native, 114 Asian Americans or Pacific Islanders, 18 Hispanic Americans), 25 international. Average age 26. 208 applicants, 74% accepted, 76 enrolled. In 2009, 60 master's awarded. *Degree requirements:* For master's, practicum, final report, oral presentation. *Entrance requirements:* For master's, GRE General Test, MCAT, GMAT, minimum GPA of 3.0. Additional exam requirements/recommendations for international students: Required—TOEFL (minimum score 600 paper-based; 250 computer-based; 100 iBT). *Application deadline:* For fall admission, 6/1 priority date for domestic and international students; for spring admission, 11/1 priority date for domestic students, 10/1 priority date for international students. Applications are processed on a rolling basis. Application fee: $85. Electronic applications accepted. *Expenses:* Tuition: Full-time $25,980; part-time $1315 per unit. Required fees: $554. One-time fee: $35 full-time. Full-time tuition and fees vary according to degree level and program. *Financial support:* In 2009–10, 175 students received support, including 20 fellowships (averaging $3,200 per year); career-related internships or fieldwork, Federal Work-Study, institutionally sponsored loans, and scholarships/grants also available. Support available to part-time students. Financial award application deadline: 5/1; financial award applicants required to submit CSS PROFILE or FAFSA. *Faculty research:* Substance abuse prevention, cancer and heart disease prevention, mass media and health communication research, health promotion, treatment compliance. *Unit head:* Dr. Thomas W. Valente, Director, 626-457-4139, Fax: 626-457-6699, E-mail: tvalente@usc.edu. *Application contact:* Chrystal Romero, Admissions Counselor, 626-457-6676, Fax: 626-457-6699, E-mail: ccromero@usc.edu.

The University of Tennessee, Graduate School, College of Education, Health and Human Sciences, Program in Health Promotion and Health Education, Knoxville, TN 37996. Offers MS. *Accreditation:* CEPH. Part-time programs available. *Degree requirements:* For master's, thesis optional. *Entrance requirements:* For master's, minimum GPA of 2.7. Additional exam requirements/recommendations for international students: Required—TOEFL. Electronic applications accepted. *Expenses:* Tuition, state resident: full-time $6826; part-time $380 per semester hour. Tuition, nonresident: full-time $21,844; part-time $1147 per semester hour. Tuition and fees vary according to program.

The University of Texas at El Paso, Graduate School, College of Health Sciences, Department of Health Promotion, El Paso, TX 79968-0001. Offers public health (MPH). Part-time and evening/weekend programs available. *Students:* 26 (21 women); includes 20 minority (all Hispanic Americans), 4 international. Average age 34. In 2009, 6 master's awarded. *Degree requirements:* For master's, thesis optional. *Entrance requirements:* For master's, GRE, minimum GPA of 3.0, resume, letters of recommendation. Additional exam requirements/recommendations for international students: Required—TOEFL; Recommended—IELTS. *Application deadline:* For fall admission, 8/1 priority date for domestic students, 3/1 for international students; for spring admission, 11/1 priority date for domestic students, 9/1 for international students. Applications are processed on a rolling basis. Application fee: $45 ($80 for international students). Electronic applications accepted. *Financial support:* In 2009–10, research assistantships (averaging $18,825 per year), teaching assistantships with partial tuition reimbursements (averaging $18,000 per year) were awarded; fellowships with partial tuition reimbursements, institutionally sponsored loans, scholarships/grants, health care benefits, tuition waivers (partial), and unspecified assistantships also available. Support available to part-time students. Financial award application deadline: 3/15; financial award applicants required to submit FAFSA. *Unit head:* Dr. Maria O. Duarte-Gardea, Chair, 915-747-8214 Ext. 7252, E-mail: moduarte@utep.edu. *Application contact:* Dr. Patricia D. Witherspoon, Dean of the Graduate School, 915-747-5491, Fax: 915-747-5788, E-mail: withersp@utep.edu.

The University of Texas at San Antonio, College of Education and Human Development, Department of Health and Kinesiology, San Antonio, TX 78249-0617. Offers health and kinesiology (MS); kinesiology and health promotion (MA Ed). Part-time programs available. *Faculty:* 12 full-time (5 women). *Students:* 22 full-time (9 women), 49 part-time (31 women); includes 40 minority (5 African Americans, 1 Asian American or Pacific Islander, 34 Hispanic Americans), 3 international. Average age 29. 43 applicants, 91% accepted, 22 enrolled. In 2009, 14 master's awarded. *Degree requirements:* For master's, comprehensive exam (for some programs), thesis (for some programs). *Entrance requirements:* For master's, GRE or GMAT, minimum GPA of 3.0. Additional exam requirements/recommendations for international students: Required—TOEFL (minimum score 500 paper-based; 173 computer-based; 61 iBT),

IELTS (minimum score 5). *Application deadline:* For fall admission, 6/1 for domestic students, 4/1 for international students; for spring admission, 11/1 for domestic students, 9/1 for international students. Applications are processed on a rolling basis. Application fee: $45 ($80 for international students). Electronic applications accepted. *Expenses:* Tuition, state resident: full-time $3975; part-time $221 per contact hour. Tuition, nonresident: full-time $13,947; part-time $775 per contact hour. Required fees: $1853. *Financial support:* In 2009–10, 3 students received support, including 14 research assistantships (averaging $10,754 per year); scholarships/grants, tuition waivers, and unspecified assistantships also available. Support available to part-time students. *Faculty research:* Motor learning/control, biomechanics, and sports psychology; exercise and military physiology; physical education and coaching; health disparities and nutrition; community and school health. Total annual research expenditures: $458,272. *Unit head:* Dr. Wanxiang Yao, Chair, 210-458-5650, E-mail: wanxiang.yao@utsa.edu. *Application contact:* Dr. Dorothy A. Flannagan, Dean of the Graduate School, 210-458-4330, Fax: 210-458-4332, E-mail: dorothy.flannagan@utsa.edu.

University of the Incarnate Word, School of Graduate Studies and Research, School of Mathematics, Science, and Engineering, Program in Nutrition, San Antonio, TX 78209-6397. Offers administration (MS); medical nutrition therapy (MS); nutrition education and health promotion (MS); nutrition services administration (MS). Part-time and evening/weekend programs available. *Students:* 11 full-time (10 women), 18 part-time (17 women); includes 14 minority (2 African Americans, 12 Hispanic Americans). Average age 27. In 2009, 5 master's awarded. *Degree requirements:* For master's, comprehensive exam, thesis or alternative. *Entrance requirements:* For master's, two letters of recommendation. Additional exam requirements/recommendations for international students: Required—TOEFL (minimum score 560 paper-based; 220 computer-based; 83 iBT). *Application deadline:* Applications are processed on a rolling basis. Application fee: $20. Electronic applications accepted. *Expenses:* Tuition: Full-time $12,150; part-time $675 per credit hour. Required fees: $83 per credit hour. *Financial support:* Federal Work-Study and scholarships/grants available. Financial award applicants required to submit FAFSA. *Faculty research:* Minority nutrition issues, child nutrition, diabetes prevention, food security and hunger, international nutrition. *Unit head:* Dr. Beth Senne-Duff, Associate Professor, 210-829-3165, Fax: 210-829-3153, E-mail: beths@uiwtx.edu. *Application contact:* Andrea Cyterski-Acosta, Dean of Enrollment, 210-829-6005, Fax: 210-829-3921, E-mail: admis@uiwtx.edu.

University of Utah, Graduate School, College of Health, Department of Health Promotion and Education, Salt Lake City, UT 84112. Offers M Phil, MS, Ed D, PhD. Part-time and evening/weekend programs available. *Faculty:* 5 full-time (2 women), 2 part-time/adjunct (1 woman). *Students:* 31 full-time (24 women), 14 part-time (11 women); includes 2 minority (1 Asian American or Pacific Islander, 1 Hispanic American), 6 international. Average age 35. 32 applicants, 69% accepted, 17 enrolled. In 2009, 7 master's, 10 doctorates awarded. Terminal master's awarded for partial completion of doctoral program. *Degree requirements:* For master's, comprehensive exam, thesis or alternative, field experience; for doctorate, comprehensive exam, thesis/dissertation, field experience. *Entrance requirements:* For master's, GRE (for thesis option), minimum GPA of 3.0; for doctorate, GRE General Test, minimum GPA of 3.2. Additional exam requirements/recommendations for international students: Required—TOEFL (minimum score 500 paper-based; 173 computer-based). *Application deadline:* For fall admission, 10/15 for domestic and international students; for spring admission, 2/15 for domestic and international students. Applications are processed on a rolling basis. Application fee: $55 ($65 for international students). *Expenses:* Tuition, state resident: full-time $4004; part-time $1674 per semester. Tuition, nonresident: full-time $14,134; part-time $5915 per semester. Required fees: $324 per semester. Tuition and fees vary according to course load, degree level and program. *Financial support:* In 2009–10, 13 students received support, including 3 research assistantships with full tuition reimbursements available (averaging $11,500 per year), 3 teaching assistantships with full tuition reimbursements available (averaging $11,500 per year); career-related internships or fieldwork, Federal Work-Study, institutionally sponsored loans, and scholarships/grants also available. Financial award application deadline: 2/15; financial award applicants required to submit FAFSA. *Faculty research:* Health behavior and counseling, health service administration, evaluation of health programs. Total annual research expenditures: $3,583. *Unit head:* Dr. Glenn E. Richardson, Department Chair, 801-581-8039, Fax: 801-585-3646, E-mail: glenn.richardson@health.utah.edu. *Application contact:* Dr. Glenn P. Trunnell, Director of Graduate Studies, 801-581-4462, Fax: 801-585-3646, E-mail: eric.trunnell@health.utah.edu.

University of Wisconsin–Stevens Point, College of Professional Studies, School of Health Promotion and Human Development, Stevens Point, WI 54481-3897. Offers human and community resources (MS); nutritional sciences (MS). Part-time programs available. *Students:* 4 full-time (all women), 2 part-time (both women); includes 2 African Americans. *Degree requirements:* For master's, thesis or alternative. *Entrance requirements:* For master's, minimum GPA of 2.75. *Application deadline:* For fall admission, 5/1 priority date for domestic students. Applications are processed on a rolling basis. Application fee: $45. *Expenses:* Tuition, state resident: full-time $7740; part-time $430 per credit hour. Tuition, nonresident: full-time $17,804; part-time $989 per credit hour. Tuition and fees vary according to course load and reciprocity agreements. *Financial support:* Research assistantships, teaching assistantships, career-related internships or fieldwork, Federal Work-Study, and unspecified assistantships available. Support available to part-time students. Financial award application deadline: 5/1; financial award applicants required to submit FAFSA. *Unit head:* Dr. Marty Loy, Head, 715-346-2830, Fax: 715-346-2720. *Application contact:* Dr. Jasia Steinmetz, Information Contact, 715-346-2830, Fax: 715-346-2720, E-mail: jsteinme@uwsp.edu.

University of Wyoming, College of Health Sciences, Division of Kinesiology and Health, Laramie, WY 82070. Offers MS. *Accreditation:* NCATE. Part-time programs available. Postbaccalaureate distance learning degree programs offered (no on-campus study). *Degree requirements:* For master's, comprehensive exam (for some programs), thesis (for some programs). *Entrance requirements:* For master's, GRE General Test, minimum GPA of 3.0. Additional exam requirements/recommendations for international students: Required—TOEFL. Electronic applications accepted. *Faculty research:* Teacher effectiveness, effects of exercising on heart function, physiological responses of overtraining, psychological benefits of physical activity, health behavior.

Walden University, Graduate Programs, School of Health Sciences, Minneapolis, MN 55401. Offers clinical research administration (MS); health informatics (MS); health services (PhD), including community health promotion and education, general program, health management and policy; healthcare administration (MHA); public health (MPH, PhD), including community health promotion and education (PhD), epidemiology (PhD). Part-time and evening/weekend programs available. Postbaccalaureate distance learning degree programs offered (minimal on-campus study). *Faculty:* 14 full-time, 136 part-time/adjunct. *Students:* 2,121 full-time (1,670 women), 724 part-time (568 women); includes 1,370 minority (1,149 African Americans, 20 American Indian/Alaska Native, 95 Asian Americans or Pacific Islanders, 106 Hispanic Americans), 134 international. Average age 40. In 2009, 232 master's, 24 doctorates awarded. *Degree requirements:* For doctorate, thesis/dissertation, residency. *Entrance requirements:* For master's, bachelor's degree or equivalent in related field, minimum GPA of 2.5; for doctorate, master's degree or equivalent in related field; minimum GPA of 3.0; official transcripts; three years of related professional/academic experience (preferred); access to computer and Internet. Additional exam requirements/recommendations for international students: Required—TOEFL (minimum score 550 paper-based; 213 computer-based), IELTS (minimum score 6.5), or Michigan English Language Assessment Battery (minimum score 82). *Application deadline:* Applications are processed on a rolling basis. Application fee: $50. Electronic applications accepted. *Expenses:* Tuition: Full-time $13,665; part-time $560 per credit. Required fees: $1375. Tuition and fees vary according to course load, degree level and program. *Financial support:* In 2009–10, 152 students received support; fellowships, Federal Work-Study, scholarships/grants, unspecified assistantships, and family tuition reduction, active duty/veteran tuition reduction, group tuition reduction, interest-free payment plans available. Support available to part-time students. Financial award applicants required to submit FAFSA. *Unit head:* Dr. Jorg Westermann, Interim Associate Dean, 800-925-3368. *Application contact:* Jennifer Hall, Director of Enrollment, 866-4-WALDEN, E-mail: info@waldenu.edu.

West Virginia University, School of Medicine, Department of Community Medicine, Morgantown, WV 26506. Offers public health (MPH), including community health/preventative medicine; public health sciences (PhD). *Accreditation:* CEPH. Part-time and evening/weekend programs available. Postbaccalaureate distance learning degree programs offered (minimal on-campus study). *Degree requirements:* For master's, thesis (for some programs). *Entrance requirements:* For master's, minimum GPA of 3.0. Additional exam requirements/recommendations for international students: Required—TOEFL. *Faculty research:* Adolescent smoking cessation, cardiovascular disease, women's health, worker's health.

Wright State University, School of Medicine, Program in Public Health, Dayton, OH 45435. Offers health promotion and education (MPH); public health management (MPH); public health nursing (MPH). *Accreditation:* CEPH.

Industrial Hygiene

California State University, Northridge, Graduate Studies, College of Health and Human Development, Department of Environmental and Occupational Health, Northridge, CA 91330. Offers environmental and occupational health (MS); industrial hygiene (MS). *Faculty:* 6 full-time (0 women), 9 part-time/adjunct (3 women). *Students:* 29 full-time (16 women), 32 part-time (21 women); includes 29 minority (5 African Americans, 1 American Indian/Alaska Native, 14 Asian Americans or Pacific Islanders, 9 Hispanic Americans), 3 international. Average age 30. 48 applicants, 67% accepted, 23 enrolled. In 2009, 21 master's awarded. *Degree requirements:* For master's, seminar, field experience, comprehensive exam or thesis. *Entrance requirements:* For master's, GRE General Test or minimum GPA of 3.0. Additional exam requirements/recommendations for international students: Required—TOEFL. *Application deadline:* For fall admission, 11/30 for domestic students. Application fee: $55. *Financial support:* Application deadline: 3/1. *Unit head:* Dr. Thomas Hatfield, Chair, 818-677-7476. *Application contact:* Dr. Thomas Hatfield, Chair, 818-677-7476.

Montana Tech of The University of Montana, Graduate School, Department of Industrial Hygiene, Butte, MT 59701-8997. Offers MS. *Accreditation:* ABET. Part-time programs available. Postbaccalaureate distance learning degree programs offered (no on-campus study). *Faculty:* 6 full-time (2 women), 4 part-time/adjunct (2 women). *Students:* 9 full-time (6 women), 31 part-time (13 women); includes 4 minority (1 African American, 1 American Indian/Alaska Native, 2 Hispanic Americans), 2 international. 25 applicants, 68% accepted, 14 enrolled. In 2009, 13 master's awarded. *Degree requirements:* For master's, comprehensive exam (for some programs), thesis. *Entrance requirements:* For master's, minimum GPA of 3.0. Additional exam requirements/recommendations for international students: Required—TOEFL (minimum score 525 paper-based; 195 computer-based; 71 iBT). *Application deadline:* For fall admission, 4/1 priority date for domestic students; for spring admission, 10/1 priority date for domestic students. Applications are processed on a rolling basis. Application fee: $30. Electronic applications accepted. *Expenses:* Tuition, state resident: full-time $5068; part-time $319 per credit. Tuition, nonresident: full-time $14,815; part-time $875 per credit. Tuition and fees vary according to course load and campus/location. *Financial support:* In 2009–10, 7 students received support, including 7 teaching assistantships with partial tuition reimbursements available (averaging $3,371 per year); research assistantships with partial tuition reimbursements available, career-related internships or fieldwork, institutionally sponsored loans, and tuition waivers (full and partial) also available. Financial award application deadline: 4/1; financial award applicants required to submit FAFSA. *Faculty research:* Ergonomics, metal bioavailability, aerosols, particulate sizing, respiration protection. *Unit head:* Dr. Terry Spear, Head, 406-496-4445, Fax: 406-496-4650, E-mail: tspear@mtech.edu. *Application contact:* Cindy Dunstan, Administrator, Graduate School, 406-496-4304, Fax: 406-496-4710, E-mail: cdunstan@mtech.edu.

Murray State University, College of Health Sciences and Human Services, Program in Occupational Safety and Health, Murray, KY 42071. Offers environmental science (MS); industrial hygiene (MS); safety management (MS). *Accreditation:* ABET. Part-time programs available. *Degree requirements:* For master's, comprehensive exam, thesis optional, professional internship. Electronic applications accepted. *Faculty research:* Light effects on plant growth, ergonomics, toxic effects of pets' pesticides, traffic safety.

New York Medical College, School of Health Sciences and Practice, Department of Environmental Health Science, Program in Industrial Hygiene, Valhalla, NY 10595-1691. Offers Graduate Certificate. *Faculty:* 4 full-time, 16 part-time/adjunct. *Students:* 13 full-time, 19 part-time. Average age 32. 10 applicants, 70% accepted, 5 enrolled. *Entrance requirements:* Additional exam requirements/recommendations for international students: Required—TOEFL (minimum score 637 paper-based; 110 iBT), IELTS (minimum score 7). *Application deadline:* For fall admission, 8/1 for domestic students; for spring admission, 12/1 for domestic students. Applications are processed on a rolling basis. Application fee: $50. Electronic applications accepted. *Expenses:* Tuition: Full-time $18,170; part-time $790 per credit. Required fees: $790 per credit. $20 per semester. One-time fee: $100. Tuition and fees vary according to class time, course level, course load, degree level, program, student level and student's religious affiliation. *Unit head:* Dr. Diane E. Heck, Chair, 914-594-3383, Fax: 914-594-4292, E-mail: diane_heck@nymc.edu. *Application contact:* Pamela Suett, Director of Recruitment, 914-594-4510, Fax: 914-594-4292, E-mail: shsp_admissions@nymc.edu.

University of Central Missouri, The Graduate School, College of Health and Human Services, Warrensburg, MO 64093. Offers criminal justice (MS); industrial hygiene (MS); occupational safety management (MS); physical education/exercise and sport science (MS); rural family nursing (MS); social gerontology (MS); sociology (MA); speech language pathology and audiology (MS). *Accreditation:* NCATE. Part-time programs available. Postbaccalaureate distance learning degree programs offered. *Faculty:* 53. *Students:* 169 full-time (107 women), 364 part-time (210 women); includes 65 minority (46 African Americans, 1 American Indian/Alaska Native, 5 Asian Americans or Pacific Islanders, 13 Hispanic Americans), 27 international. Average age 32. 236 applicants, 92% accepted, 211 enrolled. In 2009, 153 master's awarded. *Entrance requirements:* Additional exam requirements/recommendations for international students: Required—TOEFL (minimum score 550 paper-based; 79 computer-based). *Application deadline:* For fall admission, 6/1 priority date for domestic students, 5/1 for international

Industrial Hygiene

University of Central Missouri (continued)

students; for spring admission, 10/1 priority date for domestic students, 10/1 for international students. Applications are processed on a rolling basis. Application fee: $30 ($75 for international students). Electronic applications accepted. *Expenses:* Tuition, area resident: Part-time $245.80 per credit hour. Tuition, nonresident: part-time $491.60 per credit hour. Required fees: $24.20 per credit hour. Full-time tuition and fees vary according to course load, degree level, campus/location and reciprocity agreements. *Financial support:* Research assistantships with full and partial tuition reimbursements, teaching assistantships with full and partial tuition reimbursements, career-related internships or fieldwork, Federal Work-Study, scholarships/grants, and administrative and laboratory assistantships available. Support available to part-time students. Financial award application deadline: 3/1; financial award applicants required to submit FAFSA. *Unit head:* Dr. Rick Sluder, Dean, 660-543-4245, Fax: 660-543-4167, E-mail: sluder@ucmo.edu. *Application contact:* Laurie Delap, Admissions Coordinator, 660-543-4621, Fax: 660-543-4778, E-mail: gradinfo@ucmo.edu.

University of Cincinnati, Graduate School, College of Medicine, Graduate Programs in Biomedical Sciences, Department of Environmental Health, Cincinnati, OH 45221. Offers environmental and industrial hygiene (MS, PhD); environmental and occupational medicine (MS); environmental genetics and molecular toxicology (MS, PhD); epidemiology and biostatistics (MS, PhD); occupational safety and ergonomics (MS, PhD). *Accreditation:* ABET (one or more programs are accredited). Terminal master's awarded for partial completion of doctoral program. *Degree requirements:* For master's, thesis; for doctorate, thesis/dissertation, qualifying exam. *Entrance requirements:* For master's, GRE General Test, bachelor's degree in science; for doctorate, GRE General Test. Additional exam requirements/recommendations for international students: Required—TOEFL (minimum score 600 paper-based; 250 computer-based; 100 iBT). Electronic applications accepted. *Faculty research:* Carcinogens and mutagenesis, pulmonary studies, reproduction and development.

University of Massachusetts Lowell, School of Health and Environment, Department of Work Environment, Lowell, MA 01854-2881. Offers cleaner production and pollution prevention (MS, Sc D); environmental risk assessment (Certificate); epidemiology (MS, Sc D); ergonomics and safety (MS, Sc D); identification and control of ergonomic hazards (Certificate); job stress and healthy job redesign (Certificate); occupational and environmental hygiene (MS, Sc D); radiological health physics and general work environment protection (Certificate); work environment policy (MS, Sc D). *Accreditation:* ABET (one or more programs are accredited). Part-time programs available. Terminal master's awarded for partial completion of doctoral program. *Degree requirements:* For master's, thesis optional; for doctorate, thesis/dissertation. *Entrance requirements:* For master's and doctorate, GRE General Test. Additional exam requirements/recommendations for international students: Required—TOEFL.

University of Michigan, School of Public Health, Department of Environmental Health Sciences, Ann Arbor, MI 48109. Offers environmental health sciences (MS, PhD); environmental quality and health (MPH); human nutrition (MPH); industrial hygiene (MPH, MS); nutritional sciences (MS); occupational and environmental epidemiology (MPH); toxicology (MPH, MS, PhD). *Accreditation:* CEPH (one or more programs are accredited). Part-time programs available. Terminal master's awarded for partial completion of doctoral program. *Degree requirements:* For master's, thesis (for some programs); for doctorate, thesis/dissertation, qualifying exam, oral defense of dissertation, preliminary exam. *Entrance requirements:* For master's and doctorate, GRE General Test and/or MCAT. Additional exam requirements/recommendations for international students: Required—TOEFL (minimum score 560 paper-based; 220 computer-based; 100 iBT). Electronic applications accepted. *Expenses:* Tuition, state resident: full-time $17,286; part-time $1099 per credit hour. Tuition, nonresident: full-time $34,944; part-time $2080 per credit hour. Required fees: $95 per semester. Tuition and fees vary according to course load, degree level and program. *Faculty research:* Toxicology; occupational hygiene; nutrition; environmental exposure sciences; environmental epidemiology.

University of Minnesota, Twin Cities Campus, School of Public Health, Division of Environmental Health Sciences, Area in Industrial Hygiene, Minneapolis, MN 55455-0213. Offers MPH, MS, PhD. *Accreditation:* ABET (one or more programs are accredited); CEPH (one or more programs are accredited). *Degree requirements:* For doctorate, thesis/dissertation. *Entrance requirements:* For master's and doctorate, GRE General Test. Electronic applications accepted.

University of New Haven, Graduate School, Henry C. Lee College of Criminal Justice and Forensic Sciences, Program in Industrial Hygiene, West Haven, CT 06516-1916. Offers MS. In 2009, 2 master's awarded. *Degree requirements:* For master's, thesis or alternative. *Entrance requirements:* Additional exam requirements/recommendations for international students: Required—TOEFL (minimum score 520 paper-based; 190 computer-based; 70 iBT); Recommended—IELTS (minimum score 5.5). *Application deadline:* For fall admission, 5/31 for international students; for winter admission, 10/15 for international students; for spring admission, 1/15 for international students. Applications are processed on a rolling basis. Application fee: $50. *Expenses:* Tuition: Part-time $700 per credit. Required fees: $45 per term. One-time fee: $390 part-time. *Financial support:* Research assistantships with partial tuition reimbursements, teaching assistantships with partial tuition reimbursements, career-related internships or fieldwork, Federal Work-Study, scholarships/grants, tuition waivers, and unspecified assistantships available. Support available to part-time students. Financial award applicants required to submit FAFSA. *Unit head:* Dr. William Tafoya, Director, 203-932-7175. *Application contact:* Eloise Gormley, Director of Graduate Admissions, 203-932-7449, Fax: 203-932-7137, E-mail: gradinfo@newhaven.edu.

The University of North Carolina at Chapel Hill, Graduate School, School of Public Health, Department of Environmental Sciences and Engineering, Chapel Hill, NC 27599. Offers air, radiation and industrial hygiene (MPH, MS, MSEE, MSPH, PhD); aquatic and atmospheric sciences (MPH, MS, MSPH, PhD); environmental engineering (MPH, MS, MSEE, MSPH, PhD); environmental health sciences (MPH, MS, MSPH, PhD); environmental management and policy (MPH, MS, MSPH, PhD). Terminal master's awarded for partial completion of doctoral program. *Degree requirements:* For master's, comprehensive exam, thesis (for some programs), research paper; for doctorate, comprehensive exam, thesis/dissertation. *Entrance requirements:* For master's and doctorate, GRE General Test, minimum GPA of 3.0. Additional exam requirements/recommendations for international students: Required—TOEFL. Electronic applications accepted. *Faculty research:* Air, radiation and industrial hygiene, aquatic and atmospheric sciences, environmental health sciences, environmental management and policy, water resources engineering.

University of Puerto Rico, Medical Sciences Campus, Graduate School of Public Health, Program in Industrial Hygiene, San Juan, PR 00936-5067. Offers MS. Part-time programs available. *Degree requirements:* For master's, thesis. *Entrance requirements:* For master's, GRE, previous course work in biology, chemistry, mathematics, and physics. *Expenses:* Contact institution.

University of South Carolina, The Graduate School, Arnold School of Public Health, Department of Environmental Health Sciences, Program in Industrial Hygiene, Columbia, SC 29208. Offers MPH, MSPH, PhD. *Accreditation:* ABET (one or more programs are accredited); CEPH (one or more programs are accredited). *Degree requirements:* For master's, comprehensive exam, thesis (for some programs), practicum (MPH); for doctorate, one foreign language, comprehensive exam, thesis/dissertation. *Entrance requirements:* Additional exam requirements/recommendations for international students: Required—TOEFL (minimum score 570 paper-based; 230 computer-based). Electronic applications accepted. *Faculty research:* Sampling and calibration method development, exposure and risk assessment, respirator and dermal protective equipment, ergonomics, air cleaning methods and devices.

University of Wisconsin–Stout, Graduate School, College of Technology, Engineering, and Management, MS Program in Risk Control, Menomonie, WI 54751. Offers MS. Part-time programs available. *Degree requirements:* For master's, thesis. *Entrance requirements:* For master's, minimum GPA of 3.0. Additional exam requirements/recommendations for international students: Required—TOEFL (minimum score 500 paper-based; 173 computer-based; 61 iBT). Electronic applications accepted. *Faculty research:* Environmental microbiology, water supply safety, facilities planning, industrial ventilation, bioterrorist.

West Virginia University, College of Engineering and Mineral Resources, Department of Industrial and Management Systems Engineering, Program in Industrial Hygiene, Morgantown, WV 26506. Offers MS. *Accreditation:* ABET. Part-time programs available. *Degree requirements:* For master's, thesis or alternative. *Entrance requirements:* For master's, GRE General Test, minimum GPA of 3.0. Additional exam requirements/recommendations for international students: Required—TOEFL. *Faculty research:* Safety management, ergonomics and workplace design, safety and health training, construction safety.

International Health

Boston University, School of Public Health, International Health Department, Boston, MA 02215. Offers MPH, Dr PH, Certificate. *Accreditation:* CEPH (one or more programs are accredited). Part-time and evening/weekend programs available. *Students:* 125 full-time (99 women), 67 part-time (55 women); includes 32 minority (7 African Americans, 20 Asian Americans or Pacific Islanders, 5 Hispanic Americans), 22 international. Average age 27. *Degree requirements:* For master's, thesis. *Entrance requirements:* For master's, GRE, DAT, MCAT, GMAT, LSAT; for doctorate, GRE, GMAT. Additional exam requirements/recommendations for international students: Required—TOEFL (minimum score 600 paper-based; 250 computer-based; 100 iBT) or IELTS. *Application deadline:* For fall admission, 2/1 priority date for domestic and international students; for spring admission, 10/15 priority date for domestic and international students. Applications are processed on a rolling basis. Application fee: $95. Electronic applications accepted. *Expenses:* Tuition: Full-time $37,910; part-time $1184 per credit hour. Required fees: $386; $40 per semester. Part-time tuition and fees vary according to class time, course level, degree level and program. *Financial support:* Research assistantships with full tuition reimbursements, career-related internships or fieldwork, Federal Work-Study, institutionally sponsored loans, scholarships/grants, and tuition waivers (partial) available. Financial award application deadline: 3/1; financial award applicants required to submit FAFSA. *Unit head:* Dr. Jonathon Simon, Chair, 617-638-5234, E-mail: ih@bu.edu. *Application contact:* LePhan Quan, Associate Director of Admissions, 617-638-4640, Fax: 617-638-5299, E-mail: asksph@bu.edu.

Brandeis University, The Heller School for Social Policy and Management, Program in International Health Policy and Management, Waltham, MA 02454-9110. Offers MS. *Entrance requirements:* For master's, GMAT or GRE (preferred), 3 letters of recommendation, curriculum vitae or resume. Additional exam requirements/recommendations for international students: Required—TOEFL.

The Catholic University of America, School of Nursing, Washington, DC 20064. Offers adult health specialist with functional role as nurse educator (MSN); adult nurse practitioner (MSN); community/public health nurse specialist educator (MSN); family nurse practitioner (MSN); geriatric nurse practitioner (MSN); immigrant, refugee, and global health clinical nurse specialist (MSN); nursing (DNP, PhD, Certificate); pediatric nurse practitioner (MSN); promoting healthy families in vulnerable communities (MSN); psychiatric-mental health nursing (MSN). *Accreditation:* AACN. Part-time programs available. *Faculty:* 15 full-time (all women), 43 part-time/adjunct (41 women). *Students:* 28 full-time (26 women), 75 part-time (73 women); includes 37 minority (27 African Americans, 6 Asian Americans or Pacific Islanders, 4 Hispanic Americans), 4 international. Average age 42. 84 applicants, 64% accepted, 30 enrolled. In 2009, 23 master's, 7 doctorates, 3 other advanced degrees awarded. *Degree requirements:* For master's, comprehensive exam, thesis optional; for doctorate, comprehensive exam, thesis/dissertation, minimum GPA of 3.0, oral proposal defense. *Entrance requirements:* For master's, 3 letters of recommendation, BA in nursing, RN registration, official copies of academic transcripts, some post-baccalaureate nursing experience; for doctorate, GRE General Test, BA in nursing, professional portfolio (including statements, resume, copy of RN license, 3 letters of recommendation, narrative description of clinical practice, proposal), copy of research/scholarly paper related to clinical nursing. Additional exam requirements/recommendations for international students: Required—TOEFL (minimum score 580 paper-based; 237 computer-based). *Application deadline:* For fall admission, 8/1 priority date for domestic students, 7/15 for international students; for spring admission, 12/1 priority date for domestic students, 10/15 for international students. Applications are processed on a rolling basis. Application fee: $55. Electronic applications accepted. *Expenses:* Tuition: Full-time $31,740; part-time $1245 per credit hour. Required fees: $50; $25 per semester hour. One-time fee: $425. *Financial support:* Fellowships, research assistantships, teaching assistantships, Federal Work-Study, scholarships/grants, tuition waivers (full and partial), and unspecified assistantships available. Financial award application deadline: 2/1; financial award applicants required to submit FAFSA. *Faculty research:* Community involvement in health care services, primary health care services, pediatrics, chronic illness, cardiovascular disease. Total annual research expenditures: $311,172. *Unit head:* Dr. Nalini N. Jairath, Dean, 202-319-5403, Fax: 202-319-6485, E-mail: cua-deanschoolofnursing@cua.edu. *Application contact:* Julie Schwing, Director of Graduate Admissions, 202-319-5057, Fax: 202-319-6533, E-mail: cua-admissions@cua.edu.

Central Michigan University, Central Michigan University Off-Campus Programs, Program in Health Administration, Mount Pleasant, MI 48859. Offers health administration (DHA); international health (Certificate). Part-time and evening/weekend programs available. Post-baccalaureate distance learning degree programs offered (minimal on-campus study). Electronic applications accepted. *Financial support:* Scholarships/grants available. Support available to part-time students. Financial award applicants required to submit FAFSA. *Unit head:* Steven D. Berkshire, Director, 989-774-1640, E-mail: berks1sd@cmich.edu. *Application contact:* Off-Campus Programs Call Center, E-mail: cmuoffcampus@cmich.edu.

Duke University, Duke Global Health Institute, Durham, NC 27708-0586. Offers MS. *Faculty:* 49 full-time. *Students:* 17 full-time (11 women); includes 1 minority (Asian American or Pacific Islander), 5 international. 37 applicants, 68% accepted, 17 enrolled. *Degree requirements:* For master's, thesis. *Entrance requirements:* For master's, GRE or MCAT. Additional exam requirements/recommendations for international students: Required—TOEFL (minimum score 550 paper-based; 213 computer-based; 83 iBT), IELTS (minimum score 7). *Application deadline:* For fall admission, 12/8 for domestic and international students. Application fee: $75. *Unit*

head: Dr. Christopher Woods, Director of Graduate Studies, 919-681-7916, Fax: 919-681-7748, E-mail: woods004@mc.duke.edu. *Application contact:* Cynthia Robertson, Associate Dean for Enrollment Services, 919-684-3913, E-mail: grad-admissions@duke.edu.

Emory University, Rollins School of Public Health, Hubert Department of Global Health, Atlanta, GA 30322-1100. Offers global demography (MSPH); global environmental health (MPH); public nutrition (MSPH). *Accreditation:* CEPH. Part-time programs available. *Degree requirements:* For master's, thesis, practicum. *Entrance requirements:* For master's, GRE General Test. Additional exam requirements/recommendations for international students: Required—TOEFL (minimum score 550 paper-based; 213 computer-based; 80 iBT). Electronic applications accepted.

George Mason University, College of Health and Human Services, Department of Global and Community Health, Fairfax, VA 22030. Offers biostatistics (Certificate); epidemiology (Certificate); epidemiology and biostatistics (MS); gerontology (Certificate); global health (MS, Certificate); nutrition (Certificate); public health (MPH, Certificate); rehabilitation science (Certificate). *Faculty:* 14 full-time (8 women), 12 part-time/adjunct (8 women). *Students:* 93 full-time (75 women), 106 part-time (92 women); includes 87 minority (46 African Americans, 1 American Indian/Alaska Native, 31 Asian Americans or Pacific Islanders, 9 Hispanic Americans), 22 international. Average age 31. 269 applicants, 69% accepted, 146 enrolled. In 2009, 17 master's, 2 other advanced degrees awarded. *Degree requirements:* For master's, comprehensive exam (for some programs), thesis or practicum. *Entrance requirements:* For master's, GRE, BA with minimum GPA of 3.0, 2 letters of recommendation. Additional exam requirements/recommendations for international students: Required—TOEFL. *Application deadline:* For fall admission, 4/1 priority date for domestic students, 4/1 for international students; for spring admission, 11/1 for domestic and international students. Applications are processed on a rolling basis. Application fee: $75. Electronic applications accepted. *Expenses:* Tuition, state resident: full-time $7568; part-time $315.33 per credit hour. Tuition, nonresident: full-time $21,704; part-time $904.33 per credit hour. Required fees: $2184; $91 per credit hour. *Financial support:* In 2009–10, 4 students received support, including 2 research assistantships with full and partial tuition reimbursements available (averaging $3,500 per year), 2 teaching assistantships with full and partial tuition reimbursements available (averaging $2,790 per year); Federal Work-Study, scholarships/grants, unspecified assistantships, and research awards, health care benefits health care benefits (full-time research or teaching assistantship recipients) also available. Support available to part-time students. Financial award application deadline: 3/1. *Faculty research:* Providing introductory and advanced degrees in health-related disciplines centered in global and community issues, health issues and the needs of affected populations at the regional and global level. *Unit head:* Dr. Shirley S. Travis, Dean, 703-993-1918. *Application contact:* Allan Weiss, Office Manager, 703-993-3126, E-mail: aweiss2@gmu.edu.

Georgetown University, Law Center, Washington, DC 20001. Offers general (LL M); global health law (LL M); international and comparative law (LL M); international business and economic law (LL M); international legal studies (LL M); law (JD, SJD); securities and financial regulation (LL M); taxation (LL M); JD/LL M; JD/MA; JD/MBA; JD/MPH; JD/PhD. *Accreditation:* ABA. Part-time and evening/weekend programs available. *Degree requirements:* For master's, thesis; for doctorate, thesis/dissertation. *Entrance requirements:* For JD, LSAT; for master's and doctorate, JD, LL B, or first law degree earned in country of origin. Additional exam requirements/recommendations for international students: Required—TOEFL. *Expenses:* Contact institution. *Faculty research:* Constitutional law, legal history, jurisprudence.

The George Washington University, School of Public Health and Health Services, Department of Global Health, Washington, DC 20052. Offers MPH, JD/MPH, LL M/MPH, MD/MPH. *Accreditation:* CEPH. *Students:* 121 full-time (106 women), 85 part-time (72 women); includes 60 minority (17 African Americans, 2 American Indian/Alaska Native, 28 Asian Americans or Pacific Islanders, 13 Hispanic Americans), 10 international. Average age 27. 341 applicants, 87% accepted, 85 enrolled. In 2009, 52 master's awarded. *Degree requirements:* For master's, case study or special project. *Entrance requirements:* For master's, GMAT, GRE General Test, or MCAT. Additional exam requirements/recommendations for international students: Required—TOEFL. *Application deadline:* For fall admission, 4/15 priority date for domestic students, 4/15 for international students; for spring admission, 11/1 for domestic and international students. Applications are processed on a rolling basis. Application fee: $60. *Financial support:* In 2009–10, 24 students received support. Tuition waivers available. Financial award application deadline: 2/15. *Unit head:* Dr. James Sherry, Chair, 202-994-0270, Fax: 202-994-1955, E-mail: sherry@gwu.edu. *Application contact:* Jane Smith, Director of Admissions, 202-994-0248, Fax: 202-994-1860, E-mail: sphhsinfo@gwumc.edu.

Harvard University, School of Public Health, Department of Global Health and Population, Boston, MA 02115-6096. Offers SM, DPH, SD. Part-time programs available. *Faculty:* 35 full-time (8 women), 11 part-time/adjunct (2 women). *Students:* 93 full-time, 4 part-time; includes 14 minority (3 African Americans, 11 Asian Americans or Pacific Islanders), 37 international. Average age 30. 256 applicants, 24% accepted, 32 enrolled. In 2009, 22 master's, 7 doctorates awarded. *Degree requirements:* For master's, thesis; for doctorate, thesis/dissertation, qualifying exam. *Entrance requirements:* For master's and doctorate, GRE. Additional exam requirements/recommendations for international students: Required—TOEFL (minimum score 595 paper-based; 240 computer-based; 95 iBT); Recommended—IELTS (minimum score 7). *Application deadline:* For fall admission, 12/15 for domestic and international students. Application fee: $115. Electronic applications accepted. *Expenses:* Tuition: Full-time $33,696. Required fees: $1126. Full-time tuition and fees vary according to program. *Financial support:* Fellowships, research assistantships, teaching assistantships, Federal Work-Study, scholarships/grants, traineeships, tuition waivers (partial), and unspecified assistantships available. Support available to part-time students. Financial award application deadline: 2/8; financial award applicants required to submit FAFSA. *Faculty research:* International health policy, economics, reproductive health, ecology. *Unit head:* Dr. David Bloom, Chair, 617-432-1232, Fax: 617-432-6733, E-mail: dbloom@hsph.harvard.edu. *Application contact:* Vincent W. James, Director of Admissions, 617-432-1031, Fax: 617-432-7080, E-mail: admisofc@hsph.harvard.edu.

The Johns Hopkins University, Bloomberg School of Public Health, Department of International Health, Baltimore, MD 21205. Offers global disease epidemiology and control (MHS, PhD); health systems (MHS, PhD); human nutrition (MHS, PhD); international health (Dr PH); social and behavioral interventions (MHS, PhD). *Faculty:* 137 full-time (82 women), 185 part-time/adjunct (63 women). *Students:* 242 full-time (189 women), 1 (woman) part-time; includes 61 minority (9 African Americans, 41 Asian Americans or Pacific Islanders, 11 Hispanic Americans), 71 international. Average age 28. 494 applicants, 48% accepted, 100 enrolled. In 2009, 66 master's, 15 doctorates awarded. *Degree requirements:* For master's, comprehensive exam, thesis (for some programs), 1 year full-time residency, 4-9 month internship; for doctorate, comprehensive exam, thesis/dissertation or alternative, 1.5 years full-time residency, oral and written exams. *Entrance requirements:* For master's, GRE General Test or MCAT, 3 letters of recommendation, resume; for doctorate, GRE General Test or MCAT, 3 letters of recommendation, resume, transcripts. Additional exam requirements/recommendations for international students: Required—TOEFL (minimum score 600 paper-based; 250 computer-based; 100 iBT); Recommended—IELTS (minimum score 7). *Application deadline:* For fall admission, 1/2 priority date for domestic and international students. Applications are processed on a rolling basis. Application fee: $45. Electronic applications accepted. *Financial support:* In 2009–10, 188 students received support, including 15 fellowships (averaging $50,000 per year); Federal Work-Study, institutionally sponsored loans, scholarships/grants, traineeships, and stipends also available. Financial award application deadline: 1/2. *Faculty research:* Nutrition, infectious diseases, health systems, health economics, humanitarian emergencies. Total annual research expenditures: $72 million. *Unit head:* Dr. Robert E. Black, Chairman, 410-955-3934, Fax: 410-955-7159, E-mail: rblack@jhsph.edu. *Application contact:* Cristina G. Salazar, Academic Program Manager, 410-955-3734, Fax: 410-955-7159, E-mail: csalazar@jhsph.edu.

Loma Linda University, School of Public Health, Programs in Global Health, Loma Linda, CA 92350. Offers MPH. *Accreditation:* CEPH. *Entrance requirements:* Additional exam requirements/recommendations for international students: Required—Michigan English Language Assessment Battery or TOEFL.

Medical University of South Carolina, College of Health Professions, Department of Health Professions, Program in Health Administration-Global, Charleston, SC 29425. Offers MHA. *Entrance requirements:* Additional exam requirements/recommendations for international students: Required—TOEFL. *Unit head:* Dr. Emily L. Moore, Program Director, 843-792-4840, E-mail: mooreemi@musc.edu. *Application contact:* Laura Mewbourn, Student Services Coordinator, 843-792-2926, Fax: 843-792-3327, E-mail: mewbourn@musc.edu.

Morehouse School of Medicine, Master of Public Health Program, Atlanta, GA 30310-1495. Offers epidemiology (MPH); health administration, management and policy (MPH); health education/health promotion (MPH); international health (MPH). *Accreditation:* CEPH. Part-time programs available. *Faculty:* 4 full-time (1 woman), 36 part-time/adjunct (21 women). *Students:* 54 full-time (37 women), 3 part-time (2 women); includes 34 minority (33 African Americans, 1 American Indian/Alaska Native). Average age 28. 62 applicants, 48% accepted, 29 enrolled. In 2009, 13 master's awarded. *Degree requirements:* For master's, thesis, practicum, public health leadership seminar. *Entrance requirements:* For master's, GRE General Test, writing test, public health or human service experience. Additional exam requirements/recommendations for international students: Required—TOEFL (minimum score 550 paper-based; 200 computer-based). *Application deadline:* For fall admission, 3/1 for domestic and international students. Application fee: $50. Electronic applications accepted. *Expenses:* Contact institution. *Financial support:* In 2009–10, 32 students received support, including 6 research assistantships with partial tuition reimbursements available (averaging $10,000 per year); fellowships, teaching assistantships, career-related internships or fieldwork, Federal Work-Study, institutionally sponsored loans, scholarships/grants, and unspecified assistantships also available. Support available to part-time students. Financial award application deadline: 5/1; financial award applicants required to submit FAFSA. *Faculty research:* Women's and adolescent health, violence prevention, cancer epidemiology/disparities, substance abuse prevention. Total annual research expenditures: $640,176. *Unit head:* Dr. Patricia Rodney, Director/Assistant Dean for Public Health Education, 404-752-1944, Fax: 404-752-1051, E-mail: prodney@msm.edu. *Application contact:* Dr. Sterling Roaf, Director of Admissions, 404-752-1650, Fax: 404-752-1512, E-mail: mphadmissions@msm.edu.

New York Medical College, School of Health Sciences and Practice, Department of Health Policy and Management, Program in Global Health, Valhalla, NY 10595-1691. Offers Graduate Certificate. *Accreditation:* CEPH. Part-time and evening/weekend programs available. *Entrance requirements:* Additional exam requirements/recommendations for international students: Required—TOEFL (minimum score 637 paper-based; 250 computer-based; 110 iBT), IELTS (minimum score 7). *Application deadline:* For fall admission, 8/1 priority date for domestic students, 5/15 for international students; for spring admission, 12/1 priority date for domestic students, 10/15 for international students. Applications are processed on a rolling basis. Application fee: $50 ($100 for international students). Electronic applications accepted. *Expenses:* Tuition: Full-time $18,170; part-time $790 per credit. Required fees: $790 per credit. $20 per semester. One-time fee: $100. Tuition and fees vary according to class time, course level, course load, degree level, program, student level and student's religious affiliation. *Financial support:* Research assistantships, teaching assistantships, career-related internships or fieldwork, Federal Work-Study, institutionally sponsored loans, health care benefits, and tuition waivers (partial) available. Support available to part-time students. Financial award applicants required to submit FAFSA. *Unit head:* Dr. Padmini Murthy, Director, 914-594-3480, Fax: 914-594-3481, E-mail: mini_murthy@nymc.edu. *Application contact:* Pamela Suett, Director of Recruitment, 914-594-4510, Fax: 914-594-4292, E-mail: shsp_admissions@nymc.edu.

New York University, Steinhardt School of Culture, Education, and Human Development, Department of Nutrition, Food Studies, and Public Health, Program in Community Public Health, New York, NY 10012-1019. Offers community public health (MPH), including community health, international community health, public health nutrition; public health (PhD). *Accreditation:* CEPH. Part-time programs available. *Students:* 90 full-time (77 women), 45 part-time (41 women); includes 34 minority (11 African Americans, 17 Asian Americans or Pacific Islanders, 6 Hispanic Americans), 10 international. Average age 28. 257 applicants, 81% accepted, 52 enrolled. In 2009, 36 master's awarded. *Degree requirements:* For master's, thesis (for some programs). *Entrance requirements:* For master's, GRE General Test; for doctorate, GRE General Test, interview. Additional exam requirements/recommendations for international students: Required—TOEFL. *Application deadline:* For fall admission, 12/15 priority date for domestic and international students; for spring admission, 11/1 for domestic and international students. Applications are processed on a rolling basis. Application fee: $75. Electronic applications accepted. *Expenses:* Tuition: Full-time $30,528; part-time $1272 per credit. Required fees: $2177. *Financial support:* Fellowships with full and partial tuition reimbursements, career-related internships or fieldwork, Federal Work-Study, institutionally sponsored loans, scholarships/grants, and tuition waivers (partial) available. Support available to part-time students. Financial award application deadline: 2/1; financial award applicants required to submit FAFSA. *Faculty research:* Social epidemiology, primary health care, global health, immigrants and health, infectious disease prevention, HIV/AIDS. *Unit head:* Director, 212-998-5580, Fax: 212-995-4192. *Application contact:* 212-998-5030, Fax: 212-995-4328, E-mail: steinhardt.gradadmissions@nyu.edu.

San Diego State University, Graduate and Research Affairs, College of Health and Human Services, Graduate School of Public Health, San Diego, CA 92182. Offers environmental health (MPH); epidemiology (MPH, PhD), including biostatistics (MPH); global emergency preparedness and response (MS); global health (PhD); health behavior (PhD); health promotion (MPH); health services administration (MPH); toxicology (MS); MPH/MA; MSW/MPH. *Accreditation:* ABET (one or more programs are accredited); CAHME (one or more programs are accredited); CEPH (one or more programs are accredited). Part-time programs available. *Degree requirements:* For master's, comprehensive exam (for some programs), thesis (for some programs); for doctorate, thesis/dissertation. *Entrance requirements:* For master's, GMAT (MPH in health services administration), GRE General Test; for doctorate, GRE General Test. Additional exam requirements/recommendations for international students: Required—TOEFL. *Faculty research:* Evaluation of tobacco, AIDS prevalence and prevention, mammography, infant death project, Alzheimer's in elderly Chinese.

Tufts University, Fletcher School of Law and Diplomacy, Medford, MA 02155. Offers LL M, MA, MAHA, MALD, MIB, PhD, DVM/MA, JD/MALD, MALD/MA, MALD/MBA, MALD/MS, MD/MA. Postbaccalaureate distance learning degree programs offered (minimal on-campus study). *Faculty:* 34 full-time (7 women), 31 part-time/adjunct (8 women). *Students:* 443 full-time (224 women), 7 part-time (4 women); includes 51 minority (6 African Americans, 1 American Indian/Alaska Native, 26 Asian Americans or Pacific Islanders, 18 Hispanic Americans), 165 international. Average age 31. 1,866 applicants, 40% accepted, 292 enrolled. In 2009, 364 master's, 12 doctorates awarded. *Degree requirements:* For master's, one foreign language, thesis; for doctorate, one foreign language, comprehensive exam, thesis/dissertation, dissertation defense. *Entrance requirements:* For master's and doctorate, GMAT or GRE General Test. Additional exam requirements/recommendations for international students: Required—TOEFL (minimum score 600 paper-based; 250 computer-based; 100 iBT), IELTS (minimum score 7). *Application deadline:* For fall admission, 1/15 for domestic and international students; for spring admission, 10/15 for domestic and international students. Application fee: $70. Electronic applications accepted. *Expenses:* Contact institution. *Financial support:* Federal Work-Study, institutionally sponsored loans, scholarships/grants, and tuition waivers (partial) available. Financial award application deadline: 1/15; financial award applicants required to submit FAFSA. *Faculty research:* Negotiation and conflict resolution, international organizations, international business and economic law, security studies, development economics. *Unit*

International Health

Tufts University (continued)
head: Stephen W. Bosworth, Dean, 617-627-3050, Fax: 617-627-3712. *Application contact:* Laurie A. Hurley, E-mail: fletcheradmissions@tufts.edu.

TUI University, College of Health Sciences, Program in Health Sciences, Cypress, CA 90630. Offers clinical research administration (MS, Certificate); emergency and disaster management (MS, Certificate); environmental health science (Certificate); health care administration (PhD); health care management (MS), including health informatics; health education (MS, Certificate); health informatics (Certificate); health sciences (PhD); international health (MS); international health: educator or researcher option (PhD); international health: practitioner option (PhD); law and expert witness studies (MS, Certificate); public health (MS); quality assurance (Certificate). Part-time and evening/weekend programs available. Postbaccalaureate distance learning degree programs offered (no on-campus study). *Degree requirements:* For doctorate, comprehensive exam, thesis/dissertation, defense of dissertation. *Entrance requirements:* For master's, minimum GPA of 2.5 (students with GPA 3.0 or greater may transfer up to 30% of graduate level credits); for doctorate, minimum GPA of 3.4, curriculum vitae, course work in research methods or statistics. Additional exam requirements/recommendations for international students: Required—TOEFL. Electronic applications accepted.

Tulane University, School of Public Health and Tropical Medicine, Department of International Health and Development, New Orleans, LA 70118-5669. Offers MPH, Dr PH, PhD, MSW/MPH. *Accreditation:* CEPH (one or more programs are accredited). Part-time programs available. Terminal master's awarded for partial completion of doctoral program. *Degree requirements:* For master's, one foreign language; for doctorate, one foreign language, comprehensive exam, thesis/dissertation. *Entrance requirements:* For master's and doctorate, GRE General Test. Additional exam requirements/recommendations for international students: Required—TOEFL. Electronic applications accepted. *Faculty research:* Reproductive health, HIV/AIDS, nutrition and food security, health financing, program evaluation.

Uniformed Services University of the Health Sciences, School of Medicine, Graduate Programs in the Biomedical Sciences and Public Health, Bethesda, MD 20814. Offers emerging infectious diseases (PhD); medical and clinical psychology (PhD), including clinical psychology, medical and clinical psychology (clinical/dual track), medical and clinical psychology (research track); molecular and cell biology (PhD); neuroscience (PhD); preventive medicine and biometrics (MPH, MSPH, MTMH, Dr PH, PhD), including environmental health science (PhD), medical zoology (PhD), public health (MPH, MSPH, Dr PH), tropical medicine and hygiene (MTMH). *Faculty:* 372 full-time (119 women), 4,044 part-time/adjunct (908 women). *Students:* 176 full-time (96 women); includes 31 minority (6 African Americans, 4 American Indian/Alaska Native, 14 Asian Americans or Pacific Islanders, 7 Hispanic Americans), 11 international. Average age 28. 278 applicants, 20% accepted, 47 enrolled. In 2009, 36 master's, 17 doctorates awarded. Terminal master's awarded for partial completion of doctoral program. *Degree requirements:* For master's, comprehensive exam, thesis or alternative; for doctorate, comprehensive exam, thesis/dissertation, qualifying exam. *Entrance requirements:* For master's, GRE General Test; for doctorate, GRE General Test, minimum GPA of 3.0. Additional exam requirements/recommendations for international students: Required—TOEFL. *Application deadline:* For fall admission, 1/15 priority date for domestic and international students. Applications are processed on a rolling basis. Application fee: $0. Electronic applications accepted. *Financial support:* In 2009–10, fellowships with full tuition reimbursements (averaging $26,000 per year), research assistantships with full tuition reimbursements (averaging $26,000 per year) were awarded; career-related internships or fieldwork, scholarships/grants, health care benefits, and tuition waivers (full) also available. *Unit head:* Dr. Eleanor S. Metcalf, Associate Dean, 301-295-1104, E-mail: emetcalf@usuhs.mil. *Application contact:* Elena Marina Sherman, Graduate Program Coordinator, 301-295-3913, Fax: 301-295-6772, E-mail: elena.sherman@usuhs.mil.

Uniformed Services University of the Health Sciences, School of Medicine, Graduate Programs in the Biomedical Sciences and Public Health, Department of Preventive Medicine and Biometrics, Program in Tropical Medicine and Hygiene, Bethesda, MD 20814-4799. Offers MTMH. *Accreditation:* CEPH. *Faculty:* 43 full-time (14 women), 143 part-time/adjunct (25 women). *Students:* 4 full-time (0 women); includes 2 minority (1 African American, 1 Hispanic American). Average age 30. 10 applicants, 70% accepted. In 2009, 3 master's awarded. *Degree requirements:* For master's, comprehensive exam. *Entrance requirements:* For master's, GRE General Test, MD, US citizenship. *Application deadline:* For fall admission, 1/15 priority date for domestic students. Applications are processed on a rolling basis. Application fee: $0. *Financial support:* Health care benefits available. *Faculty research:* Epidemiology, biostatistics, tropical public health. *Unit head:* Dr. David Cruess, Director, 301-295-3465, Fax: 301-295-1933, E-mail: dcruess@usuhs.mil. *Application contact:* Elena Marina Sherman, Graduate Program Coordinator, 301-295-3913, Fax: 301-295-6772, E-mail: elena.sherman@usuhs.mil.

University of Alberta, School of Public Health, Department of Public Health Sciences, Edmonton, AB T6G 2E1, Canada. Offers clinical epidemiology (M Sc, MPH); environmental and occupational health (MPH); environmental health sciences (M Sc); epidemiology (M Sc); global health (M Sc, MPH); health policy and management (MPH); health policy research (M Sc); health technology assessment (MPH); occupational health (M Sc); population health (M Sc); public health leadership (MPH); public health sciences (PhD); quantitative methods (MPH). *Accreditation:* CEPH (one or more programs are accredited). *Faculty:* 24 full-time (5 women), 59 part-time/adjunct (13 women). *Students:* 49 full-time, 49 part-time. 81 applicants, 31% accepted. In 2009, 28 master's awarded. Terminal master's awarded for partial completion of doctoral program. *Degree requirements:* For master's, thesis (for some programs); for doctorate, thesis/dissertation. *Entrance requirements:* For master's, GMAT or GRE General Test. Additional exam requirements/recommendations for international students: Required—TOEFL (minimum score 550 paper-based; 213 computer-based) or IELTS (minimum score 6). *Application deadline:* For fall admission, 3/15 for domestic students, 7/1 for international students; for winter admission, 11/1 for international students; for spring admission, 3/1 for international students. Applications are processed on a rolling basis. Application fee: $0. Electronic applications accepted. Tuition and fees charges are reported in Canadian dollars. *Expenses:* Tuition, area resident: Full-time $4626 Canadian dollars; part-time $99.72 Canadian dollars per unit. International tuition: $8216 Canadian dollars full-time. Required fees: $3590 Canadian dollars; $99.72 Canadian dollars per unit. $215 Canadian dollars per term. *Financial support:* In 2009–10, 11 students received support, including 6 research assistantships with tuition reimbursements available (averaging $2,200 per year); fellowships, teaching assistantships, career-related internships or fieldwork and tuition waivers (partial) also available. Financial award application deadline: 2/1. *Faculty research:* Biostatistics, health promotion and sociobehavioral health science. Total annual research expenditures: $5.7 million. *Unit head:* L. Duncan Saunders, Acting Chair, 780-492-6814, Fax: 780-492-0364. *Application contact:* Felicity R. Hey, Graduate Programs Administrator, 780-492-6407, Fax: 780-492-0364, E-mail: felicity.hey@ualberta.ca.

University of Michigan, School of Public Health, Department of Epidemiology, Ann Arbor, MI 48109-2029. Offers dental public health (MPH); epidemiological science (PhD); epidemiology (MS); general epidemiology (MPH); hospital and molecular epidemiology (MPH); international health (MPH). PhD and MS offered through the Horace H. Rackham School of Graduate Studies. *Accreditation:* CEPH (one or more programs are accredited). Part-time programs available. *Faculty:* 33 full-time (20 women), 25 part-time/adjunct (9 women). *Students:* 192 full-time (147 women), 7 part-time (5 women); includes 48 minority (17 African Americans, 1 American Indian/Alaska Native, 24 Asian Americans or Pacific Islanders, 6 Hispanic Americans), 13 international. 587 applicants, 61% accepted, 88 enrolled. In 2009, 80 master's, 13 doctorates awarded. Terminal master's awarded for partial completion of doctoral program. *Degree requirements:* For master's, thesis (for some programs); for doctorate, comprehensive exam, thesis/dissertation, oral defense of dissertation, preliminary exam. *Entrance requirements:* For master's and doctorate, GRE General Test, MCAT. Additional exam requirements/recommendations for international students: Required—TOEFL (minimum score 560 paper-based; 220 computer-based; 100 iBT). *Application deadline:* For fall admission, 12/1 priority date for domestic students, 1/15 priority date for international students. Applications are processed on a rolling basis. Application fee: $60 ($75 for international students). Electronic applications accepted. *Expenses:* Tuition, state resident: full-time $17,286; part-time $1099 per credit hour. Tuition, nonresident: full-time $34,944; part-time $2080 per credit hour. Required fees: $95 per semester. Tuition and fees vary according to course load, degree level and program. *Financial support:* In 2009–10, 112 students received support, including 112 fellowships with full and partial tuition reimbursements available, 20 research assistantships with full tuition reimbursements available (averaging $8,400 per year), 12 teaching assistantships with full tuition reimbursements available (averaging $16,000 per year); career-related internships or fieldwork, Federal Work-Study, and scholarships/grants also available. Financial award application deadline: 3/1. *Faculty research:* Molecular virology, infectious diseases, women's health, genetics, social epidemiology. *Unit head:* Dr. Sharon Kardia, Chair, 734-764-5435, Fax: 734-764-3192. *Application contact:* Sally Musselman, Student Services Coordinator, 734-764-5415, Fax: 734-763-3192, E-mail: musselms@umich.edu.

University of Minnesota, Twin Cities Campus, School of Public Health, Division of Environmental Health Sciences, Minneapolis, MN 55455-0213. Offers environmental and occupational epidemiology (MPH, MS, PhD); environmental chemistry (MS, PhD); environmental health policy (MPH, MS, PhD); environmental infectious diseases (MPH, MS, PhD); environmental toxicology (MPH, MS, PhD); exposure sciences (MS); general environmental health (MPH, MS); global environmental health (MPH, MS, PhD); industrial hygiene (MPH, MS, PhD); occupational health nursing (MPH, MS, PhD); occupational medicine (MPH); MPH/MS. *Accreditation:* CEPH (one or more programs are accredited). Part-time programs available. *Degree requirements:* For master's, thesis optional; for doctorate, thesis/dissertation. *Entrance requirements:* For master's and doctorate, GRE General Test. Additional exam requirements/recommendations for international students: Required—TOEFL (minimum score 600 paper-based; 250 computer-based; 100 iBT). Electronic applications accepted. *Faculty research:* Behavior/measurement of airborne particles, toxicity mechanisms of environmental contaminants, health and safety interventions, foodborne disease surveillance, measuring pesticide exposures in children.

University of Pittsburgh, Graduate School of Public Health, Department of Environmental and Occupational Health, Pittsburgh, PA 15260. Offers environmental and occupational health (MPH, MS, PhD); environmental health risk assessment (Certificate); global health (Certificate); public health preparedness and disaster response (Certificate); MD/MPH. *Accreditation:* CEPH (one or more programs are accredited). Part-time programs available. *Faculty:* 28 full-time (8 women), 26 part-time/adjunct (6 women). *Students:* 23 full-time (11 women), 17 part-time (11 women); includes 3 minority (1 African American, 1 Asian American or Pacific Islander, 1 Hispanic American), 9 international. Average age 34. 69 applicants, 57% accepted, 16 enrolled. In 2009, 3 master's awarded. *Degree requirements:* For master's, comprehensive exam, thesis; for doctorate, comprehensive exam, thesis/dissertation, preliminary exams. *Entrance requirements:* For master's and Certificate, GRE General Test; for doctorate, GRE General Test, minimum GPA of 3.4; background in biology, physics, chemistry and calculus. Additional exam requirements/recommendations for international students: Required—TOEFL (minimum score 550 paper-based; 213 computer-based; 80 iBT). *Application deadline:* For fall admission, 2/15 priority date for domestic students, 2/15 for international students; for winter admission, 9/1 for international students; for spring admission, 2/1 for international students. Applications are processed on a rolling basis. Application fee: $95. Electronic applications accepted. *Expenses:* Tuition, state resident: full-time $16,402; part-time $665 per credit. Tuition, nonresident: full-time $28,694; part-time $1175 per credit. Required fees: $690; $175 per term. Tuition and fees vary according to program. *Financial support:* In 2009–10, 10 students received support, including 10 research assistantships with full tuition reimbursements available (averaging $24,000 per year); scholarships/grants and unspecified assistantships also available. *Faculty research:* Molecular toxicology, redox signaling, gene environment interaction, progenitor-progeny lineage, occupational and pulmonary medicine. Total annual research expenditures: $9.1 million. *Unit head:* Dr. Bruce R. Pitt, Chairman, 412-383-8400, Fax: 412-383-7658, E-mail: brucep@pitt.edu. *Application contact:* Eileen Penny Weiss, Student Affairs Administrator, 412-383-7297, Fax: 412-383-7658, E-mail: pweiss@pitt.edu.

University of Southern California, Keck School of Medicine and Graduate School, Graduate Programs in Medicine, Department of Preventive Medicine, Master of Public Health Program, Alhambra, CA 91803. Offers biostatistics/epidemiology (MPH); child and family health (MPH); global health leadership (MPH); health communication (MPH); health promotion (MPH). *Accreditation:* CEPH. Part-time programs available. *Faculty:* 22 full-time (12 women), 3 part-time/adjunct (0 women). *Students:* 215 full-time (158 women), 3 part-time (2 women); includes 148 minority (13 African Americans, 3 American Indian/Alaska Native, 114 Asian Americans or Pacific Islanders, 18 Hispanic Americans), 25 international. Average age 26. 208 applicants, 74% accepted, 76 enrolled. In 2009, 60 master's awarded. *Degree requirements:* For master's, practicum, final report, oral presentation. *Entrance requirements:* For master's, GRE General Test, MCAT, GMAT, minimum GPA of 3.0. Additional exam requirements/recommendations for international students: Required—TOEFL (minimum score 600 paper-based; 250 computer-based; 100 iBT). *Application deadline:* For fall admission, 6/1 priority date for domestic and international students; for spring admission, 11/1 priority date for domestic students, 10/1 priority date for international students. Applications are processed on a rolling basis. Application fee: $85. Electronic applications accepted. *Expenses:* Tuition: Full-time $25,980; part-time $1315 per unit. Required fees: $554. One-time fee: $35 full-time. Full-time tuition and fees vary according to degree level and program. *Financial support:* In 2009–10, 175 students received support, including 20 fellowships (averaging $3,200 per year); career-related internships or fieldwork, Federal Work-Study, institutionally sponsored loans, and scholarships/grants also available. Support available to part-time students. Financial award application deadline: 5/1; financial award applicants required to submit CSS PROFILE or FAFSA. *Faculty research:* Substance abuse prevention, cancer and heart disease prevention, mass media and health communication research, health promotion, treatment compliance. *Unit head:* Dr. Thomas W. Valente, Director, 626-457-4139, Fax: 626-457-6699, E-mail: tvalente@usc.edu. *Application contact:* Chrystal Romero, Admissions Counselor, 626-457-6676, Fax: 626-457-6699, E-mail: ccromero@usc.edu.

University of South Florida, Graduate School, College of Public Health, Department of Global Health, Tampa, FL 33620-9951. Offers MPH, MSPH, Dr PH, PhD. Part-time and evening/weekend programs available. *Faculty:* 15 full-time (5 women), 4 part-time/adjunct (2 women). *Students:* 114 full-time (79 women), 37 part-time (22 women); includes 42 minority (17 African Americans, 15 Asian Americans or Pacific Islanders, 10 Hispanic Americans), 27 international. Average age 29. 172 applicants, 72% accepted, 38 enrolled. In 2009, 22 master's, 1 doctorate awarded. *Degree requirements:* For master's, comprehensive exam, thesis (for some programs), minimum GPA of 3.0; for doctorate, comprehensive exam, thesis/dissertation. *Entrance requirements:* For master's, GRE General Test, minimum GPA of 3.0 in upper-level course work, goal statement letter, two professional letters of recommendation, resume/curriculum vitae; for doctorate, GRE General Test, minimum GPA of 3.0 in upper-level course work, goal statement letter, three professional letters of recommendation, resume/curriculum vitae, writing sample. Additional exam requirements/recommendations for international students: Required—TOEFL (minimum score 550 paper-based; 213 computer-based; 79 iBT). *Application deadline:* For fall admission, 6/1 for domestic students, 1/2 for international students; for spring admission, 10/15 for domestic students, 7/1 for international students. Applications are processed on a rolling basis. Application fee: $30. Electronic applications accepted. *Financial support:* In 2009–10, 4 fellowships (averaging $8,093 per year), 30 research assistantships with partial tuition reimbursements (averaging $4,227 per year), 17 teaching assistantships with full and partial tuition reimbursements (averaging $4,162 per year) were awarded; career-related internships or fieldwork, Federal Work-Study, institutionally sponsored loans, scholarships/grants, traineeships, and unspecified assistantships also available. Support available to part-time students. Total annual research expenditures: $5.4 million. *Unit head:* Boo Kwa, Chairperson,

813-974-1122, Fax: 813-974-8506. *Application contact:* Michelle Hodge, Academic Advisor, 813-974-6665, Fax: 813-974-8121, E-mail: mhodge1@health.usf.edu.

The University of Toledo, College of Graduate Studies, College of Medicine, Department of Public Health and Homeland Security, Program in Public Health, Toledo, OH 43606-3390. Offers biostatistics and epidemiology (Certificate); emergency response (Certificate); global health (Certificate); public health (MPH); MD/MPH.

University of Washington, Graduate School, School of Public Health, Department of Epidemiology, Seattle, WA 98195. Offers clinical research (MS); epidemiology (MPH, MS, PhD); global health (MPH); maternal/child health (MPH); nutritional sciences (MPH, MS, PhD); public health genetics (MPH, MS, PhD), including genetic epidemiology (MS), public health genetics (MPH, PhD). *Accreditation:* CEPH (one or more programs are accredited). Part-time programs available. *Faculty:* 66 full-time (40 women), 46 part-time/adjunct (20 women). *Students:* 145 full-time (101 women), 43 part-time (26 women); includes 33 minority (6 African Americans, 1 American Indian/Alaska Native, 18 Asian Americans or Pacific Islanders, 8 Hispanic Americans), 20 international. Average age 32. 236 applicants, 48% accepted, 60 enrolled. In 2009, 44 master's, 16 doctorates awarded. Terminal master's awarded for partial completion of doctoral program. *Degree requirements:* For master's, thesis; for doctorate, comprehensive exam, thesis/dissertation, preliminary exam, original data collection. *Entrance requirements:* For master's, GRE General Test (except applicants with U.S. doctorate); for doctorate, GRE General Test. Additional exam requirements/recommendations for international students: Required—TOEFL (minimum score 580 paper-based; 237 computer-based; 92 iBT) or IELTS (minimum score 7). *Application deadline:* For fall admission, 12/1 for domestic students, 11/1 for international students. Application fee: $50. Electronic applications accepted. *Expenses:* Contact institution. *Financial support:* In 2009–10, 90 fellowships with full tuition reimbursements (averaging $20,976 per year), 43 research assistantships with full tuition reimbursements (averaging $19,668 per year), 12 teaching assistantships with full tuition reimbursements (averaging $16,398 per year) were awarded; career-related internships or fieldwork, Federal Work-Study, institutionally sponsored loans, scholarships/grants, traineeships, health care benefits, unspecified assistantships, and tuition waiver also available. Financial award application deadline: 2/15; financial award applicants required to submit FAFSA. *Faculty research:* Chronic diseases, sexually transmitted diseases, injury, materials and child health, molecular and genetic epidemiology. *Unit head:* Dr. Scott Davis, Chair, 206-543-1065, Fax: 206-543-1065, E-mail: sdavis@fhcrc.org. *Application contact:* Kate O'Brien, Student Services Manager, 206-543-1065, Fax: 206-543-8525, E-mail: apply@u.washington.edu.

University of Washington, Graduate School, School of Public Health, Department of Global Health, Seattle, WA 98195. Offers global health (MPH); global health—peace corps international (MPH); health metrics and evaluation (MPH); leadership, policy and management (MPH); pathobiology (PhD); MPH/MAIS; MPH/MD; MPH/MN; MPH/MPA; MPH/MSW; MPH/PhD. Part-time programs available. *Faculty:* 34 full-time (16 women), 19 part-time/adjunct (13 women). *Students:* 41 full-time (24 women), 11 part-time (7 women); includes 7 minority (5 Asian Americans or Pacific Islanders, 2 Hispanic Americans), 21 international. Average age 31. 213 applicants, 19% accepted, 25 enrolled. In 2009, 9 master's awarded. *Degree requirements:* For master's, thesis, practicum. *Entrance requirements:* For master's, GRE. Additional exam requirements/recommendations for international students: Required—TOEFL (minimum score 500 paper-based; 173 computer-based; 45 iBT), IELTS (minimum score 6). *Application deadline:* For fall admission, 12/1 for domestic students, 11/1 for international students. Application fee: $50. Electronic applications accepted. *Financial support:* In 2009–10, 16 students received support, including 1 fellowship with partial tuition reimbursement available (averaging $8,000 per year), 11 research assistantships with full and partial tuition reimbursements available (averaging $21,000 per year), 7 teaching assistantships with full and partial tuition reimbursements available (averaging $10,500 per year); tuition waivers also available. Financial award applicants required to submit FAFSA. *Faculty research:* AIDS and STDs, primary healthcare, reproductive health, operations research, tuberculosis. *Unit head:* Dr. King K. Holmes, Chair, 206-744-8493, Fax: 206-744-3694, E-mail: kkh@u.washington.edu. *Application contact:* Krishna Richardson, Program Coordinator, 206-744-8493, Fax: 206-744-3694, E-mail: krishna7@u.washington.edu.

Yale University, School of Medicine, School of Public Health, Division of Global Health, New Haven, CT 06520. Offers MPH. *Accreditation:* CEPH. Part-time programs available. *Degree requirements:* For master's, one foreign language, thesis, internship. *Entrance requirements:* For master's, GMAT, GRE, or MCAT, previous undergraduate course work in mathematics and science. Additional exam requirements/recommendations for international students: Required—TOEFL. Electronic applications accepted. *Expenses:* Contact institution. *Faculty research:* International health promotion and healthy public policy, community health planning, health of elderly and disabled persons.

Maternal and Child Health

Bank Street College of Education, Graduate School, Program in Child Life, New York, NY 10025. Offers MS. *Students:* 16 full-time (all women), 13 part-time (all women); includes 3 minority (1 African American, 1 Asian American or Pacific Islander, 1 Hispanic American). Average age 28. 38 applicants, 47% accepted, 14 enrolled. In 2009, 16 master's awarded. *Degree requirements:* For master's, thesis. *Entrance requirements:* For master's, interview and 100 hours of volunteer experience in a child life setting. Additional exam requirements/recommendations for international students: Required—TOEFL (minimum score 600 paper-based; 250 computer-based; 100 iBT), IELTS (minimum score 7). *Application deadline:* For fall admission, 3/1 priority date for domestic students; for spring admission, 11/1 priority date for domestic students. Applications are processed on a rolling basis. Application fee: $65. *Expenses:* Tuition: Part-time $1120 per credit. *Financial support:* Career-related internships or fieldwork, Federal Work-Study, scholarships/grants, and unspecified assistantships available. Support available to part-time students. Financial award application deadline: 4/15; financial award applicants required to submit FAFSA. *Faculty research:* Therapeutic play in child life setting, child advocacy, psychosocial and educational intervention with care of sick children. *Unit head:* Troy Pinkney-Ragsdale, Director, 212-875-4473, Fax: 212-875-4753, E-mail: tpinkneyragsdale@bankstreet.edu. *Application contact:* Troy Pinkney-Ragsdale, Director, 212-875-4473, Fax: 212-875-4753, E-mail: tpinkneyragsdale@bankstreet.edu.

Bank Street College of Education, Graduate School, Program in Infant and Family Development and Early Intervention, New York, NY 10025. Offers early childhood special and general education (MS Ed); early childhood special education (Ed M); infant and family development (MS Ed). *Students:* 16 full-time (all women), 29 part-time (all women); includes 7 minority (3 African Americans, 1 Asian American or Pacific Islander, 3 Hispanic Americans), 1 international. Average age 31. 21 applicants, 71% accepted, 10 enrolled. In 2009, 16 master's awarded. *Degree requirements:* For master's, thesis. *Entrance requirements:* For master's, interview. Additional exam requirements/recommendations for international students: Required—TOEFL (minimum score 600 paper-based; 250 computer-based; 100 iBT), IELTS (minimum score 7). *Application deadline:* For fall admission, 3/1 priority date for domestic students; for spring admission, 11/1 priority date for domestic students. Applications are processed on a rolling basis. Application fee: $65. *Expenses:* Tuition: Part-time $1120 per credit. *Financial support:* Career-related internships or fieldwork, Federal Work-Study, scholarships/grants, and unspecified assistantships available. Support available to part-time students. Financial award application deadline: 4/15; financial award applicants required to submit FAFSA. *Faculty research:* Early intervention, early attachment practice in infant and toddler childcare, parenting skills in adolescents. *Unit head:* Sue Cabary, Director, 212-875-4509, Fax: 212-875-4753, E-mail: scarbary@bankstreet.edu. *Application contact:* Ann Morgan, Director of Graduate Admissions, 212-875-4403, Fax: 212-875-4678, E-mail: amorgan@bankstreet.edu.

Boston University, School of Public Health, Maternal and Child Health Department, Boston, MA 02215. Offers maternal and child health (MPH, Dr PH). Part-time and evening/weekend programs available. *Students:* 36 full-time (34 women), 23 part-time (all women); includes 12 minority (1 African American, 4 Asian Americans or Pacific Islanders, 7 Hispanic Americans), 2 international. Average age 28. In 2009, 28 master's, 1 doctorate awarded. *Entrance requirements:* For master's, GRE, DAT, MCAT, LSAT, or GMAT; for doctorate, GRE, GMAT. Additional exam requirements/recommendations for international students: Required—TOEFL (minimum score 600 paper-based; 250 computer-based; 100 iBT) or IELTS (minimum score 6). *Application deadline:* For fall admission, 2/1 priority date for domestic and international students; for spring admission, 10/15 priority date for domestic and international students. Applications are processed on a rolling basis. Application fee: $95. Electronic applications accepted. *Expenses:* Tuition: Full-time $37,910; part-time $1184 per credit hour. Required fees: $386; $40 per semester. Part-time tuition and fees vary according to class time, course level, degree level and program. *Financial support:* In 2009–10, 10 fellowships were awarded; career-related internships or fieldwork, Federal Work-Study, institutionally sponsored loans, scholarships/grants, traineeships, and tuition waivers (partial) also available. Financial award application deadline: 3/1; financial award applicants required to submit FAFSA. *Unit head:* Dr. Deborah Bowen, Chair, 617-638-5205, E-mail: socbeh@bu.edu. *Application contact:* LePhan Quan, Assistant Director of Admissions, 617-638-4640, Fax: 617-638-5299, E-mail: asksph@bu.edu.

Columbia University, Columbia University Mailman School of Public Health, Division of Population and Family Health, New York, NY 10032. Offers MPH. *Accreditation:* CEPH. Part-time programs available. *Students:* 92 full-time (all women), 30 part-time (26 women); includes 27 minority (7 African Americans, 9 Asian Americans or Pacific Islanders, 11 Hispanic Americans), 11 international. Average age 28. 210 applicants, 70% accepted, 61 enrolled. In 2009, 64 master's awarded. *Entrance requirements:* For master's, GRE General Test. Additional exam requirements/recommendations for international students: Required—TOEFL (minimum score 600 paper-based; 250 computer-based; 100 iBT). *Application deadline:* For fall admission, 1/5 for domestic students. Application fee: $60. *Financial support:* Research assistantships, career-related internships or fieldwork and Federal Work-Study available. Financial award application deadline: 2/1; financial award applicants required to submit FAFSA. *Faculty research:* Child and adolescent health; global health systems; health and human rights; humanitarian disasters; sexual and reproductive health. *Unit head:* Dr. John Santelli, Head, 212-304-5200. *Application contact:* Dr. John Santelli, Head, 212-304-5200.

Oakland University, Graduate Study and Lifelong Learning, School of Health Sciences, Program in Physical Therapy, Rochester, MI 48309-4401. Offers neurological rehabilitation (Certificate); orthopedic manual physical therapy (Certificate); orthopedic physical therapy (Certificate); pediatric rehabilitation (Certificate); physical therapy (MSPT, DPT, Dr Sc PT); teaching and learning for rehabilitation professionals (Certificate). *Accreditation:* APTA. *Degree requirements:* For master's, thesis (for some programs). *Entrance requirements:* For master's, acceptance in the 2-year preparatory post-baccalaureate program, minimum GPA of 3.0; for doctorate, GRE General Test. Additional exam requirements/recommendations for international students: Required—TOEFL (minimum score 550 paper-based; 213 computer-based). *Expenses:* Contact institution.

Troy University, Graduate School, College of Health and Human Services, Program in Nursing, Troy, AL 36082. Offers adult health (MSN); clinical nurse specialist adult health (DNP); clinical nurse specialist nurse practitioner (DNP); family nurse practitioner (MSN); informatics specialist (MSN); maternal infant (MSN). *Accreditation:* NLN. Part-time and evening/weekend programs available. *Students:* 28 full-time (all women), 102 part-time (93 women); includes 49 minority (48 African Americans, 1 American Indian/Alaska Native). Average age 37. 76 applicants, 86% accepted. In 2009, 25 master's awarded. *Degree requirements:* For master's, comprehensive exam, thesis optional. *Entrance requirements:* For master's, MAT (minimum score 396) or GRE (minimum score 850), minimum GPA of 2.5, BSN. Additional exam requirements/recommendations for international students: Required—TOEFL (minimum score 523 paper-based; 193 computer-based; 70 iBT), IELTS (minimum score 6), TOEFL or IELTS or ACT Compass ESL (minimum score 270 on Listening, Reading, and Grammar with no individual score below 85 and minimum score of 8 out of 12 on writing test). *Application deadline:* Applications are processed on a rolling basis. Application fee: $50. Electronic applications accepted. *Financial support:* Available to part-time students. Applicants required to submit FAFSA. *Application contact:* Brenda K. Campbell, Director of Graduate Admissions, 334-670-3178, Fax: 334-670-3733, E-mail: bcamp@troy.edu.

Tulane University, School of Public Health and Tropical Medicine, Department of Community Health Sciences, Program in Maternal and Child Health, New Orleans, LA 70118-5669. Offers MPH, Dr PH, MSW/MPH. *Accreditation:* CEPH (one or more programs are accredited). *Degree requirements:* For doctorate, comprehensive exam, thesis/dissertation. *Entrance requirements:* For master's and doctorate, GRE General Test. Additional exam requirements/recommendations for international students: Required—TOEFL.

University of California, Davis, Graduate Studies, Program in Maternal and Child Nutrition, Davis, CA 95616. Offers MAS. *Degree requirements:* For master's, comprehensive exam. *Entrance requirements:* Additional exam requirements/recommendations for international students: Required—TOEFL (minimum score 550 paper-based; 213 computer-based).

University of Maryland, College Park, Academic Affairs, School of Public Health, Department of Family Science, College Park, MD 20742. Offers family studies (PhD); marriage and family therapy (MS); maternal and child health (PhD). *Accreditation:* AAMFT/COAMFTE. Part-time and evening/weekend programs available. *Faculty:* 13 full-time (9 women), 14 part-time/adjunct (12 women). *Students:* 46 full-time (43 women), 2 part-time (both women); includes 13 minority (9 African Americans, 2 Asian Americans or Pacific Islanders, 2 Hispanic Americans), 3 international. 99 applicants, 15% accepted, 14 enrolled. In 2009, 7 master's, 4 doctorates awarded. *Degree requirements:* For master's, thesis or alternative; for doctorate, comprehensive exam, thesis/dissertation, oral defense. *Entrance requirements:* For master's, GRE General Test, minimum GPA of 3.0, 3 letters of recommendation; for doctorate, GRE General Test, minimum GPA of 3.0, 3 letters of recommendation, research sample. *Application deadline:* For fall admission, 12/1 for domestic and international students; for spring admission, 6/1 for international students. Applications are processed on a rolling basis. Application fee: $60. Electronic applications accepted. *Expenses:* Tuition, area resident: Part-time $471 per credit hour. Tuition, state resident: part-time $471 per credit hour. Tuition, nonresident: part-time $1016 per credit hour. Required fees: $337.04 per term. *Financial support:* In 2009–10, 6 fellowships with full and partial tuition reimbursements (averaging $10,021 per year), 40 teaching assistantships with tuition reimbursements (averaging $16,096 per year) were awarded;

Maternal and Child Health

University of Maryland, College Park *(continued)*
research assistantships with tuition reimbursements, career-related internships or fieldwork, Federal Work-Study, and scholarships/grants also available. Support available to part-time students. Financial award applicants required to submit FAFSA. *Faculty research:* Family life quality, interracial couples, child support, homeless families, family and child well-being. Total annual research expenditures: $346,806. *Unit head:* Elaine Anderson, Chairman, 301-405-4009, Fax: 301-314-9161, E-mail: eanders@umd.edu. *Application contact:* Dean of Graduate School, 301-405-0358.

University of Minnesota, Twin Cities Campus, School of Public Health, Major in Maternal and Child Health, Minneapolis, MN 55455-0213. Offers MPH. *Accreditation:* CEPH. Part-time programs available. *Degree requirements:* For master's, fieldwork, project. *Entrance requirements:* For master's, GRE General Test, 1 year of relevant experience. Additional exam requirements/recommendations for international students: Required—TOEFL. Electronic applications accepted. *Expenses:* Contact institution. *Faculty research:* Reproductive and perinatal health, family planning, child adolescent and family health, risk reduction and resiliency, child and family adaptation to chronic health conditions.

University of Mississippi Medical Center, School of Graduate Studies in the Health Sciences, Department of Maternal-Fetal Medicine, Jackson, MS 39216-4505. Offers MS. *Degree requirements:* For master's, thesis. *Entrance requirements:* For master's, status as obstetrician-gynecologist in the Department of Obstetrics and Gynecology's Maternal-Fetal Medicine Fellowship Program.

The University of North Carolina at Chapel Hill, Graduate School, School of Public Health, Department of Maternal and Child Health, Chapel Hill, NC 27599. Offers MPH, MSPH, Dr PH, PhD, MPH/MSW, MSPH/MSW. *Accreditation:* CEPH (one or more programs are accredited). *Degree requirements:* For master's, comprehensive exam, major paper; for doctorate, comprehensive exam, thesis/dissertation. *Entrance requirements:* For master's, GRE General Test or MCAT, minimum GPA of 3.0, paid MHCH-related work experience (preferred); for doctorate, GRE General Test, minimum GPA of 3.0, paid MHCH-related work experience (preferred). Additional exam requirements/recommendations for international students: Required—TOEFL. Electronic applications accepted. *Faculty research:* Women's health, prenatal health, family planning, program evaluation, child health policy and priorities.

University of Puerto Rico, Medical Sciences Campus, Graduate School of Public Health, Program in Maternal and Child Health, San Juan, PR 00936-5067. Offers MPH. Part-time and evening/weekend programs available. *Entrance requirements:* For master's, GRE, previous course work in algebra.

University of Washington, Graduate School, School of Public Health, Department of Epidemiology, Seattle, WA 98195. Offers clinical research (MS); epidemiology (MPH, MS, PhD); global health (MPH); maternal/child health (MPH); nutritional sciences (MPH, MS, PhD); public health genetics (MPH, MS, PhD), including genetic epidemiology (MS), public health genetics (MPH, PhD). *Accreditation:* CEPH (one or more programs are accredited). Part-time programs available. *Faculty:* 66 full-time (40 women), 46 part-time/adjunct (20 women). *Students:* 145 full-time (101 women), 43 part-time (26 women); includes 33 minority (6 African Americans, 1 American Indian/Alaska Native, 18 Asian Americans or Pacific Islanders, 8 Hispanic Americans), 20 international. Average age 32. 236 applicants, 48% accepted, 60 enrolled. In 2009, 44 master's, 16 doctorates awarded. Terminal master's awarded for partial completion of doctoral program. *Degree requirements:* For master's, thesis; for doctorate, comprehensive exam, thesis/dissertation, preliminary exam, original data collection. *Entrance requirements:* For master's, GRE General Test (except applicants with U.S. doctorate); for doctorate, GRE General Test. Additional exam requirements/recommendations for international students: Required—TOEFL (minimum score 580 paper-based; 237 computer-based; 92 iBT) or IELTS (minimum score 7). *Application deadline:* For fall admission, 12/1 for domestic students, 11/1 for international students. Application fee: $50. Electronic applications accepted. *Expenses:* Contact institution. *Financial support:* In 2009–10, 90 fellowships with full tuition reimbursements (averaging $20,976 per year), 43 research assistantships with full tuition reimbursements (averaging $19,668 per year), 12 teaching assistantships with full tuition reimbursements (averaging $16,398 per year) were awarded; career-related internships or fieldwork, Federal Work-Study, institutionally sponsored loans, scholarships/grants, traineeships, health care benefits, unspecified assistantships, and tuition waiver also available. Financial award application deadline: 2/15; financial award applicants required to submit FAFSA. *Faculty research:* Chronic diseases, sexually transmitted diseases, injury, materials and child health, molecular and genetic epidemiology. *Unit head:* Dr. Scott Davis, Chair, 206-543-1065, Fax: 206-543-1065, E-mail: sdavis@fhcrc.org. *Application contact:* Kate O'Brien, Student Services Manager, 206-543-1065, Fax: 206-543-8525, E-mail: apply@u.washington.edu.

HARVARD UNIVERSITY

School of Public Health

Programs of Study	The School of Public Health (HSPH) offers programs leading to the graduate degrees of Master of Public Health (M.P.H.), Doctor of Public Health (D.P.H.), Master of Occupational Health (M.O.H.), Master of Science in a specified field (S.M. in that field), and Doctor of Science in a specified field (S.D. in that field). Doctor of Philosophy (Ph.D.) degrees are offered in specific fields of study through the Graduate School of Arts and Sciences. Programs are offered in biostatistics, environmental health, epidemiology, genetics and complex diseases, global health and population, health policy and management, immunology and infectious diseases, nutrition, occupational health, and society, human development, and health. Some programs are designed for physicians, lawyers, managers, and other health-care professionals; some for college graduates who wish to train for health careers; and others for individuals who hold graduate degrees in medicine, law, business, government, education, and other fields who wish to apply their special skills to public health problems. Special programs include the Master of Science in maternal and child health nursing, administered jointly by HSPH and Simmons College; the combined M.D./M.P.H. program, offered in conjunction with medical schools; and the J.D./M.P.H. joint-degree program offered by HSPH and Harvard Law School. The School offers residency training leading to certification by the American Board of Preventive Medicine in occupational medicine.
Research Facilities	The main buildings of the School are the Sebastian S. Kresge Educational Facilities Building at 677 Huntington Avenue, the François-Xavier Bagnoud Building at 651 Huntington Avenue, and the Health Sciences Laboratories at 665 Huntington Avenue. The School maintains well-equipped research laboratories containing sophisticated instrumentation and supporting animal facilities. Computing and data processing resources are also available to students through the Instructional Computing Facility. The Francis A. Countway Library serves the library needs of the School. It holds more than 630,000 volumes, subscribes to 3,500 current journal titles, and houses over 10,000 noncurrent biomedical journal titles in addition to its extensive collection of historical materials, making it the largest library in the country serving a medical and health-related school.
Financial Aid	Financial aid at the School of Public Health can come from a variety of sources. Some departments have training grants that offer students full tuition plus a stipend. Through need- and merit-based programs at the School and University levels, other students are offered grants that range from half to full tuition. To supplement other aid, many students borrow through one or more of the federal educational loan programs and work at part-time jobs at Harvard and in the community.
Cost of Study	Master's program students are assessed tuition at $876 per credit. Students in a one-year master's program are required to take a minimum of 42.5 credits at $37,230, while a student in a multiple-year master's program typically take 40 credits their first year at $35,040. Doctoral students are assessed a flat tuition rate. The full-time rate for 2010–11 for a student in their first or second year is $35,040. Health insurance, health services, and registration fees are required, and total costs are $3204. Books and supplies cost approximately $1376 in 2010–11.
Living and Housing Costs	For the academic year 2010–11, it is estimated that a single student needs a minimum of $17,294 for housing and living costs: $10,017 for rent and utilities and $7277 for other expenses. Limited housing is available in the Shattuck International House, with preference given to international students. Most students arrange for housing in the adjacent communities.
Student Group	There were 1,067 graduate students (672 women and 395 men) enrolled in 2009–10. Sixty-one nations were represented.
Student Outcomes	Graduates of the Harvard School of Public Health find employment in a variety of settings, depending in part upon their previous experience and in part upon department and degree programs from which they graduate. Recent graduates have found positions in research institutes, with pharmaceutical companies and governmental and nongovernmental agencies, within the health-care industry, and as faculty members of universities.
Location	Boston is a heterogeneous metropolis rich in history and charm. Athletic, cultural, and recreational activities are abundant. The School is within walking distance of museums, colleges and universities, waterways, and parks.
The University and The School	Harvard College was founded in 1636; until the establishment of professorships in medicine in 1782, it composed the whole of the institution now called Harvard University. In addition to the college, ten graduate schools are now part of the University.
	Activity in professional education in the field of public health had been steadily increasing at Harvard University for more than two decades before the actual founding of the School in 1922. The primary mission of the School is to carry out teaching and research aimed at improving the health of population groups throughout the world. The School emphasizes not only the development and implementation of disease prevention and treatment programs but also the planning and management of systems involved in the delivery of health services in this country and abroad. The School cooperates with the Medical School in teaching and research and has close ties with other Harvard faculties. The School has more than 431 full-time and part-time faculty members and nine academic departments representing major biomedical and social disciplines.
Applying	HSPH participates in the Schools of Public Health Application Service (SOPHAS), which is an online, common application service designed to provide a more efficient application process. Students should visit the SOPHAS Web site at http://www.sophas.org for more specific information and for access to the application for admission. All applicants to the School are required to submit scores from the GRE (ETS school code: 3456); applicants are urged to take the test no later than November, since applications are not considered without the scores. Applicants may submit the DAT, GMAT, or MCAT, as appropriate to the applicant's background, in lieu of the GRE. Lawyers applying to the M.P.H. program may submit LSAT scores. Applicants with prior test scores may submit them with their application materials. In addition, applicants must persuade the Committee on Admissions and Degrees of their ability to meet academic standards and of their overall qualifications to undertake advanced study at a graduate level. Students should visit the School's Web site (http://www.hsph.harvard.edu/) for information concerning the deadline to apply for admission and to apply online.
	As a matter of policy, law, and commitment, Harvard University does not discriminate against applicants or students in admission, educational policies, or scholarship and loan programs on the basis of race, religion, sex, sexual orientation, marital or parental status, veteran status, national origin, color, creed, handicap, or age. Members of minority groups are strongly encouraged to apply.
Correspondence and Information	Catalogs and applications: Admissions Office Harvard School of Public Health 158 Longwood Avenue Boston, Massachusetts 02115-5810 Phone: 617-432-1031 Fax: 617-432-7080 E-mail: admisofc@hsph.harvard.edu Web site: http://www.hsph.harvard.edu/	Counseling and program information: Vincent W. James, Director Kerri Noonan, Associate Director Admissions Office Harvard School of Public Health 158 Longwood Avenue Boston, Massachusetts 02115-5810 Phone: 617-432-1031 E-mail: admisofc@hsph.harvard.edu

Harvard University

FACULTY CHAIRS AND DEPARTMENTAL ACTIVITIES

Biostatistics (617-432-1056)
Chair: Victor De Gruttola, Sc.D. The program combines both theory and application of statistical science to analyze public health problems and further biomedical research. Students are prepared for academic and private-sector research careers. Faculty research spans both methodological developments on new statistical techniques and important subject-matter applications that lead to significant advances in the health sciences. Current departmental research on statistical and computing methods for observational studies and clinical trials includes survival analysis, missing-data problems, and causal inference. Other areas of investigation include environmental research; statistical aspects of the study of AIDS and cancer; quantitative problems in health-risk analysis, technology assessment, and clinical decision making; statistical methodology in psychiatric research and in genetic studies; and statistical genetics and computational biology.

Environmental Health (617-432-1270)
Chair: Douglas Dockery, S.D. The mission of the Department of Environmental Health is to advance the health of all people around the world through research and training in environmental health. The department emphasizes the role of air, water, the built environment, and the workplace as critical determinants of health. Faculty members in the department study the pathogenesis and prevention of environmentally produced illnesses and act as catalysts for scientifically based public health advances. Research approaches range from the molecular studies to policy evaluation. Teaching and research activities of the department are carried out through three concentrations: exposure, epidemiology, and risk; occupational health; and molecular and integrative physiological sciences.

Epidemiology (617-432-1050)
Chair: Hans-Olov Adami, M.D., Ph.D. Epidemiology, the study of the frequency, distribution, and determinants of disease in humans, is a fundamental science of public health. Epidemiologists use many approaches, but the ultimate aim of epidemiologic research is the prevention or effective control of human disease. Current research involves the role of viruses in the etiology of cancer; the connection between diet and risk of cancer, cardiovascular disease, and other major chronic diseases; the relationship between exposure to chemicals in the workplace and the development of cancer; the epidemiology of infectious disease; factors in early life predisposing individuals to chronic diseases; and the health effects of drugs and medical devices.

Genetics and Complex Diseases (617-432-0054)
Chair: Gökhan Hotamisligil, M.D., Ph.D. The complex interplay of biological processes with environmental factors as they apply to chronic, multigenic, and multifactorial diseases is the emphasis of the Department of Genetics and Complex Diseases. Research programs in the department focus on molecular mechanisms of adaptive responses to environmental signals to elucidate the mechanisms underlying the intricate interaction between genetic determinants and their divergent responses to stress signals. Alterations in these integrated adaptive mechanisms have a major impact on the health of human populations. The diseases under study include nutritional and metabolic diseases (obesity, diabetes, and cardiovascular diseases), inflammatory bowel disease, cancer, and aging.

Global Health and Population (617-432-1232)
Chair: David Bloom, Ph.D. The department seeks to improve global health through education, research, and service from a population-based perspective. Research interests span a wide spectrum of topics, including social and economic development, health policy, and demography; design and financing of health-care systems; women's health and children's health; and prevention and control of infectious and chronic diseases. The department has a special concern with questions of health equity and human rights, particularly in relation to health and population issues in developing countries.

Health Policy and Management (617-432-1090)
Chair: Arnold Epstein, M.D. The department is mission oriented in its concern with improving the health-care delivery system and mitigating public health risks in the United States and abroad. It is dedicated to resolving major management and health policy problems through original research, advanced training, and dispute resolution. Research priorities are organized into nine broad areas, including health financing and insurance, management of health hazards, study of the causes and etiology of injury, management of health-care organizations, evaluation and management of medical technology, business and labor in health, international health, quality of health care, and health-care reform.

Immunology and Infectious Diseases (617-432-2334)
Chair: Dyann Wirth, Ph.D. The department focuses on the biological, immunological, epidemiological, and ecological aspects of viral, bacterial, protozoan, and helminthic diseases of animals and humans and the vectors that transmit some of these infectious agents. Emphasis is on research identifying basic pathogenic mechanisms that may lead to better diagnostic tools and the development of vaccines as well as the identification of new targets for antiviral and antiparasitic drugs.

Nutrition (617-432-1333)
Chair: Walter C. Willett, M.D., Dr.P.H. The department's mission is to improve human health through research aimed at understanding how diet influences health, the dissemination of new knowledge about nutrition to health professionals and the public, the development of nutritional strategies, and the education of researchers and practitioners. Department research ranges from molecular biology to human studies of cancer and heart disease, including the conduct of population-based intervention trials. Current research covers a wide range of topics, including large prospective studies of dietary factors in relation to heart disease, cancer, diabetes, and ophthalmologic disease; development of methods to assess nutritional status by analysis of body tissue; the interaction of nutritional factors with genetic determinants of disease; and the interaction of nutritional factors and infectious agents.

Society, Human Development, and Health (617-432-1135)
Chair: Ichiro Kawachi, M.D., Ph.D. The mission of the Department of Society, Human Development, and Health is to improve health throughout the lifespan, including a special emphasis on children and adolescents. This mission is achieved through research to identify the social and behavioral determinants of health, development and evaluation of interventions and policies leading to the improvement of population health, and the preparation of professionals and researchers who fill leadership positions in advocacy and public service. The department's educational mission is to train both scholars and practitioners: scholars whose research illuminates basic social determinants of health and who identify and test innovative social policy and service interventions and practitioners who are skilled in designing, implementing, and evaluating health-enhancing interventions in action settings.

Division of Biological Sciences (617-432-4470)
Director: Marianne Wessling-Resnick, Ph.D. The Division of Biological Sciences is an umbrella organization encompassing the HSPH Departments of Environmental Health, Genetics and Complex Diseases, Immunology and Infectious Diseases, and Nutrition. In most of these departments, two doctoral degrees are offered: the Doctor of Philosophy (Ph.D.) and the Doctor of Science (S.D.). The Ph.D. programs generally center on laboratory-based investigation in the biological sciences, whereas the S.D. programs emphasize epidemiological analysis. The Ph.D. programs are administered by the Division of Biological Sciences.

Master of Public Health Program (617-432-0090)
Director: Murray Mittleman, M.D.C.M., M.P.H., D.P.H. The program is designed to provide both a general background and flexibility of specialization in public health. The seven areas of concentration are clinical effectiveness, global health, health and social behavior, health-care management and policy, law and public health, occupational and environmental health, and quantitative methods.

STATE UNIVERSITY OF NEW YORK
DOWNSTATE MEDICAL CENTER
School of Public Health

Program of Study	The School of Public Health (SPH) at the State University of New York (SUNY) Downstate Medical Center offers a Master of Public Health (M.P.H.) degree and a Doctor of Public Health (Dr.P.H.) degree. The SPH has recently expanded to four new departments: Community Health Sciences, Environmental and Occupational Health Sciences, Epidemiology and Biostatistics, and Health Policy and Management, each of which offers M.P.H. and Dr.P.H. degrees. The SPH is intended for students who have completed at least a baccalaureate degree program at an accredited institution and have a strong interest in careers related to public health research and practice. Concurrent degrees with the College of Medicine, College of Nursing, and College of Health Related Professions are also available to interested public health students. Students who attend the program on a part-time basis and take approximately 6 credit hours per semester can expect to complete the Master of Public Health Program in two to four years. In addition to the academic requirements of the program, students must complete a Culminating Experience—a final requirement that integrates the academic theory with a practical public health experience.
Research Facilities	The Health Science Education Building on campus is the central location for one of the largest medical libraries in the United States. The Medical Research Library of Brooklyn offers the resources of more than 200 databases, 600 electronic full-text journals, more than seventy-five electronic books, and a constantly expanding collection of resources as well as the assistance of a professional reference staff. In addition, a Learning Resource Center provides networked workstations with a variety of software programs that access library resources, statistical programs, curriculum materials, e-mail, and the Internet. This building also houses classrooms, laboratories, and an auditorium. Clinical facilities include the University Hospital of Brooklyn, as well as the affiliated Kings County Hospital Center, other affiliated institutions throughout the New York metro area, and several community clinics operated by SUNY Downstate staff members. University Hospital is a major referral center for tertiary care and has one of the largest kidney transplantation programs in the Eastern United States.
Financial Aid	To apply for financial aid, students must be officially admitted and matriculated in a program leading to a degree (nonmatriculated students are not eligible). For the purposes of financial aid, a student must be registered for a minimum of 9 credit hours to be considered full-time. Full-time students are eligible for institutional grants and/or loans. Students registered for fewer than 9 credit hours but at least 5 credit hours are eligible for part-time financial assistance, which only includes loans. To receive assistance from the Tuition Assistance Program (TAP), a student must be registered for at least 12 credit hours; these students may be eligible for other forms of aid, depending on the credit load. Information about financial aid, including federal loans, can be obtained by calling the Office of Financial Aid at 718-270-2488 or by visiting the Web site at http://sls.downstate.edu/financialaid/index.html.
Cost of Study	Current tuition for in-state residents of New York is $349 per credit hour. It is $574 per credit hour for out-of-state residents.
Living and Housing Costs	Living expenses for full-time students attending the Downstate SPH are estimated to be approximately $14,000 per year. Students who choose to live on campus in the dormitories are charged between $2300 and $6000 per semester, depending on the size of accommodations. Additional fees are approximately $500 per year.
Student Group	Students range from faculty physicians, physician's assistants, nurses, occupational therapists, and other health professionals to attorneys, community leaders, and recent undergraduates. Students are racially and ethnically diverse and reflect Brooklyn's many ethnic communities.
Location	Located in the heart of Brooklyn, SUNY Downstate Medical Center was founded in 1860 to help people making their way in the New World by treating health problems carried from the Old. At SUNY Downstate, students live, work, and study in one of the most diverse, dynamic, and vibrant urban environments in the world. Representatives from local, state, and national organizations share their experience and knowledge in lectures, seminars, and the other special events that an international city such as New York provides.
The Medical Center	SUNY Downstate, one of only 125 academic medical centers across the country, has five colleges: Medicine, Nursing, Health Related Professions, Graduate Studies, and the School of Public Health, its most-recent addition. The School of Public Health joins these noted schools to graduate highly trained and community-minded health professionals engaged in public health. The program's faculty includes nationally respected leaders in public health who have distinguished themselves through teaching, research, and service. Located in the heart of Brooklyn, SUNY Downstate offers students the opportunity to live, study, and work in one of the most diverse, dynamic, and vibrant urban environments in the world. Students graduating from this program can expect to understand and deal with many issues facing public health professionals in diverse communities throughout the world.
Applying	Requirements for admission to the M.P.H. degree program are satisfactory completion of a baccalaureate degree from an accredited institution (an undergraduate GPA of 3.0 or better in a 4 point system, is preferred), completion of the Graduate Record Examinations (GRE) or another approved graduate entrance examination within the last five years, and completion of an M.P.H. application, including letters of recommendation, the personal statement, and the public health essay. On the application, applicants may indicate which M.P.H. track they wish to pursue: biostatistics, community health sciences (urban and immigrant health), environmental and occupational health sciences, epidemiology, or health policy and management. Applicants for concurrent degrees with other programs within the medical center must apply to and be accepted by each respective program. The admissions requirements for each respective degree apply. Students applying for concurrent degrees should indicate their intent on each application. Requirements for admission to the Dr.P.H. degree program include satisfactory completion of a Master of Public Health (M.P.H.) degree program or an equivalent master's degree (M.S.W., M.B.A., M.H.S., or other) from an accredited institution (a GPA of 3.5 or better in a 4 point system is preferred) or demonstrated competency in each of the M.P.H. core areas. Note that students accepted without an M.P.H. degree may be required to take additional course work to meet the requirements of the core M.P.H. curriculum in the chosen area of study. Course(s) completed to meet this requirement may not be used to satisfy doctoral course work requirements unless such courses are at the doctoral level. Such decisions are made on an individual basis by each department. Applicants to the Dr.P.H. degree program must also have taken the Graduate Record Examinations (GRE) or another accepted graduate entrance examination within the last five years, must complete a doctoral application including letters of recommendation and personal statement, and participate in an on-site interview with a designated faculty member. On the application, applicants must indicate which track they wish to pursue: community health sciences (urban and immigrant health), environmental and occupational health sciences, epidemiology, or health policy and management. The SUNY Downstate SPH applications for both the M.P.H. and Dr.P.H. degree programs are available and can be completed online. Supporting application documents should be sent to the Office of Admissions at SUNY Downstate Office of Admissions, 450 Clarkson Avenue, Box 60, Brooklyn, New York, 11203-2098; telephone: 718-270-2446. Further information about the programs and admission requirements is available on the University's Web site: http://www.downstate.edu/publichealth, or can be obtained by calling 718-270-1065 to speak to one of the Student Affairs staff members. The SPH accepts M.P.H. students in the summer and fall semesters of each calendar year. Deadlines for applications are February 15 for the summer semester and April 15 for the fall semester. M.D./M.P.H. students are accepted in the summer semester only. The deadline for M.D./M.P.H. applications is May 15. M.D./M.P.H. applicants must submit M.P.H. applications directly to the SUNY Downstate Office of Admissions. American Medical College Application Service (AMCAS) applications must be submitted according to the instructions for that application. The SPH accepts Dr.P.H. students in the fall semester only. The deadline for applications is April 15.
Correspondence and Information	School of Public Health State University of New York Downstate Medical Center 450 Clarkson Avenue, Box 43 Brooklyn, New York 11203-2098 Phone: 718-270-1065 Fax: 718-270-2533 E-mail: publichealth@downstate.edu Web site: http://www.downstate.edu/publichealth

State University of New York Downstate Medical Center

THE FACULTY AND THEIR RESEARCH

Pascal James Imperato, M.D., M.P.H. & T.M., Dean and Distinguished Service Professor. Served for six years as a medical epidemiologist for the Centers for Disease Control and Prevention in West Africa, directing mass immunization campaigns against smallpox, measles, yellow fever, cholera, and meningococcal meningitis; awarded the Meritorious Honor Award and Medal by the U.S. Department of State for his work in Africa; served as Commissioner of Health of New York City and Chair of the Board, New York City Health and Hospitals Corporation.

Emmanuel A. Anum, Ph.D., M.P.H., Assistant Professor in the Department of Epidemiology and Biostatistics. Previously worked as an epidemiologist with the Virginia Department of Health; his current research focuses on adverse birth outcomes among minority and disadvantaged populations in the United States. Other interests include prostate cancer and cardiovascular epidemiology.

Philippe Amstislavski, M.Arch., M.E.M., RN, Assistant Professor in the Department of Environmental and Occupational Health Sciences. His research focuses on developing spatial analysis approaches that fully include the role of behavioral, socioeconomic, and environmental variables in the study of health outcomes. His interest centers on geostatistical modeling and analysis in environmental and occupational health research.

Abraham Aragones, M.D., M.S.C.I., Assistant Professor of Community Health Sciences. His areas of research include immigrant populations and cancer, health disparities, and chronic care in these populations; colorectal cancer screening among Latinos; cancer-screening referrals among immigrants; and impact of the Chronic Care Model in the Latino immigrant population.

Karen Benker, M.D., M.P.H., Associate Dean for Community Public Health Affairs, Voluntary Attending Physician in Family Practice, and Founder and Director, Downstate's Freedom from Tobacco Project. Her research focuses on delivering primary care to inner city and immigrant populations, research and intervention on HIV-related issues, and smoking cessation.

Howard S. Berliner, Sc.D., Professor in the Department of Health Policy and Management. He has served as the Assistant State Health Commissioner for research, policy, and planning for New Jersey. His current research focuses on the needs of vulnerable populations and access to health services for the uninsured and the future of the hospital in the health care delivery system.

Denise Bruno, M.D., M.P.H., Assistant Professor of Community Health Sciences and Co-Director of the fourth-year medical student elective, Health Care in Developing Countries. Her research includes general pediatric public health issues such as immunization, asthma, perinatal hepatitis B, lead poisoning prevention, and newborn screening.

Daniel Ehlke, Ph.D., Assistant Professor in the Department of Health Policy and Management. His research focus is on recent reform episodes in the American and British health-care systems; of particular interest is the balance struck between the conflicting values associated with citizenship and consumerism, and how this shapes the contours of specific national (and subnational) reforms.

Laura Geer, Ph.D., Assistant Professor of Environmental and Occupational Health Sciences and former consultant for U.S. Environmental Protection Agency and Exposure Measurements and Analysis Branch (EMAB) at the National Exposure Research Laboratory (NERL). Her research focuses on worker dermal exposure to chemicals, environmental perinatal exposures, and infant morbidity and mortality outcomes.

Mira M. Grice, Ph.D., Assistant Professor of Environmental and Occupational Health Sciences. Her research currently involves examining how work/family conflict impacts the mental and physical health of women following childbirth. Her interests include environmental and occupational health policy, women's health, injury epidemiology, global health, and survey design.

Dr. Florence Kavaler, M.D., M.P.H., Professor and Associate Dean for Research Administration in the School of Public Health and Downstate Medical Center College of Medicine. Formerly Assistant Surgeon General and Director of the U.S. Public Health Service Hospital, Staten Island, New York; she is currently Chair of the New York State Board for Medicine.

Michael A. Joseph, Ph.D., M.P.H., Assistant Professor of Epidemiology and Biostatistics. His areas of research include chronic disease epidemiology; epidemiology of benign prostatic hyperplasia (BPH) and lower urinary tract symptoms (LUTS); morbidity in African American men; and social epidemiology, particularly issues of behavioral and cultural determinants of cancer screening practices among communities of color.

Paul Landsbergis, Ph.D., M.P.H., Ed.D., Associate Professor of Environmental and Occupational Health Sciences. His research focuses on socioeconomic position, work organization, work stress, hypertension, cardiovascular disease, psychological disorders, and musculoskeletal disorders.

Judith H. LaRosa, Ph.D., RN, Professor and Vice Dean. Was first Deputy Director of the National Institutes of Health's Office of Research on Women's Health; Professor and Chair, Department of Community Health Sciences, Tulane University School of Public Health and Tropical Medicine; and Director, Tulane Xavier National Center of Excellence in Women's Health. Her research interests encompass cultural competency, women's health, and cardiovascular disease.

Camille Ragin, M.P.H., Ph.D., Associate Professor in the Department of Epidemiology. Her research focuses on cancer mortality rates in developing countries and among populations of African descent, and infectious diseases and microbiology as important public health issues.

Rebecca Schwartz, Ph.D., Assistant Professor of Preventive Medicine and Community Health. Her research focuses on the role of psychosocial and behavioral factors in health promotion and risk prevention among low-income urban populations; clinical work with children, adolescents, and families; and therapeutic interventions for youth who are HIV-positive.

Jeanne Mager Stellman, Ph.D., Professor of Environmental and Occupational Health Sciences and Associate Dean for Research. Her research focuses on occupational and environmental health, particularly on Agent Orange exposure for Vietnam veterans. She served as editor-in-chief for the fourth edition of *ILO Encyclopaedia Occupational Safety & Health,* and editor for *Women and Health,* 1986–2004.

Michael Szarek, Ph.D., Associate Professor and Chair of the Department of Epidemiology and Biostatistics. He has been involved in the design, conduct, and analysis of several late-stage cardiovascular and oncology clinical trials. These activities have included supporting steering committees and data safety monitoring committees and interactions with worldwide regulatory agencies. He also has interests in worldwide regulatory policies and strategies for the design and conduct of clinical trials.

Emanuela Taioli, M.D., Ph.D., Professor in the Department of Biostatistics and Epidemiology. Dr. Taioli has conducted extensive studies on genetic susceptibility to environmental factors in lung and breast cancer, and differences in estrogen metabolism with ethnicity in women. Her research specialties include cardiology, cancer epidemiology and prevention, genetic susceptibility to environmental carcinogens, and population science.

Michal Tamuz, Ph.D., Associate Professor in the Department of Health Policy and Management. Her research interests include improving patient safety, health-care quality improvement, and organizational change; current research is focused on improving the quality and safety of medication management.

Tracey E. Wilson, Ph.D., Associate Professor of Community Health Sciences. Her research focuses on prevention of unintended pregnancy, STDs, HIV, and other health-related issues among women living in inner city areas of New York City; sexual and contraceptive behaviors of HIV infected and uninfected women; and issues associated with medication adherence.

For a listing of part-time faculty, please see the school's Web site at: http://www.downstate.edu/publichealth

UNIVERSITY OF SOUTHERN CALIFORNIA

Institute for Health Promotion and Disease Prevention Research
Master of Public Health Program

Program of Study

The Keck School of Medicine at the University of Southern California (USC) offers the Master of Public Health (M.P.H.) degree. The mission of the M.P.H. Program is to assist in creating healthy communities by preparing graduates to lead and collaborate with others in organized community efforts across a variety of settings, focusing on disease prevention and health promotion among diverse populations. The program addresses behavioral theory, intervention strategies, and evaluation procedures for community health promotion and primary and secondary prevention. The program is built upon the strength of its faculty members, who are world leaders in the implementation and evaluation of school- and community-based health promotion programs. Faculty members command expertise in substance use prevention, unhealthful patterns of diet and physical activity, HIV/AIDS, cancer, and cardiovascular disease. Faculty members also specialize in developing culturally tailored public health interventions.

The M.P.H. is a 47-unit program designed to give students a solid foundation in the core areas of public health theory, research, and practice. Students begin with five core courses and then pursue an area of concentrated study from one of five tracks: health promotion, biostatistics/epidemiology, health communication, child and family health, and global health leadership. To integrate concepts and skills gained in the academic program, students complete a supervised field training experience in an area of public health practice within a county, state, federal, community-based agency, or University-sponsored research project. The M.P.H. Program accommodates the needs of both full-time and part-time students. Program requirements may be completed in one year full-time or within two to four years part-time. Four dual-degree programs are available with the Schools of Psychology (Ph.D./M.P.H.), Medicine (M.D./M.P.H.), Pharmacy (Pharm.D./M.P.H.), and Physical Therapy (D.P.T./M.P.H.).

Research Facilities

Founded in 1880, USC is the oldest and largest private research university in the American West, ranking among the top ten research universities in the nation, based on federal research and development support. M.P.H. students have access to USC's numerous libraries, including the comprehensive Norris Medical Library and the Institute's own dedicated library. The Institute offers extensive research opportunities in tobacco use prevention and cessation, alcohol and drug abuse prevention, physical activity and nutrition, obesity, cancer and diabetes control and prevention, gender and cultural issues in health promotion, cardiovascular disease epidemiology and prevention, health communication, prevention of HIV/STDs, dissemination of prevention technologies, and prevention policy.

Financial Aid

Applicants pursing federal and private financial aid, grants, scholarships, and fellowships are strongly encouraged to contact the USC Keck School of Medicine Financial Aid Office at http://www.usc.edu/keckfao.

Cost of Study

Based on the 2009–10 academic year, the following are estimated two-semester costs at USC for a full-time master's student (8–14 units) living in University or non-University housing (not with parents or relatives, other than a spouse): $32,600 for tuition and fees, $20,928 for room and board, $1036 for books and supplies, $1828 for personal and miscellaneous expenses, and $2250 for transportation, for a total estimated cost of $58,642. Students should also add $30 for the orientation fee in their first semester at USC. Tuition costs vary by course load.

Living and Housing Costs

Off-campus apartment and housing rental rates vary widely by community, ranging from $800 to $2000 per month for a one-bedroom unit.

Student Group

The M.P.H. Program maintains an enrollment of approximately 200 students each semester. The student population is ethnically diverse: African American (9 percent), Hispanic/Latino (11 percent), Asian/Pacific Islander (29 percent), Native American (1 percent), and non-Hispanic white (34 percent). Women make up 70 percent of the student body, while the international student population accounts for 16 percent; 70 percent of students are full-time.

Student Outcomes

Program graduates are trained to assess health needs of individuals and communities; design, implement, and evaluate effective health promotion interventions; coordinate and manage collaborative programs in health service provision; and communicate with leaders in government and industry about public health policy. Postgraduate placements include governmental agencies (14 percent), health-care organizations (9 percent), nonprofits (13 percent), private practice (3 percent), and universities (24 percent). Nearly 30 percent of graduates pursue further education.

Location

Program offices, classrooms, and the Institute for Prevention Research (IPR) library are located at the USC Health Sciences Campus, Alhambra, a business park–like complex in the San Gabriel Valley. The city of Alhambra is a multicultural community, just minutes from USC's University Park and Health Sciences–Los Angeles Campuses. M.P.H. classes are also held at the Health Sciences and University Park Campuses. Shuttle buses connect the Alhambra Campus with neighboring campuses.

The University and The Program

The program is currently ranked twelfth among all U.S. public health programs, according to *U.S. News & World Report*. The M.P.H. Program is proud to exemplify the excellence in academics, research, and community involvement that earned USC its recognition as "College of the Year" in 2000. In 2008, USC was recognized by the *Chronicle of Higher Education* as having the fourth most productive public health faculty in the U.S. The M.P.H. Program is accredited by the Council on Education in Public Health.

Applying

The M.P.H. Program accepts applicants for fall, spring, and summer semesters. The fall application deadline is June 15. Spring application deadlines are November 15 for domestic applicants and October 15 for international applicants. The summer application deadline is February 15. Admissions requirements include the University graduate application; the M.P.H. supplemental application; a bachelor's degree from an accredited university, with a minimum cumulative GPA of 3.0; official transcripts from each college or university attended; Graduate Record Examinations (GRE) scores of at least 1000 (verbal/quantitative combined); a personal statement; three letters of recommendation (must include one academic reference); and a curriculum vitae or resume. The Test of English as a Foreign Language (TOEFL), with a minimum Internet-based score of 100 (equivalent to a computer score of 250 and paper score of 600), is required of international students.

Correspondence and Information

Oralia Gonzales, Program Manager
M.P.H. Program
Keck School of Medicine
University of Southern California/IPR
1000 South Fremont Avenue
Building A-5, Suite 5128
Alhambra, California 91803
Phone: 626-457-6676
E-mail: mphusc@usc.edu
Web site: http://www.usc.edu/medicine/mph

Financial Aid Office
Keck School of Medicine
Health Science Campus
University of Southern California
1975 Zonal Avenue, KAM B-22
Los Angeles, California 90089-9033
Phone: 323-442-1016
Fax: 323-442-2943
Web site: http://www.usc.edu/keckfao

University of Southern California

THE FACULTY AND THEIR RESEARCH

Unless otherwise noted, all faculty members are in the Department of Preventive Medicine at the Keck School of Medicine.

Stanley P. Azen, Ph.D., Professor and Co-Director, Biometry/Biostatistics Division. Biostatistical methodology with applications in the areas of atherosclerosis and cardiovascular disease, ophthalmology, diabetes, and gerontology. (sazen@usc.edu)

Lourdes Baezconde-Garbanati, Ph.D., M.P.H., Associate Professor, Preventive Medicine and Sociology. Cancer control research with special emphasis on minority populations. (baezcond@usc.edu)

Alex Y. Chen, M.D., Assistant Professor, Pediatrics and Preventive Medicine. Access and utilization of health-care services, inequalities in medical expenditures by socioeconomic factors, as well as other issues related to health and health-care disparities. (achen@chla.usc.edu)

Myles Cockburn, Ph.D., Assistant Professor. Epidemiology of melanoma, gastric cancer, and *Helicobacter;* computational methods pertaining to epidemiology; genetic and environmental aspects of disease using twins; geographical information systems (GIS) and their application to epidemiology. (cockburn@usc.edu).

Michael Cousineau, Dr.P.H., Associate Professor, Family Medicine. Issues that impact public health, in particular, access to primary care for the low-income uninsured; impact of privatization on safety-net providers, including public hospitals and community-based clinics and health centers; vulnerable populations. (cousinea@usc.edu)

Wendy Cozen, D.O., M.P.H., Professor. Epidemiology of hematologic neoplasms, particularly Hodgkin's disease, non-Hodgkin's lymphoma, and multiple myeloma; analysis of cancer clusters. (wcozen@usc.edu)

N. Tess Boley Cruz, Ph.D., M.P.H., Assistant Professor. Public health communications research, antitobacco media and pro-tobacco marketing effects. (tesscruz@usc.edu)

Jaimie Davis, Ph.D., Assistant Professor, Preventative Medicine. Designing and disseminating nutrition, physical activity, and behavioral interventions to reduce obesity and related metabolic disorders in overweight adolescents. (jaimieda@usc.edu)

William J. Gauderman, Ph.D., Professor. Biostatistical methodology, statistical methods for genetic-epidemiological analysis of pedigree data, design and analysis of studies relating health outcomes to environmental exposures. (jimg@usc.edu)

Carol Koprowski, Ph.D., RD, Assistant Professor. Diet and nutrition, relationship between diet and physical activity among adolescent girls, nutrition for dialysis patients and those with diabetes. (koprowsk@usc.edu)

Rob McConnell, M.D., Professor. Epidemiology of respiratory disease in children, studies examining causes of asthma and its relationship with indoor and outdoor air pollution. (rmcconne@usc.edu)

Roberta McKean-Cowdin, Ph.D., Assistant Professor. Epidemiology of breast cancer, including the role of endogenous sex hormones and hormone replacement therapy; epidemiology of childhood brain tumors, including developmental genetics. (mckeanco@usc.edu)

Louise Ann Rohrbach, Ph.D., M.P.H., Associate Professor. Community-based interventions for disease prevention and health promotion, with emphasis on interventions for prevention of tobacco, alcohol, and other drug abuse. (rohrbac@usc.edu)

Jonathan Samet, MD, M.S., Professor and Flora L. Thornton Chair, Department of Preventive Medicine. Cancer epidemiology, air pollution, health consequences of active and passive smoking, respiratory disease prevention, risk assessment and public policy. (jsamet@usc.edu)

Kimberly D. Siegmund, Ph.D., Associate Professor. Statistical methods for genetic-epidemiology studies. (kims@usc.edu)

Donna Spruijt-Metz, Ph.D., Assistant Professor. Adolescent health, particularly in the areas of physical activity and obesity. (dmetz@usc.edu)

Gregory D. Stevens, Ph.D., Assistant Professor, Center of Community Health Studies (CCHS). Quality of primary health care for vulnerable children and families, racial/ethnic and socioeconomic disparities in care, and patient-provider relations issues involved in the delivery of preventive care.

Ping Sun, Ph.D., Assistant Professor. Technology-facilitated interventions to prevent behavioral risk factors of cardiovascular disease and cancer (e.g., cigarette smoking and obesity). (sping@usc.edu)

Thomas W. Valente, Ph.D., Associate Professor and Director, M.P.H. Program. Evaluation of health promotion and substance abuse prevention programs, application of social network analysis and mathematical models to health-related behavior. (tvalente@usc.edu)

Heather Wipfli, Ph.D.; Assistant Professor. Global tobacco control, capacity building in developing countries, globalization and health, health security. (hwipfli@usc.edu)

The USC Institute for Health Promotion and Disease Prevention Research.

ACADEMIC AND PROFESSIONAL
PROGRAMS IN LAW

Section 32
Law

This section contains a directory of institutions offering graduate work in law, followed by in-depth entries submitted by institutions that chose to prepare detailed program descriptions. Additional information about programs listed in the directory but not augmented by an in-depth entry may be obtained by writing directly to the dean of a graduate school or chair of a department at the address given in the directory.

For programs offering related work, see also in this book *Business Administration and Management* and *Social Work*. In the other guides in this series:

Graduate Programs in the Humanities, Arts & Social Sciences
See *Criminology and Forensics; Public, Regional, and Industrial Affairs; Economics;* and *Political Science and International Affairs*

Graduate Programs in the Physical Sciences, Mathematics, Agricultural Sciences, the Environment & Natural Resources
See *Environmental Sciences and Management*

Graduate Programs in Engineering & Applied Sciences
See *Management of Engineering and Technology*

CONTENTS

Program Directories

Environmental Law

Chapman University, Graduate Studies, School of Law, Orange, CA 92866. Offers advocacy and dispute resolution (JD); entertainment law (JD); environmental, land use, and real estate (JD); international law (JD); law (LL M), including business law and economics, entertainment and media law, international and comparative law; prosecutorial science (LL M); tax law (JD); taxation (LL M); JD/MBA; JD/MFA. *Accreditation:* ABA. Part-time and evening/weekend programs available. *Faculty:* 56 full-time (21 women), 24 part-time/adjunct (4 women). *Students:* 535 full-time (260 women), 87 part-time (37 women); includes 126 minority (6 African Americans, 2 American Indian/Alaska Native, 79 Asian Americans or Pacific Islanders, 39 Hispanic Americans), 6 international. Average age 27. 2,996 applicants, 32% accepted, 226 enrolled. In 2009, 158 JDs, 7 master's awarded. *Entrance requirements:* LSAT, minimum undergraduate GPA of 2.75. Additional exam requirements/recommendations for international students: Required—TOEFL (minimum score 600 paper-based; 213 computer-based; 80 iBT). *Application deadline:* For fall admission, 4/1 priority date for domestic students. Applications are processed on a rolling basis. Application fee: $65. Electronic applications accepted. *Expenses:* Contact institution. *Financial support:* Fellowships, Federal Work-Study and scholarships/grants available. Financial award application deadline: 6/30; financial award applicants required to submit FAFSA. *Unit head:* Dr. John Eastman, Dean, 714-628-2500. *Application contact:* Marissa Vargas, Admissions Recruiter/Financial Aid Counselor, 877-CHAPLAW, E-mail: mvargas@chapman.edu.

Florida State University, College of Law, Tallahassee, FL 32306-1601. Offers American law for foreign lawyers (LL M); enviromental law and policy (LL M); JD/MBA; JD/MPA; JD/MS; JD/MSP; JD/MSW. *Accreditation:* ABA. *Faculty:* 43 full-time (19 women), 28 part-time/adjunct (6 women). *Students:* 763 full-time (314 women); includes 131 minority (64 African Americans, 3 American Indian/Alaska Native, 14 Asian Americans or Pacific Islanders, 50 Hispanic Americans), 1 international. Average age 24. 3,315 applicants, 26% accepted, 244 enrolled. In 2009, 264 JDs awarded. *Degree requirements:* For JD, upper-level writing, skills training, and pro-bono requirements. *Entrance requirements:* LSAT. Additional exam requirements/recommendations for international students: Required—TOEFL (minimum score 600 paper-based; 250 computer-based; 100 iBT). *Application deadline:* For fall admission, 4/1 priority date for domestic students. Applications are processed on a rolling basis. Application fee: $30. Electronic applications accepted. *Expenses:* Contact institution. *Financial support:* In 2009–10, 276 students received support, including 276 fellowships (averaging $2,000 per year), 58 research assistantships (averaging $3,300 per year), 12 teaching assistantships (averaging $1,034 per year); scholarships/grants also available. Financial award application deadline: 2/1; financial award applicants required to submit FAFSA. *Faculty research:* Law, business andeconomics; environmental and land use; international; criminal. *Unit head:* Donald J. Weidner, Dean, 850-644-3400, Fax: 850-644-5487, E-mail: dweidner@law.fsu.edu. *Application contact:* Jennifer L. Kessinger, Director of Admissions and Records, 850-644-3787, Fax: 850-644-7284, E-mail: jkessing@law.fsu.edu.

Golden Gate University, School of Law, San Francisco, CA 94105-2968. Offers environmental law (LL M); intellectual property law (LL M); international legal studies (LL M, SJD); law (JD); taxation (LL M); U.S. legal studies (LL M); JD/MBA; JD/PhD. *Accreditation:* ABA. Part-time and evening/weekend programs available. *Degree requirements:* For doctorate, thesis/dissertation. *Entrance requirements:* LSAT. Additional exam requirements/recommendations for international students: Required—TOEFL (minimum score 600 paper-based; 250 computer-based). Electronic applications accepted. *Expenses:* Contact institution. *Faculty research:* International law, intellectual property law, environmental law, real estate, civil rights.

Lewis & Clark College, Lewis & Clark Law School, Portland, OR 97203. Offers environmental and natural resources law (LL M); law (JD). *Accreditation:* ABA. Part-time and evening/weekend programs available. *Entrance requirements:* LSAT. Additional exam requirements/recommendations for international students: Recommended—TOEFL (minimum score 600 paper-based; 250 computer-based). Electronic applications accepted. *Expenses:* Contact institution.

Pace University, School of Law, White Plains, NY 10603. Offers comparative legal studies (LL M); environmental law (LL M, SJD); law (JD); real estate law (LL M); JD/MA; JD/MBA; JD/MEM; JD/MPA; JD/MS. *Accreditation:* ABA. Part-time and evening/weekend programs available. *Faculty:* 41 full-time (18 women), 52 part-time/adjunct (23 women). *Students:* 582 full-time (326 women), 230 part-time (145 women); includes 136 minority (33 African Americans, 1 American Indian/Alaska Native, 53 Asian Americans or Pacific Islanders, 49 Hispanic Americans), 17 international. Average age 26. 3,048 applicants, 38% accepted, 263 enrolled. In 2009, 216 first professional degrees, 20 master's, 1 doctorate awarded. *Entrance requirements:* LSAT. Additional exam requirements/recommendations for international students: Required—TOEFL (minimum score 600 paper-based; 250 computer-based); Recommended—TWE. *Application deadline:* For fall admission, 3/1 priority date for domestic students; for winter admission, 11/1 priority date for domestic students. Applications are processed on a rolling basis. Application fee: $65. Electronic applications accepted. *Expenses:* Contact institution. *Financial support:* Career-related internships or fieldwork, Federal Work-Study, institutionally sponsored loans, and scholarships/grants available. Support available to part-time students. Financial award application deadline: 2/15; financial award applicants required to submit FAFSA. *Faculty research:* Reform of energy regulations, international law, land use law, prosecutorial misconduct, corporation law, international sale of goods. Total annual research expenditures: $2.2 million. *Unit head:* Michelle S. Simon, Dean, 914-422-4407, E-mail: msimon@law.pace.edu. *Application contact:* Cathy Alexander, Assistant Dean, 914-422-4210, Fax: 914-989-8714, E-mail: calexander@law.pace.edu.

See Close-Up on page 1701.

University of Calgary, Faculty of Law, Programs in Natural Resources, Energy and Environmental Law, Calgary, AB T2N 1N4, Canada. Offers LL M, Graduate Certificate. *Entrance requirements:* Additional exam requirements/recommendations for international students: Required—TOEFL.

University of Florida, Levin College of Law, Gainesville, FL 32611. Offers comparative law (LL M); environmental law (LL M); international taxation (LL M); law (JD); taxation (LL M, SJD). *Accreditation:* ABA. *Faculty:* 77 full-time (37 women), 36 part-time/adjunct (10 women). *Students:* 1,369 full-time (620 women); includes 279 minority (69 African Americans, 8 American Indian/Alaska Native, 77 Asian Americans or Pacific Islanders, 125 Hispanic Americans), 71 international. Average age 24. 3,170 applicants, 25% accepted, 307 enrolled. In 2009, 497 JDs, 1 doctorate awarded. *Degree requirements:* For JD, thesis/dissertation or alternative. *Entrance requirements:* LSAT. Additional exam requirements/recommendations for international students: Required—TOEFL (minimum score 250 computer-based; 100 iBT). *Application deadline:* For fall admission, 1/15 for domestic and international students. Applications are processed on a rolling basis. Application fee: $30. Electronic applications accepted. *Expenses:* Contact institution. *Financial support:* In 2009–10, 299 students received support, including 25 fellowships (averaging $2,400 per year), 30 research assistantships with partial tuition reimbursements available (averaging $4,125 per year); career-related internships or fieldwork, Federal Work-Study, institutionally sponsored loans, scholarships/grants, traineeships, health care benefits, and unspecified assistantships also available. Financial award application deadline: 4/7; financial award applicants required to submit FAFSA. *Faculty research:* Environmental and land use law, taxation, family law, international law, constitutional law. *Unit head:* Robert Jerry, Dean, 352-273-0600, Fax: 352-392-8727, E-mail: jerryr@law.ufl.edu. *Application contact:* Michelle Adorno, Assistant Dean for Admissions, 352-273-0890, Fax: 352-392-4087, E-mail: madorno@law.ufl.edu.

University of Pittsburgh, School of Law, Master of Studies in Law Program, Pittsburgh, PA 15260. Offers business law (MSL), including commercial law, corporate law, general business law, international business, tax law; constitutional law (MSL); criminal law and justice (MSL); disabilities law (MSL); dispute resolution (MSL); education law (MSL); elder and estate planning law (MSL); employment and labor law (MSL); environment and real estate law (MSL); family law (MSL); general law and jurisprudence (MSL); health law (MSL); intellectual property and technology (MSL); international and comparative law (MSL); personal injury and civil litigation (MSL); regulatory law (MSL); self-designed (MSL); sports and entertainment law (MSL). Part-time programs available. *Faculty:* 43 full-time (16 women), 104 part-time/adjunct (30 women). *Students:* 3 full-time (2 women), 12 part-time (7 women); includes 3 minority (2 African Americans, 1 Asian American or Pacific Islander). Average age 31. 26 applicants, 58% accepted, 11 enrolled. In 2009, 9 master's awarded. *Entrance requirements:* Additional exam requirements/recommendations for international students: Required—TOEFL (minimum score 600 paper-based; 250 computer-based; 100 iBT). *Application deadline:* For fall admission, 6/30 for domestic students, 5/1 for international students. Applications are processed on a rolling basis. Application fee: $0. *Expenses:* Tuition, state resident: full-time $16,402; part-time $665 per credit. Tuition, nonresident: full-time $28,694; part-time $1175 per credit. Required fees: $690; $175 per term. Tuition and fees vary according to program. *Faculty research:* Law, health law, business law, contracts, intellectual property. *Unit head:* Prof. Alan Meisel, Director, 412-648-1384, Fax: 412-648-2649, E-mail: meisel@pitt.edu. *Application contact:* Bethann Pischke, Administrative Coordinator, 412-648-7120, Fax: 412-648-2649, E-mail: pischke@pitt.edu.

University of Pittsburgh, School of Law, Program in Environmental Law, Science and Policy, Pittsburgh, PA 15260. Offers Certificate. *Faculty:* 43 full-time (16 women), 104 part-time/adjunct (30 women). *Students:* 26 full-time (15 women). *Expenses:* Tuition, state resident: full-time $16,402; part-time $665 per credit. Tuition, nonresident: full-time $28,694; part-time $1175 per credit. Required fees: $690; $175 per term. Tuition and fees vary according to program. *Unit head:* Jennifer L. Poller, Director, 412-648-1408, Fax: 412-624-4843, E-mail: poller@pitt.edu. *Application contact:* Charmaine McCall, Assistant Dean of Admissions and Financial Aid, 412-648-1413, Fax: 412-648-1318, E-mail: cmccall@pitt.edu.

University of Tulsa, College of Law, Tulsa, OK 74104. Offers American Indian and indigenous law (LL M); American law for foreign lawyers (LL M); comparative and international law (Certificate); entrepreneurial law (Certificate); health law (Certificate); law (JD); Native American law (Certificate); public policy (Certificate); resources, energy, and environmental law (Certificate); JD/M Tax; JD/MA; JD/MBA; JD/MS; JD/MSF. *Accreditation:* ABA. Part-time programs available. *Faculty:* 29 full-time (14 women), 24 part-time/adjunct (8 women). *Students:* 382 full-time (148 women), 40 part-time (16 women); includes 68 minority (4 African Americans, 40 American Indian/Alaska Native, 12 Asian Americans or Pacific Islanders, 12 Hispanic Americans), 1 international. Average age 28. 1,304 applicants, 51% accepted, 140 enrolled. In 2009, 149 first professional degrees, 1 master's awarded. *Entrance requirements:* For JD, LSAT, BS or BA from accredited college/university; for master's, JD or equivalent from non-US university. Additional exam requirements/recommendations for international students: Required—TOEFL (minimum score 570 paper-based; 230 computer-based; 90 iBT), IELTS (minimum score 7). *Application deadline:* For fall admission, 2/1 priority date for domestic and international students. Applications are processed on a rolling basis. Application fee: $30. Electronic applications accepted. *Expenses:* Contact institution. *Financial support:* In 2009–10, 176 students received support. Career-related internships or fieldwork, Federal Work-Study, and scholarships/grants available. Support available to part-time students. Financial award applicants required to submit FAFSA. *Faculty research:* International law, Native American law, criminal law, commercial speech, copyright law. *Unit head:* Janet Levit, Dean, 918-631-2400, Fax: 918-631-3126, E-mail: janet-levit@utulsa.edu. *Application contact:* April M. Fox, Assistant Dean of Admissions and Financial Aid, 918-631-2406, Fax: 918-631-3630, E-mail: april-fox@utulsa.edu.

Vermont Law School, Law School, Environmental Law Center, South Royalton, VT 05068-0096. Offers LL M, MELP, JD/MELP. Part-time programs available. *Faculty:* 11 full-time (3 women), 13 part-time/adjunct (7 women). *Students:* 38 full-time (20 women), 2 part-time (1 woman); includes 1 Asian American or Pacific Islander, 1 Hispanic American. Average age 30. 86 applicants, 88% accepted, 40 enrolled. In 2009, 65 master's awarded. *Entrance requirements:* Additional exam requirements/recommendations for international students: Required—TOEFL. *Application deadline:* For fall admission, 3/1 priority date for domestic students. Applications are processed on a rolling basis. Application fee: $60. *Expenses:* Tuition: Full-time $40,420. *Financial support:* In 2009–10, 2 fellowships with full tuition reimbursements (averaging $5,000 per year) were awarded; career-related internships or fieldwork, Federal Work-Study, institutionally sponsored loans, scholarships/grants, and tuition waivers (partial) also available. Support available to part-time students. Financial award application deadline: 3/1; financial award applicants required to submit FAFSA. *Faculty research:* Environment and technology; takings; international environmental law; interaction among science, law, and environmental policy; air pollution. Total annual research expenditures: $52,000. *Unit head:* Marc Mihaly, Associate Dean, 802-831-1342, Fax: 802-763-2490, E-mail: admiss@vermontlaw.edu. *Application contact:* Anne Mansfield, Associate Director, 802-831-1338, Fax: 802-763-2940, E-mail: admiss@vermontlaw.edu.

Health Law

Boston University, School of Public Health, Health Law, Bioethics and Human Rights Department, Boston, MA 02215. Offers MPH. Part-time and evening/weekend programs available. *Students:* 10 full-time (4 women), 7 part-time (5 women); includes 3 minority (2 Asian Americans or Pacific Islanders, 1 Hispanic American), 1 international. Average age 27. *Entrance requirements:* For master's, GRE, MCAT, LSAT, GMAT, DAT. Additional exam requirements/recommendations for international students: Required—TOEFL (minimum score 600 paper-based; 250 computer-based; 100 iBT) or IELTS (minimum score 6). *Application deadline:* For fall admission, 2/1 priority date for domestic and international students; for spring admission, 10/15 priority date for domestic and international students. Applications are processed on a rolling basis. Application fee: $95. Electronic applications accepted. *Expenses:* Tuition: Full-time $37,910; part-time $1184 per credit hour. Required fees: $386; $40 per semester. Part-time tuition and fees vary according to class time, course level, degree level and program. *Financial support:* In 2009–10, 1 fellowship was awarded; career-related internships or fieldwork, Federal Work-Study, institutionally sponsored loans, scholarships/grants, and tuition waivers (partial) also available. Support available to part-time students. Financial award application deadline: 3/1; financial award applicants required to submit FAFSA. *Unit head:* Prof. George Annas, Chair, 617-638-4626. *Application contact:* LePhan Quan, Assistant Director of Admissions, 617-638-4640, Fax: 617-638-5299, E-mail: asksph@bu.edu.

DePaul University, College of Law, Chicago, IL 60604-2287. Offers health law (LL M); intellectual property law (LL M); international law (LL M); law (JD); tax law (LL M); JD/MA; JD/MAIS; JD/MBA; JD/MPS; JD/MS. *Accreditation:* ABA. Part-time and evening/weekend programs available. *Faculty:* 65 full-time (27 women), 61 part-time/adjunct (18 women). *Students:* 1,038 full-time (518 women), 16 part-time (8 women); includes 240 minority (68 African Americans, 1 American Indian/Alaska Native, 64 Asian Americans or Pacific Islanders, 107 Hispanic Americans), 15 international. Average age 27. 5,068 applicants, 39% accepted, 364 enrolled. In 2009, 320 JDs awarded. *Entrance requirements:* LSAT. Additional exam requirements/recommendations for international students: Required—TOEFL (minimum score 600 paper-based; 250 computer-based). *Application deadline:* For fall admission, 3/1 for domestic and international students. Applications are processed on a rolling basis. Application fee: $60. Electronic applications accepted. *Expenses:* Contact institution. *Financial support:* In 2009–10, 673 students received support, including 51 fellowships with partial tuition reimbursements available (averaging $5,000 per year), 106 research assistantships (averaging $1,400 per year); career-related internships or fieldwork, Federal Work-Study, scholarships/grants, and tuition waivers (partial) also available. Support available to part-time students. Financial award application deadline: 3/1; financial award applicants required to submit FAFSA. *Faculty research:* Health law, international law, constitutional law, human rights law, church-state studies. Total annual research expenditures: $152,564. *Unit head:* Warren Wolfson, Interim Dean, 312-362-8989, E-mail: wwolfson@depaul.edu. *Application contact:* Michael S. Burns, Director of Law Admission and Associate Dean, 312-362-6831, Fax: 312-362-5280, E-mail: lawinfo@depaul.edu.

DePaul University, School of Public Service, Chicago, IL 60604. Offers financial administration management (Certificate); health administration (Certificate); health law and policy (MS); international public services (MS); leadership and policy studies (MS); metropolitan planning (Certificate); public administration (MPA); public service management (MS), including association management, fundraising and philanthropy, healthcare administration, higher education administration, metropolitan planning; public services (Certificate); JD/MS. Part-time and evening/weekend programs available. Postbaccalaureate distance learning degree programs offered (minimal on-campus study). *Faculty:* 14 full-time (3 women), 43 part-time/adjunct (24 women). *Students:* 283 full-time (206 women), 298 part-time (208 women); includes 196 minority (112 African Americans, 1 American Indian/Alaska Native, 30 Asian Americans or Pacific Islanders, 53 Hispanic Americans), 18 international. Average age 26. 162 applicants, 100% accepted, 94 enrolled. In 2009, 108 master's awarded. *Degree requirements:* For master's, thesis or integrative seminar. *Entrance requirements:* For master's, minimum GPA of 2.7. Additional exam requirements/recommendations for international students: Required—TOEFL (minimum score 550 paper-based; 213 computer-based; 80 iBT), IELTS (minimum score 6.5). *Application deadline:* Applications are processed on a rolling basis. Application fee: $40. Electronic applications accepted. *Expenses:* Tuition: Full-time $37,525; part-time $620 per credit hour. *Financial support:* In 2009–10, 60 students received support, including 3 research assistantships with full tuition reimbursements available (averaging $7,000 per year); career-related internships or fieldwork, Federal Work-Study, institutionally sponsored loans, scholarships/grants, tuition waivers (partial), and unspecified assistantships also available. Support available to part-time students. Financial award application deadline: 7/1; financial award applicants required to submit FAFSA. *Faculty research:* Government financing, transportation, leadership, health care, volunteerism and organizational behavior, non-profit organizations. Total annual research expenditures: $20,000. *Unit head:* Dr. J. Patrick Murphy, Director, 312-362-5608, Fax: 312-362-5506, E-mail: jpmurphy@depaul.edu. *Application contact:* Megan B. Balderston, Director of Admissions and Marketing, 312-362-5565, Fax: 312-362-5506, E-mail: pubserv@depaul.edu.

Georgetown University, Law Center, Washington, DC 20001. Offers general (LL M); global health law (LL M); international and comparative law (LL M); international business and economic law (LL M); international legal studies (LL M); law (JD, SJD); securities and financial regulation (LL M); taxation (LL M); JD/LL M; JD/MA; JD/MBA; JD/MPH; JD/PhD. *Accreditation:* ABA. Part-time and evening/weekend programs available. *Degree requirements:* For master's, thesis; for doctorate, thesis/dissertation. *Entrance requirements:* For JD, LSAT; for master's and doctorate, JD, LL B, or first law degree earned in country of origin. Additional exam requirements/recommendations for international students: Required—TOEFL. *Expenses:* Contact institution. *Faculty research:* Constitutional law, legal history, jurisprudence.

Loyola University Chicago, School of Law, Chicago, IL 60611. Offers business law (LL M, MJ); child and family law (LL M, MJ); health law (LL M, MJ, D Law, SJD); law (JD); JD/MA; JD/MBA; JD/MSW; MJ/MSW. *Accreditation:* ABA. *Expenses:* Tuition: Full-time $14,220; part-time $790 per credit hour. Required fees: $60 per semester hour. Tuition and fees vary according to program.

Nova Southeastern University, Shepard Broad Law Center, Program in Health Law, Fort Lauderdale, FL 33314-7796. Offers MS. Part-time and evening/weekend programs available. Postbaccalaureate distance learning degree programs offered (minimal on-campus study). *Faculty:* 10 full-time (4 women), 13 part-time/adjunct (7 women). *Students:* 58 part-time (53 women); includes 27 minority (11 African Americans, 1 American Indian/Alaska Native, 1 Asian American or Pacific Islander, 14 Hispanic Americans). Average age 43. 66 applicants, 59% accepted, 35 enrolled. In 2009, 29 master's awarded. *Entrance requirements:* Additional exam requirements/recommendations for international students: Required—TOEFL (minimum score 600 paper-based; 250 computer-based). *Application deadline:* For fall admission, 5/31 priority date for domestic and international students. Applications are processed on a rolling basis. Application fee: $50. Electronic applications accepted. *Expenses:* Contact institution. *Financial support:* In 2009–10, 44 students received support. Tuition waivers (full and partial) available. Financial award application deadline: 7/4; financial award applicants required to submit FAFSA. *Unit head:* William Adams, Associate Dean, 954-262-6133, Fax: 954-262-6301, E-mail: adamsb@nsu.law.nova.edu. *Application contact:* Jennifer McIntyre, Assistant Dean for Online Programs, 954-262-6079, Fax: 954-262-6301, E-mail: mcintyrej@nsu.law.nova.edu.

Quinnipiac University, School of Law, Hamden, CT 06518. Offers health law (LL M); law (JD); JD/MBA. *Accreditation:* ABA. Part-time and evening/weekend programs available. *Faculty:* 35 full-time (14 women), 33 part-time/adjunct (7 women). *Students:* 291 full-time (154 women), 124 part-time (58 women); includes 53 minority (13 African Americans, 3 American Indian/Alaska Native, 21 Asian Americans or Pacific Islanders, 16 Hispanic Americans), 11 international. Average age 25. 2,824 applicants, 41% accepted, 160 enrolled. In 2009, 100 JDs awarded. *Entrance requirements:* LSAT. *Application deadline:* For fall admission, 3/1 priority date for domestic students. Applications are processed on a rolling basis. Application fee: $40. Electronic applications accepted. *Expenses:* Contact institution. *Financial support:* In 2009–10, 354 students received support, including 23 fellowships (averaging $1,560 per year), 38 research assistantships (averaging $680 per year); career-related internships or fieldwork, Federal Work-Study, and scholarships/grants also available. Support available to part-time students. Financial award application deadline: 4/15; financial award applicants required to submit FAFSA. *Faculty research:* Tax, health, public interest, corporate law, dispute resolution, intellectual property. *Unit head:* Brad Saxton, Dean, 203-582-3200, Fax: 203-582-3209, E-mail: ladm@quinnipiac.edu. *Application contact:* Edwin Wilkes, Executive Dean of Law School Admissions, 203-582-3400, Fax: 203-582-3339, E-mail: ladm@quinnipiac.edu.

Seton Hall University, School of Law, Newark, NJ 07102-5210. Offers health law (JD, LL M); intellectual property (JD, LL M); law (MSJ); JD/MADIR; JD/MBA; MD/JD; MD/MSJ. *Accreditation:* ABA. Part-time and evening/weekend programs available. *Faculty:* 51 full-time (23 women), 84 part-time/adjunct (36 women). *Students:* 729 full-time (329 women), 422 part-time (208 women); includes 169 minority (36 African Americans, 1 American Indian/Alaska Native, 79 Asian Americans or Pacific Islanders, 53 Hispanic Americans), 12 international. Average age 27. 3,741 applicants, 44% accepted, 393 enrolled. In 2009, 308 JDs, 18 master's awarded. *Degree requirements:* For master's, thesis optional. *Entrance requirements:* For JD, LSAT, active LSDAS registration, letters of recommendation; for master's, professional experience, letters of recommendation. *Application deadline:* For fall admission, 4/1 priority date for domestic and international students. Applications are processed on a rolling basis. Application fee: $65. Electronic applications accepted. *Expenses:* Contact institution. *Financial support:* In 2009–10, 990 students received support, including 30 fellowships (averaging $2,900 per year), 142 research assistantships (averaging $2,200 per year), 11 teaching assistantships (averaging $1,500 per year); career-related internships or fieldwork, Federal Work-Study, institutionally sponsored loans, scholarships/grants, and unspecified assistantships also available. Support available to part-time students. Financial award application deadline: 4/1; financial award applicants required to submit FAFSA. *Faculty research:* Health law, intellectual property law, science and the law, international law and employment/labor law. Total annual research expenditures: $480,700. *Unit head:* Patrick E. Hobbs, Dean and Professor of Law, 973-642-8750, Fax: 973-642-8031, E-mail: patrick.hobbs@shu.edu. *Application contact:* Gisele Joachim, Dean of Enrollment Management, 973-642-8747, Fax: 973-642-8876, E-mail: admitme@shu.edu.

Southern Illinois University Carbondale, School of Law, Program in Legal Studies, Carbondale, IL 62901-4701. Offers general law (MLS); health law and policy (MLS).

Suffolk University, Law School, Boston, MA 02108. Offers business law and financial services (JD); civil litigation (JD); global law and technology (LL M); health and biomedical law (JD); intellectual property law (JD); international law (JD); U.S. and global business law (LL M); JD/MBA; JD/MPA; JD/MSCJ; JD/MSF; JD/MSIE. *Accreditation:* ABA. Part-time and evening/weekend programs available. *Degree requirements:* For master's, legal writing. *Entrance requirements:* For JD, LSAT, LSDAS, Dean's certification, recommendation; for master's, 2 letters of recommendation, resume, personal statement. Additional exam requirements/recommendations for international students: Required—TOEFL (minimum score 600 paper-based; 250 computer-based; 100 iBT). *Application deadline:* For fall admission, 3/1 priority date for domestic and international students. Applications are processed on a rolling basis. Application fee: $60. Electronic applications accepted. *Expenses:* Contact institution. *Financial support:* Career-related internships or fieldwork, Federal Work-Study, institutionally sponsored loans, and scholarships/grants available. Support available to part-time students. Financial award application deadline: 3/1; financial award applicants required to submit FAFSA. *Faculty research:* Civil law, international law, health/biomedical law, business and finance, intellectual property. *Unit head:* Gail N. Ellis, Dean of Admissions, 617-573-8144, Fax: 617-523-1367, E-mail: gellis@suffolk.edu. *Application contact:* Ian A. Menchini, Director of Electronic Marketing and Enrollment Management, 617-573-8144, Fax: 617-523-1367, E-mail: imenchin@suffolk.edu.

Union Graduate College, Center for Bioethics and Clinical Leadership, Schenectady, NY 12308-3107. Offers bioethics (MS); clinical ethics (AC); clinical leadership in health management (MS); health, policy and law (AC). Part-time and evening/weekend programs available. Postbaccalaureate distance learning degree programs offered (minimal on-campus study). *Faculty:* 9 full-time (1 woman), 13 part-time/adjunct (6 women). *Students:* 7 full-time (3 women), 53 part-time (38 women); includes 20 minority (all Asian Americans or Pacific Islanders), 4 international. Average age 32. 69 applicants, 91% accepted, 57 enrolled. In 2009, 21 master's awarded. *Entrance requirements:* For master's, MCAT, letters of recommendation. Additional exam requirements/recommendations for international students: Required—TOEFL (minimum score 550 paper-based; 213 computer-based). *Application deadline:* Applications are processed on a rolling basis. Application fee: $60. Electronic applications accepted. *Expenses:* Contact institution. *Financial support:* Federal Work-Study, scholarships/grants, health care benefits, and tuition waivers (partial) available. Support available to part-time students. Financial award applicants required to submit FAFSA. *Faculty research:* Bioethics education, clinical ethics consultation, research ethics, history of biomedical ethics, international bioethics/research ethics. *Unit head:* Dr. Robert B. Baker, Director, 518-631-9860, Fax: 518-631-9903, E-mail: bakerr@union.edu. *Application contact:* Ann Nolte, Assistant Director, 518-631-9860, Fax: 518-631-9903, E-mail: noltea@uniongraduatecollege.edu.

Université de Sherbrooke, Faculty of Law, Sherbrooke, QC J1K 2R1, Canada. Offers alternative dispute resolution (LL M, Diploma); biotechnology (LL B); business administration (LL B); business law (Diploma); health law (LL M, Diploma); law (LL B, LL D); legal management (Diploma); notarial law (DDN); transnational law (Diploma). Part-time and evening/weekend programs available. *Degree requirements:* For master's, thesis; for other advanced degree, one foreign language. *Entrance requirements:* For master's and other advanced degree, LL B. Electronic applications accepted.

University of California, San Diego, Office of Graduate Studies, Program in Health Law, La Jolla, CA 92093. Offers MAS. Part-time programs available. *Degree requirements:* For master's, capstone project. *Entrance requirements:* For master's, undergraduate degree in healthcare, law, or related field; 3 years work experience; 3 letters of recommendation; resume.

University of Pittsburgh, School of Law, Master of Studies in Law Program, Pittsburgh, PA 15260. Offers business law (MSL), including commercial law, corporate law, general business law, international business, tax law; constitutional law (MSL); criminal law and justice (MSL); disabilities law (MSL); dispute resolution (MSL); education law (MSL); elder and estate planning law (MSL); employment and labor law (MSL); environment and real estate law (MSL); family law (MSL); general law and jurisprudence (MSL); health law (MSL); intellectual property and technology (MSL); international and comparative law (MSL); personal injury and civil litigation (MSL); regulatory law (MSL); self-designed (MSL); sports and entertainment law (MSL). Part-time programs available. *Faculty:* 43 full-time (16 women), 104 part-time/adjunct (30 women). *Students:* 3 full-time (2 women), 12 part-time (7 women); includes 3 minority (2 African Americans, 1 Asian American or Pacific Islander). Average age 31. 26 applicants, 58% accepted, 11 enrolled. In 2009, 9 master's awarded. *Entrance requirements:* Additional exam requirements/recommendations for international students: Required—TOEFL (minimum score 600 paper-based; 250 computer-based; 100 iBT). *Application deadline:* For fall admission, 6/30 for domestic students, 5/1 for international students. Applications are processed on a rolling basis. Application fee: $0. *Expenses:* Tuition, state resident: full-time $16,402; part-time $665 per credit. Tuition, nonresident: full-time $28,694; part-time $1175 per credit. Required fees: $690; $175 per term. Tuition and fees vary according to program. *Faculty research:* Law, health law, business law, contracts, intellectual property. *Unit head:* Prof. Alan Meisel, Director, 412-648-1384, Fax: 412-648-2649, E-mail: meisel@pitt.edu. *Application contact:* Bethann Pischke, Administrative Coordinator, 412-648-7120, Fax: 412-648-2649, E-mail: pischke@pitt.edu.

University of Pittsburgh, School of Law, Program in Health Law, Pittsburgh, PA 15260. Offers Certificate. *Faculty:* 46 full-time (17 women), 94 part-time/adjunct (24 women). *Students:* 33 full-time (17 women). *Application deadline:* For spring admission, 7/31 for domestic students. Applications are processed on a rolling basis. *Expenses:* Tuition, state resident: full-time $16,402; part-time $665 per credit. Tuition, nonresident: full-time $28,694; part-time $1175 per credit. Required fees: $690; $175 per term. Tuition and fees vary according to program. *Unit head:* Prof. Alan Meisel, Professor/Director, 412-648-1384, Fax: 412-648-2649, E-mail: meisel@pitt.edu. *Application contact:* Bethann Pischke, Program Administrator, 412-648-7120, Fax: 412-648-2649, E-mail: pischke@pitt.edu.

University of Tulsa, College of Law, Tulsa, OK 74104. Offers American Indian and indigenous law (LL M); American law for foreign lawyers (LL M); comparative and international law (Certificate); entrepreneurial law (Certificate); health law (Certificate); law (JD); Native American law (Certificate); public policy (Certificate); resources, energy, and environmental law (Certificate); JD/M Tax; JD/MA; JD/MBA; JD/MS; JD/MSF. *Accreditation:* ABA. Part-time programs available. *Faculty:* 29 full-time (14 women), 24 part-time/adjunct (8 women). *Students:* 382 full-time (148 women), 40 part-time (16 women); includes 68 minority (4 African Americans, 40 American Indian/Alaska Native, 12 Asian Americans or Pacific Islanders, 12 Hispanic Americans), 1 international. Average age 28. 1,304 applicants, 51% accepted, 140 enrolled. In 2009, 149 first professional degrees, 1 master's awarded. *Entrance requirements:* For JD, LSAT, BS or BA from accredited college/university; for master's, JD or equivalent from non-US university. Additional exam requirements/recommendations for international students: Required—TOEFL (minimum score 570 paper-based; 230 computer-based; 90 iBT), IELTS (minimum score 7). *Application deadline:* For fall admission, 2/1 priority date for domestic and international students. Applications are processed on a rolling basis. Application fee: $30. Electronic applications accepted. *Expenses:* Contact institution. *Financial support:* In 2009–10, 176 students received

Health Law

University of Tulsa (continued)

support. Career-related internships or fieldwork, Federal Work-Study, and scholarships/grants available. Support available to part-time students. Financial award applicants required to submit FAFSA. *Faculty research:* International law, Native American law, criminal law, commercial speech, copyright law. *Unit head:* Janet Levit, Dean, 918-631-2400, Fax: 918-631-3126, E-mail: janet-levit@utulsa.edu. *Application contact:* April M. Fox, Assistant Dean of Admissions and Financial Aid, 918-631-2406, Fax: 918-631-3630, E-mail: april-fox@utulsa.edu.

Widener University, School of Law at Wilmington, Wilmington, DE 19803-0474. Offers corporate law and finance (LL M); health law (LL M, MJ, D Law); juridical science (SJD); law (JD). *Accreditation:* ABA. Part-time programs available. *Faculty:* 58 full-time (23 women), 42 part-time/adjunct (15 women). *Students:* 961 full-time (414 women), 37 part-time (25 women); includes 128 minority (59 African Americans, 5 American Indian/Alaska Native, 52 Asian Americans or Pacific Islanders, 12 Hispanic Americans), 13 international. Average age 27. 2,376 applicants, 39% accepted, 351 enrolled. In 2009, 266 first professional degrees, 28 master's, 3 doctorates awarded. *Degree requirements:* For doctorate, thesis/dissertation. *Entrance requirements:* For JD, LSAT; for master's, GMAT; for doctorate, GRE. *Application deadline:* For fall admission, 5/15 for domestic students; for spring admission, 12/1 for domestic students. Applications are processed on a rolling basis. Application fee: $60. *Financial support:* Career-related internships or fieldwork, Federal Work-Study, institutionally sponsored loans, and scholarships/grants available. Support available to part-time students. Financial award application deadline: 2/15; financial award applicants required to submit FAFSA. *Unit head:* Linda L. Ammons, Dean, 302-477-2100, Fax: 302-477-2282, E-mail: llammons@widener.edu.

Application contact: Barbara L. Ayars, Assistant Dean of Admissions, 302-477-2210, Fax: 302-477-2224, E-mail: barbara.l.ayars@law.widener.edu.

Xavier University, College of Social Sciences, Health and Education, School of Nursing, Cincinnati, OH 45207. Offers clinical nurse leader (MSN); education (MSN); forensic nursing (MSN); healthcare law (MSN); informatics (MSN); nursing administration (MSN); school nursing (MSN); MSN/M Ed; MSN/MBA; MSN/MS. *Accreditation:* AACN. Part-time and evening/weekend programs available. Postbaccalaureate distance learning degree programs offered (no on-campus study). *Faculty:* 10 full-time (all women), 10 part-time/adjunct (9 women). *Students:* 64 full-time (55 women), 148 part-time (146 women); includes 19 minority (17 African Americans, 1 Asian American or Pacific Islander, 1 Hispanic American), 2 international. Average age 38. 141 applicants, 88% accepted, 110 enrolled. In 2009, 48 master's awarded. *Degree requirements:* For master's, thesis, scholarly project. *Entrance requirements:* For master's, GRE. Additional exam requirements/recommendations for international students: Required—TOEFL. *Application deadline:* Applications are processed on a rolling basis. Application fee: $35. Electronic applications accepted. *Expenses:* Tuition: Part-time $697 per credit hour. One-time fee: $35 part-time. *Financial support:* In 2009–10, 68 students received support. Applicants required to submit FAFSA. *Faculty research:* Clinical nurse leader, simulation, employment satisfaction, nontraditional students, holistic nursing. *Unit head:* Dr. Susan M. Schmidt, Director, 513-745-3815, Fax: 513-745-1087, E-mail: schmidt@xavier.edu. *Application contact:* Marilyn Volk Gomez, Director of Nursing Student Services, 513-745-4392, Fax: 513-745-1087, E-mail: gomez@xavier.edu.

Law

Albany Law School, Professional Program, Albany, NY 12208-3494. Offers JD, LL M, MSLS, JD/MBA, JD/MPA, JD/MRP, JD/MS, JD/MSW. *Accreditation:* ABA. Part-time programs available. *Faculty:* 49 full-time (24 women), 48 part-time/adjunct (11 women). *Students:* 726 full-time (318 women), 45 part-time (24 women); includes 93 minority (21 African Americans, 5 American Indian/Alaska Native, 37 Asian Americans or Pacific Islanders, 30 Hispanic Americans), 17 international. Average age 23. 2,215 applicants, 44% accepted, 255 enrolled. In 2009, 219 JDs, 9 master's awarded. *Entrance requirements:* For JD, LSAT; for master's, GRE or LSAT. Additional exam requirements/recommendations for international students: Recommended—TOEFL (minimum score 600 paper-based; 250 computer-based). *Application deadline:* For fall admission, 3/15 priority date for domestic students. Applications are processed on a rolling basis. Application fee: $60. *Expenses:* Contact institution. *Financial support:* In 2009–10, 473 students received support, including 50 research assistantships (averaging $2,000 per year); career-related internships or fieldwork, Federal Work-Study, institutionally sponsored loans, scholarships/grants, health care benefits, and tuition waivers (full and partial) also available. Support available to part-time students. Financial award applicants required to submit FAFSA. *Faculty research:* Federal tax, constitutional law, secured transactions, international law, American politics. *Unit head:* Thomas F. Guernsey, President and Dean, 518-445-2321, Fax: 518-472-5865. *Application contact:* Gail S. Benson, Director of Admissions, 518-445-2326, Fax: 518-445-2369, E-mail: gbens@albanylaw.edu.

American University, Washington College of Law, Program in International Legal Studies, Washington, DC 20016-8181. Offers LL M, Certificate. Part-time and evening/weekend programs available. *Students:* 42 full-time (20 women), 95 part-time (61 women); includes 8 minority (3 African Americans, 5 Hispanic Americans), 97 international. Average age 28. In 2009, 82 master's awarded. *Entrance requirements:* For master's, JD, 2 recommendations. Additional exam requirements/recommendations for international students: Required—TOEFL (minimum score 580 paper-based; 237 computer-based; 92 iBT), IELTS (minimum score 6.5). *Application deadline:* For fall admission, 6/1 for domestic students; for spring admission, 11/1 for domestic students. Applications are processed on a rolling basis. Application fee: $55. *Expenses:* Contact institution. *Financial support:* Fellowships, research assistantships, teaching assistantships, career-related internships or fieldwork and tuition waivers (partial) available. Financial award application deadline: 2/15; financial award applicants required to submit FAFSA. *Unit head:* Daniel D. Bradlow, Director, 202-274-4205. *Application contact:* Akira Shiroma, Assistant Dean of Admissions, 202-274-4101, Fax: 202-274-4107, E-mail: shiroma@wcl.american.edu.

American University, Washington College of Law, Program in Law, Washington, DC 20016-8181. Offers JD, JD/MA, JD/MBA, JD/MS. *Accreditation:* ABA. Part-time and evening/weekend programs available. *Students:* 1,247 full-time (699 women), 240 part-time (126 women); includes 537 minority (144 African Americans, 17 American Indian/Alaska Native, 167 Asian Americans or Pacific Islanders, 209 Hispanic Americans), 41 international. Average age 26. In 2009, 443 JDs awarded. *Entrance requirements:* LSAT, registration with LSDAS, 2 recommendations. *Application deadline:* For fall admission, 3/1 for domestic students. Applications are processed on a rolling basis. Application fee: $55. *Expenses:* Contact institution. *Financial support:* Fellowships, career-related internships or fieldwork, Federal Work-Study, institutionally sponsored loans, and tuition waivers (partial) available. Support available to part-time students. Financial award application deadline: 2/15. *Unit head:* Akira Shiroma, Assistant Dean of Admissions and Financial Aid, 202-274-4101, E-mail: wcladmit@wcl.american.edu. *Application contact:* Assistant Dean of Admissions.

American University, Washington College of Law, Program in Law and Government, Washington, DC 20016-8181. Offers LL M. *Students:* 25 full-time (12 women), 26 part-time (17 women); includes 11 minority (6 African Americans, 4 Asian Americans or Pacific Islanders, 1 Hispanic American), 12 international. Average age 33. In 2009, 26 master's awarded. *Degree requirements:* For master's, thesis optional. *Entrance requirements:* For master's, JD, 2 recommendations. Additional exam requirements/recommendations for international students: Required—TOEFL (minimum score 300 paper-based; 250 computer-based). *Application deadline:* For fall admission, 6/1 priority date for domestic students; for spring admission, 11/1 priority date for domestic students. Applications are processed on a rolling basis. Application fee: $55. *Expenses:* Contact institution. *Financial support:* Fellowships with partial tuition reimbursements, career-related internships or fieldwork and institutionally sponsored loans available. Support available to part-time students. Financial award application deadline: 2/15. *Unit head:* Jamin Raskin, Director, 202-885-4011, E-mail: raskin@wcl.american.edu. *Application contact:* Jamin Raskin, Director, 202-885-4011, E-mail: raskin@wcl.american.edu.

The American University of Paris, Graduate Programs, Paris, France. Offers cross-cultural and sustainable business management (MA); cultural translation (MA); global communications (MA); global communications and civil society (MA); international affairs, conflict resolution and civil society development (MA); Middle East and Islamic studies (MA); Middle East and Islamic studies and international affairs (MA); public policy and international affairs (MA); public policy and international law (MA). *Faculty:* 14 full-time (3 women). *Students:* 143 full-time (109 women). 71 applicants, 92% accepted, 34 enrolled. *Degree requirements:* For master's, thesis. *Entrance requirements:* For master's, minimum undergraduate GPA of 3.0. *Application deadline:* For fall admission, 4/15 priority date for international students; for spring admission, 11/15 priority date for international students. Applications are processed on a rolling basis. Application fee: $75. Tuition charges are reported in euros. *Expenses:* Tuition: Full-time 23,460 euros. *Financial support:* Scholarships/grants available. Financial award applicants required to submit FAFSA. *Unit head:* Celeste Schenk, President, 33 1-40620659, E-mail: president@aup.fr. *Application contact:* International Admissions Counselor, 33 1-40620720, Fax: 33 1-47053432, E-mail: admissions@aup.edu.

Appalachian School of Law, Professional Program in Law, Grundy, VA 24614. Offers JD. *Accreditation:* ABA. *Faculty:* 22 full-time (8 women), 2 part-time/adjunct (0 women). *Students:* 334 full-time (124 women); includes 32 minority (16 African Americans, 2 American Indian/Alaska Native, 6 Asian Americans or Pacific Islanders, 8 Hispanic Americans), 2 international. Average age 27. 1,617 applicants, 48% accepted, 127 enrolled. In 2009, 116 JDs awarded. *Entrance requirements:* LSAT. *Application deadline:* For fall admission, 6/1 for domestic students. Applications are processed on a rolling basis. Application fee: $60. Electronic applications accepted. *Financial support:* In 2009–10, 90 students received support; research assistantships, career-related internships or fieldwork, Federal Work-Study, institutionally sponsored loans, scholarships/grants, and tuition waivers (full and partial) available. Financial award application deadline: 7/1; financial award applicants required to submit FAFSA. *Faculty research:* Natural resources, alternative dispute resolution, constitutional law, professional ethics, intellectual property. *Unit head:* Clinton W. Shinn, Dean, 276-935-4349, Fax: 276-935-8261, E-mail: wshinn@asl.edu. *Application contact:* Nancy M. Pruitt, Director of Student Services and Registrar, 276-935-4349 Ext. 1229, Fax: 276-935-8261, E-mail: npruitt@asl.edu.

Arizona State University, Sandra Day O'Connor College of Law, Tempe, AZ 85287-7906. Offers biotechnology and genomics (LL M); law (JD); legal studies (MLS); tribal policy, law and government (LL M); JD/MBA; JD/MD; JD/PhD. *Accreditation:* ABA. *Faculty:* 57 full-time (20 women), 46 part-time/adjunct (12 women). *Students:* 591 full-time (258 women), 35 part-time (21 women); includes 131 minority (12 African Americans, 41 American Indian/Alaska Native, 19 Asian Americans or Pacific Islanders, 59 Hispanic Americans), 16 international. Average age 27. 2,400 applicants, 28% accepted, 184 enrolled. In 2009, 177 JDs awarded. *Degree requirements:* For JD, comprehensive exam, paper. *Entrance requirements:* For JD, LSAT; for master's, bachelor's degree; JD (for LL M). Additional exam requirements/recommendations for international students: Required—TOEFL (minimum score 550 paper-based; 213 computer-based; 80 iBT). *Application deadline:* For fall admission, 11/15 priority date for domestic and international students; for spring admission, 2/1 for domestic and international students. Applications are processed on a rolling basis. Application fee: $60. Electronic applications accepted. *Expenses:* Contact institution. *Financial support:* In 2009–10, 490 students received support; research assistantships, teaching assistantships, career-related internships or fieldwork, Federal Work-Study, institutionally sponsored loans, scholarships/grants, tuition waivers (full and partial), and unspecified assistantships available. Financial award application deadline: 3/5; financial award applicants required to submit FAFSA. *Faculty research:* Emerging technologies and the law, Indian law, law and philosophy, international law, intellectual property. Total annual research expenditures: $514,610. *Unit head:* Dean Paul Schiff Berman, Dean and Foundation Professor of Law, 480-965-6188, Fax: 480-965-6521, E-mail: paul.berman@asu.edu. *Application contact:* Chitra Damania, Director of Operations, 480-965-1474, Fax: 480-727-7930, E-mail: law.admissions@asu.edu.

Atlanta's John Marshall Law School, Graduate Program, Atlanta, GA 30309. Offers JD. Part-time and evening/weekend programs available. *Faculty:* 35 full-time (22 women), 25 part-time/adjunct (7 women). *Students:* 371 full-time (180 women), 184 part-time (104 women); includes 84 minority (69 African Americans, 3 American Indian/Alaska Native, 7 Asian Americans or Pacific Islanders, 5 Hispanic Americans). Average age 24. 1,789 applicants, 40% accepted, 211 enrolled. In 2009, 92 JDs awarded. *Degree requirements:* For JD, comprehensive exam. *Entrance requirements:* LSAT. Additional exam requirements/recommendations for international students: Required—TOEFL. *Application deadline:* For fall admission, 8/16 for domestic and international students. Applications are processed on a rolling basis. Application fee: $50. Electronic applications accepted. *Expenses:* Tuition: Full-time $30,720; part-time $1024 per credit. Required fees: $550 per semester. One-time fee: $150. *Financial support:* In 2009–10, 472 students received support. Applicants required to submit FAFSA. *Faculty research:* Tort reform, terrorism and the use of the U.S. military, Title VII's referral and deferral scheme, public utilities, eminent domain and land use regulations, recent films and their visions of law in Western society. *Unit head:* Michael Mears, Associate Dean for Academic Affairs, 404-872-3593 Ext. 272, Fax: 404-873-3802, E-mail: mmears@johnmarshall.edu. *Application contact:* Shannon M. Keef, Director of Admissions, 404-872-3593 Ext. 148, Fax: 404-873-3802, E-mail: skeef@johnmarshall.edu.

Ave Maria School of Law, School of Law, Ann Arbor, MI 48105-2550. Offers JD. *Faculty:* 27 full-time (7 women), 14 part-time/adjunct (3 women). *Students:* 375 full-time (160 women); includes 64 minority (13 African Americans, 2 American Indian/Alaska Native, 17 Asian Americans or Pacific Islanders, 32 Hispanic Americans), 9 international. Average age 26. 1,775 applicants, 50% accepted, 210 enrolled. In 2009, 87 JDs awarded. *Entrance requirements:* LSAT, 2 letters of recommendation. Additional exam requirements/recommendations for international students: Required—TOEFL (minimum score 600 paper-based; 250 computer-based). *Application deadline:* For fall admission, 4/1 priority date for domestic and international students. Applications are processed on a rolling basis. Application fee: $50. Electronic applications accepted. *Expenses:* Tuition: Full-time $35,948; part-time $1797.40 per credit. Required fees: $500. *Financial support:* In 2009–10, 193 students received support. Career-related internships or fieldwork, Federal Work-Study, and scholarships/grants available. Financial award application deadline: 6/1; financial award applicants required to submit FAFSA. *Application contact:* Monique McCarthy, Assistant Dean for Admissions, 239-687-5420, Fax: 239-352-2890, E-mail: info@avemarialaw.edu.

Barry University, School of Law, Orlando, FL 32807. Offers JD, JD/MS. *Accreditation:* ABA. *Entrance requirements:* LSAT.

Baylor University, School of Law, Waco, TX 76798-7288. Offers JD, JD/MBA, JD/MPPA, JD/MT. *Accreditation:* ABA. *Faculty:* 27 full-time (6 women), 13 part-time/adjunct (2 women).

Students: 465 full-time (244 women); includes 97 minority (12 African Americans, 1 American Indian/Alaska Native, 42 Asian Americans or Pacific Islanders, 42 Hispanic Americans). Average age 24. 2,360 applicants, 32% accepted, 86 enrolled. In 2009, 130 degrees awarded. *Entrance requirements:* LSAT. *Application deadline:* For fall admission, 5/1 for domestic students; for spring admission, 11/1 for domestic students. Applications are processed on a rolling basis. Application fee: $40. Electronic applications accepted. *Expenses:* Contact institution. *Financial support:* In 2009–10, 397 students received support. Career-related internships or fieldwork, Federal Work-Study, institutionally sponsored loans, and scholarships/grants available. Financial award application deadline: 2/1; financial award applicants required to submit FAFSA. *Unit head:* Dr. Bradley J. B. Toben, Dean, 254-710-1911, Fax: 254-710-2316. *Application contact:* Becky Beck, Assistant Dean of Admission, 254-710-1911, Fax: 254-710-2316, E-mail: becky_beck@baylor.edu.

Boston College, Law School, Newton, MA 02459. Offers JD, JD/MA, JD/MBA, JD/MSW. *Accreditation:* ABA. *Faculty:* 54 full-time (22 women), 47 part-time/adjunct (19 women). *Students:* 814 full-time (383 women); includes 184 minority (29 African Americans, 6 American Indian/Alaska Native, 94 Asian Americans or Pacific Islanders, 55 Hispanic Americans), 12 international. Average age 24. 7,168 applicants, 20% accepted, 264 enrolled. In 2009, 242 degrees awarded. *Entrance requirements:* LSAT. Additional exam requirements/recommendations for international students: Required—TOEFL. *Application deadline:* For fall admission, 3/1 for domestic and international students. Applications are processed on a rolling basis. Application fee: $75. Electronic applications accepted. *Expenses:* Contact institution. *Financial support:* In 2009–10, 408 students received support. Career-related internships or fieldwork, Federal Work-Study, institutionally sponsored loans, and scholarships/grants available. Financial award application deadline: 3/15; financial award applicants required to submit FAFSA. *Faculty research:* Commercial law, labor law, legal history, comparative law, international law, business law, intellectual property law, tax law, environmental law. *Application contact:* Rita C. Jones, Assistant Dean for Admissions and Financial Aid, 617-552-4351, Fax: 617-552-2917, E-mail: rita.jones@bc.edu.

Boston University, School of Law, Boston, MA 02215. Offers American law (LL M); banking (LL M); intellectual property law (LL M); law (JD); taxation (LL M); JD/LL M; JD/MA; JD/MBA; JD/MPH; JD/MS. *Accreditation:* ABA. *Faculty:* 65 full-time (26 women), 88 part-time/adjunct (32 women). *Students:* 1,014 full-time (507 women), 83 part-time (45 women); includes 211 minority (50 African Americans, 2 American Indian/Alaska Native, 104 Asian Americans or Pacific Islanders, 55 Hispanic Americans), 164 international. Average age 27. 7,660 applicants, 23% accepted, 271 enrolled. In 2009, 269 JDs, 213 master's awarded. *Degree requirements:* For master's, thesis (for some programs); for JD, thesis/dissertation, research project resulting in a paper. *Entrance requirements:* For JD, LSAT; for master's, JD. Additional exam requirements/recommendations for international students: Required—TOEFL (minimum score 600 paper-based; 250 computer-based; 100 iBT). *Application deadline:* For fall admission, 3/1 for domestic and international students. Applications are processed on a rolling basis. Application fee: $75. Electronic applications accepted. *Expenses:* Tuition: Full-time $37,910; part-time $1184 per credit hour. Required fees: $386; $40 per semester. Part-time tuition and fees vary according to class time, course level, degree level and program. *Financial support:* In 2009–10, 533 students received support. Career-related internships or fieldwork, Federal Work-Study, institutionally sponsored loans, and scholarships/grants available. Financial award application deadline: 3/1; financial award applicants required to submit FAFSA. *Faculty research:* Litigation and dispute resolution, intellectual property law, business organizations and finance law, international law, health law. *Unit head:* Maureen A. O'Rourke, Dean, 617-353-3112, Fax: 617-353-7400, E-mail: lawdean@bu.edu. *Application contact:* Alissa Leonard, Director of Admissions and Financial Aid, 617-353-3100, Fax: 617-353-0578, E-mail: bulawadm@bu.edu.

Brigham Young University, Graduate Studies, J. Reuben Clark Law School, Provo, UT 84602-8000. Offers JD, LL M, JD/M Acc, JD/M Ed, JD/MBA, JD/MPA. *Accreditation:* ABA. *Faculty:* 36 full-time (9 women), 52 part-time/adjunct (13 women). *Students:* 447 full-time (155 women); includes 70 minority (7 African Americans, 5 American Indian/Alaska Native, 35 Asian Americans or Pacific Islanders, 23 Hispanic Americans), 4 international. Average age 25. 733 applicants, 30% accepted, 147 enrolled. In 2009, 157 JDs, 8 master's awarded. *Entrance requirements:* LSAT. Additional exam requirements/recommendations for international students: Required—TOEFL (minimum score 590 paper-based; 243 computer-based; 96 iBT), IELTS (minimum score 7). *Application deadline:* For fall admission, 3/1 priority date for domestic students. Applications are processed on a rolling basis. Application fee: $50. Electronic applications accepted. *Expenses:* Contact institution. *Financial support:* In 2009–10, 252 students received support, including 151 fellowships (averaging $5,000 per year); research assistantships, teaching assistantships, career-related internships or fieldwork, institutionally sponsored loans, scholarships/grants, and health care benefits also available. Financial award application deadline: 6/1; financial award applicants required to submit FAFSA. *Faculty research:* International law, federal taxation, real property law, constitutional law, business organization law. Total annual research expenditures: $10,363. *Unit head:* James R. Rasband, Dean, 801-422-6383, Fax: 801-422-0389, E-mail: rasbandj@law.byu.edu. *Application contact:* GaeLynn Kuchar, Admissions Director, 801-422-4277, Fax: 801-422-0389, E-mail: kucharg@lawgate.byu.edu.

Brooklyn Law School, Professional Program, Brooklyn, NY 11201-3798. Offers JD, JD/MA, JD/MBA, JD/MS, JD/MUP. *Accreditation:* ABA. Part-time and evening/weekend programs available. *Entrance requirements:* LSAT, Dean's certification, 2 faculty letters of evaluation. Additional exam requirements/recommendations for international students: Required—TOEFL and TWE required for Foreign Trained Lawyers Program; Recommended—TOEFL (minimum score 600 paper-based; 250 computer-based; 100 iBT), TWE. Electronic applications accepted. *Expenses:* Tuition: Full-time $43,664; part-time $32,748 per year. Required fees: $326; $326 per year. *Faculty research:* Civil procedure, securities regulation, family law, corporate finance, international business and law, health law.

California Western School of Law, Graduate and Professional Programs, San Diego, CA 92101-3090. Offers law (JD, LL M); JD/MBA; JD/MSW; JD/PhD; MCL/LL M. *Accreditation:* ABA. Part-time programs available. *Entrance requirements:* LSAT. Additional exam requirements/recommendations for international students: Required—TOEFL. Electronic applications accepted. *Faculty research:* Biotechnology, child and family law, international law, labor and employment law, sports law.

Campbell University, Graduate and Professional Programs, Norman Adrian Wiggins School of Law, Buies Creek, NC 27506. Offers JD. *Accreditation:* ABA. *Entrance requirements:* LSAT, interview. Electronic applications accepted. *Expenses:* Contact institution. *Faculty research:* Interdisciplinary approaches to legal problems, management and planning for lawyers, church/state constitutional problems, basic research in substantive legal areas.

Capital University, Law School, Columbus, OH 43215-3200. Offers JD, LL M, MT, JD/LL M, JD/MBA, JD/MSA, JD/MSN, JD/MTS. *Accreditation:* ABA. Part-time and evening/weekend programs available. *Degree requirements:* For master's, thesis or alternative. *Entrance requirements:* For JD, LSAT, LSDAS; for master's, previous course work in accounting, business law, and taxation. Additional exam requirements/recommendations for international students: Required—TOEFL. Electronic applications accepted. *Expenses:* Contact institution. *Faculty research:* Dispute resolution, remedies, taxation, commercial law, election law.

Case Western Reserve University, School of Law, Cleveland, OH 44106. Offers law (JD); U.S. legal studies (LL M); JD/CNM; JD/MA; JD/MBA; JD/MD; JD/MNO; JD/MPH; JD/MS; JD/MSSA. *Accreditation:* ABA. Part-time programs available. *Faculty:* 56 full-time (20 women), 80 part-time/adjunct (24 women). *Students:* 673 full-time (290 women), 24 part-time (13 women); includes 81 minority (22 African Americans, 6 American Indian/Alaska Native, 45 Asian Americans or Pacific Islanders, 8 Hispanic Americans), 25 international. Average age 24. 2,667 applicants, 42% accepted, 195 enrolled. In 2009, 209 JDs, 44 master's awarded. *Entrance requirements:* LSAT, LSDAS. *Application deadline:* For fall admission, 4/1 priority date for domestic and international students. Applications are processed on a rolling basis. Application fee: $40. Electronic applications accepted. *Expenses:* Contact institution. *Financial support:* In 2009–10, 527 students received support. Career-related internships or fieldwork, Federal Work-Study, and scholarships/grants available. Financial award application deadline: 7/1; financial award applicants required to submit FAFSA. *Unit head:* Robert H. Rawson, Interim Dean, 216-368-3283. *Application contact:* Elaine Greaves, Assistant Dean for Admissions, 216-368-3600, Fax: 216-368-1042, E-mail: lawadmissions@case.edu.

The Catholic University of America, Columbus School of Law, Washington, DC 20064. Offers JD, JD/JCL, JD/MA, JD/MLS, JD/MSW. *Accreditation:* ABA. Part-time and evening/weekend programs available. *Faculty:* 48 full-time (22 women), 60 part-time/adjunct (16 women). *Students:* 596 full-time (309 women), 329 part-time (132 women); includes 181 minority (42 African Americans, 7 American Indian/Alaska Native, 88 Asian Americans or Pacific Islanders, 44 Hispanic Americans), 2 international. Average age 26. 3,299 applicants, 33% accepted, 268 enrolled. *Entrance requirements:* LSAT. Additional exam requirements/recommendations for international students: Required—TOEFL. *Application deadline:* For fall admission, 3/12 priority date for domestic students. Applications are processed on a rolling basis. Application fee: $65. Electronic applications accepted. *Expenses:* Contact institution. *Financial support:* Research assistantships, career-related internships or fieldwork, Federal Work-Study, institutionally sponsored loans, and scholarships/grants available. Support available to part-time students. Financial award application deadline: 3/12; financial award applicants required to submit FAFSA. *Unit head:* Veryl Miles, Dean, 202-319-5139, Fax: 202-319-5473. *Application contact:* Shani J. P. Butts, Director of Admissions, 202-319-5151, Fax: 202-319-6285, E-mail: butts@law.edu.

Central European University, Graduate Studies, Department of Legal Studies, Budapest, Hungary. Offers comparative constitutional law (LL M); economic and legal studies (LL M, MA); human rights (LL M, MA); international business law (LL M); legal studies (SJD). Terminal master's awarded for partial completion of doctoral program. *Degree requirements:* For master's, one foreign language, thesis; for doctorate, one foreign language, comprehensive exam, thesis/dissertation. *Entrance requirements:* For master's and doctorate, LSAT, CEU admissions exams. Additional exam requirements/recommendations for international students: Required—TOEFL (minimum score 570 paper-based; 230 computer-based). Electronic applications accepted. *Expenses:* Contact institution. *Faculty research:* Institutional, constitutional and human rights in European Union law, biomedical law and reproductive rights, data protection law, Islamic banking and finance.

Chapman University, Graduate Studies, School of Law, Orange, CA 92866. Offers advocacy and dispute resolution (JD); entertainment law (JD); environmental, land use, and real estate (JD); international law (JD); law (LL M), including business law and economics, entertainment and media law, international and comparative law; prosecutorial science (LL M); tax law (JD); taxation (LL M); JD/MBA; JD/MFA. *Accreditation:* ABA. Part-time and evening/weekend programs available. *Faculty:* 56 full-time (21 women), 24 part-time/adjunct (4 women). *Students:* 535 full-time (260 women), 87 part-time (37 women); includes 126 minority (6 African Americans, 2 American Indian/Alaska Native, 79 Asian Americans or Pacific Islanders, 39 Hispanic Americans), 6 international. Average age 27. 2,996 applicants, 32% accepted, 226 enrolled. In 2009, 158 JDs, 7 master's awarded. *Entrance requirements:* LSAT, minimum undergraduate GPA of 2.75. Additional exam requirements/recommendations for international students: Required—TOEFL (minimum score 600 paper-based; 213 computer-based; 80 iBT). *Application deadline:* For fall admission, 4/1 priority date for domestic students. Applications are processed on a rolling basis. Application fee: $65. Electronic applications accepted. *Expenses:* Contact institution. *Financial support:* Fellowships, Federal Work-Study and scholarships/grants available. Financial award application deadline: 6/30; financial award applicants required to submit FAFSA. *Unit head:* Dr. John Eastman, Dean, 714-628-2500. *Application contact:* Marissa Vargas, Admissions Recruiter/Financial Aid Counselor, 877-CHAPLAW, E-mail: mvargas@chapman.edu.

Charlotte School of Law, Professional Program, Charlotte, NC 28204. Offers JD. *Accreditation:* ABA.

City University of New York School of Law at Queens College, Professional Program, Flushing, NY 11367-1358. Offers JD. *Accreditation:* ABA. *Faculty:* 46 full-time (29 women), 10 part-time/adjunct (6 women). *Students:* 406 full-time (254 women); includes 125 minority (33 African Americans, 43 Asian Americans or Pacific Islanders, 49 Hispanic Americans), 4 international. Average age 26. 2,165 applicants, 27% accepted, 158 enrolled. In 2009, 121 JDs awarded. *Entrance requirements:* LSAT, LSDAS. *Application deadline:* For fall admission, 3/15 priority date for domestic students. Applications are processed on a rolling basis. Application fee: $50. Electronic applications accepted. *Expenses:* Tuition, state resident: full-time $10,240. Tuition, nonresident: full-time $17,020. Required fees: $1712. *Financial support:* In 2009–10, 118 students received support, including 26 fellowships (averaging $12,119 per year), 62 research assistantships (averaging $1,629 per year), 26 teaching assistantships (averaging $11,336 per year); career-related internships or fieldwork, Federal Work-Study, scholarships/grants, and tuition waivers (partial) also available. Financial award application deadline: 5/3; financial award applicants required to submit FAFSA. *Unit head:* Michelle J. Anderson, Dean/Professor of Law, 718-340-4201, Fax: 718-340-4482. *Application contact:* Yvonne Cherena-Pacheco, Assistant Dean for Enrollment Management and Director of Admissions, 718-340-4210, Fax: 718-340-4435, E-mail: admissions@mail.law.cuny.edu.

Cleveland State University, Cleveland-Marshall College of Law, Cleveland, OH 44115. Offers business law (JD); civil litigation and dispute resolution (JD); criminal law (JD); employment labor law (JD); law (JD, LL M); JD/MAES; JD/MBA; JD/MPA; JD/MSES; JD/MUPDD. *Accreditation:* ABA. Part-time and evening/weekend programs available. *Degree requirements:* For master's, thesis (for graduates of U. S. law schools); for JD, 90 credits (42 in required courses). *Entrance requirements:* For JD, LSAT, bachelor's degree; for master's, JD or LL B. Additional exam requirements/recommendations for international students: Required—TOEFL (minimum score 600 paper-based; 250 computer-based; 100 iBT). Electronic applications accepted. *Expenses:* Contact institution. *Faculty research:* Health law, international law, constitutional law, commercial law, business organizations.

The College of William and Mary, William and Mary Law School, Williamsburg, VA 23187-8795. Offers JD, LL M, JD/MA, JD/MBA, JD/MPP. *Accreditation:* ABA. *Faculty:* 35 full-time (12 women), 43 part-time/adjunct (12 women). *Students:* 658 full-time (324 women), 3 part-time (all women); includes 106 minority (80 African Americans, 1 American Indian/Alaska Native, 19 Asian Americans or Pacific Islanders, 6 Hispanic Americans), 26 international. Average age 25. 5,078 applicants, 24% accepted, 238 enrolled. In 2009, 193 JDs, 15 master's awarded. *Degree requirements:* For JD, major paper. *Entrance requirements:* LSAT, baccalaureate degree, references. Additional exam requirements/recommendations for international students: Required—TOEFL (minimum score 600 paper-based; 250 computer-based; 100 iBT) for LLM applicants. *Application deadline:* For fall admission, 3/1 priority date for domestic and international students. Application fee: $50. Electronic applications accepted. *Expenses:* Contact institution. *Financial support:* In 2009–10, 424 students received support, including 188 fellowships with partial tuition reimbursements available (averaging $4,000 per year), 11 research assistantships (averaging $2,100 per year), 28 teaching assistantships (averaging $6,000 per year); career-related internships or fieldwork, scholarships/grants, and unspecified assistantships also available. Financial award application deadline: 2/15; financial award applicants required to submit FAFSA. *Faculty research:* Criminal law, constitutional law, trial advocacy, human rights, corporate law. Total annual research expenditures: $1.2 million. *Unit head:* Davison M. Douglas, Dean/Professor, 757-221-3790, Fax: 757-221-3261, E-mail: dmdoug@wm.edu. *Application contact:* Faye F. Shealy, Associate Dean for Admission, 757-221-3785, Fax: 757-221-3261, E-mail: ffshea@wm.edu.

Columbia University, School of Law, New York, NY 10027. Offers JD, LL M, JSD, JD/M Phil, JD/MA, JD/MBA, JD/MFA, JD/MIA, JD/MPA, JD/MPH, JD/MSW. *Accreditation:* ABA. *Entrance requirements:* LSAT. Electronic applications accepted. *Expenses:* Contact institution. *Faculty research:* Human rights, law and philosophy, corporate governance, regulation of the workplace, death penalty.

Concord Law School, Program in Law, Los Angeles, CA 90024. Offers EJD, JD. Part-time and evening/weekend programs available. Postbaccalaureate distance learning degree programs

Law

Concord Law School (continued)

offered (no on-campus study). *Degree requirements:* For first professional degree, comprehensive exam. *Entrance requirements:* Online admissions test. Additional exam requirements/recommendations for international students: Required—TOEFL (minimum score 520 paper-based). Electronic applications accepted.

Cornell University, Cornell Law School, Ithaca, NY 14853-4901. Offers JD, LL M, JSD, JD/DESS, JD/LL M, JD/MA, JD/MBA, JD/MILR, JD/MLLP, JD/MLP, JD/MPA, JD/MRP, JD/Maitrise en Droit, JD/PhD. JD/MLLP offered jointly with Humboldt University, Berlin; JD/DESS offered jointly with Institut d'etudes Politiques de Paris ("Sciences Po") and Paris I. *Accreditation:* ABA. *Faculty:* 53 full-time (18 women), 54 part-time/adjunct (12 women). *Students:* 622 full-time (322 women). Average age 25. 4,204 applicants. In 2009, 188 JDs, 63 master's awarded. *Entrance requirements:* LSAT. *Application deadline:* For fall admission, 2/1 for domestic students. Applications are processed on a rolling basis. Application fee: $80. Electronic applications accepted. *Expenses:* Contact institution. *Financial support:* In 2009–10, 250 students received support. Career-related internships or fieldwork, Federal Work-Study, and scholarships/grants available. Financial award application deadline: 3/15; financial award applicants required to submit FAFSA. *Faculty research:* International law, Constitutional law, corporate laws, public interest law, feminist legal theory. *Unit head:* Stewart J. Schwab, Dean, 607-255-3527. *Application contact:* Richard D. Geiger, Associate Dean, Communications and Enrollment, 607-255-5141, Fax: 607-255-7193, E-mail: rdg9@cornell.edu.

Cornell University, Graduate School, Graduate Field in the Law School, Ithaca, NY 14853-0001. Offers JSD. *Faculty:* 49 full-time (15 women). *Students:* 12 full-time (3 women); includes 2 minority (1 Asian American or Pacific Islander, 1 Hispanic American), 8 international. Average age 32. 24 applicants, 17% accepted, 4 enrolled. In 2009, 1 doctorate awarded. *Entrance requirements:* For doctorate, JD, LL M, or equivalent; 2 letters of recommendation. Additional exam requirements/recommendations for international students: Required—TOEFL (minimum score 550 paper-based; 213 computer-based). *Application deadline:* For fall admission, 5/1 for domestic students. Application fee: $70. Electronic applications accepted. *Expenses:* Contact institution. *Financial support:* In 2009–10, 1 fellowship with full tuition reimbursement was awarded; research assistantships with full tuition reimbursements, teaching assistantships with full tuition reimbursements, institutionally sponsored loans, scholarships/grants, health care benefits, tuition waivers (full and partial), and unspecified assistantships also available. Financial award applicants required to submit FAFSA. *Faculty research:* International economic integration (WTO and EU), international commercial arbitration, feminist jurisprudence, human rights. *Unit head:* Director of Graduate Studies, 607-255-5141. *Application contact:* Graduate Field Assistant, 607-255-5141, E-mail: gradlaw@law.mail.cornell.edu.

Creighton University, School of Law, Omaha, NE 68178. Offers JD, MS, Certificate, JD/MA, JD/MBA, JD/MS. *Accreditation:* ABA. Part-time programs available. *Faculty:* 33 full-time (9 women), 35 part-time/adjunct (13 women). *Students:* 465 full-time (198 women), 9 part-time (5 women); includes 43 minority (10 African Americans, 1 American Indian/Alaska Native, 17 Asian Americans or Pacific Islanders, 15 Hispanic Americans), 2 international. Average age 24. 1,366 applicants, 56% accepted, 177 enrolled. In 2009, 147 first professional degrees awarded. *Entrance requirements:* LSAT, bachelor's degree. Additional exam requirements/recommendations for international students: Recommended—TOEFL (minimum score 600 paper-based). *Application deadline:* For fall admission, 5/1 priority date for domestic and international students. Applications are processed on a rolling basis. Application fee: $50. Electronic applications accepted. *Expenses:* Contact institution. *Financial support:* In 2009–10, 448 students received support. Career-related internships or fieldwork, institutionally sponsored loans, and scholarships/grants available. Support available to part-time students. Financial award application deadline: 7/1; financial award applicants required to submit FAFSA. *Faculty research:* Conflict of laws, international law, evidence, cyber warfare, constitutional law. *Unit head:* Marianne B. Culhane, Dean/Professor, 402-280-2874, Fax: 402-280-3161. *Application contact:* Andrea D. Bashara, Assistant Dean, 402-280-2586, Fax: 402-280-3161, E-mail: bashara@creighton.edu.

Dalhousie University, Faculty of Graduate Studies, Dalhousie Law School, Halifax, NS B3H 4H9, Canada. Offers LL M, JSD, LL B/MBA, LL B/MLIS, LL B/MPA. Part-time programs available. *Degree requirements:* For master's, thesis or alternative; for doctorate, thesis/dissertation. *Entrance requirements:* For master's, LL B; for doctorate, LL M. Additional exam requirements/recommendations for international students: Required—TOEFL, IELTS, 1 of the following 5 approved tests: TOEFL, IELTS, CANTEST, CAEL, Michigan English Language Assessment Battery. Electronic applications accepted. *Expenses:* Contact institution. *Faculty research:* Marine and environmental law, health law, the family law program.

DePaul University, College of Law, Chicago, IL 60604-2287. Offers health law (LL M); intellectual property law (LL M); international law (LL M); law (JD); tax law (LL M); JD/MA; JD/MAIS; JD/MBA; JD/MPS; JD/MS. *Accreditation:* ABA. Part-time and evening/weekend programs available. *Faculty:* 65 full-time (27 women), 61 part-time/adjunct (18 women). *Students:* 1,038 full-time (518 women), 16 part-time (8 women); includes 240 minority (68 African Americans, 1 American Indian/Alaska Native, 64 Asian Americans or Pacific Islanders, 107 Hispanic Americans), 15 international. Average age 27. 5,068 applicants, 39% accepted, 364 enrolled. In 2009, 320 JDs awarded. *Entrance requirements:* LSAT. Additional exam requirements/recommendations for international students: Required—TOEFL (minimum score 600 paper-based; 250 computer-based). *Application deadline:* For fall admission, 3/1 for domestic and international students. Applications are processed on a rolling basis. Application fee: $60. Electronic applications accepted. *Expenses:* Contact institution. *Financial support:* In 2009–10, 673 students received support, including 51 fellowships with partial tuition reimbursements available (averaging $5,000 per year), 106 research assistantships (averaging $1,400 per year); career-related internships or fieldwork, Federal Work-Study, scholarships/grants, and tuition waivers (partial) also available. Support available to part-time students. Financial award application deadline: 3/1; financial award applicants required to submit FAFSA. *Faculty research:* Health law, international law, constitutional law, human rights law, church-state studies. Total annual research expenditures: $152,564. *Unit head:* Warren Wolfson, Interim Dean, 312-362-8989, E-mail: wwolfson@depaul.edu. *Application contact:* Michael S. Burns, Director of Law Admission and Associate Dean, 312-362-6831, Fax: 312-362-5280, E-mail: lawinfo@depaul.edu.

Drake University, Law School, Des Moines, IA 50311-4505. Offers JD, JD/MA, JD/MBA, JD/MPA, JD/MS, JD/MSW, JD/Pharm D. *Accreditation:* ABA. *Faculty:* 29 full-time (10 women), 14 part-time/adjunct (6 women). *Students:* 453 full-time (195 women), 16 part-time (13 women); includes 48 minority (30 African Americans, 1 American Indian/Alaska Native, 7 Asian Americans or Pacific Islanders, 10 Hispanic Americans), 4 international. Average age 26. 1,110 applicants, 52% accepted, 156 enrolled. In 2009, 156 JDs awarded. *Degree requirements:* For JD, 2 internships. *Entrance requirements:* LSAT, LSDAS report. Additional exam requirements/recommendations for international students: Required—TOEFL (minimum score 560 paper-based; 220 computer-based), TWE. *Application deadline:* For fall admission, 4/1 priority date for domestic and international students. Applications are processed on a rolling basis. Application fee: $40. Electronic applications accepted. *Expenses:* Contact institution. *Financial support:* In 2009–10, 20 research assistantships (averaging $757 per year), 6 teaching assistantships (averaging $2,142 per year) were awarded; career-related internships or fieldwork, Federal Work-Study, institutionally sponsored loans, scholarships/grants, and tuition waivers (full and partial) also available. Support available to part-time students. Financial award application deadline: 3/1; financial award applicants required to submit FAFSA. *Faculty research:* Constitutional law, environmental law, agricultural law, computers and the law, bioethics and health law. Total annual research expenditures: $167,107. *Unit head:* David Walker, Dean, 515-271-1805, Fax: 515-271-4118, E-mail: david.walker@drake.edu. *Application contact:* Jason Allen, Director of Admission, 515-271-2040, Fax: 515-271-2530, E-mail: jason.allen@drake.edu.

Duke University, School of Law, Durham, NC 27708. Offers JD, LL M, MLS, SJD, JD/AM, JD/LL M, JD/MA, JD/MBA, JD/MEM, JD/MPP, JD/MS, JD/MTS, JD/PhD, MD/JD. LL M and SJD offered only to international students. *Accreditation:* ABA. *Degree requirements:* For doctorate, thesis/dissertation. *Entrance requirements:* LSAT. Additional exam requirements/recommendations for international students: Required—TOEFL (minimum score 600 paper-based). Electronic applications accepted. *Expenses:* Contact institution. *Faculty research:* International and comparative law; constitutional and public law; intellectual property, science and technology; business, finance, and corporate law; environmental law and policy.

Duquesne University, Bayer School of Natural and Environmental Sciences, Program in Forensic Science and Law, Pittsburgh, PA 15282-0001. Offers MS. Part-time programs available. *Faculty:* 2 full-time (1 woman), 5 part-time/adjunct (2 women). *Students:* 19 full-time (16 women). Average age 23. 19 applicants, 100% accepted, 19 enrolled. In 2009, 26 master's awarded. *Degree requirements:* For master's, comprehensive exam. *Entrance requirements:* For master's, SAT or ACT, 1 recommendation form. *Application deadline:* For fall admission, 7/1 for domestic and international students. Applications are processed on a rolling basis. Application fee: $50. Electronic applications accepted. *Expenses:* Tuition: Part-time $851 per credit. Required fees: $81 per credit. *Financial support:* In 2009–10, 2 students received support, including 1 research assistantship, 1 teaching assistantship; career-related internships or fieldwork and unspecified assistantships also available. Financial award application deadline: 5/1. *Faculty research:* Extraction protocols, mass spectrometry, synthetic fiber analysis, synthetic polymer characterization, trace analysis. *Unit head:* Dr. Frederick W. Fochtman, Director, 412-396-6373, E-mail: fochtman@duq.edu. *Application contact:* Val Lijewski, Academic Advisor, 412-396-1084, Fax: 412-396-1402, E-mail: lijewskski@duq.edu.

Duquesne University, School of Law, Pittsburgh, PA 15282-0700. Offers JD, LL M, JD/M Div, JD/MBA, JD/MS, JD/MSEM. *Accreditation:* ABA. Part-time and evening/weekend programs available. *Faculty:* 26 full-time (4 women), 51 part-time/adjunct (11 women). *Students:* 700 full-time (359 women), 1 part-time (0 women); includes 41 minority (21 African Americans, 1 American Indian/Alaska Native, 12 Asian Americans or Pacific Islanders, 7 Hispanic Americans), 5 international. Average age 26. In 2009, 182 JDs awarded. *Entrance requirements:* LSAT, minimum GPA of 3.25. Additional exam requirements/recommendations for international students: Required—TOEFL (minimum score 600 paper-based). *Application deadline:* For fall admission, 4/1 for domestic students. Applications are processed on a rolling basis. Application fee: $60. *Expenses:* Contact institution. *Financial support:* In 2009–10, 267 students received support; research assistantships, teaching assistantships, career-related internships or fieldwork, Federal Work-Study, scholarships/grants, and tuition waivers (partial) available. Support available to part-time students. Financial award application deadline: 5/31. *Faculty research:* Clinical legal education, litigation/trial advocacy. Total annual research expenditures: $100,000. *Unit head:* Ken Gormley, Interim Dean, 412-396-6300, Fax: 412-396-6659, E-mail: gormley@duq.edu. *Application contact:* Joseph P. Campion, Director, Admissions, 412-396-6296, Fax: 412-396-6659, E-mail: campion@duq.edu.

Elon University, Program in Law, Elon, NC 27244-2010. Offers JD. *Faculty:* 27 full-time (10 women), 28 part-time/adjunct (9 women). *Students:* 316 full-time (142 women); includes 11 African Americans, 1 American Indian/Alaska Native, 5 Asian Americans or Pacific Islanders, 1 international. Average age 26. 753 applicants, 42% accepted, 121 enrolled. In 2009, 107 JDs awarded. *Entrance requirements:* LSAT, LSDAS. Additional exam requirements/recommendations for international students: Required—TOEFL (minimum score 550 paper-based; 213 computer-based; 79 iBT). *Application deadline:* For spring admission, 4/1 priority date for domestic students. Applications are processed on a rolling basis. Application fee: $50. Electronic applications accepted. *Expenses:* Contact institution. *Financial support:* In 2009–10, 274 students received support. Federal Work-Study and scholarships/grants available. Financial award applicants required to submit FAFSA. *Faculty research:* Quality of life and job satisfaction, civil procedure, damages, assessment for development for instruments, psychological types. *Unit head:* George Johnson, Dean, 336-279-9201, E-mail: gjohnson8@elon.edu. *Application contact:* Alan Woodlief, Associate Dean of the School of Law/Director of Law School Admissions, 336-279-9203, E-mail: awoodlief@elon.edu.

Emory University, School of Law, Atlanta, GA 30322-2770. Offers JD, LL M, Certificate, JD/Certificate, JD/LL M, JD/M Div, JD/MA, JD/MBA, JD/MPH, JD/MTS, JD/PhD. *Accreditation:* ABA. *Faculty:* 65 full-time (29 women), 42 part-time/adjunct (11 women). *Students:* 715 full-time (342 women); includes 219 minority (65 African Americans, 8 American Indian/Alaska Native, 72 Asian Americans or Pacific Islanders, 74 Hispanic Americans), 30 international. Average age 24. 4,589 applicants, 25% accepted, 248 enrolled. In 2009, 217 first professional degrees, 7 Certificates awarded. *Entrance requirements:* LSAT, 2 letters of recommendation. Additional exam requirements/recommendations for international students: Required—TOEFL (minimum score 600 paper-based; 250 computer-based). *Application deadline:* For fall admission, 3/1 for domestic and international students. Applications are processed on a rolling basis. Application fee: $70. Electronic applications accepted. *Expenses:* Contact institution. *Financial support:* In 2009–10, 697 students received support, including 13 fellowships with full tuition reimbursements available (averaging $3,000 per year), 55 research assistantships (averaging $9,880 per year); career-related internships or fieldwork, Federal Work-Study, institutionally sponsored loans, scholarships/grants, and tuition waivers (full and partial) also available. Financial award application deadline: 3/1; financial award applicants required to submit FAFSA. *Faculty research:* Law and economics, law and religion, international law, human rights, feminism and legal theory. Total annual research expenditures: $201,645. *Unit head:* David F. Partlett, Dean, 404-712-8815, Fax: 404-727-0866, E-mail: david.partlett@emory.edu. *Application contact:* Ethan Rosenzweig, Assistant Dean for Admission, 404-727-6802, Fax: 404-727-2477, E-mail: lawinfo@law.emory.edu.

Facultad de derecho Eugenio María de Hostos, School of Law, Mayagüez, PR 00681. Offers JD. *Entrance requirements:* EXADEP, LSAT, 2 letters of recommendation.

Faulkner University, Thomas Goode Jones School of Law, Montgomery, AL 36109-3398. Offers JD. *Faculty:* 29 full-time (9 women), 6 part-time/adjunct (3 women). *Students:* 263 full-time (99 women), 41 part-time (18 women); includes 37 minority (19 African Americans, 4 American Indian/Alaska Native, 7 Asian Americans or Pacific Islanders, 7 Hispanic Americans), 2 international. Average age 26. 747 applicants, 48% accepted, 150 enrolled. *Entrance requirements:* LSAT. *Application deadline:* For fall admission, 6/15 for domestic and international students. Applications are processed on a rolling basis. Application fee: $30. Electronic applications accepted. *Financial support:* In 2009–10, 93 students received support. Career-related internships or fieldwork, scholarships/grants, and tuition waivers (full and partial) available. Financial award application deadline: 7/1; financial award applicants required to submit FAFSA. *Unit head:* Charles I. Nelson, Dean, 334-386-7220, Fax: 334-386-7545, E-mail: cnelson@faulkner.edu. *Application contact:* Joshua M. Roberts, Director of Admissions, 334-386-7210, Fax: 334-386-7908, E-mail: jmroberts@faulkner.edu.

Florida Agricultural and Mechanical University, College of Law, Tallahassee, FL 32307-3200. Offers JD. *Accreditation:* ABA. Part-time and evening/weekend programs available. *Faculty:* 42 full-time (21 women), 6 part-time/adjunct (1 woman). *Students:* 583 full-time (329 women), 24 part-time (10 women); includes 398 minority (273 African Americans, 5 American Indian/Alaska Native, 22 Asian Americans or Pacific Islanders, 98 Hispanic Americans). Average age 26. 1,807 applicants, 31% accepted, 234 enrolled. In 2009, 160 JDs awarded. *Entrance requirements:* LSAT, LSDAS, 2 letters of recommendation. Additional exam requirements/recommendations for international students: Required—TOEFL. *Application deadline:* For fall admission, 5/1 for domestic and international students. Applications are processed on a rolling basis. Application fee: $30. *Expenses:* Contact institution. *Financial support:* In 2009–10, 81 students received support. Scholarships/grants and tuition waivers available. Financial award application deadline: 3/1; financial award applicants required to submit FAFSA. *Unit head:* LeRoy Pernell, Dean/Professor, 407-254-3268, Fax: 407-254-3213, E-mail: leroy.pernell@famu.edu. *Application contact:* Dr. Chanta M. Haywood, Dean of Graduate Studies, Research, and Continuing Education, 850-599-3315, Fax: 850-599-3727, E-mail: chanta.haywood@famu.edu.

Florida Coastal School of Law, Professional Program, Jacksonville, FL 32256. Offers JD. *Accreditation:* ABA. Part-time programs available. *Entrance requirements:* LSAT. Additional exam requirements/recommendations for international students: Recommended—TOEFL (minimum score 600 paper-based; 250 computer-based). Electronic applications accepted.

Expenses: Contact institution. *Faculty research:* Law and business, law technology and intellectual property, juvenile justice and family law, constitutional law, labor law.

Florida International University, College of Law, Miami, FL 33199. Offers JD. *Accreditation:* ABA. Part-time and evening/weekend programs available. *Faculty:* 27 full-time (12 women). *Students:* 601 full-time (287 women), 19 part-time (9 women); includes 346 minority (53 African Americans, 4 American Indian/Alaska Native, 15 Asian Americans or Pacific Islanders, 274 Hispanic Americans), 4 international. Average age 32. 2,497 applicants, 26% accepted, 240 enrolled. In 2009, 123 JDs awarded. *Entrance requirements:* LSAT, 3 letters of recommendation. *Application deadline:* For fall admission, 5/1 for domestic and international students. Applications are processed on a rolling basis. Application fee: $20. Electronic applications accepted. *Expenses:* Contact institution. *Financial support:* In 2009–10, 431 students received support. *Application deadline:* 3/1. *Unit head:* Dr. R. Alex Acosta, Dean, 305-348-1118, Fax: 305-348-1159, E-mail: acosta@fiu.edu. *Application contact:* Alma Miro, Director of Admissions and Financial Aid, 305-348-8006, Fax: 305-348-2965, E-mail: lawadmit@fiu.edu.

Florida State University, College of Law, Tallahassee, FL 32306-1601. Offers American law for foreign lawyers (LL M); enviromental law and policy (LL M); JD/MBA; JD/MPA; JD/MS; JD/MSP; JD/MSW. *Accreditation:* ABA. *Faculty:* 43 full-time (19 women), 28 part-time/adjunct (6 women). *Students:* 763 full-time (314 women); includes 131 minority (64 African Americans, 3 American Indian/Alaska Native, 14 Asian Americans or Pacific Islanders, 50 Hispanic Americans), 1 international. Average age 24. 3,315 applicants, 26% accepted, 244 enrolled. In 2009, 264 JDs awarded. *Degree requirements:* For JD, upper-level writing, skills training, and pro-bono requirements. *Entrance requirements:* LSAT. Additional exam requirements/recommendations for international students: Required—TOEFL (minimum score 600 paper-based; 250 computer-based; 100 iBT). *Application deadline:* For fall admission, 4/1 priority date for domestic students. Applications are processed on a rolling basis. Application fee: $30. Electronic applications accepted. *Expenses:* Contact institution. *Financial support:* In 2009–10, 276 students received support, including 276 fellowships (averaging $2,000 per year), 58 research assistantships (averaging $3,300 per year), 12 teaching assistantships (averaging $1,034 per year); scholarships/grants also available. Financial award application deadline: 2/1; financial award applicants required to submit FAFSA. *Faculty research:* Law, business andeconomics; environmental and land use; international; criminal. *Unit head:* Donald J. Weidner, Dean, 850-644-3400, Fax: 850-644-5487, E-mail: dweidner@law.fsu.edu. *Application contact:* Jennifer L. Kessinger, Director of Admissions and Records, 850-644-3787, Fax: 850-644-7284, E-mail: jkessing@law.fsu.edu.

Fordham University, School of Law, New York, NY 10023. Offers banking, corporate and finance law (LL M); intellectual property and information law (LL M); international business and trade law (LL M); law (JD); JD/MA; JD/MBA; JD/MSW. *Accreditation:* ABA. Part-time and evening/weekend programs available. *Entrance requirements:* LSAT. Additional exam requirements/recommendations for international students: Required—TOEFL. Electronic applications accepted. *Expenses:* Contact institution. *Faculty research:* Intellectual property, business law, international law.

Franklin Pierce Law Center, Professional Program, Concord, NH 03301-4197. Offers intellectual property (Diploma); intellectual property, commerce and technology (LL M, MIP); law (JD); JD/MIP. Diploma awarded as part of Intellectual Property Summer Institute. *Accreditation:* ABA. *Entrance requirements:* LSAT. Additional exam requirements/recommendations for international students: Required—TOEFL (minimum score 600 paper-based; 250 computer-based); Recommended—TWE. Electronic applications accepted. *Expenses:* Contact institution. *Faculty research:* Legal applications of artificial intelligence, intellectual property.

Friends University, Graduate School, Division of Business, Technology, and Leadership, Program in Business Law, Wichita, KS 67213. Offers MBL. Evening/weekend programs available. *Entrance requirements:* Additional exam requirements/recommendations for international students: Required—TOEFL (minimum score 560 paper-based; 220 computer-based). Electronic applications accepted.

George Mason University, School of Law, Arlington, VA 22201. Offers intellectual property (LL M); law (JD); law and economics (LL M); JD/MA; JD/MPP; JD/PhD. *Accreditation:* ABA. Part-time and evening/weekend programs available. *Faculty:* 48 full-time (12 women), 136 part-time/adjunct (35 women). *Students:* 480 full-time (204 women), 217 part-time (87 women); includes 119 minority (18 African Americans, 3 American Indian/Alaska Native, 73 Asian Americans or Pacific Islanders, 25 Hispanic Americans), 9 international. Average age 25. 5,269 applicants, 25% accepted, 246 enrolled. In 2009, 230 JDs, 5 master's awarded. *Entrance requirements:* For JD, LSAT, baccalaureate degree; for master's, JD or international equivalent. Additional exam requirements/recommendations for international students: Required—TOEFL (minimum score 600 paper-based; 250 computer-based; 100 iBT). *Application deadline:* For fall admission, 4/1 for domestic and international students. Applications are processed on a rolling basis. Application fee: $35. Electronic applications accepted. *Expenses:* Contact institution. *Financial support:* In 2009–10, 3 fellowships with full tuition reimbursements (averaging $36,278 per year) were awarded; career-related internships or fieldwork, scholarships/grants, health care benefits, and tuition waivers (partial) also available. Support available to part-time students. Financial award applicants required to submit FAFSA. *Faculty research:* Law and economics, neuroeconomics, infrastructure protection-including homeland and national security, intellectual property. *Unit head:* Dean Daniel D. Polsby, Dean, 703-993-8006, Fax: 703-993-8088. *Application contact:* Alison H. Price, Associate Dean/Director of Admission, 703-993-8010, Fax: 703-993-8088, E-mail: lawadmit@gmu.edu.

Georgetown University, Graduate School of Arts and Sciences, Department of Government, Washington, DC 20057. Offers American government (MA, PhD); comparative government (PhD); conflict resolution (MA); democracy and governance (MA); international law and government (MA); international relations (PhD); political theory (PhD); MA/PhD. Terminal master's awarded for partial completion of doctoral program. *Degree requirements:* For master's, one foreign language, comprehensive exam; for doctorate, one foreign language, comprehensive exam, thesis/dissertation. *Entrance requirements:* For master's, GRE General Test, minimum B average; for doctorate, GRE General Test, MA. Additional exam requirements/recommendations for international students: Required—TOEFL. *Faculty research:* Western Europe, Latin America, the Middle East, political theory, international relations and law, methodology, American politics and institutions.

Georgetown University, Law Center, Washington, DC 20001. Offers general (LL M); global health law (LL M); international and comparative law (LL M); international business and economic law (LL M); international legal studies (LL M); law (JD, SJD); securities and financial regulation (LL M); taxation (LL M); JD/LL M; JD/MA; JD/MBA; JD/MPH; JD/PhD. *Accreditation:* ABA. Part-time and evening/weekend programs available. *Degree requirements:* For master's, thesis; for doctorate, thesis/dissertation. *Entrance requirements:* For JD, LSAT; for master's and doctorate, JD, LL B, or first law degree earned in country of origin. Additional exam requirements/recommendations for international students: Required—TOEFL. *Expenses:* Contact institution. *Faculty research:* Constitutional law, legal history, jurisprudence.

The George Washington University, Law School, Washington, DC 20052. Offers JD, LL M, SJD, JD/MA, JD/MBA, JD/MPA, JD/MPH, LL M/MA, LL M/MPH. *Accreditation:* ABA. Part-time and evening/weekend programs available. *Faculty:* 94 full-time (37 women), 202 part-time/adjunct (68 women). *Students:* 1,557 full-time (687 women), 417 part-time (152 women); includes 406 minority (107 African Americans, 14 American Indian/Alaska Native, 163 Asian Americans or Pacific Islanders, 122 Hispanic Americans), 118 international. Average age 27. 277 applicants, 100% accepted, 214 enrolled. In 2009, 553 JDs, 174 master's, 1 doctorate awarded. *Degree requirements:* For doctorate, thesis/dissertation. *Entrance requirements:* For JD, LSAT; for master's, JD or equivalent; for doctorate, LL M or equivalent. *Application deadline:* For fall admission, 3/1 for domestic students. Applications are processed on a rolling basis. Application fee: $65. *Expenses:* Contact institution. *Financial support:* Research assistantships, career-related internships or fieldwork, Federal Work-Study, institutionally sponsored loans, scholarships/grants, and tuition waivers (full and partial) available. Support available to

part-time students. Financial award application deadline: 3/1; financial award applicants required to submit CSS PROFILE or FAFSA. *Unit head:* Frederick M. Lawrence, Dean, 202-994-6288, Fax: 202-994-5157, E-mail: flawrence@law.gwu.edu. *Application contact:* Robert V. Stanek, Assistant Dean of Admissions and Financial Aid, 202-739-0648, Fax: 202-739-0624, E-mail: jd@admit.nlc.gwu.edu.

Georgia State University, College of Law, Atlanta, GA 30302-4037. Offers JD, JD/MA, JD/MBA, JD/MCRP, JD/MHA, JD/MPA, JD/MSHA. *Accreditation:* ABA. Part-time and evening/weekend programs available. *Entrance requirements:* LSAT, LSDAS, 2 letters of recommendation. Additional exam requirements/recommendations for international students: Recommended—TOEFL (minimum score 630 paper-based). Electronic applications accepted. *Expenses:* Contact institution. *Faculty research:* Tax law, criminal law, constitutional law, health law, metropolitan growth.

Golden Gate University, School of Law, San Francisco, CA 94105-2968. Offers environmental law (LL M); intellectual property law (LL M); international legal studies (LL M, SJD); law (JD); taxation (LL M); U.S. legal studies (LL M); JD/MBA; JD/PhD. *Accreditation:* ABA. Part-time and evening/weekend programs available. *Degree requirements:* For doctorate, thesis/dissertation. *Entrance requirements:* LSAT. Additional exam requirements/recommendations for international students: Required—TOEFL (minimum score 600 paper-based; 250 computer-based). Electronic applications accepted. *Expenses:* Contact institution. *Faculty research:* International law, intellectual property law, environmental law, real estate, civil rights.

Gonzaga University, School of Law, Spokane, WA 99220-3528. Offers JD, JD/M Acc, JD/MBA. *Accreditation:* ABA. Part-time programs available. *Faculty:* 33 full-time (16 women), 30 part-time/adjunct (7 women). *Students:* 520 full-time (203 women), 11 part-time (9 women); includes 48 minority (2 African Americans, 8 American Indian/Alaska Native, 27 Asian Americans or Pacific Islanders, 11 Hispanic Americans), 5 international. Average age 26. In 2009, 173 degrees awarded. *Entrance requirements:* LSAT. *Application deadline:* For fall admission, 4/1 priority date for domestic students. Applications are processed on a rolling basis. Application fee: $50. *Expenses:* Contact institution. *Financial support:* In 2009–10, 425 students received support. Career-related internships or fieldwork, Federal Work-Study, institutionally sponsored loans, and scholarships/grants available. Support available to part-time students. Financial award application deadline: 3/15; financial award applicants required to submit FAFSA. *Faculty research:* Environmental law, business law, public interest law, tax law. Total annual research expenditures: $28,500. *Unit head:* Earl Martin, Dean, 509-328-4220 Ext. 3700. *Application contact:* Susan Lee, Director of Admissions, 509-323-5532, Fax: 509-323-3857, E-mail: admissions@lawschool.gonzaga.edu.

Hamline University, School of Law, St. Paul, MN 55104. Offers JD, LL M, JD/MAM, JD/MANM, JD/MAOL, JD/MAPA, JD/MBA, JD/MFA, JD/MLIS. *Accreditation:* ABA. Part-time and evening/weekend programs available. *Faculty:* 43 full-time (20 women), 79 part-time/adjunct (31 women). *Students:* 468 full-time (259 women), 182 part-time (90 women); includes 85 minority (22 African Americans, 5 American Indian/Alaska Native, 32 Asian Americans or Pacific Islanders, 26 Hispanic Americans), 7 international. Average age 27. 1,506 applicants, 49% accepted, 207 enrolled. In 2009, 190 JDs, 2 master's awarded. *Entrance requirements:* LSAT, 2 letters of recommendation. Additional exam requirements/recommendations for international students: Required—TOEFL (minimum score 100 iBT). *Application deadline:* For fall admission, 5/1 priority date for domestic and international students. Applications are processed on a rolling basis. Application fee: $35. Electronic applications accepted. *Expenses:* Contact institution. *Financial support:* In 2009–10, 617 students received support, including 20 fellowships with full and partial tuition reimbursements available (averaging $3,000 per year); career-related internships or fieldwork, Federal Work-Study, and scholarships/grants also available. Support available to part-time students. Financial award applicants required to submit FAFSA. *Faculty research:* Alternative dispute resolution, intellectual property, health law, business law, ethics/public law. *Unit head:* Donald M. Lewis, Dean, 651-523-2968, Fax: 651-523-2435, E-mail: dlewis02@hamline.edu. *Application contact:* Robin C. Ingli, Director of Admissions, 800-388-3688, Fax: 651-523-3064, E-mail: ringli@hamline.edu.

Harvard University, Law School, Graduate Programs in Law, Cambridge, MA 02138. Offers LL M, SJD. *Degree requirements:* For master's, thesis optional; for doctorate, thesis/dissertation. *Entrance requirements:* Additional exam requirements/recommendations for international students: Required—TOEFL. *Expenses:* Tuition: Full-time $33,696. Required fees: $1126. Full-time tuition and fees vary according to program. *Faculty research:* Corporation finance, national and international law, legal ethics, family law, criminal law, administrative law, constitutional law.

Harvard University, Law School, Professional Programs in Law, Cambridge, MA 02138. Offers international and comparative law (JD); law and business (JD); law and government (JD); law and social change (JD); law, science and technology (JD); JD/MALD; JD/MBA; JD/MPH; JD/MPP; JD/PhD. *Accreditation:* ABA. *Degree requirements:* For JD, 3rd year paper. *Entrance requirements:* LSAT. *Expenses:* Tuition: Full-time $33,696. Required fees: $1126. Full-time tuition and fees vary according to program. *Faculty research:* Constitutional law, voting rights law, cyber law.

Hodges University, Graduate Programs, Naples, FL 34119. Offers business administration (MBA); computer information technology (MS); criminal justice (MCJ); education (MPS); information systems management (MIS); interdisciplinary (MPS); law (MPS); management (MSM); professional studies (MPS); psychology (MPS); public administration (MPA). Part-time and evening/weekend programs available. Postbaccalaureate distance learning degree programs offered (no on-campus study). *Faculty:* 14 full-time (4 women), 4 part-time/adjunct (3 women). *Students:* 37 full-time (28 women), 217 part-time (142 women); includes 76 minority (35 African Americans, 5 Asian Americans or Pacific Islanders, 36 Hispanic Americans). Average age 36. 92 applicants, 91% accepted, 81 enrolled. In 2009, 92 master's awarded. *Degree requirements:* For master's, comprehensive exam (for some programs), thesis (for some programs). *Entrance requirements:* For master's, in-house entrance exam. *Application deadline:* Applications are processed on a rolling basis. Application fee: $50. Electronic applications accepted. *Expenses:* Tuition: Full-time $16,605; part-time $615 per credit hour. Required fees: $570. *Financial support:* In 2009–10, 200 students received support. Federal Work-Study and scholarships/grants available. Financial award application deadline: 7/9; financial award applicants required to submit FAFSA. *Unit head:* Terry McMahan, President, 239-513-1122, Fax: 239-598-6253, E-mail: tmcmahan@hodges.edu. *Application contact:* Rita Lampus, Vice President of Student Enrollment Management, 239-513-1122, Fax: 239-598-6253, E-mail: rlampus@hodges.edu.

Hofstra University, School of Law, Hempstead, NY 11549. Offers American legal studies (LL M); family law (LL M); international law (LL M); law (JD); JD/MBA. *Accreditation:* ABA. Part-time programs available. *Faculty:* 59 full-time (18 women), 35 part-time/adjunct (4 women). *Students:* 943 full-time (469 women), 176 part-time (79 women); includes 301 minority (93 African Americans, 4 American Indian/Alaska Native, 112 Asian Americans or Pacific Islanders, 92 Hispanic Americans), 34 international. Average age 26. 4,934 applicants, 39% accepted, 405 enrolled. In 2009, 359 JDs, 8 master's awarded. *Entrance requirements:* LSAT, letter of recommendation. Additional exam requirements/recommendations for international students: Recommended—TOEFL (minimum score 600 paper-based; 250 computer-based; 100 iBT). *Application deadline:* For fall admission, 4/15 priority date for domestic and international students. Applications are processed on a rolling basis. Application fee: $60. Electronic applications accepted. *Expenses:* Contact institution. *Financial support:* In 2009–10, 555 students received support, including 511 fellowships with full and partial tuition reimbursements available (averaging $22,146 per year), 2 research assistantships with full and partial tuition reimbursements available (averaging $17,548 per year); Federal Work-Study, institutionally sponsored loans, scholarships/grants, tuition waivers (full and partial), and unspecified assistantships also available. Support available to part-time students. Financial award applicants required to submit FAFSA. *Faculty research:* Commercial and corporate law; constitutional law and legal history family law; gender and LGBT issues; international and comparative law; child and family advocacy. *Unit head:* Nora V. Demleitner, Dean, 516-463-5854, Fax: 516-463-6264,

Law

Hofstra University (continued)

E-mail: lawnao@hofstra.edu. *Application contact:* John Chalmers, Director of Law School Enrollment Operations, 516-463-5791, Fax: 516-463-6264, E-mail: lawadmissions@hofstra.edu.

Howard University, School of Law, Washington, DC 20008. Offers JD, LL M, JD/MBA. *Accreditation:* ABA. *Degree requirements:* For master's, one foreign language, thesis; for JD, thesis/dissertation (for some programs). *Entrance requirements:* LSAT. Additional exam requirements/recommendations for international students: Required—TOEFL. Electronic applications accepted. *Expenses:* Contact institution. *Faculty research:* Criminal law, family law, telecommunications, religion, antitrust.

Humphreys College, Laurence Drivon School of Law, Stockton, CA 95207-3896. Offers JD. Part-time and evening/weekend programs available. *Entrance requirements:* LSAT, minimum GPA of 2.5. Electronic applications accepted.

Illinois Institute of Technology, Chicago-Kent College of Law, Chicago, IL 60661-3691. Offers family law (LL M); financial services (LL M); international intellectual property (LL M); international law (LL M); law (JD); taxation (LL M); JD/LL M; JD/MBA; JD/MPA; JD/MPH; JD/MS. *Accreditation:* ABA. Part-time and evening/weekend programs available. *Faculty:* 70 full-time (26 women), 153 part-time/adjunct (29 women). *Students:* 879 full-time (428 women), 222 part-time (98 women); includes 192 minority (52 African Americans, 4 American Indian/Alaska Native, 91 Asian Americans or Pacific Islanders, 45 Hispanic Americans), 127 international. Average age 27. 3,652 applicants, 45% accepted, 388 enrolled. In 2009, 315 JDs, 140 master's awarded. *Entrance requirements:* LSAT, LSDAS. Additional exam requirements/recommendations for international students: Required—TOEFL (minimum score 600 paper-based; 250 computer-based; 100 iBT); Recommended—IELTS (minimum score 7). *Application deadline:* For fall admission, 3/1 priority date for domestic students, 2/1 priority date for international students. Applications are processed on a rolling basis. Application fee: $60 ($75 for international students). Electronic applications accepted. *Expenses:* Contact institution. *Financial support:* In 2009–10, 605 students received support. Career-related internships or fieldwork, Federal Work-Study, institutionally sponsored loans, scholarships/grants, and tuition waivers (full) available. Support available to part-time students. Financial award application deadline: 3/15; financial award applicants required to submit FAFSA. *Faculty research:* Constitutional law, bioethics, environmental law. Total annual research expenditures: $747,995. *Unit head:* Harold J. Krent, Dean, 312-906-5010, Fax: 312-906-5335, E-mail: hkrent@kentlaw.edu. *Application contact:* Nicole Vilches, Assistant Dean, 312-906-5020, Fax: 312-906-5274, E-mail: admissions@kentlaw.edu.

Indiana University Bloomington, Maurer School of Law, Bloomington, IN 47405-7000. Offers comparative law (MCL); juridical science (SJD); law (JD, LL M); law and social sciences (PhD); legal studies (Certificate); JD/MA; JD/MBA; JD/MLS; JD/MPA; JD/MS; JD/MSES. PhD offered through University Graduate School. *Accreditation:* ABA. *Faculty:* 72 full-time (28 women), 14 part-time/adjunct (4 women). *Students:* 675 full-time (274 women), 42 part-time (16 women); includes 103 minority (45 African Americans, 32 Asian Americans or Pacific Islanders, 26 Hispanic Americans), 110 international. Average age 27. 1,273 applicants, 73% accepted, 209 enrolled. In 2009, 198 first professional degrees, 66 master's, 10 doctorates, 2 other advanced degrees awarded. *Degree requirements:* For master's, thesis or practicum; for doctorate, thesis/dissertation (for some programs); for JD, research seminar. *Entrance requirements:* For JD, LSAT; for master's, LSAT, 3 letters of recommendation, law degree or license to practice; for doctorate, LSAT, 3 letters of recommendation, LL M or JD. Additional exam requirements/recommendations for international students: Required—TOEFL (minimum score 560 paper-based; 213 computer-based; 80 iBT). *Application deadline:* For fall admission, 3/1 priority date for domestic and international students. Applications are processed on a rolling basis. Application fee: $55 ($65 for international students). Electronic applications accepted. *Financial support:* In 2009–10, 301 students received support, including 278 fellowships (averaging $16,000 per year), 1 research assistantship (averaging $15,217 per year), 2 teaching assistantships (averaging $14,000 per year); career-related internships or fieldwork, Federal Work-Study, institutionally sponsored loans, scholarships/grants, health care benefits, and unspecified assistantships also available. Financial award application deadline: 3/1; financial award applicants required to submit FAFSA. *Faculty research:* Environmental risk assessment and policy analysis, information privacy and security, judicial independence, accountability, ethics. Total annual research expenditures: $1.4 million. *Unit head:* Lauren K. Robel, Dean, 812-855-8885, Fax: 812-855-7057, E-mail: lrobel@indiana.edu. *Application contact:* Kelly M. Compton, Director of Admissions, 812-855-2704, Fax: 812-855-0555, E-mail: kmcompto@indiana.edu.

Indiana University–Purdue University Indianapolis, School of Law, Indianapolis, IN 46202-2896. Offers JD, LL M, SJD, JD/M Phil, JD/MBA, JD/MHA, JD/MLS, JD/MPA, JD/MPH, JD/MSW. *Accreditation:* ABA. *Faculty:* 1 (woman) full-time. *Students:* 925 full-time (416 women), 66 part-time (36 women); includes 101 minority (48 African Americans, 1 American Indian/Alaska Native, 33 Asian Americans or Pacific Islanders, 19 Hispanic Americans), 45 international. Average age 28. 1,828 applicants, 43% accepted, 355 enrolled. In 2009, 250 JDs, 36 master's awarded. *Entrance requirements:* Additional exam requirements/recommendations for international students: Required—TOEFL. Application fee: $55 ($65 for international students). *Financial support:* Fellowships, research assistantships with full and partial tuition reimbursements, Federal Work-Study, institutionally sponsored loans, and scholarships/grants available. Support available to part-time students. Financial award applicants required to submit FAFSA. *Unit head:* Susanah M. Mead, Interim Dean, 317-274-8523. *Application contact:* Patricia Kinney, Director of Admissions, 317-274-2459, Fax: 317-278-4780, E-mail: pkkinney@iupui.edu.

Instituto Tecnológico y de Estudios Superiores de Monterrey, Campus Ciudad de México, Division of Humanities and Social Sciences, Ciudad de Mexico, Mexico. Offers LL B. Part-time and evening/weekend programs available. *Entrance requirements:* Instituto entrance exam. Additional exam requirements/recommendations for international students: Required—TOEFL. *Faculty research:* Law; politics; international relations.

Inter American University of Puerto Rico School of Law, Professional Program, San Juan, PR 00936-8351. Offers JD. *Accreditation:* ABA. Part-time and evening/weekend programs available. *Entrance requirements:* LSAT, PAEG, minimum GPA of 2.5. *Expenses:* Contact institution.

John F. Kennedy University, School of Law, Pleasant Hill, CA 94523-4817. Offers JD. Part-time and evening/weekend programs available. *Entrance requirements:* LSAT, interview. Additional exam requirements/recommendations for international students: Required—TOEFL. *Expenses:* Contact institution.

John Marshall Law School, Graduate and Professional Programs, Chicago, IL 60604-3968. Offers comparative legal studies (LL M); employee benefits (LL M, MS); information technology (LL M, MS); intellectual property (LL M); international business and trade (LL M); law (JD); real estate (LL M, MS); taxation (LL M, MS); JD/LL M; JD/MA; JD/MBA; JD/MPA. *Accreditation:* ABA. Part-time and evening/weekend programs available. *Faculty:* 73 full-time (26 women), 110 part-time/adjunct (33 women). *Students:* 1,139 full-time (505 women), 407 part-time (204 women); includes 353 minority (130 African Americans, 15 American Indian/Alaska Native, 91 Asian Americans or Pacific Islanders, 117 Hispanic Americans), 43 international. Average age 27. 3,027 applicants, 44% accepted, 385 enrolled. In 2009, 401 first professional degrees, 16 master's awarded. *Degree requirements:* For JD, 90 credits. *Entrance requirements:* For JD, LSAT; for master's, JD. Additional exam requirements/recommendations for international students: Required—TOEFL. *Application deadline:* For fall admission, 3/1 priority date for domestic and international students; for spring admission, 10/15 priority date for domestic and international students. Applications are processed on a rolling basis. Application fee: $60. Electronic applications accepted. *Expenses:* Contact institution. *Financial support:* In 2009–10, 1,350 students received support. Scholarships/grants and tuition waivers (full and partial) available. Support available to part-time students. Financial award application deadline: 6/1; financial award applicants required to submit FAFSA. *Unit head:* John Corkery, Dean, 312-

427-2737. *Application contact:* William B. Powers, Associate Dean of Admission and Student Affairs, 800-537-4280, Fax: 312-427-5136, E-mail: admission@jmls.edu.

The Judge Advocate General's School, U.S. Army, Graduate Programs, Charlottesville, VA 22903-1781. Offers military law (LL M). Only active duty military lawyers attend this school. *Accreditation:* ABA. *Degree requirements:* For master's, thesis optional. *Entrance requirements:* For master's, active duty military lawyer, international military officer, or DOD civilian attorney, JD or LL B. *Faculty research:* Criminal law, administrative and civil law, contract law, international law, legal research and writing.

Kaplan University, Davenport Campus, School of Criminal Justice, Davenport, IA 52807-2095. Offers corrections (MSCJ); global issues in criminal justice (MSCJ); law (MSCJ); leadership and executive management (MSCJ); policing (MSCJ). Part-time and evening/weekend programs available. Postbaccalaureate distance learning degree programs offered (no on-campus study). *Entrance requirements:* Additional exam requirements/recommendations for international students: Required—TOEFL (minimum score 550 paper-based; 218 computer-based; 80 iBT). Electronic applications accepted.

Lewis & Clark College, Lewis & Clark Law School, Portland, OR 97203. Offers environmental and natural resources law (LL M); law (JD). *Accreditation:* ABA. Part-time and evening/weekend programs available. *Entrance requirements:* LSAT. Additional exam requirements/recommendations for international students: Recommended—TOEFL (minimum score 600 paper-based; 250 computer-based). Electronic applications accepted. *Expenses:* Contact institution.

Liberty University, School of Law, Lynchburg, VA 24502. Offers JD. *Entrance requirements:* LSAT, 2 letters of recommendation, interview, subscription to LSDAS. Additional exam requirements/recommendations for international students: Required—TOEFL (minimum score 600 paper-based; 250 computer-based). Electronic applications accepted. *Expenses:* Tuition: Full-time $7110; part-time $415 per credit hour. Required fees: $150 per semester. Tuition and fees vary according to course load, degree level, campus/location and program.

Lincoln Memorial University, Duncan School of Law, Harrogate, TN 37752-1901. Offers JD. Part-time programs available. *Faculty:* 6 full-time (2 women). *Students:* 81 part-time (36 women); includes 5 African Americans, 2 Hispanic Americans. Average age 31. 243 applicants, 51% accepted, 81 enrolled. *Entrance requirements:* LSAT. Additional exam requirements/recommendations for international students: Required—TOEFL (minimum score 500 paper-based). *Application deadline:* For fall admission, 1/31 priority date for domestic students. Application fee: $50. Electronic applications accepted. *Expenses:* Contact institution. *Financial support:* Application deadline: 7/1. *Unit head:* Dr. Sydney Beckman, Dean, 423-869-7768, E-mail: sydney.beckman@lmunet.edu. *Application contact:* Paul Carney, Director, Office of Admissions, 423-869-7769, E-mail: paul.carney@lmunet.edu.

Louisiana State University and Agricultural and Mechanical College, Paul M. Hebert Law Center, Baton Rouge, LA 70803. Offers LL M, JD/DCL. *Accreditation:* ABA. *Faculty:* 41 full-time (10 women), 54 part-time/adjunct (6 women). *Students:* 592 full-time (266 women), 17 part-time (6 women); includes 82 minority (27 African Americans, 7 American Indian/Alaska Native, 14 Asian Americans or Pacific Islanders, 34 Hispanic Americans), 11 international. Average age 26. 1,407 applicants, 37% accepted, 236 enrolled. In 2009, 8 master's awarded. *Degree requirements:* For master's, thesis. *Entrance requirements:* Additional exam requirements/recommendations for international students: Required—TOEFL (minimum score 600 paper-based; 250 computer-based; 100 iBT). *Application deadline:* For fall admission, 3/1 priority date for domestic students, 2/1 priority date for international students. Applications are processed on a rolling basis. Application fee: $25. Electronic applications accepted. *Expenses:* Contact institution. *Financial support:* Scholarships/grants and tuition waivers (full and partial) available. Financial award applicants required to submit FAFSA. *Unit head:* Jack M. Weiss, Chancellor, 225-578-8491, Fax: 225-578-8202, E-mail: jack.weiss@law.lsu.edu. *Application contact:* Lynell Cadray, Assistant Vice Chancellor for Enrollment Services/Director of Admissions, 225-578-8646, Fax: 225-578-8647, E-mail: lynell.cadray@law.lsu.edu.

Loyola Marymount University, College of Business Administration, MBA/JD Program, Los Angeles, CA 90045-2659. Offers MBA/JD. Part-time programs available. *Faculty:* 56 full-time (15 women), 11 part-time/adjunct (1 woman). *Students:* 8 full-time (3 women), 1 (woman) part-time; includes 2 Asian Americans or Pacific Islanders. Average age 24. 18 applicants, 56% accepted, 7 enrolled. *Entrance requirements:* Additional exam requirements/recommendations for international students: Required—TOEFL (minimum score 600 paper-based; 250 computer-based; 100 iBT). *Application deadline:* For spring admission, 6/30 for domestic students. Application fee: $75. Electronic applications accepted. *Expenses:* Contact institution. *Financial support:* In 2009–10, 5 students received support. Scholarships/grants and unspecified assistantships available. Financial award application deadline: 6/30; financial award applicants required to submit FAFSA. *Unit head:* Dr. Dennis Draper, Dean, 310-338-7504, Fax: 310-338-2899, E-mail: ddraper@lmu.edu. *Application contact:* Dr. Rachelle Katz, Associate Dean and Director of MBA Program, 310-338-2848, E-mail: rkatz@lmu.edu.

Loyola Marymount University, Loyola Law School Los Angeles, Los Angeles, CA 90015. Offers law (JD); taxation (LL M); JD/MBA. *Accreditation:* ABA. Part-time and evening/weekend programs available. *Entrance requirements:* For JD, LSAT; for master's, JD (LLM). Additional exam requirements/recommendations for international students: Required—TOEFL. Electronic applications accepted.

Loyola University Chicago, School of Law, Chicago, IL 60611. Offers business law (LL M, MJ); child and family law (LL M, MJ); health law (LL M, MJ, D Law, SJD); law (JD); JD/MA; JD/MBA; JD/MSW; MJ/MSW. *Accreditation:* ABA. *Expenses:* Tuition: Full-time $14,220; part-time $790 per credit hour. Required fees: $60 per semester hour. Tuition and fees vary according to program.

Loyola University New Orleans, College of Law, New Orleans, LA 70118. Offers JD, LL M, JD/MBA, JD/MPA, JD/MURP. *Accreditation:* ABA. Part-time and evening/weekend programs available. *Students:* 737 full-time (352 women), 158 part-time (84 women); includes 233 minority (121 African Americans, 4 American Indian/Alaska Native, 32 Asian Americans or Pacific Islanders, 76 Hispanic Americans), 4 international. Average age 27. 1,788 applicants, 47% accepted, 280 enrolled. In 2009, 247 JDs awarded. *Entrance requirements:* LSAT, letters of recommendation, interview, resume. Additional exam requirements/recommendations for international students: Recommended—TOEFL (minimum score 550 paper-based; 213 computer-based). *Application deadline:* For fall admission, 2/1 priority date for domestic and international students. Applications are processed on a rolling basis. Application fee: $40. Electronic applications accepted. *Expenses:* Contact institution. *Financial support:* In 2009–10, 50 research assistantships (averaging $1,428 per year), 22 teaching assistantships (averaging $2,200 per year) were awarded; career-related internships or fieldwork and scholarships/grants also available. Support available to part-time students. Financial award application deadline: 5/1; financial award applicants required to submit FAFSA. *Faculty research:* Louisiana civil code, international law, commercial law, comparative law. *Unit head:* Dean, 504-861-5405, Fax: 504-861-5739. *Application contact:* Michele K. Allison-Davis, Assistant Dean, Admissions, 504-861-5575, Fax: 504-861-5772, E-mail: maldavis@loyno.edu.

Marquette University, Law School, Milwaukee, WI 53201-1881. Offers JD, JD/Certificate, JD/MA, JD/MBA. *Accreditation:* ABA. Part-time and evening/weekend programs available. *Entrance requirements:* LSAT. Additional exam requirements/recommendations for international students: Required—TOEFL. Electronic applications accepted. *Expenses:* Contact institution. *Faculty research:* Constitutional law, sports law, dispute resolution, intellectual property, legal ethics.

Massachusetts School of Law at Andover, Professional Program, Andover, MA 01810. Offers JD. Part-time and evening/weekend programs available. *Entrance requirements:* Massachusetts School of Law Aptitude Test (MSLAT), interview. Electronic applications accepted.

McGill University, Faculty of Graduate and Postdoctoral Studies, Faculty of Law, Department of Law, Montréal, QC H3A 2T5, Canada. Offers LL M, DCL.

McGill University, Faculty of Graduate and Postdoctoral Studies, Faculty of Law, Institute of Air and Space Law, Montréal, QC H3A 2T5, Canada. Offers LL M, DCL, Graduate Certificate.

McGill University, Faculty of Graduate and Postdoctoral Studies, Faculty of Law, Institute of Comparative Law, Montréal, QC H3A 2T5, Canada. Offers LL M, DCL, Graduate Certificate.

McGill University, Professional Program in Law, Montréal, QC H3A 2T5, Canada. Offers JD.

Mercer University, Walter F. George School of Law, Macon, GA 31207. Offers JD, JD/MBA. *Accreditation:* ABA. Part-time programs available. *Faculty:* 32 full-time (12 women), 21 part-time/adjunct (6 women). *Students:* 431 full-time (201 women); includes 71 minority (39 African Americans, 3 American Indian/Alaska Native, 22 Asian Americans or Pacific Islanders, 7 Hispanic Americans). Average age 24. 1,571 applicants, 38% accepted, 157 enrolled. In 2009, 145 JDs awarded. *Entrance requirements:* LSAT. *Application deadline:* For fall admission, 3/15 priority date for domestic students. Applications are processed on a rolling basis. Application fee: $50. Electronic applications accepted. *Expenses:* Contact institution. *Financial support:* In 2009–10, 394 students received support, including 33 fellowships (averaging $4,151 per year), 17 research assistantships (averaging $629 per year); career-related internships or fieldwork, Federal Work-Study, institutionally sponsored loans, scholarships/grants, tuition waivers (partial), and institutional work-study also available. Support available to part-time students. Financial award application deadline: 4/1; financial award applicants required to submit FAFSA. *Faculty research:* Legal ethics, environmental law, employment discrimination, statutory law, legal writing. *Unit head:* Daisy H. Floyd, Dean, 478-301-2602, Fax: 478-301-2101, E-mail: floyd_dh@law.mercer.edu. *Application contact:* Susan Martin, Admissions Assistant, 478-301-2605, Fax: 478-301-2989, E-mail: martin_sv@law.mercer.edu.

Michigan State University College of Law, Professional Program, East Lansing, MI 48824-1300. Offers American legal system (LL M); intellectual property (LL M); law (JD). *Accreditation:* ABA. Part-time and evening/weekend programs available. *Faculty:* 55 full-time (23 women), 75 part-time/adjunct (20 women). *Students:* 814 full-time (305 women), 144 part-time (71 women); includes 106 minority (39 African Americans, 12 American Indian/Alaska Native, 33 Asian Americans or Pacific Islanders, 22 Hispanic Americans), 52 international. Average age 28. 2,736 applicants, 46% accepted, 287 enrolled. In 2009, 253 JDs awarded. *Entrance requirements:* LSAT. Additional exam requirements/recommendations for international students: Required—TOEFL (minimum score 600 paper-based; 250 computer-based). *Application deadline:* For fall admission, 3/15 priority date for domestic students, 7/1 priority date for international students. Applications are processed on a rolling basis. Application fee: $60. Electronic applications accepted. *Expenses:* Contact institution. *Financial support:* In 2009–10, 288 students received support, including 301 fellowships (averaging $22,962 per year); career-related internships or fieldwork, Federal Work-Study, institutionally sponsored loans, scholarships/grants, and tuition waivers (full) also available. Support available to part-time students. Financial award application deadline: 4/15; financial award applicants required to submit FAFSA. *Faculty research:* International, constitutional, health, tax and environmental law; intellectual property, trial practice, corporate law. *Unit head:* Joan W. Howarth, Dean and Professor of Law, 517-432-6993, Fax: 517-432-6801, E-mail: howarth@law.msu.edu. *Application contact:* Charles Roboski, Assistant Dean of Admissions, 517-432-0222, Fax: 517-432-0098, E-mail: roboski@law.msu.edu.

Mississippi College, School of Law, Jackson, MS 39201. Offers civil law studies (Certificate); law (JD); JD/MBA. *Accreditation:* ABA. *Faculty:* 25 full-time (12 women), 6 part-time/adjunct (3 women). *Students:* 528 full-time (213 women); includes 42 minority (34 African Americans, 1 American Indian/Alaska Native, 2 Asian Americans or Pacific Islanders, 5 Hispanic Americans). Average age 25. 1,171 applicants, 41% accepted, 195 enrolled. In 2009, 129 first professional degrees awarded. *Degree requirements:* For JD, thesis/dissertation. *Entrance requirements:* LSAT, LDAS report. Additional exam requirements/recommendations for international students: Recommended—IELTS. *Application deadline:* For fall admission, 6/1 priority date for domestic students. Applications are processed on a rolling basis. Application fee: $50. Electronic applications accepted. *Expenses:* Contact institution. *Financial support:* In 2009–10, 490 students received support. Federal Work-Study and scholarships/grants available. Financial award applicants required to submit FAFSA. *Unit head:* James H. Rosenblatt, Dean, 601-925-7101, Fax: 601-925-7115, E-mail: rosenblatt@mc.edu. *Application contact:* Patricia H. Evans, Assistant Dean for Admissions, 601-925-7151, Fax: 601-925-7166, E-mail: pevans@mc.edu.

Montclair State University, The Graduate School, College of Humanities and Social Sciences, Department of Political Science and Law, Montclair, NJ 07043-1624. Offers law and governance (MA). Part-time and evening/weekend programs available. *Faculty:* 13 full-time (6 women), 22 part-time/adjunct (7 women). *Students:* 15 full-time (9 women), 22 part-time (16 women). Average age 33. 15 applicants, 53% accepted, 3 enrolled. In 2009, 12 master's awarded. *Degree requirements:* For master's, thesis or comprehensive exam. *Entrance requirements:* For master's, GRE, minimum cumulative GPA of 2.75 for undergraduate work. Additional exam requirements/recommendations for international students: Required—TOEFL (minimum score 83 computer-based), or IELTS. *Expenses:* Tuition, area resident: Part-time $486.74 per credit. Tuition, state resident: part-time $486.74 per credit. Tuition, nonresident: part-time $751.34 per credit. Tuition and fees vary according to degree level and program. *Financial support:* In 2009–10, 1 research assistantship with full tuition reimbursement (averaging $7,000 per year) was awarded; Federal Work-Study, scholarships/grants, and unspecified assistantships also available. Support available to part-time students. Financial award application deadline: 3/1. *Unit head:* Dr. William Berlin, Chair, 973-655-7576, E-mail: berlinw@mail.montclair.edu. *Application contact:* Amy Aiello, Director of Graduate Admissions and Operations, 973-655-5147, Fax: 973-655-7869, E-mail: graduate.school@montclair.edu.

New England LawûBoston, Professional Program, Boston, MA 02116-5687. Offers JD, LL M. *Accreditation:* ABA. Part-time and evening/weekend programs available. *Faculty:* 34 full-time (10 women), 72 part-time/adjunct (27 women). *Students:* 737 full-time (432 women), 359 part-time (176 women); includes 113 minority (18 African Americans, 3 American Indian/Alaska Native, 72 Asian Americans or Pacific Islanders, 20 Hispanic Americans). Average age 27. 2,569 applicants, 58% accepted, 255 enrolled. *Entrance requirements:* LSAT, LSDAS. Additional exam requirements/recommendations for international students: Required—TOEFL (minimum score 600 paper-based; 250 computer-based; 100 iBT). *Application deadline:* For fall admission, 3/15 for domestic students. Applications are processed on a rolling basis. Application fee: $65. Electronic applications accepted. *Expenses:* Tuition: Full-time $38,500; part-time $28,880 per year. Required fees: $80; $80 per year. *Financial support:* Federal Work-Study, scholarships/grants, and tuition waivers (full and partial) available. Support available to part-time students. Financial award applicants required to submit FAFSA. *Unit head:* John F. O'Brien, Dean, 617-422-7221, Fax: 617-422-7333, E-mail: jobrien@nesl.edu. *Application contact:* Michelle L'Etoile, Director of Admissions, 617-422-7210, Fax: 617-422-7201, E-mail: admit@nesl.edu.

New York Law School, Graduate Programs, New York, NY 10013. Offers law (JD); mental disability law (MA); real estate (LL M); taxation (LL M); JD/MBA. *Accreditation:* ABA. Part-time and evening/weekend programs available. Postbaccalaureate distance learning degree programs offered. *Entrance requirements:* LSAT, letters of recommendation, resume. Additional exam requirements/recommendations for international students: Recommended—TOEFL (minimum score 600 paper-based; 250 computer-based; 100 iBT). Electronic applications accepted.

See Close-Up on page 1699.

New York University, School of Law, New York, NY 10012-1019. Offers law (JD, LL M, JSD); law and business (Advanced Certificate); taxation (Advanced Certificate); JD/LL B; JD/LL M; JD/MA; JD/MBA; JD/MPA; JD/MPP; JD/MSW; JD/MUP; JD/PhD. *Accreditation:* ABA. Part-time programs available. *Faculty:* 125 full-time (36 women), 70 part-time/adjunct (23 women). *Students:* 1,427 full-time (628 women); includes 332 minority (88 African Americans, 3 American Indian/Alaska Native, 150 Asian Americans or Pacific Islanders, 91 Hispanic Americans), 44 international. 7,272 applicants, 450 enrolled. In 2009, 471 first professional degrees, 534 master's, 3 doctorates awarded. *Entrance requirements:* LSAT. *Application deadline:* For fall admission, 2/1 for domestic students. Application fee: $75. Electronic applications accepted. *Expenses:* Contact institution. *Financial support:* Fellowships, research assistantships, teaching assistantships, career-related internships or fieldwork, Federal Work-Study, institutionally sponsored loans, scholarships/grants, tuition waivers (partial), and loan repayment assistance available. Financial award application deadline: 4/15; financial award applicants required to submit FAFSA. *Faculty research:* International law, environmental law, corporate law, globalization of law, philosophy of law. *Unit head:* Richard L. Revesz, Dean, 212-998-6000, Fax: 212-995-3150. *Application contact:* Kenneth J. Kleinrock, Assistant Dean for Admissions, 212-998-6060, Fax: 212-995-4527.

North Carolina Central University, Division of Academic Affairs, School of Law, Durham, NC 27707. Offers JD, JD/MLS. *Accreditation:* ABA. Part-time and evening/weekend programs available. *Entrance requirements:* LSAT, LSDAS. Additional exam requirements/recommendations for international students: Required—TOEFL. *Expenses:* Contact institution.

Northeastern University, School of Law, Boston, MA 02115-5005. Offers JD, JD/MBA, JD/MPH, JD/MS/MBA, JD/PhD. *Accreditation:* ABA. *Students:* 618 full-time (368 women); includes 215 minority (69 African Americans, 9 American Indian/Alaska Native, 65 Asian Americans or Pacific Islanders, 72 Hispanic Americans), 7 international. Average age 26. In 2009, 220 JDs awarded. *Entrance requirements:* LSAT. *Application deadline:* For fall admission, 3/1 for domestic students. Applications are processed on a rolling basis. Application fee: $75. Electronic applications accepted. *Expenses:* Contact institution. *Financial support:* In 2009–10, 405 students received support; fellowships, research assistantships, teaching assistantships, career-related internships or fieldwork, Federal Work-Study, institutionally sponsored loans, scholarships/grants, and tuition waivers (full and partial) available. Financial award application deadline: 2/15; financial award applicants required to submit CSS PROFILE or FAFSA. *Faculty research:* Domestic violence, certiorari/criminal appeals, prisoners' rights, tobacco control, poverty law and practice. *Unit head:* Emily A. Spieler, Dean, 617-373-3307, Fax: 617-373-8793, E-mail: e.spieler@neu.edu. *Application contact:* Judy Cote, Information Contact, 617-373-2395, Fax: 617-373-8865, E-mail: lawweb@neu.edu.

Northern Illinois University, College of Law, De Kalb, IL 60115-2854. Offers JD. *Accreditation:* ABA. Part-time programs available. *Faculty:* 22 full-time (11 women). *Students:* 308 full-time (142 women); includes 69 minority (22 African Americans, 1 American Indian/Alaska Native, 22 Asian Americans or Pacific Islanders, 24 Hispanic Americans), 1 international. Average age 26. 1,514 applicants, 26% accepted, 105 enrolled. In 2009, 92 JDs awarded. *Entrance requirements:* LSAT. Additional exam requirements/recommendations for international students: Required—TOEFL. *Application deadline:* For fall admission, 5/15 priority date for domestic and international students. Applications are processed on a rolling basis. Application fee: $35 ($50 for international students). Electronic applications accepted. *Expenses:* Contact institution. *Financial support:* In 2009–10, 8 teaching assistantships were awarded; research assistantships, career-related internships or fieldwork, Federal Work-Study, tuition waivers (full and partial), and unspecified assistantships also available. Support available to part-time students. Financial award application deadline: 3/1; financial award applicants required to submit FAFSA. *Faculty research:* Feminist legal theory, environment law, agricultural law, administrative law, constitutional law. *Unit head:* Jennifer L. Rosato, Dean, 815-753-1380, Fax: 815-753-8552, E-mail: jrosato@niu.edu. *Application contact:* Judith L. Malen, Director of Admissions and Financial Aid, 815-753-1420, E-mail: jmalen@niu.edu.

Northern Kentucky University, Salmon P. Chase College of Law, Highland Heights, KY 41099. Offers JD, JD/MBA. *Accreditation:* ABA. Part-time and evening/weekend programs available. *Faculty:* 38 full-time (14 women), 14 part-time/adjunct (4 women). *Students:* 357 full-time (163 women), 215 part-time (106 women); includes 58 minority (33 African Americans, 2 American Indian/Alaska Native, 15 Asian Americans or Pacific Islanders, 8 Hispanic Americans). Average age 24. 1,225 applicants, 43% accepted, 194 enrolled. In 2009, 120 JDs awarded. *Entrance requirements:* LSAT. Additional exam requirements/recommendations for international students: Required—TOEFL. *Application deadline:* For fall admission, 4/1 priority date for domestic and international students. Applications are processed on a rolling basis. Application fee: $40. Electronic applications accepted. *Expenses:* Contact institution. *Financial support:* In 2009–10, 171 students received support, including 14 fellowships (averaging $3,500 per year), 33 research assistantships (averaging $1,000 per year); career-related internships or fieldwork, Federal Work-Study, scholarships/grants, and unspecified assistantships also available. Support available to part-time students. Financial award application deadline: 3/1; financial award applicants required to submit FAFSA. *Faculty research:* Transactional law; legal advocacy; alternative dispute resolution; employment and employment discrimination law; mandatory arbitration of employment disputes; local government law; tort law: libel, defamation, and privacy; constitutional and criminal law: parallels between the self-incrimination and confrontation clauses; art law: a principled approach to art restitution; business law: financing small businesses. *Unit head:* Dennis R. Honabach, Dean, 859-572-6406, Fax: 859-572-6183, E-mail: honabachd1@nku.edu. *Application contact:* Ashley Folger Gray, Director of Admissions, 859-572-5841, Fax: 859-572-6081, E-mail: graya4@nku.edu.

Northwestern University, The Graduate School, Program in Law and Social Science, Evanston, IL 60208. Offers Certificate. *Degree requirements:* For Certificate, research project. *Faculty research:* Law and social science.

Northwestern University, Law School, Chicago, IL 60611-3069. Offers executive (LL M); international human rights (LL M); law (JD, LL M); tax (LL M in Tax); two-year accelerated (JD); JD/LL M; JD/MBA; JD/PhD; LL M/Certificate. *Accreditation:* ABA. *Entrance requirements:* For JD, LSAT, 1 letter of recommendation, resume; for master's, law degree or equivalent, letter of recommendation, resume. Additional exam requirements/recommendations for international students: Required—TOEFL. Electronic applications accepted. *Expenses:* Contact institution. *Faculty research:* Constitutional law, corporate law, international law, law and social policy, ethical studies.

Nova Southeastern University, Shepard Broad Law Center, Ft. Lauderdale, FL 33314. Offers education law (MS, Certificate); employment law (MS); health law (MS); law (JD); JD/MBA; JD/MS; JD/MURP. *Accreditation:* ABA. Part-time and evening/weekend programs available. Postbaccalaureate distance learning degree programs offered (minimal on-campus study). *Faculty:* 63 full-time (35 women), 48 part-time/adjunct (18 women). *Students:* 1,080 full-time (582 women), 163 part-time (128 women); includes 394 minority (94 African Americans, 5 American Indian/Alaska Native, 57 Asian Americans or Pacific Islanders, 238 Hispanic Americans), 27 international. 2,855 applicants, 45% accepted, 384 enrolled. In 2009, 527 first professional degrees, 34 master's awarded. *Degree requirements:* For JD, thesis/dissertation. *Entrance requirements:* LSAT. *Application deadline:* For fall admission, 3/1 priority date for domestic students. Applications are processed on a rolling basis. Application fee: $50. Electronic applications accepted. *Expenses:* Contact institution. *Financial support:* In 2009–10, 58 fellowships were awarded; research assistantships, teaching assistantships, Federal Work-Study, scholarships/grants, tuition waivers (full and partial), and unspecified assistantships also available. Support available to part-time students. Financial award application deadline: 4/15; financial award applicants required to submit FAFSA. *Faculty research:* Legal issues in family law, civil rights, business associations, criminal law, law and popular culture. *Unit head:* Joseph D. Harbaugh, Dean, 954-262-6105, Fax: 954-262-3834, E-mail: harbaughj@nsu.law.nova.edu. *Application contact:* Beth Hall, Assistant Dean of Admissions, 954-262-6121, Fax: 954-262-3844, E-mail: hallb@nsu.law.nova.edu.

Ohio Northern University, Claude W. Pettit College of Law, Ada, OH 45810-1599. Offers JD, LL M. *Accreditation:* ABA. *Entrance requirements:* LSAT. Additional exam requirements/recommendations for international students: Required—TOEFL. Electronic applications accepted. *Expenses:* Contact institution. *Faculty research:* Constitutional law, environmental law, business law and taxation, criminal law, public interest law, death penalty for women and juveniles, international human rights, sports violence.

The Ohio State University, Moritz College of Law, Columbus, OH 43210. Offers JD, LL M, MSL, JD/MBA, JD/MD, JD/MHA, JD/MPH, JD/PhD. *Accreditation:* ABA. Electronic applica-

Law

The Ohio State University (continued)

tions accepted. *Expenses:* Contact institution. *Faculty research:* Alternative dispute resolution, law and policy, clinical programs, criminal law, intellectual property, cyberlaw.

Oklahoma City University, School of Law, Oklahoma City, OK 73106-1402. Offers JD, JD/MBA. *Accreditation:* ABA. Part-time and evening/weekend programs available. *Entrance requirements:* LSAT. *Application deadline:* For fall admission, 6/1 for domestic students. Application fee: $50 ($70 for international students). Electronic applications accepted. *Expenses:* Contact institution. *Financial support:* Career-related internships or fieldwork, Federal Work-Study, institutionally sponsored loans, and tuition waivers (partial) available. Support available to part-time students. Financial award application deadline: 8/1; financial award applicants required to submit FAFSA. *Faculty research:* Family law, environmental law, consumer law, alternative dispute resolution, criminal law and procedure. *Unit head:* Dr. Larry Hellman, Dean, 405-208-5337, Fax: 405-208-6041, E-mail: lhellman@okcu.edu. *Application contact:* Heidi Puckett, Associate Director, Law School Admissions, 405-208-5354, Fax: 405-208-5814, E-mail: hpuckett@okcu.edu.

Pace University, School of Law, White Plains, NY 10603. Offers comparative legal studies (LL M); environmental law (LL M, SJD); law (JD); real estate law (LL M); JD/MA; JD/MBA; JD/MEM; JD/MPA; JD/MS. *Accreditation:* ABA. Part-time and evening/weekend programs available. *Faculty:* 41 full-time (18 women), 52 part-time/adjunct (23 women). *Students:* 582 full-time (326 women), 230 part-time (145 women); includes 136 minority (33 African Americans, 1 American Indian/Alaska Native, 53 Asian Americans or Pacific Islanders, 49 Hispanic Americans), 17 international. Average age 26. 3,048 applicants, 38% accepted, 263 enrolled. In 2009, 216 first professional degrees, 20 master's, 1 doctorate awarded. *Entrance requirements:* LSAT. Additional exam requirements/recommendations for international students: Required—TOEFL (minimum score 600 paper-based; 250 computer-based); Recommended—TWE. *Application deadline:* For fall admission, 3/1 priority date for domestic students; for winter admission, 11/1 priority date for domestic students. Applications are processed on a rolling basis. Application fee: $65. Electronic applications accepted. *Expenses:* Contact institution. *Financial support:* Career-related internships or fieldwork, Federal Work-Study, institutionally sponsored loans, and scholarships/grants available. Support available to part-time students. Financial award application deadline: 2/15; financial award applicants required to submit FAFSA. *Faculty research:* Reform of energy regulations, international law, land use law, prosecutorial misconduct, corporation law, international sale of goods. Total annual research expenditures: $2.2 million. *Unit head:* Michelle S. Simon, Dean, 914-422-4407, E-mail: msimon@law.pace.edu. *Application contact:* Cathy Alexander, Assistant Dean, 914-422-4210, Fax: 914-989-8714, E-mail: calexander@law.pace.edu.

See Close-Up on page 1701.

Park University, College of Graduate and Professional Studies, Kansas City, MO 54105. Offers adult education (M Ed); at-risk students (M Ed); disaster and emergency management (MPA); educational administration (M Ed); entrepreneurship (MBA); general business (MBA); general education (M Ed); government/business relations (MPA); healthcare/services management (MBA, MPA); international business (MBA); K-12 certification (MAT); management information systems (MBA); management of information systems (MPA); middle school certification (MAT); multi-cultural education (M Ed); nonprofit management (MPA); public management (MPA); school law (M Ed); secondary school certification (MAT); special education (M Ed). Part-time and evening/weekend programs available. Postbaccalaureate distance learning degree programs offered (no on-campus study). *Degree requirements:* For master's, comprehensive exam, thesis (for some programs). *Entrance requirements:* For master's, GRE, GMAT, teacher certification (M Ed). Additional exam requirements/recommendations for international students: Required—TOEFL (minimum score 550 paper-based). Electronic applications accepted. *Faculty research:* Literacy, leadership, brain based research, multicultural education, diversity.

Penn State Dickinson School of Law, Graduate and Professional Programs, Carlisle, PA 17013-2899. Offers comparative law (LL M); law (JD). *Accreditation:* ABA. Part-time programs available. *Students:* 586 full-time (234 women), 11 part-time (5 women). Average age 25. In 2009, 212 JDs, 6 master's awarded. *Entrance requirements:* For JD, LSAT, employment record, 2 letters of recommendation; for master's, application appraisals. Additional exam requirements/recommendations for international students: Required—TOEFL (JD). *Application deadline:* For fall admission, 3/1 priority date for domestic students. Applications are processed on a rolling basis. Application fee: $60. Electronic applications accepted. *Financial support:* Research assistantships, Federal Work-Study, institutionally sponsored loans, and scholarships/grants available. Support available to part-time students. Financial award application deadline: 3/1; financial award applicants required to submit FAFSA. *Faculty research:* Arbitration, sports law, international human rights law, alternate dispute resolution. *Unit head:* Philip J. McConnaughay, Dean, 814-863-1521, E-mail: pjm30@psu.edu. *Application contact:* Barbara W. Guillaume, Director, Law Admissions, 717-240-5207, Fax: 717-241-3503, E-mail: bwg1@psu.edu.

Pepperdine University, School of Law, Professional Program, Malibu, CA 90263. Offers JD, JD/MBA. *Accreditation:* ABA. *Entrance requirements:* LSAT, 2 letters of recommendation. *Expenses:* Contact institution.

Pontifical Catholic University of Puerto Rico, School of Law, Ponce, PR 00717-0777. Offers JD. *Accreditation:* ABA. Part-time and evening/weekend programs available. *Entrance requirements:* LSAT, PAEG, 3 letters of recommendation.

Pontificia Universidad Catolica Madre y Maestra, Graduate School, Santiago, Dominican Republic. Offers administration (M Adm); architecture of interiors (M Arch); architecture of tourist lodgings (M Arch); banking and financial management (M Mgmt); civil law (LL M); construction administration (ME); corporate business law (LL M); criminal procedure law (LL M); environmental engineering (ME, MEE); finance (M Mgmt); history applied to education (M Ed); human resources (EMBA); insurance (M Mgmt); international business (M Mgmt); labor law and Social Security (LL M); logistics management (ME); marketing (M Mgmt); renewable energy (ME); strategic cost management (M Mgmt). *Entrance requirements:* For master's, curriculum vitae, interview.

Queen's University at Kingston, Faculty of Law, Kingston, ON K7L 3N6, Canada. Offers JD, LL M, JD/MBA, JD/MIR, JD/MPA. Part-time programs available. *Degree requirements:* For master's, thesis. *Entrance requirements:* LSAT, minimum 2 years of college. Additional exam requirements/recommendations for international students: Required—TOEFL, TWE. *Faculty research:* Labor relations law, tax law and policy, criminal law and policy, critical legal theories, international legal relations.

Quinnipiac University, School of Law, Hamden, CT 06518. Offers health law (LL M); law (JD); JD/MBA. *Accreditation:* ABA. Part-time and evening/weekend programs available. *Faculty:* 35 full-time (14 women), 33 part-time/adjunct (7 women). *Students:* 291 full-time (154 women), 124 part-time (58 women); includes 53 minority (13 African Americans, 3 American Indian/Alaska Native, 21 Asian Americans or Pacific Islanders, 16 Hispanic Americans), 11 international. Average age 25. 2,824 applicants, 41% accepted, 160 enrolled. In 2009, 100 JDs awarded. *Entrance requirements:* LSAT. *Application deadline:* For fall admission, 3/1 priority date for domestic students. Applications are processed on a rolling basis. Application fee: $40. Electronic applications accepted. *Expenses:* Contact institution. *Financial support:* In 2009–10, 354 students received support, including 23 fellowships (averaging $1,560 per year), 38 research assistantships (averaging $680 per year), career-related internships or fieldwork, Federal Work-Study, and scholarships/grants also available. Support available to part-time students. Financial award application deadline: 4/15; financial award applicants required to submit FAFSA. *Faculty research:* Tax, health, public interest, corporate law, dispute resolution, intellectual property. *Unit head:* Brad Saxton, Dean, 203-582-3200, Fax: 203-582-3209, E-mail: ladm@quinnipiac.edu. *Application contact:* Edwin Wilkes, Executive Dean of Law School Admissions, 203-582-3400, Fax: 203-582-3339, E-mail: ladm@quinnipiac.edu.

Regent University, Graduate School, Robertson School of Government, Virginia Beach, VA 23464. Offers American government (MA); global politics (MA); health care policy and administration (MA); international politics (MA); law and public policy (MA); Mid-East politics (MA); political leadership and management (MA); political management (MA); political theory (MA); public administration (MA); public policy (MA); terrorism and homeland defense (MA); world economies and political development (MA); JD/MA; M Div/MA; M Ed/MA; MBA/MA. Part-time and evening/weekend programs available. Postbaccalaureate distance learning degree programs offered (minimal on-campus study). *Faculty:* 6 full-time (2 women), 11 part-time/adjunct (1 woman). *Students:* 77 full-time (55 women), 65 part-time (36 women); includes 47 minority (38 African Americans, 2 Asian Americans or Pacific Islanders, 7 Hispanic Americans), 4 international. Average age 30. 131 applicants, 65% accepted, 54 enrolled. In 2009, 51 master's awarded. *Degree requirements:* For master's, thesis optional, internship. *Entrance requirements:* For master's, GRE General Test or LSAT, minimum undergraduate GPA of 3.0, writing sample, resume, interview, references. Additional exam requirements/recommendations for international students: Required—TOEFL (minimum score 577 paper-based; 233 computer-based). *Application deadline:* For fall admission, 5/1 priority date for domestic students; for spring admission, 11/1 priority date for domestic students. Applications are processed on a rolling basis. Application fee: $50. Electronic applications accepted. *Expenses:* Contact institution. *Financial support:* In 2009–10, 130 students received support. Career-related internships or fieldwork, scholarships/grants, tuition waivers (full and partial), and unspecified assistantships available. Support available to part-time students. Financial award application deadline: 9/1; financial award applicants required to submit FAFSA. *Faculty research:* Education reform, political character issues, social capital concerns, administrative ethics, Biblical law and public policy. *Unit head:* Dr. Charles W. Dunn, Dean, 757-352-4322, Fax: 757-352-4643, E-mail: cwdunn@regent.edu. *Application contact:* Matthew Chadwick, Director of Admissions, 800-373-5504, Fax: 757-352-4381, E-mail: admissions@regent.edu.

Regent University, Graduate School, School of Law, Virginia Beach, VA 23464. Offers American legal studies (LL M); law (JD); JD/MA; JD/MBA. *Accreditation:* ABA. Part-time programs available. *Faculty:* 26 full-time (8 women), 44 part-time/adjunct (8 women). *Students:* 415 full-time (204 women), 5 part-time (3 women); includes 63 minority (29 African Americans, 6 American Indian/Alaska Native, 18 Asian Americans or Pacific Islanders, 10 Hispanic Americans), 5 international. Average age 27. 892 applicants, 42% accepted, 111 enrolled. In 2009, 146 degrees awarded. *Entrance requirements:* LSAT, minimum undergraduate GPA of 2.75, 3 letters of recommendation, resume. Additional exam requirements/recommendations for international students: Required—TOEFL (minimum score 600 paper-based; 250 computer-based). *Application deadline:* For fall admission, 3/1 for domestic students. Applications are processed on a rolling basis. Application fee: $50. Electronic applications accepted. *Expenses:* Contact institution. *Financial support:* In 2009–10, 408 students received support. Career-related internships or fieldwork, scholarships/grants, and tuition waivers (full and partial) available. Support available to part-time students. Financial award application deadline: 2/1; financial award applicants required to submit FAFSA. *Faculty research:* Family law, Constitutional law, law and culture, evidence and practice, intellectual property. *Unit head:* Jeffrey Brauch, Dean, 757-352-4040, Fax: 757-352-4595, E-mail: jeffbra@regent.edu. *Application contact:* Matthew Chadwick, Director of Admissions, 800-373-5504, Fax: 757-352-4381, E-mail: admissions@regent.edu.

Roger Williams University, School of Law, Bristol, RI 02809-5171. Offers JD, JD/MLRHR, JD/MMA, JD/MSCJ. *Accreditation:* ABA. *Entrance requirements:* LSAT. Additional exam requirements/recommendations for international students: Required—TOEFL (minimum score 600 paper-based; 250 computer-based; 100 iBT). Electronic applications accepted. *Faculty research:* Civil rights, admiralty, labor, intellectual property, international and comparative law.

Rutgers, The State University of New Jersey, Camden, School of Law, Camden, NJ 08102. Offers JD, JD/DO, JD/MA, JD/MBA, JD/MCRP, JD/MD, JD/MPA, JD/MS, JD/MSW. *Accreditation:* ABA. Part-time and evening/weekend programs available. *Entrance requirements:* LSAT. Electronic applications accepted. *Expenses:* Contact institution. *Faculty research:* International law, commercial law, public law, health law, constitutional law, jurisprudence.

Rutgers, The State University of New Jersey, Newark, School of Law, Newark, NJ 07102-3094. Offers JD, JD/MA, JD/MBA, JD/MCRP, JD/MD, JD/MSW, JD/PhD. *Accreditation:* ABA. Part-time and evening/weekend programs available. *Entrance requirements:* LSAT. *Expenses:* Contact institution. *Faculty research:* Civil rights and liberties, women and the law, international human rights and world order, corporate law, employment law.

St. John's University, School of Law, Program in Law, Queens, NY 11439. Offers JD. *Students:* 745 full-time (334 women), 177 part-time (99 women); includes 222 minority (60 African Americans, 83 Asian Americans or Pacific Islanders, 79 Hispanic Americans), 10 international. Average age 26. 4,036 applicants, 37% accepted, 308 enrolled. In 2009, 285 JDs awarded. *Entrance requirements:* LSAT. Additional exam requirements/recommendations for international students: Required—TOEFL (minimum score 500 paper-based; 173 computer-based; 61 iBT), IELTS (minimum score 5.5). *Application deadline:* For fall admission, 4/1 priority date for domestic and international students. Applications are processed on a rolling basis. Application fee: $60. Electronic applications accepted. *Expenses:* Tuition: Full-time $16,290; part-time $905 per credit. Required fees: $300; $150 per semester. Tuition and fees vary according to program. *Unit head:* Michael A. Simons, Dean, 718-990-6601, Fax: 718-990-6694, E-mail: simonsm@stjohns.edu. *Application contact:* Robert Harrison, Assistant Dean and Director of Admissions, 718-990-2310, Fax: 718-990-6699, E-mail: lawinfo@stjohns.edu.

Saint Joseph's University, College of Arts and Sciences, Department of Criminal Justice, Philadelphia, PA 19131-1395. Offers administration/police executive (MS); behavior analysis (MS, Post-Master's Certificate); criminal justice (MS, Post-Master's Certificate); criminology (MS); federal law (MS); intelligence and crime (MS); probation, parole, and corrections (MS). Part-time and evening/weekend programs available. Postbaccalaureate distance learning degree programs offered (no on-campus study). *Students:* 2 full-time (0 women), 302 part-time (193 women); includes 88 minority (64 African Americans, 1 American Indian/Alaska Native, 3 Asian Americans or Pacific Islanders, 20 Hispanic Americans), 2 international. Average age 33. In 2009, 86 master's awarded. *Degree requirements:* For master's, thesis. *Entrance requirements:* For master's, GRE General Test or minimum GPA of 3.0, 2 letters of recommendation. Additional exam requirements/recommendations for international students: Required—TOEFL (minimum score 550 paper-based; 213 computer-based; 79 iBT). *Application deadline:* For fall admission, 7/15 priority date for domestic students, 4/15 for international students; for winter admission, 1/15 for international students; for spring admission, 11/15 priority date for domestic students, 10/15 for international students. Applications are processed on a rolling basis. Application fee: $35. Electronic applications accepted. *Expenses:* Tuition: Part-time $729 per credit hour. Tuition and fees vary according to degree level and program. *Financial support:* Career-related internships or fieldwork and unspecified assistantships available. Financial award applicants required to submit FAFSA. *Unit head:* Patricia Griffin, Director, 610-660-1294, E-mail: pgriffin@sju.edu. *Application contact:* Kate McConnell, Director, Graduate College of Arts and Sciences Admissions and Retention, 610-660-3184, Fax: 610-660-3230, E-mail: kate.mconnell@sju.edu.

Saint Louis University, School of Law, St. Louis, MO 63108. Offers JD, LL M. *Accreditation:* ABA. Part-time and evening/weekend programs available. *Degree requirements:* For master's, thesis (for some programs). *Entrance requirements:* For JD, LSAT/LSDAS, letters of recommendation, resumé, personal statement; for master's, JD or equivalent. Additional exam requirements/recommendations for international students: Required—TOEFL (minimum score 590 paper-based; 194 computer-based). Electronic applications accepted. *Expenses:* Contact institution. *Faculty research:* Health law, employment law, international comparative law, lawyering skills (clinical).

St. Mary's University, School of Law, San Antonio, TX 78228-8602. Offers JD, JD/MA, JD/MBA, JD/MPA, JD/MS. *Accreditation:* ABA. *Faculty:* 39 full-time (14 women), 21 part-time/adjunct (9 women). *Students:* 796 full-time (348 women), 72 part-time (27 women); includes 285 minority (30 African Americans, 7 American Indian/Alaska Native, 40 Asian Americans or

Pacific Islanders, 208 Hispanic Americans), 2 international. 1,900 applicants, 42% accepted, 292 enrolled. In 2009, 206 JDs awarded. *Entrance requirements:* LSAT. Additional exam requirements/recommendations for international students: Required—TOEFL (minimum score 600 paper-based; 213 computer-based). *Application deadline:* For fall admission, 3/1 for domestic students. Application fee: $55. Electronic applications accepted. *Expenses:* Contact institution. *Financial support:* In 2009–10, 68 research assistantships (averaging $1,900 per year), 58 teaching assistantships (averaging $1,250 per year) were awarded; career-related internships or fieldwork, Federal Work-Study, institutionally sponsored loans, scholarships/grants, and health care benefits also available. Financial award application deadline: 2/15; financial award applicants required to submit FAFSA. *Faculty research:* Ethics, church and state, exclusionary rule, civil rights, tort law. *Unit head:* Dr. Charles Cantu, Interim Dean, 210-436-3424, Fax: 210-436-3515. *Application contact:* Dr. William Charles Wilson, Assistant Dean and Director of Admissions, 210-436-3523, Fax: 210-431-4202.

St. Thomas University, School of Law, Miami Gardens, FL 33054-6459. Offers international human rights (LL M); international taxation (LL M); law (JD); JD/MBA; JD/MS. *Accreditation:* ABA. Postbaccalaureate distance learning degree programs offered (no on-campus study). *Degree requirements:* For master's, thesis (international taxation). *Entrance requirements:* LSAT. Electronic applications accepted. *Expenses:* Contact institution.

Samford University, Cumberland School of Law, Birmingham, AL 35229. Offers JD, MCL, JD/M Acc, JD/M Div, JD/MBA, JD/MPA, JD/MPH, JD/MSEM, JD/MTS. *Accreditation:* ABA. Part-time programs available. *Faculty:* 22 full-time (7 women), 13 part-time/adjunct (5 women). *Students:* 480 full-time (215 women), 9 part-time (6 women); includes 37 minority (26 African Americans, 5 American Indian/Alaska Native, 3 Asian Americans or Pacific Islanders, 3 Hispanic Americans). Average age 24. 980 applicants, 52% accepted, 178 enrolled. In 2009, 164 first professional degrees, 3 master's awarded. *Entrance requirements:* LSAT. Additional exam requirements/recommendations for international students: Required—TOEFL (minimum score 550 paper-based; 213 computer-based). *Application deadline:* For fall admission, 2/28 priority date for domestic and international students. Applications are processed on a rolling basis. Application fee: $50. Electronic applications accepted. *Expenses:* Contact institution. *Financial support:* In 2009–10, 161 students received support. Career-related internships or fieldwork, Federal Work-Study, institutionally sponsored loans, and scholarships/grants available. Financial award application deadline: 3/1; financial award applicants required to submit FAFSA. *Faculty research:* Constitutional law (commerce clause), law and literature, legal history, law and ethics, evidence. *Unit head:* John L. Carroll, Dean, 205-726-2704, Fax: 205-726-4107, E-mail: jlcarrol@samford.edu. *Application contact:* Jennifer Y. Sims, Assistant Dean of Admissions, 205-726-2702, Fax: 205-726-2057, E-mail: law.admissions@samford.edu.

San Joaquin College of Law, Law Program, Clovis, CA 93612-1312. Offers JD. Part-time and evening/weekend programs available. *Entrance requirements:* LSAT.

Santa Clara University, School of Law, Santa Clara, CA 95053. Offers high technology law (Certificate); intellectual property law (LL M); international and comparative law (LL M); international high tech law (Certificate); international law (Certificate); law (JD); public interest and social justice law (Certificate); US law for foreign lawyers (LL M); JD/MBA. *Accreditation:* ABA. Part-time and evening/weekend programs available. *Faculty:* 65 full-time (33 women), 45 part-time/adjunct (19 women). *Students:* 948 full-time (431 women), 81 part-time (40 women); includes 386 minority (28 African Americans, 10 American Indian/Alaska Native, 265 Asian Americans or Pacific Islanders, 83 Hispanic Americans), 47 international. Average age 27. 4,164 applicants, 42% accepted, 363 enrolled. In 2009, 266 first professional degrees, 19 master's awarded. *Degree requirements:* For master's, thesis; for JD, thesis/dissertation. *Entrance requirements:* LSAT. *Application deadline:* For fall admission, 2/1 for domestic and international students. Applications are processed on a rolling basis. Application fee: $75. Electronic applications accepted. *Expenses:* Contact institution. *Financial support:* In 2009–10, 847 students received support, including 841 fellowships with full and partial tuition reimbursements available (averaging $12,346 per year). Financial award application deadline: 2/1; financial award applicants required to submit FAFSA. *Unit head:* Donald Polden, Dean, 408-554-4362. *Application contact:* Jeannette Leach, Director of Admissions, 408-554-5048.

Seattle University, School of Law, Seattle, WA 98122-4340. Offers JD, JD/MATL, JD/MBA, JD/MCJ, JD/MIB, JD/MPA, JD/MSF, JD/MSL. *Accreditation:* ABA. Part-time programs available. *Entrance requirements:* LSAT. Additional exam requirements/recommendations for international students: Required—TOEFL (minimum score 600 paper-based; 250 computer-based; 100 iBT). Electronic applications accepted. *Expenses:* Contact institution. *Faculty research:* Race, postcolonial theory, and U.S. civil rights; secrecy and democratic decisions; linguistic features of police culture and the coercive impact of police officer swearing in police-citizen interaction; the imprisoned parent: differential power in same-sex families based on legal and cultural understandings of parentage; theology in public reason and legal discourse: a case for the preferential option for the poor.

Seton Hall University, School of Law, Newark, NJ 07102-5210. Offers health law (JD, LL M); intellectual property (JD, LL M); law (MSJ); JD/MADIR; JD/MBA; MD/JD; MD/MSJ. *Accreditation:* ABA. Part-time and evening/weekend programs available. *Faculty:* 51 full-time (23 women), 84 part-time/adjunct (36 women). *Students:* 729 full-time (329 women), 422 part-time (208 women); includes 169 minority (36 African Americans, 1 American Indian/Alaska Native, 79 Asian Americans or Pacific Islanders, 53 Hispanic Americans), 12 international. Average age 27. 3,741 applicants, 44% accepted, 393 enrolled. In 2009, 308 JDs, 18 master's awarded. *Degree requirements:* For master's, thesis optional. *Entrance requirements:* For JD, LSAT, active LSDAS registration, letters of recommendation; for master's, professional experience, letters of recommendation. *Application deadline:* For fall admission, 4/1 priority date for domestic and international students. Applications are processed on a rolling basis. Application fee: $65. Electronic applications accepted. *Expenses:* Contact institution. *Financial support:* In 2009–10, 990 students received support, including 30 fellowships (averaging $2,900 per year), 142 research assistantships (averaging $2,200 per year), 11 teaching assistantships (averaging $1,500 per year); career-related internships or fieldwork, Federal Work-Study, institutionally sponsored loans, scholarships/grants, and unspecified assistantships also available. Support available to part-time students. Financial award application deadline: 4/1; financial award applicants required to submit FAFSA. *Faculty research:* Health law, intellectual property law, science and the law, international law and employment/labor law. Total annual research expenditures: $480,700. *Unit head:* Patrick E. Hobbs, Dean and Professor of Law, 973-642-8750, Fax: 973-642-8031, E-mail: patrick.hobbs@shu.edu. *Application contact:* Gisele Joachim, Dean of Enrollment Management, 973-642-8747, Fax: 973-642-8876, E-mail: admitme@shu.edu.

Southern Illinois University Carbondale, School of Law, Carbondale, IL 62901-6804. Offers general law (LL M); health law and policy (LL M); law (JD); legal studies (MLS), including general law, health law and policy; JD/M Acc; JD/MBA; JD/MD; JD/MPA; JD/MSW; JD/PhD. *Accreditation:* ABA. Part-time programs available. *Entrance requirements:* LSAT. Additional exam requirements/recommendations for international students: Required—TOEFL (minimum score 600 paper-based). Electronic applications accepted. *Expenses:* Contact institution. *Faculty research:* Health care law, criminal law, environmental law, international law, tort reform.

Southern Methodist University, Dedman School of Law, Dallas, TX 75275-0110. Offers foreign law school graduates (LL M); law (JD, SJD); law-general (LL M); taxation (LL M); JD/MA; JD/MBA. *Accreditation:* ABA. Part-time and evening/weekend programs available. *Faculty:* 44 full-time (17 women), 45 part-time/adjunct (9 women). *Students:* 534 full-time (254 women), 320 part-time (143 women); includes 189 minority (43 African Americans, 10 American Indian/Alaska Native, 60 Asian Americans or Pacific Islanders, 76 Hispanic Americans). Average age 27. 3,015 applicants, 26% accepted, 309 enrolled. In 2009, 282 JDs, 77 master's, 2 doctorates awarded. *Degree requirements:* For master's, thesis optional; for doctorate, thesis/dissertation; for JD, 30 hours of public service. *Entrance requirements:* For JD, LSAT, 2 letters of recommendation, resume, personal statement; for master's, JD; for doctorate, LL M. Additional exam requirements/recommendations for international students: Required—TOEFL (minimum score 575 paper-based; 233 computer-based; 91 iBT). *Application deadline:* For fall admission, 2/15 priority date for domestic students. Applications are processed on a rolling basis. Application fee: $75. Electronic applications accepted. *Expenses:* Contact institution. *Financial support:* Career-related internships or fieldwork, Federal Work-Study, and scholarships/grants available. Financial award application deadline: 2/15; financial award applicants required to submit FAFSA. *Faculty research:* Corporate law, intellectual property, international law, commercial law, dispute resolution. *Unit head:* John B. Attanasio, Dean, 214-768-8999, Fax: 214-768-2182, E-mail: jba@mail.smu.edu. *Application contact:* Virginia Keehan, Assistant Dean for Admissions, 214-768-2550, Fax: 214-768-2549, E-mail: lawadmit@smu.edu.

Southern University and Agricultural and Mechanical College, Southern University Law Center, Baton Rouge, LA 70813. Offers JD. *Accreditation:* ABA; SACS. Part-time and evening/weekend programs available. *Entrance requirements:* LSAT. Electronic applications accepted. *Expenses:* Contact institution. *Faculty research:* Civil law, comparative law, constitutional law, civil rights law.

South Texas College of Law, Professional Program, Houston, TX 77002-7000. Offers JD. *Accreditation:* ABA. Part-time and evening/weekend programs available. *Faculty:* 54 full-time (19 women), 42 part-time/adjunct (15 women). *Students:* 973 full-time (481 women), 305 part-time (138 women); includes 332 minority (49 African Americans, 15 American Indian/Alaska Native, 129 Asian Americans or Pacific Islanders, 139 Hispanic Americans), 3 international. Average age 27. 2,377 applicants, 47% accepted, 434 enrolled. In 2009, 375 JDs awarded. *Degree requirements:* For JD, completion of 90 hours within 7 years of enrollment. *Entrance requirements:* LSAT (taken within last 4 years), degree from accredited 4-year institution. *Application deadline:* For fall admission, 2/15 for domestic and international students; for spring admission, 10/1 for domestic and international students. Application fee: $55. Electronic applications accepted. *Expenses:* Tuition: Full-time $25,110; part-time $16,740 per year. Required fees: $600; $600 per year. *Financial support:* In 2009–10, 1,222 students received support. Federal Work-Study, scholarships/grants, and tuition waivers (full and partial) available. Support available to part-time students. Financial award application deadline: 5/1; financial award applicants required to submit FAFSA. *Unit head:* Donald J. Guter, President and Dean, 713-646-1819, Fax: 713-646-2909, E-mail: dguter@stcl.edu. *Application contact:* Alicia K. Cramer, Assistant Dean of Admissions, 713-646-1810, Fax: 713-646-2906, E-mail: admissions@stcl.edu.

Southwestern Law School, Graduate Program, Los Angeles, CA 90010. Offers entertainment and media law (LL M); general studies (LL M); law (JD). *Accreditation:* ABA. Part-time and evening/weekend programs available. *Entrance requirements:* For JD, LSAT, LSDAS; for master's, JD. Additional exam requirements/recommendations for international students: Required—TOEFL. Electronic applications accepted. *Faculty research:* International trade and law, mediation/arbitration, land use and urban planning, antitrust law, entertainment and media law.

Stanford University, Law School, Stanford, CA 94305-8610. Offers JD, JSM, MLS, JSD, JD/MBA, JD/PhD. *Accreditation:* ABA. *Degree requirements:* For doctorate, thesis/dissertation. *Entrance requirements:* LSAT. Electronic applications accepted. *Expenses:* Contact institution.

Stetson University, College of Law, Gulfport, FL 33707-3299. Offers JD, LL M, JD/MBA. *Accreditation:* ABA. *Students:* 938 full-time (489 women), 197 part-time (111 women); includes 218 minority (77 African Americans, 12 American Indian/Alaska Native, 35 Asian Americans or Pacific Islanders, 94 Hispanic Americans), 13 international. Average age 27. In 2009, 311 JDs awarded. *Entrance requirements:* LSAT, LSDAS. *Application deadline:* For fall admission, 3/1 priority date for domestic students; for spring admission, 9/1 for domestic students. Application fee: $50. *Expenses:* Contact institution. *Financial support:* Research assistantships, teaching assistantships, career-related internships or fieldwork, institutionally sponsored loans, and scholarships/grants available. Financial award application deadline: 4/1; financial award applicants required to submit FAFSA. *Unit head:* Dr. Darby Dickerson, Dean, 727-562-7810. *Application contact:* Laura Zuppo, Executive Director of Admissions and Financial Aid, 727-562-7802, E-mail: lawadmit@law.stetson.edu.

Suffolk University, Law School, Boston, MA 02108. Offers business law and financial services (JD); civil litigation (JD); global law and technology (LL M); health and biomedical law (JD); intellectual property law (JD); international law (JD); U.S. and global business law (LL M); JD/MBA; JD/MPA; JD/MSCJ; JD/MSF; JD/MSIE. *Accreditation:* ABA. Part-time and evening/weekend programs available. *Degree requirements:* For master's, legal writing. *Entrance requirements:* For JD, LSAT, LSDAS, Dean's certification, recommendation; for master's, 2 letters of recommendation, resume, personal statement. Additional exam requirements/recommendations for international students: Required—TOEFL (minimum score 600 paper-based; 250 computer-based; 100 iBT). *Application deadline:* For fall admission, 3/1 priority date for domestic and international students. Applications are processed on a rolling basis. Application fee: $60. Electronic applications accepted. *Expenses:* Contact institution. *Financial support:* Career-related internships or fieldwork, Federal Work-Study, institutionally sponsored loans, and scholarships/grants available. Support available to part-time students. Financial award application deadline: 3/1; financial award applicants required to submit FAFSA. *Faculty research:* Civil law, international law, health/biomedical law, business and finance, intellectual property. *Unit head:* Gail N. Ellis, Dean of Admissions, 617-573-8144, Fax: 617-523-1367, E-mail: gellis@suffolk.edu. *Application contact:* Ian A. Menchini, Director of Electronic Marketing and Enrollment Management, 617-573-8144, Fax: 617-523-1367, E-mail: imenchin@suffolk.edu.

Syracuse University, College of Law, Syracuse, NY 13244-1030. Offers JD, JD/MA, JD/MBA, JD/MLS, JD/MPA, JD/MPS, JD/MS, JD/MS Acct, JD/MSW, JD/PhD. *Accreditation:* ABA. Part-time programs available. *Entrance requirements:* LSAT. Additional exam requirements/recommendations for international students: Required—TOEFL (minimum score 600 paper-based; 250 computer-based), TWE. Electronic applications accepted. *Expenses:* Contact institution. *Faculty research:* Interdisciplinary legal studies, law and technology, international law, advocacy training, family law.

Temple University, James E. Beasley School of Law, Philadelphia, PA 19122. Offers law (JD); legal education (SJD); taxation (LL M); transnational law (LL M); trial advocacy (LL M); JD/LL M; JD/MBA. *Accreditation:* ABA. Part-time and evening/weekend programs available. *Entrance requirements:* LSAT, LSDAS. Electronic applications accepted. *Expenses:* Contact institution. *Faculty research:* Comparative constitutional law, gender issues, immigration law, international intellectual property law and popular culture.

Texas Southern University, Thurgood Marshall School of Law, Houston, TX 77004-4584. Offers JD. *Accreditation:* ABA. *Faculty:* 35 full-time (20 women), 17 part-time/adjunct (5 women). *Students:* 541 full-time (284 women), 1 part-time (0 women); includes 438 minority (272 African Americans, 2 American Indian/Alaska Native, 35 Asian Americans or Pacific Islanders, 129 Hispanic Americans), 13 international. Average age 28. 261 applicants, 100% accepted, 230 enrolled. In 2009, 201 JDs awarded. *Entrance requirements:* LSAT. *Application deadline:* For fall admission, 4/1 for domestic and international students. Applications are processed on a rolling basis. Application fee: $55. Electronic applications accepted. *Expenses:* Contact institution. *Financial support:* In 2009–10, 75 students received support, including 2 research assistantships (averaging $5,750 per year), 93 teaching assistantships (averaging $1,835 per year); career-related internships or fieldwork, scholarships/grants, tuition waivers (partial), and unspecified assistantships also available. Financial award application deadline: 4/1; financial award applicants required to submit FAFSA. *Faculty research:* Sports law, civil rights and minors, international economics regulation, contracts principle, standards of judicial review. *Unit head:* Dr. Dannye Holley, Dean, 713-313-7388, Fax: 713-313-1049, E-mail: dholley@tsulaw.edu. *Application contact:* Edward Rene, Director of Admissions, 713-313-7115 Ext. 1004, Fax: 713-313-1049, E-mail: erene@tsulaw.edu.

Texas Tech University, School of Law, Lubbock, TX 79409-0004. Offers JD, JD/MBA, JD/MD, JD/MPA, JD/MS, JD/MSA. *Accreditation:* ABA. *Faculty:* 39 full-time (16 women), 11 part-time/adjunct (2 women). *Students:* 612 full-time (258 women), 26 part-time (8 women); includes 157 minority (24 African Americans, 6 American Indian/Alaska Native, 26 Asian Americans or Pacific Islanders, 101 Hispanic Americans), 2 international. Average age 25. 1,746 applicants,

Law

Texas Tech University (continued)
33% accepted, 184 enrolled. In 2009, 194 JDs awarded. *Entrance requirements:* LSAT. *Application deadline:* For fall admission, 2/1 priority date for domestic and international students. Applications are processed on a rolling basis. Application fee: $50 ($75 for international students). *Expenses:* Contact institution. *Financial support:* In 2009–10, 29 teaching assistantships with partial tuition reimbursements (averaging $7,427 per year) were awarded; research assistantships with partial tuition reimbursements, career-related internships or fieldwork, Federal Work-Study, and institutionally sponsored loans also available. Financial award application deadline: 4/15; financial award applicants required to submit FAFSA. *Faculty research:* Bioterrorism, water law, forensic mental health law, oil and gas law, international art law. Total annual research expenditures: $139,552. *Unit head:* Walter Burl Huffman, Dean, 806-742-3793, Fax: 806-742-4014, E-mail: walter.huffman@ttu.edu. *Application contact:* Terence Cook, Assistant Dean of Admissions and Recruitment, 806-742-3990 Ext. 273, Fax: 806-742-4617, E-mail: terence.cook@ttu.edu.

Texas Wesleyan University, School of Law, Fort Worth, TX 76102. Offers JD. *Accreditation:* ABA. Part-time and evening/weekend programs available. *Faculty:* 42 full-time (19 women), 22 part-time/adjunct (6 women). *Students:* 526 full-time (267 women), 269 part-time (135 women); includes 194 minority (51 African Americans, 12 American Indian/Alaska Native, 52 Asian Americans or Pacific Islanders, 79 Hispanic Americans), 2 international. Average age 29. 1,977 applicants, 44% accepted, 795 enrolled. In 2009, 207 JDs awarded. *Entrance requirements:* LSAT, LSDAS report, 2 letters of recommendation. Additional exam requirements/recommendations for international students: Required—TOEFL. *Application deadline:* For fall admission, 3/31 priority date for domestic students. Applications are processed on a rolling basis. Application fee: $55. Electronic applications accepted. *Expenses:* Contact institution. *Financial support:* Career-related internships or fieldwork, scholarships/grants, and tuition waivers (full and partial) available. Support available to part-time students. Financial award application deadline: 3/15; financial award applicants required to submit FAFSA. *Unit head:* Frederic White, Dean and Professor of Law, 817-212-4100, Fax: 817-212-4199. *Application contact:* Sherolyn Hurst, Assistant Dean of Admissions and Scholarships, 817-212-4040, Fax: 817-212-4141, E-mail: lawadmissions@law.txwes.edu.

Thomas Jefferson School of Law, Professional Program, San Diego, CA 92110-2905. Offers JD. *Accreditation:* ABA. Part-time and evening/weekend programs available. *Faculty:* 42 full-time (21 women), 53 part-time/adjunct (12 women). *Students:* 649 full-time (291 women), 241 part-time (114 women). Average age 26. *Entrance requirements:* LSAT. Additional exam requirements/recommendations for international students: Required—TOEFL. *Application deadline:* For fall admission, 12/1 priority date for domestic students; for spring admission, 10/1 priority date for domestic students. Applications are processed on a rolling basis. Application fee: $50. Electronic applications accepted. *Expenses:* Tuition: Full-time $36,300; part-time $24,000 per year. *Financial support:* Fellowships with full and partial tuition reimbursements, career-related internships or fieldwork, Federal Work-Study, scholarships/grants, and tuition waivers available. Support available to part-time students. Financial award application deadline: 4/30; financial award applicants required to submit FAFSA. *Faculty research:* Tenant's rights, fetal rights/medical ethics, bilateral treaties/international law, sexual harassment and gender treatment. *Unit head:* Rudolph C. Hasl, Dean and President, 619-297-9700 Ext. 1404, E-mail: hasl@tjsl.edu. *Application contact:* M. Elizabeth Kransberger, Assistant Dean for Admissions, Financial Aid, and Student Counseling Services, 619-297-9700 Ext. 1600, Fax: 619-294-4713, E-mail: bkransberger@tjsl.edu.

Thomas M. Cooley Law School, Graduate Programs, Lansing, MI 48901-3038. Offers corporate law and finance (LL M); intellectual property (LL M); law (JD); taxation (LL M). *Accreditation:* ABA. Part-time and evening/weekend programs available. *Degree requirements:* For JD, clinical experience. *Entrance requirements:* LSAT, LSDAS. Electronic applications accepted. *Faculty research:* Wrongful convictions, civil rights, environmental law, litigation techniques, death penalty.

Touro College, Jacob D. Fuchsberg Law Center, Huntington, NY 11743. Offers law (JD); U.S. law for foreign lawyers (LL M); JD/MBA; JD/MPA; JD/MSW. *Accreditation:* ABA. Part-time and evening/weekend programs available. *Entrance requirements:* LSAT. *Expenses:* Contact institution. *Faculty research:* Business law, civil rights, international law, criminal justice.

Trinity International University, Trinity Law School, Santa Ana, CA 92705. Offers JD. Part-time and evening/weekend programs available. *Entrance requirements:* LSAT. Additional exam requirements/recommendations for international students: Required—TOEFL (minimum score 580 paper-based). *Expenses:* Contact institution.

Tulane University, School of Law, New Orleans, LA 70118. Offers admiralty (LL M); American business law (LL M); energy and environment (LL M); international and comparative law (LL M); law (JD, LL M, SJD); JD/M Acct; JD/MA; JD/MBA; JD/MHA; JD/MPH; JD/MS; JD/MSW. *Accreditation:* ABA. Terminal master's awarded for partial completion of doctoral program. *Degree requirements:* For doctorate, thesis/dissertation. *Entrance requirements:* LSAT. Additional exam requirements/recommendations for international students: Required—TOEFL (minimum score 575 paper-based; 233 computer-based). Electronic applications accepted. *Expenses:* Contact institution. *Faculty research:* Civil law.

Universidad Autonoma de Guadalajara, Graduate Programs, Guadalajara, Mexico. Offers administrative law and justice (LL M); advertising and corporate communications (MA); architecture (M Arch); business (MBA); computational science (MCC); education (Ed M, Ed D); English-Spanish translation (MA); fiscal law (MA); integrated management of digital animation (MA); international business (MIB); international corporate law (LL M); internet technologies (MS); labor health (MS); manufacturing systems (MMS); philosophy (MA, PhD); power electronics (MS); quality systems (MQS); renewable energy (MS); social evaluation of projects (MBA); strategic market research (MBA); teaching mathematics (MA).

Universidad Central del Este, Law School, San Pedro de Macoris, Dominican Republic. Offers JD.

Universidad Iberoamericana, Graduate School, Santo Domingo D.N., Dominican Republic. Offers advertising management (MM); business (MBA); constitutional law (MA); dentistry (DMD); educational management (MA); integrated marketing communication (MA); psychopedagogical intervention (M Ed); strategic management of human talent (MM).

Université de Montréal, Faculty of Law, Montréal, QC H3C 3J7, Canada. Offers business law (DESS); common law (North America) (JD); international law (DESS); law (LL B, LL M, LL D, DDN, DESS); tax law (LL M). Part-time programs available. *Faculty:* 63 full-time (24 women), 6 part-time/adjunct (4 women). *Students:* 441 full-time (267 women), 85 part-time (53 women). 794 applicants, 41% accepted, 225 enrolled. In 2009, 40 master's, 7 doctorates, 105 DDNs awarded. *Degree requirements:* For master's, thesis; for doctorate, thesis/dissertation, project; for other advanced degree, thesis (for some programs). *Application deadline:* For fall admission, 2/1 priority date for domestic students; for winter admission, 11/1 priority date for domestic students; for spring admission, 2/1 priority date for domestic students. Application fee: $100. Electronic applications accepted. *Financial support:* Fellowships, research assistantships, teaching assistantships available. *Faculty research:* Legal theory; constitutional, private, and public law. *Unit head:* Gilles Trudeau, Dean, 514-343-6469, Fax: 514-343-2199, E-mail: gilles.trudeau@umontreal.ca. *Application contact:* Guy Lefebvre, Associate Dean Graduate Studies, 514-343-7202, Fax: 514-343-2199, E-mail: guy.lefebvre@umontreal.ca.

Université de Sherbrooke, Faculty of Law, Sherbrooke, QC J1K 2R1, Canada. Offers alternative dispute resolution (LL M, Diploma); biotechnology (LL B); business administration (LL B); business law (Diploma); health law (LL M, Diploma); law (LL B, LL D); legal management (Diploma); notarial law (DDN); transnational law (Diploma). Part-time and evening/weekend programs available. *Degree requirements:* For master's, thesis; for other advanced degree, one foreign language. *Entrance requirements:* For master's and other advanced degree, LL B. Electronic applications accepted.

Université du Québec à Montréal, Graduate Programs, Program in Social and Labor Law, Montréal, QC H3C 3P8, Canada. Offers Certificate.

Université Laval, Faculty of Law, Programs in Law, Québec, QC G1K 7P4, Canada. Offers environment, sustainable development and food safety (LL M); international and transnational law (LL M, Diploma); law (LL M, LL D); law of business (LL M, Diploma). Part-time programs available. Terminal master's awarded for partial completion of doctoral program. *Degree requirements:* For master's, thesis (for some programs); for doctorate, thesis/dissertation. *Entrance requirements:* For master's, doctorate, and Diploma, knowledge of French and English. Electronic applications accepted.

University at Buffalo, the State University of New York, Graduate School, Law School, Buffalo, NY 14260. Offers criminal law (LL M); general law (LL M); law (JD); JD/MA; JD/MBA; JD/MLS; JD/MPH; JD/MSW; JD/MUP; JD/PhD; JD/Pharm D. *Accreditation:* ABA. *Faculty:* 60 full-time (28 women), 123 part-time/adjunct (43 women). *Students:* 761 full-time (349 women), 1 (woman) part-time; includes 123 minority (40 African Americans, 5 American Indian/Alaska Native, 47 Asian Americans or Pacific Islanders, 31 Hispanic Americans). Average age 26. 2,104 applicants, 32% accepted, 206 enrolled. In 2009, 246 JDs awarded. *Entrance requirements:* For JD, LSAT, minimum undergraduate GPA of 2.0; for master's, JD. Additional exam requirements/recommendations for international students: Required—TOEFL (minimum score 650 paper-based; 280 computer-based; 114 iBT). *Application deadline:* For fall admission, 3/15 priority date for domestic and international students. Applications are processed on a rolling basis. Application fee: $75. Electronic applications accepted. *Expenses:* Contact institution. *Financial support:* In 2009–10, 660 students received support, including 6 fellowships with full tuition reimbursements available (averaging $16,010 per year), 21 research assistantships (averaging $519 per year); career-related internships or fieldwork, Federal Work-Study, institutionally sponsored loans, scholarships/grants, tuition waivers (full and partial), and unspecified assistantships also available. Financial award application deadline: 3/1; financial award applicants required to submit FAFSA. *Faculty research:* Criminal law, environmental law, international law, human rights, labor and employment law. Total annual research expenditures: $91,478. *Unit head:* Dr. Makau Mutua, Dean, 716-645-2311, Fax: 716-645-2064, E-mail: mutua@buffalo.edu. *Application contact:* Lillie V. Wiley-Upshaw, Vice Dean/Director of Admissions and Financial Aid, 716-645-2907, Fax: 716-645-6676, E-mail: law-admissions@buffalo.edu.

The University of Akron, School of Law, Akron, OH 44325-2901. Offers intellectual property (LL M); law (JD); JD/M Tax; JD/MAP; JD/MBA; JD/MPA; JD/MSMHR. *Accreditation:* ABA. Part-time and evening/weekend programs available. *Faculty:* 34 full-time (11 women), 36 part-time/adjunct (5 women). *Students:* 248 full-time (104 women), 249 part-time (129 women); includes 71 minority (33 African Americans, 3 American Indian/Alaska Native, 25 Asian Americans or Pacific Islanders, 10 Hispanic Americans), 3 international. Average age 26. 1,876 applicants, 39% accepted, 202 enrolled. In 2009, 144 JDs awarded. *Entrance requirements:* LSAT, LSDAS. Additional exam requirements/recommendations for international students: Required—TOEFL (minimum score 650 paper-based; 230 computer-based; 115 iBT). *Application deadline:* For fall admission, 3/1 priority date for domestic and international students. Applications are processed on a rolling basis. Application fee: $0. Electronic applications accepted. *Expenses:* Contact institution. *Financial support:* In 2009–10, 171 students received support. Career-related internships or fieldwork, scholarships/grants, and tuition waivers (full and partial) available. Support available to part-time students. Financial award applicants required to submit FAFSA. *Faculty research:* Intellectual property; law and science; trust and elder law, including taxation and retirement benefits; professional responsibility and judicial ethics; constitutional law, theory, and process. Total annual research expenditures: $46,624. *Unit head:* Martin H. Belsky, Dean, 330-972-6359, Fax: 330-258-2343, E-mail: belsky@uakron.edu. *Application contact:* Lauri S. File, Assistant Dean of Admission and Financial Aid, 330-972-7331, Fax: 330-258-2343, E-mail: lfile@uakron.edu.

The University of Alabama, School of Law, Tuscaloosa, AL 35487. Offers JD, LL M, LL M in Tax, JD/MBA. *Accreditation:* ABA. *Faculty:* 36 full-time (12 women), 45 part-time/adjunct (6 women). *Students:* 528 full-time (223 women), 182 part-time (70 women); includes 91 minority (57 African Americans, 2 American Indian/Alaska Native, 18 Asian Americans or Pacific Islanders, 14 Hispanic Americans), 4 international. Average age 29. 1,637 applicants, 21% accepted, 292 enrolled. In 2009, 162 JDs, 5 master's awarded. *Degree requirements:* For JD, 90 hours, including 3 hours of professional skills, 1 seminar, and 35 required hours. *Entrance requirements:* LSAT, undergraduate degree. Additional exam requirements/recommendations for international students: Required—TOEFL, IELTS. *Application deadline:* Applications are processed on a rolling basis. Application fee: $50 ($60 for international students). Electronic applications accepted. *Expenses:* Contact institution. *Financial support:* In 2009–10, 383 students received support. Applicants required to submit FAFSA. *Faculty research:* Public interest law, constitutional law, civil rights, international law, tax law. *Unit head:* Aaron V. Latham, Dean, 205-348-5195, Fax: 205-348-6397, E-mail: alatham@law.ua.edu. *Application contact:* Page Thead Pulliam, Assistant Director for Admissions, 205-348-7945, Fax: 205-348-3917, E-mail: ppulliam@law.ua.edu.

University of Alberta, Faculty of Law, Edmonton, AB T6G 2E1, Canada. Offers LL B, LL M, MBA/LL B. Part-time programs available. *Degree requirements:* For master's, thesis. *Entrance requirements:* For LL B, LSAT; for master's, minimum GPA of 3.0, curriculum vitae, 3 letters of recommendation. Additional exam requirements/recommendations for international students: Required—TOEFL (minimum score 600 paper-based; 250 computer-based). Electronic applications accepted. Tuition and fees charges are reported in Canadian dollars. *Expenses:* Tuition, area resident: Full-time $4626 Canadian dollars; part-time $99.72 Canadian dollars per unit. International tuition: $8216 Canadian dollars full-time. Required fees: $3590 Canadian dollars; $99.72 Canadian dollars per unit. $215 Canadian dollars per term. *Faculty research:* Health law, environmental law, native law issues, constitutional law, human rights.

The University of Arizona, James E. Rogers College of Law, Tucson, AZ 85721-0176. Offers indigenous peoples law and policy (LL M); international trade and business law (LL M); law (JD); JD/MA; JD/MBA; JD/MPA; JD/PhD. *Accreditation:* ABA. *Faculty:* 35 full-time (12 women), 40 part-time/adjunct (14 women). *Students:* 500 full-time (242 women); includes 134 minority (15 African Americans, 33 American Indian/Alaska Native, 43 Asian Americans or Pacific Islanders, 43 Hispanic Americans), 17 international. Average age 26. 2,214 applicants, 33% accepted, 155 enrolled. In 2009, 142 JDs, 15 master's awarded. *Degree requirements:* For JD, publishable paper. *Entrance requirements:* LSAT, LSDAS, resume, 2 letters of recommendation. Additional exam requirements/recommendations for international students: Required—TOEFL. *Application deadline:* For spring admission, 2/15 for domestic and international students. Applications are processed on a rolling basis. Application fee: $65. Electronic applications accepted. *Expenses:* Contact institution. *Financial support:* In 2009–10, 400 students received support, including fellowships with tuition reimbursements available (averaging $3,400 per year); career-related internships or fieldwork, Federal Work-Study, institutionally sponsored loans, scholarships/grants, and tuition waivers (full and partial) also available. Financial award application deadline: 3/1; financial award applicants required to submit FAFSA. *Faculty research:* Tax law, employment law, corporate law, torts, trial practice and skills, constitutional law, Indian law, family law, estates and trusts. *Unit head:* Lawrence Ponoroff, Dean, 520-621-1498, Fax: 520-621-9140, E-mail: lawrence.ponoroff@law.arizona.edu. *Application contact:* Eric James Eden, Assistant Dean for Admission and Financial Aid, 520-621-7666, Fax: 520-626-3436, E-mail: eric.eden@law.arizona.edu.

University of Arkansas, School of Law, Fayetteville, AR 72701. Offers agricultural law (LL M); law (JD). *Accreditation:* ABA. *Students:* 406 full-time (170 women); includes 65 minority (36 African Americans, 7 American Indian/Alaska Native, 10 Asian Americans or Pacific Islanders, 12 Hispanic Americans), 4 international. In 2009, 122 JDs, 11 master's awarded. *Entrance requirements:* LSAT. *Application deadline:* For fall admission, 4/1 for domestic students. Applications are processed on a rolling basis. Application fee: $0. *Expenses:* Contact institution. *Financial support:* In 2009–10, fellowships with full tuition reimbursements (averaging $6,000 per year), 9 research assistantships (averaging $2,500 per year) were awarded; teaching

assistantships, career-related internships or fieldwork, Federal Work-Study, and scholarships/grants also available. Support available to part-time students. Financial award application deadline: 4/1; financial award applicants required to submit FAFSA. *Unit head:* Cynthia Nance, Dean, 479-575-5601, Fax: 479-575-3320, E-mail: cnance@uark.edu. *Application contact:* James K. Miller, Associate Dean for Students, 479-575-3102, E-mail: jkmiller@uark.edu.

University of Arkansas at Little Rock, William H. Bowen School of Law, Little Rock, AR 72202-5142. Offers JD, JD/MPS. *Accreditation:* ABA. Part-time and evening/weekend programs available. *Entrance requirements:* LSAT. Electronic applications accepted. *Expenses:* Contact institution. *Faculty research:* Employment discrimination, uniform commercial code, Arkansas legal history, scientific evidence, mediation.

University of Atlanta, Graduate Programs, Atlanta, GA 30360. Offers business (MS); business administration (Exec MBA, MBA); computer science (MS); educational leadership (MS, Ed D); healthcare administration (MS, D Sc, Graduate Certificate); information technology for management (Graduate Certificate); international project management (Graduate Certificate); law (JD); managerial science (DBA); project management (Graduate Certificate); social science (MS). Postbaccalaureate distance learning degree programs offered. *Faculty:* 54 part-time/adjunct (10 women). *Students:* 251 full-time. *Entrance requirements:* For master's, minimum cumulative GPA of 2.5. *Expenses:* Tuition: Part-time $1000 per course. Part-time tuition and fees vary according to course load and degree level.

University of Baltimore, School of Law, Program in Law of the United States, Baltimore, MD 21201-5779. Offers LL M. *Entrance requirements:* Additional exam requirements/recommendations for international students: Required—TOEFL (minimum score 500 paper-based; 213 computer-based; 79 iBT). Electronic applications accepted.

The University of British Columbia, Faculty of Law, Vancouver, BC V6T 1Z1, Canada. Offers LL M, LL M CL, PhD. Part-time programs available. *Degree requirements:* For master's, variable foreign language requirement, thesis, seminar; for doctorate, variable foreign language requirement, comprehensive exam, thesis/dissertation, seminar. *Entrance requirements:* For master's, LL B or JD, thesis proposal, 3 letters of reference; for doctorate, LL B or JD, LL M, thesis proposal, 3 letters of reference. Additional exam requirements/recommendations for international students: Required—TOEFL (minimum score 600 paper-based; 250 computer-based; 100 iBT), IELTS (minimum score 7). Electronic applications accepted. *Faculty research:* Aboriginal rights/native law, Asian legal studies, criminal law, environmental law, international law, corporate, human rights, intellectual property, dispute resolution, entertainment.

University of Calgary, Faculty of Law, Calgary, AB T2N 1N4, Canada. Offers LL B, LL M, Post-Graduate Certificate. *Degree requirements:* For master's, thesis. *Entrance requirements:* For LL B, LSAT; for master's, minimum GPA of 3.0. Additional exam requirements/recommendations for international students: Required—TOEFL (minimum score 600 paper-based; 250 computer-based; 100 iBT). *Expenses:* Contact institution. *Faculty research:* Resources law, family law, legal history, taxation law, human rights.

University of California, Berkeley, Graduate Division, Haas School of Business and School of Law, Concurrent JD/MBA Program, Berkeley, CA 94720-1500. Offers JD/MBA. *Accreditation:* AACSB; ABA. *Students:* 1 full-time (0 women). *Entrance requirements:* Additional exam requirements/recommendations for international students: Required—TOEFL. Application fee: $200. Electronic applications accepted. *Financial support:* Application deadline: 3/1. *Unit head:* Julia Hwang, Director, MBA Program, 510-642-1405, Fax: 510-643-6659, E-mail: julia_hwang@haas.berkeley.edu. *Application contact:* Office of Admissions, 510-642-1405, Fax: 510-643-6659, E-mail: admissions@boalt.berkeley.edu.

University of California, Berkeley, School of Law, Berkeley, CA 94720-7200. Offers jurisprudence and social policy (PhD); law (JD, LL M, JSD); JD/MA; JD/MBA; JD/MCP; JD/MJ; JD/MPP; JD/MSW. *Accreditation:* ABA. Terminal master's awarded for partial completion of doctoral program. *Degree requirements:* For master's, thesis; for doctorate, one foreign language, thesis/dissertation, oral qualifying exam. *Entrance requirements:* For JD, LSAT, LSDAS, letters of recommendation, writing sample; for master's, letters of recommendation; for doctorate, GRE General Test, letters of recommendation. Additional exam requirements/recommendations for international students: Required—TOEFL. *Expenses:* Contact institution. *Faculty research:* Law and technology; social justice; environmental law; business, law and economics; international/comparative law.

University of California, Davis, School of Law, Davis, CA 95616-5201. Offers JD, LL M, JD/MA, JD/MBA. *Accreditation:* ABA. *Entrance requirements:* LSAT. Electronic applications accepted. *Expenses:* Contact institution. *Faculty research:* International law, international trade, immigration, environmental law, public interest law.

University of California, Hastings College of the Law, Graduate Program, San Francisco, CA 94102-4978. Offers JD, LL M. *Accreditation:* ABA. *Entrance requirements:* LSAT, LSDAS, 2 letters of recommendation. Electronic applications accepted. *Expenses:* Tuition, nonresident: full-time $11,225. Required fees: $32,468. *Faculty research:* Immigration and refugee law, civil procedure and evidence, taxation law, environmental law and policy, constitutional law and civil rights.

University of California, Los Angeles, School of Law, Los Angeles, CA 90024. Offers JD, LL M, SJD, JD/MA, JD/MBA, JD/MPH, JD/MPP, JD/MSW, JD/PhD. *Accreditation:* ABA. *Entrance requirements:* LSAT. Additional exam requirements/recommendations for international students: Required—TOEFL. Electronic applications accepted. *Expenses:* Contact institution. *Faculty research:* Business law and policy, critical race studies, entertainment and media law, law and philosophy, public interest law and policy.

University of California, San Diego, Office of Graduate Studies, Program in Health Law, La Jolla, CA 92093. Offers MAS. Part-time programs available. *Degree requirements:* For master's, capstone project. *Entrance requirements:* For master's, undergraduate degree in healthcare, law, or related field; 3 years work experience; 3 letters of recommendation; resume.

University of Chicago, The Law School, Chicago, IL 60637. Offers JD, LL M, MCL, DCL, JSD, JD/AM, JD/MBA, JD/MPP. *Accreditation:* ABA. *Faculty:* 70 full-time (20 women). *Students:* 590 full-time (264 women); includes 167 minority (37 African Americans, 2 American Indian/Alaska Native, 68 Asian Americans or Pacific Islanders, 60 Hispanic Americans), 14 international. Average age 24. 5,403 applicants, 18% accepted, 191 enrolled. In 2009, 203 first professional degrees, 50 master's, 1 doctorate awarded. *Entrance requirements:* LSAT, 2 letters of recommendation, resume. Additional exam requirements/recommendations for international students: Required—TOEFL. *Application deadline:* For fall admission, 2/1 priority date for domestic students. Applications are processed on a rolling basis. Application fee: $75. Electronic applications accepted. *Expenses:* Contact institution. *Financial support:* In 2009–10, 326 students received support, including 7 fellowships; research assistantships, teaching assistantships, career-related internships or fieldwork, institutionally sponsored loans, and scholarships/grants also available. Financial award application deadline: 3/1; financial award applicants required to submit FAFSA. *Unit head:* Michael Schill, Dean, 773-702-9494, Fax: 773-834-4409. *Application contact:* Ann K. Perry, Dean of Admissions, 773-834-4425, Fax: 773-834-0942, E-mail: admissions@law.uchicago.edu.

University of Cincinnati, College of Law, Cincinnati, OH 45221-0040. Offers JD, JD/MA, JD/MBA, JD/MCP, JD/MSW. *Accreditation:* ABA. *Faculty:* 32 full-time (16 women), 34 part-time/adjunct (10 women). *Students:* 391 full-time (165 women); includes 63 minority (23 African Americans, 1 American Indian/Alaska Native, 30 Asian Americans or Pacific Islanders, 9 Hispanic Americans). Average age 25. 1,322 applicants, 50% accepted, 138 enrolled. In 2009, 108 JDs awarded. *Entrance requirements:* LSAT. Additional exam requirements/recommendations for international students: Required—TOEFL. *Application deadline:* For fall admission, 3/1 priority date for domestic students. Applications are processed on a rolling basis. Application fee: $35. Electronic applications accepted. *Expenses:* Contact institution. *Financial support:* In 2009–10, 257 students received support, including 257 fellowships (averaging $8,450 per year); research assistantships, career-related internships or fieldwork, Federal Work-Study, scholarships/grants, tuition waivers (full and partial), and unspecified assistantships also available. Financial award application deadline: 3/1; financial award applicants required to submit FAFSA. *Faculty research:* International human rights, corporate law, intellectual property law, criminal law, law and psychiatry. *Unit head:* Louis D. Bilionois, Dean, 513-556-0121, Fax: 513-556-2391, E-mail: louis.bilionis@uc.edu. *Application contact:* Al Watson, Assistant Dean and Director of Admissions, 513-556-0077, Fax: 513-556-2391, E-mail: alfred.watson@uc.edu.

University of Colorado at Boulder, School of Law, Boulder, CO 80309-0401. Offers JD, JD/MBA, JD/MPA, JD/MS, JD/PhD. *Accreditation:* ABA. *Faculty:* 46 full-time (23 women). *Students:* 533 full-time (264 women), 2 part-time (both women); includes 108 minority (15 African Americans, 17 American Indian/Alaska Native, 37 Asian Americans or Pacific Islanders, 39 Hispanic Americans), 3 international. Average age 27. 715 applicants, 100% accepted, 182 enrolled. In 2009, 162 JDs awarded. *Entrance requirements:* LSAT, minimum undergraduate GPA of 2.75. *Application deadline:* For fall admission, 2/15 for domestic students. Applications are processed on a rolling basis. Application fee: $50 ($60 for international students). *Expenses:* Contact institution. *Financial support:* In 2009–10, 218 fellowships (averaging $8,399 per year), 1 research assistantship (averaging $432 per year) were awarded; Federal Work-Study and institutionally sponsored loans also available. Financial award applicants required to submit FAFSA. Total annual research expenditures: $443,159.

University of Connecticut, School of Law, Hartford, CT 06105. Offers JD, JD/LL M, JD/MBA, JD/MLS, JD/MPA, JD/MPH, JD/MSW. *Accreditation:* ABA. Part-time programs available. *Faculty:* 44 full-time (15 women), 44 part-time/adjunct (8 women). *Students:* 483 full-time (234 women), 232 part-time (99 women); includes 140 minority (37 African Americans, 4 American Indian/Alaska Native, 51 Asian Americans or Pacific Islanders, 48 Hispanic Americans), 34 international. Average age 25. 2,409 applicants, 28% accepted, 180 enrolled. In 2009, 208 JDs awarded. *Degree requirements:* For JD, extensive research paper. *Entrance requirements:* LSAT. Additional exam requirements/recommendations for international students: Required—TOEFL. *Application deadline:* For fall admission, 3/15 for domestic and international students. Applications are processed on a rolling basis. Application fee: $60. Electronic applications accepted. *Expenses:* Contact institution. *Financial support:* In 2009–10, 379 students received support. Federal Work-Study, scholarships/grants, and tuition waivers (full and partial) available. Financial award application deadline: 3/1; financial award applicants required to submit FAFSA. *Faculty research:* International law, intellectual property, human rights, corporate law, insurance law. *Unit head:* Jeremy Paul, Dean, 860-570-5127, Fax: 860-570-5218. *Application contact:* Karen L. DeMeola, Assistant Dean for Admissions and Student Finance, 860-570-5162, Fax: 860-570-5153, E-mail: karen.demeola@law.uconn.edu.

University of Dayton, School of Law, Dayton, OH 45469-2772. Offers JD, LL M, MSL, JD/M Ed, JD/MBA, JD/MS Ed. *Accreditation:* ABA. *Faculty:* 55 full-time (21 women), 24 part-time/adjunct (7 women). *Students:* 494 full-time (206 women), 9 part-time (7 women); includes 67 minority (35 African Americans, 3 American Indian/Alaska Native, 12 Asian Americans or Pacific Islanders, 17 Hispanic Americans), 5 international. Average age 26. 1,113 applicants, 93% accepted, 181 enrolled. In 2009, 150 JDs awarded. *Entrance requirements:* For JD, LSAT, accredited bachelor's degree or foreign equivalent; for master's, MSL. *Application deadline:* For fall admission, 5/1 priority date for domestic and international students; for spring admission, 3/1 priority date for domestic and international students. Applications are processed on a rolling basis. Application fee: $50. Electronic applications accepted. *Expenses:* Contact institution. *Financial support:* In 2009–10, 290 students received support. Career-related internships or fieldwork, institutionally sponsored loans, scholarships/grants, and tuition waivers (partial) available. Financial award application deadline: 3/1; financial award applicants required to submit FAFSA. *Faculty research:* Bankruptcy, criminal procedure, torts, computer law, intellectual property. *Unit head:* Lisa A. Kloppenberg, Dean, 937-229-3795, Fax: 937-229-2469. *Application contact:* Janet L. Hein, Assistant Dean/Director of Admissions and Financial Aid, 937-229-3555, Fax: 937-229-4194, E-mail: lawinfo@notes.udayton.edu.

University of Denver, College of Law, Professional Program, Denver, CO 80208. Offers JD. *Accreditation:* ABA. Part-time and evening/weekend programs available. *Students:* 984 full-time (472 women), 43 part-time (13 women); includes 177 minority (27 African Americans, 21 American Indian/Alaska Native, 55 Asian Americans or Pacific Islanders, 74 Hispanic Americans), 11 international. Average age 28. 3,073 applicants, 33% accepted, 318 enrolled. In 2009, 349 JDs awarded. *Entrance requirements:* LSAT. *Application deadline:* For fall admission, 3/1 priority date for domestic students. Applications are processed on a rolling basis. Application fee: $60. *Expenses:* Tuition: Full-time $34,596; part-time $961 per quarter hour. Required fees: $4 per quarter hour. Tuition and fees vary according to course load, campus/location and program. *Financial support:* Career-related internships or fieldwork, Federal Work-Study, institutionally sponsored loans, and tutorships available. Support available to part-time students. Financial award application deadline: 2/15; financial award applicants required to submit FAFSA. *Faculty research:* Lawyering skills, international and legal studies, natural resources law (domestic and international), transportation law, public interest law, business and commercial law. *Application contact:* Admissions, 303-871-6135, Fax: 303-871-6992, E-mail: admissions@law.du.edu.

University of Denver, College of Law, Programs in American and Comparative Law and International Natural Resources Law, Denver, CO 80208. Offers American and comparative law (LL M); international natural resources law (LL M, MRLS). *Students:* 36 full-time (18 women), 21 part-time (14 women); includes 5 minority (1 African American, 2 Asian Americans or Pacific Islanders, 2 Hispanic Americans), 11 international. Average age 32. 70 applicants, 94% accepted, 12 enrolled. In 2009, 34 master's awarded. *Degree requirements:* For master's, internship. *Entrance requirements:* For master's, JD from US institution. Additional exam requirements/recommendations for international students: Required—TOEFL, TWE. *Application deadline:* Applications are processed on a rolling basis. Application fee: $45. Electronic applications accepted. *Expenses:* Tuition: Full-time $34,596; part-time $961 per quarter hour. Required fees: $4 per quarter hour. Tuition and fees vary according to course load, campus/location and program. *Financial support:* Federal Work-Study and institutionally sponsored loans available. Support available to part-time students. Financial award application deadline: 2/15; financial award applicants required to submit FAFSA. *Unit head:* Don Smith, Director, 303-871-6052. *Application contact:* Lucy Daberkow, Assistant Director of Graduate Programs, 303-871-6324, Fax: 303-871-6711, E-mail: ldaberkow@law.du.edu.

University of Detroit Mercy, School of Law, Detroit, MI 48226. Offers JD, JD/LL B, JD/MBA. *Accreditation:* ABA. Part-time programs available. *Entrance requirements:* LSAT. *Expenses:* Contact institution.

University of Florida, Levin College of Law, Gainesville, FL 32611. Offers comparative law (LL M); environmental law (LL M); international taxation (LL M); law (JD); taxation (LL M, SJD). *Accreditation:* ABA. *Faculty:* 77 full-time (37 women), 36 part-time/adjunct (10 women). *Students:* 1,369 full-time (620 women); includes 279 minority (69 African Americans, 8 American Indian/Alaska Native, 77 Asian Americans or Pacific Islanders, 125 Hispanic Americans), 71 international. Average age 24. 3,170 applicants, 25% accepted, 307 enrolled. In 2009, 497 JDs, 1 doctorate awarded. *Degree requirements:* For JD, thesis/dissertation or alternative. *Entrance requirements:* LSAT. Additional exam requirements/recommendations for international students: Required—TOEFL (minimum score 250 computer-based; 100 iBT). *Application deadline:* For fall admission, 1/15 for domestic and international students. Applications are processed on a rolling basis. Application fee: $30. Electronic applications accepted. *Expenses:* Contact institution. *Financial support:* In 2009–10, 299 students received support, including 25 fellowships (averaging $2,400 per year), 30 research assistantships with partial tuition reimbursements available (averaging $4,125 per year); career-related internships or fieldwork, Federal Work-Study, institutionally sponsored loans, scholarships/grants, traineeships, health care benefits, and unspecified assistantships also available. Financial award application deadline: 4/7; financial award applicants required to submit FAFSA. *Faculty research:* Environmental and land use law, taxation, family law, international law, constitutional law. *Unit head:* Robert Jerry, Dean, 352-273-0600, Fax: 352-392-8727, E-mail: jerryr@law.ufl.edu. *Application contact:*

Law

University of Florida (continued)

Michelle Adorno, Assistant Dean for Admissions, 352-273-0890, Fax: 352-392-4087, E-mail: madorno@law.ufl.edu.

University of Georgia, Graduate School and Graduate School, Graduate Program in Law, Athens, GA 30602. Offers LL M. *Students:* 12 full-time (4 women), 3 part-time (1 woman); includes 2 minority (both African Americans), 6 international. 53 applicants, 38% accepted. In 2009, 14 master's awarded. *Degree requirements:* For master's, thesis. *Entrance requirements:* Additional exam requirements/recommendations for international students: Required—TOEFL (minimum score 600 paper-based; 250 computer-based). *Application deadline:* For fall admission, 4/15 for domestic and international students. Application fee: $50. *Expenses:* Contact institution. *Financial support:* Fellowships, research assistantships, teaching assistantships, Federal Work-Study, institutionally sponsored loans, and unspecified assistantships available. Financial award application deadline: 4/15. *Unit head:* Prof. Gabriel M. Wilner, Associate Dean, 706-542-5238, Fax: 706-542-4145, E-mail: intlgrad@uga.edu. *Application contact:* Information Contact, E-mail: intlgrad@uga.edu.

University of Georgia, School of Law, Professional Program in Law, Athens, GA 30602. Offers JD. *Accreditation:* ABA. *Students:* 688 full-time (328 women), 2 part-time (1 woman); includes 124 minority (82 African Americans, 1 American Indian/Alaska Native, 29 Asian Americans or Pacific Islanders, 12 Hispanic Americans), 1 international. In 2009, 217 JDs awarded. *Entrance requirements:* LSAT. *Expenses:* Tuition, state resident: full-time $6000; part-time $250 per credit hour. Tuition, nonresident: full-time $20,904; part-time $871 per credit hour. Required fees: $730 per semester. *Unit head:* Dean Rebecca H. White, Dean, 706-542-7140, Fax: 706-542-5283, E-mail: rhwhite@uga.edu. *Application contact:* Paul B. Rollins, Associate Director of Law Admissions, 706-542-7060, Fax: 706-542-5556, E-mail: rollins@uga.edu.

University of Hawaii at Manoa, William S. Richardson School of Law, Honolulu, HI 96822-2328. Offers JD, LL M, Graduate Certificate, JD/Certificate, JD/MA, JD/MBA, JD/MLI Sc, JD/MS, JD/MURP, JD/PhD. *Accreditation:* ABA. *Degree requirements:* For JD, 6 semesters of full-time residency. *Entrance requirements:* LSAT. Additional exam requirements/recommendations for international students: Required—TOEFL. *Expenses:* Contact institution. *Faculty research:* Law of the sea, Asian and Pacific comparative law, native Hawaiian rights, environmental law.

University of Houston, Law Center, Houston, TX 77204-6060. Offers JD, LL M, JD/MA, JD/MBA, JD/MPH, JD/PhD. *Accreditation:* ABA. Part-time and evening/weekend programs available. *Faculty:* 40 full-time (8 women), 87 part-time/adjunct (34 women). *Students:* 731 full-time (329 women), 238 part-time (108 women); includes 263 minority (76 African Americans, 2 American Indian/Alaska Native, 91 Asian Americans or Pacific Islanders, 94 Hispanic Americans), 38 international. Average age 28. 983 applicants, 99% accepted, 320 enrolled. In 2009, 290 JDs, 98 master's awarded. *Entrance requirements:* LSAT. Additional exam requirements/recommendations for international students: Required—TOEFL (minimum score 600 paper-based; 100 iBT). *Application deadline:* For fall admission, 11/1 priority date for domestic and international students; for winter admission, 2/15 for domestic and international students. Applications are processed on a rolling basis. Application fee: $70. Electronic applications accepted. *Expenses:* Contact institution. *Financial support:* Career-related internships or fieldwork, Federal Work-Study, institutionally sponsored loans, scholarships/grants, health care benefits, and unspecified assistantships available. Support available to part-time students. Financial award application deadline: 3/10; financial award applicants required to submit FAFSA. *Faculty research:* Health law, international, tax, environmental/energy, information law/intellectual property. *Unit head:* Raymond Nimmer, Dean, 713-743-2100, Fax: 713-743-2122, E-mail: rnimmer@uh.edu. *Application contact:* Jamie Hammers, Assistant Dean for Admissions, 713-743-2277, E-mail: lawadmissions@uh.edu.

University of Idaho, College of Law, Moscow, ID 83844-2321. Offers JD. *Accreditation:* ABA. *Faculty:* 23 full-time, 5 part-time/adjunct. *Students:* 319 full-time, 3 part-time. In 2009, 96 JDs awarded. *Entrance requirements:* LSAT. *Application deadline:* For fall admission, 2/1 for domestic students. Application fee: $55 ($60 for international students). *Expenses:* Tuition, state resident: full-time $6120. Tuition, nonresident: full-time $17,712. *Financial support:* Career-related internships or fieldwork, Federal Work-Study, and institutionally sponsored loans available. Financial award application deadline: 2/15. *Faculty research:* Transboundary river governance, tribal protection and stewardship, regional water issues. *Unit head:* Donald L. Burnett, Dean, 208-885-4977. *Application contact:* Donald L. Burnett, Dean, 208-885-4977.

University of Illinois at Urbana–Champaign, College of Law, Champaign, IL 61820. Offers JD, LL M, MCL, JSD, JD/DVM, JD/MBA, JD/MCS, JD/MHRIR, JD/MS, JD/MUP, MAS/JD, MD/JD. *Accreditation:* ABA. *Faculty:* 48 full-time (16 women), 32 part-time/adjunct (13 women). *Students:* 702 full-time (315 women), 4 part-time (0 women); includes 140 minority (48 African Americans, 5 American Indian/Alaska Native, 56 Asian Americans or Pacific Islanders, 31 Hispanic Americans), 114 international. 618 applicants, 68% accepted, 324 enrolled. In 2009, 193 first professional degrees, 35 master's awarded. *Entrance requirements:* For JD, LSAT; for master's and doctorate, minimum GPA of 3.0. Additional exam requirements/recommendations for international students: Required—TOEFL (minimum score 550 paper-based; 250 computer-based; 79 iBT), or IELTS (minimum score 7). *Application deadline:* Applications are processed on a rolling basis. Application fee: $75. Electronic applications accepted. *Expenses:* Contact institution. *Financial support:* In 2009–10, 1 fellowship, 2 research assistantships, 7 teaching assistantships were awarded; tuition waivers (full and partial) also available. *Unit head:* Bruce Smith, Dean, 217-244-8446, Fax: 217-244-1478, E-mail: smithb@illinois.edu. *Application contact:* Kelly J. Salefski, Director of Academic Administration and Student Records, 217-244-8663, Fax: 217-244-1478, E-mail: salefski@illinois.edu.

The University of Iowa, College of Law, Iowa City, IA 52242. Offers JD, LL M, JD/MA, JD/MBA, JD/MD, JD/MHA, JD/MPH, JD/MS, JD/PhD. *Accreditation:* ABA. *Faculty:* 48 full-time (18 women), 26 part-time/adjunct (11 women). *Students:* 590 full-time (261 women); includes 91 minority (21 African Americans, 6 American Indian/Alaska Native, 36 Asian Americans or Pacific Islanders, 28 Hispanic Americans), 19 international. Average age 24. 1,291 applicants, 44% accepted, 195 enrolled. In 2009, 206 JDs, 8 master's awarded. *Entrance requirements:* LSAT. Additional exam requirements/recommendations for international students: Required—TOEFL or IELTS. *Application deadline:* For fall admission, 3/1 for domestic and international students. Applications are processed on a rolling basis. Application fee: $60 ($85 for international students). Electronic applications accepted. *Expenses:* Contact institution. *Financial support:* In 2009–10, 345 students received support, including 198 fellowships with full and partial tuition reimbursements available (averaging $16,821 per year), 236 research assistantships with partial tuition reimbursements available (averaging $2,175 per year); career-related internships or fieldwork, Federal Work-Study, institutionally sponsored loans, scholarships/grants, health care benefits, and unspecified assistantships also available. Financial award applicants required to submit FAFSA. *Faculty research:* International and comparative law, health law, business law, intellectual property law, antitrust law. Total annual research expenditures: $228,967. *Unit head:* Gail Agrawal, Dean, 319-335-9034, E-mail: gail-agrawal@uiowa.edu. *Application contact:* Collins Byrd, Assistant Dean of Admissions, 319-335-9095, Fax: 319-335-9646, E-mail: law-admissions@uiowa.edu.

The University of Kansas, School of Law, Lawrence, KS 66045-7608. Offers law (JD); JD/MA; JD/MBA; JD/MHSA; JD/MPA; JD/MS; JD/MSW; JD/MUP. *Accreditation:* ABA. *Faculty:* 42 full-time (18 women), 14 part-time/adjunct (5 women). *Students:* 499 full-time (199 women), 16 part-time (3 women); includes 83 minority (16 African Americans, 19 American Indian/Alaska Native, 27 Asian Americans or Pacific Islanders, 21 Hispanic Americans), 35 international. Average age 25. 1,098 applicants, 35% accepted, 163 enrolled. In 2009, 159 JDs awarded. *Entrance requirements:* LSAT, 2 letters of recommendation. Additional exam requirements/recommendations for international students: Required—TOEFL. *Application deadline:* For fall admission, 3/15 for domestic and international students. Applications are processed on a rolling basis. Application fee: $55. Electronic applications accepted. *Expenses:* Contact institution. *Financial support:* In 2009–10, 482 students received support, including 51 research assistantships, 9 teaching assistantships; career-related internships or fieldwork, Federal Work-Study, institutionally sponsored loans, and scholarships/grants also available. Financial award application deadline: 3/1; financial award applicants required to submit FAFSA. *Faculty research:* International law, business law, criminal law, elder law, law and public policy. *Unit head:* Gail B. Agrawal, Dean, 785-864-4550, Fax: 785-864-5054. *Application contact:* Jacqlene Nance, Director of Admissions, 866-220-3654, E-mail: admitlaw@ku.edu.

University of Kentucky, College of Law, Lexington, KY 40506-0048. Offers JD, JD/MA, JD/MBA, JD/MPA. *Accreditation:* ABA. *Faculty:* 25 full-time (8 women), 22 part-time/adjunct (4 women). *Students:* 406 full-time (180 women); includes 56 minority (36 African Americans, 3 American Indian/Alaska Native, 9 Asian Americans or Pacific Islanders, 8 Hispanic Americans), 3 international. Average age 23. 1,074 applicants, 39% accepted, 152 enrolled. In 2009, 130 JDs awarded. *Entrance requirements:* LSAT, LSDAS. Additional exam requirements/recommendations for international students: Required—TOEFL. *Application deadline:* For fall admission, 3/1 priority date for domestic and international students. Applications are processed on a rolling basis. Application fee: $50. Electronic applications accepted. *Expenses:* Contact institution. *Financial support:* In 2009–10, 312 students received support, including 257 fellowships (averaging $4,000 per year); career-related internships or fieldwork, Federal Work-Study, and scholarships/grants also available. Support available to part-time students. Financial award application deadline: 4/1; financial award applicants required to submit FAFSA. *Faculty research:* Health law, education law, advocacy, business law, white collar crime, international trade law, corporate mergers, taxation of Internet transactions. *Unit head:* David A. Brennen, Dean, 859-257-1678, Fax: 859-323-1061. *Application contact:* Drusilla V. Bakert, Associate Dean, 859-257-6770, Fax: 859-323-1061, E-mail: dbakert@email.uky.edu.

University of La Verne, College of Law, Ontario, CA 91764. Offers JD. *Accreditation:* ABA. Part-time and evening/weekend programs available. *Faculty:* 22 full-time (11 women), 16 part-time/adjunct (5 women). *Students:* 275 full-time (119 women), 117 part-time (56 women); includes 120 minority (12 African Americans, 2 American Indian/Alaska Native, 52 Asian Americans or Pacific Islanders, 54 Hispanic Americans), 8 international. Average age 26. 1,556 applicants, 41% accepted, 131 enrolled. In 2009, 76 JDs awarded. *Entrance requirements:* LSAT. Additional exam requirements/recommendations for international students: Recommended—TOEFL (minimum score 600 paper-based; 250 computer-based; 100 iBT). *Application deadline:* For fall admission, 7/1 priority date for domestic students; for spring admission, 11/1 priority date for domestic students. Applications are processed on a rolling basis. Application fee: $50. Electronic applications accepted. *Expenses:* Contact institution. *Financial support:* In 2009–10, 317 students received support. Federal Work-Study, scholarships/grants, and health care benefits available. Support available to part-time students. Financial award application deadline: 3/2; financial award applicants required to submit FAFSA. *Unit head:* Allen K. Easley, Dean, 909-460-2000, Fax: 909-460-2081, E-mail: lawadm@laverne.edu. *Application contact:* Andrew R. Woolsey, Assistant Dean of Admissions, 909-460-2001, Fax: 909-460-2082, E-mail: lawadm@laverne.edu.

University of Louisville, Louis D. Brandeis School of Law, Louisville, KY 40292. Offers JD, JD/M Div, JD/MA, JD/MBA, JD/MSW, JD/MUP. *Accreditation:* ABA. Part-time programs available. *Faculty:* 33 full-time (14 women), 17 part-time/adjunct (6 women). *Students:* 368 full-time (173 women), 67 part-time (24 women); includes 36 minority (17 African Americans, 10 Asian Americans or Pacific Islanders, 9 Hispanic Americans), 6 international. Average age 25. 1,258 applicants, 37% accepted, 141 enrolled. In 2009, 127 JDs awarded. *Degree requirements:* For JD, 30 work hours of pro bono service. *Entrance requirements:* LSAT. Additional exam requirements/recommendations for international students: Required—TOEFL. *Application deadline:* For fall admission, 4/1 for domestic and international students. Applications are processed on a rolling basis. Application fee: $50. Electronic applications accepted. *Financial support:* In 2009–10, 197 students received support; fellowships, research assistantships, teaching assistantships, career-related internships or fieldwork, scholarships/grants, and tuition waivers (partial) available. Support available to part-time students. Financial award application deadline: 6/1; financial award applicants required to submit FAFSA. *Faculty research:* Intellectual property, environmental law, corporate law, taxation, health law, bioethics law. *Unit head:* James Ming Chen, Dean, 502-852-6879, Fax: 502-852-0862, E-mail: jim.chen@louisville.edu. *Application contact:* Brandon L. Hamilton, Assistant Dean for Admission and Financial Aid, 502-852-6365, Fax: 502-852-8971, E-mail: lawadmissions@louisville.edu.

University of Manitoba, Faculty of Graduate Studies, Faculty of Law, Winnipeg, MB R3T 2N2, Canada. Offers LL M. *Faculty:* 24 full-time (8 women). *Students:* 7 full-time (2 women), 4 part-time (1 woman). In 2009, 3 master's awarded. *Degree requirements:* For master's, thesis. *Entrance requirements:* For master's, LL B, minimum GPA of 3.0. Additional exam requirements/recommendations for international students: Required—TOEFL (minimum score 600 paper-based; 240 computer-based). *Application deadline:* For fall admission, 6/15 for domestic students, 3/15 for international students. Applications are processed on a rolling basis. Electronic applications accepted. *Financial support:* In 2009–10, 7 students received support, including 7 fellowships with full tuition reimbursements available (averaging $6,000 per year); scholarships/grants also available. Financial award application deadline: 3/15. *Faculty research:* Constitutional law, alternative dispute resolution, human rights law, international trade law, corporate law. *Unit head:* Dr. Jennifer L. Schulz, Associate Dean, Research and Graduate Studies, 204-474-7958, Fax: 204-474-7580, E-mail: j_schulz@umanitoba.ca. *Application contact:* Sonja De Gannes, Student Program Officer, 204-474-6129, Fax: 204-474-7580, E-mail: sonja_degannes@umanitoba.ca.

University of Maryland, Baltimore, School of Law, Baltimore, MD 21201. Offers JD, JD/MA, JD/MBA, JD/MCP, JD/MPH, JD/MPM, JD/MPP, JD/MS, JD/MSN, JD/MSW, JD/PhD, JD/Pharm D. *Accreditation:* ABA. Part-time and evening/weekend programs available. *Faculty:* 64 full-time (36 women), 50 part-time/adjunct (15 women). *Students:* 723 full-time (370 women), 230 part-time (106 women); includes 300 minority (120 African Americans, 4 American Indian/Alaska Native, 103 Asian Americans or Pacific Islanders, 73 Hispanic Americans), 12 international. Average age 27. 3,608 applicants, 19% accepted, 298 enrolled. In 2009, 242 JDs awarded. *Degree requirements:* For JD, writing certification. *Entrance requirements:* LSAT, LSDAS. Additional exam requirements/recommendations for international students: Required—TOEFL (minimum score 550 paper-based; 80 iBT). *Application deadline:* For fall admission, 3/15 priority date for domestic and international students. Applications are processed on a rolling basis. Application fee: $70. Electronic applications accepted. *Expenses:* Contact institution. *Financial support:* In 2009–10, 812 students received support, including 21 fellowships (averaging $4,000 per year); Federal Work-Study, institutionally sponsored loans, and scholarships/grants also available. Support available to part-time students. Financial award application deadline: 3/1; financial award applicants required to submit FAFSA. *Faculty research:* Environmental regulation, health care policy, intellectual property, civil rights and race history and policy, international and comparative law. Total annual research expenditures: $5 million. *Unit head:* Phoebe A. Haddon, Dean/Professor, 410-706-7214, Fax: 410-706-4045, E-mail: phaddon@law.umaryland.edu. *Application contact:* Connie Beals, Executive Director of Admissions and Student Recruiting, 410-706-3492, Fax: 410-706-1793, E-mail: admissions@law.umaryland.edu.

University of Maryland, College Park, Academic Affairs, Robert H. Smith School of Business, Program in Business Management/Law, College Park, MD 20742. Offers JD/MBA. *Accreditation:* AACSB. *Students:* 5 full-time (0 women), 3 part-time (0 women); includes 2 minority (1 Asian American or Pacific Islander, 1 Hispanic American). 13 applicants, 38% accepted, 5 enrolled. *Entrance requirements:* Additional exam requirements/recommendations for international students: Required—TOEFL. *Application deadline:* For fall admission, 12/15 for domestic and international students; for spring admission, 11/30 for domestic students, 6/1 for international students. Applications are processed on a rolling basis. Application fee: $60. *Expenses:* Tuition, area resident: Part-time $471 per credit hour. Tuition, state resident: part-time $471 per credit hour. Tuition, nonresident: part-time $1016 per credit hour. Required fees: $337.04 per term. *Financial support:* In 2009–10, 1 fellowship with full tuition reimbursement (averaging $15,000 per year) was awarded; teaching assistantships. Financial award applicants required

to submit FAFSA. *Unit head:* Dr. Anand Anandalingam, Dean, 301-405-0582, E-mail: ganand@umd.edu. *Application contact:* Dean of Graduate School, 301-405-0358.

University of Maryland, College Park, Academic Affairs, School of Public Policy, Joint Program in Public Policy/Law, College Park, MD 20742. Offers JD/MPM. *Students:* 3 full-time (2 women), 1 (woman) part-time. 14 applicants, 71% accepted, 2 enrolled. *Application deadline:* For fall admission, 4/1 for domestic students, 2/1 for international students; for spring admission, 10/15 for domestic students, 6/1 for international students. Applications are processed on a rolling basis. Application fee: $60. Electronic applications accepted. *Expenses:* Tuition, area resident: Part-time $471 per credit hour. Tuition, state resident: part-time $471 per credit hour. Tuition, nonresident: part-time $1016 per credit hour. Required fees: $337.04 per term. *Financial support:* In 2009–10, 1 teaching assistantship (averaging $14,000 per year) was awarded; fellowships also available. Financial award applicants required to submit FAFSA. *Application contact:* Dean of Graduate School, 301-405-0376, Fax: 301-314-9305.

University of Massachusetts Dartmouth, University of Massachusetts School of Law at Dartmouth, North Dartmouth, MA 02747-2300. Offers JD. Part-time and evening/weekend programs available. *Entrance requirements:* LSAT. *Expenses:* Tuition, state resident: full-time $2071; part-time $86.29 per credit. Tuition, nonresident: full-time $8099; part-time $337.46 per credit. Required fees: $9446. Tuition and fees vary according to class time, course load and reciprocity agreements.

University of Memphis, Cecil C. Humphreys School of Law, Memphis, TN 38103-2189. Offers JD, JD/MA, JD/MBA. *Accreditation:* ABA. Part-time programs available. *Faculty:* 19 full-time (8 women), 26 part-time/adjunct (8 women). *Students:* 392 full-time (160 women), 28 part-time (17 women); includes 59 minority (40 African Americans, 3 American Indian/Alaska Native, 9 Asian Americans or Pacific Islanders, 7 Hispanic Americans), 1 international. Average age 26. 951 applicants, 32% accepted, 143 enrolled. In 2009, 117 JDs awarded. *Entrance requirements:* LSAT, LSDAS, letters of recommendation. Additional exam requirements/recommendations for international students: Required—TOEFL. *Application deadline:* For fall admission, 3/1 priority date for domestic and international students. Applications are processed on a rolling basis. Application fee: $25 ($40 for international students). Electronic applications accepted. *Expenses:* Contact institution. *Financial support:* In 2009–10, 329 students received support, including 25 research assistantships with full and partial tuition reimbursements available (averaging $3,000 per year), 2 teaching assistantships (averaging $3,000 per year); career-related internships or fieldwork, Federal Work-Study, scholarships/grants, tuition waivers (partial), and unspecified assistantships also available. Support available to part-time students. Financial award application deadline: 4/1; financial award applicants required to submit FAFSA. *Faculty research:* Health law, civil rights, tort law, employment law, voting rights. Total annual research expenditures: $30,000. *Unit head:* Dr. Kevin H. Smith, Dean, 901-678-2421, Fax: 901-678-5210, E-mail: ksmith@memphis.edu. *Application contact:* Dr. Sue Ann McClellan, Assistant Dean for Law Admissions, Recruiting and Scholarships, 901-678-5403, Fax: 901-678-5210, E-mail: smcclell@memphis.edu.

University of Miami, Graduate School, School of Law, Coral Gables, FL 33124-8087. Offers comparative law (LL M); estate planning (LL M); international law, inter-American law, and transnational law for foreign lawyers (LL M); law (JD); ocean and coastal law (LL M); real property development (LL M); taxation (LL M); JD/LL M; JD/MBA; JD/MM; JD/MPH. *Accreditation:* ABA. *Faculty:* 65 full-time (24 women), 106 part-time/adjunct (31 women). *Students:* 1,384 full-time (597 women); includes 321 minority (94 African Americans, 4 American Indian/Alaska Native, 61 Asian Americans or Pacific Islanders, 162 Hispanic Americans), 59 international. Average age 24. 4,695 applicants, 51% accepted, 530 enrolled. In 2009, 373 JDs awarded. *Entrance requirements:* LSAT, 2 letters of recommendation. Additional exam requirements/recommendations for international students: Required—TOEFL (minimum score 600 paper-based; 250 computer-based; 75 iBT). *Application deadline:* For fall admission, 1/4 priority date for domestic and international students. Applications are processed on a rolling basis. Application fee: $60. Electronic applications accepted. *Expenses:* Contact institution. *Financial support:* In 2009–10, 1,273 students received support, including 60 fellowships (averaging $2,346 per year), 121 research assistantships (averaging $1,867 per year); career-related internships or fieldwork, Federal Work-Study, institutionally sponsored loans, scholarships/grants, and unspecified assistantships also available. Financial award application deadline: 3/1; financial award applicants required to submit FAFSA. *Faculty research:* National security law, international finance, Internet law/law of electronic commerce, law of the seas, art law/cultural heritage law. Total annual research expenditures: $349,292. *Unit head:* Michael Goodnight, Assistant Dean of Admissions, 305-284-2527, Fax: 305-284-3084, E-mail: mgoodnig@law.miami.edu. *Application contact:* Therese Lambert, Director of Student Recruiting, 305-284-6746, Fax: 305-284-3084, E-mail: tlambert@law.miami.edu.

University of Michigan, Law School, Ann Arbor, MI 48109-1215. Offers comparative law (MCL); international tax (LL M); law (JD, LL M, SJD); JD/MA; JD/MBA; JD/MHSA; JD/MPH; JD/MPP; JD/MS; JD/MSI; JD/MSW; JD/MUP; JD/PhD. *Accreditation:* ABA. *Faculty:* 87 full-time (27 women), 33 part-time/adjunct (11 women). *Students:* 1,117 full-time (486 women); includes 256 minority (57 African Americans, 17 American Indian/Alaska Native, 135 Asian Americans or Pacific Islanders, 47 Hispanic Americans), 38 international. 5,414 applicants, 22% accepted, 371 enrolled. In 2009, 410 first professional degrees, 44 master's, 4 doctorates awarded. *Entrance requirements:* For JD, master's, and doctorate, LSAT. Additional exam requirements/recommendations for international students: Required—TOEFL. *Application deadline:* For fall admission, 2/15 for domestic students. Applications are processed on a rolling basis. Application fee: $75. Electronic applications accepted. *Expenses:* Contact institution. *Financial support:* In 2009–10, 1,035 students received support. Career-related internships or fieldwork, Federal Work-Study, institutionally sponsored loans, and scholarships/grants available. Financial award applicants required to submit FAFSA. *Unit head:* Evan H. Caminker, Dean, 734-764-1358. *Application contact:* Sarah C. Zearfoss, Assistant Dean and Director of Admissions, 734-764-0537, Fax: 734-647-3218, E-mail: law.jd.admissions@umich.edu.

University of Minnesota, Twin Cities Campus, Law School, Minneapolis, MN 55455. Offers JD, LL M, JD/MA, JD/MBA, JD/MBT, JD/MCS, JD/MD, JD/MHA, JD/MP, JD/MPA, JD/MPP, JD/MS, JD/MURP, JD/PhD. *Accreditation:* ABA. *Faculty:* 64 full-time (24 women), 178 part-time/adjunct (80 women). *Students:* 794 full-time (328 women); includes 123 minority (23 African Americans, 11 American Indian/Alaska Native, 63 Asian Americans or Pacific Islanders, 26 Hispanic Americans), 45 international. Average age 25. 3,594 applicants, 25% accepted, 213 enrolled. In 2009, 255 JDs, 31 master's awarded. *Entrance requirements:* LSAT. Additional exam requirements/recommendations for international students: Required—TOEFL. *Application deadline:* For fall admission, 4/1 for domestic students. Applications are processed on a rolling basis. Application fee: $75. Electronic applications accepted. *Expenses:* Contact institution. *Financial support:* In 2009–10, 500 students received support; fellowships, research assistantships, teaching assistantships, career-related internships or fieldwork, Federal Work-Study, institutionally sponsored loans, scholarships/grants, and tuition waivers (partial) available. Financial award application deadline: 5/1; financial award applicants required to submit FAFSA. *Faculty research:* International law, corporate law, criminal law, public law, health law. Total annual research expenditures: $1.3 million. *Unit head:* David Wippman, Dean, 612-625-4841. *Application contact:* Nick Wallace, Director of Admissions, 612-625-0718, Fax: 612-625-2011, E-mail: umnlsadm@umn.edu.

University of Mississippi, School of Law, Oxford, University, MS 38677. Offers JD, JD/MBA. *Accreditation:* ABA. *Faculty:* 33 full-time (11 women), 10 part-time/adjunct (5 women). *Students:* 485 full-time (212 women), 2 part-time (0 women); includes 69 minority (59 African Americans, 3 American Indian/Alaska Native, 4 Asian Americans or Pacific Islanders, 3 Hispanic Americans), 1 international. Average age 24. 1,069 applicants, 42% accepted, 160 enrolled. In 2009, 163 JDs awarded. *Entrance requirements:* LSAT, LSDAS. Additional exam requirements/recommendations for international students: Required—TOEFL. *Application deadline:* For fall admission, 4/1 for domestic students. Application fee: $40. *Expenses:* Contact institution. *Financial support:* Fellowships, research assistantships, teaching assistantships, career-related internships or fieldwork, Federal Work-Study, institutionally sponsored loans, and

scholarships/grants available. Support available to part-time students. Financial award application deadline: 3/1; financial award applicants required to submit FAFSA. *Unit head:* Dr. Samuel Davis, Dean, 662-915-7361, Fax: 662-915-5313, E-mail: smdavis@olemiss.edu. *Application contact:* Barbara Vinson, Coordinator of Admissions, 662-915-7361, E-mail: bvinson@olemiss.edu.

University of Missouri, School of Law, Columbia, MO 65211. Offers JD, LL M, JD/MA, JD/MBA, JD/MPA. *Accreditation:* ABA. *Entrance requirements:* LSAT. Additional exam requirements/recommendations for international students: Required—TOEFL. *Expenses:* Contact institution.

University of Missouri–Kansas City, School of Law, Kansas City, MO 64110-2499. Offers law (JD, LL M), including general (LL M), taxation (LL M); JD/LL M; JD/MBA; LL M/MPA. *Accreditation:* ABA. Part-time programs available. *Faculty:* 32 full-time (14 women), 1 part-time/adjunct (0 women). *Students:* 483 full-time (191 women), 59 part-time (28 women); includes 70 minority (35 African Americans, 4 American Indian/Alaska Native, 14 Asian Americans or Pacific Islanders, 17 Hispanic Americans), 27 international. Average age 27. 984 applicants, 50% accepted, 215 enrolled. In 2009, 153 JDs, 32 master's awarded. *Degree requirements:* For master's, thesis (general). *Entrance requirements:* For JD, LSAT; for master's, LSAT, minimum GPA of 3.0 (general), 2.7 (taxation). Additional exam requirements/recommendations for international students: Required—TOEFL (minimum score 550 paper-based; 213 computer-based; 80 iBT). *Application deadline:* For fall admission, 3/1 priority date for domestic and international students. Applications are processed on a rolling basis. Application fee: $50. Electronic applications accepted. *Expenses:* Contact institution. *Financial support:* In 2009–10, 27 teaching assistantships with partial tuition reimbursements (averaging $1,944 per year) were awarded; career-related internships or fieldwork, Federal Work-Study, institutionally sponsored loans, scholarships/grants, and tuition waivers (full and partial) also available. Support available to part-time students. Financial award application deadline: 3/1; financial award applicants required to submit FAFSA. *Faculty research:* Family and children's issues, litigation, estate planning, urban law, business, tax entrepreneurial law. *Unit head:* Ellen Y. Suni, Dean, 816-235-1677, Fax: 816-235-5276, E-mail: sunie@umkc.edu. *Application contact:* Debbie Brooks, Director of Admissions, 816-325-1644, Fax: 816-235-5276, E-mail: brooksdv@umkc.edu.

The University of Montana, School of Law, Missoula, MT 59812. Offers JD, JD/MBA, JD/MPA. *Accreditation:* ABA. *Degree requirements:* For JD, oral presentation, paper. *Entrance requirements:* LSAT. *Expenses:* Contact institution. *Faculty research:* Legal education curriculum, business and probate law reform, rules of civil procedure reform, tribal courts, women's issues.

University of Nebraska–Lincoln, College of Law, Lincoln, NE 68583-0902. Offers law (JD); legal studies (MLS); space and telecommunications law (LL M); JD/MA; JD/MBA; JD/MCRP; JD/MPA; JD/PhD. *Accreditation:* ABA. *Entrance requirements:* LSAT. Electronic applications accepted. *Expenses:* Contact institution. *Faculty research:* Law and medicine, constitutional law, criminal procedure, international trade.

University of Nevada, Las Vegas, William S. Boyd School of Law, Las Vegas, NV 89154-1003. Offers JD, JD/MBA, JD/MSW, JD/PhD. *Accreditation:* ABA. Part-time and evening/weekend programs available. *Entrance requirements:* LSAT. Electronic applications accepted. *Expenses:* Contact institution. *Faculty research:* Civil procedure, constitutional law, federal courts, professional responsibility, juvenile justice.

University of New Brunswick Fredericton, Faculty of Law, Fredericton, NB E3B 5A3, Canada. Offers LL B, LL B/MBA. *Faculty:* 16 full-time (5 women), 9 part-time/adjunct (6 women). *Students:* 230 full-time (108 women). *Entrance requirements:* LSAT. *Application deadline:* For fall admission, 3/1 for domestic students. Applications are processed on a rolling basis. Application fee: $50. Electronic applications accepted. Tuition and fees charges are reported in Canadian dollars. *Expenses:* Tuition, area resident: Full-time $5562 Canadian dollars; part-time $2781 Canadian dollars per year. Required fees: $49.75 Canadian dollars per term. *Financial support:* Scholarships/grants available. *Faculty research:* Property studies, legal history, family violence, law and technology, international law. *Unit head:* David A. Townsend, Interim Dean, 506-453-4702, Fax: 506-453-4604, E-mail: townsend@unb.ca. *Application contact:* Wanda Foster, Law Admissions Officer, 506-453-4703, Fax: 506-458-7722, E-mail: wfoster@unb.ca.

University of New Mexico, School of Law, Albuquerque, NM 87131-0001. Offers JD, JD/MA, JD/MBA, JD/MPA, JD/MS, JD/PhD. *Accreditation:* ABA. *Faculty:* 33 full-time (20 women), 20 part-time/adjunct (8 women). *Students:* 351 full-time (188 women); includes 155 minority (13 African Americans, 32 American Indian/Alaska Native, 10 Asian Americans or Pacific Islanders, 100 Hispanic Americans). 1,091 applicants, 23% accepted, 117 enrolled. In 2009, 108 JDs awarded. *Degree requirements:* For JD, advanced writing piece, clinic. *Entrance requirements:* LSAT, bachelor's degree. Additional exam requirements/recommendations for international students: Required—TOEFL (minimum score 600 paper-based; 250 computer-based; 100 iBT). *Application deadline:* For fall admission, 2/15 priority date for domestic and international students. Applications are processed on a rolling basis. Application fee: $50. Electronic applications accepted. *Expenses:* Contact institution. *Financial support:* Career-related internships or fieldwork, Federal Work-Study, and scholarships/grants available. Financial award application deadline: 3/1; financial award applicants required to submit FAFSA. *Unit head:* Kevin Washburn, Dean, 505-277-4700, Fax: 505-277-9558, E-mail: washburn@law.unm.edu. *Application contact:* Susan L. Mitchell, Assistant Dean for Admissions and Financial Aid, 505-277-0959, Fax: 505-277-9958, E-mail: mitchell@law.unm.edu.

The University of North Carolina at Chapel Hill, School of Law, Chapel Hill, NC 27599-3380. Offers JD, JD/MAMC, JD/MAPPS, JD/MASA, JD/MBA, JD/MPA, JD/MPH, JD/MRP, JD/MSIS, JD/MSLS, JD/MSW. *Accreditation:* ABA. *Entrance requirements:* LSAT. Additional exam requirements/recommendations for international students: Required—TOEFL (minimum score 650 paper-based; 260 computer-based; 100 iBT). Electronic applications accepted. *Expenses:* Contact institution. *Faculty research:* Death penalty, feminist legal theory, urban reform risk-based environmental policy, state and U.S. constitutional law, health law policy.

University of North Dakota, School of Law, Grand Forks, ND 58202. Offers JD. *Accreditation:* ABA. *Entrance requirements:* LSAT. *Expenses:* Contact institution.

University of Notre Dame, Law School, Notre Dame, IN 46556-0780. Offers human rights (LL M, JSD); international and comparative law (LL M); law (JD). *Accreditation:* ABA. *Faculty:* 53 full-time (16 women), 43 part-time/adjunct (17 women). *Students:* 572 full-time (244 women); includes 128 minority (28 African Americans, 7 American Indian/Alaska Native, 46 Asian Americans or Pacific Islanders, 47 Hispanic Americans), 27 international. 3,178 applicants, 25% accepted, 186 enrolled. In 2009, 198 JDs, 20 master's, 1 doctorate awarded. *Degree requirements:* For master's, thesis, 1 year residency; for doctorate, thesis/dissertation, 2 year residency. *Entrance requirements:* For JD, LSAT; for doctorate, LL M. Additional exam requirements/recommendations for international students: Required—TOEFL. *Application deadline:* For fall admission, 11/1 priority date for domestic students; for winter admission, 3/15 for domestic students. Applications are processed on a rolling basis. Application fee: $60. Electronic applications accepted. *Expenses:* Contact institution. *Financial support:* In 2009–10, 440 students received support, including 440 fellowships with tuition reimbursements available (averaging $15,155 per year); research assistantships, teaching assistantships, career-related internships or fieldwork, Federal Work-Study, institutionally sponsored loans, scholarships/grants, health care benefits, unspecified assistantships, and university dormitory rector assistants also available. Financial award application deadline: 2/15; financial award applicants required to submit FAFSA. *Unit head:* Nell Jessup Newton, Dean, 574-631-6789, Fax: 574-631-8400, E-mail: Nell.Newton@nd.edu. *Application contact:* Melissa Ann Fruscione, Director of Admissions and Financial Aid, 574-631-6626, Fax: 574-631-5474, E-mail: lawadmit@nd.edu.

University of Oklahoma, College of Law, Norman, OK 73019. Offers JD, JD/MBA, JD/MPH, JD/MSEM, JD/MSHA, JD/MSOH. *Accreditation:* ABA. *Faculty:* 37 full-time (15 women), 18

Law

University of Oklahoma *(continued)*
part-time/adjunct (5 women). *Students:* 550 full-time (238 women); includes 115 minority (23 African Americans, 47 American Indian/Alaska Native, 25 Asian Americans or Pacific Islanders, 20 Hispanic Americans), 2 international. Average age 23. 1,151 applicants, 31% accepted, 199 enrolled. In 2009, 165 JDs awarded. *Entrance requirements:* LSAT. *Application deadline:* For fall admission, 3/15 for domestic students. Applications are processed on a rolling basis. Application fee: $50. Electronic applications accepted. *Expenses:* Contact institution. *Financial support:* In 2009–10, 401 students received support. Career-related internships or fieldwork, Federal Work-Study, institutionally sponsored loans, scholarships/grants, and tuition waivers (full and partial) available. Financial award application deadline: 3/1; financial award applicants required to submit FAFSA. *Unit head:* Dr. Andrew M. Coats, Dean, 405-325-4699, Fax: 405-325-7712, E-mail: acoats@ou.edu. *Application contact:* Vicki Ferguson, Admissions Coordinator, 405-325-4728, Fax: 405-325-0502, E-mail: admissions@law.ou.edu.

University of Oregon, School of Law, Eugene, OR 97403. Offers JD, MA, MS, JD/MBA, JD/MS. *Accreditation:* ABA. *Entrance requirements:* LSAT. *Expenses:* Contact institution.

University of Ottawa, Faculty of Graduate and Postdoctoral Studies, Faculty of Law, Ottawa, ON K1N 6N5, Canada. Offers LL M, LL D. Part-time and evening/weekend programs available. *Degree requirements:* For master's, thesis or alternative; for doctorate, thesis/dissertation. *Entrance requirements:* For master's, minimum B average, LL B; for doctorate, LL M, minimum B+ average. Electronic applications accepted. *Faculty research:* International law, human rights law, family law.

University of Pennsylvania, Law School, Philadelphia, PA 19104. Offers JD, LL CM, LL M, SJD, JD/AM, JD/M Bioethics, JD/MA, JD/MBA, JD/MCP, JD/MD, JD/MES, JD/MGA, JD/MPH, JD/MS, JD/MS Ed, JD/MSW, JD/PhD. *Accreditation:* ABA. *Faculty:* 60 full-time (16 women), 39 part-time/adjunct (14 women). *Students:* 790 full-time (373 women); includes 221 minority (58 African Americans, 2 American Indian/Alaska Native, 110 Asian Americans or Pacific Islanders, 51 Hispanic Americans), 19 international. Average age 24. 6,205 applicants, 14% accepted, 255 enrolled. In 2009, 258 JDs, 88 master's awarded. *Degree requirements:* For master's, thesis optional; for doctorate, thesis/dissertation. *Entrance requirements:* For JD, LSAT; for doctorate, LL M. Additional exam requirements/recommendations for international students: Required—TOEFL. *Application deadline:* For fall admission, 2/15 for domestic students. Applications are processed on a rolling basis. Application fee: $75. Electronic applications accepted. *Expenses:* Contact institution. *Financial support:* In 2009–10, 621 students received support, including 2 research assistantships with tuition reimbursements available (averaging $21,000 per year), 21 teaching assistantships (averaging $2,500 per year); fellowships, career-related internships or fieldwork, Federal Work-Study, institutionally sponsored loans, and scholarships/grants also available. Financial award application deadline: 3/1; financial award applicants required to submit FAFSA. *Faculty research:* Law and business, public law and the Constitution, international and comparative law, law and health sciences, intellectual property, criminal law. Total annual research expenditures: $344,352. *Unit head:* Michael A. Fitts, Dean, 215-898-7463, Fax: 215-573-2025. *Application contact:* Renee Post, Associate Dean of Admissions and Financial Aid, 215-898-7400, Fax: 215-898-9606, E-mail: admissions@law.upenn.edu.

University of Pittsburgh, Katz Graduate School of Business, MBA/Juris Doctor Dual Degree Program, Pittsburgh, PA 15260. Offers MBA/JD. *Students:* 22 full-time (4 women); includes 4 minority (1 African American, 2 Asian Americans or Pacific Islanders, 1 Hispanic American). Average age 26. 16 applicants, 100% accepted, 13 enrolled. *Entrance requirements:* Additional exam requirements/recommendations for international students: Required—TOEFL (minimum score 600 paper-based; 250 computer-based; 100 iBT), or IELTS. *Application deadline:* For fall admission, 2/1 for international students; for spring admission, 4/1 for domestic students. Application fee: $50. Electronic applications accepted. *Expenses:* Tuition, state resident: full-time $16,402; part-time $665 per credit. Tuition, nonresident: full-time $28,694; part-time $1175 per credit. Required fees: $690; $175 per term. Tuition and fees vary according to program. *Financial support:* In 2009–10, 8 students received support. Scholarships/grants available. Financial award application deadline: 6/1; financial award applicants required to submit FAFSA. *Faculty research:* Accounting statements and reporting, incentives and governance; corporate finance, mergers and acquisitions; information systems processes, structures, and decision-making; organizational structure, knowledge management, and corporate strategy; consumer behavior and marketing models. *Unit head:* William T. Valenta, Assistant Dean/Director of MBA Programs, 412-648-1610, Fax: 412-648-1659, E-mail: wtvalenta@katz.pitt.edu. *Application contact:* Cliff McCormick, Director of MBA Admissions, 412-648-1700, Fax: 412-648-1659, E-mail: mba@katz.pitt.edu.

University of Pittsburgh, School of Law, John P. Gismondi Civil Litigation Certificate Program, Pittsburgh, PA 15260. Offers Certificate. *Faculty:* 1 (woman) full-time, 26 part-time/adjunct (5 women). *Students:* 110 full-time (33 women). *Expenses:* Tuition, state resident: full-time $16,402; part-time $665 per credit. Tuition, nonresident: full-time $28,694; part-time $1175 per credit. Required fees: $690; $175 per term. Tuition and fees vary according to program. *Unit head:* Martha Mannix, Clinical Associate Professor of Law/Director, 412-648-1390, Fax: 412-648-1947, E-mail: mmannix@pitt.edu. *Application contact:* Charmaine McCall, Assistant Dean of Admissions and Financial Aid, 412-648-1413, Fax: 412-648-1318, E-mail: cmccall@pitt.edu.

University of Pittsburgh, School of Law, Professional Programs in Law, Pittsburgh, PA 15260. Offers JD, JD/MA, JD/MBA, JD/MID, JD/MPA, JD/MPH, JD/MPIA, JD/MS. *Accreditation:* ABA. *Faculty:* 43 full-time (16 women), 104 part-time/adjunct (30 women). *Students:* 688 full-time (313 women), 17 part-time (11 women); includes 108 minority (46 African Americans, 1 American Indian/Alaska Native, 43 Asian Americans or Pacific Islanders, 18 Hispanic Americans). 2,177 applicants, 37% accepted, 225 enrolled. In 2009, 230 JDs awarded. *Entrance requirements:* LSAT. Additional exam requirements/recommendations for international students: Required—TOEFL. *Application deadline:* For fall admission, 3/1 for domestic students. Applications are processed on a rolling basis. Application fee: $55. Electronic applications accepted. *Expenses:* Contact institution. *Financial support:* In 2009–10, 370 students received support, including 36 research assistantships (averaging $5,440 per year), 13 teaching assistantships (averaging $1,200 per year); career-related internships or fieldwork, Federal Work-Study, scholarships/grants, and unspecified assistantships also available. Financial award application deadline: 3/1; financial award applicants required to submit FAFSA. *Faculty research:* Civil and criminal justice, constitutional law, health law, international law, law and society. Total annual research expenditures: $397,636. *Unit head:* Mary Crossley, Dean, 412-648-1401, Fax: 412-648-2647, E-mail: crossley@pitt.edu. *Application contact:* Charmaine McCall, Assistant Dean of Admissions and Financial Aid, 412-648-1413, Fax: 412-648-1318, E-mail: cmccall@pitt.edu.

University of Pittsburgh, School of Law, Program in American Law, Pittsburgh, PA 15260. Offers international and comparative law (LL M). Program offered to international students only. *Faculty:* 43 full-time (16 women), 104 part-time/adjunct (30 women). *Students:* 12 full-time (9 women), all international. Average age 25. 44 applicants, 64% accepted, 12 enrolled. In 2009, 12 master's awarded. *Degree requirements:* For master's, seminar paper. *Entrance requirements:* For master's, law degree from foreign university. Additional exam requirements/recommendations for international students: Required—TOEFL (minimum score 600 paper-based; 250 computer-based; 100 iBT); Recommended—IELTS (minimum score 7). *Application deadline:* For fall admission, 3/30 priority date for international students. Applications are processed on a rolling basis. Application fee: $0 ($40 for international students). *Expenses:* Contact institution. *Financial support:* In 2009–10, 6 students received support, including 7 fellowships with partial tuition reimbursements available (averaging $17,000 per year); career-related internships or fieldwork and scholarships/grants also available. *Faculty research:* International business transactions, transnational litigation, international trade, international transactions. *Unit head:* Prof. Ronald A. Brand, Director, Center for International Legal Education, 412-648-7023, Fax: 412-648-2648, E-mail: rbrand@pitt.edu. *Application contact:* Gina Huggins, Program Administrator, 412-648-2023, Fax: 412-648-2648, E-mail: cile@pitt.edu.

University of Pittsburgh, School of Law, Program in Intellectual Property and Technology Law, Pittsburgh, PA 15260. Offers Certificate. *Faculty:* 4 full-time (1 woman), 10 part-time/adjunct (2 women). *Students:* 38 full-time (18 women). *Expenses:* Tuition, state resident: full-time $16,402; part-time $665 per credit. Tuition, nonresident: full-time $28,694; part-time $1175 per credit. Required fees: $690; $175 per term. Tuition and fees vary according to program. *Faculty research:* Patent, copyright, trademark, cyberspace, biotechnology. *Unit head:* Prof. Janice M. Mueller, Professor and Director, 412-648-5300, Fax: 412-648-2648, E-mail: mueller2@pitt.edu. *Application contact:* Charmaine McCall, Assistant Dean of Admissions and Financial Aid, 412-648-1413, Fax: 412-648-1318, E-mail: cmccall@pitt.edu.

University of Pittsburgh, School of Law, Program in International Law, Pittsburgh, PA 15260. Offers Certificate. *Faculty:* 43 full-time (16 women), 104 part-time/adjunct (30 women). *Students:* 110 full-time (55 women); includes 12 minority (4 African Americans, 5 Asian Americans or Pacific Islanders, 3 Hispanic Americans). Average age 24. *Expenses:* Tuition, state resident: full-time $16,402; part-time $665 per credit. Tuition, nonresident: full-time $28,694; part-time $1175 per credit. Required fees: $690; $175 per term. Tuition and fees vary according to program. *Unit head:* Prof. Ronald A. Brand, Director, Center for International Legal Education, 412-648-7023, Fax: 412-648-2648. E-mail: rbrand@pitt.edu. *Application contact:* Gina Huggins, Program Administrator, 412-648-2023, Fax: 412-648-2648, E-mail: cile@pitt.edu.

University of Puerto Rico, Río Piedras, School of Law, San Juan, PR 00931-3349. Offers JD, LL M. *Accreditation:* ABA. Part-time and evening/weekend programs available. *Entrance requirements:* For JD, GMAT, GRE, LSAT, EXADEP, minimum GPA of 3.0; for master's, LSAT, minimum GPA of 3.0, letter of recommendation. Additional exam requirements/recommendations for international students: Required—TOEFL. *Faculty research:* Civil code; Puerto Rico constitutional law; professional behavior, rules and regulations; international law; expert testimony.

University of Richmond, School of Law, Richmond, University of Richmond, VA 23173. Offers JD, JD/MA, JD/MBA, JD/MHA, JD/MPA, JD/MS, JD/MSW, JD/MURP. *Accreditation:* ABA. *Entrance requirements:* LSAT. Electronic applications accepted. *Expenses:* Contact institution.

University of St. Thomas, Graduate Studies, School of Law, Minneapolis, MN 55403-2015. Offers JD, JD/MA, JD/MBA, JD/MSW. *Accreditation:* ABA. *Faculty:* 26 full-time (10 women), 61 part-time/adjunct (21 women). *Students:* 457 full-time (208 women), 2 part-time (0 women); includes 62 minority (19 African Americans, 1 American Indian/Alaska Native, 29 Asian Americans or Pacific Islanders, 13 Hispanic Americans). Average age 26. 1,551 applicants, 51% accepted, 174 enrolled. In 2009, 145 JDs awarded. *Degree requirements:* For JD, mentor externship, public service. *Entrance requirements:* LSAT, 2 letters of recommendation. Additional exam requirements/recommendations for international students: Required—TOEFL (minimum score 550 paper-based; 213 computer-based), IELTS (minimum score 6.5), Michigan English Language Assessment Battery (minimum score 80). *Application deadline:* For fall admission, 7/1 priority date for domestic and international students. Applications are processed on a rolling basis. Application fee: $0. Electronic applications accepted. *Financial support:* In 2009–10, 269 students received support. Scholarships/grants available. Financial award application deadline: 7/1; financial award applicants required to submit FAFSA. *Faculty research:* Ethical leadership in the profession, law and religion, constitutional law, international law and litigation with the federal government. *Unit head:* Thomas M. Mengler, Dean, 651-962-4880, Fax: 651-962-4881, E-mail: tmmengler@stthomas.edu. *Application contact:* Cari Haaland, Director of Admissions, 651-962-4895, Fax: 651-962-4876, E-mail: lawschool@stthomas.edu.

University of San Diego, School of Law, San Diego, CA 92110. Offers business and corporate law (LL M); comparative law (LL M); general studies (LL M); international law (LL M); law (JD); taxation (LL M, Diploma); JD/IMBA; JD/MA; JD/MBA. *Accreditation:* ABA. Part-time and evening/weekend programs available. *Faculty:* 43 full-time (17 women), 57 part-time/adjunct (18 women). *Students:* 882 full-time (412 women), 222 part-time (96 women); includes 297 minority (15 African Americans, 12 American Indian/Alaska Native, 177 Asian Americans or Pacific Islanders, 93 Hispanic Americans), 21 international. Average age 26. 4,424 applicants, 34% accepted, 324 enrolled. In 2009, 327 first professional degrees, 59 master's awarded. *Entrance requirements:* For JD, LSAT, bachelor's degree; for master's, JD, LLB or equivalent from an ABA-accredited law school. Additional exam requirements/recommendations for international students: Required—TOEFL (minimum score 600 paper-based; 250 computer-based; 98 iBT). *Application deadline:* For fall admission, 2/1 priority date for domestic students. Applications are processed on a rolling basis. Application fee: $50. Electronic applications accepted. *Expenses:* Contact institution. *Financial support:* In 2009–10, 973 students received support. Career-related internships or fieldwork, Federal Work-Study, institutionally sponsored loans, and scholarships/grants available. Support available to part-time students. Financial award application deadline: 3/1; financial award applicants required to submit FAFSA. *Unit head:* Kevin Cole, Dean, 619-260-2330, Fax: 619-260-2218. *Application contact:* Carl J. Eging, Director of Admissions and Financial Aid, 619-260-4528, Fax: 619-260-2218, E-mail: eging@sandiego.edu.

University of San Francisco, School of Law, San Francisco, CA 94117-1080. Offers law (JD, LL M), including intellectual property and technology law (LL M), international transactions and comparative law (LL M); JD/MBA. *Accreditation:* ABA. Part-time and evening/weekend programs available. *Faculty:* 27 full-time (13 women), 49 part-time/adjunct (18 women). *Students:* 556 full-time (293 women), 158 part-time (73 women); includes 205 minority (44 African Americans, 3 American Indian/Alaska Native, 97 Asian Americans or Pacific Islanders, 61 Hispanic Americans), 33 international. Average age 28. 3,876 applicants, 37% accepted, 272 enrolled. In 2009, 224 JDs, 27 master's awarded. *Entrance requirements:* LSAT, minimum undergraduate GPA of 3.2. *Application deadline:* For fall admission, 4/1 for domestic students. Applications are processed on a rolling basis. *Expenses:* Contact institution. *Financial support:* In 2009–10, 613 students received support. Career-related internships or fieldwork, Federal Work-Study, and institutionally sponsored loans available. Support available to part-time students. Financial award application deadline: 3/2; financial award applicants required to submit FAFSA. *Unit head:* Jeffrey Brand, Dean, 415-422-6304. *Application contact:* Alan P. Guerrero, Director of Admissions, 415-422-2976, E-mail: lawadmissions@usfca.edu.

University of Saskatchewan, College of Graduate Studies and Research, College of Law, Saskatoon, SK S7N 5A2, Canada. Offers LL B, LL M. Part-time programs available. *Degree requirements:* For master's, thesis. *Entrance requirements:* For LL B, LSAT; for master's, LL B. Additional exam requirements/recommendations for international students: Required—TOEFL. Tuition and fees charges are reported in Canadian dollars. *Expenses:* Tuition, area resident: Full-time $3000 Canadian dollars; part-time $500 Canadian dollars per term. Required fees: $700 Canadian dollars; $100 Canadian dollars per term. *Faculty research:* Cooperative, native/aboriginal, constitutional, commercial, consumer, and natural resource law; criminal justice; human rights.

University of South Africa, College of Law, Pretoria, South Africa. Offers correctional services management (M Tech); criminology (MA, PhD); law (LL M, LL D); penology (MA, PhD); police science (MA, PhD); policing (M Tech); security risk management (M Tech); social science in criminology (MA).

University of South Carolina, School of Law, Columbia, SC 29208. Offers JD, JD/IMBA, JD/M Acc, JD/MCJ, JD/MEERM, JD/MHA, JD/MHR, JD/MIBS, JD/MPA, JD/MSEL, JD/MSW. *Accreditation:* ABA. *Degree requirements:* For JD, thesis/dissertation. *Entrance requirements:* LSAT. *Expenses:* Contact institution.

The University of South Dakota, School of Law, Vermillion, SD 57069-2390. Offers JD, JD/MA, JD/MBA, JD/MP Acc, JD/MPA, JD/MS. *Accreditation:* ABA. Part-time programs available. *Entrance requirements:* LSAT. Additional exam requirements/recommendations for international students: Required—TOEFL (minimum score 600 paper-based; 250 computer-based). Electronic applications accepted. *Expenses:* Contact institution. *Faculty research:* Indian law, skills training, international law, family law, evidence.

University of Southern California, Graduate School, Gould School of Law, Los Angeles, CA 90089. Offers comparative law for foreign attorneys (MCL); law (JD); law and pharmacy (JD/Pharm D); law and politics and international policy (JD/PhD); law for foreign-educated attorneys (LL M); JD/MA; JD/MBA; JD/MBT; JD/MPA; JD/MPP; JD/MRED; JD/MS; JD/MSW; JD/PhD; JD/Pharm D. *Accreditation:* ABA. *Faculty:* 55 full-time (20 women), 38 part-time/adjunct (7 women). *Students:* 752 full-time (375 women); includes 243 minority (46 African Americans, 5 American Indian/Alaska Native, 122 Asian Americans or Pacific Islanders, 70 Hispanic Americans), 126 international. 6,024 applicants, 22% accepted, 215 enrolled. In 2009, 203 first professional degrees, 96 master's awarded. *Entrance requirements:* LSAT. Additional exam requirements/recommendations for international students: Required—TOEFL. *Application deadline:* For fall admission, 2/1 for domestic and international students. Applications are processed on a rolling basis. Application fee: $75. Electronic applications accepted. *Expenses:* Tuition: Full-time $25,980; part-time $1315 per unit. Required fees: $554. One-time fee: $35 full-time. Full-time tuition and fees vary according to degree level and program. *Financial support:* In 2009–10, 370 students received support. Application deadline: 3/2. *Faculty research:* Intellectual property law, tax law, criminal law, law and psychology, law and history. *Unit head:* Dean Robert K. Rasmussen, Dean, 213-740-2523, E-mail: dean@law.usc.edu. *Application contact:* Chloe Reid, Associate Dean for Admissions, 213-740-2523, E-mail: creid@law.usc.edu.

University of Southern Maine, University of Maine School of Law, Portland, ME 04102. Offers JD, JD/MBA, JD/MPPM. Part-time programs available. *Faculty:* 16 full-time (7 women), 13 part-time/adjunct (3 women). *Students:* 264 full-time (112 women); includes 23 minority (5 African Americans, 4 American Indian/Alaska Native, 7 Asian Americans or Pacific Islanders, 7 Hispanic Americans). Average age 26. 702 applicants, 49% accepted, 90 enrolled. In 2009, 93 JDs awarded. *Entrance requirements:* LSAT. Additional exam requirements/recommendations for international students: Required—TOEFL. *Application deadline:* For fall admission, 3/1 for domestic and international students. Applications are processed on a rolling basis. Application fee: $50. Electronic applications accepted. *Expenses:* Contact institution. *Financial support:* In 2009–10, 245 students received support, including 20 fellowships (averaging $3,000 per year), 11 research assistantships (averaging $2,400 per year), 6 teaching assistantships (averaging $2,400 per year); career-related internships or fieldwork, Federal Work-Study, scholarships/grants, and tuition waivers (full and partial) also available. Support available to part-time students. Financial award application deadline: 2/15; financial award applicants required to submit FAFSA. *Faculty research:* Commercial law aspects of intellectual property; domestic violence; race, gender, and law; environmental law and climate change; bankruptcy and predatory lending. *Unit head:* Peter R. Pitegoff, Dean, 207-780-4344, Fax: 207-780-4239. *Application contact:* David Pallozzi, Assistant Dean for Admissions, 207-780-4341, Fax: 207-780-4239, E-mail: mainelaw@usm.maine.edu.

The University of Tennessee, College of Law, Knoxville, TN 37996-1810. Offers business transactions (JD); law (JD); trial advocacy and dispute resolution (JD); JD/MBA; JD/MPA. *Accreditation:* ABA. *Faculty:* 28 full-time (9 women), 41 part-time/adjunct (14 women). *Students:* 471 full-time (222 women); includes 96 minority (56 African Americans, 4 American Indian/Alaska Native, 20 Asian Americans or Pacific Islanders, 16 Hispanic Americans), 4 international. Average age 24. 1,468 applicants, 27% accepted, 158 enrolled. In 2009, 143 JDs awarded. *Entrance requirements:* LSAT. *Application deadline:* For fall admission, 3/1 priority date for domestic and international students. Applications are processed on a rolling basis. Application fee: $15. Electronic applications accepted. *Expenses:* Contact institution. *Financial support:* In 2009–10, 356 students received support, including 7 research assistantships with full tuition reimbursements available (averaging $4,400 per year); career-related internships or fieldwork, Federal Work-Study, institutionally sponsored loans, scholarships/grants, and unspecified assistantships also available. Support available to part-time students. Financial award application deadline: 3/1; financial award applicants required to submit FAFSA. *Faculty research:* Legal expert systems, medical malpractice remedies, professional ethics, insanity defense. *Unit head:* Dr. Karen R. Britton, Director of Admissions, Financial Aid and Career Services, 865-974-4131, Fax: 865-974-1572, E-mail: lawadmit@utk.edu. *Application contact:* Janet S. Hatcher, Admissions and Financial Aid Advisor, 865-974-4131, Fax: 865-974-1572, E-mail: hatcher@utk.edu.

The University of Texas at Austin, School of Law, Austin, TX 78705-3224. Offers JD, LL M, JD/MGPS, JD/MA, JD/MBA, JD/MP Aff, JD/MSCRP. *Accreditation:* ABA. *Faculty:* 88 full-time (34 women), 55 part-time/adjunct (14 women). *Students:* 1,248 full-time (566 women); includes 343 minority (71 African Americans, 7 American Indian/Alaska Native, 80 Asian Americans or Pacific Islanders, 185 Hispanic Americans), 7 international. Average age 24. 5,275 applicants, 23% accepted, 379 enrolled. In 2009, 433 JDs, 33 master's awarded. *Entrance requirements:* LSAT, minimum GPA of 2.2. *Application deadline:* For fall admission, 2/1 for domestic students. Application fee: $70. Electronic applications accepted. *Expenses:* Contact institution. *Financial support:* In 2009–10, 1,107 students received support, including 100 research assistantships, 32 teaching assistantships (averaging $3,900 per year); career-related internships or fieldwork, scholarships/grants, and tuition waivers (full) also available. Financial award application deadline: 3/31; financial award applicants required to submit FAFSA. *Faculty research:* Constitutional law, corporate law, environmental law, employment and labor law, intellectual property law. *Unit head:* Lawrence Sager, Dean, 512-232-1120, Fax: 512-471-6987, E-mail: lsager@law.utexas.edu. *Application contact:* 512-232-1200, Fax: 512-471-2765, E-mail: admissions@law.utexas.edu.

The University of Texas at Dallas, School of Economic, Political and Policy Sciences, Program in Political Science, Richardson, TX 75080. Offers constitutional law (MA); legislative studies (MA); political science (MA, PhD). Part-time and evening/weekend programs available. *Faculty:* 12 full-time (2 women). *Students:* 42 full-time (15 women), 21 part-time (10 women); includes 21 minority (4 African Americans, 2 American Indian/Alaska Native, 9 Asian Americans or Pacific Islanders, 6 Hispanic Americans), 5 international. Average age 33. 37 applicants, 65% accepted, 21 enrolled. In 2009, 18 master's, 3 doctorates awarded. *Degree requirements:* For doctorate, thesis/dissertation. *Entrance requirements:* For master's and doctorate, GRE General Test, minimum GPA of 3.0 in upper-level course work in field. Additional exam requirements/recommendations for international students: Required—TOEFL (minimum score 550 paper-based; 213 computer-based). *Application deadline:* For fall admission, 7/15 for domestic students, 5/1 priority date for international students; for spring admission, 11/15 for domestic students, 9/1 priority date for international students. Applications are processed on a rolling basis. Application fee: $50 ($100 for international students). Electronic applications accepted. *Expenses:* Tuition, state resident: full-time $11,068; part-time $461 per credit hour. Tuition, nonresident: full-time $21,178; part-time $882 per credit hour. Tuition and fees vary according to course load. *Financial support:* In 2009–10, 4 research assistantships with full tuition reimbursements (averaging $12,600 per year), 15 teaching assistantships with full tuition reimbursements (averaging $11,880 per year) were awarded; fellowships, career-related internships or fieldwork, Federal Work-Study, institutionally sponsored loans, and scholarships/grants also available. Support available to part-time students. Financial award application deadline: 4/30; financial award applicants required to submit FAFSA. *Faculty research:* Judicial politics and Congressional history, forecasting conflict, political violence and terrorism, elections and representation, international disputes. *Unit head:* Dr. Robert C. Lowry, Program Head, 972-883-6720, Fax: 972-883-2735, E-mail: robert.lowry@utdallas.edu. *Application contact:* Dr. Thomas L. Brunell, Associate Program Head, 972-883-4963, Fax: 972-883-2735, E-mail: tbrunell@utdallas.edu.

University of the District of Columbia, David A. Clarke School of Law, Washington, DC 20008. Offers JD. *Accreditation:* ABA. *Entrance requirements:* LSAT. Electronic applications accepted. *Expenses:* Contact institution. *Faculty research:* HIV law, juvenile law, legislative law, community development, small business.

University of the Pacific, McGeorge School of Law, Sacramento, CA 95817. Offers advocacy (JD); criminal justice (JD); experiential law teaching (LL M); intellectual property (JD); international legal studies (JD); international water resources law (LL M, JSD); law (JD); public law and policy (JD); public policy and law (LL M); tax (JD); transnational business practice (LL M); JD/MBA; JD/MPPA. *Accreditation:* ABA. Part-time and evening/weekend programs available. *Faculty:* 55 full-time (24 women), 57 part-time/adjunct (18 women). *Students:* 697 full-time (343 women), 377 part-time (197 women); includes 301 minority (33 African Americans, 11 American Indian/Alaska Native, 163 Asian Americans or Pacific Islanders, 94 Hispanic Americans). Average age 24. 2,659 applicants, 43% accepted, 236 enrolled. In 2009, 254 JDs, 51 master's awarded. *Degree requirements:* For master's, thesis (for some programs); for doctorate, thesis/dissertation. *Entrance requirements:* For JD, LSAT; for master's, JD; for doctorate, LL M. Additional exam requirements/recommendations for international students: Required—TOEFL (minimum score 600 paper-based; 250 computer-based; 100 iBT). *Application deadline:* For fall admission, 3/15 priority date for domestic students. Applications are processed on a rolling basis. Application fee: $50. Electronic applications accepted. *Expenses:* Contact institution. *Financial support:* In 2009–10, 887 students received support, including 1 fellowship, 114 research assistantships (averaging $1,839 per year), 12 teaching assistantships (averaging $953 per year); career-related internships or fieldwork, Federal Work-Study, institutionally sponsored loans, and scholarships/grants also available. Support available to part-time students. Financial award applicants required to submit FAFSA. *Faculty research:* International legal studies, public policy and law, advocacy, intellectual property law, taxation, criminal law. *Unit head:* Elizabeth Rindskopf Parker, Dean, 916-739-7151, E-mail: elizabeth@pacific.edu. *Application contact:* 916-739-7105, Fax: 916-739-7301, E-mail: mcgeorge@pacific.edu.

The University of Toledo, College of Law, Toledo, OH 43606. Offers JD, JD/MA, JD/MACJ, JD/MBA, JD/MPA, JD/MSE. *Accreditation:* ABA. Part-time and evening/weekend programs available. *Faculty:* 33 full-time (14 women), 18 part-time/adjunct (5 women). *Students:* 346 full-time (136 women), 147 part-time (62 women); includes 48 minority (19 African Americans, 15 Asian Americans or Pacific Islanders, 14 Hispanic Americans), 10 international. Average age 27. 869 applicants, 60% accepted, 182 enrolled. In 2009, 150 JDs awarded. *Entrance requirements:* LSAT. *Application deadline:* For fall admission, 7/31 priority date for domestic students, 7/31 for international students. Applications are processed on a rolling basis. Application fee: $0. Electronic applications accepted. *Expenses:* Contact institution. *Financial support:* In 2009–10, 493 students received support, including 16 research assistantships (averaging $867 per year), 28 teaching assistantships; career-related internships or fieldwork, Federal Work-Study, and scholarships/grants also available. Support available to part-time students. Financial award application deadline: 8/1; financial award applicants required to submit FAFSA. *Faculty research:* Concept of virtue in originalist constitutional interpretation, force of floodgates of litigation metaphor in tort law, orphan shares under CERCLA, citizen's role in state compliance with international law. Total annual research expenditures: $80,000. *Unit head:* Douglas E. Ray, Dean, 419-530-2379, Fax: 419-530-4526, E-mail: douglas.ray@utoledo.edu. *Application contact:* Lindsay Riesen, Assistant Dean of Law Admissions, 419-530-4131, Fax: 419-530-4345, E-mail: law.admissions@utoledo.edu.

University of Toronto, Faculty of Law and School of Graduate Studies, Graduate Programs in Law, Toronto, ON M5S 1A1, Canada. Offers LL M, MSL, SJD. *Degree requirements:* For master's, thesis (for some programs); for doctorate, thesis/dissertation.

University of Toronto, Faculty of Law, Professional Program in Law, Toronto, ON M5S 1A1, Canada. Offers JD, JD/Certificate, JD/M I St, JD/MA, JD/MBA, JD/MSW, JD/PhD. *Entrance requirements:* LSAT. *Expenses:* Contact institution.

University of Tulsa, College of Law, Tulsa, OK 74104. Offers American Indian and indigenous law (LL M); American law for foreign lawyers (LL M); comparative and international law (Certificate); entrepreneurial law (Certificate); health law (Certificate); law (JD); Native American law (Certificate); public policy (Certificate); resources, energy, and environmental law (Certificate); JD/M Tax; JD/MA; JD/MBA; JD/MS; JD/MSF. *Accreditation:* ABA. Part-time programs available. *Faculty:* 29 full-time (14 women), 24 part-time/adjunct (8 women). *Students:* 382 full-time (148 women), 40 part-time (16 women); includes 68 minority (4 African Americans, 40 American Indian/Alaska Native, 12 Asian Americans or Pacific Islanders, 12 Hispanic Americans), 1 international. Average age 28. 1,304 applicants, 51% accepted, 140 enrolled. In 2009, 149 first professional degrees, 1 master's awarded. *Entrance requirements:* For JD, LSAT, BS or BA from accredited college/university; for master's, JD or equivalent from non-US university. Additional exam requirements/recommendations for international students: Required—TOEFL (minimum score 570 paper-based; 230 computer-based; 90 iBT), IELTS (minimum score 7). *Application deadline:* For fall admission, 2/1 priority date for domestic and international students. Applications are processed on a rolling basis. Application fee: $30. Electronic applications accepted. *Expenses:* Contact institution. *Financial support:* In 2009–10, 176 students received support. Career-related internships or fieldwork, Federal Work-Study, and scholarships/grants available. Support available to part-time students. Financial award applicants required to submit FAFSA. *Faculty research:* International law, Native American law, criminal law, commercial speech, copyright law. *Unit head:* Janet Levit, Dean, 918-631-2400, Fax: 918-631-3126, E-mail: janet-levit@utulsa.edu. *Application contact:* April M. Fox, Assistant Dean of Admissions and Financial Aid, 918-631-2406, Fax: 918-631-3630, E-mail: april-fox@utulsa.edu.

University of Utah, S.J. Quinney College of Law, Salt Lake City, UT 84112-0730. Offers JD, LL M, JD/MBA, JD/MPA. *Accreditation:* ABA. *Entrance requirements:* LSAT, LSDAS. Additional exam requirements/recommendations for international students: Required—TOEFL (minimum score 600 paper-based; 250 computer-based). *Expenses:* Contact institution. *Faculty research:* Environmental law, natural resources law, international law, criminal law, corporate law.

University of Victoria, Faculty of Law, Victoria, BC V8W 2Y2, Canada. Offers JD, LL M, PhD, MBA/JD, MPA/JD. Part-time programs available. *Faculty:* 33 full-time (14 women), 33 part-time/adjunct (6 women). *Students:* 393 full-time, 10 part-time. Average age 28. 1,018 applicants, 30% accepted, 108 enrolled. In 2009, 125 first professional degrees, 10 master's, 1 doctorate awarded. *Degree requirements:* For master's, thesis; for doctorate, thesis/dissertation; for JD, major research paper. *Entrance requirements:* For JD, LSAT, minimum 3 years of full-time study or part-time equivalent leading toward a bachelor's degree; for master's, LL.B. or J.D.; for doctorate, LL.B. or J.D. Additional exam requirements/recommendations for international students: Required—TOEFL (minimum score 600 paper-based; 250 computer-based; 100 iBT). *Application deadline:* For fall admission, 2/1 for domestic and international students. Applications are processed on a rolling basis. Application fee: $75 Canadian dollars. Electronic applications accepted. *Expenses:* Contact institution. *Financial support:* In 2009–10, 250 students received support, including 18 fellowships (averaging $15,000 per year), 20 research assistantships (averaging $8,000 per year); career-related internships or fieldwork, Federal Work-Study, scholarships/grants, health care benefits, unspecified assistantships, and course prizes, merit-based awards also available. Support available to part-time students. Financial award application deadline: 6/1. *Faculty research:* Environmental law and policy, international law, alternative dispute resolution, intellectual property law, Aboriginal law. *Unit head:* Donna Greschner, Dean, 250-721-8147, Fax: 250-472-7299, E-mail: lawdean@uvic.ca. *Application contact:* Neela Paige, Admissions Assistant, 250-721-8151, Fax: 250-721-6390, E-mail: lawadmss@uvic.ca.

University of Virginia, School of Law, Charlottesville, VA 22903-1789. Offers JD, LL M, SJD, JD/MUEP, JD/MA, JD/MBA, JD/MP, JD/MPH, JD/MS. *Accreditation:* ABA. *Faculty:* 79 full-time (22 women), 8 part-time/adjunct (3 women). *Students:* 1,167 full-time (519 women); includes 189 minority (53 African Americans, 11 American Indian/Alaska Native, 81 Asian Americans or Pacific Islanders, 44 Hispanic Americans), 51 international. Average age 25. 8,520 applicants, 17% accepted, 418 enrolled. In 2009, 405 JDs, 30 master's, 1 doctorate awarded. *Degree requirements:* For doctorate, thesis/dissertation, oral exam. *Entrance requirements:* For JD, LSAT, 2 letters of recommendation; personal statement; for master's, 2 letters of recommendation; personal statement. Additional exam requirements/recommendations for international students: Required—TOEFL. *Application deadline:* For fall admission, 3/2 priority date for domestic students, 3/2 for international students. Applications are processed on a rolling basis. Application fee: $75. Electronic applications accepted. *Expenses:* Contact institution. *Financial support:* Fellowships, career-related internships or fieldwork, Federal Work-Study, and institutionally sponsored loans available. Financial award application deadline: 3/1; financial

Law

University of Virginia (continued)
award applicants required to submit FAFSA. *Unit head:* Paul G. Mahoney, Dean, 434-924-7351, Fax: 434-982-2128, E-mail: lawadmit@virginia.edu. *Application contact:* Jason Wu Trujillo, Senior Assistant Dean for Admissions and Financial Aid, 434-924-7351, Fax: 434-982-2128, E-mail: lawadmit@virginia.edu.

University of Washington, Graduate School, School of Law, Seattle, WA 98195-3020. Offers Asian law (LL M, PhD); intellectual property law and policy (LL M); law (JD); law of sustainable international development (LL M); taxation (LL M); JD/LL M; JD/MA; JD/MAIS; JD/MBA; JD/MPA; JD/MS; JD/PhD. *Accreditation:* ABA. *Degree requirements:* For master's, thesis; for doctorate, thesis/dissertation. *Entrance requirements:* For JD, LSAT; for master's, language proficiency (LL M in Asian law). Additional exam requirements/recommendations for international students: Required—TOEFL. *Expenses:* Contact institution. *Faculty research:* Asian, international and comparative law, intellectual property law, health law, environmental law, taxation.

The University of Western Ontario, Faculty of Law, London, ON N6A 5B8, Canada. Offers LL B, LL M, Diploma, LL B/MBA. *Entrance requirements:* For LL B, LSAT; for master's, B+ average in BA, sample of legal academic writing. Additional exam requirements/recommendations for international students: Required—TOEFL. *Expenses:* Contact institution. *Faculty research:* Taxation, administrative law, torts, drug and alcohol law and policy, property.

University of Wisconsin–Madison, Law School, Graduate Programs in Law, Madison, WI 53706-1380. Offers LL M, SJD. *Faculty:* 30 full-time (11 women), 14 part-time/adjunct (4 women). *Students:* 71 full-time (41 women), 3 part-time (0 women); includes 5 minority (2 African Americans, 1 American Indian/Alaska Native, 2 Asian Americans or Pacific Islanders), 68 international. Average age 30. 120 applicants, 55% accepted, 49 enrolled. In 2009, 33 master's, 10 doctorates awarded. *Entrance requirements:* Additional exam requirements/recommendations for international students: Required—TOEFL (minimum score 580 paper-based; 237 computer-based; 92 iBT). *Application deadline:* For fall admission, 3/1 for domestic and international students; for spring admission, 10/1 for domestic and international students. Applications are processed on a rolling basis. Application fee: $56. Electronic applications accepted. *Expenses:* Tuition, state resident: part-time $594 per credit. Tuition, nonresident: part-time $1504 per credit. Required fees: $65 per credit. Tuition and fees vary according to course load, program and reciprocity agreements. *Financial support:* In 2009–10, 5 fellowships with full tuition reimbursements (averaging $11,000 per year) were awarded; scholarships/grants and tuition waivers (partial) also available. *Faculty research:* Tax policy in emerging economics, international trade law, anti-trust law and regulation, Asian comparative law and legal history, intellectual property in business organization. *Unit head:* Prof. Gerald Thain, Chairperson, 608-262-9120. *Application contact:* Amy J. Arntsen, Program Associate, 608-262-9120, Fax: 608-265-2253, E-mail: gradprog@law.wisc.edu.

University of Wisconsin–Madison, Law School, Law Program, Madison, WI 53706. Offers JD. Part-time programs available. *Faculty:* 65 full-time (30 women), 59 part-time/adjunct (28 women). *Students:* 792 full-time (365 women), 33 part-time (15 women); includes 196 minority (58 African Americans, 20 American Indian/Alaska Native, 61 Asian Americans or Pacific Islanders, 57 Hispanic Americans), 22 international. Average age 25. 2,951 applicants, 24% accepted, 278 enrolled. In 2009, 275 JDs awarded. *Entrance requirements:* LSAT. Additional exam requirements/recommendations for international students: Required—TOEFL. *Application deadline:* For fall admission, 3/1 for domestic and international students. Applications are processed on a rolling basis. Application fee: $56. Electronic applications accepted. *Expenses:* Tuition, state resident: part-time $594 per credit. Tuition, nonresident: part-time $1504 per credit. Required fees: $65 per credit. Tuition and fees vary according to course load, program and reciprocity agreements. *Financial support:* In 2009–10, 695 students received support, including 79 fellowships with partial tuition reimbursements available (averaging $12,565 per year), 6 research assistantships with full tuition reimbursements available (averaging $10,685 per year), 1 teaching assistantship with full tuition reimbursement available (averaging $9,390 per year); career-related internships or fieldwork, Federal Work-Study, institutionally sponsored loans, scholarships/grants, tuition waivers (partial), and unspecified assistantships also available. Support available to part-time students. Financial award application deadline: 3/1; financial award applicants required to submit FAFSA. *Unit head:* Kenneth B. Davis, Dean, 608-262-0618, Fax: 608-262-5485. *Application contact:* Michael A. Hall, Department of Admissions, 608-262-5914, Fax: 608-263-3190, E-mail: admissions@law.wisc.edu.

University of Wyoming, College of Law, Laramie, WY 82071. Offers JD, JD/MPA. *Accreditation:* ABA. *Entrance requirements:* LSAT. Additional exam requirements/recommendations for international students: Required—TOEFL. Electronic applications accepted. *Expenses:* Contact institution. *Faculty research:* Environmental, public land, constitutional, securities law, criminal law.

Valparaiso University, School of Law, Valparaiso, IN 46383. Offers JD, LL M, JD/MA, JD/MALS, JD/MBA, JD/MS, JD/MSSA. *Accreditation:* ABA. Part-time programs available. *Faculty:* 40 full-time (14 women), 25 part-time/adjunct (12 women). *Students:* 3,072 applicants, 26% accepted, 214 enrolled. *Entrance requirements:* LSAT. Additional exam requirements/recommendations for international students: Required—TOEFL. *Application deadline:* For fall admission, 4/15 priority date for domestic students. Applications are processed on a rolling basis. Application fee: $60. Electronic applications accepted. *Expenses:* Contact institution. *Financial support:* In 2009–10, 500 students received support; research assistantships, teaching assistantships, career-related internships or fieldwork, Federal Work-Study, institutionally sponsored loans, scholarships/grants, and tuition waivers (partial) available. Support available to part-time students. Financial award application deadline: 3/1; financial award applicants required to submit FAFSA. *Faculty research:* International law, jurisprudence, constitutional law, animal law. *Unit head:* Jay Conison, Dean, 219-465-7834, Fax: 219-465-7872, E-mail: jay.conison@valpo.edu. *Application contact:* Tony O. Credit, Executive Director of Admissions, 219-465-7891, Fax: 219-465-7975, E-mail: tony.credit@valpo.edu.

Vanderbilt University, Vanderbilt University Law School, Nashville, TN 37203. Offers law (JD, LL M); law and economics (PhD); JD/M Div; JD/MA; JD/MBA; JD/MD; JD/MPP; JD/MTS; JD/PhD; LL M/MA. *Accreditation:* ABA. *Faculty:* 48 full-time (19 women), 75 part-time/adjunct (23 women). *Students:* 595 full-time (292 women); includes 77 minority (29 African Americans, 3 American Indian/Alaska Native, 22 Asian Americans or Pacific Islanders, 23 Hispanic Americans), 45 international. Average age 23. 4,850 applicants, 25% accepted, 195 enrolled. In 2009, 187 first professional degrees, 25 master's awarded. *Entrance requirements:* For JD, LSAT; for master's, foreign law degree. Additional exam requirements/recommendations for international students: Required—TOEFL. *Application deadline:* For fall admission, 3/15 for domestic and international students. Applications are processed on a rolling basis. Application fee: $50. Electronic applications accepted. *Expenses:* Contact institution. *Financial support:* In 2009–10, 393 students received support. Career-related internships or fieldwork, Federal Work-Study, institutionally sponsored loans, scholarships/grants, and health care benefits available. Financial award application deadline: 2/15; financial award applicants required to submit FAFSA. *Unit head:* G. Todd Morton, Assistant Dean for Admissions, 615-322-6452, Fax: 615-322-1531. *Application contact:* Admissions Office, 615-322-6452, Fax: 615-322-1531.

Vermont Law School, Law School, Professional Program, South Royalton, VT 05068-0096. Offers JD, JD/MELP. *Accreditation:* ABA. *Faculty:* 34 full-time (13 women), 39 part-time/adjunct (19 women). *Students:* Average age 27. 884 applicants, 62% accepted, 233 enrolled. In 2009, 191 JDs awarded. *Entrance requirements:* LSAT, LSDAS/registration, resume. Additional exam requirements/recommendations for international students: Required—TOEFL (minimum score 600 paper-based). *Application deadline:* For fall admission, 3/1 priority date for domestic students; for spring admission, 11/15 priority date for domestic students. Applications are processed on a rolling basis. Application fee: $60. Electronic applications accepted. *Expenses:* Contact institution. *Financial support:* Career-related internships or fieldwork, Federal Work-Study, institutionally sponsored loans, scholarships/grants, and tuition waivers (partial) available. Financial award application deadline: 3/1; financial award applicants required to submit FAFSA. *Faculty research:* Environmental law, national security, law and medicine. *Unit head:* Geoffrey B. Shields, President and Dean, 802-831-1237, Fax: 802-763-2663, E-mail: hmccarthy@vermontlaw.edu. *Application contact:* Kathy Hartman, Associate Dean for Enrollment Management, 802-831-1239, Fax: 802-831-1174, E-mail: admiss@vermontlaw.edu.

Villanova University, School of Law, Program in Law, Villanova, PA 19085-1699. Offers JD, JD/LL M, JD/MBA. *Faculty:* 58 full-time (29 women), 65 part-time/adjunct (13 women). *Students:* 754 full-time (332 women); includes 130 minority (15 African Americans, 3 American Indian/Alaska Native, 65 Asian Americans or Pacific Islanders, 47 Hispanic Americans), 6 international. Average age 25. 3,254 applicants, 43% accepted, 255 enrolled. In 2009, 226 JDs awarded. *Entrance requirements:* LSAT. *Application deadline:* For fall admission, 3/1 for domestic and international students. Applications are processed on a rolling basis. Application fee: $75. Electronic applications accepted. *Expenses:* Contact institution. *Financial support:* In 2009–10, 271 students received support, including 91 research assistantships, 13 teaching assistantships; career-related internships or fieldwork, Federal Work-Study, institutionally sponsored loans, and scholarships/grants also available. Financial award application deadline: 3/15; financial award applicants required to submit FAFSA. *Faculty research:* International law (public and private), criminal law and procedure sentencing, clinical/pro bono, tax, law and religion. *Unit head:* Doris DelTosto Brogan, Acting Dean, 610-519-7007, Fax: 610-519-6472, E-mail: brogan@law.villanova.edu. *Application contact:* Noe Bernal, Assistant Dean for Admissions, 610-519-7010, Fax: 610-519-6291, E-mail: admissions@law.villanova.edu.

Wake Forest University, School of Law, Winston-Salem, NC 27109. Offers JD, LL M, SJD, JD/M Div, JD/MA, JD/MBA. LL M for foreign law graduates in American law. *Accreditation:* ABA. *Faculty:* 38 full-time, 12 part-time/adjunct. *Students:* 463 full-time (193 women), 26 part-time (13 women); includes 80 minority (41 African Americans, 4 American Indian/Alaska Native, 16 Asian Americans or Pacific Islanders, 19 Hispanic Americans). Average age 24. 2,142 applicants, 30% accepted. In 2009, 171 JDs awarded. *Entrance requirements:* LSAT. Additional exam requirements/recommendations for international students: Required—TOEFL. *Application deadline:* For fall admission, 3/1 for domestic students. Applications are processed on a rolling basis. Application fee: $60. Electronic applications accepted. *Expenses:* Contact institution. *Financial support:* In 2009–10, 183 students received support. Career-related internships or fieldwork, Federal Work-Study, institutionally sponsored loans, and scholarships/grants available. Financial award application deadline: 4/30; financial award applicants required to submit FAFSA. *Faculty research:* Constitutional law, family law, land use planning, torts, taxation. *Unit head:* Blake D. Morant, Dean, 336-758-5435, Fax: 336-758-4632. *Application contact:* Melanie E. Nutt, Director of Admissions and Financial Aid, 336-758-5437, Fax: 336-758-3930, E-mail: admissions@law.wfu.edu.

Walden University, Graduate Programs, School of Public Policy and Administration, Minneapolis, MN 55401. Offers government management (Postbaccalaureate Certificate); health policy (MPA); homeland security policy (MPA); interdisciplinary policy studies (MPA); law and public policy (MPA); local government management for sustainable communities (MPA); nonprofit management (Postbaccalaureate Certificate); nonprofit management and leadership (MPA, MS); policy analysis (MPA); public management and leadership (MPA); public policy and administration (MPA, PhD), including criminal justice (PhD), health services (PhD), homeland security policy and coordination (PhD), international nongovernmental organizations (PhD), law and public policy (PhD), local government management for sustainable communities (PhD), nonprofit management and leadership (PhD), public management and leadership (PhD), public policy (PhD), public safety management (PhD), terrorism, mediation, and peace (PhD); terrorism, mediation, and peace (MPA). Part-time and evening/weekend programs available. Postbaccalaureate distance learning degree programs offered (minimal on-campus study). *Faculty:* 7 full-time, 62 part-time/adjunct. *Students:* 1,468 full-time (941 women), 233 part-time (162 women); includes 852 minority (761 African Americans, 9 American Indian/Alaska Native, 19 Asian Americans or Pacific Islanders, 63 Hispanic Americans), 53 international. Average age 40. In 2009, 173 master's, 13 doctorates awarded. *Degree requirements:* For doctorate, thesis/dissertation, residency. *Entrance requirements:* For master's, bachelor's degree or equivalent in related field, minimum GPA of 2.5; for doctorate, master's degree or equivalent in related field; minimum GPA of 3.0; official transcripts; three years of related professional/academic experience (preferred); access to computer and Internet. Additional exam requirements/recommendations for international students: Required—TOEFL (minimum score 550 paper-based; 213 computer-based), IELTS (minimum score 6.5), or Michigan English Language Assessment Battery (minimum score 82). *Application deadline:* Applications are processed on a rolling basis. Application fee: $50. Electronic applications accepted. *Expenses:* Tuition: Full-time $13,665; part-time $560 per credit. Required fees: $1375. Tuition and fees vary according to course load, degree level and program. *Financial support:* In 2009–10, 207 students received support; fellowships with tuition reimbursements available, Federal Work-Study, scholarships/grants, unspecified assistantships, and family tuition reduction, active duty/veteran tuition reduction, group tuition reduction, interest-free payment plans available. Support available to part-time students. Financial award applicants required to submit FAFSA. *Unit head:* Dr. Mark Gordon, Associate Dean, 800-925-3368. *Application contact:* Jennifer Hall, Director of Enrollment, 866-4-WALDEN, E-mail: info@waldenu.edu.

Washburn University, School of Law, Topeka, KS 66621. Offers JD. *Accreditation:* ABA. *Faculty:* 28 full-time (11 women), 30 part-time/adjunct (10 women). *Students:* 441 full-time (179 women); includes 57 minority (18 African Americans, 6 American Indian/Alaska Native, 13 Asian Americans or Pacific Islanders, 20 Hispanic Americans). Average age 26. 957 applicants, 47% accepted, 159 enrolled. *Entrance requirements:* LSAT. Additional exam requirements/recommendations for international students: Required—TOEFL. *Application deadline:* For fall admission, 4/1 priority date for domestic and international students; for spring admission, 11/1 priority date for domestic and international students. Applications are processed on a rolling basis. Application fee: $40. Electronic applications accepted. *Expenses:* Contact institution. *Financial support:* In 2009–10, 202 students received support. Career-related internships or fieldwork, Federal Work-Study, and scholarships/grants available. Support available to part-time students. Financial award applicants required to submit FAFSA. *Faculty research:* Constitutional law, family law, energy law, banking and securities law, agricultural law. *Unit head:* Thomas J. Romig, Dean, 785-670-1662, Fax: 785-670-3249, E-mail: thomas.romig@washburn.edu. *Application contact:* Karla Whitaker, Director of Admissions, 785-670-1185, Fax: 785-670-1120, E-mail: karla.whitaker@washburn.edu.

Washington and Lee University, School of Law, Lexington, VA 24450. Offers law (JD); U.S. law (LL M). *Accreditation:* ABA. *Entrance requirements:* LSAT. Additional exam requirements/recommendations for international students: Required—TOEFL (minimum score 560 paper-based; 220 computer-based; 83 iBT). Electronic applications accepted.

Washington University in St. Louis, School of Law, St. Louis, MO 63130-4899. Offers JD, LL M, MJS, JSD, JD/MA, JD/MBA, JD/MHA, JD/MS, JD/MSW, JD/PhD. *Accreditation:* ABA. *Entrance requirements:* LSAT. Electronic applications accepted. *Expenses:* Contact institution. *Faculty research:* International law, environmental law, employment discrimination, reproductive rights, bankruptcy and white-collar crime.

Wayne State University, Law School, Detroit, MI 48202. Offers JD, LL M, PhD, JD/MA, JD/MADR, JD/MBA. *Accreditation:* ABA. Part-time and evening/weekend programs available. *Degree requirements:* For master's, thesis. *Entrance requirements:* For JD, LSAT, Bachelor's degree from accredited institution; for master's, JD. Additional exam requirements/recommendations for international students: Required—TOEFL (minimum score 550 paper-based; 213 computer-based); Recommended—TWE (minimum score 6). Electronic applications accepted. *Expenses:* Contact institution. *Faculty research:* Constitutional law, intellectual property, commercial law, health law, tax law.

Western New England College, School of Law, Springfield, MA 01119. Offers estate planning/elder law (LL M); law (JD). *Accreditation:* ABA. Part-time and evening/weekend programs available. *Faculty:* 34 full-time (16 women), 27 part-time/adjunct (5 women). *Students:* 396 full-time (207 women), 239 part-time (131 women); includes 68 minority (19 African Americans, 2 American Indian/Alaska Native, 26 Asian Americans or Pacific Islanders, 21 Hispanic

Americans), 3 international. 1,701 applicants, 54% accepted, 180 enrolled. In 2009, 196 JDs awarded. *Entrance requirements:* LSAT, letters of recommendation. *Application deadline:* For fall admission, 3/15 priority date for domestic students. Applications are processed on a rolling basis. Application fee: $50. Electronic applications accepted. *Expenses:* Contact institution. *Financial support:* Career-related internships or fieldwork, Federal Work-Study, institutionally sponsored loans, and scholarships/grants available. Support available to part-time students. Financial award application deadline: 4/1; financial award applicants required to submit FAFSA. *Unit head:* Dean Arthur R. Gaudio, Dean, 413-782-2201, E-mail: agaudio@wnec.edu. *Application contact:* Michael A. Johnson, Director of Admissions, 413-782-1406, E-mail: admissions@law.wnec.edu.

Western State University College of Law, Professional Program, Fullerton, CA 92831-3000. Offers JD. *Accreditation:* ABA. Part-time and evening/weekend programs available. *Faculty:* 25 full-time (8 women), 23 part-time/adjunct (9 women). *Students:* 276 full-time (137 women), 141 part-time (71 women); includes 142 minority (16 African Americans, 3 American Indian/Alaska Native, 71 Asian Americans or Pacific Islanders, 52 Hispanic Americans), 7 international. Average age 27. 1,498 applicants, 50% accepted, 162 enrolled. In 2009, 84 JDs awarded. *Entrance requirements:* LSAT, 2 letters of recommendation. Additional exam requirements/recommendations for international students: Required—TOEFL (minimum score 550 paper-based; 213 computer-based; 80 iBT). *Application deadline:* For fall admission, 5/1 priority date for domestic and international students; for spring admission, 10/1 priority date for domestic and international students. Applications are processed on a rolling basis. Application fee: $50. Electronic applications accepted. *Expenses:* Tuition: Full-time $32,600; part-time $21,800 per year. Required fees: $135 per term. Tuition and fees vary according to course load. *Financial support:* In 2009–10, 8 fellowships (averaging $4,160 per year) were awarded; career-related internships or fieldwork, Federal Work-Study, and scholarships/grants also available. Support available to part-time students. Financial award application deadline: 9/15; financial award applicants required to submit FAFSA. *Faculty research:* Criminal law and practice, entrepreneurship, teaching effectiveness and student success, learning theory and legal education. *Application contact:* Gloria Switzer, Assistant Dean of Admission, 714-459-1101, Fax: 714-441-1748, E-mail: adm@wsulaw.edu.

West Virginia University, College of Law, Morgantown, WV 26506-6130. Offers JD, JD/MBA, JD/MPA. *Accreditation:* ABA. Part-time programs available. *Entrance requirements:* LSAT. Additional exam requirements/recommendations for international students: Required—TOEFL. Electronic applications accepted. *Expenses:* Contact institution. *Faculty research:* Constitutional law, public interest law, corporate law, environment and natural resources innocence project, professional skills, leadership, intellectual property, entrepreneurship, labor, sustainable development, family law, IR human rights, immigration.

Whittier College, Whittier Law School, Costa Mesa, CA 92626. Offers foreign legal studies (LL M); law (JD). *Accreditation:* ABA. Part-time and evening/weekend programs available. *Faculty:* 26 full-time (12 women), 17 part-time/adjunct (8 women). *Students:* 451 full-time (252 women), 136 part-time (69 women); includes 161 minority (16 African Americans, 2 American Indian/Alaska Native, 79 Asian Americans or Pacific Islanders, 64 Hispanic Americans), 1 international. Average age 24. 1,520 applicants, 46% accepted, 140 enrolled. In 2009, 154 JDs, 10 master's awarded. *Entrance requirements:* For JD, LSAT; for master's, first degree in law. Additional exam requirements/recommendations for international students: Required—TOEFL (minimum score 600 paper-based; 250 computer-based). *Application deadline:* For fall admission, 6/1 priority date for domestic students, 3/15 priority date for international students; for spring admission, 11/1 priority date for domestic and international students. Applications are processed on a rolling basis. Application fee: $50. Electronic applications accepted. *Expenses:* Contact institution. *Financial support:* In 2009–10, 710 students received support, including 31 fellowships with full and partial tuition reimbursements available (averaging $3,800 per year), 26 research assistantships, 47 teaching assistantships; career-related internships or fieldwork, Federal Work-Study, scholarships/grants, and unspecified assistantships also available. Financial award application deadline: 5/1; financial award applicants required to submit FAFSA. *Faculty research:* Intellectual property, international law, health law, children's rights. Total annual research expenditures: $164,629. *Unit head:* Neil H. Cogan, Dean, 714-444-4141 Ext. 111, Fax: 714-444-0855. *Application contact:* Betty Vu, Director of Admissions, 714-444-4141 Ext. 123, Fax: 714-444-0250.

Widener University, School of Human Service Professions, Institute for Graduate Clinical Psychology, Law-Psychology Program, Chester, PA 19013-5792. Offers JD/Psy D. *Faculty:* 15 full-time (6 women), 18 part-time/adjunct (10 women). *Students:* 13 full-time (9 women); includes 2 minority (1 American Indian/Alaska Native, 1 Asian American or Pacific Islander). Average age 23. 21 applicants, 19% accepted. *Application deadline:* For fall admission, 2/1 for domestic students. Applications are processed on a rolling basis. Application fee: $60. Electronic applications accepted. *Financial support:* In 2009–10, 12 students received support; research assistantships, career-related internships or fieldwork, Federal Work-Study, institutionally sponsored loans, and scholarships/grants available. Financial award application deadline: 5/31. *Unit head:* Dr. Amiram Elwork, Director, 610-499-1206, Fax: 610-499-4625, E-mail: amiram.elwork@widener.edu. *Application contact:* Maureen A. Brennan, Admissions Coordinator, 610-499-1206, Fax: 610-499-4625, E-mail: maureen.a.brennan@widener.edu.

Widener University, School of Law at Harrisburg, Harrisburg, PA 17106-9381. Offers JD. *Accreditation:* ABA. Part-time programs available. *Faculty:* 26 full-time (12 women), 18 part-time/adjunct (6 women). *Students:* 453 full-time (216 women), 58 part-time (44 women); includes 52 minority (20 African Americans, 2 American Indian/Alaska Native, 15 Asian Americans or Pacific Islanders, 15 Hispanic Americans), 1 international. Average age 26. In 2009, 120 JDs awarded. *Entrance requirements:* LSAT. *Application deadline:* For fall admission, 5/15 for domestic students. Applications are processed on a rolling basis. Application fee: $60. Electronic applications accepted. *Expenses:* Contact institution. *Financial support:* Fellowships, research assistantships, career-related internships or fieldwork, Federal Work-Study, institutionally sponsored loans, and scholarships/grants available. Support available to part-time students. Financial award application deadline: 2/15; financial award applicants required to submit FAFSA. *Faculty research:* Health law, toxic torts, constitutional law, intellectual property, corporate law. *Unit head:* Linda L. Ammons, Dean, 302-477-2100, Fax: 302-477-2282, E-mail: llammons@widener.edu. *Application contact:* Barbara L. Ayars, Assistant Dean of Admissions, 302-477-2210, Fax: 302-477-2224, E-mail: barbara.l.ayars@law.widener.edu.

Widener University, School of Law at Wilmington, Wilmington, DE 19803-0474. Offers corporate law and finance (LL M); health law (LL M, MJ, D Law); juridical science (SJD); law (JD). *Accreditation:* ABA. Part-time programs available. *Faculty:* 58 full-time (23 women), 42 part-time/adjunct (15 women). *Students:* 961 full-time (414 women), 37 part-time (25 women); includes 128 minority (59 African Americans, 5 American Indian/Alaska Native, 52 Asian Americans or Pacific Islanders, 12 Hispanic Americans), 13 international. Average age 27. 2,376 applicants, 39% accepted, 351 enrolled. In 2009, 266 first professional degrees, 28 master's, 3 doctorates awarded. *Degree requirements:* For doctorate, thesis/dissertation. *Entrance requirements:* For JD, LSAT; for master's, GMAT; for doctorate, GRE. *Application deadline:* For fall admission, 5/15 for domestic students; for spring admission, 12/1 for domestic students. Applications are processed on a rolling basis. Application fee: $60. *Financial support:* Career-related internships or fieldwork, Federal Work-Study, institutionally sponsored loans, and scholarships/grants available. Support available to part-time students. Financial award application deadline: 2/15; financial award applicants required to submit FAFSA. *Unit head:* Linda L. Ammons, Dean, 302-477-2100, Fax: 302-477-2282, E-mail: llammons@widener.edu. *Application contact:* Barbara L. Ayars, Assistant Dean of Admissions, 302-477-2210, Fax: 302-477-2224, E-mail: barbara.l.ayars@law.widener.edu.

Willamette University, College of Law, Salem, OR 97301-3922. Offers JD, LL M, JD/MBA. *Accreditation:* ABA. *Degree requirements:* For master's, thesis; for JD, thesis/dissertation. *Entrance requirements:* LSAT. Additional exam requirements/recommendations for international students: Required—TOEFL (minimum score 600 paper-based; 250 computer-based; 100 iBT); Recommended—IELTS (minimum score 7.5). Electronic applications accepted. *Expenses:* Contact institution. *Faculty research:* Dispute resolution, international law, business law, law and government.

William Howard Taft University, Graduate Programs, Bernard E. Witkin School of Law, Santa Ana, CA 92704. Offers American jurisprudence (LL M); law (JD); taxation (LL M).

William Mitchell College of Law, Professional Program, St. Paul, MN 55105-3076. Offers JD. *Accreditation:* ABA. Part-time and evening/weekend programs available. *Faculty:* 37 full-time (17 women), 253 part-time/adjunct (107 women). *Students:* 603 full-time (304 women), 374 part-time (182 women); includes 94 minority (22 African Americans, 10 American Indian/Alaska Native, 47 Asian Americans or Pacific Islanders, 15 Hispanic Americans), 4 international. Average age 29. 1,454 applicants, 58% accepted, 336 enrolled. In 2009, 327 JDs awarded. *Entrance requirements:* LSAT. Additional exam requirements/recommendations for international students: Required—TOEFL (minimum score 250 computer-based; 100 iBT). *Application deadline:* For spring admission, 5/1 for domestic and international students. Applications are processed on a rolling basis. Application fee: $0. Electronic applications accepted. *Expenses:* Tuition: Full-time $32,340; part-time $23,400 per year. *Financial support:* In 2009–10, 720 students received support, including 116 research assistantships (averaging $2,718 per year); Federal Work-Study and scholarships/grants also available. Support available to part-time students. Financial award application deadline: 3/15; financial award applicants required to submit FAFSA. *Faculty research:* Law of unincorporated associations, intellectual property law, elder law, preventive detention and post-release civil commitment, domestic violence. Total annual research expenditures: $15,000. *Unit head:* Eric S. Janus, President/Dean, 651-290-6310, Fax: 651-290-6426. *Application contact:* Kendra Dane, Assistant Dean and Director of Admissions, 651-290-6343, Fax: 651-290-6414, E-mail: admissions@wmitchell.edu.

Yale University, Yale Law School, New Haven, CT 06520-8215. Offers JD, LL M, MSL, JSD, JD/MA, JD/MAR, JD/MBA, JD/MD, JD/MES, JD/PhD. *Accreditation:* ABA. *Entrance requirements:* LSAT. Additional exam requirements/recommendations for international students: Required—TOEFL (minimum score 600 paper-based; 250 computer-based). Electronic applications accepted. *Expenses:* Contact institution.

Yeshiva University, Benjamin N. Cardozo School of Law, New York, NY 10003-4301. Offers comparative legal thought (LL M); general studies (LL M); intellectual property law (LL M); law (JD). *Accreditation:* ABA. Part-time programs available. *Faculty:* 56 full-time (19 women), 77 part-time/adjunct (52 women). *Students:* 1,076 full-time (548 women), 116 part-time (63 women); includes 235 minority (55 African Americans, 3 American Indian/Alaska Native, 104 Asian Americans or Pacific Islanders, 73 Hispanic Americans), 56 international. Average age 24. 4,827 applicants, 27% accepted, 319 enrolled. In 2009, 354 JDs, 69 master's awarded. *Entrance requirements:* LSAT, 2 letters of recommendation. *Application deadline:* For fall admission, 4/1 priority date for domestic students; for spring admission, 12/1 priority date for domestic students. Applications are processed on a rolling basis. Application fee: $70. Electronic applications accepted. *Expenses:* Contact institution. *Financial support:* In 2009–10, 964 students received support, including 91 research assistantships; career-related internships or fieldwork, Federal Work-Study, institutionally sponsored loans, scholarships/grants, health care benefits, and tuition waivers (full and partial) also available. Support available to part-time students. Financial award application deadline: 4/15; financial award applicants required to submit FAFSA. *Faculty research:* Corporate and commercial law, intellectual property law, criminal law and litigation, constitutional law, and legal theory and jurisprudence. *Unit head:* David G. Martinidez, Dean of Admissions, 212-790-0274, Fax: 212-790-0482, E-mail: lawinfo@yu.edu. *Application contact:* David G. Martinidez, Dean of Admissions, 212-790-0274, Fax: 212-790-0482, E-mail: lawinfo@yu.edu.

York University, Faculty of Graduate Studies, Atkinson Faculty of Liberal and Professional Studies, Program in Public Policy, Administration and Law, Toronto, ON M3J 1P3, Canada. Offers MPPAL.

York University, Faculty of Graduate Studies, Program in Law, Toronto, ON M3J 1P3, Canada. Offers LL B, LL M, PhD, MBA/LL B, MES/LL B, MPA/LL B. Part-time and evening/weekend programs available. *Degree requirements:* For master's, thesis; for doctorate, comprehensive exam, thesis/dissertation. *Entrance requirements:* LSAT. Electronic applications accepted.

Legal and Justice Studies

American University, Washington College of Law, Humphrey Fellows Program in Human Rights and the Law, Washington, DC 20016-8181. Offers Certificate. *Students:* 10 part-time (6 women), all international. Average age 37. *Entrance requirements:* For degree, JD. *Expenses:* Contact institution. *Unit head:* Daniel D. Bradlow, Director, 202-274-4205. *Application contact:* Akira Shiroma, Assistant Dean of Admissions, 202-274-4101, Fax: 202-274-4107, E-mail: shiroma@wcl.american.edu.

American University, Washington College of Law, Program in International Legal Studies, Washington, DC 20016-8181. Offers LL M, Certificate. Part-time and evening/weekend programs available. *Students:* 42 full-time (20 women), 95 part-time (61 women); includes 8 minority (3 African Americans, 5 Hispanic Americans), 97 international. Average age 28. In 2009, 82 master's awarded. *Entrance requirements:* For master's, JD, 2 recommendations. Additional exam requirements/recommendations for international students: Required—TOEFL (minimum score 580 paper-based; 237 computer-based; 92 iBT), IELTS (minimum score 6.5). *Application deadline:* For fall admission, 6/1 for domestic students; for spring admission, 11/1 for domestic students. Applications are processed on a rolling basis. Application fee: $55. *Expenses:* Contact institution. *Financial support:* Fellowships, research assistantships, teaching assistantships, career-related internships or fieldwork and tuition waivers (partial) available. Financial award application deadline: 2/15; financial award applicants required to submit FAFSA. *Unit head:* Daniel D. Bradlow, Director, 202-274-4205. *Application contact:* Akira Shiroma, Assistant Dean of Admissions, 202-274-4101, Fax: 202-274-4107, E-mail: shiroma@wcl.american.edu.

American University, Washington College of Law, Program in Judicial Sciences, Washington, DC 20016-8181. Offers SJD. *Students:* 4 full-time (all women), 15 part-time (5 women), 17 international. Average age 38. *Entrance requirements:* For doctorate, JD, LL M or LL B. Additional exam requirements/recommendations for international students: Required—TOEFL (minimum score 250 computer-based; 100 iBT). *Application deadline:* Applications are processed on a rolling basis. Application fee: $55. *Expenses:* Contact institution. *Application contact:* Assistant Dean of Admissions.

American University, Washington College of Law, Program in Law and Government, Washington, DC 20016-8181. Offers LL M. *Students:* 25 full-time (12 women), 26 part-time (17

Legal and Justice Studies

American University *(continued)*
women); includes 11 minority (6 African Americans, 4 Asian Americans or Pacific Islanders, 1 Hispanic American), 12 international. Average age 33. In 2009, 26 master's awarded. *Degree requirements:* For master's, thesis optional. *Entrance requirements:* For master's, JD, 2 recommendations. Additional exam requirements/recommendations for international students: Required—TOEFL (minimum score 300 paper-based; 250 computer-based). *Application deadline:* For fall admission, 6/1 priority date for domestic students; for spring admission, 11/1 priority date for domestic students. Applications are processed on a rolling basis. Application fee: $55. *Expenses:* Contact institution. *Financial support:* Fellowships with partial tuition reimbursements, career-related internships or fieldwork and institutionally sponsored loans available. Support available to part-time students. Financial award application deadline: 2/15. *Unit head:* Jamin Raskin, Director, 202-885-4011, E-mail: raskin@wcl.american.edu. *Application contact:* Jamin Raskin, Director, 202-885-4011, E-mail: raskin@wcl.american.edu.

Arizona State University, Graduate College, College of Liberal Arts and Sciences, Division of Social Sciences, School of Justice and Social Inquiry, Tempe, AZ 85287. Offers justice studies (MS, PhD); PhD/JD. *Degree requirements:* For master's, thesis optional. *Entrance requirements:* For master's, GRE. Additional exam requirements/recommendations for international students: Required—TOEFL.

Arizona State University, Graduate College, New College of Interdisciplinary Arts and Sciences, Tempe, AZ 85287. Offers communication studies (MA); interdisciplinary studies (MA); social justice and human rights (MA). Part-time and evening/weekend programs available. *Degree requirements:* For master's, applied project. *Entrance requirements:* For master's, GRE, letter of recommendation, writing sample. Additional exam requirements/recommendations for international students: Required—TOEFL (minimum score 550 paper-based; 213 computer-based; 83 iBT), IELTS (minimum score 6.5). Electronic applications accepted.

Arizona State University, Sandra Day O'Connor College of Law, Tempe, AZ 85287-7906. Offers biotechnology and genomics (LL M); law (JD); legal studies (MLS); tribal policy, law and government (LL M); JD/MBA; JD/MD; JD/PhD. *Accreditation:* ABA. *Faculty:* 57 full-time (20 women), 46 part-time/adjunct (12 women). *Students:* 591 full-time (258 women), 35 part-time (21 women); includes 131 minority (12 African Americans, 41 American Indian/Alaska Native, 19 Asian Americans or Pacific Islanders, 59 Hispanic Americans), 16 international. Average age 27. 2,400 applicants, 28% accepted, 184 enrolled. In 2009, 177 JDs awarded. *Degree requirements:* For JD, comprehensive exam, paper. *Entrance requirements:* For JD, LSAT; for master's, bachelor's degree; JD (for LL M). Additional exam requirements/recommendations for international students: Required—TOEFL (minimum score 550 paper-based; 213 computer-based; 80 iBT). *Application deadline:* For fall admission, 11/15 priority date for domestic and international students; for spring admission, 2/1 for domestic and international students. Applications are processed on a rolling basis. Application fee: $60. Electronic applications accepted. *Expenses:* Contact institution. *Financial support:* In 2009–10, 490 students received support; research assistantships, teaching assistantships, career-related internships or fieldwork, Federal Work-Study, institutionally sponsored loans, scholarships/grants, tuition waivers (full and partial), and unspecified assistantships available. Financial award application deadline: 3/5; financial award applicants required to submit FAFSA. *Faculty research:* Emerging technologies and the law, Indian law, law and philosophy, international law, intellectual property. Total annual research expenditures: $514,610. *Unit head:* Dean Paul Schiff Berman, Dean and Foundation Professor of Law, 480-965-6188, Fax: 480-965-6521, E-mail: paul.berman@asu.edu. *Application contact:* Chitra Damania, Director of Operations, 480-965-1474, Fax: 480-727-7930, E-mail: law.admissions@asu.edu.

Boston University, School of Public Health, Health Law, Bioethics and Human Rights Department, Boston, MA 02215. Offers MPH. Part-time and evening/weekend programs available. *Students:* 10 full-time (4 women), 7 part-time (5 women); includes 3 minority (2 Asian Americans or Pacific Islanders, 1 Hispanic American), 1 international. Average age 27. *Entrance requirements:* For master's, GRE, MCAT, LSAT, GMAT, DAT. Additional exam requirements/recommendations for international students: Required—TOEFL (minimum score 600 paper-based; 250 computer-based; 100 iBT) or IELTS (minimum score 6). *Application deadline:* For fall admission, 2/1 priority date for domestic and international students; for spring admission, 10/15 priority date for domestic and international students. Applications are processed on a rolling basis. Application fee: $95. Electronic applications accepted. *Expenses:* Tuition: Full-time $37,910; part-time $1184 per credit hour. Required fees: $386; $40 per semester. Part-time tuition and fees vary according to class time, course level, degree level and program. *Financial support:* In 2009–10, 1 fellowship was awarded; career-related internships or fieldwork, Federal Work-Study, institutionally sponsored loans, scholarships/grants, and tuition waivers (partial) also available. Support available to part-time students. Financial award application deadline: 3/1; financial award applicants required to submit FAFSA. *Unit head:* Prof. George Annas, Chair, 617-638-4626. *Application contact:* LePhan Quan, Assistant Director of Admissions, 617-638-4640, Fax: 617-638-5299, E-mail: asksph@bu.edu.

Brock University, Faculty of Graduate Studies, Faculty of Social Sciences, Program in Social Justice and Equity Studies, St. Catharines, ON L2S 3A1, Canada. Offers MA. Part-time programs available. *Degree requirements:* For master's, thesis optional. *Entrance requirements:* For master's, honors degree. Additional exam requirements/recommendations for international students: Required—TOEFL (minimum score 550 paper-based; 213 computer-based; 80 iBT), IELTS (minimum score 6.5), TWE (minimum score 4). Electronic applications accepted. *Faculty research:* Social inequality, social movements, gender, racism, environmental justice.

California University of Pennsylvania, School of Graduate Studies and Research, Department of Professional Studies, California, PA 15419-1394. Offers legal studies (MS), including homeland security, law and public policy. Part-time and evening/weekend programs available. Post-baccalaureate distance learning degree programs offered (no on-campus study). *Degree requirements:* For master's, thesis optional. *Entrance requirements:* For master's, interview, minimum QPA of 3.0. Additional exam requirements/recommendations for international students: Required—TOEFL (minimum score 550 paper-based; 213 computer-based; 80 iBT). Electronic applications accepted. *Faculty research:* Ethics in political practice, ethics and law, law and morality, St. Thomas Aquinas and crime, police policy.

Capital University, School of Nursing, Columbus, OH 43209-2394. Offers administration (MSN); legal studies (MSN); theological studies (MSN); JD/MSN; MBA/MSN; MSN/MTS. *Accreditation:* AACN. Part-time and evening/weekend programs available. *Degree requirements:* For master's, thesis or alternative. *Entrance requirements:* For master's, BSN, current RN license, minimum GPA of 3.0, undergraduate courses in statistics and research. Additional exam requirements/recommendations for international students: Required—TOEFL (minimum score 550 paper-based). *Expenses:* Contact institution. *Faculty research:* Bereavement, wellness/health promotion, emergency cardiac care, critical thinking, complementary and alternative healthcare.

Carleton University, Faculty of Graduate Studies, Faculty of Public Affairs and Management, Department of Law, Ottawa, ON K1S 5B6, Canada. Offers conflict resolution (Certificate); legal studies (MA). *Degree requirements:* For master's, thesis. *Entrance requirements:* For master's, honors degree. Additional exam requirements/recommendations for international students: Required—TOEFL. *Faculty research:* Legal and social theory; women, law, and gender relations; law, crime, and social order; political economy of law; international law.

Case Western Reserve University, School of Law, Cleveland, OH 44106. Offers law (JD); U.S. legal studies (LL M); JD/CNM; JD/MA; JD/MBA; JD/MD; JD/MNO; JD/MPH; JD/MS; JD/MSSA. *Accreditation:* ABA. Part-time programs available. *Faculty:* 56 full-time (20 women), 80 part-time/adjunct (24 women). *Students:* 673 full-time (290 women), 24 part-time (13 women); includes 81 minority (22 African Americans, 6 American Indian/Alaska Native, 45 Asian Americans or Pacific Islanders, 8 Hispanic Americans), 25 international. Average age 24. 2,667 applicants, 42% accepted, 195 enrolled. In 2009, 209 JDs, 44 master's awarded. *Entrance requirements:* LSAT, LSDAS. *Application deadline:* For fall admission, 4/1 priority date for domestic and international students. Applications are processed on a rolling basis.

Application fee: $40. Electronic applications accepted. *Expenses:* Contact institution. *Financial support:* In 2009–10, 527 students received support. Career-related internships or fieldwork, Federal Work-Study, and scholarships/grants available. Financial award application deadline: 7/1; financial award applicants required to submit FAFSA. *Unit head:* Robert H. Rawson, Interim Dean, 216-368-3283. *Application contact:* Elaine Greaves, Assistant Dean for Admissions, 216-368-3600, Fax: 216-368-1042, E-mail: lawadmissions@case.edu.

The Catholic University of America, School of Canon Law, Washington, DC 20064. Offers JCD, JCL, JD/JCL. Part-time programs available. *Faculty:* 7 full-time (1 woman), 1 part-time/adjunct (0 women). *Students:* 42 full-time (10 women), 48 part-time (5 women); includes 9 minority (1 African American, 3 Asian Americans or Pacific Islanders, 5 Hispanic Americans), 16 international. Average age 40. 42 applicants, 93% accepted, 30 enrolled. In 2009, 4 doctorates awarded. *Degree requirements:* For doctorate, 2 foreign languages, thesis/dissertation, fluency in canonical Latin; for JCL, one foreign language, comprehensive exam, thesis, fluency in canonical Latin. *Entrance requirements:* For doctorate, GRE General Test, 2 letters of recommendation; for JCL, GRE General Test, official copies of academic transcripts, two letters of recommendation. Additional exam requirements/recommendations for international students: Required—TOEFL (minimum score 580 paper-based; 237 computer-based). *Application deadline:* For fall admission, 8/1 priority date for domestic students, 7/15 for international students; for spring admission, 12/1 priority date for domestic students, 10/15 for international students. Applications are processed on a rolling basis. Application fee: $55. Electronic applications accepted. *Expenses:* Tuition: Full-time $31,740; part-time $1245 per credit hour. Required fees: $50; $25 per semester hour. One-time fee: $425. *Financial support:* Fellowships, research assistantships, teaching assistantships, Federal Work-Study, scholarships/grants, tuition waivers (full and partial), and unspecified assistantships available. Financial award application deadline: 2/1; financial award applicants required to submit FAFSA. *Faculty research:* Ecclesiology and the Sacrament of Orders, procedural law, temporal goods, matrimonial jurisprudence, sacramental and liturgical law. *Unit head:* Rev. Robert Kaslyn, Dean, 202-319-5492, Fax: 202-319-4187, E-mail: cua-canonlaw@cua.edu. *Application contact:* Julie Schwing, Director of Graduate Admissions, 202-319-5057, Fax: 202-319-6533, E-mail: cua-admissions@cua.edu.

Central European University, Graduate Studies, Department of Legal Studies, Budapest, Hungary. Offers comparative constitutional law (LL M); economic and legal studies (LL M, MA); human rights (LL M, MA); international business law (LL M); legal studies (SJD). Terminal master's awarded for partial completion of doctoral program. *Degree requirements:* For master's, one foreign language, thesis; for doctorate, one foreign language, comprehensive exam, thesis/dissertation. *Entrance requirements:* For master's and doctorate, LSAT, CEU admissions exams. Additional exam requirements/recommendations for international students: Required—TOEFL (minimum score 570 paper-based; 230 computer-based). Electronic applications accepted. *Expenses:* Contact institution. *Faculty research:* Institutional, constitutional and human rights in European Union law, biomedical law and reproductive rights, data protection law, Islamic banking and finance.

College of Charleston, Graduate School, School of Languages, Cultures, and World Affairs, Program in Bilingual Legal Interpreting, Charleston, SC 29424-0001. Offers MA, Certificate. *Faculty:* 4 full-time (1 woman). *Students:* 5 full-time (3 women), 5 part-time (4 women); includes 2 minority (1 African American, 1 Hispanic American), 2 international. Average age 29. 23 applicants, 35% accepted, 5 enrolled. In 2009, 1 master's, 1 other advanced degree awarded. *Entrance requirements:* For master's, GRE General Test, General Interpreting Aptitude Exam, 2 letters of recommendation; for Certificate, General Interpreting Aptitude Exam. Additional exam requirements/recommendations for international students: Required—TOEFL. *Application deadline:* For fall admission, 6/15 for domestic students; for spring admission, 11/1 for domestic students. Applications are processed on a rolling basis. Application fee: $150. Electronic applications accepted. *Expenses:* Contact institution. *Financial support:* Scholarships/grants and unspecified assistantships available. Financial award applicants required to submit FAFSA. *Unit head:* Dr. Gladys Matthews, Director, 843-953-5718, Fax: 843-953-6432, E-mail: matthewsg@corc.edu. *Application contact:* Susan Hallatt, Director of Graduate Admissions, 843-953-5614, Fax: 843-953-1434, E-mail: hallatts@cofc.edu.

College of the Humanities and Sciences, Harrison Middleton University, Graduate Program, Tempe, AZ 85282. Offers education (MA, Ed D); humanities (MA); imaginative literature (MA); interdisciplinary studies (DA); jurisprudence (MA); natural science (MA); philosophy and religion (MA); social science (MA). Part-time and evening/weekend programs available. Post-baccalaureate distance learning degree programs offered (no on-campus study). *Faculty:* 17 full-time (7 women), 14 part-time/adjunct (6 women). *Students:* 49 full-time (18 women). In 2009, 4 master's awarded. *Application deadline:* Applications are processed on a rolling basis. Application fee: $50. Electronic applications accepted. *Application contact:* Deborah Deacon, Dean of Graduate Studies, 877-248-6724, Fax: 800-762-1622, E-mail: ddeacon@chumsci.edu.

Georgetown University, Law Center, Washington, DC 20001. Offers general (LL M); global health law (LL M); international and comparative law (LL M); international business and economic law (LL M); international legal studies (LL M); law (JD, SJD); securities and financial regulation (LL M); taxation (LL M); JD/LL M; JD/MA; JD/MBA; JD/MPH; JD/PhD. *Accreditation:* ABA. Part-time and evening/weekend programs available. *Degree requirements:* For master's, thesis; for doctorate, thesis/dissertation. *Entrance requirements:* For JD, LSAT; for master's and doctorate, JD, LL B, or first law degree earned in country of origin. Additional exam requirements/recommendations for international students: Required—TOEFL. *Expenses:* Contact institution. *Faculty research:* Constitutional law, legal history, jurisprudence.

The George Washington University, College of Professional Studies, Paralegal Studies Programs, Washington, DC 20052. Offers MPS, Graduate Certificate. *Students:* 19 full-time (all women), 140 part-time (120 women); includes 44 minority (25 African Americans, 3 American Indian/Alaska Native, 5 Asian Americans or Pacific Islanders, 11 Hispanic Americans), 3 international. Average age 36. 168 applicants, 76% accepted, 67 enrolled. In 2009, 27 master's, 17 other advanced degrees awarded. *Application deadline:* For fall admission, 4/1 for domestic and international students; for spring admission, 10/1 for domestic and international students. Electronic applications accepted. *Unit head:* Toni Marsh, Director, 202-994-2844, E-mail: marsht01@gwu.edu. *Application contact:* Kristin Williams, Assistant Vice President for Graduate and Special Enrollment Management, 202-994-0467, Fax: 202-994-0371, E-mail: ksw@gwu.edu.

The George Washington University, College of Professional Studies, Program in Law Firm Management, Washington, DC 20052. Offers MPS, Graduate Certificate. Program offered in partnership with The Hildebrandt Institute and held at Alexandria, VA education center. Post-baccalaureate distance learning degree programs offered. *Students:* 20 part-time (13 women); includes 4 minority (1 African American, 1 American Indian/Alaska Native, 2 Hispanic Americans), 1 international. Average age 43. 34 applicants, 100% accepted, 11 enrolled. In 2009, 1 master's, 7 other advanced degrees awarded. *Entrance requirements:* For master's, resume, 2 references. Additional exam requirements/recommendations for international students: Required—TOEFL. *Application deadline:* For fall admission, 4/1 for domestic and international students. Electronic applications accepted. *Unit head:* Kathleen M. Burke, Dean, 202-994-9711. *Application contact:* Kristin Williams, Assistant Vice President for Graduate and Special Enrollment Management, 202-994-0467, Fax: 202-994-0371, E-mail: ksw@gwu.edu.

Golden Gate University, School of Law, San Francisco, CA 94105-2968. Offers environmental law (LL M); intellectual property law (LL M); international legal studies (LL M, SJD); law (JD); taxation (LL M); U.S. legal studies (LL M); JD/MBA; JD/PhD. *Accreditation:* ABA. Part-time and evening/weekend programs available. *Degree requirements:* For doctorate, thesis/dissertation. *Entrance requirements:* LSAT. Additional exam requirements/recommendations for international students: Required—TOEFL (minimum score 600 paper-based; 250 computer-based). Electronic applications accepted. *Expenses:* Contact institution. *Faculty research:* International law, intellectual property law, environmental law, real estate, civil rights.

Governors State University, College of Arts and Sciences, Program in Political and Justice Studies, University Park, IL 60466-0975. Offers MA. Part-time and evening/weekend programs available. *Degree requirements:* For master's, thesis or alternative. *Entrance requirements:* For master's, bachelor's degree in related field.

Harvard University, Law School, Professional Programs in Law, Cambridge, MA 02138. Offers international and comparative law (JD); law and business (JD); law and government (JD); law and social change (JD); law, science and technology (JD); JD/MALD; JD/MBA; JD/MPH; JD/MPP; JD/PhD. *Accreditation:* ABA. *Degree requirements:* For JD, 3rd year paper. *Entrance requirements:* LSAT. *Expenses:* Tuition: Full-time $33,696. Required fees: $1126. Full-time tuition and fees vary according to program. *Faculty research:* Constitutional law, voting rights law, cyber law.

Hofstra University, School of Law, Hempstead, NY 11549. Offers American legal studies (LL M); family law (LL M); international law (LL M); law (JD); JD/MBA. *Accreditation:* ABA. Part-time programs available. *Faculty:* 59 full-time (18 women), 35 part-time/adjunct (4 women). *Students:* 943 full-time (469 women), 176 part-time (79 women); includes 301 minority (93 African Americans, 4 American Indian/Alaska Native, 112 Asian Americans or Pacific Islanders, 92 Hispanic Americans), 34 international. Average age 26. 4,934 applicants, 39% accepted, 405 enrolled. In 2009, 359 JDs, 8 master's awarded. *Entrance requirements:* LSAT, letter of recommendation. Additional exam requirements/recommendations for international students: Recommended—TOEFL (minimum score 600 paper-based; 250 computer-based; 100 iBT). *Application deadline:* For fall admission, 4/15 priority date for domestic and international students. Applications are processed on a rolling basis. Application fee: $60. Electronic applications accepted. *Expenses:* Contact institution. *Financial support:* In 2009–10, 555 students received support, including 511 fellowships with full and partial tuition reimbursements available (averaging $22,146 per year), 2 research assistantships with full and partial tuition reimbursements available (averaging $17,548 per year); Federal Work-Study, institutionally sponsored loans, scholarships/grants, tuition waivers (full and partial), and unspecified assistantships also available. Support available to part-time students. Financial award applicants required to submit FAFSA. *Faculty research:* Commercial and corporate law; constitutional law and legal history family law; gender and LGBT issues; international and comparative law; child and family advocacy. *Unit head:* Nora V. Demleitner, Dean, 516-463-5854, Fax: 516-463-6264, E-mail: lawnao@hofstra.edu. *Application contact:* John Chalmers, Director of Law School Enrollment Operations, 516-463-5791, Fax: 516-463-6264, E-mail: lawadmissions@hofstra.edu.

Hollins University, Graduate Programs, Program in Liberal Studies, Roanoke, VA 24020-1603. Offers humanities (MALS); interdisciplinary studies (MALS); justice and legal studies (MALS); liberal studies (CAS); social science (MALS); visual and performing arts (MALS). Part-time and evening/weekend programs available. *Faculty:* 7 full-time (1 woman), 4 part-time/adjunct (2 women). *Students:* 23 full-time (22 women), 73 part-time (57 women); includes 15 minority (13 African Americans, 2 Asian Americans or Pacific Islanders), 4 international. Average age 39. 31 applicants, 94% accepted, 25 enrolled. In 2009, 30 master's awarded. *Degree requirements:* For master's, thesis. *Entrance requirements:* For master's, letters of recommendation, interview. Additional exam requirements/recommendations for international students: Required—TOEFL (minimum score 550 paper-based; 213 computer-based; 79 iBT). *Application deadline:* For fall admission, 7/1 priority date for domestic and international students; for spring admission, 12/10 priority date for domestic and international students. Applications are processed on a rolling basis. Application fee: $40. Electronic applications accepted. *Expenses:* Tuition: Full-time $27,780; part-time $295 per contact hour. Required fees: $280; $70 per unit. Part-time tuition and fees vary according to course load and program. *Financial support:* In 2009–10, 31 students received support, including 2 fellowships (averaging $902 per year); Federal Work-Study and scholarships/grants also available. Support available to part-time students. Financial award application deadline: 7/15; financial award applicants required to submit FAFSA. *Faculty research:* Elderly blacks, film, feminist economics, US voting patterns, Wagner, diversity. *Unit head:* Dr. Edward A. Lynch, Director, 540-362-6475, Fax: 540-362-6288, E-mail: elynch@hollins.edu. *Application contact:* Cathy S. Koon, Manager of Graduate Services, 540-362-6326, Fax: 540-362-6288, E-mail: ckoon@hollins.edu.

John Jay College of Criminal Justice of the City University of New York, Graduate Studies, Programs in Criminal Justice, New York, NY 10019-1093. Offers criminal justice (MA, PhD); criminology and deviance (PhD); forensic psychology (PhD); forensic science (PhD); law and philosophy (PhD); organizational behavior (PhD); public policy (PhD). Part-time and evening/weekend programs available. Terminal master's awarded for partial completion of doctoral program. *Degree requirements:* For master's, thesis or alternative; for doctorate, one foreign language, thesis/dissertation. *Entrance requirements:* For master's, GRE General Test, minimum B average; for doctorate, GRE General Test. Additional exam requirements/recommendations for international students: Required—TOEFL (minimum score 500 paper-based; 173 computer-based).

John Marshall Law School, Graduate and Professional Programs, Chicago, IL 60604-3968. Offers comparative legal studies (LL M); employee benefits (LL M, MS); information technology (LL M, MS); intellectual property (LL M); international business and trade (LL M); law (JD); real estate (LL M, MS); taxation (LL M, MS); JD/LL M; JD/MA; JD/MBA; JD/MPA. *Accreditation:* ABA. Part-time and evening/weekend programs available. *Faculty:* 73 full-time (26 women), 110 part-time/adjunct (33 women). *Students:* 1,139 full-time (505 women), 407 part-time (204 women); includes 353 minority (130 African Americans, 15 American Indian/Alaska Native, 91 Asian Americans or Pacific Islanders, 117 Hispanic Americans), 43 international. Average age 27. 3,027 applicants, 44% accepted, 385 enrolled. In 2009, 401 first professional degrees, 16 master's awarded. *Degree requirements:* For JD, 90 credits. *Entrance requirements:* For JD, LSAT; for master's, JD. Additional exam requirements/recommendations for international students: Required—TOEFL. *Application deadline:* For fall admission, 3/1 priority date for domestic and international students; for spring admission, 10/15 priority date for domestic and international students. Applications are processed on a rolling basis. Application fee: $60. Electronic applications accepted. *Expenses:* Contact institution. *Financial support:* In 2009–10, 1,350 students received support. Scholarships/grants and tuition waivers (full and partial) available. Support available to part-time students. Financial award application deadline: 6/1; financial award applicants required to submit FAFSA. *Unit head:* John Corkery, Dean, 312-427-2737. *Application contact:* William B. Powers, Associate Dean of Admission and Student Affairs, 800-537-4280, Fax: 312-427-5136, E-mail: admission@jmls.edu.

Kaplan University, Davenport Campus, School of Legal Studies, Davenport, IA 52807-2095. Offers health care delivery (MS); pathway to paralegal (Postbaccalaureate Certificate); state and local government (MS). Part-time and evening/weekend programs available. Postbaccalaureate distance learning degree programs offered (no on-campus study). *Entrance requirements:* Additional exam requirements/recommendations for international students: Required—TOEFL (minimum score 550 paper-based; 218 computer-based; 80 iBT).

Loyola University Chicago, Institute of Pastoral Studies, Program in Social Justice and Community Development, Chicago, IL 60660. Offers MA, Certificate. *Students:* 33 full-time (24 women), 5 part-time (4 women); includes 7 minority (5 African Americans, 2 Hispanic Americans), 1 international. Average age 30. 19 applicants, 100% accepted, 14 enrolled. In 2009, 16 master's awarded. *Degree requirements:* For master's, internship. *Expenses:* Tuition: Full-time $14,220; part-time $790 per credit hour. Required fees: $60 per semester hour. Tuition and fees vary according to program. *Unit head:* Dr. Robert A. Ludwig. *Application contact:* Randy Gibbons, Administrative Assistant, 312-915-7450, Fax: 312-915-7410, E-mail: rgibbon@luc.edu.

Marygrove College, Graduate Division, Program in Social Justice, Detroit, MI 48221-2599. Offers MA.

Marymount University, School of Business Administration, Program in Legal Administration, Arlington, VA 22207-4299. Offers legal administration (MA); paralegal studies (Certificate). Part-time and evening/weekend programs available. *Students:* 6 full-time (4 women), 20 part-time (16 women); includes 13 minority (11 African Americans, 1 Asian American or Pacific Islander, 1 Hispanic American). Average age 32. 18 applicants, 100% accepted, 11 enrolled. In 2009, 11 master's, 2 other advanced degrees awarded. *Entrance requirements:* For master's, GMAT or GRE General Test, resume; for Certificate, resume. Additional exam requirements/recommendations for international students: Required—TOEFL (minimum score 600 paper-based; 250 computer-based; 96 iBT), IELTS (minimum score 6.5). *Application deadline:* For fall admission, 7/15 for domestic students, 7/1 for international students; for spring admission, 11/15 for domestic students, 10/15 for international students. Applications are processed on a rolling basis. Application fee: $40. Electronic applications accepted. *Expenses:* Tuition: Full-time $13,050; part-time $725 per credit hour. Required fees: $135; $7.50 per credit hour. *Financial support:* Research assistantships with full tuition reimbursements, career-related internships or fieldwork, Federal Work-Study, scholarships/grants, and unspecified assistantships available. Support available to part-time students. Financial award applicants required to submit FAFSA. *Unit head:* Susan Ninassi, Director, 703-284-5934, Fax: 703-527-3830, E-mail: susanne.ninassi@marymount.edu. *Application contact:* Francesca Reed, Director, Graduate Admissions, 703-284-5901, Fax: 703-527-3815, E-mail: grad.admissions@marymount.edu.

Michigan State University College of Law, Professional Program, East Lansing, MI 48824-1300. Offers American legal system (LL M); intellectual property (LL M); law (JD). *Accreditation:* ABA. Part-time and evening/weekend programs available. *Faculty:* 55 full-time (23 women), 75 part-time/adjunct (20 women). *Students:* 814 full-time (305 women), 144 part-time (71 women); includes 106 minority (39 African Americans, 12 American Indian/Alaska Native, 33 Asian Americans or Pacific Islanders, 22 Hispanic Americans), 52 international. Average age 28. 2,736 applicants, 46% accepted, 287 enrolled. In 2009, 253 JDs awarded. *Entrance requirements:* LSAT. Additional exam requirements/recommendations for international students: Required—TOEFL (minimum score 600 paper-based; 250 computer-based). *Application deadline:* For fall admission, 3/15 priority date for domestic students, 7/1 priority date for international students. Applications are processed on a rolling basis. Application fee: $60. Electronic applications accepted. *Expenses:* Contact institution. *Financial support:* In 2009–10, 288 students received support, including 301 fellowships (averaging $22,962 per year); career-related internships or fieldwork, Federal Work-Study, institutionally sponsored loans, scholarships/grants, and tuition waivers (full) also available. Support available to part-time students. Financial award application deadline: 4/15; financial award applicants required to submit FAFSA. *Faculty research:* International, constitutional, health, tax and environmental law; intellectual property, trial practice, corporate law. *Unit head:* Joan W. Howarth, Dean and Professor of Law, 517-432-6993, Fax: 517-432-6801, E-mail: howarth@law.msu.edu. *Application contact:* Charles Roboski, Assistant Dean of Admissions, 517-432-0222, Fax: 517-432-0098, E-mail: roboski@law.msu.edu.

Mississippi College, Graduate School, College of Arts and Sciences, School of Humanities and Social Sciences, Department of History, Political Science, Administration of Justice, and Paralegal Studies, Clinton, MS 39058. Offers administration of justice (MSS); history (M Ed, MA, MSS); paralegal studies (Certificate); political science (MSS); social sciences (M Ed, MSS). Part-time programs available. *Faculty:* 4 full-time (0 women), 5 part-time/adjunct (1 woman). *Students:* 10 full-time (5 women), 27 part-time (10 women); includes 8 minority (all African Americans), 1 international. Average age 32. In 2009, 12 master's awarded. *Degree requirements:* For master's, one foreign language, comprehensive exam, thesis (for some programs). *Entrance requirements:* For master's, GRE or NTE, minimum GPA of 2.5. Additional exam requirements/recommendations for international students: Recommended—IELTS. *Application deadline:* For fall admission, 8/15 priority date for domestic students. Applications are processed on a rolling basis. Application fee: $30. Electronic applications accepted. *Expenses:* Tuition: Part-time $452 per credit hour. Required fees: $101 per semester. Tuition and fees vary according to degree level, campus/location, program and student level. *Financial support:* Teaching assistantships, Federal Work-Study, scholarships/grants, and unspecified assistantships available. Support available to part-time students. Financial award application deadline: 4/1; financial award applicants required to submit FAFSA. *Unit head:* Dr. Kirk Ford, Chair, 601-925-3326, E-mail: ford@mc.edu. *Application contact:* Elnora Lewis, Secretary, 601-925-3225, Fax: 601-925-3889, E-mail: lewis09@mc.edu.

Montclair State University, The Graduate School, College of Humanities and Social Sciences, Department of Justice Studies, Montclair, NJ 07043-1624. Offers conflict management in the workplace (Certificate); dispute resolution (MA); governance, compliance and regulation (MA); intellectual property (MA); law and governance (MA); legal management, information and technology (MA); paralegal studies (Certificate). Part-time and evening/weekend programs available. *Faculty:* 10 full-time (8 women), 17 part-time/adjunct (10 women). *Students:* 9 full-time (6 women), 17 part-time (10 women). Average age 36. 15 applicants, 100% accepted, 8 enrolled. In 2009, 12 master's, 16 other advanced degrees awarded. *Degree requirements:* For master's, comprehensive exam, thesis or alternative. *Entrance requirements:* For master's, GRE General Test, 2 letters of recommendation; for Certificate, 2 letters of recommendation. Additional exam requirements/recommendations for international students: Required—TOEFL (minimum score 83 computer-based), or IELTS. *Application deadline:* For fall admission, 6/1 for international students; for spring admission, 10/1 for international students. Applications are processed on a rolling basis. Application fee: $60. Electronic applications accepted. *Expenses:* Tuition, area resident: Part-time $486.74 per credit. Tuition, state resident: part-time $486.74 per credit. Tuition, nonresident: part-time $751.34 per credit. Tuition and fees vary according to degree level and program. *Financial support:* Federal Work-Study and scholarships/grants available. Support available to part-time students. Financial award application deadline: 3/1. *Unit head:* Dr. Norma Connolly, Chairperson, 973-655-4152, E-mail: connolyn@mail.montclair.edu. *Application contact:* Amy Aiello, Director of Graduate Admissions and Operations, 973-655-4000, E-mail: graduate.school@montclair.edu.

New York University, Graduate School of Arts and Science and School of Law, Institute for Law and Society, New York, NY 10012-1019. Offers MA, PhD, JD/MA, JD/PhD. *Faculty:* 3 full-time (1 woman). *Students:* 16 full-time (10 women), 6 part-time (4 women); includes 3 minority (1 African American, 1 Asian American or Pacific Islander, 1 Hispanic American), 5 international. Average age 32. 67 applicants, 4% accepted, 2 enrolled. In 2009, 1 master's awarded. *Degree requirements:* For doctorate, one foreign language, thesis/dissertation. *Entrance requirements:* For doctorate, GRE. Additional exam requirements/recommendations for international students: Required—TOEFL. *Application deadline:* For fall admission, 12/18 for domestic students. Application fee: $90. *Expenses:* Tuition: Full-time $30,528; part-time $1272 per credit. Required fees: $2177. *Financial support:* Fellowships with tuition reimbursements, teaching assistantships with tuition reimbursements, career-related internships or fieldwork, Federal Work-Study, institutionally sponsored loans, scholarships/grants, health care benefits, and unspecified assistantships available. Financial award application deadline: 12/18; financial award applicants required to submit FAFSA. *Faculty research:* Politics of law, law and social policy, law in comparative global perspective, rights and social movements. *Unit head:* Sally Merry, Director, 212-998-8536, Fax: 212-995-4034, E-mail: law.society@nyu.edu. *Application contact:* Jo Dixon, Director of Graduate Studies, 212-998-8536, Fax: 212-995-4034, E-mail: law.society@nyu.edu.

Northeastern University, College of Social Sciences and Humanities, Program in Law, Policy, and Society, Boston, MA 02115-5096. Offers MS, PhD, JD/PhD. Part-time and evening/weekend programs available. *Faculty:* 33 full-time (18 women), 18 part-time/adjunct (6 women). *Students:* 42 full-time (22 women), 28 part-time (13 women); includes 3 African Americans, 2 Asian Americans or Pacific Islanders, 2 Hispanic Americans, 10 international. Average age 40. 56 applicants, 41% accepted, 12 enrolled. *Degree requirements:* For master's, comprehensive exam; for doctorate, comprehensive exam, thesis/dissertation. *Entrance requirements:* For master's, GRE General Test; for doctorate, GRE General Test or LSAT. Additional exam requirements/recommendations for international students: Required—TOEFL. *Application deadline:* For fall admission, 2/1 for domestic students. Application fee: $50. *Financial support:* In 2009–10, teaching assistantships with tuition reimbursements (averaging $14,035 per year); fellowships with tuition reimbursements, research assistantships with tuition reimbursements, tuition waivers (full and partial) and unspecified assistantships also available. Financial award application deadline: 2/1; financial award applicants required to submit FAFSA. *Faculty*

Legal and Justice Studies

Northeastern University (continued)

research: Policy issues in health, crime, and labor; urban studies; education; law and environmental issues; economic development, international trade and law. *Unit head:* Dr. Joan Fitzgerald, Director, 617-373-3644, Fax: 617-373-4691, E-mail: jo.fitzgerald@neu.edu. *Application contact:* Dr. Joan Fitzgerald, Director, 617-373-3644, Fax: 617-373-4691, E-mail: jo.fitzgerald@neu.edu.

Nova Southeastern University, Shepard Broad Law Center, Program in Education Law, Fort Lauderdale, FL 33314-7796. Offers MS, Certificate. Part-time and evening/weekend programs available. Postbaccalaureate distance learning degree programs offered (minimal on-campus study). *Faculty:* 9 full-time (2 women), 15 part-time/adjunct (11 women). *Students:* 27 part-time (19 women); includes 16 minority (10 African Americans, 1 Asian American or Pacific Islander, 5 Hispanic Americans). 39 applicants, 87% accepted. *Entrance requirements:* Additional exam requirements/recommendations for international students: Required—TOEFL (minimum score 600 paper-based; 250 computer-based). *Application deadline:* For fall admission, 5/31 priority date for domestic and international students. Applications are processed on a rolling basis. Application fee: $50. Electronic applications accepted. *Expenses:* Contact institution. *Financial support:* In 2009–10, 2 students received support. *Application deadline:* 7/4. *Unit head:* William Adams, Associate Dean, 954-262-6133, Fax: 954-262-6301, E-mail: adamsb@nsu.law.nova.edu. *Application contact:* Jennifer McIntyre, Assistant Dean for Online Programs, 954-262-6079, Fax: 954-262-6301, E-mail: mcintyrej@nsu.law.nova.edu.

Nova Southeastern University, Shepard Broad Law Center, Program in Health Law, Fort Lauderdale, FL 33314-7796. Offers MS. Part-time and evening/weekend programs available. Postbaccalaureate distance learning degree programs offered (minimal on-campus study). *Faculty:* 10 full-time (4 women), 13 part-time/adjunct (7 women). *Students:* 58 part-time (53 women); includes 27 minority (11 African Americans, 1 American Indian/Alaska Native, 1 Asian American or Pacific Islander, 14 Hispanic Americans). Average age 43. 66 applicants, 59% accepted, 35 enrolled. In 2009, 29 master's awarded. *Entrance requirements:* Additional exam requirements/recommendations for international students: Required—TOEFL (minimum score 600 paper-based; 250 computer-based). *Application deadline:* For fall admission, 5/31 priority date for domestic and international students. Applications are processed on a rolling basis. Application fee: $50. Electronic applications accepted. *Expenses:* Contact institution. *Financial support:* In 2009–10, 44 students received support. Tuition waivers (full and partial) available. Financial award application deadline: 7/4; financial award applicants required to submit FAFSA. *Unit head:* William Adams, Associate Dean, 954-262-6133, Fax: 954-262-6301, E-mail: adamsb@nsu.law.nova.edu. *Application contact:* Jennifer McIntyre, Assistant Dean for Online Programs, 954-262-6079, Fax: 954-262-6301, E-mail: mcintyrej@nsu.law.nova.edu.

Pace University, School of Law, White Plains, NY 10603. Offers comparative legal studies (LL M); environmental law (LL M, SJD); law (JD); real estate law (LL M); JD/MA; JD/MBA; JD/MEM; JD/MPA; JD/MS. *Accreditation:* ABA. Part-time and evening/weekend programs available. *Faculty:* 41 full-time (18 women), 52 part-time/adjunct (23 women). *Students:* 582 full-time (326 women), 230 part-time (145 women); includes 136 minority (33 African Americans, 1 American Indian/Alaska Native, 53 Asian Americans or Pacific Islanders, 49 Hispanic Americans), 17 international. Average age 26. 3,048 applicants, 38% accepted, 263 enrolled. In 2009, 216 first professional degrees, 20 master's, 1 doctorate awarded. *Entrance requirements:* LSAT. Additional exam requirements/recommendations for international students: Required—TOEFL (minimum score 600 paper-based; 250 computer-based); Recommended—TWE. *Application deadline:* For fall admission, 3/1 priority date for domestic students; for winter admission, 11/1 priority date for domestic students. Applications are processed on a rolling basis. Application fee: $65. Electronic applications accepted. *Expenses:* Contact institution. *Financial support:* Career-related internships or fieldwork, Federal Work-Study, institutionally sponsored loans, and scholarships/grants available. Support available to part-time students. Financial award application deadline: 2/15; financial award applicants required to submit FAFSA. *Faculty research:* Reform of energy regulations, international law, land use law, prosecutorial misconduct, corporation law, international sale of goods. Total annual research expenditures: $2.2 million. *Unit head:* Michelle S. Simon, Dean, 914-422-4407, E-mail: msimon@law.pace.edu. *Application contact:* Cathy Alexander, Assistant Dean, 914-422-4210, Fax: 914-989-8714, E-mail: calexander@law.pace.edu.

See Close-Up on page 1701.

Prairie View A&M University, College of Juvenile Justice and Psychology, Prairie View, TX 77446-0519. Offers clinical adolescent psychology (PhD); juvenile forensic psychology (MSJFP); juvenile justice (MSJJ, PhD). Part-time and evening/weekend programs available. *Faculty:* 12 full-time (7 women). *Students:* 25 full-time (18 women), 50 part-time (41 women); includes 64 minority (61 African Americans, 1 Asian American or Pacific Islander, 2 Hispanic Americans), 2 international. Average age 26. 55 applicants, 60% accepted, 33 enrolled. In 2009, 5 master's, 5 doctorates awarded. *Degree requirements:* For master's, comprehensive exam (for some programs), thesis (for some programs); for doctorate, comprehensive exam, thesis/dissertation. *Entrance requirements:* For master's, GRE, minimum GPA of 2.75; for doctorate, GRE, previous course work in clinical adolescent psychology, minimum GPA of 3.5. Additional exam requirements/recommendations for international students: Required—TOEFL. *Application deadline:* For fall admission, 3/1 for domestic and international students; for spring admission, 10/1 for domestic and international students. Applications are processed on a rolling basis. Application fee: $50. *Expenses:* Tuition, state resident: full-time $2200. Tuition, nonresident: full-time $5600. Required fees: $1720. Tuition and fees vary according to course load. *Financial support:* In 2009–10, 18 students received support; research assistantships, teaching assistantships, career-related internships or fieldwork, Federal Work-Study, institutionally sponsored loans, tuition waivers (full and partial), and unspecified assistantships available. Support available to part-time students. Financial award application deadline: 3/1; financial award applicants required to submit FAFSA. *Faculty research:* Juvenile justice, juvenile forensic psychology, teen court, graduate education, capital punishment. Total annual research expenditures: $2,888. *Unit head:* Dr. Elaine Rodney, Dean, 936-261-5200, Fax: 936-261-5252, E-mail: ehrodney@pvamu.edu. *Application contact:* Sandy Siegmund, Executive Secretary, Graduate Program, 936-261-5234, Fax: 936-261-5249, E-mail: sisiegmund@pvamu.edu.

Queen's University at Kingston, School of Graduate Studies and Research, Faculty of Arts and Sciences, Department of Sociology, Kingston, ON K7L 3N6, Canada. Offers communication and information technology (MA, PhD); feminist sociology (MA, PhD); socio-legal studies (MA, PhD); sociological theory (MA, PhD). Part-time programs available. *Degree requirements:* For master's, thesis; for doctorate, comprehensive exam, thesis/dissertation. *Entrance requirements:* For master's, honors bachelors degree in sociology; for doctorate, honors bachelors degree, masters degree in sociology. Additional exam requirements/recommendations for international students: Required—TOEFL. *Faculty research:* Social change and modernization, social control, deviance and criminology, surveillance.

Regent University, Graduate School, School of Law, Virginia Beach, VA 23464. Offers American legal studies (LL M); law (JD); JD/MA; JD/MBA. *Accreditation:* ABA. Part-time programs available. *Faculty:* 26 full-time (8 women), 44 part-time/adjunct (8 women). *Students:* 415 full-time (204 women), 5 part-time (3 women); includes 63 minority (29 African Americans, 6 American Indian/Alaska Native, 18 Asian Americans or Pacific Islanders, 10 Hispanic Americans), 5 international. Average age 27. 892 applicants, 42% accepted, 111 enrolled. In 2009, 146 degrees awarded. *Entrance requirements:* LSAT, minimum undergraduate GPA of 2.75, 3 letters of recommendation, resume. Additional exam requirements/recommendations for international students: Required—TOEFL (minimum score 600 paper-based; 250 computer-based). *Application deadline:* For fall admission, 3/1 for domestic students. Applications are processed on a rolling basis. Application fee: $50. Electronic applications accepted. *Expenses:* Contact institution. *Financial support:* In 2009–10, 408 students received support. Career-related internships or fieldwork, scholarships/grants, and tuition waivers (full and partial) available. Support available to part-time students. Financial award application deadline: 2/1; financial award applicants required to submit FAFSA. *Faculty research:* Family law, Constitutional law, law and culture, evidence and practice, intellectual property. *Unit head:* Jeffrey Brauch,

Dean, 757-352-4040, Fax: 757-352-4595, E-mail: jeffbra@regent.edu. *Application contact:* Matthew Chadwick, Director of Admissions, 800-373-5504, Fax: 757-352-4381, E-mail: admissions@regent.edu.

Regis University, College for Professional Studies, MA Program, Denver, CO 80221-1099. Offers criminology (MA); fine arts administration (Certificate); language and communication (MA); mediation (Certificate); psychology (MA); self-designed major (MA); social justice, peace, and reconciliation (Certificate); social science (MA); technical communication (Certificate). Program also offered in Henderson and Las Vegas (Summerlin), NV. Part-time and evening/weekend programs available. Postbaccalaureate distance learning degree programs offered (minimal on-campus study). *Degree requirements:* For master's, thesis, research project. *Entrance requirements:* For master's, resume, recommendations. Additional exam requirements/recommendations for international students: Required—TOEFL (minimum score 213 computer-based), TWE (minimum score 5). Electronic applications accepted. *Expenses:* Contact institution. *Faculty research:* Independent/nonresidential graduate study: new methods and models, adult learning and the capstone experience, Goal Setting, behavior of Adult students, Innovative Studies for Community Colleges.

Rutgers, The State University of New Jersey, New Brunswick, Graduate School-New Brunswick, Department of Political Science, Piscataway, NJ 08854-8097. Offers American politics (PhD); comparative politics (PhD); international relations (PhD); political theory (PhD); public law (PhD); women and politics (PhD). *Degree requirements:* For doctorate, one foreign language, comprehensive exam, thesis/dissertation. *Entrance requirements:* For doctorate, GRE General Test. Additional exam requirements/recommendations for international students: Required—TOEFL.

St. John's University, College of Professional Studies, Department of Criminal Justice and Legal Studies, Queens, NY 11439. Offers MPS. *Students:* 21 full-time (8 women), 43 part-time (25 women); includes 34 minority (13 African Americans, 8 Asian Americans or Pacific Islanders, 13 Hispanic Americans), 1 international. Average age 29. 48 applicants, 81% accepted, 25 enrolled. In 2009, 25 master's awarded. *Degree requirements:* For master's, comprehensive exam, capstone project. *Entrance requirements:* For master's, bachelor's degree from a regionally-accredited college or university, minimum overall GPA of 3.0, 2 letters of recommendation. Additional exam requirements/recommendations for international students: Required—TOEFL (minimum score 500 paper-based; 173 computer-based; 61 iBT), IELTS (minimum score 5.5). *Application deadline:* For fall admission, 5/1 priority date for domestic and international students; for spring admission, 11/1 priority date for domestic and international students. Applications are processed on a rolling basis. Application fee: $70. Electronic applications accepted. *Expenses:* Tuition: Full-time $16,290; part-time $905 per credit. Required fees: $300; $150 per semester. Tuition and fees vary according to program. *Financial support:* Research assistantships available. *Faculty research:* Fire litigation, forensic psychology, organized crime, probation and parole, leadership studies, criminal justice ethics and integration control. *Unit head:* Dr. Keith Carrington, Chair, 718-390-2042, E-mail: carringk@stjohns.edu. *Application contact:* Kathleen Davis, Director of Graduate Admission, 718-990-2790, Fax: 718-990-5686, E-mail: gradhelp@stjohns.edu.

St. John's University, School of Law, Program in U.S. Legal Studies for Foreign Law School Graduates, Queens, NY 11439. Offers LL M. Part-time programs available. *Students:* 4 full-time (3 women), 3 part-time (2 women); includes 4 minority (3 Asian Americans or Pacific Islanders, 1 Hispanic American), 1 international. Average age 31. 38 applicants, 18% accepted, 7 enrolled. In 2009, 15 master's awarded. *Entrance requirements:* For master's, law degree from a non-U. S. law school, resume, 2 letters of recommendation, writing sample, interview. Additional exam requirements/recommendations for international students: Required—TOEFL (minimum score 600 paper-based; 250 computer-based; 100 iBT), IELTS (minimum score 7), TWE. *Application deadline:* For fall admission, 4/1 priority date for domestic and international students. Applications are processed on a rolling basis. Application fee: $100. Electronic applications accepted. *Expenses:* Tuition: Full-time $16,290; part-time $905 per credit. Required fees: $300; $150 per semester. Tuition and fees vary according to program. *Unit head:* Luca Melchionna, Director, 718-990-6948, E-mail: melchiol@stjohns.edu. *Application contact:* Robert Harrison, Assistant Dean and Director of Admissions, 718-990-2310, Fax: 718-990-6699, E-mail: lawinfo@stjohns.edu.

Salve Regina University, Graduate Studies, Programs in Administration of Justice, Newport, RI 02840-4192. Offers justice and homeland security (MS); law enforcement leadership (MS). Part-time and evening/weekend programs available. *Faculty:* 2 full-time (0 women), 9 part-time/adjunct (1 woman). *Students:* 26 full-time (14 women), 39 part-time (6 women); includes 2 minority (1 African American, 1 Hispanic American). Average age 30. 13 applicants, 69% accepted, 9 enrolled. In 2009, 17 master's awarded. *Entrance requirements:* For master's, GMAT, GRE General Test, or MAT. Additional exam requirements/recommendations for international students: Required—TOEFL (minimum score 600 paper-based; 250 computer-based; 100 iBT). *Application deadline:* For fall admission, 3/5 priority date for domestic students, 3/15 priority date for international students; for spring admission, 9/15 priority date for domestic students, 9/5 priority date for international students. Applications are processed on a rolling basis. Application fee: $60. Electronic applications accepted. *Expenses:* Tuition: Part-time $395 per credit. Part-time tuition and fees vary according to degree level. *Financial support:* Career-related internships or fieldwork and Federal Work-Study available. Support available to part-time students. Financial award application deadline: 3/1; financial award applicants required to submit FAFSA. *Unit head:* Dr. Daniel Knight, Director, 401-341-3255, E-mail: knightd@salve.edu. *Application contact:* Kelly Alverson, Graduate Admissions Counselor, 401-341-2153, Fax: 401-341-2973, E-mail: kelly.alverson@salve.edu.

San Francisco State University, Division of Graduate Studies, College of Education, Department of Administration and Interdisciplinary Studies, San Francisco, CA 94132-1722. Offers adult education (MA Ed, AC); educational administration (MA, AC); equity and social justice (AC); equity and social justice in education (MA Ed); special interest (MA Ed).

Southern Illinois University Carbondale, School of Law, Program in Legal Studies, Carbondale, IL 62901-4701. Offers general law (MLS); health law and policy (MLS).

State University of New York at Binghamton, Graduate School, School of Arts and Sciences, Program in Social, Political, Ethical and Legal Philosophy, Binghamton, NY 13902-6000. Offers MA, PhD. *Students:* 23 full-time (12 women), 15 part-time (4 women); includes 8 minority (3 African Americans, 1 American Indian/Alaska Native, 2 Asian Americans or Pacific Islanders, 2 Hispanic Americans), 7 international. Average age 29. 48 applicants, 40% accepted, 11 enrolled. In 2009, 5 master's, 1 doctorate awarded. Application fee: $60. *Unit head:* Dr. Bat-Ami Bar-On, Chairperson, 607-777-6198, E-mail: ami@binghamton.edu. *Application contact:* Victoria Williams, Recruiting and Admissions Coordinator, 607-777-2151, Fax: 607-777-2501, E-mail: vwilliam@binghamton.edu.

Temple University, James E. Beasley School of Law, Philadelphia, PA 19122. Offers law (JD); legal education (SJD); taxation (LL M); transnational law (LL M); trial advocacy (LL M); JD/LL M; JD/MBA. *Accreditation:* ABA. Part-time and evening/weekend programs available. *Entrance requirements:* LSAT, LSDAS. Electronic applications accepted. *Expenses:* Contact institution. *Faculty research:* Comparative constitutional law, gender issues, immigration law, international intellectual property law and popular culture.

Texas State University–San Marcos, Graduate School, College of Liberal Arts, Department of Political Science, Program in Legal Studies, San Marcos, TX 78666. Offers MA. *Faculty:* 7 full-time (2 women). *Students:* 38 full-time (21 women), 46 part-time (38 women); includes 35 minority (9 African Americans, 2 Asian Americans or Pacific Islanders, 24 Hispanic Americans), 1 international. Average age 31. 30 applicants, 100% accepted, 24 enrolled. In 2009, 19 master's awarded. *Degree requirements:* For master's, comprehensive exam. *Entrance requirements:* For master's, GRE General Test (minimum score 900, 4 analytical preferred) or LSAT, minimum GPA of 2.75 in last 60 hours of undergraduate work. Additional exam requirements/recommendations for international students: Required—TOEFL (minimum score 550 paper-based; 213 computer-based). *Application deadline:* For fall admission, 6/15 priority

date for domestic students, 6/1 priority date for international students; for spring admission, 10/15 priority date for domestic students, 10/1 priority date for international students. Applications are processed on a rolling basis. Application fee: $90 ($140 for international students). Electronic applications accepted. *Expenses:* Tuition, state resident: full-time $5784; part-time $241 per credit hour. Tuition, nonresident: full-time $13,224; part-time $551 per credit hour. Required fees: $1728; $48 per credit hour. $306. Tuition and fees vary according to course load. *Financial support:* In 2009–10, 28 students received support, including 1 research assistantship (averaging $4,928 per year), 2 teaching assistantships (averaging $5,217 per year). Financial award application deadline: 4/1; financial award applicants required to submit FAFSA. *Unit head:* Dr. Lynn Crossett, Graduate Advisor, 512-245-2233, Fax: 512-245-7815, E-mail: th10@txstate.edu. *Application contact:* Dr. J. Michael Willoughby, Dean of Graduate School, 512-245-2581, Fax: 512-245-8365, E-mail: gradcollege@txstate.edu.

TUI University, College of Health Sciences, Program in Health Sciences, Cypress, CA 90630. Offers clinical research administration (MS, Certificate); emergency and disaster management (MS, Certificate); environmental health science (Certificate); health care administration (PhD); health care management (MS), including health informatics; health education (MS, Certificate); health informatics (Certificate); health sciences (PhD); international health (MS); international health: educator or researcher option (PhD); international health: practitioner option (PhD); law and expert witness studies (MS, Certificate); public health (MS); quality assurance (Certificate). Part-time and evening/weekend programs available. Postbaccalaureate distance learning degree programs offered (no on-campus study). *Degree requirements:* For doctorate, comprehensive exam, thesis/dissertation, defense of dissertation. *Entrance requirements:* For master's, minimum GPA of 2.5 (students with GPA 3.0 or greater may transfer up to 30% of graduate level credits); for doctorate, minimum GPA of 3.4, curriculum vitae, course work in research methods or statistics. Additional exam requirements/recommendations for international students: Required—TOEFL. Electronic applications accepted.

Universidad Autonoma de Guadalajara, Graduate Programs, Guadalajara, Mexico. Offers administrative law and justice (LL M); advertising and corporate communications (MA); architecture (M Arch); business (MBA); computational science (MCC); education (Ed M, Ed D); English-Spanish translation (MA); fiscal law (MA); integrated management of digital animation (MA); international business (MIB); international corporate law (LL M); internet technologies (MS); labor health (MS); manufacturing systems (MMS); philosophy (MA, PhD); power electronics (MS); quality systems (MQS); renewable energy (MS); social evaluation of projects (MBA); strategic market research (MBA); teaching mathematics (MA).

Université Laval, Faculty of Law, Program in Notarial Law, Québec, QC G1K 7P4, Canada. Offers Diploma. Part-time programs available. *Entrance requirements:* For degree, knowledge of French. Electronic applications accepted.

University of Baltimore, Graduate School, The Yale Gordon College of Liberal Arts, Program in Legal and Ethical Studies, Baltimore, MD 21201-5779. Offers MA. Part-time and evening/weekend programs available. *Degree requirements:* For master's, thesis optional. *Entrance requirements:* For master's, minimum GPA of 3.0. Additional exam requirements/recommendations for international students: Required—TOEFL (minimum score 550 paper-based; 213 computer-based). Electronic applications accepted. *Faculty research:* Morality in law and economics, religion in lawmaking, comparative legal history, law and social change, critical issues in constitutional law, theories of justice.

University of Calgary, Faculty of Law, Programs in Natural Resources, Energy and Environmental Law, Calgary, AB T2N 1N4, Canada. Offers LL M, Graduate Certificate. *Entrance requirements:* Additional exam requirements/recommendations for international students: Required—TOEFL.

University of California, Berkeley, School of Law, Program in Jurisprudence and Social Policy, Berkeley, CA 94720-1500. Offers PhD. *Degree requirements:* For doctorate, one foreign language, thesis/dissertation, oral qualifying exam. *Entrance requirements:* For doctorate, GRE General Test, sample of written work, letters of recommendation. Electronic applications accepted. *Expenses:* Contact institution. *Faculty research:* Law and philosophy, legal history, law and economics, law and political science, law and sociology.

University of California, San Diego, Office of Graduate Studies, Program in Health Law, La Jolla, CA 92093. Offers MAS. Part-time programs available. *Degree requirements:* For master's, capstone project. *Entrance requirements:* For master's, undergraduate degree in healthcare, law, or related field; 3 years work experience; 3 letters of recommendation; resume.

University of Charleston, Executive Master of Forensic Accounting Program, Charleston, WV 25304-1099. Offers EMFA. Part-time and evening/weekend programs available. *Faculty:* 6 part-time/adjunct (1 woman). *Students:* 10 full-time (7 women). Average age 38. 14 applicants, 64% accepted, 9 enrolled. *Entrance requirements:* For master's, undergraduate degree from regionally-accredited institution; minimum GPA of 3.0 in undergraduate work (recommended); three years of work experience since receiving undergraduate degree (recommended); minimum of two professional recommendations, one from current employer, addressing career potential and ability to do graduate work. Additional exam requirements/recommendations for international students: Required—TOEFL. *Application deadline:* Applications are processed on a rolling basis. Application fee: $50. Electronic applications accepted. *Expenses:* Tuition: Full-time $25,224; part-time $875 per credit hour. Full-time tuition and fees vary according to degree level. *Financial support:* In 2009–10, 1 student received support. Applicants required to submit FAFSA. *Unit head:* Dr. Robert B. Bliss, Associate Dean, 304-357-4865, Fax: 304-357-4872, E-mail: robertbliss@ucwv.edu. *Application contact:* Dr. Robert B. Bliss, Associate Dean, 304-357-4865, Fax: 304-357-4872, E-mail: robertbliss@ucwv.edu.

University of Denver, College of Law, Program in Legal Administration, Denver, CO 80208. Offers MSLA, Certificate. Part-time and evening/weekend programs available. *Students:* 17 full-time (11 women), 26 part-time (22 women); includes 8 minority (3 African Americans, 1 American Indian/Alaska Native, 1 Asian American or Pacific Islander, 3 Hispanic Americans), 2 international. Average age 31. 33 applicants, 91% accepted, 18 enrolled. In 2009, 22 master's awarded. *Degree requirements:* For master's, internship. *Entrance requirements:* For master's, GMAT, GRE, or LSAT. *Application deadline:* Applications are processed on a rolling basis. Application fee: $25. Electronic applications accepted. *Expenses:* Tuition: Full-time $34,596; part-time $961 per quarter hour. Required fees: $4 per quarter hour. Tuition and fees vary according to course load, campus/location and program. *Financial support:* Career-related internships or fieldwork and Federal Work-Study available. Support available to part-time students. Financial award application deadline: 2/15; financial award applicants required to submit FAFSA. *Unit head:* Hope Kentnor, Director, 305-871-6308. *Application contact:* Lucy Daberkow, Admissions, 303-871-6324, Fax: 303-871-6378, E-mail: msln@law.du.edu.

University of Illinois at Springfield, Graduate Programs, College of Public Affairs and Administration, Program in Legal Studies, Springfield, IL 62703-5407. Offers MA. Part-time and evening/weekend programs available. Postbaccalaureate distance learning degree programs offered (no on-campus study). *Faculty:* 4 full-time (all women), 3 part-time/adjunct (2 women). *Students:* 7 full-time (3 women), 32 part-time (17 women); includes 7 minority (5 African Americans, 2 Hispanic Americans), 1 international. Average age 38. 48 applicants, 48% accepted, 17 enrolled. In 2009, 10 master's awarded. *Degree requirements:* For master's, thesis or seminar. *Entrance requirements:* For master's, minimum undergraduate GPA of 3.0. Additional exam requirements/recommendations for international students: Required—TOEFL (minimum score 600 paper-based; 250 computer-based; 100 iBT). *Application deadline:* Applications are processed on a rolling basis. Application fee: $50 ($60 for international students). Electronic applications accepted. *Expenses:* Tuition, state resident: full-time $6390; part-time $266.25 per credit hour. Tuition, nonresident: full-time $14,226; part-time $592.75 per credit hour. Required fees: $2044; $14.36 per credit hour. $722.50 per term. *Financial support:* In 2009–10, research assistantships with full tuition reimbursements (averaging $8,109 per year), teaching assistantships with full tuition reimbursements (averaging $8,109 per year) were awarded; career-related internships or fieldwork, Federal Work-Study, scholarships/grants, health care benefits, and unspecified assistantships also available. Support available to part-time students. Financial award application deadline: 11/15; financial award applicants required to submit FAFSA. *Unit head:* Kathryn E. Eisenhart, Program Administrator, 217-206-7882, Fax: 217-206-7807, E-mail: eisenhart.kathryn@uis.edu. *Application contact:* Dr. Lynn Pardie, Office of Graduate Studies, 800-252-8533, Fax: 217-206-7623, E-mail: pardie.lynn@uis.edu.

University of Maryland, Baltimore County, Graduate School, College of Arts, Humanities and Social Sciences, Department of Public Policy, Program in Public Policy, Baltimore, MD 21250. Offers economics (PhD); education (MPP, PhD); evaluation (MPP); health (MPP, PhD); legal (MPP, PhD); management (MPP, PhD); urban (MPP, PhD). Part-time and evening/weekend programs available. *Faculty:* 40 full-time (12 women), 2 part-time/adjunct (1 woman). *Students:* 57 full-time (34 women), 114 part-time (61 women); includes 47 minority (26 African Americans, 21 Hispanic Americans). Average age 33. 89 applicants, 47% accepted, 24 enrolled. In 2009, 12 master's, 5 doctorates awarded. Terminal master's awarded for partial completion of doctoral program. *Degree requirements:* For master's, thesis optional, public analysis paper; for doctorate, comprehensive exam, thesis/dissertation, comprehensive and field qualifying exams. *Entrance requirements:* For master's, GRE General Test, 3 academic letters of reference, transcripts, resume; for doctorate, GRE General Test, 3 academic letters of reference, transcripts, resume, research paper. Additional exam requirements/recommendations for international students: Required—TOEFL (minimum score 550 paper-based; 213 computer-based; 80 iBT). *Application deadline:* For fall admission, 1/15 priority date for domestic students, 1/1 priority date for international students; for spring admission, 11/1 priority date for domestic students, 5/1 priority date for international students. Applications are processed on a rolling basis. Application fee: $50. Electronic applications accepted. *Financial support:* In 2009–10, 32 students received support, including 1 fellowship (averaging $3,000 per year), 17 research assistantships with full tuition reimbursements available (averaging $17,400 per year); career-related internships or fieldwork, Federal Work-Study, scholarships/grants, health care benefits, and unspecified assistantships also available. Support available to part-time students. Financial award application deadline: 2/1; financial award applicants required to submit FAFSA. *Faculty research:* Health policy, education policy, urban policy, public management, evaluation and analytical method. *Unit head:* Dr. Donald Norris, Chair, 410-455-1455, E-mail: norris@umbc.edu. *Application contact:* Sally F. Helms, Administrator of Academic Affairs, 410-455-3202, Fax: 410-455-1172, E-mail: gradposi@umbc.edu.

University of Mississippi, Graduate School, School of Applied Sciences, Department of Legal Studies, Oxford, University, MS 38677. Offers MS. *Faculty:* 8 full-time (2 women), 1 part-time/adjunct (0 women). *Students:* 17 full-time (6 women), 19 part-time (5 women); includes 4 minority (3 African Americans, 1 Asian American or Pacific Islander). In 2009, 1 master's awarded. *Unit head:* Dr. David McElreath, Chair, 662-915-1635, E-mail: dhmcel@olemiss.edu. *Application contact:* Dr. Christy M. Wyandt, Associate Dean, 662-915-7474, Fax: 662-915-7577, E-mail: cwyandt@olemiss.edu.

University of Nebraska–Lincoln, College of Law, Program in Legal Studies, Lincoln, NE 68588. Offers MLS. *Entrance requirements:* For master's, GRE or LSAT. Additional exam requirements/recommendations for international students: Required—TOEFL (minimum score 600 paper-based; 250 computer-based). Electronic applications accepted.

University of Nevada, Reno, Graduate School, College of Liberal Arts, School of Social Research and Justice Studies, Program in Judicial Studies, Reno, NV 89557. Offers MJS, PhD. Offered jointly with the National Judicial College and the National Council of Juvenile and Family Court Judges. Part-time programs available. Terminal master's awarded for partial completion of doctoral program. *Degree requirements:* For master's, thesis; for doctorate, thesis/dissertation. *Entrance requirements:* For master's and doctorate, sitting judge, law degree from an accredited school. Additional exam requirements/recommendations for international students: Required—TOEFL (minimum score 500 paper-based; 173 computer-based; 61 iBT), IELTS (minimum score 6). Electronic applications accepted. *Expenses:* Contact institution. *Faculty research:* Jury research, capital punishment, expert testimony, environmental law, medical issues.

University of New Hampshire, Graduate School, College of Liberal Arts, Program in Justice Studies, Durham, NH 03824. Offers MA. Program offered in summer only. Part-time programs available. *Faculty:* 22 full-time (11 women). *Students:* 12 full-time (8 women), 12 part-time (7 women); includes 1 minority (Hispanic American). Average age 29. 1 applicant, 0% accepted, 0 enrolled. In 2009, 13 master's awarded. *Degree requirements:* For master's, thesis optional. *Entrance requirements:* For master's, GRE. Additional exam requirements/recommendations for international students: Required—TOEFL (minimum score 550 paper-based; 213 computer-based; 80 iBT); Recommended—TWE. *Application deadline:* For fall admission, 3/1 for domestic students, 3/1 priority date for international students. Applications are processed on a rolling basis. Application fee: $65. Electronic applications accepted. *Expenses:* Tuition, state resident: full-time $10,380; part-time $577 per credit hour. Tuition, nonresident: full-time $24,350; part-time $1002 per credit hour. Required fees: $1550; $387.50 per semester. Tuition and fees vary according to course load and program. *Financial support:* In 2009–10, 4 students received support, including 3 research assistantships, 1 teaching assistantship; fellowships, career-related internships or fieldwork, Federal Work-Study, scholarships/grants, and tuition waivers (full and partial) also available. Support available to part-time students. Financial award application deadline: 3/1. *Unit head:* Dr. Ellen Cohn, Chairperson, 603-862-3197, E-mail: ellen.cohn@unh.edu. *Application contact:* Deborah Briand, Administrative Assistant, 603-862-1716, E-mail: justice.studies@unh.edu.

University of Pennsylvania, Wharton School, Legal Studies and Business Ethics Department, Philadelphia, PA 19104. Offers MBA, PhD. *Expenses:* Tuition: Full-time $25,660; part-time $4758 per course. Required fees: $2152; $270 per course. Tuition and fees vary according to course load, degree level and program.

University of Pittsburgh, School of Law, Master of Studies in Law Program, Pittsburgh, PA 15260. Offers business law (MSL), including commercial law, corporate law, general business law, international business, tax law; constitutional law (MSL); criminal law and justice (MSL); disabilities law (MSL); dispute resolution (MSL); education law (MSL); elder and estate planning law (MSL); employment and labor law (MSL); environment and real estate law (MSL); family law (MSL); general law and jurisprudence (MSL); health law (MSL); intellectual property and technology (MSL); international and comparative law (MSL); personal injury and civil litigation (MSL); regulatory law (MSL); self-designed (MSL); sports and entertainment law (MSL). Part-time programs available. *Faculty:* 43 full-time (16 women), 104 part-time/adjunct (30 women). *Students:* 3 full-time (2 women), 12 part-time (7 women); includes 3 minority (2 African Americans, 1 Asian American or Pacific Islander). Average age 31. 26 applicants, 58% accepted, 11 enrolled. In 2009, 9 master's awarded. *Entrance requirements:* Additional exam requirements/recommendations for international students: Required—TOEFL (minimum score 600 paper-based; 250 computer-based; 100 iBT). *Application deadline:* For fall admission, 6/30 for domestic students, 5/1 for international students. Applications are processed on a rolling basis. Application fee: $0. *Expenses:* Tuition, state resident: full-time $16,402; part-time $665 per credit. Tuition, nonresident: full-time $28,694; part-time $1175 per credit. Required fees: $690; $175 per term. Tuition and fees vary according to program. *Faculty research:* Law, health law, business law, contracts, intellectual property. *Unit head:* Prof. Alan Meisel, Director, 412-648-1384, Fax: 412-648-2649, E-mail: meisel@pitt.edu. *Application contact:* Bethann Pischke, Administrative Coordinator, 412-648-7120, Fax: 412-648-2649, E-mail: pischke@pitt.edu.

University of Pittsburgh, School of Law, Program in Health Law, Pittsburgh, PA 15260. Offers Certificate. *Faculty:* 46 full-time (17 women), 94 part-time/adjunct (24 women). *Students:* 33 full-time (17 women). *Application deadline:* For spring admission, 7/31 for domestic students. Applications are processed on a rolling basis. *Expenses:* Tuition, state resident: full-time $16,402; part-time $665 per credit. Tuition, nonresident: full-time $28,694; part-time $1175 per credit. Required fees: $690; $175 per term. Tuition and fees vary according to program. *Unit head:* Prof. Alan Meisel, Professor/Director, 412-648-1384, Fax: 412-648-2649, E-mail: meisel@pitt.edu. *Application contact:* Bethann Pischke, Program Administrator, 412-648-7120, Fax: 412-648-2649, E-mail: pischke@pitt.edu.

Legal and Justice Studies

University of San Diego, School of Law, San Diego, CA 92110. Offers business and corporate law (LL M); comparative law (LL M); general studies (LL M); international law (LL M); law (JD); taxation (LL M, Diploma); JD/IMBA; JD/MA; JD/MBA. *Accreditation:* ABA. Part-time and evening/weekend programs available. *Faculty:* 43 full-time (17 women), 57 part-time/adjunct (18 women). *Students:* 882 full-time (412 women), 222 part-time (96 women); includes 297 minority (15 African Americans, 12 American Indian/Alaska Native, 177 Asian Americans or Pacific Islanders, 93 Hispanic Americans), 21 international. Average age 26. 4,424 applicants, 34% accepted, 324 enrolled. In 2009, 327 first professional degrees, 59 master's awarded. *Entrance requirements:* For JD, LSAT, bachelor's degree; for master's, JD, LLB or equivalent from an ABA-accredited law school. Additional exam requirements/recommendations for international students: Required—TOEFL (minimum score 600 paper-based; 250 computer-based; 98 iBT). *Application deadline:* For fall admission, 2/1 priority date for domestic students. Applications are processed on a rolling basis. Application fee: $50. Electronic applications accepted. *Expenses:* Contact institution. *Financial support:* In 2009–10, 973 students received support. Career-related internships or fieldwork, Federal Work-Study, institutionally sponsored loans, and scholarships/grants available. Support available to part-time students. Financial award application deadline: 3/1; financial award applicants required to submit FAFSA. *Unit head:* Kevin Cole, Dean, 619-260-2330, Fax: 619-260-2218. *Application contact:* Carl J. Eging, Director of Admissions and Financial Aid, 619-260-4528, Fax: 619-260-2218, E-mail: eging@sandiego.edu.

University of the Pacific, McGeorge School of Law, Sacramento, CA 95817. Offers advocacy (JD); criminal justice (JD); experiential law teaching (LL M); intellectual property (JD); international legal studies (JD); international water resources law (LL M, JSD); law (JD); public law and policy (JD); public policy and law (LL M); tax (JD); transnational business practice (LL M); JD/MBA; JD/MPPA. *Accreditation:* ABA. Part-time and evening/weekend programs available. *Faculty:* 55 full-time (24 women), 57 part-time/adjunct (18 women). *Students:* 697 full-time (343 women), 377 part-time (197 women); includes 301 minority (33 African Americans, 11 American Indian/Alaska Native, 163 Asian Americans or Pacific Islanders, 94 Hispanic Americans). Average age 24. 2,659 applicants, 43% accepted, 236 enrolled. In 2009, 254 JDs, 51 master's awarded. *Degree requirements:* For master's, thesis (for some programs); for doctorate, thesis/dissertation. *Entrance requirements:* For JD, LSAT; for master's, JD; for doctorate, LL M. Additional exam requirements/recommendations for international students: Required—TOEFL (minimum score 600 paper-based; 250 computer-based; 100 iBT). *Application deadline:* For fall admission, 3/15 priority date for domestic students. Applications are processed on a rolling basis. Application fee: $50. Electronic applications accepted. *Expenses:* Contact institution. *Financial support:* In 2009–10, 887 students received support, including 1 fellowship, 114 research assistantships (averaging $1,839 per year), 12 teaching assistantships (averaging $953 per year); career-related internships or fieldwork, Federal Work-Study, institutionally sponsored loans, and scholarships/grants also available. Support available to part-time students. Financial award applicants required to submit FAFSA. *Faculty research:* International legal studies, public policy and law, advocacy, intellectual property law, taxation, criminal law. *Unit head:* Elizabeth Rindskopf Parker, Dean, 916-739-7151, E-mail: elizabeth@pacific.edu. *Application contact:* 916-739-7105, Fax: 916-739-7301, E-mail: mcgeorge@pacific.edu.

University of the Sacred Heart, Graduate Programs, Program in Systems of Justice, San Juan, PR 00914-0383. Offers human rights and anti-discriminatory processes (MASJ); mediation and transformation of conflicts (MASJ).

University of Washington, Graduate School, School of Law, Seattle, WA 98195-3020. Offers Asian law (LL M, PhD); intellectual property law and policy (LL M); law (JD); law of sustainable international development (LL M); taxation (LL M); JD/LL M; JD/MA; JD/MAIS; JD/MBA; JD/MPA; JD/MS; JD/PhD. *Accreditation:* ABA. *Degree requirements:* For master's, thesis; for doctorate, thesis/dissertation. *Entrance requirements:* For JD, LSAT; for master's, language proficiency (LL M in Asian law). Additional exam requirements/recommendations for international students: Required—TOEFL. *Expenses:* Contact institution. *Faculty research:* Asian, international and comparative law, intellectual property law, health law, environmental law, taxation.

University of Windsor, Faculty of Graduate Studies, Faculty of Arts and Social Sciences, Department of Communication Studies, Windsor, ON N9B 3P4, Canada. Offers communication and social justice (MA). *Degree requirements:* For master's, thesis. *Entrance requirements:* For master's, writing sample/media production or multimedia portfolio. Additional exam requirements/recommendations for international students: Required—TOEFL (minimum score 600 paper-based; 250 computer-based). Electronic applications accepted. *Faculty research:* Sociology of news, media ownership and control, communication networks and social movements, issues of media representation.

University of Wisconsin–Madison, Law School, Graduate Programs in Law, Madison, WI 53706-1380. Offers LL M, SJD. *Faculty:* 30 full-time (11 women), 14 part-time/adjunct (4 women). *Students:* 71 full-time (41 women), 3 part-time (0 women); includes 5 minority (2 African Americans, 1 American Indian/Alaska Native, 2 Asian Americans or Pacific Islanders), 68 international. Average age 30. 120 applicants, 55% accepted, 49 enrolled. In 2009, 33 master's, 10 doctorates awarded. *Entrance requirements:* Additional exam requirements/recommendations for international students: Required—TOEFL (minimum score 580 paper-based; 237 computer-based; 92 iBT). *Application deadline:* For fall admission, 3/1 for domestic and international students; for spring admission, 10/1 for domestic and international students. Applications are processed on a rolling basis. Application fee: $56. Electronic applications accepted. *Expenses:* Tuition, state resident: part-time $594 per credit. Tuition, nonresident: part-time $1504 per credit. Required fees: $65 per credit. Tuition and fees vary according to course load, program and reciprocity agreements. *Financial support:* In 2009–10, 5 fellowships with full tuition reimbursements (averaging $11,000 per year) were awarded; scholarships/grants and tuition waivers (partial) also available. *Faculty research:* Tax policy in emerging economics, international trade law, anti-trust law and regulation, Asian comparative law and legal history, intellectual property in business organization. *Unit head:* Prof. Gerald Thain, Chairperson, 608-262-9120. *Application contact:* Amy J. Arntsen, Program Associate, 608-262-9120, Fax: 608-265-2253, E-mail: gradprog@law.wisc.edu.

Valparaiso University, Graduate School, Program in Legal Studies and Principles, Valparaiso, IN 46383. Offers Certificate. Part-time and evening/weekend programs available. *Students:* 1 (woman) part-time, all international. Average age 33. *Entrance requirements:* Additional exam requirements/recommendations for international students: Required—TOEFL (minimum score 550 paper-based; 213 computer-based; 80 iBT). *Application deadline:* Applications are processed on a rolling basis. Application fee: $30 ($50 for international students). Electronic applications accepted. *Financial support:* Available to part-time students. Applicants required to submit FAFSA. *Unit head:* Dr. David L. Rowland, Dean, Graduate Studies and Continuing Education/Associate Provost, 219-464-5313, Fax: 219-464-5381, E-mail: david.rowland@valpo.edu. *Application contact:* Jamie Haney, Coordinator of Graduate Admission, 219-464-5313, Fax: 219-464-5381, E-mail: jamie.haney@valpo.edu.

Vermont Law School, Law School, Environmental Law Center, South Royalton, VT 05068-0096. Offers LL M, MELP, JD/MELP. Part-time programs available. *Faculty:* 11 full-time (3 women), 13 part-time/adjunct (7 women). *Students:* 38 full-time (20 women), 2 part-time (1 woman); includes 1 Asian American or Pacific Islander, 1 Hispanic American. Average age 30. 86 applicants, 88% accepted, 40 enrolled. In 2009, 65 master's awarded. *Entrance requirements:* Additional exam requirements/recommendations for international students: Required—TOEFL. *Application deadline:* For fall admission, 3/1 priority date for domestic students. Applications are processed on a rolling basis. Application fee: $60. *Expenses:* Tuition: Full-time $40,420. *Financial support:* In 2009–10, 2 fellowships with full tuition reimbursements (averaging $5,000 per year) were awarded; career-related internships or fieldwork, Federal Work-Study, institutionally sponsored loans, scholarships/grants, and tuition waivers (partial) also available. Support available to part-time students. Financial award application deadline: 3/1; financial award applicants required to submit FAFSA. *Faculty research:* Environment and technology; takings; international environmental law; interaction among science, law, and environmental policy; air pollution. Total annual research expenditures: $52,000. *Unit head:* Marc Mihaly, Associate Dean, 802-831-1342, Fax: 802-763-2490, E-mail: admiss@vermontlaw.edu. *Application contact:* Anne Mansfield, Associate Director, 802-831-1338, Fax: 802-763-2940, E-mail: admiss@vermontlaw.edu.

Weber State University, College of Social and Behavioral Sciences, Program in Criminal Justice, Ogden, UT 84408-1001. Offers MCJ. Part-time and evening/weekend programs available. *Entrance requirements:* For master's, GRE General Test, resume.

Webster University, College of Arts and Sciences, Department of Behavioral and Social Sciences, Program in Legal Analysis, St. Louis, MO 63119-3194. Offers MA. Part-time programs available. *Entrance requirements:* Additional exam requirements/recommendations for international students: Required—TOEFL. *Expenses:* Tuition: Part-time $565 per credit hour. Tuition and fees vary according to degree level, campus/location and program.

Webster University, College of Arts and Sciences, Department of Behavioral and Social Sciences, Program in Legal Studies, St. Louis, MO 63119-3194. Offers MA. Part-time and evening/weekend programs available. *Degree requirements:* For master's, thesis optional. *Entrance requirements:* Additional exam requirements/recommendations for international students: Required—TOEFL. *Expenses:* Tuition: Part-time $565 per credit hour. Tuition and fees vary according to degree level, campus/location and program. *Faculty research:* Intellectual property rights, emerging torts, death penalty, juvenile justice, confidentiality issues in banking.

Webster University, College of Arts and Sciences, Department of Behavioral and Social Sciences, Program in Patent Agency, St. Louis, MO 63119-3194. Offers MA. Part-time and evening/weekend programs available. *Entrance requirements:* Additional exam requirements/recommendations for international students: Required—TOEFL. *Expenses:* Tuition: Part-time $565 per credit hour. Tuition and fees vary according to degree level, campus/location and program. *Faculty research:* Intellectual property rights, emerging torts, death penalty, juvenile justice, confidentiality issues in banking.

West Virginia University, Eberly College of Arts and Sciences, School of Applied Social Sciences, Division of Public Administration, Morgantown, WV 26506. Offers legal studies (MLS); public administration (MPA); JD/MPA; MSW/MPA. *Accreditation:* NASPAA. Part-time programs available. *Degree requirements:* For master's, internship. *Entrance requirements:* For master's, GRE General Test, minimum GPA of 2.75. Additional exam requirements/recommendations for international students: Required—TOEFL. Electronic applications accepted. *Faculty research:* Public management and organization, conflict resolution, work satisfaction, health administration, social policy and welfare.

Whittier College, Whittier Law School, Costa Mesa, CA 92626. Offers foreign legal studies (LL M); law (JD). *Accreditation:* ABA. Part-time and evening/weekend programs available. *Faculty:* 26 full-time (12 women), 17 part-time/adjunct (8 women). *Students:* 451 full-time (252 women), 136 part-time (69 women); includes 161 minority (16 African Americans, 2 American Indian/Alaska Native, 79 Asian Americans or Pacific Islanders, 64 Hispanic Americans), 1 international. Average age 24. 1,520 applicants, 46% accepted, 140 enrolled. In 2009, 154 JDs, 10 master's awarded. *Entrance requirements:* For JD, LSAT; for master's, first degree in law. Additional exam requirements/recommendations for international students: Required—TOEFL (minimum score 600 paper-based; 250 computer-based). *Application deadline:* For fall admission, 6/1 priority date for domestic students, 3/15 priority date for international students; for spring admission, 11/1 priority date for domestic and international students. Applications are processed on a rolling basis. Application fee: $50. Electronic applications accepted. *Expenses:* Contact institution. *Financial support:* In 2009–10, 710 students received support, including 31 fellowships with full and partial tuition reimbursements available (averaging $3,800 per year), 26 research assistantships, 47 teaching assistantships; career-related internships or fieldwork, Federal Work-Study, scholarships/grants, and unspecified assistantships also available. Financial award application deadline: 5/1; financial award applicants required to submit FAFSA. *Faculty research:* Intellectual property, international law, health law, children's rights. Total annual research expenditures: $164,629. *Unit head:* Neil H. Cogan, Dean, 714-444-4141 Ext. 111, Fax: 714-444-0855. *Application contact:* Betty Vu, Director of Admissions, 714-444-4141 Ext. 123, Fax: 714-444-0250.

William Howard Taft University, Graduate Programs, Bernard E. Witkin School of Law, Santa Ana, CA 92704. Offers American jurisprudence (LL M); law (JD); taxation (LL M).

NEW YORK LAW SCHOOL

NEW YORK LAW SCHOOL

Master of Arts in Mental Disability Law Studies
Certificate in Advanced Mental Disability Law Studies

Program of Study

New York Law School has created the nation's first online mental disability law program, offering a Master of Arts in mental disability law studies and a certificate in advanced mental disability law studies. This diverse program provides psychologists, psychiatrists, other mental health professionals, criminologists, criminal justice specialists, advocates, activists, human rights workers, social workers, and attorneys with advanced training in an important, growing field. It is the only program of its kind offered by an American Bar Association–approved law school and delivered directly through the convenience of distance learning.

Students advance their professional status and legal literacy by learning about the complexities of the law and how court decisions affect the way they handle cases, conduct research, or advocate on behalf of persons with mental disabilities. Along the way, students develops the skills required as an expert witness, administrator, clinician, researcher, advocate, or attorney in order to bring about meaningful change in the lives and treatment of persons with mental disabilities.

Designed and taught by renowned Professor Michael L. Perlin, the online mental disability law program provides the most up-to-date information and interpretation of civil, criminal, constitutional, and international human rights law via high-quality instruction and academic guidance in a multidimensional distance-learning environment. Students who are currently engaged in professional careers can further their education while maintaining their current employment since all classes meet at night and on weekends. The program utilizes the latest and most effective online learning technologies to easily disseminate legal-based education to professionals and advanced learners who may otherwise be unable to gain access to this training.

The majority of course content is completed online, where students have access to a virtual community of fellow students. Each fourteen-week course is taught by experienced, distinguished scholars and practitioners. Courses include weekly recorded lectures; weekly reading assignments; personalized e-mail access to the program's faculty and staff members; weekly synchronous classes in a virtual classroom via chat sessions where students and faculty meet in real time; weekly asynchronous threaded question-and-answer discussions through message boards; two daylong weekend seminars held at New York Law School, where students meet with professors to discuss topics addressed during the course and to emphasize skills training; and a short take-home midterm and final exam.

The Master of Arts in mental disability law studies is a 30-credit degree-bearing program that can be completed in eighteen months or up to five years, depending on whether the student is enrolled full- or part-time. Candidates are required to successfully complete six courses of the core curriculum, three elective courses, and an independent writing project supervised by the program director and/or program faculty member. (All courses are 3 credits.) To earn the M.A. degree, a candidate must have a minimum cumulative GPA of 2.5

The certificate in advanced mental disability law studies provides the opportunity to pursue graduate studies with a shorter 15-credit certificate, which can be completed in ten to eighteen months, depending on whether the student is enrolled full- or part-time. Candidates must successfully complete one required course and four elective courses. (All courses are 3 credits.) To receive the certificate, a candidate must have a minimum cumulative GPA of 2.5.

Research Facilities

The Mendik Library at New York Law School has a sizable collection in disciplines related to the area of mental disability law and provides ample staff research and reference support to the program. Resources include materials from international, federal, all fifty states, and local New York jurisdictions. The library's collection is augmented by a sophisticated range of computer research services and other technological enhancements. The online public access catalog, automated acquisitions, serials, and circulation control systems provide easy and comprehensive access to the collection. Reference librarians assist users in locating materials outside the Law School's collection and in arranging access to the most convenient sources. To maximize the range of materials and facilities available to students and faculty, the library has joined several library consortia providing access to New York metropolitan area libraries, and international and comparative law materials. Using the bibliographic databases, librarians can locate and arrange for the interlibrary loan of materials from academic, court, public, and private libraries throughout New York and the United States. The library also subscribes to e-journals and JSTOR, a resource to full articles in nonlegal, multidiscipline areas. All students have Lexis and Westlaw accounts for access to the latest state, federal, and regulatory decisions in cases related to their studies, as well as journals and newspaper resources. Although hard copy publications are available to students in the program, most of the research sources and tools used will be electronic. The combination of the library's holdings, borrowing policies, and student access to Lexis and Westlaw is allows for successful completion of student research in the program.

Financial Aid

M.A. students may be eligible for direct loans from New York Law School or private loans. For information, contact the Office of Admissions and Financial Aid at 212-431-2828 or e-mail financialaid@nyls.edu.

Cost of Study

Tuition for students in Master of Arts degree and Certificate programs is $2400 per course for the 2010–11 academic year. For students who work for nonprofit organizations or government agencies, the tuition is $1500 per course for the year.

Student Group

New York Law School reflects the cosmopolitan nature of its urban setting in New York City. The student body of more than 1,500 represents 234 undergraduate schools, thirty-three states and territories, twenty-one other countries, and several international institutions. The student body (entering class of 2008) is 51 percent female; 32 percent identify themselves as members of minority groups. In addition to the M.A. degree and certificate programs, the Law School offers Master of Laws (LL.M.) degrees in financial services law, real estate, and taxation.

It is the policy of New York Law School not to discriminate in its educational programs, admission policies, financial aid programs, employment practices, or other school-sponsored activities because of race, color, ethnicity, ancestry, citizenship, religion, sex, pregnancy, sexual orientation, gender identity, gender expression, national origin, age, disability, HIV/AIDS, predisposing genetic characteristics, marital or parental status, military status, domestic violence victim status, or any other classification protected by local, state, or federal law ("Protected Classification"). The placement facilities of the School are available only to employers whose practices are consistent with this policy. (In the wake of the 2006 U.S. Supreme Court decision affirming the Solomon Amendment, the faculty of New York Law School voted on March 27, 2006 to suspend the School's ban on military recruiting on campus.)

New York Law School complies with the Americans with Disabilities Act of 1990 and with Section 504 of the Rehabilitation Act of 1973 as amended. The Law School's Office of Student Life and Office of Academic Affairs formulate general policy on disability issues and make decisions on individual accommodation requests.

Location

New York Law School is located in the heart of Manhattan's TriBeCa district—home of the city's legal, government, and corporate headquarters, as well as a thriving cultural scene. In addition, New York Law School's first-rate campus has evolved to meet the changing needs of its students. In spring 2009, the School opened a new, state-of-the-art academic building that has nearly doubled the size of the campus. The glass-enclosed, 235,000-square-foot building extends five stories above ground and four below. With this sleek new facility, combined with the School's existing three structures, the campus reflects the Law School's past and future, symbolizing the growth and renewal of TriBeCa and all of lower Manhattan. The new building is almost exclusively student-centered, with classrooms, lounges, study rooms, dining facilities, and the library all housed within the building's central core. Students attend classes in rooms designed to maximize teaching and learning opportunities, with cutting-edge technology, top-notch lighting and acoustics, and tiered seating that promotes the open exchange of ideas.

The Law School

New York Law School, one of the oldest independent law schools in the United States, was founded in 1891 by the faculty, students, and alumni of Columbia College Law School, led by their founding dean, Theodore Dwight, a major figure in the history of legal education. In 1894, the Law School established one of the nation's first evening divisions to provide a flexible alternative to full-time legal studies to those in the workforce or with family obligations.

From its inception, New York Law School's lower Manhattan location, in the midst of the country's largest concentration of government agencies, courts, law firms, banks, corporate headquarters, and securities exchanges, has made immersion in the legal life of a great city an essential part of the School's identity and curriculum.

The Law School offers a course of study leading to the J.D. degree through full-time day and part-time evening divisions. It offers a J.D./M.B.A., with Baruch College, City University of New York; and joint bachelor's/J.D. programs with Stevens Institute of Technology, Adelphi University, New England College, and Southern Vermont College. In fall 2003 the Law School began offering the Master of Laws (LL.M.) in taxation. In 2009, the School also began offering a Master of Arts degree in mental disability law studies, a certificate in advanced mental disability law studies, an LL.M. in real estate, and an LL.M. in financial services Law.

Applying

Priority consideration is given to applications received and completed by the following dates: December 1, 2010 for spring 2011admission; April 29, 2011 for summer 2011 admission; and June 30, 2011 for fall 2011 admission. Applications received or completed after these priority deadlines are considered only if space is available. Decision notifications generally are made within one month of the receipt of a completed application. These deadlines and decision time frames also apply to transfer applications.

All candidates for the M.A. in mental disability law studies must have earned, at a minimum, an undergraduate degree from a qualifying institution prior to enrollment in the online mental disability law program. Applicants generally must have the equivalent of a B average in their undergraduate careers or in subsequent graduate work; however, applicants whose GPA is less than a 3.0 are considered on a case-by-case basis if their resumes or curricula vitae indicate a significant amount of professional experience in the field. Candidates who have completed any part of their education outside the United States may satisfy this degree requirement on the basis of an equivalent degree earned in an international jurisdiction. Applications for certification and evaluation requirements are posted on the New York Law School Web site at http://www.nyls.edu/mdl.

Applicants for whom English is a second language and who have not studied law at an institution where English is the primary language of instruction are required to take the Test of English as a Foreign Language (TOEFL). Results of the TOEFL must be forwarded to the Admissions Office for review. The minimum score requirement is 600 on the paper-based exam (with a minimum score of 60 in each of the three sections) and 250 on the computer-based scale (with a minimum score of 25 in each of the subsections.) Applicants taking the Internet-based TOEFL (iBT) must achieve a minimum score of 100, a minimum score of 26 on the reading and listening sections, and a minimum score of 22 on the writing subsection.

Applicants must submit the following: a completed and signed M.A. in mental disability law studies application form, all previous post-secondary education degree transcripts, personal statement, resume or curriculum vitae, two letters of recommendation, and a nonrefundable application fee of $65. No graduate test examination is required for admissions.

Correspondence and Information

The Online Mental Disability Law Program
Master of Arts Degree and Certificate
New York Law School
185 West Broadway
New York, New York 10013-2921
Phone: 212-431-2125
Fax: 212-343-2039
E-mail: mdl@nyls.edu
Web site: http://www.nyls.edu/mdl

Office of Admissions and Financial Aid
New York Law School
185 West Broadway
New York, New York 10013-2921
Phone: 212-431-2888
Fax: 212-966-1522
E-mail: admissions@nyls.edu
Web site: http://www.nyls.edu/mdl

New York Law School

THE FACULTY AND THEIR RESEARCH

Michael L. Perlin, Professor of law and director of the online mental disability law program and the International Mental Disability Law Reform Project of the Law School's Justice Action Center. He holds teaching appointments as adjunct professor of psychiatry and law at the University of Rochester Medical Center and at NYU School of Medicine. He is a former director of the Division of Mental Health Advocacy in the New Jersey Department of the Public Advocate, and the former deputy public defender in charge of the Mercer County Office of the Public Defender. Professor Perlin now serves on the board of advisors of Mental Disabilities Rights International and on the board of directors of the International Academy of Law and Mental Health. In conjunction with Mental Disability Rights International, a Washington, D.C.–based human rights advocacy organization, he has presented mental disability law training workshops in Hungary, Estonia, Latvia, Bulgaria, and Uruguay. Recently, he has been a visiting fellow at the European University Institute-Law in Florence, Italy; a visiting professor at Abo Akademi University/Turku University Law School in Turku, Finland; and a visiting scholar at Hebrew University in Jerusalem, Israel. Previously, Professor Perlin was an adjunct professor of law and psychology at the California School of Professional Psychology in Fresno, California; the Pfizer Distinguished Visiting Professor at Wright State University School of Medicine; and the Ida Beem Distinguished Visiting Scholar at the University of Iowa Law School and Medical College. Professor Perlin is the creator of the first Internet-based mental disability law courses to be offered by an American law school. International sections of survey of mental disability law, New York Law School's initial online course, have been offered in Japan and Nicaragua; a section of the international course has been offered in Finland. Professor Perlin's three-volume treatise, *Mental Disability Law, Civil and Criminal*, won the 1990 Walter Jeffords Writing Prize and has since been expanded into a five-volume second edition that was the recipient of the 2003 Otto Walter Writing Prize. His book *The Jurisprudence of the Insanity Defense* won the Manfred Guttmacher Award of the American Psychiatric Association and the American Academy of Psychiatry and Law as the best book of the year in law and forensic psychiatry in 1994–95. He has also written a one-volume treatise on mental health law, *Law and Mental Disability*, and has published a casebook, *Mental Disability Law: Cases and Materials*, that is now in its second edition. Another book, *The Hidden Prejudice: Mental Disability on Trial*, was published in 2000 as part of the American Psychological Association Press's Law, Society, and Psychology series, and also received the Otto Walter Writing Prize. Professor Perlin's *The Essentials of New York Mental Health Law* was published in 2003. His latest casebooks are *International Human Rights and Comparative Mental Disability Law* (2006) and *Lawyering Skills in the Representation of Persons with Mental Disabilities* (2006). He has written more than 175 articles on all aspects of mental disability law. In 1988, Professor Perlin was given the American Academy of Psychiatry and Law's Amicus Award. He graduated *magna cum laude* from Rutgers University and from Columbia University Law School, where he was a Harlan Fiske Stone Scholar.

Adjunct Faculty

Pamela S. Cohen, Adjunct Professor; J.D., Columbia, 1987. Private practice and court-appointed criminal appellate counsel.

Heather Cucolo, Adjunct Professor; J.D., New York Law, 2003.

Bruce David, Adjunct Professor; D.O., Southeastern College of Osteopathic Medicine, 1988; J.D., New York Law, 1992. Director of Forensic Psychiatry, Nassau University Medical Center.

Henry A. Dlugacz, Adjunct Professor; M.S.W., Hunter, J.D., New York Law, 1991. Attorney and expert consultant, private practice.

Deborah Dorfman, Adjunct Professor; M.A., NYU, 1989; J.D., New York Law, 1992. Senior Counsel, NYC Law Department, Office of the Corporate Counsel.

Richard Friedman, Adjunct Professor; M.S.W., Michigan; J.D., Rutgers.

Michelle Galietta, Adjunct Professor, Ph.D., Fordham, 1994. Director of Ph.D. program in forensic psychology, Director of Clinical Training, and associate professor, John Jay College.

Sarah Kerr, Adjunct Professor; J.D., Pittsburgh, 1987. Attorney, Prisoner's Rights Project, Legal Aid Society.

Shelley Mitchell, Adjunct Professor.

Patrick Reilly, Adjunct Professor.

Beth Ribet, Adjunct Professor.

Andrea Risoli, Adjunct Professor; J.D., New York Law, 2000. Sole practitioner.

David Shapiro, Adjunct Professor; Ph.D., Michigan, 1972. Associate professor of psychology, Center for Psychological Studies, Nova Southeastern University.

Eva Szeli, Adjunct Professor; Ph.D., Miami, 1994; J.D., Miami, 1999.

Karen Talley, Adjunct Professor; J.D., New York Law, 1995. Staff attorney, Disability Law Center, Boston.

New York Law School's brand-new, state-of-the-art academic building, which extends five stories above ground and four below.

PACE LAW SCHOOL
P A C E   U N I V E R S I T Y

PACE LAW SCHOOL

Programs of Study

The hallmarks of Pace Law School include experiential learning, faculty mentoring, rigorous skills training, and cutting-edge, world-class programs. The curriculum at Pace Law School is designed to transform law students into competent and ethical lawyers who can hit the ground running and can make a difference by improving society. With its intimate setting and student-centered focus, Pace Law is dedicated to excellence in teaching. The majority of classes have fewer than 35 students, which enables close faculty-student relationships. Deans, administrators, and faculty members maintain an open-door policy for students. Students participate actively in formulating law school policy through the Student Bar Association and by serving on most faculty committees.

Pace Law School attracts highly qualified students from across the country and around the world. The School offers programs of study leading to the Juris Doctor (J.D.), Master of Laws (LL.M.), and Doctor of Juridical Science (S.J.D.) degrees. There are also joint-degree and certificate program options. Students who wish to obtain the J.D. degree may choose to receive a certificate of specialization in one of two areas: environmental law or international law. Other concentrations include business law, commercial law, constitutional law, criminal law, employment law, family law, health law, intellectual property law, litigation, public interest and advocacy law, real estate and land-use law, and taxation. The joint program options allow students to work toward a degree in law while earning an M.P.A. degree from Pace's Dyson College of Arts and Sciences, an M.B.A. degree from Pace's Lubin School of Business, a joint J.D./M.E.M. degree with the Yale University School of Forestry and Environmental Studies, a J.D./M.A. degree with Sarah Lawrence College in women's studies, or a J.D./M.S. degree with Bard College Center for Environmental Policy.

Pace Law School's signature programs include the renowned Environmental Law, International Law, Criminal Law, and Public Interest Law programs, as well as unique concentrations in fields such as animal rights. The Environmental Law Program was one of the first in the country and consistently ranks as one of the best in the country in terms of academic, clinical, and other opportunities available.

Students may obtain the Master of Laws in environmental law (including new specialized tracks in climate change, and land use and sustainable development), and the Doctor of Juridical Science in environmental law.

The LL.M. in comparative legal studies is available for graduates of law schools outside the U.S. and is designed to meet the specific needs of students who want to obtain a degree in law within the U.S. that they can apply wherever they might practice. This degree can also satisfy the requirements for taking the New York State bar exam.

Students who wish to gain some international experience may also participate in the spring-semester London Law Program, the summer-semester Human Rights in Action Program at an international war crimes tribunal, or the summer International Commercial Law Externship at a foreign law firm or corporation. All three involve living, studying, and working abroad.

A mandatory first-year moot court competition is part of the First Year Legal Skills curriculum. Pace Law also competes in several interscholastic moot court competitions, including the Willem C. Vis International Commercial Arbitration Moot in Vienna. Team members are selected by professors on the basis of writing ability and oral presentation skills. The School hosts the National Environmental Moot Court Competition, the largest of its kind in the country, and the International Criminal Moot Court Competition. Pace Law also sponsors an intraschool moot, which culminates in the Grand Moot Competition each spring.

Pace Law School publishes three law reviews, the *Pace Law Review*, the *Pace Environmental Law Review*, and the *Pace International Law Review*. Admission to the reviews is based upon academic standing and a writing competition. Students also have the opportunity to work on the *Journal of Court Innovation*, a joint project of the New York State Judicial Institute (housed on the Pace Law campus), the Center for Court Innovation, and Pace Law School, to promote innovation in the courts.

Research Facilities

First-year students receive formal instruction in LexisNexis and Westlaw. Additional instruction on advanced research techniques and on research in specialized areas of law is always available. The Law Library's twenty-two computer terminals provide access to word processing and e-mail and give students free access to the information in the LexisNexis and Westlaw databases, CD-ROMs, and other Internet-based databases to which the library subscribes. In addition, the entire library facility provides wireless access to the Law School computer network.

Financial Aid

Pace Law School awards scholarships to qualified students on the basis of academic merit, leadership and work experience, community service, and financial need. A variety of scholarships are available to first-year law students, ranging from partial to full tuition. A comprehensive aid program has been developed that includes grants, employment, scholarships, and loans. Pace Law School generally dedicates over $4 million in scholarships and grants to law students annually.

Living and Housing Costs

Pace Law School offers on-campus housing for law students in Dannat Hall, located on the White Plains campus near the Law Library and an on-campus dining facility. Dannat Hall is a five-story building equipped with a kitchen, laundry room, recreation room, and weight room. Furnished single rooms were available at the rate of $6310 per semester, or $12,620 for the 2010–11 academic year. A variety of off-campus housing is available in White Plains and the surrounding area. The Admissions Office maintains a list of off-campus housing to assist Pace Law students, as well as a list of students interested in sharing apartments.

Student Group

The fall 2010 class consisted of 238 full-time day students, 5 part-time day students, and 29 part-time evening students; 52 percent of the students were women and 15 percent were members of minority groups. The average age of full-time students was 24, and the average age of part-time students was 28. The average LSAT score and GPA for students offered admission were 156 and 3.4, respectively. The inaugural January class of 2010 consisted of 30 students.

Student Outcomes

The first-time New York State bar passage rate for the 2009 graduates was 86 percent. In a survey of the class of 2009, 94.3 percent of the class was employed or pursuing an advanced degree within nine months of graduation. The Center for Career Development actively solicits law job listings and career opportunities for part-time and summer positions for students, and permanent positions for graduates. The center works closely with alumni and legal employers to expand career opportunities for students and assist alumni in their own midcareer lateral job searches. All job listings for students and alumni, as well as important career information, are maintained on the center's dedicated Web site. The Center for Career Development conducts a fall on-campus interview program for large-firm and government employers and a spring on-campus interview program for smaller to medium-sized law firms and public interest organizations. The Center for Career Development also hosts its own winter career fair, which is hugely popular with students and area employers. The center also administers more than forty career panels and programs each academic year, including a videotaped mock interview program, an intensive interview preparation workshop, an alumni mentorship program, a series on professionalism, and practice-area presentations by faculty members, alumni, and prominent practitioners.

In a recent survey of Pace Law School graduates, students had chosen the following areas of practice: law firm private practice, 42.3 percent; business, 18.1 percent; academic, 17.7 percent; government, 9.8 percent; judicial clerkships, 6 percent; and public interest, 5.1 percent.

Location

Pace Law School is located at Pace University's White Plains campus in Westchester County, New York, just 25 miles from New York City. The spacious 12-acre campus offers a combination of historic and modern buildings as well as the Judicial Institute of the State of New York. White Plains and surrounding Westchester County are home to a number of national corporations, law firms, government agencies, and county, state, and federal courts. Pace Law's location creates the ideal setting for clinical, externship, and career opportunities for students.

The University and The Law School

Pace University is a comprehensive, independent, urban, and suburban New York institution that offers a wide range of academic and professional programs at the graduate and undergraduate levels. Pace considers teaching and learning to be its highest goals. In recognizing that educational leadership implies broadening obligations, the University has become increasingly attentive to integrating scholarship and service with excellent teaching. Pace's commitment to the individual needs of its students is at the heart of its teaching mission. By offering access and opportunity to qualified men and women, Pace embraces persons of diverse talents, interests, experiences, and origins who have the will to learn and the desire to participate in University life.

Pace Law School features wireless networked classrooms, a law library, a cafeteria, an activities center, student housing, and on-site parking. It offers more than thirty-three organizations in which students can participate. Available activities include professional organizations, minority student groups, issue-centered organizations, political groups, social action groups, religious groups, a student bar association, and a student newspaper.

Applying

To apply for admission to Pace Law School, students should complete the online application. Students may submit the application for admission through the Law School Admission Council (http://www.lsac.org).

Correspondence and Information

Office of Admissions
Pace Law School
78 North Broadway
White Plains, New York 10603
Phone: 914-422-4210
Fax: 914-989-8714
E-mail: admissions@law.pace.edu
Web site: http://www.law.pace.edu

Pace University

THE FACULTY

The primary goal of the faculty at Pace Law School is to produce a high-quality educational experience for the students. The emphasis on teaching is reflected in the time devoted to class preparation and is notable in the faculty's commitment to being accessible to students outside of class. Professors make a point of being on campus at least four days a week, and an open-door policy prevails.

The majority of faculty members have had significant careers in legal practice prior to becoming legal educators. Their experience in law firms, as corporate counsel, and as federal and state regulators adds important perspectives to the theoretical principles of law.

Horace Anderson, J.D., Pennsylvania.
Barbara Atwell, J.D., Columbia.
Noa Ben-Asher, LL.B., Bar-Ilan (Israel); LL.M., NYU; J.S.D., NYU.
Adele Bernhard, J.D., NYU.
Jay Carlisle, J.D., California, Davis.
David Cassuto, J.D., Berkeley.
Luis Chiesa, LL.M., Columbia.
David Cohen, LL.M., Yale.
Karl Coplan, J.D., Columbia.
Bridget Crawford, J.D., Pennsylvania.
Don Doernberg, J.D., Columbia.
David Dorfman, J.D., Chicago.
Linda Fentiman, J.D., SUNY at Buffalo; LL.M,, Harvard.
James Fishman, J.D., NYU.
Margaret Flint, J.D., Columbia.
Leslie Yalof Garfield, J.D., Florida.
Bennett Gershman, J.D., NYU.
Steven Goldberg, J.D., Minnesota.
Shelby Green, J.D., Georgetown.
Alexander Greenwalt, J.D., Columbia.
Lissa Griffin, B.A., Michigan.
Jill Gross, J.D., Harvard.
John Humbach, J.D., Ohio State.
Ronald Jensen, LL.B., Harvard.
Irene Johnson, J.D., Columbia.
Janet Johnson, J.D., Drake; LL.M., Virginia.
R. F. Kennedy Jr., J.D., Virginia; LL.M., Pace.
Andrew Lund, J.D., NYU.
Thomas McDonnell, J.D., Fordham.
Randolph McLaughlin, J.D., Harvard.
Vanessa Merton, J.D., NYU.
Jeffrey Miller, LL.B., Harvard.
Gary Munneke, J.D., Texas.
Michael Mushlin, J.D., Northwestern.
Marie Newman, J.D., Rutgers.
John Nolon, J.D., Michigan.
Richard Ottinger, LL.B., Harvard.
Ann Powers, J.D., Georgetown.
Nicholas Robinson, J.D., Columbia.
Audrey Rogers, J.D., St. John's (New York).
Darren Rosenblum, J.D., Pennsylvania.
Michelle Simon, J.D., Syracuse.
Merril Sobie, J.D., NYU.
Ralph Stein, J.D., Hofstra.
Emily Waldman, J.D., Harvard.
Gayl Westerman, J.D., Pace; LL.M., Yale; J.S.D., Yale.

ACADEMIC AND PROFESSIONAL PROGRAMS IN LIBRARY AND INFORMATION STUDIES

Section 33
Library and Information Studies

This section contains a directory of institutions offering graduate work in library and information studies, followed by in-depth entries submitted by institutions that chose to prepare detailed program descriptions. Additional information about programs listed in the directory but not augmented by an in-depth entry may be obtained by writing directly to the dean of a graduate school or chair of a department at the address given in the directory.

For programs offering related work, see also in this book *Education*. *In another guide in this series:*
> **Graduate Programs in Engineering & Applied Sciences**
> See *Computer Science and Information Technology*

CONTENTS

Program Directories

Close-Ups

Information Studies

The Catholic University of America, School of Library and Information Science, Washington, DC 20064. Offers MSLS, JD/MSLS, MSLS/MA, MSLS/MS. *Accreditation:* ALA (one or more programs are accredited). Part-time programs available. *Faculty:* 7 full-time (5 women), 10 part-time/adjunct (4 women). *Students:* 22 full-time (19 women), 196 part-time (161 women); includes 40 minority (23 African Americans, 11 Asian Americans or Pacific Islanders, 6 Hispanic Americans), 5 international. Average age 35. 146 applicants, 82% accepted, 77 enrolled. In 2009, 78 master's awarded. *Degree requirements:* For master's, comprehensive exam. *Entrance requirements:* For master's, GRE (minimum score 1000) or minimum GPA of 3.0, 3 letters of recommendation. Additional exam requirements/recommendations for international students: Required—TOEFL (minimum score 580 paper-based; 237 computer-based). *Application deadline:* For fall admission, 8/1 priority date for domestic students, 7/15 for international students; for spring admission, 11/1 priority date for domestic students, 10/15 for international students. Applications are processed on a rolling basis. Application fee: $55. Electronic applications accepted. *Expenses:* Contact institution. *Financial support:* Fellowships, research assistantships, teaching assistantships, Federal Work-Study, scholarships/grants, tuition waivers (full and partial), and unspecified assistantships available. Financial award application deadline: 2/1; financial award applicants required to submit FAFSA. *Faculty research:* Digital collections, library and information science education, information design and architecture, cultural heritage information management, information system design and evaluation. Total annual research expenditures: $126,684. *Unit head:* Dr. Ingrid Hsieh-Yee, Acting Dean, 202-319-5085, Fax: 202-319-5574, E-mail: hsiehyee@cua.edu. *Application contact:* Julie Schwing, Director of Graduate Admissions, 202-319-5057, Fax: 202-319-6533, E-mail: cua-admissions@cua.edu.

Central Connecticut State University, School of Graduate Studies, School of Arts and Sciences, Department of Information Design, New Britain, CT 06050-4010. Offers graphic information design (MA). Part-time and evening/weekend programs available. *Faculty:* 4 full-time (3 women). *Students:* 2 full-time (both women), 4 part-time (all women); includes 1 minority (Asian American or Pacific Islander), 1 international. Average age 30. 4 applicants, 25% accepted, 1 enrolled. In 2009, 1 master's awarded. *Degree requirements:* For master's, thesis or alternative. *Entrance requirements:* For master's, portfolio, minimum undergraduate GPA of 3.0. Additional exam requirements/recommendations for international students: Required—TOEFL. *Application deadline:* For fall admission, 5/1 for domestic students; for spring admission, 12/1 for domestic students. Applications are processed on a rolling basis. Application fee: $50. Electronic applications accepted. *Expenses:* Tuition, area resident: Full-time $4662; part-time $440 per credit. Tuition, state resident: full-time $6994; part-time $440 per credit. Tuition, nonresident: full-time $12,988; part-time $440 per credit. Required fees: $3606. One-time fee: $62 part-time. *Financial support:* In 2009–10, 2 students received support, including 2 research assistantships; career-related internships or fieldwork, Federal Work-Study, scholarships/grants, and unspecified assistantships also available. Support available to part-time students. Financial award application deadline: 3/1; financial award applicants required to submit FAFSA. *Unit head:* Prof. Susan Vial, Chair, 860-832-2564. *Application contact:* James Bryant, Department Administrative Coordinator, 860-832-2564.

Claremont Graduate University, Graduate Programs, School of Arts and Humanities, Department of History, Claremont, CA 91711-6160. Offers Africana history (Certificate); American studies and U.S. history (MA, PhD); archival studies (MA); early modern studies (MA, PhD); European studies (MA, PhD); oral history (MA, PhD); MBA/MA; MBA/PhD. *Faculty:* 4 full-time (2 women). *Students:* 69 full-time (31 women), 5 part-time (3 women); includes 13 minority (1 African American, 4 Asian Americans or Pacific Islanders, 8 Hispanic Americans), 2 international. Average age 36. In 2009, 10 master's, 3 doctorates awarded. Terminal master's awarded for partial completion of doctoral program. *Entrance requirements:* For master's and doctorate, GRE General Test. Additional exam requirements/recommendations for international students: Required—TOEFL (minimum score 550 paper-based; 213 computer-based; 80 iBT). *Application deadline:* For fall admission, 2/1 priority date for domestic students. Applications are processed on a rolling basis. Application fee: $60. Electronic applications accepted. *Expenses:* Tuition: Full-time $35,046; part-time $1524 per credit. Required fees: $161 per semester. *Financial support:* Fellowships, research assistantships, Federal Work-Study, institutionally sponsored loans, and scholarships/grants available. Support available to part-time students. Financial award application deadline: 2/15; financial award applicants required to submit FAFSA. *Faculty research:* Intellectual and social history, cultural studies, gender studies, Western history, Chicano history. *Unit head:* Janet Farrell Brodie, Chair, 909-621-8880, Fax: 909-621-8609, E-mail: janet.brodie@cgu.edu. *Application contact:* Susan Hampson, Admissions Coordinator, 909-607-1278, E-mail: humanities@cgu.edu.

Columbia University, School of Continuing Education, Program in Information and Archive Management, New York, NY 10027. Offers MS. Part-time programs available. *Faculty:* 11 part-time/adjunct (5 women). *Students:* 41 part-time (22 women); includes 19 minority (7 African Americans, 4 Asian Americans or Pacific Islanders, 8 Hispanic Americans), 1 international. Average age 36. 77 applicants, 60% accepted, 30 enrolled. *Entrance requirements:* For master's, minimum undergraduate GPA of 3.0. Additional exam requirements/recommendations for international students: Required—American Language Program placement test. *Application deadline:* For fall admission, 4/15 priority date for domestic students. Application fee: $50. Electronic applications accepted. *Financial support:* Institutionally sponsored loans available. Financial award applicants required to submit FAFSA. *Faculty research:* Library science technology, information systems. *Unit head:* Dennis Green, Program Director, 212-854-7436, E-mail: dg30@columbia.edu. *Application contact:* Bryce Weinert, Admissions Adviser, 212-854-9666, E-mail: sce-apply@columbia.edu.

Cornell University, Graduate School, Graduate Fields of Arts and Sciences, Field of Information Science, Ithaca, NY 14853-0001. Offers cognition (PhD); human computer interaction (PhD); information systems (PhD); social aspects of information (PhD). *Faculty:* 35 full-time (10 women). *Students:* 14 full-time (4 women); includes 1 minority (Asian American or Pacific Islander), 6 international. Average age 31. 53 applicants, 9% accepted, 5 enrolled. In 2009, 3 doctorates awarded. *Degree requirements:* For doctorate, comprehensive exam, thesis/dissertation. *Entrance requirements:* For doctorate, GRE General Test, 3 letters of recommendation. Additional exam requirements/recommendations for international students: Required—TOEFL (minimum score 550 paper-based; 213 computer-based; 77 iBT). *Application deadline:* For fall admission, 1/1 for domestic students. Application fee: $70. Electronic applications accepted. *Expenses:* Tuition: Full-time $29,500. Required fees: $70. Full-time tuition and fees vary according to degree level, program and student level. *Financial support:* In 2009–10, 10 students received support, including 1 fellowship with full tuition reimbursement available, 2 research assistantships with full tuition reimbursements available, 2 teaching assistantships with full tuition reimbursements available; institutionally sponsored loans, scholarships/grants, tuition waivers (full and partial), and unspecified assistantships also available. Financial award applicants required to submit FAFSA. *Faculty research:* Digital libraries, game theory, data mining, human-computer interaction, computational linguistics. *Unit head:* Director of Graduate Studies, 607-255-5925. *Application contact:* Graduate Field Assistant, 607-255-5925, E-mail: info@infosci.cornell.edu.

Dalhousie University, Faculty of Management, School of Information Management, Halifax, NS B3H 3J5, Canada. Offers MIM, MLIS, LL B/MLIS, MBA/MLIS, MLIS/MPA, MLIS/MREM. *Accreditation:* ALA (one or more programs are accredited). Part-time programs available. *Faculty:* 5 full-time (3 women), 9 part-time/adjunct (6 women). *Students:* 41 full-time (30 women), 27 part-time (19 women). 59 applicants, 73% accepted. In 2009, 32 master's awarded. *Degree requirements:* For master's, one foreign language, thesis optional. *Entrance requirements:* For master's, resume, interview. Additional exam requirements/recommendations for international students: Required—TOEFL, IELTS, CANTEST, CAEL, or Michigan English Language Assessment Battery. *Application deadline:* For fall admission, 6/1 for domestic and international students. Applications are processed on a rolling basis. Application fee: $70. Electronic applications accepted. *Financial support:* In 2009–10, 25 students received support, including 15 fellowships (averaging $4,560 per year), 1 research assistantship (averaging $1,300 per year); career-related internships or fieldwork and scholarships/grants also available. Financial award application deadline: 3/1. *Faculty research:* Information-seeking behavior, electronic text design, browsing in digital environments, information diffusion among scientists. Total annual research expenditures: $55,140. *Unit head:* Dr. Fiona Black, Director, 902-494-3656, Fax: 902-494-2451, E-mail: sim@dal.ca. *Application contact:* Joann Watson, MLIS Program Coordinator, 902-494-2471, Fax: 902-494-2451, E-mail: mlis@dal.ca.

Dominican University, Graduate School of Library and Information Science, River Forest, IL 60305-1099. Offers library and information science (MLIS, PhD); special studies (CSS); MBA/MLIS; MLIS/M Div; MLIS/MA; MLIS/MM. *Accreditation:* ALA (one or more programs are accredited). Part-time and evening/weekend programs available. Postbaccalaureate distance learning degree programs offered (minimal on-campus study). *Faculty:* 16 full-time (10 women), 24 part-time/adjunct (17 women). *Students:* 162 full-time (119 women), 363 part-time (299 women); includes 70 minority (22 African Americans, 3 American Indian/Alaska Native, 14 Asian Americans or Pacific Islanders, 31 Hispanic Americans). Average age 34. In 2009, 201 master's awarded. *Entrance requirements:* For master's, minimum GPA of 3.0, GRE General Test, or MAT. Additional exam requirements/recommendations for international students: Required—TOEFL. *Application deadline:* For fall admission, 6/1 priority date for domestic students; for winter admission, 3/1 priority date for domestic students; for spring admission, 10/1 priority date for domestic students. Applications are processed on a rolling basis. Application fee: $25. *Expenses:* Contact institution. *Financial support:* Fellowships, research assistantships, career-related internships or fieldwork, Federal Work-Study, scholarships/grants, and tuition waivers (partial) available. Support available to part-time students. Financial award application deadline: 4/15; financial award applicants required to submit FAFSA. *Faculty research:* Productivity and the information environment, bibliometrics, library history, subject access, library materials and services for children. *Unit head:* Dr. Susan Roman, Dean, 708-524-6986, Fax: 708-524-6657, E-mail: sroman@dom.edu.

Drexel University, The iSchool at Drexel, College of Information Science and Technology, Master of Science in Information Systems Program, Philadelphia, PA 19104-2875. Offers MSIS. Part-time and evening/weekend programs available. Postbaccalaureate distance learning degree programs offered (no on-campus study). *Faculty:* 34 full-time (19 women), 24 part-time/adjunct (9 women). *Students:* 21 full-time (9 women), 116 part-time (36 women); includes 26 minority (12 African Americans, 9 Asian Americans or Pacific Islanders, 5 Hispanic Americans), 12 international. Average age 33. 99 applicants, 55% accepted, 37 enrolled. In 2009, 40 master's awarded. *Entrance requirements:* For master's, GRE General Test. Additional exam requirements/recommendations for international students: Required—TOEFL (minimum score 600 paper-based; 250 computer-based; 100 iBT). *Application deadline:* For fall admission, 8/1 for domestic and international students; for spring admission, 2/1 for domestic and international students. Applications are processed on a rolling basis. Electronic applications accepted. *Expenses:* Contact institution. *Financial support:* In 2009–10, 25 students received support, including 22 fellowships with partial tuition reimbursements available (averaging $225 per year); institutionally sponsored loans, scholarships/grants, and fellowships also available. Support available to part-time students. Financial award applicants required to submit FAFSA. *Faculty research:* Information retrieval/information visualization/bibliometrics, human-computer interaction, digital libraries, databases, text/data mining. Total annual research expenditures: $2 million. *Unit head:* Dr. David E. Fenske, Dean and Isaac L. Auerbach Professor of Information Science, 215-895-2475, Fax: 215-895-6378, E-mail: fenske@drexel.edu. *Application contact:* Matthew Lechtenberg, Graduate Admissions Manager, 215-895-1951, Fax: 215-895-2303, E-mail: ml333@drexel.edu.

Emporia State University, School of Graduate Studies, School of Library and Information Management, Program in Library and Information Management, Emporia, KS 66801-5087. Offers MLS, PhD, Certificate. Part-time and evening/weekend programs available. Postbaccalaureate distance learning degree programs offered (minimal on-campus study). *Faculty:* 5 full-time (4 women), 1 part-time/adjunct (0 women). *Students:* 22 full-time (16 women), 304 part-time (248 women); includes 29 minority (6 African Americans, 1 American Indian/Alaska Native, 13 Asian Americans or Pacific Islanders, 9 Hispanic Americans), 5 international. 121 applicants, 81% accepted, 86 enrolled. In 2009, 119 master's, 5 doctorates, 15 other advanced degrees awarded. *Entrance requirements:* For master's, GRE. Additional exam requirements/recommendations for international students: Required—TOEFL (minimum score 520 paper-based; 133 computer-based; 68 iBT). *Application deadline:* For fall admission, 8/15 priority date for domestic students. Applications are processed on a rolling basis. Application fee: $30 ($75 for international students). Electronic applications accepted. *Expenses:* Tuition, state resident: full-time $4154; part-time $173 per credit hour. Tuition, nonresident: full-time $12,864; part-time $536 per credit hour. Required fees: $948; $58 per credit hour. Tuition and fees vary according to campus/location. *Financial support:* In 2009–10, 6 research assistantships (averaging $7,059 per year), 4 teaching assistantships (averaging $7,059 per year) were awarded; Federal Work-Study, institutionally sponsored loans, and unspecified assistantships also available. Financial award application deadline: 3/15; financial award applicants required to submit FAFSA. *Unit head:* Dr. Gwen Alexander, Dean, School of Library and Information Management, 620-341-5203, E-mail: galexan1@emporia.edu. *Application contact:* Candace Boardman, Director, Kansas MLS Program, 620-341-6159, E-mail: cboardma@emporia.edu.

Florida State University, The Graduate School, School of Library and Information Studies, Tallahassee, FL 32306-2100. Offers library and information studies (MA). *Accreditation:* ALA (one or more programs are accredited). Part-time and evening/weekend programs available. Postbaccalaureate distance learning degree programs offered (no on-campus study). *Faculty:* 31 full-time (17 women), 13 part-time/adjunct (6 women). *Students:* 47 full-time (31 women), 716 part-time (534 women); includes 149 minority (74 African Americans, 4 American Indian/Alaska Native, 23 Asian Americans or Pacific Islanders, 48 Hispanic Americans), 47 international. Average age 35. 420 applicants, 77% accepted, 228 enrolled. In 2009, 243 master's, 4 doctorates, 3 other advanced degrees awarded. *Degree requirements:* For master's, thesis optional, minimum GPA of 3.0, 36 hours; for doctorate, comprehensive exam, thesis/dissertation, dissertation defense, manuscript clearance, minimum GPA of 3.0; for Specialist, thesis optional, culminating paper. *Entrance requirements:* For master's, GRE (minimum combined score: 1000) or minimum GPA of 3.0 on last 2 years of baccalaureate degree, resume, statement of goals, two letters of recommendation, two official transcripts from every college-level institution attended; for doctorate, GRE (minimum combined score: 1200), minimum GPA of 3.0 on last degree program, resume, 3 letters of recommendation, personal/goals statement, writing sample, brief digital video, two official transcripts from all college-level institutions attended; for Specialist, GRE (minimum combined score 1000), minimum graduate GPA of 3.2, resume, 3 letters of recommendation, writing sample. Additional exam requirements/recommendations for international students: Required—TOEFL (minimum score 585 paper-based; 94 iBT), IELTS (minimum score 6.5). *Application deadline:* For fall admission, 6/1 priority date for domestic and international students; for spring admission, 11/1 for domestic and international students. Applications are processed on a rolling basis. Application fee: $30. Electronic applications accepted. *Expenses:* Contact institution. *Financial support:* In 2009–10, 170 students received support, including 11 fellowships with full tuition reimbursements available, 88 research assistantships with full tuition reimbursements available, 69 teaching assistantships with full tuition reimbursements available; career-related internships or fieldwork, Federal Work-Study, scholarships/grants, health care benefits, and unspecified assistantships also available. Financial award application deadline: 3/1; financial award applicants required to submit FAFSA. *Faculty research:* Needs assessment, information policy, usability analysis, human information behavior, youth services. Total annual research expenditures: $1.6 million. *Unit head:* Dr. Corinne Jorgensen, Director/Associate Dean, 850-644-8126, Fax: 850-644-9763, E-mail: corinne.jorgensen@cci.fsu.edu. *Application contact:* Delores Bryant, Graduate Program Assistant, 850-645-3280, Fax: 850-644-9763, E-mail: delores.bryant@cci.fsu.edu.

Indiana University Bloomington, School of Library and Information Science, Bloomington, IN 47405-3907. Offers MIS, MLS, PhD, Sp LIS, JD/MLS, MIS/MA, MLS/MA, MPA/MIS, MPA/MLS. *Accreditation:* ALA (one or more programs are accredited). Part-time programs available. *Faculty:* 16 full-time (7 women). *Students:* 263 full-time (189 women), 82 part-time (49 women); includes 24 minority (8 African Americans, 1 American Indian/Alaska Native, 8 Asian Americans or Pacific Islanders, 7 Hispanic Americans), 38 international. Average age 29. 305 applicants, 84% accepted, 117 enrolled. In 2009, 162 master's, 1 doctorate, 3 other advanced degrees awarded. *Degree requirements:* For doctorate, thesis/dissertation. *Entrance requirements:* For master's and doctorate, GRE General Test, 3 letters of reference. Additional exam requirements/recommendations for international students: Required—TOEFL (minimum score 600 paper-based; 250 computer-based; 100 iBT). *Application deadline:* For fall admission, 5/15 priority date for domestic students, 12/1 priority date for international students; for spring admission, 10/15 priority date for domestic students, 9/1 priority date for international students. Applications are processed on a rolling basis. Application fee: $55 ($65 for international students). Electronic applications accepted. *Expenses:* Contact institution. *Financial support:* Fellowships with full and partial tuition reimbursements, research assistantships with full and partial tuition reimbursements, career-related internships or fieldwork, Federal Work-Study, institutionally sponsored loans, scholarships/grants, tuition waivers (partial), and unspecified assistantships available. Support available to part-time students. Financial award application deadline: 1/15. *Faculty research:* Scholarly communication, interface design, library and management policy, computer-mediated communication, information retrieval. *Unit head:* Dr. Blaise Cronin, Dean, 812-855-2848, Fax: 812-855-6166, E-mail: bcronin@indiana.edu. *Application contact:* Rhonda Spencer, Director of Admissions, 812-855-2018, Fax: 812-855-6166, E-mail: slis@indiana.edu.

Long Island University, C.W. Post Campus, College of Information and Computer Science, Palmer School of Library and Information Science, Brookville, NY 11548-1300. Offers archives and records management (Certificate); information studies (PhD); library and information science (MS); library media specialist (MS); public library management (Certificate). *Accreditation:* ALA (one or more programs are accredited). Part-time and evening/weekend programs available. Postbaccalaureate distance learning degree programs offered (minimal on-campus study). *Degree requirements:* For master's, thesis optional, internship; for doctorate, thesis/dissertation, qualifying exam. *Entrance requirements:* For master's, GRE or MAT, minimum undergraduate GPA of 3.0, resume. Electronic applications accepted. *Faculty research:* Information retrieval, digital libraries, scientometric and infometric studies, preservation/archiving and electronic records.

Long Island University, Westchester Graduate Campus, Program in Library and Information Science, Purchase, NY 10577. Offers MS. Part-time and evening/weekend programs available.

Louisiana State University and Agricultural and Mechanical College, Graduate School, School of Library and Information Science, Baton Rouge, LA 70803. Offers MLIS. *Accreditation:* ALA. Part-time and evening/weekend programs available. Postbaccalaureate distance learning degree programs offered (no on-campus study). *Faculty:* 10 full-time (7 women). *Students:* 58 full-time (43 women), 101 part-time (87 women); includes 19 minority (9 African Americans, 4 Asian Americans or Pacific Islanders, 6 Hispanic Americans), 4 international. Average age 34. 51 applicants, 90% accepted, 30 enrolled. In 2009, 63 master's awarded. *Degree requirements:* For master's, comprehensive exam, thesis optional. *Entrance requirements:* For master's, GRE General Test, minimum GPA of 3.0. Additional exam requirements/recommendations for international students: Required—TOEFL (minimum score 550 paper-based; 213 computer-based; 79 iBT) or IELTS (minimum score 6.5). *Application deadline:* For fall admission, 1/25 priority date for domestic students, 5/15 for international students; for spring admission, 10/15 for international students. Applications are processed on a rolling basis. Application fee: $50 ($70 for international students). Electronic applications accepted. *Financial support:* In 2009–10, 81 students received support, including 8 research assistantships with partial tuition reimbursements available (averaging $11,512 per year), 10 teaching assistantships with partial tuition reimbursements available (averaging $12,293 per year); fellowships, career-related internships or fieldwork, Federal Work-Study, institutionally sponsored loans, scholarships/grants, health care benefits, and unspecified assistantships also available. Support available to part-time students. Financial award applicants required to submit FAFSA. *Faculty research:* Information retrieval, management, collection development, public libraries. Total annual research expenditures: $22,209. *Unit head:* Dr. Beth M. Paskoff, Dean, 225-578-3158, Fax: 225-578-4581, E-mail: bpaskoff@lsu.edu. *Application contact:* LaToya Joseph, Administrative Assistant, 225-578-3150, Fax: 225-578-4581, E-mail: lcjoseph@lsu.edu.

Mansfield University of Pennsylvania, Graduate Studies, Program in School Library and Information Technologies, Mansfield, PA 16933. Offers library science (M Ed). Part-time and evening/weekend programs available. Postbaccalaureate distance learning degree programs offered. *Faculty:* 3 full-time (2 women), 11 part-time/adjunct (10 women). *Students:* 5 full-time (all women), 226 part-time (206 women); includes 21 minority (13 African Americans, 2 American Indian/Alaska Native, 1 Asian American or Pacific Islander, 5 Hispanic Americans), 1 international. Average age 38. In 2009, 77 master's awarded. *Degree requirements:* For master's, comprehensive exam, thesis optional. *Entrance requirements:* For master's, minimum GPA of 3.0. Additional exam requirements/recommendations for international students: Required—TOEFL (minimum score 550 paper-based; 220 computer-based). *Application deadline:* Applications are processed on a rolling basis. Application fee: $25. Electronic applications accepted. *Expenses:* Contact institution. *Financial support:* In 2009–10, 41 students received support. Unspecified assistantships available. Financial award application deadline: 5/1; financial award applicants required to submit FAFSA. *Unit head:* Cindy Keller, Chair, E-mail: ckeller@mansfield.edu. *Application contact:* Christina Hale, Assistant Director of Enrollment Services/Graduate Admissions, 570-662-4812, Fax: 570-662-4121, E-mail: chale@mansfield.edu.

McGill University, Faculty of Graduate and Postdoctoral Studies, Faculty of Education, School of Information Studies, Montréal, QC H3A 2T5, Canada. Offers MLIS, PhD, Certificate, Diploma. *Accreditation:* ALA (one or more programs are accredited).

Metropolitan State University, College of Management, St. Paul, MN 55106-5000. Offers business administration (MBA); information assurance security (Graduate Certificate); information management (MMIS); MIS generalist (Graduate Certificate); MIS systems analysis and design (Graduate Certificate); nonprofit management (MPNA); project management (Graduate Certificate); public administration (MPNA); systems management (MMIS). Part-time and evening/weekend programs available. *Degree requirements:* For master's, thesis optional, computer language (MMIS). *Entrance requirements:* For master's, GMAT (MBA), resume. Additional exam requirements/recommendations for international students: Required—TOEFL (minimum score 550 paper-based; 213 computer-based). *Expenses:* Tuition, state resident: full-time $5520; part-time $276 per credit hour. Tuition, nonresident: full-time $11,040; part-time $552 per credit hour. Required fees: $209; $10 per credit hour. Tuition and fees vary according to degree level. *Faculty research:* Yugoslav economic system, workers' cooperatives, participative management and job enrichment, global business systems.

North Carolina Central University, Division of Academic Affairs, School of Library and Information Sciences, Durham, NC 27707-3129. Offers MIS, MLS. *Accreditation:* ALA (one or more programs are accredited). Part-time and evening/weekend programs available. *Degree requirements:* For master's, one foreign language, thesis, research paper, or project. *Entrance requirements:* For master's, GRE, 90 hours in liberal arts. Additional exam requirements/recommendations for international students: Required—TOEFL. *Faculty research:* African-American resources, planning and evaluation, analysis of economic and physical resources, geography of information, artificial intelligence.

Pratt Institute, School of Information and Library Science, New York, NY 10011. Offers archives (Adv C); library and information science (MS, Adv C); library media specialist (Adv C); museum libraries (Adv C); JD/MS; MS/MS. *Accreditation:* ALA. Part-time programs available. *Faculty:* 9 full-time (6 women), 27 part-time/adjunct (15 women). *Students:* 143 full-time (118 women), 183 part-time (147 women); includes 51 minority (19 African Americans, 19 Asian

Americans or Pacific Islanders, 13 Hispanic Americans), 4 international. Average age 32. 379 applicants, 90% accepted, 98 enrolled. In 2009, 148 master's awarded. *Degree requirements:* For master's, thesis. *Entrance requirements:* Additional exam requirements/recommendations for international students: Required—TOEFL (minimum score 600 paper-based; 250 computer-based; 100 iBT). *Application deadline:* For fall admission, 1/5 for domestic and international students; for spring admission, 10/1 for domestic and international students. Application fee: $50 ($90 for international students). Electronic applications accepted. *Expenses:* Contact institution. *Financial support:* Career-related internships or fieldwork, Federal Work-Study, institutionally sponsored loans, scholarships/grants, health care benefits, and unspecified assistantships available. Support available to part-time students. Financial award application deadline: 2/1; financial award applicants required to submit FAFSA. *Faculty research:* Development of urban libraries and information centers, medical and law librarianship, information management. *Unit head:* Dr. Tula Giannini, Dean, 212-647-7682, E-mail: giannini@pratt.edu. *Application contact:* Young Hah, Director of Graduate Admissions, 718-636-3683, Fax: 718-399-4242, E-mail: yhah@pratt.edu.

See Close-Up on page 1721.

Queens College of the City University of New York, Division of Graduate Studies, Social Science Division, Graduate School of Library and Information Studies, Flushing, NY 11367-1597. Offers MLS, AC. *Accreditation:* ALA (one or more programs are accredited). Part-time and evening/weekend programs available. *Faculty:* 17 full-time (11 women). *Students:* 52 full-time (37 women), 444 part-time (338 women). 322 applicants, 64% accepted, 166 enrolled. In 2009, 138 master's awarded. *Degree requirements:* For master's, thesis; for AC, thesis optional. *Entrance requirements:* For master's, minimum GPA of 3.0; for AC, master's degree or equivalent. Additional exam requirements/recommendations for international students: Required—TOEFL. *Application deadline:* For fall admission, 4/1 for domestic students; for spring admission, 11/1 for domestic students. Applications are processed on a rolling basis. Application fee: $125. *Expenses:* Tuition, state resident: full-time $7360; part-time $310 per credit. Tuition, nonresident: part-time $575 per credit. One-time fee: $195 full-time; $145.25 part-time. *Financial support:* Career-related internships or fieldwork, Federal Work-Study, institutionally sponsored loans, and tuition waivers (partial) available. Support available to part-time students. Financial award application deadline: 4/1; financial award applicants required to submit FAFSA. *Faculty research:* Multimedia and video studies, ethnicity and librarianship, information science and computer applications. *Unit head:* Dr. Virgil Blake, Director/Chair, 718-997-3790. *Application contact:* Dr. Karen Smith, Graduate Adviser, 718-997-3790, E-mail: karen_smith@qc.edu.

Queen's University at Kingston, School of Graduate Studies and Research, Faculty of Arts and Sciences, Department of Sociology, Kingston, ON K7L 3N6, Canada. Offers communication and Information technology (MA, PhD); feminist sociology (MA, PhD); socio-legal studies (MA, PhD); sociological theory (MA, PhD). Part-time programs available. *Degree requirements:* For master's, thesis; for doctorate, comprehensive exam, thesis/dissertation. *Entrance requirements:* For master's, honors bachelors degree in sociology; for doctorate, honors bachelors degree, masters degree in sociology. Additional exam requirements/recommendations for international students: Required—TOEFL. *Faculty research:* Social change and modernization, social control, deviance and criminology, surveillance.

Rutgers, The State University of New Jersey, New Brunswick, School of Communication, Information and Library Studies, Program in Communication and Information Studies, Piscataway, NJ 08854-8097. Offers MCIS. Part-time programs available. *Entrance requirements:* For master's, GRE General Test. Additional exam requirements/recommendations for international students: Required—TOEFL. Electronic applications accepted. *Faculty research:* Communication processes and systems, information process and systems, human information and communication behavior.

Rutgers, The State University of New Jersey, New Brunswick, School of Communication, Information and Library Studies, Program in Communication, Library and Information Science and Media Studies, Piscataway, NJ 08854-8097. Offers PhD. Part-time programs available. *Degree requirements:* For doctorate, comprehensive exam, thesis/dissertation, qualifying exams. *Entrance requirements:* For doctorate, GRE General Test, proficiency in statistics. Additional exam requirements/recommendations for international students: Required—TOEFL (minimum score 600 paper-based; 250 computer-based). Electronic applications accepted. *Faculty research:* Information science, media studies.

St. Catherine University, Graduate Programs, Program in Library and Information Science, St. Paul, MN 55105. Offers MLIS. Part-time and evening/weekend programs available. *Faculty:* 3 full-time (all women). *Students:* 72 full-time (62 women), 89 part-time (73 women); includes 12 minority (2 African Americans, 5 Asian Americans or Pacific Islanders, 5 Hispanic Americans). Average age 34. 80 applicants, 79% accepted, 39 enrolled. In 2009, 21 master's awarded. *Degree requirements:* For master's, microcomputer competency. *Entrance requirements:* For master's, GRE or MAT, minimum GPA of 3.2 or GRE. Additional exam requirements/recommendations for international students: Required—Michigan English Language Assessment Battery or TOEFL (minimum score 600 paper-based; 250 computer-based; 100 iBT). *Application deadline:* For fall admission, 3/1 for domestic students; for winter admission, 10/1 for domestic students. Application fee: $35. Tuition and fees vary according to program. *Financial support:* In 2009–10, 117 students received support. Institutionally sponsored loans available. Support available to part-time students. Financial award application deadline: 4/1; financial award applicants required to submit FAFSA. *Unit head:* Dr. Deborah Grealy, Director, 651-690-6802. *Application contact:* 651-690-6933, Fax: 651-690-6064.

St. John's University, St. John's College of Liberal Arts and Sciences, Division of Library and Information Science, Queens, NY 11439. Offers MLS, Adv C, MA/MLS, MS/MLS. *Accreditation:* ALA (one or more programs are accredited). Part-time and evening/weekend programs available. *Students:* 39 full-time (30 women), 148 part-time (115 women); includes 40 minority (13 African Americans, 1 American Indian/Alaska Native, 7 Asian Americans or Pacific Islanders, 19 Hispanic Americans), 4 international. Average age 37. 169 applicants, 70% accepted, 63 enrolled. In 2009, 28 master's awarded. *Degree requirements:* For master's, comprehensive exam, residency. *Entrance requirements:* For master's, interview, minimum GPA of 3.0. Additional exam requirements/recommendations for international students: Required—TOEFL (minimum score 500 paper-based; 173 computer-based; 61 iBT), IELTS (minimum score 5.5). *Application deadline:* For fall admission, 5/1 priority date for domestic and international students; for spring admission, 11/1 priority date for domestic and international students. Applications are processed on a rolling basis. Application fee: $70. Electronic applications accepted. *Expenses:* Contact institution. *Financial support:* Research assistantships, career-related internships or fieldwork and scholarships/grants available. Support available to part-time students. Financial award application deadline: 3/1; financial award applicants required to submit FAFSA. *Faculty research:* Indexes and metatags, information use and users, competitive intelligence, knowledge management, database theory, young adult and children services, school media services, archives, oral history. *Unit head:* Dr. Jeffrey Olson, Director, 718-990-5705, E-mail: olsonj@stjohns.edu. *Application contact:* Kathleen Davis, Director of Graduate Admissions, 718-990-2790, Fax: 718-990-5686, E-mail: gradhelp@stjohns.edu.

San Jose State University, Graduate Studies and Research, College of Applied Sciences and Arts, School of Library and Information Science, San Jose, CA 95192-0001. Offers MLIS, PhD. *Accreditation:* ALA (one or more programs are accredited). Part-time and evening/weekend programs available. *Students:* 285 full-time (238 women), 666 part-time (528 women); includes 238 minority (18 African Americans, 7 American Indian/Alaska Native, 126 Asian Americans or Pacific Islanders, 87 Hispanic Americans), 3 international. Average age 36. 361 applicants, 44% accepted, 114 enrolled. In 2009, 437 master's awarded. *Degree requirements:* For master's, comprehensive exam. *Entrance requirements:* Additional exam requirements/recommendations for international students: Required—TOEFL (minimum score 600 paper-based). *Application deadline:* For fall admission, 6/29 for domestic students; for spring admission, 11/30 for domestic students. Applications are processed on a rolling basis. Application fee: $59. Electronic applications accepted. *Financial support:* Career-related internships or fieldwork,

Information Studies

San Jose State University (continued)

Federal Work-Study, and institutionally sponsored loans available. Support available to part-time students. Financial award application deadline: 8/20; financial award applicants required to submit FAFSA. *Faculty research:* Evaluation of information services online, search strategy, organizational behavior. *Unit head:* Dr. Ken Haycock, Director, 408-924-2491, Fax: 408-924-2476. *Application contact:* Dr. Ken Haycock, Director, 408-924-2491, Fax: 408-924-2476.

Simmons College, Graduate School of Library and Information Science, Program in Library and Information Science, Boston, MA 02115. Offers MS, PhD. Part-time and evening/weekend programs available. *Faculty:* 25 full-time (17 women), 34 part-time/adjunct (22 women). *Students:* 17 full-time (12 women), 448 part-time (341 women); includes 30 minority (8 African Americans, 16 Asian Americans or Pacific Islanders, 6 Hispanic Americans), 10 international. Average age 33. 260 applicants, 75% accepted, 105 enrolled. In 2009, 245 master's awarded. *Degree requirements:* For doctorate, comprehensive exam, thesis/dissertation. *Application deadline:* For fall admission, 3/1 for domestic and international students; for spring admission, 9/1 for domestic and international students. Applications are processed on a rolling basis. Application fee: $50. Electronic applications accepted. *Expenses:* Tuition: Part-time $925 per credit hour. Part-time tuition and fees vary according to program. *Faculty research:* Library Leadership, archives and preservation, organization, information use and users, children's literature and youth services. Total annual research expenditures: $253,656. *Unit head:* Dr. Michele V. Cloonan, Dean, 617-521-2806, Fax: 617-521-3192, E-mail: cloonan@simmons.edu. *Application contact:* Sarah Petrakos, Assistant Dean, Admission and Recruitment, 617-521-2868, Fax: 617-521-3192, E-mail: gslisadm@simmons.edu.

Southern Connecticut State University, School of Graduate Studies, School of Communication, Information and Library Science, Department of Information and Library Science, New Haven, CT 06515-1355. Offers library science (MLS); library/information studies (Diploma); JD/MLS; MLS/MA; MLS/MS. Part-time and evening/weekend programs available. Postbaccalaureate distance learning degree programs offered (no on-campus study). *Faculty:* 12 full-time, 5 part-time/adjunct. *Students:* 50 full-time (38 women), 255 part-time (223 women); includes 18 minority (5 African Americans, 10 Asian Americans or Pacific Islanders, 3 Hispanic Americans). 164 applicants, 47% accepted, 62 enrolled. In 2009, 127 master's, 12 other advanced degrees awarded. *Degree requirements:* For master's and Diploma, thesis or alternative. *Entrance requirements:* For master's, GRE General Test, interview, minimum QPA of 2.7, introductory computer science course; for Diploma, master's degree in library science or information science. *Application deadline:* For fall admission, 7/15 priority date for domestic students. Applications are processed on a rolling basis. Application fee: $50. Electronic applications accepted. Tuition and fees vary according to program. *Financial support:* Research assistantships available. Financial award application deadline: 4/15; financial award applicants required to submit FAFSA. *Unit head:* Dr. Chang Suk Kim, Chairperson, 203-392-5191, Fax: 203-392-5780, E-mail: kimc1@southernct.edu. *Application contact:* Dr. Elsie Okobi, Graduate Coordinator, 203-392-5709, E-mail: okobie1@southernct.edu.

Syracuse University, School of Information Studies, Program in Information Management, Syracuse, NY 13244. Offers MS, DPS. Part-time and evening/weekend programs available. Postbaccalaureate distance learning degree programs offered (minimal on-campus study). *Students:* 166 full-time (58 women), 125 part-time (31 women); includes 43 minority (15 African Americans, 4 American Indian/Alaska Native, 15 Asian Americans or Pacific Islanders, 9 Hispanic Americans), 137 international. Average age 30. 534 applicants, 51% accepted, 108 enrolled. In 2009, 98 master's awarded. *Entrance requirements:* For master's, GRE General Test. Additional exam requirements/recommendations for international students: Required—TOEFL (minimum score 100 iBT). *Application deadline:* For fall admission, 2/14 priority date for domestic and international students; for spring admission, 10/15 priority date for domestic and international students. Applications are processed on a rolling basis. Application fee: $75. Electronic applications accepted. *Expenses:* Tuition: Full-time $26,808; part-time $1117 per credit. Required fees: $1024. *Financial support:* Fellowships with tuition reimbursements, research assistantships with tuition reimbursements, teaching assistantships with tuition reimbursements, scholarships/grants and tuition waivers (partial) available. Financial award application deadline: 1/1; financial award applicants required to submit FAFSA. *Unit head:* David Dischiave, Director, 315-443-4681, Fax: 315-443-6886, E-mail: ddischia@syr.edu. *Application contact:* Susan Corieri, Director of Enrollment Management, 315-443-2575, E-mail: ist@syr.edu.

See Close-Up on page 1723.

Universidad del Turabo, Graduate Programs, Programs in Education, Program in Library Service and Information Technology, Gurabo, PR 00778-3030. Offers M Ed. *Students:* 70 full-time (60 women), 31 part-time (26 women); includes 86 Hispanic Americans. Average age 34. 62 applicants, 95% accepted, 43 enrolled. In 2009, 33 master's awarded. *Unit head:* Angela Candelario, Dean, 787-743-7979 Ext. 4126. *Application contact:* Virginia Gonzalez, Admissions Officer, 787-746-3009.

Université de Montréal, Faculty of Arts and Sciences, School of Library and Information Sciences, Montréal, QC H3C 3J7, Canada. Offers information sciences (MIS, PhD). *Accreditation:* ALA (one or more programs are accredited). *Faculty:* 17 full-time (6 women), 7 part-time/adjunct (4 women). *Students:* 140 full-time (95 women), 50 part-time (39 women). 199 applicants, 49% accepted, 89 enrolled. In 2009, 68 master's awarded. *Degree requirements:* For master's, thesis optional. *Entrance requirements:* For master's, interview, master's degree in library and information science or equivalent. *Application deadline:* For fall admission, 2/1 priority date for domestic students; for winter admission, 11/1 priority date for domestic students; for spring admission, 2/1 priority date for domestic students. Application fee: $100. Electronic applications accepted. *Financial support:* Fellowships available. *Unit head:* Cl??ment Arsenault, Director, 514-343-7400, Fax: 514-343-5753, E-mail: clement.arsenault@umontreal.ca. *Application contact:* James Turner, Professor/Responsible for Graduate Studies, 514-343-2454, Fax: 514-343-5753, E-mail: james.turner@umontreal.ca.

University at Albany, State University of New York, College of Computing and Information, Department of Information Studies, Albany, NY 12222-0001. Offers information science (MS, CAS). *Faculty research:* Electronic information across technologies system dynamics modeling archives, records administration.

University at Buffalo, the State University of New York, Graduate School, Graduate School of Education, Department of Library and Information Studies, Buffalo, NY 14260. Offers library and information studies (MLS, Certificate); library and information studies (online) (MLS). *Accreditation:* ALA (one or more programs are accredited). Part-time programs available. Postbaccalaureate distance learning degree programs offered (no on-campus study). *Faculty:* 10 full-time (6 women), 12 part-time/adjunct (7 women). *Students:* 157 full-time (110 women), 103 part-time (72 women); includes 21 minority (6 African Americans, 1 American Indian/Alaska Native, 10 Asian Americans or Pacific Islanders, 4 Hispanic Americans), 2 international. Average age 32. 162 applicants, 98% accepted, 99 enrolled. In 2009, 128 master's, 1 other advanced degree awarded. *Degree requirements:* For master's, thesis optional; for Certificate, thesis. *Entrance requirements:* For master's, minimum GPA of 3.0. Additional exam requirements/recommendations for international students: Required—TOEFL (minimum score 550 paper-based; 213 computer-based; 79 iBT). *Application deadline:* For fall admission, 4/1 priority date for domestic students; for spring admission, 10/15 priority date for domestic students. Applications are processed on a rolling basis. Application fee: $50. Electronic applications accepted. *Financial support:* In 2009–10, 8 fellowships with full tuition reimbursements (averaging $4,000 per year), 4 research assistantships with full tuition reimbursements (averaging $9,000 per year) were awarded; teaching assistantships, career-related internships or fieldwork, Federal Work-Study, institutionally sponsored loans, tuition waivers (full and partial), and unspecified assistantships also available. Support available to part-time students. Financial award application deadline: 3/1; financial award applicants required to submit FAFSA. *Faculty research:* Information-seeking behavior, thesauri, impact of technology, questioning behaviors, educational informatics. Total annual research expenditures: $9,929. *Unit head:* Dr. Dagobert Soergel, Chair, 716-645-2412, Fax: 716-645-3775, E-mail: ub-lis@buffalo.edu. *Application contact:* Sarah Watson, Admissions Advisor, 716-645-2110, Fax: 716-645-7937, E-mail: gse-info@buffalo.edu.

The University of Alabama, Graduate School, College of Communication and Information Sciences, School of Library and Information Studies, Tuscaloosa, AL 35487. Offers book arts (MFA); library and information studies (MLIS, PhD). *Accreditation:* ALA (one or more programs are accredited). Part-time programs available. Postbaccalaureate distance learning degree programs offered (minimal on-campus study). *Faculty:* 10 full-time (4 women), 3 part-time/adjunct (all women). *Students:* 83 full-time (64 women), 186 part-time (141 women); includes 27 minority (14 African Americans, 2 American Indian/Alaska Native, 8 Asian Americans or Pacific Islanders, 3 Hispanic Americans), 3 international. Average age 33. 295 applicants, 39% accepted, 85 enrolled. In 2009, 102 degrees awarded. *Entrance requirements:* For master's, GRE General Test or MAT, minimum GPA of 3.0. Additional exam requirements/recommendations for international students: Required—TOEFL. *Application deadline:* For fall admission, 7/1 priority date for domestic and international students; for spring admission, 11/1 priority date for domestic and international students. Applications are processed on a rolling basis. Application fee: $50 ($60 for international students). Electronic applications accepted. *Expenses:* Tuition, state resident: full-time $7000. Tuition, nonresident: full-time $19,200. *Financial support:* In 2009–10, 64 students received support, including 4 fellowships with tuition reimbursements available (averaging $14,778 per year), 13 research assistantships with full and partial tuition reimbursements available (averaging $4,912 per year), 18 teaching assistantships with full and partial tuition reimbursements available (averaging $4,912 per year); career-related internships or fieldwork, Federal Work-Study, scholarships/grants, and unspecified assistantships also available. Financial award application deadline: 3/20. *Faculty research:* Instructional design, information equity, youth services, rural information services, book history. *Unit head:* Dr. Elizabeth Aversa, Director and Professor, 205-348-4610, Fax: 205-348-3746, E-mail: eaversa@slis.ua.edu. *Application contact:* Dr. Elizabeth Aversa, 205-348-4610, E-mail: eaversa@slis.ua.edu.

University of Alberta, Faculty of Graduate Studies and Research, School of Library and Information Studies, Edmonton, AB T6G 2E1, Canada. Offers MLIS. *Accreditation:* ALA. *Faculty:* 6 full-time (5 women), 12 part-time/adjunct (7 women). *Students:* 76 full-time (65 women), 22 part-time (20 women). Average age 32. 142 applicants, 32% accepted, 42 enrolled. In 2009, 24 master's awarded. *Entrance requirements:* Additional exam requirements/recommendations for international students: Required—TOEFL, Canadian Academic English Language Assessment. *Application deadline:* For fall admission, 7/1 for domestic students, 5/1 for international students. Applications are processed on a rolling basis. Electronic applications accepted. Tuition and fees charges are reported in Canadian dollars. *Expenses:* Tuition, area resident: Full-time $4626 Canadian dollars; part-time $99.72 Canadian dollars per unit. International tuition: $8216 Canadian dollars full-time. Required fees: $3590 Canadian dollars; $99.72 Canadian dollars per unit. $215 Canadian dollars per term. *Financial support:* In 2009–10, 68 students received support, including 12 research assistantships with partial tuition reimbursements available (averaging $3,536 per year); fellowships, career-related internships or fieldwork and scholarships/grants also available. Support available to part-time students. Financial award application deadline: 7/1. *Faculty research:* Intellectual freedom, materials for children and young adults, library classification, multi-media literacy. Total annual research expenditures: $63,000. *Unit head:* Anna Altmann, Acting Director, 780-492-4140, Fax: 403-492-2430, E-mail: anna.altmann@ualberta.ca. *Application contact:* Joanne Hilger, Student Services Administrator, 780-492-4578, Fax: 780-492-2430, E-mail: slis@ualberta.ca.

The University of Arizona, Graduate College, College of Social and Behavioral Sciences, School of Information Resources and Library Science, Tucson, AZ 85721. Offers MA, PhD. *Accreditation:* ALA (one or more programs are accredited). Part-time programs available. *Faculty:* 8 full-time (5 women). *Students:* 101 full-time (74 women), 226 part-time (191 women); includes 21 minority (3 African Americans, 6 American Indian/Alaska Native, 12 Hispanic Americans), 9 international. Average age 36. 22 applicants, 36% accepted, 7 enrolled. In 2009, 121 master's awarded. *Degree requirements:* For master's, proficiency in disk operating system (DOS); for doctorate, thesis/dissertation. *Entrance requirements:* For master's and doctorate, GRE General Test, 3 letters of recommendation, resume. Additional exam requirements/recommendations for international students: Required—TOEFL (minimum score 550 paper-based; 213 computer-based; 79 iBT). *Application deadline:* For spring admission, 9/1 for domestic and international students. Applications are processed on a rolling basis. Application fee: $65. Electronic applications accepted. *Expenses:* Tuition, state resident: full-time $9028. Tuition, nonresident: full-time $24,890. *Financial support:* In 2009–10, 4 research assistantships with full tuition reimbursements (averaging $12,414 per year), 34 teaching assistantships with full tuition reimbursements (averaging $12,970 per year) were awarded; career-related internships or fieldwork, Federal Work-Study, institutionally sponsored loans, scholarships/grants, health care benefits, tuition waivers (full and partial), and unspecified assistantships also available. Financial award application deadline: 3/1. *Faculty research:* Microcomputer applications; quantitative methods systems; information transfer, planning, evaluation, and technology. Total annual research expenditures: $1.1 million. *Unit head:* Dr. Jana Bradley, Director, 520-621-3565, Fax: 520-621-3279, E-mail: janabrad@email.arizona.edu. *Application contact:* Geraldme Fragoso, Program Manager, 520-621-3565, Fax: 520-621-3279, E-mail: gfragoso@email.arizona.edu.

The University of British Columbia, Faculty of Arts, School of Library, Archival and Information Studies, Dual Master of Archival Studies/Master of Library and Information Studies Program, Vancouver, BC V6T 1Z1, Canada. Offers MLIS/MAS. *Entrance requirements:* Additional exam requirements/recommendations for international students: Required—TOEFL (minimum score 600 paper-based; 250 computer-based; 100 iBT). Electronic applications accepted. *Faculty research:* Computer systems/database design, information-seeking behaviour, archives and records management, children's literature and services, digital libraries and archives.

The University of British Columbia, Faculty of Arts, School of Library, Archival and Information Studies, Master of Library and Information Studies Program, Vancouver, BC V6T 1Z1, Canada. Offers MLIS. Part-time programs available. *Degree requirements:* For master's, thesis optional. *Entrance requirements:* For master's, minimum GPA of 3.3 in undergraduate upper-division courses. Additional exam requirements/recommendations for international students: Required—TOEFL (minimum score 600 paper-based; 250 computer-based; 100 iBT). Electronic applications accepted. *Faculty research:* Computer systems/database design; digital libraries; metadata/classification; human-computer interaction; children's literature and services.

The University of British Columbia, Faculty of Arts, School of Library, Archival and Information Studies, PhD Program in Library, Archival and Information Studies, Vancouver, BC V6T 1Z1, Canada. Offers PhD. *Degree requirements:* For doctorate, thesis/dissertation. *Entrance requirements:* For doctorate, GRE, minimum GPA of 3.3 in MAS or MLIS (other master's degrees may be considered). Additional exam requirements/recommendations for international students: Required—TOEFL (minimum score 600 paper-based; 250 computer-based; 100 iBT). Electronic applications accepted. *Faculty research:* Computer systems/database design; library and archival management; archival description and organization; children's literature and youth services; interactive information retrieval.

University of California, Berkeley, Graduate Division, School of Information Management and Systems, Berkeley, CA 94720-1500. Offers MIMS, PhD. *Students:* 98 full-time (34 women); includes 18 minority (3 African Americans, 2 American Indian/Alaska Native, 12 Asian Americans or Pacific Islanders, 1 Hispanic American), 23 international. Average age 31. In 2009, 26 master's, 5 doctorates awarded. *Degree requirements:* For doctorate, thesis/dissertation, qualifying exam. *Entrance requirements:* For master's, GRE General Test, minimum GPA of 3.0, previous course work in java or C programming, 3 letters of recommendation; for doctorate, GRE General Test, minimum GPA of 3.0. Additional exam requirements/recommendations for international students: Required—TOEFL. Application fee: $70 ($90 for international students). *Financial support:* Fellowships, research assistantships, teaching assistantships, unspecified assistantships available. *Faculty research:* Information retrieval research, design and evalu-

ation of information systems, work practice-based design of information systems, economics of information, intellectual property law. *Unit head:* Prof. AnnaLee Saxenian, Dean, 510-642-1464, E-mail: admissions@ischool.berkeley.edu. *Application contact:* Leticia Sanchez, Student Affairs Officer, 510-642-1464, Fax: 510-642-5814, E-mail: admissions@ischool.berkeley.edu.

University of California, Los Angeles, Graduate Division, Graduate School of Education and Information Studies, Department of Information Studies, Los Angeles, CA 90095. Offers archival studies (MLIS); informatics (MLIS); information studies (PhD); library and information science (Certificate); library studies (MLIS); moving image archive studies (MA); MBA/MLIS; MLIS/MA. *Accreditation:* ALA (one or more programs are accredited). *Faculty:* 14 full-time (8 women), 11 part-time/adjunct (10 women). *Students:* 171 full-time (125 women), 29 part-time (20 women); includes 76 minority (8 African Americans, 1 American Indian/Alaska Native, 44 Asian Americans or Pacific Islanders, 23 Hispanic Americans), 4 international. Average age 27. 214 applicants, 54% accepted, 82 enrolled. In 2009, 74 master's, 6 doctorates awarded. Terminal master's awarded for partial completion of doctoral program. *Degree requirements:* For master's, thesis or alternative, professional portfolio; for doctorate, thesis/dissertation, oral and written qualifying exams. *Entrance requirements:* For master's, GRE General Test, previous course work in computer programming and statistics; for doctorate, GRE General Test, previous course work in statistics, 2 samples of research writing in English. Additional exam requirements/recommendations for international students: Required—TOEFL (minimum score 613 paper-based; 220 computer-based; 87 iBT), IELTS (minimum score 7). *Application deadline:* For fall admission, 11/30 for domestic students, 10/30 for international students. Applications are processed on a rolling basis. Application fee: $60 ($80 for international students). Electronic applications accepted. *Financial support:* In 2009–10, 55 students received support, including 37 fellowships (averaging $15,750 per year), 12 research assistantships with partial tuition reimbursements available (averaging $28,600 per year), 6 teaching assistantships with partial tuition reimbursements available (averaging $54,040 per year); career-related internships or fieldwork, Federal Work-Study, institutionally sponsored loans, scholarships/grants, and unspecified assistantships also available. Financial award application deadline: 3/1; financial award applicants required to submit FAFSA. *Faculty research:* Multimedia, digital libraries, archives and electronic records, interface design, information technology and preservation, preservation, access. *Unit head:* Dr. Gregory H. Leazer, Associate Professor and Chair, 310-825-8799, E-mail: gleazer@ucla.edu. *Application contact:* Susan S. Abler, Student Affairs Officer, 310-825-5269, Fax: 310-206-4460, E-mail: abler@gseis.ucla.edu.

University of Denver, University College, Denver, CO 80208. Offers applied communication (MAS, MPS, Certificate); computer information systems (MAS, Certificate); environmental policy and management (MAS, Certificate); geographic information systems (MAS, Certificate); human resource administration (MPS, Certificate); knowledge and information technologies (MAS); liberal studies (MLS, Certificate); modern languages (MLS, Certificate); organizational leadership (MPS, Certificate); security management (Certificate); technology management (MAS, Certificate), including 21st century strategic management (MAS), international markets (MAS), project management (MAS), research and development management (MAS); telecommunications (MAS, Certificate), including broadband (MAS), telecommunications management and policy (MAS), telecommunications technology (MAS), wireless networks (MAS). Part-time and evening/weekend programs available. Postbaccalaureate distance learning degree programs offered (no on-campus study). *Faculty:* 160 part-time/adjunct (64 women). *Students:* 53 full-time (25 women), 984 part-time (551 women); includes 171 minority (72 African Americans, 10 American Indian/Alaska Native, 33 Asian Americans or Pacific Islanders, 56 Hispanic Americans), 75 international. Average age 36. 537 applicants, 96% accepted, 494 enrolled. In 2009, 229 master's, 109 Certificates awarded. *Entrance requirements:* Additional exam requirements/recommendations for international students: Required—TOEFL (minimum score 550 paper-based; 213 computer-based). *Application deadline:* Applications are processed on a rolling basis. Application fee: $75. Electronic applications accepted. *Expenses:* Contact institution. *Financial support:* Applicants required to submit FAFSA. *Unit head:* Dr. James Davis, Dean, 303-871-2291, Fax: 303-871-4047, E-mail: jdavis@du.edu. *Application contact:* Information Contact, 303-871-3155.

University of Hawaii at Manoa, Graduate Division, College of Natural Sciences, Department of Information and Computer Sciences, Library and Information Science Program, Honolulu, HI 96822-2233. Offers advanced library and information science (Graduate Certificate); library and information science (MLI Sc). *Accreditation:* ALA (one or more programs are accredited). Part-time programs available. *Degree requirements:* For master's, comprehensive exam, thesis optional. *Entrance requirements:* For master's, GRE General Test. Additional exam requirements/recommendations for international students: Required—TOEFL (minimum score 600 paper-based; 250 computer-based). Electronic applications accepted. *Expenses:* Tuition, state resident: full-time $8900; part-time $372 per credit. Tuition, nonresident: full-time $21,400; part-time $898 per credit. Required fees: $207 per semester. *Faculty research:* Information behavior, evaluation of electronic information sources, online learning, history of libraries, information literacy.

University of Illinois at Urbana–Champaign, Graduate College, Graduate School of Library and Information Science, Champaign, IL 61820. Offers bioinformatics: library and information science (MS); library and information science (MS, PhD, CAS); library and information science: digital libraries (CAS). *Accreditation:* ALA (one or more programs are accredited). Post-baccalaureate distance learning degree programs offered. *Faculty:* 26 full-time (13 women), 9 part-time/adjunct (6 women). *Students:* 321 full-time (229 women), 310 part-time (230 women); includes 101 minority (34 African Americans, 4 American Indian/Alaska Native, 36 Asian Americans or Pacific Islanders, 27 Hispanic Americans), 35 international. 747 applicants, 53% accepted, 217 enrolled. In 2009, 240 master's, 7 doctorates, 6 other advanced degrees awarded. *Entrance requirements:* For master's, GRE General Test, minimum GPA of 3.0; for doctorate, minimum GPA of 3.0; for CAS, master's degree in library and information science or related field with minimum GPA of 3.0. Additional exam requirements/recommendations for international students: Required—TOEFL (minimum score 620 paper-based; 260 computer-based; 105 iBT), or IELTS (minimum score 7). *Application deadline:* Applications are processed on a rolling basis. Application fee: $60 ($75 for international students). Electronic applications accepted. *Financial support:* In 2009–10, 52 fellowships, 41 research assistantships, 27 teaching assistantships were awarded; tuition waivers (full and partial) also available. *Unit head:* John Unsworth, Dean, 217-333-3281, Fax: 217-244-3302, E-mail: unsworth@illinois.edu. *Application contact:* Valerie Youngen, Admissions and Records Representative, 217-333-0734, Fax: 217-244-3302, E-mail: vyoungen@llinois.edu.

The University of Iowa, Graduate College, School of Library and Information Science, Iowa City, IA 52242-1316. Offers MA, MA/Certificate, MBA/MA. *Accreditation:* ALA (one or more programs are accredited). *Degree requirements:* For master's, thesis optional, exam, portfolio. *Entrance requirements:* For master's, GRE General Test, minimum GPA of 3.0. Additional exam requirements/recommendations for international students: Required—TOEFL (minimum score 550 paper-based; 213 computer-based; 81 iBT). Electronic applications accepted.

University of Maryland, College Park, Academic Affairs, College of Information Studies, College Park, MD 20742. Offers MIM, MLS, PhD, MA/MLS. *Accreditation:* ALA (one or more programs are accredited). Part-time and evening/weekend programs available. *Faculty:* 24 full-time (12 women), 14 part-time/adjunct (8 women). *Students:* 303 full-time (210 women), 211 part-time (144 women); includes 58 minority (20 African Americans, 1 American Indian/Alaska Native, 24 Asian Americans or Pacific Islanders, 13 Hispanic Americans), 113 international. 705 applicants, 56% accepted, 188 enrolled. In 2009, 156 master's, 2 doctorates awarded. Terminal master's awarded for partial completion of doctoral program. *Degree requirements:* For master's, thesis optional; for doctorate, comprehensive exam, thesis/dissertation, 1 year residency. *Entrance requirements:* For master's and doctorate, GRE General Test, minimum GPA of 3.0, 3 letters of recommendation. Additional exam requirements/recommendations for international students: Required—TOEFL. *Application deadline:* For fall admission, 2/1 for domestic and international students; for spring admission, 10/1 for domestic students, 6/1 for international students. Applications are processed on a rolling basis. Application fee: $60. Electronic applications accepted. *Expenses:* Tuition, area resident: Part-time $471

per credit hour. Tuition, state resident: part-time $471 per credit hour. Tuition, nonresident: part-time $1016 per credit hour. Required fees: $337.04 per term. *Financial support:* In 2009–10, 1 fellowship with partial tuition reimbursement (averaging $14,967 per year), 7 research assistantships (averaging $17,962 per year), 84 teaching assistantships with tuition reimbursements (averaging $16,016 per year) were awarded; career-related internships or fieldwork, Federal Work-Study, scholarships/grants, and tuition waivers (full and partial) also available. Support available to part-time students. Financial award application deadline: 2/1; financial award applicants required to submit FAFSA. Total annual research expenditures: $1.1 million. *Unit head:* Dr. Jennifer Preece, Dean, 301-405-2036, Fax: 301-314-9145, E-mail: preece@umd.edu. *Application contact:* Dean of Graduate School, 301-405-0376, Fax: 301-314-9305.

University of Michigan, Horace H. Rackham School of Graduate Studies, School of Information, Ann Arbor, MI 48109-1107. Offers archives and records management (MS); human-computer interaction (MS); information (MS, PhD); information economics, management and policy (MS); library and information services (MS). *Accreditation:* ALA (one or more programs are accredited). Part-time programs available. *Degree requirements:* For master's, variable foreign language requirement, thesis optional; for doctorate, one foreign language, thesis/dissertation, oral defense of dissertation, preliminary exam. *Entrance requirements:* For master's and doctorate, GRE General Test. Additional exam requirements/recommendations for international students: Required—TOEFL (minimum score 600 paper-based; 250 computer-based). Electronic applications accepted. *Expenses:* Tuition, state resident: full-time $17,286; part-time $1099 per credit hour. Tuition, nonresident: full-time $34,944; part-time $2080 per credit hour. Required fees: $95 per semester. Tuition and fees vary according to course load, degree level and program.

University of Missouri, Graduate School, College of Education, School of Information Science and Learning Technologies, Columbia, MO 65211. Offers educational technology (M Ed, Ed S); information science and learning technology (PhD); library science (MA). *Accreditation:* ALA (one or more programs are accredited). Part-time and evening/weekend programs available. *Entrance requirements:* For master's, GRE General Test or MAT, minimum GPA of 3.0. Additional exam requirements/recommendations for international students: Required—TOEFL (minimum score 540 paper-based; 207 computer-based; 76 iBT).

The University of North Carolina at Chapel Hill, Graduate School, School of Information and Library Science, Chapel Hill, NC 27599. Offers MSIS, MSLS, PhD, CAS. *Accreditation:* ALA (one or more programs are accredited). Part-time programs available. Terminal master's awarded for partial completion of doctoral program. *Degree requirements:* For master's, paper or project; for doctorate, thesis/dissertation. *Entrance requirements:* For master's and doctorate, GRE General Test. Additional exam requirements/recommendations for international students: Required—TOEFL (minimum score 625 paper-based; 263 computer-based). Electronic applications accepted. *Faculty research:* Information retrieval, digital libraries, management of information resources, archives and cultural heritage, information management.

The University of North Carolina at Greensboro, Graduate School, School of Education, Department of Library and Information Studies, Greensboro, NC 27412-5001. Offers MLIS. *Accreditation:* ALA. Part-time and evening/weekend programs available. Postbaccalaureate distance learning degree programs offered (no on-campus study). *Degree requirements:* For master's, portfolio. *Entrance requirements:* For master's, GRE General Test. Additional exam requirements/recommendations for international students: Required—TOEFL (minimum score 550 paper-based; 213 computer-based), IELTS (minimum score 6.5). Electronic applications accepted. *Faculty research:* Library history, gender studies, children's literature, web design, homeless, technical services.

University of North Texas, College of Information, Department of Library and Information Sciences, Denton, TX 76203-5017. Offers information science (MS, PhD); learning technologies (M Ed, Ed D), including applied technology, training and development (M Ed), computer education and cognitive systems, educational computing; library science (MS). *Accreditation:* ALA (one or more programs are accredited). Part-time and evening/weekend programs available. *Degree requirements:* For master's, comprehensive exam; for doctorate, comprehensive exam, thesis/dissertation. *Entrance requirements:* For master's, GRE General Test, MAT; for doctorate, GRE General Test. Additional exam requirements/recommendations for international students: Required—proof of English language proficiency required for non-native English speakers; Recommended—TOEFL (minimum score 550 paper-based; 213 computer-based; 79 iBT). *Application deadline:* Applications are processed on a rolling basis. Application fee: $50 ($75 for international students). Electronic applications accepted. *Expenses:* Tuition, state resident: full-time $4298; part-time $239 per contact hour. Tuition, nonresident: full-time $9878; part-time $549 per contact hour. Required fees: $265 per contact hour. *Financial support:* Fellowships, research assistantships, teaching assistantships, career-related internships or fieldwork, Federal Work-Study, institutionally sponsored loans, scholarships/grants, health care benefits, and library assistantships available. Financial award application deadline: 4/1; financial award applicants required to submit FAFSA. *Faculty research:* Information resources and services, information management and retrieval, computer-based information systems, human information behavior. *Application contact:* Graduate Academic Counselor, 940-369-2873, Fax: 940-565-3101.

University of Oklahoma, Graduate College, College of Arts and Sciences, School of Library and Information Studies, Program in Library and Information Studies, Norman, OK 73019-0390. Offers library and information studies (MLIS); school library media specialist (Certificate); M Ed/MLIS; MBA/MLIS. Part-time and evening/weekend programs available. *Students:* 31 full-time (25 women), 186 part-time (136 women); includes 34 minority (4 African Americans, 23 American Indian/Alaska Native, 2 Asian Americans or Pacific Islanders, 5 Hispanic Americans), 5 international. 73 applicants, 95% accepted, 52 enrolled. In 2009, 68 master's awarded. *Degree requirements:* For master's, comprehensive exam (MLIS). *Entrance requirements:* For master's, GRE, minimum GPA of 3.2 in last 60 hours or 3.0 overall. Additional exam requirements/recommendations for international students: Required—TOEFL (minimum score 550 paper-based; 213 computer-based). *Application deadline:* For fall admission, 3/1 priority date for domestic students, 4/1 for international students; for spring admission, 10/15 for domestic students, 9/1 for international students. Applications are processed on a rolling basis. Application fee: $40 ($90 for international students). Electronic applications accepted. *Expenses:* Tuition, state resident: full-time $3744; part-time $156 per credit hour. Tuition, nonresident: full-time $13,577; part-time $565.70 per credit hour. Required fees: $2415; $90.10 per credit hour. *Financial support:* In 2009–10, 90 students received support. Scholarships/grants and unspecified assistantships available. Financial award applicants required to submit FAFSA. *Faculty research:* Information use in the digital age, equity of access, learning organizations, education of information professionals, information services to special populations. *Unit head:* Kathy Latrobe, Director, 405-325-3921, Fax: 405-325-7648, E-mail: klatrobe@ou.edu. *Application contact:* Maggie Ryan, Coordinator of Admissions, 405-325-3921, Fax: 405-325-7648, E-mail: mryan@ou.edu.

University of Pittsburgh, School of Information Sciences, Library and Information Science Program, Pittsburgh, PA 15260. Offers health sciences librarianship (Certificate); library and information science (MLIS, PhD). *Accreditation:* ALA (one or more programs are accredited). Part-time and evening/weekend programs available. Postbaccalaureate distance learning degree programs offered (minimal on-campus study). *Faculty:* 11 full-time (6 women), 8 part-time/adjunct (7 women). *Students:* 200 full-time (163 women), 235 part-time (185 women); includes 40 minority (22 African Americans, 1 American Indian/Alaska Native, 2 Asian Americans or Pacific Islanders, 15 Hispanic Americans), 23 international. 413 applicants, 88% accepted, 217 enrolled. In 2009, 265 master's, 3 doctorates, 2 other advanced degrees awarded. *Degree requirements:* For master's, thesis optional; for doctorate, comprehensive exam, thesis/dissertation. *Entrance requirements:* For master's, bachelor's degree from accredited university; minimum GPA of 3.0; for doctorate, GRE General Test, minimum GPA of 3.5. Additional exam requirements/recommendations for international students: Required—TOEFL (minimum score 550 paper-based; 213 computer-based; 80 iBT). *Application deadline:* For fall admission, 1/15

Information Studies

University of Pittsburgh *(continued)*
priority date for domestic and international students; for winter admission, 9/15 priority date for domestic students, 6/15 priority date for international students; for spring admission, 1/15 priority date for domestic students, 12/15 priority date for international students. Applications are processed on a rolling basis. Application fee: $50. Electronic applications accepted. *Expenses:* Contact institution. *Financial support:* Fellowships with full tuition reimbursements, research assistantships with full and partial tuition reimbursements, teaching assistantships with full and partial tuition reimbursements, career-related internships or fieldwork, scholarships/grants, health care benefits, tuition waivers (full and partial), and unspecified assistantships available. Financial award application deadline: 1/15; financial award applicants required to submit FAFSA. *Faculty research:* Archives, preservation management, children's resources and services, medical informatics, digital libraries, information retrieval. *Unit head:* Dr. Mary K. Biagini, Chair, 412-624-5138, Fax: 412-624-5231, E-mail: mbiagini@sis.pitt.edu. *Application contact:* Brandi Belleau Liskey, Student Recruiting Coordinator, 412-648-3108, Fax: 412-624-5231, E-mail: lisinq@sis.pitt.edu.

University of Puerto Rico, Río Piedras, Graduate School of Information Sciences and Technologies, San Juan, PR 00931-3300. Offers administration of academic libraries (PMC); administration of public libraries (PMC); administration of special libraries (PMC); consultant in information services (PMC); documents and files administration (Post-Graduate Certificate); electronic information resources analyst (Post-Graduate Certificate); librarianship (Post-Graduate Certificate); librarianship and information services (MLS); master librarian (Post-Graduate Certificate); specialist in legal information (PMC). *Accreditation:* ALA. Part-time programs available. *Degree requirements:* For master's, comprehensive exam, thesis, portfolio. *Entrance requirements:* For master's, PAEG, GRE, interview, minimum GPA of 3.0, 3 letters of recommendation; for other advanced degree, PAEG, GRE, minimum GPA of 3.0, IST master's degree. *Faculty research:* Investigating the users needs and preferences for a specialized environmental library.

University of Rhode Island, Graduate School, College of Arts and Sciences, Graduate School of Library and Information Studies, Kingston, RI 02881. Offers MLIS, MLIS/MA, MLIS/MPA. *Accreditation:* ALA (one or more programs are accredited). Part-time programs available. *Faculty:* 7 full-time (6 women), 13 part-time/adjunct (7 women). *Students:* 56 full-time (46 women), 117 part-time (106 women); includes 4 minority (1 African American, 2 Asian Americans or Pacific Islanders, 1 Hispanic American). In 2009, 81 master's awarded. *Degree requirements:* For master's, comprehensive exam. *Entrance requirements:* For master's, GRE or MAT (if undergraduate GPA less than 3.0), 2 letters of recommendation. Additional exam requirements/recommendations for international students: Required—TOEFL (minimum score 550 paper-based; 213 computer-based). *Application deadline:* For fall admission, 6/15 for domestic students, 2/1 for international students; for spring admission, 10/15 for domestic students, 7/15 for international students. Application fee: $65. Electronic applications accepted. *Expenses:* Tuition, state resident: full-time $8828; part-time $490 per credit hour. Tuition, nonresident: full-time $22,100; part-time $1228 per credit hour. Required fees: $1118; $57 per semester. Tuition and fees vary according to program. *Financial support:* In 2009–10, 4 teaching assistantships with full and partial tuition reimbursements (averaging $9,726 per year) were awarded. Financial award application deadline: 1/15; financial award applicants required to submit FAFSA. Total annual research expenditures: $4,265. *Unit head:* Dr. Gale Eaton, Director, 401-874-4641, Fax: 401-874-4964, E-mail: geaton@uri.edu. *Application contact:* Dr. Gale Eaton, Director, 401-874-4641, Fax: 401-874-4964, E-mail: geaton@uri.edu.

University of South Carolina, The Graduate School, College of Mass Communications and Information Studies, School of Library and Information Science, Columbia, SC 29208. Offers MLIS, PhD, Certificate, Specialist, MLIS/MA. *Accreditation:* ALA (one or more programs are accredited). Part-time programs available. Postbaccalaureate distance learning degree programs offered (no on-campus study). *Degree requirements:* For master's, end of program portfolio; for doctorate, comprehensive exam, thesis/dissertation. *Entrance requirements:* For master's and other advanced degree, GRE General Test or MAT; for doctorate, GTE, writing sample. Additional exam requirements/recommendations for international students: Required—TOEFL (minimum score 570 paper-based; 230 computer-based; 75 iBT). Electronic applications accepted. *Faculty research:* Information technology management, distance education, library services for children and young adults, special libraries.

University of South Florida, Graduate School, College of Arts and Sciences, School of Library and Information Science, Tampa, FL 33620-9951. Offers MA. *Accreditation:* ALA. Part-time and evening/weekend programs available. Postbaccalaureate distance learning degree programs offered (minimal on-campus study). *Faculty:* 14 full-time (11 women), 10 part-time/adjunct (9 women). *Students:* 117 full-time (95 women), 280 part-time (235 women); includes 76 minority (25 African Americans, 2 American Indian/Alaska Native, 8 Asian Americans or Pacific Islanders, 41 Hispanic Americans), 2 international. Average age 32. 217 applicants, 67% accepted, 89 enrolled. In 2009, 174 master's awarded. *Degree requirements:* For master's, comprehensive exam, thesis. *Entrance requirements:* For master's, minimum GPA of 3.5 in upper-division course work. Additional exam requirements/recommendations for international students: Required—TOEFL (minimum score 550 paper-based; 213 computer-based). *Application deadline:* For fall admission, 6/1 for domestic students, 1/2 for international students; for spring admission, 10/15 for domestic students, 6/1 for international students. Applications are processed on a rolling basis. Application fee: $30. Electronic applications accepted. *Financial support:* In 2009–10, teaching assistantships with full tuition reimbursements (averaging $9,000 per year); unspecified assistantships also available. Financial award application deadline:

6/30; financial award applicants required to submit FAFSA. *Faculty research:* Youth services in libraries, community engagement and libraries, information architecture, biomedical informatics. Total annual research expenditures: $134,608. *Unit head:* Jim Andrews, Director, 813-974-2108, Fax: 813-974-6840, E-mail: jandrews@cas.usf.edu. *Application contact:* Jim Andrews, Director, 813-974-2108, Fax: 813-974-6840, E-mail: jandrews@cas.usf.edu.

The University of Texas at Austin, Graduate School, School of Information, Austin, TX 78712-1111. Offers MS, PhD. *Accreditation:* ALA (one or more programs are accredited). Part-time programs available. *Degree requirements:* For doctorate, 2 foreign languages, thesis/dissertation. *Entrance requirements:* For master's and doctorate, GRE General Test. Electronic applications accepted. *Faculty research:* Information retrieval and artificial intelligence, library history and administration, classification and cataloguing.

University of Toronto, School of Graduate Studies, Social Sciences Division, Faculty of Information Studies, Toronto, ON M5S 1A1, Canada. Offers MI St, PhD, G Dip. *Accreditation:* ALA (one or more programs are accredited). Part-time programs available. *Degree requirements:* For master's, thesis optional; for doctorate, thesis/dissertation, oral exam/thesis defense. *Entrance requirements:* For master's, 2 letters of reference; for doctorate, 3 letters of reference, minimum B+ average; for G Dip, MI St, MLS, or MIS degree or equivalent; minimum B+ average overall. Additional exam requirements/recommendations for international students: Required—TOEFL (minimum score 600 paper-based; 250 computer-based), TWE (minimum score 6), Michigan English Language Assessment Battery (minimum score: 95) or IELTS (minimum score: 8). *Expenses:* Contact institution.

The University of Western Ontario, Faculty of Graduate Studies, Faculty of Information and Media Studies, Programs in Library and Information Science, London, ON N6A 5B8, Canada. Offers MLIS, PhD. Program conducted on a trimester basis. *Accreditation:* ALA (one or more programs are accredited). Part-time and evening/weekend programs available. *Degree requirements:* For doctorate, comprehensive exam, thesis/dissertation. *Entrance requirements:* For master's, honors degree, minimum B average during previous 2 years of course work; for doctorate, MLIS or equivalent. Additional exam requirements/recommendations for international students: Required—TOEFL (minimum score 625 paper-based; 263 computer-based), TWE (minimum score 5). Electronic applications accepted. *Faculty research:* Information, individuals, and society; information systems, policy, power, and institutions.

University of Wisconsin–Madison, Graduate School, College of Letters and Science, School of Library and Information Studies, Madison, WI 53706-1380. Offers MA, PhD. *Accreditation:* ALA (one or more programs are accredited). Part-time programs available. *Degree requirements:* For doctorate, comprehensive exam, thesis/dissertation. Electronic applications accepted. *Expenses:* Tuition, state resident: part-time $594 per credit. Tuition, nonresident: part-time $1504 per credit. Required fees: $65 per credit. Tuition and fees vary according to course load, program and reciprocity agreements. *Faculty research:* Intellectual freedom, children's literature, print culture history, information systems design and evaluation, school library media centers.

University of Wisconsin–Milwaukee, Graduate School, School of Information Studies, Milwaukee, WI 53201-0413. Offers advanced studies in library and information science (CAS); archives and records administration (CAS); digital libraries (Certificate); information studies (MLIS, PhD); MLIS/MA; MLIS/MM; MLIS/MS. *Accreditation:* ALA (one or more programs are accredited). Part-time programs available. *Faculty:* 21 full-time (10 women). *Students:* 106 full-time (77 women), 423 part-time (351 women); includes 32 minority (8 African Americans, 13 Asian Americans or Pacific Islanders, 11 Hispanic Americans), 17 international. Average age 35. 351 applicants, 80% accepted, 73 enrolled. In 2009, 214 master's awarded. *Entrance requirements:* For master's, GRE General Test or MAT; for doctorate, GRE. Additional exam requirements/recommendations for international students: Required—TOEFL (minimum score 550 paper-based; 213 computer-based), IELTS (minimum score 6.5). *Application deadline:* For fall admission, 1/1 priority date for domestic students; for spring admission, 9/1 for domestic students. Applications are processed on a rolling basis. Application fee: $45 ($75 for international students). *Expenses:* Tuition, state resident: full-time $8800. Tuition, nonresident: full-time $20,760. Tuition and fees vary according to program and reciprocity agreements. *Financial support:* In 2009–10, 1 teaching assistantship was awarded; career-related internships or fieldwork, Federal Work-Study, and unspecified assistantships also available. Support available to part-time students. Financial award application deadline: 4/15. Total annual research expenditures: $155,942. *Unit head:* Johannes Britz, Dean, 414-229-4709, Fax: 414-229-4848. *Application contact:* Dietmar Wolfram, 414-229-6836, E-mail: dwolfram@uwm.edu.

Valdosta State University, Graduate School, Program in Library and Information Science, Valdosta, GA 31698. Offers MLIS. *Accreditation:* ALA. *Degree requirements:* For master's, comprehensive exam. *Entrance requirements:* For master's, GRE. Additional exam requirements/recommendations for international students: Required—TOEFL (minimum score 523 paper-based; 193 computer-based).

Wayne State University, Graduate School, Library and Information Science Program, Detroit, MI 48202. Offers archival administration (Certificate); library and information science (MLIS, Spec); library science (MS, Spec). *Accreditation:* ALA (one or more programs are accredited). Part-time and evening/weekend programs available. *Entrance requirements:* For master's, GRE or MAT (if undergraduate GPA is between 2.25 and 2.99), minimum undergraduate GPA of 3.0, curriculum vitae. Additional exam requirements/recommendations for international students: Required—TOEFL (minimum score 550 paper-based; 213 computer-based); Recommended—TWE (minimum score 6). Electronic applications accepted. *Faculty research:* Convergence of academic libraries and other academic services, competitive intelligence and data mining, impact of digitization on libraries, international librarianship, consumer health information.

Library Science

Appalachian State University, Cratis D. Williams Graduate School, Department of Leadership and Educational Studies, Boone, NC 28608. Offers educational administration (Ed S); educational media (MA); higher education (MA, Ed S); library science (MLS); school administration (MSA). Part-time and evening/weekend programs available. Postbaccalaureate distance learning degree programs offered (no on-campus study). *Faculty:* 25 full-time (10 women), 28 part-time/adjunct (16 women). *Students:* 48 full-time (35 women), 474 part-time (373 women); includes 24 minority (21 African Americans, 2 Asian Americans or Pacific Islanders, 1 Hispanic American), 2 international. 229 applicants, 89% accepted, 156 enrolled. In 2009, 133 master's, 32 other advanced degrees awarded. *Degree requirements:* For master's and Ed S, comprehensive exam, thesis optional. *Entrance requirements:* For master's and Ed S, GRE or MAT, 3 letters of recommendation. Additional exam requirements/recommendations for international students: Required—TOEFL (minimum score 570 paper-based; 230 computer-based; 79 iBT), IELTS (minimum score 6.5). *Application deadline:* For fall admission, 7/1 for domestic students, 2/1 for international students; for spring admission, 11/1 for domestic students, 7/1 for international students. Applications are processed on a rolling basis. Application fee: $50. Electronic applications accepted. *Expenses:* Tuition, state resident: full-time $2960. Tuition, nonresident: full-time $14,051. Required fees: $2320. *Financial support:* In 2009–10, 10 research assistantships (averaging $8,000 per year) were awarded; career-related internships or fieldwork, scholarships/grants, and unspecified assistantships also available. Financial award application deadline: 4/1; financial award applicants required to submit FAFSA. *Faculty research:* Brain, learning and meditation; leadership of teaching and learning. Total annual research expenditures: $475,000. *Unit head:* Dr. Richard Riedl, Interim

Director, 828-262-3112, E-mail: reidlr@appstate.edu. *Application contact:* Lori Dean, Graduate Student Coordinator, 828-262-6041, E-mail: deanlk@appstate.edu.

Azusa Pacific University, School of Education, Department of Advanced Studies, Program in School Librarianship, Azusa, CA 91702-7000. Offers MA.

The Catholic University of America, School of Library and Information Science, Washington, DC 20064. Offers MSLS, JD/MSLS, MSLS/MA, MSLS/MS. *Accreditation:* ALA (one or more programs are accredited). Part-time programs available. *Faculty:* 7 full-time (5 women), 10 part-time/adjunct (4 women). *Students:* 22 full-time (19 women), 196 part-time (161 women); includes 40 minority (23 African Americans, 11 Asian Americans or Pacific Islanders, 6 Hispanic Americans), 5 international. Average age 35. 146 applicants, 82% accepted, 77 enrolled. In 2009, 78 master's awarded. *Degree requirements:* For master's, comprehensive exam. *Entrance requirements:* For master's, GRE (minimum score 1000) or minimum GPA of 3.0, 3 letters of recommendation. Additional exam requirements/recommendations for international students: Required—TOEFL (minimum score 580 paper-based; 237 computer-based). *Application deadline:* For fall admission, 8/1 priority date for domestic students, 7/15 for international students; for spring admission, 11/1 priority date for domestic students, 10/15 for international students. Applications are processed on a rolling basis. Application fee: $55. Electronic applications accepted. *Expenses:* Contact institution. *Financial support:* Fellowships, research assistantships, teaching assistantships, Federal Work-Study, scholarships/grants, tuition waivers (full and partial), and unspecified assistantships available. Financial award application deadline: 2/1; financial award applicants required to submit FAFSA. *Faculty research:* Digital collections, library and information science education, information design and architecture, cultural heritage

information management, information system design and evaluation. Total annual research expenditures: $126,684. *Unit head:* Dr. Ingrid Hsieh-Yee, Acting Dean, 202-319-5085, Fax: 202-319-5574, E-mail: hsiehyee@cua.edu. *Application contact:* Julie Schwing, Director of Graduate Admissions, 202-319-5057, Fax: 202-319-6533, E-mail: cua-admissions@cua.edu.

Chicago State University, School of Graduate and Professional Studies, College of Education, Department of Reading, Elementary Education, Library Information and Media Studies, Program in Library Information and Media Studies, Chicago, IL 60628. Offers MS Ed. *Entrance requirements:* For master's, minimum GPA of 2.75.

Clarion University of Pennsylvania, Office of Research and Graduate Studies, College of Education and Human Services, Department of Library Science, Clarion, PA 16214. Offers MSLS, CAS. *Accreditation:* ALA (one or more programs are accredited). Part-time programs available. *Degree requirements:* For master's, thesis or alternative. *Entrance requirements:* For master's, minimum QPA of 3.0. Additional exam requirements/recommendations for international students: Required—TOEFL (minimum score 550 paper-based; 213 computer-based; 80 iBT). Electronic applications accepted.

Dalhousie University, Faculty of Management, School of Information Management, Halifax, NS B3H 3J5, Canada. Offers MIM, MLIS, LL B/MLIS, MBA/MLIS, MLIS/MPA, MLIS/MREM. *Accreditation:* ALA (one or more programs are accredited). Part-time programs available. *Faculty:* 5 full-time (3 women), 9 part-time/adjunct (6 women). *Students:* 41 full-time (30 women), 27 part-time (19 women). 59 applicants, 73% accepted. In 2009, 32 master's awarded. *Degree requirements:* For master's, one foreign language, thesis optional. *Entrance requirements:* For master's, resume, interview. Additional exam requirements/recommendations for international students: Required—TOEFL, IELTS, CANTEST, CAEL, or Michigan English Language Assessment Battery. *Application deadline:* For fall admission, 6/1 for domestic and international students. Applications are processed on a rolling basis. Application fee: $70. Electronic applications accepted. *Financial support:* In 2009–10, 25 students received support, including 15 fellowships (averaging $4,560 per year), 1 research assistantship (averaging $1,300 per year); career-related internships or fieldwork and scholarships/grants also available. Financial award application deadline: 3/1. *Faculty research:* Information-seeking behavior, electronic text design, browsing in digital environments, information diffusion among scientists. Total annual research expenditures: $55,140. *Unit head:* Dr. Fiona Black, Director, 902-494-3656, Fax: 902-494-2451, E-mail: sim@dal.ca. *Application contact:* Joann Watson, MLIS Program Coordinator, 902-494-2471, Fax: 902-494-2451, E-mail: mlis@dal.ca.

Dominican University, Graduate School of Library and Information Science, River Forest, IL 60305-1099. Offers library and information science (MLIS, PhD); special studies (CSS); MBA/MLIS; MLIS/M Div; MLIS/MA; MLIS/MM. *Accreditation:* ALA (one or more programs are accredited). Part-time and evening/weekend programs available. Postbaccalaureate distance learning degree programs offered (minimal on-campus study). *Faculty:* 16 full-time (10 women), 24 part-time/adjunct (17 women). *Students:* 162 full-time (119 women), 363 part-time (299 women); includes 70 minority (22 African Americans, 3 American Indian/Alaska Native, 14 Asian Americans or Pacific Islanders, 31 Hispanic Americans). Average age 34. In 2009, 201 master's awarded. *Entrance requirements:* For master's, minimum GPA of 3.0, GRE General Test, or MAT. Additional exam requirements/recommendations for international students: Required—TOEFL. *Application deadline:* For fall admission, 6/1 priority date for domestic students; for winter admission, 3/1 priority date for domestic students; for spring admission, 10/1 priority date for domestic students. Applications are processed on a rolling basis. Application fee: $25. *Expenses:* Contact institution. *Financial support:* Fellowships, research assistantships, career-related internships or fieldwork, Federal Work-Study, scholarships/grants, and tuition waivers (partial) available. Support available to part-time students. Financial award application deadline: 4/15; financial award applicants required to submit FAFSA. *Faculty research:* Productivity and the information environment, bibliometrics, library history, subject access, library materials and services for children. *Unit head:* Dr. Susan Roman, Dean, 708-524-6986, Fax: 708-524-6657, E-mail: sroman@dom.edu.

Drexel University, The iSchool at Drexel, College of Information Science and Technology, Philadelphia, PA 19104-2875. Offers healthcare informatics (Certificate); information science and technology (PMC); information studies (PhD); information studies and technology (Advanced Certificate); information systems (MSIS); library and information science (MS), including archival studies, competitive intelligence and knowledge management, digital libraries, library and information services, school library media, youth services; software engineering (MSSE). *Accreditation:* ALA (one or more programs are accredited). Part-time and evening/weekend programs available. Postbaccalaureate distance learning degree programs offered (no on-campus study). *Faculty:* 34 full-time (19 women), 24 part-time/adjunct (9 women). *Students:* 279 full-time (192 women), 571 part-time (372 women); includes 96 minority (36 African Americans, 1 American Indian/Alaska Native, 36 Asian Americans or Pacific Islanders, 23 Hispanic Americans), 48 international. Average age 34. 644 applicants, 68% accepted, 289 enrolled. In 2009, 318 master's, 12 doctorates, 15 other advanced degrees awarded. *Degree requirements:* For doctorate, thesis/dissertation. *Entrance requirements:* For master's and doctorate, GRE General Test. Additional exam requirements/recommendations for international students: Required—TOEFL (minimum score 600 paper-based; 250 computer-based; 100 iBT). *Application deadline:* For fall admission, 8/1 for domestic and international students; for spring admission, 2/1 for domestic and international students. Applications are processed on a rolling basis. Electronic applications accepted. *Expenses:* Contact institution. *Financial support:* In 2009–10, 250 students received support, including 235 fellowships with partial tuition reimbursements available (averaging $225 per year), 18 research assistantships with full tuition reimbursements available (averaging $25,000 per year), 2 teaching assistantships with full tuition reimbursements available (averaging $25,000 per year); institutionally sponsored loans, scholarships/grants, health care benefits, tuition waivers (partial), unspecified assistantships, and fellowships also available. Support available to part-time students. Financial award applicants required to submit FAFSA. *Faculty research:* Information retrieval/information visualization/bibliometrics, human-computer interaction, digital libraries, databases, text/data mining. Total annual research expenditures: $2 million. *Unit head:* Dr. David E. Fenske, Dean and Isaac L. Auerbach Professor of Information Science, 215-895-2475, Fax: 215-895-6378, E-mail: fenske@drexel.edu. *Application contact:* Matthew Lechtenberg, Graduate Admissions Manager, 215-895-1951, Fax: 215-895-2303, E-mail: ml333@drexel.edu.

See Close-Up on page 1719.

East Carolina University, Graduate School, College of Education, Department of Library Science and Instructional Technology, Greenville, NC 27858-4353. Offers instruction technology specialist (MA Ed); library science (MLS, CAS). *Accreditation:* NCATE. Part-time and evening/weekend programs available. Postbaccalaureate distance learning degree programs offered (no on-campus study). *Degree requirements:* For master's, comprehensive exam, thesis optional. *Entrance requirements:* For master's, GRE General Test or MAT, interview, minimum GPA of 2.5, bachelor's degree in related field, teaching license (MA Ed). Additional exam requirements/recommendations for international students: Required—TOEFL.

Eastern Kentucky University, The Graduate School, College of Education, Department of Curriculum and Instruction, Richmond, KY 40475-3102. Offers elementary education (MA Ed), including early elementary education, reading; library science (MA Ed); music education (MA Ed); secondary and higher education (MA Ed), including secondary education; teaching (MAT). *Accreditation:* NCATE. Part-time programs available. *Degree requirements:* For master's, portfolio is part of exam. *Entrance requirements:* For master's, GRE General Test, PRAXIS II (KY), minimum GPA of 2.5. *Faculty research:* Technology in education, reading instruction, e-portfolios, induction to teacher education, dispositions of teachers.

Emporia State University, School of Graduate Studies, School of Library and Information Management, Program in Library and Information Management, Emporia, KS 66801-5087. Offers MLS, PhD, Certificate. Part-time and evening/weekend programs available. Postbaccalaureate distance learning degree programs offered (minimal on-campus study). *Faculty:* 5 full-time (4 women), 1 part-time/adjunct (0 women). *Students:* 22 full-time (16 women), 304 part-time (248 women); includes 29 minority (6 African Americans, 1 American Indian/Alaska Native, 13 Asian Americans or Pacific Islanders, 9 Hispanic Americans), 5 international. 121 applicants, 81% accepted, 86 enrolled. In 2009, 119 master's, 5 doctorates, 15 other advanced degrees awarded. *Entrance requirements:* For master's, GRE. Additional exam requirements/recommendations for international students: Required—TOEFL (minimum score 520 paper-based; 133 computer-based; 68 iBT). *Application deadline:* For fall admission, 8/15 priority date for domestic students. Applications are processed on a rolling basis. Application fee: $30 ($75 for international students). Electronic applications accepted. *Expenses:* Tuition, state resident: full-time $4154; part-time $173 per credit hour. Tuition, nonresident: full-time $12,864; part-time $536 per credit hour. Required fees: $948; $58 per credit hour. Tuition and fees vary according to campus/location. *Financial support:* In 2009–10, 6 research assistantships (averaging $7,059 per year), 4 teaching assistantships (averaging $7,059 per year) were awarded; Federal Work-Study, institutionally sponsored loans, and unspecified assistantships also available. Financial award application deadline: 3/15; financial award applicants required to submit FAFSA. *Unit head:* Dr. Gwen Alexander, Dean, School of Library and Information Management, 620-341-5203, E-mail: galexan1@emporia.edu. *Application contact:* Candace Boardman, Director, Kansas MLS Program, 620-341-6159, E-mail: cboardma@emporia.edu.

Florida State University, The Graduate School, School of Library and Information Studies, Tallahassee, FL 32306-2100. Offers library and information studies (MA). *Accreditation:* ALA (one or more programs are accredited). Part-time and evening/weekend programs available. Postbaccalaureate distance learning degree programs offered (no on-campus study). *Faculty:* 31 full-time (17 women), 13 part-time/adjunct (6 women). *Students:* 47 full-time (31 women), 716 part-time (534 women); includes 149 minority (74 African Americans, 4 American Indian/Alaska Native, 23 Asian Americans or Pacific Islanders, 48 Hispanic Americans), 47 international. Average age 35. 420 applicants, 77% accepted, 228 enrolled. In 2009, 243 master's, 4 doctorates, 3 other advanced degrees awarded. *Degree requirements:* For master's, thesis optional, minimum GPA of 3.0, 36 hours; for doctorate, comprehensive exam, thesis/dissertation, dissertation defense, manuscript clearance, minimum GPA of 3.0; for Specialist, thesis optional, culminating paper. *Entrance requirements:* For master's, GRE (minimum combined score: 1000) or minimum GPA of 3.0 on last 2 years of baccalaureate degree, resume, statement of goals, two letters of recommendation, two official transcripts from every college-level institution attended; for doctorate, GRE (minimum combined score: 1200), minimum GPA of 3.0 on last degree program, resume, 3 letters of recommendation, personal/goals statement, writing sample, brief digital video, two official transcripts from all college-level institutions attended; for Specialist, GRE (minimum combined score 1000), minimum graduate GPA of 3.2, resume, 3 letters of recommendation, writing sample. Additional exam requirements/recommendations for international students: Required—TOEFL (minimum score 585 paper-based; 94 iBT), IELTS (minimum score 6.5). *Application deadline:* For fall admission, 6/1 priority date for domestic and international students; for spring admission, 11/1 for domestic and international students. Applications are processed on a rolling basis. Application fee: $30. Electronic applications accepted. *Expenses:* Contact institution. *Financial support:* In 2009–10, 170 students received support, including 11 fellowships with full tuition reimbursements available, 88 research assistantships with full tuition reimbursements available, 69 teaching assistantships with full tuition reimbursements available; career-related internships or fieldwork, Federal Work-Study, scholarships/grants, health care benefits, and unspecified assistantships also available. Financial award application deadline: 3/1; financial award applicants required to submit FAFSA. *Faculty research:* Needs assessment, information policy, usability analysis, human information behavior, youth services. Total annual research expenditures: $1.6 million. *Unit head:* Dr. Corinne Jorgensen, Director/Associate Dean, 850-644-8126, Fax: 850-644-9763, E-mail: corinne.jorgensen@cci.fsu.edu. *Application contact:* Delores Bryant, Graduate Program Assistant, 850-645-3280, Fax: 850-644-9763, E-mail: delores.bryant@cci.fsu.edu.

Indiana University Bloomington, School of Library and Information Science, Bloomington, IN 47405-3907. Offers MIS, MLS, PhD, Sp LIS, JD/MLS, MIS/MA, MLS/MA, MPA/MIS, MPA/MLS. *Accreditation:* ALA (one or more programs are accredited). Part-time programs available. *Faculty:* 16 full-time (7 women). *Students:* 263 full-time (189 women), 82 part-time (49 women); includes 24 minority (8 African Americans, 1 American Indian/Alaska Native, 8 Asian Americans or Pacific Islanders, 7 Hispanic Americans), 38 international. Average age 29. 305 applicants, 84% accepted, 117 enrolled. In 2009, 162 master's, 1 doctorate, 3 other advanced degrees awarded. *Degree requirements:* For doctorate, thesis/dissertation. *Entrance requirements:* For master's and doctorate, GRE General Test, 3 letters of reference. Additional exam requirements/recommendations for international students: Required—TOEFL (minimum score 600 paper-based; 250 computer-based; 100 iBT). *Application deadline:* For fall admission, 5/15 priority date for domestic students, 12/1 priority date for international students; for spring admission, 10/15 priority date for domestic students, 9/1 priority date for international students. Applications are processed on a rolling basis. Application fee: $55 ($65 for international students). Electronic applications accepted. *Expenses:* Contact institution. *Financial support:* Fellowships with full and partial tuition reimbursements, research assistantships with full and partial tuition reimbursements, career-related internships or fieldwork, Federal Work-Study, institutionally sponsored loans, scholarships/grants, tuition waivers (partial), and unspecified assistantships available. Support available to part-time students. Financial award application deadline: 1/15. *Faculty research:* Scholarly communication, interface design, library and management policy, computer-mediated communication, information retrieval. *Unit head:* Dr. Blaise Cronin, Dean, 812-855-2848, Fax: 812-855-6166, E-mail: bcronin@indiana.edu. *Application contact:* Rhonda Spencer, Director of Admissions, 812-855-2018, Fax: 812-855-6166, E-mail: slis@indiana.edu.

Indiana University–Purdue University Indianapolis, School of Library and Information Science, Indianapolis, IN 46202-2896. Offers MLS. Part-time and evening/weekend programs available. *Faculty:* 3 full-time (2 women). *Students:* 78 full-time (56 women), 232 part-time (190 women); includes 30 minority (20 African Americans, 1 American Indian/Alaska Native, 5 Asian Americans or Pacific Islanders, 4 Hispanic Americans). Average age 34. 95 applicants, 95% accepted, 79 enrolled. In 2009, 97 master's awarded. *Entrance requirements:* For master's, GRE General Test. Additional exam requirements/recommendations for international students: Required—TOEFL (minimum score 600 paper-based). *Application deadline:* For fall admission, 7/15 priority date for domestic students; for spring admission, 11/15 priority date for domestic students. Applications are processed on a rolling basis. Application fee: $55 ($65 for international students). *Financial support:* In 2009–10, 2 teaching assistantships (averaging $9,500 per year) were awarded; career-related internships or fieldwork, Federal Work-Study, institutionally sponsored loans, and scholarships/grants also available. Support available to part-time students. *Unit head:* Dr. Daniel Collison, Executive Associate Dean, 317-278-2375, Fax: 317-278-1807, E-mail: slisindy@iupui.edu. *Application contact:* Dr. Daniel Collison, Executive Associate Dean, 317-278-2375, Fax: 317-278-1807, E-mail: slisindy@iupui.edu.

Instituto Tecnológico y de Estudios Superiores de Monterrey, Campus Irapuato, Graduate Programs, Irapuato, Mexico. Offers administration (MBA); administration of information technology (MAIT); administration of telecommunications (MAT); architecture (M Arch); computer science (MCS); education (M Ed); educational administration (MEA); educational innovation and technology (DEIT); educational technology (MET); electronic commerce (MBA); environmental administration and planning (MEAP); environmental systems (MES); finances (MBA); humanistic studies (MHS); international management for Latin American executives (MIMLAE); library and information science (MLIS); manufacturing quality management (MMQM); marketing research (MBA).

Inter American University of Puerto Rico, Barranquitas Campus, Program in Education, Barranquitas, PR 00794. Offers curriculum and teaching (M Ed); educational administration and supervision (MA); elementary education (M Ed); information and library service technology (M Ed). *Degree requirements:* For master's, comprehensive exam, thesis optional. *Entrance requirements:* For master's, EXADEP, letter of recommendation. Electronic applications accepted.

Inter American University of Puerto Rico, San Germán Campus, Graduate Studies Center, Program in Library and Information Sciences, San Germán, PR 00683-5008. Offers MLS. Part-time and evening/weekend programs available. *Degree requirements:* For master's,

Library Science

Inter American University of Puerto Rico, San Germán Campus *(continued)* comprehensive exam. *Entrance requirements:* For master's, GRE General Test or EXADEP, minimum GPA of 3.0.

Kent State University, College of Communication and Information, School of Library and Information Science, Kent, OH 44242-0001. Offers MLIS. *Accreditation:* ALA. *Degree requirements:* For master's, thesis optional. *Entrance requirements:* For master's, GRE General Test, minimum GPA of 2.75.

Kutztown University of Pennsylvania, College of Education, Program in Library Science, Kutztown, PA 19530-0730. Offers MLS, Certificate. Part-time and evening/weekend programs available. *Faculty:* 6 full-time (4 women). *Students:* 12 full-time (11 women), 45 part-time (41 women). Average age 32. 36 applicants, 83% accepted, 9 enrolled. In 2009, 26 master's awarded. *Degree requirements:* For master's, comprehensive exam. *Entrance requirements:* For master's, GRE General Test. Additional exam requirements/recommendations for international students: Required—TOEFL. *Application deadline:* For fall admission, 8/15 priority date for domestic and international students; for spring admission, 12/15 priority date for domestic and international students. Applications are processed on a rolling basis. Application fee: $35. Electronic applications accepted. *Expenses:* Tuition, state resident: full-time $6666; part-time $370 per credit. Tuition, nonresident: full-time $10,666; part-time $593 per credit. Required fees: $62 per credit. $60 per semester. *Financial support:* Career-related internships or fieldwork, Federal Work-Study, scholarships/grants, and unspecified assistantships available. Financial award application deadline: 3/1; financial award applicants required to submit FAFSA. *Unit head:* Dr. Eloise Long; Chairperson, 610-683-4302, Fax: 610-683-1326, E-mail: long@kutztown.edu. *Application contact:* Kelly D. Burr, Associate Director, Graduate Admissions, 610-683-4200, Fax: 610-683-1393, E-mail: graduate@kutztown.edu.

Long Island University, C.W. Post Campus, College of Information and Computer Science, Palmer School of Library and Information Science, Brookville, NY 11548-1300. Offers archives and records management (Certificate); information studies (PhD); library and information science (MS); library media specialist (MS); public library management (Certificate). *Accreditation:* ALA (one or more programs are accredited). Part-time and evening/weekend programs available. Postbaccalaureate distance learning degree programs offered (minimal on-campus study). *Degree requirements:* For master's, thesis optional, internship; for doctorate, thesis/dissertation, qualifying exam. *Entrance requirements:* For master's, GRE or MAT, minimum undergraduate GPA of 3.0, resume. Electronic applications accepted. *Faculty research:* Information retrieval, digital libraries, scientometric and infometric studies, preservation/archiving and electronic records.

Long Island University, Westchester Graduate Campus, Program in Library and Information Science, Purchase, NY 10577. Offers MS. Part-time and evening/weekend programs available.

Louisiana State University and Agricultural and Mechanical College, Graduate School, School of Library and Information Science, Baton Rouge, LA 70803. Offers MLIS. *Accreditation:* ALA. Part-time and evening/weekend programs available. Postbaccalaureate distance learning degree programs offered (no on-campus study). *Faculty:* 10 full-time (7 women). *Students:* 58 full-time (43 women), 101 part-time (87 women); includes 19 minority (9 African Americans, 4 Asian Americans or Pacific Islanders, 6 Hispanic Americans), 4 international. Average age 34. 51 applicants, 90% accepted, 30 enrolled. In 2009, 63 master's awarded. *Degree requirements:* For master's, comprehensive exam, thesis optional. *Entrance requirements:* For master's, GRE General Test, minimum GPA of 3.0. Additional exam requirements/recommendations for international students: Required—TOEFL (minimum score 550 paper-based; 213 computer-based; 79 iBT) or IELTS (minimum score 6.5). *Application deadline:* For fall admission, 1/25 priority date for domestic students, 5/15 for international students; for spring admission, 10/15 for international students. Applications are processed on a rolling basis. Application fee: $50 ($70 for international students). Electronic applications accepted. *Financial support:* In 2009–10, 81 students received support, including 8 research assistantships with partial tuition reimbursements available (averaging $11,512 per year), 10 teaching assistantships with partial tuition reimbursements available (averaging $12,293 per year); fellowships, career-related internships or fieldwork, Federal Work-Study, institutionally sponsored loans, scholarships/grants, health care benefits, and unspecified assistantships also available. Support available to part-time students. Financial award applicants required to submit FAFSA. *Faculty research:* Information retrieval, management, collection development, public libraries. Total annual research expenditures: $22,209. *Unit head:* Dr. Beth M. Paskoff, Dean, 225-578-3158, Fax: 225-578-4581, E-mail: bpaskoff@lsu.edu. *Application contact:* LaToya Joseph, Administrative Assistant, 225-578-3150, Fax: 225-578-4581, E-mail: lcjoseph@lsu.edu.

Mansfield University of Pennsylvania, Graduate Studies, Program in School Library and Information Technologies, Mansfield, PA 16933. Offers library science (M Ed). Part-time and evening/weekend programs available. Postbaccalaureate distance learning degree programs offered. *Faculty:* 3 full-time (2 women), 11 part-time/adjunct (10 women). *Students:* 5 full-time (all women), 226 part-time (206 women); includes 21 minority (13 African Americans, 2 American Indian/Alaska Native, 1 Asian American or Pacific Islander, 5 Hispanic Americans), 1 international. Average age 38. In 2009, 77 master's awarded. *Degree requirements:* For master's, comprehensive exam, thesis optional. *Entrance requirements:* For master's, minimum GPA of 3.0. Additional exam requirements/recommendations for international students: Required—TOEFL (minimum score 550 paper-based; 220 computer-based). *Application deadline:* Applications are processed on a rolling basis. Application fee: $25. Electronic applications accepted. *Expenses:* Contact institution. *Financial support:* In 2009–10, 41 students received support. Unspecified assistantships available. Financial award application deadline: 5/1; financial award applicants required to submit FAFSA. *Unit head:* Cindy Keller, Chair, E-mail: ckeller@mansfield.edu. *Application contact:* Christina Hale, Assistant Director of Enrollment Services/Graduate Admissions, 570-662-4812, Fax: 570-662-4121, E-mail: chale@mansfield.edu.

Marywood University, Academic Affairs, Insalaco College of Creative and Performing Arts, Department of Communication Arts, Program in Information Sciences, Scranton, PA 18509-1598. Offers corporate communication (Certificate); e-business (Certificate); health communication (Certificate); information sciences (MS), including library science/information specialist; instructional technology (Certificate). *Students:* 1 full-time (0 women), 4 part-time (3 women). Average age 32. In 2009, 3 master's awarded. *Entrance requirements:* Additional exam requirements/recommendations for international students: Required—TOEFL (minimum score 550 paper-based; 213 computer-based; 79 iBT). *Application deadline:* For fall admission, 4/1 priority date for domestic students, 3/31 priority date for international students; for spring admission, 11/1 priority date for domestic students, 8/31 priority date for international students. Applications are processed on a rolling basis. Application fee: $35. Electronic applications accepted. *Expenses:* Tuition: Part-time $715 per credit. Required fees: $270 per semester. Tuition and fees vary according to degree level, campus/location and program. *Financial support:* Career-related internships or fieldwork, scholarships/grants, and unspecified assistantships available. Support available to part-time students. Financial award application deadline: 6/30; financial award applicants required to submit FAFSA. *Application contact:* Tammy Manka, Assistant Director of Graduate Admissions, 866-279-9663, E-mail: tmanka@marywood.edu.

McDaniel College, Graduate and Professional Studies, Program in Media/Library Science, Westminster, MD 21157-4390. Offers MS. Part-time and evening/weekend programs available. *Degree requirements:* For master's, comprehensive exam, thesis optional. *Entrance requirements:* For master's, GRE General Test, MAT, or NTE/PRAXIS I, letters of reference (3). Additional exam requirements/recommendations for international students: Required—TOEFL (minimum score 213 computer-based). *Expenses:* Tuition: Part-time $325 per credit hour.

McGill University, Faculty of Graduate and Postdoctoral Studies, Faculty of Education, School of Information Studies, Montréal, QC H3A 2T5, Canada. Offers MLIS, PhD, Certificate, Diploma. *Accreditation:* ALA (one or more programs are accredited).

North Carolina Central University, Division of Academic Affairs, School of Library and Information Sciences, Durham, NC 27707-3129. Offers MIS, MLS. *Accreditation:* ALA (one or more programs are accredited). Part-time and evening/weekend programs available. *Degree requirements:* For master's, one foreign language, thesis, research paper, or project. *Entrance requirements:* For master's, GRE, 90 hours in liberal arts. Additional exam requirements/recommendations for international students: Required—TOEFL. *Faculty research:* African-American resources, planning and evaluation, analysis of economic and physical resources, geography of information, artificial intelligence.

Old Dominion University, Darden College of Education, Program in Elementary/Middle Education, Norfolk, VA 23529. Offers elementary education (MS Ed); instructional technology (MS Ed); library science (MS Ed); middle school education (MS Ed). *Accreditation:* NCATE. Part-time and evening/weekend programs available. Postbaccalaureate distance learning degree programs offered (no on-campus study). *Faculty:* 20 full-time (16 women), 22 part-time/adjunct (2 women). *Students:* 109 full-time (103 women), 171 part-time (148 women); includes 41 minority (22 African Americans, 1 American Indian/Alaska Native, 10 Asian Americans or Pacific Islanders, 8 Hispanic Americans). Average age 33. 191 applicants, 76% accepted, 123 enrolled. In 2009, 155 master's awarded. *Degree requirements:* For master's, comprehensive exam. *Entrance requirements:* For master's, GRE General Test or MAT; PRAXIS I, SAT or ACT, minimum GPA of 2.8. Additional exam requirements/recommendations for international students: Required—TOEFL (minimum score 600 paper-based; 250 computer-based). *Application deadline:* For fall admission, 6/1 priority date for domestic students; for winter admission, 11/1 priority date for domestic students; for spring admission, 3/1 priority date for domestic students. Applications are processed on a rolling basis. Application fee: $50. Electronic applications accepted. *Expenses:* Tuition, state resident: full-time $8112; part-time $338 per credit. Tuition, nonresident: full-time $20,256; part-time $844 per credit. Required fees: $119 per semester. One-time fee: $50. *Financial support:* In 2009–10, 180 students received support, including teaching assistantships (averaging $9,000 per year); career-related internships or fieldwork, Federal Work-Study, institutionally sponsored loans, and scholarships/grants also available. Support available to part-time students. Financial award application deadline: 2/15; financial award applicants required to submit FAFSA. *Faculty research:* Education pre-K to 6, school librarianship. *Unit head:* Dr. Charlene Fleener, Graduate Program Director, 757-683-4374, E-mail: cfleener@odu.edu. *Application contact:* Alice McAdory, Director of Admissions, 757-683-3685, Fax: 757-683-3255, E-mail: gradadmit@odu.edu.

Old Dominion University, Darden College of Education, Programs in Secondary Education, Norfolk, VA 23529. Offers biology (MS Ed); chemistry (MS Ed); English (MS Ed); instructional technology (MS Ed); library science (MS Ed); secondary education (MS Ed). *Accreditation:* NCATE. Part-time and evening/weekend programs available. Postbaccalaureate distance learning degree programs offered (minimal on-campus study). *Faculty:* 20 full-time (16 women). *Students:* 74 full-time (54 women), 137 part-time (92 women); includes 41 minority (22 African Americans, 1 American Indian/Alaska Native, 11 Asian Americans or Pacific Islanders, 7 Hispanic Americans). Average age 33. 67 applicants, 79% accepted, 53 enrolled. In 2009, 131 master's awarded. *Degree requirements:* For master's, comprehensive exam, thesis. *Entrance requirements:* For master's, GRE General Test or MAT, PRAXIS I (for licensure), minimum GPA of 2.8, teaching certificate. Additional exam requirements/recommendations for international students: Required—TOEFL. *Application deadline:* For fall admission, 6/1 for domestic and international students; for winter admission, 11/1 for domestic and international students; for spring admission, 3/1 for domestic and international students. Applications are processed on a rolling basis. Application fee: $50. Electronic applications accepted. *Expenses:* Tuition, state resident: full-time $8112; part-time $338 per credit. Tuition, nonresident: full-time $20,256; part-time $844 per credit. Required fees: $119 per semester. One-time fee: $50. *Financial support:* In 2009–10, 56 students received support, including fellowships (averaging $15,000 per year), 2 research assistantships with tuition reimbursements available (averaging $9,000 per year), 3 teaching assistantships with tuition reimbursements available (averaging $12,500 per year); career-related internships or fieldwork, Federal Work-Study, institutionally sponsored loans, scholarships/grants, and tuition waivers (partial) also available. Support available to part-time students. Financial award application deadline: 2/15; financial award applicants required to submit FAFSA. *Faculty research:* Use of technology, writing project for teachers, geography teaching, reading. *Unit head:* Dr. Robert Lucking, Graduate Program Director, 757-683-5545, Fax: 757-683-5862, E-mail: rlucking@odu.edu. *Application contact:* Dr. Robert Lucking, Graduate Program Director, 757-683-5545, Fax: 757-683-5862, E-mail: rlucking@odu.edu.

Olivet Nazarene University, Graduate School, Division of Education, Program in Library Information Specialist, Bourbonnais, IL 60914. Offers MAE.

Pratt Institute, School of Information and Library Science, New York, NY 10011. Offers archives (Adv C); library and information science (MS, Adv C); library media specialist (Adv C); museum libraries (Adv C); JD/MS; MS/MS. *Accreditation:* ALA. Part-time programs available. *Faculty:* 9 full-time (6 women), 27 part-time/adjunct (15 women). *Students:* 143 full-time (118 women), 183 part-time (147 women); includes 51 minority (19 African Americans, 19 Asian Americans or Pacific Islanders, 13 Hispanic Americans), 4 international. Average age 32. 379 applicants, 90% accepted, 98 enrolled. In 2009, 148 master's awarded. *Degree requirements:* For master's, thesis. *Entrance requirements:* Additional exam requirements/recommendations for international students: Required—TOEFL (minimum score 600 paper-based; 250 computer-based; 100 iBT). *Application deadline:* For fall admission, 1/5 for domestic and international students; for spring admission, 10/1 for domestic and international students. Application fee: $50 ($90 for international students). Electronic applications accepted. *Expenses:* Contact institution. *Financial support:* Career-related internships or fieldwork, Federal Work-Study, institutionally sponsored loans, scholarships/grants, health care benefits, and unspecified assistantships available. Support available to part-time students. Financial award application deadline: 2/1; financial award applicants required to submit FAFSA. *Faculty research:* Development of urban libraries and information centers, medical and law librarianship, information management. *Unit head:* Dr. Tula Giannini, Dean, 212-647-7682, E-mail: giannini@pratt.edu. *Application contact:* Young Hah, Director of Graduate Admissions, 718-636-3683, Fax: 718-399-4242, E-mail: yhah@pratt.edu.

See Close-Up on page 1721.

Queens College of the City University of New York, Division of Graduate Studies, Social Science Division, Graduate School of Library and Information Studies, Flushing, NY 11367-1597. Offers MLS, AC. *Accreditation:* ALA (one or more programs are accredited). Part-time and evening/weekend programs available. *Faculty:* 17 full-time (11 women). *Students:* 52 full-time (37 women), 444 part-time (338 women). 322 applicants, 64% accepted, 166 enrolled. In 2009, 138 master's awarded. *Degree requirements:* For master's, thesis; for AC, thesis optional. *Entrance requirements:* For master's, minimum GPA of 3.0; for AC, master's degree or equivalent. Additional exam requirements/recommendations for international students: Required—TOEFL. *Application deadline:* For fall admission, 4/1 for domestic students; for spring admission, 11/1 for domestic students. Applications are processed on a rolling basis. Application fee: $125. *Expenses:* Tuition, state resident: full-time $7360; part-time $310 per credit. Tuition, nonresident: part-time $575 per credit. One-time fee: $195 full-time; $145.25 part-time. *Financial support:* Career-related internships or fieldwork, Federal Work-Study, institutionally sponsored loans, and tuition waivers (partial) available. Support available to part-time students. Financial award application deadline: 4/1; financial award applicants required to submit FAFSA. *Faculty research:* Multimedia and video studies, ethnicity and librarianship, information science and computer applications. *Unit head:* Dr. Virgil Blake, Director/Chair, 718-997-3790. *Application contact:* Dr. Karen Smith, Graduate Adviser, 718-997-3790, E-mail: karen_smith@qc.edu.

Rowan University, Graduate School, College of Education, Department of Special Educational Services/Instruction, Program in School and Public Librarianship, Glassboro, NJ 08028-1701. Offers MA. *Accreditation:* NCATE. Part-time and evening/weekend programs available. *Students:* 17 part-time (all women); includes 2 minority (1 African American, 1 Hispanic American). Average age 41. In 2009, 13 master's awarded. *Degree requirements:* For master's,

comprehensive exam, thesis. *Entrance requirements:* For master's, GRE General Test, minimum GPA of 2.8. Additional exam requirements/recommendations for international students: Required—TOEFL. *Application deadline:* Applications are processed on a rolling basis. Application fee: $50. Electronic applications accepted. *Expenses:* Tuition, state resident: full-time $10,624; part-time $590 per semester hour. Tuition, nonresident: full-time $10,624; part-time $590 per semester hour. Required fees: $2320; $125 per semester hour. *Financial support:* Career-related internships or fieldwork, scholarships/grants, health care benefits, and unspecified assistantships available. Support available to part-time students. *Unit head:* Dr. Mira Lalovic-Hand, Interim Associate Provost/Director of Graduate School, 856-256-5120, E-mail: lalovic-hand@rowan.edu. *Application contact:* Karen Haynes, Graduate Coordinator, 856-256-4052, E-mail: haynes@rowan.edu.

Rutgers, The State University of New Jersey, New Brunswick, School of Communication, Information and Library Studies, Department of Library and Information Science, Piscataway, NJ 08854-8097. Offers MLS. *Accreditation:* ALA. Part-time programs available. Postbaccalaureate distance learning degree programs offered (no on-campus study). *Entrance requirements:* For master's, GRE General Test. Additional exam requirements/recommendations for international students: Required—TOEFL. Electronic applications accepted. *Faculty research:* Information science, library services, management of information services.

Rutgers, The State University of New Jersey, New Brunswick, School of Communication, Information and Library Studies, Program in Communication, Library and Information Science and Media Studies, Piscataway, NJ 08854-8097. Offers PhD. Part-time programs available. *Degree requirements:* For doctorate, comprehensive exam, thesis/dissertation, qualifying exams. *Entrance requirements:* For doctorate, GRE General Test, proficiency in statistics. Additional exam requirements/recommendations for international students: Required—TOEFL (minimum score 600 paper-based; 250 computer-based). Electronic applications accepted. *Faculty research:* Information science, media studies.

St. Catherine University, Graduate Programs, Program in Library and Information Science, St. Paul, MN 55105. Offers MLIS. Part-time and evening/weekend programs available. *Faculty:* 3 full-time (all women). *Students:* 72 full-time (62 women), 89 part-time (73 women); includes 12 minority (2 African Americans, 5 Asian Americans or Pacific Islanders, 5 Hispanic Americans). Average age 34. 80 applicants, 79% accepted, 39 enrolled. In 2009, 21 master's awarded. *Degree requirements:* For master's, microcomputer competency. *Entrance requirements:* For master's, GRE or MAT, minimum GPA of 3.2 or GRE. Additional exam requirements/recommendations for international students: Required—Michigan English Language Assessment Battery or TOEFL (minimum score 600 paper-based; 250 computer-based; 100 iBT). *Application deadline:* For fall admission, 3/1 for domestic students; for winter admission, 10/1 for domestic students. Application fee: $35. Tuition and fees vary according to program. *Financial support:* In 2009–10, 117 students received support. Institutionally sponsored loans available. Support available to part-time students. Financial award application deadline: 4/1; financial award applicants required to submit FAFSA. *Unit head:* Dr. Deborah Grealy, Director, 651-690-6802. *Application contact:* 651-690-6933, Fax: 651-690-6064.

St. John's University, St. John's College of Liberal Arts and Sciences, Division of Library and Information Science, Queens, NY 11439. Offers MLS, Adv C, MA/MLS, MS/MLS. *Accreditation:* ALA (one or more programs are accredited). Part-time and evening/weekend programs available. *Students:* 39 full-time (30 women), 148 part-time (115 women); includes 40 minority (13 African Americans, 1 American Indian/Alaska Native, 7 Asian Americans or Pacific Islanders, 19 Hispanic Americans), 4 international. Average age 37. 169 applicants, 70% accepted, 63 enrolled. In 2009, 28 master's awarded. *Degree requirements:* For master's, comprehensive exam, residency. *Entrance requirements:* For master's, interview, minimum GPA of 3.0. Additional exam requirements/recommendations for international students: Required—TOEFL (minimum score 500 paper-based; 173 computer-based; 61 iBT), IELTS (minimum score 5.5). *Application deadline:* For fall admission, 5/1 priority date for domestic and international students; for spring admission, 11/1 priority date for domestic and international students. Applications are processed on a rolling basis. Application fee: $70. Electronic applications accepted. *Expenses:* Contact institution. *Financial support:* Research assistantships, career-related internships or fieldwork and scholarships/grants available. Support available to part-time students. Financial award application deadline: 3/1; financial award applicants required to submit FAFSA. *Faculty research:* Indexes and metatags, information use and users, competitive intelligence, knowledge management, database theory, young adult and children services, school media services, archives, oral history. *Unit head:* Dr. Jeffrey Olson, Director, 718-990-5705, E-mail: olsonj@stjohns.edu. *Application contact:* Kathleen Davis, Director of Graduate Admissions, 718-990-2790, Fax: 718-990-5686, E-mail: gradhelp@stjohns.edu.

Sam Houston State University, College of Education and Applied Science, Department of Library Science, Huntsville, TX 77341. Offers MLS. Part-time and evening/weekend programs available. *Faculty:* 8 full-time (7 women), 2 part-time/adjunct (both women). *Students:* 3 full-time (all women), 202 part-time (188 women); includes 80 minority (5 African Americans, 3 Asian Americans or Pacific Islanders, 72 Hispanic Americans). Average age 37. 97 applicants, 98% accepted, 72 enrolled. In 2009, 70 master's awarded. *Entrance requirements:* For master's, GRE General Test, minimum GPA of 2.8. Additional exam requirements/recommendations for international students: Required—TOEFL (minimum score 550 paper-based; 213 computer-based; 79 iBT). *Application deadline:* For fall admission, 8/1 for domestic students; for spring admission, 12/1 for domestic students. Applications are processed on a rolling basis. Application fee: $20. *Expenses:* Tuition, state resident: full-time $3690; part-time $205 per credit hour. Tuition, nonresident: full-time $8676; part-time $482 per credit hour. Required fees: $1474. Tuition and fees vary according to course load and campus/location. *Financial support:* Teaching assistantships, career-related internships or fieldwork and Federal Work-Study available. Support available to part-time students. Financial award application deadline: 5/31; financial award applicants required to submit FAFSA. *Unit head:* Dr. Mary Bell, Acting Chair, 936-294-1150, Fax: 936-294-1153, E-mail: lis_mah@shsu.edu. *Application contact:* Molly Doughtie, Advisor, 936-294-1105, E-mail: edu_mxd@shsu.edu.

San Jose State University, Graduate Studies and Research, College of Applied Sciences and Arts, School of Library and Information Science, San Jose, CA 95192-0001. Offers MLIS, PhD. *Accreditation:* ALA (one or more programs are accredited). Part-time and evening/weekend programs available. *Students:* 285 full-time (238 women), 666 part-time (528 women); includes 238 minority (18 African Americans, 7 American Indian/Alaska Native, 126 Asian Americans or Pacific Islanders, 87 Hispanic Americans), 3 international. Average age 36. 361 applicants, 44% accepted, 114 enrolled. In 2009, 437 master's awarded. *Degree requirements:* For master's, comprehensive exam. *Entrance requirements:* Additional exam requirements/recommendations for international students: Required—TOEFL (minimum score 600 paper-based). *Application deadline:* For fall admission, 6/29 for domestic students; for spring admission, 11/30 for domestic students. Applications are processed on a rolling basis. Application fee: $59. Electronic applications accepted. *Financial support:* Career-related internships or fieldwork, Federal Work-Study, and institutionally sponsored loans available. Support available to part-time students. Financial award application deadline: 8/20; financial award applicants required to submit FAFSA. *Faculty research:* Evaluation of information services online, search strategy, organizational behavior. *Unit head:* Dr. Ken Haycock, Director, 408-924-2491, Fax: 408-924-2476. *Application contact:* Dr. Ken Haycock, Director, 408-924-2491, Fax: 408-924-2476.

Simmons College, Graduate School of Library and Information Science, Program in Library and Information Science, Boston, MA 02115. Offers MS, PhD. Part-time and evening/weekend programs available. *Faculty:* 25 full-time (17 women), 34 part-time/adjunct (22 women). *Students:* 17 full-time (12 women), 448 part-time (341 women); includes 30 minority (8 African Americans, 16 Asian Americans or Pacific Islanders, 6 Hispanic Americans), 10 international. Average age 33. 260 applicants, 75% accepted, 105 enrolled. In 2009, 245 master's awarded. *Degree requirements:* For doctorate, comprehensive exam, thesis/dissertation. *Application deadline:* For fall admission, 3/1 for domestic and international students; for spring admission, 9/1 for domestic and international students. Applications are processed on a rolling basis. Application fee: $50. Electronic applications accepted. *Expenses:* Tuition: Part-time $925 per credit hour. Part-time tuition and fees vary according to program. *Faculty research:* Library Leadership, archives and preservation, organization, information use and users, children's literature and youth services. Total annual research expenditures: $253,656. *Unit head:* Dr. Michele V. Cloonan, Dean, 617-521-2806, Fax: 617-521-3192, E-mail: cloonan@simmons.edu. *Application contact:* Sarah Petrakos, Assistant Dean, Admission and Recruitment, 617-521-2868, Fax: 617-521-3192, E-mail: gslisadm@simmons.edu.

Southern Arkansas University–Magnolia, Graduate Programs, Magnolia, AR 71753. Offers agriculture (MS); business administration (MBA); computer and information sciences (MS); counseling (MS); education (M Ed), including counseling and development, curriculum and instruction emphasis, educational administration and supervision, elementary education, middle level emphasis, reading emphasis, secondary education, TESOL emphasis; kinesiology (MS); library media and information specialist (M Ed); mental health and clinical counseling (MS); public administration (EMPA); school counseling (M Ed); teaching (MAT). *Accreditation:* NCATE. Part-time and evening/weekend programs available. *Faculty:* 43 full-time (24 women), 12 part-time/adjunct (7 women). *Students:* 116 full-time (78 women), 333 part-time (255 women); includes 105 minority (98 African Americans, 3 American Indian/Alaska Native, 3 Asian Americans or Pacific Islanders, 1 Hispanic American), 11 international. Average age 33. In 2009, 88 master's awarded. *Degree requirements:* For master's, comprehensive exam, thesis optional. *Entrance requirements:* For master's, GRE, MAT or GMAT, minimum GPA of 2.75. *Application deadline:* For fall admission, 8/15 for domestic students; for winter admission, 1/8 for domestic students; for spring admission, 1/8 for domestic students. Applications are processed on a rolling basis. Application fee: $0. *Expenses:* Tuition, state resident: full-time $3798; part-time $211 per hour. Tuition, nonresident: full-time $5580; part-time $310 per hour. Required fees: $584. *Financial support:* Career-related internships or fieldwork, Federal Work-Study, scholarships/grants, tuition waivers (full), and unspecified assistantships available. Financial award applicants required to submit FAFSA. *Faculty research:* Alternative certification for teachers, supervision of instruction, instructional leadership, counseling. *Unit head:* Dr. Kim Bloss, Dean, Graduate Studies, 870-235-4150, Fax: 870-235-5227, E-mail: kkbloss@saumag.edu. *Application contact:* Dr. Kim Bloss, Dean, Graduate Studies, 870-235-4150, Fax: 870-235-5227, E-mail: kkbloss@saumag.edu.

Southern Connecticut State University, School of Graduate Studies, School of Communication, Information and Library Science, Department of Information and Library Science, New Haven, CT 06515-1355. Offers library science (MLS); library/information studies (Diploma); JD/MLS; MLS/MA; MLS/MS. Part-time and evening/weekend programs available. Postbaccalaureate distance learning degree programs offered (no on-campus study). *Faculty:* 12 full-time, 5 part-time/adjunct. *Students:* 50 full-time (38 women), 255 part-time (223 women); includes 18 minority (5 African Americans, 10 Asian Americans or Pacific Islanders, 3 Hispanic Americans). 164 applicants, 47% accepted, 62 enrolled. In 2009, 127 master's, 12 other advanced degrees awarded. *Degree requirements:* For master's and Diploma, thesis or alternative. *Entrance requirements:* For master's, GRE General Test, interview, minimum QPA of 2.7, introductory computer science course; for Diploma, master's degree in library science or information science. *Application deadline:* For fall admission, 7/15 priority date for domestic students. Applications are processed on a rolling basis. Application fee: $50. Electronic applications accepted. Tuition and fees vary according to program. *Financial support:* Research assistantships available. Financial award application deadline: 4/15; financial award applicants required to submit FAFSA. *Unit head:* Dr. Chang Suk Kim, Chairperson, 203-392-5191, Fax: 203-392-5780, E-mail: kimc1@southernct.edu. *Application contact:* Dr. Elsie Okobi, Graduate Coordinator, 203-392-5709, E-mail: okobie1@southernct.edu.

Syracuse University, School of Information Studies, Program in Digital Libraries, Syracuse, NY 13244. Offers CAS. Part-time and evening/weekend programs available. Postbaccalaureate distance learning degree programs offered (minimal on-campus study). *Students:* 1 (woman) full-time, 8 part-time (7 women); includes 2 minority (1 Asian American or Pacific Islander, 1 Hispanic American), 2 international. Average age 47. 13 applicants, 92% accepted, 2 enrolled. In 2009, 20 CASs awarded. *Entrance requirements:* Additional exam requirements/recommendations for international students: Required—TOEFL (minimum score 100 iBT). *Application deadline:* For fall admission, 2/1 priority date for domestic and international students; for spring admission, 10/15 priority date for domestic and international students. Applications are processed on a rolling basis. Application fee: $75. Electronic applications accepted. *Expenses:* Tuition: Full-time $26,808; part-time $1117 per credit. Required fees: $1024. *Financial support:* Fellowships with full and partial tuition reimbursements, research assistantships with full and partial tuition reimbursements, teaching assistantships with full and partial tuition reimbursements, scholarships/grants and tuition waivers (partial) available. Financial award application deadline: 1/1; financial award applicants required to submit FAFSA. *Unit head:* R. David Lankes, Head, 315-443-1707, Fax: 315-443-6886, E-mail: rdlankes@iis.syr.edu. *Application contact:* Susan Corieri, Director of Enrollment Management, 315-443-2575, E-mail: ist@syr.edu.

Syracuse University, School of Information Studies, Program in Library and Information Science, Syracuse, NY 13244. Offers MS. *Accreditation:* ALA. Part-time and evening/weekend programs available. Postbaccalaureate distance learning degree programs offered (minimal on-campus study). *Students:* 77 full-time (59 women), 99 part-time (83 women); includes 10 minority (1 African American, 1 American Indian/Alaska Native, 4 Asian Americans or Pacific Islanders, 4 Hispanic Americans), 8 international. Average age 32. 196 applicants, 89% accepted, 80 enrolled. In 2009, 71 master's awarded. *Degree requirements:* For master's, fieldwork or research paper. *Entrance requirements:* For master's, GRE General Test. Additional exam requirements/recommendations for international students: Required—TOEFL (minimum score 100 iBT). *Application deadline:* For fall admission, 2/1 priority date for domestic and international students; for spring admission, 10/15 priority date for domestic and international students. Application fee: $75. Electronic applications accepted. *Expenses:* Tuition: Full-time $26,808; part-time $1117 per credit. Required fees: $1024. *Financial support:* Fellowships with tuition reimbursements, tuition waivers (full and partial) available. Financial award application deadline: 1/1; financial award applicants required to submit FAFSA. *Unit head:* R. David Lankes, Head, 315-443-1707, Fax: 315-443-6886, E-mail: rdlankes@iis.syr.edu. *Application contact:* Susan Corieri, Director of Enrollment Management, 315-443-2575, E-mail: ist@syr.edu.

See Close-Up on page 1723.

Tennessee Technological University, Graduate School, College of Education, Department of Curriculum and Instruction, Program in Library Science, Cookeville, TN 38505. Offers MA. *Students:* 9 full-time (all women), 5 part-time (4 women). 8 applicants, 88% accepted, 4 enrolled. In 2009, 7 master's awarded. *Degree requirements:* For master's, comprehensive exam, thesis or alternative. *Entrance requirements:* For master's, MAT or GRE. Additional exam requirements/recommendations for international students: Required—TOEFL (minimum score 550 paper-based; 79 iBT), IELTS (minimum score 5.5). *Application deadline:* For fall admission, 8/1 for domestic students, 5/1 for international students; for spring admission, 12/1 for domestic students, 10/1 for international students. Application fee: $25 ($30 for international students). Electronic applications accepted. *Expenses:* Tuition, state resident: full-time $7034; part-time $368 per credit hour. *Financial support:* In 2009–10, research assistantships (averaging $4,000 per year), 2 teaching assistantships (averaging $4,000 per year) were awarded. Financial award application deadline: 4/1. *Unit head:* Dr. Matthew R. Smith, Chairperson, 931-372-3181, Fax: 931-372-6270. *Application contact:* Shelia K. Kendrick, Coordinator of Graduate Studies, 931-372-3808, Fax: 931-372-3497, E-mail: skendrick@tntech.edu.

Texas Woman's University, Graduate School, College of Professional Education, School of Library and Information Studies, Denton, TX 76201. Offers library science (MA, MLS, PhD). *Accreditation:* ALA (one or more programs are accredited). Part-time and evening/weekend programs available. Postbaccalaureate distance learning degree programs offered (minimal on-campus study). *Faculty:* 13 full-time (9 women). *Students:* 72 full-time (64 women), 498 part-time (472 women); includes 131 minority (32 African Americans, 5 American Indian/Alaska Native, 12 Asian Americans or Pacific Islanders, 82 Hispanic Americans), 6 international.

Library Science

Texas Woman's University (continued)
Average age 38. 163 applicants, 81% accepted, 102 enrolled. In 2009, 226 master's awarded. *Degree requirements:* For doctorate, comprehensive exam, thesis/dissertation. *Entrance requirements:* For master's, GRE (preferred), GMAT, MCAT, MAT, 3 letters of recommendation, 2-page statement of intent; for doctorate, GRE (preferred), GMAT, MCAT, MAT, curriculum vitae/resume, 3 letters of reference, interview. Additional exam requirements/recommendations for international students: Required—TOEFL (minimum score 550 paper-based; 213 computer-based; 79 iBT). *Application deadline:* For fall admission, 2/15 priority date for domestic students, 2/15 for international students. Applications are processed on a rolling basis. Application fee: $50. Electronic applications accepted. *Expenses:* Tuition, state resident: full-time $3564; part-time $198 per credit hour. Tuition, nonresident: full-time $8550; part-time $475 per credit hour. Required fees: $69.26 per credit hour. Tuition and fees vary according to course load. *Financial support:* In 2009–10, 71 students received support, including 18 research assistantships (averaging $11,862 per year), 1 teaching assistantship (averaging $11,862 per year); career-related internships or fieldwork, Federal Work-Study, institutionally sponsored loans, scholarships/grants, traineeships, health care benefits, and unspecified assistantships also available. Support available to part-time students. Financial award application deadline: 3/1; financial award applicants required to submit FAFSA. *Faculty research:* Children's literature, health information, information needs analysis, information policy, library management. *Unit head:* Dr. Ling Hwey Jeng, Director, 940-898-2602, Fax: 940-898-2611, E-mail: slis@twu.edu. *Application contact:* Samuel Wheeler, Assistant Director of Admissions, 940-898-3188, Fax: 940-898-3081, E-mail: wheelersr@twu.edu.

Trevecca Nazarene University, Graduate Division, School of Education, Major in Library and Information Science, Nashville, TN 37210-2877. Offers MLI Sc. Evening/weekend programs available. *Students:* 36 full-time (all women). Average age 39. In 2009, 15 master's awarded. *Degree requirements:* For master's, exit assessment. *Entrance requirements:* For master's, GRE General Test, MAT, technology pre-assessment, minimum GPA of 2.7, 2 reference forms. Additional exam requirements/recommendations for international students: Required—TOEFL (minimum score 550 paper-based; 213 computer-based). *Application deadline:* Applications are processed on a rolling basis. Application fee: $25. *Expenses:* Contact institution. *Financial support:* Applicants required to submit FAFSA. *Unit head:* Dr. Esther Swink, Dean, School of Education/Director of Graduate Education Program, 615-248-1201, Fax: 615-248-1597, E-mail: admissions_ged@trevecca.edu. *Application contact:* Admissions Office, 615-248-1201, Fax: 615-248-1597, E-mail: admissions_ged@trevecca.edu.

Universidad del Turabo, Graduate Programs, Programs in Education, Program in Administration of School Libraries, Gurabo, PR 00778-3030. Offers Certificate. *Students:* 1 (woman) full-time; minority (Hispanic American). Average age 39.*Unit head:* Angela Candelario, Dean, 787-743-7979 Ext. 4126. *Application contact:* Virginia Gonzalez, Admissions Officer, 787-746-3009.

Universidad del Turabo, Graduate Programs, Programs in Education, Program in Library Service and Information Technology, Gurabo, PR 00778-3030. Offers M Ed. *Students:* 70 full-time (60 women), 31 part-time (26 women); includes 86 Hispanic Americans. Average age 34. 62 applicants, 95% accepted, 43 enrolled. In 2009, 33 master's awarded. *Unit head:* Angela Candelario, Dean, 787-743-7979 Ext. 4126. *Application contact:* Virginia Gonzalez, Admissions Officer, 787-746-3009.

Université de Montréal, Faculty of Arts and Sciences, School of Library and Information Sciences, Montréal, QC H3C 3J7, Canada. Offers information sciences (MIS, PhD). *Accreditation:* ALA (one or more programs are accredited). *Faculty:* 17 full-time (6 women), 7 part-time/adjunct (4 women). *Students:* 140 full-time (95 women), 50 part-time (39 women). 199 applicants, 49% accepted, 89 enrolled. In 2009, 68 master's awarded. *Degree requirements:* For master's, thesis optional. *Entrance requirements:* For master's, interview, master's degree in library and information science or equivalent. *Application deadline:* For fall admission, 2/1 priority date for domestic students; for winter admission, 11/1 priority date for domestic students; for spring admission, 2/1 priority date for domestic students. Application fee: $100. Electronic applications accepted. *Financial support:* Fellowships available. *Unit head:* Cl??ment Arsenault, Director, 514-343-7400, Fax: 514-343-5753, E-mail: clement.arsenault@umontreal.ca. *Application contact:* James Turner, Professor/Responsible for Graduate Studies, 514-343-2454, Fax: 514-343-5753, E-mail: james.turner@umontreal.ca.

University at Buffalo, the State University of New York, Graduate School, Graduate School of Education, Department of Library and Information Studies, Buffalo, NY 14260. Offers library and information studies (MLS, Certificate); library and information studies (online) (MLS). *Accreditation:* ALA (one or more programs are accredited). Part-time programs available. Postbaccalaureate distance learning degree programs offered (no on-campus study). *Faculty:* 10 full-time (6 women), 12 part-time/adjunct (7 women). *Students:* 157 full-time (110 women), 103 part-time (72 women); includes 21 minority (6 African Americans, 1 American Indian/Alaska Native, 10 Asian Americans or Pacific Islanders, 4 Hispanic Americans), 2 international. Average age 32. 162 applicants, 98% accepted, 99 enrolled. In 2009, 128 master's, 1 other advanced degree awarded. *Degree requirements:* For master's, thesis optional; for Certificate, thesis. *Entrance requirements:* For master's, minimum GPA of 3.0. Additional exam requirements/recommendations for international students: Required—TOEFL (minimum score 550 paper-based; 213 computer-based; 79 iBT). *Application deadline:* For fall admission, 4/1 priority date for domestic students; for spring admission, 10/15 priority date for domestic students. Applications are processed on a rolling basis. Application fee: $50. Electronic applications accepted. *Financial support:* In 2009–10, 8 fellowships with full tuition reimbursements (averaging $4,000 per year), 4 research assistantships with full tuition reimbursements (averaging $9,000 per year) were awarded; teaching assistantships, career-related internships or fieldwork, Federal Work-Study, institutionally sponsored loans, tuition waivers (full and partial), and unspecified assistantships also available. Support available to part-time students. Financial award application deadline: 3/1; financial award applicants required to submit FAFSA. *Faculty research:* Information-seeking behavior, thesauri, impact of technology, questioning behaviors, educational informatics. Total annual research expenditures: $9,929. *Unit head:* Dr. Dagobert Soergel, Chair, 716-645-2412, Fax: 716-645-3775, E-mail: ub-lis@buffalo.edu. *Application contact:* Sarah Watson, Admissions Advisor, 716-645-2110, Fax: 716-645-7937, E-mail: gse-info@buffalo.edu.

The University of Alabama, Graduate School, College of Communication and Information Sciences, School of Library and Information Studies, Tuscaloosa, AL 35487. Offers book arts (MFA); library and information studies (MLIS, PhD). *Accreditation:* ALA (one or more programs are accredited). Part-time programs available. Postbaccalaureate distance learning degree programs offered (minimal on-campus study). *Faculty:* 10 full-time (4 women), 3 part-time/adjunct (all women). *Students:* 83 full-time (64 women), 186 part-time (141 women); includes 27 minority (14 African Americans, 2 American Indian/Alaska Native, 8 Asian Americans or Pacific Islanders, 3 Hispanic Americans), 3 international. Average age 33. 295 applicants, 39% accepted, 85 enrolled. In 2009, 102 degrees awarded. *Entrance requirements:* For master's, GRE General Test or MAT, minimum GPA of 3.0. Additional exam requirements/recommendations for international students: Required—TOEFL. *Application deadline:* For fall admission, 7/1 priority date for domestic and international students; for spring admission, 11/1 priority date for domestic and international students. Applications are processed on a rolling basis. Application fee: $50 ($60 for international students). Electronic applications accepted. *Expenses:* Tuition, state resident: full-time $7000. Tuition, nonresident: full-time $19,200. *Financial support:* In 2009–10, 64 students received support, including 4 fellowships with tuition reimbursements available (averaging $14,778 per year), 13 research assistantships with full and partial tuition reimbursements available (averaging $4,912 per year), 18 teaching assistantships with full and partial tuition reimbursements available (averaging $4,912 per year); career-related internships or fieldwork, Federal Work-Study, scholarships/grants, and unspecified assistantships also available. Financial award application deadline: 3/20. *Faculty research:* Instructional design, information equity, youth services, rural information services, book history. *Unit head:* Dr. Elizabeth Aversa, Director and Professor, 205-348-4610, Fax: 205-348-3746, E-mail: eaversa@slis.ua.edu. *Application contact:* Dr. Elizabeth Aversa, 205-348-4610, E-mail: eaversa@slis.ua.edu.

University of Alberta, Faculty of Graduate Studies and Research, School of Library and Information Studies, Edmonton, AB T6G 2E1, Canada. Offers MLIS. *Accreditation:* ALA. *Faculty:* 6 full-time (5 women), 12 part-time/adjunct (7 women). *Students:* 76 full-time (65 women), 22 part-time (20 women). Average age 32. 142 applicants, 32% accepted, 42 enrolled. In 2009, 24 master's awarded. *Entrance requirements:* Additional exam requirements/recommendations for international students: Required—TOEFL, Canadian Academic English Language Assessment. *Application deadline:* For fall admission, 7/1 for domestic students, 5/1 for international students. Applications are processed on a rolling basis. Electronic applications accepted. Tuition and fees charges are reported in Canadian dollars. *Expenses:* Tuition, area resident: Full-time $4626 Canadian dollars; part-time $99.72 Canadian dollars per unit. International tuition: $8216 Canadian dollars full-time. Required fees: $3590 Canadian dollars; $99.72 Canadian dollars per unit. $215 Canadian dollars per term. *Financial support:* In 2009–10, 68 students received support, including 12 research assistantships with partial tuition reimbursements available (averaging $3,536 per year); fellowships, career-related internships or fieldwork and scholarships/grants also available. Support available to part-time students. Financial award application deadline: 7/1. *Faculty research:* Intellectual freedom, materials for children and young adults, library classification, multi-media literacy. Total annual research expenditures: $63,000. *Unit head:* Anna Altmann, Acting Director, 780-492-4140, Fax: 403-492-2430, E-mail: anna.altmann@ualberta.ca. *Application contact:* Joanne Hilger, Student Services Administrator, 780-492-4578, Fax: 780-492-2430, E-mail: slis@ualberta.ca.

The University of Arizona, Graduate College, College of Social and Behavioral Sciences, School of Information Resources and Library Science, Tucson, AZ 85721. Offers MA, PhD. *Accreditation:* ALA (one or more programs are accredited). Part-time programs available. *Faculty:* 8 full-time (5 women). *Students:* 101 full-time (74 women), 226 part-time (191 women); includes 21 minority (3 African Americans, 6 American Indian/Alaska Native, 12 Hispanic Americans), 9 international. Average age 36. 22 applicants, 36% accepted, 7 enrolled. In 2009, 121 master's awarded. *Degree requirements:* For master's, proficiency in disk operating system (DOS); for doctorate, thesis/dissertation. *Entrance requirements:* For master's and doctorate, GRE General Test, 3 letters of recommendation, resume. Additional exam requirements/recommendations for international students: Required—TOEFL (minimum score 550 paper-based; 213 computer-based; 79 iBT). *Application deadline:* For spring admission, 9/1 for domestic and international students. Applications are processed on a rolling basis. Application fee: $65. Electronic applications accepted. *Expenses:* Tuition, state resident: full-time $9028. Tuition, nonresident: full-time $24,890. *Financial support:* In 2009–10, 4 research assistantships with full tuition reimbursements (averaging $12,414 per year), 34 teaching assistantships with full tuition reimbursements (averaging $12,970 per year) were awarded; career-related internships or fieldwork, Federal Work-Study, institutionally sponsored loans, scholarships/grants, health care benefits, tuition waivers (full and partial), and unspecified assistantships also available. Financial award application deadline: 3/1. *Faculty research:* Microcomputer applications; quantitative methods systems; information transfer, planning, evaluation, and technology. Total annual research expenditures: $1.1 million. *Unit head:* Dr. Jana Bradley, Director, 520-621-3565, Fax: 520-621-3279, E-mail: janabrad@email.arizona.edu. *Application contact:* Geraldme Fragoso, Program Manager, 520-621-3565, Fax: 520-621-3279, E-mail: gfragoso@email.arizona.edu.

The University of British Columbia, Faculty of Arts, School of Library, Archival and Information Studies, Dual Master of Archival Studies/Master of Library and Information Studies Program, Vancouver, BC V6T 1Z1, Canada. Offers MLIS/MAS. *Entrance requirements:* Additional exam requirements/recommendations for international students: Required—TOEFL (minimum score 600 paper-based; 250 computer-based; 100 iBT). Electronic applications accepted. *Faculty research:* Computer systems/database design, information-seeking behaviour, archives and records management, children's literature and services, digital libraries and archives.

The University of British Columbia, Faculty of Arts, School of Library, Archival and Information Studies, Master of Library and Information Studies Program, Vancouver, BC V6T 1Z1, Canada. Offers MLIS. Part-time programs available. *Degree requirements:* For master's, thesis optional. *Entrance requirements:* For master's, minimum GPA of 3.3 in undergraduate upper-division courses. Additional exam requirements/recommendations for international students: Required—TOEFL (minimum score 600 paper-based; 250 computer-based; 100 iBT). Electronic applications accepted. *Faculty research:* Computer systems/database design; digital libraries; metadata/classification; human-computer interaction; children's literature and services.

The University of British Columbia, Faculty of Arts, School of Library, Archival and Information Studies, PhD Program in Library, Archival and Information Studies, Vancouver, BC V6T 1Z1, Canada. Offers PhD. *Degree requirements:* For doctorate, thesis/dissertation. *Entrance requirements:* For doctorate, GRE, minimum GPA of 3.3 in MAS or MLIS (other master's degrees may be considered). Additional exam requirements/recommendations for international students: Required—TOEFL (minimum score 600 paper-based; 250 computer-based; 100 iBT). Electronic applications accepted. *Faculty research:* Computer systems/database design; library and archival management; archival description and organization; children's literature and youth services; interactive information retrieval.

University of California, Los Angeles, Graduate Division, Graduate School of Education and Information Studies, Department of Information Studies, Los Angeles, CA 90095. Offers archival studies (MLIS); informatics (MLIS); information studies (PhD); library and information science (Certificate); library studies (MLIS); moving image archive studies (MA); MBA/MLIS; MLIS/MA. *Accreditation:* ALA (one or more programs are accredited). *Faculty:* 14 full-time (8 women), 11 part-time/adjunct (10 women). *Students:* 171 full-time (125 women), 29 part-time (20 women); includes 76 minority (8 African Americans, 1 American Indian/Alaska Native, 44 Asian Americans or Pacific Islanders, 23 Hispanic Americans), 4 international. Average age 27. 214 applicants, 54% accepted, 82 enrolled. In 2009, 74 master's, 6 doctorates awarded. Terminal master's awarded for partial completion of doctoral program. *Degree requirements:* For master's, thesis or alternative, professional portfolio; for doctorate, thesis/dissertation, oral and written qualifying exams. *Entrance requirements:* For master's, GRE General Test, previous course work in computer programming and statistics; for doctorate, GRE General Test, previous course work in statistics, 2 samples of research writing in English. Additional exam requirements/recommendations for international students: Required—TOEFL (minimum score 613 paper-based; 220 computer-based; 87 iBT), IELTS (minimum score 7). *Application deadline:* For fall admission, 11/30 for domestic students, 10/30 for international students. Applications are processed on a rolling basis. Application fee: $60 ($80 for international students). Electronic applications accepted. *Financial support:* In 2009–10, 55 students received support, including 37 fellowships (averaging $15,750 per year), 12 research assistantships with partial tuition reimbursements available (averaging $28,600 per year), 6 teaching assistantships with partial tuition reimbursements available (averaging $54,040 per year); career-related internships or fieldwork, Federal Work-Study, institutionally sponsored loans, scholarships/grants, and unspecified assistantships also available. Financial award application deadline: 3/1; financial award applicants required to submit FAFSA. *Faculty research:* Multimedia, digital libraries, archives and electronic records, interface design, information technology and preservation, preservation, access. *Unit head:* Dr. Gregory H. Leazer, Associate Professor and Chair, 310-825-8799, E-mail: gleazer@ucla.edu. *Application contact:* Susan S. Abler, Student Affairs Officer, 310-825-5269, Fax: 310-206-4460, E-mail: abler@gseis.ucla.edu.

University of Central Arkansas, Graduate School, College of Education, Department of Teaching, Learning, and Technology, Program in Education Media and Library Science, Conway, AR 72035-0001. Offers MS. Part-time programs available. *Students:* 4 full-time (0 women), 5 part-time (4 women). Average age 37. 29 applicants, 100% accepted. In 2009, 41 master's awarded. *Degree requirements:* For master's, comprehensive exam. *Entrance requirements:* For master's, GRE General Test, minimum GPA of 2.7. Additional exam requirements/recommendations for international students: Required—TOEFL (minimum score 550 paper-

based; 213 computer-based). *Application deadline:* For fall admission, 3/1 priority date for domestic and international students; for spring admission, 10/1 priority date for domestic and international students. Applications are processed on a rolling basis. Application fee: $25 ($50 for international students). *Expenses:* Tuition, state resident: full-time $5136; part-time $214 per credit hour. Required fees: $379.50; $127 per term. Tuition and fees vary according to course level, course load and campus/location. *Financial support:* Federal Work-Study, scholarships/grants, and tuition waivers (partial) available. Financial award application deadline: 2/15; financial award applicants required to submit FAFSA. *Unit head:* Stephanie Huffman, Head, 501-450-5430, Fax: 501-450-5680, E-mail: stephanieh@uca.edu. *Application contact:* Brenda Herring, Admissions Assistant, 501-450-5065, Fax: 501-450-5678, E-mail: bherring@uca.edu.

University of Central Missouri, The Graduate School, College of Education, Warrensburg, MO 64093. Offers career and technical education administration (MS); career and technical education industry training (MS); career and technical education leadership/teaching (MS); college student personnel administration (MS); counseling (MS); curriculum and instruction (Ed S); educational leadership (Ed D); educational technology (MS); elementary education/educational foundations and literacy (MSE); elementary school administration (MSE); elementary school principalship (Ed S); human services/learning resources (Ed S); human services/professional counseling (Ed S); human services/special education (Ed S); human services/technology and occupational education (Ed S); K-12 education/educational foundations and literacy (MSE); K-12 special education (MSE); library science and information services (MS); literacy education (MSE); secondary education/educational foundations & literacy (MSE); secondary school administration (MSE); secondary school principalship (Ed S); superintendency (Ed S); teaching (MAT). Part-time programs available. Postbaccalaureate distance learning degree programs offered. *Faculty:* 42. *Students:* 123 full-time (82 women), 721 part-time (552 women); includes 58 minority (38 African Americans, 3 American Indian/Alaska Native, 6 Asian Americans or Pacific Islanders, 11 Hispanic Americans), 6 international. Average age 34. 229 applicants, 88% accepted, 190 enrolled. In 2009, 212 master's, 47 other advanced degrees awarded. *Entrance requirements:* Additional exam requirements/recommendations for international students: Required—TOEFL (minimum score 550 paper-based; 79 computer-based). *Application deadline:* For fall admission, 6/1 priority date for domestic students, 5/1 for international students; for spring admission, 10/1 priority date for domestic students, 10/1 for international students. Applications are processed on a rolling basis. Application fee: $30 ($75 for international students). Electronic applications accepted. *Expenses:* Tuition, area resident: Part-time $245.80 per credit hour. Tuition, nonresident: part-time $491.60 per credit hour. Required fees: $24.20 per credit hour. Full-time tuition and fees vary according to course load, degree level, campus/location and reciprocity agreements. *Financial support:* Research assistantships with full and partial tuition reimbursements, teaching assistantships with full and partial tuition reimbursements, career-related internships or fieldwork, Federal Work-Study, scholarships/grants, and administrative and laboratory assistantships available. Support available to part-time students. Financial award application deadline: 3/1; financial award applicants required to submit FAFSA. *Unit head:* Dr. Michael Wright, Dean, 660-543-4272, Fax: 660-543-8753, E-mail: mwright@ucmo.edu. *Application contact:* Laurie Delap, Admissions Coordinator, 660-543-4621, Fax: 660-543-4778, E-mail: gradinfo@ucmo.edu.

University of Denver, College of Education, Denver, CO 80208. Offers counseling psychology (MA, PhD); curriculum and instruction (MA, PhD, Certificate), including curriculum leadership (MA, PhD); educational administration and policy studies (Certificate); educational psychology (MA, PhD, Ed S), including child and family studies (MA, PhD), quantitative research methods (MA, PhD), school psychology (PhD, Ed S); higher education and adult studies (MA, PhD); library and information science (MLIS); library and information sciences (Certificate); school administration (PhD). *Accreditation:* ALA; APA (one or more programs are accredited). Part-time and evening/weekend programs available. Postbaccalaureate distance learning degree programs offered (no on-campus study). *Faculty:* 33 full-time (24 women), 62 part-time/adjunct (41 women). *Students:* 384 full-time (305 women), 453 part-time (336 women); includes 164 minority (47 African Americans, 8 American Indian/Alaska Native, 14 Asian Americans or Pacific Islanders, 95 Hispanic Americans), 20 international. Average age 34. 1,065 applicants, 59% accepted, 433 enrolled. In 2009, 206 master's, 38 doctorates, 117 other advanced degrees awarded. Terminal master's awarded for partial completion of doctoral program. *Degree requirements:* For master's, comprehensive exam; for doctorate, 2 foreign languages, comprehensive exam, thesis/dissertation. *Entrance requirements:* For master's and doctorate, GRE General Test or MAT. *Application deadline:* Applications are processed on a rolling basis. Application fee: $50. Electronic applications accepted. *Expenses:* Tuition: Full-time $34,596; part-time $961 per quarter hour. Required fees: $4 per quarter hour. Tuition and fees vary according to course load, campus/location and program. *Financial support:* In 2009–10, 78 teaching assistantships with full and partial tuition reimbursements (averaging $11,700 per year) were awarded; career-related internships or fieldwork, Federal Work-Study, institutionally sponsored loans, and scholarships/grants also available. Support available to part-time students. Financial award application deadline: 3/1; financial award applicants required to submit FAFSA. *Faculty research:* Parkinson's disease, personnel training, development and assessments, gifted education, service-learning, transportation, public schools. Total annual research expenditures: $340,000. *Unit head:* Dr. Gregory M. Anderson, Dean, 303-871-3665. *Application contact:* Janet Erickson, Director of Graduate Admission, 303-871-2485, E-mail: edinfo@du.edu.

University of Hawaii at Manoa, Graduate Division, College of Natural Sciences, Department of Information and Computer Sciences, Library and Information Science Program, Honolulu, HI 96822-2233. Offers advanced library and information science (Graduate Certificate); library and information science (MLI Sc). *Accreditation:* ALA (one or more programs are accredited). Part-time programs available. *Degree requirements:* For master's, comprehensive exam, thesis optional. *Entrance requirements:* For master's, GRE General Test. Additional exam requirements/recommendations for international students: Required—TOEFL (minimum score 600 paper-based; 250 computer-based). Electronic applications accepted. *Expenses:* Tuition, state resident: full-time $8900; part-time $372 per credit. Tuition, nonresident: full-time $21,400; part-time $898 per credit. Required fees: $207 per semester. *Faculty research:* Information behavior, evaluation of electronic information sources, online learning, history of libraries, information literacy.

University of Houston–Clear Lake, School of Education, Program in Curriculum and Instruction, Houston, TX 77058-1098. Offers curriculum and instruction (MS); early childhood education (MS); reading (MS); school library and information science (MS). Part-time and evening/weekend programs available. *Degree requirements:* For master's, thesis (for some programs). *Entrance requirements:* For master's, GRE or minimum GPA of 3.0 in last 60 hours. Additional exam requirements/recommendations for international students: Required—TOEFL (minimum score 550 paper-based; 213 computer-based). Electronic applications accepted.

University of Illinois at Urbana–Champaign, Graduate College, Graduate School of Library and Information Science, Champaign, IL 61820. Offers bioinformatics: library and information science (MS); library and information science (MS, PhD, CAS); library and information science: digital libraries (CAS). *Accreditation:* ALA (one or more programs are accredited). Postbaccalaureate distance learning degree programs offered. *Faculty:* 26 full-time (13 women), 9 part-time/adjunct (6 women). *Students:* 321 full-time (229 women), 310 part-time (230 women); includes 101 minority (34 African Americans, 4 American Indian/Alaska Native, 36 Asian Americans or Pacific Islanders, 27 Hispanic Americans), 35 international. 747 applicants, 53% accepted, 217 enrolled. In 2009, 240 master's, 7 doctorates, 6 other advanced degrees awarded. *Entrance requirements:* For master's, GRE General Test, minimum GPA of 3.0; for doctorate, minimum GPA of 3.0; for CAS, master's degree in library and information science or related field with minimum GPA of 3.0. Additional exam requirements/recommendations for international students: Required—TOEFL (minimum score 620 paper-based; 260 computer-based; 105 iBT), or IELTS (minimum score 7). *Application deadline:* Applications are processed on a rolling basis. Application fee: $60 ($75 for international students). Electronic applications accepted. *Financial support:* In 2009–10, 52 fellowships, 41 research assistantships, 27 teaching assistantships were awarded; tuition waivers (full and partial) also available. *Unit head:* John Unsworth, Dean, 217-333-3281, Fax: 217-244-3302, E-mail: unsworth@illinois.edu. *Application contact:* Valerie Youngen, Admissions and Records Representative, 217-333-0734, Fax: 217-244-3302, E-mail: vyoungen@llinois.edu.

The University of Iowa, Graduate College, School of Library and Information Science, Iowa City, IA 52242-1316. Offers MA, MA/Certificate, MBA/MA. *Accreditation:* ALA (one or more programs are accredited). *Degree requirements:* For master's, thesis optional, exam, portfolio. *Entrance requirements:* For master's, GRE General Test, minimum GPA of 3.0. Additional exam requirements/recommendations for international students: Required—TOEFL (minimum score 550 paper-based; 213 computer-based; 81 iBT). Electronic applications accepted.

University of Kentucky, Graduate School, College of Communications and Information Studies, Program in Library and Information Science, Lexington, KY 40506-0032. Offers library science (MA, MSLS). *Accreditation:* ALA (one or more programs are accredited). Part-time programs available. *Degree requirements:* For master's, variable foreign language requirement, comprehensive exam. *Entrance requirements:* For master's, GRE General Test, minimum undergraduate GPA of 2.75. Additional exam requirements/recommendations for international students: Required—TOEFL (minimum score 550 paper-based; 213 computer-based). *Faculty research:* Information retrieval systems, information-seeking behavior, organizational behavior, computer cataloging, library resource sharing.

University of Maryland, College Park, Academic Affairs, Program in Geography, Library, and Information Services, College Park, MD 20742. Offers MA/MLS. *Application deadline:* For fall admission, 1/15 for domestic and international students. Applications are processed on a rolling basis. Application fee: $60. Electronic applications accepted. *Expenses:* Tuition, area resident: Part-time $471 per credit hour. Tuition, state resident: part-time $471 per credit hour. Tuition, nonresident: part-time $1016 per credit hour. Required fees: $337.04 per term. *Financial support:* Fellowships, research assistantships, teaching assistantships available. Financial award application deadline: 2/1; financial award applicants required to submit FAFSA. *Unit head:* Dr. Diane Barlow, Associate Dean, 301-405-2042, Fax: 301-314-9145, E-mail: dbarlow@umd.edu. *Application contact:* Dean of Graduate School, 301-405-0376, Fax: 301-314-9305.

University of Maryland, College Park, Academic Affairs, Program in History, Library, and Information Services, College Park, MD 20742. Offers MA/MLS. *Students:* 15 full-time (13 women), 4 part-time (all women); includes 2 minority (1 Asian American or Pacific Islander, 1 Hispanic American), 2 international. 35 applicants, 57% accepted, 6 enrolled. *Entrance requirements:* Additional exam requirements/recommendations for international students: Required—TOEFL. *Application deadline:* For fall admission, 12/15 for domestic and international students. Applications are processed on a rolling basis. Application fee: $60. Electronic applications accepted. *Expenses:* Tuition, area resident: Part-time $471 per credit hour. Tuition, state resident: part-time $471 per credit hour. Tuition, nonresident: part-time $1016 per credit hour. Required fees: $337.04 per term. *Financial support:* In 2009–10, 1 research assistantship (averaging $17,182 per year), 4 teaching assistantships (averaging $15,524 per year) were awarded; fellowships also available. Financial award applicants required to submit FAFSA. *Unit head:* Dr. Diane Barlow, Associate Dean, 301-405-2042, Fax: 301-314-9145, E-mail: dbarlow@umd.edu. *Application contact:* Dean of Graduate School, 301-405-0376, Fax: 301-314-9305.

University of Michigan, Horace H. Rackham School of Graduate Studies, School of Information, Ann Arbor, MI 48109-1107. Offers archives and records management (MS); human-computer interaction (MS); information (MS, PhD); information economics, management and policy (MS); library and information services (MS). *Accreditation:* ALA (one or more programs are accredited). Part-time programs available. *Degree requirements:* For master's, variable foreign language requirement, thesis optional; for doctorate, one foreign language, thesis/dissertation, oral defense of dissertation, preliminary exam. *Entrance requirements:* For master's and doctorate, GRE General Test. Additional exam requirements/recommendations for international students: Required—TOEFL (minimum score 600 paper-based; 250 computer-based). Electronic applications accepted. *Expenses:* Tuition, state resident: full-time $17,286; part-time $1099 per credit hour. Tuition, nonresident: full-time $34,944; part-time $2080 per credit hour. Required fees: $95 per semester. Tuition and fees vary according to course load, degree level and program.

University of Missouri, Graduate School, College of Education, School of Information Science and Learning Technologies, Columbia, MO 65211. Offers educational technology (M Ed, Ed S); information science and learning technology (PhD); library science (MA). *Accreditation:* ALA (one or more programs are accredited). Part-time and evening/weekend programs available. *Entrance requirements:* For master's, GRE General Test or MAT, minimum GPA of 3.0. Additional exam requirements/recommendations for international students: Required—TOEFL (minimum score 540 paper-based; 207 computer-based; 76 iBT).

The University of North Carolina at Chapel Hill, Graduate School, School of Information and Library Science, Chapel Hill, NC 27599. Offers MSIS, MSLS, PhD, CAS. *Accreditation:* ALA (one or more programs are accredited). Part-time programs available. Terminal master's awarded for partial completion of doctoral program. *Degree requirements:* For master's, paper or project; for doctorate, thesis/dissertation. *Entrance requirements:* For master's and doctorate, GRE General Test. Additional exam requirements/recommendations for international students: Required—TOEFL (minimum score 625 paper-based; 263 computer-based). Electronic applications accepted. *Faculty research:* Information retrieval, digital libraries, management of information resources, archives and cultural heritage, information management.

The University of North Carolina at Greensboro, Graduate School, School of Education, Department of Library and Information Studies, Greensboro, NC 27412-5001. Offers MLIS. *Accreditation:* ALA. Part-time and evening/weekend programs available. Postbaccalaureate distance learning degree programs offered (no on-campus study). *Degree requirements:* For master's, portfolio. *Entrance requirements:* For master's, GRE General Test. Additional exam requirements/recommendations for international students: Required—TOEFL (minimum score 550 paper-based; 213 computer-based), IELTS (minimum score 6.5). Electronic applications accepted. *Faculty research:* Library history, gender studies, children's literature, web design, homeless, technical services.

University of Northern Colorado, Graduate School, College of Education and Behavioral Sciences, School of Educational Research, Leadership and Technology, Program in School Library Education, Greeley, CO 80639. Offers MA. Part-time programs available. *Faculty:* 5 full-time (1 woman). *Students:* 2 full-time (both women), 20 part-time (11 women); includes 1 minority (Asian American or Pacific Islander). Average age 34. 6 applicants, 100% accepted, 5 enrolled. In 2009, 8 master's awarded. *Application deadline:* Applications are processed on a rolling basis. Application fee: $50 ($60 for international students). Electronic applications accepted. *Expenses:* Tuition, state resident: full-time $5770; part-time $320.55 per credit hour. Tuition, nonresident: full-time $13,847; part-time $769.27 per credit hour. Required fees: $948.78; $52.72 per credit. *Financial support:* Application deadline: 3/1. *Unit head:* Berlinda Saenz, Program Coordinator, 970-351-2816. *Application contact:* Linda Sisson, Graduate Student Admission Coordinator, 970-351-1807, Fax: 970-351-2371, E-mail: linda.sisson@unco.edu.

University of North Texas, College of Information, Department of Library and Information Sciences, Denton, TX 76203-5017. Offers information science (MS, PhD); learning technologies (M Ed, Ed D), including applied technology, training and development (M Ed), computer education and cognitive systems, educational computing; library science (MS). *Accreditation:* ALA (one or more programs are accredited). Part-time and evening/weekend programs available. *Degree requirements:* For master's, comprehensive exam; for doctorate, comprehensive exam, thesis/dissertation. *Entrance requirements:* For master's, GRE General Test, MAT; for doctorate, GRE General Test. Additional exam requirements/recommendations for international students: Required—proof of English language proficiency required for non-native English speakers; Recommended—TOEFL (minimum score 550 paper-based; 213 computer-based; 79 iBT). *Application deadline:* Applications are processed on a rolling basis. Application fee: $50 ($75

Library Science

University of North Texas (continued)
for international students). Electronic applications accepted. *Expenses:* Tuition, state resident: full-time $4298; part-time $239 per contact hour. Tuition, nonresident: full-time $9878; part-time $549 per contact hour. Required fees: $265 per contact hour. *Financial support:* Fellowships, research assistantships, teaching assistantships, career-related internships or fieldwork, Federal Work-Study, institutionally sponsored loans, scholarships/grants, health care benefits, and library assistantships available. Financial award application deadline: 4/1; financial award applicants required to submit FAFSA. *Faculty research:* Information resources and services, information management and retrieval, computer-based information systems, human information behavior. *Application contact:* Graduate Academic Counselor, 940-369-2873, Fax: 940-565-3101.

University of Oklahoma, Graduate College, College of Arts and Sciences, School of Library and Information Studies, Program in Knowledge Management, Norman, OK 73019-0390. Offers MSKM. Part-time and evening/weekend programs available. *Students:* 1 full-time (0 women), 10 part-time (6 women); includes 2 minority (both Hispanic Americans). 3 applicants, 100% accepted, 3 enrolled. In 2009, 3 master's awarded. *Degree requirements:* For master's, comprehensive exam, thesis. *Entrance requirements:* For master's, GRE, minimum GPA of 3.2 in last 60 hours or 3.0 overall. *Application deadline:* For fall admission, 3/1 priority date for domestic students, 4/1 for international students; for spring admission, 10/15 for domestic students, 9/1 for international students. Applications are processed on a rolling basis. Application fee: $40 ($90 for international students). Electronic applications accepted. *Expenses:* Tuition, state resident: full-time $3744; part-time $156 per credit hour. Tuition, nonresident: full-time $13,577; part-time $565.70 per credit hour. Required fees: $2415; $90.10 per credit hour. *Financial support:* In 2009–10, 3 students received support. Unspecified assistantships available. Financial award applicants required to submit FAFSA. *Faculty research:* Best practices, communities of practice, learning organization, knowledge and management technologies. *Unit head:* Kathy Latrobe, Director, 405-325-3921, Fax: 405-325-7648, E-mail: klatrobe@ou.edu. *Application contact:* Maggie Ryan, Coordinator of Admissions, 405-325-3921, Fax: 405-325-7648, E-mail: mryan@ou.edu.

University of Oklahoma, Graduate College, College of Arts and Sciences, School of Library and Information Studies, Program in Library and Information Studies, Norman, OK 73019-0390. Offers library and information studies (MLIS); school library media specialist (Certificate); M Ed/MLIS; MBA/MLIS. Part-time and evening/weekend programs available. *Students:* 31 full-time (25 women), 186 part-time (136 women); includes 34 minority (4 African Americans, 23 American Indian/Alaska Native, 2 Asian Americans or Pacific Islanders, 5 Hispanic Americans), 5 international. 73 applicants, 95% accepted, 52 enrolled. In 2009, 68 master's awarded. *Degree requirements:* For master's, comprehensive exam (MLIS). *Entrance requirements:* For master's, GRE, minimum GPA of 3.2 in last 60 hours or 3.0 overall. Additional exam requirements/recommendations for international students: Required—TOEFL (minimum score 550 paper-based; 213 computer-based). *Application deadline:* For fall admission, 3/1 priority date for domestic students, 4/1 for international students; for spring admission, 10/15 for domestic students, 9/1 for international students. Applications are processed on a rolling basis. Application fee: $40 ($90 for international students). Electronic applications accepted. *Expenses:* Tuition, state resident: full-time $3744; part-time $156 per credit hour. Tuition, nonresident: full-time $13,577; part-time $565.70 per credit hour. Required fees: $2415; $90.10 per credit hour. *Financial support:* In 2009–10, 90 students received support. Scholarships/grants and unspecified assistantships available. Financial award applicants required to submit FAFSA. *Faculty research:* Information use in the digital age, equity of access, learning organizations, education of information professionals, information services to special populations. *Unit head:* Kathy Latrobe, Director, 405-325-3921, Fax: 405-325-7648, E-mail: klatrobe@ou.edu. *Application contact:* Maggie Ryan, Coordinator of Admissions, 405-325-3921, Fax: 405-325-7648, E-mail: mryan@ou.edu.

University of Pittsburgh, School of Information Sciences, Library and Information Science Program, Pittsburgh, PA 15260. Offers health sciences librarianship (Certificate); library and information science (MLIS, PhD). *Accreditation:* ALA (one or more programs are accredited). Part-time and evening/weekend programs available. Postbaccalaureate distance learning degree programs offered (minimal on-campus study). *Faculty:* 11 full-time (6 women), 8 part-time/adjunct (7 women). *Students:* 200 full-time (163 women), 235 part-time (185 women); includes 40 minority (22 African Americans, 1 American Indian/Alaska Native, 2 Asian Americans or Pacific Islanders, 15 Hispanic Americans), 23 international. 413 applicants, 88% accepted, 217 enrolled. In 2009, 265 master's, 3 doctorates, 2 other advanced degrees awarded. *Degree requirements:* For master's, thesis optional; for doctorate, comprehensive exam, thesis/dissertation. *Entrance requirements:* For master's, bachelor's degree from accredited university; minimum GPA of 3.0; for doctorate, GRE General Test, minimum GPA of 3.5. Additional exam requirements/recommendations for international students: Required—TOEFL (minimum score 550 paper-based; 213 computer-based; 80 iBT). *Application deadline:* For fall admission, 1/15 priority date for domestic and international students; for winter admission, 9/15 priority date for domestic students, 6/15 priority date for international students; for spring admission, 1/15 priority date for domestic students, 12/15 priority date for international students. Applications are processed on a rolling basis. Application fee: $50. Electronic applications accepted. *Expenses:* Contact institution. *Financial support:* Fellowships with full tuition reimbursements, research assistantships with full and partial tuition reimbursements, teaching assistantships with full and partial tuition reimbursements, career-related internships or fieldwork, scholarships/grants, health care benefits, tuition waivers (full and partial), and unspecified assistantships available. Financial award application deadline: 1/15; financial award applicants required to submit FAFSA. *Faculty research:* Archives, preservation management, children's resources and services, medical informatics, digital libraries, information retrieval. *Unit head:* Dr. Mary K. Biagini, Chair, 412-624-5138, Fax: 412-624-5231, E-mail: mbiagini@sis.pitt.edu. *Application contact:* Brandi Belleau Liskey, Student Recruiting Coordinator, 412-648-3108, Fax: 412-624-5231, E-mail: lisinq@sis.pitt.edu.

University of Puerto Rico, Río Piedras, Graduate School of Information Sciences and Technologies, San Juan, PR 00931-3300. Offers administration of academic libraries (PMC); administration of public libraries (PMC); administration of special libraries (PMC); consultant in information services (PMC); documents and files administration (Post-Graduate Certificate); electronic information resources analyst (Post-Graduate Certificate); librarianship (Post-Graduate Certificate); librarianship and information services (MLS); master librarian (Post-Graduate Certificate); specialist in legal information (PMC). *Accreditation:* ALA. Part-time programs available. *Degree requirements:* For master's, comprehensive exam, thesis, portfolio. *Entrance requirements:* For master's, PAEG, GRE, interview, minimum GPA of 3.0, 3 letters of recommendation; for other advanced degree, PAEG, GRE, minimum GPA of 3.0, IST master's degree. *Faculty research:* Investigating the users needs and preferences for a specialized environmental library.

University of Rhode Island, Graduate School, College of Arts and Sciences, Graduate School of Library and Information Studies, Kingston, RI 02881. Offers MLIS, MLIS/MA, MLIS/MPA. *Accreditation:* ALA (one or more programs are accredited). Part-time programs available. *Faculty:* 7 full-time (6 women), 13 part-time/adjunct (7 women). *Students:* 56 full-time (46 women), 117 part-time (106 women); includes 4 minority (1 African American, 2 Asian Americans or Pacific Islanders, 1 Hispanic American). In 2009, 81 master's awarded. *Degree requirements:* For master's, comprehensive exam. *Entrance requirements:* For master's, GRE or MAT (if undergraduate GPA less than 3.0), 2 letters of recommendation. Additional exam requirements/recommendations for international students: Required—TOEFL (minimum score 550 paper-based; 213 computer-based). *Application deadline:* For fall admission, 6/15 for domestic students, 2/1 for international students; for spring admission, 10/15 for domestic students, 7/15 for international students. Application fee: $65. Electronic applications accepted. *Expenses:* Tuition, state resident: full-time $8828; part-time $490 per credit hour. Tuition, nonresident: full-time $22,100; part-time $1228 per credit hour. Required fees: $1118; $57 per semester. Tuition and fees vary according to program. *Financial support:* In 2009–10, 4 teaching assistantships with full and partial tuition reimbursements (averaging $9,726 per year) were awarded. Financial award application deadline: 1/15; financial award applicants required to submit FAFSA. Total annual research expenditures: $4,265. *Unit head:* Dr. Gale Eaton, Director, 401-874-4641, Fax: 401-874-4964, E-mail: geaton@uri.edu. *Application contact:* Dr. Gale Eaton, Director, 401-874-4641, Fax: 401-874-4964, E-mail: geaton@uri.edu.

University of South Carolina, The Graduate School, College of Mass Communications and Information Studies, School of Library and Information Science, Columbia, SC 29208. Offers MLIS, PhD, Certificate, Specialist, MLIS/MA. *Accreditation:* ALA (one or more programs are accredited). Part-time programs available. Postbaccalaureate distance learning degree programs offered (no on-campus study). *Degree requirements:* For master's, end of program portfolio; for doctorate, comprehensive exam, thesis/dissertation. *Entrance requirements:* For master's and other advanced degree, GRE General Test or MAT; for doctorate, GTE, writing sample. Additional exam requirements/recommendations for international students: Required—TOEFL (minimum score 570 paper-based; 230 computer-based; 75 iBT). Electronic applications accepted. *Faculty research:* Information technology management, distance education, library services for children and young adults, special libraries.

University of Southern Mississippi, Graduate School, College of Education and Psychology, School of Library and Information Science, Hattiesburg, MS 39406-0001. Offers MLIS, SLS. *Accreditation:* ALA (one or more programs are accredited). Part-time and evening/weekend programs available. Postbaccalaureate distance learning degree programs offered (minimal on-campus study). *Faculty:* 8 full-time (7 women), 1 part-time/adjunct (0 women). *Students:* 24 full-time (18 women), 140 part-time (123 women); includes 18 minority (17 African Americans, 1 Hispanic American), 1 international. Average age 37. 51 applicants, 69% accepted, 30 enrolled. In 2009, 60 master's awarded. *Degree requirements:* For master's, comprehensive exam, thesis optional, research project; for SLS, comprehensive exam, thesis optional, field project. *Entrance requirements:* For master's, GRE General Test, minimum GPA of 3.0; for SLS, GRE General Test, MLIS, minimum graduate GPA of 3.25. Additional exam requirements/recommendations for international students: Required—TOEFL. *Application deadline:* For fall admission, 3/15 priority date for domestic students, 3/15 for international students. Applications are processed on a rolling basis. Application fee: $35. Electronic applications accepted. *Expenses:* Tuition, state resident: full-time $5096; part-time $284 per hour. Tuition, nonresident: full-time $13,052; part-time $726 per hour. Required fees: $402. Tuition and fees vary according to course level and course load. *Financial support:* In 2009–10, 8 students received support, including 6 research assistantships with full tuition reimbursements available (averaging $6,100 per year), 1 teaching assistantship with full tuition reimbursement available (averaging $6,100 per year); fellowships with tuition reimbursements available, career-related internships or fieldwork, Federal Work-Study, institutionally sponsored loans, scholarships/grants, tuition waivers (full and partial), and unspecified assistantships also available. Financial award application deadline: 3/15; financial award applicants required to submit FAFSA. *Faculty research:* Printing, library history, children's literature, telecommunications, management. Total annual research expenditures: $14,185. *Unit head:* Dr. Melanie J. Norton, Director, 601-266-4228, Fax: 601-266-5774. *Application contact:* Shonna Breland, Manager of Graduate Admissions, 601-266-6563, Fax: 601-266-5138.

University of South Florida, Graduate School, College of Arts and Sciences, School of Library and Information Science, Tampa, FL 33620-9951. Offers MA. *Accreditation:* ALA. Part-time and evening/weekend programs available. Postbaccalaureate distance learning degree programs offered (minimal on-campus study). *Faculty:* 14 full-time (11 women), 10 part-time/adjunct (9 women). *Students:* 117 full-time (95 women), 280 part-time (235 women); includes 76 minority (25 African Americans, 2 American Indian/Alaska Native, 8 Asian Americans or Pacific Islanders, 41 Hispanic Americans), 2 international. Average age 32. 217 applicants, 67% accepted, 89 enrolled. In 2009, 174 master's awarded. *Degree requirements:* For master's, comprehensive exam, thesis. *Entrance requirements:* For master's, minimum GPA of 3.5 in upper-division course work. Additional exam requirements/recommendations for international students: Required—TOEFL (minimum score 550 paper-based; 213 computer-based). *Application deadline:* For fall admission, 6/1 for domestic students, 1/2 for international students; for spring admission, 10/15 for domestic students, 6/1 for international students. Applications are processed on a rolling basis. Application fee: $30. Electronic applications accepted. *Financial support:* In 2009–10, teaching assistantships with full tuition reimbursements (averaging $9,000 per year); unspecified assistantships also available. Financial award application deadline: 6/30; financial award applicants required to submit FAFSA. *Faculty research:* Youth services in libraries, community engagement and libraries, information architecture, biomedical informatics. Total annual research expenditures: $134,608. *Unit head:* Jim Andrews, Director, 813-974-2108, Fax: 813-974-6840, E-mail: jandrews@cas.usf.edu. *Application contact:* Jim Andrews, Director, 813-974-2108, Fax: 813-974-6840, E-mail: jandrews@cas.usf.edu.

University of Toronto, School of Graduate Studies, Social Sciences Division, Faculty of Information Studies, Toronto, ON M5S 1A1, Canada. Offers MI St, PhD, G Dip. *Accreditation:* ALA (one or more programs are accredited). Part-time programs available. *Degree requirements:* For master's, thesis optional; for doctorate, thesis/dissertation, oral exam/thesis defense. *Entrance requirements:* For master's, 2 letters of reference; for doctorate, 3 letters of reference, minimum B+ average; for G Dip, MI St, MLS, or MIS degree or equivalent; minimum B+ average overall. Additional exam requirements/recommendations for international students: Required—TOEFL (minimum score 600 paper-based; 250 computer-based), TWE (minimum score 6), Michigan English Language Assessment Battery (minimum score: 95) or IELTS (minimum score: 8). *Expenses:* Contact institution.

University of Washington, Graduate School, The Information School, Seattle, WA 98195. Offers information management (MSIM); information science (PhD); library and information science (MLIS). *Accreditation:* ALA (one or more programs are accredited). Part-time and evening/weekend programs available. Postbaccalaureate distance learning degree programs offered (minimal on-campus study). *Faculty:* 39 full-time (16 women), 14 part-time/adjunct (11 women). *Students:* 258 full-time (169 women), 277 part-time (191 women); includes 77 minority (13 African Americans, 7 American Indian/Alaska Native, 41 Asian Americans or Pacific Islanders, 16 Hispanic Americans), 68 international. Average age 33. 733 applicants, 53% accepted, 219 enrolled. In 2009, 164 master's, 4 doctorates awarded. Terminal master's awarded for partial completion of doctoral program. *Degree requirements:* For master's, comprehensive exam (for some programs), culminating experience project (thesis, capstone or portfolio), internship; for doctorate, comprehensive exam, thesis/dissertation. *Entrance requirements:* For master's, GRE General Test, GMAT, minimum GPA of 3.0; for doctorate, GRE General Test, minimum GPA of 3.0. Additional exam requirements/recommendations for international students: Required—TOEFL (minimum score 580 paper-based; 237 computer-based; 92 iBT), IELTS (minimum score 7), MLT (minimum score 90). *Application deadline:* For fall admission, 12/15 for domestic students, 11/1 for international students. Application fee: $65. Electronic applications accepted. *Expenses:* Contact institution. *Financial support:* In 2009–10, 98 students received support, including 5 fellowships with full tuition reimbursements available (averaging $15,204 per year), 15 research assistantships with full and partial tuition reimbursements available (averaging $16,608 per year), 13 teaching assistantships with full tuition reimbursements available (averaging $17,350 per year); career-related internships or fieldwork, Federal Work-Study, institutionally sponsored loans, scholarships/grants, health care benefits, tuition waivers (full and partial), and unspecified assistantships also available. Support available to part-time students. Financial award application deadline: 2/28; financial award applicants required to submit FAFSA. *Faculty research:* Human computer interaction, information policy and ethics, knowledge organization, information literacy and access, information assurance and cyber security. Total annual research expenditures: $4.7 million. *Unit head:* Dr. Harry Bruce, Dean. *Application contact:* Kari Brothers, Admissions Counselor, 206-616-5541, Fax: 206-616-3152, E-mail: kari683@uw.edu.

The University of Western Ontario, Faculty of Graduate Studies, Faculty of Information and Media Studies, Programs in Library and Information Science, London, ON N6A 5B8, Canada. Offers MLIS, PhD. Program conducted on a trimester basis. *Accreditation:* ALA (one or more programs are accredited). Part-time and evening/weekend programs available. *Degree requirements:* For doctorate, comprehensive exam, thesis/dissertation. *Entrance requirements:*

For master's, honors degree, minimum B average during previous 2 years of course work; for doctorate, MLIS or equivalent. Additional exam requirements/recommendations for international students: Required—TOEFL (minimum score 625 paper-based; 263 computer-based), TWE (minimum score 5). Electronic applications accepted. *Faculty research:* Information, individuals, and society; information systems, policy, power, and institutions.

University of Wisconsin–Eau Claire, College of Education and Human Sciences, Program in Secondary Education, Eau Claire, WI 54702-4004. Offers English (MST); professional development (MEPD), including library science, professional educator. Part-time and evening/weekend programs available. Postbaccalaureate distance learning degree programs offered. *Faculty:* 13 full-time (8 women). *Students:* 3 full-time (2 women), 9 part-time (5 women); includes 1 minority (African American). Average age 31. 8 applicants, 50% accepted, 3 enrolled. In 2009, 14 master's awarded. *Degree requirements:* For master's, thesis optional, oral exam, portfolio, written exam. *Entrance requirements:* For master's, certification to teach, minimum GPA of 2.75. Additional exam requirements/recommendations for international students: Required—TOEFL (minimum score 550 paper-based; 213 computer-based; 79 iBT). *Application deadline:* For fall admission, 7/1 priority date for domestic students, 6/1 priority date for international students; for spring admission, 12/1 priority date for domestic students, 11/1 priority date for international students. Applications are processed on a rolling basis. Application fee: $56. Electronic applications accepted. *Expenses:* Tuition, state resident: full-time $6705.90; part-time $372.55 per credit. Tuition, nonresident: full-time $16,771; part-time $931.74 per credit. Required fees: $925.50; $51.19 per credit. One-time fee: $56. *Financial support:* In 2009–10, 6 students received support, including 4 fellowships (averaging $3,125 per year); Federal Work-Study and unspecified assistantships also available. Financial award application deadline: 3/1; financial award applicants required to submit FAFSA. *Unit head:* Dr. Dwight Watson, Chair, 715-836-2013, Fax: 715-836-4868, E-mail: watsondc@uwec.edu. *Application contact:* Kristina Anderson, Director of Admissions, 715-836-5415, Fax: 715-836-2409, E-mail: admissions@uwec.edu.

University of Wisconsin–Madison, Graduate School, College of Letters and Science, School of Library and Information Studies, Madison, WI 53706-1380. Offers MA, PhD. *Accreditation:* ALA (one or more programs are accredited). Part-time programs available. *Degree requirements:* For doctorate, comprehensive exam, thesis/dissertation. Electronic applications accepted. *Expenses:* Tuition, state resident: part-time $594 per credit. Tuition, nonresident: part-time $1504 per credit. Required fees: $65 per credit. Tuition and fees vary according to course load, program and reciprocity agreements. *Faculty research:* Intellectual freedom, children's literature, print culture history, information systems design and evaluation, school library media centers.

University of Wisconsin–Milwaukee, Graduate School, School of Information Studies, Milwaukee, WI 53201-0413. Offers advanced studies in library and information science (CAS); archives and records administration (CAS); digital libraries (Certificate); information studies (MLIS, PhD); MLIS/MA; MLIS/MM; MLIS/MS. *Accreditation:* ALA (one or more programs are accredited). Part-time programs available. *Faculty:* 21 full-time (10 women). *Students:* 106 full-time (77 women), 423 part-time (351 women); includes 32 minority (8 African Americans, 13 Asian Americans or Pacific Islanders, 11 Hispanic Americans), 17 international. Average age 35. 351 applicants, 80% accepted, 73 enrolled. In 2009, 214 master's awarded. *Entrance requirements:* For master's, GRE General Test or MAT; for doctorate, GRE. Additional exam requirements/recommendations for international students: Required—TOEFL (minimum score 550 paper-based; 213 computer-based), IELTS (minimum score 6.5). *Application deadline:* For fall admission, 1/1 priority date for domestic students; for spring admission, 9/1 for domestic students. Applications are processed on a rolling basis. Application fee: $45 ($75 for international students). *Expenses:* Tuition, state resident: full-time $8800. Tuition, nonresident: full-time $20,760. Tuition and fees vary according to program and reciprocity agreements. *Financial support:* In 2009–10, 1 teaching assistantship was awarded; career-related internships or fieldwork, Federal Work-Study, and unspecified assistantships also available. Support

available to part-time students. Financial award application deadline: 4/15. Total annual research expenditures: $155,942. *Unit head:* Johannes Britz, Dean, 414-229-4709, Fax: 414-229-4848. *Application contact:* Dietmar Wolfram, 414-229-6836, E-mail: dwolfram@uwm.edu.

Valdosta State University, Graduate School, Program in Library and Information Science, Valdosta, GA 31698. Offers MLIS. *Accreditation:* ALA. *Degree requirements:* For master's, comprehensive exam. *Entrance requirements:* For master's, GRE. Additional exam requirements/recommendations for international students: Required—TOEFL (minimum score 523 paper-based; 193 computer-based).

Valley City State University, School of Education and Graduate Studies, Valley City, ND 58072. Offers English language learners (ELL) (M Ed); library and information technologies (M Ed); teaching and technology (M Ed); technology education (M Ed). *Accreditation:* NCATE. Part-time and evening/weekend programs available. Postbaccalaureate distance learning degree programs offered (no on-campus study). *Faculty:* 19 full-time (13 women), 4 part-time/adjunct (3 women). *Students:* 7 full-time (4 women), 115 part-time (73 women); includes 4 minority (1 African American, 1 American Indian/Alaska Native, 1 Asian American or Pacific Islander, 1 Hispanic American). Average age 36. 33 applicants, 97% accepted, 22 enrolled. In 2009, 22 master's awarded. *Degree requirements:* For master's, action research report, comprehensive portfolio. *Entrance requirements:* For master's, GRE, MAT, PRAXIS II or National Teaching Board for Professional Standards (if GPA less than 3.0). Additional exam requirements/recommendations for international students: Required—TOEFL (minimum score 525 paper-based; 193 computer-based). *Application deadline:* For fall admission, 5/24 priority date for domestic and international students; for winter admission, 12/11 priority date for domestic and international students; for spring admission, 4/24 priority date for domestic and international students. Applications are processed on a rolling basis. Application fee: $35. Electronic applications accepted. *Expenses:* Tuition, state resident: full-time $4266; part-time $237.40 per credit hour. Tuition, nonresident: full-time $4266; part-time $237.40 per credit hour. Required fees: $237.40 per credit hour. One-time fee: $35. *Financial support:* In 2009–10, 30 students received support. Applicants required to submit FAFSA. *Faculty research:* Academically at-risk students in higher education, communication pedagogy and technology, gender communication, computer mediated communication, creativity in music. Total annual research expenditures: $26,000. *Unit head:* Dr. Gary Thompson, Dean, 701-845-7197, E-mail: gary.thompson@vcsu.edu. *Application contact:* Misty Lindgren, 701-845-7303, Fax: 701-845-7305, E-mail: misty.lindgren@vcsu.edu.

Wayne State University, Graduate School, Library and Information Science Program, Detroit, MI 48202. Offers archival administration (Certificate); library and information science (MLIS, Spec); library science (MS, Spec). *Accreditation:* ALA (one or more programs are accredited). Part-time and evening/weekend programs available. *Entrance requirements:* For master's, GRE or MAT (if undergraduate GPA is between 2.25 and 2.99), minimum undergraduate GPA of 3.0, curriculum vitae. Additional exam requirements/recommendations for international students: Required—TOEFL (minimum score 550 paper-based; 213 computer-based); Recommended—TWE (minimum score 6). Electronic applications accepted. *Faculty research:* Convergence of academic libraries and other academic services, competitive intelligence and data mining, impact of digitization on libraries, international librarianship, consumer health information.

Wright State University, School of Graduate Studies, College of Education and Human Services, Department of Teacher Education, Programs in Workforce Education, Dayton, OH 45435. Offers career, technology and vocational education (M Ed, MA); computer/technology education (M Ed, MA); library/media (M Ed, MA); vocational education (M Ed, MA). *Accreditation:* NCATE. *Degree requirements:* For master's, thesis (for some programs). *Entrance requirements:* For master's, GRE General Test, MAT. Additional exam requirements/recommendations for international students: Required—TOEFL.

DREXEL UNIVERSITY

The iSchool at Drexel
College of Information Science and Technology

Programs of Study

The *iSchool* at Drexel, College of Information Science and Technology, prepares students for careers in the information field (iField) through coursework, research, and real-world experience. With an *iSchool* education, graduates learn to connect people with information through technology, to deliver the right information at the right time to the right people in the right form.

The *iSchool* offers four graduate degree programs: the Master of Science (M.S.) in library and information science, offered online and/or on campus in Philadelphia or at Drexel's Center for Graduate Studies in Sacramento, with optional concentrations available in library and information services, competitive intelligence and knowledge management, digital libraries, archival studies, youth services, and school library media; the Master of Science in Information Systems (M.S.I.S.), offered online and/or on campus in Philadelphia or at Drexel's Center for Graduate Studies in Sacramento; the Master of Science in Software Engineering (M.S.S.E.), offered online and/or on campus; and the Doctor of Philosophy (Ph.D.) in information studies, which is offered on campus only. Each of the three master's programs requires fifteen courses that may be completed on a full- or part-time basis. Post-master's professional development programs are also available. The advanced certificate in information studies and technology provides specialized education in information science. This program is open to anyone holding a master's degree in such areas as library science, computer or information science, information systems, instructional technology, software engineering, or other appropriate degrees from a suitable accredited program that has prepared them for advanced study in the chosen area of specialization. The five-course post-master's specialist program is available to those holding an ALA-accredited master's degree, or a graduate degree closely related to the chosen specialization who wish to futher focus their studies in one of four specific subject areas: archival studies, competitive intelligence and knowledge management, digital libraries, and youth services.

The *iSchool's* M.S. is one of just sixty-two programs accredited by the American Library Association (ALA). It was ranked ninth nationally in *U.S. News & World Report's* America's Best Graduate Schools, with specialties in information systems and digital librarianship ranking third and sixth respectively. The College also ranked fifth under the library and information studies specialty rankings for health librarianship.

Through the M.S. program, students must complete six required courses, five of which are taken at the outset of the program. The balance of the program can be completed either through a range of electives or through an optional concentration, which consists of five courses plus four electives of the student's choice. Concentrations are currently available in library and information services, competitive intelligence and knowledge management, digital libraries, archival studies, youth services, and school library media. A certificate in healthcare informatics is also available. Course work is offered relating to legal, medical, scientific, and business settings, as well as studies in medical informatics, computerized library information systems, Web-mastery, and print-oriented information services. The College also offers a practicum, which provides the opportunity to earn credit for work experience along with associated academic course work.

The Ph.D. in Information Studies comprises advanced course work, research apprenticeships, a portfolio, journal club, and a dissertation. The program requires minimum of three consecutive terms of full-time residency. An impartial ranking by Academics Analytics Faculty Scholarly Productivity Index (FSP index) rated Ph.D. faculty productivity eighth nationally for overall productivity in information science/studies, fifth in citations per faculty, and seventh in percentage of faculty with a journal publication.

The *iSchool* at Drexel, College of Information Science and Technology is a founding member of iSchools, an alliance of more than twenty-five prominent colleges dedicated to immersing students in the information field—connecting people, information, and technology. Its purpose is to raise awareness and understanding of the information sciences as a cutting-edge and progressive field of study.

Research Facilities

The iCommons has two major functions at the *iSchool*. First, the facility itself provides a computer lab and collaboration space solely for *iSchool* student use. There is also a fully equipped conference room for student use, with plasma display and videoconferencing capabilities. Second, iCommons staff serves and supports *iSchool* faculty, administrative personnel, and individuals using iCommons resources by offering access to computing equipment, information systems software, audio-visual presentation equipment, and bibliographic resources. The iCommons staff also provides technical support for the College's seven presentation classrooms, two student computer laboratories, and a usability lab. The iCommons student labs, and classrooms have access to networked databases, print and file resources within the College, and the Internet via the University's wireless network, DragonFly.

The *iSchool* is also home to Drexel's Institute for Healthcare Informatics and the Data Mining and Bioinformatics Lab. The ipl2, hosted at the *iSchool*, represents the merger of the Internet Public Library and the Librarians' Internet Index, two of the most widely used library-based technological resources connecting individuals, businesses, and society with information. The ipl2 offers students and faculty a unique platform for teaching and research.

The University's four libraries share an extensive collection of materials for all major areas of library and information science, computer science, systems engineering, information systems, and technology. Electronic resources compose the majority of the collection, delivered to the desktop on or off campus, with more than 450 research databases holding more than 21,500 full-text electronic journal titles and more than 110,000 electronics books. Students also have easy access to the many libraries and information centers in the Philadelphia area. Professional librarian assistance is available throughout the week, 114 hours, with specialist consultations by appointment. The main library now offers 24/7 study space in the new library café.

Financial Aid

The College of Information Science and Technology awards scholarships one time per year in the fall term, and only accepts online scholarship applications from the Web site. The College offers many different types of assistance, including research assistantships for new, full-time Ph.D. students (there are no assistantships for master's-level students); endowed scholarships; and full-time and part-time Dean's Fellowships. Dean's Fellowships are awarded to students applying for both admissions terms (fall and spring). There is no application for Dean's Fellowship as all full-time applications are automatically considered for this award on a merit basis. There are three merit scholarships awarded in the spring to graduating students. All eligible, degree-seeking, continuing students, and newly accepted, degree-seeking applicants are encouraged to apply. The *iSchool* scholarship committee generally awards the scholarships evenly between new and continuing students. There is no distinction made between online and on-campus students; all who are eligible are encouraged to apply. Prospective students should visit the Web site at http://www.ischool.drexel.edu for complete information, deadlines, and additional criteria. Online students may also be eligible for discounts through Drexel's Educational Partner Network. Visit http://www.drexel.com/drexelpro to learn more.

Cost of Study

In 2010–11, tuition is $960 per credit. Each term, on-campus students are also charged a general University fee based on full-time ($250) or part-time ($125) status.

Living and Housing Costs

Ample housing is available in the neighborhood bordering the campus. Drexel University also has graduate apartments available just three blocks from the center of Drexel's campus.

Student Group

The College's graduate students represent diverse academic and professional backgrounds and have varied career expectations. Many of the more than 900 master's students come from the mid-Atlantic region; other regions and countries are also represented. Many students are career changers, have professional work experience, or have pursued graduate studies in other disciplines. The College offers graduate programs both online and on campus in Philadelphia or at Drexel's Center for Graduate Studies in Sacramento, California. Students have the option of completing programs in either mode, and many students enroll in both online and on-campus classes throughout their degree programs. The College also enrolls undergraduates pursuing B.S. degrees in information systems, software engineering, and information technology.

The *iSchool* maintains its own Career Services Office. The office helps students find preprofessional positions and internships and assists graduates in locating professional employment. The M.S. qualifies students for a variety of positions in traditional and nontraditional settings, including academic librarian, children's or young adult librarian, knowledge management specialist, systems librarian, Web developer, digital librarian, law librarian, and competitive intelligence analyst.

Location

Drexel's 60-acre University City Main Campus is located in the University City district of Philadelphia, Pennsylvania, about a 10-minute walk from Center City, Philadelphia. As one of the nation's oldest and largest cities, Philadelphia is rich in cultural, historical, and academic institutions and is a leading center for business, industry, and government. These resources provide ample opportunities for information science and technology students to pursue preprofessional employment, internships, and permanent employment. The M.S. and M.S.I.S. are also available on campus at Drexel's Center for Graduate Studies in Sacramento, California, a unique, state-of-the-art, professional learning environment.

The University

Drexel is a private institution with an enrollment of 7,488 graduate and professional students and 13,197 undergraduate students. In addition to the information science and technology curricula, degree programs are offered in arts and sciences, biomedical engineering, business, education, engineering, law, media and design arts, medicine, nursing and health services, professional studies, and public health.

With College approval, graduate students may include courses from other Drexel units in their program of study. Related curricula include computer science, management, neuropsychology, and technical and science communication.

Applying

Graduate students may apply for admission in the fall and spring terms; doctoral students are admitted in the fall term. An application and fee, transcripts, a resume, letters of recommendation, and a personal statement are required. Scores for the GRE General Test are required for all master's and Ph.D. applicants. Master's applicants are automatically reviewed for a GRE waiver at the College's discretion based on the GPA of a previous degree. Generally the GPA threshold needed to receive a waiver is an overall 3.2 cumulative GPA or a half cumulative GPA of 3.2 on a 4.0 scale. Exceptions may apply. Official Test of English as a Foreign Language (TOEFL) scores are required for applicants whose bachelor's degree is from a non-U.S. institution. Students must obtain a minimum score of 600 on the written exam, 250 on the computer-based test, or 100 on the Internet-based exam. Students should visit the College's Web site at http://www.ischool.drexel.edu for additional requirements.

Correspondence and Information

The *iSchool* at Drexel
College of Information Science and Technology
Drexel University
3141 Chestnut Street
Philadelphia, Pennsylvania 19104-2875

Phone: 215-895-2474
Fax: 215-895-2494
Web site: http://www.ischool.drexel.edu
E-mail: istinfo@drexel.edu

Drexel University

THE FACULTY AND THEIR RESEARCH

Eileen G. Abels, Professor and Associate Dean for Academic Affairs; Ph.D., UCLA. Digital reference, information-seeking behaviors, information access, business information needs.

Denise E. Agosto, Associate Professor; Ph.D., Rutgers. Information behavior, public libraries, gender, children, young adults, multicultural materials.

Robert B. Allen, Associate Professor; Ph.D., California, San Diego. Digital libraries, information organization, knowledge management, scholarly publishing, information retrieval, decision processes.

Yuan An, Assistant Professor; Ph.D., Toronto. Conceptual modeling, schema and ontology mapping, information integration, knowledge representation, requirements engineering, healthcare information systems, and Semantic Web.

Michael E. Atwood, Professor and Associate Dean for Research and for Undergraduate Education; Ph.D., Colorado. Human-computer interaction, computer-supported cooperative work, organizational memory.

Glenn Booker, Assistant Teaching Professor; M.S., Berkeley. Software engineering, systems analysis and design, software and process measurement, process improvement, object-oriented analysis and design, bioinformatics, modeling of biological systems.

Toni Carbo, Professor and Program Leader Sacramento Program; Ph.D., Drexel. Information policy, information ethics, academic librarianship, LIS education.

Chaomei Chen, Associate Professor; Ph.D., Liverpool. Information visualization, visual analytics, knowledge domain visualization, network analysis and modeling, scientific discovery, science mapping, scientometrics, citation analysis, human-computer interaction.

Thomas A. Childers, Professor Emeritus; Ph.D., Rutgers. Measurement, evaluation, and planning of information and library services; effectiveness of information organizations.

Catherine D. Collins, Assistant Teaching Professor; M.L.I.S., Simmons. Knowledge management, collection development, management of information organizations, information sources and services, international development.

Prudence W. Dalrymple, Research and Teaching Professor and Director of the Institute for Healthcare Informatics; Ph.D., Wisconsin–Madison. User-centered information behaviors, particularly in the health arena; health informatics; evidence-based practice; education for the information professions and evaluation and translation of research into practice.

Susan E. Davis, Associate Teaching Professor; Ph.D., Wisconsin–Madison. Archives and special collections management, organization of and access to archival records, archival education, leadership in professions.

Belinha De Abreu, Assistant Teaching Professor; Ph.D., Connecticut. Media literacy, media effects, information literacy, critical thinking, teacher training, young adults, children services, middle school, school libraries.

Martin Donaldson, Associate Teaching Professor; M.B.A., Pennsylvania; M.A., Cambridge (England). Planning and design of information systems, human-computer design, information architecture.

M. Carl Drott, Associate Professor; Ph.D., Michigan. Systems analysis techniques, Web usage, competitive intelligence.

David E. Fenske, Isaac L. Auerbach Professor of Information Science and Dean of the College; Ph.D., Wisconsin–Madison. Digital libraries, informatics, knowledge management and information technologies.

Andrea Forte, Assistant Professor; Ph.D., Georgia Tech. Social computing, human-computer interaction, computer-supported cooperative work, computer-supported collaborative learning, information literacy.

Susan Gasson, Associate Professor; Ph.D., Warwick. Codesign of business and IT systems, early requirements analysis for boundary-spanning information systems, human-centered collaborative systems design, social informatics, distributed cognition and knowledge management, wicked problems.

Sean P. Goggins, Assistant Professor; Ph.D., Missouri. Computer-supported cooperative work, computer-supported collaborative learning, social computing, collaborative information behavior, distributed work, small group research, software engineering.

Peter Grillo, Assistant Teaching Professor; Ph.D., Temple. Strategic applications of technology within organizations.

John B. Hall, Professor Emeritus; Ph.D., Florida State. Academic library service, library administration, organization of materials.

Gregory W. Hislop, Associate Professor; Ph.D., Drexel. Information technology for teaching and learning, online education, structure and organization of the information disciplines, computing education research, software evaluation and characterization.

Xiaohua Tony Hu, Associate Professor; Ph.D., Regina (Canada). Data mining and databases, including data-mining algorithms and methods; Web mining; bioinformatics; data-mining applications in biomedical systems; real-time data warehousing and OLAP.

Michael Khoo, Assistant Professor; Ph.D., Colorado at Boulder. The understandings and practices that users bring to their interactions with information systems, with a focus on the evaluation of digital libraries and educational technologies.

Lee Leitner, Associate Teaching Professor; Ph.D., Nova Southeastern. Information security and assurance, software engineering, networking and distributed computing, systems analysis and programming languages.

Alison M. Lewis, Assistant Teaching Professor; Ph.D., Temple. Ethics of librarianship, collection development, services to humanists and social scientists.

Jiexun Jason Li, Assistant Professor; Ph.D., Arizona. Knowledge discovery, data mining, text mining, Web mining, machine learning, network analysis.

Xia Lin, Associate Professor; Ph.D., Maryland. Digital libraries, information visualization, visual interface design, knowledge mapping, human-computer interaction, object-oriented programming, information retrieval, information architecture, information-seeking behaviors in digital environments.

Jacqueline C. Mancall, Professor Emeritus; Ph.D., Drexel. Information resources and services for children and young adults, collection development, school media centers, instructional role of the information specialist.

Linda S. Marion, Associate Teaching Professor; Ph.D., Drexel. Formal and informal communication, bibliometric studies of scholarly communication, diffusion of information, information use in the social sciences, academic and public libraries, information science education.

Katherine W. McCain, Professor; Ph.D., Drexel. Scholarly communication, information production and use in the research process, development and structure of scientific specialties, diffusion of innovation, bibliometrics, evaluation of information retrieval systems.

Carol Hansen Montgomery, Research Professor and Dean of Libraries Emeritus; Ph.D., Drexel. Selection and use of electronic collections, evaluation of library and information systems, digital libraries, economics of libraries and digital collections.

Vanessa J. Irvin Morris, Assistant Teaching Professor; M.S.L.S., Clarion. Library anthropology, social epistemology, youth services, multicultural literature, reader response, cultural competency.

Delia Neuman, Associate Professor and Director of the School Library Media Program; Ph.D., Ohio State. Learning in information-rich environments, instructional systems design, the use of media for learning, school library media.

Danuta A. Nitecki, Professor and Dean of Libraries; Ph.D., Maryland, College Park. Library metrics and use in management, library as place, academic library service models.

Jung-ran Park, Assistant Professor; Ph.D., Hawaii. Knowledge organization and representation (cataloging and classification, metadata, image indexing, thesauri, lexicons, ontologies, Semantic Web), computer-mediated communication, cross-cultural communication, multilingual information access, discourse, pragmatics.

Jennifer A. Rode, Assistant Professor; Ph.D., California, Irvine. Human-computer interaction; ubiquitous computing; digital anthropology; gender, security and privacy.

Michelle L. Rogers, Assistant Professor, Ph.D., Wisconsin–Madison. Human-computer interaction, healthcare informatics, human factors engineering, socio-technical systems, health services research, patient safety.

Thomas J. Smith, Assistant Teaching Professor; M.S., Iowa; M.B.A., St. Thomas (Minnesota); M.A., Pennsylvania. Internet technologies, programming languages, software design and development processes, software engineering, information science education.

Il-Yeol Song, Professor; Ph.D., LSU. Conceptual modeling, ontology and patterns, data warehouse and OLAP, object-oriented analysis and design with UML, medical and bioinformatics data modeling and integration, digital forensics.

Gerry Stahl, Associate Professor; Ph.D., Colorado; Ph.D., Northwestern. Human-computer interaction, computer-supported cooperative work, computer-supported collaborative learning, theory of collaboration.

Deborah Turner, Assistant Professor; Ph.D., Washington (Seattle). Information behavior/interaction, management of information institutions, orality and information.

Rosina Weber, Associate Professor; Ph.D., Federal University of Santa Catarina (Brazil). Knowledge-based systems; case-based reasoning; textual case-based reasoning; computational intelligence; knowledge discovery; uncertainty, mainly targeting knowledge management goals in different domains, e.g., software engineering, military, finance, law, bioinformatics, and health sciences.

Howard D. White, Professor Emeritus and Visiting Research Professor; Ph.D., Berkeley. Literature information systems, bibliometrics, research methods, collection development, online searching.

Susan Wiedenbeck, Professor and Ph.D. Program Director; Ph.D., Pittsburgh. Human-computer interaction, end-user programming/end-user development, empirical studies of programmers, interface design and evaluation.

Christopher C. Yang, Associate Professor; Ph.D., Arizona. Web search and mining, security informatics, social media analytics, knowledge management, cross-lingual information retrieval, text summarization, multimedia retrieval, information visualization, information sharing and privacy, artificial intelligence, digital library, electronic commerce.

Valerie Ann Yonker, Associate Teaching Professor; Ph.D., Drexel. Human service information systems, telemedicine, measurement in software evaluation, knowledge engineering.

Lisl Zach, Assistant Professor; Ph.D., Maryland. Knowledge management/competitive intelligence, disaster-related information services, information-seeking behavior of decision makers, measuring and communicating the value of information, organizational use of information.

The *iSchool* at Drexel's Rush Building.

The Alumni Garden.

PRATT INSTITUTE

School of Information and Library Science

Programs of Study

Distinguished as the only ALA-accredited graduate school of information and library science based in Manhattan and the oldest library and information science (LIS) school in North America, Pratt's School of Information and Library Science (SILS) was established in 1890 and has been continuously accredited since 1923, when accreditation was first introduced to the field.

Building upon Pratt's national reputation as a leading school in art and design, Pratt brings creativity and innovation to library science education to offer students exciting and cutting-edge programs and courses from archives and digital libraries, to special libraries and school library media.

In addition to the 36-credit Master of Science in Library and Information Science (M.S.L.I.S.) degree, Pratt offers three joint-degree programs, one with Pratt's History of Art Department (M.S.L.I.S./M.S. in history of art, 60 credits), one with Pratt's Digital Arts M.F.A. (M.S.L.I.S./M.F.A. in digital arts, 75 credits), and one with the Brooklyn Law School (M.S.L.I.S./J.D., 86 credits); a 12-credit Archives Certificate Program within the M.S.L.I.S.; a 12-credit Museum Libraries Certificate; and an M.S. with Library Media Specialist certification.

The School of Information and Library Science prepares students for leadership positions in the information professions, including special opportunities in arts and humanities librarianship for students pursuing careers in academic and research libraries, art and museum libraries, and archives and special collections. The program combines a core curriculum (information professions, information services and sources, information technologies, and knowledge organization) with elective courses, such as advanced Web design, digital libraries, human information behavior, information architecture, information policy, and projects in digital archives. Some courses are taught on location in museums and libraries, such as the New York Public Library, the Watson Library, and the Metropolitan Museum of Art. Other courses are held on the Brooklyn Campus in the Pratt Library, and students in the library and media specialist (LMS) studies program take courses in the Art and Design Education Department. SILS maintains a dean's office in North Hall. Students carry out practicum internships at many of New York's leading cultural institutions. Students may choose from a number of program concentrations, depending on their interests and career goals, including business, cultural informatics, digital technology and knowledge organization, legal and health information, library media specialist studies, management and leadership, public urban libraries, and reference and information literacy.

The master's program may be completed in as little as two semesters and one summer and must be completed within four years of enrollment. Courses are offered in the evening, during the day, and on Saturday and Sunday to accommodate students who work.

Research Facilities

The program's teaching and research facilities occupy the entire sixth floor of a seven-story facility in its home at 144 West 14th Street, Manhattan, in a beautifully restored landmark building, designated the Pratt Manhattan Center (PMC). Here, students find faculty and staff offices, smart classrooms, large computer labs, an elegant conference room, and the student cyber place. The fifth-floor computer lab adds to SILS resources, and a separate scanning lab supports digital library projects. The fourth floor is home to the PMC library, containing extensive LIS collections of books, journals, and full-text online databases. Special SILS events and lectures are held in a 150-person lecture hall adjoining the second-floor gallery space. This rich complex of facilities, all with wireless access and convenient to students and faculty members, adds greatly to effective operations and enhances the learning environment.

Financial Aid

Graduate scholarships ranging in amount are awarded to all eligible applicants. There is no application required. Financial aid is available through a variety of programs funded by institutions, New York State, and the federal government. These include the Federal Perkins Loan and the Federal Work-Study Program, the Tuition Assistance Program of New York State, and Pratt scholarships, loans, and student aid. Continuing students in all departments may apply for fellowships and assistantships on a competitive basis. Special alumni-sponsored fellowships are also available.

Cost of Study

In 2009–10, tuition was $960 per credit for the M.S.L.I.S. degree, and student fees were approximately $1280 per year. The cost of books and supplies varies widely among the different programs.

Living and Housing Costs

Housing is available for single students on the Brooklyn Campus. The cost averages $15,984 per year. The Office of Residential Life maintains listings of off-campus housing to help students find suitable accommodations.

Student Group

Graduate students at Pratt are drawn from all parts of the United States (forty-nine states) and more than sixty other countries. The SILS graduate program average age is 31, with most students working full-time while taking M.S.L.I.S. courses. The employment outlook for Pratt graduates is bright. At present, more than 95 percent of the graduates obtain positions in a broad range of work environments from academic libraries and museums, to special libraries, including those in the corporate, business, and medical fields. The growth potential of the job market is seemingly unlimited. Job opportunities have been increasing for graduates of the information and library science program.

Location

Pratt-SILS is headquartered in the heart of Manhattan. Here, most SILS courses are offered at times convenient to those students who wish to work and pursue their M.S.L.I.S. The main campus of Pratt Institute is located in the Clinton Hill section of Brooklyn. Some courses are offered there to support programs such as the joint degree with Brooklyn Law School and program courses in urban librarianship at Brooklyn Public Library. In Manhattan, courses are taught at Cornell Medical Center for health sciences specialization and the New York Public Library/Research Libraries for special collections.

SILS students enjoy the advantages of New York's position as a world center for the information professions. Students also benefit from the wealth of professional experience and expertise that complements their formal study. A vast variety of cultural and recreational activities are available in the neighborhood, in Brooklyn, in the city, and in the region. Pratt has a parklike campus in a quiet neighborhood of Victorian buildings set in the midst of one of the most vibrant cities in the world.

The Institute

A private, nonsectarian institute of higher education, Pratt was founded in 1887 by industrialist and philanthropist Charles Pratt. Changing with the requirements of the professions for which it educates, Pratt today prepares a student body of approximately 4,700 undergraduate and graduate students for a wide range of careers in architecture and planning, design and fine arts, and information science.

Applying

Applications should be submitted by January 5 for anticipated entrance in the fall semester and by October 1 for anticipated entrance in the spring semester. Applications received after these deadlines are considered if there is available space. Information and application forms may be obtained from the Graduate Admissions Office or the Web site. Applications may also be submitted online at http://www.pratt.edu/admiss/apply.

Correspondence and Information

Graduate Admissions Office
Pratt Institute
200 Willoughby Avenue
Brooklyn, New York 11205
Phone: 718-636-3514
      800-331-0834 (toll-free)
Fax: 718-399-4242
Web site: http://www.pratt.edu/admiss

School of Information and Library Science
Pratt Institute
144 West 14th Street, 6th Floor
New York, New York 10011
Phone: 212-647-7682
E-mail: infosils@pratt.edu
Web site: http://www.pratt.edu/sils

Pratt Institute

THE FACULTY

Tula Giannini, Dean; M.L.S., Rutgers; Ph.D., Bryn Mawr.
Virginia L. Bartow, Visiting Assistant Professor; M.L.S., Columbia.
Jason Baumann, Visiting Assistant Professor; M.L.S., CUNY, Queens.
John Berry III, Visiting Professor; M.L.S., Simmons.
Rick Block, Visiting Associate Professor; M.L.S., Wisconsin–Madison.
Helen-Ann Brown, Visiting Assistant Professor; M.L.S., Maryland, College Park.
Gilok Choi, Assistant Professor; Ph.D., Texas at Austin.
Anthony M. Cucchiara, Visiting Assistant Professor; M.L.S., Pratt; M.B.A., LIU, Brooklyn.
Joseph Dalton, Visiting Assistant Professor; M.S.in L.I.S., Illinois at Urbana-Champaign.
Ernest DiMattia, Visiting Associate Professor; M.L.S., Simmons; M.B.A., Connecticut.
Susan S. DiMattia, Visiting Associate Professor; M.L.S., Simmons; M.B.A., Connecticut.
Deirdre Donohue, Visiting Assistant Professor; M.L.I.S., Pratt.
Richard Eiger, Visiting Professor; M.B.A., NYU.
Donna Fleming, Visiting Assistant Professor; postgraduate diploma, Library and Information Science, University of the West Indies.
Clare Flemming, Visiting Assistant Professor; M.L.S., Pratt.
Judy Freeman, Visiting Professor; M.L.S., Rutgers.
Nancy Friedland, Visiting Associate Professor; M.L.S., Rutgers.
Barbara Genco, Visiting Associate Professor; M.L.S., Pratt.
Sharareh Goldsmith, Visiting Assistant Professor; M.L.S., Pratt.
Denise Hibay, Visiting Associate Professor; M.L.S., Pittsburgh.
Jessica Lee Hochman, Assistant Professor; M.A., Columbia.
Alice Hudson, Visiting Associate Professor; M.L.S., Vanderbilt.
Michael Inman, Visiting Assistant Professor; M.L.S., Pratt.
Scott Johnston, Visiting Assistant Professor; M.L.S., Western Ontario.
Anne Kelly, Associate Professor; M.L.S., Columbia.
Alice Knapp, Visiting Assistant Professor; M.L.S., SUNY at Albany.
Elyssa Kroski, Visiting Assistant Professor; M.S.L.I.S., LIU, C.W. Post.
Deidre Lawrence, Visiting Assistant Professor; M.L.S., Pratt.
Irene Lopatovska, Assistant Professor; M.L.S., North Texas.
Ellen Loughran, Assistant Professor; B.A., Marymount Manhattan.
Barbara Mathe, Visiting Assistant Professor; M.L.S., Columbia.
Seoud M. Matta, Dean Emeritus; D.L.S., Columbia.
Ron Miller, Visiting Associate Professor; M.L.S., Pratt.
William Mills, Visiting Associate Professor; M.L.S., Columbia.
Elena Dana Neacsu, Visiting Assistant Professor; J.D., Bucharest School of Law; M.L.S., CUNY, Queens.
Maria Cristina Pattuelli, Assistant Professor; Ph.D., North Carolina at Chapel Hill.
Deborah Rabina, Assistant Professor; Ph.D., Rutgers.
Lee Robinson, Visiting Associate Professor; M.L.S., Columbia.
Pamela Rollo, Visiting Professor; M.L.S., Columbia.
Caroline Romans, Visiting Professor; M.L.S., Drexel.
Charles Rubenstein, Professor; Ph.D., Polytechnic of New York; M.L.S., Pratt.
Shelby Sanett, Visiting Assistant Professor; Ph.D., Charles Sturt University (Australia).
Harriet Selverstone, Visiting Associate Professor; M.L.S., Pratt.
Nasser Sharify, Dean Emeritus, Distinguished Professor of Library and Information Science; D.L.S., Columbia.
Kenneth Soehner, Visiting Associate Professor; M.L.S., Columbia.
David Walczyk, Assistant Professor; Ed.D., Columbia.
Gary Wasdin, Visiting Associate Professor; M.L.S, Southern Connecticut State.
Kevin B. Winkler, Visiting Assistant Professor; M.L.S., Columbia.
Philip Yockey, Visiting Associate Professor; M.L.S., Columbia.

School of Information Studies
SYRACUSE UNIVERSITY

SYRACUSE UNIVERSITY

School of Information Studies
Master of Science in Information Management
Master of Science in Library and Information Science
Master of Science in Telecommunications and Network Management

Programs of Study

The Syracuse University School of Information Studies (iSchool) offers M.S. degree programs in three areas to prepare students for a growing number of dynamic careers that involve the management and use of information: digital librarianship, eScience, global enterprise technologies, virtual environments, databases, information security and IT governance, information and communication technologies, wireless networks, mobile and Web applications, and telecommunications technologies. Students can earn any of these degrees on campus or online with limited residency requirements.

Ranked number one in information systems by *U.S. News & World Report,* the iSchool offers an M.S. in information management (IM), which requires the completion of 42 credit hours. Each student completes course work in management approaches and strategies, user information needs, technological infrastructures, and elective subjects. There is also an exit requirement. The program provides an integrated approach to the effective management and use of information and communication technologies within organizations. Many IM students concurrently pursue a certificate of advanced study in information security management.

The iSchool also offers a 30-credit Executive Track for the M.S. in information management geared toward mid-career professionals looking to advance their organizations and their job prospects. This track can be completed online or on campus.

Accredited by the American Library Association (ALA), the M.S. in library and information science (LIS) program requires the completion of 36 credit hours. The program is dedicated to educating students to become leaders in the evolution of the library and information profession. LIS students work with interdisciplinary faculty advisers to plan their programs of study, which may include course work in other academic areas. The program offers a concentration in school media and certificates of advanced study in digital libraries and school media, which were ranked fourth in the 2009 *U.S. News & World Report* rankings, as well as a new certificate in cultural heritage and preservation.

The M.S. in telecommunications and network management (TNM) requires the completion of 36 credit hours. It provides an integrated approach to the effective management, operation, and implementation of telecommunication systems, including voice, data, and wireless networks, within organizations. Faculty members engage students in research and classroom lessons in a wide variety of areas, including international telecommunications policy and Internet governance, information assurance/security, eCollaboration, enterprise architecture, wireless systems, information policy, information systems management, online retrieval systems, project management, strategic planning, and telecommunications management. Many TNM students also pursue a certificate of advanced study in information systems and telecommunications management.

All three degree programs focus on employing technology and digital tools to find, evaluate, organize, and use information for the betterment of people. Graduates of the iSchool at Syracuse work in a broad range of managerial and technical positions in business, government, education, health care, and other fields.

The iSchool also offers two doctoral-level programs: a research-oriented Ph.D. in information science and technology for those individuals interested in becoming researchers, professors, and consultants (i.e., more theoretically oriented positions) and the Doctorate of Professional Studies in Information Management, a part-time distance-learning executive degree program for working professionals who are interested in the applied aspects of the information field.

The iSchool's certificates of advanced study have broad appeal and attract students across disciplines. Options include information security management, information systems and telecommunications management, e-government management and leadership, cultural heritage and preservation, digital libraries, and school media. These certificates can be earned on campus or online, and provide a valuable development opportunity both for emerging and experienced professionals in the information field.

Research Facilities

Ranked as one of the most connected campuses by Princeton Review/forbes.com and a 2010 Campus Technology Innovator award recipient, Syracuse University offers wireless capabilities from most buildings and public spaces on campus and provides students with hundreds of computer workstations in public clusters. The School of Information Studies is located in a recently renovated building, Hinds Hall, in the heart of the University's Main Campus Quad. The facility features the latest technologies and innovative instructional and meeting spaces to encourage collaborative and interactive learning. The iSchool's research and development centers, which have achieved national and international distinction, allow students to apply classroom lessons to authentic problems, sometimes using technologies that have not yet made it to market.

The University's library system includes collections of 3.1 million volumes, more than 24,000 online and print journals, and extensive collections of microforms, maps, images, music scores, videos, rare books, and manuscripts. Many of these resources can be accessed from academic and residence hall computer clusters. Among its special collections is the Belfer Audio Laboratory and Archive, which contains more than 340,000 historical sound recordings in all formats, including a collection of 22,000 cylinder records, the largest held by any private institution in North America.

Financial Aid

Fellowships, scholarships, and assistantships are available to full-time students both on campus and online. The most prestigious and competitive are Syracuse University graduate fellowships, which include a scholarship and a stipend for the academic year. University scholarships provide 24 credit hours of tuition, and graduate assistantships provide tuition and a stipend for the academic year. The University also participates in the federal Scholarship for Service program, which awards full scholarships plus a stipend and paid internship opportunities to U.S. citizens who are interested in earning graduate degrees in fields related to information assurance and security. Syracuse also offers fellowships through the McNair Scholars program and Graduate Education for Minorities (GEM) program. Tuition scholarships and other small scholarships are available to part-time students.

Loans are available through the University financial aid office. For Federal Work-Study Program contracts, students work through the University student employment office. Financial aid is awarded according to federal financial need guidelines.

Cost of Study

Tuition for 2010–11 is $1162 per graduate credit hour. Fees are approximately $1424 for one year of full-time study.

Living and Housing Costs

Academic-year living expenses are about $17,870 for single students. The University has residence hall rooms and on-campus apartments for single and married graduate students. Many graduate students choose to live off campus.

Student Group

Syracuse University has about 12,000 students, including about 4,500 graduate students. Approximately 650 graduate students are enrolled in the School of Information Studies. Thirty percent are international students, with the remainder coming from all parts of the United States. Students have diverse backgrounds, with undergraduate majors in the liberal arts, natural sciences, fine arts, business administration, computer science, and engineering. They participate in more than 300 student groups and extracurricular activities, including Women in Information Technology, Information Studies Graduate Organization, Black and Latino Information Studies Support, iOrange Toastmasters, iVenture Upstate, and chapters of national information and library associations.

Student Outcomes

Career opportunities for graduates of the programs are excellent. Information management graduates find lucrative professional positions in a wide variety of organizations, with responsibilities ranging from information systems analysis, database design, and consulting, to risk assessment, social media strategy, and systems management. Library and information science graduates not only work in library settings, but also hold professional positions in corporations, media and communications outlets, museums, government agencies, and universities. Telecommunications and network management graduates find success in four main sectors of industry: information systems positions within organizations requiring data and voice network management and strategies; telecommunications organizations involved in voice, data, or video transmissions; large voice and data network communication vendors such as Cisco and Nortel; and large consulting companies.

Location

The Syracuse metropolitan area is home to more than a half million people and is the commercial, industrial, medical, and cultural center of central New York State. The 200-acre Main Campus is spacious and attractive, and new University facilities extend the campus into the heart of downtown Syracuse, which is only a 20-minute walk from the University. Winters are snowy and summers are pleasant. Lake Ontario, the Finger Lakes, and the Adirondack and Catskill Mountains are nearby. Boston, Toronto, New York, and Philadelphia are within a 5-hour drive.

The School

The School of Information Studies is a leading center for innovative graduate programs in information fields. The school's focus on information users and understanding user information needs sets it apart from other institutions that offer computer science, management, and related programs. The interdisciplinary faculty combines expertise in information science, telecommunications, public administration, education, school media, business management and management information systems, social science, design, linguistics, computer science, library science, and communications. The iSchool also offers a unique undergraduate degree program in information management and technology.

Applying

Applicants for the master's degree programs must have a bachelor's degree from an accredited undergraduate institution and an academic record that is satisfactory for admission to the graduate school. Two letters of recommendation, a resume, and an essay on academic plans and professional goals are also required. Applicants for the master's degree and doctoral programs are required to submit scores from the Graduate Record Examinations (GRE). Whenever possible, an interview is recommended. International students should plan to take the Test of English as a Foreign Language (TOEFL); a score of at least 580 on the paper-based test is expected. Students interested in University fellowships must apply by January 8. Other financial aid applicants must submit all materials by February 12.

For additional information please visit the School of Information Studies Web site, http://ischool.syr.edu or e-mail ischool@syr.edu. Follow the School on Facebook or Twitter at http://facebook.com/su.ischool and http://twitter.com/syracuseischool. Videos about the School can be found at http://www.youtube.com/user/syracuseischool.

Correspondence and Information

School of Information Studies
343 Hinds Hall
Syracuse University
Syracuse, New York 13244-4100

Phone: 315-443-2911
E-mail: ischool@syr.edu
Web site: http://ischool.syr.edu
http://facebook.com/su.ischool (Facebook)
http://twitter.com/syracuseischool (Twitter)

Syracuse University

THE FACULTY AND THEIR RESEARCH

Marilyn Arnone, Research Associate Professor; Ph.D. (instructional design, development, and evaluation), Syracuse. Information literacy education, children's learning and curiosity in interactive multimedia environments.

Bahram Attaie, Assistant Professor of Practice. Microsoft and Cisco certification, business information technology, networking and database programming for the corporate world.

Susan Bonzi, Director of Instructional Quality and Associate Professor; Ph.D. (library and information science), Illinois. Image retrieval systems, bibliometrics, linguistics applications in information science. Received the first Information Science Doctoral Dissertation Award from the American Society for Information Science (ASIS), 1982.

Carlos E. Caicedo, Assistant Professor; Ph.D. (telecommunications), Pittsburgh. Security in future data environments, spectrum trading markets and technology, security management, telecommunication and network systems management.

Derrick L. Cogburn, Associate Professor; Ph.D. (political science), Howard. Global information and communication technology (ICT) policy, global governance, use of ICTs for socioeconomic development.

Kevin Crowston, Ph.D. (information technologies), MIT. Organizational implications of technology, free/libre open source software development, coordination in distributed teams, ICT in real estate.

Jason Dedrick, Associate Professor; Ph.D. (management information systems), California, Irvine. Globalization of information technology, national technology policy, offshoring of knowledge work, personal computing industry, green information technologies.

Michael D'Eredita, Assistant Professor; Ph.D. (experimental/cognitive psychology), Syracuse. Enterprise skill acquisition, collective expertise, virtual apprenticeship, organizational behavior, collaboration.

David Dischiave, Assistant Professor of Practice; M.S. (computer information technology), Regis. Systems analysis and design, database management and design, project management, computer hardware and operating system architecture.

Susan Dischiave, Assistant Professor of Practice; M.B.A. (business administration), Le Moyne. Enterprise systems analysis and design, database management and design, application development.

Renee Franklin, Assistant Professor; Ph.D. (information studies), Florida State. School library media, intellectual freedom in K–12 schools, increasing the level of participation of underrepresented ethnic groups in library and information science education.

Paul Gandel, Professor; Ph.D. (information studies), Syracuse. Digital libraries; digital services; information organization and retrieval; information technology and development; information, organizations, and society knowledge.

Martha A. Garcia-Murillo, Associate Professor; Ph.D. (international political economy and telecommunications), USC. Digital divide, economics of the information industry, information and communications policy and regulations.

Robert Heckman, Senior Associate Dean; Ph.D. (information systems), Pittsburgh. Strategy and planning for information resources, teaching and learning strategies for professionals, collaboration in virtual communities and teams, open source software development.

Jill Hurst-Wahl, Assistant Professor of Practice; M.L.S., Maryland. Digitization, digital libraries, copyright, online social networking, Web 2.0, virtual worlds.

Michelle Lynn Kaarst-Brown, Associate Professor; Ph.D. (organizational theory and management information systems), York. Information technology culture, strategic alignment of information technology with business strategy, perceptions of risk and opportunity in IT adoption, influences on IT governance, Internet-based business.

Bruce Kingma, Professor and Associate Provost for Innovation and Entrepreneurship; Ph.D. (economics), Rochester. Economics of online education, digital libraries, scholarly publishing, library and nonprofit management.

Barbara Kwasnik, Professor; Ph.D. (library and information studies), Rutgers. Classification research, knowledge representation and organization, research methods, information-related behavior.

R. David Lankes, Associate Professor; Ph.D. (information transfer), Syracuse. Participatory librarianship, digital reference, digital libraries, credibility.

Kenneth Lavender, Assistant Professor of Practice; Ph.D. (English), California, Santa Barbara. Digital reference, rare books, archives, preservation of cultural heritage, distance education pedagogy, context of information services.

Elizabeth D. Liddy, Dean and Trustee Professor; Ph.D. (information transfer), Syracuse. Indexing, data mining, natural-language processing, information retrieval.

Ian MacInnes, Associate Dean for Academic Affairs; Ph.D. (political economy and public policy), USC. Electronic commerce, competition policy, information technology and globalization, public policy, standardization, network economics, microeconomics.

Nancy McCracken, Research Associate Professor; Ph.D. (computer and information science), Syracuse. Computational linguistics, natural language processing, data mining, information extraction and retrieval, question answering, knowledge representation.

Lee McKnight, Associate Professor; Ph.D. (political science, communication, and international relations), MIT. Wireless grids, nomadicity, social networking of devices, Internet economics and policy, national and international technology policy.

David Molta, Assistant Dean, Technology Integration; M.P.A., North Texas. Mobile and wireless information systems; interoperability and performance testing; impact of mobile communications technologies on individuals, organizations, and society.

Milton L. Mueller, Professor; Ph.D. (telecommunication), Pennsylvania. Internet governance, telecommunication policy, transnational civil society, global governance institutions in communication and information, digital identity, digital convergence.

Scott Nicholson, Associate Professor; Ph.D. (information studies), North Texas. Gaming in libraries, evaluation and assessment of library services, data mining for libraries, Web search tools.

Michael Nilan, Associate Professor; Ph.D. (communication research), Washington (Seattle). Virtual communities, cognitive behavior, information seeking and using, information system design and evaluation, user-based research methods.

Megan Oakleaf, Assistant Professor; Ph.D. (information and library science), North Carolina at Chapel Hill. Evolution and assessment of information services, outcomes-based assessment, evidence-based decision making, digital reference, digital libraries, information services.

Carsten Osterlund, Associate Professor; Ph.D. (organization studies and behavioral policy science), MIT. Medical informatics, documenting work, distributed work, organizational implications of information technology, indoor tracking systems, qualitative research techniques.

Joon S. Park, Associate Professor; Ph.D. (information technology and information security), George Mason. Information and systems security; security policies, models, mechanisms, evaluation, survivability, and applications.

Jian Qin, Associate Professor; Ph.D. (library and information science), Illinois at Urbana-Champaign. Knowledge organization, information organization, information technology applications in managing knowledge and information.

Anthony Rotolo, Assistant Professor of Practice and Social Media Strategist; M.S. (information management), Syracuse. Social media and Web 2.0, instructional technologies, online safety, augmented reality, e-democracy, social implications of technology.

Jeffrey Rubin, Assistant Professor of Practice; M.S. (telecommunications and network management), Syracuse. Managing Web sites, e-business, content management systems, information architecture, designing Internet services, Web analytics.

Steven B. Sawyer, Associate Professor; D.B.A. (management information systems), Boston. Social informatics, design and development of information systems, project management, role of information and communication technologies relative to organizational and social change.

Ruth V. Small, Meredith Professor; Ph.D. (instructional design, development, and evaluation), Syracuse. Motivational aspects of information literacy, design and use of information and information technologies in education, role of school media specialist, information components of inventive thinking.

Jeffrey Stanton, Associate Dean for Research and Doctoral Programs; Ph.D. (information studies), Connecticut. Organizational psychology and data collection; behavioral information security; statistical models to predict attitudes, motivation, and behavior; interactions between people and technology.

Zixiang (Alex) Tan, Associate Professor; Ph.D. (telecommunications management and policy), Rutgers. Telecommunications policy and regulations, new technology development and applications, industry restructure and competition.

Arthur Thomas, Assistant Professor of Practice; Ph.D. (research and evaluation/instructional systems design and management), SUNY at Buffalo. Performance improvement, project management, data networking engineering, instructional design, information systems management.

Howard Turtle, Associate Research Professor; Ph.D. (computer science), Massachusetts Amherst. Design and implementation of retrieval systems, operating system support for large databases, text representation techniques, automatic classification, text and data mining, and automated inference techniques.

Murali Venkatesh, Associate Professor; Ph.D. (management), Indiana. Civic network design, group-based decision support systems, sociological analyses of administrative documents, human-computer interaction, telecommunications.

Carlos Villalba, Assistant Professor of Practice; Ph.D. candidate (instructional design, development, and evaluation), Syracuse. Oracle database administration, IT security, open source application development, search engine optimization, e-commerce.

Jun Wang, Assistant Research Professor; Ph.D. (library and information science), Illinois at Urbana-Champaign. Human computation, machine learning, computational neuroscience, computational language evolution.

Ozgur Yilmazel, Assistant Research Professor; Ph.D. (electrical engineering), Syracuse. Natural language processing, information retrieval, text categorization, software engineering.

Bei Yu, Assistant Professor; Ph.D. (library and information science), Illinois at Urbana-Champaign. Text classification and analysis, natural language processing, political linguistics, language and social behavior, automated language extraction and classification development.

Ping Zhang, Professor; Ph.D. (information systems), Texas at Austin. Human computer interaction, information management, intellectual development of information-related fields.

The iSchool is located on the Main Campus Quad in the heart of the Syracuse University campus.

ACADEMIC AND PROFESSIONAL PROGRAMS IN THE MEDICAL PROFESSIONS AND SCIENCES

Section 34
Acupuncture and Oriental Medicine

This section contains a directory of institutions offering graduate work in acupuncture and oriental medicine. Additional information about programs listed in the directory may be obtained by writing directly to the dean of a graduate school or chair of a department at the address given in the directory.

CONTENTS

Program Directory

Close-Up

Acupuncture and Oriental Medicine

Academy for Five Element Acupuncture, Graduate Program, Hallandale, FL 33009. Offers M Ac. *Accreditation:* ACAOM.

Academy of Chinese Culture and Health Sciences, Program in Traditional Chinese Medicine, Oakland, CA 94612. Offers MS. *Accreditation:* ACAOM. Part-time and evening/weekend programs available. *Degree requirements:* For master's, comprehensive exam, thesis. *Entrance requirements:* Additional exam requirements/recommendations for international students: Required—TOEFL (minimum score 500 paper-based; 173 computer-based). *Faculty research:* Herbs, acupuncture.

Academy of Oriental Medicine at Austin, Master of Acupuncture and Oriental Medicine Program, Austin, TX 78757. Offers MAcOM. *Accreditation:* ACAOM. *Faculty:* 9 full-time (2 women), 15 part-time/adjunct (6 women). *Students:* 161 full-time (133 women), 49 part-time (23 women); includes 46 minority (6 African Americans, 22 Asian Americans or Pacific Islanders, 18 Hispanic Americans). Average age 35. 43 applicants, 93% accepted, 35 enrolled. In 2009, 34 master's awarded. *Degree requirements:* For master's, comprehensive exam, clinical rotations (42 credits). *Entrance requirements:* For master's, minimum of 90 credits at the baccalaureate level from a regionally-accredited institution with 30 credits of general education coursework, or BA or higher; minimum GPA of 2.5. Additional exam requirements/recommendations for international students: Required—TOEFL (minimum score 85 iBT). *Application deadline:* For fall admission, 7/19 priority date for domestic students; for winter admission, 11/1 priority date for domestic students; for spring admission, 5/17 priority date for domestic students. Applications are processed on a rolling basis. Application fee: $75. Electronic applications accepted. *Expenses:* Tuition: Full-time $12,361; part-time $189 per credit. Required fees: $330; $130 per quarter. Part-time tuition and fees vary according to course load. *Financial support:* Scholarships/grants available. Financial award applicants required to submit FAFSA. *Faculty research:* Acupuncture, Chinese herbal medicine, integrative medicine, pulse diagnosis. *Unit head:* Dr. William R. Morris, President, 512-454-1188, Fax: 512-454-7001, E-mail: info@aoma.edu. *Application contact:* Hannah Thornton, Director of Admissions and Student Services, 512-492-3017, Fax: 512-454-7001, E-mail: admissions@aoma.edu.

Acupuncture & Integrative Medicine College, Berkeley, Program in Oriental Medicine, Berkeley, CA 94704. Offers MS. *Accreditation:* ACAOM. Part-time and evening/weekend programs available. *Degree requirements:* For master's, comprehensive exam. *Entrance requirements:* For master's, interview, minimum GPA of 2.5, 60 semester units of course work at the baccalaureate level. Additional exam requirements/recommendations for international students: Required—TOEFL (minimum score 500 paper-based; 173 computer-based). *Faculty research:* Stimulus therapy, oxygen hemoglobin, acupuncture needling, classical Chinese medicine.

Acupuncture and Massage College, Program in Oriental Medicine, Miami, FL 33176. Offers MOM. *Accreditation:* ACAOM.

American College of Acupuncture and Oriental Medicine, Graduate Studies, Houston, TX 77063. Offers MAOM. *Accreditation:* ACAOM. Part-time programs available. *Entrance requirements:* For master's, 60 undergraduate credit hours. Additional exam requirements/recommendations for international students: Required—TOEFL.

American College of Traditional Chinese Medicine, Graduate Program, San Francisco, CA 94107. Offers acupuncture and Oriental medicine (DAOM); shiatsu massage (Certificate); traditional Chinese medicine (MSTCM); tui na massage (Certificate). *Accreditation:* ACAOM. Part-time programs available. *Faculty:* 20 full-time (10 women), 58 part-time/adjunct (25 women). *Students:* 208 full-time (150 women), 88 part-time (67 women); includes 85 minority (3 African Americans, 65 Asian Americans or Pacific Islanders, 17 Hispanic Americans), 7 international. Average age 34. 60 applicants, 95% accepted, 40 enrolled. In 2009, 58 master's, 13 doctorates awarded. *Degree requirements:* For master's, one foreign language, comprehensive exam, internship; for doctorate, thesis/dissertation, clinical experience. *Entrance requirements:* For master's, minimum of 90 semester or 135 quarter units from an accredited institution, minimum GPA of 3.0, interview; for doctorate, received or equivalent to MSTCM (master degree in Traditional Chinese Medicine), interview, and State or National licensee. Additional exam requirements/recommendations for international students: Required—TOEFL (minimum score 550 paper-based; 213 computer-based; 79 iBT); Recommended—IELTS (minimum score 6.5). *Application deadline:* For fall admission, 9/1 for domestic and international students; for winter admission, 12/1 for domestic and international students; for spring admission, 3/1 for domestic and international students. Applications are processed on a rolling basis. Application fee: $100 ($150 for international students). *Expenses:* Tuition: Full-time $18,700; part-time $2338 per quarter. Required fees: $222; $237 per unit. $51 per quarter. *Financial support:* In 2009–10, 190 students received support, including 8 teaching assistantships (averaging $250 per year); Federal Work-Study, institutionally sponsored loans, and scholarships/grants also available. Support available to part-time students. Financial award applicants required to submit FAFSA. *Unit head:* Lixin Huang, President, 415-282-7600 Ext. 12, Fax: 415-282-0856, E-mail: lixinhuang@actcm.edu. *Application contact:* Gina Rossi, Admissions Counselor, 415-282-7600 Ext. 14, Fax: 415-282-0856, E-mail: admissions@actcm.edu.

Arizona School of Acupuncture and Oriental Medicine, Graduate Programs, Tucson, AZ 85712. Offers M Ac, M Ac OM.

Atlantic Institute of Oriental Medicine, Graduate Program, Fort Lauderdale, FL 33301. Offers MS. *Accreditation:* ACAOM. Evening/weekend programs available. *Faculty:* 6 full-time (0 women), 16 part-time/adjunct (7 women). *Students:* 110 full-time (78 women); includes 23 minority (3 African Americans, 7 Asian Americans or Pacific Islanders, 13 Hispanic Americans), 7 international. *Entrance requirements:* Additional exam requirements/recommendations for international students: Required—TOEFL (minimum score 500 paper-based). *Application deadline:* For fall admission, 7/1 for domestic students, 5/1 for international students; for spring admission, 11/30 for domestic students, 2/28 for international students. Applications are processed on a rolling basis. Application fee: $20 ($100 for international students). *Expenses:* Tuition: Full-time $13,000. *Unit head:* Dr. Johanna C. Yen, President, 954-763-9840 Ext. 202, Fax: 954-763-9844, E-mail: president@atom.edu. *Application contact:* Milagros Ferreira, Registrar, 954-763-9840 Ext. 207, Fax: 954-763-9844, E-mail: registrar@atom.edu.

Bastyr University, School of Acupuncture and Oriental Medicine, Kenmore, WA 98028-4966. Offers acupuncture (MS); acupuncture and Oriental medicine (MS, DAOM); Chinese herbal medicine (Certificate). *Accreditation:* ACAOM. *Students:* 87 full-time (62 women), 31 part-time (21 women). Average age 32. In 2009, 57 master's, 3 doctorates awarded. *Entrance requirements:* For master's, course work in biology, chemistry, college algebra and psychology; for doctorate, MS in acupuncture or certificate and 10 years clinical experience. Additional exam requirements/recommendations for international students: Required—TOEFL (minimum score 550 paper-based; 213 computer-based; 79 iBT). *Application deadline:* For fall admission, 3/15 priority date for domestic and international students. Applications are processed on a rolling basis. Application fee: $75. *Expenses:* Tuition: Full-time $23,478. Tuition and fees vary according to course level, course load and program. *Financial support:* Career-related internships or fieldwork, Federal Work-Study, and scholarships/grants available. Support available to part-time students. Financial award application deadline: 3/15; financial award applicants required to submit FAFSA. *Unit head:* Terry Courtney, Dean, 425-823-1300, Fax: 425-823-6222. *Application contact:* Admissions Office, 425-602-3330, Fax: 425-602-3090, E-mail: admissions@bastyr.edu.

Canadian Memorial Chiropractic College, Certificate Programs, Toronto, ON M2H 3J1, Canada. Offers chiropractic clinical sciences (Certificate); chiropractic radiology (Certificate); chiropractic sports sciences (Certificate); clinical acupuncture (Certificate). *Degree requirements:* For Certificate, thesis. *Entrance requirements:* For degree, DC, board certification. *Faculty research:* Theories and concepts of chiropractic, sciences related to chiropractic, assessments of the efficacy and efficiency of chiropractic.

Colorado School of Traditional Chinese Medicine, Graduate Program, Denver, CO 80206-2127. Offers traditional Chinese medicine (MS). *Accreditation:* ACAOM. Part-time and evening/weekend programs available. *Faculty:* 36 part-time/adjunct (11 women). *Students:* 91 full-time (73 women), 13 part-time (9 women); includes 23 minority (2 African Americans, 2 American Indian/Alaska Native, 13 Asian Americans or Pacific Islanders, 6 Hispanic Americans), 3 international. Average age 33. 28 applicants, 100% accepted, 28 enrolled. In 2009, 22 master's awarded. *Entrance requirements:* For master's, 60 semester credits or 90 quarter credits from an accredited college. Additional exam requirements/recommendations for international students: Required—TOEFL (minimum score 500 paper-based; 173 computer-based; 61 iBT). *Application deadline:* For fall admission, 8/26 for domestic students, 8/15 for international students; for winter admission, 12/24 for domestic students, 12/1 for international students; for spring admission, 4/26 for domestic students, 4/15 for international students. Applications are processed on a rolling basis. Application fee: $50 ($100 for international students). *Financial support:* In 2009–10, 86 students received support. Scholarships/grants available. Financial award applicants required to submit FAFSA. *Unit head:* Vladimir Dibrigida, Administrative Director, 303-329-6355 Ext. 11, Fax: 303-388-8165, E-mail: director@cstcm.edu. *Application contact:* Lera Atwater, Registrar, 303-329-6355 Ext. 12, Fax: 303-388-8165, E-mail: registrar@cstcm.edu.

Dongguk Royal University, Program in Oriental Medicine, Los Angeles, CA 90020. Offers MS. *Accreditation:* ACAOM. Part-time and evening/weekend programs available.

East West College of Natural Medicine, Graduate Programs, Sarasota, FL 34234. Offers MSOM. *Accreditation:* ACAOM.

Emperor's College of Traditional Oriental Medicine, Graduate Programs, Santa Monica, CA 90403. Offers MTOM, DAOM. *Accreditation:* ACAOM. Part-time and evening/weekend programs available. *Entrance requirements:* For master's, minimum 2 years of undergraduate course work, interview; for doctorate, CA acupuncture licensure. *Faculty research:* Menopause, dysmenorrhea.

Five Branches University: Graduate School of Traditional Chinese Medicine, Program in Traditional Chinese Medicine, Santa Cruz, CA 95062. Offers MTCM. *Accreditation:* ACAOM. *Degree requirements:* For master's, comprehensive exam. *Entrance requirements:* For master's, 6 units in anatomy and physiology, 9 units in basic sciences, minimum GPA of 2.5. Electronic applications accepted.

Florida College of Integrative Medicine, Graduate Program, Orlando, FL 32809. Offers MSOM. *Accreditation:* ACAOM. Evening/weekend programs available. *Entrance requirements:* For master's, minimum 60 semester hours of undergraduate coursework. Electronic applications accepted.

Institute of Clinical Acupuncture and Oriental Medicine, Program in Oriental Medicine, Honolulu, HI 96817. Offers MSOM. *Accreditation:* ACAOM.

Midwest College of Oriental Medicine, Graduate Programs, Racine, WI 53403-9747. Offers acupuncture (Certificate); oriental medicine (MSOM). *Accreditation:* ACAOM. Part-time and evening/weekend programs available. *Degree requirements:* For master's and Certificate, comprehensive exam, thesis. *Entrance requirements:* For master's and Certificate, 60 semester credit hours from accredited school, 2 letters of recommendation, interview. Additional exam requirements/recommendations for international students: Required—TOEFL. *Faculty research:* Pharmacology.

Midwest College of Oriental Medicine, Graduate Programs-Chicago, Chicago, IL 60613. Offers acupuncture (Certificate); oriental medicine (MSOM). Part-time and evening/weekend programs available. *Degree requirements:* For master's and Certificate, comprehensive exam, thesis. *Entrance requirements:* For master's and Certificate, 60 semester credit hours from accredited school, 2 letters of recommendation, interview. Additional exam requirements/recommendations for international students: Required—TOEFL.

National College of Natural Medicine, Classical Chinese Medicine School, Portland, OR 97201. Offers MSOM. *Accreditation:* ACAOM. *Faculty:* 8 full-time (2 women), 27 part-time/adjunct (10 women). *Students:* 85 full-time (55 women), 8 part-time (5 women); includes 9 minority (2 African Americans, 4 Asian Americans or Pacific Islanders, 3 Hispanic Americans). Average age 29. 51 applicants, 88% accepted, 34 enrolled. In 2009, 26 master's awarded. *Degree requirements:* For master's, thesis. *Entrance requirements:* Additional exam requirements/recommendations for international students: Required—TOEFL (minimum score 550 paper-based; 213 computer-based). *Application deadline:* For fall admission, 11/1 priority date for domestic and international students; for winter admission, 2/1 priority date for domestic and international students. Applications are processed on a rolling basis. Application fee: $75. *Expenses:* Contact institution. *Financial support:* In 2009–10, 77 students received support. Federal Work-Study and scholarships/grants available. Financial award application deadline: 4/30; financial award applicants required to submit FAFSA. *Faculty research:* Cases on herbs and acupuncture for asthma, diabetes, depression associated with menopause, Qi Gong to maintain weight loss. *Unit head:* Dr. Laurie Regan, Dean, 503-552-1775, Fax: 503-499-0027, E-mail: admissions@ncnm.edu. *Application contact:* Hang Nguyen, Admissions Coordinator, 503-552-1660, Fax: 503-499-0027, E-mail: admissions@ncnm.edu.

National University of Health Sciences, College of Professional Studies, Lombard, IL 60148-4583. Offers acupuncture (MSAC); chiropractic medicine (DC); naturopathic medicine (ND); Oriental medicine (MSOM). *Accreditation:* CCE. *Faculty:* 62 full-time (19 women), 60 part-time/adjunct (30 women). *Students:* 588 full-time (299 women), 65 part-time (32 women); includes 120 minority (45 African Americans, 41 Asian Americans or Pacific Islanders, 34 Hispanic Americans), 10 international. Average age 26. 271 applicants, 80% accepted, 120 enrolled. In 2009, 290 DCs awarded. *Degree requirements:* For master's and DC, comprehensive exam, internship, community service. *Entrance requirements:* For DC, bachelor's degree, character references, undergraduate transcripts, written essay; for master's, character references. Additional exam requirements/recommendations for international students: Required—TOEFL (minimum score 550 paper-based; 213 computer-based; 79 iBT). *Application deadline:* For fall admission, 8/13 for domestic students, 8/1 for international students; for winter admission, 12/10 for domestic students, 12/1 for international students; for spring admission, 4/6 for domestic students, 4/1 for international students. Applications are processed on a rolling basis. Application fee: $55. Electronic applications accepted. *Expenses:* Tuition: Part-time $370 per credit hour. Required fees: $84 per trimester. Tuition and fees vary according to course load, degree level and program. *Financial support:* In 2009–10, 622 students received support, including 10 fellowships (averaging $5,500 per year), 15 research assistantships (averaging $2,500 per year); teaching assistantships, Federal Work-Study, scholarships/grants, and tuition waivers (partial) also available. Support available to part-time students. Financial award applicants required to submit FAFSA. *Faculty research:* Mechanisms of action of CAM therapies, clinical trials of CAM therapies, practice-based research networks for CAM therapies, evidence-based practice for CAM therapies, educational research in CAM teaching institutions. Total annual research expenditures: $472,975. *Unit head:* Dr. Nicholas A. Trongale, Dean, College of Professional Studies, 630-889-6673, Fax: 630-889-6499, E-mail: ntrongale@nuhs.edu. *Application contact:* Teri Hatfield, Assistant Director of Admissions, 800-826-6285, Fax: 630-889-6566, E-mail: thatfield@nuhs.edu.

See Close-Up on page 1735.

New England School of Acupuncture, Program in Acupuncture and Oriental Medicine, Newton, MA 02458. Offers acupuncture (M Ac); acupuncture and Oriental medicine (MAOM). *Accreditation:* ACAOM (one or more programs are accredited). Part-time programs available. *Degree requirements:* For master's, comprehensive exam. *Entrance requirements:* For master's, previous course work in anatomy, biology, physiology, and psychology. Additional exam requirements/recommendations for international students: Required—TOEFL (minimum score

550 paper-based; 213 computer-based). *Faculty research:* Acupuncture and women's health, acupuncture and stroke rehabilitation, tai chi and cardiovascular health, tai chi and balance, cancer.

New York Chiropractic College, Acupuncture and Oriental Medicine Programs, Seneca Falls, NY 13148-0800. Offers acupuncture (MS); acupuncture and oriental medicine (MS). *Accreditation:* ACAOM. *Faculty:* 8 full-time (6 women), 7 part-time/adjunct (4 women). *Students:* 48 full-time (40 women), 26 part-time (19 women); includes 5 minority (1 African American, 4 Asian Americans or Pacific Islanders). Average age 32. 66 applicants, 80% accepted, 37 enrolled. In 2009, 24 master's awarded. *Degree requirements:* For master's, clinical internship. *Entrance requirements:* For master's, interview, minimum GPA of 2.5, writing example, references. Additional exam requirements/recommendations for international students: Recommended—TOEFL (minimum score 550 paper-based; 213 computer-based). *Application deadline:* Applications are processed on a rolling basis. Application fee: $60. Electronic applications accepted. *Expenses:* Tuition: Full-time $18,320; part-time $426 per credit hour. Required fees: $680. Tuition and fees vary according to course load and program. *Financial support:* In 2009–10, 42 students received support, including 1 fellowship with tuition reimbursement available (averaging $30,000 per year); Federal Work-Study and scholarships/grants also available. Financial award applicants required to submit FAFSA. *Unit head:* Jason Wright, Dean of Finger Lakes School of Acupuncture and Oriental Medicine, 315-568-3268, E-mail: jwright@nycc.edu. *Application contact:* Michael Lynch, Director of Admissions, 315-568-3040, Fax: 315-568-3087, E-mail: mlynch@nycc.edu.

New York College of Health Professions, Graduate School of Oriental Medicine, Syosset, NY 11791-4413. Offers acupuncture (MS); Oriental medicine (MS). *Accreditation:* ACAOM. Part-time programs available. *Degree requirements:* For master's, thesis. *Entrance requirements:* For master's, minimum GPA of 2.5, 60 semester credits in undergraduate course work. Additional exam requirements/recommendations for international students: Required—TOEFL. *Faculty research:* Breast cancer, diabetic neuropathy hemolysis.

New York College of Traditional Chinese Medicine, Graduate Programs, Mineola, NY 11501. Offers oriental medicine (MAOM). *Accreditation:* ACAOM.

Northwestern Health Sciences University, Minnesota College of Acupuncture and Oriental Medicine, Bloomington, MN 55431-1599. Offers acupuncture (M Ac); oriental medicine (MOM). *Accreditation:* ACAOM. *Entrance requirements:* Additional exam requirements/recommendations for international students: Required—TOEFL (minimum score 540 paper-based; 207 computer-based). Electronic applications accepted.

Oregon College of Oriental Medicine, Graduate Program in Acupuncture and Oriental Medicine, Portland, OR 97216. Offers M Ac OM, MAcOM, DAOM. *Accreditation:* ACAOM. Part-time programs available. *Entrance requirements:* For master's, minimum 3 years of college; course work in chemistry, biology, and psychology; for doctorate, documentation of clinical practice, 3 years of clinical experience. Additional exam requirements/recommendations for international students: Required—TOEFL (minimum score 550 paper-based).

Pacific College of Oriental Medicine, Graduate Program, San Diego, CA 92108. Offers MSTOM, DAOM. *Accreditation:* ACAOM. Part-time and evening/weekend programs available. *Entrance requirements:* For master's, 2 letters of reference, interviews, minimum GPA of 3.0. *Faculty research:* PMS, acupuncture, herbs, Tai Ji Quan, sports medicine.

Pacific College of Oriental Medicine-Chicago, Graduate Program, Chicago, IL 60613. Offers MTOM. *Accreditation:* ACAOM. Part-time and evening/weekend programs available. *Entrance requirements:* For master's, 2 letters of reference, interview, minimum GPA of 3.0. *Faculty research:* AIDS, cancer, mental health, clinical counseling.

Pacific College of Oriental Medicine-New York, Graduate Program, New York, NY 10010. Offers MSTOM. *Accreditation:* ACAOM. Part-time and evening/weekend programs available. *Entrance requirements:* For master's, 2 letters of reference, interview, minimum GPA of 3.0. *Faculty research:* Energy medicine, acupuncture in the treatment of neurological disorders.

Samra University of Oriental Medicine, Program in Oriental Medicine, Los Angeles, CA 90015. Offers MS, DAOM. *Accreditation:* ACAOM. Part-time and evening/weekend programs available. *Degree requirements:* For master's, comprehensive exam. *Entrance requirements:* For master's, 60 semester (90 quarter) units with a 'C' average in general education from an accredited college. *Faculty research:* Herbal therapy; alleviation of AIDS symptoms, cancer, colds, flu.

Seattle Institute of Oriental Medicine, Graduate Program, Seattle, WA 98115. Offers M Ac OM. *Accreditation:* ACAOM. *Degree requirements:* For master's, one foreign language, comprehensive exam. *Entrance requirements:* For master's, course work in biology, psychology, chemistry, anatomy, physiology; CPR/first aid certification; 3 years (90 semester credits) post secondary coursework. Additional exam requirements/recommendations for international students: Recommended—TOEFL (minimum score 500 paper-based).

South Baylo University, Program in Oriental Medicine and Acupuncture, Anaheim, CA 92801-1701. Offers MS. *Accreditation:* ACAOM. Evening/weekend programs available. *Degree requirements:* For master's, 3 foreign languages, comprehensive exam. *Entrance requirements:* Additional exam requirements/recommendations for international students: Required—TOEFL (minimum score 500 paper-based; 173 computer-based). Electronic applications accepted. *Faculty research:* Effectiveness of acupuncture therapy.

Southern California University of Health Sciences, College of Acupuncture and Oriental Medicine, Whittier, CA 90609-1166. Offers MAOM. *Accreditation:* ACAOM. Part-time and evening/weekend programs available. *Faculty:* 10 full-time (6 women), 19 part-time/adjunct (6 women). *Students:* 115 full-time (61 women), 68 part-time (35 women); includes 89 minority (3 African Americans, 3 American Indian/Alaska Native, 74 Asian Americans or Pacific Islanders, 9 Hispanic Americans). Average age 28. 118 applicants, 66% accepted, 46 enrolled. In 2009, 33 master's awarded. *Entrance requirements:* For master's, 60 semester hours or 90 quarter credits of undergraduate course work, interview. Additional exam requirements/recommendations for international students: Required—TOEFL (minimum score 500 paper-based; 173 computer-based). *Application deadline:* Applications are processed on a rolling basis. Application fee: $50. Electronic applications accepted. *Financial support:* In 2009–10, 104 students received support. Federal Work-Study available. Financial award applicants required to submit FAFSA. *Unit head:* Dr. Wen-Shuo Wu, Dean, 562-947-8755 Ext. 7028, E-mail: wen-shuowu@scuhs.edu. *Application contact:* Debra Mitchell, Director of Admissions, 562-902-3309, Fax: 562-902-3321, E-mail: debramitchell@scuhs.edu.

Southwest Acupuncture College, Program in Oriental Medicine, Albuquerque Campus, Albuquerque, NM 87109, Armenia. Offers MS. *Accreditation:* ACAOM. Part-time programs available. *Entrance requirements:* For master's, minimum 2 years of college general education. Additional exam requirements/recommendations for international students: Required—TOEFL (minimum score 500 paper-based; 173 computer-based). Electronic applications accepted.

Southwest Acupuncture College, Program in Oriental Medicine, Boulder Campus, Boulder, CO 80301. Offers MS. *Accreditation:* ACAOM. Part-time programs available. *Entrance requirements:* For master's, minimum 2 years of college general education.

Southwest Acupuncture College, Program in Oriental Medicine, Santa Fe Campus, Santa Fe, NM 87505. Offers MS. *Accreditation:* ACAOM. Part-time programs available. *Entrance requirements:* For master's, minimum 2 years of college general education. Additional exam requirements/recommendations for international students: Required—TOEFL (minimum score 500 paper-based; 173 computer-based). Electronic applications accepted.

Swedish Institute, College of Health Sciences, Graduate Program, New York, NY 10001-6700. Offers acupuncture (MS). *Accreditation:* ACAOM. Part-time and evening/weekend programs available. *Entrance requirements:* Additional exam requirements/recommendations for international students: Required—TOEFL (minimum score 72 iBT).

Tai Sophia Institute, Chinese Herb Certificate Program, Laurel, MD 20723. Offers Certificate. Part-time and evening/weekend programs available. *Entrance requirements:* Additional exam requirements/recommendations for international students: Required—TOEFL.

Tai Sophia Institute, Program in Acupuncture, Laurel, MD 20723. Offers M Ac. *Accreditation:* ACAOM. *Degree requirements:* For master's, comprehensive exam, 500 clinical hours, oral exams. *Entrance requirements:* Additional exam requirements/recommendations for international students: Required—TOEFL. *Faculty research:* Philosophical roots of oriental medicine, meridian pathways, points, pulses.

Tai Sophia Institute, Program in Applied Healing Arts, Laurel, MD 20723. Offers MA. *Entrance requirements:* Additional exam requirements/recommendations for international students: Required—TOEFL. *Faculty research:* Healing habits of mind and heart, an expanded vision, bringing of one's vision and practices to a special arena.

Tai Sophia Institute, Program in Herbal Medicine, Laurel, MD 20723. Offers MS. *Entrance requirements:* Additional exam requirements/recommendations for international students: Required—TOEFL. *Faculty research:* Philosophical roots of holistic healing, botany, herbal pharmacology; materia medica, holistic healing.

Texas College of Traditional Chinese Medicine, Program in Acupuncture and Oriental Medicine, Austin, TX 78704. Offers MAOM. *Accreditation:* ACAOM. Part-time and evening/weekend programs available. *Entrance requirements:* For master's, minimum GPA of 2.0. Additional exam requirements/recommendations for international students: Required—TOEFL (minimum score 500 paper-based; 173 computer-based), TWE. Electronic applications accepted.

Touro College, School of Health Sciences, Bay Shore, NY 11706. Offers acupuncture (MS); occupational therapy (MS); oriental medicine (MSOM); physical therapy (DPT); public health (MPH); speech-language pathology (MS). *Expenses:* Contact institution.

Traditional Chinese Medical College of Hawaii, Graduate Programs, Kamuela, HI 96743-2288. Offers MSOM. *Accreditation:* ACAOM.

Tri-State College of Acupuncture, Program in Acupuncture, New York, NY 10011. Offers acupuncture (MS); oriental medicine (MS); traditional Chinese herbology (Certificate). *Accreditation:* ACAOM. Evening/weekend programs available.

University of Bridgeport, Acupuncture Institute, Bridgeport, CT 06604. Offers MS. *Accreditation:* ACAOM. Part-time programs available. *Entrance requirements:* Additional exam requirements/recommendations for international students: Recommended—TOEFL (minimum score 550 paper-based; 213 computer-based; 80 iBT), IELTS (minimum score 6.5). Electronic applications accepted. *Expenses:* Contact institution.

World Medicine Institute of Acupuncture and Herbal Medicine, Program in Acupuncture and Oriental Medicine, Honolulu, HI 96828. Offers M Ac OM. *Accreditation:* ACAOM. Part-time and evening/weekend programs available. *Entrance requirements:* For master's, minimum 60 college credits.

Yo San University of Traditional Chinese Medicine, Program in Acupuncture and Traditional Chinese Medicine, Los Angeles, CA 90066. Offers MATCM. *Accreditation:* ACAOM. Part-time programs available. Postbaccalaureate distance learning degree programs offered (no on-campus study). *Degree requirements:* For master's, observation and practice internships, exam. *Entrance requirements:* For master's, minimum 2 years of college, interview, minimum GPA of 2.5.

Section 35
Chiropractic

This section contains a directory of institutions offering graduate work in chiropractic, followed by in-depth entries submitted by institutions that chose to prepare detailed program descriptions. Additional information about programs listed in the directory but not augmented by an in-depth entry may be obtained by writing directly to the dean of a graduate school or chair of a department at the address given in the directory.

CONTENTS

Chiropractic

Canadian Memorial Chiropractic College, Certificate Programs, Toronto, ON M2H 3J1, Canada. Offers chiropractic clinical sciences (Certificate); chiropractic radiology (Certificate); chiropractic sports sciences (Certificate); clinical acupuncture (Certificate). *Degree requirements:* For Certificate, thesis. *Entrance requirements:* For degree, DC, board certification. *Faculty research:* Theories and concepts of chiropractic, sciences related to chiropractic, assessments of the efficacy and efficiency of chiropractic.

Canadian Memorial Chiropractic College, Professional Program, Toronto, ON M2H 3J1, Canada. Offers DC. *Entrance requirements:* 3 full years of university (15 full courses or 90 hours). *Faculty research:* Theories and concepts of chiropractic, sciences related to chiropractic, assessment of the efficacy and efficiency of chiropractic.

Cleveland Chiropractic College–Kansas City Campus, Professional Program, Overland Park, KS 66210. Offers DC. *Accreditation:* CCE. Part-time programs available. *Degree requirements:* For DC, comprehensive exam. *Entrance requirements:* 90 semester hours of pre-professional study. Additional exam requirements/recommendations for international students: Required—TOEFL (minimum score 550 paper-based; 213 computer-based; 79 iBT). Electronic applications accepted. *Faculty research:* Effectiveness and efficacy of chiropractic care.

Cleveland Chiropractic College–Los Angeles Campus, Professional Program, Los Angeles, CA 90004-2196. Offers DC. *Accreditation:* CCE. *Faculty:* 23 full-time (9 women), 10 part-time/adjunct (2 women). *Students:* 240 full-time (99 women), 33 part-time (11 women); includes 85 minority (10 African Americans, 1 American Indian/Alaska Native, 48 Asian Americans or Pacific Islanders, 26 Hispanic Americans), 14 international. Average age 29. 41 applicants, 76% accepted, 31 enrolled. *Degree requirements:* For DC, internship. *Entrance requirements:* 90 semester units of course work in liberal arts; 2 semesters of biology, general chemistry, organic chemistry, and general physics. Additional exam requirements/recommendations for international students: Required—TOEFL (minimum score 550 paper-based; 213 computer-based; 80 iBT). *Application deadline:* For fall admission, 8/10 priority date for domestic and international students; for spring admission, 12/7 priority date for domestic and international students. Applications are processed on a rolling basis. Application fee: $50. Electronic applications accepted. *Expenses:* Tuition: Full-time $17,472; part-time $8736 per year. Required fees: $825 per year. *Financial support:* Fellowships, research assistantships with partial tuition reimbursements, Federal Work-Study and scholarships/grants available. Financial award application deadline: 7/1. *Faculty research:* Chiropractic care for extremity disorders, hip osteoarthritis, pre and post manipulation for MG and functional MRI studies, the effect of gait abnormalities on LBP. *Unit head:* Dr. Ruth Sandefur, Vice President for Academic Affairs, 816-501-0100, Fax: 323-660-5387. *Application contact:* Brian Kane, Director of Admission, 800-466-CCLA, Fax: 323-906-2094, E-mail: brian.kane@cleveland.edu.

D'Youville College, Department of Holistic Health Studies, Buffalo, NY 14201-1084. Offers chiropractic (DC). *Accreditation:* CCE. *Entrance requirements:* Minimum GPA of 2.0, 90 undergraduate credits earned. *Expenses:* Contact institution.

Institut Franco-Européen de Chiropratique, Professional Program, 94200 Ivry-sur-Seine, France. Offers DC.

Life Chiropractic College West, Professional Program, Hayward, CA 94545. Offers DC. *Accreditation:* CCE. *Entrance requirements:* Minimum GPA of 2.5. Additional exam requirements/recommendations for international students: Required—TOEFL (minimum score 550 paper-based). *Faculty research:* Imaging, ergonomics, upper cervical adjusting, academics.

Life University, College of Chiropractic, Marietta, GA 30060-2903. Offers DC. *Accreditation:* CCE. Part-time programs available. *Degree requirements:* For DC, comprehensive exam, thesis/dissertation or alternative. *Entrance requirements:* Minimum 3 years of college; course work in biology, chemistry, physics, humanities, psychology, and English; minimum GPA of 2.5. Additional exam requirements/recommendations for international students: Required—TOEFL (minimum score 500 paper-based; 173 computer-based). Electronic applications accepted. *Faculty research:* Chiropractic clinical trial, spinal modeling, biomechanics, clinical evaluation studies, chiropractic technique development, sports performance.

Logan University–College of Chiropractic, Chiropractic Program, Chesterfield, MO 63006-1065. Offers DC. *Accreditation:* CCE. *Faculty:* 52 full-time (15 women), 45 part-time/adjunct (20 women). *Students:* 879 full-time (341 women), 82 part-time (33 women); includes 77 minority (29 African Americans, 5 American Indian/Alaska Native, 25 Asian Americans or Pacific Islanders, 18 Hispanic Americans), 24 international. Average age 26. 207 applicants, 98% accepted, 134 enrolled. In 2009, 250 DCs awarded. *Degree requirements:* For DC, comprehensive exam. *Entrance requirements:* 90 hours of pre-chiropractic including biology, chemistry, physics, and social sciences; minimum GPA of 2.5. Additional exam requirements/recommendations for international students: Required—TOEFL (minimum score 79 iBT). *Application deadline:* For fall admission, 7/15 priority date for domestic and international students; for winter admission, 11/15 priority date for domestic and international students; for spring admission, 3/15 priority date for domestic students, 3/15 for international students. Applications are processed on a rolling basis. Application fee: $50. Electronic applications accepted. *Financial support:* In 2009–10, 100 students received support. Federal Work-Study and scholarships/grants available. Support available to part-time students. Financial award applicants required to submit FAFSA. *Faculty research:* Effects of injury on proprioception as measured by joint position sense, interventions for older adults with low back pain, interventions affecting heart rate variability, finite element computer modeling of spinal biomechanics, electrophysiological diagnosis of common neuromusculoskeletal conditions, the effects of spinal manipulation on posture and postural control. *Unit head:* Dr. Robert Scott, Vice President, Academic Affairs, 636-227-2100 Ext. 1745, Fax: 636-207-2431, E-mail: robert.scott@logan.edu. *Application contact:* Dr. Tom Huebner, Vice President, Enrollment Management, 636-227-2100 Ext. 1752, Fax: 636-207-2425, E-mail: loganadm@logan.edu.

Logan University–College of Chiropractic, University Programs, Chesterfield, MO 63006-1065. Offers MS. *Faculty:* 6 full-time (2 women), 12 part-time/adjunct (3 women). *Students:* 16 full-time (5 women), 33 part-time (6 women); includes 5 minority (2 African Americans, 1 American Indian/Alaska Native, 1 Asian American or Pacific Islander, 1 Hispanic American), 3 international. Average age 29. 35 applicants, 97% accepted, 28 enrolled. In 2009, 25 master's awarded. *Degree requirements:* For master's, comprehensive exam. *Entrance requirements:* For master's, GRE or National Board of Chiropractic Examiners test, minimum GPA of 2.5. Additional exam requirements/recommendations for international students: Required—TOEFL (minimum score 79 iBT). *Application deadline:* For fall admission, 7/15 priority date for domestic and international students; for winter admission, 11/15 priority date for domestic and international students; for spring admission, 3/15 priority date for domestic students, 3/15 for international students. Application fee: $50. *Expenses:* Contact institution. *Financial support:* Federal Work-Study available. Support available to part-time students. Financial award applicants required to submit FAFSA. *Faculty research:* Effects of spinal manipulation on somato-sensory integration, shoulder rehabilitation, low back pain in college football linemen, short arc banding and low back pain, interventions to improve core stability. *Unit head:* Dr. Elizabeth A. Goodman, Dean, 636-227-2100, Fax: 636-207-2431, E-mail: elizabeth.goodman@logan.edu. *Application contact:* Felicia Linear, Assistant Director, Admissions, 636-227-2100 Ext. 1754, Fax: 636-207-2425, E-mail: loganadm@logan.edu.

National University of Health Sciences, Chiropractic Program in Florida, Seminole, FL 33772. Offers DC. *Faculty:* 4 full-time (1 woman), 2 part-time/adjunct (both women). *Students:* 11 full-time (6 women); includes 1 African American, 3 Asian Americans or Pacific Islanders, 1 Hispanic American. Average age 26. 19 applicants, 84% accepted, 11 enrolled. *Degree requirements:* For DC, comprehensive exam, internship, community service. *Entrance requirements:* Bachelor's degree, character references, undergraduate transcripts, written essay. Additional exam requirements/recommendations for international students: Required—TOEFL (minimum score 550 paper-based; 213 computer-based; 79 iBT). *Application deadline:* For fall admission, 8/15 for domestic students, 8/1 for international students; for winter admission, 12/12 for domestic students, 12/1 for international students; for spring admission, 4/17 for domestic students, 4/1 for international students. Applications are processed on a rolling basis. Application fee: $55. Electronic applications accepted. *Expenses:* Tuition: Part-time $370 per credit hour. Required fees: $84 per trimester. Tuition and fees vary according to course load, degree level and program. *Financial support:* Fellowships, research assistantships, teaching assistantships, Federal Work-Study and scholarships/grants available. Support available to part-time students. Financial award applicants required to submit FAFSA. *Unit head:* Dr. Joseph Stiefel, Dean, College of Professional Studies—Florida, 727-394-6058, Fax: 727-394-6210, E-mail: jstiefel@nuhs.edu. *Application contact:* Teri Hatfield, Assistant Director of Admissions, 800-826-6285, Fax: 630-889-6566, E-mail: thatfield@nuhs.edu.

National University of Health Sciences, College of Professional Studies, Lombard, IL 60148-4583. Offers acupuncture (MSAC); chiropractic medicine (DC); naturopathic medicine (ND); Oriental medicine (MSOM). *Accreditation:* CCE. *Faculty:* 62 full-time (19 women), 60 part-time/adjunct (30 women). *Students:* 588 full-time (299 women), 65 part-time (32 women); includes 120 minority (45 African Americans, 41 Asian Americans or Pacific Islanders, 34 Hispanic Americans), 10 international. Average age 26. 271 applicants, 80% accepted, 120 enrolled. In 2009, 290 DCs awarded. *Degree requirements:* For master's and DC, comprehensive exam, internship, community service. *Entrance requirements:* For DC, bachelor's degree, character references, undergraduate transcripts, written essay; for master's, character references. Additional exam requirements/recommendations for international students: Required—TOEFL (minimum score 550 paper-based; 213 computer-based; 79 iBT). *Application deadline:* For fall admission, 8/13 for domestic students, 8/1 for international students; for winter admission, 12/10 for domestic students, 12/1 for international students; for spring admission, 4/6 for domestic students, 4/1 for international students. Applications are processed on a rolling basis. Application fee: $55. Electronic applications accepted. *Expenses:* Tuition: Part-time $370 per credit hour. Required fees: $84 per trimester. Tuition and fees vary according to course load, degree level and program. *Financial support:* In 2009–10, 622 students received support, including 10 fellowships (averaging $5,500 per year), 15 research assistantships (averaging $2,500 per year); teaching assistantships, Federal Work-Study, scholarships/grants, and tuition waivers (partial) also available. Support available to part-time students. Financial award applicants required to submit FAFSA. *Faculty research:* Mechanisms of action of CAM therapies, clinical trials of CAM therapies, practice-based research networks for CAM therapies, evidence-based practice for CAM therapies, educational research in CAM teaching institutions. Total annual research expenditures: $472,975. *Unit head:* Dr. Nicholas A. Trongale, Dean, College of Professional Studies, 630-889-6673, Fax: 630-889-6499, E-mail: ntrongale@nuhs.edu. *Application contact:* Teri Hatfield, Assistant Director of Admissions, 800-826-6285, Fax: 630-889-6566, E-mail: thatfield@nuhs.edu.

See Close-Up on page 1735.

New York Chiropractic College, Doctor of Chiropractic Program, Seneca Falls, NY 13148-0800. Offers DC. *Accreditation:* CCE. *Faculty:* 54 full-time (23 women), 19 part-time/adjunct (6 women). *Students:* 648 full-time (256 women); includes 66 minority (11 African Americans, 4 American Indian/Alaska Native, 29 Asian Americans or Pacific Islanders, 22 Hispanic Americans), 96 international. Average age 26. 244 applicants, 80% accepted, 123 enrolled. In 2009, 159 DCs awarded. *Degree requirements:* For DC, internship in health center (clinic). *Entrance requirements:* 24 credit hours of course work in science (90 credit hours with minimum GPA of 2.5), references, interview. Additional exam requirements/recommendations for international students: Recommended—TOEFL (minimum score 550 paper-based; 213 computer-based). *Application deadline:* Applications are processed on a rolling basis. Application fee: $60. Electronic applications accepted. *Expenses:* Tuition: Full-time $18,320; part-time $426 per credit hour. Required fees: $680. Tuition and fees vary according to course load and program. *Financial support:* In 2009–10, 610 students received support, including 5 fellowships with full tuition reimbursements available (averaging $30,000 per year), 1 research assistantship with full tuition reimbursement available (averaging $30,000 per year); Federal Work-Study and scholarships/grants also available. Financial award applicants required to submit FAFSA. *Faculty research:* Anatomy, pathophysiology, neurophysiology biomechanics, musculoskeletal pain syndrome, nutrition. Total annual research expenditures: $525,260. *Unit head:* Dr. Karen A. Bobak, Dean, 315-568-3864, Fax: 315-568-3087. *Application contact:* Michael Lynch, Director of Admissions, 315-568-3040, Fax: 315-568-3087, E-mail: mlynch@nycc.edu.

See Display on next page and Close-Up on page 1737.

Northwestern Health Sciences University, Northwestern College of Chiropractic, Bloomington, MN 55431-1599. Offers DC. *Accreditation:* CCE. *Entrance requirements:* 90 semester hours of course work in health or science, minimum GPA of 2.5. Additional exam requirements/recommendations for international students: Required—TOEFL (minimum score 540 paper-based; 207 computer-based). Electronic applications accepted. *Faculty research:* Headache, low back pain, neck pain, sciatica, rehabilitative exercise.

Palmer College of Chiropractic, Professional Program, Davenport, IA 52803-5287. Offers DC. *Accreditation:* CCE. Part-time programs available. *Faculty:* 133 full-time (40 women). *Students:* 1,331 full-time (466 women), 22 part-time (5 women); includes 125 minority (12 African Americans, 7 American Indian/Alaska Native, 72 Asian Americans or Pacific Islanders, 34 Hispanic Americans). Average age 25. 380 applicants, 36% accepted, 134 enrolled. In 2009, 381 DCs awarded. *Entrance requirements:* Previous course work in science, minimum GPA of 2.5. Additional exam requirements/recommendations for international students: Required—TOEFL (minimum score 500 paper-based; 178 computer-based; 61 iBT). *Application deadline:* For fall admission, 10/1 priority date for domestic students; for spring admission, 2/1 priority date for domestic students. Applications are processed on a rolling basis. Application fee: $50. *Financial support:* Federal Work-Study, institutionally sponsored loans, scholarships/grants, and tuition waivers available. Support available to part-time students. Financial award applicants required to submit FAFSA. *Faculty research:* Studies to advance the understanding of chiropractic. *Unit head:* Dr. Dennis Marchiori, Chancellor, 563-884-5466, Fax: 563-884-5624, E-mail: marchiori_d@palmer.edu. *Application contact:* Karen Eden, Director of Admissions, 563-884-5656, Fax: 563-884-5414, E-mail: pcadmit@palmer.edu.

Palmer College of Chiropractic, Professional Program–Florida Campus, Davenport, IA 52803-5287. Offers DC. *Accreditation:* CCE. *Degree requirements:* For DC, clinical internship. *Entrance requirements:* Minimum GPA of 2.5. Additional exam requirements/recommendations for international students: Recommended—TOEFL (minimum score 500 paper-based; 61 iBT).

Palmer College of Chiropractic, Professional Program–West Campus, San Jose, CA 95134-1617. Offers DC. *Accreditation:* CCE. *Faculty:* 26 full-time (5 women), 14 part-time/adjunct (4 women). *Students:* 308 full-time (112 women), 6 part-time (2 women); includes 99 minority (4 African Americans, 3 American Indian/Alaska Native, 64 Asian Americans or Pacific Islanders, 28 Hispanic Americans), 3 international. Average age 28. 73 applicants, 60% accepted, 35 enrolled. In 2009, 117 DCs awarded. *Degree requirements:* For DC, clinical internship. *Entrance requirements:* Minimum GPA of 2.5. Additional exam requirements/recommendations for international students: Required—TOEFL. *Application deadline:* Applications are processed on a rolling basis. Application fee: $50. Electronic applications accepted. *Financial support:* Career-related internships or fieldwork, Federal Work-Study, and scholarships/grants available. Support available to part-time students. Financial award applicants required to submit FAFSA. *Faculty research:* Low back pain complaints, spinal manipulation therapy, cervical biomechanics, clinical trials, practice guidelines. *Unit head:* Julie Behn, Campus Enrollment Director, 408-

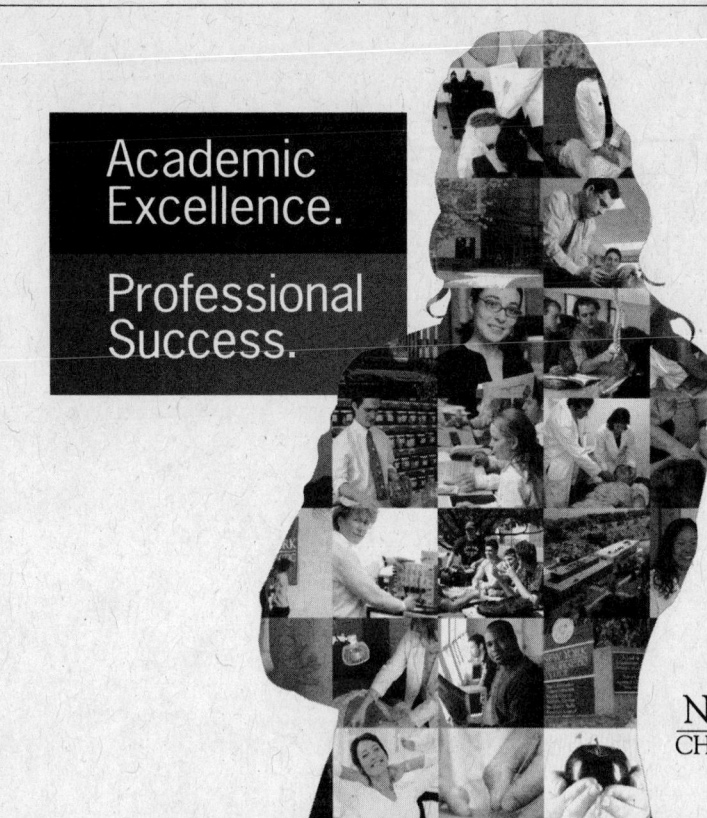

944-6121, Fax: 908-944-6032, E-mail: julie.behn@palmer.edu. *Application contact:* Julie Behn, Campus Enrollment Director, 408-944-6121, Fax: 408-944-6032, E-mail: julie.behn@palmer.edu.

Parker College of Chiropractic, Doctor of Chiropractic Program, Dallas, TX 75229-5668. Offers DC. *Accreditation:* CCE. Part-time programs available. *Entrance requirements:* Minimum GPA of 2.65. Additional exam requirements/recommendations for international students: Required—TOEFL (minimum score 550 paper-based; 213 computer-based). Electronic applications accepted. *Faculty research:* Arterial tonometry, bioenergetics, outcome assessment for clinical care.

Sherman College of Straight Chiropractic, Professional Program, Spartanburg, SC 29304-1452. Offers DC. *Accreditation:* CCE. Electronic applications accepted. *Faculty research:* Chiropractic effect of immune response, biomechanics, videofluoroscopy, dynamic motion.

Southern California University of Health Sciences, Los Angeles College of Chiropractic, Whittier, CA 90609-1166. Offers DC. *Accreditation:* CCE. *Faculty:* 17 full-time (5 women), 29 part-time/adjunct (13 women). *Students:* 346 full-time (129 women), 3 part-time (0 women); includes 166 minority (8 African Americans, 6 American Indian/Alaska Native, 107 Asian Americans or Pacific Islanders, 45 Hispanic Americans). Average age 28. 212 applicants, 60% accepted, 85 enrolled. In 2009, 131 DCs awarded. *Degree requirements:* For DC, clinical internship. *Entrance requirements:* Minimum GPA of 2.5, 90 incoming units in pre-requisite coursework. Additional exam requirements/recommendations for international students: Required—TOEFL (minimum score 500 paper-based; 173 computer-based). *Application deadline:* Applications are processed on a rolling basis. Application fee: $50. Electronic applications accepted. *Financial support:* Career-related internships or fieldwork, Federal Work-Study, and scholarships/grants available. Financial award applicants required to submit FAFSA. *Faculty research:* X-rays, motion palpation. *Unit head:* Dr. Michael Sackett, Dean, 562-947-8755 Ext. 522, Fax: 562-947-5724, E-mail: mikesackett@scuhs.edu. *Application contact:* Dr. Peter Hanna, Interim Director of Admissions, 562-947-8755 Ext. 384, Fax: 562-902-3321, E-mail: peterhanna@scuhs.edu.

Texas Chiropractic College, Professional Program, Pasadena, TX 77505-1699. Offers DC. *Accreditation:* CCE. Part-time programs available. *Faculty:* 31 full-time (11 women), 11 part-time/adjunct (2 women). *Students:* 331 full-time (147 women), 12 part-time (4 women); includes 148 minority (54 African Americans, 1 American Indian/Alaska Native, 46 Asian Americans or Pacific Islanders, 47 Hispanic Americans). Average age 30. 196 applicants, 85% accepted, 128 enrolled. In 2009, 104 DCs awarded. *Degree requirements:* For DC, clinical internship. *Entrance requirements:* 2 years of college (90 hours with 30 upper-level hours), minimum GPA of 2.5 in last 3 years (90 hours). Additional exam requirements/recommendations for international students: Required—TOEFL. *Application deadline:* For fall admission, 9/1 priority date for domestic students; for spring admission, 12/1 priority date for domestic students. Applications are processed on a rolling basis. Application fee: $50. *Expenses:* Tuition: Full-time $25,200; part-time $700 per credit hour. Required fees: $810. Tuition and fees vary according to class time, course level, course load, degree level, campus/location, program and student level. *Financial support:* Career-related internships or fieldwork, Federal Work-Study, institutionally sponsored loans, and tuition waivers (partial) available. Support available to part-time students. Financial award application deadline: 4/15; financial award applicants required to submit FAFSA. *Faculty research:* Range of motion comparison male vs. female student stress levels. *Unit head:* Dr. Richard G. Brassard, President, 281-487-1170, Fax: 281-487-0329, E-mail: rbrassard@txchiro.edu. *Application contact:* Dr. David Anderson, Director of Admissions, 281-998-6098, Fax: 281-991-4871, E-mail: shughes@txchiro.edu.

Université du Québec à Trois-Rivières, Graduate Programs, Program in Chiropractic, Trois-Rivières, QC G9A 5H7, Canada. Offers DC.

University of Bridgeport, College of Chiropractic, Bridgeport, CT 06604. Offers DC. *Accreditation:* CCE. *Degree requirements:* For DC, thesis/dissertation, National Board of Chiropractic Exam Parts I and II. *Entrance requirements:* Additional exam requirements/recommendations for international students: Recommended—TOEFL (minimum score 550 paper-based; 213 computer-based; 80 iBT), IELTS (minimum score 6.5). Electronic applications accepted. *Expenses:* Contact institution.

Western States Chiropractic College, Professional Program, Portland, OR 97230-3099. Offers DC. *Accreditation:* CCE. *Degree requirements:* For DC, comprehensive exam, internship. *Entrance requirements:* 3 years of pre-chiropractic study in biological sciences, minimum GPA of 2.5. *Faculty research:* Low back pain.

NATIONAL UNIVERSITY OF HEALTH SCIENCES

Doctor of Chiropractic Medicine
Doctor of Naturopathic Medicine
Master of Science in Acupuncture
Master of Science in Oriental Medicine

Programs of Study

National University of Health Sciences (NUHS), formerly The National College of Chiropractic, was founded in 1906 and proudly claims over a hundred years of history in educating practitioners of natural health care. As the institution moves into its second century, National has become a hub of complementary health-care education. National's goal is to develop, encourage, and promote collegiality among members of the complementary and alternative professions and allopathic medicine.

In addition to its ten-trimester Doctor of Chiropractic degree, National University is accredited by the Higher Learning Commission of the North Central Association of Colleges and Schools to offer a ten-trimester Doctor of Naturopathic Medicine degree, a seven-trimester Master of Science in Acupuncture, a nine-trimester Master of Science in Oriental Medicine, a Bachelor of Biomedical Science completion degree, an Associate of Applied Science in Massage Therapy, a Massage Therapy Certificate, and a Chiropractic Assistant Certificate. National's massage program is accredited by the Commission on Massage Therapy Accreditation (COMTA).

As one of the only two institutions in the U.S. to combine chiropractic, oriental, and naturopathic medicine on one campus, National students have the unique opportunity to participate in integrated learning situations. While these professions often compete with each other, NUHS students are able to dialogue together, share collaborative research and clinical-care opportunities, and take a leading role in mainstream health care.

NUHS also offers its Doctor of Chiropractic graduates the opportunity to enter residency programs in family practice and clinical research, as well as residencies in diagnostic imaging and clinical practice, which can lead to a Master of Science in Diagnostic Imaging and a Master of Science in Advanced Clinical Practice.

In the fall of 2009, National became part of the University Partnership Center of St. Petersburg College. This innovative campus-sharing program allows NUHS to offer its Doctor of Chiropractic degree on site at the St. Petersburg College campus.

Research Facilities

National University has one of the most prestigious research facilities among chiropractic colleges, with laboratories dedicated to spinal biomechanics, interdisciplinary research, and biological resources. The NUHS Department of Research promotes the advancement of knowledge pertaining to the practice of chiropractic and other aspects of complementary and alternative medicine by performing and encouraging high-quality, efficiently conducted ethical research. In the last seven years alone, NUHS researchers and faculty have received more than twenty-one grants for research and have written over eighty-eight journal articles and sixty abstract and submission presentations. National is the only chiropractic college to publish three scientific journals: the *Journal of Chiropractic Humanities*, the *Journal of Chiropractic Medicine*, and the *Journal of Manipulative and Physiological Therapeutics (JMPT)*, the official research journal of the American Chiropractic Association.

The first chiropractic college to own its own Magnetic Resonance Imaging (MRI), the University's MRI Center is utilized for student, patient, and research purposes.

Financial Aid

The University's Office of Financial Aid helps students finance their chiropractic education through grants, loans, scholarships, and employment on campus. Federal funds for higher education become available when there is a gap between educational costs and the ability of the student to pay. The principal responsibility for educational costs rests with the student. Most of the University's students take advantage of financial aid in one form or another and augment their income with employment. A comprehensive packet of information on all financial aid programs is available from the Office of Financial Aid. The University's institutional loan default rate is 1.2 percent.

Cost of Study

For the 2009–10 academic year, tuition in the doctoral and master's programs was $370 per credit hour. Tuition for the certificate programs was $15.40 per clock hour. Additional costs that students incur during their study are for books, diagnostic instruments, equipment, and supplies.

Living and Housing Costs

The Lombard, Illinois campus offers on-campus dormitory and apartment-style housing. Costs range from $2330 per trimester for an efficiency apartment to $3700 per trimester for a two-bedroom apartment. Private apartments and rental homes are also available in nearby suburbs.

The St. Petersburg, Florida campus does not offer on-campus housing. However, detailed information is provided for many affordable rental complexes in St. Petersburg.

Student Group

The total student enrollment for all programs stands at approximately 798 students with 53 percent women. The average age of an NUHS student is about 29. The majority of the professional degree students are recent college graduates or career changers, with men making up approximately 39 percent of this group. The majority of the certificate program students are women.

Location

National's Lombard, Illinois campus is just 20 miles from Chicago, a cultural and industrial hub and home to some of the nation's finest museums, entertainment and sports centers, zoos, restaurants, stores, beaches, and other recreation areas. National's location in west suburban Lombard places it in a community of 42,000 that is characterized by a broad-based economy and a moderate cost-of-living level, excellent public and private schools, diverse employment opportunities, and an abundance of shopping, restaurants, and sports and entertainment venues.

National's St. Petersburg, Florida campus enjoys proximity to three airports and the vibrant city of Tampa. The Bay Area, home to several major sports teams, museums, and an aquarium, and close to several major amusement parks, offers many outdoor and family recreational opportunities.

The University

The 32-acre Lombard, Illinois campus has a student center, lecture halls, a fitness center, teaching and research laboratories, and housing facilities. A Training and Assessment Center (TAC) allows for remote observation and recording of student-patient interactions with standardized patients and assessment of their clinical competency. The Learning Resource Center offers bibliographic collections and services carefully tailored to meet the needs of health-care students, faculty members, and professionals.

National's teaching clinics include a campus student health-care center and three Whole Health Centers located in Lombard, Chicago, and suburban Aurora. In addition, there are two nonprofit clinics serving the uninsured and underprivileged in downtown Chicago.

Approximately thirty clubs are active under the auspices of the Student Council, ranging from sports clubs to religious organizations and professional fraternities. Also available to students are an academic advising program, a tutorial service, and many health services at no charge.

The campuses of St. Petersburg College offer five student cafes, five bookstores, three libraries, and over thirty-six student social, athletic, professional, service, and religious organizations. There are also wellness centers equipped with a variety of fitness equipment.

Applying

NUHS admits new classes in January, May, and September. Students are encouraged to apply one year in advance. All doctoral and master's degree students must have earned a bachelor's degree in the arts or sciences from an accredited college or university, with a minimum cumulative grade point average of 2.5 on a 4.0 scale.

In order for chiropractic students to be successful at National, the University maintains specific course requirements, including 6 semester hours of English language skills, 3 of psychology, 15 of social sciences or humanities, 6 of biological sciences, 12 of chemistry, and 6 of physics and related studies. For details on the required science courses, prospective students should consult the University Bulletin. A Prerequisite Program is available for applicants who do not meet specific science requirements.

Correspondence and Information

Office of Admissions
National University of Health Sciences
200 East Roosevelt Road
Lombard, Illinois 60148-4583
Phone: 630-629-2000
          800-826-6285 (toll-free)
E-mail: admissions@nuhs.edu
Web site: http://www.nuhs.edu

National University of Health Sciences

THE FACULTY

Faculty of the University
Corrine Acosta, B.A.A., CMT.
Joe Adkins, CMT.
Kristine Aikenhead, D.C.
Brian Anderson, D.C., CCN.
Robert F. Appleyard, Ph.D.
Zhaid Arfeen, M.B.B.S.
Kelly Baltazar, N.D., D.C., M.S.
Jim Betinis, M.S.
Antonio Bifero, D.C.
Edward J. Bifulco, D.C., DAAIM.
Mary Binyamin, Pharm. D.
Therese Black, D.C.
William Bogar, D.C., DACBR.
Francine Burke, D.C.
Hui Yan Cai, Ph.D., LAc.
Jerrilyn A. Cambron, D.C., M.P.H., Ph.D., LMT.
Nick Chancellor, D.C.
Puramo Woncho Chong, Ph.D., LAc.
James A. Christiansen, Ph.D.
Patricia Coe, D.C.
Ezra Cohen, D.C., CMT.
Kristina Conner, N.D.
Nicole Corradetti, M.S.O.M.
Gregory D. Cramer, D.C., Ph.D.
Susan A. Darby, Ph.D.
Vincent F. DeBono, D.C., CSCS.
Dennis Delfosse, M.A.
Daniel R. Driscoll, Ph.D.
Manuel A. Duarte, D.C., DABCO, DACBSP, CCSP, CSCS.
Laura Dupler, C.M.T., C.A.
Louise Edwards, N.D. LAc.
Terry M. Elder, D.C.
Stephanie Fall-Harris, D.C.
Kelly Fallon, D.C.
Robin Fan, M.D. (China), LAc.
Michael Fergus, D.C. DACBR.
Timothy Fior, M.D.
Marcy Forgeron, M.A., CMT.
Robert Frysztak, Ph.D.
Judy Fulop, M.S., N.D.
David A. Gidcumb, D.C., DABCO.
Kenneth Gieser, CMT.
Bart Green, D.C., M.S.E., DACBSP.
Thomas Grieve, D.C.
Shellee A. Handley, D.C.
Keith Hartley, B.A.
Mark Hartsuyker, D.C.
Larry L. Hill, D.C., CCSP.
Bruce Hodges, D.C.
Ann Hoeffel, B.S., CMT.
William J. Hogan, D.C., D.N., DABCI.
C. Robert Humphreys, D.C., DACNB.
Russell A. Iwami, M.A.L.S.
James Jedlicka, D.C.
James Jenkins, D.C.
Claire Johnson, D.C.
Theodore L. Johnson Jr., D.C., DABCI.
Simone J. Joseph, D.C., DACO.
Anna Jurik, D.C., RD., LDN.
Muhammad A. Khan, M.D., DTCD, MCPS.
Hyunbae Kim, Ph.D.

Hyundo Franz Kim, M.S.O.M., Ph.D., LAc.
Janina Kojak, PT.
Charles J. Kuehner, D.C.
Yihyun Kwon, D.C., LAc., M.S.O.M.
Peter Lamkin, B.S.
Heather Lantry, M.A.
Evelyn Laptook, D.C., DACBR.
Thomas Lotus, D.C.
Chad Maola, D.C.
Marc McRae, D.C., DACBN, CNS, FACN.
Erika Mennerick, D.C.
Heather Miley, D.C., M.S.D.I.
Alicia Miller, N.D.
April Miller, D.C.
Nathan Miller, D.C.
Steven Moore, D.C.
Ernest Mounce, CMT.
Donald Myers, M.S.
Jin-Hong Ngan, M.S.O.M., LAc.
Nicholas Nowicki, D.C.
Albert Ockerse, M.B.Ch.B.
David Parish, D.C., DACBSP, CSCS, CCSP.
Candi Parkin, M.S.
Julie Patterson, M.B.A.
Lisa Patterson, B.S., CMT.
Sandy Pearce, CMT.
Theresa Peter, M.S.
Josephine Polich, D.C., DCAH.
Jaya Prakash, M.D.
Tari S. Reinke, D.C.
Daniel L. Richardson, Ph.D., D.N., DAANC.
Kathryn Rioch, R.D.
Terri Robery, M.S.
Michelle Rogers, M.S., N.D.
Matthew Schipma, Ph.D.
Daniel Schuh, B.S.
Scott Selby, D.C.
Karen Selph, CMT.
Preety Shah, N.D.
William D. Shelton, D.C.
Joel Shepperd, M.D.
Robert C. Shiel, Ph.D.
Jamie Shish, B.S.
Gina Sirchio, D.C.
Evangelia Skokas, D.C.
Fraser Smith, N.D.
Thomas Solecki, D.C.
Jonathan Soltys, D.C., DABFP.
Lorinda Sorensen
Nancy Steinke, M.A.
Joseph Stiefel, D.C.
Frank Strehl, D.C., DABCI.
George Stretch, D.N., LAc.
Barbara Sullivan, Ph.D.
Jarmila Svoboda, Thai Bodywork
Randy L. Swenson, D.C., M.H.P.E.
Derek Talbot, D.C., CNS.
Charles C. Tasharski, D.C.
Nicholas A. Trongale, M.A., A.M., Ed.D.
Mark Vavra, D.C.
Vrajlal H. Vyas, M.D.
Rebecca Walter, Ph.D.
Lurlean Washington, CMT.

Leah Weber, D.C.
Keith Werosh, Ph.D.
Joyce E. Whitehead, M.A.L.S.
Debbie Wilkonski, D.C., CMT.
James F. Winterstein, D.C., DACBR.
Heather Wisniewski, D.C.
Frank Yurasek, Ph.D., N.M.D.
Guang Xie, M.D., LAc.
Jia Xu, M.S.O.M.
Yu Zhu, M.D., LAc.

Postprofessional Faculty
Shawn Allen, D.C., DABCO.
Edward J. Bifulco, D.C.
Jerrilyn Cambron, D.C., M.P.H., Ph.D., LMT.
Corey Campbell, D.C.
Joseph R. Carter, D.C.
James M. Cox, D.C., DACBR.
Gregory D. Cramer, D.C., Ph.D.
Susan A. Darby, Ph.D.
Vincent DeBono, D.C., CSCS.
Eric J. Deppert, M.D., F.A.C.P.
Manuel A. Duarte, D.C., DABCO., DACBSP, CCSP, CSCS.
Terry M. Elder, D.C.
Scott D. Fonda, D.C., DABCO.
Nicholas Gatto, D.C., NCCAOM.
Zhengang Guo, D.O.M.
Leena Guptha, N.D., D.O., LAc, Ph.D.
David Gursky, Ph.D.
Steven L. Heffner, D.C.
Ann Hoeffel, B.S., CMT.
Robert Humphreys, D.C., DACBN.
Gary Jacob, D.C., D.O.M., M.P.H.
Warren T. Jahn, D.C., DABCC, DABCO, DABFP, DABIME, DACBSP.
Mary Jennings, D.C., DNCCAOM.
Kathy Joy, M.B.A.
Leo M. Kenney, D.C., CCSP.
Hyunbae Kim, Ph.D.
Matthew Kowalski, D.C., DABCO.
Evelyn Laptook, D.C., DACBR.
Robert Lardner, B.S., PT.
Craig Liebenson, D.C.
David W. Miller, M.D., F.A.A.P.
Donald R. Murphy, D.C., CCSP.
David B. Parish, D.C., DACBSP, CCSP, CSCS.
David Radford, D.C., DAAPM.
Daniel L. Richardson, Ph.D., D.N., DAANC.
David Seaman, D.C., DABCN, DACBN.
Dennis R. Skogsbergh, D.C., DABCO, DACBR.
Jonathan Soltys, D.C., DABFP.
Louis Sportelli, D.C.
Jon A. Sunderlage, D.C., DNCCAOM.
Joy L. Sunderlage, D.C., DNCCAOM, DICACCP.
Rand S. Swenson, Ph.D., D.C., M.D.
Kristine Tohtz, D.C.
Ryan Van Matre, D.C.
Scott Varley, D.C., LAc.
Alex Vasquez, D.C., N.D.
Brett Winchester, D.C.
James F. Winterstein, D.C., DACBR.
Steven Yeomans, D.C., DABCO.

National University of Health Sciences.

NEW YORK CHIROPRACTIC COLLEGE

Program of Study

New York Chiropractic College offers a rigorous but highly rewarding program leading to the degree of Doctor of Chiropractic (D.C.) and prepares students for a professional career in chiropractic health care as well as in related research and teaching. The program is ten trimesters in length and takes five academic years to complete. New York Chiropractic College offers classes year-round, and students generally complete the program in forty months of continuous study. The program is open only to full-time students. It includes three trimesters of internship at one of the College's three health centers.

Several 3+1 joint-degree B.S./D.C. programs, which enable the student to save a year in the completion of the two degrees, are offered. NYCC's Postgraduate Division offers continuing education for chiropractors to further their professional development and to satisfy the license renewal requirements of various states.

Research Facilities

NYCC research department activity encompasses a wide variety of research interests. The research programs incorporate sports medicine and chiropractic geriatric studies, biomechanics, nutrition, and pathophysiology. The College supports three primary research laboratories: a biochemistry laboratory; a biodynamics laboratory, where sports chiropractic and related ergonomic and neurophysiology research is conducted; and a biomechanical/gait research laboratory. All laboratories are equipped with state-of-the-art technology capable of supporting extensive research activity in those respective areas. The laboratories are housed in an 8,000-square-foot research facility that contains administrative offices as well as a bone histology and microscopy laboratory and several computer graphics and data analysis workstations.

Financial Aid

Financial aid is generally available on the basis of need, as evidenced by information supplied on the FAFSA as well as an institutional application. Federal sources of aid include Federal Perkins Loans, Federal Work-Study, and veterans' benefits to eligible students. Limited grants are available under New York State's Tuition Assistance Program (TAP). Students may obtain Federal Stafford Student Loans and may compete for scholarships offered by chiropractic associations, private foundations, and NYCC.

Cost of Study

Only full-time students are admitted into the doctoral program. For 2009–10, tuition was $9000 per trimester; tuition and fees for the calendar year (three trimesters) from September 2008 through summer 2009 were estimated at $27,000. The estimated cost of textbooks, equipment, and supplies is an additional $900 per trimester.

Living and Housing Costs

NYCC offers excellent on-campus housing in eight residence halls. The cost of a suite for married students is $2790 (these are trimester rates). Meal plans are additional and range from $325 to $950 per trimester. Off-campus housing is available and comparatively priced. The cost of living in the area is substantially lower than that of urban areas.

Student Group

New York Chiropractic College's 700 students (including senior interns) come from more than twenty states and several other countries. The majority are residents of the Northeast. Students range in age from 21 to over 55, with the largest age group consisting of those in their mid-20s. Thirty percent of the students are women, and 80 percent of all students hold a baccalaureate or higher degree. Many students participate in intramural sports and student government as well as in the more than thirty student organizations that pursue such special interests as nutrition, sports injuries, publications, and research. Numerous technique clubs (e.g., Applied Kinesiology, Gonstead) are active on campus.

Location

New York Chiropractic College is located in Seneca Falls, New York, in the scenic wine-growing region of the Finger Lakes, a popular vacation spot less than a 45-minute drive from Syracuse, Rochester, and Ithaca. Outpatient clinics are located in Buffalo, Seneca Falls, and Levittown (Long Island). The 286-acre campus has 250 feet of frontage property on Cayuga Lake, the largest of the Finger Lakes. The College borders a state park and has a nine-hole, par 3 golf course on the campus.

The College

Established in 1919 in New York City as Columbia Institute of Chiropractic, the College is the oldest chiropractic institution in the Northeast. In 1976, it moved to Nassau County on suburban Long Island and moved again to a larger campus in upstate New York in 1991. The College is accredited by the Middle States Association of Colleges and Schools and by the Council on Chiropractic Education. It holds an Absolute Charter from the Board of Regents of the University of the State of New York.

Applying

Information and application forms may be obtained by visiting NYCC's Web site or by calling 800-234-6922 (toll-free). Admission is a continuous process; there are entering classes in September, January, and May of each year. Approximately 300 students are admitted for each year, and applicants are encouraged to apply ten to twelve months in advance of their desired entrance date. Reference forms are supplied upon receipt of an application.

Correspondence and Information

Admissions Office
New York Chiropractic College
2360 Route 89
Seneca Falls, New York 13148-0800
Phone: 315-568-3040
         800-234-6922 (toll-free)
E-mail: enrolnow@nycc.edu
Web site: http://www.nycc.edu

New York Chiropractic College

THE FACULTY

Anatomy
M. Elizabeth Bedford, Ph.D., Kent State, 1994.
Andrew S. Choi, D.C., New York Chiropractic, 2000.
Michael L. Lentini, D.C., National Chiropractic, 1991.
Raj J. Philomin, Ph.D., Madras Medical College (India), 1986.
Maria Thomadaki, D.C., New York Chiropractic, 1994.
Robert A. Walker, Ph.D., Kent State, 1989.
Michael P. Zumpano, Ph.D., SUNY at Buffalo, 1997.

Physiopathology
David S. Aberant, M.S., LIU, C.W. Post, 1970.
Mary E. Balliett, D.C., New York Chiropractic, 1988.
Deborah A. Barr, Sc.D., Boston University, 1988.
Scott Coon, D.C., New York Chiropractic, 1994.
Chithambaram S. Philomin, M.B.B.S., Stanley Medical College, 1989.
Carolyn M. Pover, Ph.D., Bristol, 1986.
Veronica M. Sciotti, Ph.D., SUNY at Buffalo, 1988.
Lee C. VanDusen, D.C., National Chiropractic, 1985.

Diagnosis and Clinical Practice
Lisa K. Bloom, D.C., New York Chiropractic, 1990.
Susan E. Conley, D.C., New York Chiropractic, 1995.
Christine M. Cunningham, M.S., SUNY at Stony Brook, 1988.
Paul E. Dougherty, D.C., Logan Chiropractic, 1990.
Margaret M. Finn, D.C., New York Chiropractic, 1992.
Fiona Jarrett-Thelwell, D.C., New York Chiropractic, 1994.
Stephen J. Mesiti, D.C., New York Chiropractic, 1997.
Joseph A. Miller, D.C., National Chiropractic, 1991.
Michael J. O'Connor, D.C., New York Chiropractic, 1982.
Julie A. Plezbert, D.C., National Chiropractic, 1986.
Robert Ruddy, D.C., New York Chiropractic, 1996.
Fred L. SanFilipo, D.C., New York Chiropractic, 1982.
Judy M. Silvestrone, D.C., Palmer Chiropractic, 1984.
John A. M. Taylor, D.C., Canadian Memorial Chiropractic, 1979.
Meghan B. VanLoon, D.C., Northwestern Chiropractic, 1991.
Jeneen L. Wallace, D.C., New York Chiropractic, 1997.

Technique and Principles
Karen A. Bobak, D.C., National Chiropractic, 1986.
Brian M. Cunningham, D.C., New York Chiropractic, 1986.
John L. DeCicco, D.C., New York Chiropractic, 1982.
James R. Ebbets, D.C., New York Chiropractic, 1992.
Lillian M. Ford, D.C., New York Chiropractic, 1985.

Christopher J. Good, D.C., Palmer Chiropractic, 1982.
Sandra Hartwell-Ford, D.C., New York Chiropractic, 1996.
Lloyd E. Henby, D.C., National Chiropractic, 1952.
Michael E. Howard, D.C., Life Chiropractic, 1981.
Thomas McCloughan, D.C., New York Chiropractic, 1993.
Hunter A. Mollin, D.C., New York Chiropractic, 1980.
David F. Petters, D.C., New York Chiropractic, 1986.
Christopher P. Ryan, D.C., New York Chiropractic, 1987.
Paul W. Ryan, D.C., New York Chiropractic, 1989.
Eileen C. Santipadri, D.C., Palmer Chiropractic, 1981.
David A. Shinherr, D.C., New York Chiropractic, 1995.
Edward J. Sullivan, D.C., Northwestern Chiropractic, 1991.
Michael S. Young, D.C., New York Chiropractic, 1996.

Research
JeanMarie Burke, Ph.D., Indiana, 1991.

Depew Health Center
Margaret M. Anticola, D.C., Life Chiropractic, 1986.
Charles D. Coyle, D.C., National Chiropractic, 1988.
Mark A. Dux, D.C., Western States Chiropractic, 1980.
Daniel R. Johnson, D.C., Logan Chiropractic, 1981.
Sherri L. LaShomb, D.C., Palmer Chiropractic, 1988.
David L. Ribakove, D.C., New York Chiropractic, 1992.
Mark D. Sokolowski, D.C., Palmer Chiropractic, 1985.
Mercedes M. Trzcinski, D.C., Palmer Chiropractic, 1981.

Levittown Health Center
Patricia M. Flynn, D.C., National Chiropractic, 1996.
Charles A. Hemsey, D.C., Life Chiropractic, 1981.
Lloyd H. Kupferman, D.C., New York Chiropractic, 1981.
Frank S. Lizzio, D.C., New York Chiropractic, 1980.
Mariangela Penna, D.C., New York Chiropractic, 1986.
Michael G. Perillo, D.C., National Chiropractic, 1978.
Joseph E. Pfeifer, D.C., New York Chiropractic, 1984.
Lana K. Slinkard, D.C., National Chiropractic, 1985.
Veronica A. Wicks, D.C., New York Chiropractic, 1988.

Seneca Falls Health Center
Steven Feldman, D.C., New York Chiropractic, 1981.
Dennis M. Homack, D.C., New York Chiropractic, 1997.
Wendy L. Maneri, D.C., New York Chiropractic, 1999.
William H. Sherwood, D.C., National Chiropractic, 1990.

NYCC's newest academic building.

A radiology faculty member reviews X-rays with students.

Section 36
Dentistry and Dental Sciences

This section contains a directory of institutions offering graduate work in dentistry and dental sciences, followed by an in-depth entry submitted by an institution that chose to prepare a detailed program description. Additional information about programs listed in the directory but not augmented by an in-depth entry may be obtained by writing directly to the dean of a graduate school or chair of a department at the address given in the directory.

For programs offering related work, see also in this book *Allied Health*. In another guide in this series:
Graduate Programs in the Biological Sciences
See *Anatomy; Biological and Biomedical Sciences; Cell, Molecular, and Structural Biology; Microbiological Sciences;* and *Pathology and Pathobiology*

CONTENTS

Program Directories

Close-Up

Dentistry

Boston University, Goldman School of Dental Medicine, Graduate Programs in Dentistry, Boston, MA 02215. Offers advanced general dentistry (CAGS); dental public health (MS, MSD, D Sc D, CAGS); dentistry (DMD); endodontics (MSD, D Sc D, CAGS); implantology (CAGS); operative dentistry (MSD, D Sc D, CAGS); oral and maxillofacial surgery (MSD, D Sc D, CAGS); oral biology (MSD, D Sc, D Sc D, PhD); orthodontics (MSD, D Sc D, CAGS); pediatric dentistry (MSD, D Sc D, CAGS); periodontology (MSD, D Sc D, CAGS); prosthodontics (MSD, D Sc D, CAGS). *Students:* 606 full-time (295 women); includes 149 minority (7 African Americans, 3 American Indian/Alaska Native, 113 Asian Americans or Pacific Islanders, 26 Hispanic Americans), 209 international. Average age 26. In 2009, 175 first professional degrees awarded. *Degree requirements:* For master's, thesis; for doctorate, thesis/dissertation; for CAGS, thesis (for some programs). *Entrance requirements:* For DMD, DAT, minimum GPA of 3.0; for CAGS, dental degree. *Application deadline:* For fall admission, 5/1 for domestic students. Applications are processed on a rolling basis. Application fee: $60. *Expenses:* Contact institution. *Financial support:* Career-related internships or fieldwork and institutionally sponsored loans available. Financial award application deadline: 4/15; financial award applicants required to submit CSS PROFILE or FAFSA. *Faculty research:* Defensive mechanisms, bone-cell regulation, protein biochemistry, molecular biology, biomaterials. *Unit head:* Dr. Jeffrey W. Hutter, Interim Dean, 617-638-4780. *Application contact:* 617-638-4787, Fax: 617-638-4798.

Case Western Reserve University, School of Dental Medicine, Professional Program in Dentistry, Cleveland, OH 44106. Offers DMD. *Accreditation:* ADA. *Degree requirements:* For DMD, thesis/dissertation. *Entrance requirements:* DAT. Additional exam requirements/recommendations for international students: Required—TOEFL (minimum score 550 paper-based; 213 computer-based). *Expenses:* Contact institution. *Faculty research:* Periodontal disease; overall health; natural antibodies; obesity and periodontal disease; 3D cone beam computerized tomography.

Columbia University, College of Dental Medicine, Professional Program in Dental and Oral Surgery, New York, NY 10032. Offers DDS, DDS/MBA, DDS/MPH. *Accreditation:* ADA. *Entrance requirements:* DAT, previous course work in biology, organic chemistry, inorganic chemistry, physics, and English.

Creighton University, School of Dentistry, Omaha, NE 68178-0001. Offers DDS. *Accreditation:* ADA. *Entrance requirements:* DAT. *Expenses:* Contact institution. *Faculty research:* Dental implants, bone calcification, dental materials, laser usage in dentistry.

Harvard University, School of Dental Medicine, Advanced Graduate Programs in Dentistry, Cambridge, MA 02138. Offers advanced general dentistry (Certificate); dental public health (Certificate); endodontics (Certificate); general practice residency (Certificate); oral biology (M Med Sc, D Med Sc); oral implantology (Certificate); oral medicine (Certificate); oral pathology (Certificate); oral surgery (Certificate); orthodontics (Certificate); pediatric dentistry (Certificate); periodontics (Certificate); prosthodontics (Certificate). *Expenses:* Tuition: Full-time $33,696. Required fees: $1126. Full-time tuition and fees vary according to program.

Harvard University, School of Dental Medicine, Professional Program in Dental Medicine, Cambridge, MA 02138. Offers DMD. *Accreditation:* ADA. *Entrance requirements:* Dental Admissions Test, 1 year each: biology, general chemistry, organic chemistry, physics, calculus, English. *Expenses:* Tuition: Full-time $33,696. Required fees: $1126. Full-time tuition and fees vary according to program.

Howard University, College of Dentistry, Washington, DC 20059-0002. Offers advanced education program general dentistry (Certificate); dentistry (DDS); general dentistry (Certificate); oral and maxillofacial surgery (Certificate); orthodontics (Certificate); pediatric dentistry (Certificate). *Accreditation:* ADA (one or more programs are accredited). *Degree requirements:* For DDS, comprehensive exam, didactic and clinical exams. *Entrance requirements:* DAT, 8 semester hours of course work in each biology, inorganic chemistry, organic chemistry. *Expenses:* Contact institution. *Faculty research:* Epidemiological, biomaterial, molecular genetic, behavioral modification, and clinical trial studies.

Idaho State University, Office of Graduate Studies, Kasiska College of Health Professions, Department of Dental Sciences, Pocatello, ID 83209-8088. Offers advanced general dentistry (Post-Doctoral Certificate). First year of Idaho Dental Education Program available in conjunction with Creighton University's School of Dentistry. *Students:* 15 full-time (3 women); includes 2 minority (both Asian Americans or Pacific Islanders). Average age 28. In 2009, 2 Post-Doctoral Certificates awarded. *Degree requirements:* For Post-Doctoral Certificate, comprehensive exam, thesis optional, 1-year residency. *Entrance requirements:* For degree, DAT, 3 dental application forms. Additional exam requirements/recommendations for international students: Required—TOEFL (minimum score 600 paper-based; 213 computer-based). *Application deadline:* For fall admission, 7/1 for domestic students, 6/1 for international students; for spring admission, 12/1 for domestic students, 11/1 for international students. Applications are processed on a rolling basis. Application fee: $55. Electronic applications accepted. *Expenses:* Contact institution. *Financial support:* Career-related internships or fieldwork, Federal Work-Study, institutionally sponsored loans, scholarships/grants, traineeships, and health care benefits available. Financial award application deadline: 1/1; financial award applicants required to submit FAFSA. *Unit head:* Dr. Brian Crawford, Chair, 208-282-5275, Fax: 208-282-5834, E-mail: crawbri3@isu.edu. *Application contact:* Tami Carson, Graduate School Technical Records Specialist, 208-282-2150, Fax: 208-282-4847, E-mail: carstami@isu.edu.

Indiana University–Purdue University Indianapolis, School of Dentistry, Indianapolis, IN 46202-2896. Offers DDS, MS, MSD, PhD, Certificate. *Accreditation:* ADA (one or more programs are accredited). *Faculty:* 96 full-time (28 women). *Students:* 498 full-time (185 women), 50 part-time (21 women); includes 60 minority (5 African Americans, 1 American Indian/Alaska Native, 43 Asian Americans or Pacific Islanders, 11 Hispanic Americans), 65 international. Average age 28. 56 applicants, 4% accepted, 1 enrolled. In 2009, 98 first professional degrees, 30 master's, 2 doctorates awarded. *Degree requirements:* For master's, thesis or manuscript, qualifying exam; for doctorate, thesis/dissertation, completion of all coursework with a passing grade, minimum GPA of 3.0, qualifying examination; for DDS, completion of all coursework with passing grades, minimum GPA of 2.0, passing scores for Part I and II of National Board of Dental Examinations; for Certificate, completion of all coursework with passing grades, minimum GPA of 3.0. *Entrance requirements:* For DDS, DAT; for master's, DDS or DMD; for doctorate, GRE, DDS or DMD. Additional exam requirements/recommendations for international students: Required—TOEFL (minimum score 550 paper-based; 213 computer-based). Application fee: $55 ($65 for international students). *Expenses:* Contact institution. *Financial support:* In 2009–10, 43 students received support, including 25 fellowships (averaging $9,864 per year); research assistantships, teaching assistantships, Federal Work-Study, institutionally sponsored loans, and scholarships/grants also available. Financial award application deadline: 3/1; financial award applicants required to submit FAFSA. *Faculty research:* Caries research: early caries detection and management, secondary caries, remineralization, oral biofilms, fluoride, dental erosion; oral biology: molecular biology and immunobiology of streptococcus mutans, oral biofilms, infection control, actinobaccillus actinomycetemcomitans; orthodontics and oral facial genetics: orthodontics biomechanics; oral pathology and immunology program: chronic inflammation and autoimmunity, innate immunity in oral pathology; periodontal disease and implants. Total annual research expenditures: $7.8 million. *Unit head:* Lawrence I. Goldblatt, Dean, 317-274-7461. *Application contact:* Robert Kasberg, Associate Dean for Student Affairs and Director of Admissions, 317-274-8173, Fax: 317-274-2419, E-mail: blerner@iupui.edu.

Loma Linda University, School of Dentistry, Loma Linda, CA 92350. Offers DDS, MS, Certificate, DDS/MS, DDS/PhD, MS/Certificate. *Accreditation:* ADA. *Entrance requirements:* For DDS, DAT; for master's, GRE, minimum 3.0 GPA. Additional exam requirements/recommendations for international students: Required—TOEFL (minimum score 550 paper-based; 213 computer-based). *Expenses:* Contact institution.

Louisiana State University Health Sciences Center, School of Dentistry, New Orleans, LA 70112-2223. Offers DDS. *Accreditation:* ADA. *Entrance requirements:* DAT, interview. *Expenses:* Contact institution. *Faculty research:* HIV/AIDS, implants, metallurgy, lipids, DNA.

Marquette University, School of Dentistry, Professional Program in Dentistry, Milwaukee, WI 53201-1881. Offers DDS. *Accreditation:* ADA. *Entrance requirements:* DAT, 1 year course work in each biology, inorganic chemistry, organic chemistry, physics, and English. Additional exam requirements/recommendations for international students: Required—TOEFL. *Faculty research:* Biomaterials, wound healing, diabetes, biocompatibility, cancer, aging, lasers.

McGill University, Faculty of Graduate and Postdoctoral Studies, Faculty of Dentistry, Montréal, QC H3A 2T5, Canada. Offers forensic dentistry (Certificate); oral and maxillofacial surgery (M Sc, PhD).

McGill University, Professional Program in Dentistry, Montréal, QC H3A 2T5, Canada. Offers DMD. *Accreditation:* ADA. Electronic applications accepted.

Medical College of Georgia, School of Dentistry, Augusta, GA 30912. Offers DMD, DMD/MS, DMD/PhD. *Accreditation:* ADA. *Faculty:* 53 full-time (10 women), 14 part-time/adjunct (4 women). *Students:* 255 full-time (107 women), 2 part-time (0 women); includes 66 minority (24 African Americans, 2 American Indian/Alaska Native, 28 Asian Americans or Pacific Islanders, 12 Hispanic Americans). Average age 25. 296 applicants, 25% accepted, 65 enrolled. In 2009, 60 DMDs awarded. *Degree requirements:* For DMD, comprehensive exam. *Entrance requirements:* DAT, previous course work in biology, English, organic chemistry, and general chemistry; 1 semester of course work in physics. Additional exam requirements/recommendations for international students: Required—TOEFL (minimum score 100 iBT). *Application deadline:* For fall admission, 10/15 for domestic students. Application fee: $30. Electronic applications accepted. *Expenses:* Contact institution. *Financial support:* Federal Work-Study and scholarships/grants available. Financial award application deadline: 5/1; financial award applicants required to submit FAFSA. *Faculty research:* Biocompatibility, dentin bonding, oral cancer, ceramic strengthening, resin polymerization. Total annual research expenditures: $1.1 million. *Unit head:* Connie Drisko, Dean, 706-721-2117, Fax: 706-721-6276, E-mail: cdrisko@mcg.edu. *Application contact:* Dr. Carole M. Hanes, Associate Dean for Student and Alumni Affairs, 706-721-3587, Fax: 706-721-6276, E-mail: chanes@mcg.edu.

Medical University of South Carolina, College of Dental Medicine, Charleston, SC 29425. Offers DMD, DMD/PhD. *Accreditation:* ADA. *Faculty:* 47 full-time (10 women), 33 part-time/adjunct (5 women). *Students:* 235 full-time (98 women); includes 18 minority (6 African Americans, 1 American Indian/Alaska Native, 9 Asian Americans or Pacific Islanders, 2 Hispanic Americans), 1 international. Average age 26. 793 applicants, 10% accepted, 66 enrolled. In 2009, 58 DMDs awarded. *Degree requirements:* For DMD, National Board of Dental Examinations Part I and II. *Entrance requirements:* DAT, interview, 52 hours of specific pre-dental course work. Additional exam requirements/recommendations for international students: Required—TOEFL (minimum score 600 paper-based; 250 computer-based). *Application deadline:* For spring admission, 1/15 for domestic and international students. Application fee: $85. Electronic applications accepted. *Expenses:* Contact institution. *Financial support:* Federal Work-Study, scholarships/grants, and tuition waivers (partial) available. Support available to part-time students. Financial award application deadline: 3/10; financial award applicants required to submit FAFSA. *Faculty research:* South Carolina oral health, genetics, health disparities, chlamydia, oral cancer. *Unit head:* Dr. John J. Sanders, Dean, 843-792-3811, Fax: 843-792-1376, E-mail: sandersjj@musc.edu. *Application contact:* William H. Liner, Dental Admissions Counselor, 843-792-4892, Fax: 843-792-6615, E-mail: linerw@musc.edu.

Meharry Medical College, School of Dentistry, Nashville, TN 37208-9989. Offers DDS. *Accreditation:* ADA. *Entrance requirements:* DAT.

Midwestern University, Glendale Campus, College of Dental Medicine, Glendale, AZ 85308. Offers DMD. *Accreditation:* ADA. *Faculty:* 18 full-time (6 women), 2 part-time/adjunct (0 women). *Students:* 221 full-time (106 women); includes 42 minority (5 African Americans, 1 American Indian/Alaska Native, 32 Asian Americans or Pacific Islanders, 4 Hispanic Americans), 9 international. Average age 27. 2,328 applicants, 9% accepted, 112 enrolled. *Unit head:* Dr. Richard Simonsen, Dean, 623-572-3801. *Application contact:* James Walter, Director of Admissions, 888-247-9277, Fax: 623-572-3229, E-mail: admissaz@midwestern.edu.

New York University, College of Dentistry, Professional Program in Dentistry, New York, NY 10010. Offers DDS. *Accreditation:* ADA. *Faculty:* 235 full-time, 690 part-time/adjunct. *Students:* 1,306 full-time (642 women); includes 805 minority (35 African Americans, 3 American Indian/Alaska Native, 714 Asian Americans or Pacific Islanders, 53 Hispanic Americans). Average age 25. 4,986 applicants, 13% accepted, 236 enrolled. In 2009, 336 DDSs awarded. *Entrance requirements:* DAT. Additional exam requirements/recommendations for international students: Required—TOEFL (minimum score 230 computer-based). *Application deadline:* For fall admission, 4/1 priority date for domestic students. Applications are processed on a rolling basis. Application fee: $75. *Expenses:* Tuition: Full-time $30,528; part-time $1272 per credit. Required fees: $2177. *Financial support:* In 2009–10, 1,134 students received support, including fellowships with tuition reimbursements available (averaging $25,000 per year); Federal Work-Study, institutionally sponsored loans, and scholarships/grants also available. Support available to part-time students. Financial award application deadline: 3/1; financial award applicants required to submit FAFSA. *Unit head:* Dr. Anthony Palatta, Assistant Dean for Admissions and Student Affairs, 212-998-9918, Fax: 212-995-4240, E-mail: ap16@nyu.edu. *Application contact:* Dr. Eugenia Mejia, Director for Admissions, 212-998-5333, Fax: 212-995-4302, E-mail: ak96@nyu.edu.

Nova Southeastern University, Health Professions Division, College of Dental Medicine, Fort Lauderdale, FL 33314-7796. Offers dental medicine (DMD); dentistry (MS). *Accreditation:* ADA. *Faculty:* 83 full-time (23 women), 200 part-time/adjunct (44 women). *Students:* 507 full-time (255 women); includes 196 minority (10 African Americans, 1 American Indian/Alaska Native, 78 Asian Americans or Pacific Islanders, 107 Hispanic Americans), 43 international. Average age 24. 2,774 applicants, 6% accepted, 105 enrolled. In 2009, 123 first professional degrees, 2 master's awarded. *Degree requirements:* For master's, thesis. *Entrance requirements:* DAT, minimum GPA of 3.0. Additional exam requirements/recommendations for international students: Required—TOEFL (minimum score 550 paper-based; 225 computer-based). *Application deadline:* For fall admission, 1/15 for domestic students, 2/15 for international students. Applications are processed on a rolling basis. Application fee: $50. *Expenses:* Contact institution. *Financial support:* In 2009–10, 372 students received support, including 1 fellowship with full tuition reimbursement available, 11 teaching assistantships with full tuition reimbursements available. Financial award application deadline: 4/3; financial award applicants required to submit FAFSA. *Faculty research:* Tissue engineering, dental materials. *Unit head:* Dr. Robert A. Uchin, Dean, 954-262-7312, Fax: 954-262-1782, E-mail: ruchin@nova.edu. *Application contact:* Su-Ann Zarrett, Associate Director, 954-262-1108, Fax: 954-262-2282, E-mail: zarrett@nsu.nova.edu.

The Ohio State University, College of Dentistry, Programs in Dentistry, Columbus, OH 43210. Offers DDS, MS, DDS/PhD. *Accreditation:* ADA. *Faculty:* 97 full-time (29 women), 155 part-time/adjunct (30 women). *Students:* 488 full-time (188 women), 28 part-time (13 women); includes 73 minority (18 African Americans, 5 American Indian/Alaska Native, 36 Asian Americans or Pacific Islanders, 14 Hispanic Americans), 14 international. Average age 26. In 2009, 106 first professional degrees, 30 master's awarded. *Entrance requirements:* DAT. Additional exam requirements/recommendations for international students: Required—TOEFL. *Application deadline:* For fall admission, 11/15 for domestic students. Applications are processed on a rolling basis. Application fee: $60 ($70 for international students). Electronic applications accepted. *Expenses:* Tuition, state resident: full-time $10,683. Tuition, nonresident: full-time $25,923. Tuition and fees vary according to course load and program. *Financial support:* Fellowships, teaching assistantships, Federal Work-Study and institutionally sponsored loans

available. Financial award application deadline: 3/1; financial award applicants required to submit FAFSA. Total annual research expenditures: $3.4 million. *Unit head:* Ann L. Griffen, Graduate Studies Committee Chair, 614-292-1150, Fax: 614-292-7619, E-mail: griffen.l@osu.edu. *Application contact:* Graduate Admissions, 614-292-9444, Fax: 614-292-3895, E-mail: domestic.grad@osu.edu.

Oregon Health & Science University, School of Dentistry, Professional Program in Dentistry, Portland, OR 97239-3098. Offers dentistry (DMD); oral and maxillofacial surgery (Certificate); MD/DMD. *Accreditation:* ADA. *Entrance requirements:* DAT. Electronic applications accepted. Tuition and fees vary according to course level, course load, degree level, program and reciprocity agreements. *Faculty research:* Dentin permeability, tooth sensations, fluoride metabolism, immunology of periodontal disease, craniofacial growth.

Saint Louis University, Graduate School, Center for Advanced Dental Education, St. Louis, MO 63103-2097. Offers endodontics (MSD); orthodontics (MSD); periodontics (MSD). *Degree requirements:* For master's, comprehensive exam, thesis, teaching practicum. *Entrance requirements:* For master's, GRE General Test, NBDE (National Board Dental Exam), DDS or DMD, interview, letters of recommendation. Additional exam requirements/recommendations for international students: Required—TOEFL (minimum score 525 paper-based; 194 computer-based). Electronic applications accepted. *Faculty research:* Craniofacial growth.

Southern Illinois University Edwardsville, School of Dental Medicine, Edwardsville, IL 62026-0001. Offers DMD. *Accreditation:* ADA. *Faculty:* 21 full-time (2 women). *Students:* 195 full-time (78 women); includes 35 minority (10 African Americans, 1 American Indian/Alaska Native, 16 Asian Americans or Pacific Islanders, 8 Hispanic Americans). Average age 25. In 2009, 45 DMDs awarded. *Entrance requirements:* DAT. *Application deadline:* For fall admission, 6/1 priority date for domestic students, 6/1 for international students. Application fee: $20. Electronic applications accepted. *Expenses:* Contact institution. *Financial support:* Application deadline: 3/1. *Unit head:* Dr. Ann Boyle, Dean, 618-474-7249, E-mail: sdmapps@siue.edu. *Application contact:* Dr. Ann Boyle, Dean, 618-474-7249, E-mail: sdmapps@siue.edu.

Stony Brook University, State University of New York, Stony Brook University Medical Center, Health Sciences Center, School of Dental Medicine, Professional Program in Dental Medicine, Stony Brook, NY 11794. Offers dental medicine (DDS); endodontics (Certificate); orthodontics (Certificate); periodontics (Certificate). *Accreditation:* ADA (one or more programs are accredited). *Faculty:* 25 full-time (9 women), 68 part-time/adjunct (19 women). *Students:* 157 full-time (72 women), 21 part-time (5 women); includes 54 minority (2 African Americans, 45 Asian Americans or Pacific Islanders, 7 Hispanic Americans), 1 international. Average age 25. 1,456 applicants, 3% accepted. In 2009, 39 first professional degrees, 15 Certificates awarded. *Entrance requirements:* DAT. *Application deadline:* For fall admission, 1/15 for domestic students. Application fee: $75. *Expenses:* Tuition, state resident: full-time $8370; part-time $349 per credit. Tuition, nonresident: full-time $13,250; part-time $552 per credit. Required fees: $933. *Financial support:* In 2009–10, 1 research assistantship was awarded; Federal Work-Study also available. Support available to part-time students. Total annual research expenditures: $937,856. *Unit head:* Dr. Ray C. Williams, Dean, 631-632-8950, Fax: 631-632-9105. *Application contact:* Dr. Marcia Simon, Associate Dean for Graduate Studies, 631-632-8922.

Teachers College, Columbia University, Graduate Faculty of Education, Department of Math, Science and Technology, Program in Science and Dental Management, New York, NY 10027-6696. Offers MA.

Temple University, Health Sciences Center, School of Dentistry, Professional Program in Dentistry, Philadelphia, PA 19122-6096. Offers DMD, DMD/MBA. *Accreditation:* ADA. *Entrance requirements:* DAT, 6 credits of course work in each biology, chemistry, organic chemistry, physics, and English. *Expenses:* Contact institution.

Texas A&M Health Science Center, Baylor College of Dentistry, Professional Program in Dentistry, College Station, TX 77840. Offers DDS. *Entrance requirements:* DAT. *Expenses:* Contact institution. *Faculty research:* Bleaching, implants, craniofacial growth, oral oncology, pulp biology.

Tufts University, School of Dental Medicine, International Student Program in Dental Medicine, Medford, MA 02155. Offers DMD. *Accreditation:* ADA. *Entrance requirements:* National Dental Hygiene Board Exam Part I, BDS, DDS, or equivalent. Additional exam requirements/recommendations for international students: Required—TOEFL. *Expenses:* Tuition: Full-time $38,096; part-time $3962 per credit. Required fees: $686; $40 per year. Tuition and fees vary according to course level, course load, degree level, program and student level.

Tufts University, School of Dental Medicine, Professional Program in Dental Medicine, Medford, MA 02155. Offers DMD, DMD/PhD. *Accreditation:* ADA. *Entrance requirements:* DAT. *Expenses:* Tuition: Full-time $38,096; part-time $3962 per credit. Required fees: $686; $40 per year. Tuition and fees vary according to course level, course load, degree level, program and student level.

Universidad Central del Este, Graduate School, San Pedro de Macoris, Dominican Republic. Offers administration (M Ad); dentistry (DMD); development of educational and social policies (PhD); environmental engineering (ME); financial management (M Ad); higher education (M Ed); human resources (M Ad); public health (MPH). *Entrance requirements:* For master's, letters of recommendation.

Universidad Iberoamericana, Graduate School, Santo Domingo D.N., Dominican Republic. Offers advertising management (MM); business (MBA); constitutional law (MA); dentistry (DMD); educational management (MA); integrated marketing communication (MA); psychopedagogical intervention (M Ed); strategic management of human talent (MM).

Universidad Nacional Pedro Henriquez Urena, School of Dentistry, Santo Domingo, Dominican Republic. Offers DDS.

Université Laval, Faculty of Dentistry, Professional Programs in Dentistry, Québec, QC G1K 7P4, Canada. Offers DMD. *Accreditation:* ADA. *Entrance requirements:* Visual perception exam, manual dexterity exam, interview, knowledge of French. Electronic applications accepted.

University at Buffalo, the State University of New York, Graduate School, School of Dental Medicine, Graduate Programs in Dental Medicine, Buffalo, NY 14214. Offers advanced education in general dentistry (Certificate); combined prosthodontics (Certificate); endodontics (Certificate); general practice residency (Certificate); oral and maxillofacial pathology (Certificate); oral and maxillofacial surgery (Certificate); oral biology (PhD); oral diagnostic sciences (MS), including biomaterials; oral sciences (MS); orthodontics (MS); pediatric dentistry (Certificate); periodontics (Certificate); temporomandibular disorders and oralfacial pain (Certificate). *Degree requirements:* For master's, thesis; for doctorate, thesis/dissertation; for Certificate, comprehensive exam (for some programs). *Entrance requirements:* For doctorate, GRE General Test, GRE Subject Test in biology or DDS; for Certificate, DDS, DMD or equivalent. Additional exam requirements/recommendations for international students: Required—TOEFL (minimum score 79 iBT). Electronic applications accepted. *Expenses:* Contact institution. *Faculty research:* Immunology and microbiology of dental disease, surface science, saliva biochemistry, bone biology.

University at Buffalo, the State University of New York, Graduate School, School of Dental Medicine, Professional Program in Dental Medicine, Buffalo, NY 14260. Offers DDS. *Accreditation:* ADA. *Faculty:* 69 full-time (25 women), 109 part-time/adjunct (26 women). *Students:* 356 full-time (137 women); includes 82 minority (2 African Americans, 73 Asian Americans or Pacific Islanders, 7 Hispanic Americans), 22 international. Average age 26. 1,905 applicants, 10% accepted. In 2009, 83 DDSs awarded. *Degree requirements:* For DDS, National Dental Board Exams. *Entrance requirements:* DAT. *Application deadline:* For fall admission, 2/1 for domestic and international students. Applications are processed on a rolling basis. Application fee: $50. *Financial support:* Federal Work-Study, institutionally sponsored loans, and scholarships/grants available. Financial award application deadline: 3/1; financial award applicants required to submit FAFSA. *Unit head:* Dr. Michael Glick, Dean, 716-829-2836, Fax: 716-833-3517, E-mail: sdm-dean@buffalo.edu. *Application contact:* Dr. David H. Brown, Director of Admissions, 716-829-2839, Fax: 716-833-3517, E-mail: dhbrown@buffalo.edu.

The University of Alabama at Birmingham, School of Dentistry, Professional Program in Dentistry, Birmingham, AL 35294. Offers DMD. *Accreditation:* ADA. *Entrance requirements:* DAT. Electronic applications accepted. *Faculty research:* Etiology and pathogenesis of dental diseases, dental biomaterials, therapy of dental diseases.

University of Alberta, Faculty of Medicine and Dentistry, Department of Dentistry, Professional Program in Dentistry, Edmonton, AB T6G 2E1, Canada. Offers DDS. *Accreditation:* ADA. *Faculty:* 29 full-time (6 women), 113 part-time/adjunct (28 women). *Students:* 138 full-time (62 women). 322 applicants, 12% accepted, 34 enrolled. In 2009, 35 DDSs awarded. *Entrance requirements:* DAT (Canadian version), interview. Additional exam requirements/recommendations for international students: Required—TOEFL. *Application deadline:* For fall admission, 11/1 for domestic and international students. Application fee: $75. Electronic applications accepted. Tuition and fees charges are reported in Canadian dollars. *Expenses:* Tuition, area resident: Full-time $4626 Canadian dollars; part-time $99.72 Canadian dollars per unit. International tuition: $8216 Canadian dollars full-time. Required fees: $3590 Canadian dollars; $99.72 Canadian dollars per unit. $215 Canadian dollars per term. *Faculty research:* Oral biology, biochemistry of connective tissues, preventive dentistry, applied clinical orthodontics, biomaterials. *Unit head:* Dr. Nadine C. Milos, Acting Department Chair, 780-492-3312, Fax: 780-492-7536, E-mail: nmilos@ualberta.ca. *Application contact:* Melanie Grams, Administrative Assistant, 780-492-6437, Fax: 780-492-7536, E-mail: melanie.grams@ualberta.ca.

The University of British Columbia, Faculty of Dentistry, Professional Program in Dentistry, Vancouver, BC V6T 1Z1, Canada. Offers DMD. *Accreditation:* ADA. *Entrance requirements:* DAT, ACFD Eligibility Exam, interview, psychomotor assessment. Additional exam requirements/recommendations for international students: Required—IELTS. Electronic applications accepted. *Expenses:* Contact institution.

University of California, Los Angeles, School of Dentistry, Professional Program in Dentistry, Los Angeles, CA 90095. Offers DDS, Certificate, DDS/MS, DDS/PhD, MS/Certificate, PhD/Certificate. *Accreditation:* ADA (one or more programs are accredited). *Entrance requirements:* DAT.

University of California, San Francisco, School of Dentistry, San Francisco, CA 94143-0150. Offers DDS. *Accreditation:* ADA. *Entrance requirements:* DAT. *Expenses:* Contact institution.

University of Colorado Denver, School of Dental Medicine, Denver, CO 80217-3364. Offers DDS. *Accreditation:* ADA. *Faculty:* 72 full-time (23 women), 51 part-time/adjunct (25 women). *Students:* 202 full-time (79 women); includes 32 minority (3 African Americans, 2 American Indian/Alaska Native, 17 Asian Americans or Pacific Islanders, 10 Hispanic Americans). Average age 26. In 2009, 70 DDSs awarded. *Entrance requirements:* DAT, 1 semester of course work in English composition; 2 semesters of course work each in chemistry/lab, organic chemistry/lab, general biology/lab, general physics/lab, and humanities; 3 letters of recommendation. Additional exam requirements/recommendations for international students: Required—TOEFL (minimum score 580 paper-based; 237 computer-based). *Application deadline:* For fall admission, 1/1 for domestic students, 3/31 for international students. Application fee: $50 ($125 for international students). *Expenses:* Contact institution. *Financial support:* Federal Work-Study and institutionally sponsored loans available. Financial award application deadline: 3/15; financial award applicants required to submit FAFSA. *Faculty research:* Pain control, materials research, geriatric dentistry, restorative dentistry, periodontics. Total annual research expenditures: $6.2 million. *Unit head:* Dr. Denise K. Kassebaum, Dean, 303-724-7100, Fax: 303-724-7109, E-mail: denise.kassebaum@ucdenver.edu. *Application contact:* Dr. Randy L. Kluender, Assistant Dean for Admissions and Student Affairs, 303-724-7124, E-mail: randy.kluender@ucdenver.edu.

University of Connecticut Health Center, School of Dental Medicine, Professional Program in Dental Medicine, Farmington, CT 06030. Offers DMD, Certificate. *Accreditation:* ADA. *Faculty:* 85 full-time (28 women). *Students:* 102 full-time (46 women); includes 21 minority (2 African Americans, 1 American Indian/Alaska Native, 18 Hispanic Americans), 39 international. Average age 34. 855 applicants, 5% accepted, 40 enrolled. *Entrance requirements:* For degree, National Board Dental Examination. Additional exam requirements/recommendations for international students: Required—TOEFL (minimum score 550 paper-based; 215 computer-based). *Application deadline:* For fall admission, 10/15 for domestic students. Applications are processed on a rolling basis. Application fee: $75. *Financial support:* In 2009–10, 24 students received support. Application deadline: 4/1. *Unit head:* Dr. Steven Lepowsky, Associate Dean for Education and Patient Care, 860-679-4885, Fax: 860-679-3201, E-mail: lepowsky@nso.uchc.edu. *Application contact:* Margaret Sweet-Hoffman, Administrative Program Coordinator, 860-679-2574, Fax: 860-679-1899, E-mail: sweethoffm@nso1.uchc.edu.

University of Detroit Mercy, School of Dentistry, Professional Program in Dentistry, Detroit, MI 48221. Offers DDS. *Accreditation:* ADA. *Entrance requirements:* DAT. *Faculty research:* Peer evaluation in teaching, evaluation of restorative materials, HIV and periodontal disease.

University of Florida, College of Dentistry, Professional Programs in Dentistry, Gainesville, FL 32611. Offers dentistry (DMD); foreign trained dentistry (Certificate). *Degree requirements:* For Certificate, National Dental Boards Parts I and II. *Entrance requirements:* For DMD, DAT, interview; for Certificate, interview. Additional exam requirements/recommendations for international students: Required—TOEFL (minimum score 550 paper-based; 213 computer-based). *Faculty research:* Actinobacillus, critical thinking, DNA adenine, methylase, LJP.

University of Illinois at Chicago, College of Dentistry, Professional Program in Dentistry, Chicago, IL 60607-7128. Offers DDS, DDS/MPH, DDS/PhD. *Accreditation:* ADA. *Entrance requirements:* DAT. Additional exam requirements/recommendations for international students: Required—TOEFL. Electronic applications accepted.

The University of Iowa, College of Dentistry and Graduate College, Graduate Programs in Dentistry, Iowa City, IA 52242-1316. Offers endodontics (MS, Certificate); operative dentistry (MS, Certificate); oral and maxillofacial surgery (MS, Certificate); oral pathology, radiology and medicine (MS, Certificate), including oral and maxillofacial pathology (Certificate), oral and maxillofacial radiology (Certificate), stomatology (MS); oral science (MS, PhD); orthodontics (MS, Certificate); pediatric dentistry (Certificate); periodontics (MS, Certificate); preventive and community dentistry (MS), including dental public health; prosthodontics (MS, Certificate). *Accreditation:* ADA. *Degree requirements:* For master's, thesis; for doctorate, thesis/dissertation. *Entrance requirements:* For master's, GRE, DDS; for Certificate, DDS. Additional exam requirements/recommendations for international students: Required—TOEFL. *Expenses:* Contact institution.

The University of Iowa, College of Dentistry, Professional Program in Dentistry, Iowa City, IA 52242-1316. Offers DDS. *Accreditation:* ADA. *Entrance requirements:* DAT, minimum 90 semester hours with minimum GPA of 2.5.

University of Kentucky, College of Dentistry, Lexington, KY 40506-0032. Offers DMD. *Accreditation:* ADA. *Entrance requirements:* DAT, minimum undergraduate GPA of 3.0. *Faculty research:* Dental amalgams and mercury, Alzheimer's and aging in oral health.

University of Louisville, School of Dentistry, Louisville, KY 40202. Offers oral biology (MS). *Accreditation:* ADA (one or more programs are accredited). Part-time programs available. *Faculty:* 63 full-time (20 women), 84 part-time/adjunct (22 women). *Students:* 360 full-time (171 women), 6 part-time (5 women); includes 59 minority (29 African Americans, 7 American Indian/Alaska Native, 19 Asian Americans or Pacific Islanders, 4 Hispanic Americans), 10 international. Average age 26. 2,895 applicants, 11% accepted, 196 enrolled. In 2009, 78 first professional degrees, 10 master's awarded. *Degree requirements:* For master's, thesis; for DMD, National Board exams. *Entrance requirements:* For DMD, DAT, 32 hours of course work in science; for master's, DAT or GRE General Test, minimum GPA of 2.75. Additional exam requirements/recommendations for international students: Required—TOEFL (minimum score 100 iBT). *Application deadline:* For fall admission, 1/1 for domestic and international students.

Dentistry

University of Louisville (continued)

Applications are processed on a rolling basis. Application fee: $50. Electronic applications accepted. *Expenses:* Contact institution. *Financial support:* In 2009–10, 88 students received support, including 1 research assistantship with full tuition reimbursement available (averaging $20,000 per year). Financial award application deadline: 3/15. *Faculty research:* Inflammation and periondontitis, birth defects and developmental biology, biomaterials, oral infections, digital imaging. *Unit head:* Dr. John J. Sauk, Dean, 502-852-1304, Fax: 502-852-3364, E-mail: jjsauk01@louisville.edu. *Application contact:* Robin Benningfield, Admissions Counselor, 502-852-5081, Fax: 502-852-1210, E-mail: dmdadms@louisville.edu.

University of Manitoba, Faculty of Dentistry, Professional Program in Dentistry, Winnipeg, MB R3T 2N2, Canada. Offers DMD. *Accreditation:* ADA. *Entrance requirements:* DAT, interview. *Faculty research:* Oral physiology, microbiology, and biochemistry of the oral cavity in health and disease; application of clinical research.

University of Maryland, Baltimore, Professional and Advanced Education Programs in Dentistry, Baltimore, MD 21201-1627. Offers advanced general dentistry (Certificate); dentistry (DDS); endodontics (Certificate); oral and experimental pathology (Certificate); oral biology (MS); oral-maxillofacial surgery (Certificate); orthodontics (Certificate); pediatric dentistry (Certificate); periodontics (Certificate); prosthodontics (Certificate); DDS/MBA; DDS/PhD. *Accreditation:* ADA. *Entrance requirements:* DAT. Additional exam requirements/recommendations for international students: Required—TOEFL. *Application deadline:* For fall admission, 1/1 for domestic students. Applications are processed on a rolling basis. Application fee: $75. *Expenses:* Contact institution. *Financial support:* Career-related internships or fieldwork, Federal Work-Study, institutionally sponsored loans, scholarships/grants, and unspecified assistantships available. Financial award application deadline: 3/1; financial award applicants required to submit FAFSA. *Faculty research:* Pain, neuroscience, cancer biology. *Unit head:* Dr. Christian S. Stohler, Dean, 410-706-7461. *Application contact:* Dr. Patricia Meehan, Assistant Dean for Admissions, 410-706-7472, Fax: 410-706-0945, E-mail: ddsadmissions@umaryland.edu.

University of Medicine and Dentistry of New Jersey, New Jersey Dental School, Newark, NJ 07101-1709. Offers dental science (MS); dentistry (DMD); endodontics (Certificate); oral medicine (Certificate); orthodontics (Certificate); pediatric dentistry (Certificate); periodontics (Certificate); prosthodontics (Certificate); DMD/MPH; DMD/PhD; MD/Certificate; MS/Certificate. *Accreditation:* ADA (one or more programs are accredited). *Entrance requirements:* DAT. Electronic applications accepted. *Expenses:* Contact institution.

University of Michigan, School of Dentistry, Professional Program in Dentistry, Ann Arbor, MI 48109. Offers DDS. *Accreditation:* ADA. *Degree requirements:* For DDS, Parts I and II of National Board Exams. *Entrance requirements:* DAT, 6 credits of course work in English; 8 credits of course work in each chemistry, organic chemistry, biology, and physics; 3 credits of biochemistry, microbiology, psychology, sociology. Electronic applications accepted. *Expenses:* Contact institution.

University of Minnesota, Twin Cities Campus, School of Dentistry, Professional Program in Dentistry, Minneapolis, MN 55455-0213. Offers DDS. *Accreditation:* ADA. *Entrance requirements:* DAT. Additional exam requirements/recommendations for international students: Required—TOEFL.

University of Mississippi Medical Center, School of Dentistry, Jackson, MS 39216-4505. Offers DMD, MS, PhD. *Accreditation:* ADA. *Entrance requirements:* DAT. *Expenses:* Contact institution. *Faculty research:* Bone growth factors, salivary markers of disease, biomaterial synthesis and evaluation, metabolic bone disease, periodontal disease.

University of Missouri–Kansas City, School of Dentistry, Kansas City, MO 64110-2499. Offers advanced education in dentistry (Graduate Dental Certificate); dental hygiene education (MS); dental specialties (Graduate Dental Certificate); dentistry (DDS); diagnostic sciences (Graduate Dental Certificate); oral and maxillofacial surgery (Graduate Dental Certificate); oral biology (MS, PhD); orthodontics and dentofacial orthopedics (Graduate Dental Certificate); pediatric dentistry (Graduate Dental Certificate); periodontics (Graduate Dental Certificate); prosthodontics (Graduate Dental Certificate). PhD (interdisciplinary) offered through the School of Graduate Studies. *Accreditation:* ADA (one or more programs are accredited). *Faculty:* 101 full-time (40 women), 77 part-time/adjunct (25 women). *Students:* 402 full-time (177 women), 50 part-time (28 women); includes 54 minority (8 African Americans, 3 American Indian/Alaska Native, 29 Asian Americans or Pacific Islanders, 14 Hispanic Americans), 1 international. Average age 27. 536 applicants, 24% accepted, 126 enrolled. In 2009, 102 first professional degrees, 9 master's awarded. *Degree requirements:* For master's, thesis; for doctorate, thesis/dissertation. *Entrance requirements:* For DDS, DAT; for master's, DAT, letters of evaluation, personal interview; for Graduate Dental Certificate, DDS. Additional exam requirements/recommendations for international students: Required—TOEFL (minimum score 550 paper-based; 213 computer-based; 80 iBT). *Application deadline:* For fall admission, 2/1 for domestic and international students. Application fee: $45 ($50 for international students). *Expenses:* Contact institution. *Financial support:* In 2009–10, 4 fellowships (averaging $60,500 per year), 3 research assistantships (averaging $17,728 per year) were awarded; career-related internships or fieldwork, Federal Work-Study, institutionally sponsored loans, and tuition waivers (full and partial) also available. Support available to part-time students. Financial award application deadline: 3/1; financial award applicants required to submit FAFSA. *Faculty research:* Biomaterials, dental use of lasers, effectiveness of periodontal treatments, temporomandibular joint dysfunction. Total annual research expenditures: $5.9 million. *Unit head:* Dr. Marsha Pyle, Dean, 816-235-2010. *Application contact:* 816-235-2080.

University of Nebraska Medical Center, College of Dentistry, Professional Program in Dentistry, Omaha, NE 68198. Offers DDS. *Accreditation:* ADA. *Entrance requirements:* DAT. *Expenses:* Contact institution.

University of Nebraska Medical Center, College of Dentistry, Program in Dentistry, Omaha, NE 68198. Offers MS, PhD, Certificate. *Accreditation:* ADA. *Degree requirements:* For Certificate, thesis or alternative. *Entrance requirements:* For degree, GRE or National Board Dental Exam, DDS or DMD.

The University of North Carolina at Chapel Hill, School of Dentistry, Professional Program in Dentistry, Chapel Hill, NC 27599. Offers DDS, DDS/PhD. *Accreditation:* ADA. *Entrance requirements:* DAT, interview. Additional exam requirements/recommendations for international students: Required—TOEFL (minimum score 550 paper-based; 213 computer-based). Electronic applications accepted. *Expenses:* Contact institution.

University of Oklahoma Health Sciences Center, College of Dentistry, Advanced Education in General Dentistry Program, Oklahoma City, OK 73190. Offers Certificate. *Accreditation:* ADA. *Faculty:* 1 full-time (0 women), 5 part-time/adjunct (1 woman). *Students:* 6 full-time (2 women). Average age 28. 45 applicants, 13% accepted, 6 enrolled. *Application deadline:* For fall admission, 11/1 for domestic students. Electronic applications accepted. *Expenses:* Tuition, state resident: full-time $3120; part-time $156 per credit hour. Tuition, nonresident: full-time $11,314; part-time $409.70 per credit hour. Required fees: $1471; $51.20 per credit hour. $223.25 per term. *Financial support:* Salaried residencies available. *Unit head:* Dr. J. David Buxton, DDS, Director, 405-271-2380, E-mail: david-buxton@ouhsc.edu. *Application contact:* Dr. J. David Buxton, DDS, Director, 405-271-2380, E-mail: david-buxton@ouhsc.edu.

University of Oklahoma Health Sciences Center, College of Dentistry, Professional Program in Dentistry, Oklahoma City, OK 73190. Offers DDS. *Accreditation:* ADA. *Faculty:* 71 full-time (25 women), 61 part-time/adjunct (11 women). *Students:* 228 full-time (69 women); includes 52 minority (21 American Indian/Alaska Native, 23 Asian Americans or Pacific Islanders, 8 Hispanic Americans), 3 international. Average age 25. 755 applicants, 7% accepted, 56 enrolled. In 2009, 60 DDSs awarded. *Degree requirements:* For DDS, National Board Dental Exam Part I and Part II. *Entrance requirements:* DAT, minimum GPA of 2.5; course work in English, general psychology, biology, general chemistry, organic chemistry, physics, and biochemistry. Additional exam requirements/recommendations for international students: Required—TOEFL (minimum score 570 paper-based; 230 computer-based). *Application deadline:* For fall admission, 10/1 for domestic and international students. Applications are processed on a rolling basis. Application fee: $75. Electronic applications accepted. *Expenses:* Tuition, state resident: full-time $3120; part-time $156 per credit hour. Tuition, nonresident: full-time $11,314; part-time $409.70 per credit hour. Required fees: $1471; $51.20 per credit hour. $223.25 per term. *Financial support:* In 2009–10, 205 students received support. Institutionally sponsored loans available. Financial award application deadline: 5/1; financial award applicants required to submit FAFSA. *Faculty research:* Dental caries, microwave sterilization, dental care delivery systems, dental materials, oral health of Native Americans. *Unit head:* Dr. Randy P. Jones, Director of Admissions and Student Affairs, 405-271-3530, Fax: 405-271-3423, E-mail: randolph-jones@ouhsc.edu. *Application contact:* Sally J. Davenport, Admissions Coordinator, 405-271-3530, Fax: 405-271-3423, E-mail: sally-davenport@ouhsc.edu.

University of Pennsylvania, School of Dental Medicine, Philadelphia, PA 19104. Offers DMD, DMD/MS Ed. *Accreditation:* ADA. *Entrance requirements:* DAT. *Expenses:* Contact institution. *Faculty research:* Bone, teeth and extracellular matrix; craniofacial genetic anomalies; infection and host response; periodonatal diseases; stem cells.

University of Pittsburgh, School of Dental Medicine, Professional Program in Dental Medicine, Pittsburgh, PA 15260. Offers DMD. *Accreditation:* ADA. *Faculty:* 90 full-time (39 women), 191 part-time/adjunct (48 women). *Students:* 315 full-time (117 women); includes 97 minority (5 African Americans, 3 American Indian/Alaska Native, 62 Asian Americans or Pacific Islanders, 27 Hispanic Americans), 13 international. Average age 26. 2,048 applicants, 11% accepted, 80 enrolled. In 2009, 81 DMDs awarded. *Entrance requirements:* DAT, minimum GPA of 3.2 (science and non-science). Additional exam requirements/recommendations for international students: Required—TOEFL (minimum score 100 iBT). *Application deadline:* For fall admission, 12/1 for domestic and international students. Applications are processed on a rolling basis. Application fee: $35 ($50 for international students). *Expenses:* Contact institution. *Financial support:* In 2009–10, 275 students received support; fellowships, teaching assistantships with full tuition reimbursements available, scholarships/grants available. Financial award application deadline: 4/30; financial award applicants required to submit FAFSA. *Faculty research:* Human genetics, tissue engineering, public health, periodontal disease, cardiology. Total annual research expenditures: $5.1 million. *Unit head:* Dr. Kenneth Etzel, Associate Dean for Student Services and Admissions, 412-648-8422, Fax: 412-648-9751, E-mail: kre@pitt.edu. *Application contact:* Rosemary Mangold, Assistant Director of Admissions, 412-648-8437, Fax: 412-648-9571, E-mail: mangold@pitt.edu.

University of Pittsburgh, School of Dental Medicine, Residency Programs in Dental Medicine, Advanced Education Program in General Practice Residency, Pittsburgh, PA 15260. Offers Certificate. *Accreditation:* ADA. *Faculty:* 3 full-time (1 woman), 5 part-time/adjunct (2 women). *Students:* 3 full-time (all women); includes 1 minority (African American). Average age 27. 11 applicants, 27% accepted, 3 enrolled. In 2009, 2 Certificates awarded. *Application deadline:* For fall admission, 10/15 for domestic students. Application fee: $0. Electronic applications accepted. *Expenses:* Tuition, state resident: full-time $16,402; part-time $665 per credit. Tuition, nonresident: full-time $28,694; part-time $1175 per credit. Required fees: $690; $175 per term. Tuition and fees vary according to program. *Financial support:* Fellowships, research assistantships, teaching assistantships available. *Unit head:* Mary Ellen Cuccaro, Program Director, 412-648-6730, Fax: 412-648-6798, E-mail: mec11@pitt.edu. *Application contact:* Pamela A. Edwards, Administrator, Office of Resident Education, 412-648-8406, Fax: 412-648-8219, E-mail: pae3@pitt.edu.

University of Pittsburgh, School of Dental Medicine, Residency Programs in Dental Medicine, Department of Pediatric Dentistry, Pittsburgh, PA 15260. Offers MDS, Certificate. *Accreditation:* ADA. *Faculty:* 3 full-time (all women), 2 part-time/adjunct (1 woman). *Students:* 4 full-time (3 women). Average age 28. 48 applicants, 4% accepted, 2 enrolled. *Degree requirements:* For Certificate, clinical research. *Entrance requirements:* For degree, National Dental Board Exam Parts I and II, US or Canadian dental degree. *Application deadline:* For fall admission, 10/1 for domestic students. Application fee: $35. Electronic applications accepted. *Expenses:* Tuition, state resident: full-time $16,402; part-time $665 per credit. Tuition, nonresident: full-time $28,694; part-time $1175 per credit. Required fees: $690; $175 per term. Tuition and fees vary according to program. *Financial support:* In 2009–10, 4 students received support, including 4 fellowships (averaging $24,000 per year). Financial award application deadline: 7/30; financial award applicants required to submit FAFSA. *Faculty research:* Sports dentistry, behavior management, women's oral health, adolescent oral health, infant oral health and cariology. *Unit head:* Dr. Deborah A. Studen-Pavlovich, Chair and Professor, 412-648-8183, Fax: 412-648-8435, E-mail: das12@pitt.edu. *Application contact:* Sharon Hohman, Department Secretary, 412-648-8416, Fax: 412-648-8435, E-mail: sah10@pitt.edu.

University of Pittsburgh, School of Dental Medicine, Residency Programs in Dental Medicine, Program in Advanced Education in General Dentistry, Pittsburgh, PA 15260. Offers Certificate. *Accreditation:* ADA. *Faculty:* 4 part-time/adjunct (1 woman). *Students:* 3 full-time (2 women); includes 2 minority (1 Asian American or Pacific Islander, 1 Hispanic American). Average age 34. 35 applicants, 9% accepted, 3 enrolled. In 2009, 1 Certificate awarded. *Entrance requirements:* For degree, National Dental Board Parts I and II, American or Canadian DDS or DMD. *Application deadline:* For fall admission, 12/15 for domestic students. Applications are processed on a rolling basis. Application fee: $50. Electronic applications accepted. *Expenses:* Tuition, state resident: full-time $16,402; part-time $665 per credit. Tuition, nonresident: full-time $28,694; part-time $1175 per credit. Required fees: $690; $175 per term. Tuition and fees vary according to program. *Financial support:* In 2009–10, 3 fellowships (averaging $23,000 per year) were awarded. *Unit head:* Dr. Maribeth Krzesinski, Director, 412-648-8093, Fax: 412-383-7796, E-mail: mbk3@pitt.edu. *Application contact:* Pamela A. Edwards, Administrator, Office of Resident Education, 412-648-8406, Fax: 412-648-8219, E-mail: pae3@pitt.edu.

University of Puerto Rico, Medical Sciences Campus, School of Dental Medicine, Professional Program in Dentistry, San Juan, PR 00936-5067. Offers DMD. *Accreditation:* ADA. *Entrance requirements:* DAT, interview. *Expenses:* Contact institution. *Faculty research:* Analgesic drugs, anti-inflammatory drugs, saliva cytoanalysis, dental material and cariology, oral health condition of school-age population.

University of Saskatchewan, College of Dentistry, Saskatoon, SK S7N 5A2, Canada. Offers DMD. *Accreditation:* ADA. *Entrance requirements:* DAT. Additional exam requirements/recommendations for international students: Required—TOEFL (minimum score 550 paper-based; 213 computer-based; 80 iBT), IELTS (minimum score 6.5), Michigan English Language Assessment Battery (85); CanTEST (4.0); CAEL (60); CPE (C). Electronic applications accepted. *Expenses:* Contact institution. *Faculty research:* Protein structure, oral cavity, immunology, bone densitometry, biological sciences.

University of Southern California, Graduate School, School of Dentistry, Professional Programs in Dentistry, Los Angeles, CA 90089. Offers DDS, DDS/MBA, DDS/MS. *Accreditation:* ADA (one or more programs are accredited). *Students:* 717 full-time (310 women), 1 part-time (0 women); includes 302 minority (21 African Americans, 1 American Indian/Alaska Native, 239 Asian Americans or Pacific Islanders, 41 Hispanic Americans), 68 international. In 2009, 182 DDSs awarded. Application fee: $85. *Expenses:* Tuition: Full-time $25,980; part-time $1315 per unit. Required fees: $554. One-time fee: $35 full-time. Full-time tuition and fees vary according to degree level and program.

The University of Tennessee Health Science Center, College of Dentistry, Memphis, TN 38163-0002. Offers dentistry (DDS); oral and maxillofacial surgery (Certificate); orthodontics (MS); pediatric dentistry (MS, Certificate); periodontics (MS); prosthodontics (Certificate). *Accreditation:* ADA (one or more programs are accredited). *Degree requirements:* For master's, thesis. *Entrance requirements:* For DDS, DAT, interview, pre-professional evaluation; for master's, GRE, interviews. Additional exam requirements/recommendations for international students: Required—TOEFL (minimum score 275 computer-based). Electronic applications accepted.

Expenses: Contact institution. *Faculty research:* Oral cancer, proteomics, inflammation mechanisms, defensins, periopathogens, dental material.

The University of Texas Health Science Center at Houston, The University of Texas Dental Branch at Houston, Houston, TX 77225-0036. Offers DDS, MS. *Accreditation:* ADA. *Faculty:* 91 full-time (35 women), 93 part-time/adjunct (33 women). *Students:* 331 full-time (162 women); includes 151 minority (4 African Americans, 1 American Indian/Alaska Native, 89 Asian Americans or Pacific Islanders, 57 Hispanic Americans). Average age 25. 1,136 applicants, 15% accepted, 84 enrolled. In 2009, 76 first professional degrees awarded. *Entrance requirements:* DAT, 90 semester hours of prerequisite courses. *Application deadline:* For fall admission, 10/1 for domestic students. Applications are processed on a rolling basis. Application fee: $80. Electronic applications accepted. *Financial support:* In 2009–10, 287 students received support. Institutionally sponsored loans and scholarships/grants available. Financial award application deadline: 3/9; financial award applicants required to submit FAFSA. *Faculty research:* Salivary diagnostics, autoimmune disease, mucosal immunity, craniofacial anomalies, molecular imaging, bioengineering. *Unit head:* Dr. John A. Valenza, Interim Dean, 713-500-4021, Fax: 713-500-4089. *Application contact:* Dr. H. Philip Pierpont, Associate Dean for Student and Alumni Affairs, 713-500-4151, Fax: 713-500-4425, E-mail: dbstudentaffairs@uthouston.edu.

The University of Texas Health Science Center at San Antonio, Dental School, San Antonio, TX 78229-3900. Offers DDS, MS, Certificate, DDS/PhD. *Accreditation:* ADA (one or more programs are accredited). *Degree requirements:* For master's, thesis; for DDS, comprehensive exam. *Entrance requirements:* For DDS, DAT; for master's, GRE General Test, DDS; for Certificate, DDS. Electronic applications accepted. *Expenses:* Tuition, state resident: full-time $2832; part-time $118 per credit hour. Tuition, nonresident: full-time $10,896; part-time $454 per credit hour. Required fees: $884 per semester. One-time fee: $70. *Faculty research:* Nutrition and oral health, periodontal disease, biomaterials, bone mineralization, caries prevention.

University of Toronto, Faculty of Dentistry, Professional Program in Dentistry, Toronto, ON M5S 1A1, Canada. Offers DDS. *Accreditation:* ADA. *Entrance requirements:* Canadian Dental Aptitude Test or equivalent, minimum GPA of 2.7; completion of at least 2 courses in life sciences and 1 course in humanities or social sciences. Additional exam requirements/recommendations for international students: Required—Michigan English Language Assessment Battery, TOEFL, IELTS or COPE. *Expenses:* Contact institution.

University of Washington, Graduate School, School of Dentistry, Program in Dental Surgery, Seattle, WA 98195. Offers DDS. *Accreditation:* ADA. *Entrance requirements:* DAT.

The University of Western Ontario, Schulich School of Medicine and Dentistry, School of Dentistry, Professional Program in Dentistry, London, ON N6A 5B8, Canada. Offers DDS. *Accreditation:* ADA. *Entrance requirements:* DAT (Canadian version), minimum B average.

Virginia Commonwealth University, Medical College of Virginia-Professional Programs, School of Dentistry, Richmond, VA 23284-9005. Offers DDS, MS, DDS/MS, DDS/PhD. *Accreditation:* ADA. *Entrance requirements:* DAT. Electronic applications accepted. *Expenses:* Contact institution.

Western University of Health Sciences, College of Dental Medicine, Pomona, CA 91766-1854. Offers DMD. *Accreditation:* ADA.

West Virginia University, School of Dentistry, Professional Program in Dentistry, Morgantown, WV 26506. Offers DDS. *Accreditation:* ADA. *Degree requirements:* For DDS, comprehensive exam. *Entrance requirements:* DAT, Letters of recommendation, interview, and pre-requisite courses. Additional exam requirements/recommendations for international students: Required—TOEFL (minimum score 500 paper-based; 173 computer-based).

Oral and Dental Sciences

A.T. Still University of Health Sciences, Arizona School of Dentistry and Oral Health, Mesa, AZ 85206. Offers dental medicine (DMD); orthodontics (Certificate). *Faculty:* 38 full-time (14 women), 109 part-time/adjunct (37 women). *Students:* 260 full-time (130 women); includes 66 minority (6 African Americans, 12 American Indian/Alaska Native, 33 Asian Americans or Pacific Islanders, 15 Hispanic Americans). Average age 25. 3,199 applicants, 3% accepted, 68 enrolled. In 2009, 49 first professional degrees, 4 Certificates awarded. *Degree requirements:* For DMD, National Board Exams I and II. *Entrance requirements:* DAT, minimum GPA of 2.5 overall and in science. *Application deadline:* For fall admission, 12/1 for domestic and international students. Applications are processed on a rolling basis. Application fee: $60. Electronic applications accepted. *Expenses:* Contact institution. *Financial support:* In 2009–10, 231 students received support. Federal Work-Study and scholarships/grants available. Financial award application deadline: 5/1; financial award applicants required to submit FAFSA. *Faculty research:* EBD in clinical practice, xerostomia and malnutrition in assisted living settings, medical screening in the dental office: patient attitudes, rapid oral HIV screening in the dental setting, dental public health: early childhood caries. *Unit head:* Dr. Jack Dillenberg, Dean, 480-219-6000, Fax: 480-219-6110, E-mail: jdillenberg@atsu.edu. *Application contact:* Donna Sparks, Associate Director for Admissions, 660-626-2237, Fax: 660-626-2969, E-mail: admissions@atsu.edu.

Boston University, Goldman School of Dental Medicine, Graduate Programs in Dentistry, Boston, MA 02215. Offers advanced general dentistry (CAGS); dental public health (MS, MSD, D Sc D, CAGS); dentistry (DMD); endodontics (MSD, D Sc D, CAGS); implantology (CAGS); operative dentistry (MSD, D Sc D, CAGS); oral and maxillofacial surgery (MSD, D Sc D, CAGS); oral biology (MSD, D Sc, D Sc D, PhD); orthodontics (MSD, D Sc D, CAGS); pediatric dentistry (MSD, D Sc D, CAGS); periodontology (MSD, D Sc D, CAGS); prosthodontics (MSD, D Sc D, CAGS). *Students:* 606 full-time (295 women); includes 149 minority (7 African Americans, 3 American Indian/Alaska Native, 113 Asian Americans or Pacific Islanders, 26 Hispanic Americans), 209 international. Average age 26. In 2009, 175 first professional degrees awarded. *Degree requirements:* For master's, thesis; for doctorate, thesis/dissertation; for CAGS, thesis (for some programs). *Entrance requirements:* For DMD, DAT, minimum GPA of 3.0; for CAGS, dental degree. *Application deadline:* For fall admission, 5/1 for domestic students. Applications are processed on a rolling basis. Application fee: $60. *Expenses:* Contact institution. *Financial support:* Career-related internships or fieldwork and institutionally sponsored loans available. Financial award application deadline: 4/15; financial award applicants required to submit CSS PROFILE or FAFSA. *Faculty research:* Defensive mechanisms, bone-cell regulation, protein biochemistry, molecular biology, biomaterials. *Unit head:* Dr. Jeffrey W. Hutter, Interim Dean, 617-638-4780. *Application contact:* 617-638-4787, Fax: 617-638-4798.

Case Western Reserve University, School of Dental Medicine and School of Graduate Studies, Advanced Specialty Education Programs in Dentistry, Cleveland, OH 44106. Offers advanced general dentistry (Certificate); endodontics (MSD, Certificate); oral surgery (Certificate); orthodontics (MSD, Certificate); pedodontics (MSD, Certificate); periodontics (MSD, Certificate). *Degree requirements:* For master's, thesis. *Entrance requirements:* For master's, National Dental Board Exam, DDS, minimum GPA of 3.0; for Certificate, DDS. Additional exam requirements/recommendations for international students: Required—TOEFL (minimum score 550 paper-based; 213 computer-based; 79 iBT). *Expenses:* Contact institution. *Faculty research:* Natural antibiotics, obesity and periodontal disease, perioninfection and CV disease, periodontal disease and overall health, 3D cone beam computerized tomography.

Columbia University, College of Dental Medicine and Graduate School of Arts and Sciences, Programs in Dental Specialties, New York, NY 10027. Offers advanced education in general dentistry (Certificate); biomedical informatics (MA, PhD); endodontics (Certificate); orthodontics (MS, Certificate); periodontics (MS, Certificate); prosthodontics (MS, Certificate); science education (MA). *Degree requirements:* For master's, thesis, presentation of seminar. *Entrance requirements:* For master's, GRE General Test, DDS or equivalent. *Expenses:* Contact institution. *Faculty research:* Analysis of growth/form, pulpal microcirculation, implants, microbiology of oral environment, calcified tissues.

Dalhousie University, Faculty of Dentistry, Department of Oral and Maxillofacial Surgery, Halifax, NS B3H 3J5, Canada. Offers MD/M Sc. *Application deadline:* For spring admission, 8/31 priority date for domestic students. Applications are processed on a rolling basis. Application fee: $70. Electronic applications accepted. *Expenses:* Contact institution. *Financial support:* Career-related internships or fieldwork available. *Faculty research:* Cleft lip/palate, jaw biomechanics. *Unit head:* Dr. Chad Robertson, Graduate Coordinator, 902-494-6778, Fax: 902-494-6411, E-mail: denadmis@dal.ca. *Application contact:* Lesley Partanen, Secretary, 902-494-1679, Fax: 902-494-6411, E-mail: lesley.partanen@dal.ca.

Harvard University, Graduate School of Arts and Sciences, Program in Biological Sciences in Dental Medicine, Cambridge, MA 02138. Offers PhD. *Expenses:* Tuition: Full-time $33,696. Required fees: $1126. Full-time tuition and fees vary according to program.

Harvard University, School of Dental Medicine, Advanced Graduate Programs in Dentistry, Cambridge, MA 02138. Offers advanced general dentistry (Certificate); dental public health (Certificate); endodontics (Certificate); general practice residency (Certificate); oral biology (M Med Sc, D Med Sc); oral implantology (Certificate); oral medicine (Certificate); oral pathology (Certificate); oral surgery (Certificate); orthodontics (Certificate); pediatric dentistry (Certificate); periodontics (Certificate); prosthodontics (Certificate). *Expenses:* Tuition: Full-time $33,696. Required fees: $1126. Full-time tuition and fees vary according to program.

Howard University, College of Dentistry, Washington, DC 20059-0002. Offers advanced education program general dentistry (Certificate); dentistry (DDS); general dentistry (Certificate); oral and maxillofacial surgery (Certificate); orthodontics (Certificate); pediatric dentistry (Certificate). *Accreditation:* ADA (one or more programs are accredited). *Degree requirements:* For DDS, comprehensive exam, didactic and clinical exams. *Entrance requirements:* DAT, 8 semester hours of course work in each biology, inorganic chemistry, organic chemistry. *Expenses:* Contact institution. *Faculty research:* Epidemiological, biomaterial, molecular genetic, behavioral modification, and clinical trial studies.

Idaho State University, Office of Graduate Studies, Kasiska College of Health Professions, Department of Dental Sciences, Pocatello, ID 83209-8088. Offers advanced general dentistry (Post-Doctoral Certificate). First year of Idaho Dental Education Program available in conjunction with Creighton University's School of Dentistry. *Students:* 15 full-time (3 women); includes 2 minority (both Asian Americans or Pacific Islanders). Average age 28. In 2009, 2 Post-Doctoral Certificates awarded. *Degree requirements:* For Post-Doctoral Certificate, comprehensive exam, thesis optional, 1-year residency. *Entrance requirements:* For degree, DAT, 3 dental application forms. Additional exam requirements/recommendations for international students: Required—TOEFL (minimum score 600 paper-based; 213 computer-based). *Application deadline:* For fall admission, 7/1 for domestic students, 6/1 for international students; for spring admission, 12/1 for domestic students, 11/1 for international students. Applications are processed on a rolling basis. Application fee: $55. Electronic applications accepted. *Expenses:* Contact institution. *Financial support:* Career-related internships or fieldwork, Federal Work-Study, institutionally sponsored loans, scholarships/grants, traineeships, and health care benefits available. Financial award application deadline: 1/1; financial award applicants required to submit FAFSA. *Unit head:* Dr. Brian Crawford, Chair, 208-282-5275, Fax: 208-282-5834, E-mail: crawbri3@isu.edu. *Application contact:* Tami Carson, Graduate School Technical Records Specialist, 208-282-2150, Fax: 208-282-4847, E-mail: carstami@isu.edu.

Jacksonville University, College of Arts and Sciences, School of Orthodontics, Jacksonville, FL 32211. Offers Certificate. *Entrance requirements:* Additional exam requirements/recommendations for international students: Required—TOEFL. *Expenses:* Contact institution.

Loma Linda University, School of Dentistry, Program in Endodontics, Loma Linda, CA 92350. Offers MS, Certificate, MS/Certificate. *Degree requirements:* For master's, thesis. *Entrance requirements:* For master's, GRE General Test, DDS or DMD, minimum GPA of 3.0, National Boards. Additional exam requirements/recommendations for international students: Required—TOEFL (minimum score 550 paper-based; 213 computer-based).

Loma Linda University, School of Dentistry, Program in Implant Dentistry, Loma Linda, CA 92350. Offers MS, Certificate, MS/Certificate. *Degree requirements:* For master's, thesis. *Entrance requirements:* For master's, GRE General Test, DDS or DMD, minimum GPA of 3.0.

Loma Linda University, School of Dentistry, Program in Oral and Maxillofacial Surgery, Loma Linda, CA 92350. Offers MS, Certificate, MS/Certificate. *Degree requirements:* For master's, thesis. *Entrance requirements:* For master's, GRE General Test, DDS or DMD, minimum GPA of 3.0.

Loma Linda University, School of Dentistry, Program in Orthodontics, Loma Linda, CA 92350. Offers MS, Certificate, MS/Certificate. *Degree requirements:* For master's, thesis. *Entrance requirements:* For master's, GRE General Test, DDS or DMD, minimum GPA of 3.0. Additional exam requirements/recommendations for international students: Required—TOEFL (minimum score 550 paper-based; 213 computer-based).

Loma Linda University, School of Dentistry, Program in Periodontics, Loma Linda, CA 92350. Offers MS. *Degree requirements:* For master's, thesis. *Entrance requirements:* For master's, GRE General Test, DDS or DMD, minimum GPA of 3.0. Additional exam requirements/recommendations for international students: Required—TOEFL (minimum score 550 paper-based; 213 computer-based).

Marquette University, School of Dentistry and Graduate School, Graduate Programs in Dentistry, Program in Advanced Training in General Dentistry, Milwaukee, WI 53201-1881. Offers MS. *Entrance requirements:* Additional exam requirements/recommendations for international students: Required—TOEFL. *Faculty research:* Biochemistry.

Marquette University, School of Dentistry and Graduate School, Graduate Programs in Dentistry, Program in Dental Biomaterials, Milwaukee, WI 53201-1881. Offers MS. Part-time programs available. *Degree requirements:* For master's, thesis. *Entrance requirements:* For master's, GRE General Test. Additional exam requirements/recommendations for international students: Required—TOEFL. *Faculty research:* Composite resins, dentin bonding agents.

Marquette University, School of Dentistry and Graduate School, Graduate Programs in Dentistry, Program in Endodontics, Milwaukee, WI 53201-1881. Offers MS. *Degree requirements:* For master's, thesis or alternative. *Entrance requirements:* For master's, DDS or equivalent. Additional exam requirements/recommendations for international students: Required—TOEFL. *Faculty research:* Mechanical properties of endodontic files, use of lasers in endodontics.

Oral and Dental Sciences

Marquette University, School of Dentistry and Graduate School, Graduate Programs in Dentistry, Program in Orthodontics, Milwaukee, WI 53201-1881. Offers MS. *Degree requirements:* For master's, thesis or alternative. *Entrance requirements:* For master's, DDS or equivalent. Additional exam requirements/recommendations for international students: Required—TOEFL. *Faculty research:* Biomaterials, adhesion.

Marquette University, School of Dentistry and Graduate School, Graduate Programs in Dentistry, Program in Prosthodontics, Milwaukee, WI 53201-1881. Offers MS. *Degree requirements:* For master's, thesis or alternative. *Entrance requirements:* For master's, DDS or equivalent. Additional exam requirements/recommendations for international students: Required—TOEFL. *Faculty research:* Biomaterials, implants.

Massachusetts College of Pharmacy and Health Sciences, Graduate Studies, Program in Community Oral Health, Boston, MA 02115-5896. Offers MS. Part-time programs available. Postbaccalaureate distance learning degree programs offered (minimal on-campus study). *Students:* 9 part-time (all women); includes 1 African American. Average age 37. 12 applicants, 100% accepted, 9 enrolled. *Entrance requirements:* For master's, 2 years of work experience in health care. Additional exam requirements/recommendations for international students: Required—TOEFL (minimum score 550 paper-based; 213 computer-based; 79 iBT). *Application deadline:* For fall admission, 7/1 priority date for domestic students. Application fee: $70. *Expenses:* Tuition: Full-time $28,000; part-time $875 per credit hour. Required fees: $750; $190 per semester. Part-time tuition and fees vary according to course load, campus/location, program and student level. *Unit head:* Becky DeSpain Eden, Assistant Dean of Graduate Studies, 617-735-1594, E-mail: becky.eden@mcphs.edu. *Application contact:* Tara Hennesey, Coordinator of Graduate Admission, 617-732-2850, E-mail: admissions@mcphs.edu.

McGill University, Faculty of Graduate and Postdoctoral Studies, Faculty of Dentistry, Montréal, QC H3A 2T5, Canada. Offers forensic dentistry (Certificate); oral and maxillofacial surgery (M Sc, PhD).

Medical College of Georgia, School of Graduate Studies, Program in Oral Biology and Maxillofacial Pathology, Augusta, GA 30912. Offers MS, PhD. Part-time programs available. *Degree requirements:* For master's, thesis; for doctorate, thesis/dissertation. *Entrance requirements:* For master's and doctorate, GRE General Test or DAT, DDS, DMD, or equivalent degree. Additional exam requirements/recommendations for international students: Required—TOEFL (minimum score 550 paper-based; 213 computer-based; 79 iBT). Electronic applications accepted. Full-time tuition and fees vary according to campus/location, program and student level. *Faculty research:* Oral cancer and chemoprevention, properties of biomaterials including oxidative stress, mechanical stress and shear stress responses, taurine and blood pressure in diabetes, bone and dentin biology, induction of periodontal regeneration.

New York University, College of Dentistry, Postgraduate Programs in Dentistry, New York, NY 10010. Offers endodontics (Advanced Certificate); oral and maxillofacial surgery (Advanced Certificate); orthodontics (Advanced Certificate); pediatric dentistry (Advanced Certificate); periodontics (Advanced Certificate); prosthodontics (Advanced Certificate); prosthodontics (implantology) (Advanced Certificate). Part-time programs available. *Faculty:* 235 full-time, 690 part-time/adjunct. *Students:* 110 full-time (52 women), 13 part-time (3 women); includes 45 minority (2 African Americans, 36 Asian Americans or Pacific Islanders, 7 Hispanic Americans). Average age 32. 570 applicants, 9% accepted, 49 enrolled. In 2009, 42 Advanced Certificates awarded. *Entrance requirements:* For degree, National Dental Boards Exam Part I, DDS. Additional exam requirements/recommendations for international students: Required—TOEFL (minimum score 570 paper-based; 230 computer-based; 90 iBT). *Application deadline:* For fall admission, 12/1 for domestic students. Application fee: $100. Electronic applications accepted. *Expenses:* Tuition: Full-time $30,528; part-time $1272 per credit. Required fees: $2177. *Financial support:* Scholarships/grants and unspecified assistantships available. Financial award application deadline: 3/1; financial award applicants required to submit FAFSA. *Unit head:* Dr. David Sirois, Dean, College of Dentistry, 212-998-9540, Fax: 212-995-4240, E-mail: david.sirois@nyu.edu. *Application contact:* Dr. Anthony M. Palatta, Assistant Dean for Student Affairs and Admissions, 212-998-9918, Fax: 212-995-4240, E-mail: ap16@nyu.edu.

New York University, Graduate School of Arts and Science, Department of Biology, New York, NY 10012-1019. Offers biology (PhD); biomedical journalism (MS); cancer and molecular biology (PhD); computational biology (PhD); computers in biological research (MS); developmental genetics (PhD); general biology (MS); immunology and microbiology (PhD); molecular genetics (PhD); neurobiology (PhD); oral biology (MS); plant biology (PhD); recombinant DNA technology (MS); MS/MBA. Part-time programs available. *Faculty:* 24 full-time (5 women). *Students:* 142 full-time (79 women), 44 part-time (28 women); includes 34 minority (1 African American, 25 Asian Americans or Pacific Islanders, 8 Hispanic Americans), 82 international. Average age 27. 362 applicants, 71% accepted, 72 enrolled. In 2009, 43 master's, 9 doctorates awarded. Terminal master's awarded for partial completion of doctoral program. *Degree requirements:* For master's, thesis or alternative, qualifying paper; for doctorate, comprehensive exam, thesis/dissertation. *Entrance requirements:* For master's, GRE General Test; for doctorate, GRE General Test, GRE Subject Test. Additional exam requirements/recommendations for international students: Required—TOEFL. *Application deadline:* For fall admission, 12/12 priority date for domestic students. Application fee: $90. *Expenses:* Tuition: Full-time $30,528; part-time $1272 per credit. Required fees: $2177. *Financial support:* Fellowships with tuition reimbursements, research assistantships with tuition reimbursements, teaching assistantships with tuition reimbursements, career-related internships or fieldwork, Federal Work-Study, institutionally sponsored loans, scholarships/grants, health care benefits, and unspecified assistantships available. Financial award application deadline: 12/12; financial award applicants required to submit FAFSA. *Faculty research:* Genomics, molecular and cell biology, development and molecular genetics, molecular evolution of plants and animals. *Unit head:* Gloria Coruzzi, Chair, 212-998-8200, Fax: 212-995-4015, E-mail: biology@nyu.edu. *Application contact:* Stephen Small, Director of Graduate Studies, 212-998-8200, Fax: 212-995-4015, E-mail: biology@nyu.edu.

New York University, Graduate School of Arts and Science and College of Dentistry, Department of Biomaterials and Biomimetics, New York, NY 10012-1019. Offers biomaterials science (MS). *Faculty:* 5 full-time (2 women). *Students:* 12 full-time (7 women), 14 part-time (7 women); includes 2 minority (both Asian Americans or Pacific Islanders), 11 international. Average age 30. 13 applicants, 92% accepted, 8 enrolled. In 2009, 5 master's awarded. *Degree requirements:* For master's, thesis. *Entrance requirements:* For master's, DDS or DMD. Additional exam requirements/recommendations for international students: Required—TOEFL. *Application deadline:* For fall admission, 4/15 for domestic students. Application fee: $90. *Expenses:* Tuition: Full-time $30,528; part-time $1272 per credit. Required fees: $2177. *Financial support:* Application deadline: 4/1. *Faculty research:* Calcium phosphate, composite restoratives, surfactants, dental metallurgy, impression materials. *Unit head:* Dr. John L. Ricci, Director of Graduate Studies, 212-998-9703, Fax: 212-995-4244, E-mail: gsas.graduate.biomaterials@nyu.edu. *Application contact:* Carmen Chilsom, Administrator, 212-998-9703, Fax: 212-995-4244, E-mail: graduate.biomaterials@nyu.edu.

The Ohio State University, College of Dentistry, Program in Oral Biology, Columbus, OH 43210. Offers PhD, DDS/PhD. *Faculty:* 29 full-time (6 women). *Students:* 4 full-time (1 woman), 4 part-time (1 woman), 6 international. Average age 30. In 2009, 4 doctorates awarded. *Degree requirements:* For doctorate, thesis/dissertation. *Entrance requirements:* For doctorate, GRE General Test, GRE Subject Test in biology (recommended). Additional exam requirements/recommendations for international students: Required—TOEFL (minimum score 600 paper-based; 250 computer-based). *Application deadline:* For fall admission, 10/1 priority date for domestic and international students. Applications are processed on a rolling basis. Application fee: $40 ($50 for international students). Electronic applications accepted. *Expenses:* Tuition, state resident: full-time $10,683. Tuition, nonresident: full-time $25,923. Tuition and fees vary according to course load and program. *Financial support:* In 2009–10, 7 fellowships with tuition reimbursements, 13 research assistantships with tuition reimbursements were awarded; teaching assistantships. Financial award application deadline: 3/1. *Faculty research:* Neurobiology, inflammation and immunity, materials science. Total annual research expenditures: $3.4 million. *Unit head:* M. Scott Herness, Graduate Studies Committee Chair, 614-292-1322, Fax: 614-292-7619, E-mail: herness.1@osu.edu. *Application contact:* Graduate Admissions, 614-292-9444, Fax: 614-292-3895, E-mail: domestic.grad@osu.edu.

Oregon Health & Science University, School of Dentistry, Graduate Programs in Dentistry, Department of Endodontics, Portland, OR 97239-3098. Offers Certificate. *Entrance requirements:* For degree, GRE General Test. Additional exam requirements/recommendations for international students: Required—TOEFL. Tuition and fees vary according to course level, course load, degree level, program and reciprocity agreements.

Oregon Health & Science University, School of Dentistry, Graduate Programs in Dentistry, Department of Orthodontics, Portland, OR 97239-3098. Offers MS, Certificate. *Degree requirements:* For master's, thesis. *Entrance requirements:* For master's and Certificate, GRE General Test, DMD/DDS. Additional exam requirements/recommendations for international students: Required—TOEFL. Tuition and fees vary according to course level, course load, degree level, program and reciprocity agreements.

Oregon Health & Science University, School of Dentistry, Graduate Programs in Dentistry, Department of Pediatric Dentistry, Portland, OR 97239-3098. Offers Certificate. Tuition and fees vary according to course level, course load, degree level, program and reciprocity agreements.

Oregon Health & Science University, School of Dentistry, Graduate Programs in Dentistry, Department of Periodontology, Portland, OR 97239-3098. Offers MS, Certificate. *Degree requirements:* For master's, thesis. *Entrance requirements:* For master's and Certificate, GRE General Test, DMD/DDS. Additional exam requirements/recommendations for international students: Required—TOEFL. Tuition and fees vary according to course level, course load, degree level, program and reciprocity agreements.

Oregon Health & Science University, School of Dentistry, Graduate Programs in Dentistry, Department of Restorative Dentistry, Division of Biomaterials and Biomechanics, Portland, OR 97239-3098. Offers MS. Tuition and fees vary according to course level, course load, degree level, program and reciprocity agreements.

Oregon Health & Science University, School of Dentistry, Graduate Programs in Dentistry, Program in Oral Molecular Biology, Portland, OR 97239-3098. Offers MS. Tuition and fees vary according to course level, course load, degree level, program and reciprocity agreements.

Oregon Health & Science University, School of Dentistry, Professional Program in Dentistry, Portland, OR 97239-3098. Offers dentistry (DMD); oral and maxillofacial surgery (Certificate); MD/DMD. *Accreditation:* ADA. *Entrance requirements:* DAT. Electronic applications accepted. Tuition and fees vary according to course level, course load, degree level, program and reciprocity agreements. *Faculty research:* Dentin permeability, tooth sensations, fluoride metabolism, immunology of periodontal disease, craniofacial growth.

Saint Louis University, Graduate School, Center for Advanced Dental Education, St. Louis, MO 63103-2097. Offers endodontics (MSD); orthodontics (MSD); periodontics (MSD). *Degree requirements:* For master's, comprehensive exam, thesis, teaching practicum. *Entrance requirements:* For master's, GRE General Test, NBDE (National Board Dental Exam), DDS or DMD, interview, letters of recommendation. Additional exam requirements/recommendations for international students: Required—TOEFL (minimum score 525 paper-based; 194 computer-based). Electronic applications accepted. *Faculty research:* Craniofacial growth.

Stony Brook University, State University of New York, Stony Brook University Medical Center, Health Sciences Center, School of Dental Medicine and Graduate School, Department of Oral Biology and Pathology, Stony Brook, NY 11794. Offers MS, PhD. *Faculty:* 8 full-time (5 women). *Students:* 1 (woman) full-time, 1 part-time (0 women); includes 1 minority (Asian American or Pacific Islander), 1 international. Average age 34. 12 applicants, 0% accepted. In 2009, 1 doctorate awarded. *Entrance requirements:* For doctorate, GRE General Test. Additional exam requirements/recommendations for international students: Required—TOEFL. *Application deadline:* For fall admission, 1/15 for domestic students. Application fee: $60. *Expenses:* Contact institution. *Financial support:* In 2009–10, 2 research assistantships were awarded; fellowships, teaching assistantships, Federal Work-Study also available. Financial award application deadline: 3/15. *Faculty research:* Collagen metabolism, periodontal disease and diabetes, salivary antimicrobial proteins, dental plaque metabolism and dental caries. Total annual research expenditures: $1.4 million. *Unit head:* Dr. Ray Williams, Chair, 631-632-8950. *Application contact:* Dr. Marcia Simon, 631-632-8922.

Stony Brook University, State University of New York, Stony Brook University Medical Center, Health Sciences Center, School of Dental Medicine, Professional Program in Dental Medicine, Stony Brook, NY 11794. Offers dental medicine (DDS); endodontics (Certificate); orthodontics (Certificate); periodontics (Certificate). *Accreditation:* ADA (one or more programs are accredited). *Faculty:* 25 full-time (9 women), 68 part-time/adjunct (19 women). *Students:* 157 full-time (72 women), 21 part-time (5 women); includes 54 minority (2 African Americans, 45 Asian Americans or Pacific Islanders, 7 Hispanic Americans), 1 international. Average age 25. 1,456 applicants, 3% accepted. In 2009, 39 first professional degrees, 15 Certificates awarded. *Entrance requirements:* DAT. *Application deadline:* For fall admission, 1/15 for domestic students. Application fee: $75. *Expenses:* Tuition, state resident: full-time $8370; part-time $349 per credit. Tuition, nonresident: full-time $13,250; part-time $552 per credit. Required fees: $933. *Financial support:* In 2009–10, 1 research assistantship was awarded; Federal Work-Study also available. Support available to part-time students. Total annual research expenditures: $937,856. *Unit head:* Dr. Ray C. Williams, Dean, 631-632-8950, Fax: 631-632-9105. *Application contact:* Dr. Marcia Simon, Associate Dean for Graduate Studies, 631-632-8922.

Temple University, Health Sciences Center, School of Dentistry and Graduate School, Graduate Programs in Dentistry, Philadelphia, PA 19122-6096. Offers advanced education in general dentistry (Certificate); endodontology (Certificate); oral biology (MS); orthodontics (Certificate); periodontology (Certificate). *Degree requirements:* For master's, thesis; for Certificate, comprehensive exam. *Entrance requirements:* For master's, GRE; for Certificate, National Boards Parts I and II, DMD or DDS, 3 letters of recommendation. Additional exam requirements/recommendations for international students: Required—TOEFL (minimum score 650 paper-based). *Expenses:* Contact institution. *Faculty research:* Saliva and salivary glands, implantology, material science, periodontal disease, geriatric dentistry.

Texas A&M Health Science Center, Baylor College of Dentistry, Graduate Division, Department of Biomaterials Science, College Station, TX 77840. Offers MS. Part-time programs available. *Degree requirements:* For master's, thesis. *Entrance requirements:* For master's, GRE General Test, DDS or DMD or BS in engineering. Additional exam requirements/recommendations for international students: Required—TOEFL. *Faculty research:* Titanium casting for dental applications, mechanical properties of dental ceramics, metal-ceramic adhesion, fatigue failure of dental implants, orthodontic materials, laser welding.

Texas A&M Health Science Center, Baylor College of Dentistry, Graduate Division, Department of Oral and Maxillofacial Surgery, College Station, TX 77840. Offers MD, Certificate. *Degree requirements:* For Certificate, thesis. *Entrance requirements:* For MD, DAT, MCAT; for Certificate, GRE General Test, National Board Dental Examination, DDS or DMD. Additional exam requirements/recommendations for international students: Required—TOEFL. *Faculty research:* Dental implants, temporomandibular joint, recombinant BMP-2.

Texas A&M Health Science Center, Baylor College of Dentistry, Graduate Division, Department of Orthodontics, College Station, TX 77840. Offers MS, Certificate. *Degree requirements:* For master's and Certificate, thesis. *Entrance requirements:* For master's and Certificate, GRE General Test, National Board Dental Examination, DDS or DMD. Additional exam requirements/recommendations for international students: Required—TOEFL. *Faculty research:* Craniofacial biology, distraction osteogenesis, clinical orthodontics, function and shape memory alloys.

Texas A&M Health Science Center, Baylor College of Dentistry, Graduate Division, Department of Pediatric Dentistry, College Station, TX 77840. Offers MS, Certificate. Part-time programs available. *Degree requirements:* For master's and Certificate, thesis. *Entrance requirements:* For master's and Certificate, GRE General Test, National Board Dental Examination, DDS or DMD. Additional exam requirements/recommendations for international students: Required—TOEFL. *Faculty research:* Pulp biology, pharmacological methods of behavior management.

Texas A&M Health Science Center, Baylor College of Dentistry, Graduate Division, Department of Periodontics, College Station, TX 77840. Offers MS, Certificate. Part-time programs available. *Degree requirements:* For master's and Certificate, thesis. *Entrance requirements:* For master's and Certificate, GRE General Test, National Board Dental Examination, DDS or DMD. Additional exam requirements/recommendations for international students: Required—TOEFL. *Faculty research:* Dental implants, quantification of *candida albicans* in adult periodontitis: a survey, smoking, wound healing, stomatology, gingival overgrowth, diabetes mellitus.

Texas A&M Health Science Center, Baylor College of Dentistry, Graduate Division, Department of Restorative Sciences, Field of Endodontics, College Station, TX 77840. Offers endodontics (Certificate); oral biology (MS, PhD). *Degree requirements:* For master's, thesis; for doctorate, thesis/dissertation. *Entrance requirements:* For master's and Certificate, GRE General Test, National Board Dental Examination, DDS or DMD; for doctorate, GRE General Test, DDS or DMD. Additional exam requirements/recommendations for international students: Required—TOEFL. *Faculty research:* Periradicular healing in response to a biologically inductive root-end filling material.

Texas A&M Health Science Center, Baylor College of Dentistry, Graduate Division, Department of Restorative Sciences, Field of Prosthodontics, College Station, TX 77840. Offers MS, Certificate. Part-time programs available. *Degree requirements:* For master's, thesis. *Entrance requirements:* For master's and Certificate, GRE General Test, National Board Dental Examination, DDS or DMD. Additional exam requirements/recommendations for international students: Required—TOEFL. *Faculty research:* Biomaterials, implants.

Texas A&M Health Science Center, Baylor College of Dentistry, Graduate Division, Program in Oral and Maxillofacial Pathology, College Station, TX 77840. Offers MS, PhD, Certificate. Part-time programs available. Terminal master's awarded for partial completion of doctoral program. *Degree requirements:* For master's, thesis; for doctorate, thesis/dissertation. *Entrance requirements:* For master's and doctorate, GRE General Test, DDS or DMD; for Certificate, GRE General Test, National Board Dental Examination, DDS or DMD. Additional exam requirements/recommendations for international students: Required—TOEFL. *Faculty research:* Oral cancer and precancer, odontogenic tumors, stomatology.

Tufts University, School of Dental Medicine, Advanced Education Programs in Dental Medicine, Medford, MA 02155. Offers dentistry (Certificate), including endodontics, oral and maxillofacial surgery, orthodontics, pediatric dentistry, periodontology, prosthodontics. *Entrance requirements:* Additional exam requirements/recommendations for international students: Required—TOEFL. *Expenses:* Contact institution.

Tufts University, School of Dental Medicine, Graduate Programs in Dental Medicine, Medford, MA 02155. Offers MS. *Degree requirements:* For master's, thesis. *Entrance requirements:* For master's, DDS, DMD, or equivalent; minimum B average. Additional exam requirements/recommendations for international students: Required—TOEFL. *Expenses:* Contact institution. *Faculty research:* Periodontal research, dental materials, salivary research, epidemiology, bone biology.

Université de Montréal, Faculty of Dental Medicine, Program in Multidisciplinary Residency, Montréal, QC H3C 3J7, Canada. Offers Certificate. *Students:* 7 full-time (5 women). In 2009, 6 Certificates awarded. *Application deadline:* For fall admission, 10/1 for domestic students. Application fee: $100. Electronic applications accepted. *Unit head:* Gilles Lavigne, Dean, 514-343-6005, Fax: 514-343-2233, E-mail: gilles.lavigne@umontreal.ca. *Application contact:* Anne Charbonneau, Associate Dean for Studies, 514-343-5761, Fax: 514-343-2233, E-mail: anne.charbonneau@umontreal.ca.

Université de Montréal, Faculty of Dental Medicine, Program in Oral and Dental Sciences, Montréal, QC H3C 3J7, Canada. Offers M Sc. *Students:* 7 full-time (2 women). In 2009, 5 master's awarded. *Application deadline:* For fall admission, 10/1 for domestic students. Application fee: $100. Electronic applications accepted. *Unit head:* Gilles Lavigne, Dean, 514-343-6005, Fax: 514-343-2233, E-mail: gilles.lavigne@umontreal.ca. *Application contact:* Anne Charbonneau, Associate Dean, Graduate Studies, 514-343-5761, Fax: 514-343-2233, E-mail: anne.charbonneau@umontreal.ca.

Université de Montréal, Faculty of Dental Medicine, Program in Orthodontics, Montréal, QC H3C 3J7, Canada. Offers M Sc. *Students:* 12 full-time (5 women). *Application deadline:* For fall admission, 10/1 for domestic students. Application fee: $100. Electronic applications accepted. *Unit head:* Gilles Lavigne, Dean, 514-343-6005, Fax: 514-343-2233, E-mail: gilles.lavigne@umontreal.ca. *Application contact:* Anne Charbonneau, Associate Dean for Graduate Studies, 514-343-5761, Fax: 514-343-2233, E-mail: anne.charbonneau@umontreal.ca.

Université de Montréal, Faculty of Dental Medicine, Program in Pediatric Dentistry, Montréal, QC H3C 3J7, Canada. Offers M Sc. *Students:* 5 full-time (all women). *Application deadline:* For fall admission, 10/1 for domestic students. Application fee: $100. Electronic applications accepted. *Unit head:* Gilles Lavigne, Dean, 514-343-6005, Fax: 514-343-2233, E-mail: gilles.lavigne@umontreal.ca. *Application contact:* Anne Charbonneau, Associate Dean for Graduate Studies, 514-343-5761, Fax: 514-343-2233, E-mail: anne.charbonneau@umontreal.ca.

Université de Montréal, Faculty of Dental Medicine, Program in Prosthodontics Rehabilitation, Montréal, QC H3C 3J7, Canada. Offers M Sc. *Application deadline:* For fall admission, 10/1 for domestic students. Application fee: $100. Electronic applications accepted. *Unit head:* Pierre Boudrias, Director, 514-343-5830, Fax: 514-343-2233, E-mail: pierre.boudrias@umontreal.ca. *Application contact:* Pierre de Grandmont, Responsible for graduate studies, 514-343-2268, Fax: 514-343-2233, E-mail: pierre.de.grandmont@umontreal.ca.

Université Laval, Faculty of Dentistry, Diploma Program in Buccal and Maxillofacial Surgery, Québec, QC G1K 7P4, Canada. Offers DESS. *Degree requirements:* For DESS, comprehensive exam. *Entrance requirements:* For degree, interview, knowledge of French. Electronic applications accepted.

Université Laval, Faculty of Dentistry, Diploma Program in Gerodontology, Québec, QC G1K 7P4, Canada. Offers DESS. Part-time programs available. *Entrance requirements:* For degree, interview, good knowledge of French. Electronic applications accepted.

Université Laval, Faculty of Dentistry, Diploma Program in Multidisciplinary Dentistry, Québec, QC G1K 7P4, Canada. Offers DESS. *Entrance requirements:* For degree, interview, knowledge of French. Electronic applications accepted.

Université Laval, Faculty of Dentistry, Diploma Program in Periodontics, Québec, QC G1K 7P4, Canada. Offers DESS. *Entrance requirements:* For degree, interview, knowledge of French. Electronic applications accepted.

Université Laval, Faculty of Dentistry, Graduate Program in Dentistry, Québec, QC G1K 7P4, Canada. Offers M Sc. *Degree requirements:* For master's, thesis (for some programs). Electronic applications accepted.

University at Buffalo, the State University of New York, Graduate School, School of Dental Medicine, Graduate Programs in Dental Medicine, Department of Oral Biology, Buffalo, NY 14260. Offers PhD. *Degree requirements:* For doctorate, thesis/dissertation. *Entrance requirements:* For doctorate, GRE General Test, GRE Subject Test in biology or DDS. Additional exam requirements/recommendations for international students: Required—TOEFL (minimum score 79 iBT). Electronic applications accepted. *Faculty research:* Oral immunology and microbiology, bone physiology, biochemistry, molecular genetics, neutrophil biology.

University at Buffalo, the State University of New York, Graduate School, School of Dental Medicine, Graduate Programs in Dental Medicine, Department of Oral Diagnostic Sciences, Buffalo, NY 14260. Offers biomaterials (MS). Part-time programs available. *Degree requirements:* For master's, thesis. *Entrance requirements:* Additional exam requirements/recommendations for international students: Required—TOEFL (minimum score 79 iBT). Electronic applications accepted. *Faculty research:* Bioengineering, surface science, bioadhesion, regulatory sterilization.

University at Buffalo, the State University of New York, Graduate School, School of Dental Medicine, Graduate Programs in Dental Medicine, Department of Orthodontics, Buffalo, NY 14260. Offers MS. *Faculty:* 3 full-time (1 woman), 4 part-time/adjunct (1 woman). *Students:* 6 full-time (4 women); includes 1 minority (Asian American or Pacific Islander), 1 international. Average age 25. 200 applicants, 3% accepted, 6 enrolled. In 2009, 6 master's awarded. *Degree requirements:* For master's, thesis. *Entrance requirements:* For master's, DDS or equivalent. Additional exam requirements/recommendations for international students: Required—TOEFL (minimum score 500 paper-based; 79 iBT). *Application deadline:* For fall admission, 9/1 for domestic and international students. Application fee: $50. Electronic applications accepted. *Faculty research:* Stem cell, clinical respiration, growth and development. *Unit head:* Dr. C. Brian Preston, Chairman, 716-829-2845, Fax: 716-829-2572, E-mail: cbp@buffalo.edu. *Application contact:* Kristin Yager, Admissions Secretary, 716-829-2839, Fax: 716-833-3517, E-mail: kmyager2@buffalo.edu.

University at Buffalo, the State University of New York, Graduate School, School of Dental Medicine, Graduate Programs in Dental Medicine, Program in Oral Sciences, Buffalo, NY 14260. Offers MS. *Degree requirements:* For master's, thesis. *Entrance requirements:* For master's, DDS, DMD, or equivalent foreign degree. Additional exam requirements/recommendations for international students: Required—TOEFL (minimum score 79 iBT). Electronic applications accepted. *Faculty research:* Oral biology and pathology, behavioral sciences, neuromuscular physiology, facial pain, oral microbiology.

The University of Alabama at Birmingham, School of Dentistry, Graduate Programs in Dentistry, Birmingham, AL 35294. Offers MS. *Degree requirements:* For master's, thesis. Electronic applications accepted.

University of Alberta, Faculty of Medicine and Dentistry, Department of Dentistry, Program in Orthodontics, Edmonton, AB T6G 2E1, Canada. Offers M Sc, PhD. *Faculty:* 4 full-time (1 woman), 10 part-time/adjunct (1 woman). *Students:* 17 full-time (6 women). Average age 30. 70 applicants, 6% accepted, 4 enrolled. In 2009, 3 master's awarded. *Degree requirements:* For master's, thesis; for doctorate, thesis/dissertation. *Entrance requirements:* Additional exam requirements/recommendations for international students: Required—TOEFL (minimum score 580 paper-based; 237 computer-based). *Application deadline:* For fall admission, 10/1 for domestic and international students. Application fee: $100. Electronic applications accepted. Tuition and fees charges are reported in Canadian dollars. *Expenses:* Tuition, area resident: Full-time $4626 Canadian dollars; part-time $99.72 Canadian dollars per unit. International tuition: $8216 Canadian dollars full-time. Required fees: $3590 Canadian dollars; $99.72 Canadian dollars per unit. $215 Canadian dollars per term. *Financial support:* In 2009–10, 1 student received support, including research assistantships (averaging $3,000 per year); institutionally sponsored loans and scholarships/grants also available. *Unit head:* Dr. Paul Major, Head, 780-492-4469, Fax: 780-492-1624, E-mail: major@ualberta.ca. *Application contact:* Dr. Paul Major, Head, 780-492-4469, Fax: 780-492-1624, E-mail: major@ualberta.ca.

The University of British Columbia, Faculty of Dentistry and Faculty of Graduate Studies, Graduate/Postgraduate and Professional Specialty Programs in Dentistry, Vancouver, BC V6T 1Z1, Canada. Offers dental science (M Sc, PhD); periodontics (Diploma). *Degree requirements:* For master's, thesis; for doctorate, comprehensive exam, thesis/dissertation. *Entrance requirements:* For degree, dental license, interview. Additional exam requirements/recommendations for international students: Required—TOEFL (minimum score 580 paper-based; 237 computer-based). Electronic applications accepted. *Expenses:* Contact institution. *Faculty research:* Cell biology, oral physiology, microbiology, immunology, biomaterials.

University of California, Los Angeles, Graduate Division, College of Letters and Science and David Geffen School of Medicine, UCLA ACCESS to Programs in the Molecular, Cellular and Integrative Life Sciences, Los Angeles, CA 90095. Offers biochemistry and molecular biology (PhD); biological chemistry (PhD); cellular and molecular pathology (PhD); human genetics (PhD); microbiology, immunology, and molecular genetics (PhD); molecular biology (PhD); molecular toxicology (PhD); molecular, cellular and integrative physiology (PhD); neurobiology (PhD); oral biology (PhD); physiology (PhD). ACCESS is an umbrella program for first-year coursework in 12 PhD programs. *Students:* 39 full-time (25 women); includes 14 minority (1 African American, 1 American Indian/Alaska Native, 8 Asian Americans or Pacific Islanders, 4 Hispanic Americans), 10 international. Average age 25. 437 applicants, 22% accepted, 30 enrolled. *Degree requirements:* For doctorate, thesis/dissertation, oral and written qualifying exams. *Entrance requirements:* For doctorate, GRE General Test, minimum undergraduate GPA of 3.0. Additional exam requirements/recommendations for international students: Required—TOEFL. *Application deadline:* For fall admission, 12/15 for domestic and international students. Application fee: $70 ($90 for international students). Electronic applications accepted. *Financial support:* In 2009–10, 56 fellowships with full and partial tuition reimbursements, 16 research assistantships with full and partial tuition reimbursements were awarded; teaching assistantships with full and partial tuition reimbursements, Federal Work-Study, institutionally sponsored loans, scholarships/grants, health care benefits, tuition waivers (full and partial), and unspecified assistantships also available. Financial award application deadline: 3/1; financial award applicants required to submit FAFSA. *Faculty research:* Molecular, cellular, and developmental biology; immunology; microbiology; integrative biology. *Unit head:* Dr. Greg I. Payne, Chair, 310-206-3121. *Application contact:* Coordinator, 310-206-3121, Fax: 310-206-5280, E-mail: uclaaccess@mednet.ucla.edu.

University of California, Los Angeles, School of Dentistry and Graduate Division, Graduate Programs in Dentistry, Program in Oral Biology, Los Angeles, CA 90095. Offers MS, PhD, DDS/MS, DDS/PhD, MD/PhD, MS/Certificate, PhD/Certificate. *Degree requirements:* For master's, thesis; for doctorate, thesis/dissertation, oral and written qualifying exams. *Entrance requirements:* For doctorate, GRE General Test. *Faculty research:* Neurophysiology, immunology of periodontal disease.

University of California, San Francisco, Graduate Division, Program in Oral and Craniofacial Sciences, San Francisco, CA 94143. Offers MS, PhD. Terminal master's awarded for partial completion of doctoral program. *Degree requirements:* For master's, thesis; for doctorate, thesis/dissertation. *Entrance requirements:* For master's and doctorate, GRE General Test.

University of Connecticut, Graduate School, University of Connecticut Health Center, Field of Dental Science, Storrs, CT 06269. Offers M Dent Sc. *Faculty:* 50 full-time (17 women). *Students:* 2 full-time (0 women), 40 part-time (18 women); includes 8 minority (1 African American, 7 Asian Americans or Pacific Islanders), 13 international. Average age 31. 16 applicants, 25% accepted, 1 enrolled. In 2009, 11 master's awarded. *Degree requirements:* For master's, comprehensive exam. *Entrance requirements:* For master's, GRE General Test. Additional exam requirements/recommendations for international students: Required—TOEFL (minimum score 550 paper-based; 213 computer-based). *Application deadline:* For fall admission, 2/1 priority date for domestic and international students; for spring admission, 11/1 for domestic students, 10/1 for international students. Applications are processed on a rolling basis. Application fee: $55. Electronic applications accepted. *Expenses:* Tuition, state resident: full-time $4725; part-time $525 per credit. Tuition, nonresident: full-time $12,267; part-time $1363 per credit. Required fees: $346 per semester. Tuition and fees vary according to course load. *Financial support:* In 2009–10, 1 research assistantship with full tuition reimbursement was awarded; Federal Work-Study, scholarships/grants, health care benefits, and unspecified assistantships also available. Financial award application deadline: 2/1; financial award applicants required to submit FAFSA. *Application contact:* Margaret Sweet-Hoffman, Administrative Assistant, 860-679-2574, Fax: 860-679-1899, E-mail: sweethoffm@nso.uchc.edu.

Oral and Dental Sciences

University of Connecticut Health Center, Graduate School, Programs in Biomedical Sciences, Combined Degree Programs in Oral Biology, Farmington, CT 06030. Offers DMD/PhD. *Faculty:* 172 full-time. *Students:* 8 full-time (4 women); includes 1 minority (Asian American or Pacific Islander). Average age 30. *Entrance requirements:* Additional exam requirements/recommendations for international students: Required—TOEFL (minimum score 600 paper-based; 250 computer-based). *Application deadline:* For fall admission, 2/1 for domestic students. Applications are processed on a rolling basis. Application fee: $75. *Financial support:* In 2009–10, 8 students received support, including 8 research assistantships with full tuition reimbursements available (averaging $27,000 per year); fellowships also available. *Unit head:* Dr. Alan Lurie, Director, 860-679-4049, Fax: 860-679-4760, E-mail: lurie@nso.uchc.edu. *Application contact:* Dr. Alan Lurie, Director, 860-679-4049, Fax: 860-679-4760, E-mail: lurie@nso.uchc.edu.

University of Connecticut Health Center, Graduate School, Programs in Biomedical Sciences, Program in Skeletal, Craniofacial and Oral Biology, Farmington, CT 06030. Offers PhD, DMD/PhD, MD/PhD. *Faculty:* 24. *Students:* 16 full-time (11 women); includes 4 minority (1 African American, 1 Asian American or Pacific Islander, 2 Hispanic Americans), 5 international. Average age 29. 165 applicants, 35% accepted. In 2009, 5 doctorates awarded. *Degree requirements:* For doctorate, comprehensive exam, thesis/dissertation. *Entrance requirements:* For doctorate, GRE General Test. Additional exam requirements/recommendations for international students: Required—TOEFL (minimum score 600 paper-based; 250 computer-based). *Application deadline:* For fall admission, 12/15 for domestic students. Application fee: $55. Electronic applications accepted. *Financial support:* In 2009–10, 16 students received support, including 16 research assistantships with tuition reimbursements available (averaging $27,000 per year); fellowships, health care benefits also available. *Faculty research:* Skeletal development and patterning, bone biology, connective tissue biology, neurophysiology of taste and smell, microbiological aspects of caries. *Unit head:* Dr. Mina Mina, Director, 860-679-4081, Fax: 860-679-4078, E-mail: mina@ns01.uchc.edu. *Application contact:* Tricia Avolt, Graduate Admissions Coordinator, 860-679-2175, Fax: 860-679-1899, E-mail: robertson@nso2.uchc.edu.

See Close-Up on page 1751.

University of Connecticut Health Center, School of Dental Medicine, Program in Dental Science, Farmington, CT 06030. Offers MDS. Part-time programs available. *Faculty:* 85 full-time (28 women). *Students:* 2 full-time (0 women), 39 part-time (18 women); includes 8 minority (1 African American, 7 Asian Americans or Pacific Islanders), 12 international. Average age 31. 184 applicants, 10% accepted, 17 enrolled. In 2009, 9 master's awarded. *Degree requirements:* For master's, comprehensive exam, thesis. *Entrance requirements:* For master's, National Board Dental Examination Parts I and II. Application fee: $75. *Expenses:* Contact institution. *Financial support:* In 2009–10, 1 research assistantship with full tuition reimbursement (averaging $27,000 per year) was awarded. Financial award application deadline: 4/15; financial award applicants required to submit FAFSA. *Unit head:* Dr. Steven Lepowsky, Associate Dean for Education and Patient Care, 860-679-4885, Fax: 860-679-3201, E-mail: lepowsky@nso.uchc.edu. *Application contact:* Cindy Phoenix, Administrative Program Coordinator, 860-679-2574, Fax: 860-679-1899, E-mail: sweethoffm@nso1.uchc.edu.

University of Detroit Mercy, School of Dentistry, Department of Endodontics, Detroit, MI 48221. Offers MS, Certificate. *Degree requirements:* For master's, thesis. *Entrance requirements:* For master's, DDS or DMD; for Certificate, DAT, DDS or DMD. *Faculty research:* Roof and filling materials, cavity preparations, pulp biology.

University of Detroit Mercy, School of Dentistry, Department of Orthodontics, Detroit, MI 48221. Offers MS, Certificate. *Degree requirements:* For master's, thesis. *Entrance requirements:* For master's, DDS or DMD; for Certificate, DAT, DDS or DMD. *Faculty research:* Changes in oral flora due to fixed orthodontic appliances, cranioskeletal osteogenesis.

University of Detroit Mercy, School of Dentistry, Department of Periodontology and Dental Hygiene, Detroit, MI 48221. Offers periodontics (MS, Certificate).

University of Florida, College of Dentistry and Graduate School, Graduate Programs in Dentistry, Department of Endodontics, Gainesville, FL 32611. Offers MS, Certificate. *Entrance requirements:* For master's, DAT, GRE General Test, National Board Dental Examination Parts I and II, minimum GPA of 3.0, interview; for Certificate, DAT. Additional exam requirements/recommendations for international students: Required—TOEFL (minimum score 550 paper-based; 213 computer-based). *Faculty research:* Canal cleanliness, antibiotics, resilon, lasers, microbes.

University of Florida, College of Dentistry and Graduate School, Graduate Programs in Dentistry, Department of Oral Biology, Gainesville, FL 32611. Offers PhD. *Degree requirements:* For doctorate, thesis/dissertation. *Entrance requirements:* For doctorate, GRE General Test, minimum GPA of 3.0. Additional exam requirements/recommendations for international students: Required—TOEFL. Electronic applications accepted. *Faculty research:* Bacterial genetics, cell adhesion, salivary glands, cell proliferation.

University of Florida, College of Dentistry and Graduate School, Graduate Programs in Dentistry, Department of Orthodontics, Gainesville, FL 32611. Offers MS, Certificate. *Degree requirements:* For master's, thesis. *Entrance requirements:* For master's, DAT, GRE General Test, National Board Dental Examination Parts I and II, minimum GPA of 3.0, interview. Additional exam requirements/recommendations for international students: Required—TOEFL (minimum score 550 paper-based; 213 computer-based). *Faculty research:* Bone biology, osteoclasts, clinical research, root resorption, pain control.

University of Florida, College of Dentistry and Graduate School, Graduate Programs in Dentistry, Department of Periodontology, Gainesville, FL 32611. Offers MS, Certificate. *Degree requirements:* For master's, thesis. *Entrance requirements:* For master's, DAT, GRE General Test, National Board Dental Examination Parts I and II, minimum GPA of 3.0, interview. Additional exam requirements/recommendations for international students: Required—TOEFL (minimum score 550 paper-based; 213 computer-based). *Faculty research:* Gingival grafting, periodontal plastic surgery, regenerative periodontal surgery, dental implant complications, osteogenic fibroma.

University of Florida, College of Dentistry and Graduate School, Graduate Programs in Dentistry, Department of Prosthodontics, Gainesville, FL 32611. Offers MS, Certificate. *Degree requirements:* For master's, thesis. *Entrance requirements:* For master's, DAT, GRE General Test, National Board Dental Examination Parts I and II, minimum GPA of 3.0, interview. Additional exam requirements/recommendations for international students: Required—TOEFL (minimum score 550 paper-based; 213 computer-based). *Faculty research:* Computer panograph, dental implants, resin provisional materials wear rate, implant surface variation, Sjorgen's Syndrome.

University of Illinois at Chicago, College of Dentistry and Graduate College, Graduate Programs in Oral Sciences, Chicago, IL 60607-7128. Offers MS, PhD. *Degree requirements:* For master's, thesis. *Entrance requirements:* For master's, GRE General Test, DDS, DVM, or MD. Additional exam requirements/recommendations for international students: Required—TOEFL. Electronic applications accepted. *Expenses:* Contact institution.

The University of Iowa, College of Dentistry and Graduate College, Graduate Programs in Dentistry, Department of Endodontics, Iowa City, IA 52242-1316. Offers MS, Certificate. *Degree requirements:* For master's, thesis. *Entrance requirements:* For master's, GRE, DDS; for Certificate, DDS. Additional exam requirements/recommendations for international students: Required—TOEFL.

The University of Iowa, College of Dentistry and Graduate College, Graduate Programs in Dentistry, Department of Operative Dentistry, Iowa City, IA 52242-1316. Offers MS, Certificate. *Degree requirements:* For master's, thesis. *Entrance requirements:* For master's, GRE, DDS; for Certificate, DDS. Additional exam requirements/recommendations for international students: Required—TOEFL.

The University of Iowa, College of Dentistry and Graduate College, Graduate Programs in Dentistry, Department of Oral and Maxillofacial Surgery, Iowa City, IA 52242-1316. Offers MS, Certificate. *Degree requirements:* For master's, thesis. *Entrance requirements:* For master's, GRE, DDS; for Certificate, DDS.

The University of Iowa, College of Dentistry and Graduate College, Graduate Programs in Dentistry, Department of Oral Pathology, Radiology and Medicine, Iowa City, IA 52242-1316. Offers oral and maxillofacial pathology (Certificate); oral and maxillofacial radiology (Certificate); stomatology (MS). *Degree requirements:* For master's, thesis. *Entrance requirements:* For master's, GRE, DDS, minimum GPA of 2.7. Additional exam requirements/recommendations for international students: Required—TOEFL.

The University of Iowa, College of Dentistry and Graduate College, Graduate Programs in Dentistry, Department of Orthodontics, Iowa City, IA 52242-1316. Offers MS, Certificate. *Degree requirements:* For master's, thesis. *Entrance requirements:* For master's, GRE, DDS; for Certificate, DDS. Additional exam requirements/recommendations for international students: Required—TOEFL.

The University of Iowa, College of Dentistry and Graduate College, Graduate Programs in Dentistry, Department of Pediatric Dentistry, Iowa City, IA 52242-1316. Offers Certificate. *Entrance requirements:* For degree, DDS. Additional exam requirements/recommendations for international students: Required—TOEFL.

The University of Iowa, College of Dentistry and Graduate College, Graduate Programs in Dentistry, Department of Periodontics, Iowa City, IA 52242-1316. Offers MS, Certificate. *Degree requirements:* For master's, thesis. *Entrance requirements:* For master's, GRE, DDS; for Certificate, DDS. Additional exam requirements/recommendations for international students: Required—TOEFL.

The University of Iowa, College of Dentistry and Graduate College, Graduate Programs in Dentistry, Department of Preventive and Community Dentistry, Iowa City, IA 52242-1316. Offers dental public health (MS). *Degree requirements:* For master's, thesis. *Entrance requirements:* For master's, GRE, DDS. Additional exam requirements/recommendations for international students: Required—TOEFL.

The University of Iowa, College of Dentistry and Graduate College, Graduate Programs in Dentistry, Department of Prosthodontics, Iowa City, IA 52242-1316. Offers MS, Certificate. *Degree requirements:* For master's, thesis. *Entrance requirements:* For master's, GRE, DDS; for Certificate, DDS. Additional exam requirements/recommendations for international students: Required—TOEFL.

The University of Iowa, College of Dentistry and Graduate College, Graduate Programs in Dentistry, Oral Science Graduate Program, Iowa City, IA 52242-1316. Offers MS, PhD. *Degree requirements:* For master's, thesis; for doctorate, thesis/dissertation. *Entrance requirements:* For master's, GRE, DDS. Additional exam requirements/recommendations for international students: Required—TOEFL.

University of Kentucky, Graduate School, Graduate Program in Dentistry, Lexington, KY 40506-0032. Offers MS. *Degree requirements:* For master's, comprehensive exam, thesis. *Entrance requirements:* For master's, GRE General Test, minimum undergraduate GPA of 2.5. Additional exam requirements/recommendations for international students: Required—TOEFL (minimum score 550 paper-based; 213 computer-based). Electronic applications accepted.

University of Louisville, School of Dentistry, Louisville, KY 40202. Offers oral biology (MS). *Accreditation:* ADA (one or more programs are accredited). Part-time programs available. *Faculty:* 63 full-time (20 women), 84 part-time/adjunct (22 women). *Students:* 360 full-time (171 women), 6 part-time (5 women); includes 59 minority (29 African Americans, 7 American Indian/Alaska Native, 19 Asian Americans or Pacific Islanders, 4 Hispanic Americans), 10 international. Average age 26. 2,895 applicants, 11% accepted, 196 enrolled. In 2009, 78 first professional degrees, 10 master's awarded. *Degree requirements:* For master's, thesis; for DMD, National Board exams. *Entrance requirements:* For DMD, DAT, 32 hours of course work in science; for master's, DAT or GRE General Test, minimum GPA of 2.75. Additional exam requirements/recommendations for international students: Required—TOEFL (minimum score 100 iBT). *Application deadline:* For fall admission, 1/1 for domestic and international students. Applications are processed on a rolling basis. Application fee: $50. Electronic applications accepted. *Expenses:* Contact institution. *Financial support:* In 2009–10, 88 students received support, including 1 research assistantship with full tuition reimbursement available (averaging $20,000 per year). Financial award application deadline: 3/15. *Faculty research:* Inflammation and periondontitis, birth defects and developmental biology, biomaterials, oral infections, digital imaging. *Unit head:* Dr. John J. Sauk, Dean, 502-852-1304, Fax: 502-852-3364, E-mail: jjsauk01@louisville.edu. *Application contact:* Robin Benningfield, Admissions Counselor, 502-852-5081, Fax: 502-852-1210, E-mail: dmdadms@louisville.edu.

University of Manitoba, Faculty of Dentistry and Faculty of Graduate Studies, Graduate Programs in Dentistry, Department of Dental Diagnostic and Surgical Sciences, Winnipeg, MB R3T 2N2, Canada. Offers oral and maxillofacial surgery (M Dent); periodontology (M Dent). *Entrance requirements:* For master's, dental degree. *Faculty research:* Implantology, clinical trials, tobacco use, periodontal disease.

University of Manitoba, Faculty of Dentistry and Faculty of Graduate Studies, Graduate Programs in Dentistry, Department of Oral Biology, Winnipeg, MB R3T 2N2, Canada. Offers M Sc, PhD. *Degree requirements:* For master's, thesis; for doctorate, comprehensive exam, thesis/dissertation. *Entrance requirements:* For master's, B Sc or pre-M Sc. Additional exam requirements/recommendations for international students: Required—TOEFL (minimum score 250 computer-based). *Faculty research:* Oral bacterial ecology and metabolism, biofilms, saliva and oral health, secretory mechanisms.

University of Manitoba, Faculty of Dentistry and Faculty of Graduate Studies, Graduate Programs in Dentistry, Department of Preventive Dental Science, Winnipeg, MB R3T 2N2, Canada. Offers orthodontics (M Sc). *Degree requirements:* For master's, thesis. *Entrance requirements:* For master's, dental degree. Electronic applications accepted.

University of Maryland, Baltimore, Graduate School, Graduate Programs in Dentistry, Department of Oral Pathology, Baltimore, MD 21201. Offers MS, PhD. *Students:* 5 full-time (2 women); includes 1 minority (American Indian/Alaska Native), 4 international. Average age 31. 6 applicants, 17% accepted, 0 enrolled. In 2009, 1 doctorate awarded. *Degree requirements:* For master's, thesis or alternative; for doctorate, comprehensive exam, thesis/dissertation. *Entrance requirements:* For master's and doctorate, GRE General Test, DDS, DMD. Additional exam requirements/recommendations for international students: Required—TOEFL (minimum score 550 paper-based; 80 iBT), or IELTS (minimum score 7). *Application deadline:* For fall admission, 7/1 for domestic students, 1/15 for international students. Application fee: $50. Electronic applications accepted. *Expenses:* Tuition, state resident: full-time $7290; part-time $405 per credit hour. Tuition, nonresident: full-time $12,780; part-time $710 per credit hour. Required fees: $774; $10 per credit hour. $297 per semester. Tuition and fees vary according to course load, degree level and program. *Financial support:* Fellowships, research assistantships, teaching assistantships available. Support available to part-time students. Financial award application deadline: 2/15. *Faculty research:* Histopathology, epidemiology of oral lesions, embryology. *Unit head:* Dr. John J. Sauk, Chairman, 410-706-7936, Fax: 410-706-0193, E-mail: jjs001@dental.umaryland.edu. *Application contact:* Dr. Bernard A. Levy, Director, 410-706-7936, Fax: 410-706-0193, E-mail: bal002@dental.umaryland.edu.

University of Maryland, Baltimore, Graduate School, Graduate Programs in Dentistry, Graduate Program in Biomedical Sciences—Dental School, Baltimore, MD 21201. Offers MS, PhD, DDS/PhD. *Students:* 2 full-time (both women), 3 part-time (2 women); includes 1 minority (African American), 3 international. Average age 35. 12 applicants, 0% accepted, 0 enrolled. In 2009, 13 master's, 4 doctorates awarded. *Degree requirements:* For master's, thesis optional; for doctorate, comprehensive exam, thesis/dissertation. *Entrance requirements:* For master's and doctorate, GRE General Test. Additional exam requirements/recommendations for inter-

national students: Required—TOEFL (minimum score 550 paper-based; 80 iBT), or IELTS (minimum score 7). *Application deadline:* For fall admission, 7/1 for domestic students, 1/15 for international students. *Application fee:* $50. Electronic applications accepted. *Expenses:* Tuition, state resident: full-time $7290; part-time $405 per credit hour. Tuition, nonresident: full-time $12,780; part-time $710 per credit hour. Required fees: $774; $10 per credit hour. $297 per semester. Tuition and fees vary according to course load, degree level and program. *Financial support:* In 2009–10, research assistantships with full tuition reimbursements (averaging $23,000 per year). *Faculty research:* Neuroscience, molecular and cell biology, infectious diseases. *Unit head:* Dr. Ronald Dubner, Professor and Chair, 410-706-0860, Fax: 410-706-0865, E-mail: rdubner@dental.umaryland.edu. *Application contact:* Dr. Norman Capra, Graduate Program Director, 410-706-4219, Fax: 410-706-0865, E-mail: ncapra@umaryland.edu.

University of Maryland, Baltimore, Professional and Advanced Education Programs in Dentistry, Baltimore, MD 21201-1627. Offers advanced general dentistry (Certificate); dentistry (DDS); endodontics (Certificate); oral and experimental pathology (Certificate); oral biology (MS); oral-maxillofacial surgery (Certificate); orthodontics (Certificate); pediatric dentistry (Certificate); periodontics (Certificate); prosthodontics (Certificate); DDS/MBA; DDS/PhD. *Accreditation:* ADA. *Entrance requirements:* DAT. Additional exam requirements/recommendations for international students: Required—TOEFL. *Application deadline:* For fall admission, 1/1 for domestic students. Applications are processed on a rolling basis. Application fee: $75. *Expenses:* Contact institution. *Financial support:* Career-related internships or fieldwork, Federal Work-Study, institutionally sponsored loans, scholarships/grants, and unspecified assistantships available. Financial award application deadline: 3/1; financial award applicants required to submit FAFSA. *Faculty research:* Pain, neuroscience, cancer biology. *Unit head:* Dr. Christian S. Stohler, Dean, 410-706-7461. *Application contact:* Dr. Patricia Meehan, Assistant Dean for Admissions, 410-706-7472, Fax: 410-706-0945, E-mail: ddsadmissions@umaryland.edu.

University of Medicine and Dentistry of New Jersey, New Jersey Dental School, Newark, NJ 07101-1709. Offers dental science (MS); dentistry (DMD); endodontics (Certificate); oral medicine (Certificate); orthodontics (Certificate); pediatric dentistry (Certificate); periodontics (Certificate); prosthodontics (Certificate); DMD/MPH; DMD/PhD; MD/Certificate; MS/Certificate. *Accreditation:* ADA (one or more programs are accredited). *Entrance requirements:* DAT. Electronic applications accepted. *Expenses:* Contact institution.

University of Michigan, School of Dentistry and Horace H. Rackham School of Graduate Studies, Graduate Programs in Dentistry, Biomaterials Program, Ann Arbor, MI 48109-1078. Offers MS. Part-time and evening/weekend programs available. Postbaccalaureate distance learning degree programs offered (minimal on-campus study). Terminal master's awarded for partial completion of doctoral program. *Degree requirements:* For master's, thesis. *Entrance requirements:* Additional exam requirements/recommendations for international students: Required—TOEFL (minimum score 84 iBT). Electronic applications accepted. *Expenses:* Tuition, state resident: full-time $17,286; part-time $1099 per credit hour. Tuition, nonresident: full-time $34,944; part-time $2080 per credit hour. Required fees: $95 per semester. Tuition and fees vary according to course load, degree level and program.

University of Michigan, School of Dentistry and Horace H. Rackham School of Graduate Studies, Graduate Programs in Dentistry, Endodontics Program, Ann Arbor, MI 48109-1078. Offers MS. *Degree requirements:* For master's, thesis. *Entrance requirements:* For master's, DDS. Additional exam requirements/recommendations for international students: Required—TOEFL (minimum score 84 iBT). Electronic applications accepted. *Expenses:* Tuition, state resident: full-time $17,286; part-time $1099 per credit hour. Tuition, nonresident: full-time $34,944; part-time $2080 per credit hour. Required fees: $95 per semester. Tuition and fees vary according to course load, degree level and program.

University of Michigan, School of Dentistry and Horace H. Rackham School of Graduate Studies, Graduate Programs in Dentistry, Orthodontics Program, Ann Arbor, MI 48109-1078. Offers MS. Part-time and evening/weekend programs available. Postbaccalaureate distance learning degree programs offered (minimal on-campus study). Terminal master's awarded for partial completion of doctoral program. *Degree requirements:* For master's, thesis. *Entrance requirements:* For master's, GRE, National Dental Board Exam, DDS. Additional exam requirements/recommendations for international students: Required—TOEFL (minimum score 84 iBT). Electronic applications accepted. *Expenses:* Tuition, state resident: full-time $17,286; part-time $1099 per credit hour. Tuition, nonresident: full-time $34,944; part-time $2080 per credit hour. Required fees: $95 per semester. Tuition and fees vary according to course load, degree level and program.

University of Michigan, School of Dentistry and Horace H. Rackham School of Graduate Studies, Graduate Programs in Dentistry, Pediatric Dentistry Program, Ann Arbor, MI 48109-1078. Offers MS. Part-time and evening/weekend programs available. Postbaccalaureate distance learning degree programs offered (minimal on-campus study). Terminal master's awarded for partial completion of doctoral program. *Degree requirements:* For master's, thesis. *Entrance requirements:* For master's, DDS. Additional exam requirements/recommendations for international students: Required—TOEFL (minimum score 84 iBT). Electronic applications accepted. *Expenses:* Tuition, state resident: full-time $17,286; part-time $1099 per credit hour. Tuition, nonresident: full-time $34,944; part-time $2080 per credit hour. Required fees: $95 per semester. Tuition and fees vary according to course load, degree level and program.

University of Michigan, School of Dentistry and Horace H. Rackham School of Graduate Studies, Graduate Programs in Dentistry, Periodontics Program, Ann Arbor, MI 48109-1078. Offers MS. *Degree requirements:* For master's, thesis. *Entrance requirements:* For master's, DDS. Additional exam requirements/recommendations for international students: Required—TOEFL (minimum score 84 iBT). Electronic applications accepted. *Expenses:* Tuition, state resident: full-time $17,286; part-time $1099 per credit hour. Tuition, nonresident: full-time $34,944; part-time $2080 per credit hour. Required fees: $95 per semester. Tuition and fees vary according to course load, degree level and program.

University of Michigan, School of Dentistry and Horace H. Rackham School of Graduate Studies, Graduate Programs in Dentistry, Prosthodontics Program, Ann Arbor, MI 48109-1078. Offers MS. Part-time and evening/weekend programs available. Postbaccalaureate distance learning degree programs offered (minimal on-campus study). Terminal master's awarded for partial completion of doctoral program. *Degree requirements:* For master's, thesis. *Entrance requirements:* For master's, DDS. Additional exam requirements/recommendations for international students: Required—TOEFL (minimum score 84 iBT). Electronic applications accepted. *Expenses:* Tuition, state resident: full-time $17,286; part-time $1099 per credit hour. Tuition, nonresident: full-time $34,944; part-time $2080 per credit hour. Required fees: $95 per semester. Tuition and fees vary according to course load, degree level and program.

University of Michigan, School of Dentistry and Horace H. Rackham School of Graduate Studies, Graduate Programs in Dentistry, Restorative Dentistry Program, Ann Arbor, MI 48109-1078. Offers MS. Part-time programs available. *Degree requirements:* For master's, thesis. *Entrance requirements:* Additional exam requirements/recommendations for international students: Required—TOEFL (minimum score 84 iBT). Electronic applications accepted. *Expenses:* Tuition, state resident: full-time $17,286; part-time $1099 per credit hour. Tuition, nonresident: full-time $34,944; part-time $2080 per credit hour. Required fees: $95 per semester. Tuition and fees vary according to course load, degree level and program.

University of Michigan, School of Dentistry, Oral Health Sciences PhD Program, Ann Arbor, MI 48109-1078. Offers PhD. *Faculty:* 32 full-time (8 women). *Students:* 15 full-time (10 women). Average age 30. 20 applicants, 25% accepted, 2 enrolled. In 2009, 2 doctorates awarded. *Degree requirements:* For doctorate, thesis/dissertation, preliminary exam, oral defense of dissertation. *Entrance requirements:* For doctorate, GRE. Additional exam requirements/recommendations for international students: Required—TOEFL. *Application deadline:* For fall admission, 1/5 priority date for domestic and international students. Applications are processed on a rolling basis. Application fee: $60 ($75 for international students).

Electronic applications accepted. *Expenses:* Tuition, state resident: full-time $17,286; part-time $1099 per credit hour. Tuition, nonresident: full-time $34,944; part-time $2080 per credit hour. Required fees: $95 per semester. Tuition and fees vary according to course load, degree level and program. *Financial support:* In 2009–10, 11 fellowships with full tuition reimbursements (averaging $22,000 per year), 3 research assistantships with full tuition reimbursements (averaging $22,000 per year) were awarded; scholarships/grants, traineeships, and health care benefits also available. *Faculty research:* Craniofacial development; oral and pharyngeal cancer; mineralized tissue biology and musculoskeletal disorders; tissue engineering and regeneration; oral infectious and immunologic diseases; oral sensory systems and central circuits. Total annual research expenditures: $16.2 million. *Unit head:* Dr. Charlotte M. Mistretta, Associate Dean for Research and PhD Training, 734-615-1970, E-mail: ohsphd@umich.edu. *Application contact:* Patricia E. Schultz, PhD Training Manager, 734-615-1970, E-mail: ohsphd@umich.edu.

University of Minnesota, Twin Cities Campus, School of Dentistry and Graduate School, Graduate Programs in Dentistry, Advanced Education Program in Periodontology, Minneapolis, MN 55455-0213. Offers MS. *Degree requirements:* For master's, comprehensive exam, thesis. *Entrance requirements:* For master's, DDS/DMD, letter from Dental Dean, specific GGP/class rank, two letters of recommendation. Additional exam requirements/recommendations for international students: Required—TOEFL (minimum score 590 paper-based; 243 computer-based). *Faculty research:* Periodontitis, risk factors, regenerating, diabetes immunology.

University of Minnesota, Twin Cities Campus, School of Dentistry and Graduate School, Graduate Programs in Dentistry, Division of Endodontics, Minneapolis, MN 55455-0213. Offers MS, Certificate. *Degree requirements:* For master's, thesis. *Entrance requirements:* Additional exam requirements/recommendations for international students: Required—TOEFL. *Faculty research:* Pain, inflammation, neuropharmacology, neuropeptides, cytokines.

University of Minnesota, Twin Cities Campus, School of Dentistry and Graduate School, Graduate Programs in Dentistry, Division of Orthodontics, Minneapolis, MN 55455-0213. Offers MS. *Degree requirements:* For master's, thesis. *Entrance requirements:* Additional exam requirements/recommendations for international students: Required—TOEFL (minimum score 587 paper-based; 240 computer-based). *Faculty research:* Bone biology, 3-D imaging.

University of Minnesota, Twin Cities Campus, School of Dentistry and Graduate School, Graduate Programs in Dentistry, Division of Pediatric Dentistry, Minneapolis, MN 55455-0213. Offers MS. *Degree requirements:* For master's, thesis. *Entrance requirements:* Additional exam requirements/recommendations for international students: Required—TOEFL. *Faculty research:* Molecular genetics of facial growth, dental material/adhesion, expanded functions dental auxiliary utilization.

University of Minnesota, Twin Cities Campus, School of Dentistry and Graduate School, Graduate Programs in Dentistry, Division of Prosthodontics, Minneapolis, MN 55455-0213. Offers MS. *Degree requirements:* For master's, thesis, clinical. *Entrance requirements:* Additional exam requirements/recommendations for international students: Required—TOEFL.

University of Minnesota, Twin Cities Campus, School of Dentistry and Graduate School, Graduate Programs in Dentistry, Program in Oral Biology, Minneapolis, MN 55455-0213. Offers MS, PhD. *Degree requirements:* For master's, thesis. *Faculty research:* Microbiology, neuroscience, biomaterials, biochemistry, cancer biology.

University of Minnesota, Twin Cities Campus, School of Dentistry and Graduate School, Graduate Programs in Dentistry, Program in Oral Health Services for Older Adults (Geriatrics), Minneapolis, MN 55455-0213. Offers MS, Certificate. *Degree requirements:* For master's, thesis (for some programs). *Entrance requirements:* For master's, DDS degree or equivalent. Additional exam requirements/recommendations for international students: Required—TOEFL (minimum score 560 paper-based; 233 computer-based). Electronic applications accepted. *Faculty research:* Geriatrics dental care, long-term care dental services, oral-systemic health relationships, utilization of care by older adults.

University of Minnesota, Twin Cities Campus, School of Dentistry and Graduate School, Graduate Programs in Dentistry, Program in Temporomandibular Joint Disorders, Minneapolis, MN 55455-0213. Offers MS. *Degree requirements:* For master's, comprehensive exam, thesis. *Entrance requirements:* Additional exam requirements/recommendations for international students: Required—TOEFL. Electronic applications accepted. *Faculty research:* Clinical trials, TMJ mechanicals, diagnostic criteria, biomarkers, genetics.

University of Mississippi Medical Center, School of Dentistry, Department of Craniofacial and Dental Research, Jackson, MS 39216-4505. Offers MS, PhD.

University of Missouri–Kansas City, School of Dentistry, Kansas City, MO 64110-2499. Offers advanced education in dentistry (Graduate Dental Certificate); dental hygiene education (MS); dental specialties (Graduate Dental Certificate); dentistry (DDS); diagnostic sciences (Graduate Dental Certificate); oral and maxillofacial surgery (Graduate Dental Certificate); oral biology (MS, PhD); orthodontics and dentofacial orthopedics (Graduate Dental Certificate); pediatric dentistry (Graduate Dental Certificate); periodontics (Graduate Dental Certificate); prosthodontics (Graduate Dental Certificate). PhD (interdisciplinary) offered through the School of Graduate Studies. *Accreditation:* ADA (one or more programs are accredited). *Faculty:* 101 full-time (40 women), 77 part-time/adjunct (25 women). *Students:* 402 full-time (177 women), 50 part-time (28 women); includes 54 minority (8 African Americans, 3 American Indian/Alaska Native, 29 Asian Americans or Pacific Islanders, 14 Hispanic Americans), 1 international. Average age 27. 536 applicants, 24% accepted, 126 enrolled. In 2009, 102 first professional degrees, 9 master's awarded. *Degree requirements:* For master's, thesis; for doctorate, thesis/dissertation. *Entrance requirements:* For DDS, DAT; for master's, DAT, letters of evaluation, personal interview; for Graduate Dental Certificate, DDS. Additional exam requirements/recommendations for international students: Required—TOEFL (minimum score 550 paper-based; 213 computer-based; 80 iBT). *Application deadline:* For fall admission, 2/1 for domestic and international students. Application fee: $45 ($50 for international students). *Expenses:* Contact institution. *Financial support:* In 2009–10, 4 fellowships (averaging $60,500 per year), 3 research assistantships (averaging $17,728 per year) were awarded; career-related internships or fieldwork, Federal Work-Study, institutionally sponsored loans, and tuition waivers (full and partial) also available. Support available to part-time students. Financial award application deadline: 3/1; financial award applicants required to submit FAFSA. *Faculty research:* Biomaterials, dental use of lasers, effectiveness of periodontal treatments, temporomandibular joint dysfunction. Total annual research expenditures: $5.9 million. *Unit head:* Dr. Marsha Pyle, Dean, 816-235-2010. *Application contact:* 816-235-2080.

The University of North Carolina at Chapel Hill, School of Dentistry and Graduate School, Graduate Programs in Dentistry, Chapel Hill, NC 27599. Offers dental hygiene (MS); endodontics (MS); epidemiology (PhD); operative dentistry (MS); oral and maxillofacial pathology (MS); oral and maxillofacial radiology (MS); oral biology (PhD); orthodontics (MS); pediatric dentistry (MS); periodontology (MS); prosthodontics (MS). *Degree requirements:* For master's, thesis; for doctorate, thesis/dissertation. *Entrance requirements:* For master's, dental degree; for doctorate, GRE General Test. Additional exam requirements/recommendations for international students: Required—TOEFL (minimum score 550 paper-based; 213 computer-based). Electronic applications accepted. *Expenses:* Contact institution. *Faculty research:* Inflammation, cell biology, immunology, microbiology, neuroscience, molecular biology.

University of Oklahoma Health Sciences Center, College of Dentistry and Graduate College, Graduate Programs in Dentistry, Department of Orthodontics, Oklahoma City, OK 73190. Offers MS. *Faculty:* 4 full-time (0 women), 17 part-time/adjunct (2 women). *Students:* 148 applicants, 3% accepted, 5 enrolled. In 2009, 4 master's awarded. *Degree requirements:* For master's, thesis. *Entrance requirements:* For master's, minimum GPA of 3.0, DDS/DMD. Additional exam requirements/recommendations for international students: Required—TOEFL. *Application deadline:* For fall admission, 9/1 priority date for domestic and international students. Applications are processed on a rolling basis. Application fee: $65. Electronic applications

Oral and Dental Sciences

University of Oklahoma Health Sciences Center (continued)
accepted. *Expenses:* Tuition, state resident: full-time $3120; part-time $156 per credit hour. Tuition, nonresident: full-time $11,314; part-time $409.70 per credit hour. Required fees: $1471; $51.20 per credit hour. $223.25 per term. *Financial support:* In 2009–10, 8 teaching assistantships (averaging $6,000 per year) were awarded; institutionally sponsored loans also available. Financial award application deadline: 3/1; financial award applicants required to submit FAFSA. *Faculty research:* Craniofacial growth and development, biomechanical principles in orthodontics. Total annual research expenditures: $10,000. *Unit head:* Dr. G. Frans Currier, Director, 405-271-6087, Fax: 405-271-1178, E-mail: frans-currier@ouhsc.edu. *Application contact:* Angel Miller, Senior Administrative Assistant/Admissions Coordinator, 405-271-4271, Fax: 405-271-1178, E-mail: angel-miller@ouhsc.edu.

University of Oklahoma Health Sciences Center, College of Dentistry and Graduate College, Graduate Programs in Dentistry, Department of Periodontics, Oklahoma City, OK 73190. Offers MS. *Faculty:* 4 full-time (1 woman), 8 part-time/adjunct (0 women). *Students:* 6 full-time (1 woman); includes 1 minority (Hispanic American). 35 applicants, 6% accepted, 2 enrolled. In 2009, 2 master's awarded. *Degree requirements:* For master's, thesis. *Entrance requirements:* For master's, DDS/DMD, minimum GPA of 3.0. Additional exam requirements/recommendations for international students: Required—TOEFL (minimum score 550 paper-based; 213 computer-based). *Application deadline:* For fall admission, 9/15 for domestic and international students. Applications are processed on a rolling basis. Application fee: $65. Electronic applications accepted. *Expenses:* Tuition, state resident: full-time $3120; part-time $156 per credit hour. Tuition, nonresident: full-time $11,314; part-time $409.70 per credit hour. Required fees: $1471; $51.20 per credit hour. $223.25 per term. *Financial support:* In 2009–10, 6 students received support, including 6 teaching assistantships (averaging $6,000 per year); institutionally sponsored loans and tuition waivers (partial) also available. Financial award application deadline: 3/1; financial award applicants required to submit FAFSA. *Unit head:* Dr. Robert E. Carson, Director, 405-271-6531, Fax: 405-271-3794, E-mail: robert-carson@ouhsc.edu. *Application contact:* Rizalina Goldston, Office Manager, 405-271-6531, Fax: 405-271-3794.

University of Pittsburgh, School of Dental Medicine, Residency Programs in Dental Medicine, Advanced Education Program in Prosthodontics, Pittsburgh, PA 15261. Offers MDS, Certificate. *Faculty:* 3 full-time (0 women), 6 part-time/adjunct (0 women). *Students:* 8 full-time (2 women); includes 2 minority (both Asian Americans or Pacific Islanders), 4 international. Average age 28. 39 applicants, 8% accepted, 3 enrolled. In 2009, 1 master's awarded. *Degree requirements:* For master's, comprehensive exam, thesis. *Entrance requirements:* Additional exam requirements/recommendations for international students: Required—TOEFL. *Application deadline:* For fall admission, 11/15 for domestic and international students. Applications are processed on a rolling basis. Application fee: $50. Electronic applications accepted. *Expenses:* Tuition, state resident: full-time $16,402; part-time $665 per credit. Tuition, nonresident: full-time $28,694; part-time $1175 per credit. Required fees: $690; $175 per term. Tuition and fees vary according to program. *Financial support:* In 2009–10, 5 students received support, including 5 fellowships (averaging $25,000 per year); monthly stipends also available. *Faculty research:* Implant dentistry, occlusion, biomechanics, microbiology, genetics. *Unit head:* Dr. Mohsen Azarbal, Program Director, 412-624-8840, Fax: 412-624-8850, E-mail: moa5@pitt.edu. *Application contact:* Pamela A. Edwards, Administrator, Office of Resident Education, 412-648-8406, Fax: 412-648-8219, E-mail: pae3@pitt.edu.

University of Pittsburgh, School of Dental Medicine, Residency Programs in Dental Medicine, Department of Dental Anesthesia, Pittsburgh, PA 15260. Offers Certificate. *Faculty:* 4 full-time (0 women), 4 part-time/adjunct (0 women). *Students:* 5 full-time (1 woman); includes 2 Hispanic Americans. Average age 34. 26 applicants, 8% accepted, 2 enrolled. In 2009, 1 Certificate awarded. *Entrance requirements:* For degree, National Board Dental Exam Parts I and II, DMD or DDS. *Application deadline:* For fall admission, 10/30 for domestic students. Application fee: $50. Electronic applications accepted. *Expenses:* Tuition, state resident: full-time $16,402; part-time $665 per credit. Tuition, nonresident: full-time $28,694; part-time $1175 per credit. Required fees: $690; $175 per term. Tuition and fees vary according to program. *Financial support:* In 2009–10, 5 fellowships (averaging $34,000 per year) were awarded; health care benefits also available. *Faculty research:* Clinical pharmacology and random controlled trials. *Unit head:* Dr. Michael A. Cuddy, Program Director, 412-648-8609, Fax: 412-648-2591, E-mail: mc2@pitt.edu. *Application contact:* Lisa R. Lehman, Department Administrator, 412-648-8609, Fax: 412-648-2591, E-mail: lrl12@pitt.edu.

University of Pittsburgh, School of Dental Medicine, Residency Programs in Dental Medicine, Department of Endodontics, Pittsburgh, PA 15260. Offers MDS, Certificate. *Faculty:* 1 full-time (0 women), 7 part-time/adjunct (2 women). *Students:* 6 full-time (1 woman); includes 1 minority (Asian American or Pacific Islander). Average age 27. 77 applicants, 4% accepted. In 2009, 3 Certificates awarded. *Degree requirements:* For master's, comprehensive exam, thesis. *Entrance requirements:* For master's and Certificate, National Boards Part 1 and 2. *Application deadline:* For fall admission, 11/1 for domestic students. Application fee: $50. *Expenses:* Tuition, state resident: full-time $16,402; part-time $665 per credit. Tuition, nonresident: full-time $28,694; part-time $1175 per credit. Required fees: $690; $175 per term. Tuition and fees vary according to program. *Financial support:* Application deadline: 4/15. *Faculty research:* Pulpal neurobiology, root canal therapy, root fracture/resorption repair, osseous grafts related to endodontics, endodontic surgery. Total annual research expenditures: $10,000. *Unit head:* Dr. Herbert L. Ray, Director, 412-648-8647, Fax: 412-383-7796, E-mail: skipp@pitt.edu. *Application contact:* Pamela A. Edwards, Administrator, Office of Resident Education, 412-648-8406, Fax: 412-648-8219, E-mail: pae3@pitt.edu.

University of Pittsburgh, School of Dental Medicine, Residency Programs in Dental Medicine, Department of Oral and Maxillofacial Surgery, Pittsburgh, PA 15260. Offers craniofacial and maxillofacial surgery (Certificate); oral and maxillofacial surgery (Certificate). *Faculty:* 12 full-time (3 women). *Students:* 13 full-time (0 women); includes 1 minority (Asian American or Pacific Islander). Average age 25. 142 applicants, 2% accepted, 3 enrolled. In 2009, 4 Certificates awarded. *Degree requirements:* For Certificate, comprehensive exam. *Entrance requirements:* For degree, National Boards Part I, US or Canadian dental degree (DDS or DMD). *Application deadline:* For fall admission, 10/15 for domestic students. Applications are processed on a rolling basis. Application fee: $0. Electronic applications accepted. *Expenses:* Contact institution. *Financial support:* In 2009–10, 8 students received support, including 4 fellowships with partial tuition reimbursements available (averaging $36,000 per year); scholarships/grants, health care benefits, and tuition waivers also available. *Faculty research:* Clefts, craniofacial anomalies, facial trauma, head and neck cancer, pain management. Total annual research expenditures: $54,000. *Unit head:* Dr. Bernard J. Costello, Program Director, 412-648-6801, Fax: 412-648-6835. *Application contact:* Andrea M. Ford, Residency and Fellowship Coordinator, 412-648-6801, Fax: 412-648-6835, E-mail: fordam@upmc.edu.

University of Pittsburgh, School of Dental Medicine, Residency Programs in Dental Medicine, Department of Orthodontics and Dentofacial Orthopedics, Pittsburgh, PA 15261. Offers MDS, Certificate. *Faculty:* 2 full-time (1 woman), 8 part-time/adjunct (0 women). *Students:* 12 full-time (3 women); includes 4 minority (all Asian Americans or Pacific Islanders). Average age 27. 186 applicants, 2% accepted. In 2009, 1 master's, 2 Certificates awarded. *Degree requirements:* For master's, comprehensive exam, thesis; for Certificate, comprehensive exam. *Entrance requirements:* For master's and Certificate, National Boards Parts I and II. *Application deadline:* For fall admission, 10/1 for domestic students. Application fee: $135. *Expenses:* Tuition, state resident: full-time $16,402; part-time $665 per credit. Tuition, nonresident: full-time $28,694; part-time $1175 per credit. Required fees: $690; $175 per term. Tuition and fees vary according to program. *Faculty research:* Muscle physiology, orthodontic outcomes. *Unit head:* Dr. Joseph F. A. Petrone, Director of Residency Education, 412-648-8638, Fax: 412-648-8817, E-mail: jfap@pitt.edu. *Application contact:* Lauren M. Breskovich, Department Administrator, 412-648-8419, Fax: 412-648-8817, E-mail: lmb111@pitt.edu.

University of Pittsburgh, School of Dental Medicine, Residency Programs in Dental Medicine, Department of Periodontics, Pittsburgh, PA 15261. Offers MDS, Certificate. *Faculty:* 4 full-time (1 woman), 8 part-time/adjunct (2 women). *Students:* 9 full-time (3 women); includes 1 minority (Asian American or Pacific Islander), 3 international. Average age 28. 36 applicants, 8% accepted, 3 enrolled. In 2009, 2 Certificates awarded. *Entrance requirements:* For degree, DMD, DDS. *Application deadline:* For fall admission, 8/15 priority date for domestic and international students. Applications are processed on a rolling basis. *Expenses:* Tuition, state resident: full-time $16,402; part-time $665 per credit. Tuition, nonresident: full-time $28,694; part-time $1175 per credit. Required fees: $690; $175 per term. Tuition and fees vary according to program. *Financial support:* In 2009–10, 2 fellowships (averaging $23,000 per year) were awarded. *Faculty research:* Bone tissue engineering, transcriptional regulation, periodontics, implantology, gene delivery. Total annual research expenditures: $50,000. *Unit head:* Dr. Pouran Famili, Director/Chair, 412-648-8598, Fax: 412-648-8594, E-mail: pof@pitt.edu. *Application contact:* Dr. Pouran Famili, Director/Chair, 412-648-8598, Fax: 412-648-8594, E-mail: pof@pitt.edu.

University of Puerto Rico, Medical Sciences Campus, School of Dental Medicine, Graduate Programs in Dentistry, San Juan, PR 00936-5067. Offers general dentistry (Certificate); oral and maxillofacial surgery (Certificate); orthodontics (Certificate); pediatric dentistry (Certificate); prosthodontics (Certificate). *Degree requirements:* For Certificate, comprehensive exam (for some programs). *Entrance requirements:* For degree, National Board Dental Exam I, National Board Dental Exam II, DDS or DMD, interview. Electronic applications accepted. *Expenses:* Contact institution. *Faculty research:* Analgesic drugs, anti-inflammatory drugs, saliva cytoanalysis, dental materials, oral epidemiology and dental caries.

University of Rochester, School of Medicine and Dentistry, Graduate Programs in Medicine and Dentistry, Center for Oral Biology, Rochester, NY 14627. Offers MS. *Degree requirements:* For master's, thesis. *Entrance requirements:* For master's, GRE General Test, DDS or equivalent.

University of Southern California, Graduate School, School of Dentistry and Graduate School, Department of Craniofacial Biology, Los Angeles, CA 90089. Offers MS, PhD, Graduate Certificate. *Faculty:* 34 full-time (9 women), 2 part-time/adjunct (1 woman). *Students:* 32 full-time (17 women); includes 14 minority (1 African American, 12 Asian Americans or Pacific Islanders, 1 Hispanic American), 9 international. 20 applicants, 75% accepted, 15 enrolled. In 2009, 13 master's, 3 doctorates awarded. Terminal master's awarded for partial completion of doctoral program. *Degree requirements:* For master's, comprehensive exam, thesis; for doctorate, comprehensive exam, thesis/dissertation. *Entrance requirements:* For master's and doctorate, GRE; for Graduate Certificate, DDS. Additional exam requirements/recommendations for international students: Required—TOEFL. *Application deadline:* Applications are processed on a rolling basis. Application fee: $145. Electronic applications accepted. *Expenses:* Tuition: Full-time $25,980; part-time $1315 per unit. Required fees: $554. One-time fee: $35 full-time. Full-time tuition and fees vary according to degree level and program. *Financial support:* In 2009–10, 4 students received support, including 4 fellowships with full tuition reimbursements available (averaging $5,000 per year); traineeships and health care benefits also available. *Faculty research:* Orthodontics, periodontics, tooth development, biomineralization, stem cell biology. *Unit head:* Dr. Michael Paine, Associate Professor, 323-442-1728, Fax: 323-442-2981, E-mail: paine@usc.edu. *Application contact:* Dr. Michael Katherine Paine, Associate Professor, 323-442-1728, Fax: 323-442-2981, E-mail: paine@usc.edu.

University of Southern Nevada, College of Dental Medicine, Henderson, NV 89014. Offers advanced education in orthodontics and dentofacial orthopedics (Graduate Certificate). *Faculty:* 3 full-time (1 woman), 7 part-time/adjunct (0 women). *Students:* 22 full-time (6 women); includes 12 minority (2 African Americans, 1 American Indian/Alaska Native, 8 Asian Americans or Pacific Islanders, 1 Hispanic American), 1 international. Average age 28. 105 applicants, 10% accepted, 10 enrolled. *Degree requirements:* For Graduate Certificate, comprehensive exam, thesis or alternative. *Application deadline:* For fall admission, 9/15 for domestic students. Applications are processed on a rolling basis. Application fee: $50. *Expenses:* Tuition: Full-time $37,900. Full-time tuition and fees vary according to program. *Financial support:* In 2009–10, 22 students received support. Scholarships/grants available. Financial award application deadline: 6/30; financial award applicants required to submit FAFSA. *Unit head:* Dr. Jaleh Pourhamidi, Program Director, AEODO/MBA Residency Program/Associate Professor of Dental Medicine, 702-968-1652, Fax: 702-968-5277, E-mail: jpourhamidi@usn.edu. *Application contact:* Lore Loiacono, Administrative Assistant to the Program Director, 702-968-1682, Fax: 702-968-5277, E-mail: lloiacano@usn.edu.

The University of Tennessee Health Science Center, College of Dentistry, Memphis, TN 38163-0002. Offers dentistry (DDS); oral and maxillofacial surgery (Certificate); orthodontics (MS); pediatric dentistry (MS, Certificate); periodontics (MS); prosthodontics (Certificate). *Accreditation:* ADA (one or more programs are accredited). *Degree requirements:* For master's, thesis. *Entrance requirements:* For DDS, DAT, interview, pre-professional evaluation; for master's, GRE, interviews. Additional exam requirements/recommendations for international students: Required—TOEFL (minimum score 275 computer-based). Electronic applications accepted. *Expenses:* Contact institution. *Faculty research:* Oral cancer, proteomics, inflammation mechanisms, defensins, periopathogens, dental material.

The University of Texas Health Science Center at San Antonio, Dental School and Graduate School of Biomedical Sciences, Graduate Program in Dentistry, San Antonio, TX 78229-3900. Offers MS, Certificate. *Degree requirements:* For master's, thesis. *Entrance requirements:* For master's, GRE General Test, DDS; for Certificate, DDS. *Expenses:* Tuition, state resident: full-time $2832; part-time $118 per credit hour. Tuition, nonresident: full-time $10,896; part-time $454 per credit hour. Required fees: $884 per semester. One-time fee: $70. *Faculty research:* Nutrition and oral health, peridontal disease, biomaterials, bone mineralization, cavities prevention.

The University of Toledo, College of Graduate Studies, College of Medicine, Biomedical Science Programs, Department of Oral Biology, Toledo, OH 43606-3390. Offers MSBS. Part-time programs available. *Degree requirements:* For master's, thesis, qualifying exam. *Entrance requirements:* For master's, GRE General Test, minimum undergraduate GPA of 3.0. *Faculty research:* Oral biology-tissue cultures.

University of Toronto, Faculty of Dentistry, Graduate Programs in Dentistry, Toronto, ON M5S 1A1, Canada. Offers M Sc, PhD. Part-time programs available. Terminal master's awarded for partial completion of doctoral program. *Degree requirements:* For master's, thesis; for doctorate, thesis/dissertation. *Entrance requirements:* For master's, honors B Sc., minimum B average, 2 letters of reference; for doctorate, M Sc., minimum B+ average. Additional exam requirements/recommendations for international students: Required—Michigan English Language Assessment Battery, IELTS, TOEFL or COPE. Electronic applications accepted. *Expenses:* Contact institution. *Faculty research:* Plaque, periodontal biology, biomaterials/dental implants, community dentistry, growth and development.

University of Toronto, Faculty of Dentistry, Specialty Master's Programs, Toronto, ON M5S 1A1, Canada. Offers dental anesthesia (M Sc); dental public health (M Sc); endodontics (M Sc); oral and maxillofacial surgery and anesthesia (M Sc); oral pathology (M Sc); oral radiology (M Sc); orthodontics (M Sc); pediatric dentistry (M Sc); periodontology (M Sc); prosthodontics (M Sc). *Degree requirements:* For master's, thesis. *Entrance requirements:* For master's, completion of professional degree of DDS/BDS, DMD, minimum B average, 2 letters of reference. Additional exam requirements/recommendations for international students: Required—TOEFL, Michigan English Language Assessment Battery, IELTS or COPE. *Expenses:* Contact institution. *Faculty research:* Plaque and periodontal biology, biomaterials/dental implants, community dentistry, growth development, neurophysiology.

University of Washington, Graduate School, School of Dentistry and Graduate School, Graduate Programs in Dentistry, Department of Endodontics, Seattle, WA 98195. Offers MSD, Certificate.

University of Washington, Graduate School, School of Dentistry and Graduate School, Graduate Programs in Dentistry, Department of Orthodontics, Seattle, WA 98195. Offers MSD, Certificate.

Oral and Dental Sciences

University of Washington, Graduate School, School of Dentistry, Program in Dental Surgery, Seattle, WA 98195. Offers DDS. *Accreditation:* ADA. *Entrance requirements:* DAT.

The University of Western Ontario, Schulich School of Medicine and Dentistry, School of Dentistry, Division of Graduate Orthodontics, London, ON N6A 5B8, Canada. Offers M Cl D. *Degree requirements:* For master's, thesis. *Entrance requirements:* For master's, GRE General Test, minimum B average, 1 year of general practice preferred. Additional exam requirements/recommendations for international students: Required—TOEFL (minimum score 600 paper-based; 250 computer-based).

West Virginia University, School of Dentistry, Division of Dental Hygiene, Morgantown, WV 26506. Offers MS. Part-time programs available. *Degree requirements:* For master's, thesis.

Entrance requirements: For master's, GRE, MAT, BS in dental hygiene or equivalent, minimum GPA of 2.75. Additional exam requirements/recommendations for international students: Required—TOEFL. *Faculty research:* Curriculum and instruction, infection control, special patient care, diversity and cultural sensitivity, oral health disparities.

West Virginia University, School of Dentistry, Graduate Programs in Dentistry, Morgantown, WV 26506. Offers endodontics (MS); orthodontics (MS); prosthodontics (MS). *Degree requirements:* For master's, thesis. *Entrance requirements:* For master's, National Dental Board Exam Parts I and II, DDS/DMD from accredited U.S. or Canadian Dental School, minimum GPA of 3.0. Additional exam requirements/recommendations for international students: Required—TOEFL. *Expenses:* Contact institution. *Faculty research:* Growth and development, cephalographics, endodontic interpretation and therapy.

UNIVERSITY OF CONNECTICUT HEALTH CENTER

Graduate Program in Skeletal, Craniofacial, and Oral Biology

Programs of Study	The Graduate Program in Skeletal, Craniofacial, and Oral Biology provides students with interdisciplinary research training in the areas of skeletal, craniofacial, and oral biology, emphasizing contemporary research technologies in cell, molecular, and developmental biology; genetics; and biochemistry. Trainees may enter a Ph.D. program or a combined D.M.D./Ph.D., M.D./Ph.D., or dental residency/Ph.D. program. The program prepares trainees for academic or industrial careers in the basic biomedical sciences or for academic careers in medicine or dental medicine.
	Areas of research include regulation of the formation, outgrowth, and patterning of the developing limb; control of cartilage differentiation, endochondral ossification, osteogenesis, and joint formation; molecular regulation of gene expression in bone; homeobox gene regulation of osteoblast differentiation; gene therapy of bone diseases; hormonal and cytokine regulation of bone growth, formation, and remodeling; control of craniofacial skeletogenesis and tooth development; signal transduction and intracellular signaling pathways; cellular and molecular aspects of the pathogenesis of inflammatory disease; microbiology, pathogenesis, and immunology of caries and periodontal disease; neural structure and function in the gustatory system; biomaterial development for tissue engineering; bone cell–implant interactions; differentiation of human embryonic stem cells into skeletal tissues; and analysis of oral and mucosal function and disease.
Research Facilities	The University complex provides excellent physical facilities for research in both basic and clinical sciences. The Health Center Library is well equipped with extensive journal and book holdings and rapid electronic access to database searching, the World Wide Web, and library holdings. The library also contains the Computer Education Center and the End User Support Center. The Center for Laboratory Animal Care contains a transgenic mouse production facility fully equipped for gene targeting studies and with special facilities for housing immunodeficient animals. Facilities include the Center for Biomaterials, the General Clinical Research Center, the Center for Cell Analysis and Modeling (confocal microscopy, low light level microscopy, two photon microscopy), the Center for Bone Histology and Histomorphometry; the Molecular Imaging Laboratory, the Fluorescence Flow Cytometry Facility, the Electron Microscopy Facility, Gene Targeting and Transgenic Facility, the Microarray Core Facility, the Molecular Core Facility, NMR Structural Biology Facility, National Resource for Cell Analysis and Modeling, and the Center for Molecular Medicine (laser capture microdissection).
Financial Aid	Support for doctoral students engaged in full-time degree programs at the Health Center is provided on a competitive basis. Graduate research assistantships for 2010–11 provide a stipend of $28,000 per year, which includes a waiver of tuition/University fees for the fall and spring semesters and a student health-insurance plan. While financial aid is offered competitively, the Health Center makes every possible effort to address the financial needs of all students during their period of training.
Cost of Study	For 2010–11, tuition is $4455 per semester ($8910 per year) for full-time students (Connecticut residents) and $11,565 per semester ($23,130 per year) for full-time out-of-state residents. General University fees are added to the cost of tuition for students who do not receive a tuition waiver. These costs are usually met by traineeships or research assistantships for doctoral students.
Living and Housing Costs	There is a wide range of affordable housing options in the Greater Hartford area within easy commuting distance of the campus, including an extensive complex that is adjacent to the Health Center. Costs range from $600 to $900 per month for a one-bedroom unit; two or more students sharing an apartment usually pay less. University housing is not available at the Health Center.
Student Group	The Program in Skeletal, Craniofacial, and Oral Biology has approximately 20 trainees. At the Health Center there are about 500 students in the Schools of Medicine and Dental Medicine, 150 Ph.D. students, and about 50 postdoctoral fellows. Graduate students are represented on various administrative committees concerned with curricular affairs. A graduate student organization fosters social contact among graduate students in the Health Center and represents graduate students' needs and concerns to the faculty and administration.
Location	The Health Center is located in the historic town of Farmington, Connecticut. Set in the beautiful New England countryside, on a hill overlooking the Farmington Valley, it is close to ski areas, hiking trails, and facilities for boating, fishing, and swimming. Connecticut's capital city of Hartford, 7 miles east of Farmington, is the center of an urban region of approximately 800,000 people. The beaches of the Long Island Sound are about 50 minutes away to the south, and the beautiful Berkshires are a short drive to the northwest. New York City and Boston can be reached within 2½ hours by car.
	Hartford is the home of the acclaimed Hartford Stage Company, TheatreWorks, the Hartford Symphony and Chamber orchestras, two ballet companies, an opera company, the Wadsworth Atheneum (the oldest public art museum in the nation), the Mark Twain house, the Hartford Civic Center, and many other interesting cultural and recreational facilities. The area is also home to several branches of the University of Connecticut, Trinity College, and the University of Hartford, which includes the Hartt School of Music. Bradley International Airport (about 30 minutes from campus) serves the Hartford/Springfield area with frequent airline connections to major cities in this country and abroad. Frequent bus and rail service is also available from Hartford.
The Health Center	The 200-acre Health Center campus at Farmington houses a division of the University of Connecticut Graduate School, as well as the Schools of Medicine and Dental Medicine. The campus also includes the John Dempsey Hospital, associated clinics, and extensive medical research facilities, all in a centralized facility with more than 1 million square feet of floor space. The Health Center's newest research addition, the Academic Research Building, opened in 1999. This impressive eleven-story structure provides 170,000 square feet of state-of-the-art laboratory space. The faculty at the center includes more than 260 full-time members. The institution has a strong commitment to graduate study within an environment that promotes social and intellectual interaction among the various educational programs. Graduate students are represented on various administrative committees concerned with curricular affairs, and the Graduate Student Organization (GSO) represents graduate students' needs and concerns to the faculty and administration, in addition to fostering social contact among graduate students in the Health Center.
Applying	Applications for admission should be submitted on standard forms that can be obtained from the Graduate Admissions Office at the University of Connecticut (UConn) Health Center or from the Web site at http://grad.uchc.edu/oral_bio/oralbio_intro.html. Applications should be filed together with transcripts, three letters of recommendation, a personal statement, and recent results from the General Test of the Graduate Record Examinations. International students must take the Test of English as a Foreign Language (TOEFL) to satisfy Graduate School requirements.
	The deadline for completed applications and receipt of all supplemental materials is December 15. Deadlines and application procedures for combined programs vary depending on the program. For further information on combined programs, prospective students should contact Dr. Mina Mina in the Department of Reconstructive Sciences.
	In accordance with the laws of the state of Connecticut and of the United States, the University of Connecticut Health Center does not discriminate against any person in its educational and employment activities on the grounds of race, color, creed, national origin, sex, age, or physical disability.
Correspondence and Information	Dr. Mina Mina Craniofacial Sciences and Pediatric Dentistry Department of Reconstructive Sciences University of Connecticut Health Center Farmington, Connecticut 06030-3705 Phone: 860-679-4081 E-mail: mina@nso1.uchc.edu Web site: http://grad.uchc.edu/oral_bio/oralbio_intro.html

University of Connecticut Health Center

THE FACULTY AND THEIR RESEARCH

Andrew Arnold, Professor of Medicine and Murray-Heilig Chair in Molecular Medicine; M.D., Harvard. The molecular genetic underpinnings of tumors of the endocrine glands, role of the cyclin D1 oncogene, animal modeling of hyperparathyroidism.

Caroline N. Dealy, Associate Professor of Reconstructive Sciences, Center for Regenerative Medicine and Skeletal Development; Ph.D., Connecticut. Roles of various growth factors and signaling molecules, particularly IGF-I and insulin, in the regulation of chick limb development.

Anne Delany, Assistant Professor of Medicine; Ph.D., Dartmouth. Study of noncollagenous matrix proteins and metalloproteinases important in bone remodeling, including investigation of function and posttranscriptional regulation of osteonectin or SPARC in bone and function and regulation of the metastasis-associated metalloproteinase, stromelysyin-3, in bone.

Anna Dongari-Bagtzoglou, Assistant Professor, Department of Oral Health and Diagnostic Sciences, Division of Periodontology; D.D.S., Ph.D., Texas Health Science Center at San Antonio. Host-pathogen interactions, with emphasis on the pathogenesis of inflammation and the innate immune functions of oral mucosal cells.

Paul M. Epstein, Associate Professor of Cell Biology; Ph.D., Yeshiva (Einstein). Second messengers and signal transduction, with particular focus on cyclic nucleotide metabolism and protein phosphorylation, with emphasis on analysis of cyclic nucleotide phosphodiesterase (PDE).

Marion Frank, Professor of Oral Health and Diagnostic Sciences and Director, Center for Neurosciences; Ph.D., Brown. Study of the sense of taste, using basic and clinical research; development of a fundamental understanding of gustatory systems in mammals at all levels from receptors to cerebral cortex; application of basic knowledge of gustatory systems to the diagnosis and treatment of taste disorders in humans.

A. Jon Goldberg, Professor of Reconstructive Sciences, Center for Regenerative Medicine and Skeletal Development; Ph.D., Michigan. Biomaterials, with studies involving structure-property relationships, development of novel systems, clinical evaluations, and surface analysis.

Gloria Gronowicz, Professor of Surgery; Ph.D., Columbia. Effects of hormones and growth factors on the production of extracellular matrix (ECM) proteins, on the regulation of integrins (receptors for ECM proteins), and on apoptosis in bone; response of bone cells to implant biomaterials.

Arthur R. Hand, Professor of Craniofacial Sciences, Division of Pediatric Dentistry; D.D.S., UCLA. Study of gene expression in rodent salivary glands during normal growth and development and in various experimental conditions employing morphological, immunological, and biochemical methodology.

Marc Hansen, Professor of Medicine, Center for Molecular Medicine; Ph.D., Cincinnati. Molecular genetics of osteosarcoma and related bone diseases.

John R. Harrison, Professor of Craniofacial Sciences, Division of Orthodontics; Ph.D., Connecticut. Hormonal regulation of bone remodeling.

Marja M. Hurley, Associate Professor of Medicine; M.D., Connecticut. Molecular mechanisms regulating the expression of fibroblast growth factors in bone, mechanisms of signal transduction by growth factors in bone cells, and role of fibroblast growth factors in bone remodeling.

Robert A. Kosher, Professor of Reconstructive Sciences, Center for Regenerative Medicine and Skeletal Development; Ph.D., Temple. Limb development; roles and relationships among regulatory genes, particularly homeobox-containing genes, secreted signaling molecules, and the extracellular matrix in the regulation of limb formation, outgrowth, patterning, cartilage differentiation, osteogenesis, and joint formation.

Barbara E. Kream, Professor of Medicine; Ph.D., Yale. Hormonal regulation of bone remodeling.

Liisa T. Kuhn, Assistant Professor of Reconstructive Sciences, Center for Regenerative Medicine and Skeletal Development; Ph.D., California, Santa Barbara. Biomaterials for drug delivery and bone regeneration and repair.

Marc Lalande, Professor and Head, Department of Genetics and Developmental Biology; Ph.D., Toronto. Genomic imprinting of human chromosome 15q.

Leo Lefrancois, Professor of Immunology; Ph.D., Wake Forest. T-lymphocyte development, mucosal immunology, intestinal intraepithelial T lymphocytes, gamma/delta T cells.

Alexander Lichtler, Associate Professor of Reconstructive Sciences, Center for Regenerative Medicine and Skeletal Development; Ph.D., Florida. Hormone regulation of bone collagen synthesis.

Alan G. Lurie, Professor of Oral Health and Diagnostic Sciences and Chairperson, Division of Oral and Maxillofacial Radiology; D.D.S., UCLA; Ph.D., Rochester. Actions and interactions of radiation and chemical carcinogens during epithelial carcinogenesis, DNA mutagenesis and repair by gamma radiation in lymphoblasts from both normal and ataxia telangiectatic humans, clinical research digital imaging.

Sanjay Mallya, Assistant Professor of Oral Health and Diagnostic Sciences, Division of Oral Diagnosis; M.D.S., Bombay; Ph.D., Connecticut. Molecular genetics of oral cancer, effects of parathyroid hormone on bone.

Mina Mina, Professor of Craniofacial Sciences; Chairperson, Division of Pediatric Dentistry; and Director, Skeletal, Craniofacial, and Oral Biology Graduate Program; D.M.D., National University of Iran; Ph.D., Connecticut Health Center. Development of the mandibular arch, including the elongation and polarized outgrowth of the mandibular primordia and subsequent differentiation of the skeletal tissues in spatially defined patterns; characterization of genetic and epigenetic influences involved in the pattern formation and skeletogenesis of the chick mandible and mouse tooth germ; regulation of patterning in the developing mandible and developing teeth by mandibular epithelium, extracellular matrix molecules, growth factors, and transcription factors.

Carol C. Pilbeam, Professor of Medicine; Ph.D., Yale. Mechanisms of regulation of bone formation and resorption.

Ernst Reichenberger, Assistant Professor of Reconstructive Sciences, Center for Regenerative Medicine and Skeletal Development; Ph.D., Erlangen (Germany). Study of complex processes required for generating and maintaining the skin and bones through characterization of human genetic disorders in which they are disrupted, including aplasia cutis congenita (ACC), cherubism, and craniometaphyseal dysplasia (CMD).

Blanka Rogina, Assistant Professor of Genetics and Developmental Biology; Ph.D., Zagreb (Croatia). Molecular and genetic mechanisms underlying aging and cost of reproduction.

David W. Rowe, Professor of Reconstructive Sciences and Director, Center for Regenerative Medicine and Skeletal Development; M.D., Vermont. Genetic and hormonal control of type I collagen production, development of strategies for somatic gene therapy for heritable diseases of bone built upon the structural and regulatory principles of collagen production.

Jason M. Tanzer, Professor of Oral Health and Diagnostic Sciences and Chairperson, Division of Microbiology and Oral Medicine; D.M.D., Tufts; Ph.D., Georgetown. Physiological/biochemical/genetic bases of virulence by the mutans streptococci and their expression and modification in both humans and experimental animals; secretion of saliva, its regulation by novel and old cholinomimetic agents, and associated characterization of the pharmacokinetics of these agents and pharmacodynamics of cardiovascular, salivary, and lachrymal responses in experimental animals and humans.

William B. Upholt, Professor of Reconstructive Sciences, Center for Regenerative Medicine and Skeletal Development; Ph.D., Cal Tech. Molecular mechanisms regulating differentiation and pattern formation during embryonic skeletal development in the limb and mandible, use of transgenic mouse model systems, study of the regulation of the process of chondrogenesis.

Sunil Wadhwa, Assistant Professor of Craniofacial Sciences, Division of Orthodontics; D.D.S., Columbia; Ph.D., Connecticut. Bone biology and temporomandibular joint development and function.

Section 37
Medicine

This section contains a directory of institutions offering graduate work in medicine, followed by in-depth entries submitted by institutions that chose to prepare detailed program descriptions. Additional information about programs listed in the directory but not augmented by an in-depth entry may be obtained by writing directly to the dean of a graduate school or chair of a department at the address given in the directory.

CONTENTS

Allopathic Medicine

Albany Medical College, Professional Program, Albany, NY 12208-3479. Offers MD. *Accreditation:* LCME/AMA. *Faculty:* 84 full-time (22 women), 29 part-time/adjunct (9 women). *Students:* 560 full-time (281 women); includes 186 minority (13 African Americans, 1 American Indian/Alaska Native, 159 Asian Americans or Pacific Islanders, 13 Hispanic Americans), 16 international. Average age 27. 9,503 applicants, 3% accepted, 133 enrolled. In 2009, 138 MDs awarded. *Degree requirements:* For MD, United States Medical Licensing Exam Steps 1 and 2, clinical skills. *Entrance requirements:* MCAT, letters of recommendation, interview. *Application deadline:* For fall admission, 11/15 for domestic and international students. Applications are processed on a rolling basis. Application fee: $105. Electronic applications accepted. *Expenses:* Contact institution. *Financial support:* Federal Work-Study, institutionally sponsored loans, and tuition waivers (partial) available. Financial award application deadline: 3/15; financial award applicants required to submit FAFSA. *Unit head:* Dr. Vincent Verdile, Dean, 518-262-6008. *Application contact:* Joanne H. Nanos, Director of Admissions and Student Records, 518-262-5521, Fax: 518-262-5887.

Albert Einstein College of Medicine, Professional Program in Medicine, Bronx, NY 10461. Offers MD, MD/PhD. *Accreditation:* LCME/AMA. *Degree requirements:* For MD, independent scholars project. *Entrance requirements:* MCAT, interview. *Faculty research:* Cancer, diabetes mellitus, liver disease, infectious disease, neuroscience.

American University of Beirut, Graduate Programs, Faculty of Medicine, Beirut, Lebanon. Offers biochemistry (MS); human morphology (MS); medicine (MD); microbiology and immunology (MS); neuroscience (MS); pharmacology and therapeutics (MS); physiology (MS). Part-time programs available. *Degree requirements:* For master's, one foreign language, comprehensive exam, thesis (for some programs). *Entrance requirements:* For MD, MCAT, bachelor's degree; for master's, letter of recommendation. Additional exam requirements/recommendations for international students: Required—TOEFL (minimum score 600 paper-based; 250 computer-based; 100 iBT), IELTS (minimum score 7.5). *Faculty research:* Cancer research, stem cell research, genetic research, neuroscience research, bone research.

Baylor College of Medicine, Medical School, Professional Program in Medicine, Houston, TX 77030-3498. Offers MD, MD/PhD. *Accreditation:* LCME/AMA. *Students:* 698 full-time (358 women); includes 413 minority (38 African Americans, 12 American Indian/Alaska Native, 255 Asian Americans or Pacific Islanders, 108 Hispanic Americans), 1 international. Average age 24. 4,588 applicants, 7% accepted, 186 enrolled. In 2009, 157 MDs awarded. *Entrance requirements:* MCAT, 90 hours of pre-med course work. *Application deadline:* For fall admission, 11/1 for domestic students. Applications are processed on a rolling basis. Application fee: $90. Electronic applications accepted. *Expenses:* Contact institution. *Financial support:* In 2009–10, 503 students received support. Federal Work-Study, institutionally sponsored loans, and scholarships/grants available. Financial award application deadline: 5/11; financial award applicants required to submit FAFSA. *Unit head:* Dr. Stephen B. Greenberg, Senior Vice President and Dean of Medical Education, 713-798-8878, Fax: 713-798-3096, E-mail: stepheng@bcm.edu. *Application contact:* Dr. Florence F. Eddins-Folensbee, Senior Associate Dean of the Medical School, 713-798-4842, Fax: 713-798-5563, E-mail: florence@bcm.edu.

Boston University, School of Medicine, Professional Program in Medicine, Boston, MA 02215. Offers MD, MD/MA, MD/MPH, MD/PhD. *Accreditation:* LCME/AMA. Part-time programs available. *Students:* 663 full-time (349 women), 49 part-time (32 women); includes 212 minority (57 African Americans, 1 American Indian/Alaska Native, 122 Asian Americans or Pacific Islanders, 32 Hispanic Americans), 32 international. Average age 25. In 2009, 154 MDs awarded. *Application deadline:* For fall admission, 11/1 for domestic students. Application fee: $95. *Expenses:* Tuition: Full-time $37,910; part-time $1184 per credit hour. Required fees: $386; $40 per semester. Part-time tuition and fees vary according to class time, course level, degree level and program. *Financial support:* Fellowships, Federal Work-Study available. Support available to part-time students. *Unit head:* Dr. Karen H. Antman, Dean, 617-638-5300. *Application contact:* Dr. Robert Witzburg, Associate Dean for Admissions, 617-638-4630.

Brown University, Program in Medicine, Providence, RI 02912. Offers MD, MD/PhD. *Accreditation:* LCME/AMA. *Expenses:* Contact institution.

Case Western Reserve University, School of Medicine, Professional Program in Medicine, Cleveland, OH 44106. Offers MD, MD/JD, MD/MA, MD/MBA, MD/MPH, MD/MS, MD/PhD. *Accreditation:* LCME/AMA. *Entrance requirements:* MCAT, interview. Electronic applications accepted.

Charles Drew University of Medicine and Science, Professional Program in Medicine, Los Angeles, CA 90059. Offers MD. *Entrance requirements:* MCAT.

Columbia University, College of Physicians and Surgeons, Professional Program in Medicine, New York, NY 10032. Offers MD, MD/DDS, MD/MPH, MD/MS, MD/PhD. *Accreditation:* LCME/AMA. Part-time programs available. *Entrance requirements:* MCAT.

Columbia University, School of Continuing Education, Program in Narrative Medicine, New York, NY 10027. Offers MS. *Faculty:* 9. Application fee: $65. Electronic applications accepted. *Financial support:* Applicants required to submit FAFSA. *Application contact:* Bryce Weinert, 212-854-9666, E-mail: ce-info@columbia.edu.

Creighton University, School of Medicine, Professional Program in Medicine, Omaha, NE 68178-0001. Offers MD, MD/PhD. *Accreditation:* LCME/AMA. *Entrance requirements:* MCAT. Electronic applications accepted. *Expenses:* Tuition: Full-time $11,700; part-time $650 per credit hour. Required fees: $126 per semester. *Faculty research:* Hereditary cancer, osteoporosis, diabetes, immunology, microbiology.

Dalhousie University, Faculty of Medicine, Halifax, NS B3H 4H7, Canada. Offers MD, M Sc, PhD, M Sc/PhD, MD/M Sc, MD/PhD. *Accreditation:* LCME/AMA. *Entrance requirements:* For MD and master's, MCAT. Electronic applications accepted.

Dartmouth College, Dartmouth Medical School, Hanover, NH 03755. Offers MD, MD/MBA, MD/PhD. *Accreditation:* LCME/AMA. *Faculty:* 252 full-time (81 women), 64 part-time/adjunct (33 women). *Students:* 339 full-time (168 women), 4 part-time (3 women); includes 85 minority (6 African Americans, 3 American Indian/Alaska Native, 62 Asian Americans or Pacific Islanders, 14 Hispanic Americans), 40 international. Average age 26. 5,074 applicants, 5% accepted, 81 enrolled. In 2009, 63 MDs awarded. *Unit head:* Dr. William Green, Dean, 603-650-1200. *Application contact:* Andrew Welch, Director, DMS Admissions, 603-650-1505, Fax: 603-650-1560.

Drexel University, College of Medicine, Professional Program in Medicine, Philadelphia, PA 19104-2875. Offers MD, MD/PhD. *Accreditation:* LCME/AMA. *Degree requirements:* For MD, National Board Exam Parts I and II. *Entrance requirements:* MCAT. Electronic applications accepted.

Duke University, School of Medicine, Professional Program in Medicine, Durham, NC 27708-0586. Offers MD, MD/JD, MD/MALS, MD/MBA, MD/MHS, MD/MLS, MD/MPH, MD/MPP, MD/MSIS, MD/PhD. *Accreditation:* LCME/AMA. *Faculty:* 1,427 full-time (455 women). *Students:* 421 full-time (205 women); includes 188 minority (78 African Americans, 6 American Indian/Alaska Native, 93 Asian Americans or Pacific Islanders, 11 Hispanic Americans), 16 international. Average age 25. 4,966 applicants, 4% accepted, 100 enrolled. *Entrance requirements:* MCAT. *Application deadline:* For fall admission, 11/1 for domestic students. Application fee: $80. Electronic applications accepted. *Expenses:* Contact institution. *Financial support:* In 2009–10, 119 students received support. Institutionally sponsored loans and scholarships/grants available. Financial award application deadline: 5/1; financial award applicants required to submit FAFSA. *Application contact:* Dr. Brenda E. Armstrong, Director of Admissions, 919-684-2985, Fax: 919-684-8893, E-mail: medadm@mc.duke.edu.

East Carolina University, Brody School of Medicine, Department of Medicine, Greenville, NC 27858-4353. Offers MD. *Accreditation:* LCME/AMA. *Entrance requirements:* MCAT, pre-med courses, interviews, faculty evaluations. Electronic applications accepted. *Faculty research:* Diabetes, cardiovascular disease, cancer, neurological disorders.

Eastern Virginia Medical School, Professional Program in Medicine, Norfolk, VA 23501-1980. Offers MD, MD/PhD. *Accreditation:* LCME/AMA. *Students:* 447 full-time (203 women); includes 27 African Americans, 93 Asian Americans or Pacific Islanders, 6 Hispanic Americans. 4,997 applicants, 118 enrolled. In 2009, 108 MDs awarded. *Entrance requirements:* MCAT, bachelor's degree or equivalent, course work in sciences. *Application deadline:* For fall admission, 11/15 priority date for domestic students. Applications are processed on a rolling basis. Application fee: $95. Electronic applications accepted. Tuition and fees vary according to program. *Unit head:* Dr. Michael J. Solhaug, Associate Dean for Medical Admissions and Students, 757-446-5805, Fax: 757-446-5896, E-mail: solhaumj@evms.edu. *Application contact:* Susan Castora, Director of Admissions, 757-446-5812, Fax: 757-446-5896, E-mail: castorsl@evms.edu.

East Tennessee State University, James H. Quillen College of Medicine, Professional Programs in Medicine, Johnson City, TN 37614. Offers MD. *Accreditation:* LCME/AMA. *Entrance requirements:* MCAT. Additional exam requirements/recommendations for international students: Required—TOEFL (minimum score 550 paper-based; 213 computer-based).

Emory University, School of Medicine, Professional Program in Medicine, Atlanta, GA 30322-4510. Offers MD, MD/MPH, MD/MSCR, MD/PhD. *Accreditation:* LCME/AMA. *Faculty:* 2,032 full-time (706 women), 1,200 part-time/adjunct (426 women). *Students:* 517 full-time (274 women); includes 153 minority (42 African Americans, 1 American Indian/Alaska Native, 91 Asian Americans or Pacific Islanders, 19 Hispanic Americans), 13 international. Average age 25. 3,971 applicants, 8% accepted, 136 enrolled. In 2009, 109 MDs awarded. *Degree requirements:* For MD, United States Medical Licensing Exam Step 1 and 2. *Entrance requirements:* MCAT. *Application deadline:* For fall admission, 10/15 for domestic and international students. Applications are processed on a rolling basis. Application fee: $100. Electronic applications accepted. *Expenses:* Contact institution. *Financial support:* In 2009–10, 379 students received support. Institutionally sponsored loans and scholarships/grants available. Financial award application deadline: 3/1; financial award applicants required to submit CSS PROFILE or FAFSA. *Faculty research:* Immunology and pathogenesis of chronic viral infections, immunological memory and vaccine development, development of antiviral agents to treat infections caused by human immunodeficiency and hepatitus viruses, development of therapeutic and diagnostic approaches to improve outcomes after transplantation genetic mechanisms of neuropsychiatric disease, Fragile X Syndrome, immune system ontogeny and phylogeny. Total annual research expenditures: $269.4 million. *Application contact:* Dr. Ira K. Schwartz, Associate Dean of Student Affairs/Director of Admissions, 404-727-5660, Fax: 404-727-5456, E-mail: medadmissions@emory.edu.

Florida International University, Herbert Wertheim College of Medicine, Miami, FL 33199. Offers MD. *Faculty:* 30 full-time (11 women), 6 part-time/adjunct (0 women). *Students:* 43 full-time (16 women); includes 25 minority (2 African Americans, 1 American Indian/Alaska Native, 8 Asian Americans or Pacific Islanders, 14 Hispanic Americans). Average age 25. 3,247 applicants, 4% accepted, 43 enrolled. *Entrance requirements:* MCAT (minimum score of 25), minimum overall GPA of 3.0; 3 letters of recommendation, 2 from basic science faculty (biology, chemistry, physics, math) and 1 from any other faculty member. *Application deadline:* For fall admission, 12/15 for domestic students. Application fee: $160. Electronic applications accepted. *Expenses:* Contact institution. *Financial support:* Institutionally sponsored loans and scholarships/grants available. Financial award application deadline: 3/1; financial award applicants required to submit FAFSA. *Unit head:* Dr. John Rock, Dean, 305-348-0644, Fax: 305-348-0650, E-mail: med.admissions@fiu.edu. *Application contact:* Betty Monfort, Director of Admissions and Records, 305-348-0644, Fax: 305-348-0650, E-mail: med.admissions@fiu.edu.

Georgetown University, School of Medicine, Washington, DC 20057. Offers MD, MD/MBA, MD/PhD. *Accreditation:* LCME/AMA. *Entrance requirements:* MCAT, minimum 90 credit hours with 1 year of course work in biology, organic chemistry, inorganic chemistry, physics, mathematics, and English. *Expenses:* Contact institution.

The George Washington University, School of Medicine and Health Sciences, Professional Program in Medicine, Washington, DC 20052. Offers MD, MD/MPH, MD/PhD. *Accreditation:* LCME/AMA. *Students:* 717 full-time (425 women); includes 265 minority (85 African Americans, 1 American Indian/Alaska Native, 172 Asian Americans or Pacific Islanders, 7 Hispanic Americans), 1 international. Average age 26. In 2009, 164 MDs awarded. *Entrance requirements:* MCAT, minimum 90 undergraduate semester hours, specific pre-med courses equal to 38 semester hours. *Application deadline:* For fall admission, 12/1 for domestic students. Applications are processed on a rolling basis. Application fee: $80. *Financial support:* Career-related internships or fieldwork, Federal Work-Study, and institutionally sponsored loans available. *Unit head:* Dr. Alan Wasserman, Chair, 202-741-2302. *Application contact:* Diane P. McQuail, Director of Admissions, 202-994-3507, E-mail: maeve@gwu.edu.

Harvard University, Harvard Medical School and Graduate School of Arts and Sciences, Division of Health Sciences and Technology, Program in Medical Sciences, Cambridge, MA 02138. Offers MD, MD/MM Sc. *Accreditation:* LCME/AMA. *Students:* 179 full-time (66 women); includes 103 minority (4 African Americans, 1 American Indian/Alaska Native, 89 Asian Americans or Pacific Islanders, 9 Hispanic Americans), 10 international. Average age 26. 683 applicants, 6% accepted, 30 enrolled. In 2009, 38 MDs awarded. *Degree requirements:* For MD, thesis/dissertation. *Entrance requirements:* MCAT. *Application deadline:* For fall admission, 10/15 for domestic students. Application fee: $85. *Expenses:* Contact institution. *Financial support:* In 2009–10, 61 students received support, including 8 fellowships with partial tuition reimbursements available (averaging $39,792 per year), 39 research assistantships with partial tuition reimbursements available (averaging $21,343 per year), 24 teaching assistantships with partial tuition reimbursements available (averaging $6,034 per year); career-related internships or fieldwork, scholarships/grants, health care benefits, and unspecified assistantships also available. Financial award application deadline: 10/15; financial award applicants required to submit FAFSA. *Unit head:* Dr. David Earl Cohen, Director of Health Sciences and Technology, 617-726-5576. *Application contact:* Zara Smith, MD Admissions Coordinator, 617-432-7195, E-mail: hstadmissions@hms.harvard.edu.

Harvard University, Harvard Medical School, Professional Program in Medicine, Cambridge, MA 02138. Offers MD, PhD, MD/MBA, MD/MM Sc, MD/MPH, MD/MPP, MD/PhD. *Accreditation:* LCME/AMA. *Faculty:* 8,259 full-time, 2,758 part-time/adjunct. *Students:* 705 full-time (346 women); includes 345 minority (71 African Americans, 6 American Indian/Alaska Native, 210 Asian Americans or Pacific Islanders, 58 Hispanic Americans), 45 international. Average age 26. 5,031 applicants, 4% accepted, 165 enrolled. In 2009, 175 first professional degrees awarded. *Entrance requirements:* MCAT, previous course work in biology, chemistry, physics, calculus, and expository writing. *Application deadline:* For fall admission, 10/15 for domestic students. Application fee: $85. Electronic applications accepted. *Expenses:* Tuition: Full-time $33,696. Required fees: $1126. Full-time tuition and fees vary according to program. *Financial support:* In 2009–10, 571 students received support; fellowships, research assistantships, teaching assistantships, career-related internships or fieldwork, Federal Work-Study, institutionally sponsored loans, scholarships/grants, and tuition waivers (partial) available. Financial award application deadline: 4/15; financial award applicants required to submit CSS PROFILE or FAFSA. *Unit head:* Dr. Jules Dienstag, Dean for Medical Education, 617-432-6250. *Application contact:* Admissions Office, 617-432-1550, Fax: 617-432-3307, E-mail: admissions_office@hms.harvard.edu.

Howard University, College of Medicine, Professional Program in Medicine, Washington, DC 20059-0002. Offers MD, PhD, MD/PhD. *Accreditation:* LCME/AMA. *Degree requirements:* For MD, U. S. Medical Licensing Exam Steps 1 and 2. *Entrance requirements:* MCAT, previous course work in biology, English, general and organic chemistry, mathematics, and physics. *Faculty research:* Infectious diseases, protein modeling, neuropsychopharmacology.

Indiana University–Purdue University Indianapolis, Indiana University School of Medicine, Indianapolis, IN 46202-5114. Offers MD, MPH, MS, DPT, PhD, MD/MA, MD/MBA, MD/MS, MD/PhD. *Accreditation:* LCME/AMA. *Faculty:* 270 full-time (56 women). *Students:* 1,740 full-time (899 women), 113 part-time (82 women); includes 302 minority (98 African Americans, 9 American Indian/Alaska Native, 154 Asian Americans or Pacific Islanders, 41 Hispanic Americans), 113 international. Average age 26. 1,071 applicants, 39% accepted, 375 enrolled. In 2009, 258 first professional degrees, 43 master's awarded. *Degree requirements:* For doctorate, thesis/dissertation. *Entrance requirements:* For MD, MCAT; for master's and doctorate, GRE General Test. Additional exam requirements/recommendations for international students: Required—TOEFL. *Application deadline:* For fall admission, 8/1 priority date for domestic students. Applications are processed on a rolling basis. Application fee: $55 ($65 for international students). *Expenses:* Contact institution. *Financial support:* Fellowships with full and partial tuition reimbursements, research assistantships with full and partial tuition reimbursements, teaching assistantships with full tuition reimbursements, Federal Work-Study, institutionally sponsored loans, scholarships/grants, tuition waivers (full and partial), and stipends available. Support available to part-time students. Total annual research expenditures: $94.3 million. *Unit head:* Dr. D. Craig Brater, Dean, 317-274-5000, Fax: 317-278-5211. *Application contact:* Robert M. Stump, Director of Admissions, 317-274-3772, E-mail: inmedadm@iupui.edu.

Instituto Tecnologico de Santo Domingo, School of Medicine, Santo Domingo, Dominican Republic. Offers MD, M Bioethics.

The Johns Hopkins University, School of Medicine, Professional Program in Medicine, Baltimore, MD 21218-2699. Offers MD, MD/PhD. *Accreditation:* LCME/AMA. *Faculty:* 2,384 full-time (906 women), 1,244 part-time/adjunct (408 women). *Students:* 480 full-time (231 women); includes 220 minority (38 African Americans, 3 American Indian/Alaska Native, 163 Asian Americans or Pacific Islanders, 16 Hispanic Americans), 16 international. Average age 24. 3,655 applicants, 7% accepted, 120 enrolled. In 2009, 125 MDs awarded. *Entrance requirements:* MCAT. *Application deadline:* For fall admission, 10/15 for domestic and international students. Applications are processed on a rolling basis. Application fee: $80. Electronic applications accepted. *Financial support:* Fellowships, research assistantships, teaching assistantships available. *Unit head:* Dr. Edward D. Miller, Dean of Medical Faculty and Chief Executive Officer, 410-955-3180. *Application contact:* Dr. James L. Weiss, Associate Dean for Admissions, 410-955-3182, Fax: 410-516-5188.

Loma Linda University, School of Medicine, Loma Linda, CA 92350. Offers MD, MS, PhD. *Accreditation:* LCME/AMA. *Degree requirements:* For master's, thesis optional; for doctorate, thesis/dissertation. *Entrance requirements:* MCAT, 1 year course work in biology, chemistry, organic chemistry, and physics. Additional exam requirements/recommendations for international students: Required—TOEFL (minimum score 550 paper-based; 213 computer-based). *Expenses:* Contact institution.

Louisiana State University Health Sciences Center, School of Medicine in New Orleans, New Orleans, LA 70112-2223. Offers MD, MPH, MD/PhD. Open only to Louisiana residents. *Accreditation:* LCME/AMA. *Entrance requirements:* MCAT. Electronic applications accepted. *Expenses:* Contact institution. *Faculty research:* Medical and basic sciences.

Louisiana State University Health Sciences Center at Shreveport, School of Medicine, Shreveport, LA 71130-3932. Offers MD, MD/PhD. *Accreditation:* LCME/AMA. *Entrance requirements:* MCAT. *Expenses:* Contact institution. *Faculty research:* Biomedical science, molecular biology, cardiovascular science.

Loyola University Chicago, Stritch School of Medicine, Maywood, IL 60153. Offers MD. *Accreditation:* LCME/AMA. *Degree requirements:* For MD, passing scores on U. S. Medical Licensing Exam Step 1, Step 2CS, and Step 2CK. *Entrance requirements:* MCAT, 1 full academic year of general biology or zoology, organic chemistry, physics and inorganic chemistry all with labs. *Expenses:* Contact institution. *Faculty research:* Cardiovascular pathophysiology, cancer biology, neuroscience, burn injury, infectious disease.

Marshall University, Joan C. Edwards School of Medicine, Professional Program in Medicine, Huntington, WV 25755. Offers MD. *Accreditation:* LCME/AMA. *Degree requirements:* For MD, U. S. Medical Licensing Exam, Steps 1 and 2. *Entrance requirements:* MCAT, 1 year of course work in biology, physics, chemistry, organic chemistry, English, and social or behavioral sciences. *Expenses:* Contact institution.

Mayo Medical School, Professional Program, Rochester, MN 55905. Offers MD, MD/Certificate, MD/PhD. MD offered through the Mayo Foundation's Division of Education. *Accreditation:* LCME/AMA. *Entrance requirements:* MCAT, previous undergraduate course work in biology, chemistry, physics, and biochemistry. Electronic applications accepted.

McGill University, Faculty of Graduate and Postdoctoral Studies, Faculty of Medicine, Department of Surgery, Montréal, QC H3A 2T5, Canada. Offers M Sc, PhD.

McGill University, Professional Program in Medicine, Montréal, QC H3A 2T5, Canada. Offers MD/CM, MD/MBA, MD/PhD. *Accreditation:* LCME/AMA.

Medical College of Georgia, School of Medicine, Augusta, GA 30912. Offers MD, MD/PhD. *Accreditation:* LCME/AMA. *Faculty:* 438 full-time (133 women), 80 part-time/adjunct (37 women). *Students:* 762 full-time (335 women); includes 223 minority (46 African Americans, 161 Asian Americans or Pacific Islanders, 16 Hispanic Americans). Average age 25. 2,055 applicants, 15% accepted, 190 enrolled. In 2009, 179 MDs awarded. *Degree requirements:* For MD, comprehensive exam. *Entrance requirements:* MCAT, minimum GPA of 3.6 in sciences, 3.64 overall. *Application deadline:* For fall admission, 11/1 for domestic students. Applications are processed on a rolling basis. Application fee: $0. *Expenses:* Contact institution. *Financial support:* Fellowships with tuition reimbursements, career-related internships or fieldwork, Federal Work-Study, institutionally sponsored loans, and scholarships/grants available. Support available to part-time students. Financial award application deadline: 5/1; financial award applicants required to submit FAFSA. *Faculty research:* Cancer, cardiovascular diseases, diabetes, neurological diseases, infection and inflammation. Total annual research expenditures: $50 million. *Unit head:* Dr. Douglas Miller, Senior Vice President for Health Affairs/Dean, 706-721-2231, Fax: 706-721-7035, E-mail: ddmiller@mcg.edu. *Application contact:* Dr. Geoffrey H. Young, Associate Dean for Admissions, 706-721-3186, Fax: 706-721-0959, E-mail: geyoung@mcg.edu.

Medical College of Wisconsin, Medical School, Professional Program in Medicine, Milwaukee, WI 53226-0509. Offers MD, MD/MA, MD/MS, MD/PhD. *Accreditation:* LCME/AMA. *Entrance requirements:* MCAT, interview, minimum 4 years of college.

Medical University of South Carolina, College of Medicine, Charleston, SC 29425. Offers MD, MD/MBA, MD/MHA, MD/MPH, MD/MSCR, MD/PhD. *Accreditation:* LCME/AMA. *Faculty:* 1,083 full-time (402 women), 151 part-time/adjunct (64 women). *Students:* 670 full-time (280 women); includes 162 minority (89 African Americans, 7 American Indian/Alaska Native, 48 Asian Americans or Pacific Islanders, 18 Hispanic Americans), 7 international. Average age 26. 2,667 applicants, 7% accepted, 155 enrolled. In 2009, 136 MDs awarded. *Degree requirements:* For MD, Steps 1 and 2 of Clinical Performance Exam and U. S. Medical Licensing Examination. *Entrance requirements:* MCAT, interview. *Application deadline:* For fall admission, 12/1 for domestic students. Applications are processed on a rolling basis. Application fee: $85. Electronic applications accepted. *Expenses:* Contact institution. *Financial support:* Federal Work-Study and scholarships/grants available. Financial award application deadline: 3/10; financial award applicants required to submit FAFSA. *Faculty research:* Cardiovascular proteomics, translational cancer research, diabetes mellitus, neurodegenerative diseases, addiction. Total annual research expenditures: $114 million. *Unit head:* Dr. Etta D. Pisano, Dean, 843-792-2842, Fax: 843-792-2967, E-mail: pisanoe@musc.edu. *Application contact:* Joan M. Graesch, Admissions Counselor, 843-792-3283, Fax: 843-792-0204, E-mail: jmg26@musc.edu.

Meharry Medical College, School of Medicine, Nashville, TN 37208-9989. Offers MD. *Accreditation:* LCME/AMA. *Entrance requirements:* MCAT. Electronic applications accepted. *Faculty research:* Signal transduction, membrane biology, neurophysiology, tropical medicine.

Mercer University, School of Medicine, Macon, GA 31207. Offers MD, MFT, MPH, MSA. *Accreditation:* AAMFT/COAMFTE; LCME/AMA (one or more programs are accredited). *Faculty:* 203 full-time, 931 part-time/adjunct. *Students:* 465 full-time (254 women), 1 (woman) part-time. 1,060 applicants, 24% accepted, 174 enrolled. In 2009, 58 first professional degrees, 36 master's awarded. *Entrance requirements:* Additional exam requirements/recommendations for international students: Required—TOEFL. *Application deadline:* For fall admission, 1/15 for domestic students, 10/1 for international students. Applications are processed on a rolling basis. Application fee: $50 ($150 for international students). *Financial support:* Institutionally sponsored loans available. Financial award application deadline: 4/1; financial award applicants required to submit FAFSA. *Faculty research:* Anatomy, biochemistry/nutrition, genetics, microbiology/immunology, neuroscience. *Unit head:* Dr. William Bina, Dean, 478-301-5570, Fax: 478-301-2547. *Application contact:* Mary C. Putnam, Enrollment Associate, 478-301-2542, Fax: 478-301-2547, E-mail: putnam_mc@mercer.edu.

Michigan State University, College of Human Medicine, Professional Program in Human Medicine, East Lansing, MI 48824. Offers human medicine (MD); human medicine/medical scientist training program (MD). *Accreditation:* LCME/AMA. *Students:* 566 full-time (288 women), 38 part-time (21 women); includes 182 minority (45 African Americans, 7 American Indian/Alaska Native, 102 Asian Americans or Pacific Islanders, 28 Hispanic Americans), 9 international. Average age 26. 316 applicants, 99% accepted. In 2009, 95 MDs awarded. *Entrance requirements:* Additional exam requirements/recommendations for international students: Required—TOEFL, Michigan State University ELT (minimum score 85), Michigan Michigan English Language Assessment Battery (minimum score 83). *Application deadline:* For fall admission, 11/15 for domestic students. Electronic applications accepted. *Expenses:* Tuition, state resident: part-time $478.25 per credit hour. Tuition, nonresident: part-time $966.50 per credit hour. Part-time tuition and fees vary according to program. *Financial support:* In 2009–10, 4 research assistantships with tuition reimbursements (averaging $7,019 per year) were awarded. *Unit head:* Dr. Marsha D. Rappley, Dean, 517-353-1730, E-mail: rappley@msu.edu. *Application contact:* Admissions Officer, 517-353-9620, Fax: 517-432-0021, E-mail: mdadmissions@msu.edu.

Morehouse School of Medicine, Professional Program, Atlanta, GA 30310-1495. Offers MD, MD/MPH. *Accreditation:* LCME/AMA. *Faculty:* 220 full-time (105 women), 41 part-time/adjunct (16 women). *Students:* 217 full-time (133 women); includes 196 minority (156 African Americans, 22 American Indian/Alaska Native, 11 Asian Americans or Pacific Islanders, 7 Hispanic Americans). Average age 26. 3,753 applicants, 4% accepted, 56 enrolled. In 2009, 56 MDs awarded. *Degree requirements:* For MD, U. S. Medical Licensing Exam Steps 1 and 2. *Entrance requirements:* MCAT. *Application deadline:* For fall admission, 12/1 for domestic students. Applications are processed on a rolling basis. Application fee: $50. Electronic applications accepted. *Expenses:* Contact institution. *Financial support:* In 2009–10, 200 students received support. Career-related internships or fieldwork, Federal Work-Study, institutionally sponsored loans, and scholarships/grants available. Financial award application deadline: 5/1; financial award applicants required to submit FAFSA. *Faculty research:* Cardiovascular disease and related sequela, infectious diseases/HIV-AIDS, neurological diseases, cancer. Total annual research expenditures: $6.9 million. *Unit head:* Dr. Martha Elks, Senior Associate Dean for Education and Faculty Affairs, 404-752-1881, Fax: 404-752-1594, E-mail: melks@msm.edu. *Application contact:* Dr. Sterling Roaf, Director of Admissions, 404-752-1650, Fax: 404-752-1512, E-mail: mdadmission@msm.edu.

Mount Sinai School of Medicine of New York University, Medical School, New York, NY 10029-6504. Offers MD, MD/PhD. *Accreditation:* LCME/AMA. *Degree requirements:* For MD, comprehensive exam, United States Medical Licensing Examination Steps 1 and 2. *Entrance requirements:* MCAT. Additional exam requirements/recommendations for international students: Required—TOEFL. *Expenses:* Contact institution. *Faculty research:* Academic medicine, translational research.

New York Medical College, Professional Program, Vahalla, NY 10595-1691. Offers MD, MD/MPH, MD/PhD. *Accreditation:* LCME/AMA. *Entrance requirements:* MCAT, 2 semesters of course work in general biology, general chemistry, organic chemistry, physics, and English. Electronic applications accepted. *Expenses:* Contact institution. *Faculty research:* Vascular function, hormonal regulation of blood pressure, physiological and molecular control of heart failure, neuroscience, adult stem cells.

New York University, School of Medicine, Professional Program in Medicine, New York, NY 10012-1019. Offers MD, MD/MA, MD/MPA, MD/PhD. *Accreditation:* LCME/AMA. *Faculty:* 1,126 full-time (395 women), 384 part-time/adjunct (139 women). *Students:* 670 full-time (331 women); includes 236 minority (31 African Americans, 4 American Indian/Alaska Native, 157 Asian Americans or Pacific Islanders, 44 Hispanic Americans), 3 international. Average age 24. 7,573 applicants, 6% accepted, 160 enrolled. In 2009, 158 MDs awarded. *Entrance requirements:* MCAT. *Application deadline:* For fall admission, 10/15 for domestic students. Application fee: $100. *Expenses:* Contact institution. *Financial support:* In 2009–10, 365 students received support. Federal Work-Study, institutionally sponsored loans, and scholarships/grants available. Financial award application deadline: 7/21; financial award applicants required to submit FAFSA. *Faculty research:* Vascular biology, cancer genetics, molecular pathogenesis, epithelial pathobiology, microbial pathogenesis/host defense. Total annual research expenditures: $141.6 million. *Unit head:* Dr. Veronica Catanese, Senior Associate Dean for Education and Student Affairs, 212-263-0794, Fax: 212-263-0520, E-mail: veronica.catanese@med.nyu.edu. *Application contact:* Dr. Nancy Genieser, Associate Dean, Admissions, 212-263-5290, Fax: 212-263-0720, E-mail: nancy.genieser@nyumc.org.

Northeastern Ohio Universities College of Medicine and Pharmacy, College of Medicine, Rootstown, OH 44272-0095. Offers MD, MD/PhD. *Accreditation:* LCME/AMA. *Faculty:* 344 full-time (107 women), 1,727 part-time/adjunct (390 women). *Students:* 460 full-time (227 women); includes 174 minority (15 African Americans, 1 American Indian/Alaska Native, 145 Asian Americans or Pacific Islanders, 13 Hispanic Americans). Average age 23. 555 applicants, 34% accepted, 108 enrolled. In 2009, 120 MDs awarded. *Entrance requirements:* MCAT, 2 semesters of course work in organic chemistry and physics. *Application deadline:* For fall admission, 8/1 priority date for domestic students; for winter admission, 10/1 for domestic students. Applications are processed on a rolling basis. Application fee: $40. Electronic applications accepted. *Financial support:* In 2009–10, 133 students received support. Institutionally sponsored loans and scholarships/grants available. Financial award application deadline: 4/15; financial award applicants required to submit FAFSA. *Faculty research:* Lipid metabolism/cardiovascular disease, bone diseases/skeletal biology, virology/infectious diseases, clinical outcomes, sensory neurobiology. Total annual research expenditures: $4.3 million. *Unit head:* Dr. Jay Williamson, Interim Dean, 330-325-6255. *Application contact:* Julie Grove, Assistant Director of Admissions, 330-325-6270, E-mail: admission@neoucom.edu.

Northwestern University, Northwestern University Feinberg School of Medicine, Combined MD/PhD Medical Scientist Training Program, Evanston, IL 60208. Offers MD/PhD. Application must be made to both The Graduate School and the Medical School. *Accreditation:* LCME/AMA. Electronic applications accepted. *Faculty research:* Cardiovascular epidemiology, cancer epidemiology, nutritional interventions for the prevention of cardiovascular disease and cancer, women's health, outcomes research.

The Ohio State University, College of Medicine, School of Biomedical Science, Professional Program in Medicine, Columbus, OH 43210. Offers MD. *Accreditation:* LCME/AMA. *Entrance requirements:* MCAT. Electronic applications accepted. *Expenses:* Tuition, state resident: full-time $10,683. Tuition, nonresident: full-time $25,923. Tuition and fees vary according to course load

Allopathic Medicine

The Ohio State University (continued)
and program. *Faculty research:* Molecular genetics, stress and the immune system, molecular cardiology, transplantation biology.

Oregon Health & Science University, School of Medicine, Professional Program in Medicine, Portland, OR 97239-3098. Offers MD, MD/DMD. *Accreditation:* LCME/AMA. *Degree requirements:* For MD, National Board Exam Parts I and II. *Entrance requirements:* MCAT, 1 year of course work in biology, English, social science and physics; 2 years of course work in chemistry and genetics. Tuition and fees vary according to course level, course load, degree level, program and reciprocity agreements.

Penn State Hershey Medical Center, College of Medicine, Hershey, PA 17033. Offers MD, MS, PhD, MD/PhD, PhD/MBA. *Accreditation:* LCME/AMA. Terminal master's awarded for partial completion of doctoral program. *Degree requirements:* For master's, thesis optional; for doctorate, comprehensive exam, thesis/dissertation, minimum GPA of 3.0. *Entrance requirements:* For MD, MCAT; for master's and doctorate, GRE. Additional exam requirements/recommendations for international students: Required—TOEFL (minimum score 560 paper-based; 220 computer-based). *Application deadline:* Applications are processed on a rolling basis. Application fee: $65. Electronic applications accepted. *Expenses:* Contact institution. *Financial support:* In 2009–10, 99 students received support, including research assistantships with full tuition reimbursements available (averaging $22,260 per year); fellowships with full tuition reimbursements available, career-related internships or fieldwork, scholarships/grants, health care benefits, and unspecified assistantships also available. *Unit head:* Dr. Michael Verderame, Assistant Dean for Graduate Studies, 717-531-8892, Fax: 717-531-0786, E-mail: grad-hmc@psu.edu. *Application contact:* Dr. Michael Verderame, Assistant Dean for Graduate Studies, 717-531-8892, Fax: 717-531-0786, E-mail: grad-hmc@psu.edu.

Ponce School of Medicine, Professional Program, Ponce, PR 00732-7004. Offers MD. *Accreditation:* LCME/AMA. *Faculty:* 128 full-time (47 women), 206 part-time/adjunct (52 women). *Students:* 288 full-time (142 women); includes 1 African American, 6 Asian Americans or Pacific Islanders, 253 Hispanic Americans. Average age 26. 1,346 applicants, 12% accepted, 66 enrolled. In 2009, 85 MDs awarded. *Degree requirements:* For MD, one foreign language, comprehensive exam, United States Medical Licensing Exam. *Entrance requirements:* MCAT, coursework in Spanish language, proficiency in Spanish/English, 3 letters of recommendation, criminal backgound check. Additional exam requirements/recommendations for international students: Required—TOEFL. *Application deadline:* For fall admission, 12/15 for domestic and international students. Applications are processed on a rolling basis. Application fee: $100. Electronic applications accepted. *Expenses:* Tuition: Part-time $225 per credit hour. Part-time tuition and fees vary according to program. *Financial support:* In 2009–10, 280 students received support; fellowships, scholarships/grants available. Financial award application deadline: 4/30; financial award applicants required to submit FAFSA. *Unit head:* Dr. Joxel Garcia, President and Dean, 787-844-3710, Fax: 787-840-9756, E-mail: jgarcia@psm.edu. *Application contact:* Maria Colon, Admissions Officer, 787-840-2575 Ext. 2143, E-mail: mcolon@psm.edu.

Pontificia Universidad Catolica Madre y Maestra, Department of Medicine, Santiago, Dominican Republic. Offers MD.

Queen's University at Kingston, School of Medicine, Professional Program in Medicine, Kingston, ON K7L 3N6, Canada. Offers MD. *Accreditation:* LCME/AMA. *Entrance requirements:* MCAT.

Rosalind Franklin University of Medicine and Science, The Chicago Medical School, North Chicago, IL 60064-3095. Offers MD, MD/MS, MD/PhD. *Accreditation:* LCME/AMA. *Degree requirements:* For MD, clerkship, step 1 and step 2 exams. *Entrance requirements:* MCAT, 3 years of course work with lab in biology, physics, inorganic chemistry, and organic chemistry. *Expenses:* Contact institution. *Faculty research:* Neurosciences, structural biology, cancer biology, cell biology, developmental biology.

Rush University, Rush Medical College, Chicago, IL 60612. Offers MD, MD/PhD. *Accreditation:* LCME/AMA. *Entrance requirements:* MCAT, interview. Electronic applications accepted. *Expenses:* Contact institution.

Saint Louis University, Graduate School, School of Medicine, Program in Medicine, St. Louis, MO 63103-2097. Offers MD. *Accreditation:* LCME/AMA. *Degree requirements:* For MD, U. S. Medical Licensing Exam Steps 1 and 2. *Entrance requirements:* MCAT, photograph, letters of recommendation, interview. Additional exam requirements/recommendations for international students: Required—TOEFL (minimum score 525 paper-based; 199 computer-based). Electronic applications accepted. *Expenses:* Contact institution. *Faculty research:* Geriatric medicine, organ transplantation, chronic disease prevention, vaccine research.

San Juan Bautista School of Medicine, Professional Program, Caguas, PR 00726-4968. Offers MD. *Accreditation:* LCME/AMA. *Faculty:* 35 full-time (19 women), 20 part-time/adjunct (4 women). *Students:* 253 full-time (164 women); all minorities (all Hispanic Americans). 204 applicants, 50% accepted, 60 enrolled. In 2009, 69 MDs awarded. *Degree requirements:* For MD, comprehensive exam, United States Medical Licensing Exam Steps I and II. *Entrance requirements:* MCAT, interview. *Application deadline:* For fall admission, 7/20 priority date for domestic students. Applications are processed on a rolling basis. Application fee: $75. *Expenses:* Tuition: Full-time $8500. *Financial support:* Applicants required to submit FAFSA. *Faculty research:* Protein structure, Cl tissue inflammations, bacterial metabolism, human hormone. *Unit head:* Dr. Yocasta Brugal, President/Dean, 787-743-3038, Fax: 787-746-3093, E-mail: xbrugal@sanjuanbautista.edu. *Application contact:* Jaymi Sanchez, Admissions, 787-743-3038 Ext. 236, Fax: 787-746-3093, E-mail: jsanchez@sanjuanbautista.edu.

Stanford University, School of Medicine, Professional Program in Medicine, Stanford, CA 94305-9991. Offers MD. *Accreditation:* LCME/AMA. *Entrance requirements:* MCAT. Electronic applications accepted. *Expenses:* Contact institution.

State University of New York Downstate Medical Center, College of Medicine, Brooklyn, NY 11203-2098. Offers MD, MPH, MD/MPH, MD/PhD. *Accreditation:* LCME/AMA. *Entrance requirements:* MCAT. *Expenses:* Contact institution. *Faculty research:* AIDS epidemiology, virus/host interaction, molecular genetics, developmental neurobiology, prostate cancer.

State University of New York Downstate Medical Center, School of Graduate Studies, MD/PhD Program, Brooklyn, NY 11203-2098. Offers MD/PhD.

State University of New York Upstate Medical University, College of Medicine, Syracuse, NY 13210-2334. Offers MD, MD/PhD. *Accreditation:* LCME/AMA. *Degree requirements:* For MD, comprehensive exam. *Entrance requirements:* MCAT. Additional exam requirements/recommendations for international students: Required—TOEFL. Electronic applications accepted. *Expenses:* Contact institution.

Stony Brook University, State University of New York, Stony Brook University Medical Center, School of Medicine, Medical Scientist Training Program, Stony Brook, NY 11794. Offers MD/PhD. *Application deadline:* For fall admission, 1/15 for domestic students. *Expenses:* Tuition, state resident: full-time $8370; part-time $349 per credit. Tuition, nonresident: full-time $13,250; part-time $552 per credit. Required fees: $933. *Financial support:* Tuition waivers (full) available. *Unit head:* Dr. Richard N. Fine, Dean, 631-444-2113. *Application contact:* Dr. Richard N. Fine, Dean, 631-444-2113.

Stony Brook University, State University of New York, Stony Brook University Medical Center, School of Medicine, Professional Program in Medicine, Stony Brook, NY 11794. Offers MD, MD/PhD. *Accreditation:* LCME/AMA. *Faculty:* 518 full-time (171 women), 92 part-time/adjunct (43 women). *Students:* 474 full-time (227 women); includes 216 minority (39 African Americans, 3 American Indian/Alaska Native, 152 Asian Americans or Pacific Islanders, 22 Hispanic Americans), 1 international. Average age 26. 3,498 applicants, 7% accepted. In 2009, 108 MDs awarded. *Entrance requirements:* MCAT, interview. *Application deadline:* For fall admission, 1/15 for domestic students. Application fee: $75. *Expenses:* Tuition, state resident: full-time $8370; part-time $349 per credit. Tuition, nonresident: full-time $13,250; part-time $552 per credit. Required fees: $933. *Financial support:* Fellowships, teaching assistantships available. Total annual research expenditures: $33.2 million. *Unit head:* Dr. Richard Fine, Dean, 631-444-1785. *Application contact:* Dr. Jack Fuhrer, Associate Dean for Admissions, 631-444-2113, Fax: 631-444-6032, E-mail: admissions@dean.som.sunysb.edu.

Temple University, Health Sciences Center, School of Medicine, Professional Program in Medicine, Philadelphia, PA 19140. Offers MD, MD/MPH, MD/PhD. *Accreditation:* LCME/AMA. *Faculty:* 428 full-time (116 women), 55 part-time/adjunct (19 women). *Students:* 741 full-time (345 women); includes 277 minority (54 African Americans, 7 American Indian/Alaska Native, 152 Asian Americans or Pacific Islanders, 64 Hispanic Americans). Average age 24. 9,179 applicants, 6% accepted, 196 enrolled. In 2009, 163 MDs awarded. *Degree requirements:* For MD, United States Medical Licensing Exam Step 1, Step 2CK, and Step 2CS. *Entrance requirements:* MCAT. *Application deadline:* For fall admission, 12/15 for domestic students. Applications are processed on a rolling basis. Application fee: $75. Electronic applications accepted. *Expenses:* Contact institution. *Financial support:* In 2009–10, 673 students received support, including 12 fellowships with full tuition reimbursements available (averaging $15,300 per year), 8 research assistantships with full tuition reimbursements available (averaging $22,000 per year); Federal Work-Study, institutionally sponsored loans, and scholarships/grants also available. Financial award application deadline: 3/1; financial award applicants required to submit FAFSA. *Faculty research:* Translational medicine, molecular biology and immunology of autoimmune diseases and cancer, cardiovascular and pulmonary disease pathophysiology, biology of substance abuse, causes and consequences of obesity, molecular mechanisms of neurological dysfunction. Total annual research expenditures: $52.8 million. *Unit head:* Dr. John M. Daly, Dean, 215-707-7000, Fax: 215-707-8431, E-mail: johndaly@temple.edu. *Application contact:* Information Contact, 215-707-3656, E-mail: medadmissions@temple.edu.

Texas Tech University Health Sciences Center, School of Medicine, Lubbock, TX 79430-0002. Offers MD, MD/MBA, MD/PhD. Open only to residents of Texas, eastern New Mexico, and southwestern Oklahoma. *Accreditation:* LCME/AMA. *Entrance requirements:* MCAT. Additional exam requirements/recommendations for international students: Required—TOEFL. Electronic applications accepted. *Expenses:* Contact institution.

Thomas Jefferson University, Jefferson College of Graduate Studies, MD/PhD Program, Philadelphia, PA 19107. Offers MD/PhD. *Students:* 17 full-time (8 women); includes 4 minority (2 African Americans, 2 Asian Americans or Pacific Islanders), 3 international. 140 applicants, 7% accepted, 5 enrolled. *Entrance requirements:* Additional exam requirements/recommendations for international students: Required—IELTS or TOEFL (minimum score 250 computer-based; 100 iBT). *Application deadline:* For fall admission, 11/1 for domestic and international students. Applications are processed on a rolling basis. Application fee: $0. Electronic applications accepted. *Expenses:* Tuition: Full-time $26,858; part-time $879 per credit. Required fees: $525. *Financial support:* In 2009–10, 17 fellowships with full tuition reimbursements were awarded; Federal Work-Study and institutionally sponsored loans also available. Financial award application deadline: 5/1; financial award applicants required to submit FAFSA. *Faculty research:* Signal transduction, tumorigenesis, apoptosis, molecular immunology, structural biology. *Unit head:* Dr. Scott A. Waldman, Academic Director, 215-955-6086, Fax: 215-955-5681, E-mail: scott.waldman@jefferson.edu. *Application contact:* Marc E. Stearns, Director of Admissions, 215-503-0155, Fax: 215-503-9920, E-mail: jcgs-info@jefferson.edu.

Thomas Jefferson University, Jefferson Medical College, Philadelphia, PA 19107. Offers MD, MD/PhD. *Accreditation:* LCME/AMA. *Faculty:* 743 full-time (225 women), 42 part-time/adjunct (21 women). *Students:* 1,018 full-time (512 women); includes 312 minority (21 African Americans, 2 American Indian/Alaska Native, 240 Asian Americans or Pacific Islanders, 49 Hispanic Americans), 56 international. Average age 26. 9,713 applicants, 5% accepted, 255 enrolled. In 2009, 256 MDs awarded. *Entrance requirements:* MCAT. *Application deadline:* For fall admission, 11/15 for domestic and international students. Applications are processed on a rolling basis. Application fee: $80. Electronic applications accepted. *Expenses:* Contact institution. *Financial support:* In 2009–10, 856 students received support. Federal Work-Study and institutionally sponsored loans available. Financial award application deadline: 3/1; financial award applicants required to submit FAFSA. *Faculty research:* Translational medicine, Alzheimer's research, pancreatic cancer, oncology and endocrinology. Total annual research expenditures: $67.7 million. *Unit head:* Dr. Mark Tykowcinski, Interim Dean, 215-955-6980, Fax: 215-923-6939. *Application contact:* Dr. Clara Callahan, Dean for Admissions, 215-955-6983, Fax: 215-923-6939, E-mail: clara.callahan@jefferson.edu.

Tufts University, School of Medicine, Professional Program in Medicine, Medford, MA 02155. Offers MD, MD/MA, MD/MBA, MD/MPH, MD/MSE, MD/PhD. *Accreditation:* LCME/AMA. *Students:* 748 full-time (332 women); includes 242 minority (25 African Americans, 2 American Indian/Alaska Native, 179 Asian Americans or Pacific Islanders, 36 Hispanic Americans), 5 international. 9,044 applicants, 6% accepted, 200 enrolled. In 2009, 169 MDs awarded. *Entrance requirements:* MCAT. *Application deadline:* For fall admission, 1/15 for domestic students. Application fee: $105. *Expenses:* Contact institution. *Financial support:* Federal Work-Study, institutionally sponsored loans, and scholarships/grants available. Financial award application deadline: 3/13; financial award applicants required to submit FAFSA. *Unit head:* Dr. Harris Berman, Interim Dean, 617-636-6565. *Application contact:* Thomas Slavin, Director of Admissions, 617-636-6571, E-mail: med-admissions@tufts.edu.

Tulane University, School of Medicine, Professional Programs in Medicine, New Orleans, LA 70118-5669. Offers MD, MD/MBA, MD/MPH, MD/MPHTM, MD/MSPH, MD/PhD. *Accreditation:* LCME/AMA. *Entrance requirements:* MCAT.

Universidad Autonoma de Guadalajara, School of Medicine, Guadalajara, Mexico. Offers MD. *Entrance requirements:* MCAT, minimum GPA of 3.0.

Universidad Central del Caribe, School of Medicine, Bayamón, PR 00960-6032. Offers MD, MA, MS. *Accreditation:* LCME/AMA. *Degree requirements:* For MD, one foreign language. *Entrance requirements:* MCAT, interview, minimum GPA of 2.5, letter of recommendation. *Faculty research:* Membrane neurotransmitter receptors, brain neurotransmission, cocaine toxicology, membrane transport, antimetabolite pharmacology.

Universidad Central del Este, Medical School, San Pedro de Macoris, Dominican Republic. Offers MD.

Universidad de Ciencias Medicas, Graduate Programs, San Jose, Costa Rica. Offers dermatology (SP); family health (MS); health service center administration (MHA); human anatomy (MS); medical and surgery (MD); occupational medicine (MS); pharmacy (Pharm D). Part-time programs available. *Degree requirements:* For master's, thesis; for first professional degree and SP, comprehensive exam. *Entrance requirements:* For first professional degree, admissions test; for master's, MD or bachelors degree; for SP, admissions test, MD degree.

Universidad de Iberoamerica, Graduate School, San Jose, Costa Rica. Offers clinical neuropsychology (PhD); clinical psychology (M Psych); educational psychology (M Psych); forensic psychology (M Psych); hospital management (MHA); intensive care nursing (MN); medicine (MD). *Entrance requirements:* For master's, 2 letters of recommendation, interview.

Universidad Iberoamericana, School of Medicine, Santo Domingo D.N., Dominican Republic. Offers MD. *Entrance requirements:* 3 letters of recommendation.

Universidad Nacional Pedro Henriquez Urena, School of Medicine, Santo Domingo, Dominican Republic. Offers MD.

Université de Montréal, Faculty of Medicine, Professional Program in Medicine, Montréal, QC H3C 3J7, Canada. Offers MD. Open only to Canadian residents. *Accreditation:* LCME/AMA. *Students:* 901 full-time (593 women), 12 part-time (9 women). 876 applicants, 26% accepted, 231 enrolled. *Entrance requirements:* Proficiency in French. *Application deadline:* For fall admission, 2/1 priority date for domestic students; for winter admission, 11/1 priority date for domestic students; for spring admission, 2/1 priority date for domestic students. Application

fee: $100. Electronic applications accepted. *Unit head:* Francyne Poulin, Assistant to the Vice Dean, 514-343-6111 Ext. 4139, Fax: 514-343-6629, E-mail: francyne.poulin@umontreal.ca. *Application contact:* Dr. Christian Bourdy, Vice Dean Graduate Studies, 514-343-6723, Fax: 514-343-6629, E-mail: christian.bourdy@umontreal.ca.

Université de Montréal, Faculty of Medicine, Program in Specialized Studies, Montréal, QC H3C 3J7, Canada. Offers anesthesia (DES); diagnostic radiology (DES); family medicine (DES); gastroenterology (DES); geriatry (DES); intensive care (DES); medical biochemistry (DES); medical genetics (DES); medicine (DES); microbiology and infectious diseases (DES); nuclear medicine (DES); obstetrics and gynecology (DES); ophthalmology (DES); pediatrics (DES); pneumology (DES); psychiatry (DES); radiology-oncology (DES); rheumatology (DES); surgery (DES). *Faculty:* 154 full-time (40 women), 333 part-time/adjunct (100 women). *Students:* 930 full-time (580 women), 7 part-time (all women). 74 applicants, 77% accepted, 29 enrolled. *Application deadline:* For fall admission, 2/1 priority date for domestic students; for winter admission, 11/1 priority date for domestic students; for spring admission, 2/1 priority date for domestic students. Application fee: $100. Electronic applications accepted. *Unit head:* Lorraine Locas, Assistant to the Vice Dean of Graduate Studies, 514-343-6269, Fax: 514-343-5751, E-mail: lorraine.locas@umontreal.ca. *Application contact:* Dr. Andre Ferron, Vice Dean Graduate Studies, 514-343-6111 Ext. 0933, Fax: 514-343-5751, E-mail: andre.ferron@umontreal.ca.

Université de Sherbrooke, Faculty of Medicine and Health Sciences, Professional Program in Medicine, Sherbrooke, QC J1K 2R1, Canada. Offers MD. *Accreditation:* LCME/AMA. Electronic applications accepted.

Université Laval, Faculty of Medicine, Post-Professional Programs in Medical Studies, Québec, QC G1K 7P4, Canada. Offers anatomy–pathology (DESS); anesthesiology (DESS); cardiology (DESS); care of older people (Diploma); clinical research (DESS); community health (DESS); dermatology (DESS); diagnostic radiology (DESS); emergency medicine (Diploma); family medicine (DESS); general surgery (DESS); geriatrics (DESS); hematology (DESS); internal medicine (DESS); maternal and fetal medicine (Diploma); medical biochemistry (DESS); medical microbiology and infectious diseases (DESS); medical oncology (DESS); nephrology (DESS); neurology (DESS); neurosurgery (DESS); obstetrics and gynecology (DESS); ophthalmology (DESS); orthopedic surgery (DESS); oto-rhino-laryngology (DESS); palliative medicine (Diploma); pediatrics (DESS); plastic surgery (DESS); psychiatry (DESS); pulmonary medicine (DESS); radiology–oncology (DESS); thoracic surgery (DESS); urology (DESS). *Degree requirements:* For other advanced degree, comprehensive exam. *Entrance requirements:* For degree, knowledge of French. Electronic applications accepted.

Université Laval, Faculty of Medicine, Professional Program in Medicine, Québec, QC G1K 7P4, Canada. Offers MD. *Accreditation:* LCME/AMA. *Entrance requirements:* Interview, proficiency in French. Electronic applications accepted.

University at Buffalo, the State University of New York, Graduate School, School of Medicine and Biomedical Sciences, Professional Program in Medicine, Buffalo, NY 14260. Offers MD, MD/MBA, MD/MPH, MD/PhD. *Accreditation:* LCME/AMA. *Students:* 566 full-time (309 women); includes 151 minority (13 African Americans, 2 American Indian/Alaska Native, 130 Asian Americans or Pacific Islanders, 6 Hispanic Americans). Average age 26. 3,824 applicants, 10% accepted, 140 enrolled. In 2009, 131 MDs awarded. *Entrance requirements:* MCAT, interview. *Application deadline:* For fall admission, 11/15 for domestic students. Applications are processed on a rolling basis. Application fee: $65. Electronic applications accepted. *Financial support:* In 2009–10, 551 students received support. Career-related internships or fieldwork, Federal Work-Study, and institutionally sponsored loans available. Financial award application deadline: 3/1; financial award applicants required to submit FAFSA. *Faculty research:* Microbial pathogenesis, neuronal plasticity, structural biology of ion channels, structural development, cell biology of development. Total annual research expenditures: $117.3 million. *Unit head:* Dr. Charles Severin, Dean for Admissions, 716-829-2803, Fax: 716-829-2798, E-mail: severin@buffalo.edu. *Application contact:* James J. Rosso, Admissions Advisor, 716-829-3466, Fax: 716-829-3849, E-mail: jjrosso@buffalo.edu.

The University of Alabama at Birmingham, School of Medicine, Birmingham, AL 35294. Offers MD, MD/PhD. *Accreditation:* LCME/AMA (one or more programs are accredited). *Entrance requirements:* MCAT, interview. Electronic applications accepted. *Expenses:* Contact institution.

The University of Arizona, College of Medicine, Professional Programs in Medicine, Tucson, AZ 85721. Offers MD, MD/PhD. MD program open only to state residents. *Accreditation:* LCME/AMA. *Entrance requirements:* MCAT, previous course work in general chemistry, organic chemistry, biology/zoology, physics, and English. *Expenses:* Tuition, state resident: full-time $9028. Tuition, nonresident: full-time $24,890. *Faculty research:* Developmental biology, cellular structure and function, immunology, clinical cancer research, heart and respiratory disease.

University of Arkansas for Medical Sciences, College of Medicine, Little Rock, AR 72205-7199. Offers MD, MD/PhD. *Students:* 618 full-time. *Entrance requirements:* MCAT. *Expenses:* Contact institution. *Financial support:* Fellowships, research assistantships, teaching assistantships, Federal Work-Study and unspecified assistantships available. Support available to part-time students. *Unit head:* Dr. Debra Fiser, Dean, 501-686-5350. *Application contact:* Linda Dupuy, Director of Medical Student Recruitment and Admissions, 501-686-5355, E-mail: dupuylinda@uams.edu.

The University of British Columbia, Faculty of Medicine, Department of Surgery, Vancouver, BC V6T 1Z1, Canada. Offers M Sc. Part-time programs available. *Degree requirements:* For master's, thesis. *Entrance requirements:* Additional exam requirements/recommendations for international students: Required—TOEFL. Electronic applications accepted. *Faculty research:* Photodynamic therapy, transplantation immunobiology, isolated cell culture, neurophysiology.

The University of British Columbia, Faculty of Medicine, Professional Program in Medicine, Vancouver, BC V6T 1Z1, Canada. Offers MD, MD/PhD. *Accreditation:* LCME/AMA. *Entrance requirements:* MCAT.

University of Calgary, Faculty of Medicine, Professional Program in Medicine, Calgary, AB T2N 1N4, Canada. Offers MD. *Accreditation:* LCME/AMA. *Students:* 465 full-time (244 women). Average age 25. 1,832 applicants, 20% accepted, 180 enrolled. In 2009, 127 MDs awarded. *Entrance requirements:* MCAT. *Application deadline:* For fall admission, 10/15 for domestic students. Application fee: $150. Electronic applications accepted. *Financial support:* Career-related internships or fieldwork available. *Unit head:* Dr. B. Wright, Associate Dean (Medical Education), 403-220-3843, Fax: 403-270-2681, E-mail: umeadm4@ucalgary.ca. *Application contact:* Adele Meyers, Coordinator, Admissions and Student Affairs, 403-220-4357, Fax: 403-210-8148, E-mail: meyers@ucalgary.ca.

University of California, Berkeley, Graduate Division, School of Public Health, Group in Health and Medical Sciences, Berkeley, CA 94720-1500. Offers MD/MS. *Students:* 79 full-time (47 women). Average age 28. 60 applicants, 16 enrolled. *Application deadline:* For fall admission, 10/15 for domestic students. Applications are processed on a rolling basis. Application fee: $70 ($90 for international students). *Financial support:* Fellowships, research assistantships, teaching assistantships, Federal Work-Study and unspecified assistantships available. Financial award application deadline: 2/1; financial award applicants required to submit FAFSA. *Unit head:* Prof. John Swartzberg, Chair, 510-642-5479, E-mail: jmp@berkeley.edu. *Application contact:* Mary Rita Algazalli, Student Affairs Officer, 510-642-5482, Fax: 510-643-8771, E-mail: maryrita@berkeley.edu.

University of California, Davis, School of Medicine, Davis, CA 95616. Offers MD, MD/MBA, MD/MPH, MD/MS, MD/PhD. *Accreditation:* LCME/AMA. *Entrance requirements:* MCAT. Electronic applications accepted. *Expenses:* Contact institution. *Faculty research:* Cancer, neuroscience, health disparities, stem cell, cardiovascular disease.

University of California, Irvine, School of Medicine, Professional Program in Medicine, Irvine, CA 92697. Offers MD, MD/MBA, MD/MPH, MD/PhD. *Accreditation:* LCME/AMA. *Students:* 388 full-time (188 women); includes 158 minority (9 African Americans, 112 Asian Americans or Pacific Islanders, 37 Hispanic Americans). Average age 26. In 2009, 95 MDs awarded. *Entrance requirements:* MCAT. Additional exam requirements/recommendations for international students: Required—TOEFL (minimum score 550 paper-based; 213 computer-based). *Application deadline:* For fall admission, 11/1 for domestic students. Application fee: $70 ($90 for international students). Electronic applications accepted. *Financial support:* Fellowships, institutionally sponsored loans, traineeships, health care benefits, and unspecified assistantships available. Financial award application deadline: 3/2; financial award applicants required to submit FAFSA. *Unit head:* Dr. Thomas Cesario, Dean, 949-824-5926. *Application contact:* Peggy Harvey-Lee, Director of Outreach, 949-824-4618, Fax: 949-824-2485, E-mail: pharveyl@uci.edu.

University of California, Los Angeles, David Geffen School of Medicine, Professional Program in Medicine, Los Angeles, CA 90095. Offers MD, MD/MBA, MD/PhD. *Accreditation:* LCME/AMA. *Entrance requirements:* MCAT.

University of California, San Diego, School of Medicine, Professional Program in Medicine, La Jolla, CA 92093. Offers MD, MD/PhD. *Accreditation:* LCME/AMA. *Entrance requirements:* MCAT.

University of California, San Francisco, School of Medicine, San Francisco, CA 94143-0408. Offers MD, MD/MPH, MD/MS, MD/PhD. *Accreditation:* LCME/AMA (one or more programs are accredited). *Entrance requirements:* MCAT, interview. Electronic applications accepted. *Expenses:* Contact institution. *Faculty research:* Neurosciences, human genetics, developmental biology, social/behavioral/policy sciences, immunology.

University of Chicago, Division of the Biological Sciences, Pritzker School of Medicine, Chicago, IL 60637-1513. Offers MD, MD/PhD. *Accreditation:* LCME/AMA. *Faculty:* 884 full-time. *Students:* 394 full-time (193 women); includes 155 minority (36 African Americans, 2 American Indian/Alaska Native, 90 Asian Americans or Pacific Islanders, 27 Hispanic Americans), 11 international. Average age 25. 6,439 applicants, 4% accepted, 88 enrolled. In 2009, 113 MDs awarded. *Entrance requirements:* MCAT, one year of each with lab: chemistry, physics, biology and organic chemistry. *Application deadline:* For fall admission, 10/15 for domestic and international students. Applications are processed on a rolling basis. Application fee: $75. Electronic applications accepted. *Financial support:* In 2009–10, 354 students received support, including 8 fellowships with full tuition reimbursements available (averaging $27,000 per year), 75 teaching assistantships; career-related internships or fieldwork, Federal Work-Study, institutionally sponsored loans, and scholarships/grants also available. Financial award application deadline: 4/1; financial award applicants required to submit FAFSA. *Faculty research:* Human genetics, diabetes, developmental biology, structural biology, neurobiology. Total annual research expenditures: $224.6 million. *Application contact:* Sylvia Robertson, Assistant Dean for Admissions and Financial Aid, 773-702-1937, Fax: 773-834-5412, E-mail: sroberts@bsd.uchicago.edu.

University of Cincinnati, Graduate School, College of Allied Health Sciences, Program in Transfusion and Transplantation Sciences, Cincinnati, OH 45221. Offers blood transfusion medicine (MS); cellular therapies (MS). *Degree requirements:* For master's, comprehensive exam, thesis. *Entrance requirements:* For master's, GRE General Test. Additional exam requirements/recommendations for international students: Required—TOEFL (minimum score 570 paper-based). Electronic applications accepted. *Faculty research:* Preservation of red cells, red cell oxidation and delivery to tissues, cellular therapies, coagulopathies.

University of Cincinnati, Graduate School, College of Medicine, Physician Scientist Training Program, Cincinnati, OH 45221. Offers MD/PhD. *Entrance requirements:* Additional exam requirements/recommendations for international students: Required—TOEFL. Electronic applications accepted.

University of Cincinnati, Graduate School, College of Medicine, Professional Program in Medicine, Cincinnati, OH 45221. Offers MD. *Accreditation:* LCME/AMA. *Entrance requirements:* MCAT. Electronic applications accepted. *Faculty research:* Molecular genetics, environmental health, neuroscience and cell biology, cardiovascular science, developmental biology.

University of Colorado Denver, School of Medicine, Professional Program in Medicine, Denver, CO 80217-3364. Offers MD, MD/MBA, MD/PhD. *Students:* 604 full-time (292 women), 8 part-time (1 woman); includes 104 minority (11 African Americans, 6 American Indian/Alaska Native, 56 Asian Americans or Pacific Islanders, 31 Hispanic Americans), 1 international. In 2009, 133 MDs awarded. *Entrance requirements:* MCAT. Additional exam requirements/recommendations for international students: Required—TOEFL (minimum score 550 paper-based). Application fee: $100. *Unit head:* Dr. Richard Krugman, Dean, 303-724-0882. *Application contact:* Dr. Norma Wagoner, Associate Dean for Admissions, 303-724-8025, E-mail: somadmin@ucdenver.edu.

University of Connecticut Health Center, School of Medicine, Farmington, CT 06030. Offers MD, MD/MBA, MD/MPH, MD/PhD. *Accreditation:* LCME/AMA. *Faculty:* 393 full-time (124 women), 116 part-time/adjunct (65 women). *Students:* 342 full-time (192 women), 4 part-time (1 woman); includes 112 minority (39 African Americans, 4 American Indian/Alaska Native, 52 Asian Americans or Pacific Islanders, 17 Hispanic Americans), 5 international. Average age 26. 2,760 applicants, 7% accepted, 85 enrolled. In 2009, 76 MDs awarded. *Entrance requirements:* MCAT. *Application deadline:* For fall admission, 12/15 for domestic and international students. Application fee: $85. Electronic applications accepted. *Expenses:* Contact institution. *Financial support:* In 2009–10, 307 students received support. Institutionally sponsored loans and tuition waivers (partial) available. Financial award application deadline: 4/15; financial award applicants required to submit FAFSA. *Unit head:* Dr. Cato Laurencin, Dean, 860-679-2413, Fax: 860-679-1282. *Application contact:* Dr. Richard Zeff, Assistant Dean and Director, 860-679-2112, Fax: 860-679-1282, E-mail: zeff@neuron.uchc.edu.

University of Florida, College of Medicine, Professional Program in Medicine, Gainesville, FL 32611. Offers MD, MD/PhD. *Accreditation:* LCME/AMA. *Entrance requirements:* MCAT, 8 semester hours of course work in biology, general chemistry, and general physics; 4 semester hours of course work in geochemistry and organic chemistry. Electronic applications accepted. *Faculty research:* Neurobiology, gene therapy and genetic imaging technologies, diabetes and autoimmune diseases, transplantation.

University of Hawaii at Manoa, John A. Burns School of Medicine, Professional Program in Medicine, Honolulu, HI 96822. Offers MD. *Accreditation:* LCME/AMA. *Entrance requirements:* MCAT. Electronic applications accepted. *Expenses:* Contact institution.

University of Illinois at Chicago, College of Medicine, Professional Program in Medicine, Chicago, IL 60607-7128. Offers MD, MD/MS, MD/PhD. Part-time programs available. *Entrance requirements:* MCAT. Electronic applications accepted. *Faculty research:* Biomedical and clinical sciences.

University of Illinois at Urbana–Champaign, Graduate College, Medical Scholars Program, Urbana, IL 61801. Offers MD/MBA, MD/PhD. *Students:* 152 full-time (65 women); includes 48 minority (4 African Americans, 35 Asian Americans or Pacific Islanders, 9 Hispanic Americans). 141 applicants, 28% accepted, 27 enrolled. *Application deadline:* For fall admission, 12/31 for domestic students. Application fee: $0. Electronic applications accepted. *Expenses:* Contact institution. *Financial support:* Fellowships, research assistantships, teaching assistantships, institutionally sponsored loans available. Financial award applicants required to submit FAFSA. *Unit head:* Dr. James Hall, Associate Dean, 217-333-8146, Fax: 217-333-2640. *Application contact:* Tony Jimenez, Coordinator, 217-333-8146, Fax: 217-333-2640, E-mail: ojimenez@ad.uiuc.edu.

The University of Iowa, Roy J. and Lucille A. Carver College of Medicine and Graduate College, Medical Scientist Training Program, Iowa City, IA 52242-1316. Offers MD/PhD. *Faculty:* 137 full-time (32 women), 3 part-time/adjunct (0 women). *Students:* 61 full-time (25 women); includes 17 minority (1 American Indian/Alaska Native, 9 Asian Americans or Pacific Islanders, 7 Hispanic Americans). Average age 24. 139 applicants, 19% accepted, 9 enrolled. *Application deadline:* For fall admission, 11/15 priority date for domestic students. Applications

Allopathic Medicine

The University of Iowa (continued)
are processed on a rolling basis. Application fee: $50. Electronic applications accepted. *Financial support:* In 2009–10, 25 students received support, including 8 fellowships with full tuition reimbursements available (averaging $20,976 per year), 25 research assistantships with full tuition reimbursements available (averaging $2,764 per year); scholarships/grants, traineeships, health care benefits, and unspecified assistantships also available. *Faculty research:* Structure and function of ion channels, molecular genetics of human disease, neurobiology of pain, viral immunology and immunopathology, epidemiology of aging and cancer, human learning and memory, structural enzymology. Total annual research expenditures: $2 million. *Unit head:* Dr. C. Michael Knudson, Director, 319-335-8147, Fax: 319-335-6634, E-mail: c-knudson@uiowa.edu. *Application contact:* Leslie Harrington, Program Associate, 319-335-8304, Fax: 319-335-6634, E-mail: mstp@uiowa.edu.

The University of Iowa, Roy J. and Lucille A. Carver College of Medicine, Professional Program in Medicine, Iowa City, IA 52242-1316. Offers MD, MD/JD, MD/MBA, MD/MPH, MD/PhD. *Accreditation:* LCME/AMA. *Faculty:* 891 full-time (254 women). *Students:* 576 full-time (289 women); includes 104 minority (28 African Americans, 1 American Indian/Alaska Native, 48 Asian Americans or Pacific Islanders, 27 Hispanic Americans). Average age 26. 2,763 applicants, 10% accepted, 148 enrolled. In 2009, 143 MDs awarded. *Entrance requirements:* MCAT, course work in biology, chemistry, physics, mathematics, English, and social sciences, bachelor's degree. *Application deadline:* For fall admission, 11/1 for domestic students. Applications are processed on a rolling basis. Application fee: $60. Electronic applications accepted. *Expenses:* Contact institution. *Financial support:* In 2009–10, 576 students received support, including 62 fellowships with full tuition reimbursements available (averaging $23,500 per year); institutionally sponsored loans, scholarships/grants, and unspecified assistantships also available. Support available to part-time students. Financial award applicants required to submit FAFSA. *Unit head:* Dr. Christopher Cooper, Associate Dean, 319-335-8435, Fax: 319-335-8643. *Application contact:* Kathi J. Huebner, Director of Admissions, 319-335-6703, Fax: 319-335-8049, E-mail: medical-admissions@uiowa.edu.

The University of Kansas, University of Kansas Medical Center, School of Medicine, Lawrence, KS 66045. Offers MD, MA, MHSA, MPH, MS, PhD, JD/MHSA, MBA/MHSA, MD/MHS, MD/MHSA, MD/MPH, MD/MS, MD/PhD, MHSA/MS. *Accreditation:* LCME/AMA. *Faculty:* 850. *Students:* 819 full-time (430 women), 173 part-time (104 women); includes 179 minority (47 African Americans, 11 American Indian/Alaska Native, 80 Asian Americans or Pacific Islanders, 41 Hispanic Americans), 78 international. Average age 27. 2,549 applicants, 14% accepted, 259 enrolled. In 2009, 157 first professional degrees, 64 master's, 17 doctorates awarded. *Degree requirements:* For MD, comprehensive exam, NBME basic science subject exam, 3rd-year clinical exam, clinical skills assessment exams. *Entrance requirements:* MCAT, letters of recommendation, interviews, AMCAS application. Additional exam requirements/recommendations for international students: Required—TOEFL. *Application deadline:* For fall admission, 10/15 for domestic students. Applications are processed on a rolling basis. Application fee: $50. Electronic applications accepted. *Expenses:* Tuition, state resident: full-time $6492; part-time $270.50 per credit hour. Tuition, nonresident: full-time $15,510; part-time $646.25 per credit hour. Required fees: $847; $70.56 per credit hour. Tuition and fees vary according to course load and program. *Financial support:* In 2009–10, 690 students received support. Institutionally sponsored loans available. Financial award application deadline: 2/15; financial award applicants required to submit FAFSA. *Faculty research:* Reproductive biology (fertility, ovulation, embryo implantation, pregnancy maintenance), multidisciplinary research on the basic mechanisms of cancer, renal research, neurological research, liver research. Total annual research expenditures: $74.1 million. *Unit head:* Dr. Barbara Atkinson, Executive Dean, 913-588-1440, E-mail: batkinson@kumc.edu. *Application contact:* Dr. Barbara Atkinson, Executive Dean, 913-588-1440, E-mail: batkinson@kumc.edu.

University of Kentucky, College of Medicine, Professional Program in Medicine, Lexington, KY 40506-0032. Offers MD, MD/PhD. *Accreditation:* LCME/AMA. *Entrance requirements:* MCAT. Electronic applications accepted.

University of Louisville, School of Medicine, Professional Programs in Medicine, Louisville, KY 40292-0001. Offers MD, MD/MBA, MD/MS, MD/PhD. *Accreditation:* LCME/AMA. *Students:* 613 full-time (265 women), 2 part-time (both women); includes 116 minority (44 African Americans, 1 American Indian/Alaska Native, 64 Asian Americans or Pacific Islanders, 7 Hispanic Americans), 1 international. Average age 25. 2,495 applicants, 10% accepted, 165 enrolled. In 2009, 133 MDs awarded. *Entrance requirements:* MCAT. *Application deadline:* For fall admission, 1/15 for domestic students. Application fee: $100. *Unit head:* Dr. Edward C. Halperin, Dean, 502-852-1499, Fax: 502-852-1484, E-mail: edward.halperin@louisville.edu. *Application contact:* Director of Admissions, 502-852-5793, Fax: 502-852-6849.

University of Maryland, Baltimore, School of Medicine, Professional Program in Medicine, Baltimore, MD 21201. Offers MD, MD/PhD. *Accreditation:* LCME/AMA. *Entrance requirements:* MCAT, 1 year lecture and laboratory work in biology, general chemistry, organic chemistry, and physics; 1 year course work in English. *Application deadline:* For fall admission, 11/1 for domestic students. Applications are processed on a rolling basis. Application fee: $70. Electronic applications accepted. *Expenses:* Contact institution. *Financial support:* Fellowships with full tuition reimbursements, research assistantships with full tuition reimbursements, Federal Work-Study, institutionally sponsored loans, and scholarships/grants available. Financial award application deadline: 3/15; financial award applicants required to submit FAFSA. *Faculty research:* Vaccine development, genetics, diabetes, schizophrenia, cancer. *Application contact:* Dr. Milford M. Foxwell, Associate Dean for Admissions, 410-706-7478, Fax: 410-706-0467, E-mail: mfoxwell@som.umaryland.edu.

University of Massachusetts Worcester, School of Medicine, Worcester, MA 01655-0115. Offers MD, MD/PhD. *Accreditation:* LCME/AMA. *Faculty:* 1,048 full-time (347 women), 138 part-time/adjunct (101 women). *Students:* 469 full-time (258 women); includes 101 minority (23 African Americans, 69 Asian Americans or Pacific Islanders, 9 Hispanic Americans). Average age 27. 865 applicants, 22% accepted, 125 enrolled. In 2009, 99 MDs awarded. *Entrance requirements:* MCAT, state residency. *Application deadline:* For fall admission, 12/15 for domestic students. Application fee: $75. Electronic applications accepted. *Expenses:* Contact institution. *Financial support:* In 2009–10, 396 students received support. Institutionally sponsored loans, scholarships/grants, health care benefits, tuition waivers (partial), and unspecified assistantships available. Financial award application deadline: 4/15; financial award applicants required to submit FAFSA. *Faculty research:* RNA interference, cell dynamics, immunology and virology, chemical biology, stem cell research. Total annual research expenditures: $223.8 million. *Unit head:* Dr. Terence R. Flotte, Dean/Provost/Executive Deputy Chancellor, 508-856-8000. *Application contact:* Karen Lawton, Director of Admissions, 508-856-2303, E-mail: karen.lawton@umassmed.edu.

University of Medicine and Dentistry of New Jersey, New Jersey Medical School, Newark, NJ 07101-1709. Offers MD, MD/Certificate, MD/JD, MD/MBA, MD/MPH, MD/PhD. *Accreditation:* LCME/AMA. *Entrance requirements:* MCAT. Additional exam requirements/recommendations for international students: Required—TOEFL. Electronic applications accepted. *Expenses:* Contact institution.

University of Medicine and Dentistry of New Jersey, Robert Wood Johnson Medical School, Piscataway, NJ 08822. Offers MD, MD/JD, MD/MBA, MD/MPH, MD/MS, MD/MSJ, MD/PhD. *Accreditation:* LCME/AMA (one or more programs are accredited). *Entrance requirements:* MCAT. Additional exam requirements/recommendations for international students: Required—TOEFL. Electronic applications accepted. *Expenses:* Contact institution.

University of Miami, Graduate School, Miller School of Medicine, Professional Program in Medicine, Coral Gables, FL 33124. Offers MD. *Accreditation:* LCME/AMA. *Faculty:* 1,315 full-time (454 women), 7 part-time/adjunct (1 woman). *Students:* 740 full-time (334 women); includes 284 minority (45 African Americans, 2 American Indian/Alaska Native, 143 Asian Americans or Pacific Islanders, 94 Hispanic Americans). Average age 23. 4,922 applicants, 7% accepted, 195 enrolled. *Entrance requirements:* MCAT, 90 pre-med semester hours. *Application deadline:* For fall admission, 12/1 for domestic students. Applications are processed on a rolling basis. Application fee: $75. Electronic applications accepted. *Financial support:* In 2009–10, 570 students received support. Federal Work-Study, institutionally sponsored loans, and scholarships/grants available. Financial award application deadline: 4/1; financial award applicants required to submit FAFSA. *Faculty research:* AIDS, cancer, diabetes, neuroscience, wound healing. Total annual research expenditures: $196.3 million. *Unit head:* Dr. Richard S. Weisman, Associate Dean for Admissions, 305-243-3234, Fax: 305-243-6548, E-mail: med.admissions@miami.edu. *Application contact:* Agnes Murphy, Director of Admissions, 305-243-3234, Fax: 305-243-6548, E-mail: med.admissions@miami.edu.

University of Michigan, Medical School and Horace H. Rackham School of Graduate Studies, Medical Scientist Training Program, Ann Arbor, MI 48109. Offers MD/PhD. *Accreditation:* LCME/AMA. *Students:* 88 full-time (22 women); includes 6 minority (5 African Americans, 1 Hispanic American). 222 applicants, 18% accepted, 13 enrolled. *Application deadline:* For fall admission, 10/15 for domestic students. Applications are processed on a rolling basis. Application fee: $60. Electronic applications accepted. *Expenses:* Tuition, state resident: full-time $17,286; part-time $1099 per credit hour. Tuition, nonresident: full-time $34,944; part-time $2080 per credit hour. Required fees: $95 per semester. Tuition and fees vary according to course load, degree level and program. *Financial support:* In 2009–10, 88 students received support, including 71 fellowships with full tuition reimbursements available (averaging $26,500 per year), 14 research assistantships with full tuition reimbursements available (averaging $26,500 per year), 3 teaching assistantships with full tuition reimbursements available (averaging $26,500 per year); scholarships/grants, traineeships, and health care benefits also available. *Unit head:* Dr. Ronald J. Koenig, Director, 734-764-6176, Fax: 734-764-8180, E-mail: rkoenig@umich.edu. *Application contact:* Laurie Koivupalo, Administrative Associate, 734-764-6176, Fax: 734-764-8180, E-mail: lkoivupl@umich.edu.

University of Michigan, Medical School, Professional Program in Medicine, Ann Arbor, MI 48109. Offers MD, MD/MA Edu, MD/MBA, MD/MPH, MD/MPP, MD/MSI, MD/PhD. *Accreditation:* LCME/AMA. *Students:* 670 full-time (349 women); includes 245 minority (36 African Americans, 5 American Indian/Alaska Native, 168 Asian Americans or Pacific Islanders, 36 Hispanic Americans). 5,134 applicants, 170 enrolled. In 2009, 161 MDs awarded. *Entrance requirements:* MCAT. *Application deadline:* For fall admission, 11/15 for domestic students. Applications are processed on a rolling basis. Application fee: $80. Electronic applications accepted. *Expenses:* Tuition, state resident: full-time $17,286; part-time $1099 per credit hour. Tuition, nonresident: full-time $34,944; part-time $2080 per credit hour. Required fees: $95 per semester. Tuition and fees vary according to course load, degree level and program. *Financial support:* In 2009–10, 605 students received support. Application deadline: 3/31. *Unit head:* Dr. James S. Woolliscroft, Dean, 734-764-8175, Fax: 734-936-3510, E-mail: wolli@umich.edu. *Application contact:* Robert F. Ruiz, Director of Admissions, 734-764-6317, Fax: 734-936-3510, E-mail: rfruiz@umich.edu.

University of Minnesota, Duluth, Medical School, Professional Program in Medicine, Duluth, MN 55812-2496. Offers MD. *Entrance requirements:* MCAT. Electronic applications accepted.

University of Minnesota, Twin Cities Campus, Medical School, Professional Program in Medicine, Minneapolis, MN 55455-0213. Offers MD, JD/MD, MD/MBA, MD/MHI, MD/MPH, MD/MS, MD/PhD. *Accreditation:* LCME/AMA. *Entrance requirements:* MCAT, 1 semester each of biology, chemistry, 4 other life sciences, and a humanity or social science. Electronic applications accepted. *Expenses:* Contact institution.

University of Mississippi Medical Center, School of Medicine, Jackson, MS 39216-4505. Offers MD, MD/PhD. *Accreditation:* LCME/AMA. *Entrance requirements:* MCAT. *Faculty research:* Cardiovascular physiology (computer simulation), transplant immunology, reproductive endocrinology, protein structure, neurotransmitter vesicle structure.

University of Missouri, School of Medicine, Professional Program in Medicine, Columbia, MO 65211. Offers MD, MD/MS, MD/PhD. *Accreditation:* LCME/AMA. *Entrance requirements:* MCAT, minimum GPA of 3.49, specified pre-med courses. *Faculty research:* Basic and clinical biomedical sciences.

University of Missouri–Kansas City, School of Medicine, Kansas City, MO 64110-2499. Offers MD, MD/PhD. *Accreditation:* LCME/AMA. *Faculty:* 36 full-time (10 women), 9 part-time/adjunct (4 women). *Students:* 393 full-time (207 women), 2 part-time (both women); includes 188 minority (18 African Americans, 1 American Indian/Alaska Native, 154 Asian Americans or Pacific Islanders, 15 Hispanic Americans). Average age 23. 748 applicants, 12% accepted, 92 enrolled. In 2009, 87 MDs awarded. *Degree requirements:* For MD, one foreign language, United States Medical Licensing Exam Step 1 and 2. *Entrance requirements:* Interview. *Application deadline:* For fall admission, 11/15 for domestic and international students. Application fee: $50. *Expenses:* Contact institution. *Financial support:* Career-related internships or fieldwork, Federal Work-Study, institutionally sponsored loans, scholarships/grants, and tuition waivers (partial) available. Financial award application deadline: 3/1; financial award applicants required to submit FAFSA. *Faculty research:* Cardiovascular disease, women's and children's health, trauma and infectious diseases, neurological, metabolic disease. Total annual research expenditures: $4.7 million. *Unit head:* Dr. Betty Drees, Dean, 816-235-1808, E-mail: dreesb@umkc.edu. *Application contact:* MaryAnne Morgenegg, Selection Administrative Assistant, 816-235-1870, Fax: 816-235-6579, E-mail: morgeneggm@umkc.edu.

University of Nebraska Medical Center, College of Medicine, Omaha, NE 68198-5527. Offers MD, Certificate, MD/MPH, MD/PhD. *Accreditation:* LCME/AMA. *Entrance requirements:* MCAT. Electronic applications accepted. *Expenses:* Contact institution.

University of New Mexico, School of Medicine, Professional Program in Medicine, Albuquerque, NM 87131-2039. Offers MD. *Degree requirements:* For MD, research. *Entrance requirements:* MCAT, previous course work in biology, general chemistry, organic chemistry, and physics. *Expenses:* Contact institution.

The University of North Carolina at Chapel Hill, School of Medicine, Professional Program in Medicine, Chapel Hill, NC 27599. Offers MD, MD/MPH, MD/PhD. *Accreditation:* LCME/AMA. *Entrance requirements:* MCAT.

University of North Dakota, School of Medicine and Health Sciences, Professional Program in Medicine, Grand Forks, ND 58202. Offers MD, MD/PhD. *Accreditation:* LCME/AMA. *Entrance requirements:* MCAT, minimum GPA of 3.0. Additional exam requirements/recommendations for international students: Required—TOEFL (minimum score 550 paper-based; 213 computer-based; 79 iBT), IELTS (minimum score 6.5). Electronic applications accepted.

University of Oklahoma Health Sciences Center, College of Medicine, Professional Program in Medicine, Oklahoma City, OK 73190. Offers MD, MD/PhD. *Accreditation:* LCME/AMA. *Faculty:* 106 full-time (32 women), 3 part-time/adjunct (1 woman). *Students:* 653 full-time (258 women); includes 151 minority (8 African Americans, 45 American Indian/Alaska Native, 93 Asian Americans or Pacific Islanders, 5 Hispanic Americans), 5 international. Average age 25. 1,170 applicants, 18% accepted, 167 enrolled. In 2009, 147 MDs awarded. *Entrance requirements:* MCAT. *Application deadline:* For fall admission, 10/31 for domestic students. Application fee: $25 ($50 for international students). *Expenses:* Tuition, state resident: full-time $3120; part-time $156 per credit hour. Tuition, nonresident: full-time $11,314; part-time $409.70 per credit hour. Required fees: $1471; $51.20 per credit hour. $223.25 per term. *Financial support:* Fellowships available. *Faculty research:* Behavior and drugs, structure and function of endothelium, genetics and behavior, gene structure and function, action of antibiotics. *Unit head:* Dr. Dewayne Andrews, Executive Dean, 405-271-2265. *Application contact:* Dr. Nancy Hall, Associate Dean, 405-271-2339, E-mail: nancy-hall@ouhsc.edu.

University of Oklahoma—Tulsa, School of Community Medicine, Tulsa, OK 74135-2512. Offers MD.

University of Ottawa, Faculty of Graduate and Postdoctoral Studies, Faculty of Medicine, Ottawa, ON K1N 6N5, Canada. Offers MD, M Sc, PhD. *Accreditation:* LCME/AMA. *Degree requirements:* For master's, thesis; for doctorate, thesis/dissertation. *Entrance requirements:*

For master's, honors degree or equivalent, minimum B average; for doctorate, master's degree, minimum B+ average. Electronic applications accepted.

University of Pennsylvania, School of Medicine, Professional Program in Medicine, Philadelphia, PA 19104. Offers MD, MD/MBE, MD/MSCE, MD/JD, MD/MBA, MD/MS, MD/PhD. *Accreditation:* LCME/AMA. *Faculty:* 2,390 full-time (837 women), 1,274 part-time/adjunct (566 women). *Students:* 738 full-time (353 women); includes 240 minority (50 African Americans, 7 American Indian/Alaska Native, 129 Asian Americans or Pacific Islanders, 54 Hispanic Americans), 13 international. Average age 25. 6,217 applicants, 4% accepted, 161 enrolled. In 2009, 153 MDs awarded. *Entrance requirements:* MCAT. *Application deadline:* For fall admission, 10/15 for domestic students. Application fee: $80. Electronic applications accepted. *Expenses:* Tuition: Full-time $25,660; part-time $4758 per course. Required fees: $2152; $270 per course. Tuition and fees vary according to course load, degree level and program. *Financial support:* In 2009–10, 620 students received support; fellowships, research assistantships, teaching assistantships, career-related internships or fieldwork, Federal Work-Study, institutionally sponsored loans, and scholarships/grants available. Financial award application deadline: 5/1; financial award applicants required to submit FAFSA. *Unit head:* Dr. Gail Morrison, Vice Dean, 215-898-8034, E-mail: morrisog@mail.med.upenn.edu. *Application contact:* Gaye Sheffler, Director, Admissions, 215-898-8001, Fax: 215-898-0833, E-mail: sheffler@mail.med.upenn.edu.

University of Pittsburgh, School of Medicine, Professional Program in Medicine, Pittsburgh, PA 15261. Offers MD. *Accreditation:* LCME/AMA. *Faculty:* 2,093 full-time (674 women), 77 part-time/adjunct (50 women). *Students:* 569 full-time (257 women); includes 235 minority (49 African Americans, 156 Asian Americans or Pacific Islanders, 30 Hispanic Americans). Average age 26. 5,202 applicants, 8% accepted, 148 enrolled. In 2009, 145 MDs awarded. *Entrance requirements:* MCAT. *Application deadline:* For fall admission, 11/1 for domestic students. Applications are processed on a rolling basis. Application fee: $85. Electronic applications accepted. *Expenses:* Contact institution. *Financial support:* In 2009–10, 380 students received support. Institutionally sponsored loans and scholarships/grants available. Financial award application deadline: 4/16; financial award applicants required to submit FAFSA. *Faculty research:* Drug discovery and vaccine development; regenerative medicine; artificial organ and medical device development; psychiatry and neuroscience; structural, computational and developmental biology. Total annual research expenditures: $432 million. *Unit head:* Dr. Beth Piraino, Associate Dean, 412-648-9891, Fax: 412-648-8768, E-mail: admissions@medschool.pitt.edu. *Application contact:* Cynthia May Bonetti, Executive Director for Admissions and Financial Aid, 412-648-9891, Fax: 412-648-8768, E-mail: admissions@medschool.pitt.edu.

University of Puerto Rico, Medical Sciences Campus, School of Medicine, Professional Program in Medicine, San Juan, PR 00936-5067. Offers MD. *Accreditation:* LCME/AMA. *Degree requirements:* For MD, one foreign language. *Entrance requirements:* MCAT, minimum GPA of 2.5, computer literacy.

University of Rochester, School of Medicine and Dentistry, Professional Program in Medicine, Rochester, NY 14627. Offers MD, MD/MPH, MD/MS, MD/PhD. *Accreditation:* LCME/AMA. *Entrance requirements:* MCAT.

University of Saskatchewan, College of Medicine, Professional Program in Medicine, Saskatoon, SK S7N 5A2, Canada. Offers MD. *Accreditation:* LCME/AMA. Tuition and fees charges are reported in Canadian dollars. *Expenses:* Tuition, area resident: Full-time $3000 Canadian dollars; part-time $500 Canadian dollars per term. Required fees: $700 Canadian dollars; $100 Canadian dollars per term.

University of South Alabama, College of Medicine, Professional Program in Medicine, Mobile, AL 36688-0002. Offers MD, MD/PhD. *Accreditation:* LCME/AMA. *Faculty:* 51 full-time (10 women), 1 part-time/adjunct (0 women). *Students:* 290 full-time (135 women); includes 46 minority (18 African Americans, 2 American Indian/Alaska Native, 26 Asian Americans or Pacific Islanders), 2 international. In 2009, 63 MDs awarded. *Entrance requirements:* MCAT. Additional exam requirements/recommendations for international students: Required—TOEFL. *Application deadline:* For fall admission, 6/1 for domestic students, 6/15 for international students. Application fee: $75. Electronic applications accepted. *Expenses:* Tuition, state resident: part-time $218 per contact hour. Required fees: $1102 per year. *Financial support:* Scholarships/grants available. Financial award applicants required to submit FAFSA. *Unit head:* Mark Scott, Academic Advisor/Director of Admissions, 251-460-7176, E-mail: mscott@usouthal.edu. *Application contact:* Dr. B. Keith Harrison, Dean of the Graduate School, 251-460-6310, Fax: 251-461-1513, E-mail: kharriso@usouthal.edu.

University of South Carolina, School of Medicine, Professional Program in Medicine, Columbia, SC 29208. Offers MD, MD/MPH, MD/PhD. *Accreditation:* LCME/AMA. *Entrance requirements:* MCAT. Electronic applications accepted. *Faculty research:* Cardiovascular diseases, oncology, reproductive biology, vision, neuroscience.

The University of South Dakota, School of Medicine and Health Sciences, Professional Program in Medicine, Vermillion, SD 57069-2390. Offers MD. *Accreditation:* LCME/AMA. *Degree requirements:* For MD, USMLE-Step 1 USMLE-Step 2, CK OSCE. *Entrance requirements:* MCAT, previous course work in biology, chemistry, organic chemistry, mathematics and physics. Electronic applications accepted.

University of Southern California, Keck School of Medicine, Professional Program in Medicine, Los Angeles, CA 90089. Offers MD, MD/MBA, MD/MPH, MD/PhD. *Accreditation:* LCME/AMA. *Faculty:* 1,251 full-time (470 women), 112 part-time/adjunct (60 women). *Students:* 670 full-time (321 women); includes 277 minority (27 African Americans, 4 American Indian/Alaska Native, 160 Asian Americans or Pacific Islanders, 86 Hispanic Americans), 13 international. Average age 24. 6,310 applicants, 6% accepted, 166 enrolled. In 2009, 174 MDs awarded. *Entrance requirements:* MCAT, 2 semesters or 3 quarters of course work in biology, chemistry, organic chemistry, physics (all with lab); 1 course in molecular biology; 30 units of course work in social sciences. *Application deadline:* For fall admission, 11/1 for domestic and international students. Applications are processed on a rolling basis. Application fee: $90. Electronic applications accepted. *Expenses:* Contact institution. *Financial support:* In 2009–10, 346 students received support, including 7 research assistantships (averaging $22,000 per year), 24 teaching assistantships with partial tuition reimbursements available (averaging $4,134 per year); institutionally sponsored loans and scholarships/grants also available. Financial award application deadline: 4/15; financial award applicants required to submit FAFSA. *Unit head:* Dr. Erin A. Quinn, Associate Dean for Admissions, 323-442-2552, Fax: 323-442-2433, E-mail: medadmit@usc.edu. *Application contact:* Director of Admissions, 323-442-2552, Fax: 323-442-2433, E-mail: medadmit@usc.edu.

The University of Tennessee Health Science Center, College of Medicine, Memphis, TN 38163-0002. Offers MD, MS, PhD, MD/PhD. *Accreditation:* LCME/AMA. *Entrance requirements:* MCAT, interview, pre-professional evaluation. Electronic applications accepted. *Expenses:* Contact institution.

The University of Texas Health Science Center at Houston, Medical School, Houston, TX 77225-0036. Offers MD, MD/MPH, MD/PhD. *Accreditation:* LCME/AMA. *Entrance requirements:* MCAT. Electronic applications accepted. *Expenses:* Contact institution. *Faculty research:* Stroke, infectious diseases, cardiovascular disease, neoplastic disease (cancer), molecular medicine for the prevention of diseases.

The University of Texas Health Science Center at San Antonio, School of Medicine, San Antonio, TX 78229-3900. Offers MD, MPH. *Accreditation:* LCME/AMA. *Entrance requirements:* MCAT. *Expenses:* Contact institution. *Faculty research:* Geriatrics, diabetes, cancer, AIDS, obesity.

The University of Texas Medical Branch, School of Medicine, Galveston, TX 77555. Offers MD. *Accreditation:* LCME/AMA. *Students:* 920 full-time (422 women); includes 396 minority (92 African Americans, 5 American Indian/Alaska Native, 146 Asian Americans or Pacific Islanders, 153 Hispanic Americans), 7 international. Average age 25. In 2009, 200 MDs awarded. *Entrance requirements:* MCAT. *Application deadline:* For fall admission, 10/1 for domestic students. Application fee: $75 ($120 for international students). *Expenses:* Contact institution. *Financial support:* Federal Work-Study, institutionally sponsored loans, scholarships/grants, and tuition waivers (full and partial) available. Financial award applicants required to submit FAFSA. *Unit head:* Dr. Garland D. Anderson, Dean, 409-772-4793, Fax: 409-772-9598, E-mail: ganderso@utmb.edu. *Application contact:* Dr. Lauree Thomas, Associate Dean for Admissions and Student Affairs, 409-772-1442, Fax: 409-772-5148, E-mail: lauthoma@utmb.edu.

The University of Texas Southwestern Medical Center at Dallas, Southwestern Medical School, Dallas, TX 75390. Offers MD, MD/PhD. *Accreditation:* LCME/AMA. *Faculty:* 1,464 full-time, 402 part-time/adjunct. *Students:* 896 full-time (413 women); includes 461 minority (46 African Americans, 1 American Indian/Alaska Native, 288 Asian Americans or Pacific Islanders, 126 Hispanic Americans), 20 international. Average age 25. 3,788 applicants, 10% accepted, 227 enrolled. In 2009, 233 MDs awarded. *Entrance requirements:* MCAT. *Application deadline:* For fall admission, 10/15 for domestic students. Applications are processed on a rolling basis. Application fee: $65. Electronic applications accepted. *Expenses:* Contact institution. *Financial support:* In 2009–10, 700 students received support. Federal Work-Study and institutionally sponsored loans available. Financial award application deadline: 3/15; financial award applicants required to submit FAFSA. *Faculty research:* Endocrinology, molecular biology, immunology, cancer biology, neuroscience. Total annual research expenditures: $206,000. *Unit head:* Dr. Alfred Gilman, Dean, 214-648-2509. *Application contact:* Anne Mclane, Associate Director of Admissions, 214-648-5617, Fax: 214-648-3289, E-mail: admissions@utsouthwestern.edu.

University of Toronto, Faculty of Medicine, Toronto, ON M5S 1A1, Canada. Offers MD, M Sc, M Sc BMC, M Sc OT, M Sc PT, MH Sc, PhD, MD/PhD. *Accreditation:* LCME/AMA. *Entrance requirements:* For MD, MCAT, at least 2 courses in life sciences, one course in humanities, social sciences or languages; minimum GPA of 3.6; for doctorate, master's degree in related area, minimum B+ average. *Expenses:* Contact institution.

University of Utah, School of Medicine, MD/PhD Program in Medicine, Salt Lake City, UT 84112-1107. Offers MD/PhD. Part-time programs available. Electronic applications accepted. *Expenses:* Tuition, state resident: full-time $4004; part-time $1674 per semester. Tuition, nonresident: full-time $14,134; part-time $5915 per semester. Required fees: $324 per semester. Tuition and fees vary according to course load, degree level and program. *Faculty research:* Molecular biology, biochemistry, cell biology, immunology, bioengineering.

University of Utah, School of Medicine, Professional Program in Medicine, Salt Lake City, UT 84112-1107. Offers MD. *Accreditation:* LCME/AMA. *Entrance requirements:* MCAT, 2 years chemistry with lab, 1 year physics with lab, writing/speech, 2 courses biology, 1 course cell biology or biochemistry, 1 course humanities, 1 course diversity, 1 course social science. Electronic applications accepted. *Expenses:* Contact institution. *Faculty research:* Molecular biology, genetics, immunology, cardiology, endocrinology.

University of Vermont, College of Medicine, Professional Program in Medicine, Burlington, VT 05405. Offers MD, MD/MS, MD/PhD. *Accreditation:* LCME/AMA. *Students:* 458 (246 women); includes 102 minority (8 African Americans, 65 Asian Americans or Pacific Islanders, 29 Hispanic Americans), 12 international. 5,797 applicants, 4% accepted, 115 enrolled. In 2009, 104 MDs awarded. *Entrance requirements:* MCAT. Additional exam requirements/recommendations for international students: Required—TOEFL (minimum score 550 paper-based; 213 computer-based; 80 iBT). *Application deadline:* For fall admission, 11/1 for domestic and international students. Applications are processed on a rolling basis. Application fee: $85. Electronic applications accepted. *Expenses:* Contact institution. *Financial support:* In 2009–10, 340 students received support. Institutionally sponsored loans and scholarships/grants available. Support available to part-time students. Financial award application deadline: 2/28; financial award applicants required to submit FAFSA. *Unit head:* Dr. G. Scott Waterman, Associate Dean for Student Affairs, 802-656-2150, Fax: 802-656-9377. *Application contact:* Janice M. Gallant, Associate Dean for Admissions, 802-656-2150.

University of Virginia, School of Medicine, Charlottesville, VA 22903. Offers MD, MPH, MS, PhD, JD/MPH, MD/PhD. *Accreditation:* LCME/AMA. *Faculty:* 926 full-time (282 women), 89 part-time/adjunct (56 women). *Students:* 896 full-time (438 women), 21 part-time (13 women); includes 223 minority (52 African Americans, 1 American Indian/Alaska Native, 117 Asian Americans or Pacific Islanders, 53 Hispanic Americans), 62 international. Average age 26. 4,467 applicants, 11% accepted, 181 enrolled. In 2009, 142 first professional degrees, 50 master's, 38 doctorates awarded. *Entrance requirements:* MCAT. Additional exam requirements/recommendations for international students: Required—TOEFL. *Application deadline:* Applications are processed on a rolling basis. Application fee: $80. Electronic applications accepted. *Financial support:* Institutionally sponsored loans and scholarships/grants available. Financial award applicants required to submit FAFSA. *Unit head:* Steven T. DeKosky, Vice President and Dean, 434-924-5118, E-mail: slh2m@virginia.edu. *Application contact:* Lesley L. Thomas, Director, Admissions Office, 434-924-5571, Fax: 434-982-2586, E-mail: medsch-adm@virginia.edu.

University of Washington, Graduate School, School of Medicine, Professional Program in Medicine, Seattle, WA 98195. Offers MD, MD/MPH, MD/PhD. *Accreditation:* LCME/AMA. *Entrance requirements:* MCAT or GRE, minimum 3 years of college. Electronic applications accepted.

The University of Western Ontario, Faculty of Graduate Studies, Biosciences Division, Department of Family Medicine, London, ON N6A 5B8, Canada. Offers M Cl Sc. *Accreditation:* LCME/AMA. Part-time programs available. Postbaccalaureate distance learning degree programs offered (minimal on-campus study). *Degree requirements:* For master's, thesis. *Entrance requirements:* For master's, medical degree, minimum B average. Additional exam requirements/recommendations for international students: Required—TOEFL. *Faculty research:* Family medicine education, dietary counseling, alcohol problems, palliative care support, multicultural health care.

The University of Western Ontario, Schulich School of Medicine and Dentistry, Professional Program in Medicine, London, ON N6A 5B8, Canada. Offers MD. *Accreditation:* LCME/AMA.

University of Wisconsin–Madison, School of Medicine and Public Health, Professional Program in Medicine, Madison, WI 53705. Offers MD. *Accreditation:* LCME/AMA. *Expenses:* Tuition, state resident: part-time $594 per credit. Tuition, nonresident: part-time $1504 per credit. Required fees: $65 per credit. Tuition and fees vary according to course load, program and reciprocity agreements. *Unit head:* Dr. Robert N. Golden, Dean, 608-263-4910, Fax: 608-265-3286, E-mail: rngolden@wisc.edu. *Application contact:* Information Contact, 608-265-6344.

Vanderbilt University, School of Medicine, Nashville, TN 37240-1001. Offers MD, MDE, MMP, MPH, MS, MSCI, Au D, DMP. *Accreditation:* LCME/AMA (one or more programs are accredited). *Faculty:* 2,052 full-time (736 women), 987 part-time/adjunct (352 women). *Students:* 636 full-time (338 women); includes 146 minority (52 African Americans, 2 American Indian/Alaska Native, 87 Asian Americans or Pacific Islanders, 5 Hispanic Americans), 41 international. Average age 24. 4,892 applicants, 6% accepted, 111 enrolled. In 2009, 103 first professional degrees, 59 master's, 8 doctorates awarded. *Entrance requirements:* MCAT, 6 hours of English/composition; 8 hours each of general biology, inorganic biology, organic biology, and physics. *Application deadline:* For fall admission, 11/15 for domestic and international students. Applications are processed on a rolling basis. Application fee: $50. Electronic applications accepted. *Expenses:* Contact institution. *Financial support:* In 2009–10, 333 students received support. Institutionally sponsored loans and scholarships/grants available. Financial award application deadline: 3/1; financial award applicants required to submit FAFSA. Total annual research expenditures: $260 million. *Unit head:* Dr. Jeffrey R. Balser, Interim Dean, 615-322-5191, E-mail: steven.gabbe@vanderbilt.edu. *Application contact:* Dr. John A. Zic, Associate Dean for Admissions, 615-322-2145, Fax: 615-343-8397.

Virginia Commonwealth University, Medical College of Virginia-Professional Programs, School of Medicine, Professional Program in Medicine, Richmond, VA 23284-9005. Offers MD,

Allopathic Medicine

Virginia Commonwealth University (continued)
MD/PhD. *Accreditation:* LCME/AMA. *Entrance requirements:* MCAT. Electronic applications accepted. *Expenses:* Contact institution.

Wake Forest University, School of Medicine, Professional Program in Medicine, Winston-Salem, NC 27109. Offers MD, MD/MA, MD/MBA, MD/MS, MD/PhD. *Accreditation:* LCME/AMA. *Entrance requirements:* MCAT, 32 hours of course work in science. Electronic applications accepted. *Faculty research:* Cancer, stroke, infectious diseases, membrane biology, nutrition.

Washington University in St. Louis, School of Medicine, Professional Program in Medicine, St. Louis, MO 63130-4899. Offers MD, MD/MA, MD/MS, MD/PhD. *Accreditation:* LCME/AMA. *Faculty:* 1,356 full-time (444 women), 1,749 part-time/adjunct (548 women). *Students:* 607 full-time (285 women), 5 part-time (3 women); includes 225 minority (34 African Americans, 3 American Indian/Alaska Native, 164 Asian Americans or Pacific Islanders, 24 Hispanic Americans), 17 international. Average age 23. 3,892 applicants, 8% accepted, 121 enrolled. In 2009, 113 MDs awarded. *Entrance requirements:* MCAT. *Application deadline:* For fall admission, 12/31 for domestic and international students. Applications are processed on a rolling basis. Application fee: $65. Electronic applications accepted. *Expenses:* Contact institution. *Financial support:* Career-related internships or fieldwork and institutionally sponsored loans available. *Unit head:* Dr. Larry Shapiro, Dean, 314-362-6827. *Application contact:* Dr. W. Edwin Dodson, Associate Dean, 314-362-6848, Fax: 314-362-4658, E-mail: wumscoa@msnotes.wustl.edu.

Wayne State University, School of Medicine, Professional Program in Medicine, Detroit, MI 48202. Offers MD, MD/PhD. *Accreditation:* LCME/AMA. Part-time programs available. *Entrance requirements:* MCAT. Additional exam requirements/recommendations for international students: Required—TOEFL (minimum score 550 paper-based; 213 computer-based); Recommended—TWE (minimum score 6). Electronic applications accepted.

West Virginia University, School of Medicine, Professional Program in Medicine, Morgantown, WV 26506. Offers MD, MD/PhD. *Accreditation:* LCME/AMA. *Entrance requirements:* MCAT.

Wright State University, School of Medicine, Professional Program in Medicine, Dayton, OH 45435. Offers MD. *Accreditation:* LCME/AMA. *Entrance requirements:* MCAT.

Yale University, School of Medicine, Professional Program in Medicine, New Haven, CT 06510. Offers MD. *Accreditation:* LCME/AMA. *Degree requirements:* For MD, thesis/dissertation. *Entrance requirements:* MCAT. Electronic applications accepted.

Bioethics

Albany Medical College, Alden March Bioethics Institute, Albany, NY 12208-3479. Offers bioethics (MS); clinical ethics (Certificate). Part-time programs available. Postbaccalaureate distance learning degree programs offered (no on-campus study). *Degree requirements:* For master's, thesis. *Entrance requirements:* For master's, essay, official transcripts, 2 letters of reference. *Application deadline:* Applications are processed on a rolling basis. Application fee: $100. Electronic applications accepted. *Expenses:* Tuition: Full-time $18,820. *Faculty research:* Ethics in nanotechnology, ethics in genetics, ethics in transplants, philosophy and bioethics, the states and bioethics. *Unit head:* Dr. Bruce D. White, Director, 518-262-6082, Fax: 518-262-6856, E-mail: whiteb@mail.amc.edu. *Application contact:* Coordinator of Graduate Studies, 518-262-2639, Fax: 518-262-6856, E-mail: bioethics@mail.amc.edu.

Boston University, School of Public Health, Health Law, Bioethics and Human Rights Department, Boston, MA 02215. Offers MPH. Part-time and evening/weekend programs available. *Students:* 10 full-time (4 women), 7 part-time (5 women); includes 3 minority (2 Asian Americans or Pacific Islanders, 1 Hispanic American), 1 international. Average age 27. *Entrance requirements:* For master's, GRE, MCAT, LSAT, GMAT, DAT. Additional exam requirements/recommendations for international students: Required—TOEFL (minimum score 600 paper-based; 250 computer-based; 100 iBT) or IELTS (minimum score 6). *Application deadline:* For fall admission, 2/1 priority date for domestic and international students; for spring admission, 10/15 priority date for domestic and international students. Applications are processed on a rolling basis. Application fee: $95. Electronic applications accepted. *Expenses:* Tuition: Full-time $37,910; part-time $1184 per credit hour. Required fees: $386; $40 per semester. Part-time tuition and fees vary according to class time, course level, degree level and program. *Financial support:* In 2009–10, 1 fellowship was awarded; career-related internships or fieldwork, Federal Work-Study, institutionally sponsored loans, scholarships/grants, and tuition waivers (partial) also available. Support available to part-time students. Financial award application deadline: 3/1; financial award applicants required to submit FAFSA. *Unit head:* Prof. George Annas, Chair, 617-638-4626. *Application contact:* LePhan Quan, Assistant Director of Admissions, 617-638-4640, Fax: 617-638-5299, E-mail: asksph@bu.edu.

Case Western Reserve University, Frances Payne Bolton School of Nursing, Nursing/Bioethics Program, Cleveland, OH 44106. Offers MSN/MA.

Case Western Reserve University, School of Medicine and School of Graduate Studies, Graduate Programs in Medicine, Department of Bioethics, Cleveland, OH 44106. Offers MA, JD/MA, MA/MD, MA/MPH, MA/PhD, MSN/MA, MSSA/MA. *Entrance requirements:* For master's, GRE General Test or MCAT or MAT or LSAT or GMAT. Additional exam requirements/recommendations for international students: Required—TOEFL (minimum score 550 paper-based). Electronic applications accepted. *Faculty research:* Ethical issues in genetics, conflicts of interest, organ donation, end-of-life decision making, clinical ethics consultation.

Cleveland State University, College of Graduate Studies, College of Liberal Arts and Social Sciences, Department of Philosophy, Cleveland, OH 44115. Offers bioethics (MA, Certificate), including bioethics (MA); philosophy (MA), including philosophy. Part-time and evening/weekend programs available. *Degree requirements:* For master's, comprehensive exam, thesis optional. *Entrance requirements:* For master's, minimum GPA of 2.75. Additional exam requirements/recommendations for international students: Required—TOEFL (minimum score 525 paper-based; 197 computer-based). *Faculty research:* Ethics, history of philosophy, bioethics, social and political philosophy.

Columbia University, School of Continuing Education, Program in Bioethics, New York, NY 10027. Offers MS. Part-time programs available. *Faculty:* 4. *Degree requirements:* For master's, thesis. *Application deadline:* For fall admission, 4/15 for domestic students. Application fee: $50. Electronic applications accepted. *Unit head:* Robert Klitzman, Associate Professor of Clinical Psychiatry, E-mail: rlk2@columbia.edu. *Application contact:* Bryce Weinert, Admissions Adviser, 212-854-9666, E-mail: sce-apply@columbia.edu.

Drew University, Caspersen School of Graduate Studies, Program in Medical Humanities, Madison, NJ 07940-1493. Offers MMH, DMH, CMH. Part-time and evening/weekend programs available. *Students:* 14 full-time (11 women), 68 part-time (54 women); includes 12 minority (6 African Americans, 3 Asian Americans or Pacific Islanders, 3 Hispanic Americans). 20 applicants, 90% accepted, 9 enrolled. In 2009, 6 master's, 9 doctorates, 9 CMHs awarded. *Degree requirements:* For master's, thesis; for doctorate, thesis/dissertation. *Entrance requirements:* For master's and doctorate, transcripts, writing sample, personal statement, recommendations. Additional exam requirements/recommendations for international students: Required—TOEFL (minimum score 585 paper-based; 240 computer-based; 95 iBT), TWE (minimum score 4). *Application deadline:* For fall admission, 8/1 priority date for domestic students; for spring admission, 1/15 priority date for domestic students. Applications are processed on a rolling basis. Application fee: $35. *Expenses:* Contact institution. *Financial support:* In 2009–10, 38 students received support. Federal Work-Study, scholarships/grants, and tuition waivers (full and partial) available. Financial award application deadline: 2/15; financial award applicants required to submit FAFSA. *Faculty research:* Biomedical ethics, medical narrative, history of medicine, medicine and the arts. *Unit head:* Dr. Phil Scibilia, 973-408-3138, E-mail: pscibili@drew.edu. *Application contact:* Carla J. Burns, Director of Graduate Admissions, 973-408-3110, Fax: 973-408-3040, E-mail: gradm@drew.edu.

Duquesne University, Graduate School of Liberal Arts, Program in Health Care Ethics, Pittsburgh, PA 15282-0001. Offers MA, DHCE, PhD, Certificate. Part-time programs available. Postbaccalaureate distance learning degree programs offered (no on-campus study). *Faculty:* 2 full-time (0 women), 2 part-time/adjunct (both women). *Students:* 26 full-time (14 women), 11 part-time (8 women); includes 1 minority (African American), 7 international. Average age 42. 14 applicants, 100% accepted, 11 enrolled. In 2009, 5 master's, 3 doctorates awarded. Terminal master's awarded for partial completion of doctoral program. *Degree requirements:* For doctorate, 2 foreign languages, comprehensive exam, thesis/dissertation. *Entrance requirements:* For master's, GRE General Test; for doctorate, master's degree in health care ethics. Additional exam requirements/recommendations for international students: Required—TOEFL. *Application deadline:* For fall admission, 8/1 for domestic students, 5/1 for international students. Applications are processed on a rolling basis. Electronic applications accepted. *Expenses:* Tuition: Part-time $851 per credit. Required fees: $81 per credit. *Financial support:* Federal Work-Study available. Support available to part-time students. Financial award application deadline: 5/1. *Unit head:* Dr. Gerard Magill, Acting Director. *Application contact:* Linda L. Rendulic, Assistant to the Dean, 412-396-6400, Fax: 412-396-5265, E-mail: rendulic@duq.edu.

Indiana University–Purdue University Indianapolis, School of Liberal Arts, Department of Philosophy, Indianapolis, IN 46202-2896. Offers American philosophy (Certificate); bioethics (Certificate); philosophy (MA); JD/MA; MD/MA. Part-time programs available. *Faculty:* 13 full-time (2 women), 1 part-time/adjunct (0 women). *Students:* 3 full-time (0 women), 15 part-time (7 women); includes 1 minority (Hispanic American). Average age 32. 7 applicants, 14% accepted, 0 enrolled. *Degree requirements:* For master's, thesis optional. *Entrance requirements:* For master's, GRE. Additional exam requirements/recommendations for international students: Required—TOEFL. *Application deadline:* For fall admission, 3/1 priority date for domestic and international students; for spring admission, 11/15 for domestic and international students. Applications are processed on a rolling basis. Application fee: $55 ($65 for international students). Electronic applications accepted. *Financial support:* In 2009–10, 6 students received support, including 1 fellowship (averaging $1,000 per year), 4 teaching assistantships (averaging $4,330 per year); research assistantships with full tuition reimbursements available. Financial award application deadline: 1/15; financial award applicants required to submit FAFSA. *Faculty research:* American philosophy, Peirce bioethics, metaphysics, ethical theory. *Unit head:* Dr. John Tilley, Associate Professor and Chair, 317-274-4690, Fax: 317-278-4579, E-mail: jtilley@iupui.edu. *Application contact:* Dr. Jason Thomas Eberl, Assistant Professor and Graduate Co-Director, 317-278-9239, Fax: 317-278-4579, E-mail: jeberl@iupui.edu.

The Johns Hopkins University, Bloomberg School of Public Health, Department of Health Policy and Management, Baltimore, MD 21205-1996. Offers bioethics and policy (PhD); health and public policy (PhD); health care management and leadership (Dr PH); health economics (MHS); health economics and policy (PhD); health finance and management (MHA); health policy (MHS); health services research and policy (PhD). *Accreditation:* CAHME (one or more programs are accredited). Part-time programs available. *Faculty:* 60 full-time (32 women), 178 part-time/adjunct (66 women). *Students:* 136 full-time (95 women), 55 part-time (21 women); includes 53 minority (14 African Americans, 36 Asian Americans or Pacific Islanders, 3 Hispanic Americans), 48 international. Average age 32. 299 applicants, 39% accepted, 64 enrolled. In 2009, 49 master's, 19 doctorates awarded. *Degree requirements:* For master's, thesis (for some programs), internship (for some programs); for doctorate, comprehensive exam, thesis/dissertation, 1 year full-time residency (for some programs), oral and written exams. *Entrance requirements:* For master's, GRE General Test or GMAT, 3 letters of recommendation, curriculum vitae/resume; for doctorate, GRE General Test or GMAT, 3 letters of recommendation, curriculum vitae, transcripts. Additional exam requirements/recommendations for international students: Recommended—TOEFL (minimum score 600 paper-based; 250 computer-based; 100 iBT), IELTS. *Application deadline:* For fall admission, 12/1 for domestic and international students. Applications are processed on a rolling basis. Application fee: $45. Electronic applications accepted. *Financial support:* In 2009–10, 145 students received support; fellowships, research assistantships, teaching assistantships, career-related internships or fieldwork, Federal Work-Study, institutionally sponsored loans, scholarships/grants, traineeships, and stipends available. Support available to part-time students. Financial award application deadline: 3/15; financial award applicants required to submit FAFSA. *Faculty research:* Quality of care and health outcomes, health care finance and technology, health disparities and vulnerable populations, injury prevention, health policy and health care policy. Total annual research expenditures: $14.2 million. *Unit head:* Dr. Ellen J. MacKenzie, Chairman, 410-955-3625, E-mail: emackenz@jhsph.edu. *Application contact:* Mary Sewell, Coordinator, 410-955-2489, Fax: 410-614-9152, E-mail: msewell@jhsph.edu.

Kansas City University of Medicine and Biosciences, College of Biosciences, Kansas City, MO 64106-1453. Offers bioethics (MA); biomedical sciences (MS).

Loma Linda University, Faculty of Religion, Program in Biomedical and Clinical Ethics, Loma Linda, CA 92350. Offers MA, Certificate. *Degree requirements:* For master's, comprehensive exam, thesis optional. *Entrance requirements:* For master's, GRE General Test, baccalaureate degree. Additional exam requirements/recommendations for international students: Required—TOEFL. Electronic applications accepted.

Loyola Marymount University, College of Liberal Arts, The Bioethics Institute, Program in Bioethics, Los Angeles, CA 90045. Offers MA. *Faculty:* 2 full-time (0 women), 3 part-time/adjunct (2 women). *Students:* 13 full-time (6 women), 18 part-time (10 women); includes 6 minority (1 African American, 1 American Indian/Alaska Native, 2 Asian Americans or Pacific Islanders, 2 Hispanic Americans), 2 international. Average age 43. 15 applicants, 80% accepted, 7 enrolled. In 2009, 11 master's awarded. *Entrance requirements:* For master's, GRE or MAT, personal statement, interview, letters of recommendation. Additional exam requirements/recommendations for international students: Required—TOEFL (minimum score 600 paper-based; 250 computer-based; 100 iBT). *Application deadline:* For fall admission, 3/1 for domestic students; for spring admission, 10/1 for domestic students. Applications are processed on a rolling basis. Application fee: $50. Electronic applications accepted. *Financial support:* In 2009–10, 27 students received support, including 1 research assistantship (averaging $1,440 per year). Financial award application deadline: 6/1; financial award applicants required to submit FAFSA. *Unit head:* Dr. James J. Walter, Chair, 310-258-8621, Fax: 310-258-8642, E-mail: jwalter@lmu.edu. *Application contact:* Chake H. Kouyoumjian, Associate Dean of Graduate Studies, 310-338-2721, Fax: 310-338-6086, E-mail: ckouyoum@lmu.edu.

McGill University, Faculty of Graduate and Postdoctoral Studies, Faculty of Arts, Department of Philosophy, Montréal, QC H3A 2T5, Canada. Offers bioethics (MA); philosophy (PhD).

McGill University, Faculty of Graduate and Postdoctoral Studies, Faculty of Law, Montréal, QC H3A 2T5, Canada. Offers air and space law (LL M, DCL, Graduate Certificate); bioethics (LL M); comparative law (LL M, DCL, Graduate Certificate); law (LL M, DCL). Applications for LL M with specialization in bioethics are made initially through the Biomedical Ethics Unit in the Faculty of Medicine.

McGill University, Faculty of Graduate and Postdoctoral Studies, Faculty of Medicine, Department of Medicine, Montréal, QC H3A 2T5, Canada. Offers experimental medicine (M Sc, PhD), including bioethics (M Sc), experimental medicine.

Medical College of Wisconsin, Graduate School of Biomedical Sciences, Department of Population Health, Program in Bioethics, Milwaukee, WI 53226-0509. Offers AMA and MCW professionalism and bioethics (Graduate Certificate); clinical bioethics (Graduate Certificate); research bioethics (Graduate Certificate). Part-time programs available. *Degree requirements:* For master's, thesis. *Entrance requirements:* For master's, GRE General Test. Additional exam requirements/recommendations for international students: Required—TOEFL. *Faculty research:* Ethics committees and consultation, ethics of managed care, discussion of code status by physicians.

Midwestern University, Glendale Campus, College of Health Sciences, Arizona Campus, Program in Bioethics, Glendale, AZ 85308. Offers MA, Certificate. *Students:* 4 part-time (2 women); includes 1 minority (African American). Average age 53. 5 applicants, 60% accepted, 2 enrolled. In 2009, 9 master's awarded. Application fee: $50. *Unit head:* Dr. Gregory S. Loeben, Director, 623-572-3625. *Application contact:* James Walter, Director of Admissions, 888-247-9277, Fax: 623-572-3229, E-mail: admissaz@midwestern.edu.

Mount Sinai School of Medicine of New York University, Graduate School of Biological Sciences, The Bioethics Program, New York, NY 10029-6504. Offers MS.

New York University, Graduate School of Arts and Science, Program in Bioethics, New York, NY 10012-1019. Offers MA. Part-time programs available. *Students:* 13 full-time (11 women), 14 part-time (9 women); includes 1 African American, 3 Asian Americans or Pacific Islanders, 6 international. Average age 28. 21 applicants, 90% accepted, 15 enrolled. In 2009, 8 master's awarded. *Degree requirements:* For master's, one foreign language. *Entrance requirements:* For master's, GRE General Test. Additional exam requirements/recommendations for international students: Required—TOEFL. *Application deadline:* For fall admission, 4/1 priority date for domestic students; for spring admission, 11/1 priority date for domestic students. Application fee: $90. *Expenses:* Tuition: Full-time $30,528; part-time $1272 per credit. Required fees: $2177. *Financial support:* Application deadline: 4/1. *Unit head:* Dr. William Ruddick, Director, 212-992-7999, Fax: 212-995-4157, E-mail: bioethics@nyu.edu. *Application contact:* Zahra Ali, Program Coordinator, 212-992-7999, Fax: 212-995-4157, E-mail: bioethics@nyu.edu.

Rush University, College of Health Sciences, Program in Healthcare Ethics, Chicago, IL 60612-3832. Offers MA, Graduate Certificate. Part-time programs available. *Degree requirements:* For master's, oral presentation of thesis. *Entrance requirements:* For master's, GRE General Test, minimum GPA of 3.0. Electronic applications accepted. *Faculty research:* Daily spirituality in the disease process, training psychiatry residents in spirituality, defining and screening for spiritual struggle.

Saint Louis University, Graduate School, Center for Health Care Ethics, St. Louis, MO 63103-2097. Offers clinical health care ethics (Certificate); health care ethics (PhD). *Degree requirements:* For doctorate, comprehensive exam, thesis/dissertation. *Entrance requirements:* For doctorate, GRE General Test, master's degree in ethics or a field related to health care, basic competencies in philosophical and applied ethics, transcripts. Additional exam requirements/recommendations for international students: Required—TOEFL (minimum score 525 paper-based; 194 computer-based). Electronic applications accepted. *Faculty research:* Health policy, clinical ethics, research ethics, empirical bioethics, ethics education and assessment.

Trinity International University, Trinity Graduate School, Deerfield, IL 60015-1284. Offers bioethics (MA); communication and culture (MA); counseling psychology (MA); instructional leadership (M Ed); teaching (MA). Part-time and evening/weekend programs available. Post-baccalaureate distance learning degree programs offered (minimal on-campus study). *Degree requirements:* For master's, comprehensive exam. *Entrance requirements:* For master's, GRE General Test or MAT, minimum undergraduate GPA of 3.0. Additional exam requirements/recommendations for international students: Required—TOEFL (minimum score 580 paper-based; 237 computer-based), TWE (minimum score 4). Electronic applications accepted.

Union Graduate College, Center for Bioethics and Clinical Leadership, Schenectady, NY 12308-3107. Offers bioethics (MS); clinical ethics (AC); clinical leadership in health management (MS); health, policy and law (AC). Part-time and evening/weekend programs available. Post-baccalaureate distance learning degree programs offered (minimal on-campus study). *Faculty:* 9 full-time (1 woman), 13 part-time/adjunct (6 women). *Students:* 7 full-time (3 women), 53 part-time (38 women); includes 20 minority (all Asian Americans or Pacific Islanders), 4 international. Average age 32. 69 applicants, 91% accepted, 57 enrolled. In 2009, 21 master's awarded. *Entrance requirements:* For master's, MCAT, letters of recommendation. Additional exam requirements/recommendations for international students: Required—TOEFL (minimum score 550 paper-based; 213 computer-based). *Application deadline:* Applications are processed on a rolling basis. Application fee: $60. Electronic applications accepted. *Expenses:* Contact institution. *Financial support:* Federal Work-Study, scholarships/grants, health care benefits,

and tuition waivers (partial) available. Support available to part-time students. Financial award applicants required to submit FAFSA. *Faculty research:* Bioethics education, clinical ethics consultation, research ethics, history of biomedical ethics, international bioethics/research ethics. *Unit head:* Dr. Robert B. Baker, Director, 518-631-9860, Fax: 518-631-9903, E-mail: bakerr@union.edu. *Application contact:* Ann Nolte, Assistant Director, 518-631-9860, Fax: 518-631-9903, E-mail: noltea@uniongraduatecollege.edu.

Université de Montréal, Faculty of Medicine, Programs in Bioethics, Montréal, QC H3C 3J7, Canada. Offers MA, DESS. *Students:* 6 full-time (all women), 50 part-time (40 women). 26 applicants, 65% accepted, 13 enrolled. In 2009, 2 master's, 4 other advanced degrees awarded. *Application deadline:* For fall admission, 2/1 priority date for domestic students; for winter admission, 11/1 priority date for domestic students; for spring admission, 2/1 priority date for domestic students. Application fee: $100. Electronic applications accepted. *Unit head:* Marie-France Raynault, Director, 514-343-6140, Fax: 514-343-5738, E-mail: marie-france.raynault@umontreal.ca. *Application contact:* Williams-Jones Bryn, Responsible for program, 514-343-6111 Ext. 4881, Fax: 514-343-5738, E-mail: bryn.williams-jones@umontreal.ca.

Université de Montréal, Faculty of Theology and Sciences of Religions, Montréal, QC H3C 3J7, Canada. Offers health, spirituality and bioethics (DESS); practical theology (MA, PhD); religious sciences (MA, PhD); theology (MA, D Th, PhD, L Th); theology-Biblical studies (PhD). *Faculty:* 23 full-time (7 women), 5 part-time/adjunct (1 woman). *Students:* 83 full-time (20 women), 17 part-time (12 women). 74 applicants, 36% accepted, 24 enrolled. In 2009, 14 master's, 7 doctorates awarded. *Degree requirements:* For master's, one foreign language; for doctorate, 2 foreign languages, thesis/dissertation, general exam. *Application deadline:* For fall admission, 2/1 priority date for domestic students; for winter admission, 11/1 priority date for domestic students; for spring admission, 2/1 priority date for domestic students. Application fee: $100. Electronic applications accepted. *Financial support:* Research assistantships, teaching assistantships, institutionally sponsored loans and tuition waivers (partial) available. *Unit head:* Jean-Claude Breton, Dean, 514-343-7160, Fax: 514-343-5738, E-mail: jean-claude.breton@umontreal.ca. *Application contact:* Jean-Francois Roussel, Associate Dean of Graduate Studies, 514-343-6840, Fax: 514-343-5738, E-mail: jean-francois.roussel@umontreal.ca.

University of Pittsburgh, School of Arts and Sciences, Center for Bioethics and Health Law, Pittsburgh, PA 15213. Offers bioethics (MA). Part-time programs available. *Faculty:* 4 full-time (1 woman), 3 part-time/adjunct (1 woman). *Students:* 4 full-time (3 women), 14 part-time (9 women). Average age 34. 11 applicants, 73% accepted, 8 enrolled. In 2009, 2 master's awarded. *Degree requirements:* For master's, thesis. *Entrance requirements:* For master's, GRE General Test, letters of recommendation, writing sample. Additional exam requirements/recommendations for international students: Required—TOEFL. *Application deadline:* For fall admission, 2/1 priority date for domestic students, 6/30 for international students. Applications are processed on a rolling basis. Application fee: $50. Electronic applications accepted. *Expenses:* Tuition, state resident: full-time $16,402; part-time $665 per credit. Tuition, nonresident: full-time $28,694; part-time $1175 per credit. Required fees: $690; $175 per term. Tuition and fees vary according to program. *Financial support:* Tuition waivers (partial) available. *Faculty research:* End of life care, ethics and genetics, health law and policy, organ donation and transplantation, research ethics. *Unit head:* Dr. Lisa S. Parker, Director of Graduate Education, 412-647-5780, Fax: 412-647-5877, E-mail: lisap@pitt.edu. *Application contact:* Janet E. Malis, Administrative Assistant, 412-647-5785, Fax: 412-647-5877, E-mail: bioethic@pitt.edu.

The University of Tennessee, Graduate School, College of Arts and Sciences, Department of Philosophy, Knoxville, TN 37996. Offers medical ethics (MA, PhD); philosophy (MA, PhD); religious studies (MA). Part-time programs available. *Degree requirements:* For master's, thesis or alternative; for doctorate, one foreign language, thesis/dissertation. *Entrance requirements:* For master's and doctorate, GRE General Test, minimum GPA of 2.7. Additional exam requirements/recommendations for international students: Required—TOEFL. Electronic applications accepted. *Expenses:* Tuition, state resident: full-time $6826; part-time $380 per semester hour. Tuition, nonresident: full-time $21,844; part-time $1147 per semester hour. Tuition and fees vary according to program.

University of Toronto, School of Graduate Studies, Life Sciences Division, Institute of Medical Science, Toronto, ON M5S 1A1, Canada. Offers bioethics (MH Sc); biomedical communications (M Sc BMC); medical science (M Sc, PhD). *Degree requirements:* For master's, thesis; for doctorate, thesis/dissertation, thesis defense. *Entrance requirements:* For master's, minimum GPA of 3.7 in 3 of 4 years (M Sc), interview; for doctorate, M Sc or equivalent, defended thesis, minimum A– average, interview.

University of Virginia, College and Graduate School of Arts and Sciences, Center for Biomedical Ethics, Charlottesville, VA 22903. Offers bioethics (MA). *Students:* 5 applicants, 20% accepted, 0 enrolled. *Degree requirements:* For master's, thesis. *Entrance requirements:* For master's, GRE General Test. *Application deadline:* Applications are processed on a rolling basis. Application fee: $60. Electronic applications accepted. *Financial support:* Applicants required to submit FAFSA. *Unit head:* Margaret Mohrmann, Director, 434-924-5974, E-mail: mem7e@virginia.edu. *Application contact:* Margaret Mohrmann, Director, 434-924-5974, E-mail: mem7e@virginia.edu.

University of Washington, Graduate School, School of Medicine and Graduate School, Graduate Programs in Medicine, Department of Medical History and Ethics, Seattle, WA 98195. Offers bioethics (MA).

Naturopathic Medicine

Bastyr University, School of Naturopathic Medicine, Kenmore, WA 98028-4966. Offers ND. *Accreditation:* CNME; MEAC. *Students:* 465 full-time (377 women), 32 part-time (27 women); includes 74 minority (13 African Americans, 2 American Indian/Alaska Native, 41 Asian Americans or Pacific Islanders, 18 Hispanic Americans), 36 international. Average age 30. 233 applicants, 72% accepted, 107 enrolled. *Degree requirements:* For doctorate, comprehensive exam. *Entrance requirements:* For doctorate, 1 year of course work in biology, chemistry, organic chemistry and physics. Additional exam requirements/recommendations for international students: Required—TOEFL (minimum score 550 paper-based; 213 computer-based; 79 iBT). *Application deadline:* For fall admission, 2/1 priority date for domestic and international students. Applications are processed on a rolling basis. Application fee: $75. *Expenses:* Tuition: Full-time $23,478. Tuition and fees vary according to course level, course load and program. *Financial support:* Career-related internships or fieldwork, Federal Work-Study, and scholarships/grants available. Support available to part-time students. Financial award application deadline: 4/15; financial award applicants required to submit FAFSA. *Unit head:* Dr. Jane Guiltinan, Dean, 425-823-1300, Fax: 425-823-6222. *Application contact:* Admissions Office, 425-602-3330, Fax: 425-602-3090, E-mail: admissions@bastyr.edu.

Canadian College of Naturopathic Medicine, Doctor of Naturopathic Medicine Program, Toronto, ON M2K 1E2, Canada. Offers ND. *Accreditation:* CNME. *Faculty:* 16 full-time, 105 part-time/adjunct. *Students:* 452 full-time (392 women), 100 part-time (79 women). Average age 25. 199 applicants, 78% accepted, 115 enrolled. *Entrance requirements:* Additional exam requirements/recommendations for international students: Recommended—TOEFL (minimum score 580 paper-based; 257 computer-based). *Application deadline:* For fall admission, 1/31 priority date for domestic and international students; for winter admission, 5/31 priority date for domestic and international students. Applications are processed on a rolling basis. Application

fee: $150. Tuition and fees charges are reported in Canadian dollars. *Expenses:* Tuition: Full-time $18,815 Canadian dollars. Required fees: $450 Canadian dollars. *Financial support:* In 2009–10, 42 students received support. Career-related internships or fieldwork, institutionally sponsored loans, scholarships/grants, and health care benefits available. Support available to part-time students. Financial award application deadline: 7/31; financial award applicants required to submit FAFSA. *Faculty research:* Natural health products for lung cancer: a series of 10 systematic reviews, the use of habanero chili pepper for cancer: a systematic review, melatonin as an anticancer agent with and without chemotherapy: systematic review and meta-analysis, interactions between natural health products and pharmaceuticals: a systematic review, the use of selenium for patients with HIV/AIDS: a systematic review and meta-analysis. *Unit head:* Bob Bernhardt, President/CEO, 416-498-1255, Fax: 416-498-3197, E-mail: bbernhardt@ccnm.edu. *Application contact:* Student Services and Admissions Department, 416-498-1225 Ext. 245, Fax: 416-498-3197, E-mail: info@ccnm.edu.

See Close-Up on page 1765.

National College of Natural Medicine, Naturopathic School, Portland, OR 97201. Offers ND. *Accreditation:* CNME. *Faculty:* 18 full-time (9 women), 62 part-time/adjunct (37 women). *Students:* 405 full-time (324 women), 19 part-time (18 women); includes 44 minority (9 African Americans, 2 American Indian/Alaska Native, 23 Asian Americans or Pacific Islanders, 10 Hispanic Americans), 11 international. Average age 29. 220 applicants, 60% accepted, 104 enrolled. In 2009, 60 doctorates awarded. *Entrance requirements:* Additional exam requirements/recommendations for international students: Required—TOEFL (minimum score 550 paper-based; 213 computer-based). *Application deadline:* For fall admission, 11/1 priority date for domestic and international students; for winter admission, 2/1 priority date for domestic and international students. Applications are processed on a rolling basis. Application fee: $75.

Naturopathic Medicine

National College of Natural Medicine (continued)
Expenses: Tuition: Full-time $24,150. Tuition and fees vary according to course load. *Financial support:* In 2009–10, 308 students received support. Federal Work-Study and scholarships/grants available. Financial award application deadline: 4/30; financial award applicants required to submit FAFSA. *Faculty research:* Diet and diabetes, whole practice research, cruciferous vegetables and cancer, natural medicine and immune function, taraxacum and diuretics. Total annual research expenditures: $350,000. *Unit head:* Dr. Rita Bettenburg, Dean, 503-552-1761, Fax: 503-499-0022, E-mail: rbettenburg@ncnm.edu. *Application contact:* Hang Nguyen, Admissions Coordinator, 503-552-1660, Fax: 503-499-0027, E-mail: admissions@ncmn.edu.

National University of Health Sciences, College of Professional Studies, Lombard, IL 60148-4583. Offers acupuncture (MSAC); chiropractic medicine (DC); naturopathic medicine (ND); Oriental medicine (MSOM). *Accreditation:* CCE. *Faculty:* 62 full-time (19 women), 60 part-time/adjunct (30 women). *Students:* 588 full-time (299 women), 65 part-time (32 women); includes 120 minority (45 African Americans, 41 Asian Americans or Pacific Islanders, 34 Hispanic Americans), 10 international. Average age 26. 271 applicants, 80% accepted, 120 enrolled. In 2009, 290 DCs awarded. *Degree requirements:* For master's and DC, comprehensive exam, internship, community service. *Entrance requirements:* For DC, bachelor's degree, character references, undergraduate transcripts, written essay; for master's, character references. Additional exam requirements/recommendations for international students: Required—TOEFL (minimum score 550 paper-based; 213 computer-based; 79 iBT). *Application deadline:* For fall admission, 8/13 for domestic students, 8/1 for international students; for winter admission, 12/10 for domestic students, 12/1 for international students; for spring admission, 4/6 for domestic students, 4/1 for international students. Applications are processed on a rolling basis. Application fee: $55. Electronic applications accepted. *Expenses:* Tuition: Part-time $370 per credit hour. Required fees: $84 per trimester. Tuition and fees vary according to course load, degree level and program. *Financial support:* In 2009–10, 622 students received support, including 10 fellowships (averaging $5,500 per year), 15 research assistantships (averaging $2,500 per year); teaching assistantships, Federal Work-Study, scholarships/grants, and tuition waivers (partial) also available. Support available to part-time students. Financial award applicants required to submit FAFSA. *Faculty research:* Mechanisms of action of CAM therapies, clinical trials of CAM therapies, practice-based research networks for CAM therapies, evidence-based practice for CAM therapies, educational research in CAM teaching institutions. Total annual research expenditures: $472,975. *Unit head:* Dr. Nicholas A. Trongale, Dean, College of Professional Studies, 630-889-6673, Fax: 630-889-6499, E-mail: ntrongale@nuhs.edu. *Application contact:* Teri Hatfield, Assistant Director of Admissions, 800-826-6285, Fax: 630-889-6566, E-mail: thatfield@nuhs.edu.

See Close-Up on page 1735.

Southwest College of Naturopathic Medicine and Health Sciences, Program in Naturopathic Medicine, Tempe, AZ 85282. Offers ND. *Accreditation:* CNME. *Entrance requirements:* For doctorate, minimum GPA of 3.0, letters of recommendation. Additional exam requirements/recommendations for international students: Recommended—TOEFL (minimum score 550 paper-based; 213 computer-based). *Expenses:* Tuition: Full-time $24,200; part-time $19,208 per year. *Faculty research:* Environmental toxicology, microbial infection, diabetes, homeopathy.

See Close-Up on page 1767.

Universidad del Turabo, Graduate Programs, School of Health Sciences, Program in Naturopathy, Gurabo, PR 00778-3030. Offers ND. *Students:* 9 full-time (5 women), 1 (woman) part-time; includes 6 Hispanic Americans. Average age 33. 4 applicants, 100% accepted, 3 enrolled. *Unit head:* David Mendez, Head, 787-743-7979. *Application contact:* Virginia Gonzalez, Admissions Officer, 787-746-3009.

University of Bridgeport, College of Naturopathic Medicine, Bridgeport, CT 06604. Offers ND. *Accreditation:* CNME. *Degree requirements:* For doctorate, NPLEX Part I. *Entrance requirements:* For doctorate, minimum GPA of 2.5. Additional exam requirements/recommendations for international students: Recommended—TOEFL (minimum score 550 paper-based; 213 computer-based; 80 iBT), IELTS. Electronic applications accepted.

Osteopathic Medicine

A.T. Still University of Health Sciences, Kirksville College of Osteopathic Medicine, Kirksville, MO 63501. Offers biomedical sciences (MS); osteopathic medicine (DO). *Faculty:* 53 full-time (12 women), 33 part-time/adjunct (9 women). *Students:* 698 full-time (270 women), 25 part-time (11 women); includes 106 minority (12 African Americans, 6 American Indian/Alaska Native, 73 Asian Americans or Pacific Islanders, 15 Hispanic Americans), 12 international. Average age 27. 3,241 applicants, 11% accepted, 172 enrolled. In 2009, 166 first professional degrees, 7 master's awarded. *Degree requirements:* For master's, thesis; for DO, Level 1 and 2 COMLEX-PE exams. *Entrance requirements:* For DO, MCAT, bachelor's degree with minimum undergraduate GPA of 2.5 (cumulative and science) or 90 semester hours with minimum GPA of 3.5 (cumulative and science) and minimum MCAT of 28; for master's, GRE, MCAT, or DAT, minimum undergraduate GPA of 2.5 (cumulative and science). *Application deadline:* For fall admission, 2/1 for domestic and international students. Applications are processed on a rolling basis. Application fee: $60. Electronic applications accepted. *Expenses:* Contact institution. *Financial support:* In 2009–10, 630 students received support, including 12 fellowships with full tuition reimbursements available (averaging $16,000 per year); research assistantships, teaching assistantships, Federal Work-Study and scholarships/grants also available. Financial award application deadline: 5/1; financial award applicants required to submit FAFSA. *Faculty research:* Osteopathic palpatory procedures, Duchenne muscular dystrophy, gene array studies of pain remediation, thoracic lymphatic pump techniques. Total annual research expenditures: $338,806. *Unit head:* Dr. Philip C. Slocum, Dean, 660-626-2354, Fax: 660-626-2080, E-mail: pslocum@atsu.edu. *Application contact:* Donna Sparks, Associate Director for Admissions, 660-626-2237, Fax: 660-626-2969, E-mail: admissions@atsu.edu.

A.T. Still University of Health Sciences, School of Osteopathic Medicine in Arizona, Mesa, AZ 85206. Offers DO. *Faculty:* 36 full-time (12 women), 510 part-time/adjunct (200 women). *Students:* 309 full-time (148 women); includes 114 minority (9 African Americans, 13 American Indian/Alaska Native, 63 Asian Americans or Pacific Islanders, 29 Hispanic Americans). Average age 26. 3,287 applicants, 8% accepted, 107 enrolled. *Degree requirements:* For DO, Level 1 and 2 COMLEX-PE exams. *Entrance requirements:* MCAT, minimum undergraduate GPA of 2.5 (cumulative and science) with bachelor's degree. *Application deadline:* For fall admission, 3/1 for domestic students. Applications are processed on a rolling basis. Application fee: $60. Electronic applications accepted. *Expenses:* Tuition: Full-time $30,145. Required fees: $1050. Full-time tuition and fees vary according to degree level, campus/location, program and student level. *Financial support:* In 2009–10, 284 students received support. Federal Work-Study and scholarships/grants available. Financial award application deadline: 5/1; financial award applicants required to submit FAFSA. *Faculty research:* Medical education research, osteopathic medicine research. Total annual research expenditures: $2,240. *Unit head:* Dr. Douglas Wood, Dean, 480-219-6000, Fax: 480-219-6110, E-mail: dwood@atsu.edu. *Application contact:* Donna Sparks, Associate Director for Admissions, 660-626-2237, Fax: 660-626-2969, E-mail: admissions@atsu.edu.

Des Moines University, College of Osteopathic Medicine, Des Moines, IA 50312-4104. Offers DO. *Accreditation:* AOsA. *Faculty:* 40 full-time (16 women), 22 part-time/adjunct (4 women). *Students:* 872 full-time (413 women); includes 104 minority (5 African Americans, 1 American Indian/Alaska Native, 80 Asian Americans or Pacific Islanders, 18 Hispanic Americans), 16 international. Average age 25. 3,204 applicants, 15% accepted, 221 enrolled. In 2009, 204 DOs awarded. *Degree requirements:* For DO, National Board of Osteopathic Medical Examiners Exam Level 1 and 2. *Entrance requirements:* MCAT, minimum GPA of 3.0; 8 hours of course work in biology, chemistry, organic chemistry, and physics; 3 hours of biochemistry; 6 hours of course work in English; interview. *Application deadline:* For fall admission, 2/1 for domestic students, 2/1 priority date for international students. Applications are processed on a rolling basis. Application fee: $50. Electronic applications accepted. *Expenses:* Contact institution. *Financial support:* In 2009–10, 102 students received support, including 9 fellowships with tuition reimbursements available (averaging $6,000 per year); institutionally sponsored loans, scholarships/grants, and university employment also available. Support available to part-time students. Financial award application deadline: 7/15; financial award applicants required to submit FAFSA. *Faculty research:* Cardiovascular, infectious disease, cancer immunology, cell signaling nociception. *Unit head:* Dr. Kendall Reed, Dean, 515-271-1515, Fax: 515-271-1532, E-mail: kendall.reed@dmu.edu. *Application contact:* Jamie Rehmann, Director of Admissions, 515-271-1451, Fax: 515-271-7163, E-mail: doadmit@dmu.edu.

Edward Via Virginia College of Osteopathic Medicine, Graduate Program, Blacksburg, VA 24060. Offers DO. *Accreditation:* AOsA. *Faculty:* 41 full-time (16 women), 451 part-time/adjunct (104 women). *Students:* 689 full-time (348 women). Average age 25. 2,364 applicants, 11% accepted, 162 enrolled. *Degree requirements:* For DO, thesis/dissertation. *Entrance requirements:* MCAT, 8 hours of biology, general chemistry, and organic chemistry; 6 hours each of additional science and English; minimum overall science GPA of 2.75. *Application deadline:* For fall admission, 2/1 for domestic and international students. Applications are processed on a rolling basis. Application fee: $75. *Expenses:* Tuition: Full-time $33,558. Required fees: $827.50. *Financial support:* In 2009–10, 610 students received support. Scholarships/grants available. *Faculty research:* Nanobiology of aging, calcium transport regulation, prescription drug abuse, oxidative stress and inflammation, immune protection. *Application contact:* Megan R. Price, Director of Admissions, 540-231-6138, Fax: 540-231-5252, E-mail: admissions@vcom.vt.edu.

Georgia Campus–Philadelphia College of Osteopathic Medicine, Program in Osteopathic Medicine, Suwanee, GA 30024. Offers DO. *Accreditation:* AOsA.

Kansas City University of Medicine and Biosciences, College of Osteopathic Medicine, Kansas City, MO 64106-1453. Offers DO, DO/MA, DO/MBA. *Accreditation:* AOsA. *Degree requirements:* For DO, National Board Exam. *Entrance requirements:* MCAT, interview. *Faculty research:* 2-Chloroadenine in DNA use in controlling leukemia, dietary isoprenoids role in tumor cell control, preventive medicine and public health research of maternal and child health, nonenzymatic glycosylation in cardiac tissue.

Lake Erie College of Osteopathic Medicine, Professional Programs, Erie, PA 16509-1025. Offers biomedical sciences (Postbaccalaureate Certificate); medical education (MS); osteopathic medicine (DO); pharmacy (Pharm D). *Accreditation:* ACPE; AOsA. *Degree requirements:* For first professional degree, comprehensive exam, National Osteopathic Medical Licensing Exam, Levels 1 and 2; for Postbaccalaureate Certificate, comprehensive exam, North American Pharmacist Licensure Examination (NAPLEX). *Entrance requirements:* For first professional degree, MCAT, minimum GPA of 3.2, letters of recommendation; for Postbaccalaureate Certificate, PCAT, letters of recommendation, minimum GPA of 3.5. Electronic applications accepted. *Faculty research:* Cardiac smooth and skeletal muscle mechanics, chemotherapeutics and vitamins, osteopathic manipulation.

Lincoln Memorial University, DeBusk College of Osteopathic Medicine, Harrogate, TN 37752-1901. Offers DO. *Students:* 166 full-time (78 women); includes 17 minority (2 African Americans, 13 Asian Americans or Pacific Islanders, 2 Hispanic Americans). Average age 26. 2,305 applicants, 8% accepted, 166 enrolled. *Entrance requirements:* MCAT. Additional exam requirements/recommendations for international students: Required—TOEFL (minimum score 600 paper-based; 250 computer-based; 100 iBT). *Application deadline:* For fall admission, 4/1 for domestic students. Applications are processed on a rolling basis. Application fee: $50. *Expenses:* Tuition: Full-time $11,700; part-time $390 per hour. *Financial support:* In 2009–10, 5 students received support. Applicants required to submit FAFSA. *Unit head:* Dr. Ray Stowers, Vice President and Dean, 423-869-7077, E-mail: ray.stowers@lmunet.edu. *Application contact:* Janette Martin, Director of Admissions, 423-869-7102, Fax: 423-869-7172, E-mail: janette.martin@lmunet.edu.

Michigan State University, College of Osteopathic Medicine, Professional Program in Osteopathic Medicine, East Lansing, MI 48824. Offers DO. *Accreditation:* AOsA. *Students:* 940 full-time (450 women), 17 part-time (9 women); includes 183 minority (31 African Americans, 5 American Indian/Alaska Native, 129 Asian Americans or Pacific Islanders, 18 Hispanic Americans), 5 international. Average age 25. In 2009, 197 DOs awarded. *Application deadline:* Applications are processed on a rolling basis. Application fee: $155. Electronic applications accepted. *Expenses:* Tuition, state resident: part-time $478.25 per credit hour. Tuition, nonresident: part-time $966.50 per credit hour. Part-time tuition and fees vary according to program. *Financial support:* In 2009–10, 23 research assistantships with tuition reimbursements (averaging $7,607 per year) were awarded. *Unit head:* Dr. Gail Riegle, Associate Dean, Academic Programs, 517-355-9616, E-mail: riegle@msu.edu. *Application contact:* Information Contact, 517-353-7740, Fax: 517-355-3296, E-mail: comadm@com.msu.edu.

Midwestern University, Downers Grove Campus, Chicago College of Osteopathic Medicine, Downers Grove, IL 60515-1235. Offers DO. *Accreditation:* AOsA. *Faculty:* 37 full-time (15 women), 30 part-time/adjunct (11 women). *Students:* 680 full-time (351 women); includes 101 minority (3 African Americans, 96 Asian Americans or Pacific Islanders, 2 Hispanic Americans), 1 international. Average age 26. 4,930 applicants, 8% accepted, 176 enrolled. In 2009, 178 DOs awarded. *Entrance requirements:* MCAT, 1 year course work each in organic chemistry, general chemistry, biology, physics, and English. *Application deadline:* For fall admission, 1/1 for domestic students. Applications are processed on a rolling basis. Application fee: $50. *Expenses:* Contact institution. *Financial support:* In 2009–10, 568 students received support; fellowships with partial tuition reimbursements available, career-related internships or fieldwork, Federal Work-Study, institutionally sponsored loans, and tuition waivers (full and partial) available. Financial award application deadline: 6/1; financial award applicants required to submit FAFSA. *Faculty research:* Cadmium toxicity, amino acid transport, metabolic actions of vanadium, diabetes and obesity. Total annual research expenditures: $1.2 million. *Unit head:* Dr. Karen J. Nichols, Dean, 630-515-6159, E-mail: knicho@midwestern.edu. *Application contact:* Michael Laken, Director of Admissions, 630-515-6171, Fax: 630-971-6086, E-mail: admissil@midwestern.edu.

Midwestern University, Glendale Campus, Arizona College of Osteopathic Medicine, Glendale, AZ 85308. Offers DO. *Accreditation:* AOsA. *Faculty:* 43 full-time (14 women), 12 part-time/adjunct (5 women). *Students:* 797 full-time (306 women), 2 part-time (0 women); includes 29 minority (2 African Americans, 3 American Indian/Alaska Native, 21 Asian Americans or Pacific Islanders, 3 Hispanic Americans), 7 international. Average age 27. 3,211 applicants, 19% accepted, 255 enrolled. In 2009, 135 DOs awarded. *Entrance requirements:* MCAT. *Application deadline:* For fall admission, 11/1 priority date for domestic students; for winter admission, 2/1 for domestic students. Applications are processed on a rolling basis. Application fee: $50. Electronic applications accepted. *Expenses:* Contact institution. *Financial support:* Fellowships

with partial tuition reimbursements, career-related internships or fieldwork, Federal Work-Study, institutionally sponsored loans, and tuition waivers (full and partial) available. Financial award application deadline: 6/12; financial award applicants required to submit FAFSA. *Unit head:* Dr. Lori Kemper, Dean, 623-572-3202. *Application contact:* James Walter, Director of Admissions, 888-247-9277, Fax: 623-572-3229, E-mail: admissaz@midwestern.edu.

New York Institute of Technology, New York College of Osteopathic Medicine, Old Westbury, NY 11568-8000. Offers DO, DO/MBA, DO/MS. *Accreditation:* AOsA. *Students:* 1,182 full-time (625 women); includes 375 minority (48 African Americans, 286 Asian Americans or Pacific Islanders, 41 Hispanic Americans). Average age 26. In 2009, 303 DOs awarded. *Degree requirements:* For DO, comprehensive exam. *Entrance requirements:* MCAT, 6 hours of course work in biology, English, general chemistry, organic chemistry, and physics; minimum GPA of 2.75. *Application deadline:* For fall admission, 2/1 for domestic students. Application fee: $60. *Expenses:* Contact institution. *Financial support:* In 2009–10, 914 students received support, including fellowships with partial tuition reimbursements available (averaging $17,200 per year); tuition waivers (full and partial) also available. Financial award application deadline: 4/1; financial award applicants required to submit FAFSA. *Faculty research:* Osteopathic manipulation therapy, paleodiet of fossil horses, effect of OMT on range motion of arthritic knee, osteopathic treatment of muscle with compromised innervation, cycling smooth muscle crossbridges as substrates for myosin light chain kinase and phosphatase. *Unit head:* Dr. Thomas Scandalis, Dean, 516-686-3722, Fax: 516-686-3830, E-mail: tscandal@nyit.edu. *Application contact:* Rodika Zaika, Director of NYCOM Admissions, 516-686-3792, Fax: 516-686-3831, E-mail: rzaika@nyit.edu.

Nova Southeastern University, Health Professions Division, College of Osteopathic Medicine, Fort Lauderdale, FL 33314-7796. Offers biomedical informatics (MS, Graduate Certificate), including biomedical informatics (MS), clinical informatics (Graduate Certificate), public health informatics (Graduate Certificate); osteopathic medicine (DO); public health (MPH). *Accreditation:* AOsA. *Faculty:* 82 full-time (33 women), 983 part-time/adjunct (212 women). *Students:* 993 full-time (472 women), 77 part-time (44 women); includes 404 minority (65 African Americans, 4 American Indian/Alaska Native, 220 Asian Americans or Pacific Islanders, 115 Hispanic Americans), 25 international. 3,427 applicants, 11% accepted, 232 enrolled. In 2009, 228 first professional degrees, 30 master's awarded. *Entrance requirements:* MCAT. *Application deadline:* For fall admission, 1/15 for domestic students. Applications are processed on a rolling basis. Application fee: $50. Electronic applications accepted. *Expenses:* Contact institution. *Financial support:* In 2009–10, 815 students received support, including 18 fellowships with full tuition reimbursements available (averaging $13,000 per year); research assistantships, teaching assistantships, career-related internships or fieldwork, Federal Work-Study, institutionally sponsored loans, and scholarships/grants also available. Financial award application deadline: 6/1; financial award applicants required to submit FAFSA. *Faculty research:* Teaching strategies, simulated patient use, HIV-AIDS education, minority health issues, managed care education. *Unit head:* Dr. Anthony J. Silavgni, Dean, 954-262-1407, E-mail: silvagni@hpd.nova.edu. *Application contact:* Ellen Rondino, College of Osteopathic Medicine Admissions Counselor, 866-817-4068.

Ohio University, College of Osteopathic Medicine, Athens, OH 45701-2979. Offers DO, DO/MA, DO/MBA, DO/MHA, DO/MS, DO/PhD. *Accreditation:* AOsA. *Faculty:* 81 full-time (32 women), 33 part-time/adjunct (9 women). *Students:* 462 full-time (248 women); includes 116 minority (49 African Americans, 6 American Indian/Alaska Native, 42 Asian Americans or Pacific Islanders, 19 Hispanic Americans). Average age 24. 3,379 applicants, 6% accepted, 120 enrolled. In 2009, 106 DOs awarded. *Degree requirements:* For DO, comprehensive exam, thesis/dissertation (for some programs), National Board Exam Parts I and II, COMLEX-PE. *Entrance requirements:* MCAT, interview; course work in English, physics, biology, general chemistry, organic chemistry, and behavioral sciences. *Application deadline:* For fall admission, 2/1 for domestic students. Applications are processed on a rolling basis. Application fee: $40. Electronic applications accepted. *Expenses:* Contact institution. *Financial support:* In 2009–10, 436 students received support, including 8 fellowships with full tuition reimbursements available (averaging $43,055 per year); career-related internships or fieldwork, Federal Work-Study, institutionally sponsored loans, scholarships/grants, and tuition waivers (partial) also available. Financial award applicants required to submit FAFSA. *Faculty research:* Strong emphasis in diabetes research and cancer research, cardiovascular disease, drug development, biomechanics, international medicine. Total annual research expenditures: $1.8 million. *Unit head:* Dr. John A. Brose, Dean, 740-593-9350, Fax: 740-593-0761, E-mail: wilcox@ohio.edu. *Application contact:* Dr. John D. Schriner, Director of Admissions, 740-593-4313, Fax: 740-593-2256, E-mail: admissions@exchange.oucom.ohiou.edu.

Oklahoma State University Center for Health Sciences, College of Osteopathic Medicine, Tulsa, OK 74107-1898. Offers DO, DO/MS, DO/PhD. *Accreditation:* AOsA. *Entrance requirements:* MCAT, interview, minimum 90 hours of college course work, minimum GPA of 3.0. *Faculty research:* Neuroscience, artificial vision, mechanisms of hormone action, vaccines and immunotherapy, pathogenic free-living amoebae.

Philadelphia College of Osteopathic Medicine, Graduate and Professional Programs, Program in Osteopathic Medicine, Philadelphia, PA 19131-1694. Offers DO, DO/MBA, DO/MPH, DO/PhD. *Accreditation:* AOsA. *Faculty:* 57 full-time (23 women), 942 part-time/adjunct (73 women). *Students:* 1,422 full-time (748 women); includes 424 minority (101 African Americans, 1 American Indian/Alaska Native, 184 Asian Americans or Pacific Islanders, 138 Hispanic Americans), 610 international. Average age 26. 4,397 applicants, 9% accepted, 268 enrolled.

In 2009, 241 DOs awarded. *Entrance requirements:* MCAT, minimum GPA of 3.2; course work in biology, chemistry, English, and physics. *Application deadline:* For fall admission, 2/1 priority date for domestic students. Applications are processed on a rolling basis. Application fee: $50. *Financial support:* In 2009–10, 905 students received support, including 12 fellowships with partial tuition reimbursements available; Federal Work-Study, institutionally sponsored loans, and scholarships/grants also available. Financial award application deadline: 4/15; financial award applicants required to submit FAFSA. *Faculty research:* Alzheimer's disease, non-human stem cells, inflammatory diseases, pain management, physical activity. Total annual research expenditures: $957,475. *Unit head:* Dr. Kenneth J. Veit, Dean, 215-871-6770, Fax: 215-871-6781, E-mail: kenv@pcom.edu. *Application contact:* Carol A. Fox, Associate Vice President for Enrollment Management, 215-871-6700, Fax: 215-871-6719, E-mail: carolf@pcom.edu.

Pikeville College, School of Osteopathic Medicine, Pikeville, KY 41501. Offers DO. *Accreditation:* AOsA. *Entrance requirements:* MCAT. *Faculty research:* Primary care in medically underserved areas.

Touro University, Graduate Programs, Vallejo, CA 94592. Offers education (MA); osteopathic medicine (DO); pharmacy (Pharm D); physical therapy (DPT); physician assistant studies (MS); public health (MPH). *Accreditation:* AOsA; ARC-PA. Part-time and evening/weekend programs available. *Faculty:* 91 full-time (52 women), 51 part-time/adjunct (28 women). *Students:* 1,439 full-time (891 women). 6,914 applicants, 12% accepted, 503 enrolled. In 2009, 229 first professional degrees, 103 master's awarded. *Degree requirements:* For master's, comprehensive exam, thesis; for first professional degree, comprehensive exam. *Entrance requirements:* BS/BA. *Application deadline:* For fall admission, 3/15 for domestic students; for winter admission, 12/1 for domestic students. Applications are processed on a rolling basis. Application fee: $100. Electronic applications accepted. *Financial support:* In 2009–10, 1,236 students received support, including 119 fellowships (averaging $1,535 per year), 24 research assistantships (averaging $3,686 per year), 13 teaching assistantships (averaging $4,058 per year); Federal Work-Study and scholarships/grants also available. Support available to part-time students. Financial award applicants required to submit FAFSA. *Faculty research:* Cancer, heart disease. *Application contact:* Steve Davis, Associate Director of Admissions, 707-638-5270, Fax: 707-638-5250, E-mail: steven.davis@tu.edu.

University of Medicine and Dentistry of New Jersey, School of Osteopathic Medicine, Stratford, NJ 08084-1501. Offers DO, DO/MPA, DO/MPH, DO/PhD, JD/DO. *Accreditation:* AOsA. *Entrance requirements:* MCAT. Electronic applications accepted. *Expenses:* Contact institution.

University of New England, College of Osteopathic Medicine, Program in Osteopathic Medicine, Biddeford, ME 04005-9526. Offers DO. *Faculty:* 21 full-time (9 women), 25 part-time/adjunct (9 women). *Students:* 498 full-time (269 women); includes 3 African Americans, 22 Asian Americans or Pacific Islanders, 7 Hispanic Americans. Average age 28. In 2009, 119 DOs awarded. *Entrance requirements:* MCAT, interview. *Application deadline:* For fall admission, 3/1 for domestic students. *Expenses:* Contact institution. *Financial support:* Fellowships, institutionally sponsored loans and scholarships/grants available. Financial award application deadline: 5/1; financial award applicants required to submit FAFSA. *Unit head:* Dr. Marc Hahn, Interim Dean, 207-602-2340, Fax: 207-878-2434, E-mail: deanunecom@une.edu. *Application contact:* Stacy Gato, Director, Graduate Admissions, 207-221-4225 Ext. 2292, Fax: 207-221-4898, E-mail: gradadmissions@une.edu.

University of North Texas Health Science Center at Fort Worth, Texas College of Osteopathic Medicine, Fort Worth, TX 76107-2699. Offers osteopathic medicine (DO); physician assistant studies (MPAS); DO/MPH; DO/MS; DO/PhD; MPAS/MPH. *Accreditation:* AOsA. *Entrance requirements:* MCAT, 1 year course work in each biology, physics and English; 2 years course work in chemistry. Electronic applications accepted. *Faculty research:* Tuberculosis, aging, cardiovascular disease, cancer.

Western University of Health Sciences, College of Osteopathic Medicine of the Pacific, Pomona, CA 91766-1854. Offers DO. *Accreditation:* AOsA. *Entrance requirements:* MCAT, minimum GPA of 3.3, interview, letters of recommendation.

West Virginia School of Osteopathic Medicine, Professional Program, Lewisburg, WV 24901-1196. Offers DO. *Accreditation:* AOsA. *Faculty:* 46 full-time (16 women), 11 part-time/adjunct (4 women). *Students:* 778 full-time (369 women); includes 146 minority (11 African Americans, 3 American Indian/Alaska Native, 108 Asian Americans or Pacific Islanders, 24 Hispanic Americans). Average age 26. 2,879 applicants, 18% accepted, 204 enrolled. In 2009, 104 DOs awarded. *Entrance requirements:* MCAT, 3 hours of English; 8 hours each of biology, physics, inorganic chemistry, and organic chemistry. *Application deadline:* For fall admission, 2/15 for domestic students. Applications are processed on a rolling basis. Electronic applications accepted. *Expenses:* Tuition, state resident: full-time $19,950. Tuition, nonresident: full-time $49,950. *Financial support:* In 2009–10, 55 students received support; teaching assistantships with full and partial tuition reimbursements available, Federal Work-Study, scholarships/grants, tuition waivers (full), and unspecified assistantships available. Financial award application deadline: 4/1; financial award applicants required to submit FAFSA. *Faculty research:* Cardiac hypertrophy, diabetic population, myocardial ischemia reperfusion, computer animations. *Unit head:* Dr. Michael D. Adelman, Acting President/Dean/Vice President of Academic Affairs, 304-645-6295, Fax: 304-645-4859, E-mail: madelman@osteo.wvsom.edu. *Application contact:* Donna S. Varney, Director of Admissions, 304-647-6373, Fax: 304-647-6384, E-mail: dvarney@wvsom.edu.

Podiatric Medicine

Barry University, School of Graduate Medical Sciences, Podiatric Medicine and Surgery Program, Miami Shores, FL 33161-6695. Offers DPM, DPM/MBA, DPM/MPH. *Accreditation:* APMA. *Entrance requirements:* MCAT, GRE General Test, previous course work in science and English. Additional exam requirements/recommendations for international students: Required—TOEFL. Electronic applications accepted. *Expenses:* Contact institution.

California School of Podiatric Medicine at Samuel Merritt College, Graduate and Professional Programs, Oakland, CA 94609. Offers DPM. *Accreditation:* APMA. *Faculty:* 17 full-time (3 women), 6 part-time/adjunct (0 women). *Students:* 161 full-time (64 women); includes 69 minority (4 African Americans, 1 American Indian/Alaska Native, 56 Asian Americans or Pacific Islanders, 8 Hispanic Americans). Average age 27. 361 applicants, 30% accepted, 48 enrolled. In 2009, 31 DPMs awarded. *Entrance requirements:* MCAT, 90 hours of undergraduate course work; 1 year of course work in organic chemistry, inorganic chemistry, and physics; 2 years of course work in biological sciences. *Application deadline:* For fall admission, 4/1 priority date for domestic students. Applications are processed on a rolling basis. Application fee: $50. *Expenses:* Tuition: Full-time $29,635. *Financial support:* Fellowships, Federal Work-Study and institutionally sponsored loans available. Financial award application deadline: 3/2; financial award applicants required to submit FAFSA. *Faculty research:* Biomechanics, surgery, diabetics, sports medicine. *Unit head:* Irma Walker-Adame, Associate Dean for Administrative Affairs, 510-869-8742, E-mail: iadame@samuelmerritt.edu. *Application contact:* Dr. David Tran, Assistant Director of Admission, 510-869-6789, Fax: 510-869-6525, E-mail: dtran@samuelmerritt.edu.

Des Moines University, College of Podiatric Medicine and Surgery, Des Moines, IA 50312-4104. Offers DPM. *Accreditation:* APMA. *Faculty:* 5 full-time (1 woman), 1 part-time/adjunct (0 women). *Students:* 226 full-time (77 women); includes 17 minority (3 African Americans, 1 American Indian/Alaska Native, 9 Asian Americans or Pacific Islanders, 4 Hispanic Americans),

3 international. Average age 24. 392 applicants, 27% accepted, 58 enrolled. In 2009, 45 DPMs awarded. *Entrance requirements:* MCAT, interview; minimum GPA of 2.5; 1 year of organic chemistry, inorganic chemistry, physics, biology, and English. *Application deadline:* For fall admission, 6/1 for domestic and international students. Applications are processed on a rolling basis. Application fee: $0. Electronic applications accepted. *Expenses:* Contact institution. *Financial support:* In 2009–10, 82 students received support. Institutionally sponsored loans, scholarships/grants, and university employment available. Support available to part-time students. Financial award application deadline: 7/15; financial award applicants required to submit FAFSA. *Faculty research:* Physics of equines, gait analysis. *Unit head:* Dr. Robert Yoho, Dean, 515-271-1464, Fax: 515-271-1521, E-mail: robert.yoho@dmu.edu. *Application contact:* Gina Smith, Admissions Coordinator, 515-271-7497, E-mail: cpmsadmit@dmu.edu.

Midwestern University, Glendale Campus, College of Health Sciences, Arizona Campus, Program in Podiatric Medicine, Glendale, AZ 85308. Offers DPM. *Accreditation:* APMA. *Faculty:* 9 full-time (3 women), 1 part-time/adjunct (0 women). *Students:* 121 full-time (33 women); includes 17 minority (2 African Americans, 2 American Indian/Alaska Native, 10 Asian Americans or Pacific Islanders, 3 Hispanic Americans), 4 international. Average age 28. 418 applicants, 21% accepted, 33 enrolled. *Entrance requirements:* MCAT or PCAT, 90 semester hours at an accredited college or university, minimum GPA of 2.75. *Application deadline:* For fall admission, 6/1 for domestic students. Applications are processed on a rolling basis. Application fee: $50. *Expenses:* Contact institution. *Unit head:* Jeffrey C. Page, Director, 623-572-3451. *Application contact:* James Walter, Director of Admissions, 888-247-9277, Fax: 623-572-3229, E-mail: admissaz@midwestern.edu.

New York College of Podiatric Medicine, Professional Program, New York, NY 10035. Offers DPM, DPM/MPH. *Accreditation:* APMA. *Degree requirements:* For DPM, comprehensive

Podiatric Medicine

New York College of Podiatric Medicine (continued)
exam. *Entrance requirements:* MCAT or DAT, 1 year course work in biology, physics, English, and general and organic chemistry. Additional exam requirements/recommendations for international students: Required—TOEFL.

Ohio College of Podiatric Medicine, Ohio College of Podiatric Medicine, Independence, OH 44131. Offers DPM. *Accreditation:* APMA. *Faculty:* 14 full-time (5 women), 13 part-time/adjunct (6 women). *Students:* 433 full-time (170 women), 2 part-time (1 woman); includes 84 minority (41 African Americans, 4 American Indian/Alaska Native, 25 Asian Americans or Pacific Islanders, 14 Hispanic Americans), 11 international. Average age 26. 467 applicants, 32% accepted, 113 enrolled. In 2009, 68 DPMs awarded. *Entrance requirements:* MCAT, previous course work in biology, chemistry, and physics. Additional exam requirements/recommendations for international students: Recommended—TOEFL (minimum score 81 iBT). *Application deadline:* For fall admission, 4/1 priority date for domestic students. Applications are processed on a rolling basis. Application fee: $50. Electronic applications accepted. *Expenses:* Tuition: Full-time $27,250. Required fees: $1834. One-time fee: $450 full-time.

Tuition and fees vary according to student level. *Financial support:* In 2009–10, 66 students received support. Career-related internships or fieldwork, Federal Work-Study, institutionally sponsored loans, and scholarships/grants available. Financial award application deadline: 6/30; financial award applicants required to submit FAFSA. *Unit head:* Dr. Thomas Melillo, President, 216-231-3300. *Application contact:* Dean Lois Lott, Dean of Student Affairs, 216-231-3300 Ext. 7486, Fax: 216-447-0210, E-mail: llott@ocpm.edu.

Rosalind Franklin University of Medicine and Science, The Dr. William M. Scholl College of Podiatric Medicine, North Chicago, IL 60064-3095. Offers DPM. *Accreditation:* APMA. *Entrance requirements:* MCAT (or GRE on approval), 12 semester hours of biology; 8 semester hours of inorganic chemistry, organic chemistry and physics; 6 semester hours of English. Additional exam requirements/recommendations for international students: Required—TOEFL.

Temple University, Health Sciences Center, School of Podiatric Medicine, Philadelphia, PA 19107-2496. Offers DPM, DPM/MBA, DPM/PhD. *Accreditation:* APMA. *Degree requirements:* For DPM, National Board Exam. *Entrance requirements:* MCAT, GRE, or DAT, interview, 8 hours of organic chemistry, inorganic chemistry, physics, biology. *Faculty research:* Gait analysis, infectious diseases, diabetic neuropathy, peripheral vascular disease.

THE CANADIAN COLLEGE OF NATUROPATHIC MEDICINE

Doctor of Naturopathic Medicine Program

CCNM
CANADIAN COLLEGE OF
NATUROPATHIC MEDICINE

Programs of Study

The Canadian College of Naturopathic Medicine (CCNM) is Canada's premier institute for education and research in naturopathic medicine. Naturopathic doctors are highly educated primary-care providers who integrate standard medical diagnostics with a broad range of natural therapies. CCNM offers a rigorous four-year, full-time Doctor of Naturopathic Medicine (N.D.) program. CCNM is also home to the Robert Schad Naturopathic Clinic, a dynamic naturopathic teaching clinic where senior clinicians and N.D. supervisors conduct more than 25,000 patient visits per year. CCNM's intensive four-year program involves more than 4,200 hours (classroom and clinic) and is accredited by the Council on Naturopathic Medical Education (CNME), which is the North American accrediting agency for naturopathic programs recognized by the U.S. Department of Education. CCNM is a member of the Association of Accredited Naturopathic Medical Colleges.

The N.D. curriculum involves three major areas of study: basic sciences, clinical sciences, and naturopathic disciplines. Students take courses in the basic sciences of anatomy, histopathology, physiology, biochemistry, microbiology, and immunology. Development of problem-solving skills in applied basic life sciences is achieved through lectures, case discussion, tutorial groups, and clinical simulations. Some of these courses have a laboratory component. Laboratory resources include diagnostic test kits and access to human cadavers for gross anatomy study. A variety of audiovisual resources are also available.

Clinical science disciplines include physical and clinical diagnosis, differential and laboratory diagnosis, advanced imaging, physical assessment, health psychology, primary care, and pathology. The principles and philosophy of naturopathic medicine form the bridgework between the academic and clinical parts of the curriculum. Six major disciplines define the areas of naturopathic practice: acupuncture/traditional Chinese medicine (TCM), botanical medicine, physical medicine (massage, hydrotherapy, etc.), clinical nutrition, homeopathic medicine, and lifestyle counseling.

Research Facilities

CCNM has collaborated with many major medical research institutions, including McMaster University, University of Oxford, the Hospital for Sick Children, the University of Toronto, the Ottawa Regional Cancer Centre, the Ottawa General Hospital, the Centre for Addiction and Mental Health, the Mayo Clinic, and the Johns Hopkins University, to advance the state of knowledge in naturopathic medicine. Researchers from CCNM have published numerous systematic reviews and research articles on naturopathic therapies in a wide variety of peer-reviewed journals, including *BMJ, JAMA, Lancet Oncology, the Archives of Internal Medicine*, and *PloS One*. CCNM is a leader in the conduct of clinical trials investigating naturopathic medical approaches for the diagnosis and treatment of disease, including recent studies on melatonin for non-small-cell lung cancer, cinnamon for type 2 diabetes, and naturopathic interventions for chronic low-back pain, anxiety, rotator cuff dysfunction, and risk for cardiovascular disease. The Scientific Review Board and Research Ethics Board at CCNM provide expert review on the conduct of research in complementary and alternative medicines.

Results from CCNM research studies help improve treatment options and access to health care and help to influence policy makers on better international health-care policies. This makes CCNM a natural home for the Centre for International Health and Human Rights Studies, the nonprofit research organization dedicated to providing evidence to support equal access to health care for all individuals. For more information on this organization, students should visit http://www.cihhrs.org.

The Learning Resources Centre houses more than 11,000 resources on naturopathic and complementary health care. CCNM's Department of Research and Clinical Epidemiology is advancing the state of medicine through a better understanding of complementary and alternative medical science. Research department faculty members educate students in their first years in epidemiology, encouraging them to investigate evidence-based medicine throughout their years at the college and to consider a research project of their own. This commitment to evidence-based medicine cultivates research initiatives within the CCNM community, including student and faculty initiatives, through teaching, experiential learning, and mentorship. By fostering this culture of research, CCNM has become a leader in naturopathic and complementary medicine worldwide, investigating topics that not only improve naturopathic treatment practices but also have widespread relevance and international impact.

Financial Aid

Canadian students enrolled in the Doctor of Naturopathic Medicine program may be eligible for federal and provincial financial assistance. Students must apply in their province of residence and submit a new loan application each year. Students should apply as early as possible. For more information, students can contact their provincial loan office or Student Services. Students may also be eligible for scholarships and bursaries and should contact Student Services for more information.

Canadian College of Naturopathic Medicine participates in the Federal Family Education Loan Program (FFEL) as well as Stafford loans, available to eligible students who are citizens of the United States. Sallie Mae Signature Student Loans are available for students who are either U.S. citizens/residents or who have a co-borrower who is a U.S. citizen/resident. Students may qualify for up to US$25,000.

Bank loans through the Canadian Imperial Bank of Commerce (CIBC) are another possibility. Students enrolled in the N.D. program at CCNM can apply for a professional line of credit without the need of a co-signatory. The four-year program limit is Can$140,000. There is no annual limit—students are assessed each academic year on the basis of their need. Interest is the prime rate plus 1 percent; the line of credit is converted to a personal loan twelve months after graduation. (Note: This information was correct at the time of publication. As policies at financial institutions are subject to change, students should contact their institution of choice to confirm details).

Cost of Study

In-state and out-of-state tuition for the 2010–11 academic year is Can$18,815; international tuition is Can$21,990. Books, materials, and miscellaneous expenses cost approximately Can$1500–$3000.

Living and Housing Costs

On-campus residence is $475 per month.

Student Group

Currently, over 550 students are enrolled at CCNM. Students come from every province in Canada; with significant numbers from the United States and abroad. The ratio of women to men at CCNM is approximately 4:1. Student ages range from 20 to 50 years and older.

Student Outcomes

Upon graduation, many naturopathic doctors open their own practice. CCNM graduates are building successful practices throughout North America, including remote areas. Some graduates, however, choose to partner with existing naturopathic practices, multidisciplinary clinics, wellness centres, fitness centres, spas, or corporate wellness programs. Many naturopathic doctors conduct special lectures and workshops, represent natural health product companies as spokespeople, develop natural health products, and perform medical and scientific research.

Location

CCNM's 4.43-acre, 176,000-square-foot campus is conveniently located in Toronto's North York region at the Leslie subway station. It is also close to major highways. Toronto is Canada's largest city, with a population of 4.4 million. Toronto is well maintained, with excellent public transportation and comparatively low living costs. Rated the safest large North American city, Toronto is a welcoming multicultural mosaic. Toronto offers students a wealth of entertainment, leisure, and cultural activities. Whether tastes lead to exotic cuisines, multicultural festivals, sports events, or the theatre district, there is always something to capture interest in Toronto.

The College

Naturopathic medical education began in Canada in 1978 with the founding of the Ontario College of Naturopathic Medicine in Toronto. In 1992, the college became the Canadian College of Naturopathic Medicine to better reflect its mandate to educate students from across Canada.

Applying

The Canadian College of Naturopathic Medicine evaluates each candidate regarding academic achievement, motivation, character, community service, and life experience. The admission decision is based primarily on the applicant's undergraduate grade point average, but additional criteria may include the applicant's academic history, essay, references, autobiographical sketch, and interview. Historically, the average cumulative GPA of accepted students has been 3.3 on a 4.0 scale, encompassing a range of 2.7 to 4.0.

Applicants must have completed a baccalaureate degree. Prerequisite courses include biology, organic chemistry, biochemistry, psychology, physiology, and humanities, as well as recommended courses in anatomy, environmental science, microbiology, physics, sociology, and statistics. Students should submit the completed application form and nonrefundable Can$150 application fee. Official transcripts should be mailed directly to CCNM's Student Services Department by the institutions attended. International transcripts of academic records from outside North America must be translated and evaluated by an approved credential evaluation service and mailed directly to CCNM.

Applicants must also provide proof of current course enrolment, if applicable; a copy of government-issued photo ID and proof of citizenship; two letters of reference from an academic (postsecondary), professional (previous employer), and/or naturopathic doctor (nonrelative); and a written personal statement explaining the motivation and desire to become a naturopathic doctor.

Correspondence and Information

Student Services
The Canadian College of Naturopathic Medicine
1255 Sheppard Avenue East
Toronto, Ontario M2K 1E2
Canada

Phone: 416-498-1255 Ext. 245
866-241-2266 Ext. 245 (toll-free)
E-mail: info@ccnm.edu
Web site: http://www.ccnm.edu

The Canadian College of Naturopathic Medicine

THE FACULTY AND THEIR RESEARCH

Nadia Bakir, N.D., FCAH, DHANP; Associate Professor, Clinic Supervisor, and Coordinator, Robert Schad Naturopathic Clinic (RSNC) Homeopathy Shifts. Nadia Bakir designed, developed, and implemented the Homeopathy Specialty Clinic at the Robert Schad Naturopathic Clinic, which is now an integral part of the RSNC curriculum. She has committed herself to updating and improving the College's homeopathic curriculum and coordinates an annual student trip to India to study homeopathy. Bakir believes that maintaining a private practice in addition to her position at CCNM enriches her contribution to students.

Kimberlee Blyden-Taylor, N.D.; Assistant Professor and Associate Dean of Clinical Education. Kimberlee Blyden-Taylor oversees the second-, third-, and fourth-year clinical education component of CCNM's academic program. Blyden-Taylor also supervises fourth-year clinic interns, clinical faculty and staff members, and the RSNC's homeopathic medicine specialty groups. In addition to working within the RSNC, Blyden-Taylor teaches and facilitates group studies for a number of CCNM's academic courses. She is also the founder and director of Redhawk Healing Arts in Toronto, where she runs her private practice.

Jasmine Carino, N.D.; Associate Dean of the Curriculum and Residency Program. Jasmine Carino is a graduate of Laurentian University and CCNM.

Nick De Groot, N.D.; Dean. Nick De Groot is responsible for overseeing the day-to-day operations of the clinic. In addition to monitoring and developing the quality of patient care, De Groot supervises the clinical education of students in every stage of the naturopathic program.

Shehab El-hashemy, M.B.Ch.B, N.D.; Associate Dean of Academic Delivery. Shehab El-hashemy is a graduate of Cairo University (Egypt), Lakehead University, and CCNM.

Matthew Gowan, N.D.; Research Resident. Matt Gowan graduated from CCNM in 2003 and completed the college resident program in 2005. Gowan has also completed the contemporary medical acupuncture course from McMaster University. Before studying naturopathic medicine, Gowan completed his Honours Bachelor of Science degree in co-op biochemistry at the University of Waterloo and spent two years performing research for two leading pharmaceutical companies. His interest in natural medicine inspired him to travel throughout Asia, learning about Eastern healing traditions, such as yoga and meditation. Gowan is currently a clinic supervisor and a resident contributor to CCNM's research department.

Jennifer Hillier, N.D.; Assistant Professor. An enthusiastic member of the clinic faculty, Jennifer Hillier supervises fourth-year interns in their care of patients at the RSNC and at Anishnawbe Health Toronto, an interdisciplinary satellite clinic dedicated to improving the health and well-being of aboriginal people. She works with second- and third-year students in physical and clinical diagnosis tutorials and primary-care analysis. Hillier has a family practice in Mississauga, with a focus on family medicine and traditional Asian therapies. Inspired by inner-city need, she has also established a free HIV clinic in Vancouver, along with a community-based research project investigating the efficacy of alternative medicine in the treatment of HIV.

Hal Huff, N.D., Clinic Faculty and Head Supervisor, Sherbourne Health Centre, Naturopathic HIV/AIDS Clinic. Hal Huff directs the College's HIV/AIDS specialty clinic and frequently lectures on the use of naturopathic medicine for the treatment of HIV and hepatitis C. He participates in several Ontario government-funded initiatives to investigate the use of complementary and alternative medicine to treat HIV/AIDS. Huff also participates in CCNM's institutional review board (IRB), established to set and enforce the ethical standards of CCNM's research activities.

Deborah Kennedy, M.B.A., N.D.; Research Fellow. Deborah Kennedy is a resident naturopathic doctor at the RSNC. Kennedy supervises fourth-year interns at the RSNC and Sherbourne Health Centre satellite clinic, as well as the RSNC second-year clinical rotations in hydrotherapy and massage. She also assists second-year students with their skills development. Kennedy operates a general naturopathic practice from the RSNC.

Afsoun Khalili, N.D.; Clinic Faculty. Afsoun Khalili teaches, observes, and evaluates fourth-year student interns during their clinic shifts, both at the Robert Schad Naturopathic Clinic and the Sherbourne Health Centre. Khalili is the creator and coordinator of Be Your Best Self, an RSNC support-group program that helps clinic patients lose weight and maintain their weight loss with healthy lifestyle habits. In addition, Khalili promotes CCNM's corporate wellness program, delivering presentations explaining the bottom-line benefits of institutionalized health strategies. Khalili maintains a private practice located in the Robert Schad Naturopathic Clinic.

Nellie Pachkovskaja, M.D., Ph.D., CMS; Professor, Clinical Sciences, and Associate Dean, Academics. Dr. Nellie Pachkovskaja designs, develops, reviews, and delivers academic curriculum content, course structure, and program-related learning materials. In addition, Dr. Pachkovskaja monitors the program's overall integration and consistency, prepares timetables and exam schedules, and monitors student academic performance. She acts as an academic liaison between students and faculty members.

Jonathan Prousky, N.D., FRSH; Associate Professor of Clinical Nutrition and Chief Naturopathic Medical Officer. In addition to ensuring the delivery of safe and effective naturopathic medical care, Jonathan Prousky develops clinical curriculum for the N.D. program and coordinates educational activities and operations within the Robert Schad Naturopathic Clinic to ensure the competency of all graduates. He coordinates the monthly grand rounds program and supervises the postgraduate residency program in naturopathic medicine. Prousky has also been published in numerous lay publications and peer-reviewed medical journals.

Paul Saunders, N.D., Ph.D., DHANP, CCH; Adjunct Faculty. After earning a Ph.D. in plant ecology from Duke University, Paul Saunders graduated from the Ontario (now the Canadian) College of Naturopathic Medicine and then earned an additional N.D. diploma at National College of Naturopathic Medicine, Portland, Oregon. Dr. Saunders introduced the practice of peer reviewing during his tenure as editor of the *Canadian Journal of Herbalism* (2000–02). He has participated in numerous conferences, delivered lectures for prominent groups, and been honoured with various awards and distinctions. Dr. Saunders currently teaches botanical medicine, parenteral therapy, venipuncture, and art and practice of naturopathic medicine. He currently runs a private practice in Dundas, Ontario.

Dugald Seely, N.D.; Assistant Professor and Research Fellow. As a research fellow in CCNM's Department of Clinical Epidemiology, Dugald Seely is involved in developing clinical trials and research methodology to assess natural health products and therapies used by naturopathic doctors. He also secures funding for conducting and disseminating research projects at CCNM and in collaboration with other institutions. As Assistant Professor, Seely teaches the principles of research and clinical epidemiology and assists student research initiatives.

Ljubisa Terzic, M.D.; Associate Professor. Ljubisa Terzic practised as a resident neurosurgeon in the University Medical Centre in Sarajevo while completing a postgraduate program in ear, nose, and throat (ENT) and maxillofacial surgery at the University of Zagreb and teaching anatomy and general surgery at the local university. Having relocated to Canada, Dr. Terzic teaches anatomy, embryology, and minor surgical procedures at CCNM. A favourite with students, he has been presented with several teaching awards. Dr. Terzic has authored and coauthored a number of published articles and textbooks.

Jonathan Wilde, M.B.A.; Senior Academic Administrator. Jonathan Wilde has dedicated the academic administrative team to restructuring processes, including exam marking, grade reporting, and student/faculty evaluation, thereby improving the office's accessibility and responsiveness to students. In addition, Wilde is committed to continuously evaluating and updating the College's academic program.

CURRENT RESEARCH PROJECTS

Clinical trial to assess the effect of melatonin on lung cancer recurrence and mortality. This study, funded by the Lotte and John Hecht Memorial Foundation, is expected to be completed by 2012.

Clinical trial to test the efficacy of cinnamon as an aid in diabetes to reduce blood sugar levels.

Clinical trial to compare the effectiveness of two naturopathic-based treatments on shoulder pain in workers at Canada Post.

When time permits and when funding initiatives dictate, the department is also involved in conducting and publishing secondary research in the form of systematic reviews. Current work in this area includes a comparison of trials that have tested *Panax ginseng* for diabetes from a Western-versus-Eastern medicine perspective, a systematic review of all clinical trials that assess for the effect of melatonin on chemotherapy toxicity, and a systematic review of English and Chinese language studies that assess acupuncture as a treatment aid for poststroke rehabilitation.

SOUTHWEST COLLEGE OF NATUROPATHIC MEDICINE AND HEALTH SCIENCES
Doctor of Naturopathic Medicine Program

Programs of Study

Southwest College of Naturopathic Medicine and Health Sciences (SCNM), founded in 1992, offers a four-year professional degree program leading to the Doctor of Naturopathic Medicine (N.D.). Graduates are educated in the same basic sciences as an M.D., in addition to studying holistic and less-toxic approaches to therapy, with a strong emphasis on disease prevention and optimizing wellness. As part of the N.D. program at Southwest College, students have extensive experience with local hospitals, M.D.'s, and other health-care practitioners. The mission of SCNM is to provide a school of medicine and health sciences grounded in naturopathic principles. Dedicated to the ideal that everyone deserves high quality health care, SCNM engages students in rigorous innovative academic programs, discovers and expands knowledge, and empowers individuals and communities to achieve optimal health.

SCNM is accredited by the Council on Naturopathic Medical Education, the accrediting agency for naturopathic colleges and programs in the United States and Canada. The College is also accredited by the Higher Learning Commission of the North Central Association of Colleges and Schools. In states that license naturopathic physicians, including Arizona, the profession is regulated. In these states, naturopathic physicians must pass either national or state board examinations and must have received an education from an accredited four-year professional-level, naturopathic medical school. Naturopathic physicians are subject to review by a state board of examiners to ensure protection of the patients.

Research Facilities

SCNM's Research Department serves the public by conducting and promoting research on natural therapies and advancing the knowledge of complimentary/alternative medicine. It provides scientific evidence to the empirical findings experienced, documented, and practiced by individuals around the world, along with fundamental and scientific reasons for the effectiveness of natural therapeutics. SCNM provides naturopathic physicians, researchers, and academicians the opportunity to scientifically demonstrate the medicinal value of complimentary/alternative medicine. Biomedical research programs include human subject research, basic sciences research, public health projects, epidemiological studies, and quality assurance of natural products.

SCNM has the facilities to support faculty and student research projects. There is an adequate administrative area and a faculty area with computer networks. The basic sciences research area may also be available in the future at the College's planned off-site location in the Biomedical Institute at Arizona State University in Tempe, about 5 miles from SCNM.

Human subject research projects are conducted at the teaching clinic of SCNM and at the Southwest Naturopathic Medical Center located at 8010 East McDowell Road in Scottsdale, about 5 miles from SCNM.

The SCNM Medical Center offers multidisciplinary primary medical care for common, serious, and chronic health conditions while providing an engaging clinical experience for students with patients in the community. SCNM requires a great amount of patient contact and numerous clinical training hours. The College's Medical Center and affiliated off-site and extended-site clinics are centers for learning for hundreds of clinical training students pursuing their naturopathic degree, for clinical or research fellows conducting research, and for house staff members facilitating patient care. The Medical Center has numerous off-site facilities and maintains strong business ties in an integrative community.

The SCNM library provides the campus community with books, journals, and other information resources; teaches bibliographic and other research skills; and provides the larger community with a major information resource, the best of its kind in the Southwest. The size of the library normally increases by approximately100 cataloged items per month. The library's collection is unique, and its arrangements and access are customized to meet the unique needs and interests of the clientele. The library's catalog is Internet-accessible and its collections include more than 15,000 items, with about 1,750 additional volumes and extra copies, the largest naturopathic collection in the Southwest. There are approximately 200 journal titles currently in the library, of which 100 are current subscriptions, including approximately 14,000 separate issues. Several years ago, the library received a major donation of environmental medicine books from the late Dr. Theron G. Randolph, known as the father of clinical ecology. Harvard University received his manuscript collection, and SCNM received his personal book collection. The library also provides access to software and online resources including Alt HealthWatch, AMED, Biopac Student Lab, Clinical Pharmacology, Encyclopedia Homeopathica, EndNote, First Consult, FoodWorks, Herbal Medicine II, MD Consult, Natural Medicines Comprehensive Database, Natural Standard, PubMed, QPuncture, and RADAR. The library houses 3,400 audio shelf items; 500 video shelf items; and many professional conferences, seminars, and workshops. Library hours, schedules, and further information are available at http://69.63.217.13/S20040.

Financial Aid

Approximately 90 percent of Southwest College students receive some type of financial aid. The Financial Aid Office assists students in financing their professional education. Financial resources include scholarships, direct subsidized loans, direct unsubsidized loand, and Federal Graduate PLUS loans.

Cost of Study

Tuition for the 2009–10 academic year was $24,200. Tuition cost per quarter was $6050. Books and supplies cost $1000 per quarter.

Living and Housing Costs

Arizona has one of the lowest costs of living in the United States. Housing is readily available in the Phoenix area. A two-bedroom, two-bath apartment in Phoenix costs between $800 and $1000 per month.

Student Group

The total enrollment is 330 students. Each year, the fall class has approximately 75 students and the winter class has approximately 30 students. The College's last incoming class hailed from no fewer than fifty-five different colleges, forty different states, and five different countries. The average age of students who are enrolled is 30.

Student Outcomes

Sixty-five percent of SCNM graduates continue to practice in Arizona. The N.D. program prepares graduates for a wide range of career opportunities, mostly as primary-care physicians, respecting the integral relationship of body, mind, and spirit while combining the wisdom of ancient healing with the rigor of modern scientific methods. Some practitioners have a private general practice; some concentrate on disease-specific practices such as cancer, cardiac disease, or arthritis; while others focus on specific populations such as men's health, women's health, or pediatrics. Many N.D. graduates work in clinics, wellness centers, and other integrative settings, and are part of a patient's integrative health care team, using their naturopathic medical expertise to create a wealth of health options for their patients;.

The Doctor of Naturopathic Medicine degree sets the stage for careers in scientific research, professional media and scientific writing, public health education, and academia. The N.D. is a sought-after credential in product development, sales/marketing, and professional education within the environmental, neutraceutical, and natural product industries.

Location

SCNM is situated in the tri-city area of Scottsdale, Mesa, and Tempe, Arizona. The environment of the College fosters a positive learning community. The 15-acre campus in Tempe and the medical center in Scottsdale convey the excitement and enthusiasm that the students and faculty and staff members bring to naturopathic medical education. In addition to its beautiful weather, Arizona has much to offer residents. Recreational activities include hiking, mountain biking, walking, water sports, winter sports, golfing, spring training baseball games, and skydiving. Arizona has its share of lakes and rivers as well, including Saguaro Lake, Roosevelt Lake, Lake Powell, Tempe Town Lake, and the Salt River.

The College

SCNM is an accredited, nonprofit, private coeducational naturopathic medical college. The College is one of the best academic and technological leaders of the naturopathic medical schools. The College prepares students to be conscientious and caring naturopathic health-care providers. The SCNM experience is characterized by a high degree of student-faculty interaction, teamwork, practical application, and contact with external organizations. The Naturopathic Residency Program at SCNM is one of the most integrated residency programs available to naturopathic medical school graduates. The program exposes residents to private practice, community clinic, research, and teaching environments. Affiliation agreements with area hospitals and medical clinics allow the College's residents access to hospital facilities, including emergency rooms. The residency program provides broad-based training in diagnostic and treatment strategies, patient management, case presentation, public speaking, teaching, student supervision, and research.

Applying

Applicants are evaluated on their overall academic record, including transcripts, letters of recommendation, personal essay, and work experience. Admission decisions are based on academic performance, occupational history, professional potential, level of maturity, concern for others, and previous experience with natural medicine. Applications are accepted on a year-round basis, and students are admitted for either the fall or the spring start. Applications are available at http://my.scnm.edu/ics.

Correspondence and Information

Admissions Department
Southwest College of Naturopathic Medicine and Health Sciences
2140 East Broadway
Tempe, Arizona 85282

Phone: 888-882-7266
Fax: 480-858-9116
E-mail: admissions@scnm.edu
Web site: http://www.scnm.edu

Southwest College of Naturopathic Medicine and Health Sciences

THE FACULTY AND THEIR RESEARCH

Leslie Axelrod, Professor; N.D., Bastyr, 1987; Southwest Acupuncture, 1999. Dr. Axelrod offers medical services, including acupuncture, homeopathy, craniosacral therapy, nutrition, botanical medicine, family medicine, and women's health. She is also nationally certified in acupuncture.

Matthew Baral, Assistant Professor; N.D., Bastyr, 2000. Dr. Baral is medical director of the Hamilton Elementary School Clinic and teaches pediatrics and nutrition courses at the College. He has a particular interest in childhood diseases and has published papers on ear infection, childhood obesity, and autism. His focus is general pediatric medicine, nutrition, autism, and attention deficit/hyperactivity.

Nick Buratovich, Associate Professor and Chair of Physical Medicine; N.D., National College of Naturopathic Medicine, 1983. Dr. Buratovich specializes in manipulation, acupuncture, and nutrition as well as homeopathy and botanical medicine. In addition to maintaining two busy practices, Dr. Buratovich teaches physical medicine at SCNM and is an active member of the SCNM's Board of Trustees.

Boyd Campbell, Professor of Anatomy and Division Director; M.D., 1963, Ph.D. (anatomy), 1965, Illinois. Dr. Campbell completed a surgical internship at Rush-Presbyterian-St. Luke's Medical Center in Chicago and has done residency training in neurology, neurosurgery, and neuroradiology. He was a faculty member at Indiana University, University of Maryland, University of Puerto Rico, California Institute of Technology, Georgetown University, and the Uniformed Services University of the Health Sciences. He is a retired colonel in the U.S. Army Medical Corps, where he served as a research neurologist at the Walter Reed Army Institute of Research. He teaches gross human anatomy, neuroanatomy, and human histology at SCNM.

Walter J. Crinnion, Professor of Naturopathic Medicine and Director, Environmental Medicine Center of Excellence; N.D., Bastyr, 1982. Dr. Crinnion developed a specialty in environmental medicine and opened a comprehensive cleansing center in the Seattle area for twenty years. In addition to directing SCNM's Environmental Medicine Center of Excellence, he is an adjunct faculty member at the National College of Naturopathic Medicine, Bastyr University, and the University of Bridgeport, where he teaches environmental medicine to all four U.S. naturopathic medical schools.

Yong Deng, Professor of Acupuncture and Oriental Medicine; M.D., Chengdu University of Traditional Chinese Medicine (China), 1983; L.Ac. (Arizona), Dipl.Ac., National Certification Commission for Acupuncture and Oriental Medicine. From 1983 through 1996, Dr. Deng taught and practiced acupuncture and Chinese herbal medicine at Chengdu University of Traditional Chinese Medicine and its teaching hospital. He has a practice at Southwest Naturopathic Medical Center. Dr. Deng has more than eighteen years' experience in practicing acupuncture, Chinese herbs, and Tiu Na (Chinese therapeutic massage) for a wide range of diseases and conditions.

John Dye, Professor of Naturopathic Medicine and Department Chair of Mind-Body Medicine; N.D., National College of Naturopathic Medicine, 1979. Dr. Dye teaches endocrinology, mind-body medicine, and geriatrics at SCNM. He is a nationally recognized speaker in the fields of natural hormone replacement, diabetes, and longevity medicine. He is an attending physician and also teaches classes in mind-body healing and stress management and integrates techniques such as imagery, meditation, and stress-release into medical practice.

Patricia Gaines, Assistant Professor, Division of Naturopathic Therapeutics; Chair, Department of Botanical Medicine; N.D., Bastyr, 2002.

Richard Laherty, Associate Professor of Anatomy and Chair of Basic Medical Sciences; Ph.D. (human anatomy), Berkeley, 1978. Dr. Laherty's research interest in reproductive endocrinology led him to the Reproductive Endocrinology Center in the Department of Obstetrics and Gynecology at the University of California, San Francisco, School of Medicine. There, he served on the faculties of the School of Dentistry and the School of Medicine and taught histology, gross anatomy, and neuroanatomy. He next served on the faculty of Indiana University School of Medicine where he taught histology and did research in reproductive endocrinology and on the endocrine regulation of the immune system. Dr. Laherty then moved to Kentucky, where he was a faculty member at the University of Kentucky before settling in Arizona. He teaches gross human anatomy, neuroanatomy, and endocrinology.

Jeffrey Langland, Associate Professor of Microbiology and Co-Chair of the Research Department; Ph.D. (virology), Arizona State, 1990. Dr. Langland's area of interest is investigating and understanding the complex cellular defenses against microorganisms. After graduating from Arizona State University (ASU) Dr. Langland did a postdoctoral fellowship at the University of California, Davis studying oncolytic viruses, followed by a postdoctoral position at the University of Wyoming comparing similarities between plant and human defenses against viruses. In 1995, he returned to ASU as a research assistant professor. In this capacity, he has instructed several courses including general virology and the biology of AIDS.

Arben Lasku, Associate Professor of Pathology and Laboratory Medicine; M.D., 1985, Ph.D. (tumor markers), 1994, Tirana (Albania). Dr. Lasku completed a specialization in nuclear medicine at the University of Genoa Medical Center, Italy. He has trained in clinical chemistry, clinical pathology, and nuclear medicine and has been a faculty member at the University of Tirana. Dr. Lasku teaches human pathology, laboratory diagnosis, and immunology at SCNM.

Pamela Martin, Assistant Professor; M.D., Texas Tech Health Sciences Center. Dr. Martin completed a residency in pediatrics at the Texas Tech Health Sciences Center, Lubbock, Texas. Dr. Martin was in practice for ten years in Amarillo, Texas, and has been an adjunct faculty member at SCNM for several years. Dr. Martin teaches medical ethics, hematology, musculoskeletal and connective tissue disorders, and HEENT.

Stephen Messer, Dolisos Professor of Homeopathy and Director, Division of Naturopathic Therapeutics; N.D., National College of Naturopathic Medicine, 1979. Dr. Messer offers medical services, including nutrition, homeopathy, and family medicine. He has been in practice for twenty-three years and is well known in the world of homeopathy as one the founders of the Homeopathic Academy of Naturopathic Physicians, a board member of the National Center for Homeopathy (NCH), and the dean of the NCH's summer school program.

Mona Morstein, Associate Professor and Chair of Department of Nutrition; N.D., National College of Naturopathic Medicine, 1988; DHANP. Dr. Morstein did her residency in family practice from 1988 to 1989; and then had a private practice in Great Falls, Montana, from 1989 to 2002 before joining SCNM in 2002. She specializes in the treatment of diabetes, women's medicine, and gastrointestinal disorders, although her private practice encompassed a broad spectrum of family medicine. Dr. Morstein teaches gastroenterology, nutrition, and the grand rounds courses.

Timothy Schwaiger, Assistant Professor of Physical Assessment and Director of Clinical Sciences; N.M.D., Southwest College of Naturopathic Medicine and Health Sciences, 1999. Dr. Schwaiger holds a master's degree in health services management and has over 24 years of health-related experience. Dr. Schwaiger has a private practice and teaching rotations at Southwest Naturopathic Medical Center. His practice focuses on family medicine in treating both acute and chronic conditions. Dr. Schwaiger treats patients with allergies/asthma, anxiety, depression, sleep disorders, cardiovascular disease, high blood pressure/cholesterol, prostate conditions, headaches, gastrointestinal disorders, hormone problems, and skin problems. He has had extensive training in prolotherapy used in the treatment of pain. Among many treatment modalities, he uses nutrition and supplementation, botanical medicine, acupuncture and Chinese medicine, pharmacology, hormone replacement, homeopathy, IV therapy, lifestyle modification, and vertebral manipulation.

Christine Sorensen, Full-time Clinical Faculty and Residency Director; N.D., Southwest College of Naturopathic Medicine and Health Sciences, 2001; RN, Arizona State, 1980.

Jessica Tran, Fellow, Department of Environmental Medicine; N.D., Bastyr. Dr. Tran graduated with a B.S. in biological sciences and B.A. in social ecology with a concentration in epidemiology and public health from the University of California, Irvine. She practices general family medicine with a special interest in the pediatric and geriatric population. Her focus is environmental medicine, homeopathy, and naturopathic oncology. She completed a one-year family medicine residency at Southwest Naturopathic Medical Center and is completing an environmental medicine fellowship under the directorship of Dr. Crinnion.

Robert Waters, Professor of Biochemistry, Genetics, and Statistics and Chair of the Research Department; Ph.D., Montana State, 1975. Dr. Waters earned his doctorate in genetics with graduate minors in biochemistry and statistics. Postdoctoral training and a faculty appointment were added at Kansas State University (KSU) in Manhattan, Kansas. Research duties at KSU included radioactive tracing of DNA involving intergeneric hybridization with publications. During his tenure at KSU, Dr. Waters had the privilege of working with Nobel Prize Laureate Dr. Norman E. Borlaug in genetics with the International Maize and Wheat Improvement Center near Mexico City (Toluca) and Ciudad Obregón in Sonora, Mexico. Following KSU, Dr. Waters received extensive training in computer science, communications, and programming from IBM, DEC, and many other companies. In computer science, he consulted with the Mexican Ministry of Agriculture in Mexico City and British Petroleum in London. With his varied background he designed, developed, and implemented an extensive emergency medical software system and was a coprincipal investigator for a multimillion-dollar federal DOT/NHTSA grant to rewrite the EMT basic curriculum. Following twenty years in private industry, Dr. Waters joined the faculty at the SCNM in 1993 as an Associate Professor of Medical Biochemistry and Medical Genetics. He teaches biochemistry, research methods, and medical genetics.

Debra Wollner, Associate Professor of Physiology and Pharmacology; Ph.D. (pharmacology), Washington (Seattle), 1987. Dr. Wollner teaches physiology, endocrinology, pharmacology, and research. She performed postdoctoral research in the Department of Cell Biology at New York University School of Medicine, the Institute for Cancer Research at the Fox Chase Cancer Center, and the Department of Molecular and Cellular Physiology at Stanford University Medical Center. She has published her research on the development of epithelial polarity, cellular adhesion, and the diversity of the voltage sensitive sodium channel, work that was funded by the NSF, the NIH, and the Cystic Fibrosis Foundation. She currently serves as Chair of the Southwest College Institutional Review Board (IRB).

Section 38
Optometry and Vision Sciences

This section contains a directory of institutions offering graduate work in optometry and vision sciences. Additional information about programs listed in the directory may be obtained by writing directly to the dean of a graduate school or chair of a department at the address given in the directory.

In the other guides in this series:
Graduate Programs in the Humanities, Arts & Social Sciences
See *Psychology and Counseling*
Graduate Programs in the Biological Sciences
See *Biological and Biomedical Sciences, Biophysics, Neuroscience and Neurobiology,* and *Physiology*

Graduate Programs in the Physical Sciences, Mathematics, Agricultural Sciences, the Environment & Natural Resources
See *Physics*
Graduate Programs in Engineering & Applied Sciences
See *Biomedical Engineering* and *Biotechnology*

CONTENTS

Program Directories

Optometry

Ferris State University, Michigan College of Optometry, Big Rapids, MI 49307. Offers OD. *Accreditation:* AOA. *Faculty:* 19 full-time (4 women), 101 part-time/adjunct (39 women). *Students:* 145 full-time (85 women), 1 part-time (0 women); includes 10 minority (9 Asian Americans or Pacific Islanders, 1 Hispanic American), 7 international. Average age 24. 247 applicants, 12% accepted, 29 enrolled. In 2009, 33 ODs awarded. *Entrance requirements:* OAT. Additional exam requirements/recommendations for international students: Required—TOEFL (minimum score 500 paper-based; 173 computer-based; 61 iBT). *Application deadline:* For fall admission, 3/1 for domestic and international students. Applications are processed on a rolling basis. Application fee: $30. Electronic applications accepted. *Financial support:* Fellowships, research assistantships, teaching assistantships, career-related internships or fieldwork, Federal Work-Study, and scholarships/grants available. Financial award application deadline: 3/15; financial award applicants required to submit FAFSA. *Faculty research:* Corneal reshaping, spatial vision and vision science, reading disabilities, vision development, vision care access. *Unit head:* Dr. Michael Cron, Dean, 231-591-3706, Fax: 231-591-2394, E-mail: cronm@ferris.edu. *Application contact:* Dr. Nancy Peterson-Klein, Associate Dean, 231-591-3703, Fax: 231-591-2394, E-mail: peterson@ferris.edu.

Illinois College of Optometry, Professional Program, Chicago, IL 60616-3878. Offers OD. *Accreditation:* AOA. *Entrance requirements:* OAT. Electronic applications accepted. *Faculty research:* Eye disease treatment, binocular vision, cataract development, pediatric vision, genetic eye disease.

Indiana University Bloomington, School of Optometry, Bloomington, IN 47405-3680. Offers OD, MS, PhD. *Accreditation:* AOA (one or more programs are accredited). *Faculty:* 36 full-time (11 women), 7 part-time/adjunct (5 women). *Students:* 321 full-time (189 women), 4 part-time (2 women); includes 40 minority (13 African Americans, 2 American Indian/Alaska Native, 24 Asian Americans or Pacific Islanders, 1 Hispanic American), 27 international. Average age 25. 432 applicants, 29% accepted, 59 enrolled. In 2009, 91 first professional degrees, 2 master's, 4 doctorates awarded. Terminal master's awarded for partial completion of doctoral program. *Degree requirements:* For master's, thesis; for doctorate, comprehensive exam, thesis/dissertation. *Entrance requirements:* For OD, OAT; for master's, GRE, BA in science; for doctorate, GRE, BA in science (master's degree preferred). Additional exam requirements/recommendations for international students: Required—TOEFL (minimum score 550 paper-based; 213 computer-based; 80 iBT). *Application deadline:* For fall admission, 1/15 for domestic students; for winter admission, 2/1 for domestic and international students; for spring admission, 9/1 for domestic students. Applications are processed on a rolling basis. Application fee: $55 ($65 for international students). Electronic applications accepted. *Expenses:* Contact institution. *Financial support:* In 2009–10, 48 students received support; fellowships with full tuition reimbursements available, research assistantships with full tuition reimbursements available, Federal Work-Study, institutionally sponsored loans, scholarships/grants, health care benefits, and research assistantships available. Support available to part-time students. Financial award application deadline: 12/1; financial award applicants required to submit FAFSA. *Faculty research:* Corneal physiology, contact lenses, adaptive optics, dry eye, low vision, refractive anomalies, ophthalmic imaging, glaucoma, ocular physiology, infant vision, retinal disease. Total annual research expenditures: $5.6 million. *Unit head:* Dr. P. Sarita Soni, Interim Dean, 812-855-4440, Fax: 812-855-8664, E-mail: sonip@indiana.edu. *Application contact:* Patricia Reyes, Associate Director of Student Services, 812-855-1292, Fax: 812-855-4389, E-mail: patreyes@indiana.edu.

Inter American University of Puerto Rico School of Optometry, Professional Program, Bayam¾n, PR 00957. Offers OD. *Accreditation:* AOA. *Degree requirements:* For OD, thesis/dissertation, research project. *Entrance requirements:* OAT, interview, minimum GPA of 2.5, 2 letters of recommendation. Electronic applications accepted. *Expenses:* Contact institution. *Faculty research:* Visual characteristics of special populations, contact lenses, refraction and diabetes.

Midwestern University, Glendale Campus, Arizona College of Optometry, Glendale, AZ 85308. Offers OD. *Accreditation:* AOA. *Faculty:* 4 full-time (0 women). *Students:* 52 full-time (21 women); includes 16 minority (2 African Americans, 1 American Indian/Alaska Native, 10 Asian Americans or Pacific Islanders, 3 Hispanic Americans). Average age 25. 178 applicants, 39% accepted, 52 enrolled. *Entrance requirements:* OAT, bachelor's degree, minimum overall cumulative and science GPA of 2.75, 2 letters of recommendation. *Unit head:* Hector Santiago, Dean, 623-572-3901, Fax: 623-572-3911, E-mail: azoptometry@midwestern.edu. *Application contact:* James Walter, Director of Admissions, 888-247-9277, Fax: 623-572-3229, E-mail: admissaz@midwestern.edu.

The New England College of Optometry, Professional Program, Boston, MA 02115-1100. Offers optometry (OD); vision science (MS). *Accreditation:* AOA. *Entrance requirements:* OAT. Electronic applications accepted.

Northeastern State University, College of Optometry, Tahlequah, OK 74464. Offers OD. Applicants must be residents of Oklahoma, Arkansas, Kansas, Colorado, New Mexico, Missouri, Texas, or Nebraska. *Accreditation:* AOA. *Degree requirements:* For OD, research project. *Entrance requirements:* OAT. *Expenses:* Contact institution. *Faculty research:* Extended-wear and bifocal contact lenses, methods of vision therapy, glaucoma, low vision, diabetes.

Nova Southeastern University, Health Professions Division, College of Optometry, Fort Lauderdale, FL 33328. Offers clinical vision research (MS); optometry (OD). *Accreditation:* AOA. Postbaccalaureate distance learning degree programs offered (no on-campus study). *Faculty:* 48 full-time (32 women), 11 part-time/adjunct (10 women). *Students:* 450 full-time (294 women), 2 part-time (1 woman); includes 181 minority (13 African Americans, 123 Asian Americans or Pacific Islanders, 45 Hispanic Americans), 36 international. Average age 23. 746 applicants, 25% accepted, 106 enrolled. In 2009, 103 first professional degrees, 2 master's awarded. *Degree requirements:* For master's, comprehensive exam (for some programs), thesis. *Entrance requirements:* For OD, OAT, minimum GPA of 3.0; for master's, OAT or GRE, BA. Additional exam requirements/recommendations for international students: Required—TOEFL (minimum score 79 iBT). *Application deadline:* For fall admission, 4/1 for domestic and international students. Applications are processed on a rolling basis. Application fee: $50. Electronic applications accepted. *Expenses:* Contact institution. *Financial support:* In 2009–10, 393 students received support. Federal Work-Study, institutionally sponsored loans, and scholarships/grants available. Financial award applicants required to submit FAFSA. *Faculty research:* Retinal disease, low vision, binocular vision, contact lenses, accommodation. *Unit head:* Dr. David Loshin, Dean, 954-262-1404, Fax: 954-262-1818. *Application contact:* Fran Franconeri, Admissions Counselor, 954-262-1132, Fax: 954-262-2282.

The Ohio State University, College of Optometry, Professional Program in Optometry, Columbus, OH 43210. Offers OD. *Accreditation:* AOA. *Faculty:* 33 full-time (14 women). *Students:* 252 full-time (138 women); includes 29 minority (6 African Americans, 1 American Indian/Alaska Native, 20 Asian Americans or Pacific Islanders, 2 Hispanic Americans), 1 international. Average age 25. In 2009, 68 ODs awarded. *Entrance requirements:* OAT. Additional exam requirements/recommendations for international students: Required—TOEFL. *Application deadline:* For fall admission, 3/1 for domestic and international students. Applications are processed on a rolling basis. Application fee: $40 ($50 for international students). Electronic applications accepted. *Expenses:* Tuition, state resident: full-time $10,683. Tuition, nonresident: full-time $25,923. Tuition and fees vary according to course load and program. *Financial support:* In 2009–10, 220 students received support. Federal Work-Study and scholarships/grants available. Financial award application deadline: 3/1; financial award applicants required to submit FAFSA. *Application contact:* Professional Admissions, 614-292-9444, Fax: 614-292-3895, E-mail: professional@osu.edu.

Salus University, Professional Program, Elkins Park, PA 19027-1598. Offers OD, OD/MS. *Accreditation:* AOA. *Faculty:* 49 full-time (26 women), 23 part-time/adjunct (11 women). *Students:* 619 full-time (419 women); includes 270 minority (43 African Americans, 2 American Indian/Alaska Native, 214 Asian Americans or Pacific Islanders, 11 Hispanic Americans), 4 international. Average age 25. 880 applicants, 29% accepted, 157 enrolled. In 2009, 155 ODs awarded. *Degree requirements:* For OD, comprehensive exam (for some programs). *Entrance requirements:* OAT, interview. Additional exam requirements/recommendations for international students: Required—TOEFL. *Application deadline:* For fall admission, 3/31 priority date for domestic students, 3/31 for international students. Applications are processed on a rolling basis. Electronic applications accepted. *Expenses:* Tuition: Full-time $31,700. Required fees: $550. Full-time tuition and fees vary according to degree level and program. *Financial support:* Career-related internships or fieldwork, Federal Work-Study, institutionally sponsored loans, and scholarships/grants available. Financial award application deadline: 3/31; financial award applicants required to submit FAFSA. *Faculty research:* Vision research, visual perception, ocular motility, electrodiagnosis, photobiology glaucoma, myopia, keratoconus. Total annual research expenditures: $635,000. *Unit head:* Robert E. Horne, Vice President of Student Affairs, 215-780-1312, Fax: 215-780-1396, E-mail: rhorne@salus.edu. *Application contact:* Dr. James Caldwell, Director of Admissions, 215-780-1300, E-mail: jcaldwell@Salus.edu.

Southern California College of Optometry, Professional Program, Fullerton, CA 92831-1615. Offers OD. *Accreditation:* AOA. *Degree requirements:* For OD, thesis/dissertation. *Entrance requirements:* OAT. Electronic applications accepted. *Faculty research:* Structure and function of the human visual system.

Southern College of Optometry, Professional Program, Memphis, TN 38104-2222. Offers OD. *Accreditation:* AOA. *Degree requirements:* For OD, clinical experience. *Entrance requirements:* OAT, 3 years of undergraduate pre-optometry course work.

State University of New York College of Optometry, Professional Program, New York, NY 10036. Offers OD, OD/MPH, OD/MS, OD/PhD. *Accreditation:* AOA. *Faculty:* 45 full-time (10 women), 102 part-time/adjunct (28 women). *Students:* 281 full-time (196 women); includes 130 minority (9 African Americans, 114 Asian Americans or Pacific Islanders, 7 Hispanic Americans), 19 international. Average age 24. 499 applicants, 28% accepted, 74 enrolled. In 2009, 68 ODs awarded. *Entrance requirements:* OAT. Additional exam requirements/recommendations for international students: Required—TOEFL (minimum score 550 paper-based; 220 computer-based). *Application deadline:* For fall admission, 2/15 priority date for domestic and international students. Applications are processed on a rolling basis. Application fee: $75. Electronic applications accepted. *Expenses:* Tuition, state resident: full-time $16,520. Tuition, nonresident: full-time $31,720. Required fees: $395. *Financial support:* In 2009–10, 234 students received support; fellowships, career-related internships or fieldwork, Federal Work-Study, and tuition waivers (full and partial) available. Financial award application deadline: 4/15; financial award applicants required to submit FAFSA. *Faculty research:* Vision research. *Unit head:* Dr. Edward Johnston, Vice President for Student Affairs and Director of Admissions, 212-938-5500, Fax: 212-938-5504, E-mail: johnston@sunyopt.edu. *Application contact:* Dr. Edward Johnston, Vice President for Student Affairs and Director of Admissions, 212-938-5500, Fax: 212-938-5504, E-mail: johnston@sunyopt.edu.

Université de Montréal, School of Optometry, Professional Program in Optometry, Montréal, QC H3C 3J7, Canada. Offers residency (DESS); visual impairment intervention-orientation and mobility (DESS); visual impairment intervention-readaptation (DESS). Open only to Canadian residents. *Accreditation:* AOA. *Students:* 19 full-time (16 women), 9 part-time (8 women). In 2009, 13 DESSs awarded. *Application deadline:* For fall admission, 2/1 priority date for domestic students; for winter admission, 11/1 priority date for domestic students; for spring admission, 2/1 priority date for domestic students. Application fee: $100. Electronic applications accepted. *Application contact:* Christian Casanova, Chairperson, 514-343-2407, Fax: 514-343-2382, E-mail: christian.casanova@umontreal.ca.

The University of Alabama at Birmingham, School of Optometry, Professional Program in Optometry, Birmingham, AL 35294. Offers OD. *Entrance requirements:* OAT, interview.

University of California, Berkeley, School of Optometry, Berkeley, CA 94720-1500. Offers OD, Certificate. *Accreditation:* AOA. *Faculty:* 21 full-time, 86 part-time/adjunct. *Students:* 252 full-time (205 women); includes 176 minority (2 African Americans, 1 American Indian/Alaska Native, 163 Asian Americans or Pacific Islanders, 10 Hispanic Americans). Average age 23. 273 applicants, 28% accepted, 67 enrolled. In 2009, 54 first professional degrees awarded. *Entrance requirements:* OAT. Additional exam requirements/recommendations for international students: Required—TOEFL (minimum score 570 paper-based; 230 computer-based). *Application deadline:* For fall admission, 12/1 for domestic and international students. Application fee: $70 ($90 for international students). Electronic applications accepted. *Financial support:* In 2009–10, 54 students received support. Career-related internships or fieldwork, Federal Work-Study, institutionally sponsored loans, scholarships/grants, unspecified assistantships, and departmental awards available. Financial award application deadline: 3/2; financial award applicants required to submit FAFSA. *Faculty research:* Low vision, spatial vision, psychophysics of vision, clinical optics, patient care. Total annual research expenditures: $34 million. *Unit head:* Dr. Dennis M. Levi, Dean, 510-642-3414, Fax: 510-642-7806, E-mail: optometry-admissions@berkeley.edu. *Application contact:* Dr. Richard C. Van Sluyters, Associate Dean for Student Affairs/Head Graduate Adviser, 510-642-9537, Fax: 510-643-5109, E-mail: optometry-admissions@berkeley.edu.

University of Houston, College of Optometry, Professional Program in Optometry, Houston, TX 77204. Offers OD. *Accreditation:* AOA. *Expenses:* Tuition, state resident: full-time $7676; part-time $320 per credit hour. Tuition, nonresident: full-time $14,324; part-time $597 per credit hour. Required fees: $3034. *Financial support:* Fellowships, research assistantships, teaching assistantships, career-related internships or fieldwork, Federal Work-Study, institutionally sponsored loans, scholarships/grants, health care benefits, and unspecified assistantships available. Support available to part-time students. *Faculty research:* Refractive error development, corneal physiology, low vision, binocular vision.

University of Missouri–St. Louis, College of Optometry, Professional Program in Optometry, St. Louis, MO 63121. Offers OD. *Accreditation:* AOA. *Faculty:* 23 full-time (6 women), 14 part-time/adjunct (4 women). *Students:* 176 full-time (99 women); includes 26 minority (8 African Americans, 1 American Indian/Alaska Native, 15 Asian Americans or Pacific Islanders, 2 Hispanic Americans), 4 international. Average age 23. 349 applicants, 21% accepted, 44 enrolled. In 2009, 43 ODs awarded. *Entrance requirements:* OAT, 90 hours of undergraduate course work. *Application deadline:* For fall admission, 2/15 for domestic and international students. Applications are processed on a rolling basis. Application fee: $50. Electronic applications accepted. *Expenses:* Tuition, state resident: full-time $5377; part-time $297.70 per credit hour. Tuition, nonresident: full-time $13,882; part-time $771.20 per credit hour. Required fees: $220; $12.20 per credit hour. One-time fee: $12. Tuition and fees vary according to course level, campus/location and program. *Financial support:* In 2009–10, 175 students received support, including 3 research assistantships (averaging $500 per year), 3 teaching assistantships (averaging $500 per year); Federal Work-Study, institutionally sponsored loans, and scholarships/grants also available. Financial award application deadline: 4/1; financial award applicants required to submit FAFSA. *Faculty research:* Visual psychophysics and perception, noninvasive assessment of visual processing, aging and Alzheimer's disease, orthokeratology. *Unit head:* Dr. Edward S. Bennett, Director, Student Services, 314-516-6263, Fax: 314-516-6708, E-mail: optstuaff@umsl.edu. *Application contact:* Linda L. Stein, Administrative Assistant, 314-516-5905, Fax: 314-516-6708, E-mail: linda_stein@umsl.edu.

University of the Incarnate Word, School of Optometry, San Antonio, TX 78209-6397. Offers OD. *Accreditation:* AOA. *Students:* 62 full-time (34 women); includes 24 minority (2 African Americans, 17 Asian Americans or Pacific Islanders, 5 Hispanic Americans), 3 international. Average age 25. *Degree requirements:* For OD, clinical contact hours. *Entrance requirements:* OAT (minimum score 300 recommended), 90 credit hours of prerequisite course work, interview.

Additional exam requirements/recommendations for international students: Required—TOEFL (minimum score 560 paper-based; 220 computer-based; 83 iBT). *Application deadline:* For fall admission, 7/15 for domestic students. Applications are processed on a rolling basis. Application fee: $50. Electronic applications accepted. *Expenses:* Contact institution. *Financial support:* Federal Work-Study and scholarships/grants available. Financial award applicants required to submit FAFSA. *Unit head:* Dr. Hani Ghazi-Birry, Founding Dean, 210-883-1190, Fax: 210-883-1191, E-mail: optometry@uiwtx.edu. *Application contact:* Henry Cantu, Director of Optometry Admissions and Student Services, 210-883-1193, Fax: 210-883-1191, E-mail: hmcantu@uiwtx.edu.

University of Waterloo, Graduate Studies, Faculty of Science, School of Optometry, Waterloo, ON N2L 3G1, Canada. Offers vision science (M Sc, PhD). *Accreditation:* AOA. Part-time programs available. *Degree requirements:* For master's, thesis; for doctorate, thesis/dissertation. *Entrance requirements:* For master's, honors degree, minimum B average; for doctorate, master's degree, minimum B average. Additional exam requirements/recommendations for international students: Required—TOEFL (minimum score 580 paper-based; 237 computer-based), TWE (minimum score 4). Electronic applications accepted. *Faculty research:* Vision science, fundamental and clinical vision, physiological optics, psycho-physics, perception.

Western University of Health Sciences, College of Optometry, Pomona, CA 91766-1854. Offers OD. *Accreditation:* AOA.

Vision Sciences

Eastern Virginia Medical School, Ophthalmic Technology Program, Norfolk, VA 23501-1980. Offers Certificate. *Faculty:* 1 (woman) full-time, 1 (woman) part-time/adjunct. *Students:* 6 full-time (all women); includes 3 minority (2 African Americans, 1 Asian American or Pacific Islander). 12 applicants, 42% accepted, 5 enrolled. *Application deadline:* For fall admission, 4/1 for domestic students. Applications are processed on a rolling basis. Application fee: $60. Electronic applications accepted. *Expenses:* Contact institution. *Unit head:* Lori J. Williams, Director, 757-388-3747, E-mail: optech@evms.edu. *Application contact:* Rose Mwayungu, Executive Director of Operations and Compliance, 757-446-7153, Fax: 757-446-6179, E-mail: mwayunra@evms.edu.

Emory University, School of Medicine, Programs in Allied Health Professions, The Emory Ophthalmic Technology Program, Atlanta, GA 30322-1100. Offers MM Sc. *Faculty:* 1 full-time (0 women). In 2009, 1 master's awarded. *Degree requirements:* For master's, thesis. Application fee: $0. *Expenses:* Contact institution. *Financial support:* Institutionally sponsored loans and scholarships/grants available. Financial award application deadline: 3/1; financial award applicants required to submit FAFSA. *Unit head:* Paul M. Larson, Director, 404-778-4305, Fax: 404-778-5128, E-mail: plarson@emory.edu. *Application contact:* Paul M. Larson, Director, 404-778-4305, Fax: 404-778-5128, E-mail: plarson@emory.edu.

The New England College of Optometry, Professional Program, Boston, MA 02115-1100. Offers optometry (OD); vision science (MS). *Accreditation:* AOA. *Entrance requirements:* OAT. Electronic applications accepted.

Nova Southeastern University, Health Professions Division, College of Optometry, Fort Lauderdale, FL 33328. Offers clinical vision research (MS); optometry (OD). *Accreditation:* AOA. Postbaccalaureate distance learning degree programs offered (no on-campus study). *Faculty:* 48 full-time (32 women), 11 part-time/adjunct (10 women). *Students:* 450 full-time (294 women), 2 part-time (1 woman); includes 181 minority (13 African Americans, 123 Asian Americans or Pacific Islanders, 45 Hispanic Americans), 36 international. Average age 23. 746 applicants, 25% accepted, 106 enrolled. In 2009, 103 first professional degrees, 2 master's awarded. *Degree requirements:* For master's, comprehensive exam (for some programs), thesis. *Entrance requirements:* For OD, OAT, minimum GPA of 3.0; for master's, OAT or GRE, BA. Additional exam requirements/recommendations for international students: Required—TOEFL (minimum score 79 iBT). *Application deadline:* For fall admission, 4/1 for domestic and international students. Applications are processed on a rolling basis. Application fee: $50. Electronic applications accepted. *Expenses:* Contact institution. *Financial support:* In 2009–10, 393 students received support. Federal Work-Study, institutionally sponsored loans, and scholarships/grants available. Financial award applicants required to submit FAFSA. *Faculty research:* Retinal disease, low vision, binocular vision, contact lenses, accommodation. *Unit head:* Dr. David Loshin, Dean, 954-262-1404, Fax: 954-262-1818. *Application contact:* Fran Franconeri, Admissions Counselor, 954-262-1132, Fax: 954-262-2282.

Salus University, Graduate Studies in Vision Impairment and Audiology, Elkins Park, PA 19027-1598. Offers education of children and youth with visual and multiple impairments (M Ed, Certificate); low vision rehabilitation (MS, Certificate); orientation and mobility therapy (MS, Certificate); vision rehabilitation therapy (MS, Certificate); OD/MS. Part-time programs available. Postbaccalaureate distance learning degree programs offered. *Faculty:* 8 full-time (7 women), 1 (woman) part-time/adjunct. *Students:* 4 full-time (all women), 64 part-time (58 women); includes 7 minority (5 African Americans, 1 American Indian/Alaska Native, 1 Hispanic American). Average age 37. In 2009, 14 master's, 12 other advanced degrees awarded. *Entrance requirements:* For master's, GRE or MAT, letters of reference (3), interviews (2). Additional exam requirements/recommendations for international students: Required—TOEFL, TWE. *Application deadline:* For fall admission, 6/1 for domestic students. Applications are processed on a rolling basis. *Expenses:* Contact institution. *Financial support:* Federal Work-Study and scholarships/grants available. Financial award applicants required to submit FAFSA. *Faculty research:* Knowledge utilization, technology transfer. *Unit head:* Dr. Audrey Smith, Associate Dean, 215-780-1361, Fax: 215-780-1357, E-mail: ASmith@Salus.edu. *Application contact:* Dr. Audrey Smith, Associate Dean, 215-780-1361, Fax: 215-780-1357, E-mail: ASmith@Salus.edu.

State University of New York College of Optometry, Graduate Programs, New York, NY 10036. Offers MS, PhD, OD/MS, OD/PhD. Part-time programs available. *Faculty:* 28 full-time (3 women), 1 (woman) part-time/adjunct. *Students:* 11 full-time (5 women), 14 part-time (9 women). 11 applicants, 36% accepted, 3 enrolled. In 2009, 4 master's, 1 doctorate awarded. Terminal master's awarded for partial completion of doctoral program. *Degree requirements:* For master's, thesis; for doctorate, comprehensive exam, thesis/dissertation, specialty exam. *Entrance requirements:* For master's and doctorate, GRE General Test. Additional exam requirements/recommendations for international students: Required—TOEFL. *Application deadline:* For fall admission, 3/1 priority date for domestic and international students. Applications are processed on a rolling basis. Application fee: $75. *Expenses:* Contact institution. *Financial support:* In 2009–10, 9 students received support, including 7 teaching assistantships with full tuition reimbursements available (averaging $18,000 per year); fellowships, research assistantships, Federal Work-Study, tuition waivers (full and partial), and unspecified assistantships also available. Financial award application deadline: 3/1. *Faculty research:* Oculomotor systems, perception, physiological optics, ocular biochemistry, accommodation, color and motion. *Unit head:* Dr. Jerry Feldman, Associate Dean, 212-938-5541, Fax: 212-938-5537, E-mail: jfeldman@sunyopt.edu. *Application contact:* Debra Berger, Assistant to Associate Dean, 212-938-5544, Fax: 212-938-5537, E-mail: dberger@sunyopt.edu.

Université de Montréal, Faculty of Medicine, Program in Specialized Studies, Montréal, QC H3C 3J7, Canada. Offers anesthesia (DES); diagnostic radiology (DES); family medicine (DES); gastroenterology (DES); geriatry (DES); intensive care (DES); medical biochemistry (DES); medical genetics (DES); medicine (DES); microbiology and infectious diseases (DES); nuclear medicine (DES); obstetrics and gynecology (DES); ophthalmology (DES); pediatrics (DES); pneumology (DES); psychiatry (DES); radiology-oncology (DES); rheumatology (DES); surgery (DES). *Faculty:* 154 full-time (40 women), 333 part-time/adjunct (100 women). *Students:* 930 full-time (580 women), 7 part-time (all women). 74 applicants, 77% accepted, 29 enrolled. *Application deadline:* For fall admission, 2/1 priority date for domestic students; for winter admission, 11/1 priority date for domestic students; for spring admission, 2/1 priority date for domestic students. Application fee: $100. Electronic applications accepted. *Unit head:* Lorraine Locas, Assistant to the Vice Dean of Graduate Studies, 514-343-6269, Fax: 514-343-5751, E-mail: lorraine.locas@umontreal.ca. *Application contact:* Dr. Andre Ferron, Vice Dean Graduate Studies, 514-343-6111 Ext. 0933, Fax: 514-343-5751, E-mail: andre.ferron@umontreal.ca.

Université de Montréal, School of Optometry, Graduate Programs in Optometry, Montréal, QC H3C 3J7, Canada. Offers vision sciences (M Sc). Part-time programs available. *Students:* 11 full-time (9 women), 14 part-time (8 women). In 2009, 7 master's awarded. *Degree requirements:* For master's, thesis. *Entrance requirements:* For master's, OD or appropriate bachelor's degree, minimum GPA of 2.7. *Application deadline:* For fall admission, 2/1 priority date for domestic students; for winter admission, 11/1 priority date for domestic students; for spring admission, 2/1 priority date for domestic students. Application fee: $100. Electronic applications accepted. *Financial support:* Research assistantships, teaching assistantships, career-related internships or fieldwork available. Support available to part-time students. *Faculty research:* Binocular vision, visual electrophysiology, eye movements, corneal metabolism, glare sensitivity. *Application contact:* Christian Casanova, Chairperson, 514-343-2407, Fax: 514-343-2382, E-mail: christian.casanova@umontreal.ca.

The University of Alabama at Birmingham, School of Optometry, Graduate Program in Vision Science, Birmingham, AL 35294. Offers MS, PhD. Terminal master's awarded for partial completion of doctoral program. *Degree requirements:* For master's, thesis; for doctorate, thesis/dissertation. *Entrance requirements:* For master's and doctorate, GRE General Test, OAT, interview. Electronic applications accepted.

The University of Alabama in Huntsville, School of Graduate Studies, College of Engineering, Department of Electrical and Computer Engineering, Huntsville, AL 35899. Offers computer engineering (MSE, PhD); electrical engineering (MSE, PhD); optical science and engineering (PhD); optics and photonics (MSE); software engineering (MSSE). Part-time and evening/weekend programs available. *Faculty:* 22 full-time (2 women), 3 part-time/adjunct (0 women). *Students:* 42 full-time (10 women), 147 part-time (18 women); includes 16 minority (7 African Americans, 6 Asian Americans or Pacific Islanders, 3 Hispanic Americans), 28 international. Average age 31. 205 applicants, 53% accepted, 58 enrolled. In 2009, 53 master's, 4 doctorates awarded. *Degree requirements:* For master's, comprehensive exam, thesis or alternative, oral and written exams; for doctorate, comprehensive exam, thesis/dissertation, oral and written exams. *Entrance requirements:* For master's, GRE General Test, appropriate bachelor's degree, minimum GPA of 3.0; for doctorate, GRE General Test, minimum GPA of 3.0. Additional exam requirements/recommendations for international students: Required—TOEFL (minimum score 500 paper-based; 173 computer-based; 62 iBT). *Application deadline:* For fall admission, 7/15 for domestic students, 4/1 for international students; for spring admission, 11/30 for domestic students, 9/1 for international students. Applications are processed on a rolling basis. Application fee: $40 ($50 for international students). Electronic applications accepted. *Expenses:* Tuition, state resident: part-time $355.75 per credit hour. Tuition, nonresident: part-time $847.10 per credit hour. Required fees: $210.80 per semester. Tuition and fees vary according to course load and program. *Financial support:* In 2009–10, 28 students received support, including 11 research assistantships with full and partial tuition reimbursements available (averaging $11,113 per year), 16 teaching assistantships with full and partial tuition reimbursements available (averaging $10,479 per year); career-related internships or fieldwork, Federal Work-Study, institutionally sponsored loans, scholarships/grants, health care benefits, tuition waivers, and unspecified assistantships also available. Support available to part-time students. Financial award application deadline: 4/1; financial award applicants required to submit FAFSA. *Faculty research:* Optical signal processing, electromagnetics, photonics, nonlinear waves, computer architecture. Total annual research expenditures: $3.4 million. *Unit head:* Dr. Reza Adhami, Chair, 256-824-6316, Fax: 256-824-6803, E-mail: adhami@ece.uah.edu. *Application contact:* Kathy Biggs, Graduate Studies Admissions Manager, 256-824-6199, Fax: 256-824-6405, E-mail: deangrad@uah.edu.

University of Alberta, Faculty of Medicine and Dentistry and Faculty of Graduate Studies and Research, Graduate Programs in Medicine, Department of Ophthalmology, Edmonton, AB T6G 2E1, Canada. Offers M Sc, PhD. Part-time programs available. *Faculty:* 1 full-time (0 women), 1 part-time/adjunct (0 women). *Students:* 2 full-time (1 woman). Average age 25. In 2009, 1 master's awarded. Terminal master's awarded for partial completion of doctoral program. *Degree requirements:* For master's, thesis; for doctorate, comprehensive exam, thesis/dissertation. *Application deadline:* For fall admission, 4/1 priority date for domestic students. Applications are processed on a rolling basis. Application fee: $60. Tuition and fees charges are reported in Canadian dollars. *Expenses:* Tuition, area resident: Full-time $4626 Canadian dollars; part-time $99.72 Canadian dollars per unit. International tuition: $8216 Canadian dollars full-time. Required fees: $3590 Canadian dollars; $99.72 Canadian dollars per unit. $215 Canadian dollars per term. *Financial support:* In 2009–10, 1 student received support; research assistantships available. *Faculty research:* Ocular genetics. Total annual research expenditures: $240,500. *Unit head:* Dr. G. T. Drummond, Acting Chair, 780-477-4924, Fax: 780-477-4969. *Application contact:* Dr. G. T. Drummond, Acting Chair, 780-477-4924, Fax: 780-477-4969.

University of California, Berkeley, Graduate Division, Group in Vision Science, Berkeley, CA 94720-1500. Offers MS, PhD. *Students:* 35 full-time (15 women). Average age 34. 39 applicants, 7 enrolled. In 2009, 1 master's, 5 doctorates awarded. *Degree requirements:* For master's, thesis; for doctorate, thesis/dissertation. *Entrance requirements:* For master's and doctorate, GRE General Test, GRE Subject Test, minimum GPA of 3.0, 3 letters of recommendation. *Application deadline:* For fall admission, 1/5 for domestic students. Application fee: $70 ($90 for international students). *Financial support:* Fellowships, research assistantships, teaching assistantships, Federal Work-Study, institutionally sponsored loans, scholarships/grants, tuition waivers (partial), and unspecified assistantships available. Financial award applicants required to submit FAFSA. *Faculty research:* Visual neuroscience, bioengineering, computational vision, molecular cell biology, basic and clinical psychophysics. *Unit head:* Prof. Austin Roorda, Chair, 510-643-8670, E-mail: aroorda@berkeley.edu. *Application contact:* Inez Bailey, Graduate Student Affairs, 510-642-9804, Fax: 510-643-5109, E-mail: vision@berkeley.edu.

University of Chicago, Division of the Biological Sciences, Department of Ophthalmology and Visual Science, Chicago, IL 60637-1513. Offers PhD. *Faculty:* 12 full-time (5 women). *Degree requirements:* For doctorate, thesis/dissertation, ethics class, 2 teaching assistantships. *Entrance requirements:* For doctorate, GRE General Test. Additional exam requirements/recommendations for international students: Required—TOEFL (minimum score 600 paper-based; 250 computer-based; 104 iBT), IELTS (minimum score 7). *Application deadline:* For fall admission, 12/1 priority date for domestic and international students. Application fee: $55. *Financial support:* In 2009–10, fellowships with tuition reimbursements (averaging $29,053 per year), research assistantships with tuition reimbursements (averaging $29,053 per year) were awarded; institutionally sponsored loans, scholarships/grants, traineeships, and health care

Vision Sciences

University of Chicago *(continued)*
benefits also available. Financial award applicants required to submit FAFSA. *Faculty research:* Visual psychophysics, visual molecular biology, immunology, transplantation, infections. Total annual research expenditures: $1.2 million. *Unit head:* Dr. Mark Greenwald, Chairman, 773-702-3838, Fax: 773-702-8094, E-mail: wmieler@bsd.chicago.edu. *Application contact:* Sandra Wallace, Residency Program Coordinator, 773-795-7286, E-mail: swallace@bsd.uchicago.edu.

University of Guelph, Ontario Veterinary College and Graduate Program Services, Graduate Programs in Veterinary Sciences, Department of Clinical Studies, Guelph, ON N1G 2W1, Canada. Offers anesthesiology (M Sc, DV Sc); cardiology (DV Sc, Diploma); clinical studies (Diploma); dermatology (M Sc); diagnostic imaging (M Sc, DV Sc); emergency/critical care (M Sc, DV Sc, Diploma); medicine (M Sc, DV Sc); neurology (M Sc, DV Sc); ophthalmology (M Sc, DV Sc); surgery (M Sc, DV Sc). *Degree requirements:* For master's, thesis; for doctorate, comprehensive exam, thesis/dissertation. *Entrance requirements:* Additional exam requirements/recommendations for international students: Required—TOEFL (minimum score 550 paper-based; 213 computer-based), IELTS (minimum score 6.5). Electronic applications accepted. *Faculty research:* Orthopedics, respirology, oncology, exercise physiology, cardiology.

University of Houston, College of Optometry, Program in Physiological Optics/Vision Science, Houston, TX 77204. Offers MS Phys Op, PhD. Application fee: $0. *Expenses:* Tuition, state resident: full-time $7676; part-time $320 per credit hour. Tuition, nonresident: full-time $14,324; part-time $597 per credit hour. Required fees: $3034. *Financial support:* Fellowships, research assistantships, teaching assistantships, career-related internships or fieldwork, Federal Work-Study, institutionally sponsored loans, scholarships/grants, health care benefits, and unspecified assistantships available. Support available to part-time students. *Faculty research:* Space perception, amblyopia, binocular vision, development of visual skills, strabismus, visual cell biology, refractive error.

University of Missouri–St. Louis, College of Optometry and Graduate School, Program in Vision Science, St. Louis, MO 63121. Offers MS, PhD. *Faculty:* 11 full-time (1 woman). *Students:* 2 full-time (1 woman), 1 (woman) part-time; includes 2 minority (1 African American, 1 Asian American or Pacific Islander). Average age 29. 9 applicants, 11% accepted, 1 enrolled. *Degree requirements:* For master's, thesis; for doctorate, comprehensive exam, thesis/dissertation. *Entrance requirements:* Additional exam requirements/recommendations for international students: Required—TOEFL (minimum score 570 paper-based). *Application deadline:* For fall admission, 3/15 for domestic and international students. Applications are processed on a rolling basis. Application fee: $25 ($40 for international students). Electronic applications accepted. *Expenses:* Contact institution. *Financial support:* In 2009–10, 1 research assistantship with full tuition reimbursement (averaging $23,000 per year), 3 teaching assistantships with full tuition reimbursements (averaging $23,000 per year) were awarded; fellowships with full tuition reimbursements, Federal Work-Study, institutionally sponsored loans, and unspecified assistantships also available. Financial award application deadline: 3/15; financial award applicants required to submit FAFSA. *Faculty research:* Theoretical and applied optics, theoretical and applied psychophysics, eye movements, binocular vision, contact lenses. *Unit head:* Dr. Carl J. Bassi, Director, Research and Graduate Studies, 314-516-6029, Fax: 314-516-5150, E-mail: bassi@umsl.edu. *Application contact:* Dr. Edward S. Bennett, Director, Student Services, 314-516-6263, Fax: 314-516-6708, E-mail: optstuaff@umsl.edu.

University of Waterloo, Graduate Studies, Faculty of Science, School of Optometry, Waterloo, ON N2L 3G1, Canada. Offers vision science (M Sc, PhD). *Accreditation:* AOA. Part-time programs available. *Degree requirements:* For master's, thesis; for doctorate, thesis/dissertation. *Entrance requirements:* For master's, honors degree, minimum B average; for doctorate, master's degree, minimum B average. Additional exam requirements/recommendations for international students: Required—TOEFL (minimum score 580 paper-based; 237 computer-based), TWE (minimum score 4). Electronic applications accepted. *Faculty research:* Vision science, fundamental and clinical vision, physiological optics, psycho-physics, perception.

Section 39
Pharmacy and Pharmaceutical Sciences

This section contains a directory of institutions offering graduate work in pharmacy and pharmaceutical sciences, followed by in-depth entries submitted by institutions that chose to prepare detailed program descriptions. Additional information about programs listed in the directory but not augmented by an in-depth entry may be obtained by writing directly to the dean of a graduate school or chair of a department at the address given in the directory.

For programs offering related work, see also in this book *Allied Health*. In the other guides in this series:

Graduate Programs in the Biological Sciences

See *Biochemistry, Biological and Biomedical Sciences, Nutrition, Pharmacology and Toxicology,* and *Physiology*

Graduate Programs in the Physical Sciences, Mathematics, Agricultural Sciences, the Environment & Natural Resources

See *Chemistry*

Graduate Programs in Engineering & Applied Sciences

See *Biomedical Engineering and Biotechnology,* and *Chemical Engineering*

CONTENTS

Medicinal and Pharmaceutical Chemistry

Duquesne University, Mylan School of Pharmacy/Graduate School of Pharmaceutical Sciences, Graduate School of Pharmaceutical Sciences, Program in Medicinal Chemistry, Pittsburgh, PA 15282-0001. Offers MS, PhD. *Faculty:* 4 full-time (0 women). *Students:* 18 full-time (7 women), 1 part-time (0 women), all international. 27 applicants, 26% accepted, 3 enrolled. In 2009, 2 master's, 3 doctorates awarded. *Degree requirements:* For master's, thesis; for doctorate, comprehensive exam, thesis/dissertation. *Entrance requirements:* For master's and doctorate, GRE General Test. Additional exam requirements/recommendations for international students: Required—TOEFL. *Application deadline:* For fall admission, 2/1 priority date for domestic and international students; for spring admission, 10/1 priority date for domestic and international students. Applications are processed on a rolling basis. Application fee: $50. Electronic applications accepted. *Expenses:* Tuition: Part-time $851 per credit. Required fees: $81 per credit. *Financial support:* In 2009–10, 19 students received support, including 6 research assistantships with full tuition reimbursements available, 12 teaching assistantships with full tuition reimbursements available. *Unit head:* Dr. Aleem Gangjee, Head, 412-396-6070. *Application contact:* Information Contact, 412-396-1172, E-mail: gsps-adm@duq.edu.

See Close-Up on page 1791.

Florida Agricultural and Mechanical University, Division of Graduate Studies, Research, and Continuing Education, College of Pharmacy and Pharmaceutical Sciences, Graduate Programs in Pharmaceutical Sciences, Tallahassee, FL 32307-3200. Offers environmental toxicology (PhD); medicinal chemistry (MS, PhD); pharmaceutics (MS, PhD); pharmacology/toxicology (MS, PhD); pharmacy administration (MS). *Accreditation:* CEPH. *Faculty:* 21 full-time (6 women). *Students:* 438 full-time (296 women), 21 part-time (13 women); includes 417 minority (380 African Americans, 1 American Indian/Alaska Native, 30 Asian Americans or Pacific Islanders, 6 Hispanic Americans), 5 international. In 2009, 4 master's, 7 doctorates awarded. *Degree requirements:* For master's, comprehensive exam, thesis, publishable paper; for doctorate, comprehensive exam, thesis/dissertation, publishable paper. *Entrance requirements:* For master's and doctorate, GRE General Test, minimum GPA of 3.0 in last 60 hours. Additional exam requirements/recommendations for international students: Required—TOEFL. *Application deadline:* For fall admission, 4/1 for domestic students. Application fee: $20. *Financial support:* Fellowships, research assistantships, Federal Work-Study and scholarships/grants available. *Faculty research:* Anticancer agents, anti-inflammatory drugs, chronopharmacology, neuroendocrinology, microbiology. *Unit head:* Dr. Thomas J. Fitzgerald, Chairman, Graduate Committee, 850-599-3301. *Application contact:* Gloria James, Graduate Coordinator, 850-599-3144.

Idaho State University, Office of Graduate Studies, College of Pharmacy, Department of Biomedical and Pharmaceutical Sciences, Pocatello, ID 83209-8334. Offers biopharmaceutical analysis (PhD); drug delivery (PhD); medicinal chemistry (PhD); pharmaceutical sciences (MS); pharmacology (PhD). Part-time programs available. *Faculty:* 9 full-time (1 woman). *Students:* 13 full-time (5 women), 7 part-time (3 women); includes 2 minority (both Asian Americans or Pacific Islanders), 14 international. Average age 29. In 2009, 7 master's, 2 doctorates awarded. *Degree requirements:* For master's, one foreign language, comprehensive exam, thesis, thesis research, classes in speech and technical writing; for doctorate, comprehensive exam, thesis/dissertation, written and oral exams, classes in speech and technical writing. *Entrance requirements:* For master's, GRE General Test, minimum GPA of 3.0, 3 letters of recommendation; for doctorate, GRE General Test, BS in pharmacy or related field, minimum GPA of 3.0, 3 letters of recommendation. Additional exam requirements/recommendations for international students: Required—TOEFL (minimum score 550 paper-based; 213 computer-based; 80 iBT). *Application deadline:* For fall admission, 7/1 for domestic students, 6/1 for international students; for spring admission, 12/1 for domestic students, 11/1 for international students. Applications are processed on a rolling basis. Application fee: $55. Electronic applications accepted. *Expenses:* Contact institution. *Financial support:* Research assistantships with full and partial tuition reimbursements, teaching assistantships with full and partial tuition reimbursements, career-related internships or fieldwork, Federal Work-Study, institutionally sponsored loans, scholarships/grants, traineeships, health care benefits, tuition waivers (full and partial), and unspecified assistantships available. Support available to part-time students. Financial award application deadline: 1/1; financial award applicants required to submit FAFSA. *Faculty research:* Metabolic toxicity of heavy metals, neuroendocrine pharmacology, cardiovascular pharmacology, cancer biology, immunopharmacology. *Unit head:* Dr. Timothy Hunt, Chair, 208-282-2682, Fax: 208-282-4305, E-mail: thunt@pharmacy.isu.edu. *Application contact:* Tami Carson, Graduate School Technical Records Specialist, 208-282-2150, Fax: 208-282-4847, E-mail: carstami@isu.edu.

Long Island University, C.W. Post Campus, School of Health Professions and Nursing, Department of Biomedical Sciences, Brookville, NY 11548-1300. Offers cardiovascular perfusion (MS); clinical laboratory management (MS); medical biology (MS), including hematology, immunology, medical biology, medical chemistry, medical microbiology. Part-time and evening/weekend programs available. Postbaccalaureate distance learning degree programs offered. *Degree requirements:* For master's, thesis. *Entrance requirements:* For master's, minimum GPA of 2.75 in major. Electronic applications accepted.

Medical University of South Carolina, College of Graduate Studies, Department of Pharmaceutical and Biomedical Sciences, Charleston, SC 29425. Offers cell injury and repair (PhD); drug discovery (PhD); medicinal chemistry (PhD); toxicology (PhD); DMD/PhD; MD/PhD; Pharm D/PhD. *Faculty:* 8 full-time (1 woman), 1 part-time/adjunct (0 women). *Students:* 7 full-time (3 women); includes 1 minority (African American), 1 international. Average age 30. In 2009, 2 doctorates awarded. *Degree requirements:* For doctorate, thesis/dissertation, oral and written exams, teaching and research seminar. *Entrance requirements:* For doctorate, GRE General Test, interview, minimum GPA of 3.0. Additional exam requirements/recommendations for international students: Required—TOEFL (minimum score 600 paper-based; 250 computer-based; 100 iBT). *Application deadline:* For fall admission, 1/15 priority date for domestic and international students. Applications are processed on a rolling basis. Application fee: $0 ($85 for international students). Electronic applications accepted. *Financial support:* In 2009–10, 7 students received support, including 7 research assistantships with partial tuition reimbursements available (averaging $23,000 per year); Federal Work-Study and scholarships/grants also available. Support available to part-time students. Financial award application deadline: 3/10; financial award applicants required to submit FAFSA. *Faculty research:* Drug discovery, toxicology, metabolomics, cell stress and injury. *Unit head:* Dr. Rick Schnellmann, Eminent Scholar, Professor and Chair, 843-792-3754, Fax: 843-792-6590, E-mail: schnell@musc.edu. *Application contact:* Dr. Craig C. Beeson, Associate Professor, 843-876-5091, Fax: 843-792-6590, E-mail: beesonc@musc.edu.

The Ohio State University, College of Pharmacy and Graduate School, Graduate Programs in Pharmacy, Division of Medicinal Chemistry and Pharmacognosy, Columbus, OH 43210. Offers MS, PhD. *Degree requirements:* For master's, thesis; for doctorate, thesis/dissertation. *Entrance requirements:* For master's and doctorate, GRE General Test, minimum GPA of 3.0. Additional exam requirements/recommendations for international students: Required—TOEFL (minimum score 620 paper-based; 250 computer-based; 100 iBT). Electronic applications accepted. *Expenses:* Tuition, state resident: full-time $10,683. Tuition, nonresident: full-time $25,923. Tuition and fees vary according to course load and program. *Faculty research:* Drug design, natural products, synthesis of enzyme inhibitors, drug metabolism and anticancer agents.

Purdue University, College of Pharmacy and Pharmacal Sciences and Graduate School, Graduate Programs in Pharmacy and Pharmacal Sciences, Department of Medicinal Chemistry and Molecular Pharmacology, West Lafayette, IN 47907. Offers analytical medicinal chemistry (PhD); computational and biophysical medicinal chemistry (PhD); medicinal and bioorganic chemistry (PhD); medicinal biochemistry and molecular biology (PhD); molecular pharmacology and toxicology (PhD); natural products and pharmacognosy (PhD); nuclear pharmacy (MS); radiopharmaceutical chemistry and nuclear pharmacy (PhD); MS/PhD. Terminal master's awarded for partial completion of doctoral program. *Degree requirements:* For master's, thesis; for doctorate, thesis/dissertation. *Entrance requirements:* For master's, GRE General Test, minimum B average; BS in biology, chemistry, or pharmacy; for doctorate, GRE General Test, minimum B average; BS in biology, chemistry, or pharmacology. Additional exam requirements/recommendations for international students: Required—TOEFL. Electronic applications accepted. *Faculty research:* Drug design and development, cancer research, drug synthesis and analysis, chemical pharmacology, environmental toxicology.

Rutgers, The State University of New Jersey, New Brunswick, Ernest Mario School of Pharmacy, Program in Medicinal Chemistry, Piscataway, NJ 08854-8097. Offers MS, PhD. Part-time programs available. *Degree requirements:* For master's, comprehensive exam, thesis; for doctorate, comprehensive exam, thesis/dissertation. *Entrance requirements:* For master's and doctorate, GRE General Test. Additional exam requirements/recommendations for international students: Required—TOEFL (minimum score 600 paper-based; 250 computer-based; 90 iBT). Electronic applications accepted. *Faculty research:* Synthesis and design of anticancer drugs, synthesis of pro-drugs for prostate cancer, natural product synthesis, natural product isolation and structure elucidation, computational chemistry.

Temple University, Health Sciences Center, School of Pharmacy, Department of Pharmaceutical Sciences, Program in Medicinal Chemistry, Philadelphia, PA 19122-6096. Offers MS, PhD. *Degree requirements:* For master's, thesis; for doctorate, 2 foreign languages, thesis/dissertation. *Entrance requirements:* For master's and doctorate, GRE General Test, minimum undergraduate GPA of 3.0. Additional exam requirements/recommendations for international students: Required—TOEFL (minimum score 550 paper-based; 213 computer-based; 79 iBT). Electronic applications accepted.

University at Buffalo, the State University of New York, Graduate School, College of Arts and Sciences, Department of Chemistry, Buffalo, NY 14260. Offers chemistry (MA, PhD); medicinal chemistry (MS, PhD). Part-time programs available. *Faculty:* 34 full-time (5 women), 2 part-time/adjunct (1 woman). *Students:* 143 full-time (62 women), 4 part-time (1 woman); includes 21 minority (9 African Americans, 5 Asian Americans or Pacific Islanders, 7 Hispanic Americans), 43 international. Average age 26. 260 applicants, 30% accepted, 34 enrolled. In 2009, 10 master's, 20 doctorates awarded. Terminal master's awarded for partial completion of doctoral program. *Degree requirements:* For master's, thesis or alternative, project; for doctorate, thesis/dissertation, synopsis proposal. *Entrance requirements:* For master's and doctorate, GRE General Test, GRE Subject Test. Additional exam requirements/recommendations for international students: Required—TOEFL (minimum score 550 paper-based; 213 computer-based; 79 iBT). *Application deadline:* For fall admission, 3/1 priority date for domestic students, 3/1 for international students; for spring admission, 11/1 priority date for domestic students. Applications are processed on a rolling basis. Application fee: $50. Electronic applications accepted. *Financial support:* In 2009–10, 10 students received support, including 10 fellowships with full tuition reimbursements available (averaging $21,500 per year), 50 research assistantships with full tuition reimbursements available (averaging $21,500 per year), 75 teaching assistantships with full tuition reimbursements available (averaging $21,500 per year); Federal Work-Study, institutionally sponsored loans, and unspecified assistantships also available. Financial award application deadline: 6/15; financial award applicants required to submit FAFSA. *Faculty research:* Synthesis, measurements, structure theory, translation. Total annual research expenditures: $9.5 million. *Unit head:* Dr. Luis A. Colon, Chairman, 716-645-6824, Fax: 716-645-6963, E-mail: chechair@buffalo.edu. *Application contact:* Dr. Steven T. Diver, Director of Graduate Studies, 716-645-4208, Fax: 716-645-6963, E-mail: diver@buffalo.edu.

University of California, San Francisco, School of Pharmacy and Graduate Division, Chemistry and Chemical Biology Graduate Program, San Francisco, CA 94143. Offers PhD. *Faculty:* 45 full-time (9 women). *Students:* 48 full-time (23 women); includes 18 minority (2 African Americans, 9 Asian Americans or Pacific Islanders, 7 Hispanic Americans), 4 international. Average age 27. 111 applicants, 19% accepted, 9 enrolled. In 2009, 8 doctorates awarded. *Degree requirements:* For doctorate, thesis/dissertation. *Entrance requirements:* For doctorate, GRE General Test, GRE Subject Test, minimum GPA of 3.0. Additional exam requirements/recommendations for international students: Required—TOEFL (minimum score 550 paper-based; 213 computer-based; 80 iBT). *Application deadline:* For fall admission, 12/1 for domestic and international students. Applications are processed on a rolling basis. Application fee: $70 ($90 for international students). Electronic applications accepted. *Financial support:* In 2009–10, 48 students received support, including 41 fellowships with partial tuition reimbursements available (averaging $19,365 per year), 16 research assistantships with full tuition reimbursements available (averaging $27,000 per year), 2 teaching assistantships with partial tuition reimbursements available (averaging $16,000 per year); institutionally sponsored loans, scholarships/grants, traineeships, and tuition waivers (full) also available. Financial award application deadline: 5/15. *Faculty research:* Biochemistry, macromolecular structure, cellular and molecular pharmacology, physical chemistry and computational biology, synthetic chemistry. *Unit head:* Dr. Charles S. Craik, Director, 415-476-8146, E-mail: craik@cgl.ucsf.edu. *Application contact:* Christine Olson, Senior Administrative Analyst, 415-476-1914, Fax: 415-514-1546, E-mail: olson@cmp.ucsf.edu.

University of Connecticut, Graduate School, School of Pharmacy, Department of Pharmaceutical Sciences, Program in Medicinal Chemistry, Storrs, CT 06269. Offers MS, PhD. *Faculty:* 10 full-time (3 women). *Students:* 14 full-time (7 women); includes 2 minority (both Asian Americans or Pacific Islanders), 7 international. Average age 27. 25 applicants, 12% accepted, 1 enrolled. In 2009, 4 doctorates awarded. Terminal master's awarded for partial completion of doctoral program. *Degree requirements:* For master's, comprehensive exam, thesis; for doctorate, thesis/dissertation. *Entrance requirements:* Additional exam requirements/recommendations for international students: Required—TOEFL (minimum score 550 paper-based; 213 computer-based). *Application deadline:* For fall admission, 2/1 priority date for domestic and international students; for spring admission, 11/1 for domestic students, 10/1 for international students. Applications are processed on a rolling basis. Application fee: $55. Electronic applications accepted. *Expenses:* Tuition, state resident: full-time $4725; part-time $525 per credit. Tuition, nonresident: full-time $12,267; part-time $1363 per credit. Required fees: $346 per semester. Tuition and fees vary according to course load. *Financial support:* In 2009–10, 10 research assistantships with full tuition reimbursements, 4 teaching assistantships with full tuition reimbursements were awarded; fellowships, Federal Work-Study, scholarships/grants, traineeships, health care benefits, and unspecified assistantships also available. Financial award application deadline: 2/1; financial award applicants required to submit FAFSA. *Unit head:* Robin Bogner, Chairperson, 860-486-2136, Fax: 860-486-4998, E-mail: robin.bogner@uconn.edu. *Application contact:* Leslie Lebel, Administrative Assistant, 860-486-4066, Fax: 860-486-4998, E-mail: leslie.lebel@uconn.edu.

University of Florida, College of Pharmacy and Graduate School, Graduate Programs in Pharmacy, Department of Medicinal Chemistry, Gainesville, FL 32611. Offers medicinal chemistry (Pharm D); pharmaceutical sciences (MSP, PhD). *Degree requirements:* For doctorate, thesis/dissertation. *Entrance requirements:* For doctorate, GRE General Test, minimum GPA of 3.0. Additional exam requirements/recommendations for international students: Required—TOEFL. *Faculty research:* Iron chelation, anticancer drug development, drug metabolism and toxicity, dermal delivery of drug and prodrugs.

The University of Kansas, Graduate Studies, School of Pharmacy, Department of Medicinal Chemistry, Lawrence, KS 66045. Offers MS, PhD. *Students:* 38 full-time (14 women), 1 part-time (0 women); includes 1 minority (Asian American or Pacific Islander), 14 international. Average age 26. 92 applicants, 10% accepted, 6 enrolled. In 2009, 11 master's, 2 doctorates awarded. Terminal master's awarded for partial completion of doctoral program. *Degree requirements:* For master's, comprehensive exam, thesis (for some programs); for doctorate,

comprehensive exam, thesis/dissertation, cumulative exams. *Entrance requirements:* For master's and doctorate, GRE General Test. Additional exam requirements/recommendations for international students: Required—TOEFL. *Application deadline:* For fall admission, 3/1 priority date for domestic and international students. Applications are processed on a rolling basis. Application fee: $45 ($55 for international students). Electronic applications accepted. *Expenses:* Tuition, state resident: full-time $6492; part-time $270.50 per credit hour. Tuition, nonresident: full-time $15,510; part-time $646.25 per credit hour. Required fees: $847; $70.56 per credit hour. Tuition and fees vary according to course load and program. *Financial support:* Fellowships with full tuition reimbursements, research assistantships with full tuition reimbursements, teaching assistantships with full tuition reimbursements, health care benefits and unspecified assistantships available. Financial award application deadline: 3/1. *Faculty research:* Drug design and synthesis, natural products chemistry, drug metabolism and toxicity, enzyme mechanism and inhibition, antiinfective and chemotherapeutic agents. *Unit head:* Prof. Barbara Timmermann, University Distinguished Professor and Chair, 785-864-4495, Fax: 785-864-5326, E-mail: btimmer@ku.edu. *Application contact:* Prof. Apurba Dutta, Director of Graduate Studies, 785-864-4495, Fax: 785-864-5326, E-mail: medchem@ku.edu.

The University of Kansas, Graduate Studies, School of Pharmacy, Department of Pharmaceutical Chemistry, Lawrence, KS 66047. Offers MS, PhD. Part-time and evening/weekend programs available. Postbaccalaureate distance learning degree programs offered (no on-campus study). *Faculty:* 15 full-time (2 women). *Students:* 46 full-time (18 women), 20 part-time (18 women); includes 6 minority (1 American Indian/Alaska Native, 3 Asian Americans or Pacific Islanders, 2 Hispanic Americans), 25 international. Average age 29. 68 applicants, 16% accepted, 8 enrolled. In 2009, 3 master's, 7 doctorates awarded. Terminal master's awarded for partial completion of doctoral program. *Degree requirements:* For master's, thesis, qualifying exam; for doctorate, comprehensive exam, thesis/dissertation, qualifying exam. *Entrance requirements:* For master's, GRE General Test, bachelor's degree in biological sciences, chemical engineering, chemistry, or pharmacy; for doctorate, GRE General Test. Additional exam requirements/recommendations for international students: Required—TOEFL. *Application deadline:* For fall admission, 1/15 priority date for domestic and international students. Applications are processed on a rolling basis. Application fee: $45 ($55 for international students). Electronic applications accepted. *Expenses:* Tuition, state resident: full-time $6492; part-time $270.50 per credit hour. Tuition, nonresident: full-time $15,510; part-time $646.25 per credit hour. Required fees: $847; $70.56 per credit hour. Tuition and fees vary according to course load and program. *Financial support:* Fellowships with full tuition reimbursements, research assistantships with full and partial tuition reimbursements, career-related internships or fieldwork, scholarships/grants, traineeships, and unspecified assistantships available. Financial award application deadline: 1/20. *Faculty research:* Drug delivery, drug analysis, biotechnology, nanomaterials, protein structure. *Unit head:* Dr. Christian Schoneich, Chair, 785-864-4880, Fax: 785-864-5736, E-mail: schoneic@ku.edu. *Application contact:* Jeffrey Krise, Graduate Director, 785-864-2626, Fax: 785-864-5736, E-mail: krise@ku.edu.

University of Michigan, College of Pharmacy and University of Michigan, Department of Medicinal Chemistry, Ann Arbor, MI 48109. Offers PhD. *Degree requirements:* For doctorate, oral defense of dissertation, preliminary exam. *Entrance requirements:* For doctorate, GRE. Additional exam requirements/recommendations for international students: Required—TOEFL or IELTS. *Expenses:* Contact institution.

University of Minnesota, Twin Cities Campus, College of Pharmacy and Graduate School, Graduate Programs in Pharmacy, Graduate Program in Medicinal Chemistry, Minneapolis, MN 55455-0213. Offers MS, PhD. Terminal master's awarded for partial completion of doctoral program. *Degree requirements:* For master's, thesis; for doctorate, thesis/dissertation. *Entrance requirements:* For master's and doctorate, GRE General Test, BS in biology, chemistry, or pharmacy. Additional exam requirements/recommendations for international students: Required—TOEFL. *Faculty research:* Drug design and synthesis, molecular modeling, chemical aspects of drug metabolism and toxicity.

University of Mississippi, Graduate School, School of Pharmacy, Graduate Programs in Pharmacy, Oxford, University, MS 38677. Offers medicinal chemistry (PhD); pharmaceutical sciences (MS); pharmaceutics (PhD); pharmacognosy (PhD); pharmacology (PhD); pharmacy administration (PhD). *Faculty:* 32 full-time (9 women), 8 part-time/adjunct (5 women). *Students:* 84 full-time (37 women), 8 part-time (6 women); includes 6 minority (3 African Americans, 2 Asian Americans or Pacific Islanders, 1 Hispanic American), 64 international. In 2009, 2 master's, 12 doctorates awarded. *Unit head:* Dr. Barbara G. Wells, Dean, 662-915-7265, Fax: 662-915-5704, E-mail: pharmacy@olemiss.edu. *Application contact:* Dr. Christy M. Wyandt, Associate Dean, 662-915-7474, Fax: 662-915-7577, E-mail: cwyandt@olemiss.edu.

University of Rhode Island, Graduate School, College of Pharmacy, Department of Biomedical and Pharmaceutical Sciences, Kingston, RI 02881. Offers medicinal chemistry and pharmacognosy (MS, PhD); pharmaceutics and pharmacokinetics (MS, PhD); pharmacology and toxicology (MS, PhD). Part-time programs available. *Faculty:* 17 full-time (5 women), 1 part-time/adjunct (0 women). *Students:* 33 full-time (16 women), 20 part-time (7 women); includes 12 minority (2 African Americans, 10 Asian Americans or Pacific Islanders), 19 international. In 2009, 6 master's, 6 doctorates awarded. *Entrance requirements:* For master's and doctorate, GRE, 2 letters of recommendation. Additional exam requirements/recommendations for international students: Required—TOEFL (minimum score 550 paper-based; 213 computer-based). Application fee: $65. Electronic applications accepted. *Expenses:* Tuition, state resident: full-time $8828; part-time $490 per credit hour. Tuition, nonresident: full-time $22,100; part-time $1228 per credit hour. Required fees: $1118; $57 per semester. Tuition and fees vary according to program. *Financial support:* In 2009–10, 6 research assistantships with partial tuition reimbursements (averaging $7,119 per year), 12 teaching assistantships with full and partial tuition reimbursements (averaging $10,115 per year) were awarded. Financial award applicants required to submit FAFSA. *Faculty research:* Chemical carcinogenesis with a major emphasis on the structural and synthetic aspects of DNA-adduct formation, drug-drug/herb interaction, drug-genetic interaction, signaling of nuclear receptors, transcriptional regulation, oncogenesis. Total annual research expenditures: $6.2 million. *Unit head:* Dr. Clinton O. Chichester, Chair, 401-874-5034, Fax: 401-874-5787, E-mail: chichester@uri.edu. *Application contact:* Dr. David C. Rowley, Graduate Coordinator, 401-874-9228, Fax: 401-874-2516, E-mail: drowley@uri.edu.

University of the Sciences in Philadelphia, College of Graduate Studies, Program in Chemistry, Biochemistry and Pharmacognosy, Philadelphia, PA 19104-4495. Offers biochemistry (MS, PhD); chemistry (MS, PhD); pharmacognosy (MS, PhD). Part-time programs available. *Degree requirements:* For master's, thesis, qualifying exams; for doctorate, comprehensive exam, thesis/dissertation, qualifying exams. *Entrance requirements:* For master's and doctorate, GRE General Test, GRE Subject Test. Additional exam requirements/recommendations for international students: Required—TOEFL, TWE. *Expenses:* Contact institution. *Faculty research:* Organic and medicinal synthesis, mass spectroscopy use in protein analysis, study of analogues of taxol, cholesteryl esters.

The University of Toledo, College of Graduate Studies, College of Pharmacy, Program in Medicinal and Biological Chemistry, Toledo, OH 43606-3390. Offers MS, PhD. Terminal master's awarded for partial completion of doctoral program. *Degree requirements:* For master's, thesis; for doctorate, thesis/dissertation. *Entrance requirements:* For master's and doctorate, GRE General Test. Additional exam requirements/recommendations for international students: Required—TOEFL (minimum score 550 paper-based; 213 computer-based; 80 iBT). Electronic applications accepted. *Faculty research:* Neuroscience, molecular modeling, immunotoxicology, organic synthesis, peptide biochemistry.

University of Utah, Graduate School, College of Pharmacy, Department of Medicinal Chemistry, Salt Lake City, UT 84112-5820. Offers MS, PhD. *Faculty:* 8 full-time (1 woman). *Students:* 9 full-time (0 women), 4 part-time (2 women), 4 international. Average age 30. 42 applicants, 5% accepted, 0 enrolled. In 2009, 2 master's awarded. *Degree requirements:* For doctorate, thesis/dissertation. *Entrance requirements:* For doctorate, GRE, minimum GPA of 3.0. Additional exam requirements/recommendations for international students: Required—TOEFL. *Application deadline:* For fall admission, 1/15 priority date for domestic and international students. Application fee: $55 ($65 for international students). Electronic applications accepted. *Expenses:* Tuition, state resident: full-time $4004; part-time $1674 per semester. Tuition, nonresident: full-time $14,134; part-time $5915 per semester. Required fees: $324 per semester. Tuition and fees vary according to course load, degree level and program. *Financial support:* In 2009–10, 11 students received support, including 1 fellowship with full tuition reimbursement available (averaging $15,000 per year), 10 research assistantships with full tuition reimbursements available (averaging $25,000 per year); teaching assistantships. *Faculty research:* Anticancer and anti-infective drug discovery, assays for high-throughput screening, neuroactive peptides, bioinorganic chemistry, structure-based drug design and modeling. Total annual research expenditures: $4.4 million. *Unit head:* Dr. Darrell R. Davis, Chair, 801-581-7063, E-mail: darrell.davis@utah.edu. *Application contact:* Dr. Darrell R. Davis, Chair, 801-581-7063, E-mail: darrell.davis@utah.edu.

University of Utah, Graduate School, College of Pharmacy, Department of Pharmaceutics and Pharmaceutical Chemistry, Salt Lake City, UT 84112. Offers MS, PhD. *Faculty:* 9 full-time (1 woman), 3 part-time/adjunct (1 woman). *Students:* 26 full-time (17 women), 7 part-time (2 women); includes 2 minority (both Asian Americans or Pacific Islanders), 18 international. Average age 29. 80 applicants, 8% accepted, 6 enrolled. In 2009, 1 master's, 7 doctorates awarded. Terminal master's awarded for partial completion of doctoral program. *Degree requirements:* For master's, thesis; for doctorate, comprehensive exam, thesis/dissertation, peer reviewed scientific publications and oral presentations. *Entrance requirements:* For master's and doctorate, GRE. Additional exam requirements/recommendations for international students: Required—TOEFL (minimum score 550 paper-based; 100 computer-based). *Application deadline:* For fall admission, 12/1 priority date for domestic and international students. Applications are processed on a rolling basis. Application fee: $55 ($65 for international students). Electronic applications accepted. *Expenses:* Tuition, state resident: full-time $4004; part-time $1674 per semester. Tuition, nonresident: full-time $14,134; part-time $5915 per semester. Required fees: $324 per semester. Tuition and fees vary according to course load, degree level and program. *Financial support:* In 2009–10, 2 fellowships (averaging $600 per year), 22 research assistantships (averaging $23,000 per year), 1 teaching assistantship (averaging $15,000 per year) were awarded; scholarships/grants, health care benefits, tuition waivers (full), and unspecified assistantships also available. *Faculty research:* Drug delivery, biopharmaceutics, nano medicine, pharmacokinetics, polymeric biomaterials. Total annual research expenditures: $2.5 million. *Unit head:* Dr. David W. Grainger, Chairperson, 801-581-7831, Fax: 801-581-3674, E-mail: phceu@pharm.utah.edu. *Application contact:* Office of Admissions, 801-581-7281, Fax: 801-585-3034, E-mail: admissionweb_grad@saff.utah.edu.

University of Washington, School of Pharmacy, Department of Medicinal Chemistry, Seattle, WA 98195. Offers PhD, Pharm D/PhD. *Faculty:* 9 full-time (1 woman), 1 part-time/adjunct (0 women). *Students:* 26 full-time (15 women); includes 2 minority (1 Asian American or Pacific Islander, 1 Hispanic American), 1 international. 54 applicants, 7% accepted, 2 enrolled. In 2009, 3 doctorates awarded. *Degree requirements:* For doctorate, thesis/dissertation. *Entrance requirements:* For doctorate, GRE General Test, minimum GPA of 3.0, 3 letters of recommendation. Additional exam requirements/recommendations for international students: Required—TOEFL. *Application deadline:* For fall admission, 1/15 for domestic and international students. Application fee: $20 ($34 for international students). Electronic applications accepted. *Financial support:* Fellowships, research assistantships, Federal Work-Study and institutionally sponsored loans available. *Faculty research:* Chemical and molecular aspects of drug action, metabolism and drug toxicity, theoretical studies on protein folding, NMR of macromolecules and biomedical mass spectrometry. *Unit head:* Dr. Allan E. Rettie, Chairman, 206-685-0615, E-mail: rettie@u.washington.edu. *Application contact:* Meg Running, Graduate Program Assistant, 206-543-2224, E-mail: medchem@u.washington.edu.

Wayne State University, Eugene Applebaum College of Pharmacy and Health Sciences, Department of Pharmacy Practice, Detroit, MI 48202. Offers medicinal chemistry (MS, PhD); pharmaceutical sciences (MS, PhD); pharmaceutics (MS, PhD); pharmacology (MS, PhD); pharmacy (Pharm D). Terminal master's awarded for partial completion of doctoral program. *Degree requirements:* For master's, thesis; for doctorate, thesis/dissertation. *Entrance requirements:* For master's, GRE General Test, minimum GPA of 2.6; for doctorate, GRE General Test, minimum GPA of 3.0. Additional exam requirements/recommendations for international students: Required—TOEFL (minimum score 550 paper-based; 213 computer-based); Recommended—TWE (minimum score 6). Electronic applications accepted. *Faculty research:* Pharmacodynamics and pharmacokinetics of anti-infective agents; efficacy of drug treatments for traumatic head injury and stroke; cultural difference in Arab-Americans related to diabetes treatment and prevention; drug disposition and effect in pediatrics; evaluation of anticoagulation regimens.

West Virginia University, School of Pharmacy, Program in Pharmaceutical and Pharmacological Sciences, Morgantown, WV 26506. Offers administrative pharmacy (PhD); behavioral pharmacy (MS, PhD); biopharmaceutics/pharmacokinetics (MS, PhD); industrial pharmacy (MS); medicinal chemistry (MS, PhD); pharmaceutical chemistry (MS, PhD); pharmaceutics (MS, PhD); pharmacology and toxicology (MS); pharmacy (MS); pharmacy administration (MS). Part-time programs available. Terminal master's awarded for partial completion of doctoral program. *Degree requirements:* For master's, thesis; for doctorate, one foreign language, comprehensive exam, thesis/dissertation. *Entrance requirements:* For master's and doctorate, GRE General Test, minimum GPA of 2.75. Additional exam requirements/recommendations for international students: Required—TOEFL; Recommended—TWE. Electronic applications accepted. *Expenses:* Contact institution. *Faculty research:* Pharmaceutics, medicinal chemistry, biopharmaceutics/pharmacokinetics, health outcomes research.

Pharmaceutical Administration

Columbia University, Graduate School of Business, MBA Program, New York, NY 10027. Offers accounting (MBA); decision, risk, and operations (MBA); entrepreneurship (MBA); finance and economics (MBA); healthcare and pharmaceutical management (MBA); human resource management (MBA); international business (MBA); leadership and ethics (MBA); management (MBA); marketing (MBA); media (MBA); private equity (MBA); real estate (MBA); social enterprise (MBA); value investing (MBA); DDS/MBA; JD/MBA; MBA/MIA; MBA/MPH; MBA/MS; MD/MBA. *Faculty:* 149 full-time (23 women), 134 part-time/adjunct (16 women). *Students:* 1,293 full-time (435 women); includes 235 minority (65 African Americans, 4 American Indian/Alaska Native, 135 Asian Americans or Pacific Islanders, 31 Hispanic Americans), 417 international. Average age 28. 6,885 applicants, 15% accepted, 737 enrolled. In 2009, 696 master's awarded. *Entrance requirements:* For master's, GMAT, 2 letters of recommendation. Additional exam requirements/recommendations for international students: Required—TOEFL. *Application deadline:* For fall admission, 4/14 for domestic students, 3/3 for international students; for spring admission, 10/7 for domestic and international students. Applications are processed on a rolling basis. Application fee: $250. Electronic applications accepted. *Expenses:* Contact institution. *Financial support:* In 2009–10, 358 students received support, including 101 fellowships (averaging $23,250 per year); research assistantships, teaching assistantships, career-related internships or fieldwork, institutionally sponsored loans, and scholarships/grants also available. Financial award application deadline: 3/1; financial award applicants required to submit CSS PROFILE or FAFSA. *Faculty research:* Human decision making and behavioral research; real estate market and mortgage defaults; financial crisis and corporate governance; international business; security analysis and accounting. *Unit head:* Prof. Amir Ziv, Vice Dean of Students and the MBA Program, 212-854-3485, Fax: 212-932-0545, E-mail: az50@columbia.edu. *Application contact:* Mary J. Miller, Assistant Dean of Admissions, 212-854-1961, Fax: 212-662-6754, E-mail: apply@gsb.columbia.edu.

Duquesne University, Mylan School of Pharmacy/Graduate School of Pharmaceutical Sciences, Graduate School of Pharmaceutical Sciences, Program in Pharmaceutical Administration, Pittsburgh, PA 15282-0001. Offers pharmacy administration (MS). *Faculty:* 4 full-time (1 woman). *Students:* 2 full-time (1 woman), 3 part-time (all women), 4 international. 59 applicants, 3% accepted, 0 enrolled. *Degree requirements:* For master's, thesis optional. *Entrance requirements:* For master's, GRE General Test. Additional exam requirements/recommendations for international students: Required—TOEFL. *Application deadline:* For fall admission, 2/1 priority date for domestic and international students. Applications are processed on a rolling basis. Application fee: $50. Electronic applications accepted. *Expenses:* Tuition: Part-time $851 per credit. Required fees: $81 per credit. *Financial support:* In 2009–10, 2 students received support, including 2 teaching assistantships with full tuition reimbursements available. *Unit head:* Dr. David J. Tipton, Head, 412-396-5458. *Application contact:* Information Contact, 412-396-1172, E-mail: gsps-adm@duq.edu.

Emmanuel College, Graduate Programs, Program in Management, Boston, MA 02115. Offers biopharmaceutical leadership (MSM); management (MSM); management and leadership (Certificate); research administration (MSM, Certificate). Part-time and evening/weekend programs available. Postbaccalaureate distance learning degree programs offered. *Faculty:* 1 (woman) full-time, 18 part-time/adjunct (4 women). *Students:* 7 full-time (6 women), 139 part-time (102 women); includes 30 minority (17 African Americans, 4 Asian Americans or Pacific Islanders, 9 Hispanic Americans). Average age 36. 66 applicants, 76% accepted, 50 enrolled. In 2009, 24 master's, 3 other advanced degrees awarded. *Degree requirements:* For master's, thesis or alternative. *Entrance requirements:* For master's, interview, essay, resume, 2 letters of recommendation, bachelor's degree. Additional exam requirements/recommendations for international students: Required—TOEFL (minimum score 600 paper-based; 250 computer-based). *Application deadline:* For fall admission, 8/15 priority date for domestic students; for spring admission, 12/8 priority date for domestic students. Applications are processed on a rolling basis. Application fee: $50. Electronic applications accepted. *Expenses:* Tuition: Part-time $665 per credit. *Unit head:* Dr. Judith Marley, Dean, Graduate and Professional Programs, 617-735-9700, Fax: 617-507-0434, E-mail: gpp@emmanuel.edu. *Application contact:* Enrollment Counselor, 617-735-9700, Fax: 617-507-0434, E-mail: gpp@emmanuel.edu.

Fairleigh Dickinson University, Metropolitan Campus, Silberman College of Business, Program in Pharmaceutical Studies, Teaneck, NJ 07666-1914. Offers chemical studies (Certificate); pharmaceutical studies (MBA, Certificate). *Students:* 68 full-time (20 women), 8 part-time (3 women), 68 international. Average age 24. 194 applicants, 74% accepted, 31 enrolled. In 2009, 6 master's awarded. *Application deadline:* Applications are processed on a rolling basis. *Application contact:* Susan Brooman, University Director of Graduate Admissions, 201-692-2554, Fax: 201-692-2560, E-mail: globaleducation@fdu.edu.

Florida Agricultural and Mechanical University, Division of Graduate Studies, Research, and Continuing Education, College of Pharmacy and Pharmaceutical Sciences, Graduate Programs in Pharmaceutical Sciences, Tallahassee, FL 32307-3200. Offers environmental toxicology (PhD); medicinal chemistry (MS, PhD); pharmaceutics (MS, PhD); pharmacology/toxicology (MS, PhD); pharmacy administration (MS). *Accreditation:* CEPH. *Faculty:* 21 full-time (6 women). *Students:* 438 full-time (296 women), 21 part-time (13 women); includes 417 minority (380 African Americans, 1 American Indian/Alaska Native, 30 Asian Americans or Pacific Islanders, 6 Hispanic Americans), 5 international. In 2009, 4 master's, 7 doctorates awarded. *Degree requirements:* For master's, comprehensive exam, thesis, publishable paper; for doctorate, comprehensive exam, thesis/dissertation, publishable paper. *Entrance requirements:* For master's and doctorate, GRE General Test, minimum GPA of 3.0 in last 60 hours. Additional exam requirements/recommendations for international students: Required—TOEFL. *Application deadline:* For fall admission, 4/1 for domestic students. Application fee: $20. *Financial support:* Fellowships, research assistantships, Federal Work-Study and scholarships/grants available. *Faculty research:* Anticancer agents, anti-inflammatory drugs, chronopharmacology, neuroendocrinology, microbiology. *Unit head:* Dr. Thomas J. Fitzgerald, Chairman, Graduate Committee, 850-599-3301. *Application contact:* Gloria James, Graduate Coordinator, 850-599-3144.

Idaho State University, Office of Graduate Studies, College of Pharmacy, Department of Pharmacy Practice and Administrative Sciences, Pocatello, ID 83209-8333. Offers pharmacy (Pharm D); pharmacy administration (MS, PhD). *Accreditation:* ACPE (one or more programs are accredited). Part-time programs available. *Faculty:* 8 full-time (3 women). *Students:* 244 full-time (96 women), 17 part-time (5 women); includes 32 minority (6 African Americans, 4 American Indian/Alaska Native, 14 Asian Americans or Pacific Islanders, 8 Hispanic Americans), 3 international. Average age 29. In 2009, 67 first professional degrees, 1 master's awarded. *Degree requirements:* For master's, one foreign language, comprehensive exam, thesis, thesis research, speech and technical writing classes; for doctorate, comprehensive exam, thesis/dissertation, oral and written exams, speech and technical writing classes; for Pharm D, comprehensive exam, thesis/dissertation, written and oral exams. *Entrance requirements:* For Pharm D, GRE General Test, minimum GPA of 3.0, 2 years of pre-pharmacy, BS degree in pharmacy or related field, 3 letters of recommendation; for master's, GRE General Test, minimum GPA of 3.0, 3 letters of recommendation; for doctorate, GRE General Test, BS in pharmacy or related field, minimum GPA of 3.0, 3 letters of recommendation. Additional exam requirements/recommendations for international students: Required—TOEFL (minimum score 550 paper-based; 213 computer-based; 80 iBT). *Application deadline:* For fall admission, 7/1 for domestic students, 6/1 for international students; for spring admission, 12/1 for domestic students, 11/1 for international students. Applications are processed on a rolling basis. Application fee: $55. Electronic applications accepted. *Expenses:* Contact institution. *Financial support:* In 2009–10, 4 teaching assistantships with full and partial tuition reimbursements (averaging $10,841 per year) were awarded; research assistantships with full and partial tuition reimbursements, career-related internships or fieldwork, Federal Work-Study, institutionally sponsored loans, scholarships/grants, traineeships, health care benefits, tuition waivers (full and partial), and unspecified assistantships also available. Support available to part-time students. Financial award application deadline: 1/1; financial award applicants required to submit FAFSA. *Faculty research:* Pharmaceutical care outcomes, drug use review, pharmacoeconomics. *Unit head:* Dr. Christopher Owens, Interim Chairman, 208-282-2586, Fax: 208-282-4482, E-mail: ctowens@pharmacy.isu.edu. *Application contact:* Tami Carson, Graduate School Technical Records Specialist, 208-282-2150, Fax: 208-282-4847, E-mail: carstami@isu.edu.

Long Island University, Brooklyn Campus, Arnold and Marie Schwartz College of Pharmacy and Health Sciences, Graduate Programs in Pharmacy, Division of Social and Administrative Sciences, Brooklyn, NY 11201-8423. Offers drug regulatory affairs (MS); pharmacy administration (MS). Part-time and evening/weekend programs available. *Degree requirements:* For master's, thesis optional. *Entrance requirements:* For master's, minimum GPA of 3.0.

The Ohio State University, College of Pharmacy and Graduate School, Graduate Programs in Pharmacy, Division of Pharmacy Practice and Administration, Columbus, OH 43210. Offers pharmaceutical administration (MS, PhD). Part-time programs available. *Degree requirements:* For doctorate, one foreign language, thesis/dissertation. *Entrance requirements:* For master's and doctorate, GRE General Test, minimum GPA of 3.0. Additional exam requirements/recommendations for international students: Required—TOEFL (minimum score 600 paper-based; 250 computer-based; 100 iBT). Electronic applications accepted. *Expenses:* Tuition, state resident: full-time $10,683. Tuition, nonresident: full-time $25,923. Tuition and fees vary according to course load and program. *Faculty research:* Pharmacoeconomic analysis, finance, institutional behavior, drug distribution and public policy.

Purdue University, College of Pharmacy and Pharmacal Sciences and Graduate School, Graduate Programs in Pharmacy and Pharmacal Sciences, Department of Industrial and Physical Pharmacy, West Lafayette, IN 47907. Offers pharmaceutics (PhD); regulatory quality compliance (MS, Certificate). *Degree requirements:* For doctorate, thesis/dissertation. *Entrance requirements:* For doctorate, GRE General Test, minimum B average; BS in biology, chemistry, or pharmacy. Additional exam requirements/recommendations for international students: Required—TOEFL. Electronic applications accepted. *Faculty research:* Controlled drug delivery systems, liposomes, antacids, coating technology.

St. John's University, College of Pharmacy and Allied Health Professions, Graduate Programs in Pharmacy, Program in Pharmacy Administration, Queens, NY 11439. Offers MS. Part-time and evening/weekend programs available. *Students:* 57 full-time (23 women), 8 part-time (2 women); includes 2 minority (both Asian Americans or Pacific Islanders), 60 international. Average age 24. 130 applicants, 37% accepted, 10 enrolled. In 2009, 11 master's awarded. *Degree requirements:* For master's, comprehensive exam, thesis optional, one-year residency. *Entrance requirements:* For master's, GRE General Test, bachelor's degree in pharmacy, minimum GPA of 3.0, 2 letters of recommendation. Additional exam requirements/recommendations for international students: Required—TOEFL (minimum score 500 paper-based; 173 computer-based; 61 iBT), IELTS (minimum score 5.5). *Application deadline:* For fall admission, 3/1 priority date for domestic students, 5/1 priority date for international students; for spring admission, 11/1 priority date for domestic and international students. Applications are processed on a rolling basis. Application fee: $70. Electronic applications accepted. *Expenses:* Contact institution. *Financial support:* Fellowships, research assistantships, career-related internships or fieldwork available. Support available to part-time students. Financial award application deadline: 3/1; financial award applicants required to submit FAFSA. *Unit head:* Dr. Wenchen Wu, Chair, 718-990-5690, E-mail: wuw@stjohns.edu. *Application contact:* Kathleen Davis, Director of Graduate Admissions, 718-990-2790, E-mail: gradhelp@stjohns.edu.

San Diego State University, Graduate and Research Affairs, College of Sciences, Program in Regulatory Affairs, San Diego, CA 92182. Offers MS. *Degree requirements:* For master's, thesis. *Entrance requirements:* For master's, GRE General Test, 3 letters of recommendation, employment/volunteer experience list. Additional exam requirements/recommendations for international students: Required—TOEFL. Electronic applications accepted.

Temple University, Graduate School, Fox School of Business, MBA Programs, Philadelphia, PA 19122-6096. Offers accounting (MBA); business management (MBA); financial management (MBA); healthcare and life sciences innovation (MBA); human resource management (MBA); international business (IMBA); IT management (MBA); marketing management (MBA); pharmaceutical management (MBA); strategic management (EMBA, MBA). EMBA offered in Philadelphia, PA and Tokyo, Japan. *Accreditation:* AACSB. Part-time and evening/weekend programs available. Postbaccalaureate distance learning degree programs offered (minimal on-campus study). *Entrance requirements:* For master's, GMAT, minimum undergraduate GPA of 3.0. Additional exam requirements/recommendations for international students: Required—TOEFL (minimum score 600 paper-based; 250 computer-based; 100 iBT), IELTS (minimum score 7.5).

University of Arkansas for Medical Sciences, College of Pharmacy, Program in Pharmaceutical Evaluation and Policy, Little Rock, AR 72205-7199. Offers MS. *Students:* 6 full-time (2 women). *Degree requirements:* For master's, thesis. *Entrance requirements:* For master's, GRE, 3 letters of recommendation, resume. Additional exam requirements/recommendations for international students: Required—TOEFL. *Application deadline:* For fall admission, 3/1 for domestic and international students. Application fee: $0. *Unit head:* Dr. Bradley C. Martin, Program Director, E-mail: bmartin@uams.edu. *Application contact:* Dr. Bradley C. Martin, Program Director, E-mail: bmartin@uams.edu.

University of Florida, College of Pharmacy and Graduate School, Graduate Programs in Pharmacy, Department of Pharmacy Health Care Administration, Gainesville, FL 32611. Offers MSP, PhD. Part-time programs available. *Degree requirements:* For doctorate, thesis/dissertation. *Entrance requirements:* For master's, minimum GPA of 3.0; for doctorate, GRE General Test, minimum GPA of 3.0. Additional exam requirements/recommendations for international students: Required—TOEFL. Electronic applications accepted. *Faculty research:* Pharmaceutical care, drug use systems, drug-related morbidity, pharmacy law.

University of Houston, College of Pharmacy, Houston, TX 77204. Offers hospital pharmacy (MSPHR); pharmacy administration (MSPHR). *Accreditation:* ACPE. Part-time programs available. *Faculty:* 25 full-time (5 women), 13 part-time/adjunct (8 women). *Students:* 541 full-time (339 women), 38 part-time (22 women); includes 293 minority (26 African Americans, 1 American Indian/Alaska Native, 229 Asian Americans or Pacific Islanders, 37 Hispanic Americans), 86 international. Average age 25. 736 applicants, 26% accepted, 147 enrolled. In 2009, 123 first professional degrees, 13 master's, 4 doctorates awarded. Terminal master's awarded for partial completion of doctoral program. *Degree requirements:* For master's, thesis; for doctorate, thesis/dissertation; for Pharm D, comprehensive exam. *Entrance requirements:* For Pharm D, PCAT, community service, letter of recommendation; for master's and doctorate, GRE (preferred), GMAT. Additional exam requirements/recommendations for international students: Required—TOEFL. *Application deadline:* For fall admission, 2/1 for domestic and international students. Applications are processed on a rolling basis. Application fee: $25 ($75 for international students). Electronic applications accepted. *Expenses:* Tuition, state resident: full-time $7676; part-time $320 per credit hour. Tuition, nonresident: full-time $14,324; part-time $597 per credit hour. Required fees: $3034. *Financial support:* In 2009–10, 18 research assistantships with full tuition reimbursements (averaging $14,350 per year), 37 teaching assistantships with full tuition reimbursements (averaging $14,350 per year) were awarded; career-related internships or fieldwork, Federal Work-Study, institutionally sponsored loans, scholarships/grants, health care benefits, and unspecified assistantships also available. Support available to part-time students. Financial award application deadline: 2/1. *Faculty research:* Drug screening and design, cardiovascular pharmacology, infectious disease, asthma research, herbal medicine. *Unit head:* Dr. Lamar Pritchard, Dean, 713-743-1253, Fax: 713-743-1259, E-mail: flpritchard@uh.edu. *Application contact:* Morgan Ely, Director of Admissions, 713-743-1291, Fax: 713-743-1237, E-mail: pharmacyadmissions@uh.edu.

University of Illinois at Chicago, College of Pharmacy and Graduate College, Graduate Programs in Pharmacy, Chicago, IL 60607-7128. Offers biopharmaceutical sciences (PhD); forensic science (MS); medicinal chemistry (MS, PhD); pharmacognosy (MS, PhD); pharmacy administration (MS, PhD). Terminal master's awarded for partial completion of doctoral program. *Degree requirements:* For master's, variable foreign language requirement, thesis; for doctorate, variable foreign language requirement, thesis/dissertation. *Entrance requirements:* For master's and doctorate, GRE General Test. Additional exam requirements/recommendations for international students: Required—TOEFL. Electronic applications accepted. *Expenses:* Contact institution.

University of Maryland, Baltimore, Graduate School, Graduate Programs in Pharmacy, Department of Pharmaceutical Health Service Research, Baltimore, MD 21201. Offers epidemiology (MS); pharmacy administration (PhD); Pharm D/PhD. *Degree requirements:* For doctorate, comprehensive exam, thesis/dissertation. *Entrance requirements:* For doctorate, GRE General Test. Additional exam requirements/recommendations for international students: Required—TOEFL, IELTS. Electronic applications accepted. *Expenses:* Tuition, state resident: full-time $7290; part-time $405 per credit hour. Tuition, nonresident: full-time $12,780; part-time $710 per credit hour. Required fees: $774; $10 per credit hour. $297 per semester. Tuition and fees vary according to course load, degree level and program. *Faculty research:* Pharmacoeconomics, outcomes research, public health policy, drug therapy and aging.

University of Michigan, College of Pharmacy and Horace H. Rackham School of Graduate Studies, Department of Social and Administrative Sciences, Ann Arbor, MI 48109. Offers PhD. Terminal master's awarded for partial completion of doctoral program. *Degree requirements:* For doctorate, oral defense of dissertation, preliminary exam. *Entrance requirements:* For doctorate, GRE General Test. Additional exam requirements/recommendations for international students: Required—TOEFL or IELTS. Electronic applications accepted. *Expenses:* Tuition, state resident: full-time $17,286; part-time $1099 per credit hour. Tuition, nonresident: full-time $34,944; part-time $2080 per credit hour. Required fees: $95 per semester. Tuition and fees vary according to course load, degree level and program.

University of Minnesota, Twin Cities Campus, College of Pharmacy and Graduate School, Graduate Programs in Pharmacy, Graduate Program in Social, Administrative and Clinical Pharmacy, Minneapolis, MN 55455-0213. Offers experimental and clinical pharmacology (MS, PhD); social and administrative pharmacy (MS, PhD). *Degree requirements:* For master's, thesis (for some programs); for doctorate, thesis/dissertation. *Entrance requirements:* For master's, GRE General Test, BS in science; for doctorate, GRE General Test. Additional exam requirements/recommendations for international students: Required—TOEFL. *Faculty research:* Pharmaceutical economics, pharmaceutical policy, pharmaceutical social/behavioral sciences.

University of Mississippi, Graduate School, School of Pharmacy, Graduate Programs in Pharmacy, Oxford, University, MS 38677. Offers medicinal chemistry (PhD); pharmaceutical sciences (MS); pharmaceutics (PhD); pharmacognosy (PhD); pharmacology (PhD); pharmacy administration (PhD). *Faculty:* 32 full-time (9 women), 8 part-time/adjunct (5 women). *Students:* 84 full-time (37 women), 8 part-time (6 women); includes 6 minority (3 African Americans, 2 Asian Americans or Pacific Islanders, 1 Hispanic American), 64 international. In 2009, 2 master's, 12 doctorates awarded. *Unit head:* Dr. Barbara G. Wells, Dean, 662-915-7265, Fax: 662-915-5704, E-mail: pharmacy@olemiss.edu. *Application contact:* Dr. Christy M. Wyandt, Associate Dean, 662-915-7474, Fax: 662-915-7577, E-mail: cwyandt@olemiss.edu.

University of Pittsburgh, School of Pharmacy, Pittsburgh, PA 15260. Offers pharmaceutical sciences (MS, PhD); pharmacy (Pharm D); pharmacy administration/residency (MS). *Faculty:* 79 full-time (37 women), 84 part-time/adjunct (39 women). *Students:* 469 full-time (285 women), 1 part-time (0 women); includes 56 minority (15 African Americans, 2 American Indian/Alaska Native, 34 Asian Americans or Pacific Islanders, 5 Hispanic Americans), 20 international. Average age 23. 981 applicants, 15% accepted, 116 enrolled. In 2009, 100 first professional degrees, 1 master's, 2 doctorates awarded. Terminal master's awarded for partial completion of doctoral program. *Degree requirements:* For master's, comprehensive exam, thesis; for doctorate, comprehensive exam, thesis/dissertation. *Entrance requirements:* For Pharm D, PCAT; for master's and doctorate, GRE General Test. Additional exam requirements/recommendations for international students: Required—TOEFL (minimum score 550 paper-based; 215 computer-based; 80 iBT). Electronic applications accepted. *Expenses:* Contact institution. *Financial support:* In 2009–10, 163 students received support, including 3 fellowships with full tuition reimbursements available (averaging $18,000 per year), 9 research assistantships with full tuition reimbursements available (averaging $15,675 per year), 14 teaching assistantships with full tuition reimbursements available (averaging $15,675 per year); career-related internships or fieldwork, Federal Work-Study, institutionally sponsored loans, scholarships/grants, and health care benefits also available. Financial award application deadline: 10/1. *Faculty research:* Drug delivery and targeting; neuroendocrine pharmacology; genomics, proteomics, and drug discovery; clinical pharmaceutical sciences. Total annual research expenditures: $7.8 million. *Unit head:* Dr. Patricia Dowley Kroboth, Dean, 412-624-2400, Fax: 412-648-1086. *Application contact:* Marcia L. Borrelli, Director of Student Services, 412-383-9000, Fax: 412-383-9996, E-mail: borrelli@pitt.edu.

University of the Sciences in Philadelphia, College of Graduate Studies, Program in Pharmaceutical Business, Philadelphia, PA 19104-4495. Offers MBA. Part-time and evening/weekend programs available. *Entrance requirements:* Additional exam requirements/recommendations for international students: Required—TOEFL, TWE. *Expenses:* Contact institution.

University of the Sciences in Philadelphia, College of Graduate Studies, Program in Pharmacy Administration, Philadelphia, PA 19104-4495. Offers MS. Part-time programs available. *Entrance requirements:* Additional exam requirements/recommendations for international students: Required—TOEFL, TWE. *Expenses:* Contact institution. *Faculty research:* Cost-effect analysis, pharmaceutical economics, pharmaceutical care, marketing research, health communications.

The University of Toledo, College of Graduate Studies, College of Pharmacy, Program in Pharmaceutical Sciences, Toledo, OH 43606-3390. Offers administrative pharmacy (MSPS); industrial pharmacy (MSPS); pharmacology toxicology (MSPS). *Degree requirements:* For master's, thesis. *Entrance requirements:* For master's, GRE General Test. Additional exam requirements/recommendations for international students: Required—TOEFL (minimum score 550 paper-based; 213 computer-based; 80 iBT). Electronic applications accepted.

University of West Florida, College of Professional Studies, Department of Professional and Community Leadership, Program in Administration, Pensacola, FL 32514-5750. Offers acquisition and contract administration (MSA); biomedical/pharmaceutical (MSA); criminal justice administration (MSA); database administration (MSA); education leadership (MSA); healthcare administration (MSA); human performance technology (MSA); leadership (MSA); nursing administration (MSA); public administration (MSA); software engineering administration (MSA). Part-time and evening/weekend programs available. Postbaccalaureate distance learning degree programs offered (no on-campus study). *Students:* 33 full-time (21 women), 168 part-time (97 women); includes 53 minority (32 African Americans, 2 American Indian/Alaska Native, 5 Asian Americans or Pacific Islanders, 14 Hispanic Americans), 1 international. Average age 34. 103 applicants, 74% accepted, 64 enrolled. In 2009, 47 master's awarded. *Entrance requirements:* For master's, GRE General Test, letter of intent, names of references. Additional exam requirements/recommendations for international students: Required—TOEFL (minimum score 550 paper-based; 213 computer-based). *Application deadline:* For fall admission, 6/1 for domestic students, 5/15 for international students; for spring admission, 11/1 for domestic students, 10/1 for international students. Applications are processed on a rolling basis. Application fee: $30. *Expenses:* Tuition, state resident: full-time $4982; part-time $260 per credit hour. Tuition, nonresident: full-time $20,059; part-time $919 per credit hour. Required fees: $1247; $52 per credit hour. *Financial support:* Unspecified assistantships available. Financial award application deadline: 4/15; financial award applicants required to submit FAFSA. *Unit head:* Dr. Karen Rasmussen, Chairperson, 850-474-2301, Fax: 850-474-2804. *Application contact:* Terry McCray, Assistant Director of Graduate Admissions, 850-473-7718, Fax: 850-473-7714, E-mail: gradadmissions@uwf.edu.

University of Wisconsin–Madison, School of Pharmacy and Graduate School, Graduate Programs in Pharmacy, Madison, WI 53706-1380. Offers pharmaceutical sciences (PhD); social and administrative sciences in pharmacy (MS, PhD). Terminal master's awarded for partial completion of doctoral program. *Degree requirements:* For master's, thesis (for some programs); for doctorate, comprehensive exam (for some programs), thesis/dissertation. *Entrance requirements:* For master's and doctorate, GRE. Additional exam requirements/recommendations for international students: Required—TOEFL. Electronic applications accepted. *Expenses:* Contact institution.

Wayne State University, Eugene Applebaum College of Pharmacy and Health Sciences, Department of Pharmaceutical Sciences, Detroit, MI 48202. Offers experimental technology in pharmaceutical sciences (Certificate); health systems pharmacy management (MS); hospital pharmacy (MS); pharmaceutical administration (MS, PhD); pharmacy (Pharm D). *Accreditation:* ACPE (one or more programs are accredited). Part-time programs available. *Degree requirements:* For master's, thesis optional. *Entrance requirements:* For Pharm D, bachelor's degree in pharmacy; for master's, GRE General Test, bachelor's degree in pharmacy. Additional exam requirements/recommendations for international students: Required—TOEFL (minimum score 550 paper-based; 213 computer-based); Recommended—TWE (minimum score 6). Electronic applications accepted. *Faculty research:* Mechanisms of resistance of bacteria to anti-microbial agents, drug metabolism and disposition in children, treatment strategies for stroke/neurovascular disease, prevalence and treatment of diabetes in Arab-Americans, ethnic variability in development of osteoporosis.

West Virginia University, School of Pharmacy, Program in Pharmaceutical and Pharmacological Sciences, Morgantown, WV 26506. Offers administrative pharmacy (PhD); behavioral pharmacy (MS, PhD); biopharmaceutics/pharmacokinetics (MS, PhD); industrial pharmacy (MS); medicinal chemistry (MS, PhD); pharmaceutical chemistry (MS, PhD); pharmaceutics (MS, PhD); pharmacology and toxicology (MS); pharmacy (MS); pharmacy administration (MS). Part-time programs available. Terminal master's awarded for partial completion of doctoral program. *Degree requirements:* For master's, thesis; for doctorate, one foreign language, comprehensive exam, thesis/dissertation. *Entrance requirements:* For master's and doctorate, GRE General Test, minimum GPA of 2.75. Additional exam requirements/recommendations for international students: Required—TOEFL; Recommended—TWE. Electronic applications accepted. *Expenses:* Contact institution. *Faculty research:* Pharmaceutics, medicinal chemistry, biopharmaceutics/pharmacokinetics, health outcomes research.

Pharmaceutical Sciences

Auburn University, Harrison School of Pharmacy and Graduate School, Graduate Program in Pharmacy, Auburn University, AL 36849. Offers pharmacal sciences (MS, PhD); pharmaceutical sciences (PhD); pharmacy care systems (MS, PhD). Part-time programs available. *Faculty:* 48 full-time (27 women), 1 (woman) part-time/adjunct. *Students:* 16 full-time (9 women), 10 part-time (4 women); includes 1 minority (African American), 19 international. Average age 32. 133 applicants, 8% accepted, 8 enrolled. In 2009, 2 master's, 4 doctorates awarded. *Degree requirements:* For master's, thesis; for doctorate, thesis/dissertation. *Entrance requirements:* For master's and doctorate, GRE General Test. *Application deadline:* For fall admission, 7/7 for domestic students; for spring admission, 11/24 for domestic students. Applications are processed on a rolling basis. Application fee: $50 ($60 for international students). Electronic applications accepted. *Expenses:* Tuition, state resident: full-time $6240. Tuition, nonresident: full-time $18,720. International tuition: $18,938 full-time. Required fees: $492. Tuition and fees vary according to course load, program and reciprocity agreements. *Financial support:* Fellowships, research assistantships, teaching assistantships available. *Faculty research:* Communications, facilities design, substance abuse. Total annual research expenditures: $600,000. *Unit head:* Dr. R. Lee Evans, Dean and Professor, Harrison School of Pharmacy, 334-844-8348, Fax: 334-844-8353. *Application contact:* Dr. George Flowers, Dean of the Graduate School, 334-844-2125.

Boston University, School of Medicine, Division of Graduate Medical Sciences, Department of Pharmacology and Experimental Therapeutics, Boston, MA 02118. Offers MA, PhD, MD/PhD. Terminal master's awarded for partial completion of doctoral program. *Degree requirements:* For master's, thesis; for doctorate, thesis/dissertation. *Entrance requirements:* For master's and doctorate, GRE General Test, GRE Subject Test. Additional exam requirements/recommendations for international students: Required—TOEFL. *Application deadline:* For fall admission, 1/15 priority date for domestic students; for spring admission, 10/15 priority date for domestic students. Electronic applications accepted. *Expenses:* Tuition: Full-time $37,910; part-time $1184 per credit hour. Required fees: $386; $40 per semester. Part-time tuition and fees vary according to class time, course level, degree level and program. *Financial support:* In 2009–10, fellowships with tuition reimbursements (averaging $19,000 per year), research assistantships with tuition reimbursements (averaging $19,000 per year) were awarded; Federal Work-Study, scholarships/grants, traineeships, tuition waivers, and research stipends also available. *Faculty research:* Molecular pharmacology, neuropharmacology, peptide receptors, psychopharmacology. *Unit head:* Dr. David H. Farb, Chairman, 617-638-4300, Fax: 617-638-4329, E-mail: dfarb@bu.edu. *Application contact:* Dr. Carol T. Walsh, Graduate Director, 617-638-4326, Fax: 617-638-4329, E-mail: ctwalsh@bu.edu.

Butler University, College of Pharmacy, Indianapolis, IN 46208-3485. Offers pharmaceutical science (Pharm D, MS); physician assistance studies (MS). *Accreditation:* ACPE (one or more programs are accredited). Part-time and evening/weekend programs available. *Faculty:* 24 full-time (11 women), 2 part-time/adjunct (1 woman). *Students:* 274 full-time (194 women), 10 part-time (6 women); includes 19 minority (4 African Americans, 9 Asian Americans or Pacific Islanders, 6 Hispanic Americans), 11 international. Average age 24. 107 applicants, 6% accepted, 6 enrolled. In 2009, 129 first professional degrees, 51 master's awarded. *Degree requirements:* For master's, research paper or thesis. *Application deadline:* For fall admission, 8/1 priority date for domestic students; for spring admission, 12/15 for domestic students. Applications are processed on a rolling basis. Application fee: $35. Electronic applications accepted. *Expenses:* Contact institution. *Financial support:* Applicants required to submit FAFSA. *Faculty research:* Anti-seizure drugs, casein kinase inhibitors, speech recognition interface for prescribing drugs, pharmacoeconomics. Total annual research expenditures: $92,000. *Unit head:* Dr. Mary Andritz, Dean, 317-940-9451, Fax: 317-940-6172, E-mail: mandritz@butler.edu. *Application contact:* Dr. Bruce Clayton, Professor, 317-940-9830, E-mail: bclayton@butler.edu.

Pharmaceutical Sciences

Campbell University, Graduate and Professional Programs, School of Pharmacy, Buies Creek, NC 27506. Offers clinical research (MS); pharmaceutical science (MS); pharmacy (Pharm D). *Accreditation:* ACPE. Part-time and evening/weekend programs available. *Entrance requirements:* For Pharm D, PCAT; for master's, MCAT, PCAT, GRE, bachelor's degree in health sciences or related field. Additional exam requirements/recommendations for international students: Required—TOEFL (minimum score 550 paper-based; 213 computer-based; 79 iBT). Electronic applications accepted. *Expenses:* Contact institution. *Faculty research:* Immunology, medicinal chemistry, pharmaceutics, applied pharmacology.

Creighton University, School of Medicine and Graduate School, Graduate Programs in Medicine, Department of Pharmacology, Omaha, NE 68178-0001. Offers pharmaceutical sciences (MS); pharmacology (MS, PhD); Pharm D/MS. Terminal master's awarded for partial completion of doctoral program. *Degree requirements:* For master's, comprehensive exam, thesis; for doctorate, comprehensive exam, thesis/dissertation, oral and written preliminary exams. *Entrance requirements:* For master's and doctorate, GRE General Test, minimum GPA of 3.0, undergraduate degree in sciences. Additional exam requirements/recommendations for international students: Required—TOEFL. Electronic applications accepted. *Expenses:* Tuition: Full-time $11,700; part-time $650 per credit hour. Required fees: $126 per semester. *Faculty research:* Pharmacology secretion, cardiovascular-renal pharmacology, adrenergic receptors, signal transduction, genetic regulation of receptors.

Creighton University, School of Pharmacy and Health Professions and Department of Pharmacology, Program in Pharmaceutical Sciences, Omaha, NE 68178-0001. Offers MS, Pharm D/MS. *Faculty:* 22 full-time (4 women). *Students:* 9 full-time (4 women), all international. Average age 23. 81 applicants, 19% accepted, 3 enrolled. In 2009, 3 master's awarded. *Degree requirements:* For master's, thesis. *Entrance requirements:* For master's, GRE, three recommendations. Additional exam requirements/recommendations for international students: Required—TOEFL (minimum score 550 paper-based; 213 computer-based; 80 iBT). *Application deadline:* For fall admission, 3/30 for domestic and international students. Application fee: $50. Electronic applications accepted. *Expenses:* Tuition: Full-time $11,700; part-time $650 per credit hour. Required fees: $126 per semester. *Financial support:* In 2009–10, 8 students received support. Tuition waivers (full) available. Financial award application deadline: 5/1; financial award applicants required to submit FAFSA. *Unit head:* Dr. Manzoor M. Khan, Professor, 402-280-5576, E-mail: mmkhan@creighton.edu. *Application contact:* Taunya Plater, Senior Program Coordinator, 402-280-2870, Fax: 402-280-2899, E-mail: taunyaplater@creighton.edu.

Dartmouth College, Program in Experimental and Molecular Medicine, Molecular Pharmacology, Toxicology and Experimental Therapeutics Track, Hanover, NH 03755. Offers PhD.

Duquesne University, Mylan School of Pharmacy/Graduate School of Pharmaceutical Sciences, Graduate School of Pharmaceutical Sciences, Program in Pharmaceutics, Pittsburgh, PA 15282-0001. Offers MS, PhD, MBA/MS. *Faculty:* 8 full-time (2 women). *Students:* 19 full-time (6 women), 3 part-time (0 women); includes 1 minority (Asian American or Pacific Islander), 14 international. 100 applicants, 6% accepted, 3 enrolled. In 2009, 1 master's, 3 doctorates awarded. *Degree requirements:* For master's, thesis; for doctorate, comprehensive exam, thesis/dissertation. *Entrance requirements:* For master's and doctorate, GRE General Test. Additional exam requirements/recommendations for international students: Required—TOEFL. *Application deadline:* For fall admission, 2/1 priority date for domestic and international students; for spring admission, 10/1 priority date for domestic and international students. Applications are processed on a rolling basis. Application fee: $50. Electronic applications accepted. *Expenses:* Tuition: Part-time $851 per credit. Required fees: $81 per credit. *Financial support:* In 2009–10, 17 students received support, including 19 teaching assistantships with full tuition reimbursements available; research assistantships with full tuition reimbursements available, unspecified assistantships also available. *Unit head:* Dr. Wilson S. Meng, Head, 412-396-6366. *Application contact:* Information Contact, 412-396-1172, E-mail: gsps-adm@duq.edu.

See Close-Up on page 1791.

Florida Agricultural and Mechanical University, Division of Graduate Studies, Research, and Continuing Education, College of Pharmacy and Pharmaceutical Sciences, Graduate Programs in Pharmaceutical Sciences, Tallahassee, FL 32307-3200. Offers environmental toxicology (PhD); medicinal chemistry (MS, PhD); pharmaceutics (MS, PhD); pharmacology/toxicology (MS, PhD); pharmacy administration (MS). *Accreditation:* CEPH. *Faculty:* 21 full-time (6 women). *Students:* 438 full-time (296 women), 21 part-time (13 women); includes 417 minority (380 African Americans, 1 American Indian/Alaska Native, 30 Asian Americans or Pacific Islanders, 6 Hispanic Americans), 5 international. In 2009, 4 master's, 7 doctorates awarded. *Degree requirements:* For master's, comprehensive exam, thesis, publishable paper; for doctorate, comprehensive exam, thesis/dissertation, publishable paper. *Entrance requirements:* For master's and doctorate, GRE General Test, minimum GPA of 3.0 in last 60 hours. Additional exam requirements/recommendations for international students: Required—TOEFL. *Application deadline:* For fall admission, 4/1 for domestic students. Application fee: $20. *Financial support:* Fellowships, research assistantships, Federal Work-Study and scholarships/grants available. *Faculty research:* Anticancer agents, anti-inflammatory drugs, chronopharmacology, neuroendocrinology, microbiology. *Unit head:* Dr. Thomas J. Fitzgerald, Chairman, Graduate Committee, 850-599-3301. *Application contact:* Gloria James, Graduate Coordinator, 850-599-3144.

Idaho State University, Office of Graduate Studies, College of Pharmacy, Department of Biomedical and Pharmaceutical Sciences, Pocatello, ID 83209-8334. Offers biopharmaceutical analysis (PhD); drug delivery (PhD); medicinal chemistry (PhD); pharmaceutical sciences (MS); pharmacology (PhD). Part-time programs available. *Faculty:* 9 full-time (1 woman). *Students:* 13 full-time (5 women), 7 part-time (3 women); includes 2 minority (both Asian Americans or Pacific Islanders), 14 international. Average age 29. In 2009, 7 master's, 2 doctorates awarded. *Degree requirements:* For master's, one foreign language, comprehensive exam, thesis, thesis research, classes in speech and technical writing; for doctorate, comprehensive exam, thesis/dissertation, written and oral exams, classes in speech and technical writing. *Entrance requirements:* For master's, GRE General Test, minimum GPA of 3.0, 3 letters of recommendation; for doctorate, GRE General Test, BS in pharmacy or related field, minimum GPA of 3.0, 3 letters of recommendation. Additional exam requirements/recommendations for international students: Required—TOEFL (minimum score 550 paper-based; 213 computer-based; 80 iBT). *Application deadline:* For fall admission, 7/1 for domestic students, 6/1 for international students; for spring admission, 12/1 for domestic students, 11/1 for international students. Applications are processed on a rolling basis. Application fee: $55. Electronic applications accepted. *Expenses:* Contact institution. *Financial support:* Research assistantships with full and partial tuition reimbursements, teaching assistantships with full and partial tuition reimbursements, career-related internships or fieldwork, Federal Work-Study, institutionally sponsored loans, scholarships/grants, traineeships, health care benefits, tuition waivers (full and partial), and unspecified assistantships available. Support available to part-time students. Financial award application deadline: 1/1; financial award applicants required to submit FAFSA. *Faculty research:* Metabolic toxicity of heavy metals, neuroendocrine pharmacology, cardiovascular pharmacology, cancer biology, immunopharmacology. *Unit head:* Dr. Timothy Hunt, Chair, 208-282-2682, Fax: 208-282-4305, E-mail: thunt@pharmacy.isu.edu. *Application contact:* Tami Carson, Graduate School Technical Records Specialist, 208-282-2150, Fax: 208-282-4847, E-mail: carstami@isu.edu.

The Johns Hopkins University, Zanvyl Krieger School of Arts and Sciences, Advanced Academic Programs, Program in Bioscience Regulatory Affairs, Baltimore, MD 21218-2699. Offers MS. *Faculty:* 8 full-time (4 women), 99 part-time/adjunct (21 women). *Students:* 139 part-time (95 women); includes 61 minority (21 African Americans, 36 Asian Americans or Pacific Islanders, 4 Hispanic Americans), 20 international. Average age 34. 70 applicants, 56% accepted, 30 enrolled. In 2009, 26 degrees awarded. *Degree requirements:* For master's, practicum. *Entrance requirements:* For master's, undergraduate degree in the life sciences or engineering from a four-year college with minimum GPA of 3.0. Application fee: $75. *Financial support:* Scholarships/grants available. *Unit head:* Kirsty Gharavi, Director, 301-294-7162, E-mail: kgharavi@jhu.edu. *Application contact:* Valana M. McMickens, Admissions Manager, 202-452-1941, Fax: 202-452-1970, E-mail: aapadmissions@jhu.edu.

Long Island University, Brooklyn Campus, Arnold and Marie Schwartz College of Pharmacy and Health Sciences, Graduate Programs in Pharmacy, Division of Pharmaceutical Sciences, Brooklyn, NY 11201-8423. Offers cosmetic science (MS); industrial pharmacy (MS); pharmaceutics (PhD); pharmacology/toxicology (MS). Part-time and evening/weekend programs available. Terminal master's awarded for partial completion of doctoral program. *Degree requirements:* For master's, thesis optional; for doctorate, thesis/dissertation, candidacy exam. *Entrance requirements:* For master's and doctorate, minimum GPA of 3.0.

Long Island University, Rockland Graduate Campus, Graduate School, Program in Pharmaceutics, Orangeburg, NY 10962. Offers cosmetic science (MS); industrial pharmacy (MS). *Expenses:* Tuition: Part-time $930 per credit. Required fees: $200 per semester. *Unit head:* Carmen L. Bowen, Program Director, 845-359-7200 Ext. 5435, E-mail: carmen.bowen@liu.edu. *Application contact:* Peter S. Reiner, Director of Admissions and Marketing, 845-359-7200, Fax: 845-359-7248, E-mail: peter.reiner@liu.edu.

Massachusetts College of Pharmacy and Health Sciences, Graduate Studies, Program in Pharmaceutics/Industrial Pharmacy, Boston, MA 02115-5896. Offers MS, PhD. *Students:* 1 full-time (0 women), 14 part-time (11 women); includes 1 minority (Asian American or Pacific Islander), 13 international. Average age 28. 48 applicants, 15% accepted, 4 enrolled. In 2009, 1 doctorate awarded. Terminal master's awarded for partial completion of doctoral program. *Degree requirements:* For master's, thesis, oral defense of thesis; for doctorate, one foreign language, comprehensive exam, thesis/dissertation, oral defense of dissertation, qualifying exam. *Entrance requirements:* For master's and doctorate, GRE General Test, minimum QPA of 3.0. Additional exam requirements/recommendations for international students: Required—TOEFL (minimum score 550 paper-based; 213 computer-based; 79 iBT). *Application deadline:* For fall admission, 2/1 priority date for domestic students, 2/1 for international students. Application fee: $70. *Expenses:* Tuition: Full-time $28,000; part-time $875 per credit hour. Required fees: $750; $190 per semester. Part-time tuition and fees vary according to course load, campus/location, program and student level. *Financial support:* Fellowships with partial tuition reimbursements, research assistantships with partial tuition reimbursements, teaching assistantships with full tuition reimbursements, tuition waivers (partial) and library assistantships available. Financial award application deadline: 3/15. *Faculty research:* Pharmacokinetics and drug metabolism, pharmaceutics and physical pharmacy, dosage forms. *Unit head:* Dr. Eman Atef, Assistant Professor, Pharmaceutics, 617-732-2980, E-mail: eman.atef@mcphs.edu. *Application contact:* Tara Hennesey, Coordinator of Graduate Admission, 617-732-2850, E-mail: admissions@mcphs.edu.

Memorial University of Newfoundland, School of Graduate Studies, School of Pharmacy, St. John's, NL A1C 5S7, Canada. Offers MSCPharm, PhD. Part-time programs available. *Degree requirements:* For master's, thesis, seminar; for doctorate, comprehensive exam, thesis/dissertation, oral defense of thesis. *Entrance requirements:* For master's, B Sc in pharmacy or related area. Electronic applications accepted. *Faculty research:* Pharmaceutics, medicinal chemistry, physical pharmacy, pharmacology, toxicology.

Mercer University, Graduate Studies, Cecil B. Day Campus, College of Pharmacy and Health Sciences, Macon, GA 31207-0003. Offers medical sciences (MS); pharmacy (Pharm D, PhD); Pharm D/MBA; Pharm D/PhD. *Accreditation:* ACPE (one or more programs are accredited). *Faculty:* 22 full-time (14 women), 3 part-time/adjunct (1 woman). *Students:* 676 full-time (440 women), 4 part-time (1 woman); includes 170 minority (68 African Americans, 91 Asian Americans or Pacific Islanders, 11 Hispanic Americans), 41 international. Average age 26. In 2009, 139 first professional degrees, 6 doctorates awarded. *Degree requirements:* For doctorate, thesis/dissertation. *Entrance requirements:* For Pharm D, PCAT, minimum GPA of 3.0; for master's, GRE, minimum GPA of 2.75; for doctorate, GRE, Pharm D or BS in pharmacy or science, minimum GPA of 3.0. Additional exam requirements/recommendations for international students: Required—TOEFL. *Application deadline:* For fall admission, 1/1 for domestic students. Applications are processed on a rolling basis. Application fee: $25. Electronic applications accepted. *Expenses:* Contact institution. *Financial support:* In 2009–10, 350 students received support; teaching assistantships with tuition reimbursements available, career-related internships or fieldwork, Federal Work-Study, institutionally sponsored loans, scholarships/grants, and tuition waivers available. Support available to part-time students. Financial award application deadline: 5/1; financial award applicants required to submit FAFSA. *Faculty research:* Stability and compatibility of steroids, synthesis of antihypertensives, disposition of cyclosporine, DUZ-drug research, synthesis of enzyme inhibitors. *Unit head:* Dr. Hewitt W. Matthews, Dean, 678-547-6304, Fax: 678-547-6315, E-mail: matthews_h@mercer.edu. *Application contact:* Dr. James W. Bartling, Associate Dean for Student Affairs and Admissions, 678-547-6181, Fax: 678-547-6063, E-mail: bartling_jw@mercer.edu.

North Dakota State University, College of Graduate and Interdisciplinary Studies, College of Pharmacy, Nursing and Allied Sciences, Department of Pharmaceutical Sciences, Fargo, ND 58108. Offers MS, PhD. *Accreditation:* ACPE. Part-time programs available. *Faculty:* 8 full-time (0 women), 2 part-time/adjunct (1 woman). *Students:* 17 full-time (8 women), 3 part-time (all women), 18 international. Average age 25. 80 applicants, 5% accepted. In 2009, 6 doctorates awarded. Terminal master's awarded for partial completion of doctoral program. *Degree requirements:* For master's, thesis; for doctorate, thesis/dissertation. *Entrance requirements:* For master's and doctorate, GRE General Test. Additional exam requirements/recommendations for international students: Required—TOEFL. *Application deadline:* For fall admission, 4/15 for domestic students. Applications are processed on a rolling basis. Application fee: $45 ($60 for international students). *Financial support:* In 2009–10, 19 research assistantships with full tuition reimbursements (averaging $14,000 per year) were awarded; institutionally sponsored loans also available. Financial award application deadline: 4/15. *Faculty research:* Subcellular pharmacokinetics, cancer, cardiovascular drug design, iontophonesis, neuropharmacology. *Unit head:* Dr. Jagdish Singh, Chair, 701-231-7943, E-mail: jagdishsingh@ndsu.edu. *Application contact:* Dr. Jonathan Sheng, Assistant Professor, 701-231-6140, Fax: 701-231-8333, E-mail: jonathan.sheng@ndsu.edu.

Northeastern University, Bouvé College of Health Sciences Graduate School, Department of Pharmaceutical Sciences, Boston, MA 02115-5096. Offers MS, PhD. Part-time and evening/weekend programs available. *Faculty:* 18 full-time (3 women). *Students:* 49 full-time (17 women), 3 part-time (all women). Average age 30. 294 applicants, 28% accepted, 52 enrolled. In 2009, 32 master's, 5 doctorates awarded. *Degree requirements:* For master's, comprehensive exam, thesis optional; for doctorate, comprehensive exam. *Entrance requirements:* For master's, GRE, bachelor's degree in science, minimum GPA of 3.0. Additional exam requirements/recommendations for international students: Required—TOEFL (minimum score 100 iBT). *Application deadline:* For fall admission, 6/1 for domestic students, 4/1 for international students; for winter admission, 12/15 for domestic students. Applications are processed on a rolling basis. Application fee: $50. Electronic applications accepted. *Financial support:* Research assistantships, Federal Work-Study and tuition waivers (partial) available. Support available to part-time students. Financial award application deadline: 3/1; financial award applicants required to submit FAFSA. *Faculty research:* Bioanalytical chemistry, cardiovascular targeting, neuroopharmacology, immunology, nanomedicide, nicotinic receptor subtypes, G-protein coupled receptors, dopamine receptor pharmacology, path-clamping of ion channel. *Unit head:* Prof. Ralph H. Loring, Program Coordinator, 617-373-3216, Fax: 617-373-8886, E-mail: r.loring@neu.edu. *Application contact:* Prof. Margaret Schnabel, Director of Graduate Admissions, 617-373-2708, E-mail: bouvegrad@neu.edu.

Northeastern University, Bouvé College of Health Sciences Graduate School, School of Pharmacy, Boston, MA 02115-5096. Offers Pharm D, MS, PhD. Students enter program as undergraduates. *Accreditation:* ACPE. *Students:* 85 full-time (38 women), 4 part-time (all women); includes 2 Asian Americans or Pacific Islanders, 67 international. 313 applicants, 31% accepted, 54 enrolled. In 2009, 113 first professional degrees, 42 master's, 3 doctorates awarded. *Degree requirements:* For doctorate, comprehensive exam, thesis/dissertation. *Entrance requirements:* For Pharm D, prior admission to undergraduate pharmacy program;

for master's and doctorate, GRE. Additional exam requirements/recommendations for international students: Required—TOEFL (minimum score 100 iBT). *Application deadline:* For fall admission, 3/1 for domestic students, 6/1 for international students. Electronic applications accepted. *Financial support:* In 2009–10, 18 research assistantships, 20 teaching assistantships were awarded; scholarships/grants also available. *Unit head:* Ralph Loring, Professor, 617-373-3216, Fax: 617-373-7655, E-mail: r.loring@neu.edu. *Application contact:* Margaret Schnabel, Director of Graduate Admission, 617-373-2708, Fax: 617-373-8780, E-mail: admissions@neu.edu.

The Ohio State University, College of Pharmacy and Graduate School, Graduate Programs in Pharmacy, Division of Medicinal Chemistry and Pharmacognosy, Columbus, OH 43210. Offers MS, PhD. *Degree requirements:* For master's, thesis; for doctorate, thesis/dissertation. *Entrance requirements:* For master's and doctorate, GRE General Test, minimum GPA of 3.0. Additional exam requirements/recommendations for international students: Required—TOEFL (minimum score 620 paper-based; 250 computer-based; 100 iBT). Electronic applications accepted. *Expenses:* Tuition, state resident: full-time $10,683. Tuition, nonresident: full-time $25,923. Tuition and fees vary according to course load and program. *Faculty research:* Drug design, natural products, synthesis of enzyme inhibitors, drug metabolism and anticancer agents.

The Ohio State University, College of Pharmacy and Graduate School, Graduate Programs in Pharmacy, Division of Pharmaceutics, Columbus, OH 43210. Offers MS, PhD. Terminal master's awarded for partial completion of doctoral program. *Degree requirements:* For doctorate, thesis/dissertation. *Entrance requirements:* For master's and doctorate, GRE General Test, minimum GPA of 3.0. Additional exam requirements/recommendations for international students: Required—TOEFL (minimum score 600 paper-based; 250 computer-based; 100 iBT). Electronic applications accepted. *Expenses:* Tuition, state resident: full-time $10,683. Tuition, nonresident: full-time $25,923. Tuition and fees vary according to course load and program. *Faculty research:* Absorption, metabolism, and elimination of drugs; drug release from emulsions, liposomes, and liquid crystals; clinical and forensic research application.

Oregon State University, College of Pharmacy, Corvallis, OR 97331. Offers Pharm D, MS, PhD. *Accreditation:* ACPE (one or more programs are accredited). Part-time programs available. *Faculty:* 31 full-time (13 women). *Students:* 379 full-time (215 women), 12 part-time (5 women); includes 141 minority (5 African Americans, 123 Asian Americans or Pacific Islanders, 13 Hispanic Americans), 29 international. Average age 27. In 2009, 80 first professional degrees, 5 doctorates awarded. Terminal master's awarded for partial completion of doctoral program. *Degree requirements:* For master's, thesis; for doctorate, thesis/dissertation. *Entrance requirements:* For master's, GRE General Test, minimum GPA of 3.0 in last 90 hours; for doctorate, GRE General Test, minimum GPA of 3.0 in last 90 hours, pre-pharmacy curriculum. Additional exam requirements/recommendations for international students: Required—TOEFL. *Application deadline:* For fall admission, 3/1 for domestic students. Applications are processed on a rolling basis. Application fee: $50. *Expenses:* Tuition, state resident: full-time $9774; part-time $362 per credit. Tuition, nonresident: full-time $15,849; part-time $587 per credit. Required fees: $1639. Full-time tuition and fees vary according to course load and program. *Financial support:* Fellowships, research assistantships, teaching assistantships, career-related internships or fieldwork, Federal Work-Study, and institutionally sponsored loans available. Support available to part-time students. Financial award application deadline: 2/1. *Faculty research:* Pharmacology/toxicology, pharmacokinetics, biopharmaceutics, neuroscience, natural products. *Unit head:* Dr. Wayne A. Kradjan, Dean, 541-737-3424, Fax: 541-737-3424, E-mail: wayne.kradjan@orst.edu.

Purdue University, College of Pharmacy and Pharmacal Sciences and Graduate School, Graduate Programs in Pharmacy and Pharmacal Sciences, Department of Medicinal Chemistry and Molecular Pharmacology, West Lafayette, IN 47907. Offers analytical medicinal chemistry (PhD); computational and biophysical medicinal chemistry (PhD); medicinal and bioorganic chemistry (PhD); medicinal biochemistry and molecular biology (PhD); molecular pharmacology and toxicology (PhD); natural products and pharmacognosy (PhD); nuclear pharmacy (MS); radiopharmaceutical chemistry and nuclear pharmacy (PhD); MS/PhD. Terminal master's awarded for partial completion of doctoral program. *Degree requirements:* For master's, thesis; for doctorate, thesis/dissertation. *Entrance requirements:* For master's, GRE General Test, minimum B average; BS in biology, chemistry, or pharmacy; for doctorate, GRE General Test, minimum B average; BS in biology, chemistry, or pharmacology. Additional exam requirements/recommendations for international students: Required—TOEFL. Electronic applications accepted. *Faculty research:* Drug design and development, cancer research, drug synthesis and analysis, chemical pharmacology, environmental toxicology.

Purdue University, College of Pharmacy and Pharmacal Sciences and Graduate School, Graduate Programs in Pharmacy and Pharmacal Sciences, Department of Pharmacy Practice, West Lafayette, IN 47907. Offers clinical pharmacy (MS, PhD); pharmacy administration (MS, PhD). Terminal master's awarded for partial completion of doctoral program. *Degree requirements:* For master's, thesis optional; for doctorate, thesis/dissertation. *Entrance requirements:* For master's, GRE General Test, BS in pharmacy or Pharm D; for doctorate, GRE General Test, BS in pharmacy or Pharm D, minimum B average. Additional exam requirements/recommendations for international students: Required—TOEFL. Electronic applications accepted. *Faculty research:* Clinical drug studies, pharmacy education advancement, administrative studies.

Queen's University at Kingston, School of Graduate Studies and Research, Faculty of Health Sciences, Department of Anatomy and Cell Biology, Kingston, ON K7L 3N6, Canada. Offers biology of reproduction (M Sc, PhD); cancer (M Sc, PhD); cardiovascular pathophysiology (M Sc, PhD); cell and molecular biology (M Sc, PhD); drug metabolism (M Sc, PhD); endocrinology (M Sc, PhD); motor control (M Sc, PhD); neural regeneration (M Sc, PhD); neurophysiology (M Sc, PhD). Part-time programs available. *Degree requirements:* For master's, thesis; for doctorate, one foreign language, comprehensive exam, thesis/dissertation. *Entrance requirements:* Additional exam requirements/recommendations for international students: Required—TOEFL. Electronic applications accepted. *Faculty research:* Human kinetics, neuroscience, reproductive biology, cardiovascular.

Rush University, Graduate College, Division of Pharmacology, Chicago, IL 60612-3832. Offers clinical research (MS); pharmacology (MS, PhD); MD/PhD. Terminal master's awarded for partial completion of doctoral program. *Degree requirements:* For master's, thesis; for doctorate, thesis/dissertation. *Entrance requirements:* For master's and doctorate, GRE General Test, interview. Additional exam requirements/recommendations for international students: Required—TOEFL (minimum score 550 paper-based; 213 computer-based). *Faculty research:* Dopamine neurobiology and Parkinson's disease; cardiac electrophysiology and clinical pharmacology; neutrophil motility, apoptosis, and adhesion; angiogenesis; pulmonary vascular physiology.

Rutgers, The State University of New Jersey, New Brunswick, Ernest Mario School of Pharmacy, Program in Pharmaceutical Science, Piscataway, NJ 08854-8097. Offers MS, PhD. Part-time programs available. Terminal master's awarded for partial completion of doctoral program. *Degree requirements:* For master's, thesis; for doctorate, thesis/dissertation. *Entrance requirements:* For master's and doctorate, GRE General Test, 3 letters of recommendation. Additional exam requirements/recommendations for international students: Required—TOEFL (minimum score 550 paper-based; 213 computer-based; 83 iBT). Electronic applications accepted. *Faculty research:* Drug transport, drug delivery, pharmacokinetics, cancer chemoprevention, pharmacogenomics.

St. John's University, College of Pharmacy and Allied Health Professions, Graduate Programs in Pharmacy, Program in Pharmaceutical Sciences, Queens, NY 11439. Offers MS, PhD. Part-time and evening/weekend programs available. *Students:* 110 full-time (56 women), 66 part-time (31 women); includes 15 minority (1 African American, 12 Asian Americans or Pacific Islanders, 2 Hispanic Americans), 142 international. Average age 26. 361 applicants, 35% accepted, 26 enrolled. In 2009, 44 master's, 12 doctorates awarded. Terminal master's awarded

for partial completion of doctoral program. *Degree requirements:* For master's, comprehensive exam, thesis optional, residency; for doctorate, comprehensive exam, thesis/dissertation, qualifying exams, residency. *Entrance requirements:* For master's, GRE General Test, minimum GPA of 3.0; for doctorate, GRE General Test, minimum GPA of 3.5 (undergraduate), 3.0 (graduate). Additional exam requirements/recommendations for international students: Required—TOEFL (minimum score 500 paper-based; 173 computer-based; 61 iBT), IELTS (minimum score 5.5). *Application deadline:* For fall admission, 3/1 priority date for domestic students, 5/1 priority date for international students; for spring admission, 11/1 priority date for domestic and international students. Applications are processed on a rolling basis. Application fee: $70. Electronic applications accepted. *Expenses:* Contact institution. *Financial support:* Fellowships, research assistantships, career-related internships or fieldwork and scholarships/grants available. Support available to part-time students. Financial award application deadline: 3/1; financial award applicants required to submit FAFSA. *Faculty research:* Neurotoxicology, biochemical toxicology, molecular pharmacology, neuropharmacology, intermediary metabolism. *Unit head:* Dr. Louis Trombetta, Chair, 718-990-6025; E-mail: trombetl@stjohns.edu. *Application contact:* Kathleen Davis, Director of Graduate Admission, 718-990-2790, Fax: 718-990-5686, E-mail: gradhelp@stjohns.edu.

South Dakota State University, Graduate School, College of Pharmacy, Department of Pharmaceutical Sciences, Brookings, SD 57007. Offers biological science (MS); pharmaceutical sciences (PhD). *Degree requirements:* For master's, thesis, oral exam; for doctorate, comprehensive exam, thesis/dissertation, oral exam. *Entrance requirements:* For master's and doctorate, GRE General Test. Additional exam requirements/recommendations for international students: Required—TOEFL (minimum score 550 paper-based; 213 computer-based). *Faculty research:* Drugs of abuse, anti-cancer drugs, sustained drug delivery, drug metabolism.

Stevens Institute of Technology, Graduate School, Charles V. Schaefer Jr. School of Engineering, Department of Mechanical Engineering, Program in Pharmaceutical Manufacturing, Hoboken, NJ 07030. Offers M Eng, MS, Certificate. *Expenses:* Tuition: Full-time $9900; part-time $1100 per credit. Required fees: $286 per semester.

Stevens Institute of Technology, Graduate School, Wesley J. Howe School of Technology Management, Program in Business Administration, Hoboken, NJ 07030. Offers engineering management (MBA); financial engineering (MBA); information management (MBA); information technology in financial services (MBA); information technology in the pharmaceutical industry (MBA); information technology outsourcing (MBA); pharmaceutical management (MBA); project management (MBA); technology management (MBA); telecommunications management (MBA). *Expenses:* Tuition: Full-time $9900; part-time $1100 per credit. Required fees: $286 per semester.

Temple University, Health Sciences Center, School of Pharmacy, Department of Pharmaceutical Sciences, Program in Pharmaceutics, Philadelphia, PA 19122-6096. Offers MS, PhD. *Degree requirements:* For master's, thesis; for doctorate, 2 foreign languages, thesis/dissertation. *Entrance requirements:* For master's, GRE General Test, minimum undergraduate GPA of 3.0; for doctorate, GRE General Test, minimum GPA of 3.0. Additional exam requirements/recommendations for international students: Required—TOEFL (minimum score 550 paper-based; 213 computer-based; 79 iBT). Electronic applications accepted.

Temple University, Health Sciences Center, School of Pharmacy, Department of Pharmaceutical Sciences, Program in Quality Assurance/Regulatory Affairs, Philadelphia, PA 19122-6096. Offers MS. Part-time and evening/weekend programs available. Postbaccalaureate distance learning degree programs offered (minimal on-campus study). *Degree requirements:* For master's, thesis. *Entrance requirements:* For master's, GRE or GMAT, minimum undergraduate GPA of 3.0. Additional exam requirements/recommendations for international students: Required—TOEFL (minimum score 550 paper-based; 213 computer-based; 79 iBT). Electronic applications accepted.

Texas Tech University Health Sciences Center, Graduate School of Biomedical Sciences, Department of Pharmaceutical Sciences, Lubbock, TX 79430. Offers MS, PhD. *Accreditation:* ACPE. *Faculty:* 19 full-time (2 women), 8 part-time/adjunct (1 woman). *Students:* 37 full-time (12 women), 1 (woman) part-time; includes 33 minority (32 Asian Americans or Pacific Islanders, 1 Hispanic American). Average age 26. 72 applicants, 8% accepted, 6 enrolled. In 2009, 5 doctorates awarded. Terminal master's awarded for partial completion of doctoral program. *Degree requirements:* For master's, thesis; for doctorate, thesis/dissertation. *Entrance requirements:* For master's and doctorate, GRE General Test, minimum GPA of 3.0. Additional exam requirements/recommendations for international students: Required—TOEFL (minimum score 550 paper-based; 213 computer-based; 79 iBT). *Application deadline:* For fall admission, 3/1 priority date for domestic and international students. Application fee: $45. Electronic applications accepted. *Financial support:* In 2009–10, 36 students received support, including research assistantships (averaging $23,000 per year); scholarships/grants also available. Financial award application deadline: 3/1. *Faculty research:* Drug design and delivery, pharmacology, pharmacokinetics, drug receptor modeling, molecular and reproductive biology. Total annual research expenditures: $2.2 million. *Unit head:* Dr. Thomas J. Abbruscato, Associate Dean for Graduate School of Biomedical Sciences/Graduate Program Advisor/Associate Professor/Interim Chair, 806-356-4016 Ext. 320, Fax: 806-356-4021, E-mail: thomas.abbruscato@ttuhsc.edu. *Application contact:* Teresa Carol Carlisle, Director of Graduate Program, 806-356-4015 Ext. 287, Fax: 806-356-4021, E-mail: teresa.carlisle@ttuhsc.edu.

Université de Montréal, Faculty of Pharmacy, Montréal, QC H3C 3J7, Canada. Offers drugs development (DESS); pharmaceutical care (DESS); pharmaceutical practice (M Sc); pharmaceutical sciences (M Sc, PhD); pharmacist-supervisor teacher (DESS). Part-time programs available. *Faculty:* 29 full-time (14 women), 32 part-time/adjunct (16 women). *Students:* 198 full-time (130 women), 113 part-time (76 women). 299 applicants, 47% accepted, 17 enrolled. In 2009, 18 master's, 11 doctorates, 45 other advanced degrees awarded. Terminal master's awarded for partial completion of doctoral program. *Degree requirements:* For master's, thesis; for doctorate, thesis/dissertation. *Entrance requirements:* For master's and doctorate, proficiency in French. *Application deadline:* For fall admission, 2/1 priority date for domestic students; for winter admission, 11/1 priority date for domestic students; for spring admission, 2/1 priority date for domestic students. Application fee: $100. Electronic applications accepted. *Financial support:* Fellowships, teaching assistantships, career-related internships or fieldwork, Federal Work-Study, and institutionally sponsored loans available. *Faculty research:* Novel drug delivery systems, immunoassay development, medicinal chemistry of CNS compounds, pharmacokinetics and biopharmaceutical compounds. *Unit head:* Pierre Moreau, Dean, 514-343-6440, Fax: 514-343-2102, E-mail: pierre.moreau@umontreal.edu. *Application contact:* Daniel Lamontagne, Associate Dean for Graduate Studies, 514-343-6467, Fax: 514-343-2102, E-mail: daniel.lamontagne@umontreal.ca.

Université Laval, Faculty of Pharmacy, Program in Hospital Pharmacy, Québec, QC G1K 7P4, Canada. Offers M Sc. *Entrance requirements:* For master's, knowledge of French, interview. Electronic applications accepted.

Université Laval, Faculty of Pharmacy, Programs in Community Pharmacy, Québec, QC G1K 7P4, Canada. Offers DESS. Part-time programs available. *Entrance requirements:* For degree, knowledge of French. Electronic applications accepted.

Université Laval, Faculty of Pharmacy, Programs in Pharmacy, Québec, QC G1K 7P4, Canada. Offers M Sc, PhD. Part-time programs available. Terminal master's awarded for partial completion of doctoral program. *Degree requirements:* For master's, thesis; for doctorate, comprehensive exam, thesis/dissertation. *Entrance requirements:* For master's and doctorate, knowledge of French. Electronic applications accepted.

University at Buffalo, the State University of New York, Graduate School, School of Pharmacy and Pharmaceutical Sciences, Department of Pharmaceutical Sciences, Buffalo, NY 14260. Offers MS, PhD, Pharm D/MS. Postbaccalaureate distance learning degree programs offered (minimal on-campus study). *Faculty:* 17 full-time (4 women), 2 part-time/adjunct (0

Pharmaceutical Sciences

University at Buffalo, the State University of New York (continued)
women). *Students:* 28 full-time (16 women), 29 part-time (16 women); includes 9 minority (2 African Americans, 7 Asian Americans or Pacific Islanders), 34 international. Average age 27. 266 applicants, 7% accepted, 17 enrolled. In 2009, 5 master's, 6 doctorates awarded. Terminal master's awarded for partial completion of doctoral program. *Degree requirements:* For master's, comprehensive exam (for some programs), thesis optional, project; for doctorate, comprehensive exam, thesis/dissertation. *Entrance requirements:* For master's, GRE, BS, B Eng, or Pharm D; for doctorate, GRE, BS, MS, B Eng, M Eng, or Pharm D. Additional exam requirements/recommendations for international students: Required—TOEFL (minimum score 550 paper-based; 213 computer-based; 79 iBT). *Application deadline:* For fall admission, 2/15 for domestic and international students. Applications are processed on a rolling basis. Application fee: $50. Electronic applications accepted. *Financial support:* In 2009–10, 37 students received support, including 37 research assistantships with full tuition reimbursements available (averaging $23,500 per year); health care benefits and unspecified assistantships also available. Financial award application deadline: 3/1; financial award applicants required to submit FAFSA. *Faculty research:* Pharmacokinetics, biopharmaceutics, drug delivery systems, pharmacodynamics, drug metabolism and analysis. *Unit head:* Dr. William J. Jusko, Chair, 716-645-2855 Ext. 225, Fax: 716-645-3693, E-mail: wjjusko@acsu.buffalo.edu. *Application contact:* Dr. Murali Ramanathan, Director of Graduate Studies, 716-645-4846, Fax: 716-645-3690, E-mail: murali@buffalo.edu.

University of Alberta, Faculty of Graduate Studies and Research, Department of Pharmacy and Pharmaceutical Sciences, Edmonton, AB T6G 2E1, Canada. Offers M Sc, PhD. *Faculty:* 35. *Students:* 47. Average age 30. 562 applicants, 2% accepted, 11 enrolled. In 2009, 3 master's, 5 doctorates awarded. Terminal master's awarded for partial completion of doctoral program. *Degree requirements:* For master's, thesis; for doctorate, thesis/dissertation. *Entrance requirements:* Additional exam requirements/recommendations for international students: Required—Michigan English Language Assessment Battery or IELTS. *Application deadline:* For fall admission, 6/1 for international students; for winter admission, 9/15 for international students. Applications are processed on a rolling basis. Electronic applications accepted. Tuition and fees charges are reported in Canadian dollars. *Expenses:* Tuition, area resident: Full-time $4626 Canadian dollars; part-time $99.72 Canadian dollars per unit. International tuition: $8216 Canadian dollars full-time. Required fees: $3590 Canadian dollars; $99.72 Canadian dollars per unit. $215 Canadian dollars per term. *Financial support:* In 2009–10, 13 students received support, including 6 teaching assistantships; research assistantships, tuition waivers (partial) also available. *Faculty research:* Radiopharmacy, pharmacokinetics, bionucleonics, medicinal chemistry, microbiology. Total annual research expenditures: $2 million. *Unit head:* Dr. Nathaniel Jackson. *Application contact:* Dr. Edward E. Knaus, Director of Graduate Affairs, 780-492-5993, Fax: 780-492-1217.

The University of Arizona, Graduate College, College of Pharmacy, Program in Pharmaceutical Sciences, Tucson, AZ 85721. Offers medicinal and natural products chemistry (MS, PhD); pharmaceutical economics (MS, PhD); pharmaceutics and pharmacokinetics (MS, PhD). *Faculty:* 13 full-time (2 women). *Students:* 36 full-time (20 women), 7 part-time (6 women); includes 9 minority (2 African Americans, 3 Asian Americans or Pacific Islanders, 4 Hispanic Americans), 17 international. Average age 31. 89 applicants, 13% accepted, 12 enrolled. In 2009, 1 master's, 6 doctorates awarded. *Degree requirements:* For master's, thesis; for doctorate, one foreign language, thesis/dissertation. *Entrance requirements:* For master's, GRE General Test, 3 letters of recommendation, bachelor's degree in related field; for doctorate, GRE General Test, 3 letters of recommendation, statement of purpose, bachelor's degree in related field. Additional exam requirements/recommendations for international students: Required—TOEFL (minimum score 550 paper-based; 213 computer-based; 79 iBT). *Application deadline:* For fall admission, 1/1 for domestic students, 12/1 for international students. Applications are processed on a rolling basis. Application fee: $65. Electronic applications accepted. *Expenses:* Tuition, state resident: full-time $9028. Tuition, nonresident: full-time $24,890. *Financial support:* In 2009–10, 18 research assistantships with full tuition reimbursements (averaging $20,939 per year) were awarded; scholarships/grants, health care benefits, tuition waivers (full), and unspecified assistantships also available. Financial award application deadline: 3/1. *Faculty research:* Drug design, natural products isolation, biological applications of NMR and mass spectrometry, drug formulation and delivery, pharmacokinetics. *Unit head:* Brian L. Erstad, Department Head, 520-694-5600, Fax: 520-626-4063, E-mail: erstad@pharmacy.arizona.edu. *Application contact:* Nancy F. Colbert, Information Contact, 520-626-7265, Fax: 520-626-2466, E-mail: colbert@pharmacy.arizona.edu.

University of Arkansas for Medical Sciences, College of Pharmacy, Program in Pharmaceutical Evaluation and Policy, Little Rock, AR 72205-7199. Offers MS. *Students:* 6 full-time (2 women). *Degree requirements:* For master's, thesis. *Entrance requirements:* For master's, GRE, 3 letters of recommendation, resume. Additional exam requirements/recommendations for international students: Required—TOEFL. *Application deadline:* For fall admission, 3/1 for domestic and international students. Application fee: $0. *Unit head:* Dr. Bradley C. Martin, Program Director, E-mail: bmartin@uams.edu. *Application contact:* Dr. Bradley C. Martin, Program Director, E-mail: bmartin@uams.edu.

The University of British Columbia, Faculty of Pharmaceutical Sciences, Vancouver, BC V6T 1Z3, Canada. Offers Pharm D, M Sc, PhD. *Degree requirements:* For master's, thesis, seminar; for doctorate, comprehensive exam, thesis/dissertation, seminar. *Entrance requirements:* B Sc in pharmacy, Canadian pharmacy license, interview. Additional exam requirements/recommendations for international students: Required—TOEFL (minimum score 600 paper-based; 250 computer-based; 100 iBT). Electronic applications accepted. *Faculty research:* Biopharmaceutics, pharmaceutical chemistry, pharmacology, toxicology, formulation.

University of California, San Francisco, School of Pharmacy and Graduate Division, Pharmaceutical Sciences and Pharmacogenomics Graduate Group, San Francisco, CA 94158-0775. Offers PhD. *Faculty:* 51 full-time (14 women). *Students:* 43 full-time (22 women); includes 15 minority (14 Asian Americans or Pacific Islanders, 1 Hispanic American). Average age 24. 69 applicants, 23% accepted, 6 enrolled. In 2009, 5 doctorates awarded. *Degree requirements:* For doctorate, comprehensive exam, thesis/dissertation. *Entrance requirements:* For doctorate, GRE General Test, minimum GPA of 3.0. Additional exam requirements/recommendations for international students: Required—TOEFL. *Application deadline:* For fall admission, 12/31 for domestic students. Application fee: $60 ($80 for international students). Electronic applications accepted. *Financial support:* In 2009–10, 4 fellowships with full tuition reimbursements (averaging $27,000 per year), 23 research assistantships with full tuition reimbursements (averaging $27,000 per year), 6 teaching assistantships with full tuition reimbursements (averaging $27,000 per year) were awarded; career-related internships or fieldwork, institutionally sponsored loans, scholarships/grants, traineeships, tuition waivers (full), and unspecified assistantships also available. Financial award application deadline: 4/6. *Faculty research:* Drug development, drug delivery, molecular pharmacology. *Unit head:* Francis C. Szoka, Program Director, 415-476-3895, Fax: 415-476-0688, E-mail: szoka@cgl.ucsf.edu. *Application contact:* Debbie Acoba-Idlebi, Program Coordinator, 415-476-1947, Fax: 415-476-6022, E-mail: debbie.acoba@ucsf.edu.

University of Cincinnati, College of Pharmacy, Division of Pharmaceutical Sciences, Cincinnati, OH 45221. Offers MS, PhD. *Degree requirements:* For master's, thesis; for doctorate, thesis/dissertation. *Entrance requirements:* For master's and doctorate, GRE General Test, minimum GPA of 3.0. Additional exam requirements/recommendations for international students: Required—TOEFL.

University of Colorado Denver, School of Pharmacy, Doctor of Pharmacy Program, Denver, CO 80217-3364. Offers Pharm D. *Students:* 563 full-time (346 women), 8 part-time (4 women); includes 179 minority (35 African Americans, 3 American Indian/Alaska Native, 110 Asian Americans or Pacific Islanders, 31 Hispanic Americans), 4 international. In 2009, 163 Pharm Ds awarded. *Entrance requirements:* Additional exam requirements/recommendations for international students: Required—TOEFL (minimum score 550 paper-based; 213 computer-based). Application fee: $50. Electronic applications accepted. *Financial support:* Career-related internships or fieldwork, Federal Work-Study, and institutionally sponsored loans available. Support available to part-time students. Financial award application deadline: 3/15; financial award applicants required to submit FAFSA. *Faculty research:* Mechanistic studies of viral assembly, synthetic gene delivery systems for use in gene therapy, mechanisms of toxicity, pulmonary drug delivery. *Application contact:* Jackie Milowski, Information Contact, 303-724-7263, E-mail: jackie.milowski@ucdenver.edu.

University of Connecticut, Graduate School, School of Pharmacy, Department of Pharmaceutical Sciences, Program in Pharmaceutics, Storrs, CT 06269. Offers MS, PhD. *Faculty:* 10 full-time (2 women). *Students:* 19 full-time (12 women), 2 part-time (both women); includes 3 minority (2 Asian Americans or Pacific Islanders, 1 Hispanic American), 15 international. Average age 28. 86 applicants, 3% accepted, 3 enrolled. In 2009, 6 doctorates awarded. Terminal master's awarded for partial completion of doctoral program. *Degree requirements:* For master's, comprehensive exam, thesis; for doctorate, thesis/dissertation. *Entrance requirements:* For master's and doctorate, GRE General Test. Additional exam requirements/recommendations for international students: Required—TOEFL (minimum score 550 paper-based; 213 computer-based). *Application deadline:* For fall admission, 2/1 priority date for domestic and international students; for spring admission, 11/1 for domestic students, 10/1 for international students. Applications are processed on a rolling basis. Application fee: $55. Electronic applications accepted. *Expenses:* Tuition, state resident: full-time $4725; part-time $525 per credit. Tuition, nonresident: full-time $12,267; part-time $1363 per credit. Required fees: $346 per semester. Tuition and fees vary according to course load. *Financial support:* In 2009–10, 12 research assistantships with full tuition reimbursements, 7 teaching assistantships with full tuition reimbursements were awarded; fellowships, Federal Work-Study, scholarships/grants, health care benefits, and unspecified assistantships also available. Financial award application deadline: 2/1; financial award applicants required to submit FAFSA. *Unit head:* Robin Bogner, Chairperson, 860-486-2136, Fax: 860-486-4998, E-mail: robin.bogner@uconn.edu. *Application contact:* Leslie Lebel, Administrative Assistant, 860-486-4066, Fax: 860-486-4998, E-mail: leslie.lebel@uconn.edu.

University of Florida, College of Pharmacy and Graduate School, Graduate Programs in Pharmacy, Department of Pharmaceutics, Gainesville, FL 32611. Offers pharmaceutical sciences (PhD). *Degree requirements:* For doctorate, thesis/dissertation. *Entrance requirements:* For doctorate, GRE General Test, minimum GPA of 3.0. Additional exam requirements/recommendations for international students: Required—TOEFL. Electronic applications accepted.

University of Florida, College of Pharmacy and Graduate School, Graduate Programs in Pharmacy, Department of Pharmacy Practice, Gainesville, FL 32611. Offers clinical pharmaceutical sciences (PhD).

University of Georgia, College of Pharmacy, Graduate Programs in Pharmacy, Athens, GA 30602. Offers clinical trials design and management (Certificate); pharmacy (MS, PhD); pharmacy and biomedical regulatory affairs (Certificate). *Faculty:* 21 full-time (6 women), 3 part-time/adjunct (0 women). *Students:* 38 full-time (23 women), 11 part-time (8 women); includes 10 minority (7 African Americans, 3 Asian Americans or Pacific Islanders), 22 international. Average age 25. 51 applicants, 45% accepted, 14 enrolled. In 2009, 3 master's, 7 doctorates awarded. Terminal master's awarded for partial completion of doctoral program. *Degree requirements:* For master's, thesis; for doctorate, comprehensive exam, thesis/dissertation. *Entrance requirements:* For master's and doctorate, GRE General Test, minimum GPA of 3.0. Additional exam requirements/recommendations for international students: Required—TOEFL (minimum score 550 paper-based; 213 computer-based). *Application deadline:* For fall admission, 5/15 for domestic students; for spring admission, 10/15 for domestic students. Application fee: $50. Electronic applications accepted. *Expenses:* Tuition, state resident: full-time $6000; part-time $250 per credit hour. Tuition, nonresident: full-time $20,904; part-time $871 per credit hour. Required fees: $730 per semester. *Financial support:* In 2009–10, 14 teaching assistantships (averaging $11,509 per year) were awarded; tuition waivers (full) and unspecified assistantships also available. Financial award application deadline: 2/15. *Faculty research:* Pharmacy care administration, pharmacoeconomics, cardiovascular therapeutics, central nervous system therapeutics, drug use in populations.

University of Georgia, College of Pharmacy, Program in Pharmaceutical and Biomedical Regulatory Affairs, Athens, GA 30602. Offers Certificate. *Faculty:* 18 full-time (4 women), 2 part-time/adjunct (0 women). *Students:* 2 full-time (1 woman), both international. 13 applicants, 77% accepted. Application fee: $50. *Expenses:* Tuition, state resident: full-time $6000; part-time $250 per credit hour. Tuition, nonresident: full-time $20,904; part-time $871 per credit hour. Required fees: $730 per semester. *Unit head:* Dr. Paul Brooks, Head, 706-542-5343, Fax: 706-542-5285, E-mail: pbrooks@rx.uga.edu. *Application contact:* Dr. Paul Brooks, Head, 706-542-5343, Fax: 706-542-5285, E-mail: pbrooks@rx.uga.edu.

University of Illinois at Chicago, College of Pharmacy and Graduate College, Graduate Programs in Pharmacy, Chicago, IL 60607-7128. Offers biopharmaceutical sciences (PhD); forensic science (MS); medicinal chemistry (MS, PhD); pharmacognosy (MS, PhD); pharmacy administration (MS, PhD). Terminal master's awarded for partial completion of doctoral program. *Degree requirements:* For master's, variable foreign language requirement, thesis; for doctorate, variable foreign language requirement, thesis/dissertation. *Entrance requirements:* For master's and doctorate, GRE General Test. Additional exam requirements/recommendations for international students: Required—TOEFL. Electronic applications accepted. *Expenses:* Contact institution.

The University of Kansas, Graduate Studies, School of Pharmacy, Department of Pharmacy Practice, Lawrence, KS 66045. Offers MS. *Faculty:* 5 full-time (2 women), 13 part-time/adjunct (8 women). *Students:* 4 full-time (2 women), 3 part-time (2 women), 1 international. Average age 27. 2 applicants, 100% accepted, 2 enrolled. In 2009, 3 master's awarded. *Degree requirements:* For master's, thesis. *Entrance requirements:* For master's, GRE General Test, Pharm D, Kansas pharmacy license, ASHP Resident Matching Program. *Application deadline:* For fall admission, 2/1 priority date for domestic students. Application fee: $45 ($55 for international students). Electronic applications accepted. *Expenses:* Tuition, state resident: full-time $6492; part-time $270.50 per credit hour. Tuition, nonresident: full-time $15,510; part-time $646.25 per credit hour. Required fees: $847; $70.56 per credit hour. Tuition and fees vary according to course load and program. *Financial support:* Fellowships with partial tuition reimbursements, health care benefits and residencies available. Financial award application deadline: 2/15. *Faculty research:* Drug trials, drug stability, pharmacoeconomics, education, outcomes. *Unit head:* Dr. Dennis W. Grauer, Graduate Director, 785-864-3262, Fax: 785-864-2399, E-mail: dgrauer@kumc.edu. *Application contact:* Dr. Dennis W. Grauer, Graduate Director, 785-864-3262, Fax: 785-864-2399, E-mail: dgrauer@kumc.edu.

University of Kentucky, Graduate School, Graduate Programs in Pharmaceutical Sciences, Lexington, KY 40506-0032. Offers MS, PhD. *Faculty:* 47 full-time (14 women), 9 part-time/adjunct (2 women). *Students:* 74 full-time (45 women); includes 11 minority (4 African Americans, 6 Asian Americans or Pacific Islanders, 1 Hispanic American), 39 international. Average age 28. 216 applicants, 6% accepted, 13 enrolled. In 2009, 14 doctorates awarded. Terminal master's awarded for partial completion of doctoral program. *Degree requirements:* For master's, thesis optional; for doctorate, comprehensive exam, thesis/dissertation. *Entrance requirements:* For master's, GRE General Test, minimum undergraduate GPA of 3.2; for doctorate, GRE General Test, minimum graduate GPA of 3.2. Additional exam requirements/recommendations for international students: Required—TOEFL (minimum score 550 paper-based; 213 computer-based; 79 iBT). *Application deadline:* For fall admission, 1/14 priority date for domestic students, 2/1 priority date for international students. Applications are processed on a rolling basis. Application fee: $50 ($65 for international students). Electronic applications accepted. *Financial support:* In 2009–10, 68 students received support, including 11 fellowships with full tuition reimbursements available (averaging $20,000 per year), 42 research assistantships with full tuition reimbursements available (averaging $20,000 per year), 15 teaching assistantships with full tuition reimbursements available (averaging $20,000 per year). *Faculty research:* Drug development, biotechnology, medicinal chemistry, cardiology, pharmacokinetics, CNS pharmacology, clinical pharmacology, pharmacotherapy and health outcomes, pharmaceutical

policy. Total annual research expenditures: $19.9 million. *Unit head:* Dr. Robert Yokel, Director of Graduate Studies, 859-257-4855, Fax: 859-257-7585, E-mail: ryokel@email.uky.edu. *Application contact:* Catina Rossoll, Graduate Program Student Affairs Coordinator, 859-257-1998, Fax: 859-257-7564, E-mail: cross2@email.uky.edu.

University of Louisiana at Monroe, Graduate School, College of Pharmacy, Program in Pharmaceutical Sciences, Monroe, LA 71209-0001. Offers MS. *Students:* 2 full-time (0 women), both international. Average age 24. *Entrance requirements:* For master's, GRE General Test or GMAT, minimum GPA of 2.5. Additional exam requirements/recommendations for international students: Required—TOEFL (minimum score 500 paper-based; 173 computer-based; 61 iBT). *Application deadline:* For fall admission, 8/24 for domestic students, 7/1 for international students; for winter admission, 12/14 for domestic students; for spring admission, 1/19 for domestic students, 11/1 for international students. Applications are processed on a rolling basis. Application fee: $20 ($30 for international students). Electronic applications accepted. *Expenses:* Tuition, state resident: part-time $159 per credit hour. Tuition, nonresident: part-time $159 per credit hour. Required fees: $1300 per year. Tuition and fees vary according to course load. *Financial support:* Federal Work-Study and unspecified assistantships available. Financial award application deadline: 4/1; financial award applicants required to submit FAFSA. *Unit head:* Dr. Karen Briski, Interim Head, 318-342-3283, E-mail: briski@ulm.edu. *Application contact:* Dr. Karen Briski, Interim Head, 318-342-3283, E-mail: briski@ulm.edu.

University of Manitoba, Faculty of Graduate Studies, Faculty of Pharmacy, Winnipeg, MB R3T 2N2, Canada. Offers M Sc, PhD. *Degree requirements:* For master's, one foreign language, thesis.

University of Maryland, Baltimore, Graduate School, Graduate Programs in Pharmacy, Department of Pharmaceutical Sciences, Baltimore, MD 21201. Offers PhD. *Degree requirements:* For doctorate, comprehensive exam, thesis/dissertation. *Entrance requirements:* For doctorate, GRE General Test. Additional exam requirements/recommendations for international students: Required—TOEFL (minimum score 600 paper-based; 260 computer-based), IELTS. Electronic applications accepted. *Expenses:* Tuition, state resident: full-time $7290; part-time $405 per credit hour. Tuition, nonresident: full-time $12,780; part-time $710 per credit hour. Required fees: $774; $10 per credit hour. $297 per semester. Tuition and fees vary according to course load, degree level and program. *Faculty research:* Drug delivery, cellular and biological chemistry, clinical pharmaceutical sciences, biopharmaceutics, neuroscience.

University of Michigan, College of Pharmacy and Horace H. Rackham School of Graduate Studies, Department of Pharmaceutical Sciences, Ann Arbor, MI 48109. Offers PhD. Terminal master's awarded for partial completion of doctoral program. *Degree requirements:* For doctorate, oral defense of dissertation, preliminary exam. *Entrance requirements:* For doctorate, GRE General Test. Additional exam requirements/recommendations for international students: Required—TOEFL or IELTS. Electronic applications accepted. *Expenses:* Tuition, state resident: full-time $17,286; part-time $1099 per credit hour. Tuition, nonresident: full-time $34,944; part-time $2080 per credit hour. Required fees: $95 per semester. Tuition and fees vary according to course load, degree level and program. *Faculty research:* New drug design, new drug delivery systems, new biotechnology, pharmacy and the public sector.

University of Minnesota, Twin Cities Campus, College of Pharmacy and Graduate School, Graduate Programs in Pharmacy, Graduate Program in Pharmaceutics, Minneapolis, MN 55455-0213. Offers PhD. Terminal master's awarded for partial completion of doctoral program. *Degree requirements:* For doctorate, thesis/dissertation. *Entrance requirements:* For doctorate, GRE General Test, BS in biology, biomedical engineering, chemical engineering, chemistry, pharmacy, or other science. Additional exam requirements/recommendations for international students: Required—TOEFL. *Faculty research:* Molecular biopharmaceutics, pharmacokinetics, drug delivery, drug metabolism, pharmacodynamics, crystal engineering, biophysical chemistry.

University of Minnesota, Twin Cities Campus, College of Pharmacy and Graduate School, Graduate Programs in Pharmacy, Graduate Program in Social, Administrative and Clinical Pharmacy, Minneapolis, MN 55455-0213. Offers experimental and clinical pharmacology (MS, PhD); social and administrative pharmacy (MS, PhD). *Degree requirements:* For master's, thesis (for some programs); for doctorate, thesis/dissertation. *Entrance requirements:* For master's, GRE General Test, BS in science; for doctorate, GRE General Test. Additional exam requirements/recommendations for international students: Required—TOEFL. *Faculty research:* Pharmaceutical economics, pharmaceutical policy, pharmaceutical social/behavioral sciences.

University of Mississippi, Graduate School, School of Pharmacy, Graduate Programs in Pharmacy, Oxford, University, MS 38677. Offers medicinal chemistry (PhD); pharmaceutical sciences (MS); pharmaceutics (PhD); pharmacognosy (PhD); pharmacology (PhD); pharmacy administration (PhD). *Faculty:* 32 full-time (9 women), 8 part-time/adjunct (5 women). *Students:* 84 full-time (37 women), 8 part-time (6 women); includes 6 minority (3 African Americans, 2 Asian Americans or Pacific Islanders, 1 Hispanic American), 64 international. In 2009, 2 master's, 12 doctorates awarded. *Unit head:* Dr. Barbara G. Wells, Dean, 662-915-7265, Fax: 662-915-5704, E-mail: pharmacy@olemiss.edu. *Application contact:* Dr. Christy M. Wyandt, Associate Dean, 662-915-7474, Fax: 662-915-7577, E-mail: cwyandt@olemiss.edu.

University of Missouri–Kansas City, School of Pharmacy, Kansas City, MO 64110-2499. Offers pharmaceutical sciences (MS, PhD); pharmacy (Pharm D). *Accreditation:* ACPE (one or more programs are accredited). Postbaccalaureate distance learning degree programs offered (minimal on-campus study). *Faculty:* 49 full-time (23 women), 8 part-time/adjunct (3 women). *Students:* 339 full-time (210 women), 2 part-time (1 woman); includes 46 minority (10 African Americans, 1 American Indian/Alaska Native, 32 Asian Americans or Pacific Islanders, 3 Hispanic Americans), 7 international. Average age 26. 599 applicants, 26% accepted, 114 enrolled. In 2009, 70 first professional degrees, 1 master's awarded. *Degree requirements:* For master's, comprehensive exam (for some programs), thesis. *Entrance requirements:* For Pharm D, PCAT, interview, minimum GPA of 2.5, specified pre-pharmacy course work; for master's, GRE General Test, minimum undergraduate GPA of 3.0, graduate 3.5, 3 letters of reference. Additional exam requirements/recommendations for international students: Required—TOEFL (minimum score 550 paper-based; 213 computer-based; 80 iBT). *Application deadline:* For fall admission, 12/5 for domestic students, 12/15 for international students; for spring admission, 10/1 for domestic students. Applications are processed on a rolling basis. Application fee: $45 ($50 for international students). Electronic applications accepted. *Expenses:* Contact institution. *Financial support:* In 2009–10, 39 research assistantships with full and partial tuition reimbursements (averaging $9,397 per year), 18 teaching assistantships with full tuition reimbursements (averaging $11,300 per year) were awarded; career-related internships or fieldwork, Federal Work-Study, institutionally sponsored loans, tuition waivers (full and partial), and unspecified assistantships also available. Financial award application deadline: 3/1; financial award applicants required to submit FAFSA. *Faculty research:* Bio-organic and medicinal chemistry, drug delivery, pharmaceutics, molecular neurobiology, neurology. Total annual research expenditures: $1.4 million. *Unit head:* Dr. Robert W. Piepho, Dean, 816-235-1609, Fax: 816-235-5190, E-mail: piephor@umkc.edu. *Application contact:* Shelly M. Janasz, Director, Student Services, 816-235-2400, Fax: 816-235-5190, E-mail: janaszs@umkc.edu.

The University of Montana, Graduate School, College of Health Professions and Biomedical Sciences, Skaggs School of Pharmacy, Department of Biomedical and Pharmaceutical Sciences, Missoula, MT 59812-0002. Offers biomedical sciences (PhD); neuroscience (MS, PhD); pharmaceutical sciences (MS); toxicology (MS, PhD). *Accreditation:* ACPE. *Degree requirements:* For master's, oral defense of thesis; for doctorate, research dissertation defense. *Entrance requirements:* For master's and doctorate, GRE General Test. Additional exam requirements/recommendations for international students: Required—TOEFL (minimum score 540 paper-based; 210 computer-based). Electronic applications accepted. *Faculty research:* Cardiovascular pharmacology, medicinal chemistry, neurosciences, environmental toxicology, pharmacogenetics, cancer.

University of Nebraska Medical Center, Graduate Studies, Department of Pharmaceutical Sciences, Omaha, NE 68198. Offers MS, PhD. Terminal master's awarded for partial completion of doctoral program. *Degree requirements:* For master's, thesis; for doctorate, comprehensive exam, thesis/dissertation. *Entrance requirements:* For master's, GRE General Test; for doctorate, GRE. Additional exam requirements/recommendations for international students: Required—TOEFL (minimum score 550 paper-based; 213 computer-based). Electronic applications accepted. *Faculty research:* Pharmaceutics, medicinal chemistry, toxicology, chemical carcinogenesis, pharmacokinetics.

University of New Mexico, Graduate School, College of Pharmacy, Graduate Programs in Pharmaceutical Sciences, Albuquerque, NM 87131-2039. Offers MS, PhD. Part-time programs available. *Faculty:* 49 full-time (28 women), 2 part-time/adjunct (both women). *Students:* 5 full-time (1 woman), 8 part-time (5 women); includes 1 minority (Hispanic American), 8 international. Average age 32. 51 applicants, 12% accepted, 4 enrolled. *Degree requirements:* For master's, comprehensive exam, thesis; for doctorate, comprehensive exam, thesis/dissertation. *Entrance requirements:* For master's and doctorate, GRE General Test (for some concentrations), 3 letters of recommendation, letter of intent, resume. Additional exam requirements/recommendations for international students: Required—TOEFL (minimum score 580 paper-based; 237 computer-based; 93 iBT). *Application deadline:* For fall admission, 2/1 for domestic students. Application fee: $50. Electronic applications accepted. *Expenses:* Tuition, state resident: full-time $2099; part-time $233.20 per credit hour. Tuition, nonresident: full-time $6650. Required fees: $25 per semester. Tuition and fees vary according to course load, program and reciprocity agreements. *Financial support:* In 2009–10, 3 students received support, including 10 research assistantships (averaging $23,000 per year); health care benefits and residencies also available. Financial award application deadline: 3/1; financial award applicants required to submit FAFSA. *Faculty research:* Pharmaceutical research, cancer research, pharmacy administration, radiopharmacy, toxicology. Total annual research expenditures: $2 million. *Unit head:* Donald Godwin, Assistant Dean for Professional and Graduate Education, 505-272-3241, Fax: 505-272-5782, E-mail: dgodwin@salud.unm.edu. *Application contact:* Krystal McCutchen, Supervisor, Student Advisement, 505-272-3241, Fax: 505-272-5782, E-mail: kweaver@salud.unm.edu.

The University of North Carolina at Chapel Hill, Eshelman School of Pharmacy, Chapel Hill, NC 27599. Offers MS, PhD. *Accreditation:* ACPE (one or more programs are accredited). Part-time programs available. Postbaccalaureate distance learning degree programs offered (minimal on-campus study). Terminal master's awarded for partial completion of doctoral program. *Degree requirements:* For master's, comprehensive exam, thesis; for doctorate, comprehensive exam, thesis/dissertation. *Entrance requirements:* For master's and doctorate, GRE General Test, minimum GPA of 3.0. Additional exam requirements/recommendations for international students: Required—TOEFL (minimum score 550 paper-based; 213 computer-based). Electronic applications accepted. *Faculty research:* Health services research, pharmacokinetics, molecular modeling, infectious disease, genomics/proteomics, translational research.

University of Oklahoma Health Sciences Center, College of Pharmacy and Graduate College, Graduate Programs in Pharmacy, Oklahoma City, OK 73190. Offers MS, PhD, MS/MBA. *Faculty:* 9 full-time (1 woman), 1 part-time/adjunct (0 women). *Students:* 3 full-time (2 women), 15 part-time (7 women); includes 1 minority (Asian American or Pacific Islander), 5 international. Average age 32. 25 applicants, 8% accepted, 2 enrolled. In 2009, 3 master's awarded. Terminal master's awarded for partial completion of doctoral program. *Degree requirements:* For master's, comprehensive exam, thesis; for doctorate, comprehensive exam, thesis/dissertation. *Entrance requirements:* For master's and doctorate, GRE General Test. Additional exam requirements/recommendations for international students: Required—TOEFL. *Application deadline:* For fall admission, 4/1 priority date for domestic students. Application fee: $50. *Expenses:* Tuition, state resident: full-time $3120; part-time $156 per credit hour. Tuition, nonresident: full-time $11,314; part-time $409.70 per credit hour. Required fees: $1471; $51.20 per credit hour. $223.25 per term. *Financial support:* In 2009–10, 9 research assistantships (averaging $17,000 per year) were awarded; fellowships, teaching assistantships, career-related internships or fieldwork and institutionally sponsored loans also available. *Faculty research:* Medicinal chemistry, pharmacokinetics/biopharmaceutics, nuclear pharmacy, pharmacy administration, pharmacodynamics and toxicology. *Unit head:* Dr. Lester Reinke, Graduate Liaison, 405-271-6598, E-mail: lester-reinke@ouhsc.edu. *Application contact:* Dr. Keith Swanson, Director of Student Services, 405-271-6598, E-mail: keith-swanson@ouhsc.edu.

University of Pittsburgh, School of Pharmacy, Department of Pharmaceutical Sciences, Pittsburgh, PA 15260. Offers MS, PhD. *Faculty:* 79 full-time (37 women), 84 part-time/adjunct (39 women). *Students:* 31 full-time (12 women), 1 part-time (0 women); includes 4 minority (2 African Americans, 1 American Indian/Alaska Native, 1 Asian American or Pacific Islander), 17 international. Average age 30. 174 applicants, 6% accepted, 8 enrolled. In 2009, 1 master's, 2 doctorates awarded. Terminal master's awarded for partial completion of doctoral program. *Degree requirements:* For master's, comprehensive exam, thesis; for doctorate, comprehensive exam, thesis/dissertation. *Entrance requirements:* For master's and doctorate, GRE General Test. Additional exam requirements/recommendations for international students: Required—TOEFL (minimum score 550 paper-based; 215 computer-based; 80 iBT). *Application deadline:* For fall admission, 3/31 priority date for domestic and international students. Applications are processed on a rolling basis. Application fee: $50. Electronic applications accepted. *Expenses:* Contact institution. *Financial support:* In 2009–10, 3 fellowships with full tuition reimbursements (averaging $18,000 per year), 9 research assistantships with full tuition reimbursements (averaging $15,675 per year), 14 teaching assistantships with full tuition reimbursements (averaging $15,675 per year) were awarded; Federal Work-Study, institutionally sponsored loans, and health care benefits also available. Financial award application deadline: 9/1. *Faculty research:* Drug delivery and targeting, neuroendocrine pharmacology, genomics, proteomics and drug discovery, clinical pharmaceutical sciences. Total annual research expenditures: $7.8 million. *Unit head:* Dr. M. Maggie Folan, Chair, Graduate Program Council, 412-648-8555, Fax: 412-383-9996, E-mail: folanm@pitt.edu. *Application contact:* Robie Gosney, Program Coordinator, 412-383-9000, Fax: 412-383-9996, E-mail: rog8@pitt.edu.

University of Puerto Rico, Medical Sciences Campus, School of Pharmacy, San Juan, PR 00936-5067. Offers industrial pharmacy (MS); pharmaceutical sciences (MS); pharmacy (Pharm D). The MS in Pharmacy program is not admitting students in the academic year 2010-2011. *Accreditation:* ACPE. Part-time and evening/weekend programs available. *Degree requirements:* For master's, thesis; for Pharm D, portfolio, research project. *Entrance requirements:* For Pharm D, PCAT, interview; for master's, GRE, interview. Electronic applications accepted. *Expenses:* Contact institution. *Faculty research:* Controlled release, solid dosage form, screening of anti-HIV drugs, pharmacokinetic/pharmacodynamic of drugs.

University of Rhode Island, Graduate School, College of Pharmacy, Department of Biomedical and Pharmaceutical Sciences, Kingston, RI 02881. Offers medicinal chemistry and pharmacognosy (MS, PhD); pharmaceutics and pharmacokinetics (MS, PhD); pharmacology and toxicology (MS, PhD). Part-time programs available. *Faculty:* 17 full-time (5 women), 1 part-time/adjunct (0 women). *Students:* 33 full-time (16 women), 20 part-time (7 women); includes 12 minority (2 African Americans, 10 Asian Americans or Pacific Islanders), 19 international. In 2009, 6 master's, 6 doctorates awarded. *Entrance requirements:* For master's and doctorate, GRE, 2 letters of recommendation. Additional exam requirements/recommendations for international students: Required—TOEFL (minimum score 550 paper-based; 213 computer-based). Application fee: $65. Electronic applications accepted. *Expenses:* Tuition, state resident: full-time $8828; part-time $490 per credit hour. Tuition, nonresident: full-time $22,100; part-time $1228 per credit hour. Required fees: $1118; $57 per semester. Tuition and fees vary according to program. *Financial support:* In 2009–10, 6 research assistantships with partial tuition reimbursements (averaging $7,119 per year), 12 teaching assistantships with full and partial tuition reimbursements (averaging $10,115 per year) were awarded. Financial award applicants required to submit FAFSA. *Faculty research:* Chemical carcinogenesis with a major emphasis on the structural and synthetic aspects of DNA-adduct formation, drug-drug/herb interaction, drug-genetic interaction, signaling of nuclear receptors, transcriptional regulation, oncogenesis. Total annual research expenditures: $6.2 million. *Unit head:* Dr. Clinton O. Chichester, Chair,

Pharmaceutical Sciences

University of Rhode Island (continued)
401-874-5034, Fax: 401-874-5787, E-mail: chichester@uri.edu. *Application contact:* Dr. David C. Rowley, Graduate Coordinator, 401-874-9228, Fax: 401-874-2516, E-mail: drowley@uri.edu.

University of Rhode Island, Graduate School, College of Pharmacy, Department of Pharmacy Practice, Kingston, RI 02881. Offers pharmaceutical sciences (MS, PhD), including pharmacoepidemiology and pharmacoeconomics; MS/PhD; PhD/MBA. *Accreditation:* ACPE. *Faculty:* 24 full-time (18 women). *Students:* 602 full-time (358 women), 1 part-time (0 women); includes 71 minority (11 African Americans, 51 Asian Americans or Pacific Islanders, 9 Hispanic Americans), 16 international. *Entrance requirements:* For master's and doctorate, 2 letters of recommendation. Additional exam requirements/recommendations for international students: Required—TOEFL (minimum score 550 paper-based; 213 computer-based). Application fee: $65. Electronic applications accepted. *Expenses:* Tuition, state resident: full-time $8828; part-time $490 per credit hour. Tuition, nonresident: full-time $22,100; part-time $1228 per credit hour. Required fees: $1118; $57 per semester. Tuition and fees vary according to program. *Financial support:* Applicants required to submit FAFSA. *Faculty research:* Treatment, virulence inhibition (toxin and biofilm), colonization and control of methicillin-resistant Staphylococcus aureus (MRSA); investigating activity of catheter lock solutions against biofilm producing bacteria. Total annual research expenditures: $507,319. *Unit head:* Dr. Stephen Kogut, Chair, 401-874-5370, Fax: 401-874-2181, E-mail: kogut@uri.edu. *Application contact:* Dr. Stephen Kogut, Chair, 401-874-5370, Fax: 401-874-2181, E-mail: kogut@uri.edu.

University of Saskatchewan, College of Graduate Studies and Research, College of Pharmacy and Nutrition, Saskatoon, SK S7N 5A2, Canada. Offers M Sc, PhD. *Degree requirements:* For master's, thesis; for doctorate, thesis/dissertation. *Entrance requirements:* Additional exam requirements/recommendations for international students: Required—TOEFL. Tuition and fees charges are reported in Canadian dollars. *Expenses:* Tuition, area resident: Full-time $3000 Canadian dollars; part-time $500 Canadian dollars per term. Required fees: $700 Canadian dollars; $100 Canadian dollars per term.

University of South Carolina, South Carolina College of Pharmacy and The Graduate School, Department of Basic Pharmaceutical Sciences, Columbia, SC 29208. Offers MS, PhD. Part-time programs available. Terminal master's awarded for partial completion of doctoral program. *Degree requirements:* For master's, one foreign language, comprehensive exam, thesis; for doctorate, one foreign language, comprehensive exam, thesis/dissertation. *Entrance requirements:* For master's, GRE General Test, BS in biology, chemistry, pharmacy, or related field; for doctorate, GRE General Test, BS in biology, chemistry, or related field. Additional exam requirements/recommendations for international students: Required—TOEFL. Electronic applications accepted. *Faculty research:* Cancer treatment and prevention, Ion channels, DNA damage repair, inflammation.

University of Southern California, Graduate School, School of Pharmacy, Department of Pharmaceutical Economics and Policy, Los Angeles, CA 90089. Offers MS, PhD. *Faculty:* 7 full-time (1 woman), 1 (woman) part-time/adjunct. *Students:* 25 full-time (17 women); includes 11 minority (10 Asian Americans or Pacific Islanders, 1 Hispanic American), 9 international. In 2009, 1 master's, 4 doctorates awarded. Terminal master's awarded for partial completion of doctoral program. *Degree requirements:* For master's, comprehensive exam; for doctorate, thesis/dissertation, 64 units of coursework (excluding seminar and research courses). *Entrance requirements:* For master's and doctorate, GRE. Additional exam requirements/recommendations for international students: Required—TOEFL (minimum score 603 paper-based; 250 computer-based; 100 iBT). *Application deadline:* For fall admission, 1/15 for domestic and international students; for spring admission, 10/15 for domestic and international students. Application fee: $75. Electronic applications accepted. *Expenses:* Tuition: Full-time $25,980; part-time $1315 per unit. Required fees: $554. One-time fee: $35 full-time. Full-time tuition and fees vary according to degree level and program. *Financial support:* In 2009–10, 24 students received support, including 2 fellowships with full tuition reimbursements available (averaging $28,565 per year), 13 research assistantships (averaging $30,144 per year), 9 teaching assistantships with full tuition reimbursements available (averaging $29,400 per year); health care benefits also available. *Faculty research:* Cost-effective analyses/modeling, retrospective data analysis of comparative effectiveness, quality of life measurement, competitive pricing systems in health care. *Unit head:* Dr. Kathleen Johnson, Professor and Department Chair, 323-442-1393, E-mail: rbjones@usc.edu. *Application contact:* Wade Thompson-Harper, Coordinator of Graduate Affairs, 323-442-1474, E-mail: wharper@usc.edu.

See Close-Up on page 1797.

University of Southern California, Graduate School, School of Pharmacy, Department of Pharmaceutical Sciences, Los Angeles, CA 90089. Offers pharmacology and pharmaceutical sciences (MS, PhD). *Faculty:* 19 full-time (4 women), 4 part-time/adjunct (2 women). *Students:* 40 full-time (19 women); includes 7 minority (4 Asian Americans or Pacific Islanders, 3 Hispanic Americans), 24 international. 123 applicants, 12% accepted, 10 enrolled. In 2009, 3 master's, 4 doctorates awarded. *Degree requirements:* For master's, thesis; for doctorate, thesis/dissertation, 24 units of formal course work (excluding research and seminar courses). *Entrance requirements:* For master's and doctorate, GRE. Additional exam requirements/recommendations for international students: Required—TOEFL (minimum score 603 paper-based; 250 computer-based; 100 iBT). *Application deadline:* For fall admission, 1/15 for domestic and international students; for spring admission, 10/15 for domestic and international students. Application fee: $75. Electronic applications accepted. *Expenses:* Tuition: Full-time $25,980; part-time $1315 per unit. Required fees: $554. One-time fee: $35 full-time. Full-time tuition and fees vary according to degree level and program. *Financial support:* In 2009–10, 27 students received support, including 3 fellowships with full tuition reimbursements available (averaging $28,656 per year), 11 research assistantships with full tuition reimbursements available (averaging $30,144 per year), 13 teaching assistantships with full tuition reimbursements available (averaging $29,400 per year); health care benefits also available. *Faculty research:* Drug design, drug delivery, pharmaceutical sciences. *Unit head:* Dr. Sarah Hamm-Alvarez, Associate Dean and Department Chair, 323-442-3269, E-mail: gongora@usc.edu. *Application contact:* Wade Thompson-Harper, Coordinator of Graduate Affairs, 323-442-1474, E-mail: pharmgrad@usc.edu.

See Close-Up on page 1797.

University of Southern California, Graduate School, School of Pharmacy, Regulatory Science Programs, Los Angeles, CA 90089. Offers clinical research design and management (Graduate Certificate); food safety (Graduate Certificate); patient and product safety (Graduate Certificate); preclinical drug development (Graduate Certificate); regulatory and clinical affairs (Graduate Certificate); regulatory science (MS, DRSc). Part-time and evening/weekend programs available. Postbaccalaureate distance learning degree programs offered (minimal on-campus study). *Faculty:* 6 full-time (2 women), 7 part-time/adjunct (5 women). *Students:* 23 full-time (11 women), 80 part-time (52 women); includes 38 minority (7 African Americans, 1 American Indian/Alaska Native, 25 Asian Americans or Pacific Islanders, 5 Hispanic Americans), 19 international. 57 applicants, 54% accepted, 31 enrolled. In 2009, 32 master's, 28 other advanced degrees awarded. Terminal master's awarded for partial completion of doctoral program. *Degree requirements:* For master's, thesis optional; for doctorate, comprehensive exam, thesis/dissertation. *Entrance requirements:* For master's, GRE. Additional exam requirements/recommendations for international students: Required—TOEFL (minimum score 250 computer-based; 100 iBT). *Application deadline:* For fall admission, 6/15 priority date for domestic and international students; for winter admission, 2/15 priority date for domestic and international students; for spring admission, 10/15 priority date for domestic and international students. Application fee: $85. Electronic applications accepted. *Expenses:* Tuition: Full-time $25,980; part-time $1315 per unit. Required fees: $554. One-time fee: $35 full-time. Full-time tuition and fees vary according to degree level and program. *Unit head:* Dr. Frances J. R. Richmond, Director, 323-442-3531, Fax: 323-442-2333, E-mail: fjr@hsc.usc.edu. *Application contact:* Dr. Kathy Rolle, Program Manager, 323-442-3102, Fax: 323-442-2333, E-mail: regsci@usc.edu.

The University of Tennessee Health Science Center, College of Graduate Health Sciences and College of Pharmacy, Department of Pharmaceutical Sciences, Memphis, TN 38163-0002. Offers MS, PhD, Pharm D/PhD. *Degree requirements:* For master's, comprehensive exam, thesis; for doctorate, thesis/dissertation, oral and written preliminary and comprehensive exams. *Entrance requirements:* For master's and doctorate, GRE General Test, minimum GPA of 3.0. Additional exam requirements/recommendations for international students: Required—TOEFL. Electronic applications accepted.

The University of Texas at Austin, Graduate School, College of Pharmacy, Graduate Programs in Pharmacy, Austin, TX 78712-1111. Offers MS, PhD. *Degree requirements:* For master's, thesis; for doctorate, thesis/dissertation. *Entrance requirements:* For master's and doctorate, GRE General Test. Electronic applications accepted. *Faculty research:* Synthetic medical chemistry, synthetic molecular biology, bio-organic chemistry, pharmacoeconomics, pharmacy practice.

University of the Pacific, School of Pharmacy and Health Sciences, Pharmaceutical and Chemical Sciences Graduate Program, Stockton, CA 95211-0197. Offers MS, PhD. *Faculty:* 10 full-time (1 woman), 1 part-time/adjunct (0 women). *Students:* 2 full-time (1 woman), 47 part-time (24 women); includes 4 minority (all Asian Americans or Pacific Islanders), 41 international. Average age 24. 125 applicants, 15% accepted, 13 enrolled. In 2009, 6 master's, 7 doctorates awarded. *Entrance requirements:* Additional exam requirements/recommendations for international students: Required—TOEFL (minimum score 475 paper-based; 150 computer-based). Application fee: $75. *Financial support:* Application deadline: 3/1. *Unit head:* Dr. Xiaolin Li, Head, 209-946-3162, E-mail: bjasti@pacific.edu. *Application contact:* Cyndi Porter, Outreach Officer, 209-946-3957, Fax: 209-946-2410, E-mail: cporter@pacific.edu.

University of the Sciences in Philadelphia, College of Graduate Studies, Program in Pharmaceutics, Philadelphia, PA 19104-4495. Offers MS, PhD. Part-time programs available. Terminal master's awarded for partial completion of doctoral program. *Degree requirements:* For master's, thesis (for some programs); for doctorate, comprehensive exam, thesis/dissertation, oral defense. *Entrance requirements:* For master's and doctorate, GRE General Test. Additional exam requirements/recommendations for international students: Required—TOEFL, TWE. *Expenses:* Tuition: Full-time $22,230; part-time $1235 per credit. Tuition and fees vary according to program. *Faculty research:* Pharmacodynamics, disperse systems, peptide-biomembranes interactions, in vitro/in vivo correlations, cellular drug delivery.

The University of Toledo, College of Graduate Studies, College of Pharmacy, Program in Pharmaceutical Sciences, Toledo, OH 43606-3390. Offers administrative pharmacy (MSPS); industrial pharmacy (MSPS); pharmacology toxicology (MSPS). *Degree requirements:* For master's, thesis. *Entrance requirements:* For master's, GRE General Test. Additional exam requirements/recommendations for international students: Required—TOEFL (minimum score 550 paper-based; 213 computer-based; 80 iBT). Electronic applications accepted.

University of Toronto, School of Graduate Studies, Life Sciences Division, Department of Pharmaceutical Sciences, Toronto, ON M5S 1A1, Canada. Offers M Sc, PhD. Part-time programs available. *Degree requirements:* For master's, thesis, poster presentation, oral thesis defense; for doctorate, thesis/dissertation, oral presentation, qualifying examination. *Entrance requirements:* For master's, minimum B average in last 2 years of full-time study, 3 letters of reference, resume; for doctorate, minimum B+ average, M Sc or equivalent, 3 letters of reference, resumé. Additional exam requirements/recommendations for international students: Required—TOEFL (600 paper-based, 250 computer-based), Michigan English Language Assessment Battery (88) or IELTS (7); GRE General Test.

University of Utah, Graduate School, College of Pharmacy, Department of Pharmacotherapy, Salt Lake City, UT 84112. Offers MS. *Faculty:* 16 full-time (9 women), 29 part-time/adjunct (14 women). *Students:* 4 full-time (3 women), 5 part-time (1 woman), 4 international. Average age 27. 15 applicants, 33% accepted, 5 enrolled. In 2009, 2 master's awarded. *Degree requirements:* For master's, comprehensive exam, thesis. *Entrance requirements:* Additional exam requirements/recommendations for international students: Required—TOEFL (minimum score 550 paper-based; 213 computer-based; 80 iBT). *Application deadline:* For fall admission, 1/10 for domestic and international students. Application fee: $55 ($65 for international students). *Expenses:* Tuition, state resident: full-time $4004; part-time $1674 per semester. Tuition, nonresident: full-time $14,134; part-time $5915 per semester. Required fees: $324 per semester. Tuition and fees vary according to course load, degree level and program. *Financial support:* In 2009–10, 3 students received support, including 3 research assistantships with full tuition reimbursements available (averaging $11,500 per year); health care benefits also available. Financial award application deadline: 1/10. *Faculty research:* Outcomes in pharmacy, pharmacotherapy. Total annual research expenditures: $36,530. *Unit head:* Dr. Diana I. Brixner, Department Chair and Professor, 801-581-6731. *Application contact:* Sara Ray, Academic Program Manager, 801-581-5984, Fax: 801-585-6160, E-mail: sara.ray@pharm.utah.edu.

University of Washington, School of Pharmacy, Department of Pharmaceutics, Seattle, WA 98195. Offers MS, PhD, Pharm D/PhD. *Faculty:* 11 full-time (3 women), 1 part-time/adjunct (0 women). *Students:* 26 full-time (15 women); includes 13 minority (12 Asian Americans or Pacific Islanders, 1 Hispanic American). Average age 29. 58 applicants, 10% accepted, 5 enrolled. In 2009, 1 master's, 3 doctorates awarded. Terminal master's awarded for partial completion of doctoral program. *Degree requirements:* For master's, thesis; for doctorate, thesis/dissertation. *Entrance requirements:* For master's and doctorate, GRE General Test. Additional exam requirements/recommendations for international students: Required—TOEFL. *Application deadline:* For fall admission, 1/15 for domestic and international students. Application fee: $65. Electronic applications accepted. *Financial support:* In 2009–10, 25 students received support, including 5 fellowships with full tuition reimbursements available (averaging $26,676 per year), 21 research assistantships with full tuition reimbursements available (averaging $26,676 per year); institutionally sponsored loans, scholarships/grants, and health care benefits also available. *Faculty research:* Pharmacokinetics, drug delivery, drug metabolism, pharmacogenetics, transporters. *Unit head:* Dr. Kenneth E. Thummel, Chair, 206-543-9434, Fax: 206-543-3204, E-mail: thummel@u.washington.edu. *Application contact:* Colleen McCallum, Program Coordinator, 206-616-2797, Fax: 206-543-3204, E-mail: pceut@u.washington.edu.

University of Wisconsin–Madison, School of Pharmacy and Graduate School, Graduate Programs in Pharmacy, Pharmaceutical Sciences Division, Madison, WI 53706-1380. Offers PhD. Terminal master's awarded for partial completion of doctoral program. *Degree requirements:* For doctorate, comprehensive exam, thesis/dissertation. *Entrance requirements:* For doctorate, GRE. Additional exam requirements/recommendations for international students: Required—TOEFL. Electronic applications accepted. *Expenses:* Tuition, state resident: part-time $594 per credit. Tuition, nonresident: part-time $1504 per credit. Required fees: $65 per credit. Tuition and fees vary according to course load, program and reciprocity agreements. *Faculty research:* Drug action, drug delivery, drug discovery.

University of Wisconsin–Madison, School of Pharmacy and Graduate School, Graduate Programs in Pharmacy, Social and Administrative Sciences in Pharmacy Division, Madison, WI 53706-1380. Offers MS, PhD. Terminal master's awarded for partial completion of doctoral program. *Degree requirements:* For master's, comprehensive exam (for some programs), thesis optional; for doctorate, comprehensive exam, thesis/dissertation. *Entrance requirements:* For master's and doctorate, GRE. Additional exam requirements/recommendations for international students: Required—TOEFL. Electronic applications accepted. *Expenses:* Tuition, state resident: part-time $594 per credit. Tuition, nonresident: part-time $1504 per credit. Required fees: $65 per credit. Tuition and fees vary according to course load, program and reciprocity agreements. *Faculty research:* Patient-provider communication, economics, patient care systems.

Virginia Commonwealth University, Medical College of Virginia-Professional Programs, School of Pharmacy, Department of Pharmaceutics, Richmond, VA 23284-9005. Offers Pharm D, MS, PhD. Terminal master's awarded for partial completion of doctoral program. *Degree requirements:* For master's, thesis; for doctorate, thesis/dissertation. *Entrance requirements:*

For master's and doctorate, GRE General Test. Additional exam requirements/recommendations for international students: Required—TOEFL. *Faculty research:* Drug delivery systems, drug development.

Wayne State University, Eugene Applebaum College of Pharmacy and Health Sciences, Department of Pharmaceutical Sciences, Detroit, MI 48202. Offers experimental technology in pharmaceutical sciences (Certificate); health systems pharmacy management (MS); hospital pharmacy (MS); pharmaceutical administration (MS, PhD); pharmacy (Pharm D). *Accreditation:* ACPE (one or more programs are accredited). Part-time programs available. *Degree requirements:* For master's, thesis optional. *Entrance requirements:* For Pharm D, bachelor's degree in pharmacy; for master's, GRE General Test, bachelor's degree in pharmacy. Additional exam requirements/recommendations for international students: Required—TOEFL (minimum score 550 paper-based; 213 computer-based); Recommended—TWE (minimum score 6). Electronic applications accepted. *Faculty research:* Mechanisms of resistance of bacteria to anti-microbial agents, drug metabolism and disposition in children, treatment strategies for stroke/neurovascular disease, prevalence and treatment of diabetes in Arab-Americans, ethnic variability in development of osteoporosis.

Western University of Health Sciences, College of Pharmacy, Program in Pharmaceutical Sciences, Pomona, CA 91766-1854. Offers MS. *Entrance requirements:* Additional exam requirements/recommendations for international students: Required—TOEFL (minimum score 500 paper-based; 213 computer-based; 89 iBT). *Expenses:* Contact institution.

West Virginia University, School of Medicine, Graduate Programs at the Health Sciences Center, Interdisciplinary Graduate Programs in Biomedical Sciences, Program in Pharmaceutical and Pharmacological Sciences, Morgantown, WV 26506. Offers MS, PhD, MD/PhD. *Degree requirements:* For doctorate, comprehensive exam, thesis/dissertation. *Entrance requirements:* For doctorate, GRE General Test, minimum GPA of 3.0. Additional exam requirements/recommendations for international students: Required—TOEFL. Electronic applications accepted. *Faculty research:* Medicinal chemistry, pharmacokinetics, nano-pharmaceutics, polymer-based drug delivery, molecular therapeutics.

West Virginia University, School of Pharmacy, Program in Pharmaceutical and Pharmacological Sciences, Morgantown, WV 26506. Offers administrative pharmacy (PhD); behavioral pharmacy (MS, PhD); biopharmaceutics/pharmacokinetics (MS, PhD); industrial pharmacy (MS); medicinal chemistry (MS, PhD); pharmaceutical chemistry (MS, PhD); pharmaceutics (MS, PhD); pharmacology and toxicology (MS); pharmacy (MS); pharmacy administration (MS). Part-time programs available. Terminal master's awarded for partial completion of doctoral program. *Degree requirements:* For master's, thesis; for doctorate, one foreign language, comprehensive exam, thesis/dissertation. *Entrance requirements:* For master's and doctorate, GRE General Test, minimum GPA of 2.75. Additional exam requirements/recommendations for international students: Required—TOEFL; Recommended—TWE. Electronic applications accepted. *Expenses:* Contact institution. *Faculty research:* Pharmaceutics, medicinal chemistry, biopharmaceutics/pharmacokinetics, health outcomes research.

Pharmacy

Albany College of Pharmacy and Health Sciences, Program in Pharmacy, Albany, NY 12208. Offers health outcomes research (MS); pharmaceutical sciences (MS); pharmacy (Pharm D); pharmacy administration (MS). *Accreditation:* ACPE. *Faculty:* 60 full-time (24 women), 10 part-time/adjunct (6 women). *Students:* 452 full-time (245 women); includes 78 minority (21 African Americans, 54 Asian Americans or Pacific Islanders, 3 Hispanic Americans), 46 international. Average age 26. 1,223 applicants, 12% accepted, 79 enrolled. In 2009, 211 first professional degrees awarded. *Degree requirements:* For master's, thesis (for some programs); for Pharm D, comprehensive exam (for some programs), practice experience. *Entrance requirements:* For Pharm D, PCAT, minimum GPA of 3.0; for master's, GRE, minimum GPA of 3.0. Additional exam requirements/recommendations for international students: Required—TOEFL (minimum score 600 paper-based; 250 computer-based; 100 iBT). *Application deadline:* For fall admission, 2/1 for domestic and international students. Applications are processed on a rolling basis. Application fee: $75. Electronic applications accepted. *Expenses:* Tuition: Full-time $23,260; part-time $775 per credit hour. Required fees: $1150. *Financial support:* In 2009–10, 185 students received support, including 1 fellowship (averaging $40,000 per year); Federal Work-Study and scholarships/grants also available. Support available to part-time students. Financial award application deadline: 3/1; financial award applicants required to submit FAFSA. *Faculty research:* Therapeutic use of drugs, pharmacokinetics, pharmaceutical care, health outcomes, drug delivery. *Unit head:* Dr. Mehdi Boroujerdi, Dean, 518-694-7212, Fax: 518-694-7063. *Application contact:* Donna Myers, Pharmacy and Graduate Admissions Counselor, 518-694-7186, Fax: 518-694-7063.

See Close-Up on page 1789.

Auburn University, Harrison School of Pharmacy, Professional Program in Pharmacy, Auburn University, AL 36849. Offers Pharm D. *Accreditation:* ACPE. Part-time programs available. *Faculty:* 48 full-time (27 women), 1 (woman) part-time/adjunct. *Students:* 519 full-time (352 women), 43 part-time (30 women); includes 83 minority (39 African Americans, 8 American Indian/Alaska Native, 33 Asian Americans or Pacific Islanders, 3 Hispanic Americans), 3 international. Average age 25. In 2009, 119 Pharm Ds awarded. Application fee: $0. *Expenses:* Contact institution. *Financial support:* Federal Work-Study available. Support available to part-time students. Financial award applicants required to submit FAFSA. *Unit head:* Dr. R. Lee Evans, Dean and Professor, Harrison School of Pharmacy, 334-844-8348, Fax: 334-844-8353. *Application contact:* Dr. R. Lee Evans, Dean and Professor, Harrison School of Pharmacy, 334-844-8348, Fax: 334-844-8353.

Belmont University, College of Health Sciences, School of Pharmacy, Nashville, TN 37212-3757. Offers Pharm D. *Entrance requirements:* PCAT. Additional exam requirements/recommendations for international students: Required—TOEFL. Electronic applications accepted. *Faculty research:* Academic innovation, cultural competency, medication errors, patient safety.

Butler University, College of Pharmacy, Indianapolis, IN 46208-3485. Offers pharmaceutical science (Pharm D, MS); physician assistance studies (MS). *Accreditation:* ACPE (one or more programs are accredited). Part-time and evening/weekend programs available. *Faculty:* 24 full-time (11 women), 2 part-time/adjunct (1 woman). *Students:* 274 full-time (194 women), 10 part-time (6 women); includes 19 minority (4 African Americans, 9 Asian Americans or Pacific Islanders, 6 Hispanic Americans), 11 international. Average age 24. 107 applicants, 6% accepted, 6 enrolled. In 2009, 129 first professional degrees, 51 master's awarded. *Degree requirements:* For master's, research paper or thesis. *Application deadline:* For fall admission, 8/1 priority date for domestic students; for spring admission, 12/15 for domestic students. Applications are processed on a rolling basis. Application fee: $35. Electronic applications accepted. *Expenses:* Contact institution. *Financial support:* Applicants required to submit FAFSA. *Faculty research:* Anti-seizure drugs, casein kinase inhibitors, speech recognition interface for prescribing drugs, pharmacoeconomics. Total annual research expenditures: $92,000. *Unit head:* Dr. Mary Andritz, Dean, 317-940-9451, Fax: 317-940-6172, E-mail: mandritz@butler.edu. *Application contact:* Dr. Bruce Clayton, Professor, 317-940-9830, E-mail: bclayton@butler.edu.

Campbell University, Graduate and Professional Programs, School of Pharmacy, Buies Creek, NC 27506. Offers clinical research (MS); pharmaceutical science (MS); pharmacy (Pharm D). *Accreditation:* ACPE. Part-time and evening/weekend programs available. *Entrance requirements:* For Pharm D, PCAT; for master's, MCAT, PCAT, GRE, bachelor's degree in health sciences or related field. Additional exam requirements/recommendations for international students: Required—TOEFL (minimum score 550 paper-based; 213 computer-based; 79 iBT). Electronic applications accepted. *Expenses:* Contact institution. *Faculty research:* Immunology, medicinal chemistry, pharmaceutics, applied pharmacology.

Creighton University, School of Pharmacy and Health Professions, Professional Program in Pharmacy, Omaha, NE 68178-0001. Offers Pharm D. *Accreditation:* ACPE. Postbaccalaureate distance learning degree programs offered (no on-campus study). *Entrance requirements:* PCAT. Electronic applications accepted. *Expenses:* Tuition: Full-time $11,700; part-time $650 per credit hour. Required fees: $126 per semester. *Faculty research:* Patient safety in health services research, health information technology and health services research, nanotechnology and drug development, pharmacy practice outcomes research, cross-cultural care of patients in pharmacy practice.

Duquesne University, Mylan School of Pharmacy/Graduate School of Pharmaceutical Sciences, Professional Program in Pharmacy, Pittsburgh, PA 15282. Offers Pharm D. Students enter program as first-year undergraduates. *Accreditation:* ACPE. Evening/weekend programs available. *Faculty:* 48 full-time (20 women), 2 part-time/adjunct (0 women). *Students:* 1,141 full-time (715 women); includes 46 minority (14 African Americans, 27 Asian Americans or Pacific Islanders, 5 Hispanic Americans), 9 international. 990 applicants, 55% accepted, 172 enrolled. In 2009, 212 Pharm Ds awarded. *Entrance requirements:* PCAT (for professional

phase). Additional exam requirements/recommendations for international students: Required—TOEFL. *Application deadline:* For fall admission, 12/1 priority date for domestic and international students. Applications are processed on a rolling basis. Application fee: $50. Electronic applications accepted. *Expenses:* Tuition: Part-time $851 per credit. Required fees: $81 per credit. *Financial support:* Federal Work-Study and scholarships/grants available. Financial award application deadline: 5/1; financial award applicants required to submit FAFSA. *Unit head:* Dr. Thomas J. Mattei, Associate Dean for Professional Programs, 412-396-6393. *Application contact:* Admissions/Recruitment Coordinator, 412-396-6393, Fax: 412-396-4375, E-mail: pharmadmission@duq.edu.

Ferris State University, College of Pharmacy, Big Rapids, MI 49307. Offers Pharm D. *Accreditation:* ACPE. *Faculty:* 39 full-time (24 women), 4 part-time/adjunct (3 women). *Students:* 536 full-time (296 women), 21 part-time (12 women); includes 60 minority (13 African Americans, 2 American Indian/Alaska Native, 41 Asian Americans or Pacific Islanders, 4 Hispanic Americans), 34 international. Average age 24. 427 applicants, 25% accepted, 24 enrolled. In 2009, 142 Pharm Ds awarded. *Entrance requirements:* PCAT, 2 years of pre-pharmacy course work. *Application deadline:* For fall admission, 12/15 for domestic students. Application fee: $0. *Expenses:* Contact institution. *Financial support:* Institutionally sponsored loans and scholarships/grants available. Financial award applicants required to submit FAFSA. *Faculty research:* Diabetes, rural health education, managed care practice, antimicrobial pharmacotherapy, medicinal flora. *Unit head:* Dr. Ian Mathison, Dean, 231-591-2254, Fax: 231-591-3829, E-mail: mathisol@ferris.edu. *Application contact:* Tara M. Lee, Assistant Dean, 231-591-3780, Fax: 231-591-3829, E-mail: leet@ferris.edu.

Florida Agricultural and Mechanical University, Division of Graduate Studies, Research, and Continuing Education, College of Pharmacy and Pharmaceutical Sciences, Professional Program in Pharmacy and Pharmaceutical Sciences, Tallahassee, FL 32307-3200. Offers Pharm D, Ex Doc. *Accreditation:* ACPE. *Faculty:* 31 full-time (12 women). *Students:* 1,133 full-time (790 women), 50 part-time (29 women); includes 1,071 minority (968 African Americans, 2 American Indian/Alaska Native, 82 Asian Americans or Pacific Islanders, 19 Hispanic Americans), 8 international. In 2009, 116 Pharm Ds awarded. *Entrance requirements:* Minimum GPA of 2.5. Additional exam requirements/recommendations for international students: Required—TOEFL. *Application deadline:* For fall admission, 2/1 for domestic students. Application fee: $20. *Unit head:* Carlton Bailey, Director, 850-599-3301, Fax: 850-599-3347. *Application contact:* Carlton Bailey, Director, 850-599-3301, Fax: 850-599-3347.

Harding University, College of Pharmacy, Searcy, AR 72147-2230. Offers Pharm D. *Faculty:* 20 full-time (10 women), 2 part-time/adjunct (1 woman). *Students:* 118 full-time (55 women); includes 42 minority (11 African Americans, 3 American Indian/Alaska Native, 28 Asian Americans or Pacific Islanders), 1 international. Average age 26. *Degree requirements:* For Pharm D, licensure as a pharmacy intern in AR, completion of 300 hours of introductory pharmacy practice experience and 1,440 hours of advanced pharmacy practice experience. *Entrance requirements:* PCAT, 90 semester hours of undergraduate work. Additional exam requirements/recommendations for international students: Required—TOEFL (minimum score 550 paper-based). *Application deadline:* For fall admission, 3/1 priority date for domestic and international students. Applications are processed on a rolling basis. Application fee: $50. Electronic applications accepted. *Expenses:* Contact institution. *Financial support:* In 2009–10, 18 students received support. Scholarships/grants available. Financial award applicants required to submit FAFSA. *Faculty research:* Drug alteration of neural conduction, micro-encapsulation techniques, solid and liquid dosage forms, extraction of microbial nucleic acids. Total annual research expenditures: $50,000. *Unit head:* Dr. Julie Ann Hixson-Wallace, Dean, 501-279-5205, Fax: 501-279-5525, E-mail: jahixson@harding.edu. *Application contact:* Carol Kell, Director of Admissions, 501-279-5523, Fax: 501-279-5525, E-mail: ckell@harding.edu.

Howard University, College of Pharmacy, Nursing and Allied Health Sciences, School of Pharmacy, Washington, DC 20059-0002. Offers Pharm D, Pharm D/MBA. *Accreditation:* ACPE. Postbaccalaureate distance learning degree programs offered (minimal on-campus study). *Degree requirements:* For Pharm D, comprehensive exam. *Entrance requirements:* PCAT, minimum GPA of 2.5. Electronic applications accepted. *Expenses:* Contact institution. *Faculty research:* Kinetics of drug absorption, stealth liposomes, synthesis, opiate analgesics.

Idaho State University, Office of Graduate Studies, College of Pharmacy, Department of Pharmacy Practice and Administrative Sciences, Pocatello, ID 83209-8333. Offers pharmacy (Pharm D); pharmacy administration (MS, PhD). *Accreditation:* ACPE (one or more programs are accredited). Part-time programs available. *Faculty:* 8 full-time (3 women). *Students:* 244 full-time (96 women), 17 part-time (5 women); includes 32 minority (6 African Americans, 4 American Indian/Alaska Native, 14 Asian Americans or Pacific Islanders, 8 Hispanic Americans), 3 international. Average age 29. In 2009, 67 first professional degrees, 1 master's awarded. *Degree requirements:* For master's, one foreign language, comprehensive exam, thesis, thesis research, speech and technical writing classes; for doctorate, comprehensive exam, thesis/dissertation, oral and written exams, speech and technical writing classes; for Pharm D, comprehensive exam, thesis/dissertation, written and oral exams. *Entrance requirements:* For Pharm D, GRE General Test, minimum GPA of 3.0, 2 years of pre-pharmacy, BS degree in pharmacy or related field, 3 letters of recommendation; for master's, GRE General Test, minimum GPA of 3.0, 3 letters of recommendation; for doctorate, GRE General Test, BS in pharmacy or related field, minimum GPA of 3.0, 3 letters of recommendation. Additional exam requirements/recommendations for international students: Required—TOEFL (minimum score 550 paper-based; 213 computer-based; 80 iBT). *Application deadline:* For fall admission, 7/1 for domestic students, 6/1 for international students; for spring admission, 12/1 for domestic students, 11/1 for international students. Applications are processed on a rolling basis. Application fee: $55. Electronic applications accepted. *Expenses:* Contact institution. *Financial support:* In

Pharmacy

Idaho State University *(continued)*
2009–10, 4 teaching assistantships with full and partial tuition reimbursements (averaging $10,841 per year) were awarded; research assistantships with full and partial tuition reimbursements, career-related internships or fieldwork, Federal Work-Study, institutionally sponsored loans, scholarships/grants, traineeships, health care benefits, tuition waivers (full and partial), and unspecified assistantships also available. Support available to part-time students. Financial award application deadline: 1/1; financial award applicants required to submit FAFSA. *Faculty research:* Pharmaceutical care outcomes, drug use review, pharmacoeconomics. *Unit head:* Dr. Christopher Owens, Interim Chairman, 208-282-2586, Fax: 208-282-4482, E-mail: ctowens@pharmacy.isu.edu. *Application contact:* Tami Carson, Graduate School Technical Records Specialist, 208-282-2150, Fax: 208-282-4847, E-mail: carstami@isu.edu.

Lake Erie College of Osteopathic Medicine, Professional Programs, Erie, PA 16509-1025. Offers biomedical sciences (Postbaccalaureate Certificate); medical education (MS); osteopathic medicine (DO); pharmacy (Pharm D). *Accreditation:* ACPE; AOsA. *Degree requirements:* For first professional degree, comprehensive exam, National Osteopathic Medical Licensing Exam, Levels 1 and 2; for Postbaccalaureate Certificate, comprehensive exam, North American Pharmacist Licensure Examination (NAPLEX). *Entrance requirements:* For first professional degree, MCAT, minimum GPA of 3.2, letters of recommendation; for Postbaccalaureate Certificate, PCAT, letters of recommendation, minimum GPA of 3.5. Electronic applications accepted. *Faculty research:* Cardiac smooth and skeletal muscle mechanics, chemotherapeutics and vitamins, osteopathic manipulation.

Lebanese American University, School of Pharmacy, Beirut, Lebanon. Offers Pharm D. *Accreditation:* ACPE.

Lipscomb University, Program in Pharmacy, Nashville, TN 37204-3951. Offers). *Faculty:* 9 full-time (5 women), 9 part-time/adjunct (1 woman). *Students:* 149 full-time (93 women); includes 7 African Americans, 1 American Indian/Alaska Native, 11 Asian Americans or Pacific Islanders. Average age 25. 883 applicants, 13% accepted, 75 enrolled. *Entrance requirements:* PCAT. *Application deadline:* For fall admission, 2/7 for domestic students. Applications are processed on a rolling basis. Application fee: $50. *Expenses:* Tuition: Full-time $16,002; part-time $889 per credit hour. Tuition and fees vary according to program. *Financial support:* Application deadline: 2/15. *Unit head:* Dr. Roger Davis, Dean of College of Pharmacy/Professor of Pharmacy Practice, 615-966-7161. *Application contact:* Kathryne Chanell, Administrative Assistant, E-mail: kathryne.channell@lipscomb.edu.

Loma Linda University, School of Pharmacy, Loma Linda, CA 92350. Offers Pharm D. *Accreditation:* ACPE. *Degree requirements:* For Pharm D, intern pharmacist license.

Massachusetts College of Pharmacy and Health Sciences, Graduate Studies, School of Pharmacy–Boston, Postbaccalaureate Doctor of Pharmacy Pathway Program, Boston, MA 02115-5896. Offers Pharm D. Part-time programs available. Postbaccalaureate distance learning degree programs offered (minimal on-campus study). *Students:* 78 part-time (47 women); includes 23 Asian Americans or Pacific Islanders, 4 international. Average age 39. 54 applicants, 85% accepted, 38 enrolled. In 2009, 21 Pharm Ds awarded. *Entrance requirements:* Registered pharmacist status in the U.S.; working at or have access to a site that provides opportunities to practice pharmaceutical care; curriculum vitae; letter of recommendation. Additional exam requirements/recommendations for international students: Required—TOEFL (minimum score 550 paper-based; 213 computer-based; 79 iBT). *Application deadline:* For fall admission, 5/1 priority date for domestic students. Applications are processed on a rolling basis. Application fee: $70. Electronic applications accepted. *Expenses:* Tuition: Full-time $28,000; part-time $875 per credit hour. Required fees: $750; $190 per semester. Part-time tuition and fees vary according to course load, campus/location, program and student level. *Unit head:* Kathy Grams, Director, 617-732-2830, E-mail: kathy.grams@mcphs.edu. *Application contact:* Tara Hennesey, Coordinator of Graduate Admission, 617-732-2850, E-mail: admissions@mcphs.edu.

Massachusetts College of Pharmacy and Health Sciences, Graduate Studies, School of Pharmacy–Boston, Program in Pharmacy, Boston, MA 02115-5896. Offers Pharm D. Post-baccalaureate distance learning degree programs offered. *Students:* 1,745 full-time (1,103 women), 40 part-time (31 women); includes 652 minority (48 African Americans, 7 American Indian/Alaska Native, 567 Asian Americans or Pacific Islanders, 30 Hispanic Americans), 69 international. Average age 22. 2,836 applicants, 35% accepted, 378 enrolled. In 2009, 255 Pharm Ds awarded. *Entrance requirements:* SAT (if fewer than 30 semester hours completed), minimum GPA of 2.5, interview. Additional exam requirements/recommendations for international students: Required—TOEFL (minimum score 550 paper-based; 213 computer-based; 79 iBT). *Application deadline:* For fall admission, 2/1 priority date for domestic and international students. Application fee: $70. Electronic applications accepted. *Expenses:* Tuition: Full-time $28,000; part-time $875 per credit hour. Required fees: $750; $190 per semester. Part-time tuition and fees vary according to course load, campus/location, program and student level. *Financial support:* Application deadline: 3/15. *Unit head:* Dr. Douglas Pisano, Dean, School of Pharmacy, 617-732-2781. *Application contact:* Kathleen Ryan, Coordinator of Transfer Admissions, Pharmacy and Nursing, 617-732-5042.

Massachusetts College of Pharmacy and Health Sciences, School of Pharmacy–Worcester/Manchester, Accelerated Program in Pharmacy, Boston, MA 02115-5896. Offers Pharm D. *Students:* 636 full-time (386 women), 21 part-time (6 women); includes 251 minority (67 African Americans, 3 American Indian/Alaska Native, 175 Asian Americans or Pacific Islanders, 6 Hispanic Americans), 41 international. Average age 27. 2,135 applicants, 18% accepted, 250 enrolled. In 2009, 162 Pharm Ds awarded. *Entrance requirements:* Minimum GPA of 2.5, interview. Additional exam requirements/recommendations for international students: Required—TOEFL (minimum score 550 paper-based; 213 computer-based; 79 iBT). *Application deadline:* For fall admission, 2/1 priority date for domestic students, 2/1 for international students. Application fee: $70. *Expenses:* Tuition: Full-time $28,000; part-time $875 per credit hour. Required fees: $750; $190 per semester. Part-time tuition and fees vary according to course load, campus/location, program and student level. *Financial support:* Scholarships/grants available. Financial award application deadline: 3/15. *Unit head:* Michael Malloy, Dean, School of Pharmacy-Worcester/Manchester, 508-373-5603, E-mail: michael.malloy@mcphs.edu. *Application contact:* Bryan Witham, Director of Admissions, Worcester and Manchester, 508-373-5623, E-mail: bryanwitham@mcphs.edu.

Medical University of South Carolina, South Carolina College of Pharmacy, Charleston, SC 29425. Offers Pharm D. *Accreditation:* ACPE. *Faculty:* 36 full-time (15 women), 3 part-time/adjunct (2 women). *Students:* 314 full-time (211 women), 1 part-time (0 women); includes 49 minority (17 African Americans, 2 American Indian/Alaska Native, 22 Asian Americans or Pacific Islanders, 8 Hispanic Americans), 1 international. Average age 25. 526 applicants, 43% accepted, 192 enrolled. In 2009, 78 Pharm Ds awarded. *Entrance requirements:* PCAT, 2 years pre-professional course work, interview, minimum GPA of 2.5. Additional exam requirements/recommendations for international students: Required—TOEFL (minimum score 600 paper-based; 250 computer-based). *Application deadline:* For fall admission, 1/1 for domestic and international students. Application fee: $85. Electronic applications accepted. *Expenses:* Contact institution. *Financial support:* Career-related internships or fieldwork, Federal Work-Study, institutionally sponsored loans, and scholarships/grants available. Financial award application deadline: 3/10; financial award applicants required to submit FAFSA. *Faculty research:* Rational and computer aided drug design; drug metabolism and transport; molecular immunology and cellular toxicology; cell injury, death and regeneration; outcome sciences. *Unit head:* Dr. Joseph T. DiPiro, Executive Dean, 843-792-8452, Fax: 843-792-9081, E-mail: jdipiro@sccp.sc.edu. *Application contact:* Dr. Philip D. Hall, Associate Dean, 843-792-8979, Fax: 843-792-9081, E-mail: hallpd@sccp.sc.edu.

Mercer University, Graduate Studies, Cecil B. Day Campus, College of Pharmacy and Health Sciences, Macon, GA 31207-0003. Offers medical sciences (MS); pharmacy (Pharm D, PhD); Pharm D/MBA; Pharm D/PhD. *Accreditation:* ACPE (one or more programs are accredited). *Faculty:* 22 full-time (14 women), 3 part-time/adjunct (1 woman). *Students:* 676 full-time (440 women), 4 part-time (1 woman); includes 170 minority (68 African Americans, 91 Asian

Americans or Pacific Islanders, 11 Hispanic Americans), 41 international. Average age 26. In 2009, 139 first professional degrees, 6 doctorates awarded. *Degree requirements:* For doctorate, thesis/dissertation. *Entrance requirements:* For Pharm D, PCAT, minimum GPA of 3.0; for master's, GRE, minimum GPA of 2.75; for doctorate, GRE, Pharm D or BS in pharmacy or science, minimum GPA of 3.0. Additional exam requirements/recommendations for international students: Required—TOEFL. *Application deadline:* For fall admission, 1/1 for domestic students. Applications are processed on a rolling basis. Application fee: $25. Electronic applications accepted. *Expenses:* Contact institution. *Financial support:* In 2009–10, 350 students received support; teaching assistantships with tuition reimbursements available, career-related internships or fieldwork, Federal Work-Study, institutionally sponsored loans, scholarships/grants, and tuition waivers available. Support available to part-time students. Financial award application deadline: 5/1; financial award applicants required to submit FAFSA. *Faculty research:* Stability and compatibility of steroids, synthesis of antihypertensives, disposition of cyclosporine, DUZ-drug research, synthesis of enzyme inhibitors. *Unit head:* Dr. Hewitt W. Matthews, Dean, 678-547-6304, Fax: 678-547-6315, E-mail: matthews_h@mercer.edu. *Application contact:* Dr. James W. Bartling, Associate Dean for Student Affairs and Admissions, 678-547-6181, Fax: 678-547-6063, E-mail: bartling_jw@mercer.edu.

Midwestern University, Downers Grove Campus, Chicago College of Pharmacy, Downers Grove, IL 60515-1235. Offers Pharm D. *Accreditation:* ACPE. Part-time programs available. Postbaccalaureate distance learning degree programs offered (minimal on-campus study). *Faculty:* 50 full-time (35 women). *Students:* 735 full-time (448 women), 28 part-time (17 women); includes 255 minority (9 African Americans, 1 American Indian/Alaska Native, 229 Asian Americans or Pacific Islanders, 16 Hispanic Americans), 11 international. Average age 25. 2,499 applicants, 19% accepted, 201 enrolled. In 2009, 217 Pharm Ds awarded. *Entrance requirements:* PCAT. *Application deadline:* For fall admission, 2/3 for domestic students. Application fee: $50. *Expenses:* Contact institution. *Financial support:* Federal Work-Study and institutionally sponsored loans available. Support available to part-time students. Financial award applicants required to submit FAFSA. *Unit head:* Dr. Nancy Fjortoft, Dean, 630-971-6408. *Application contact:* Michael Laken, Director of Admissions, 630-515-6171, Fax: 630-971-6086, E-mail: admissil@midwestern.edu.

Midwestern University, Glendale Campus, College of Pharmacy-Glendale, Glendale, AZ 85308. Offers Pharm D. *Accreditation:* ACPE. *Faculty:* 28 full-time (17 women), 1 part-time/adjunct (0 women). *Students:* 386 full-time (201 women), 4 part-time (0 women); includes 129 minority (4 African Americans, 1 American Indian/Alaska Native, 101 Asian Americans or Pacific Islanders, 23 Hispanic Americans), 11 international. Average age 27. 1,550 applicants, 15% accepted, 134 enrolled. In 2009, 133 Pharm Ds awarded. *Entrance requirements:* PCAT. *Application deadline:* For fall admission, 2/1 for domestic students. Application fee: $50. *Expenses:* Contact institution. *Financial support:* Applicants required to submit FAFSA. *Unit head:* Dr. Dennis McCallian, Interim Dean, 623-572-3501. *Application contact:* James Walter, Director of Admissions, 888-247-9277, Fax: 623-572-3229, E-mail: admissaz@midwestern.edu.

Northeastern Ohio Universities College of Medicine and Pharmacy, College of Pharmacy, Rootstown, OH 44272-0095. Offers Pharm D. *Faculty:* 40 full-time (16 women), 161 part-time/adjunct (64 women). *Students:* 142 full-time (81 women); includes 31 minority (9 African Americans, 1 American Indian/Alaska Native, 19 Asian Americans or Pacific Islanders, 2 Hispanic Americans). Average age 25. 546 applicants, 23% accepted, 81 enrolled. *Entrance requirements:* PCAT. *Application deadline:* For fall admission, 9/20 priority date for domestic students; for winter admission, 1/5 for domestic students. Applications are processed on a rolling basis. Application fee: $50. Electronic applications accepted. *Expenses:* Contact institution. *Financial support:* In 2009–10, 26 students received support. Scholarships/grants available. Financial award application deadline: 4/15; financial award applicants required to submit FAFSA. *Unit head:* Dr. David D. Allen, Dean, 330-325-6467, Fax: 330-325-5930. *Application contact:* Julie Grove, Assistant Director of Admissions, 330-325-6270, E-mail: admission@neoucom.edu.

Nova Southeastern University, Health Professions Division, College of Pharmacy, Fort Lauderdale, FL 33314-7796. Offers Pharm D. *Accreditation:* ACPE. Postbaccalaureate distance learning degree programs offered (minimal on-campus study). *Faculty:* 52 full-time (32 women), 9 part-time/adjunct (3 women). *Students:* 917 full-time (605 women), 52 part-time (41 women); includes 604 minority (62 African Americans, 3 American Indian/Alaska Native, 178 Asian Americans or Pacific Islanders, 361 Hispanic Americans), 97 international. Average age 25. 1,177 applicants, 22% accepted, 189 enrolled. In 2009, 248 Pharm Ds awarded. *Degree requirements:* For Pharm D, comprehensive exam, thesis/dissertation (for some programs). *Entrance requirements:* PCAT. Additional exam requirements/recommendations for international students: Required—TOEFL (minimum score 550 paper-based; 213 computer-based). *Application deadline:* For fall admission, 3/1 for domestic students, 2/1 for international students. Applications are processed on a rolling basis. Application fee: $50. Electronic applications accepted. *Expenses:* Contact institution. *Financial support:* Career-related internships or fieldwork, Federal Work-Study, institutionally sponsored loans, and scholarships/grants available. Financial award application deadline: 4/15; financial award applicants required to submit FAFSA. *Faculty research:* Neovascularization, health care delivery, pharmacoeconomics, cardiovascular/metabolic metastasis. Total annual research expenditures: $526,388. *Unit head:* Dr. Andres Malave, Dean, 954-262-1300, Fax: 954-262-2278. *Application contact:* Tracy Templin, Admissions Counselor, 954-262-1112, Fax: 954-262-2282, E-mail: dpetracy@nsu.nova.edu.

Ohio Northern University, Raabe College of Pharmacy, Ada, OH 45810-1599. Offers Pharm D. Students enter the program as undergraduates. *Accreditation:* ACPE. *Degree requirements:* For Pharm D, 9 clinical rotations, capstone course. *Entrance requirements:* ACT or SAT. Additional exam requirements/recommendations for international students: Required—TOEFL (minimum score 550 paper-based; 213 computer-based; 80 iBT). Electronic applications accepted. *Expenses:* Contact institution. *Faculty research:* Alcohol and substance abuse, women in pharmacy, non-traditional educations, continuing pharmaceutical education, medicinal chemistry.

The Ohio State University, College of Pharmacy, Professional Program in Pharmacy, Columbus, OH 43210. Offers Pharm D. *Accreditation:* ACPE. *Entrance requirements:* PCAT. Additional exam requirements/recommendations for international students: Required—TOEFL (minimum score 577 paper-based; 233 computer-based). Electronic applications accepted. *Expenses:* Tuition, state resident: full-time $10,683. Tuition, nonresident: full-time $25,923. Tuition and fees vary according to course load and program. *Faculty research:* Clinical pharmacokinetics, drug metabolism, critical care therapeutics, drug interactions, stereoselective drug dispositions.

Oregon State University, College of Pharmacy, Corvallis, OR 97331. Offers Pharm D, MS, PhD. *Accreditation:* ACPE (one or more programs are accredited). Part-time programs available. *Faculty:* 31 full-time (13 women). *Students:* 379 full-time (215 women), 12 part-time (5 women); includes 141 minority (5 African Americans, 123 Asian Americans or Pacific Islanders, 13 Hispanic Americans), 29 international. Average age 27. In 2009, 80 first professional degrees, 5 doctorates awarded. Terminal master's awarded for partial completion of doctoral program. *Degree requirements:* For master's, thesis; for doctorate, thesis/dissertation. *Entrance requirements:* For master's, GRE General Test, minimum GPA of 3.0, in last 90 hours; for doctorate, GRE General Test, minimum GPA of 3.0 in last 90 hours, pre-pharmacy curriculum. Additional exam requirements/recommendations for international students: Required—TOEFL. *Application deadline:* For fall admission, 3/1 for domestic students. Applications are processed on a rolling basis. Application fee: $50. *Expenses:* Tuition, state resident: full-time $9774; part-time $362 per credit. Tuition, nonresident: full-time $15,849; part-time $587 per credit. Required fees: $1639. Full-time tuition and fees vary according to course load and program. *Financial support:* Fellowships, research assistantships, teaching assistantships, career-related internships or fieldwork, Federal Work-Study, and institutionally sponsored loans available. Support available to part-time students. Financial award application deadline: 2/1. *Faculty research:* Pharmacology/toxicology, pharmacokinetics, biopharmaceutics, neuroscience, natural

products. *Unit head:* Dr. Wayne A. Kradjan, Dean, 541-737-3424, Fax: 541-737-3424, E-mail: wayne.kradjan@orst.edu.

Pacific University, School of Pharmacy, Forest Grove, OR 97116-1797. Offers Pharm D. *Accreditation:* ACPE. *Entrance requirements:* Additional exam requirements/recommendations for international students: Required—TOEFL (minimum score 600 paper-based; 250 computer-based). Electronic applications accepted. *Expenses:* Contact institution. *Faculty research:* Informatics, enzyme metabolism, apostosis/cell cycle, neurophysiology of chronic pain, neurophysiology of Alzheimer's.

Palm Beach Atlantic University, Gregory School of Pharmacy, West Palm Beach, FL 33416-4708. Offers Pharm D. *Accreditation:* ACPE. *Faculty:* 18 full-time (13 women), 2 part-time/adjunct (0 women). *Students:* 297 full-time (192 women), 14 part-time (6 women); includes 94 minority (19 African Americans, 1 American Indian/Alaska Native, 30 Asian Americans or Pacific Islanders, 44 Hispanic Americans), 10 international. Average age 25. In 2009, 61 Pharm Ds awarded. *Entrance requirements:* PCAT, minimum GPA of 2.75. Additional exam requirements/recommendations for international students: Required—TOEFL (minimum score 550 paper-based; 213 computer-based). *Application deadline:* For fall admission, 5/31 priority date for domestic and international students. Applications are processed on a rolling basis. Application fee: $80. Electronic applications accepted. *Expenses:* Contact institution. *Financial support:* Unspecified assistantships available. Financial award applicants required to submit FAFSA. *Unit head:* Dr. Daniel Brown, Dean, 561-803-2700, E-mail: daniel_brown@pba.edu. *Application contact:* Pharmacy Admissions, 561-803-2150.

Purdue University, College of Pharmacy and Pharmacal Sciences, Professional Program in Pharmacy and Pharmacal Sciences, West Lafayette, IN 47907. Offers Pharm D. *Accreditation:* ACPE. *Entrance requirements:* Minimum 2 years of pre-pharmacy course work, interview. *Expenses:* Contact institution. *Faculty research:* Medicinal chemistry, pharmacology, pharmaceutics, clinical pharmacy, pharmacy administration.

Regis University, Rueckert-Hartman School for Health Professions, Denver, CO 80221-1099. Offers clinical leadership for physician assistants (MS); family nurse practitioner (MSN); health informatics (Postbaccalaureate Certificate); health services administration (MS); healthcare education (Certificate); leadership in healthcare systems (MSN); neonatal nurse practitioner (MSN); nursing (MSN); pharmacy (Pharm D); physical therapy (DPT, TDPT). *Entrance requirements:* Additional exam requirements/recommendations for international students: Required—TOEFL (minimum score 550 paper-based; 213 computer-based; 82 iBT). Electronic applications accepted. *Expenses:* Contact institution. *Faculty research:* Normal and pathological balance and gait research, normal/pathological upper limb motor control/biomechanics, exercise energy/metabolism research, optical treatment protocols for therapeutic modalities.

Rutgers, The State University of New Jersey, New Brunswick, Ernest Mario School of Pharmacy, Piscataway, NJ 08854-8097. Offers medicinal chemistry (MS, PhD); pharamceutical science (PhD); pharmaceutical science (MS); pharmacy (Pharm D). *Accreditation:* ACPE. *Degree requirements:* For Pharm D, one foreign language. *Entrance requirements:* SAT or PCAT, interview, criminal background check. Additional exam requirements/recommendations for international students: Recommended—TOEFL (minimum score 550 paper-based; 213 computer-based). Electronic applications accepted. *Expenses:* Contact institution. *Faculty research:* Pharmacokinetics, cancer prevention, cardiology, neurology, pharmacodynamics.

St. John Fisher College, Wegmans School of Pharmacy, Doctor of Pharmacy Program, Rochester, NY 14618-3597. Offers Pharm D. *Accreditation:* ACPE. *Faculty:* 19 full-time (11 women). *Students:* 264 full-time (134 women); includes 43 minority (3 African Americans, 34 Asian Americans or Pacific Islanders, 6 Hispanic Americans), 6 international. Average age 25. 1,431 applicants, 11% accepted, 76 enrolled. *Degree requirements:* For Pharm D, advanced pharmacy practice experience. *Entrance requirements:* PCAT, 2 letters of recommendation, interview, minimum of 62 credit hours of specific undergraduate courses. Additional exam requirements/recommendations for international students: Required—TOEFL (minimum score 575 paper-based; 233 computer-based; 80 iBT). *Application deadline:* For fall admission, 2/1 for domestic students. Applications are processed on a rolling basis. Application fee: $50. Electronic applications accepted. *Expenses:* Contact institution. *Financial support:* In 2009–10, 246 students received support. Federal Work-Study and scholarships/grants available. Financial award applicants required to submit FAFSA. *Faculty research:* Opioid pharmacology, heavy metal toxicology. *Unit head:* Dr. Scott A. Swigart, Dean of the School of Pharmacy, 585-385-8201, Fax: 585-385-8453, E-mail: sswigart@sjfc.edu. *Application contact:* Jose Perales, Director of Graduate Admissions, 585-385-8067, E-mail: jperales@sjfc.edu.

St. John's University, College of Pharmacy and Allied Health Professions, Professional Program in Pharmacy, Queens, NY 11439. Offers Pharm D. *Accreditation:* ACPE. *Students:* 482 full-time (304 women), 20 part-time (10 women); includes 312 minority (9 African Americans, 298 Asian Americans or Pacific Islanders, 5 Hispanic Americans), 16 international. Average age 23. 29 applicants, 0% accepted, 0 enrolled. In 2009, 240 Pharm Ds awarded. *Degree requirements:* For Pharm D, comprehensive exam, 1-year residency. *Entrance requirements:* Bachelor's degree from an ACPE-accredited program or BS in pharmacy and license, clinical experience, interview. Additional exam requirements/recommendations for international students: Required—TOEFL (minimum score 500 paper-based; 173 computer-based; 61 iBT), IELTS (minimum score 5.5). *Application deadline:* For fall admission, 3/15 priority date for domestic students, 5/1 priority date for international students; for spring admission, 11/1 priority date for domestic and international students. Applications are processed on a rolling basis. Application fee: $70. Electronic applications accepted. *Expenses:* Contact institution. *Financial support:* Research assistantships, career-related internships or fieldwork and unspecified assistantships available. Support available to part-time students. Financial award application deadline: 3/1; financial award applicants required to submit FAFSA. *Faculty research:* Patient outcomes, drug-drug-infections, pharmacokinetics, pharmcodynamics. *Unit head:* Dr. Candace Smith, Chair, 718-990-5374, E-mail: smithc@stjohns.edu. *Application contact:* Kathleen Davis, Director of Graduate Admission, 718-990-2790, Fax: 718-990-5686, E-mail: gradhelp@stjohns.edu.

St. Louis College of Pharmacy, Professional Program in Pharmacy, St. Louis, MO 63110-1088. Offers Pharm D. *Accreditation:* ACPE. *Entrance requirements:* PCAT, 2 letters of recommendation. Additional exam requirements/recommendations for international students: Required—TOEFL (minimum score 550 paper-based; 220 computer-based). Electronic applications accepted. *Faculty research:* Geriatrics, cardiology, psychobiology, infectious diseases.

Samford University, McWhorter School of Pharmacy, Birmingham, AL 35229. Offers Pharm D. *Accreditation:* ACPE. *Faculty:* 39 full-time (18 women), 1 (woman) part-time/adjunct. *Students:* 498 full-time (309 women), 3 part-time (2 women); includes 50 minority (18 African Americans, 3 American Indian/Alaska Native, 21 Asian Americans or Pacific Islanders, 8 Hispanic Americans), 7 international. Average age 23. 910 applicants, 20% accepted, 128 enrolled. In 2009, 125 Pharm Ds awarded. *Entrance requirements:* PCAT, minimum GPA of 2.75. Additional exam requirements/recommendations for international students: Required—TOEFL (minimum score 550 paper-based; 213 computer-based; 80 iBT). *Application deadline:* For fall admission, 2/1 for domestic students. Applications are processed on a rolling basis. Application fee: $50. Electronic applications accepted. *Expenses:* Contact institution. *Financial support:* In 2009–10, 224 students received support. Career-related internships or fieldwork, Federal Work-Study, and institutionally sponsored loans available. Financial award application deadline: 5/2; financial award applicants required to submit FAFSA. *Faculty research:* Biotechnology, transdermal drug delivery, vaccines, human skin models, genetic mapping of disease. *Unit head:* Dr. Charles D. Sands, Dean, 205-726-2820, Fax: 205-726-2759, E-mail: ccsands@samford.edu. *Application contact:* C. Bruce Foster, Director of External Relations and Pharmacy Admissions, 205-726-2982, Fax: 205-726-4141, E-mail: cbfoster@samford.edu.

Shenandoah University, School of Pharmacy, Winchester, VA 22601-5195. Offers pharmacy and non-traditional pharmacy (Pharm D). *Accreditation:* ACPE. Part-time programs available. Postbaccalaureate distance learning degree programs offered (minimal on-campus study). *Faculty:* 22 full-time (11 women), 2 part-time/adjunct (both women). *Students:* 309 full-time (168 women), 125 part-time (68 women); includes 111 minority (18 African Americans, 1 American Indian/Alaska Native, 88 Asian Americans or Pacific Islanders, 4 Hispanic Americans), 2 international. Average age 31. 1,077 applicants, 28% accepted, 157 enrolled. *Entrance requirements:* PCAT, interview, minimum GPA of 2.8, 3 letters of recommendation. Additional exam requirements/recommendations for international students: Required—TOEFL (minimum score 550 paper-based; 213 computer-based; 79 iBT), IELTS (minimum score 6.5). *Application deadline:* For fall admission, 2/1 for domestic and international students. Applications are processed on a rolling basis. Application fee: $30. Electronic applications accepted. *Expenses:* Contact institution. *Financial support:* Application deadline: 3/15. *Unit head:* Dr. Alan McKay, Dean, 540-665-1280, Fax: 540-665-1283, E-mail: amckay@su.edu. *Application contact:* David Anthony, Dean of Admissions, 540-665-4581, Fax: 540-665-4627, E-mail: admit@su.edu.

South Dakota State University, Graduate School, College of Pharmacy, Professional Program in Pharmacy, Brookings, SD 57007. Offers Pharm D. *Accreditation:* ACPE. *Entrance requirements:* ACT or PCAT, bachelor's degree in pharmacy. Additional exam requirements/recommendations for international students: Required—TOEFL (minimum score 550 paper-based; 213 computer-based). *Faculty research:* Geriatric medicine, drugs of abuse, anti-cancer drugs, drug metabolism, sustained drug delivery.

Southern Illinois University Edwardsville, School of Pharmacy, Edwardsville, IL 62026-0001. Offers Pharm D. *Accreditation:* ACPE. *Faculty:* 20 full-time (6 women). *Students:* 316 full-time (182 women); includes 36 minority (10 African Americans, 19 Asian Americans or Pacific Islanders, 7 Hispanic Americans), 1 international. Average age 26. *Entrance requirements:* PCAT. *Application deadline:* For fall admission, 12/1 for domestic and international students. Application fee: $40. Electronic applications accepted. *Expenses:* Tuition, state resident: part-time $1252.50 per semester. Tuition, nonresident: part-time $3131.25 per semester. Required fees: $586.85 per semester. Tuition and fees vary according to course load. *Financial support:* Career-related internships or fieldwork, Federal Work-Study, institutionally sponsored loans, scholarships/grants, and traineeships available. Support available to part-time students. Financial award application deadline: 3/1; financial award applicants required to submit FAFSA. *Unit head:* Dr. Philip J. Medon, Head, 618-650-5150, E-mail: pharmacy@siue.edu. *Application contact:* Dr. Philip J. Medon, Head, 618-650-5150, E-mail: pharmacy@siue.edu.

South University, Graduate Programs, School of Pharmacy, Savannah, GA 31406. Offers Pharm D. *Accreditation:* ACPE.

See Close-Up on page 1795.

South University, Program in Pharmacy, Columbia, SC 29203. Offers Pharm D.

See Close-Up on page 1793.

Southwestern Oklahoma State University, College of Pharmacy, Weatherford, OK 73096-3098. Offers Pharm D. *Accreditation:* ACPE. *Entrance requirements:* PCAT.

Temple University, Health Sciences Center, School of Pharmacy, Professional Program in Pharmacy, Philadelphia, PA 19122-6096. Offers Pharm D. *Accreditation:* ACPE. *Expenses:* Contact institution.

Texas Southern University, College of Pharmacy and Health Sciences, Houston, TX 77004-4584. Offers Pharm D, MS, PhD. *Accreditation:* ACPE. Postbaccalaureate distance learning degree programs offered. *Faculty:* 13 full-time (5 women), 1 (woman) part-time/adjunct. *Students:* 363 full-time (216 women), 152 part-time (89 women); includes 425 minority (228 African Americans, 177 Asian Americans or Pacific Islanders, 20 Hispanic Americans), 54 international. Average age 29. 139 applicants, 100% accepted, 129 enrolled. In 2009, 116 first professional degrees, 2 master's awarded. *Entrance requirements:* For Pharm D, GRE General Test, PCAT; for master's, PCAT. *Application deadline:* For fall admission, 2/15 for domestic and international students. Applications are processed on a rolling basis. Application fee: $50 ($75 for international students). Electronic applications accepted. *Expenses:* Tuition, state resident: full-time $1805; part-time $100 per credit hour. Tuition, nonresident: full-time $6470; part-time $343 per credit hour. Tuition and fees vary according to course level, course load and degree level. *Financial support:* In 2009–10, 1 research assistantship (averaging $22,000 per year), 11 teaching assistantships (averaging $18,521 per year) were awarded; fellowships, career-related internships or fieldwork, scholarships/grants, and tuition waivers (partial) also available. Financial award application deadline: 5/1; financial award applicants required to submit FAFSA. *Faculty research:* Basic and clinical pharmacokinetics, metabolism studies, diabetes, hypertension, sickle cell. *Unit head:* Dr. Barbara Hayes, Dean, 713-313-7164, Fax: 713-313-1091, E-mail: hayes_bc@tsu.edu. *Application contact:* LaJoy Kay, Director, 713-313-1880, E-mail: kay_lj@tsu.edu.

Thomas Jefferson University, Jefferson College of Health Professions, School of Pharmacy, Philadelphia, PA 19107. Offers Pharm D. *Expenses:* Tuition: Full-time $26,858; part-time $879 per credit. Required fees: $525.

Touro University, Graduate Programs, Vallejo, CA 94592. Offers education (MA); osteopathic medicine (DO); pharmacy (Pharm D); physical therapy (DPT); physician assistant studies (MS); public health (MPH). *Accreditation:* AOsA; ARC-PA. Part-time and evening/weekend programs available. *Faculty:* 91 full-time (52 women), 51 part-time/adjunct (28 women). *Students:* 1,439 full-time (891 women). 6,914 applicants, 12% accepted, 503 enrolled. In 2009, 229 first professional degrees, 103 master's awarded. *Degree requirements:* For master's, comprehensive exam, thesis; for first professional degree, comprehensive exam. *Entrance requirements:* BS/BA. *Application deadline:* For fall admission, 3/15 for domestic students; for winter admission, 12/1 for domestic students. Applications are processed on a rolling basis. Application fee: $100. Electronic applications accepted. *Financial support:* In 2009–10, 1,236 students received support, including 119 fellowships (averaging $1,535 per year), 24 research assistantships (averaging $3,686 per year), 13 teaching assistantships (averaging $4,058 per year); Federal Work-Study and scholarships/grants also available. Support available to part-time students. Financial award applicants required to submit FAFSA. *Faculty research:* Cancer, heart disease. *Application contact:* Steve Davis, Associate Director of Admissions, 707-638-5270, Fax: 707-638-5250, E-mail: steven.davis@tu.edu.

Universidad de Ciencias Medicas, Graduate Programs, San Jose, Costa Rica. Offers dermatology (SP); family health (MS); health service center administration (MHA); human anatomy (MS); medical and surgery (MD); occupational medicine (MS); pharmacy (Pharm D). Part-time programs available. *Degree requirements:* For master's, thesis; for first professional degree and SP, comprehensive exam. *Entrance requirements:* For first professional degree, admissions test; for master's, MD or bachelors degree; for SP, admissions test, MD degree.

University at Buffalo, the State University of New York, Graduate School, School of Pharmacy and Pharmaceutical Sciences, Professional Program in Pharmacy, Buffalo, NY 14260. Offers Pharm D, Pharm D/JD, Pharm D/MBA, Pharm D/MPH, Pharm D/MS, Pharm D/PhD. *Accreditation:* ACPE. *Faculty:* 23 full-time (8 women), 9 part-time/adjunct (3 women). *Students:* 351 full-time (215 women); includes 98 minority (15 African Americans, 4 American Indian/Alaska Native, 71 Asian Americans or Pacific Islanders, 8 Hispanic Americans), 21 international. Average age 25. 1,472 applicants, 8% accepted, 125 enrolled. In 2009, 114 Pharm Ds awarded. *Degree requirements:* For Pharm D, project. *Entrance requirements:* PCAT. *Application deadline:* For fall admission, 2/1 priority date for domestic and international students. Applications are processed on a rolling basis. Application fee: $50. Electronic applications accepted. *Financial support:* In 2009–10, 29 students received support. Health care benefits and merit and disadvantaged scholarships available. Financial award application deadline: 3/1; financial award applicants required to submit FAFSA. *Faculty research:* Pharmacokinetics, pharmacoepidemiology, AIDS, renal transplant, Attention Deficit Hyperactivity Disorder (ADHD), HIV/AIDS, oncology, critical care, PKPD, renal transplantation. Total annual research expenditures: $2.6 million. *Unit head:* Dr. Edward M. Bednarczyk, Chairman, 716-645-2828 Ext. 357, Fax: 716-645-2886, E-mail: eb@buffalo.edu. *Application contact:* Dr. Jennifer M. Hess, Assistant Dean, 716-645-2825 Ext. 1, Fax: 716-645-3688, E-mail: pharm-admin@buffalo.edu.

University of Alberta, Faculty of Graduate Studies and Research, Department of Pharmacy and Pharmaceutical Sciences, Edmonton, AB T6G 2E1, Canada. Offers M Sc, PhD. *Faculty:*

Pharmacy

University of Alberta (continued)
35. *Students:* 47. Average age 30. 562 applicants, 2% accepted, 11 enrolled. In 2009, 3 master's, 5 doctorates awarded. Terminal master's awarded for partial completion of doctoral program. *Degree requirements:* For master's, thesis; for doctorate, thesis/dissertation. *Entrance requirements:* Additional exam requirements/recommendations for international students: Required—Michigan English Language Assessment Battery or IELTS. *Application deadline:* For fall admission, 6/1 for international students; for winter admission, 9/15 for international students. Applications are processed on a rolling basis. Electronic applications accepted. Tuition and fees charges are reported in Canadian dollars. *Expenses:* Tuition, area resident: Full-time $4626 Canadian dollars; part-time $99.72 Canadian dollars per unit. International tuition: $8216 Canadian dollars full-time. Required fees: $3590 Canadian dollars; $99.72 Canadian dollars per unit. $215 Canadian dollars per term. *Financial support:* In 2009–10, 13 students received support, including 6 teaching assistantships; research assistantships, tuition waivers (partial) also available. *Faculty research:* Radiopharmacy, pharmacokinetics, bionucleonics, medicinal chemistry, microbiology. Total annual research expenditures: $2 million. *Unit head:* Dr. Nathaniel Jackson. *Application contact:* Dr. Edward E. Knaus, Director of Graduate Affairs, 780-492-5993, Fax: 780-492-1217.

The University of Arizona, Graduate College, College of Pharmacy, Pharmacy Professional Program, Tucson, AZ 85721. Offers Pharm D. *Accreditation:* ACPE. Part-time programs available. *Faculty:* 9. *Students:* 367 full-time (230 women), 6 part-time (3 women); includes 36 minority (2 African Americans, 1 American Indian/Alaska Native, 25 Asian Americans or Pacific Islanders, 8 Hispanic Americans), 29 international. Average age 29. In 2009, 78 Pharm Ds awarded. *Entrance requirements:* PCAT, 4-6 months of pharmacy experience. Additional exam requirements/recommendations for international students: Required—TOEFL (minimum score 550 paper-based; 213 computer-based; 79 iBT). Application fee: $65. Electronic applications accepted. *Expenses:* Tuition, state resident: full-time $9028. Tuition, nonresident: full-time $24,890. *Financial support:* In 2009–10, 11 research assistantships (averaging $20,700 per year) were awarded; career-related internships or fieldwork, scholarships/grants, health care benefits, and unspecified assistantships also available. *Faculty research:* Health/service administrative pharmacy education, geriatric pharmacy, social and behavioral pharmacy management and economics. Total annual research expenditures: $1.8 million. *Unit head:* Dr. Marie A. Chisholm-Burns, Head, 520-626-2298, E-mail: chilholm@pharmacy.arizona.edu. *Application contact:* General Information, 520-626-4311, E-mail: admissionsinfo@pharmacy.arizona.edu.

University of Arkansas for Medical Sciences, College of Pharmacy, Little Rock, AR 72205-7199. Offers Pharm D, MS. *Accreditation:* ACPE (one or more programs are accredited). *Students:* 473 full-time, 8 part-time. *Degree requirements:* For master's, thesis. *Entrance requirements:* For Pharm D, PCAT; for master's, GRE. Additional exam requirements/recommendations for international students: Required—TOEFL. Application fee: $0. *Expenses:* Contact institution. *Financial support:* Research assistantships available. Support available to part-time students. *Unit head:* Dr. Stephanie Gardner, Dean, 501-686-5558. *Application contact:* Dr. Kim Light, Graduate Program Director, E-mail: kelight@uams.edu.

The University of British Columbia, Faculty of Pharmaceutical Sciences, Vancouver, BC V6T 1Z3, Canada. Offers Pharm D, M Sc, PhD. *Degree requirements:* For master's, thesis, seminar; for doctorate, comprehensive exam, thesis/dissertation, seminar. *Entrance requirements:* B Sc in pharmacy, Canadian pharmacy license, interview. Additional exam requirements/recommendations for international students: Required—TOEFL (minimum score 600 paper-based; 250 computer-based; 100 iBT). Electronic applications accepted. *Faculty research:* Biopharmaceutics, pharmaceutical chemistry, pharmacology, toxicology, formulation.

University of California, San Diego, School of Pharmacy and Pharmaceutical Sciences, La Jolla, CA 92093. Offers Pharm D. *Accreditation:* ACPE.

University of California, San Francisco, School of Pharmacy, Program in Pharmacy, San Francisco, CA 94143. Offers Pharm D. *Accreditation:* ACPE. *Faculty:* 87 full-time (38 women), 15 part-time/adjunct (6 women). *Students:* 484 full-time (345 women); includes 281 minority (7 African Americans, 247 Asian Americans or Pacific Islanders, 27 Hispanic Americans). Average age 25. 1,673 applicants, 8% accepted, 122 enrolled. In 2009, 122 Pharm Ds awarded. *Degree requirements:* For Pharm D, comprehensive exam, supervised practice experience. *Entrance requirements:* 2 years of preparatory course work in basic sciences. *Application deadline:* For fall admission, 11/1 for domestic and international students. Application fee: $60 ($80 for international students). Electronic applications accepted. *Financial support:* In 2009–10, 431 students received support; teaching assistantships, career-related internships or fieldwork, Federal Work-Study, institutionally sponsored loans, and scholarships/grants available. Financial award application deadline: 2/1; financial award applicants required to submit FAFSA. *Faculty research:* Drug delivery, drug metabolism and chemical toxicology, macromolecular structure, molecular parasitology, pharmacokinetics. *Unit head:* Cynthia B. Watchmaker, Associate Dean & Director, Office of Student & Curricular Affairs, 415-476-8025, Fax: 415-476-6805, E-mail: watchmakerc@pharmacy.ucsf.edu. *Application contact:* Joel Gonzales, Admissions Coordinator, 415-502-5368, Fax: 415-476-6805, E-mail: osaca@pharmacy.ucsf.edu.

University of Charleston, Robert C. Byrd School of Pharmacy, Charleston, WV 25304-1099. Offers Pharm D. *Accreditation:* ACPE. *Faculty:* 22 full-time (11 women), 2 part-time/adjunct (1 woman). *Students:* 307 full-time (160 women), 6 part-time (5 women); includes 52 minority (18 African Americans, 32 Asian Americans or Pacific Islanders, 2 Hispanic Americans), 4 international. Average age 26. 670 applicants, 22% accepted, 80 enrolled. *Entrance requirements:* PCAT (taken within 2 years of the date of application), minimum GPA of 2.75, completion of 66 credit hours of pre-pharmacy prerequisite course work, 2 letters of recommendation (at least one from a practicing pharmacist). Additional exam requirements/recommendations for international students: Required—TOEFL. *Application deadline:* For fall admission, 2/1 priority date for domestic and international students. Applications are processed on a rolling basis. Application fee: $50. Electronic applications accepted. *Expenses:* Tuition: Full-time $25,224; part-time $875 per credit hour. Full-time tuition and fees vary according to degree level. *Financial support:* Application deadline: 3/1. *Unit head:* Dr. Michelle Easton, Dean, 304-357-4858, Fax: 304-357-4868, E-mail: michelleeaston@ucwv.edu. *Application contact:* Dr. Michelle Easton, Assistant Dean, Professional and Student Affairs, 304-357-4879, Fax: 304-357-4868, E-mail: michelleeaston@ucwv.edu.

University of Cincinnati, College of Pharmacy, Division of Pharmacy Practice, Cincinnati, OH 45221. Offers Pharm D. *Accreditation:* ACPE. *Entrance requirements:* GRE General Test, BS in pharmacy or equivalent, minimum GPA of 3.0. Additional exam requirements/recommendations for international students: Required—TOEFL.

University of Colorado Denver, School of Pharmacy, Denver, CO 80217-3364. Offers Pharm D, PhD. *Accreditation:* ACPE (one or more programs are accredited). *Faculty:* 101 full-time (48 women), 58 part-time/adjunct (35 women). *Students:* 618 full-time (372 women), 8 part-time (4 women); includes 183 minority (35 African Americans, 3 American Indian/Alaska Native, 112 Asian Americans or Pacific Islanders, 33 Hispanic Americans), 23 international. Average age 27. In 2009, 163 first professional degrees, 5 doctorates awarded. *Entrance requirements:* Minimum GPA of 2.75 in pre-pharmacy course work, 3 letters of recommendation. Additional exam requirements/recommendations for international students: Required—TOEFL (minimum score 550 paper-based; 213 computer-based). *Application deadline:* For fall admission, 12/1 for domestic students. Application fee: $50. *Expenses:* Contact institution. *Financial support:* Fellowships, research assistantships, teaching assistantships, career-related internships or fieldwork, Federal Work-Study, and institutionally sponsored loans available. Support available to part-time students. Financial award application deadline: 3/15; financial award applicants required to submit FAFSA. *Faculty research:* Antiviral clinical pharmacology, beriatric pharmacology, pharmacoepidemiology, pharmacogenomics, smoking cessation. Total annual research expenditures: $14.3 million. *Unit head:* Ralpha Altiere, Dean, 303-724-2631, E-mail: ralph.altiere@ucdenver.edu. *Application contact:* Beverly Brunson, Director, 303-724-2881, E-mail: beverly.brunson@ucdenver.edu.

University of Connecticut, Graduate School, School of Pharmacy, Professional Program in Pharmacy, Storrs, CT 06269. Offers Pharm D. *Expenses:* Tuition, state resident: full-time $4725; part-time $525 per credit. Tuition, nonresident: full-time $12,267; part-time $1363 per credit. Required fees: $346 per semester. Tuition and fees vary according to course load.

The University of Findlay, Graduate and Professional Studies, College of Pharmacy, Findlay, OH 45840-3653. Offers Pharm D. *Accreditation:* ACPE.

University of Florida, College of Pharmacy, Professional Program in Pharmacy, Gainesville, FL 32611. Offers Pharm D, MBA/Pharm D, Pharm D/MPA, Pharm D/MPH, Pharm D/PhD. *Accreditation:* ACPE. Part-time programs available. Postbaccalaureate distance learning degree programs offered (no on-campus study). *Entrance requirements:* PCAT, minimum GPA of 2.5. Additional exam requirements/recommendations for international students: Required—TOEFL. Electronic applications accepted. *Faculty research:* Drug discovery, drug delivery, pharmacodynamics, socioeconomics of pharmacy, neurobiology of aging.

University of Georgia, College of Pharmacy, Professional Program in Pharmacy, Athens, GA 30602. Offers Pharm D. *Accreditation:* ACPE. *Faculty:* 38 full-time (11 women), 4 part-time/adjunct (0 women). *Students:* 517 full-time (326 women), 3 part-time (1 woman); includes 121 minority (30 African Americans, 2 American Indian/Alaska Native, 82 Asian Americans or Pacific Islanders, 7 Hispanic Americans), 8 international. In 2009, 120 Pharm Ds awarded. *Expenses:* Tuition, state resident: full-time $6000; part-time $250 per credit hour. Tuition, nonresident: full-time $20,904; part-time $871 per credit hour. Required fees: $730 per semester. *Unit head:* Dr. Svein Oie, Dean, 706-542-1914, Fax: 706-542-5269, E-mail: soie@mail.rx.uga.edu. *Application contact:* Dr. Alan Wolfgang, Assistant Dean, 706-542-5278, Fax: 706-542-5269, E-mail: wolfgang@rx.uga.edu.

University of Houston, College of Pharmacy, Houston, TX 77204. Offers hospital pharmacy (MSPHR); pharmacy administration (MSPHR). *Accreditation:* ACPE. Part-time programs available. *Faculty:* 25 full-time (5 women), 13 part-time/adjunct (8 women). *Students:* 541 full-time (339 women), 38 part-time (22 women); includes 293 minority (26 African Americans, 1 American Indian/Alaska Native, 229 Asian Americans or Pacific Islanders, 37 Hispanic Americans), 86 international. Average age 25. 736 applicants, 26% accepted, 147 enrolled. In 2009, 123 first professional degrees, 13 master's, 4 doctorates awarded. Terminal master's awarded for partial completion of doctoral program. *Degree requirements:* For master's, thesis; for doctorate, thesis/dissertation; for Pharm D, comprehensive exam. *Entrance requirements:* For Pharm D, PCAT, community service, letter of recommendation; for master's and doctorate, GRE (preferred), GMAT. Additional exam requirements/recommendations for international students: Required—TOEFL. *Application deadline:* For fall admission, 2/1 for domestic and international students. Applications are processed on a rolling basis. Application fee: $25 ($75 for international students). Electronic applications accepted. *Expenses:* Tuition, state resident: full-time $7676; part-time $320 per credit hour. Tuition, nonresident: full-time $14,324; part-time $597 per credit hour. Required fees: $3034. *Financial support:* In 2009–10, 18 research assistantships with full tuition reimbursements (averaging $14,350 per year), 37 teaching assistantships with full tuition reimbursements (averaging $14,350 per year) were awarded; career-related internships or fieldwork, Federal Work-Study, institutionally sponsored loans, scholarships/grants, health care benefits, and unspecified assistantships also available. Support available to part-time students. Financial award application deadline: 2/1. *Faculty research:* Drug screening and design, cardiovascular pharmacology, infectious disease, asthma research, herbal medicine. *Unit head:* Dr. Lamar Pritchard, Dean, 713-743-1253, Fax: 713-743-1259, E-mail: flpritchard@uh.edu. *Application contact:* Morgan Ely, Director of Admissions, 713-743-1291, Fax: 713-743-1237, E-mail: pharmacyadmissions@uh.edu.

University of Illinois at Chicago, College of Pharmacy, Center for Pharmaceutical Biotechnology, Chicago, IL 60607-7173. Offers PhD.

University of Illinois at Chicago, College of Pharmacy, Professional Program in Pharmacy, Chicago, IL 60607-7128. Offers Pharm D. *Accreditation:* ACPE. *Entrance requirements:* PCAT.

The University of Iowa, College of Pharmacy, Iowa City, IA 52242-1316. Offers MS, PhD, Pharm D/MPH. *Accreditation:* ACPE (one or more programs are accredited). *Degree requirements:* For master's, thesis optional, exam; for doctorate, comprehensive exam, thesis/dissertation. *Entrance requirements:* For master's and doctorate, GRE General Test, minimum GPA of 3.0. Additional exam requirements/recommendations for international students: Required—TOEFL (minimum score 550 paper-based; 213 computer-based; 81 iBT). Electronic applications accepted.

University of Kentucky, College of Pharmacy, Professional Program in Pharmacy, Lexington, KY 40506-0032. Offers Pharm D. *Accreditation:* ACPE. *Faculty:* 71 full-time (26 women), 23 part-time/adjunct (9 women). *Students:* 514 full-time (319 women); includes 53 minority (25 African Americans, 28 Asian Americans or Pacific Islanders), 8 international. Average age 24. 688 applicants, 19% accepted, 132 enrolled. In 2009, 120 Pharm Ds awarded. *Entrance requirements:* PCAT, interview, minimum GPA of 2.5. Additional exam requirements/recommendations for international students: Required—TOEFL (minimum score 550 paper-based; 213 computer-based). *Application deadline:* For fall admission, 1/1 for domestic and international students. Applications are processed on a rolling basis. Application fee: $75. *Expenses:* Contact institution. *Financial support:* In 2009–10, 366 students received support, including 130 fellowships (averaging $1,300 per year); career-related internships or fieldwork, Federal Work-Study, institutionally sponsored loans, and scholarships/grants also available. Financial award application deadline: 9/15; financial award applicants required to submit FAFSA. *Faculty research:* Cardiology, pharmacokinetics, pediatrics, critical care, nutrition, infectious disease. *Unit head:* Dr. Kelly M. Smith, Associate Dean for Academic Affairs, 859-257-5304, Fax: 859-257-7297, E-mail: ksmit1@email.uky.edu. *Application contact:* Dr. Kelly M. Smith, Associate Dean for Academic Affairs, 859-257-5304, Fax: 859-257-7297, E-mail: ksmit1@email.uky.edu.

University of Louisiana at Monroe, Graduate School, College of Pharmacy, Program in Pharmacy, Monroe, LA 71209-0001. Offers PhD. *Accreditation:* ACPE. *Faculty:* 19 full-time (5 women), 9 part-time/adjunct (2 women). *Students:* 355 full-time (209 women), 10 part-time (4 women); includes 57 minority (19 African Americans, 1 American Indian/Alaska Native, 34 Asian Americans or Pacific Islanders, 3 Hispanic Americans), 42 international. Average age 24. In 2009, 90 doctorates awarded. *Degree requirements:* For doctorate, comprehensive exam, thesis/dissertation. *Entrance requirements:* For doctorate, GRE General Test or GMAT. Additional exam requirements/recommendations for international students: Required—TOEFL (minimum score 500 paper-based; 173 computer-based; 61 iBT). *Application deadline:* For fall admission, 8/24 priority date for domestic students, 7/1 for international students; for winter admission, 12/14 priority date for domestic students; for spring admission, 1/19 priority date for domestic students, 11/1 for international students. Applications are processed on a rolling basis. Application fee: $20 ($30 for international students). Electronic applications accepted. *Expenses:* Tuition, state resident: part-time $159 per credit hour. Tuition, nonresident: part-time $159 per credit hour. Required fees: $1300 per year. Tuition and fees vary according to course load. *Financial support:* In 2009–10, 16 research assistantships with full tuition reimbursements (averaging $5,655 per year), 18 teaching assistantships with full tuition reimbursements (averaging $5,655 per year) were awarded; Federal Work-Study and unspecified assistantships also available. Financial award application deadline: 4/1; financial award applicants required to submit FAFSA. *Unit head:* Dr. Wallace G. Leader, Dean, 318-342-1600, Fax: 318-342-1606, E-mail: pritchard@ulm.edu. *Application contact:* Dr. Paul W. Sylvester, Director of Research and Graduate Studies, 318-342-1958, Fax: 318-342-1606, E-mail: sylvester@ulm.edu.

University of Maryland, Baltimore, Graduate School, Graduate Programs in Pharmacy, Baltimore, MD 21201. Offers pharmaceutical health service research (MS, PhD), including epidemiology (MS), pharmacy administration (PhD); pharmaceutical sciences (PhD); Pharm D/PhD. *Accreditation:* ACPE (one or more programs are accredited). *Degree requirements:* For doctorate, comprehensive exam, thesis/dissertation. *Entrance requirements:* For doctorate, GRE General Test. Additional exam requirements/recommendations for international students:

Required—TOEFL (minimum score 550 paper-based; 215 computer-based), IELTS. Electronic applications accepted. *Expenses:* Tuition, state resident: full-time $7290; part-time $405 per credit hour. Tuition, nonresident: full-time $12,780; part-time $710 per credit hour. Required fees: $774; $10 per credit hour. $297 per semester. Tuition and fees vary according to course load, degree level and program. *Faculty research:* Drug discovery, pharmacokinetics, drug delivery, pharmaceutical outcomes and policy, pharmaceutical sciences.

University of Maryland, Baltimore, Professional Program in Pharmacy, Baltimore, MD 21201. Offers Pharm D, JD/Pharm D, Pharm D/MBA, Pharm D/MPH, Pharm D/PhD. *Accreditation:* ACPE. *Faculty:* 81 full-time (46 women), 594 part-time/adjunct (174 women). *Students:* 592 full-time (383 women); includes 294 minority (66 African Americans, 1 American Indian/Alaska Native, 220 Asian Americans or Pacific Islanders, 7 Hispanic Americans). Average age 25. 973 applicants, 17% accepted, 167 enrolled. In 2009, 117 first professional degrees awarded. *Entrance requirements:* PCAT, 65 hours in pre-pharmacy course work, on-site interview. Additional exam requirements/recommendations for international students: Required—TOEFL (minimum score 550 paper-based; 213 computer-based; 80 iBT). *Application deadline:* For fall admission, 1/5 for domestic and international students. Application fee: $45. Electronic applications accepted. *Expenses:* Tuition, state resident: full-time $7290; part-time $405 per credit hour. Tuition, nonresident: full-time $12,780; part-time $710 per credit hour. Required fees: $774; $10 per credit hour. $297 per semester. Tuition and fees vary according to course load, degree level and program. *Financial support:* In 2009–10, 362 students received support. Career-related internships or fieldwork, Federal Work-Study, institutionally sponsored loans, and scholarships/grants available. Support available to part-time students. Financial award application deadline: 3/1; financial award applicants required to submit FAFSA. *Faculty research:* Pharmaceutics, molecular biology, pharmacology, pharmacoepidemiology, pharmocoeconomics. Total annual research expenditures: $16.4 million. *Unit head:* Dr. Jill Morgan, Associate Dean for Student Affairs, 410-706-4332, Fax: 410-706-2158, E-mail: jmorgan@rx.umaryland.edu. *Application contact:* Patrice Sharp, Admissions Officer, 410-706-7653, Fax: 410-706-2158, E-mail: pharmdhelp@umaryland.edu.

University of Michigan, College of Pharmacy, Professional Program in Pharmacy, Ann Arbor, MI 48109. Offers Pharm D, Pharm D/PhD. *Accreditation:* ACPE. *Entrance requirements:* PCAT. *Expenses:* Tuition, state resident: full-time $17,286; part-time $1099 per credit hour. Tuition, nonresident: full-time $34,944; part-time $2080 per credit hour. Required fees: $95 per semester. Tuition and fees vary according to course load, degree level and program.

University of Minnesota, Duluth, Medical School, Department of Biochemistry, Molecular Biology and Biophysics, Duluth, MN 55812-2496. Offers biochemistry, molecular biology and biophysics (MS); biology and biophysics (PhD); social, administrative, and clinical pharmacy (MS, PhD); toxicology (MS, PhD). *Faculty:* 10 full-time (3 women). *Students:* 16 full-time (5 women); includes 3 minority (all Asian Americans or Pacific Islanders). Average age 29. 7 applicants, 29% accepted, 2 enrolled. In 2009, 1 master's, 1 doctorate awarded. Terminal master's awarded for partial completion of doctoral program. *Degree requirements:* For master's, comprehensive exam, thesis; for doctorate, comprehensive exam, thesis/dissertation. *Entrance requirements:* For master's and doctorate, GRE General Test. Additional exam requirements/recommendations for international students: Required—TOEFL. *Application deadline:* For winter admission, 1/3 for domestic students, 1/2 for international students; for spring admission, 3/15 priority date for domestic and international students. Application fee: $75 ($95 for international students). Electronic applications accepted. *Financial support:* In 2009–10, 8 students received support, including research assistantships with full tuition reimbursements available (averaging $27,300 per year), teaching assistantships with full tuition reimbursements available (averaging $27,300 per year); career-related internships or fieldwork, scholarships/grants, health care benefits, and unspecified assistantships also available. Financial award application deadline: 9/1. *Faculty research:* Intestinal cancer biology; hepatotoxins and mitochondriopathies; toxicology; cell cycle regulation in stem cells; neurobiology of brain development, trace metal function and blood-brain barrier; hibernation biology. Total annual research expenditures: $1.5 million. *Unit head:* Dr. Lester R. Drewes, Professor/Head, 218-726-7925, Fax: 218-726-8014, E-mail: ldrewes@d.umn.edu. *Application contact:* Cheryl Beeman, Administrative Assistant, 218-726-6354, Fax: 218-726-8014, E-mail: ahcd@d.umn.edu.

University of Minnesota, Twin Cities Campus, College of Pharmacy and Graduate School, Graduate Programs in Pharmacy, Graduate Program in Social, Administrative and Clinical Pharmacy, Minneapolis, MN 55455-0213. Offers experimental and clinical pharmacology (MS, PhD); social and administrative pharmacy (MS, PhD). *Degree requirements:* For master's, thesis (for some programs); for doctorate, thesis/dissertation. *Entrance requirements:* For master's, GRE General Test, BS in science; for doctorate, GRE General Test. Additional exam requirements/recommendations for international students: Required—TOEFL. *Faculty research:* Pharmaceutical economics, pharmaceutical policy, pharmaceutical social/behavioral sciences.

University of Minnesota, Twin Cities Campus, College of Pharmacy, Professional Program in Pharmacy, Minneapolis, MN 55455-0213. Offers Pharm D. *Accreditation:* ACPE. *Degree requirements:* For Pharm D, paper and seminar presentation. *Entrance requirements:* 2 years of pharmacy-related course work.

University of Mississippi, Graduate School, School of Pharmacy, Professional Program in Pharmacy, Oxford, University, MS 38677. Offers Pharm D. *Accreditation:* ACPE. *Faculty:* 12 full-time (5 women). *Students:* 173 full-time (115 women), 6 part-time (2 women); includes 16 minority (7 African Americans, 8 Asian Americans or Pacific Islanders, 1 Hispanic American). In 2009, 75 Pharm Ds awarded. *Application deadline:* For fall admission, 4/1 for domestic students. Applications are processed on a rolling basis. Application fee: $25. *Expenses:* Contact institution. *Financial support:* Scholarships/grants available. Financial award application deadline: 3/1; financial award applicants required to submit FAFSA. *Unit head:* Dr. Barbara G. Wells, Dean, 662-915-7265, Fax: 662-915-5704, E-mail: pharmacy@olemiss.edu. *Application contact:* Dr. Christy M. Wyandt, Associate Dean, 662-915-7474, Fax: 662-915-7577, E-mail: cwyandt@olemiss.edu.

University of Missouri–Kansas City, School of Pharmacy, Kansas City, MO 64110-2499. Offers pharmaceutical sciences (MS, PhD); pharmacy (Pharm D). *Accreditation:* ACPE (one or more programs are accredited). Postbaccalaureate distance learning degree programs offered (minimal on-campus study). *Faculty:* 49 full-time (23 women), 8 part-time/adjunct (3 women). *Students:* 339 full-time (210 women), 2 part-time (1 woman); includes 46 minority (10 African Americans, 1 American Indian/Alaska Native, 32 Asian Americans or Pacific Islanders, 3 Hispanic Americans), 7 international. Average age 26. 599 applicants, 26% accepted, 114 enrolled. In 2009, 70 first professional degrees, 1 master's awarded. *Degree requirements:* For master's, comprehensive exam (for some programs), thesis. *Entrance requirements:* For Pharm D, PCAT, interview, minimum GPA of 2.5, specified pre-pharmacy course work; for master's, GRE General Test, minimum undergraduate GPA of 3.0, graduate 3.5, 3 letters of reference. Additional exam requirements/recommendations for international students: Required—TOEFL (minimum score 550 paper-based; 213 computer-based; 80 iBT). *Application deadline:* For fall admission, 12/5 for domestic students, 12/15 for international students; for spring admission, 10/1 for domestic students. Applications are processed on a rolling basis. Application fee: $45 ($50 for international students). Electronic applications accepted. *Expenses:* Contact institution. *Financial support:* In 2009–10, 39 research assistantships with full and partial tuition reimbursements (averaging $9,397 per year), 18 teaching assistantships with full tuition reimbursements (averaging $11,300 per year) were awarded; career-related internships or fieldwork, Federal Work-Study, institutionally sponsored loans, tuition waivers (full and partial), and unspecified assistantships also available. Financial award application deadline: 3/1; financial award applicants required to submit FAFSA. *Faculty research:* Bio-organic and medicinal chemistry, drug delivery, pharmaceutics, molecular neurobiology, neurology. Total annual research expenditures: $1.4 million. *Unit head:* Dr. Robert W. Piepho, Dean, 816-235-1609, Fax: 816-235-5190, E-mail: piephor@umkc.edu. *Application contact:* Shelly M. Janasz, Director, Student Services, 816-235-2400, Fax: 816-235-5190, E-mail: janaszs@umkc.edu.

The University of Montana, Graduate School, College of Health Professions and Biomedical Sciences, Skaggs School of Pharmacy, Missoula, MT 59812-0002. Offers biomedical and pharmaceutical sciences (MS, PhD), including biomedical sciences (PhD), neuroscience, pharmaceutical sciences (MS), toxicology; pharmacy (Pharm D). Electronic applications accepted. *Faculty research:* Neuroendocrinology, neuropharmacology, molecular biochemistry, cardiovascular pharmacology, pharmacognosy.

University of Nebraska Medical Center, College of Pharmacy, Omaha, NE 68198. Offers Pharm D. *Accreditation:* ACPE. *Faculty:* 27 full-time (4 women), 4 part-time/adjunct (0 women). *Students:* 263 full-time (173 women); includes 24 minority (4 African Americans, 16 Asian Americans or Pacific Islanders, 4 Hispanic Americans). Average age 23. 139 applicants, 47% accepted, 65 enrolled. In 2009, 61 Pharm Ds awarded. *Entrance requirements:* PCAT, 90 semester hours of pre-pharmacy work. *Application deadline:* For fall admission, 1/1 for domestic students. Application fee: $45. Electronic applications accepted. *Expenses:* Contact institution. *Financial support:* Career-related internships or fieldwork, Federal Work-Study, institutionally sponsored loans, and scholarships/grants available. Financial award application deadline: 4/1; financial award applicants required to submit FAFSA. *Faculty research:* Biopharmaceutics, nanomedicine, drug design, pharmaceutics, pharmacokinetics. *Unit head:* Dr. Courtney V. Fletcher, Dean, 402-559-4333, Fax: 402-559-5060, E-mail: cfletcher@unmc.edu. *Application contact:* Dr. Charles H. Krobot, Associate Dean for Student Affairs, 402-559-4333, Fax: 402-559-5060, E-mail: ckrobot@unmc.edu.

University of New England, College of Pharmacy, Biddeford, ME 04005-9526. Offers Pharm D. *Accreditation:* ACPE. *Faculty:* 13 full-time (3 women), 1 part-time/adjunct (0 women). *Students:* 99 full-time (55 women); includes 11 African Americans, 16 Asian Americans or Pacific Islanders. *Unit head:* Douglas H. Kay, Dean, 207-221-4500, Fax: 207-523-1927, E-mail: dkay@une.edu. *Application contact:* Stacy Gato, Assistant Director of Graduate Admissions, 207-221-4225, Fax: 207-221-4898, E-mail: gradadmissions@une.edu.

University of New Mexico, Graduate School, College of Pharmacy, Professional Program in Pharmacy, Albuquerque, NM 87131-2039. Offers Pharm D. Registered pharmacists may pursue the non-traditional Pharm D degree. *Accreditation:* ACPE. *Students:* 344 full-time (196 women), 3 part-time (1 woman); includes 167 minority (11 African Americans, 17 American Indian/Alaska Native, 37 Asian Americans or Pacific Islanders, 102 Hispanic Americans), 18 international. Average age 27. In 2009, 93 Pharm Ds awarded. *Entrance requirements:* PCAT, 3 letters of recommendation, interview, 91 credit hours of prerequisites, letter of intent, Pharmcas application. *Application deadline:* For fall admission, 2/1 for domestic students. Applications are processed on a rolling basis. Application fee: $50. Electronic applications accepted. *Expenses:* Contact institution. *Financial support:* In 2009–10, 278 students received support. Federal Work-Study, institutionally sponsored loans, and scholarships/grants available. Financial award application deadline: 3/1; financial award applicants required to submit FAFSA. Total annual research expenditures: $107,864. *Unit head:* Dr. Donald Godwin, Assistant Dean for Professional and Graduate Education, 505-272-3241, Fax: 505-272-8324, E-mail: dgodwin@salud.unm.edu. *Application contact:* Krystal Weaver, Coordinator, Student Advisement, 505-272-0583, Fax: 505-272-5782, E-mail: kweaver@salud.unm.edu.

University of Oklahoma Health Sciences Center, College of Pharmacy, Professional Program in Pharmacy, Oklahoma City, OK 73190. Offers Pharm D. *Accreditation:* ACPE. *Faculty:* 39 full-time (22 women), 1 part-time/adjunct (0 women). *Students:* 491 full-time (285 women), 5 part-time (3 women); includes 170 minority (16 African Americans, 43 American Indian/Alaska Native, 97 Asian Americans or Pacific Islanders, 14 Hispanic Americans), 12 international. Average age 26. 282 applicants, 49% accepted, 112 enrolled. In 2009, 129 Pharm Ds awarded. Application fee: $25 ($50 for international students). *Expenses:* Tuition, state resident: full-time $3120; part-time $156 per credit hour. Tuition, nonresident: full-time $11,314; part-time $409.70 per credit hour. Required fees: $1471; $51.20 per credit hour. $223.25 per term. *Unit head:* Dr. Keith Swanson, Director of Student Services, 405-271-6598, E-mail: keith-swanson@ouhsc.edu. *Application contact:* Dr. Keith Swanson, Director of Student Services, 405-271-6598, E-mail: keith-swanson@ouhsc.edu.

University of Pittsburgh, School of Pharmacy, Professional Program in Pharmacy, Pittsburgh, PA 15260. Offers Pharm D. *Accreditation:* ACPE. *Faculty:* 79 full-time (37 women), 84 part-time/adjunct (39 women). *Students:* 430 full-time (269 women); includes 51 minority (12 African Americans, 1 American Indian/Alaska Native, 33 Asian Americans or Pacific Islanders, 5 Hispanic Americans), 3 international. Average age 22. 807 applicants, 17% accepted, 108 enrolled. In 2009, 100 Pharm Ds awarded. *Entrance requirements:* PCAT. *Application deadline:* For fall admission, 12/1 for domestic students. Application fee: $205. Electronic applications accepted. *Expenses:* Contact institution. *Financial support:* In 2009–10, 163 students received support. Career-related internships or fieldwork, Federal Work-Study, and scholarships/grants available. Financial award application deadline: 10/1. *Faculty research:* Drug delivery and targeting; neuroendocrine pharmacology; genomics, proteomics, and drug discovery; clinical pharmaceutical sciences. Total annual research expenditures: $7.8 million. *Unit head:* Dr. Sharon Corey, Assistant Dean of Students, 412-648-9157, Fax: 412-383-9996, E-mail: coreys@pitt.edu. *Application contact:* Marcia L. Borrelli, Director of Student Services, 412-383-9000, Fax: 412-383-9996, E-mail: borrelli@pitt.edu.

University of Puerto Rico, Medical Sciences Campus, School of Pharmacy, San Juan, PR 00936-5067. Offers industrial pharmacy (MS); pharmaceutical sciences (MS); pharmacy (Pharm D). The MS in Pharmacy program is not admitting students in the academic year 2010-2011. *Accreditation:* ACPE. Part-time and evening/weekend programs available. *Degree requirements:* For master's, thesis; for Pharm D, portfolio, research project. *Entrance requirements:* For Pharm D, PCAT, interview; for master's, GRE, interview. Electronic applications accepted. *Expenses:* Contact institution. *Faculty research:* Controlled release, solid dosage form, screening of anti-HIV drugs, pharmacokinetic/pharmacodynamic of drugs.

University of Rhode Island, Graduate School, College of Pharmacy, Department of Pharmacy Practice, Kingston, RI 02881. Offers pharmaceutical sciences (MS, PhD), including pharmacoepidemiology and pharmacoeconomics; MS/PhD; PhD/MBA. *Accreditation:* ACPE. *Faculty:* 24 full-time (18 women). *Students:* 602 full-time (358 women), 1 part-time (0 women); includes 71 minority (11 African Americans, 51 Asian Americans or Pacific Islanders, 9 Hispanic Americans), 16 international. *Entrance requirements:* For master's and doctorate, 2 letters of recommendation. Additional exam requirements/recommendations for international students: Required—TOEFL (minimum score 550 paper-based; 213 computer-based). Application fee: $65. Electronic applications accepted. *Expenses:* Tuition, state resident: full-time $8828; part-time $490 per credit hour. Tuition, nonresident: full-time $22,100; part-time $1228 per credit hour. Required fees: $1118; $57 per semester. Tuition and fees vary according to program. *Financial support:* Applicants required to submit FAFSA. *Faculty research:* Treatment, virulence inhibition (toxin and biofilm), colonization and control of methicillin-resistant Staphylococcus aureus (MRSA); investigating activity of catheter lock solutions against biofilm producing bacteria. Total annual research expenditures: $507,319. *Unit head:* Dr. Stephen Kogut, Chair, 401-874-5370, Fax: 401-874-2181, E-mail: kogut@uri.edu. *Application contact:* Dr. Stephen Kogut, Chair, 401-874-5370, Fax: 401-874-2181, E-mail: kogut@uri.edu.

University of South Carolina, South Carolina College of Pharmacy, Professional Program in Pharmacy, Columbia, SC 29208. Offers Pharm D. *Accreditation:* ACPE. *Degree requirements:* For Pharm D, one foreign language. *Entrance requirements:* PCAT, 2 years of preprofessional study, interview. Electronic applications accepted. *Faculty research:* Cancer treatment and prevention, Ion channels, DNA damage repair, inflammation.

University of Southern California, Graduate School, School of Pharmacy, Professional Program in Pharmacy, Los Angeles, CA 90089. Offers Pharm D, Pharm D/MBA, Pharm D/MS, Pharm D/PhD. *Accreditation:* ACPE. *Students:* 725 full-time (513 women); includes 502 minority (18 African Americans, 3 American Indian/Alaska Native, 448 Asian Americans or Pacific Islanders, 33 Hispanic Americans), 8 international. In 2009, 169 Pharm Ds awarded. Application fee: $85. Electronic applications accepted. *Expenses:* Tuition: full-time $25,980; part-time $1315 per unit. Required fees: $554. One-time fee: $35 full-time. Full-time tuition and fees vary according to degree level and program. *Faculty research:* Infectious diseases, health services research, geriatric pharmacology, clinical psychopharmacology.

Pharmacy

University of Southern Nevada, College of Pharmacy, Henderson, NV 89014. Offers Pharm D. *Accreditation:* ACPE. *Faculty:* 52 full-time (28 women), 18 part-time/adjunct (5 women). *Students:* 663 full-time (361 women); includes 309 minority (56 African Americans, 3 American Indian/Alaska Native, 234 Asian Americans or Pacific Islanders, 16 Hispanic Americans), 19 international. Average age 27. 1,611 applicants, 17% accepted, 227 enrolled. In 2009, 176 Pharm Ds awarded. *Degree requirements:* For Pharm D, comprehensive exam. *Entrance requirements:* PCAT. *Application deadline:* For fall admission, 12/8 for domestic and international students. Applications are processed on a rolling basis. Application fee: $150. *Expenses:* Tuition: Full-time $37,900. Full-time tuition and fees vary according to program. *Financial support:* In 2009–10, 639 students received support. Scholarships/grants available. Financial award application deadline: 3/2; financial award applicants required to submit FAFSA. *Unit head:* Dr. Renee Coffman, Dean, 702-968-2017, Fax: 702-990-4435, E-mail: rcoffman@usn.edu. *Application contact:* Dr. Michael DeYoung, Associate Dean for Admissions, 702-968-2006, Fax: 702-968-1644, E-mail: mdeyoung@usn.edu.

The University of Tennessee Health Science Center, College of Pharmacy, Memphis, TN 38163-0002. Offers Pharm D, MS, PhD, Pharm D/PhD. *Accreditation:* ACPE (one or more programs are accredited). Terminal master's awarded for partial completion of doctoral program. *Degree requirements:* For master's, thesis; for doctorate, thesis/dissertation. *Entrance requirements:* For Pharm D, PCAT; for master's and doctorate, GRE General Test, minimum GPA of 3.0. Additional exam requirements/recommendations for international students: Required—TOEFL. Electronic applications accepted. *Expenses:* Contact institution.

The University of Texas at Austin, Graduate School, College of Pharmacy, Professional Program in Pharmacy, Austin, TX 78712-1111. Offers Pharm D. *Accreditation:* ACPE. *Entrance requirements:* GRE General Test.

University of the Incarnate Word, Feik School of Pharmacy, San Antonio, TX 78209-6397. Offers Pharm D. *Accreditation:* ACPE. *Faculty:* 21 full-time (11 women). *Students:* 352 full-time (256 women), 3 part-time (1 woman); includes 229 minority (31 African Americans, 2 American Indian/Alaska Native, 82 Asian Americans or Pacific Islanders, 114 Hispanic Americans), 7 international. Average age 27. *Entrance requirements:* PCAT, 80 hours documented pharmacy observational experience. Additional exam requirements/recommendations for international students: Required—TOEFL (minimum score 560 paper-based). *Application deadline:* For fall admission, 1/5 for domestic students. Application fee: $100. *Expenses:* Contact institution. *Financial support:* Federal Work-Study and scholarships/grants available. Financial award applicants required to submit FAFSA. *Unit head:* Dr. Arcelia Johnson-Fannin, Founding Dean, 210-883-1015, Fax: 210-822-1516, E-mail: johnsonf@uiwtx.edu. *Application contact:* Dr. Carmita A. Coleman, Assistant Dean, Office of Student Affairs, 210-883-1060, Fax: 210-822-1521, E-mail: cacolema@uiwtx.edu.

University of the Pacific, School of Pharmacy and Health Sciences, Professional Program in Pharmacy, Stockton, CA 95211-0197. Offers Pharm D. *Accreditation:* ACPE. *Faculty:* 34 full-time (17 women), 7 part-time/adjunct (3 women). *Students:* 633 full-time (390 women), 17 part-time (10 women); includes 447 minority (12 African Americans, 2 American Indian/Alaska Native, 408 Asian Americans or Pacific Islanders, 25 Hispanic Americans), 10 international. Average age 24. 2,185 applicants, 13% accepted, 209 enrolled. In 2009, 208 Pharm Ds awarded. *Entrance requirements:* Additional exam requirements/recommendations for international students: Required—TOEFL. *Application deadline:* For fall admission, 2/1 for domestic students. Application fee: $75. *Financial support:* Career-related internships or fieldwork, Federal Work-Study, institutionally sponsored loans, and tuition waivers (partial) available. Support available to part-time students. Financial award application deadline: 3/1; financial award applicants required to submit FAFSA. *Application contact:* Cyndi Porter, Outreach Officer, 209-946-3957, Fax: 209-946-2410, E-mail: cporter@pacific.edu.

University of Utah, Graduate School, College of Pharmacy, Professional Program in Pharmacy, Salt Lake City, UT 84112-5820. Offers Pharm D. *Accreditation:* ACPE. *Students:* 201 full-time (94 women), 1 (woman) part-time; includes 15 minority (2 African Americans, 1 American Indian/Alaska Native, 6 Asian Americans or Pacific Islanders, 6 Hispanic Americans), 1 international. Average age 27. 126 applicants, 48% accepted, 59 enrolled. In 2009, 48 Pharm Ds awarded. *Entrance requirements:* PCAT. *Application deadline:* For fall admission, 1/5 for domestic and international students. Application fee: $55 ($65 for international students). *Expenses:* Tuition, state resident: full-time $4004; part-time $1674 per semester. Tuition, nonresident: full-time $14,134; part-time $5915 per semester. Required fees: $324 per semester. Tuition and fees vary according to course load, degree level and program. *Financial support:* Teaching assistantships available. *Faculty research:* Pain management, pharmacokinetic aspects of antiarrhythmics and anticoagulants, patient compliance. *Unit head:* Dr. John W. Mauger, Dean, 801-581-6731. *Application contact:* Sarah Lindsey, Academic Advisor, 801-581-5384, E-mail: pharmd.admissions@pharm.utah.edu.

University of Washington, School of Pharmacy and Graduate School, Department of Pharmacy, Seattle, WA 98195-7630. Offers MS, PhD. *Faculty:* 12 full-time (3 women), 3 part-time/adjunct (1 woman). *Students:* 21 full-time (9 women); includes 4 minority (all Asian Americans or Pacific Islanders), 5 international. 19 applicants, 26% accepted, 5 enrolled. In 2009, 2 master's, 3 doctorates awarded. Terminal master's awarded for partial completion of doctoral program. *Degree requirements:* For master's, thesis; for doctorate, thesis/dissertation. *Entrance requirements:* For master's and doctorate, GRE General Test. Additional exam requirements/recommendations for international students: Required—TOEFL. *Application deadline:* For winter admission, 1/15 priority date for domestic students, 1/15 for international students. Application fee: $50 ($100 for international students). Electronic applications accepted. *Financial support:* In 2009–10, 6 students received support, including 2 fellowships with full tuition reimbursements available (averaging $14,679 per year), 1 research assistantship with full tuition reimbursement available (averaging $14,679 per year), 3 teaching assistantships with full tuition reimbursements available (averaging $14,679 per year); institutionally sponsored loans, scholarships/grants, and tuition waivers (full) also available. *Faculty research:* Pharmacoeconomics, pharmacoepidemiology, drug policy, outcomes research. Total annual research expenditures: $1.2 million. *Unit head:* Dr. Danny Shen, Chair, 206-543-6788, Fax: 206-543-3835, E-mail: ds@u.washington.edu. *Application contact:* Dr. David Veenstra, Director, 206-543-6788, Fax: 206-543-3835, E-mail: veenstra@u.washington.edu.

University of Washington, School of Pharmacy, Professional Program in Pharmacy, Seattle, WA 98195-7631. Offers Pharm D, Pharm D/PhD. *Accreditation:* ACPE. *Students:* 344 full-time (221 women); includes 151 minority (2 African Americans, 2 American Indian/Alaska Native, 139 Asian Americans or Pacific Islanders, 8 Hispanic Americans). Average age 25. 396 applicants, 27% accepted, 81 enrolled. In 2009, 90 Pharm Ds awarded. *Entrance requirements:* PCAT. *Application deadline:* For fall admission, 1/5 for domestic students. Application fee: $45. *Financial support:* In 2009–10, 152 students received support. Career-related internships or fieldwork, scholarships/grants, and tuition waivers (partial) available. Financial award application deadline: 8/1; financial award applicants required to submit FAFSA. *Unit head:* Dr. Nanci Murphy, Associate Dean, Academic and Student Programs, 206-685-2715, Fax: 206-616-2740, E-mail: pharminf@u.washington.edu. *Application contact:* Admissions Coordinator, 206-543-6100, Fax: 206-616-2740, E-mail: pharminf@u.washington.edu.

University of Wisconsin–Madison, School of Pharmacy, Professional Program in Pharmacy, Madison, WI 53706-1380. Offers Pharm D. *Accreditation:* ACPE. *Expenses:* Tuition, state resident: part-time $594 per credit. Tuition, nonresident: part-time $1504 per credit. Required fees: $65 per credit. Tuition and fees vary according to course load, program and reciprocity agreements.

University of Wyoming, College of Health Sciences, School of Pharmacy, Laramie, WY 82070. Offers Pharm D. *Accreditation:* ACPE. *Entrance requirements:* PCAT. Additional exam requirements/recommendations for international students: Required—TOEFL.

Virginia Commonwealth University, Medical College of Virginia-Professional Programs, School of Pharmacy, Professional Program in Pharmacy, Richmond, VA 23284-9005. Offers Pharm D, Pharm D/PhD. *Accreditation:* ACPE. Part-time programs available. *Degree requirements:* For Pharm D, research project. *Entrance requirements:* PCAT. *Faculty research:* Oncology, cardiology, infectious diseases, epilepsy, connective tissue.

Washington State University, Graduate School, College of Pharmacy, Department of Pharmaceutical Science, Pullman, WA 99164. Offers Pharm D. *Accreditation:* ACPE. *Entrance requirements:* GRE, minimum GPA of 3.0, interview, minimum 60 hours documented pharmacy experience. *Faculty research:* Enzymes, quality assurance, practices, tumor biology of metastasis, heart disease, anxiety and pain control.

Washington State University Spokane, Program in Pharmacy, Spokane, WA 99210-1495. Offers Pharm D. *Faculty:* 39. *Students:* 408. *Degree requirements:* For Pharm D, comprehensive exam, thesis/dissertation. *Entrance requirements:* GRE, 3 letters of recommendation, supplemental pharmacy CAS form, interview. *Application deadline:* For fall admission, 1/10 priority date for domestic students, 1/10 for international students; for spring admission, 7/1 priority date for domestic students, 7/1 for international students. Applications are processed on a rolling basis. Application fee: $50. *Expenses:* Contact institution. *Financial support:* Career-related internships or fieldwork, Federal Work-Study, and scholarships/grants available. Financial award application deadline: 2/15. *Faculty research:* Infectious disease, neuroopsychopharmacology, biotechnology/gene therapy. Total annual research expenditures: $5.2 million. *Unit head:* Dr. William Campbell, Interim Dean, 509-335-4750, E-mail: vburnham@wsu.edu. *Application contact:* Teresa Woolverton, Academic Coordinator, 509-335-2356, E-mail: twool@wsu.edu.

Wayne State University, Eugene Applebaum College of Pharmacy and Health Sciences, Department of Pharmaceutical Sciences, Detroit, MI 48202. Offers experimental technology in pharmaceutical sciences (Certificate); health systems pharmacy management (MS); hospital pharmacy (MS); pharmaceutical administration (MS, PhD); pharmacy (Pharm D). *Accreditation:* ACPE (one or more programs are accredited). Part-time programs available. *Degree requirements:* For master's, thesis optional. *Entrance requirements:* For Pharm D, bachelor's degree in pharmacy; for master's, GRE General Test, bachelor's degree in pharmacy. Additional exam requirements/recommendations for international students: Required—TOEFL (minimum score 550 paper-based; 213 computer-based); Recommended—TWE (minimum score 6). Electronic applications accepted. *Faculty research:* Mechanisms of resistance of bacteria to anti-microbial agents, drug metabolism and disposition in children, treatment strategies for stroke/neurovascular disease, prevalence and treatment of diabetes in Arab-Americans, ethnic variability in development of osteoporosis.

Wayne State University, Eugene Applebaum College of Pharmacy and Health Sciences, Department of Pharmacy Practice, Detroit, MI 48202. Offers medicinal chemistry (MS, PhD); pharmaceutical sciences (MS, PhD); pharmaceutics (MS, PhD); pharmacology (MS, PhD); pharmacy (Pharm D). Terminal master's awarded for partial completion of doctoral program. *Degree requirements:* For master's, thesis; for doctorate, thesis/dissertation. *Entrance requirements:* For master's, GRE General Test, minimum GPA of 2.6; for doctorate, GRE General Test, minimum GPA of 3.0. Additional exam requirements/recommendations for international students: Required—TOEFL (minimum score 550 paper-based; 213 computer-based); Recommended—TWE (minimum score 6). Electronic applications accepted. *Faculty research:* Pharmacodynamics and pharmacokinetics of anti-infective agents; efficacy of drug treatments for traumatic head injury and stroke; cultural difference in Arab-Americans related to diabetes treatment and prevention; drug disposition and effect in pediatrics; evaluation of anticoagulation regimens.

Western University of Health Sciences, College of Pharmacy, Program in Pharmacy, Pomona, CA 91766-1854. Offers Pharm D. *Accreditation:* ACPE. *Entrance requirements:* Minimum GPA of 2.5, interview, letters of recommendation. Additional exam requirements/recommendations for international students: Required—TOEFL (minimum score 500 paper-based; 213 computer-based). *Expenses:* Contact institution.

West Virginia University, School of Pharmacy, Professional Program in Pharmacy, Morgantown, WV 26506. Offers clinical pharmacy (Pharm D). Students enter program as undergraduates. *Accreditation:* ACPE. *Degree requirements:* For Pharm D, 100 hours of community service. *Entrance requirements:* PCAT, minimum GPA of 3.1. Electronic applications accepted.

West Virginia University, School of Pharmacy, Program in Pharmaceutical and Pharmacological Sciences, Morgantown, WV 26506. Offers administrative pharmacy (PhD); behavioral pharmacy (MS, PhD); biopharmaceutics/pharmacokinetics (MS, PhD); industrial pharmacy (MS); medicinal chemistry (MS, PhD); pharmaceutical chemistry (MS, PhD); pharmaceutics (MS, PhD); pharmacology and toxicology (MS); pharmacy (MS); pharmacy administration (MS). Part-time programs available. Terminal master's awarded for partial completion of doctoral program. *Degree requirements:* For master's, thesis; for doctorate, one foreign language, comprehensive exam, thesis/dissertation. *Entrance requirements:* For master's and doctorate, GRE General Test, minimum GPA of 2.75. Additional exam requirements/recommendations for international students: Required—TOEFL; Recommended—TWE. Electronic applications accepted. *Expenses:* Contact institution. *Faculty research:* Pharmaceutics, medicinal chemistry, biopharmaceutics/pharmacokinetics, health outcomes research.

Wilkes University, College of Graduate and Professional Studies, Nesbitt College of Pharmacy and Nursing, School of Pharmacy, Wilkes-Barre, PA 18766-0002. Offers Pharm D. *Students:* 279 full-time (164 women); includes 12 minority (1 African American, 10 Asian Americans or Pacific Islanders, 1 Hispanic American), 2 international. Average age 22. In 2009, 61 Pharm Ds awarded. *Entrance requirements:* PCAT. Additional exam requirements/recommendations for international students: Required—TOEFL (minimum score 500 paper-based; 173 computer-based; 79 iBT). *Unit head:* Dr. Bernard Graham, Dean, 570-408-4280, Fax: 570-408-7729, E-mail: bernard.graham@wilkes.edu. *Application contact:* Dr. Bernard Graham, Dean, 570-408-4280, Fax: 570-408-7729, E-mail: bernard.graham@wilkes.edu.

Wingate University, School of Pharmacy, Wingate, NC 28174-0159. Offers Pharm D. *Accreditation:* ACPE. *Degree requirements:* For Pharm D, comprehensive exam. *Entrance requirements:* PCAT. Electronic applications accepted. *Expenses:* Contact institution. *Faculty research:* Stress response in aging, arthritis therapy educational processes, professional development, sarcopenia in aging, geriatric–psych drug therapy.

Xavier University of Louisiana, College of Pharmacy, New Orleans, LA 70125-1098. Offers Pharm D. *Accreditation:* ACPE. *Entrance requirements:* Additional exam requirements/recommendations for international students: Required—TOEFL. Electronic applications accepted. *Expenses:* Contact institution.

Albany College of Pharmacy
AND HEALTH SCIENCES

ALBANY COLLEGE OF PHARMACY AND HEALTH SCIENCES
Pharmacy Program

Programs of Study

Albany College of Pharmacy and Health Sciences (ACPHS) offers a range of master's degree programs in the health sciences, spanning areas that include pharmaceutics, diagnostics, management, and comparative effectiveness research.

Students interested in these disciplines may pursue graduate degrees in the following programs: M.S. in Pharmacy Administration, M.S. in Health Outcomes Research, M.S. in Pharmaceutical Sciences, M.S. in Biotechnology, and M.S. in Cytotechnology and Molecular Cytology. Each of these programs may be completed in two years by full-time students, although options exist for working professionals interested in pursuing a degree program on a part-time basis.

Regardless of the program, students have opportunities to work side-by-side with faculty members on research across a range of subjects. Whether it is performing drug discovery and development, conducting molecular clinical case studies, or examining how people will pay for health care in the future, ACPHS has experts and resources to help students gain the knowledge necessary to succeed in their chosen careers.

The graduate programs at ACPHS are further differentiated from those of many other colleges and universities by small class sizes and the individualized attention afforded to each student. This environment allows students to work with faculty members who are most closely aligned with their interests and who are able to help them reach their goals.

Graduates of these programs are well positioned to accelerate their current career paths, transition to new careers in the health sciences, advance into executive level positions, or gain the academic foundation needed to pursue a Ph.D. or M.D.

Research Facilities

The Pharmaceutical Research Institute at Albany College of Pharmacy and Health Sciences (PRI-Albany) is a research and development institute dedicated to cutting-edge research, pharmaceutical services, and education, in partnership with pharmaceutical and biotechnology companies and academic and research centers in New York State, across the nation, and around the world.

ACPHS students benefit from the knowledge and experience of PRI-Albany Vice Provost and Chairman Shaker A. Mousa, Ph.D., formerly a senior researcher at DuPont Pharmaceuticals Company. Dr. Mousa holds thirty U.S. patents and 200 international patents, and his work has been reported in more than 700 publications.

PRI-Albany's primary objective is to enrich and advance pharmaceutical education by providing hands-on access to the full spectrum of drug development. The Institute strives to demonstrate, through the full range of its capabilities and expertise, how medicines advance from the "bench to the bedside," presenting students with a broad array of career options.

The Biomedical Research Building houses the Pharmaceutical Sciences department. Laboratory space exists for research in pharmacology and pharmaceutics. During the 2009–10 academic year, an animal research facility was opened. Animals are used to research the cause and effect of medications on sepsis and bladder disease as well as other disorders. Applications for accreditation and animal welfare assurance are in the process of being approved.

The Research Institute for Health Outcomes (RIHO) conducts research and disseminates findings in the areas of health outcomes, comparative effectiveness, pharmacoeconomics, and health technology assessment. Outcomes research is a type of study that measures the results of various medical interventions and options including drug treatments, therapies, health-care services, and diagnostic tools in actual clinical practice situations. The results of outcomes research can guide health-care decision makers in selecting and utilizing the most appropriate treatment strategies to optimize patient care.

Financial Aid

Students may apply for financial aid through the federal student financial aid program as well as alternative lending sources. Students performing research for funded faculty members have opportunities to secure additional financial support. International students seeking loans through a U.S. lender must have a sponsor or cosigner who is a U.S. citizen.

Cost of Study

For the 2010–11 academic year, full-time tuition for M.S. students is $7335 per semester or $815 per credit hour. General fees, including the meal plan, are $4047 per year. Cost of books will vary depending on the program.

Living and Housing Costs

Although most graduate students live off-campus, a limited amount of housing exists for graduate students on campus. For on-campus housing information, students should contact the Office of Residence Life at 518-694-7352. Requests for on-campus housing should be made no later than February for the fall semester. Students may contact the Graduate Admissions Office at 518-694-7149 for off-campus housing information.

Student Group

The College has more than 1,600 undergraduate and graduate students enrolled full-time at its Albany and Vermont campuses. ACPHS has a diverse student body representing fourteen countries and twenty states. ACPHS encourages individuals from all races, religions, national origin, sex and sexual preference, marital status, disability, and age to apply for admission to the College.

Location

The College's main campus is located in Albany, New York. Albany has garnered several honors in the past two years as an excellent place to live. These include being ranked by *Business Week* magazine as one of the top 20 cities for Generation Y based on its high percentage of creative workers and high income growth; ranked 15th on Forbes' list of America's most innovative cities; and ranked 18th by Portfolio.com for quality of life among the largest U.S. metro areas. The city's location—known as the crossroads of the Northeast—puts it within a 3- to 4-hour drive from New York City, Montreal, Boston, and Philadelphia.

ACPHS has a satellite campus in Colchester, Vermont.

The College

Established in 1881, Albany College of Pharmacy and Health Sciences is a private, independent institution with more than 1,600 students and approximately 100 full- and part-time faculty members. The College offers academic programs spanning the full spectrum of pharmacy and health sciences from drug discovery to patient care.

ACPHS has significantly expanded its research capabilities in recent years, leading to increased opportunities for students to work with faculty on government- and industry-funded research.

Students interested in research have an array of resources at their disposal, including an animal research facility and two research institutes. The College also has interdepartmental groups of faculty members dedicated to the study of infectious disease and nephrology.

Applying

The deadline for application is April 1 for the fall semester and November 1 for the spring. Students should contact the Graduate Admissions Office to confirm if a particular program allows spring admission. As with most graduate programs, admission is competitive and space is limited. Serious applicants should apply early and submit a complete application.

Students must submit the graduate admissions application along with a $75 application fee, GRE scores, transcripts, and a personal statement. International applicants must also include a WES or ECE evaluation for international transcripts and a TOEFL score. Highly qualified applicants will be invited for an in-person or telephone interview. All admissions materials should be sent to the Graduate Admissions Office or e-mailed to graduateeducation@acphs.edu.

Correspondence and Information

Albany College of Pharmacy and Health Sciences
106 New Scotland Avenue
Albany, New York 12208-3492

Phone: 518-694-7149
888-203-8010 (toll-free)
E-mail: graduate@acphs.edu
Web site: http://www.acphs.edu

Albany College of Pharmacy and Health Sciences

FACULTY HEADS AND PROGRAMS

Mehdi Boroujerdi, Ph.D., Provost and Dean.
Shaker A. Mousa, Ph.D., Vice Provost for Research.
William Millington, Ph.D., Director of Graduate Education and Chair, Pharmaceutical Sciences.
Hassan El-Fawal, Ph.D., Director of Biotechnology and Chair, Department of Health Sciences.
David Kile, R.Ph., M.S., Director of Pharmacy Administration and Health Outcomes Research.

M.S. in Pharmaceutical Sciences: The M.S. in Pharmaceutical Sciences program educates students in the scientific disciplines required for the discovery, development, and evaluation of new drugs and other pharmaceutical products. The thesis option trains students in basic and translational research under the supervision of a thesis advisor and committee of research faculty. This path is ideal for students interested in working as research scientists or pursuing a Ph.D. or M.D. The non-thesis option is geared toward individuals in the pharmaceutical or biomedical industry who would like to accelerate their careers with a graduate degree but who are not necessarily interested in laboratory research.

M.S. in Biotechnology: Designed to meet the needs of laboratory diagnosticians or basic research scientists, the M.S. in Biotechnology program integrates the basic sciences and laboratory innovation. Graduates of this program will improve their opportunity for advancement in their current field, in addition to gaining flexibility to pursue careers in areas such as molecular diagnostics, oncology research, forensic science, and environmental toxicology.

M.S. in Pharmacy Administration: The M.S. in Pharmacy Administration program is targeted to those current pharmacists aspiring to advance to a pharmacy management position. Unlike a traditional business degree program, the M.S. in pharmacy administration offers course work built around pharmacy and clinical experiences.

M.S. in Health Outcomes Research: The M.S. in Health Outcomes Research program provides the knowledge and unique skills necessary for evaluating outcomes of commonly prescribed therapies in order to guide the selection of the most effective treatments. This field will play an increasingly important role in finding better ways to provide the best care at the lowest cost.

M.S. in Cytotechnology and Molecular Cytology: The M.S. in Cytotechnology and Molecular Cytology program is designed to train students and diagnosticians to become leaders in the field of tissue and cell-based diagnostics. Students who enter this program learn to utilize traditional and innovative technologies such as image analysis, flow cytometry, and immunohistochemistry to diagnose cancer and other diseases in their early stages.

ACPHS Student Center.

Small class sizes at ACPHS allow students to work closely with faculty members.

DUQUESNE UNIVERSITY

Graduate School of Pharmaceutical Sciences

Programs of Study

The Graduate School of Pharmaceutical Sciences (GSPS) offers the M.S. and Ph.D. degrees in pharmaceutics, medicinal chemistry, and pharmacology and the M.S. degree in pharmacy administration. M.S. programs require a minimum of 30 postbaccalaureate semester hours (36 credits are required for the M.S. in pharmacy administration), including 6 credits in thesis research. Ph.D. programs require a minimum of 60 postbaccalaureate semester hours, including at least 12 credits in dissertation research.

Research Facilities

The Graduate School of Pharmaceutical Sciences is centered in the Richard King Mellon Hall of Science. A broad range of analytical instrumentation is available for students and faculty to carry out research in each discipline of study. Modern cell culture facilities are available for the pharmacology discipline. Modern animal facilities in adjacent Bayer Learning Center provide the opportunity for physiological, pharmacological, and toxicological evaluations of drugs and chemicals.

Mellon Hall facilities include the Duquesne University Center for Pharmaceutical Technology (DCPT) with a well-equipped manufacturing laboratory/pilot plant. The pharmaceutical manufacturing laboratory and DCPT house equipment for research into the manufacturing of solid dosage forms and an internationally regarded capability in analytical spectroscopy/process analytical technology/quality by design/process control.

The Gumberg Library at Duquesne houses a state-of-the-art integrated, online library system complete with a computerized card catalog, advanced computer disk (CD-ROM) system, online networked databases, and an array of technical support functions. The system enables students to access extensive local, national, and international databases and library catalogs around the world. Students have direct access to other university and research libraries in the Pittsburgh area.

Financial Aid

Teaching and research assistantships, which may include full remission of tuition and fees, are available.

Cost of Study

In 2010–11, tuition is $1098 per credit plus a University fee of $84 per credit.

Living and Housing Costs

For 2010–11, room and board in University dormitories cost $9476 per student per academic year for double occupancy. Food and clothing costs are similar to those in other cities of comparable size. The University offers a Student Health Care package, required for all graduate students.

Student Group

The University enrolls more than 10,300 students; typically, 70 students, representing a mix of U.S. (30 percent) and international (70 percent), are enrolled in graduate programs in the Graduate School of Pharmaceutical Sciences.

Student Outcomes

Most recent M.S. graduates have continued studies at the doctoral level or are employed in a variety of research laboratory settings. Graduates of Ph.D. programs are employed in research and administrative positions in industry and in research and teaching in academia.

Location

Allegheny County has a population of about 1.2 million; one third live in the city of Pittsburgh. Downtown is headquarters for several major corporations and the hub of cultural and recreational activities. Pittsburgh fields professional teams in football, baseball, and hockey. Perhaps the most engaging quality is the hometown flavor of the many neighborhoods that make up Pittsburgh.

The University

Duquesne is a private, Catholic, coeducational university. The 49-acre self-enclosed campus overlooks the Monongahela River. Students and 472 full-time faculty members are organized into the College and Graduate School of Liberal Arts and the Schools of Pharmacy, Nursing, Law, Business Administration, Education, Music, Health Sciences, Natural and Environmental Sciences, and Leadership and Professional Advancement. All campus facilities have been refurbished, with recent additions of current computer labs, a multipurpose athletic complex, and student living-learning centers. The University supports many intercollegiate and intramural athletics programs. The Tamburitzans and the Red Masquers are well-established ethnic dance and theatrical groups.

Applying

Students are admitted for the fall or spring semester. Assistantships are normally awarded in spring for the following academic year. Applicants should have earned a baccalaureate degree in chemistry, biology, pharmacy, engineering, allied health sciences, or social/behavioral or business sciences, depending on the proposed field of study. The completed application and supporting documents (official transcripts of all undergraduate and graduate course work, a brief statement of purpose and intent with regard to the specific area of graduate study chosen, three letters of recommendation from persons acquainted with the academic abilities of the applicant, and results of the GRE General Test) must be sent to the Associate Dean, Research and Graduate Programs. Applicants whose native language or principal language of instruction is not English are required to submit TOEFL scores to the Graduate School and to sit for on-campus English language competency testing. International students who are applying for a teaching assistantship are required to submit TSE scores.

Correspondence and Information

Associate Dean, Research and Graduate Programs
Graduate School of Pharmaceutical Sciences
Mylan School of Pharmacy
409 Mellon Hall
Duquesne University
Pittsburgh, Pennsylvania 15282
Phone: 412-396-1172
E-mail: gsps-adm@duq.edu
Web site: http://www.pharmacy.duq.edu

Duquesne University

THE FACULTY AND THEIR RESEARCH

Medicinal Chemistry

Patrick Flaherty, Assistant Professor of Medicinal Chemistry; Ph.D., Iowa. Synthetic medicinal chemistry and rational drug design, with emphasis on emerging biochemical targets relevant to human disease states, modern synthetic methodology, and iterative rounds of computation, synthesis, then biochemical analysis; general therapeutic areas of CNS agents and anticancer agents; current biological targets of CDK5, microtubules, MEK/ERK, alpha-synuclein, and GPI.

Aleem Gangjee, Professor of Medicinal Chemistry and Mylan School of Pharmacy Distinguished Professor; Adrian Van Kaam, C.S.Sp. Chair in Scholarly Excellence; Ph.D., Iowa. Synthetic medicinal chemistry, computer-assisted drug design, inhibitors of folate-metabolizing enzymes, receptor tyrosine kinase inhibitors, antimitotic agents, antitumor agents, design of combination chemotherapeutic potential in signal agents, antiopportunistic infection agents, heterocyclic chemistry, stereochemistry.

Marc W. Harrold, Professor of Medicinal Chemistry; Ph.D., Ohio State. Development of computer-based educational tools, instructional strategies in medicinal chemistry, drug design.

David J. Lapinsky, Assistant Professor of Medicinal Chemistry; Ph.D., Ohio State. Synthetic organic medicinal chemistry, rational drug design, computer-assisted drug design, emphasis on irreversible probes for characterizing monoamine transporter structure/function, development of drug candidates for treating psychostimulant abuse.

Pharmaceutical Administration

Vincent J. Giannetti, Professor of Pharmaceutical Administration; Ph.D., Pittsburgh. Prescription drug adherence, mental health, substance abuse, pharmacist counseling behaviors, health-care policy and ethics, coping with medication errors.

Khalid M. Kamal, Assistant Professor of Pharmaceutical Administration; Ph.D., West Virginia. Application of decision and cost-effectiveness analysis in health policy and medicine; health outcomes assessment in chronic conditions such as rheumatoid arthritis, ankylosing spondylitis, and chronic obstructive pulmonary disease; and use of Electronic Medical Records as a tool for quality improvement in the health-care system.

Andrea R. Pfalzgraf, Assistant Professor of Pharmaceutical Administration; M.P.H., Emory; Ph.D., West Virginia. Physician prescribing decisions, child and adolescent mental health.

David J. Tipton, Associate Professor of Pharmaceutical Administration; Ph.D., St. Louis. Medication errors, services marketing.

Pharmaceutics

Carl A. Anderson, Associate Professor of Pharmaceutical Sciences; Ph.D., Texas at Austin. Sensor technology for the study and control of pharmaceutical manufacturing, near-infrared and raman imaging, multivariate data analysis, process monitoring/control.

Lawrence H. Block, Professor of Pharmaceutics; Ph.D., Maryland. Pharmaceutic aspects of macromolecular/polymeric excipients (e.g., alginates, chitosan, and xanthan gum with an emphasis on the rheological properties of their solutions); pharmaceutical engineering, especially scale-up of processing of nonparenteral liquids and semisolids; hydrophilic gels as drug delivery systems; controlled and modified release drug and cosmetic delivery system development.

Ira Buckner, Assistant Professor of Pharmaceutical Sciences; Ph.D., Iowa. Investigation of the interactions between pharmaceutical materials and mechanical energy to facilitate advanced product development.

James K. Drennen III, Associate Professor of Pharmaceutics; Associate Dean of Research and Graduate Programs; Director, Center for Pharmaceutical Technology; Noble J. Dick Endowed Chair in Academic Leadership; and Editor-in-Chief of the *Journal of Pharmaceutical Innovation*; Ph.D., Kentucky. Pharmaceutical and medical applications of near-infrared spectroscopy, process control, quality by design, process analytical technology.

Jelena Janjic, Assistant Professor of Pharmaceutics; Ph.D., Pittsburgh. Fluorine chemistry applied to design and synthesis of multimodal nanoparticles for molecular imaging and diagnostics; rational design of nanoparticles as drug delivery vehicles for DNA, RNA, and small molecules in cancer and inflammation disease models.

Wilson S. Meng, Associate Professor of Pharmaceutical Sciences; Ph.D., USC. Self-assembling materials and polymeric particles as platforms for protein and nucleic acids delivery in mouse models of transplant rejection and tumor immunity.

Peter L. D. Wildfong, Associate Professor of Pharmaceutics; Ph.D., Purdue. Pharmaceutical materials science, with current research projects exploring how specific physicochemical and structural properties of small molecule organic solid materials impact large-scale manufacturing and final-dosage-form performance; emphasis on mechanically activated solid-state phase transformations of APIs and excipients; potential for high-shear induction of polymorphism and amorphization.

Pharmacology

J. Douglas Bricker, Professor of Pharmacology and Dean of the Mylan School of Pharmacy; Ph.D., Duquesne. Effects of drugs, chemicals, and disease states on the regulation of calcium uptake mechanisms, development, and screening of antidotal agents for clinical use and in vitro toxicity testing methods.

Jane E. Cavanaugh, Assistant Professor of Pharmacology; Ph.D., Penn State Hershey Medical Center. Mechanisms of cell death and survival in the diseased (Parkinson's disease, Alzheimer's disease) and nondiseased (normal aging) brain.

David A. Johnson, Associate Professor of Pharmacology and Director of Graduate Studies; Ph.D., Massachusetts College of Pharmacy. Drugs that enhance the function of neuronal pathways involved with learning and memory, neuropathology and treatment of eating disorders.

Rehana Leak, Assistant Professor of Pharmacology; Ph.D., Pittsburgh. Cellular adaptations to sublethal stress in models of neurodegenerative diseases are examined at the in vitro and in vivo level, with an emphasis on Parkinson's pathology.

Lauren O'Donnell, Assistant Professor of Pharmacology; Ph.D., Pennsylvania. Mechanisms of cytokine-mediated viral clearance from neurons, with a focus on the impact of inflammation on neurodevelopment.

Christopher K. Surratt, Associate Professor of Pharmacology and Division Head of Pharmaceutical Sciences; Ph.D., Virginia. Molecular mechanisms of brain receptors that recognize antidepressants, anxiolytics, and psychostimulant drugs of abuse.

Paula A. Witt-Enderby, Professor of Pharmacology; Ph.D., Arizona. Molecular pharmacology of melatonin receptors, and its associated signaling cascades, with emphasis on the role of melatonin in stem cell differentiation.

SouthUniversity℠

SOUTH UNIVERSITY

Columbia Campus
School of Pharmacy
Doctor of Pharmacy

Program of Study

The South University School of Pharmacy, accredited by the Accreditation Council for Pharmacy Education (ACPE), is one of only three schools of pharmacy in the state of Georgia and one of less than a dozen in the United States to offer an accelerated three-year curriculum. The mission of the South University School of Pharmacy is to serve the public's health-care needs by preparing pharmacists to provide pharmaceutical care that improves health outcomes for patients.

The Doctor of Pharmacy degree program at South University's campus in Columbia, South Carolina, is designed to provide progressive, quality postgraduate education for the pharmacy profession's future practitioners. The role of pharmacists in the medical field is changing and evolving to meet the demands of the profession and society. The Pharmacy degree curriculum at South University–Columbia is structured to produce graduates who can adapt to the profession's changes while also maintaining high standards of pharmacy practice. This is the third Doctor of Pharmacy program in South Carolina.

The School of Pharmacy strives for excellence in teaching, scholarship, professional service, and community service. Faculty members provide students with the knowledge, skills, abilities, and values necessary to become a successful practitioner. While at South University, students are encouraged to foster a desire for lifelong learning, engage in scholarship, learn about the process of research, and develop an understanding of the value of interdisciplinary care. At South University, students are encouraged to become involved in their community and develop an understanding of the importance of volunteerism and its impact on the community.

Students learn the skills needed to assess, monitor, initiate, or adjust drug therapy programs. In those roles, they are prepared to educate patients on the proper use of pharmaceuticals, develop drug therapy plans through data evaluation, and partner with other health-care providers to contribute to a patient's well-being.

Research Facilities

South University's Columbia campus recently celebrated the opening of its new satellite campus facility for the School of Pharmacy program. In addition to the new facility and its classroom and lab facilities, South University–Columbia includes a bookstore, student lounge, and career services center. Students may retrieve periodicals in paper or electronic form. The South University Library provides in-library and remote access to electronic databases. Both bibliographic and full-text databases are available via EBSCOhost (e.g., Academic Search Premier, SocINDEX, PsycINFO, PsycARTICLES, and Mental Measurements Yearbook), the search and retrieval system of EBSCO Information Services, and via the Library and Information Resources Network (e.g., Infotrac and ProQuest databases). Infotrac databases include counseling sources such as Expanded Academic ASAP, Academic OneFile, and InfotracOneFile, and ProQuest databases include counseling sources such as ProQuest Psychology Journals and ProQuest Research Library. Internet access is available on all computers throughout the campus.

Financial Aid

A wide range of financial aid options is available to students who qualify. The Savannah campus of South University offers access to federal and state aid, including grants, loans, and work-study programs. Eligible students may apply for veterans' educational benefits and are encouraged to investigate the availability of grants and scholarships through community resources. As a first step, students should complete the Free Application for Federal Student Aid (FAFSA). Students may apply electronically at http://www.fafsa.ed.gov or at the campus Student Financial Services department. Applications should be submitted promptly to receive consideration for the maximum amount of aid.

Cost of Study

Tuition information for the Doctor of Pharmacy program may be obtained by contacting the School of Pharmacy via the South University Web site at http://www.southuniversity.edu.

Living and Housing Costs

South University does not offer or operate student housing. Pharmacy students typically live in apartments in the Columbia area. Students who commute from long distances can arrange to stay at nearby hotels that offer long-term rates. More information is available by contacting the Admissions Department.

Student Group

The Columbia campus of South University has a diverse student body enrolled in both day and evening classes. Students are primarily commuters who live within 50 miles of the city.

Student Outcomes

The South University Career Services Department has been established to assist currently enrolled students in developing their career plans and reaching their employment goals. Career services include, but are not limited to, one-on-one career counseling, special career-related workshops and programs, coaching for resume and cover letter development, and resume referral to employers.

Location

South University recently relocated its Columbia campus to the growing east side of Columbia, just minutes from downtown. The new campus is conveniently located off of I-77 at Farrow Road and Parklane.

The campus surroundings are highlighted by a natural wooded landscape and vast green space featuring a tranquil campus courtyard. Convenient to malls, shopping, and the growing east side of Columbia, the new campus location provides easier access to students from throughout the greater Columbia area.

The School

The School of Pharmacy is accredited by the American Council on Pharmaceutical Education (ACPE). South University is accredited by the Commission on Colleges of the Southern Association of Colleges and Schools (SACS) to award associate, bachelor's, master's, and doctoral degrees. Students should contact the Commission on Colleges at 1866 Southern Lane, Decatur, Georgia 30033-4097 or call 404-679-4500 with questions about the accreditation of South University.

Applying

Students are accepted into the Doctor of Pharmacy program once each year, in the fall quarter that begins in June. Entrance into the program is gained through a formal application review and assessment of the applicant's potential for professional and academic achievement. Prospective students must complete a minimum of two years of prescribed prepharmacy course requirements at a regionally accredited U.S. college or university. A grade of C or better must be earned in each prerequisite course. The cumulative GPA for the current first-year class was 3.41, and their average science GPA was 3.15. Applicants also must submit scores from the Pharmacy College Admissions Test (PCAT).

The South University School of Pharmacy utilizes the Pharmacy College Application Service (PharmCAS), a centralized application service for prospective students applying to colleges and schools of pharmacy. In addition, a supplemental application is required to complete the application process, along with a fee of $50. The application is available at http://www.southuniversity.edu/Pharmacy/

Correspondence and Information

Applications for admission to the South University Doctor of Pharmacy program are available by contacting:

School of Pharmacy
South University
709 Mall Boulevard
Savannah, Georgia 31406-4805

Phone: 912-201-8120
866-629-2901 (toll-free)
Fax: 912-201-8070
E-mail: pharmd@southuniversity.edu
Web site: http://www.southuniversity.edu/pharmacy

South University

THE FACULTY

One of the most outstanding aspects of South University's Doctor of Pharmacy program is the dedication of the faculty members and their ability to cultivate a supportive learning environment. Faculty members are committed to their roles as mentors, teachers, and colearners. They are also dedicated to the training of students who can assume positions of leadership within the field of pharmacy. A current list of program faculty members is available at the South University Web site (http://www.southuniversity.edu/pharmacy).

South University's School of Pharmacy is one of less than a dozen schools in the country to offer an accelerated three-year Doctor of Pharmacy degree program.

SouthUniversity℠

SOUTH UNIVERSITY

Savannah Campus
School of Pharmacy
Doctor of Pharmacy

Program of Study	The South University School of Pharmacy, accredited by the Accreditation Council for Pharmacy Education (ACPE), is one of only three schools of pharmacy in the state of Georgia and one of less than a dozen in the U.S. to offer an accelerated three-year curriculum. The mission of the South University School of Pharmacy is to serve the public's health-care needs by preparing pharmacists to provide pharmaceutical care that improves health outcomes for patients.
	The School of Pharmacy strives for excellence in teaching, scholarship, professional service, and community service. Faculty members provide students with the knowledge, skills, abilities, and values necessary to become a successful practitioner. While at South University, students are encouraged to foster a desire for lifelong learning, engage in scholarship, learn about the process of research, and develop an understanding of the value of interdisciplinary care. At South University, students are encouraged to become involved in their community and develop an understanding of the importance of volunteerism and its impact on the community.
	Following acceptance into the program, Pharm.D. students begin an accelerated, full-time, twelve-quarter schedule designed to provide four academic years of study within three calendar years. This accelerated pace is only available at a handful of institutions across the country. South University's program was designed to meet the increasing demand for well-trained pharmacists. The program is tailored to accentuate the future of the pharmacy profession while also developing pharmacists who are familiar with contemporary practice. The curriculum is structured to educate and prepare competent pharmaceutical practitioners who can provide care in a variety of institutional, community, and other settings. Students learn the skills needed to assess, monitor, initiate, or adjust drug therapy programs. In those roles, they are prepared to educate patients on the proper use of pharmaceuticals, develop drug therapy plans through data evaluation, and partner with other health-care providers to contribute to a patient's well-being.
Research Facilities	South University's Savannah campus is home to the College of Arts and Sciences, College of Business, the College of Health Professions, the College of Nursing, and the School of Pharmacy. The campus houses classroom and laboratory facilities for the health sciences and pharmacy programs. In addition, the University opened an $8-million School of Pharmacy building in December 2004. This facility provides wireless instructional, laboratory, and office facilities for pharmacy students, faculty members, and administrators. In addition to eight small classrooms, two large tiered lecture halls, and two 50-seat classrooms, the building houses two general-purpose laboratories that accommodate 34 students each, a sterile dilutions facility, six patient examination rooms equipped with audio/video monitoring, a drug information center, and a suite of eight laboratories to accommodate basic faculty research. Practice sites to provide both intermediate and advanced practice experiences include community pharmacies, hospitals, long-term-care facilities, pharmaceutical companies, and other venues that have been recruited to support the experiential component of the curriculum. South University's facilities are designed to offer personalized and technically sophisticated instructional delivery.
	The campus library provides comfortable study space for students, wireless Internet capabilities for laptop network connectivity, a separate computer lab, and reference and interlibrary loan services.
Financial Aid	A wide range of financial aid options is available to students who qualify. The Savannah campus of South University offers access to federal and state aid, including grants, loans, and work-study programs. Eligible students may apply for veterans' educational benefits and are encouraged to investigate the availability of grants and scholarships through community resources. As a first step, students should complete the Free Application for Federal Student Aid (FAFSA). Students may apply electronically at http://www.fafsa.ed.gov or at the campus Student Financial Services department. Applications should be submitted promptly to receive consideration for the maximum amount of aid.
Cost of Study	Tuition information for the Doctor of Pharmacy program may be obtained by contacting the School of Pharmacy via the South University Web site at http://www.southuniversity.edu.
Living and Housing Costs	South University offers school-sponsored student housing at its Savannah campus in conjunction with a local apartment complex. Due to the full-time nature of the program, pharmacy students typically live in rental homes or apartments in the Savannah area. More information is available by contacting the Director of Student Housing at 912-201-8000.
Student Group	The Savannah campus of South University has a diverse student body enrolled in both day and evening classes. Students are primarily commuters who live within 50 miles of the city.
Student Outcomes	The South University Career Services Department has been established to assist currently enrolled students in developing their career plans and reaching their employment goals. Career services include, but are not limited to, one-on-one career counseling, special career-related workshops and programs, coaching for resume and cover letter development, and resume referral to employers.
Location	Located on the south side of the historic city of Savannah, the campus is convenient to the city's bustling midtown section and a full range of educational and cultural activities. The Atlantic Ocean and recreational amenities of Tybee Island, including beaches and numerous outdoor activities, are just a short drive away. In addition, the campus is located just a short drive from Hilton Head Island and Charleston, South Carolina.
The School	The School of Pharmacy is accredited by the American Council on Pharmaceutical Education (ACPE). South University is accredited by the Commission on Colleges of the Southern Association of Colleges and Schools (SACS) to award associate, bachelor's, master's, and doctoral degrees. Students should contact the Commission on Colleges at 1866 Southern Lane, Decatur, Georgia 30033-4097 or call 404-679-4500 with questions about the accreditation of South University.
Applying	Students are accepted into the Doctor of Pharmacy program once each year, in the fall quarter that begins in June. Entrance into the program is gained through a formal application review and assessment of the applicant's potential for professional and academic achievement. Prospective students must complete a minimum of two years of prescribed prepharmacy course requirements at a regionally accredited U.S. college or university. A grade of C or better must be earned in each prerequisite course. The cumulative GPA for the current first-year class was 3.41, and their average science GPA was 3.15. Applicants also must submit scores from the Pharmacy College Admissions Test (PCAT).
	The South University School of Pharmacy utilizes the Pharmacy College Application Service (PharmCAS), a centralized application service for prospective students applying to colleges and schools of pharmacy. In addition, a supplemental application is required to complete the application process, along with a fee of $50. The application is available at http://www.southuniversity.edu/Pharmacy/
Correspondence and Information	Applications for admission to the South University Doctor of Pharmacy program are available by contacting:

School of Pharmacy
South University
709 Mall Boulevard
Savannah, Georgia 31406-4805
Phone: 912-201-8120
   866-629-2901 (toll-free)
Fax: 912-201-8070
E-mail: pharmd@southuniversity.edu
Web site: http://www.southuniversity.edu/pharmacy

South University

THE FACULTY

One of the most outstanding aspects of South University's Doctor of Pharmacy program is the dedication of the faculty members and their ability to cultivate a supportive learning environment. Faculty members are committed to their roles as mentors, teachers, and colearners. They are also dedicated to the training of students who can assume positions of leadership within the field of pharmacy. A current list of program faculty members is available at the South University Web site (http://www.southuniversity.edu/pharmacy).

South University's School of Pharmacy is one of less than a dozen schools in the country to offer an accelerated three-year Doctor of Pharmacy degree program.

UNIVERSITY OF SOUTHERN CALIFORNIA

School of Pharmacy

Programs of Study	The School of Pharmacy at the University of Southern California (USC) offers graduate programs in molecular pharmacology and toxicology, pharmaceutical economics and policy, and pharmaceutical sciences. The School also offers an interdisciplinary M.S. in regulatory science.
	The programs that lead to the M.S. and Ph.D. degrees in molecular pharmacology and toxicology have an emphasis on molecular pharmacology, gene regulation, neuropharmacology, free-radical biochemistry, toxicology, and neurotoxicology. The molecular pharmacology and toxicology program offers superb interdisciplinary educational opportunities. Faculty members are engaged in research directed toward understanding the mechanisms of drug action, gene regulation, neurobiology of behavior, learning and memory, neurobiology of drug tolerance, and the induction and regulation of signal transduction systems. A major focus of research of the toxicology faculty is the role of free-radical mechanisms in metabolic regulation, carcinogenesis, and membrane-associated disorders. All areas of research emphasize the potential for development of therapeutic agents.
	The programs that lead to the Master of Science (M.S.) and Doctor of Philosophy (Ph.D.) degrees in pharmaceutical economics and policy focus on economics and outcomes assessment of pharmaceuticals, pharmacy services, and medical technology. The programs also include research into the finance and delivery of pharmaceuticals and pharmacy services. Graduates have the capability to conduct research and provide training and expertise in assisting health-care organizations to make decisions regarding the costs and benefits of alternative therapeutic strategies.
	The programs that lead to the M.S. and Ph.D. degrees in pharmaceutical sciences have an emphasis on cancer pharmacology, cell biology, computational drug design, drug targeting and delivery, medicinal chemistry, membrane biophysics, molecular pharmacology, and pharmacokinetics. The pharmaceutical sciences program provides highly interdisciplinary educational opportunities. Utilizing a broad spectrum of state-of-the-art techniques, faculty members are engaged in research directed toward understanding the mechanisms of drug interactions at transport barriers and target sites and developing new strategies in the design, functional analysis, delivery, and optimization of therapeutic agents.
	Regulatory science relates to the regulatory and legal requirements of biomedical product development to the scientific testing and oversight needed to establish product safety and efficacy. The program provides an opportunity for advanced preparation in the fields of regulatory affairs, quality assurance, and clinical research. Offerings include a full- and part-time stand-alone program and a dual Pharm.D./M.S. program.
Research Facilities	The graduate programs of the School of Pharmacy are housed in the seven-story Pharmaceutical Sciences Center and the three-story Center for Health Professionals on the University's Health Science Campus. There are collaborative research programs with the USC Comprehensive Cancer Center, the USC Research Center for Liver Disease, the Doheny Eye Institute and Hospital, and the L.A. County–USC Medical Center, all of which are adjacent to the School of Pharmacy; with the science, public administration, and economics departments on the University Park Campus; and with a number of other prestigious clinical research facilities in the Los Angeles area. The School has the full range of equipment found in any modern research facility. The Norris Medical Library, located on the Health Science Campus, supports computerized searches through Ovid Online. With the University Park Campus libraries, the number of volumes exceeds 1.5 million.
Financial Aid	Fellowships, teaching assistantships, and research assistantships are available. These assistantships come with an annual stipend award, and assistants also receive full-tuition remission (up to 12 units per semester), while quarter-time positions receive up to 8 units of tuition remission per semester and health insurance and mandatory health center fees for the year.
Cost of Study	Tuition fees for 2010 are $1383 per semester unit.
Living and Housing Costs	A limited number of double rooms are available in Seaver Hall, located next to the School. Rents vary in range (students should contact USC Housing Services for exact costs). Off-campus housing is also available.
Student Group	Of a total University population of 28,000 full-time and part-time students, almost 12,500 are pursuing graduate or professional degrees. Within the School of Pharmacy there are more than 120 graduate students. Approximately 75 percent of the students receive some form of financial assistance. The demand from the pharmaceutical industry, academia, and government for graduates in selected areas is high.
Location	The health sciences campus is 5 miles from downtown Los Angeles and is easily accessible from all parts of greater Los Angeles. The ocean, mountains, and deserts are all close by. Recreational and sporting facilities are excellent. Cultural and entertainment attractions are numerous, including the Los Angeles Philharmonic, the Los Angeles Chamber Orchestra, the Hollywood Bowl, numerous theaters, and the Music Center. Los Angeles supports professional basketball, hockey, soccer, and baseball teams, and numerous college sporting events are held throughout the year. The southern California climate, with mild winters and warm, dry summers, is renowned.
The University	Founded in 1880, the University is the oldest major independent, coeducational, nonsectarian university in the West. The modern health sciences campus, 7 miles from the main campus and adjacent to the L.A. County–USC Medical Center, houses not only the School of Pharmacy but also the School of Medicine, the Doheny Eye Institute and Hospital, and the USC Comprehensive Cancer Center, all of which have active research programs. There are excellent opportunities for collaborative work.
Applying	Applicants must have, or expect to receive, a bachelor's or higher-level degree in an appropriate field prior to beginning graduate studies (students should contact the respective department for details). A GPA of at least 3.0 and qualifying verbal and quantitative GRE test scores are required. International applicants must also submit a TOEFL score. Applicants who meet graduate admission standards are notified of acceptance by the end of May. Fellowships and teaching assistantships are offered to top applicants who have expressed the desire for financial aid. The application deadline for some of the fellowships is February 1.
Correspondence and Information	Graduate Affairs Office School of Pharmacy University of Southern California 1985 Zonal Avenue, PSC 713 Los Angeles, California 90089-9121 Phone: 323-442-1474 Fax: 323-442-2258 E-mail: pharmgrd@hsc.usc.edu Web site: http://www.usc.edu/schools/pharmacy

University of Southern California

THE FACULTY AND THEIR RESEARCH

R. Pete Vanderveen, Dean, USC School of Pharmacy; Ph.D., Michigan State, 1987.

Pharmaceutical Economics and Policy

Richard L. Ernst, Assistant Research Professor; Ph.D., Berkeley, 1970. Theoretical foundations of cost-effective analysis for the planning of pharmaceutical formularies, provision of health care in general.

Denise R. Globe, Assistant Professor; Ph.D., UCLA, 1998. Health services research, quality of life, utility measurement, health-care finance.

Joel W. Hay, Associate Professor; Ph.D., Yale, 1980. Health economics, pharmaceutical economics, HIV/AIDS medical costs and epidemiology, health insurance reform, economic assessment of medical technology, medical interventions.

Kathleen A. Johnson, Associate Professor and Director, Clinical Pharmacy; Ph.D., UCLA, 1991. Health services research, clinical pharmacy, pharmaceutical economics, health economics, OTC nonprescription drugs, women's health issues.

Jeffrey S. McCombs, Associate Professor; Ph.D., California, San Diego, 1982. Health economics, pharmaceutical economics, capitated medical systems, noncompliance with drug therapies and with drug formularies.

Michael B. Nichol, Associate Professor and Chairman; Ph.D., USC, 1987. State health policy, pharmaceutical economics, cost-effectiveness, outcomes research.

Pharmaceutical Sciences

M. B. Bolger, Associate Professor; Ph.D., California, San Francisco, 1978. Molecular mechanisms of drug and hormone action; biophysical, biochemical, and computational study of ligand-receptor interaction.

S. F. Hamm-Alvarez, Associate Dean and Director, Pharmacology and Pharmaceutical Sciences; Ph.D., Duke, 1990. Role of kinesin and cytoplasmic dynein in vesicle transport along microtubules, regulation of microtubule-dependent vesicle transport in intact cells, regulation of cytoskeletal processes.

I. S. Haworth, Associate Professor; Ph.D., Liverpool, 1989. Computational drug design, NMR spectroscopy, structure and dynamics of DNA and DNA-ligand complexes, molecular modeling, molecular dynamics.

E. J. Lien, Professor; Ph.D., California, San Francisco, 1966. Quantitative structure-activity correlation of chemotherapeutic agents, centrally acting drugs and natural products, design synthesis and testing of new antiviral and antitumor agents, isolation and testing of immunostimulating polysaccharides from plants, especially Chinese medicinal plants.

C. McKenna, Professor of Chemistry and of Pharmaceutical Sciences (secondary appointment); Ph.D., California, San Diego, 1971. Synthetic and biological chemistry of phosphonocarboxylates, phosphinophophonates, and bisphosphonates.

N. Neamati, Assistant Professor; Ph.D., Texas, 1995. Structure- and mechanism-based drug design, computer modeling, cellular and molecular pharmacology of anti-cancer and anti-viral drugs, pharmacogenomics and target identification.

Curtis T. Okamoto, Associate Professor and Assistant Director, Pharmacology and Pharmaceutical Sciences; Ph.D., Berkeley, 1989. Protein sorting in epithelial cells.

W. C. Shen, Professor; Ph.D., Boston University, 1972. Endocytosis and transcytosis of proteins in epithelial cells and its applications in oral drug delivery.

W. Wolf, Distinguished Professor; Ph.D., Paris, 1956. Pharmacokinetic imaging, noninvasive studies of drug biodistribution, targeting and metabolism using NMRS and nuclear medicine imaging (including PET) techniques, pharmacokinetics of antitumor agents, synthesis and mechanism of action of radiopharmaceuticals.

Molecular Pharmacology and Toxicology

J. D. Adams Jr., Associate Professor; Ph.D., California, San Francisco, 1981. Bioactivation of drugs and toxins in Parkinson's disease and other diseases.

R. L. Alkana, Professor and Associate Dean, Curriculum and Interdisciplinary Programs; Pharm.D., USC, 1970; Ph.D., California, Irvine, 1975. Mechanisms of psychoactive drug action, neuropharmacology and behavioral pharmacology/toxicology, pharmacogenetics, allosteric signal transduction.

D. K. Ann, Professor; Ph.D., Purdue, 1984. Molecular mechanism(s) governing tissue-specific and inducible gene expression and signal transduction.

R. E. Brinton, Associate Professor (also with Neurosciences); Ph.D., Arizona, 1984. Neurobiology of learning and memory; peptide and steroid induction of morphological, biochemical, and genomic plasticity in cultured nerve cells.

E. Cadenas, Professor and Associate Dean (also with Biochemistry and Molecular Biology); Ph.D., Buenos Aires, 1977. Free-radical chemistry and biology, cell-cycle regulation by oxidants and antioxidants.

T. M. Chan, Professor; Ph.D., California, Davis, 1972. Metabolic toxicology, metabolic and hormonal abnormalities in obesity and diabetes, perturbation of cell growth and intermediary metabolism by free radicals and related oxidants.

K. Chen, Research Associate Professor; Ph.D., UCLA, 1976. Mitochondria genesis and protein targeting, serotonin and brain developmental abnormality.

N. S. Cohen, Research Assistant Professor; Ph.D., NYU, 1965. Intracellular organization of the proteins of enzymatic pathways, mRNA transport and localization, protein-protein interactions.

D. L. Davies, Research Assistant Professor and Director of the Alcohol and Brain Research Laboratory; Ph.D., USC, 1996. Neuropharmacology, with an emphasis on alcohol and other psychoactive drugs that act on GABA-A and other ligand-gated ion channels in the central nervous system.

R. F. Duncan, Associate Professor (also with Microbiology); Ph.D., Hawaii, 1978. Function of stress proteins in cell regulation and cell survival during stress, molecular mechanisms that regulate the rate of protein synthesis.

D. Johnson, Professor (also with Biochemistry and Molecular Biology); Ph.D., Georgetown, 1980. Regulation of gene expression by viral proteins and by activation of signal transduction pathways.

F. J. R. Richmond, Research Professor and Director of Regulatory and Clinical Science, Alfred E. Mann Institute of Biomedical Engineering; Ph.D., Queen's University, 1976. Neural control of movement, medical product development and testing, regulatory aspects of product development and commercialization.

J. C. Shih, Professor; Ph.D., California, Riverside, 1968. Biochemistry and molecular biology of serotonin receptors and enzymes related to catecholamine metabolism, molecular basis of mental disorders, neurodegeneration and aggressive behavior.

R. S. Sohal, Professor; Ph.D., Tulane, 1965. Role of oxidative stress in the aging process.

Section 40
Veterinary Medicine and Sciences

This section contains a directory of institutions offering graduate work in veterinary medicine and sciences, followed by in-depth entries submitted by institutions that chose to prepare detailed program descriptions. Additional information about programs listed in the directory but not augmented by an in-depth entry may be obtained by writing directly to the dean of a graduate school or chair of a department at the address given in the directory.

In the other guides in this series:

Graduate Programs in the Humanities, Arts & Social Sciences
See *Economics (Agricultural Economics and Agribusiness)*
Graduate Programs in the Biological Sciences
See *Biological and Biomedical Sciences* and *Zoology*
Graduate Programs in the Physical Sciences, Mathematics, Agricultural Sciences, the Environment & Natural Resources

See *Agricultural and Food Sciences, Marine Sciences and Oceanography,* and *Natural Resources*
Graduate Programs in Engineering & Applied Sciences
See *Agricultural Engineering and Bioengineering* and *Biomedical Engineering and Biotechnology*

CONTENTS

Program Directories

Veterinary Medicine

Auburn University, College of Veterinary Medicine, Professional Program in Veterinary Medicine, Auburn University, AL 36849. Offers DVM, DVM/MS. *Accreditation:* AVMA. *Faculty:* 100 full-time (40 women), 5 part-time/adjunct (1 woman). *Students:* 372 full-time (264 women), 20 part-time (14 women); includes 17 minority (7 African Americans, 1 American Indian/Alaska Native, 2 Asian Americans or Pacific Islanders, 7 Hispanic Americans). Average age 25. In 2009, 96 DVMs awarded. *Degree requirements:* For DVM, preceptorship. *Application deadline:* For fall admission, 7/7 for domestic students; for spring admission, 11/24 for domestic students. Applications are processed on a rolling basis. Application fee: $50 ($60 for international students). *Expenses:* Contact institution. *Financial support:* Fellowships available. Financial award application deadline: 3/15; financial award applicants required to submit FAFSA. *Unit head:* Dr. Timothy R. Boosinger, Dean, 334-844-4546. *Application contact:* Dr. George Flowers, Interim Dean of the Graduate School, 334-844-2125.

Colorado State University, College of Veterinary Medicine and Biomedical Sciences, Professional Program in Veterinary Medicine, Fort Collins, CO 80523-1601. Offers DVM, DVM/PhD, MBA/DVM. *Accreditation:* AVMA. *Students:* 538 full-time (408 women); includes 81 minority (6 African Americans, 6 American Indian/Alaska Native, 32 Asian Americans or Pacific Islanders, 37 Hispanic Americans), 2 international. Average age 27. 1,831 applicants, 8% accepted, 140 enrolled. In 2009, 125 DVMs awarded. *Entrance requirements:* GRE General Test. Additional exam requirements/recommendations for international students: Required—TOEFL. *Application deadline:* For fall admission, 10/1 for domestic students. Application fee: $60. Electronic applications accepted. *Expenses:* Tuition, state resident: full-time $6434; part-time $359.10 per credit. Tuition, nonresident: full-time $18,116; part-time $1006.45 per credit. Required fees: $1496; $83 per credit. *Financial support:* Fellowships, research assistantships, teaching assistantships, Federal Work-Study, scholarships/grants, and unspecified assistantships available. Financial award application deadline: 3/1; financial award applicants required to submit FAFSA. *Faculty research:* Animal reproduction, infectious diseases, cancer biology, musculoskeletal research, neurobiology. Total annual research expenditures: $1.4 million. *Unit head:* Peter Hellyer, Associate Dean, 970-491-2009, E-mail: peter.hellyer@colostate.edu. *Application contact:* Dr. Sherry Stewart, Assistant Dean of Admissions and Student Affairs, 970-491-7054, Fax: 970-491-2250, E-mail: sherry.stewart@colostate.edu.

Cornell University, College of Veterinary Medicine, Ithaca, NY 14853-0001. Offers veterinary medicine (DVM). *Accreditation:* AVMA. *Faculty:* 184 full-time (71 women). *Students:* 349 full-time (269 women); includes 62 minority (14 African Americans, 1 American Indian/Alaska Native, 18 Asian Americans or Pacific Islanders, 29 Hispanic Americans), 1 international. Average age 26. 901 applicants, 14% accepted, 92 enrolled. *Entrance requirements:* GRE General Test or MCAT, required prerequisite courses, animal or veterinary experience, letters of recommendation. Additional exam requirements/recommendations for international students: Required—TOEFL. *Application deadline:* For fall admission, 10/1 for domestic and international students. Application fee: $60. Electronic applications accepted. *Expenses:* Contact institution. *Financial support:* In 2009–10, 331 students received support; fellowships, research assistantships, teaching assistantships, Federal Work-Study, institutionally sponsored loans, and scholarships/grants available. Financial award application deadline: 2/1; financial award applicants required to submit CSS PROFILE or FAFSA. *Faculty research:* Biomedical research, comparative cancer, food safety. Total annual research expenditures: $44 million. *Unit head:* Dr. Michael Kotlikoff, Dean, 607-253-3771, Fax: 607-253-3701. *Application contact:* Jennifer A. Mailey, Director of Admissions, 607-253-3700, Fax: 607-253-3709, E-mail: jam333@cornell.edu.

Iowa State University of Science and Technology, College of Veterinary Medicine and Graduate College, Graduate Programs in Veterinary Medicine, Department of Veterinary Diagnostic and Production Animal Medicine, Ames, IA 50011. Offers veterinary diagnostic and production animal medicine (MS); veterinary preventative medicine (MS). *Faculty:* 26 full-time (3 women), 7 part-time/adjunct (1 woman). *Students:* 6 full-time (1 woman), 9 part-time (5 women), 3 international. 6 applicants, 33% accepted, 2 enrolled. In 2009, 3 master's awarded. *Degree requirements:* For master's, thesis or alternative. *Entrance requirements:* Additional exam requirements/recommendations for international students: Required—TOEFL (minimum score 550 paper-based; 79 iBT) or IELTS (minimum score 6.5). *Application deadline:* Applications are processed on a rolling basis. Application fee: $40 ($90 for international students). Electronic applications accepted. *Expenses:* Tuition, state resident: full-time $6716. Tuition, nonresident: full-time $8908. Tuition and fees vary according to course level, course load, program and student level. *Financial support:* In 2009–10, 4 research assistantships with partial tuition reimbursements (averaging $20,830 per year) were awarded; teaching assistantships with partial tuition reimbursements, institutionally sponsored loans, scholarships/grants, health care benefits, and unspecified assistantships also available. *Unit head:* Dr. Patrick Halbur, Chair, 515-294-8790. *Application contact:* Dr. Patrick Halbur, Chair, 515-294-8790.

Iowa State University of Science and Technology, College of Veterinary Medicine, Professional Program in Veterinary Medicine, Ames, IA 50011. Offers DVM. *Accreditation:* AVMA. *Students:* 563 full-time (412 women); includes 13 minority (1 American Indian/Alaska Native, 2 Asian Americans or Pacific Islanders, 10 Hispanic Americans), 297 international. In 2009, 105 DVMs awarded. *Expenses:* Tuition, state resident: full-time $6716. Tuition, nonresident: full-time $8908. Tuition and fees vary according to course level, course load, program and student level. *Financial support:* Federal Work-Study available. *Unit head:* Dr. John Thomson, Dean, 515-294-1250. *Application contact:* Dr. John Thomson, Dean, 515-294-1250.

Louisiana State University and Agricultural and Mechanical College, School of Veterinary Medicine, Professional Program in Veterinary Medicine, Baton Rouge, LA 70803. Offers DVM. Available to state and contract students and a limited number of highly qualified out-of-state applicants. *Students:* 324 full-time (248 women), 3 part-time (all women); includes 30 minority (4 African Americans, 2 American Indian/Alaska Native, 7 Asian Americans or Pacific Islanders, 17 Hispanic Americans), 1 international. Average age 26. 94 applicants, 100% accepted, 90 enrolled. In 2009, 81 DVMs awarded. *Entrance requirements:* GRE General Test or MCAT. Additional exam requirements/recommendations for international students: Required—TOEFL. *Application deadline:* For fall admission, 3/1 priority date for domestic students. Applications are processed on a rolling basis. *Expenses:* Contact institution. *Financial support:* In 2009–10, 289 students received support, including 6 fellowships with full and partial tuition reimbursements available (averaging $13,646 per year); research assistantships with full and partial tuition reimbursements available, teaching assistantships with full and partial tuition reimbursements available, Federal Work-Study, institutionally sponsored loans, health care benefits, tuition waivers (full and partial), and unspecified assistantships also available. Financial award applicants required to submit FAFSA. *Faculty research:* Veterinary microbiology, pathology, immunology, anatomy, epidemiology. Total annual research expenditures: $6.8 million. *Application contact:* Dr. Thomas R. Klei, Associate Dean for Research and Advanced Studies, 225-578-9727, Fax: 225-578-9916, E-mail: klei@vetmed.lsu.edu.

Michigan State University, College of Veterinary Medicine, Professional Program in Veterinary Medicine, East Lansing, MI 48824. Offers veterinary medicine (DVM); veterinary medicine/medical scientist training program (DVM). *Accreditation:* AVMA. *Students:* 428 full-time (364 women), 5 part-time (4 women); includes 42 minority (5 African Americans, 6 American Indian/Alaska Native, 20 Asian Americans or Pacific Islanders, 11 Hispanic Americans), 3 international. Average age 25. 112 applicants, 99% accepted. In 2009, 104 DVMs awarded. *Entrance requirements:* Additional exam requirements/recommendations for international students: Required—TOEFL. Application fee: $144. Electronic applications accepted. *Expenses:* Contact institution. *Financial support:* In 2009–10, 2 research assistantships with tuition reimbursements (averaging $8,089 per year) were awarded. *Unit head:* Dr. David J. Sprecher, Associate Dean for Professional Academic Programs, 517-355-7624, Fax: 517-432-1037, E-mail: sprecher@cvm.msu.edu. *Application contact:* Admissions Office, 517-353-9793, Fax: 517-353-3041, E-mail: admiss@cvm.msu.edu.

Mississippi State University, College of Veterinary Medicine, Professional Program in Veterinary Medicine, Mississippi State, MS 39762. Offers DVM. *Accreditation:* AVMA. *Entrance requirements:* VCAT, GRE, minimum GPA of 3.0 in math and science coursework, 2.8 overall. *Application deadline:* For fall admission, 10/1 for domestic students. *Expenses:* Contact institution. *Financial support:* Federal Work-Study and institutionally sponsored loans available. Financial award application deadline: 4/1; financial award applicants required to submit FAFSA. *Unit head:* Dr. Philip Bushby, Academic Director, 662-325-5157, Fax: 662-325-8714, E-mail: bushby@cvm.msstate.edu. *Application contact:* Dr. Philip Bushby, Academic Director, 662-325-5157, Fax: 662-325-8714, E-mail: bushby@cvm.msstate.edu.

North Carolina State University, College of Veterinary Medicine, Professional Program, Raleigh, NC 27695. Offers DVM. *Entrance requirements:* GRE. Additional exam requirements/recommendations for international students: Required—TOEFL.

North Carolina State University, College of Veterinary Medicine, Program in Specialized Veterinary Medicine, Raleigh, NC 27695. Offers MSpVM. *Accreditation:* AVMA. *Degree requirements:* For master's, thesis optional. *Entrance requirements:* For master's, GRE General Test. Additional exam requirements/recommendations for international students: Required—TOEFL (minimum score 550 paper-based; 213 computer-based). Electronic applications accepted. *Faculty research:* Cell biology, infectious diseases, pharmacology and toxicology, genomics, pathology and population medicine.

North Carolina State University, College of Veterinary Medicine, Program in Veterinary Public Health, Raleigh, NC 27695. Offers MVPH. *Degree requirements:* For master's, thesis optional. Electronic applications accepted.

The Ohio State University, College of Veterinary Medicine, Professional Program in Veterinary Medicine, Columbus, OH 43210. Offers DVM, DVM/MS, DVM/PhD. *Accreditation:* AVMA. *Students:* 560 full-time (434 women), 3 part-time (all women); includes 39 minority (3 African Americans, 3 American Indian/Alaska Native, 22 Asian Americans or Pacific Islanders, 11 Hispanic Americans), 1 international. Average age 25. In 2009, 139 DVMs awarded. *Entrance requirements:* GRE General Test, MCAT, or VCAT, 96 hours of pre-veterinary course work. *Application deadline:* For fall admission, 10/1 for domestic students. Applications are processed on a rolling basis. Application fee: $60 ($70 for international students). Electronic applications accepted. *Expenses:* Tuition, state resident: full-time $10,683. Tuition, nonresident: full-time $25,923. Tuition and fees vary according to course load and program. *Financial support:* Fellowships, Federal Work-Study and institutionally sponsored loans available. Support available to part-time students. *Unit head:* Lonnie King, 614-688-8749, Fax: 614-292-3544, E-mail: king.1518@osu.edu. *Application contact:* Professional Admissions, 614-292-9444, Fax: 614-292-3895, E-mail: professional@osu.edu.

Oklahoma State University, Center for Veterinary Health Sciences, Professional Program in Veterinary Medicine, Stillwater, OK 74078. Offers DVM. *Accreditation:* AVMA. *Students:* 328 full-time (243 women); includes 35 minority (1 African American, 23 American Indian/Alaska Native, 5 Asian Americans or Pacific Islanders, 6 Hispanic Americans). Average age 24. 452 applicants, 18% accepted, 82 enrolled. In 2009, 74 DVMs awarded. *Entrance requirements:* GRE General Test, GRE Subject Test (biology). *Application deadline:* For fall admission, 10/1 for domestic students. Application fee: $50. Electronic applications accepted. *Expenses:* Tuition, state resident: full-time $3716; part-time $154.85 per credit hour. Tuition, nonresident: full-time $14,448; part-time $602 per credit hour. Required fees: $1772; $73.85 per credit hour. One-time fee: $50. Tuition and fees vary according to course load and campus/location. *Financial support:* Career-related internships or fieldwork, Federal Work-Study, scholarships/grants, and tuition waivers (partial) available. Support available to part-time students. Financial award application deadline: 3/1. *Faculty research:* Infectious diseases, physiology, toxicology, biomedical lasers, clinical studies. *Application contact:* Robin K. Wilson, Manager of Admissions, 405-744-6653, Fax: 405-744-0356, E-mail: robin.wilson@okstate.edu.

Oregon State University, College of Veterinary Medicine, Veterinary Medicine Professional Graduate Program, Corvallis, OR 97331. Offers DVM. DVM admissions open only to residents of Oregon and other states participating in the Western Interstate Commission for Higher Education. *Accreditation:* AVMA. *Students:* 211 full-time (170 women); includes 13 minority (1 American Indian/Alaska Native, 6 Asian Americans or Pacific Islanders, 6 Hispanic Americans), 6 international. Average age 27. In 2009, 47 DVMs awarded. *Entrance requirements:* VCAT and/or GRE, minimum GPA of 3.3 during previous 2 years, 3.2 overall. *Application deadline:* For fall admission, 11/1 for domestic students. Application fee: $50. *Expenses:* Tuition, state resident: full-time $9774; part-time $362 per credit. Tuition, nonresident: full-time $15,849; part-time $587 per credit. Required fees: $1639. Full-time tuition and fees vary according to course load and program. *Financial support:* Federal Work-Study, institutionally sponsored loans, and scholarships/grants available. Support available to part-time students. Financial award application deadline: 2/1. *Unit head:* Dr. Christine V. Loehr, Program Director, 541-737-9673, Fax: 541-737-6817, E-mail: christine.loehre@oregonstate.edu. *Application contact:* Dr. Christine V. Loehr, Program Director, 541-737-9673, Fax: 541-737-6817, E-mail: christine.loehre@oregonstate.edu.

Purdue University, School of Veterinary Medicine, Professional Program in Veterinary Medicine, West Lafayette, IN 47907. Offers DVM, DVM/MS, DVM/PhD. *Accreditation:* AVMA. *Students:* 269 full-time (213 women), 1 part-time (0 women); includes 35 minority (6 African Americans, 3 American Indian/Alaska Native, 15 Asian Americans or Pacific Islanders, 11 Hispanic Americans), 2 international. Average age 23. 665 applicants, 15% accepted. In 2009, 63 DVMs awarded. *Entrance requirements:* GRE General Test. Additional exam requirements/recommendations for international students: Required—TOEFL. *Application deadline:* For fall admission, 10/1 for domestic and international students. Electronic applications accepted. *Financial support:* Federal Work-Study, institutionally sponsored loans, and scholarships/grants available. Support available to part-time students. Financial award application deadline: 3/1; financial award applicants required to submit FAFSA. *Unit head:* J. F. Van Vleet, Associate Dean, 765-494-9185. *Application contact:* Denise A. Ottinger, Admissions Coordinator, 765-494-7893, Fax: 765-496-2891, E-mail: vetadmissions@purdue.edu.

Texas A&M University, College of Veterinary Medicine, Department of Veterinary Large Animal Clinical Sciences, College Station, TX 77843. Offers veterinary medicine and surgery (MS). *Faculty:* 2. *Students:* 1 (woman) full-time, 3 part-time (all women). Average age 30. *Degree requirements:* For master's, thesis (for some programs). *Entrance requirements:* For master's, GRE General Test. Additional exam requirements/recommendations for international students: Required—TOEFL. Application fee: $50 ($75 for international students). *Expenses:* Tuition, state resident: full-time $3991; part-time $221.74 per credit hour. Tuition, nonresident: full-time $9049; part-time $502.74 per credit hour. *Financial support:* In 2009–10, fellowships with tuition reimbursements (averaging $37,500 per year), research assistantships (averaging $30,700 per year), teaching assistantships (averaging $37,500 per year) were awarded. Financial award application deadline: 4/1; financial award applicants required to submit FAFSA. *Faculty research:* Epidemiology including environmental and food safety, veterinary clinical studies. *Unit head:* Dr. William Moyer, Head, 979-845-9127, Fax: 979-847-8863, E-mail: wmoyer@tamu.edu. *Application contact:* Dr. James A. Thompson, Graduate Advisor, 979-845-9158, Fax: 979-847-8863, E-mail: jthompson@cvm.tamu.edu.

Texas A&M University, College of Veterinary Medicine, Professional Programs in Veterinary Medicine, College Station, TX 77843. Offers DVM, DVM/PhD. *Accreditation:* AVMA. *Students:* 536 full-time (396 women), 4 part-time (3 women); includes 75 minority (4 African Americans, 2 American Indian/Alaska Native, 14 Asian Americans or Pacific Islanders, 55 Hispanic Americans), 5 international. Average age 24. In 2009, 119 DVMs awarded. *Entrance requirements:* GRE. *Application deadline:* For fall admission, 9/1 for domestic students. Application fee: $100. *Expenses:* Contact institution. *Financial support:* Application deadline: 4/1. *Faculty research:* Reproductive biology, theriogenology, genetics, endocrinology, animal behavior. *Unit head:* Dr. Eleanor Green, Dean, 979-845-5053, E-mail: emgreen@tamu.edu.

Application contact: Yolanda Brinkman, Coordinator of Admissions, 979-845-5038, Fax: 979-845-5088, E-mail: ymbrinkman@cvm.tamu.edu.

Tufts University, Cummings School of Veterinary Medicine, North Grafton, MA 01536. Offers comparative biomedical sciences (PhD); veterinary medicine (DVM, MS); DVM/MPH; DVM/MS. *Accreditation:* AVMA (one or more programs are accredited). *Faculty:* 85 full-time (32 women), 164 part-time/adjunct (79 women). *Students:* 355 full-time (309 women); includes 20 minority (6 African Americans, 1 American Indian/Alaska Native, 6 Asian Americans or Pacific Islanders, 7 Hispanic Americans), 6 international. Average age 25. 747 applicants, 25% accepted, 97 enrolled. In 2009, 78 first professional degrees, 13 master's, 1 doctorate awarded. *Degree requirements:* For master's, thesis (for some programs); for doctorate, comprehensive exam, thesis/dissertation; for DVM, thesis/dissertation optional. *Entrance requirements:* For DVM, master's, and doctorate, GRE General Test. Additional exam requirements/recommendations for international students: Required—TOEFL, IELTS. *Application deadline:* For fall admission, 11/1 for domestic and international students. Application fee: $70. Electronic applications accepted. *Expenses:* Contact institution. *Financial support:* In 2009–10, 69 students received support, including 6 research assistantships with full tuition reimbursements available (averaging $25,000 per year), 2 teaching assistantships (averaging $5,000 per year); career-related internships or fieldwork, Federal Work-Study, institutionally sponsored loans, scholarships/grants, and institutional aid awards also available. Financial award application deadline: 3/10; financial award applicants required to submit FAFSA. *Faculty research:* Equine sports medicine, oncology, veterinary ethics, international veterinary medicine, veterinary genomics. *Unit head:* Dr. Deborah T. Kochevar, Dean, 508-839-5302, Fax: 508-839-2953, E-mail: deborah.kochevar@tufts.edu. *Application contact:* Rebecca Russo, Director of Admissions, 508-839-7920, Fax: 508-887-4820, E-mail: rebecca.russo@tufts.edu.

Tuskegee University, Graduate Programs, College of Veterinary Medicine, Nursing and Allied Health, School of Veterinary Medicine, Tuskegee, AL 36088. Offers DVM, MS. *Faculty:* 62 full-time (6 women). *Students:* 249 full-time (193 women); includes 143 minority (128 African Americans, 1 American Indian/Alaska Native, 3 Asian Americans or Pacific Islanders, 11 Hispanic Americans), 4 international. Average age 31. 281 applicants, 26% accepted. In 2009, 50 first professional degrees, 4 master's awarded. *Degree requirements:* For master's, thesis. *Entrance requirements:* For DVM, VCAT; for master's, GRE General Test. Additional exam requirements/recommendations for international students: Required—TOEFL (minimum score 500 paper-based; 69 computer-based). *Application deadline:* For fall admission, 7/15 for domestic students. Applications are processed on a rolling basis. Application fee: $25 ($35 for international students). *Expenses:* Tuition: Full-time $15,630; part-time $940 per credit hour. Required fees: $650. *Financial support:* Application deadline: 4/15. *Unit head:* Dr. Tsegaye Habtemariam, Dean, 334-727-8174, Fax: 334-727-8177. *Application contact:* Dr. Robert L. Laney, Vice President/Director of Admissions and Enrollment Management, 334-727-8580, Fax: 334-727-5750, E-mail: planey@tuskegee.edu.

Universidad Nacional Pedro Henriquez Urena, Graduate School, Santo Domingo, Dominican Republic. Offers administrative sciences (PhD); business administration (MBA); environmental engineering (MEE); project management (M Man, MPM); sanitation engineering (ME); veterinary medicine (DVM).

Université de Montréal, Faculty of Veterinary Medicine, Professional Program in Veterinary Medicine, Montréal, QC H3C 3J7, Canada. Offers DES. Open only to Canadian residents. *Accreditation:* AVMA. Part-time programs available. *Application deadline:* For fall admission, 2/1 priority date for domestic students; for winter admission, 11/1 priority date for domestic students; for spring admission, 2/1 priority date for domestic students. Application fee: $100. Electronic applications accepted. *Financial support:* Teaching assistantships, career-related internships or fieldwork available. *Faculty research:* Animal reproduction, infectious diseases of swine, physiology of exercise in horses, viral diseases of cattle, health management and epidemiology. *Unit head:* Andre Vrins, Unit Head, 514-343-6111 Ext. 0084, Fax: 450-778-8102, E-mail: andre.vrins@umontreal.ca. *Application contact:* Isabelle Codo-Jarry, 514-343-6111 Ext. 8224, Fax: 450-778-8137, E-mail: isabelle.codo@umontreal.ca.

University of California, Davis, School of Veterinary Medicine, Program in Veterinary Medicine, Davis, CA 95616. Offers DVM, DVM/MPVM. *Accreditation:* AVMA. *Entrance requirements:* GRE General Test. Additional exam requirements/recommendations for international students: Required—TOEFL. Electronic applications accepted.

University of Florida, College of Veterinary Medicine, Professional Program in Veterinary Medicine, Gainesville, FL 32611. Offers DVM. *Accreditation:* AVMA. *Entrance requirements:* GRE General Test.

University of Georgia, College of Veterinary Medicine and Graduate School, Graduate Programs in Veterinary Medicine, Department of Population Health, Athens, GA 30602. Offers food animal medicine (MFAM); population health (MAM). *Faculty:* 26 full-time (5 women), 1 part-time/adjunct (0 women). *Students:* 5 full-time (2 women), 2 international. 1 applicant, 100% accepted, 0 enrolled. In 2009, 2 master's awarded. *Entrance requirements:* For master's, GRE General Test. *Application deadline:* For fall admission, 7/1 priority date for domestic students; for spring admission, 11/15 for domestic students. Application fee: $50. Electronic applications accepted. *Expenses:* Tuition, state resident: full-time $6000; part-time $250 per credit hour. Tuition, nonresident: full-time $20,904; part-time $871 per credit hour. Required fees: $730 per semester. *Financial support:* Fellowships, research assistantships, teaching assistantships, unspecified assistantships available. *Unit head:* Dr. John R. Glisson, Head, 706-542-5629, Fax: 706-542-5630, E-mail: jglisson@uga.edu. *Application contact:* Dr. Margie D. Lee, Graduate Coordinator, 706-583-0797, Fax: 706-542-5630, E-mail: leem@uga.edu.

University of Georgia, College of Veterinary Medicine, Professional Program in Veterinary Medicine, Athens, GA 30602. Offers DVM. *Accreditation:* AVMA. *Entrance requirements:* GRE General Test, GRE Subject Test (biology). *Application deadline:* For fall admission, 10/1 for domestic students. Application fee: $155. Electronic applications accepted. *Expenses:* Tuition, state resident: full-time $6000; part-time $250 per credit hour. Tuition, nonresident: full-time $20,904; part-time $871 per credit hour. Required fees: $730 per semester. *Financial support:* Career-related internships or fieldwork and scholarships/grants available. Financial award application deadline: 8/1; financial award applicants required to submit FAFSA. *Faculty research:* Vascular biomedicine, environmental toxicology, food safety, vaccines and emerging diseases. *Application contact:* Admissions Counselor, 706-542-5727, Fax: 706-542-1004.

University of Guelph, Ontario Veterinary College and Graduate Program Services, Graduate Programs in Veterinary Sciences, Department of Clinical Studies, Guelph, ON N1G 2W1, Canada. Offers anesthesiology (M Sc, DV Sc); cardiology (DV Sc, Diploma); clinical studies (Diploma); dermatology (M Sc); diagnostic imaging (M Sc, DV Sc); emergency/critical care (M Sc, DV Sc, Diploma); medicine (M Sc, DV Sc); neurology (M Sc, DV Sc); ophthalmology (M Sc, DV Sc); surgery (M Sc, DV Sc). *Degree requirements:* For master's, thesis; for doctorate, comprehensive exam, thesis/dissertation. *Entrance requirements:* Additional exam requirements/recommendations for international students: Required—TOEFL (minimum score 550 paper-based; 213 computer-based), IELTS (minimum score 6.5). Electronic applications accepted. *Faculty research:* Orthopedics, respirology, oncology, exercise physiology, cardiology.

University of Illinois at Urbana–Champaign, College of Veterinary Medicine, Professional Program in Veterinary Medicine, Champaign, IL 61820. Offers veterinary medical science (DVM). *Accreditation:* AVMA. *Faculty:* 65 full-time (26 women), 7 part-time/adjunct (2 women). *Students:* 463 full-time (367 women); includes 29 minority (3 African Americans, 1 American Indian/Alaska Native, 13 Asian Americans or Pacific Islanders, 12 Hispanic Americans), 3 international. 251 applicants, 93% accepted, 119 enrolled. In 2009, 104 DVMs awarded. *Entrance requirements:* GRE. Application fee: $60 ($75 for international students). Electronic applications accepted. *Expenses:* Contact institution. *Financial support:* In 2009–10, 6 fellowships, 3 research assistantships were awarded; teaching assistantships, tuition waivers (full and partial) also available. *Unit head:* Herbert Whiteley, Dean, 217-333-2760, Fax: 217-333-4628, E-mail: hwhitele@illinois.edu. *Application contact:* Mary Anna Kelm, Assistant Dean for Academic and Student Affairs, 217-333-1192, Fax: 217-333-4628, E-mail: marykelm@illinois.edu.

University of Maryland, College Park, Academic Affairs, College of Agriculture and Natural Resources, Maryland Campus of VA/MD Regional College of Veterinary Medicine, Professional Program in Veterinary Medicine, College Park, MD 20742. Offers DVM. *Accreditation:* AVMA. *Students:* 115 full-time (91 women); includes 5 minority (1 African American, 3 Asian Americans or Pacific Islanders, 1 Hispanic American). 29 applicants, 100% accepted, 29 enrolled. In 2009, 28 DVMs awarded. *Degree requirements:* For DVM, thesis/dissertation, oral exam, public seminar. *Application deadline:* For fall admission, 5/1 for domestic students, 2/1 for international students; for spring admission, 10/1 for domestic students, 6/1 for international students. Application fee: $60. *Expenses:* Tuition, area resident: Part-time $471 per credit hour. Tuition, state resident: part-time $471 per credit hour. Tuition, nonresident: part-time $1016 per credit hour. Required fees: $337.04 per term. *Financial support:* Fellowships available. *Unit head:* Dr. Siba K. Samal, Chair, 301-314-6813, Fax: 301-314-6855, E-mail: ssamal@umd.edu. *Application contact:* Dean of Graduate School, 301-405-0358, Fax: 301-314-9305.

University of Minnesota, Twin Cities Campus, College of Veterinary Medicine, Professional Program in Veterinary Medicine, Minneapolis, MN 55455-0213. Offers DVM, DVM/PhD. *Accreditation:* AVMA. *Entrance requirements:* GRE General Test. Electronic applications accepted. *Expenses:* Contact institution. *Faculty research:* Infectious toxic diseases of animals, zoonotic animal models of human disease, epidemiologic and preventive medicine.

University of Missouri, College of Veterinary Medicine, Professional Program in Veterinary Medicine, Columbia, MO 65211. Offers DVM. *Accreditation:* AVMA. *Faculty:* 113 full-time (37 women), 8 part-time/adjunct (3 women). *Students:* 322 full-time (250 women); includes 13 minority (1 African American, 1 American Indian/Alaska Native, 4 Asian Americans or Pacific Islanders, 7 Hispanic Americans). Average age 24. 334 applicants, 34% accepted, 111 enrolled. In 2009, 70 DVMs awarded. *Entrance requirements:* VCAT, minimum GPA of 2.5 for state residents, 3.0 for nonresidents. *Application deadline:* For fall admission, 11/1 for domestic students. Electronic applications accepted. *Financial support:* In 2009–10, 58 students received support; fellowships, research assistantships, career-related internships or fieldwork, institutionally sponsored loans, tuition waivers (full), and research associateships available. *Faculty research:* Cardiovascular physiology, food safety, infectious diseases, laboratory animal medicine, ophthalmology. Total annual research expenditures: $4 million. *Unit head:* Dr. Neil C. Olson, Dean, E-mail: olsonne@missouri.edu. *Application contact:* Dr. C. B. Chastain, Associate Dean of Academic Affairs, E-mail: chastainc@missouri.edu.

University of Pennsylvania, School of Veterinary Medicine, Philadelphia, PA 19104. Offers VMD, VMD/MBA, VMD/PhD. *Accreditation:* AVMA. *Entrance requirements:* GRE. Additional exam requirements/recommendations for international students: Required—TOEFL. *Expenses:* Contact institution.

University of Prince Edward Island, Atlantic Veterinary College, Professional Program in Veterinary Medicine, Charlottetown, PE C1A 4P3, Canada. Offers DVM. *Accreditation:* AVMA. *Entrance requirements:* GRE. Additional exam requirements/recommendations for international students: Required—TOEFL (minimum score 550 paper-based; 213 computer-based; 80 iBT), Canadian Academic English Language Assessment, Michigan English Language Assessment Battery, Canadian Test of English for Scholars and Trainees. *Faculty research:* Shellfish toxicology, animal nutrition, fish health, toxicology, animal health management.

University of Saskatchewan, Western College of Veterinary Medicine and College of Graduate Studies and Research, Graduate Programs in Veterinary Medicine, Department of Large Animal Clinical Sciences, Saskatoon, SK S7N 5A2, Canada. Offers M Sc, M Vet Sc, PhD. *Faculty:* 30. *Students:* 20; includes 1 minority (African American). In 2009, 7 master's, 2 doctorates awarded. *Degree requirements:* For master's, thesis (for some programs); for doctorate, comprehensive exam (for some programs), thesis/dissertation. *Entrance requirements:* Additional exam requirements/recommendations for international students: Required—TOEFL (minimum score 80 iBT); Recommended—IELTS (minimum score 6.5). Electronic applications accepted. Tuition and fees charges are reported in Canadian dollars. *Expenses:* Tuition, area resident: Full-time $3000 Canadian dollars; part-time $500 Canadian dollars per term. Required fees: $700 Canadian dollars; $100 Canadian dollars per term. *Faculty research:* Reproduction, infectious diseases, epidemiology, food safety. *Unit head:* Dr. David Wilson, Head, 306-966-7145, Fax: 306-966-7159, E-mail: david.wilson@usask.ca. *Application contact:* Dr. Joseph Stookey, Associate Dean, Research, 306-966-7145, Fax: 306-966-7159, E-mail: joseph.stookey@usask.ca.

University of Saskatchewan, Western College of Veterinary Medicine and College of Graduate Studies and Research, Graduate Programs in Veterinary Medicine, Department of Small Animal Clinical Sciences, Saskatoon, SK S7N 5A2, Canada. Offers small animal clinical sciences (M Sc, PhD); veterinary anesthesiology, radiology and surgery (M Vet Sc); veterinary internal medicine (M Vet Sc). *Faculty:* 6 full-time (4 women). *Students:* 7. In 2009, 5 master's awarded. *Degree requirements:* For master's, thesis (for some programs); for doctorate, comprehensive exam (for some programs), thesis/dissertation. *Entrance requirements:* Additional exam requirements/recommendations for international students: Required—TOEFL (minimum score 80 iBT); Recommended—IELTS (minimum score 6.5). Application fee: $75. Electronic applications accepted. Tuition and fees charges are reported in Canadian dollars. *Expenses:* Tuition, area resident: Full-time $3000 Canadian dollars; part-time $500 Canadian dollars per term. Required fees: $700 Canadian dollars; $100 Canadian dollars per term. *Faculty research:* Orthopedics, wildlife, cardiovascular exercise/myelopathy, ophthalmology. *Unit head:* Dr. Klaas Post, Head, 306-966-7084, Fax: 306-966-7174, E-mail: klaas.post@usask.ca. *Application contact:* Dr. Klaas Post, Graduate Chair, 306-966-7084, Fax: 306-966-7174, E-mail: klaas.post@usask.ca.

University of Saskatchewan, Western College of Veterinary Medicine, Professional Program in Veterinary Medicine, Saskatoon, SK S7N 5A2, Canada. Offers DVM. *Accreditation:* AVMA. *Degree requirements:* For DVM, thesis/dissertation. Tuition and fees charges are reported in Canadian dollars. *Expenses:* Tuition, area resident: Full-time $3000 Canadian dollars; part-time $500 Canadian dollars per term. Required fees: $700 Canadian dollars; $100 Canadian dollars per term.

The University of Tennessee, Graduate School, College of Veterinary Medicine, Knoxville, TN 37996. Offers DVM. *Accreditation:* AVMA. *Entrance requirements:* VCAT, interview, minimum GPA of 2.7. Additional exam requirements/recommendations for international students: Required—TOEFL. *Expenses:* Contact institution.

University of Wisconsin–Madison, School of Veterinary Medicine, Professional Program in Veterinary Medicine, Madison, WI 53706. Offers DVM. *Accreditation:* AVMA. *Entrance requirements:* GRE General Test. Additional exam requirements/recommendations for international students: Required—TOEFL (minimum score 600 paper-based; 250 computer-based; 100 iBT), IELTS (minimum score 7), MELAB: 84. Electronic applications accepted. *Expenses:* Tuition, state resident: part-time $594 per credit. Tuition, nonresident: part-time $1504 per credit. Required fees: $65 per credit. Tuition and fees vary according to course load, program and reciprocity agreements.

Virginia Polytechnic Institute and State University, Virginia-Maryland Regional College of Veterinary Medicine, Professional Programs in Veterinary Medicine, Blacksburg, VA 24061. Offers DVM. *Accreditation:* AVMA. *Students:* 364 full-time (279 women), 1 (woman) part-time; includes 8 minority (1 African American, 1 American Indian/Alaska Native, 2 Asian Americans or Pacific Islanders, 4 Hispanic Americans), 119 international. Average age 26. In 2009, 86 DVMs awarded. *Entrance requirements:* Additional exam requirements/recommendations for international students: Required—TOEFL. *Expenses:* Contact institution. *Financial support:* Career-related internships or fieldwork, Federal Work-Study, scholarships/grants, and unspecified assistantships available. Total annual research expenditures: $3 million. *Unit head:* Dr. Roger

Virginia Polytechnic Institute and State University (continued)
Avery, Associate Dean of Research and Graduate Studies, 540-231-5649, Fax: 540-231-7367, E-mail: avery@vt.edu. *Application contact:* Becky Jones, Information Contact, 540-231-4992, Fax: 540-231-7367, E-mail: vmsgrad@vt.edu.

Washington State University, College of Veterinary Medicine, Professional Program in Veterinary Medicine, Pullman, WA 99164. Offers DVM, DVM/MS, DVM/PhD. *Accreditation:* AVMA. *Faculty:* 45 full-time (8 women), 15 part-time/adjunct (4 women). *Students:* 392 full-time (320 women); includes 36 minority (6 American Indian/Alaska Native, 18 Asian Americans or Pacific Islanders, 12 Hispanic Americans), 2 international. Average age 25. 952 applicants, 16% accepted, 97 enrolled. In 2009, 96 DVMs awarded. *Entrance requirements:* GRE General Test. Additional exam requirements/recommendations for international students: Required—TOEFL. *Application deadline:* For fall admission, 10/1 for domestic and international students. Application fee: $60. Electronic applications accepted. *Financial support:* In 2009–10, 270 students received support; research assistantships, teaching assistantships, career-related internships or fieldwork, Federal Work-Study, institutionally sponsored loans, scholarships/grants, traineeships, and tuition waivers (partial) available. Support available to part-time students. Financial award application deadline: 2/15; financial award applicants required to submit FAFSA. *Faculty research:* Biotechnology, immunology, pathology, neurosciences, clinical sciences. *Unit head:* Dr. Patricia Talcott, Director of Admissions, 509-355-1532. *Application contact:* Barbara Hodson, Program Coordinator, 509-335-1532, Fax: 509-335-6133, E-mail: bhodson@vetmed.wsu.edu.

Western University of Health Sciences, College of Veterinary Medicine, Pomona, CA 91766-1854. Offers DVM. *Accreditation:* AVMA. *Entrance requirements:* MCAT or GRE General Test, minimum GPA of 2.5, letters of recommendation, interview. Additional exam requirements/recommendations for international students: Required—TOEFL (minimum score 550 paper-based; 213 computer-based). *Expenses:* Contact institution.

Veterinary Sciences

Auburn University, College of Veterinary Medicine and Graduate School, Graduate Programs in Veterinary Medicine, Auburn University, AL 36849. Offers biomedical sciences (MS, PhD), including anatomy, physiology and pharmacology (MS), biomedical sciences (PhD), clinical sciences (MS), large animal surgery and medicine (MS), pathobiology (MS), radiology (MS), small animal surgery and medicine (MS); DVM/MS. Part-time programs available. *Faculty:* 100 full-time (40 women), 5 part-time/adjunct (1 woman). *Students:* 17 full-time (6 women), 51 part-time (35 women); includes 8 minority (2 African Americans, 1 American Indian/Alaska Native, 3 Asian Americans or Pacific Islanders, 2 Hispanic Americans), 22 international. Average age 31. 70 applicants, 34% accepted, 10 enrolled. In 2009, 12 master's, 7 doctorates awarded. *Degree requirements:* For doctorate, thesis/dissertation. *Entrance requirements:* For master's, GRE General Test; for doctorate, GRE General Test, GRE Subject Test. *Application deadline:* For fall admission, 7/7 for domestic students; for spring admission, 11/24 for domestic students. Applications are processed on a rolling basis. Application fee: $50 ($60 for international students). Electronic applications accepted. *Expenses:* Tuition, state resident: full-time $6240. Tuition, nonresident: full-time $18,720. International tuition: $18,938 full-time. Required fees: $492. Tuition and fees vary according to course load, program and reciprocity agreements. *Financial support:* Research assistantships, teaching assistantships, Federal Work-Study available. Support available to part-time students. Financial award application deadline: 3/15; financial award applicants required to submit FAFSA. *Unit head:* Dr. Timothy R. Boosinger, Dean, 334-844-4546. *Application contact:* Dr. George Flowers, Dean of the Graduate School, 334-844-2125.

Clemson University, Graduate School, College of Agriculture, Forestry and Life Sciences, Department of Animal and Veterinary Sciences, Clemson, SC 29634. Offers animal and veterinary sciences (MS, PhD). *Faculty:* 13 full-time (5 women), 1 part-time/adjunct (0 women). *Students:* 17 full-time (13 women), 4 part-time (2 women), 4 international. Average age 26. 19 applicants, 42% accepted, 5 enrolled. In 2009, 1 master's, 1 doctorate awarded. *Degree requirements:* For doctorate, thesis/dissertation. *Entrance requirements:* For master's and doctorate, GRE General Test. Additional exam requirements/recommendations for international students: Required—TOEFL. *Application deadline:* For fall admission, 4/15 for international students; for spring admission, 9/15 for international students. Applications are processed on a rolling basis. Application fee: $70 ($80 for international students). Electronic applications accepted. *Expenses:* Contact institution. *Financial support:* In 2009–10, 13 students received support, including 5 fellowships with full and partial tuition reimbursements available (averaging $8,533 per year), 6 research assistantships with partial tuition reimbursements available (averaging $16,578 per year), 7 teaching assistantships with partial tuition reimbursements available (averaging $14,643 per year); career-related internships or fieldwork, Federal Work-Study, institutionally sponsored loans, scholarships/grants, and unspecified assistantships also available. Financial award applicants required to submit FAFSA. Total annual research expenditures: $574,478. *Unit head:* Dr. Susan K. Duckett, Chair, 864-656-2570, Fax: 864-656-3131, E-mail: sducket@clemson.edu. *Application contact:* Dr. Denzil Maurice, 864-656-4023, E-mail: dmrc@clemson.edu.

Colorado State University, College of Veterinary Medicine and Biomedical Sciences, Department of Clinical Sciences, Fort Collins, CO 80523-1678. Offers MS, PhD. Part-time programs available. *Faculty:* 57 full-time (21 women). *Students:* 28 full-time (22 women), 46 part-time (33 women); includes 4 minority (1 Asian American or Pacific Islander, 3 Hispanic Americans), 17 international. Average age 32. 18 applicants, 83% accepted, 15 enrolled. In 2009, 13 master's, 3 doctorates awarded. Terminal master's awarded for partial completion of doctoral program. *Degree requirements:* For master's, thesis (for some programs), exam; for doctorate, thesis/dissertation, exam. *Entrance requirements:* For master's, GRE General Test, minimum GPA of 3.0, DVM or other equivalent medical degree, 3 letters of recommendation; for doctorate, GRE General Test, DVM or other equivalent medical degree, 3 letters of recommendation, biographical statement. Additional exam requirements/recommendations for international students: Required—TOEFL (minimum score 550 paper-based). *Application deadline:* For fall admission, 2/1 priority date for domestic students. Applications are processed on a rolling basis. Application fee: $50. Electronic applications accepted. *Expenses:* Tuition, state resident: full-time $6434; part-time $359.10 per credit. Tuition, nonresident: full-time $18,116; part-time $1006.45 per credit. Required fees: $1496; $83 per credit. *Financial support:* In 2009–10, 33 students received support, including 16 fellowships (averaging $34,159 per year), 17 research assistantships with full and partial tuition reimbursements available (averaging $24,462 per year); teaching assistantships, Federal Work-Study, institutionally sponsored loans, and traineeships also available. Financial award application deadline: 2/15; financial award applicants required to submit FAFSA. *Faculty research:* Orthopedics, oncology, epidemiology, infectious diseases, equine medicine. Total annual research expenditures: $8.5 million. *Unit head:* D. Paul Lunn, Head, 970-297-1274, Fax: 970-297-1275, E-mail: david.lunn@colostate.edu. *Application contact:* Morna J. Mynard, Information Contact, 970-297-4030, Fax: 970-297-1275, E-mail: morna.mynard@colostate.edu.

Drexel University, College of Medicine, Biomedical Graduate Programs, Program in Laboratory Animal Science, Philadelphia, PA 19104-2875. Offers MLAS. Part-time programs available. *Degree requirements:* For master's, comprehensive exam. *Entrance requirements:* For master's, GRE General Test, minimum GPA of 3.0. Additional exam requirements/recommendations for international students: Required—TOEFL. Electronic applications accepted. *Faculty research:* Laboratory animal medicine, experimental surgery, development of animal models for human diseases.

Iowa State University of Science and Technology, College of Veterinary Medicine and Graduate College, Graduate Programs in Veterinary Medicine, Department of Veterinary Clinical Sciences, Ames, IA 50011. Offers MS. Part-time programs available. *Faculty:* 24 full-time (7 women), 1 part-time/adjunct (0 women). *Students:* 1 (woman) full-time. 1 applicant, 0% accepted, 0 enrolled. In 2009, 1 master's awarded. *Degree requirements:* For master's, thesis or alternative. *Entrance requirements:* For master's, GRE. Additional exam requirements/recommendations for international students: Required—TOEFL (minimum score 590 paper-based; 94 iBT) or IELTS (minimum score 6.5). *Application deadline:* Applications are processed on a rolling basis. Application fee: $40 ($90 for international students). Electronic applications accepted. *Expenses:* Tuition, state resident: full-time $6716. Tuition, nonresident: full-time $8908. Tuition and fees vary according to course level, course load, program and student level. *Financial support:* Fellowships, research assistantships with partial tuition reimbursements, teaching assistantships with partial tuition reimbursements, career-related internships or fieldwork, scholarships/grants, health care benefits, and unspecified assistantships available. *Faculty research:* Theriogenology, veterinary medicine, veterinary surgery, extracorporeal shock waves, therapy, orthopedic research in animals. *Unit head:* Dr. Rodney Bagley, Chair, 515-294-2199, E-mail: rsbagley@iastate.edu. *Application contact:* Dr. Rodney Bagley, Chair, 515-294-2199, E-mail: rsbagley@iastate.edu.

Iowa State University of Science and Technology, College of Veterinary Medicine and Graduate College, Graduate Programs in Veterinary Medicine, Department of Veterinary Microbiology and Preventive Medicine, Ames, IA 50011. Offers veterinary microbiology (MS, PhD). *Faculty:* 20 full-time (5 women), 8 part-time/adjunct (4 women). *Students:* 27 full-time (10 women), 14 part-time (6 women); includes 4 minority (1 African American, 3 Asian Americans or Pacific Islanders), 11 international. 14 applicants, 21% accepted, 2 enrolled. In 2009, 2 master's, 4 doctorates awarded. *Degree requirements:* For master's, thesis or alternative; for doctorate, thesis/dissertation. *Entrance requirements:* For master's and doctorate, GRE General Test. Additional exam requirements/recommendations for international students: Required—TOEFL (minimum score 550 paper-based; 79 iBT) or IELTS (minimum score 6.5). *Application deadline:* For fall admission, 2/1 priority date for domestic and international students. Applications are processed on a rolling basis. Application fee: $40 ($90 for international students). Electronic applications accepted. *Expenses:* Tuition, state resident: full-time $6716. Tuition, nonresident: full-time $8908. Tuition and fees vary according to course level, course load, program and student level. *Financial support:* In 2009–10, 8 research assistantships with full and partial tuition reimbursements (averaging $16,480 per year) were awarded; fellowships, teaching assistantships with full and partial tuition reimbursements, scholarships/grants, health care benefits, and unspecified assistantships also available. *Faculty research:* Bacteriology, immunology, virology, public health and food safety. *Unit head:* Dr. Michael Wannemuehler, Chair, 515-294-5776, E-mail: vetmicro@iastate.edu. *Application contact:* Dr. Michael Wannemuehler, Chair, 515-294-5776, E-mail: vetmicro@iastate.edu.

Kansas State University, College of Veterinary Medicine, Department of Clinical Sciences, Manhattan, KS 66506. Offers MPH. *Faculty:* 31 full-time (10 women), 4 part-time/adjunct (3 women). *Students:* 19 full-time (17 women), 14 part-time (9 women); includes 2 minority (1 African American, 1 Hispanic American), 4 international. Average age 31. 38 applicants, 76% accepted, 14 enrolled. In 2009, 9 master's awarded. *Degree requirements:* For master's, thesis. *Entrance requirements:* For master's, GRE, DVM. Additional exam requirements/recommendations for international students: Required—TOEFL (minimum score 550 paper-based; 213 computer-based). *Application deadline:* For fall admission, 2/1 priority date for domestic and international students; for spring admission, 8/1 priority date for domestic and international students. Applications are processed on a rolling basis. Application fee: $40 ($55 for international students). Electronic applications accepted. *Financial support:* In 2009–10, 6 research assistantships (averaging $19,185 per year) were awarded; teaching assistantships, institutionally sponsored loans and scholarships/grants also available. Financial award application deadline: 3/1; financial award applicants required to submit FAFSA. *Faculty research:* Clinical trials, equine gastrointestinal ulceration, leptospirosis, food animal pharmacology, equine immunology, diabetes. Total annual research expenditures: $762,126. *Unit head:* Bonnie Rush, Department Head, 785-532-4249, E-mail: brush@ksu.edu. *Application contact:* Michael Kenney, Director, 785-532-4513, Fax: 785-432-4557, E-mail: kkenney@ksu.edu.

Louisiana State University and Agricultural and Mechanical College, School of Veterinary Medicine and Graduate School, Department of Comparative Biomedical Sciences, Baton Rouge, LA 70803. Offers MS, PhD. *Faculty:* 17 full-time (0 women). *Students:* 21 full-time (10 women), 2 part-time (both women); includes 1 American Indian/Alaska Native, 12 international. Average age 29. 13 applicants, 23% accepted, 2 enrolled. In 2009, 1 doctorate awarded. *Degree requirements:* For master's, thesis; for doctorate, thesis/dissertation, final exam. *Entrance requirements:* For master's and doctorate, GRE, minimum GPA of 3.0. Additional exam requirements/recommendations for international students: Required—TOEFL (minimum score 550 paper-based; 213 computer-based; 79 iBT) or IELTS (minimum score 6.5). *Application deadline:* For fall admission, 5/15 for international students; for spring admission, 10/15 for international students. Electronic applications accepted. *Financial support:* In 2009–10, 23 students received support, including 3 fellowships with full and partial tuition reimbursements available (averaging $33,288 per year), 18 research assistantships with full and partial tuition reimbursements available (averaging $22,571 per year); teaching assistantships, Federal Work-Study, institutionally sponsored loans, scholarships/grants, health care benefits, and unspecified assistantships also available. Support available to part-time students. Financial award applicants required to submit FAFSA. *Faculty research:* Gene therapy, metastasis, DNA repair, cytokines in cardiovascular function, aquatic toxicology. Total annual research expenditures: $2.4 million. *Unit head:* Dr. Gary E. Wise, Head, 225-578-9889, Fax: 225-578-9895, E-mail: gwise@mail.vetmed.lsu.edu. *Application contact:* Dr. George M. Strain, Graduate Adviser, 225-578-9758, Fax: 225-578-9895, E-mail: strain@lsu.edu.

Louisiana State University and Agricultural and Mechanical College, School of Veterinary Medicine and Graduate School, Department of Pathobiological Sciences, Baton Rouge, LA 70803. Offers MS, PhD. *Faculty:* 29 full-time (7 women). *Students:* 28 full-time (17 women), 5 part-time (2 women); includes 2 Asian Americans or Pacific Islanders, 1 Hispanic American, 16 international. Average age 31. 20 applicants, 40% accepted, 7 enrolled. In 2009, 2 master's, 6 doctorates awarded. *Degree requirements:* For doctorate, thesis/dissertation. *Entrance requirements:* Additional exam requirements/recommendations for international students: Required—TOEFL (minimum score 550 paper-based; 213 computer-based; 79 iBT) or IELTS (minimum score 6.5). *Application deadline:* For fall admission, 5/15 for international students; for spring admission, 10/15 for international students. Application fee: $50 ($70 for international students). Electronic applications accepted. *Financial support:* In 2009–10, 26 students received support, including 4 fellowships with full tuition reimbursements available (averaging $27,427 per year), 26 research assistantships with full and partial tuition reimbursements available (averaging $25,061 per year); teaching assistantships with full and partial tuition reimbursements available, Federal Work-Study, scholarships/grants, health care benefits, and unspecified assistantships also available. Support available to part-time students. Financial award applicants required to submit FAFSA. *Faculty research:* Infectious disease, host-

pathogen interaction, vaccinology. Total annual research expenditures: $4.1 million. *Unit head:* Dr. Ronald Thune, Head, 225-578-9680, Fax: 225-578-9701, E-mail: thune@mail.vetmed.lsu.edu. *Application contact:* Dr. James E. Miller, Graduate Adviser, 225-578-9652, Fax: 225-578-9701, E-mail: jmille1@lsu.edu.

Louisiana State University and Agricultural and Mechanical College, School of Veterinary Medicine and Graduate School, Department of Veterinary Clinical Sciences, Baton Rouge, LA 70803. Offers MS, PhD. *Faculty:* 31 full-time (13 women). *Students:* 6 full-time (5 women), 8 part-time (4 women); includes 1 African American, 8 international. Average age 30. 5 applicants, 80% accepted, 2 enrolled. In 2009, 3 master's, 1 doctorate awarded. *Entrance requirements:* For master's and doctorate, GRE, DVM or equivalent degree. Additional exam requirements/recommendations for international students: Required—TOEFL (minimum score 550 paper-based; 213 computer-based; 79 iBT) or IELTS (minimum score 6.5). *Application deadline:* For fall admission, 5/15 for domestic and international students; for spring admission, 10/15 for international students. Application fee: $50 ($70 for international students). Electronic applications accepted. *Financial support:* In 2009–10, 13 students received support, including 3 research assistantships with full and partial tuition reimbursements available (averaging $22,000 per year); fellowships, teaching assistantships, Federal Work-Study, institutionally sponsored loans, scholarships/grants, health care benefits, and unspecified assistantships also available. Support available to part-time students. Financial award applicants required to submit FAFSA. *Faculty research:* Urology/nephrology, equine arthroscopy orthopedics and laser surgery, physical rehabilitation on companion animals, cardiology, gastroenterology, infectious diseases, medical oncology, mare infertility. Total annual research expenditures: $316,773. *Unit head:* Dr. Dale Paccamonti, Head, 225-578-9551, Fax: 225-578-9559, E-mail: pacc@lsu.edu. *Application contact:* Dr. Susan Eades, Graduate Adviser, 225-578-9512, Fax: 225-578-9559, E-mail: sceades@vetmed.lsu.edu.

Michigan State University, College of Veterinary Medicine and The Graduate School, Graduate Programs in Veterinary Medicine, East Lansing, MI 48824. Offers comparative medicine and integrative biology (MS, PhD), including comparative medicine and integrative biology, comparative medicine and integrative biology–environmental toxicology (PhD); food safety and toxicology (MS), including food safety; integrative toxicology (PhD), including animal science–environmental toxicology, biochemistry and molecular biology–environmental toxicology, chemistry–environmental toxicology, crop and soil sciences–environmental toxicology, environmental engineering–environmental toxicology, environmental geosciences–environmental toxicology, fisheries and wildlife–environmental toxicology, food science–environmental toxicology, forestry–environmental toxicology, genetics–environmental toxicology, human nutrition–environmental toxicology, microbiology–environmental toxicology, pharmacology and toxicology–environmental toxicology, zoology–environmental toxicology; large animal clinical sciences (MS, PhD); microbiology and molecular genetics (MS, PhD), including industrial microbiology, microbiology, microbiology and molecular genetics, microbiology–environmental toxicology (PhD); pathobiology and diagnostic investigation (MS, PhD), including pathology, pathology–environmental toxicology (PhD); pharmacology and toxicology (MS, PhD); pharmacology and toxicology–environmental toxicology (PhD); physiology (MS, PhD); small animal clinical sciences (MS). *Students:* 66 full-time (40 women), 90 part-time (56 women); includes 24 minority (14 African Americans, 6 Asian Americans or Pacific Islanders, 4 Hispanic Americans), 51 international. Average age 33. In 2009, 22 master's, 16 doctorates awarded. *Application deadline:* For fall admission, 12/27 for domestic students. Applications are processed on a rolling basis. Application fee: $50. Electronic applications accepted. *Expenses:* Tuition, state resident: part-time $478.25 per credit hour. Tuition, nonresident: part-time $966.50 per credit hour. Part-time tuition and fees vary according to program. *Financial support:* In 2009–10, 32 research assistantships with tuition reimbursements (averaging $8,131 per year) were awarded. *Faculty research:* Molecular genetics, food safety/toxicology, comparative orthopedics, airway disease, population medicine. *Unit head:* Dr. Susan L. Ewart, Associate Dean for Research and Graduate Studies, 517-432-2388, Fax: 517-432-1037, E-mail: ewart@cvm.msu.edu. *Application contact:* Dr. Susan L. Ewart, Associate Dean for Research and Graduate Studies, 517-432-2388, Fax: 517-432-1037, E-mail: ewart@cvm.msu.edu.

Mississippi State University, College of Veterinary Medicine, Graduate Programs in Veterinary Medical Science, Mississippi State, MS 39762. Offers environmental toxicology (PhD); veterinary medical sciences (MS, PhD). Part-time programs available. Terminal master's awarded for partial completion of doctoral program. *Degree requirements:* For master's, thesis (for some programs); for doctorate, thesis/dissertation. *Entrance requirements:* For master's and doctorate, minimum GPA of 3.0. Additional exam requirements/recommendations for international students: Required—TOEFL. *Application deadline:* For fall admission, 3/1 priority date for domestic students, 1/1 priority date for international students; for spring admission, 8/1 priority date for domestic students, 7/1 priority date for international students. Applications are processed on a rolling basis. Electronic applications accepted. *Expenses:* Contact institution. *Financial support:* Fellowships with full tuition reimbursements, research assistantships with full tuition reimbursements, career-related internships or fieldwork available. *Faculty research:* Food animal health (poultry and warm-water aquaculture) using immunology, microbiology, molecular biology, parasitology, pathology, pharmacology, and environmental toxicology. *Unit head:* Dr. Larry Hanson, Graduate Coordinator, 662-325-1202, Fax: 662-325-1031, E-mail: hanson@cvm.msstate.edu. *Application contact:* Tia Peay, Administrative Assistant, 662-325-1417, Fax: 662-325-1193, E-mail: peay@cvm.msstate.edu.

Montana State University, College of Graduate Studies, College of Agriculture, Department of Veterinary Molecular Biology, Bozeman, MT 59717. Offers MS, PhD. Part-time programs available. *Faculty:* 7 full-time (2 women), 1 (woman) part-time/adjunct. *Students:* 2 full-time (both women), 9 part-time (4 women), 2 international. Average age 29. 5 applicants. In 2009, 5 doctorates awarded. *Degree requirements:* For master's, comprehensive exam; for doctorate, comprehensive exam, thesis/dissertation. *Entrance requirements:* For master's, GRE General Test; for doctorate, GRE General Test, BS or BA. Additional exam requirements/recommendations for international students: Required—TOEFL (minimum score 550 paper-based; 213 computer-based). *Application deadline:* For fall admission, 7/15 priority date for domestic students, 5/15 for international students; for spring admission, 12/1 priority date for domestic students, 10/1 priority date for international students. Applications are processed on a rolling basis. Application fee: $30. Electronic applications accepted. *Expenses:* Tuition, state resident: full-time $5635; part-time $3492 per year. Tuition, nonresident: full-time $17,212; part-time $7865.10 per year. Required fees: $1441; $153.15 per credit. Tuition and fees vary according to course load and program. *Financial support:* In 2009–10, 11 students received support, including 2 fellowships with full tuition reimbursements available (averaging $21,000 per year), 4 teaching assistantships with full tuition reimbursements available (averaging $5,700 per year); health care benefits and unspecified assistantships also available. Financial award application deadline: 3/1; financial award applicants required to submit FAFSA. *Faculty research:* Infectious disease pathogenesis, immunology, developmental biology, vaccine development, complementary and alternative medicine. Total annual research expenditures: $7.8 million. *Unit head:* Dr. Mark G. Quinn, Head, 406-994-5721, Fax: 406-994-4303, E-mail: mquinn@montana.edu. *Application contact:* Dr. Carl A. Fox, Vice Provost for Graduate Education, 406-994-4145, Fax: 406-994-7433, E-mail: gradstudy@montana.edu.

North Carolina State University, College of Veterinary Medicine, Program in Comparative Biomedical Sciences, Raleigh, NC 27695. Offers cell biology (MS, PhD); infectious disease (MS, PhD); pathology (MS, PhD); pharmacology (MS, PhD); population medicine (MS, PhD). Part-time programs available. *Degree requirements:* For master's, thesis; for doctorate, thesis/dissertation. *Entrance requirements:* For master's and doctorate, GRE General Test. Additional exam requirements/recommendations for international students: Required—TOEFL (minimum score 550 paper-based; 213 computer-based). Electronic applications accepted. *Expenses:* Contact institution. *Faculty research:* Infectious diseases, cell biology, pharmacology and toxicology, genomics, pathology and population medicine.

North Dakota State University, College of Graduate and Interdisciplinary Studies, College of Agriculture, Food Systems, and Natural Resources, Department of Veterinary and Microbiological Sciences, Fargo, ND 58108. Offers food safety (MS); microbiology (MS); molecular pathogenesis (PhD). Part-time programs available. *Students:* 4 full-time (all women), 3 part-time (1 woman). *Degree requirements:* For master's, thesis; for doctorate, thesis/dissertation, oral and written preliminary exams. *Entrance requirements:* For master's and doctorate, GRE. Additional exam requirements/recommendations for international students: Required—TOEFL (minimum score 525 paper-based; 197 computer-based; 71 iBT). *Application deadline:* For fall admission, 3/15 priority date for domestic students. Applications are processed on a rolling basis. Application fee: $25. *Financial support:* Fellowships with full tuition reimbursements, research assistantships with full tuition reimbursements, teaching assistantships with full tuition reimbursements, Federal Work-Study and institutionally sponsored loans available. Financial award application deadline: 4/15. *Faculty research:* Bacterial gene regulation, antibiotic resistance, molecular virology, mechanisms of bacterial pathogenesis, immunology of animals. *Unit head:* Dr. Doug Freeman, Head, 701-231-7511, E-mail: douglas.freeman@ndsu.nodak.edu. *Application contact:* Dr. Eugene S. Berry, Associate Professor, 701-231-7520, Fax: 701-231-7514, E-mail: eugene.berry@ndsu.edu.

The Ohio State University, College of Veterinary Medicine, Department of Veterinary Biosciences, Columbus, OH 43210. Offers anatomy and cellular biology (MS, PhD); pathobiology (MS, PhD); pharmacology (MS, PhD); toxicology (MS, PhD); veterinary physiology (MS, PhD). *Faculty:* 45. *Students:* 18 full-time (14 women), 20 part-time (16 women); includes 3 minority (1 African American, 1 Asian American or Pacific Islander, 1 Hispanic American), 16 international. Average age 30. In 2009, 1 master's, 9 doctorates awarded. *Entrance requirements:* For master's and doctorate, GRE General Test. Additional exam requirements/recommendations for international students: Required—TOEFL. *Application deadline:* Applications are processed on a rolling basis. Application fee: $40 ($50 for international students). Electronic applications accepted. *Expenses:* Tuition, state resident: full-time $10,683. Tuition, nonresident: full-time $25,923. Tuition and fees vary according to course load and program. *Faculty research:* Microvasculature, muscle biology, neonatal lung and bone development. *Unit head:* Dr. Michael J. Oglesbee, Graduate Studies Committee Chair, 614-292-5661, Fax: 614-292-6473, E-mail: oglesbee.1@osu.edu. *Application contact:* Graduate Admissions, 614-292-9444, Fax: 614-292-3895, E-mail: domestic.grad@osu.edu.

The Ohio State University, College of Veterinary Medicine, Department of Veterinary Clinical Sciences, Columbus, OH 43210. Offers MS, PhD. *Faculty:* 54. *Students:* 38 full-time (25 women), 3 part-time (all women), 10 international. Average age 30. In 2009, 12 master's awarded. *Entrance requirements:* For master's and doctorate, GRE (for graduates of institutions not accredited by the AVMA). *Application deadline:* For fall admission, 1/2 for domestic students. Applications are processed on a rolling basis. Application fee: $40 ($50 for international students). Electronic applications accepted. *Expenses:* Tuition, state resident: full-time $10,683. Tuition, nonresident: full-time $25,923. Tuition and fees vary according to course load and program. *Faculty research:* Equine exercise physiology, orthopedic surgery, oncology. *Unit head:* Rustin M. Moore, Chair, 614-292-7105, Fax: 614-292-0895, E-mail: moore.66@osu.edu. *Application contact:* Graduate Admissions, 614-292-9444, Fax: 614-292-3895, E-mail: domestic.grad@osu.edu.

The Ohio State University, College of Veterinary Medicine, Department of Veterinary Preventive Medicine, Columbus, OH 43210. Offers MS, PhD. *Faculty:* 34. *Students:* 8 full-time (5 women), 10 part-time (5 women), 11 international. Average age 32. In 2009, 4 master's, 5 doctorates awarded. *Entrance requirements:* For master's and doctorate, GRE (for graduates of institutions not accredited by the AVMA). *Application deadline:* Applications are processed on a rolling basis. Application fee: $40 ($50 for international students). Electronic applications accepted. *Expenses:* Tuition, state resident: full-time $10,683. Tuition, nonresident: full-time $25,923. Tuition and fees vary according to course load and program. *Faculty research:* Epidemiology; herd health; environmental health; animal health research pertaining to diagnosis, prevention, and control. *Unit head:* Dr. Willi J. A. Saville, Graduate Studies Committee Chair, 614-292-1206, Fax: 614-292-4142, E-mail: saville.4@osu.edu. *Application contact:* Graduate Admissions, 614-292-9444, Fax: 614-292-3895, E-mail: domestic.grad@osu.edu.

Oklahoma State University, Center for Veterinary Health Sciences and Graduate College, Graduate Program in Veterinary Biomedical Sciences, Stillwater, OK 74078. Offers MS, PhD. Postbaccalaureate distance learning degree programs offered (no on-campus study). *Faculty:* 82 full-time (20 women). *Students:* 35 full-time (18 women); includes 2 minority (1 American Indian/Alaska Native, 1 Hispanic American), 14 international. Average age 28. 30 applicants, 33% accepted, 10 enrolled. In 2009, 5 master's, 3 doctorates awarded. Terminal master's awarded for partial completion of doctoral program. *Degree requirements:* For master's, thesis; for doctorate, comprehensive exam, thesis/dissertation. *Entrance requirements:* For master's and doctorate, GRE General Test. Additional exam requirements/recommendations for international students: Required—TOEFL (minimum score 80 iBT). *Application deadline:* For fall admission, 7/1 priority date for domestic students, 2/15 priority date for international students; for spring admission, 10/1 priority date for domestic students, 7/1 priority date for international students. Applications are processed on a rolling basis. Application fee: $50 ($75 for international students). Electronic applications accepted. *Expenses:* Contact institution. *Financial support:* In 2009–10, 33 students received support, including 5 fellowships with partial tuition reimbursements available (averaging $8,000 per year), 9 research assistantships with full and partial tuition reimbursements available (averaging $23,376 per year), 13 teaching assistantships with full and partial tuition reimbursements available (averaging $23,376 per year); career-related internships or fieldwork, scholarships/grants, tuition waivers (full and partial), and unspecified assistantships also available. Financial award application deadline: 3/15; financial award applicants required to submit FAFSA. *Faculty research:* Infectious and parasitic diseases, physiology, toxicology, biomedical lasers, clinical studies. Total annual research expenditures: $5 million. *Unit head:* Dr. Ken D. Clinkenbeard, Coordinator, Veterinary Biomedical Sciences Graduate Program, 405-744-6750, Fax: 405-744-5275, E-mail: ken.clinkenbeard@okstate.edu. *Application contact:* Paula Seale, Assistant, 405-744-6750, Fax: 405-744-5275, E-mail: paula.seales@okstate.edu.

Oregon State University, College of Veterinary Medicine, Program in Comparative Veterinary Medicine, Corvallis, OR 97331. Offers PhD. *Students:* 3 full-time (2 women), 1 (woman) part-time, 2 international. Average age 31. *Degree requirements:* For doctorate, one foreign language, thesis/dissertation. *Entrance requirements:* For doctorate, minimum GPA of 3.0 in last 90 hours of course work. Additional exam requirements/recommendations for international students: Required—TOEFL. *Application deadline:* For fall admission, 11/1 for domestic students. Application fee: $50. *Expenses:* Tuition, state resident: full-time $9774; part-time $362 per credit. Tuition, nonresident: full-time $15,849; part-time $587 per credit. Required fees: $1639. Full-time tuition and fees vary according to course load and program. *Financial support:* Fellowships, research assistantships, Federal Work-Study and institutionally sponsored loans available. Support available to part-time students. Financial award application deadline: 2/1. *Faculty research:* Microbiology, virology, toxicology. *Unit head:* Dr. Luiz E. Bermudez, Department Head, 541-737-6538, Fax: 541-737-8035. *Application contact:* Dr. Susan J. Tornquist, Associate Dean, 541-737-2098, Fax: 541-737-4245, E-mail: susan.tornquist@oregonstate.edu.

Penn State Hershey Medical Center, College of Medicine, Graduate School Programs in the Biomedical Sciences, Graduate Program in Laboratory Animal Medicine, Hershey, PA 17033. Offers MS. *Degree requirements:* For master's, thesis or alternative. *Entrance requirements:* For master's, GRE, DVM. Additional exam requirements/recommendations for international students: Required—TOEFL (minimum score 550 paper-based; 213 computer-based). *Application deadline:* For fall admission, 1/31 priority date for domestic students, 2/1 priority date for international students. Applications are processed on a rolling basis. Application fee: $65. Electronic applications accepted. *Expenses:* Tuition, state resident: part-time $644 per credit. Tuition, nonresident: part-time $1142 per credit. Required fees: $22 per semester. *Financial support:* In 2009–10, 2 students received support; fellowships with full tuition reimbursements available, research assistantships with full tuition reimbursements available, scholarships/grants, traineeships, health care benefits, and unspecified assistantships available. Financial award applicants required to submit FAFSA. *Faculty research:* Veterinary pathology; pain, analgesia and anesthesia of lab animals; genetically modified animal models of cancer; transgenic animals. *Unit head:* Dr. Ronald P. Wilson, Chair, 717-531-8460, Fax: 717-531-5001,

Veterinary Sciences

Penn State Hershey Medical Center (continued)
E-mail: grad-hmc@psu.edu. *Application contact:* Nannette Kirst, Program Aide, 717-531-8460, Fax: 717-531-5001, E-mail: nkirst@psu.edu.

Penn State University Park, Graduate School, College of Agricultural Sciences, Department of Veterinary and Biomedical Sciences, State College, University Park, PA 16802-1503. Offers pathobiology (PhD).

Purdue University, School of Veterinary Medicine and Graduate School, Graduate Programs in Veterinary Medicine, Department of Basic Medical Sciences, West Lafayette, IN 47907. Offers anatomy (MS, PhD); pharmacology (MS, PhD); physiology (MS, PhD). Part-time programs available. *Faculty:* 23 full-time (7 women), 2 part-time/adjunct (1 woman). *Students:* 23 full-time (15 women), 1 (woman) part-time; includes 3 minority (1 African American, 2 Asian Americans or Pacific Islanders), 14 international. Average age 32. 15 applicants, 27% accepted, 4 enrolled. In 2009, 2 master's, 2 doctorates awarded. Terminal master's awarded for partial completion of doctoral program. *Degree requirements:* For master's, thesis; for doctorate, thesis/dissertation. *Entrance requirements:* For master's and doctorate, GRE General Test. Additional exam requirements/recommendations for international students: Required—TOEFL. *Application deadline:* For fall admission, 12/15 priority date for domestic students, 12/15 for international students. Application fee: $55. Electronic applications accepted. *Financial support:* In 2009–10, 14 research assistantships with partial tuition reimbursements (averaging $17,420 per year), 8 teaching assistantships with partial tuition reimbursements (averaging $15,000 per year) were awarded; fellowships with partial tuition reimbursements also available. Financial award application deadline: 3/1; financial award applicants required to submit FAFSA. *Faculty research:* Development and regeneration, tissue injury and shock, biomedical engineering, ovarian function, bone and cartilage biology, cell and molecular biology. *Unit head:* Dr. Laurie A. Jaeger, Head, 765-494-7348, Fax: 765-494-0781, E-mail: ljaeger@purdue.edu. *Application contact:* Dr. Kevin M. Hannon, Chairman, Graduate Committee, 765-494-5949, Fax: 765-494-0781, E-mail: bmsgrad@purdue.edu.

Purdue University, School of Veterinary Medicine and Graduate School, Graduate Programs in Veterinary Medicine, Department of Comparative Pathobiology, West Lafayette, IN 47907-2027. Offers comparative epidemiology and public health (MS); comparative epidemiology and public heath (PhD); comparative microbiology and immunology (MS, PhD); comparative pathobiology (MS, PhD); interdisciplinary studies (PhD), including microbial pathogenesis, molecular signaling and cancer biology, molecular virology; lab animal medicine (MS); veterinary anatomic pathology (MS); veterinary clinical pathology (MS). *Faculty:* 37 full-time (10 women), 4 part-time/adjunct (2 women). *Students:* 53 full-time (31 women), 2 part-time (1 woman); includes 3 minority (2 African Americans, 1 Hispanic American), 32 international. Average age 35. In 2009, 6 master's, 2 doctorates awarded. Terminal master's awarded for partial completion of doctoral program. *Degree requirements:* For master's, thesis (for some programs); for doctorate, thesis/dissertation. *Entrance requirements:* For master's and doctorate, GRE General Test. Additional exam requirements/recommendations for international students: Required—TOEFL (minimum score 575 paper-based; 232 computer-based), IELTS (minimum score 6.5), TWE (minimum score 4). *Application deadline:* For fall admission, 8/12 for domestic students, 6/15 for international students; for spring admission, 1/12 for domestic students, 10/15 for international students. Application fee: $55. Electronic applications accepted. *Financial support:* Fellowships, research assistantships, teaching assistantships available. Financial award application deadline: 3/1; financial award applicants required to submit FAFSA. *Unit head:* Dr. Suresh Mittal, Interim Head, 765-494-7543. *Application contact:* Denise A. Ottinger, Director, Student Services and Admissions, 765-494-7893, Fax: 765-496-2891, E-mail: vetadmissions@purdue.edu.

Purdue University, School of Veterinary Medicine and Graduate School, Graduate Programs in Veterinary Medicine, Department of Veterinary Clinical Sciences, West Lafayette, IN 47907. Offers MS, PhD. Degrees offered are post-DVM. Terminal master's awarded for partial completion of doctoral program. *Degree requirements:* For master's, thesis (for some programs); for doctorate, thesis/dissertation. *Entrance requirements:* For master's and doctorate, DVM. *Faculty research:* Flow cytometry, chemotherapy, biologic response modifiers, broncho-alveolar lavage, lithotripsy.

South Dakota State University, Graduate School, College of Agriculture and Biological Sciences, Department of Veterinary Science, Brookings, SD 57007. Offers biological sciences (MS, PhD). Part-time and evening/weekend programs available. *Degree requirements:* For master's, thesis (for some programs), oral exam; for doctorate, comprehensive exam, thesis/dissertation, preliminary oral and written exams. *Entrance requirements:* Additional exam requirements/recommendations for international students: Required—TOEFL (minimum score 525 paper-based; 197 computer-based; 71 iBT). *Faculty research:* Infectious disease, food animal, virology, immunology.

Texas A&M University, College of Veterinary Medicine, Department of Veterinary Small Animal Medicine and Surgery, College Station, TX 77843. Offers veterinary medicine and surgery (MS). *Faculty:* 2. *Students:* 7 full-time (2 women), 1 part-time (0 women); includes 1 minority (Hispanic American), 6 international. Average age 25. *Degree requirements:* For master's, thesis. *Entrance requirements:* For master's, GRE General Test. Additional exam requirements/recommendations for international students: Required—TOEFL. Application fee: $50 ($75 for international students). *Expenses:* Tuition, state resident: full-time $3991; part-time $221.74 per credit hour. Tuition, nonresident: full-time $9049; part-time $502.74 per credit hour. *Financial support:* In 2009–10, research assistantships with full tuition reimbursements (averaging $13,800 per year); fellowships, teaching assistantships also available. Financial award application deadline: 3/1; financial award applicants required to submit FAFSA. *Faculty research:* Gastroenterology, anesthesiology, nephrology and urology, cardiology, nutrition. *Unit head:* Dr. Sandee Hartsfield, Head, 979-845-2351, Fax: 979-845-6978, E-mail: shartsfield@tamu.edu. *Application contact:* Dr. Sandee Hartsfield, Head, 979-845-2351, Fax: 979-845-6978, E-mail: shartsfield@tamu.edu.

Tuskegee University, Graduate Programs, College of Veterinary Medicine, Nursing and Allied Health, School of Veterinary Medicine, Tuskegee, AL 36088. Offers DVM, MS. *Faculty:* 62 full-time (6 women). *Students:* 249 full-time (193 women); includes 143 minority (128 African Americans, 1 American Indian/Alaska Native, 3 Asian Americans or Pacific Islanders, 11 Hispanic Americans), 4 international. Average age 31. 281 applicants, 26% accepted. In 2009, 50 first professional degrees, 4 master's awarded. *Degree requirements:* For master's, thesis. *Entrance requirements:* For DVM, VCAT; for master's, GRE General Test. Additional exam requirements/recommendations for international students: Required—TOEFL (minimum score 500 paper-based; 69 computer-based). *Application deadline:* For fall admission, 7/15 for domestic students. Applications are processed on a rolling basis. Application fee: $25 ($35 for international students). *Expenses:* Tuition: Full-time $15,630; part-time $940 per credit hour. Required fees: $650. *Financial support:* Application deadline: 4/15. *Unit head:* Dr. Tsegaye Habtemariam, Dean, 334-727-8174, Fax: 334-727-8177. *Application contact:* Dr. Robert L. Laney, Vice President/Director of Admissions and Enrollment Management, 334-727-8580, Fax: 334-727-5750, E-mail: planey@tuskegee.edu.

Université de Montréal, Faculty of Veterinary Medicine and Faculty of Graduate Studies, Graduate Programs in Veterinary Sciences, Montréal, QC H3C 3J7, Canada. Offers M Sc, PhD. *Students:* Average age 29. In 2009, 24 master's, 4 doctorates awarded. *Degree requirements:* For master's, one foreign language, thesis optional. *Application deadline:* For fall admission, 2/1 priority date for domestic students; for winter admission, 11/1 priority date for domestic students; for spring admission, 2/1 priority date for domestic students. Application fee: $100. Electronic applications accepted. *Financial support:* Research assistantships, teaching assistantships, career-related internships or fieldwork and scholarships/grants available. *Faculty research:* Animal reproduction, infectious diseases of swine, physiology of exercise in horses, viral diseases of cattle, health management and epidemiology. *Unit head:* Michel Carrier, Dean, 514-345-8521, Fax: 450-778-8101, E-mail: michel.carrier@umontreal.ca. *Application contact:* Sylvain Quessy, Associate Dean, Responsible for Graduate Studies, 514-343-6111 Ext. 8398, Fax: 450-778-8105, E-mail: sylvain.quessy@umontreal.ca.

University of California, Davis, School of Veterinary Medicine and Graduate Studies, Program in Preventive Veterinary Medicine, Davis, CA 95616. Offers MPVM, DVM/MPVM. Part-time programs available. *Degree requirements:* For master's, thesis. *Entrance requirements:* For master's, DVM or equivalent. Additional exam requirements/recommendations for international students: Required—TOEFL (minimum score 550 paper-based; 213 computer-based). *Faculty research:* Epidemiology, zoonoses, veterinary public health, wildlife and ecosystem health.

University of California, Davis, School of Veterinary Medicine, Residency Training Program, Davis, CA 95616. Offers Certificate. *Entrance requirements:* For degree, DVM or equivalent, 1 year of related experience. *Faculty research:* Small animal and large animal medicine, surgery, infectious diseases, pathology.

University of Florida, College of Veterinary Medicine, Graduate Program in Veterinary Medical Sciences, Gainesville, FL 32611. Offers forensic toxicology (Certificate); veterinary medical sciences (MS, PhD), including forensic toxicology (MS). Postbaccalaureate distance learning degree programs offered (no on-campus study). Terminal master's awarded for partial completion of doctoral program. *Degree requirements:* For master's, thesis; for doctorate, thesis/dissertation. *Entrance requirements:* For master's and doctorate, GRE General Test, minimum GPA of 3.0. Additional exam requirements/recommendations for international students: Required—TOEFL (minimum score 550 paper-based; 213 computer-based). Electronic applications accepted. *Expenses:* Contact institution.

University of Georgia, College of Veterinary Medicine and Graduate School, Graduate Programs in Veterinary Medicine, Athens, GA 30602. Offers infectious diseases (MS, PhD); pathology (MS, PhD); physiology and pharmacology (MS, PhD), including pharmacology, physiology; population health (MAM, MFAM), including food animal medicine (MFAM), population health (MAM); toxicology (MS, PhD); veterinary anatomy and radiology (MS), including veterinary anatomy. *Faculty:* 101 full-time (35 women), 9 part-time/adjunct (2 women). *Students:* 449 full-time (307 women), 9 part-time (7 women); includes 41 minority (17 African Americans, 1 American Indian/Alaska Native, 9 Asian Americans or Pacific Islanders, 14 Hispanic Americans), 30 international. Average age 27. 88 applicants, 39% accepted, 13 enrolled. In 2009, 14 master's, 104 doctorates awarded. *Degree requirements:* For master's, comprehensive exam, thesis; for doctorate, comprehensive exam, thesis/dissertation. *Entrance requirements:* For master's and doctorate, GRE General Test, 3 letters of recommendation. Additional exam requirements/recommendations for international students: Required—TOEFL (minimum score 550 paper-based; 213 computer-based). *Application deadline:* For fall admission, 7/1 for domestic students, 4/15 for international students; for spring admission, 11/15 for domestic students, 10/15 for international students. Applications are processed on a rolling basis. Application fee: $50. *Expenses:* Contact institution. *Financial support:* In 2009–10, 102 research assistantships with full tuition reimbursements (averaging $23,000 per year) were awarded; unspecified assistantships also available. Financial award application deadline: 3/1; financial award applicants required to submit FAFSA. *Faculty research:* Vascular biomedicine, environmental toxicology, food safety, vaccines and emergency diseases. Total annual research expenditures: $11.3 million. *Unit head:* Dr. Harry W. Dickerson, Associate Dean for Research and Graduate Affairs, 706-542-5734, Fax: 706-542-8254, E-mail: hwd@vet.uga.edu. *Application contact:* Director of Graduate Admissions.

University of Guelph, Ontario Veterinary College and Graduate Program Services, Graduate Programs in Veterinary Sciences, Guelph, ON N1G 2W1, Canada. Offers M Sc, DV Sc, PhD, Diploma. *Accreditation:* AVMA (one or more programs are accredited). *Degree requirements:* For master's, thesis; for doctorate, comprehensive exam, thesis/dissertation. *Entrance requirements:* Additional exam requirements/recommendations for international students: Required—TOEFL. *Faculty research:* Veterinary and comparative medicine, biomedical science, population medicine, pathology, microbiology.

University of Idaho, College of Graduate Studies, College of Agricultural and Life Sciences, Department of Animal and Veterinary Science, Moscow, ID 83844-2282. Offers animal physiology (PhD); animal science (MS, PhD), including production. *Faculty:* 7 full-time. *Students:* 23 full-time, 13 part-time, 8 international. In 2009, 3 master's, 2 doctorates awarded. *Degree requirements:* For doctorate, thesis/dissertation. *Entrance requirements:* For master's, GRE General Test, minimum GPA of 2.8; for doctorate, minimum undergraduate GPA of 2.8, graduate 3.0. *Application deadline:* For fall admission, 8/1 for domestic students; for spring admission, 12/15 for domestic students. Application fee: $55 ($60 for international students). *Expenses:* Tuition, state resident: full-time $6120. Tuition, nonresident: full-time $17,712. *Financial support:* Research assistantships, teaching assistantships available. Financial award application deadline: 2/15. *Faculty research:* Reproductive biology, muscle and growth physiology, meat science, aquaculture, ruminant nutrition. *Unit head:* Dr. Carl W. Hunt, Head, 208-885-6932. *Application contact:* Dr. Carl W. Hunt, Head, 208-885-6932.

University of Illinois at Urbana–Champaign, College of Veterinary Medicine, Department of Pathobiology, Urbana, IL 61802. Offers MS, PhD, DVM/PhD. Part-time programs available. *Faculty:* 21 full-time (6 women). *Students:* 10 full-time (6 women), 5 part-time (1 woman); includes 3 minority (1 African American, 1 Asian American or Pacific Islander, 1 Hispanic American), 6 international. 34 applicants, 21% accepted, 6 enrolled. In 2009, 3 doctorates awarded. Terminal master's awarded for partial completion of doctoral program. *Entrance requirements:* For master's and doctorate, GRE, minimum GPA of 3.0. Additional exam requirements/recommendations for international students: Required—TOEFL (minimum score 590 paper-based; 243 computer-based). *Application deadline:* Applications are processed on a rolling basis. Application fee: $60 ($75 for international students). Electronic applications accepted. *Financial support:* In 2009–10, 3 fellowships, 5 research assistantships, 1 teaching assistantship were awarded; tuition waivers (full and partial) also available. *Faculty research:* Epidemiology, immunology, microbiology, parasitology, clinical pathology. *Unit head:* Daniel L. Rock, Head, 217-333-2449, Fax: 217-244-7421, E-mail: dlrock@illinois.edu. *Application contact:* Paula Moxley, Administrative Aide, 217-244-8924, Fax: 217-244-7421, E-mail: pkm@illinois.edu.

University of Illinois at Urbana–Champaign, College of Veterinary Medicine, Department of Veterinary Biosciences, Urbana, IL 61802. Offers MS, PhD, DVM/PhD. *Faculty:* 18 full-time (7 women), 3 part-time/adjunct (2 women). *Students:* 18 full-time (12 women), 1 (woman) part-time; includes 1 minority (Hispanic American), 11 international. 10 applicants, 30% accepted, 3 enrolled. In 2009, 1 master's awarded. *Entrance requirements:* For master's and doctorate, GRE, minimum GPA of 3.0. Additional exam requirements/recommendations for international students: Required—TOEFL (minimum score 600 paper-based; 250 computer-based). *Application deadline:* Applications are processed on a rolling basis. Application fee: $60 ($75 for international students). Electronic applications accepted. *Financial support:* In 2009–10, 5 fellowships, 10 research assistantships, 1 teaching assistantship were awarded; tuition waivers (full and partial) also available. *Unit head:* Dr. Duncan Ferguson, Head, 217-333-2506, Fax: 217-244-1652, E-mail: dcf@illinois.edu. *Application contact:* Carla Manuel, Administrative Aide, 217-333-8781, Fax: 217-244-1652, E-mail: cmanuel@illinois.edu.

University of Illinois at Urbana–Champaign, College of Veterinary Medicine, Department of Veterinary Clinical Medicine, Urbana, IL 61801. Offers MS, PhD, DVM/PhD. *Faculty:* 23 full-time (12 women), 1 part-time/adjunct (0 women). *Students:* 23 full-time (15 women), 6 part-time (3 women); includes 2 minority (both Hispanic Americans), 13 international. 11 applicants, 73% accepted, 5 enrolled. In 2009, 6 master's awarded. *Entrance requirements:* For master's, GRE (if applicant does not have a DVM), minimum GPA of 3.0; for doctorate, GRE if applicant does not have a DVM, minimum GPA of 3.0. Additional exam requirements/recommendations for international students: Required—TOEFL (minimum score 550 paper-based; 213 computer-based). *Application deadline:* Applications are processed on a rolling basis. Application fee: $60 ($75 for international students). Electronic applications accepted. *Financial support:* In 2009–10, 1 fellowship, 7 research assistantships were awarded; teaching assistantships, tuition waivers (full and partial) also available. *Unit head:* David A. Williams,

Head, 217-333-5310, Fax: 217-244-1475, E-mail: daw@illinois.edu. *Application contact:* Barbara Huffman, Staff Secretary, 217-333-5343, Fax: 217-244-1475, E-mail: bhuffman@illinois.edu.

University of Kentucky, Graduate School, College of Agriculture, Program in Veterinary Science, Lexington, KY 40506-0032. Offers MS, PhD. *Degree requirements:* For master's, comprehensive exam, thesis; for doctorate, comprehensive exam, thesis/dissertation. *Entrance requirements:* For master's, GRE General Test, minimum undergraduate GPA of 2.75; for doctorate, GRE General Test, minimum graduate GPA of 3.0. Additional exam requirements/recommendations for international students: Required—TOEFL (minimum score 550 paper-based; 213 computer-based). Electronic applications accepted. *Faculty research:* Microbiology, reproductive physiology, genetics, pharmacology/toxicology, parasitology.

University of Maryland, College Park, Academic Affairs, College of Agriculture and Natural Resources, Maryland Campus of VA/MD Regional College of Veterinary Medicine, Veterinary Medical Sciences Program, College Park, MD 20742. Offers MS, PhD. *Students:* 16 full-time (4 women); includes 1 minority (Asian American or Pacific Islander), 13 international. 7 applicants, 29% accepted, 2 enrolled. In 2009, 1 master's, 2 doctorates awarded. *Degree requirements:* For master's, thesis, oral exam; for doctorate, thesis/dissertation, oral exam, public seminar. *Entrance requirements:* For doctorate, GRE General Test. *Application deadline:* For fall admission, 5/1 for domestic students, 2/1 for international students; for spring admission, 10/1 for domestic students, 6/1 for international students. Applications are processed on a rolling basis. Application fee: $60. Electronic applications accepted. *Expenses:* Tuition, area resident: Part-time $471 per credit hour. Tuition, state resident: part-time $471 per credit hour. Tuition, nonresident: part-time $1016 per credit hour. Required fees: $337.04 per term. *Financial support:* In 2009–10, 8 research assistantships (averaging $17,944 per year), 1 teaching assistantship (averaging $18,912 per year) were awarded; fellowships also available. *Unit head:* Dr. Siba K. Samal, Chair, 301-314-6813, Fax: 301-314-6855, E-mail: ssamal@umd.edu. *Application contact:* Dean of Graduate School, 301-405-0376, Fax: 301-314-9305.

University of Minnesota, Twin Cities Campus, College of Veterinary Medicine and Graduate School, Graduate Programs in Veterinary Medicine, Program in Comparative and Molecular Bioscience, Minneapolis, MN 55455-0213. Offers MS, PhD, DVM/PhD. Terminal master's awarded for partial completion of doctoral program. *Degree requirements:* For master's, comprehensive exam, thesis; for doctorate, comprehensive exam, thesis/dissertation. *Entrance requirements:* For master's and doctorate, GRE. Additional exam requirements/recommendations for international students: Required—TOEFL (minimum score 550 paper-based; 213 computer-based; 79 iBT). Electronic applications accepted. *Faculty research:* Molecular regulation of immunity; mechanisms of bacterial, viral, and parasite pathogenesis; structural and functional comparative physiology and pathology.

University of Minnesota, Twin Cities Campus, College of Veterinary Medicine and Graduate School, Graduate Programs in Veterinary Medicine, Program in Veterinary Medicine, Minneapolis, MN 55455-0213. Offers MS, PhD, DVM/PhD. Terminal master's awarded for partial completion of doctoral program. *Degree requirements:* For master's, comprehensive exam, thesis; for doctorate, comprehensive exam, thesis/dissertation. *Entrance requirements:* Additional exam requirements/recommendations for international students: Required—TOEFL (minimum score 550 paper-based; 213 computer-based; 79 iBT). Electronic applications accepted. *Faculty research:* Infectious diseases, internal medicine, population medicine, surgery/radiology/anesthesiology, theriogenology.

University of Missouri, College of Veterinary Medicine and Graduate School, Graduate Programs in Veterinary Medicine, Columbia, MO 65211. Offers veterinary biomedical sciences (MS, PhD), including biomedical sciences (PhD); veterinary medicine and surgery (MS), including veterinary biomedical sciences; veterinary pathobiology (MS, PhD), including laboratory animal medicine (MS), pathobiology. *Faculty:* 188 full-time (83 women), 26 part-time/adjunct (11 women). *Students:* 16 full-time (6 women), 27 part-time (16 women); includes 2 minority (1 African American, 1 Hispanic American), 8 international. Average age 30. 33 applicants, 45% accepted, 11 enrolled. In 2009, 26 master's, 11 doctorates awarded. *Degree requirements:* For master's, thesis; for doctorate, 2 foreign languages, comprehensive exam, thesis/dissertation. *Entrance requirements:* For master's and doctorate, GRE General Test, minimum GPA of 3.0. Additional exam requirements/recommendations for international students: Required—TOEFL (minimum score 600 paper-based; 250 computer-based; 100 iBT). Application fee: $45 ($60 for international students). Electronic applications accepted. *Expenses:* Contact institution. *Financial support:* Fellowships with full tuition reimbursements, research assistantships with full tuition reimbursements, teaching assistantships with full tuition reimbursements, institutionally sponsored loans available. *Faculty research:* Exercise physiology, cardiovascular science, comparative medicine, biodefense-related organisms, vector borne infectious diseases. *Unit head:* Dr. Ronald Terjung, Associate Dean for Research and Postdoctoral Studies, 573-882-2635, E-mail: terjungr@missouri.edu. *Application contact:* Dr. Ronald Terjung, Associate Dean for Research and Postdoctoral Studies, 573-882-2635, E-mail: terjungr@missouri.edu.

University of Nebraska–Lincoln, Graduate College, College of Agricultural Sciences and Natural Resources, Department of Veterinary and Biomedical Sciences, Lincoln, NE 68588. Offers veterinary science (MS). Postbaccalaureate distance learning degree programs offered (minimal on-campus study). *Degree requirements:* For master's, thesis optional; for doctorate, comprehensive exam, thesis/dissertation. *Entrance requirements:* For master's, GRE General Test; for doctorate, GRE General Test, MCAT, or VCAT. Additional exam requirements/recommendations for international students: Required—TOEFL (minimum score 550 paper-based; 213 computer-based). Electronic applications accepted. *Faculty research:* Virology, immunobiology, molecular biology, mycotoxins, ocular degeneration.

University of Prince Edward Island, Atlantic Veterinary College, Graduate Program in Veterinary Medicine, Charlottetown, PE C1A 4P3, Canada. Offers anatomy (M Sc, PhD); bacteriology (M Sc, PhD); clinical pharmacology (M Sc, PhD); clinical sciences (M Sc, PhD); epidemiology (M Sc, PhD), including reproduction; fish health (M Sc, PhD); food animal nutrition (M Sc, PhD); immunology (M Sc, PhD); microanatomy (M Sc, PhD); parasitology (M Sc, PhD); pathology (M Sc, PhD); pharmacology (M Sc, PhD); physiology (M Sc, PhD); toxicology (M Sc, PhD); veterinary science (M Vet Sc); virology (M Sc, PhD). Part-time programs available. *Degree requirements:* For master's, thesis; for doctorate, thesis/dissertation. *Entrance requirements:* For master's, DVM, B Sc honors degree, or equivalent; for doctorate, M Sc. Additional exam requirements/recommendations for international students: Required—TOEFL (minimum score 550 paper-based; 213 computer-based; 80 iBT). *Expenses:* Contact institution. *Faculty research:* Animal health management, infectious diseases, fin fish and shellfish health, basic biomedical sciences, ecosystem health.

University of Saskatchewan, Western College of Veterinary Medicine and College of Graduate Studies and Research, Graduate Programs in Veterinary Medicine, Saskatoon, SK S7N 5A2, Canada. Offers large animal clinical sciences (M Sc, M Vet Sc, PhD); small animal clinical sciences (M Sc, M Vet Sc, PhD), including small animal clinical sciences (M Sc, PhD), veterinary anesthesiology, radiology and surgery (M Vet Sc), veterinary internal medicine (M Vet Sc); veterinary biomedical sciences (M Sc, M Vet Sc, PhD), including veterinary anatomy (M Sc), veterinary biomedical sciences (M Vet Sc), veterinary physiological sciences (M Sc, PhD); veterinary medicine (M Sc, PhD); veterinary microbiology (M Sc, M Vet Sc, PhD); veterinary pathology (M Sc, M Vet Sc, PhD). *Faculty:* 125. *Students:* 108. In 2009, 24 master's, 11 doctorates awarded. *Degree requirements:* For master's, comprehensive exam, thesis (for some programs); for doctorate, comprehensive exam, thesis/dissertation. *Entrance requirements:* Additional exam requirements/recommendations for international students: Required—TOEFL (minimum score 80 iBT) or IELTS (minimum score 6.5). *Application deadline:* For fall admission, 7/1 priority date for domestic students. Application fee: $75. Electronic applications accepted. *Expenses:* Contact institution. *Financial support:* Fellowships, teaching assistantships available. Financial award application deadline: 1/31. *Faculty research:* Reproduction, toxicology, wildlife diseases, food animal medicine, equine health. *Unit head:* Dr. C. S. Rhodes, Dean, 306-966-7447, Fax: 306-966-8747, E-mail: charles.rhodes@usask.ca. *Application contact:* Dr. Norman C. Rawlings, Associate Dean, Research, 306-966-7068, Fax: 306-966-8747, E-mail: norman.rawlings@usask.ca.

University of Washington, Graduate School, School of Medicine and Graduate School, Graduate Programs in Medicine, Department of Comparative Medicine, Seattle, WA 98195. Offers MS.

University of Wisconsin–Madison, School of Veterinary Medicine, Graduate Program in Comparative Biomedical Sciences, Madison, WI 53706. Offers MS, PhD. Terminal master's awarded for partial completion of doctoral program. *Degree requirements:* For master's, thesis; for doctorate, thesis/dissertation, 32 credits (15 didactic) plus seminars. *Entrance requirements:* For master's and doctorate, GRE, minimum GPA of 3.0. Additional exam requirements/recommendations for international students: Required—TOEFL (minimum score 550 paper-based; 213 computer-based; 80 iBT), IELTS (minimum score 6), MELAB: 77. Electronic applications accepted. *Expenses:* Tuition, state resident: part-time $594 per credit. Tuition, nonresident: part-time $1504 per credit. Required fees: $65 per credit. Tuition and fees vary according to course load, program and reciprocity agreements. *Faculty research:* Cell and molecular biology, genomics, immunology, infectious disease, medical technology, oncology, pharmacology and toxicology, physiology, virology.

Utah State University, School of Graduate Studies, College of Agriculture, Department of Animal, Dairy and Veterinary Sciences, Logan, UT 84322. Offers animal science (MS, PhD); bioveterinary science (MS, PhD); dairy science (MS). Part-time programs available. *Degree requirements:* For master's, thesis (for some programs); for doctorate, comprehensive exam, thesis/dissertation. *Entrance requirements:* For master's and doctorate, GRE General Test, minimum GPA of 3.0. Additional exam requirements/recommendations for international students: Required—TOEFL. Electronic applications accepted. *Faculty research:* Monoclonal antibodies, antiviral chemotherapy, management systems, biotechnology, rumen fermentation manipulation.

Virginia Polytechnic Institute and State University, Virginia-Maryland Regional College of Veterinary Medicine and Graduate School, Graduate Programs in Biomedical and Veterinary Sciences, Blacksburg, VA 24061. Offers MS, PhD. Part-time programs available. *Faculty:* 31 full-time (8 women). *Students:* 61 full-time (39 women), 27 part-time (20 women); includes 36 minority (27 American Indian/Alaska Native, 3 Asian Americans or Pacific Islanders, 6 Hispanic Americans), 1 international. Average age 29. 51 applicants, 37% accepted, 18 enrolled. In 2009, 13 master's, 7 doctorates awarded. *Degree requirements:* For master's, thesis; for doctorate, thesis/dissertation. *Entrance requirements:* Additional exam requirements/recommendations for international students: Required—TOEFL. *Application deadline:* For fall admission, 5/15 for international students; for spring admission, 10/15 for international students. Applications are processed on a rolling basis. Application fee: $65. Electronic applications accepted. *Expenses:* Contact institution. *Financial support:* In 2009–10, 5 fellowships with full tuition reimbursements (averaging $37,350 per year), 18 research assistantships with full tuition reimbursements (averaging $16,373 per year), 44 teaching assistantships with full tuition reimbursements (averaging $22,737 per year) were awarded; career-related internships or fieldwork, Federal Work-Study, scholarships/grants, health care benefits, and unspecified assistantships also available. Financial award application deadline: 1/15. *Faculty research:* Infectious diseases, nanotechnology and neuroscience, immunology, nutrition, toxicology and pharmacology. *Unit head:* Dr. Roger Avery, Associate Dean of Research and Graduate Studies, 540-231-5649, Fax: 540-231-7367, E-mail: avery@vt.edu. *Application contact:* Becky Jones, Information Contact, 540-231-4992, Fax: 540-231-7367, E-mail: vmsgrad@vt.edu.

Washington State University, College of Veterinary Medicine and Graduate School, Graduate Programs in Veterinary Science, Department of Veterinary and Comparative Anatomy, Pharmacology, and Physiology, Pullman, WA 99164-6520. Offers neuroscience (MS, PhD); veterinary science (MS, PhD). Part-time programs available. *Faculty:* 24 full-time (7 women), 1 part-time/adjunct (0 women). *Students:* 2 full-time (1 woman), 1 part-time (0 women), 2 international. Average age 43. 1 applicant, 100% accepted, 1 enrolled. *Degree requirements:* For master's, thesis, written exam; for doctorate, thesis/dissertation, written exam, oral exam. *Entrance requirements:* For master's and doctorate, GRE General Test or MCAT, minimum GPA of 3.0. Additional exam requirements/recommendations for international students: Required—TOEFL (minimum score 550 paper-based; 213 computer-based; 80 iBT). *Application deadline:* For fall admission, 12/31 priority date for domestic and international students; for spring admission, 8/1 for domestic and international students. Applications are processed on a rolling basis. Application fee: $50. Electronic applications accepted. *Financial support:* In 2009–10, 1 student received support, including 1 fellowship with full tuition reimbursement available (averaging $28,000 per year), research assistantships with full tuition reimbursements available (averaging $21,588 per year), teaching assistantships with full tuition reimbursements available (averaging $21,588 per year); Federal Work-Study, scholarships/grants, health care benefits, and unspecified assistantships also available. Financial award application deadline: 4/15. *Faculty research:* Addiction, sleep and performance, body weight and energy balance, emotion and well being, learning and memory, reproduction, vision, movement. Total annual research expenditures: $5 million. *Unit head:* Dr. Steven K. Simasko, Chairman, 509-335-6624, Fax: 509-335-4650, E-mail: simasko@vetmed.wsu.edu. *Application contact:* Heather Cochran, Academic Coordinator, 509-335-7675, Fax: 509-335-4650, E-mail: hcochran@vetmed.wsu.edu.

Washington State University, College of Veterinary Medicine and Graduate School, Graduate Programs in Veterinary Science, Department of Veterinary Clinical Sciences, Pullman, WA 99164. Offers MS. Part-time programs available. *Faculty:* 25 full-time (3 women). *Students:* 32 full-time (18 women), 1 (woman) part-time; includes 1 minority (Asian American or Pacific Islander), 12 international. Average age 30. 9 applicants, 100% accepted, 9 enrolled. In 2009, 7 master's awarded. *Degree requirements:* For master's, thesis, oral exam. *Entrance requirements:* For master's, GRE General Test, minimum GPA of 3.0, DVM or equivalent. *Application deadline:* For fall admission, 12/31 priority date for domestic students. Application fee: $50. Electronic applications accepted. *Financial support:* In 2009–10, research assistantships with full tuition reimbursements (averaging $20,800 per year). Financial award application deadline: 3/1. *Faculty research:* Oncology, mastitis, nuclear medicine, neuroanesthesia, exercise physiology. Total annual research expenditures: $500,000. *Unit head:* Dr. William Dernell, Chair, 509-335-0738, Fax: 509-335-0880. *Application contact:* Theresa A. Pfaff, Administrative Manager, 509-335-0723, Fax: 509-335-0880, E-mail: tpfaff@vetmed.wsu.edu.

Washington State University, College of Veterinary Medicine and Graduate School, Graduate Programs in Veterinary Science, Department of Veterinary Microbiology and Pathology, Pullman, WA 99164. Offers veterinary science (MS, PhD). *Faculty:* 27 full-time (4 women), 3 part-time/adjunct (1 woman). *Students:* 48 full-time (28 women); includes 2 minority (both Asian Americans or Pacific Islanders), 22 international. Average age 31. 44 applicants, 23% accepted, 7 enrolled. In 2009, 2 doctorates awarded. Terminal master's awarded for partial completion of doctoral program. *Degree requirements:* For master's, thesis, oral exam; for doctorate, thesis/dissertation, oral exam. *Entrance requirements:* For master's and doctorate, minimum GPA of 3.0. Additional exam requirements/recommendations for international students: Required—TOEFL (minimum score 550 paper-based; 213 computer-based). *Application deadline:* Applications are processed on a rolling basis. Application fee: $50. Electronic applications accepted. *Financial support:* In 2009–10, 32 research assistantships (averaging $27,024 per year) were awarded; scholarships/grants, traineeships, health care benefits, and unspecified assistantships also available. Financial award application deadline: 3/1. *Faculty research:* Microbial pathogenesis, veterinary and wildlife parasitology, laboratory animal pathology, immune responses to infectious diseases. *Unit head:* Dr. David J. Prieur, Chair, 509-335-6030, Fax: 509-335-8529, E-mail: dprieur@vetmed.wsu.edu. *Application contact:* Dr. Guy Palmer, Professor, 509-335-6033, Fax: 509-335-8529, E-mail: gpalmer@vetmed.wsu.edu.

ACADEMIC AND PROFESSIONAL PROGRAMS IN PHYSICAL EDUCATION, SPORTS, AND RECREATION

Section 41
Leisure Studies and Recreation

This section contains a directory of institutions offering graduate work in leisure studies and recreation. Additional information about programs listed in the directory may be obtained by writing directly to the dean of a graduate school or chair of a department at the address given in the directory.

In the other guides in this series:

Graduate Programs in the Humanities, Arts & Social Sciences
See *Performing Arts*

Graduate Programs in the Physical Sciences, Mathematics, Agricultural Sciences, the Environment & Natural Resources
See *Natural Resources*

CONTENTS

Program Directories

Leisure Studies

Aurora University, George Williams College of Aurora University, School of Experiential Leadership, Aurora, IL 60506-4892. Offers administration of leisure services (MS); outdoor pursuits recreation administration (MS). Part-time and evening/weekend programs available. *Degree requirements:* For master's, thesis optional. *Entrance requirements:* For master's, minimum GPA of 2.75. Additional exam requirements/recommendations for international students: Required—TOEFL (minimum score 550 paper-based; 213 computer-based). Electronic applications accepted. *Expenses:* Contact institution.

Bowling Green State University, Graduate College, College of Education and Human Development, School of Human Movement, Sport, and Leisure Studies, Bowling Green, OH 43403. Offers developmental kinesiology (M Ed); recreation and leisure (M Ed); sport administration (M Ed). Part-time programs available. *Degree requirements:* For master's, thesis or alternative. *Entrance requirements:* For master's, GRE General Test, minimum GPA of 2.7. Additional exam requirements/recommendations for international students: Required—TOEFL. Electronic applications accepted. *Faculty research:* Teacher-learning process, travel and tourism, sport marketing and management, exercise physiology and sport psychology, life-span motor development.

California State University, Long Beach, Graduate Studies, College of Health and Human Services, Department of Recreation and Leisure Studies, Long Beach, CA 90840. Offers recreation administration (MS). Part-time programs available. *Faculty:* 2 full-time (1 woman). *Students:* 17 full-time (12 women), 21 part-time (13 women); includes 8 minority (4 African Americans, 2 Asian Americans or Pacific Islanders, 2 Hispanic Americans), 10 international. Average age 30. 27 applicants, 67% accepted, 12 enrolled. *Degree requirements:* For master's, comprehensive exam or thesis. *Entrance requirements:* For master's, GRE General Test. *Application deadline:* For fall admission, 7/1 for domestic students. Applications are processed on a rolling basis. Application fee: $55. Electronic applications accepted. *Expenses:* Required fees: $1802 per semester. Part-time tuition and fees vary according to course load. *Financial support:* Federal Work-Study, institutionally sponsored loans, and scholarships/grants available. Financial award application deadline: 3/2. *Unit head:* Dr. Maridith Janssen, Chair, 562-985-4079, Fax: 562-985-8154, E-mail: mjanssen@csulb.edu. *Application contact:* Dr. Katherine James, Graduate Advisor, 562-985-8077, Fax: 562-985-8154, E-mail: kjames@csulb.edu.

Central Michigan University, College of Graduate Studies, College of Education and Human Services, Department of Recreation, Parks, and Leisure Services Administration, Mount Pleasant, MI 48859. Offers recreation and park administration (MA); therapeutic recreation (MA). Part-time programs available. *Degree requirements:* For master's, thesis or alternative. Electronic applications accepted. *Faculty research:* Commercial recreation and facilities management; study of ethics in parks and recreation professionals; computer touch-tone information services at visitor centers; creative play spaces for children; therapeutic recreation.

The College at Brockport, State University of New York, School of Health and Human Performance, Department of Recreation and Leisure Studies, Brockport, NY 14420-2997. Offers recreation and leisure (MS), including recreation and leisure service management, therapeutic recreation. Part-time programs available. *Students:* 15 full-time (10 women), 8 part-time (2 women); includes 3 minority (1 African American, 1 Asian American or Pacific Islander, 1 Hispanic American). 13 applicants, 100% accepted, 13 enrolled. In 2009, 9 master's awarded. *Degree requirements:* For master's, thesis or alternative. *Entrance requirements:* For master's, minimum GPA of 3.0, letters of recommendation, written critical analysis. Additional exam requirements/recommendations for international students: Required—TOEFL (minimum score 550 paper-based; 213 computer-based; 79 iBT). *Application deadline:* For fall admission, 7/15 priority date for domestic and international students; for spring admission, 11/15 priority date for domestic and international students. Application fee: $50. Electronic applications accepted. *Expenses:* Tuition, state resident: full-time $8370; part-time $349 per credit. Tuition, nonresident: full-time $13,250; part-time $522 per credit. *Financial support:* Federal Work-Study, scholarships/grants, and unspecified assistantships available. Support available to part-time students. Financial award application deadline: 3/15; financial award applicants required to submit FAFSA. *Faculty research:* Leisure service delivery systems; therapeutic recreation; international issues in recreation and leisure; tourism; customer service, customer behavior and perceived value/satisfaction; leisure motivation among Baby Boomers. *Unit head:* Dr. Joel Frater, Chairperson, 585-395-2994, Fax: 585-395-5246, E-mail: jfrater@brockport.edu. *Application contact:* Dr. Lynda Sperazza, Graduate Director, 585-395-5490, Fax: 585-395-5246, E-mail: lsperazza@brockport.edu.

Dalhousie University, Faculty of Health Professions, School of Health and Human Performance, Program in Leisure Studies, Halifax, NS B3H 1T8, Canada. Offers MA. Part-time programs available. *Faculty:* 6 full-time (4 women). *Students:* 15 full-time (13 women), 2 part-time (1 woman); includes 1 minority (American Indian/Alaska Native). 6 applicants, 67% accepted. In 2009, 2 master's awarded. *Degree requirements:* For master's, thesis. *Entrance requirements:* For master's, minimum GPA of 3.3. Additional exam requirements/recommendations for international students: Required—TOEFL, IELTS, CANTEST, CAEL, or Michigan English Language Assessment Battery. *Application deadline:* For fall admission, 6/1 priority date for domestic and international students. Applications are processed on a rolling basis. Application fee: $70. Electronic applications accepted. *Financial support:* In 2009–10, 6 students received support; research assistantships, teaching assistantships available. Financial award application deadline: 3/1. *Faculty research:* Leisure and lifestyles of social groups such as older adults, women, and persons with health problems or disabilities; historical analysis of leisure; sport and leisure administration. *Unit head:* Dr. Carol Putnam, Graduate Coordinator, 902-494-1167, Fax: 902-494-5120, E-mail: susan.tirone@dal.ca. *Application contact:* Tracy Powell, Graduate Administrative Secretary, 902-494-1154, Fax: 902-494-5120, E-mail: tracy.powell@dal.ca.

East Carolina University, Graduate School, College of Health and Human Performance, Department of Recreation and Leisure Studies, Greenville, NC 27858-4353. Offers recreation and leisure services administration (MS); therapeutic recreation administration (MS). Part-time and evening/weekend programs available. Postbaccalaureate distance learning degree programs offered (minimal on-campus study). *Degree requirements:* For master's, comprehensive exam, thesis optional. *Entrance requirements:* For master's, GRE General Test or MAT. Additional exam requirements/recommendations for international students: Required—TOEFL. *Faculty research:* Therapeutic recreation, stress and coping behavior, medicine carrying capacity, choice behavior, tourism preferences.

Florida International University, College of Education, Department of Health, Physical Education, and Recreation, Program in Parks and Recreation Management, Miami, FL 33199. Offers leisure services (MS); therapeutic recreation (MS). Part-time and evening/weekend programs available. *Entrance requirements:* For master's, GRE General Test or minimum GPA of 3.0. Additional exam requirements/recommendations for international students: Required—TOEFL (minimum score 550 paper-based; 213 computer-based; 80 iBT), IELTS (minimum score 6.3). Electronic applications accepted. *Expenses:* Tuition, state resident: full-time $8008; part-time $4004 per year. Tuition, nonresident: full-time $20,104; part-time $10,052 per year. Required fees: $298; $149 per term. *Faculty research:* Effects of prosocial behavior interventions on children and adolescents with behavior disorders or who are considered to be at risk.

Gallaudet University, The Graduate School, Department of Physical Education and Recreation, Washington, DC 20002-3625. Offers leisure services administration (MS). *Entrance requirements:* For master's, GRE General Test or MAT. Electronic applications accepted.

Howard University, Graduate School, Department of Health, Human Performance and Leisure Studies, Washington, DC 20059-0002. Offers exercise physiology (MS); health education (MS); sports studies (MS), including sociology of sports, sports management; urban recreation (MS), including leisure studies. Part-time and evening/weekend programs available. *Degree requirements:* For master's, comprehensive exam, thesis. *Entrance requirements:* For master's, BS in human performance or related field. Electronic applications accepted. *Faculty research:* Health promotion, cardiovascular hypertension, physical activity, sport and human rights issues.

Indiana University Bloomington, School of Health, Physical Education and Recreation, Department of Recreation, Park, and Tourism Studies, Bloomington, IN 47405-7000. Offers leisure behavior (PhD); outdoor recreation (MS); recreation (Re Dir); recreation administration (MS); recreational sports administration (MS); therapeutic recreation (MS); tourism management (MS). *Faculty:* 16 full-time (6 women), 2 part-time/adjunct (both women). *Students:* 55 full-time (29 women), 17 part-time (15 women); includes 8 minority (2 African Americans, 2 American Indian/Alaska Native, 3 Asian Americans or Pacific Islanders, 1 Hispanic American), 22 international. Average age 31. 62 applicants, 69% accepted, 23 enrolled. In 2009, 11 master's, 5 doctorates awarded. Terminal master's awarded for partial completion of doctoral program. *Degree requirements:* For master's and Re Dir, thesis optional; for doctorate, thesis/dissertation. *Entrance requirements:* For master's, GRE General Test, minimum GPA of 2.8; for doctorate, GRE General Test, minimum GPA of 3.0 (undergraduate), 3.5 (graduate). Additional exam requirements/recommendations for international students: Required—TOEFL. *Application deadline:* For fall admission, 1/1 for international students; for spring admission, 9/1 for international students. Applications are processed on a rolling basis. Application fee: $55 ($65 for international students). *Financial support:* In 2009–10, 30 students received support, including 7 fellowships (averaging $4,723 per year), 17 research assistantships (averaging $10,002 per year), 13 teaching assistantships with partial tuition reimbursements available (averaging $11,565 per year); career-related internships or fieldwork, Federal Work-Study, institutionally sponsored loans, scholarships/grants, tuition waivers (partial), unspecified assistantships, and fee remissions also available. Financial award application deadline: 3/1. *Faculty research:* Leisure counseling, gerontology, special populations, planning and development. *Unit head:* Dr. Craig Ross, Chairperson, 812-855-4711, E-mail: cmross@indiana.edu. *Application contact:* Program Office, 812-855-4711, Fax: 812-855-3998, E-mail: recpark@indiana.edu.

Murray State University, College of Health Sciences and Human Services, Department of Wellness and Therapeutic Sciences, Program in Exercise and Leisure Studies, Murray, KY 42071. Offers MS. Part-time programs available. *Degree requirements:* For master's, thesis optional. *Entrance requirements:* For master's, GRE General Test or MAT. Additional exam requirements/recommendations for international students: Required—TOEFL. *Faculty research:* Exercise and cancer recovery.

Penn State University Park, Graduate School, College of Health and Human Development, Department of Recreation, Park and Tourism Management, State College, University Park, PA 16802-1503. Offers MS, PhD.

Prescott College, Graduate Programs, Program in Adventure Education/Wilderness Leadership, Prescott, AZ 86301. Offers adventure education (MA); student-directed concentrations (MA). Part-time programs available. Postbaccalaureate distance learning degree programs offered (minimal on-campus study). *Faculty:* 16 part-time/adjunct (9 women). *Students:* 16 full-time (10 women), 14 part-time (8 women); includes 1 minority (American Indian/Alaska Native), 3 international. Average age 32. 22 applicants, 86% accepted, 14 enrolled. In 2009, 10 master's awarded. *Degree requirements:* For master's, thesis, fieldwork or internship, practicum. *Entrance requirements:* For master's, 2 letters of recommendation, resume. Additional exam requirements/recommendations for international students: Required—TOEFL (minimum score 500 paper-based; 173 computer-based). *Application deadline:* For fall admission, 4/15 priority date for domestic and international students; for spring admission, 9/15 priority date for domestic and international students. Applications are processed on a rolling basis. Application fee: $40. Electronic applications accepted. *Expenses:* Tuition: Full-time $14,712; part-time $613 per credit. Required fees: $50 per term. One-time fee: $150. Tuition and fees vary according to course load and degree level. *Financial support:* Career-related internships or fieldwork, Federal Work-Study, and scholarships/grants available. Financial award applicants required to submit FAFSA. *Unit head:* Dr. Shari Leach, Interim Chair, 303-823-5138, E-mail: sleach@prescott.edu. *Application contact:* Kerstin Alicki, Admissions Counselor, 877-412-8705, Fax: 928-277-4695, E-mail: admissions@prescott.edu.

San Francisco State University, Division of Graduate Studies, College of Health and Human Services, Department of Recreation and Leisure Studies, San Francisco, CA 94132-1722. Offers recreation (MS). Part-time programs available.

Southeast Missouri State University, School of Graduate Studies, Department of Health, Human Performance and Recreation, Cape Girardeau, MO 63701-4799. Offers community wellness and leisure (MPA); nutrition and exercise science (MS). Part-time and evening/weekend programs available. *Degree requirements:* For master's, comprehensive exam (for some programs), thesis or alternative. *Entrance requirements:* For master's, GRE General Test (minimum score 1000 verbal and quantitative) for nutrition and exercise science (MS), minimum undergraduate GPA of 3.0 (MS), 2.7 (MPA). Additional exam requirements/recommendations for international students: Required—TOEFL (minimum score 550 paper-based; 213 computer-based); Recommended—IELTS (minimum score 6). Electronic applications accepted. *Expenses:* Tuition, state resident: full-time $4266; part-time $237 per credit hour. Tuition, nonresident: full-time $7506; part-time $417 per credit hour. Required fees: $427; $427. *Faculty research:* Health issues of athletes, body composition assessment, exercise testing, exercise training, perceptual responses to physical activity.

Southern Connecticut State University, School of Graduate Studies, School of Health and Human Services, Department of Recreation and Leisure Studies, New Haven, CT 06515-1355. Offers MS. Part-time and evening/weekend programs available. *Faculty:* 2 full-time, 1 part-time/adjunct. *Students:* 11 full-time (8 women), 22 part-time (12 women); includes 2 minority (1 Asian American or Pacific Islander, 1 Hispanic American). 20 applicants, 65% accepted, 12 enrolled. In 2009, 10 master's awarded. *Degree requirements:* For master's, thesis or alternative. *Entrance requirements:* For master's, interview, minimum undergraduate QPA of 3.0 in graduate major field or 2.5 overall. *Application deadline:* For fall admission, 7/15 priority date for domestic students. Applications are processed on a rolling basis. Application fee: $50. Electronic applications accepted. Tuition and fees vary according to program. *Financial support:* In 2009–10, 1 teaching assistantship was awarded; career-related internships or fieldwork also available. Financial award application deadline: 4/15; financial award applicants required to submit FAFSA. *Unit head:* Dr. James MacGregor, Chairperson, 203-392-6385, Fax: 203-392-6965, E-mail: macgregorj1@southernct.edu. *Application contact:* Dr. Jan Louise Jones, Graduate Coordinator, 203-392-8837, Fax: 203-392-6147, E-mail: jonesj39@southernct.edu.

Temple University, Graduate School, School of Tourism and Hospitality Management, Program in Sport and Recreation Administration, Philadelphia, PA 19122-6096. Offers Ed M. Part-time and evening/weekend programs available. *Entrance requirements:* For master's, GRE General Test or MAT, minimum undergraduate GPA of 3.0. Additional exam requirements/recommendations for international students: Required—TOEFL (minimum score 550 paper-based; 213 computer-based; 79 iBT). Electronic applications accepted.

Texas State University–San Marcos, Graduate School, College of Education, Department of Health and Human Performance, Program in Recreation and Leisure Services, San Marcos, TX 78666. Offers MSRLS. *Faculty:* 3 full-time (2 women), 1 (woman) part-time/adjunct. *Students:* 28 full-time (12 women), 16 part-time (11 women); includes 8 minority (1 African American, 1 Asian American or Pacific Islander, 6 Hispanic Americans). Average age 28. 26 applicants, 100% accepted, 18 enrolled. In 2009, 7 master's awarded. *Degree requirements:* For master's, comprehensive exam, thesis optional. *Entrance requirements:* For master's, GRE General Test, minimum GPA of 2.75 in last 60 hours of course work. Additional exam requirements/recommendations for international students: Required—TOEFL (minimum score 550 paper-based; 213 computer-based). *Application deadline:* For fall admission, 6/15 priority date for domestic students; for spring admission, 10/15 priority date for domestic students. Applications

are processed on a rolling basis. Application fee: $40 ($90 for international students). Electronic applications accepted. *Expenses:* Tuition, state resident: full-time $5784; part-time $241 per credit hour. Tuition, nonresident: full-time $13,224; part-time $551 per credit hour. Required fees: $1728; $48 per credit hour. $306. Tuition and fees vary according to course load. *Financial support:* In 2009–10, 34 students received support, including 4 research assistantships (averaging $5,234 per year), 4 teaching assistantships (averaging $5,414 per year). Financial award application deadline: 4/1; financial award applicants required to submit FAFSA. *Unit head:* Dr. Duane Knudson, Graduate Advisor, 512-245-2561, Fax: 512-245-8678, E-mail: dk19@txstate.edu. *Application contact:* Dr. Stephen Awonly, Head, 512-245-2561, Fax: 512-245-8678, E-mail: sa11@txstate.edu.

Universidad Metropolitana, Graduate Programs in Education, Program in Managing Leisure Services, San Juan, PR 00928-1150. Offers M Ed. Part-time programs available. *Degree requirements:* For master's, thesis or alternative. *Entrance requirements:* For master's, EXADEP, interview. Electronic applications accepted.

Université du Québec à Trois-Rivières, Graduate Programs, Program in Leisure, Culture and Tourism Sciences, Trois-Rivières, QC G9A 5H7, Canada. Offers MA, DESS. Part-time programs available. *Degree requirements:* For master's, thesis optional. *Entrance requirements:* For master's, appropriate bachelor's degree, proficiency in French.

University of Connecticut, Graduate School, Neag School of Education, Department of Kinesiology, Program in Sport Management and Sociology, Storrs, CT 06269. Offers MA, PhD. *Faculty:* 16 full-time (8 women). *Students:* 21 full-time (9 women), 7 part-time (5 women); includes 9 minority (all African Americans), 3 international. Average age 26. 46 applicants, 26% accepted, 4 enrolled. In 2009, 4 master's, 2 doctorates awarded. Terminal master's awarded for partial completion of doctoral program. *Degree requirements:* For master's, comprehensive exam, thesis or alternative; for doctorate, thesis/dissertation. *Entrance requirements:* For doctorate, GRE General Test. Additional exam requirements/recommendations for international students: Required—TOEFL (minimum score 550 paper-based; 213 computer-based). *Application deadline:* For fall admission, 2/1 priority date for domestic and international students; for spring admission, 11/1 for domestic students, 10/1 for international students. Applications are processed on a rolling basis. Application fee: $55. Electronic applications accepted. *Expenses:* Tuition, state resident: full-time $4725; part-time $525 per credit. Tuition, nonresident: full-time $12,267; part-time $1363 per credit. Required fees: $346 per semester. Tuition and fees vary according to course load. *Financial support:* In 2009–10, 13 research assistantships with full tuition reimbursements, 3 teaching assistantships with full tuition reimbursements were awarded; fellowships, Federal Work-Study, scholarships/grants, health care benefits, and unspecified assistantships also available. Financial award application deadline: 2/1; financial award applicants required to submit FAFSA. *Unit head:* Carl Maresh, Head, 860-486-3623, Fax: 860-486-1123. *Application contact:* Lisa Rasicot, Graduate Coordinator, 860-486-3065, Fax: 860-486-0210, E-mail: l.rasicot@uconn.edu.

University of Georgia, Graduate School, College of Education, Department of Counseling and Human Development Services, Athens, GA 30602. Offers college student affairs administration (M Ed, PhD); counseling and student personnel (PhD); counseling psychology (PhD); professional counseling (M Ed); professional school counseling (Ed S); recreation and leisure studies (M Ed, MA, PhD). *Accreditation:* ACA (one or more programs are accredited); APA (one or more programs are accredited); NCATE. *Faculty:* 22 full-time (13 women). *Students:* 147 full-time (102 women), 56 part-time (30 women); includes 45 minority (36 African Americans, 5 Asian Americans or Pacific Islanders, 4 Hispanic Americans), 1 international. 278 applicants, 27% accepted, 69 enrolled. In 2009, 49 master's, 13 doctorates, 4 other advanced degrees awarded. *Degree requirements:* For master's, thesis (MA); for doctorate, variable foreign language requirement, thesis/dissertation. *Entrance requirements:* For master's, GRE General Test or MAT; for doctorate, GRE General Test. *Application deadline:* For fall admission, 7/1 priority date for domestic students; for spring admission, 11/15 for domestic students. Application fee: $50. Electronic applications accepted. *Expenses:* Tuition, state resident: full-time $6000; part-time $250 per credit hour. Tuition, nonresident: full-time $20,904; part-time $871 per credit hour. Required fees: $730 per semester. *Financial support:* Fellowships, research assistantships, teaching assistantships, unspecified assistantships available. *Unit head:* Dr. Rosemary E. Phelps, Head, 706-542-4221, Fax: 706-542-4130, E-mail: rephelps@uga.edu. *Application contact:* Dr. Georgia B. Calhoun, Graduate Coordinator, 706-542-4103, Fax: 706-542-4130, E-mail: gcalhoun@uga.edu.

University of Illinois at Urbana–Champaign, Graduate College, College of Applied Health Sciences, Department of Recreation, Sport and Tourism, Champaign, IL 61820. Offers MS, PhD. Part-time and evening/weekend programs available. Postbaccalaureate distance learning degree programs offered (no on-campus study). *Faculty:* 12 full-time (8 women). *Students:* 30 full-time (18 women), 37 part-time (11 women); includes 10 minority (4 African Americans, 2 Asian Americans or Pacific Islanders, 4 Hispanic Americans), 19 international. 60 applicants, 43% accepted, 16 enrolled. In 2009, 20 master's, 2 doctorates awarded. *Entrance requirements:* For master's, GRE General Test, minimum GPA of 3.0; for doctorate, GRE, minimum GPA of 3.0. Additional exam requirements/recommendations for international students: Required—TOEFL (minimum score 600 paper-based; 250 computer-based). *Application deadline:* Applications are processed on a rolling basis. Application fee: $60 ($75 for international students). Electronic applications accepted. *Financial support:* In 2009–10, 19 research assistantships, 21 teaching assistantships were awarded; fellowships, tuition waivers (full and partial) also available. *Unit head:* Cary D. McDonald, Head, 217-333-4410, Fax: 217-244-1935, E-mail: carym@illinois.edu. *Application contact:* Jill M. Gurk, Secretary, 217-333-4410, Fax: 217-244-1935, E-mail: jgurke@illinois.edu.

The University of Iowa, Graduate College, College of Liberal Arts and Sciences, Program in Leisure Studies, Iowa City, IA 52242-1316. Offers leisure and recreational sport management (MA); therapeutic recreation (MA). *Degree requirements:* For master's, thesis optional, exam. *Entrance requirements:* For master's, minimum GPA of 3.0. Additional exam requirements/recommendations for international students: Required—TOEFL (minimum score 550 paper-based; 213 computer-based; 81 iBT). Electronic applications accepted.

University of Memphis, Graduate School, College of Education, Department of Health and Sport Sciences, Memphis, TN 38152. Offers clinical nutrition (MS); exercise and sport science (MS); health promotion (MS); physical education teacher education (MS), including teacher education; sport and leisure commerce (MS). Part-time and evening/weekend programs available. *Faculty:* 18 full-time (9 women), 3 part-time/adjunct (1 woman). *Students:* 64 full-time (35 women), 36 part-time (23 women); includes 17 African Americans, 1 Asian American or Pacific Islander, 1 Hispanic American, 4 international. Average age 27. 99 applicants, 72% accepted, 50 enrolled. In 2009, 35 master's awarded. *Degree requirements:* For master's, comprehensive exam, thesis. *Entrance requirements:* For master's, GRE General Test or GMAT (sport and leisure commerce). *Application deadline:* For fall admission, 5/1 priority date for domestic students; for spring admission, 11/1 for domestic students. Applications are processed on a rolling basis. Application fee: $35 ($60 for international students). *Expenses:* Tuition, state resident: full-time $6246; part-time $347 per credit hour. Tuition, nonresident: full-time $15,894; part-time $883 per credit hour. Required fees: $1160. Full-time tuition and fees vary according to course load, degree level and program. *Financial support:* In 2009–10, 59 students received support; research assistantships with full tuition reimbursements available, teaching assistantships with full tuition reimbursements available, career-related internships or fieldwork, Federal Work-Study, scholarships/grants, tuition waivers (partial), and unspecified assistantships available. Financial award application deadline: 2/15; financial award applicants required to submit FAFSA. *Faculty research:* Sport marketing and consumer analysis, health psychology, smoking cessation, psychosocial aspects of cardiovascular disease, global health promotion. *Unit head:* Linda H. Clemens, Interim Chair, 901-678-2324, Fax: 901-678-3591, E-mail: lhclemns@memphis.edu. *Application contact:* Dr. Kenneth Ward, Graduate Studies Coordinator, 901-678-1714, E-mail: kdward@memphis.edu.

University of Minnesota, Twin Cities Campus, Graduate School, College of Education and Human Development, School of Kinesiology, Division of Recreation, Park, and Leisure Studies, Minneapolis, MN 55455-0213. Offers M Ed, MA, PhD. Part-time programs available. *Students:* 2 full-time (both women), 6 part-time (3 women), 4 international. Average age 34. 8 applicants, 75% accepted, 3 enrolled. In 2009, 9 master's, 3 doctorates awarded. Terminal master's awarded for partial completion of doctoral program. *Degree requirements:* For master's, thesis (for some programs), final oral exam; for doctorate, thesis/dissertation, preliminary written/oral exam, final oral exam. *Entrance requirements:* For master's, GRE or MAT, minimum GPA of 3.0; for doctorate, GRE or MAT, minimum GPA of 3.0, writing sample. *Application deadline:* For fall admission, 7/15 for domestic students; for spring admission, 12/15 for domestic students. Applications are processed on a rolling basis. *Financial support:* Fellowships, research assistantships, teaching assistantships, career-related internships or fieldwork, Federal Work-Study, institutionally sponsored loans, and tuition waivers (full and partial) available. Support available to part-time students. *Application contact:* Dr. Mary Trettin, Associate Dean, 612-625-3339, Fax: 612-626-1580, E-mail: mtrettin@umn.edu.

University of Mississippi, Graduate School, School of Applied Sciences, Department of Health, Exercise Science, and Recreation Management, Oxford, University, MS 38677. Offers exercise science (MS); exercise science and leisure management (PhD); park and recreation management (MA); wellness (MS). *Faculty:* 10 full-time (2 women), 2 part-time/adjunct (both women). *Students:* 37 full-time (22 women), 8 part-time (5 women); includes 8 minority (7 African Americans, 1 Hispanic American), 5 international. In 2009, 5 master's, 3 doctorates awarded. *Degree requirements:* For master's, thesis (for some programs); for doctorate, thesis/dissertation. *Entrance requirements:* For master's, GRE General Test, minimum GPA of 3.0; for doctorate, GRE General Test. Additional exam requirements/recommendations for international students: Required—TOEFL. *Application deadline:* For fall admission, 4/1 for domestic students; for spring admission, 10/1 for domestic students. Applications are processed on a rolling basis. Application fee: $25. *Financial support:* Scholarships/grants available. Financial award application deadline: 3/1; financial award applicants required to submit FAFSA. *Unit head:* Dr. Mark Loftin, Interim Chair, 662-915-5844, Fax: 662-915-5525, E-mail: mloftin@olemiss.edu. *Application contact:* Dr. Christy M. Wyandt, Associate Dean, 662-915-7474, Fax: 662-915-7577, E-mail: cwyandt@olemiss.edu.

University of Nevada, Las Vegas, Graduate College, William F. Harrah College of Hotel Administration, Department of Leisure Studies, Las Vegas, NV 89154-6013. Offers sport and leisure services management (MS). Part-time programs available. *Faculty:* 6 full-time (2 women). *Students:* 11 full-time (2 women), 7 part-time (4 women); includes 3 minority (2 Asian Americans or Pacific Islanders, 1 Hispanic American). Average age 29. 35 applicants, 71% accepted, 15 enrolled. In 2009, 5 master's awarded. *Degree requirements:* For master's, thesis (for some programs), professional paper. *Entrance requirements:* For master's, GRE General Test. Additional exam requirements/recommendations for international students: Required—TOEFL (minimum score 550 paper-based; 213 computer-based; 80 iBT), IELTS (minimum score 7). *Application deadline:* For fall admission, 6/15 priority date for domestic students, 5/1 for international students; for spring admission, 11/15 priority date for domestic students, 10/1 for international students. Applications are processed on a rolling basis. Application fee: $60 ($95 for international students). Electronic applications accepted. *Financial support:* In 2009–10, 5 students received support, including 5 research assistantships with partial tuition reimbursements available (averaging $10,000 per year); institutionally sponsored loans, scholarships/grants, health care benefits, and unspecified assistantships also available. Financial award application deadline: 3/1. *Faculty research:* Volunteerism in natural resource settings, sport tourism, achieving well-being through leisure, impact of youth sport on youth participants, sport marketing research. *Unit head:* Dr. Pearl Brewer, Chair/ Professor, 702-895-3643, Fax: 702-895-4872, E-mail: pearl.brewer@unlv.edu. *Application contact:* Graduate College Admissions Evaluator, 702-895-3320, Fax: 702-895-4180, E-mail: gradcollege@unlv.edu.

The University of North Carolina at Chapel Hill, Graduate School, College of Arts and Sciences, Department of Recreation and Leisure Studies, Chapel Hill, NC 27599. Offers MSRA. Part-time programs available. *Degree requirements:* For master's, comprehensive exam, thesis or alternative. *Entrance requirements:* For master's, GRE General Test, minimum GPA of 3.0. Additional exam requirements/recommendations for international students: Required—TOEFL. Electronic applications accepted. *Faculty research:* Leisure research related to gender, youth, inclusion, and family; social psychology of leisure; leisure democracy.

University of Northern Iowa, Graduate College, College of Education, School of Health, Physical Education, and Leisure Services, Program in Leisure Services, Cedar Falls, IA 50614. Offers leisure services (Ed D); program administration (MA); youth/human services administration (MA). *Students:* 23 full-time (14 women), 25 part-time (13 women); includes 16 minority (14 African Americans, 1 Asian American or Pacific Islander, 1 Hispanic American), 8 international. 20 applicants. In 2009, 8 master's awarded. *Degree requirements:* For master's, comprehensive exam, thesis or alternative; for doctorate, thesis/dissertation. *Entrance requirements:* For master's, minimum GPA of 3.0; for doctorate, GRE, minimum GPA of 3.5. Additional exam requirements/recommendations for international students; Required—TOEFL (minimum score 500 paper-based; 180 computer-based; 61 iBT). *Application deadline:* Applications are processed on a rolling basis. Application fee: $30 ($50 for international students). Electronic applications accepted. *Financial support:* Career-related internships or fieldwork, Federal Work-Study, institutionally sponsored loans, tuition waivers (full), and unspecified assistantships available. Financial award application deadline: 2/1. *Unit head:* Dr. Samuel Lankford, Interim Director, 319-273-6840, Fax: 319-273-5958, E-mail: sam.lankford@uni.edu. *Application contact:* Laurie S. Russell, Record Analyst, 319-273-2623, Fax: 319-273-6792, E-mail: laurie.russell@uni.edu.

University of North Texas, Robert B. Toulouse School of Graduate Studies, College of Education, Department of Kinesiology, Health Promotion, and Recreation, Program in Recreation and Leisure Studies, Denton, TX 76203. Offers recreation and leisure studies (MS); recreation management (Certificate). Part-time programs available. *Degree requirements:* For master's, thesis or alternative, culminating project or field placement. *Entrance requirements:* For master's, GRE General Test or MAT, resume, 2 letters of reference, 300-word statement. Additional exam requirements/recommendations for international students: Required—proof of English language proficiency required for non-native English speakers; Recommended—TOEFL (minimum score 550 paper-based; 213 computer-based). *Application deadline:* Applications are processed on a rolling basis. Application fee: $50 ($75 for international students). Electronic applications accepted. *Expenses:* Tuition, state resident: full-time $4298; part-time $239 per contact hour. Tuition, nonresident: full-time $9878; part-time $549 per contact hour. Required fees: $265 per contact hour. *Financial support:* Teaching assistantships, career-related internships or fieldwork, Federal Work-Study, institutionally sponsored loans, and unspecified assistantships available. Financial award application deadline: 4/1. *Faculty research:* Physically active leisure, trail use, community recreation programming, inclusion of persons with disabilities, therapeutic recreation.

University of South Alabama, Graduate School, College of Education, Department of Health, Physical Education and Leisure Services, Mobile, AL 36688-0002. Offers exercise science (MS); health education (M Ed); physical education (M Ed); therapeutic recreation (MS). *Accreditation:* NCATE (one or more programs are accredited). Part-time programs available. *Degree requirements:* For master's, comprehensive exam. *Entrance requirements:* For master's, GRE General Test or MAT. *Expenses:* Tuition, state resident: part-time $218 per contact hour. Required fees: $1102 per year.

University of Southern Mississippi, Graduate School, College of Health, School of Human Performance and Recreation, Hattiesburg, MS 39406-0001. Offers human performance (MS, Ed D, PhD); interscholastic athletic administration (MS); recreation and leisure management (MS); sport administration (MS); sport and coaching education (MS); sport management (MS); sports and high performance materials (MS). Part-time and evening/weekend programs available. *Faculty:* 13 full-time (5 women). *Students:* 62 full-time (27 women), 40 part-time (10 women); includes 13 minority (10 African Americans, 1 Asian American or Pacific Islander, 2 Hispanic Americans), 4 international. Average age 29. 79 applicants, 59% accepted, 33 enrolled. In 2009, 43 master's, 4 doctorates awarded. *Degree requirements:* For master's, comprehensive

Leisure Studies

University of Southern Mississippi *(continued)*
exam, thesis optional; for doctorate, comprehensive exam, thesis/dissertation. *Entrance requirements:* For master's, GRE General Test, minimum GPA of 2.75 in last 60 hours; for doctorate, GRE General Test, minimum GPA of 3.5. Additional exam requirements/recommendations for international students: Required—TOEFL. *Application deadline:* For fall admission, 3/1 priority date for domestic students, 3/1 for international students. Applications are processed on a rolling basis. *Application fee:* $35. Electronic applications accepted. *Expenses:* Tuition, state resident: full-time $5096; part-time $284 per hour. Tuition, nonresident: full-time $13,052; part-time $726 per hour. Required fees: $402. Tuition and fees vary according to course level and course load. *Financial support:* In 2009–10, 1 fellowship (averaging $16,000 per year), 6 research assistantships with full tuition reimbursements (averaging $7,492 per year), 5 teaching assistantships with full tuition reimbursements (averaging $7,330 per year) were awarded; career-related internships or fieldwork, Federal Work-Study, institutionally sponsored loans, and tuition waivers (partial) also available. Financial award application deadline: 3/15. *Faculty research:* Exercise physiology, health behaviors, resource management, activity interaction, site development. *Unit head:* Dr. Louis Marciani, Director, 601-266-5379, Fax: 601-266-4445. *Application contact:* Dr. Dennis Phillips, Graduate Coordinator, 601-266-5379, Fax: 601-266-4445.

The University of Tennessee, Graduate School, College of Education, Health and Human Sciences, Department of Exercise, Sport, and Leisure Studies, Knoxville, TN 37996. Offers exercise science (MS, PhD), including biomechanics/sports medicine, exercise physiology; recreation and leisure studies (MS); sport management (MS); sport studies (MS, PhD); therapeutic recreation (MS). Part-time and evening/weekend programs available. *Degree requirements:* For master's, thesis optional. *Entrance requirements:* For master's, minimum GPA of 2.7. Additional exam requirements/recommendations for international students: Required—TOEFL. Electronic applications accepted. *Expenses:* Tuition, state resident: full-time $6826; part-time $380 per semester hour. Tuition, nonresident: full-time $21,844; part-time $1147 per semester hour. Tuition and fees vary according to program.

The University of Toledo, College of Graduate Studies, College of Health Science and Human Service, Division of Human Services, Department of Recreation and Leisure, Toledo, OH 43606-3390. Offers MA.

University of Utah, Graduate School, College of Health, Department of Parks, Recreation, and Tourism, Salt Lake City, UT 84112-1107. Offers M Phil, MS, Ed D, PhD. *Faculty:* 11 full-time (4 women). *Students:* 36 full-time (20 women), 14 part-time (5 women), 11 international. Average age 31. 53 applicants, 51% accepted, 20 enrolled. In 2009, 10 master's, 5 doctorates awarded. Terminal master's awarded for partial completion of doctoral program. *Degree requirements:* For master's, comprehensive exam, thesis or alternative; for doctorate, thesis/dissertation. *Entrance requirements:* For master's, minimum GPA of 3.0; for doctorate, GRE General Test or MAT, minimum GPA of 3.2. Additional exam requirements/recommendations for international students: Required—TOEFL (minimum score 500 paper-based; 173 computer-based). *Application deadline:* For fall admission, 4/1 for domestic students, 2/15 for international students; for spring admission, 11/1 for domestic students. Application fee: $55 ($65 for international students). Electronic applications accepted. *Expenses:* Tuition, state resident: full-time $4004; part-time $1674 per semester. Tuition, nonresident: full-time $14,134; part-time $5915 per semester. Required fees: $324 per semester. Tuition and fees vary according to course load, degree level and program. *Financial support:* Teaching assistantships with full

tuition reimbursements, career-related internships or fieldwork available. Financial award application deadline: 2/15; financial award applicants required to submit FAFSA. *Faculty research:* Commercial, therapeutic, community, and outdoor recreation; tourism. Total annual research expenditures: $98,598. *Unit head:* Dr. Dan Dustin, Chair, 801-581-7560, E-mail: daniel.dustin@health.utah.edu. *Application contact:* Dr. Edward J. Ruddell, Director of Graduate Studies, 801-585-8085, Fax: 801-581-4930, E-mail: edward.ruddell@health.utah.edu.

University of Victoria, Faculty of Graduate Studies, Faculty of Education, School of Exercise Science, Physical, and Health Education, Victoria, BC V8W 2Y2, Canada. Offers coaching studies (co-operative education) (M Ed); kinesiology (M Sc, MA); leisure service administration (MA); physical education (MA). Part-time programs available. *Degree requirements:* For master's, comprehensive exam (for some programs), thesis (for some programs). *Entrance requirements:* For master's, minimum B average. Additional exam requirements/recommendations for international students: Required—TOEFL (minimum score 575 paper-based; 233 computer-based), IELTS (minimum score 7). Electronic applications accepted. *Faculty research:* Children and exercise, mental skills in sports, teaching effectiveness, neural control of human movement, physical performance and health.

University of Waterloo, Graduate Studies, Faculty of Applied Health Sciences, Department of Recreation and Leisure Studies, Waterloo, ON N2L 3G1, Canada. Offers MA, PhD. Part-time programs available. *Degree requirements:* For master's, thesis; for doctorate, comprehensive exam, thesis/dissertation. *Entrance requirements:* For master's, honors degree, minimum B average, writing sample, resume; for doctorate, GRE (recommended), master's degree, minimum B average, writing sample, resumé. Additional exam requirements/recommendations for international students: Required—TOEFL, TWE. Electronic applications accepted. *Faculty research:* Tourism, leisure behavior, special populations, leisure service management, outdoor resources, aging, health and well-being, work and health.

University of West Florida, College of Professional Studies, Division of Health, Leisure, and Exercise Science, Program in Health, Leisure, and Exercise Science, Pensacola, FL 32514-5750. Offers exercise science (MS); physical education (MS). Part-time and evening/weekend programs available. *Faculty:* 5 full-time (2 women), 2 part-time/adjunct (1 woman). *Students:* 20 full-time (9 women), 23 part-time (10 women); includes 6 minority (3 African Americans, 1 Asian American or Pacific Islander, 2 Hispanic Americans), 4 international. Average age 28. 30 applicants, 83% accepted, 11 enrolled. In 2009, 26 master's awarded. *Degree requirements:* For master's, thesis or alternative. *Entrance requirements:* For master's, GRE General Test, minimum GPA of 3.0. Additional exam requirements/recommendations for international students: Required—TOEFL (minimum score 550 paper-based; 213 computer-based). *Application deadline:* For fall admission, 6/1 for domestic students, 5/15 for international students; for spring admission, 11/1 for domestic students, 10/1 for international students. Applications are processed on a rolling basis. Application fee: $30. Electronic applications accepted. *Expenses:* Tuition, state resident: full-time $4982; part-time $260 per credit hour. Tuition, nonresident: full-time $20,059; part-time $919 per credit hour. Required fees: $1247; $52 per credit hour. *Financial support:* Career-related internships or fieldwork, Federal Work-Study, scholarships/grants, and tuition waivers (partial) available. Support available to part-time students. Financial award application deadline: 4/15; financial award applicants required to submit FAFSA. *Unit head:* Dr. John Todorovich, Chairperson, 850-473-7248, Fax: 850-474-2106. *Application contact:* Terry McCray, Assistant Director of Graduate Admissions, 850-473-7718, Fax: 850-473-7714, E-mail: gradadmissions@uwf.edu.

Recreation and Park Management

Acadia University, Faculty of Professional Studies, School of Recreation Management and Kinesiology, Wolfville, NS B4P 2R6, Canada. Offers MR. *Students:* 2 full-time (both women), 1 part-time (0 women). 5 applicants, 40% accepted, 2 enrolled. In 2009, 1 master's awarded. *Degree requirements:* For master's, thesis. *Entrance requirements:* Additional exam requirements/recommendations for international students: Required—TOEFL (minimum score 580 paper-based; 237 computer-based; 93 iBT), IELTS (minimum score 6.5). *Application deadline:* For fall admission, 2/1 for domestic and international students. Applications are processed on a rolling basis. Application fee: $50. *Financial support:* In 2009–10, teaching assistantships (averaging $9,000 per year); unspecified assistantships also available. *Unit head:* Dr. Rene Murphy, Director, 902-585-1559, Fax: 902-585-1702, E-mail: rene.murphy@acadiau.ca. *Application contact:* Krista Robertson, Secretary, 902-585-1457, Fax: 902-585-1702, E-mail: krista.robertson@acadiau.ca.

Arizona State University, Graduate College, College of Public Programs, School of Community Resources and Development, Tempe, AZ 85287. Offers community resources and development (PhD); nonprofit studies (MNpS); recreation and tourism studies (MS). *Degree requirements:* For master's, thesis or alternative.

Bowling Green State University, Graduate College, College of Education and Human Development, School of Human Movement, Sport, and Leisure Studies, Bowling Green, OH 43403. Offers developmental kinesiology (M Ed); recreation and leisure (M Ed); sport administration (M Ed). Part-time programs available. *Degree requirements:* For master's, thesis or alternative. *Entrance requirements:* For master's, GRE General Test, minimum GPA of 2.7. Additional exam requirements/recommendations for international students: Required—TOEFL. Electronic applications accepted. *Faculty research:* Teacher-learning process, travel and tourism, sport marketing and management, exercise physiology and sport psychology, life-span motor development.

Brigham Young University, Graduate Studies, Marriott School of Management, Department of Recreation Management and Youth Leadership, Provo, UT 84602. Offers youth and family recreation (MS). *Faculty:* 8 full-time (1 woman). *Students:* 8 full-time (all women), 6 part-time (4 women), 1 international. Average age 28. 6 applicants, 83% accepted, 4 enrolled. In 2009, 3 master's awarded. *Degree requirements:* For master's, thesis, oral defense. *Entrance requirements:* For master's, GRE General Test, minimum GPA of 3.0 in last 60 hours. Additional exam requirements/recommendations for international students: Required—TOEFL (minimum score 580 paper-based; 237 computer-based; 85 iBT), IELTS (minimum score 7). *Application deadline:* For fall admission, 2/1 priority date for domestic and international students. Application fee: $50. Electronic applications accepted. *Expenses:* Contact institution. *Financial support:* In 2009–10, 9 students received support, including 9 research assistantships with full tuition reimbursements available (averaging $2,200 per year); fellowships, teaching assistantships with tuition reimbursements available, career-related internships or fieldwork, institutionally sponsored loans, scholarships/grants, tuition waivers (full and partial), unspecified assistantships, and administrative aides also available. Support available to part-time students. Financial award application deadline: 3/1. *Faculty research:* Family recreation, adolescent development, leisure behavior, families with child with disability inclusive and adaptive recreation. *Unit head:* Dr. Patti Ann Freeman, Chair, 801-422-1286, Fax: 801-422-0609, E-mail: patti_freeman@byu.edu. *Application contact:* Dr. Brian Jack Hill, Graduate Coordinator, 801-422-1287, Fax: 801-422-0609, E-mail: brian_hill@byu.edu.

California State University, Chico, Graduate School, College of Communication and Education, Department of Recreation and Parks Management, Chico, CA 95929-0722. Offers recreation administration (MA). Part-time programs available. *Students:* 4 full-time (2 women), 6 part-time (4 women), 2 international. Average age 34. 5 applicants, 60% accepted, 1 enrolled. In 2009, 1 master's awarded. *Degree requirements:* For master's, thesis or alternative. *Entrance*

requirements: For master's, GRE General Test, 3 letters of recommendation, resume. Additional exam requirements/recommendations for international students: Required—TOEFL (minimum score 550 paper-based; 213 computer-based; 80 iBT), IELTS (minimum score 6.5). *Application deadline:* For fall admission, 3/1 priority date for domestic students, 3/1 for international students; for spring admission, 9/15 priority date for domestic students, 9/15 for international students. Applications are processed on a rolling basis. Application fee: $55. Electronic applications accepted. *Financial support:* Fellowships, career-related internships or fieldwork and stipends available. *Unit head:* Dr. James Fletcher, Graduate Coordinator, 530-898-4365. *Application contact:* School of Graduate, International, and Interdisciplinary Studies, 530-898-6880, Fax: 530-898-6889, E-mail: grin@csuchico.edu.

California State University, East Bay, Graduate Programs, College of Education and Allied Studies, Department of Hospitality, Recreation and Tourism, Hayward, CA 94542-3000. Offers recreation and tourism (MS). Part-time and evening/weekend programs available. Post-baccalaureate distance learning degree programs offered (no on-campus study). *Faculty:* 7 full-time (4 women). *Students:* 16 full-time (12 women), 8 part-time (5 women); includes 19 minority (1 African American, 17 Asian Americans or Pacific Islanders, 1 Hispanic American). Average age 31. 18 applicants, 44% accepted, 4 enrolled. *Entrance requirements:* For master's, minimum GPA of 2.75; 2 years' related work experience. Additional exam requirements/recommendations for international students: Required—TOEFL (minimum score 550 paper-based; 237 computer-based). *Application deadline:* For fall admission, 6/30 for domestic and international students. Applications are processed on a rolling basis. Application fee: $55. Electronic applications accepted. *Financial support:* Federal Work-Study, institutionally sponsored loans, and scholarships/grants available. Support available to part-time students. Financial award application deadline: 3/1; financial award applicants required to submit FAFSA. *Unit head:* Dr. Melany Spielman, Chair, 510-885-3043, E-mail: melany.spielman@csueastbay.edu. *Application contact:* Donna Wiley, Interim Associate Director, 510-885-2928, Fax: 510-885-4777, E-mail: donna.wiley@csueastbay.edu.

California State University, Long Beach, Graduate Studies, College of Health and Human Services, Department of Recreation and Leisure Studies, Long Beach, CA 90840. Offers recreation administration (MS). Part-time programs available. *Faculty:* 2 full-time (1 woman). *Students:* 17 full-time (12 women), 21 part-time (13 women); includes 8 minority (4 African Americans, 2 Asian Americans or Pacific Islanders, 2 Hispanic Americans), 10 international. Average age 30. 27 applicants, 67% accepted, 12 enrolled. *Degree requirements:* For master's, comprehensive exam or thesis. *Entrance requirements:* For master's, GRE General Test. *Application deadline:* For fall admission, 7/1 for domestic students. Applications are processed on a rolling basis. Application fee: $55. Electronic applications accepted. *Expenses:* Required fees: $1802 per semester. Part-time tuition and fees vary according to course load. *Financial support:* Federal Work-Study, institutionally sponsored loans, and scholarships/grants available. Financial award application deadline: 3/2. *Unit head:* Dr. Maridith Janssen, Chair, 562-985-4079, Fax: 562-985-8154, E-mail: mjanssen@csulb.edu. *Application contact:* Dr. Katherine James, Graduate Advisor, 562-985-8077, Fax: 562-985-8154, E-mail: kjames@csulb.edu.

California State University, Northridge, Graduate Studies, College of Health and Human Development, Department of Recreation and Tourism Management, Northridge, CA 91330. Offers hospitality and tourism (MS); recreational sport management/campus recreation (MS). *Faculty:* 6 full-time (4 women), 11 part-time/adjunct (7 women). *Students:* 29 full-time (17 women), 21 part-time (11 women); includes 6 minority (4 African Americans, 1 Asian American or Pacific Islander, 1 Hispanic American), 9 international. Average age 27. 53 applicants, 77% accepted, 31 enrolled. In 2009, 8 master's awarded. *Degree requirements:* For master's, thesis (for some programs). *Entrance requirements:* For master's, GRE (if cumulative undergraduate GPA less than 3.0). Additional exam requirements/recommendations for inter-

national students: Required—TOEFL. *Application deadline:* For fall admission, 11/30 for domestic students. Application fee: $55. *Financial support:* Application deadline: 3/1. *Unit head:* Dr. Craig Finney, Chair, 818-677-3202, E-mail: cfinney@csun.edu. *Application contact:* Dr. Craig Finney, Chair, 818-677-3202, E-mail: cfinney@csun.edu.

California State University, Sacramento, Graduate Studies, College of Health and Human Services, Department of Recreation and Leisure Studies, Sacramento, CA 95819. Offers recreation administration (MS). Part-time programs available. *Degree requirements:* For master's, thesis or alternative, writing proficiency exam. *Entrance requirements:* Additional exam requirements/recommendations for international students: Required—TOEFL. Electronic applications accepted.

Central Michigan University, College of Graduate Studies, College of Education and Human Services, Department of Recreation, Parks, and Leisure Services Administration, Mount Pleasant, MI 48859. Offers recreation and park administration (MA); therapeutic recreation (MA). Part-time programs available. *Degree requirements:* For master's, thesis or alternative. Electronic applications accepted. *Faculty research:* Commercial recreation and facilities management; study of ethics in parks and recreation professionals; computer touch-tone information services at visitor centers; creative play spaces for children; therapeutic recreation.

Central Michigan University, College of Graduate Studies, Interdisciplinary Administration Programs, Mount Pleasant, MI 48859. Offers acquisitions administration (MSA, Graduate Certificate); general administration (MSA, Graduate Certificate); health services administration (MSA, Graduate Certificate); human resource administration (Graduate Certificate); human resources administration (MSA); information resource management (MSA, Graduate Certificate); international administration (MSA, Graduate Certificate); leadership (MSA); organizational communication (MSA, Graduate Certificate); public administration (MSA, Graduate Certificate); recreation and park administration (MSA); sport administration (MSA). *Accreditation:* AACSB. Part-time and evening/weekend programs available. Postbaccalaureate distance learning degree programs offered (no on-campus study). *Degree requirements:* For master's, thesis or alternative. *Entrance requirements:* For master's, bachelor's degree with minimum GPA of 2.7. Electronic applications accepted. *Faculty research:* Interdisciplinary studies in acquisitions administration, health services administration, sport administration, recreation and park administration, and international administration.

Clemson University, Graduate School, College of Health, Education, and Human Development, Department of Parks, Recreation, and Tourism Management, Clemson, SC 29634. Offers MPRTM, MS, PhD. Part-time programs available. *Faculty:* 16 full-time (6 women). *Students:* 49 full-time (27 women), 14 part-time (8 women); includes 4 minority (2 African Americans, 2 American Indian/Alaska Native), 14 international. Average age 32. 60 applicants, 42% accepted, 12 enrolled. In 2009, 3 master's, 5 doctorates awarded. *Degree requirements:* For master's, thesis (for some programs); for doctorate, thesis/dissertation. *Entrance requirements:* For master's, GRE General Test, minimum undergraduate GPA of 3.0; for doctorate, GRE General Test, minimum graduate GPA of 3.0. Additional exam requirements/recommendations for international students: Required—TOEFL. *Application deadline:* For fall admission, 5/1 priority date for domestic students; for spring admission, 10/1 for domestic students. Applications are processed on a rolling basis. Application fee: $70 ($80 for international students). Electronic applications accepted. *Expenses:* Tuition, state resident: full-time $8684; part-time $528 per credit hour. Tuition, nonresident: full-time $15,330; part-time $1078 per credit hour. Required fees: $736; $37 per semester. Part-time tuition and fees vary according to course load and program. *Financial support:* In 2009–10, 41 students received support, including 3 research assistantships with partial tuition reimbursements available (averaging $19,587 per year), 16 teaching assistantships with partial tuition reimbursements available (averaging $10,735 per year); fellowships with full and partial tuition reimbursements available, career-related internships or fieldwork, scholarships/grants, health care benefits, tuition waivers (partial), and unspecified assistantships also available. Support available to part-time students. Financial award application deadline: 4/15; financial award applicants required to submit FAFSA. *Faculty research:* Recreation resource management, leisure behavior, therapeutic recreation, community leisure services. Total annual research expenditures: $370,389. *Unit head:* Dr. Brett A. Wright, Chair, 864-656-3036, Fax: 864-656-2226, E-mail: wright@clemson.edu. *Application contact:* Dr. Denise M. Anderson, Graduate Coordinator, 864-656-5679, Fax: 864-656-2226, E-mail: dander2@clemson.edu.

The College at Brockport, State University of New York, School of Health and Human Performance, Department of Recreation and Leisure Studies, Brockport, NY 14420-2997. Offers recreation and leisure (MS), including recreation and leisure service management, therapeutic recreation. Part-time programs available. *Students:* 15 full-time (10 women), 8 part-time (2 women); includes 3 minority (1 African American, 1 Asian American or Pacific Islander, 1 Hispanic American). 13 applicants, 100% accepted, 13 enrolled. In 2009, 9 master's awarded. *Degree requirements:* For master's, thesis or alternative. *Entrance requirements:* For master's, minimum GPA of 3.0, letters of recommendation, written critical analysis. Additional exam requirements/recommendations for international students: Required—TOEFL (minimum score 550 paper-based; 213 computer-based; 79 iBT). *Application deadline:* For fall admission, 7/15 priority date for domestic and international students; for spring admission, 11/15 priority date for domestic and international students. Application fee: $50. Electronic applications accepted. *Expenses:* Tuition, state resident: full-time $8370; part-time $349 per credit. Tuition, nonresident: full-time $13,250; part-time $522 per credit. *Financial support:* Federal Work-Study, scholarships/grants, and unspecified assistantships available. Support available to part-time students. Financial award application deadline: 3/15; financial award applicants required to submit FAFSA. *Faculty research:* Leisure service delivery systems; therapeutic recreation; international issues in recreation and leisure; tourism; customer service, customer behavior and perceived value/satisfaction; leisure motivation among Baby Boomers. *Unit head:* Dr. Joel Frater, Chairperson, 585-395-2994, Fax: 585-395-5246, E-mail: jfrater@brockport.edu. *Application contact:* Dr. Lynda Sperazza, Graduate Director, 585-395-5490, Fax: 585-395-5246, E-mail: lsperazza@brockport.edu.

Colorado State University, Graduate School, Warner College of Natural Resources, Department of Human Dimensions of Natural Resources, Fort Collins, CO 80523-1480. Offers MS, PhD. Part-time programs available. *Faculty:* 10 full-time (3 women), 1 part-time/adjunct (0 women). *Students:* 21 full-time (11 women), 12 part-time (6 women); includes 5 minority (1 American Indian/Alaska Native, 1 Asian American or Pacific Islander, 3 Hispanic Americans), 2 international. Average age 31. 25 applicants, 32% accepted, 7 enrolled. In 2009, 9 master's, 1 doctorate awarded. Terminal master's awarded for partial completion of doctoral program. *Degree requirements:* For master's, comprehensive exam, thesis or alternative; for doctorate, comprehensive exam, thesis/dissertation. *Entrance requirements:* For master's, minimum GPA of 3.0, 3 letters of recommendation; for doctorate, GRE General Test (combined minimum score of 1000 on the Verbal and Quantitative sections), minimum GPA of 3.0, 3 letters of recommendation, copy of master's thesis or professional paper, interview, statement of interest. Additional exam requirements/recommendations for international students: Required—TOEFL. *Application deadline:* For fall admission, 3/1 priority date for domestic students. Applications are processed on a rolling basis. Application fee: $50. Electronic applications accepted. *Expenses:* Tuition, state resident: full-time $6434; part-time $359.10 per credit. Tuition, nonresident: full-time $18,116; part-time $1006.45 per credit. Required fees: $1496; $83 per credit. *Financial support:* In 2009–10, 19 students received support, including 1 fellowship (averaging $41,667 per year), 11 research assistantships with tuition reimbursements available (averaging $11,087 per year), 7 teaching assistantships with tuition reimbursements available (averaging $5,820 per year); career-related internships or fieldwork, Federal Work-Study, scholarships/grants, traineeships, and unspecified assistantships also available. Support available to part-time students. Financial award application deadline: 3/1; financial award applicants required to submit FAFSA. *Faculty research:* International tourism, wilderness preservation, resource interpretation, human dimensions in natural resources, protected areas management. Total annual research expenditures: $925,755. *Unit head:* Dr. Michael J. Manfredo, Head, 970-491-0474, Fax: 970-491-2255, E-mail: manfredo@cnr.colostate.edu. *Application contact:* Linda Adams, Coordinator of Administration, 970-491-6591, Fax: 970-491-2255, E-mail: linda.adams@colostate.edu.

Delta State University, Graduate Programs, College of Education, Division of Health, Physical Education and Recreation, Cleveland, MS 38733-0001. Offers physical education and recreation (M Ed). Part-time and evening/weekend programs available. *Degree requirements:* For master's, thesis optional. *Entrance requirements:* For master's, GRE General Test or MAT, Class A teaching certificate. *Expenses:* Tuition, state resident: full-time $4450; part-time $247 per credit hour. Tuition, nonresident: full-time $11,520; part-time $640 per credit hour. *Faculty research:* Blood pressure, body fat, power and reaction time, learning disorders for athletes, effects of walking.

East Carolina University, Graduate School, College of Health and Human Performance, Department of Recreation and Leisure Studies, Greenville, NC 27858-4353. Offers recreation and leisure services administration (MS); therapeutic recreation administration (MS). Part-time and evening/weekend programs available. Postbaccalaureate distance learning degree programs offered (minimal on-campus study). *Degree requirements:* For master's, comprehensive exam, thesis optional. *Entrance requirements:* For master's, GRE General Test or MAT. Additional exam requirements/recommendations for international students: Required—TOEFL. *Faculty research:* Therapeutic recreation, stress and coping behavior, medicine carrying capacity, choice behavior, tourism preferences.

Eastern Kentucky University, The Graduate School, College of Health Sciences, Department of Recreation and Park Administration, Richmond, KY 40475-3102. Offers MS. Part-time programs available. *Degree requirements:* For master's, comprehensive exam, thesis optional. *Entrance requirements:* For master's, GRE General Test, MAT, minimum GPA of 2.5. *Faculty research:* Marketing, at risk youth, outdoor education, event planning, TR in schools.

Florida Agricultural and Mechanical University, Division of Graduate Studies, Research, and Continuing Education, College of Education, Department of Health, Physical Education, and Recreation, Tallahassee, FL 32307-3200. Offers M Ed, MS Ed. *Accreditation:* NCATE. Part-time and evening/weekend programs available. *Faculty:* 10 full-time (6 women). *Students:* 11 full-time (9 women), 3 part-time (2 women); all minorities (all African Americans). In 2009, 2 master's awarded. *Degree requirements:* For master's, thesis optional. *Entrance requirements:* For master's, GRE General Test, minimum GPA of 3.0. Additional exam requirements/recommendations for international students: Required—TOEFL. *Application deadline:* For fall admission, 5/18 for domestic students, 12/18 for international students; for spring admission, 11/12 for domestic students, 5/12 for international students. Application fee: $20. *Financial support:* Teaching assistantships, Federal Work-Study and institutionally sponsored loans available. *Faculty research:* Administration/curriculum, work behavior, psychology. *Unit head:* Dr. E. Newton Jackson, Chairperson, 850-599-3135. *Application contact:* Dr. Chanta M. Haywood, Dean of Graduate Studies, Research, and Continuing Education, 850-599-3315, Fax: 850-599-3727.

Florida International University, College of Education, Department of Health, Physical Education, and Recreation, Program in Parks and Recreation Management, Miami, FL 33199. Offers leisure services (MS); therapeutic recreation (MS). Part-time and evening/weekend programs available. *Entrance requirements:* For master's, GRE General Test or minimum GPA of 3.0. Additional exam requirements/recommendations for international students: Required—TOEFL (minimum score 550 paper-based; 213 computer-based; 80 iBT), IELTS (minimum score 6.3). Electronic applications accepted. *Expenses:* Tuition, state resident: full-time $8008; part-time $4004 per year. Tuition, nonresident: full-time $20,104; part-time $10,052 per year. Required fees: $298; $149 per term. *Faculty research:* Effects of prosocial behavior interventions on children and adolescents with behavior disorders or who are considered to be at risk.

Florida State University, The Graduate School, College of Education, Department of Sport Management, Tallahassee, FL 32306. Offers MS, Ed D, PhD. *Faculty:* 14 full-time (8 women), 1 (woman) part-time/adjunct. *Students:* 117 full-time (42 women), 49 part-time (20 women); includes 28 minority (15 African Americans, 1 American Indian/Alaska Native, 5 Asian Americans or Pacific Islanders, 7 Hispanic Americans), 24 international. 166 applicants, 66% accepted, 58 enrolled. In 2009, 30 master's, 1 doctorate awarded. *Degree requirements:* For master's, comprehensive exam, thesis optional; for doctorate, comprehensive exam, thesis/dissertation. *Entrance requirements:* For master's and doctorate, GRE General Test, minimum GPA of 3.0. Additional exam requirements/recommendations for international students: Required—TOEFL (minimum score 550 paper-based; 213 computer-based; 80 iBT). *Application deadline:* For fall admission, 7/1 priority date for domestic students, 7/1 for international students; for spring admission, 11/1 for domestic and international students. Applications are processed on a rolling basis. Application fee: $30. Electronic applications accepted. *Expenses:* Tuition, state resident: full-time $7413. Tuition, nonresident: full-time $22,567. *Financial support:* In 2009–10, 2 fellowships with full and partial tuition reimbursements, 51 research assistantships with full and partial tuition reimbursements, 15 teaching assistantships with full and partial tuition reimbursements were awarded; career-related internships or fieldwork and Federal Work-Study also available. Financial award applicants required to submit FAFSA. *Faculty research:* Sport marketing, gender issues in sport, finances in sport industry, coaching. *Unit head:* Dr. Jeffrey James, Chair, 850-644-9214, Fax: 850-644-0975, E-mail: jdjames@fsu.edu. *Application contact:* Cynthia Bailey, Program Assistant, 850-644-4813, Fax: 850-644-0975, E-mail: bailey@coe.fsu.edu.

Frostburg State University, Graduate School, College of Education, Program in Parks and Recreational Management, Frostburg, MD 21532-1099. Offers MS. Part-time and evening/weekend programs available. *Faculty:* 2 full-time (1 woman). *Students:* 1 (woman) full-time, 16 part-time (10 women); includes 3 minority (all African Americans). Average age 36. 6 applicants, 33% accepted, 2 enrolled. *Degree requirements:* For master's, thesis. *Entrance requirements:* For master's, resume. Additional exam requirements/recommendations for international students: Required—TOEFL. *Application deadline:* For fall admission, 7/15 priority date for domestic students. Applications are processed on a rolling basis. Application fee: $30. Electronic applications accepted. *Expenses:* Tuition, state resident: full-time $5706; part-time $317 per credit hour. Tuition, nonresident: full-time $6948; part-time $386 per credit hour. Required fees: $1476; $82 per credit hour. $11 per term. One-time fee: $30 full-time. *Financial support:* In 2009–10, 1 research assistantship with full tuition reimbursement (averaging $5,000 per year) was awarded; career-related internships or fieldwork and Federal Work-Study also available. Financial award application deadline: 4/1; financial award applicants required to submit FAFSA. *Unit head:* Dr. Maureen Dougherty, Coordinator, 410-869-1103, E-mail: mdougherty@frostburg.edu. *Application contact:* Vickie Mazer, Director, Graduate Services, 301-687-7053, Fax: 301-687-4597, E-mail: vmmazer@frostburg.edu.

Georgia College & State University, Graduate School, College of Health Sciences, Department of Kinesiology, Milledgeville, GA 31061. Offers health promotion (M Ed); human performance (M Ed); kinesiology (MAT); outdoor education (M Ed). *Accreditation:* NCATE (one or more programs are accredited). Part-time and evening/weekend programs available. *Faculty:* 12 full-time (5 women). *Students:* 25 full-time (13 women), 7 part-time (5 women); includes 4 minority (2 African Americans, 2 Hispanic Americans), 3 international. Average age 26. 23 applicants, 87% accepted, 19 enrolled. In 2009, 7 master's awarded. *Degree requirements:* For master's, thesis optional. *Entrance requirements:* For master's, GRE General Test or MAT, minimum GPA of 2.75 in upper-level undergraduate courses, 2 letters of reference. Additional exam requirements/recommendations for international students: Recommended—TOEFL (minimum score 550 paper-based; 213 computer-based; 79 iBT). *Application deadline:* For fall admission, 7/15 priority date for domestic students; for spring admission, 11/15 for domestic students. Applications are processed on a rolling basis. Application fee: $40. Electronic applications accepted. *Expenses:* Tuition, area resident: Part-time $241 per credit hour. Tuition, state resident: full-time $4338. Tuition, nonresident: full-time $17,352; part-time $964 per credit hour. Required fees: $609 per semester. Tuition and fees vary according to course load and campus/location. *Financial support:* In 2009–10, 20 research assistantships with full tuition reimbursements were awarded; career-related internships or fieldwork and unspecified assistantships also available. Support available to part-time students. Financial award applicants

Recreation and Park Management

Georgia College & State University (continued)
required to submit FAFSA. *Unit head:* Dr. Jude Hirsch, Chair, 478-445-4072, Fax: 478-445-1790, E-mail: jude.hirsch@gcsu.edu. *Application contact:* Dr. Jude Hirsch, Chair, 478-445-4072, Fax: 478-445-1790, E-mail: jude.hirsch@gcsu.edu.

Georgia Southern University, Jack N. Averitt College of Graduate Studies, College of Health and Human Sciences, Department of Hospitality, Tourism, and Family and Consumer Sciences, Program in Recreation Administration, Statesboro, GA 30460. Offers MS. Part-time and evening/weekend programs available. In 2009, 4 master's awarded. *Degree requirements:* For master's, thesis optional, exam. *Entrance requirements:* For master's, GMAT, GRE General Test, or MAT, minimum GPA of 2.75, undergraduate major in recreation or related field, faculty interview. Additional exam requirements/recommendations for international students: Required—TOEFL (minimum score 550 paper-based; 213 computer-based; 80 iBT). *Application deadline:* For fall admission, 3/1 priority date for domestic and international students; for spring admission, 10/1 priority date for domestic students, 10/1 for international students. Applications are processed on a rolling basis. Application fee: $50. Electronic applications accepted. *Expenses:* Tuition, state resident: full-time $5040; part-time $210 per credit hour. Tuition, nonresident: full-time $20,136; part-time $839 per credit hour. Required fees: $1644. *Financial support:* In 2009–10, research assistantships with partial tuition reimbursements (averaging $6,850 per year), teaching assistantships with partial tuition reimbursements (averaging $6,850 per year) were awarded; Federal Work-Study, scholarships/grants, tuition waivers (partial), and unspecified assistantships also available. Support available to part-time students. Financial award application deadline: 4/15; financial award applicants required to submit FAFSA. *Faculty research:* Tourism management, economic development, urban planning and design, commercial recreation, clinical therapeutic recreation. Total annual research expenditures: $1,583. *Application contact:* 912-478-5384, Fax: 912-478-0740, E-mail: gradadmissions@georgiasouthern.edu.

Hardin-Simmons University, Graduate School, Irvin School of Education, Department of Fitness and Sport Sciences, Program in Kinesiology, Sport, and Recreation, Abilene, TX 79698-0001. Offers M Ed. Part-time programs available. *Faculty:* 5 full-time (2 women), 2 part-time/adjunct (1 woman). *Students:* 8 full-time (1 woman), 16 part-time (6 women); includes 8 minority (4 African Americans, 4 Hispanic Americans), 1 international. Average age 25. 11 applicants, 100% accepted, 7 enrolled. In 2009, 12 master's awarded. *Degree requirements:* For master's, comprehensive exam, thesis optional, internship, project. *Entrance requirements:* For master's, minimum undergraduate GPA of 3.0 in major, 2.7 overall; interview; writing sample; letters of recommendation; resume. Additional exam requirements/recommendations for international students: Required—TOEFL (minimum score 550 paper-based; 213 computer-based; 75 iBT). *Application deadline:* For fall admission, 8/15 priority date for domestic students, 4/1 for international students; for spring admission, 1/5 priority date for domestic students, 9/1 for international students. Applications are processed on a rolling basis. Application fee: $50. *Expenses:* Tuition: Full-time $11,430; part-time $635 per credit hour. Required fees: $650; $110 per semester. Tuition and fees vary according to degree level. *Financial support:* In 2009–10, 10 students received support, including 19 fellowships (averaging $1,000 per year); career-related internships or fieldwork, scholarships/grants, and recreation assistantships also available. Support available to part-time students. Financial award application deadline: 6/30; financial award applicants required to submit FAFSA. *Unit head:* Dr. Robert Moore, Director, 325-670-1265, Fax: 325-670-1218, E-mail: bemoore@hsutx.edu. *Application contact:* Dr. Gary Stanlake, Dean of Graduate Studies, 325-670-1298, Fax: 325-670-1564, E-mail: gradoff@hsutx.edu.

Indiana University Bloomington, School of Health, Physical Education and Recreation, Department of Recreation, Park, and Tourism Studies, Bloomington, IN 47405-7000. Offers leisure behavior (PhD); outdoor recreation (MS); recreation (Re Dir); recreation administration (MS); recreational sports administration (MS); therapeutic recreation (MS); tourism management (MS). *Faculty:* 16 full-time (6 women), 2 part-time/adjunct (both women). *Students:* 55 full-time (29 women), 17 part-time (15 women); includes 8 minority (2 African Americans, 2 American Indian/Alaska Native, 3 Asian Americans or Pacific Islanders, 1 Hispanic American), 22 international. Average age 31. 62 applicants, 69% accepted, 23 enrolled. In 2009, 11 master's, 5 doctorates awarded. Terminal master's awarded for partial completion of doctoral program. *Degree requirements:* For master's and Re Dir, thesis optional; for doctorate, thesis/dissertation. *Entrance requirements:* For master's, GRE General Test, minimum GPA of 2.8; for doctorate, GRE General Test, minimum GPA of 3.0 (undergraduate), 3.5 (graduate). Additional exam requirements/recommendations for international students: Required—TOEFL. *Application deadline:* For fall admission, 1/1 for international students; for spring admission, 9/1 for international students. Applications are processed on a rolling basis. Application fee: $55 ($65 for international students). *Financial support:* In 2009–10, 30 students received support, including 7 fellowships (averaging $4,723 per year), 17 research assistantships (averaging $10,002 per year), 13 teaching assistantships with partial tuition reimbursements available (averaging $11,565 per year); career-related internships or fieldwork, Federal Work-Study, institutionally sponsored loans, scholarships/grants, tuition waivers (partial), unspecified assistantships, and fee remissions also available. Financial award application deadline: 3/1. *Faculty research:* Leisure counseling, gerontology, special populations, planning and development. *Unit head:* Dr. Craig Ross, Chairperson, 812-855-4711, E-mail: cmross@indiana.edu. *Application contact:* Program Office, 812-855-4711, Fax: 812-855-3998, E-mail: recpark@indiana.edu.

Kent State University, Graduate School of Education, Health, and Human Services, School of Foundations, Leadership and Administration, Program in Exercise, Leisure and Sport, Kent, OH 44242-0001. Offers sport and recreation management (MA); sports studies (MA). *Faculty:* 11 full-time (6 women), 4 part-time/adjunct (0 women). *Students:* 50 full-time (17 women), 16 part-time (6 women); includes 7 minority (6 African Americans, 1 Asian American or Pacific Islander), 1 international. 48 applicants, 100% accepted. In 2009, 31 master's awarded. Application fee: $30. *Financial support:* In 2009–10, 10 research assistantships (averaging $8,500 per year) were awarded; Federal Work-Study, scholarships/grants, and unspecified assistantships also available. *Unit head:* Mark Lyberger, Coordinator, 330-672-0228, E-mail: mlyberge@kent.edu. *Application contact:* Nancy Miller, Academic Program Coordinator, Office of Graduate Student Services, 330-672-2576, Fax: 330-672-9162, E-mail: ogs@kent.edu.

Lehman College of the City University of New York, Division of Natural and Social Sciences, Department of Health Sciences, Program in Recreation, Bronx, NY 10468-1589. Offers recreation education (MA, MS Ed). Part-time and evening/weekend programs available. *Degree requirements:* For master's, comprehensive exam, thesis or alternative. *Entrance requirements:* For master's, minimum GPA of 2.7. *Faculty research:* Therapeutic recreation philosophy, curriculum, current approaches to treatment, impact of societal trends, ethical issues.

Michigan State University, The Graduate School, College of Agriculture and Natural Resources, Department of Community, Agriculture, Recreation, and Resource Studies, East Lansing, MI 48824. Offers MS, PhD. *Faculty:* 29 full-time (9 women). *Students:* 60 full-time (34 women), 18 part-time (14 women); includes 8 minority (3 African Americans, 4 Asian Americans or Pacific Islanders, 1 Hispanic American), 29 international. Average age 34. 27 applicants, 67% accepted. In 2009, 13 master's, 8 doctorates awarded. *Entrance requirements:* Additional exam requirements/recommendations for international students: Required—TOEFL. Electronic applications accepted. *Expenses:* Tuition, state resident: part-time $478.25 per credit hour. Tuition, nonresident: part-time $966.50 per credit hour. Part-time tuition and fees vary according to program. *Financial support:* In 2009–10, 27 research assistantships with tuition reimbursements (averaging $6,894 per year), 2 teaching assistantships with tuition reimbursements (averaging $6,229 per year) were awarded. Total annual research expenditures: $2.7 million. *Unit head:* Dr. David E. Wright, Chairperson, 517-432-0263, Fax: 517-432-3597, E-mail: dewrite@msu.edu. *Application contact:* Diane Davis, Graduate Secretary, 517-432-0275, Fax: 517-432-3597, E-mail: davisdia@msu.edu.

Middle Tennessee State University, College of Graduate Studies, College of Education and Behavioral Science, Department of Health and Human Performance, Program in Health, Physical Education and Recreation, Murfreesboro, TN 37132. Offers MS. Part-time and evening/weekend programs available. Postbaccalaureate distance learning degree programs offered. *Students:* 9 full-time (6 women), 59 part-time (27 women); includes 22 minority (19 African Americans, 2 Asian Americans or Pacific Islanders, 1 Hispanic American). 54 applicants, 74% accepted, 40 enrolled. In 2009, 36 master's awarded. *Degree requirements:* For master's, comprehensive exam, thesis optional. *Entrance requirements:* For master's, GRE or MAT. Additional exam requirements/recommendations for international students: Required—TOEFL (minimum score 525 paper-based; 195 computer-based; 71 iBT) or IELTS (minimum score 6). *Application deadline:* For fall admission, 6/1 for domestic and international students. Applications are processed on a rolling basis. Application fee: $25 ($30 for international students). *Expenses:* Tuition, state resident: full-time $4404. Tuition, nonresident: full-time $10,956. *Financial support:* In 2009–10, 14 students received support. Career-related internships or fieldwork and institutionally sponsored loans available. Support available to part-time students. Financial award application deadline: 5/1. *Unit head:* Dr. Scott Colclough, Interim Chair, 615-898-5073, Fax: 615-898-5020, E-mail: scolclou@mtsu.edu. *Application contact:* Dr. Michael Allen, Dean and Vice Provost for Research, 615-898-2840, Fax: 615-904-8020, E-mail: mallen@mtsu.edu.

Naropa University, Graduate Programs, Program in Transpersonal Counseling Psychology, Concentration in Wilderness Therapy, Boulder, CO 80302-6697. Offers MA. *Degree requirements:* For master's, internship, field work. *Entrance requirements:* For master's, in-person interview, outdoor experience, course work in psychology, resume, letter of interest, 3 letters of recommendation. Additional exam requirements/recommendations for international students: Required—TOEFL (minimum score 600 paper-based; 250 computer-based). Electronic applications accepted.

New England College, Program in Sports and Recreation Management: Coaching, Henniker, NH 03242-3293. Offers MS. *Entrance requirements:* For master's, resume, 2 letters of reference.

North Carolina Central University, Division of Academic Affairs, College of Behavioral and Social Sciences, Department of Physical Education and Recreation, Durham, NC 27707-3129. Offers athletic administration (MS); physical education (MS); recreation administration (MS); therapeutic recreation (MS). Part-time and evening/weekend programs available. *Degree requirements:* For master's, one foreign language, comprehensive exam, thesis. *Entrance requirements:* For master's, GRE, minimum GPA of 3.0 in major, 2.5 overall. Additional exam requirements/recommendations for international students: Required—TOEFL. *Faculty research:* Physical activity patterns of children with disabilities, physical fitness test of North Carolina school children, exercise physiology, motor learning/development.

North Carolina State University, Graduate School, College of Natural Resources, Department of Parks, Recreation and Tourism Management, Raleigh, NC 27695. Offers natural resource management (MPRTM, MS); park and recreation management (MPRTM, MS); parks, recreation and tourism management (PhD); recreational sport management (MPRTM, MS); spatial information science (MPRTM, MS); tourism policy and development (MPRTM, MS). *Degree requirements:* For master's, thesis (for some programs); for doctorate, thesis/dissertation. *Entrance requirements:* For master's and doctorate, GRE General Test. Additional exam requirements/recommendations for international students: Required—TOEFL. Electronic applications accepted. *Faculty research:* Tourism policy and development, spatial information systems, natural resource management, recreational sports management, park and recreation management.

Northwest Missouri State University, Graduate School, College of Education and Human Services, Department of Health, Physical Education, Recreation and Dance, Maryville, MO 64468-6001. Offers applied health science (MS); health and physical education (MS Ed); recreation (MS). *Accreditation:* NCATE. Part-time programs available. *Faculty:* 10 full-time (5 women). *Students:* 38 full-time (10 women), 12 part-time (5 women); includes 3 minority (2 African Americans, 1 Hispanic American), 2 international. 35 applicants, 77% accepted, 20 enrolled. In 2009, 10 master's awarded. *Degree requirements:* For master's, comprehensive exam. *Entrance requirements:* For master's, GRE General Test, minimum undergraduate GPA of 2.75, teaching certificate, writing sample. Additional exam requirements/recommendations for international students: Required—TOEFL (minimum score 550 paper-based; 213 computer-based). *Application deadline:* For fall admission, 7/1 for domestic and international students; for spring admission, 11/15 for domestic and international students. Applications are processed on a rolling basis. Application fee: $0 ($50 for international students). *Expenses:* Tuition, state resident: part-time $296.34 per credit hour. Tuition, nonresident: part-time $510.43 per credit hour. *Financial support:* In 2009–10, 27 teaching assistantships with full tuition reimbursements (averaging $6,000 per year) were awarded; unspecified assistantships also available. Financial award application deadline: 4/1; financial award applicants required to submit FAFSA. *Unit head:* Dr. Terry Robertson, Program Director, 660-562-1781. *Application contact:* Dr. Gregory Haddock, Dean of Graduate School, 660-562-1145, Fax: 660-562-1096, E-mail: gradsch@nwmissouri.edu.

Ohio University, Graduate College, College of Health and Human Services, School of Recreation and Sport Sciences, Program in Recreation Studies, Athens, OH 45701-2979. Offers MS. Part-time programs available. *Faculty:* 4 full-time (3 women), 5 part-time/adjunct (1 woman). *Students:* 16 full-time (6 women), 2 part-time (0 women); includes 1 minority (Hispanic American). 19 applicants, 74% accepted, 11 enrolled. In 2009, 8 master's awarded. *Degree requirements:* For master's, thesis or alternative. *Entrance requirements:* For master's, GRE. Additional exam requirements/recommendations for international students: Required—TOEFL (minimum score 550 paper-based; 80 iBT) or IELTS Academic (minimum score 6.5). *Application deadline:* For fall admission, 3/1 priority date for domestic and international students; for winter admission, 11/1 priority date for domestic and international students; for spring admission, 1/1 priority date for domestic and international students. Application fee: $50 ($55 for international students). Electronic applications accepted. *Expenses:* Tuition, state resident: full-time $7839; part-time $323 per quarter hour. Tuition, nonresident: full-time $15,831; part-time $654 per quarter hour. Required fees: $2931. *Financial support:* In 2009–10, teaching assistantships with full tuition reimbursements (averaging $7,900 per year); Federal Work-Study, scholarships/grants, tuition waivers (full), and unspecified assistantships also available. Financial award application deadline: 3/15. *Faculty research:* Recreation, leisure studies, physical education, national parks. Total annual research expenditures: $7,500. *Unit head:* Dr. Ming Li, Coordinator, 740-593-4656, Fax: 740-593-0284, E-mail: lim1@ohio.edu. *Application contact:* Dr. Ming Li, Coordinator, 740-593-4656, Fax: 740-593-0284, E-mail: lim1@ohio.edu.

Old Dominion University, Darden College of Education, Program in Physical Education, Recreation and Tourism Studies Emphasis, Norfolk, VA 23529. Offers MS Ed. Part-time and evening/weekend programs available. Postbaccalaureate distance learning degree programs offered (minimal on-campus study). *Faculty:* 1 full-time (0 women). *Students:* 9 full-time (6 women), 6 part-time (4 women); includes 5 minority (4 African Americans, 1 Asian American or Pacific Islander). Average age 26. 10 applicants, 60% accepted, 5 enrolled. In 2009, 1 master's awarded. *Degree requirements:* For master's, comprehensive exam, thesis or alternative, internship, research project. *Entrance requirements:* For master's, GRE, minimum GPA of 2.8 overall, 3.0 in major. Additional exam requirements/recommendations for international students: Required—TOEFL (minimum score 500 paper-based; 200 computer-based). *Application deadline:* For fall admission, 6/1 for domestic students. Application fee: $40. Electronic applications accepted. *Expenses:* Tuition, state resident: full-time $8112; part-time $338 per credit. Tuition, nonresident: full-time $20,256; part-time $844 per credit. Required fees: $119 per semester. One-time fee: $50. *Financial support:* In 2009–10, 1 student received support, including 1 research assistantship with partial tuition reimbursement available (averaging $9,000 per year); career-related internships or fieldwork, scholarships/grants, and unspecified assistantships also available. Financial award application deadline: 3/1; financial award applicants required to submit FAFSA. *Faculty research:* Ethnicity and recreation, recreation programming, recreation and resiliency, tourism development, dog parks, sense of community and urban parks. Total annual research expenditures: $12,000. *Unit head:* Dr. Edwin Gomez, Graduate Program Director, 757-683-4995, Fax: 757-683-4270, E-mail: egomez@odu.edu. *Application contact:* Dr. Edwin Gomez, Graduate Program Director, 757-683-4995, Fax: 757-683-4270, E-mail: egomez@odu.edu.

Penn State University Park, Graduate School, College of Health and Human Development, Department of Recreation, Park and Tourism Management, State College, University Park, PA 16802-1503. Offers MS, PhD.

San Francisco State University, Division of Graduate Studies, College of Health and Human Services, Department of Recreation and Leisure Studies, San Francisco, CA 94132-1722. Offers recreation (MS). Part-time programs available.

San Jose State University, Graduate Studies and Research, College of Applied Sciences and Arts, Department of Hospitality, Recreation and Tourism Management, San Jose, CA 95192-0001. Offers recreation (MS). *Students:* 17 full-time (16 women), 23 part-time (16 women); includes 10 minority (2 African Americans, 2 Asian Americans or Pacific Islanders, 6 Hispanic Americans), 9 international. Average age 30. 37 applicants, 51% accepted, 13 enrolled. In 2009, 8 master's awarded. *Application deadline:* For fall admission, 6/27 for domestic students; for spring admission, 11/30 for domestic students. Applications are processed on a rolling basis. Application fee: $59. Electronic applications accepted. *Financial support:* Applicants required to submit FAFSA. *Unit head:* Dr. Randy Virden, Chair, 408-924-3000, Fax: 408-924-3061. *Application contact:* Dr. Randy Virden, Chair, 408-924-3000, Fax: 408-924-3061.

South Dakota State University, Graduate School, College of Education and Human Sciences, Department of Health, Physical Education and Recreation, Brookings, SD 57007. Offers MS. Part-time programs available. *Degree requirements:* For master's, thesis, oral and written exams. *Entrance requirements:* Additional exam requirements/recommendations for international students: Required—TOEFL (minimum score 550 paper-based; 213 computer-based; 71 iBT). *Faculty research:* Effective teaching behaviors in physical education, sports nutrition, muscle/bone interaction, hormonal response to exercise.

Southern Adventist University, School of Business and Management, Collegedale, TN 37315-0370. Offers accounting (MBA); church administration (MSA); church and nonprofit leadership (MBA); financial management (MFM); healthcare administration (MBA); management (MBA); marketing management (MBA); outdoor education (MSA); MFM. Part-time and evening/weekend programs available. Postbaccalaureate distance learning degree programs offered (no on-campus study). *Faculty:* 2 full-time (0 women), 8 part-time/adjunct (1 woman). *Students:* 55 full-time (32 women), 30 part-time (22 women); includes 23 minority (14 African Americans, 1 American Indian/Alaska Native, 1 Asian American or Pacific Islander, 7 Hispanic Americans). Average age 35. In 2009, 20 master's awarded. *Entrance requirements:* For master's, GMAT. Additional exam requirements/recommendations for international students: Required—TOEFL (minimum score 600 paper-based; 250 computer-based; 100 iBT). *Application deadline:* For fall admission, 8/1 priority date for domestic students, 7/1 for international students; for winter admission, 12/1 priority date for domestic students, 11/1 for international students; for spring admission, 4/1 priority date for domestic students, 3/1 for international students. Applications are processed on a rolling basis. Application fee: $25. Electronic applications accepted. *Expenses:* Tuition: Full-time $13,149; part-time $487 per credit hour. *Financial support:* In 2009–10, 32 students received support. Scholarships/grants and unspecified assistantships available. Financial award application deadline: 9/1; financial award applicants required to submit FAFSA. *Unit head:* Dr. Don Van Ornam, Dean, 423-236-2750, Fax: 423-236-1527, E-mail: dvanorna@southern.edu. *Application contact:* Linda Wilhelm, Admissions Coordinator, 423-236-2751, Fax: 423-236-1527, E-mail: sbm@southern.edu.

Southern Connecticut State University, School of Graduate Studies, School of Health and Human Services, Department of Recreation and Leisure Studies, New Haven, CT 06515-1355. Offers MS. Part-time and evening/weekend programs available. *Faculty:* 2 full-time, 1 part-time/adjunct. *Students:* 11 full-time (8 women), 22 part-time (12 women); includes 2 minority (1 Asian American or Pacific Islander, 1 Hispanic American). 20 applicants, 65% accepted, 12 enrolled. In 2009, 10 master's awarded. *Degree requirements:* For master's, thesis or alternative. *Entrance requirements:* For master's, interview, minimum undergraduate QPA of 3.0 in graduate major field or 2.5 overall. *Application deadline:* For fall admission, 7/15 priority date for domestic students. Applications are processed on a rolling basis. Application fee: $50. Electronic applications accepted. Tuition and fees vary according to program. *Financial support:* In 2009–10, 1 teaching assistantship was awarded; career-related internships or fieldwork also available. Financial award application deadline: 4/15; financial award applicants required to submit FAFSA. *Unit head:* Dr. James MacGregor, Chairperson, 203-392-6385, Fax: 203-392-6965, E-mail: macgregorj1@southernct.edu. *Application contact:* Dr. Jan Louise Jones, Graduate Coordinator, 203-392-8837, Fax: 203-392-6147, E-mail: jonesj39@southernct.edu.

Southern Illinois University Carbondale, Graduate School, College of Education, Department of Health Education and Recreation, Program in Recreation, Carbondale, IL 62901-4701. Offers MS Ed. Part-time programs available. *Degree requirements:* For master's, thesis. *Entrance requirements:* For master's, minimum GPA of 2.7. Additional exam requirements/recommendations for international students: Required—TOEFL. *Faculty research:* Leisure across the life span, outdoor recreation, recreation therapy, leisure service administration.

Southern University and Agricultural and Mechanical College, Graduate School, College of Education, Program in Leisure and Recreation Studies, Baton Rouge, LA 70813. Offers therapeutic recreation (MS). *Degree requirements:* For master's, comprehensive exam, thesis optional. *Entrance requirements:* For master's, GMAT or GRE General Test. Additional exam requirements/recommendations for international students: Required—TOEFL (minimum score 525 paper-based; 193 computer-based).

Southwestern Oklahoma State University, College of Professional and Graduate Studies, School of Behavioral Sciences and Education, Specialization in Parks and Recreation Management, Weatherford, OK 73096-3098. Offers M Ed.

Springfield College, Graduate Programs, Programs in Sport Management and Recreation, Springfield, MA 01109-3797. Offers recreational management (M Ed, MS); sport management (M Ed, MS); therapeutic recreational management (M Ed, MS). Part-time programs available. *Degree requirements:* For master's, comprehensive exam, research project. *Entrance requirements:* Additional exam requirements/recommendations for international students: Required—TOEFL (minimum score 550 paper-based; 213 computer-based). Electronic applications accepted. *Expenses:* Tuition: Full-time $19,800; part-time $825 per credit hour. Required fees: $150.

State University of New York College at Cortland, Graduate Studies, School of Professional Studies, Department of Recreation and Leisure Studies, Cortland, NY 13045. Offers MS, MS Ed. Part-time and evening/weekend programs available. *Degree requirements:* For master's, comprehensive exam, thesis (for some programs). *Entrance requirements:* Additional exam requirements/recommendations for international students: Required—TOEFL.

State University of New York College of Environmental Science and Forestry, Department of Forest and Natural Resources Management, Syracuse, NY 13210-2779. Offers environmental and natural resource policy (MS, PhD); environmental and natural resources policy (MPS); forest management and operations (MF); forestry ecosystems science and applications (MPS, MS, PhD); natural resources management (MPS, MS, PhD); quantitative methods and management in forest science (MPS, MS, PhD); recreation and resource management (MPS, MS, PhD); watershed management and forest hydrology (MPS, MS, PhD). *Degree requirements:* For master's, thesis (for some programs); for doctorate, comprehensive exam, thesis/dissertation. *Entrance requirements:* For master's and doctorate, GRE General Test, minimum GPA of 3.0. Additional exam requirements/recommendations for international students: Required—TOEFL (minimum score 550 paper-based; 213 computer-based; 80 iBT), IELTS (minimum score 6). *Faculty research:* Silviculture recreation management, tree improvement, operations management, economics.

Temple University, Graduate School, School of Tourism and Hospitality Management, Program in Sport and Recreation Administration, Philadelphia, PA 19122-6096. Offers Ed M. Part-time and evening/weekend programs available. *Entrance requirements:* For master's, GRE General Test or MAT, minimum undergraduate GPA of 3.0. Additional exam requirements/recommendations for international students: Required—TOEFL (minimum score 550 paper-based; 213 computer-based; 79 iBT). Electronic applications accepted.

Temple University, Health Sciences Center and Graduate School, College of Health Professions, Department of Therapeutic Recreation, Philadelphia, PA 19122-6096. Offers Ed M. Part-time and evening/weekend programs available. *Degree requirements:* For master's, comprehensive exam, thesis optional. *Entrance requirements:* For master's, GRE or MAT. Additional exam requirements/recommendations for international students: Required—TOEFL (minimum score 550 paper-based; 213 computer-based; 79 iBT). Electronic applications accepted. *Faculty research:* Quality of life, curriculum issues, disability issues, adaptive equipment/technology.

Texas A&M University, College of Agriculture and Life Sciences, Department of Recreation, Park and Tourism Sciences, College Station, TX 77843. Offers natural resources development (M Agr); recreation resources development (M Agr); recreation, park, and tourism sciences (MS, PhD). *Faculty:* 15. *Students:* 46 full-time (28 women), 17 part-time (10 women); includes 7 minority (3 African Americans, 1 American Indian/Alaska Native, 3 Hispanic Americans), 26 international. Average age 28. In 2009, 8 master's, 15 doctorates awarded. *Degree requirements:* For master's, thesis (for some programs), internship and professional paper (M Agr); for doctorate, thesis/dissertation. *Entrance requirements:* For master's and doctorate, GRE General Test. Additional exam requirements/recommendations for international students: Required—TOEFL. *Application deadline:* For fall admission, 4/15 priority date for domestic students; for spring admission, 10/15 priority date for domestic students. Applications are processed on a rolling basis. Application fee: $50 ($75 for international students). Electronic applications accepted. *Expenses:* Tuition, state resident: full-time $3991; part-time $221.74 per credit hour. Tuition, nonresident: full-time $9049; part-time $502.74 per credit hour. *Financial support:* Fellowships, research assistantships, teaching assistantships, career-related internships or fieldwork, institutionally sponsored loans, and scholarships/grants available. Financial award application deadline: 4/15; financial award applicants required to submit FAFSA. *Faculty research:* Administration and tourism, outdoor recreation, commercial recreation, environmental law, system planning. *Unit head:* Head, 979-845-7324. *Application contact:* Graduate Recruitment Coordinator, 979-845-5412, Fax: 979-845-0446, E-mail: majohnson@ag.tamu.edu.

Texas State University–San Marcos, Graduate School, College of Education, Department of Health and Human Performance, Program in Recreation and Leisure Services, San Marcos, TX 78666. Offers MSRLS. *Faculty:* 3 full-time (2 women), 1 (woman) part-time/adjunct. *Students:* 28 full-time (12 women), 16 part-time (11 women); includes 8 minority (1 African American, 1 Asian American or Pacific Islander, 6 Hispanic Americans). Average age 28. 26 applicants, 100% accepted, 18 enrolled. In 2009, 7 master's awarded. *Degree requirements:* For master's, comprehensive exam, thesis optional. *Entrance requirements:* For master's, GRE General Test, minimum GPA of 2.75 in last 60 hours of course work. Additional exam requirements/recommendations for international students: Required—TOEFL (minimum score 550 paper-based; 213 computer-based). *Application deadline:* For fall admission, 6/15 priority date for domestic students; for spring admission, 10/15 priority date for domestic students. Applications are processed on a rolling basis. Application fee: $40 ($90 for international students). Electronic applications accepted. *Expenses:* Tuition, state resident: full-time $5784; part-time $241 per credit hour. Tuition, nonresident: full-time $13,224; part-time $551 per credit hour. Required fees: $1728; $48 per credit hour. $306. Tuition and fees vary according to course load. *Financial support:* In 2009–10, 34 students received support, including 4 research assistantships (averaging $5,234 per year), 4 teaching assistantships (averaging $5,414 per year). Financial award application deadline: 4/1; financial award applicants required to submit FAFSA. *Unit head:* Dr. Duane Knudson, Graduate Advisor, 512-245-2561, Fax: 512-245-8678, E-mail: dk19@txstate.edu. *Application contact:* Dr. Stephen Awonly, Head, 512-245-2561, Fax: 512-245-8678, E-mail: sa11@txstate.edu.

Texas State University–San Marcos, Graduate School, Interdisciplinary Studies Program in Health, Physical Education, and Recreation, San Marcos, TX 78666. Offers MAIS. Part-time and evening/weekend programs available. *Students:* 7 full-time (5 women), 4 part-time (0 women); includes 1 minority (Hispanic American). Average age 28. 5 applicants, 100% accepted, 5 enrolled. In 2009, 1 master's awarded. *Degree requirements:* For master's, comprehensive exam, thesis optional. *Entrance requirements:* For master's, GRE General Test, minimum GPA of 2.75 in last 60 hours of course work. Additional exam requirements/recommendations for international students: Required—TOEFL (minimum score 550 paper-based; 213 computer-based). *Application deadline:* For fall admission, 6/15 priority date for domestic students, 6/1 for international students; for spring admission, 10/15 priority date for domestic students, 10/1 for international students. Applications are processed on a rolling basis. Application fee: $40 ($90 for international students). *Expenses:* Tuition, state resident: full-time $5784; part-time $241 per credit hour. Tuition, nonresident: full-time $13,224; part-time $551 per credit hour. Required fees: $1728; $48 per credit hour. $306. Tuition and fees vary according to course load. *Financial support:* In 2009–10, 8 students received support, including 2 teaching assistantships (averaging $5,751 per year); career-related internships or fieldwork, Federal Work-Study, and institutionally sponsored loans also available. Support available to part-time students. Financial award application deadline: 4/1; financial award applicants required to submit FAFSA. *Unit head:* Dr. Tinker Murray, Head, 512-245-2561, Fax: 512-245-8678, E-mail: tm05@txstate.edu. *Application contact:* Dr. J. Michael Willoughby, Dean of Graduate School, 512-245-2581, Fax: 512-245-8365, E-mail: gradcollege@txstate.edu.

Universidad Metropolitana, Graduate Programs in Education, Program in Managing Leisure Services, San Juan, PR 00928-1150. Offers M Ed. Part-time programs available. *Degree requirements:* For master's, thesis or alternative. *Entrance requirements:* For master's, EXADEP, interview. Electronic applications accepted.

University of Alberta, Faculty of Graduate Studies and Research, Department of Physical Education and Recreation, Edmonton, AB T6G 2E1, Canada. Offers physical education (M Sc); recreation and physical education (MA, PhD). Part-time programs available. *Faculty:* 30 full-time (10 women). *Students:* 60 full-time (34 women), 55 part-time (28 women). 69 applicants, 36% accepted. In 2009, 13 master's, 7 doctorates awarded. Terminal master's awarded for partial completion of doctoral program. *Degree requirements:* For master's, thesis (for some programs); for doctorate, thesis/dissertation. *Entrance requirements:* For master's, bachelor's degree in related field; for doctorate, master's degree in related field with thesis. Additional exam requirements/recommendations for international students: Required—TOEFL. *Application deadline:* For fall admission, 1/1 priority date for domestic students. Applications are processed on a rolling basis. Tuition and fees charges are reported in Canadian dollars. *Expenses:* Tuition, area resident: Full-time $4626 Canadian dollars; part-time $99.72 Canadian dollars per unit. International tuition: $8216 Canadian dollars full-time. Required fees: $3590 Canadian dollars; $99.72 Canadian dollars per unit. $215 Canadian dollars per term. *Financial support:* In 2009–10, 63 students received support, including 28 research assistantships, 35 teaching assistantships; career-related internships or fieldwork and scholarships/grants also available. Support available to part-time students. *Faculty research:* Motivation and adherence to physical ability, performance enhancement, adapted physical activity, exercise physiology, sport administration, tourism. *Unit head:* Dr. D. Marshall, Assistant Dean, 780-492-3198, Fax: 403-492-2364. *Application contact:* Anne Jordan, Department Office, 403-492-3198, Fax: 403-492-2364, E-mail: pergrad@ualberta.ca.

University of Arkansas, Graduate School, College of Education and Health Professions, Department of Health Science, Kinesiology, Recreation and Dance, Program in Recreation, Fayetteville, AR 72701-1201. Offers M Ed, Ed D. *Students:* 9 full-time (6 women), 23 part-time (10 women); includes 3 minority (1 African American, 1 American Indian/Alaska Native, 1 Hispanic American). In 2009, 12 master's awarded. *Degree requirements:* For master's, thesis optional; for doctorate, thesis/dissertation. *Entrance requirements:* For doctorate, GRE General Test. Application fee: $40 ($50 for international students). *Expenses:* Tuition, state resident: full-time $7355; part-time $356.58 per hour. Tuition, nonresident: full-time $17,401; part-time $775.17 per hour. Required fees: $1203. *Financial support:* In 2009–10, 4 research assistant-

Recreation and Park Management

University of Arkansas (continued)
ships, 3 teaching assistantships were awarded; fellowships with tuition reimbursements, career-related internships or fieldwork and Federal Work-Study also available. Support available to part-time students. Financial award application deadline: 4/1; financial award applicants required to submit FAFSA. *Unit head:* Dr. Sharon Hunt, Department Chairperson, 479-575-2857, Fax: 479-575-5728, E-mail: sbhunt@uark.edu. *Application contact:* Dr. Dean Gorman, Coordinator of Graduate Studies, 479-575-2890, E-mail: dgorman@uark.edu.

University of Florida, Graduate School, College of Health and Human Performance, Department of Tourism, Recreation and Sport Management, Gainesville, FL 32611. Offers health and human performance (PhD), including natural resource recreation (MS, PhD), sport management (MS, PhD), therapeutic recreation (MS, PhD), tourism; recreational studies (MS), including campus recreation programming and administration, natural resource recreation (MS, PhD), recreation administration and supervision, sport management (MS, PhD), therapeutic recreation (MS, PhD), tourism and commercial recreation. *Degree requirements:* For master's, thesis optional. *Entrance requirements:* For master's, GRE General Test, minimum GPA of 3.0. Additional exam requirements/recommendations for international students: Required—TOEFL (minimum score 550 paper-based; 213 computer-based). Electronic applications accepted. *Faculty research:* Recreation resource planning, commercial recreation, campus recreation.

University of Idaho, College of Graduate Studies, College of Education, Department of Health, Physical Education, Recreation, and Dance, Program in Recreation, Moscow, ID 83844-2282. Offers MS. *Students:* 10 full-time, 4 part-time. In 2009, 16 master's awarded. *Entrance requirements:* For master's, minimum GPA of 2.8. *Application deadline:* For fall admission, 8/1 for domestic students; for spring admission, 12/15 for domestic students. Application fee: $55 ($60 for international students). *Expenses:* Tuition, state resident: full-time $6120. Tuition, nonresident: full-time $17,712. *Financial support:* Research assistantships available. Financial award application deadline: 2/15. *Unit head:* Dr. Kathy Browder, Chair, 208-885-2192. *Application contact:* Dr. Kathy Browder, Chair, 208-885-2192.

The University of Iowa, Graduate College, College of Liberal Arts and Sciences, Program in Leisure Studies, Iowa City, IA 52242-1316. Offers leisure and recreational sport management (MA); therapeutic recreation (MA). *Degree requirements:* For master's, thesis optional, exam. *Entrance requirements:* For master's, minimum GPA of 3.0. Additional exam requirements/recommendations for international students: Required—TOEFL (minimum score 550 paper-based; 213 computer-based; 81 iBT). Electronic applications accepted.

University of Manitoba, Faculty of Graduate Studies, Faculty of Kinesiology and Recreation Management, Winnipeg, MB R3T 2N2, Canada. Offers kinesiology and recreation management (M Sc); recreation studies (MA).

University of Minnesota, Twin Cities Campus, Graduate School, College of Education and Human Development, School of Kinesiology, Division of Recreation, Park, and Leisure Studies, Minneapolis, MN 55455-0213. Offers M Ed, MA, PhD. Part-time programs available. *Students:* 2 full-time (both women), 6 part-time (3 women), 4 international. Average age 34. 8 applicants, 75% accepted, 3 enrolled. In 2009, 9 master's, 3 doctorates awarded. Terminal master's awarded for partial completion of doctoral program. *Degree requirements:* For master's, thesis (for some programs), final oral exam; for doctorate, thesis/dissertation, preliminary written/oral exam, final oral exam. *Entrance requirements:* For master's, GRE or MAT, minimum GPA of 3.0; for doctorate, GRE or MAT, minimum GPA of 3.0, writing sample. *Application deadline:* For fall admission, 7/15 for domestic students; for spring admission, 12/15 for domestic students. Applications are processed on a rolling basis. *Financial support:* Fellowships, research assistantships, teaching assistantships, career-related internships or fieldwork, Federal Work-Study, institutionally sponsored loans, and tuition waivers (full and partial) available. Support available to part-time students. *Application contact:* Dr. Mary Trettin, Associate Dean, 612-625-3339, Fax: 612-626-1580, E-mail: mtrettin@umn.edu.

University of Mississippi, Graduate School, School of Applied Sciences, Department of Health, Exercise Science, and Recreation Management, Oxford, University, MS 38677. Offers exercise science (MS); exercise science and leisure management (PhD); park and recreation management (MA); wellness (MS). *Faculty:* 10 full-time (2 women), 2 part-time/adjunct (both women). *Students:* 37 full-time (22 women), 8 part-time (5 women); includes 8 minority (7 African Americans, 1 Hispanic American), 5 international. In 2009, 5 master's, 3 doctorates awarded. *Degree requirements:* For master's, thesis (for some programs); for doctorate, thesis/dissertation. *Entrance requirements:* For master's, GRE General Test, minimum GPA of 3.0; for doctorate, GRE General Test. Additional exam requirements/recommendations for international students: Required—TOEFL. *Application deadline:* For fall admission, 4/1 for domestic students; for spring admission, 10/1 for domestic students. Applications are processed on a rolling basis. Application fee: $25. *Financial support:* Scholarships/grants available. Financial award application deadline: 3/1; financial award applicants required to submit FAFSA. *Unit head:* Dr. Mark Loftin, Interim Chair, 662-915-5844, Fax: 662-915-5525, E-mail: mloftin@olemiss.edu. *Application contact:* Dr. Christy M. Wyandt, Associate Dean, 662-915-7474, Fax: 662-915-7577, E-mail: cwyandt@olemiss.edu.

University of Missouri, Graduate School, School of Natural Resources, Department of Parks, Recreation and Tourism, Columbia, MO 65211. Offers MS. *Entrance requirements:* For master's, GRE General Test, minimum GPA of 3.0. Additional exam requirements/recommendations for international students: Required—TOEFL (minimum score 500 paper-based; 173 computer-based; 61 iBT).

The University of Montana, Graduate School, College of Forestry and Conservation, Missoula, MT 59812-0002. Offers ecosystem management (MEM, MS); fish and wildlife biology (PhD); forestry (MS, PhD); recreation management (MS); resource conservation (MS); wildlife biology (MS). *Degree requirements:* For doctorate, thesis/dissertation. *Entrance requirements:* For master's and doctorate, GRE General Test. Additional exam requirements/recommendations for international students: Required—TOEFL (minimum score 575 paper-based; 213 computer-based).

University of Nebraska at Omaha, Graduate Studies, College of Education, School of Health, Physical Education, and Recreation, Omaha, NE 68182. Offers MA, MS. Part-time and evening/weekend programs available. *Faculty:* 12 full-time (4 women). *Students:* 43 full-time (25 women), 38 part-time (23 women); includes 5 minority (4 African Americans, 1 Asian American or Pacific Islander), 12 international. Average age 29. 49 applicants, 53% accepted, 16 enrolled. In 2009, 30 master's awarded. *Degree requirements:* For master's, comprehensive exam, thesis (for some programs). *Entrance requirements:* For master's, minimum GPA of 3.0. Additional exam requirements/recommendations for international students: Required—TOEFL (minimum score 550 paper-based; 213 computer-based; 80 iBT). *Application deadline:* For fall admission, 7/1 priority date for domestic students; for spring admission, 12/1 priority date for domestic students. Applications are processed on a rolling basis. Application fee: $45. Electronic applications accepted. *Financial support:* In 2009–10, 48 students received support, including 8 research assistantships with tuition reimbursements available; fellowships, Federal Work-Study, institutionally sponsored loans, scholarships/grants, tuition waivers (full), and unspecified assistantships also available. Support available to part-time students. Financial award application deadline: 3/1; financial award applicants required to submit FAFSA. *Unit head:* Dr. Dan Blanke, Director, 402-554-2670. *Application contact:* Penny Harmoney, Director, Graduate Studies, 402-554-2341, Fax: 402-554-3143, E-mail: graduate@unomaha.edu.

University of New Brunswick Fredericton, School of Graduate Studies, Faculty of Kinesiology, Fredericton, NB E3B 5A3, Canada. Offers exercise and sport science (M Sc); sport and recreation management (MBA); sport and recreation studies (MA). Part-time programs available. *Faculty:* 17 full-time (7 women). *Students:* 35 full-time (16 women), 6 part-time (5 women). In 2009, 10 master's awarded. *Degree requirements:* For master's, thesis (for some programs). *Entrance requirements:* For master's, minimum GPA of 3.0, written statement of research goals and interests. Additional exam requirements/recommendations for international students: Required—TOEFL (minimum score 600 paper-based; 250 computer-based), TWE (minimum score 4). *Application deadline:* For winter admission, 1/31 for domestic students; for spring admission, 3/31 for domestic students. Applications are processed on a rolling basis. Application fee: $50 Canadian dollars. Electronic applications accepted. Tuition and fees charges are reported in Canadian dollars. *Expenses:* Tuition, area resident: Full-time $5562 Canadian dollars; part-time $2781 Canadian dollars per year. Required fees: $49.75 Canadian dollars per term. *Financial support:* In 2009–10, 2 fellowships with tuition reimbursements were awarded; research assistantships, teaching assistantships, career-related internships or fieldwork and scholarships/grants also available. *Unit head:* Dr. Wayne Albert, Acting Director of Graduate Studies, 506-447-3254, Fax: 506-453-3511, E-mail: walbert@unb.ca. *Application contact:* Linda O'Brien, Graduate Secretary, 506-453-4576, Fax: 506-453-3511, E-mail: lobrien@unb.ca.

University of New Hampshire, Graduate School, School of Health and Human Services, Department of Recreation Management and Policy, Durham, NH 03824. Offers recreation administration (MS); therapeutic recreation (MS). Part-time programs available. *Faculty:* 4 full-time (3 women). *Students:* 8 full-time (all women), 8 part-time (4 women); includes 1 minority (American Indian/Alaska Native). Average age 29. 17 applicants, 65% accepted, 8 enrolled. In 2009, 5 master's awarded. *Degree requirements:* For master's, thesis optional. *Entrance requirements:* For master's, GRE. Additional exam requirements/recommendations for international students: Required—TOEFL (minimum score 550 paper-based; 213 computer-based; 80 iBT); Recommended—TWE. *Application deadline:* For fall admission, 6/1 priority date for domestic students, 4/1 priority date for international students; for spring admission, 12/1 for domestic students. Application fee: $65. Electronic applications accepted. *Expenses:* Tuition, state resident: full-time $10,380; part-time $577 per credit hour. Tuition, nonresident: full-time $24,350; part-time $1002 per credit hour. Required fees: $1550; $387.50 per semester. Tuition and fees vary according to course load and program. *Financial support:* In 2009–10, 5 students received support, including 5 teaching assistantships; fellowships, research assistantships also available. *Unit head:* Dr. Janet Sable, Chairperson, 603-862-3401. *Application contact:* Louise Craig, Administrative Assistant, 603-862-2391, E-mail: rmp.graduate@unh.edu.

The University of North Carolina at Chapel Hill, Graduate School, College of Arts and Sciences, Department of Recreation and Leisure Studies, Chapel Hill, NC 27599. Offers MSRA. Part-time programs available. *Degree requirements:* For master's, comprehensive exam, thesis or alternative. *Entrance requirements:* For master's, GRE General Test, minimum GPA of 3.0. Additional exam requirements/recommendations for international students: Required—TOEFL. Electronic applications accepted. *Faculty research:* Leisure research related to gender, youth, inclusion, and family; social psychology of leisure; leisure democracy.

The University of North Carolina at Greensboro, Graduate School, School of Health and Human Performance, Department of Recreation, Tourism, and Hospitality Management, Greensboro, NC 27412-5001. Offers parks and recreation management (MS). *Degree requirements:* For master's, thesis. *Entrance requirements:* For master's, GRE General Test. Additional exam requirements/recommendations for international students: Required—TOEFL. Electronic applications accepted.

University of North Texas, Robert B. Toulouse School of Graduate Studies, College of Education, Department of Kinesiology, Health Promotion, and Recreation, Program in Recreation and Leisure Studies, Denton, TX 76203. Offers recreation and leisure studies (MS); recreation management (Certificate). Part-time programs available. *Degree requirements:* For master's, thesis or alternative, culminating project or field placement. *Entrance requirements:* For master's, GRE General Test or MAT, resume, 2 letters of reference, 300-word statement. Additional exam requirements/recommendations for international students: Required—proof of English language proficiency required for non-native English speakers; Recommended—TOEFL (minimum score 550 paper-based; 213 computer-based). *Application deadline:* Applications are processed on a rolling basis. Application fee: $50 ($75 for international students). Electronic applications accepted. *Expenses:* Tuition, state resident: full-time $4298; part-time $239 per contact hour. Tuition, nonresident: full-time $9878; part-time $549 per contact hour. Required fees: $265 per contact hour. *Financial support:* Teaching assistantships, career-related internships or fieldwork, Federal Work-Study, institutionally sponsored loans, and unspecified assistantships available. Financial award application deadline: 4/1. *Faculty research:* Physically active leisure, trail use, community recreation programming, inclusion of persons with disabilities, therapeutic recreation.

University of Rhode Island, Graduate School, College of Human Science and Services, Department of Kinesiology, Kingston, RI 02881. Offers cultural studies of sport and physical culture (MS); exercise science (MS); physical education pedagogy (MS); psychosocial/behavioral aspects of physical activity (MS). *Accreditation:* NCATE. Part-time programs available. *Faculty:* 13 full-time (7 women). *Students:* 16 full-time (8 women), 2 part-time (1 woman), 1 international. In 2009, 6 master's awarded. *Degree requirements:* For master's, thesis optional. *Entrance requirements:* For master's, GRE, 2 letters of recommendation. Additional exam requirements/recommendations for international students: Required—TOEFL (minimum score 550 paper-based; 213 computer-based). *Application deadline:* For fall admission, 4/15 for domestic students, 2/1 for international students; for spring admission, 11/15 for domestic students, 7/15 for international students. Application fee: $65. Electronic applications accepted. *Expenses:* Tuition, state resident: full-time $8828; part-time $490 per credit hour. Tuition, nonresident: full-time $22,100; part-time $1228 per credit hour. Required fees: $1118; $57 per semester. Tuition and fees vary according to program. *Financial support:* In 2009–10, 4 teaching assistantships with full and partial tuition reimbursements (averaging $7,939 per year) were awarded. Financial award application deadline: 4/15; financial award applicants required to submit FAFSA. *Faculty research:* Strength training and older adults, interventions to promote a healthy lifestyle as well as analysis of the psychosocial outcomes of those interventions, effects of exercise and nutrition on skeletal muscle of aging healthy adults with CVD and other metabolic related diseases, physical activity and fitness of deaf children and youth. Total annual research expenditures: $92,479. *Unit head:* Dr. Deborah Riebe, Chair, 401-874-5444, Fax: 401-874-4215, E-mail: debriebe@uri.edu. *Application contact:* Dr. Lori Ciccomascolo, Director of Graduate Studies, 401-874-5454, Fax: 401-874-4215, E-mail: lecicco@uri.edu.

University of South Alabama, Graduate School, College of Education, Department of Health, Physical Education and Leisure Services, Mobile, AL 36688-0002. Offers exercise science (MS); health education (M Ed); physical education (M Ed); therapeutic recreation (MS). *Accreditation:* NCATE (one or more programs are accredited). Part-time programs available. *Degree requirements:* For master's, comprehensive exam. *Entrance requirements:* For master's, GRE General Test or MAT. *Expenses:* Tuition, state resident: part-time $218 per contact hour. Required fees: $1102 per year.

University of Southern Mississippi, Graduate School, College of Health, School of Human Performance and Recreation, Hattiesburg, MS 39406-0001. Offers human performance (MS, Ed D, PhD); interscholastic athletic administration (MS); recreation and leisure management (MS); sport administration (MS); sport and coaching education (MS); sport management (MS); sports and high performance materials (MS). Part-time and evening/weekend programs available. *Faculty:* 13 full-time (5 women). *Students:* 62 full-time (27 women), 40 part-time (10 women); includes 13 minority (10 African Americans, 1 Asian American or Pacific Islander, 2 Hispanic Americans), 4 international. Average age 29. 79 applicants, 59% accepted, 33 enrolled. In 2009, 43 master's, 4 doctorates awarded. *Degree requirements:* For master's, comprehensive exam, thesis optional; for doctorate, comprehensive exam, thesis/dissertation. *Entrance requirements:* For master's, GRE General Test, minimum GPA of 2.75 in last 60 hours; for doctorate, GRE General Test, minimum GPA of 3.5. Additional exam requirements/recommendations for international students: Required—TOEFL. *Application deadline:* For fall admission, 3/1 priority date for domestic students, 3/1 for international students. Applications are processed on a rolling basis. Application fee: $35. Electronic applications accepted. *Expenses:* Tuition, state resident: full-time $5096; part-time $284 per hour. Tuition, nonresident: full-time $13,052; part-time $726 per hour. Required fees: $402. Tuition and fees vary according to course load and course load. *Financial support:* In 2009–10, 1 fellowship (averaging $16,000 per year), 6 research assistantships with full tuition reimbursements (averaging

$7,492 per year), 5 teaching assistantships with full tuition reimbursements (averaging $7,330 per year) were awarded; career-related internships or fieldwork, Federal Work-Study, institutionally sponsored loans, and tuition waivers (partial) also available. Financial award application deadline: 3/15. *Faculty research:* Exercise physiology, health behaviors, resource management, activity interaction, site development. *Unit head:* Dr. Louis Marciani, Director, 601-266-5379, Fax: 601-266-4445. *Application contact:* Dr. Dennis Phillips, Graduate Coordinator, 601-266-5379, Fax: 601-266-4445.

The University of Tennessee, Graduate School, College of Education, Health and Human Sciences, Department of Exercise, Sport, and Leisure Studies, Knoxville, TN 37996. Offers exercise science (MS, PhD), including biomechanics/sports medicine, exercise physiology; recreation and leisure studies (MS); sport management (MS); sport studies (MS, PhD); therapeutic recreation (MS). Part-time and evening/weekend programs available. *Degree requirements:* For master's, thesis optional. *Entrance requirements:* For master's, minimum GPA of 2.7. Additional exam requirements/recommendations for international students: Required—TOEFL. Electronic applications accepted. *Expenses:* Tuition, state resident: full-time $6826; part-time $380 per semester hour. Tuition, nonresident: full-time $21,844; part-time $1147 per semester hour. Tuition and fees vary according to program.

University of Utah, Graduate School, College of Health, Department of Parks, Recreation, and Tourism, Salt Lake City, UT 84112-1107. Offers M Phil, MS, Ed D, PhD. *Faculty:* 11 full-time (4 women). *Students:* 36 full-time (20 women), 14 part-time (5 women), 11 international. Average age 31. 53 applicants, 51% accepted, 20 enrolled. In 2009, 10 master's, 5 doctorates awarded. Terminal master's awarded for partial completion of doctoral program. *Degree requirements:* For master's, comprehensive exam, thesis or alternative; for doctorate, thesis/dissertation. *Entrance requirements:* For master's, minimum GPA of 3.0; for doctorate, GRE General Test or MAT, minimum GPA of 3.2. Additional exam requirements/recommendations for international students: Required—TOEFL (minimum score 500 paper-based; 173 computer-based). *Application deadline:* For fall admission, 4/1 for domestic students, 2/15 for international students; for spring admission, 11/1 for domestic students. Application fee: $55 ($65 for international students). Electronic applications accepted. *Expenses:* Tuition, state resident: full-time $4004; part-time $1674 per semester. Tuition, nonresident: full-time $14,134; part-time $5915 per semester. Required fees: $324 per semester. Tuition and fees vary according to course load, degree level and program. *Financial support:* Teaching assistantships with full tuition reimbursements, career-related internships or fieldwork available. Financial award application deadline: 2/15; financial award applicants required to submit FAFSA. *Faculty research:* Commercial, therapeutic, community, and outdoor recreation; tourism. Total annual research expenditures: $98,598. *Unit head:* Dr. Dan Dustin, Chair, 801-581-7560, E-mail: daniel.dustin@health.utah.edu. *Application contact:* Dr. Edward J. Ruddell, Director of Graduate Studies, 801-585-8085, Fax: 801-581-4930, E-mail: edward.ruddell@health.utah.edu.

University of Waterloo, Graduate Studies, Faculty of Applied Health Sciences, Department of Recreation and Leisure Studies, Waterloo, ON N2L 3G1, Canada. Offers MA, PhD. Part-time programs available. *Degree requirements:* For master's, thesis; for doctorate, comprehensive exam, thesis/dissertation. *Entrance requirements:* For master's, honors degree, minimum B average, writing sample, resume; for doctorate, GRE (recommended), master's degree, minimum B average, writing sample, resumé. Additional exam requirements/recommendations for international students: Required—TOEFL, TWE. Electronic applications accepted. *Faculty research:* Tourism, leisure behavior, special populations, leisure service management, outdoor resources, aging, health and well-being, work and health.

University of Wisconsin–La Crosse, Office of University Graduate Studies, College of Science and Health, Department of Recreation Management and Therapeutic Recreation, Program in Recreation Management, La Crosse, WI 54601-3742. Offers MS. *Students:* 15 full-time (10 women), 4 part-time (2 women), 4 international. Average age 25. 24 applicants, 71% accepted, 10 enrolled. In 2009, 8 master's awarded. *Entrance requirements:* Additional exam requirements/recommendations for international students: Required—TOEFL (minimum score 550 paper-based; 213 computer-based; 79 iBT). *Application deadline:* For fall admission, 3/15 priority date for domestic students. Applications are processed on a rolling basis. Application fee: $56. Electronic applications accepted. *Financial support:* Research assistantships, career-related internships or fieldwork, Federal Work-Study, health care benefits, and unspecified assistantships available. Support available to part-time students. Financial award applicants required to submit FAFSA. *Unit head:* Dr. Steven Simpson, Graduate Program Director, 608-785-8216, E-mail: simpson.stev@uwlax.edu. *Application contact:* Kathryn Kiefer, Director of Admissions, 608-785-8939, E-mail: admissions@uwlax.edu.

University of Wisconsin–La Crosse, Office of University Graduate Studies, College of Science and Health, Department of Recreation Management and Therapeutic Recreation, Program in Therapeutic Recreation, La Crosse, WI 54601-3742. Offers MS. *Students:* 6 full-time (5 women). Average age 25. 12 applicants, 75% accepted, 4 enrolled. In 2009, 3 master's awarded. *Entrance requirements:* Additional exam requirements/recommendations for international students: Required—TOEFL (minimum score 550 paper-based; 213 computer-based; 79 iBT). *Application deadline:* For fall admission, 3/15 priority date for domestic students. Applications are processed on a rolling basis. Application fee: $56. Electronic applications accepted. *Financial support:* Research assistantships, career-related internships or fieldwork, Federal Work-Study, health care benefits, and unspecified assistantships available. Support available to part-time students. Financial award applicants required to submit FAFSA. *Unit head:* Dr. Steven Simpson, Graduate Program Director, 608-785-8216, E-mail: simpson. stev@uwlax.edu. *Application contact:* Kathryn Kiefer, Director of Admissions, 608-785-8939, E-mail: admissions@uwlax.edu.

University of Wisconsin–Milwaukee, Graduate School, College of Health Sciences, Department of Occupational Therapy, Milwaukee, WI 53201-0413. Offers ergonomics (Certificate); occupational therapy (MS); therapeutic recreation (Certificate). *Accreditation:* AOTA. *Faculty:* 7 full-time (3 women). *Students:* 40 full-time (37 women), 3 part-time (all women), 6 international. Average age 25. 19 applicants, 37% accepted, 1 enrolled. In 2009, 38 master's awarded. *Degree requirements:* For master's, thesis or alternative. *Entrance requirements:* Additional exam requirements/recommendations for international students: Required—TOEFL (minimum score 550 paper-based; 79 iBT), IELTS (minimum score 6.5). *Application deadline:* For fall admission, 1/1 priority date for domestic students; for spring admission, 9/1 for domestic students. Applications are processed on a rolling basis. Application fee: $45 ($75 for international students). *Expenses:* Tuition, state resident: full-time $8800. Tuition, nonresident: full-time $20,760. Tuition and fees vary according to program and reciprocity agreements. *Financial support:* Fellowships, research assistantships, teaching assistantships, unspecified assistantships available. Support available to part-time students. Financial award application deadline: 4/15. Total annual research expenditures: $778,000. *Unit head:* Virginia Stoffel, Chair, 414-229-5583, Fax: 414-229-5100, E-mail: stoffelv@uwm.edu. *Application contact:* Virginia Stoffel, Chair, 414-229-5583, Fax: 414-229-5100, E-mail: stoffelv@uwm.edu.

Utah State University, School of Graduate Studies, College of Natural Resources, Department of Environment and Society, Logan, UT 84322. Offers bioregional planning (MS); geography (MA, MS); human dimensions of ecosystem science and management (MS, PhD); recreation resource management (MS, PhD). *Degree requirements:* For master's, comprehensive exam, thesis (for some programs). *Entrance requirements:* For master's and doctorate, GRE General Test, minimum GPA of 3.0. Additional exam requirements/recommendations for international students: Required—TOEFL. Electronic applications accepted. *Faculty research:* Geographic information systems/geographic and environmental education, bioregional planning, natural resource and environmental policy, outdoor recreation and tourism, natural resource and environmental management.

Virginia Commonwealth University, Graduate School, School of Education, Program in Recreation, Parks and Sports Leadership, Richmond, VA 23284-9005. Offers MS. *Entrance requirements:* For master's, GRE General Test or MAT.

Virginia Polytechnic Institute and State University, Graduate School, College of Natural Resources, Department of Forestry, Blacksburg, VA 24061. Offers forest biology (MF, MS, PhD); forest biometry (MF, MS, PhD); forest management/economics (MF, MS, PhD); industrial forestry operations (MF, MS, PhD); outdoor recreation (MF, MS, PhD). *Faculty:* 25 full-time (5 women), 1 (woman) part-time/adjunct. *Students:* 48 full-time (16 women), 8 part-time (2 women); includes 13 minority (all American Indian/Alaska Native), 1 international. Average age 30. 41 applicants, 37% accepted, 14 enrolled. In 2009, 16 master's, 9 doctorates awarded. *Entrance requirements:* For master's and doctorate, GRE, GMAT. Additional exam requirements/recommendations for international students: Required—TOEFL (minimum score 550 paper-based; 213 computer-based). *Application deadline:* For fall admission, 5/15 for international students; for spring admission, 10/15 for international students. Applications are processed on a rolling basis. Application fee: $65. Electronic applications accepted. *Expenses:* Tuition, area resident: full-time $10,228; part-time $459 per credit hour. Tuition, nonresident: full-time $17,892; part-time $865 per credit hour. Required fees: $1966; $451 per semester. *Financial support:* In 2009–10, 28 research assistantships with full tuition reimbursements (averaging $19,721 per year), 8 teaching assistantships with full tuition reimbursements (averaging $18,232 per year) were awarded; career-related internships or fieldwork, Federal Work-Study, scholarships/grants, and unspecified assistantships also available. Financial award application deadline: 1/15. Total annual research expenditures: $1.8 million. *Unit head:* Dr. Janaki Alavalapati, Head, 540-231-5676, Fax: 540-231-3698, E-mail: jrra@vt.edu. *Application contact:* Dr. Janaki Alavalapati, Head, 540-231-5676, Fax: 540-231-3698, E-mail: jrra@vt.edu.

Wayne State University, College of Education, Division of Kinesiology, Health and Sports Studies, Detroit, MI 48202. Offers health education (M Ed); kinesiology (M Ed); physical education (M Ed); recreation and park services (MA); sports administration (MA). *Degree requirements:* For master's, thesis (for some programs). *Entrance requirements:* Additional exam requirements/recommendations for international students: Required—TOEFL; Recommended—TWE (minimum score 6). Electronic applications accepted. *Faculty research:* Fitness in urban children, motor development of crack babies, effects of caffeine on metabolism/exercise, body composition of elite youth sports participants, systematic observation of teaching.

Western Illinois University, School of Graduate Studies, College of Education and Human Services, Department of Recreation, Park, and Tourism Administration, Macomb, IL 61455-1390. Offers MS. Part-time programs available. *Students:* 35 full-time (19 women), 10 part-time (9 women); includes 4 minority (2 African Americans, 2 Hispanic Americans), 3 international. Average age 27. 34 applicants, 74% accepted. In 2009, 25 master's awarded. *Degree requirements:* For master's, thesis or alternative. *Entrance requirements:* Additional exam requirements/recommendations for international students: Required—TOEFL (minimum score 550 paper-based; 213 computer-based; 80 iBT). *Application deadline:* Applications are processed on a rolling basis. Application fee: $30. Electronic applications accepted. *Expenses:* Tuition, state resident: full-time $4486; part-time $249.21 per credit hour. Tuition, nonresident: full-time $8972; part-time $498.42 per credit hour. Required fees: $72.62 per credit hour. *Financial support:* In 2009–10, 28 students received support, including 28 research assistantships with full tuition reimbursements available (averaging $7,280 per year). Financial award applicants required to submit FAFSA. *Unit head:* Dr. K. Dale Adkins, Chairperson, 309-298-1967. *Application contact:* Evelyn Hoing, Assistant Director of Graduate Studies, 309-298-1806, Fax: 309-298-2345, E-mail: grad-office@wiu.edu.

Western Kentucky University, Graduate Studies, College of Health and Human Services, Department of Physical Education and Recreation, Bowling Green, KY 42101. Offers physical education (MS); recreation (MS). Part-time and evening/weekend programs available. *Degree requirements:* For master's, comprehensive exam, thesis optional. *Entrance requirements:* For master's, GRE General Test, minimum GPA of 2.75. Additional exam requirements/recommendations for international students: Required—TOEFL (minimum score 555 paper-based; 213 computer-based; 79 iBT). *Expenses:* Tuition, state resident: full-time $4160; part-time $416 per credit hour. Tuition, nonresident: full-time $9550; part-time $506 per credit hour. Tuition and fees vary according to campus/location and reciprocity agreements. *Faculty research:* Orthopedic rehabilitation, fitness center coordination, heat acclimation, biomechanical and physiological parameters.

West Virginia University, Davis College of Agriculture, Forestry and Consumer Sciences, Division of Forestry, Program in Recreation, Parks and Tourism Resources, Morgantown, WV 26506. Offers MS. Part-time programs available. *Degree requirements:* For master's, thesis (for some programs). *Entrance requirements:* For master's, GRE, minimum GPA of 3.0. Additional exam requirements/recommendations for international students: Required—TOEFL. *Faculty research:* Attitudes, use patterns and impacts of outdoor recreation in West Virginia.

Winona State University, College of Education, Department of Educational Leadership, Winona, MN 55987-5838. Offers educational leadership (Ed S), including general superintendency, K-12 prinicpalship; general school leadership (MS); K-12 principalship (MS); outdoor education/adventure based leadership (MS); sports management (MS); teacher leadership (MS). *Accreditation:* NCATE. Part-time and evening/weekend programs available. *Degree requirements:* For master's, comprehensive exam, thesis optional; for Ed S, thesis optional. *Faculty research:* Financial equity, democratic practices in the classroom.

Wright State University, School of Graduate Studies, College of Education and Human Services, Department of Health, Physical Education, and Recreation, Dayton, OH 45435. Offers M Ed, MA. *Accreditation:* NCATE. *Degree requirements:* For master's, comprehensive exam, thesis (for some programs). *Entrance requirements:* For master's, GRE General Test, MAT. Additional exam requirements/recommendations for international students: Required—TOEFL. *Faculty research:* Motor learning, motor development, exercise physiology, adapted physical education.

Section 42
Physical Education and Kinesiology

This section contains a directory of institutions offering graduate work in physical education and kinesiology, followed by in-depth entries submitted by institutions that chose to prepare detailed program descriptions. Additional information about programs listed in the directory but not augmented by an in-depth entry may be obtained by writing directly to the dean of a graduate school or chair of a department at the address given in the directory.

For programs offering related work, see also in this book *Business Administration and Management, Education,* and *Sports Management.* In another guide in this series:

Graduate Programs in the Humanities, Arts & Social Sciences
See *Performing Arts*

CONTENTS

Program Directories

Athletic Training and Sports Medicine

Armstrong Atlantic State University, School of Graduate Studies, Program in Sports Medicine, Savannah, GA 31419-1997. Offers sports health sciences (MSSM). Part-time programs available. *Degree requirements:* For master's, comprehensive exam, thesis optional, project. *Entrance requirements:* For master's, GRE General Test, MAT, GMAT, minimum GPA of 2.5. Additional exam requirements/recommendations for international students: Required—TOEFL (minimum score 523 paper-based; 193 computer-based).

A.T. Still University of Health Sciences, Arizona School of Health Sciences, Mesa, AZ 85206. Offers advanced occupational therapy (MS); advanced physician assistant (MS); athletic training (MS); audiology (Au D); health sciences (DHSc); human movement (MS); occupational therapy (MS); physical therapy (MS, DPT); physician assistant (MS); transitional audiology (Au D); transitional physical therapy (DPT). *Accreditation:* AOTA (one or more programs are accredited); ASHA. Postbaccalaureate distance learning degree programs offered (no on-campus study). *Faculty:* 53 full-time (30 women), 205 part-time/adjunct (117 women). *Students:* 491 full-time (353 women), 1,251 part-time (874 women); includes 319 minority (70 African Americans, 11 American Indian/Alaska Native, 176 Asian Americans or Pacific Islanders, 62 Hispanic Americans), 3 international. Average age 31. 2,697 applicants, 22% accepted, 420 enrolled. In 2009, 225 master's, 523 doctorates awarded. *Degree requirements:* For master's, thesis (for some programs); for doctorate, thesis/dissertation (for some programs). *Entrance requirements:* For master's, GRE General Test; for doctorate, GRE, Evaluation of Practicing Audiologists Capabilities (Au D), Physical Therapy Evaluation Tool (DPT), current state licensure, master's degree or equivalent (Au D), minimum GPA of 2.7. Additional exam requirements/recommendations for international students: Recommended—TOEFL (minimum score 550 paper-based; 213 computer-based; 80 iBT). *Application deadline:* For fall admission, 2/1 priority date for domestic and international students. Applications are processed on a rolling basis. Application fee: $60. *Expenses:* Contact institution. *Financial support:* In 2009–10, 651 students received support. Federal Work-Study and scholarships/grants available. Financial award application deadline: 5/1; financial award applicants required to submit FAFSA. *Faculty research:* Adolescent health-related quality of life, clinical outcomes following sport related injury, pediatric concussion, shoulder stability and neuromuscular control, sport conditioning, exercise and sport psychology, geriatric exercise and wellness. Total annual research expenditures: $61,527. *Unit head:* Dr. Randy Danielsen, Dean, 480-219-6000, Fax: 480-219-6110, E-mail: rdanielsen@atsu.edu. *Application contact:* Donna Sparks, Associate Director for Admissions, 660-626-2237, Fax: 660-626-2969, E-mail: admissions@atsu.edu.

Barry University, School of Human Performance and Leisure Sciences, Programs in Movement Science, Specialization in Athletic Training, Miami Shores, FL 33161-6695. Offers MS. Part-time and evening/weekend programs available. *Degree requirements:* For master's, comprehensive exam, project or thesis. *Entrance requirements:* For master's, GRE General Test, minimum GPA of 3.0. Electronic applications accepted. *Faculty research:* Pain management, prevention and injury analysis, low energy static magnetic field therapy, upper extremity biomechanics.

Bloomsburg University of Pennsylvania, School of Graduate Studies, College of Liberal Arts, Department of Exercise Science and Athletics, Bloomsburg, PA 17815-1301. Offers clinical athletic training (MS); exercise science (MS). *Degree requirements:* For master's, thesis, practical clinical experience. *Entrance requirements:* For master's, GRE General Test or MAT, minimum QPA of 3.0. Additional exam requirements/recommendations for international students: Required—TOEFL (minimum score 550 paper-based; 213 computer-based; 79 iBT). Electronic applications accepted.

Boston University, College of Health and Rehabilitation Sciences—Sargent College, Department of Physical Therapy and Athletic Training, Boston, MA 02215. Offers physical therapy (DPT); rehabilitation sciences (D Sc). *Accreditation:* APTA (one or more programs are accredited). Postbaccalaureate distance learning degree programs offered (minimal on-campus study). *Faculty:* 13 full-time (10 women), 26 part-time/adjunct (12 women). *Students:* 142 full-time (116 women); includes 20 minority (1 African American, 14 Asian Americans or Pacific Islanders, 5 Hispanic Americans). Average age 26. 177 applicants, 46% accepted, 31 enrolled. In 2009, 93 doctorates awarded. *Degree requirements:* For doctorate, comprehensive exam (for some programs), thesis/dissertation (for some programs). *Entrance requirements:* For doctorate, GRE General Test, master's degree (for ScD), bachelor's degree (for DPT). Additional exam requirements/recommendations for international students: Required—TOEFL (minimum score 550 paper-based; 84 computer-based). *Application deadline:* For fall admission, 1/7 priority date for domestic students. Applications are processed on a rolling basis. Application fee: $70. Electronic applications accepted. *Expenses:* Tuition: Full-time $37,910; part-time $1184 per credit hour. Required fees: $386; $40 per semester. Part-time tuition and fees vary according to class time, course level, degree level and program. *Financial support:* In 2009–10, 125 students received support, including 14 fellowships (averaging $16,000 per year), 10 teaching assistantships with partial tuition reimbursements available (averaging $3,000 per year); career-related internships or fieldwork, Federal Work-Study, institutionally sponsored loans, scholarships/grants, and tuition waivers (partial) also available. Financial award application deadline: 4/15; financial award applicants required to submit FAFSA. *Faculty research:* Gait, balance, motor control, dynamical systems. *Unit head:* Dr. Wendy Coster, Chairman, 617-353-2720, E-mail: wjcoster@bu.edu. *Application contact:* Sharon Sankey, Director, Student Services, 617-353-2713, Fax: 617-353-7500, E-mail: ssankey@bu.edu.

Brigham Young University, Graduate Studies, College of Life Sciences, Department of Exercise Sciences, Provo, UT 84602. Offers athletic training (MS); exercise physiology (MS, PhD); exercise science (MS); health promotion (MS, PhD); physical medicine and rehabilitation (PhD). *Faculty:* 19 full-time (2 women). *Students:* 22 full-time (13 women), 41 part-time (19 women); includes 1 American Indian/Alaska Native, 3 Asian Americans or Pacific Islanders, 2 international. Average age 32. 30 applicants, 80% accepted, 22 enrolled. In 2009, 21 master's, 7 doctorates awarded. *Degree requirements:* For master's, thesis, oral defense; for doctorate, comprehensive exam, thesis/dissertation, oral defense, oral and written exams. *Entrance requirements:* For master's, GRE General Test, minimum GPA of 3.0 in last 60 hours of course work; for doctorate, GRE General Test, minimum GPA of 3.5 in last 60 hours of course work. Additional exam requirements/recommendations for international students: Required—TOEFL (minimum score 580 paper-based; 237 computer-based; 85 iBT), IELTS (minimum score 7). *Application deadline:* For fall admission, 2/1 for domestic and international students. Application fee: $50. Electronic applications accepted. *Expenses:* Tuition: Full-time $5580; part-time $301 per credit hour. Tuition and fees vary according to student's religious affiliation. *Financial support:* In 2009–10, 46 students received support, including 15 research assistantships with full and partial tuition reimbursements available (averaging $5,615 per year), 34 teaching assistantships with full and partial tuition reimbursements available (averaging $10,106 per year); fellowships, career-related internships or fieldwork, institutionally sponsored loans, tuition waivers (full and partial), and unspecified assistantships also available. Financial award application deadline: 3/1. *Faculty research:* Injury prevention and rehabilitation, human skeletal muscle adaptation, cardiovascular health and fitness, lifestyle modification and health promotion. Total annual research expenditures: $18,096. *Unit head:* Dr. Larry Hall, Chair, 801-422-7303, Fax: 801-422-0543, E-mail: larry_hall@byu.edu. *Application contact:* Dr. Jeffrey Brent Feland, Graduate Coordinator, 801-422-1182, Fax: 801-422-0543, E-mail: brent_feland@byu.edu.

California Baptist University, Program in Athletic Training, Riverside, CA 92504-3206. Offers MS. *Faculty:* 1 (woman) full-time. *Students:* 22 full-time (13 women), 1 (woman) part-time; includes 6 minority (2 African Americans, 2 Asian Americans or Pacific Islanders, 2 Hispanic Americans), 3 international. 31 applicants, 45% accepted, 10 enrolled. In 2009, 8 master's awarded. *Entrance requirements:* For master's, minimum GPA of 2.5, 7 classes of prerequisite coursework. Additional exam requirements/recommendations for international students: Required—TOEFL (minimum score 575 paper-based; 230 computer-based; 89 iBT). *Application deadline:* For fall admission, 8/1 priority date for domestic students, 7/1 for international students; for spring admission, 12/1 priority date for domestic students, 10/15 for international students. Applications are processed on a rolling basis. Application fee: $45. Electronic applica-

tions accepted. *Expenses:* Tuition: Full-time $8352; part-time $464 per semester hour. Required fees: $125 per semester. Tuition and fees vary according to course load, campus/location and program. *Financial support:* Federal Work-Study and scholarships/grants available. Financial award applicants required to submit FAFSA. *Unit head:* Dr. Nicole MacDonald, Director, 951-343-4379. *Application contact:* Gail Ronveaux, Dean of Graduate Enrollment, 951-343-5045, Fax: 951-343-5095, E-mail: graduateadmissions@calbaptist.edu.

California State University, Long Beach, Graduate Studies, College of Health and Human Services, Department of Kinesiology, Long Beach, CA 90840. Offers adapted physical education (MA); coaching and student athlete development (MA); exercise physiology and nutrition (MS); exercise science (MS); individualized studies (MA); kinesiology (MA); pedagogical studies (MA); sport and exercise psychology (MS); sport management (MA); sports medicine and injury studies (MS). Part-time programs available. *Faculty:* 9 full-time (6 women), 1 part-time/adjunct (0 women). *Students:* 34 full-time (22 women), 23 part-time (14 women); includes 22 minority (4 African Americans, 2 American Indian/Alaska Native, 8 Asian Americans or Pacific Islanders, 8 Hispanic Americans), 9 international. Average age 27. 143 applicants, 59% accepted, 20 enrolled. *Degree requirements:* For master's, oral and written comprehensive exams or thesis. *Entrance requirements:* For master's, GRE General Test, minimum GPA of 2.75 during previous 2 years of course work. *Application deadline:* For fall admission, 6/1 for domestic students. Applications are processed on a rolling basis. Application fee: $55. Electronic applications accepted. *Expenses:* Required fees: $1802 per semester. Part-time tuition and fees vary according to course load. *Financial support:* Federal Work-Study, institutionally sponsored loans, and scholarships/grants available. Financial award application deadline: 3/2. *Faculty research:* Pulmonary functioning, feedback and practice structure, strength training, history and politics of sports, special population research issues. *Unit head:* Dr. Sharon R. Guthrie, Chair, 562-985-7487, Fax: 562-985-8067, E-mail: guthrie@csulb.edu. *Application contact:* Dr. Grant Hill, Graduate Advisor, 562-985-8856, Fax: 562-985-8067, E-mail: ghill@csulb.edu.

California University of Pennsylvania, School of Graduate Studies and Research, School of Education, Department of Athletic Training, California, PA 15419-1394. Offers athletic training (MS); exercise science and health promotion (MS), including fitness and wellness, performance enhancement and injury prevention, rehabilitation sciences, sport management, sport psychology. Summer admission only. *Degree requirements:* For master's, comprehensive exam, thesis. *Entrance requirements:* For master's, minimum GPA of 3.0. Additional exam requirements/recommendations for international students: Required—TOEFL (minimum score 550 paper-based; 213 computer-based; 80 iBT). *Faculty research:* Exercise physiology, pedagogy, athletic training, biomechanical engineering, case studies in injury and athletic medicine.

Eastern Michigan University, Graduate School, College of Health and Human Services, School of Health Promotion and Human Performance, Programs in Exercise Physiology, Ypsilanti, MI 48197. Offers exercise physiology (MS); sports medicine-biomechanics (MS); sports medicine-corporate adult fitness (MS); sports medicine-exercise physiology (MS). Part-time and evening/weekend programs available. *Students:* 10 full-time (5 women), 32 part-time (10 women); includes 6 minority (2 African Americans, 4 Hispanic Americans), 2 international. Average age 29. In 2009, 12 master's awarded. *Degree requirements:* For master's, comprehensive exam, thesis or 450-hour internship. *Entrance requirements:* Additional exam requirements/recommendations for international students: Required—TOEFL. *Application deadline:* For fall admission, 8/1 for domestic students, 5/1 for international students; for winter admission, 12/1 for domestic students, 10/1 for international students; for spring admission, 3/15 for domestic students, 3/1 for international students. Application fee: $35. Tuition and fees vary according to course level. *Unit head:* Dr. Steve McGregor, Program Coordinator, 734-487-0090, Fax: 734-487-2024, E-mail: stephen.mcgregor@emich.edu. *Application contact:* Dr. Steve McGregor, Program Coordinator, 734-487-0090, Fax: 734-487-2024, E-mail: stephen.mcgregor@emich.edu.

Eastern Michigan University, Graduate School, College of Health and Human Services, School of Health Promotion and Human Performance, Programs in Orthotics and Prosthetics, Ypsilanti, MI 48197. Offers orthotics (Graduate Certificate); orthotics/prosthetics (MS); prosthetics (Graduate Certificate). *Students:* 30 full-time (11 women), 4 part-time (3 women); includes 3 minority (2 African Americans, 1 Asian American or Pacific Islander). Average age 29. In 2009, 14 master's, 3 other advanced degrees awarded. *Degree requirements:* For master's, comprehensive exam, thesis or project, 500 hours of clinicals. *Entrance requirements:* For master's, MAT. Additional exam requirements/recommendations for international students: Required—TOEFL. *Application deadline:* For fall admission, 5/1 for domestic and international students. Applications are processed on a rolling basis. Application fee: $35. Tuition and fees vary according to course level. *Financial support:* Fellowships, research assistantships with full tuition reimbursements, teaching assistantships with full tuition reimbursements, career-related internships or fieldwork, Federal Work-Study, institutionally sponsored loans, scholarships/grants, tuition waivers (partial), and unspecified assistantships available. Support available to part-time students. Financial award applicants required to submit FAFSA. *Unit head:* Robert Rhodes, Program Coordinator, 734-487-7120 Ext. 2724, Fax: 734-487-2024, E-mail: rrhodes4@emich.edu. *Application contact:* Robert Rhodes, Program Coordinator, 734-487-7120 Ext. 2724, Fax: 734-487-2024, E-mail: rrhodes4@emich.edu.

Florida International University, College of Education, Department of Health, Physical Education, and Recreation, Program in Exercise and Sports Science, Miami, FL 33199. Offers advanced athletic injury training/sports medicine (MS); strength and conditioning (MS). *Accreditation:* NCATE. Part-time and evening/weekend programs available. *Entrance requirements:* Additional exam requirements/recommendations for international students: Required—TOEFL (minimum score 550 paper-based; 213 computer-based; 80 iBT), IELTS (minimum score 6.3). Electronic applications accepted. *Expenses:* Tuition, state resident: full-time $8008; part-time $4004 per year. Tuition, nonresident: full-time $20,104; part-time $10,052 per year. Required fees: $298; $149 per term. *Faculty research:* Strength and conditioning, women in athletic training, celiac disease.

Florida International University, College of Nursing and Health Sciences, Department of Athletic Training, Miami, FL 33199. Offers MS. *Faculty:* 1 (woman) full-time. *Students:* 16 full-time (10 women), 2 part-time (both women); includes 14 minority (4 African Americans, 10 Hispanic Americans), 1 international. Average age 25. 32 applicants, 0% accepted, 0 enrolled. In 2009, 7 master's awarded. *Degree requirements:* For master's, 800 clinical education hours. *Entrance requirements:* For master's, bachelor's degree from accredited institution; minimum GPA of 3.0 overall and in last 60 credits of upper-division courses of the bachelor's degree; three letters of recommendation; resume; personal statement of professional/educational goals. Additional exam requirements/recommendations for international students: Required—TOEFL (minimum score 550 paper-based; 80 iBT). *Application deadline:* For fall admission, 2/15 for domestic and international students. Application fee: $30. Electronic applications accepted. *Expenses:* Contact institution. *Financial support:* In 2009–10, 1 student received support. Institutionally sponsored loans and scholarships/grants available. Financial award application deadline: 3/1; financial award applicants required to submit FAFSA. *Faculty research:* Continuing professional education, leadership styles and outcomes, professionalism and professional Image. *Unit head:* Dr. Jennifer Doherty-Restrepo, Director, 305-348-3398, Fax: 305-348-2125, E-mail: dohertyj@fiu.edu. *Application contact:* Nanett Rojas, Assistant Director of Graduate Admissions, 305-348-7441, Fax: 305-348-7442, E-mail: gradadm@fiu.edu.

Georgia State University, College of Education, Department of Kinesiology and Health, Program in Sports Medicine, Atlanta, GA 30302-3083. Offers MS. *Degree requirements:* For master's, comprehensive exam. *Entrance requirements:* For master's, GRE General Test, minimum GPA of 2.5. *Faculty research:* Athletic training.

Humboldt State University, Graduate Studies, College of Professional Studies, Department of Kinesiology, Arcata, CA 95521-8299. Offers athletic training education (MS); exercise

science/wellness management (MS); pre-physical therapy (MS); teaching/coaching (MS). *Students:* 24 full-time (13 women), 8 part-time (5 women); includes 5 minority (2 African Americans, 1 American Indian/Alaska Native, 2 Hispanic Americans). Average age 30. 25 applicants, 80% accepted, 15 enrolled. In 2009, 4 master's awarded. *Degree requirements:* For master's, thesis or alternative. *Entrance requirements:* For master's, GMAT, minimum GPA of 2.5. Additional exam requirements/recommendations for international students: Required—TOEFL. *Application deadline:* For fall admission, 6/1 for domestic students; for spring admission, 12/2 for domestic students. Applications are processed on a rolling basis. Application fee: $55. *Expenses:* Tuition, nonresident: full-time $8928. Required fees: $6102. Tuition and fees vary according to program. *Financial support:* Teaching assistantships, career-related internships or fieldwork, Federal Work-Study, and institutionally sponsored loans available. Financial award application deadline: 3/1; financial award applicants required to submit FAFSA. *Faculty research:* Human performance, adapted physical education, physical therapy. *Unit head:* Dr. Kathy Munoz, Chair, 707-826-3840, Fax: 707-826-5451, E-mail: kdm1@humboldt.edu. *Application contact:* Dr. T. K. Koesterer, Coordinator, 707-826-5967, Fax: 707-826-5451, E-mail: tjk17@humboldt.edu.

Indiana State University, School of Graduate Studies, College of Nursing, Health and Human Services, Department of Athletic Training, Terre Haute, IN 47809. Offers MS. *Degree requirements:* For master's, thesis or alternative. *Entrance requirements:* For master's, GRE General Test. Electronic applications accepted.

Indiana University Bloomington, School of Health, Physical Education and Recreation, Department of Kinesiology, Bloomington, IN 47405-7000. Offers adapted physical education (MS); applied sport science (MS); athletic administration/sport management (MS); athletic training (MS); biomechanics (MS); ergonomics (MS); exercise physiology (MS); fitness management (MS); human performance (PhD); motor learning/control (MS). Part-time programs available. *Faculty:* 28 full-time (11 women). *Students:* 132 full-time (55 women), 37 part-time (7 women); includes 16 minority (13 African Americans, 1 Asian American or Pacific Islander, 2 Hispanic Americans), 29 international. Average age 28. 179 applicants, 60% accepted, 72 enrolled. In 2009, 59 master's awarded. Terminal master's awarded for partial completion of doctoral program. *Degree requirements:* For master's, thesis optional; for doctorate, variable foreign language requirement, thesis/dissertation. *Entrance requirements:* For master's, GRE General Test, minimum GPA of 2.8; for doctorate, GRE General Test, minimum graduate GPA of 3.5, undergraduate 3.0. *Application deadline:* For fall admission, 1/1 for international students; for spring admission, 9/1 for international students. Applications are processed on a rolling basis. Application fee: $55 ($65 for international students). *Financial support:* In 2009–10, 71 students received support, including 9 fellowships (averaging $1,400 per year), 28 research assistantships with full tuition reimbursements available (averaging $10,131 per year), 38 teaching assistantships with full tuition reimbursements available (averaging $10,390 per year); career-related internships or fieldwork, Federal Work-Study, institutionally sponsored loans, scholarships/grants, tuition waivers (partial), and fee remissions also available. Financial award application deadline: 3/1. *Faculty research:* Exercise physiology and biochemistry, sports biomechanics, human motor control, adaptation of fitness and exercise to special populations. *Unit head:* Dr. Donetta Cothran, Chairperson, 812-855-3114. *Application contact:* Program Office, 812-855-5523, Fax: 812-855-9417, E-mail: kines@indiana.edu.

Inter American University of Puerto Rico, Metropolitan Campus, Graduate Programs, Program in Physical Education, San Juan, PR 00919-1293. Offers teaching of physical education (MA); training and sport performance (MA). *Degree requirements:* For master's, comprehensive exam. *Entrance requirements:* For master's, GRE or EXADEP, interview. Electronic applications accepted.

Kent State University, Graduate School of Education, Health, and Human Services, School of Health Sciences, Program in Exercise, Leisure and Sport, Kent, OH 44242-0001. Offers athletic training (MA); exercise physiology (MA). *Faculty:* 6 full-time (3 women). *Students:* 10 full-time (5 women), 1 (woman) part-time; includes 1 Asian American or Pacific Islander. 29 applicants, 66% accepted. In 2009, 7 master's awarded. *Financial support:* In 2009–10, 8 research assistantships (averaging $8,313 per year) were awarded; Federal Work-Study, scholarships/grants, and unspecified assistantships also available. *Unit head:* Dr. Lynne B. Rowan, Interim Director, 330-672-9785, E-mail: lrowan@kent.edu. *Application contact:* Nancy Miller, Academic Program Coordinator, Office of Graduate Student Services, 330-672-2576, Fax: 330-672-9162, E-mail: ogs@kent.edu.

Lenoir-Rhyne University, Graduate Programs, School of Health, Exercise and Sport Science, Hickory, NC 28601. Offers athletic training (MS).

Long Island University, Brooklyn Campus, School of Health Professions, Division of Sports Sciences, Brooklyn, NY 11201-8423. Offers adapted physical education (MS); athletic training and sports sciences (MS); exercise physiology (MS); health sciences (MS). Part-time and evening/weekend programs available. *Entrance requirements:* For master's, 2 letters of recommendation. Additional exam requirements/recommendations for international students: Required—TOEFL (minimum score 500 paper-based; 173 computer-based). Electronic applications accepted.

Montana State University Billings, College of Allied Health Professions, Department of Health and Human Performance, Program in Athletic Training, Billings, MT 59101-0298. Offers MS.

Ohio University, Graduate College, College of Health and Human Services, School of Recreation and Sport Sciences, Program in Athletic Training, Athens, OH 45701-2979. Offers MS. *Faculty:* 4 full-time (2 women). *Students:* 29 full-time (16 women); includes 1 minority (Hispanic American). 13 applicants, 31% accepted, 4 enrolled. In 2009, 15 master's awarded. *Entrance requirements:* For master's, GRE. Additional exam requirements/recommendations for international students: Required—TOEFL (minimum score 550 paper-based; 80 iBT) or IELTS Academic (minimum score 7.5). Application fee: $50 ($55 for international students). *Expenses:* Tuition, state resident: full-time $7839; part-time $323 per quarter hour. Tuition, nonresident: full-time $15,831; part-time $654 per quarter hour. Required fees: $2931. *Financial support:* In 2009–10, teaching assistantships with full tuition reimbursements (averaging $9,000 per year); Federal Work-Study and unspecified assistantships also available. Financial award application deadline: 2/15. *Faculty research:* Athletic training, heart, injuries, health, muscles, exercise, sport. *Unit head:* Dr. Chad Starkey, Coordinator, 740-593-1217, Fax: 740-593-0284, E-mail: starkeyc@ohio.edu. *Application contact:* Graduate Admissions, 740-593-2800, Fax: 740-593-4625, E-mail: graduate@ohio.edu.

Old Dominion University, Darden College of Education, Program in Physical Education, Athletic Training Emphasis, Norfolk, VA 23529. Offers MS Ed. Part-time programs available. *Faculty:* 1 (woman) full-time. *Students:* 23 full-time (18 women); includes 2 minority (1 African American, 1 Asian American or Pacific Islander). Average age 23. 40 applicants, 33% accepted, 3 enrolled. In 2009, 15 master's awarded. *Degree requirements:* For master's, comprehensive exam, thesis or research project. *Entrance requirements:* For master's, GRE, minimum GPA of 3.0. Additional exam requirements/recommendations for international students: Required—TOEFL (minimum score 500 paper-based; 200 computer-based). *Application deadline:* For spring admission, 2/1 priority date for domestic and international students. Applications are processed on a rolling basis. Application fee: $40. Electronic applications accepted. *Expenses:* Tuition, state resident: full-time $8112; part-time $338 per credit. Tuition, nonresident: full-time $20,256; part-time $844 per credit. Required fees: $119 per semester. One-time fee: $50. *Financial support:* In 2009–10, 23 research assistantships with partial tuition reimbursements (averaging $12,000 per year), 1 teaching assistantship with partial tuition reimbursement (averaging $9,000 per year) were awarded; career-related internships or fieldwork, scholarships/grants, and unspecified assistantships also available. Financial award application deadline: 4/15; financial award applicants required to submit FAFSA. *Faculty research:* ACL injury prevention, lower extremity biomechanical program satisfaction, manual therapy, evidence based practice in education. *Unit head:* Dr. Bonnie L. Van Lunen, Graduate Program Director, 757-683-3516, Fax: 757-683-4270, E-mail: bvanlune@odu.edu. *Application contact:* Dr. Bonnie L. Van Lunen, Graduate Program Director, 757-683-3516, Fax: 757-683-4270, E-mail: bvanlune@odu.edu.

Plymouth State University, College of Graduate Studies, Graduate Studies in Education, Program in Athletic Training, Plymouth, NH 03264-1595. Offers M Ed, MS. Part-time and evening/weekend programs available. *Entrance requirements:* For master's, MAT, GRE General Test.

Saint Louis University, Graduate School, Doisy College of Health Sciences, Department of Physical Therapy, St. Louis, MO 63103-2097. Offers athletic training (MAT); physical therapy (DPT). *Accreditation:* APTA. Part-time programs available. *Entrance requirements:* Additional exam requirements/recommendations for international students: Required—TOEFL (minimum score 525 paper-based; 194 computer-based; 55 iBT). Electronic applications accepted. *Faculty research:* Patellofemoral pain and associated risk factors; prevalence of disordered eating in physical therapy students; effects of selected interventions for children with cerebral palsy on gait and posture: hippotherapy, ankle strengthening, supported treadmill training, spirituality in physical therapy/patient care, risk factors for exercise-related leg pain in running athletes.

Seton Hall University, School of Health and Medical Sciences, Program in Athletic Training, South Orange, NJ 07079-2697. Offers MS. *Degree requirements:* For master's, research project. *Entrance requirements:* Additional exam requirements/recommendations for international students: Required—TOEFL. Electronic applications accepted. *Faculty research:* Electrotherapy.

Shenandoah University, School of Health Professions, Division of Athletic Training, Winchester, VA 22601-5195. Offers MS. *Faculty:* 2 full-time (1 woman), 1 part-time/adjunct (0 women). *Students:* 18 full-time (11 women), 4 part-time (all women); includes 1 minority (American Indian/Alaska Native), 1 international. Average age 26. 17 applicants, 100% accepted, 11 enrolled. In 2009, 9 master's awarded. *Degree requirements:* For master's, clinical field experience. *Entrance requirements:* For master's, SAT or GRE General Test, minimum GPA of 2.8, interview, athletic experience, 3 letters of recommendation. Additional exam requirements/recommendations for international students: Required—TOEFL (minimum score 550 paper-based; 213 computer-based; 79 iBT), IELTS (minimum score 6.5). *Application deadline:* Applications are processed on a rolling basis. Application fee: $30. Electronic applications accepted. *Expenses:* Contact institution. *Financial support:* Application deadline: 3/15. *Unit head:* Dr. Rose A. Schmieg, Director, 540-665-5534, Fax: 540-545-7387, E-mail: rschmieg@su.edu. *Application contact:* David Anthony, Dean of Admissions, 540-665-4581, Fax: 540-665-4627, E-mail: admit@su.edu.

Springfield College, Graduate Programs, Programs in Exercise Science and Sport Studies, Springfield, MA 01109-3797. Offers athletic training (MS); exercise physiology (MS), including clinical exercise physiology, science and research; exercise science and sport studies (PhD); health promotion and disease prevention (MS); sport psychology (MS). Part-time programs available. Terminal master's awarded for partial completion of doctoral program. *Degree requirements:* For master's, comprehensive exam, research project or thesis; for doctorate, comprehensive exam, thesis/dissertation. *Entrance requirements:* For master's and doctorate, GRE General Test. Additional exam requirements/recommendations for international students: Required—TOEFL (minimum score 550 paper-based; 213 computer-based). Electronic applications accepted. *Expenses:* Tuition: Full-time $19,800; part-time $825 per credit hour. Required fees: $150.

Stephen F. Austin State University, Graduate School, College of Education, Department of Kinesiology and Health Science, Nacogdoches, TX 75962. Offers athletic training (MS); kinesiology (M Ed). *Degree requirements:* For master's, comprehensive exam. *Entrance requirements:* For master's, GRE General Test. Additional exam requirements/recommendations for international students: Required—TOEFL.

Texas State University–San Marcos, Graduate School, College of Education, Department of Health and Human Performance, Program in Athletic Training, San Marcos, TX 78666. Offers MS. *Faculty:* 2 full-time (1 woman). *Students:* 10 full-time (4 women), 7 part-time (1 woman); includes 6 minority (1 African American, 5 Hispanic Americans). Average age 24. 9 applicants, 89% accepted, 6 enrolled. In 2009, 1 master's awarded. *Degree requirements:* For master's, comprehensive exam, thesis optional. *Entrance requirements:* For master's, athletic trainer certification or eligibility for certification exam. Additional exam requirements/recommendations for international students: Required—TOEFL (minimum score 550 paper-based; 213 computer-based). Application fee: $40 ($90 for international students). *Expenses:* Tuition, state resident: full-time $5784; part-time $241 per credit hour. Tuition, nonresident: full-time $13,224; part-time $551 per credit hour. Required fees: $1728; $48 per credit hour. $306. Tuition and fees vary according to course load. *Financial support:* In 2009–10, 16 students received support, including 9 research assistantships (averaging $6,102 per year), 8 teaching assistantships (averaging $5,913 per year). *Unit head:* Dr. Jack Ransone, Coordinator, 512-245-8176, E-mail: jr41@txstate.edu. *Application contact:* Dr. John Walker, Head, 512-245-2561, Fax: 512-245-8678, E-mail: jw18@txstate.edu.

Texas Tech University Health Sciences Center, School of Allied Health Sciences, Program in Athletic Training, Lubbock, TX 79430. Offers MAT. *Faculty:* 5 full-time (2 women). *Students:* 46 full-time (21 women); includes 18 minority (5 African Americans, 2 American Indian/Alaska Native, 2 Asian Americans or Pacific Islanders, 9 Hispanic Americans), 1 international. Average age 29. 50 applicants, 52% accepted, 26 enrolled. In 2009, 20 master's awarded. *Entrance requirements:* Additional exam requirements/recommendations for international students: Required—TOEFL, IELTS. *Application deadline:* For fall admission, 10/15 priority date for domestic students; for spring admission, 2/1 priority date for domestic students. Application fee: $35. Electronic applications accepted. *Financial support:* Career-related internships or fieldwork, institutionally sponsored loans, and scholarships/grants available. Financial award applicants required to submit FAFSA. *Unit head:* Dr. Steve Sawyer, Chair, 806-743-3226, Fax: 806-743-3249, E-mail: steve.sawyer@ttuhsc.edu. *Application contact:* Jeri Moravcik, Assistant Director of Admissions and Student Affairs, 806-743-3220, Fax: 806-743-2994, E-mail: jeri.moravcik@ttuhsc.edu.

United States Sports Academy, Graduate Programs, Program in Sports Medicine, Daphne, AL 36526-7055. Offers MSS. Part-time programs available. Postbaccalaureate distance learning degree programs offered (no on-campus study). *Degree requirements:* For master's, comprehensive exam, thesis optional. *Entrance requirements:* For master's, GRE General Test, GMAT, or MAT, minimum GPA of 2.5, 3 letters of recommendation, resume. Additional exam requirements/recommendations for international students: Required—TOEFL (minimum score 500 paper-based; 213 computer-based). *Application deadline:* Applications are processed on a rolling basis. Application fee: $50 ($125 for international students). Electronic applications accepted. *Financial support:* Career-related internships or fieldwork, Federal Work-Study, scholarships/grants, and service assistantships available. Support available to part-time students. Financial award application deadline: 8/15; financial award applicants required to submit FAFSA. *Faculty research:* Psychiatric aspects of injury rehabilitation, geriatric exercises and mobility. *Unit head:* Dr. Enrico Esposito, Chair, 251-626-3303 Ext. 7155, Fax: 251-626-1149, E-mail: esposito@ussa.edu. *Application contact:* Craig T. Bogar, Assistant Dean of Student Services, 251-626-3303 Ext. 7147, Fax: 251-625-1035, E-mail: cbogar@ussa.edu.

Universidad del Turabo, Graduate Programs, Programs in Education, Program in Athletic Training, Gurabo, PR 00778-3030. Offers MPHE. *Students:* 21 full-time (5 women), 12 part-time (7 women); includes 30 Hispanic Americans. Average age 29. 16 applicants, 94% accepted, 12 enrolled. In 2009, 13 master's awarded. *Unit head:* Angela Candelario, Dean, 787-743-7979 Ext. 4126. *Application contact:* Virginia Gonzalez, Admissions Officer, 787-746-3009.

The University of Findlay, Graduate and Professional Studies, College of Health Professions, Program in Athletic Training, Findlay, OH 45840-3653. Offers MAT. *Entrance requirements:* For master's, minimum GPA of 3.0, 75 hours of supervised clinical experience, 3 letters of recommendation. Additional exam requirements/recommendations for international students:

Athletic Training and Sports Medicine

The University of Findlay (continued)
Required—TOEFL (minimum score 550 paper-based; 213 computer-based; 80 iBT). Electronic applications accepted.

University of Florida, Graduate School, College of Health and Human Performance, Department of Applied Physiology and Kinesiology, Gainesville, FL 32611. Offers athletic training/sport medicine (MS, PhD); biomechanics (MS, PhD); clinical exercise physiology (MS); exercise physiology (MS, PhD); health and human performance (PhD); human performance (MS); motor learning/control (MS, PhD); sport and exercise psychology (MS). *Degree requirements:* For doctorate, thesis/dissertation. *Entrance requirements:* For doctorate, GRE General Test. Electronic applications accepted.

University of Miami, Graduate School, School of Education, Department of Exercise and Sport Sciences, Program in Sports Medicine, Coral Gables, FL 33124. Offers MS Ed. Part-time and evening/weekend programs available. *Students:* 2 full-time (1 woman), 1 part-time (0 women); includes 2 minority (1 African American, 1 Hispanic American). Average age 23. 4 applicants, 75% accepted, 3 enrolled. In 2009, 2 master's awarded. *Degree requirements:* For master's, thesis optional, special project. *Entrance requirements:* For master's, GRE General Test. Additional exam requirements/recommendations for international students: Required—TOEFL (minimum score 550 paper-based; 80 iBT); Recommended—IELTS (minimum score 6.5). *Application deadline:* Applications are processed on a rolling basis. Application fee: $65. Electronic applications accepted. *Financial support:* In 2009–10, 2 students received support. Career-related internships or fieldwork and institutionally sponsored loans available. Financial award application deadline: 3/1; financial award applicants required to submit FAFSA. *Faculty research:* Care, prevention, and treatment of athletic injuries. *Unit head:* Dr. Arlette Perry, Department Chairperson, 305-284-3025, Fax: 305-284-5168, E-mail: aperry@miami.edu. *Application contact:* Marissa Stevenson-Jacobs, Graduate Admissions Coordinator, 305-284-2167, Fax: 305-284-3003, E-mail: mstevenson@miami.edu.

The University of North Carolina at Chapel Hill, Graduate School, College of Arts and Sciences, Department of Exercise and Sport Science, Chapel Hill, NC 27599. Offers athletic training (MA); exercise physiology (MA); sport administration (MA). *Degree requirements:* For master's, comprehensive exam, thesis. *Entrance requirements:* For master's, GRE General Test, minimum GPA of 3.0. Additional exam requirements/recommendations for international students: Required—TOEFL (minimum score 550 paper-based). Electronic applications accepted. *Faculty research:* Mild head injury in sport, endocrine system's response to exercise, obesity and children, effect of aerobic exercise on cerebral bloodflow in elderly population.

University of Pittsburgh, School of Health and Rehabilitation Sciences, Master's Programs in Health and Rehabilitation Sciences, Pittsburgh, PA 15260. Offers health and rehabilitation sciences (MS), including clinical dietetics and nutrition, health care supervision and management, health information systems, occupational therapy, physical therapy, rehabilitation counseling, rehabilitation science and technology, sports medicine, wellness and human performance. *Accreditation:* APTA. Part-time and evening/weekend programs available. *Faculty:* 30 full-time (14 women), 4 part-time/adjunct (3 women). *Students:* 81 full-time (47 women), 54 part-time (27 women); includes 10 minority (6 African Americans, 4 Asian Americans or Pacific Islanders), 44 international. Average age 29. 326 applicants, 65% accepted, 130 enrolled. In 2009, 93 master's awarded. *Degree requirements:* For master's, comprehensive exam (for some programs), thesis optional. *Entrance requirements:* For master's, minimum GPA of 3.0. Additional exam requirements/recommendations for international students: Required—TOEFL, IELTS. *Application deadline:* For fall admission, 1/31 for international students; for spring admission, 7/31 for international students. Applications are processed on a rolling basis. Application fee: $50. Electronic applications accepted. *Expenses:* Contact institution. *Financial support:* In 2009–10, 3 research assistantships with full tuition reimbursements (averaging $18,450 per year) were awarded; teaching assistantships, Federal Work-Study, institutionally sponsored loans, traineeships, and unspecified assistantships also available. Financial award applicants required to submit FAFSA. *Faculty research:* Assistive technology, seating and wheeled mobility, cellular neurophysiology, low back syndrome, augmentative communication. Total annual research expenditures: $6.5 million. *Unit head:* Dr. Clifford E. Brubaker, Dean, 412-383-6560, Fax: 412-383-6535, E-mail: cliffb@pitt.edu. *Application contact:* Shameem Gangjee, Director of Admissions, 412-383-6558, Fax: 412-383-6535, E-mail: admissions@shrs.pitt.edu.

The University of Tennessee, Graduate School, College of Education, Health and Human Sciences, Department of Exercise, Sport, and Leisure Studies, Program in Exercise Science, Knoxville, TN 37996. Offers biomechanics/sports medicine (MS, PhD); exercise physiology (MS, PhD). *Accreditation:* CEPH (one or more programs are accredited). Part-time programs available. *Degree requirements:* For master's, thesis optional. *Entrance requirements:* For master's, minimum GPA of 2.7. Additional exam requirements/recommendations for international students: Required—TOEFL. Electronic applications accepted. *Expenses:* Tuition, state resident: full-time $6826; part-time $380 per semester hour. Tuition, nonresident: full-time $21,844; part-time $1147 per semester hour. Tuition and fees vary according to program.

The University of Tennessee at Chattanooga, Graduate School, College of Health, Education and Professional Studies, Department of Health and Human Performance, Program in Athletic Training, Chattanooga, TN 37403. Offers MSAT. *Faculty:* 4 full-time (1 woman). *Students:* 26 full-time (19 women); includes 3 minority (1 African American, 1 Asian American or Pacific Islander, 1 Hispanic American), 1 international. Average age 25. 1 applicant, 100% accepted, 0 enrolled. *Entrance requirements:* For master's, GRE. Additional exam requirements/recommendations for international students: Required—TOEFL (minimum score 550 paper-based; 213 computer-based; 79 iBT), IELTS (minimum score 6). *Application deadline:* For fall admission, 8/1 for domestic students, 6/1 for international students; for spring admission, 12/1 for domestic students, 10/1 for international students. Applications are processed on a rolling basis. Application fee: $35. Electronic applications accepted. *Expenses:* Tuition, state resident: full-time $5404; part-time $300 per credit hour. Tuition, nonresident: full-time $16,702; part-time $928 per credit hour. Required fees: $1150; $130 per credit hour. *Financial support:* In 2009–10, 7 research assistantships with full and partial tuition reimbursements (averaging $5,500 per year) were awarded; career-related internships or fieldwork, scholarships/grants, and unspecified assistantships also available. Support available to part-time students. *Faculty research:* Ankle biomechanics, lumbar spine injury prevention and mechanics, therapeutic exercise, clinical prediction rules, ethical considerations of athletic training. *Unit head:* Dr. Gregory Heath, Head, 423-425-4432, Fax: 423-425-4457, E-mail: gatp@utc.edu. *Application contact:* Dr. Stephanie Bellar, Dean of Graduate Studies, 423-425-4666, Fax: 423-425-5223, E-mail: stephanie-bellar@utc.edu.

The University of West Alabama, School of Graduate Studies, College of Education, Department of Physical Education and Athletic Training, Livingston, AL 35470. Offers physical education (M Ed, MAT). Part-time programs available. *Entrance requirements:* For master's, GRE General Test, MAT, minimum GPA of 2.75.

University of Wisconsin–La Crosse, Office of University Graduate Studies, College of Science and Health, Department of Exercise and Sport Science, Program in Human Performance, La Crosse, WI 54601-3742. Offers athletic training (MS); human performance (MS). Part-time and evening/weekend programs available. *Students:* 17 full-time (8 women), 3 part-time (1 woman). Average age 24. 24 applicants, 67% accepted, 9 enrolled. In 2009, 11 master's awarded. *Degree requirements:* For master's, comprehensive exam (for some programs), thesis optional. *Entrance requirements:* For master's, GRE, course work in anatomy, physiology, biomechanics, and exercise physiology. Additional exam requirements/recommendations for international students: Required—TOEFL (minimum score 550 paper-based; 213 computer-based; 79 iBT). *Application deadline:* For fall admission, 2/1 priority date for domestic students. Application fee: $56. Electronic applications accepted. *Financial support:* Research assistantships, career-related internships or fieldwork, Federal Work-Study, institutionally sponsored loans, scholarships/grants, health care benefits, tuition waivers (full and partial), unspecified assistantships, and grant-funded positions available. Support available to part-time students. Financial award application deadline: 3/15; financial award applicants required to submit FAFSA. *Unit head:* Dr. Glenn Wright, Director, 608-785-8689, Fax: 608-785-6520, E-mail: wright.glen@uwlax.edu. *Application contact:* Kathryn Kiefer, Director of Admissions, 608-785-8939, E-mail: admissions@uwlax.edu.

Virginia Commonwealth University, Graduate School, School of Education, Department of Health and Human Performance, Program in Athletic Training, Richmond, VA 23284-9005. Offers MSAT.

Weber State University, Jerry and Vickie Moyes College of Education, Program in Athletic Training, Ogden, UT 84408-1001. Offers MSAT. Part-time programs available. *Degree requirements:* For master's, thesis. *Entrance requirements:* For master's, GRE (if GPA less than 3.0), physical, immunizations. Additional exam requirements/recommendations for international students: Required—TOEFL (minimum score 550 paper-based; 213 computer-based). *Faculty research:* Pedagogy, heat illness, electrical stimulation.

Western Michigan University, Graduate College, College of Education, Department of Health, Physical Education and Recreation, Kalamazoo, MI 49008. Offers exercise and sports medicine (MS), including athletic training, exercise physiology; physical education (MA), including coaching sport performance, pedagogy, special physical education, sport management. *Faculty:* 20 full-time (9 women). *Students:* 60 full-time (27 women), 53 part-time (25 women); includes 9 minority (6 African Americans, 2 Asian Americans or Pacific Islanders, 1 Hispanic American), 6 international. 69 applicants, 81% accepted, 21 enrolled. In 2009, 42 master's awarded. *Application deadline:* For fall admission, 2/15 priority date for domestic students. Applications are processed on a rolling basis. Application fee: $25. *Financial support:* Fellowships, research assistantships, teaching assistantships, Federal Work-Study available. Financial award application deadline: 2/15; financial award applicants required to submit FAFSA. *Unit head:* Lee deLisle, Chair, 269-387-2669. *Application contact:* Admissions and Orientation, 269-387-2000, Fax: 269-387-2355.

West Virginia University, School of Physical Education, Morgantown, WV 26506. Offers athletic coaching education (MS); athletic training (MS); physical education/teacher education (MS, PhD), including curriculum and instruction (PhD), motor behavior (PhD), physical education supervision (PhD); sport and exercise psychology (PhD); sport management (MS). *Degree requirements:* For doctorate, comprehensive exam, thesis/dissertation, oral exam. *Entrance requirements:* For master's, GRE or MAT, minimum GPA of 3.0; for doctorate, GRE General Test or MAT, minimum GPA of 3.5. Additional exam requirements/recommendations for international students: Required—TOEFL (minimum score 550 paper-based; 213 computer-based). Electronic applications accepted. *Faculty research:* Sport psychosociology, teacher education, exercise psychology, counseling.

West Virginia Wesleyan College, Department of Exercise Science, Buckhannon, WV 26201. Offers athletic training (MS). *Expenses:* Tuition: Part-time $360 per credit hour.

Exercise and Sports Science

American University, College of Arts and Sciences, School of Education, Teaching, and Health, Program in Health Promotion Management, Washington, DC 22016-8030. Offers MS. *Students:* 8 full-time (6 women), 26 part-time (21 women); includes 8 minority (5 African Americans, 3 Hispanic Americans). Average age 27. 27 applicants, 67% accepted, 8 enrolled. In 2009, 12 master's awarded. *Degree requirements:* For master's, comprehensive exam, thesis or alternative, tools of research. *Entrance requirements:* For master's, GRE. Application fee: $80. *Expenses:* Tuition: Full-time $22,266; part-time $1237 per credit hour. Required fees: $430. Tuition and fees vary according to program. *Unit head:* Dr. Robert Karch, Director, 202-885-6285, Fax: 202-885-6288. *Application contact:* Kathleen Clowery, Director, Graduate Admissions, 202-885-3621, Fax: 202-885-1505.

Appalachian State University, Cratis D. Williams Graduate School, Department of Health, Leisure, and Exercise Science, Boone, NC 28608. Offers exercise science (MS), including cardiorehab, research, strength and conditioning. *Faculty:* 19 full-time (3 women), 4 part-time/adjunct (2 women). *Students:* 31 full-time (10 women), 1 (woman) part-time, 2 international. 48 applicants, 42% accepted, 14 enrolled. In 2009, 14 master's awarded. *Degree requirements:* For master's, comprehensive exam, thesis optional. *Entrance requirements:* For master's, GRE General Test, 3 letters of recommendation. Additional exam requirements/recommendations for international students: Required—TOEFL (minimum score 570 paper-based; 230 computer-based; 79 iBT), IELTS (minimum score 6.5). *Application deadline:* For fall admission, 3/1 priority date for domestic students, 2/1 for international students; for spring admission, 11/1 for domestic students, 7/1 for international students. Applications are processed on a rolling basis. Application fee: $50. Electronic applications accepted. *Expenses:* Tuition, state resident: full-time $2960. Tuition, nonresident: full-time $14,051. Required fees: $2320. *Financial support:* In 2009–10, 22 research assistantships (averaging $9,500 per year) were awarded; career-related internships or fieldwork, Federal Work-Study, scholarships/grants, and unspecified assistantships also available. Financial award application deadline: 4/1; financial award applicants required to submit FAFSA. *Faculty research:* Exercise immunology, biomechanics, exercise and chronic disease, muscle damage, strength and conditioning. Total annual research expenditures: $350,000. *Unit head:* Dr. Paul Gaskill, Head, 828-262-6336, E-mail: gaskillpl@appstate.edu. *Application contact:* Dr. Travis Triplett, Director, 828-262-7148, E-mail: triplttnt@appstate.edu.

Arizona State University, Graduate College, College of Nursing and Healthcare Innovation, Department of Exercise and Wellness, Tempe, AZ 85287. Offers exercise and wellness (MS); physical activity, nutrition and wellness (PhD). *Degree requirements:* For master's, thesis, oral defense. *Entrance requirements:* For master's, GRE, letters of recommendation. Additional exam requirements/recommendations for international students: Required—TOEFL (minimum score 550 paper-based; 213 computer-based; 83 iBT); Recommended—TWE. Electronic applications accepted. *Faculty research:* Fitness, health and wellness benefits of healthy lifestyles; disease prevention and fitness; physical activity and fitness program effectiveness; women's health issues; motivation, assessment, environmental health and fitness.

Arkansas State University—Jonesboro, Graduate School, College of Education, Department of Health, Physical Education, and Sport Sciences, Jonesboro, State University, AR 72467. Offers exercise science (MS); physical education (MSE, SCCT). Part-time programs available. *Faculty:* 6 full-time (1 woman). *Students:* 9 full-time (7 women), 14 part-time (7 women); includes 3 minority (2 African Americans, 1 Hispanic American), 8 international. Average age 27. 21 applicants, 86% accepted, 12 enrolled. In 2009, 4 master's awarded. *Degree requirements:* For master's, comprehensive exam, thesis or alternative; for SCCT, comprehensive exam. *Entrance requirements:* For master's, GRE General Test or MAT, appropriate bachelor's degree; for SCCT, GRE General Test or MAT, interview, master's degree, official transcript,

immunization records. Additional exam requirements/recommendations for international students: Required—TOEFL (minimum score 550 paper-based; 213 computer-based; 79 iBT), IELTS (minimum score 6). *Application deadline:* For fall admission, 7/15 for domestic students, 7/1 for international students; for spring admission, 12/1 for domestic students, 11/13 for international students. Applications are processed on a rolling basis. Application fee: $30 ($40 for international students). Electronic applications accepted. *Expenses:* Tuition, state resident: full-time $3744; part-time $208 per credit hour. Tuition, nonresident: full-time $9540; part-time $530 per credit hour. Required fees: $896; $47 per credit hour. $25 per term. One-time fee: $50. Tuition and fees vary according to course load and program. *Financial support:* In 2009–10, 13 students received support; teaching assistantships, career-related internships or fieldwork, scholarships/grants, and unspecified assistantships available. Financial award application deadline: 7/1; financial award applicants required to submit FAFSA. *Unit head:* Dr. Jim Stillwell, Chair, 870-972-3066, Fax: 870-972-3096, E-mail: jstillwel@astate.edu. *Application contact:* Dr. Andrew Sustich, Dean of the Graduate School, 870-972-3029, Fax: 870-972-3857, E-mail: sustich@astate.edu.

Armstrong Atlantic State University, School of Graduate Studies, Program in Sports Medicine, Savannah, GA 31419-1997. Offers sports health sciences (MSSM). Part-time programs available. *Degree requirements:* For master's, comprehensive exam, thesis optional, project. *Entrance requirements:* For master's, GRE General Test, MAT, GMAT, minimum GPA of 2.5. Additional exam requirements/recommendations for international students: Required—TOEFL (minimum score 523 paper-based; 193 computer-based).

Ashland University, Dwight Schar College of Education, Department of Sport Sciences, Ashland, OH 44805-3702. Offers adapted physical education (M Ed); applied exercise science (M Ed); sport education (M Ed); sport management (M Ed). Part-time programs available. *Faculty:* 5 full-time (3 women), 2 part-time/adjunct (both women). *Students:* 24 full-time (9 women), 31 part-time (12 women); includes 4 minority (all African Americans), 4 international. Average age 30. 15 applicants, 100% accepted, 15 enrolled. In 2009, 26 master's awarded. *Degree requirements:* For master's, practicum, inquiry seminar, thesis, or internship. *Entrance requirements:* For master's, teaching certificate or license, bachelor's degree, minimum cumulative GPA of 2.75. Additional exam requirements/recommendations for international students: Required—TOEFL. *Application deadline:* For fall admission, 8/27 for domestic students; for spring admission, 1/14 for domestic students. Applications are processed on a rolling basis. Application fee: $30. *Financial support:* In 2009–10, 32 students received support; teaching assistantships, institutionally sponsored loans and scholarships/grants available. Financial award application deadline: 4/15. *Faculty research:* Coaching, legal issues, strength and conditioning, sport management rating of perceived exertion, youth fitness, geriatric exercise science. *Unit head:* Dr. Randall F. Gearhart, Chair, 419-289-6198, E-mail: rgearhar@ashland.edu. *Application contact:* Dr. Randall F. Gearhart, Chair, 419-289-6198, E-mail: rgearhar@ashland.edu.

Auburn University, Graduate School, College of Education, Department of Kinesiology, Auburn University, AL 36849. Offers exercise science (M Ed, MS, PhD); health promotion (M Ed, MS); kinesiology (PhD); physical education/teacher education (M Ed, MS, Ed D, Ed S). *Accreditation:* NCATE. Part-time programs available. *Faculty:* 16 full-time (7 women), 1 part-time/adjunct (0 women). *Students:* 70 full-time (46 women), 21 part-time (8 women); includes 10 minority (8 African Americans, 2 Asian Americans or Pacific Islanders), 10 international. Average age 26. 109 applicants, 68% accepted, 53 enrolled. In 2009, 26 master's, 7 doctorates awarded. *Degree requirements:* For master's, thesis (for some programs); for doctorate, thesis/dissertation; for Ed S, exam, field project. *Entrance requirements:* For master's, GRE General Test; for doctorate and Ed S, GRE General Test, interview, master's degree. *Application deadline:* For fall admission, 7/7 for domestic students; for spring admission, 11/24 for domestic students. Applications are processed on a rolling basis. Application fee: $50 ($60 for international students). Electronic applications accepted. *Expenses:* Tuition, state resident: full-time $6240. Tuition, nonresident: full-time $18,720. International tuition: $18,938 full-time. Required fees: $492. Tuition and fees vary according to course load, program and reciprocity agreements. *Financial support:* Research assistantships, teaching assistantships, Federal Work-Study available. Support available to part-time students. Financial award application deadline: 3/15; financial award applicants required to submit FAFSA. *Faculty research:* Biomechanics, exercise physiology, motor skill learning, school health, curriculum development. *Unit head:* Dr. Mary E. Rudisill, Head, 334-844-4483. *Application contact:* Dr. George Flowers, Dean of the Graduate School, 334-844-2125.

Austin Peay State University, College of Graduate Studies, College of Behavioral and Health Sciences, Department of Health and Human Performance, Clarksville, TN 37044. Offers health leadership (MS). Part-time and evening/weekend programs available. Postbaccalaureate distance learning degree programs offered (no on-campus study). *Faculty:* 5 full-time (3 women). *Students:* 28 full-time (19 women), 45 part-time (35 women); includes 33 minority (28 African Americans, 1 Asian American or Pacific Islander, 4 Hispanic Americans). Average age 32. 72 applicants, 96% accepted, 39 enrolled. In 2009, 23 master's awarded. *Degree requirements:* For master's, comprehensive exam, thesis optional. *Entrance requirements:* For master's, GRE General Test, 3 letters of recommendation, minimum undergraduate GPA of 2.5. Additional exam requirements/recommendations for international students: Required—TOEFL (minimum score 500 paper-based; 173 computer-based). *Application deadline:* For fall admission, 7/27 priority date for domestic students; for spring admission, 12/17 priority date for domestic students. Applications are processed on a rolling basis. Application fee: $25. Electronic applications accepted. *Expenses:* Tuition, state resident: full-time $6160; part-time $608 per credit hour. Tuition, nonresident: full-time $17,080; part-time $854 per credit hour. Required fees: $1224; $61.20 per credit hour. *Financial support:* In 2009–10, 9 students received support, including 9 research assistantships with full tuition reimbursements available (averaging $5,184 per year); career-related internships or fieldwork, Federal Work-Study, institutionally sponsored loans, scholarships/grants, and unspecified assistantships also available. Support available to part-time students. Financial award application deadline: 3/1; financial award applicants required to submit FAFSA. *Faculty research:* Aging and physical activity. *Unit head:* Dr. Marcy Maurer, Interim Chair, 931-221-6105, Fax: 931-221-7040, E-mail: maurerm@apsu.edu. *Application contact:* Dr. Dixie Dennis, Dean, College of Graduate Studies, 931-221-7662, Fax: 931-221-7641, E-mail: dennisdi@apsu.edu.

Ball State University, Graduate School, College of Applied Science and Technology, Interdepartmental Program in Human Bioenergetics, Muncie, IN 47306-1099. Offers PhD. *Degree requirements:* For doctorate, thesis/dissertation. *Entrance requirements:* For doctorate, GRE General Test, interview, minimum graduate GPA of 3.2, resume.

Barry University, School of Human Performance and Leisure Sciences, Programs in Movement Science, Specialization in Exercise Science, Miami Shores, FL 33161-6695. Offers MS. *Degree requirements:* For master's, comprehensive exam, thesis. *Entrance requirements:* For master's, GRE, minimum GPA of 3.0. Electronic applications accepted. *Faculty research:* Physiological adaptations to exercise.

Baylor University, Graduate School, School of Education, Department of Health, Human Performance and Recreation, Waco, TX 76798. Offers exercise, nutrition and preventive health (PhD); health, human performance and recreation (MS Ed). *Accreditation:* NCATE. Part-time programs available. *Faculty:* 13 full-time (5 women), 3 part-time/adjunct (1 woman). *Students:* 66 full-time (35 women), 42 part-time (21 women); includes 14 minority (7 African Americans, 3 Asian Americans or Pacific Islanders, 4 Hispanic Americans), 5 international. 30 applicants, 87% accepted. In 2009, 48 master's, 6 doctorates awarded. *Degree requirements:* For master's, thesis optional. *Entrance requirements:* For master's, GRE General Test. *Application deadline:* For fall admission, 4/1 priority date for domestic students; for spring admission, 10/1 for domestic students. Applications are processed on a rolling basis. Application fee: $25. Electronic applications accepted. *Financial support:* In 2009–10, 35 students received support, including 22 teaching assistantships; career-related internships or fieldwork, Federal Work-Study, institutionally sponsored loans, tuition waivers (partial), and recreation supplements also available. *Faculty research:* Behavior change theory, pedagogy, nutrition and enzyme therapy, exercise testing, health planning. *Unit head:* Dr. Glenn Miller, Graduate Program Director, 254-710-4001, Fax: 254-710-3527, E-mail: glenn_miller@baylor.edu. *Application contact:* Eva Berger-Rhodes, Administrative Assistant, 254-710-4945, Fax: 254-710-3870, E-mail: eva_rhodes@baylor.edu.

Bemidji State University, School of Graduate Studies, College of Professional Studies, Field of Sport Studies, Bemidji, MN 56601-2699. Offers MS. Part-time programs available. *Degree requirements:* For master's, thesis, departmental qualifying exam. *Entrance requirements:* For master's, letters of recommendation. Additional exam requirements/recommendations for international students: Required—TOEFL. Electronic applications accepted. *Faculty research:* Performance training for athletes, sport biomechanics for throwing and pitching, faith based fitness programs.

Benedictine University, Graduate Programs, Program in Clinical Exercise Physiology, Lisle, IL 60532-0900. Offers MS. Part-time programs available. *Faculty:* 1 full-time (0 women), 3 part-time/adjunct (1 woman). *Students:* 3 full-time (2 women), 29 part-time (19 women); includes 1 minority (Hispanic American). Average age 28. 30 applicants, 67% accepted, 16 enrolled. In 2009, 7 master's awarded. *Entrance requirements:* Additional exam requirements/recommendations for international students: Required—TOEFL (minimum score 550 paper-based; 213 computer-based). *Application deadline:* For fall admission, 9/1 for domestic students; for winter admission, 12/1 for domestic students; for spring admission, 2/15 for domestic students. Applications are processed on a rolling basis. Application fee: $40. Electronic applications accepted. *Expenses:* Tuition: Part-time $750 per credit hour. Tuition and fees vary according to campus/location and program. *Financial support:* Career-related internships or fieldwork and health care benefits available. Support available to part-time students. *Faculty research:* Protein synthesis cell signaling control, aging. *Unit head:* Regina Schurman, Program and Research Coordinator, 630-725-6563, Fax: 630-960-1126, E-mail: rschurman@ben.edu. *Application contact:* Kari Gibbons, Director, Admissions, 630-829-6200, Fax: 630-829-6584, E-mail: kgibbons@ben.edu.

Bloomsburg University of Pennsylvania, School of Graduate Studies, College of Liberal Arts, Department of Exercise Science and Athletics, Bloomsburg, PA 17815-1301. Offers clinical athletic training (MS); exercise science (MS). *Degree requirements:* For master's, thesis, practical clinical experience. *Entrance requirements:* For master's, GRE General Test or MAT, minimum QPA of 3.0. Additional exam requirements/recommendations for international students: Required—TOEFL (minimum score 550 paper-based; 213 computer-based; 79 iBT). Electronic applications accepted.

Boise State University, Graduate College, College of Education, Department of Kinesiology, Program in Exercise and Sports Studies, Boise, ID 83725-0399. Offers MS. Part-time programs available. *Degree requirements:* For master's, thesis. *Entrance requirements:* For master's, minimum GPA of 3.0. Electronic applications accepted. *Expenses:* Tuition, state resident: full-time $3106; part-time $209 per credit. Tuition, nonresident: part-time $284 per credit.

Brigham Young University, Graduate Studies, College of Life Sciences, Department of Exercise Sciences, Provo, UT 84602. Offers athletic training (MS); exercise physiology (MS, PhD); exercise science (MS); health promotion (MS, PhD); physical medicine and rehabilitation (PhD). *Faculty:* 19 full-time (2 women). *Students:* 22 full-time (13 women), 41 part-time (19 women); includes 1 American Indian/Alaska Native, 3 Asian Americans or Pacific Islanders, 2 international. Average age 32. 30 applicants, 80% accepted, 22 enrolled. In 2009, 21 master's, 7 doctorates awarded. *Degree requirements:* For master's, thesis, oral defense; for doctorate, comprehensive exam, thesis/dissertation, oral defense, oral and written exams. *Entrance requirements:* For master's, GRE General Test, minimum GPA of 3.0 in last 60 hours of course work; for doctorate, GRE General Test, minimum GPA of 3.5 in last 60 hours of course work. Additional exam requirements/recommendations for international students: Required—TOEFL (minimum score 580 paper-based; 237 computer-based; 85 iBT), IELTS (minimum score 7). *Application deadline:* For fall admission, 2/1 for domestic and international students. Application fee: $50. Electronic applications accepted. *Expenses:* Tuition: Full-time $5580; part-time $301 per credit hour. Tuition and fees vary according to student's religious affiliation. *Financial support:* In 2009–10, 46 students received support, including 15 research assistantships with full and partial tuition reimbursements available (averaging $5,615 per year), 34 teaching assistantships with full and partial tuition reimbursements available (averaging $10,106 per year); fellowships, career-related internships or fieldwork, institutionally sponsored loans, tuition waivers (full and partial), and unspecified assistantships also available. Financial award application deadline: 3/1. *Faculty research:* Injury prevention and rehabilitation, human skeletal muscle adaptation, cardiovascular health and fitness, lifestyle modification and health promotion. Total annual research expenditures: $18,096. *Unit head:* Dr. Larry Hall, Chair, 801-422-7303, Fax: 801-422-0543, E-mail: larry_hall@byu.edu. *Application contact:* Dr. Jeffrey Brent Feland, Graduate Coordinator, 801-422-1182, Fax: 801-422-0543, E-mail: brent_feland@byu.edu.

Brooklyn College of the City University of New York, Division of Graduate Studies, Department of Physical Education and Exercise Science, Brooklyn, NY 11210-2889. Offers exercise science and rehabilitation (MS); physical education (MS), including sports management. Part-time programs available. *Students:* 15 full-time (7 women), 127 part-time (58 women); includes 39 minority (23 African Americans, 3 Asian Americans or Pacific Islanders, 13 Hispanic Americans), 65 international. Average age 27. 127 applicants, 96% accepted, 57 enrolled. In 2009, 15 master's awarded. *Degree requirements:* For master's, comprehensive exam or thesis. *Entrance requirements:* For master's, previous course work in physical education and education, minimum GPA of 3.0, 2 letters of recommendation, essay. Additional exam requirements/recommendations for international students: Required—TOEFL (minimum score 500 paper-based; 173 computer-based; 61 iBT). *Application deadline:* For fall admission, 3/1 priority date for domestic students, 2/1 priority date for international students; for spring admission, 11/1 priority date for domestic students, 10/1 priority date for international students. Applications are processed on a rolling basis. Application fee: $125. Electronic applications accepted. *Expenses:* Tuition, state resident: full-time $7360; part-time $310 per credit hour. Tuition, nonresident: full-time $13,800; part-time $575 per credit hour. Required fees: $140.10 per semester. *Financial support:* Career-related internships or fieldwork, Federal Work-Study, institutionally sponsored loans, and scholarships/grants available. Support available to part-time students. Financial award application deadline: 5/1; financial award applicants required to submit FAFSA. *Faculty research:* Exercise physiology, motor learning, sports psychology, women in athletics. *Unit head:* Dr. Artis Smith, Chairperson, 718-951-5514, E-mail: basmith@brooklyn.cuny.edu. *Application contact:* Hernan Sierra, Graduate Admissions Coordinator, 718-951-4536, Fax: 718-951-4506, E-mail: grads@brooklyn.cuny.edu.

California Baptist University, Program in Kinesiology, Riverside, CA 92504-3206. Offers exercise science (MS); physical education pedagogy (MS); sport management (MS). Part-time programs available. *Faculty:* 3 full-time (0 women). *Students:* 17 full-time (8 women), 14 part-time (8 women); includes 10 minority (1 African American, 1 American Indian/Alaska Native, 3 Asian Americans or Pacific Islanders, 5 Hispanic Americans), 2 international. 45 applicants, 49% accepted, 15 enrolled. In 2009, 15 master's awarded. *Degree requirements:* For master's, thesis or alternative, field experience. *Entrance requirements:* For master's, 12 semester units of course work in kinesiology, including basic movement anatomy or a related course; minimum undergraduate GPA of 2.75 (physical education pedagogy). Additional exam requirements/recommendations for international students: Required—TOEFL (minimum score 575 paper-based; 230 computer-based; 89 iBT). *Application deadline:* For fall admission, 8/1 priority date for domestic students, 7/1 for international students; for spring admission, 12/1 priority date for domestic students, 10/15 for international students. Applications are processed on a rolling basis. Application fee: $45. Electronic applications accepted. *Expenses:* Tuition: Full-time $8352; part-time $464 per semester hour. Required fees: $125 per semester. Tuition and fees vary according to course load, campus/location and program. *Financial support:* Federal Work-Study and scholarships/grants available. Support available to part-time students. Financial award applicants required to submit FAFSA. *Unit head:* Dr. Sean Sullivan, Chair, Department of Kinesiology, 951-343-4528, E-mail: ssullivan@calbaptist.edu. *Application contact:*

Exercise and Sports Science

California Baptist University *(continued)*
Gail Ronveaux, Dean of Graduate Enrollment, 951-343-5045, Fax: 951-343-5095, E-mail: graduateadmissions@calbaptist.edu.

California State University, Fresno, Division of Graduate Studies, College of Health and Human Services, Department of Kinesiology, Fresno, CA 93740-8027. Offers exercise science (MA); sport psychology (MA). Part-time and evening/weekend programs available. *Degree requirements:* For master's, thesis or alternative. *Entrance requirements:* For master's, GRE General Test, minimum GPA of 2.7. Additional exam requirements/recommendations for international students: Required—TOEFL. Electronic applications accepted. *Faculty research:* Refugee education, homeless, geriatrics, fitness.

California State University, Long Beach, Graduate Studies, College of Health and Human Services, Department of Kinesiology, Long Beach, CA 90840. Offers adapted physical education (MA); coaching and student athlete development (MA); exercise physiology and nutrition (MS); exercise science (MS); individualized studies (MA); kinesiology (MA); pedagogical studies (MA); sport and exercise psychology (MS); sport management (MA); sports medicine and injury studies (MS). Part-time programs available. *Faculty:* 9 full-time (6 women), 1 part-time/adjunct (0 women). *Students:* 34 full-time (22 women), 23 part-time (14 women); includes 22 minority (4 African Americans, 2 American Indian/Alaska Native, 8 Asian Americans or Pacific Islanders, 8 Hispanic Americans), 9 international. Average age 27. 143 applicants, 59% accepted, 20 enrolled. *Degree requirements:* For master's, oral and written comprehensive exams or thesis. *Entrance requirements:* For master's, GRE General Test, minimum GPA of 2.75 during previous 2 years of course work. *Application deadline:* For fall admission, 6/1 for domestic students. Applications are processed on a rolling basis. Application fee: $55. Electronic applications accepted. *Expenses:* Required fees: $1802 per semester. Part-time tuition and fees vary according to course load. *Financial support:* Federal Work-Study, institutionally sponsored loans, and scholarships/grants available. Financial award application deadline: 3/2. *Faculty research:* Pulmonary functioning, feedback and practice structure, strength training, history and politics of sports, special population research issues. *Unit head:* Dr. Sharon R. Guthrie, Chair, 562-985-7487, Fax: 562-985-8067, E-mail: guthrie@csulb.edu. *Application contact:* Dr. Grant Hill, Graduate Advisor, 562-985-8856, Fax: 562-985-8067, E-mail: ghill@csulb.edu.

California University of Pennsylvania, School of Graduate Studies and Research, School of Education, Department of Athletic Training, Program in Exercise Science and Health Promotion, California, PA 15419-1394. Offers fitness and wellness (MS); performance enhancement and injury prevention (MS); rehabilitation sciences (MS); sport management (MS); sport psychology (MS). Part-time and evening/weekend programs available. Postbaccalaureate distance learning degree programs offered (no on-campus study). *Degree requirements:* For master's, comprehensive exam, thesis optional. *Entrance requirements:* For master's, minimum QPA of 3.0. Additional exam requirements/recommendations for international students: Required—TOEFL (minimum score 550 paper-based; 213 computer-based; 80 iBT). Electronic applications accepted. *Expenses:* Contact institution. *Faculty research:* Reducing obesity in children, sport performance, creating unique biomechanical assessment techniques, Web-based training for fitness professionals, Webcams.

Central Connecticut State University, School of Graduate Studies, School of Education and Professional Studies, Department of Physical Education and Human Performance, New Britain, CT 06050-4010. Offers physical education (MS, Certificate). Part-time and evening/weekend programs available. *Faculty:* 17 full-time (8 women), 24 part-time/adjunct (15 women). *Students:* 27 full-time (15 women), 43 part-time (17 women); includes 5 minority (1 African American, 1 American Indian/Alaska Native, 3 Hispanic Americans), 1 international. Average age 28. 34 applicants, 53% accepted, 11 enrolled. In 2009, 12 master's, 4 other advanced degrees awarded. *Degree requirements:* For master's, comprehensive exam, thesis or alternative; for Certificate, qualifying exam. *Entrance requirements:* For master's, minimum GPA of 2.7, bachelor's degree in physical education (preferred). Additional exam requirements/recommendations for international students: Required—TOEFL. *Application deadline:* For fall admission, 7/1 for domestic students; for spring admission, 12/1 for domestic students. Applications are processed on a rolling basis. Application fee: $50. Electronic applications accepted. *Expenses:* Tuition, area resident: Full-time $4662; part-time $440 per credit. Tuition, state resident: full-time $6994; part-time $440 per credit. Tuition, nonresident: full-time $12,988; part-time $440 per credit. Required fees: $3606. One-time fee: $62 part-time. *Financial support:* In 2009–10, 11 students received support, including 8 research assistantships; career-related internships or fieldwork, Federal Work-Study, scholarships/grants, and unspecified assistantships also available. Support available to part-time students. Financial award application deadline: 3/1; financial award applicants required to submit FAFSA. *Faculty research:* Exercise science, athletic training, preparation of physical education for schools. *Unit head:* Dr. David Harackiewicz, Chair, 860-832-2155. *Application contact:* Dr. David Harackiewicz, Chair, 860-832-2155.

Central Michigan University, College of Graduate Studies, The Herbert H. and Grace A. Dow College of Health Professions, Department of Physical Education and Sport, Mount Pleasant, MI 48859. Offers physical education (MA), including athletic administration, coaching, exercise science, teaching; sport education (MA). Part-time programs available. *Degree requirements:* For master's, thesis or alternative. Electronic applications accepted. *Faculty research:* Athletic administration and sport management; performance enhancing substance use in sport; computer applications for sport managers; mental skill development for ultimate performance; teaching methods.

Central Washington University, Graduate Studies and Research, College of Education and Professional Studies, Department of Nutrition, Exercise and Health Services, Ellensburg, WA 98926. Offers exercise science (MS); nutrition (MS). *Accreditation:* NCATE. Part-time programs available. *Faculty:* 21 full-time (5 women). *Students:* 26 full-time (13 women), 6 part-time (1 woman), 1 international. 30 applicants, 63% accepted, 19 enrolled. In 2009, 9 master's awarded. *Degree requirements:* For master's, thesis or alternative. *Entrance requirements:* For master's, GRE (nutrition), minimum GPA of 3.0. Additional exam requirements/recommendations for international students: Required—TOEFL (minimum score 550 paper-based; 213 computer-based; 79 iBT). *Application deadline:* For fall admission, 2/1 priority date for domestic students; for winter admission, 10/1 for domestic students; for spring admission, 1/1 for domestic students. Applications are processed on a rolling basis. Application fee: $50. Electronic applications accepted. *Expenses:* Tuition, state resident: full-time $7353; part-time $245 per credit. Tuition, nonresident: full-time $16,383; part-time $546 per credit. Required fees: $882. Tuition and fees vary according to degree level. *Financial support:* In 2009–10, 17 teaching assistantships with full and partial tuition reimbursements (averaging $9,145 per year) were awarded; research assistantships, Federal Work-Study and health care benefits also available. Financial award application deadline: 3/1; financial award applicants required to submit FAFSA. *Unit head:* Dr. Vince Nethery, Chair, 509-963-1911. *Application contact:* Justine Eason, Admissions Program Coordinator, 509-963-3103, Fax: 509-963-1799, E-mail: masters@cwu.edu.

Cleveland State University, College of Graduate Studies, College of Education and Human Services, Department of Health, Physical Education, Recreation and Dance, Cleveland, OH 44115. Offers community health education (M Ed); exercise science (M Ed); human performance (M Ed); physical education pedagogy (M Ed); public health (MPH); school health education (M Ed); sport and exercise psychology (M Ed); sports management (M Ed). Part-time programs available. *Degree requirements:* For master's, comprehensive exam, thesis optional. *Entrance requirements:* For master's, GRE General Test or MAT (if undergraduate GPA less than 2.75), minimum undergraduate GPA of 2.75. Additional exam requirements/recommendations for international students: Required—TOEFL (minimum score 525 paper-based; 197 computer-based), IELTS (minimum score 6). Electronic applications accepted. *Faculty research:* Bone density, marketing fitness centers, motor development of disabled, online learning and survey research.

The College of St. Scholastica, Graduate Studies, Department of Exercise Physiology, Duluth, MN 55811-4199. Offers MA. Part-time programs available. *Degree requirements:* For master's, thesis (for some programs). *Entrance requirements:* For master's, minimum GPA of 2.7. Additional exam requirements/recommendations for international students: Required—TOEFL (minimum score 550 paper-based; 213 computer-based; 79 iBT). Electronic applications accepted. *Faculty research:* Cardiovascular and metabolic responses, cardiorespiratory effects, orthostatic intolerance, lower extremity asymmetry.

Colorado State University, Graduate School, College of Applied Human Sciences, Department of Health and Exercise Science, Fort Collins, CO 80523-1582. Offers health and exercise science (MS); human bioenergetics (PhD). Part-time programs available. *Faculty:* 15 full-time (3 women). *Students:* 30 full-time (18 women), 12 part-time (8 women); includes 3 minority (1 American Indian/Alaska Native, 2 Hispanic Americans), 3 international. Average age 28. 86 applicants, 23% accepted, 13 enrolled. In 2009, 9 master's awarded. *Degree requirements:* For master's, thesis; for doctorate, comprehensive exam, thesis/dissertation, publication of dissertation. *Entrance requirements:* For master's, GRE General Test, minimum GPA of 3.0; for doctorate, bachelor's or master's degree. Additional exam requirements/recommendations for international students: Required—TOEFL (minimum score 550 paper-based; 213 computer-based; 80 iBT). *Application deadline:* For fall admission, 1/31 priority date for domestic and international students; for spring admission, 9/30 priority date for domestic and international students. Application fee: $50. Electronic applications accepted. *Expenses:* Tuition, state resident: full-time $6434; part-time $359.10 per credit. Tuition, nonresident: full-time $18,116; part-time $1006.45 per credit. Required fees: $1496; $83 per credit. *Financial support:* In 2009–10, 29 students received support, including 7 research assistantships with full tuition reimbursements available (averaging $9,718 per year), 22 teaching assistantships with full tuition reimbursements available (averaging $13,269 per year); fellowships, unspecified assistantships also available. Financial award application deadline: 1/31; financial award applicants required to submit FAFSA. *Faculty research:* Metabolism and metabolic disease, obesity, diabetes, hypertension, physical activity and health across the lifespan, bioenergetics. Total annual research expenditures: $964,249. *Unit head:* Richard Gay Israel, Head, 970-491-3785, Fax: 970-491-0216, E-mail: richard.israel@colostate.edu. *Application contact:* Robin Noehl, Department Operations, 970-491-7161, Fax: 970-491-0445, E-mail: robin.noehl@colostate.edu.

Concordia University, School of Graduate Studies, Faculty of Arts and Science, Department of Exercise Science, Montréal, QC H3G 1M8, Canada. Offers M Sc.

Concordia University Chicago, College of Graduate and Innovative Programs, Program in Human Services, River Forest, IL 60305-1499. Offers human services (MA), including administration, exercise science. Part-time and evening/weekend programs available. *Degree requirements:* For master's, comprehensive exam, thesis. *Entrance requirements:* For master's, minimum GPA of 2.9. Additional exam requirements/recommendations for international students: Required—TOEFL (minimum score 550 paper-based; 195 computer-based). Electronic applications accepted.

Delaware State University, Graduate Programs, Department of Sport Sciences, Dover, DE 19901-2277. Offers sport administration (MS). *Entrance requirements:* Additional exam requirements/recommendations for international students: Required—TOEFL (minimum score 550 paper-based). Electronic applications accepted.

East Carolina University, Graduate School, College of Health and Human Performance, Department of Exercise and Sports Science, Greenville, NC 27858-4353. Offers bioenergetics (PhD); exercise and sport science (MA, MA Ed). *Degree requirements:* For master's, comprehensive exam, thesis optional; for doctorate, comprehensive exam, thesis/dissertation. *Entrance requirements:* For master's, GRE General Test or MAT; for doctorate, GRE. Additional exam requirements/recommendations for international students: Required—TOEFL. *Faculty research:* Diabetes metabolism, pediatric obesity, biomechanics of arthritis, physical activity measurement.

Eastern Illinois University, Graduate School, College of Education and Professional Studies, Department of Kinesiology and Sports Studies, Charleston, IL 61920-3099. Offers MS. Part-time programs available. *Faculty:* 15 full-time (3 women). In 2009, 33 master's awarded. *Application deadline:* For fall admission, 3/31 priority date for domestic students. Applications are processed on a rolling basis. Application fee: $30. *Expenses:* Tuition, state resident: full-time $9434; part-time $239 per credit hour. Tuition, nonresident: full-time $23,774; part-time $717 per credit hour. Required fees: $802.63. *Financial support:* In 2009–10, 9 teaching assistantships with tuition reimbursements (averaging $8,100 per year) were awarded; Federal Work-Study also available. Support available to part-time students. *Unit head:* Dr. Jill Owen, Chairperson, 217-581-2215, E-mail: jdowen@eiu.edu. *Application contact:* Dr. Brent Walker, Coordinator, 217-581-2215, E-mail: bwalker@eiu.edu.

Eastern Michigan University, Graduate School, College of Health and Human Services, School of Health Promotion and Human Performance, Programs in Exercise Physiology, Ypsilanti, MI 48197. Offers exercise physiology (MS); sports medicine-biomechanics (MS); sports medicine-corporate adult fitness (MS); sports medicine-exercise physiology (MS). Part-time and evening/weekend programs available. *Students:* 10 full-time (5 women), 32 part-time (10 women); includes 6 minority (2 African Americans, 4 Hispanic Americans), 2 international. Average age 29. In 2009, 12 master's awarded. *Degree requirements:* For master's, comprehensive exam, thesis or 450-hour internship. *Entrance requirements:* Additional exam requirements/recommendations for international students: Required—TOEFL. *Application deadline:* For fall admission, 8/1 for domestic students, 5/1 for international students; for winter admission, 12/1 for domestic students, 10/1 for international students; for spring admission, 3/15 for domestic students, 3/1 for international students. Application fee: $35. Tuition and fees vary according to course level. *Unit head:* Dr. Steve McGregor, Program Coordinator, 734-487-0090, Fax: 734-487-2024, E-mail: stephen.mcgregor@emich.edu. *Application contact:* Dr. Steve McGregor, Program Coordinator, 734-487-0090, Fax: 734-487-2024, E-mail: stephen.mcgregor@emich.edu.

Eastern Washington University, Graduate Studies, College of Education and Human Development, Department of Physical Education, Health and Recreation, Cheney, WA 99004-2431. Offers exercise science (MS); sport and exercise psychology (MS); sports administration/pedagogy (MS). *Degree requirements:* For master's, comprehensive exam, thesis or alternative. *Entrance requirements:* For master's, minimum GPA of 3.0. *Expenses:* Tuition, state resident: full-time $7476; part-time $249 per quarter hour. Tuition, nonresident: full-time $18,030; part-time $601 per quarter hour. Required fees: $3.50 per quarter hour. $142 per quarter.

East Stroudsburg University of Pennsylvania, Graduate School, College of Health Sciences, Department of Exercise Science, East Stroudsburg, PA 18301-2999. Offers cardiac rehabilitation and exercise science (MS). Part-time and evening/weekend programs available. *Faculty:* 3 full-time (1 woman). *Students:* 38 full-time (18 women), 3 part-time (2 women); includes 1 minority (Hispanic American), 4 international. Average age 25. In 2009, 35 master's awarded. *Degree requirements:* For master's, comprehensive exam, thesis or alternative, computer literacy. *Entrance requirements:* Additional exam requirements/recommendations for international students: Required—TOEFL (minimum score 560 paper-based; 220 computer-based; 83 iBT). *Application deadline:* For fall admission, 7/31 priority date for domestic students, 5/1 priority date for international students; for spring admission, 11/30 for domestic students, 10/1 for international students. Applications are processed on a rolling basis. Application fee: $50. *Expenses:* Tuition, state resident: full-time $9942; part-time $387 per credit. Tuition, nonresident: full-time $14,240; part-time $619 per credit. *Financial support:* In 2009–10, 57 research assistantships with full and partial tuition reimbursements (averaging $1,749 per year) were awarded; Federal Work-Study and institutionally sponsored loans also available. Financial award application deadline: 3/1. *Unit head:* Dr. Shala Davis, Graduate Coordinator, 570-422-3302, Fax: 570-422-3616, E-mail: sdavis@po-box.esu.edu. *Application contact:* Kevin Quintero, Graduate Admissions Coordinator, 570-422-3890, Fax: 570-422-2711, E-mail: kquintero@po-box.esu.edu.

East Tennessee State University, School of Graduate Studies, College of Education, Department of Physical Education, Exercise and Sport Sciences, Johnson City, TN 37614. Offers exercise physiology (MA); fitness leadership (MA); physical education (M Ed, MA); sports management (MA); sports sciences (MA). Part-time and evening/weekend programs available. *Degree requirements:* For master's, comprehensive exam (M Ed), oral and written comprehensive exams, thesis (MA). *Entrance requirements:* For master's, GRE General Test, major or minor in physical education or equivalent, interview, minimum GPA of 2.7. Additional exam requirements/recommendations for international students: Required—TOEFL (minimum score 550 paper-based; 213 computer-based). *Faculty research:* Resistance training for various populations, self actualization using challenging courses, park and recreation industry needs relative to recent university graduates, funding sport operations.

Florida Atlantic University, College of Education, Department of Exercise Science and Health Promotion, Boca Raton, FL 33431-0991. Offers MS. Part-time and evening/weekend programs available. *Faculty:* 8 full-time (3 women), 13 part-time/adjunct (7 women). *Students:* 31 full-time (13 women), 17 part-time (10 women); includes 13 minority (6 African Americans, 1 Asian American or Pacific Islander, 6 Hispanic Americans), 1 international. Average age 26. 56 applicants, 68% accepted, 5 enrolled. In 2009, 15 master's awarded. *Degree requirements:* For master's, comprehensive exam, thesis optional. *Entrance requirements:* For master's, GRE General Test, minimum GPA of 3.0 during last 60 hours of course work. Additional exam requirements/recommendations for international students: Required—TOEFL (minimum score 500 paper-based). *Application deadline:* For fall admission, 7/1 priority date for domestic students, 2/15 for international students; for spring admission, 11/1 priority date for domestic students, 7/15 for international students. Applications are processed on a rolling basis. Application fee: $30. *Expenses:* Tuition, state resident: full-time $7055; part-time $293.94 per credit hour. Tuition, nonresident: full-time $22,096; part-time $920.66 per credit hour. *Financial support:* Research assistantships with partial tuition reimbursements, teaching assistantships with partial tuition reimbursements, career-related internships or fieldwork available. *Faculty research:* Pulmonary limitations during exercise, metabolism regulation, determinants of performance, age related change in functional mobility and geriatric exercise, behavioral change aimed at promoting active lifestyles. *Unit head:* Dr. Sue Graves, Chair, 954-236-1261, Fax: 954-236-1259. *Application contact:* Dr. Joseph A. O'Kroy, Graduate Coordinator, 954-236-1266, Fax: 954-236-1259, E-mail: okroy@fau.edu.

Florida International University, College of Education, Department of Health, Physical Education, and Recreation, Program in Exercise and Sports Science, Miami, FL 33199. Offers advanced athletic injury training/sports medicine (MS); strength and conditioning (MS). *Accreditation:* NCATE. Part-time and evening/weekend programs available. *Entrance requirements:* Additional exam requirements/recommendations for international students: Required—TOEFL (minimum score 550 paper-based; 213 computer-based; 80 iBT), IELTS (minimum score 6.3). Electronic applications accepted. *Expenses:* Tuition, state resident: full-time $8008; part-time $4004 per year. Tuition, nonresident: full-time $20,104; part-time $10,052 per year. Required fees: $298; $149 per term. *Faculty research:* Strength and conditioning, women in athletic training, celiac disease.

Florida State University, The Graduate School, College of Human Sciences, Department of Nutrition, Food, and Exercise Sciences, Tallahassee, FL 32306-1493. Offers exercise science (MS, PhD), including exercise physiology; nutrition and food sciences (MS, PhD), including clinical nutrition (MS), food science, human nutrition (PhD), nutrition and sport (MS), nutrition science (MS), nutrition, education and health promotion (MS). Part-time programs available. *Faculty:* 13 full-time (8 women). *Students:* 88 full-time (58 women), 21 part-time (14 women); includes 28 minority (10 African Americans, 5 Asian Americans or Pacific Islanders, 13 Hispanic Americans), 23 international. 128 applicants, 52% accepted, 35 enrolled. In 2009, 30 master's, 8 doctorates awarded. *Degree requirements:* For master's, comprehensive exam (for some programs), thesis optional; for doctorate, thesis/dissertation. *Entrance requirements:* For master's, GRE General Test, minimum upper-division GPA of 3.0; for doctorate, GRE General Test, minimum upper-division GPA of 3.0, MS. Additional exam requirements/recommendations for international students: Required—TOEFL (minimum score 570 paper-based; 80 iBT). *Application deadline:* For fall admission, 7/1 for domestic students, 3/1 for international students; for spring admission, 11/1 for domestic students, 5/1 for international students. Application fee: $30. Electronic applications accepted. *Expenses:* Tuition, state resident: full-time $7413. Tuition, nonresident: full-time $22,567. *Financial support:* In 2009–10, 42 students received support, including 5 fellowships with partial tuition reimbursements available (averaging $10,000 per year), 8 research assistantships with partial tuition reimbursements available (averaging $8,000 per year), 31 teaching assistantships with partial tuition reimbursements available (averaging $8,000 per year); career-related internships or fieldwork, Federal Work-Study, institutionally sponsored loans, scholarships/grants, and unspecified assistantships also available. Financial award application deadline: 1/15; financial award applicants required to submit FAFSA. *Faculty research:* Body composition, functional food, chronic disease and aging response; food safety, food allergy, and safety/quality detection methods; sports nutrition, energy and human performance. *Unit head:* Dr. Bahram H. Arjmandi, Margaret A. Sitton Professor and Chair, 850-645-1517, Fax: 850-645-5000, E-mail: barjmandi@fsu.edu. *Application contact:* Ursula M. Tate, Administrative Support Assistant, 850-644-4800, Fax: 850-645-5000, E-mail: utate@fsu.edu.

Gardner-Webb University, Graduate School, Department of Physical Education, Wellness, and Sport Studies, Boiling Springs, NC 28017. Offers sport science and pedagogy (MA). Part-time and evening/weekend programs available. *Faculty:* 2 full-time (0 women). *Students:* 7 full-time (3 women), 9 part-time (5 women); includes 2 minority (both African Americans). Average age 26. 11 applicants, 100% accepted, 11 enrolled. In 2009, 8 master's awarded. *Degree requirements:* For master's, comprehensive exam. *Entrance requirements:* For master's, GRE General Test or NTE, PRAXIS, minimum GPA of 2.5. *Application deadline:* For fall admission, 8/1 priority date for domestic students. Applications are processed on a rolling basis. Application fee: $25. Electronic applications accepted. *Expenses:* Tuition: Part-time $305 per credit hour. *Financial support:* Unspecified assistantships available. *Unit head:* Dr. Ken Baker, Chair, 704-406-4481, Fax: 704-406-4739. *Application contact:* Dr. Franki Burch, Dean, Graduate School, 704-406-4724, Fax: 704-406-4329, E-mail: gradschool@gardner-webb.edu.

George Mason University, College of Education and Human Development, School of Recreation, Health and Tourism, Manassas, VA 20110. Offers exercise, fitness, and health promotion (MS). *Faculty:* 26 full-time (10 women), 50 part-time/adjunct (29 women). *Students:* 3 full-time (1 woman), 13 part-time (7 women); includes 1 minority (Asian American or Pacific Islander). Average age 32. 16 applicants, 56% accepted, 5 enrolled. In 2009, 7 master's awarded. *Degree requirements:* For master's, thesis (for some programs). *Entrance requirements:* For master's, GRE or MAT, 3 letters of recommendation. Additional exam requirements/recommendations for international students: Required—TOEFL. *Application deadline:* For fall admission, 11/1 priority date for domestic students, 11/1 for international students; for spring admission, 4/1 for domestic and international students. Application fee: $75. Electronic applications accepted. *Expenses:* Tuition, state resident: full-time $7568; part-time $315.33 per credit hour. Tuition, nonresident: full-time $21,704; part-time $904.33 per credit hour. Required fees: $2184; $91 per credit hour. *Financial support:* In 2009–10, 2 students received support, including 2 research assistantships with full and partial tuition reimbursements available (averaging $5,374 per year); Federal Work-Study, scholarships/grants, unspecified assistantships, and health care benefits (full-time research or teaching assistantship recipients) also available. Support available to part-time students. Financial award application deadline: 3/1; financial award applicants required to submit FAFSA. *Faculty research:* Informing policy; promoting economic development; advocating stewardship of natural resources; improving the quality of life of individuals, families, and communities at the local, national and international levels. Total annual research expenditures: $77,515. *Unit head:* David Wiggins, Director, 703-993-2057, E-mail: dwiggin1@gmu.edu. *Application contact:* Dr. Pierre Rodgers, Associate Professor/Co-Coordinator of the Graduate Program, 703-993-8317, E-mail: prodgers@gmu.edu.

George Mason University, College of Health and Human Services, Program in Health Science, Fairfax, VA 22030. Offers exercise, science and health (MS). *Students:* 2 full-time (both women), 10 part-time (8 women); includes 6 minority (4 African Americans, 2 Asian Americans or Pacific Islanders), 2 international. Average age 36. In 2009, 12 master's awarded. *Degree requirements:* For master's, comprehensive exam, thesis optional. *Entrance requirements:* For master's, minimum GPA of 3.0 in last 60 hours of course work. *Application deadline:* For fall admission, 5/1 for domestic students; for spring admission, 11/1 for domestic students. Application fee: $60 ($75 for international students). Electronic applications accepted. *Expenses:* Tuition, state resident: full-time $7568; part-time $315.33 per credit hour. Tuition, nonresident: full-time $21,704; part-time $904.33 per credit hour. Required fees: $2184; $91 per credit hour. *Financial support:* Available to part-time students. Application deadline: 3/1. *Unit head:* Dr. David Wiggins, Chair, 703-993-2057, E-mail: dwiggin1@gmu.edu. *Application contact:* Dr. David Wiggins, Chair, 703-993-2057, E-mail: dwiggin1@gmu.edu.

The George Washington University, School of Public Health and Health Services, Department of Exercise Science, Washington, DC 20052. Offers MS. *Faculty:* 6 full-time (3 women), 56 part-time/adjunct (34 women). *Students:* 40 full-time (28 women), 26 part-time (22 women); includes 11 minority (5 African Americans, 1 Asian American or Pacific Islander, 5 Hispanic Americans), 3 international. Average age 27. 50 applicants, 90% accepted, 27 enrolled. In 2009, 16 master's awarded. *Degree requirements:* For master's, comprehensive exam, thesis. *Entrance requirements:* For master's, GRE General Test or MAT. Additional exam requirements/recommendations for international students: Required—TOEFL. *Application deadline:* For fall admission, 4/15 priority date for domestic students, 4/15 for international students; for spring admission, 11/1 for domestic and international students. Applications are processed on a rolling basis. Application fee: $60. *Financial support:* In 2009–10, 12 students received support. Tuition waivers available. Financial award application deadline: 2/15. *Faculty research:* Fitness and cardiac rehabilitation, exercise testing, women in exercise. *Unit head:* Dr. Loretta DiPietro, Chair, 202-994-4910, Fax: 202-994-1420, E-mail: esclxd@gwumc.edu. *Application contact:* Jane Smith, Director of Admissions, 202-994-0248, Fax: 202-994-1860, E-mail: sphhsinfo@gwumc.edu.

Georgia College & State University, Graduate School, College of Health Sciences, Department of Kinesiology, Milledgeville, GA 31061. Offers health promotion (M Ed); human performance (M Ed); kinesiology (MAT); outdoor education (M Ed). *Accreditation:* NCATE (one or more programs are accredited). Part-time and evening/weekend programs available. *Faculty:* 12 full-time (5 women). *Students:* 25 full-time (13 women), 7 part-time (5 women); includes 4 minority (2 African Americans, 2 Hispanic Americans), 3 international. Average age 26. 23 applicants, 87% accepted, 19 enrolled. In 2009, 7 master's awarded. *Degree requirements:* For master's, thesis optional. *Entrance requirements:* For master's, GRE General Test or MAT, minimum GPA of 2.75 in upper-level undergraduate courses, 2 letters of reference. Additional exam requirements/recommendations for international students: Recommended—TOEFL (minimum score 550 paper-based; 213 computer-based; 79 iBT). *Application deadline:* For fall admission, 7/15 priority date for domestic students; for spring admission, 11/15 for domestic students. Applications are processed on a rolling basis. Application fee: $40. Electronic applications accepted. *Expenses:* Tuition, area resident: Part-time $241 per credit hour. Tuition, state resident: full-time $4338. Tuition, nonresident: full-time $17,352; part-time $964 per credit hour. Required fees: $609 per semester. Tuition and fees vary according to course load and campus/location. *Financial support:* In 2009–10, 20 research assistantships with full tuition reimbursements were awarded; career-related internships or fieldwork and unspecified assistantships also available. Support available to part-time students. Financial award applicants required to submit FAFSA. *Unit head:* Dr. Jude Hirsch, Chair, 478-445-4072, Fax: 478-445-1790, E-mail: jude.hirsch@gcsu.edu. *Application contact:* Dr. Jude Hirsch, Chair, 478-445-4072, Fax: 478-445-1790, E-mail: jude.hirsch@gcsu.edu.

Georgia State University, College of Education, Department of Kinesiology and Health, Program in Exercise Science, Atlanta, GA 30302-3083. Offers MS. *Degree requirements:* For master's, comprehensive exam. *Entrance requirements:* For master's, GRE General Test, minimum GPA of 2.5. *Faculty research:* Aging, exercise metabolism, biomechanics and ergonomics, blood pressure regulation, exercise performance.

High Point University, Norcross Graduate School, High Point, NC 27262-3598. Offers business administration (MBA); educational leadership (M Ed); elementary education (M Ed); history (MA); nonprofit management (MA); special education (M Ed); sport studies (MS). *Accreditation:* ACBSP; NCATE. Part-time and evening/weekend programs available. *Degree requirements:* For master's, comprehensive exam (for some programs), thesis (for some programs). *Entrance requirements:* For master's, GMAT (MBA), GRE General Test, MAT, minimum GPA of 3.0. Additional exam requirements/recommendations for international students: Required—TOEFL (minimum score 550 paper-based). Electronic applications accepted.

Hofstra University, School of Education, Health, and Human Services, Department of Physical Education and Sports Sciences, Hempstead, NY 11549. Offers physical education (MA, MS), including adventure education, curriculum (MA), strength and conditioning; sport science (MS), including adventure education (MA, MS), strength and conditioning (MA, MS). Part-time and evening/weekend programs available. *Faculty:* 6 full-time (3 women), 11 part-time/adjunct (5 women). *Students:* 76 full-time (23 women), 28 part-time (11 women); includes 8 minority (5 African Americans, 3 Hispanic Americans). Average age 28. 47 applicants, 89% accepted, 29 enrolled. In 2009, 25 master's awarded. *Degree requirements:* For master's, electronic portfolio, capstone project. *Entrance requirements:* For master's, 2 letters of recommendation, interview. Additional exam requirements/recommendations for international students: Required—TOEFL (minimum score 550 paper-based; 213 computer-based; 80 iBT). *Application deadline:* Applications are processed on a rolling basis. Application fee: $60. Electronic applications accepted. *Expenses:* Tuition: Full-time $16,200; part-time $900 per credit hour. Required fees: $970; $145 per term. Tuition and fees vary according to program. *Financial support:* In 2009–10, 30 students received support, including 9 fellowships with full and partial tuition reimbursements available (averaging $2,944 per year), 4 research assistantships with full and partial tuition reimbursements available (averaging $16,784 per year); Federal Work-Study, institutionally sponsored loans, scholarships/grants, and tuition waivers (full and partial) also available. Support available to part-time students. Financial award applicants required to submit FAFSA. *Faculty research:* After school programming; energy expenditures in physical activities; group cohesion; childhood obesity. Total annual research expenditures: $8,500. *Unit head:* Dr. Nancy E. Halliday, Chairperson, 516-463-5811, Fax: 516-463-6275, E-mail: hprneh@hofstra.edu. *Application contact:* Carol Drummer, Dean of Graduate Admissions, 516-463-4876, Fax: 516-463-4664, E-mail: gradstudent@hofstra.edu.

Howard University, Graduate School, Department of Health, Human Performance and Leisure Studies, Washington, DC 20059-0002. Offers exercise physiology (MS); health education (MS); sports studies (MS), including sociology of sports, sports management; urban recreation (MS), including leisure studies. Part-time and evening/weekend programs available. *Degree requirements:* For master's, comprehensive exam, thesis. *Entrance requirements:* For master's, BS in human performance or related field. Electronic applications accepted. *Faculty research:* Health promotion, cardiovascular hypertension, physical activity, sport and human rights issues.

Humboldt State University, Graduate Studies, College of Professional Studies, Department of Kinesiology, Arcata, CA 95521-8299. Offers athletic training education (MS); exercise science/wellness management (MS); pre-physical therapy (MS); teaching/coaching (MS). *Students:* 24 full-time (13 women), 8 part-time (5 women); includes 5 minority (2 African Americans, 1 American Indian/Alaska Native, 2 Hispanic Americans). Average age 30. 25 applicants, 80% accepted, 15 enrolled. In 2009, 4 master's awarded. *Degree requirements:* For master's, thesis or alternative. *Entrance requirements:* For master's, GMAT, minimum GPA of 2.5. Additional exam requirements/recommendations for international students: Required—TOEFL. *Application deadline:* For fall admission, 6/1 for domestic students; for spring admission, 12/2 for domestic students. Applications are processed on a rolling basis. Application fee: $55. *Expenses:* Tuition, nonresident: full-time $8928. Required fees: $6102. Tuition and fees vary according to program. *Financial support:* Teaching assistantships, career-related internships

Exercise and Sports Science

Humboldt State University (continued)

or fieldwork, Federal Work-Study, and institutionally sponsored loans available. Financial award application deadline: 3/1; financial award applicants required to submit FAFSA. *Faculty research:* Human performance, adapted physical education, physical therapy. *Unit head:* Dr. Kathy Munoz, Chair, 707-826-3840, Fax: 707-826-5451, E-mail: kdm1@humboldt.edu. *Application contact:* Dr. T. K. Koesterer, Coordinator, 707-826-5967, Fax: 707-826-5451, E-mail: tjk17@humboldt.edu.

Indiana State University, School of Graduate Studies, College of Nursing, Health and Human Services, Department of Physical Education, Terre Haute, IN 47809. Offers adult fitness (MA, MS); coaching (MA, MS); exercise science (MA, MS). *Degree requirements:* For master's, thesis (for some programs). *Entrance requirements:* For master's, minor in physical education. Electronic applications accepted. *Faculty research:* Exercise science.

Indiana University Bloomington, School of Health, Physical Education and Recreation, Department of Kinesiology, Bloomington, IN 47405-7000. Offers adapted physical education (MS); applied sport science (MS); athletic administration/sport management (MS); athletic training (MS); biomechanics (MS); ergonomics (MS); exercise physiology (MS); fitness management (MS); human performance (PhD); motor learning/control (MS). Part-time programs available. *Faculty:* 28 full-time (11 women). *Students:* 132 full-time (55 women), 37 part-time (7 women); includes 16 minority (13 African Americans, 1 Asian American or Pacific Islander, 2 Hispanic Americans), 29 international. Average age 28. 179 applicants, 60% accepted, 72 enrolled. In 2009, 59 master's awarded. Terminal master's awarded for partial completion of doctoral program. *Degree requirements:* For master's, thesis optional; for doctorate, variable foreign language requirement, thesis/dissertation. *Entrance requirements:* For master's, GRE General Test, minimum GPA of 2.8; for doctorate, GRE General Test, minimum graduate GPA of 3.5, undergraduate 3.0. *Application deadline:* For fall admission, 1/1 for international students; for spring admission, 9/1 for international students. Applications are processed on a rolling basis. Application fee: $55 ($65 for international students). *Financial support:* In 2009–10, 71 students received support, including 9 fellowships (averaging $1,400 per year), 28 research assistantships with full tuition reimbursements available (averaging $10,131 per year), 38 teaching assistantships with full tuition reimbursements available (averaging $10,390 per year); career-related internships or fieldwork, Federal Work-Study, institutionally sponsored loans, scholarships/grants, tuition waivers (partial), and fee remissions also available. Financial award application deadline: 3/1. *Faculty research:* Exercise physiology and biochemistry, sports biomechanics, human motor control, adaptation of fitness and exercise to special populations. *Unit head:* Dr. Donetta Cothran, Chairperson, 812-855-3114. *Application contact:* Program Office, 812-855-5523, Fax: 812-855-9417, E-mail: kines@indiana.edu.

Indiana University of Pennsylvania, School of Graduate Studies and Research, College of Health and Human Services, Department of Health and Physical Education, Program in Sport Science, Indiana, PA 15705-1087. Offers MS. Part-time programs available. *Faculty:* 8 full-time (4 women). *Students:* 32 full-time (15 women), 15 part-time (6 women); includes 7 minority (all African Americans), 14 international. Average age 25. 113 applicants, 38% accepted, 25 enrolled. In 2009, 30 master's awarded. *Degree requirements:* For master's, thesis optional. *Entrance requirements:* For master's, 2 letters of recommendation. Additional exam requirements/recommendations for international students: Required—TOEFL. *Application deadline:* For fall admission, 7/1 priority date for domestic students; for spring admission, 11/1 for domestic students. Applications are processed on a rolling basis. Application fee: $40. *Expenses:* Tuition, state resident: full-time $6666; part-time $370 per credit hour. Tuition, nonresident: full-time $10,666; part-time $593 per credit hour. Required fees: $813 per semester. *Financial support:* In 2009–10, 1 fellowship (averaging $500 per year), 8 research assistantships (averaging $4,451 per year) were awarded. Financial award application deadline: 3/15; financial award applicants required to submit FAFSA. *Unit head:* Dr. Robert Kostelnik, E-mail: robert.kostelnik@iup.edu. *Application contact:* Dr. Robert Kostelnik, E-mail: robert.kostelnik@iup.edu.

Inter American University of Puerto Rico, Metropolitan Campus, Graduate Programs, Program in Physical Education, San Juan, PR 00919-1293. Offers teaching of physical education (MA); training and sport performance (MA). *Degree requirements:* For master's, comprehensive exam. *Entrance requirements:* For master's, GRE or EXADEP, interview. Electronic applications accepted.

Ithaca College, Division of Graduate and Professional Studies, School of Health Sciences and Human Performance, Program in Exercise and Sport Sciences, Ithaca, NY 14850. Offers MS. Part-time programs available. *Faculty:* 11 full-time (4 women). *Students:* 33 full-time (17 women), 7 part-time (6 women); includes 3 minority (1 Asian American or Pacific Islander, 2 Hispanic Americans), 6 international. Average age 23. 93 applicants, 65% accepted, 25 enrolled. In 2009, 14 master's awarded. *Degree requirements:* For master's, comprehensive exam (for some programs), thesis optional. *Entrance requirements:* For master's, GRE General Test, minimum GPA of 3.0. Additional exam requirements/recommendations for international students: Required—TOEFL (minimum score 550 paper-based; 213 computer-based; 80 iBT). *Application deadline:* Applications are processed on a rolling basis. Application fee: $40. Electronic applications accepted. *Expenses:* Tuition: Full-time $18,960; part-time $632 per credit hour. *Financial support:* In 2009–10, 32 students received support, including 22 teaching assistantships (averaging $10,757 per year); career-related internships or fieldwork, Federal Work-Study, scholarships/grants, and unspecified assistantships also available. Support available to part-time students. Financial award application deadline: 3/1; financial award applicants required to submit CSS PROFILE or FAFSA. *Faculty research:* Coach and athlete behavior and performance, strength and conditioning for athletes, exercise physiology across the age spectrum, psychophysiology, sport psychology. *Unit head:* Dr. Jeff Ives, Chairperson, 607-274-3527, Fax: 607-274-1263, E-mail: gps@ithaca.edu. *Application contact:* Rob Gearhart, Dean, Graduate and Professional Studies, 607-274-3527, Fax: 607-274-1263, E-mail: gps@ithaca.edu.

Kean University, College of Education, Program in Exercise Science, Union, NJ 07083. Offers MS. *Faculty:* 16 full-time (10 women). *Students:* 7 full-time (1 woman), 10 part-time (4 women); includes 3 minority (1 Asian American or Pacific Islander, 2 Hispanic Americans), 2 international. Average age 27. 13 applicants, 92% accepted, 6 enrolled. In 2009, 2 master's awarded. *Degree requirements:* For master's, comprehensive exam, thesis. *Entrance requirements:* For master's, GRE General Test, minimum GPA of 3.0, interview, 2 letters of recommendation, minimum B average in undergraduate prerequisites. *Application deadline:* For fall admission, 5/1 for domestic students; for spring admission, 11/1 for domestic students. Application fee: $60 ($150 for international students). Electronic applications accepted. *Expenses:* Tuition, state resident: full-time $10,440; part-time $435 per credit. Tuition, nonresident: full-time $14,160; part-time $590 per credit. Required fees: $2642; $110 per credit. Part-time tuition and fees vary according to course load and degree level. *Financial support:* In 2009–10, 1 research assistantship with full tuition reimbursement (averaging $3,263 per year) was awarded; unspecified assistantships also available. *Unit head:* Dr. Walter D. Andzel, Program Coordinator, 908-737-0662, E-mail: wandzel@kean.edu. *Application contact:* Steven Koch, Pre-Admissions Coordinator, 908-737-5924, Fax: 908-737-5965, E-mail: skoch@kean.edu.

Kennesaw State University, College of Health and Human Services, Program in Applied Exercise and Health Science, Kennesaw, GA 30144-5591. Offers MS. Part-time and evening/weekend programs available. *Students:* 13 full-time (7 women), 10 part-time (6 women); includes 2 minority (both African Americans), 3 international. Average age 29. 18 applicants, 61% accepted, 9 enrolled. *Entrance requirements:* For master's, GRE, resume. Additional exam requirements/recommendations for international students: Required—TOEFL (minimum score 550 paper-based; 218 computer-based; 80 iBT), IELTS (minimum score 6). *Application deadline:* For fall admission, 6/1 for domestic and international students; for winter admission, 12/1 for domestic and international students; for spring admission, 4/1 for domestic and international students. Applications are processed on a rolling basis. Application fee: $60. *Expenses:* Tuition, state resident: full-time $2341; part-time $196 per credit hour. Tuition, nonresident: full-time $9396; part-time $783 per credit hour. Required fees: $573 per semester. *Financial support:* In 2009–10, 2 research assistantships (averaging $4,000 per year) were

awarded. Financial award applicants required to submit FAFSA. *Unit head:* Dr. Ping Johnson, Program Director, 770-499-3149, E-mail: pjohnso2@kennesaw.edu. *Application contact:* Vilma Marquez, Admissions Counselor, 770-420-4377, Fax: 770-423-6885, E-mail: vmarquez@kennesaw.edu.

Kent State University, Graduate School of Education, Health, and Human Services, School of Foundations, Leadership and Administration, Program in Exercise, Leisure and Sport, Kent, OH 44242-0001. Offers sport and recreation management (MA); sports studies (MA). *Faculty:* 11 full-time (6 women), 4 part-time/adjunct (0 women). *Students:* 50 full-time (17 women), 16 part-time (6 women); includes 7 minority (6 African Americans, 1 Asian American or Pacific Islander), 1 international. 48 applicants, 100% accepted. In 2009, 31 master's awarded. Application fee: $30. *Financial support:* In 2009–10, 10 research assistantships (averaging $8,500 per year) were awarded; Federal Work-Study, scholarships/grants, and unspecified assistantships also available. *Unit head:* Mark Lyberger, Coordinator, 330-672-0228, E-mail: mlyberge@kent.edu. *Application contact:* Nancy Miller, Academic Program Coordinator, Office of Graduate Student Services, 330-672-2576, Fax: 330-672-9162, E-mail: ogs@kent.edu.

Kent State University, Graduate School of Education, Health, and Human Services, School of Health Sciences, Program in Exercise, Leisure and Sport, Kent, OH 44242-0001. Offers athletic training (MA); exercise physiology (MA). *Faculty:* 6 full-time (3 women). *Students:* 10 full-time (5 women), 1 (woman) part-time; includes 1 Asian American or Pacific Islander. 29 applicants, 66% accepted. In 2009, 7 master's awarded. *Financial support:* In 2009–10, 8 research assistantships (averaging $8,313 per year) were awarded; Federal Work-Study, scholarships/grants, and unspecified assistantships also available. *Unit head:* Dr. Lynne B. Rowan, Interim Director, 330-672-9785, E-mail: lrowan@kent.edu. *Application contact:* Nancy Miller, Academic Program Coordinator, Office of Graduate Student Services, 330-672-2576, Fax: 330-672-9162, E-mail: ogs@kent.edu.

Kent State University, Graduate School of Education, Health, and Human Services, School of Health Sciences, Program in Physical Education, Kent, OH 44242-0001. Offers exercise physiology (PhD). *Faculty:* 4 full-time (2 women). *Students:* 21 full-time (8 women), 4 part-time (1 woman); includes 4 minority (2 African Americans, 2 Asian Americans or Pacific Islanders), 1 international. 9 applicants, 67% accepted. In 2009, 2 doctorates awarded. Application fee: $30. *Financial support:* In 2009–10, 5 fellowships (averaging $10,952 per year) were awarded; Federal Work-Study, scholarships/grants, and unspecified assistantships also available. *Unit head:* Ellen Glickman, Coordinator, 330-672-2930, E-mail: eglickma@kent.edu. *Application contact:* Nancy Miller, Academic Program Coordinator, Office of Graduate Student Services, 330-672-2576, Fax: 330-672-9162, E-mail: ogs@kent.edu.

Lakehead University, Graduate Studies, School of Kinesiology, Thunder Bay, ON P7B 5E1, Canada. Offers kinesiology (M Sc); kinesiology and gerontology (M Sc). Part-time programs available. *Degree requirements:* For master's, thesis. *Entrance requirements:* For master's, minimum B average. Additional exam requirements/recommendations for international students: Required—TOEFL. *Faculty research:* Social psychology and physical education, sport history, sports medicine, exercise physiology, gerontology.

Life University, College of Arts and Sciences, Program in Sport Health Science, Marietta, GA 30060-2903. Offers chiropractic sport science (MS); exercise and sport science (MS); sport coaching (MS); sport injury management (MS). Part-time programs available. *Degree requirements:* For master's, comprehensive exam (for some programs), thesis optional. *Entrance requirements:* For master's, GRE General Test or MAT, minimum GPA of 3.0, 3 letters of recommendation. Additional exam requirements/recommendations for international students: Required—TOEFL (minimum score 500 paper-based; 173 computer-based). Electronic applications accepted.

Long Island University, Brooklyn Campus, School of Health Professions, Division of Sports Sciences, Brooklyn, NY 11201-8423. Offers adapted physical education (MS); athletic training and sports sciences (MS); exercise physiology (MS); health sciences (MS). Part-time and evening/weekend programs available. *Entrance requirements:* For master's, 2 letters of recommendation. Additional exam requirements/recommendations for international students: Required—TOEFL (minimum score 500 paper-based; 173 computer-based). Electronic applications accepted.

Louisiana Tech University, Graduate School, College of Education, Department of Health and Exercise Sciences, Ruston, LA 71272. Offers MS. *Accreditation:* NCATE. Part-time programs available. *Degree requirements:* For master's, thesis or alternative. *Entrance requirements:* For master's, GRE General Test.

Manhattanville College, Graduate Programs, School of Education, Program in Physical Education and Sport Pedagogy, Purchase, NY 10577-2132. Offers MAT. Part-time and evening/weekend programs available. *Students:* 94 full-time (28 women), 116 part-time (27 women); includes 8 African Americans, 3 Asian Americans or Pacific Islanders, 6 Hispanic Americans, 2 international. In 2009, 50 master's awarded. *Entrance requirements:* Additional exam requirements/recommendations for international students: Required—TOEFL. *Application deadline:* Applications are processed on a rolling basis. Application fee: $70. Electronic applications accepted. *Financial support:* Career-related internships or fieldwork, Federal Work-Study, institutionally sponsored loans, scholarships/grants, and unspecified assistantships available. Support available to part-time students. Financial award application deadline: 3/1; financial award applicants required to submit FAFSA. *Unit head:* Dr. Shelley Wepner, Dean, 914-323-5192, Fax: 914-694-2386, E-mail: wepners@mville.edu. *Application contact:* Jeanine Pardey-Levine, Director of Admissions, 914-373-3208, Fax: 914-694-1732, E-mail: edschool@mville.edu.

Marshall University, Academic Affairs Division, College of Education and Human Services, School of Kinesiology, Program in Exercise Science, Huntington, WV 25755. Offers MS. *Faculty:* 7 full-time (2 women), 5 part-time/adjunct (2 women). *Students:* 39 full-time (19 women), 6 part-time (2 women); includes 5 minority (4 African Americans, 1 Asian American or Pacific Islander). Average age 25. In 2009, 15 master's awarded. *Degree requirements:* For master's, thesis optional, comprehensive assessment. *Entrance requirements:* For master's, GRE General Test. Application fee: $40. *Unit head:* Dr. William Marley, Director, Human Performance Laboratory Programs, 304-696-2936, E-mail: marley@marshall.edu. *Application contact:* Information Contact, 304-746-1900, Fax: 304-746-1902, E-mail: services@marshall.edu.

Marywood University, Academic Affairs, College of Health and Human Services, Department of Nutrition and Dietetics, Program in Sports Nutrition and Exercise Science, Scranton, PA 18509-1598. Offers MS. *Students:* 11 full-time (8 women), 5 part-time (3 women). Average age 26. In 2009, 4 master's awarded. *Entrance requirements:* Additional exam requirements/recommendations for international students: Required—TOEFL (minimum score 550 paper-based; 213 computer-based; 79 iBT). *Application deadline:* For fall admission, 4/1 priority date for domestic students, 3/31 priority date for international students; for spring admission, 11/1 priority date for domestic students, 8/31 priority date for international students. Applications are processed on a rolling basis. Application fee: $35. Electronic applications accepted. *Expenses:* Tuition: Part-time $715 per credit. Required fees: $270 per semester. Tuition and fees vary according to degree level, campus/location and program. *Financial support:* Career-related internships or fieldwork, scholarships/grants, and unspecified assistantships available. Support available to part-time students. Financial award application deadline: 6/30; financial award applicants required to submit FAFSA. *Faculty research:* Lung function studies (pulmonary diffusing capacity of nitric oxide). *Unit head:* Dr. Kathleen Mckee, Co-Chair, 570-348-6211 Ext. 2632, E-mail: khmckee@es.marywood.edu. *Application contact:* Tammy Manka, Assistant Director of Graduate Admissions, 866-279-9663, E-mail: tmanka@marywood.edu.

McNeese State University, Doré School of Graduate Studies, Burton College of Education, Department of Health and Human Performance, Lake Charles, LA 70609. Offers exercise physiology (MS); health promotion (MS); nutrition and wellness (MS). *Accreditation:* NCATE. Evening/weekend programs available. *Faculty:* 5 full-time (2 women). *Students:* 40 full-time (32 women), 6 part-time (4 women); includes 6 minority (all African Americans), 4 international.

In 2009, 22 master's awarded. *Entrance requirements:* For master's, GRE, undergraduate major or minor in health and human performance or related field of study. *Application deadline:* For fall admission, 5/15 priority date for domestic and international students; for spring admission, 10/15 priority date for domestic and international students. Applications are processed on a rolling basis. Application fee: $20 ($30 for international students). *Expenses:* Tuition, area resident: Full-time $2556. Tuition, state resident: full-time $2556. Required fees: $1031. Tuition and fees vary according to course load. *Financial support:* Application deadline: 5/1. *Unit head:* Dr. Michael Soileau, Head, 337-475-5374, Fax: 337-475-5947, E-mail: msoileau@mcneese.edu. *Application contact:* Dr. George F. Mead, Interim Dean of Dore' School of Graduate Studies, 337-475-5396, Fax: 337-475-5397, E-mail: admissions@mcneese.edu.

Memorial University of Newfoundland, School of Graduate Studies, School of Human Kinetics and Recreation, St. John's, NL A1C 5S7, Canada. Offers administration, curriculum and supervision (MPE); biomechanics/ergonomics (MS Kin); exercise and work physiology (MS Kin); sport psychology (MS Kin). Part-time programs available. *Degree requirements:* For master's, thesis optional, seminars, thesis presentations. *Entrance requirements:* For master's, bachelor's degree in a related field, minimum B average. Electronic applications accepted. *Faculty research:* Administration, sociology of sports, kinesiology, physiology/recreation.

Miami University, Graduate School, School of Education and Allied Professions, Department of Physical Education, Health, and Sports Studies, Oxford, OH 45056. Offers exercise and health studies (MS); sport studies (MS). Part-time programs available. *Students:* 45 full-time (27 women), 7 part-time (3 women); includes 5 minority (3 African Americans, 1 Asian American or Pacific Islander, 1 Hispanic American), 2 international. *Entrance requirements:* For master's, GRE or MAT, minimum undergraduate GPA of 3.0 during previous 2 years or 2.75 overall. Additional exam requirements/recommendations for international students: Required—TOEFL. Application fee: $50. *Expenses:* Tuition, state resident: full-time $11,280. Tuition, nonresident: full-time $24,912. Required fees: $516. *Financial support:* Fellowships with full tuition reimbursements, research assistantships, teaching assistantships, Federal Work-Study, health care benefits, tuition waivers (full), and unspecified assistantships available. Financial award application deadline: 3/1. *Unit head:* Dr. Helaine Alessio, Chair, 513-529-2700, E-mail: knhdept@muohio.edu. *Application contact:* Dr. Robin Vealey, Coordinator, Graduate Program, 513-529-2700, E-mail: knhdept@muohio.edu.

Middle Tennessee State University, College of Graduate Studies, College of Education and Behavioral Science, Department of Health and Human Performance, Program in Exercise Science, Murfreesboro, TN 37132. Offers MS. Part-time and evening/weekend programs available. Postbaccalaureate distance learning degree programs offered. *Students:* 2 full-time (0 women), 24 part-time (12 women); includes 6 minority (4 African Americans, 1 Asian American or Pacific Islander, 1 Hispanic American). 32 applicants, 91% accepted. In 2009, 6 master's awarded. *Degree requirements:* For master's, comprehensive exam. *Entrance requirements:* For master's, GRE or MAT. Additional exam requirements/recommendations for international students: Required—TOEFL (minimum score 525 paper-based; 195 computer-based; 71 iBT) or IELTS (minimum score 6). *Application deadline:* For fall admission, 6/1 for domestic and international students. Applications are processed on a rolling basis. Application fee: $25 ($30 for international students). *Expenses:* Tuition, state resident: full-time $4404. Tuition, nonresident: full-time $10,956. *Financial support:* Application deadline: 5/1. *Unit head:* Dr. Scott Colclough, Interim Chair, 615-898-5073, Fax: 615-898-5020, E-mail: scolclou@mtsu.edu. *Application contact:* Dr. Michael Allen, Dean and Vice Provost for Research, 615-898-2840, Fax: 615-904-8020, E-mail: mallen@mtsu.edu.

Middle Tennessee State University, College of Graduate Studies, College of Education and Behavioral Science, Department of Health and Human Performance, Program in Human Performance, Murfreesboro, TN 37132. Offers PhD. Part-time and evening/weekend programs available. Postbaccalaureate distance learning degree programs offered. *Students:* 1 full-time (0 women), 34 part-time (22 women); includes 9 minority (3 African Americans, 5 Asian Americans or Pacific Islanders, 1 Hispanic American). 22 applicants, 50% accepted, 11 enrolled. In 2009, 11 doctorates awarded. *Degree requirements:* For doctorate, comprehensive exam, thesis/dissertation. *Entrance requirements:* For doctorate, GRE. Additional exam requirements/recommendations for international students: Required—TOEFL (minimum score 525 paper-based; 195 computer-based; 71 iBT) or IELTS (minimum score 6). *Application deadline:* For fall admission, 6/1 for domestic and international students. Applications are processed on a rolling basis. Application fee: $25 ($30 for international students). *Expenses:* Tuition, state resident: full-time $4404. Tuition, nonresident: full-time $10,956. *Financial support:* In 2009–10, 15 students received support. Application deadline: 5/1. *Unit head:* Dr. Scott Colclough, Interim Chair, 615-898-5073, Fax: 615-898-5020, E-mail: scolclou@mtsu.edu. *Application contact:* Dr. Michael Allen, Dean and Vice Provost for Research, 615-898-2840, Fax: 615-904-8020, E-mail: mallen@mtsu.edu.

Mississippi State University, College of Education, Department of Kinesiology, MS State, MS 39762. Offers physical education (MS), including exercise science, sport administration, teaching/coaching. Part-time programs available. Postbaccalaureate distance learning degree programs offered (minimal on-campus study). *Faculty:* 7 full-time (1 woman). *Students:* 56 full-time (22 women), 11 part-time (6 women); includes 20 minority (18 African Americans, 1 American Indian/Alaska Native, 1 Asian American or Pacific Islander), 2 international. Average age 25. 58 applicants, 72% accepted, 36 enrolled. In 2009, 22 master's awarded. *Degree requirements:* For master's, comprehensive exam, thesis optional. *Entrance requirements:* For master's, GRE General Test, minimum GPA of 3.0. Additional exam requirements/recommendations for international students: Required—TOEFL (minimum score 550 paper-based; 213 computer-based; 79 iBT); Recommended—IELTS (minimum score 6.5). *Application deadline:* For fall admission, 7/1 for domestic students, 5/1 for international students; for spring admission, 11/1 for domestic students, 9/1 for international students. Applications are processed on a rolling basis. Application fee: $40. Electronic applications accepted. *Expenses:* Tuition, state resident: full-time $2575.50; part-time $286.25 per credit hour. Tuition, nonresident: full-time $6510; part-time $723.50 per credit hour. Tuition and fees vary according to course load. *Financial support:* In 2009–10, 7 teaching assistantships (averaging $8,772 per year) were awarded; career-related internships or fieldwork, Federal Work-Study, institutionally sponsored loans, and unspecified assistantships also available. Financial award application deadline: 4/1; financial award applicants required to submit FAFSA. *Faculty research:* Static balance and stepping performance of older adults, organizational justice, public health, strength training and recovery drinks, high risk drinking perceptions and behaviors. *Unit head:* Dr. Stanley Brown, Head, 662-325-2963, Fax: 662-325-4525, E-mail: spb107@msstate.edu. *Application contact:* Dr. John G. Lamberth, Associate Professor and Graduate Coordinator, 662-325-0906, Fax: 662-325-4525, E-mail: jgl@ra.msstate.edu.

Montana State University, College of Graduate Studies, College of Education, Health, and Human Development, Department of Health and Human Development, Bozeman, MT 59717. Offers health and human development (MS), including counseling, exercise and nutrition sciences, family and consumer sciences, family financial planning, health promotion and education. *Accreditation:* ACA. Part-time programs available. Postbaccalaureate distance learning degree programs offered (no on-campus study). *Faculty:* 27 full-time (18 women), 7 part-time/adjunct (6 women). *Students:* 54 full-time (47 women), 18 part-time (15 women); includes 1 minority (Hispanic American). Average age 30. 32 applicants, 34% accepted, 10 enrolled. In 2009, 26 master's awarded. *Degree requirements:* For master's, comprehensive exam. *Entrance requirements:* For master's, GRE General Test. Additional exam requirements/recommendations for international students: Required—TOEFL (minimum score 550 paper-based; 213 computer-based). *Application deadline:* For fall admission, 7/15 priority date for domestic students, 5/15 priority date for international students; for spring admission, 12/1 priority date for domestic students, 10/1 priority date for international students. Applications are processed on a rolling basis. Application fee: $30. Electronic applications accepted. *Expenses:* Tuition, state resident: full-time $5635; part-time $3492 per year. Tuition, nonresident: full-time $17,212; part-time $7865.10 per year. Required fees: $1441; $153.15 per credit. Tuition and fees vary according to course load and program. *Financial support:* In 2009–10, 24 students received support, including 7 research assistantships (averaging $1,000 per year), 17 teaching assistantships with full tuition reimbursements available (averaging $8,000 per year). Financial award application deadline: 3/1; financial award applicants required to submit FAFSA. *Faculty research:* Gait analysis, cancer prevention, obesity prevention, energy expenditure, decision making. Total annual research expenditures: $2.8 million. *Unit head:* Dr. Tim Dunnagan, Head, 404-994-3242, Fax: 404-994-2013, E-mail: dunnagan@montana.edu. *Application contact:* Dr. Carl Fox.

Montclair State University, The Graduate School, College of Education and Human Services, Department of Exercise Science and Physical Education, Montclair, NJ 07043-1624. Offers health and physical education (Certificate); nutrition and exercise science (Certificate); physical education (MA, Certificate), including coaching and sports administration (MA), exercise science (MA), physical education (MA), teaching and supervision of physical education (MA). Part-time and evening/weekend programs available. *Faculty:* 15 full-time (9 women), 17 part-time/adjunct (10 women). *Students:* 8 full-time (3 women), 38 part-time (19 women). Average age 30. 34 applicants, 56% accepted, 13 enrolled. In 2009, 9 master's awarded. *Degree requirements:* For master's, comprehensive exam. *Entrance requirements:* For master's, GRE General Test, 2 letters of recommendation; for Certificate, 2 letters of recommendation (nutrition and exercise science concentration). Additional exam requirements/recommendations for international students: Required—TOEFL (minimum score 83 computer-based), or IELTS. *Application deadline:* For fall admission, 6/1 for international students; for spring admission, 10/1 for international students. Applications are processed on a rolling basis. Application fee: $60. Electronic applications accepted. *Expenses:* Tuition, area resident: Part-time $486.74 per credit. Tuition, state resident: part-time $486.74 per credit. Tuition, nonresident: part-time $751.34 per credit. Tuition and fees vary according to degree level and program. *Financial support:* In 2009–10, 5 research assistantships with full tuition reimbursements (averaging $7,000 per year) were awarded; Federal Work-Study, scholarships/grants, and unspecified assistantships also available. Support available to part-time students. Financial award application deadline: 3/1; financial award applicants required to submit FAFSA. *Unit head:* Dr. Susana Juniu, Chairperson, 973-655-7093. *Application contact:* Amy Aliello, Director of Graduate Admissions and Operations, 973-655-5147, Fax: 973-655-7869, E-mail: graduate.school@montclair.edu.

Morehead State University, Graduate Programs, College of Science and Technology, Department of Health, Wellness and Human Performance, Morehead, KY 40351. Offers health/physical education (MA). *Accreditation:* NCATE. Part-time and evening/weekend programs available. *Faculty:* 5 full-time (4 women). *Students:* 8 full-time (4 women), 6 part-time (4 women); includes 1 African American. Average age 28. 9 applicants, 78% accepted, 6 enrolled. In 2009, 3 master's awarded. *Degree requirements:* For master's, comprehensive exam, thesis, oral exam, written core exam. *Entrance requirements:* For master's, GRE General Test or MAT, minimum GPA of 2.5; undergraduate major/minor in health, physical education, or recreation. Additional exam requirements/recommendations for international students: Required—TOEFL (minimum score 500 paper-based; 173 computer-based). *Application deadline:* For fall admission, 8/1 priority date for domestic and international students; for spring admission, 12/1 priority date for domestic and international students. Applications are processed on a rolling basis. Application fee: $30. Electronic applications accepted. *Expenses:* Tuition, state resident: full-time $6318; part-time $351 per credit hour. Tuition, nonresident: full-time $15,804; part-time $878 per credit hour. *Financial support:* In 2009–10, 1 research assistantship (averaging $10,000 per year), 3 teaching assistantships (averaging $10,000 per year) were awarded; career-related internships or fieldwork, Federal Work-Study, and unspecified assistantships also available. Financial award application deadline: 3/15; financial award applicants required to submit FAFSA. *Faculty research:* Child growth and performance, instructional strategies, outdoor leadership qualities, exercise science, athletic training. *Unit head:* Dr. Lynne Fitzgerald, Chair, 606-783-2466, Fax: 606-783-5058, E-mail: l.fitzgerald@moreheadstate.edu. *Application contact:* Michelle Barber, Graduate Recruitment and Retention Assistant Director, 606-783-5127, Fax: 606-783-5061, E-mail: m.barber@moreheadstate.edu.

Murray State University, College of Health Sciences and Human Services, Department of Wellness and Therapeutic Sciences, Program in Exercise and Leisure Studies, Murray, KY 42071. Offers MS. Part-time programs available. *Degree requirements:* For master's, thesis optional. *Entrance requirements:* For master's, GRE General Test or MAT. Additional exam requirements/recommendations for international students: Required—TOEFL. *Faculty research:* Exercise and cancer recovery.

New Mexico Highlands University, Graduate Studies, School of Education, Department of Exercise and Sport Sciences, Las Vegas, NM 87701. Offers human performance and sport (MA); sports administration (MA); teacher education (MA). Part-time programs available. *Degree requirements:* For master's, comprehensive exam, thesis or alternative. *Entrance requirements:* For master's, minimum undergraduate GPA of 3.0. Additional exam requirements/recommendations for international students: Required—TOEFL (minimum score 540 paper-based; 207 computer-based). *Faculty research:* Child obesity and physical inactivity, body composition and fitness assessment, motor development, sport marketing, sport finance.

North Dakota State University, College of Graduate and Interdisciplinary Studies, College of Human Development and Education, Department of Health, Nutrition, and Exercise Sciences, Fargo, ND 58108. Offers dietetics (MS); entry level athletic training (MS); exercise science (MS); nutrition science (MS); public health (MS); sport pedagogy (MS); sports recreation management (MS). Part-time and evening/weekend programs available. Postbaccalaureate distance learning degree programs offered (no on-campus study). *Faculty:* 12 full-time (6 women). *Students:* 28 full-time (18 women), 23 part-time (16 women); includes 1 African American, 1 Asian American or Pacific Islander, 3 international. 19 applicants, 100% accepted, 15 enrolled. In 2009, 27 master's awarded. *Degree requirements:* For master's, thesis (for some programs). *Entrance requirements:* For master's, minimum GPA of 3.0. Additional exam requirements/recommendations for international students: Required—TOEFL (minimum score 525 paper-based; 197 computer-based; 71 iBT). *Application deadline:* For fall admission, 3/1 priority date for domestic and international students. Application fee: $45 ($60 for international students). Electronic applications accepted. *Financial support:* In 2009–10, 28 students received support, including 18 teaching assistantships with full tuition reimbursements available (averaging $6,500 per year). Financial award application deadline: 3/31. *Faculty research:* Biomechanics, sport specialization, recreation, nutrition, athletic training. Total annual research expenditures: $10,000. *Unit head:* Brad Strand, Head, 701-231-7474, Fax: 701-231-8872, E-mail: bradford.strand@ndsu.edu. *Application contact:* Brad Strand, Head, 701-231-7474, Fax: 701-231-8872, E-mail: bradford.strand@ndsu.edu.

Northeastern University, Bouvé College of Health Sciences Graduate School, Program in Clinical Exercise Physiology, Boston, MA 02115-5096. Offers MS. Part-time and evening/weekend programs available. *Students:* 21 full-time (15 women); includes 2 Hispanic Americans, 3 international. 35 applicants, 71% accepted, 13 enrolled. In 2009, 9 master's awarded. *Degree requirements:* For master's, comprehensive exam, thesis optional. *Entrance requirements:* For master's, GRE General Test. Additional exam requirements/recommendations for international students: Required—TOEFL (minimum score 100 iBT). *Application deadline:* For fall admission, 6/1 for domestic students. Applications are processed on a rolling basis. Application fee: $50. Electronic applications accepted. *Financial support:* Research assistantships with tuition reimbursements, teaching assistantships with tuition reimbursements, career-related internships or fieldwork, Federal Work-Study, scholarships/grants, tuition waivers (partial), and unspecified assistantships available. Support available to part-time students. Financial award application deadline: 3/1; financial award applicants required to submit FAFSA. *Faculty research:* Exercise in cardiovascular pulmonary and metabolic diseases, mechanisms related to lactate and ventilation threshold, body composition assessment techniques. *Unit head:* Prof. William J. Gillespie, Director, 617-373-5695, Fax: 617-373-2968, E-mail: w.gillespie@neu.edu. *Application contact:* Margaret Schnabel, Director of Graduate Admissions, 617-373-2708, E-mail: bouvegrad@neu.edu.

Northern Michigan University, College of Graduate Studies, College of Professional Studies, Department of Health, Physical Education and Recreation, Marquette, MI 49855-5301. Offers

Exercise and Sports Science

Northern Michigan University (continued)
exercise science (MS). Part-time programs available. *Degree requirements:* For master's, thesis or alternative. *Entrance requirements:* For master's, GRE General Test, minimum GPA of 3.0 in major, 2.75 overall; 9 hours of course work in human anatomy, physiology, kinesiology.

Oakland University, Graduate Study and Lifelong Learning, School of Health Sciences, Program in Exercise Science, Rochester, MI 48309-4401. Offers MS, Certificate. *Degree requirements:* For master's, thesis (for some programs). *Entrance requirements:* For master's, minimum GPA of 3.0 for unconditional admission. Additional exam requirements/recommendations for international students: Required—TOEFL (minimum score 550 paper-based; 213 computer-based). Electronic applications accepted. *Expenses:* Contact institution.

Ohio University, Graduate College, College of Arts and Sciences, Department of Biological Sciences, Athens, OH 45701-2979. Offers biological sciences (MS, PhD); cell biology and physiology (MS, PhD); ecology and evolutionary biology (MS, PhD); exercise physiology and muscle biology (MS, PhD); microbiology (MS, PhD); neuroscience (MS, PhD). *Faculty:* 50 full-time (14 women), 6 part-time/adjunct (1 woman). *Students:* 44 full-time (19 women), 8 part-time (3 women); includes 2 minority (1 African American, 1 Hispanic American), 21 international. 95 applicants, 24% accepted, 10 enrolled. In 2009, 4 master's, 9 doctorates awarded. Terminal master's awarded for partial completion of doctoral program. *Degree requirements:* For master's, comprehensive exam, thesis, 1 quarter of teaching experience; for doctorate, comprehensive exam, thesis/dissertation, 2 quarters of teaching experience. *Entrance requirements:* For master's, GRE General Test, names of three faculty members whose research interests most closely match the applicant's interest; for doctorate, GRE General Test, essay concerning prior training, research interest and career goals, plus names of three faculty members whose research interests most closely match the applicant's interest. Additional exam requirements/recommendations for international students: Required—TOEFL (minimum score 620 paper-based; 105 iBT) or IELTS Academic (minimum score 7.5). *Application deadline:* For fall admission, 1/15 for domestic and international students. Application fee: $50 ($55 for international students). Electronic applications accepted. *Expenses:* Tuition, state resident: full-time $7839; part-time $323 per quarter hour. Tuition, nonresident: full-time $15,831; part-time $654 per quarter hour. Required fees: $2931. *Financial support:* In 2009–10, 1 fellowship with full tuition reimbursement (averaging $18,957 per year), 10 research assistantships with full tuition reimbursements (averaging $18,957 per year), 42 teaching assistantships with full tuition reimbursements (averaging $18,957 per year) were awarded; Federal Work-Study and institutionally sponsored loans also available. Financial award application deadline: 1/15. *Faculty research:* Ecology and evolutionary biology, exercise physiology and muscle biology, neurobiology, cell biology, physiology. Total annual research expenditures: $2.8 million. *Unit head:* Dr. Ralph DiCaprio, Chair, 740-593-2290, Fax: 740-593-0300, E-mail: dicapri@ohio.edu. *Application contact:* Dr. Donald Holzschu, Graduate Chair, 740-593-0425, Fax: 740-593-0300, E-mail: holzschu@ohio.edu.

Ohio University, Graduate College, College of Health and Human Services, School of Recreation and Sport Sciences, Program in Physiology of Exercise, Athens, OH 45701-2979. Offers MS. *Faculty:* 5 full-time (2 women), 2 part-time/adjunct (0 women). *Students:* 15 full-time (6 women), 1 part-time (0 women). 74 applicants, 47% accepted. In 2009, 6 master's awarded. *Degree requirements:* For master's, thesis or alternative. *Entrance requirements:* For master's, GRE, minimum GPA of 3.0. Additional exam requirements/recommendations for international students: Required—TOEFL (minimum score 550 paper-based; 80 iBT) or IELTS Academic (minimum score 6.5). *Application deadline:* For fall admission, 3/1 priority date for domestic and international students. Application fee: $50 ($55 for international students). Electronic applications accepted. *Expenses:* Tuition, state resident: full-time $7839; part-time $323 per quarter hour. Tuition, nonresident: full-time $15,831; part-time $654 per quarter hour. Required fees: $2931. *Financial support:* In 2009–10, research assistantships with tuition reimbursements (averaging $8,577 per year), teaching assistantships with full tuition reimbursements (averaging $8,577 per year) were awarded; Federal Work-Study, institutionally sponsored loans, and scholarships/grants also available. Financial award application deadline: 3/15. *Faculty research:* Blood pressure, heart rate, health skeleton, muscles, training. *Unit head:* Dr. Roger Gilders, Coordinator, 740-593-0101, Fax: 740-593-0285, E-mail: gilders@ohio.edu. *Application contact:* Graduate Records.

Old Dominion University, Darden College of Education, Program in Physical Education, Exercise and Wellness Emphasis, Norfolk, VA 23529. Offers MS Ed. Part-time and evening/weekend programs available. *Faculty:* 7 full-time (4 women). *Students:* 19 full-time (13 women), 7 part-time (5 women); includes 4 minority (3 African Americans, 1 Hispanic American), 3 international. Average age 27. 12 applicants, 100% accepted, 10 enrolled. In 2009, 11 master's awarded. *Degree requirements:* For master's, comprehensive exam, thesis or alternative, internship, research project. *Entrance requirements:* For master's, GRE, minimum GPA of 2.8 overall, 3.0 in major. Additional exam requirements/recommendations for international students: Required—TOEFL (minimum score 500 paper-based; 200 computer-based). *Application deadline:* For fall admission, 7/1 for domestic students; for spring admission, 11/1 for domestic students. Applications are processed on a rolling basis. Application fee: $40. *Expenses:* Tuition, state resident: full-time $8112; part-time $338 per credit. Tuition, nonresident: full-time $20,256; part-time $844 per credit. Required fees: $119 per semester. One-time fee: $50. *Financial support:* In 2009–10, 1 teaching assistantship (averaging $9,000 per year) was awarded; career-related internships or fieldwork and scholarships/grants also available. Financial award application deadline: 4/15. *Faculty research:* Diabetes, exercise, prescription, gait and balance. Total annual research expenditures: $105,000. *Unit head:* Liz Dowling, Graduate Program Director, 757-683-4995, E-mail: ldowling@odu.edu. *Application contact:* Liz Dowling, Graduate Program Director, 757-683-4995, E-mail: ldowling@odu.edu.

Oregon State University, Graduate School, College of Health and Human Sciences, Department of Nutrition and Exercise Sciences, Corvallis, OR 97331. Offers exercise and sport science (MS, PhD); movement studies in disabilities (MAIS, MS); nutrition and exercise sciences (MAIS); nutrition and food management (MS). *Faculty:* 26 full-time (16 women), 3 part-time/adjunct (all women). *Students:* 47 full-time (26 women), 6 part-time (3 women); includes 2 minority (1 American Indian/Alaska Native, 1 Hispanic American), 7 international. Average age 29. In 2009, 20 master's, 9 doctorates awarded. Terminal master's awarded for partial completion of doctoral program. *Degree requirements:* For master's, thesis; for doctorate, thesis/dissertation. *Entrance requirements:* For master's and doctorate, minimum GPA of 3.0 in last 90 hours. Additional exam requirements/recommendations for international students: Required—TOEFL. Application fee: $50. *Expenses:* Tuition, state resident: full-time $9774; part-time $362 per credit. Tuition, nonresident: full-time $15,849; part-time $587 per credit. Required fees: $1639. Full-time tuition and fees vary according to course load and program. *Financial support:* Research assistantships, teaching assistantships, career-related internships or fieldwork, Federal Work-Study, and institutionally sponsored loans available. Support available to part-time students. Financial award application deadline: 2/1. *Faculty research:* Motor control, sports medicine, exercise physiology, sport psychology, biomechanics. *Unit head:* Dr. Anthony R. Wilcox, Chair, 541-737-2643, Fax: 541-737-6914, E-mail: anthony.wilcox@oregonstate.edu. *Application contact:* Dr. Anthony R. Wilcox, Chair, 541-737-2643, Fax: 541-737-6914, E-mail: anthony.wilcox@oregonstate.edu.

Purdue University, Graduate School, College of Liberal Arts, Department of Health and Kinesiology, West Lafayette, IN 47907. Offers exercise, human physiology of movement and sport (PhD); health and fitness (MS); health promotion (MS); health promotion and disease prevention (PhD); movement and sport science (MS); pedagogy and administration (MS); pedagogy of physical activity and health (PhD); psychology of sport and exercise, and motor behavior (PhD). Part-time programs available. *Degree requirements:* For master's, thesis (for some programs); for doctorate, thesis/dissertation. *Entrance requirements:* For master's and doctorate, GRE General Test. Additional exam requirements/recommendations for international students: Required—TOEFL. Electronic applications accepted. *Faculty research:* Wellness, motivation, teaching effectiveness, learning and development.

Queens College of the City University of New York, Division of Graduate Studies, Mathematics and Natural Sciences Division, Department of Family, Nutrition and Exercise Sciences, Flushing, NY 11367-1597. Offers home economics (MS Ed); physical education and exercise sciences (MS Ed). Part-time and evening/weekend programs available. *Faculty:* 12 full-time (7 women). *Students:* 13 full-time (all women), 68 part-time (44 women). 58 applicants, 78% accepted, 25 enrolled. In 2009, 9 master's awarded. *Degree requirements:* For master's, research project. *Entrance requirements:* For master's, minimum GPA of 3.0. Additional exam requirements/recommendations for international students: Required—TOEFL. *Application deadline:* For fall admission, 4/1 for domestic students; for spring admission, 11/1 for domestic students. Applications are processed on a rolling basis. Application fee: $125. *Expenses:* Tuition, state resident: full-time $7360; part-time $310 per credit. Tuition, nonresident: part-time $575 per credit. One-time fee: $195 full-time; $145.25 part-time. *Financial support:* Career-related internships or fieldwork, Federal Work-Study, institutionally sponsored loans, and tuition waivers (partial) available. Support available to part-time students. Financial award application deadline: 4/1; financial award applicants required to submit FAFSA. *Faculty research:* Exercise and environmental physiology, interdisciplinary approaches to school curricula using outdoor education, program development in cardiac rehabilitation and adult fitness, nutrition education. *Unit head:* Dr. Elizabeth Lowe, Chairperson, 718-997-4168. *Application contact:* Mario Caruso, Director of Graduate Admissions, 718-997-5200, Fax: 718-997-5193, E-mail: graduate_admissions@qc.edu.

Queen's University at Kingston, School of Graduate Studies and Research, School of Kinesiology and Health Studies, Kingston, ON K7L 3N6, Canada. Offers applied exercise science (PhD); biomechanics/ergonomics (M Sc); exercise physiology (M Sc); social psychology of sport and exercise rehabilitation (MA); sociology of sport (MA). Part-time programs available. *Degree requirements:* For master's, thesis (for some programs); for doctorate, comprehensive exam, thesis/dissertation. *Entrance requirements:* For master's and doctorate, minimum B+ average. Additional exam requirements/recommendations for international students: Required—TOEFL. Electronic applications accepted. *Faculty research:* Expert performance ergonomics, obesity research, pregnancy and exercise, gender and sport participation.

Sacred Heart University, Graduate Programs, College of Education and Health Professions, Department of Physical Therapy and Human Movement and Sports Science, Fairfield, CT 06825-1000. Offers exercise science and nutrition (MS); physical therapy (DPT). *Accreditation:* APTA. *Faculty:* 9 full-time (5 women). *Students:* 146 full-time (95 women); includes 17 minority (4 African Americans, 1 American Indian/Alaska Native, 7 Asian Americans or Pacific Islanders, 5 Hispanic Americans), 2 international. Average age 25. 205 applicants, 58% accepted, 63 enrolled. *Entrance requirements:* Additional exam requirements/recommendations for international students: Required—TOEFL (minimum score 550 paper-based; 213 computer-based). *Application deadline:* For fall admission, 1/15 priority date for domestic students. Applications are processed on a rolling basis. Application fee: $50 ($100 for international students). Electronic applications accepted. *Expenses:* Contact institution. *Financial support:* Career-related internships or fieldwork, institutionally sponsored loans, and unspecified assistantships available. Support available to part-time students. Financial award applicants required to submit FAFSA. *Unit head:* Dr. Michael Emery, Director, 203-365-7656. *Application contact:* Kathy Dilks, Assistant Dean of Graduate Admissions, Health Professions, 203-396-8259, Fax: 203-365-4732, E-mail: gradstudies@sacredheart.edu.

St. Cloud State University, School of Graduate Studies, College of Education, Department of Health, Physical Education, Recreation, and Sport Science, St. Cloud, MN 56301-4498. Offers exercise science (MS); physical education (MS); sports management (MS). *Faculty:* 16 full-time (8 women), 1 (woman) part-time/adjunct. *Students:* 21 full-time (10 women), 39 part-time (13 women); includes 7 minority (3 African Americans, 4 Asian Americans or Pacific Islanders), 2 international. 31 applicants, 71% accepted. In 2009, 17 master's awarded. *Degree requirements:* For master's, thesis or alternative. *Entrance requirements:* For master's, GRE General Test, minimum GPA of 2.75. Additional exam requirements/recommendations for international students: Required—Michigan English Language Assessment Battery; Recommended—TOEFL (minimum score 550 paper-based; 213 computer-based), IELTS (minimum score 6.5). *Application deadline:* For fall admission, 6/1 priority date for domestic students, 4/1 for international students; for spring admission, 10/1 priority date for domestic students, 8/1 for international students. Applications are processed on a rolling basis. Application fee: $35. Electronic applications accepted. *Financial support:* Federal Work-Study, scholarships/grants, and unspecified assistantships available. Financial award application deadline: 3/1. *Unit head:* Dr. Caryl Martin, Chairperson, 320-308-4251, E-mail: clmartin@stcloudstate.edu. *Application contact:* Linda Lou Krueger, School of Graduate Studies, 320-308-2113, Fax: 320-308-5371, E-mail: lekrueger@stcloudstate.edu.

Saint Mary's College of California, School of Liberal Arts, Department of Kinesiology, Moraga, CA 94556. Offers sport management (MA); sport studies (MA). Part-time programs available. *Faculty:* 6 full-time (1 woman), 3 part-time/adjunct (1 woman). *Students:* 30 full-time (15 women); includes 7 minority (5 African Americans, 1 Asian American or Pacific Islander, 1 Hispanic American). Average age 28. 23 applicants, 65% accepted, 14 enrolled. In 2009, 28 master's awarded. *Degree requirements:* For master's, thesis or special project. *Entrance requirements:* For master's, minimum GPA of 2.75, BA in physical education or related field, or professional experience. Application fee: $25. Electronic applications accepted. *Expenses:* Contact institution. *Financial support:* In 2009–10, 15 students received support, including research assistantships (averaging $6,000 per year); career-related internships or fieldwork, institutionally sponsored loans, scholarships/grants, tuition waivers (partial), and unspecified assistantships also available. Support available to part-time students. Financial award applicants required to submit FAFSA. *Faculty research:* Moral development in sport, applied motor learning, achievement motivation, sport history. Total annual research expenditures: $1,500. *Unit head:* William Manning, Chair, 925-631-4969, Fax: 925-631-4965, E-mail: wmanning@stmarys-ca.edu. *Application contact:* Jeanne Abate, Administrative Assistant, 925-631-4377, Fax: 925-631-4965, E-mail: jabate@stmarys-ca.edu.

San Diego State University, Graduate and Research Affairs, College of Professional Studies and Fine Arts, Department of Exercise and Nutritional Sciences, Program in Exercise Physiology, San Diego, CA 92182. Offers MS, MS/MS. *Degree requirements:* For master's, thesis. *Entrance requirements:* For master's, GRE General Test, 2 letters of reference. Additional exam requirements/recommendations for international students: Required—TOEFL. Electronic applications accepted.

Smith College, Graduate and Special Programs, Department of Exercise and Sport Studies, Northampton, MA 01063. Offers MS. Part-time programs available. *Faculty:* 4 full-time (2 women), 1 part-time/adjunct (0 women). *Students:* 23 full-time (19 women), 1 (woman) part-time; includes 2 minority (1 African American, 1 Hispanic American). Average age 26. 31 applicants, 52% accepted, 11 enrolled. In 2009, 6 master's awarded. *Degree requirements:* For master's, thesis or special studies. *Entrance requirements:* For master's, GRE General Test. Additional exam requirements/recommendations for international students: Required—TOEFL (minimum score 590 paper-based; 243 computer-based; 97 iBT). *Application deadline:* For fall admission, 4/1 for domestic students, 1/15 for international students; for spring admission, 12/1 for domestic students. Application fee: $60. *Financial support:* In 2009–10, 23 students received support, including 10 teaching assistantships with full tuition reimbursements available (averaging $11,910 per year); career-related internships or fieldwork, institutionally sponsored loans, scholarships/grants, and tuition waivers (partial) also available. Support available to part-time students. Financial award application deadline: 1/15; financial award applicants required to submit CSS PROFILE or FAFSA. *Faculty research:* Women in sport, perceived exertion, motor programming, race in sport, stress management. *Unit head:* Jane Stangl, Graduate Student Adviser, 413-585-3972, E-mail: jstangl@smith.edu. *Application contact:* Jane Stangl, Graduate Student Adviser, 413-585-3972, E-mail: jstangl@smith.edu.

Southeast Missouri State University, School of Graduate Studies, Department of Health, Human Performance and Recreation, Cape Girardeau, MO 63701-4799. Offers community wellness and leisure (MPA); nutrition and exercise science (MS). Part-time and evening/

weekend programs available. *Degree requirements:* For master's, comprehensive exam (for some programs), thesis or alternative. *Entrance requirements:* For master's, GRE General Test (minimum score 1000 verbal and quantitative) for nutrition and exercise science (MS), minimum undergraduate GPA of 3.0 (MS), 2.7 (MPA). Additional exam requirements/recommendations for international students: Required—TOEFL (minimum score 550 paper-based; 213 computer-based); Recommended—IELTS (minimum score 6). Electronic applications accepted. *Expenses:* Tuition, state resident: full-time $4266; part-time $237 per credit hour. Tuition, nonresident: full-time $7506; part-time $417 per credit hour. Required fees: $427; $427. *Faculty research:* Health issues of athletes, body composition assessment, exercise testing, exercise training, perceptual responses to physical activity.

Southern Connecticut State University, School of Graduate Studies, School of Education, Department of Exercise Science, New Haven, CT 06515-1355. Offers human performance (MS); physical education (MS); school health education (MS); sport psychology (MS). Part-time and evening/weekend programs available. *Faculty:* 8 full-time. *Students:* 28 full-time (13 women), 54 part-time (28 women); includes 6 minority (2 African Americans, 4 Hispanic Americans), 1 international. 20 applicants, 55% accepted, 10 enrolled. In 2009, 18 master's awarded. *Degree requirements:* For master's, thesis or alternative. *Entrance requirements:* For master's, interview. *Application deadline:* For fall admission, 7/15 priority date for domestic students. Applications are processed on a rolling basis. Application fee: $50. Electronic applications accepted. Tuition and fees vary according to program. *Financial support:* In 2009–10, 8 teaching assistantships were awarded. Financial award application deadline: 4/15; financial award applicants required to submit FAFSA. *Unit head:* Dr. Daniel Swartz, Chairperson, 203-392-8721, Fax: 203-392-6911, E-mail: swartzd1@southernct.edu. *Application contact:* Dr. Robert Axtell, Coordinator, 203-392-6037, Fax: 203-392-6093, E-mail: axtell@southernct.edu.

Southern Utah University, College of Education, Program in Sports Conditioning, Cedar City, UT 84720-2498. Offers MS. *Faculty:* 5 full-time (2 women). *Students:* 8 full-time (4 women), 55 part-time (21 women); includes 7 minority (2 African Americans, 2 Asian Americans or Pacific Islanders, 3 Hispanic Americans). 18 applicants, 83% accepted, 15 enrolled. *Application deadline:* Applications are processed on a rolling basis. Application fee: $50 ($65 for international students). Electronic applications accepted. *Financial support:* In 2009–10, 2 teaching assistantships (averaging $2,390 per year) were awarded. *Unit head:* Dr. Prent Klag, Dean, 435-586-7803, Fax: 435-865-8485, E-mail: klag@suu.edu. *Application contact:* Joan Anderson, Administrative Assistant, 435-586-7816, Fax: 435-865-8057, E-mail: anderson_j@suu.edu.

Springfield College, Graduate Programs, Programs in Exercise Science and Sport Studies, Springfield, MA 01109-3797. Offers athletic training (MS); exercise physiology (MS), including clinical exercise physiology, science and research; exercise science and sport studies (PhD); health promotion and disease prevention (MS); sport psychology (MS). Part-time programs available. Terminal master's awarded for partial completion of doctoral program. *Degree requirements:* For master's, comprehensive exam, research project or thesis; for doctorate, comprehensive exam, thesis/dissertation. *Entrance requirements:* For master's and doctorate, GRE General Test. Additional exam requirements/recommendations for international students: Required—TOEFL (minimum score 550 paper-based; 213 computer-based). Electronic applications accepted. *Expenses:* Tuition: Full-time $19,800; part-time $825 per credit hour. Required fees: $150.

State University of New York College at Cortland, Graduate Studies, School of Professional Studies, Department of Exercise Science and Sport Studies, Cortland, NY 13045. Offers MS.

Syracuse University, School of Education, Program in Exercise Science, Syracuse, NY 13244. Offers MS. Part-time programs available. *Students:* 21 full-time (10 women), 1 (woman) part-time; includes 2 minority (1 African American, 1 Asian American or Pacific Islander), 3 international. Average age 25. 26 applicants, 69% accepted, 13 enrolled. In 2009, 13 master's awarded. *Degree requirements:* For master's, thesis or alternative. *Entrance requirements:* For master's, GRE, resume. Additional exam requirements/recommendations for international students: Required—TOEFL (minimum score 100 iBT). *Application deadline:* For fall admission, 2/1 priority date for domestic and international students; for spring admission, 10/15 priority date for domestic and international students. Applications are processed on a rolling basis. Application fee: $75. Electronic applications accepted. *Expenses:* Tuition: Full-time $26,808; part-time $1117 per credit. Required fees: $1024. *Financial support:* Fellowships, research assistantships with full and partial tuition reimbursements, teaching assistantships with full and partial tuition reimbursements available. Financial award application deadline: 1/1; financial award applicants required to submit FAFSA. *Faculty research:* Bone density, obesity in females, cardiovascular functioning, attitudes toward physical education, sports management and psychology. *Unit head:* Dr. Tom Brutsaert, Chair, 315-443-2114, E-mail: tdbrutsa@syr.edu. *Application contact:* Liza Rochelson, Graduate Recruiter, School of Education, 315-443-2505, E-mail: e-gradrcrt@syr.edu.

Tennessee State University, The School of Graduate Studies and Research, College of Education, Department of Human Performance and Sports Science, Nashville, TN 37209-1561. Offers MA Ed. *Degree requirements:* For master's, thesis optional. *Entrance requirements:* For master's, GRE General Test or MAT.

Texas A&M University–Commerce, Graduate School, College of Education and Human Services, Department of Health and Human Performance, Commerce, TX 75429-3011. Offers exercise physiology (MS); health and human performance (M Ed); health promotion (MS); health, kinesiology and sports studies (Ed D); motor performance (MS); sport studies (MS). Part-time programs available. *Degree requirements:* For master's, comprehensive exam, thesis (for some programs). *Entrance requirements:* For master's, GRE General Test. Electronic applications accepted. *Faculty research:* Teaching, physical fitness.

Texas Tech University, Graduate School, College of Arts and Sciences, Department of Health, Exercise and Sport Sciences, Lubbock, TX 79409. Offers exercise and sport sciences (MS). Part-time programs available. *Faculty:* 10 full-time (6 women). *Students:* 57 full-time (15 women), 19 part-time (4 women); includes 11 minority (3 African Americans, 1 Asian American or Pacific Islander, 7 Hispanic Americans), 5 international. Average age 25. 116 applicants, 50% accepted, 31 enrolled. In 2009, 23 master's awarded. *Degree requirements:* For master's, thesis or alternative. *Entrance requirements:* For master's, GRE General Test. Additional exam requirements/recommendations for international students: Required—TOEFL (minimum score 550 paper-based; 213 computer-based). *Application deadline:* For fall admission, 3/1 priority date for international students; for spring admission, 11/1 priority date for international students. Applications are processed on a rolling basis. Application fee: $50 ($75 for international students). Electronic applications accepted. *Expenses:* Tuition, state resident: full-time $5100; part-time $213 per credit hour. Tuition, nonresident: full-time $11,748; part-time $490 per credit hour. Required fees: $2298; $50 per credit hour. $555 per semester. *Financial support:* In 2009–10, 1 research assistantship with partial tuition reimbursement (averaging $18,155 per year), 26 teaching assistantships with partial tuition reimbursements (averaging $10,423 per year) were awarded; Federal Work-Study and institutionally sponsored loans also available. Support available to part-time students. Financial award application deadline: 4/15; financial award applicants required to submit FAFSA. *Faculty research:* Cardiopulmonary physiology; physical activity in children; motivation for exercise participation; muscle physiology; sport injury. Total annual research expenditures: $5,009. *Unit head:* Dr. Melanie Hart, Interim Chair, 806-742-3371, Fax: 806-742-1688. *Application contact:* Monica Luna, Graduate Program Secretary, 806-742-3371, Fax: 806-742-1688.

Texas Woman's University, Graduate School, College of Health Sciences, Department of Nutrition and Food Sciences, Program in Exercise and Sports Nutrition, Denton, TX 76201. Offers MS. Part-time programs available. *Students:* 14 full-time (13 women), 13 part-time (9 women); includes 5 minority (3 African Americans, 2 Hispanic Americans), 3 international. Average age 27. 14 applicants, 71% accepted, 6 enrolled. In 2009, 2 master's awarded. *Degree requirements:* For master's, comprehensive exam, thesis. *Entrance requirements:* For master's, GRE General Test (minimum score 500 verbal, 400 quantitative), 9 hours each of chemistry, nutrition, and kinesiology; 3 hours of human physiology; minimum GPA of 3.0 in last 60 hours; resume; 2 letters of recommendation. Additional exam requirements/recommendations for international students: Required—TOEFL (minimum score 550 paper-based; 213 computer-based; 79 iBT). *Application deadline:* For fall admission, 7/1 priority date for domestic students, 3/1 for international students; for spring admission, 11/1 priority date for domestic students, 7/1 for international students. Applications are processed on a rolling basis. Application fee: $50. Electronic applications accepted. *Expenses:* Tuition, state resident: full-time $3564; part-time $198 per credit hour. Tuition, nonresident: full-time $8550; part-time $475 per credit hour. Required fees: $69.26 per credit hour. Tuition and fees vary according to course load. *Financial support:* In 2009–10, 9 students received support. Career-related internships or fieldwork, Federal Work-Study, institutionally sponsored loans, scholarships/grants, traineeships, health care benefits, and unspecified assistantships available. Support available to part-time students. Financial award application deadline: 3/1; financial award applicants required to submit FAFSA. *Faculty research:* Metabolism of lipoproteins, insulin, bone, childhood obesity. *Unit head:* Dr. Chandan Prasad, Program Director, 940-898-2636, Fax: 940-898-2634, E-mail: nutrfdsci@twu.edu. *Application contact:* Samuel Wheeler, Assistant Director of Admissions, 940-898-3188, Fax: 940-898-3081, E-mail: wheelersr@twu.edu.

Troy University, Graduate School, College of Education, Program in Postsecondary Education, Troy, AL 36082. Offers adult education (M Ed); biology (M Ed); criminal justice (M Ed); english (M Ed); foundations of education (M Ed); general science (M Ed); higher education administration (M Ed); history (M Ed); instructional technology (M Ed); mathematics (M Ed); music industry (M Ed); physical fitness (M Ed); political science (M Ed); public administration (M Ed); social science (M Ed); teaching english (M Ed). Also offered through the University College. *Accreditation:* NCATE. Part-time and evening/weekend programs available. *Students:* 267 full-time (192 women), 381 part-time (293 women); includes 326 minority (309 African Americans, 4 American Indian/Alaska Native, 5 Asian Americans or Pacific Islanders, 8 Hispanic Americans). Average age 34. 343 applicants, 90% accepted. In 2009, 480 master's awarded. *Degree requirements:* For master's, comprehensive exam, thesis. *Entrance requirements:* For master's, MAT (minimum score 385), minimum GPA of 2.5. Additional exam requirements/recommendations for international students: Required—TOEFL (minimum score 523 paper-based; 193 computer-based; 70 iBT), IELTS, or ACT Compass ESL (minimum score 270 on Listening, Reading, and Grammar with no individual score below 85 and a minimum score of 8 out of 12 on writing test). *Application deadline:* Applications are processed on a rolling basis. Application fee: $50. Electronic applications accepted. *Financial support:* Available to part-time students. Applicants required to submit FAFSA. *Unit head:* Dr. Andrew Creamer, Chair, 334-670-3350, E-mail: drcreamer@troy.edu. *Application contact:* Brenda K. Campbell, Director of Graduate Admissions, 334-670-3178, Fax: 334-670-3733, E-mail: bcamp@troy.edu.

United States Sports Academy, Graduate Programs, Program in Sports Fitness and Health, Daphne, AL 36526-7055. Offers MSS. Part-time programs available. Postbaccalaureate distance learning degree programs offered (no on-campus study). *Degree requirements:* For master's, comprehensive exam, thesis optional. *Entrance requirements:* For master's, GRE General Test, GMAT, or MAT, minimum GPA of 2.5, 3 letters of recommendation, resume. Additional exam requirements/recommendations for international students: Required—TOEFL (minimum score 500 paper-based; 213 computer-based). *Application deadline:* Applications are processed on a rolling basis. Application fee: $50 ($125 for international students). Electronic applications accepted. *Financial support:* Application deadline: 8/15. *Faculty research:* Exercise physiology, conditioning. *Unit head:* Dr. Brian Wallace, Chair, 251-626-3303 Ext. 7156, Fax: 251-625-1035, E-mail: bwallace@ussa.edu. *Application contact:* Craig T. Bogar, Assistant Dean of Student Services, 251-626-3303 Ext. 7147, Fax: 251-625-1035, E-mail: cbogar@ussa.edu.

United States Sports Academy, Graduate Programs, Program in Sport Studies, Daphne, AL 36526-7055. Offers MSS. Part-time programs available. Postbaccalaureate distance learning degree programs offered (no on-campus study). *Degree requirements:* For master's, comprehensive exam, thesis optional. *Entrance requirements:* For master's, GRE General Test, GMAT, or MAT, minimum GPA of 2.5, 3 letters of recommendation, resume. Additional exam requirements/recommendations for international students: Required—TOEFL (minimum score 500 paper-based; 213 computer-based). *Application deadline:* Applications are processed on a rolling basis. Application fee: $50 ($125 for international students). Electronic applications accepted. *Unit head:* Dr. Kelly Flanagan, Department Chair, 251-626-3303 Ext. 7151, Fax: 251-625-1035, E-mail: flanagan@ussa.edu. *Application contact:* Craig T. Bogar, Assistant Dean of Student Services, 251-626-3303 Ext. 7147, Fax: 251-625-1035, E-mail: cbogar@ussa.edu.

University at Buffalo, the State University of New York, Graduate School, School of Public Health and Health Professions, Department of Exercise and Nutrition Sciences, Buffalo, NY 14260. Offers exercise science (MS, PhD); nutrition (MS). Part-time programs available. *Faculty:* 16 full-time (4 women), 14 part-time/adjunct (12 women). *Students:* 93 full-time (51 women), 29 part-time (24 women); includes 16 minority (4 African Americans, 9 Asian Americans or Pacific Islanders, 3 Hispanic Americans), 24 international. Average age 24. 72 applicants, 60% accepted. In 2009, 19 master's, 3 doctorates awarded. *Degree requirements:* For master's, comprehensive exam or thesis; for doctorate, comprehensive exam, thesis/dissertation. *Entrance requirements:* For master's, GRE General Test (nutrition), minimum GPA of 3.0; for doctorate, GRE General Test, minimum GPA of 3.0 (PhD). Additional exam requirements/recommendations for international students: Required—TOEFL (minimum score 550 paper-based; 213 computer-based; 79 iBT), IELTS (minimum score 6.5). *Application deadline:* For fall admission, 1/31 for domestic students, 2/1 for international students. Applications are processed on a rolling basis. Application fee: $50. Electronic applications accepted. *Financial support:* In 2009–10, 10 students received support, including 1 research assistantship with tuition reimbursement available (averaging $18,000 per year), 10 teaching assistantships with full and partial tuition reimbursements available (averaging $11,000 per year); career-related internships or fieldwork, Federal Work-Study, institutionally sponsored loans, scholarships/grants, health care benefits, tuition waivers (full and partial), unspecified assistantships, and stipends also available. Financial award application deadline: 3/15; financial award applicants required to submit FAFSA. *Faculty research:* Cardiovascular disease-diet and exercise, respiratory control and muscle function, plasticity of connective and neural tissue, exercise nutrition, diet and cancer. Total annual research expenditures: $409,473. *Unit head:* Dr. Joan Dorn, Chair, 716-829-2975 Ext. 619, Fax: 716-829-2979, E-mail: jdorn@buffalo.edu. *Application contact:* Dr. Gaspar Farkas, Director of Graduate Studies, 76-829-2941 Ext. 311, Fax: 716-829-2428, E-mail: farkas@buffalo.edu.

The University of Akron, Graduate School, College of Education, Department of Sport Science and Wellness Education, Program in Exercise Physiology/Adult Fitness, Akron, OH 44325. Offers MA, MS. *Students:* 34 full-time (14 women), 19 part-time (7 women); includes 7 minority (5 African Americans, 1 Asian American or Pacific Islander, 1 Hispanic American), 3 international. Average age 30. 25 applicants, 96% accepted, 14 enrolled. In 2009, 20 master's awarded. *Degree requirements:* For master's, comprehensive exam, thesis optional. *Entrance requirements:* For master's, minimum GPA of 2.75, letters of recommendation. Additional exam requirements/recommendations for international students: Required—TOEFL (minimum score 550 paper-based; 213 computer-based; 79 iBT). *Application deadline:* Applications are processed on a rolling basis. Application fee: $30 ($40 for international students). Electronic applications accepted. *Expenses:* Tuition, state resident: full-time $6570; part-time $365 per credit hour. Tuition, nonresident: full-time $11,250; part-time $625 per credit hour. *Unit head:* Dr. Ron Otterstetter, Coordinator, 330-972-7738, E-mail: ro5@uakron.edu. *Application contact:* Dr. Ron Otterstetter, Coordinator, 330-972-7738, E-mail: ro5@uakron.edu.

The University of Akron, Graduate School, College of Education, Department of Sport Science and Wellness Education, Program in Sports Science/Coaching, Akron, OH 44325. Offers MA, MS. *Students:* 34 full-time (8 women), 16 part-time (4 women); includes 12 minority (9 African Americans, 1 Asian American or Pacific Islander, 2 Hispanic Americans), 1 international. Average age 29. 29 applicants, 93% accepted, 21 enrolled. In 2009, 31 master's awarded. *Degree requirements:* For master's, comprehensive exam, thesis optional. *Entrance requirements:* For master's, minimum GPA of 2.75, letters of recommendation. Additional exam requirements/recommendations for international students: Required—TOEFL (minimum score 550 paper-based; 213 computer-based; 79 iBT). *Application deadline:* Applications are processed on a

Exercise and Sports Science

The University of Akron *(continued)*
rolling basis. Application fee: $30 ($40 for international students). Electronic applications accepted. *Expenses:* Tuition, state resident: full-time $6570; part-time $365 per credit hour. Tuition, nonresident: full-time $11,250; part-time $625 per credit hour. *Unit head:* Dr. Alan Kornspan, Head, 330-972-8145, E-mail: alan3@uakron.edu. *Application contact:* Dr. Alan Kornspan, Head, 330-972-8145, E-mail: alan3@uakron.edu.

The University of Alabama, Graduate School, College of Education, Department of Kinesiology, Tuscaloosa, AL 35487. Offers alternative sport pedagogy (MA); exercise science (MA, PhD); human performance (MA); sport management (MA); sport pedagogy (MA, PhD). Part-time programs available. *Faculty:* 7 full-time (1 woman). *Students:* 63 full-time (30 women), 17 part-time (4 women); includes 5 minority (3 African Americans, 1 American Indian/Alaska Native, 1 Hispanic American), 11 international. Average age 28. 74 applicants, 64% accepted, 29 enrolled. In 2009, 22 master's, 5 doctorates awarded. *Median time to degree:* Of those who began their doctoral program in fall 2001, 100% received their degree in 8 years or less. *Degree requirements:* For master's, comprehensive exam, thesis optional; for doctorate, comprehensive exam, thesis/dissertation. *Entrance requirements:* For master's and doctorate, GRE, MAT, minimum GPA of 3.0. Additional exam requirements/recommendations for international students: Required—TOEFL. *Application deadline:* Applications are processed on a rolling basis. Application fee: $50 ($60 for international students). Electronic applications accepted. *Expenses:* Tuition, state resident: full-time $7000. Tuition, nonresident: full-time $19,200. *Financial support:* In 2009–10, 14 students received support, including 13 teaching assistantships with full tuition reimbursements available (averaging $8,678 per year). *Faculty research:* Race, gender and sexuality in sports; physical education curriculum reform; disability sports; physical activity and health; environmental physiology. Total annual research expenditures: $46,329. *Unit head:* Dr. Matt Curtner-Smith, Department Head and Professor, 205-348-9209, Fax: 205-348-0867, E-mail: msmith@bamaed.ua.edu. *Application contact:* Dr. Kathy S. Wetzel, Assistant Dean for Student Services, 205-348-1154, Fax: 205-348-0080, E-mail: kwetzel@bamaed.ua.edu.

University of Alberta, Faculty of Graduate Studies and Research, Department of Physical Education and Recreation, Edmonton, AB T6G 2E1, Canada. Offers physical education (M Sc); recreation and physical education (MA, PhD). Part-time programs available. *Faculty:* 30 full-time (10 women). *Students:* 60 full-time (34 women), 55 part-time (28 women). 69 applicants, 36% accepted. In 2009, 13 master's, 7 doctorates awarded. Terminal master's awarded for partial completion of doctoral program. *Degree requirements:* For master's, thesis (for some programs); for doctorate, thesis/dissertation. *Entrance requirements:* For master's, bachelor's degree in related field; for doctorate, master's degree in related field with thesis. Additional exam requirements/recommendations for international students: Required—TOEFL. *Application deadline:* For fall admission, 1/1 priority date for domestic students. Applications are processed on a rolling basis. Tuition and fees charges are reported in Canadian dollars. *Expenses:* Tuition, area resident: Full-time $4626 Canadian dollars; part-time $99.72 Canadian dollars per unit. International tuition: $8216 Canadian dollars full-time. Required fees: $3590 Canadian dollars; $99.72 Canadian dollars per unit. $215 Canadian dollars per term. *Financial support:* In 2009–10, 63 students received support, including 28 research assistantships, 35 teaching assistantships; career-related internships or fieldwork and scholarships/grants also available. Support available to part-time students. *Faculty research:* Motivation and adherence to physical ability, performance enhancement, adapted physical activity, exercise physiology, sport administration, tourism. *Unit head:* Dr. D. Marshall, Assistant Dean, 780-492-3198, Fax: 403-492-2364. *Application contact:* Anne Jordan, Department Office, 403-492-3198, Fax: 403-492-2364, E-mail: pergrad@ualberta.ca.

University of Calgary, Faculty of Graduate Studies, Faculty of Kinesiology, Calgary, AB T2N 1N4, Canada. Offers biomedical engineering (M Sc, PhD); kinesiology (M Kin, M Sc, PhD), including biomechanics (PhD), health and exercise physiology (PhD). *Degree requirements:* For master's, thesis (M Sc); for doctorate, thesis/dissertation. *Entrance requirements:* Additional exam requirements/recommendations for international students: Required—TOEFL. Electronic applications accepted. *Faculty research:* Load acting on the human body, muscle mechanics and physiology, optimizing high performance athlete performance, eye movement in sports, analysis of body composition.

University of California, Davis, Graduate Studies, Graduate Group in Exercise Science, Davis, CA 95616. Offers MS. *Degree requirements:* For master's, thesis. *Entrance requirements:* For master's, GRE, minimum GPA of 3.25. Additional exam requirements/recommendations for international students: Required—TOEFL (minimum score 550 paper-based; 213 computer-based). Electronic applications accepted.

University of Central Florida, College of Education, Department of Child, Family and Community Sciences, Program in Sport and Fitness, Orlando, FL 32816. Offers sport and fitness (MA); sport leadership (Certificate). Part-time and evening/weekend programs available. *Students:* 31 full-time (14 women), 42 part-time (21 women); includes 15 minority (10 African Americans, 5 Hispanic Americans). Average age 26. 78 applicants, 77% accepted, 33 enrolled. In 2009, 17 master's awarded. *Entrance requirements:* For master's, GRE General Test. Additional exam requirements/recommendations for international students: Required—TOEFL. *Application deadline:* For fall admission, 7/15 for domestic students; for spring admission, 12/1 for domestic students. Application fee: $30. Electronic applications accepted. *Expenses:* Tuition, state resident: part-time $306.31 per credit hour. Tuition, nonresident: part-time $1099.01 per credit hour. Part-time tuition and fees vary according to degree level and program. *Financial support:* In 2009–10, 5 students received support, including 2 fellowships with partial tuition reimbursements available (averaging $7,500 per year), 1 research assistantship with partial tuition reimbursement available (averaging $6,900 per year), 3 teaching assistantships with partial tuition reimbursements available (averaging $4,700 per year); career-related internships or fieldwork, Federal Work-Study, institutionally sponsored loans, tuition waivers (partial), and unspecified assistantships also available. Financial award application deadline: 3/1; financial award applicants required to submit FAFSA.

University of Central Missouri, The Graduate School, College of Health and Human Services, Warrensburg, MO 64093. Offers criminal justice (MS); industrial hygiene (MS); occupational safety management (MS); physical education/exercise and sport science (MS); rural family nursing (MS); social gerontology (MS); sociology (MA); speech language pathology and audiology (MS). *Accreditation:* NCATE. Part-time programs available. Postbaccalaureate distance learning degree programs offered. *Faculty:* 53. *Students:* 169 full-time (107 women), 364 part-time (210 women); includes 65 minority (46 African Americans, 1 American Indian/Alaska Native, 5 Asian Americans or Pacific Islanders, 13 Hispanic Americans), 27 international. Average age 32. 236 applicants, 92% accepted, 211 enrolled. In 2009, 153 master's awarded. *Entrance requirements:* Additional exam requirements/recommendations for international students: Required—TOEFL (minimum score 550 paper-based; 79 computer-based). *Application deadline:* For fall admission, 6/1 priority date for domestic students, 5/1 for international students; for spring admission, 10/1 priority date for domestic students, 10/1 for international students. Applications are processed on a rolling basis. Application fee: $30 ($75 for international students). Electronic applications accepted. *Expenses:* Tuition, area resident: part-time $245.80 per credit hour. Tuition, nonresident: part-time $491.60 per credit hour. Required fees: $24.20 per credit hour. Full-time tuition and fees vary according to course load, degree level, campus/location and reciprocity agreements. *Financial support:* Research assistantships with full and partial tuition reimbursements, teaching assistantships with full and partial tuition reimbursements, career-related internships or fieldwork, Federal Work-Study, scholarships/grants, and administrative and laboratory assistantships available. Support available to part-time students. Financial award application deadline: 3/1; financial award applicants required to submit FAFSA. *Unit head:* Dr. Rick Sluder, Dean, 660-543-4245, Fax: 660-543-4167, E-mail: sluder@ucmo.edu. *Application contact:* Laurie Delap, Admissions Coordinator, 660-543-4621, Fax: 660-543-4778, E-mail: gradinfo@ucmo.edu.

University of Connecticut, Graduate School, Neag School of Education, Department of Kinesiology, Program in Exercise Science, Storrs, CT 06269. Offers MA, PhD. *Faculty:* 6 full-time (3 women). *Students:* 48 full-time (32 women), 2 part-time (both women); includes 9 minority (3 African Americans, 3 Asian Americans or Pacific Islanders, 3 Hispanic Americans), 1 international. Average age 26. 97 applicants, 27% accepted, 12 enrolled. In 2009, 14 master's, 7 doctorates awarded. Terminal master's awarded for partial completion of doctoral program. *Degree requirements:* For master's, comprehensive exam, thesis or alternative; for doctorate, thesis/dissertation. *Entrance requirements:* For doctorate, GRE General Test. Additional exam requirements/recommendations for international students: Required—TOEFL (minimum score 550 paper-based; 213 computer-based). *Application deadline:* For fall admission, 2/1 priority date for domestic and international students; for spring admission, 11/1 for domestic students, 10/1 for international students. Applications are processed on a rolling basis. Application fee: $55. Electronic applications accepted. *Expenses:* Tuition, state resident: full-time $4725; part-time $525 per credit. Tuition, nonresident: full-time $12,267; part-time $1363 per credit. Required fees: $346 per semester. Tuition and fees vary according to course load. *Financial support:* In 2009–10, 44 research assistantships with full tuition reimbursements, 1 teaching assistantship with full tuition reimbursement were awarded; Federal Work-Study, scholarships/grants, health care benefits, and unspecified assistantships also available. Financial award application deadline: 2/1; financial award applicants required to submit FAFSA. *Unit head:* Carl Maresh, Head, 860-486-3623, Fax: 860-486-1123. *Application contact:* Lisa Rasicot, Graduate Coordinator, 860-486-3065, Fax: 860-486-0210, E-mail: l.rasicot@uconn.edu.

University of Dayton, Graduate School, School of Education and Allied Professions, Department of Health and Sport Science, Dayton, OH 45469-1300. Offers exercise science (MS Ed); physical therapy (DPT). Part-time and evening/weekend programs available. *Faculty:* 16 full-time (7 women). *Students:* 116 full-time (79 women), 3 part-time (all women); includes 9 minority (5 African Americans, 3 Asian Americans or Pacific Islanders, 1 Hispanic American), 2 international. Average age 25. 200 applicants, 37% accepted, 43 enrolled. In 2009, 3 master's awarded. *Degree requirements:* For master's, thesis; for doctorate, thesis/dissertation. *Entrance requirements:* For master's, GRE General Test, MAT, minimum GPA of 2.75; for doctorate, GRE General Test, minimum GPA of 3.0, 80 observation hours. Additional exam requirements/recommendations for international students: Required—TOEFL (minimum score 550 paper-based; 213 computer-based; 80 iBT). *Application deadline:* For fall admission, 2/15 priority date for domestic students, 3/1 priority date for international students; for winter admission, 7/1 priority date for international students; for spring admission, 1/1 priority date for international students. Applications are processed on a rolling basis. Application fee: $0 ($50 for international students). Electronic applications accepted. *Expenses:* Tuition: Full-time $8412; part-time $701 per credit hour. Required fees: $325; $65 per course. $25 per semester. Tuition and fees vary according to course load, degree level and program. *Financial support:* In 2009–10, 4 students received support, including 4 teaching assistantships with tuition reimbursements available (averaging $8,000 per year); research assistantships, career-related internships or fieldwork, institutionally sponsored loans, health care benefits, and unspecified assistantships also available. Financial award applicants required to submit FAFSA. *Faculty research:* Energy expenditure, strength, training, teaching nutrition and calcium intake of children and families in Head-Start. *Unit head:* Dr. Lloyd Laubach, Interim Chair, 937-229-4240, Fax: 937-229-4244, E-mail: lloyd.laubach@notes.udayton.edu. *Application contact:* Graduate Admissions, 937-229-4411, Fax: 937-229-4729, E-mail: gradadmission@udayton.edu.

University of Delaware, College of Health Sciences, Department of Health, Nutrition, and Exercise Sciences, Newark, DE 19716. Offers exercise science (MS), including biomechanics, exercise physiology, motor control; health promotion (MS); human nutrition (MS). Part-time programs available. *Degree requirements:* For master's, thesis. *Entrance requirements:* For master's, GRE General Test, interview, minimum GPA of 3.0. Additional exam requirements/recommendations for international students: Required—TOEFL (minimum score 550 paper-based; 213 computer-based). Electronic applications accepted. *Faculty research:* Sport biomechanics, rehabilitation biomechanics, vascular dynamics.

University of Florida, Graduate School, College of Health and Human Performance, Department of Applied Physiology and Kinesiology, Gainesville, FL 32611. Offers athletic training/sport medicine (MS, PhD); biomechanics (MS, PhD); clinical exercise physiology (MS); exercise physiology (MS, PhD); health and human performance (PhD); human performance (MS); motor learning/control (MS, PhD); sport and exercise psychology (MS). *Degree requirements:* For doctorate, thesis/dissertation. *Entrance requirements:* For doctorate, GRE General Test. Electronic applications accepted.

University of Houston, College of Education, Department of Health and Human Performance, Houston, TX 77204. Offers allied health education and administration (M Ed, Ed D); exercise science (MS); health education (M Ed); human nutrition (MS); human space exploration sciences (MS); kinesiology (PhD); physical education (M Ed). *Accreditation:* NCATE (one or more programs are accredited). Part-time and evening/weekend programs available. *Faculty:* 12 full-time (4 women), 4 part-time/adjunct (3 women). *Students:* 53 full-time (26 women), 39 part-time (25 women); includes 21 minority (12 African Americans, 6 Asian Americans or Pacific Islanders, 3 Hispanic Americans), 14 international. Average age 29. 78 applicants, 64% accepted, 26 enrolled. In 2009, 20 master's, 2 doctorates awarded. *Degree requirements:* For master's, comprehensive exam, thesis (for some programs); for doctorate, comprehensive exam, thesis/dissertation, qualifying exam, candidacy paper. *Entrance requirements:* For master's, GRE (minimum 35th percentile on each section), minimum cumulative GPA of 3.0; for doctorate, GRE (minimum 35th percentile on each section), minimum cumulative GPA of 3.3. Additional exam requirements/recommendations for international students: Required—TOEFL (minimum score 550 paper-based; 79 iBT). *Application deadline:* For fall admission, 5/1 for domestic students, 4/1 for international students; for spring admission, 10/1 for domestic and international students. Applications are processed on a rolling basis. Application fee: $45 ($75 for international students). Electronic applications accepted. *Expenses:* Tuition, state resident: full-time $7676; part-time $320 per credit hour. Tuition, nonresident: full-time $14,324; part-time $597 per credit hour. Required fees: $3034. *Financial support:* In 2009–10, 7 fellowships with full tuition reimbursements (averaging $9,500 per year), 8 research assistantships with full tuition reimbursements (averaging $9,850 per year), 12 teaching assistantships with full tuition reimbursements (averaging $9,850 per year) were awarded; career-related internships or fieldwork, Federal Work-Study, institutionally sponsored loans, scholarships/grants, health care benefits, and unspecified assistantships also available. Support available to part-time students. Financial award application deadline: 2/1. *Faculty research:* Biomechanics, exercise physiology, obesity, nutrition, space exploration science. *Unit head:* Dr. Charles Layne, Chairperson, 713-743-9868, Fax: 713-743-9860, E-mail: clayne2@uh.edu. *Application contact:* Todd Boutte, Graduate Admission Counselor, 713-743-0571, Fax: 713-743-0123, E-mail: tboutte@mail.coe.uh.edu.

University of Houston–Clear Lake, School of Human Sciences and Humanities, Programs in Human Sciences, Houston, TX 77058-1098. Offers behavioral sciences (MA), including criminology, cross cultural studies, general psychology, sociology; clinical psychology (MA); criminology (MA); cross cultural studies (MA); family therapy (MA); fitness and human performance (MA); school psychology (MA). *Accreditation:* AAMFT/COAMFTE. Part-time and evening/weekend programs available. Postbaccalaureate distance learning degree programs offered (minimal on-campus study). *Degree requirements:* For master's, thesis or alternative. *Entrance requirements:* For master's, GRE General Test. Additional exam requirements/recommendations for international students: Required—TOEFL (minimum score 550 paper-based; 213 computer-based). Electronic applications accepted. *Faculty research:* Smoking cessation, adolescent sexuality, white collar crime, serial murder, human factors/human computer interaction.

The University of Iowa, Graduate College, College of Liberal Arts and Sciences, Department of Health and Sport Studies, Iowa City, IA 52242-1316. Offers psychology of sport and physical activity (MA, PhD); sports studies (MA, PhD). *Degree requirements:* For master's, thesis optional, exam; for doctorate, comprehensive exam, thesis/dissertation. *Entrance requirements:* For master's and doctorate, GRE General Test, minimum GPA of 3.0. Additional exam requirements/recommendations for international students: Required—TOEFL (minimum score 600 paper-based; 250 computer-based; 100 iBT). Electronic applications accepted.

The University of Iowa, Graduate College, College of Liberal Arts and Sciences, Department of Integrative Physiology, Iowa City, IA 52242-1316. Offers exercise science (MS); integrative physiology (PhD). *Degree requirements:* For master's, thesis optional, exam; for doctorate, comprehensive exam, thesis/dissertation. *Entrance requirements:* For master's and doctorate, GRE General Test, minimum GPA of 3.0. Additional exam requirements/recommendations for international students: Required—TOEFL (minimum score 550 paper-based; 213 computer-based; 81 iBT). Electronic applications accepted.

University of Kentucky, Graduate School, College of Education, Program in Kinesiology and Health Promotion, Lexington, KY 40506-0032. Offers exercise science (PhD); kinesiology (MS, Ed D). Terminal master's awarded for partial completion of doctoral program. *Degree requirements:* For master's, comprehensive exam, thesis optional; for doctorate, comprehensive exam, thesis/dissertation. *Entrance requirements:* For master's, GRE General Test, minimum undergraduate GPA of 2.75; for doctorate, GRE General Test, minimum graduate GPA of 3.0. Additional exam requirements/recommendations for international students: Required—TOEFL (minimum score 550 paper-based; 213 computer-based). Electronic applications accepted.

University of Lethbridge, School of Graduate Studies, Lethbridge, AB T1K 3M4, Canada. Offers accounting (MScM); addictions counseling (M Sc); agricultural biotechnology (M Sc); agricultural studies (M Sc, MA); anthropology (MA); archaeology (MA); art (MA, MFA); biochemistry (M Sc); biological sciences (M Sc); biomolecular science (PhD); biosystems and biodiversity (PhD); Canadian studies (MA); chemistry (M Sc); computer science (M Sc); computer science and geographical information science (M Sc); counseling psychology (M Ed); dramatic arts (MA); earth, space, and physical science (PhD); economics (MA); educational leadership (M Ed); English (MA); environmental science (M Sc); evolution and behavior (PhD); exercise science (M Sc); finance (MScM); French (MA); French/German (MA); French/Spanish (MA); general education (M Ed); general management (MScM); geography (M Sc, MA); German (MA); health science (M Sc); health sciences (MA); history (MA); human resource management and labour relations (MScM); individualized multidisciplinary (M Sc, MA); information systems (MScM); international management (MScM); kinesiology (M Sc, MA); management (M Sc, MA); marketing (MScM); mathematics (M Sc); music (M Mus, MA); Native American studies (MA); neuroscience (M Sc, PhD); new media (MA); nursing (M Sc); philosophy (MA); physics (M Sc); policy and strategy (MScM); political science (MA); psychology (M Sc, MA); religious studies (MA); social sciences (MA); sociology (MA); theatre and dramatic arts (MFA); theoretical and computational science (PhD); urban and regional studies (MA); women's studies (MA). Part-time and evening/weekend programs available. *Degree requirements:* For doctorate, comprehensive exam, thesis/dissertation. *Entrance requirements:* For master's, GMAT (M Sc in management), bachelor's degree in related field, minimum GPA of 3.0 during previous 20 graded semester courses, 2 years teaching or related experience (M Ed); for doctorate, master's degree, minimum graduate GPA of 3.5. Additional exam requirements/recommendations for international students: Required—TOEFL. *Faculty research:* Movement and brain plasticity, gibberellin physiology, photosynthesis, carbon cycling, molecular properties of main-group ring components.

University of Louisiana at Monroe, Graduate School, College of Education and Human Development, Department of Kinesiology, Monroe, LA 71209-0001. Offers applied exercise physiology (MS); clinical exercise physiology (MS). Part-time and evening/weekend programs available. *Faculty:* 8 full-time (4 women). *Students:* 13 full-time (6 women), 11 part-time (6 women); includes 2 minority (both African Americans), 1 international. Average age 24. In 2009, 15 master's awarded. *Degree requirements:* For master's, comprehensive exam, thesis, 6-hour internship. *Entrance requirements:* For master's, GRE General Test. Additional exam requirements/recommendations for international students: Required—TOEFL (minimum score 500 paper-based; 173 computer-based; 61 iBT). *Application deadline:* For fall admission, 8/24 priority date for domestic students, 7/1 for international students; for winter admission, 12/14 priority date for domestic students; for spring admission, 1/19 for domestic students, 11/1 for international students. Applications are processed on a rolling basis. Application fee: $20 ($30 for international students). Electronic applications accepted. *Expenses:* Tuition, state resident: part-time $159 per credit hour. Tuition, nonresident: part-time $159 per credit hour. Required fees: $1300 per year. Tuition and fees vary according to course load. *Financial support:* In 2009–10, 2 teaching assistantships with full tuition reimbursements (averaging $5,000 per year) were awarded; career-related internships or fieldwork, Federal Work-Study, and unspecified assistantships also available. Financial award application deadline: 4/1; financial award applicants required to submit FAFSA. *Faculty research:* Cardiovascular disease risk factors; exercise and immunological system; attitude, exercise, and the aged. *Unit head:* Dr. Mark Doherty, Chair, 318-342-3155, E-mail: doherty@ulm.edu. *Application contact:* Dr. Mark Doherty, Chair, 318-342-3155, E-mail: doherty@ulm.edu.

University of Louisville, Graduate School, College of Education and Human Development, Department of Health and Sport Sciences, Louisville, KY 40292-0001. Offers community health education (M Ed); exercise physiology (MS); health and physical education (MAT); sport administration (MS). Part-time and evening/weekend programs available. *Faculty:* 17 full-time (8 women), 1 part-time/adjunct (0 women). *Students:* 73 full-time (28 women), 28 part-time (17 women); includes 13 minority (11 African Americans, 2 Asian Americans or Pacific Islanders), 8 international. Average age 26. 154 applicants, 67% accepted, 59 enrolled. In 2009, 42 master's awarded. *Entrance requirements:* For master's, GRE General Test. Additional exam requirements/recommendations for international students: Required—TOEFL (minimum score 560 paper-based; 210 computer-based; 83 iBT). Application fee: $50. Electronic applications accepted. *Financial support:* In 2009–10, 21 students received support; fellowships, research assistantships, teaching assistantships, career-related internships or fieldwork, Federal Work-Study, scholarships/grants, and unspecified assistantships available. Financial award application deadline: 6/1; financial award applicants required to submit FAFSA. *Faculty research:* Impact of sports and sport marketing on society, factors associated with school and community health, cardiac and pulmonary rehabilitation, impact of participation in activities on student retention and graduation, strength and conditioning. Total annual research expenditures: $58,888. *Unit head:* Dr. David W. Britt, Chair, 502-852-6645, Fax: 502-852-4534, E-mail: david.britt@louisville.edu. *Application contact:* Libby Leggett, Director, Graduate Admissions, 502-852-3101, Fax: 502-852-6536, E-mail: gradadm@louisville.edu.

University of Mary Hardin-Baylor, Graduate Studies in Education, Belton, TX 76513. Offers educational administration (M Ed, Ed D); educational psychology (M Ed); exercise and sport science (M Ed); general studies (M Ed); reading education (M Ed). Part-time and evening/weekend programs available. *Degree requirements:* For master's, comprehensive exam; for doctorate, thesis/dissertation. *Entrance requirements:* For master's, GRE General Test, minimum GPA of 2.75, Texas teaching certificate. Electronic applications accepted.

University of Memphis, Graduate School, College of Education, Department of Health and Sport Sciences, Memphis, TN 38152. Offers clinical nutrition (MS); exercise and sport science (MS); health promotion (MS); physical education teacher education (MS), including teacher education; sport and leisure commerce (MS). Part-time and evening/weekend programs available. *Faculty:* 18 full-time (9 women), 3 part-time/adjunct (1 woman). *Students:* 64 full-time (35 women), 36 part-time (23 women); includes 17 African Americans, 1 Asian American or Pacific Islander, 1 Hispanic American, 4 international. Average age 27. 99 applicants, 72% accepted, 50 enrolled. In 2009, 35 master's awarded. *Degree requirements:* For master's, comprehensive exam, thesis. *Entrance requirements:* For master's, GRE General Test or GMAT (sport and leisure commerce). *Application deadline:* For fall admission, 5/1 priority date for domestic students; for spring admission, 11/1 for domestic students. Applications are processed on a rolling basis. Application fee: $35 ($60 for international students). *Expenses:* Tuition, state resident: full-time $6246; part-time $347 per credit hour. Tuition, nonresident: full-time $15,894; part-time $883 per credit hour. Required fees: $1160. Full-time tuition and fees vary according to course load, degree level and program. *Financial support:* In 2009–10, 59 students received support; research assistantships with full tuition reimbursements available, teaching assistantships with full tuition reimbursements available, career-related internships or fieldwork, Federal Work-Study, scholarships/grants, tuition waivers (partial), and unspecified assistantships available. Financial award application deadline: 2/15; financial award applicants required to submit FAFSA. *Faculty research:* Sport marketing and consumer analysis, health psychology, smoking cessation, psychosocial aspects of cardiovascular disease, global health promotion. *Unit head:* Linda H. Clemens, Interim Chair, 901-678-2324, Fax: 901-678-3591, E-mail: lhclemns@memphis.edu. *Application contact:* Dr. Kenneth Ward, Graduate Studies Coordinator, 901-678-1714, E-mail: kdward@memphis.edu.

University of Miami, Graduate School, School of Education, Department of Exercise and Sport Sciences, Program in Exercise Physiology, Coral Gables, FL 33124. Offers MS Ed, PhD. Part-time and evening/weekend programs available. *Students:* 19 full-time (11 women), 3 part-time (all women); includes 5 minority (1 African American, 4 Hispanic Americans), 5 international. Average age 32. 23 applicants, 57% accepted, 5 enrolled. In 2009, 5 master's, 3 doctorates awarded. Terminal master's awarded for partial completion of doctoral program. *Degree requirements:* For master's, special project; for doctorate, thesis/dissertation, qualifying exam. *Entrance requirements:* For master's and doctorate, GRE General Test. Additional exam requirements/recommendations for international students: Required—TOEFL (minimum score 550 paper-based; 80 iBT); Recommended—IELTS (minimum score 6.5). *Application deadline:* For fall admission, 1/5 for domestic and international students. Applications are processed on a rolling basis. Application fee: $65. Electronic applications accepted. *Financial support:* In 2009–10, 15 students received support. Career-related internships or fieldwork, institutionally sponsored loans, health care benefits, and unspecified assistantships available. Support available to part-time students. Financial award application deadline: 3/1; financial award applicants required to submit FAFSA. *Faculty research:* Women's health, cardiovascular health, aging, metabolism, obesity. *Unit head:* Dr. Arlette Perry, Department Chairperson, 305-284-3025, Fax: 305-284-5168, E-mail: aperry@miami.edu. *Application contact:* Marissa Stevenson-Jacobs, Graduate Admissions Coordinator, 305-284-2167, Fax: 305-284-3003, E-mail: mstevenson@miami.edu.

University of Minnesota, Twin Cities Campus, Graduate School, College of Education and Human Development, School of Kinesiology, Minneapolis, MN 55455-0213. Offers adapted physical education (MA, PhD); biomechanics (MA); biomechanics and neural control (PhD); coaching (Certificate); developmental adapted physical education (M Ed); exercise physiology (MA, PhD); human factors/ergonomics (MA, PhD); international/comparative sport (MA, PhD); kinesiology (M Ed, MA, PhD); leisure services/management (MA, PhD); motor development (MA, PhD); motor learning/control (MA, PhD); outdoor education/recreation (MA, PhD); physical education (M Ed); recreation, park, and leisure studies (M Ed, MA, PhD); sport and exercise science (M Ed); sport management (M Ed, MA, PhD); sport psychology (MA, PhD); sport sociology (MA, PhD); therapeutic recreation (MA, PhD). Part-time programs available. *Faculty:* 15 full-time (8 women). *Students:* 139 full-time (67 women), 55 part-time (19 women); includes 24 minority (12 African Americans, 3 American Indian/Alaska Native, 4 Asian Americans or Pacific Islanders, 5 Hispanic Americans), 18 international. Average age 29. 173 applicants, 53% accepted, 74 enrolled. In 2009, 66 master's, 4 doctorates, 18 other advanced degrees awarded. Terminal master's awarded for partial completion of doctoral program. *Degree requirements:* For master's, final oral exam; for doctorate, thesis/dissertation, preliminary written/oral exam, final oral exam. *Entrance requirements:* For master's, GRE or MAT, minimum GPA of 3.0; for doctorate, GRE or MAT, minimum GPA of 3.0, writing sample. *Financial support:* In 2009–10, 2 fellowships (averaging $22,500 per year), 11 research assistantships with full tuition reimbursements (averaging $26,599 per year), 34 teaching assistantships with full tuition reimbursements (averaging $26,081 per year) were awarded; career-related internships or fieldwork, Federal Work-Study, institutionally sponsored loans, and tuition waivers (full and partial) also available. Support available to part-time students. *Faculty research:* Exercise for health promotion and disease prevention and management, female athletes and bone health, affordance perception-action, gender and youth sport and psychosocial outcomes, neurological movement disorders. Total annual research expenditures: $294,676. *Unit head:* Dr. Mary Jo Kane, Director, 612-625-3870, Fax: 612-626-7700, E-mail: maryjo@umn.edu. *Application contact:* Dr. Mary Trettin, Associate Dean, 612-625-6501, Fax: 612-626-1580, E-mail: mtrettin@umn.edu.

University of Mississippi, Graduate School, School of Applied Sciences, Department of Health, Exercise Science, and Recreation Management, Oxford, University, MS 38677. Offers exercise science (MS); exercise science and leisure management (PhD); park and recreation management (MA); wellness (MS). *Faculty:* 10 full-time (2 women), 2 part-time/adjunct (both women). *Students:* 37 full-time (22 women), 8 part-time (5 women); includes 8 minority (7 African Americans, 1 Hispanic American), 5 international. In 2009, 5 master's, 3 doctorates awarded. *Degree requirements:* For master's, thesis (for some programs); for doctorate, thesis/dissertation. *Entrance requirements:* For master's, GRE General Test, minimum GPA of 3.0; for doctorate, GRE General Test. Additional exam requirements/recommendations for international students: Required—TOEFL. *Application deadline:* For fall admission, 4/1 for domestic students; for spring admission, 10/1 for domestic students. Applications are processed on a rolling basis. Application fee: $25. *Financial support:* Scholarships/grants available. Financial award application deadline: 3/1; financial award applicants required to submit FAFSA. *Unit head:* Dr. Mark Loftin, Interim Chair, 662-915-5844, Fax: 662-915-5525, E-mail: mloftin@olemiss.edu. *Application contact:* Dr. Christy M. Wyandt, Associate Dean, 662-915-7474, Fax: 662-915-7577, E-mail: cwyandt@olemiss.edu.

University of Missouri, Graduate School, College of Human Environmental Science, Department of Nutritional Sciences, Columbia, MO 65211. Offers exercise physiology (MA, PhD); nutritional sciences (MS, PhD). *Degree requirements:* For doctorate, thesis/dissertation. *Entrance requirements:* For master's and doctorate, GRE General Test, minimum GPA of 3.0. Additional exam requirements/recommendations for international students: Required—TOEFL (minimum score 500 paper-based; 173 computer-based; 61 iBT).

The University of Montana, Graduate School, School of Education, Department of Health and Human Performance, Missoula, MT 59812-0002. Offers exercise science (MS); health and human performance (MS); health promotion (MS). Part-time programs available. *Entrance requirements:* For master's, GRE General Test. Additional exam requirements/recommendations for international students: Required—TOEFL. *Faculty research:* Exercise physiology, performance psychology, nutrition, pre-employment physical screening, program evaluation.

University of Nebraska at Kearney, College of Graduate Study, College of Education, Department of Health, Physical Education, Recreation, and Leisure Studies, Kearney, NE 68849-0001. Offers adapted physical education (MA Ed); exercise science (MA Ed); master teacher (MA Ed). Part-time and evening/weekend programs available. *Degree requirements:* For master's, comprehensive exam, thesis optional. *Entrance requirements:* For master's, GRE General Test. Additional exam requirements/recommendations for international students: Required—TOEFL (minimum score 550 paper-based; 213 computer-based). Electronic applications accepted. *Faculty research:* Ergonomic aids, nutrition, motor development, sports pedagogy, applied behavior analysis.

University of Nebraska–Lincoln, Graduate College, College of Education and Human Sciences, Department of Nutrition and Health Sciences, Lincoln, NE 68588. Offers community nutrition and health promotion (MS); nutrition (MS, PhD); nutrition and exercise (MS); nutrition and health sciences (MS, PhD). *Degree requirements:* For master's, thesis optional. *Entrance requirements:* For master's, GRE General Test. Additional exam requirements/recommendations for international students: Required—TOEFL (minimum score 550 paper-based; 213 computer-based). Electronic applications accepted. *Faculty research:* Foods/food service administration, community nutrition science, diet-health relationships.

University of Nevada, Las Vegas, Graduate College, School of Allied Health Sciences, Department of Kinesiology, Las Vegas, NV 89154-3034. Offers exercise physiology (MS); kinesiology (MS). Part-time programs available. *Faculty:* 11 full-time (4 women), 2 part-time/adjunct (1 woman). *Students:* 32 full-time (19 women), 18 part-time (7 women); includes 4 minority (2 Asian Americans or Pacific Islanders, 2 Hispanic Americans), 6 international. Average age 29. 50 applicants, 96% accepted, 19 enrolled. In 2009, 10 master's awarded. *Degree requirements:* For master's, comprehensive exam (for some programs), thesis (for some programs). *Entrance requirements:* For master's, GRE General Test. Additional exam

Exercise and Sports Science

University of Nevada, Las Vegas (continued)
requirements/recommendations for international students: Required—TOEFL (minimum score 550 paper-based; 213 computer-based; 80 iBT), IELTS (minimum score 7). *Application deadline:* For fall admission, 3/15 priority date for domestic and international students; for spring admission, 9/15 priority date for domestic and international students. Applications are processed on a rolling basis. Application fee: $60 ($95 for international students). Electronic applications accepted. *Financial support:* In 2009–10, 22 students received support, including 19 research assistantships with partial tuition reimbursements available (averaging $10,957 per year), 3 teaching assistantships with partial tuition reimbursements available (averaging $10,000 per year); institutionally sponsored loans, scholarships/grants, health care benefits, and unspecified assistantships also available. Financial award application deadline: 3/1. *Faculty research:* Lower limb biomechanics, dietary supplements, motor skill acquisition, human performance, injury assessment and rehabilitation techniques. *Unit head:* Dr. John Young, Chair/ Professor, 702-895-4626, Fax: 702-895-1500, E-mail: john.young@unlv.edu. *Application contact:* Graduate College Admissions Evaluator, 702-895-3320, Fax: 702-895-4180, E-mail: gradcollege@unlv.edu.

University of New Brunswick Fredericton, School of Graduate Studies, Faculty of Kinesiology, Fredericton, NB E3B 5A3, Canada. Offers exercise and sport science (M Sc); sport and recreation management (MBA); sport and recreation studies (MA). Part-time programs available. *Faculty:* 17 full-time (7 women). *Students:* 35 full-time (16 women), 6 part-time (5 women). In 2009, 10 master's awarded. *Degree requirements:* For master's, thesis (for some programs). *Entrance requirements:* For master's, minimum GPA of 3.0, written statement of research goals and interests. Additional exam requirements/recommendations for international students: Required—TOEFL (minimum score 600 paper-based; 250 computer-based), TWE (minimum score 4). *Application deadline:* For winter admission, 1/31 for domestic students; for spring admission, 3/31 for domestic students. Applications are processed on a rolling basis. Application fee: $50 Canadian dollars. Electronic applications accepted. Tuition and fees charges are reported in Canadian dollars. *Expenses:* Tuition, area resident: Full-time $5562 Canadian dollars; part-time $2781 Canadian dollars per year. Required fees: $49.75 Canadian dollars per term. *Financial support:* In 2009–10, 2 fellowships with tuition reimbursements were awarded; research assistantships, teaching assistantships, career-related internships or fieldwork and scholarships/grants also available. *Unit head:* Dr. Wayne Albert, Acting Director of Graduate Studies, 506-447-3254, Fax: 506-453-3511, E-mail: walbert@unb.ca. *Application contact:* Linda O'Brien, Graduate Secretary, 506-453-4576, Fax: 506-453-3511, E-mail: lobrien@unb.ca.

University of New Mexico, Graduate School, College of Education, Department of Health, Exercise and Sports Sciences, Program in Physical Education, Sports and Exercise Science, Albuquerque, NM 87131-2039. Offers PhD. Part-time programs available. *Faculty:* 19 full-time (10 women), 20 part-time/adjunct (10 women). *Students:* 29 full-time (8 women), 14 part-time (3 women); includes 9 minority (4 African Americans, 2 Asian Americans or Pacific Islanders, 3 Hispanic Americans), 11 international. Average age 35. 35 applicants, 51% accepted, 13 enrolled. In 2009, 7 doctorates awarded. *Degree requirements:* For doctorate, comprehensive exam, thesis/dissertation, inquiry skills, 24 credits in supporting area. *Entrance requirements:* For doctorate, GRE, letter of intent, 3 letters of reference, minimum cumulative GPA of 3.0 in last 2 years of bachelor's degree. Additional exam requirements/recommendations for international students: Required—TOEFL (minimum score 550 paper-based; 213 computer-based). *Application deadline:* For fall admission, 3/1 priority date for domestic students; for spring admission, 11/1 priority date for domestic students. Application fee: $50. Electronic applications accepted. *Expenses:* Tuition, state resident: full-time $2099; part-time $233.20 per credit hour. Tuition, nonresident: full-time $6650. Required fees: $25 per semester. Tuition and fees vary according to course load, program and reciprocity agreements. *Financial support:* In 2009–10, 29 students received support, including 20 teaching assistantships with full tuition reimbursements available (averaging $10,815 per year); career-related internships or fieldwork, Federal Work-Study, institutionally sponsored loans, scholarships/grants, health care benefits, tuition waivers, and unspecified assistantships also available. Financial award application deadline: 3/1; financial award applicants required to submit FAFSA. *Faculty research:* Facility risk management, physical education pedagogy practices, physiological adaptations to exercise, physiological adaptations to heat. *Unit head:* Dr. Gloria Napper-Owen, Chair, 505-277-8173, Fax: 505-277-6227, E-mail: napperow@unm.edu. *Application contact:* Carol Catania, Program Office, 505-277-5151, Fax: 505-277-6227, E-mail: catania@unm.edu.

The University of North Carolina at Chapel Hill, Graduate School, College of Arts and Sciences, Department of Exercise and Sport Science, Chapel Hill, NC 27599. Offers athletic training (MA); exercise physiology (MA); sport administration (MA). *Degree requirements:* For master's, comprehensive exam, thesis. *Entrance requirements:* For master's, GRE General Test, minimum GPA of 3.0. Additional exam requirements/recommendations for international students: Required—TOEFL (minimum score 550 paper-based). Electronic applications accepted. *Faculty research:* Mild head injury in sport, endocrine system's response to exercise, obesity and children, effect of aerobic exercise on cerebral bloodflow in elderly population.

The University of North Carolina at Charlotte, Graduate School, College of Health and Human Services, Department of Kinesiology, Charlotte, NC 28223-0001. Offers clinical exercise physiology (MS). *Faculty:* 9 full-time (3 women). *Students:* 11 full-time (7 women), 15 part-time (12 women); includes 6 minority (3 African Americans, 1 American Indian/Alaska Native, 2 Asian Americans or Pacific Islanders), 1 international. Average age 26. 21 applicants, 71% accepted, 9 enrolled. In 2009, 9 master's awarded. *Degree requirements:* For master's, thesis or practicum. *Entrance requirements:* For master's, GRE or MAT. Additional exam requirements/recommendations for international students: Required—TOEFL (minimum score 557 paper-based; 220 computer-based; 83 iBT). *Application deadline:* For fall admission, 7/1 for domestic students, 5/1 for international students; for spring admission, 11/1 for domestic students, 10/1 for international students. Applications are processed on a rolling basis. Application fee: $55. Electronic applications accepted. *Financial support:* In 2009–10, 8 students received support, including 1 fellowship (averaging $41,796 per year), 2 research assistantships (averaging $19,419 per year), 5 teaching assistantships (averaging $9,931 per year); career-related internships or fieldwork, Federal Work-Study, institutionally sponsored loans, scholarships/grants, traineeships, and unspecified assistantships also available. Support available to part-time students. Financial award application deadline: 4/1; financial award applicants required to submit FAFSA. *Faculty research:* Genetic determinants of physical activity, cardiac muscle apoptosis with aging, sensorimotor deficits in knee osteoarthritis, mechanical laxity in functional ankle instability. Total annual research expenditures: $363,717. *Unit head:* Dr. Mitchell L. Cordova, Chair, 704-687-4695, Fax: 704-687-3180, E-mail: mcordova@uncc.edu. *Application contact:* Kathy B. Giddings, Director of Graduate Admissions, 704-687-5503, Fax: 704-687-3279, E-mail: gradadm@uncc.edu.

The University of North Carolina at Greensboro, Graduate School, School of Health and Human Performance, Department of Exercise and Sports Science, Greensboro, NC 27412-5001. Offers M Ed, MS, Ed D, PhD. *Degree requirements:* For master's, thesis (for some programs); for doctorate, thesis/dissertation. *Entrance requirements:* For master's and doctorate, GRE General Test. Additional exam requirements/recommendations for international students: Required—TOEFL. Electronic applications accepted.

University of Northern Colorado, Graduate School, College of Natural and Health Sciences, School of Sport and Exercise Science, Greeley, CO 80639. Offers exercise science (MS, PhD); sport administration (MS, PhD); sport pedagogy (MS, PhD). Part-time and evening/weekend programs available. *Faculty:* 14 full-time (7 women). *Students:* 66 full-time (37 women), 24 part-time (11 women); includes 11 minority (1 African American, 3 American Indian/Alaska Native, 3 Asian Americans or Pacific Islanders, 4 Hispanic Americans), 16 international. Average age 28. 175 applicants, 56% accepted, 31 enrolled. In 2009, 65 master's, 10 doctorates awarded. *Degree requirements:* For master's, comprehensive exam; for doctorate, comprehensive exam, thesis/dissertation. *Entrance requirements:* For master's, 2 letters of recommendation, resume; for doctorate, GRE General Test, 3 letters of recommendation, resume. *Application deadline:* Applications are processed on a rolling basis. Application fee: $50 ($60 for international students). Electronic applications accepted. *Expenses:* Tuition, state resident: full-time $5770; part-time $320.55 per credit hour. Tuition, nonresident: full-time $13,847; part-time $769.27 per credit hour. Required fees: $948.78; $52.72 per credit. *Financial support:* In 2009–10, 7 research assistantships (averaging $3,876 per year), 17 teaching assistantships (averaging $8,928 per year) were awarded; fellowships, unspecified assistantships also available. Financial award application deadline: 3/1; financial award applicants required to submit FAFSA. *Unit head:* Dr. David Stotlar, Director, 970-351-2535, Fax: 970-351-1762. *Application contact:* Linda Sisson, Graduate Student Admission Coordinator, 970-351-1807, Fax: 970-351-2371, E-mail: linda.sisson@unco.edu.

University of Oklahoma, Graduate College, College of Arts and Sciences, Department of Health and Exercise Science, Norman, OK 73019. Offers MS, PhD. *Faculty:* 11 full-time (4 women), 1 part-time/adjunct (0 women). *Students:* 35 full-time (15 women), 6 part-time (2 women); includes 3 minority (1 African American, 1 American Indian/Alaska Native, 1 Hispanic American), 8 international. 23 applicants, 65% accepted, 15 enrolled. In 2009, 8 master's, 2 doctorates awarded. *Degree requirements:* For master's, comprehensive exam (for some programs), thesis. *Entrance requirements:* For master's, GRE General Test, minimum GPA of 3.0 in last 60 hours of undergraduate course work, interview, 3 letters of recommendation; for doctorate, GRE General Test, 3 letters of recommendation, curriculum vitae. Additional exam requirements/recommendations for international students: Required—TOEFL (minimum score 550 paper-based; 213 computer-based). *Application deadline:* For fall admission, 4/1 priority date for domestic students, 4/1 for international students; for spring admission, 11/1 for domestic students, 9/1 for international students. Applications are processed on a rolling basis. Application fee: $40 ($90 for international students). Electronic applications accepted. *Expenses:* Tuition, state resident: full-time $3744; part-time $156 per credit hour. Tuition, nonresident: full-time $13,577; part-time $565.70 per credit hour. Required fees: $2415; $90.10 per credit hour. *Financial support:* In 2009–10, 40 teaching assistantships with partial tuition reimbursements (averaging $11,483 per year) were awarded; health care benefits, tuition waivers (partial), and unspecified assistantships also available. Financial award applicants required to submit FAFSA. *Faculty research:* Aging, supplements, osteoporosis, barriers to exercise, muscle function. Total annual research expenditures: $478,491. *Unit head:* Michael Bemben, Chair, 405-325-5211, Fax: 405-325-0594, E-mail: mgbemben@ou.edu. *Application contact:* Dr. Joel Cramer, Graduate Liaison, 405-325-1371, Fax: 405-325-0594, E-mail: jcramer@ou.edu.

University of Pittsburgh, School of Education, Department of Health and Physical Activity, Program in Developmental Movement, Pittsburgh, PA 15260. Offers MS. *Students:* 1 (woman) full-time, 2 part-time (1 woman); includes 1 minority (African American). Average age 40. 3 applicants, 67% accepted, 2 enrolled. In 2009, 2 master's awarded. *Degree requirements:* For master's, thesis. *Entrance requirements:* Additional exam requirements/recommendations for international students: Required—TOEFL. *Application deadline:* For fall admission, 2/1 for domestic students. Application fee: $50. Electronic applications accepted. *Expenses:* Tuition, state resident: full-time $16,402; part-time $665 per credit. Tuition, nonresident: full-time $28,694; part-time $1175 per credit. Required fees: $690; $175 per term. Tuition and fees vary according to program. *Financial support:* Traineeships and unspecified assistantships available. Financial award application deadline: 3/1; financial award applicants required to submit FAFSA. *Unit head:* Dr. John M. Jakicic, Chair, 412-648-8914, E-mail: jjakicic@pitt.edu. *Application contact:* Graduate Enrollment Manager, 412-648-2230, Fax: 412-648-1899, E-mail: soeinfo@pitt.edu.

University of Pittsburgh, School of Education, Department of Health and Physical Activity, Program in Exercise Physiology, Pittsburgh, PA 15260. Offers MS, PhD. *Students:* 56 full-time (31 women), 25 part-time (17 women); includes 9 minority (5 African Americans, 1 American Indian/Alaska Native, 2 Asian Americans or Pacific Islanders, 1 Hispanic American), 2 international. Average age 29. 65 applicants, 78% accepted, 37 enrolled. In 2009, 42 master's, 7 doctorates awarded. *Entrance requirements:* Additional exam requirements/recommendations for international students: Required—TOEFL (minimum score 550 paper-based; 213 computer-based; 80 iBT). *Application deadline:* Applications are processed on a rolling basis. Application fee: $50. Electronic applications accepted. *Expenses:* Tuition, state resident: full-time $16,402; part-time $665 per credit. Tuition, nonresident: full-time $28,694; part-time $1175 per credit. Required fees: $690; $175 per term. Tuition and fees vary according to program. *Unit head:* Dr. John M. Jakicic, Chair, 412-648-8914, E-mail: jjakicic@pitt.edu. *Application contact:* Graduate Enrollment Manager, 412-648-2230, Fax: 412-648-1899, E-mail: soeinfo@pitt.edu.

University of Puerto Rico, Río Piedras, College of Education, Program in Exercise Sciences, San Juan, PR 00931-3300. Offers MS. *Entrance requirements:* For master's, PAEG or GRE, minimum GPA of 3.0.

University of Rhode Island, Graduate School, College of Human Science and Services, Department of Kinesiology, Kingston, RI 02881. Offers cultural studies of sport and physical culture (MS); exercise science (MS); physical education pedagogy (MS); psychosocial/behavioral aspects of physical activity (MS). *Accreditation:* NCATE. Part-time programs available. *Faculty:* 13 full-time (7 women). *Students:* 16 full-time (8 women), 2 part-time (1 woman), 1 international. In 2009, 6 master's awarded. *Degree requirements:* For master's, thesis optional. *Entrance requirements:* For master's, GRE, 2 letters of recommendation. Additional exam requirements/recommendations for international students: Required—TOEFL (minimum score 550 paper-based; 213 computer-based). *Application deadline:* For fall admission, 4/15 for domestic students, 2/1 for international students; for spring admission, 11/15 for domestic students, 7/15 for international students. Application fee: $65. Electronic applications accepted. *Expenses:* Tuition, state resident: full-time $8828; part-time $490 per credit hour. Tuition, nonresident: full-time $22,100; part-time $1228 per credit hour. Required fees: $1118; $57 per semester. Tuition and fees vary according to program. *Financial support:* In 2009–10, 4 teaching assistantships with full and partial tuition reimbursements (averaging $7,939 per year) were awarded. Financial award application deadline: 4/15; financial award applicants required to submit FAFSA. *Faculty research:* Strength training and older adults, interventions to promote a healthy lifestyle as well as analysis of the psychosocial outcomes of those interventions, effects of exercise and nutrition on skeletal muscle of aging healthy adults with CVD and other metabolic related diseases, physical activity and fitness of deaf children and youth. Total annual research expenditures: $92,479. *Unit head:* Dr. Deborah Riebe, Chair, 401-874-5444, Fax: 401-874-4215, E-mail: debriebe@uri.edu. *Application contact:* Dr. Lori Ciccomascolo, Director of Graduate Studies, 401-874-5454, Fax: 401-874-4215, E-mail: lecicco@uri.edu.

University of South Alabama, Graduate School, College of Education, Department of Health, Physical Education and Leisure Services, Mobile, AL 36688-0002. Offers exercise science (MS); health education (M Ed); physical education (M Ed); therapeutic recreation (MS). *Accreditation:* NCATE (one or more programs are accredited). Part-time programs available. *Degree requirements:* For master's, comprehensive exam. *Entrance requirements:* For master's, GRE General Test or MAT. *Expenses:* Tuition, state resident: part-time $218 per contact hour. Required fees: $1102 per year.

University of South Carolina, The Graduate School, Arnold School of Public Health, Department of Exercise Science, Columbia, SC 29208. Offers MS, DPT, PhD. Part-time programs available. *Degree requirements:* For master's, comprehensive exam, thesis (for some programs), project; for doctorate, comprehensive exam, thesis/dissertation. *Entrance requirements:* For master's and doctorate, GRE General Test. Additional exam requirements/recommendations for international students: Required—TOEFL (minimum score 570 paper-based; 230 computer-based). Electronic applications accepted. *Faculty research:* Effects of acute and chronic exercise on human function and health, motor control.

University of Southern Mississippi, Graduate School, College of Health, School of Human Performance and Recreation, Hattiesburg, MS 39406-0001. Offers human performance (MS, Ed D, PhD); interscholastic athletic administration (MS); recreation and leisure management (MS); sport administration (MS); sport and coaching education (MS); sport management (MS); sports and high performance materials (MS). Part-time and evening/weekend programs available.

Faculty: 13 full-time (5 women). *Students:* 62 full-time (27 women), 40 part-time (10 women); includes 13 minority (10 African Americans, 1 Asian American or Pacific Islander, 2 Hispanic Americans), 4 international. Average age 29. 79 applicants, 59% accepted, 33 enrolled. In 2009, 43 master's, 4 doctorates awarded. *Degree requirements:* For master's, comprehensive exam, thesis optional; for doctorate, comprehensive exam, thesis/dissertation. *Entrance requirements:* For master's, GRE General Test, minimum GPA of 2.75 in last 60 hours; for doctorate, GRE General Test, minimum GPA of 3.5. Additional exam requirements/recommendations for international students: Required—TOEFL. *Application deadline:* For fall admission, 3/1 priority date for domestic students, 3/1 for international students. Applications are processed on a rolling basis. Application fee: $35. Electronic applications accepted. *Expenses:* Tuition, state resident: full-time $5096; part-time $284 per hour. Tuition, nonresident: full-time $13,052; part-time $726 per hour. Required fees: $402. Tuition and fees vary according to course level and course load. *Financial support:* In 2009–10, 1 fellowship (averaging $16,000 per year), 6 research assistantships with full tuition reimbursements (averaging $7,492 per year), 5 teaching assistantships with full tuition reimbursements (averaging $7,330 per year) were awarded; career-related internships or fieldwork, Federal Work-Study, institutionally sponsored loans, and tuition waivers (partial) also available. Financial award application deadline: 3/15. *Faculty research:* Exercise physiology, health behaviors, resource management, activity interaction, site development. *Unit head:* Dr. Louis Marciani, Director, 601-266-5379, Fax: 601-266-4445. *Application contact:* Dr. Dennis Phillips, Graduate Coordinator, 601-266-5379, Fax: 601-266-4445.

University of South Florida, Graduate School, College of Education–Main Campus, School of Physical Education and Exercise Science, Tampa, FL 33620-9951. Offers exercise science (MA); physical education teacher preparation (MA). Part-time and evening/weekend programs available. Postbaccalaureate distance learning degree programs offered (no on-campus study). *Faculty:* 9 full-time (6 women). *Students:* 43 full-time (22 women), 57 part-time (30 women); includes 18 minority (8 African Americans, 2 American Indian/Alaska Native, 1 Asian American or Pacific Islander, 7 Hispanic Americans), 1 international. Average age 30. 59 applicants, 66% accepted, 27 enrolled. In 2009, 27 master's awarded. *Degree requirements:* For master's, comprehensive exam, thesis optional. *Entrance requirements:* For master's, GRE General Test, minimum GPA of 3.0 in last 60 hours of coursework. Additional exam requirements/recommendations for international students: Required—TOEFL (minimum score 500 paper-based; 213 computer-based). *Application deadline:* For fall admission, 2/15 for domestic students, 1/2 for international students; for spring admission, 10/15 for domestic students, 6/1 for international students. Applications are processed on a rolling basis. Application fee: $30. Electronic applications accepted. *Financial support:* In 2009–10, 5 teaching assistantships with full tuition reimbursements (averaging $9,200 per year) were awarded; unspecified assistantships also available. Financial award application deadline: 7/3; financial award applicants required to submit FAFSA. *Faculty research:* Physical education pedagogy, active gaming, exercise motivation, heat stress research, strength and nutrition research, physical activity risk management. Total annual research expenditures: $20,482. *Unit head:* Dr. Steve Sanders, Director, 813-974-4871, Fax: 813-974-4979, E-mail: sanders@usf.edu. *Application contact:* Dr. Steve Sanders, Director, 813-974-4871, Fax: 813-974-4979, E-mail: sanders@usf.edu.

The University of Tennessee, Graduate School, College of Education, Health and Human Sciences, Department of Exercise, Sport, and Leisure Studies, Program in Exercise Science, Knoxville, TN 37996. Offers biomechanics/sports medicine (MS, PhD); exercise physiology (MS, PhD). *Accreditation:* CEPH (one or more programs are accredited). Part-time programs available. *Degree requirements:* For master's, thesis optional. *Entrance requirements:* For master's, minimum GPA of 2.7. Additional exam requirements/recommendations for international students: Required—TOEFL. Electronic applications accepted. *Expenses:* Tuition, state resident: full-time $6826; part-time $380 per semester hour. Tuition, nonresident: full-time $21,844; part-time $1147 per semester hour. Tuition and fees vary according to program.

The University of Tennessee, Graduate School, College of Education, Health and Human Sciences, Program in Education, Knoxville, TN 37996. Offers art education (MS); counseling education (PhD); cultural studies in education (PhD); curriculum (MS, Ed S); curriculum, educational research and evaluation (Ed D, PhD); early childhood education (PhD); early childhood special education (MS); education of deaf and hard of hearing (MS); educational administration and policy studies (Ed D, PhD); educational administration and supervision (Ed S); educational psychology (Ed D, PhD); elementary education (MS, Ed S); elementary teaching (MS); English education (MS, Ed S); exercise science (PhD); foreign language/ESL education (MS, Ed S); instructional technology (MS, Ed D, PhD, Ed S); literacy, language and ESL education (PhD); literacy, language education, and ESL education (Ed D); mathematics education (MS, Ed S); modified and comprehensive special education (MS); reading education (MS, Ed S); school counseling (Ed S); school psychology (PhD, Ed S); science education (MS, Ed S); secondary teaching (MS); social foundations (MS); social science education (MS, Ed S); socio-cultural foundations of sports and education (PhD); special education (Ed S); teacher education (Ed D, PhD). *Accreditation:* NCATE. Part-time and evening/weekend programs available. *Degree requirements:* For master's and Ed S, thesis optional; for doctorate, variable foreign language requirement, thesis/dissertation. *Entrance requirements:* For master's, minimum GPA of 2.7; for doctorate and Ed S, GRE General Test, minimum GPA of 2.7. Additional exam requirements/recommendations for international students: Required—TOEFL. Electronic applications accepted. *Expenses:* Tuition, state resident: full-time $6826; part-time $380 per semester hour. Tuition, nonresident: full-time $21,844; part-time $1147 per semester hour. Tuition and fees vary according to program.

The University of Texas at Arlington, Graduate School, College of Education, Arlington, TX 76019. Offers curriculum and instruction (M Ed); educational leadership and policy studies (M Ed); K-16 educational, leadership and policy studies (PhD); physiology of exercise (MS); teaching (M Ed T). *Accreditation:* NCATE. Part-time and evening/weekend programs available. *Faculty:* 35 full-time (22 women), 4 part-time/adjunct (2 women). *Students:* 125 full-time (83 women), 586 part-time (479 women); includes 283 minority (125 African Americans, 4 American Indian/Alaska Native, 19 Asian Americans or Pacific Islanders, 135 Hispanic Americans), 15 international. Average age 35. 601 applicants, 99% accepted, 238 enrolled. In 2009, 161 degrees awarded. *Degree requirements:* For master's, comprehensive exam (for some programs), thesis (for some programs), comprehensive activity, research project; for doctorate, comprehensive exam, thesis/dissertation. *Entrance requirements:* For master's, GRE General Test, minimum undergraduate GPA of 3.0 in last 60 hours of course work, writing sample, 3 letters of recommendation; for doctorate, GRE General Test, interview, minimum GPA of 3.5, master's degree in education or other appropriate field, 3 years of documented experience in an education related work environment. Additional exam requirements/recommendations for international students: Required—TOEFL (minimum score 550 paper-based; 213 computer-based). *Application deadline:* For fall admission, 6/5 priority date for domestic students, 4/3 priority date for international students; for spring admission, 10/17 priority date for domestic students, 9/5 priority date for international students. Applications are processed on a rolling basis. Application fee: $35 ($50 for international students). Electronic applications accepted. *Financial support:* In 2009–10, 9 fellowships (averaging $1,000 per year), 6 research assistantships (averaging $6,250 per year), 10 teaching assistantships with full tuition reimbursements (averaging $5,200 per year) were awarded; career-related internships or fieldwork, Federal Work-Study, scholarships/grants, and unspecified assistantships also available. Financial award application deadline: 6/1; financial award applicants required to submit FAFSA. *Unit head:* Dr. Jeanne M. Gerlach, Dean, 817-272-2591, Fax: 817-272-2530, E-mail: coeadvising@uta.edu. *Application contact:* Kas McConnell, Graduate Advisor, 817-272-7489, Fax: 817-272-7624, E-mail: coedadvising@uta.edu.

University of the Pacific, College of the Pacific, Department of Sport Sciences, Stockton, CA 95211-0197. Offers MA. *Faculty:* 9 full-time (4 women), 1 (woman) part-time/adjunct. *Students:* 1 (woman) full-time, 14 part-time (9 women); includes 1 minority (Asian American or Pacific Islander), 1 international. Average age 23. 17 applicants, 59% accepted, 8 enrolled. In 2009, 3 master's awarded. *Degree requirements:* For master's, comprehensive exam (for some programs), thesis (for some programs). *Entrance requirements:* For master's, GRE General Test. Additional exam requirements/recommendations for international students: Required—TOEFL (minimum score 475 paper-based; 150 computer-based). *Application deadline:* For fall admission, 3/1 priority date for domestic students; for spring admission, 10/1 for domestic students. Applications are processed on a rolling basis. Application fee: $75. *Financial support:* In 2009–10, 7 teaching assistantships were awarded; institutionally sponsored loans also available. Support available to part-time students. Financial award application deadline: 3/1; financial award applicants required to submit FAFSA. *Unit head:* Dr. Christopher Snell, Chairperson, 209-946-2703, E-mail: csnell@pacific.edu. *Application contact:* Information Contact, 209-946-2261.

The University of Toledo, College of Graduate Studies, College of Health Science and Human Service, Division of Human Services, Department of Kinesiology, Toledo, OH 43606-3390. Offers exercise science (MSX, PhD).

University of Utah, Graduate School, College of Health, Department of Exercise and Sport Science, Salt Lake City, UT 84112. Offers MS, PhD. *Faculty:* 17 full-time (8 women), 1 (woman) part-time/adjunct. *Students:* 72 full-time (33 women), 16 part-time (5 women); includes 5 minority (3 Asian Americans or Pacific Islanders, 2 Hispanic Americans), 10 international. Average age 30. 121 applicants, 47% accepted, 32 enrolled. In 2009, 18 master's, 4 doctorates awarded. Terminal master's awarded for partial completion of doctoral program. *Degree requirements:* For master's, comprehensive exam, thesis (for some programs); for doctorate, comprehensive exam, thesis/dissertation. *Entrance requirements:* For master's and doctorate, GRE General Test, curriculum vitae, 2 letters of recommendation, minimum GPA of 3.0. Additional exam requirements/recommendations for international students: Required—TOEFL (minimum score 500 paper-based; 173 computer-based; 61 iBT). *Application deadline:* For fall admission, 1/15 for domestic and international students. Application fee: $55 ($65 for international students). Electronic applications accepted. *Expenses:* Tuition, state resident: full-time $4004; part-time $1674 per semester. Tuition, nonresident: full-time $14,134; part-time $5915 per semester. Required fees: $324 per semester. Tuition and fees vary according to course load, degree level and program. *Financial support:* In 2009–10, 44 students received support, including 3 fellowships with full tuition reimbursements available (averaging $13,000 per year), 14 research assistantships with full and partial tuition reimbursements available (averaging $13,000 per year), 27 teaching assistantships with full and partial tuition reimbursements available (averaging $12,000 per year); career-related internships or fieldwork, scholarships/grants, traineeships, health care benefits, and unspecified assistantships also available. Financial award application deadline: 4/15; financial award applicants required to submit FAFSA. *Faculty research:* Exercise physiology, psychosocial aspects of sports and physical education, special physical education, elementary/secondary physical education. Total annual research expenditures: $229,947. *Unit head:* Dr. Barry B. Shultz, Chair, 801-581-4440, Fax: 801-585-3992, E-mail: barry.shultz@health.utah.edu. *Application contact:* Dr. James C. Hannon, Director of Graduate Studies, 801-581-7646, Fax: 801-585-3992, E-mail: james.hannon@hsc.utah.edu.

University of West Florida, College of Professional Studies, Department of Professional and Community Leadership, Program in Administration, Pensacola, FL 32514-5750. Offers acquisition and contract administration (MSA); biomedical/pharmaceutical (MSA); criminal justice administration (MSA); database administration (MSA); education leadership (MSA); healthcare administration (MSA); human performance technology (MSA); leadership (MSA); nursing administration (MSA); public administration (MSA); software engineering administration (MSA). Part-time and evening/weekend programs available. Postbaccalaureate distance learning degree programs offered (no on-campus study). *Students:* 33 full-time (21 women), 168 part-time (97 women); includes 53 minority (32 African Americans, 2 American Indian/Alaska Native, 5 Asian Americans or Pacific Islanders, 14 Hispanic Americans), 1 international. Average age 34. 103 applicants, 74% accepted, 64 enrolled. In 2009, 47 master's awarded. *Entrance requirements:* For master's, GRE General Test, letter of intent, names of references. Additional exam requirements/recommendations for international students: Required—TOEFL (minimum score 550 paper-based; 213 computer-based). *Application deadline:* For fall admission, 6/1 for domestic students, 5/15 for international students; for spring admission, 11/1 for domestic students, 10/1 for international students. Applications are processed on a rolling basis. Application fee: $30. *Expenses:* Tuition, state resident: full-time $4982; part-time $260 per credit hour. Tuition, nonresident: full-time $20,059; part-time $919 per credit hour. Required fees: $1247; $52 per credit hour. *Financial support:* Unspecified assistantships available. Financial award application deadline: 4/15; financial award applicants required to submit FAFSA. *Unit head:* Dr. Karen Rasmussen, Chairperson, 850-474-2301, Fax: 850-474-2804. *Application contact:* Terry McCray, Assistant Director of Graduate Admissions, 850-473-7718, Fax: 850-473-7714, E-mail: gradadmissions@uwf.edu.

University of West Florida, College of Professional Studies, Division of Health, Leisure, and Exercise Science, Program in Health, Leisure, and Exercise Science, Pensacola, FL 32514-5750. Offers exercise science (MS); physical education (MS). Part-time and evening/weekend programs available. *Faculty:* 5 full-time (2 women), 2 part-time/adjunct (1 woman). *Students:* 20 full-time (9 women), 23 part-time (10 women); includes 6 minority (3 African Americans, 1 Asian American or Pacific Islander, 2 Hispanic Americans), 4 international. Average age 28. 30 applicants, 83% accepted, 11 enrolled. In 2009, 26 master's awarded. *Degree requirements:* For master's, thesis or alternative. *Entrance requirements:* For master's, GRE General Test, minimum GPA of 3.0. Additional exam requirements/recommendations for international students: Required—TOEFL (minimum score 550 paper-based; 213 computer-based). *Application deadline:* For fall admission, 6/1 for domestic students, 5/15 for international students; for spring admission, 11/1 for domestic students, 10/1 for international students. Applications are processed on a rolling basis. Application fee: $30. Electronic applications accepted. *Expenses:* Tuition, state resident: full-time $4982; part-time $260 per credit hour. Tuition, nonresident: full-time $20,059; part-time $919 per credit hour. Required fees: $1247; $52 per credit hour. *Financial support:* Career-related internships or fieldwork, Federal Work-Study, scholarships/grants, and tuition waivers (partial) available. Support available to part-time students. Financial award application deadline: 4/15; financial award applicants required to submit FAFSA. *Unit head:* Dr. John Todorovich, Chairperson, 850-473-7248, Fax: 850-474-2106. *Application contact:* Terry McCray, Assistant Director of Graduate Admissions, 850-473-7718, Fax: 850-473-7714, E-mail: gradadmissions@uwf.edu.

University of Wisconsin–La Crosse, Office of University Graduate Studies, College of Science and Health, Department of Exercise and Sport Science, Program in Clinical Exercise Physiology, La Crosse, WI 54601-3742. Offers MS. *Students:* 15 full-time (10 women); includes 1 minority (African American). Average age 23. 45 applicants, 44% accepted. In 2009, 15 master's awarded. *Degree requirements:* For master's, thesis optional. *Entrance requirements:* Additional exam requirements/recommendations for international students: Required—TOEFL (minimum score 550 paper-based; 213 computer-based; 79 iBT). *Application deadline:* For fall admission, 2/1 priority date for domestic students. Application fee: $56. Electronic applications accepted. *Financial support:* Research assistantships, career-related internships or fieldwork, Federal Work-Study, institutionally sponsored loans, health care benefits, tuition waivers (full and partial), and unspecified assistantships available. Financial award application deadline: 2/1; financial award applicants required to submit FAFSA. *Unit head:* Dr. John Porcari, Director, 608-785-8684, Fax: 608-785-8686, E-mail: porcari.john@uwlax.edu. *Application contact:* Kathryn Kiefer, Director of Admissions, 608-785-8939, E-mail: admissions@uwlax.edu.

University of Wisconsin–La Crosse, Office of University Graduate Studies, College of Science and Health, Department of Exercise and Sport Science, Program in Human Performance, La Crosse, WI 54601-3742. Offers athletic training (MS); human performance (MS). Part-time and evening/weekend programs available. *Students:* 17 full-time (8 women), 3 part-time (1 woman). Average age 24. 24 applicants, 67% accepted, 9 enrolled. In 2009, 11 master's awarded. *Degree requirements:* For master's, comprehensive exam (for some programs), thesis optional. *Entrance requirements:* For master's, GRE, course work in anatomy, physiology, biomechanics, and exercise physiology. Additional exam requirements/recommendations for international students: Required—TOEFL (minimum score 550 paper-based; 213 computer-based; 79 iBT). *Application deadline:* For fall admission, 2/1 priority date for domestic students. Application fee: $56. Electronic applications accepted. *Financial support:*

Exercise and Sports Science

University of Wisconsin–La Crosse *(continued)*
Research assistantships, career-related internships or fieldwork, Federal Work-Study, institutionally sponsored loans, scholarships/grants, health care benefits, tuition waivers (full and partial), unspecified assistantships, and grant-funded positions available. Support available to part-time students. Financial award application deadline: 3/15; financial award applicants required to submit FAFSA. *Unit head:* Dr. Glenn Wright, Director, 608-785-8689, Fax: 608-785-6520, E-mail: wright.glen@uwlax.edu. *Application contact:* Kathryn Kiefer, Director of Admissions, 608-785-8939, E-mail: admissions@uwlax.edu.

University of Wyoming, College of Health Sciences, Division of Kinesiology and Health, Laramie, WY 82070. Offers MS. *Accreditation:* NCATE. Part-time programs available. Post-baccalaureate distance learning degree programs offered (no on-campus study). *Degree requirements:* For master's, comprehensive exam (for some programs), thesis (for some programs). *Entrance requirements:* For master's, GRE General Test, minimum GPA of 3.0. Additional exam requirements/recommendations for international students: Required—TOEFL. Electronic applications accepted. *Faculty research:* Teacher effectiveness, effects of exercising on heart function, physiological responses of overtraining, psychological benefits of physical activity, health behavior.

Virginia Commonwealth University, Graduate School, School of Education, Department of Health and Human Performance, Program in Health and Movement Sciences, Richmond, VA 23284-9005. Offers MS.

Wake Forest University, Graduate School of Arts and Sciences, Department of Health and Exercise Science, Winston-Salem, NC 27109. Offers MS. *Degree requirements:* For master's, one foreign language, thesis. *Entrance requirements:* For master's, GRE General Test, resume. Additional exam requirements/recommendations for international students: Required—TOEFL (minimum score 213 computer-based; 79 iBT). Electronic applications accepted. *Faculty research:* Cardiac rehabilitation, biomechanics, health psychology, exercise physiology.

Washington State University, Graduate School, College of Education, Department of Teaching and Learning, Pullman, WA 99164. Offers curriculum and instruction (Ed D, PhD); diverse languages (M Ed, MA); elementary education (M Ed, MA, MIT); exercise science (MS); literacy education (M Ed, MA, PhD); math education (PhD); secondary education (M Ed, MA). *Accreditation:* NCATE. *Degree requirements:* For master's, comprehensive exam (for some programs), thesis (for some programs), oral or written exam; for doctorate, comprehensive exam, thesis/dissertation, oral, written exam. *Entrance requirements:* For master's and doctorate, GRE General Test, minimum GPA of 3.0, 3 letters of recommendation. Additional exam requirements/recommendations for international students: Required—TOEFL. *Faculty research:* Evolution of middle school education issues in special education, computer-assisted language learning.

Washington State University Spokane, Graduate Programs, Program in Exercise Science, Spokane, WA 99210-1495. Offers MS. *Faculty:* 4. *Degree requirements:* For master's, comprehensive exam, thesis optional. *Entrance requirements:* For master's, GRE, minimum GPA of 3.0. Additional exam requirements/recommendations for international students: Required—TOEFL (minimum score 550 paper-based; 213 computer-based). *Application deadline:* For fall admission, 7/15 priority date for domestic students, 3/1 for international students; for spring admission, 10/15 priority date for domestic students, 7/1 for international students. Application fee: $50. *Expenses:* Tuition, state resident: part-time $423 per credit. Tuition, nonresident: part-time $1032 per credit. *Financial support:* In 2009–10, 4 students received support, including 3 research assistantships with full and partial tuition reimbursements available (averaging $13,917 per year), teaching assistantships with full and partial tuition reimbursements available (averaging $13,056 per year); career-related internships or fieldwork, Federal Work-Study; scholarships/grants, health care benefits, and unspecified assistantships also available. *Faculty research:* Experimental exercise physiology, cellular and molecular mechanisms. *Unit head:* Dr. Sally Blank, Associate Professor/Director, 509-358-7633, E-mail: seblank@wsu.edu. *Application contact:* Graduate School Admissions, 800-GRADWSU, Fax: 509-335-1949, E-mail: gradsch@wsu.edu.

Wayne State College, Department of Health, Human Performance and Sport, Wayne, NE 68787. Offers exercise science (MSE); organizational management (MS), including sport management. Part-time and evening/weekend programs available. *Degree requirements:* For master's, comprehensive exam, thesis optional. *Entrance requirements:* For master's, GRE General Test, minimum GPA of 3.0. Additional exam requirements/recommendations for international students: Required—TOEFL (minimum score 550 paper-based; 213 computer-based). Electronic applications accepted.

West Chester University of Pennsylvania, Office of Graduate Studies, College of Health Sciences, Department of Kinesiology, West Chester, PA 19383. Offers adapted physical education (Certificate); health and physical education (MS, Teaching Certificate), including exercise physiology (MS); physical education (MS); sport and athletic administration (MSA). Part-time and evening/weekend programs available. *Students:* 2 full-time (1 woman), 37 part-time (15 women); includes 2 minority (both African Americans), 3 international. Average age 25. 39 applicants, 90% accepted, 11 enrolled. In 2009, 25 master's awarded. *Degree requirements:* For master's, thesis (for some programs), thesis or report (MS), 2 internships (MSA). *Entrance requirements:* For master's, GRE (MS); GMAT, GRE General Test, or MAT

(MSA), minimum GPA of 3.0 with interview (MS) or letters of recommendation (MSA). Additional exam requirements/recommendations for international students: Required—TOEFL (minimum score 550 paper-based; 213 computer-based; 80 iBT). *Application deadline:* For fall admission, 4/15 priority date for domestic students, 3/15 for international students; for spring admission, 10/15 for domestic students, 9/1 for international students. Applications are processed on a rolling basis. Application fee: $35. Electronic applications accepted. *Expenses:* Tuition, state resident: full-time $6666; part-time $370 per credit. Tuition, nonresident: full-time $10,666; part-time $593 per credit. Required fees: $122.56 per credit. *Financial support:* In 2009–10, 11 research assistantships with full and partial tuition reimbursements (averaging $5,000 per year) were awarded; unspecified assistantships also available. Support available to part-time students. Financial award application deadline: 2/15; financial award applicants required to submit FAFSA. *Faculty research:* Weight lifting and type 1 diabetes mellitus, martial arts, sexual harassment in sports. *Unit head:* Dr. Frank Fry, Chair, 610-436-2832, E-mail: ffry@wcupa.edu. *Application contact:* Dr. Sheri Melton, Graduate Coordinator, 610-436-2260, E-mail: smelton@wcupa.edu.

Western Michigan University, Graduate College, College of Education, Department of Health, Physical Education and Recreation, Kalamazoo, MI 49008. Offers exercise and sports medicine (MS), including athletic training, exercise physiology; physical education (MA), including coaching sport performance, pedagogy, special physical education, sport management. *Faculty:* 20 full-time (9 women). *Students:* 60 full-time (27 women), 53 part-time (25 women); includes 9 minority (6 African Americans, 2 Asian Americans or Pacific Islanders, 1 Hispanic American), 6 international. 69 applicants, 81% accepted, 21 enrolled. In 2009, 42 master's awarded. *Application deadline:* For fall admission, 2/15 priority date for domestic students. Applications are processed on a rolling basis. Application fee: $25. *Financial support:* Fellowships, research assistantships, teaching assistantships, Federal Work-Study available. Financial award application deadline: 2/15; financial award applicants required to submit FAFSA. *Unit head:* Lee deLisle, Chair, 269-387-2669. *Application contact:* Admissions and Orientation, 269-387-2000, Fax: 269-387-2355.

Western Washington University, Graduate School, College of Humanities and Social Sciences, Department of Physical Education, Health, and Recreation, Bellingham, WA 98225-5996. Offers exercise science (MS); sport psychology (MS). Part-time programs available. *Degree requirements:* For master's, thesis. *Entrance requirements:* For master's, GRE General Test, minimum GPA of 3.0 in last 60 semester hours or last 90 quarter hours. Additional exam requirements/recommendations for international students: Required—TOEFL (minimum score 567 paper-based; 227 computer-based). Electronic applications accepted. *Faculty research:* Spinal motor control, biomechanics/kinesiology, biomechanics of aging, mobility of older adults, fall prevention, exercise interventions and function, magnesium and inspiratory muscle training (IMT).

West Texas A&M University, College of Education and Social Sciences, Department of Sports and Exercise Science, Canyon, TX 79016-0001. Offers MS. Part-time and evening/weekend programs available. *Degree requirements:* For master's, comprehensive exam, thesis or alternative. *Entrance requirements:* For master's, GRE General Test, minimum GPA of 3.0. Additional exam requirements/recommendations for international students: Required—TOEFL (minimum score 550 paper-based). Electronic applications accepted. *Faculty research:* Coronary heart disease, athletic performance, pain coping, cardiovascular fitness, nutritional status of NCAA athletes.

West Virginia University, School of Medicine, Graduate Programs at the Health Sciences Center, Interdisciplinary Graduate Programs in Biomedical Sciences, Exercise Physiology Program, Morgantown, WV 26506. Offers MS, PhD, MD/PhD. *Degree requirements:* For doctorate, comprehensive exam, thesis/dissertation. *Entrance requirements:* For doctorate, GRE General Test, minimum GPA of 3.0. Additional exam requirements/recommendations for international students: Required—TOEFL. Electronic applications accepted. *Faculty research:* Cardiovascular function in health and disease, circulatory adaptations to exercise training, aging, microgravity, muscle adaptation and injury.

West Virginia University, School of Physical Education, Morgantown, WV 26506. Offers athletic coaching education (MS); athletic training (MS); physical education/teacher education (MS, PhD), including curriculum and instruction (PhD), motor behavior (PhD), physical education supervision (PhD); sport and exercise psychology (PhD); sport management (MS). *Degree requirements:* For doctorate, comprehensive exam, thesis/dissertation, oral exam. *Entrance requirements:* For master's, GRE or MAT, minimum GPA of 3.0; for doctorate, GRE General Test or MAT, minimum GPA of 3.5. Additional exam requirements/recommendations for international students: Required—TOEFL (minimum score 550 paper-based; 213 computer-based). Electronic applications accepted. *Faculty research:* Sport psychosociology, teacher education, exercise psychology, counseling.

Wichita State University, Graduate School, College of Education, Department of Human Performance Studies, Wichita, KS 67260. Offers exercise science (M Ed). Part-time programs available. *Expenses:* Tuition, state resident: full-time $4247; part-time $235.95 per credit hour. Tuition, nonresident: full-time $11,171; part-time $620.60 per credit hour. Required fees: $34; $3.60 per credit hour. $17 per term. Tuition and fees vary according to campus/location and program. *Unit head:* Dr. Mike Rogers, Chairperson, 316-978-3340, Fax: 316-978-3302, E-mail: mike.rogers@wichita.edu. *Application contact:* Dr. Mike Rogers, Chairperson, 316-978-3340, Fax: 316-978-3302, E-mail: mike.rogers@wichita.edu.

Kinesiology and Movement Studies

Acadia University, Faculty of Professional Studies, School of Recreation Management and Kinesiology, Wolfville, NS B4P 2R6, Canada. Offers MR. *Students:* 2 full-time (both women), 1 part-time (0 women). 5 applicants, 40% accepted, 2 enrolled. In 2009, 1 master's awarded. *Degree requirements:* For master's, thesis. *Entrance requirements:* Additional exam requirements/recommendations for international students: Required—TOEFL (minimum score 580 paper-based; 237 computer-based; 93 iBT), IELTS (minimum score 6.5). *Application deadline:* For fall admission, 2/1 for domestic and international students. Applications are processed on a rolling basis. Application fee: $50. *Financial support:* In 2009–10, teaching assistantships (averaging $9,000 per year); unspecified assistantships also available. *Unit head:* Dr. Rene Murphy, Director, 902-585-1559, Fax: 902-585-1702, E-mail: rene.murphy@acadiau.ca. *Application contact:* Krista Robertson, Secretary, 902-585-1457, Fax: 902-585-1702, E-mail: krista.robertson@acadiau.ca.

Angelo State University, College of Graduate Studies, College of Education, Department of Kinesiology, San Angelo, TX 76909. Offers MS. Part-time and evening/weekend programs available. *Faculty:* 3 full-time (0 women). *Students:* 2 full-time (0 women), 19 part-time (6 women); includes 5 minority (1 African American, 4 Hispanic Americans). Average age 24. 20 applicants, 95% accepted, 10 enrolled. In 2009, 9 master's awarded. *Degree requirements:* For master's, comprehensive exam. *Entrance requirements:* For master's, GRE General Test. Additional exam requirements/recommendations for international students: Required—TOEFL or IELTS. *Application deadline:* For fall admission, 7/15 priority date for domestic students, 6/10 for international students; for spring admission, 12/1 priority date for domestic students, 11/1 for international students. Applications are processed on a rolling basis. Application fee: $40 ($50 for international students). Electronic applications accepted. *Expenses:* Tuition, state resident: full-time $3396; part-time $142 per credit hour. Tuition, nonresident: full-time $10,152; part-time $423 per credit hour. Required fees: $1786; $36.25 per credit hour. $494 per

semester. Full-time tuition and fees vary according to course load, degree level and program. *Financial support:* In 2009–10, 2 teaching assistantships (averaging $10,251 per year) were awarded; career-related internships or fieldwork, Federal Work-Study, scholarships/grants, and unspecified assistantships also available. Support available to part-time students. Financial award application deadline: 3/1; financial award applicants required to submit FAFSA. *Unit head:* Dr. Doyle Carter, Department Head, 325-942-2365 Ext. 225, Fax: 325-942-2129, E-mail: doyle.carter@angelo.edu. *Application contact:* Dr. Warren Simpson, Graduate Advisor, 325-942-2173 Ext. 224, Fax: 325-942-2129, E-mail: warren.simpson@angelo.edu.

Arizona State University, Graduate College, College of Liberal Arts and Sciences, Division of Natural Sciences, Department of Kinesiology, Tempe, AZ 85287. Offers PhD. *Degree requirements:* For doctorate, thesis/dissertation.

A.T. Still University of Health Sciences, Arizona School of Health Sciences, Mesa, AZ 85206. Offers advanced occupational therapy (MS); advanced physician assistant (MS); athletic training (MS); audiology (Au D); health sciences (DHSc); human movement (MS); occupational therapy (MS); physical therapy (MS, DPT); physician assistant (MS); transitional audiology (Au D); transitional physical therapy (DPT). *Accreditation:* AOTA (one or more programs are accredited); ASHA. Postbaccalaureate distance learning degree programs offered (no on-campus study). *Faculty:* 53 full-time (30 women), 205 part-time/adjunct (117 women). *Students:* 491 full-time (353 women), 1,251 part-time (874 women); includes 319 minority (70 African Americans, 11 American Indian/Alaska Native, 176 Asian Americans or Pacific Islanders, 62 Hispanic Americans), 3 international. Average age 31. 2,697 applicants, 22% accepted, 420 enrolled. In 2009, 225 master's, 523 doctorates awarded. *Degree requirements:* For master's, thesis (for some programs); for doctorate, thesis/dissertation (for some programs). *Entrance requirements:* For master's, GRE General Test; for doctorate, GRE, Evaluation of Practicing Audiologists Capabilities (Au D), Physical Therapy Evaluation Tool (DPT), current state licensure, master's

degree or equivalent (Au D), minimum GPA of 2.7. Additional exam requirements/recommendations for international students: Recommended—TOEFL (minimum score 550 paper-based; 213 computer-based; 80 iBT). *Application deadline:* For fall admission, 2/1 priority date for domestic and international students. Applications are processed on a rolling basis. Application fee: $60. *Expenses:* Contact institution. *Financial support:* In 2009–10, 651 students received support. Federal Work-Study and scholarships/grants available. Financial award application deadline: 5/1; financial award applicants required to submit FAFSA. *Faculty research:* Adolescent health-related quality of life, clinical outcomes following sport related injury, pediatric concussion, shoulder stability and neuromuscular control, sport conditioning, exercise and sport psychology, geriatric exercise and wellness. Total annual research expenditures: $61,527. *Unit head:* Dr. Randy Danielsen, Dean, 480-219-6000, Fax: 480-219-6110, E-mail: rdanielsen@atsu.edu. *Application contact:* Donna Sparks, Associate Director for Admissions, 660-626-2237, Fax: 660-626-2969, E-mail: admissions@atsu.edu.

Auburn University, Graduate School, College of Education, Department of Kinesiology, Auburn University, AL 36849. Offers exercise science (M Ed, MS, PhD); health promotion (M Ed, MS); kinesiology (PhD); physical education/teacher education (M Ed, MS, Ed D, Ed S). *Accreditation:* NCATE. Part-time programs available. *Faculty:* 16 full-time (7 women), 1 part-time/adjunct (0 women). *Students:* 70 full-time (46 women), 21 part-time (8 women); includes 10 minority (8 African Americans, 2 Asian Americans or Pacific Islanders), 10 international. Average age 26. 109 applicants, 68% accepted, 53 enrolled. In 2009, 26 master's, 7 doctorates awarded. *Degree requirements:* For master's, thesis (for some programs); for doctorate, thesis/dissertation; for Ed S, exam, field project. *Entrance requirements:* For master's, GRE General Test; for doctorate and Ed S, GRE General Test, interview, master's degree. *Application deadline:* For fall admission, 7/7 for domestic students; for spring admission, 11/24 for domestic students. Applications are processed on a rolling basis. Application fee: $50 ($60 for international students). Electronic applications accepted. *Expenses:* Tuition, state resident: full-time $6240. Tuition, nonresident: full-time $18,720. International tuition: $18,938 full-time. Required fees: $492. Tuition and fees vary according to course load, program and reciprocity agreements. *Financial support:* Research assistantships, teaching assistantships, Federal Work-Study available. Support available to part-time students. Financial award application deadline: 3/15; financial award applicants required to submit FAFSA. *Faculty research:* Biomechanics, exercise physiology, motor skill learning, school health, curriculum development. *Unit head:* Dr. Mary E. Rudisill, Head, 334-844-4483. *Application contact:* Dr. George Flowers, Dean of the Graduate School, 334-844-2125.

Barry University, School of Human Performance and Leisure Sciences, Programs in Movement Science, General Movement Science Program, Miami Shores, FL 33161-6695. Offers MS.

Barry University, School of Human Performance and Leisure Sciences, Programs in Movement Science, Specialization in Biomechanics, Miami Shores, FL 33161-6695. Offers MS. *Entrance requirements:* For master's, GRE General Test, minimum GPA of 3.0. Electronic applications accepted. *Faculty research:* Upper extremity biomechanics, orthopedic biomechanics.

Bowling Green State University, Graduate College, College of Education and Human Development, School of Human Movement, Sport, and Leisure Studies, Bowling Green, OH 43403. Offers developmental kinesiology (M Ed); recreation and leisure (M Ed); sport administration (M Ed). Part-time programs available. *Degree requirements:* For master's, thesis or alternative. *Entrance requirements:* For master's, GRE General Test, minimum GPA of 2.7. Additional exam requirements/recommendations for international students: Required—TOEFL. Electronic applications accepted. *Faculty research:* Teacher-learning process, travel and tourism, sport marketing and management, exercise physiology and sport psychology, life-span motor development.

California Baptist University, Program in Kinesiology, Riverside, CA 92504-3206. Offers exercise science (MS); physical education pedagogy (MS); sport management (MS). Part-time programs available. *Faculty:* 3 full-time (0 women). *Students:* 17 full-time (8 women), 14 part-time (8 women); includes 10 minority (1 African American, 1 American Indian/Alaska Native, 3 Asian Americans or Pacific Islanders, 5 Hispanic Americans), 2 international. 45 applicants, 49% accepted, 15 enrolled. In 2009, 15 master's awarded. *Degree requirements:* For master's, thesis or alternative, field experience. *Entrance requirements:* For master's, 12 semester units of course work in kinesiology, including basic movement anatomy or a related course; minimum undergraduate GPA of 2.75 (physical education pedagogy). Additional exam requirements/recommendations for international students: Required—TOEFL (minimum score 575 paper-based; 230 computer-based; 89 iBT). *Application deadline:* For fall admission, 8/1 priority date for domestic students, 7/1 for international students; for spring admission, 12/1 priority date for domestic students, 10/15 for international students. Applications are processed on a rolling basis. Application fee: $45. Electronic applications accepted. *Expenses:* Tuition: Full-time $8352; part-time $464 per semester hour. Required fees: $125 per semester. Tuition and fees vary according to course load, campus/location and program. *Financial support:* Federal Work-Study and scholarships/grants available. Support available to part-time students. Financial award applicants required to submit FAFSA. *Unit head:* Dr. Sean Sullivan, Chair, Department of Kinesiology, 951-343-4528, E-mail: ssullivan@calbaptist.edu. *Application contact:* Gail Ronveaux, Dean of Graduate Enrollment, 951-343-5045, Fax: 951-343-5095, E-mail: graduateadmissions@calbaptist.edu.

California Polytechnic State University, San Luis Obispo, College of Science and Mathematics, Department of Kinesiology, San Luis Obispo, CA 93407. Offers MS. Part-time programs available. *Faculty:* 8 full-time (5 women), 1 (woman) part-time/adjunct. *Students:* 17 full-time (10 women), 10 part-time (5 women); includes 7 minority (1 African American, 3 Asian Americans or Pacific Islanders, 3 Hispanic Americans). Average age 26. 23 applicants, 74% accepted, 11 enrolled. In 2009, 8 master's awarded. *Degree requirements:* For master's, comprehensive exam (for some programs), thesis (for some programs). *Entrance requirements:* For master's, minimum GPA of 2.75 in last 90 quarter units of course work. Additional exam requirements/recommendations for international students: Required—TOEFL (minimum score 550 paper-based; 213 computer-based), or IELTS (minimum score 6). *Application deadline:* For fall admission, 5/1 for domestic students, 11/30 for international students; for winter admission, 9/1 for domestic students, 6/30 for international students; for spring admission, 1/1 for domestic students. Application fee: $55. *Expenses:* Tuition, nonresident: full-time $11,160; part-time $248 per unit. Required fees: $7134; $1553 per quarter. *Financial support:* Teaching assistantships, career-related internships or fieldwork, Federal Work-Study, and scholarships/grants available. Support available to part-time students. Financial award application deadline: 3/2; financial award applicants required to submit FAFSA. *Faculty research:* Biomechanics, motor learning and control, physiology of exercise, commercial fitness, cardiac rehabilitation. *Unit head:* Dr. Kris Jankovitz, Graduate Coordinator, 805-756-2534, Fax: 805-756-7273, E-mail: kjankovi@calpoly.edu. *Application contact:* Dr. Kris Jankovitz, Graduate Coordinator, 805-756-2534, Fax: 805-756-7273, E-mail: kjankovi@calpoly.edu.

California State Polytechnic University, Pomona, Academic Affairs, College of Letters, Arts, and Social Sciences, Program in Kinesiology, Pomona, CA 91768-2557. Offers MS. Part-time programs available. *Students:* 6 full-time (5 women), 22 part-time (15 women); includes 6 minority (2 African Americans, 1 Asian American or Pacific Islander, 3 Hispanic Americans), 4 international. Average age 28. 19 applicants, 68% accepted, 6 enrolled. In 2009, 3 master's awarded. *Degree requirements:* For master's, thesis or alternative. *Application deadline:* For fall admission, 5/1 priority date for domestic students; for winter admission, 10/15 priority date for domestic students; for spring admission, 1/20 priority date for domestic students. Applications are processed on a rolling basis. Application fee: $55. Electronic applications accepted. *Expenses:* Tuition, nonresident: full-time $6696; part-time $248 per credit. Required fees: $5487; $3237 per term. Tuition and fees vary according to course load, degree level and program. *Financial support:* Federal Work-Study and institutionally sponsored loans available. Support available to part-time students. Financial award application deadline: 3/2; financial award applicants required to submit FAFSA. *Unit head:* Dr. Wanda Rainbolt, Graduate Coordinator, 909-869-2788, E-mail: wjrainbolt@csupomona.edu. *Application contact:* Scott J. Duncan, Director, Admissions, 909-869-3258, Fax: 909-869-4529, E-mail: sjduncan@csupomona.edu.

California State University, Chico, Graduate School, College of Communication and Education, Department of Kinesiology, Chico, CA 95929-0722. Offers MA. Part-time programs available. *Students:* 23 full-time (10 women), 18 part-time (8 women); includes 7 minority (1 African American, 1 American Indian/Alaska Native, 1 Asian American or Pacific Islander, 4 Hispanic Americans), 2 international. Average age 27. 24 applicants, 92% accepted, 18 enrolled. In 2009, 18 master's awarded. *Entrance requirements:* For master's, GRE General Test, 2 letters of recommendation. Additional exam requirements/recommendations for international students: Required—TOEFL (minimum score 550 paper-based; 213 computer-based; 80 iBT), IELTS (minimum score 6.5). *Application deadline:* For fall admission, 3/1 priority date for domestic students, 3/1 for international students; for spring admission, 9/15 priority date for domestic students, 9/15 for international students. Applications are processed on a rolling basis. Application fee: $55. Electronic applications accepted. *Financial support:* Fellowships, teaching assistantships available. *Unit head:* David Swanson, Graduate Coordinator, 530-898-4841. *Application contact:* David Swanson, Graduate Coordinator, 530-898-4841.

California State University, Fresno, Division of Graduate Studies, College of Health and Human Services, Department of Kinesiology, Fresno, CA 93740-8027. Offers exercise science (MA); sport psychology (MA). Part-time and evening/weekend programs available. *Degree requirements:* For master's, thesis or alternative. *Entrance requirements:* For master's, GRE General Test, minimum GPA of 2.7. Additional exam requirements/recommendations for international students: Required—TOEFL. Electronic applications accepted. *Faculty research:* Refugee education, homeless, geriatrics, fitness.

California State University, Long Beach, Graduate Studies, College of Health and Human Services, Department of Kinesiology, Long Beach, CA 90840. Offers adapted physical education (MA); coaching and student athlete development (MA); exercise physiology and nutrition (MS); exercise science (MS); individualized studies (MA); kinesiology (MA); pedagogical studies (MA); sport and exercise psychology (MS); sport management (MA); sports medicine and injury studies (MS). Part-time programs available. *Faculty:* 9 full-time (6 women), 1 part-time/adjunct (0 women). *Students:* 34 full-time (22 women), 23 part-time (14 women); includes 22 minority (4 African Americans, 2 American Indian/Alaska Native, 8 Asian Americans or Pacific Islanders, 8 Hispanic Americans), 9 international. Average age 27. 143 applicants, 59% accepted, 20 enrolled. *Degree requirements:* For master's, oral and written comprehensive exams or thesis. *Entrance requirements:* For master's, GRE General Test, minimum GPA of 2.75 during previous 2 years of course work. *Application deadline:* For fall admission, 6/1 for domestic students. Applications are processed on a rolling basis. Application fee: $55. Electronic applications accepted. *Expenses:* Required fees: $1802 per semester. Part-time tuition and fees vary according to course load. *Financial support:* Federal Work-Study, institutionally sponsored loans, and scholarships/grants available. Financial award application deadline: 3/2. *Faculty research:* Pulmonary functioning, feedback and practice structure, strength training, history and politics of sports, special population research issues. *Unit head:* Dr. Sharon R. Guthrie, Chair, 562-985-7487, Fax: 562-985-8067, E-mail: guthrie@csulb.edu. *Application contact:* Dr. Grant Hill, Graduate Advisor, 562-985-8856, Fax: 562-985-8067, E-mail: ghill@csulb.edu.

California State University, Los Angeles, Graduate Studies, College of Health and Human Services, Department of Kinesiology and Nutritional Sciences, Los Angeles, CA 90032-8530. Offers nutritional science (MS); physical education and kinesiology (MA, MS). *Accreditation:* ADtA. Part-time and evening/weekend programs available. *Faculty:* 6 full-time (3 women), 1 part-time/adjunct (0 women). *Students:* 64 full-time (57 women), 49 part-time (38 women); includes 58 minority (10 African Americans, 29 Asian Americans or Pacific Islanders, 19 Hispanic Americans), 11 international. Average age 31. 55 applicants, 100% accepted, 17 enrolled. In 2009, 17 master's awarded. *Degree requirements:* For master's, comprehensive exam, project or thesis. *Entrance requirements:* For master's, minimum GPA of 2.75. Additional exam requirements/recommendations for international students: Required—TOEFL (minimum score 500 paper-based; 173 computer-based). *Application deadline:* For fall admission, 5/1 for domestic and international students. Applications are processed on a rolling basis. Application fee: $55. *Financial support:* Federal Work-Study available. Support available to part-time students. Financial award application deadline: 3/1. *Unit head:* Dr. Nazareth Khodiguian, Chair, 323-343-4650, Fax: 323-343-6482, E-mail: nkhodig@calstatela.edu. *Application contact:* Dr. Cheryl L. Ney, Associate Vice President for Academic Affairs and Dean of Graduate Studies, 323-343-3820, Fax: 323-343-5653, E-mail: cney@cslanet.calstatela.edu.

California State University, Northridge, Graduate Studies, College of Health and Human Development, Department of Kinesiology, Northridge, CA 91330. Offers MS. Part-time and evening/weekend programs available. *Faculty:* 21 full-time (11 women), 30 part-time/adjunct (18 women). *Students:* 13 full-time (3 women), 29 part-time (16 women); includes 1 African American, 3 Asian Americans or Pacific Islanders, 5 Hispanic Americans, 6 international. Average age 31. 50 applicants, 40% accepted, 14 enrolled. In 2009, 16 master's awarded. *Degree requirements:* For master's, thesis or alternative. *Entrance requirements:* For master's, GRE General Test or minimum GPA of 3.0, 3 letters of recommendation. Additional exam requirements/recommendations for international students: Required—TOEFL. *Application deadline:* For fall admission, 11/30 for domestic students. Application fee: $55. *Financial support:* Teaching assistantships, unspecified assistantships available. Financial award application deadline: 3/1. *Unit head:* Dr. Shane Frehlich, Chair, 818-677-3205, E-mail: shane.g.frehlich@csun.edu. *Application contact:* Dr. William Whiting, Graduate Coordinator, 818-677-4917, E-mail: william.whiting@csun.edu.

California State University, San Bernardino, Graduate Studies, College of Natural Sciences, Department of Kinesiology, San Bernardino, CA 92407-2397. Offers MA Ed. Part-time and evening/weekend programs available. *Faculty:* 1 full-time (0 women). *Students:* 12 full-time (1 woman), 9 part-time (4 women); includes 9 minority (4 African Americans, 5 Hispanic Americans), 2 international. Average age 28. 20 applicants, 90% accepted, 9 enrolled. In 2009, 6 master's awarded. *Degree requirements:* For master's, advancement to candidacy. *Entrance requirements:* For master's, minimum GPA of 3.0. *Application deadline:* Applications are processed on a rolling basis. Application fee: $55. *Financial support:* Career-related internships or fieldwork, Federal Work-Study, and institutionally sponsored loans available. Support available to part-time students. *Unit head:* Dr. Terry Rizzo, Chair, 909-537-5355, Fax: 909-537-2397, E-mail: trizzo@csusb.edu. *Application contact:* Olivia Rosas, Director of Admissions, 909-537-7577, Fax: 909-537-7034, E-mail: orosas@csusb.edu.

Columbia University, College of Physicians and Surgeons, Programs in Occupational Therapy, New York, NY 10032. Offers movement science (Ed D), including occupational therapy; occupational therapy (professional) (MS); occupational therapy administration or education (post-professional) (MS); MPH/MS. *Accreditation:* AOTA. *Faculty:* 10 full-time (9 women), 7 part-time/adjunct (4 women). *Students:* 98 full-time (91 women), 4 part-time (all women); includes 17 minority (3 African Americans, 9 Asian Americans or Pacific Islanders, 5 Hispanic Americans). Average age 26. In 2009, 48 master's awarded. *Degree requirements:* For master's, project, 6 months of fieldwork, thesis (for post-professional students); for doctorate, comprehensive exam, thesis/dissertation. *Entrance requirements:* For master's, undergraduate course work in anatomy, physiology, statistics, psychology, social sciences, humanities, English composition; NBCOT eligibility; for doctorate, NBCOT certification, MS. Additional exam requirements/recommendations for international students: Required—TOEFL (minimum score 250 computer-based; 100 iBT), TWE (minimum score 4). *Application deadline:* For fall admission, 1/3 for domestic and international students. Application fee: $75. Electronic applications accepted. *Expenses:* Contact institution. *Financial support:* In 2009–10, 80 students received support. Career-related internships or fieldwork, Federal Work-Study, institutionally sponsored loans, and scholarships/grants available. Financial award application deadline: 4/15; financial award applicants required to submit FAFSA. *Faculty research:* Community mental health, developmental tasks of late life, infant play, cognition, obesity, motor learning. Total annual research expenditures: $35,000. *Unit head:* Dr. Janet Falk-Kessler, Director, 212-305-5267, Fax: 212-305-4569, E-mail: jf6@columbia.edu. *Application contact:* Marilyn Harper, Administrative Assistant, 212-305-5267, Fax: 212-305-4569, E-mail: mh15@columbia.edu.

Kinesiology and Movement Studies

Dalhousie University, Faculty of Health Professions, School of Health and Human Performance, Program in Kinesiology, Halifax, NS B3H 3J5, Canada. Offers M Sc. Part-time programs available. *Faculty:* 8 full-time (2 women). *Students:* 11 full-time (4 women), 3 part-time (2 women); includes 1 minority (Asian American or Pacific Islander). 11 applicants, 64% accepted. In 2009, 5 master's awarded. *Degree requirements:* For master's, thesis. *Entrance requirements:* Additional exam requirements/recommendations for international students: Required—TOEFL, IELTS, CANTEST, CAEL, or Michigan English Language Assessment Battery. *Application deadline:* For fall admission, 6/1 for domestic students. Applications are processed on a rolling basis. Application fee: $70. Electronic applications accepted. *Financial support:* In 2009–10, 10 students received support; research assistantships, teaching assistantships, institutionally sponsored loans available. *Faculty research:* Sport science, fitness, neuromuscular physiology, biomechanics, ergonomics, sport psychology. *Unit head:* Dr. Carol Putnam, Graduate Coordinator, 902-494-1167, Fax: 902-494-5120, E-mail: hahp@dal.ca. *Application contact:* Tracy Powell, Graduate Administrative Secretary, 902-494-1154, Fax: 902-494-5120, E-mail: tracy.powell@dal.ca.

Dallas Baptist University, Dorothy M. Bush College of Education, Program in Kinesiology, Dallas, TX 75211-9299. Offers M Ed. *Entrance requirements:* For master's, GRE General Test, minimum GPA of 3.0. Additional exam requirements/recommendations for international students: Required—TOEFL, IELTS. *Expenses:* Tuition: Full-time $10,674; part-time $593 per credit hour.

Eastern Illinois University, Graduate School, College of Education and Professional Studies, Department of Kinesiology and Sports Studies, Charleston, IL 61920-3099. Offers MS. Part-time programs available. *Faculty:* 15 full-time (3 women). In 2009, 33 master's awarded. *Application deadline:* For fall admission, 3/31 priority date for domestic students. Applications are processed on a rolling basis. Application fee: $30. *Expenses:* Tuition, state resident: full-time $9434; part-time $239 per credit hour. Tuition, nonresident: full-time $23,774; part-time $717 per credit hour. Required fees: $802.63. *Financial support:* In 2009–10, 9 teaching assistantships with tuition reimbursements (averaging $8,100 per year) were awarded; Federal Work-Study also available. Support available to part-time students. *Unit head:* Dr. Jill Owen, Chairperson, 217-581-2215, E-mail: jdowen@eiu.edu. *Application contact:* Dr. Brent Walker, Coordinator, 217-581-2215, E-mail: bwalker@eiu.edu.

Eastern Michigan University, Graduate School, College of Health and Human Services, School of Health Promotion and Human Performance, Programs in Exercise Physiology, Ypsilanti, MI 48197. Offers exercise physiology (MS); sports medicine-biomechanics (MS); sports medicine-corporate adult fitness (MS); sports medicine-exercise physiology (MS). Part-time and evening/weekend programs available. *Students:* 10 full-time (5 women), 32 part-time (10 women); includes 6 minority (2 African Americans, 4 Hispanic Americans), 2 international. Average age 29. In 2009, 12 master's awarded. *Degree requirements:* For master's, comprehensive exam, thesis or 450-hour internship. *Entrance requirements:* Additional exam requirements/recommendations for international students: Required—TOEFL. *Application deadline:* For fall admission, 8/1 for domestic students, 5/1 for international students; for winter admission, 12/1 for domestic students, 10/1 for international students; for spring admission, 3/15 for domestic students, 3/1 for international students. Application fee: $35. Tuition and fees vary according to course level. *Unit head:* Dr. Steve McGregor, Program Coordinator, 734-487-0090, Fax: 734-487-2024, E-mail: stephen.mcgregor@emich.edu. *Application contact:* Dr. Steve McGregor, Program Coordinator, 734-487-0090, Fax: 734-487-2024, E-mail: stephen.mcgregor@emich.edu.

Fresno Pacific University, Graduate Programs, Program in Kinesiology, Fresno, CA 93702-4709. Offers MA. *Entrance requirements:* Additional exam requirements/recommendations for international students: Required—TOEFL (minimum score 550 paper-based; 213 computer-based).

Georgia College & State University, Graduate School, College of Health Sciences, Department of Kinesiology, Milledgeville, GA 31061. Offers health promotion (M Ed); human performance (M Ed); kinesiology (MAT); outdoor education (M Ed). *Accreditation:* NCATE (one or more programs are accredited). Part-time and evening/weekend programs available. *Faculty:* 12 full-time (5 women). *Students:* 25 full-time (13 women), 7 part-time (5 women); includes 4 minority (2 African Americans, 2 Hispanic Americans), 3 international. Average age 26. 23 applicants, 87% accepted, 19 enrolled. In 2009, 7 master's awarded. *Degree requirements:* For master's, thesis optional. *Entrance requirements:* For master's, GRE General Test or MAT, minimum GPA of 2.75 in upper-level undergraduate courses, 2 letters of reference. Additional exam requirements/recommendations for international students: Recommended—TOEFL (minimum score 550 paper-based; 213 computer-based; 79 iBT). *Application deadline:* For fall admission, 7/15 priority date for domestic students; for spring admission, 11/15 for domestic students. Applications are processed on a rolling basis. Application fee: $40. Electronic applications accepted. *Expenses:* Tuition, area resident: Part-time $241 per credit hour. Tuition, state resident: full-time $4338. Tuition, nonresident: full-time $17,352; part-time $964 per credit hour. Required fees: $609 per semester. Tuition and fees vary according to course load and campus/location. *Financial support:* In 2009–10, 20 research assistantships with full tuition reimbursements were awarded; career-related internships or fieldwork and unspecified assistantships also available. Support available to part-time students. Financial award applicants required to submit FAFSA. *Unit head:* Dr. Jude Hirsch, Chair, 478-445-4072, Fax: 478-445-1790, E-mail: jude.hirsch@gcsu.edu. *Application contact:* Dr. Jude Hirsch, Chair, 478-445-4072, Fax: 478-445-1790, E-mail: jude.hirsch@gcsu.edu.

Georgia Southern University, Jack N. Averitt College of Graduate Studies, College of Health and Human Sciences, Department of Health and Kinesiology, Statesboro, GA 30460. Offers MS. Part-time and evening/weekend programs available. Postbaccalaureate distance learning degree programs offered. *Students:* 68 full-time (34 women), 42 part-time (9 women); includes 16 minority (14 African Americans, 2 Hispanic Americans), 3 international. Average age 26. 67 applicants, 76% accepted, 36 enrolled. In 2009, 31 master's awarded. *Degree requirements:* For master's, comprehensive exam (for some programs), thesis optional. *Entrance requirements:* For master's, GRE, minimum GPA of 2.75, resume, letters of reference. Additional exam requirements/recommendations for international students: Required—TOEFL (minimum score 550 paper-based; 213 computer-based; 80 iBT). *Application deadline:* For fall admission, 3/1 priority date for domestic and international students; for spring admission, 10/1 priority date for domestic students, 10/1 for international students. Applications are processed on a rolling basis. Application fee: $50. Electronic applications accepted. *Expenses:* Tuition, state resident: full-time $5040; part-time $210 per credit hour. Tuition, nonresident: full-time $20,136; part-time $839 per credit hour. Required fees: $1644. *Financial support:* In 2009–10, 101 students received support, including research assistantships with partial tuition reimbursements available (averaging $7,200 per year), teaching assistantships with partial tuition reimbursements available (averaging $7,200 per year); tuition waivers (partial) and unspecified assistantships also available. Financial award application deadline: 4/15; financial award applicants required to submit FAFSA. *Faculty research:* Overtraining in collegiate athletes, positive sport psychology interventions, ankle and knee injuries in collegiate athletes, conclusion knowledge of coaches, obesity issues for college females, concussion injuries in athletics. *Unit head:* Dr. Barry A. Joyner, Chair, 912-478-0495, E-mail: joyner@georgiasouthern.edu. *Application contact:* Dr. Charles Ziglar, Coordinator for Graduate Student Recruitment, 912-478-5635, Fax: 912-478-0740, E-mail: gradadmissions@georgiasouthern.edu.

Georgia State University, College of Education, Department of Kinesiology and Health, Program in Kinesiology, Atlanta, GA 30302-3083. Offers PhD. *Degree requirements:* For doctorate, comprehensive exam, thesis/dissertation. *Entrance requirements:* For doctorate, GRE General Test or MAT, minimum GPA of 3.3. *Faculty research:* Aging, exercise metabolism, biomechanics and ergonomics, blood pressure regulation, exercise performance.

Hardin-Simmons University, Graduate School, Irvin School of Education, Department of Fitness and Sport Sciences, Program in Kinesiology, Sport, and Recreation, Abilene, TX 79698-0001. Offers M Ed. Part-time programs available. *Faculty:* 5 full-time (2 women), 2 part-time/adjunct (1 woman). *Students:* 8 full-time (1 woman), 16 part-time (6 women); includes 8 minority (4 African Americans, 4 Hispanic Americans), 1 international. Average age 25. 11 applicants, 100% accepted, 7 enrolled. In 2009, 12 master's awarded. *Degree requirements:* For master's, comprehensive exam, thesis optional, internship, project. *Entrance requirements:* For master's, minimum undergraduate GPA of 3.0 in major, 2.7 overall; interview; writing sample; letters of recommendation; resume. Additional exam requirements/recommendations for international students: Required—TOEFL (minimum score 550 paper-based; 213 computer-based; 75 iBT). *Application deadline:* For fall admission, 8/15 priority date for domestic students, 4/1 for international students; for spring admission, 1/5 priority date for domestic students, 9/1 for international students. Applications are processed on a rolling basis. Application fee: $50. *Expenses:* Tuition: Full-time $11,430; part-time $635 per credit hour. Required fees: $650; $110 per semester. Tuition and fees vary according to degree level. *Financial support:* In 2009–10, 10 students received support, including 19 fellowships (averaging $1,000 per year); career-related internships or fieldwork, scholarships/grants, and recreation assistantships also available. Support available to part-time students. Financial award application deadline: 6/30; financial award applicants required to submit FAFSA. *Unit head:* Dr. Robert Moore, Director, 325-670-1265, Fax: 325-670-1218, E-mail: bemoore@hsutx.edu. *Application contact:* Dr. Gary Stanlake, Dean of Graduate Studies, 325-670-1298, Fax: 325-670-1564, E-mail: gradoff@hsutx.edu.

Humboldt State University, Graduate Studies, College of Professional Studies, Department of Kinesiology, Arcata, CA 95521-8299. Offers athletic training education (MS); exercise science/wellness management (MS); pre-physical therapy (MS); teaching/coaching (MS). *Students:* 24 full-time (13 women), 8 part-time (5 women); includes 5 minority (2 African Americans, 1 American Indian/Alaska Native, 2 Hispanic Americans). Average age 30. 25 applicants, 80% accepted, 15 enrolled. In 2009, 4 master's awarded. *Degree requirements:* For master's, thesis or alternative. *Entrance requirements:* For master's, GMAT, minimum GPA of 2.5. Additional exam requirements/recommendations for international students: Required—TOEFL. *Application deadline:* For fall admission, 6/1 for domestic students; for spring admission, 12/2 for domestic students. Applications are processed on a rolling basis. Application fee: $55. *Expenses:* Tuition, nonresident: full-time $8928. Required fees: $6102. Tuition and fees vary according to program. *Financial support:* Teaching assistantships, career-related internships or fieldwork, Federal Work-Study, and institutionally sponsored loans available. Financial award application deadline: 3/1; financial award applicants required to submit FAFSA. *Faculty research:* Human performance, adapted physical education, physical therapy. *Unit head:* Dr. Kathy Munoz, Chair, 707-826-3840, Fax: 707-826-5451, E-mail: kdm1@humboldt.edu. *Application contact:* Dr. T. K. Koesterer, Coordinator, 707-826-5967, Fax: 707-826-5451, E-mail: tjk17@humboldt.edu.

Indiana University Bloomington, School of Health, Physical Education and Recreation, Department of Kinesiology, Bloomington, IN 47405-7000. Offers adapted physical education (MS); applied sport science (MS); athletic administration/sport management (MS); athletic training (MS); biomechanics (MS); ergonomics (MS); exercise physiology (MS); fitness management (MS); human performance (PhD); motor learning/control (MS). Part-time programs available. *Faculty:* 28 full-time (11 women). *Students:* 132 full-time (55 women), 37 part-time (7 women); includes 16 minority (13 African Americans, 1 Asian American or Pacific Islander, 2 Hispanic Americans), 29 international. Average age 28. 179 applicants, 60% accepted, 72 enrolled. In 2009, 59 master's awarded. Terminal master's awarded for partial completion of doctoral program. *Degree requirements:* For master's, thesis optional; for doctorate, variable foreign language requirement, thesis/dissertation. *Entrance requirements:* For master's, GRE General Test, minimum GPA of 2.8; for doctorate, GRE General Test, minimum graduate GPA of 3.5, undergraduate 3.0. *Application deadline:* For fall admission, 1/1 for international students; for spring admission, 9/1 for international students. Applications are processed on a rolling basis. Application fee: $55 ($65 for international students). *Financial support:* In 2009–10, 71 students received support, including 9 fellowships (averaging $1,400 per year), 28 research assistantships with full tuition reimbursements available (averaging $10,131 per year), 38 teaching assistantships with full tuition reimbursements available (averaging $10,390 per year); career-related internships or fieldwork, Federal Work-Study, institutionally sponsored loans, scholarships/grants, tuition waivers (partial), and fee remissions also available. Financial award application deadline: 3/1. *Faculty research:* Exercise physiology and biochemistry, sports biomechanics, human motor control, adaptation of fitness and exercise to special populations. *Unit head:* Dr. Donetta Cothran, Chairperson, 812-855-3114. *Application contact:* Program Office, 812-855-5523, Fax: 812-855-9417, E-mail: kines@indiana.edu.

Inter American University of Puerto Rico, San Germán Campus, Graduate Studies Center, Program in Physical Education and Scientific Analysis of Human Body Movement, San Germán, PR 00683-5008. Offers MA. Part-time and evening/weekend programs available. *Degree requirements:* For master's, comprehensive exam. *Entrance requirements:* For master's, GRE General Test or EXADEP, minimum GPA of 3.0.

Iowa State University of Science and Technology, Graduate College, College of Human Sciences, Department of Kinesiology, Ames, IA 50011. Offers MS, PhD. *Faculty:* 16 full-time (5 women). *Students:* 36 full-time (20 women), 5 part-time (3 women); includes 3 minority (2 African Americans, 1 Hispanic American), 13 international. 40 applicants, 33% accepted, 10 enrolled. In 2009, 8 master's, 2 doctorates awarded. *Degree requirements:* For master's, thesis or alternative; for doctorate, thesis/dissertation. *Entrance requirements:* For master's and doctorate, GRE General Test. Additional exam requirements/recommendations for international students: Required—TOEFL (minimum score 550 paper-based; 79 iBT) or IELTS (minimum score 6.5). *Application deadline:* For fall admission, 1/1 priority date for domestic and international students; for spring admission, 10/1 priority date for domestic and international students. Application fee: $40 ($90 for international students). Electronic applications accepted. *Expenses:* Tuition, state resident: full-time $6716. Tuition, nonresident: full-time $8908. Tuition and fees vary according to course level, course load, program and student level. *Financial support:* In 2009–10, 14 research assistantships with full and partial tuition reimbursements (averaging $15,560 per year), 17 teaching assistantships with full and partial tuition reimbursements (averaging $14,440 per year) were awarded; fellowships, career-related internships or fieldwork, scholarships/grants, health care benefits, and unspecified assistantships also available. *Unit head:* Dr. Philip E. Martin, Chair, 515-294-8009, Fax: 515-294-8740. *Application contact:* Dr. Philip E. Martin, Chair, 515-294-8009, Fax: 515-294-8740.

James Madison University, The Graduate School, College of Integrated Science and Technology, Department of Kinesiology, Harrisonburg, VA 22807. Offers MS. Part-time and evening/weekend programs available. *Faculty:* 10 full-time (2 women), 2 part-time/adjunct (0 women). *Students:* 73 full-time (41 women), 10 part-time (3 women); includes 10 minority (6 African Americans, 1 American Indian/Alaska Native, 3 Asian Americans or Pacific Islanders), 2 international. Average age 27. In 2009, 40 master's awarded. *Degree requirements:* For master's, thesis or alternative. *Entrance requirements:* For master's, GRE General Test. Additional exam requirements/recommendations for international students: Required—TOEFL. *Application deadline:* For fall admission, 5/1 priority date for domestic students; for spring admission, 9/1 priority date for domestic students. Applications are processed on a rolling basis. Application fee: $55. Electronic applications accepted. *Expenses:* Tuition, area resident: Part-time $305 per credit hour. Tuition, state resident: part-time $305 per credit hour. Tuition, nonresident: part-time $890 per credit hour. *Financial support:* In 2009–10, 29 students received support, including 13 teaching assistantships with full tuition reimbursements available (averaging $8,664 per year); Federal Work-Study also available. Financial award application deadline: 3/1; financial award applicants required to submit FAFSA. *Unit head:* Dr. Michael S. Goldberger, Academic Unit Head, 540-568-6145. *Application contact:* Dr. M. Kent Todd, Graduate Coordinator, 540-568-6145.

Kansas State University, Graduate School, College of Arts and Sciences, Department of Kinesiology, Manhattan, KS 66506. Offers MS. Part-time programs available. *Faculty:* 8 full-time (3 women), 2 part-time/adjunct (0 women). *Students:* 12 full-time (9 women). Average age 24. 23 applicants, 48% accepted, 6 enrolled. In 2009, 13 master's awarded. *Degree requirements:* For master's, thesis optional. *Entrance requirements:* For master's, GRE General Test, bachelor's

degree in kinesiology or exercise science, minimum GPA of 3.0. Additional exam requirements/recommendations for international students: Required—TOEFL. *Application deadline:* For fall admission, 2/1 priority date for domestic and international students; for spring admission, 8/1 priority date for domestic and international students. Applications are processed on a rolling basis. Application fee: $40 ($55 for international students). Electronic applications accepted. *Financial support:* In 2009–10, 1 research assistantship (averaging $9,723 per year), 8 teaching assistantships (averaging $10,472 per year) were awarded; fellowships, career-related internships or fieldwork, Federal Work-Study, institutionally sponsored loans, scholarships/grants, and tuition waivers (full) also available. Support available to part-time students. Financial award application deadline: 3/1; financial award applicants required to submit FAFSA. *Faculty research:* Exercise physiology, vascular function, cardiorespiratory disease, exercise adherence and compliance, public health/physical activity. *Unit head:* David Dzewahowski, Head, 785-532-7795, Fax: 785-532-6486, E-mail: dadx@ksu.edu. *Application contact:* Tom Barstow, Director, 785-532-0712, Fax: 785-532-6486, E-mail: tbarsto@ksu.edu.

Lakehead University, Graduate Studies, School of Kinesiology, Thunder Bay, ON P7B 5E1, Canada. Offers kinesiology (M Sc); kinesiology and gerontology (M Sc). Part-time programs available. *Degree requirements:* For master's, thesis. *Entrance requirements:* For master's, minimum B average. Additional exam requirements/recommendations for international students: Required—TOEFL. *Faculty research:* Social psychology and physical education, sport history, sports medicine, exercise physiology, gerontology.

Lamar University, College of Graduate Studies, College of Education and Human Development, Department of Health and Kinesiology, Beaumont, TX 77710. Offers kinesiology (MS). *Faculty:* 6 full-time (3 women). *Students:* 17 full-time (11 women), 7 part-time (6 women); includes 7 minority (5 African Americans, 2 Hispanic Americans), 10 international. Average age 25. 36 applicants, 28% accepted, 10 enrolled. In 2009, 8 master's awarded. *Degree requirements:* For master's, comprehensive exam (for some programs), thesis optional. *Entrance requirements:* For master's, GRE General Test, minimum GPA of 2.5. Additional exam requirements/recommendations for international students: Required—TOEFL. *Application deadline:* For fall admission, 8/1 for domestic students; for spring admission, 12/1 for domestic students. Applications are processed on a rolling basis. Application fee: $25. *Financial support:* In 2009–10, 4 teaching assistantships (averaging $7,500 per year) were awarded. Financial award application deadline: 4/1. *Faculty research:* Motor learning, exercise physiology, pedagogy. *Unit head:* Dr. Charles L. Nix, Chair, 409-880-2226, Fax: 409-880-1761, E-mail: nixcl@hal.lamar.edu. *Application contact:* Dr. Daniel R. Chilek, Graduate Coordinator, 409-880-8090, Fax: 409-880-1761, E-mail: chilekdr@hal.lamar.edu.

Louisiana State University and Agricultural and Mechanical College, Graduate School, College of Education, Department of Kinesiology, Baton Rouge, LA 70803. Offers MS, PhD. *Faculty:* 22 full-time (7 women). *Students:* 65 full-time (27 women), 36 part-time (11 women); includes 14 minority (8 African Americans, 2 Asian Americans or Pacific Islanders, 4 Hispanic Americans), 10 international. Average age 27. 80 applicants, 63% accepted, 38 enrolled. In 2009, 34 master's, 7 doctorates awarded. Terminal master's awarded for partial completion of doctoral program. *Degree requirements:* For master's, thesis (for some programs); for doctorate, one foreign language, thesis/dissertation, residency. *Entrance requirements:* For master's and doctorate, GRE General Test, minimum GPA of 3.0. Additional exam requirements/recommendations for international students: Required—TOEFL (minimum score 550 paper-based; 213 computer-based; 79 iBT) or IELTS (minimum score 6.5). *Application deadline:* For fall admission, 1/25 priority date for domestic students, 5/15 for international students; for spring admission, 10/15 for international students. Applications are processed on a rolling basis. Application fee: $50 ($70 for international students). Electronic applications accepted. *Financial support:* In 2009–10, 80 students received support, including 3 fellowships with full and partial tuition reimbursements available (averaging $28,186 per year), 21 teaching assistantships with full and partial tuition reimbursements available (averaging $24,091 per year); research assistantships with full and partial tuition reimbursements available, career-related internships or fieldwork, Federal Work-Study, health care benefits, tuition waivers (full and partial), and unspecified assistantships also available. Financial award applicants required to submit FAFSA. *Faculty research:* Physical activity promotion in schools, wellness centers, hospitals and sports settings, healthy aging, rehabilitation studies. Total annual research expenditures: $336,903. *Unit head:* Dr. Gilmore M. Reeves, Chair, 225-578-2036, Fax: 225-578-3680, E-mail: tgreeve@lsu.edu. *Application contact:* Dr. Melinda Solmon, Coordinator of Graduate Studies, 225-578-2639, Fax: 225-578-3680, E-mail: msolmo1@lsu.edu.

Louisiana State University in Shreveport, College of Education and Human Development, Program in Kinesiology and Wellness, Shreveport, LA 71115-2399. Offers MS. Part-time and evening/weekend programs available. *Students:* 6 full-time (3 women), 6 part-time (3 women); includes 3 minority (all African Americans). 11 applicants, 82% accepted, 6 enrolled. In 2009, 1 master's awarded. *Entrance requirements:* For master's, GRE, baccalaureate degree with minimum GPA of 2.5 or 2.75 on last 60 credit hours attempted in degree program. Additional exam requirements/recommendations for international students: Required—TOEFL (minimum score 500 paper-based; 173 computer-based; 61 iBT). *Application deadline:* For fall admission, 6/30 for domestic and international students; for spring admission, 11/30 for domestic and international students. Application fee: $10 ($20 for international students). *Financial support:* Unspecified assistantships available. *Unit head:* Dr. Timothy P. Winter, Program Director, 318-797-5264, Fax: 318-797-5386, E-mail: timothy.winter@lsus.edu. *Application contact:* Dr. Timothy P. Winter, Program Director, 318-797-5264, Fax: 318-797-5386, E-mail: timothy.winter@lsus.edu.

Marywood University, Academic Affairs, College of Health and Human Services, Department of Health and Physical Education, Scranton, PA 18509-1598. Offers kinesiology (MS). *Expenses:* Tuition: Part-time $715 per credit. Required fees: $270 per semester. Tuition and fees vary according to degree level, campus/location and program.

McGill University, Faculty of Graduate and Postdoctoral Studies, Faculty of Education, Department of Kinesiology and Physical Education, Montréal, QC H3A 2T5, Canada. Offers M Sc, MA, PhD, Certificate, Diploma.

McMaster University, School of Graduate Studies, Faculty of Social Sciences, Department of Kinesiology, Hamilton, ON L8S 4M2, Canada. Offers human biodynamics (M Sc, PhD). *Degree requirements:* For master's, thesis. *Entrance requirements:* For master's, minimum B+ average in undergraduate course work. Additional exam requirements/recommendations for international students: Required—TOEFL (minimum score 580 paper-based; 237 computer-based). *Faculty research:* Motor learning and control, neuromuscular physiology, exercise rehabilitation, cellular responses to exercise, management.

Memorial University of Newfoundland, School of Graduate Studies, School of Human Kinetics and Recreation, St. John's, NL A1C 5S7, Canada. Offers administration, curriculum and supervision (MPE); biomechanics/ergonomics (MS Kin); exercise and work physiology (MS Kin); sport psychology (MS Kin). Part-time programs available. *Degree requirements:* For master's, thesis optional, seminars, thesis presentations. *Entrance requirements:* For master's, bachelor's degree in a related field, minimum B average. Electronic applications accepted. *Faculty research:* Administration, sociology of sports, kinesiology, physiology/recreation.

Michigan State University, The Graduate School, College of Education, Department of Kinesiology, East Lansing, MI 48824. Offers MS, PhD. *Faculty:* 9 full-time (6 women). *Students:* 73 full-time (42 women), 30 part-time (10 women); includes 8 minority (4 African Americans, 1 Asian American or Pacific Islander, 3 Hispanic Americans), 17 international. Average age 27. 142 applicants, 37% accepted. In 2009, 36 master's, 9 doctorates awarded. *Entrance requirements:* Additional exam requirements/recommendations for international students: Required—TOEFL. Electronic applications accepted. *Expenses:* Tuition, state resident: part-time $478.25 per credit hour. Tuition, nonresident: part-time $966.50 per credit hour. Part-time tuition and fees vary according to program. *Financial support:* In 2009–10, 31 research assistantships with tuition reimbursements (averaging $7,318 per year), 36 teaching assistantships with tuition reimbursements (averaging $6,946 per year) were awarded. Total annual research expenditures: $396,499. *Unit head:* Dr. Deborah L. Feltz, Chairperson, 517-355-4732, Fax: 517-353-2944, E-mail: dfeltz@msu.edu. *Application contact:* Verna Lyon, Graduate Studies Secretary, 517-355-1824, Fax: 517-353-2944, E-mail: kingrad@msu.edu.

Midwestern State University, Graduate Studies, College of Health Sciences and Human Services, Program in Kinesiology, Wichita Falls, TX 76308. Offers MSK. Part-time and evening/weekend programs available. *Degree requirements:* For master's, comprehensive exam, thesis optional. *Entrance requirements:* For master's, GRE General Test or MAT. Additional exam requirements/recommendations for international students: Required—TOEFL (minimum score 550 paper-based; 213 computer-based). Electronic applications accepted. *Expenses:* Tuition, state resident: full-time $1620; part-time $90 per credit hour. Tuition, nonresident: full-time $2160; part-time $120 per credit hour. International tuition: $7506 full-time. Required fees: $3068.80; $145.60 per credit hour. $179 per semester.

Mississippi College, Graduate School, School of Education, Department of Kinesiology, Clinton, MS 39058. Offers athletic administration (MS). *Faculty:* 1 part-time/adjunct (0 women). *Students:* 4 full-time (3 women), 18 part-time (3 women); includes 3 minority (2 African Americans, 1 Asian American or Pacific Islander), 4 international. Average age 25. In 2009, 4 master's awarded. *Degree requirements:* For master's, comprehensive exam, thesis optional. *Entrance requirements:* For master's, GRE, GMAT, or PRAXIS, minimum GPA of 2.5. Additional exam requirements/recommendations for international students: Recommended—IELTS. *Application deadline:* For fall admission, 8/15 priority date for domestic students. Applications are processed on a rolling basis. Application fee: $30. Electronic applications accepted. *Expenses:* Tuition: Part-time $452 per credit hour. Required fees: $101 per semester. Tuition and fees vary according to degree level, campus/location, program and student level. *Financial support:* Teaching assistantships, career-related internships or fieldwork, Federal Work-Study, and unspecified assistantships available. Support available to part-time students. Financial award application deadline: 4/1; financial award applicants required to submit FAFSA. *Unit head:* Dr. Christopher Washam, Chair, 601-925-3302, E-mail: washam@mc.edu. *Application contact:* Elnora Lewis, Secretary, 601-925-3225, Fax: 601-925-3889, E-mail: lewis09@mc.edu.

Mississippi State University, College of Education, Department of Kinesiology, MS State, MS 39762. Offers physical education (MS), including exercise science, sport administration, teaching/coaching. Part-time programs available. Postbaccalaureate distance learning degree programs offered (minimal on-campus study). *Faculty:* 7 full-time (1 woman). *Students:* 56 full-time (22 women), 11 part-time (6 women); includes 20 minority (18 African Americans, 1 American Indian/Alaska Native, 1 Asian American or Pacific Islander), 2 international. Average age 25. 58 applicants, 72% accepted, 36 enrolled. In 2009, 22 master's awarded. *Degree requirements:* For master's, comprehensive exam, thesis optional. *Entrance requirements:* For master's, GRE General Test, minimum GPA of 3.0. Additional exam requirements/recommendations for international students: Required—TOEFL (minimum score 550 paper-based; 213 computer-based; 79 iBT); Recommended—IELTS (minimum score 6.5). *Application deadline:* For fall admission, 7/1 for domestic students, 5/1 for international students; for spring admission, 11/1 for domestic students, 9/1 for international students. Applications are processed on a rolling basis. Application fee: $40. Electronic applications accepted. *Expenses:* Tuition, state resident: full-time $2575.50; part-time $286.25 per credit hour. Tuition, nonresident: full-time $6510; part-time $723.50 per credit hour. Tuition and fees vary according to course load. *Financial support:* In 2009–10, 7 teaching assistantships (averaging $8,772 per year) were awarded; career-related internships or fieldwork, Federal Work-Study, institutionally sponsored loans, and unspecified assistantships also available. Financial award application deadline: 4/1; financial award applicants required to submit FAFSA. *Faculty research:* Static balance and stepping performance of older adults, organizational justice, public health, strength training and recovery drinks, high risk drinking perceptions and behaviors. *Unit head:* Dr. Stanley Brown, Head, 662-325-2963, Fax: 662-325-4525, E-mail: spb107@msstate.edu. *Application contact:* Dr. John G. Lamberth, Associate Professor and Graduate Coordinator, 662-325-0906, Fax: 662-325-4525, E-mail: jgl@ra.msstate.edu.

New York University, Steinhardt School of Culture, Education, and Human Development, Department of Physical Therapy, New York, NY 10010-5615. Offers orthopedic physical therapy (Advanced Certificate); physical therapy (MA, DPT), including pathokinesiology (MA); physical therapy for practicing physical therapists (DPT); research in physical therapy (PhD). *Accreditation:* APTA (one or more programs are accredited). Part-time programs available. *Faculty:* 12 full-time (6 women), 14 part-time/adjunct (8 women). *Students:* 124 full-time (93 women), 7 part-time (5 women); includes 43 minority (10 African Americans, 23 Asian Americans or Pacific Islanders, 10 Hispanic Americans), 15 international. Average age 27. 125 applicants, 70% accepted, 41 enrolled. In 2009, 3 master's, 42 doctorates awarded. *Degree requirements:* For master's, thesis (for some programs); for doctorate, thesis/dissertation. *Entrance requirements:* For master's, physical therapy certificate; for doctorate, GRE General Test, interview, physical therapy certificate. Additional exam requirements/recommendations for international students: Required—TOEFL. *Application deadline:* For fall admission, 12/1 priority date for domestic and international students; for spring admission, 11/1 for domestic and international students. Applications are processed on a rolling basis. Application fee: $75. Electronic applications accepted. *Expenses:* Tuition: Full-time $30,528; part-time $1272 per credit. Required fees: $2177. *Financial support:* Fellowships with full and partial tuition reimbursements, research assistantships with full and partial tuition reimbursements, career-related internships or fieldwork, Federal Work-Study, scholarships/grants, tuition waivers (partial), and unspecified assistantships available. Support available to part-time students. Financial award application deadline: 2/1; financial award applicants required to submit FAFSA. *Faculty research:* Motor learning and control, neuromuscular disorders, biomechanics and ergonomics, movement analysis, exercise physiology; neurocognitive function in joint instability; pathomechanics. *Unit head:* Dr. Wen K. Ling, Chairperson, 212-998-9400, Fax: 212-995-4190. *Application contact:* 212-998-5030, Fax: 212-995-4328, E-mail: steinhardt.gradadmissions@nyu.edu.

Northwestern University, Northwestern University Feinberg School of Medicine, Department of Physical Therapy and Human Movement Sciences, Chicago, IL 60611-2814. Offers movement and rehabilitation science (PhD); physical therapy (DPT). *Accreditation:* APTA. *Faculty:* 22 full-time (13 women), 4 part-time/adjunct (3 women). *Students:* 209 full-time (172 women); includes 16 minority (7 African Americans, 5 Asian Americans or Pacific Islanders, 4 Hispanic Americans). Average age 24. 375 applicants, 42% accepted, 64 enrolled. *Degree requirements:* For doctorate, synthesis project. *Entrance requirements:* Additional exam requirements/recommendations for international students: Required—TOEFL (minimum score 265 computer-based). *Application deadline:* For fall admission, 10/15 for domestic students. Applications are processed on a rolling basis. Application fee: $40. Electronic applications accepted. *Expenses:* Contact institution. *Financial support:* In 2009–10, 184 students received support. Federal Work-Study, institutionally sponsored loans, and scholarships/grants available. Financial award application deadline: 2/15; financial award applicants required to submit FAFSA. *Faculty research:* Neuromuscular control, student performance (academic/professional), clinical outcomes, human performance. Total annual research expenditures: $2.8 million. *Unit head:* Dr. Julius P. A. Dewald, Associate Professor and Chair, 312-908-6788, Fax: 312-908-0741, E-mail: j-dewald@northwestern.edu. *Application contact:* Dr. Jane Sullivan, Assistant Professor and Assistant Chair for Recruitment and Admissions, 312-908-6789, Fax: 312-908-0741, E-mail: j-sullivan@northwestern.edu.

Old Dominion University, Darden College of Education, Program in Human Movement Science, Norfolk, VA 23529. Offers PhD. *Faculty:* 2 full-time (both women). *Students:* 9 full-time (6 women), 4 part-time (3 women); includes 2 minority (both African Americans), 1 international. Average age 33. 9 applicants, 44% accepted, 4 enrolled. *Degree requirements:* For doctorate, comprehensive exam, thesis/dissertation. *Entrance requirements:* For doctorate, GRE, minimum GPA of 3.0. Additional exam requirements/recommendations for international students: Required—TOEFL. *Application deadline:* For spring admission, 2/1 priority date for domestic and international students. Applications are processed on a rolling basis. Application fee: $40. Electronic applications accepted. *Expenses:* Tuition, state resident: full-time $8112; part-time $338 per credit. Tuition, nonresident: full-time $20,256; part-time $844 per credit.

Kinesiology and Movement Studies

Old Dominion University (continued)

Required fees: $119 per semester. One-time fee: $50. *Financial support:* In 2009–10, 6 students received support, including 1 fellowship with full tuition reimbursement available (averaging $15,000 per year), 5 teaching assistantships with full tuition reimbursements available (averaging $15,000 per year); career-related internships or fieldwork, scholarships/grants, and unspecified assistantships also available. Financial award application deadline: 5/1. *Faculty research:* Prevention of ACL injury, lower extremity mechanics, manual therapy, athletic training education, evidence-based practice outcomes. Total annual research expenditures: $10,000. *Unit head:* Dr. Bonnie L. Van Lunen, Graduate Program Director, 757-683-3516, Fax: 757-683-4270, E-mail: bvanlune@odu.edu. *Application contact:* Alice McAdory, Director of Admissions, 757-683-3685, Fax: 757-683-3255, E-mail: gradadmit@odu.edu.

Oregon State University, Graduate School, College of Health and Human Sciences, Department of Nutrition and Exercise Sciences, Program in Movement Studies in Disabilities, Corvallis, OR 97331. Offers MAIS, MS. *Students:* 5 full-time (2 women), 1 (woman) part-time; includes 1 minority (Hispanic American). Average age 26. In 2009, 1 master's awarded. *Degree requirements:* For master's, thesis. *Entrance requirements:* For master's, minimum GPA of 3.0 in last 90 hours. Additional exam requirements/recommendations for international students: Required—TOEFL. *Application deadline:* For fall admission, 3/1 for domestic students. Applications are processed on a rolling basis. Application fee: $50. *Expenses:* Tuition, state resident: full-time $9774; part-time $362 per credit. Tuition, nonresident: full-time $15,849; part-time $587 per credit. Required fees: $1639. Full-time tuition and fees vary according to course load and program. *Financial support:* Research assistantships, teaching assistantships, career-related internships or fieldwork, Federal Work-Study, and institutionally sponsored loans available. Support available to part-time students. Financial award application deadline: 2/1. *Faculty research:* Fitness testing of disabled, biomechanics of disabled, assessment of disabled athletes, biomechanics of wheeling, energy cost of wheeling. *Unit head:* Dr. Jeffrey A. McCubbin, Associate Dean, 541-737-5921, Fax: 541-737-4230, E-mail: jeff.mccubbin@oregonstate.edu. *Application contact:* Dr. Jeffrey A. McCubbin, Associate Dean, 541-737-5921, Fax: 541-737-4230, E-mail: jeff.mccubbin@oregonstate.edu.

Penn State University Park, Graduate School, College of Health and Human Development, Department of Kinesiology, State College, University Park, PA 16802-1503. Offers MS, PhD.

Saint Mary's College of California, School of Liberal Arts, Department of Kinesiology, Moraga, CA 94556. Offers sport management (MA); sport studies (MA). Part-time programs available. *Faculty:* 6 full-time (1 woman), 3 part-time/adjunct (1 woman). *Students:* 30 full-time (15 women); includes 7 minority (5 African Americans, 1 Asian American or Pacific Islander, 1 Hispanic American). Average age 28. 23 applicants, 65% accepted, 14 enrolled. In 2009, 28 master's awarded. *Degree requirements:* For master's, thesis or special project. *Entrance requirements:* For master's, minimum GPA of 2.75, BA in physical education or related field, or professional experience. Application fee: $25. Electronic applications accepted. *Expenses:* Contact institution. *Financial support:* In 2009–10, 15 students received support, including research assistantships (averaging $6,000 per year); career-related internships or fieldwork, institutionally sponsored loans, scholarships/grants, tuition waivers (partial), and unspecified assistantships also available. Support available to part-time students. Financial award applicants required to submit FAFSA. *Faculty research:* Moral development in sport, applied motor learning, achievement motivation, sport history. Total annual research expenditures: $1,500. *Unit head:* William Manning, Chair, 925-631-4969, Fax: 925-631-4965, E-mail: wmanning@stmarys-ca.edu. *Application contact:* Jeanne Abate, Administrative Assistant, 925-631-4377, Fax: 925-631-4965, E-mail: jabate@stmarys-ca.edu.

Sam Houston State University, College of Education and Applied Science, Department of Health and Kinesiology, Huntsville, TX 77341. Offers health (M Ed, MA); kinesiology (M Ed, MA). Part-time and evening/weekend programs available. *Faculty:* 6 full-time (2 women). *Students:* 14 full-time (5 women), 27 part-time (11 women); includes 10 minority (all African Americans), 3 international. Average age 27. 26 applicants, 100% accepted, 23 enrolled. In 2009, 7 master's awarded. *Entrance requirements:* For master's, GRE, MAT. Additional exam requirements/recommendations for international students: Required—TOEFL (minimum score 550 paper-based; 213 computer-based; 79 iBT). *Application deadline:* For fall admission, 8/1 for domestic students; for spring admission, 12/1 for domestic students. Application fee: $20. *Expenses:* Tuition, state resident: full-time $3690; part-time $205 per credit hour. Tuition, nonresident: full-time $8676; part-time $482 per credit hour. Required fees: $1474. Tuition and fees vary according to course load and campus/location. *Financial support:* Research assistantships, teaching assistantships, career-related internships or fieldwork, Federal Work-Study, and institutionally sponsored loans available. Financial award application deadline: 5/31; financial award applicants required to submit FAFSA. *Unit head:* Dr. Alice Fisher, Chair, 936-294-1165, Fax: 936-294-3891. *Application contact:* Molly Doughtie, Advisor, 936-294-1105, E-mail: edu_mxd@shsu.edu.

San Diego State University, Graduate and Research Affairs, College of Professional Studies and Fine Arts, Department of Exercise and Nutritional Sciences, Program in Physical Education/Kinesiology, San Diego, CA 92182. Offers MS. *Degree requirements:* For master's, thesis. *Entrance requirements:* For master's, GRE General Test, 2 letters of reference. Additional exam requirements/recommendations for international students: Required—TOEFL. Electronic applications accepted.

San Francisco State University, Division of Graduate Studies, College of Health and Human Services, Department of Kinesiology, San Francisco, CA 94132-1722. Offers MS.

San Jose State University, Graduate Studies and Research, College of Applied Sciences and Arts, Department of Kinesiology, San Jose, CA 95192-0001. Offers MA. *Students:* 56 full-time (28 women), 47 part-time (28 women); includes 37 minority (9 African Americans, 13 Asian Americans or Pacific Islanders, 15 Hispanic Americans), 9 international. Average age 28. 116 applicants, 44% accepted, 35 enrolled. In 2009, 37 master's awarded. *Degree requirements:* For master's, comprehensive exam. *Entrance requirements:* For master's, bachelor's degree in physical education. *Application deadline:* For fall admission, 6/27 for domestic students; for spring admission, 11/30 for domestic students. Applications are processed on a rolling basis. Application fee: $59. Electronic applications accepted. *Financial support:* Applicants required to submit FAFSA. *Unit head:* Dr. Shirley Reekie, Chair, 408-924-3010, Fax: 408-924-3053, E-mail: sreekie@kin.sjsu.edu. *Application contact:* Dr. Ted Butryn, Graduate Coordinator, 408-924-3068, E-mail: tbutryn1@kin.sjsu.edu.

Simon Fraser University, Graduate Studies, Faculty of Applied Sciences, School of Kinesiology, Burnaby, BC V5A 1S6, Canada. Offers M Sc, PhD. *Degree requirements:* For master's, thesis; for doctorate, thesis/dissertation. *Entrance requirements:* For master's, minimum GPA of 3.0; for doctorate, minimum GPA of 3.5. Additional exam requirements/recommendations for international students: Required—TOEFL or IELTS. *Faculty research:* Biomechanics, human factors/ergonomics, behavioral neuroscience/motor control, cardiovascular/respiratory physiology, endocrine and immune systems.

Sonoma State University, School of Science and Technology, Department of Kinesiology, Rohnert Park, BC 94928. Offers MA. Part-time programs available. *Faculty:* 2 full-time (both women). *Students:* 11 part-time (4 women). Average age 27. 8 applicants, 25% accepted, 2 enrolled. In 2009, 3 master's awarded. *Degree requirements:* For master's, thesis, oral exam. *Entrance requirements:* For master's, minimum GPA of 2.8. Additional exam requirements/recommendations for international students: Required—TOEFL (minimum score 500 paper-based; 173 computer-based). *Application deadline:* For fall admission, 11/30 for domestic students; for spring admission, 9/1 for domestic students. Applications are processed on a rolling basis. Application fee: $55. *Expenses:* Tuition, nonresident: full-time $11,160. Required fees: $6226. Full-time tuition and fees vary according to course load. *Financial support:* Career-related internships or fieldwork available. Financial award application deadline: 3/2; financial award applicants required to submit FAFSA. *Unit head:* Dr. Steven Winter, Chair, 707-664-2357, E-mail: steven.winter@sonoma.edu. *Application contact:* Dr. Wanda Boda, Graduate Coordinator, 707-664-3938, E-mail: wanda.boda@sonoma.edu.

Southeastern Louisiana University, College of Nursing and Health Sciences, Department of Kinesiology and Health Studies, Hammond, LA 70402. Offers health and kinesiology (MA), including exercise science, health promotion and exercise science, health studies, kinesiology. *Accreditation:* NCATE. Part-time and evening/weekend programs available. *Faculty:* 9 full-time (3 women). *Students:* 34 full-time (22 women), 18 part-time (11 women); includes 14 minority (13 African Americans, 1 Hispanic American), 10 international. Average age 26. 20 applicants, 95% accepted, 14 enrolled. In 2009, 11 master's awarded. *Degree requirements:* For master's, comprehensive exam (for some programs), thesis optional. *Entrance requirements:* For master's, GRE General Test (minimum score 800), minimum undergraduate cumulative GPA of 2.5 or 2.75 during last 60 hours of coursework. Additional exam requirements/recommendations for international students: Required—TOEFL (minimum score 500 paper-based; 173 computer-based; 61 iBT). *Application deadline:* For fall admission, 7/15 priority date for domestic students, 6/1 priority date for international students; for spring admission, 12/1 priority date for domestic students, 10/1 priority date for international students. Applications are processed on a rolling basis. Application fee: $20 ($30 for international students). Electronic applications accepted. *Expenses:* Tuition, state resident: full-time $3086; part-time $225 per credit hour. Tuition, nonresident: part-time $529 per credit hour. Required fees: $1195. Tuition and fees vary according to course level and course load. *Financial support:* In 2009–10, 12 students received support, including 8 research assistantships (averaging $9,412 per year), 4 teaching assistantships (averaging $9,412 per year); Federal Work-Study, institutionally sponsored loans, and administrative assistantships also available. Support available to part-time students. Financial award application deadline: 5/1; financial award applicants required to submit FAFSA. *Faculty research:* Relationship of exercise on body hormones, sexuality knowledge–attitudes and behaviors, drug and tobacco use and abuse, relationship of health and spirituality, exercise adherence and motivation. *Unit head:* Dr. Edward Hebert, Department Head, 985-549-2129, Fax: 985-549-5119, E-mail: ehebert@selu.edu. *Application contact:* Sandra Meyers, Graduate Admissions Analyst, 985-549-5620, Fax: 985-549-5632, E-mail: admissions@selu.edu.

Southern Arkansas University–Magnolia, Graduate Programs, Magnolia, AR 71753. Offers agriculture (MS); business administration (MBA); computer and information sciences (MS); counseling (MS); education (M Ed), including counseling and development, curriculum and instruction emphasis, educational administration and supervision, elementary education, middle level emphasis, reading emphasis, secondary education, TESOL emphasis; kinesiology (MS); library media and information specialist (M Ed); mental health and clinical counseling (MS); public administration (EMPA); school counseling (M Ed); teaching (MAT). *Accreditation:* NCATE. Part-time and evening/weekend programs available. *Faculty:* 43 full-time (24 women), 12 part-time/adjunct (7 women). *Students:* 116 full-time (78 women), 333 part-time (255 women); includes 105 minority (98 African Americans, 3 American Indian/Alaska Native, 3 Asian Americans or Pacific Islanders, 1 Hispanic American), 11 international. Average age 33. In 2009, 88 master's awarded. *Degree requirements:* For master's, comprehensive exam, thesis optional. *Entrance requirements:* For master's, GRE, MAT or GMAT, minimum GPA of 2.75. *Application deadline:* For fall admission, 8/15 for domestic students; for winter admission, 1/8 for domestic students; for spring admission, 1/8 for domestic students. Applications are processed on a rolling basis. Application fee: $0. *Expenses:* Tuition, state resident: full-time $3798; part-time $211 per hour. Tuition, nonresident: full-time $5580; part-time $310 per hour. Required fees: $584. *Financial support:* Career-related internships or fieldwork, Federal Work-Study, scholarships/grants, tuition waivers (full), and unspecified assistantships available. Financial award applicants required to submit FAFSA. *Faculty research:* Alternative certification for teachers, supervision of instruction, instructional leadership, counseling. *Unit head:* Dr. Kim Bloss, Dean, Graduate Studies, 870-235-4150, Fax: 870-235-5227, E-mail: kkbloss@saumag.edu. *Application contact:* Dr. Kim Bloss, Dean, Graduate Studies, 870-235-4150, Fax: 870-235-5227, E-mail: kkbloss@saumag.edu.

Southern Illinois University Edwardsville, Graduate Studies and Research, School of Education, Department of Kinesiology and Health Education, Edwardsville, IL 62026-0001. Offers kinesiology (MS Ed). *Accreditation:* NCATE. Part-time and evening/weekend programs available. *Faculty:* 12 full-time (5 women). *Students:* 25 full-time (16 women), 50 part-time (21 women); includes 6 minority (5 African Americans, 1 Hispanic American), 4 international. Average age 26. 81 applicants, 60% accepted. In 2009, 30 master's awarded. *Degree requirements:* For master's, thesis (for some programs), final exam. *Entrance requirements:* Additional exam requirements/recommendations for international students: Required—TOEFL (minimum score 550 paper-based; 213 computer-based; 79 iBT), IELTS (minimum score 6.5). *Application deadline:* For fall admission, 7/23 for domestic students, 6/1 for international students; for spring admission, 12/11 for domestic students, 10/1 for international students. Applications are processed on a rolling basis. Application fee: $30. Electronic applications accepted. *Expenses:* Tuition, state resident: part-time $1252.50 per semester. Tuition, nonresident: part-time $3131.25 per semester. Required fees: $586.85 per semester. Tuition and fees vary according to course load. *Financial support:* In 2009–10, 17 teaching assistantships with full tuition reimbursements (averaging $8,064 per year) were awarded; fellowships; research assistantships with full tuition reimbursements, career-related internships or fieldwork, Federal Work-Study, institutionally sponsored loans, scholarships/grants, traineeships, and unspecified assistantships also available. Support available to part-time students. Financial award application deadline: 3/1; financial award applicants required to submit FAFSA. *Unit head:* Dr. Curt Lox, Director, 618-650-2938, E-mail: clox@siue.edu. *Application contact:* Dr. Curt Lox, Director, 618-650-2938, E-mail: clox@siue.edu.

Southwestern Oklahoma State University, College of Professional and Graduate Studies, School of Behavioral Sciences and Education, Specialization in Kinesiology, Weatherford, OK 73096-3098. Offers M Ed. Part-time programs available. *Degree requirements:* For master's, exam. *Entrance requirements:* For master's, GRE General Test or minimum undergraduate GPA of 3.0. Additional exam requirements/recommendations for international students: Required—TOEFL.

Stephen F. Austin State University, Graduate School, College of Education, Department of Kinesiology and Health Science, Nacogdoches, TX 75962. Offers athletic training (MS); kinesiology (M Ed). *Degree requirements:* For master's, comprehensive exam. *Entrance requirements:* For master's, GRE General Test. Additional exam requirements/recommendations for international students: Required—TOEFL.

Teachers College, Columbia University, Graduate Faculty of Education, Department of Biobehavioral Studies, Program in Kinesiology, New York, NY 10027-6696. Offers PhD.

Teachers College, Columbia University, Graduate Faculty of Education, Department of Biobehavioral Studies, Program in Motor Learning/Movement Science, New York, NY 10027-6696. Offers Ed M, MA, Ed D. Part-time and evening/weekend programs available. *Faculty:* 4 full-time (1 woman). *Students:* 6 full-time (4 women), 21 part-time (15 women); includes 4 minority (2 Asian Americans or Pacific Islanders, 2 Hispanic Americans), 7 international. Average age 33. 45 applicants, 67% accepted, 17 enrolled. In 2009, 8 master's, 1 doctorate awarded. Terminal master's awarded for partial completion of doctoral program. *Degree requirements:* For master's, integrative paper; for doctorate, thesis/dissertation. *Entrance requirements:* For doctorate, GRE General Test. *Application deadline:* For fall admission, 5/15 for domestic students; for spring admission, 12/1 for domestic students. Application fee: $65. *Financial support:* Teaching assistantships, career-related internships or fieldwork, Federal Work-Study, institutionally sponsored loans, traineeships, and tuition waivers (full and partial) available. Support available to part-time students. Financial award application deadline: 2/1. *Faculty research:* Motor control, analysis of tasks, biomechanical aspect of learning, skill acquisition, recovery of motor behavior. *Unit head:* John H. Saxman, Chair, 212-678-3895, E-mail: jhs37@columbia.edu. *Application contact:* Debbie Lesperance, Assistant Director of Admission, 212-678-3710, Fax: 212-678-4171.

Teachers College, Columbia University, Graduate Faculty of Education, Department of Biobehavioral Studies, Program in Movement Sciences and Education, New York, NY 10027-6696. Offers Ed D.

Kinesiology and Movement Studies

Temple University, Health Sciences Center and Graduate School, College of Health Professions, Department of Kinesiology, Philadelphia, PA 19122-6096. Offers kinesiology (Ed M, PhD), including behavioral sciences, somatic sciences. Part-time programs available. Terminal master's awarded for partial completion of doctoral program. *Degree requirements:* For master's, thesis; for doctorate, thesis/dissertation. *Entrance requirements:* For master's, GRE General Test or MAT, minimum undergraduate GPA of 3.0; for doctorate, GRE General Test, minimum undergraduate GPA of 3.0. Additional exam requirements/recommendations for international students: Required—TOEFL (minimum score 550 paper-based; 213 computer-based; 79 iBT).

Tennessee Technological University, Graduate School, College of Education, Department of Exercise Science, Physical Education and Wellness, Cookeville, TN 38505. Offers MA. *Accreditation:* NCATE. Part-time programs available. *Faculty:* 7 full-time (0 women). *Students:* 14 full-time (8 women), 32 part-time (17 women); includes 5 minority (4 African Americans, 1 American Indian/Alaska Native). Average age 27. 27 applicants, 93% accepted, 20 enrolled. In 2009, 17 master's awarded. *Degree requirements:* For master's, comprehensive exam, thesis or alternative. *Entrance requirements:* For master's, MAT or GRE. Additional exam requirements/recommendations for international students: Required—TOEFL (minimum score 550 paper-based; 79 iBT), IELTS (minimum score 5.5). *Application deadline:* For fall admission, 8/1 for domestic students, 5/1 for international students; for spring admission, 12/1 for domestic students, 10/1 for international students. Application fee: $25 ($30 for international students). Electronic applications accepted. *Expenses:* Tuition, state resident: full-time $7034; part-time $368 per credit hour. *Financial support:* In 2009–10, fellowships (averaging $8,000 per year), 3 research assistantships (averaging $4,000 per year), 4 teaching assistantships (averaging $4,000 per year) were awarded; career-related internships or fieldwork also available. Financial award application deadline: 4/1. *Unit head:* Dr. Patricia Jordan, Interim Chairperson, 931-372-3467, Fax: 931-372-6319. *Application contact:* Shelia K. Kendrick, Coordinator of Graduate Studies, 931-372-3808, Fax: 931-372-3497, E-mail: skendrick@tntech.edu.

Texas A&M University, College of Education and Human Development, Department of Health and Kinesiology, College Station, TX 77843. Offers health education (M Ed, MS, Ed D, PhD); kinesiology (M Ed, MS, Ed D, PhD), including kinesiology (MS, PhD), physical education (M Ed, Ed D). Part-time programs available. *Faculty:* 33. *Students:* 132 full-time (57 women), 25 part-time (15 women); includes 26 minority (9 African Americans, 1 American Indian/Alaska Native, 7 Asian Americans or Pacific Islanders, 9 Hispanic Americans), 32 international. Average age 23. In 2009, 42 master's, 10 doctorates awarded. *Degree requirements:* For master's, thesis (for some programs); for doctorate, comprehensive exam, thesis/dissertation. *Entrance requirements:* For master's and doctorate, GRE General Test. Additional exam requirements/recommendations for international students: Required—TOEFL. *Application deadline:* Applications are processed on a rolling basis. Application fee: $50 ($75 for international students). Electronic applications accepted. *Expenses:* Tuition, state resident: full-time $3991; part-time $221.74 per credit hour. Tuition, nonresident: full-time $9049; part-time $502.74 per credit hour. *Financial support:* Fellowships with partial tuition reimbursements, research assistantships, teaching assistantships, career-related internships or fieldwork and institutionally sponsored loans available. Financial award application deadline: 2/15; financial award applicants required to submit FAFSA. *Unit head:* Head, 979-845-3491, Fax: 979-847-8987, E-mail: info@hlkn.tamu.edu. *Application contact:* Information Contact, 979-458-2673, Fax: 979-847-8987, E-mail: info@hlkn.tamu.edu.

Texas A&M University–Commerce, Graduate School, College of Education and Human Services, Department of Health and Human Performance, Commerce, TX 75429-3011. Offers exercise physiology (MS); health and human performance (M Ed); health promotion (MS); health, kinesiology and sports studies (Ed D); motor performance (MS); sport studies (MS). Part-time programs available. *Degree requirements:* For master's, comprehensive exam, thesis (for some programs). *Entrance requirements:* For master's, GRE General Test. Electronic applications accepted. *Faculty research:* Teaching, physical fitness.

Texas A&M University–Corpus Christi, Graduate Studies and Research, College of Education, Corpus Christi, TX 78412-5503. Offers counseling (MS, PhD), including counseling (MS); counselor education (PhD); curriculum and instruction (MS, Ed D); early childhood education (MS); educational administration (MS); educational leadership (Ed D); educational technology (MS); elementary education (MS); kinesiology (MS); reading (MS); secondary education (MS); special education (MS). Part-time and evening/weekend programs available. *Degree requirements:* For master's, comprehensive exam, thesis (for some programs); for doctorate, comprehensive exam, thesis/dissertation. *Entrance requirements:* For master's, GRE General Test. Additional exam requirements/recommendations for international students: Required—TOEFL. Electronic applications accepted.

Texas A&M University–Kingsville, College of Graduate Studies, College of Education, Department of Health and Kinesiology, Kingsville, TX 78363. Offers MA, MS. Part-time programs available. *Degree requirements:* For master's, comprehensive exam, thesis or alternative. *Entrance requirements:* For master's, GRE General Test, minimum GPA of 3.0. *Faculty research:* Body composition, electromyography.

Texas Christian University, Harris College of Nursing and Health Sciences, Department of Kinesiology, Fort Worth, TX 76129-0002. Offers MS. Part-time programs available. *Degree requirements:* For master's, thesis. *Entrance requirements:* For master's, GRE General Test, course work in kinesiology. Additional exam requirements/recommendations for international students: Required—TOEFL. *Application deadline:* For fall admission, 3/1 for domestic and international students; for spring admission, 12/1 for domestic and international students. Applications are processed on a rolling basis. Application fee: $50. *Expenses:* Tuition: full-time $17,640; part-time $980 per credit hour. Tuition and fees vary according to program. *Financial support:* In 2009–10, 8 research assistantships with full tuition reimbursements (averaging $7,500 per year) were awarded; unspecified assistantships also available. Financial award application deadline: 3/1. *Unit head:* Dr. Joel Mitchell, Chairperson, 817-257-7665, E-mail: j.mitchell@tcu.edu. *Application contact:* Admissions, TCU Graduate Studies Office, 817-257-7515, Fax: 817-257-7484, E-mail: frogmail@tcu.edu.

Texas Woman's University, Graduate School, College of Health Sciences, Department of Kinesiology, Denton, TX 76201. Offers MS, PhD. Part-time and evening/weekend programs available. *Faculty:* 14 full-time (7 women). *Students:* 46 full-time (29 women), 89 part-time (53 women); includes 22 minority (10 African Americans, 1 American Indian/Alaska Native, 1 Asian American or Pacific Islander, 10 Hispanic Americans), 34 international. Average age 31. 115 applicants, 80% accepted, 37 enrolled. In 2009, 33 master's, 4 doctorates awarded. Terminal master's awarded for partial completion of doctoral program. *Degree requirements:* For master's, thesis or alternative; for doctorate, comprehensive exam, thesis/dissertation, qualifying exam. *Entrance requirements:* For master's, 2 letters of reference, curriculum vitae; for doctorate, interview, 3 letters of reference, curriculum vitae, statement of commitment. Additional exam requirements/recommendations for international students: Required—TOEFL (minimum score 550 paper-based; 213 computer-based; 79 iBT). *Application deadline:* For fall admission, 7/1 priority date for domestic students, 3/1 for international students; for spring admission, 11/1 priority date for domestic students, 7/1 for international students. Applications are processed on a rolling basis. Application fee: $50. Electronic applications accepted. *Expenses:* Tuition, state resident: full-time $3564; part-time $198 per credit hour. Tuition, nonresident: full-time $8550; part-time $475 per credit hour. Required fees: $69.26 per credit hour. Tuition and fees vary according to course load. *Financial support:* In 2009–10, 20 students received support, including 9 research assistantships (averaging $10,746 per year), 13 teaching assistantships (averaging $10,746 per year); fellowships, career-related internships or fieldwork, Federal Work-Study, institutionally sponsored loans, scholarships/grants, traineeships, health care benefits, and unspecified assistantships also available. Support available to part-time students. Financial award application deadline: 3/1; financial award applicants required to submit FAFSA. *Faculty research:* Kinematics and kinetics of sport activities, autism students, lipoprotein-cholesterol metabolism, obesity in children, bone mineral density in children. *Unit head:* Dr. Barney Sanborn, Chair, 940-898-2575, Fax: 940-898-2581, E-mail: csanborn@twu.edu.

Application contact: Samuel Wheeler, Assistant Director of Admissions, 940-898-3188, Fax: 940-898-3081, E-mail: wheelersr@twu.edu.

Towson University, College of Graduate Studies and Research, Program in Kinesiology, Towson, MD 21252-0001. Offers MS.

Université de Montréal, Department of Kinesiology, Montréal, QC H3C 3J7, Canada. Offers kinesiology (M Sc, DESS); physical activity (M Sc, PhD). *Faculty:* 15 full-time (3 women), 15 part-time/adjunct (3 women). *Students:* 68 full-time (42 women), 14 part-time (8 women). Average age 26. 103 applicants, 31% accepted, 17 enrolled. In 2009, 10 master's, 3 doctorates, 2 other advanced degrees awarded. *Degree requirements:* For master's, one foreign language, thesis (for some programs); for doctorate, one foreign language, thesis/dissertation, general exam. *Application deadline:* For fall admission, 2/1 priority date for domestic students; for winter admission, 11/1 priority date for domestic students; for spring admission, 2/1 priority date for domestic students. Application fee: $100. Electronic applications accepted. *Financial support:* In 2009–10, 3 fellowships (averaging $20,000 per year), 10 research assistantships (averaging $5,000 per year), 6 teaching assistantships (averaging $7,000 per year) were awarded. Financial award application deadline: 2/1. *Faculty research:* Physiology of exercise, psychology of sports, biomechanics, dance, sociology of sports. Total annual research expenditures: $600,000. *Unit head:* Francois Prince, Director, 514-343-6116, Fax: 514-343-2181, E-mail: francois.prince@umontreal.ca. *Application contact:* Francine Normandeau, Information Contact, 514-343-6152, E-mail: francine.normandeau@umontreal.ca.

Université de Sherbrooke, Faculty of Physical Education and Sports, Program in Physical Education, Sherbrooke, QC J1K 2R1, Canada. Offers kinanthropology (M Sc); physical activity (Diploma). *Degree requirements:* For master's, thesis. *Entrance requirements:* For master's, minimum GPA of 2.7; for Diploma, bachelor's degree in physical education. *Faculty research:* Physical fitness, nutrition, human factors, sociology, teaching.

Université du Québec à Montréal, Graduate Programs, Program in Human Movement Studies, Montréal, QC H3C 3P8, Canada. Offers M Sc. Part-time programs available. *Degree requirements:* For master's, thesis optional. *Entrance requirements:* For master's, appropriate bachelor's degree or equivalent and proficiency in French.

Université Laval, Faculty of Medicine, Graduate Programs in Medicine, Programs in Kinesiology, Québec, QC G1K 7P4, Canada. Offers M Sc, PhD. Terminal master's awarded for partial completion of doctoral program. *Degree requirements:* For master's, thesis; for doctorate, comprehensive exam, thesis/dissertation. *Entrance requirements:* For master's and doctorate, French exam, knowledge of French, comprehension of written English. Electronic applications accepted.

The University of Alabama, Graduate School, College of Education, Department of Kinesiology, Tuscaloosa, AL 35487. Offers alternative sport pedagogy (MA); exercise science (MA, PhD); human performance (MA); sport management (MA); sport pedagogy (MA, PhD). Part-time programs available. *Faculty:* 7 full-time (1 woman). *Students:* 63 full-time (30 women), 17 part-time (4 women); includes 5 minority (3 African Americans, 1 American Indian/Alaska Native, 1 Hispanic American), 11 international. Average age 28. 74 applicants, 64% accepted, 29 enrolled. In 2009, 22 master's, 5 doctorates awarded. *Median time to degree:* Of those who began their doctoral program in fall 2001, 100% received their degree in 8 years or less. *Degree requirements:* For master's, comprehensive exam, thesis optional; for doctorate, comprehensive exam, thesis/dissertation. *Entrance requirements:* For master's and doctorate, GRE, MAT, minimum GPA of 3.0. Additional exam requirements/recommendations for international students: Required—TOEFL. *Application deadline:* Applications are processed on a rolling basis. Application fee: $50 ($60 for international students). Electronic applications accepted. *Expenses:* Tuition, state resident: full-time $7000. Tuition, nonresident: full-time $19,200. *Financial support:* In 2009–10, 14 students received support, including 13 teaching assistantships with full tuition reimbursements available (averaging $8,678 per year). *Faculty research:* Race, gender and sexuality in sports; physical education curriculum reform; disability sports; physical activity and health; environmental physiology. Total annual research expenditures: $46,329. *Unit head:* Dr. Matt Curtner-Smith, Department Head and Professor, 205-348-9209, Fax: 205-348-0867, E-mail: msmith@bamaed.ua.edu. *Application contact:* Dr. Kathy S. Wetzel, Assistant Dean for Student Services, 205-348-1154, Fax: 205-348-0080, E-mail: kwetzel@bamaed.ua.edu.

University of Arkansas, Graduate School, College of Education and Health Professions, Department of Health Science, Kinesiology, Recreation and Dance, Program in Kinesiology, Fayetteville, AR 72701-1201. Offers MS, PhD. *Students:* 54 full-time (28 women), 23 part-time (11 women); includes 11 minority (6 African Americans, 1 American Indian/Alaska Native, 4 Asian Americans or Pacific Islanders), 6 international. In 2009, 19 master's, 5 doctorates awarded. *Degree requirements:* For doctorate, thesis/dissertation. *Entrance requirements:* For doctorate, GRE General Test. Application fee: $40 ($50 for international students). *Expenses:* Tuition, state resident: full-time $7355; part-time $356.58 per hour. Tuition, nonresident: full-time $17,401; part-time $775.17 per hour. Required fees: $1203. *Financial support:* In 2009–10, 6 fellowships with tuition reimbursements, 10 research assistantships, 6 teaching assistantships were awarded; career-related internships or fieldwork and Federal Work-Study also available. Support available to part-time students. Financial award application deadline: 4/1; financial award applicants required to submit FAFSA. *Unit head:* Dr. Sharon Hunt, Department Chairperson, 479-575-2857, Fax: 479-575-5778, E-mail: sbhunt@uark.edu. *Application contact:* Dr. Dean Gorman, Coordinator of Graduate Studies, 479-575-2890, E-mail: dgorman@uark.edu.

The University of British Columbia, Faculty of Education, School of Human Kinetics, Vancouver, BC V6T 1Z1, Canada. Offers M Sc, MA, MHK, PhD. Part-time programs available. *Degree requirements:* For master's, thesis (for some programs); for doctorate, comprehensive exam, thesis/dissertation. *Entrance requirements:* For doctorate, thesis-based master's degree. Additional exam requirements/recommendations for international students: Required—TOEFL (minimum score 550 paper-based; 213 computer-based), IELTS. Electronic applications accepted. *Faculty research:* Exercise physiology, biomechanics, motor learning, natural sciences, socio-managerial.

University of Calgary, Faculty of Graduate Studies, Faculty of Kinesiology, Calgary, AB T2N 1N4, Canada. Offers biomedical engineering (M Sc, PhD); kinesiology (M Kin, M Sc, PhD), including biomechanics (PhD), health and exercise physiology (PhD). *Degree requirements:* For master's, thesis (M Sc); for doctorate, thesis/dissertation. *Entrance requirements:* Additional exam requirements/recommendations for international students: Required—TOEFL. Electronic applications accepted. *Faculty research:* Load acting on the human body, muscle mechanics and physiology, optimizing high performance athlete performance, eye movement in sports, analysis of body composition.

University of Central Arkansas, Graduate School, College of Health and Behavioral Sciences, Department of Kinesiology, Conway, AR 72035-0001. Offers MS. *Faculty:* 3 full-time (1 woman), 1 (woman) part-time/adjunct. *Students:* 6 full-time (3 women), 3 part-time (2 women); includes 3 minority (all African Americans). Average age 26. 3 applicants, 100% accepted, 1 enrolled. In 2009, 6 master's awarded. *Degree requirements:* For master's, comprehensive exam, thesis optional. *Entrance requirements:* For master's, GRE General Test, minimum GPA of 2.7. Additional exam requirements/recommendations for international students: Required—TOEFL (minimum score 550 paper-based; 213 computer-based). *Application deadline:* For fall admission, 3/1 priority date for domestic students; for spring admission, 10/1 for domestic students. Applications are processed on a rolling basis. Application fee: $25 ($50 for international students). *Expenses:* Tuition, state resident: full-time $5136; part-time $214 per credit hour. Required fees: $379.50; $127 per term. Tuition and fees vary according to course level, course load and campus/location. *Financial support:* Federal Work-Study, scholarships/grants, tuition waivers (partial), and unspecified assistantships available. Financial award application deadline: 2/15; financial award applicants required to submit FAFSA. *Unit head:* Dr. Deborah Howell-Creswell, Chairperson, 501-450-3148, Fax: 501-450-5503, E-mail: debbieh@uca.edu.

Kinesiology and Movement Studies

University of Central Arkansas (continued)
Application contact: Patti Hornor, Administrative Assistant, 501-450-5063, Fax: 501-450-5678, E-mail: pattih@uca.edu.

University of Colorado at Boulder, Graduate School, College of Arts and Sciences, Department of Integrative Physiology, Boulder, CO 80309. Offers MS, PhD. *Faculty:* 22 full-time (6 women). *Students:* 50 full-time (18 women), 11 part-time (4 women); includes 4 minority (1 African American, 2 Asian Americans or Pacific Islanders, 1 Hispanic American), 5 international. Average age 27. 67 applicants, 28% accepted, 17 enrolled. In 2009, 19 master's, 5 doctorates awarded. *Degree requirements:* For master's, comprehensive exam, thesis or alternative; for doctorate, thesis/dissertation. *Entrance requirements:* For master's, GRE General Test, minimum undergraduate GPA of 2.75. *Application deadline:* For fall admission, 1/15 priority date for domestic students, 12/15 for international students. Applications are processed on a rolling basis. Application fee: $50 ($60 for international students). *Financial support:* In 2009–10, 24 fellowships (averaging $15,189 per year), 33 research assistantships (averaging $6,975 per year) were awarded. Financial award application deadline: 2/1. *Faculty research:* Integrative or cellular kinesiology. Total annual research expenditures: $8.8 million.

University of Delaware, College of Arts and Sciences, Interdisciplinary Program in Biomechanics and Movement Science, Newark, DE 19716. Offers MS, PhD. Part-time programs available. Terminal master's awarded for partial completion of doctoral program. *Degree requirements:* For master's, thesis; for doctorate, thesis/dissertation. *Entrance requirements:* For master's and doctorate, GRE General Test, minimum undergraduate GPA of 3.0. Additional exam requirements/recommendations for international students: Required—TOEFL (minimum score 550 paper-based; 213 computer-based). Electronic applications accepted. *Faculty research:* Muscle modeling, gait, motor control, human movement.

University of Delaware, College of Health Sciences, Department of Health, Nutrition, and Exercise Sciences, Newark, DE 19716. Offers exercise science (MS), including biomechanics, exercise physiology, motor control; health promotion (MS); human nutrition (MS). Part-time programs available. *Degree requirements:* For master's, thesis. *Entrance requirements:* For master's, GRE General Test, interview, minimum GPA of 3.0. Additional exam requirements/recommendations for international students: Required—TOEFL (minimum score 550 paper-based; 213 computer-based). Electronic applications accepted. *Faculty research:* Sport biomechanics, rehabilitation biomechanics, vascular dynamics.

University of Delaware, College of Health Sciences, Department of Kinesiology and Applied Physiology, Newark, DE 19716. Offers MS, PhD.

University of Florida, Graduate School, College of Health and Human Performance, Department of Applied Physiology and Kinesiology, Gainesville, FL 32611. Offers athletic training/sport medicine (MS, PhD); biomechanics (MS, PhD); clinical exercise physiology (MS); exercise physiology (MS, PhD); health and human performance (PhD); human performance (MS); motor learning/control (MS, PhD); sport and exercise psychology (MS). *Degree requirements:* For doctorate, thesis/dissertation. *Entrance requirements:* For doctorate, GRE General Test. Electronic applications accepted.

University of Georgia, Graduate School, College of Education, Department of Kinesiology, Athens, GA 30602. Offers MS, PhD. *Faculty:* 20 full-time (5 women). *Students:* 103 full-time (48 women), 22 part-time (7 women); includes 17 minority (10 African Americans, 2 Asian Americans or Pacific Islanders, 5 Hispanic Americans), 14 international. Average age 27. 175 applicants, 41% accepted, 44 enrolled. In 2009, 29 master's, 8 doctorates awarded. *Entrance requirements:* For master's, GRE General Test or MAT; for doctorate, GRE General Test. Additional exam requirements/recommendations for international students: Required—TOEFL. *Application deadline:* For fall admission, 7/1 priority date for domestic students; for spring admission, 11/15 for domestic students. Application fee: $50. Electronic applications accepted. *Expenses:* Tuition, state resident: full-time $6000; part-time $250 per credit hour. Tuition, nonresident: full-time $20,904; part-time $871 per credit hour. Required fees: $730 per semester. *Unit head:* Dr. Kirk J. Cureton, Head, 706-542-4387, Fax: 706-542-3148, E-mail: kcureton@uga.edu. *Application contact:* Dr. Ted A. Baumgartner, Graduate Coordinator, 706-542-4424, Fax: 706-542-3148, E-mail: tbaumgar@uga.edu.

University of Hawaii at Manoa, Graduate Division, College of Education, Department of Kinesiology and Rehabilitation Science, Honolulu, HI 96822. Offers kinesiology (MS). Part-time programs available. *Students:* 51 full-time (33 women), 24 part-time (15 women); includes 31 minority (1 American Indian/Alaska Native, 28 Asian Americans or Pacific Islanders, 2 Hispanic Americans), 2 international. Average age 30. 97 applicants, 41% accepted, 29 enrolled. In 2009, 26 master's awarded. *Degree requirements:* For master's, thesis optional. *Entrance requirements:* For master's, GRE General Test. Additional exam requirements/recommendations for international students: Required—TOEFL (minimum score 540 paper-based; 207 computer-based; 76 iBT), IELTS (minimum score 5). *Application deadline:* For fall admission, 4/1 for domestic and international students; for spring admission, 11/1 for domestic and international students. Application fee: $60. *Expenses:* Tuition, state resident: full-time $8900; part-time $372 per credit. Tuition, nonresident: full-time $21,400; part-time $898 per credit. Required fees: $207 per semester. *Financial support:* In 2009–10, 4 students received support, including 3 fellowships (averaging $7,184 per year), 4 research assistantships (averaging $17,672 per year), 9 teaching assistantships (averaging $14,382 per year). *Application contact:* Julienne Maeda, Graduate Chair, 808-956-7606, Fax: 808-956-7976, E-mail: julienne@hawaii.edu.

University of Hawaii at Manoa, Graduate Division, College of Education, Doctorate in Education Program, Honolulu, HI 96822. Offers curriculum and instruction (PhD); educational administration (PhD); educational foundations (PhD); educational policy studies (PhD); educational technology (PhD); exceptionalities (PhD); kinesiology (PhD). Part-time and evening/weekend programs available. *Faculty:* 65 full-time (40 women), 28 part-time/adjunct (17 women). *Students:* 74 full-time (44 women), 119 part-time (77 women); includes 101 minority (5 African Americans, 2 American Indian/Alaska Native, 86 Asian Americans or Pacific Islanders, 8 Hispanic Americans), 17 international. Average age 38. 98 applicants, 53% accepted, 35 enrolled. In 2009, 11 doctorates awarded. *Degree requirements:* For doctorate, thesis/dissertation. *Entrance requirements:* For doctorate, GRE General Test, sample of written work. Additional exam requirements/recommendations for international students: Required—TOEFL (minimum score 600 paper-based; 250 computer-based; 100 iBT), IELTS (minimum score 7). *Application deadline:* For fall admission, 2/1 for domestic students, 1/15 for international students. Application fee: $50. *Expenses:* Tuition, state resident: full-time $8900; part-time $372 per credit. Tuition, nonresident: full-time $21,400; part-time $898 per credit. Required fees: $207 per semester. *Financial support:* In 2009–10, 1 student received support, including 11 fellowships (averaging $4,147 per year), 17 research assistantships (averaging $17,392 per year), 4 teaching assistantships (averaging $14,670 per year); career-related internships or fieldwork, Federal Work-Study, and tuition waivers (full and partial) also available. *Application contact:* Dr. Helen Slaughter, Chairperson, 808-956-7913, Fax: 808-956-9905, E-mail: slaughte@hawaii.edu.

University of Houston, College of Education, Department of Health and Human Performance, Houston, TX 77204. Offers allied health education and administration (M Ed, Ed D); exercise science (MS); health education (M Ed); human nutrition (MS); human space exploration sciences (MS); kinesiology (PhD); physical education (M Ed). *Accreditation:* NCATE (one or more programs are accredited). Part-time and evening/weekend programs available. *Faculty:* 12 full-time (4 women), 4 part-time/adjunct (3 women). *Students:* 53 full-time (26 women), 39 part-time (25 women); includes 21 minority (12 African Americans, 6 Asian Americans or Pacific Islanders, 3 Hispanic Americans), 14 international. Average age 29. 78 applicants, 64% accepted, 26 enrolled. In 2009, 20 master's, 2 doctorates awarded. *Degree requirements:* For master's, comprehensive exam, thesis (for some programs); for doctorate, comprehensive exam, thesis/dissertation, qualifying exam, candidacy paper. *Entrance requirements:* For master's, GRE (minimum 35th percentile on each section), minimum cumulative GPA of 3.0; for doctorate, GRE (minimum 35th percentile on each section), minimum cumulative GPA of 3.3. Additional exam requirements/recommendations for international students: Required—

TOEFL (minimum score 550 paper-based; 79 iBT). *Application deadline:* For fall admission, 5/1 for domestic students, 4/1 for international students; for spring admission, 10/1 for domestic and international students. Applications are processed on a rolling basis. Application fee: $45 ($75 for international students). Electronic applications accepted. *Expenses:* Tuition, state resident: full-time $7676; part-time $320 per credit hour. Tuition, nonresident: full-time $14,324; part-time $597 per credit hour. Required fees: $3034. *Financial support:* In 2009–10, 7 fellowships with full tuition reimbursements (averaging $9,500 per year), 8 research assistantships with full tuition reimbursements (averaging $9,850 per year), 12 teaching assistantships with full tuition reimbursements (averaging $9,850 per year) were awarded; career-related internships or fieldwork, Federal Work-Study, institutionally sponsored loans, scholarships/grants, health care benefits, and unspecified assistantships also available. Support available to part-time students. Financial award application deadline: 2/1. *Faculty research:* Biomechanics, exercise physiology, obesity, nutrition, space exploration science. *Unit head:* Dr. Charles Layne, Chairperson, 713-743-9868, Fax: 713-743-9860, E-mail: clayne2@uh.edu. *Application contact:* Todd Boutte, Graduate Admission Counselor, 713-743-0571, Fax: 713-743-0123, E-mail: tboutte@mail.coe.uh.edu.

University of Illinois at Chicago, Graduate College, College of Applied Health Sciences, Program in Kinesiology, Chicago, IL 60607-7128. Offers MS, PhD. Part-time programs available. *Degree requirements:* For master's, thesis. *Entrance requirements:* For master's, GRE General Test, minimum GPA of 2.75. Additional exam requirements/recommendations for international students: Required—TOEFL. Electronic applications accepted. *Faculty research:* Mitochondrial biogenesis, glucocorticoid lipid metabolism, at-risk youth, motor control.

University of Illinois at Urbana–Champaign, Graduate College, College of Applied Health Sciences, Department of Kinesiology and Community Health, Champaign, IL 61820. Offers community health (MS, MSPH, PhD); kinesiology (MS, PhD); public health (MPH); rehabilitation (MS). *Faculty:* 31 full-time (16 women). *Students:* 110 full-time (62 women), 17 part-time (9 women); includes 26 minority (15 African Americans, 1 American Indian/Alaska Native, 8 Asian Americans or Pacific Islanders, 2 Hispanic Americans), 23 international. 139 applicants, 28% accepted, 26 enrolled. In 2009, 26 master's, 9 doctorates awarded. *Entrance requirements:* For master's, GRE, minimum GPA of 3.0; for doctorate, GRE, minimum graduate GPA of 3.5. Additional exam requirements/recommendations for international students: Required—TOEFL. *Application deadline:* Applications are processed on a rolling basis. Application fee: $60 ($75 for international students). Electronic applications accepted. *Financial support:* In 2009–10, 13 fellowships, 55 research assistantships, 71 teaching assistantships were awarded; tuition waivers (full and partial) also available. *Unit head:* Wojciech Chodzko-Zajko, Head, 217-244-0823, Fax: 217-244-7322, E-mail: wojtek@illinois.edu. *Application contact:* Tina M. Candler, Office Manager, 217-333-1083, Fax: 217-244-7322, E-mail: tcandler@illinois.edu.

University of Kentucky, Graduate School, College of Education, Program in Kinesiology and Health Promotion, Lexington, KY 40506-0032. Offers exercise science (PhD); kinesiology (MS, Ed D). Terminal master's awarded for partial completion of doctoral program. *Degree requirements:* For master's, comprehensive exam, thesis optional; for doctorate, comprehensive exam, thesis/dissertation. *Entrance requirements:* For master's, GRE General Test, minimum undergraduate GPA of 2.75; for doctorate, GRE General Test, minimum graduate GPA of 3.0. Additional exam requirements/recommendations for international students: Required—TOEFL (minimum score 550 paper-based; 213 computer-based). Electronic applications accepted.

University of Lethbridge, School of Graduate Studies, Lethbridge, AB T1K 3M4, Canada. Offers accounting (MScM); addictions counseling (M Sc); agricultural biotechnology (M Sc); agricultural studies (M Sc, MA); anthropology (MA); archaeology (MA); art (MA, MFA); biochemistry (M Sc); biological sciences (M Sc); biomolecular science (PhD); biosystems and biodiversity (PhD); Canadian studies (MA); chemistry (M Sc); computer science (M Sc); computer science and geographical information science (M Sc); counseling psychology (M Ed); dramatic arts (MA); earth, space, and physical science (PhD); economics (MA); educational leadership (M Ed); English (MA); environmental science (M Sc); evolution and behavior (PhD); exercise science (M Sc); finance (MScM); French (MA); French/German (MA); French/Spanish (MA); general education (M Ed); general management (MScM); geography (M Sc, MA); German (MA); health science (M Sc); health sciences (MA); history (MA); human resource management and labour relations (MScM); individualized multidisciplinary (M Sc, MA); information systems (MScM); international management (MScM); kinesiology (M Sc, MA); management (M Sc, MA); marketing (MScM); mathematics (M Sc); music (M Mus, MA); Native American studies (MA); neuroscience (M Sc, PhD); new media (MA); nursing (M Sc); philosophy (MA); physics (M Sc); policy and strategy (MScM); political science (MA); psychology (M Sc, MA); religious studies (MA); social sciences (MA); sociology (MA); theatre and dramatic arts (MFA); theoretical and computational science (PhD); urban and regional studies (MA); women's studies (MA). Part-time and evening/weekend programs available. *Degree requirements:* For doctorate, comprehensive exam, thesis/dissertation. *Entrance requirements:* For master's, GMAT (M Sc in management), bachelor's degree in related field, minimum GPA of 3.0 during previous 20 graded semester courses, 2 years teaching or related experience (M Ed); for doctorate, master's degree, minimum graduate GPA of 3.5. Additional exam requirements/recommendations for international students: Required—TOEFL. *Faculty research:* Movement and brain plasticity, gibberellin physiology, photosynthesis, carbon cycling, molecular properties of main-group ring components.

University of Maine, Graduate School, College of Education and Human Development, Program in Kinesiology and Physical Education, Orono, ME 04469. Offers M Ed, MS. Part-time and evening/weekend programs available. *Students:* 11 full-time (1 woman), 5 part-time (0 women); includes 1 minority (Hispanic American). Average age 28. 16 applicants, 56% accepted, 5 enrolled. In 2009, 22 master's awarded. *Degree requirements:* For master's, thesis or alternative. *Entrance requirements:* For master's, MAT. Additional exam requirements/recommendations for international students: Required—TOEFL. *Application deadline:* For fall admission, 2/1 priority date for domestic students. Applications are processed on a rolling basis. Application fee: $65. Electronic applications accepted. *Financial support:* Career-related internships or fieldwork, Federal Work-Study, institutionally sponsored loans, tuition waivers (full and partial), and unspecified assistantships available. Support available to part-time students. Financial award application deadline: 3/1. *Unit head:* Dr. Janet Spector, Coordinator, 207-581-2444, Fax: 207-581-2423. *Application contact:* Scott G. Delcourt, Associate Dean of the Graduate School, 207-581-3291, Fax: 207-581-3232, E-mail: graduate@maine.edu.

University of Manitoba, Faculty of Graduate Studies, Faculty of Kinesiology and Recreation Management, Winnipeg, MB R3T 2N2, Canada. Offers kinesiology and recreation management (M Sc); recreation studies (MA).

University of Maryland, College Park, Academic Affairs, School of Public Health, Department of Kinesiology, College Park, MD 20742. Offers MA, PhD. Part-time and evening/weekend programs available. *Faculty:* 27 full-time (9 women), 10 part-time/adjunct (5 women). *Students:* 62 full-time (34 women), 6 part-time (3 women); includes 7 minority (3 African Americans, 1 American Indian/Alaska Native, 2 Asian Americans or Pacific Islanders, 1 Hispanic American), 15 international. 71 applicants, 14% accepted, 10 enrolled. In 2009, 10 master's, 10 doctorates awarded. *Degree requirements:* For master's, thesis optional; for doctorate, thesis/dissertation. *Entrance requirements:* For master's, GRE General Test, minimum GPA of 3.0, 3 letters of recommendation; for doctorate, GRE General Test, minimum GPA of 3.5, 3 letters of recommendation. *Application deadline:* For fall admission, 3/15 for domestic students, 2/1 for international students; for spring admission, 10/1 for domestic students, 6/1 for international students. Applications are processed on a rolling basis. Application fee: $60. Electronic applications accepted. *Expenses:* Tuition, area resident: Part-time $471 per credit hour. Tuition, state resident: part-time $471 per credit hour. Tuition, nonresident: part-time $1016 per credit hour. Required fees: $337.04 per term. *Financial support:* In 2009–10, 8 fellowships with full and partial tuition reimbursements (averaging $15,886 per year), 3 research assistantships with tuition reimbursements (averaging $16,522 per year), 22 teaching assistantships with tuition reimbursements (averaging $15,906 per year) were awarded; career-related internships or fieldwork, Federal Work-Study, and scholarships/grants also available. Support available to

part-time students. Financial award applicants required to submit CSS PROFILE or FAFSA. *Faculty research:* Sports, biophysical and professional studies, cognitive motor behavior, exercise physiology. Total annual research expenditures: $1.7 million. *Unit head:* Dr. Jane E. Clark, Chairman, 301-405-2450, Fax: 301-405-5578, E-mail: jeclark@umd.edu. *Application contact:* Dean of Graduate School, 301-405-0358.

University of Massachusetts Amherst, Graduate School, School of Public Health and Health Sciences, Department of Kinesiology, Amherst, MA 01003. Offers MS, PhD. Part-time programs available. *Faculty:* 17 full-time (7 women). *Students:* 36 full-time (21 women), 7 part-time (2 women); includes 3 minority (1 African American, 2 Hispanic Americans), 8 international. Average age 29. 63 applicants, 21% accepted, 10 enrolled. In 2009, 11 master's, 5 doctorates awarded. Terminal master's awarded for partial completion of doctoral program. *Degree requirements:* For master's, thesis optional; for doctorate, comprehensive exam, thesis/dissertation. *Entrance requirements:* For master's and doctorate, GRE General Test. Additional exam requirements/recommendations for international students: Required—TOEFL (minimum score 550 paper-based; 213 computer-based; 80 iBT), IELTS (minimum score 6.5). *Application deadline:* For fall admission, 2/1 for domestic and international students. Applications are processed on a rolling basis. Application fee: $50 ($65 for international students). Electronic applications accepted. *Expenses:* Tuition, state resident: full-time $2640; part-time $110 per credit. Tuition, nonresident: full-time $9936; part-time $414 per credit. Tuition and fees vary according to course load. *Financial support:* In 2009–10, 1 fellowship with full tuition reimbursement (averaging $9,190 per year), 36 research assistantships with full tuition reimbursements (averaging $10,061 per year), 25 teaching assistantships with full tuition reimbursements (averaging $8,013 per year) were awarded; career-related internships or fieldwork, Federal Work-Study, scholarships/grants, traineeships, health care benefits, tuition waivers (full), and unspecified assistantships also available. Support available to part-time students. Financial award application deadline: 2/1. *Unit head:* Dr. Graham E. Caldwell, Graduate Program Director, 413-545-6070, Fax: 413-545-2906. *Application contact:* Jean M. Ames, Supervisor of Admissions, 413-545-0722, Fax: 413-577-0010, E-mail: gradadm@grad.umass.edu.

University of Medicine and Dentistry of New Jersey, School of Health Related Professions, Department of Interdisciplinary Studies, Program in Health Sciences, Newark, NJ 07107-1709. Offers cardiopulmonary sciences (PhD); clinical laboratory sciences (PhD); health sciences (MS); interdisciplinary studies (PhD); nutrition (PhD); physical therapy/movement science (PhD). *Degree requirements:* For doctorate, thesis/dissertation. *Entrance requirements:* For doctorate, interview, writing sample. Additional exam requirements/recommendations for international students: Required—TOEFL. Electronic applications accepted.

University of Michigan, Horace H. Rackham School of Graduate Studies, School of Kinesiology, Ann Arbor, MI 48109. Offers kinesiology (MS, PhD); sport management (AM). Terminal master's awarded for partial completion of doctoral program. *Degree requirements:* For master's, thesis (for some programs); for doctorate, comprehensive exam, thesis/dissertation, oral defense of dissertation. *Entrance requirements:* For master's and doctorate, GRE General Test. Additional exam requirements/recommendations for international students: Required—TOEFL. Electronic applications accepted. *Expenses:* Contact institution. *Faculty research:* Motor development, exercise physiology, biomechanics, sport medicine, sport management.

University of Minnesota, Twin Cities Campus, Graduate School, College of Education and Human Development, School of Kinesiology, Division of Kinesiology, Minneapolis, MN 55455-0213. Offers M Ed, MA, PhD. Part-time programs available. *Students:* 137 full-time (65 women), 49 part-time (16 women); includes 24 minority (12 African Americans, 3 American Indian/Alaska Native, 4 Asian Americans or Pacific Islanders, 5 Hispanic Americans), 14 international. Average age 29. 173 applicants, 53% accepted, 74 enrolled. In 2009, 66 master's, 4 doctorates awarded. Terminal master's awarded for partial completion of doctoral program. *Degree requirements:* For master's, thesis (for some programs), final oral exam; for doctorate, thesis/dissertation, preliminary written/oral exam, final oral exam. *Entrance requirements:* For master's, GRE or MAT, minimum GPA of 3.0; for doctorate, GRE or MAT, minimum GPA of 3.0, writing sample. *Application deadline:* Applications are processed on a rolling basis. *Financial support:* Fellowships, research assistantships, teaching assistantships, career-related internships or fieldwork, Federal Work-Study, institutionally sponsored loans, and tuition waivers (full and partial) available. Support available to part-time students. *Application contact:* Dr. Mary Trettin, Associate Dean, 612-625-6501, Fax: 612-626-1580, E-mail: mtrettin@umn.edu.

University of Nevada, Las Vegas, Graduate College, School of Allied Health Sciences, Department of Kinesiology, Las Vegas, NV 89154-3034. Offers exercise physiology (MS); kinesiology (MS). Part-time programs available. *Faculty:* 11 full-time (4 women), 2 part-time/adjunct (1 woman). *Students:* 32 full-time (19 women), 18 part-time (7 women); includes 4 minority (2 Asian Americans or Pacific Islanders, 2 Hispanic Americans), 6 international. Average age 29. 50 applicants, 96% accepted, 19 enrolled. In 2009, 10 master's awarded. *Degree requirements:* For master's, comprehensive exam (for some programs), thesis (for some programs). *Entrance requirements:* For master's, GRE General Test. Additional exam requirements/recommendations for international students: Required—TOEFL (minimum score 550 paper-based; 213 computer-based; 80 iBT), IELTS (minimum score 7). *Application deadline:* For fall admission, 3/15 priority date for domestic and international students; for spring admission, 9/15 priority date for domestic and international students. Applications are processed on a rolling basis. Application fee: $60 ($95 for international students). Electronic applications accepted. *Financial support:* In 2009–10, 22 students received support, including 19 research assistantships with partial tuition reimbursements available (averaging $10,957 per year), 3 teaching assistantships with partial tuition reimbursements available (averaging $10,000 per year); institutionally sponsored loans, scholarships/grants, health care benefits, and unspecified assistantships also available. Financial award application deadline: 3/1. *Faculty research:* Lower limb biomechanics, dietary supplements, motor skill acquisition, human performance, injury assessment and rehabilitation techniques. *Unit head:* Dr. John Young, Chair/ Professor, 702-895-4626, Fax: 702-895-1500, E-mail: john.young@unlv.edu. *Application contact:* Graduate College Admissions Evaluator, 702-895-3320, Fax: 702-895-4180, E-mail: gradcollege@unlv.edu.

University of New Hampshire, Graduate School, School of Health and Human Services, Department of Kinesiology, Durham, NH 03824. Offers MS. Part-time programs available. *Faculty:* 13 full-time (3 women). *Students:* 7 full-time (4 women), 8 part-time (3 women), 1 international. Average age 27. 27 applicants, 56% accepted, 8 enrolled. In 2009, 4 master's awarded. *Degree requirements:* For master's, thesis or alternative. *Entrance requirements:* For master's, GRE General Test. Additional exam requirements/recommendations for international students: Required—TOEFL (minimum score 550 paper-based; 213 computer-based; 80 iBT). *Application deadline:* For fall admission, 6/1 priority date for domestic students, 4/1 for international students; for spring admission, 12/1 for domestic students. Applications are processed on a rolling basis. Application fee: $65. *Expenses:* Tuition, state resident: full-time $10,380; part-time $577 per credit hour. Tuition, nonresident: full-time $24,350; part-time $1002 per credit hour. Required fees: $1550; $387.50 per semester. Tuition and fees vary according to course load and program. *Financial support:* In 2009–10, 8 students received support, including 7 teaching assistantships; fellowships, research assistantships, career-related internships or fieldwork, Federal Work-Study, scholarships/grants, and tuition waivers (full and partial) also available. Support available to part-time students. Financial award application deadline: 2/15. *Faculty research:* Exercise specialist, sports studies, special physical education, pediatric exercises and motor behavior. *Unit head:* Dr. Ron Croce, Chairperson, 603-862-2080. *Application contact:* Allison Dwyer, Administrative Assistant, 603-862-2071, E-mail: kinesiology.dept@unh.edu.

The University of North Carolina at Chapel Hill, School of Medicine and Graduate School, Graduate Programs in Medicine, Chapel Hill, NC 27599. Offers allied health sciences (MPT, MS, Au D, DPT, PhD), including human movement science (MS, PhD), occupational science (MS, PhD), physical therapy (MPT, MS, DPT), rehabilitation counseling and psychology (MS), speech and hearing sciences (MS, Au D, PhD); biochemistry and biophysics (MS, PhD); biomedical engineering (MS, PhD); cell and developmental biology (PhD); cell and molecular physiology (PhD); genetics and molecular biology (PhD); microbiology and immunology (MS, PhD), including immunology, microbiology; neurobiology (PhD); pathology and laboratory medicine (PhD), including experimental pathology; pharmacology (PhD); MD/PhD. Post-baccalaureate distance learning degree programs offered. Terminal master's awarded for partial completion of doctoral program. *Degree requirements:* For master's, comprehensive exam; for doctorate, thesis/dissertation. Electronic applications accepted. *Expenses:* Contact institution.

The University of North Carolina at Chapel Hill, School of Medicine and Graduate School, Graduate Programs in Medicine, Department of Allied Health Sciences, Curriculum in Human Movement Science, Chapel Hill, NC 27599. Offers PhD. *Faculty:* 9 full-time (5 women). *Students:* 18 full-time (9 women), 1 (woman) part-time; includes 6 minority (1 African American, 4 Asian Americans or Pacific Islanders, 1 Hispanic American). Average age 33. 21 applicants, 38% accepted, 7 enrolled. In 2009, 4 doctorates awarded. *Degree requirements:* For doctorate, comprehensive exam, thesis/dissertation or alternative. *Entrance requirements:* For doctorate, GRE General Test, curriculum vitae, minimum GPA of 3.0. Additional exam requirements/recommendations for international students: Required—TOEFL (minimum score 550 paper-based; 79 computer-based). *Application deadline:* For fall admission, 12/1 priority date for domestic students, 12/1 for international students. Applications are processed on a rolling basis. Application fee: $75. Electronic applications accepted. *Financial support:* In 2009–10, 5 research assistantships with tuition reimbursements (averaging $5,100 per year), 5 teaching assistantships (averaging $7,000 per year) were awarded; fellowships with tuition reimbursements, career-related internships or fieldwork also available. Financial award application deadline: 12/1. *Faculty research:* Orthopaedics, neuromuscular, biomedical endocrinology, postural control developmental disabilities. Total annual research expenditures: $583,574. *Unit head:* Carol A. Giuliani, Director, 919-843-8792, Fax: 919-966-3678, E-mail: carol-giuliani@med.unc.edu. *Application contact:* Shauni Lowrance, Registrar, 919-966-4708, Fax: 919-966-3678, E-mail: shauni-lowrance@med.unc.edu.

The University of North Carolina at Chapel Hill, School of Medicine and Graduate School, Graduate Programs in Medicine, Department of Allied Health Sciences, Program in Human Movement Science, Chapel Hill, NC 27599. Offers PhD. *Faculty:* 14 full-time (10 women), 3 part-time/adjunct (2 women). *Students:* 1 full-time (0 women). Average age 33. *Entrance requirements:* Additional exam requirements/recommendations for international students: Required—TOEFL (minimum score 550 paper-based; 79 computer-based). *Application deadline:* For fall admission, 12/1 priority date for domestic students, 12/1 for international students. Applications are processed on a rolling basis. Application fee: $0. Electronic applications accepted. *Financial support:* Fellowships, research assistantships, teaching assistantships, career-related internships or fieldwork available. Financial award application deadline: 12/1; financial award applicants required to submit FAFSA. Total annual research expenditures: $583,574. *Unit head:* Rick Segal, Associate Professor, Director, 919-843-8660, Fax: 919-966-3678, E-mail: richard_segal@med.unc.edu. *Application contact:* Shauni Lowrance, Registrar, 919-966-4708, Fax: 919-966-3678, E-mail: shauni-lowrance@med.unc.edu.

The University of North Carolina at Charlotte, Graduate School, College of Health and Human Services, Department of Kinesiology, Charlotte, NC 28223-0001. Offers clinical exercise physiology (MS). *Faculty:* 9 full-time (3 women). *Students:* 11 full-time (7 women), 15 part-time (12 women); includes 6 minority (3 African Americans, 1 American Indian/Alaska Native, 2 Asian Americans or Pacific Islanders), 1 international. Average age 26. 21 applicants, 71% accepted, 9 enrolled. In 2009, 9 master's awarded. *Degree requirements:* For master's, thesis or practicum. *Entrance requirements:* For master's, GRE or MAT. Additional exam requirements/recommendations for international students: Required—TOEFL (minimum score 557 paper-based; 220 computer-based; 83 iBT). *Application deadline:* For fall admission, 7/1 for domestic students, 5/1 for international students; for spring admission, 11/1 for domestic students, 10/1 for international students. Applications are processed on a rolling basis. Application fee: $55. Electronic applications accepted. *Financial support:* In 2009–10, 8 students received support, including 1 fellowship (averaging $41,796 per year), 2 research assistantships (averaging $19,419 per year), 5 teaching assistantships (averaging $9,931 per year); career-related internships or fieldwork, Federal Work-Study, institutionally sponsored loans, scholarships/grants, traineeships, and unspecified assistantships also available. Support available to part-time students. Financial award application deadline: 4/1; financial award applicants required to submit FAFSA. *Faculty research:* Genetic determinants of physical activity, cardiac muscle apoptosis with aging, sensorimotor deficits in knee osteoarthritis, mechanical laxity in functional ankle instability. Total annual research expenditures: $363,717. *Unit head:* Dr. Mitchell L. Cordova, Chair, 704-687-4695, Fax: 704-687-3180, E-mail: mcordova@uncc.edu. *Application contact:* Kathy B. Giddings, Director of Graduate Admissions, 704-687-5503, Fax: 704-687-3279, E-mail: gradadm@uncc.edu.

University of North Dakota, Graduate School, College of Education and Human Development, Department of Kinesiology, Grand Forks, ND 58202. Offers MS. Part-time programs available. *Degree requirements:* For master's, thesis or alternative, final exam or comprehensive examination. *Entrance requirements:* For master's, GRE General Test, minimum GPA of 3.0. Additional exam requirements/recommendations for international students: Required—TOEFL (minimum score 550 paper-based; 213 computer-based; 79 iBT), IELTS (minimum score 6.5). Electronic applications accepted. *Faculty research:* Exercise physiology, exercise biomechanics, anatomy and physiology, exercise psychology.

University of North Texas, Robert B. Toulouse School of Graduate Studies, College of Education, Department of Kinesiology, Health Promotion, and Recreation, Program in Kinesiology, Denton, TX 76203. Offers MS. Part-time programs available. *Degree requirements:* For master's, comprehensive exam, thesis optional. *Entrance requirements:* For master's, GRE General Test, GMAT or MAT, minimum overall GPA of 2.8, 300-word essay. Additional exam requirements/recommendations for international students: Required—proof of English language proficiency required for non-native English speakers; Recommended—TOEFL (minimum score 550 paper-based; 213 computer-based; 79 iBT). *Application deadline:* Applications are processed on a rolling basis. Application fee: $50 ($75 for international students). Electronic applications accepted. *Expenses:* Tuition, state resident: full-time $4298; part-time $239 per contact hour. Tuition, nonresident: full-time $9878; part-time $549 per contact hour. Required fees: $265 per contact hour. *Financial support:* Fellowships, teaching assistantships, career-related internships or fieldwork, Federal Work-Study, and institutionally sponsored loans available. Financial award application deadline: 4/1; financial award applicants required to submit FAFSA. *Faculty research:* Exercise science, sports psychology, sport management, health fitness management, physical activity. Total annual research expenditures: $330,000. *Application contact:* Graduate Adviser, 940-565-2651, Fax: 940-565-4904.

University of Ottawa, Faculty of Graduate and Postdoctoral Studies, Faculty of Health Sciences, School of Human Kinetics, Ottawa, ON K1N 6N5, Canada. Offers MA. *Degree requirements:* For master's, thesis or alternative. *Entrance requirements:* For master's, honors degree or equivalent, minimum B average. Electronic applications accepted. *Faculty research:* Psychosocial sciences, physical and health administration of sport and physical activity, intervention and consultation in sport, physical activity and health.

University of Regina, Faculty of Graduate Studies and Research, Faculty of Kinesiology and Health Studies, Regina, SK S4S 0A2, Canada. Offers kinesiology and health studies (PhD); physical activity studies (M Sc). *Faculty:* 15 full-time (5 women), 3 part-time/adjunct (0 women). *Students:* 21 full-time (8 women), 10 part-time (8 women). 17 applicants, 76% accepted. *Degree requirements:* For master's, thesis; for doctorate, thesis/dissertation. *Entrance requirements:* Additional exam requirements/recommendations for international students: Required—TOEFL (minimum score 580 paper-based; 237 computer-based; 80 iBT). *Application deadline:* Applications are processed on a rolling basis. Application fee: $90 ($100 for international students). *Financial support:* In 2009–10, 3 fellowships (averaging $19,000 per year), 2 research assistantships (averaging $16,910 per year), 5 teaching assistantships (averaging $6,650 per year) were awarded; scholarships/grants also available. *Unit head:* Dr. Shanthi

Kinesiology and Movement Studies

University of Regina (continued)
Johnson, Dean, 306-585-3180, Fax: 306-585-4854, E-mail: shanthi.johnson@uregina.ca. *Application contact:* Shannon Morrison, Graduate Program Coordinator, 306-585-5005, E-mail: shannon.morrison@uregina.ca.

University of Saskatchewan, College of Graduate Studies and Research, College of Kinesiology, Saskatoon, SK S7N 5A2, Canada. Offers M Sc, PhD, Diploma. *Degree requirements:* For master's, thesis; for doctorate, thesis/dissertation. *Entrance requirements:* Additional exam requirements/recommendations for international students: Required—TOEFL. Tuition and fees charges are reported in Canadian dollars. *Expenses:* Tuition, area resident: Full-time $3000 Canadian dollars; part-time $500 Canadian dollars per term. Required fees: $700 Canadian dollars; $100 Canadian dollars per term.

University of Southern California, Graduate School, School of Dentistry, Division of Biokinesiology and Physical Therapy, Graduate Programs in Biokinesiology, Los Angeles, CA 90089. Offers MS, PhD. *Faculty:* 18 full-time (10 women). *Students:* 33 full-time (16 women), 1 (woman) part-time; includes 3 minority (1 American Indian/Alaska Native, 1 Asian American or Pacific Islander, 1 Hispanic American), 16 international. 33 applicants, 48% accepted, 12 enrolled. In 2009, 2 master's, 6 doctorates awarded. Terminal master's awarded for partial completion of doctoral program. *Degree requirements:* For master's, comprehensive exam; for doctorate, thesis/dissertation. *Entrance requirements:* For master's and doctorate, GRE. Additional exam requirements/recommendations for international students: Required—TOEFL (minimum score 600 paper-based; 250 computer-based; 100 iBT). *Application deadline:* For fall admission, 11/1 for domestic and international students. Application fee: $85. Electronic applications accepted. *Expenses:* Contact institution. *Financial support:* In 2009–10, research assistantships with full tuition reimbursements (averaging $24,000 per year), teaching assistantships with full tuition reimbursements (averaging $24,000 per year) were awarded; health care benefits also available. Financial award applicants required to submit FAFSA. *Faculty research:* Exercise and aging biomechanics, musculoskeletal biomechanics, exercise and hormones related to muscle wasting, computational neurorehabilitation, motor behavior and neurorehabilitation, stroke rehabilitation, motor development, infant motor performance. *Unit head:* Christopher Powers, Chair/Associate Professor, 323-442-1928, Fax: 323-442-1515, E-mail: powers@usc.edu. *Application contact:* Virginia Orcasitas, Admission Coordinator, 323-442-2890, Fax: 323-442-1515, E-mail: vorcas@usc.edu.

The University of Tennessee, Graduate School, College of Education, Health and Human Sciences, Department of Exercise, Sport, and Leisure Studies, Program in Exercise Science, Knoxville, TN 37996. Offers biomechanics/sports medicine (MS, PhD); exercise physiology (MS, PhD). *Accreditation:* CEPH (one or more programs are accredited). Part-time programs available. *Degree requirements:* For master's, thesis optional. *Entrance requirements:* For master's, minimum GPA of 2.7. Additional exam requirements/recommendations for international students: Required—TOEFL. Electronic applications accepted. *Expenses:* Tuition, state resident: full-time $6826; part-time $380 per semester hour. Tuition, nonresident: full-time $21,844; part-time $1147 per semester hour. Tuition and fees vary according to program.

The University of Texas at Austin, Graduate School, College of Education, Department of Kinesiology and Health Education, Austin, TX 78712-1111. Offers behavioral health (PhD); exercise and sport psychology (M Ed, MA); health education (M Ed, MA, Ed D, PhD); kinesiology (M Ed, MA). Part-time programs available. Terminal master's awarded for partial completion of doctoral program. *Degree requirements:* For master's, thesis (for some programs); for doctorate, thesis/dissertation. *Entrance requirements:* For master's and doctorate, GRE General Test. Additional exam requirements/recommendations for international students: Required—TOEFL. Electronic applications accepted. *Faculty research:* Health promotion, human performance and exercise biochemistry, motor behavior and biomechanics, sport management, aging and pediatric development.

The University of Texas at El Paso, Graduate School, College of Health Sciences, Department of Kinesiology, El Paso, TX 79968-0001. Offers kinesiology (MS); kinesiology on-line (MS). Part-time and evening/weekend programs available. Postbaccalaureate distance learning degree programs offered. *Students:* 17 (9 women); includes 7 minority (all Hispanic Americans), 3 international. Average age 34. In 2009, 3 master's awarded. *Degree requirements:* For master's, thesis optional. *Entrance requirements:* For master's, GRE. Additional exam requirements/recommendations for international students: Required—TOEFL; Recommended—IELTS. *Application deadline:* For fall admission, 8/1 priority date for domestic students, 3/1 for international students; for spring admission, 11/1 priority date for domestic students, 9/1 for international students. Applications are processed on a rolling basis. Application fee: $45 ($80 for international students). Electronic applications accepted. *Financial support:* In 2009–10, research assistantships (averaging $18,825 per year), teaching assistantships with partial tuition reimbursements (averaging $18,000 per year) were awarded; fellowships with tuition reimbursements, institutionally sponsored loans, scholarships/grants, health care benefits, tuition waivers (partial), and unspecified assistantships also available. Support available to part-time students. Financial award application deadline: 3/15; financial award applicants required to submit FAFSA. *Unit head:* Dr. Darla Smith, Chair, 915-747-7245, Fax: 915-747-8211, E-mail: darsmith@utep.edu. *Application contact:* Dr. Patricia D. Witherspoon, Dean of the Graduate School, 915-747-5491, Fax: 915-747-5788, E-mail: withersp@utep.edu.

The University of Texas at San Antonio, College of Education and Human Development, Department of Health and Kinesiology, San Antonio, TX 78249-0617. Offers health and kinesiology (MS); kinesiology and health promotion (MA Ed). Part-time programs available. *Faculty:* 12 full-time (5 women). *Students:* 22 full-time (9 women), 49 part-time (31 women); includes 40 minority (5 African Americans, 1 Asian American or Pacific Islander, 34 Hispanic Americans), 3 international. Average age 29. 43 applicants, 91% accepted, 22 enrolled. In 2009, 14 master's awarded. *Degree requirements:* For master's, comprehensive exam (for some programs), thesis (for some programs). *Entrance requirements:* For master's, GRE or GMAT, minimum GPA of 3.0. Additional exam requirements/recommendations for international students: Required—TOEFL (minimum score 500 paper-based; 173 computer-based; 61 iBT), IELTS (minimum score 5). *Application deadline:* For fall admission, 6/1 for domestic students, 4/1 for international students; for spring admission, 11/1 for domestic students, 9/1 for international students. Applications are processed on a rolling basis. Application fee: $45 ($80 for international students). Electronic applications accepted. *Expenses:* Tuition, state resident: full-time $3975; part-time $221 per contact hour. Tuition, nonresident: full-time $13,947; part-time $775 per contact hour. Required fees: $1853. *Financial support:* In 2009–10, 3 students received support, including 14 research assistantships (averaging $10,754 per year); scholarships/grants, tuition waivers, and unspecified assistantships also available. Support available to part-time students. *Faculty research:* Motor learning/control, biomechanics, and sports psychology; exercise and military physiology; physical education and coaching; health disparities and nutrition; community and school health. Total annual research expenditures: $458,272. *Unit head:* Dr. Wanxiang Yao, Chair, 210-458-5650, E-mail: wanxiang.yao@utsa.edu. *Application contact:* Dr. Dorothy A. Flannagan, Dean of the Graduate School, 210-458-4330, Fax: 210-458-4332, E-mail: dorothy.flannagan@utsa.edu.

The University of Texas at Tyler, College of Nursing and Health Sciences, Department of Health and Kinesiology, Tyler, TX 75799-0001. Offers health and kinesiology (M Ed, MA); health sciences (MS); kinesiology (MS). Part-time programs available. Postbaccalaureate distance learning degree programs offered. *Faculty:* 7 full-time (2 women). *Students:* 23 full-time (16 women), 36 part-time (24 women); includes 9 minority (8 African Americans, 1 Hispanic American). Average age 29. 44 applicants, 100% accepted, 27 enrolled. In 2009, 13 master's awarded. *Degree requirements:* For master's, comprehensive exam (for some programs), thesis (for some programs). *Entrance requirements:* Additional exam requirements/recommendations for international students: Required—TOEFL (minimum score 79 computer-based). *Application deadline:* For fall admission, 8/17 priority date for domestic students, 7/1 priority date for international students; for spring admission, 12/21 priority date for domestic students, 11/1 priority date for international students. Applications are processed on a rolling basis. Application fee: $25 ($50 for international students). Electronic applications accepted. *Expenses:* Tuition, state resident: part-time $665 per semester hour. Tuition, nonresident: part-time $942 per semester hour. Part-time tuition and fees vary according to degree level and program. *Financial support:* In 2009–10, 2 teaching assistantships (averaging $6,000 per year) were awarded; research assistantships, Federal Work-Study and scholarships/grants also available. Financial award application deadline: 7/1. *Faculty research:* Osteoporosis, muscle soreness, economy of locomotion, adoption of rehabilitation programs, effect of inactivity and aging on muscle blood vessels, territoriality. *Unit head:* Dr. Scott Marzilli, Chair/Professor, 903-566-7178, Fax: 903-566-7065, E-mail: smarzilli@uttyler.edu. *Application contact:* Dr. Scott Marzilli.

The University of Texas of the Permian Basin, Office of Graduate Studies, College of Arts and Sciences, Department of Kinesiology, Odessa, TX 79762-0001. Offers MS. Part-time and evening/weekend programs available. Postbaccalaureate distance learning degree programs offered (no on-campus study). *Degree requirements:* For master's, comprehensive exam (for some programs), thesis (for some programs). *Entrance requirements:* For master's, GRE General Test, minimum GPA of 2.5. Additional exam requirements/recommendations for international students: Required—TOEFL (minimum score 550 paper-based; 213 computer-based).

The University of Texas–Pan American, College of Education, Department of Health and Kinesiology, Edinburg, TX 78539. Offers kinesiology (MS). Part-time and evening/weekend programs available. Postbaccalaureate distance learning degree programs offered (no on-campus study). *Degree requirements:* For master's, comprehensive exam, thesis optional, oral exam. *Entrance requirements:* For master's, minimum GPA of 3.0 in last 60 hours. *Expenses:* Tuition, state resident: full-time $3630.60; part-time $201.70 per credit hour. Tuition, nonresident: full-time $8617; part-time $478.70 per credit hour. Required fees: $806.50. *Faculty research:* History, physiology of exercise, fitness levels, Mexican-American children, winter tourist profiles, sports psychology.

University of the Incarnate Word, School of Graduate Studies and Research, Dreeben School of Education, Programs in Education, San Antonio, TX 78209-6397. Offers adult education (M Ed, MA); cross-cultural education (M Ed, MA); early childhood literacy (M Ed, MA); general education (M Ed, MA); Higher Education (PhD); instructional technology (M Ed, MA); international education and entrepreneurship (PhD); kinesiology (M Ed, MA); literacy (M Ed, MA); organizational leadership (PhD); organizational learning and learning (M Ed, MA); reading (M Ed, MA); special education (M Ed, MA); teacher leadership (M Ed, MA). Part-time and evening/weekend programs available. *Students:* 20 full-time (11 women), 201 part-time (122 women); includes 113 minority (29 African Americans, 2 American Indian/Alaska Native, 2 Asian Americans or Pacific Islanders, 80 Hispanic Americans), 30 international. Average age 41. In 2009, 26 master's, 19 doctorates awarded. *Degree requirements:* For master's, capstone; for doctorate, thesis/dissertation, qualifying exam. *Entrance requirements:* For master's, baccalaureate degree; minimum foundation GPA of 2.5; interview; for doctorate, master's degree; interview; supervised writing sample. Additional exam requirements/recommendations for international students: Required—TOEFL (minimum score 560 paper-based; 220 computer-based; 83 iBT). *Application deadline:* Applications are processed on a rolling basis. Application fee: $20. Electronic applications accepted. *Expenses:* Tuition: Full-time $12,150; part-time $675 per credit hour. Required fees: $83 per credit hour. *Financial support:* Federal Work-Study and scholarships/grants available. Financial award applicants required to submit FAFSA. *Unit head:* Dr. Denise Staudt, Dean, Dreeben School of Education, 210-829-2762, E-mail: staudt@uiwtx.edu. *Application contact:* Andrea Cyterski-Acosta, Dean of Enrollment, 210-829-6005, Fax: 210-829-3921, E-mail: admis@uiwtx.edu.

University of the Incarnate Word, School of Graduate Studies and Research, School of Nursing and Health Professions, Programs in Kinesiology, San Antonio, TX 78209-6397. Offers MS. Part-time and evening/weekend programs available. *Students:* 9 full-time (4 women), 15 part-time (11 women); includes 20 minority (all Hispanic Americans), 1 international. Average age 27. In 2009, 5 master's awarded. *Degree requirements:* For master's, capstone. *Entrance requirements:* For master's, GRE, baccalaureate degree in kinesiology or related field; teacher certification in physical education or other teaching field plus athletic coaching experience, or letter of recommendation from professional in field. Additional exam requirements/recommendations for international students: Required—TOEFL (minimum score 560 paper-based; 220 computer-based; 83 iBT). *Application deadline:* Applications are processed on a rolling basis. Application fee: $20. Electronic applications accepted. *Expenses:* Tuition: Full-time $12,150; part-time $675 per credit hour. Required fees: $83 per credit hour. *Financial support:* Federal Work-Study and scholarships/grants available. *Unit head:* Dr. William Carleton, Chair, 210-829-3966, Fax: 210-829-3174, E-mail: carleton@uiwtx.edu. *Application contact:* Andrea Cyterski-Acosta, Dean of Enrollment, 210-829-6005, Fax: 210-829-3921, E-mail: admis@uiwtx.edu.

University of Victoria, Faculty of Graduate Studies, Faculty of Education, School of Exercise Science, Physical, and Health Education, Victoria, BC V8W 2Y2, Canada. Offers coaching studies (co-operative education) (M Ed); kinesiology (M Sc, MA); leisure service administration (MA); physical education (MA). Part-time programs available. *Degree requirements:* For master's, comprehensive exam (for some programs), thesis (for some programs). *Entrance requirements:* For master's, minimum B average. Additional exam requirements/recommendations for international students: Required—TOEFL (minimum score 575 paper-based; 233 computer-based), IELTS (minimum score 7). Electronic applications accepted. *Faculty research:* Children and exercise, mental skills in sports, teaching effectiveness, neural control of human movement, physical performance and health.

University of Virginia, Curry School of Education, Department of Human Services, Program in Health and Physical Education, Charlottesville, VA 22903. Offers kinesiology (M Ed, Ed D). *Students:* 38 full-time (27 women), 6 part-time (3 women); includes 3 minority (2 African Americans, 1 Hispanic American). Average age 24. 13 applicants, 92% accepted, 8 enrolled. In 2009, 43 master's, 1 doctorate awarded. *Entrance requirements:* For master's and doctorate, GRE General Test, 2 letters of recommendation. Additional exam requirements/recommendations for international students: Required—TOEFL (minimum score 600 paper-based; 250 computer-based; 90 iBT), IELTS (minimum score 7). *Application deadline:* Applications are processed on a rolling basis. Application fee: $60. Electronic applications accepted. *Financial support:* Applicants required to submit FAFSA.

University of Virginia, Curry School of Education, Program in Education, Charlottesville, VA 22903. Offers administration and supervision (PhD); applied developmental science (PhD); counselor education (PhD); curriculum and instruction (PhD); early childhood-developmental risk (MT); education evaluation (PhD); educational psychology (PhD); educational research (PhD); elementary (MT, PhD); English education (MT, PhD); foreign language education (MT); higher education (PhD); instructional technology (PhD); kinesiology (MT, PhD); math education (PhD); reading education (PhD); research statistics and evaluation (PhD); school psychology (PhD); science education (PhD); social studies education (MT, PhD); special education (PhD); world languages education (MT). *Students:* 336 full-time (239 women), 88 part-time (54 women); includes 43 minority (24 African Americans, 2 American Indian/Alaska Native, 11 Asian Americans or Pacific Islanders, 6 Hispanic Americans), 18 international. Average age 27. 199 applicants, 48% accepted, 55 enrolled. In 2009, 127 master's, 52 doctorates awarded. *Degree requirements:* For master's, comprehensive exam (for some programs), field project; for doctorate, comprehensive exam, thesis/dissertation. *Entrance requirements:* For doctorate, GRE General Test. Additional exam requirements/recommendations for international students: Required—TOEFL (minimum score 600 paper-based; 250 computer-based; 90 iBT), IELTS (minimum score 7). *Application deadline:* Applications are processed on a rolling basis. Application fee: $60. Electronic applications accepted. *Financial support:* Fellowships, research assistantships, teaching assistantships available. Financial award application deadline: 1/5; financial award applicants required to submit FAFSA.

University of Waterloo, Graduate Studies, Faculty of Applied Health Sciences, Department of Kinesiology, Waterloo, ON N2L 3G1, Canada. Offers M Sc, PhD. Part-time programs available. *Degree requirements:* For master's, thesis; for doctorate, comprehensive exam, thesis/

dissertation. *Entrance requirements:* For master's, honors degree, minimum B average, writing sample; for doctorate, GRE (recommended), master's degree, minimum B average, writing sample. Additional exam requirements/recommendations for international students: Required—TOEFL, TWE. Electronic applications accepted. *Faculty research:* Work physiology, biomechanics and neural control of human movement, psychomotor learning and performance, aging, health and well-being, work and health.

The University of Western Ontario, Faculty of Graduate Studies, Health Sciences Division, School of Kinesiology, London, ON N6A 5B8, Canada. Offers M Sc, MA, PhD. *Degree requirements:* For master's, thesis optional; for doctorate, comprehensive exam, thesis/dissertation. *Entrance requirements:* For doctorate, MA in physical education or kinesiology. Additional exam requirements/recommendations for international students: Required—Michigan English Language Assessment Battery, TOEFL or IELTS. *Faculty research:* Exercise physiology/biochemistry, sports injuries, sport psychology, sport history, sport philosophy.

University of Windsor, Faculty of Graduate Studies, Faculty of Human Kinetics, Windsor, ON N9B 3P4, Canada. Offers MHK. Part-time programs available. *Degree requirements:* For master's, thesis optional. *Entrance requirements:* For master's, minimum B average. Additional exam requirements/recommendations for international students: Required—TOEFL (minimum score 600 paper-based; 250 computer-based). Electronic applications accepted. *Faculty research:* Movement sciences, sport and lifestyle management, historical and sociological studies of sport.

University of Wisconsin–Madison, Graduate School, School of Education, Department of Kinesiology, Madison, WI 53706-1380. Offers kinesiology (MS, PhD); occupational therapy (MS, PhD); therapeutic science (MS). *Accreditation:* AOTA. *Degree requirements:* For doctorate, thesis/dissertation. *Entrance requirements:* For master's and doctorate, GRE General Test. Application fee: $56. Electronic applications accepted. *Expenses:* Tuition, state resident: part-time $594 per credit. Tuition, nonresident: part-time $1504 per credit. Required fees: $65 per credit. Tuition and fees vary according to course load, program and reciprocity agreements. *Financial support:* Fellowships with full tuition reimbursements, research assistantships with full tuition reimbursements, teaching assistantships with full tuition reimbursements, project assistantships available. *Unit head:* Dr. Dorothy Edwards, Chair, 608-262-0048. *Application contact:* Dr. Dorothy Edwards, Chair, 608-262-0048.

University of Wisconsin–Milwaukee, Graduate School, College of Health Sciences, Program in Kinesiology/Human Movement Sciences, Milwaukee, WI 53201-0413. Offers MS. Part-time programs available. *Faculty:* 14 full-time (6 women). *Students:* 9 full-time (3 women), 11 part-time (7 women), 1 international. Average age 26. 40 applicants, 40% accepted, 6 enrolled. In 2009, 5 master's awarded. *Degree requirements:* For master's, comprehensive exam, thesis optional. *Entrance requirements:* For master's, GRE General Test. Additional exam requirements/recommendations for international students: Required—TOEFL (minimum score 550 paper-based; 79 iBT), IELTS (minimum score 6.5). *Application deadline:* For fall admission, 1/1 priority date for domestic students; for spring admission, 9/1 for domestic students. Applications are processed on a rolling basis. Application fee: $45 ($75 for international students). *Expenses:* Tuition, state resident: full-time $8800. Tuition, nonresident: full-time $20,760. Tuition and fees vary according to program and reciprocity agreements. *Financial support:* In 2009–10, 4 research assistantships, 8 teaching assistantships were awarded; fellowships, career-related internships or fieldwork and unspecified assistantships also available. Support available to part-time students. Financial award application deadline: 4/15. Total annual research expenditures: $1.1 million. *Unit head:* Barbara B. Meyer, Chair, 414-229-4591, Fax: 414-906-3935, E-mail: bbmeyer@uwm.edu. *Application contact:* Ann Swartz, General Information Contact (Kinesiology), 414-229-4242, Fax: 414-229-6967, E-mail: gradschool@uwm.edu.

University of Wyoming, College of Health Sciences, Division of Kinesiology and Health, Laramie, WY 82070. Offers MS. *Accreditation:* NCATE. Part-time programs available. Post-baccalaureate distance learning degree programs offered (no on-campus study). *Degree requirements:* For master's, comprehensive exam (for some programs), thesis (for some programs). *Entrance requirements:* For master's, GRE General Test, minimum GPA of 3.0. Additional exam requirements/recommendations for international students: Required—TOEFL. Electronic applications accepted. *Faculty research:* Teacher effectiveness, effects of exercising on heart function, physiological responses of overtraining, psychological benefits of physical activity, health behavior.

Washington University in St. Louis, Graduate School of Arts and Sciences, Interdisciplinary Program in Movement Science, St. Louis, MO 63130-4899. Offers PhD. *Degree requirements:* For doctorate, thesis/dissertation. *Entrance requirements:* For doctorate, GRE General Test. Electronic applications accepted.

Wayne State University, College of Education, Division of Kinesiology, Health and Sports Studies, Detroit, MI 48202. Offers health education (M Ed); kinesiology (M Ed); physical education (M Ed); recreation and park services (MA); sports administration (MA). *Degree requirements:* For master's, thesis (for some programs). *Entrance requirements:* Additional exam requirements/recommendations for international students: Required—TOEFL; Recommended—TWE (minimum score 6). Electronic applications accepted. *Faculty research:* Fitness in urban children, motor development of crack babies, effects of caffeine on metabolism/exercise, body composition of elite youth sports participants, systematic observation of teaching.

West Chester University of Pennsylvania, Office of Graduate Studies, College of Health Sciences, Department of Kinesiology, West Chester, PA 19383. Offers adapted physical education (Certificate); health and physical education (MS, Teaching Certificate), including exercise physiology (MS); physical education (MS); sport and athletic administration (MSA). Part-time and evening/weekend programs available. *Students:* 2 full-time (1 woman), 37 part-time (15 women); includes 2 minority (both African Americans), 3 international. Average age 25. 39 applicants, 90% accepted, 11 enrolled. In 2009, 25 master's awarded. *Degree requirements:* For master's, thesis (for some programs), thesis or report (MS), 2 internships (MSA). *Entrance requirements:* For master's, GRE (MS); GMAT, GRE General Test, or MAT (MSA), minimum GPA of 3.0 with interview (MS) or letters of recommendation (MSA). Additional exam requirements/recommendations for international students: Required—TOEFL (minimum score 550 paper-based; 213 computer-based; 80 iBT). *Application deadline:* For fall admission, 4/15 priority date for domestic students, 3/15 for international students; for spring admission, 10/15 for domestic students, 9/1 for international students. Applications are processed on a rolling basis. Application fee: $35. Electronic applications accepted. *Expenses:* Tuition, state resident: full-time $6666; part-time $370 per credit. Tuition, nonresident: full-time $10,666; part-time $593 per credit. Required fees: $122.56 per credit. *Financial support:* In 2009–10, 11 research assistantships with full and partial tuition reimbursements (averaging $5,000 per year) were awarded; unspecified assistantships also available. Support available to part-time students. Financial award application deadline: 2/15; financial award applicants required to submit FAFSA. *Faculty research:* Weight lifting and type 1 diabetes mellitus, martial arts, sexual harassment in sports. *Unit head:* Dr. Frank Fry, Chair, 610-436-2832, E-mail: ffry@wcupa.edu. *Application contact:* Dr. Sheri Melton, Graduate Coordinator, 610-436-2260, E-mail: smelton@wcupa.edu.

Western Illinois University, School of Graduate Studies, College of Education and Human Services, Department of Kinesiology, Program in Kinesiology, Macomb, IL 61455-1390. Offers MS. Part-time programs available. *Students:* 32 full-time (14 women), 6 part-time (2 women); includes 2 minority (1 African American, 1 Hispanic American), 2 international. Average age 26. 55 applicants, 51% accepted. In 2009, 17 master's awarded. *Entrance requirements:* For master's, minimum GPA of 3.0. Additional exam requirements/recommendations for international students: Required—TOEFL (minimum score 550 paper-based; 213 computer-based; 80 iBT). *Application deadline:* Applications are processed on a rolling basis. Application fee: $30. Electronic applications accepted. *Expenses:* Tuition, state resident: full-time $4486; part-time $249.21 per credit hour. Tuition, nonresident: full-time $8972; part-time $498.42 per credit hour. Required fees: $72.62 per credit hour. *Financial support:* In 2009–10, 20 students received support, including 12 research assistantships with full tuition reimbursements available (averaging $7,280 per year), 8 teaching assistantships with full tuition reimbursements available (averaging $8,400 per year). Financial award applicants required to submit FAFSA. *Unit head:* Dr. Chris Kovacs, Graduate Committee Chairperson, 309-298-1981. *Application contact:* Evelyn Hoing, Assistant Director of Graduate Studies, 309-298-1806, Fax: 309-298-2345, E-mail: grad-office@wiu.edu.

Wilfrid Laurier University, Faculty of Graduate Studies, Faculty of Science, Department of Kinesiology and Physical Education, Waterloo, ON N2L 3C5, Canada. Offers M Sc. *Degree requirements:* For master's, thesis. *Entrance requirements:* For master's, honours degree in kinesiology, health, physical education with a minimum B+ in kinesiology and health-related courses. Additional exam requirements/recommendations for international students: Required—TOEFL (minimum score 230 computer-based; 89 iBT). Electronic applications accepted. *Faculty research:* Biomechanics, health, exercise physiology, motor control, sport psychology.

York University, Faculty of Graduate Studies, Faculty of Health, Program in Kinesiology and Health Science, Toronto, ON M3J 1P3, Canada. Offers M Sc, MA, PhD. Part-time programs available. *Degree requirements:* For master's, thesis or alternative; for doctorate, comprehensive exam, thesis/dissertation. Electronic applications accepted.

Physical Education

Adams State College, The Graduate School, Department of Human Performance and Physical Education, Alamosa, CO 81102. Offers MA. *Accreditation:* Teacher Education Accreditation Council. Part-time programs available. *Degree requirements:* For master's, comprehensive exam. *Entrance requirements:* For master's, GRE General Test or MAT, minimum undergraduate GPA of 2.75.

Adelphi University, School of Education, Program in Physical Education and Human Performance Science, Garden City, NY 11530-0701. Offers aging (Certificate); physical/educational human performance science (MA). Part-time and evening/weekend programs available. *Students:* 39 full-time (20 women), 107 part-time (42 women); includes 12 minority (6 African Americans, 3 Asian Americans or Pacific Islanders, 3 Hispanic Americans), 4 international. Average age 29. In 2009, 60 master's awarded. *Degree requirements:* For master's, internship. *Entrance requirements:* For master's, 3 letters of recommendation, resume. Additional exam requirements/recommendations for international students: Required—TOEFL (minimum score 550 paper-based; 213 computer-based; 80 iBT). *Application deadline:* For fall admission, 4/1 for international students; for spring admission, 11/1 for international students. Applications are processed on a rolling basis. Application fee: $50. Electronic applications accepted. *Expenses:* Tuition: Full-time $28,340; part-time $830 per credit. Required fees: $600; $250 per credit. Full-time tuition and fees vary according to course load and program. *Financial support:* Fellowships, research assistantships with full and partial tuition reimbursements, teaching assistantships, career-related internships or fieldwork, Federal Work-Study, institutionally sponsored loans, and tuition waivers (full) available. Support available to part-time students. Financial award application deadline: 2/15; financial award applicants required to submit FAFSA. *Faculty research:* Physical education for the handicapped, sport sociology, sport pedagogy. *Unit head:* Dr. Stephen J. Virgilio, Chair, 516-877-4262, E-mail: virgilio@adelphi.edu. *Application contact:* Christine Murphy, Director of Admissions, 516-877-3050, Fax: 516-877-3039, E-mail: graduateadmissions@adelphi.edu.

Alabama Agricultural and Mechanical University, School of Graduate Studies, School of Education, Area in Health and Physical Education, Huntsville, AL 35811. Offers physical education (M Ed, MS). Part-time and evening/weekend programs available. *Degree requirements:* For master's, comprehensive exam. *Entrance requirements:* For master's, GRE General Test. Additional exam requirements/recommendations for international students: Required—TOEFL (minimum score 500 paper-based; 173 computer-based; 61 iBT). Electronic applications accepted. *Faculty research:* Cardiorespiratory assessment.

Alabama State University, School of Graduate Studies, College of Education, Department of Health, Physical Education, and Recreation, Montgomery, AL 36101-0271. Offers health education (M Ed); physical education (M Ed). Part-time programs available. *Degree requirements:* For master's, comprehensive exam. *Entrance requirements:* For master's, GRE General Test, MAT, graduate writing competency test. Additional exam requirements/recommendations for international students: Required—TOEFL (minimum score 500 paper-based; 173 computer-based). *Faculty research:* Risk factors for heart disease in the college-age population, cardiovascular reactivity for the Cold Pressor Test.

Albany State University, College of Education, Program in Health and Physical Education, Albany, GA 31705-2717. Offers M Ed. *Accreditation:* NCATE. Part-time programs available. *Students:* 5 full-time (2 women), 17 part-time (6 women); includes 19 minority (all African Americans). Average age 32. 4 applicants, 100% accepted, 3 enrolled. In 2009, 1 master's awarded. *Degree requirements:* For master's, comprehensive exam, thesis optional. *Entrance requirements:* For master's, GRE General Test, MAT or NTE (GACE II). Additional exam requirements/recommendations for international students: Required—TOEFL. *Application deadline:* For fall admission, 11/16 for domestic students, 9/16 for international students; for spring admission, 4/19 for domestic students, 2/19 for international students. Applications are processed on a rolling basis. Application fee: $20. Electronic applications accepted. *Expenses:* Tuition, state resident: full-time $2970; part-time $162 per credit hour. Tuition, nonresident: full-time $12,168; part-time $676 per credit hour. Required fees: $962; $75 per credit hour. *Financial support:* Application deadline: 6/30. *Faculty research:* Neuromuscular function, nutrition, health, recreation, and physical education. *Unit head:* Dr. Richard H. Williams, Chair, 229-430-4762, Fax: 229-430-3020, E-mail: richard.williams@asurams.edu. *Application contact:* Dr. Rani George, Interim Graduate Admissions Officer, 229-430-4862, Fax: 229-430-6398, E-mail: nicole.lane@asurams.edu.

Alcorn State University, School of Graduate Studies, School of Psychology and Education, Alcorn State, MS 39096-7500. Offers agricultural education (MS Ed); elementary education (MS Ed, Ed S); guidance and counseling (MS Ed); industrial education (MS Ed); secondary education (MS Ed), including health and physical education; special education (MS Ed). *Accreditation:* NCATE. *Degree requirements:* For master's, thesis optional.

American University of Puerto Rico, Program in Education, Bayamón, PR 00960-2037. Offers art history (M Ed); elementary education (4-6) (M Ed); elementary education (k-3) (M Ed); general science education (M Ed); physical education (k-12) (M Ed); special education at secondary level (transition) (M Ed). *Faculty:* 1 full-time (0 women), 22 part-time/adjunct (6 women). *Students:* 121 full-time (98 women), 64 part-time (50 women); includes all Hispanic Americans. Average age 30. 250 applicants, 80% accepted, 185 enrolled. *Entrance*

Physical Education

American University of Puerto Rico (continued)

requirements: For master's, EXADEP or GRE or MAT, 2 letters of recommendation, minimum GPA of 2.5. *Application deadline:* For fall admission, 8/4 for domestic students; for winter admission, 10/18 for domestic students; for spring admission, 3/22 for domestic students. Applications are processed on a rolling basis. Application fee: $50. *Application contact:* Information Contact, E-mail: oficnaadmisiones@aupr.edu.

Arizona State University, Graduate College, College of Teacher Education and Leadership, Tempe, AZ 85287. Offers educational administration and supervision (M Ed); elementary education (M Ed, Certificate); leadership/innovation (administration) (Ed D); leadership/innovation (teaching) (Ed D); physical education (MPE); secondary education (M Ed, Certificate); special education (M Ed). Part-time and evening/weekend programs available. *Degree requirements:* For master's, applied project or comprehensive exams; for doctorate, comprehensive exam, thesis/dissertation. *Entrance requirements:* For master's, 3 letters of recommendation, minimum undergraduate GPA of 3.0, resume; for doctorate, master's degree in education or related field, 3 professional references, resumé, graduate GPA of 3.0, 3 letters of recommendation. Additional exam requirements/recommendations for international students: Required—TOEFL (minimum score 550 paper-based; 213 computer-based; 83 iBT), IELTS (minimum score 6.5). Electronic applications accepted. *Expenses:* Contact institution. *Faculty research:* Self-regulated learning in students, collaboration and consultation skills for educators, school reform and restructuring, hands-on science and mathematics programs, educational technology.

Arkansas State University—Jonesboro, Graduate School, College of Education, Department of Health, Physical Education, and Sport Sciences, Jonesboro, State University, AR 72467. Offers exercise science (MS); physical education (MSE, SCCT). Part-time programs available. *Faculty:* 6 full-time (1 woman). *Students:* 9 full-time (7 women), 14 part-time (7 women); includes 3 minority (2 African Americans, 1 Hispanic American), 8 international. Average age 27. 21 applicants, 86% accepted, 12 enrolled. In 2009, 4 master's awarded. *Degree requirements:* For master's, comprehensive exam, thesis or alternative; for SCCT, comprehensive exam. *Entrance requirements:* For master's, GRE General Test or MAT, appropriate bachelor's degree; for SCCT, GRE General Test or MAT, interview, master's degree, official transcript, immunization records. Additional exam requirements/recommendations for international students: Required—TOEFL (minimum score 550 paper-based; 213 computer-based; 79 iBT), IELTS (minimum score 6). *Application deadline:* For fall admission, 7/15 for domestic students, 7/1 for international students; for spring admission, 12/1 for domestic students, 11/13 for international students. Applications are processed on a rolling basis. Application fee: $30 ($40 for international students). Electronic applications accepted. *Expenses:* Tuition, state resident: full-time $3744; part-time $208 per credit hour. Tuition, nonresident: full-time $9540; part-time $530 per credit hour. Required fees: $896; $47 per credit hour. $25 per term. One-time fee: $50. Tuition and fees vary according to course load and program. *Financial support:* In 2009–10, 13 students received support; teaching assistantships, career-related internships or fieldwork, scholarships/grants, and unspecified assistantships available. Financial award application deadline: 7/1; financial award applicants required to submit FAFSA. *Unit head:* Dr. Jim Stillwell, Chair, 870-972-3066, Fax: 870-972-3096, E-mail: jstillwel@astate.edu. *Application contact:* Dr. Andrew Sustich, Dean of the Graduate School, 870-972-3029, Fax: 870-972-3857, E-mail: sustich@astate.edu.

Ashland University, Dwight Schar College of Education, Department of Sport Sciences, Ashland, OH 44805-3702. Offers adapted physical education (M Ed); applied exercise science (M Ed); sport education (M Ed); sport management (M Ed). Part-time programs available. *Faculty:* 5 full-time (3 women), 2 part-time/adjunct (both women). *Students:* 24 full-time (9 women), 31 part-time (12 women); includes 4 minority (all African Americans), 4 international. Average age 30. 15 applicants, 100% accepted, 15 enrolled. In 2009, 26 master's awarded. *Degree requirements:* For master's, practicum, inquiry seminar, thesis, or internship. *Entrance requirements:* For master's, teaching certificate or license, bachelor's degree, minimum cumulative GPA of 2.75. Additional exam requirements/recommendations for international students: Required—TOEFL. *Application deadline:* For fall admission, 8/27 for domestic students; for spring admission, 1/14 for domestic students. Applications are processed on a rolling basis. Application fee: $30. *Financial support:* In 2009–10, 32 students received support; teaching assistantships, institutionally sponsored loans and scholarships/grants available. Financial award application deadline: 4/15. *Faculty research:* Coaching, legal issues, strength and conditioning, sport management rating of perceived exertion, youth fitness, geriatric exercise science. *Unit head:* Dr. Randall F. Gearhart, Chair, 419-289-6198, E-mail: rgearhar@ashland.edu. *Application contact:* Dr. Randall F. Gearhart, Chair, 419-289-6198, E-mail: rgearhar@ashland.edu.

Auburn University, Graduate School, College of Education, Department of Kinesiology, Auburn University, AL 36849. Offers exercise science (M Ed, MS, PhD); health promotion (M Ed, MS); kinesiology (PhD); physical education/teacher education (M Ed, MS, Ed D, Ed S). *Accreditation:* NCATE. Part-time programs available. *Faculty:* 16 full-time (7 women), 1 part-time/adjunct (0 women). *Students:* 70 full-time (46 women), 21 part-time (8 women); includes 10 minority (8 African Americans, 2 Asian Americans or Pacific Islanders), 10 international. Average age 26. 109 applicants, 68% accepted, 53 enrolled. In 2009, 26 master's, 7 doctorates awarded. *Degree requirements:* For master's, thesis (for some programs); for doctorate, thesis/dissertation; for Ed S, exam, field project. *Entrance requirements:* For master's, GRE General Test; for doctorate and Ed S, GRE General Test, interview, master's degree. *Application deadline:* For fall admission, 7/7 for domestic students; for spring admission, 11/24 for domestic students. Applications are processed on a rolling basis. Application fee: $50 ($60 for international students). Electronic applications accepted. *Expenses:* Tuition, state resident: full-time $6240. Tuition, nonresident: full-time $18,720. International tuition: $18,938 full-time. Required fees: $492. Tuition and fees vary according to course load, program and reciprocity agreements. *Financial support:* Research assistantships, teaching assistantships, Federal Work-Study available. Support available to part-time students. Financial award application deadline: 3/15; financial award applicants required to submit FAFSA. *Faculty research:* Biomechanics, exercise physiology, motor skill learning, school health, curriculum development. *Unit head:* Dr. Mary E. Rudisill, Head, 334-844-4483. *Application contact:* Dr. George Flowers, Dean of the Graduate School, 334-844-2125.

Auburn University Montgomery, School of Education, Department of Foundations, Secondary, and Physical Education, Montgomery, AL 36124-4023. Offers physical education (M Ed); secondary education (M Ed, Ed S). *Accreditation:* NCATE. Part-time and evening/weekend programs available. *Faculty:* 12 full-time (8 women), 2 part-time/adjunct (both women). *Students:* 58 full-time (43 women), 101 part-time (78 women); includes 60 minority (56 African Americans, 2 American Indian/Alaska Native, 2 Asian Americans or Pacific Islanders), 3 international. Average age 32. In 2009, 38 master's awarded. *Degree requirements:* For master's and Ed S, comprehensive exam, thesis optional. *Entrance requirements:* For master's, GRE General Test or MAT, certification, BS in teaching; for Ed S, GRE General Test or MAT, certification. *Application deadline:* Applications are processed on a rolling basis. Electronic applications accepted. *Expenses:* Tuition, state resident: full-time $2841; part-time $225 per credit hour. Tuition, nonresident: full-time $8241; part-time $675 per credit hour. Required fees: $282; $8 per hour. $45 per term. *Financial support:* In 2009–10, 3 teaching assistantships were awarded; career-related internships or fieldwork and scholarships/grants also available. Support available to part-time students. Financial award application deadline: 3/1; financial award applicants required to submit FAFSA. *Unit head:* Dr. Henry N. Williford, Head, 334-244-3548, Fax: 334-244-3547, E-mail: hwilliford@mail.aum.edu. *Application contact:* Dr. Sam Flynt, Associate Graduate Coordinator, 334-244-3270, Fax: 334-244-3835, E-mail: sflynt@mail.aum.edu.

Augusta State University, Graduate Studies, College of Education, Program in Health and Physical Education, Augusta, GA 30904-2200. Offers M Ed. *Entrance requirements:* For master's, GRE, MAT, minimum GPA of 2.5.

Austin College, Program in Education, Sherman, TX 75090-4400. Offers art education (MA); elementary education (MA); middle school education (MA); music education (MA); physical education and coaching (MA); secondary education (MA); theatre education (MA). Part-time programs available. *Faculty:* 5 full-time (3 women), 1 (woman) part-time/adjunct. *Students:* 29 full-time (21 women); includes 3 minority (1 Asian American or Pacific Islander, 2 Hispanic Americans). Average age 23. In 2009, 23 master's awarded. *Degree requirements:* For master's, one foreign language, thesis or alternative. *Entrance requirements:* For master's, Texas Academic Skills Program Test. *Application deadline:* For fall admission, 5/1 priority date for domestic students; for spring admission, 1/15 priority date for domestic students. Applications are processed on a rolling basis. Application fee: $35. Electronic applications accepted. *Expenses:* Tuition: Full-time $31,575. Required fees: $160. *Financial support:* Career-related internships or fieldwork, Federal Work-Study, scholarships/grants, and unspecified assistantships available. Support available to part-time students. Financial award application deadline: 4/1; financial award applicants required to submit FAFSA. *Unit head:* Dr. Barbara Sylvester, Director of Teaching Program, 903-813-2327, Fax: 903-813-2326, E-mail: bsylvester@austincollege.edu. *Application contact:* Dr. Barbara Sylvester, Director of Teaching Program, 903-813-2327, Fax: 903-813-2326, E-mail: bsylvester@austincollege.edu.

Averett University, Master in Education Program, Danville, VA 24541-3692. Offers art education (M Ed); biology (M Ed); biology education (M Ed); chemistry (M Ed); chemistry education (M Ed); curriculum and instruction (M Ed); elementary education (M Ed); English (M Ed); English education (M Ed); health and physical education (M Ed); history and social studies education (M Ed); math (M Ed); mathematics education (M Ed); physical science (M Ed); reading specialization (M Ed); special education (learning disabilities specialization PK-12) (M Ed). Program also offered at Richmond, VA regional campus location. Part-time and evening/weekend programs available. *Faculty:* 4 full-time (3 women), 36 part-time/adjunct (22 women). *Students:* 182 full-time (160 women), 142 part-time (94 women); includes 113 minority (94 African Americans, 1 American Indian/Alaska Native, 7 Asian Americans or Pacific Islanders, 11 Hispanic Americans). Average age 37. 119 applicants, 99% accepted, 98 enrolled. In 2009, 92 master's awarded. *Degree requirements:* For master's, comprehensive exam, thesis optional. *Entrance requirements:* For master's, PRAXIS, GRE General Test, MAT or NTE, writing proficiency exam, 3 letters of recommendation, current teacher's licensure or eligibility for licensure, minimum undergraduate GPA of 3.0 in previous 2 years. Additional exam requirements/recommendations for international students: Required—TOEFL (minimum score 600 paper-based; 200 computer-based). *Application deadline:* Applications are processed on a rolling basis. *Expenses:* Contact institution. *Financial support:* Career-related internships or fieldwork, Federal Work-Study, and scholarships/grants available. Financial award application deadline: 4/1; financial award applicants required to submit FAFSA. *Faculty research:* Literary assessment-PreK-6, handwriting instruction and assessment-PreK-6, written language instruction and assessment-PreK-6 and special needs students learning styles, curriculum and instruction processes. *Unit head:* Dr. Lynn H. Wolf, Chair/Associate Professor/Director, 434-793-3995, Fax: 434-791-4392, E-mail: lynn.wolf@averett.edu. *Application contact:* Dr. Lynn H. Wolf, Chair/Associate Professor/Director, 434-793-3995, Fax: 434-791-4392, E-mail: lynn.wolf@averett.edu.

Azusa Pacific University, School of Education, Department of Advanced Studies, Program in Physical Education, Azusa, CA 91702-7000. Offers M Ed. Evening/weekend programs available. *Degree requirements:* For master's, core exams, oral exam, oral presentation. *Entrance requirements:* For master's, BA in physical education or 12 units of course work in education, minimum GPA of 3.0.

Ball State University, Graduate School, College of Applied Science and Technology, School of Physical Education, Muncie, IN 47306-1099. Offers MA, MAE, MS, PhD. *Degree requirements:* For doctorate, thesis/dissertation. *Entrance requirements:* For master's, resumé; for doctorate, GRE General Test, minimum graduate GPA of 3.2.

Baylor University, Graduate School, School of Education, Department of Health, Human Performance and Recreation, Waco, TX 76798. Offers exercise, nutrition and preventive health (PhD); health, human performance and recreation (MS Ed). *Accreditation:* NCATE. Part-time programs available. *Faculty:* 13 full-time (5 women), 3 part-time/adjunct (1 woman). *Students:* 66 full-time (35 women), 42 part-time (21 women); includes 14 minority (7 African Americans, 3 Asian Americans or Pacific Islanders, 4 Hispanic Americans), 5 international. 30 applicants, 87% accepted. In 2009, 48 master's, 6 doctorates awarded. *Degree requirements:* For master's, thesis optional. *Entrance requirements:* For master's, GRE General Test. *Application deadline:* For fall admission, 4/1 priority date for domestic students; for spring admission, 10/1 for domestic students. Applications are processed on a rolling basis. Application fee: $25. Electronic applications accepted. *Financial support:* In 2009–10, 35 students received support, including 22 teaching assistantships; career-related internships or fieldwork, Federal Work-Study, institutionally sponsored loans, tuition waivers (partial), and recreation supplements also available. *Faculty research:* Behavior change theory, pedagogy, nutrition and enzyme therapy, exercise testing, health planning. *Unit head:* Dr. Glenn Miller, Graduate Program Director, 254-710-4001, Fax: 254-710-3527, E-mail: glenn_miller@baylor.edu. *Application contact:* Eva Berger-Rhodes, Administrative Assistant, 254-710-4945, Fax: 254-710-3870, E-mail: eva_rhodes@baylor.edu.

Bethel University, Program in Education, McKenzie, TN 38201. Offers administration and supervision (MA Ed); biology education K8-12 (MAT); elementary education (MAT); English education K8-12 (MAT); history education K8-12 (MAT); physical education K8-12 (MAT); special education K8-12 (MAT). Part-time and evening/weekend programs available. *Degree requirements:* For master's, thesis (for some programs). *Entrance requirements:* For master's, GRE General Test or MAT, minimum undergraduate GPA of 2.5.

Boston University, School of Education, Department of Curriculum and Teaching, Program in Physical Education and Coaching, Boston, MA 02215. Offers Ed M, Ed D, CAGS. *Degree requirements:* For master's, thesis optional; for doctorate, comprehensive exam, thesis/dissertation; for CAGS, comprehensive exam. *Entrance requirements:* For master's, doctorate, and CAGS, GRE General Test or MAT. Additional exam requirements/recommendations for international students: Required—TOEFL. Electronic applications accepted. *Expenses:* Tuition: Full-time $37,910; part-time $1184 per credit hour. Required fees: $386; $40 per semester. Part-time tuition and fees vary according to class time, course level, degree level and program. *Faculty research:* Sports theory, biofeedback, exercise.

Bridgewater State University, School of Graduate Studies, School of Education and Allied Science, Department of Movement Arts, Health Promotion, and Leisure Studies, Program in Physical Education, Bridgewater, MA 02325-0001. Offers MS. Part-time and evening/weekend programs available. *Degree requirements:* For master's, thesis or alternative. *Entrance requirements:* For master's, GRE General Test.

Brooklyn College of the City University of New York, Division of Graduate Studies, Department of Physical Education and Exercise Science, Brooklyn, NY 11210-2889. Offers exercise science and rehabilitation (MS); physical education (MS), including sports management. Part-time programs available. *Students:* 15 full-time (7 women), 127 part-time (58 women); includes 39 minority (23 African Americans, 3 Asian Americans or Pacific Islanders, 13 Hispanic Americans), 65 international. Average age 27. 127 applicants, 96% accepted, 57 enrolled. In 2009, 15 master's awarded. *Degree requirements:* For master's, comprehensive exam or thesis. *Entrance requirements:* For master's, previous course work in physical education and education, minimum GPA of 3.0, 2 letters of recommendation, essay. Additional exam requirements/recommendations for international students: Required—TOEFL (minimum score 500 paper-based; 173 computer-based; 61 iBT). *Application deadline:* For fall admission, 3/1 priority date for domestic students, 2/1 priority date for international students; for spring admission, 11/1 priority date for domestic students, 10/1 priority date for international students. Applications are processed on a rolling basis. Application fee: $125. Electronic applications accepted. *Expenses:* Tuition, state resident: full-time $7360; part-time $310 per credit hour. Tuition, nonresident: full-time $13,800; part-time $575 per credit hour. Required fees: $140.10 per semester. *Financial support:* Career-related internships or fieldwork, Federal Work-Study, institutionally sponsored loans, and scholarships/grants available. Support available to part-time students. Financial award application deadline: 5/1; financial award applicants required to

submit FAFSA. *Faculty research:* Exercise physiology, motor learning, sports psychology, women in athletics. *Unit head:* Dr. Artis Smith, Chairperson, 718-951-5514, E-mail: basmith@brooklyn.cuny.edu. *Application contact:* Hernan Sierra, Graduate Admissions Coordinator, 718-951-4536, Fax: 718-951-4506, E-mail: grads@brooklyn.cuny.edu.

Brooklyn College of the City University of New York, Division of Graduate Studies, School of Education, Program in Adolescence Education and Special Subjects, Brooklyn, NY 11210-2889. Offers adolescence science education (MAT); art teacher (MA); biology teacher (MA); chemistry teacher (MA); earth science teacher (MAT); English teacher (MA); French teacher (MA); health and nutrition sciences: health teacher (MS Ed); mathematics teacher (MA); music education (CAS); music teacher (MA); physical education teacher (MS Ed); physics teacher (MA); social studies teacher (MA); Spanish teacher (MA). Part-time and evening/weekend programs available. *Students:* 23 full-time (15 women), 449 part-time (256 women); includes 147 minority (96 African Americans, 1 American Indian/Alaska Native, 18 Asian Americans or Pacific Islanders, 32 Hispanic Americans), 12 international. Average age 30. 251 applicants, 80% accepted, 141 enrolled. In 2009, 163 master's, 2 other advanced degrees awarded. *Degree requirements:* For master's, comprehensive exam (for some programs), thesis (for some programs). *Entrance requirements:* For master's, LAST, previous course work in education, resume, 2 letters of recommendation, essay. Additional exam requirements/recommendations for international students: Required—TOEFL (minimum score 500 paper-based; 173 computer-based; 61 iBT). *Application deadline:* For fall admission, 7/15 for domestic students, 7/1 for international students; for spring admission, 11/15 for domestic students, 10/1 for international students. Applications are processed on a rolling basis. Application fee: $125. Electronic applications accepted. *Expenses:* Tuition, state resident: full-time $7360; part-time $310 per credit hour. Tuition, nonresident: full-time $13,800; part-time $575 per credit hour. Required fees: $140.10 per semester. *Financial support:* Career-related internships or fieldwork, Federal Work-Study, institutionally sponsored loans, and scholarships/grants available. Support available to part-time students. Financial award application deadline: 5/1; financial award applicants required to submit FAFSA. *Faculty research:* Interdisciplinary education, semiotics, discourse analysis, autobiography, teacher identity. *Unit head:* Prof. Stephen Phillips, Program Head, 718-951-5214, E-mail: phillips@brooklyn.cuny.edu. *Application contact:* Hernan Sierra, Graduate Admissions Coordinator, 718-951-4536, Fax: 718-951-4506, E-mail: grads@brooklyn.cuny.edu.

California Baptist University, Program in Kinesiology, Riverside, CA 92504-3206. Offers exercise science (MS); physical education pedagogy (MS); sport management (MS). Part-time programs available. *Faculty:* 3 full-time (0 women). *Students:* 17 full-time (8 women), 14 part-time (8 women); includes 10 minority (1 African American, 1 American Indian/Alaska Native, 3 Asian Americans or Pacific Islanders, 5 Hispanic Americans), 2 international. 45 applicants, 49% accepted, 15 enrolled. In 2009, 15 master's awarded. *Degree requirements:* For master's, thesis or alternative, field experience. *Entrance requirements:* For master's, 12 semester units of course work in kinesiology, including basic movement anatomy or a related course; minimum undergraduate GPA of 2.75 (physical education pedagogy). Additional exam requirements/recommendations for international students: Required—TOEFL (minimum score 575 paper-based; 230 computer-based; 89 iBT). *Application deadline:* For fall admission, 8/1 priority date for domestic students, 7/1 for international students; for spring admission, 12/1 priority date for domestic students, 10/15 for international students. Applications are processed on a rolling basis. Application fee: $45. Electronic applications accepted. *Expenses:* Tuition: Full-time $8352; part-time $464 per semester hour. Required fees: $125 per semester. Tuition and fees vary according to course load, campus/location and program. *Financial support:* Federal Work-Study and scholarships/grants available. Support available to part-time students. Financial award applicants required to submit FAFSA. *Unit head:* Dr. Sean Sullivan, Chair, Department of Kinesiology, 951-343-4528, E-mail: ssullivan@calbaptist.edu. *Application contact:* Gail Ronveaux, Dean of Graduate Enrollment, 951-343-5045, Fax: 951-343-5095, E-mail: graduateadmissions@calbaptist.edu.

California State University, Dominguez Hills, College of Professional Studies, School of Health and Human Services, Program in Physical Education Administration, Carson, CA 90747-0001. Offers MA. Part-time programs available. *Faculty:* 5 full-time (2 women). *Students:* 2 full-time (both women), 9 part-time (2 women); includes 8 minority (3 African Americans, 3 Asian Americans or Pacific Islanders, 2 Hispanic Americans). Average age 33. 10 applicants, 100% accepted, 2 enrolled. In 2009, 13 master's awarded. *Degree requirements:* For master's, comprehensive exam. *Entrance requirements:* For master's, minimum GPA of 2.75. Additional exam requirements/recommendations for international students: Required—TOEFL, IELTS. *Application deadline:* For fall admission, 6/1 for domestic students. Applications are processed on a rolling basis. Application fee: $55. *Expenses:* Tuition, nonresident: full-time $6696; part-time $372 per unit. Required fees: $5946; $1752 per semester. *Faculty research:* Teaching pedagogy, physical activity. *Unit head:* Dr. Ben Zhou, Chair, 310-243-2223, E-mail: bzhou@csudh.edu. *Application contact:* 310-243-3600.

California State University, East Bay, Graduate Programs, College of Education and Allied Studies, Department of Kinesiology, Hayward, CA 94542-3000. Offers humanities/cultural studies (MS). *Faculty:* 6 full-time (3 women). *Students:* 8 full-time (2 women), 35 part-time (28 women); includes 20 minority (4 African Americans, 1 American Indian/Alaska Native, 7 Asian Americans or Pacific Islanders, 8 Hispanic Americans). Average age 30. 46 applicants, 67% accepted, 19 enrolled. In 2009, 16 master's awarded. *Degree requirements:* For master's, exam or thesis. *Entrance requirements:* For master's, BA in kinesiology or related discipline, minimum major course work GPA of 3.0. Additional exam requirements/recommendations for international students: Required—TOEFL (minimum score 550 paper-based; 213 computer-based). *Application deadline:* For fall admission, 6/30 for domestic and international students. Applications are processed on a rolling basis. Application fee: $55. Electronic applications accepted. *Financial support:* Fellowships, Federal Work-Study, institutionally sponsored loans, and scholarships/grants available. Support available to part-time students. Financial award application deadline: 3/1; financial award applicants required to submit FAFSA. *Unit head:* Dr. Calvin Caplan, Graduate Coordinator, 510-885-3089, Fax: 510-885-2282, E-mail: calvin.caplan@csueastbay.edu. *Application contact:* Donna Wiley, Interim Associate Director, 510-885-2928, Fax: 510-885-4777, E-mail: donna.wiley@csueastbay.edu.

California State University, Fullerton, Graduate Studies, College of Health and Human Development, Department of Kinesiology, Fullerton, CA 92834-9480. Offers MS. Part-time programs available. *Students:* 38 full-time (17 women), 60 part-time (30 women); includes 37 minority (2 African Americans, 14 Asian Americans or Pacific Islanders, 21 Hispanic Americans), 2 international. Average age 27. 94 applicants, 54% accepted, 36 enrolled. In 2009, 33 master's awarded. *Degree requirements:* For master's, project or thesis. *Entrance requirements:* For master's, minimum GPA of 3.0 in field, 2.5 overall. Application fee: $55. *Expenses:* Tuition, nonresident: full-time $11,160; part-time $373 per credit. Required fees: $1440 per term. Tuition and fees vary according to course load, degree level and program. *Financial support:* Career-related internships or fieldwork, Federal Work-Study, institutionally sponsored loans, and scholarships/grants available. Support available to part-time students. Financial award application deadline: 3/1; financial award applicants required to submit FAFSA. *Unit head:* Dr. Stephen Walk, Head, 657-278-3320. *Application contact:* Admissions/Applications, 657-278-2371.

California State University, Long Beach, Graduate Studies, College of Health and Human Services, Department of Kinesiology, Long Beach, CA 90840. Offers adapted physical education (MA); coaching and student athlete development (MA); exercise physiology and nutrition (MS); exercise science (MS); individualized studies (MA); kinesiology (MA); pedagogical studies (MA); sport and exercise psychology (MS); sport management (MA); sports medicine and injury studies (MS). Part-time programs available. *Faculty:* 9 full-time (6 women), 1 part-time/adjunct (0 women). *Students:* 34 full-time (22 women), 23 part-time (14 women); includes 22 minority (4 African Americans, 2 American Indian/Alaska Native, 8 Asian Americans or Pacific Islanders, 8 Hispanic Americans), 9 international. Average age 27. 143 applicants, 59% accepted, 20 enrolled. *Degree requirements:* For master's, oral and written comprehensive exams or thesis. *Entrance requirements:* For master's, GRE General Test, minimum GPA of 2.75 during previous 2 years of course work. *Application deadline:* For fall admission, 6/1 for domestic students. Applications are processed on a rolling basis. Application fee: $55. Electronic applications accepted. *Expenses:* Required fees: $1802 per semester. Part-time tuition and fees vary according to course load. *Financial support:* Federal Work-Study, institutionally sponsored loans, and scholarships/grants available. Financial award application deadline: 3/2. *Faculty research:* Pulmonary functioning, feedback and practice structure, strength training, history and politics of sports, special population research issues. *Unit head:* Dr. Sharon R. Guthrie, Chair, 562-985-7487, Fax: 562-985-8067, E-mail: guthrie@csulb.edu. *Application contact:* Dr. Grant Hill, Graduate Advisor, 562-985-8856, Fax: 562-985-8067, E-mail: ghill@csulb.edu.

California State University, Los Angeles, Graduate Studies, College of Health and Human Services, Department of Kinesiology and Nutritional Sciences, Los Angeles, CA 90032-8530. Offers nutritional science (MS); physical education and kinesiology (MA, MS). *Accreditation:* ADtA. Part-time and evening/weekend programs available. *Faculty:* 6 full-time (3 women), 1 part-time/adjunct (0 women). *Students:* 64 full-time (57 women), 49 part-time (38 women); includes 58 minority (10 African Americans, 29 Asian Americans or Pacific Islanders, 19 Hispanic Americans), 11 international. Average age 31. 55 applicants, 100% accepted, 17 enrolled. In 2009, 17 master's awarded. *Degree requirements:* For master's, comprehensive exam, project or thesis. *Entrance requirements:* For master's, minimum GPA of 2.75. Additional exam requirements/recommendations for international students: Required—TOEFL (minimum score 500 paper-based; 173 computer-based). *Application deadline:* For fall admission, 5/1 for domestic and international students. Applications are processed on a rolling basis. Application fee: $55. *Financial support:* Federal Work-Study available. Support available to part-time students. Financial award application deadline: 3/1. *Unit head:* Dr. Nazareth Khodiguian, Chair, 323-343-4650, Fax: 323-343-6482, E-mail: nkhodig@calstatela.edu. *Application contact:* Dr. Cheryl L. Ney, Associate Vice President for Academic Affairs and Dean of Graduate Studies, 323-343-3820, Fax: 323-343-5653, E-mail: cney@cslanet.calstatela.edu.

California State University, Sacramento, Graduate Studies, College of Health and Human Services, Department of Kinesiology and Health Science, Sacramento, CA 95819. Offers physical education (MS). *Accreditation:* APTA. Part-time programs available. *Degree requirements:* For master's, thesis or alternative, writing proficiency exam. *Entrance requirements:* Additional exam requirements/recommendations for international students: Required—TOEFL. Electronic applications accepted.

California State University, Stanislaus, College of Education, Department of Physical Education and Health, Turlock, CA 95382. Offers education (MA); physical education (MA). *Degree requirements:* For master's, thesis. *Entrance requirements:* For master's, MAT, GPA by formula, 3 letters of reference. Additional exam requirements/recommendations for international students: Required—TOEFL (minimum score 550 paper-based; 213 computer-based). Electronic applications accepted. *Faculty research:* Girls and wrestling team, sex education, culture and physical education, sports psychology and coaching, water safety K-12.

Campbell University, Graduate and Professional Programs, School of Education, Buies Creek, NC 27506. Offers administration (MSA); community counseling (MA); elementary education (M Ed); English education (M Ed); interdisciplinary studies (M Ed); mathematics education (M Ed); middle grades education (M Ed); physical education (M Ed); school counseling (M Ed); secondary education (M Ed); social science education (M Ed). *Accreditation:* NCATE. Part-time and evening/weekend programs available. *Degree requirements:* For master's, comprehensive exam. *Entrance requirements:* For master's, GRE General Test, minimum GPA of 2.7. *Faculty research:* Spiritual values and wellness issues in counseling, stress and professional burnout among counselors, thinking strategies, leadership, adaptive technology.

Canisius College, Graduate Division, School of Education and Human Services, Department of Physical Education, Buffalo, NY 14208-1098. Offers physical education (MS); physical education (Pre-K to Grade 12) (MS). Part-time and evening/weekend programs available. Postbaccalaureate distance learning degree programs offered (minimal on-campus study). *Faculty:* 8 full-time (1 woman), 15 part-time/adjunct (5 women). *Students:* 72 full-time (27 women), 145 part-time (55 women); includes 8 minority (5 African Americans, 1 Asian American or Pacific Islander, 2 Hispanic Americans), 28 international. Average age 28. 96 applicants, 77% accepted, 55 enrolled. In 2009, 80 master's awarded. *Degree requirements:* For master's, research project or thesis. *Entrance requirements:* For master's, GRE General Test, minimum GPA of 2.5. *Application deadline:* Applications are processed on a rolling basis. Application fee: $25. *Financial support:* Research assistantships, career-related internships or fieldwork, institutionally sponsored loans, scholarships/grants, health care benefits, tuition waivers (full and partial), and unspecified assistantships available. Financial award application deadline: 7/1; financial award applicants required to submit FAFSA. *Faculty research:* Sport psychology, adapted physical education, current health issues, teaching methods. *Unit head:* Dr. Gregory K. Reeds, Chair, 716-888-2952, Fax: 716-888-3219, E-mail: reedsg@canisius.edu. *Application contact:* James D. Bagwell, Director of Graduate Recruitment and Admissions, 716-888-2544, Fax: 716-888-3290, E-mail: bagwellj@canisius.edu.

Caribbean University, Graduate School, Bayamón, PR 00960-0493. Offers administration and supervision (MA Ed); criminal justice (MA); curriculum and instruction (MA Ed), including elementary education, English education, history education, mathematics education, primary education, science education, Spanish education; education (PhD); gerontology (MSN); human resources (MBA); museology, archiving and art history (MA Ed); neonatal pediatrics (MSN); physical education (MA Ed); special education (MA Ed). *Entrance requirements:* For master's, interview, minimum GPA of 2.5.

Central Connecticut State University, School of Graduate Studies, School of Education and Professional Studies, Department of Physical Education and Human Performance, New Britain, CT 06050-4010. Offers physical education (MS, Certificate). Part-time and evening/weekend programs available. *Faculty:* 17 full-time (8 women), 24 part-time/adjunct (15 women). *Students:* 27 full-time (15 women), 43 part-time (17 women); includes 5 minority (1 African American, 1 American Indian/Alaska Native, 3 Hispanic Americans), 1 international. Average age 28. 34 applicants, 53% accepted, 11 enrolled. In 2009, 12 master's, 4 other advanced degrees awarded. *Degree requirements:* For master's, comprehensive exam, thesis or alternative; for Certificate, qualifying exam. *Entrance requirements:* For master's, minimum GPA of 2.7, bachelor's degree in physical education (preferred). Additional exam requirements/recommendations for international students: Required—TOEFL. *Application deadline:* For fall admission, 7/1 for domestic students; for spring admission, 12/1 for domestic students. Applications are processed on a rolling basis. Application fee: $50. Electronic applications accepted. *Expenses:* Tuition, area resident: Full-time $4662; part-time $440 per credit. Tuition, state resident: full-time $6994; part-time $440 per credit. Tuition, nonresident: full-time $12,988; part-time $440 per credit. Required fees: $3606. One-time fee: $62 part-time. *Financial support:* In 2009–10, 11 students received support, including 8 research assistantships; career-related internships or fieldwork, Federal Work-Study, scholarships/grants, and unspecified assistantships also available. Support available to part-time students. Financial award application deadline: 3/1; financial award applicants required to submit FAFSA. *Faculty research:* Exercise science, athletic training, preparation of physical education for schools. *Unit head:* Dr. David Harackiewicz, Chair, 860-832-2155. *Application contact:* Dr. David Harackiewicz, Chair, 860-832-2155.

Central Michigan University, College of Graduate Studies, The Herbert H. and Grace A. Dow College of Health Professions, Department of Physical Education and Sport, Mount Pleasant, MI 48859. Offers physical education (MA), including athletic administration, coaching, exercise science, teaching; sport education (MA). Part-time programs available. *Degree requirements:* For master's, thesis or alternative. Electronic applications accepted. *Faculty research:* Athletic administration and sport management; performance enhancing substance use in sport; computer applications for sport managers; mental skill development for ultimate performance; teaching methods.

Chicago State University, School of Graduate and Professional Studies, College of Education, Department of Health, Physical Education and Recreation, Chicago, IL 60628. Offers physical

Physical Education

Chicago State University (continued)
education (MS Ed). Part-time and evening/weekend programs available. Postbaccalaureate distance learning degree programs offered. *Degree requirements:* For master's, thesis optional. *Entrance requirements:* For master's, minimum GPA of 2.75. *Faculty research:* Sports psychology, recreation and leisure studies administration.

The Citadel, The Military College of South Carolina, Citadel Graduate College, Department of Health, Exercise, and Sport Science, Charleston, SC 29409. Offers health, exercise, and sport science (MS); physical education (MAT). *Accreditation:* NCATE. Part-time and evening/weekend programs available. *Faculty:* 6 full-time (3 women), 2 part-time/adjunct (0 women). *Students:* 12 full-time (9 women), 49 part-time (22 women); includes 8 minority (6 African Americans, 1 American Indian/Alaska Native, 1 Hispanic American), 2 international. Average age 26. In 2009, 9 master's awarded. *Degree requirements:* For master's, comprehensive exam, thesis optional. *Entrance requirements:* For master's, GRE (minimum score 900) or MAT (minimum score 396), minimum undergraduate GPA of 2.5, 3 letters of recommendation, resume detailing previous work experience (for MS only). Additional exam requirements/recommendations for international students: Required—TOEFL (minimum score 550 paper-based; 213 computer-based; 79 iBT). *Application deadline:* Applications are processed on a rolling basis. Application fee: $30. Electronic applications accepted. *Expenses:* Tuition, state resident: part-time $400 per credit hour. Tuition, nonresident: part-time $657 per credit hour. Required fees: $40 per term. *Financial support:* Career-related internships or fieldwork, health care benefits, and unspecified assistantships available. Support available to part-time students. Financial award application deadline: 7/1; financial award applicants required to submit FAFSA. *Faculty research:* Risk management in sport and physical activity programs, legal aspects of sport (gender equity/interscholastic athletics), comparison of dietary habits of Greek vs. American hs students, school-wide physical activity programs, exercise intervention among HIV-infected individuals, exercise and dietary intervention among breast cancer survivors, factors influencing motor skill in SC physical education programs, physical activity influences on inflammation and risk of recurrent colorectal neoplasia. *Unit head:* Dr. John S. Carter, Department Head, 843-953-7953, Fax: 843-953-6798, E-mail: john.carter@citadel.edu. *Application contact:* Dr. Steve A. Nida, Associate Provost, The Citadel Graduate College, 843-953-5089, Fax: 843-953-7630, E-mail: cgc@citadel.edu.

Cleveland State University, College of Graduate Studies, College of Education and Human Services, Department of Health, Physical Education, Recreation and Dance, Cleveland, OH 44115. Offers community health education (M Ed); exercise science (M Ed); human performance (M Ed); physical education pedagogy (M Ed); public health (MPH); school health education (M Ed); sport and exercise psychology (M Ed); sports management (M Ed). Part-time programs available. *Degree requirements:* For master's, comprehensive exam, thesis optional. *Entrance requirements:* For master's, GRE General Test or MAT (if undergraduate GPA less than 2.75), minimum undergraduate GPA of 2.75. Additional exam requirements/recommendations for international students: Required—TOEFL (minimum score 525 paper-based; 197 computer-based), IELTS (minimum score 6). Electronic applications accepted. *Faculty research:* Bone density, marketing fitness centers, motor development of disabled, online learning and survey research.

The College at Brockport, State University of New York, School of Health and Human Performance, Department of Kinesiology, Sports Studies and Physical Education, Brockport, NY 14420-2997. Offers physical education (MS Ed), including adapted physical education, athletic administration, teacher education/pedagogy. Part-time programs available. *Students:* 14 full-time (12 women), 69 part-time (26 women); includes 4 minority (all Hispanic Americans). 36 applicants, 83% accepted, 30 enrolled. In 2009, 45 master's awarded. *Degree requirements:* For master's, thesis or alternative. *Entrance requirements:* For master's, minimum GPA of 3.0. Additional exam requirements/recommendations for international students: Required—TOEFL (minimum score 550 paper-based; 213 computer-based; 79 iBT). *Application deadline:* For fall admission, 3/15 priority date for domestic and international students; for spring admission, 10/15 priority date for domestic and international students. Application fee: $80. Electronic applications accepted. *Expenses:* Tuition, state resident: full-time $8370; part-time $349 per credit. Tuition, nonresident: full-time $13,250; part-time $522 per credit. *Financial support:* In 2009–10, 1 research assistantship with full tuition reimbursement (averaging $6,200 per year), 5 teaching assistantships with full tuition reimbursements (averaging $6,000 per year) were awarded; Federal Work-Study, scholarships/grants, and unspecified assistantships also available. Support available to part-time students. Financial award application deadline: 3/15; financial award applicants required to submit FAFSA. *Faculty research:* Athletic administration, adapted physical education, physical education curriculum, physical education teaching/coaching, children's physical activity. *Unit head:* Dr. Susan C. Petersen, Chairperson, 585-395-5332, Fax: 585-395-2771, E-mail: speterse@brockport.edu. *Application contact:* Dr. Alisa James, Graduate Program Director, 585-395-5330, Fax: 585-395-2771, E-mail: ajames@brockport.edu.

The College of New Jersey, Graduate Division, School of Nursing, Health and Exercise Science, Department of Health and Exercise Science, Program in Health Education, Ewing, NJ 08628. Offers health (MAT); physical education (M Ed). *Accreditation:* NCATE. Part-time programs available. *Students:* 2 full-time (0 women), 4 part-time (all women); includes 1 minority (Hispanic American). 5 applicants, 60% accepted. In 2009, 4 master's awarded. *Degree requirements:* For master's, comprehensive exam. *Entrance requirements:* For master's, GRE, minimum GPA of 3.0 in field or 2.75 overall. Additional exam requirements/recommendations for international students: Required—TOEFL. *Application deadline:* For fall admission, 2/1 priority date for domestic students; for spring admission, 10/1 priority date for domestic students. Application fee: $70. Electronic applications accepted. *Expenses:* Tuition, state resident: part-time $573.70 per credit. Tuition, nonresident: part-time $887.75 per credit. Required fees: $140.85 per credit. One-time fee: $10 part-time. *Financial support:* Tuition waivers (partial) and unspecified assistantships available. Financial award application deadline: 5/1; financial award applicants required to submit FAFSA. *Unit head:* Dr. Aristomen Chilakos, Coordinator, 609-771-3160, Fax: 609-637-5153, E-mail: chilako@tcnj.edu. *Application contact:* Susan L. Hydro, Assistant Dean, Office of Graduate Studies, 609-771-2300, Fax: 609-637-5105, E-mail: graduate@tcnj.edu.

The College of New Jersey, Graduate Division, School of Nursing, Health and Exercise Science, Department of Health and Exercise Science, Program in Physical Education, Ewing, NJ 08628. Offers M Ed, MAT. Part-time programs available. *Students:* 4 full-time (2 women), 4 part-time (3 women); includes 1 minority (African American). 9 applicants, 78% accepted. In 2009, 4 master's awarded. *Degree requirements:* For master's, comprehensive exam. *Entrance requirements:* For master's, GRE, minimum GPA of 2.75 overall or 3.0 in field. Additional exam requirements/recommendations for international students: Required—TOEFL. *Application deadline:* For fall admission, 2/1 priority date for domestic students; for spring admission, 10/1 priority date for domestic students. Application fee: $70. Electronic applications accepted. *Expenses:* Tuition, state resident: part-time $573.70 per credit. Tuition, nonresident: part-time $887.75 per credit. Required fees: $140.85 per credit. One-time fee: $10 part-time. *Financial support:* Tuition waivers (partial) and unspecified assistantships available. Financial award application deadline: 5/1; financial award applicants required to submit FAFSA. *Unit head:* Dr. Aristomen Chilakos, Coordinator, 609-771-3160, Fax: 609-637-5153, E-mail: chilako@tcnj.edu. *Application contact:* Susan L. Hydro, Assistant Dean, Office of Graduate Studies, 609-771-2300, Fax: 609-637-5105, E-mail: graduate@tcnj.edu.

Colorado State University–Pueblo, College of Education, Engineering and Professional Studies, Education Program, Pueblo, CO 81001-4901. Offers art education (M Ed); foreign language education (M Ed); health and physical education (M Ed); instructional technology (M Ed); linguistically diverse education (M Ed); music education (M Ed); special education (M Ed). *Accreditation:* Teacher Education Accreditation Council. Part-time programs available. *Degree requirements:* For master's, portfolio. *Entrance requirements:* For master's, 3 recommendations, teaching license. Additional exam requirements/recommendations for international students: Required—TOEFL (minimum score 500 paper-based; 173 computer-based). Electronic applications accepted. *Faculty research:* Portfolio assessment, math education, science education.

Columbus State University, Graduate Studies, College of Education and Health Professions, Department of Teacher Education, Columbus, GA 31907-5645. Offers accomplished teaching (M Ed); early childhood education (M Ed, Ed S); health administration (MPA); instructional technology (MS); middle grades education (M Ed, Ed S); physical education (M Ed); secondary education (M Ed, MAT, Ed S), including English/language arts (M Ed, Ed S), general science (M Ed), mathematics (M Ed), social science (M Ed); special education (M Ed), including behavior disorders, mental retardation. *Accreditation:* NCATE. Part-time and evening/weekend programs available. Postbaccalaureate distance learning degree programs offered (minimal on-campus study). *Faculty:* 18 full-time (15 women), 14 part-time/adjunct (10 women). *Students:* 146 full-time (113 women), 312 part-time (261 women); includes 142 minority (120 African Americans, 1 American Indian/Alaska Native, 8 Asian Americans or Pacific Islanders, 13 Hispanic Americans), 2 international. Average age 31. 248 applicants, 64% accepted, 114 enrolled. In 2009, 103 master's, 22 other advanced degrees awarded. *Degree requirements:* For master's, thesis, exit exam; for Ed S, thesis or alternative. *Entrance requirements:* For master's, GRE General Test, minimum GPA of 2.75; for Ed S, GRE General Test. Additional exam requirements/recommendations for international students: Required—TOEFL (minimum score 550 paper-based; 213 computer-based; 79 iBT). *Application deadline:* For fall admission, 5/1 priority date for domestic students, 5/1 for international students; for spring admission, 11/1 for domestic and international students. Applications are processed on a rolling basis. Application fee: $30. Electronic applications accepted. *Financial support:* In 2009–10, 305 students received support, including 36 research assistantships with partial tuition reimbursements available (averaging $3,000 per year); career-related internships or fieldwork, Federal Work-Study, institutionally sponsored loans, scholarships/grants, tuition waivers (partial), and unspecified assistantships also available. Support available to part-time students. Financial award application deadline: 5/1; financial award applicants required to submit FAFSA. *Unit head:* Dr. Deborah Gober, Acting Chair, 706-568-2255, Fax: 706-568-3134, E-mail: gober_deborah@colstate.edu. *Application contact:* Katie Thornton, Graduate Admissions Specialist, 706-568-2035, Fax: 706-568-2462, E-mail: thornton_katie@colstate.edu.

Concordia University, School of Arts and Sciences, Irvine, CA 92612-3299. Offers coaching and athletic administration (MA). Part-time and evening/weekend programs available. Postbaccalaureate distance learning degree programs offered. *Faculty:* 8 full-time (3 women), 19 part-time/adjunct (1 woman). *Students:* 236 full-time (42 women), 73 part-time (17 women); includes 50 minority (20 African Americans, 3 American Indian/Alaska Native, 4 Asian Americans or Pacific Islanders, 23 Hispanic Americans). Average age 34. 126 applicants, 100% accepted, 119 enrolled. In 2009, 85 master's awarded. *Degree requirements:* For master's, culminating project. *Entrance requirements:* Additional exam requirements/recommendations for international students: Required—TOEFL. *Application deadline:* For fall admission, 8/10 for domestic students, 6/1 for international students; for spring admission, 2/14 for domestic students, 10/1 for international students. Application fee: $50 ($125 for international students). Electronic applications accepted. *Expenses:* Tuition: Full-time $6000; part-time $400 per unit. One-time fee: $125. Tuition and fees vary according to campus/location and program. *Financial support:* In 2009–10, 271 students received support. Tuition waivers (full and partial) and unspecified assistantships available. Financial award applicants required to submit FAFSA. *Unit head:* Dr. Timothy Preuss, Dean, 949-854-8002 Ext. 1349, E-mail: tim.preuss@cui.edu. *Application contact:* Chris Lewis, Associate Director of Graduate Admissions, 877-854-1194, Fax: 949-854-6894, E-mail: chris.lewis@cui.edu.

Defiance College, Program in Education, Defiance, OH 43512-1610. Offers adolescent and young adult (MA); mild and moderate intervention specialist (MA); sport science (MA). Part-time programs available. *Degree requirements:* For master's, thesis (for some programs). *Entrance requirements:* For master's, teaching certificate.

Delta State University, Graduate Programs, College of Education, Division of Health, Physical Education and Recreation, Cleveland, MS 38733-0001. Offers physical education and recreation (M Ed). Part-time and evening/weekend programs available. *Degree requirements:* For master's, thesis optional. *Entrance requirements:* For master's, GRE General Test or MAT, Class A teaching certificate. *Expenses:* Tuition, state resident: full-time $4450; part-time $247 per credit hour. Tuition, nonresident: full-time $11,520; part-time $640 per credit hour. *Faculty research:* Blood pressure, body fat, power and reaction time, learning disorders for athletes, effects of walking.

DePaul University, School of Education, Chicago, IL 60106. Offers bilingual and bicultural education (M Ed, MA); curriculum studies (M Ed, MA, Ed D); educational leadership (M Ed, MA, Ed D), including administration and supervision (M Ed, MA), Catholic school leadership (M Ed, MA), physical education (M Ed, MA); human development and learning (MA); human services and counseling (M Ed, MA), including agencies, family concerns, and higher education, elementary schools, human services management, secondary schools; reading and learning disabilities (M Ed, MA); social culture studies in education and development (M Ed, MA), including curriculum studies/development; teaching and learning (early childhood, elementary and secondary) (M Ed), including elementary education (M Ed, MA), secondary education (M Ed, MA); teaching and learning (early childhood, elementary, and secondary) (MA), including elementary education (M Ed, MA), secondary education (M Ed, MA). *Accreditation:* NCATE. Part-time and evening/weekend programs available. *Faculty:* 61 full-time (40 women), 66 part-time/adjunct (41 women). *Students:* 799 full-time (779 women), 470 part-time (365 women); includes 319 minority (153 African Americans, 3 American Indian/Alaska Native, 48 Asian Americans or Pacific Islanders, 115 Hispanic Americans), 15 international. Average age 30. 635 applicants, 74% accepted, 318 enrolled. In 2009, 604 master's, 5 doctorates awarded. *Degree requirements:* For doctorate, thesis/dissertation. *Entrance requirements:* For master's, interview, minimum GPA of 2.75, 2 letters of recommendation; for doctorate, interview, master's degree, writing sample, 3 letters of recommendation. Additional exam requirements/recommendations for international students: Required—TOEFL (minimum score 550 paper-based; 213 computer-based; 80 iBT). *Application deadline:* Applications are processed on a rolling basis. Application fee: $40. Electronic applications accepted. *Expenses:* Tuition: Full-time $37,525; part-time $620 per credit hour. *Financial support:* In 2009–10, 14 research assistantships with tuition reimbursements (averaging $5,800 per year) were awarded; career-related internships or fieldwork also available. *Faculty research:* Reflective teaching, children at risk, loss, ethnicity, urban education. Total annual research expenditures: $1.6 million. *Unit head:* Dr. Marie Donovan, Dean, 773-325-7581, Fax: 773-325-7713, E-mail: mdonovan@depaul.edu. *Application contact:* Brandon Washington, Data Project Manager, 773-325-1152, Fax: 773-325-2270, E-mail: bwashin3@depaul.edu.

Eastern Kentucky University, The Graduate School, College of Education, Department of Curriculum and Instruction, Program in Secondary and Higher Education, Richmond, KY 40475-3102. Offers secondary education (MA Ed), including agricultural education, art education, biological sciences education, business education, English education, geography education, history education, home economics education, industrial education, mathematical sciences education, physical education, school health education. *Accreditation:* NCATE. Part-time programs available. *Entrance requirements:* For master's, GRE General Test, minimum GPA of 2.5.

Eastern Kentucky University, The Graduate School, College of Health Sciences, Department of Exercise and Sport Science, Richmond, KY 40475-3102. Offers exercise and sport science (MS); exercise and wellness (MS); sports administration (MS). Part-time programs available. *Entrance requirements:* For master's, GRE General Test (minimum score 700 verbal and quantitative), minimum GPA of 2.5 (for most), minimum GPA of 3.0 (analytical writing). *Faculty research:* Nutrition and exercise.

Eastern Michigan University, Graduate School, College of Health and Human Services, School of Health Promotion and Human Performance, Programs in Physical Education, Ypsilanti, MI 48197. Offers adapted physical education (MS); physical education pedagogy (MS). Part-time and evening/weekend programs available. Postbaccalaureate distance learning degree programs

offered (minimal on-campus study). *Students:* 9 part-time (3 women); includes 1 minority (African American). Average age 31. In 2009, 4 master's awarded. *Degree requirements:* For master's, thesis or independant study project and comprehensive exams. *Entrance requirements:* Additional exam requirements/recommendations for international students: Required—TOEFL. *Application deadline:* For fall admission, 8/1 for domestic students, 5/1 for international students; for winter admission, 12/1 for domestic students, 10/1 for international students; for spring admission, 4/15 for domestic students, 3/1 for international students. Applications are processed on a rolling basis. Application fee: $35. Tuition and fees vary according to course level. *Financial support:* Fellowships, research assistantships with full tuition reimbursements, teaching assistantships with full tuition reimbursements, career-related internships or fieldwork, Federal Work-Study, institutionally sponsored loans, scholarships/grants, tuition waivers (partial), and unspecified assistantships available. Support available to part-time students. Financial award applicants required to submit FAFSA. *Unit head:* Dr. Roberta Faust, Program Coordinator, 734-487-7210 Ext. 2712, Fax: 734-487-2024, E-mail: rfaust@emich.edu. *Application contact:* Dr. Roberta Faust, Program Coordinator, 734-487-7210 Ext. 2712, Fax: 734-487-2024, E-mail: rfaust@emich.edu.

Eastern New Mexico University, Graduate School, College of Education and Technology, Department of Health and Physical Education, Portales, NM 88130. Offers physical education (MS). Part-time programs available. *Faculty:* 2 full-time (both women), 1 (woman) part-time/adjunct. *Students:* 38 part-time (12 women); includes 12 minority (2 African Americans, 10 Hispanic Americans), 2 international. Average age 28. 28 applicants, 71% accepted, 15 enrolled. In 2009, 11 master's awarded. *Degree requirements:* For master's, comprehensive exam, thesis optional. *Entrance requirements:* For master's, minimum GPA of 3.0. Additional exam requirements/recommendations for international students: Required—TOEFL (minimum score 550 paper-based; 213 computer-based; 79 iBT), IELTS (minimum score 6). *Application deadline:* For fall admission, 7/20 priority date for domestic students, 6/20 priority date for international students. Applications are processed on a rolling basis. Application fee: $10. Electronic applications accepted. *Expenses:* Tuition, state resident: full-time $2922; part-time $121.75 per credit hour. Tuition, nonresident: full-time $8454; part-time $352.25 per credit hour. Required fees: $1038; $43.25 per credit hour. *Financial support:* In 2009–10, fellowships (averaging $1,025 per year), 1 research assistantship with tuition reimbursement (averaging $8,500 per year), 14 teaching assistantships with tuition reimbursements (averaging $8,500 per year) were awarded; career-related internships or fieldwork, tuition waivers (partial), and unspecified assistantships also available. Support available to part-time students. Financial award applicants required to submit FAFSA. *Unit head:* Dr. Sarah Wall, Graduate Coordinator, 575-562-2915, E-mail: sarah.wall@enmu.edu. *Application contact:* Dr. Sarah Wall, Graduate Coordinator, 575-562-2915, E-mail: sarah.wall@enmu.edu.

Eastern Washington University, Graduate Studies, College of Education and Human Development, Department of Physical Education, Health and Recreation, Cheney, WA 99004-2431. Offers exercise science (MS); sport and exercise psychology (MS); sports administration/pedagogy (MS). *Degree requirements:* For master's, comprehensive exam, thesis or alternative. *Entrance requirements:* For master's, minimum GPA of 3.0. *Expenses:* Tuition, state resident: full-time $7476; part-time $249 per quarter hour. Tuition, nonresident: full-time $18,030; part-time $601 per quarter hour. Required fees: $3.50 per quarter hour. $142 per quarter.

East Stroudsburg University of Pennsylvania, Graduate School, College of Health Sciences, Department of Exercise Science, East Stroudsburg, PA 18301-2999. Offers cardiac rehabilitation and exercise science (MS). Part-time and evening/weekend programs available. *Faculty:* 3 full-time (1 woman). *Students:* 38 full-time (18 women), 3 part-time (2 women); includes 1 minority (Hispanic American), 4 international. Average age 25. In 2009, 35 master's awarded. *Degree requirements:* For master's, comprehensive exam, thesis or alternative, computer literacy. *Entrance requirements:* Additional exam requirements/recommendations for international students: Required—TOEFL (minimum score 560 paper-based; 220 computer-based; 83 iBT). *Application deadline:* For fall admission, 7/31 priority date for domestic students, 5/1 priority date for international students; for spring admission, 11/30 for domestic students, 10/1 for international students. Applications are processed on a rolling basis. Application fee: $50. *Expenses:* Tuition, state resident: full-time $9942; part-time $387 per credit. Tuition, nonresident: full-time $14,240; part-time $619 per credit. *Financial support:* In 2009–10, 57 research assistantships with full and partial tuition reimbursements (averaging $1,749 per year) were awarded; Federal Work-Study and institutionally sponsored loans also available. Financial award application deadline: 3/1. *Unit head:* Dr. Shala Davis, Graduate Coordinator, 570-422-3302, Fax: 570-422-3616, E-mail: sdavis@po-box.esu.edu. *Application contact:* Kevin Quintero, Graduate Admissions Coordinator, 570-422-3890, Fax: 570-422-2711, E-mail: kquintero@po-box.esu.edu.

East Stroudsburg University of Pennsylvania, Graduate School, College of Health Sciences, Department of Physical Education, East Stroudsburg, PA 18301-2999. Offers health and physical education (M Ed). *Faculty:* 1 (woman) full-time. *Students:* 2 full-time (1 woman), 6 part-time (3 women); includes 1 minority (African American). Average age 35. In 2009, 11 master's awarded. *Degree requirements:* For master's, computer literacy, portfolio exhibition as exiting research project. *Entrance requirements:* For master's, teacher certification in physical education or health and physical education. Additional exam requirements/recommendations for international students: Required—TOEFL (minimum score 560 paper-based; 220 computer-based; 83 iBT), or IELTS. *Application deadline:* For fall admission, 7/31 for domestic students, 5/1 for international students; for spring admission, 11/30 for domestic students, 10/1 for international students. Applications are processed on a rolling basis. Application fee: $50. *Expenses:* Tuition, state resident: full-time $9942; part-time $387 per credit. Tuition, nonresident: full-time $14,240; part-time $619 per credit. *Financial support:* Federal Work-Study and unspecified assistantships available. Financial award application deadline: 3/1; financial award applicants required to submit FAFSA. *Unit head:* Dr. Caroline Kuchinski, Graduate Admissions Coordinator, 570-422-3293, Fax: 570-422-3824, E-mail: ckuchinski@po-box.esu.edu. *Application contact:* Kevin Quintero, Graduate Admissions Coordinator, 570-422-3890, Fax: 570-422-2711, E-mail: kquintero@po-box.esu.edu.

East Tennessee State University, School of Graduate Studies, College of Education, Department of Physical Education, Exercise and Sport Sciences, Johnson City, TN 37614. Offers exercise physiology (MA); fitness leadership (MA); physical education (M Ed, MA); sports management (MA); sports sciences (MA). Part-time and evening/weekend programs available. *Degree requirements:* For master's, comprehensive exam (M Ed), oral and written comprehensive exams, thesis (MA). *Entrance requirements:* For master's, GRE General Test, major or minor in physical education or equivalent, interview, minimum GPA of 2.7. Additional exam requirements/recommendations for international students: Required—TOEFL (minimum score 550 paper-based; 213 computer-based). *Faculty research:* Resistance training for various populations, self actualization using challenging courses, park and recreation industry needs relative to recent university graduates, funding sport operations.

Emporia State University, School of Graduate Studies, The Teachers College, Department of Health, Physical Education and Recreation, Emporia, KS 66801-5087. Offers physical education (MS). Part-time programs available. Postbaccalaureate distance learning degree programs offered (no on-campus study). *Faculty:* 16 full-time (10 women), 2 part-time/adjunct (both women). *Students:* 19 full-time (10 women), 167 part-time (59 women); includes 13 minority (5 African Americans, 3 American Indian/Alaska Native, 1 Asian American or Pacific Islander, 4 Hispanic Americans), 1 international. In 2009, 74 master's awarded. *Degree requirements:* For master's, comprehensive exam or thesis. *Entrance requirements:* For master's, bachelor's degree in physical education, health, and recreation; letters of recommendation. Additional exam requirements/recommendations for international students: Required—TOEFL (minimum score 520 paper-based; 133 computer-based; 68 iBT). *Application deadline:* For fall admission, 8/15 priority date for domestic students. Applications are processed on a rolling basis. Application fee: $30 ($75 for international students). Electronic applications accepted. *Expenses:* Tuition, state resident: full-time $4154; part-time $173 per credit hour. Tuition, nonresident: full-time $12,864; part-time $536 per credit hour. Required fees: $948; $58 per credit hour. Tuition and fees vary according to campus/location. *Financial support:* In 2009–10, 5 teaching assistant-

ships with full tuition reimbursements (averaging $7,059 per year) were awarded; career-related internships or fieldwork, Federal Work-Study, institutionally sponsored loans, health care benefits, and unspecified assistantships also available. Financial award application deadline: 3/15; financial award applicants required to submit FAFSA. *Unit head:* Dr. Kathy Ermler, Chair, 620-341-5926, E-mail: kermler@emporia.edu. *Application contact:* Dr. Kathy Ermler, Chair, 620-341-5926, E-mail: kermler@emporia.edu.

Florida Agricultural and Mechanical University, Division of Graduate Studies, Research, and Continuing Education, College of Education, Department of Health, Physical Education, and Recreation, Tallahassee, FL 32307-3200. Offers M Ed, MS Ed. *Accreditation:* NCATE. Part-time and evening/weekend programs available. *Faculty:* 10 full-time (6 women). *Students:* 11 full-time (9 women), 3 part-time (2 women); all minorities (all African Americans). In 2009, 2 master's awarded. *Degree requirements:* For master's, thesis optional. *Entrance requirements:* For master's, GRE General Test, minimum GPA of 3.0. Additional exam requirements/recommendations for international students: Required—TOEFL. *Application deadline:* For fall admission, 5/18 for domestic students, 12/18 for international students; for spring admission, 11/12 for domestic students, 5/12 for international students. Application fee: $20. *Financial support:* Teaching assistantships, Federal Work-Study and institutionally sponsored loans available. *Faculty research:* Administration/curriculum, work behavior, psychology. *Unit head:* Dr. E. Newton Jackson, Chairperson, 850-599-3135. *Application contact:* Dr. Chanta M. Haywood, Dean of Graduate Studies, Research, and Continuing Education, 850-599-3315, Fax: 850-599-3727.

Florida International University, College of Education, Department of Curriculum and Instruction, Miami, FL 33199. Offers art education (MAT, MS, Ed D); curriculum and instruction (Ed S); curriculum development (MS); curriculum studies (PhD); early childhood education (MS, Ed D); elementary education (MS, Ed D); English education (MAT, MS, Ed D); foreign language education—teaching English to speakers of other languages (TESOL) (Certificate), including foreign language education; foreign language education– teaching English to speakers of other languages (TESOL) (MS), including teaching English; French education—initial teacher preparation (MAT); international and intercultural development education (Ed D); international and intercultural developmental education (MS); language, literacy and culture (PhD); learning technologies (MS, Ed D, PhD); mathematics education (MAT, MS, Ed D, PhD); modern language education/bilingual education (MS, Ed D); physical education (MS); reading education (MS, Ed D); science education (MAT, MS, Ed D, PhD); social studies education (MAT, MS, Ed D); Spanish education—initial teacher preparation (MAT); special education (MS). Part-time and evening/weekend programs available. *Degree requirements:* For doctorate, comprehensive exam, thesis/dissertation. *Entrance requirements:* For master's, GRE General Test, Florida General Knowledge Test or Florida College Level Academic Skills Test; for doctorate and other advanced degree, GRE General Test. Additional exam requirements/recommendations for international students: Required—TOEFL (minimum score 550 paper-based; 213 computer-based; 80 iBT), IELTS (minimum score 6.3). Electronic applications accepted. *Expenses:* Tuition, state resident: full-time $8008; part-time $4004 per year. Tuition, nonresident: full-time $20,104; part-time $10,052 per year. Required fees: $298; $149 per term.

Florida International University, College of Education, Department of Health, Physical Education, and Recreation, Program in Physical Education, Miami, FL 33199. Offers advanced teacher preparation (MS); sports management (MS). Part-time and evening/weekend programs available. *Entrance requirements:* For master's, GRE General Test or minimum GPA of 3.0, teaching certificate in physical education. Additional exam requirements/recommendations for international students: Required—TOEFL (minimum score 550 paper-based; 213 computer-based; 80 iBT), IELTS (minimum score 6.3). Electronic applications accepted. *Expenses:* Tuition, state resident: full-time $8008; part-time $4004 per year. Tuition, nonresident: full-time $20,104; part-time $10,052 per year. Required fees: $298; $149 per term.

Florida State University, The Graduate School, College of Education, Department of Sport Management, Tallahassee, FL 32306. Offers MS, Ed D, PhD. *Faculty:* 14 full-time (8 women), 1 (woman) part-time/adjunct. *Students:* 117 full-time (42 women), 49 part-time (20 women); includes 28 minority (15 African Americans, 1 American Indian/Alaska Native, 5 Asian Americans or Pacific Islanders, 7 Hispanic Americans), 24 international. 166 applicants, 66% accepted, 58 enrolled. In 2009, 30 master's, 1 doctorate awarded. *Degree requirements:* For master's, comprehensive exam, thesis optional; for doctorate, comprehensive exam, thesis/dissertation. *Entrance requirements:* For master's and doctorate, GRE General Test, minimum GPA of 3.0. Additional exam requirements/recommendations for international students: Required—TOEFL (minimum score 550 paper-based; 213 computer-based; 80 iBT). *Application deadline:* For fall admission, 7/1 priority date for domestic students, 7/1 for international students; for spring admission, 11/1 for domestic and international students. Applications are processed on a rolling basis. Application fee: $30. Electronic applications accepted. *Expenses:* Tuition, state resident: full-time $7413. Tuition, nonresident: full-time $22,567. *Financial support:* In 2009–10, 2 fellowships with full and partial tuition reimbursements, 51 research assistantships with full and partial tuition reimbursements, 15 teaching assistantships with full and partial tuition reimbursements were awarded; career-related internships or fieldwork and Federal Work-Study also available. Financial award applicants required to submit FAFSA. *Faculty research:* Sport marketing, gender issues in sport, finances in sport industry, coaching. *Unit head:* Dr. Jeffrey James, Chair, 850-644-9214, Fax: 850-644-0975, E-mail: jdjames@fsu.edu. *Application contact:* Cynthia Bailey, Program Assistant, 850-644-4813, Fax: 850-644-0975, E-mail: bailey@coe.fsu.edu.

Fort Hays State University, Graduate School, College of Health and Life Sciences, Department of Health and Human Performance, Hays, KS 67601-4099. Offers MS. Part-time programs available. *Degree requirements:* For master's, comprehensive exam, thesis optional. *Entrance requirements:* For master's, GRE General Test or MAT. Additional exam requirements/recommendations for international students: Required—TOEFL (minimum score 550 paper-based; 213 computer-based). Electronic applications accepted. *Faculty research:* Isoproterenol hydrochloride and exercise, dehydrogenase and high-density lipoprotein levels in athletics, venous blood parameters to adipose fat.

Gardner-Webb University, Graduate School, Department of Physical Education, Wellness, and Sport Studies, Boiling Springs, NC 28017. Offers sport science and pedagogy (MA). Part-time and evening/weekend programs available. *Faculty:* 2 full-time (0 women). *Students:* 7 full-time (3 women), 9 part-time (5 women); includes 2 minority (both African Americans). Average age 26. 11 applicants, 100% accepted, 11 enrolled. In 2009, 8 master's awarded. *Degree requirements:* For master's, comprehensive exam. *Entrance requirements:* For master's, GRE General Test or NTE, PRAXIS, minimum GPA of 2.5. *Application deadline:* For fall admission, 8/1 priority date for domestic students. Applications are processed on a rolling basis. Application fee: $25. Electronic applications accepted. *Expenses:* Tuition: Part-time $305 per credit hour. *Financial support:* Unspecified assistantships available. *Unit head:* Dr. Ken Baker, Chair, 704-406-4481, Fax: 704-406-4739. *Application contact:* Dr. Franki Burch, Dean, Graduate School, 704-406-4724, Fax: 704-406-4329, E-mail: gradschool@gardner-webb.edu.

Georgia College & State University, Graduate School, College of Health Sciences, Department of Kinesiology, Milledgeville, GA 31061. Offers health promotion (M Ed); human performance (M Ed); kinesiology (MAT); outdoor education (M Ed). *Accreditation:* NCATE (one or more programs are accredited). Part-time and evening/weekend programs available. *Faculty:* 12 full-time (5 women). *Students:* 25 full-time (13 women), 7 part-time (5 women); includes 4 minority (2 African Americans, 2 Hispanic Americans), 3 international. Average age 26. 23 applicants, 87% accepted, 19 enrolled. In 2009, 7 master's awarded. *Degree requirements:* For master's, thesis optional. *Entrance requirements:* For master's, GRE General Test or MAT, minimum GPA of 2.75 in upper-level undergraduate courses, 2 letters of reference. Additional exam requirements/recommendations for international students: Recommended—TOEFL (minimum score 550 paper-based; 213 computer-based; 79 iBT). *Application deadline:* For fall admission, 7/15 priority date for domestic students; for spring admission, 11/15 for domestic students. Applications are processed on a rolling basis. Application fee: $40. Electronic applica-

Physical Education

Georgia College & State University (continued)
tions accepted. *Expenses:* Tuition, area resident: Part-time $241 per credit hour. Tuition, state resident: full-time $4338. Tuition, nonresident: full-time $17,352; part-time $964 per credit hour. Required fees: $609 per semester. Tuition and fees vary according to course load and campus/location. *Financial support:* In 2009–10, 20 research assistantships with full tuition reimbursements were awarded; career-related internships or fieldwork and unspecified assistantships also available. Support available to part-time students. Financial award applicants required to submit FAFSA. *Unit head:* Dr. Jude Hirsch, Chair, 478-445-4072, Fax: 478-445-1790, E-mail: jude.hirsch@gcsu.edu. *Application contact:* Dr. Jude Hirsch, Chair, 478-445-4072, Fax: 478-445-1790, E-mail: jude.hirsch@gcsu.edu.

Georgia Southern University, Jack N. Averitt College of Graduate Studies, College of Education, Department of Teaching and Learning, Program in Health and Physical Education, Statesboro, GA 30460. Offers M Ed. *Accreditation:* NCATE. Part-time and evening/weekend programs available. In 2009, 4 master's awarded. *Degree requirements:* For master's, comprehensive exam. *Entrance requirements:* For master's, GRE General Test or MAT, minimum GPA of 2.5. Additional exam requirements/recommendations for international students: Required—TOEFL (minimum score 550 paper-based; 213 computer-based; 80 iBT). *Application deadline:* For fall admission, 3/1 priority date for domestic and international students; for spring admission, 10/1 priority date for domestic students, 10/1 for international students. Applications are processed on a rolling basis. Application fee: $50. Electronic applications accepted. *Expenses:* Tuition, state resident: full-time $5040; part-time $210 per credit hour. Tuition, nonresident: full-time $20,136; part-time $839 per credit hour. Required fees: $1644. *Financial support:* In 2009–10, research assistantships with partial tuition reimbursements (averaging $6,850 per year), teaching assistantships with partial tuition reimbursements (averaging $6,850 per year) were awarded; career-related internships or fieldwork, Federal Work-Study, and tuition waivers (partial) also available. Support available to part-time students. Financial award application deadline: 4/15; financial award applicants required to submit FAFSA. *Unit head:* Dr. Tony Pritchard, Coordinator, 912-478-1323, Fax: 912-478-0026, E-mail: tpritchard@georgiasouthern.edu. *Application contact:* 912-478-5384, Fax: 912-478-0740, E-mail: gradadmissions@georgiasouthern.edu.

Georgia Southwestern State University, Graduate Studies, School of Education, Americus, GA 31709-4693. Offers early childhood education (M Ed, Ed S); health and physical education (M Ed); middle grades education (M Ed, Ed S); reading (M Ed); secondary education (M Ed); special education (M Ed). *Accreditation:* NCATE. *Degree requirements:* For master's, comprehensive exam. *Entrance requirements:* For master's, GRE General Test or MAT, minimum GPA of 2.5; for Ed S, GRE General Test or MAT, minimum graduate GPA of 3.25, M Ed from accredited college or university, 3 years teaching experience. Electronic applications accepted.

Georgia State University, College of Education, Department of Kinesiology and Health, Program in Health and Physical Education, Atlanta, GA 30302-3083. Offers M Ed. Part-time and evening/weekend programs available. *Degree requirements:* For master's, comprehensive exam. *Entrance requirements:* For master's, GRE General Test, minimum GPA of 2.5. *Faculty research:* Exercise science, teacher behavior.

Henderson State University, Graduate Studies, School of Education, Department of Health, Physical Education, Recreation and Athletic Training, Arkadelphia, AR 71999-0001. Offers recreation (MS); sports administration (MS). Part-time programs available. *Faculty:* 4 full-time (1 woman). *Students:* 16 full-time (3 women), 27 part-time (12 women); includes 10 minority (8 African Americans, 2 Hispanic Americans), 6 international. Average age 27. 17 applicants, 100% accepted, 17 enrolled. In 2009, 26 master's awarded. *Entrance requirements:* For master's, GRE General Test or MAT, minimum GPA of 2.7. Additional exam requirements/recommendations for international students: Required—TOEFL (minimum score 550 paper-based; 213 computer-based); Recommended—IELTS (minimum score 6). *Application deadline:* For fall admission, 8/1 priority date for domestic students, 6/30 priority date for international students; for spring admission, 1/1 priority date for domestic students, 11/30 priority date for international students. Application fee: $25 ($75 for international students). Electronic applications accepted. *Expenses:* Tuition, state resident: full-time $3798; part-time $211 per credit hour. Tuition, nonresident: full-time $7596; part-time $422 per credit hour. Required fees: $903. *Unit head:* Dr. Lynn Glover-Stanley, Chair, 870-230-5200, E-mail: stanlel@hsu.edu. *Application contact:* Dr. Marck L. Beggs, Graduate Dean, 870-230-5126, Fax: 870-230-5479, E-mail: beggsm@hsu.edu.

Hofstra University, School of Education, Health, and Human Services, Department of Curriculum and Teaching, Program in Learning and Teaching, Hempstead, NY 11549. Offers learning and teaching (Ed D), including applied linguistics, art education, arts and humanities, early childhood education, English education, human development, math education, math, science, and technology, multicultural education, physical education, science education, social studies education, special education. Part-time and evening/weekend programs available. *Students:* 5 full-time (all women), 21 part-time (17 women); includes 2 minority (1 African American, 1 Hispanic American), 1 international. Average age 38. 22 applicants, 68% accepted, 11 enrolled. *Degree requirements:* For doctorate, comprehensive exam, thesis/dissertation. *Entrance requirements:* For doctorate, GRE, 3 letters of recommendation, interview, 2 years full-time teaching experience. Additional exam requirements/recommendations for international students: Required—TOEFL (minimum score 550 paper-based; 213 computer-based; 80 iBT). *Application deadline:* Applications are processed on a rolling basis. Application fee: $60. Electronic applications accepted. *Expenses:* Tuition: Full-time $16,200; part-time $900 per credit hour. Required fees: $970; $145 per term. Tuition and fees vary according to program. *Financial support:* In 2009–10, 24 students received support, including 20 fellowships with full and partial tuition reimbursements available (averaging $4,906 per year); research assistantships with full and partial tuition reimbursements available, Federal Work-Study, institutionally sponsored loans, scholarships/grants, and tuition waivers (full and partial) also available. Support available to part-time students. Financial award applicants required to submit FAFSA. *Faculty research:* Critical thinking, professional development, teacher quality, quantitative research. *Unit head:* Dr. Bruce A. Torff, Director, 516-463-5803, Fax: 516-463-6196, E-mail: catajs@hofstra.edu. *Application contact:* Carol Drummer, Dean of Graduate Admissions, 516-463-4876, Fax: 516-463-4664, E-mail: gradstudent@hofstra.edu.

Hofstra University, School of Education, Health, and Human Services, Department of Physical Education and Sports Sciences, Hempstead, NY 11549. Offers physical education (MA, MS), including adventure education, curriculum (MA), strength and conditioning; sport science (MS), including adventure education (MA, MS), strength and conditioning (MA, MS). Part-time and evening/weekend programs available. *Faculty:* 6 full-time (3 women), 11 part-time/adjunct (5 women). *Students:* 76 full-time (23 women), 28 part-time (11 women); includes 8 minority (5 African Americans, 3 Hispanic Americans). Average age 28. 47 applicants, 89% accepted, 29 enrolled. In 2009, 25 master's awarded. *Degree requirements:* For master's, electronic portfolio, capstone project. *Entrance requirements:* For master's, 2 letters of recommendation, interview. Additional exam requirements/recommendations for international students: Required—TOEFL (minimum score 550 paper-based; 213 computer-based; 80 iBT). *Application deadline:* Applications are processed on a rolling basis. Application fee: $60. Electronic applications accepted. *Expenses:* Tuition: Full-time $16,200; part-time $900 per credit hour. Required fees: $970; $145 per term. Tuition and fees vary according to program. *Financial support:* In 2009–10, 30 students received support, including 9 fellowships with full and partial tuition reimbursements available (averaging $2,944 per year), 4 research assistantships with full and partial tuition reimbursements available (averaging $16,784 per year); Federal Work-Study, institutionally sponsored loans, scholarships/grants, and tuition waivers (full and partial) also available. Support available to part-time students. Financial award applicants required to submit FAFSA. *Faculty research:* After school programming; energy expenditures in physical activities; group cohesion; childhood obesity. Total annual research expenditures: $8,500. *Unit head:* Dr. Nancy E. Halliday, Chairperson, 516-463-5811, Fax: 516-463-6275, E-mail: hprneh@hofstra.edu. *Application contact:* Carol Drummer, Dean of Graduate Admissions, 516-463-4876, Fax: 516-463-4664, E-mail: gradstudent@hofstra.edu.

Howard University, Graduate School, Department of Health, Human Performance and Leisure Studies, Washington, DC 20059-0002. Offers exercise physiology (MS); health education (MS); sports studies (MS), including sociology of sports, sports management; urban recreation (MS), including leisure studies. Part-time and evening/weekend programs available. *Degree requirements:* For master's, comprehensive exam, thesis. *Entrance requirements:* For master's, BS in human performance or related field. Electronic applications accepted. *Faculty research:* Health promotion, cardiovascular hypertension, physical activity, sport and human rights issues.

Humboldt State University, Graduate Studies, College of Professional Studies, Department of Kinesiology, Arcata, CA 95521-8299. Offers athletic training education (MS); exercise science/wellness management (MS); pre-physical therapy (MS); teaching/coaching (MS). *Students:* 24 full-time (13 women), 8 part-time (5 women); includes 5 minority (2 African Americans, 1 American Indian/Alaska Native, 2 Hispanic Americans). Average age 30. 25 applicants, 80% accepted, 15 enrolled. In 2009, 4 master's awarded. *Degree requirements:* For master's, thesis or alternative. *Entrance requirements:* For master's, GMAT, minimum GPA of 2.5. Additional exam requirements/recommendations for international students: Required—TOEFL. *Application deadline:* For fall admission, 6/1 for domestic students; for spring admission, 12/2 for domestic students. Applications are processed on a rolling basis. Application fee: $55. *Expenses:* Tuition, nonresident: full-time $8928. Required fees: $6102. Tuition and fees vary according to program. *Financial support:* Teaching assistantships, career-related internships or fieldwork, Federal Work-Study, and institutionally sponsored loans available. Financial award application deadline: 3/1; financial award applicants required to submit FAFSA. *Faculty research:* Human performance, adapted physical education, physical therapy. *Unit head:* Dr. Kathy Munoz, Chair, 707-826-3840, Fax: 707-826-5451, E-mail: kdm1@humboldt.edu. *Application contact:* Dr. T. K. Koesterer, Coordinator, 707-826-5967, Fax: 707-826-5451, E-mail: tjk17@humboldt.edu.

Idaho State University, Office of Graduate Studies, College of Education, Department of Sports Science and Physical Education, Pocatello, ID 83209-8105. Offers physical education (MPE). Part-time programs available. *Faculty:* 4 full-time (1 woman). *Students:* 20 full-time (9 women), 49 part-time (17 women); includes 7 minority (2 African Americans, 1 American Indian/Alaska Native, 2 Asian Americans or Pacific Islanders, 2 Hispanic Americans), 2 international. Average age 31. In 2009, 24 master's awarded. *Degree requirements:* For master's, comprehensive exam (for some programs), thesis optional, internship, oral defense of dissertation, or written exams. *Entrance requirements:* For master's, MAT or GRE General Test, minimum GPA of 3.0 in upper division classes. Additional exam requirements/recommendations for international students: Required—TOEFL (minimum score 550 paper-based; 213 computer-based; 80 iBT). *Application deadline:* For fall admission, 7/1 for domestic students, 6/1 for international students; for spring admission, 12/1 for domestic students, 11/1 for international students. Applications are processed on a rolling basis. Application fee: $55. Electronic applications accepted. *Expenses:* Tuition, state resident: full-time $3318; part-time $297 per credit hour. Tuition, nonresident: full-time $13,120; part-time $437 per credit hour. Required fees: $2530. Tuition and fees vary according to program. *Financial support:* Teaching assistantships with full and partial tuition reimbursements, career-related internships or fieldwork, Federal Work-Study, institutionally sponsored loans, scholarships/grants, health care benefits, tuition waivers (full and partial), and unspecified assistantships available. Support available to part-time students. Financial award application deadline: 1/1; financial award applicants required to submit FAFSA. *Faculty research:* Gender and diversity; concussion awareness/sports medicine; legal aspects of athletic health care; sports psychology; exercise physiology; sports management and leadership; adapted activities; fitness, wellness, and nutrition; coaching perspectives; critical features of athletic activities. *Unit head:* Dr. Michael Lester, Chair, 208-282-2657, Fax: 208-282-4697, E-mail: lestmich@isu.edu. *Application contact:* Dr. Peter Denner, Assistant Dean, 208-282-3807, Fax: 208-282-4697, E-mail: dennpete@isu.edu.

Illinois State University, Graduate School, College of Applied Science and Technology, School of Kinesiology and Recreation, Normal, IL 61790-2200. Offers health education (MS); physical education (MS). *Degree requirements:* For master's, thesis or alternative. *Entrance requirements:* For master's, GRE General Test, minimum GPA of 2.6 in last 60 hours of course work. *Faculty research:* Influences on positive youth development through sport, country-wide health fitness project, graduate practicum in athletic training, perceived exertion and self-selected intensity during resistance exercise in younger and older.

Indiana State University, School of Graduate Studies, College of Nursing, Health and Human Services, Department of Physical Education, Terre Haute, IN 47809. Offers adult fitness (MA, MS); coaching (MA, MS); exercise science (MA, MS). *Degree requirements:* For master's, thesis (for some programs). *Entrance requirements:* For master's, minor in physical education. Electronic applications accepted. *Faculty research:* Exercise science.

Indiana University Bloomington, School of Health, Physical Education and Recreation, Department of Kinesiology, Bloomington, IN 47405-7000. Offers adapted physical education (MS); applied sport science (MS); athletic administration/sport management (MS); athletic training (MS); biomechanics (MS); ergonomics (MS); exercise physiology (MS); fitness management (MS); human performance (PhD); motor learning/control (MS). Part-time programs available. *Faculty:* 28 full-time (11 women). *Students:* 132 full-time (55 women), 37 part-time (7 women); includes 16 minority (13 African Americans, 1 Asian American or Pacific Islander, 2 Hispanic Americans), 29 international. Average age 28. 179 applicants, 60% accepted, 72 enrolled. In 2009, 59 master's awarded. Terminal master's awarded for partial completion of doctoral program. *Degree requirements:* For master's, thesis optional; for doctorate, variable foreign language requirement, thesis/dissertation. *Entrance requirements:* For master's, GRE General Test, minimum GPA of 2.8; for doctorate, GRE General Test, minimum graduate GPA of 3.5, undergraduate 3.0. *Application deadline:* For fall admission, 1/1 for international students; for spring admission, 9/1 for international students. Applications are processed on a rolling basis. Application fee: $55 ($65 for international students). *Financial support:* In 2009–10, 71 students received support, including 9 fellowships (averaging $1,400 per year), 28 research assistantships with full tuition reimbursements available (averaging $10,131 per year), 38 teaching assistantships with full tuition reimbursements available (averaging $10,390 per year); career-related internships or fieldwork, Federal Work-Study, institutionally sponsored loans, scholarships/grants, tuition waivers (partial), and fee remissions also available. Financial award application deadline: 3/1. *Faculty research:* Exercise physiology and biochemistry, sports biomechanics, human motor control, adaptation of fitness and exercise to special populations. *Unit head:* Dr. Donetta Cothran, Chairperson, 812-855-3114. *Application contact:* Program Office, 812-855-5523, Fax: 812-855-9417, E-mail: kines@indiana.edu.

Indiana University of Pennsylvania, School of Graduate Studies and Research, College of Health and Human Services, Department of Health and Physical Education, Indiana, PA 15705-1087. Offers aquatics administration and facilities management (MS); exercise science (MS); sport management (MS); sport science (MS). Part-time programs available. *Faculty:* 8 full-time (4 women). *Students:* 55 full-time (24 women), 33 part-time (10 women); includes 8 minority (all African Americans), 14 international. Average age 25. 154 applicants, 48% accepted, 48 enrolled. In 2009, 54 master's awarded. *Degree requirements:* For master's, thesis optional. *Entrance requirements:* For master's, 2 letters of recommendation. Additional exam requirements/recommendations for international students: Required—TOEFL. *Application deadline:* For fall admission, 7/1 priority date for domestic students; for spring admission, 11/1 for domestic students. Applications are processed on a rolling basis. Application fee: $40. *Expenses:* Tuition, state resident: full-time $6666; part-time $370 per credit hour. Tuition, nonresident: full-time $10,666; part-time $593 per credit hour. Required fees: $813 per semester. *Financial support:* In 2009–10, 1 fellowship (averaging $500 per year), 16 research assistantships with full and partial tuition reimbursements (averaging $4,335 per year) were awarded. Financial award application deadline: 3/15; financial award applicants required to submit FAFSA. *Unit head:* Dr. Elaine Blair, Chairperson, 724-357-2770, E-mail: eblair@iup.edu. *Application contact:* Dr. Elaine Blair, Chairperson, 724-357-2770, E-mail: eblair@iup.edu.

Indiana University–Purdue University Indianapolis, School of Physical Education and Tourism Management, Indianapolis, IN 46202-2896. Offers physical education (MS). *Faculty:* 4

full-time (2 women). *Students:* 9 full-time (2 women), 12 part-time (4 women); includes 1 minority (African American). Average age 33. 14 applicants, 79% accepted, 8 enrolled. In 2009, 5 master's awarded. Application fee: $55 ($65 for international students). *Financial support:* Career-related internships or fieldwork, Federal Work-Study, institutionally sponsored loans, and scholarships/grants available. Support available to part-time students. *Application contact:* Dr. Sherry Queener, Director, Graduate Studies and Associate Dean, 317-274-1577, Fax: 317-278-2380.

Inter American University of Puerto Rico, Metropolitan Campus, Graduate Programs, Program in Physical Education, San Juan, PR 00919-1293. Offers teaching of physical education (MA); training and sport performance (MA). *Degree requirements:* For master's, comprehensive exam. *Entrance requirements:* For master's, GRE or EXADEP, interview. Electronic applications accepted.

Inter American University of Puerto Rico, San Germán Campus, Graduate Studies Center, Program in Physical Education and Scientific Analysis of Human Body Movement, San Germán, PR 00683-5008. Offers MA. Part-time and evening/weekend programs available. *Degree requirements:* For master's, comprehensive exam. *Entrance requirements:* For master's, GRE General Test or EXADEP, minimum GPA of 3.0.

Ithaca College, Division of Graduate and Professional Studies, School of Health Sciences and Human Performance, Program in Physical Education, Ithaca, NY 14850. Offers MS. Part-time programs available. *Faculty:* 8 full-time (6 women), 1 (woman) part-time/adjunct. *Students:* 3 full-time (1 woman). Average age 21. 5 applicants, 60% accepted, 3 enrolled. In 2009, 1 master's awarded. *Degree requirements:* For master's, comprehensive exam (for some programs), thesis optional. *Entrance requirements:* For master's, GRE General Test, minimum GPA of 3.0. Additional exam requirements/recommendations for international students: Required—TOEFL (minimum score 550 paper-based; 213 computer-based; 80 iBT). *Application deadline:* For fall admission, 3/1 for domestic and international students; for spring admission, 12/1 for domestic and international students. Applications are processed on a rolling basis. Application fee: $40. Electronic applications accepted. *Expenses:* Contact institution. *Financial support:* In 2009–10, 2 students received support, including 2 teaching assistantships (averaging $5,630 per year); career-related internships or fieldwork, Federal Work-Study, scholarships/grants, and unspecified assistantships also available. Support available to part-time students. Financial award application deadline: 3/1; financial award applicants required to submit CSS PROFILE or FAFSA. *Faculty research:* Needs assessment evaluation of health education programs, minority health (includes diversity), employee health assessment and program planning, youth at risk/families, multicultural/international health, program planning/health behaviors, sexuality education in the family and school setting, parent-teacher and student-teacher relationships, attitude/interest/motivation, teaching effectiveness, student learning/achievement. *Unit head:* Dr. Srijana Bajracharya, Chairperson, 607-274-3527, Fax: 607-274-1263, E-mail: gps@ithaca.edu. *Application contact:* Rob Gearhart, Dean, Graduate and Professional Studies, 607-274-3527, Fax: 607-274-1263, E-mail: gps@ithaca.edu.

Jackson State University, Graduate School, School of Education, Department of Health, Physical Education and Recreation, Jackson, MS 39217. Offers MS Ed. *Accreditation:* NCATE. Part-time and evening/weekend programs available. *Degree requirements:* For master's, comprehensive exam, thesis or alternative. *Entrance requirements:* For master's, GRE General Test. Additional exam requirements/recommendations for international students: Required—TOEFL.

Jacksonville State University, College of Graduate Studies and Continuing Education, College of Education and Professional Studies, Program in Health and Physical Education, Jacksonville, AL 36265-1602. Offers MS Ed. *Accreditation:* NCATE. Part-time and evening/weekend programs available. *Degree requirements:* For master's, comprehensive exam, thesis (for some programs). *Entrance requirements:* For master's, GRE General Test or MAT. Electronic applications accepted.

Kent State University, Graduate School of Education, Health, and Human Services, School of Health Sciences, Program in Physical Education, Kent, OH 44242-0001. Offers exercise physiology (PhD). *Faculty:* 4 full-time (2 women). *Students:* 21 full-time (8 women), 4 part-time (1 woman); includes 4 minority (2 African Americans, 2 Asian Americans or Pacific Islanders), 1 international. 9 applicants, 67% accepted. In 2009, 2 doctorates awarded. Application fee: $30. *Financial support:* In 2009–10, 5 fellowships (averaging $10,952 per year) were awarded; Federal Work-Study, scholarships/grants, and unspecified assistantships also available. *Unit head:* Ellen Glickman, Coordinator, 330-672-2930, E-mail: eglickma@kent.edu. *Application contact:* Nancy Miller, Academic Program Coordinator, Office of Graduate Student Services, 330-672-2576, Fax: 330-672-9162, E-mail: ogs@kent.edu.

Long Island University, Brooklyn Campus, School of Health Professions, Division of Sports Sciences, Brooklyn, NY 11201-8423. Offers adapted physical education (MS); athletic training and sports sciences (MS); exercise physiology (MS); health sciences (MS). Part-time and evening/weekend programs available. *Entrance requirements:* For master's, 2 letters of recommendation. Additional exam requirements/recommendations for international students: Required—TOEFL (minimum score 500 paper-based; 173 computer-based). Electronic applications accepted.

Louisiana Tech University, Graduate School, College of Education, Department of Curriculum, Instruction and Leadership, Ruston, LA 71272. Offers curriculum and instruction (MS, Ed D); educational leadership (Ed D); secondary education (M Ed), including business education, English education, foreign language education, health and physical education, mathematics education, science education, social studies education, speech education. *Accreditation:* NCATE. Part-time programs available. *Degree requirements:* For doctorate, thesis/dissertation. *Entrance requirements:* For master's and doctorate, GRE General Test.

McDaniel College, Graduate and Professional Studies, Program in Physical Education, Westminster, MD 21157-4390. Offers MS. Part-time and evening/weekend programs available. *Degree requirements:* For master's, comprehensive exam, thesis optional. *Entrance requirements:* For master's, letters of reference (3). Additional exam requirements/recommendations for international students: Required—TOEFL (minimum score 213 computer-based). *Expenses:* Tuition: Part-time $325 per credit hour.

McGill University, Faculty of Graduate and Postdoctoral Studies, Faculty of Education, Department of Kinesiology and Physical Education, Montréal, QC H3A 2T5, Canada. Offers M Sc, MA, PhD, Certificate, Diploma.

Memorial University of Newfoundland, School of Graduate Studies, School of Human Kinetics and Recreation, St. John's, NL A1C 5S7, Canada. Offers administration, curriculum and supervision (MPE); biomechanics/ergonomics (MS Kin); exercise and work physiology (MS Kin); sport psychology (MS Kin). Part-time programs available. *Degree requirements:* For master's, thesis optional, seminars, thesis presentations. *Entrance requirements:* For master's, bachelor's degree in a related field, minimum B average. Electronic applications accepted. *Faculty research:* Administration, sociology of sports, kinesiology, physiology/recreation.

Middle Tennessee State University, College of Graduate Studies, College of Education and Behavioral Science, Department of Health and Human Performance, Program in Health, Physical Education and Recreation, Murfreesboro, TN 37132. Offers MS. Part-time and evening/weekend programs available. Postbaccalaureate distance learning degree programs offered. *Students:* 9 full-time (6 women), 59 part-time (27 women); includes 22 minority (19 African Americans, 2 Asian Americans or Pacific Islanders, 1 Hispanic American). 54 applicants, 74% accepted, 40 enrolled. In 2009, 36 master's awarded. *Degree requirements:* For master's, comprehensive exam, thesis optional. *Entrance requirements:* For master's, GRE or MAT. Additional exam requirements/recommendations for international students: Required—TOEFL (minimum score 525 paper-based; 195 computer-based; 71 iBT) or IELTS (minimum score 6). *Application deadline:* For fall admission, 6/1 for domestic and international students. Applications are processed on a rolling basis. Application fee: $25 ($30 for international students). *Expenses:* Tuition, state resident: full-time $4404. Tuition, nonresident: full-time $10,956.

Financial support: In 2009–10, 14 students received support. Career-related internships or fieldwork and institutionally sponsored loans available. Support available to part-time students. Financial award application deadline: 5/1. *Unit head:* Dr. Scott Colclough, Interim Chair, 615-898-5073, Fax: 615-898-5020, E-mail: scolclou@mtsu.edu. *Application contact:* Dr. Michael Allen, Dean and Vice Provost for Research, 615-898-2840, Fax: 615-904-8020, E-mail: mallen@mtsu.edu.

Minnesota State University Mankato, College of Graduate Studies, College of Allied Health and Nursing, Department of Human Performance, Mankato, MN 56001. Offers MA, MS, MT, SP. Part-time programs available. *Students:* 60 full-time (34 women), 66 part-time (25 women). *Degree requirements:* For master's, comprehensive exam, thesis; for SP, thesis. *Entrance requirements:* For master's, minimum GPA of 3.0 during previous 2 years; for SP, minimum GPA of 3.0. Additional exam requirements/recommendations for international students: Required—TOEFL. *Application deadline:* For fall admission, 3/1 priority date for domestic and international students. Applications are processed on a rolling basis. Application fee: $40. *Expenses:* Tuition, state resident: full-time $5364. Tuition, nonresident: full-time $8314. *Financial support:* Research assistantships with full tuition reimbursements, teaching assistantships with full tuition reimbursements, career-related internships or fieldwork, Federal Work-Study, institutionally sponsored loans, and unspecified assistantships available. Support available to part-time students. Financial award application deadline: 3/15; financial award applicants required to submit FAFSA. *Faculty research:* Exercise physiology. *Unit head:* Dr. Cindra Kamphoff, Graduate Coordinator, 507-389-6313. *Application contact:* 507-389-2321, E-mail: grad@mnsu.edu.

Mississippi State University, College of Education, Department of Kinesiology, MS State, MS 39762. Offers physical education (MS), including exercise science, sport administration, teaching/coaching. Part-time programs available. Postbaccalaureate distance learning degree programs offered (minimal on-campus study). *Faculty:* 7 full-time (1 woman). *Students:* 56 full-time (22 women), 11 part-time (6 women); includes 20 minority (18 African Americans, 1 American Indian/Alaska Native, 1 Asian American or Pacific Islander), 2 international. Average age 25. 58 applicants, 72% accepted, 36 enrolled. In 2009, 22 master's awarded. *Degree requirements:* For master's, comprehensive exam, thesis optional. *Entrance requirements:* For master's, GRE General Test, minimum GPA of 3.0. Additional exam requirements/recommendations for international students: Required—TOEFL (minimum score 550 paper-based; 213 computer-based; 79 iBT); Recommended—IELTS (minimum score 6.5). *Application deadline:* For fall admission, 7/1 for domestic students, 5/1 for international students; for spring admission, 11/1 for domestic students, 9/1 for international students. Applications are processed on a rolling basis. Application fee: $40. Electronic applications accepted. *Expenses:* Tuition, state resident: full-time $2575.50; part-time $286.25 per credit hour. Tuition, nonresident: full-time $6510; part-time $723.50 per credit hour. Tuition and fees vary according to course load. *Financial support:* In 2009–10, 7 teaching assistantships (averaging $8,772 per year) were awarded; career-related internships or fieldwork, Federal Work-Study, institutionally sponsored loans, and unspecified assistantships also available. Financial award application deadline: 4/1; financial award applicants required to submit FAFSA. *Faculty research:* Static balance and stepping performance of older adults, organizational justice, public health, strength training and recovery drinks, high risk drinking perceptions and behaviors. *Unit head:* Dr. Stanley Brown, Head, 662-325-2963, Fax: 662-325-4525, E-mail: spb107@msstate.edu. *Application contact:* Dr. John G. Lamberth, Associate Professor and Graduate Coordinator, 662-325-0906, Fax: 662-325-4525, E-mail: jgl@ra.msstate.edu.

Missouri State University, Graduate College, College of Health and Human Services, Department of Health, Physical Education, and Recreation, Springfield, MO 65897. Offers health promotion and wellness management (MS); secondary education (MS Ed), including physical education. Part-time programs available. *Faculty:* 13 full-time (5 women). *Students:* 20 full-time (10 women), 10 part-time (6 women), 1 international. Average age 27. 17 applicants, 94% accepted, 12 enrolled. In 2009, 10 master's awarded. *Degree requirements:* For master's, comprehensive exam, thesis or alternative. *Entrance requirements:* For master's, GRE (MS), minimum GPA of 2.8 (MS); 9-12 teaching certification (MS Ed). Additional exam requirements/recommendations for international students: Required—TOEFL (minimum score 550 paper-based; 213 computer-based; 79 iBT). *Application deadline:* For fall admission, 7/20 priority date for domestic students, 5/1 for international students; for spring admission, 12/20 priority date for domestic students, 9/1 for international students. Applications are processed on a rolling basis. Application fee: $35 ($50 for international students). Electronic applications accepted. *Expenses:* Tuition, state resident: full-time $3852; part-time $214 per credit hour. Tuition, nonresident: full-time $7524; part-time $418 per credit hour. Required fees: $696; $172 per semester. Tuition and fees vary according to course level, course load, degree level and program. *Financial support:* In 2009–10, 5 teaching assistantships with full tuition reimbursements (averaging $7,340 per year) were awarded; Federal Work-Study, institutionally sponsored loans, scholarships/grants, and unspecified assistantships also available. Financial award application deadline: 3/31; financial award applicants required to submit FAFSA. *Unit head:* Dr. Sarah McCallister, Acting Head, 417-836-6582, Fax: 417-836-5371, E-mail: sarahmccallister@missouristate.edu. *Application contact:* Eric Eckert, Coordinator of Graduate Admissions and Recruitment, 417-836-5331, Fax: 417-836-6200, E-mail: ericeckert@missouristate.edu.

Montana State University Billings, College of Allied Health Professions, Department of Health and Human Performance, Billings, MT 59101-0298. Offers athletic training (MS); sport management (MS). *Degree requirements:* For master's, thesis optional. *Entrance requirements:* For master's, GRE General Test, minimum undergraduate GPA of 3.0.

Montclair State University, The Graduate School, College of Education and Human Services, Department of Curriculum and Teaching, Montclair, NJ 07043-1624. Offers education (M Ed); educational technology (M Ed); learning disabled teacher consultant (Certificate); school library media specialist (Certificate); teaching (MAT, Certificate), including art (MAT), biological science (MAT), early childhood education (P-3) (MAT), earth science (MAT), elementary education (K-8) (MAT), English (MAT), French (MAT), health and physical education (MAT), health education (MAT), home economics (MAT), mathematics (MAT), music (MAT), physical education (MAT), physical science (MAT), social studies (MAT), Spanish (MAT), teacher of ESL (MAT), teacher of students with disabilities (MAT). Part-time and evening/weekend programs available. *Faculty:* 17 full-time (12 women), 29 part-time/adjunct (21 women). *Students:* 124 full-time (63 women), 174 part-time (126 women). Average age 31. 112 applicants, 69% accepted, 59 enrolled. In 2009, 179 master's, 2 other advanced degrees awarded. *Degree requirements:* For master's, comprehensive exam, field experience. *Entrance requirements:* For master's, GRE, 2 letters of recommendation. Additional exam requirements/recommendations for international students: Required—TOEFL (minimum score 83 computer-based), or IELTS. *Application deadline:* For fall admission, 2/15 for domestic and international students; for spring admission, 9/15 for domestic and international students. Applications are processed on a rolling basis. Application fee: $60. Electronic applications accepted. *Expenses:* Tuition, area resident: Part-time $486.74 per credit. Tuition, state resident: part-time $486.74 per credit. Tuition, nonresident: part-time $751.34 per credit. Tuition and fees vary according to degree level and program. *Financial support:* In 2009–10, 12 research assistantships with full tuition reimbursements (averaging $7,000 per year) were awarded; Federal Work-Study, scholarships/grants, and unspecified assistantships also available. Support available to part-time students. Financial award application deadline: 3/1; financial award applicants required to submit FAFSA. *Unit head:* Dr. David Schwarzer, Chairperson, 973-655-5187. *Application contact:* Amy Aiello, Director of Graduate Admissions and Operations, 973-655-5147, Fax: 973-655-7869, E-mail: graduate.school@montclair.edu.

Montclair State University, The Graduate School, College of Education and Human Services, Department of Exercise Science and Physical Education, Montclair, NJ 07043-1624. Offers health and physical education (Certificate); nutrition and exercise science (Certificate); physical education (MA, Certificate), including coaching and sports administration (MA), exercise science (MA), physical education (MA); teaching and supervision of physical education (MA). Part-time and evening/weekend programs available. *Faculty:* 15 full-time (9 women), 17 part-time/adjunct (10 women). *Students:* 8 full-time (3 women), 38 part-time (19 women). Average age

Physical Education

Montclair State University (continued)

30. 34 applicants, 56% accepted, 13 enrolled. In 2009, 9 master's awarded. *Degree requirements:* For master's, comprehensive exam. *Entrance requirements:* For master's, GRE General Test, 2 letters of recommendation; for Certificate, 2 letters of recommendation (nutrition and exercise science concentration). Additional exam requirements/recommendations for international students: Required—TOEFL (minimum score 83 computer-based), or IELTS. *Application deadline:* For fall admission, 6/1 for international students; for spring admission, 10/1 for international students. Applications are processed on a rolling basis. Application fee: $60. Electronic applications accepted. *Expenses:* Tuition, area resident: Part-time $486.74 per credit. Tuition, state resident: part-time $486.74 per credit. Tuition, nonresident: part-time $751.34 per credit. Tuition and fees vary according to degree level and program. *Financial support:* In 2009–10, 5 research assistantships with full tuition reimbursements (averaging $7,000 per year) were awarded; Federal Work-Study, scholarships/grants, and unspecified assistantships also available. Support available to part-time students. Financial award application deadline: 3/1; financial award applicants required to submit FAFSA. *Unit head:* Dr. Susana Juniu, Chairperson, 973-655-7093. *Application contact:* Amy Aliello, Director of Graduate Admissions and Operations, 973-655-5147, Fax: 973-655-7869, E-mail: graduate.school@montclair.edu.

Morehead State University, Graduate Programs, College of Education, Department of Middle Grades and Secondary Education, Morehead, KY 40351. Offers business and marketing education (MAT); English/language arts 5-9 (MAT); French (MAT); health P-12 (MAT); mathematics 5-9 (MAT); physical education P-12 (MAT); science 5-9 (MAT); secondary biology (MAT); secondary chemistry (MAT); secondary earth science (MAT); secondary English (MAT); secondary math (MAT); secondary physics (MAT); secondary social studies (MAT); social studies 5-9 (MAT); Spanish (MAT). Part-time and evening/weekend programs available. *Students:* 54 full-time (31 women), 233 part-time (142 women); includes 11 minority (5 African Americans, 1 American Indian/Alaska Native, 1 Asian American or Pacific Islander, 4 Hispanic Americans). Average age 32. 206 applicants, 71% accepted, 79 enrolled. In 2009, 101 master's awarded. *Degree requirements:* For master's, portfolio. *Entrance requirements:* For master's, GRE or PRAXIS II content exam, minimum overall undergraduate GPA of 2.5. Additional exam requirements/recommendations for international students: Required—TOEFL (minimum score 500 paper-based; 173 computer-based). *Application deadline:* For fall admission, 8/1 priority date for domestic and international students; for spring admission, 12/1 priority date for domestic and international students. Applications are processed on a rolling basis. Application fee: $30. Electronic applications accepted. *Expenses:* Tuition, state resident: full-time $6318; part-time $351 per credit hour. Tuition, nonresident: full-time $15,804; part-time $878 per credit hour. *Financial support:* In 2009–10, 1 research assistantship (averaging $10,000 per year) was awarded; career-related internships or fieldwork, Federal Work-Study, and unspecified assistantships also available. Financial award application deadline: 3/15; financial award applicants required to submit FAFSA. *Unit head:* Dr. Cathy Gunn, Dean, 606-783-2040, Fax: 606-783-5029, E-mail: c.gunn@moreheadstate.edu. *Application contact:* Michelle Barber, Graduate Recruitment and Retention Assistant Director, 606-783-5127, Fax: 606-783-5061, E-mail: m.barber@moreheadstate.edu.

Morehead State University, Graduate Programs, College of Science and Technology, Department of Health, Wellness and Human Performance, Morehead, KY 40351. Offers health/physical education (MA). *Accreditation:* NCATE. Part-time and evening/weekend programs available. *Faculty:* 5 full-time (4 women). *Students:* 8 full-time (4 women), 6 part-time (4 women); includes 1 African American. Average age 28. 9 applicants, 78% accepted, 6 enrolled. In 2009, 3 master's awarded. *Degree requirements:* For master's, comprehensive exam, thesis, oral exam, written core exam. *Entrance requirements:* For master's, GRE General Test or MAT, minimum GPA of 2.5; undergraduate major/minor in health, physical education, or recreation. Additional exam requirements/recommendations for international students: Required—TOEFL (minimum score 500 paper-based; 173 computer-based). *Application deadline:* For fall admission, 8/1 priority date for domestic and international students; for spring admission, 12/1 priority date for domestic and international students. Applications are processed on a rolling basis. Application fee: $30. Electronic applications accepted. *Expenses:* Tuition, state resident: full-time $6318; part-time $351 per credit hour. Tuition, nonresident: full-time $15,804; part-time $878 per credit hour. *Financial support:* In 2009–10, 1 research assistantship (averaging $10,000 per year), 3 teaching assistantships (averaging $10,000 per year) were awarded; career-related internships or fieldwork, Federal Work-Study, and unspecified assistantships also available. Financial award application deadline: 3/15; financial award applicants required to submit FAFSA. *Faculty research:* Child growth and performance, instructional strategies, outdoor leadership qualities, exercise science, athletic training. *Unit head:* Dr. Lynne Fitzgerald, Chair, 606-783-2466, Fax: 606-783-5058, E-mail: l.fitzgerald@moreheadstate.edu. *Application contact:* Michelle Barber, Graduate Recruitment and Retention Assistant Director, 606-783-5127, Fax: 606-783-5061, E-mail: m.barber@moreheadstate.edu.

Murray State University, College of Education, Department of Adolescent, Career and Special Education, Murray, KY 42071. Offers health, physical education, and recreation (MA), including physical education; industrial and technical education (MS); middle school education (MA Ed, Ed S); secondary education (MA Ed, Ed S); special education (MA Ed), including advanced learning behavior disorders, learning disabilities, moderate/severe disorders. *Accreditation:* NCATE. Part-time programs available. *Entrance requirements:* Additional exam requirements/recommendations for international students: Required—TOEFL.

North Carolina Agricultural and Technical State University, Graduate School, School of Education, Department of Human Performance and Leisure Studies, Greensboro, NC 27411. Offers physical education (MAT, MS). *Accreditation:* NCATE. Part-time and evening/weekend programs available. *Degree requirements:* For master's, comprehensive exam, thesis or alternative, qualifying exam. *Entrance requirements:* For master's, GRE General Test, minimum GPA of 3.0.

North Carolina Central University, Division of Academic Affairs, College of Behavioral and Social Sciences, Department of Physical Education and Recreation, Durham, NC 27707-3129. Offers athletic administration (MS); physical education (MS); recreation administration (MS); therapeutic recreation (MS). Part-time and evening/weekend programs available. *Degree requirements:* For master's, one foreign language, comprehensive exam, thesis. *Entrance requirements:* For master's, GRE, minimum GPA of 3.0 in major, 2.5 overall. Additional exam requirements/recommendations for international students: Required—TOEFL. *Faculty research:* Physical activity patterns of children with disabilities, physical fitness test of North Carolina school children, exercise physiology, motor learning/development.

North Dakota State University, College of Graduate and Interdisciplinary Studies, College of Human Development and Education, School of Education, Program in Curriculum and Instruction, Fargo, ND 58108. Offers pedagogy (M Ed, MS); physical education and athletic administration (M Ed, MS). *Faculty:* 10 full-time (3 women). *Students:* 1 (woman) full-time, 11 part-time (10 women). Average age 27. 8 applicants, 75% accepted, 6 enrolled. In 2009, 1 master's awarded. *Degree requirements:* For master's, comprehensive exam, thesis (for some programs). *Entrance requirements:* For master's, Cooperative English Test, GRE General Test, MAT. Additional exam requirements/recommendations for international students: Required—TOEFL. *Application deadline:* For fall admission, 5/1 for domestic students. Applications are processed on a rolling basis. Application fee: $45 ($60 for international students). *Financial support:* Teaching assistantships, career-related internships or fieldwork, Federal Work-Study, institutionally sponsored loans, and tuition waivers (full) available. Financial award application deadline: 4/15. *Unit head:* Dr. William Martin, Chair, 701-231-7202, Fax: 701-231-7416, E-mail: william.martin@ndsu.edu. *Application contact:* Dr. Justin Wageman, Associate Professor, 701-231-7108, Fax: 701-231-9685, E-mail: justin.wageman@ndsu.edu.

Northern Illinois University, Graduate School, College of Education, Department of Kinesiology and Physical Education, De Kalb, IL 60115-2854. Offers physical education (MS Ed); sport management (MS). Part-time and evening/weekend programs available. *Faculty:* 21 full-time (12 women). *Students:* 63 full-time (25 women), 97 part-time (39 women); includes 13 minority (7 African Americans, 4 Asian Americans or Pacific Islanders, 2 Hispanic Americans), 7 international. Average age 28. 78 applicants, 69% accepted, 26 enrolled. In 2009, 68 master's awarded. *Degree requirements:* For master's, comprehensive exam, thesis optional. *Entrance requirements:* For master's, GRE General Test, minimum GPA of 2.75, undergraduate major in related area. Additional exam requirements/recommendations for international students: Required—TOEFL (minimum score 550 paper-based; 213 computer-based). *Application deadline:* For fall admission, 6/1 for domestic students, 5/1 for international students; for spring admission, 11/1 for domestic students, 10/1 for international students. Applications are processed on a rolling basis. Application fee: $30. Electronic applications accepted. *Expenses:* Tuition, state resident: full-time $6576; part-time $274 per credit hour. Tuition, nonresident: full-time $13,152; part-time $548 per credit hour. Required fees: $1813; $75.53 per credit hour. Part-time tuition and fees vary according to course load. *Financial support:* In 2009–10, 35 teaching assistantships with full tuition reimbursements were awarded; fellowships with full tuition reimbursements, research assistantships with full tuition reimbursements, career-related internships or fieldwork, Federal Work-Study, scholarships/grants, tuition waivers (full), and unspecified assistantships also available. Support available to part-time students. Financial award applicants required to submit FAFSA. *Faculty research:* Leadership in athletic training, motor development, dance education, gait analysis, fat phobia. *Unit head:* Dr. Paul Carpenter, Chair, 815-753-1407, Fax: 815-753-1413, E-mail: chowell@niu.edu. *Application contact:* Dr. Laurie Zittel, Director, Graduate Studies, 815-753-3907, E-mail: lzape@niu.edu.

Northern State University, Division of Graduate Studies in Education, Program in Teaching and Learning, Aberdeen, SD 57401-7198. Offers educational studies (MS Ed); elementary classroom teaching (MS Ed); health, physical education, and coaching (MS Ed); language and literacy (MS Ed); secondary classroom teaching (MS Ed); special education (MS Ed). *Accreditation:* NCATE. Part-time and evening/weekend programs available. *Faculty:* 10 full-time (8 women). *Students:* 23 full-time (16 women), 35 part-time (17 women); includes 2 minority (1 African American, 1 American Indian/Alaska Native, 1 Asian American or Pacific Islander). Average age 32. In 2009, 26 master's awarded. *Degree requirements:* For master's, thesis optional. *Entrance requirements:* For master's, minimum GPA of 2.75. Additional exam requirements/recommendations for international students: Required—TOEFL (minimum score 550 paper-based; 213 computer-based; 76 iBT). *Application deadline:* For fall admission, 8/15 priority date for domestic students; for spring admission, 12/15 for domestic students. Applications are processed on a rolling basis. Application fee: $35. Electronic applications accepted. *Financial support:* In 2009–10, 18 teaching assistantships with partial tuition reimbursements (averaging $5,558 per year) were awarded; career-related internships or fieldwork, Federal Work-Study, institutionally sponsored loans, scholarships/grants, and unspecified assistantships also available. Support available to part-time students. Financial award application deadline: 3/1; financial award applicants required to submit FAFSA. *Application contact:* Tammy K. Griffith, Program Assistant, 605-626-2558, Fax: 605-626-7190, E-mail: griffith@northern.edu.

North Georgia College & State University, Graduate Studies, Program in Teacher Education, Dahlonega, GA 30597. Offers early childhood education (M Ed); educational leadership (Ed S); middle grades education (M Ed); secondary education (M Ed), including art education, biology education, chemistry education, English education, history education, mathematics education, physical education, science education; special education (M Ed), including interrelated special education, learning disabilities. *Accreditation:* NCATE. Part-time and evening/weekend programs available. Postbaccalaureate distance learning degree programs offered (minimal on-campus study). *Degree requirements:* For master's, comprehensive exam, thesis optional. *Entrance requirements:* For master's, GRE General Test or MAT, minimum GPA of 2.75; for Ed S, GRE General Test or MAT, 3 years of teaching experience, master's degree, minimum graduate GPA of 3.25. Electronic applications accepted. *Faculty research:* Computers and teachers' attitudes, rural versus urban teacher attitudes, teacher leadership roles, minority recruitment in teaching force.

Northwest Missouri State University, Graduate School, College of Education and Human Services, Department of Health, Physical Education, Recreation and Dance, Maryville, MO 64468-6001. Offers applied health science (MS); health and physical education (MS Ed); recreation (MS). *Accreditation:* NCATE. Part-time programs available. *Faculty:* 10 full-time (5 women). *Students:* 38 full-time (10 women), 12 part-time (5 women); includes 3 minority (2 African Americans, 1 Hispanic American), 2 international. 35 applicants, 77% accepted, 20 enrolled. In 2009, 10 master's awarded. *Degree requirements:* For master's, comprehensive exam. *Entrance requirements:* For master's, GRE General Test, minimum undergraduate GPA of 2.75, teaching certificate, writing sample. Additional exam requirements/recommendations for international students: Required—TOEFL (minimum score 550 paper-based; 213 computer-based). *Application deadline:* For fall admission, 7/1 for domestic and international students; for spring admission, 11/15 for domestic and international students. Applications are processed on a rolling basis. Application fee: $0 ($50 for international students). *Expenses:* Tuition, state resident: part-time $296.34 per credit hour. Tuition, nonresident: part-time $510.43 per credit hour. *Financial support:* In 2009–10, 27 teaching assistantships with full tuition reimbursements (averaging $6,000 per year) were awarded; unspecified assistantships also available. Financial award application deadline: 4/1; financial award applicants required to submit FAFSA. *Unit head:* Dr. Terry Robertson, Program Director, 660-562-1781. *Application contact:* Dr. Gregory Haddock, Dean of Graduate School, 660-562-1145, Fax: 660-562-1096, E-mail: gradsch@nwmissouri.edu.

The Ohio State University, Graduate School, College of Education and Human Ecology, School of Physical Activity and Educational Services, Columbus, OH 43210. Offers M Ed, MA, PhD. Part-time programs available. *Faculty:* 57. *Students:* 150 full-time (95 women), 181 part-time (136 women); includes 56 minority (35 African Americans, 2 American Indian/Alaska Native, 7 Asian Americans or Pacific Islanders, 12 Hispanic Americans), 25 international. Average age 33. In 2009, 93 master's, 30 doctorates awarded. *Degree requirements:* For master's, thesis optional; for doctorate, thesis/dissertation. *Entrance requirements:* Additional exam requirements/recommendations for international students: Required—TOEFL (minimum score 600 paper-based; 250 computer-based). *Application deadline:* For fall admission, 8/15 priority date for domestic students, 7/1 priority date for international students; for winter admission, 12/1 priority date for domestic students, 11/1 priority date for international students; for spring admission, 3/1 priority date for domestic students, 2/1 priority date for international students. Applications are processed on a rolling basis. Application fee: $40 ($50 for international students). Electronic applications accepted. *Expenses:* Tuition, state resident: full-time $10,683. Tuition, nonresident: full-time $25,923. Tuition and fees vary according to course load and program. *Financial support:* Fellowships, research assistantships, teaching assistantships, Federal Work-Study and institutionally sponsored loans available. Support available to part-time students. *Unit head:* Donna Pastore, Director, 614-688-6787, Fax: 614-292-7229, E-mail: ward.116@osu.edu. *Application contact:* 614-292-9444, Fax: 614-292-3895, E-mail: domestic.grad@osu.edu.

Ohio University, Graduate College, College of Health and Human Services, School of Recreation and Sport Sciences, Program in Coaching Education, Athens, OH 45701-2979. Offers MS. *Faculty:* 5 full-time (2 women). *Students:* 23 full-time (6 women), 2 part-time (0 women), 2 international. 18 applicants, 89% accepted, 11 enrolled. In 2009, 15 master's awarded. *Entrance requirements:* For master's, GRE. Additional exam requirements/recommendations for international students: Required—TOEFL (minimum score 550 paper-based; 80 iBT) or IELTS Academic (minimum score 6.5). *Application deadline:* For fall admission, 3/1 priority date for domestic and international students. Applications are processed on a rolling basis. Application fee: $50 ($55 for international students). Electronic applications accepted. *Expenses:* Tuition, state resident: full-time $7839; part-time $323 per quarter hour. Tuition, nonresident: full-time $15,831; part-time $654 per quarter hour. Required fees: $2931. *Financial support:* In 2009–10, research assistantships with full tuition reimbursements (averaging $8,835 per year), teaching assistantships with full tuition reimbursements (averaging $8,835 per year) were awarded; scholarships/grants and stipends also available. Financial award application deadline: 3/1. *Faculty research:* Sports, physical activity, athletes. *Unit head:* Dr. David Carr, Assistant Professor and Coordinator, 740-593-4651, Fax: 740-593-0284, E-mail:

carr@ohio.edu. *Application contact:* Dr. David Carr, Assistant Professor and Coordinator, 740-593-4651, Fax: 740-593-0284, E-mail: carr@ohio.edu.

Old Dominion University, Darden College of Education, Program in Physical Education, Norfolk, VA 23529. Offers athletic training (MS Ed); curriculum and instruction (MS Ed); exercise and wellness (MS Ed); physical education (MS Ed); recreation and tourism studies (MS Ed); sport management (MS Ed). Part-time and evening/weekend programs available. *Faculty:* 12 full-time (6 women), 6 part-time/adjunct (4 women). *Students:* 87 full-time (51 women), 34 part-time (16 women); includes 23 minority (17 African Americans, 3 Asian Americans or Pacific Islanders, 3 Hispanic Americans), 6 international. Average age 26. 105 applicants, 72% accepted, 55 enrolled. In 2009, 54 master's awarded. *Degree requirements:* For master's, comprehensive exam, thesis or alternative, internship, research project. *Entrance requirements:* For master's, GRE General Test, minimum GPA of 2.8. Additional exam requirements/recommendations for international students: Required—TOEFL (minimum score 500 paper-based; 200 computer-based). *Application deadline:* For fall admission, 7/1 for domestic students; for spring admission, 11/1 for domestic students. Applications are processed on a rolling basis. Application fee: $40. *Expenses:* Tuition, state resident: full-time $8112; part-time $338 per credit. Tuition, nonresident: full-time $20,256; part-time $844 per credit. Required fees: $119 per semester. One-time fee: $50. *Financial support:* In 2009–10, 1 fellowship (averaging $1,500 per year), 2 research assistantships with partial tuition reimbursements (averaging $9,000 per year), 5 teaching assistantships with tuition reimbursements (averaging $9,000 per year) were awarded; career-related internships or fieldwork and scholarships/grants also available. Financial award application deadline: 4/15; financial award applicants required to submit FAFSA. *Faculty research:* Exercise physiology, nutrition and sports, motion analysis, sports management. Total annual research expenditures: $183,251. *Unit head:* Robert Spina, Chair, 757-683-6029, Fax: 757-683-4270, E-mail: rspina@odu.edu. *Application contact:* Robert Spina, Chair, 757-683-6029, Fax: 757-683-4270, E-mail: rspina@odu.edu.

Pittsburg State University, Graduate School, College of Education, Department of Health, Physical Education and Recreation, Pittsburg, KS 66762. Offers physical education (MS). *Degree requirements:* For master's, thesis or alternative. *Expenses:* Tuition, state resident: full-time $4212; part-time $176 per credit. Tuition, nonresident: full-time $11,530; part-time $480 per credit. Required fees: $940; $43 per credit. Tuition and fees vary according to course level, course load, degree level, campus/location, reciprocity agreements and student level. *Faculty research:* Personality of athletes, fitness activities for children, aerobic conditioning, fitness evaluation.

Prairie View A&M University, College of Education, Department of Health and Human Performance, Prairie View, TX 77446-0519. Offers health education (M Ed, MS); physical education (M Ed, MS). *Accreditation:* NCATE. Part-time and evening/weekend programs available. *Faculty:* 3 full-time (0 women). *Students:* 14 part-time (8 women); includes 10 African Americans, 1 Hispanic American. Average age 31. 36 applicants, 100% accepted. In 2009, 6 master's awarded. *Entrance requirements:* For master's, GRE General Test. Additional exam requirements/recommendations for international students: Required—TOEFL. *Application deadline:* For fall admission, 10/2 priority date for domestic students; for spring admission, 2/19 for domestic students. Applications are processed on a rolling basis. Application fee: $50. *Expenses:* Tuition, state resident: full-time $2200. Tuition, nonresident: full-time $5600. Required fees: $1720. Tuition and fees vary according to course load. *Financial support:* In 2009–10, 8 fellowships with tuition reimbursements (averaging $1,200 per year), 10 research assistantships with tuition reimbursements (averaging $15,000 per year) were awarded; teaching assistantships with tuition reimbursements, career-related internships or fieldwork, Federal Work-Study, and institutionally sponsored loans also available. Support available to part-time students. Financial award application deadline: 4/1. *Unit head:* Dr. Patricia Hoffman-Miller, Interim Department Head, 936-261-3530, Fax: 936-261-3617. *Application contact:* Dr. William H. Parker, Dean of Graduate School, 936-261-3500, Fax: 936-261-3529, E-mail: whparker@pvamu.edu.

Purdue University, Graduate School, College of Liberal Arts, Department of Health and Kinesiology, West Lafayette, IN 47907. Offers exercise, human physiology of movement and sport (PhD); health and fitness (MS); health promotion (MS); health promotion and disease prevention (PhD); movement and sport science (MS); pedagogy and administration (MS); pedagogy of physical activity and health (PhD); psychology of sport and exercise, and motor behavior (PhD). Part-time programs available. *Degree requirements:* For master's, thesis (for some programs); for doctorate, thesis/dissertation. *Entrance requirements:* For master's and doctorate, GRE General Test. Additional exam requirements/recommendations for international students: Required—TOEFL. Electronic applications accepted. *Faculty research:* Wellness, motivation, teaching effectiveness, learning and development.

Rhode Island College, School of Graduate Studies, Feinstein School of Education and Human Development, Department of Health and Physical Education, Providence, RI 02908-1991. Offers health education (M Ed); physical education (CGS). *Accreditation:* NCATE. Part-time and evening/weekend programs available. *Faculty:* 3 full-time (2 women). *Students:* 15 part-time (13 women). Average age 39. In 2009, 9 master's awarded. *Degree requirements:* For master's, comprehensive assessment. *Entrance requirements:* For master's, GRE General Test or MAT, undergraduate transcripts; minimum undergraduate GPA of 3.0; copy of teaching certificate (when applicable); 3 letters of recommendation; for CGS, GRE or MAT (for most programs), undergraduate transcripts; minimum undergraduate GPA of 3.0; copy of teaching certificate (when applicable); 3 letters of recommendation. Additional exam requirements/recommendations for international students: Recommended—TOEFL (minimum score 550 paper-based; 213 computer-based; 79 iBT). *Application deadline:* For fall admission, 3/15 for domestic students; for spring admission, 11/1 for domestic students. Applications are processed on a rolling basis. Application fee: $50. *Expenses:* Tuition, state resident: full-time $7440; part-time $310 per credit hour. Tuition, nonresident: full-time $14,784; part-time $616 per credit hour. Required fees: $552; $20 per credit. $70 per term. *Financial support:* Teaching assistantships with full tuition reimbursements, Federal Work-Study, scholarships/grants, health care benefits, and unspecified assistantships available. Support available to part-time students. Financial award application deadline: 5/15; financial award applicants required to submit FAFSA. *Unit head:* Dr. Betty Rauhe, Chair, 401-456-8046. *Application contact:* Graduate Studies, 401-456-8700.

Saginaw Valley State University, College of Education, Program in Adapted Physical Activity, University Center, MI 48710. Offers MAT. Part-time and evening/weekend programs available. *Students:* 2 part-time (1 woman). Average age 32. 1 applicant, 100% accepted, 1 enrolled. *Degree requirements:* For master's, capstone course. *Entrance requirements:* For master's, minimum GPA of 3.0. Additional exam requirements/recommendations for international students: Required—TOEFL (minimum score 525 paper-based; 197 computer-based; 71 iBT). *Application deadline:* Applications are processed on a rolling basis. Application fee: $25. Electronic applications accepted. *Financial support:* Federal Work-Study and scholarships/grants available. Support available to part-time students. Financial award applicants required to submit FAFSA. *Unit head:* Dr. Steve P. Barbus, Dean, 989-964-6067, Fax: 989-790-4385, E-mail: barbus@svsu.edu. *Application contact:* Dr. Steve P. Barbus, Dean, 989-964-6067, Fax: 989-790-4385, E-mail: barbus@svsu.edu.

St. Cloud State University, School of Graduate Studies, College of Education, Department of Health, Physical Education, Recreation, and Sport Science, St. Cloud, MN 56301-4498. Offers exercise science (MS); physical education (MS); sports management (MS). *Faculty:* 16 full-time (8 women), 1 (woman) part-time/adjunct. *Students:* 21 full-time (10 women), 39 part-time (13 women); includes 7 minority (3 African Americans, 4 Asian Americans or Pacific Islanders), 2 international. 31 applicants, 71% accepted. In 2009, 17 master's awarded. *Degree requirements:* For master's, thesis or alternative. *Entrance requirements:* For master's, GRE General Test, minimum GPA of 2.75. Additional exam requirements/recommendations for international students: Required—Michigan English Language Assessment Battery; Recommended—TOEFL (minimum score 550 paper-based; 213 computer-based), IELTS (minimum score 6.5). *Application deadline:* For fall admission, 6/1 priority date for domestic students, 4/1 for international students; for spring admission, 10/1 priority date for domestic students, 8/1 for international students. Applications are processed on a rolling basis. Application fee: $35. Electronic applications accepted. *Financial support:* Federal Work-Study, scholarships/grants, and unspecified assistantships available. Financial award application deadline: 3/1. *Unit head:* Dr. Caryl Martin, Chairperson, 320-308-4251, E-mail: clmartin@stcloudstate.edu. *Application contact:* Linda Lou Krueger, School of Graduate Studies, 320-308-2113, Fax: 320-308-5371, E-mail: lekrueger@stcloudstate.edu.

Salem State College, School of Graduate Studies, Program in Physical Education, Salem, MA 01970-5353. Offers M Ed. Part-time and evening/weekend programs available. *Students:* 25 part-time (12 women); includes 1 minority (Hispanic American). Average age 36. 4 applicants, 100% accepted, 4 enrolled. In 2009, 14 master's awarded. *Entrance requirements:* For master's, GRE or MAT. Additional exam requirements/recommendations for international students: Required—TOEFL (minimum score 550 paper-based; 80 iBT), or IELTS (minimum score 5.5). *Application deadline:* For fall admission, 5/1 for domestic students; for spring admission, 10/1 for domestic students. Applications are processed on a rolling basis. Application fee: $50. *Expenses:* Tuition, state resident: full-time $2520; part-time $275 per credit hour. Tuition, nonresident: full-time $4140; part-time $365 per credit hour. Required fees: $2430. *Financial support:* In 2009–10, 1 student received support. Career-related internships or fieldwork, Federal Work-Study, scholarships/grants, and unspecified assistantships available. Support available to part-time students. Financial award application deadline: 5/1; financial award applicants required to submit FAFSA. *Unit head:* Phil Kelly, Program Coordinator, 978-542-6310, Fax: 978-542-7215, E-mail: pkelly@salemstate.edu. *Application contact:* Dr. Lee A. Brossoit, Assistant Dean of Graduate Admissions, 978-542-6675, Fax: 978-542-7215, E-mail: lbrossoit@salemstate.edu.

San Diego State University, Graduate and Research Affairs, College of Professional Studies and Fine Arts, Department of Exercise and Nutritional Sciences, Program in Physical Education/Kinesiology, San Diego, CA 92182. Offers MS. *Degree requirements:* For master's, thesis. *Entrance requirements:* For master's, GRE General Test, 2 letters of reference. Additional exam requirements/recommendations for international students: Required—TOEFL. Electronic applications accepted.

Slippery Rock University of Pennsylvania, Graduate Studies (Recruitment), College of Education, Department of Physical Education, Slippery Rock, PA 16057-1383. Offers adapted physical activity (MS). *Degree requirements:* For master's, thesis optional, internship. *Entrance requirements:* For master's, GRE General Test, MAT, minimum GPA of 2.75 (3.0 for initial certification programs). Additional exam requirements/recommendations for international students: Required—TOEFL (minimum score 550 paper-based; 213 computer-based). *Application deadline:* For fall admission, 3/1 priority date for domestic students, 5/1 priority date for international students; for spring admission, 11/1 priority date for domestic students, 9/1 priority date for international students. Applications are processed on a rolling basis. Application fee: $25 ($30 for international students). Electronic applications accepted. *Expenses:* Tuition, state resident: full-time $6666; part-time $370 per credit. Tuition, nonresident: full-time $10,666; part-time $593 per credit. Required fees: $2184; $182 per credit. *Financial support:* Career-related internships or fieldwork, institutionally sponsored loans, scholarships/grants, and unspecified assistantships available. Support available to part-time students. Financial award application deadline: 5/1; financial award applicants required to submit FAFSA. *Unit head:* Dr. Robert Arnhold, Graduate Coordinator, 724-738-2847, Fax: 724-738-4987, E-mail: robert.arnhold@sru.edu. *Application contact:* Angela Piverotto, Director of Graduate Studies, 724-738-2051, Fax: 724-738-2146, E-mail: graduate.admissions@sru.edu.

South Dakota State University, Graduate School, College of Education and Human Sciences, Department of Health, Physical Education and Recreation, Brookings, SD 57007. Offers MS. Part-time programs available. *Degree requirements:* For master's, thesis, oral and written exams. *Entrance requirements:* Additional exam requirements/recommendations for international students: Required—TOEFL (minimum score 550 paper-based; 213 computer-based; 71 iBT). *Faculty research:* Effective teaching behaviors in physical education, sports nutrition, muscle/bone interaction, hormonal response to exercise.

Southern Connecticut State University, School of Graduate Studies, School of Education, Department of Exercise Science, New Haven, CT 06515-1355. Offers human performance (MS); physical education (MS); school health education (MS); sport psychology (MS). Part-time and evening/weekend programs available. *Faculty:* 8 full-time. *Students:* 28 full-time (13 women), 54 part-time (28 women); includes 6 minority (2 African Americans, 4 Hispanic Americans), 1 international. 20 applicants, 55% accepted, 10 enrolled. In 2009, 18 master's awarded. *Degree requirements:* For master's, thesis or alternative. *Entrance requirements:* For master's, interview. *Application deadline:* For fall admission, 7/15 priority date for domestic students. Applications are processed on a rolling basis. Application fee: $50. Electronic applications accepted. Tuition and fees vary according to program. *Financial support:* In 2009–10, 8 teaching assistantships were awarded. Financial award application deadline: 4/15; financial award applicants required to submit FAFSA. *Unit head:* Dr. Daniel Swartz, Chairperson, 203-392-8721, Fax: 203-392-6911, E-mail: swartzd1@southernct.edu. *Application contact:* Dr. Robert Axtell, Coordinator, 203-392-6037, Fax: 203-392-6093, E-mail: axtell@southernct.edu.

Southern Illinois University Carbondale, Graduate School, College of Education, Department of Physical Education, Carbondale, IL 62901-4701. Offers MS Ed. Part-time programs available. *Degree requirements:* For master's, thesis. *Entrance requirements:* For master's, GRE, minimum GPA of 2.7. Additional exam requirements/recommendations for international students: Required—TOEFL. *Faculty research:* Caffeine and exercise effects, ground reaction forces in walking and running, social psychology of sports.

Springfield College, Graduate Programs, Programs in Physical Education, Springfield, MA 01109-3797. Offers adapted physical education (M Ed, MPE, MS); advanced level coaching (M Ed, MPE, MS); athletic administration (M Ed, MPE, MS); general physical education (PhD, CAGS); health education licensure (MPE, MS); health education licensure program (M Ed); physical education licensure (MPE, MS); physical education licensure program (M Ed); teaching and administration (MS). Part-time programs available. *Degree requirements:* For master's, comprehensive exam, thesis (for some programs). *Entrance requirements:* For master's and doctorate, GRE General Test. Additional exam requirements/recommendations for international students: Required—TOEFL (minimum score 550 paper-based; 213 computer-based). Electronic applications accepted. *Expenses:* Tuition: Full-time $19,800; part-time $825 per credit hour. Required fees: $150.

State University of New York College at Cortland, Graduate Studies, School of Professional Studies, Department of Physical Education, Cortland, NY 13045. Offers MS Ed. Part-time and evening/weekend programs available. *Entrance requirements:* Additional exam requirements/recommendations for international students: Required—TOEFL.

Stony Brook University, State University of New York, School of Professional Development, Stony Brook, NY 11794. Offers biology-grade 7-12 (MAT); chemistry-grade 7-12 (MAT); coaching (Graduate Certificate); computer integrated engineering (Graduate Certificate); earth science-grade 7-12 (MAT); educational computing (Graduate Certificate); educational leadership (Advanced Certificate); English-grade 7-12 (MAT); environmental management (Graduate Certificate); environmental/occupational health and safety (Graduate Certificate); French-grade 7-12 (MAT); German-grade 7-12 (MAT); human resource management (Graduate Certificate); information systems management (Graduate Certificate); Italian-grade 7-12 (MAT); liberal studies (MA); mathematics-grade 7-12 (MAT); operation research (Graduate Certificate); physics-grade 7-12 (MAT); school administration and supervision (Graduate Certificate); school building leadership (Graduate Certificate); school district administration (Graduate Certificate); school district business leadership (Advanced Certificate); school district leadership (Graduate Certificate); social science and the professions (MPS), including environmental waste management, human resource management; social studies-grade 7-12 (MAT); Spanish-grade 7-12 (MAT); waste management (Graduate Certificate). Part-time and evening/weekend programs available. Postbaccalaureate distance learning degree programs offered. *Faculty:* 5 full-time (3 women), 131 part-time/adjunct (53 women). *Students:* 317 full-time (187 women),

Physical Education

Stony Brook University, State University of New York (continued)
1,200 part-time (773 women); includes 187 minority (77 African Americans, 2 American Indian/Alaska Native, 22 Asian Americans or Pacific Islanders, 86 Hispanic Americans), 11 international. Average age 28. In 2009, 597 master's, 234 other advanced degrees awarded. *Degree requirements:* For master's, one foreign language, thesis or alternative. *Application deadline:* Applications are processed on a rolling basis. Application fee: $62. *Expenses:* Tuition, state resident: full-time $8370; part-time $349 per credit. Tuition, nonresident: full-time $13,250; part-time $552 per credit. Required fees: $933. *Financial support:* Fellowships, research assistantships, teaching assistantships, career-related internships or fieldwork available. Support available to part-time students. *Unit head:* Dr. Paul J. Edelson, Dean, 631-632-7052, Fax: 631-632-9046, E-mail: paul.edelson@stonybrook.edu. *Application contact:* Dr. Paul J. Edelson, Dean, 631-632-7052, Fax: 631-632-9046, E-mail: paul.edelson@stonybrook.edu.

Sul Ross State University, School of Professional Studies, Department of Physical Education, Alpine, TX 79832. Offers M Ed. Part-time programs available. *Entrance requirements:* For master's, GMAT or GRE General Test, minimum GPA of 2.5 in last 60 hours of undergraduate work.

Tarleton State University, College of Graduate Studies, College of Education, Department of Health and Physical Education, Stephenville, TX 76402. Offers physical education (M Ed). Part-time and evening/weekend programs available. *Degree requirements:* For master's, comprehensive exam, thesis optional. *Entrance requirements:* For master's, GRE General Test, minimum GPA of 3.0. Additional exam requirements/recommendations for international students: Required—TOEFL (minimum score 550 paper-based; 213 computer-based; 80 iBT). Electronic applications accepted.

Teachers College, Columbia University, Graduate Faculty of Education, Department of Biobehavioral Studies, Program in Curriculum and Teaching in Physical Education, New York, NY 10027-6696. Offers Ed M, MA, Ed D. Part-time and evening/weekend programs available. *Faculty:* 1 full-time (0 women). *Students:* 1 full-time (0 women), 25 part-time (11 women); includes 6 minority (3 African Americans, 3 Hispanic Americans), 1 international. Average age 34. 8 applicants, 63% accepted, 4 enrolled. In 2009, 5 master's, 2 doctorates awarded. Terminal master's awarded for partial completion of doctoral program. *Degree requirements:* For master's, integrative paper; for doctorate, thesis/dissertation. *Entrance requirements:* For doctorate, GRE General Test. *Application deadline:* For fall admission, 5/15 for domestic students; for spring admission, 12/1 for domestic students. Application fee: $65. *Financial support:* Career-related internships or fieldwork, Federal Work-Study, institutionally sponsored loans, and tuition waivers (full and partial) available. Support available to part-time students. Financial award application deadline: 2/1. *Faculty research:* Analysis of teaching, teacher performance, program development, data bank project in physical education. *Unit head:* John H. Saxman, Chair, 212-678-3895, E-mail: jhs37@columbia.edu. *Application contact:* Debbie Lesperance, Assistant Director of Admission, 212-678-3710, Fax: 212-678-4171.

Teachers College, Columbia University, Graduate Faculty of Education, Department of Biobehavioral Studies, Program in Physical Education, New York, NY 10027-6696. Offers MA.

Temple University, Health Sciences Center and Graduate School, College of Health Professions, Department of Kinesiology, Philadelphia, PA 19122-6096. Offers kinesiology (Ed M, PhD), including behavioral sciences, somatic sciences. Part-time programs available. Terminal master's awarded for partial completion of doctoral program. *Degree requirements:* For master's, thesis; for doctorate, thesis/dissertation. *Entrance requirements:* For master's, GRE General Test or MAT, minimum undergraduate GPA of 3.0; for doctorate, GRE General Test, minimum undergraduate GPA of 3.0. Additional exam requirements/recommendations for international students: Required—TOEFL (minimum score 550 paper-based; 213 computer-based; 79 iBT).

Tennessee State University, The School of Graduate Studies and Research, College of Education, Department of Human Performance and Sports Science, Nashville, TN 37209-1561. Offers MA Ed. *Degree requirements:* For master's, thesis optional. *Entrance requirements:* For master's, GRE General Test or MAT.

Tennessee Technological University, Graduate School, College of Education, Department of Exercise Science, Physical Education and Wellness, Cookeville, TN 38505. Offers MA. *Accreditation:* NCATE. Part-time programs available. *Faculty:* 7 full-time (0 women). *Students:* 14 full-time (8 women), 32 part-time (17 women); includes 5 minority (4 African Americans, 1 American Indian/Alaska Native). Average age 27. 27 applicants, 93% accepted, 20 enrolled. In 2009, 17 master's awarded. *Degree requirements:* For master's, comprehensive exam, thesis or alternative. *Entrance requirements:* For master's, MAT or GRE. Additional exam requirements/recommendations for international students: Required—TOEFL (minimum score 550 paper-based; 79 iBT), IELTS (minimum score 5.5). *Application deadline:* For fall admission, 8/1 for domestic students, 5/1 for international students; for spring admission, 12/1 for domestic students, 10/1 for international students. Application fee: $25 ($30 for international students). Electronic applications accepted. *Expenses:* Tuition, state resident: full-time $7034; part-time $368 per credit hour. *Financial support:* In 2009–10, fellowships (averaging $8,000 per year), 3 research assistantships (averaging $4,000 per year), 4 teaching assistantships (averaging $4,000 per year) were awarded; career-related internships or fieldwork also available. Financial award application deadline: 4/1. *Unit head:* Dr. Patricia Jordan, Interim Chairperson, 931-372-3467, Fax: 931-372-6319. *Application contact:* Shelia K. Kendrick, Coordinator of Graduate Studies, 931-372-3808, Fax: 931-372-3497, E-mail: skendrick@tntech.edu.

Texas A&M University, College of Education and Human Development, Department of Health and Kinesiology, College Station, TX 77843. Offers health education (M Ed, MS, Ed D, PhD); kinesiology (M Ed, MS, Ed D, PhD), including kinesiology (MS, PhD), physical education (M Ed, Ed D). Part-time programs available. *Faculty:* 33. *Students:* 132 full-time (57 women), 25 part-time (15 women); includes 26 minority (9 African Americans, 1 American Indian/Alaska Native, 7 Asian Americans or Pacific Islanders, 9 Hispanic Americans), 32 international. Average age 23. In 2009, 42 master's, 10 doctorates awarded. *Degree requirements:* For master's, thesis (for some programs); for doctorate, comprehensive exam, thesis/dissertation. *Entrance requirements:* For master's and doctorate, GRE General Test. Additional exam requirements/recommendations for international students: Required—TOEFL. *Application deadline:* Applications are processed on a rolling basis. Application fee: $50 ($75 for international students). Electronic applications accepted. *Expenses:* Tuition, state resident: full-time $3991; part-time $221.74 per credit hour. Tuition, nonresident: full-time $9049; part-time $502.74 per credit hour. *Financial support:* Fellowships with partial tuition reimbursements, research assistantships, teaching assistantships, career-related internships or fieldwork and institutionally sponsored loans available. Financial award application deadline: 2/15; financial award applicants required to submit FAFSA. *Unit head:* Head, 979-845-3491, Fax: 979-847-8987, E-mail: info@hlkn.tamu.edu. *Application contact:* Information Contact, 979-458-2673, Fax: 979-847-8987, E-mail: info@hlkn.tamu.edu.

Texas A&M University–Commerce, Graduate School, College of Education and Human Services, Department of Health and Human Performance, Commerce, TX 75429-3011. Offers exercise physiology (MS); health and human performance (M Ed); health promotion (MS); health, kinesiology and sports studies (Ed D); motor performance (MS); sport studies (MS). Part-time programs available. *Degree requirements:* For master's, comprehensive exam, thesis (for some programs). *Entrance requirements:* For master's, GRE General Test. Electronic applications accepted. *Faculty research:* Teaching, physical fitness.

Texas Southern University, College of Education, Department of Health and Kinesiology, Houston, TX 77004-4584. Offers health education (MS); human performance (MS). Part-time and evening/weekend programs available. *Faculty:* 5 full-time (2 women). *Students:* 13 full-time (7 women), 17 part-time (12 women); includes 26 minority (25 African Americans, 1 Hispanic American), 2 international. Average age 32. 13 applicants, 92% accepted, 10 enrolled. In 2009, 8 master's awarded. *Degree requirements:* For master's, comprehensive exam, thesis optional. *Entrance requirements:* For master's, GRE General Test, minimum GPA of 2.5. Additional exam requirements/recommendations for international students: Required—TOEFL. *Application deadline:* For fall admission, 7/1 for domestic and international students; for spring admission, 11/1 for domestic and international students. Applications are processed on a rolling basis. Application fee: $50 ($75 for international students). Electronic applications accepted. *Expenses:* Tuition; state resident: full-time $1805; part-time $100 per credit hour. Tuition, nonresident: full-time $6470; part-time $343 per credit hour. Tuition and fees vary according to course level, course load and degree level. *Financial support:* In 2009–10, 3 teaching assistantships (averaging $4,041 per year) were awarded; scholarships/grants and unspecified assistantships also available. Support available to part-time students. Financial award application deadline: 5/1. *Unit head:* Dr. Marie Horton, Interim Chair, 713-313-7087, E-mail: horton_mr@tsu.edu. *Application contact:* Dr. Gregory Maddox, Interim Dean of the Graduate School, 713-313-7011 Ext. 4410, Fax: 713-639-1876, E-mail: maddox_gh@tsu.edu.

Texas State University–San Marcos, Graduate School, College of Education, Department of Health and Human Performance, Program in Physical Education, San Marcos, TX 78666. Offers M Ed. Part-time and evening/weekend programs available. *Faculty:* 6 full-time (3 women). *Students:* 57 full-time (18 women), 48 part-time (20 women); includes 48 minority (14 African Americans, 2 Asian Americans or Pacific Islanders, 32 Hispanic Americans), 1 international. Average age 27. 56 applicants, 95% accepted, 35 enrolled. In 2009, 36 master's awarded. *Degree requirements:* For master's, comprehensive exam, thesis optional. *Entrance requirements:* For master's, GRE General Test, minimum GPA of 2.75 in last 60 hours of course work. Additional exam requirements/recommendations for international students: Required—TOEFL (minimum score 550 paper-based; 213 computer-based). *Application deadline:* For fall admission, 6/15 priority date for domestic students; for spring admission, 10/15 priority date for domestic students. Applications are processed on a rolling basis. Application fee: $40 ($90 for international students). Electronic applications accepted. *Expenses:* Tuition, state resident: full-time $5784; part-time $241 per credit hour. Tuition, nonresident: full-time $13,224; part-time $551 per credit hour. Required fees: $1728; $48 per credit hour. $306. Tuition and fees vary according to course load. *Financial support:* In 2009–10, 86 students received support, including 7 research assistantships (averaging $5,385 per year), 12 teaching assistantships (averaging $5,301 per year); career-related internships or fieldwork, Federal Work-Study, and institutionally sponsored loans also available. Support available to part-time students. Financial award application deadline: 4/1; financial award applicants required to submit FAFSA. *Faculty research:* AIDS education, employee wellness, isometric strength evaluation. *Unit head:* Dr. Duane Knudson, Head, 512-245-2561, Fax: 512-245-8678, E-mail: dk19@txstate.edu. *Application contact:* Dr. John Walker, Head, 512-245-2561, Fax: 512-245-8678, E-mail: jw18@txstate.edu.

Texas State University–San Marcos, Graduate School, Interdisciplinary Studies Program in Health, Physical Education, and Recreation, San Marcos, TX 78666. Offers MAIS. Part-time and evening/weekend programs available. *Students:* 7 full-time (5 women), 4 part-time (0 women); includes 1 minority (Hispanic American). Average age 28. 5 applicants, 100% accepted, 5 enrolled. In 2009, 1 master's awarded. *Degree requirements:* For master's, comprehensive exam, thesis optional. *Entrance requirements:* For master's, GRE General Test, minimum GPA of 2.75 in last 60 hours of course work. Additional exam requirements/recommendations for international students: Required—TOEFL (minimum score 550 paper-based; 213 computer-based). *Application deadline:* For fall admission, 6/15 priority date for domestic students, 6/1 for international students; for spring admission, 10/15 priority date for domestic students, 10/1 for international students. Applications are processed on a rolling basis. Application fee: $40 ($90 for international students). *Expenses:* Tuition, state resident: full-time $5784; part-time $241 per credit hour. Tuition, nonresident: full-time $13,224; part-time $551 per credit hour. Required fees: $1728; $48 per credit hour. $306. Tuition and fees vary according to course load. *Financial support:* In 2009–10, 8 students received support, including 2 teaching assistantships (averaging $5,751 per year); career-related internships or fieldwork, Federal Work-Study, and institutionally sponsored loans also available. Support available to part-time students. Financial award application deadline: 4/1; financial award applicants required to submit FAFSA. *Unit head:* Dr. Tinker Murray, Head, 512-245-2561, Fax: 512-245-8678, E-mail: tm05@txstate.edu. *Application contact:* Dr. J. Michael Willoughby, Dean of Graduate School, 512-245-2581, Fax: 512-245-8365, E-mail: gradcollege@txstate.edu.

Troy University, Graduate School, College of Education, Program in Teacher Education-Multiple Levels, Troy, AL 36082. Offers alternative 5th year art education (MS); alternative 5th year instrumental (MS); alternative 5th year physical education (MS); alternative 5th year vocal/choral (MS); traditional art education (MS); traditional gifted education (MS); traditional instrumental (MS); traditional physical education (MS); traditional reading specialist (MS); traditional vocal/choral (MS). Part-time and evening/weekend programs available. *Students:* 5 full-time (3 women), 21 part-time (12 women); includes 11 minority (9 African Americans, 1 American Indian/Alaska Native, 1 Asian American or Pacific Islander). Average age 30. 2 applicants, 50% accepted. In 2009, 8 master's awarded. *Degree requirements:* For master's, comprehensive exam, thesis. *Entrance requirements:* For master's, minimum GPA of 2.5. Additional exam requirements/recommendations for international students: Required—TOEFL (minimum score 523 paper-based; 193 computer-based; 70 iBT), IELTS (minimum score 6). *Application deadline:* Applications are processed on a rolling basis. Application fee: $50. Electronic applications accepted. *Financial support:* Available to part-time students. Applicants required to submit FAFSA. *Unit head:* Dr. Marian Parker, Coordinator, 334-670-5661, Fax: 334-670-3548, E-mail: mjparker@troy.edu. *Application contact:* Brenda K. Campbell, Director of Graduate Admissions, 334-670-3178, Fax: 334-670-3733, E-mail: bcamp@troy.edu.

Union College, Graduate Programs, Department of Education, Barbourville, KY 40906-1499. Offers elementary education (MA); health and physical education (MA); middle grades (MA); music education (MA); principalship (MA); reading specialist (MA); secondary education (MA); special education (MA). *Degree requirements:* For master's, thesis optional. *Entrance requirements:* For master's, GRE General Test, NTE.

United States Sports Academy, Graduate Programs, Program in Sports Coaching, Daphne, AL 36526-7055. Offers MSS. Part-time programs available. Postbaccalaureate distance learning degree programs offered (no on-campus study). *Degree requirements:* For master's, comprehensive exam, thesis optional. *Entrance requirements:* For master's, GRE General Test, GMAT, or MAT, minimum GPA of 2.5, 3 letters of recommendation, resume. Additional exam requirements/recommendations for international students: Required—TOEFL (minimum score 500 paper-based; 213 computer-based). *Application deadline:* Applications are processed on a rolling basis. Application fee: $50 ($125 for international students). Electronic applications accepted. *Financial support:* Career-related internships or fieldwork, Federal Work-Study, scholarships/grants, and service assistantships available. Support available to part-time students. Financial award application deadline: 8/15; financial award applicants required to submit FAFSA. *Faculty research:* Effect of attentional skill on sports performance, survey of coaching qualifications, coaching certification. Total annual research expenditures: $2,500. *Unit head:* Chair, 251-626-3303 Ext. 7139, Fax: 251-626-1149. *Application contact:* Craig T. Bogar, Assistant Dean of Student Services, 251-626-3303 Ext. 7147, Fax: 251-625-1035, E-mail: cbogar@ussa.edu.

Universidad del Turabo, Graduate Programs, Programs in Education, Program in Coaching, Gurabo, PR 00778-3030. Offers MPHE. *Students:* 30 full-time (6 women), 9 part-time (0 women); includes 36 Hispanic Americans. Average age 30. 25 applicants, 92% accepted, 18 enrolled. In 2009, 11 master's awarded. *Unit head:* Angela Candelario, Dean, 787-743-7979 Ext. 4126. *Application contact:* Virginia Gonzalez, Admissions Officer, 787-746-3009.

Universidad Metropolitana, Graduate Programs in Education, Program in Teaching of Physical Education, San Juan, PR 00928-1150. Offers M Ed. *Degree requirements:* For master's, thesis or alternative. *Entrance requirements:* For master's, EXADEP, interview. Electronic applications accepted.

Université de Montréal, Department of Kinesiology, Montréal, QC H3C 3J7, Canada. Offers kinesiology (M Sc, DESS); physical activity (M Sc, PhD). *Faculty:* 15 full-time (3 women), 15 part-time/adjunct (3 women). *Students:* 68 full-time (42 women), 14 part-time (8 women). Average age 26. 103 applicants, 31% accepted, 17 enrolled. In 2009, 10 master's, 3 doctorates, 2 other advanced degrees awarded. *Degree requirements:* For master's, one foreign language,

thesis (for some programs); for doctorate, one foreign language, thesis/dissertation, general exam. *Application deadline:* For fall admission, 2/1 priority date for domestic students; for winter admission, 11/1 priority date for domestic students; for spring admission, 2/1 priority date for domestic students. Application fee: $100. Electronic applications accepted. *Financial support:* In 2009–10, 3 fellowships (averaging $20,000 per year), 10 research assistantships (averaging $5,000 per year), 6 teaching assistantships (averaging $7,000 per year) were awarded. Financial award application deadline: 2/1. *Faculty research:* Physiology of exercise, psychology of sports, biomechanics, dance, sociology of sports. Total annual research expenditures: $600,000. *Unit head:* Francois Prince, Director, 514-343-6116, Fax: 514-343-2181, E-mail: francois.prince@umontreal.ca. *Application contact:* Francine Normandeau, Information Contact, 514-343-6152, E-mail: francine.normandeau@umontreal.ca.

Université de Sherbrooke, Faculty of Physical Education and Sports, Program in Physical Education, Sherbrooke, QC J1K 2R1, Canada. Offers kinanthropology (M Sc); physical activity (Diploma). *Degree requirements:* For master's, thesis. *Entrance requirements:* For master's, minimum GPA of 2.7; for Diploma, bachelor's degree in physical education. *Faculty research:* Physical fitness, nutrition, human factors, sociology, teaching.

Université du Québec à Trois-Rivières, Graduate Programs, Program in Physical Education, Trois-Rivières, QC G9A 5H7, Canada. Offers M Sc. Part-time programs available. *Degree requirements:* For master's, thesis. *Entrance requirements:* For master's, appropriate bachelor's degree, proficiency in French.

The University of Akron, Graduate School, College of Education, Department of Sport Science and Wellness Education, Program in Sports Science/Coaching, Akron, OH 44325. Offers MA, MS. *Students:* 34 full-time (8 women), 16 part-time (4 women); includes 12 minority (9 African Americans, 1 Asian American or Pacific Islander, 2 Hispanic Americans), 1 international. Average age 29. 29 applicants, 93% accepted, 21 enrolled. In 2009, 31 master's awarded. *Degree requirements:* For master's, comprehensive exam, thesis optional. *Entrance requirements:* For master's, minimum GPA of 2.75, letters of recommendation. Additional exam requirements/recommendations for international students: Required—TOEFL (minimum score 550 paper-based; 213 computer-based; 79 iBT). *Application deadline:* Applications are processed on a rolling basis. Application fee: $30 ($40 for international students). Electronic applications accepted. *Expenses:* Tuition, state resident: full-time $6570; part-time $365 per credit hour. Tuition, nonresident: full-time $11,250; part-time $625 per credit hour. *Unit head:* Dr. Alan Kornspan, Head, 330-972-8145, E-mail: alan3@uakron.edu. *Application contact:* Dr. Alan Kornspan, Head, 330-972-8145, E-mail: alan3@uakron.edu.

The University of Alabama, Graduate School, College of Education, Department of Kinesiology, Tuscaloosa, AL 35487. Offers alternative sport pedagogy (MA); exercise science (MA, PhD); human performance (MA); sport management (MA); sport pedagogy (MA, PhD). Part-time programs available. *Faculty:* 7 full-time (1 woman). *Students:* 63 full-time (30 women), 17 part-time (4 women); includes 5 minority (3 African Americans, 1 American Indian/Alaska Native, 1 Hispanic American), 11 international. Average age 28. 74 applicants, 64% accepted, 29 enrolled. In 2009, 22 master's, 5 doctorates awarded. *Median time to degree:* Of those who began their doctoral program in fall 2001, 100% received their degree in 8 years or less. *Degree requirements:* For master's, comprehensive exam, thesis optional; for doctorate, comprehensive exam, thesis/dissertation. *Entrance requirements:* For master's and doctorate, GRE, MAT, minimum GPA of 3.0. Additional exam requirements/recommendations for international students: Required—TOEFL. *Application deadline:* Applications are processed on a rolling basis. Application fee: $50 ($60 for international students). Electronic applications accepted. *Expenses:* Tuition, state resident: full-time $7000. Tuition, nonresident: full-time $19,200. *Financial support:* In 2009–10, 14 students received support, including 13 teaching assistantships with full tuition reimbursements available (averaging $8,678 per year). *Faculty research:* Race, gender and sexuality in sports; physical education curriculum reform; disability sports; physical activity and health; environmental physiology. Total annual research expenditures: $46,329. *Unit head:* Dr. Matt Curtner-Smith, Department Head and Professor, 205-348-9209, Fax: 205-348-0867, E-mail: msmith@bamaed.ua.edu. *Application contact:* Dr. Kathy S. Wetzel, Assistant Dean for Student Services, 205-348-1154, Fax: 205-348-0080, E-mail: kwetzel@bamaed.ua.edu.

The University of Alabama at Birmingham, College of Arts and Sciences, School of Education, Program in Physical Education, Birmingham, AL 35294. Offers MA Ed. Evening/weekend programs available. *Degree requirements:* For master's, thesis optional. *Entrance requirements:* For master's, GRE General Test, MAT, or NTE, minimum GPA of 3.0. Electronic applications accepted.

University of Alberta, Faculty of Graduate Studies and Research, Department of Physical Education and Recreation, Edmonton, AB T6G 2E1, Canada. Offers physical education (M Sc); recreation and physical education (MA, PhD). Part-time programs available. *Faculty:* 30 full-time (10 women). *Students:* 60 full-time (34 women), 55 part-time (28 women). 69 applicants, 36% accepted. In 2009, 13 master's, 7 doctorates awarded. Terminal master's awarded for partial completion of doctoral program. *Degree requirements:* For master's, thesis (for some programs); for doctorate, thesis/dissertation. *Entrance requirements:* For master's, bachelor's degree in related field; for doctorate, master's degree in related field with thesis. Additional exam requirements/recommendations for international students: Required—TOEFL. *Application deadline:* For fall admission, 1/1 priority date for domestic students. Applications are processed on a rolling basis. Tuition and fees charges are reported in Canadian dollars. *Expenses:* Tuition, area resident: Full-time $4626 Canadian dollars; part-time $99.72 Canadian dollars per unit. International tuition: $8216 Canadian dollars full-time. Required fees: $3590 Canadian dollars; $99.72 Canadian dollars per unit. $215 Canadian dollars per term. *Financial support:* In 2009–10, 63 students received support, including 28 research assistantships, 35 teaching assistantships; career-related internships or fieldwork and scholarships/grants also available. Support available to part-time students. *Faculty research:* Motivation and adherence to physical ability, performance enhancement, adapted physical activity, exercise physiology, sport administration, tourism. *Unit head:* Dr. D. Marshall, Assistant Dean, 780-492-3198, Fax: 403-492-2364. *Application contact:* Anne Jordan, Department Office, 403-492-3198, Fax: 403-492-2364, E-mail: pergrad@ualberta.ca.

University of Arkansas, Graduate School, College of Education and Health Professions, Department of Health Science, Kinesiology, Recreation and Dance, Program in Physical Education, Fayetteville, AR 72701-1201. Offers M Ed, MAT. *Students:* 1 full-time (0 women), 17 part-time (8 women); includes 1 minority (African American). In 2009, 10 master's awarded. *Degree requirements:* For master's, thesis optional. Application fee: $40 ($50 for international students). *Expenses:* Tuition, state resident: full-time $7355; part-time $356.58 per hour. Tuition, nonresident: full-time $17,401; part-time $775.17 per hour. Required fees: $1203. *Financial support:* Fellowships with tuition reimbursements, research assistantships, teaching assistantships, career-related internships or fieldwork and Federal Work-Study available. Support available to part-time students. Financial award application deadline: 4/1; financial award applicants required to submit FAFSA. *Unit head:* Dr. Sharon Hunt, Department Chairperson, 479-575-2890, Fax: 479-575-5778, E-mail: sbhunt@uark.edu. *Application contact:* Dr. Dean Gorman, Coordinator of Graduate Studies, 479-575-2890, E-mail: dgorman@uark.edu.

University of Arkansas at Pine Bluff, Program in Education, Pine Bluff, AR 71601-2799. Offers elementary education (M Ed); secondary education (M Ed), including general science, physical education, social studies. *Accreditation:* NCATE. Part-time and evening/weekend programs available. *Degree requirements:* For master's, comprehensive exam. *Entrance requirements:* For master's, GRE, minimum GPA of 2.75, NTE or Standard Arkansas Teaching Certificate. *Faculty research:* Teacher certification, accreditation, assessment, standards, portfolio development, rehabilitation, technology.

The University of British Columbia, Faculty of Education, Department of Curriculum and Pedagogy, Vancouver, BC V6T 1Z4, Canada. Offers art education (M Ed, MA); business education (MA); curriculum studies (M Ed, MA, PhD); home economics education (M Ed, MA); math education (M Ed, MA); music education (M Ed, MA); physical education (M Ed, MA); science education (M Ed, MA); social studies education (M Ed, MA); technology studies education (M Ed, MA). Part-time programs available. *Degree requirements:* For master's, thesis (MA); for doctorate, comprehensive exam, thesis/dissertation. *Entrance requirements:* Additional exam requirements/recommendations for international students: Required—TOEFL (minimum score 580 paper-based; 237 computer-based; 92 iBT). Electronic applications accepted. *Expenses:* Contact institution. *Faculty research:* School subjects, teaching and learning.

University of Central Florida, College of Education, Department of Child, Family and Community Sciences, Program in Sport and Fitness, Orlando, FL 32816. Offers sport and fitness (MA); sport leadership (Certificate). Part-time and evening/weekend programs available. *Students:* 31 full-time (14 women), 42 part-time (21 women); includes 15 minority (10 African Americans, 5 Hispanic Americans). Average age 26. 78 applicants, 77% accepted, 33 enrolled. In 2009, 17 master's awarded. *Entrance requirements:* For master's, GRE General Test. Additional exam requirements/recommendations for international students: Required—TOEFL. *Application deadline:* For fall admission, 7/15 for domestic students; for spring admission, 12/1 for domestic students. Application fee: $30. Electronic applications accepted. *Expenses:* Tuition, state resident: part-time $306.31 per credit hour. Tuition, nonresident: part-time $1099.01 per credit hour. Part-time tuition and fees vary according to degree level and program. *Financial support:* In 2009–10, 5 students received support, including 2 fellowships with partial tuition reimbursements available (averaging $7,500 per year), 1 research assistantship with partial tuition reimbursement available (averaging $6,900 per year), 3 teaching assistantships with partial tuition reimbursements available (averaging $4,700 per year); career-related internships or fieldwork, Federal Work-Study, institutionally sponsored loans, tuition waivers (partial), and unspecified assistantships also available. Financial award application deadline: 3/1; financial award applicants required to submit FAFSA.

University of Central Missouri, The Graduate School, College of Health and Human Services, Warrensburg, MO 64093. Offers criminal justice (MS); industrial hygiene (MS); occupational safety management (MS); physical education/exercise and sport science (MS); rural family nursing (MS); social gerontology (MS); sociology (MA); speech language pathology and audiology (MS). *Accreditation:* NCATE. Part-time programs available. Postbaccalaureate distance learning degree programs offered. *Faculty:* 53. *Students:* 169 full-time (107 women), 364 part-time (210 women); includes 65 minority (46 African Americans, 1 American Indian/Alaska Native, 5 Asian Americans or Pacific Islanders, 13 Hispanic Americans), 27 international. Average age 32. 236 applicants, 92% accepted, 211 enrolled. In 2009, 153 master's awarded. *Entrance requirements:* Additional exam requirements/recommendations for international students: Required—TOEFL (minimum score 550 paper-based; 79 computer-based). *Application deadline:* For fall admission, 6/1 priority date for domestic students, 5/1 for international students; for spring admission, 10/1 priority date for domestic students, 10/1 for international students. Applications are processed on a rolling basis. Application fee: $30 ($75 for international students). Electronic applications accepted. *Expenses:* Tuition, area resident: Part-time $245.80 per credit hour. Tuition, nonresident: part-time $491.60 per credit hour. Required fees: $24.20 per credit hour. Full-time tuition and fees vary according to course load, degree level, campus/location and reciprocity agreements. *Financial support:* Research assistantships with full and partial tuition reimbursements, teaching assistantships with full and partial tuition reimbursements, career-related internships or fieldwork, Federal Work-Study, scholarships/grants, and administrative and laboratory assistantships available. Support available to part-time students. Financial award application deadline: 3/1; financial award applicants required to submit FAFSA. *Unit head:* Dr. Rick Sluder, Dean, 660-543-4245, Fax: 660-543-4167, E-mail: sluder@ucmo.edu. *Application contact:* Laurie Delap, Admissions Coordinator, 660-543-4621, Fax: 660-543-4778, E-mail: gradinfo@ucmo.edu.

University of Dayton, Graduate School, School of Education and Allied Professions, Department of Health and Sport Science, Dayton, OH 45469-1300. Offers exercise science (MS Ed); physical therapy (DPT). Part-time and evening/weekend programs available. *Faculty:* 16 full-time (7 women). *Students:* 116 full-time (79 women), 3 part-time (all women); includes 9 minority (5 African Americans, 3 Asian Americans or Pacific Islanders, 1 Hispanic American), 2 international. Average age 25. 200 applicants, 37% accepted, 43 enrolled. In 2009, 3 master's awarded. *Degree requirements:* For master's, thesis; for doctorate, thesis/dissertation. *Entrance requirements:* For master's, GRE General Test, MAT, minimum GPA of 2.75; for doctorate, GRE General Test, minimum GPA of 3.0, 80 observation hours. Additional exam requirements/recommendations for international students: Required—TOEFL (minimum score 550 paper-based; 213 computer-based; 80 iBT). *Application deadline:* For fall admission, 2/15 priority date for domestic students, 3/1 priority date for international students; for winter admission, 7/1 priority date for international students; for spring admission, 1/1 priority date for international students. Applications are processed on a rolling basis. Application fee: $0 ($50 for international students). Electronic applications accepted. *Expenses:* Tuition: Full-time $8412; part-time $701 per credit hour. Required fees: $325; $65 per course. $25 per semester. Tuition and fees vary according to course load, degree level and program. *Financial support:* In 2009–10, 4 students received support, including 4 teaching assistantships with tuition reimbursements available (averaging $8,000 per year); research assistantships, career-related internships or fieldwork, institutionally sponsored loans, health care benefits, and unspecified assistantships also available. Financial award applicants required to submit FAFSA. *Faculty research:* Energy expenditure, strength, training, teaching nutrition and calcium intake of children and families in Head-Start. *Unit head:* Dr. Lloyd Laubach, Interim Chair, 937-229-4240, Fax: 937-229-4244, E-mail: lloyd.laubach@notes.udayton.edu. *Application contact:* Graduate Admissions, 937-229-4411, Fax: 937-229-4729, E-mail: gradadmission@udayton.edu.

University of Florida, Graduate School, College of Health and Human Performance, Department of Applied Physiology and Kinesiology, Gainesville, FL 32611. Offers athletic training/sport medicine (MS, PhD); biomechanics (MS, PhD); clinical exercise physiology (MS); exercise physiology (MS, PhD); health and human performance (PhD); human performance (MS); motor learning/control (MS, PhD); sport and exercise psychology (MS). *Degree requirements:* For doctorate, thesis/dissertation. *Entrance requirements:* For doctorate, GRE General Test. Electronic applications accepted.

University of Georgia, Graduate School, College of Education, Department of Kinesiology, Athens, GA 30602. Offers MS, PhD. *Faculty:* 20 full-time (5 women). *Students:* 103 full-time (48 women), 22 part-time (7 women); includes 17 minority (10 African Americans, 2 Asian Americans or Pacific Islanders, 5 Hispanic Americans), 14 international. Average age 27. 175 applicants, 41% accepted, 44 enrolled. In 2009, 29 master's, 8 doctorates awarded. *Entrance requirements:* For master's, GRE General Test or MAT; for doctorate, GRE General Test. Additional exam requirements/recommendations for international students: Required—TOEFL. *Application deadline:* For fall admission, 7/1 priority date for domestic students; for spring admission, 11/15 for domestic students. Application fee: $50. Electronic applications accepted. *Expenses:* Tuition, state resident: full-time $6000; part-time $250 per credit hour. Tuition, nonresident: full-time $20,904; part-time $871 per credit hour. Required fees: $730 per semester. *Unit head:* Dr. Kirk J. Cureton, Head, 706-542-4387, Fax: 706-542-3148, E-mail: kcureton@uga.edu. *Application contact:* Dr. Ted A. Baumgartner, Graduate Coordinator, 706-542-4424, Fax: 706-542-3148, E-mail: tbaumgar@uga.edu.

University of Houston, College of Education, Department of Health and Human Performance, Houston, TX 77204. Offers allied health education and administration (M Ed, Ed D); exercise science (MS); health education (M Ed); human nutrition (MS); human space exploration sciences (MS); kinesiology (PhD); physical education (M Ed). *Accreditation:* NCATE (one or more programs are accredited). Part-time and evening/weekend programs available. *Faculty:* 12 full-time (4 women), 4 part-time/adjunct (3 women). *Students:* 53 full-time (26 women), 39 part-time (25 women); includes 21 minority (12 African Americans, 6 Asian Americans or Pacific Islanders, 3 Hispanic Americans), 14 international. Average age 29. 78 applicants, 64% accepted, 26 enrolled. In 2009, 20 master's, 2 doctorates awarded. *Degree requirements:* For master's, comprehensive exam, thesis (for some programs); for doctorate, comprehensive exam, thesis/dissertation, qualifying exam, candidacy paper. *Entrance requirements:* For master's, GRE (minimum 35th percentile on each section), minimum cumulative GPA of 3.0;

Physical Education

University of Houston *(continued)*
for doctorate, GRE (minimum 35th percentile on each section), minimum cumulative GPA of 3.3. Additional exam requirements/recommendations for international students: Required—TOEFL (minimum score 550 paper-based; 79 iBT). *Application deadline:* For fall admission, 5/1 for domestic students, 4/1 for international students; for spring admission, 10/1 for domestic and international students. Applications are processed on a rolling basis. Application fee: $45 ($75 for international students). Electronic applications accepted. *Expenses:* Tuition, state resident: full-time $7676; part-time $320 per credit hour. Tuition, nonresident: full-time $14,324; part-time $597 per credit hour. Required fees: $3034. *Financial support:* In 2009–10, 7 fellowships with full tuition reimbursements (averaging $9,500 per year), 8 research assistantships with full tuition reimbursements (averaging $9,850 per year), 12 teaching assistantships with full tuition reimbursements (averaging $9,850 per year) were awarded; career-related internships or fieldwork, Federal Work-Study, institutionally sponsored loans, scholarships/grants, health care benefits, and unspecified assistantships also available. Support available to part-time students. Financial award application deadline: 2/1. *Faculty research:* Biomechanics, exercise physiology, obesity, nutrition, space exploration science. *Unit head:* Dr. Charles Layne, Chairperson, 713-743-9868, Fax: 713-743-9860, E-mail: clayne2@uh.edu. *Application contact:* Todd Boutte, Graduate Admission Counselor, 713-743-0571, Fax: 713-743-0123, E-mail: tboutte@mail.coe.uh.edu.

University of Idaho, College of Graduate Studies, College of Education, Department of Health, Physical Education, Recreation, and Dance, Program in Physical Education, Moscow, ID 83844-2282. Offers M Ed. *Students:* 11 full-time, 10 part-time. In 2009, 6 master's awarded. *Entrance requirements:* For master's, minimum GPA of 2.8. *Application deadline:* For fall admission, 8/1 for domestic students; for spring admission, 12/15 for domestic students. Application fee: $55 ($60 for international students). *Expenses:* Tuition, state resident: full-time $6120. Tuition, nonresident: full-time $17,712. *Financial support:* Research assistantships, teaching assistantships available. Financial award application deadline: 2/15. *Unit head:* Dr. Kathy Browder, Chair, 208-885-2192. *Application contact:* Dr. Kathy Browder, Chair, 208-885-2192.

University of Indianapolis, Graduate Programs, School of Education, Indianapolis, IN 46227-3697. Offers art education (MAT); biology (MAT); chemistry (MAT); curriculum and instruction (MA); earth sciences (MAT); education (MA, MAT); educational leadership (MA); elementary education (MA); English (MAT); French (MAT); math (MAT); physical education (MAT); physics (MAT); secondary education (MA), including art education, education, English education, social studies education; social studies (MAT); Spanish (MAT). *Accreditation:* NCATE. Part-time and evening/weekend programs available. *Faculty:* 4 full-time (3 women), 3 part-time/adjunct (2 women). *Students:* 52 full-time (28 women), 110 part-time (67 women); includes 3 minority (all African Americans), 2 international. Average age 33. *Entrance requirements:* For master's, GRE Subject Test, PRAXIS I, minimum GPA of 2.5, 3 letters of recommendation, interview, writing exercise. Additional exam requirements/recommendations for international students: Required—TOEFL (minimum score 550 paper-based; 213 computer-based). *Application deadline:* Applications are processed on a rolling basis. Application fee: $50. *Financial support:* Federal Work-Study available. Financial award application deadline: 5/1; financial award applicants required to submit FAFSA. *Faculty research:* Assessment of teacher education, perceptions of prospective teachers by parents. *Unit head:* Dr. Kathy Moran, Dean, 317-788-3285, Fax: 317-788-3300, E-mail: kmoran@uindy.edu. *Application contact:* Chemain Slater, 317-788-2051, E-mail: slaterc@uindy.edu.

The University of Iowa, Graduate College, College of Liberal Arts and Sciences, Department of Health and Sport Studies, Iowa City, IA 52242-1316. Offers psychology of sport and physical activity (MA, PhD); sports studies (MA, PhD). *Degree requirements:* For master's, thesis optional, exam; for doctorate, comprehensive exam, thesis/dissertation. *Entrance requirements:* For master's and doctorate, GRE General Test, minimum GPA of 3.0. Additional exam requirements/recommendations for international students: Required—TOEFL (minimum score 600 paper-based; 250 computer-based; 100 iBT). Electronic applications accepted.

The University of Kansas, Graduate Studies, School of Education, Department of Health, Sport, and Exercise Sciences, Lawrence, KS 66045. Offers health and physical education (MS Ed, Ed D, PhD). *Accreditation:* NCATE. Part-time and evening/weekend programs available. *Students:* 53 full-time (28 women), 21 part-time (9 women); includes 5 minority (2 American Indian/Alaska Native, 2 Asian Americans or Pacific Islanders, 1 Hispanic American), 4 international. Average age 26. 73 applicants, 56% accepted, 31 enrolled. In 2009, 40 master's, 3 doctorates awarded. *Degree requirements:* For master's, comprehensive exam, thesis (for some programs); for doctorate, variable foreign language requirement, comprehensive exam, thesis/dissertation. *Entrance requirements:* For master's, GRE General Test (minimum score 1000, 450 verbal, 450 quantitative, 4.0 analytical), minimum GPA of 3.0; for doctorate, GRE General Test (minimum score 1100: verbal 500, quantitative 500, analytical 5.0), minimum graduate GPA of 3.5, undergraduate 3.0. Additional exam requirements/recommendations for international students: Required—TOEFL (minimum score 570 paper-based; 230 computer-based). *Application deadline:* For fall admission, 3/15 priority date for domestic students; for spring admission, 10/15 priority date for domestic students. Applications are processed on a rolling basis. Application fee: $45 ($55 for international students). Electronic applications accepted. *Expenses:* Tuition, state resident: full-time $6492; part-time $270.50 per credit hour. Tuition, nonresident: full-time $15,510; part-time $646.25 per credit hour. Required fees: $847; $70.56 per credit hour. Tuition and fees vary according to course load and program. *Financial support:* Research assistantships with full and partial tuition reimbursements, teaching assistantships with full and partial tuition reimbursements available. Financial award application deadline: 4/1. *Faculty research:* Character education, health education, ACE genotype, obesity prevention, force and torque production. *Unit head:* Dr. Andy Fry, Chair, 785-864-0784, Fax: 785-864-3343, E-mail: acfry@ku.edu. *Application contact:* Dr. Keith D. Tennant, Graduate Coordinator, 785-864-4656, Fax: 785-864-3343, E-mail: ktennant@ku.edu.

University of Louisville, Graduate School, College of Education and Human Development, Department of Health and Sport Sciences, Louisville, KY 40292-0001. Offers community health education (M Ed); exercise physiology (MS); health and physical education (MAT); sport administration (MS). Part-time and evening/weekend programs available. *Faculty:* 17 full-time (8 women), 1 part-time/adjunct (0 women). *Students:* 73 full-time (28 women), 28 part-time (17 women); includes 13 minority (11 African Americans, 2 Asian Americans or Pacific Islanders), 8 international. Average age 26. 154 applicants, 67% accepted, 59 enrolled. In 2009, 42 master's awarded. *Entrance requirements:* For master's, GRE General Test. Additional exam requirements/recommendations for international students: Required—TOEFL (minimum score 560 paper-based; 210 computer-based; 83 iBT). Application fee: $50. Electronic applications accepted. *Financial support:* In 2009–10, 21 students received support; fellowships, research assistantships, teaching assistantships, career-related internships or fieldwork, Federal Work-Study, scholarships/grants, and unspecified assistantships available. Financial award application deadline: 6/1; financial award applicants required to submit FAFSA. *Faculty research:* Impact of sports and sport marketing on society, factors associated with school and community health, cardiac and pulmonary rehabilitation, impact of participation in activities on student retention and graduation, strength and conditioning. Total annual research expenditures: $58,888. *Unit head:* Dr. David W. Britt, Chair, 502-852-6645, Fax: 502-852-4534, E-mail: david.britt@louisville.edu. *Application contact:* Libby Leggett, Director, Graduate Admissions, 502-852-3101, Fax: 502-852-6536, E-mail: gradadm@louisville.edu.

University of Maine, Graduate School, College of Education and Human Development, Program in Kinesiology and Physical Education, Orono, ME 04469. Offers M Ed, MS. Part-time and evening/weekend programs available. *Students:* 11 full-time (1 woman), 5 part-time (0 women); includes 1 minority (Hispanic American). Average age 28. 16 applicants, 56% accepted, 5 enrolled. In 2009, 22 master's awarded. *Degree requirements:* For master's, thesis or alternative. *Entrance requirements:* For master's, MAT. Additional exam requirements/recommendations for international students: Required—TOEFL. *Application deadline:* For fall admission, 2/1 priority date for domestic students. Applications are processed on a rolling

basis. Application fee: $65. Electronic applications accepted. *Financial support:* Career-related internships or fieldwork, Federal Work-Study, institutionally sponsored loans, tuition waivers (full and partial), and unspecified assistantships available. Support available to part-time students. Financial award application deadline: 3/1. *Unit head:* Dr. Janet Spector, Coordinator, 207-581-2444, Fax: 207-581-2423. *Application contact:* Scott G. Delcourt, Associate Dean of the Graduate School, 207-581-3291, Fax: 207-581-3232, E-mail: graduate@maine.edu.

University of Manitoba, Faculty of Graduate Studies, Faculty of Kinesiology and Recreation Management, Winnipeg, MB R3T 2N2, Canada. Offers kinesiology and recreation management (M Sc); recreation studies (MA).

University of Memphis, Graduate School, College of Education, Department of Health and Sport Sciences, Memphis, TN 38152. Offers clinical nutrition (MS); exercise and sport science (MS); health promotion (MS); physical education teacher education (MS), including teacher education; sport and leisure commerce (MS). Part-time and evening/weekend programs available. *Faculty:* 18 full-time (9 women), 3 part-time/adjunct (1 woman). *Students:* 64 full-time (35 women), 36 part-time (23 women); includes 17 African Americans, 1 Asian American or Pacific Islander, 1 Hispanic American, 4 international. Average age 27. 99 applicants, 72% accepted, 50 enrolled. In 2009, 35 master's awarded. *Degree requirements:* For master's, comprehensive exam, thesis. *Entrance requirements:* For master's, GRE General Test or GMAT (sport and leisure commerce). *Application deadline:* For fall admission, 5/1 priority date for domestic students; for spring admission, 11/1 for domestic students. Applications are processed on a rolling basis. Application fee: $35 ($60 for international students). *Expenses:* Tuition, state resident: full-time $6246; part-time $347 per credit hour. Tuition, nonresident: full-time $15,894; part-time $883 per credit hour. Required fees: $1160. Full-time tuition and fees vary according to course load, degree level and program. *Financial support:* In 2009–10, 59 students received support; research assistantships with full tuition reimbursements available, teaching assistantships with full tuition reimbursements available, career-related internships or fieldwork, Federal Work-Study, scholarships/grants, tuition waivers (partial), and unspecified assistantships available. Financial award application deadline: 2/15; financial award applicants required to submit FAFSA. *Faculty research:* Sport marketing and consumer analysis, health psychology, smoking cessation, psychosocial aspects of cardiovascular disease, global health promotion. *Unit head:* Linda H. Clemens, Interim Chair, 901-678-2324, Fax: 901-678-3591, E-mail: lhclemns@memphis.edu. *Application contact:* Dr. Kenneth Ward, Graduate Studies Coordinator, 901-678-1714, E-mail: kdward@memphis.edu.

University of Minnesota, Twin Cities Campus, Graduate School, College of Education and Human Development, School of Kinesiology, Minneapolis, MN 55455-0213. Offers adapted physical education (MA, PhD); biomechanics (MA); biomechanics and neural control (PhD); coaching (Certificate); developmental adapted physical education (M Ed); exercise physiology (MA, PhD); human factors/ergonomics (MA, PhD); international/comparative sport (MA, PhD); kinesiology (M Ed, MA, PhD); leisure services/management (MA, PhD); motor development (MA, PhD); motor learning/control (MA, PhD); outdoor education/recreation (MA, PhD); physical education (M Ed); recreation, park, and leisure studies (M Ed, MA, PhD); sport and exercise science (M Ed); sport management (M Ed, MA, PhD); sport psychology (MA, PhD); sport sociology (MA, PhD); therapeutic recreation (MA, PhD). Part-time programs available. *Faculty:* 15 full-time (8 women). *Students:* 139 full-time (67 women), 55 part-time (19 women); includes 24 minority (12 African Americans, 3 American Indian/Alaska Native, 4 Asian Americans or Pacific Islanders, 5 Hispanic Americans), 18 international. Average age 29. 173 applicants, 53% accepted, 74 enrolled. In 2009, 66 master's, 4 doctorates, 18 other advanced degrees awarded. Terminal master's awarded for partial completion of doctoral program. *Degree requirements:* For master's, final oral exam; for doctorate, thesis/dissertation, preliminary written/oral exam, final oral exam. *Entrance requirements:* For master's, GRE or MAT, minimum GPA of 3.0; for doctorate, GRE or MAT, minimum GPA of 3.0, writing sample. *Financial support:* In 2009–10, 2 fellowships (averaging $22,500 per year), 11 research assistantships with full tuition reimbursements (averaging $26,599 per year), 34 teaching assistantships with full tuition reimbursements (averaging $26,081 per year) were awarded; career-related internships or fieldwork, Federal Work-Study, institutionally sponsored loans, and tuition waivers (full and partial) also available. Support available to part-time students. *Faculty research:* Exercise for health promotion and disease prevention and management, female athletes and bone health, affordance perception-action, gender and youth sport and psychosocial outcomes, neurological movement disorders. Total annual research expenditures: $294,676. *Unit head:* Dr. Mary Jo Kane, Director, 612-625-3870, Fax: 612-626-7700, E-mail: maryjo@umn.edu. *Application contact:* Dr. Mary Trettin, Associate Dean, 612-625-6501, Fax: 612-626-1580, E-mail: mtrettin@umn.edu.

The University of Montana, Graduate School, School of Education, Department of Health and Human Performance, Missoula, MT 59812-0002. Offers exercise science (MS); health and human performance (MS); health promotion (MS). Part-time programs available. *Entrance requirements:* For master's, GRE General Test. Additional exam requirements/recommendations for international students: Required—TOEFL. *Faculty research:* Exercise physiology, performance psychology, nutrition, pre-employment physical screening, program evaluation.

University of Nebraska at Kearney, College of Graduate Study, College of Education, Department of Health, Physical Education, Recreation, and Leisure Studies, Kearney, NE 68849-0001. Offers adapted physical education (MA Ed); exercise science (MA Ed); master teacher (MA Ed). Part-time and evening/weekend programs available. *Degree requirements:* For master's, comprehensive exam, thesis optional. *Entrance requirements:* For master's, GRE General Test. Additional exam requirements/recommendations for international students: Required—TOEFL (minimum score 550 paper-based; 213 computer-based). Electronic applications accepted. *Faculty research:* Ergonomic aids, nutrition, motor development, sports pedagogy, applied behavior analysis.

University of Nebraska at Omaha, Graduate Studies, College of Education, School of Health, Physical Education, and Recreation, Omaha, NE 68182. Offers MA, MS. Part-time and evening/weekend programs available. *Faculty:* 12 full-time (4 women). *Students:* 43 full-time (25 women), 38 part-time (23 women); includes 5 minority (4 African Americans, 1 Asian American or Pacific Islander), 12 international. Average age 29. 49 applicants, 53% accepted, 16 enrolled. In 2009, 30 master's awarded. *Degree requirements:* For master's, comprehensive exam, thesis (for some programs). *Entrance requirements:* For master's, minimum GPA of 3.0. Additional exam requirements/recommendations for international students: Required—TOEFL (minimum score 550 paper-based; 213 computer-based; 80 iBT). *Application deadline:* For fall admission, 7/1 priority date for domestic students; for spring admission, 12/1 priority date for domestic students. Applications are processed on a rolling basis. Application fee: $45. Electronic applications accepted. *Financial support:* In 2009–10, 48 students received support, including 8 research assistantships with tuition reimbursements available; fellowships, Federal Work-Study, institutionally sponsored loans, scholarships/grants, tuition waivers (full), and unspecified assistantships also available. Support available to part-time students. Financial award application deadline: 3/1; financial award applicants required to submit FAFSA. *Unit head:* Dr. Dan Blanke, Director, 402-554-2670. *Application contact:* Penny Harmoney, Director, Graduate Studies, 402-554-2341, Fax: 402-554-3143, E-mail: graduate@unomaha.edu.

University of Nevada, Las Vegas, Graduate College, College of Education, Department of Sports Education Leadership, Las Vegas, NV 89154-3031. Offers physical education (M Ed, MS); sports education leadership (PhD). *Faculty:* 8 full-time (5 women), 12 part-time/adjunct (5 women). *Students:* 22 full-time (7 women), 20 part-time (7 women); includes 6 minority (5 African Americans, 1 Hispanic American), 2 international. Average age 31. 42 applicants, 74% accepted, 21 enrolled. In 2009, 9 master's, 5 doctorates awarded. *Degree requirements:* For doctorate, comprehensive exam, thesis/dissertation, scholarly product. *Entrance requirements:* For master's and doctorate, GRE General Test. Additional exam requirements/recommendations for international students: Required—TOEFL (minimum score 550 paper-based; 213 computer-based; 80 iBT), IELTS (minimum score 7). *Application deadline:* For fall admission, 3/1 priority date for domestic and international students; for spring admission, 11/15 priority date for domestic students, 10/1 for international students. Applications are processed on a rolling

basis. Application fee: $60 ($95 for international students). Electronic applications accepted. *Financial support:* In 2009–10, 9 students received support, including 3 research assistantships (averaging $11,333 per year), 6 teaching assistantships (averaging $12,000 per year); institutionally sponsored loans, scholarships/grants, health care benefits, and unspecified assistantships also available. Financial award application deadline: 3/1. *Faculty research:* Physical activity and policy, physical education teacher education, sport marketing, sport policy, sport coaching and administration. *Unit head:* Dr. Monica Lounsbery, Chair/Associate Professor, 702-895-5057, Fax: 702-895-5056, E-mail: monica.lounsbery@unlv.edu. *Application contact:* Graduate College Admissions Evaluator, 702-895-3320, Fax: 702-895-4180, E-mail: gradcollege@unlv.edu.

University of New Brunswick Fredericton, School of Graduate Studies, Faculty of Kinesiology, Fredericton, NB E3B 5A3, Canada. Offers exercise and sport science (M Sc); sport and recreation management (MBA); sport and recreation studies (MA). Part-time programs available. *Faculty:* 17 full-time (7 women). *Students:* 35 full-time (16 women), 6 part-time (5 women). In 2009, 10 master's awarded. *Degree requirements:* For master's, thesis (for some programs). *Entrance requirements:* For master's, minimum GPA of 3.0, written statement of research goals and interests. Additional exam requirements/recommendations for international students: Required—TOEFL (minimum score 600 paper-based; 250 computer-based), TWE (minimum score 4). *Application deadline:* For winter admission, 1/31 for domestic students; for spring admission, 3/31 for domestic students. Applications are processed on a rolling basis. Application fee: $50 Canadian dollars. Electronic applications accepted. Tuition and fees charges are reported in Canadian dollars. *Expenses:* Tuition, area resident: Full-time $5562 Canadian dollars; part-time $2781 Canadian dollars per year. Required fees: $49.75 Canadian dollars per term. *Financial support:* In 2009–10, 2 fellowships with tuition reimbursements were awarded; research assistantships, teaching assistantships, career-related internships or fieldwork and scholarships/grants also available. *Unit head:* Dr. Wayne Albert, Acting Director of Graduate Studies, 506-447-3254, Fax: 506-453-3511, E-mail: walbert@unb.ca. *Application contact:* Linda O'Brien, Graduate Secretary, 506-453-4576, Fax: 506-453-3511, E-mail: lobrien@unb.ca.

University of New Mexico, Graduate School, College of Education, Department of Health, Exercise and Sports Sciences, Program in Physical Education, Albuquerque, NM 87131-2039. Offers MS. Part-time programs available. *Students:* 53 full-time (22 women), 27 part-time (11 women); includes 23 minority (3 African Americans, 3 American Indian/Alaska Native, 17 Hispanic Americans), 12 international. Average age 28. 57 applicants, 72% accepted, 27 enrolled. In 2009, 30 master's awarded. Terminal master's awarded for partial completion of doctoral program. *Degree requirements:* For master's, comprehensive exam, thesis optional. *Entrance requirements:* For master's, GRE, 3 letters of reference, minimum cumulative GPA of 3.0 in last 2 years of bachelor's degree, letter of intent. Additional exam requirements/recommendations for international students: Required—TOEFL (minimum score 550 paper-based; 213 computer-based). *Application deadline:* For fall admission, 3/1 priority date for domestic students; for spring admission, 11/1 priority date for domestic students. Application fee: $50. Electronic applications accepted. *Expenses:* Tuition, state resident: full-time $2099; part-time $233.20 per credit hour. Tuition, nonresident: full-time $6650. Required fees: $25 per semester. Tuition and fees vary according to course load, program and reciprocity agreements. *Financial support:* In 2009–10, 29 students received support, including 20 teaching assistantships with full tuition reimbursements available (averaging $10,815 per year); career-related internships or fieldwork, Federal Work-Study, institutionally sponsored loans, scholarships/grants, health care benefits, tuition waivers, and unspecified assistantships also available. Financial award application deadline: 3/1; financial award applicants required to submit FAFSA. *Faculty research:* Physical education pedagogy, sports psychology, sports administration, cardiac rehabilitation, sports physiology, physical fitness assessment, exercise prescription. *Unit head:* Dr. Gloria Napper-Owen, Chair, 505-277-8173, Fax: 505-277-6227, E-mail: napperow@unm.edu. *Application contact:* Carol Catania, Department Office, 505-277-5151, Fax: 505-277-6227, E-mail: catania@unm.edu.

University of New Mexico, Graduate School, College of Education, Department of Health, Exercise and Sports Sciences, Program in Physical Education, Sports and Exercise Science, Albuquerque, NM 87131-2039. Offers PhD. Part-time programs available. *Faculty:* 19 full-time (10 women), 20 part-time/adjunct (10 women). *Students:* 29 full-time (8 women), 14 part-time (3 women); includes 9 minority (4 African Americans, 2 Asian Americans or Pacific Islanders, 3 Hispanic Americans), 11 international. Average age 35. 35 applicants, 51% accepted, 13 enrolled. In 2009, 7 doctorates awarded. *Degree requirements:* For doctorate, comprehensive exam, thesis/dissertation, inquiry skills, 24 credits in supporting area. *Entrance requirements:* For doctorate, GRE, letter of intent, 3 letters of reference, minimum cumulative GPA of 3.0 in last 2 years of bachelor's degree. Additional exam requirements/recommendations for international students: Required—TOEFL (minimum score 550 paper-based; 213 computer-based). *Application deadline:* For fall admission, 3/1 priority date for domestic students; for spring admission, 11/1 priority date for domestic students. Application fee: $50. Electronic applications accepted. *Expenses:* Tuition, state resident: full-time $2099; part-time $233.20 per credit hour. Tuition, nonresident: full-time $6650. Required fees: $25 per semester. Tuition and fees vary according to course load, program and reciprocity agreements. *Financial support:* In 2009–10, 29 students received support, including 20 teaching assistantships with full tuition reimbursements available (averaging $10,815 per year); career-related internships or fieldwork, Federal Work-Study, institutionally sponsored loans, scholarships/grants, health care benefits, tuition waivers, and unspecified assistantships also available. Financial award application deadline: 3/1; financial award applicants required to submit FAFSA. *Faculty research:* Facility risk management, physical education pedagogy practices, physiological adaptations to exercise, physiological adaptations to heat. *Unit head:* Dr. Gloria Napper-Owen, Chair, 505-277-8173, Fax: 505-277-6227, E-mail: napperow@unm.edu. *Application contact:* Carol Catania, Program Office, 505-277-5151, Fax: 505-277-6227, E-mail: catania@unm.edu.

The University of North Carolina at Chapel Hill, Graduate School, College of Arts and Sciences, Department of Exercise and Sport Science, Chapel Hill, NC 27599. Offers athletic training (MA); exercise physiology (MA); sport administration (MA). *Degree requirements:* For master's, comprehensive exam, thesis. *Entrance requirements:* For master's, GRE General Test, minimum GPA of 3.0. Additional exam requirements/recommendations for international students: Required—TOEFL (minimum score 550 paper-based). Electronic applications accepted. *Faculty research:* Mild head injury in sport, endocrine system's response to exercise, obesity and children, effect of aerobic exercise on cerebral bloodflow in elderly population.

The University of North Carolina at Pembroke, Graduate Studies, Department of Health, Physical Education, and Recreation, Pembroke, NC 28372-1510. Offers physical education (MA, MAT). Part-time and evening/weekend programs available. *Degree requirements:* For master's, comprehensive exam, thesis optional. *Entrance requirements:* For master's, MAT or GRE, minimum GPA of 3.0 in major, 2.5 overall. Additional exam requirements/recommendations for international students: Required—TOEFL.

University of Northern Colorado, Graduate School, College of Natural and Health Sciences, School of Sport and Exercise Science, Greeley, CO 80639. Offers exercise science (MS, PhD); sport administration (MS, PhD); sport pedagogy (MS, PhD). Part-time and evening/weekend programs available. *Faculty:* 14 full-time (7 women). *Students:* 66 full-time (37 women), 24 part-time (11 women); includes 11 minority (1 African American, 3 American Indian/Alaska Native, 3 Asian Americans or Pacific Islanders, 4 Hispanic Americans), 16 international. Average age 28. 175 applicants, 56% accepted, 31 enrolled. In 2009, 65 master's, 10 doctorates awarded. *Degree requirements:* For master's, comprehensive exam; for doctorate, comprehensive exam, thesis/dissertation. *Entrance requirements:* For master's, 2 letters of recommendation, resume; for doctorate, GRE General Test, 3 letters of recommendation, resume. *Application deadline:* Applications are processed on a rolling basis. Application fee: $50 ($60 for international students). Electronic applications accepted. *Expenses:* Tuition, state resident: full-time $5770; part-time $320.55 per credit hour. Tuition, nonresident: full-time $13,847; part-time $769.27 per credit hour. Required fees: $948.78; $52.72 per credit. *Financial support:* In 2009–10, 7 research assistantships (averaging $3,876 per year), 17 teaching assistantships (averaging $8,928 per year) were awarded; fellowships, unspecified assistantships also available. Financial award application deadline: 3/1; financial award applicants required to submit FAFSA. *Unit head:* Dr. David Stotlar, Director, 970-351-2535, Fax: 970-351-1762. *Application contact:* Linda Sisson, Graduate Student Admission Coordinator, 970-351-1807; Fax: 970-351-2371, E-mail: linda.sisson@unco.edu.

University of Northern Iowa, Graduate College, College of Education, School of Health, Physical Education, and Leisure Services, Program in Physical Education, Cedar Falls, IA 50614. Offers physical education (MA); scientific basis of physical education (MA); teaching/coaching (MA). Part-time and evening/weekend programs available. *Students:* 45 full-time (20 women), 8 part-time (1 woman); includes 4 minority (3 African Americans, 1 Hispanic American), 3 international. 52 applicants, 85% accepted, 26 enrolled. In 2009, 19 master's awarded. *Degree requirements:* For master's, comprehensive exam, thesis or alternative. *Entrance requirements:* For master's, minimum GPA of 3.0. Additional exam requirements/recommendations for international students: Required—TOEFL (minimum score 500 paper-based; 180 computer-based; 61 iBT). *Application deadline:* For fall admission, 8/1 priority date for domestic students. Applications are processed on a rolling basis. Application fee: $30 ($50 for international students). Electronic applications accepted. *Financial support:* Career-related internships or fieldwork, Federal Work-Study, and tuition waivers (full and partial) available. Support available to part-time students. Financial award application deadline: 2/1. *Unit head:* Dr. Jody Brucker, Coordinator, 319-273-6477, Fax: 319-273-5958, E-mail: jody.brucker@uni.edu. *Application contact:* Laurie S. Russell, Record Analyst, 319-273-2623, Fax: 319-273-6792, E-mail: laurie.russell@uni.edu.

University of Rhode Island, Graduate School, College of Human Science and Services, Department of Kinesiology, Kingston, RI 02881. Offers cultural studies of sport and physical culture (MS); exercise science (MS); physical education pedagogy (MS); psychosocial/behavioral aspects of physical activity (MS). *Accreditation:* NCATE. Part-time programs available. *Faculty:* 13 full-time (7 women). *Students:* 16 full-time (8 women), 2 part-time (1 woman), 1 international. In 2009, 6 master's awarded. *Degree requirements:* For master's, thesis optional. *Entrance requirements:* For master's, GRE, 2 letters of recommendation. Additional exam requirements/recommendations for international students: Required—TOEFL (minimum score 550 paper-based; 213 computer-based). *Application deadline:* For fall admission, 4/15 for domestic students, 2/1 for international students; for spring admission, 11/15 for domestic students, 7/15 for international students. Application fee: $65. Electronic applications accepted. *Expenses:* Tuition, state resident: full-time $8828; part-time $490 per credit hour. Tuition, nonresident: full-time $22,100; part-time $1228 per credit hour. Required fees: $1118; $57 per semester. Tuition and fees vary according to program. *Financial support:* In 2009–10, 4 teaching assistantships with full and partial tuition reimbursements (averaging $7,939 per year) were awarded. Financial award application deadline: 4/15; financial award applicants required to submit FAFSA. *Faculty research:* Strength training and older adults, interventions to promote a healthy lifestyle as well as analysis of the psychosocial outcomes of those interventions, effects of exercise and nutrition on skeletal muscle of aging healthy adults with CVD and other metabolic related diseases, physical activity and fitness of deaf children and youth. Total annual research expenditures: $92,479. *Unit head:* Dr. Deborah Riebe, Chair, 401-874-5444, Fax: 401-874-4215, E-mail: debriebe@uri.edu. *Application contact:* Dr. Lori Ciccomascolo, Director of Graduate Studies, 401-874-5454, Fax: 401-874-4215, E-mail: lecicco@uri.edu.

University of South Alabama, Graduate School, College of Education, Department of Health, Physical Education and Leisure Services, Mobile, AL 36688-0002. Offers exercise science (MS); health education (M Ed); physical education (M Ed); therapeutic recreation (MS). *Accreditation:* NCATE (one or more programs are accredited). Part-time programs available. *Degree requirements:* For master's, comprehensive exam. *Entrance requirements:* For master's, GRE General Test or MAT. *Expenses:* Tuition, state resident: part-time $218 per contact hour. Required fees: $1102 per year.

University of South Carolina, The Graduate School, College of Education, Department of Physical Education, Columbia, SC 29208. Offers IMA, MAT, MS, PhD. Part-time programs available. *Degree requirements:* For master's, comprehensive exam, thesis (for some programs); for doctorate, comprehensive exam, thesis/dissertation. *Entrance requirements:* For master's, GRE General Test, or Miller Analogies Test, writing sample, letter of intent, letters of recommendation; for doctorate, GRE General Test or Miller Analogies Test, writing sample, interview, letter of intent, letters of recommendation. *Faculty research:* Teaching/learning processes, anthropometric measurement, growth and development, motor development.

The University of South Dakota, Graduate School, School of Education, Division of Health, Physical Education and Recreation, Vermillion, SD 57069-2390. Offers MA. *Accreditation:* NCATE. Part-time programs available. *Degree requirements:* For master's, comprehensive exam, thesis or alternative. *Entrance requirements:* For master's, GRE General Test, MAT, minimum GPA of 2.7. Additional exam requirements/recommendations for international students: Required—TOEFL (minimum score 550 paper-based; 213 computer-based; 79 iBT). Electronic applications accepted.

University of Southern Mississippi, Graduate School, College of Health, School of Human Performance and Recreation, Hattiesburg, MS 39406-0001. Offers human performance (MS, Ed D, PhD); interscholastic athletic administration (MS); recreation and leisure management (MS); sport administration (MS); sport and coaching education (MS); sport management (MS); sports and high performance materials (MS). Part-time and evening/weekend programs available. *Faculty:* 13 full-time (5 women). *Students:* 62 full-time (27 women), 40 part-time (10 women); includes 13 minority (10 African Americans, 1 Asian American or Pacific Islander, 2 Hispanic Americans), 4 international. Average age 29. 79 applicants, 59% accepted, 33 enrolled. In 2009, 43 master's, 4 doctorates awarded. *Degree requirements:* For master's, comprehensive exam, thesis optional; for doctorate, comprehensive exam, thesis/dissertation. *Entrance requirements:* For master's, GRE General Test, minimum GPA of 2.75 in last 60 hours; for doctorate, GRE General Test, minimum GPA of 3.5. Additional exam requirements/recommendations for international students: Required—TOEFL. *Application deadline:* For fall admission, 3/1 priority date for domestic students, 3/1 for international students. Applications are processed on a rolling basis. Application fee: $35. Electronic applications accepted. *Expenses:* Tuition, state resident: full-time $5096; part-time $284 per hour. Tuition, nonresident: full-time $13,052; part-time $726 per hour. Required fees: $402. Tuition and fees vary according to course level and course load. *Financial support:* In 2009–10, 1 fellowship (averaging $16,000 per year), 6 research assistantships with full tuition reimbursements (averaging $7,492 per year), 5 teaching assistantships with full tuition reimbursements (averaging $7,330 per year) were awarded; career-related internships or fieldwork, Federal Work-Study, institutionally sponsored loans, and tuition waivers (partial) also available. Financial award application deadline: 3/15. *Faculty research:* Exercise physiology, health behaviors, resource management, activity interaction, site development. *Unit head:* Dr. Louis Marciani, Director, 601-266-5379, Fax: 601-266-4445. *Application contact:* Dr. Dennis Phillips, Graduate Coordinator, 601-266-5379, Fax: 601-266-4445.

University of South Florida, Graduate School, College of Education–Main Campus, School of Physical Education and Exercise Science, Tampa, FL 33620-9951. Offers exercise science (MA); physical education teacher preparation (MA). Part-time and evening/weekend programs available. Postbaccalaureate distance learning degree programs offered (no on-campus study). *Faculty:* 9 full-time (6 women). *Students:* 43 full-time (22 women), 57 part-time (30 women); includes 18 minority (8 African Americans, 2 American Indian/Alaska Native, 1 Asian American or Pacific Islander, 7 Hispanic Americans), 1 International. Average age 30. 59 applicants, 66% accepted, 27 enrolled. In 2009, 27 master's awarded. *Degree requirements:* For master's, comprehensive exam, thesis optional. *Entrance requirements:* For master's, GRE General Test, minimum GPA of 3.0 in last 60 hours of coursework. Additional exam requirements/recommendations for international students: Required—TOEFL (minimum score 500 paper-based; 213 computer-based). *Application deadline:* For fall admission, 2/15 for domestic students, 1/2 for international students; for spring admission, 10/15 for domestic students, 6/1 for international students. Applications are processed on a rolling basis. Application fee: $30.

Physical Education

University of South Florida (continued)

Electronic applications accepted. *Financial support:* In 2009–10, 5 teaching assistantships with full tuition reimbursements (averaging $9,200 per year) were awarded; unspecified assistantships also available. Financial award application deadline: 7/3; financial award applicants required to submit FAFSA. *Faculty research:* Physical education pedagogy, active gaming, exercise motivation, heat stress research, strength and nutrition research, physical activity risk management. Total annual research expenditures: $20,482. *Unit head:* Dr. Steve Sanders, Director, 813-974-4871, Fax: 813-974-4979, E-mail: sanders@usf.edu. *Application contact:* Dr. Steve Sanders, Director, 813-974-4871, Fax: 813-974-4979, E-mail: sanders@usf.edu.

The University of Tennessee at Chattanooga, Graduate School, College of Health, Education and Professional Studies, Department of Health and Human Performance, Program in Health and Human Performance, Chattanooga, TN 37403. Offers MS. *Faculty:* 4 full-time (1 woman). *Students:* 9 full-time (6 women), 1 part-time (0 women), 2 international. Average age 26. 36 applicants, 36% accepted, 4 enrolled. In 2009, 21 master's awarded. *Degree requirements:* For master's, thesis or alternative, clinical rotations. *Entrance requirements:* For master's, GRE General Test or MAT, minimum GPA of 2.75 overall or 3.0 in last 60 hours; CPR and First Aid certification. Additional exam requirements/recommendations for international students: Required—TOEFL (minimum score 550 paper-based; 213 computer-based; 79 iBT), IELTS (minimum score 6). *Application deadline:* For fall admission, 8/1 priority date for domestic students, 6/1 for international students; for spring admission, 12/1 priority date for domestic students, 10/1 for international students. Applications are processed on a rolling basis. Application fee: $35. Electronic applications accepted. *Expenses:* Tuition, state resident: full-time $5404; part-time $300 per credit hour. Tuition, nonresident: full-time $16,702; part-time $928 per credit hour. Required fees: $1150; $130 per credit hour. *Financial support:* In 2009–10, 7 research assistantships with full and partial tuition reimbursements (averaging $5,500 per year) were awarded; fellowships, career-related internships or fieldwork, scholarships/grants, and unspecified assistantships also available. Support available to part-time students. *Faculty research:* Therapeutic exercise, lumbar spine biomechanics, functional rehabilitation outcomes, metabolic health. *Unit head:* Dr. Gary Wilkerson, Coordinator, 423-425-5394, E-mail: gary-wilkerson@utc.edu. *Application contact:* Dr. Stephanie Bellar, Dean of Graduate Studies, 423-425-4666, Fax: 423-425-5223, E-mail: stephanie-bellar@utc.edu.

The University of Texas at Arlington, Graduate School, College of Education, Arlington, TX 76019. Offers curriculum and instruction (M Ed); educational leadership and policy studies (M Ed); K-16 educational, leadership and policy studies (PhD); physiology of exercise (MS); teaching (M Ed T). *Accreditation:* NCATE. Part-time and evening/weekend programs available. *Faculty:* 35 full-time (22 women), 4 part-time/adjunct (2 women). *Students:* 125 full-time (83 women), 586 part-time (479 women); includes 283 minority (125 African Americans, 4 American Indian/Alaska Native, 19 Asian Americans or Pacific Islanders, 135 Hispanic Americans), 15 international. Average age 35. 601 applicants, 99% accepted, 238 enrolled. In 2009, 161 degrees awarded. *Degree requirements:* For master's, comprehensive exam (for some programs), thesis (for some programs), comprehensive activity, research project; for doctorate, comprehensive exam, thesis/dissertation. *Entrance requirements:* For master's, GRE General Test, minimum undergraduate GPA of 3.0 in last 60 hours of course work, writing sample, 3 letters of recommendation; for doctorate, GRE General Test, interview, minimum GPA of 3.5, master's degree in education or other appropriate field, 3 years of documented experience in an education related work environment. Additional exam requirements/recommendations for international students: Required—TOEFL (minimum score 550 paper-based; 213 computer-based). *Application deadline:* For fall admission, 6/5 priority date for domestic students, 4/3 priority date for international students; for spring admission, 10/17 priority date for domestic students, 9/5 priority date for international students. Applications are processed on a rolling basis. Application fee: $35 ($50 for international students). Electronic applications accepted. *Financial support:* In 2009–10, 9 fellowships (averaging $1,000 per year), 6 research assistantships (averaging $6,250 per year), 10 teaching assistantships with full tuition reimbursements (averaging $5,200 per year) were awarded; career-related internships or fieldwork, Federal Work-Study, scholarships/grants, and unspecified assistantships also available. Financial award application deadline: 6/1; financial award applicants required to submit FAFSA. *Unit head:* Dr. Jeanne M. Gerlach, Dean, 817-272-2591, Fax: 817-272-2530, E-mail: coeadvising@uta.edu. *Application contact:* Kas McConnell, Graduate Advisor, 817-272-7489, Fax: 817-272-7624, E-mail: coedadvising@uta.edu.

University of the Incarnate Word, School of Graduate Studies and Research, School of Nursing and Health Professions, Programs in Sports Management, San Antonio, TX 78209-6397. Offers sport management (MS, Certificate); sport pedagogy (Certificate). Part-time and evening/weekend programs available. *Students:* 5 full-time (2 women), 3 part-time (2 women); includes 3 minority (1 African American, 2 Hispanic Americans). Average age 28. *Degree requirements:* For master's, internship. *Entrance requirements:* For master's, GRE, letter of recommendation from professional in field. Additional exam requirements/recommendations for international students: Required—TOEFL (minimum score 560 paper-based; 220 computer-based; 83 iBT). *Application deadline:* Applications are processed on a rolling basis. Application fee: $20. Electronic applications accepted. *Expenses:* Tuition: Full-time $12,150; part-time $675 per credit hour. Required fees: $83 per credit hour. *Financial support:* Federal Work-Study and scholarships/grants available. Financial award applicants required to submit FAFSA. *Unit head:* Dr. Timothy Henrich, Professor, 210-829-6036, Fax: 210-829-3174, E-mail: henrich@uiwtx.edu. *Application contact:* Andrea Cyterski-Acosta, Dean of Enrollment, 210-829-6005, Fax: 210-829-3921, E-mail: admis@uiwtx.edu.

The University of Toledo, College of Graduate Studies, College of Education, Department of Early Childhood, Physical and Special Education, Program in Physical Education, Toledo, OH 43606-3390. Offers ME.

University of Toronto, School of Graduate Studies, Life Sciences Division, Faculty of Physical Education and Health, Toronto, ON M5S 1A1, Canada. Offers M Sc, PhD. *Degree requirements:* For master's, thesis, oral defense of thesis; for doctorate, comprehensive exam, defense of thesis. *Entrance requirements:* For master's, background in physical education and health, minimum B+ average in final year of undergraduate study, 2 letters of reference, resume, 2 writing samples; for doctorate, master's degree with successful defense of thesis, background in exercise sciences, minimum A– average, 2 letters of reference.

University of Victoria, Faculty of Graduate Studies, Faculty of Education, School of Exercise Science, Physical, and Health Education, Victoria, BC V8W 2Y2, Canada. Offers coaching studies (co-operative education) (M Ed); kinesiology (M Sc, MA); leisure service administration (MA); physical education (MA). Part-time programs available. *Degree requirements:* For master's, comprehensive exam (for some programs), thesis (for some programs). *Entrance requirements:* For master's, minimum B average. Additional exam requirements/recommendations for international students: Required—TOEFL (minimum score 575 paper-based; 233 computer-based), IELTS (minimum score 7). Electronic applications accepted. *Faculty research:* Children and exercise, mental skills in sports, teaching effectiveness, neural control of human movement, physical performance and health.

University of Virginia, Curry School of Education, Department of Human Services, Program in Health and Physical Education, Charlottesville, VA 22903. Offers kinesiology (M Ed, Ed D). *Students:* 38 full-time (27 women), 6 part-time (3 women); includes 3 minority (2 African Americans, 1 Hispanic American). Average age 24. 13 applicants, 92% accepted, 8 enrolled. In 2009, 43 master's, 1 doctorate awarded. *Entrance requirements:* For master's and doctorate, GRE General Test, 2 letters of recommendation. Additional exam requirements/recommendations for international students: Required—TOEFL (minimum score 600 paper-based; 250 computer-based; 90 iBT), IELTS (minimum score 7). *Application deadline:* Applications are processed on a rolling basis. Application fee: $60. Electronic applications accepted. *Financial support:* Applicants required to submit FAFSA.

University of Washington, Graduate School, College of Education, Seattle, WA 98195. Offers curriculum and instruction (M Ed, Ed D, PhD), including educational technology, general

curriculum (Ed D, PhD), language, literacy, and culture, mathematics education, multicultural education, reading and language arts education (Ed D), science education, social studies education, teaching and curriculum (M Ed); educational leadership and policy studies (M Ed, Ed D, PhD), including administration (Ed D), educational policy, organization, and leadership (M Ed, PhD), higher education, leadership for learning (Ed D), social and cultural foundations of education (M Ed, PhD); educational psychology (M Ed, PhD), including educational psychology (PhD), human development and cognition (M Ed), learning sciences, measurement, statistics and research design (M Ed), school psychology (M Ed); instructional leadership (M Ed); intercollegiate athletic leadership (M Ed); special education (M Ed, Ed D, PhD), including early childhood special education (M Ed), emotional and behavioral disabilities (M Ed), learning disabilities (M Ed), low-incidence disabilities (M Ed), severe disabilities (M Ed), special education (Ed D, PhD); teacher education (MIT). *Accreditation:* APA. Part-time and evening/weekend programs available. *Degree requirements:* For master's, thesis optional; for doctorate, thesis/dissertation. *Entrance requirements:* For master's and doctorate, GRE General Test, minimum GPA of 3.0. Additional exam requirements/recommendations for international students: Required—TOEFL. Electronic applications accepted. *Faculty research:* School restructuring/effective schools, special education interventions, literacy and writing, technology, school partnerships, teacher preparation.

The University of West Alabama, School of Graduate Studies, College of Education, Department of Physical Education and Athletic Training, Livingston, AL 35470. Offers physical education (M Ed, MAT). Part-time programs available. *Entrance requirements:* For master's, GRE General Test, MAT, minimum GPA of 2.75.

University of West Florida, College of Professional Studies, Division of Health, Leisure, and Exercise Science, Program in Health, Leisure, and Exercise Science, Pensacola, FL 32514-5750. Offers exercise science (MS); physical education (MS). Part-time and evening/weekend programs available. *Faculty:* 5 full-time (2 women), 2 part-time/adjunct (1 woman). *Students:* 20 full-time (9 women), 23 part-time (10 women); includes 6 minority (3 African Americans, 1 Asian American or Pacific Islander, 2 Hispanic Americans), 4 international. Average age 28. 30 applicants, 83% accepted, 11 enrolled. In 2009, 26 master's awarded. *Degree requirements:* For master's, thesis or alternative. *Entrance requirements:* For master's, GRE General Test, minimum GPA of 3.0. Additional exam requirements/recommendations for international students: Required—TOEFL (minimum score 550 paper-based; 213 computer-based). *Application deadline:* For fall admission, 6/1 for domestic students, 5/15 for international students; for spring admission, 11/1 for domestic students, 10/1 for international students. Applications are processed on a rolling basis. Application fee: $30. Electronic applications accepted. *Expenses:* Tuition, state resident: full-time $4982; part-time $260 per credit hour. Tuition, nonresident: full-time $20,059; part-time $919 per credit hour. Required fees: $1247; $52 per credit hour. *Financial support:* Career-related internships or fieldwork, Federal Work-Study, scholarships/grants, and tuition waivers (partial) available. Support available to part-time students. Financial award application deadline: 4/15; financial award applicants required to submit FAFSA. *Unit head:* Dr. John Todorovich, Chairperson, 850-473-7248, Fax: 850-474-2106. *Application contact:* Terry McCray, Assistant Director of Graduate Admissions, 850-473-7718, Fax: 850-473-7714, E-mail: gradadmissions@uwf.edu.

University of West Georgia, Graduate School, College of Education, Department of Health, Physical Education, and Sport Studies, Carrollton, GA 30118. Offers physical education (M Ed). Part-time programs available. Postbaccalaureate distance learning degree programs offered (minimal on-campus study). *Faculty:* 6 full-time (3 women). *Students:* 9 full-time (3 women), 1 part-time (0 women); includes 2 minority (both African Americans). Average age 29. 6 applicants, 50% accepted, 1 enrolled. In 2009, 7 master's awarded. *Degree requirements:* For master's, comprehensive exam, action research project. *Entrance requirements:* For master's, GACE Basic Skills Test, minimum GPA of 2.7. Additional exam requirements/recommendations for international students: Required—GACE Basic Skills. *Application deadline:* For fall admission, 7/17 for domestic students; for spring admission, 11/20 for domestic students. Applications are processed on a rolling basis. Application fee: $30. Electronic applications accepted. *Expenses:* Tuition, state resident: full-time $2952; part-time $164 per semester hour. Tuition, nonresident: full-time $11,808; part-time $656 per semester hour. Required fees: $42.90 per semester hour. $307 per semester. Tuition and fees vary according to course load. *Financial support:* In 2009–10, 3 students received support, including 4 research assistantships with full tuition reimbursements available (averaging $3,000 per year); career-related internships or fieldwork, scholarships/grants, and unspecified assistantships also available. Support available to part-time students. Financial award applicants required to submit FAFSA. *Faculty research:* Biomechanics, physical education pedagogy, sport management, sport marketing. Total annual research expenditures: $3,000. *Unit head:* Dr. Deborah Bainer Jenkins, Interim Chair, 678-839-6181, Fax: 678-839-6185, E-mail: djenkins@westga.edu. *Application contact:* Dr. Charles W. Clark, Dean, 678-839-6508, E-mail: cclark@westga.edu.

University of Wisconsin–La Crosse, Office of University Graduate Studies, College of Science and Health, Department of Exercise and Sport Science, Program in Physical Education Teaching, La Crosse, WI 54601-3742. Offers MS. Part-time and evening/weekend programs available. *Students:* 11 full-time (7 women), 24 part-time (15 women); includes 2 minority (both Hispanic Americans). Average age 28. 24 applicants, 63% accepted, 13 enrolled. In 2009, 21 master's awarded. *Degree requirements:* For master's, thesis optional. *Entrance requirements:* For master's, minimum GPA of 3.0 during previous 2 years, 2.85 overall; BA in physical education. Additional exam requirements/recommendations for international students: Required—TOEFL (minimum score 550 paper-based; 213 computer-based; 79 iBT). *Application deadline:* Applications are processed on a rolling basis. Application fee: $56. Electronic applications accepted. *Financial support:* Research assistantships, career-related internships or fieldwork, Federal Work-Study, institutionally sponsored loans, health care benefits, and tuition waivers (full and partial) available. Financial award application deadline: 3/15; financial award applicants required to submit FAFSA. *Unit head:* Dr. Jeff Steffen, Director, 608-785-6535, E-mail: steffen.jeff@uwlax.edu. *Application contact:* Kathryn Kiefer, Director of Admissions, 608-785-8939, E-mail: admissions@uwlax.edu.

University of Wyoming, College of Health Sciences, Division of Kinesiology and Health, Laramie, WY 82070. Offers MS. *Accreditation:* NCATE. Part-time programs available. Postbaccalaureate distance learning degree programs offered (no on-campus study). *Degree requirements:* For master's, comprehensive exam (for some programs), thesis (for some programs). *Entrance requirements:* For master's, GRE General Test, minimum GPA of 3.0. Additional exam requirements/recommendations for international students: Required—TOEFL. Electronic applications accepted. *Faculty research:* Teacher effectiveness, effects of exercising on heart function, physiological responses of overtraining, psychological benefits of physical activity, health behavior.

Utah State University, School of Graduate Studies, College of Education and Human Services, Department of Health, Physical Education and Recreation, Logan, UT 84322. Offers M Ed, MS. Part-time and evening/weekend programs available. Postbaccalaureate distance learning degree programs offered (minimal on-campus study). *Degree requirements:* For master's, thesis (for some programs). *Entrance requirements:* For master's, GRE General Test or MAT, minimum GPA of 3.0. Additional exam requirements/recommendations for international students: Required—TOEFL. *Faculty research:* Sport psychology intervention, motor learning biomechanics, pedagogy, physiology.

Virginia Commonwealth University, Graduate School, School of Education, Department of Health and Human Performance, Richmond, VA 23284-9005. Offers athletic training (MSAT); health and movement sciences (MS); rehabilitation and movement science (PhD). *Entrance requirements:* For master's, GRE General Test or MAT.

Virginia Polytechnic Institute and State University, Graduate School, College of Liberal Arts and Human Sciences, School of Education, Department of Teaching and Learning, Blacksburg, VA 24061. Offers career and technical education (MS Ed, Ed D, PhD, Ed S); curriculum and instruction (MA Ed, Ed D, PhD, Ed S); health and physical education (MS Ed); mathematics education (MA Ed, PhD); secondary English education (MA Ed). *Accreditation:*

NCATE. Postbaccalaureate distance learning degree programs offered (no on-campus study). *Students:* 295 full-time (186 women), 374 part-time (272 women); includes 104 minority (1 African American, 39 American Indian/Alaska Native, 54 Asian Americans or Pacific Islanders, 10 Hispanic Americans), 23 international. Average age 34. 324 applicants, 85% accepted, 205 enrolled. In 2009, 235 master's, 34 doctorates, 1 other advanced degree awarded. *Entrance requirements:* For master's and doctorate, GRE, GMAT. Additional exam requirements/recommendations for international students: Required—TOEFL (minimum score 550 paper-based; 213 computer-based). *Application deadline:* For fall admission, 5/15 for international students; for spring admission, 10/15 for international students. Applications are processed on a rolling basis. Application fee: $65. Electronic applications accepted. *Expenses:* Tuition, area resident: Full-time $10,228; part-time $459 per credit hour. Tuition, nonresident: full-time $17,892; part-time $865 per credit hour. Required fees: $1966; $451 per semester. *Financial support:* Career-related internships or fieldwork, Federal Work-Study, scholarships/grants, and unspecified assistantships available. Financial award application deadline: 1/15. *Faculty research:* Instructional technology, teacher evaluation, school change, literacy, teaching strategies. *Unit head:* Dr. Daisy L. Stewart, Dean, 540-231-8180, Fax: 540-231-3717, E-mail: daisys@vt.edu. *Application contact:* Dr. Daisy L. Stewart, Dean, 540-231-8180, Fax: 540-231-3717, E-mail: daisys@vt.edu.

Wayne State College, Department of Health, Human Performance and Sport, Wayne, NE 68787. Offers exercise science (MSE); organizational management (MS), including sport management. Part-time and evening/weekend programs available. *Degree requirements:* For master's, comprehensive exam, thesis optional. *Entrance requirements:* For master's, GRE General Test, minimum GPA of 3.0. Additional exam requirements/recommendations for international students: Required—TOEFL (minimum score 550 paper-based; 213 computer-based). Electronic applications accepted.

Wayne State University, College of Education, Division of Kinesiology, Health and Sports Studies, Detroit, MI 48202. Offers health education (M Ed); kinesiology (M Ed); physical education (M Ed); recreation and park services (MA); sports administration (MA). *Degree requirements:* For master's, thesis (for some programs). *Entrance requirements:* Additional exam requirements/recommendations for international students: Required—TOEFL; Recommended—TWE (minimum score 6). Electronic applications accepted. *Faculty research:* Fitness in urban children, motor development of crack babies, effects of caffeine on metabolism/exercise, body composition of elite youth sports participants, systematic observation of teaching.

West Chester University of Pennsylvania, Office of Graduate Studies, College of Health Sciences, Department of Kinesiology, West Chester, PA 19383. Offers adapted physical education (Certificate); health and physical education (MS, Teaching Certificate), including exercise physiology (MS); physical education (MS); sport and athletic administration (MSA). Part-time and evening/weekend programs available. *Students:* 2 full-time (1 woman), 37 part-time (15 women); includes 2 minority (both African Americans), 3 international. Average age 25. 39 applicants, 90% accepted, 11 enrolled. In 2009, 25 master's awarded. *Degree requirements:* For master's, thesis (for some programs), thesis or report (MS), 2 internships (MSA). *Entrance requirements:* For master's, GRE (MS); GMAT, GRE General Test, or MAT (MSA), minimum GPA of 3.0 with interview (MS) or letters of recommendation (MSA). Additional exam requirements/recommendations for international students: Required—TOEFL (minimum score 550 paper-based; 213 computer-based; 80 iBT). *Application deadline:* For fall admission, 4/15 priority date for domestic students, 3/15 for international students; for spring admission, 10/15 for domestic students, 9/1 for international students. Applications are processed on a rolling basis. Application fee: $35. Electronic applications accepted. *Expenses:* Tuition, state resident: full-time $6666; part-time $370 per credit. Tuition, nonresident: full-time $10,666; part-time $593 per credit. Required fees: $122.56 per credit. *Financial support:* In 2009–10, 11 research assistantships with full and partial tuition reimbursements (averaging $5,000 per year) were awarded; unspecified assistantships also available. Support available to part-time students. Financial award application deadline: 2/15; financial award applicants required to submit FAFSA. *Faculty research:* Weight lifting and type 1 diabetes mellitus, martial arts, sexual harassment in sports. *Unit head:* Dr. Frank Fry, Chair, 610-436-2832, E-mail: ffry@wcupa.edu. *Application contact:* Dr. Sheri Melton, Graduate Coordinator, 610-436-2260, E-mail: smelton@wcupa.edu.

Western Carolina University, Graduate School, College of Education and Allied Professions, Department of Educational Leadership and Foundations, Teaching Degree Programs, Cullowhee, NC 28723. Offers comprehensive education (MA Ed); physical education (MA Ed); teaching (MAT). *Accreditation:* NCATE. Part-time and evening/weekend programs available. Postbaccalaureate distance learning degree programs offered. *Students:* 62 full-time (46 women), 172 part-time (148 women). Average age 33. 125 applicants, 77% accepted, 64 enrolled. In 2009, 46 master's awarded. *Degree requirements:* For master's, comprehensive exam. *Entrance requirements:* For master's, GRE General Test or MAT, appropriate undergraduate degree, letters of recommendation. Additional exam requirements/recommendations for international students: Required—TOEFL (minimum score 550 paper-based; 270 computer-based; 79 iBT). *Application deadline:* For fall admission, 5/1 priority date for domestic students; for spring admission, 9/1 priority date for domestic students. Applications are processed on a rolling basis. Application fee: $45. *Financial support:* In 2009–10, 35 students received support, including 1 fellowship (averaging $6,000 per year), 20 research assistantships with full and partial tuition reimbursements available (averaging $7,716 per year), 14 teaching assistantships with full and partial tuition reimbursements available (averaging $7,143 per year); career-related internships or fieldwork, institutionally sponsored loans, scholarships/grants, and unspecified assistantships also available. Financial award application deadline: 3/31; financial award applicants required to submit FAFSA. *Faculty research:* Educational leadership; organizational theory and practice; women's access to leadership positions; preparation, evaluation and professional development of teachers. *Unit head:* Dr. Jacqueline Jacobs, Head, 828-227-7415, Fax: 828-227-7607, E-mail: jjacobs@email.wcu.edu. *Application contact:* Admissions Specialist for Teaching Degrees, 828-227-7398, Fax: 828-227-7480, E-mail: gradsch@email.wcu.edu.

Western Kentucky University, Graduate Studies, College of Health and Human Services, Department of Physical Education and Recreation, Bowling Green, KY 42101. Offers physical education (MS); recreation (MS). Part-time and evening/weekend programs available. *Degree requirements:* For master's, comprehensive exam, thesis optional. *Entrance requirements:* For master's, GRE General Test, minimum GPA of 2.75. Additional exam requirements/recommendations for international students: Required—TOEFL (minimum score 555 paper-based; 213 computer-based; 79 iBT). *Expenses:* Tuition, state resident: full-time $4160; part-time $416 per credit hour. Tuition, nonresident: full-time $9550; part-time $506 per credit hour. Tuition and fees vary according to campus/location and reciprocity agreements. *Faculty research:* Orthopedic rehabilitation, fitness center coordination, heat acclimation, biomechanical and physiological parameters.

Western Michigan University, Graduate College, College of Education, Department of Health, Physical Education and Recreation, Kalamazoo, MI 49008. Offers exercise and sports medicine (MS), including athletic training, exercise physiology; physical education (MA), including coaching sport performance, pedagogy, special physical education, sport management. *Faculty:* 20 full-time (9 women). *Students:* 60 full-time (27 women), 53 part-time (25 women); includes 9 minority (6 African Americans, 2 Asian Americans or Pacific Islanders, 1 Hispanic American), 6 international. 69 applicants, 81% accepted, 21 enrolled. In 2009, 42 master's awarded. *Application deadline:* For fall admission, 2/15 priority date for domestic students. Applications are processed on a rolling basis. Application fee: $25. *Financial support:* Fellowships, research assistantships, teaching assistantships, Federal Work-Study available. Financial award application deadline: 2/15; financial award applicants required to submit FAFSA. *Unit head:* Lee deLisle, Chair, 269-387-2669. *Application contact:* Admissions and Orientation, 269-387-2000, Fax: 269-387-2355.

Western Washington University, Graduate School, College of Humanities and Social Sciences, Department of Physical Education, Health, and Recreation, Bellingham, WA 98225-5996. Offers exercise science (MS); sport psychology (MS). Part-time programs available. *Degree requirements:* For master's, thesis. *Entrance requirements:* For master's, GRE General Test, minimum GPA of 3.0 in last 60 semester hours or last 90 quarter hours. Additional exam requirements/recommendations for international students: Required—TOEFL (minimum score 567 paper-based; 227 computer-based). Electronic applications accepted. *Faculty research:* Spinal motor control, biomechanics/kinesiology, biomechanics of aging, mobility of older adults, fall prevention, exercise interventions and function, magnesium and inspiratory muscle training (IMT).

Westfield State College, Division of Graduate and Continuing Education, Department of Movement Science, Sport, and Leisure, Westfield, MA 01086. Offers physical education (M Ed). Part-time and evening/weekend programs available. *Degree requirements:* For master's, comprehensive exam. *Entrance requirements:* For master's, GRE General Test or MAT, minimum GPA of 2.7.

West Virginia University, School of Physical Education, Morgantown, WV 26506. Offers athletic coaching education (MS); athletic training (MS); physical education/teacher education (MS, PhD), including curriculum and instruction (PhD), motor behavior (PhD), physical education supervision (PhD); sport and exercise psychology (PhD); sport management (MS). *Degree requirements:* For doctorate, comprehensive exam, thesis/dissertation, oral exam. *Entrance requirements:* For master's, GRE or MAT, minimum GPA of 3.0; for doctorate, GRE General Test or MAT, minimum GPA of 3.5. Additional exam requirements/recommendations for international students: Required—TOEFL (minimum score 550 paper-based; 213 computer-based). Electronic applications accepted. *Faculty research:* Sport psychosociology, teacher education, exercise psychology, counseling.

Wilfrid Laurier University, Faculty of Graduate Studies, Faculty of Science, Department of Kinesiology and Physical Education, Waterloo, ON N2L 3C5, Canada. Offers M Sc. *Degree requirements:* For master's, thesis. *Entrance requirements:* For master's, honours degree in kinesiology, health, physical education with a minimum B+ in kinesiology and health-related courses. Additional exam requirements/recommendations for international students: Required—TOEFL (minimum score 230 computer-based; 89 iBT). Electronic applications accepted. *Faculty research:* Biomechanics, health, exercise physiology, motor control, sport psychology.

William Woods University, Graduate and Adult Studies, Fulton, MO 65251-1098. Offers administration (Ed S); agriculture (MBA); athletic/activities administration (M Ed); curriculum and instruction (M Ed); curriculum leadership (Ed S); elementary administration (M Ed); health management (MBA); human resources (MBA); principalship (Ed S); secondary administration (M Ed); special education director (M Ed). Evening/weekend programs available. *Degree requirements:* For master's, capstone course (MBA), action research (M Ed); for Ed S, field experience. *Entrance requirements:* For master's, 2 recommendations, resumé, BA/BS; teaching certification (M Ed); course work in economics and accounting (MBA); for Ed S, M Ed, 2 letters of recommendation, resume, teaching certification. Additional exam requirements/recommendations for international students: Required—TOEFL (minimum score 550 paper-based). Electronic applications accepted.

Wingate University, Program in Education, Wingate, NC 28174-0159. Offers educational leadership (MA Ed); elementary education (MA Ed, MAT); physical education (MA Ed); sport administration (MA Ed). *Accreditation:* NCATE. Part-time and evening/weekend programs available. *Degree requirements:* For master's, portfolio. *Entrance requirements:* For master's, GRE General Test or MAT, teaching certificate (MA Ed).

Winthrop University, College of Education, Program in Physical Education, Rock Hill, SC 29733. Offers MS. Part-time programs available. *Degree requirements:* For master's, comprehensive exam, thesis optional. *Entrance requirements:* For master's, GRE General Test or PRAXIS. Electronic applications accepted.

Wright State University, School of Graduate Studies, College of Education and Human Services, Department of Health, Physical Education, and Recreation, Dayton, OH 45435. Offers M Ed, MA. *Accreditation:* NCATE. *Degree requirements:* For master's, comprehensive exam, thesis (for some programs). *Entrance requirements:* For master's, GRE General Test, MAT. Additional exam requirements/recommendations for international students: Required—TOEFL. *Faculty research:* Motor learning, motor development, exercise physiology, adapted physical education.

Section 43
Sports Management

This section contains a directory of institutions offering graduate work in sports management. Additional information about programs listed in the directory may be obtained by writing directly to the dean of a graduate school or chair of a department at the address given in the directory.

For programs offering related work, see also in this book *Business Administration and Management, Education,* and *Physical Education and Kinesiology.*

CONTENTS

Program Directory

Close-Up

Sports Management

American Public University System, AMU/APU Graduate Programs, Charles Town, WV 25414. Offers air warfare (MA Military Studies); American Revolution (MA Military Studies); business administration (MBA); Civil War (MA Military Studies); criminal justice (MA); defense management (MA Military Studies); emergency and disaster management (MA); environmental policy and management (MS); fire science management (MA); global engagement (MA); history (MA); homeland security (MA); humanities (MA); intelligence (MA Military Studies, MA Strategic Intelligence); international peace and conflict resolution (MA); international relations and conflict resolution (MA); joint warfare (MA Military Studies); land warfare international perspective (MA Military Studies); management (MA); military history (MA); military leadership (MA Military Studies); national security studies (MA); naval warfare international (MA Military Studies); naval warfare US (MA Military Studies); political science (MA); public administration (MA); public health (MA); security management (MA); space studies (MS); special ops/LIC (MA Military Studies); sports management (MA); transportation and logistics management (MA); transportation management (MA); unconventional warfare (MA Military Studies); World War II (MA Military Studies). Programs offered via distance learning only. Part-time and evening/weekend programs available. Postbaccalaureate distance learning degree programs offered (no on-campus study). *Students:* 788 full-time (330 women), 6,916 part-time (2,050 women); includes 1,767 minority (908 African Americans, 70 American Indian/Alaska Native, 223 Asian Americans or Pacific Islanders, 566 Hispanic Americans), 77 international. Average age 35. *Degree requirements:* For master's, comprehensive exam or practicum. *Entrance requirements:* For master's, bachelor's degree or equivalent, minimum GPA of 2.7 in last 60 hours of course work. *Application deadline:* Applications are processed on a rolling basis. Application fee: $0. Electronic applications accepted. *Financial support:* Applicants required to submit FAFSA. *Faculty research:* Military history, criminal justice, management performance, national security. *Unit head:* Dr. Frank McCluskey, Provost, 877-468-6268, Fax: 304-724-3780. *Application contact:* Terry Grant, Director of Enrollment Management, 877-468-6268, Fax: 304-724-3780, E-mail: info@apus.edu.

Ashland University, Dwight Schar College of Education, Department of Sport Sciences, Ashland, OH 44805-3702. Offers adapted physical education (M Ed); applied exercise science (M Ed); sport education (M Ed); sport management (M Ed). Part-time programs available. *Faculty:* 5 full-time (3 women), 2 part-time/adjunct (both women). *Students:* 24 full-time (9 women), 31 part-time (12 women); includes 4 minority (all African Americans), 4 international. Average age 30. 15 applicants, 100% accepted, 15 enrolled. In 2009, 26 master's awarded. *Degree requirements:* For master's, practicum, inquiry seminar, thesis, or internship. *Entrance requirements:* For master's, teaching certificate or license, bachelor's degree, minimum cumulative GPA of 2.75. Additional exam requirements/recommendations for international students: Required—TOEFL. *Application deadline:* For fall admission, 8/27 for domestic students; for spring admission, 1/14 for domestic students. Applications are processed on a rolling basis. Application fee: $30. *Financial support:* In 2009–10, 32 students received support; teaching assistantships, institutionally sponsored loans and scholarships/grants available. Financial award application deadline: 4/15. *Faculty research:* Coaching, legal issues, strength and conditioning, sport management rating of perceived exertion, youth fitness, geriatric exercise science. *Unit head:* Dr. Randall F. Gearhart, Chair, 419-289-6198, E-mail: rgearhar@ashland.edu. *Application contact:* Dr. Randall F. Gearhart, Chair, 419-289-6198, E-mail: rgearhar@ashland.edu.

Augustana College, Program in Sports Administration and Leadership, Sioux Falls, SD 57197. Offers MA. *Expenses:* Tuition: Full-time $25,422; part-time $427 per credit hour. Required fees: $274. Part-time tuition and fees vary according to course load and program.

Barry University, School of Human Performance and Leisure Sciences, Program in Sport Management, Miami Shores, FL 33161-6695. Offers MS. Part-time and evening/weekend programs available. *Degree requirements:* For master's, comprehensive exam, project or thesis. *Entrance requirements:* For master's, GMAT or GRE General Test, minimum GPA of 3.0. Electronic applications accepted. *Faculty research:* Economic impact of professional sports, sport marketing.

Barry University, School of Human Performance and Leisure Sciences and Andreas School of Business, Program in Sport Management and Business Administration, Miami Shores, FL 33161-6695. Offers MS/MBA. Part-time and evening/weekend programs available. Electronic applications accepted. *Faculty research:* Economic impact of professional sports, sport marketing.

Belmont University, College of Arts and Sciences, School of Education, Nashville, TN 37212-3757. Offers education (M Ed); elementary education (MAT), including early childhood education, elementary education, language arts education; English (MAT); history (MAT); mathematics (MAT); middle grade education (MAT); science (MAT); secondary education (MAT); special education (MAT); sports administration (MSA). *Accreditation:* NCATE. Part-time and evening/weekend programs available. *Degree requirements:* For master's, comprehensive exam, thesis, culminating portfolio. *Entrance requirements:* For master's, MAT or GRE and/or LSAT or GMAT, minimum GPA of 2.75. Additional exam requirements/recommendations for international students: Required—TOEFL. *Expenses:* Contact institution. *Faculty research:* Improving secondary literacy, Montessori, classroom management strategies, teacher residency programs, online professional development, mentoring, leadership, sociological issues in sport, faculty development, coaching.

Boise State University, Graduate College, College of Education, Department of Kinesiology, Program in Physical Education, Boise, ID 83725-0399. Offers athletic administration (MPE). Part-time programs available. *Degree requirements:* For master's, thesis. *Entrance requirements:* For master's, minimum GPA of 3.0. Electronic applications accepted. *Expenses:* Tuition, state resident: full-time $3106; part-time $209 per credit. Tuition, nonresident: part-time $284 per credit.

Bowling Green State University, Graduate College, College of Education and Human Development, School of Human Movement, Sport, and Leisure Studies, Bowling Green, OH 43403. Offers developmental kinesiology (M Ed); recreation and leisure (M Ed); sport administration (M Ed). Part-time programs available. *Degree requirements:* For master's, thesis or alternative. *Entrance requirements:* For master's, GRE General Test, minimum GPA of 2.7. Additional exam requirements/recommendations for international students: Required—TOEFL. Electronic applications accepted. *Faculty research:* Teacher-learning process, travel and tourism, sport marketing and management, exercise physiology and sport psychology, life-span motor development.

Brooklyn College of the City University of New York, Division of Graduate Studies, Department of Physical Education and Exercise Science, Brooklyn, NY 11210-2889. Offers exercise science and rehabilitation (MS); physical education (MS), including sports management. Part-time programs available. *Students:* 15 full-time (7 women), 127 part-time (58 women); includes 39 minority (23 African Americans, 3 Asian Americans or Pacific Islanders, 13 Hispanic Americans), 65 international. Average age 27. 127 applicants, 96% accepted, 57 enrolled. In 2009, 15 master's awarded. *Degree requirements:* For master's, comprehensive exam or thesis. *Entrance requirements:* For master's, previous course work in physical education and education, minimum GPA of 3.0, 2 letters of recommendation, essay. Additional exam requirements/recommendations for international students: Required—TOEFL (minimum score 500 paper-based; 173 computer-based; 61 iBT). *Application deadline:* For fall admission, 3/1 priority date for domestic students, 2/1 priority date for international students; for spring admission, 11/1 priority date for domestic students, 10/1 priority date for international students. Applications are processed on a rolling basis. Application fee: $125. Electronic applications accepted. *Expenses:* Tuition, state resident: full-time $7360; part-time $310 per credit hour. Tuition, nonresident: full-time $13,800; part-time $575 per credit hour. Required fees: $140.10 per semester. *Financial support:* Career-related internships or fieldwork, Federal Work-Study, institutionally sponsored loans, and scholarships/grants available. Support available to part-time students. Financial award application deadline: 5/1; financial award applicants required to submit FAFSA. *Faculty research:* Exercise physiology, motor learning, sports psychology, women in athletics. *Unit head:* Dr. Artis Smith, Chairperson, 718-951-5514, E-mail: basmith@brooklyn.cuny.edu. *Application contact:* Hernan Sierra, Graduate Admissions Coordinator, 718-951-4536, Fax: 718-951-4506, E-mail: grads@brooklyn.cuny.edu.

California Baptist University, Program in Kinesiology, Riverside, CA 92504-3206. Offers exercise science (MS); physical education pedagogy (MS); sport management (MS). Part-time programs available. *Faculty:* 3 full-time (0 women). *Students:* 17 full-time (8 women), 14 part-time (8 women); includes 10 minority (1 African American, 1 American Indian/Alaska Native, 3 Asian Americans or Pacific Islanders, 5 Hispanic Americans), 2 international. 45 applicants, 49% accepted, 15 enrolled. In 2009, 15 master's awarded. *Degree requirements:* For master's, thesis or alternative, field experience. *Entrance requirements:* For master's, 12 semester units of course work in kinesiology, including basic movement anatomy or a related course; minimum undergraduate GPA of 2.75 (physical education pedagogy). Additional exam requirements/recommendations for international students: Required—TOEFL (minimum score 575 paper-based; 230 computer-based; 89 iBT). *Application deadline:* For fall admission, 8/1 priority date for domestic students, 7/1 for international students; for spring admission, 12/1 priority date for domestic students, 10/15 for international students. Applications are processed on a rolling basis. Application fee: $45. Electronic applications accepted. *Expenses:* Tuition: Full-time $8352; part-time $464 per semester hour. Required fees: $125 per semester. Tuition and fees vary according to course load, campus/location and program. *Financial support:* Federal Work-Study and scholarships/grants available. Support available to part-time students. Financial award applicants required to submit FAFSA. *Unit head:* Dr. Sean Sullivan, Chair, Department of Kinesiology, 951-343-4528, E-mail: ssullivan@calbaptist.edu. *Application contact:* Gail Ronveaux, Dean of Graduate Enrollment, 951-343-5045, Fax: 951-343-5095, E-mail: graduateadmissions@calbaptist.edu.

California State University, Long Beach, Graduate Studies, College of Health and Human Services, Department of Kinesiology, Long Beach, CA 90840. Offers adapted physical education (MA); coaching and student athlete development (MA); exercise physiology and nutrition (MS); exercise science (MS); individualized studies (MA); kinesiology (MA); pedagogical studies (MA); sport and exercise psychology (MS); sport management (MA); sports medicine and injury studies (MS). Part-time programs available. *Faculty:* 9 full-time (6 women), 1 part-time/adjunct (0 women). *Students:* 34 full-time (22 women), 23 part-time (14 women); includes 22 minority (4 African Americans, 2 American Indian/Alaska Native, 8 Asian Americans or Pacific Islanders, 8 Hispanic Americans), 9 international. Average age 27. 143 applicants, 59% accepted, 20 enrolled. *Degree requirements:* For master's, oral and written comprehensive exams or thesis. *Entrance requirements:* For master's, GRE General Test, minimum GPA of 2.75 during previous 2 years of course work. *Application deadline:* For fall admission, 6/1 for domestic students. Applications are processed on a rolling basis. Application fee: $55. Electronic applications accepted. *Expenses:* Required fees: $1802 per semester. Part-time tuition and fees vary according to course load. *Financial support:* Federal Work-Study, institutionally sponsored loans, and scholarships/grants available. Financial award application deadline: 3/2. *Faculty research:* Pulmonary functioning, feedback and practice structure, strength training, history and politics of sports, special population research issues. *Unit head:* Dr. Sharon R. Guthrie, Chair, 562-985-7487, Fax: 562-985-8067, E-mail: guthrie@csulb.edu. *Application contact:* Dr. Grant Hill, Graduate Advisor, 562-985-8856, Fax: 562-985-8067, E-mail: ghill@csulb.edu.

California University of Pennsylvania, School of Graduate Studies and Research, School of Education, Department of Athletic Training, Program in Exercise Science and Health Promotion, California, PA 15419-1394. Offers fitness and wellness (MS); performance enhancement and injury prevention (MS); rehabilitation sciences (MS); sport management (MS); sport psychology (MS). Part-time and evening/weekend programs available. Postbaccalaureate distance learning degree programs offered (no on-campus study). *Degree requirements:* For master's, comprehensive exam, thesis optional. *Entrance requirements:* For master's, minimum QPA of 3.0. Additional exam requirements/recommendations for international students: Required—TOEFL (minimum score 550 paper-based; 213 computer-based; 80 iBT). Electronic applications accepted. *Expenses:* Contact institution. *Faculty research:* Reducing obesity in children, sport performance, creating unique biomechanical assessment techniques, Web-based training for fitness professionals, Webcams.

Canisius College, Graduate Division, School of Education and Human Services, Department of Sport Administration, Buffalo, NY 14208-1098. Offers MS. *Faculty:* 5 part-time/adjunct (1 woman). *Students:* 67 full-time (30 women), 62 part-time (17 women); includes 9 minority (8 African Americans, 1 American Indian/Alaska Native), 3 international. Average age 25. 117 applicants, 77% accepted, 65 enrolled. In 2009, 55 master's awarded. *Degree requirements:* For master's, research project. *Entrance requirements:* For master's, GRE General Test. *Application deadline:* Applications are processed on a rolling basis. Application fee: $25. *Financial support:* Research assistantships with full tuition reimbursements, career-related internships or fieldwork, institutionally sponsored loans, scholarships/grants, health care benefits, tuition waivers (full and partial), and unspecified assistantships available. *Faculty research:* Organizational effectiveness, economic impact, sponsorship and marketing, ethics, leadership. *Unit head:* Staci C. Carney Studesville, Director, 716-888-3165, Fax: 716-888-3174, E-mail: studesvs@canisius.edu. *Application contact:* James D. Bagwell, Director of Graduate Recruitment and Admissions, 716-888-2544, Fax: 716-888-3290, E-mail: bagwellj@canisius.edu.

Cardinal Stritch University, College of Arts and Sciences, Program in Sport Management, Milwaukee, WI 53217-3985. Offers MS.

Central Michigan University, Central Michigan University Off-Campus Programs, Program in Sport Administration, Mount Pleasant, MI 48859. Offers MA. Part-time and evening/weekend programs available. *Entrance requirements:* For master's, minimum GPA of 3.0. *Unit head:* Scott J. Smith, Director, 989-774-6525, E-mail: smith5sj@cmich.edu. *Application contact:* 877-268-4636, E-mail: cmuoffcampus@cmich.edu.

Central Michigan University, College of Graduate Studies, The Herbert H. and Grace A. Dow College of Health Professions, Department of Physical Education and Sport, Mount Pleasant, MI 48859. Offers physical education (MA), including athletic administration, coaching, exercise science, teaching; sport education (MA). Part-time programs available. *Degree requirements:* For master's, thesis or alternative. Electronic applications accepted. *Faculty research:* Athletic administration and sport management; performance enhancing substance use in sport; computer applications for sport managers; mental skill development for ultimate performance; teaching methods.

Central Michigan University, College of Graduate Studies, Interdisciplinary Administration Programs, Mount Pleasant, MI 48859. Offers acquisitions administration (MSA, Graduate Certificate); general administration (MSA, Graduate Certificate); health services administration (MSA, Graduate Certificate); human resource administration (Graduate Certificate); human resources administration (MSA); information resource management (MSA, Graduate Certificate); international administration (MSA, Graduate Certificate); leadership (MSA); organizational communication (MSA, Graduate Certificate); public administration (MSA, Graduate Certificate); recreation and park administration (MSA); sport administration (MSA). *Accreditation:* AACSB. Part-time and evening/weekend programs available. Postbaccalaureate distance learning degree programs offered (no on-campus study). *Degree requirements:* For master's, thesis or alternative. *Entrance requirements:* For master's, bachelor's degree with minimum GPA of 2.7. Electronic applications accepted. *Faculty research:* Interdisciplinary studies in acquisitions administration, health services administration, sport administration, recreation and park administration, and international administration.

Cleveland State University, College of Graduate Studies, College of Education and Human Services, Department of Health, Physical Education, Recreation and Dance, Cleveland, OH 44115. Offers community health education (M Ed); exercise science (M Ed); human performance (M Ed); physical education pedagogy (M Ed); public health (MPH); school health education (M Ed); sport and exercise psychology (M Ed); sports management (M Ed). Part-time programs available. *Degree requirements:* For master's, comprehensive exam, thesis optional. *Entrance requirements:* For master's, GRE General Test or MAT (if undergraduate GPA less than 2.75), minimum undergraduate GPA of 2.75. Additional exam requirements/recommendations for international students: Required—TOEFL (minimum score 525 paper-based; 197 computer-based), IELTS (minimum score 6). Electronic applications accepted. *Faculty research:* Bone density, marketing fitness centers, motor development of disabled, online learning and survey research.

The College at Brockport, State University of New York, School of Health and Human Performance, Department of Kinesiology, Sports Studies and Physical Education, Brockport, NY 14420-2997. Offers physical education (MS Ed), including adapted physical education, athletic administration, teacher education/pedagogy. Part-time programs available. *Students:* 14 full-time (12 women), 69 part-time (26 women); includes 4 minority (all Hispanic Americans). 36 applicants, 83% accepted, 30 enrolled. In 2009, 45 master's awarded. *Degree requirements:* For master's, thesis or alternative. *Entrance requirements:* For master's, minimum GPA of 3.0. Additional exam requirements/recommendations for international students: Required—TOEFL (minimum score 550 paper-based; 213 computer-based; 79 iBT). *Application deadline:* For fall admission, 3/15 priority date for domestic and international students; for spring admission, 10/15 priority date for domestic and international students. Application fee: $80. Electronic applications accepted. *Expenses:* Tuition, state resident: full-time $8370; part-time $349 per credit. Tuition, nonresident: full-time $13,250; part-time $522 per credit. *Financial support:* In 2009–10, 1 research assistantship with full tuition reimbursement (averaging $6,200 per year), 5 teaching assistantships with full tuition reimbursements (averaging $6,000 per year) were awarded; Federal Work-Study, scholarships/grants, and unspecified assistantships also available. Support available to part-time students. Financial award application deadline: 3/15; financial award applicants required to submit FAFSA. *Faculty research:* Athletic administration, adapted physical education, physical education curriculum, physical education teaching/coaching, children's physical activity. *Unit head:* Dr. Susan C. Petersen, Chairperson, 585-395-5332, Fax: 585-395-2771, E-mail: spetersе@brockport.edu. *Application contact:* Dr. Alisa James, Graduate Program Director, 585-395-5330, Fax: 585-395-2771, E-mail: ajames@brockport.edu.

Columbia University, School of Continuing Education, Program in Sports Management, New York, NY 10027. Offers MS. Part-time programs available. *Faculty:* 20 part-time/adjunct (4 women). *Students:* 1 full-time (0 women), 64 part-time (23 women); includes 19 minority (7 African Americans, 6 Asian Americans or Pacific Islanders, 6 Hispanic Americans), 1 international. Average age 28. 70 applicants, 53% accepted, 25 enrolled. *Entrance requirements:* For master's, minimum GPA of 3.0, 2 letters of recommendation, professional resume. *Application deadline:* For fall admission, 6/15 for domestic students. Application fee: $50. Electronic applications accepted. *Financial support:* Institutionally sponsored loans available. Financial award applicants required to submit FAFSA. *Unit head:* Lucas Rubin, Program Director, 212-854-5855, E-mail: lr2008@columbia.edu. *Application contact:* Bryce Weinert, Admissions Adviser, 212-854-9666, E-mail: sce-apply@columbia.edu.

Concordia University, School of Arts and Sciences, Irvine, CA 92612-3299. Offers coaching and athletic administration (MA). Part-time and evening/weekend programs available. Post-baccalaureate distance learning degree programs offered. *Faculty:* 8 full-time (3 women), 19 part-time/adjunct (1 woman). *Students:* 236 full-time (42 women), 73 part-time (17 women); includes 50 minority (20 African Americans, 3 American Indian/Alaska Native, 4 Asian Americans or Pacific Islanders, 23 Hispanic Americans). Average age 34. 126 applicants, 100% accepted, 119 enrolled. In 2009, 85 master's awarded. *Degree requirements:* For master's, culminating project. *Entrance requirements:* Additional exam requirements/recommendations for international students: Required—TOEFL. *Application deadline:* For fall admission, 8/10 for domestic students, 6/1 for international students; for spring admission, 2/14 for domestic students, 10/1 for international students. Application fee: $50 ($125 for international students). Electronic applications accepted. *Expenses:* Tuition: Full-time $6000; part-time $400 per unit. One-time fee: $125. Tuition and fees vary according to campus/location and program. *Financial support:* In 2009–10, 271 students received support. Tuition waivers (full and partial) and unspecified assistantships available. Financial award applicants required to submit FAFSA. *Unit head:* Dr. Timothy Preuss, Dean, 949-854-8002 Ext. 1349, E-mail: tim.preuss@cui.edu. *Application contact:* Chris Lewis, Associate Director of Graduate Admissions, 877-854-1194, Fax: 949-854-6894, E-mail: chris.lewis@cui.edu.

Concordia University, School of Graduate Studies, John Molson School of Business, Montréal, QC H3G 1M8, Canada. Offers administration (M Sc, Diploma); aviation management (Certificate, Diploma); business administration (MBA, UA Undergraduate Associate, PhD), including international aviation (UA Undergraduate Associate); chartered accountancy (Diploma); community organizational development (Certificate); event management and fundraising (Certificate); executive business administration (EMBA); investment management (Diploma); investment management option (MBA); management accounting (Certificate); management of healthcare organizations (Certificate); sport administration (Diploma). *Accreditation:* AACSB. Part-time and evening/weekend programs available. *Degree requirements:* For master's, one foreign language, thesis (for some programs), research project; for doctorate, one foreign language, thesis/dissertation; for other advanced degree, one foreign language. *Entrance requirements:* For master's and doctorate, GMAT. Additional exam requirements/recommendations for international students: Required—TOEFL. *Expenses:* Contact institution. *Faculty research:* General business, capital markets, international business.

Concordia University, St. Paul, College of Education, St. Paul, MN 55104-5494. Offers curriculum and instruction (MA Ed), including K-12 reading endorsement; differentiated instruction (MA Ed); early childhood education (MA Ed); educational leadership (MA Ed); family life education (MA); K-12 reading endorsement (Certificate); special education (Certificate); sports management (MA). *Accreditation:* NCATE. Evening/weekend programs available. Post-baccalaureate distance learning degree programs offered (minimal on-campus study). *Faculty:* 12 full-time (8 women), 59 part-time/adjunct (47 women). *Students:* 697 full-time (571 women), 13 part-time (12 women); includes 64 minority (31 African Americans, 1 American Indian/Alaska Native, 21 Asian Americans or Pacific Islanders, 11 Hispanic Americans), 1 international. Average age 34. In 2009, 402 master's, 29 other advanced degrees awarded. *Application deadline:* Applications are processed on a rolling basis. Application fee: $50. Electronic applications accepted. *Financial support:* Applicants required to submit FAFSA. *Unit head:* Dr. Donald Helmstetter, Dean, 651-641-8227, Fax: 651-641-8807, E-mail: helmstetter@csp.edu. *Application contact:* Kimberly Craig, Director of Graduate and Cohort Admission, 651-603-6223, Fax: 651-603-6320, E-mail: craig@csp.edu.

Drexel University, School of Technology and Professional Studies, Philadelphia, PA 19104-2875. Offers construction management (MS); engineering technology (MS); food science (MS); hospitality management (MS); professional studies: creativity studies (MS); professional studies: e-learning leadership (MS); professional studies: homeland security management (MS); project management (MS); property management (MS); sport management (MS). Post-baccalaureate distance learning degree programs offered.

Duquesne University, School of Leadership and Professional Advancement, Pittsburgh, PA 15282-0001. Offers leadership (MS), including business ethics, community leadership, global leadership, information technology, leadership, liberal studies, professional administration, sports leadership. Part-time and evening/weekend programs available. Postbaccalaureate distance learning degree programs offered (no on-campus study). *Faculty:* 1 full-time (0 women), 70 part-time/adjunct (35 women). *Students:* 654 (307 women); includes 68 minority (57 African Americans, 1 American Indian/Alaska Native, 6 Asian Americans or Pacific Islanders, 4 Hispanic Americans). 161 applicants, 73% accepted, 103 enrolled. In 2009, 108 master's awarded. *Degree requirements:* For master's, capstone course. *Entrance requirements:* For master's, professional work experience, 500-word essay. Additional exam requirements/recommendations for international students: Required—TOEFL. *Application deadline:* Applications are processed on a rolling basis. Application fee: $0. Electronic applications accepted. *Expenses:* Tuition: Part-time $851 per credit. Required fees: $81 per credit. *Financial support:* Applicants required to submit FAFSA. *Unit head:* Dr. Dorothy Bassett, Dean, 412-396-2141, Fax: 412-396-4711, E-mail: bassettd@duq.edu. *Application contact:* Marianne Leister, Director of Student Services, 412-396-4933, Fax: 412-396-5072, E-mail: leister@duq.edu.

Eastern Kentucky University, The Graduate School, College of Health Sciences, Department of Exercise and Sport Science, Richmond, KY 40475-3102. Offers exercise and sport science (MS); exercise and wellness (MS); sports administration (MS). Part-time programs available. *Entrance requirements:* For master's, GRE General Test (minimum score 700 verbal and quantitative), minimum GPA of 2.5 (for most), minimum GPA of 3.0 (analytical writing). *Faculty research:* Nutrition and exercise.

Eastern Michigan University, Graduate School, College of Health and Human Services, School of Health Promotion and Human Performance, Program in Sports Management, Ypsilanti, MI 48197. Offers MS. Part-time and evening/weekend programs available. *Students:* 13 full-time (7 women), 46 part-time (16 women); includes 12 minority (10 African Americans, 1 American Indian/Alaska Native, 1 Hispanic American). Average age 28. In 2009, 10 master's awarded. *Degree requirements:* For master's, comprehensive exams or thesis. *Entrance requirements:* For master's, minimum GPA of 2.75. Additional exam requirements/recommendations for international students: Required—TOEFL. *Application deadline:* For fall admission, 8/1 for domestic students, 5/1 for international students; for winter admission, 12/1 for domestic students, 10/1 for international students; for spring admission, 4/15 for domestic students, 3/1 for international students. Applications are processed on a rolling basis. Application fee: $35. Tuition and fees vary according to course level. *Financial support:* Fellowships, research assistantships with full tuition reimbursements, teaching assistantships with full tuition reimbursements, career-related internships or fieldwork, Federal Work-Study, institutionally sponsored loans, scholarships/grants, tuition waivers (partial), and unspecified assistantships available. Support available to part-time students. Financial award applicants required to submit FAFSA. *Unit head:* Dr. Brenda Riemer, Program Coordinator, 734-487-7120 Ext. 2745, Fax: 734-487-2024, E-mail: briemer@emich.edu. *Application contact:* Dr. Brenda Riemer, Program Coordinator, 734-487-7120 Ext. 2745, Fax: 734-487-2024, E-mail: briemer@emich.edu.

Eastern Washington University, Graduate Studies, College of Education and Human Development, Department of Physical Education, Health and Recreation, Cheney, WA 99004-2431. Offers exercise science (MS); sport and exercise psychology (MS); sports administration/pedagogy (MS). *Degree requirements:* For master's, comprehensive exam, thesis or alternative. *Entrance requirements:* For master's, minimum GPA of 3.0. *Expenses:* Tuition, state resident: full-time $7476; part-time $249 per quarter hour. Tuition, nonresident: full-time $18,030; part-time $601 per quarter hour. Required fees: $3.50 per quarter hour. $142 per quarter.

East Stroudsburg University of Pennsylvania, Graduate School, College of Business and Management, Department of Sport Management, East Stroudsburg, PA 18301-2999. Offers management and leadership (MS); sports management (MS). Part-time and evening/weekend programs available. *Faculty:* 5 full-time (3 women). *Students:* 29 full-time (12 women), 15 part-time (0 women); includes 2 minority (1 African American, 1 Hispanic American), 2 international. Average age 26. In 2009, 22 master's awarded. *Degree requirements:* For master's, comprehensive exam. *Entrance requirements:* For master's, GRE and/or GMAT. Additional exam requirements/recommendations for international students: Required—TOEFL (minimum score 560 paper-based; 220 computer-based; 83 iBT), or IELTS. *Application deadline:* For fall admission, 3/15 priority date for domestic students, 5/1 priority date for international students; for spring admission, 11/30 for domestic students, 10/1 for international students. Application fee: $50. *Expenses:* Tuition, state resident: full-time $9942; part-time $387 per credit. Tuition, nonresident: full-time $14,240; part-time $619 per credit. *Financial support:* In 2009–10, 36 research assistantships (averaging $2,127 per year) were awarded; Federal Work-Study and unspecified assistantships also available. Financial award application deadline: 3/1; financial award applicants required to submit FAFSA. *Unit head:* Dr. Robert Fleischman, Graduate Coordinator, 570-422-3316, Fax: 570-422-3824, E-mail: bfleischman@po-box.esu.edu. *Application contact:* Kevin Quintero, Graduate Admissions Coordinator, 570-422-3890, Fax: 570-422-2711, E-mail: kquintero@po-box.esu.edu.

East Tennessee State University, School of Graduate Studies, College of Education, Department of Physical Education, Exercise and Sport Sciences, Johnson City, TN 37614. Offers exercise physiology (MA); fitness leadership (MA); physical education (M Ed, MA); sports management (MA); sports sciences (MA). Part-time and evening/weekend programs available. *Degree requirements:* For master's, comprehensive exam (M Ed), oral and written comprehensive exams, thesis (MA). *Entrance requirements:* For master's, GRE General Test, major or minor in physical education or equivalent, interview, minimum GPA of 2.7. Additional exam requirements/recommendations for international students: Required—TOEFL (minimum score 550 paper-based; 213 computer-based). *Faculty research:* Resistance training for various populations, self actualization using challenging courses, park and recreation industry needs relative to recent university graduates, funding sport operations.

Endicott College, Van Loan School of Graduate and Professional Studies, Program in Athletic Administration, Beverly, MA 01915-2096. Offers M Ed. Part-time and evening/weekend programs available. *Faculty:* 6 part-time/adjunct (2 women). *Students:* 3 full-time (1 woman), 20 part-time (6 women). Average age 28. 15 applicants, 100% accepted, 15 enrolled. In 2009, 5 master's awarded. *Degree requirements:* For master's, thesis, practicum. *Entrance requirements:* For master's, GRE or MAT, letters of recommendation. Additional exam requirements/recommendations for international students: Required—TOEFL. Application fee: $50. *Expenses:* Contact institution. *Unit head:* Richard Benedetto, Associate Dean of Graduate School, 978-232-2744, Fax: 978-232-3000, E-mail: rbenedet@endicott.edu. *Application contact:* Richard Benedetto, Associate Dean of Graduate School, 978-232-2744, Fax: 978-232-3000, E-mail: rbenedet@endicott.edu.

Fairleigh Dickinson University, Metropolitan Campus, Anthony J. Petrocelli College of Continuing Studies, Department of Sports Administration, Program in Sports Administration, Teaneck, NJ 07666-1914. Offers MSA. *Students:* 21 full-time (9 women), 30 part-time (10 women), 1 international. Average age 30. 26 applicants, 92% accepted, 18 enrolled. *Application deadline:* Applications are processed on a rolling basis. Application fee: $40. *Unit head:* Kenneth T. Vehrkens, Dean, 201-692-2000. *Application contact:* Susan Brooman, University Director of Graduate Admissions, 201-692-2554, Fax: 201-692-2560, E-mail: globaleducation@fdu.edu.

Florida International University, College of Education, Department of Health, Physical Education, and Recreation, Program in Physical Education, Miami, FL 33199. Offers advanced teacher preparation (MS); sports management (MS). Part-time and evening/weekend programs available. *Entrance requirements:* For master's, GRE General Test or minimum GPA of 3.0, teaching certificate in physical education. Additional exam requirements/recommendations for international students: Required—TOEFL (minimum score 550 paper-based; 213 computer-based; 80 iBT), IELTS (minimum score 6.3). Electronic applications accepted. *Expenses:* Tuition, state resident: full-time $8008; part-time $4004 per year. Tuition, nonresident: full-time $20,104; part-time $10,052 per year. Required fees: $298; $149 per term.

Florida State University, The Graduate School, College of Education, Department of Sport Management, Tallahassee, FL 32306. Offers MS, Ed D, PhD. *Faculty:* 14 full-time (8 women), 1 (woman) part-time/adjunct. *Students:* 117 full-time (42 women), 49 part-time (20 women); includes 28 minority (15 African Americans, 1 American Indian/Alaska Native, 5 Asian Americans or Pacific Islanders, 7 Hispanic Americans), 24 international. 166 applicants, 66% accepted, 58 enrolled. In 2009, 30 master's, 1 doctorate awarded. *Degree requirements:* For master's, comprehensive exam, thesis optional; for doctorate, comprehensive exam, thesis/dissertation. *Entrance requirements:* For master's and doctorate, GRE General Test, minimum GPA of 3.0. Additional exam requirements/recommendations for international students: Required—TOEFL

Sports Management

Florida State University (continued)
(minimum score 550 paper-based; 213 computer-based; 80 iBT). *Application deadline:* For fall admission, 7/1 priority date for domestic students, 7/1 for international students; for spring admission, 11/1 for domestic and international students. Applications are processed on a rolling basis. Application fee: $30. Electronic applications accepted. *Expenses:* Tuition, state resident: full-time $7413. Tuition, nonresident: full-time $22,567. *Financial support:* In 2009–10, 2 fellowships with full and partial tuition reimbursements, 51 research assistantships with full and partial tuition reimbursements, 15 teaching assistantships with full and partial tuition reimbursements were awarded; career-related internships or fieldwork and Federal Work-Study also available. Financial award applicants required to submit FAFSA. *Faculty research:* Sport marketing, gender issues in sport, finances in sport industry, coaching. *Unit head:* Dr. Jeffrey James, Chair, 850-644-9214, Fax: 850-644-0975, E-mail: jdjames@fsu.edu. *Application contact:* Cynthia Bailey, Program Assistant, 850-644-4813, Fax: 850-644-0975, E-mail: bailey@coe.fsu.edu.

Franklin Pierce University, Graduate Studies, Rindge, NH 03461-0060. Offers emerging network technology (Graduate Certificate); health practice management (MBA, Graduate Certificate); human resource management (MBA); human resources management (Graduate Certificate); information technology management (MS); leadership (MBA, DA), including transformational leadership (DA); nursing (MS); physical therapy (DPT); physician assistant (MPAS); sports facilities management (MS); teacher education (M Ed). *Accreditation:* APTA. Part-time programs available. Postbaccalaureate distance learning degree programs offered (no on-campus study). *Faculty:* 27 full-time (16 women), 18 part-time/adjunct (4 women). *Students:* 296 full-time (172 women), 249 part-time (165 women); includes 18 minority (5 African Americans, 7 Asian Americans or Pacific Islanders, 6 Hispanic Americans), 31 international. Average age 38. 227 applicants, 97% accepted, 185 enrolled. In 2009, 76 master's, 46 doctorates awarded. *Degree requirements:* For master's, concentrated original research projects; student teaching; fieldwork and/or internship; leadership project; for doctorate, concentrated original research projects, clinical fieldwork and/or internship, leadership project. *Entrance requirements:* For master's, minimum GPA of 2.5, 3 letters of recommendation; for doctorate, demonstrated success at previous academic institutions (minimum GPA of 2.5), 3 letters of recommendation, personal mission statement, interview; writing sample (for DA program). Additional exam requirements/recommendations for international students: Required—TOEFL (minimum score 550 paper-based; 195 computer-based). *Application deadline:* Applications are processed on a rolling basis. Application fee: $0. Electronic applications accepted. *Expenses:* Tuition: Part-time $1560 per course. Part-time tuition and fees vary according to degree level, campus/location and program. *Financial support:* In 2009–10, 36 students received support, including 22 teaching assistantships with full and partial tuition reimbursements available; career-related internships or fieldwork and unspecified assistantships also available. Support available to part-time students. Financial award applicants required to submit FAFSA. *Faculty research:* Evidence based practice in sports physical therapy, human resource management in economic crisis, leadership in nursing, innovation in sports facility management, differentiated learning and understanding by design. *Unit head:* Dr. Robert G. Goddard, Assistant Dean, 603-899-4361, Fax: 603-229-4580, E-mail: goddardr@franklinpierce.edu. *Application contact:* 800-325-1090, Fax: 603-898-0827, E-mail: gpsadmin@franklinpierce.edu.

Georgetown University, Graduate School of Arts and Sciences, School of Continuing Studies, Washington, DC 20057. Offers American studies (MALS); Catholic studies (MALS); classical civilizations (MALS); ethics and the professions (MALS); human resources management (MPS); humanities (MALS); individualized study (MALS); international affairs (MALS); Islam and Muslim-Christian relations (MALS); journalism (MPS); liberal studies (DLS); literature and society (MALS); medieval and early modern European studies (MALS); public relations (MPS); real estate (MPS); religious studies (MALS); social and public policy (MALS); sports industry management (MPS); the theory and practice of American democracy (MALS); visual culture (MALS). *Entrance requirements:* Additional exam requirements/recommendations for international students: Required—TOEFL.

The George Washington University, School of Business, Department of Tourism and Hospitality Management, Washington, DC 20052. Offers event and meeting management (MTA); event management (Professional Certificate); hospitality management (MTA, Professional Certificate); sports business management (Professional Certificate); sports management (MTA); sustainable destination management (MTA); tourism administration (MTA); tourism and hospitality management (MBA); tourism destination management (Professional Certificate). Part-time programs available. Postbaccalaureate distance learning degree programs offered. *Faculty:* 8 full-time (3 women), 5 part-time/adjunct (2 women). *Students:* 71 full-time (51 women), 110 part-time (86 women); includes 43 minority (23 African Americans, 3 American Indian/Alaska Native, 4 Asian Americans or Pacific Islanders, 13 Hispanic Americans), 42 international. Average age 30. 115 applicants, 83% accepted, 59 enrolled. In 2009, 74 master's awarded. *Degree requirements:* For master's, comprehensive exam, thesis. *Entrance requirements:* For master's, GRE General Test. Additional exam requirements/recommendations for international students: Required—TOEFL. *Application deadline:* For fall admission, 4/1 priority date for domestic students; for spring admission, 10/1 for domestic students. Applications are processed on a rolling basis. Application fee: $60. *Financial support:* In 2009–10, 32 students received support; fellowships, teaching assistantships, career-related internships or fieldwork, Federal Work-Study, institutionally sponsored loans, and tuition waivers (partial) available. Financial award application deadline: 4/1. *Faculty research:* Tourism policy, tourism impact forecasting, geotourism. *Unit head:* Susan M. Phillips, Dean, 202-994-6380, E-mail: gwsbdean@gwu.edu. *Application contact:* Kristin Williams, Assistant Vice President for Graduate and Special Enrollment Management, 202-994-0467, Fax: 202-994-0371, E-mail: ksw@gwu.edu.

Georgia Southern University, Jack N. Averitt College of Graduate Studies, College of Health and Human Sciences, Department of Hospitality, Tourism, and Family and Consumer Sciences, Program in Sport Management, Statesboro, GA 30460. Offers MS. Part-time programs available. *Students:* 29 full-time (10 women), 1 part-time (0 women); includes 7 minority (6 African Americans, 1 Hispanic American), 2 international. Average age 24. 37 applicants, 68% accepted, 18 enrolled. In 2009, 11 master's awarded. *Degree requirements:* For master's, terminal exam. *Entrance requirements:* For master's, GMAT, GRE, resume. Additional exam requirements/recommendations for international students: Required—TOEFL (minimum score 550 paper-based; 213 computer-based; 80 iBT). *Application deadline:* For fall admission, 3/1 priority date for domestic and international students; for spring admission, 10/1 priority date for domestic students, 10/1 for international students. Applications are processed on a rolling basis. Application fee: $50. Electronic applications accepted. *Expenses:* Tuition, state resident: full-time $5040; part-time $210 per credit hour. Tuition, nonresident: full-time $20,136; part-time $839 per credit hour. Required fees: $1644. *Financial support:* In 2009–10, 22 students received support. Career-related internships or fieldwork, Federal Work-Study, scholarships/grants, and tuition waivers (partial) available. Support available to part-time students. Financial award application deadline: 4/15; financial award applicants required to submit FAFSA. *Faculty research:* Sport marketing, sport sociology, sport law, sports finance and economics. *Unit head:* Dr. Sam Todd, Coordinator, 912-478-5054, Fax: 912-478-0386, E-mail: sytodd@georgiasouthern.edu. *Application contact:* Dr. Charles Ziglar, Coordinator for Graduate Student Recruitment, 912-478-5635, Fax: 912-478-0740, E-mail: gradadmissions@georgiasouthern.edu.

Georgia State University, College of Education, Department of Kinesiology and Health, Program in Sports Administration, Atlanta, GA 30302-3083. Offers MS. *Degree requirements:* For master's, comprehensive exam. *Entrance requirements:* For master's, GRE General Test, minimum GPA of 2.5. *Faculty research:* Sports marketing.

Gonzaga University, School of Education, Program in Sports and Athletic Administration, Spokane, WA 99258. Offers MASPAA. *Faculty:* 4 full-time (2 women), 2 part-time/adjunct (0 women). *Students:* 5 full-time (2 women), 25 part-time (5 women); includes 3 minority (all Hispanic Americans). Average age 27. In 2009, 20 master's awarded. *Degree requirements:* For master's, comprehensive exam. *Entrance requirements:* Additional exam requirements/recommendations for international students: Required—TOEFL. Application fee: $50. Tuition and fees vary according to course level, course load, degree level, campus/location and program. *Unit head:* Dr. Diane Tunnell, Chair, 509-328-4220 Ext. 3479, E-mail: tunnell@gonzaga.edu. *Application contact:* Julie McCulloh, Dean of Admissions, 509-323-6592, Fax: 509-323-5780, E-mail: mcculloh@gu.gonzaga.edu.

Grambling State University, School of Graduate Studies and Research, College of Education, Department of Kinesiology, Sports and Leisure Studies, Grambling, LA 71245. Offers sports administration (MS). Part-time programs available. *Faculty:* 3 full-time (1 woman). *Students:* 46 full-time (19 women), 5 part-time (3 women); includes 48 minority (47 African Americans, 1 American Indian/Alaska Native), 1 international. Average age 26. 20 applicants, 85% accepted, 12 enrolled. In 2009, 15 master's awarded. *Degree requirements:* For master's, comprehensive exam. *Entrance requirements:* For master's, GRE General Test, minimum GPA of 2.5 on last degree. Additional exam requirements/recommendations for international students: Required—TOEFL (minimum score 500 paper-based; 173 computer-based; 61 iBT). *Application deadline:* For fall admission, 7/1 for domestic and international students; for spring admission, 12/1 for domestic and international students. Applications are processed on a rolling basis. Application fee: $20 ($30 for international students). Electronic applications accepted. *Expenses:* Tuition, state resident: full-time $2610. Tuition, nonresident: full-time $2610. *Financial support:* In 2009–10, 8 research assistantships (averaging $8,671 per year) were awarded; career-related internships or fieldwork, health care benefits, tuition waivers (full and partial), and unspecified assistantships also available. Financial award application deadline: 5/31; financial award applicants required to submit FAFSA. *Faculty research:* Administrative relations and organization, measuring human performance, sport history from ancient times through current date, learning dynamics of personality and sports selection. *Unit head:* Dr. Willie Daniel, Head, 318-274-2294, Fax: 318-274-6053. *Application contact:* Shelia Griffin, Secretary, 318-274-2294, Fax: 318-274-6053, E-mail: griffins@gram.edu.

Henderson State University, Graduate Studies, School of Education, Department of Health, Physical Education, Recreation and Athletic Training, Arkadelphia, AR 71999-0001. Offers recreation (MS); sports administration (MS). Part-time programs available. *Faculty:* 4 full-time (1 woman). *Students:* 16 full-time (3 women), 27 part-time (12 women); includes 10 minority (8 African Americans, 2 Hispanic Americans), 6 international. Average age 27. 17 applicants, 100% accepted, 17 enrolled. In 2009, 26 master's awarded. *Entrance requirements:* For master's, GRE General Test or MAT, minimum GPA of 2.7. Additional exam requirements/recommendations for international students: Required—TOEFL (minimum score 550 paper-based; 213 computer-based); Recommended—IELTS (minimum score 6). *Application deadline:* For fall admission, 8/1 priority date for domestic students, 6/30 priority date for international students; for spring admission, 1/1 priority date for domestic students, 11/30 priority date for international students. Application fee: $25 ($75 for international students). Electronic applications accepted. *Expenses:* Tuition, state resident: full-time $3798; part-time $211 per credit hour. Tuition, nonresident: full-time $7596; part-time $422 per credit hour. Required fees: $903. *Unit head:* Dr. Lynn Glover-Stanley, Chair, 870-230-5200, E-mail: stanlel@hsu.edu. *Application contact:* Dr. Marck L. Beggs, Graduate Dean, 870-230-5126, Fax: 870-230-5479, E-mail: beggsm@hsu.edu.

Hofstra University, Frank G. Zarb School of Business, Department of Management, Entrepreneurship and General Management, Hempstead, NY 11549. Offers business administration (MBA), including health services management, management, sports and entertainment management; human resource management (MS). Part-time and evening/weekend programs available. *Faculty:* 6 full-time (2 women), 4 part-time/adjunct (0 women). *Students:* 75 full-time (35 women), 185 part-time (72 women); includes 55 minority (19 African Americans, 24 Asian Americans or Pacific Islanders, 12 Hispanic Americans), 26 international. Average age 33. 215 applicants, 61% accepted, 71 enrolled. In 2009, 53 master's awarded. *Degree requirements:* For master's, capstone course (MBA), thesis (MS). *Entrance requirements:* For master's, GMAT or GRE, 2 letters of recommendation, resume. Additional exam requirements/recommendations for international students: Required—TOEFL (minimum score 550 paper-based; 213 computer-based; 80 iBT); Recommended—IELTS (minimum score 6). *Application deadline:* Applications are processed on a rolling basis. Application fee: $60. Electronic applications accepted. *Expenses:* Contact institution. *Financial support:* In 2009–10, 23 students received support, including 20 fellowships with full and partial tuition reimbursements available (averaging $10,251 per year), 2 research assistantships with full and partial tuition reimbursements available (averaging $20,788 per year); career-related internships or fieldwork, Federal Work-Study, institutionally sponsored loans, scholarships/grants, tuition waivers (full and partial), and unspecified assistantships also available. Support available to part-time students. Financial award applicants required to submit FAFSA. *Faculty research:* Business/personal ethics; emotion in workplace; gender issues; learning and pedagogical issues; family business. *Unit head:* Dr. Mamdouh I. Farid, Chairperson, 516-463-5735, Fax: 516-463-4834, E-mail: mgbmif@hofstra.edu. *Application contact:* Carol Drummer, Dean of Graduate Admissions, 516-463-4876, Fax: 516-463-4664, E-mail: gradstudent@hofstra.edu.

Holy Names University, Graduate Division, Department of Business, Oakland, CA 94619-1699. Offers energy and environment management (MBA); finance (MBA); management and leadership (MBA); marketing (MBA); sports management (MBA). Part-time and evening/weekend programs available. *Entrance requirements:* For master's, minimum undergraduate GPA of 2.6 overall, 3.0 in major. Additional exam requirements/recommendations for international students: Required—TOEFL (minimum score 550 paper-based; 213 computer-based; 80 iBT). *Faculty research:* Business ethics, sustainable economics, accounting models, cross-cultural management, diversity in organizations.

Howard University, Graduate School, Department of Health, Human Performance and Leisure Studies, Washington, DC 20059-0002. Offers exercise physiology (MS); health education (MS); sports studies (MS), including sociology of sports, sports management; urban recreation (MS), including leisure studies. Part-time and evening/weekend programs available. *Degree requirements:* For master's, comprehensive exam, thesis. *Entrance requirements:* For master's, BS in human performance or related field. Electronic applications accepted. *Faculty research:* Health promotion, cardiovascular hypertension, physical activity, sport and human rights issues.

Indiana State University, School of Graduate Studies, College of Nursing, Health and Human Services, Department of Physical Education, Terre Haute, IN 47809. Offers adult fitness (MA, MS); coaching (MA, MS); exercise science (MA, MS). *Degree requirements:* For master's, thesis (for some programs). *Entrance requirements:* For master's, minor in physical education. Electronic applications accepted. *Faculty research:* Exercise science.

Indiana State University, School of Graduate Studies, College of Nursing, Health and Human Services, Department of Recreation and Sport Management, Terre Haute, IN 47809. Offers MA, MS. *Degree requirements:* For master's, comprehensive exam (for some programs), thesis (for some programs). *Entrance requirements:* For master's, GRE General Test, undergraduate major in related field. Electronic applications accepted.

Indiana University Bloomington, School of Health, Physical Education and Recreation, Department of Kinesiology, Bloomington, IN 47405-7000. Offers adapted physical education (MS); applied sport science (MS); athletic administration/sport management (MS); athletic training (MS); biomechanics (MS); ergonomics (MS); exercise physiology (MS); fitness management (MS); human performance (PhD); motor learning/control (MS). Part-time programs available. *Faculty:* 28 full-time (11 women). *Students:* 132 full-time (55 women), 37 part-time (7 women); includes 16 minority (13 African Americans, 1 Asian American or Pacific Islander, 2 Hispanic Americans), 29 international. Average age 28. 179 applicants, 60% accepted, 72 enrolled. In 2009, 59 master's awarded. Terminal master's awarded for partial completion of doctoral program. *Degree requirements:* For master's, thesis optional; for doctorate, variable foreign language requirement, thesis/dissertation. *Entrance requirements:* For master's, GRE General Test, minimum GPA of 2.8; for doctorate, GRE General Test, minimum graduate GPA of 3.5, undergraduate 3.0. *Application deadline:* For fall admission, 1/1 for international students; for spring admission, 9/1 for international students. Applications are processed on a rolling basis. Application fee: $55 ($65 for international students). *Financial support:* In 2009–10, 71

students received support, including 9 fellowships (averaging $1,400 per year), 28 research assistantships with full tuition reimbursements available (averaging $10,131 per year), 38 teaching assistantships with full tuition reimbursements available (averaging $10,390 per year); career-related internships or fieldwork, Federal Work-Study, institutionally sponsored loans, scholarships/grants, tuition waivers (partial), and fee remissions also available. Financial award application deadline: 3/1. *Faculty research:* Exercise physiology and biochemistry, sports biomechanics, human motor control, adaptation of fitness and exercise to special populations. *Unit head:* Dr. Donetta Cothran, Chairperson, 812-855-3114. *Application contact:* Program Office, 812-855-5523, Fax: 812-855-9417, E-mail: kines@indiana.edu.

Indiana University Bloomington, School of Health, Physical Education and Recreation, Department of Recreation, Park, and Tourism Studies, Bloomington, IN 47405-7000. Offers leisure behavior (PhD); outdoor recreation (MS); recreation (Re Dir); recreation administration (MS); recreational sports administration (MS); therapeutic recreation (MS); tourism management (MS). *Faculty:* 16 full-time (6 women), 2 part-time/adjunct (both women). *Students:* 55 full-time (29 women), 17 part-time (15 women); includes 8 minority (2 African Americans, 2 American Indian/Alaska Native, 3 Asian Americans or Pacific Islanders, 1 Hispanic American), 22 international. Average age 31. 62 applicants, 69% accepted, 23 enrolled. In 2009, 11 master's, 5 doctorates awarded. Terminal master's awarded for partial completion of doctoral program. *Degree requirements:* For master's and Re Dir, thesis optional; for doctorate, thesis/dissertation. *Entrance requirements:* For master's, GRE General Test, minimum GPA of 2.8; for doctorate, GRE General Test, minimum GPA of 3.0 (undergraduate), 3.5 (graduate). Additional exam requirements/recommendations for international students: Required—TOEFL. *Application deadline:* For fall admission, 1/1 for international students; for spring admission, 9/1 for international students. Applications are processed on a rolling basis. Application fee: $55 ($65 for international students). *Financial support:* In 2009–10, 30 students received support, including 7 fellowships (averaging $4,723 per year), 17 research assistantships (averaging $10,002 per year), 13 teaching assistantships with partial tuition reimbursements available (averaging $11,565 per year); career-related internships or fieldwork, Federal Work-Study, institutionally sponsored loans, scholarships/grants, tuition waivers (partial), unspecified assistantships, and fee remissions also available. Financial award application deadline: 3/1. *Faculty research:* Leisure counseling, gerontology, special populations, planning and development. *Unit head:* Dr. Craig Ross, Chairperson, 812-855-4711, E-mail: cmross@indiana.edu. *Application contact:* Program Office, 812-855-4711, Fax: 812-855-3998, E-mail: recpark@indiana.edu.

Indiana University of Pennsylvania, School of Graduate Studies and Research, College of Health and Human Services, Department of Health and Physical Education, Indiana, PA 15705-1087. Offers aquatics administration and facilities management (MS); exercise science (MS); sport management (MS); sport science (MS). Part-time programs available. *Faculty:* 8 full-time (4 women). *Students:* 55 full-time (24 women), 33 part-time (10 women); includes 8 minority (all African Americans), 14 international. Average age 25. 154 applicants, 48% accepted, 48 enrolled. In 2009, 54 master's awarded. *Degree requirements:* For master's, thesis optional. *Entrance requirements:* For master's, 2 letters of recommendation. Additional exam requirements/recommendations for international students: Required—TOEFL. *Application deadline:* For fall admission, 7/1 priority date for domestic students; for spring admission, 11/1 for domestic students. Applications are processed on a rolling basis. Application fee: $40. *Expenses:* Tuition, state resident: full-time $6666; part-time $370 per credit hour. Tuition, nonresident: full-time $10,666; part-time $593 per credit hour. Required fees: $813 per semester. *Financial support:* In 2009–10, 1 fellowship (averaging $500 per year), 16 research assistantships with full and partial tuition reimbursements (averaging $4,335 per year) were awarded. Financial award application deadline: 3/15; financial award applicants required to submit FAFSA. *Unit head:* Dr. Elaine Blair, Chairperson, 724-357-2770, E-mail: eblair@iup.edu. *Application contact:* Dr. Elaine Blair, Chairperson, 724-357-2770, E-mail: eblair@iup.edu.

Ithaca College, Division of Graduate and Professional Studies, School of Health Sciences and Human Performance, Program in Sport Management, Ithaca, NY 14850. Offers MS. Part-time programs available. *Faculty:* 5 full-time (2 women). *Students:* 15 full-time (7 women), 4 part-time (1 woman); includes 1 minority (Asian American or Pacific Islander), 2 international. Average age 25. 42 applicants, 67% accepted, 15 enrolled. In 2009, 13 master's awarded. *Degree requirements:* For master's, comprehensive exam (for some programs), thesis optional. *Entrance requirements:* For master's, GRE General Test, minimum GPA of 3.0. Additional exam requirements/recommendations for international students: Required—TOEFL (minimum score 550 paper-based; 213 computer-based; 80 iBT). *Application deadline:* For fall admission, 4/1 priority date for domestic and international students; for spring admission, 12/1 for domestic and international students. Applications are processed on a rolling basis. Application fee: $40. Electronic applications accepted. *Expenses:* Tuition: Full-time $18,960; part-time $632 per credit hour. *Financial support:* In 2009–10, 14 students received support, including 12 teaching assistantships (averaging $8,216 per year); career-related internships or fieldwork, Federal Work-Study, scholarships/grants, and unspecified assistantships also available. Support available to part-time students. Financial award application deadline: 4/1; financial award applicants required to submit CSS PROFILE or FAFSA. *Faculty research:* Consumer behavior in sport, legal issues in sport, Title IX and gender equity in sport, college sport finances, policy and governance, American Indians and sport. *Unit head:* Dr. Ellen Staurowsky, Chairperson, 607-274-3527, Fax: 607-274-1263, E-mail: gps@ithaca.edu. *Application contact:* Rob Gearhart, Dean, Graduate and Professional Studies, 607-274-3527, Fax: 607-274-1263, E-mail: gps@ithaca.edu.

Kansas Wesleyan University, Program in Business Administration, Salina, KS 67401-6196. Offers business administration (MBA); sports management (MBA). Part-time and evening/weekend programs available. *Entrance requirements:* For master's, GMAT, minimum graduate GPA of 3.0 or undergraduate GPA of 3.25.

Kent State University, Graduate School of Education, Health, and Human Services, School of Foundations, Leadership and Administration, Program in Exercise, Leisure and Sport, Kent, OH 44242-0001. Offers sport and recreation management (MA); sports studies (MA). *Faculty:* 11 full-time (6 women), 4 part-time/adjunct (0 women). *Students:* 50 full-time (17 women), 16 part-time (6 women); includes 7 minority (6 African Americans, 1 Asian American or Pacific Islander), 1 international. 48 applicants, 100% accepted. In 2009, 31 master's awarded. Application fee: $30. *Financial support:* In 2009–10, 10 research assistantships (averaging $8,500 per year) were awarded; Federal Work-Study, scholarships/grants, and unspecified assistantships also available. *Unit head:* Mark Lyberger, Coordinator, 330-672-0228, E-mail: mlyberge@kent.edu. *Application contact:* Nancy Miller, Academic Program Coordinator, Office of Graduate Student Services, 330-672-2576, Fax: 330-672-9162, E-mail: ogs@kent.edu.

Lasell College, Graduate and Professional Studies in Sport Management, Newton, MA 02466-2709. Offers sport hospitality management (MS, Graduate Certificate); sport leadership (MS, Graduate Certificate); sport non-profit management (MS, Graduate Certificate). Part-time programs available. Postbaccalaureate distance learning degree programs offered (no on-campus study). *Entrance requirements:* For master's and Graduate Certificate, bachelor's degree from an accredited institution. Additional exam requirements/recommendations for international students: Required—TOEFL (minimum score 550 paper-based; 213 computer-based; 75 iBT) or IELTS. *Application deadline:* For fall admission, 8/31 priority date for domestic students, 6/30 priority date for international students; for spring admission, 12/31 priority date for domestic students, 10/31 priority date for international students. Applications are processed on a rolling basis. Electronic applications accepted. *Expenses:* Tuition: Full-time $4890; part-time $525 per credit hour. Required fees: $55 per term. *Financial support:* Available to part-time students. Application deadline: 8/31. *Unit head:* Dr. Joan Dolamore, Dean of Graduate and Professional Studies, 617-243-2485, Fax: 617-243-2450, E-mail: gradinfo@lasell.edu. *Application contact:* Adrienne Franciosi, Director of Graduate Admission, 617-243-2214, Fax: 617-243-2450, E-mail: gradinfo@lasell.edu.

Lindenwood University, Graduate Programs, School of Business and Entrepreneurship, St. Charles, MO 63301-1695. Offers accounting (MBA, MS); business administration (MBA); entrepreneurial studies (MBA, MS); finance (MBA, MS); human resource management (MBA); human resources (MS); international business (MBA, MS); management (MBA, MS); management information systems (MBA, MS); marketing (MBA, MS); public management (MBA, MS); sport management (MA). *Accreditation:* ACBSP. Part-time and evening/weekend programs available. *Faculty:* 20 full-time (8 women), 17 part-time/adjunct (5 women). *Students:* 129 full-time (60 women), 138 part-time (61 women); includes 15 minority (11 African Americans, 2 Asian Americans or Pacific Islanders, 2 Hispanic Americans), 84 international. Average age 28. 149 applicants, 73 enrolled. In 2009, 142 master's awarded. *Degree requirements:* For master's, comprehensive exam (for some programs), thesis (for some programs). *Entrance requirements:* For master's, interview, minimum GPA of 3.0, letter of recommendation. Additional exam requirements/recommendations for international students: Required—TOEFL (minimum score 550 paper-based; 213 computer-based; 80 iBT). *Application deadline:* For fall admission, 7/30 priority date for domestic students, 9/16 priority date for international students; for winter admission, 12/19 priority date for domestic students, 12/17 priority date for international students; for spring admission, 2/25 priority date for domestic students, 2/11 priority date for international students. Applications are processed on a rolling basis. Application fee: $30 ($100 for international students). Electronic applications accepted. *Expenses:* Tuition: Full-time $12,960; part-time $370 per credit hour. Required fees: $340. One-time fee: $30 full-time. Tuition and fees vary according to course level and course load. *Financial support:* In 2009–10, 209 students received support. Career-related internships or fieldwork, Federal Work-Study, institutionally sponsored loans, and tuition waivers (partial) available. Financial award application deadline: 6/30; financial award applicants required to submit FAFSA. *Unit head:* Ed Morris, Dean of Management, 636-949-4832, E-mail: emorris@lindenwood.edu. *Application contact:* Brett Barger, Dean of Evening Admissions and Extension Campuses, 636-949-4934, Fax: 636-949-4109, E-mail: adultadmissions@lindenwood.edu.

Lipscomb University, MBA Program, Nashville, TN 37204-3951. Offers accounting (MBA); business administration (general) (MBA); conflict management (MBA); financial services (MBA); healthcare management (MBA); leadership (MBA); nonprofit management (MBA); sports administration (MBA); sustainable practice (MBA). *Accreditation:* ACBSP. Part-time and evening/weekend programs available. *Faculty:* 10 full-time (1 woman), 7 part-time/adjunct (2 women). *Students:* 43 full-time (23 women), 86 part-time (38 women); includes 23 minority (18 African Americans, 1 Asian American or Pacific Islander, 4 Hispanic Americans), 1 international. Average age 31. 95 applicants, 64% accepted, 35 enrolled. In 2009, 59 master's awarded. *Entrance requirements:* For master's, GMAT, interview, 2 references, resume. Additional exam requirements/recommendations for international students: Required—TOEFL (minimum score 570 paper-based; 230 computer-based). *Application deadline:* For fall admission, 2/1 for international students; for winter admission, 6/1 for international students. Applications are processed on a rolling basis. Application fee: $50 ($75 for international students). Electronic applications accepted. *Expenses:* Contact institution. *Financial support:* Career-related internships or fieldwork, Federal Work-Study, scholarships/grants, tuition waivers (partial), and unspecified assistantships available. Support available to part-time students. Financial award application deadline: 7/1; financial award applicants required to submit FAFSA. *Faculty research:* Impact of spirituality on organization commitment, leadership, psychological empowerment, training. *Unit head:* Dr. Mike Kendrick, Interim Chair of Graduate Business Studies, 615-966-1833, Fax: 615-966-1818, E-mail: mikekendrick@lipscomb.edu. *Application contact:* Emily Landsdell, 615-966-5284, E-mail: emily.lansdell@lipscomb.edu.

Lynn University, College of Business and Management, Boca Raton, FL 33431-5598. Offers aviation management (MBA); financial valuation and investment management (MBA); hospitality management (MBA); international business (MBA); marketing (MBA); mass communication and media management (MBA); sports and athletics administration (MBA). Part-time and evening/weekend programs available. Postbaccalaureate distance learning degree programs offered. *Degree requirements:* For master's, project. *Entrance requirements:* For master's, GMAT or GRE, minimum undergraduate GPA of 3.0, resume, 2 letters of recommendation. Additional exam requirements/recommendations for international students: Required—TOEFL (minimum score 550 paper-based; 213 computer-based). *Application deadline:* Applications are processed on a rolling basis. Application fee: $50. Electronic applications accepted. *Expenses:* Tuition: Part-time $580 per credit. One-time fee: $200 part-time. Part-time tuition and fees vary according to degree level. *Financial support:* Career-related internships or fieldwork, Federal Work-Study, institutionally sponsored loans, scholarships/grants, tuition waivers (full and partial), and unspecified assistantships available. Support available to part-time students. Financial award application deadline: 8/1; financial award applicants required to submit FAFSA. *Faculty research:* Labor relations, dynamic balance in leisure-time skills, ethics in athletics, hotel development. *Unit head:* Dr. Ralph Norcio, Associate Dean, 561-237-7010, Fax: 561-237-7014, E-mail: rnorcio@lynn.edu. *Application contact:* Dr. Larissa Baia, Assistant Director of Graduate Admissions, 561-237-7916, Fax: 561-237-7100, E-mail: admissionpm@lynn.edu.

Manhattanville College, Graduate Programs, Humanities and Social Sciences Programs, Program in Sport Business Management, Purchase, NY 10577-2132. Offers MS. Part-time and evening/weekend programs available. *Students:* 32 full-time (6 women), 31 part-time (6 women); includes 5 minority (2 African Americans, 3 Hispanic Americans), 3 international. In 2009, 15 master's awarded. *Entrance requirements:* Additional exam requirements/recommendations for international students: Required—TOEFL. *Application deadline:* Applications are processed on a rolling basis. Application fee: $70. *Financial support:* Career-related internships or fieldwork, Federal Work-Study, institutionally sponsored loans, and unspecified assistantships available. Financial award application deadline: 3/1; financial award applicants required to submit FAFSA. *Unit head:* Dr. Don Richards, Interim Dean, School of Graduate and Professional Studies, 914-323-5469, Fax: 914-694-3488, E-mail: gps@mville.edu. *Application contact:* Office of Admissions for Graduate and Professional Studies, 914-323-5418, E-mail: gps@mville.edu.

Marshall University, Academic Affairs Division, College of Education and Human Services, School of Kinesiology, Program in Sport Administration, Huntington, WV 25755. Offers MS. *Faculty:* 5 full-time (2 women), 5 part-time/adjunct (2 women). *Students:* 33 full-time (8 women), 5 part-time (0 women); includes 4 minority (3 African Americans, 1 Hispanic American), 2 international. Average age 25. In 2009, 20 master's awarded. *Degree requirements:* For master's, thesis optional, comprehensive assessment. *Entrance requirements:* For master's, GRE General Test. Application fee: $40. *Unit head:* Dr. Jennifer Mak, Graduate Program Director, 304-696-2927, E-mail: mak@marshall.edu. *Application contact:* Information Contact, 304-746-1900, Fax: 304-746-1902, E-mail: services@marshall.edu.

Millersville University of Pennsylvania, College of Graduate and Professional Studies, School of Education, Department of Wellness and Sport Science, Program in Sport Management, Millersville, PA 17551-0302. Offers athletic coaching (M Ed); athletic management (M Ed). Part-time and evening/weekend programs available. *Faculty:* 11 full-time (4 women), 1 part-time/adjunct (0 women). *Students:* 10 full-time (6 women), 35 part-time (10 women); includes 1 minority (African American). Average age 27. 30 applicants, 87% accepted, 18 enrolled. In 2009, 21 master's awarded. *Degree requirements:* For master's, comprehensive exam, thesis optional. *Entrance requirements:* For master's, GRE or MAT, 3 letters of recommendation. Additional exam requirements/recommendations for international students: Required—TOEFL (minimum score 500 paper-based; 183 computer-based; 65 iBT) or IELTS (minimum score 6). *Application deadline:* For fall admission, 1/15 priority date for domestic and international students; for winter admission, 10/1 priority date for domestic and international students; for spring admission, 10/1 priority date for domestic and international students. Applications are processed on a rolling basis. Application fee: $40 ($50 for international students). Electronic applications accepted. *Expenses:* Tuition, state resident: full-time $6666; part-time $370 per credit. Tuition, nonresident: full-time $10,666; part-time $593 per credit. Required fees: $1578.50; $76.25 per credit. One-time fee: $60 part-time. Tuition and fees vary according to course load. *Financial support:* In 2009–10, 12 students received support, including 12 research assistantships with full tuition reimbursements available (averaging $5,067 per year); institutionally sponsored loans and unspecified assistantships also available. Support available to part-time students. Financial award application deadline: 3/15; financial award

Sports Management

Millersville University of Pennsylvania (continued)

applicants required to submit FAFSA. *Faculty research:* Dispute resolution, restorative justice, emotional intelligence, pediatric and early childhood obesity, sport governance. Total annual research expenditures: $76,432. *Unit head:* Dr. Rebecca J. Mowrey, Coordinator, 717-872-3794, Fax: 717-871-2393, E-mail: rebecca.mowrey@millersville.edu. *Application contact:* Dr. Victor S. DeSantis, Dean of Graduate and Professional Studies, 717-872-3099, Fax: 717-872-3453, E-mail: victor.desantis@millersville.edu.

Mississippi State University, College of Education, Department of Kinesiology, MS State, MS 39762. Offers physical education (MS), including exercise science, sport administration, teaching/coaching. Part-time programs available. Postbaccalaureate distance learning degree programs offered (minimal on-campus study). *Faculty:* 7 full-time (1 woman). *Students:* 56 full-time (22 women), 11 part-time (6 women); includes 20 minority (18 African Americans, 1 American Indian/Alaska Native, 1 Asian American or Pacific Islander), 2 international. Average age 25. 58 applicants, 72% accepted, 36 enrolled. In 2009, 22 master's awarded. *Degree requirements:* For master's, comprehensive exam, thesis optional. *Entrance requirements:* For master's, GRE General Test, minimum GPA of 3.0. Additional exam requirements/recommendations for international students: Required—TOEFL (minimum score 550 paper-based; 213 computer-based; 79 iBT); Recommended—IELTS (minimum score 6.5). *Application deadline:* For fall admission, 7/1 for domestic students, 5/1 for international students; for spring admission, 11/1 for domestic students, 9/1 for international students. Applications are processed on a rolling basis. Application fee: $40. Electronic applications accepted. *Expenses:* Tuition, state resident: full-time $2575.50; part-time $286.25 per credit hour. Tuition, nonresident: full-time $6510; part-time $723.50 per credit hour. Tuition and fees vary according to course load. *Financial support:* In 2009–10, 7 teaching assistantships (averaging $8,772 per year) were awarded; career-related internships or fieldwork, Federal Work-Study, institutionally sponsored loans, and unspecified assistantships also available. Financial award application deadline: 4/1; financial award applicants required to submit FAFSA. *Faculty research:* Static balance and stepping performance of older adults, organizational justice, public health, strength training and recovery drinks, high risk drinking perceptions and behaviors. *Unit head:* Dr. Stanley Brown, Head, 662-325-2963, Fax: 662-325-4525, E-mail: spb107@msstate.edu. *Application contact:* Dr. John G. Lamberth, Associate Professor and Graduate Coordinator, 662-325-0906, Fax: 662-325-4525, E-mail: jgl@ra.msstate.edu.

Missouri State University, Graduate College, Interdisciplinary Program in Administrative Studies, Springfield, MO 65897. Offers applied communication (MS); criminal justice (MS); environmental management (MS); project management (MS); sports management (MS). Part-time and evening/weekend programs available. Postbaccalaureate distance learning degree programs offered (no on-campus study). *Students:* 17 full-time (11 women), 60 part-time (26 women); includes 6 minority (4 African Americans, 1 Asian American or Pacific Islander, 1 Hispanic American), 2 international. Average age 35. 24 applicants, 100% accepted, 19 enrolled. In 2009, 16 master's awarded. *Degree requirements:* For master's, comprehensive exam, thesis or alternative. *Entrance requirements:* For master's, GRE, GMAT, 3 years of work experience. Additional exam requirements/recommendations for international students: Required—TOEFL (minimum score 550 paper-based; 213 computer-based; 79 iBT). *Application deadline:* For fall admission, 7/20 priority date for domestic students; for spring admission, 12/20 priority date for domestic students. Applications are processed on a rolling basis. Application fee: $35 ($50 for international students). Electronic applications accepted. *Expenses:* Tuition, state resident: full-time $3852; part-time $214 per credit hour. Tuition, nonresident: full-time $7524; part-time $418 per credit hour. Required fees: $696; $172 per semester. Tuition and fees vary according to course level, course load, degree level and program. *Financial support:* In 2009–10, 1 teaching assistantship with full tuition reimbursement (averaging $7,340 per year) was awarded; career-related internships or fieldwork, Federal Work-Study, institutionally sponsored loans, scholarships/grants, and unspecified assistantships also available. Support available to part-time students. Financial award application deadline: 3/31; financial award applicants required to submit FAFSA. *Unit head:* John Bourhis, Director, 417-836-6390, E-mail: johnbourhis@missouristate.edu. *Application contact:* Eric Eckert, Coordinator of Graduate Admissions and Recruitment, 417-836-5331, Fax: 417-836-6200, E-mail: ericeckert@missouristate.edu.

Montana State University Billings, College of Allied Health Professions, Department of Health and Human Performance, Billings, MT 59101-0298. Offers athletic training (MS); sport management (MS). *Degree requirements:* For master's, thesis optional. *Entrance requirements:* For master's, GRE General Test, minimum undergraduate GPA of 3.0.

Montclair State University, The Graduate School, College of Education and Human Services, Department of Exercise Science and Physical Education, Montclair, NJ 07043-1624. Offers health and physical education (Certificate); nutrition and exercise science (Certificate); physical education (MA, Certificate), including coaching and sports administration (MA), exercise science (MA), physical education (MA), teaching and supervision of physical education (MA). Part-time and evening/weekend programs available. *Faculty:* 15 full-time (9 women), 17 part-time/adjunct (10 women). *Students:* 8 full-time (3 women), 38 part-time (19 women). Average age 30. 34 applicants, 56% accepted, 13 enrolled. In 2009, 9 master's awarded. *Degree requirements:* For master's, comprehensive exam. *Entrance requirements:* For master's, GRE General Test, 2 letters of recommendation; for Certificate, 2 letters of recommendation (nutrition and exercise science concentration). Additional exam requirements/recommendations for international students: Required—TOEFL (minimum score 83 computer-based), or IELTS. *Application deadline:* For fall admission, 6/1 for international students; for spring admission, 10/1 for international students. Applications are processed on a rolling basis. Application fee: $60. Electronic applications accepted. *Expenses:* Tuition, area resident: Part-time $486.74 per credit. Tuition, state resident: part-time $486.74 per credit. Tuition, nonresident: part-time $751.34 per credit. Tuition and fees vary according to degree level and program. *Financial support:* In 2009–10, 5 research assistantships with full tuition reimbursements (averaging $7,000 per year) were awarded; Federal Work-Study, scholarships/grants, and unspecified assistantships also available. Support available to part-time students. Financial award application deadline: 3/1; financial award applicants required to submit FAFSA. *Unit head:* Dr. Susana Juniu, Chairperson, 973-655-7093. *Application contact:* Amy Aiello, Director of Graduate Admissions and Operations, 973-655-5147, Fax: 973-655-7869, E-mail: graduate.school@montclair.edu.

Morehead State University, Graduate Programs, College of Business and Public Affairs, School of Business Administration, Morehead, KY 40351. Offers business administration (MBA); information systems (MSIS); sport management (MA). Part-time and evening/weekend programs available. *Faculty:* 21 full-time (8 women). *Students:* 41 full-time (17 women), 198 part-time (99 women); includes 16 minority (10 African Americans, 4 Asian Americans or Pacific Islanders, 2 Hispanic Americans), 4 international. Average age 32. 118 applicants, 71% accepted, 53 enrolled. In 2009, 60 master's awarded. *Entrance requirements:* For master's, GRE or GMAT. Additional exam requirements/recommendations for international students: Required—TOEFL (minimum score 500 paper-based; 173 computer-based). *Application deadline:* For fall admission, 8/1 priority date for domestic and international students; for spring admission, 12/1 priority date for domestic and international students. Applications are processed on a rolling basis. Application fee: $30. Electronic applications accepted. *Expenses:* Tuition, state resident: full-time $6318; part-time $351 per credit hour. Tuition, nonresident: full-time $15,804; part-time $878 per credit hour. *Financial support:* In 2009–10, 1 research assistantship (averaging $10,000 per year), 9 teaching assistantships (averaging $10,000 per year) were awarded; career-related internships or fieldwork, Federal Work-Study, and unspecified assistantships also available. Financial award application deadline: 3/15; financial award applicants required to submit FAFSA. *Unit head:* Dr. Robert L. Albert, Dean, 606-783-2174, Fax: 606-783-5025, E-mail: r.albert@moreheadstate.edu. *Application contact:* Michelle Barber, Graduate Recruitment and Retention Assistant Director, 606-783-5127, Fax: 606-783-5061, E-mail: m.barber@moreheadstate.edu.

Neumann University, Program in Sports Management, Aston, PA 19014-1298. Offers MS. Part-time programs available. *Faculty:* 2 full-time (both women), 3 part-time/adjunct (2 women). *Students:* 3 full-time (0 women), 11 part-time (5 women). Average age 28. 10 applicants, 100% accepted, 8 enrolled. In 2009, 11 master's awarded. *Degree requirements:* For master's, thesis or alternative, experiential component. *Application deadline:* Applications are processed on a rolling basis. Application fee: $50. Electronic applications accepted. *Expenses:* Tuition: Full-time $10,260; part-time $570 per credit hour. *Financial support:* Available to part-time students. Application deadline: 3/15. *Unit head:* Dr. Sandra L. Slabik, Coordinator, 610-361-5291, Fax: 610-558-5574, E-mail: slabiks@neumann.edu. *Application contact:* Kittie D. Pain, Associate Director of Admissions, Graduate and Adult Programs, 610-558-5613, Fax: 610-558-5652, E-mail: paink@neumann.edu.

New England College, Program in Sports and Recreation Management: Coaching, Henniker, NH 03242-3293. Offers MS. *Entrance requirements:* For master's, resume, 2 letters of reference.

New Mexico Highlands University, Graduate Studies, School of Education, Department of Exercise and Sport Sciences, Las Vegas, NM 87701. Offers human performance and sport (MA); sports administration (MA); teacher education (MA). Part-time programs available. *Degree requirements:* For master's, comprehensive exam, thesis or alternative. *Entrance requirements:* For master's, minimum undergraduate GPA of 3.0. Additional exam requirements/recommendations for international students: Required—TOEFL (minimum score 540 paper-based; 207 computer-based). *Faculty research:* Child obesity and physical inactivity, body composition and fitness assessment, motor development, sport marketing, sport finance.

New York University, School of Continuing and Professional Studies, The Preston Robert Tisch Center for Hospitality, Tourism, and Sports Management, Program in Sports Business, New York, NY 10012-1019. Offers finance and development (MS); marketing and media (MS); sports business (Advanced Certificate). Part-time and evening/weekend programs available. *Faculty:* 13 full-time (5 women), 11 part-time/adjunct (2 women). *Students:* 43 full-time (10 women), 65 part-time (21 women); includes 10 minority (5 African Americans, 2 Asian Americans or Pacific Islanders, 3 Hispanic Americans). Average age 28. 140 applicants, 49% accepted, 42 enrolled. In 2009, 45 master's, 6 other advanced degrees awarded. *Degree requirements:* For master's, comprehensive exam (for some programs), thesis. *Entrance requirements:* For master's, GMAT or GRE General Test (for recent graduates), resume, 2 letters of recommendation, essay. Additional exam requirements/recommendations for international students: Required—TOEFL (minimum score 600 paper-based; 250 computer-based; 100 iBT), TWE. *Application deadline:* For fall admission, 2/1 priority date for domestic and international students; for spring admission, 10/15 priority date for domestic students, 8/15 priority date for international students. Applications are processed on a rolling basis. Application fee: $75. Electronic applications accepted. *Expenses:* Tuition: Full-time $30,528; part-time $1272 per credit. Required fees: $2177. *Financial support:* In 2009–10, 39 students received support, including 39 fellowships (averaging $3,408 per year); career-related internships or fieldwork, Federal Work-Study, institutionally sponsored loans, and scholarships/grants also available. Support available to part-time students. Financial award application deadline: 3/1; financial award applicants required to submit FAFSA. *Faculty research:* Implications of college football's bowl coalition series from a legal, economic, and academic perspective; social history of sports. *Unit head:* Lalia Rach, Divisional Dean, 212-998-9100, Fax: 212-995-4676, E-mail: lalia.rach@nyu.edu. *Application contact:* Sandra Dove-Lowther, Academic Services Director, 212-998-9106, Fax: 212-995-4676, E-mail: sd2@nyu.edu.

Nichols College, Graduate Program in Business Administration, Dudley, MA 01571-5000. Offers business administration (MBA, MOL); security management (MBA); sport management (MBA). Part-time and evening/weekend programs available. Postbaccalaureate distance learning degree programs offered (no on-campus study). *Entrance requirements:* For master's, 2 letters of recommendation. Additional exam requirements/recommendations for international students: Required—TOEFL (minimum score 500 paper-based; 213 computer-based). Electronic applications accepted.

North Carolina Central University, Division of Academic Affairs, College of Behavioral and Social Sciences, Department of Physical Education and Recreation, Durham, NC 27707-3129. Offers athletic administration (MS); physical education (MS); recreation administration (MS); therapeutic recreation (MS). Part-time and evening/weekend programs available. *Degree requirements:* For master's, one foreign language, comprehensive exam, thesis. *Entrance requirements:* For master's, GRE, minimum GPA of 3.0 in major, 2.5 overall. Additional exam requirements/recommendations for international students: Required—TOEFL. *Faculty research:* Physical activity patterns of children with disabilities, physical fitness test of North Carolina school children, exercise physiology, motor learning/development.

North Carolina State University, Graduate School, College of Natural Resources, Department of Parks, Recreation and Tourism Management, Raleigh, NC 27695. Offers natural resource management (MPRTM, MS); park and recreation management (MPRTM, MS); parks, recreation and tourism management (PhD); recreational sport management (MPRTM, MS); spatial information science (MPRTM, MS); tourism policy and development (MPRTM, MS). *Degree requirements:* For master's, thesis (for some programs); for doctorate, thesis/dissertation. *Entrance requirements:* For master's and doctorate, GRE General Test. Additional exam requirements/recommendations for international students: Required—TOEFL. Electronic applications accepted. *Faculty research:* Tourism policy and development, spatial information systems, natural resource management, recreational sports management, park and recreation management.

North Dakota State University, College of Graduate and Interdisciplinary Studies, College of Human Development and Education, Department of Health, Nutrition, and Exercise Sciences, Fargo, ND 58108. Offers dietetics (MS); entry level athletic training (MS); exercise science (MS); nutrition science (MS); public health (MS); sport pedagogy (MS); sports recreation management (MS). Part-time and evening/weekend programs available. Postbaccalaureate distance learning degree programs offered (no on-campus study). *Faculty:* 12 full-time (6 women). *Students:* 28 full-time (18 women), 23 part-time (16 women); includes 1 African American, 1 Asian American or Pacific Islander, 3 international. 19 applicants, 100% accepted, 15 enrolled. In 2009, 27 master's awarded. *Degree requirements:* For master's, thesis (for some programs). *Entrance requirements:* For master's, minimum GPA of 3.0. Additional exam requirements/recommendations for international students: Required—TOEFL (minimum score 525 paper-based; 197 computer-based; 71 iBT). *Application deadline:* For fall admission, 3/1 priority date for domestic and international students. Application fee: $45 ($60 for international students). Electronic applications accepted. *Financial support:* In 2009–10, 28 students received support, including 18 teaching assistantships with full tuition reimbursements available (averaging $6,500 per year). Financial award application deadline: 3/31. *Faculty research:* Biomechanics, sport specialization, recreation, nutrition, athletic training. Total annual research expenditures: $10,000. *Unit head:* Brad Strand, Head, 701-231-7474, Fax: 701-231-8872, E-mail: bradford.strand@ndsu.edu. *Application contact:* Brad Strand, Head, 701-231-7474, Fax: 701-231-8872, E-mail: bradford.strand@ndsu.edu.

North Dakota State University, College of Graduate and Interdisciplinary Studies, College of Human Development and Education, School of Education, Program in Curriculum and Instruction, Fargo, ND 58108. Offers pedagogy (M Ed, MS); physical education and athletic administration (M Ed, MS). *Faculty:* 10 full-time (3 women). *Students:* 1 (woman) full-time, 11 part-time (10 women). Average age 27. 8 applicants, 75% accepted, 6 enrolled. In 2009, 1 master's awarded. *Degree requirements:* For master's, comprehensive exam, thesis (for some programs). *Entrance requirements:* For master's, Cooperative English Test, GRE General Test, MAT. Additional exam requirements/recommendations for international students: Required—TOEFL. *Application deadline:* For fall admission, 5/1 for domestic students. Applications are processed on a rolling basis. Application fee: $45 ($60 for international students). *Financial support:* Teaching assistantships, career-related internships or fieldwork, Federal Work-Study, institutionally sponsored loans, and tuition waivers (full) available. Financial award application deadline: 4/15. *Unit head:* Dr. William Martin, Chair, 701-231-7202, Fax: 701-231-7416, E-mail: william.martin@ndsu.edu. *Application contact:* Dr. Justin Wageman, Associate Professor, 701-231-7108, Fax: 701-231-9685, E-mail: justin.wageman@ndsu.edu.

Northern Illinois University, Graduate School, College of Education, Department of Kinesiology and Physical Education, De Kalb, IL 60115-2854. Offers physical education (MS Ed); sport management (MS). Part-time and evening/weekend programs available. *Faculty:* 21 full-time (12 women). *Students:* 63 full-time (25 women), 97 part-time (39 women); includes 13 minority (7 African Americans, 4 Asian Americans or Pacific Islanders, 2 Hispanic Americans), 7 international. Average age 28. 78 applicants, 69% accepted, 26 enrolled. In 2009, 68 master's awarded. *Degree requirements:* For master's, comprehensive exam, thesis optional. *Entrance requirements:* For master's, GRE General Test, minimum GPA of 2.75, undergraduate major in related area. Additional exam requirements/recommendations for international students: Required—TOEFL (minimum score 550 paper-based; 213 computer-based). *Application deadline:* For fall admission, 6/1 for domestic students, 5/1 for international students; for spring admission, 11/1 for domestic students, 10/1 for international students. Applications are processed on a rolling basis. Application fee: $30. Electronic applications accepted. *Expenses:* Tuition, state resident: full-time $6576; part-time $274 per credit hour. Tuition, nonresident: full-time $13,152; part-time $548 per credit hour. Required fees: $1813; $75.53 per credit hour. Part-time tuition and fees vary according to course load. *Financial support:* In 2009–10, 35 teaching assistantships with full tuition reimbursements were awarded; fellowships with full tuition reimbursements, research assistantships with full tuition reimbursements, career-related internships or fieldwork, Federal Work-Study, scholarships/grants, tuition waivers (full), and unspecified assistantships also available. Support available to part-time students. Financial award applicants required to submit FAFSA. *Faculty research:* Leadership in athletic training, motor development, dance education, gait analysis, fat phobia. *Unit head:* Dr. Paul Carpenter, Chair, 815-753-1407, Fax: 815-753-1413, E-mail: chowell@niu.edu. *Application contact:* Dr. Laurie Zittel, Director, Graduate Studies, 815-753-3907, E-mail: lzape@niu.edu.

Northwestern University, School of Continuing Studies, Program in Sports Administration, Evanston, IL 60208. Offers sports management (MA); sports marketing and public relations (MA).

Nova Southeastern University, Fischler School of Education and Human Services, Graduate Teacher Education Program, Fort Lauderdale, FL 33314-7796. Offers athletic administration (MS); brain research (MS, Ed S); charter school education/leadership (MS); cognitive and behavioral disabilities (MS); computer science education (Ed S); computer science education (K-12) (MS); curriculum and teaching (Ed S); curriculum, instruction and technology (MS); curriculum, instruction, management and administration (Ed S); early childhood education (MS); early literacy and reading (Ed S); early literacy education (MS); education technology (MS); educational leadership (administration K–12) (MS, Ed S); educational media (Ed S); educational media (K-12) (MS); elementary education (MS, Ed S), including ESOL endorsement (MS); English education (MS, Ed S); environmental education (MS); exceptional student education (MS), including ESOL endorsement; gifted education (MS, Ed S); interdisciplinary arts education (MS); management and administration of educational programs (MS); mathematics (MS); mathematics education (Ed S); multicultural early intervention (MS); pre-kindergarten/primary (MS); preschool education (MS); reading (MS); reading and TESOL (MS); reading education (Ed S); science (MS); science education (Ed S); secondary education (MS); social studies (MS, Ed S); Spanish language (MS); special education and reading (MS); teaching and learning (MA, MS), including curriculum and instruction (MA), elementary mathematics (MA), elementary reading (MA), K-12 technology integration (MA); teaching English to speakers of other languages (MS, Ed S); technology management and administration (Ed S); urban studies education (MS). Part-time and evening/weekend programs available. Postbaccalaureate distance learning degree programs offered (minimal on-campus study). *Faculty:* 72 full-time (43 women), 385 part-time/adjunct (252 women). *Students:* 196 full-time (175 women), 1,304 part-time (1,128 women); includes 594 minority (471 African Americans, 5 American Indian/Alaska Native, 18 Asian Americans or Pacific Islanders, 100 Hispanic Americans). Average age 37. 2,610 applicants, 72% accepted, 1352 enrolled. In 2009, 836 other advanced degrees awarded. *Degree requirements:* For master's and Ed S, thesis, practicum, internship. *Entrance requirements:* For master's, MAT, GRE, CLAST, CBEST, PRAXIS I, General Knowledge Test, minimum GPA of 2.5; for Ed S, MAT or GRE, master's degree, teaching certificate, minimum GPA of 3.0. Additional exam requirements/recommendations for international students: Required—TSE (recommended, minimum score 50); Recommended—TOEFL (minimum score 550 paper-based; 213 computer-based; 80 iBT), IELTS (minimum score 6). *Application deadline:* For fall admission, 9/25 priority date for domestic and international students; for winter admission, 2/23 priority date for domestic and international students; for spring admission, 4/25 priority date for domestic and international students. Applications are processed on a rolling basis. Application fee: $50. Electronic applications accepted. *Financial support:* Federal Work-Study available. Support available to part-time students. Financial award application deadline: 4/15; financial award applicants required to submit FAFSA. *Faculty research:* School effectiveness, critical thinking, leadership skills acquisition, child education, multicultural education. *Unit head:* Dr. Ronald Kern, Dean of Academic Affairs, 800-986-3223 Ext. 7809, Fax: 954-262-3606, E-mail: rk429@nsu.nova.edu. *Application contact:* Dr. Jennifer Quinones Nottingham, Dean of Student Affairs, 800-986-3223 Ext. 1559.

Ohio University, Graduate College, College of Health and Human Services, School of Recreation and Sport Sciences, Program in Coaching Education, Athens, OH 45701-2979. Offers MS. *Faculty:* 5 full-time (2 women). *Students:* 23 full-time (6 women), 2 part-time (0 women), 2 international. 18 applicants, 89% accepted, 11 enrolled. In 2009, 15 master's awarded. *Entrance requirements:* For master's, GRE. Additional exam requirements/recommendations for international students: Required—TOEFL (minimum score 550 paper-based; 80 iBT) or IELTS Academic (minimum score 6.5). *Application deadline:* For fall admission, 3/1 priority date for domestic and international students. Applications are processed on a rolling basis. Application fee: $50 ($55 for international students). Electronic applications accepted. *Expenses:* Tuition, state resident: full-time $7839; part-time $323 per quarter hour. Tuition, nonresident: full-time $15,831; part-time $654 per quarter hour. Required fees: $2931. *Financial support:* In 2009–10, research assistantships with full tuition reimbursements (averaging $8,835 per year), teaching assistantships with full tuition reimbursements (averaging $8,835 per year) were awarded; scholarships/grants and stipends also available. Financial award application deadline: 3/1. *Faculty research:* Sports, physical activity, athletes. *Unit head:* Dr. David Carr, Assistant Professor and Coordinator, 740-593-4651, Fax: 740-593-0284, E-mail: carr@ohio.edu. *Application contact:* Dr. David Carr, Assistant Professor and Coordinator, 740-593-4651, Fax: 740-593-0284, E-mail: carr@ohio.edu.

Ohio University, Graduate College, College of Health and Human Services, School of Recreation and Sport Sciences, Program in Sports Administration and Facility Management, Athens, OH 45701-2979. Offers MSA. Postbaccalaureate distance learning degree programs offered (minimal on-campus study). *Faculty:* 6 full-time (2 women), 3 part-time/adjunct (0 women). *Students:* 41 full-time (11 women), 2 part-time (1 woman); includes 6 minority (3 African Americans, 1 Asian American or Pacific Islander, 2 Hispanic Americans), 3 international. 52 applicants, 21% accepted, 9 enrolled. In 2009, 32 master's awarded. *Degree requirements:* For master's, 11-week internship. *Entrance requirements:* For master's, GMAT or LSAT, interview. Additional exam requirements/recommendations for international students: Required—TOEFL (minimum score 600 paper-based; 250 computer-based; 100 iBT) or IELTS Academic (minimum score 7.5). *Application deadline:* For fall admission, 2/1 for domestic and international students. Application fee: $50 ($55 for international students). Electronic applications accepted. *Expenses:* Tuition, state resident: full-time $7839; part-time $323 per quarter hour. Tuition, nonresident: full-time $15,831; part-time $654 per quarter hour. Required fees: $2931. *Financial support:* Fellowships with full tuition reimbursements, research assistantships with full and partial tuition reimbursements, Federal Work-Study, institutionally sponsored loans, scholarships/grants, tuition waivers (partial), and stipends available. Financial award application deadline: 2/1. *Faculty research:* Sport management, sport marketing, sports and technology, career development. *Unit head:* James Kahler, Executive Director, 740-593-4666, Fax: 740-593-0539, E-mail: kahler@ohio.edu. *Application contact:* Teresa Tedrow, Administrative Associate, 740-593-4666, Fax: 740-593-0539, E-mail: tedrow@ohio.edu.

Old Dominion University, Darden College of Education, Program in Physical Education, Sport Management Emphasis, Norfolk, VA 23529. Offers MS Ed. Part-time and evening/weekend programs available. *Faculty:* 3 full-time (1 woman), 2 part-time/adjunct (both women). *Students:* 27 full-time (10 women), 15 part-time (3 women); includes 8 minority (7 African Americans, 1 Hispanic American), 2 international. Average age 25. 42 applicants, 71% accepted, 28 enrolled. In 2009, 19 master's awarded. *Degree requirements:* For master's, comprehensive exam, thesis or alternative, internship, research project. *Entrance requirements:* For master's, GRE, minimum GPA of 2.8 overall, 3.0 in major. Additional exam requirements/recommendations for international students: Required—TOEFL (minimum score 500 paper-based; 200 computer-based). *Application deadline:* For fall admission, 7/1 for domestic students; for spring admission, 11/1 for domestic students. Applications are processed on a rolling basis. Application fee: $40. *Expenses:* Tuition, state resident: full-time $8112; part-time $338 per credit. Tuition, nonresident: full-time $20,256; part-time $844 per credit. Required fees: $119 per semester. One-time fee: $50. *Financial support:* In 2009–10, fellowships (averaging $15,000 per year), 1 research assistantship with partial tuition reimbursement (averaging $10,000 per year), teaching assistantships with partial tuition reimbursements (averaging $10,000 per year) were awarded; career-related internships or fieldwork and scholarships/grants also available. Financial award application deadline: 4/15; financial award applicants required to submit FAFSA. *Faculty research:* Leadership, fan motives, sport communications, curriculum development in sport management, violence in sport. Total annual research expenditures: $185,000. *Unit head:* Robert Case, Graduate Program Director, 757-683-5962, Fax: 757-683-4270, E-mail: rcase@odu.edu. *Application contact:* Robert Case, Graduate Program Director, 757-683-5962, Fax: 757-683-4270, E-mail: rcase@odu.edu.

St. Cloud State University, School of Graduate Studies, College of Education, Department of Health, Physical Education, Recreation, and Sport Science, St. Cloud, MN 56301-4498. Offers exercise science (MS); physical education (MS); sports management (MS). *Faculty:* 16 full-time (8 women), 1 (woman) part-time/adjunct. *Students:* 21 full-time (10 women), 39 part-time (13 women); includes 7 minority (3 African Americans, 4 Asian Americans or Pacific Islanders), 2 international. 31 applicants, 71% accepted. In 2009, 17 master's awarded. *Degree requirements:* For master's, thesis or alternative. *Entrance requirements:* For master's, GRE General Test, minimum GPA of 2.75. Additional exam requirements/recommendations for international students: Required—Michigan English Language Assessment Battery; Recommended—TOEFL (minimum score 550 paper-based; 213 computer-based), IELTS (minimum score 6.5). *Application deadline:* For fall admission, 6/1 priority date for domestic students, 4/1 for international students; for spring admission, 10/1 priority date for domestic students, 8/1 for international students. Applications are processed on a rolling basis. Application fee: $35. Electronic applications accepted. *Financial support:* Federal Work-Study, scholarships/grants, and unspecified assistantships available. Financial award application deadline: 3/1. *Unit head:* Dr. Caryl Martin, Chairperson, 320-308-4251, E-mail: clmartin@stcloudstate.edu. *Application contact:* Linda Lou Krueger, School of Graduate Studies, 320-308-2113, Fax: 320-308-5371, E-mail: lekrueger@stcloudstate.edu.

St. Edward's University, School of Education, Program in Teaching, Austin, TX 78704. Offers curriculum leadership (Certificate); instructional technology (Certificate); mentoring and supervision (Certificate); sports management (Certificate); teaching (MA), including conflict resolution, initial teacher certification, liberal arts, organization development and training, sports management, teacher leadership. Part-time and evening/weekend programs available. *Students:* 5 full-time (4 women), 36 part-time (26 women); includes 10 minority (1 African American, 9 Hispanic Americans). Average age 30. 23 applicants, 70% accepted, 12 enrolled. In 2009, 9 master's awarded. *Degree requirements:* For master's, minimum of 24 resident hours. *Entrance requirements:* For master's, GRE General Test, minimum GPA of 3.0 in last 60 hours or 2.75 overall. Additional exam requirements/recommendations for international students: Required—TOEFL (minimum score 550 paper-based; 213 computer-based; 79 iBT) or IELTS (minimum score 6). *Application deadline:* For fall admission, 7/1 for domestic and international students; for spring admission, 11/1 for domestic and international students. Applications are processed on a rolling basis. Application fee: $45 ($50 for international students). Electronic applications accepted. *Expenses:* Tuition: Full-time $14,922; part-time $829 per credit hour. Required fees: $50 per trimester. Full-time tuition and fees vary according to course load and program. *Financial support:* In 2009–10, 3 students received support. Scholarships/grants available. *Unit head:* Dr. David Hollier, Director, 512-448-8666, Fax: 512-428-1372, E-mail: davidrh@stedwards.edu. *Application contact:* Kay L. Arnold, Assistant Director of Admissions, 512-233-1636, Fax: 512-428-1032, E-mail: kayla@stedwards.edu.

St. John's University, College of Professional Studies, Department of Sport Management, Queens, NY 11439. Offers MPS. *Students:* 32 full-time (12 women), 13 part-time (6 women); includes 12 minority (6 African Americans, 1 Asian American or Pacific Islander, 5 Hispanic Americans), 4 international. Average age 25. 72 applicants, 64% accepted, 20 enrolled. In 2009, 6 master's awarded. *Degree requirements:* For master's, comprehensive exam, capstone project. *Entrance requirements:* For master's, bachelor's degree from a regionally-accredited college or university, minimum GPA of 3.0, 2 letters of recommendation. Additional exam requirements/recommendations for international students: Required—TOEFL (minimum score 500 paper-based; 173 computer-based; 61 iBT), IELTS (minimum score 5.5). *Application deadline:* For fall admission, 5/1 priority date for domestic and international students; for spring admission, 11/1 priority date for domestic and international students. Applications are processed on a rolling basis. Application fee: $70. Electronic applications accepted. *Expenses:* Tuition: Full-time $16,290; part-time $905 per credit. Required fees: $300; $150 per semester. Tuition and fees vary according to program. *Faculty research:* The Olympic Movement, sports economics, administration of intercollegiate athletics, sport management education. *Unit head:* Prof. Glenn Gerstner, Director, Graduate Sport Management Program, 718-990-7474, E-mail: gerstneg@stjohns.edu. *Application contact:* Kathleen Davis, Director of Graduate Admissions, 718-990-2790, Fax: 718-990-5686, E-mail: gradhelp@stjohns.edu.

Saint Leo University, Graduate Business Studies, Saint Leo, FL 33574-6665. Offers accounting (MBA); business (MBA); criminal justice (MBA); health services management (MBA); human resource administration (MBA); information security management (MBA); marketing (MBA); sport business (MBA). Part-time and evening/weekend programs available. Postbaccalaureate distance learning degree programs offered (no on-campus study). *Faculty:* 31 full-time (5 women), 48 part-time/adjunct (17 women). *Students:* 1,433 full-time (856 women), 3 part-time (1 woman); includes 601 minority (429 African Americans, 8 American Indian/Alaska Native, 75 Asian Americans or Pacific Islanders, 89 Hispanic Americans), 11 international. Average age 37. In 2009, 405 master's awarded. *Entrance requirements:* For master's, GMAT (minimum score 500 if applicant does not have 5 years of professional work experience), bachelor's degree from regionally-accredited college or university with minimum GPA of 3.0 in the last 60 hours of coursework; 5 years of professional work experience; resume; 2 letters of recommendation. Additional exam requirements/recommendations for international students: Required—TOEFL (minimum score 550 paper-based; 213 computer-based; 80 iBT). *Application deadline:* For fall admission, 7/1 priority date for domestic students; for spring admission, 11/12 priority date for domestic students. Applications are processed on a rolling basis. Application fee: $75. Electronic applications accepted. *Expenses:* Contact institution. *Financial support:* In 2009–10, 1 student received support. Career-related internships or fieldwork, Federal Work-Study, and health care benefits available. Financial award application deadline: 3/1; financial award applicants required to submit FAFSA. *Unit head:* Dr. Robert Robertson, Director, 352-588-7390, Fax: 352-588-8585, E-mail: mba@saintleo.edu. *Application contact:* Jared Welling, Director, Graduate/Weekend and Evening Admission, 800-707-8846, Fax: 352-588-7873, E-mail: grad.admissions@saintleo.edu.

Saint Mary's College of California, School of Liberal Arts, Department of Kinesiology, Moraga, CA 94556. Offers sport management (MA); sport studies (MA). Part-time programs available. *Faculty:* 6 full-time (1 woman), 3 part-time/adjunct (1 woman). *Students:* 30 full-time (15 women); includes 7 minority (5 African Americans, 1 Asian American or Pacific Islander, 1 Hispanic American). Average age 28. 23 applicants, 65% accepted, 14 enrolled. In 2009, 28 master's awarded. *Degree requirements:* For master's, thesis or special project. *Entrance*

Sports Management

Saint Mary's College of California (continued)

requirements: For master's, minimum GPA of 2.75, BA in physical education or related field, or professional experience. Application fee: $25. Electronic applications accepted. *Expenses:* Contact institution. *Financial support:* In 2009–10, 15 students received support, including research assistantships (averaging $6,000 per year); career-related internships or fieldwork, institutionally sponsored loans, scholarships/grants, tuition waivers (partial), and unspecified assistantships also available. Support available to part-time students. Financial award applicants required to submit FAFSA. *Faculty research:* Moral development in sport, applied motor learning, achievement motivation, sport history. Total annual research expenditures: $1,500. *Unit head:* William Manning, Chair, 925-631-4969, Fax: 925-631-4965, E-mail: wmanning@stmarys-ca.edu. *Application contact:* Jeanne Abate, Administrative Assistant, 925-631-4377, Fax: 925-631-4965, E-mail: jabate@stmarys-ca.edu.

St. Thomas University, School of Business, Department of Management, Miami Gardens, FL 33054-6459. Offers accounting (MBA); general management (MSM, Certificate); health management (MBA, MSM, Certificate); human resource management (MBA, MSM, Certificate); international business (MBA, MIB, MSM, Certificate); justice administration (MSM, Certificate); management accounting (MSM, Certificate); public management (MSM, Certificate); sports administration (MS). Part-time and evening/weekend programs available. *Degree requirements:* For master's, comprehensive exam. *Entrance requirements:* For master's, interview, minimum GPA of 3.0 or GMAT. Additional exam requirements/recommendations for international students: Required—TOEFL (minimum score 550 paper-based; 213 computer-based; 79 iBT). Electronic applications accepted.

San Diego State University, Graduate and Research Affairs, College of Business Administration, Sports Business Management Program, San Diego, CA 92182. Offers MBA.

Seattle University, College of Arts and Sciences, Center for the Study of Sport and Exercise, Seattle, WA 98122-1090. Offers MSAL.

Seton Hall University, Stillman School of Business, Programs in Business Administration, South Orange, NJ 07079-2697. Offers accounting (MBA); finance (MBA); information technology management (MBA); international business (MBA); management (MBA); marketing (MBA); sport management (MBA). Part-time and evening/weekend programs available. *Faculty:* 57 full-time (13 women), 30 part-time/adjunct (3 women). *Students:* 69 full-time (26 women), 217 part-time (91 women); includes 53 minority (11 African Americans, 35 Asian Americans or Pacific Islanders, 7 Hispanic Americans), 38 international. Average age 29. 286 applicants, 70% accepted, 130 enrolled. In 2009, 110 master's awarded. *Degree requirements:* For master's, 20 hours of community service (Social Responsibility Project). *Entrance requirements:* For master's, GMAT, minimum GPA of 3.0. Additional exam requirements/recommendations for international students: Required—TOEFL (minimum score 607 paper-based; 254 computer-based; 102 iBT), or IELTS, or Pearson Test of English (PTE). *Application deadline:* For fall admission, 5/31 priority date for domestic students, 3/31 priority date for international students; for spring admission, 10/31 priority date for domestic students, 4/30 priority date for international students. Applications are processed on a rolling basis. Application fee: $75. Electronic applications accepted. *Financial support:* In 2009–10, research assistantships with full tuition reimbursements (averaging $34,404 per year); career-related internships or fieldwork, Federal Work-Study, scholarships/grants, and unspecified assistantships also available. Support available to part-time students. Financial award application deadline: 6/30; financial award applicants required to submit FAFSA. *Faculty research:* Financial, hedge funds, international business, legal issues, disclosure and branding. *Unit head:* Dr. Joyce A. Strawser, Associate Dean for Undergraduate and MBA Curricula, 973-761-9225, Fax: 973-761-9217, E-mail: strawsjo@shu.edu. *Application contact:* Catherine Bianchi, Director of Graduate Admissions, 973-761-9262, Fax: 973-761-9208, E-mail: catherine.bianchi@shu.edu.

Slippery Rock University of Pennsylvania, Graduate Studies (Recruitment), College of Education, Department of Sport Management, Slippery Rock, PA 16057-1383. Offers MS. Part-time and evening/weekend programs available. *Degree requirements:* For master's, comprehensive exam (for some programs), thesis (for some programs). *Entrance requirements:* For master's, GRE General Test, MAT, minimum GPA of 2.75. Additional exam requirements/recommendations for international students: Required—TOEFL (minimum score 550 paper-based; 213 computer-based). *Application deadline:* For fall admission, 3/1 priority date for domestic students, 5/1 priority date for international students; for spring admission, 11/1 priority date for domestic students, 9/1 priority date for international students. Applications are processed on a rolling basis. Application fee: $25 ($30 for international students). Electronic applications accepted. *Expenses:* Tuition, state resident: full-time $6666; part-time $370 per credit. Tuition, nonresident: full-time $10,666; part-time $593 per credit. Required fees: $2184; $182 per credit. *Financial support:* Career-related internships or fieldwork, Federal Work-Study, scholarships/grants, and unspecified assistantships available. Support available to part-time students. Financial award application deadline: 5/1. *Unit head:* Dr. Brian Crow, Graduate Coordinator, 724-738-2392, Fax: 724-738-2921, E-mail: brain.crow@sru.edu. *Application contact:* Angela Piverotto, Director of Graduate Studies, 724-738-2051, Fax: 724-738-2146, E-mail: graduate.admissions@sru.edu.

Southeast Missouri State University, School of Graduate Studies, Harrison College of Business, Cape Girardeau, MO 63701-4799. Offers accounting (MBA); entrepreneurship (MBA); environmental management (MBA); financial management (MBA); general management (MBA); health administration (MBA); industrial management (MBA); international business (MBA); sport management (MBA). *Accreditation:* AACSB. Part-time and evening/weekend programs available. Postbaccalaureate distance learning degree programs offered (no on-campus study). *Degree requirements:* For master's, applied research project. *Entrance requirements:* For master's, GMAT, minimum undergraduate GPA of 2.5. Additional exam requirements/recommendations for international students: Required—TOEFL (minimum score 550 paper-based; 213 computer-based); Recommended—IELTS (minimum score 6). *Expenses:* Tuition, state resident: full-time $4266; part-time $237 per credit hour. Tuition, nonresident: full-time $7506; part-time $417 per credit hour. Required fees: $427; $427. *Faculty research:* Human resources, laws impacting accounting, advertising.

Southern New Hampshire University, School of Business, Manchester, NH 03106-1045. Offers accounting (MS); business administration (MBA, Certificate), including accounting (Certificate), business administration (MBA), finance (Certificate), forensic accounting (Certificate), human resources management (Certificate), international business (Certificate), international sport management (Certificate), leadership of not for profit organizations (Certificate), marketing (Certificate), operations management (Certificate), sport management (Certificate), taxation (Certificate); finance (MS); hospitality and tourism leadership (Certificate); information technology (MS, Certificate); information technology/international business (Certificate); integrated marketing communications (Certificate); international business (MS, DBA); marketing (MS); operations and project management (MS); organizational leadership (MS); project management (Certificate); sport management (MS); MBA/Certificate. *Accreditation:* ACBSP. Part-time and evening/weekend programs available. Postbaccalaureate distance learning degree programs offered (no on-campus study). Terminal master's awarded for partial completion of doctoral program. *Degree requirements:* For master's, one foreign language, comprehensive exam (for some programs), thesis or alternative; for doctorate, one foreign language, comprehensive exam, thesis/dissertation. *Entrance requirements:* For master's, minimum GPA of 2.5; for doctorate, GMAT. Additional exam requirements/recommendations for international students: Required—TOEFL (minimum score 500 paper-based). Electronic applications accepted.

Springfield College, Graduate Programs, Programs in Physical Education, Springfield, MA 01109-3797. Offers adapted physical education (M Ed, MPE, MS); advanced level coaching (M Ed, MPE, MS); athletic administration (M Ed, MPE, MS); general physical education (PhD, CAGS); health education licensure (MPE, MS); health education licensure program (M Ed); physical education licensure (MPE, MS); physical education licensure program (M Ed); teaching and administration (MS). Part-time programs available. *Degree requirements:* For master's, comprehensive exam, thesis (for some programs). *Entrance requirements:* For master's and doctorate, GRE General Test. Additional exam requirements/recommendations for international students: Required—TOEFL (minimum score 550 paper-based; 213 computer-based). Electronic applications accepted. *Expenses:* Tuition: Full-time $19,800; part-time $825 per credit hour. Required fees: $150.

Springfield College, Graduate Programs, Programs in Sport Management and Recreation, Springfield, MA 01109-3797. Offers recreational management (M Ed, MS); sport management (M Ed, MS); therapeutic recreational management (M Ed, MS). Part-time programs available. *Degree requirements:* For master's, comprehensive exam, research project. *Entrance requirements:* Additional exam requirements/recommendations for international students: Required—TOEFL (minimum score 550 paper-based; 213 computer-based). Electronic applications accepted. *Expenses:* Tuition: Full-time $19,800; part-time $825 per credit hour. Required fees: $150.

State University of New York College at Cortland, Graduate Studies, School of Professional Studies, Department of Sport Management, Cortland, NY 13045. Offers international sport management (MS); sport management (MS). *Entrance requirements:* For master's, GMAT or GRE, 2 letters of recommendation.

Temple University, Graduate School, Fox School of Business, Doctoral Programs in Business, Philadelphia, PA 19122-6096. Offers accounting (PhD); entrepreneurship (PhD); finance (PhD); human resource administration (PhD); international business (PhD); management information systems (PhD); marketing (PhD); risk management and insurance (PhD); statistics (PhD); strategic management (PhD); tourism and sport (PhD). *Accreditation:* AACSB. *Degree requirements:* For doctorate, thesis/dissertation. *Entrance requirements:* For doctorate, GRE General Test, GMAT, minimum GPA of 3.0, master's degree. Additional exam requirements/recommendations for international students: Required—TOEFL (minimum score 600 paper-based; 250 computer-based; 100 iBT), IELTS (minimum score 7.5). Electronic applications accepted.

Temple University, Graduate School, School of Tourism and Hospitality Management, Program in Sport and Recreation Administration, Philadelphia, PA 19122-6096. Offers Ed M. Part-time and evening/weekend programs available. *Entrance requirements:* For master's, GRE General Test or MAT, minimum undergraduate GPA of 3.0. Additional exam requirements/recommendations for international students: Required—TOEFL (minimum score 550 paper-based; 213 computer-based; 79 iBT). Electronic applications accepted.

Tiffin University, Program in Business Administration, Tiffin, OH 44883-2161. Offers general management (MBA); leadership (MBA); safety and security management (MBA); sports management (MBA). *Accreditation:* ACBSP. Part-time and evening/weekend programs available. Postbaccalaureate distance learning degree programs offered (no on-campus study). *Entrance requirements:* For master's, minimum undergraduate GPA of 2.5, work experience. Additional exam requirements/recommendations for international students: Required—TOEFL (minimum score 550 paper-based; 213 computer-based). Electronic applications accepted. *Faculty research:* Small business, executive development operations, research and statistical analysis, market research, management information systems.

Troy University, Graduate School, College of Health and Human Services, Program in Sport and Fitness Management, Troy, AL 36082. Offers MS. Part-time and evening/weekend programs available. *Students:* 35 full-time (10 women), 48 part-time (14 women); includes 34 minority (31 African Americans, 2 Asian Americans or Pacific Islanders, 1 Hispanic American). Average age 26. 85 applicants, 46% accepted. In 2009, 31 master's awarded. *Degree requirements:* For master's, comprehensive exam, thesis optional. *Entrance requirements:* For master's, GRE or MAT. Additional exam requirements/recommendations for international students: Required—TOEFL (minimum score 523 paper-based; 193 computer-based; 70 iBT), IELTS (minimum score 6), or ACT Compass ESL (minimum score 270 on Listening, Reading, and Grammar with no individual score below 85 and a minimum score of 8 out of 12 on writing test). *Application deadline:* Applications are processed on a rolling basis. Application fee: $50. Electronic applications accepted. *Financial support:* Career-related internships or fieldwork and unspecified assistantships available. *Faculty research:* Sport marketing, fitness, sport law. *Unit head:* Dr. Fred Green, Interim Chairman, 334-670-3764, Fax: 334-670-3936, E-mail: fegreen@troy.edu. *Application contact:* Brenda K. Campbell, Director of Graduate Admissions, 334-670-3178, Fax: 334-670-3733, E-mail: bcamp@troy.edu.

United States Sports Academy, Graduate Programs, Program in Sport Management, Daphne, AL 36526-7055. Offers MSS, Ed D. Part-time programs available. Postbaccalaureate distance learning degree programs offered (no on-campus study). *Degree requirements:* For master's, comprehensive exam, thesis optional; for doctorate, comprehensive exam, thesis/dissertation. *Entrance requirements:* For master's, GRE General Test, GMAT, or MAT, minimum GPA of 2.5, 3 letters of recommendation, resume; for doctorate, GRE General Test, GMAT, or MAT, master's degree, 3 letters of recommendation, resume. Additional exam requirements/recommendations for international students: Required—TOEFL (minimum score 500 paper-based; 213 computer-based). *Application deadline:* Applications are processed on a rolling basis. Application fee: $50 ($125 for international students). Electronic applications accepted. *Financial support:* Research assistantships with full tuition reimbursements, career-related internships or fieldwork, Federal Work-Study, scholarships/grants, and service assistantships available. Support available to part-time students. Financial award application deadline: 8/15; financial award applicants required to submit FAFSA. *Faculty research:* Sport law, leadership behavior, personnel evaluation. *Unit head:* Dr. Fred Cromartie, Chair, 251-626-3303 Ext. 7140, Fax: 251-625-1035, E-mail: cromarti@ussa.edu. *Application contact:* Craig T. Bogar, Assistant Dean of Student Services, 251-626-3303 Ext. 7147, Fax: 251-625-1035, E-mail: cbogar@ussa.edu.

The University of Alabama, Graduate School, College of Education, Department of Kinesiology, Tuscaloosa, AL 35487. Offers alternative sport pedagogy (MA); exercise science (MA, PhD); human performance (MA); sport management (MA); sport pedagogy (MA, PhD). Part-time programs available. *Faculty:* 7 full-time (1 woman). *Students:* 63 full-time (30 women), 17 part-time (4 women); includes 5 minority (3 African Americans, 1 American Indian/Alaska Native, 1 Hispanic American), 11 international. Average age 28. 74 applicants, 64% accepted, 29 enrolled. In 2009, 22 master's, 5 doctorates awarded. *Median time to degree:* Of those who began their doctoral program in fall 2001, 100% received their degree in 8 years or less. *Degree requirements:* For master's, comprehensive exam, thesis optional; for doctorate, comprehensive exam, thesis/dissertation. *Entrance requirements:* For master's and doctorate, GRE, MAT, minimum GPA of 3.0. Additional exam requirements/recommendations for international students: Required—TOEFL. *Application deadline:* Applications are processed on a rolling basis. Application fee: $50 ($60 for international students). Electronic applications accepted. *Expenses:* Tuition, state resident: full-time $7000. Tuition, nonresident: full-time $19,200. *Financial support:* In 2009–10, 14 students received support, including 13 teaching assistantships with full tuition reimbursements available (averaging $8,678 per year). *Faculty research:* Race, gender and sexuality in sports; physical education curriculum reform; disability sports; physical activity and health; environmental physiology. Total annual research expenditures: $46,329. *Unit head:* Dr. Matt Curtner-Smith, Department Head and Professor, 205-348-9209, Fax: 205-348-0867, E-mail: msmith@bamaed.ua.edu. *Application contact:* Dr. Kathy S. Wetzel, Assistant Dean for Student Services, 205-348-1154, Fax: 205-348-0080, E-mail: kwetzel@bamaed.ua.edu.

The University of Alabama, Graduate School, College of Human Environmental Sciences, Program in Human Environmental Science, Tuscaloosa, AL 35487. Offers family financial planning and counseling (MS); interactive technology (MS); quality management (MS); restaurant and meeting management (MS); rural community health (MS); sport management (MS). *Students:* 70 full-time (40 women), 99 part-time (45 women); includes 44 minority (42 African Americans, 2 Hispanic Americans), 1 international. Average age 33. 124 applicants, 71% accepted, 71 enrolled. In 2009, 70 degrees awarded. *Degree requirements:* For master's, comprehensive exam. *Entrance requirements:* For master's, GRE (for some specializations),

minimum GPA of 3.0. Additional exam requirements/recommendations for international students: Required—TOEFL. *Application deadline:* Applications are processed on a rolling basis. Application fee: $50 ($60 for international students). Electronic applications accepted. *Expenses:* Tuition, state resident: full-time $7000. Tuition, nonresident: full-time $19,200. *Faculty research:* Hospitality management, sports medicine education, technology and education. *Unit head:* Dr. Milla D. Boschung, Dean, 205-348-6250, Fax: 205-348-1786, E-mail: mboschun@ches.ua.edu. *Application contact:* Dr. Stuart Usdan, Associate Dean, 205-348-6150, Fax: 205-348-3789, E-mail: susdan@ches.ua.edu.

University of Alberta, Faculty of Graduate Studies and Research, Program in Business Administration, Edmonton, AB T6G 2E1, Canada. Offers international business (MBA); leisure and sport management (MBA); natural resources and energy (MBA); technology commercialization (MBA); MBA/LL B; MBA/M Ag; MBA/M Eng; MBA/MF; MBA/PhD. *Accreditation:* AACSB. Part-time and evening/weekend programs available. *Faculty:* 77 full-time, 20 part-time/adjunct. *Students:* 131 full-time (56 women), 109 part-time (51 women). Average age 29. 525 applicants, 30% accepted, 90 enrolled. In 2009, 114 master's awarded. *Degree requirements:* For master's, thesis or alternative. *Entrance requirements:* For master's, GMAT. Additional exam requirements/recommendations for international students: Required—TOEFL (minimum score 600 paper-based; 250 computer-based). *Application deadline:* For fall admission, 4/30 priority date for domestic students, 4/30 for international students. Applications are processed on a rolling basis. Application fee: $0. Electronic applications accepted. Tuition and fees charges are reported in Canadian dollars. *Expenses:* Tuition, area resident: Full-time $4626 Canadian dollars; part-time $99.72 Canadian dollars per unit. International tuition: $8216 Canadian dollars full-time. Required fees: $3590 Canadian dollars; $99.72 Canadian dollars per unit. $215 Canadian dollars per term. *Financial support:* Fellowships, research assistantships, teaching assistantships, career-related internships or fieldwork, scholarships/grants, health care benefits, and unspecified assistantships available. *Faculty research:* Natural resources and energy/management and policy/family enterprise/international business/healthcare research management. Total annual research expenditures: $1 million. *Unit head:* Dr. Douglas Olsen, Associate Dean, 780-492-5412, Fax: 780-492-7825. *Application contact:* Joan A. White, Secretary, 780-492-3679, Fax: 780-492-2024, E-mail: mba@ualberta.ca.

University of Central Florida, College of Business Administration, Department of Sport Business Management, Orlando, FL 32816. Offers MSBM. *Faculty:* 3 full-time (0 women), 3 part-time/adjunct (1 woman). *Students:* 56 full-time (24 women), 3 part-time (2 women); includes 21 minority (13 African Americans, 1 American Indian/Alaska Native, 3 Asian Americans or Pacific Islanders, 4 Hispanic Americans), 7 international. Average age 24. 79 applicants, 42% accepted, 28 enrolled. In 2009, 30 master's awarded. *Degree requirements:* For master's, thesis or alternative, internship. *Entrance requirements:* For master's, GMAT, minimum GPA of 3.0, letters of recommendation. Additional exam requirements/recommendations for international students: Required—TOEFL. *Application deadline:* For fall admission, 2/15 priority date for domestic students. Application fee: $30. Electronic applications accepted. *Expenses:* Tuition, state resident: part-time $306.31 per credit hour. Tuition, nonresident: part-time $1099.01 per credit hour. Part-time tuition and fees vary according to degree level and program. *Financial support:* In 2009–10, 45 students received support, including 38 fellowships with partial tuition reimbursements available (averaging $4,400 per year), 8 research assistantships with partial tuition reimbursements available (averaging $7,000 per year), 2 teaching assistantships (averaging $7,000 per year). *Unit head:* Dr. Richard Lapchick, Director, 407-823-4887, E-mail: richard.lapchick@bus.ucf.edu. *Application contact:* Dr. Richard Lapchick, Director, 407-823-4887, E-mail: richard.lapchick@bus.ucf.edu.

University of Dallas, Graduate School of Management, Irving, TX 75062-4736. Offers accounting (MBA, MM, MS); business management (MBA, MM); corporate finance (MBA, MM); financial services (MBA); global business (MBA, MM); health services management (MBA, MM); human resource management (MBA, MM); information assurance (MBA, MM, MS); information technology (MBA, MM, MS); information technology service management (MBA, MM, MS); marketing management (MBA, MM); organization development (MBA, MM); project management (MBA, MM); sports and entertainment management (MBA, MM); strategic leadership (MBA, MM); supply chain management (MBA); supply chain management and market logistics (MM). *Accreditation:* ACBSP. Part-time and evening/weekend programs available. Postbaccalaureate distance learning degree programs offered (no on-campus study). *Faculty:* 25 full-time (6 women), 31 part-time/adjunct (6 women). *Students:* 232 full-time (95 women), 923 part-time (365 women); includes 462 minority (184 African Americans, 14 American Indian/Alaska Native, 153 Asian Americans or Pacific Islanders, 111 Hispanic Americans), 184 international. Average age 34. 474 applicants, 85% accepted, 237 enrolled. In 2009, 399 master's awarded. *Entrance requirements:* Additional exam requirements/recommendations for international students: Required—TOEFL. *Application deadline:* Applications are processed on a rolling basis. Application fee: $50. Electronic applications accepted. *Expenses:* Contact institution. *Financial support:* In 2009–10, 399 students received support. Scholarships/grants and unspecified assistantships available. Financial award application deadline: 2/15; financial award applicants required to submit FAFSA. *Unit head:* Alounda Joseph, Director of Enrollment Processes, 972-721-5356, E-mail: admiss@gsm.udallas.edu. *Application contact:* Alounda Joseph, Director of Enrollment Processes, 972-721-5356, E-mail: admiss@gsm.udallas.edu.

University of Florida, Graduate School, College of Health and Human Performance, Department of Tourism, Recreation and Sport Management, Gainesville, FL 32611. Offers health and human performance (PhD), including natural resource recreation (MS, PhD), sport management (MS, PhD), therapeutic recreation (MS, PhD), tourism; recreational studies (MS), including campus recreation programming and administration, natural resource recreation (MS, PhD), recreation administration and supervision, sport management (MS, PhD), therapeutic recreation (MS, PhD), tourism and commercial recreation. *Degree requirements:* For master's, thesis optional. *Entrance requirements:* For master's, GRE General Test, minimum GPA of 3.0. Additional exam requirements/recommendations for international students: Required—TOEFL (minimum score 550 paper-based; 213 computer-based). Electronic applications accepted. *Faculty research:* Recreation resource planning, commercial recreation, campus recreation.

University of Florida, Graduate School, Warrington College of Business Administration, Hough Graduate School of Business, Programs in Business Administration, Gainesville, FL 32611. Offers accounting (MBA); arts administration (MBA); business strategy and public policy (MBA); competitive strategy (MBA); decision and information sciences (MBA); electronic commerce (MBA); finance (MBA); general business (MBA); global management (MBA); Graham-Buffett security analysis (MBA); health administration (MBA); human resources management (MBA); international studies (MBA); Latin American business (MBA); management (MBA); marketing (MBA); sports administration (MBA); JD/MBA; MBA/MS; MBA/PhD; MBA/Pharm D; MD/MBA. *Accreditation:* AACSB. Part-time and evening/weekend programs available. Postbaccalaureate distance learning degree programs offered. *Entrance requirements:* For master's, GMAT, minimum GPA of 3.0, interview. Additional exam requirements/recommendations for international students: Required—TOEFL (minimum score 550 paper-based; 213 computer-based). Electronic applications accepted. *Faculty research:* Accounting, finance, insurance, management, real estate and urban analysis marketing.

The University of Iowa, Graduate College, College of Liberal Arts and Sciences, Program in Leisure Studies, Iowa City, IA 52242-1316. Offers leisure and recreational sport management (MA); therapeutic recreation (MA). *Degree requirements:* For master's, thesis optional, exam. *Entrance requirements:* For master's, minimum GPA of 3.0. Additional exam requirements/recommendations for international students: Required—TOEFL (minimum score 550 paper-based; 213 computer-based; 81 iBT). Electronic applications accepted.

University of Louisville, Graduate School, College of Education and Human Development, Department of Health and Sport Sciences, Louisville, KY 40292-0001. Offers community health education (M Ed); exercise physiology (MS); health and physical education (MAT); sport administration (MS). Part-time and evening/weekend programs available. *Faculty:* 17 full-time (8 women), 1 part-time/adjunct (0 women). *Students:* 73 full-time (28 women), 28 part-time (17 women); includes 13 minority (11 African Americans, 2 Asian Americans or

Pacific Islanders), 8 international. Average age 26. 154 applicants, 67% accepted, 59 enrolled. In 2009, 42 master's awarded. *Entrance requirements:* For master's, GRE General Test. Additional exam requirements/recommendations for international students: Required—TOEFL (minimum score 560 paper-based; 210 computer-based; 83 iBT). Application fee: $50. Electronic applications accepted. *Financial support:* In 2009–10, 21 students received support; fellowships, research assistantships, teaching assistantships, career-related internships or fieldwork, Federal Work-Study, scholarships/grants, and unspecified assistantships available. Financial award application deadline: 6/1; financial award applicants required to submit FAFSA. *Faculty research:* Impact of sports and sport marketing on society, factors associated with school and community health, cardiac and pulmonary rehabilitation, impact of participation in activities on student retention and graduation, strength and conditioning. Total annual research expenditures: $58,888. *Unit head:* Dr. David W. Britt, Chair, 502-852-6645, Fax: 502-852-4534, E-mail: david.britt@louisville.edu. *Application contact:* Libby Leggett, Director, Graduate Admissions, 502-852-3101, Fax: 502-852-6536, E-mail: gradadm@louisville.edu.

University of Massachusetts Amherst, Graduate School, Interdisciplinary Programs, Program in Sports Management and Business Administration, Amherst, MA 01003. Offers MS/MBA. Part-time programs available. *Students:* 19 full-time (7 women); includes 3 minority (all Asian Americans or Pacific Islanders). Average age 26. 52 applicants, 38% accepted, 10 enrolled. *Entrance requirements:* Additional exam requirements/recommendations for international students: Required—TOEFL (minimum score 600 paper-based; 250 computer-based; 100 iBT), IELTS (minimum score 7). *Application deadline:* For fall admission, 2/1 for domestic and international students. Applications are processed on a rolling basis. Application fee: $50 ($65 for international students). Electronic applications accepted. *Expenses:* Tuition, state resident: full-time $2640; part-time $110 per credit. Tuition, nonresident: full-time $9936; part-time $414 per credit. Tuition and fees vary according to course load. *Financial support:* Career-related internships or fieldwork, Federal Work-Study, scholarships/grants, traineeships, health care benefits, tuition waivers (full), and unspecified assistantships available. Support available to part-time students. Financial award application deadline: 2/1. *Unit head:* Dr. Stephen M. McKelvey, Graduate Program Director, 413-545-0471, Fax: 413-545-0642. *Application contact:* Jean M. Ames, Supervisor of Admissions, 413-545-0722, Fax: 413-577-0010, E-mail: gradadm@grad.umass.edu.

University of Massachusetts Amherst, Graduate School, Isenberg School of Management, Department of Sport Management, Amherst, MA 01003. Offers MS, PhD, MBA/MS. Part-time programs available. *Faculty:* 11 full-time (3 women). *Students:* 16 full-time (5 women), 11 part-time (2 women); includes 1 minority (African American), 3 international. Average age 28. 47 applicants, 36% accepted, 13 enrolled. In 2009, 24 master's, 1 doctorate awarded. Terminal master's awarded for partial completion of doctoral program. *Degree requirements:* For master's, thesis or alternative; for doctorate, comprehensive exam, thesis/dissertation. *Entrance requirements:* For master's, GMAT; for doctorate, GMAT or GRE. Additional exam requirements/recommendations for international students: Required—TOEFL (minimum score 550 paper-based; 213 computer-based; 80 iBT), IELTS (minimum score 6.5). *Application deadline:* For fall admission, 2/1 for domestic and international students. Applications are processed on a rolling basis. Application fee: $50 ($65 for international students). Electronic applications accepted. *Expenses:* Tuition, state resident: full-time $2640; part-time $110 per credit. Tuition, nonresident: full-time $9936; part-time $414 per credit. Tuition and fees vary according to course load. *Financial support:* In 2009–10, 1 fellowship with full tuition reimbursement (averaging $7,364 per year), 21 research assistantships with full tuition reimbursements (averaging $5,079 per year), 14 teaching assistantships with full tuition reimbursements (averaging $6,112 per year) were awarded; career-related internships or fieldwork, Federal Work-Study, scholarships/grants, traineeships, health care benefits, tuition waivers (full), and unspecified assistantships also available. Support available to part-time students. Financial award application deadline: 2/1. *Unit head:* Dr. Stephen McKelvey, Graduate Program Director, 413-545-0471, Fax: 413-577-0642. *Application contact:* Jean M. Ames, Supervisor of Admissions, 413-545-0722, Fax: 413-577-0010, E-mail: gradadm@grad.umass.edu.

University of Miami, Graduate School, School of Education, Department of Exercise and Sport Sciences, Program in Sport Administration, Coral Gables, FL 33124. Offers MS Ed. Part-time and evening/weekend programs available. *Students:* 26 full-time (12 women), 5 part-time (0 women); includes 8 minority (4 African Americans, 1 Asian American or Pacific Islander, 3 Hispanic Americans), 3 international. Average age 24. 85 applicants, 66% accepted, 29 enrolled. In 2009, 23 master's awarded. *Degree requirements:* For master's, special project. *Entrance requirements:* For master's, GRE General Test. Additional exam requirements/recommendations for international students: Required—TOEFL (minimum score 550 paper-based; 80 iBT); Recommended—IELTS (minimum score 6.5). *Application deadline:* Applications are processed on a rolling basis. Application fee: $65. Electronic applications accepted. *Financial support:* In 2009–10, 21 students received support. Career-related internships or fieldwork, institutionally sponsored loans, scholarships/grants, and unspecified assistantships available. Financial award application deadline: 3/1; financial award applicants required to submit FAFSA. *Faculty research:* Constitutional procedural due process, legal liability, tort law, moral development in sports administration, ethics intervention. *Unit head:* Dr. Warren Whisenant, Associate Department Chairperson, 305-284-5622, Fax: 305-284-5168, E-mail: wwhisenant@miami.edu. *Application contact:* Marissa Stevenson-Jacobs, Graduate Admissions Coordinator, 305-284-2167, Fax: 305-284-3003, E-mail: mstevenson@miami.edu.

University of Michigan, Horace H. Rackham School of Graduate Studies, School of Kinesiology, Ann Arbor, MI 48109. Offers kinesiology (MS, PhD); sport management (AM). Terminal master's awarded for partial completion of doctoral program. *Degree requirements:* For master's, thesis (for some programs); for doctorate, comprehensive exam, thesis/dissertation, oral defense of dissertation. *Entrance requirements:* For master's and doctorate, GRE General Test. Additional exam requirements/recommendations for international students: Required—TOEFL. Electronic applications accepted. *Expenses:* Contact institution. *Faculty research:* Motor development, exercise physiology, biomechanics, sport medicine, sport management.

University of Minnesota, Twin Cities Campus, Graduate School, College of Education and Human Development, School of Kinesiology, Minneapolis, MN 55455-0213. Offers adapted physical education (MA, PhD); biomechanics (MA); biomechanics and neural control (PhD); coaching (Certificate); developmental adapted physical education (M Ed); exercise physiology (MA, PhD); human factors/ergonomics (MA, PhD); international/comparative sport (MA, PhD); kinesiology (M Ed, MA, PhD); leisure services/management (MA, PhD); motor development (MA, PhD); motor learning/control (MA, PhD); outdoor education/recreation (MA, PhD); physical education (M Ed); recreation, park, and leisure studies (M Ed, MA, PhD); sport and exercise science (M Ed); sport management (M Ed, MA, PhD); sport psychology (MA, PhD); sport sociology (MA, PhD); therapeutic recreation (MA, PhD). Part-time programs available. *Faculty:* 15 full-time (8 women). *Students:* 139 full-time (67 women), 55 part-time (19 women); includes 24 minority (12 African Americans, 3 American Indian/Alaska Native, 4 Asian Americans or Pacific Islanders, 5 Hispanic Americans), 18 international. Average age 29. 173 applicants, 53% accepted, 74 enrolled. In 2009, 66 master's, 4 doctorates, 18 other advanced degrees awarded. Terminal master's awarded for partial completion of doctoral program. *Degree requirements:* For master's, final oral exam; for doctorate, thesis/dissertation, preliminary written/oral exam, final oral exam. *Entrance requirements:* For master's, GRE or MAT, minimum GPA of 3.0; for doctorate, GRE or MAT, minimum GPA of 3.0, writing sample. *Financial support:* In 2009–10, 2 fellowships (averaging $22,500 per year), 11 research assistantships with full tuition reimbursements (averaging $26,599 per year), 34 teaching assistantships with full tuition reimbursements (averaging $26,081 per year) were awarded; career-related internships or fieldwork, Federal Work-Study, institutionally sponsored loans, and tuition waivers (full and partial) also available. Support available to part-time students. *Faculty research:* Exercise for health promotion and disease prevention and management, female athletes and bone health, affordance perception-action, gender and youth sport and psychosocial outcomes, neurological movement disorders. Total annual research expenditures: $294,676. *Unit head:* Dr. Mary Jo Kane, Director, 612-625-3870, Fax: 612-626-7700, E-mail: maryjo@umn.edu. *Application contact:* Dr. Mary Trettin, Associate Dean, 612-625-6501, Fax: 612-626-1580, E-mail: mtrettin@umn.edu.

Sports Management

University of Nevada, Las Vegas, Graduate College, College of Education, Department of Sports Education Leadership, Las Vegas, NV 89154-3031. Offers physical education (M Ed, MS); sports education leadership (PhD). *Faculty:* 8 full-time (5 women), 12 part-time/adjunct (5 women). *Students:* 22 full-time (7 women), 20 part-time (7 women); includes 6 minority (5 African Americans, 1 Hispanic American), 2 international. Average age 31. 42 applicants, 74% accepted, 21 enrolled. In 2009, 9 master's, 5 doctorates awarded. *Degree requirements:* For doctorate, comprehensive exam, thesis/dissertation, scholarly product. *Entrance requirements:* For master's and doctorate, GRE General Test. Additional exam requirements/recommendations for international students: Required—TOEFL (minimum score 550 paper-based; 213 computer-based; 80 iBT), IELTS (minimum score 7). *Application deadline:* For fall admission, 3/1 priority date for domestic and international students; for spring admission, 11/15 priority date for domestic students, 10/1 for international students. Applications are processed on a rolling basis. Application fee: $60 ($95 for international students). Electronic applications accepted. *Financial support:* In 2009–10, 9 students received support, including 3 research assistantships (averaging $11,333 per year), 6 teaching assistantships (averaging $12,000 per year); institutionally sponsored loans, scholarships/grants, health care benefits, and unspecified assistantships also available. Financial award application deadline: 3/1. *Faculty research:* Physical activity and policy, physical education teacher education, sport marketing, sport policy, sport coaching and administration. *Unit head:* Dr. Monica Lounsbery, Chair/Associate Professor, 702-895-5057, Fax: 702-895-5056, E-mail: monica.lounsbery@unlv.edu. *Application contact:* Graduate College Admissions Evaluator, 702-895-3320, Fax: 702-895-4180, E-mail: gradcollege@unlv.edu.

University of New Brunswick Fredericton, School of Graduate Studies, Faculty of Business Administration, Fredericton, NB E3B 5A3, Canada. Offers business administration (MBA); engineering management (MBA); entrepreneurship (MBA); sports and recreation management (MBA); MBA/LL B. Part-time programs available. *Faculty:* 37 full-time (13 women). *Students:* 27 full-time (10 women), 51 part-time (25 women). In 2009, 72 master's awarded. *Degree requirements:* For master's, thesis optional. *Entrance requirements:* For master's, GMAT (550 minimum score), minimum GPA of 3.0; 3-5 years work experience. Additional exam requirements/recommendations for international students: Required—TOEFL (minimum score 580 paper-based; 92 iBT), IELTS (minimum score 7), TOEFL or IELTS. *Application deadline:* For fall admission, 3/1 priority date for domestic students. Applications are processed on a rolling basis. Application fee: $50 Canadian dollars. Tuition and fees charges are reported in Canadian dollars. *Expenses:* Tuition, area resident: Full-time $5562 Canadian dollars; part-time $2781 Canadian dollars per year. Required fees: $49.75 Canadian dollars per term. *Financial support:* In 2009–10, 4 research assistantships (averaging $4,500 per year), 11 teaching assistantships (averaging $2,250 per year) were awarded. *Faculty research:* Strategic management, entrepreneurship, investment practices, marketing and supply chain management, operations management. *Unit head:* Judy Roy, Director of Graduate Studies, 506-458-7307, Fax: 506-453-3561, E-mail: jroy@unb.ca. *Application contact:* Marilyn Davis, Acting Graduate Secretary, 506-453-4766, Fax: 506-453-3561, E-mail: mbacontact@unb.ca.

University of New Brunswick Fredericton, School of Graduate Studies, Faculty of Kinesiology, Fredericton, NB E3B 5A3, Canada. Offers exercise and sport science (M Sc); sport and recreation management (MBA); sport and recreation studies (MA). Part-time programs available. *Faculty:* 17 full-time (7 women). *Students:* 35 full-time (16 women), 6 part-time (5 women). In 2009, 10 master's awarded. *Degree requirements:* For master's, thesis (for some programs). *Entrance requirements:* For master's, minimum GPA of 3.0, written statement of research goals and interests. Additional exam requirements/recommendations for international students: Required—TOEFL (minimum score 600 paper-based; 250 computer-based), TWE (minimum score 4). *Application deadline:* For winter admission, 1/31 for domestic students; for spring admission, 3/31 for domestic students. Applications are processed on a rolling basis. Application fee: $50 Canadian dollars. Electronic applications accepted. Tuition and fees charges are reported in Canadian dollars. *Expenses:* Tuition, area resident: Full-time $5562 Canadian dollars; part-time $2781 Canadian dollars per year. Required fees: $49.75 Canadian dollars per term. *Financial support:* In 2009–10, 2 fellowships with tuition reimbursements were awarded; research assistantships, teaching assistantships, career-related internships or fieldwork and scholarships/grants also available. *Unit head:* Dr. Wayne Albert, Acting Director of Graduate Studies, 506-447-3254, Fax: 506-453-3511, E-mail: walbert@unb.ca. *Application contact:* Linda O'Brien, Graduate Secretary, 506-453-4576, Fax: 506-453-3511, E-mail: lobrien@unb.ca.

University of New Haven, Graduate School, School of Business, Program in Business Administration, West Haven, CT 06516-1916. Offers accounting (MBA, Certificate), including CPA (MBA); business management (Certificate); business policy and strategy (MBA); finance (MBA), including CFA; global marketing (MBA); human resource management (Certificate); human resources management (MBA); international business (Certificate); marketing (Certificate); sports management (MBA); telcommunications management (Certificate); MBA/MPA. Part-time and evening/weekend programs available. *Faculty:* 26 full-time (3 women), 23 part-time/adjunct (5 women). *Students:* 302 full-time (120 women), 194 part-time (101 women); includes 109 minority (56 African Americans, 3 American Indian/Alaska Native, 28 Asian Americans or Pacific Islanders, 22 Hispanic Americans), 110 international. Average age 31. 372 applicants, 83% accepted, 172 enrolled. In 2009, 194 master's, 31 other advanced degrees awarded. *Degree requirements:* For master's, thesis or alternative. *Entrance requirements:* For master's, GMAT. Additional exam requirements/recommendations for international students: Required—TOEFL (minimum score 520 paper-based; 190 computer-based; 70 iBT), IELTS (minimum score 5.5). *Application deadline:* For fall admission, 5/31 for international students; for winter admission, 10/15 for international students; for spring admission, 1/15 for international students. Applications are processed on a rolling basis. Application fee: $50. Electronic applications accepted. *Expenses:* Contact institution. *Financial support:* Research assistantships with partial tuition reimbursements, teaching assistantships with partial tuition reimbursements, Federal Work-Study, scholarships/grants, health care benefits, tuition waivers, and unspecified assistantships available. Support available to part-time students. Financial award applicants required to submit FAFSA. *Unit head:* Charles Coleman, Chairman, 203-932-7375. *Application contact:* Eloise Gormley, Director of Graduate Admissions, 203-932-7449, Fax: 203-932-7137, E-mail: gradinfo@newhaven.edu.

University of New Haven, Graduate School, School of Business, Program in Sports Management, West Haven, CT 06516-1916. Offers facility management (MS); management of sports industries (Certificate); sports management (MS). *Faculty:* 2 full-time (0 women), 11 part-time/adjunct (4 women). *Students:* 19 full-time (7 women), 12 part-time (5 women); includes 2 minority (both African Americans), 5 international. Average age 26. 31 applicants, 94% accepted, 15 enrolled. In 2009, 17 master's awarded. *Entrance requirements:* For master's, GMAT, minimum GPA of 2.7. Additional exam requirements/recommendations for international students: Required—TOEFL (minimum score 520 paper-based; 190 computer-based; 70 iBT); Recommended—IELTS (minimum score 5.5). *Application deadline:* For fall admission, 5/31 for international students; for winter admission, 10/15 for international students; for spring admission, 1/15 for international students. Applications are processed on a rolling basis. Application fee: $50. Electronic applications accepted. *Expenses:* Tuition: Part-time $700 per credit. Required fees: $45 per term. One-time fee: $390 part-time. *Financial support:* Research assistantships with partial tuition reimbursements, teaching assistantships with partial tuition reimbursements, career-related internships or fieldwork, Federal Work-Study, scholarships/grants, tuition waivers, and unspecified assistantships available. Support available to part-time students. Financial award applicants required to submit FAFSA. *Unit head:* Dr. Gil B. Fried, Head, 203-932-7081. *Application contact:* Eloise Gormley, Director of Graduate Admissions, 203-932-7449, Fax: 203-932-7137, E-mail: gradinfo@newhaven.edu.

The University of North Carolina at Chapel Hill, Graduate School, College of Arts and Sciences, Department of Exercise and Sport Science, Chapel Hill, NC 27599. Offers athletic training (MA); exercise physiology (MA); sport administration (MA). *Degree requirements:* For master's, comprehensive exam, thesis. *Entrance requirements:* For master's, GRE General Test, minimum GPA of 3.0. Additional exam requirements/recommendations for international students: Required—TOEFL (minimum score 550 paper-based). Electronic applications accepted. *Faculty research:* Mild head injury in sport, endocrine system's response to exercise, obesity and children, effect of aerobic exercise on cerebral bloodflow in elderly population.

The University of North Carolina at Charlotte, Graduate School, Belk College of Business, Program in Sports Marketing Management, Charlotte, NC 28223-0001. Offers MBA. *Faculty:* 11 full-time (2 women), 1 part-time/adjunct (0 women). *Students:* 22 full-time (6 women), 1 part-time (0 women); includes 3 African Americans, 1 international. Average age 25. 51 applicants, 41% accepted, 14 enrolled. *Degree requirements:* For master's, thesis or alternative, internship. Application fee: $55. Total annual research expenditures: $2,699. *Unit head:* Dr. Linda Swayne, Director, 704-687-7663, Fax: 704-687-4014, E-mail: leswayne@uncc.edu. *Application contact:* Kathy B. Giddings, Director of Graduate Admissions, 704-687-5503, Fax: 704-687-3279, E-mail: gradadm@uncc.edu.

University of Northern Colorado, Graduate School, College of Natural and Health Sciences, School of Sport and Exercise Science, Greeley, CO 80639. Offers exercise science (MS, PhD); sport administration (MS, PhD); sport pedagogy (MS, PhD). Part-time and evening/weekend programs available. *Faculty:* 14 full-time (7 women). *Students:* 66 full-time (37 women), 24 part-time (11 women); includes 11 minority (1 African American, 3 American Indian/Alaska Native, 3 Asian Americans or Pacific Islanders, 4 Hispanic Americans), 16 international. Average age 28. 175 applicants, 56% accepted, 31 enrolled. In 2009, 65 master's, 10 doctorates awarded. *Degree requirements:* For master's, comprehensive exam; for doctorate, comprehensive exam, thesis/dissertation. *Entrance requirements:* For master's, 2 letters of recommendation, resume; for doctorate, GRE General Test, 3 letters of recommendation, resume. *Application deadline:* Applications are processed on a rolling basis. Application fee: $50 ($60 for international students). Electronic applications accepted. *Expenses:* Tuition, state resident: full-time $5770; part-time $320.55 per credit hour. Tuition, nonresident: full-time $13,847; part-time $769.27 per credit hour. Required fees: $948.78; $52.72 per credit. *Financial support:* In 2009–10, 7 research assistantships (averaging $3,876 per year), 17 teaching assistantships (averaging $8,928 per year) were awarded; fellowships, unspecified assistantships also available. Financial award application deadline: 3/1; financial award applicants required to submit FAFSA. *Unit head:* Dr. David Stotlar, Director, 970-351-2535, Fax: 970-351-1762. *Application contact:* Linda Sisson, Graduate Student Admission Coordinator, 970-351-1807, Fax: 970-351-2371, E-mail: linda.sisson@unco.edu.

University of Northern Iowa, Graduate College, College of Education, School of Health, Physical Education, and Leisure Services, Program in Leisure Services, Cedar Falls, IA 50614. Offers leisure services (Ed D); program administration (MA); youth/human services administration (MA). *Students:* 23 full-time (14 women), 25 part-time (13 women); includes 16 minority (14 African Americans, 1 Asian American or Pacific Islander, 1 Hispanic American), 8 international. 20 applicants. In 2009, 8 master's awarded. *Degree requirements:* For master's, comprehensive exam, thesis or alternative; for doctorate, thesis/dissertation. *Entrance requirements:* For master's, minimum GPA of 3.0; for doctorate, GRE, minimum GPA of 3.5. Additional exam requirements/recommendations for international students: Required—TOEFL (minimum score 500 paper-based; 180 computer-based; 61 iBT). *Application deadline:* Applications are processed on a rolling basis. Application fee: $30 ($50 for international students). Electronic applications accepted. *Financial support:* Career-related internships or fieldwork, Federal Work-Study, institutionally sponsored loans, tuition waivers (full), and unspecified assistantships available. Financial award application deadline: 2/1. *Unit head:* Dr. Samuel Lankford, Interim Director, 319-273-6840, Fax: 319-273-5958, E-mail: sam.lankford@uni.edu. *Application contact:* Laurie S. Russell, Record Analyst, 319-273-2623, Fax: 319-273-6792, E-mail: laurie.russell@uni.edu.

University of San Francisco, College of Arts and Sciences, Program in Sport Management, San Francisco, CA 94117-1080. Offers MA. Evening/weekend programs available. *Faculty:* 4 full-time (0 women), 11 part-time/adjunct (1 woman). *Students:* 133 full-time (46 women), 70 part-time (20 women); includes 47 minority (15 African Americans, 13 Asian Americans or Pacific Islanders, 19 Hispanic Americans), 24 international. Average age 27. 262 applicants, 43% accepted, 72 enrolled. In 2009, 72 master's awarded. *Degree requirements:* For master's, thesis or alternative. *Entrance requirements:* For master's, interview, minimum GPA of 2.75. *Application deadline:* For fall admission, 3/31 priority date for domestic students. Applications are processed on a rolling basis. Application fee: $55 ($65 for international students). *Expenses:* Tuition: Full-time $19,710; part-time $1095 per unit. Part-time tuition and fees vary according to degree level, campus/location and program. *Financial support:* In 2009–10, 146 students received support. Career-related internships or fieldwork, Federal Work-Study, and institutionally sponsored loans available. Financial award application deadline: 3/2; financial award applicants required to submit FAFSA. *Faculty research:* Media and sports, sports marketing, sports law, management and organization. *Unit head:* Dr. Stan Fasci, Graduate Director, 415-422-2678, Fax: 415-422-6267. *Application contact:* Information Contact, 415-422-5135, Fax: 415-422-2217, E-mail: asgraduate@usfca.edu.

University of South Carolina, The Graduate School, College of Hospitality, Retail, and Sport Management, Department of Sport and Entertainment Management, Columbia, SC 29208. Offers live sport and entertainment events (MS); public assembly facilities management (MS). Part-time programs available. *Degree requirements:* For master's, comprehensive exam, thesis optional. *Entrance requirements:* For master's, GRE General Test or GMAT (preferred), minimum GPA of 3.0. Additional exam requirements/recommendations for international students: Required—TOEFL (minimum score 570 paper-based; 230 computer-based; 70 iBT). Electronic applications accepted. *Expenses:* Contact institution. *Faculty research:* Public assembly marketing, operations, box office, booking and scheduling, law/economic impacts.

University of Southern Maine, College of Education and Human Development, Educational Leadership Program, Portland, ME 04104-9300. Offers assistant principal (Certificate); athletic administration (Certificate); educational leadership (MS Ed, CAS); middle-level education (Certificate). Part-time and evening/weekend programs available. Postbaccalaureate distance learning degree programs offered (minimal on-campus study). *Faculty:* 5 full-time (0 women), 2 part-time/adjunct (1 woman). *Students:* 15 full-time (6 women), 42 part-time (23 women); includes 1 minority (American Indian/Alaska Native). 20 applicants, 85% accepted, 10 enrolled. In 2009, 26 master's, 11 CASs awarded. *Degree requirements:* For master's, thesis or alternative, practicum, internship; for other advanced degree, thesis or alternative. *Entrance requirements:* For master's, three years of documented teaching; for other advanced degree, master's degree. Additional exam requirements/recommendations for international students: Required—TOEFL (minimum score 550 paper-based; 213 computer-based; 79 iBT). *Application deadline:* For fall admission, 5/1 priority date for domestic students; for spring admission, 10/15 priority date for domestic students. Applications are processed on a rolling basis. Application fee: $50. Electronic applications accepted. *Financial support:* Research assistantships with partial tuition reimbursements, career-related internships or fieldwork, Federal Work-Study, institutionally sponsored loans, scholarships/grants, and unspecified assistantships available. Financial award application deadline: 3/1; financial award applicants required to submit FAFSA. *Unit head:* Dr. James Curry, Chair, Professional Education Department, 270-780-5400, Fax: 270-780-5674, E-mail: jcurry@usm.maine.edu. *Application contact:* Mary Sloan, Director of Graduate Admissions, 207-780-4386, Fax: 207-780-4969, E-mail: msloan@usm.maine.edu.

University of Southern Mississippi, Graduate School, College of Health, School of Human Performance and Recreation, Hattiesburg, MS 39406-0001. Offers human performance (MS, Ed D, PhD); interscholastic athletic administration (MS); recreation and leisure management (MS); sport administration (MS); sport and coaching education (MS); sport management (MS); sports and high performance materials (MS). Part-time and evening/weekend programs available. *Faculty:* 13 full-time (5 women). *Students:* 62 full-time (27 women), 40 part-time (10 women); includes 13 minority (10 African Americans, 1 Asian American or Pacific Islander, 2 Hispanic Americans), 4 international. Average age 29. 79 applicants, 59% accepted, 33 enrolled. In 2009, 43 master's, 4 doctorates awarded. *Degree requirements:* For master's, comprehensive exam, thesis optional; for doctorate, comprehensive exam, thesis/dissertation. *Entrance requirements:* For master's, GRE General Test, minimum GPA of 2.75 in last 60 hours; for doctorate, GRE General Test, minimum GPA of 3.5. Additional exam requirements/

recommendations for international students: Required—TOEFL. *Application deadline:* For fall admission, 3/1 priority date for domestic students, 3/1 for international students. Applications are processed on a rolling basis. Application fee: $35. Electronic applications accepted. *Expenses:* Tuition, state resident: full-time $5096; part-time $284 per hour. Tuition, nonresident: full-time $13,052; part-time $726 per hour. Required fees: $402. Tuition and fees vary according to course level and course load. *Financial support:* In 2009–10, 1 fellowship (averaging $16,000 per year), 6 research assistantships with full tuition reimbursements (averaging $7,492 per year), 5 teaching assistantships with full tuition reimbursements (averaging $7,330 per year) were awarded; career-related internships or fieldwork, Federal Work-Study, institutionally sponsored loans, and tuition waivers (partial) also available. Financial award application deadline: 3/15. *Faculty research:* Exercise physiology, health behaviors, resource management, activity interaction, site development. *Unit head:* Dr. Louis Marciani, Director, 601-266-5379, Fax: 601-266-4445. *Application contact:* Dr. Dennis Phillips, Graduate Coordinator, 601-266-5379, Fax: 601-266-4445.

The University of Tennessee, Graduate School, College of Education, Health and Human Sciences, Department of Exercise, Sport, and Leisure Studies, Knoxville, TN 37996. Offers exercise science (MS, PhD), including biomechanics/sports medicine, exercise physiology; recreation and leisure studies (MS); sport management (MS); sport studies (MS, PhD); therapeutic recreation (MS). Part-time and evening/weekend programs available. *Degree requirements:* For master's, thesis optional. *Entrance requirements:* For master's, minimum GPA of 2.7. Additional exam requirements/recommendations for international students: Required—TOEFL. Electronic applications accepted. *Expenses:* Tuition, state resident: full-time $6826; part-time $380 per semester hour. Tuition, nonresident: full-time $21,844; part-time $1147 per semester hour. Tuition and fees vary according to program.

University of the Incarnate Word, School of Graduate Studies and Research, H-E-B School of Business and Administration, Programs in Administration, San Antonio, TX 78209-6397. Offers adult education (MAA); applied administration (MAA); communication arts (MAA); healthcare administration (MAA); instructional technology (MAA); international business (Certificate); nutrition (MAA); organizational development (MAA, Certificate); project management (Certificate); sports management (MAA). Part-time and evening/weekend programs available. Postbaccalaureate distance learning degree programs offered (no on-campus study). *Students:* 30 full-time (17 women), 163 part-time (114 women); includes 128 minority (18 African Americans, 3 Asian Americans or Pacific Islanders, 107 Hispanic Americans), 8 international. Average age 35. In 2009, 68 master's awarded. *Degree requirements:* For master's, capstone. *Entrance requirements:* For master's, GRE, GMAT, undergraduate degree, minimum GPA of 2.5. Additional exam requirements/recommendations for international students: Required—TOEFL (minimum score 560 paper-based; 220 computer-based; 83 iBT). *Application deadline:* Applications are processed on a rolling basis. Application fee: $20. Electronic applications accepted. *Expenses:* Tuition: Full-time $12,150; part-time $675 per credit hour. Required fees: $83 per credit hour. *Financial support:* Federal Work-Study and scholarships/grants available. Financial award applicants required to submit FAFSA. *Unit head:* Dr. Daniel Dominguez, MAA Director, 210-829-3180, Fax: 210-805-3564, E-mail: domingue@uiwtx.edu. *Application contact:* Andrea Cyterski-Acosta, Dean of Enrollment, 210-829-6005, Fax: 210-829-3921, E-mail: admis@uiwtx.edu.

University of the Incarnate Word, School of Graduate Studies and Research, H-E-B School of Business and Administration, Programs in Business Administration, San Antonio, TX 78209-6397. Offers general business (MBA); international business (MBA); international business strategy (MBA); sports management (MBA). *Accreditation:* ACBSP. Part-time and evening/weekend programs available. Postbaccalaureate distance learning degree programs offered. *Students:* 100 full-time (55 women), 255 part-time (155 women); includes 196 minority (19 African Americans, 1 American Indian/Alaska Native, 14 Asian Americans or Pacific Islanders, 162 Hispanic Americans), 41 international. Average age 32. In 2009, 111 master's awarded. *Degree requirements:* For master's, capstone. *Entrance requirements:* For master's, GMAT (minimum score 450), undergraduate degree with minimum overall GPA of 2.5. Additional exam requirements/recommendations for international students: Required—TOEFL (minimum score 560 paper-based; 220 computer-based; 83 iBT). *Application deadline:* Applications are processed on a rolling basis. Application fee: $20. Electronic applications accepted. *Expenses:* Tuition: Full-time $12,150; part-time $675 per credit hour. Required fees: $83 per credit hour. *Financial support:* Federal Work-Study and scholarships/grants available. Financial award applicants required to submit FAFSA. *Unit head:* Dr. Jeannie Scott, MBA Director, 210-283-5002, Fax: 210-805-3564, E-mail: scott@uiwtx.edu. *Application contact:* Andrea Cyterski-Acosta, Dean of Enrollment, 210-829-6005, Fax: 210-829-3921, E-mail: admis@uiwtx.edu.

University of the Incarnate Word, School of Graduate Studies and Research, School of Nursing and Health Professions, Programs in Sports Management, San Antonio, TX 78209-6397. Offers sport management (MS, Certificate); sport pedagogy (Certificate). Part-time and evening/weekend programs available. *Students:* 5 full-time (2 women), 3 part-time (2 women); includes 3 minority (1 African American, 2 Hispanic Americans). Average age 28. *Degree requirements:* For master's, internship. *Entrance requirements:* For master's, GRE, letter of recommendation from professional in field. Additional exam requirements/recommendations for international students: Required—TOEFL (minimum score 560 paper-based; 220 computer-based; 83 iBT). *Application deadline:* Applications are processed on a rolling basis. Application fee: $20. Electronic applications accepted. *Expenses:* Tuition: Full-time $12,150; part-time $675 per credit hour. Required fees: $83 per credit hour. *Financial support:* Federal Work-Study and scholarships/grants available. Financial award applicants required to submit FAFSA. *Unit head:* Dr. Timothy Henrich, Professor, 210-829-6036, Fax: 210-829-3174, E-mail: henrich@uiwtx.edu. *Application contact:* Andrea Cyterski-Acosta, Dean of Enrollment, 210-829-6005, Fax: 210-829-3921, E-mail: admis@uiwtx.edu.

University of Wisconsin–La Crosse, Office of University Graduate Studies, College of Science and Health, Department of Exercise and Sport Science, Program in Sport Administration, La Crosse, WI 54601-3742. Offers MS. Part-time programs available. *Students:* 20 full-time (11 women), 13 part-time (4 women); includes 1 minority (African American), 4 international. Average age 27. 50 applicants, 44% accepted, 13 enrolled. In 2009, 24 master's awarded. *Degree requirements:* For master's, comprehensive exam, thesis optional, internship. *Entrance requirements:* For master's, minimum GPA of 2.85, course work in anatomy and physiology. Additional exam requirements/recommendations for international students: Required—TOEFL (minimum score 550 paper-based; 213 computer-based; 79 iBT). *Application deadline:* For fall admission, 3/1 priority date for domestic students. Applications are processed on a rolling basis. Application fee: $56. Electronic applications accepted. *Financial support:* Research assistantships, career-related internships or fieldwork, Federal Work-Study, institutionally sponsored loans, health care benefits, and unspecified assistantships available. Financial award application deadline: 3/15; financial award applicants required to submit FAFSA. *Unit head:* Dr. Patrick DiRocco, Chair, 608-785-8171, E-mail: dirocco.patr@uwlax.edu. *Application contact:* Kathryn Kiefer, Director of Admissions, 608-785-8939, E-mail: admissions@uwlax.edu.

Valparaiso University, Graduate School, Program in Sports Administration, Valparaiso, IN 46383. Offers MS, JD/MS. Part-time and evening/weekend programs available. *Students:* 26 full-time (6 women), 19 part-time (8 women); includes 10 minority (6 African Americans, 1 Asian American or Pacific Islander, 3 Hispanic Americans), 2 international. Average age 26. In 2009, 33 master's awarded. *Entrance requirements:* For master's, minimum GPA of 3.0. Additional exam requirements/recommendations for international students: Required—TOEFL (minimum score 550 paper-based; 213 computer-based; 80 iBT). *Application deadline:* Applications are processed on a rolling basis. Application fee: $30 ($50 for international students). Electronic applications accepted. *Financial support:* Available to part-time students. Applicants required to submit FAFSA. *Unit head:* Dr. David L. Rowland, Dean, Graduate Studies and Continuing Education/Associate Provost, 219-464-5313, Fax: 219-464-5381, E-mail: david.rowland@valpo.edu. *Application contact:* Jamie Haney, Coordinator of Graduate Admission, 219-464-5313, Fax: 219-464-5381, E-mail: jamie.haney@valpo.edu.

Washington State University, Graduate School, College of Education, Department of Educational Leadership and Counseling Psychology, Pullman, WA 99164. Offers counseling psychology (Ed M, MA, PhD, Certificate), including counseling psychology (Ed M, MA, PhD); school psychologist (Certificate); educational leadership (M Ed, MA, Ed D, PhD); educational psychology (Ed M, MA, PhD); higher education (Ed M, MA, Ed D, PhD), including higher education administration (PhD), sport management (PhD), student affairs (PhD); higher education with sport management (Ed M). *Accreditation:* NCATE. Terminal master's awarded for partial completion of doctoral program. *Degree requirements:* For master's, comprehensive exam (for some programs), thesis (for some programs), oral exam or written exam; for doctorate, comprehensive exam, thesis/dissertation, oral and written exams. *Entrance requirements:* For master's and doctorate, GRE General Test, minimum GPA of 3.0, 3 letters of recommendation. Additional exam requirements/recommendations for international students: Required—TOEFL (minimum score 550 paper-based; 213 computer-based). *Faculty research:* Attentional processes, cross cultural psychology, faculty development in higher education.

Wayne State College, Department of Health, Human Performance and Sport, Wayne, NE 68787. Offers exercise science (MSE); organizational management (MS), including sport management. Part-time and evening/weekend programs available. *Degree requirements:* For master's, comprehensive exam, thesis optional. *Entrance requirements:* For master's, GRE General Test, minimum GPA of 3.0. Additional exam requirements/recommendations for international students: Required—TOEFL (minimum score 550 paper-based; 213 computer-based). Electronic applications accepted.

Wayne State University, College of Education, Division of Kinesiology, Health and Sports Studies, Detroit, MI 48202. Offers health education (M Ed); kinesiology (M Ed); physical education (M Ed); recreation and park services (MA); sports administration (MA). *Degree requirements:* For master's, thesis (for some programs). *Entrance requirements:* Additional exam requirements/recommendations for international students: Required—TOEFL; Recommended—TWE (minimum score 6). Electronic applications accepted. *Faculty research:* Fitness in urban children, motor development of crack babies, effects of caffeine on metabolism/exercise, body composition of elite youth sports participants, systematic observation of teaching.

Webber International University, Graduate School of Business, Babson Park, FL 33827-0096. Offers accounting (MBA); management (MBA); security management (MBA); sports management (MBA). Part-time and evening/weekend programs available. *Degree requirements:* For master's, thesis or alternative. *Entrance requirements:* For master's, previous course work in financial and managerial accounting. Additional exam requirements/recommendations for international students: Required—TOEFL. *Faculty research:* Finance strategy, market research, investments, intranet.

See Close-Up on page 281.

West Chester University of Pennsylvania, Office of Graduate Studies, College of Health Sciences, Department of Kinesiology, West Chester, PA 19383. Offers adapted physical education (Certificate); health and physical education (MS, Teaching Certificate), including exercise physiology (MS); physical education (MS); sport and athletic administration (MSA). Part-time and evening/weekend programs available. *Students:* 2 full-time (1 woman), 37 part-time (15 women); includes 2 minority (both African Americans), 3 international. Average age 25. 39 applicants, 90% accepted, 11 enrolled. In 2009, 25 master's awarded. *Degree requirements:* For master's, thesis (for some programs), thesis or report (MS), 2 internships (MSA). *Entrance requirements:* For master's, GRE (MS); GMAT, GRE General Test, or MAT (MSA), minimum GPA of 3.0 with interview (MS) or letters of recommendation (MSA). Additional exam requirements/recommendations for international students: Required—TOEFL (minimum score 550 paper-based; 213 computer-based; 80 iBT). *Application deadline:* For fall admission, 4/15 priority date for domestic students, 3/15 for international students; for spring admission, 10/15 for domestic students, 9/1 for international students. Applications are processed on a rolling basis. Application fee: $35. Electronic applications accepted. *Expenses:* Tuition, state resident: full-time $6666; part-time $370 per credit. Tuition, nonresident: full-time $10,666; part-time $593 per credit. Required fees: $122.56 per credit. *Financial support:* In 2009–10, 11 research assistantships with full and partial tuition reimbursements (averaging $5,000 per year) were awarded; unspecified assistantships also available. Support available to part-time students. Financial award application deadline: 2/15; financial award applicants required to submit FAFSA. *Faculty research:* Weight lifting and type 1 diabetes mellitus, martial arts, sexual harassment in sports. *Unit head:* Dr. Frank Fry, Chair, 610-436-2832, E-mail: ffry@wcupa.edu. *Application contact:* Dr. Sheri Melton, Graduate Coordinator, 610-436-2260, E-mail: smelton@wcupa.edu.

Western Illinois University, School of Graduate Studies, College of Education and Human Services, Department of Kinesiology, Program in Sport Management, Macomb, IL 61455-1390. Offers MS. Part-time programs available. *Students:* 43 full-time (14 women), 9 part-time (2 women); includes 4 minority (3 African Americans, 1 Hispanic American), 3 international. Average age 25. 53 applicants, 62% accepted. In 2009, 28 master's awarded. *Entrance requirements:* For master's, minimum GPA of 3.0. Additional exam requirements/recommendations for international students: Required—TOEFL (minimum score 550 paper-based; 213 computer-based; 80 iBT). *Application deadline:* Applications are processed on a rolling basis. Application fee: $30. Electronic applications accepted. *Expenses:* Tuition, state resident: full-time $4486; part-time $249.21 per credit hour. Tuition, nonresident: full-time $8972; part-time $498.42 per credit hour. Required fees: $72.62 per credit hour. *Financial support:* In 2009–10, 23 students received support, including 21 research assistantships with full tuition reimbursements available (averaging $7,280 per year), 2 teaching assistantships with full tuition reimbursements available (averaging $8,400 per year). *Unit head:* Dr. Darlene Young, Graduate Committee Chairperson, 309-298-1981. *Application contact:* Evelyn Hoing, Assistant Director of Graduate Studies, 309-298-1806, Fax: 309-298-2345, E-mail: grad-office@wiu.edu.

Western Michigan University, Graduate College, College of Education, Department of Health, Physical Education and Recreation, Kalamazoo, MI 49008. Offers exercise and sports medicine (MS), including athletic training, exercise physiology; physical education (MA), including coaching sport performance, pedagogy, special physical education, sport management. *Faculty:* 20 full-time (9 women). *Students:* 60 full-time (27 women), 53 part-time (25 women); includes 9 minority (6 African Americans, 2 Asian Americans or Pacific Islanders, 1 Hispanic American), 6 international. 69 applicants, 81% accepted, 21 enrolled. In 2009, 42 master's awarded. *Application deadline:* For fall admission, 2/15 priority date for domestic students. Applications are processed on a rolling basis. Application fee: $25. *Financial support:* Fellowships, research assistantships, teaching assistantships, Federal Work-Study available. Financial award application deadline: 2/15; financial award applicants required to submit FAFSA. *Unit head:* Lee deLisle, Chair, 269-387-2669. *Application contact:* Admissions and Orientation, 269-387-2000, Fax: 269-387-2355.

Western New England College, School of Business, Program in Business Administration (General), Springfield, MA 01119. Offers general business (MBA); sport management (MBA). *Accreditation:* AACSB. Part-time and evening/weekend programs available. *Students:* 103 part-time (43 women); includes 5 African Americans, 2 Asian Americans or Pacific Islanders, 2 Hispanic Americans. In 2009, 22 master's awarded. *Entrance requirements:* For master's, GMAT, 2 letters of reference, resume. *Application deadline:* Applications are processed on a rolling basis. Application fee: $30. *Expenses:* Tuition: Part-time $552 per credit hour. Part-time tuition and fees vary according to program. *Financial support:* Available to part-time students. Applicants required to submit FAFSA. *Unit head:* Dr. Julie Siciliano, Dean, 413-782-1231. *Application contact:* Matt Fox, Director of Recruiting and Marketing for Adult Learners, 413-782-1249, Fax: 413-782-1779, E-mail: ce@wnec.edu.

West Virginia University, School of Physical Education, Morgantown, WV 26506. Offers athletic coaching education (MS); athletic training (MS); physical education/teacher education (MS, PhD), including curriculum and instruction (PhD), motor behavior (PhD), physical education supervision (PhD); sport and exercise psychology (PhD); sport management (MS). *Degree requirements:* For doctorate, comprehensive exam, thesis/dissertation, oral exam. *Entrance requirements:* For master's, GRE or MAT, minimum GPA of 3.0; for doctorate, GRE General Test or MAT, minimum GPA of 3.5. Additional exam requirements/recommendations for inter-

Sports Management

West Virginia University (continued)
national students: Required—TOEFL (minimum score 550 paper-based; 213 computer-based). Electronic applications accepted. *Faculty research:* Sport psychosociology, teacher education, exercise psychology, counseling.

Wichita State University, Graduate School, College of Education, Department of Sport Management, Wichita, KS 67260. Offers M Ed. *Expenses:* Tuition, state resident: full-time $4247; part-time $235.95 per credit hour. Tuition, nonresident: full-time $11,171; part-time $620.60 per credit hour. Required fees: $34; $3.60 per credit hour. $17 per term. Tuition and fees vary according to campus/location and program.

Wingate University, Program in Education, Wingate, NC 28174-0159. Offers educational leadership (MA Ed); elementary education (MA Ed, MAT); physical education (MA Ed); sport administration (MA Ed). *Accreditation:* NCATE. Part-time and evening/weekend programs available. *Degree requirements:* For master's, portfolio. *Entrance requirements:* For master's, GRE General Test or MAT, teaching certificate (MA Ed).

Winona State University, College of Education, Department of Educational Leadership, Winona, MN 55987-5838. Offers educational leadership (Ed S), including general superintendency, K-12 prinicpalship; general school leadership (MS); K-12 principalship (MS); outdoor education/adventure based leadership (MS); sports management (MS); teacher leadership (MS).

Accreditation: NCATE. Part-time and evening/weekend programs available. *Degree requirements:* For master's, comprehensive exam, thesis optional; for Ed S, thesis optional. *Faculty research:* Financial equity, democratic practices in the classroom.

Xavier University, College of Social Sciences, Health and Education, Department of Sports Studies, Cincinnati, OH 45207. Offers sport administration (M Ed). Part-time and evening/weekend programs available. *Faculty:* 3 full-time (1 woman), 6 part-time/adjunct (1 woman). *Students:* 40 full-time (10 women), 29 part-time (13 women); includes 7 minority (6 African Americans, 1 Hispanic American). Average age 26. 67 applicants, 97% accepted, 32 enrolled. In 2009, 24 master's awarded. *Degree requirements:* For master's, thesis optional, internship. *Entrance requirements:* For master's, GRE or MAT. Additional exam requirements/recommendations for international students: Required—TOEFL. *Application deadline:* For fall admission, 2/15 priority date for domestic and international students; for spring admission, 9/15 priority date for domestic and international students. Applications are processed on a rolling basis. Application fee: $35. Electronic applications accepted. *Expenses:* Tuition: Part-time $697 per credit hour. One-time fee: $35 part-time. *Financial support:* In 2009–10, 43 students received support. Applicants required to submit FAFSA. *Faculty research:* Coaching education, brand equity, strategic management, economic impact, place marketing. *Unit head:* Dr. Douglas Olberding, Chair, 513-745-1085, Fax: 513-745-4291, E-mail: olberdin@xavier.edu. *Application contact:* Roger Bosse, Interim Director of Graduate Studies, 513-745-3360, Fax: 513-745-1048, E-mail: bosse@xavier.edu.

ACADEMIC AND PROFESSIONAL PROGRAMS IN SOCIAL WORK

Section 44
Social Work

This section contains a directory of institutions offering graduate work in social work, followed by in-depth entries submitted by institutions that chose to prepare detailed program descriptions. Additional information about programs listed in the directory but not augmented by an in-depth entry may be obtained by writing directly to the dean of a graduate school or chair of a department at the address given in the directory.

For programs offering related work, see also in this book *Allied Health* and *Education*. In another guide in this series:
Graduate Programs in the Humanities, Arts & Social Sciences
See *Criminology and Forensics, Family and Consumer Sciences, Psychology and Counseling,* and *Sociology, Anthropology, and Archaeology*

CONTENTS

Program Directories

Close-Ups

Human Services

Abilene Christian University, Graduate School, College of Arts and Sciences, Department of Sociology and Family Studies, Abilene, TX 79699-9100. Offers gerontology (MS, Certificate). Part-time programs available. *Faculty:* 3 part-time/adjunct (0 women). *Students:* 2 full-time (both women), 1 (woman) part-time; includes 2 minority (1 African American, 1 Hispanic American), 1 international. 2 applicants, 100% accepted, 1 enrolled. In 2009, 2 master's, 1 other advanced degree awarded. *Degree requirements:* For master's, comprehensive exam. *Entrance requirements:* For master's, GRE General Test or MAT. *Application deadline:* For fall admission, 4/1 priority date for domestic students; for spring admission, 11/1 for domestic students. Applications are processed on a rolling basis. Application fee: $40 ($45 for international students). Electronic applications accepted. *Expenses:* Tuition: Full-time $11,520; part-time $640 per hour. Required fees: $1090; $53.50 per hour. $10 per term. Tuition and fees vary according to program. *Financial support:* In 2009–10, 3 students received support. Career-related internships or fieldwork and Federal Work-Study available. Support available to part-time students. Financial award application deadline: 4/1; financial award applicants required to submit FAFSA. *Unit head:* Department Chair, 325-674-2349, Fax: 325-674-6524. *Application contact:* William Horn, Graduate Admissions Counselor, 325-674-2656, Fax: 325-674-6717, E-mail: gradinfo@acu.edu.

Abilene Christian University, Graduate School, College of Education and Human Services, Abilene, TX 79699-9100. Offers M Ed, MS, MSSW. *Faculty:* 20 part-time/adjunct (12 women). *Students:* 89 full-time (68 women), 229 part-time (168 women); includes 38 minority (23 African Americans, 2 Asian Americans or Pacific Islanders, 13 Hispanic Americans), 9 international. 235 applicants, 51% accepted, 114 enrolled. In 2009, 39 master's awarded. *Degree requirements:* For master's, comprehensive exam. *Application deadline:* For fall admission, 4/1 priority date for domestic students; for spring admission, 11/1 for domestic students. Applications are processed on a rolling basis. Application fee: $40. Electronic applications accepted. *Expenses:* Tuition: Full-time $11,520; part-time $640 per hour. Required fees: $1090; $53.50 per hour. $10 per term. Tuition and fees vary according to program. *Financial support:* In 2009–10, 236 students received support. Application deadline: 4/1. *Unit head:* Dr. Malesa Breeding, Dean, 325-674-2700. *Application contact:* William Horn, Graduate Admissions Counselor, 325-674-2656, Fax: 325-674-6717, E-mail: gradinfo@acu.edu.

Andrews University, School of Graduate Studies, College of Arts and Sciences, Department of Behavioral Science, Berrien Springs, MI 49104. Offers community services management (MSA); international development (MSA). *Students:* 9 full-time (7 women), 3 part-time (all women); includes 5 minority (2 African Americans, 1 Asian American or Pacific Islander, 2 Hispanic Americans), 5 international. Average age 31. 17 applicants, 47% accepted, 4 enrolled. In 2009, 3 master's awarded. *Entrance requirements:* For master's, GRE. Additional exam requirements/recommendations for international students: Required—TOEFL (minimum score 550 paper-based). Application fee: $40. *Unit head:* Dr. Duane C. McBride, Chair, 269-471-3152. *Application contact:* Carolyn Hurst, Supervisor of Graduate Admission, 800-253-2874, Fax: 269-471-6321, E-mail: graduate@andrews.edu.

Bellevue University, Graduate School, Programs in Healthcare Administration, Bellevue, NE 68005-3098. Offers healthcare administration (MHA); human services (MA, MS). Postbaccalaureate distance learning degree programs offered.

Boricua College, Program in Human Services (Brooklyn Campus), New York, NY 10032-1560. Offers MS. Evening/weekend programs available. *Degree requirements:* For master's, thesis. *Entrance requirements:* For master's, interview by the faculty.

Boricua College, Program in Human Services (Manhattan Campus), New York, NY 10032-1560. Offers MS. Evening/weekend programs available. *Degree requirements:* For master's, thesis. *Entrance requirements:* For master's, interview by the faculty.

Brandeis University, The Heller School for Social Policy and Management, Program in Nonprofit Management, Waltham, MA 02454-9110. Offers aging services management (MBA); child, youth, and family management (MBA); health care management (MBA); social impact management (MBA); social policy and management (MBA); sustainable development (MBA); MBA/MA. *Accreditation:* AACSB. Part-time and evening/weekend programs available. *Degree requirements:* For master's, team consulting project. *Entrance requirements:* For master's, GMAT. Additional exam requirements/recommendations for international students: Required—TOEFL (minimum score 600 paper-based). Electronic applications accepted. *Expenses:* Contact institution. *Faculty research:* Health care, child and family, elder and disabled services, general human services.

California State University, Sacramento, Graduate Studies, College of Health and Human Services, Division of Social Work, Sacramento, CA 95819. Offers family and children's services (MSW); health care (MSW); mental health (MSW); social justice and corrections (MSW). *Accreditation:* CSWE. *Degree requirements:* For master's, thesis or alternative, writing proficiency exam. *Entrance requirements:* For master's, minimum GPA of 2.5 during previous 2 years of course work. Additional exam requirements/recommendations for international students: Required—TOEFL. Electronic applications accepted.

Capella University, School of Human Services, Minneapolis, MN 55402. Offers addictions counseling (Certificate); counseling studies (MS, PhD); criminal justice (MS, PhD, Certificate); diversity studies (Certificate); general human services (MS, PhD); health care administration (MS, PhD, Certificate); management of nonprofit agencies (MS, PhD, Certificate); marital, couple and family counseling/therapy (MS); marriage and family services (Certificate); mental health counseling (MS); professional counseling (Certificate); social and community services (MS, PhD, Certificate). Part-time and evening/weekend programs available. Postbaccalaureate distance learning degree programs offered (minimal on-campus study). Terminal master's awarded for partial completion of doctoral program. *Degree requirements:* For master's, thesis optional, integrative project; for doctorate, comprehensive exam, thesis/dissertation. *Entrance requirements:* Additional exam requirements/recommendations for international students: Required—TOEFL (minimum score 550 paper-based; 213 computer-based), TWE (minimum score 4). Electronic applications accepted. *Faculty research:* Compulsive and addictive behaviors, substance abuse, assessment of psychopathology and neuropsychology.

Capella University, School of Public Service Leadership, Minneapolis, MN 55402. Offers criminal justice (MS, PhD); emergency management (MS, PhD); general human services (MS, PhD); general public administration (MPA, DPA); gerontology (MS); health care administration (MS, PhD); health management and policy (MSPH); management of nonprofit agencies (MS, PhD); nurse educator (MS); public safety leadership (MS, PhD); social and community services (MS, PhD); social behavioral sciences (MSPH).

Chestnut Hill College, School of Graduate Studies, Program in Administration of Human Services, Philadelphia, PA 19118-2693. Offers administration of human services (MS); adult and aging services (CAS); leadership development (CAS). Part-time and evening/weekend programs available. *Degree requirements:* For master's, special projects or internship. *Entrance requirements:* For master's, GRE General Test or MAT, 100 volunteer hours or 1 year work-related human services experience, statement of professional goals, writing sample, transcripts, letters of recommendation; for CAS, GRE or MAT, letters of recommendation. Additional exam requirements/recommendations for international students: Required—TOEFL (minimum score 500 paper-based; 213 computer-based).

Concordia University Chicago, College of Graduate and Innovative Programs, Program in Human Services, River Forest, IL 60305-1499. Offers human services (MA), including administration, exercise science. Part-time and evening/weekend programs available. *Degree requirements:* For master's, comprehensive exam, thesis. *Entrance requirements:* For master's, minimum GPA of 2.9. Additional exam requirements/recommendations for international students: Required—TOEFL (minimum score 550 paper-based; 195 computer-based). Electronic applications accepted.

Concordia University Wisconsin, Graduate Programs, School of Health and Human Services, Mequon, WI 53097-2402. Offers MOT, MSN, MSPT, MSRS, DPT.

Coppin State University, Division of Graduate Studies, Division of Arts and Sciences, Department of Social Sciences, Baltimore, MD 21216-3698. Offers human services administration (MS). Part-time and evening/weekend programs available. *Entrance requirements:* For master's, resume, references, interview.

DePaul University, School of Education, Chicago, IL 60106. Offers bilingual and bicultural education (M Ed, MA); curriculum studies (M Ed, MA, Ed D); educational leadership (M Ed, MA, Ed D), including administration and supervision (M Ed, MA), Catholic school leadership (M Ed, MA), physical education (M Ed, MA); human development and learning (MA); human services and counseling (M Ed, MA), including agencies, family concerns, and higher education, elementary schools, human services management, secondary schools; reading and learning disabilities (M Ed, MA); social culture studies in education and development (M Ed, MA), including curriculum studies/development; teaching and learning (early childhood, elementary and secondary) (M Ed), including elementary education (M Ed, MA), secondary education (M Ed, MA); teaching and learning (early childhood, elementary, and secondary) (MA), including elementary education (M Ed, MA), secondary education (M Ed, MA). *Accreditation:* NCATE. Part-time and evening/weekend programs available. *Faculty:* 61 full-time (40 women), 66 part-time/adjunct (41 women). *Students:* 799 full-time (779 women), 470 part-time (365 women); includes 319 minority (153 African Americans, 3 American Indian/Alaska Native, 48 Asian Americans or Pacific Islanders, 115 Hispanic Americans), 15 international. Average age 30. 635 applicants, 74% accepted, 318 enrolled. In 2009, 604 master's, 5 doctorates awarded. *Degree requirements:* For doctorate, thesis/dissertation. *Entrance requirements:* For master's, interview, minimum GPA of 2.75, 2 letters of recommendation; for doctorate, interview, master's degree, writing sample, 3 letters of recommendation. Additional exam requirements/recommendations for international students: Required—TOEFL (minimum score 550 paper-based; 213 computer-based; 80 iBT). *Application deadline:* Applications are processed on a rolling basis. Application fee: $40. Electronic applications accepted. *Expenses:* Tuition: Full-time $37,525; part-time $620 per credit hour. *Financial support:* In 2009–10, 14 research assistantships with tuition reimbursements (averaging $5,800 per year) were awarded; career-related internships or fieldwork also available. *Faculty research:* Reflective teaching, children at risk, loss, ethnicity, urban education. Total annual research expenditures: $1.6 million. *Unit head:* Dr. Marie Donovan, Dean, 773-325-7581, Fax: 773-325-7713, E-mail: mdonovan@depaul.edu. *Application contact:* Brandon Washington, Data Project Manager, 773-325-1152, Fax: 773-325-2270, E-mail: bwashin3@depaul.edu.

Drury University, Graduate Programs in Education, Springfield, MO 65802. Offers elementary education (M Ed); gifted education (M Ed); human services (M Ed); instructional mathematics K-8 (M Ed); instructional technology (M Ed); middle school teaching (M Ed); secondary education (M Ed); special education (M Ed); special reading (M Ed). *Accreditation:* NCATE. Part-time and evening/weekend programs available. *Degree requirements:* For master's, thesis. *Entrance requirements:* For master's, GRE or MAT, minimum GPA of 2.75. Additional exam requirements/recommendations for international students: Required—TOEFL. Electronic applications accepted. *Faculty research:* Cultural enrichment, research skills, parental involvement relating to reading skills, reading strategies for mainstreaming children.

Eastern Michigan University, Graduate School, College of Health and Human Services, Interdisciplinary Program in Health and Human Services, Ypsilanti, MI 48197. Offers community building (Graduate Certificate); nonprofit management (Graduate Certificate). Part-time and evening/weekend programs available. In 2009, 1 other advanced degree awarded. *Entrance requirements:* Additional exam requirements/recommendations for international students: Required—TOEFL. Application fee: $35. Tuition and fees vary according to course level. *Unit head:* Dr. Marcia Bombyk, Program Coordinator, 734-487-4173, Fax: 734-487-8536, E-mail: marcia.bombyk@emich.edu. *Application contact:* Dr. Marcia Bombyk, Program Coordinator, 734-487-4173, Fax: 734-487-8536, E-mail: marcia.bombyk@emich.edu.

Eastern New Mexico University, Graduate School, College of Liberal Arts and Sciences, Department of Health and Human Services, Portales, NM 88130. Offers speech pathology and audiology (MS). *Accreditation:* ASHA. Part-time programs available. Postbaccalaureate distance learning degree programs offered (minimal on-campus study). *Faculty:* 4 full-time (3 women). *Students:* 11 full-time (10 women), 41 part-time (39 women); includes 22 minority (1 African American, 2 American Indian/Alaska Native, 1 Asian American or Pacific Islander, 18 Hispanic Americans). Average age 29. 33 applicants, 58% accepted, 19 enrolled. In 2009, 11 master's awarded. *Degree requirements:* For master's, comprehensive exam, thesis optional, professional portfolio. *Entrance requirements:* For master's, GRE, minimum GPA of 3.0, 3 letters of recommendation. Additional exam requirements/recommendations for international students: Required—TOEFL (minimum score 550 paper-based; 213 computer-based; 79 iBT), IELTS (minimum score 6). *Application deadline:* For fall admission, 3/1 priority date for domestic and international students; for spring admission, 10/15 priority date for domestic and international students. Applications are processed on a rolling basis. Application fee: $10. Electronic applications accepted. *Expenses:* Tuition, state resident: full-time $2922; part-time $121.75 per credit hour. Tuition, nonresident: full-time $8454; part-time $352.25 per credit hour. Required fees: $1038; $43.25 per credit hour. *Financial support:* In 2009–10, 6 research assistantships with full tuition reimbursements (averaging $4,250 per year) were awarded; fellowships, teaching assistantships, unspecified assistantships also available. Support available to part-time students. Financial award applicants required to submit FAFSA. *Unit head:* Dr. Adrienne Bratcher, Graduate Coordinator, 575-562-2159, E-mail: adrienne.bratcher@enmu.edu. *Application contact:* Dean, Graduate School.

Fairfield University, Graduate School of Education and Allied Professions, Department of Psychological and Educational Consultation, Fairfield, CT 06824-5195. Offers applied psychology (MA), including foundations of advanced psychology, human services, industrial/organizational/personnel; media/educational technology (MA); school media specialist (MA); school psychology (MA, CAS); special education (MA, CAS). Part-time and evening/weekend programs available. *Degree requirements:* For master's, comprehensive exam, thesis optional. *Entrance requirements:* For master's, PRAXIS I (PPST), minimum QPA of 3.0, 2 recommendations, resume. Additional exam requirements/recommendations for international students: Required—TOEFL (minimum score 550 paper-based; 213 computer-based; 80 iBT). Electronic applications accepted. *Faculty research:* Child neuropsychology, disabilities, effect of pre-treatment orientation on treatment, autism, technology in business and classroom, collaboration with schools, communities and industry.

Fairmont State University, Graduate Studies, Program in Human Services, Fairmont, WV 26554. Offers human and community service administration (MS). *Degree requirements:* For master's, comprehensive exam, 400-hour supervised internship. *Entrance requirements:* For master's, GRE, minimum undergraduate cumulative GPA of 3.0; 3 letters of reference; baccalaureate degree in psychology, sociology, or similar social/behavioral field.

Ferris State University, College of Education and Human Services, Big Rapids, MI 49307. Offers M Ed, MSCJ, MSCTE. Part-time and evening/weekend programs available. Postbaccalaureate distance learning degree programs offered. *Faculty:* 15 full-time (10 women), 12 part-time/adjunct (5 women). *Students:* 31 full-time (19 women), 229 part-time (146 women); includes 37 minority (32 African Americans, 1 American Indian/Alaska Native, 1 Asian American or Pacific Islander, 3 Hispanic Americans), 2 international. Average age 36. 49 applicants, 41% accepted, 18 enrolled. In 2009, 111 master's awarded. *Entrance requirements:* For master's, minimum GPA of 3.0 (MSCJ), 2.75 (MSCTE, M Ed). Additional exam requirements/recommendations for international students: Required—TOEFL (minimum score 500 paper-based; 173 computer-based; 61 iBT). *Application deadline:* For fall admission, 7/1 priority date for domestic students; for spring admission, 11/1 priority date for domestic students. Applications are processed on a rolling basis. Application fee: $30. *Financial support:* In 2009–10, 8

students received support, including 2 research assistantships (averaging $4,800 per year); career-related internships or fieldwork, Federal Work-Study, scholarships/grants, and unspecified assistantships also available. Support available to part-time students. *Faculty research:* Competency testing, teaching methodologies, assessment of teaching effectiveness, suicide prevention, women in education, special needs. *Unit head:* Michelle Johnston, Dean, 231-591-3646, Fax: 231-592-3792, E-mail: michelle_johnston@ferris.edu. *Application contact:* Michelle Johnston, Dean, 231-591-3646, Fax: 231-592-3792, E-mail: michelle_johnston@ferris.edu.

Georgia State University, College of Health and Human Sciences, School of Social Work, Atlanta, GA 30294. Offers community partnerships (MSW). *Accreditation:* CSWE. Part-time programs available. *Degree requirements:* For master's, community project. *Entrance requirements:* For master's, GRE General Test. Additional exam requirements/recommendations for international students: Required—TOEFL (minimum score 550 paper-based; 213 computer-based). Electronic applications accepted. *Faculty research:* Child welfare, labor unions and child care workers, secondary victimization in death penalty cases, aging.

Indiana University Northwest, School of Public and Environmental Affairs, Gary, IN 46408-1197. Offers criminal justice (MPA); environmental affairs (Graduate Certificate); health services administration (MPA); human services administration (MPA); nonprofit management (Graduate Certificate); public management (MPA, Graduate Certificate). *Accreditation:* NASPAA (one or more programs are accredited). Part-time programs available. *Faculty:* 5 full-time (3 women). *Students:* 19 full-time (14 women), 121 part-time (100 women); includes 100 minority (84 African Americans, 1 American Indian/Alaska Native, 1 Asian American or Pacific Islander, 14 Hispanic Americans). Average age 39. In 2009, 29 master's, 27 other advanced degrees awarded. *Entrance requirements:* For master's, GRE General Test or GMAT, letters of recommendation. *Application deadline:* For fall admission, 8/15 priority date for domestic students. Applications are processed on a rolling basis. Application fee: $25. *Financial support:* Career-related internships or fieldwork, Federal Work-Study, and tuition waivers (partial) available. Support available to part-time students. Financial award application deadline: 3/1. *Faculty research:* Employment in income security policies, evidence in criminal justice, equal employment law, social welfare policy and welfare reform, public finance in developing countries. *Unit head:* George Assibey-Mensah, Interim Dean/Division Director, 219-980-6695, Fax: 219-980-6737. *Application contact:* Sandra Hall Smith, Secretary, 219-980-6695, Fax: 219-980-6737, E-mail: shsmith@iun.edu.

Kansas State University, Graduate School, College of Human Ecology, School of Family Studies and Human Services, Manhattan, KS 66506. Offers communication sciences and disorders (MS); early childhood education (MS); family studies (MS); life span human development (MS); marriage and family therapy (MS). *Accreditation:* AAMFT/COAMFTE; ASHA. Part-time programs available. *Faculty:* 25 full-time (15 women), 3 part-time/adjunct (2 women). *Students:* 76 full-time (67 women), 101 part-time (61 women); includes 17 minority (7 African Americans, 1 American Indian/Alaska Native, 2 Asian Americans or Pacific Islanders, 7 Hispanic Americans), 1 international. Average age 32. 117 applicants, 68% accepted, 47 enrolled. In 2009, 63 master's awarded. *Degree requirements:* For master's, thesis or alternative, oral exam, residency. *Entrance requirements:* For master's, GRE, minimum GPA of 3.0 in last 2 years of undergraduate study. Additional exam requirements/recommendations for international students: Required—TOEFL (minimum score 600 paper-based; 250 computer-based). *Application deadline:* For fall admission, 2/1 priority date for domestic and international students; for spring admission, 8/1 priority date for domestic and international students. Applications are processed on a rolling basis. Application fee: $40 ($55 for international students). Electronic applications accepted. *Financial support:* In 2009–10, 26 research assistantships (averaging $10,867 per year), 17 teaching assistantships with full and partial tuition reimbursements (averaging $11,635 per year) were awarded; Federal Work-Study, institutionally sponsored loans, scholarships/grants, and unspecified assistantships also available. Support available to part-time students. Financial award application deadline: 3/1; financial award applicants required to submit FAFSA. *Faculty research:* Health and security of military families, personal and family risk assessment and evaluation, disorders of communication and swallowing, families and health. Total annual research expenditures: $10.1 million. *Unit head:* Dr. Maurice McDonald, Head, 785-532-1472, E-mail: morey@ksu.edu. *Application contact:* Connie Fechter, Administrative Specialist, 785-532-1473, Fax: 785-532-5505, E-mail: fechter@ksu.edu.

Kent State University, Graduate School of Education, Health, and Human Services, Kent, OH 44242-0001. Offers M Ed, MA, MAT, MPH, MS, Au D, PhD, Ed S. *Accreditation:* NCATE. Part-time and evening/weekend programs available. Postbaccalaureate distance learning degree programs offered. *Faculty:* 235 full-time (148 women), 166 part-time/adjunct (120 women). *Students:* 896 full-time (711 women), 806 part-time (638 women); includes 200 minority (145 African Americans, 1 American Indian/Alaska Native, 31 Asian Americans or Pacific Islanders, 23 Hispanic Americans), 29 international. 1,138 applicants, 45% accepted. In 2009, 534 master's, 35 doctorates, 28 other advanced degrees awarded. *Degree requirements:* For master's, thesis (for some programs); for doctorate, comprehensive exam, thesis/dissertation. *Entrance requirements:* For doctorate and Ed S, GRE General Test. Additional exam requirements/recommendations for international students: Required—TOEFL (minimum score 525 paper-based; 197 computer-based). *Application deadline:* Applications are processed on a rolling basis. Application fee: $30 ($60 for international students). Electronic applications accepted. *Financial support:* In 2009–10, 28 fellowships with full tuition reimbursements (averaging $11,889 per year), 85 research assistantships with full tuition reimbursements (averaging $8,429 per year), 26 teaching assistantships with full tuition reimbursements (averaging $11,889 per year) were awarded; Federal Work-Study, scholarships/grants, and unspecified assistantships also available. Financial award application deadline: 4/1; financial award applicants required to submit FAFSA. *Unit head:* Dr. Daniel Mahony, Dean, 330-672-2202, Fax: 330-672-3407, E-mail: dmahony@kent.edu. *Application contact:* Nancy Miller, Academic Program Coordinator, Office of Graduate Student Services, 330-672-2576, Fax: 330-672-9162, E-mail: nmiller1@kent.edu.

Lehigh University, College of Education, Program in Counseling Psychology, Bethlehem, PA 18015. Offers counseling and human services (M Ed); counseling psychology (PhD); elementary counseling with certification (M Ed); international counseling (Certificate); international counseling with certification (M Ed); secondary school counseling (M Ed). *Accreditation:* APA (one or more programs are accredited). Part-time and evening/weekend programs available. Postbaccalaureate distance learning degree programs offered (minimal on-campus study). *Faculty:* 6 full-time (4 women), 10 part-time/adjunct (5 women). *Students:* 40 full-time (33 women), 37 part-time (32 women); includes 13 minority (7 African Americans, 1 American Indian/Alaska Native, 3 Asian Americans or Pacific Islanders, 2 Hispanic Americans), 4 international. Average age 29. 194 applicants, 24% accepted, 17 enrolled. In 2009, 34 master's, 3 doctorates awarded. *Degree requirements:* For doctorate, comprehensive exam, thesis/dissertation. *Entrance requirements:* For master's, minimum GPA of 3.0, 2 letters of recommendation, essay, transcript; for doctorate, GRE General Test (Verbal and Quantitative), 2 letters of recommendation, supplemental application, transcript, essay; for Certificate, minimum GPA of 3.0. Additional exam requirements/recommendations for international students: Required—TOEFL (minimum score 600 paper-based; 250 computer-based; 93 iBT). *Application deadline:* For fall admission, 11/15 for domestic and international students; for winter admission, 2/1 for international students. Application fee: $65. Electronic applications accepted. *Financial support:* In 2009–10, 11 students received support, including 2 fellowships with full and partial tuition reimbursements available (averaging $24,000 per year), 2 research assistantships with full and partial tuition reimbursements available (averaging $13,000 per year); career-related internships or fieldwork, Federal Work-Study, institutionally sponsored loans, scholarships/grants, and tuition waivers (full and partial) also available. Financial award application deadline: 1/31; financial award applicants required to submit FAFSA. *Faculty research:* Supervision, violence prevention, multicultural training and counseling, career development and health interventions. *Unit head:* Dr. Arpana Inman, Coordinator, 610-758-4443, Fax: 610-758-3227, E-mail: agi2@lehigh.edu. *Application contact:* Donna M. Johnson, Coordinator, 610-758-3231, Fax: 610-758-6223, E-mail: dmj4@lehigh.edu.

Lincoln University, Graduate Center, Lincoln University, PA 19352. Offers administration (MSA), including finance, human resources management; early childhood education (M Ed); elementary education (M Ed); human services (M Hum Svcs); reading (MSR). Evening/weekend programs available. *Degree requirements:* For master's, thesis. *Entrance requirements:* For master's, 5 years of work experience in human services. *Faculty research:* Gerontology/minority aging, computers in composition instruction.

Louisiana State University in Shreveport, College of Liberal Arts, Program in Human Services Administration, Shreveport, LA 71115-2399. Offers MS. Part-time and evening/weekend programs available. *Students:* 4 full-time (all women), 8 part-time (all women); includes 2 minority (both African Americans). Average age 34. 9 applicants, 100% accepted, 6 enrolled. In 2009, 6 master's awarded. *Degree requirements:* For master's, final project. *Entrance requirements:* For master's, GRE, minimum GPA of 3.0 in last 2 undergraduate years, interview, recommendations. Additional exam requirements/recommendations for international students: Required—TOEFL (minimum score 500 paper-based; 173 computer-based; 61 iBT). *Application deadline:* For fall admission, 6/30 for domestic and international students; for spring admission, 11/30 for domestic and international students. Applications are processed on a rolling basis. Application fee: $10 ($20 for international students). *Financial support:* In 2009–10, 3 research assistantships with partial tuition reimbursements (averaging $30,000 per year) were awarded. *Unit head:* Dr. Helen Wise, Program Director, 318-797-5333, Fax: 318-797-5358, E-mail: helen.wise@lsus.edu. *Application contact:* Yvonne Yarbrough, Secretary, Graduate Studies, 318-797-5247, Fax: 318-798-4120, E-mail: yyarbrou@lsus.edu.

McDaniel College, Graduate and Professional Studies, Program in Human Services Management in Special Education, Westminster, MD 21157-4390. Offers MS. *Accreditation:* NCATE. Evening/weekend programs available. *Degree requirements:* For master's, internship. *Entrance requirements:* For master's, letters of reference (3). Additional exam requirements/recommendations for international students: Required—TOEFL (minimum score 213 computer-based). *Expenses:* Tuition: Part-time $325 per credit hour.

Minnesota State University Mankato, College of Graduate Studies, College of Social and Behavioral Sciences, Department of Sociology and Corrections, Mankato, MN 56001. Offers sociology (MA); sociology: corrections (MS); sociology: human services planning and administration (MS). Part-time programs available. *Students:* 10 full-time (5 women), 41 part-time (25 women). *Degree requirements:* For master's, comprehensive exam, thesis or alternative. *Entrance requirements:* For master's, minimum GPA of 3.0 during previous 2 years, 3 letters of reference, resume. Additional exam requirements/recommendations for international students: Required—TOEFL. *Application deadline:* For fall admission, 7/1 priority date for domestic students; for spring admission, 11/1 for domestic students. Applications are processed on a rolling basis. Application fee: $40. Electronic applications accepted. *Expenses:* Tuition, state resident: full-time $5364. Tuition, nonresident: full-time $8314. *Financial support:* Research assistantships with full tuition reimbursements, teaching assistantships with full tuition reimbursements, career-related internships or fieldwork, Federal Work-Study, institutionally sponsored loans, and unspecified assistantships available. Support available to part-time students. Financial award application deadline: 3/15; financial award applicants required to submit FAFSA. *Faculty research:* Women's suffrage movements. *Unit head:* Dr. Barbara Keating, Chairperson, 507-389-1561. *Application contact:* 507-389-2321, E-mail: grad@mnsu.edu.

Minnesota State University Moorhead, Graduate Studies, College of Education and Human Services, Moorhead, MN 56563-0002. Offers counseling and student affairs (MS); curriculum and instruction (MS); educational leadership (MS, Ed S); nursing (MS); reading (MS); special education (MS); speech-language pathology (MS). *Accreditation:* NCATE. Part-time and evening/weekend programs available. *Degree requirements:* For master's, comprehensive exam, final oral exam, project or thesis. *Entrance requirements:* Additional exam requirements/recommendations for international students: Required—TOEFL. Electronic applications accepted.

Minnesota State University Moorhead, Graduate Studies, College of Social and Natural Sciences, Program in Public, Human Services, and Health Administration, Moorhead, MN 56563-0002. Offers MS. Part-time and evening/weekend programs available. *Degree requirements:* For master's, final oral exam, final project paper or thesis. *Entrance requirements:* For master's, GRE General Test, minimum GPA of 2.75. Additional exam requirements/recommendations for international students: Required—TOEFL (minimum score 550 paper-based; 213 computer-based). Electronic applications accepted.

Montana State University Billings, College of Allied Health Professions, Department of Rehabilitation and Human Services, Billings, MT 59101-0298. Offers MSRC. *Accreditation:* CORE. Part-time programs available. *Degree requirements:* For master's, thesis or professional paper and/or field experience. *Entrance requirements:* For master's, GRE General Test or MAT, minimum GPA of 3.0.

Murray State University, College of Education, Department of Educational Studies, Leadership and Counseling, Program in Human Development and Leadership, Murray, KY 42071. Offers MS. Part-time programs available. *Degree requirements:* For master's, thesis optional. *Entrance requirements:* Additional exam requirements/recommendations for international students: Required—TOEFL.

National-Louis University, College of Arts and Sciences, Department of Counseling and Human Services, Chicago, IL 60603. Offers community counseling (MS); school counseling (MS). Part-time programs available. *Degree requirements:* For master's, internship. *Entrance requirements:* For master's, GRE General Test, MAT, or Watson-Glaser Critical Thinking Appraisal, interview, minimum GPA of 3.0. *Expenses:* Tuition: Full-time $17,160; part-time $715 per semester hour. Tuition and fees vary according to course load, degree level, campus/location and program. *Faculty research:* Religion and aging, drug abuse prevention, hunger, homelessness, multicultural diversity.

National University, Academic Affairs, School of Health and Human Services, La Jolla, CA 92037-1011. Offers MHA, MHCA, MIH, MS. Part-time and evening/weekend programs available. Postbaccalaureate distance learning degree programs offered (no on-campus study). *Faculty:* 2 full-time (1 woman), 2 part-time/adjunct (both women). *Students:* 12 full-time (7 women), 50 part-time (37 women); includes 23 minority (6 African Americans, 9 Asian Americans or Pacific Islanders, 8 Hispanic Americans), 20 international. Average age 31. 75 applicants, 100% accepted, 55 enrolled. In 2009, 3 master's awarded. *Degree requirements:* For master's, thesis. *Entrance requirements:* For master's, interview, minimum GPA of 2.5. Additional exam requirements/recommendations for international students: Required—TOEFL (minimum score 550 paper-based; 213 computer-based; 79 iBT), IELTS (minimum score 6). *Application deadline:* Applications are processed on a rolling basis. Application fee: $60 ($65 for international students). Electronic applications accepted. *Expenses:* Tuition: Part-time $338 per quarter hour. *Financial support:* Career-related internships or fieldwork, institutionally sponsored loans, and scholarships/grants available. Support available to part-time students. Financial award application deadline: 6/30; financial award applicants required to submit FAFSA. *Faculty research:* Nursing education, obesity prevention, workforce diversity. *Unit head:* Dr. Michael Lacourse, Dean, 858-309-3472, Fax: 858-309-3480, E-mail: mlacourse@nu.edu. *Application contact:* Dominick Giovanniello, Associate Regional Dean—San Diego, 800-NAT-UNIV, Fax: 858-541-7792, E-mail: dgiovann@nu.edu.

New England College, Program in Community Mental Health Counseling, Henniker, NH 03242-3293. Offers human services (MS); mental health counseling (MS). Part-time and evening/weekend programs available. *Degree requirements:* For master's, internship.

Nova Southeastern University, Fischler School of Education and Human Services, Program in Education, Fort Lauderdale, FL 33314-7796. Offers educational leadership (Ed D); health care education (Ed D); higher education leadership (Ed D); human services administration (Ed D); instructional leadership (Ed D); instructional technology and distance education (Ed D); organizational leadership (Ed D); special education (Ed D); speech language pathology (Ed D). Part-time and evening/weekend programs available. Postbaccalaureate distance learning degree programs offered (minimal on-campus study). *Faculty:* 88 full-time (46 women), 132 part-time/

Human Services

Nova Southeastern University (continued)

adjunct (63 women). *Students:* 2,805 full-time (2,128 women), 1,411 part-time (1,081 women); includes 2,629 minority (2,034 African Americans, 19 American Indian/Alaska Native, 62 Asian Americans or Pacific Islanders, 514 Hispanic Americans), 30 international. Average age 41. 964 applicants, 69% accepted, 513 enrolled. In 2009, 445 doctorates awarded. *Degree requirements:* For doctorate, thesis/dissertation. *Entrance requirements:* For doctorate, MAT or GRE, master's degree, 2 letters of recommendation, work experience. Additional exam requirements/recommendations for international students: Required—TSE (recommended, minimum score 50); Recommended—TOEFL (minimum score 550 paper-based; 213 computer-based; 80 iBT), IELTS (minimum score 6). *Application deadline:* For fall admission, 8/20 priority date for domestic and international students; for winter admission, 12/19 priority date for domestic and international students; for spring admission, 4/26 priority date for domestic students, 4/25 priority date for international students. Applications are processed on a rolling basis. Application fee: $50. Electronic applications accepted. *Financial support:* In 2009–10, 2 fellowships with full tuition reimbursements (averaging $30,000 per year) were awarded; scholarships/grants and tuition waivers (full) also available. Support available to part-time students. Financial award application deadline: 4/15; financial award applicants required to submit FAFSA. *Unit head:* Dr. Ronald Kern, Dean of Academic Affairs, 800-986-3223 Ext. 7809, Fax: 954-262-3606, E-mail: rk429@nsu.nova.edu. *Application contact:* Dr. Jennifer Quinones Nottingham, Dean of Student Affairs, 800-986-3223 Ext. 1546.

Nova Southeastern University, Fischler School of Education and Human Services, Programs in Human Services, Fort Lauderdale, FL 33314-7796. Offers child and youth studies (Ed D); child protection (MHS); education (MS), including human services; health professions education (MS); substance abuse counseling and education (MS). Part-time and evening/weekend programs available. *Students:* 1,867 full-time (1,442 women), 1,273 part-time (976 women); includes 1,866 minority (1,545 African Americans, 16 American Indian/Alaska Native, 48 Asian Americans or Pacific Islanders, 257 Hispanic Americans), 27 international. In 2009, 118 doctorates awarded. *Degree requirements:* For master's, thesis, practicum; for doctorate, thesis/dissertation, practicum. *Entrance requirements:* For master's, GRE or MAT, work experience in field, minimum GPA of 2.5; for doctorate, GRE or MAT, master's degree, minimum GPA of 3.0, work experience. Additional exam requirements/recommendations for international students: Recommended—TOEFL (minimum score 550 paper-based; 213 computer-based), IELTS (minimum score 6). *Application deadline:* Applications are processed on a rolling basis. Application fee: $50. Electronic applications accepted. *Expenses:* Contact institution. *Financial support:* Career-related internships or fieldwork and Federal Work-Study available. Support available to part-time students. Financial award application deadline: 4/15; financial award applicants required to submit FAFSA. *Unit head:* Dr. Elda Veloso, Associate Dean, 954-262-8538, Fax: 954-262-2917, E-mail: veloso@nova.edu. *Application contact:* Dr. Jennifer Quinones Nottingham, Dean of Student Affairs, 800-986-3223 Ext. 8500.

Pontifical Catholic University of Puerto Rico, Institute of Graduate Studies in Behavioral Science and Community Affairs, Ponce, PR 00717-0777. Offers clinical psychology (MA, MS, PhD, Psy D); clinical social work (MSW); criminology (MA); industrial psychology (MS, PhD); psychology (PhD); public administration (MA); vocational rehabilitation counseling (MSS). Part-time and evening/weekend programs available. *Degree requirements:* For master's, thesis; for doctorate, comprehensive exam, thesis/dissertation. *Entrance requirements:* For master's, EXADEP, GRE General Test, 3 letters of recommendation, interview, minimum GPA of 2.75.

Post University, Program in Human Services, Waterbury, CT 06723-2540. Offers human services (MS); human services/clinical (MS); human services/management (MS). Part-time programs available. Postbaccalaureate distance learning degree programs offered.

Purdue University Calumet, Graduate School, School of Education, Program in Counseling, Hammond, IN 46323-2094. Offers human services (MS Ed); mental health counseling (MS Ed); school counseling (MS Ed). *Entrance requirements:* Additional exam requirements/recommendations for international students: Required—TOEFL.

Roberts Wesleyan College, Division of Social Work, Rochester, NY 14624-1997. Offers child and family practice (MSW); congregational and community practice (MSW); mental health practice (MSW). *Accreditation:* CSWE. *Entrance requirements:* For master's, minimum GPA of 2.75. *Faculty research:* Religion and social work, family studies, values and ethics.

Rosemont College, Schools of Graduate and Professional Studies, Program in Counseling Psychology, Rosemont, PA 19010-1699. Offers human services (MA); school counseling (MA). Part-time and evening/weekend programs available. *Degree requirements:* For master's, thesis or alternative, practicum. *Entrance requirements:* For master's, minimum undergraduate GPA of 3.0, 3 letters of recommendation. Additional exam requirements/recommendations for international students: Required—TOEFL. Electronic applications accepted. *Expenses:* Contact institution. *Faculty research:* Addictions counseling.

St. Edward's University, School of Management and Business, Program in Human Services, Austin, TX 78704. Offers administration (Certificate); conflict resolution (Certificate); family mediation (Certificate); human services (MA), including administration, conflict resolution, human resource management, organization development and training, social and psychological services; mediation (Certificate); organization development and training (Certificate). Part-time and evening/weekend programs available. *Students:* 4 full-time (3 women), 51 part-time (43 women); includes 24 minority (9 African Americans, 2 Asian Americans or Pacific Islanders, 13 Hispanic Americans). Average age 34. 23 applicants, 96% accepted, 18 enrolled. In 2009, 19 master's awarded. *Degree requirements:* For master's, minimum of 24 resident hours. *Entrance requirements:* For master's, GRE General Test, GMAT, minimum GPA of 2.75 in last 60 hours of course work. Additional exam requirements/recommendations for international students: Required—TOEFL (minimum score 550 paper-based; 213 computer-based; 79 iBT) or IELTS (minimum score 6). *Application deadline:* For fall admission, 7/1 for domestic and international students; for spring admission, 11/1 for domestic and international students. Applications are processed on a rolling basis. Application fee: $45 ($50 for international students). Electronic applications accepted. *Expenses:* Tuition: Full-time $14,922; part-time $829 per credit hour. Required fees: $50 per trimester. Full-time tuition and fees vary according to course load and program. *Financial support:* In 2009–10, 2 students received support. Scholarships/grants available. *Faculty research:* Leadership development, organizational management, public policy. *Unit head:* Dr. Constance D. Porter, Director, 512-416-5827, Fax: 512-448-8492, E-mail: constanp@stedwards.edu. *Application contact:* Kay L. Arnold, Assistant Director of Admissions, 512-233-1636, Fax: 512-428-1032, E-mail: kayla@stedwards.edu.

St. Joseph's College, New York, Graduate Programs, Program in Human Services Management and Leadership, Brooklyn, NY 11205-3688. Offers MS.

Saint Joseph's University, College of Arts and Sciences, Program in Gerontological Services, Philadelphia, PA 19131-1395. Offers gerontological counseling (MS); gerontological services (Post-Master's Certificate); human services administration (MS). Part-time and evening/weekend programs available. *Students:* 2 full-time (0 women), 8 part-time (all women); includes 2 minority (both African Americans), 2 international. Average age 34. In 2009, 5 master's awarded. *Entrance requirements:* For master's, 2 letters of recommendation. Additional exam requirements/recommendations for international students: Required—TOEFL (minimum score 550 paper-based; 213 computer-based; 79 iBT). *Application deadline:* For fall admission, 7/15 priority date for domestic students, 4/15 for international students; for winter admission, 1/15 for international students; for spring admission, 11/15 priority date for domestic students, 10/15 for international students. Applications are processed on a rolling basis. Application fee: $35. Electronic applications accepted. *Expenses:* Tuition: Part-time $729 per credit hour. Tuition and fees vary according to degree level and program. *Financial support:* Fellowships available. Financial award applicants required to submit FAFSA. *Unit head:* Dr. Catherine Murray, Director, 610-660-1805, E-mail: cmurray@sju.edu. *Application contact:* Kate McConnell, Director, Graduate College of Arts and Sciences Admissions and Retention, 610-660-3184, Fax: 610-660-3230, E-mail: kate.mcconnell@sju.edu.

St. Mary's University, Graduate School, Department of Counseling and Human Services, San Antonio, TX 78228-8507. Offers community counseling (MA); counseling (Sp C); counseling education and supervision (PhD); marriage and family relations (Certificate); marriage and family therapy (MA, PhD); mental health (MA); mental health and substance abuse counseling (Certificate); substance abuse (MA). *Accreditation:* AAMFT/COAMFTE (one or more programs are accredited); ACA (one or more programs are accredited). Postbaccalaureate distance learning degree programs offered (minimal on-campus study). *Degree requirements:* For master's, comprehensive exam, internship; for doctorate, comprehensive exam, thesis/dissertation, internship. *Entrance requirements:* For master's, GRE General Test, MAT; for doctorate, GRE General Test, recommendation from employers, admissions committee and department faculty. Additional exam requirements/recommendations for international students: Required—TOEFL (minimum score 550 paper-based; 213 computer-based; 80 iBT). Electronic applications accepted. *Expenses:* Contact institution.

Sojourner-Douglass College, Graduate Program, Baltimore, MD 21205-1814. Offers human services (MASS); public administration (MASS); urban education (reading) (MASS). Part-time and evening/weekend programs available. *Degree requirements:* For master's, comprehensive exam, written proposal oral defense. *Entrance requirements:* For master's, Graduate Examination.

South Carolina State University, School of Graduate Studies, Department of Human Services, Orangeburg, SC 29117-0001. Offers elementary counselor education (M Ed); rehabilitation counseling (MA); secondary counselor education (M Ed). *Accreditation:* CORE. Part-time and evening/weekend programs available. *Degree requirements:* For master's, comprehensive exam (for some programs), departmental qualifying exam, internship. *Entrance requirements:* For master's, GRE, MAT, minimum GPA of 2.7. Electronic applications accepted. *Expenses:* Tuition, state resident: part-time $470 per credit hour. Tuition, nonresident: part-time $924 per credit hour. *Faculty research:* Handicap, disability, rehabilitation evaluation, vocation.

Southeastern University, Department of Behavioral and Social Sciences, Lakeland, FL 33801-6099. Offers human services (MA); professional counseling (MS); school counseling (MS). Evening/weekend programs available.

Springfield College, Graduate Programs, Program in Human Services, Springfield, MA 01109-3797. Offers human services (MS), including community counseling psychology, mental health counseling, organizational management and leadership. Part-time programs available. *Degree requirements:* For master's, comprehensive exam, thesis (for some programs), research project. *Entrance requirements:* For master's, GRE. Additional exam requirements/recommendations for international students: Required—TOEFL (minimum score 550 paper-based; 213 computer-based). Electronic applications accepted. *Expenses:* Contact institution.

State University of New York at Oswego, Graduate Studies, School of Education, Department of Counseling and Psychological Services, Program in Human Services/Counseling, Oswego, NY 13126. Offers MS. Part-time programs available. *Degree requirements:* For master's, comprehensive exam. *Entrance requirements:* For master's, GRE General Test, interview, minimum GPA of 3.0. Additional exam requirements/recommendations for international students: Required—TOEFL (minimum score 560 paper-based; 220 computer-based).

Syracuse University, School of Education, Program in Educational Technology, Syracuse, NY 13244. Offers CAS. *Accreditation:* ACA. Part-time programs available. *Students:* 1 (woman) part-time; minority (African American). Average age 47. In 2009, 1 CAS awarded. *Degree requirements:* For CAS, thesis or alternative. *Entrance requirements:* Additional exam requirements/recommendations for international students: Required—TOEFL (minimum score 100 iBT). *Application deadline:* For fall admission, 2/1 priority date for domestic and international students; for spring admission, 10/15 priority date for domestic and international students. Applications are processed on a rolling basis. Application fee: $75. Electronic applications accepted. *Expenses:* Tuition: Full-time $26,808; part-time $1117 per credit. Required fees: $1024. *Financial support:* Fellowships, research assistantships, teaching assistantships available. Financial award application deadline: 1/1. *Faculty research:* Academics and athletics, drug free schools, group counseling, prejudice prevention, culture-centered counseling. *Unit head:* Dr. Janine Bernard, Chair, 315-443-5266, Fax: 315-443-5732, E-mail: bernard@syr.edu. *Application contact:* Liza Rochelson, Graduate Recruiter, School of Education, 315-443-2505, E-mail: e-gradrcrt@syr.edu.

Texas Southern University, College of Liberal Arts and Behavioral Sciences, Department of Human Services and Consumer Sciences, Houston, TX 77004-4584. Offers MS. Part-time and evening/weekend programs available. *Faculty:* 2 full-time (both women). *Students:* 7 full-time (6 women), 25 part-time (23 women); includes all African Americans. Average age 34. 13 applicants, 100% accepted, 5 enrolled. In 2009, 10 master's awarded. *Degree requirements:* For master's, comprehensive exam, thesis (for some programs). *Entrance requirements:* For master's, GRE General Test, minimum GPA of 2.5. Additional exam requirements/recommendations for international students: Required—TOEFL. *Application deadline:* For fall admission, 7/1 for domestic and international students; for spring admission, 11/1 for domestic and international students. Applications are processed on a rolling basis. Application fee: $50 ($75 for international students). Electronic applications accepted. *Expenses:* Tuition, state resident: full-time $1805; part-time $100 per credit hour. Tuition, nonresident: full-time $6470; part-time $343 per credit hour. Tuition and fees vary according to course level, course load and degree level. *Financial support:* In 2009–10, 1 teaching assistantship (averaging $6,400 per year) was awarded; research assistantships, scholarships/grants and unspecified assistantships also available. Financial award application deadline: 5/1. *Faculty research:* Food radiation/food for space travel, adolescent parenting, gerontology/grandparenting. *Unit head:* Dr. Shirley R. Nealy, Chair, 713-313-7638, Fax: 713-313-7228, E-mail: nealy_sr@tsu.edu. *Application contact:* Dr. Gregory Maddox, Interim Dean of the Graduate School, 713-313-7011 Ext. 4410, Fax: 713-639-1876, E-mail: maddox_gh@tsu.edu.

Thomas University, Department of Human Services, Thomasville, GA 31792-7499. Offers community counseling (MSCC); rehabilitation counseling (MRC). *Accreditation:* CORE. Part-time programs available. *Entrance requirements:* For master's, resume, 3 academic/professional references. Additional exam requirements/recommendations for international students: Required—TOEFL (minimum score 600 paper-based; 250 computer-based). Electronic applications accepted.

Universidad del Turabo, Graduate Programs, School of Social Sciences and Humanities, Programs in Public Affairs, Program in Human Services Administration, Gurabo, PR 00778-3030. Offers MPA. *Students:* 28 full-time (23 women), 17 part-time (8 women); includes 35 Hispanic Americans. Average age 31. 17 applicants, 100% accepted, 16 enrolled. In 2009, 23 master's awarded. *Entrance requirements:* For master's, GRE, EXADEP, interview. *Application deadline:* For fall admission, 8/5 for domestic students. Application fee: $25. *Unit head:* Dr. Marco A. Gil Dela Madrid, Dean, 787-743-7979. *Application contact:* Virginia Gonzalez, Admissions Officer, 787-746-3009.

Université de Montréal, Faculty of Arts and Sciences, Programs in Applied Human Sciences, Montréal, QC H3C 3J7, Canada. Offers PhD. *Students:* 22 full-time (16 women), 38 part-time (23 women). 20 applicants, 40% accepted, 6 enrolled. In 2009, 5 doctorates awarded. *Degree requirements:* For doctorate, thesis/dissertation, general exam. *Application deadline:* For fall admission, 2/1 priority date for domestic students; for winter admission, 11/1 priority date for domestic students; for spring admission, 2/1 priority date for domestic students. Application fee: $100. Electronic applications accepted. *Unit head:* Violaine Lemay, Director, 514-343-7165, Fax: 514-343-2314, E-mail: violaine.lemay@umontreal.ca. *Application contact:* Manon Lebrun, Student Files Management Technician, 514-343-7165, Fax: 514-343-2314, E-mail: manon.lebrun@umontreal.ca.

University of Baltimore, Graduate School, The Yale Gordon College of Liberal Arts, Program in Human Services Administration, Baltimore, MD 21201-5779. Offers MS. Part-time and evening/weekend programs available. *Entrance requirements:* For master's, interview. Additional

exam requirements/recommendations for international students: Required—TOEFL (minimum score 550 paper-based; 213 computer-based). Electronic applications accepted.

University of Bridgeport, School of Education and Human Resources, Division of Human Resources, Bridgeport, CT 06604. Offers college student personnel (MS); community counseling (MS); human resource development (MS); human service (MS). Part-time and evening/weekend programs available. *Degree requirements:* For master's, thesis, project. *Entrance requirements:* Additional exam requirements/recommendations for international students: Recommended—TOEFL (minimum score 550 paper-based; 213 computer-based; 80 iBT), IELTS (minimum score 6.5). Electronic applications accepted. *Faculty research:* Corporate elder care programs.

University of Central Missouri, The Graduate School, College of Education, Warrensburg, MO 64093. Offers career and technical education administration (MS); career and technical education industry training (MS); career and technical education leadership/teaching (MS); college student personnel administration (MS); counseling (MS); curriculum and instruction (Ed S); educational leadership (Ed D); educational technology (MS); elementary education/educational foundations and literacy (MSE); elementary school administration (MSE); elementary school principalship (Ed S); human services/learning resources (Ed S); human services/professional counseling (Ed S); human services/special education (Ed S); human services/technology and occupational education (Ed S); K-12 education/educational foundations and literacy (MSE); K-12 special education (MSE); library science and information services (MS); literacy education (MSE); secondary education/educational foundations & literacy (MSE); secondary school administration (MSE); secondary school principalship (Ed S); superintendency (Ed S); teaching (MAT). Part-time programs available. Postbaccalaureate distance learning degree programs offered. *Faculty:* 42. *Students:* 123 full-time (82 women), 721 part-time (552 women); includes 58 minority (38 African Americans, 3 American Indian/Alaska Native, 6 Asian Americans or Pacific Islanders, 11 Hispanic Americans), 6 international. Average age 34. 229 applicants, 88% accepted, 190 enrolled. In 2009, 212 master's, 47 other advanced degrees awarded. *Entrance requirements:* Additional exam requirements/recommendations for international students: Required—TOEFL (minimum score 550 paper-based; 79 computer-based). *Application deadline:* For fall admission, 6/1 priority date for domestic students, 5/1 for international students; for spring admission, 10/1 priority date for domestic students, 10/1 for international students. Applications are processed on a rolling basis. Application fee: $30 ($75 for international students). Electronic applications accepted. *Expenses:* Tuition, area resident: Part-time $245.80 per credit hour. Tuition, nonresident: part-time $491.60 per credit hour. Required fees: $24.20 per credit hour. Full-time tuition and fees vary according to course load, degree level, campus/location and reciprocity agreements. *Financial support:* Research assistantships with full and partial tuition reimbursements, teaching assistantships with full and partial tuition reimbursements, career-related internships or fieldwork, Federal Work-Study, scholarships/grants, and administrative and laboratory assistantships available. Support available to part-time students. Financial award application deadline: 3/1; financial award applicants required to submit FAFSA. *Unit head:* Dr. Michael Wright, Dean, 660-543-4272, Fax: 660-543-8753, E-mail: mwright@ucmo.edu. *Application contact:* Laurie Delap, Admissions Coordinator, 660-543-4621, Fax: 660-543-4778, E-mail: gradinfo@ucmo.edu.

University of Colorado at Colorado Springs, Graduate School, College of Education, Colorado Springs, CO 80933-7150. Offers counseling and human services (MA); curriculum and instruction (MA); educational administration (MA); educational leadership (MA, PhD); special education (MA). *Accreditation:* ACA; NCATE. Part-time and evening/weekend programs available. Postbaccalaureate distance learning degree programs offered (minimal on-campus study). *Faculty:* 23 full-time (15 women), 11 part-time/adjunct (8 women). *Students:* 317 full-time (243 women), 160 part-time (132 women); includes 81 minority (23 African Americans, 3 American Indian/Alaska Native, 13 Asian Americans or Pacific Islanders, 42 Hispanic Americans), 2 international. Average age 36. 375 applicants, 94% accepted, 254 enrolled. In 2009, 203 master's awarded. *Degree requirements:* For master's, comprehensive exam, thesis or alternative, microcomputer proficiency; for doctorate, comprehensive exam, research lab. *Entrance requirements:* For master's, GRE General Test, MAT. *Application deadline:* For fall admission, 6/15 for domestic students; for spring admission, 10/15 for domestic students. Applications are processed on a rolling basis. Application fee: $60 ($75 for international students). *Expenses:* Tuition, state resident: full-time $8922; part-time $639 per credit hour. Tuition, nonresident: full-time $19,372; part-time $1154 per credit hour. Tuition and fees vary according to course level, course load, degree level, program, reciprocity agreements and student level. *Financial support:* Fellowships, career-related internships or fieldwork, Federal Work-Study, and scholarships/grants available. Support available to part-time students. Financial award application deadline: 3/1; financial award applicants required to submit FAFSA. *Faculty research:* Job training for special populations, materials development for classroom. Total annual research expenditures: $1.4 million. *Unit head:* Dr. LaVonne Neal, Dean, 719-255-4111, Fax: 719-262-4110, E-mail: lneal@uccs.edu. *Application contact:* Melissa Schecter, Student Services Manager, 719-255-4526, Fax: 719-255-4110, E-mail: mschedte@uccs.edu.

University of Great Falls, Graduate Studies, Program in Organization Management, Great Falls, MT 59405. Offers human development (MSM); management (MSM). Part-time and evening/weekend programs available. Postbaccalaureate distance learning degree programs offered (minimal on-campus study). *Degree requirements:* For master's, thesis optional. *Entrance requirements:* For master's, GRE General Test or MAT, 3 letters of recommendation. Additional exam requirements/recommendations for international students: Required—TOEFL (minimum score 500 paper-based; 205 computer-based). Electronic applications accepted.

University of Illinois at Springfield, Graduate Programs, College of Education and Human Services, Program in Human Services, Springfield, IL 62703-5407. Offers alcoholism and substance abuse (MA); child and family services (MA); gerontology (MA); social services administration (MA). Part-time and evening/weekend programs available. Postbaccalaureate distance learning degree programs offered (no on-campus study). *Faculty:* 4 full-time (3 women), 1 (woman) part-time/adjunct. *Students:* 34 full-time (32 women), 91 part-time (76 women); includes 34 minority (31 African Americans, 1 American Indian/Alaska Native, 1 Asian American or Pacific Islander, 1 Hispanic American), 1 international. Average age 36. 76 applicants, 54% accepted, 33 enrolled. In 2009, 20 master's awarded. *Degree requirements:* For master's, internship; project or thesis. *Entrance requirements:* For master's, minimum undergraduate GPA of 3.0, 2 letters of recommendation. Additional exam requirements/recommendations for international students: Required—TOEFL (minimum score 500 paper-based; 176 computer-based; 61 iBT). Application fee: $50 ($60 for international students). Electronic applications accepted. *Expenses:* Tuition, state resident: full-time $6390; part-time $266.25 per credit hour. Tuition, nonresident: full-time $14,226; part-time $592.75 per credit hour. Required fees: $2044; $14.36 per credit hour. $722.50 per term. *Financial support:* In 2009–10, research assistantships with full tuition reimbursements (averaging $8,109 per year), teaching assistantships with full tuition reimbursements (averaging $8,109 per year) were awarded; career-related internships or fieldwork, scholarships/grants, health care benefits, and unspecified assistantships also available. Support available to part-time students. Financial award application deadline: 11/15. *Unit head:* Dr. Carolyn Peck, Program Administrator, 217-206-7577, Fax: 217-206-6775, E-mail: peck.carolyn@uis.edu. *Application contact:* Dr. Lynn Pardie, Office of Graduate Studies, 800-252-8533, Fax: 217-206-7623, E-mail: pardie.lynn@uis.edu.

University of Maryland, Baltimore County, Graduate School, College of Arts, Humanities and Social Sciences, Department of Psychology, Program in Human Services Psychology, Baltimore, MD 21250. Offers applied behavioral analysis (MA); human services psychology/clinical (PhD). *Faculty:* 17 full-time (5 women), 11 part-time/adjunct (4 women). *Students:* 75 full-time (64 women), 25 part-time (19 women); includes 29 minority (11 African Americans, 11 Asian Americans or Pacific Islanders, 7 Hispanic Americans). Average age 29. 133 applicants, 28% accepted, 21 enrolled. In 2009, 19 master's, 12 doctorates awarded. Terminal master's awarded for partial completion of doctoral program. *Degree requirements:* For master's, thesis; for doctorate, comprehensive exam, thesis/dissertation. *Entrance requirements:* For master's, GRE General Test, minimum GPA of 3.0; for doctorate, GRE General Test, GRE Subject Test, minimum GPA of 3.0. Additional exam requirements/recommendations for international students: Required—TOEFL. *Application deadline:* For fall admission, 12/1 for domestic and international students. Application fee: $70. Electronic applications accepted. *Financial support:* In 2009–10, fellowships with full and partial tuition reimbursements (averaging $2,200 per year), 18 research assistantships with full and partial tuition reimbursements (averaging $14,857 per year), 32 teaching assistantships with full and partial tuition reimbursements (averaging $14,857 per year) were awarded; career-related internships or fieldwork, Federal Work-Study, scholarships/grants, health care benefits, tuition waivers (full and partial), and unspecified assistantships also available. Financial award application deadline: 3/1; financial award applicants required to submit FAFSA. *Faculty research:* Addictive behaviors, cardiovascular and cerebrovascular disease, family violence, pediatric psychology, community prevention. Total annual research expenditures: $2.3 million. *Unit head:* Dr. Shari Waldstein, Director, 410-455-2567, Fax: 410-455-1055, E-mail: waldstei@umbc.edu. *Application contact:* Nicole Mooney, Program Management Specialist, 410-455-2567, Fax: 410-455-1055, E-mail: psycdept@umbc.edu.

University of Massachusetts Boston, Office of Graduate Studies, College of Public and Community Service, Program in Human Services, Boston, MA 02125-3393. Offers MS. Part-time and evening/weekend programs available. *Degree requirements:* For master's, practicum, final project. *Entrance requirements:* For master's, MAT, GRE, minimum GPA of 2.75. *Faculty research:* Institutional and policy context of human services, ethics and social policy, public law and human services, social welfare, politics and human services.

University of Oklahoma, Graduate College, College of Arts and Sciences, Department of Human Relations, Norman, OK 73019-0390. Offers MHR. Part-time and evening/weekend programs available. Postbaccalaureate distance learning degree programs offered (minimal on-campus study). *Faculty:* 30 full-time (20 women), 41 part-time/adjunct (18 women). *Students:* 307 full-time (194 women), 641 part-time (410 women); includes 346 minority (204 African Americans, 40 American Indian/Alaska Native, 55 Asian Americans or Pacific Islanders, 47 Hispanic Americans), 26 international. 223 applicants, 98% accepted, 204 enrolled. In 2009, 416 master's awarded. *Degree requirements:* For master's, thesis optional. *Entrance requirements:* For master's, minimum GPA of 3.0 in last 60 hours of undergraduate course work, resume, 3 letters of reference. Additional exam requirements/recommendations for international students: Required—TOEFL (minimum score 550 paper-based; 213 computer-based). *Application deadline:* For fall admission, 4/1 priority date for domestic students, 4/1 for international students; for spring admission, 11/1 for domestic students, 9/1 for international students. Applications are processed on a rolling basis. Application fee: $40 ($90 for international students). Electronic applications accepted. *Expenses:* Tuition, state resident: full-time $3744; part-time $156 per credit hour. Tuition, nonresident: full-time $13,577; part-time $565.70 per credit hour. Required fees: $2415; $90.10 per credit hour. *Financial support:* In 2009–10, 217 students received support, including 25 research assistantships with partial tuition reimbursements available (averaging $10,161 per year), 3 teaching assistantships (averaging $10,724 per year); career-related internships or fieldwork, Federal Work-Study, institutionally sponsored loans, scholarships/grants, health care benefits, tuition waivers (partial), and unspecified assistantships also available. Financial award applicants required to submit FAFSA. *Faculty research:* Counseling and adolescent issues, child welfare, women's criminality, substance abuse, diversity, leadership and organization. Total annual research expenditures: $169,548. *Unit head:* Dr. Dorscine S. Spigner-Littles, Acting Director, 405-325-1756, Fax: 405-325-4405, E-mail: dslittles@ou.edu. *Application contact:* Jacob Smith, Admissions Coordinator, 405-325-1756, Fax: 405-325-1756, E-mail: jacosmith@ou.edu.

University of Oklahoma, Graduate College, College of Liberal Studies, Norman, OK 73019-0390. Offers administrative leadership (MLS); integrated studies (MLS); interprofessional human and health services (MLS); museum studies (MLS). Part-time programs available. Postbaccalaureate distance learning degree programs offered (no on-campus study). *Faculty:* 15 full-time (8 women), 26 part-time/adjunct (16 women). *Students:* 17 full-time (11 women), 326 part-time (169 women); includes 71 minority (33 African Americans, 24 American Indian/Alaska Native, 4 Asian Americans or Pacific Islanders, 10 Hispanic Americans). 126 applicants, 90% accepted, 75 enrolled. In 2009, 94 master's awarded. *Degree requirements:* For master's, thesis, research project, internship. *Entrance requirements:* For master's, minimum GPA of 3.0 in last 60 hours, writing sample. Additional exam requirements/recommendations for international students: Required—TOEFL (minimum score 550 paper-based; 213 computer-based). *Application deadline:* For fall admission, 7/15 priority date for domestic students, 4/1 for international students; for spring admission, 12/1 for domestic students, 9/1 for international students. Applications are processed on a rolling basis. Application fee: $40 ($90 for international students). Electronic applications accepted. *Expenses:* Tuition, state resident: full-time $3744; part-time $156 per credit hour. Tuition, nonresident: full-time $13,577; part-time $565.70 per credit hour. Required fees: $2415; $90.10 per credit hour. *Financial support:* In 2009–10, 163 students received support. Career-related internships or fieldwork, scholarships/grants, and tuition waivers (partial) available. Support available to part-time students. Financial award applicants required to submit FAFSA. *Faculty research:* Distance education, adult learning processes, student satisfaction, administrative leadership, organizations, museum studies. *Unit head:* Dr. James Pappas, Dean and Vice President for University Outreach, 405-325-6361, Fax: 405-325-7196, E-mail: jpappas@ou.edu. *Application contact:* Dr. Julie Raadschelders, MA Program Coordinator, 405-325-1061, Fax: 405-325-9632, E-mail: jraadschelders@ou.edu.

University of Phoenix–Maryland Campus, The Artemis School, College of Health and Human Services, Columbia, MD 21045-5424. Offers administration of justice and security (MS); health administration (MHA); health care education (MSN); health care management (MBA); nursing (MSN); psychology (MS); MSN/MBA; MSN/MHA. Evening/weekend programs available. *Degree requirements:* For master's, thesis (for some programs). *Entrance requirements:* For master's, minimum undergraduate GPA of 2.5, 3 years work experience. Additional exam requirements/recommendations for international students: Required—TOEFL (minimum score 550 paper-based; 213 computer-based; 79 iBT). Electronic applications accepted.

University of Phoenix–Richmond Campus, The Artemis School, College of Health and Human Services, Richmond, VA 23230. Offers administration of justice and security (MS); health administration (MHA); health care education (MSN); health care management (MBA); nursing (MSN); psychology (MS); MSN/MBA; MSN/MHA. Evening/weekend programs available. *Degree requirements:* For master's, thesis (for some programs). *Entrance requirements:* For master's, minimum undergraduate GPA of 2.5, 3 years work experience, current RN license for nursing programs. Additional exam requirements/recommendations for international students: Required—TOEFL (minimum score 500 paper-based; 213 computer-based; 79 iBT). Electronic applications accepted.

Upper Iowa University, Online Master's Programs, Fayette, IA 52142-1857. Offers accounting (MBA); corporate financial management (MBA); global business (MBA); health and human services (MPA); higher education administration (MHEA); homeland security (MPA); human resources management (MBA); justice administration (MPA); organizational development (MBA); public personnel management (MPA); quality management (MBA). MBA also available at Madison, WI campus. Part-time programs available. Postbaccalaureate distance learning degree programs offered (no on-campus study). *Faculty:* 3 full-time (0 women), 66 part-time/adjunct (27 women). *Students:* 723 full-time (442 women). *Degree requirements:* For master's, research project. *Entrance requirements:* For master's, GMAT, GRE, or minimum GPA of 2.7 during last 60 hours. Additional exam requirements/recommendations for international students: Required—TOEFL (minimum score 570 paper-based; 230 computer-based). *Application deadline:* Applications are processed on a rolling basis. Application fee: $50. Electronic applications accepted. *Expenses:* Tuition: Full-time $6948; part-time $386 per credit hour. *Financial support:* Available to part-time students. Applicants required to submit FAFSA. *Faculty research:* Total quality management, CQI, teams, organization culture and climate, management. *Application contact:* David Hannum, Admissions Advisor, 800-603-3756, E-mail: hannumd@uiu.edu.

Human Services

Walden University, Graduate Programs, School of Counseling and Social Service, Minneapolis, MN 55401. Offers counselor education and supervision (PhD), including consultation, counseling and social change, forensic mental health counseling, general program, nonprofit management and leadership, trauma and crisis; human services (PhD), including clinical social work, counseling, criminal justice, family studies and intervention strategies, general program, human services administration, self-designed, social policy analysis and planning; marriage, couple, and family counseling (MS), including forensic counseling, trauma and crisis counseling; mental health counseling (MS), including forensic counseling. Part-time and evening/weekend programs available. Postbaccalaureate distance learning degree programs offered (minimal on-campus study). *Faculty:* 13 full-time, 78 part-time/adjunct. *Students:* 1,932 full-time (1,624 women), 210 part-time (181 women); includes 945 minority (817 African Americans, 24 American Indian/Alaska Native, 24 Asian Americans or Pacific Islanders, 80 Hispanic Americans), 34 international. Average age 39. In 2009, 55 master's, 5 doctorates awarded. *Degree requirements:* For master's, residency (for some programs); for doctorate, thesis/dissertation, residency. *Entrance requirements:* For master's, bachelor's degree or equivalent in related field, minimum GPA of 2.5; for doctorate, master's degree or equivalent in related field; minimum GPA of 3.0; official transcripts; three years' related professional/academic experience (preferred); access to computer and Internet. Additional exam requirements/recommendations for international students: Required—TOEFL (minimum score 550 paper-based; 213 computer-based), IELTS (minimum score 6.5), or Michigan English Language Assessment Battery (minimum score 82). *Application deadline:* Applications are processed on a rolling basis. Application fee: $50. Electronic applications accepted. *Expenses:* Tuition: Full-time $13,665; part-time $560 per credit. Required fees: $1375. Tuition and fees vary according to course load, degree level and program. *Financial support:* In 2009–10, 200 students received support; fellowships, Federal Work-Study, scholarships/grants, unspecified assistantships, and family tuition reduction, active duty/veteran tuition reduction, group tuition reduction, interest-free payment plans available. Support available to part-time students. Financial award applicants required to submit FAFSA. *Unit head:* Dr. Savitri Dixon-Saxon, Associate Dean, 800-925-3368. *Application contact:* Jennifer Hall, Director of Enrollment, 866-4-WALDEN, E-mail: info@waldenu.edu.

Wayne State University, Graduate School, Interdisciplinary Program in Developmental Disabilities, Detroit, MI 48202. Offers Certificate. *Entrance requirements:* Additional exam requirements/recommendations for international students: Required—TOEFL (minimum score

550 paper-based; 213 computer-based); Recommended—TWE (minimum score 6). Electronic applications accepted.

West Virginia University, Eberly College of Arts and Sciences, School of Applied Social Sciences, Division of Social Work, Morgantown, WV 26506. Offers aging and health care (MSW); children and families (MSW); community mental health (MSW); community organization and social administration (MSW); direct (clinical) social work practice (MSW). *Accreditation:* CSWE. Part-time programs available. *Degree requirements:* For master's, fieldwork. *Entrance requirements:* For master's, GRE, minimum GPA of 2.75, 2 letters of reference. Additional exam requirements/recommendations for international students: Required—TOEFL. *Faculty research:* Rural and small town social work practice, gerontology, health and mental health, welfare reform, child welfare.

Wichita State University, Graduate School, Fairmount College of Liberal Arts and Sciences, School of Community Affairs, Wichita, KS 67260. Offers criminal justice (MA); gerontology (MA). Part-time programs available. *Expenses:* Tuition, state resident: full-time $4247; part-time $235.95 per credit hour. Tuition, nonresident: full-time $11,171; part-time $620.60 per credit hour. Required fees: $34; $3.60 per credit hour. $17 per term. Tuition and fees vary according to campus/location and program. *Unit head:* Dr. Michael Birzer, Director, 316-978-7200, Fax: 316-978-3626, E-mail: michael.birzer@wichita.edu. *Application contact:* Dr. Michael Birzer, Director, 316-978-7200, Fax: 316-978-3626, E-mail: michael.birzer@wichita.edu.

Wilmington University, College of Social and Behavioral Sciences, New Castle, DE 19720-6491. Offers administration of human services (MS); administration of justice (MS); community counseling (MS). *Accreditation:* ACA. Part-time and evening/weekend programs available. *Entrance requirements:* Additional exam requirements/recommendations for international students: Required—TOEFL (minimum score 500 paper-based; 173 computer-based). Electronic applications accepted.

Youngstown State University, Graduate School, Bitonte College of Health and Human Services, Department of Health Professions, Youngstown, OH 44555-0001. Offers health and human services (MHHS); public health (MPH). *Accreditation:* NAACLS. Part-time and evening/weekend programs available. *Degree requirements:* For master's, thesis optional. *Entrance requirements:* For master's, GRE General Test, minimum GPA of 3.0. Additional exam requirements/recommendations for international students: Required—TOEFL. *Faculty research:* Drug prevention, multiskilling in health care, organizational behavior, health care management, health behaviors, research management.

Social Work

Abilene Christian University, Graduate School, College of Education and Human Services, School of Social Work, Abilene, TX 79699-9100. Offers MSSW. Part-time programs available. *Faculty:* 8 part-time/adjunct (3 women). *Students:* 24 full-time (21 women), 2 part-time (1 woman); includes 7 minority (3 African Americans, 4 Hispanic Americans), 4 international. 26 applicants, 69% accepted, 18 enrolled. In 2009, 13 master's awarded. *Entrance requirements:* For master's, GRE if undergraduate GPA less than 3.0. *Application deadline:* For fall admission, 4/1 priority date for domestic students; for spring admission, 11/1 for domestic students. Applications are processed on a rolling basis. Application fee: $40. Electronic applications accepted. *Expenses:* Tuition: Full-time $11,520; part-time $640 per hour. Required fees: $1090; $53.50 per hour. $10 per term. Tuition and fees vary according to program. *Financial support:* In 2009–10, 21 students received support, including 2 research assistantships with partial tuition reimbursements available (averaging $5,800 per year); career-related internships or fieldwork, Federal Work-Study, and tuition waivers (partial) also available. Financial award application deadline: 4/1; financial award applicants required to submit FAFSA. *Unit head:* Dr. Stephanie Hamm, Director of Graduate Program, 325-674-2072, Fax: 325-674-6525, E-mail: socialwork@acu.edu. *Application contact:* William Horn, Graduate Admissions Counselor, 325-674-2656, Fax: 325-674-6717, E-mail: gradinfo@acu.edu.

Adelphi University, School of Social Work, Garden City, NY 11530-0701. Offers social welfare (DSW); social work (MSW, PhD). *Accreditation:* CSWE (one or more programs are accredited). Part-time and evening/weekend programs available. *Faculty:* 28 full-time (20 women), 61 part-time/adjunct (45 women). *Students:* 217 full-time (187 women), 646 part-time (564 women); includes 377 minority (253 African Americans, 4 American Indian/Alaska Native, 21 Asian Americans or Pacific Islanders, 99 Hispanic Americans), 5 international. Average age 35. 591 applicants, 78% accepted, 294 enrolled. In 2009, 307 master's, 7 doctorates awarded. *Degree requirements:* For master's, field internships; for doctorate, thesis/dissertation. *Entrance requirements:* For master's, minimum undergraduate GPA of 3.0, paid or volunteer work experience, 3 letters of recommendation, interview; for doctorate, GRE, MSW with minimum GPA of 3.3, 3 years post-MSW work experience, 3 letters of reference, 3 examples of professional writing. Additional exam requirements/recommendations for international students: Required—TOEFL (minimum score 550 paper-based; 213 computer-based; 80 iBT). *Application deadline:* For fall admission, 4/1 for international students; for spring admission, 12/1 for domestic students, 11/1 for international students. Application fee: $50. Electronic applications accepted. *Expenses:* Tuition: Full-time $28,340; part-time $830 per credit. Required fees: $600; $250 per credit. Full-time tuition and fees vary according to course load and program. *Financial support:* In 2009–10, 23 teaching assistantships (averaging $3,888 per year) were awarded; career-related internships or fieldwork, Federal Work-Study, institutionally sponsored loans, scholarships/grants, traineeships, tuition waivers (full and partial), and unspecified assistantships also available. Financial award application deadline: 2/15; financial award applicants required to submit FAFSA. *Faculty research:* Services for rape victims, immigrants research methods, remarriage and step families, social health indicators. *Unit head:* Dr. Andrew Safyer, Dean, 516-877-4300, E-mail: asafyer@adelphi.edu. *Application contact:* Christine Murphy, Director of Admissions, 516-877-3050, Fax: 516-877-3039, E-mail: graduateadmissions@adelphi.edu.

Alabama Agricultural and Mechanical University, School of Graduate Studies, School of Arts and Sciences, Department of Social Work, Huntsville, AL 35811. Offers MSW. *Accreditation:* CSWE. *Degree requirements:* For master's, thesis. *Entrance requirements:* For master's, GRE General Test, portfolio. Additional exam requirements/recommendations for international students: Required—TOEFL (minimum score 500 paper-based; 173 computer-based; 61 iBT). Electronic applications accepted.

American Jewish University, Graduate School, David Lieber School of Graduate Studies, Program in Jewish Communal Studies, Bel Air, CA 90077-1599. Offers MAJCS. *Degree requirements:* For master's, thesis. *Entrance requirements:* For master's, GMAT or GRE General Test, interview.

Andrews University, School of Graduate Studies, College of Arts and Sciences, Department of Social Work, Berrien Springs, MI 49104. Offers MSW. *Accreditation:* CSWE. *Students:* 28 full-time (25 women), 3 part-time (2 women); includes 15 minority (10 African Americans, 5 Hispanic Americans), 4 international. Average age 32. 48 applicants, 63% accepted, 15 enrolled. In 2009, 24 master's awarded. *Entrance requirements:* For master's, GRE. Additional exam requirements/recommendations for international students: Required—TOEFL (minimum score 550 paper-based). *Application deadline:* Applications are processed on a rolling basis. Application fee: $40. *Unit head:* Dr. Curtis VanderWaal, Chair, 269-471-6196. *Application contact:* Carolyn Hurst, Supervisor of Graduate Admission, 800-253-2874, Fax: 269-471-6321, E-mail: graduate@andrews.edu.

Appalachian State University, Cratis D. Williams Graduate School, Department of Social Work, Boone, NC 28608. Offers MSW. *Accreditation:* CSWE. Part-time and evening/weekend programs available. Postbaccalaureate distance learning degree programs offered (no on-campus study). *Faculty:* 5 full-time (4 women), 5 part-time/adjunct (all women). *Students:* 25 full-time (22 women), 31 part-time (23 women). 76 applicants, 63% accepted, 34 enrolled. *Degree requirements:* For master's, comprehensive exam. *Entrance requirements:* For master's, GRE General Test, 3 letters of recommendation. Additional exam requirements/recommendations for international students: Required—TOEFL (minimum score 550 paper-based; 230 computer-based; 79 iBT), IELTS (minimum score 6.5). *Application deadline:* For fall admission, 3/1 for domestic students, 2/1 for international students; for spring admission, 7/1 for international students. Applications are processed on a rolling basis. Application fee: $50. Electronic applications accepted. *Expenses:* Tuition, state resident: full-time $2960. Tuition, nonresident: full-time $14,051. Required fees: $2320. *Financial support:* In 2009–10, 6 research assistantships (averaging $8,000 per year) were awarded; career-related internships or fieldwork, Federal Work-Study, scholarships/grants, and unspecified assistantships also available. Financial award application deadline: 4/1; financial award applicants required to submit FAFSA. *Unit head:* Dr. Gail Leedy, Chairperson, E-mail: leedyg@appstate.edu. *Application contact:* Dr. Julie Sprinkle, Graduate Program Director, 828-262-6399, E-mail: sprinkleje@appstate.edu.

Arizona State University, Graduate College, College of Public Programs, School of Social Work, Tempe, AZ 85287. Offers MSW, PhD. *Accreditation:* CSWE (one or more programs are accredited). *Degree requirements:* For doctorate, thesis/dissertation. *Entrance requirements:* For master's, GRE or MAT.

Arkansas State University—Jonesboro, Graduate School, College of Nursing and Health Professions, Department of Social Work, Jonesboro, State University, AR 72467. Offers MSW. Part-time programs available. *Faculty:* 7 full-time (5 women). *Students:* 8 full-time (7 women), 41 part-time (40 women); includes 11 minority (10 African Americans, 1 Asian American or Pacific Islander). Average age 36. 63 applicants, 63% accepted, 37 enrolled. *Degree requirements:* For master's, comprehensive exam, thesis (for some programs). *Entrance requirements:* For master's, GRE or MAT, appropriate bachelor's degree, letters of reference, interview. Additional exam requirements/recommendations for international students: Required—TOEFL (minimum score 550 paper-based; 213 computer-based; 79 iBT), IELTS (minimum score 6). *Application deadline:* For fall admission, 7/1 for domestic and international students; for spring admission, 11/15 for domestic students, 11/13 for international students. Applications are processed on a rolling basis. Application fee: $30 ($40 for international students). Electronic applications accepted. *Expenses:* Contact institution. *Financial support:* In 2009–10, 3 students received support. Career-related internships or fieldwork, scholarships/grants, and unspecified assistantships available. Financial award application deadline: 7/1; financial award applicants required to submit FAFSA. *Unit head:* Dr. Barbara Turnage, Chair, 870-972-3984, Fax: 870-972-3987, E-mail: bturnage@astate.edu. *Application contact:* Dr. Andrew Sustich, Dean of the Graduate School, 870-972-3029, Fax: 870-972-3857, E-mail: sustich@astate.edu.

Asbury University, School of Graduate and Professional Studies, Master of Social Work Program, Wilmore, KY 40390-1198. Offers child and family services (MSW). *Faculty:* 6 full-time (3 women). *Students:* 36 full-time (24 women); includes 2 African Americans, 1 Hispanic American, 1 international. 27 applicants, 81% accepted, 20 enrolled. *Degree requirements:* For master's, comprehensive exam, 954 praticum hours completed in agency. *Entrance requirements:* For master's, prerequisite courses in psychology, sociology, and statistics. Additional exam requirements/recommendations for international students: Required—TOEFL. *Application deadline:* Applications are processed on a rolling basis. Application fee: $25. Electronic applications accepted. *Expenses:* Contact institution. *Financial support:* Applicants required to submit FAFSA. *Faculty research:* Integration of faith and practice, survivors of family violence, program evaluation, cross-cultural counseling. *Unit head:* Dr. William Descoteaux, Program Director, 859-858-3511 Ext. 2206, Fax: 859-858-3921, E-mail: bill.descoteaux@asbury.edu. *Application contact:* Aaron D. Wilkinson, Coordinator of Admissions and Marketing, 859-858-3511 Ext. 25256, Fax: 859-858-3921, E-mail: aaron.wilkinson@asbury.edu.

Augsburg College, Program in Social Work, Minneapolis, MN 55454-1351. Offers MSW. *Accreditation:* CSWE. Part-time and evening/weekend programs available. *Degree requirements:* For master's, thesis optional. *Entrance requirements:* For master's, previous course work in human biology and statistics. *Expenses:* Tuition: Full-time $16,713; part-time $1857 per course. Required fees: $450; $50 per course. Tuition and fees vary according to course load and program.

Aurora University, College of Professional Studies, School of Social Work, Aurora, IL 60506-4892. Offers MSW. *Accreditation:* CSWE. Part-time and evening/weekend programs available. *Degree requirements:* For master's, thesis optional. *Entrance requirements:* For master's,

minimum GPA of 3.0. Additional exam requirements/recommendations for international students: Required—TOEFL (minimum score 550 paper-based; 213 computer-based). Electronic applications accepted. *Expenses:* Contact institution.

Austin Peay State University, College of Graduate Studies, College of Behavioral and Health Sciences, Department of Social Work, Clarksville, TN 37044. Offers MSW. Part-time and evening/weekend programs available. *Faculty:* 2 full-time (1 woman). *Students:* 9 full-time (8 women), 3 part-time (all women); includes 4 minority (3 African Americans, 1 Hispanic American). Average age 35. 24 applicants, 63% accepted, 12 enrolled. *Degree requirements:* For master's, internship of 400-500 hours. *Entrance requirements:* For master's, GRE General Test, letters of recommendation. Additional exam requirements/recommendations for international students: Required—TOEFL (minimum score 500 paper-based; 173 computer-based). *Application deadline:* For fall admission, 3/1 priority date for domestic students. Application fee: $25. *Expenses:* Tuition, state resident: full-time $6160; part-time $608 per credit hour. Tuition, nonresident: full-time $17,080; part-time $854 per credit hour. Required fees: $1224; $61.20 per credit hour. *Financial support:* In 2009–10, 1 student received support, including 1 research assistantship (averaging $5,184 per year); career-related internships or fieldwork, Federal Work-Study, institutionally sponsored loans, scholarships/grants, and unspecified assistantships also available. Support available to part-time students. *Unit head:* Joyce Hargrove, Chair, 931-221-7730, E-mail: hargrovej@apsu.edu. *Application contact:* Dr. Dixie Dennis, Dean, College of Graduate Studies, 931-221-7662, Fax: 931-221-7641, E-mail: dennisdi@apsu.edu.

Barry University, School of Social Work, Doctoral Program in Social Work, Miami Shores, FL 33161-6695. Offers PhD. Part-time and evening/weekend programs available. *Degree requirements:* For doctorate, thesis/dissertation. *Entrance requirements:* For doctorate, GRE, MSW from an accredited school of social work, 2 years of professional experience. Electronic applications accepted. *Faculty research:* Family and children services, homelessness, gerontology, school social work.

Barry University, School of Social Work, Master's Program in Social Work, Miami Shores, FL 33161-6695. Offers MSW. *Accreditation:* CSWE. Part-time and evening/weekend programs available. *Degree requirements:* For master's, fieldwork. *Entrance requirements:* For master's, minimum GPA of 3.0, minimum of 30 liberal arts credits. Additional exam requirements/recommendations for international students: Required—TOEFL (minimum score 550 paper-based; 173 computer-based). Electronic applications accepted. *Faculty research:* Family and children services, homelessness, gerontology, school social work.

Baylor University, School of Social Work, Waco, TX 76798-7320. Offers MSW, M Div/MSW, MTS/MSW. *Accreditation:* CSWE. Part-time programs available. *Faculty:* 11 full-time (5 women), 13 part-time/adjunct (7 women). *Students:* 115 full-time (94 women), 7 part-time (6 women); includes 28 minority (10 African Americans, 3 American Indian/Alaska Native, 5 Asian Americans or Pacific Islanders, 10 Hispanic Americans), 7 international. Average age 27. 190 applicants, 72% accepted, 77 enrolled. In 2009, 57 master's awarded. *Degree requirements:* For master's, research project. *Entrance requirements:* For master's, writing sample. Additional exam requirements/recommendations for international students: Required—TOEFL (minimum score 550 paper-based; 213 computer-based; 80 iBT) or IELTS (minimum score 6.5). *Application deadline:* For spring admission, 3/15 for domestic and international students. Applications are processed on a rolling basis. Application fee: $45. Electronic applications accepted. *Financial support:* In 2009–10, 114 students received support, including 12 research assistantships with tuition reimbursements available (averaging $6,800 per year); career-related internships or fieldwork, Federal Work-Study, institutionally sponsored loans, scholarships/grants, traineeships, tuition waivers (full and partial), and unspecified assistantships also available. Support available to part-time students. Financial award application deadline: 6/1; financial award applicants required to submit FAFSA. *Faculty research:* Healthy marriage, family literacy, Alzheimer's and grief, congregational community service, clergy sexual abuse, older volunteers. Total annual research expenditures: $533,412. *Unit head:* Dr. Dennis Myers, Associate Dean for Graduate Studies, 254-710-6404, E-mail: dennis_myers@baylor.edu. *Application contact:* Tracey Kelley, Director of Recruitment/Career Services, 254-710-4479, Fax: 254-710-6455, E-mail: tracey_kelley@baylor.edu.

Boise State University, Graduate College, College of Social Sciences and Public Affairs, School of Social Work, Boise, ID 83725-0399. Offers MSW. *Accreditation:* CSWE. Part-time programs available. *Entrance requirements:* For master's, GRE General Test, minimum GPA of 3.0. Electronic applications accepted. *Expenses:* Tuition, state resident: full-time $3106; part-time $209 per credit. Tuition, nonresident: part-time $284 per credit.

Boston College, Graduate School of Social Work, Chestnut Hill, MA 02467-3800. Offers MSW, PhD, JD/MSW, MSW/MA, MSW/MBA. *Accreditation:* CSWE (one or more programs are accredited). Part-time programs available. *Faculty:* 15 full-time (9 women), 44 part-time/adjunct (32 women). *Students:* 386 full-time (340 women), 138 part-time (121 women); includes 100 minority (42 African Americans, 3 American Indian/Alaska Native, 27 Asian Americans or Pacific Islanders, 28 Hispanic Americans), 19 international. 779 applicants, 66% accepted, 210 enrolled. In 2009, 188 master's, 6 doctorates awarded. *Degree requirements:* For master's, 2 internships; for doctorate, comprehensive exam, thesis/dissertation. *Entrance requirements:* For doctorate, GRE. Additional exam requirements/recommendations for international students: Required—TOEFL (minimum score 550 paper-based; 213 computer-based). *Application deadline:* For fall admission, 3/1 for domestic students. Applications are processed on a rolling basis. Application fee: $40. *Expenses:* Contact institution. *Financial support:* In 2009–10, 401 students received support, including 16 fellowships with full tuition reimbursements available (averaging $18,000 per year), 2 research assistantships (averaging $5,000 per year); teaching assistantships, career-related internships or fieldwork, Federal Work-Study, institutionally sponsored loans, scholarships/grants, traineeships, health care benefits, tuition waivers (partial), and unspecified assistantships also available. Support available to part-time students. Financial award applicants required to submit FAFSA. *Faculty research:* Well-being of children and families, health and mental health issues, aging and work, consumer-directed services, international social work practice. Total annual research expenditures: $4 million. *Unit head:* Dr. Alberto Godenzi, Dean, 617-552-0866, Fax: 617-552-2374, E-mail: godenzi@bc.edu. *Application contact:* Dr. William Howard, Director of Admission, 617-552-4024, Fax: 617-552-1690, E-mail: william.howard@bc.edu.

Boston University, Graduate School of Arts and Sciences, Interdisciplinary Program in Sociology and Social Work, Boston, MA 02215. Offers PhD. *Students:* 18 full-time (14 women), 7 part-time (6 women); includes 7 minority (2 African Americans, 2 Asian Americans or Pacific Islanders, 3 Hispanic Americans), 2 international. Average age 37. 30 applicants, 30% accepted, 3 enrolled. *Degree requirements:* For doctorate, one foreign language, comprehensive exam, thesis/dissertation, critical essay. *Entrance requirements:* For doctorate, GRE General Test or MAT, sample of written work. Additional exam requirements/recommendations for international students: Required—TOEFL. *Application deadline:* For fall admission, 1/15 for domestic and international students. Application fee: $70. Electronic applications accepted. *Expenses:* Tuition: Full-time $37,910; part-time $1184 per credit hour. Required fees: $386; $40 per semester. Part-time tuition and fees vary according to class time, course level, degree level and program. *Financial support:* In 2009–10, 22 students received support, including 2 research assistantships with full tuition reimbursements available (averaging $18,400 per year); career-related internships or fieldwork, Federal Work-Study, and scholarships/grants also available. Support available to part-time students. Financial award application deadline: 1/15; financial award applicants required to submit FAFSA. *Faculty research:* Mental health, child welfare, aging, substance abuse. *Unit head:* Sara Bachman, Director, 617-353-1415, Fax: 617-353-5612, E-mail: sbachman@bu.edu. *Application contact:* Brook Davis, Staff Coordinator, 617-353-9675, Fax: 617-353-5612, E-mail: davis@bu.edu.

Boston University, School of Social Work, Boston, MA 02215. Offers clinical practice with groups (MSW); clinical practice with individuals and families (MSW); macro social work practice (MSW); social work and sociology (PhD); D Min/MSW; M Div/MSW; MSW/Ed M; MSW/Ed M; MSW/MPH; MSW/MTS. *Accreditation:* CSWE (one or more programs are accredited). Part-time programs available. *Faculty:* 22 full-time (16 women), 29 part-time/adjunct (23 women). *Students:* 187 full-time (162 women), 183 part-time (157 women); includes 57 minority (21 African Americans, 13 Asian Americans or Pacific Islanders, 23 Hispanic Americans), 6 international. Average age 29. 685 applicants, 81% accepted, 176 enrolled. In 2009, 123 master's awarded. *Degree requirements:* For doctorate, one foreign language, thesis/dissertation, critical essay. *Entrance requirements:* For master's, minimum GPA of 3.0, GRE General Test, or MAT; for doctorate, GRE General Test or MAT, writing sample. Additional exam requirements/recommendations for international students: Required—TOEFL (minimum score 550 paper-based; 213 computer-based; 80 iBT). *Application deadline:* For fall admission, 3/1 for domestic and international students. Applications are processed on a rolling basis. Application fee: $70. Electronic applications accepted. *Expenses:* Contact institution. *Financial support:* In 2009–10, 1 research assistantship with full tuition reimbursement (averaging $8,000 per year) was awarded; career-related internships or fieldwork, Federal Work-Study, institutionally sponsored loans, and scholarships/grants also available. Support available to part-time students. Financial award application deadline: 3/1; financial award applicants required to submit FAFSA. *Faculty research:* Health and aging, child and adolescent substance abuse, mental health. Total annual research expenditures: $1.3 million. *Unit head:* Gail Steketee, Dean, 617-353-3760, Fax: 617-353-5612. *Application contact:* Edward M. Greene, Director of Admissions, 617-353-3750, Fax: 617-353-5612, E-mail: busswad@bu.edu.

Bridgewater State University, School of Graduate Studies, School of Arts and Sciences, Department of Social Work, Bridgewater, MA 02325-0001. Offers MSW. *Accreditation:* CSWE.

Brigham Young University, Graduate Studies, College of Family, Home, and Social Sciences, School of Social Work, Provo, UT 84602-1001. Offers MSW. *Accreditation:* CSWE. *Faculty:* 9 full-time (5 women), 5 part-time/adjunct (4 women). *Students:* 79 full-time (55 women); includes 10 minority (1 African American, 3 Asian Americans or Pacific Islanders, 6 Hispanic Americans), 1 international. Average age 28. 130 applicants, 41% accepted, 38 enrolled. In 2009, 40 master's awarded. *Degree requirements:* For master's, thesis optional. *Entrance requirements:* Additional exam requirements/recommendations for international students: Required—TOEFL (minimum score 580 paper-based; 237 computer-based; 85 iBT), IELTS (minimum score 7). *Application deadline:* For fall admission, 1/15 for domestic and international students. Application fee: $50. Electronic applications accepted. *Expenses:* Tuition: Full-time $5580; part-time $301 per credit hour. Tuition and fees vary according to student's religious affiliation. *Financial support:* In 2009–10, 21 students received support, including 5 fellowships with tuition reimbursements available (averaging $5,420 per year), 14 research assistantships (averaging $2,300 per year); teaching assistantships, career-related internships or fieldwork, tuition waivers (partial), and administrative aides, paid field practicum also available. Financial award application deadline: 1/15. *Faculty research:* Adoptions, depression, spirituality, child welfare, marriage and family. Total annual research expenditures: $100,000. *Unit head:* Dr. Gordon E. Limb, Director, 801-422-3282, Fax: 801-422-0624, E-mail: socialwork@byu.edu. *Application contact:* Lisa Willey, Graduate Secretary, 801-422-5681, Fax: 801-422-0624, E-mail: lisa_willey@byu.edu.

Bryn Mawr College, Graduate School of Social Work and Social Research, Bryn Mawr, PA 19010. Offers MLSP, MSS, PhD. *Accreditation:* CSWE (one or more programs are accredited). Part-time and evening/weekend programs available. *Faculty:* 14 full-time (7 women), 16 part-time/adjunct (2 women). *Students:* 145 full-time (128 women), 73 part-time (65 women); includes 46 minority (39 African Americans, 5 Asian Americans or Pacific Islanders, 2 Hispanic Americans), 2 international. Average age 35. 182 applicants, 85% accepted, 91 enrolled. In 2009, 84 master's, 3 doctorates awarded. *Degree requirements:* For master's, fieldwork; for doctorate, comprehensive exam, thesis/dissertation. *Entrance requirements:* For master's, interview, 3 letters of reference; for doctorate, GRE General Test, interview, 3 letters of reference, master's degree. Additional exam requirements/recommendations for international students: Required—TOEFL (minimum score 620 paper-based). *Application deadline:* For fall admission, 3/31 priority date for domestic and international students. Applications are processed on a rolling basis. Application fee: $50. Electronic applications accepted. *Expenses:* Contact institution. *Financial support:* In 2009–10, 193 students received support, including 29 fellowships with full and partial tuition reimbursements available (averaging $2,517 per year), 1 research assistantship with full and partial tuition reimbursement available (averaging $9,333 per year), 7 teaching assistantships with full and partial tuition reimbursements available (averaging $8,680 per year); career-related internships or fieldwork, Federal Work-Study, institutionally sponsored loans, scholarships/grants, tuition waivers (full and partial), and dissertation award (PhD) also available. Support available to part-time students. Financial award application deadline: 3/1; financial award applicants required to submit FAFSA. *Faculty research:* Ethical issues, children and adolescents, poverty, mental health, child and family welfare. Total annual research expenditures: $7.1 million. *Unit head:* Dr. Marcia L. Martin, Director, 610-520-2603, Fax: 610-520-2613, E-mail: mmartin@brynmawr.edu. *Application contact:* Nancy J. Kirby, Assistant Dean and Director of Admissions, 610-520-2601, Fax: 610-520-2655, E-mail: swadmiss@brynmawr.edu.

California State University, Bakersfield, Division of Graduate Studies, School of Humanities and Social Sciences, Program in Social Work, Bakersfield, CA 93311. Offers MSW. *Accreditation:* CSWE.

California State University, Chico, Graduate School, College of Behavioral and Social Sciences, School of Social Work, Chico, CA 95929-0722. Offers MSW. *Accreditation:* CSWE. Evening/weekend programs available. *Students:* 71 full-time (61 women), 43 part-time (34 women); includes 34 minority (2 African Americans, 3 American Indian/Alaska Native, 7 Asian Americans or Pacific Islanders, 22 Hispanic Americans), 1 international. Average age 32. 141 applicants, 62% accepted, 68 enrolled. In 2009, 64 master's awarded. *Entrance requirements:* For master's, 3 letters of recommendation on departmental form. Additional exam requirements/recommendations for international students: Required—TOEFL (minimum score 550 paper-based; 213 computer-based; 80 iBT), IELTS (minimum score 6.5). *Application deadline:* For fall admission, 3/1 for domestic and international students. Application fee: $55. Electronic applications accepted. *Unit head:* Jean Schuldberg, Graduate Coordinator, 530-898-4187. *Application contact:* School of Graduate, International, and Interdisciplinary Studies, 530-898-6880, Fax: 530-898-6889, E-mail: grin@csuchico.edu.

California State University, Dominguez Hills, College of Professional Studies, School of Health and Human Services, Program in Social Work, Carson, CA 90747-0001. Offers MSW. *Accreditation:* CSWE. Part-time and evening/weekend programs available. *Faculty:* 8 full-time (6 women), 5 part-time/adjunct (3 women). *Students:* 80 full-time (67 women), 58 part-time (45 women); includes 111 minority (54 African Americans, 17 Asian Americans or Pacific Islanders, 40 Hispanic Americans). Average age 33. 229 applicants, 44% accepted, 54 enrolled. In 2009, 15 master's awarded. *Degree requirements:* For master's, thesis. *Entrance requirements:* For master's, minimum GPA of 2.75 in last 60 units; 3 courses in behavioral science, 2 in humanities, 1 in English composition, 1 in elementary statistics, and 1 in human biology. *Application deadline:* For fall admission, 4/30 for domestic students. Applications are processed on a rolling basis. *Expenses:* Tuition, nonresident: full-time $6696; part-time $372 per unit. Required fees: $5946; $1752 per semester. *Faculty research:* HIV/AIDS, community capacity, program evaluation. *Unit head:* Dr. Larry Ortiz, Professor and Director, 310-243-5464, E-mail: lortiz@csudh.edu. *Application contact:* Susan Nakaoka, Director of Admissions, 310-243-2181, Fax: 310-217-6800, E-mail: snakaoka@csudh.edu.

California State University, East Bay, Graduate Programs, College of Letters, Arts, and Social Sciences, Department of Social Work, Hayward, CA 94542-3000. Offers MSW. *Accreditation:* CSWE. *Faculty:* 10 full-time (7 women), 9 part-time/adjunct (6 women). *Students:* 167 full-time (136 women), 68 part-time (58 women); includes 149 minority (60 African Americans, 2 American Indian/Alaska Native, 31 Asian Americans or Pacific Islanders, 56 Hispanic Americans). Average age 32. 366 applicants, 49% accepted, 122 enrolled. In 2009, 103 master's awarded. *Entrance requirements:* For master's, minimum GPA of 2.8; course in statistics; course in human biology, physiology or anatomy; liberal arts or social science background. Additional exam requirements/recommendations for international students:

Social Work

California State University, East Bay (continued)

Required—TOEFL (minimum score 550 paper-based; 213 computer-based). *Application deadline:* For fall admission, 3/15 for domestic and international students. Applications are processed on a rolling basis. Application fee: $55. Electronic applications accepted. *Financial support:* Fellowships, career-related internships or fieldwork, Federal Work-Study, institutionally sponsored loans, and scholarships/grants available. Support available to part-time students. Financial award application deadline: 3/1; financial award applicants required to submit FAFSA. *Unit head:* Dr. Dianne Rush Woods, Chair, 510-885-4916, Fax: 510-885-7580, E-mail: dianne.woods@csueastbay.edu. *Application contact:* Donna Wiley, Interim Associate Director, 510-885-2928, Fax: 510-885-4777, E-mail: donna.wiley@csueastbay.edu.

California State University, Fresno, Division of Graduate Studies, College of Health and Human Services, Department of Social Work Education, Fresno, CA 93740-8027. Offers MSW. *Accreditation:* CSWE. Part-time and evening/weekend programs available. *Degree requirements:* For master's, thesis or alternative. *Entrance requirements:* For master's, GRE General Test, minimum GPA of 2.5. Additional exam requirements/recommendations for international students: Required—TOEFL. Electronic applications accepted. *Faculty research:* Children at risk, international cooperation, child welfare training, nutrition.

California State University, Fullerton, Graduate Studies, College of Health and Human Development, Program of Social Work, Fullerton, CA 92834-9480. Offers MSW. Part-time programs available. *Students:* 68 full-time (63 women), 14 part-time (11 women); includes 48 minority (4 African Americans, 12 Asian Americans or Pacific Islanders, 32 Hispanic Americans), 2 international. Average age 29. 213 applicants, 25% accepted, 46 enrolled. In 2009, 18 master's awarded. *Entrance requirements:* For master's, minimum GPA of 3.0 for last 60 semester or 90 quarter units. Application fee: $55. *Expenses:* Tuition, nonresident: full-time $11,160; part-time $373 per credit. Required fees: $1440 per term. Tuition and fees vary according to course load, degree level and program. *Financial support:* Career-related internships or fieldwork, Federal Work-Study, institutionally sponsored loans, and scholarships/grants available. Support available to part-time students. Financial award application deadline: 3/1; financial award applicants required to submit FAFSA. *Unit head:* Dr. David Cherin, Director, 657-278-2790. *Application contact:* Admissions/Applications, 657-278-2371.

California State University, Long Beach, Graduate Studies, College of Health and Human Services, Department of Social Work, Long Beach, CA 90840. Offers MSW. *Accreditation:* CSWE. Part-time and evening/weekend programs available. Postbaccalaureate distance learning degree programs offered (no on-campus study). *Faculty:* 35 full-time (22 women), 20 part-time/adjunct (18 women). *Students:* 252 full-time (216 women), 215 part-time (186 women); includes 332 minority (57 African Americans, 5 American Indian/Alaska Native, 45 Asian Americans or Pacific Islanders, 225 Hispanic Americans), 5 international. Average age 32. 763 applicants, 39% accepted, 229 enrolled. *Degree requirements:* For master's, thesis. *Application deadline:* For fall admission, 3/1 for domestic students. Applications are processed on a rolling basis. Application fee: $55. Electronic applications accepted. *Expenses:* Required fees: $1802 per semester. Part-time tuition and fees vary according to course load. *Financial support:* Federal Work-Study, institutionally sponsored loans, and scholarships/grants available. Financial award application deadline: 3/2. *Unit head:* Dr. John Oliver, Director, 562-985-5655, Fax: 562-985-5514, E-mail: joliver@csulb.edu. *Application contact:* Dr. Rebecca Lopez, Coordinator of Academic Programs, 562-985-5655, Fax: 562-985-5514, E-mail: rlopez@csulb.edu.

California State University, Los Angeles, Graduate Studies, College of Health and Human Services, School of Social Work, Los Angeles, CA 90032-8530. Offers MSW. *Accreditation:* CSWE. *Faculty:* 11 full-time (8 women), 24 part-time/adjunct (17 women). *Students:* 182 full-time (148 women), 72 part-time (56 women); includes 177 minority (19 African Americans, 27 Asian Americans or Pacific Islanders, 131 Hispanic Americans), 13 international. Average age 32. 306 applicants, 100% accepted, 103 enrolled. In 2009, 100 master's awarded. *Entrance requirements:* Additional exam requirements/recommendations for international students: Required—TOEFL (minimum score 500 paper-based; 173 computer-based). *Application deadline:* For fall admission, 5/1 for domestic and international students. Applications are processed on a rolling basis. Application fee: $55. *Financial support:* Application deadline: 3/1. *Unit head:* Dr. Karin Elliott-Brown, Chair, 323-343-4680, Fax: 323-343-5009, E-mail: kbrown5@calstatela.edu. *Application contact:* Dr. Cheryl L. Ney, Associate Vice President for Academic Affairs and Dean of Graduate Studies, 323-343-3820, Fax: 323-343-5653, E-mail: cney@cslanet.calstatela.edu.

California State University, Northridge, Graduate Studies, College of Social and Behavioral Sciences, Department of Social Work, Northridge, CA 91330. Offers MSW. Part-time programs available. *Faculty:* 6 full-time (5 women), 15 part-time/adjunct (10 women). *Entrance requirements:* For master's, GRE (if cumulative undergraduate GPA less than 3.0). *Application deadline:* For fall admission, 1/15 for domestic students. *Unit head:* Dr. James T. Decker, Chair, 818-677-7630. *Application contact:* Dr. James T. Decker, Chair, 818-677-7630.

California State University, Sacramento, Graduate Studies, College of Health and Human Services, Division of Social Work, Sacramento, CA 95819. Offers family and children's services (MSW); health care (MSW); mental health (MSW); social justice and corrections (MSW). *Accreditation:* CSWE. *Degree requirements:* For master's, thesis or alternative, writing proficiency exam. *Entrance requirements:* For master's, minimum GPA of 2.5 during previous 2 years of course work. Additional exam requirements/recommendations for international students: Required—TOEFL. Electronic applications accepted.

California State University, San Bernardino, Graduate Studies, College of Social and Behavioral Sciences, Department of Social Work, San Bernardino, CA 92407-2397. Offers MSW. *Accreditation:* CSWE. Part-time and evening/weekend programs available. *Faculty:* 7 full-time (5 women), 10 part-time/adjunct (3 women). *Students:* 169 full-time (142 women), 10 part-time (8 women); includes 104 minority (27 African Americans, 2 American Indian/Alaska Native, 5 Asian Americans or Pacific Islanders, 70 Hispanic Americans), 3 international. Average age 33. 224 applicants, 76% accepted, 117 enrolled. In 2009, 56 master's awarded. *Degree requirements:* For master's, field practicum, research project. *Entrance requirements:* For master's, minimum GPA of 2.75 in last 2 years of course work, liberal arts background. *Application deadline:* For fall admission, 8/31 priority date for domestic students. Application fee: $55. *Financial support:* Fellowships, research assistantships, career-related internships or fieldwork, Federal Work-Study, institutionally sponsored loans, and stipends for practicum available. Support available to part-time students. Financial award application deadline: 5/1. *Faculty research:* Addiction, computers in social work practice, minority issues, gerontology. *Unit head:* Laurie Smith, Director/Associate Professor/Graduate Coordinator, 909-537-3837, Fax: 909-537-7029, E-mail: lasmith@csusb.edu. *Application contact:* Olivia Rosas, Director of Admissions, 909-537-7577, Fax: 909-537-7034, E-mail: orosas@csusb.edu.

California State University, Stanislaus, College of Human and Health Sciences, Department of Social Work, Turlock, CA 95382. Offers MSW. *Accreditation:* CSWE. *Degree requirements:* For master's, thesis. *Entrance requirements:* For master's, minimum GPA of 3.0, 3 letters of reference. Electronic applications accepted. *Faculty research:* Mental health supervision, health issues on adulthood and aging, geriatric social work, effects of violence on children, rural mental health.

California University of Pennsylvania, School of Graduate Studies and Research, School of Education, Department of Social Work and Gerontology, California, PA 15419-1394. Offers social work (MSW). *Accreditation:* CSWE. Part-time programs available. *Degree requirements:* For master's, comprehensive exam. *Entrance requirements:* For master's, GRE, letters of reference. Additional exam requirements/recommendations for international students: Required—TOEFL. Electronic applications accepted. *Faculty research:* Social welfare and policy, housing and community development, health and mental health, Black Appalachian, aging.

Campbellsville University, Carver School of Social Work, Campbellsville, KY 42718-2799. Offers M Ed/MLIS. Evening/weekend programs available. Electronic applications accepted. *Expenses:* Tuition: Full-time $6750; part-time $375 per credit hour.

Carleton University, Faculty of Graduate Studies, Faculty of Public Affairs and Management, School of Social Work, Ottawa, ON K1S 5B6, Canada. Offers MSW. Part-time programs available. *Degree requirements:* For master's, thesis optional. *Entrance requirements:* For master's, basic research methods course. Additional exam requirements/recommendations for international students: Required—TOEFL. *Faculty research:* Social administration, program evaluation, history of Canadian social welfare, women's issues, education in social work.

Case Western Reserve University, Mandel School of Applied Social Sciences, Cleveland, OH 44106. Offers social administration (MSSA); social welfare (PhD); JD/MSSA; MSSA/MA; MSSA/MBA; MSSA/MNO. *Accreditation:* CSWE (one or more programs are accredited). Evening/weekend programs available. *Degree requirements:* For master's, fieldwork; for doctorate, thesis/dissertation. *Entrance requirements:* For master's, GRE General Test, MAT, or minimum GPA of 2.7; for doctorate, GRE General Test. Additional exam requirements/recommendations for international students: Required—TOEFL (minimum score 550 paper-based; 213 computer-based; 79 iBT). Electronic applications accepted. *Expenses:* Contact institution. *Faculty research:* Urban poverty, community social development, substance abuse, health, child welfare, aging, mental health.

The Catholic University of America, National Catholic School of Social Service, Washington, DC 20064. Offers clinical (MSW); combined (clinical and macro) (MSW); contract research and theory in clinical social work (PhD); macro (MSW), including policy analysis, social planning, social work management; research and theory in macro social work (PhD); MSW/JD. *Accreditation:* CSWE (one or more programs are accredited). Part-time programs available. *Faculty:* 19 full-time (16 women), 27 part-time/adjunct (22 women). *Students:* 108 full-time (93 women), 186 part-time (161 women); includes 67 minority (38 African Americans, 11 Asian Americans or Pacific Islanders, 18 Hispanic Americans), 35 international. Average age 34. 278 applicants, 81% accepted, 140 enrolled. In 2009, 80 master's, 4 doctorates awarded. *Degree requirements:* For master's, comprehensive exam, thesis or alternative; for doctorate, comprehensive exam, thesis/dissertation, minimum GPA of 3.0. *Entrance requirements:* For master's, GRE or MAT if undergraduate GPA less than 3.0, statement of purpose, official copies of academic transcripts, three letters of recommendation, resume; for doctorate, GRE, statement of purpose, official copies of academic transcripts, three letters of recommendation, resume, writing sample. Additional exam requirements/recommendations for international students: Required—TOEFL (minimum score 600 paper-based; 250 computer-based). *Application deadline:* For fall admission, 6/1 priority date for domestic students, 7/15 for international students; for spring admission, 11/30 priority date for domestic students, 10/15 for international students. Applications are processed on a rolling basis. Application fee: $55. Electronic applications accepted. *Expenses:* Contact institution. *Financial support:* Fellowships, research assistantships, teaching assistantships, Federal Work-Study, scholarships/grants, tuition waivers (full and partial), and unspecified assistantships available. Financial award application deadline: 2/1; financial award applicants required to submit FAFSA. *Faculty research:* International social development, spirituality and social work, advancement of children, youth, and families, global aging, community development and social justice, promotion of health, mental health well-being. Total annual research expenditures: $290,084. *Unit head:* Dr. James R. Zabora, Dean, 202-319-5454, Fax: 202-319-5093, E-mail: zabora@cua.edu. *Application contact:* Julie Schwing, Director of Graduate Admissions, 202-319-5057, Fax: 202-319-6533, E-mail: cua-admissions@cua.edu.

Chicago State University, School of Graduate and Professional Studies, College of Arts and Sciences, Program in Social Work, Chicago, IL 60628. Offers MSW. *Accreditation:* CSWE. Electronic applications accepted.

Clark Atlanta University, School of Social Work, Atlanta, GA 30314. Offers MSW, PhD. *Accreditation:* CSWE (one or more programs are accredited). Part-time programs available. *Faculty:* 9 full-time (7 women), 9 part-time/adjunct (4 women). *Students:* 121 full-time (107 women), 55 part-time (50 women); includes 156 minority (all African Americans), 2 international. Average age 32. 107 applicants, 90% accepted, 59 enrolled. In 2009, 54 master's, 1 doctorate awarded. Terminal master's awarded for partial completion of doctoral program. *Degree requirements:* For master's, one foreign language; for doctorate, one foreign language, comprehensive exam, thesis/dissertation. *Entrance requirements:* For master's, GRE General Test, minimum undergraduate GPA of 3.0; for doctorate, GRE General Test. Additional exam requirements/recommendations for international students: Required—TOEFL (minimum score 500 paper-based; 173 computer-based). *Application deadline:* For fall admission, 4/1 for domestic and international students; for spring admission, 11/1 for domestic and international students. Applications are processed on a rolling basis. Application fee: $40 ($55 for international students). Electronic applications accepted. *Expenses:* Tuition: Full-time $12,240; part-time $680 per credit hour. Required fees: $710; $355 per semester. *Financial support:* Fellowships, career-related internships or fieldwork, Federal Work-Study, scholarships/grants, and unspecified assistantships available. Support available to part-time students. Financial award application deadline: 4/30; financial award applicants required to submit FAFSA. *Unit head:* Dr. Vimala Pillari, Interim Dean, 404-880-8006, E-mail: rlyle@cau.edu. *Application contact:* Michelle Clark-Davis, Graduate Program Admissions, 404-880-6605, E-mail: cauadmissions@cau.edu.

Cleveland State University, College of Graduate Studies, College of Liberal Arts and Social Sciences, School of Social Work, Cleveland, OH 44115. Offers MSW. *Accreditation:* CSWE. Part-time and evening/weekend programs available. Postbaccalaureate distance learning degree programs offered (no on-campus study). *Entrance requirements:* For master's, 3 letters of reference. Additional exam requirements/recommendations for international students: Required—TOEFL (minimum score 525 paper-based; 197 computer-based); Recommended—IELTS (minimum score 6). *Faculty research:* Mental health, aging.

The College at Brockport, State University of New York, School of Education and Human Services, Greater Rochester Collaborative Master of Social Work Program, Brockport, NY 14420-2997. Offers social work (MSW), including family and community practice, interdisciplinary health practice. Part-time programs available. *Students:* 58 full-time (53 women), 72 part-time (56 women); includes 28 minority (22 African Americans, 2 Asian Americans or Pacific Islanders, 4 Hispanic Americans). 50 applicants, 100% accepted, 50 enrolled. In 2009, 42 master's awarded. *Degree requirements:* For master's, thesis or alternative. *Entrance requirements:* For master's, minimum GPA of 3.0, letters of recommendation. Additional exam requirements/recommendations for international students: Required—TOEFL (minimum score 550 paper-based; 213 computer-based; 79 iBT). *Application deadline:* For fall admission, 3/15 priority date for domestic and international students. Application fee: $50. Electronic applications accepted. *Expenses:* Contact institution. *Financial support:* Federal Work-Study, scholarships/grants, and unspecified assistantships available. Support available to part-time students. Financial award application deadline: 3/15; financial award applicants required to submit FAFSA. *Faculty research:* Care giving, child welfare, gerontological social work, home-school-community partnerships, domestic violence. *Unit head:* Dr. Carol Brownstein-Evans, Director, 585-395-8450, Fax: 585-395-8603, E-mail: grcmsw@brockport.edu. *Application contact:* Dr. Carol Brownstein-Evans, Director, 585-395-8450, Fax: 585-395-8603, E-mail: grcmsw@brockport.edu.

Colorado State University, Graduate School, College of Applied Human Sciences, School of Social Work, Fort Collins, CO 80523-1586. Offers MSW. *Accreditation:* CSWE. Part-time and evening/weekend programs available. Postbaccalaureate distance learning degree programs offered (minimal on-campus study). *Faculty:* 10 full-time (6 women), 1 part-time/adjunct (0 women). *Students:* 73 full-time (66 women), 37 part-time (33 women); includes 11 minority (1 African American, 2 American Indian/Alaska Native, 1 Asian American or Pacific Islander, 7 Hispanic Americans). Average age 31. 121 applicants, 36% accepted, 23 enrolled. In 2009, 79 master's awarded. Terminal master's awarded for partial completion of doctoral program. *Degree requirements:* For master's, variable foreign language requirement, thesis or alternative, research report. *Entrance requirements:* For master's, minimum GPA of 3.0; 18 credits of course work in social or behavioral science, human biology, statistics, and human development; 450 hours of verifiable human service work and/or volunteer experience; bachelor's degree.

Additional exam requirements/recommendations for international students: Required—TOEFL (minimum score 550 paper-based; 213 computer-based; 80 iBT). *Application deadline:* For fall admission, 1/31 priority date for domestic and international students; for spring admission, 6/1 priority date for domestic students, 6/1 for international students. Application fee: $50. Electronic applications accepted. *Expenses:* Tuition, state resident: full-time $6434; part-time $359.10 per credit. Tuition, nonresident: full-time $18,116; part-time $1006.45 per credit. Required fees: $1496; $83 per credit. *Financial support:* In 2009–10, 1 student received support, including 1 research assistantship with partial tuition reimbursement available (averaging $15,364 per year); fellowships with partial tuition reimbursements available, teaching assistantships with partial tuition reimbursements available, career-related internships or fieldwork, scholarships/grants, unspecified assistantships, and AmeriCorps also available. Financial award application deadline: 12/15; financial award applicants required to submit FAFSA. *Faculty research:* Environmental health, child welfare, mental health, international social work, disabilities, social advocacy. Total annual research expenditures: $783,600. *Unit head:* Dr. Deborah P. Valentine, Director, 970-491-1893, Fax: 970-491-7280, E-mail: deborah.valentine@colostate.edu. *Application contact:* Peter Friedrichsen, MSW Program Coordinator, 970-491-2536, Fax: 970-491-7280, E-mail: peter.friedrichsen@colostate.edu.

Columbia University, School of Social Work, New York, NY 10027. Offers MSSW, PhD, JD/MS, MBA/MS, MPA/MS, MPH/MS, MS/M Div, MS/MA, MS/MS, MS/MS Ed. PhD offered through the Graduate School of Arts and Sciences. *Accreditation:* CSWE (one or more programs are accredited). *Degree requirements:* For doctorate, thesis/dissertation. *Entrance requirements:* For master's, 3 letters of reference; for doctorate, GRE General Test, 3 letters of recommendation. Additional exam requirements/recommendations for international students: Required—TOEFL, TWE, TSE. Electronic applications accepted. *Expenses:* Contact institution.

Cornell University, Graduate School, Graduate Fields of Human Ecology, Field of Policy Analysis and Management, Ithaca, NY 14853-0001. Offers consumer policy (PhD); evaluation (PhD); family and social welfare policy (PhD); health administration (MHA); health management and policy (PhD). *Faculty:* 40 full-time (17 women). *Students:* 51 full-time (27 women); includes 13 minority (4 African Americans, 8 Asian Americans or Pacific Islanders, 1 Hispanic American), 7 international. Average age 26. 130 applicants, 38% accepted, 31 enrolled. In 2009, 25 master's, 5 doctorates awarded. *Degree requirements:* For master's, thesis; for doctorate, thesis/dissertation. *Entrance requirements:* For master's, GRE General Test or GMAT, 2 letters of recommendation; for doctorate, GRE General Test, 2 letters of recommendation. Additional exam requirements/recommendations for international students: Required—TOEFL (minimum score 550 paper-based; 213 computer-based; 77 iBT). *Application deadline:* For fall admission, 1/15 for domestic students. Application fee: $70. Electronic applications accepted. *Expenses:* Tuition: Full-time $29,500. Required fees: $70. Full-time tuition and fees vary according to degree level, program and student level. *Financial support:* In 2009–10, 17 students received support, including 1 fellowship with full and partial tuition reimbursement available, 8 teaching assistantships with full and partial tuition reimbursements available; research assistantships with full and partial tuition reimbursements available, institutionally sponsored loans, scholarships/grants, health care benefits, tuition waivers (full and partial), and unspecified assistantships also available. Financial award applicants required to submit FAFSA. *Faculty research:* Health policy, family policy, social welfare policy, program evaluation, consumer policy. *Unit head:* Director of Graduate Studies, 607-255-7772. *Application contact:* Graduate Field Assistant, 607-255-7772, Fax: 607-255-4071, E-mail: pam_phd@cornell.edu.

Dalhousie University, Faculty of Health Professions, School of Social Work, Halifax, NS B3H3J5, Canada. Offers MSW. Part-time programs available. Postbaccalaureate distance learning degree programs offered (minimal on-campus study). *Faculty:* 12 full-time (8 women), 3 part-time/adjunct (all women). *Students:* 26 full-time (24 women), 65 part-time (50 women); includes 12 minority (4 African Americans, 8 American Indian/Alaska Native). Average age 37. 50 applicants, 32% accepted. In 2009, 19 master's awarded. *Degree requirements:* For master's, thesis optional, field placement. *Entrance requirements:* For master's, bachelor's degree in social work, 2 years work experience in social work, minimum GPA of 3.0. Additional exam requirements/recommendations for international students: Required—TOEFL, IELTS, CANTEST, CAEL, or Michigan English Language Assessment Battery. *Application deadline:* For spring admission, 12/1 priority date for domestic and international students. Application fee: $70. Electronic applications accepted. *Expenses:* Contact institution. *Financial support:* In 2009–10, 13 students received support, including 4 fellowships with tuition reimbursements available, 3 teaching assistantships (averaging $2,520 per year); institutionally sponsored loans, scholarships/grants, and bursaries also available. *Faculty research:* Family and child welfare, physical and mental health, public policy, elder abuse, violence against women, community practice. *Unit head:* Catrina Brown, Graduate Coordinator, 902-494-7150, Fax: 902-494-6709, E-mail: social.work@dal.ca. *Application contact:* Lisa Calda, Admissions Coordinator, 902-494-1361, Fax: 902-494-6709, E-mail: social.work@dal.ca.

Delaware State University, Graduate Programs, Department of Social Work, Program in Social Work, Dover, DE 19901-2277. Offers MSW. *Accreditation:* CSWE. Evening/weekend programs available. *Entrance requirements:* For master's, GRE, minimum GPA of 3.0 in major, 2.75 overall. Additional exam requirements/recommendations for international students: Required—TOEFL. Electronic applications accepted. *Faculty research:* Gerontology, human behavior, corrections, child welfare, adolescent behavior policy.

Dominican University, Graduate School of Social Work, River Forest, IL 60305. Offers MSW. *Accreditation:* CSWE. Part-time programs available. *Faculty:* 7 full-time (4 women), 18 part-time/adjunct (5 women). *Students:* 117 full-time (103 women), 89 part-time (79 women); includes 58 minority (38 African Americans, 4 Asian Americans or Pacific Islanders, 16 Hispanic Americans), 1 international. Average age 32. In 2009, 32 master's awarded. *Entrance requirements:* For master's, minimum GPA of 2.75 for regular standing, 3.0 for advanced standing. Additional exam requirements/recommendations for international students: Required—TOEFL (minimum score 83 iBT); Recommended—IELTS (minimum score 7). *Application deadline:* For fall admission, 7/1 for domestic and international students; for spring admission, 11/1 for domestic and international students. Applications are processed on a rolling basis. Application fee: $25. Electronic applications accepted. *Expenses:* Tuition: Part-time $681 per credit hour. Required fees: $10 per course. Tuition and fees vary according to program. *Financial support:* In 2009–10, 45 students received support, including 4 research assistantships (averaging $4,000 per year); scholarships/grants and unspecified assistantships also available. *Faculty research:* Human trafficking, domestic violence, gerontology, school social work, child welfare. *Unit head:* Dr. Mark Rodgers, Dean, 708-366-3316, E-mail: mrodgers@dom.edu. *Application contact:* Felicia L. Townsend, Assistant Dean of Recruitment, Admissions and Marketing, 708-771-5298, Fax: 708-366-3446, E-mail: ftownsend@dom.edu.

East Carolina University, Graduate School, College of Human Ecology, School of Social Work, Greenville, NC 27858-4353. Offers MSW. *Accreditation:* CSWE. Postbaccalaureate distance learning degree programs offered (no on-campus study). *Degree requirements:* For master's, comprehensive exam. *Entrance requirements:* For master's, GRE or MAT. Additional exam requirements/recommendations for international students: Required—TOEFL. *Faculty research:* Social research, gerontology, women's issues, social services in schools, human behavior.

Eastern Michigan University, Graduate School, College of Health and Human Services, School of Social Work, Ypsilanti, MI 48197. Offers family and children's services (MSW); mental health and chemical dependency (MSW); services to the aging (MSW). *Accreditation:* CSWE. Part-time and evening/weekend programs available. *Faculty:* 20 full-time (16 women). *Students:* 34 full-time (30 women), 179 part-time (159 women); includes 69 minority (63 African Americans, 2 American Indian/Alaska Native, 2 Asian Americans or Pacific Islanders, 2 Hispanic Americans), 1 international. Average age 35. 220 applicants, 54% accepted, 99 enrolled. In 2009, 56 master's awarded. *Entrance requirements:* Additional exam requirements/recommendations for international students: Required—TOEFL. *Application deadline:* For fall admission, 1/15 priority date for domestic students. Applications are processed on a rolling basis. Application fee: $35. Tuition and fees vary according to course level. *Financial support:* Fellowships, research assistantships with full tuition reimbursements, teaching assistantships with full tuition reimbursements, career-related internships or fieldwork, Federal Work-Study, institutionally sponsored loans, scholarships/grants, tuition waivers (partial), and unspecified assistantships available. Support available to part-time students. Financial award applicants required to submit FAFSA. *Unit head:* Dr. Ann Alvarez, Director, 734-487-0393, Fax: 734-487-6832, E-mail: aalvare4@emich.edu. *Application contact:* Julie Harkema, Admissions Director, 734-487-4206, Fax: 734-487-6832, E-mail: jharkema@emich.edu.

Eastern Washington University, Graduate Studies, School of Social Work and Human Services, Cheney, WA 99004-2431. Offers MSW, MPA/MSW. *Accreditation:* CSWE. Part-time programs available. *Degree requirements:* For master's, comprehensive exam. *Entrance requirements:* For master's, minimum GPA of 3.0. *Expenses:* Tuition, state resident: full-time $7476; part-time $249 per quarter hour. Tuition, nonresident: full-time $18,030; part-time $601 per quarter hour. Required fees: $3.50 per quarter hour. $142 per quarter.

East Tennessee State University, School of Graduate Studies, College of Arts and Sciences, Department of Social Work, Johnson City, TN 37614. Offers MSW. *Accreditation:* CSWE. *Entrance requirements:* For master's, GRE. Additional exam requirements/recommendations for international students: Required—TOEFL (minimum score 550 paper-based; 213 computer-based).

Edinboro University of Pennsylvania, School of Graduate Studies and Research, School of Liberal Arts, Department of Social Work, Edinboro, PA 16444. Offers MSW. *Accreditation:* CSWE. Evening/weekend programs available. *Faculty:* 5 full-time (3 women), 3 part-time/adjunct (2 women). *Students:* 40 full-time (36 women), 34 part-time (25 women); includes 9 minority (6 African Americans, 1 American Indian/Alaska Native, 1 Asian American or Pacific Islander, 1 Hispanic American). Average age 34. In 2009, 25 master's awarded. *Degree requirements:* For master's, competency exam. *Application deadline:* Applications are processed on a rolling basis. Application fee: $30. Electronic applications accepted. *Expenses:* Tuition, state resident: full-time $6666; part-time $370 per credit. Tuition, nonresident: full-time $10,666; part-time $593 per credit. Required fees: $2206.28. One-time fee: $204 part-time. *Financial support:* In 2009–10, 5 research assistantships with full and partial tuition reimbursements (averaging $4,050 per year) were awarded; career-related internships or fieldwork, Federal Work-Study, scholarships/grants, and unspecified assistantships also available. Support available to part-time students. Financial award application deadline: 2/15; financial award applicants required to submit FAFSA. *Unit head:* Dr. Suzanne McDevitt, Program Head, 814-732-1585, E-mail: smcdevitt@edinboro.edu. *Application contact:* Dr. Suzanne McDevitt, Program Head, 814-732-1585, E-mail: smcdevitt@edinboro.edu.

Fayetteville State University, Graduate School, Program in Social Work, Fayetteville, NC 28301-4298. Offers MSW. *Accreditation:* CSWE. *Faculty:* 10 full-time (7 women), 2 part-time/adjunct (1 woman). *Students:* 61 full-time (56 women), 13 part-time (10 women); includes 59 minority (54 African Americans, 1 American Indian/Alaska Native, 4 Hispanic Americans). Average age 36. 36 applicants, 100% accepted, 36 enrolled. In 2009, 38 master's awarded. *Application deadline:* For fall admission, 1/15 for domestic students. Application fee: $35. *Unit head:* Dr. Terri Moore-Brown, Department Chair, 910-672-1853, E-mail: tmbrown@uncfsu.edu. *Application contact:* Katrina Hoffman, Associate Vice-Chancellor for Enrollment Management, 910-672-1374, Fax: 910-672-1470, E-mail: khoffma1@uncfsu.edu.

Florida Agricultural and Mechanical University, Division of Graduate Studies, Research, and Continuing Education, College of Arts and Sciences, Division of History and Political Sciences, Program in Applied Social Science, Tallahassee, FL 32307-3200. Offers African American history (MASS); criminal justice (MASS); economics (MASS); history (MASS); political science (MASS); public administration (MASS); public management (MASS); social work (MASS); sociology (MASS). Part-time programs available. *Faculty:* 17 full-time (2 women). *Students:* 54 full-time (42 women), 4 part-time (2 women); includes 57 minority (all African Americans). In 2009, 14 master's awarded. *Degree requirements:* For master's, thesis optional. *Entrance requirements:* For master's, GRE General Test, minimum GPA of 3.0. *Application deadline:* For fall admission, 5/18 for domestic students, 12/18 for international students; for spring admission, 11/12 for domestic students, 5/12 for international students. Application fee: $20. *Financial support:* Fellowships, research assistantships, career-related internships or fieldwork, Federal Work-Study, and tuition waivers (full) available. Financial award application deadline: 4/1. *Faculty research:* Southern history, black history, election trends, presidential history. *Unit head:* Dr. Gary Paul, Director, 850-599-3447. *Application contact:* Dr. Chanta M. Haywood, Dean of Graduate Studies, Research, and Continuing Education, 850-599-3315, Fax: 850-599-3727.

Florida Agricultural and Mechanical University, Division of Graduate Studies, Research, and Continuing Education, College of Arts and Sciences, Division of History and Political Sciences, Program in Social Work, Tallahassee, FL 32307-3200. Offers MSW. *Accreditation:* CSWE. *Faculty:* 12 full-time (9 women). *Students:* 44 full-time (42 women), 14 part-time (12 women); includes 57 African Americans. In 2009, 14 master's awarded. *Entrance requirements:* For master's, GRE General Test, minimum GPA of 3.0, 3 letters of recommendation. Additional exam requirements/recommendations for international students: Required—TOEFL. *Application deadline:* For fall admission, 5/18 for domestic students, 12/18 for international students; for spring admission, 11/12 for domestic students, 5/12 for international students. Application fee: $30. *Unit head:* Dr. Gary Paul, Director, 850-599-3447. *Application contact:* Dr. Chanta M. Haywood, Dean of Graduate Studies, Research, and Continuing Education, 850-599-3315, Fax: 850-599-3727.

Florida Atlantic University, College of Architecture, Urban and Public Affairs, School of Social Work, Boca Raton, FL 33431-0991. Offers MSW. *Accreditation:* CSWE. Part-time and evening/weekend programs available. *Faculty:* 18 full-time (8 women), 19 part-time/adjunct (15 women). *Students:* 78 full-time (58 women), 82 part-time (71 women); includes 52 minority (26 African Americans, 2 Asian Americans or Pacific Islanders, 24 Hispanic Americans). Average age 34. 213 applicants, 55% accepted, 57 enrolled. In 2009, 60 master's awarded. *Application deadline:* For fall admission, 5/1 priority date for domestic students, 2/15 for international students. Applications are processed on a rolling basis. Application fee: $30. *Expenses:* Tuition, state resident: full-time $7055; part-time $293.94 per credit hour. Tuition, nonresident: full-time $22,096; part-time $920.66 per credit hour. *Financial support:* Fellowships with tuition reimbursements, research assistantships with tuition reimbursements, career-related internships or fieldwork, Federal Work-Study, institutionally sponsored loans, and tuition waivers (partial) available. Financial award application deadline: 4/1. *Faculty research:* Child welfare, special work education. *Unit head:* Dr. Michele Hawkins, Director, 561-297-3234, Fax: 561-297-2866, E-mail: mhawkins@fau.edu. *Application contact:* Dr. Elwood Hamlin, Coordinator, 501-297-3234, E-mail: ehamlin@fau.edu.

Florida Gulf Coast University, College of Professional Studies, Program in Social Work, Fort Myers, FL 33965-6565. Offers MSW. *Accreditation:* CSWE. Part-time and evening/weekend programs available. *Faculty:* 32 full-time (11 women), 29 part-time/adjunct (12 women). *Students:* 21 full-time (18 women), 29 part-time (27 women); includes 11 minority (4 African Americans, 7 Hispanic Americans). Average age 32. 62 applicants, 69% accepted, 34 enrolled. In 2009, 27 master's awarded. *Entrance requirements:* For master's, GRE General Test, MAT, minimum GPA of 3.0. Additional exam requirements/recommendations for international students: Required—TOEFL (minimum score 550 paper-based; 213 computer-based). *Application deadline:* For fall admission, 4/1 priority date for domestic students. Applications are processed on a rolling basis. Application fee: $30. Electronic applications accepted. *Financial support:* In 2009–10, 6 research assistantships were awarded; career-related internships or fieldwork and tuition waivers (partial) also available. Support available to part-time students. *Faculty research:* Gerontology, clinical case management, domestic violence, homelessness, migrant workers. *Unit head:* Dr. Sakinah Salahu-Din, Director, 239-590-7867, Fax: 239-590-7842, E-mail: ssalahud@fgcu.edu. *Application contact:* Dr. Sakinah Salahu-Din, Director, 239-590-7867, Fax: 239-590-7842, E-mail: ssalahud@fgcu.edu.

Social Work

Florida International University, Stempel College of Public Health and Social Work, School of Social Work, Miami, FL 33199. Offers social welfare (PhD); social work (MSW). *Accreditation:* CSWE (one or more programs are accredited). Part-time and evening/weekend programs available. *Faculty:* 16 full-time (7 women). *Students:* 117 full-time (105 women), 65 part-time (58 women); includes 157 minority (68 African Americans, 1 Asian American or Pacific Islander, 88 Hispanic Americans), 3 international. Average age 34. 144 applicants, 45% accepted, 62 enrolled. In 2009, 97 master's, 1 doctorate awarded. *Degree requirements:* For doctorate, comprehensive exam, thesis/dissertation. *Entrance requirements:* For master's, minimum undergraduate GPA of 3.0 in upper-level coursework; letters of recommendation; undergraduate courses in biology (including human biology), statistics, and social/behavioral science (12 credits); BSW from accredited program; for doctorate, GRE, minimum graduate GPA of 3.5, 3 letters of recommendation, resume, writing samples, 2 examples of scholarly work. Additional exam requirements/recommendations for international students: Required—TOEFL (minimum score 550 paper-based; 80 iBT). *Application deadline:* For fall admission, 6/1 for domestic students, 4/1 for international students; for spring admission, 10/1 for domestic students, 9/1 for international students. Applications are processed on a rolling basis. Application fee: $30. Electronic applications accepted. *Expenses:* Tuition, state resident: full-time $8008; part-time $4004 per year. Tuition, nonresident: full-time $20,104; part-time $10,052 per year. Required fees: $298; $149 per term. *Financial support:* Institutionally sponsored loans and scholarships/grants available. Financial award application deadline: 3/1; financial award applicants required to submit FAFSA. *Unit head:* Dr. Paul Stuart, Director, 305-348-5880, Fax: 305-348-5312, E-mail: paul.stuart@fiu.edu. *Application contact:* Nanett Rojas, Assistant Director of Graduate Admissions, 305-348-7442, Fax: 305-348-7441, E-mail: gradadm@fiu.edu.

Florida State University, The Graduate School, College of Social Work, Tallahassee, FL 32306. Offers clinical social work (MSW); social policy and administration (MSW); social work (PhD); JD/MSW; MPA/MSW; MS/MSW; MSW/MBA. *Accreditation:* CSWE (one or more programs are accredited). Part-time and evening/weekend programs available. Post-baccalaureate distance learning degree programs offered (no on-campus study). *Faculty:* 33 full-time (23 women), 5 part-time/adjunct (all women). *Students:* 152 full-time (135 women), 252 part-time (222 women); includes 103 minority (76 African Americans, 5 American Indian/Alaska Native, 4 Asian Americans or Pacific Islanders, 18 Hispanic Americans). Average age 31. 237 applicants, 70% accepted, 149 enrolled. In 2009, 193 master's, 7 doctorates awarded. *Degree requirements:* For doctorate, comprehensive exam, thesis/dissertation. *Entrance requirements:* For master's and doctorate, GRE General Test, minimum GPA of 3.0. Additional exam requirements/recommendations for international students: Required—TOEFL. *Application deadline:* For fall admission, 5/1 priority date for domestic students; for winter admission, 3/1 priority date for domestic students; for spring admission, 10/1 priority date for domestic students. Applications are processed on a rolling basis. Application fee: $30. Electronic applications accepted. *Expenses:* Tuition, state resident: full-time $7413. Tuition, nonresident: full-time $22,567. *Financial support:* In 2009–10, 25 students received support, including 4 fellowships with partial tuition reimbursements available, 49 research assistantships with partial tuition reimbursements available (averaging $3,500 per year), 2 teaching assistantships with full tuition reimbursements available (averaging $15,000 per year); career-related internships or fieldwork, Federal Work-Study, institutionally sponsored loans, scholarships/grants, trainee-ships, health care benefits, and unspecified assistantships also available. Support available to part-time students. Financial award application deadline: 3/1; financial award applicants required to submit FAFSA. *Faculty research:* Family violence, AIDS, aging, family therapy, substance abuse. Total annual research expenditures: $2.6 million. *Unit head:* Dr. Nicholas Mazza, Dean, 850-644-4752, Fax: 850-644-9750. *Application contact:* Craig Stanley, Director of the MSW Program, 800-378-9550, Fax: 850-644-1201, E-mail: grad@csw.fsu.edu.

Fordham University, Graduate School of Social Service, New York, NY 10023. Offers social work (MSW, PhD); JD/MSW. *Accreditation:* CSWE (one or more programs are accredited). Part-time and evening/weekend programs available. *Faculty:* 48 full-time (36 women), 78 part-time/adjunct (61 women). *Students:* 884 full-time (787 women), 366 part-time (327 women); includes 355 minority (198 African Americans, 1 American Indian/Alaska Native, 19 Asian Americans or Pacific Islanders, 137 Hispanic Americans). Average age 32. In 2009, 539 master's, 4 doctorates awarded. *Degree requirements:* For master's, 1200 hours of field placement; for doctorate, comprehensive exam, thesis/dissertation. *Entrance requirements:* For master's, BA in liberal arts; for doctorate, GRE, master's degree in social work or related field. Additional exam requirements/recommendations for international students: Required—TOEFL (minimum score 575 paper-based; 231 computer-based; 90 iBT). *Application deadline:* For fall admission, 6/1 priority date for domestic students; for spring admission, 12/1 priority date for domestic students. Applications are processed on a rolling basis. Application fee: $60. Electronic applications accepted. *Expenses:* Contact institution. *Financial support:* In 2009–10, 838 students received support, including 39 research assistantships with partial tuition reimbursements available (averaging $1,980 per year); fellowships with partial tuition reimbursements available, career-related internships or fieldwork, scholarships/grants, tuition waivers (partial), and unspecified assistantships also available. Support available to part-time students. Financial award application deadline: 9/1; financial award applicants required to submit FAFSA. *Faculty research:* Aging, children and family, healthcare, domestic violence, substance abuse. *Unit head:* Dr. Peter B. Vaughan, Dean, 212-636-6616. *Application contact:* Elaine Gerald, Assistant Dean, 212-636-6600, Fax: 212-636-6613, E-mail: gssadmission@fordham.edu.

Gallaudet University, The Graduate School, College of Arts and Sciences, Department of Social Work, Washington, DC 20002-3625. Offers MSW. *Accreditation:* CSWE. *Degree requirements:* For master's, thesis optional. *Entrance requirements:* For master's, GRE General Test or MAT. Electronic applications accepted.

George Mason University, College of Health and Human Services, Department of Social Work, Fairfax, VA 22030. Offers MSW. *Accreditation:* CSWE. *Faculty:* 13 full-time (8 women), 19 part-time/adjunct (18 women). *Students:* 98 full-time (86 women), 29 part-time (24 women); includes 34 minority (15 African Americans, 1 American Indian/Alaska Native, 10 Asian Americans or Pacific Islanders, 8 Hispanic Americans), 2 international. Average age 29. 193 applicants, 76% accepted, 64 enrolled. In 2009, 22 master's awarded. *Entrance requirements:* For master's, undergraduate degree from a regionally-accredited college/university; minimum GPA of 3.0 for last 60 hours of undergraduate work; at least 30 hours of undergraduate liberal arts credits with at least 3 credits each in statistics, English composition, history or government, and social sciences; resume; 3 letters of recommendation. Additional exam requirements/recommendations for international students: Required—TOEFL. *Application deadline:* For fall admission, 2/1 for domestic students. Application fee: $75. Electronic applications accepted. *Expenses:* Tuition, state resident: full-time $7568; part-time $315.33 per credit hour. Tuition, nonresident: full-time $21,704; part-time $904.33 per credit hour. Required fees: $2184; $91 per credit hour. *Financial support:* In 2009–10, 5 students received support, including 5 research assistantships with full and partial tuition reimbursements available (averaging $3,346 per year); Federal Work-Study, scholarships/grants, unspecified assistantships, and health care benefits (full-time research or teaching assistantship recipients) also available. Support available to part-time students. Financial award application deadline: 3/1. *Faculty research:* Social work methods, child welfare, social work ethics, field education, supervision. Total annual research expenditures: $45,833. *Unit head:* Cathleen Lewandowski, Chair, 703-993-7017, E-mail: clewando@gmu.edu. *Application contact:* Breana Bayraktar, Administrative Support Specialist, 703-993-4247, E-mail: bbayrakt@gmu.edu.

Georgia State University, College of Health and Human Sciences, School of Social Work, Atlanta, GA 30294. Offers community partnerships (MSW). *Accreditation:* CSWE. Part-time programs available. *Degree requirements:* For master's, community project. *Entrance requirements:* For master's, GRE General Test. Additional exam requirements/recommendations for international students: Required—TOEFL (minimum score 550 paper-based; 213 computer-based). Electronic applications accepted. *Faculty research:* Child welfare, labor unions and child care workers, secondary victimization in death penalty cases, aging.

Governors State University, College of Health Professions, Program in Social Work, University Park, IL 60466-0975. Offers MSW. *Accreditation:* CSWE.

Graduate School and University Center of the City University of New York, Graduate Studies, Program in Social Welfare, New York, NY 10016-4039. Offers DSW, PhD. *Faculty:* 17 full-time (7 women). *Students:* 83 full-time (61 women); includes 21 minority (9 African Americans, 5 Asian Americans or Pacific Islanders, 7 Hispanic Americans), 3 international. Average age 43. 53 applicants, 23% accepted, 12 enrolled. In 2009, 9 doctorates awarded. *Degree requirements:* For doctorate, thesis/dissertation, project, qualifying exam. *Entrance requirements:* For doctorate, MSW or equivalent, 3 years of post-master's work experience. Additional exam requirements/recommendations for international students: Required—TOEFL. *Application deadline:* For fall admission, 3/1 for domestic students. Application fee: $125. Electronic applications accepted. *Financial support:* In 2009–10, 52 students received support, including 36 fellowships, 1 teaching assistantship; research assistantships, career-related internships or fieldwork, Federal Work-Study, institutionally sponsored loans, and tuition waivers (full and partial) also available. Financial award application deadline: 2/1; financial award applicants required to submit FAFSA. *Unit head:* Dr. Michael Fabricant, Executive Officer, 212-452-7023, Fax: 212-452-7440, E-mail: mfabrica@hunter.cuny.edu. *Application contact:* Les Gribben, Director of Admissions, 212-817-7470, Fax: 212-817-1624, E-mail: lgribben@gc.cuny.edu.

Grambling State University, School of Graduate Studies and Research, College of Professional Studies, School of Social Work, Grambling, LA 71245. Offers MSW. *Accreditation:* CSWE. Part-time programs available. *Faculty:* 6 full-time (5 women), 1 part-time/adjunct (0 women). *Students:* 51 full-time (43 women), 7 part-time (all women); includes 48 minority (all African Americans). Average age 33. 10 applicants, 40% accepted, 3 enrolled. In 2009, 25 master's awarded. *Degree requirements:* For master's, comprehensive exam, research project or thesis. *Entrance requirements:* For master's, GRE, minimum GPA of 3.0 on last degree, 36 hours in liberal arts, autobiography, interview. Additional exam requirements/recommendations for international students: Required—TOEFL (minimum score 500 paper-based; 173 computer-based; 61 iBT). *Application deadline:* For fall admission, 5/15 priority date for domestic and international students. Applications are processed on a rolling basis. Electronic applications accepted. *Expenses:* Tuition, state resident: full-time $2610. Tuition, nonresident: full-time $2610. *Financial support:* In 2009–10, 5 research assistantships (averaging $8,163 per year) were awarded; health care benefits, tuition waivers (full and partial), and unspecified assistantships also available. Financial award application deadline: 5/31; financial award applicants required to submit FAFSA. *Faculty research:* Welfare history, aging, end of life issues, stress and child abuse; African-American families, rurality. *Unit head:* Dr. Larry Grubbs, Acting Coordinator, MSW Program, 318-274-3162, Fax: 318-274-3254, E-mail: grubbsl@gram.edu. *Application contact:* LaVerne Junior, Secretary, 318-274-3166, Fax: 318-274-3254, E-mail: juniorls@gram.edu.

Grand Valley State University, College of Community and Public Service, School of Social Work, Allendale, MI 49401-9403. Offers MSW. *Accreditation:* CSWE. Part-time programs available. *Faculty:* 10 full-time (6 women), 15 part-time/adjunct (11 women). *Students:* 141 full-time (121 women), 211 part-time (179 women); includes 55 minority (24 African Americans, 9 American Indian/Alaska Native, 3 Asian Americans or Pacific Islanders, 19 Hispanic Americans), 16 international. Average age 31. 173 applicants, 97% accepted, 124 enrolled. In 2009, 104 master's awarded. *Entrance requirements:* Additional exam requirements/recommendations for international students: Required—TOEFL. *Application deadline:* For fall admission, 5/1 priority date for domestic students; for winter admission, 10/1 priority date for domestic students; for spring admission, 3/15 priority date for domestic students. Applications are processed on a rolling basis. Application fee: $30. Electronic applications accepted. *Expenses:* Tuition, state resident: part-time $471 per credit hour. Tuition, nonresident: part-time $646 per credit hour. Tuition and fees vary according to course level. *Financial support:* In 2009–10, 47 fellowships (averaging $2,235 per year), 19 research assistantships with full and partial tuition reimbursements (averaging $6,000 per year) were awarded; career-related internships or fieldwork, Federal Work-Study, institutionally sponsored loans, and unspecified assistantships also available. *Faculty research:* Drug addiction, aging, management, effectiveness of therapy. *Unit head:* Dr. Gwendolyn Adam, Dept. Chair, 616-331-6561, Fax: 616-331-6550, E-mail: adamg@gvsu.edu. *Application contact:* Joan Borst, Chair, Admissions, 616-331-6581, E-mail: borstj@gvsu.edu.

Gratz College, Graduate Programs, Program in Jewish Communal Service, Melrose Park, PA 19027. Offers MA, Certificate, MSW/Certificate. Part-time and evening/weekend programs available. Postbaccalaureate distance learning degree programs offered. *Degree requirements:* For master's, one foreign language, internship.

Hawai'i Pacific University, College of Humanities and Social Sciences, Program in Social Work, Honolulu, HI 96813. Offers MSW. *Accreditation:* CSWE. *Faculty:* 6 full-time (3 women), 2 part-time/adjunct (0 women). *Students:* 53 full-time (40 women), 35 part-time (27 women); includes 51 minority (8 African Americans, 1 American Indian/Alaska Native, 35 Asian Americans or Pacific Islanders, 7 Hispanic Americans), 7 international. 73 applicants, 89% accepted, 41 enrolled. In 2009, 11 master's awarded. *Expenses:* Tuition: Full-time $12,600; part-time $700 per credit hour. Tuition and fees vary according to program. *Unit head:* Dr. William Potter, Associate Vice President and Dean, 808-544-0228, Fax: 808-544-1424, E-mail: wpotter@hpu.edu. *Application contact:* Danny Lam, Assistant Director of Graduate Admissions, 808-544-1135, Fax: 808-544-0280, E-mail: graduate@hpu.edu.

Hebrew Union College–Jewish Institute of Religion, School of Jewish Communal Service, Los Angeles, CA 90007-3796. Offers MAJCS, Certificate, MAJCS/MA, MAJCS/MAJE, MAJCS/MAJS, MAJCS/MBA, MAJCS/MPA, MAJCS/MPAS, MAJCS/MSW, MCM/MAJCS. *Degree requirements:* For master's, one foreign language, project or thesis, Hebrew. *Entrance requirements:* For master's, GRE General Test, interview, minimum undergraduate GPA of 3.0. Additional exam requirements/recommendations for international students: Required—TOEFL (minimum score 550 paper-based). Electronic applications accepted. *Faculty research:* Language and culture of Jews.

Howard University, School of Social Work, Washington, DC 20059. Offers MSW, PhD. *Accreditation:* CSWE (one or more programs are accredited). Part-time programs available. *Degree requirements:* For doctorate, comprehensive exam, thesis/dissertation, qualifying exam. *Entrance requirements:* For master's, minimum GPA of 2.5; for doctorate, GRE General Test, minimum GPA of 3.3, MSW or master's in related field. Additional exam requirements/recommendations for international students: Required—TOEFL. *Faculty research:* Infant mortality, child and family services, displaced populations, social work practice, domestic violence, black males, mental health.

Humboldt State University, Graduate Studies, College of Professional Studies, Department of Social Work, Arcata, CA 95521-8299. Offers MSW. *Accreditation:* CSWE. *Students:* 64 full-time (52 women); includes 15 minority (1 African American, 7 American Indian/Alaska Native, 3 Asian Americans or Pacific Islanders, 4 Hispanic Americans). Average age 35. 92 applicants, 32% accepted, 20 enrolled. In 2009, 32 master's awarded. *Entrance requirements:* For master's, 3 letters of recommendation. Additional exam requirements/recommendations for international students: Required—TOEFL (minimum score 500 paper-based; 173 computer-based). *Application deadline:* For fall admission, 2/1 for domestic and international students. Application fee: $55. *Expenses:* Tuition, nonresident: full-time $8928. Required fees: $6102. Tuition and fees vary according to program. *Financial support:* Application deadline: 3/1. *Unit head:* Dr. Ronnie Swartz, Chair, 707-826-4443, Fax: 707-826-4418, E-mail: rjs19@humboldt.edu. *Application contact:* Dr. Christian Itin, Coordinator, 707-826-4451, E-mail: ci3@humboldt.edu.

Hunter College of the City University of New York, Graduate School, School of Social Work, New York, NY 10021-5085. Offers MSW, DSW. *Accreditation:* CSWE (one or more programs are accredited). *Faculty:* 34 full-time (17 women), 64 part-time/adjunct (42 women). *Students:* 655 full-time (536 women), 299 part-time (230 women); includes 308 minority (157 African Americans, 1 American Indian/Alaska Native, 34 Asian Americans or Pacific Islanders, 116 Hispanic Americans). Average age 33. 1,208 applicants, 30% accepted, 282 enrolled. In 2009, 331 master's awarded. *Degree requirements:* For master's, major paper. *Entrance requirements:* Additional exam requirements/recommendations for international students: Required—TOEFL. *Application deadline:* For fall admission, 1/15 for domestic and inter-

national students. Applications are processed on a rolling basis. Application fee: $125. *Expenses:* Tuition, state resident: full-time $7360; part-time $310 per credit. Required fees: $250 per semester. *Financial support:* In 2009–10, 120 fellowships (averaging $1,000 per year) were awarded; career-related internships or fieldwork, Federal Work-Study, and tuition waivers (partial) also available. Support available to part-time students. *Faculty research:* Child welfare, AIDS, homeless, aging, mental health. *Unit head:* Dr. Jacqueline B. Mondros, Dean/Professor, 212-452-7085, Fax: 212-452-7150, E-mail: jmondros@hunter.cuny.edu. *Application contact:* Raymond Montero, Coordinator of Admissions, 212-452-7005, E-mail: grad.socworkadvisor@hunter.cuny.edu.

Illinois State University, Graduate School, College of Arts and Sciences, School of Social Work, Normal, IL 61790-2200. Offers MSW. *Accreditation:* CSWE. *Faculty research:* Developing professional careers in child welfare, research and policy work for the Evan B. Donaldson Adoption Institute, evidence-based practice training pilot evaluation.

Indiana University East, School of Social Work, Richmond, IN 47374-1289. Offers MSW.

Indiana University Northwest, Division of Social Work, Gary, IN 46408-1197. Offers MSW. Part-time and evening/weekend programs available. *Faculty:* 1 full-time (0 women). *Students:* 29 full-time (28 women), 79 part-time (68 women); includes 40 minority (32 African Americans, 8 Hispanic Americans). Average age 37. *Entrance requirements:* For master's, minimum GPA of 3.0. *Application deadline:* For fall admission, 2/1 for domestic students. Application fee: $25. *Expenses:* Contact institution. *Financial support:* In 2009–10, 43 students received support. Career-related internships or fieldwork, Federal Work-Study, and tuition waivers (partial) available. Support available to part-time students. Financial award application deadline: 6/1; financial award applicants required to submit FAFSA. *Faculty research:* Educational outcomes, generalist practice, homelessness. Total annual research expenditures: $1,000. *Unit head:* Dr. Frank Caucci, Director, 219-985-4286, Fax: 219-981-4264, E-mail: fcaucci@iun.edu. *Application contact:* Dr. Frank Caucci, Director, 219-985-4286, Fax: 219-981-4264, E-mail: fcaucci@iun.edu.

Indiana University–Purdue University Indianapolis, School of Social Work, Indianapolis, IN 46202-2896. Offers MSW, PhD, Certificate. *Accreditation:* CSWE (one or more programs are accredited). Part-time and evening/weekend programs available. *Faculty:* 40 full-time. *Students:* 240 full-time (220 women), 260 part-time (221 women); includes 87 minority (71 African Americans, 3 American Indian/Alaska Native, 3 Asian Americans or Pacific Islanders, 10 Hispanic Americans). Average age 33. 182 applicants, 75% accepted, 99 enrolled. In 2009, 250 master's, 2 doctorates awarded. Terminal master's awarded for partial completion of doctoral program. *Degree requirements:* For master's, field practicum; for doctorate, thesis/dissertation, residential internship. *Entrance requirements:* For master's, minimum GPA of 2.5; course work in social behavior, statistics, research methodology, and human biology; for doctorate, GRE General Test. Additional exam requirements/recommendations for international students: Required—TOEFL. Application fee: $55 ($65 for international students). *Expenses:* Contact institution. *Financial support:* In 2009–10, 27 students received support, including 2 fellowships with full tuition reimbursements available (averaging $8,313 per year), 10 teaching assistantships (averaging $8,847 per year); research assistantships with partial tuition reimbursements available, Federal Work-Study, institutionally sponsored loans, scholarships/grants, and tuition waivers (partial) also available. Support available to part-time students. Financial award applicants required to submit FAFSA. *Faculty research:* Social justice, institutional child welfare, mental health, aging, AIDS/HIV disease. Total annual research expenditures: $145,580. *Unit head:* Dr. Margaret Adamek, Dean, 317-274-6730, Fax: 317-274-8630. *Application contact:* Susan Larimer, Information Contact for MSW, 317-274-6966, Fax: 317-274-8630.

Indiana University South Bend, School of Social Work, South Bend, IN 46634-7111. Offers MSW. Part-time and evening/weekend programs available. *Faculty:* 4 full-time (2 women). *Students:* 35 full-time (30 women), 67 part-time (56 women); includes 17 minority (16 African Americans, 1 Hispanic American). Average age 37. *Application deadline:* For fall admission, 2/1 priority date for domestic students. Application fee: $46 ($58 for international students). *Expenses:* Contact institution. *Financial support:* Career-related internships or fieldwork and Federal Work-Study available. Support available to part-time students. Financial award application deadline: 3/1; financial award applicants required to submit FAFSA. *Unit head:* Dr. Marilynne Ramsey, Program Director, 574-520-4880, Fax: 574-520-4876, E-mail: mjramsey@iusb.edu. *Application contact:* Admissions Counselor, 574-520-4839, Fax: 574-520-4834, E-mail: graduate@iusb.edu.

Institute for Clinical Social Work, Graduate Programs, Chicago, IL 60601. Offers PhD. Part-time programs available. *Degree requirements:* For doctorate, thesis/dissertation, supervised practicum. *Entrance requirements:* For doctorate, 2 years of experience. *Faculty research:* Impact of AIDS on partners, effects of learning disabilities on children and families, clinical social work issues.

Inter American University of Puerto Rico, Metropolitan Campus, Graduate Programs, Program in Social Work, San Juan, PR 00919-1293. Offers advanced clinical services (MSW); advanced social work administration (MSW); clinical services (MSW); social work administration (MSW). *Accreditation:* CSWE. Evening/weekend programs available. *Degree requirements:* For master's, comprehensive exam. *Entrance requirements:* For master's, GRE or EXADEP, interview. Electronic applications accepted.

Jackson State University, Graduate School, School of Social Work, Jackson, MS 39217. Offers MSW, PhD. *Accreditation:* CSWE (one or more programs are accredited). Evening/weekend programs available. *Degree requirements:* For master's, comprehensive exam; for doctorate, comprehensive exam, thesis/dissertation. *Entrance requirements:* For master's, GRE General Test; for doctorate, MAT. Additional exam requirements/recommendations for international students: Required—TOEFL.

Kean University, Nathan Weiss Graduate College, Program in Social Work, Union, NJ 07083. Offers advanced standing (MSW); social work (MSW). *Accreditation:* CSWE. Part-time and evening/weekend programs available. *Faculty:* 6 full-time (all women). *Students:* 108 full-time (95 women), 5 part-time (all women); includes 56 minority (32 African Americans, 4 Asian Americans or Pacific Islanders, 20 Hispanic Americans), 1 international. Average age 30. 144 applicants, 77% accepted, 60 enrolled. In 2009, 41 master's awarded. *Degree requirements:* For master's, thesis optional, field work. *Entrance requirements:* For master's, minimum GPA of 3.0, undergraduate course work in social sciences, 3 letters of recommendation. *Application deadline:* For fall admission, 3/15 for domestic students. Application fee: $60 ($150 for international students). Electronic applications accepted. *Expenses:* Tuition, state resident: full-time $10,440; part-time $435 per credit. Tuition, nonresident: full-time $14,160; part-time $590 per credit. Required fees: $2642; $110 per credit. Part-time tuition and fees vary according to course load and degree level. *Financial support:* In 2009–10, 6 research assistantships with full tuition reimbursements (averaging $3,263 per year) were awarded; unspecified assistantships also available. *Unit head:* Dr. Carol Williams, Program Coordinator, 908-737-4030, E-mail: cwilliams@kean.edu. *Application contact:* Dorothy Rowe, Pre-Admissions Coordinator, 908-737-5928, E-mail: drowe@kean.edu.

Kennesaw State University, College of Health and Human Services, Program in Social Work, Kennesaw, GA 30144-5591. Offers MSW. *Accreditation:* CSWE. *Students:* 63 full-time (51 women), 2 part-time (1 woman); includes 24 minority (18 African Americans, 1 American Indian/Alaska Native, 5 Hispanic Americans), 2 international. Average age 30. 73 applicants, 62% accepted, 33 enrolled. In 2009, 32 master's awarded. *Entrance requirements:* For master's, GRE, criminal history check, minimum GPA of 2.75, 3 letters of recommendation, resume. Additional exam requirements/recommendations for international students: Required—TOEFL (minimum score 550 paper-based; 213 computer-based; 80 iBT), IELTS (minimum score 6). *Application deadline:* For fall admission, 3/15 for domestic and international students. Application fee: $60. Electronic applications accepted. *Expenses:* Tuition, state resident: full-time $2341; part-time $196 per credit hour. Tuition, nonresident: full-time $9396; part-time $783 per credit hour. Required fees: $573 per semester. *Financial support:* In 2009–10, 2 research assistantships (averaging $4,000 per year) were awarded; unspecified assistantships also available. Financial award applicants required to submit FAFSA. *Unit head:* Dr. Alan Kirk, Department Chair, 770-423-6630, E-mail: akirk@kennesaw.edu. *Application contact:* Vilma Marquez, Admissions Counselor, 770-420-4377, Fax: 770-423-6885, E-mail: vmarquez@kennesaw.edu.

Kutztown University of Pennsylvania, College of Liberal Arts and Sciences, Program in Social Work, Kutztown, PA 19530-0730. Offers MSW. *Accreditation:* CSWE. Part-time and evening/weekend programs available. *Faculty:* 9 full-time (5 women). *Students:* 44 full-time (34 women), 7 part-time (all women); includes 8 minority (2 African Americans, 1 Asian American or Pacific Islander, 5 Hispanic Americans), 2 international. Average age 30. 53 applicants, 77% accepted, 21 enrolled. In 2009, 15 master's awarded. *Degree requirements:* For master's, comprehensive exam. *Entrance requirements:* For master's, GRE. Additional exam requirements/recommendations for international students: Required—TOEFL. *Application deadline:* For fall admission, 8/15 priority date for domestic and international students; for spring admission, 12/15 priority date for domestic and international students. Applications are processed on a rolling basis. Application fee: $35. Electronic applications accepted. *Expenses:* Tuition, state resident: full-time $6666; part-time $370 per credit. Tuition, nonresident: full-time $10,666; part-time $593 per credit. Required fees: $62 per credit. $60 per semester. *Financial support:* Career-related internships or fieldwork, Federal Work-Study, scholarships/grants, and unspecified assistantships available. Financial award application deadline: 3/1; financial award applicants required to submit FAFSA. *Unit head:* Dr. John Vafeas, Chairperson, 610-683-4235, E-mail: vafeas@kutztown.edu. *Application contact:* Kelly D. Burr, Associate Director, Graduate Admissions, 610-683-4200, Fax: 610-683-1393, E-mail: graduate@kutztown.edu.

Lakehead University, Graduate Studies, Gerontology Collaborative Program-Northern Educational Center for Aging and Health, Thunder Bay, ON P7B 5E1, Canada. Offers specialization gerontology (M Ed, M Sc, MA, MSW). Part-time programs available. *Degree requirements:* For master's, thesis (for some programs). *Entrance requirements:* Additional exam requirements/recommendations for international students: Required—TOEFL. *Faculty research:* Integrated health information systems.

Lakehead University, Graduate Studies, School of Social Work, Thunder Bay, ON P7B 5E1, Canada. Offers gerontology (MSW); social work (MSW); women's studies (MSW). Part-time programs available. *Degree requirements:* For master's, thesis or project. *Entrance requirements:* For master's, minimum B average. Additional exam requirements/recommendations for international students: Required—TOEFL. *Faculty research:* Clinical psychology, social work and practice theory, long-term care, health care for frail elderly, women's studies.

Laurentian University, School of Graduate Studies and Research, School of Social Work, Sudbury, ON P3E 2C6, Canada. Offers MSW. Open only to French-speaking students. Part-time programs available. *Degree requirements:* For master's, thesis. *Faculty research:* Income security, poverty, violence against women, child poverty, effects of economic crisis on families.

Loma Linda University, School of Science and Technology, Department of Social Work and Social Ecology, Loma Linda, CA 92350. Offers social policy and research (PhD); social work (MSW). *Accreditation:* CSWE. *Degree requirements:* For master's, comprehensive exam, thesis optional; for doctorate, comprehensive exam, thesis/dissertation. *Entrance requirements:* For master's and doctorate, GRE General Test. Additional exam requirements/recommendations for international students: Required—TOEFL, Michigan English Language Assessment Battery. Electronic applications accepted.

Long Island University, C.W. Post Campus, College of Management, Department of Social Work, Brookville, NY 11548-1300. Offers MSW. *Accreditation:* CSWE.

Louisiana State University and Agricultural and Mechanical College, Graduate School, School of Social Work, Baton Rouge, LA 70803. Offers MSW, PhD. *Accreditation:* CSWE (one or more programs are accredited). Part-time programs available. *Faculty:* 14 full-time (5 women). *Students:* 141 full-time (120 women), 60 part-time (57 women); includes 67 minority (59 African Americans, 1 American Indian/Alaska Native, 3 Asian Americans or Pacific Islanders, 4 Hispanic Americans), 2 international. Average age 31. 112 applicants, 75% accepted, 67 enrolled. In 2009, 90 master's, 3 doctorates awarded. *Degree requirements:* For master's, thesis, field instruction; for doctorate, comprehensive exam, thesis/dissertation. *Entrance requirements:* For master's and doctorate, GRE General Test, minimum GPA of 3.0. Additional exam requirements/recommendations for international students: Required—TOEFL (minimum score 550 paper-based; 213 computer-based; 79 iBT) or IELTS (minimum score 6.5). *Application deadline:* For fall admission, 2/15 for domestic and international students. Application fee: $50 ($70 for international students). Electronic applications accepted. *Financial support:* In 2009–10, 144 students received support, including 3 research assistantships with partial tuition reimbursements available (averaging $15,533 per year), 19 teaching assistantships with partial tuition reimbursements available (averaging $10,626 per year); fellowships, career-related internships or fieldwork, Federal Work-Study, scholarships/grants, health care benefits, and unspecified assistantships also available. Support available to part-time students. Financial award applicants required to submit FAFSA. *Faculty research:* Child welfare, gerontology addictions, mental health. Total annual research expenditures: $714,665. *Unit head:* Dr. Christian Molidor, Dean, 225-578-5875, Fax: 225-578-1357, E-mail: cmolidor@lsu.edu. *Application contact:* Denise Chiasson, Assistant Dean, 225-578-1234, Fax: 225-578-1357, E-mail: dchiass@lsu.edu.

Marywood University, Academic Affairs, College of Health and Human Services, School of Social Work, Scranton, PA 18509-1598. Offers MSW. *Accreditation:* CSWE. *Faculty:* 18 full-time (12 women). *Students:* 181 full-time (161 women), 140 part-time (127 women); includes 31 minority (10 African Americans, 1 Asian American or Pacific Islander, 20 Hispanic Americans). Average age 33. In 2009, 125 master's awarded. *Entrance requirements:* Additional exam requirements/recommendations for international students: Required—TOEFL (minimum score 550 paper-based; 213 computer-based; 79 iBT). *Application deadline:* For fall admission, 4/1 priority date for domestic students, 3/31 priority date for international students; for spring admission, 11/1 priority date for domestic students, 8/31 priority date for international students. Applications are processed on a rolling basis. Application fee: $35. Electronic applications accepted. *Expenses:* Contact institution. *Financial support:* Research assistantships, career-related internships or fieldwork, scholarships/grants, and unspecified assistantships available. Support available to part-time students. Financial award application deadline: 6/30; financial award applicants required to submit FAFSA. *Faculty research:* Impaired professionals, ethics, child welfare, communities, professional gatekeeping. *Unit head:* Dr. LLoyd Lyter, Director, 570-348-6211 Ext. 2388, E-mail: lyter@marywood.edu. *Application contact:* Tammy Manka, Assistant Director of Graduate Admissions, 866-279-9663, E-mail: tmanka@marywood.edu.

Marywood University, Academic Affairs, Reap College of Education and Human Development, Department of Human Development, Emphasis in Social Work, Scranton, PA 18509-1598. Offers PhD. *Students:* 9 part-time (7 women). Average age 40. In 2009, 3 doctorates awarded. *Entrance requirements:* Additional exam requirements/recommendations for international students: Required—TOEFL (minimum score 550 paper-based; 213 computer-based; 79 iBT). *Application deadline:* For fall admission, 1/30 priority date for domestic and international students. Application fee: $35. Electronic applications accepted. *Expenses:* Contact institution. *Financial support:* Career-related internships or fieldwork, scholarships/grants, and unspecified assistantships available. Support available to part-time students. Financial award application deadline: 6/30; financial award applicants required to submit FAFSA. *Unit head:* Dr. Brook Cannon, Director, 570-348-6211 Ext. 2324, E-mail: lcannon@marywood.edu. *Application contact:* Tammy Manka, Assistant Director of Graduate Admissions, 866-279-9663, E-mail: tmanka@marywood.edu.

McGill University, Faculty of Graduate and Postdoctoral Studies, Faculty of Arts, School of Social Work, Montréal, QC H3A 2T5, Canada. Offers MSW, PhD, Diploma, MSW/LL B.

McMaster University, School of Graduate Studies, Faculty of Social Sciences, School of Social Work, Hamilton, ON L8S 4M2, Canada. Offers analysis of social welfare policy (MSW); analysis of social work practice (MSW). Part-time programs available. *Entrance requirements:* For master's, minimum B+ average in final year, BSW from accredited program, half course

Social Work

McMaster University (continued)

each in introductory statistics and introductory social research methods. Additional exam requirements/recommendations for international students: Required—TOEFL (minimum score 580 paper-based; 237 computer-based). *Faculty research:* Health policy, income maintenance, child welfare, native issues, immigration policies, racism.

Memorial University of Newfoundland, School of Graduate Studies, School of Social Work, St. John's, NL A1C 5S7, Canada. Offers MSW. Part-time and evening/weekend programs available. *Degree requirements:* For master's, thesis optional, internship. *Entrance requirements:* For master's, BSW with a minimum of 2nd-class standing or equivalent. Electronic applications accepted. *Faculty research:* Violence, child abuse, sexual abuse, social policy, gerontology.

Michigan State University, The Graduate School, College of Social Science, School of Social Work, East Lansing, MI 48824. Offers clinical social work (MSW); organizational and community practice (MSW); social work (PhD). *Accreditation:* CSWE. Part-time programs available. Postbaccalaureate distance learning degree programs offered (minimal on-campus study). *Faculty:* 19 full-time (11 women). *Students:* 213 full-time (187 women), 217 part-time (185 women); includes 84 minority (49 African Americans, 6 American Indian/Alaska Native, 11 Asian Americans or Pacific Islanders, 18 Hispanic Americans), 7 international. Average age 32. 251 applicants, 70% accepted. In 2009, 124 master's, 3 doctorates awarded. *Entrance requirements:* Additional exam requirements/recommendations for international students: Required—TOEFL. Electronic applications accepted. *Expenses:* Tuition, state resident: part-time $478.25 per credit hour. Tuition, nonresident: part-time $966.50 per credit hour. Part-time tuition and fees vary according to program. *Financial support:* In 2009–10, 10 research assistantships with tuition reimbursements (averaging $5,865 per year), 3 teaching assistantships with tuition reimbursements (averaging $5,874 per year) were awarded. Total annual research expenditures: $817,051. *Unit head:* Dr. Gary R. Anderson, Director, 517-355-7515, Fax: 517-353-3038, E-mail: gary.anderson@ssc.msu.edu. *Application contact:* Nancy Gray, Graduate Office Assistant, 517-353-8632, Fax: 517-353-3038, E-mail: nancy.gray@ssc.msu.edu.

Middle Tennessee State University, College of Graduate Studies, College of Liberal Arts, Department of Social Work, Murfreesboro, TN 37132. Offers MSW. *Students:* 8 full-time (7 women), 10 part-time (7 women); includes 4 minority (3 African Americans, 1 Asian American or Pacific Islander). *Expenses:* Tuition, state resident: full-time $4404. Tuition, nonresident: full-time $10,956. *Unit head:* Dr. Rebecca Smith, Chair, 615-898-2868, E-mail: resmith@mtsu.edu. *Application contact:* Dr. Michael Allen, Dean and Vice Provost for Research, 615-898-2840, Fax: 615-904-8020, E-mail: mallen@mtsu.edu.

Millersville University of Pennsylvania, College of Graduate and Professional Studies, School of Humanities and Social Sciences, Department of Social Work, Millersville, PA 17551-0302. Offers MSW. *Accreditation:* CSWE. Part-time programs available. *Faculty:* 8 full-time (6 women), 5 part-time/adjunct (all women). *Students:* 28 full-time (26 women), 40 part-time (37 women); includes 7 minority (6 African Americans, 1 Hispanic American), 1 international. Average age 31. 28 applicants, 100% accepted, 28 enrolled. In 2009, 24 master's awarded. *Entrance requirements:* For master's, GRE or MAT (if GPA less than 2.8), 3 letters of recommendation, resume. Additional exam requirements/recommendations for international students: Required—TOEFL (minimum score 500 paper-based; 183 computer-based; 65 iBT) or IELTS (minimum score 6). *Application deadline:* For fall admission, 2/1 for domestic and international students. Application fee: $40 ($50 for international students). Electronic applications accepted. *Expenses:* Tuition, state resident: full-time $6666; part-time $370 per credit. Tuition, nonresident: full-time $10,666; part-time $593 per credit. Required fees: $1578.50; $76.25 per credit. One-time fee: $60 part-time. Tuition and fees vary according to course load. *Financial support:* In 2009–10, 15 students received support, including 15 research assistantships with full and partial tuition reimbursements available (averaging $4,613 per year); institutionally sponsored loans and unspecified assistantships also available. Support available to part-time students. Financial award application deadline: 3/15; financial award applicants required to submit FAFSA. *Unit head:* Dr. Kathryn A. Gregoire, Chairperson, 717-871-2475, Fax: 717-872-3959, E-mail: kathryn.gregoire@millersville.edu. *Application contact:* Dr. Victor S. DeSantis, Dean of Graduate and Professional Studies, 717-872-3099, Fax: 717-872-3453, E-mail: victor.desantis@millersville.edu.

Minnesota State University Mankato, College of Graduate Studies, College of Social and Behavioral Sciences, Department of Social Work, Mankato, MN 56001. Offers MSW. *Expenses:* Tuition, state resident: full-time $5364. Tuition, nonresident: full-time $8314.

Missouri State University, Graduate College, College of Health and Human Services, School of Social Work, Springfield, MO 65897. Offers MSW. *Accreditation:* CSWE. Part-time programs available. *Faculty:* 11 full-time (9 women), 17 part-time/adjunct (12 women). *Students:* 58 full-time (48 women), 34 part-time (29 women); includes 4 minority (2 African Americans, 2 Asian Americans or Pacific Islanders), 1 international. Average age 33. 38 applicants, 97% accepted, 29 enrolled. In 2009, 43 master's awarded. *Degree requirements:* For master's, comprehensive exam, thesis or alternative. *Entrance requirements:* For master's, GRE, minimum GPA of 3.0. Additional exam requirements/recommendations for international students: Required—TOEFL (minimum score 550 paper-based; 213 computer-based; 79 iBT). *Application deadline:* For fall admission, 2/15 priority date for domestic and international students. Application fee: $35 ($50 for international students). Electronic applications accepted. *Expenses:* Tuition, state resident: full-time $3852; part-time $214 per credit hour. Tuition, nonresident: full-time $7524; part-time $418 per credit hour. Required fees: $696; $172 per semester. Tuition and fees vary according to course level, course load, degree level and program. *Financial support:* Federal Work-Study, institutionally sponsored loans, scholarships/grants, and unspecified assistantships available. Financial award application deadline: 3/31; financial award applicants required to submit FAFSA. *Faculty research:* Child and family therapy, rural social work, adolescent social issues, domestic violence. *Unit head:* Dr. Susan Dollar, Acting Director, 417-836-6967, Fax: 417-836-7688, E-mail: socialwork@missouristate.edu. *Application contact:* Eric Eckert, Coordinator of Graduate Admissions and Recruitment, 417-836-5331, Fax: 417-836-6200, E-mail: ericeckert@missouristate.edu.

Molloy College, Graduate Social Work Program, Rockville Centre, NY 11571-5002. Offers MSW. *Expenses:* Tuition: Part-time $765 per credit. Required fees: $340 per semester. *Unit head:* Jennifer S. McKinnon, Coordinator, 516-678-5000 Ext. 6957, E-mail: jmckinnon@molloy.edu. *Application contact:* Jennifer S. McKinnon, Coordinator, 516-678-5000 Ext. 6957, E-mail: jmckinnon@molloy.edu.

Monmouth University, Graduate School, School of Social Work, West Long Branch, NJ 07764-1898. Offers clinical practice with families and children (MSW); international and community development (MSW); play therapy (Post-Master's Certificate). *Accreditation:* CSWE. Part-time and evening/weekend programs available. *Faculty:* 11 full-time (10 women), 16 part-time/adjunct (13 women). *Students:* 130 full-time (116 women), 118 part-time (108 women); includes 40 minority (20 African Americans, 4 Asian Americans or Pacific Islanders, 16 Hispanic Americans). Average age 32. 217 applicants, 95% accepted, 119 enrolled. In 2009, 95 master's awarded. *Degree requirements:* For master's, thesis, internship. *Entrance requirements:* For master's, minimum GPA of 3.0 in major, 2.75 overall. Additional exam requirements/recommendations for international students: Required—TOEFL (minimum score 550 paper-based; 213 computer-based; 79 iBT), IELTS (minimum score 5), Michigan English Language Assessment Battery (minimum score 77), Cambridge A, B, C. *Application deadline:* For fall admission, 3/15 priority date for domestic students, 3/15 for international students. Applications are processed on a rolling basis. Application fee: $50. Electronic applications accepted. *Expenses:* Tuition: Part-time $773 per credit. Required fees: $157 per semester. *Financial support:* In 2009–10, 113 students received support, including 106 fellowships (averaging $3,390 per year), 4 research assistantships (averaging $7,668 per year); career-related internships or fieldwork, scholarships/grants, and unspecified assistantships also available. Support available to part-time students. Financial award applicants required to submit FAFSA. *Faculty research:* Child welfare citizen participation, cultural diversity, diversity issues, employee help. *Unit head:* Dr. Mary Swigonski, Program Director, 732-263-5536, Fax: 732-263-5217, E-mail: swdept@monmouth.edu. *Application contact:* Kevin Roane, Director, Office of Graduate Admission, 732-571-3452, Fax: 732-263-5123, E-mail: gradadm@monmouth.edu.

Morgan State University, School of Graduate Studies, School of Education and Urban Studies, Department of Social Work, Baltimore, MD 21251. Offers MSW, PhD. *Accreditation:* CSWE. *Entrance requirements:* For doctorate, GRE.

Nazareth College of Rochester, Graduate Studies, Department of Social Work, Rochester, NY 14618-3790. Offers MSW. *Entrance requirements:* For master's, minimum GPA of 3.0.

Newman University, School of Social Work, Wichita, KS 67213-2097. Offers MSW. *Accreditation:* CSWE. Postbaccalaureate distance learning degree programs offered (no on-campus study). *Faculty:* 8 full-time (4 women), 4 part-time/adjunct (1 woman). *Students:* 49 full-time (46 women), 100 part-time (88 women); includes 28 minority (14 African Americans, 2 American Indian/Alaska Native, 3 Asian Americans or Pacific Islanders, 9 Hispanic Americans), 1 international. Average age 36. 118 applicants, 73% accepted, 71 enrolled. In 2009, 55 master's awarded. *Degree requirements:* For master's, comprehensive exam (for some programs), thesis optional, fieldwork. *Entrance requirements:* For master's, minimum GPA of 3.0, 3 letters of reference. Additional exam requirements/recommendations for international students: Required—TOEFL (minimum score 600 paper-based; 250 computer-based; 100 iBT). *Application deadline:* For fall admission, 8/15 for domestic students, 7/15 priority date for international students. Applications are processed on a rolling basis. Application fee: $25 ($40 for international students). *Expenses:* Tuition: Full-time $11,016; part-time $459 per credit hour. Required fees: $10 per credit hour. Tuition and fees vary according to course load, campus/location and program. *Financial support:* In 2009–10, 7 students received support. Federal Work-Study and scholarships/grants available. Financial award application deadline: 8/15; financial award applicants required to submit FAFSA. *Unit head:* Dr. Kevin Brown, Director, 316-942-4291 Ext. 2458, Fax: 316-942-4483. *Application contact:* Linda Kay Sabala, Director of Graduate Admissions, 316-942-4291 Ext. 2230, Fax: 316-942-4483, E-mail: sabalal@newmanu.edu.

New Mexico Highlands University, Graduate Studies, School of Social Work, Las Vegas, NM 87701. Offers bilingual/bicultural social work practice (MSW); clinical practice (MSW); government non-profit management (MSW). *Accreditation:* CSWE. Part-time programs available. *Degree requirements:* For master's, comprehensive exam, thesis or alternative. *Entrance requirements:* For master's, minimum undergraduate GPA of 3.0. Additional exam requirements/recommendations for international students: Required—TOEFL (minimum score 540 paper-based; 207 computer-based). *Faculty research:* Treatment attrition among domestic violence batterers, children's health and mental health, Dejando Huellas: meeting the bilingual/bicultural needs of the Latino mental health patient, impact of culture on the therapeutic process, effects of generational gang involvement on adolescents' future.

New Mexico State University, Graduate School, College of Health and Social Services, School of Social Work, Las Cruces, NM 88003-8001. Offers MSW. *Accreditation:* CSWE. Part-time and evening/weekend programs available. *Faculty:* 9 full-time (3 women), 8 part-time/adjunct (4 women). *Students:* 154 full-time (128 women), 57 part-time (48 women); includes 117 minority (7 African Americans, 8 American Indian/Alaska Native, 5 Asian Americans or Pacific Islanders, 97 Hispanic Americans), 2 international. Average age 33. 193 applicants, 96% accepted, 121 enrolled. In 2009, 81 master's awarded. *Degree requirements:* For master's, comprehensive exam, thesis optional, research project, oral exam. *Entrance requirements:* For master's, minimum GPA of 3.0. Additional exam requirements/recommendations for international students: Required—TOEFL (minimum score 637 paper-based; 270 computer-based). *Application deadline:* For fall admission, 1/15 priority date for domestic and international students. Applications are processed on a rolling basis. Application fee: $30 ($50 for international students). Electronic applications accepted. *Expenses:* Tuition, state resident: full-time $4080; part-time $223 per credit. Tuition, nonresident: full-time $14,256; part-time $647 per credit. Required fees: $1278; $639 per semester. *Financial support:* In 2009–10, 5 research assistantships (averaging $5,865 per year), 18 teaching assistantships with tuition reimbursements (averaging $4,903 per year) were awarded; fellowships, career-related internships or fieldwork, traineeships, health care benefits, and unspecified assistantships also available. Financial award application deadline: 3/1. *Faculty research:* Attachment issues, border issues, substance abuse, sexual orientation, family diversity. *Unit head:* Dr. Shelly Bucher, Head, 575-646-4300, Fax: 575-646-4343, E-mail: bucher@nmsu.edu. *Application contact:* Dr. Alice Chornesky, Graduate Program Coordinator, 575-646-2143, Fax: 575-646-4116, E-mail: achornes@nmsu.edu.

New York University, Silver School of Social Work, New York, NY 10012-1019. Offers MSW, PhD, MSW/JD, MSW/MA, MSW/MS. *Accreditation:* CSWE (one or more programs are accredited). Part-time and evening/weekend programs available. *Faculty:* 40 full-time (32 women), 146 part-time/adjunct (109 women). *Students:* 704 full-time (618 women), 448 part-time (376 women); includes 342 minority (110 African Americans, 2 American Indian/Alaska Native, 100 Asian Americans or Pacific Islanders, 130 Hispanic Americans). Average age 27. 1,381 applicants, 71% accepted, 450 enrolled. In 2009, 442 master's, 12 doctorates awarded. *Degree requirements:* For doctorate, comprehensive exam, thesis/dissertation. *Entrance requirements:* For master's, bachelor's degree; for doctorate, GRE or MAT, MSW. Additional exam requirements/recommendations for international students: Required—TOEFL, TWE. *Application deadline:* For fall admission, 2/8 priority date for domestic and international students; for spring admission, 11/2 priority date for domestic and international students. Applications are processed on a rolling basis. Application fee: $50. Electronic applications accepted. *Expenses:* Contact institution. *Financial support:* In 2009–10, 898 students received support. Career-related internships or fieldwork, Federal Work-Study, scholarships/grants, health care benefits, tuition waivers (partial), and unspecified assistantships available. Support available to part-time students. Financial award application deadline: 3/1; financial award applicants required to submit FAFSA. *Faculty research:* Social welfare policies, foster care, aging, mental health, substance abuse. *Unit head:* Dr. Lynn Videka, Dean, 212-998-5959, Fax: 212-995-4172. *Application contact:* Robert W. Sommo, Assistant Dean for Enrollment Services, 212-998-5910, Fax: 212-995-4171, E-mail: ssw.admissions@nyu.edu.

See Close-Up on page 1895.

Norfolk State University, School of Graduate Studies, School of Social Work, Norfolk, VA 23504. Offers MSW, PhD. *Accreditation:* CSWE (one or more programs are accredited). Part-time programs available. *Degree requirements:* For doctorate, thesis/dissertation. *Entrance requirements:* For master's, minimum GPA of 2.7. Additional exam requirements/recommendations for international students: Required—TOEFL.

North Carolina Agricultural and Technical State University, Graduate School, College of Arts and Sciences, Department of Sociology and Social Work, Greensboro, NC 27411. Offers MSW. *Accreditation:* CSWE. Part-time and evening/weekend programs available. *Degree requirements:* For master's, comprehensive exam, qualifying exam. *Entrance requirements:* For master's, GRE General Test.

North Carolina State University, Graduate School, College of Humanities and Social Sciences, Department of Social Work, Raleigh, NC 27695. Offers MSW. *Accreditation:* CSWE.

Northwest Nazarene University, Graduate Studies, Program in Social Work, Nampa, ID 83686-5897. Offers MSW. *Accreditation:* CSWE. *Degree requirements:* For master's, comprehensive exam. Electronic applications accepted.

The Ohio State University, Graduate School, College of Social Work, Columbus, OH 43210. Offers MSW, PhD. *Accreditation:* CSWE (one or more programs are accredited). Part-time programs available. *Faculty:* 31. *Students:* 294 full-time (258 women), 224 part-time (195 women); includes 87 minority (66 African Americans, 5 American Indian/Alaska Native, 6 Asian Americans or Pacific Islanders, 10 Hispanic Americans), 15 international. Average age 32. In 2009, 186 master's, 1 doctorate awarded. *Degree requirements:* For master's, thesis optional; for doctorate, thesis/dissertation. *Entrance requirements:* Additional exam requirements/

recommendations for international students: Required—TOEFL (minimum score 550 paper-based; 213 computer-based) or IELTS (minimum score 7) or Michigan English Language Assessment Battery (minimum score 82). *Application deadline:* For fall admission, 8/15 priority date for domestic students, 7/1 priority date for international students; for winter admission, 12/1 priority date for domestic students, 11/1 priority date for international students; for spring admission, 3/1 priority date for domestic students, 2/1 priority date for international students. Applications are processed on a rolling basis. Application fee: $40 ($50 for international students). Electronic applications accepted. *Expenses:* Tuition, state resident: full-time $10,683. Tuition, nonresident: full-time $25,923. Tuition and fees vary according to course load and program. *Financial support:* Fellowships, research assistantships, teaching assistantships, Federal Work-Study, institutionally sponsored loans, and unspecified assistantships available. Support available to part-time students. *Unit head:* Tom Gregoire, Interim Dean, 614-292-6288, Fax: 614-292-6940, E-mail: gregoire.5@osu.edu. *Application contact:* 614-292-9444, Fax: 614-292-3895, E-mail: domestic.grad@osu.edu.

The Ohio State University at Lima, Graduate Programs, Lima, OH 45804. Offers early childhood education (M Ed); education (MA); middle childhood education (M Ed); social work (MSW). *Students:* 23 full-time (18 women), 83 part-time (72 women); includes 1 minority (African American). Average age 34. *Degree requirements:* For master's, comprehensive exam (for some programs), thesis (for some programs). *Entrance requirements:* For master's, GRE, minimum GPA of 3.0. Additional exam requirements/recommendations for international students: Required—TOEFL, IELTS or Michigan English Language Assessment Battery. *Application deadline:* For fall admission, 8/15 priority date for domestic students, 7/1 priority date for international students; for winter admission, 12/1 priority date for domestic students, 11/1 priority date for international students; for spring admission, 3/1 priority date for domestic students, 2/1 priority date for international students. Applications are processed on a rolling basis. Application fee: $40 ($50 for international students). Electronic applications accepted. *Expenses:* Tuition, state resident: full-time $10,155. Tuition, nonresident: full-time $25,395. Tuition and fees vary according to course load. *Unit head:* Dr. John Snyder, Dean/Director, 419-995-8481, E-mail: snyder.4@osu.edu. *Application contact:* Graduate Admissions, 614-292-9444, Fax: 614-292-3895, E-mail: domestic.grad@osu.edu.

The Ohio State University at Marion, Graduate Programs, Marion, OH 43302-5695. Offers early childhood education (pre-K to grade 3) (M Ed); integrated teaching and learning (MA); middle childhood education (grades 4-9) (M Ed); nursing (MS, PhD); social work (MSW); MS/PhD. Part-time programs available. *Students:* 49 full-time (38 women), 34 part-time (25 women); includes 2 minority (both African Americans). Average age 31. *Degree requirements:* For master's, comprehensive exam (for some programs), thesis (for some programs). *Entrance requirements:* For master's and doctorate, GRE, minimum undergraduate GPA of 3.0. Additional exam requirements/recommendations for international students: Required—TOEFL, IELTS or Michigan English Language Assessment Battery. *Application deadline:* For fall admission, 8/15 priority date for domestic students, 7/1 priority date for international students; for winter admission, 12/1 priority date for domestic students, 11/1 priority date for international students; for spring admission, 3/1 priority date for domestic students, 2/1 priority date for international students. Applications are processed on a rolling basis. Application fee: $40 ($50 for international students). Electronic applications accepted. *Expenses:* Tuition, state resident: full-time $10,155. Tuition, nonresident: full-time $25,395. Tuition and fees vary according to course load. *Unit head:* Gregory S. Rose, Dean/Director, 740-389-6786 Ext. 6218, E-mail: rose.9@osu.edu. *Application contact:* Graduate Admissions, 614-292-9444, Fax: 614-292-3895, E-mail: domestic.grad@osu.edu.

The Ohio State University–Mansfield Campus, Graduate Programs, Mansfield, OH 44906-1599. Offers early and middle childhood education (MA); early childhood education (M Ed); middle childhood education (M Ed); social work (MSW). *Faculty:* 8 full-time (4 women). *Students:* 31 full-time (29 women), 32 part-time (29 women); includes 1 minority (Asian American or Pacific Islander), 1 international. Average age 31. *Degree requirements:* For master's, comprehensive exam (for some programs), thesis (for some programs). *Entrance requirements:* For master's, GRE, minimum GPA of 3.0. Additional exam requirements/recommendations for international students: Required—TOEFL (minimum score 550 paper-based; 213 computer-based). *Application deadline:* For fall admission, 8/15 priority date for domestic students, 7/1 priority date for international students; for winter admission, 12/1 priority date for domestic students, 11/1 priority date for international students; for spring admission, 3/1 priority date for domestic students, 2/1 priority date for international students. Applications are processed on a rolling basis. Application fee: $40 ($50 for international students). Electronic applications accepted. *Expenses:* Tuition, state resident: full-time $10,155. Tuition, nonresident: full-time $25,395. Tuition and fees vary according to course load. *Financial support:* In 2009–10, 14 students received support, including 3 teaching assistantships with full tuition reimbursements available (averaging $9,000 per year); Federal Work-Study and scholarships/grants also available. Support available to part-time students. Financial award application deadline: 7/1. *Application contact:* Graduate Admissions, 614-292-9444, Fax: 614-292-3895, E-mail: domestic.grad@osu.edu.

The Ohio State University–Newark Campus, Graduate Programs, Newark, OH 43055-1797. Offers early/middle childhood education (M Ed); integrated teaching and learning (MA); social work (MSW). *Students:* 40 full-time (36 women), 64 part-time (59 women); includes 5 minority (4 African Americans, 1 Asian American or Pacific Islander), 1 international. Average age 31. *Degree requirements:* For master's, comprehensive exam (for some programs), thesis (for some programs). *Entrance requirements:* For master's, GRE, minimum GPA of 3.0. Additional exam requirements/recommendations for international students: Required—TOEFL, IELTS or Michigan English Language Assessment Battery. *Application deadline:* For fall admission, 8/15 priority date for domestic students, 7/1 priority date for international students; for winter admission, 12/1 priority date for domestic students, 11/1 priority date for international students; for spring admission, 3/1 priority date for domestic students, 2/1 priority date for international students. Applications are processed on a rolling basis. Application fee: $40 ($50 for international students). Electronic applications accepted. *Expenses:* Tuition, state resident: full-time $10,155. Tuition, nonresident: full-time $25,395. Tuition and fees vary according to course load. *Unit head:* Dr. William L. MacDonald, Dean/Director, 740-366-9333 Ext. 330, E-mail: macdonald.24@osu.edu. *Application contact:* Graduate Admissions, 614-292-9444, Fax: 614-292-3985, E-mail: domestic.grad@osu.edu.

Ohio University, Graduate College, College of Arts and Sciences, Department of Social Work, Athens, OH 45701-2979. Offers MSW. *Accreditation:* CSWE. Part-time programs available. *Faculty:* 6 full-time (4 women), 2 part-time/adjunct (0 women). *Students:* 20 full-time (19 women), 11 part-time (10 women); includes 2 minority (1 African American, 1 American Indian/Alaska Native), 1 international. Average age 28. 12 applicants, 8% accepted, 0 enrolled. In 2009, 13 master's awarded. *Degree requirements:* For master's, fieldwork. *Entrance requirements:* For master's, GRE General Test or minimum GPA of 3.0, liberal arts background with coursework in human biology, statistics, and three social science areas; paid or volunteer work in human services. Additional exam requirements/recommendations for international students: Required—TOEFL (minimum score 620 paper-based; 105 iBT) or IELTS Academic (minimum score 7.5). *Application deadline:* For fall admission, 2/1 for domestic students, 8/15 for international students. Application fee: $50 ($55 for international students). Electronic applications accepted. *Expenses:* Tuition, state resident: full-time $7839; part-time $323 per quarter hour. Tuition, nonresident: full-time $15,831; part-time $654 per quarter hour. Required fees: $2931. *Financial support:* In 2009–10, teaching assistantships with full tuition reimbursements (averaging $9,000 per year); research assistantships with full tuition reimbursements, career-related internships or fieldwork, Federal Work-Study, tuition waivers (partial), and unspecified assistantships also available. Financial award application deadline: 2/1; financial award applicants required to submit FAFSA. *Faculty research:* Violence, families, rural life. Total annual research expenditures: $100,000. *Unit head:* Dr. Susan Kiss Sarnoff, Chair, 740-593-1301, Fax: 740-593-0427, E-mail: sarnoff@ohio.edu. *Application contact:* Dr. Karen Carlson, 740-593-1297, E-mail: carlsonk@ohio.edu.

Our Lady of the Lake University of San Antonio, Worden School of Social Service, San Antonio, TX 78207-4689. Offers MSW. *Accreditation:* CSWE. Part-time programs available. *Students:* 31 full-time (30 women), 18 part-time (15 women); includes 32 minority (9 African Americans, 1 Asian American or Pacific Islander, 22 Hispanic Americans). Average age 34. In 2009, 32 master's awarded. *Degree requirements:* For master's, thesis optional, practicum. *Entrance requirements:* For master's, GRE General Test or MAT. Additional exam requirements/recommendations for international students: Required—TOEFL. *Application deadline:* For fall admission, 4/2 priority date for domestic and international students; for spring admission, 11/1 priority date for domestic and international students. Applications are processed on a rolling basis. Application fee: $25 ($50 for international students). Electronic applications accepted. *Expenses:* Tuition: Full-time $12,330; part-time $685 per contact hour. Required fees: $139; $12 per contact hour. $57 per semester. Tuition and fees vary according to campus/location. *Financial support:* In 2009–10, 11 research assistantships were awarded; career-related internships or fieldwork, Federal Work-Study, institutionally sponsored loans, and tuition waivers (partial) also available. Financial award application deadline: 4/15. *Faculty research:* Cross-cultural social work practice, mental health, adult literacy, spirituality, maternal health care, experiential learning. *Unit head:* Dr. Walter Calvo, Director, 210-431-3969, Fax: 210-431-4028, E-mail: wecalvo@lake.ollusa.edu. *Application contact:* 210-434-6711 Ext. 2314, Fax: 210-431-4036, E-mail: gradadm@lake.ollusa.edu.

Phillips Theological Seminary, Programs in Theology, Tulsa, OK 74116. Offers administration of church agencies (M Div); campus ministry (M Div); church-related social work (M Div); college and seminary teaching (M Div); global mission work (M Div); institutional chaplaincy (M Div); ministerial vocations in Christian education (M Div); ministry (D Min), including parish ministry, pastoral counseling, practices of ministry; ministry and culture (MAMC), including Christian education, congregational leadership, history and practice of Christian spirituality, theology, ethics, and culture; ministry of music (M Div); pastoral care and counseling (M Div); pastoral ministry (M Div); theological studies (MTS). *Accreditation:* ATS. Part-time programs available. Postbaccalaureate distance learning degree programs offered (minimal on-campus study). *Degree requirements:* For master's, thesis (for some programs); for doctorate, thesis/dissertation. *Entrance requirements:* For master's, minimum GPA of 2.5; for doctorate, M Div, minimum GPA of 3.0. *Faculty research:* Biblical studies, historical studies, theology and culture, practical theology, theology and film.

Pontifical Catholic University of Puerto Rico, Institute of Graduate Studies in Behavioral Science and Community Affairs, Program in Clinical Social Work, Ponce, PR 00717-0777. Offers MSW. Part-time and evening/weekend programs available. *Entrance requirements:* For master's, EXADEP, 3 letters of recommendation, interview, minimum GPA of 2.75.

Portland State University, Graduate Studies, Graduate School of Social Work, Portland, OR 97207-0751. Offers social work (MSW); social work and social research (PhD). *Accreditation:* CSWE (one or more programs are accredited). Part-time programs available. *Degree requirements:* For doctorate, comprehensive exam, thesis/dissertation, residency. *Entrance requirements:* For master's, minimum GPA of 3.0 in upper-division course work or 2.75 overall; for doctorate, GRE General Test, 4 references. Additional exam requirements/recommendations for international students: Required—TOEFL (minimum score 550 paper-based; 213 computer-based). *Faculty research:* Child welfare; child mental health; social welfare policies and services; work, family, and dependent care; adult mental health.

Radford University, College of Graduate and Professional Studies, Waldron College of Health and Human Services, School of Social Work, Radford, VA 24142. Offers MSW. *Accreditation:* CSWE. Part-time programs available. *Faculty:* 10 full-time (9 women), 15 part-time/adjunct (10 women). *Students:* 51 full-time (43 women), 63 part-time (55 women); includes 21 minority (14 African Americans, 1 Asian American or Pacific Islander, 6 Hispanic Americans). Average age 33. 96 applicants, 80% accepted, 55 enrolled. In 2009, 59 master's awarded. *Degree requirements:* For master's, comprehensive exam. *Entrance requirements:* For master's, minimum GPA of 2.75; 3 letters of reference, personal essay, previous experience in the field of human services. Additional exam requirements/recommendations for international students: Required—TOEFL (minimum score 550 paper-based; 213 computer-based; 79 iBT). *Application deadline:* For fall admission, 4/1 priority date for domestic students, 12/1 for international students. Applications are processed on a rolling basis. Application fee: $50. Electronic applications accepted. *Expenses:* Tuition, state resident: full-time $5086; part-time $211 per credit hour. Tuition, nonresident: full-time $12,608; part-time $525 per credit hour. Required fees: $2508; $105 per credit hour. *Financial support:* In 2009–10, 19 students received support, including 14 research assistantships with partial tuition reimbursements available (averaging $8,000 per year); career-related internships or fieldwork, Federal Work-Study, institutionally sponsored loans, scholarships/grants, and unspecified assistantships also available. Financial award application deadline: 3/1; financial award applicants required to submit FAFSA. *Unit head:* Dr. Elise M. Fullmer, Director, 540-831-7691, Fax: 540-831-7670, E-mail: efullmer@radford.edu. *Application contact:* Graduate Admissions, 540-831-5431, Fax: 540-831-6061, E-mail: gradcollege@radford.edu.

Rhode Island College, School of Graduate Studies, School of Social Work, Providence, RI 02908-1991. Offers MSW. *Accreditation:* CSWE. Part-time programs available. *Faculty:* 5 full-time (3 women), 12 part-time/adjunct (9 women). *Students:* 130 full-time (114 women), 67 part-time (56 women); includes 22 minority (15 African Americans, 7 Hispanic Americans). Average age 33. In 2009, 62 master's awarded. *Entrance requirements:* For master's, official transcripts, personal statement, 3 letters of recommendation. Additional exam requirements/recommendations for international students: Recommended—TOEFL (minimum score 550 paper-based; 213 computer-based; 79 iBT). *Application deadline:* For fall admission, 2/15 for domestic students. Applications are processed on a rolling basis. Application fee: $50. *Expenses:* Contact institution. *Financial support:* Career-related internships or fieldwork, Federal Work-Study, scholarships/grants, health care benefits, and unspecified assistantships available. Support available to part-time students. Financial award application deadline: 5/15; financial award applicants required to submit FAFSA. *Unit head:* Sue Pearlmutter, Interim Dean, 401-456-8042, E-mail: spearlmutter@ric.edu. *Application contact:* Graduate Studies, 401-456-8700.

Roberts Wesleyan College, Division of Social Work, Rochester, NY 14624-1997. Offers child and family practice (MSW); congregational and community practice (MSW); mental health practice (MSW). *Accreditation:* CSWE. *Entrance requirements:* For master's, minimum GPA of 2.75. *Faculty research:* Religion and social work, family studies, values and ethics.

Rutgers, The State University of New Jersey, New Brunswick, School of Social Work, Piscataway, NJ 08854-8097. Offers MSW, PhD, JD/MSW, M Div/MSW. *Accreditation:* CSWE (one or more programs are accredited). Part-time programs available. *Degree requirements:* For doctorate, comprehensive exam, thesis/dissertation. *Entrance requirements:* For doctorate, GRE General Test. Additional exam requirements/recommendations for international students: Required—TOEFL. Electronic applications accepted. *Faculty research:* Family theory, adolescent development, child and adolescent mental health delivery systems, poverty and employment policy.

St. Ambrose University, College of Arts and Sciences, Program in Social Work, Davenport, IA 52803-2898. Offers MSW. *Accreditation:* CSWE. Part-time and evening/weekend programs available. *Faculty:* 6 full-time (2 women), 4 part-time/adjunct (all women). *Students:* 55 full-time (48 women), 19 part-time (18 women); includes 2 minority (both African Americans). Average age 29. 42 applicants, 100% accepted, 42 enrolled. In 2009, 36 master's awarded. *Degree requirements:* For master's, comprehensive exam (for some programs), thesis or alternative, integration projects. *Entrance requirements:* For master's, minimum GPA of 3.0, course work in statistics, bachelor's degree in liberal arts. Additional exam requirements/recommendations for international students: Required—TOEFL. *Application deadline:* For fall admission, 8/1 priority date for domestic students; for winter admission, 12/15 priority date for domestic students; for spring admission, 1/1 priority date for domestic students. Applications are processed on a rolling basis. Application fee: $25. Electronic applications accepted. *Expenses:* Tuition: Part-time $702 per credit hour. Tuition and fees vary according to degree level, program and reciprocity agreements. *Financial support:* In 2009–10, 71 students received support, including 8 research assistantships with partial tuition reimbursements available (averaging $3,600 per

Social Work

St. Ambrose University (continued)

year); career-related internships or fieldwork, scholarships/grants, tuition waivers (partial), and unspecified assistantships also available. Financial award application deadline: 8/15; financial award applicants required to submit FAFSA. *Faculty research:* Social work practice, cults/sects, family therapy, developmental disabilities. *Unit head:* Dr. Katherine VanBlair, Associate Director, 563-333-6484, Fax: 563-333-6243, E-mail: vanblairkatherine@sau.edu. *Application contact:* Tonita M. Wamsley, Administrative Assistant and Admissions Coordinator, 563-333-6379, Fax: 563-333-6243, E-mail: wamsleytonitam@sau.edu.

St. Catherine University, Graduate Programs, Program in Social Work, St. Paul, MN 55105. Offers MSW. *Accreditation:* CSWE. Part-time and evening/weekend programs available. *Faculty:* 29 full-time (24 women). *Students:* 369 full-time (337 women), 26 part-time (21 women); includes 33 minority (14 African Americans, 2 American Indian/Alaska Native, 11 Asian Americans or Pacific Islanders, 6 Hispanic Americans), 1 international. Average age 32. 185 applicants, 83% accepted, 103 enrolled. In 2009, 114 master's awarded. *Degree requirements:* For master's, clinical research paper. *Entrance requirements:* For master's, minimum GPA of 3.0. Additional exam requirements/recommendations for international students: Required—Michigan English Language Assessment Battery or TOEFL (minimum score 600 paper-based; 250 computer-based; 100 iBT). *Application deadline:* For fall admission, 1/10 for domestic students. Application fee: $35. *Expenses:* Contact institution. *Financial support:* Career-related internships or fieldwork and institutionally sponsored loans available. Support available to part-time students. Financial award application deadline: 4/1; financial award applicants required to submit FAFSA. *Unit head:* Barbara Shank, Director, 651-690-6704, Fax: 651-690-6024. *Application contact:* 651-690-6933, Fax: 651-690-6064.

St. Cloud State University, School of Graduate Studies, College of Social Sciences, Department of Social Work, St. Cloud, MN 56301-4498. Offers MSW. *Students:* 40 full-time (35 women), 1 (woman) part-time; includes 3 minority (all Asian Americans or Pacific Islanders), 1 international. 31 applicants, 100% accepted, 0 enrolled. In 2009, 14 master's awarded. *Entrance requirements:* For master's, GRE General Test, minimum GPA of 2.75. *Application deadline:* For fall admission, 6/1 priority date for domestic students, 3/1 for international students. Applications are processed on a rolling basis. Application fee: $35. *Unit head:* Dr. Jeanne Lacourt, Chairperson, 320-308-1048, E-mail: jalacourt@stcloudstate.edu. *Application contact:* Linda Lou Krueger, School of Graduate Studies, 320-308-2113, Fax: 320-308-5371, E-mail: lekrueger@stcloudstate.edu.

Saint Leo University, Graduate Studies in Social Work, Saint Leo, FL 33574-6665. Offers advanced clinical practice (MSW); management (MSW). Postbaccalaureate distance learning degree programs offered (minimal on-campus study). *Faculty:* 3 full-time (all women). *Students:* 17 full-time (14 women); includes 8 minority (7 African Americans, 1 Hispanic American). *Entrance requirements:* For master's, GRE (minimum score 1000) or MAT (minimum score 410) if undergraduate GPA less than 3.0, 3 recommendations; minimum GPA of 3.0 in undergraduate work, resume (for regular two-year full-time MSW); BSW from CSWE-accredited program with minimum GPA of 3.25 in social work completed in the last 5 years, minimum B average in upper-level social work courses (for one-year full-time advanced standing MSW). *Application deadline:* For fall admission, 7/15 for domestic students. Application fee: $75. *Expenses:* Tuition: Part-time $1767 per course. Required fees: $115 per course. *Financial support:* Career-related internships or fieldwork, Federal Work-Study, and health care benefits available. *Unit head:* Dr. Cindy Lee, Director, 352-588-8869, Fax: 352-588-8289, E-mail: cindy.lee@saintleo.edu. *Application contact:* Jared Welling, Director, Graduate/Weekend and Evening Admission, 800-707-8846, Fax: 352-588-7873, E-mail: grad.admissions@saintleo.edu.

Saint Louis University, Graduate School, College of Education and Public Service, School of Social Work, St. Louis, MO 63103-2097. Offers MSW. *Accreditation:* CSWE. Part-time programs available. *Entrance requirements:* For master's, minimum GPA of 3.0, letters of recommendation. Additional exam requirements/recommendations for international students: Required—TOEFL (minimum score 550 paper-based; 215 computer-based). *Expenses:* Contact institution. *Faculty research:* Gerontology, mental health issues, child welfare (especially abuse and neglect), social justice, and peace making, homelessness.

Salem State College, School of Graduate Studies, Program in Social Work, Salem, MA 01970-5353. Offers MSW. *Accreditation:* CSWE. Part-time and evening/weekend programs available. *Students:* 88 full-time (81 women), 134 part-time (112 women); includes 22 minority (10 African Americans, 1 American Indian/Alaska Native, 2 Asian Americans or Pacific Islanders, 9 Hispanic Americans), 4 international. Average age 35. 90 applicants, 98% accepted, 88 enrolled. In 2009, 65 master's awarded. *Entrance requirements:* For master's, GRE, MAT. Additional exam requirements/recommendations for international students: Required—TOEFL (minimum score 550 paper-based; 80 iBT), or IELTS (minimum score 5.5). *Application deadline:* For fall admission, 2/15 for domestic students. Applications are processed on a rolling basis. Application fee: $50. *Expenses:* Tuition, state resident: full-time $2520; part-time $275 per credit hour. Tuition, nonresident: full-time $4140; part-time $365 per credit hour. Required fees: $2430. *Financial support:* In 2009–10, 119 students received support. Career-related internships or fieldwork, Federal Work-Study, scholarships/grants, and unspecified assistantships available. Support available to part-time students. Financial award application deadline: 5/1; financial award applicants required to submit FAFSA. *Unit head:* Mary Byrne, Associate Professor, 978-542-6997, E-mail: mbyrne@salemstate.edu. *Application contact:* Dr. Lee A. Brossoit, Assistant Dean of Graduate Admissions, 978-542-6675, Fax: 978-542-7215, E-mail: lbrossoit@salemstate.edu.

Salisbury University, Graduate Division, Program in Social Work, Salisbury, MD 21801-6837. Offers MSW. *Accreditation:* CSWE. Part-time and evening/weekend programs available. *Faculty:* 15 full-time (12 women), 9 part-time/adjunct (8 women). *Students:* 118 full-time (108 women), 34 part-time (32 women); includes 26 minority (22 African Americans, 1 American Indian/Alaska Native, 3 Asian Americans or Pacific Islanders). Average age 31. 107 applicants, 77% accepted, 63 enrolled. In 2009, 46 master's awarded. *Degree requirements:* For master's, comprehensive exam (for some programs). *Entrance requirements:* Additional exam requirements/recommendations for international students: Required—TOEFL (minimum score 550 paper-based; 213 computer-based). *Application deadline:* For fall admission, 2/2 for domestic students. Applications are processed on a rolling basis. Application fee: $45. Electronic applications accepted. *Expenses:* Tuition, area resident: Part-time $278 per credit hour. Tuition, state resident: part-time $278 per credit hour. Tuition, nonresident: part-time $574 per credit hour. Required fees: $57 per credit hour. *Financial support:* In 2009–10, 101 students received support. Applicants required to submit FAFSA. *Unit head:* Dr. Vicki Root, Program Coordinator, 410-677-3948, E-mail: vbroot@salisbury.edu. *Application contact:* Susan Mareski, Program Admissions Coordinator, 410-677-5363, E-mail: smmareski@salisbury.edu.

San Diego State University, Graduate and Research Affairs, College of Health and Human Services, School of Social Work, San Diego, CA 92182. Offers MSW, JD/MSW, MSW/MPH. *Accreditation:* CSWE. Part-time programs available. *Degree requirements:* For master's, comprehensive exam, thesis optional. *Entrance requirements:* For master's, GRE General Test. Additional exam requirements/recommendations for international students: Required—TOEFL. Electronic applications accepted. *Faculty research:* Child maltreatment, substance abuse, neighborhood studies, child welfare.

San Francisco State University, Division of Graduate Studies, College of Health and Human Services, School of Social Work, San Francisco, CA 94132-1722. Offers MSW. *Accreditation:* CSWE. Part-time programs available. *Degree requirements:* For master's, thesis optional.

San Jose State University, Graduate Studies and Research, College of Applied Sciences and Arts, School of Social Work, San Jose, CA 95192-0001. Offers MSW, Certificate. *Accreditation:* CSWE. *Students:* 269 full-time (229 women), 75 part-time (64 women); includes 199 minority (20 African Americans, 1 American Indian/Alaska Native, 55 Asian Americans or Pacific Islanders, 123 Hispanic Americans), 6 international. Average age 31. 351 applicants, 49% accepted, 143 enrolled. In 2009, 128 master's awarded. *Application deadline:* For fall admission, 6/29 for domestic students; for spring admission, 11/30 for domestic students. Applications are processed on a rolling basis. Application fee: $59. Electronic applications accepted. *Financial support:* Application deadline: 5/31. *Unit head:* Alice Hines, Director, 408-924-5847. *Application contact:* Alice Hines, Director, 408-924-5847.

Savannah State University, Master of Social Work Program, Savannah, GA 31404. Offers MSW. *Accreditation:* CSWE. *Faculty:* 11 full-time (7 women). *Students:* 50 full-time (46 women), 6 part-time (5 women); includes 40 African Americans, 2 Hispanic Americans. In 2009, 17 master's awarded. *Entrance requirements:* For master's, GRE General Test. Additional exam requirements/recommendations for international students: Required—TOEFL. *Application deadline:* For fall admission, 7/1 for domestic students, 7/15 for international students; for spring admission, 10/31 for domestic students, 10/1 for international students. Applications are processed on a rolling basis. *Expenses:* Tuition, state resident: full-time $3662; part-time $153 per credit hour. Tuition, nonresident: full-time $14,648. Required fees: $450 per term. *Financial support:* Career-related internships or fieldwork, Federal Work-Study, institutionally sponsored loans, scholarships/grants, and unspecified assistantships available. Financial award applicants required to submit FAFSA. *Faculty research:* Clinical and administrative social work. *Unit head:* Dr. Roenia Deloach, Chair, 912-358-3247, E-mail: deloachr@savannahstate.edu. *Application contact:* Dr. Emily Crawford, Interim Dean of Graduate Studies, 912-356-2244, Fax: 912-356-2299, E-mail: crawford@savannahstate.edu.

Shippensburg University of Pennsylvania, School of Graduate Studies, College of Education and Human Services, Department of Social Work and Gerontology, Shippensburg, PA 17257-2299. Offers aging (Certificate); social work (MSW). *Accreditation:* CSWE. Part-time and evening/weekend programs available. Postbaccalaureate distance learning degree programs offered. *Degree requirements:* For master's, thesis, practicum. *Entrance requirements:* For master's, GRE or MAT, 3 letters of reference; resume; minimum GPA of 2.8; course work in human biology, economics, government/political science, psychology, sociology/anthropology and statistics. Additional exam requirements/recommendations for international students: Required—TOEFL (minimum score 560 paper-based; 220 computer-based); Recommended—IELTS (minimum score 6). Electronic applications accepted.

Simmons College, School of Social Work, Boston, MA 02115. Offers clinical social work (MSW, PhD); social work (CAGS); MSW/Certificate. *Accreditation:* CSWE (one or more programs are accredited). Part-time programs available. *Faculty:* 26 full-time (19 women), 53 part-time/adjunct (41 women). *Students:* 292 full-time (262 women), 190 part-time (173 women); includes 63 minority (41 African Americans, 8 Asian Americans or Pacific Islanders, 14 Hispanic Americans), 5 international. Average age 27. 532 applicants, 83% accepted, 191 enrolled. In 2009, 146 master's, 2 doctorates, 35 other advanced degrees awarded. *Degree requirements:* For master's, thesis or alternative; for doctorate, thesis/dissertation. *Entrance requirements:* For master's, minimum GPA of 3.0 in last 2 years of undergraduate course work; for doctorate, MAT, interview, minimum GPA of 3.0 in last 2 years of undergraduate course work. Additional exam requirements/recommendations for international students: Required—TOEFL (minimum score 600 paper-based; 250 computer-based; 105 iBT). *Application deadline:* For fall admission, 2/15 for domestic and international students; for spring admission, 10/15 for domestic students. Applications are processed on a rolling basis. Application fee: $45. Electronic applications accepted. *Expenses:* Contact institution. *Financial support:* Application deadline: 3/1. *Faculty research:* Domestic violence, trauma, multicultural practice, gerontology, aging and disabilities, child welfare. *Unit head:* Dr. Stefan Krug, Dean, 617-521-3929, Fax: 617-521-3980, E-mail: stefan.krug@simmons.edu. *Application contact:* Carlos Frontado, Director of Admissions, 617-521-3920, Fax: 617-521-3980, E-mail: carlos.frontado@simmons.edu.

Smith College, School for Social Work, Northampton, MA 01063. Offers MSW, PhD. *Accreditation:* CSWE (one or more programs are accredited). *Faculty:* 15 full-time (11 women), 90 part-time/adjunct (68 women). *Students:* 346 full-time (301 women), 52 part-time (44 women); includes 78 minority (28 African Americans, 3 American Indian/Alaska Native, 17 Asian Americans or Pacific Islanders, 30 Hispanic Americans), 8 international. Average age 34. 363 applicants, 68% accepted, 116 enrolled. In 2009, 109 master's, 6 doctorates awarded. *Degree requirements:* For master's, thesis; for doctorate, thesis/dissertation. *Entrance requirements:* For doctorate, MAT. Additional exam requirements/recommendations for international students: Required—TOEFL. *Application deadline:* For fall admission, 2/21 for domestic students. Applications are processed on a rolling basis. Application fee: $60. *Expenses:* Contact institution. *Financial support:* In 2009–10, 205 students received support. Career-related internships or fieldwork, institutionally sponsored loans, and scholarships/grants available. Financial award application deadline: 3/20; financial award applicants required to submit FAFSA. *Faculty research:* Social work practice, human behavior in the social environment, social welfare policy, social work research. *Unit head:* Dr. Carolyn Jacobs, Dean and Elizabeth Marting Truehaft Professor, 413-585-7977, E-mail: cjacobs@smith.edu. *Application contact:* Irene Rodriguez Martin, Director of Enrollment Management and Continuing Education, 413-585-7960, Fax: 413-585-7994, E-mail: imartin@smith.edu.

Southern Connecticut State University, School of Graduate Studies, School of Health and Human Services, Department of Social Work, New Haven, CT 06515-1355. Offers MSW, MSW/MS. *Accreditation:* CSWE. Part-time and evening/weekend programs available. *Faculty:* 16 full-time, 7 part-time/adjunct. *Students:* 87 full-time (73 women), 57 part-time (47 women); includes 24 minority (11 African Americans, 2 Asian Americans or Pacific Islanders, 11 Hispanic Americans), 1 international. 277 applicants, 23% accepted, 58 enrolled. In 2009, 49 master's awarded. *Degree requirements:* For master's, thesis. *Entrance requirements:* For master's, minimum undergraduate QPA of 3.0 in graduate major field, interview. *Application deadline:* For fall admission, 3/1 for domestic students; for spring admission, 12/1 for domestic students. Application fee: $50. Electronic applications accepted. Tuition and fees vary according to program. *Financial support:* Application deadline: 4/15. *Faculty research:* Social work practice; social service development; services for women, the aging, children, and families in educational and health care systems. *Unit head:* Dr. Todd Rofuth, Chairperson, 203-392-6557, Fax: 203-392-6580, E-mail: rofutht1@southernct.edu. *Application contact:* Dr. Barbara Worden, Graduate Coordinator, 203-392-6563, Fax: 203-392-6580, E-mail: wordenb1@southernct.edu.

Southern Illinois University Carbondale, Graduate School, College of Education, School of Social Work, Carbondale, IL 62901-4701. Offers MSW, JD/MSW. *Accreditation:* CSWE. *Entrance requirements:* For master's, GRE General Test, minimum GPA of 2.7. Additional exam requirements/recommendations for international students: Required—TOEFL. *Faculty research:* Service delivery systems, comparative race relations, advocacy research, gerontology, child welfare and health.

Southern Illinois University Edwardsville, Graduate Studies and Research, College of Arts and Sciences, Department of Social Work, Edwardsville, IL 62026-0001. Offers school social work (MSW); social work (MSW). *Accreditation:* CSWE. Part-time and evening/weekend programs available. *Faculty:* 8 full-time (3 women). *Students:* 63 full-time (58 women), 30 part-time (29 women); includes 13 minority (12 African Americans, 1 Hispanic American). Average age 26. 128 applicants, 61% accepted. In 2009, 33 master's awarded. *Degree requirements:* For master's, thesis or alternative, final exam. *Entrance requirements:* Additional exam requirements/recommendations for international students: Required—TOEFL (minimum score 550 paper-based; 213 computer-based; 79 iBT), IELTS (minimum score 6.5). *Application deadline:* For fall admission, 2/15 for domestic and international students. Application fee: $30. Electronic applications accepted. *Expenses:* Tuition, state resident: part-time $1252.50 per semester. Tuition, nonresident: part-time $3131.25 per semester. Required fees: $586.85 per semester. Tuition and fees vary according to course load. *Financial support:* In 2009–10, 1 fellowship with full tuition reimbursement (averaging $8,370 per year), 9 teaching assistantships with full tuition reimbursements (averaging $8,064 per year) were awarded; research assistantships with full tuition reimbursements, career-related internships or fieldwork, Federal Work-Study, institutionally sponsored loans, scholarships/grants, traineeships, and unspecified assistantships also available. Support available to part-time students. Financial award application deadline: 3/1; financial award applicants required to submit FAFSA. *Unit head:* Dr. Larry Kreuger, Chair, 618-650-5758, E-mail: lkreuge@siue.edu. *Application contact:* Dr. Carl Bentelspacher, Director, 618-650-5758, E-mail: cbentel@siue.edu.

Southern University at New Orleans, School of Social Work, New Orleans, LA 70126-1009. Offers MSW. *Accreditation:* CSWE. Part-time and evening/weekend programs available. *Degree requirements:* For master's, thesis. *Faculty research:* Service needs of people with AIDS, suicidal rate of people with AIDS.

Spalding University, Graduate Studies, College of Social Sciences and Humanities, School of Social Work, Louisville, KY 40203-2188. Offers MSW. *Accreditation:* CSWE. Evening/weekend programs available. *Faculty:* 6 full-time (5 women), 12 part-time/adjunct (8 women). *Students:* 42 full-time (36 women), 3 part-time (all women); includes 24 minority (23 African Americans, 1 Hispanic American). Average age 35. 37 applicants, 68% accepted, 24 enrolled. In 2009, 15 master's awarded. *Degree requirements:* For master's, thesis or alternative, project presentation. *Entrance requirements:* For master's, GRE General Test (if undergraduate GPA less than 2.8), 18 hours of course work in social sciences including statistics, human biology. Additional exam requirements/recommendations for international students: Required—TOEFL (minimum score 535 paper-based; 203 computer-based). *Application deadline:* For fall admission, 5/15 priority date for domestic students. Applications are processed on a rolling basis. Application fee: $30. Electronic applications accepted. *Expenses:* Tuition: Full-time $11,340; part-time $630 per credit hour. Tuition and fees vary according to program. *Financial support:* In 2009–10, 32 students received support, including 2 research assistantships with partial tuition reimbursements available (averaging $5,085 per year); career-related internships or fieldwork, Federal Work-Study, and scholarships/grants also available. Financial award application deadline: 3/15; financial award applicants required to submit FAFSA. *Faculty research:* Addictions, spirituality, feminist studies, mental retardation, action research. *Unit head:* Dr. Rita Valade, Chair, 502-585-9911 Ext. 2281, E-mail: rvalade@spalding.edu. *Application contact:* Susan Grace, Administrative Assistant, 502-588-7183, Fax: 502-585-7158, E-mail: sgrace@spalding.edu.

Springfield College, Graduate Programs, School of Social Work, Springfield, MA 01109-3797. Offers advanced generalist (weekday and weekend) (MSW); advanced standing (MSW); JD/MSW. *Accreditation:* CSWE. Part-time programs available. *Degree requirements:* For master's, comprehensive exam. *Entrance requirements:* Additional exam requirements/recommendations for international students: Required—TOEFL (minimum score 550 paper-based; 213 computer-based). Electronic applications accepted. *Expenses:* Tuition: Full-time $19,800; part-time $825 per credit hour. Required fees: $150.

State University of New York at Binghamton, Graduate School, College of Community and Public Affairs, Department of Social Work, Binghamton, NY 13902-6000. Offers MSW, MSW/MPA. *Accreditation:* CSWE. Part-time and evening/weekend programs available. *Students:* 68 full-time (47 women), 64 part-time (56 women); includes 22 minority (16 African Americans, 2 Asian Americans or Pacific Islanders, 4 Hispanic Americans), 2 international. Average age 34. 156 applicants, 53% accepted, 62 enrolled. In 2009, 48 master's awarded. *Degree requirements:* For master's, thesis. *Entrance requirements:* For master's, GRE General Test. Additional exam requirements/recommendations for international students: Required—TOEFL (minimum score 550 paper-based; 213 computer-based; 80 iBT). *Application deadline:* For fall admission, 2/1 priority date for domestic and international students. Applications are processed on a rolling basis. Application fee: $60. Electronic applications accepted. *Financial support:* In 2009–10, 11 students received support, including 2 fellowships with full and partial tuition reimbursements available (averaging $10,000 per year), teaching assistantships with full tuition reimbursements available (averaging $10,000 per year); research assistantships, career-related internships or fieldwork, Federal Work-Study, institutionally sponsored loans, scholarships/grants, health care benefits, and unspecified assistantships also available. Financial award application deadline: 2/15; financial award applicants required to submit FAFSA. *Unit head:* Dr. Laura Bronstein, Chairperson, 607-777-9162, E-mail: lbronst@binghamton.edu. *Application contact:* Victoria Williams, Recruiting and Admissions Coordinator, 607-777-2151, Fax: 607-777-2501, E-mail: vwilliam@binghamton.edu.

Stephen F. Austin State University, Graduate School, College of Applied Arts and Science, School of Social Work, Nacogdoches, TX 75962. Offers MSW. *Accreditation:* CSWE. *Degree requirements:* For master's, comprehensive exam, thesis optional. *Entrance requirements:* For master's, GRE General Test, interview. Additional exam requirements/recommendations for international students: Required—TOEFL (minimum score 550 paper-based).

Stony Brook University, State University of New York, Stony Brook University Medical Center, Health Sciences Center, School of Social Welfare, Doctoral Program in Social Welfare, Stony Brook, NY 11794. Offers PhD. *Faculty:* 28 full-time (15 women), 26 part-time/adjunct (12 women). *Students:* 33 full-time (22 women), 4 part-time (all women); includes 13 minority (7 African Americans, 5 Asian Americans or Pacific Islanders, 1 Hispanic American), 3 international. 25 applicants, 36% accepted. In 2009, 5 doctorates awarded. *Degree requirements:* For doctorate, thesis/dissertation. *Entrance requirements:* For doctorate, GRE General Test. *Application deadline:* For fall admission, 2/1 for domestic students. Application fee: $60. *Expenses:* Tuition, state resident: full-time $8370; part-time $349 per credit. Tuition, nonresident: full-time $13,250; part-time $552 per credit. Required fees: $933. *Financial support:* Fellowships, teaching assistantships available. Financial award application deadline: 2/1. *Unit head:* Dr. Joel Blau, Director, 631-444-3149, Fax: 631-444-7565, E-mail: jblau@notes.cc.sunysb.edu. *Application contact:* Edie Lundgren, Administrative Assistant, 631-444-8361, Fax: 631-444-7565, E-mail: elundgr@notes.cc.sunysb.edu.

Stony Brook University, State University of New York, Stony Brook University Medical Center, Health Sciences Center, School of Social Welfare, Master's Program in Social Work, Stony Brook, NY 11794. Offers MSW. *Accreditation:* CSWE. *Faculty:* 28 full-time (15 women), 26 part-time/adjunct (12 women). *Students:* 336 full-time (283 women), 9 part-time (all women); includes 116 minority (61 African Americans, 2 American Indian/Alaska Native, 13 Asian Americans or Pacific Islanders, 40 Hispanic Americans). Average age 35. 407 applicants, 86% accepted. In 2009, 201 master's awarded. *Degree requirements:* For master's, project or thesis. *Entrance requirements:* For master's, interview. *Application deadline:* For fall admission, 3/1 for domestic students. Application fee: $60. *Expenses:* Tuition, state resident: full-time $8370; part-time $349 per credit. Tuition, nonresident: full-time $13,250; part-time $552 per credit. Required fees: $933. *Financial support:* In 2009–10, 1 teaching assistantship was awarded. Financial award application deadline: 3/1. *Unit head:* Dr. Frances L. Brisbane, Dean, 631-444-2139, Fax: 631-444-7565, E-mail: fbrisbane@notes.cc.sunysb.edu. *Application contact:* Dr. Linda Francis, Director, 631-444-3166, Fax: 631-444-7565, E-mail: linda.francis@sunysb.edu.

Syracuse University, College of Human Ecology, Program in Social Work, Syracuse, NY 13244. Offers MSW. *Accreditation:* CSWE. Part-time and evening/weekend programs available. *Students:* 130 full-time (118 women), 85 part-time (74 women); includes 25 minority (19 African Americans, 1 American Indian/Alaska Native, 1 Asian American or Pacific Islander, 4 Hispanic Americans), 4 international. Average age 31. 38 applicants, 84% accepted, 15 enrolled. In 2009, 92 master's awarded. *Entrance requirements:* Additional exam requirements/recommendations for international students: Required—TOEFL (minimum score 100 iBT). *Application deadline:* For fall admission, 3/15 for domestic students, 3/15 priority date for international students. Applications are processed on a rolling basis. Application fee: $75. Electronic applications accepted. *Expenses:* Tuition: Full-time $26,808; part-time $1117 per credit. Required fees: $1024. *Financial support:* Fellowships with tuition reimbursements, research assistantships with partial tuition reimbursements, teaching assistantships with tuition reimbursements, tuition waivers (partial) available. Financial award application deadline: 1/1; financial award applicants required to submit FAFSA. *Faculty research:* Aging policy, healthcare, criminal justice, disability, rights of passage. *Unit head:* Dr. Carrie Jefferson Smith, Director, 315-443-5555, E-mail: inquire@hshp.syr.edu. *Application contact:* Amy Pangborn, Information Contact, 315-443-5555, E-mail: inquire@hshp.syr.edu.

Temple University, Graduate School, School of Social Administration, Program in Social Work, Philadelphia, PA 19122-6096. Offers MSW. *Accreditation:* CSWE. Part-time and evening/weekend programs available. *Entrance requirements:* For master's, minimum GPA of 3.0. Additional exam requirements/recommendations for international students: Required—TOEFL (minimum score 550 paper-based; 213 computer-based; 79 iBT). Electronic applications accepted.

Texas A&M University–Commerce, Graduate School, College of Education and Human Services, Department of Social Work, Commerce, TX 75429-3011. Offers MSW. *Accreditation:* CSWE. *Entrance requirements:* For master's, GRE General Test.

Texas State University–San Marcos, Graduate School, College of Applied Arts, School of Social Work, San Marcos, TX 78666. Offers MSW. *Accreditation:* CSWE. *Faculty:* 13 full-time (10 women), 2 part-time/adjunct (1 woman). *Students:* 75 full-time (70 women), 94 part-time (83 women); includes 61 minority (13 African Americans, 2 American Indian/Alaska Native, 2 Asian Americans or Pacific Islanders, 44 Hispanic Americans). Average age 32. 188 applicants, 55% accepted, 56 enrolled. In 2009, 58 master's awarded. *Degree requirements:* For master's, comprehensive exam. *Entrance requirements:* For master's, minimum GPA of 3.0 in last 60 hours of course work, 3 recommendation forms, curriculum vitae. Additional exam requirements/recommendations for international students: Required—TOEFL (minimum score 550 paper-based; 213 computer-based). *Application deadline:* For fall admission, 2/1 priority date for domestic students, 2/1 for international students. Applications are processed on a rolling basis. Application fee: $40 ($90 for international students). Electronic applications accepted. *Expenses:* Tuition, state resident: full-time $5784; part-time $241 per credit hour. Tuition, nonresident: full-time $13,224; part-time $551 per credit hour. Required fees: $1728; $48 per credit hour. $306. Tuition and fees vary according to course load. *Financial support:* In 2009–10, 159 students received support, including 6 research assistantships (averaging $4,973 per year), 5 teaching assistantships (averaging $5,102 per year); career-related internships or fieldwork, Federal Work-Study, institutionally sponsored loans, and unspecified assistantships also available. Support available to part-time students. Financial award application deadline: 4/1; financial award applicants required to submit FAFSA. *Unit head:* Dr. Mary Tijeirina, Program Advisor, 512-245-8835, E-mail: mt01@txstate.edu. *Application contact:* Dr. Mary Tijeirina, Program Advisor, 512-245-8835, E-mail: mt01@txstate.edu.

Thompson Rivers University, Program in Social Work, Kamloops, BC V2C 5N3, Canada. Offers MSW.

Troy University, Graduate School, College of Education, Program in Counseling and Psychology, Troy, AL 36082. Offers agency counseling (Ed S); clinical mental health (MS); community counseling (MS, Ed S); corrections counseling (MS); rehabilitation counseling (MS); school psychology (MS, Ed S); school psychometry (MS); social service counseling (MS); student affairs counseling (MS); substance abuse counseling (MS). *Accreditation:* ACA; CORE; NCATE. Part-time and evening/weekend programs available. *Students:* 375 full-time (302 women), 753 part-time (642 women); includes 664 minority (610 African Americans, 8 American Indian/Alaska Native, 9 Asian Americans or Pacific Islanders, 37 Hispanic Americans). Average age 33. 493 applicants, 92% accepted. In 2009, 102 master's, 191 other advanced degrees awarded. *Degree requirements:* For master's, comprehensive exam, thesis. *Entrance requirements:* For master's, MAT, minimum GPA of 2.5. Additional exam requirements/recommendations for international students: Required—TOEFL (minimum score 523 paper-based; 193 computer-based; 70 iBT), IELTS (minimum score 6). *Application deadline:* Applications are processed on a rolling basis. Application fee: $50. Electronic applications accepted. *Unit head:* Dr. Andrew Creamer, Chair, 334-670-3350, Fax: 334-670-32961, E-mail: drcreamer@troy.edu. *Application contact:* Brenda K. Campbell, Director of Graduate Admissions, 334-670-3178, Fax: 334-670-3733, E-mail: bcamp@troy.edu.

Tulane University, School of Social Work, New Orleans, LA 70118-5669. Offers MSW, JD/MSW, MSW/MPH. *Accreditation:* CSWE (one or more programs are accredited). Part-time programs available. *Degree requirements:* For master's, thesis. *Entrance requirements:* Additional exam requirements/recommendations for international students: Required—TOEFL. Electronic applications accepted.

Universidad del Este, Graduate School, Carolina, PR 00984. Offers accounting (MBA); adult education (M Ed); agribusiness (MBA); bilingual education (M Ed); criminal justice and criminology (MA); early education (M Ed); elementary education (M Ed); human resources (MBA); information security management (MBA); information technology and Web business development (MBA); management (MBA); public policy (MPA); social work (MA), including clinical social work; special education (M Ed); strategic leadership (MBA); teaching English (M Ed); teaching Spanish (M Ed).

Université de Moncton, Faculty of Arts and Social Sciences, School of Social Work, Moncton, NB E1A 3E9, Canada. Offers MSW. *Degree requirements:* For master's, one foreign language, major paper. *Entrance requirements:* For master's, minimum GPA of 3.0. *Faculty research:* Burnout and education, mental health (institutionalization), unemployment's effect on youth, women and health services.

Université de Montréal, Faculty of Arts and Sciences, School of Social Service, Program in Social Administration, Montréal, QC H3C 3J7, Canada. Offers DESS. *Students:* 5 part-time (4 women). 47 applicants, 36% accepted, 11 enrolled. *Application deadline:* For fall admission, 2/1 priority date for domestic students; for winter admission, 11/1 priority date for domestic students; for spring admission, 2/1 priority date for domestic students. Application fee: $100. Electronic applications accepted. *Unit head:* Dominique Damant, Director, 514-343-6596, Fax: 514-343-2493, E-mail: dominique.damant@umontreal.ca. *Application contact:* Helene Durocher, Student Files Management Technician, 514-343-6606, Fax: 514-343-2493, E-mail: helene.durocher@umontreal.ca.

Université de Sherbrooke, Faculty of Letters and Human Sciences, Department of Social Service, Sherbrooke, QC J1K 2R1, Canada. Offers MSS.

Université du Québec à Montréal, Graduate Programs, Program in Social Intervention, Montréal, QC H3C 3P8, Canada. Offers MA. Part-time programs available. *Degree requirements:* For master's, thesis. *Entrance requirements:* For master's, appropriate bachelor's degree or equivalent, proficiency in French.

Université du Québec en Abitibi-Témiscamingue, Graduate Programs, Program in Social Work, Rouyn-Noranda, QC J9X 5E4, Canada. Offers MSW.

Université du Québec en Outaouais, Graduate Programs, Program in Social Work, Gatineau, QC J8X 3X7, Canada. Offers MA.

Université Laval, Faculty of Social Sciences, School of Social Work, Programs in Social Work, Québec, QC G1K 7P4, Canada. Offers M Serv Soc, PhD. Terminal master's awarded for partial completion of doctoral program. *Degree requirements:* For master's, thesis (for some programs); for doctorate, comprehensive exam, thesis/dissertation. *Entrance requirements:* For master's and doctorate, knowledge of French, comprehension of written English. Electronic applications accepted.

University at Albany, State University of New York, School of Social Welfare, Albany, NY 12222-0001. Offers MSW, PhD, MSW/MA. *Accreditation:* CSWE (one or more programs are accredited). Part-time and evening/weekend programs available. *Degree requirements:* For doctorate, thesis/dissertation. *Entrance requirements:* For doctorate, GRE General Test. Additional exam requirements/recommendations for international students: Required—TOEFL (minimum score 550 paper-based; 213 computer-based). Electronic applications accepted. *Faculty research:* Welfare reform, homelessness, children and families, mental health, substance abuse.

University at Buffalo, the State University of New York, Graduate School, School of Social Work, Buffalo, NY 14260. Offers MSW, PhD, JD/MSW, MBA/MSW, MPH/MSW. *Accreditation:* CSWE (one or more programs are accredited). Part-time programs available. *Faculty:* 23 full-time (16 women), 36 part-time/adjunct (28 women). *Students:* 263 full-time (224 women), 240 part-time (215 women); includes 69 minority (41 African Americans, 3 American Indian/Alaska Native, 10 Asian Americans or Pacific Islanders, 15 Hispanic Americans), 19 international.

Social Work

University at Buffalo, the State University of New York (continued)
Average age 30. 498 applicants, 69% accepted, 216 enrolled. In 2009, 160 master's, 3 doctorates awarded. *Degree requirements:* For master's, 900 hours of field work; for doctorate, comprehensive exam, thesis/dissertation. *Entrance requirements:* For master's, 24 credits of course work in liberal arts; for doctorate, GRE General Test, MSW or equivalent. Additional exam requirements/recommendations for international students: Required—TOEFL (minimum score 600 paper-based; 250 computer-based; 100 iBT). *Application deadline:* For fall admission, 3/1 priority date for domestic and international students. Applications are processed on a rolling basis. Application fee: $50. Electronic applications accepted. *Financial support:* In 2009–10, 44 students received support, including 1 fellowship with full tuition reimbursement available (averaging $7,500 per year), 4 research assistantships with full tuition reimbursements available (averaging $15,000 per year), 5 teaching assistantships with full tuition reimbursements available (averaging $3,000 per year); Federal Work-Study, scholarships/grants, health care benefits, tuition waivers (partial), unspecified assistantships, and instructorships and research grants (PhD) also available. Financial award application deadline: 4/30; financial award applicants required to submit FAFSA. *Faculty research:* Trauma, substance abuse, child welfare, aging, human rights. *Unit head:* Dr. Nancy J. Smyth, Dean, 716-645-3381, Fax: 716-645-3883, E-mail: sw-dean@buffalo.edu. *Application contact:* Maria Soos, Admissions Processor, 716-645-3381, Fax: 716-645-3456, E-mail: sw-info@buffalo.edu.

The University of Akron, Graduate School, College of Health Sciences and Human Services, School of Social Work, Akron, OH 44325. Offers MS. *Accreditation:* CSWE. *Faculty:* 5 full-time (3 women), 43 part-time/adjunct (31 women). *Students:* 80 full-time (70 women), 15 part-time (13 women); includes 16 minority (15 African Americans, 1 Hispanic American). Average age 33. 61 applicants, 84% accepted, 37 enrolled. In 2009, 43 master's awarded. *Entrance requirements:* For master's, undergraduate major in social work or related field, letters of recommendation, resume. Additional exam requirements/recommendations for international students: Required—TOEFL (minimum score 550 paper-based; 213 computer-based; 79 iBT). *Application deadline:* For fall admission, 2/15 for domestic and international students. Application fee: $30 ($40 for international students). Electronic applications accepted. *Expenses:* Tuition, state resident: full-time $6570; part-time $365 per credit hour. Tuition, nonresident: full-time $11,250; part-time $625 per credit hour. *Financial support:* In 2009–10, 4 research assistantships with full tuition reimbursements, 3 teaching assistantships with full tuition reimbursements were awarded; Federal Work-Study also available. *Faculty research:* Spirituality and alternative healing, child welfare education and training, ethics and social work practice, evidence-based social work practice, social work continuing education. *Unit head:* Dr. Timothy McCarragher, Director, 330-972-5976, E-mail: mccarra@uakron.edu. *Application contact:* Associate Dean.

The University of Alabama, Graduate School, School of Social Work, Tuscaloosa, AL 35487-0314. Offers MSW, PhD. *Accreditation:* CSWE (one or more programs are accredited). Postbaccalaureate distance learning degree programs offered (no on-campus study). *Faculty:* 12 full-time (7 women). *Students:* 235 full-time (212 women), 53 part-time (50 women); includes 104 minority (98 African Americans, 2 American Indian/Alaska Native, 3 Asian Americans or Pacific Islanders, 1 Hispanic American), 7 international. Average age 30. 336 applicants, 58% accepted, 134 enrolled. In 2009, 141 master's, 6 doctorates awarded. *Median time to degree:* Of those who began their doctoral program in fall 2001, 83% received their degree in 8 years or less. *Degree requirements:* For doctorate, comprehensive exam, thesis/dissertation. *Entrance requirements:* For master's, GRE or MAT (if GPA less than 3.0), minimum GPA of 2.5; for doctorate, GRE, minimum GPA of 3.0. Additional exam requirements/recommendations for international students: Required—TOEFL, IELTS. *Application deadline:* For fall admission, 2/1 priority date for domestic students; for spring admission, 9/1 priority date for domestic students. Applications are processed on a rolling basis. Application fee: $50 ($60 for international students). Electronic applications accepted. *Expenses:* Tuition, state resident: full-time $7000. Tuition, nonresident: full-time $19,200. *Financial support:* In 2009–10, 113 students received support, including 4 fellowships (averaging $3,750 per year), 9 research assistantships with full tuition reimbursements available (averaging $9,394 per year), 3 teaching assistantships with full tuition reimbursements available (averaging $9,396 per year); career-related internships or fieldwork, scholarships/grants, health care benefits, tuition waivers (partial), and unspecified assistantships also available. Financial award application deadline: 2/1; financial award applicants required to submit FAFSA. *Faculty research:* Children, adolescents, and their families; gerontology; juvenile justice; addictions; health. Total annual research expenditures: $146,257. *Unit head:* Dr. James A. Hall, Dean, 205-348-3924, Fax: 205-348-9419, E-mail: jhall1@sw.ua.edu. *Application contact:* Casey Barnes, Admissions Coordinator, 205-348-8413, Fax: 205-348-9419, E-mail: credmill@sw.ua.edu.

University of Alaska Anchorage, College of Health and Social Welfare, School of Social Work, Anchorage, AK 99508. Offers clinical social work practice (Certificate); social work (MSW); social work management (Certificate). *Accreditation:* CSWE. Part-time and evening/weekend programs available. Postbaccalaureate distance learning degree programs offered (no on-campus study). *Degree requirements:* For master's, comprehensive exam (for some programs), thesis or alternative, research project. *Entrance requirements:* For master's, GRE General Test, writing sample. Additional exam requirements/recommendations for international students: Required—TOEFL (minimum score 550 paper-based; 213 computer-based). Electronic applications accepted. *Expenses:* Contact institution.

University of Arkansas, Graduate School, J. William Fulbright College of Arts and Sciences, School of Social Work, Fayetteville, AR 72701-1201. Offers MSW. *Accreditation:* CSWE. *Students:* 29 full-time (26 women), 7 part-time (all women); includes 3 minority (1 African American, 1 Asian American or Pacific Islander, 1 Hispanic American), 2 international. In 2009, 22 master's awarded. *Entrance requirements:* For master's, GRE General Test. Application fee: $40 ($50 for international students). *Expenses:* Tuition, state resident: full-time $7355; part-time $356.58 per hour. Tuition, nonresident: full-time $17,401; part-time $775.17 per hour. Required fees: $1203. *Financial support:* In 2009–10, 4 research assistantships were awarded; fellowships with tuition reimbursements, teaching assistantships also available. *Unit head:* Dr. Marcia Shobe, Department Chairperson, 479-575-5039, Fax: 479-575-4145, E-mail: mshobe@uark.edu. *Application contact:* Dr. Glenda House, Graduate Coordinator, 479-575-3783, E-mail: ghouse@uark.edu.

University of Arkansas at Little Rock, Graduate School, College of Professional Studies, School of Social Work, Program in Social Work, Little Rock, AR 72204-1099. Offers advanced direct practice (MSW); management and community practice (MSW). *Accreditation:* CSWE. *Entrance requirements:* For master's, GRE General Test or MAT.

The University of British Columbia, Faculty of Arts and Faculty of Graduate Studies, School of Social Work, Vancouver, BC V6T 1Z2, Canada. Offers MSW, PhD. *Degree requirements:* For master's, thesis or essay; for doctorate, comprehensive exam, thesis/dissertation. *Entrance requirements:* For master's, BSW; for doctorate, MSW. Additional exam requirements/recommendations for international students: Required—TOEFL (minimum score 580 paper-based; 237 computer-based; 93 iBT). Electronic applications accepted. *Faculty research:* Gerontology, family resources, diversity, social inequality.

University of Calgary, Faculty of Graduate Studies, Faculty of Social Work, Calgary, AB T2N 1N4, Canada. Offers MSW, PhD, Postgraduate Diploma. *Degree requirements:* For master's, thesis (for some programs); for doctorate, thesis/dissertation, candidacy exam. *Entrance requirements:* For master's, BSW, minimum undergraduate GPA of 3.4 (1 year program), minimum GPA of 3.5 (2 year program); for doctorate, minimum graduate GPA of 3.5, MSW (preferred); for Postgraduate Diploma, MSW, minimum graduate GPA of 3.5. Additional exam requirements/recommendations for international students: Required—TOEFL (paper-based 550; computer-based 213) or IELTS (paper-based 7). Electronic applications accepted. *Faculty research:* Family violence, direct practice, gerontology, child welfare, community development.

University of California, Berkeley, Graduate Division, School of Social Welfare, Berkeley, CA 94720-1500. Offers MSW, PhD, MSW/PhD. *Accreditation:* CSWE (one or more programs are accredited). *Students:* 230 full-time (195 women); includes 75 minority (12 African Americans, 3 American Indian/Alaska Native, 28 Asian Americans or Pacific Islanders, 32 Hispanic Americans), 3 international. Average age 31. 434 applicants, 96 enrolled. In 2009, 93 master's, 5 doctorates awarded. Terminal master's awarded for partial completion of doctoral program. *Degree requirements:* For master's, thesis optional; for doctorate, thesis/dissertation, qualifying exam. *Entrance requirements:* For master's and doctorate, GRE General Test, minimum GPA of 3.0, 3 letters of recommendation. Additional exam requirements/recommendations for international students: Required—TOEFL, TWE. *Application deadline:* Applications are processed on a rolling basis. Application fee: $70 ($90 for international students). *Financial support:* Fellowships, research assistantships with partial tuition reimbursements, teaching assistantships with partial tuition reimbursements, career-related internships or fieldwork, Federal Work-Study, scholarships/grants, traineeships, health care benefits, and unspecified assistantships available. Financial award applicants required to submit FAFSA. *Faculty research:* Child welfare, law and social welfare, minority mental health, social welfare policy analysis, health services. *Unit head:* Prof. Lorraine Midanik, Dean, 510-642-4341, E-mail: swdean@berkeley.edu. *Application contact:* Lupe Lopez, Administrative Assistant, 510-642-9042, E-mail: socwelf@berkeley.edu.

University of California, Los Angeles, Graduate Division, School of Public Affairs, Program in Social Welfare, Los Angeles, CA 90095. Offers MSW, PhD, JD/MSW. *Accreditation:* CSWE (one or more programs are accredited). *Degree requirements:* For master's, comprehensive exam, research project; for doctorate, thesis/dissertation, oral and written qualifying exams. *Entrance requirements:* For master's, GRE General Test, minimum GPA of 3.0; for doctorate, GRE General Test, minimum undergraduate GPA of 3.0. Additional exam requirements/recommendations for international students: Required—TOEFL. Electronic applications accepted.

University of Central Florida, College of Health and Public Affairs, School of Social Work, Orlando, FL 32816. Offers aging studies (Certificate); children's services (Certificate); social work (MSW); social work administration (Certificate). *Accreditation:* CSWE. Part-time and evening/weekend programs available. *Faculty:* 16 full-time (11 women), 18 part-time/adjunct (14 women). *Students:* 149 full-time (129 women), 118 part-time (99 women); includes 91 minority (58 African Americans, 3 Asian Americans or Pacific Islanders, 30 Hispanic Americans), 4 international. Average age 31. 270 applicants, 80% accepted, 170 enrolled. In 2009, 79 master's, 10 other advanced degrees awarded. *Degree requirements:* For master's, thesis or alternative, field education. *Entrance requirements:* For master's, resume. Additional exam requirements/recommendations for international students: Required—TOEFL. *Application deadline:* For fall admission, 3/1 for domestic students. Application fee: $30. Electronic applications accepted. *Expenses:* Tuition, state resident: part-time $306.31 per credit hour. Tuition, nonresident: part-time $1099.01 per credit hour. Part-time tuition and fees vary according to degree level and program. *Financial support:* In 2009–10, 5 students received support, including 2 fellowships with partial tuition reimbursements available (averaging $10,000 per year), 1 research assistantship with partial tuition reimbursement available (averaging $7,100 per year), 2 teaching assistantships with partial tuition reimbursements available (averaging $3,200 per year); career-related internships or fieldwork, Federal Work-Study, institutionally sponsored loans, and unspecified assistantships also available. Financial award application deadline: 3/1; financial award applicants required to submit FAFSA. *Unit head:* Dr. John Ronnau, Director, 407-823-2114, Fax: 407-823-5697, E-mail: jronnau@mail.ucf.edu. *Application contact:* Dr. John Ronnau, Director, 407-823-2114, Fax: 407-823-5697, E-mail: jronnau@mail.ucf.edu.

University of Chicago, School of Social Service Administration, Chicago, IL 60637. Offers social service administration (PhD); social work (AM); AM/M Div; MBA/AM; MPP/AM. *Accreditation:* CSWE (one or more programs are accredited). Part-time and evening/weekend programs available. *Degree requirements:* For master's, 2 field placements; for doctorate, comprehensive exam, thesis/dissertation. *Entrance requirements:* For master's, 4 letters of recommendation; for doctorate, writing sample, 4 letters of recommendation. Additional exam requirements/recommendations for international students: Required—TOEFL (minimum score 600 paper-based; 250 computer-based). Electronic applications accepted. *Expenses:* Contact institution. *Faculty research:* Family treatment, mental health, the aged, child welfare, health administration.

University of Cincinnati, Graduate School, School of Social Work, Cincinnati, OH 45221. Offers MSW. *Accreditation:* CSWE. Part-time programs available. *Entrance requirements:* Additional exam requirements/recommendations for international students: Required—TOEFL. Electronic applications accepted. *Faculty research:* Fatherhood, mediation, mental illness, child welfare, elderly.

University of Denver, Graduate School of Social Work, Denver, CO 80208. Offers MSW, PhD, Certificate. *Accreditation:* CSWE (one or more programs are accredited). Part-time and evening/weekend programs available. *Faculty:* 25 full-time (17 women), 75 part-time/adjunct (61 women). *Students:* 421 full-time (382 women), 20 part-time (19 women); includes 81 minority (18 African Americans, 13 American Indian/Alaska Native, 17 Asian Americans or Pacific Islanders, 33 Hispanic Americans), 3 international. Average age 28. 633 applicants, 400 enrolled. In 2009, 206 master's, 5 doctorates, 67 other advanced degrees awarded. *Degree requirements:* For doctorate, thesis/dissertation. *Entrance requirements:* For doctorate, GRE General Test, MSW. *Application deadline:* Applications are processed on a rolling basis. Application fee: $60. Electronic applications accepted. *Expenses:* Tuition: Full-time $34,596; part-time $961 per quarter hour. Required fees: $4 per quarter hour. Tuition and fees vary according to course load, campus/location and program. *Financial support:* 13 teaching assistantships with full and partial tuition reimbursements (averaging $12,700 per year) for PhD students available. *Faculty research:* Children, youth, and families; mental health; drug dependency; gerontology; child welfare. Total annual research expenditures: $2.3 million. *Application contact:* Colin Schneider, Director of Admission and Financial Aid, 303-871-2841, Fax: 303-871-2845, E-mail: gssw-admission@du.edu.

University of Georgia, Graduate School, School of Social Work, Athens, GA 30602. Offers MA, MSW, PhD, Certificate. *Accreditation:* CSWE (one or more programs are accredited). Part-time and evening/weekend programs available. *Faculty:* 23 full-time (14 women). *Students:* 258 full-time (215 women), 20 part-time (15 women); includes 55 minority (44 African Americans, 8 Asian Americans or Pacific Islanders, 3 Hispanic Americans), 11 international. Average age 34. 351 applicants, 62% accepted, 128 enrolled. In 2009, 130 master's, 8 doctorates awarded. *Degree requirements:* For master's, thesis or alternative; for doctorate, one foreign language, thesis/dissertation. *Entrance requirements:* For master's and doctorate, GRE General Test. *Application deadline:* For fall admission, 7/1 priority date for domestic students, 7/1 for international students; for spring admission, 11/15 for domestic and international students. Applications are processed on a rolling basis. Application fee: $50. Electronic applications accepted. *Expenses:* Tuition, state resident: full-time $6000; part-time $250 per credit hour. Tuition, nonresident: full-time $20,904; part-time $871 per credit hour. Required fees: $730 per semester. *Financial support:* In 2009–10, 39 students received support, including 4 fellowships (averaging $25,000 per year), 35 research assistantships with tuition reimbursements available (averaging $7,500 per year); teaching assistantships with tuition reimbursements available, career-related internships or fieldwork, Federal Work-Study, scholarships/grants, tuition waivers (full and partial), and unspecified assistantships also available. Support available to part-time students. Financial award application deadline: 2/10; financial award applicants required to submit FAFSA. *Faculty research:* Juvenile justice, substance abuse, civil rights and social justice, gerontology, social policy. Total annual research expenditures: $2.6 million. *Unit head:* Dr. Maurice C. Daniels, Dean, 706-542-5424, Fax: 706-542-3282, E-mail: sswdean@uga.edu. *Application contact:* Dr. Brian Bride, Graduate Coordinator, 706-542-5471, Fax: 706-542-3282, E-mail: bbride@uga.edu.

University of Guam, Office of Graduate Studies, College of Natural and Applied Sciences, Program in Social Work, Mangilao, GU 96923. Offers MSW.

University of Hawaii at Manoa, Graduate Division, School of Social Work, Honolulu, HI 96822. Offers social welfare (PhD); social work (MSW). *Accreditation:* CSWE (one or more programs are accredited). Part-time programs available. *Faculty:* 14 full-time (7 women), 13

part-time/adjunct (9 women). *Students:* 193 full-time (165 women), 31 part-time (23 women); includes 114 minority (6 African Americans, 1 American Indian/Alaska Native, 98 Asian Americans or Pacific Islanders, 9 Hispanic Americans), 11 international. Average age 33. 192 applicants, 59% accepted, 69 enrolled. In 2009, 70 master's, 3 doctorates awarded. *Degree requirements:* For doctorate, comprehensive exam, thesis/dissertation. *Entrance requirements:* For doctorate, master's degree (MSW preferred), minimum GPA of 3.0. Additional exam requirements/recommendations for international students: Required—TOEFL (minimum score 560 paper-based; 220 computer-based; 83 iBT), IELTS (minimum score 5). *Application deadline:* For fall admission, 1/15 for domestic and international students. Applications are processed on a rolling basis. Application fee: $60. *Expenses:* Tuition, state resident: full-time $8900; part-time $372 per credit. Tuition, nonresident: full-time $21,400; part-time $898 per credit. Required fees: $207 per semester. *Financial support:* In 2009–10, 6 students received support, including 25 fellowships with full and partial tuition reimbursements available (averaging $2,021 per year), 9 research assistantships with full and partial tuition reimbursements available (averaging $16,647 per year); career-related internships or fieldwork, Federal Work-Study, institutionally sponsored loans, and tuition waivers (full) also available. Support available to part-time students. Financial award application deadline: 2/1; financial award applicants required to submit FAFSA. *Faculty research:* Health, mental health, AIDS, substance abuse, rural health, community-based research, social policy. Total annual research expenditures: $4.5 million. *Unit head:* Jon Matsuoka, Dean, 808-956-6300, E-mail: jmatsuok@hawaii.edu. *Application contact:* Crystal Mills, Graduate Chair, 808-956-3831, Fax: 808-956-5964, E-mail: millsc@hawaii.edu.

University of Houston, Graduate School of Social Work, Houston, TX 77204. Offers MSW, PhD. *Accreditation:* CSWE (one or more programs are accredited). Part-time programs available. *Faculty:* 13 full-time (6 women), 28 part-time/adjunct (23 women). *Students:* 305 full-time (275 women), 57 part-time (47 women); includes 184 minority (100 African Americans, 1 American Indian/Alaska Native, 20 Asian Americans or Pacific Islanders, 63 Hispanic Americans), 8 international. Average age 32. 317 applicants, 57% accepted, 157 enrolled. In 2009, 134 master's, 4 doctorates awarded. *Degree requirements:* For master's, 900 clock hours of field experience, integrative paper. *Entrance requirements:* For master's, GRE, minimum GPA of 3.0 in last 60 hours, bachelor's degree. Additional exam requirements/recommendations for international students: Required—TOEFL (minimum score 550 paper-based; 79 iBT). *Application deadline:* For fall admission, 2/1 priority date for domestic and international students. Applications are processed on a rolling basis. Application fee: $40 ($115 for international students). *Expenses:* Tuition, state resident: full-time $7676; part-time $320 per credit hour. Tuition, nonresident: full-time $14,324; part-time $597 per credit hour. Required fees: $3034. *Financial support:* In 2009–10, 17 fellowships with full tuition reimbursements (averaging $12,850 per year), 9 research assistantships with full tuition reimbursements (averaging $8,800 per year), 2 teaching assistantships with full tuition reimbursements (averaging $8,800 per year) were awarded; career-related internships or fieldwork, Federal Work-Study, institutionally sponsored loans, scholarships/grants, health care benefits, and unspecified assistantships also available. Support available to part-time students. Financial award application deadline: 3/10; financial award applicants required to submit FAFSA. *Faculty research:* Health care, gerontology, political social work, mental health, children and families. *Unit head:* Dr. Ira C. Colby, Dean, 713-743-8075, Fax: 713-743-3267, E-mail: icolby@uh.edu. *Application contact:* Amber Mollhagen, Director of Recruitment and Admissions, 713-743-8082, Fax: 713-743-8149, E-mail: amollhagen@uh.edu.

University of Illinois at Chicago, Graduate College, Jane Addams College of Social Work, Chicago, IL 60607-7128. Offers MSW, PhD. *Accreditation:* CSWE (one or more programs are accredited). Part-time programs available. Terminal master's awarded for partial completion of doctoral program. *Degree requirements:* For doctorate, thesis/dissertation. *Entrance requirements:* For master's, GMAT, minimum GPA of 2.75; for doctorate, GRE General Test or MAT, minimum GPA of 2.75. Additional exam requirements/recommendations for international students: Required—TOEFL. Electronic applications accepted.

University of Illinois at Urbana–Champaign, Graduate College, School of Social Work, Champaign, IL 61820. Offers advocacy, leadership, and social change (MSW); children, youth and family services (MSW); social work (PhD); MS/MSW. *Accreditation:* CSWE (one or more programs are accredited). *Faculty:* 19 full-time (12 women), 2 part-time/adjunct (both women). *Students:* 235 full-time (207 women), 77 part-time (65 women); includes 53 minority (32 African Americans, 1 American Indian/Alaska Native, 10 Asian Americans or Pacific Islanders, 10 Hispanic Americans), 22 international. 339 applicants, 57% accepted, 116 enrolled. In 2009, 123 master's, 2 doctorates awarded. *Entrance requirements:* For master's and doctorate, minimum GPA of 3.0. Additional exam requirements/recommendations for international students: Required—TOEFL (minimum score 580 paper-based; 237 computer-based). *Application deadline:* Applications are processed on a rolling basis. Application fee: $60 ($75 for international students). Electronic applications accepted. *Financial support:* In 2009–10, 4 fellowships, 14 research assistantships, 7 teaching assistantships were awarded; tuition waivers (full and partial) also available. *Unit head:* Wynne S. Korr, Dean, 217-333-2260, Fax: 217-244-5220, E-mail: wkorr@illinois.edu. *Application contact:* Cheryl M. Street, Admissions and Records Officer, 217-333-2261, Fax: 217-244-5220, E-mail: street@illinois.edu.

The University of Iowa, Graduate College, College of Liberal Arts and Sciences, School of Social Work, Iowa City, IA 52242-1316. Offers MSW, PhD, JD/MSW, MSW/MA, MSW/MS, MSW/PhD. *Accreditation:* CSWE. *Degree requirements:* For master's, thesis optional; for doctorate, comprehensive exam, thesis/dissertation. *Entrance requirements:* For master's, minimum GPA of 3.0; for doctorate, GRE General Test, minimum GPA of 3.0. Additional exam requirements/recommendations for international students: Required—TOEFL (minimum score 600 paper-based; 250 computer-based; 100 iBT). Electronic applications accepted.

University of Kentucky, Graduate School, College of Social Work, Program in Social Work, Lexington, KY 40506-0032. Offers MSW, PhD. *Accreditation:* CSWE (one or more programs are accredited). *Degree requirements:* For master's, comprehensive exam; for doctorate, comprehensive exam, thesis/dissertation. *Entrance requirements:* For master's, GRE General Test, minimum undergraduate GPA of 2.75; for doctorate, GRE General Test, minimum undergraduate GPA of 3.0. Additional exam requirements/recommendations for international students: Required—TOEFL (minimum score 550 paper-based; 213 computer-based). Electronic applications accepted. *Faculty research:* Aging, family and children, domestic violence, delinquency, health and mental health.

University of Louisville, Graduate School, Raymond A. Kent School of Social Work, Louisville, KY 40292-0001. Offers marriage and family therapy (PMC); social work (MSSW, PhD), including alcohol and drug counseling (MSSW), gerontology (MSSW), school social work (MSSW). *Accreditation:* AAMFT/COAMFTE; CSWE (one or more programs are accredited). Part-time and evening/weekend programs available. *Faculty:* 23 full-time (15 women), 38 part-time/adjunct (21 women). *Students:* 279 full-time (221 women), 64 part-time (52 women); includes 79 minority (70 African Americans, 2 American Indian/Alaska Native, 2 Asian Americans or Pacific Islanders, 5 Hispanic Americans), 5 international. Average age 32. 288 applicants, 74% accepted, 145 enrolled. In 2009, 137 master's, 4 doctorates awarded. *Degree requirements:* For doctorate, comprehensive exam, thesis/dissertation. *Entrance requirements:* For master's, GRE or minimum GPA of 2.75; for doctorate, GRE General Test, interview, writing sample. Additional exam requirements/recommendations for international students: Required—TOEFL (minimum score 550 paper-based; 213 computer-based; 79 iBT). *Application deadline:* For fall admission, 7/31 for domestic and international students. Applications are processed on a rolling basis. Application fee: $50. Electronic applications accepted. *Financial support:* In 2009–10, 70 students received support, including 9 research assistantships with full tuition reimbursements available (averaging $19,000 per year), 1 teaching assistantship (averaging $19,000 per year); Federal Work-Study, institutionally sponsored loans, scholarships/grants, health care benefits, and unspecified assistantships also available. Support available to part-time students. Financial award application deadline: 5/15; financial award applicants required to submit FAFSA. *Faculty research:* Child welfare, substance abuse, gerontology, family functioning, health behavior. Total annual research expenditures: $2.8 million. *Unit head:* Dr. Terry Singer, Dean, 502-852-6402, Fax: 502-852-0422, E-mail: terry.singer@louisville.edu. *Application contact:* Libby Leggett, Director, Graduate Admissions, 502-852-3101, Fax: 502-852-6536, E-mail: gradadm@louisville.edu.

University of Maine, Graduate School, College of Business, Public Policy and Health, School of Social Work, Orono, ME 04469. Offers MSW. *Accreditation:* CSWE. *Faculty:* 8 full-time (4 women), 1 (woman) part-time/adjunct. *Students:* 126 full-time (106 women), 7 part-time (5 women); includes 10 minority (1 African American, 7 American Indian/Alaska Native, 2 Asian Americans or Pacific Islanders), 5 international. Average age 37. 66 applicants, 64% accepted, 37 enrolled. In 2009, 27 master's awarded. *Entrance requirements:* For master's, GRE General Test. Additional exam requirements/recommendations for international students: Required—TOEFL. *Application deadline:* For fall admission, 2/1 priority date for domestic students. Applications are processed on a rolling basis. Application fee: $65. Electronic applications accepted. *Financial support:* Application deadline: 3/1. *Unit head:* Dr. Sandra Butler, Director, 207-581-2382, Fax: 207-581-2396. *Application contact:* Scott G. Delcourt, Associate Dean of the Graduate School, 207-581-3291, Fax: 207-581-3232, E-mail: graduate@maine.edu.

University of Manitoba, Faculty of Graduate Studies, Faculty of Social Work, Winnipeg, MB R3T 2N2, Canada. Offers MSW, PhD. *Degree requirements:* For master's, thesis or alternative.

University of Maryland, Baltimore, Graduate School, School of Social Work, Doctoral Program in Social Work, Baltimore, MD 21201. Offers PhD. Part-time programs available. *Degree requirements:* For doctorate, thesis/dissertation. *Entrance requirements:* For doctorate, GRE General Test, minimum GPA of 3.5, MSW. *Expenses:* Tuition, state resident: full-time $7290; part-time $405 per credit hour. Tuition, nonresident: full-time $12,780; part-time $710 per credit hour. Required fees: $774; $10 per credit hour. $297 per semester. Tuition and fees vary according to course load, degree level and program. *Faculty research:* Social work research, social work teaching.

University of Maryland, Baltimore, Graduate School, School of Social Work, Master's Program in Social Work, Baltimore, MD 21201. Offers MSW, MBA/MSW, MSW/JD, MSW/MA, MSW/MPH. *Accreditation:* CSWE. *Entrance requirements:* For master's, minimum GPA of 3.0. Additional exam requirements/recommendations for international students: Required—TOEFL. Electronic applications accepted. *Expenses:* Tuition, state resident: full-time $7290; part-time $405 per credit hour. Tuition, nonresident: full-time $12,780; part-time $710 per credit hour. Required fees: $774; $10 per credit hour. $297 per semester. Tuition and fees vary according to course load, degree level and program. *Faculty research:* Aging, families and children, health, mental health, social action and community development.

University of Maryland, College Park, Academic Affairs, Robert H. Smith School of Business, Combined MSW/MBA Program, College Park, MD 20742. Offers MSW/MBA. *Accreditation:* AACSB. *Students:* 1 part-time (0 women). 4 applicants, 50% accepted, 0 enrolled. *Entrance requirements:* Additional exam requirements/recommendations for international students: Required—TOEFL. *Application deadline:* For fall admission, 12/15 priority date for domestic students, 12/15 for international students; for spring admission, 11/30 for domestic students, 6/1 for international students. Application fee: $60. *Expenses:* Tuition, area resident: Part-time $471 per credit hour. Tuition, state resident: part-time $471 per credit hour. Tuition, nonresident: part-time $1016 per credit hour. Required fees: $337.04 per term. *Financial support:* Fellowships available. *Unit head:* Dr. Robert Krapfel, Associate Dean, 301-405-2198, E-mail: bkrapfel@umd.edu. *Application contact:* Dean of Graduate School, 301-405-0358.

University of Michigan, School of Social Work, Ann Arbor, MI 48109. Offers MSW, PhD, MSW/JD, MSW/MBA, MSW/MPH, MSW/MPP, MSW/MSI, MSW/MUP. PhD offered through the Horace H. Rackham School of Graduate Studies. *Accreditation:* CSWE (one or more programs are accredited). *Degree requirements:* For doctorate, oral defense of dissertation, preliminary exam. *Entrance requirements:* For doctorate, GRE General Test. Additional exam requirements/recommendations for international students: Required—TOEFL (minimum score 600 paper-based; 250 computer-based; 100 iBT), IELTS (minimum score 7), TWE. Electronic applications accepted. *Expenses:* Contact institution. *Faculty research:* Children and adults, aging, community organization, health and mental health, policy and evaluation.

University of Minnesota, Duluth, Graduate School, College of Education and Human Service Professions, Department of Social Work, Duluth, MN 55812-2496. Offers MSW. *Accreditation:* CSWE. Part-time and evening/weekend programs available. Postbaccalaureate distance learning degree programs offered (minimal on-campus study). *Entrance requirements:* For master's, minimum GPA of 3.0. Additional exam requirements/recommendations for international students: Required—TOEFL (minimum score 550 paper-based; 213 computer-based). *Faculty research:* Domestic abuse, substance abuse, minority health, child welfare, gerontology.

University of Minnesota, Twin Cities Campus, Graduate School, College of Education and Human Development, School of Social Work, Minneapolis, MN 55455-0213. Offers MSW, PhD. *Accreditation:* CSWE (one or more programs are accredited). Part-time and evening/weekend programs available. Postbaccalaureate distance learning degree programs offered. *Faculty:* 20 full-time (9 women). *Students:* 262 full-time (231 women), 59 part-time (48 women); includes 58 minority (25 African Americans, 4 American Indian/Alaska Native, 23 Asian Americans or Pacific Islanders, 6 Hispanic Americans), 12 international. Average age 33. 496 applicants, 44% accepted, 216 enrolled. In 2009, 125 master's, 4 doctorates awarded. *Degree requirements:* For doctorate, thesis/dissertation. *Entrance requirements:* For master's, minimum GPA of 3.0, 1 year of work experience; for doctorate, GRE, minimum GPA of 3.0, MSW. *Application deadline:* For fall admission, 1/15 for domestic students. Application fee: $40 ($50 for international students). *Financial support:* In 2009–10, 142 students received support, including 3 fellowships (averaging $35,667 per year), 39 research assistantships (averaging $27,198 per year); teaching assistantships, career-related internships or fieldwork, Federal Work-Study, institutionally sponsored loans, and tuition waivers (full and partial) also available. Support available to part-time students. Financial award applicants required to submit FAFSA. *Faculty research:* Mental health, aging and disability, work with youth, family violence, New American and immigrant populations, child welfare. Total annual research expenditures: $3.6 million. *Unit head:* James Reinardy, Director, 612-624-3673, Fax: 612-624-3746, E-mail: jreinard@umn.edu. *Application contact:* Rachel Grewell, Information Contact, 612-625-0477.

University of Mississippi, Graduate School, School of Applied Sciences, Department of Social Work, Oxford, University, MS 38677. Offers MSW. *Faculty:* 13 full-time (10 women), 1 (woman) part-time/adjunct. *Students:* 22 full-time (19 women), 18 part-time (15 women); includes 11 minority (10 African Americans, 1 American Indian/Alaska Native). *Unit head:* Dr. Carol Minor Boyd, Chair, 662-915-7336, Fax: 662-915-1288, E-mail: socialwk@olemiss.edu. *Application contact:* Dr. Christy M. Wyandt, Associate Dean, 662-915-7474, Fax: 662-915-7577, E-mail: cwyandt@olemiss.edu.

University of Missouri, Graduate School, School of Social Work, Columbia, MO 65211. Offers MSW. *Accreditation:* CSWE. Part-time programs available. *Entrance requirements:* For master's, GRE General Test, minimum GPA of 3.0. Additional exam requirements/recommendations for international students: Required—TOEFL (minimum score 500 paper-based; 173 computer-based; 61 iBT).

University of Missouri–Kansas City, College of Arts and Sciences, School of Social Work, Kansas City, MO 64110-2499. Offers MSW. *Accreditation:* CSWE. Part-time and evening/weekend programs available. *Faculty:* 11 full-time (8 women), 9 part-time/adjunct (4 women). *Students:* 95 full-time (83 women), 112 part-time (94 women); includes 50 minority (37 African Americans, 2 American Indian/Alaska Native, 2 Asian Americans or Pacific Islanders, 9 Hispanic Americans), 1 international. Average age 34. 121 applicants, 85% accepted, 97 enrolled. In 2009, 72 master's awarded. *Entrance requirements:* For master's, minimum GPA of 3.0, 3 letters of reference. Additional exam requirements/recommendations for international students: Recommended—TOEFL (minimum score 550 paper-based; 213 computer-based; 80 iBT). *Application deadline:* For fall admission, 4/30 for domestic and international students; for spring admission, 12/1 for domestic and international students. Applications are processed on a rolling basis. Application fee: $45 ($50 for international students). *Expenses:* Tuition, state

Social Work

University of Missouri–Kansas City (continued)
resident: full-time $5378; part-time $299 per credit hour. Tuition, nonresident: full-time $13,881; part-time $771 per credit hour. Required fees: $641; $71 per credit hour. Tuition and fees vary according to course load and program. *Financial support:* In 2009–10, 3 research assistantships with partial tuition reimbursements (averaging $11,280 per year) were awarded; career-related internships or fieldwork and institutionally sponsored loans also available. Financial award application deadline: 3/1; financial award applicants required to submit FAFSA. *Faculty research:* Social justice, LGBT issues, deinstitutionalization, community collaboration and partnerships, evaluation of strengths model with addiction model. Total annual research expenditures: $133,978. *Unit head:* Dr. Michael Smith, Program Director, 816-235-1025, E-mail: soc-wk@umkc.edu. *Application contact:* Dr. Michael Smith, Program Director, 816-235-1025, E-mail: soc-wk@umkc.edu.

University of Missouri–St. Louis, College of Arts and Sciences, School of Social Work, St. Louis, MO 63121. Offers MS, MSW, Certificate. *Accreditation:* CSWE. *Faculty:* 10 full-time (8 women), 5 part-time/adjunct (3 women). *Students:* 64 full-time (57 women), 65 part-time (57 women); includes 17 minority (15 African Americans, 1 American Indian/Alaska Native, 1 Hispanic American), 1 international. Average age 32. In 2009, 33 master's awarded. *Entrance requirements:* For master's, 3 letters of recommendation. Additional exam requirements/recommendations for international students: Required—TOEFL (minimum score 550 paper-based; 213 computer-based). *Application deadline:* For fall admission, 2/15 for domestic and international students. Application fee: $35 ($40 for international students). Electronic applications accepted. *Expenses:* Tuition, state resident: full-time $5377; part-time $297.70 per credit hour. Tuition, nonresident: full-time $13,882; part-time $771.20 per credit hour. Required fees: $220; $12.20 per credit hour. One-time fee: $12. Tuition and fees vary according to course level, campus/location and program. *Financial support:* In 2009–10, 2 research assistantships with full and partial tuition reimbursements (averaging $8,550 per year), 6 teaching assistantships with full and partial tuition reimbursements (averaging $8,438 per year) were awarded. Financial award applicants required to submit FAFSA. *Faculty research:* Family violence, child abuse/neglect, immigration, community economic development. *Unit head:* Dr. Lois Pierce, Graduate Program Director, 314-516-6364, Fax: 314-516-5816, E-mail: socialwork@umsl.edu. *Application contact:* 314-516-5458, Fax: 314-516-6996, E-mail: gradadm@umsl.edu.

The University of Montana, Graduate School, College of Health Professions and Biomedical Sciences, School of Social Work, Missoula, MT 59812-0002. Offers MSW. *Accreditation:* CSWE.

University of Nebraska at Omaha, Graduate Studies, College of Public Affairs and Community Service, School of Social Work, Omaha, NE 68182. Offers MSW. *Accreditation:* CSWE. *Faculty:* 11 full-time (9 women). *Students:* 103 full-time (90 women), 78 part-time (68 women); includes 13 minority (3 African Americans, 1 American Indian/Alaska Native, 3 Asian Americans or Pacific Islanders, 6 Hispanic Americans), 4 international. Average age 29. 128 applicants, 73% accepted, 58 enrolled. In 2009, 44 master's awarded. *Degree requirements:* For master's, comprehensive exam, thesis (for some programs). *Entrance requirements:* For master's, minimum GPA of 3.0, letters of recommendation, resume. Additional exam requirements/recommendations for international students: Required—TOEFL (minimum score 500 paper-based; 173 computer-based; 61 iBT). *Application deadline:* For fall admission, 3/1 for domestic students. Applications are processed on a rolling basis. Application fee: $45. Electronic applications accepted. *Financial support:* In 2009–10, 94 students received support; fellowships, research assistantships with tuition reimbursements available, career-related internships or fieldwork, Federal Work-Study, institutionally sponsored loans, scholarships/grants, tuition waivers (full), and unspecified assistantships available. Support available to part-time students. Financial award application deadline: 3/1; financial award applicants required to submit FAFSA. *Unit head:* Dr. Theresa Barron-McKeagney, Director, 402-554-2791. *Application contact:* Penny Harmoney, Director, Graduate Studies, 402-554-2341, Fax: 402-554-3143, E-mail: graduate@unomaha.edu.

University of Nevada, Las Vegas, Graduate College, Greenspun College of Urban Affairs, School of Social Work, Las Vegas, NV 89154-5032. Offers forensic social work (Advanced Certificate); social work (MSW); MSW/JD. *Accreditation:* CSWE. *Faculty:* 14 full-time (11 women), 11 part-time/adjunct (7 women). *Students:* 116 full-time (97 women), 66 part-time (51 women); includes 60 minority (20 African Americans, 2 American Indian/Alaska Native, 10 Asian Americans or Pacific Islanders, 28 Hispanic Americans), 1 international. Average age 34. 206 applicants, 45% accepted, 65 enrolled. In 2009, 66 master's, 3 other advanced degrees awarded. *Degree requirements:* For master's, comprehensive exam, thesis optional. *Entrance requirements:* Additional exam requirements/recommendations for international students: Required—TOEFL (minimum score 550 paper-based; 231 computer-based; 80 iBT), IELTS (minimum score 7). *Application deadline:* For fall admission, 2/1 priority date for domestic and international students. Applications are processed on a rolling basis. Application fee: $60 ($95 for international students). Electronic applications accepted. *Financial support:* In 2009–10, 4 students received support, including 4 teaching assistantships with partial tuition reimbursements available (averaging $10,000 per year); institutionally sponsored loans, scholarships/grants, health care benefits, and unspecified assistantships also available. Financial award application deadline: 3/1. *Faculty research:* Child welfare, mental health, substance abuse, youth services and wrap-around services, poverty and TANF. *Unit head:* Dr. Joanne Thompson, Director/ Professor, 702-895-0521, Fax: 702-895-4079, E-mail: joanne.thompson@unlv.edu. *Application contact:* Graduate College Admissions Evaluator, 702-895-3320, Fax: 702-895-4180, E-mail: gradcollege@unlv.edu.

University of Nevada, Reno, Graduate School, Division of Health Sciences, School of Social Work, Reno, NV 89557. Offers MSW. *Accreditation:* CSWE. *Degree requirements:* For master's, thesis optional. *Entrance requirements:* For master's, GRE General Test, minimum GPA of 2.75, statistics course. Additional exam requirements/recommendations for international students: Required—TOEFL (minimum score 500 paper-based; 173 computer-based; 61 iBT), IELTS (minimum score 6). Electronic applications accepted. *Faculty research:* Policy practice, poverty, women's issues, race and diversity, vulnerable family, social justice, social change, diversity.

University of New England, Westbrook College of Health Professions, School of Social Work, Biddeford, ME 04005-9526. Offers addictions counseling (Certificate); gerontology (Certificate); social work (MSW). *Accreditation:* CSWE. Part-time programs available. *Faculty:* 12 full-time (8 women), 4 part-time/adjunct (all women). *Students:* 159 full-time (134 women), 2 part-time (both women); includes 6 minority (5 African Americans, 1 American Indian/Alaska Native), 3 international. In 2009, 44 master's awarded. *Degree requirements:* For master's, field internships. *Entrance requirements:* Additional exam requirements/recommendations for international students: Required—TOEFL (minimum score 550 paper-based; 213 computer-based). *Application deadline:* For fall admission, 1/15 priority date for domestic students; for spring admission, 3/31 priority date for domestic students, 3/31 for international students. Applications are processed on a rolling basis. Application fee: $40. Electronic applications accepted. *Financial support:* In 2009–10, 40 students received support. Scholarships/grants and tuition waivers (partial) available. Financial award application deadline: 5/1; financial award applicants required to submit FAFSA. *Faculty research:* Domestic violence, solution-focused practice, empowerment models, adverse childhood experiences. *Unit head:* Martha Wilson, Director, 207-221-4513, E-mail: mwilson@une.edu. *Application contact:* Stacy Gato, Assistant Director of Graduate Admissions, 207-221-4225, Fax: 207-221-4898, E-mail: gradadmissions@une.edu.

University of New Hampshire, Center for Graduate and Professional Studies, Manchester, NH 03101. Offers business administration (MBA); counseling (M Ed); education (M Ed, MAT); educational administration and supervision (M Ed, CAGS); industrial statistics (Certificate); public administration (MPA); public health (MPH, Certificate); social work (MSW). Part-time and evening/weekend programs available. *Students:* 86 full-time (57 women), 150 part-time (87 women); includes 13 minority (3 African Americans, 6 Asian Americans or Pacific Islanders, 4 Hispanic Americans), 7 international. 127 applicants, 73% accepted, 60 enrolled. In 2009, 81 master's, 5 other advanced degrees awarded. *Degree requirements:* For master's, thesis or

alternative. *Entrance requirements:* Additional exam requirements/recommendations for international students: Required—TOEFL (minimum score 550 paper-based; 213 computer-based; 80 iBT), TOEIC, TSE. *Application deadline:* For fall admission, 6/1 for domestic students, 4/1 for international students; for spring admission, 12/1 for domestic students. Applications are processed on a rolling basis. Application fee: $65. Electronic applications accepted. *Expenses:* Tuition, state resident: full-time $10,380; part-time $577 per credit hour. Tuition, nonresident: full-time $24,350; part-time $1002 per credit hour. Required fees: $1550; $387.50 per semester. Tuition and fees vary according to course load and program. *Financial support:* In 2009–10, 20 students received support, including 1 fellowship, 1 teaching assistantship; research assistantships, Federal Work-Study, scholarships/grants, health care benefits, and unspecified assistantships also available. Support available to part-time students. Financial award application deadline: 3/1; financial award applicants required to submit FAFSA. *Unit head:* Kate Ferreira, Director, 603-641-4313, E-mail: unhm.gradcenter@unh.edu. *Application contact:* Graduate Admissions Office, 603-862-3000, Fax: 603-862-0275, E-mail: grad.school@unh.edu.

University of New Hampshire, Graduate School, School of Health and Human Services, Department of Social Work, Durham, NH 03824. Offers MSW, Postbaccalaureate Certificate. *Accreditation:* CSWE. Part-time programs available. *Faculty:* 11 full-time (8 women). *Students:* 106 full-time (91 women), 31 part-time (29 women); includes 6 minority (2 African Americans, 2 Asian Americans or Pacific Islanders, 2 Hispanic Americans), 2 international. Average age 34. 136 applicants, 76% accepted, 61 enrolled. In 2009, 40 master's, 3 other advanced degrees awarded. *Entrance requirements:* Additional exam requirements/recommendations for international students: Required—TOEFL (minimum score 550 paper-based; 213 computer-based; 80 iBT). *Application deadline:* For fall admission, 2/1 for domestic and international students. Applications are processed on a rolling basis. Application fee: $65. Electronic applications accepted. *Expenses:* Tuition, state resident: full-time $10,380; part-time $577 per credit hour. Tuition, nonresident: full-time $24,350; part-time $1002 per credit hour. Required fees: $1550; $387.50 per semester. Tuition and fees vary according to course load and program. *Financial support:* In 2009–10, 14 students received support, including 7 teaching assistantships; fellowships, research assistantships, career-related internships or fieldwork, Federal Work-Study, and scholarships/grants also available. Support available to part-time students. Financial award application deadline: 2/15. *Unit head:* Dr. Jerry Marx, Chairperson, 603-862-0274. *Application contact:* Karen Frarie, Application Contact, 603-862-0215, E-mail: kfrarie@cisunix.unh.edu.

The University of North Carolina at Chapel Hill, Graduate School, School of Social Work, Chapel Hill, NC 27599. Offers MSW, PhD, JD/MSW, MPA/MSW, MSPH/MSW. *Accreditation:* CSWE (one or more programs are accredited). Part-time programs available. Terminal master's awarded for partial completion of doctoral program. *Degree requirements:* For doctorate, thesis/dissertation, qualifying exam. *Entrance requirements:* For master's and doctorate, GRE General Test, minimum GPA of 3.0. Electronic applications accepted. *Faculty research:* School success, risk and resiliency, welfare reform, aging, substance abuse.

The University of North Carolina at Charlotte, Graduate School, College of Health and Human Services, Department of Social Work, Charlotte, NC 28223-0001. Offers MSW. *Accreditation:* CSWE. Part-time programs available. *Faculty:* 12 full-time (8 women), 5 part-time/adjunct (all women). *Students:* 94 full-time (81 women), 8 part-time (all women); includes 29 minority (25 African Americans, 1 Asian American or Pacific Islander, 3 Hispanic Americans). Average age 31. 124 applicants, 66% accepted, 48 enrolled. In 2009, 54 master's awarded. *Entrance requirements:* For master's, GRE, minimum GPA of 2.7 overall, 3.0 in last 30 hours of course work. Additional exam requirements/recommendations for international students: Required—TOEFL (minimum score 557 paper-based; 220 computer-based; 83 iBT). *Application deadline:* For fall admission, 7/1 for domestic students, 5/1 for international students; for spring admission, 11/1 for domestic students, 10/1 for international students. Applications are processed on a rolling basis. Application fee: $55. Electronic applications accepted. *Financial support:* In 2009–10, 3 students received support, including 1 research assistantship (averaging $4,500 per year), 2 teaching assistantships (averaging $4,529 per year); career-related internships or fieldwork, Federal Work-Study, institutionally sponsored loans, scholarships/grants, and unspecified assistantships also available. Support available to part-time students. Financial award application deadline: 4/1; financial award applicants required to submit FAFSA. *Faculty research:* Social work practice with lesbian and gay youth, aging, welfare reform, non-custodial fathers, grandparents as caregivers of grandchildren. Total annual research expenditures: $351,640. *Unit head:* Dr. Dennis Long, Interim Chair, 704-687-7935, Fax: 704-687-2343, E-mail: ddlong@uncc.edu. *Application contact:* Kathy B. Giddings, Director of Graduate Admissions, 704-687-5503, Fax: 704-687-3279, E-mail: gradadm@uncc.edu.

The University of North Carolina at Greensboro, Graduate School, School of Human Environmental Sciences, Department of Social Work, Greensboro, NC 27412-5001. Offers MSW. *Accreditation:* CSWE. *Entrance requirements:* For master's, GRE General Test. Additional exam requirements/recommendations for international students: Required—TOEFL. Electronic applications accepted.

The University of North Carolina Wilmington, College of Arts and Sciences, Department of Social Work, Wilmington, NC 28403-3297. Offers MSW. *Accreditation:* CSWE. *Degree requirements:* For master's, comprehensive exam, thesis or alternative. *Entrance requirements:* For master's, GMAT, GRE General Test. Additional exam requirements/recommendations for international students: Required—TOEFL (minimum score 550 paper-based; 217 computer-based; 79 iBT), IELTS (minimum score 6.5).

University of North Dakota, Graduate School, College of Education and Human Development, School of Social Work, Grand Forks, ND 58202. Offers MSW. *Accreditation:* CSWE. *Degree requirements:* For master's, comprehensive exam, thesis or alternative. *Entrance requirements:* For master's, minimum GPA of 3.0. Additional exam requirements/recommendations for international students: Required—TOEFL (minimum score 550 paper-based; 213 computer-based; 79 iBT), IELTS (minimum score 6.5). Electronic applications accepted. *Faculty research:* Mental health, gerontology, chemical abuse, children and families.

University of Northern British Columbia, Office of Graduate Studies, Prince George, BC V2N 4Z9, Canada. Offers business administration (Diploma); community health science (M Sc); disability management (MA); education (M Ed); first nations studies (MA); gender studies (MA); history (MA); interdisciplinary studies (MA); international studies (MA); mathematical, computer and physical sciences (M Sc); natural resources and environmental studies (M Sc, MA, MNRES, PhD); political science (MA); psychology (M Sc, PhD); social work (MSW). Part-time and evening/weekend programs available. Postbaccalaureate distance learning degree programs offered (no on-campus study). *Degree requirements:* For master's, thesis; for doctorate, thesis/dissertation. *Entrance requirements:* For master's, GRE, minimum B average in undergraduate course work; for doctorate, candidacy exam, minimum A average in graduate course work.

University of Northern Iowa, Graduate College, College of Social and Behavioral Sciences, Department of Social Work, Cedar Falls, IA 50614. Offers MSW. *Accreditation:* CSWE. *Students:* 54 full-time (51 women), 7 part-time (all women); includes 6 minority (3 African Americans, 1 Asian American or Pacific Islander, 2 Hispanic Americans). 42 applicants, 45% accepted, 14 enrolled. In 2009, 27 master's awarded. *Entrance requirements:* For master's, minimum GPA of 3.0; department application; 3 letters of recommendation; personal autobiographical statement. Additional exam requirements/recommendations for international students: Required—TOEFL (minimum score 500 paper-based; 180 computer-based; 61 iBT). *Application deadline:* For fall admission, 8/1 priority date for domestic students. Applications are processed on a rolling basis. Application fee: $30 ($50 for international students). Electronic applications accepted. *Financial support:* Application deadline: 2/1. *Unit head:* Dr. Thomas W. Keefe, Department Head/Professor, 319-273-6249, Fax: 319-273-6976, E-mail: thomas.keefe@uni.edu. *Application contact:* Laurie S. Russell, Record Analyst, 319-273-2623, Fax: 319-273-6792, E-mail: laurie.russell@uni.edu.

University of Oklahoma, Graduate College, College of Arts and Sciences, School of Social Work, Norman, OK 73019. Offers MSW. *Accreditation:* CSWE. Part-time programs available. *Faculty:* 20 full-time (11 women), 18 part-time/adjunct (12 women). *Students:* 194 full-time (170 women), 140 part-time (119 women); includes 109 minority (53 African Americans, 31 American Indian/Alaska Native, 12 Asian Americans or Pacific Islanders, 13 Hispanic Americans), 2 international. 143 applicants, 74% accepted, 91 enrolled. In 2009, 104 master's awarded. *Entrance requirements:* For master's, GRE, minimum GPA of 3.0, 3 letters of reference. Additional exam requirements/recommendations for international students: Required—TOEFL (minimum score 550 paper-based; 213 computer-based). *Application deadline:* For fall admission, 3/1 priority date for domestic students, 4/1 for international students; for spring admission, 11/1 for domestic students, 9/1 for international students. Application fee: $40 ($90 for international students). Electronic applications accepted. *Expenses:* Tuition, state resident: full-time $3744; part-time $156 per credit hour. Tuition, nonresident: full-time $13,577; part-time $565.70 per credit hour. Required fees: $2415; $90.10 per credit hour. *Financial support:* In 2009–10, 147 students received support, including 15 research assistantships with partial tuition reimbursements available (averaging $9,586 per year), 4 teaching assistantships with partial tuition reimbursements available (averaging $9,586 per year); career-related internships or fieldwork, institutionally sponsored loans, scholarships/grants, traineeships, health care benefits, tuition waivers (partial), and unspecified assistantships also available. Support available to part-time students. Financial award application deadline: 3/1; financial award applicants required to submit FAFSA. *Faculty research:* Homelessness, co-occurring disorders, prevention of substance abuse, social justice, HIV/AIDS. Total annual research expenditures: $134,184. *Unit head:* Dr. Donald R. Baker, Director, 405-325-2821, Fax: 405-325-7072, E-mail: drralph@ou.edu. *Application contact:* Dr. James Rosenthal, Graduate Coordinator, 405-325-1399, Fax: 405-325-7072, E-mail: jimar@ou.edu.

University of Ottawa, Faculty of Graduate and Postdoctoral Studies, Faculty of Social Sciences, School of Social Work, Ottawa, ON K1N 6N5, Canada. Offers MSS. Program offered in French. *Degree requirements:* For master's, thesis or alternative. *Entrance requirements:* For master's, honors bachelor's degree or equivalent, minimum B average. Electronic applications accepted. *Faculty research:* Family-children, health.

University of Pennsylvania, School of Social Policy and Practice, Graduate Group on Social Welfare, Philadelphia, PA 19104. Offers PhD. *Faculty:* 23 full-time, 14 part-time/adjunct. *Students:* 55 full-time (44 women); includes 21 minority (11 African Americans, 7 Asian Americans or Pacific Islanders, 3 Hispanic Americans). Average age 30. 53 applicants, 9% accepted, 4 enrolled. In 2009, 4 doctorates awarded. *Degree requirements:* For doctorate, thesis/dissertation. *Entrance requirements:* For doctorate, GRE General Test, MSW or master's degree in related field. Additional exam requirements/recommendations for international students: Required—TOEFL (minimum score 600 paper-based; 213 computer-based; 100 iBT). *Application deadline:* For fall admission, 12/15 for domestic and international students. Application fee: $70. Electronic applications accepted. *Expenses:* Tuition: Full-time $25,660; part-time $4758 per course. Required fees: $2152; $270 per course. Tuition and fees vary according to course load, degree level and program. *Financial support:* In 2009–10, 55 students received support, including 4 fellowships with full tuition reimbursements available (averaging $19,000 per year), 16 research assistantships with full tuition reimbursements available (averaging $19,000 per year); teaching assistantships with full tuition reimbursements available, career-related internships or fieldwork, institutionally sponsored loans, and unspecified assistantships also available. Financial award application deadline: 2/1; financial award applicants required to submit FAFSA. *Faculty research:* Mental health, child welfare, organizational behavior, urban poverty, comparative social welfare. Total annual research expenditures: $3.5 million. *Unit head:* Dr. Susan Sorenson, Director, Doctoral Program, 215-893-1169, Fax: 215-573-2099, E-mail: sorenson@sp2.upenn.edu. *Application contact:* Mary C. Mazzola, Associate Dean, Enrollment Management, 215-898-5550, Fax: 215-573-2099, E-mail: mmazzola@sp2.upenn.edu.

See Close-Up on page 1897.

University of Pennsylvania, School of Social Policy and Practice, Program in Social Work, Philadelphia, PA 19104. Offers MSW, DSW, JD/MSW, MSW/Certificate, MSW/MBA, MSW/MBE, MSW/MCP, MSW/MGA, MSW/MPH, MSW/MS Ed, MSW/MSC, MSW/PhD. *Accreditation:* CSWE. Part-time programs available. *Faculty:* 21 full-time, 49 part-time/adjunct. *Students:* 197 full-time (181 women), 72 part-time (62 women); includes 75 minority (43 African Americans, 3 American Indian/Alaska Native, 21 Asian Americans or Pacific Islanders, 8 Hispanic Americans), 3 international. Average age 24. 527 applicants, 63% accepted, 180 enrolled. In 2009, 111 master's awarded. Terminal master's awarded for partial completion of doctoral program. *Degree requirements:* For master's, fieldwork. *Entrance requirements:* For doctorate, GRE General Test, MSW or Masters Degree in Related Field. Additional exam requirements/recommendations for international students: Required—TOEFL (minimum score 600 paper-based; 213 computer-based; 100 iBT). *Application deadline:* For fall admission, 4/15 priority date for domestic and international students. Applications are processed on a rolling basis. Application fee: $65. Electronic applications accepted. *Expenses:* Tuition: Full-time $25,660; part-time $4758 per course. Required fees: $2152; $270 per course. Tuition and fees vary according to course load, degree level and program. *Financial support:* In 2009–10, 225 students received support. Federal Work-Study and scholarships/grants available. Support available to part-time students. Financial award applicants required to submit FAFSA. *Faculty research:* Homelessness, juvenile justice, mental health/children's mental health, child welfare, domestic and family violence. Total annual research expenditures: $3.5 million. *Unit head:* Richard Gelles, Dean, 215-898-5541, Fax: 215-573-2099, E-mail: gelles@sp2.upenn.edu. *Application contact:* Mary C. Mazzola, Associate Dean, Enrollment Management, 215-898-5550, Fax: 215-573-2099, E-mail: mmazzola@sp2.upenn.edu.

See Close-Up on page 1897.

University of Pittsburgh, School of Social Work, Pittsburgh, PA 15260. Offers gerontology (Certificate); social work (MSW, PhD); M Div/MSW; MPA/MSW; MPH/PhD; MPIA/MSW; MSW/JD; MSW/MAJCS; MSW/MPH. *Accreditation:* CSWE (one or more programs are accredited). Part-time programs available. *Faculty:* 21 full-time (12 women), 35 part-time/adjunct (29 women). *Students:* 392 full-time (325 women), 242 part-time (200 women); includes 114 minority (83 African Americans, 2 American Indian/Alaska Native, 15 Asian Americans or Pacific Islanders, 14 Hispanic Americans). Average age 28. 500 applicants, 86% accepted, 255 enrolled. In 2009, 174 master's, 4 doctorates awarded. *Degree requirements:* For master's, practicum; for doctorate, comprehensive exam, thesis/dissertation; for Certificate, thesis. *Entrance requirements:* For master's, minimum QPA of 3.0, course work in statistics; for doctorate, GRE, MSW or related degree, course work in statistics. Additional exam requirements/recommendations for international students: Required—TOEFL (minimum score 550 paper-based; 213 computer-based; 80 iBT). *Application deadline:* For fall admission, 5/1 for domestic and international students. Applications are processed on a rolling basis. Application fee: $40 ($50 for international students). Electronic applications accepted. *Expenses:* Tuition, state resident: full-time $16,402; part-time $665 per credit. Tuition, nonresident: full-time $28,694; part-time $1175 per credit. Required fees: $690; $175 per term. Tuition and fees vary according to program. *Financial support:* In 2009–10, 213 students received support, including 1 research assistantship with full tuition reimbursement available (averaging $11,830 per year), 3 teaching assistantships with full tuition reimbursements available (averaging $15,065 per year); fellowships, career-related internships or fieldwork, institutionally sponsored loans, scholarships/grants, traineeships, tuition waivers (full), and unspecified assistantships also available. Financial award application deadline: 3/31; financial award applicants required to submit FAFSA. *Faculty research:* Mental health services research, child abuse and neglect, geriatrics, criminal justice race issues. Total annual research expenditures: $595,476. *Unit head:* Dr. Larry E. Davis, Dean, 412-624-6304, Fax: 412-624-6323, E-mail: ledavis@pitt.edu. *Application contact:* Philip Mack, Director of Admissions, 412-624-6346, Fax: 412-624-6323, E-mail: psm8@pitt.edu.

University of Puerto Rico, Río Piedras, College of Social Sciences, Graduate School of Social Work, San Juan, PR 00931-3300. Offers MSW, PhD. *Accreditation:* CSWE. Part-time programs available. *Degree requirements:* For master's, comprehensive exam, thesis; for doctorate, comprehensive exam, thesis/dissertation. *Entrance requirements:* For master's, PAEG or GRE, interview, minimum GPA of 3.0, letter of recommendation; for doctorate, PAEG or GRE, interview, minimum GPA of 3.0, 3 letters of recommendation, social work experience. *Faculty research:* Social work in Puerto Rico, Cuba, and the Dominican Republic; migration; poverty in Puerto Rico.

University of Regina, Faculty of Graduate Studies and Research, Faculty of Social Work, Regina, SK S4S 0A2, Canada. Offers MASW, MSW, PhD. Part-time programs available. *Faculty:* 13 full-time (6 women), 3 part-time/adjunct (2 women). *Students:* 44 full-time (38 women), 30 part-time (25 women). 59 applicants, 71% accepted. In 2009, 9 master's, 1 doctorate awarded. *Degree requirements:* For doctorate, thesis/dissertation. *Entrance requirements:* For master's, BSW. Additional exam requirements/recommendations for international students: Required—TOEFL (minimum score 580 paper-based; 237 computer-based; 80 iBT). *Application deadline:* For fall admission, 2/15 for domestic students. Application fee: $90 ($100 for international students). *Expenses:* Contact institution. *Financial support:* In 2009–10, 2 fellowships (averaging $19,000 per year), 2 teaching assistantships (averaging $6,650 per year) were awarded; research assistantships, career-related internships or fieldwork and scholarships/grants also available. Financial award application deadline: 6/15. *Faculty research:* Social research, social planning, social policy implementation, policy planning, social administration. *Unit head:* Dr. David Broad, Dean, 306-585-4588, E-mail: david.broad@uregina.ca. *Application contact:* Dr. Miguel Sanchez, Graduate Program Coordinator, 306-585-4848, Fax: 306-585-4872, E-mail: miguel.sanchez@uregina.ca.

University of St. Francis, College of Arts and Sciences, Joliet, IL 60435-6169. Offers physician assistant practice (MS); social work (MSW). *Faculty:* 9 full-time (7 women). *Students:* 78 full-time (58 women), 9 part-time (all women); includes 24 minority (11 African Americans, 2 American Indian/Alaska Native, 2 Asian Americans or Pacific Islanders, 9 Hispanic Americans). Average age 31. 50 applicants, 44% accepted, 10 enrolled. In 2009, 44 master's awarded. *Entrance requirements:* Additional exam requirements/recommendations for international students: Required—TOEFL (minimum score 550 paper-based; 213 computer-based). *Application deadline:* Applications are processed on a rolling basis. Application fee: $30. Electronic applications accepted. *Expenses:* Tuition: Part-time $589 per credit hour. Tuition and fees vary according to degree level, campus/location and program. *Financial support:* In 2009–10, 86 students received support. Federal Work-Study, scholarships/grants, and tuition waivers (partial) available. Support available to part-time students. Financial award applicants required to submit FAFSA. *Unit head:* Dr. Robert Kase, Dean, 815-740-3367, Fax: 815-740-6366. *Application contact:* Sandra Sloka, Director of Admissions for Graduate and Degree Completion Programs, 800-735-7500, Fax: 815-740-5032, E-mail: ssloka@stfrancis.edu.

University of St. Thomas, Graduate Studies, School of Social Work, St. Paul, MN 55105-1096. Offers MSW. *Accreditation:* CSWE. Part-time and evening/weekend programs available. Postbaccalaureate distance learning degree programs offered (minimal on-campus study). *Faculty:* 15 full-time (11 women), 18 part-time/adjunct (12 women). *Students:* 207 full-time (189 women), 184 part-time (166 women); includes 32 minority (14 African Americans, 2 American Indian/Alaska Native, 10 Asian Americans or Pacific Islanders, 6 Hispanic Americans). Average age 31. 263 applicants, 82% accepted, 158 enrolled. In 2009, 110 master's awarded. *Degree requirements:* For master's, thesis, fieldwork. *Entrance requirements:* For master's, previous course work in developmental psychology, human biology, and statistics/methods. Additional exam requirements/recommendations for international students: Required—TOEFL (minimum score 600 paper-based; 250 computer-based; 100 iBT), Michigan English Language Assessment Battery (minimum score 90). *Application deadline:* For fall admission, 1/10 for domestic students. Application fee: $35. Electronic applications accepted. *Expenses:* Contact institution. *Financial support:* In 2009–10, 339 students received support, including 8 fellowships, 16 research assistantships; career-related internships or fieldwork, Federal Work-Study, institutionally sponsored loans, scholarships/grants, and unspecified assistantships also available. Support available to part-time students. Financial award application deadline: 7/1; financial award applicants required to submit FAFSA. *Faculty research:* Clinical supervision and practice, group work, child welfare and social work. *Unit head:* Dr. Barbara W. Shank, Dean and Professor, 651-962-5801, Fax: 651-962-5819, E-mail: bwshank@stthomas.edu. *Application contact:* Lisa Dalsin, Program Manager, 651-962-5810, Fax: 651-962-5819, E-mail: msw@stthomas.edu.

University of South Africa, College of Human Sciences, Pretoria, South Africa. Offers adult education (M Ed); African languages (MA, PhD); African politics (MA, PhD); Afrikaans (MA, PhD); ancient history (MA, PhD); ancient Near Eastern studies (MA, PhD); anthropology (MA, PhD); applied linguistics (MA); Arabic (MA, PhD); archaeology (MA); art history (MA); Biblical archaeology (MA); Biblical studies (M Th, D Th, PhD); Christian spirituality (M Th, D Th); church history (M Th, D Th); classical studies (MA, PhD); clinical psychology (MA); communication (MA, PhD); comparative education (M Ed, Ed D); consulting psychology (D Admin, D Com, PhD); curriculum studies (M Ed, Ed D); development studies (M Admin, MA, D Admin, PhD); didactics (M Ed, Ed D); education (M Tech); education management (M Ed, Ed D); educational psychology (M Ed); English (MA); environmental education (M Ed); French (MA, PhD); German (MA, PhD); Greek (MA); guidance and counseling (M Ed); health studies (MA, PhD), including health sciences education (MA), health services management (MA), medical and surgical nursing science (critical care general) (MA), midwifery and neonatal nursing science (MA), trauma and emergency care (MA); history (MA, PhD); history of education (Ed D); inclusive education (M Ed, Ed D); information and communications technology policy and regulation (MA); information science (MA, MIS, PhD); international politics (MA, PhD); Islamic studies (MA, PhD); Italian (MA, PhD); Judaica (MA, PhD); linguistics (MA, PhD); mathematical education (M Ed); mathematics education (MA); missiology (M Th, D Th); modern Hebrew (MA, PhD); musicology (MA, MMus, D Mus, PhD); natural science education (M Ed); New Testament (M Th, D Th); Old Testament (D Th); pastoral therapy (M Th, D Th); philosophy (MA); philosophy of education (M Ed, Ed D); politics (MA, PhD); Portuguese (MA, PhD); practical theology (M Th, D Th); psychology (MA, MS, PhD); psychology of education (M Ed, Ed D); public health (MA); religious studies (MA, D Th, PhD); Romance languages (MA); Russian (MA, PhD); Semitic languages (MA, PhD); social behavior studies in HIV/AIDS (MA); social science (mental health) (MA); social science in development studies (MA); social science in psychology (MA); social science in social work (MA); social science in sociology (MA); social work (MSW, DSW, PhD); socio-education (M Ed, Ed D); sociolinguistics (MA); sociology (MA, PhD); Spanish (MA, PhD); systematic theology (M Th, D Th); TESOL (teaching English to speakers of other languages) (MA); theological ethics (M Th, D Th); theory of literature (MA, PhD); urban ministries (D Th); urban ministry (M Th).

University of South Carolina, The Graduate School, College of Social Work, Columbia, SC 29208. Offers MSW, PhD, JD/MSW, MSW/MPA, MSW/MPH. *Accreditation:* CSWE (one or more programs are accredited). Part-time programs available. *Degree requirements:* For master's, comprehensive exam; for doctorate, thesis/dissertation. *Entrance requirements:* For master's, GRE (minimum combined score 800), minimum undergraduate GPA of 3.0. Additional exam requirements/recommendations for international students: Required—TOEFL (minimum score 570 paper-based; 230 computer-based). Electronic applications accepted. *Expenses:* Contact institution. *Faculty research:* Victimization, child abuse and neglect, families.

University of Southern California, Graduate School, School of Social Work, Los Angeles, CA 90089. Offers community organization, planning and administration (MSW); families and children (MSW); health (MSW); mental health (MSW); military social work and veterans services (MSW); older adults (MSW); public child welfare (MSW); school settings (MSW); social work (MSW, PhD); systems of mental illness recovery (MSW); work and life (MSW); JD/MSW; M Pl/MSW; MPA/MSW; MSW/MAJCS; MSW/MBA; MSW/MS. *Accreditation:* CSWE (one or more programs are accredited). Part-time programs available. Postbaccalaureate distance learning degree programs offered. *Faculty:* 72 full-time (50 women), 75 part-time/adjunct (53 women). *Students:* 766 full-time (650 women), 155 part-time (131 women); includes 606 minority (132 African Americans, 3 American Indian/Alaska Native, 115 Asian Americans or Pacific Islanders, 356 Hispanic Americans), 37 international. 1,634 applicants, 49% accepted, 476 enrolled. In 2009, 288 master's, 7 doctorates awarded. *Degree requirements:* For doctorate, comprehensive exam, thesis/dissertation, qualifying exam/publishable paper. *Entrance*

Social Work

University of Southern California (continued)

requirements: For doctorate, GRE General Test. Additional exam requirements/recommendations for international students: Recommended—TOEFL (minimum score 600 paper-based; 250 computer-based; 100 iBT). *Application deadline:* For fall admission, 3/15 for domestic and international students. Electronic applications accepted. *Expenses:* Tuition: Full-time $25,980; part-time $1315 per unit. Required fees: $554. One-time fee: $35 full-time. Full-time tuition and fees vary according to degree level and program. *Financial support:* In 2009–10, 738 students received support, including fellowships with full tuition reimbursements available (averaging $35,000 per year), teaching assistantships with full tuition reimbursements available (averaging $30,000 per year); Federal Work-Study and scholarships/grants also available. Financial award application deadline: 5/3; financial award applicants required to submit FAFSA. *Faculty research:* Military social work, homelessness, health disparities, school violence, depression and chronic diseases. *Unit head:* Dean Marilyn Flynn, Dean and Professor, 213-740-8311. *Application contact:* Janine M. Luzano, Director of Admissions and Financial Aid, 213-740-2013, Fax: 213-821-1235, E-mail: janinelu@usc.edu.

University of Southern Indiana, Graduate Studies, College of Education and Human Services, Program in Social Work, Evansville, IN 47712-3590. Offers MSW. *Accreditation:* CSWE. Part-time and evening/weekend programs available. *Faculty:* 7 full-time (5 women), 1 part-time/adjunct (0 women). *Students:* 77 full-time (67 women), 40 part-time (34 women); includes 12 minority (7 African Americans, 3 Asian Americans or Pacific Islanders, 2 Hispanic Americans), 1 international. Average age 31. 63 applicants, 100% accepted, 50 enrolled. In 2009, 35 master's awarded. *Entrance requirements:* For master's, minimum GPA of 2.8. Additional exam requirements/recommendations for international students: Required—TOEFL (minimum score 550 paper-based; 213 computer-based; 79 iBT), IELTS (minimum score 6). *Application deadline:* For fall admission, 1/12 for domestic and international students. Application fee: $25. Electronic applications accepted. *Expenses:* Tuition, state resident: full-time $4592; part-time $255 per credit hour. Tuition, nonresident: full-time $9060; part-time $503 per credit hour. Required fees: $220; $22.75 per term. Tuition and fees vary according to course load and reciprocity agreements. *Financial support:* In 2009–10, 82 students received support. Federal Work-Study, scholarships/grants, tuition waivers (full and partial), and unspecified assistantships available. Financial award application deadline: 3/1; financial award applicants required to submit FAFSA. *Unit head:* Dr. Wendy Turner, Director, 812-465-1201, E-mail: wturner@usi.edu. *Application contact:* Dr. Wendy Turner, Director, 812-465-1201, E-mail: wturner@usi.edu.

University of Southern Maine, College of Arts and Sciences, Program in Social Work, Portland, ME 04104-9300. Offers MSW. *Accreditation:* CSWE. Part-time and evening/weekend programs available. *Entrance requirements:* For master's, GRE or MAT. Electronic applications accepted. *Faculty research:* Social inequality, immigrants and refugees, aging, sexual harassment, service learning, technology and social service.

University of Southern Mississippi, Graduate School, College of Health, School of Social Work, Hattiesburg, MS 39406-0001. Offers MSW. *Accreditation:* CSWE. Part-time programs available. *Faculty:* 13 full-time (7 women). *Students:* 79 full-time (68 women), 69 part-time (64 women); includes 79 minority (all African Americans). Average age 35. 96 applicants, 49% accepted, 44 enrolled. In 2009, 48 master's awarded. *Degree requirements:* For master's, comprehensive exam, thesis or alternative, practicum. *Entrance requirements:* For master's, GRE General Test, minimum GPA of 2.75 in last 60 hours. Additional exam requirements/recommendations for international students: Required—TOEFL. *Application deadline:* For fall admission, 4/1 priority date for domestic students, 4/1 for international students. Applications are processed on a rolling basis. Application fee: $35. Electronic applications accepted. *Expenses:* Tuition, state resident: full-time $5096; part-time $284 per hour. Tuition, nonresident: full-time $13,052; part-time $726 per hour. Required fees: $402. Tuition and fees vary according to course level and course load. *Financial support:* In 2009–10, 16 research assistantships (averaging $7,643 per year) were awarded; teaching assistantships, career-related internships or fieldwork, Federal Work-Study, and scholarships/grants also available. Financial award application deadline: 3/15; financial award applicants required to submit FAFSA. *Faculty research:* Delinquency prevention, risk and resiliency in youth, successful aging, women in social service management, social work and the law. *Unit head:* Dr. Tim Rehner, Director, 601-266-4171, Fax: 601-266-4165, E-mail: tim.rehner@usm.edu. *Application contact:* Shonna Breland, 601-266-6563.

University of South Florida, Graduate School, College of Behavioral and Community Sciences, School of Social Work, Tampa, DE 33620. Offers MSW, PhD. *Accreditation:* CSWE. Part-time and evening/weekend programs available. *Faculty:* 9 full-time (7 women), 45 part-time/adjunct (39 women). *Students:* 119 full-time (110 women), 74 part-time (61 women); includes 44 minority (17 African Americans, 1 American Indian/Alaska Native, 6 Asian Americans or Pacific Islanders, 20 Hispanic Americans), 1 international. Average age 32. 205 applicants, 37% accepted, 56 enrolled. In 2009, 81 master's, 2 doctorates awarded. *Degree requirements:* For master's, comprehensive exam, thesis; for doctorate, comprehensive exam, thesis/dissertation. *Entrance requirements:* For master's, GRE General Test, minimum GPA of 3.0 in last 60 hours of course work; for doctorate, GRE General Test. Additional exam requirements/recommendations for international students: Required—TOEFL (minimum score 550 paper-based; 213 computer-based). *Application deadline:* For fall admission, 2/15 priority date for domestic students, 1/2 for international students. Applications are processed on a rolling basis. Application fee: $30. Electronic applications accepted. *Financial support:* In 2009–10, teaching assistantships (averaging $19,251 per year); unspecified assistantships also available. Financial award application deadline: 3/15; financial award applicants required to submit FAFSA. *Faculty research:* Kinship care, child trauma, juvenile delinquency, end-of-life issues, aging issues, child welfare. Total annual research expenditures: $7.7 million. *Unit head:* Dr. Anne L. Strozier, Chair, 813-974-1379, Fax: 813-974-4675, E-mail: strozier@bcs.usf.edu. *Application contact:* Yvonne Wallace, Receptionist, 813-974-2063, Fax: 813-974-4675, E-mail: ywallace@bcs.usf.edu.

The University of Tennessee, Graduate School, College of Social Work, Knoxville, TN 37996. Offers clinical social work practice (MSSW); social welfare management and community practice (MSSW); social work (PhD). *Accreditation:* CSWE (one or more programs are accredited). Part-time programs available. *Degree requirements:* For master's, thesis or alternative; for doctorate, thesis/dissertation. *Entrance requirements:* For master's and doctorate, GRE General Test, minimum GPA of 2.7. Additional exam requirements/recommendations for international students: Required—TOEFL. Electronic applications accepted. *Expenses:* Tuition, state resident: full-time $6826; part-time $380 per semester hour. Tuition, nonresident: full-time $21,844; part-time $1147 per semester hour. Tuition and fees vary according to program.

The University of Texas at Arlington, Graduate School, School of Social Work, Arlington, TX 76019. Offers MSSW, PhD. *Accreditation:* CSWE (one or more programs are accredited). Part-time and evening/weekend programs available. Postbaccalaureate distance learning degree programs offered (no on-campus study). *Faculty:* 27 full-time (13 women), 3 part-time/adjunct (2 women). *Students:* 321 full-time (293 women), 241 part-time (218 women); includes 225 minority (124 African Americans, 2 American Indian/Alaska Native, 21 Asian Americans or Pacific Islanders, 78 Hispanic Americans), 16 international. Average age 32. 274 applicants, 98% accepted, 174 enrolled. In 2009, 217 master's, 10 doctorates awarded. *Degree requirements:* For master's, thesis optional; for doctorate, comprehensive exam, thesis/dissertation. *Entrance requirements:* For master's, GRE General Test (if GPA less than 3.0), 3 letters of recommendation; for doctorate, GRE General Test (if GPA is below 3.4), minimum graduate GPA of 3.4. Additional exam requirements/recommendations for international students: Required—TOEFL (minimum score 550 paper-based; 213 computer-based). *Application deadline:* For fall admission, 6/5 for domestic students; for winter admission, 10/17 for domestic students. Applications are processed on a rolling basis. Application fee: $35 ($50 for international students). Electronic applications accepted. *Financial support:* In 2009–10, 355 students received support, including 40 fellowships (averaging $2,000 per year), 10 research assistantships (averaging $6,000 per year), 10 teaching assistantships (averaging $6,000 per year); career-related internships or fieldwork, Federal Work-Study, institutionally sponsored loans, scholarships/grants, and unspecified assistantships also available. Support available to part-time students. Financial award application deadline: 6/1; financial award applicants required to submit FAFSA. *Faculty research:* Community practice, administrative practice, mental health and children and families. Total annual research expenditures: $4.4 million. *Unit head:* Dr. Phillip Popple, Interim Dean, 817-272-3181, Fax: 817-272-5229, E-mail: popplepr@uta.edu. *Application contact:* Darlene Santee, Director of admissions, 817-272-3613, Fax: 817-272-5229.

The University of Texas at Austin, Graduate School, School of Social Work, Austin, TX 78712-1111. Offers MSSW, PhD. *Accreditation:* CSWE (one or more programs are accredited). Part-time programs available. *Degree requirements:* For doctorate, thesis/dissertation. *Entrance requirements:* For master's and doctorate, GRE General Test. Additional exam requirements/recommendations for international students: Required—TOEFL. *Faculty research:* Substance abuse, child welfare, gerontology, mental health, public policy.

The University of Texas at El Paso, Graduate School, College of Health Sciences, Social Work Program, El Paso, TX 79968-0001. Offers MSW.

The University of Texas at San Antonio, College of Public Policy, Department of Social Work, San Antonio, TX 78249-0617. Offers MSW. *Accreditation:* CSWE. Part-time and evening/weekend programs available. *Faculty:* 9 full-time (7 women), 2 part-time/adjunct (both women). *Students:* 42 full-time (34 women), 82 part-time (64 women); includes 72 minority (12 African Americans, 1 American Indian/Alaska Native, 3 Asian Americans or Pacific Islanders, 56 Hispanic Americans), 1 international. Average age 34. 58 applicants, 76% accepted, 36 enrolled. In 2009, 36 master's awarded. *Degree requirements:* For master's, comprehensive exam (for some programs), thesis (for some programs). *Entrance requirements:* For master's, GRE. Additional exam requirements/recommendations for international students: Required—TOEFL (minimum score 500 paper-based; 173 computer-based; 91 iBT), IELTS (minimum score 5). *Application deadline:* For fall admission, 7/1 for domestic students, 4/1 for international students; for spring admission, 11/1 for domestic students, 9/1 for international students. Applications are processed on a rolling basis. Application fee: $45 ($80 for international students). Electronic applications accepted. *Expenses:* Tuition, state resident: full-time $3975; part-time $221 per contact hour. Tuition, nonresident: full-time $13,947; part-time $775 per contact hour. Required fees: $1853. *Financial support:* In 2009–10, 7 students received support, including 11 research assistantships (averaging $6,476 per year); career-related internships or fieldwork, scholarships/grants, tuition waivers, and unspecified assistantships also available. Support available to part-time students. *Faculty research:* Hispanic female adolescents and problematic behavior, military sociology, child welfare abuse and neglect prevention and intervention, religion and spirituality. *Unit head:* Dr. Dennis Haynes, Chair, 210-458-3000, E-mail: dennis.haynes@utsa.edu. *Application contact:* Rosalie Ambrosino, Graduate Advisor, 210-458-2918, E-mail: rosalie.ambrosino@utsa.edu.

The University of Texas–Pan American, College of Health Sciences and Human Services, Department of Social Work, Edinburg, TX 78539. Offers MSSW. *Accreditation:* CSWE. Part-time programs available. *Entrance requirements:* For master's, minimum GPA of 3.0, basic statistics course completed within 5 years of admission. Additional exam requirements/recommendations for international students: Recommended—TOEFL (minimum score 500 paper-based). *Expenses:* Tuition, state resident: full-time $3630.60; part-time $201.70 per credit hour. Tuition, nonresident: full-time $8617; part-time $478.70 per credit hour. Required fees: $806.50. *Faculty research:* Child welfare, family violence, social justice, Hispanic traditional healing (curanderismo and spirituality), community development.

The University of Toledo, College of Graduate Studies, College of Health Science and Human Service, Division of Human Services, Department of Social Work, Toledo, OH 43606-3390. Offers MSW. *Accreditation:* CSWE.

University of Toronto, School of Graduate Studies, Social Sciences Division, Faculty of Social Work, Toronto, ON M5S 1A1, Canada. Offers MSW, PhD. Part-time programs available. *Degree requirements:* For doctorate, thesis/dissertation, oral exam/thesis defense. *Entrance requirements:* For master's, minimum mid-B average in last 2 years of full-time study, 3 full courses in social sciences, experience in social services recommended, 3 letters of reference, resume; for doctorate, MSW or equivalent, minimum B+ average, competency in basic statistical methods. Additional exam requirements/recommendations for international students: Required—TOEFL (minimum score 580 paper-based; 237 computer-based), TWE (minimum score 5), IELTS (minimum score: 7) or Michigan English Language Assessment Battery (minimum score: 85). *Expenses:* Contact institution.

University of Utah, Graduate School, College of Social Work, Salt Lake City, UT 84112. Offers MSW, PhD, MPA/PhD. *Accreditation:* CSWE (one or more programs are accredited). Part-time programs available. Postbaccalaureate distance learning degree programs offered (minimal on-campus study). *Faculty:* 32 full-time (19 women), 6 part-time/adjunct (2 women). *Students:* 331 full-time (248 women), 31 part-time (20 women); includes 38 minority (3 African Americans, 4 American Indian/Alaska Native, 8 Asian Americans or Pacific Islanders, 23 Hispanic Americans), 9 international. Average age 34. 401 applicants, 44% accepted, 138 enrolled. In 2009, 148 master's, 4 doctorates awarded. *Degree requirements:* For master's, thesis or alternative; for doctorate, comprehensive exam, thesis/dissertation. *Entrance requirements:* For master's, GRE General Test, MAT, minimum GPA of 3.0; for doctorate, GRE General Test. Additional exam requirements/recommendations for international students: Required—TOEFL (minimum score 600 paper-based; 173 computer-based). *Application deadline:* For fall admission, 4/1 for domestic and international students; for spring admission, 11/1 for domestic and international students. Applications are processed on a rolling basis. Application fee: $55 ($65 for international students). *Expenses:* Tuition, state resident: full-time $4004; part-time $1674 per semester. Tuition, nonresident: full-time $14,134; part-time $5915 per semester. Required fees: $324 per semester. Tuition and fees vary according to course load, degree level and program. *Financial support:* In 2009–10, 158 fellowships with full and partial tuition reimbursements (averaging $3,500 per year), 34 research assistantships with full and partial tuition reimbursements (averaging $7,000 per year), 6 teaching assistantships with full and partial tuition reimbursements (averaging $5,000 per year) were awarded; Federal Work-Study and institutionally sponsored loans also available. Support available to part-time students. Financial award application deadline: 3/15; financial award applicants required to submit FAFSA. *Faculty research:* Clinical/direct practice, health and mental health, gerontology, child welfare, prevention of substance abuse. Total annual research expenditures: $711,076. *Unit head:* Dr. Jannah H. Mather, Dean, 801-581-6194, Fax: 801-585-3219, E-mail: jannah.mather@socwk.utah.edu. *Application contact:* Dr. Mary Jane Taylor, Associate Dean, 801-581-8828, Fax: 801-585-3219, E-mail: maryjane.taylor@socwk.utah.edu.

University of Vermont, Graduate College, College of Education and Social Services, Department of Social Work, Burlington, VT 05405. Offers MSW. *Accreditation:* CSWE. *Students:* 65 (54 women); includes 4 minority (1 African American, 2 Asian Americans or Pacific Islanders, 1 Hispanic American). 82 applicants, 76% accepted, 30 enrolled. In 2009, 24 master's awarded. *Entrance requirements:* For master's, GRE General Test, resume. Additional exam requirements/recommendations for international students: Required—TOEFL (minimum score 550 paper-based; 213 computer-based; 80 iBT). *Application deadline:* For fall admission, 2/1 priority date for domestic students. Applications are processed on a rolling basis. Application fee: $40. Electronic applications accepted. *Expenses:* Tuition, state resident: part-time $508 per credit hour. Tuition, nonresident: part-time $1281 per credit hour. *Financial support:* Application deadline: 2/1. *Unit head:* B. Solomon, Coordinator, 802-656-8800. *Application contact:* B. Solomon, Coordinator, 802-656-8800.

University of Victoria, Faculty of Graduate Studies, Faculty of Human and Social Development, School of Social Work, Victoria, BC V8W 2Y2, Canada. Offers MSW. *Entrance requirements:* For master's, BSW. Additional exam requirements/recommendations for international students: Required—TOEFL (minimum score 575 paper-based; 233 computer-based), IELTS (minimum

score 7). Electronic applications accepted. *Faculty research:* Women's issues, public policy formation and implementation, child welfare, First Nations, community development.

University of Victoria, Faculty of Graduate Studies, Faculty of Human and Social Development, Studies in Policy and Practice Program, Victoria, BC V8W 2Y2, Canada. Offers MA. Part-time programs available. *Degree requirements:* For master's, thesis. *Entrance requirements:* For master's, resume. Additional exam requirements/recommendations for international students: Required—TOEFL (minimum score 575 paper-based; 233 computer-based), IELTS (minimum score 7). Electronic applications accepted. *Faculty research:* Women's issues, public policy formation and implementation, health promotion and education, children, youth and families.

University of Washington, Graduate School, School of Social Work, Seattle, WA 98195. Offers MSW, PhD, MPH/MSW. *Accreditation:* CSWE (one or more programs are accredited). Evening/weekend programs available. Postbaccalaureate distance learning degree programs offered (minimal on-campus study). *Degree requirements:* For master's, thesis optional; for doctorate, thesis/dissertation. *Entrance requirements:* For master's, GRE General Test, minimum GPA of 3.0; for doctorate, master's degree, sample of scholarly work, minimum GPA of 3.0. Additional exam requirements/recommendations for international students: Required—TOEFL. *Faculty research:* Health and mental health; children, youth, and families; multicultural issues; reducing risk and enhancing protective factors in children; etrology of substance use.

University of Washington, Graduate School, School of Social Work, Tacoma Campus, Seattle, WA 98195. Offers MSW. Part-time and evening/weekend programs available. *Entrance requirements:* For master's, GRE General Test, minimum GPA of 3.0 for last 90 undergraduate credits. Electronic applications accepted. *Faculty research:* Aging, diversity, feminism, spirituality, medical social work.

University of Washington, Tacoma, Graduate Programs, Program in Social Work, Tacoma, WA 98402-3100. Offers MSW. Part-time and evening/weekend programs available. *Faculty:* 10 full-time (6 women), 7 part-time/adjunct (5 women). *Students:* 44 full-time (39 women), 82 part-time (75 women); includes 37 minority (16 African Americans, 1 American Indian/Alaska Native, 7 Asian Americans or Pacific Islanders, 13 Hispanic Americans). Average age 36. 142 applicants, 44% accepted, 41 enrolled. In 2009, 42 master's awarded. *Degree requirements:* For master's, 360 hours of practicum. *Application deadline:* For fall admission, 3/1 priority date for domestic students; for winter admission, 6/30 priority date for domestic students. Applications are processed on a rolling basis. *Application fee:* $65. Electronic applications accepted. *Expenses:* Tuition, state resident: full-time $10,660; part-time $484 per credit. Tuition, nonresident: full-time $24,000; part-time $1119 per credit. Required fees: $150 per term. Tuition and fees vary according to course load and program. *Faculty research:* Violence, gerontology, gender in social work, cultural competence. *Unit head:* Dr. Rich Furman, Director, 253-692-5820, Fax: 253-692-5825, E-mail: tsocial@u.washington.edu. *Application contact:* Terri Simonsen, Program Adviser and Administrator, 253-692-5820, Fax: 253-692-5825, E-mail: tsocial@u.washington.edu.

University of West Florida, College of Professional Studies, School of Justice Studies and Social Work, Department of Social Work, Pensacola, FL 32514-5750. Offers MSW. Part-time and evening/weekend programs available. *Faculty:* 8 full-time (4 women). *Students:* 45 full-time (37 women), 2 part-time (1 woman); includes 14 minority (10 African Americans, 1 American Indian/Alaska Native, 1 Asian American or Pacific Islander, 2 Hispanic Americans). Average age 37. 35 applicants, 77% accepted, 21 enrolled. *Entrance requirements:* For master's, GRE or MAT, 3 letters of recommendation. Additional exam requirements/recommendations for international students: Required—TOEFL (minimum score 550 paper-based; 213 computer-based). *Application deadline:* For fall admission, 6/1 for domestic students, 5/1 for international students; for spring admission, 11/1 for domestic students, 10/1 for international students. Applications are processed on a rolling basis. Electronic applications accepted. *Expenses:* Tuition, state resident: full-time $4982; part-time $260 per credit hour. Tuition, nonresident: full-time $20,059; part-time $919 per credit hour. Required fees: $1247; $52 per credit hour. *Financial support:* In 2009–10, 4 research assistantships (averaging $3,280 per year) were awarded; unspecified assistantships also available. *Unit head:* Dr. Glenn Rohrer, Chair, 850-474-2154, E-mail: grohrer@uwf.edu. *Application contact:* Terry McCray, Assistant Director of Graduate Admissions, 850-473-7718, Fax: 850-473-7714, E-mail: gradadmissions@uwf.edu.

University of Windsor, Faculty of Graduate Studies, Faculty of Arts and Social Sciences, School of Social Work, Windsor, ON N9B 3P4, Canada. Offers MSW. Part-time programs available. *Degree requirements:* For master's, thesis or alternative. *Entrance requirements:* For master's, minimum B+ average in last year of undergraduate study. Additional exam requirements/recommendations for international students: Required—TOEFL (minimum score 600 paper-based; 250 computer-based). Electronic applications accepted. *Faculty research:* Addiction, social policy analysis, gerontology and health care.

University of Wisconsin–Green Bay, Graduate Studies, Program in Social Work, Green Bay, WI 54311-7001. Offers MSW. *Accreditation:* CSWE. *Faculty:* 2 full-time (both women), 1 (woman) part-time/adjunct. *Students:* 17 full-time (14 women), 21 part-time (19 women); includes 6 minority (3 American Indian/Alaska Native, 2 Asian Americans or Pacific Islanders, 1 Hispanic American). Average age 33. 24 applicants, 96% accepted, 21 enrolled. In 2009, 16 master's awarded. *Degree requirements:* For master's, thesis or alternative. *Entrance requirements:* For master's, GRE, minimum GPA of 2.75. *Application deadline:* For fall admission, 8/1 priority date for domestic students; for spring admission, 11/1 priority date for domestic students. Applications are processed on a rolling basis. *Application fee:* $56. Electronic applications accepted. *Expenses:* Tuition, state resident: full-time $6706; part-time $373 per credit. Tuition, nonresident: full-time $16,722; part-time $932 per credit. Required fees: $1250; $52 per credit. Tuition and fees vary according to degree level and reciprocity agreements. *Faculty research:* Child welfare. *Unit head:* Dr. Judith Martin, Coordinator, 920-465-2049, E-mail: martinj@uwgb.edu. *Application contact:* Pam Harvey-Jacobs, Director of Admissions, 920-465-2111, Fax: 920-465-5754, E-mail: uwgb@uwgb.edu.

University of Wisconsin–Madison, Graduate School, College of Letters and Science, School of Social Work, Madison, WI 53706-1380. Offers social welfare (PhD); social work (MSW). *Accreditation:* CSWE (one or more programs are accredited). Terminal master's awarded for partial completion of doctoral program. *Degree requirements:* For doctorate, thesis/dissertation. *Entrance requirements:* For master's, minimum GPA of 3.0 on last 60 credits; for doctorate, GRE General Test, minimum GPA of 3.0 on last 60 credits. Electronic applications accepted. *Expenses:* Contact institution. *Faculty research:* Poverty, caregiving, child welfare, developmental disabilities, mental health, severe mental illnesses, adolescence, family, social policy, child support.

University of Wisconsin–Milwaukee, Graduate School, School of Social Welfare, Department of Social Work, Milwaukee, WI 53201-0413. Offers applied gerontology (Certificate); marriage and family therapy (Certificate); non-profit management (Certificate); social work (MSW, PhD). *Accreditation:* CSWE. Part-time programs available. *Faculty:* 18 full-time (11 women). *Students:* 173 full-time (157 women), 101 part-time (92 women); includes 55 minority (38 African Americans, 2 American Indian/Alaska Native, 7 Asian Americans or Pacific Islanders, 8 Hispanic Americans). Average age 31. 303 applicants, 62% accepted, 93 enrolled. In 2009, 105 master's awarded. *Degree requirements:* For master's, thesis or alternative. *Entrance requirements:* For doctorate, GRE, bachelor's degree. Additional exam requirements/recommendations for international students: Required—TOEFL (minimum score 550 paper-based; 79 iBT), IELTS (minimum score 6.5). *Application deadline:* For fall admission, 1/1 priority date for domestic students; for spring admission, 9/1 for domestic students. Applications are processed on a rolling basis. *Application fee:* $45 ($75 for international students). *Expenses:* Tuition, state resident: full-time $8800. Tuition, nonresident: full-time $20,760. Tuition and fees vary according to program and reciprocity agreements. *Financial support:* In 2009–10, 3 fellowships, 4 teaching assistantships were awarded; research assistantships, career-related internships or fieldwork and unspecified assistantships also available. Support available to part-time students. Financial award application deadline: 4/15. Total annual research expenditures: $806,977. *Unit head:* Deborah Padgett, Representative, 414-229-4851, Fax: 414-229-5311, E-mail: dpadgett@

uwm.edu. *Application contact:* Steve McMurtry, General Information Contact, 414-229-2249, Fax: 414-229-6967, E-mail: mcmurtry@uwm.edu.

University of Wisconsin–Oshkosh, The Office of Graduate Studies, Department of Social Work, Oshkosh, WI 54901. Offers MSW. *Accreditation:* CSWE. Part-time programs available. *Entrance requirements:* For master's, GRE, letters of recommendation, previous courses in statistics and human biology, work experience. Additional exam requirements/recommendations for international students: Required—TOEFL (minimum score 550 paper-based; 213 computer-based; 79 iBT).

University of Wyoming, College of Health Sciences, Division of Social Work, Laramie, WY 82070. Offers MSW. *Accreditation:* CSWE. *Degree requirements:* For master's, comprehensive exam, thesis or alternative. *Entrance requirements:* For master's, minimum GPA of 3.0. Additional exam requirements/recommendations for international students: Required—TOEFL. *Expenses:* Contact institution. *Faculty research:* Social work education, child welfare, mental health, diversity, school social work.

Valdosta State University, Graduate School, Division of Social Work, Valdosta, GA 31698. Offers MSW. *Accreditation:* CSWE. Part-time and evening/weekend programs available. *Degree requirements:* For master's, comprehensive exam, 5 practica. *Entrance requirements:* For master's, GRE General Test, MAT, minimum GPA of 3.0 in last 2 years of course work. Additional exam requirements/recommendations for international students: Required—TOEFL (minimum score 523 paper-based; 193 computer-based).

Virginia Commonwealth University, Graduate School, School of Social Work, Doctoral Program in Social Work, Richmond, VA 23284-9005. Offers PhD. *Degree requirements:* For doctorate, comprehensive exam, thesis/dissertation. *Entrance requirements:* For doctorate, GRE General Test, MSW or related degree.

Virginia Commonwealth University, Graduate School, School of Social Work, Master's Program in Social Work, Richmond, VA 23284-9005. Offers MSW, JD/MSW, MSW/MA. *Accreditation:* CSWE.

Walden University, Graduate Programs, School of Counseling and Social Service, Minneapolis, MN 55401. Offers counselor education and supervision (PhD), including consultation, counseling and social change, forensic mental health counseling, general program, nonprofit management and leadership, trauma and crisis; human services (PhD), including clinical social work, counseling, criminal justice, family studies and intervention strategies, general program, human services administration, self-designed, social policy analysis and planning; marriage, couple, and family counseling (MS), including forensic counseling, trauma and crisis counseling; mental health counseling (MS), including forensic counseling. Part-time and evening/weekend programs available. Postbaccalaureate distance learning degree programs offered (minimal on-campus study). *Faculty:* 13 full-time, 78 part-time/adjunct. *Students:* 1,932 full-time (1,624 women), 210 part-time (181 women); includes 945 minority (817 African Americans, 24 American Indian/Alaska Native, 24 Asian Americans or Pacific Islanders, 80 Hispanic Americans), 34 international. Average age 39. In 2009, 55 master's, 5 doctorates awarded. *Degree requirements:* For master's, residency (for some programs); for doctorate, thesis/dissertation, residency. *Entrance requirements:* For master's, bachelor's degree or equivalent in related field, minimum GPA of 2.5; for doctorate, master's degree or equivalent in related field; minimum GPA of 3.0; official transcripts; three years' related professional/academic experience (preferred); access to computer and Internet. Additional exam requirements/recommendations for international students: Required—TOEFL (minimum score 550 paper-based; 213 computer-based), IELTS (minimum score 6.5), or Michigan English Language Assessment Battery (minimum score 82). *Application deadline:* Applications are processed on a rolling basis. *Application fee:* $50. Electronic applications accepted. *Expenses:* Tuition: Full-time $13,665; part-time $560 per credit. Required fees: $1375. Tuition and fees vary according to course load, degree level and program. *Financial support:* In 2009–10, 200 students received support; fellowships, Federal Work-Study, scholarships/grants, unspecified assistantships, and family tuition reduction, active duty/veteran tuition reduction, group tuition reduction, interest-free payment plans available. Support available to part-time students. Financial award applicants required to submit FAFSA. *Unit head:* Dr. Savitri Dixon-Saxon, Associate Dean, 800-925-3368. *Application contact:* Jennifer Hall, Director of Enrollment, 866-4-WALDEN, E-mail: info@waldenu.edu.

Walla Walla University, Graduate School, Wilma Hepker School of Social Work and Sociology, College Place, WA 99324-1198. Offers social work (MSW). *Accreditation:* CSWE. Part-time programs available. *Faculty:* 13 full-time (9 women), 17 part-time/adjunct (13 women). *Students:* 173 full-time (129 women), 14 part-time (11 women); includes 35 minority (4 African Americans, 22 American Indian/Alaska Native, 4 Asian Americans or Pacific Islanders, 5 Hispanic Americans). Average age 37. 178 applicants, 74% accepted, 95 enrolled. In 2009, 115 master's awarded. *Entrance requirements:* For master's, minimum GPA of 2.75. Additional exam requirements/recommendations for international students: Required—TOEFL (minimum score 550 paper-based; 213 computer-based; 79 iBT). *Application deadline:* For fall admission, 7/15 priority date for domestic students. Applications are processed on a rolling basis. *Application fee:* $50. Electronic applications accepted. *Expenses:* Tuition: Full-time $19,929. *Financial support:* In 2009–10, 150 students received support. Career-related internships or fieldwork, Federal Work-Study, and scholarships/grants available. Support available to part-time students. Financial award application deadline: 4/1; financial award applicants required to submit FAFSA. *Unit head:* Dr. Pamela Cress, Dean, 509-527-2273, Fax: 509-527-2270, E-mail: pam.cress@wallawalla.edu. *Application contact:* Dr. Joe G. Galusha, Dean of Graduate Studies, 509-527-2421, Fax: 509-527-2237, E-mail: joe.galusha@wallawalla.edu.

Washburn University, School of Applied Studies, Department of Social Work, Topeka, KS 66621. Offers clinical social work (MSW). *Accreditation:* CSWE. Part-time and evening/weekend programs available. *Faculty:* 10 full-time (4 women), 2 part-time/adjunct (1 woman). *Students:* 51 full-time (44 women), 64 part-time (56 women); includes 15 minority (9 African Americans, 6 Hispanic Americans). Average age 36. 84 applicants, 88% accepted, 74 enrolled. In 2009, 61 master's awarded. *Entrance requirements:* For master's, coursework in human biology and cultural anthropology (or multiculturalism or human diversity). Additional exam requirements/recommendations for international students: Required—TOEFL (minimum score 520 paper-based; 193 computer-based; 69 iBT). *Application deadline:* For fall admission, 1/15 priority date for domestic and international students; for spring admission, 10/15 priority date for domestic and international students. Applications are processed on a rolling basis. *Application fee:* $25. Electronic applications accepted. *Financial support:* Career-related internships or fieldwork, Federal Work-Study, institutionally sponsored loans, and scholarships/grants available. Support available to part-time students. Financial award applicants required to submit FAFSA. *Unit head:* Dr. Jay L. Memmott, Chair/Director, 785-670-1616, Fax: 785-670-1027, E-mail: jay.memmott@washburn.edu. *Application contact:* Dr. Jay L. Memmott, Chair/Director, 785-670-1616, Fax: 785-670-1027, E-mail: jay.memmott@washburn.edu.

Washington University in St. Louis, George Warren Brown School of Social Work, St. Louis, MO 63130-4899. Offers public health (MPH); social work (MSW, PhD); JD/MSW; M Arch/MSW; MBA/MSW; MSW/M Div; MSW/MAJCS; MSW/MAPS; MSW/MPH. *Accreditation:* CSWE (one or more programs are accredited). *Faculty:* 44 full-time, 48 part-time/adjunct. *Students:* 504 full-time (428 women); includes 89 minority (48 African Americans, 10 American Indian/Alaska Native, 20 Asian Americans or Pacific Islanders, 11 Hispanic Americans), 98 international. Average age 27. 716 applicants, 63% accepted, 225 enrolled. In 2009, 212 master's, 13 doctorates awarded. *Degree requirements:* For master's, 60 credit hours, including practicum (MSW); 45 credit hours, including practicum (MPH); for doctorate, comprehensive exam, thesis/dissertation. *Entrance requirements:* For master's, GRE, GMAT, LSAT, or MCAT (public health program), minimum GPA of 3.0; for doctorate, GRE, MA or MSW. Additional exam requirements/recommendations for international students: Required—TOEFL (minimum score 575 paper-based; 233 computer-based; 90 iBT). *Application deadline:* For fall admission, 12/15 priority date for domestic and international students. Applications are processed on a rolling basis. *Application fee:* $40. Electronic applications accepted. *Expenses:* Contact institution.

Social Work

Washington University in St. Louis (continued)
Financial support: In 2009–10, 486 students received support. Federal Work-Study, institutionally sponsored loans, scholarships/grants, health care benefits, tuition waivers (partial), and research assistantships, partial tuition waivers available. Support available to part-time students. Financial award applicants required to submit FAFSA. *Faculty research:* Mental health services, social development, child welfare, at-risk teens, autism, environmental health, health policy, health communications, obesity, violence and injury prevention, chronic disease prevention, poverty, public health, productive aging/gerontology, social work, civic engagement, school social work, program evaluation, health disparities. Total annual research expenditures: $14.7 million. *Unit head:* Dr. Edward F. Lawlor, Dean and William E. Gordon Professor, 314-935-6693, Fax: 314-935-8511, E-mail: elawlor@wustl.edu. *Application contact:* Richard Sigg, Director of Admissions and Recruiting, 314-935-6676, Fax: 314-935-4859, E-mail: rsigg@wustl.edu.

See Close-Up on page 1899.

Washington University in St. Louis, Graduate School of Arts and Sciences, Program in Social Work, St. Louis, MO 63130-4899. Offers PhD. Electronic applications accepted.

Wayne State University, School of Social Work, Detroit, MI 48202. Offers interdisciplinary studies (PhD); social work (MSW); social work practice with families and couples (Certificate). *Accreditation:* CSWE (one or more programs are accredited). Part-time and evening/weekend programs available. *Degree requirements:* For master's, thesis optional. *Entrance requirements:* Additional exam requirements/recommendations for international students: Required—TOEFL (minimum score 550 paper-based; 213 computer-based); Recommended—TWE (minimum score 6). Electronic applications accepted. *Faculty research:* Child welfare; interpersonal and relationship violence; aging; homelessness and at-risk youth; community-planning and development; international social work; re-entry and re-integration of ex-offenders.

West Chester University of Pennsylvania, Office of Graduate Studies, College of Business and Public Affairs, Department of Social Work, West Chester, PA 19383. Offers MSW. *Accreditation:* CSWE. Part-time and evening/weekend programs available. *Students:* 46 full-time (43 women), 37 part-time (35 women); includes 13 minority (10 African Americans, 1 American Indian/Alaska Native, 1 Asian American or Pacific Islander, 1 Hispanic American). Average age 31. 106 applicants, 83% accepted, 46 enrolled. In 2009, 31 master's awarded. *Degree requirements:* For master's, research paper. *Entrance requirements:* For master's, minimum GPA of 3.0. Additional exam requirements/recommendations for international students: Required—TOEFL (minimum score 550 paper-based; 213 computer-based; 80 iBT). *Application deadline:* For fall admission, 4/15 priority date for domestic students, 3/16 for international students; for spring admission, 10/15 for domestic students, 9/1 for international students. Applications are processed on a rolling basis. Application fee: $35. Electronic applications accepted. *Expenses:* Tuition, state resident: full-time $6666; part-time $370 per credit. Tuition, nonresident: full-time $10,666; part-time $593 per credit. Required fees: $122.56 per credit. *Financial support:* In 2009–10, 4 research assistantships with full and partial tuition reimbursements (averaging $5,000 per year) were awarded; unspecified assistantships also available. Support available to part-time students. Financial award application deadline: 2/15; financial award applicants required to submit FAFSA. *Faculty research:* Teen pregnancy/parenting, adoption, health care advocacy, welfare-to-work, mentoring/alternative education. *Unit head:* Dr. Ann Abbott, Chair and Graduate Coordinator, 610-738-0351, E-mail: aabbott@wcupa.edu. *Application contact:* Dr. Ann Abbott, Chair and Graduate Coordinator, 610-738-0351, E-mail: aabbott@wcupa.edu.

Western Carolina University, Graduate School, College of Health and Human Sciences, Department of Social Work, Cullowhee, NC 28723. Offers MSW. *Accreditation:* CSWE. Part-time programs available. *Students:* 39 full-time (32 women), 3 part-time (1 woman). Average age 33. 43 applicants, 65% accepted, 20 enrolled. *Entrance requirements:* For master's, appropriate undergraduate major with minimum GPA of 3.0, 3 recommendations, resume. Additional exam requirements/recommendations for international students: Required—TOEFL (minimum score 550 paper-based; 270 computer-based; 79 iBT). *Application deadline:* For fall admission, 2/1 for domestic students. Applications are processed on a rolling basis. Application fee: $45. *Financial support:* In 2009–10, 6 students received support, including 1 fellowship (averaging $6,000 per year), 5 research assistantships with full and partial tuition reimbursements available (averaging $3,500 per year); teaching assistantships with full and partial tuition reimbursements available, institutionally sponsored loans, scholarships/grants, and unspecified assistantships also available. Financial award application deadline: 3/31. *Unit head:* Dr. Marie Huff, Head, 828-227-7112, Fax: 828-227-7061, E-mail: mhuff@email.wcu.edu. *Application contact:* Admissions Specialist for Social Work, 828-227-7398, Fax: 828-227-7480, E-mail: gradsch@email.wcu.edu.

Western Kentucky University, Graduate Studies, College of Health and Human Services, Department of Social Work, Bowling Green, KY 42101. Offers MSW. *Accreditation:* CSWE. *Entrance requirements:* Additional exam requirements/recommendations for international students: Required—TOEFL (minimum score 555 paper-based; 213 computer-based; 79 iBT). *Expenses:* Tuition, state resident: full-time $4160; part-time $416 per credit hour. Tuition, nonresident: full-time $9550; part-time $506 per credit hour. Tuition and fees vary according to campus/location and reciprocity agreements.

Western Michigan University, Graduate College, College of Health and Human Services, School of Social Work, Kalamazoo, MI 49008. Offers MSW. *Accreditation:* CSWE. Part-time programs available. *Faculty:* 18 full-time (10 women). *Students:* 219 full-time (183 women), 15 part-time (11 women); includes 39 minority (32 African Americans, 3 Asian Americans or Pacific Islanders, 4 Hispanic Americans), 2 international. 138 applicants, 88% accepted, 51 enrolled. In 2009, 83 master's awarded. *Application deadline:* For fall admission, 3/1 for domestic students. Application fee: $25. *Financial support:* Fellowships, research assistantships, teaching assistantships, Federal Work-Study available. Financial award application deadline: 2/15; financial award applicants required to submit FAFSA. *Unit head:* Dr. Linwood H. Cousins, Director, 269-387-3172. *Application contact:* Admissions and Orientation, 269-387-2000, Fax: 269-387-2355.

Western New Mexico University, Graduate Division, Department of Social Work, Silver City, NM 88062-0680. Offers MSW. Part-time programs available. Postbaccalaureate distance learning degree programs offered. Electronic applications accepted.

West Virginia University, Eberly College of Arts and Sciences, School of Applied Social Sciences, Division of Social Work, Morgantown, WV 26506. Offers aging and health care (MSW); children and families (MSW); community mental health (MSW); community organization and social administration (MSW); direct (clinical) social work practice (MSW). *Accreditation:* CSWE. Part-time programs available. *Degree requirements:* For master's, fieldwork. *Entrance requirements:* For master's, GRE, minimum GPA of 2.75, 2 letters of reference. Additional exam requirements/recommendations for international students: Required—TOEFL. *Faculty research:* Rural and small town social work practice, gerontology, health and mental health, welfare reform, child welfare.

Wheelock College, Graduate Programs, Division of Social Work, Boston, MA 02215-4176. Offers MSW. *Accreditation:* CSWE. *Degree requirements:* For master's, comprehensive exam, thesis. *Entrance requirements:* For master's, minimum GPA of 3.0; undergraduate course work in human biology, statistics. Additional exam requirements/recommendations for international students: Required—TOEFL. Electronic applications accepted.

Wichita State University, Graduate School, Fairmount College of Liberal Arts and Sciences, School of Social Work, Wichita, KS 67260. Offers MSW. *Accreditation:* CSWE. *Expenses:* Tuition, state resident: full-time $4247; part-time $235.95 per credit hour. Tuition, nonresident: full-time $11,171; part-time $620.60 per credit hour. Required fees: $34; $3.60 per credit hour. $17 per term. Tuition and fees vary according to campus/location and program. *Unit head:* Dr. Linnea GlenMaye, Director, 316-978-7250, Fax: 316-978-3328, E-mail: linnea.glenmaye@wichita.edu. *Application contact:* Dr. Linnea GlenMaye, Director, 316-978-7250, Fax: 316-978-3328, E-mail: linnea.glenmaye@wichita.edu.

Widener University, School of Human Service Professions, Center for Social Work Education, Chester, PA 19013-5792. Offers MSW, PhD. *Accreditation:* CSWE. Part-time programs available. *Faculty:* 15 full-time (9 women), 16 part-time/adjunct (9 women). *Students:* 54 full-time (49 women), 226 part-time (199 women); includes 78 minority (71 African Americans, 2 Asian Americans or Pacific Islanders, 5 Hispanic Americans), 1 international. Average age 33. 184 applicants, 95% accepted. In 2009, 117 master's awarded. *Degree requirements:* For master's, field practica. *Entrance requirements:* For master's, minimum GPA of 3.0. *Application deadline:* For fall admission, 3/1 for domestic students. Applications are processed on a rolling basis. Application fee: $25 ($300 for international students). Electronic applications accepted. *Expenses:* Contact institution. *Financial support:* In 2009–10, 11 students received support, including 6 fellowships; career-related internships or fieldwork, Federal Work-Study, institutionally sponsored loans, and unspecified assistantships also available. Support available to part-time students. Financial award applicants required to submit FAFSA. *Faculty research:* Clinical practice, clinical supervision, gerontology, child welfare, self-psychology. Total annual research expenditures: $85,000. *Unit head:* Dr. Paula T. Silver, Associate Dean and Director, 610-499-1150, Fax: 610-499-4617, E-mail: socialwork@widener.edu. *Application contact:* Jill L. Brinker, Secretary, 610-499-1513, Fax: 610-499-4617, E-mail: socialwork@widener.edu.

Wilfrid Laurier University, Faculty of Graduate Studies, Faculty of Social Work, Waterloo, ON N2L 3C5, Canada. Offers MSW, PhD. Part-time programs available. *Degree requirements:* For master's, thesis optional; for doctorate, thesis/dissertation. *Entrance requirements:* For master's, course work in social science, research methodology, and statistics; honors BA with a minimum B average; for doctorate, master's degree in social work, minimum A- average. Additional exam requirements/recommendations for international students: Required—TOEFL (minimum score 230 computer-based; 89 iBT). Electronic applications accepted. *Expenses:* Contact institution. *Faculty research:* Individuals, families, and groups/community, policy, planning and organizations/integrated concentration/aboriginal fields of study.

Winthrop University, College of Arts and Sciences, Program in Social Work, Rock Hill, SC 29733. Offers MA. *Accreditation:* CSWE. *Entrance requirements:* For master's, GRE or MAT, minimum GPA of 3.0, 3 letters of recommendation, resume. Electronic applications accepted.

Yeshiva University, Wurzweiler School of Social Work, New York, NY 10033-3201. Offers MSW, PhD, MSW/Certificate. *Accreditation:* CSWE (one or more programs are accredited). Part-time and evening/weekend programs available. *Faculty:* 26 full-time (14 women), 55 part-time/adjunct (41 women). *Students:* 189 full-time (152 women), 184 part-time (135 women); includes 118 minority (71 African Americans, 4 Asian Americans or Pacific Islanders, 43 Hispanic Americans). Average age 42. 355 applicants, 69% accepted, 169 enrolled. In 2009, 158 master's, 5 doctorates awarded. *Degree requirements:* For master's, thesis, comprehensive essay or integrative room; for doctorate, comprehensive exam, thesis/dissertation. *Entrance requirements:* For master's, interview, minimum GPA of 3.0, letters of reference; for doctorate, GRE, interview, letters of reference, writing sample, MSW, minimum 2 years professional social work experience. Additional exam requirements/recommendations for international students: Required—TOEFL (minimum score 550 paper-based; 213 computer-based). *Application deadline:* For fall admission, 5/1 priority date for domestic students; for spring admission, 10/31 for domestic students. Applications are processed on a rolling basis. Application fee: $50. *Expenses:* Contact institution. *Financial support:* In 2009–10, 167 students received support, including 2 teaching assistantships (averaging $5,000 per year); career-related internships or fieldwork, Federal Work-Study, institutionally sponsored loans, and scholarships/grants also available. Financial award application deadline: 4/15; financial award applicants required to submit FAFSA. *Faculty research:* Child abuse, AIDS, day care, nonprofits, gerontology. Total annual research expenditures: $300,000. *Unit head:* Dr. Sheldon R. Gelman, Dean, 212-960-0820, Fax: 212-960-0822, E-mail: srgelman@yu.edu. *Application contact:* Ruth Bigman, Director of Admissions, 212-960-0811, Fax: 212-960-0822, E-mail: rbigman@yu.edu.

York University, Faculty of Graduate Studies, Atkinson Faculty of Liberal and Professional Studies, Program in Social Work, Toronto, ON M3J 1P3, Canada. Offers MSW, PhD. Part-time and evening/weekend programs available. *Degree requirements:* For master's, thesis or alternative. Electronic applications accepted.

NEW YORK UNIVERSITY

Silver School of Social Work

Programs of Study	The New York University (NYU) Silver School of Social Work is widely known for professional education in direct practice with individuals, groups, and families. The School offers B.S., M.S.W., and Ph.D. degrees in social work. The School's programs are fully accredited by the Council on Social Work Education.

The M.S.W. program is offered in several formats to accommodate the differing circumstances of its highly diverse student body. The Two-Year Program requires four semesters of study. The 16-Month Accelerated Program, an intensive route to a master's degree, provides a concentrated two-year course of study over four continuous semesters, including summer. The Extended M.S.W. Program allows students to complete their M.S.W. over three to four years, with one year of full-time study. The Extended One-Year Residence Program (typically three to four years, with one year of full-time study) is designed for individuals who are employed in social service agencies. Graduates of an accredited undergraduate social work program may apply for advanced standing admission into the second year of the Two-Year Program. The 32-Month Program for Working Professionals is designed for those who work full-time. This program allows students to earn an M.S.W. over a thirty-two month period through evening, weekend, and summer study. All programs may be completed at the main Washington Square campus. All M.S.W. programs can be completed at the School's Rockland County and Westchester County campuses, with the exception of the 16-Month Accelerated Program and the 32-Month Program. Foundation courses may be taken at the School's Staten Island and Westchester sites.

The School offers dual-degree programs with the School of Law and the Wagner Graduate School of Public Service at NYU, and with Sarah Lawrence College. A dual-degree M.S.W./M.P.H. in global public health is also available.

Study for all programs features small classes, articulation of hands-on field placement and academic work, experienced faculty members who practice what they teach, and a uniquely supportive advisement system. The curriculum includes foundation courses that build a knowledge base for work with individuals, families, and groups; an advanced concentration in clinical practice, providing intensive training in human behavior and intervention strategies for direct practice; and a wide selection of electives through which students may pursue individual professional interests. Students in all programs are trained at two or more of the 600 field instruction sites at which the School has arranged experienced on-site supervision.

The Ph.D. program in social work at New York University focuses on practice-informed research and prepares students for leadership in the study, design, and development of clinical social work practice. The program, which is offered on a full- or part-time basis, combines contemporary theory and knowledge related to practice in the urban environment, with content related to diversity, the opportunity for interdisciplinary study, and a global perspective on social work. Graduates of the program are faculty members in social work education, scholars of practice, and/or leaders in policy implementation.

Research Facilities	Bobst Library at NYU is one of the largest open-stack research libraries in the nation, with an extraordinary assemblage of accessible print/video/audio resources, ample reading room and individual study spaces, and long, convenient hours of operation. NYU is a wired university, and students and faculty members alike have free, high-powered access for research and study (from campus or home) to computing resources that include e-mail, the Internet, and major databases. The School itself is home to the widely used international Web site for social work research and education, Information for Practice. The School houses initiatives for research focused on poverty and social services, including the McSilver Institute for Poverty Policy and Research. Students participate with faculty members on research and program development projects with community service agencies.
Financial Aid	The School offers a comprehensive program of both merit-based and need-based financial assistance. Nearly 85 percent of eligible M.S.W. students receive School-based scholarships, and 97 percent of M.S.W. students receive some level of financial assistance. Amounts of financial assistance vary per student and are contingent on the availability of funding each academic year.
Cost of Study	Graduate tuition for 2010–11 was $954 per point plus a $60 nonreturnable registration and services fee, per point, for registration after the first point. There are additional health insurance fees for graduate students, which vary based on coverage.
Living and Housing Costs	Graduate student housing at NYU provides the advantages of apartment-style living, with the convenience, security, activities, and supportive environment of residence hall life. Several types of accommodations are offered to suit different preferences and budgets, including shared studios, double rooms in one- and two-bedroom apartments, and a limited number of private rooms in 2- and 3-person suites. Monthly costs for on-campus housing options range from $950 to $1500. Off-campus housing is also available at market rates. Meal plans are available but not required. For further information, students may contact NYU Housing at 212-998-4600 or visit the Web at http://www.nyu.edu/housing.
Student Group	The School's commitment to diversity is the governing philosophy that is reflected in every aspect of the student experience. The School's student body, like its faculty, is composed of individuals of varied ages, ethnicities, cultural backgrounds, and interests. Great emphasis is placed on keeping the mix vital.
Student Outcomes	According to the most recent report, more than 92 percent of the School's graduates have jobs in social work within three months of graduation. They work in all areas of social work, with the greatest proportion going into mental health services. Significant numbers find employment in the areas of aging, school social work, hospital social work, child welfare and adoption services, and AIDS/HIV support services.
Location	NYU is an integral part of the metropolitan community of New York City, an international capital of art, culture, business, and finance and home of the United Nations. Located in historic Washington Square in the heart of Greenwich Village, NYU allows students to have the city's extraordinary resources at their doorstep. Museums, art galleries, and theaters enrich both academic programs and life experience and contribute to a dynamic environment for study and learning.
The School	The School is, in many respects, an intimate school within the larger University—in its educational philosophy, program structure, and physical setting. Faculty members and students interact in a teaching culture where faculty members are very accessible. Small classes predominate, typically with 25 or fewer students. Three nineteenth-century town houses facing Washington Square Park are the educational and social center of the Silver School, where students gather for classes, seminars, advisement sessions, and informal meetings.

Established in 1953, the School is one of the few in the country to provide a continuum of social work education from undergraduate through doctoral levels. The School maintains affiliations with more than 600 mental health, social services, and health agencies in the tristate area that serve as teaching centers for students in field internships.

Applying	Application forms are available from the School's Office of Admissions as well as at the School's Web site and should be returned with a nonrefundable fee of $50. Programs begin in the fall and spring only. The Ph.D. program begins in the fall only. Prospective students should consult the School's Web site for application deadlines at http://www.socialwork.nyu.edu. International applications are welcomed. All applications should be sent to Office of Social Work Admissions, Graduate Processing Center, New York University, P.O. Box 919, New York, New York 10003-0919.

For more information and application forms, prospective students should contact:

Correspondence and Information	Silver School of Social Work New York University One Washington Square North New York, New York 10003-6654 Phone: 212-998-5910 E-mail: ssw.admissions@nyu.edu Web site: http://www.socialwork.nyu.edu

New York University

THE FACULTY AND THEIR RESEARCH

Theresa Aiello, Associate Professor; Ph.D., NYU. Child and adolescent treatment, object relations theory, history of psychoanalysis and social work, HIV/AIDS.

Alison Aldrich, Clinical Assistant Professor; M.S.W., Columbia. Harm reduction strategies, disclosure issues in the LGBT and transgender communities, substance abuse in individuals with HIV and AIDS.

Patti Aldredge, Clinical Associate Professor; Ph.D., Houston. Pedagogy in social work education, field education, drama-based methodologies.

Jeane W. Anastas, Professor; Ph.D., Brandeis. Women's issues, mental health and substance-abuse services research, gay and lesbian issues, research methodology.

Karra Bikson, Assistant Professor; Ph.D., UCLA. Organizational change and innovation in health and human services, hospice and palliative care, improving access to services for underserved populations, politics of aging and health policy.

Alma J. Carten, Associate Professor; Ph.D., CUNY, Hunter. Child welfare, welfare reform, elderly kinship caretakers, adolescent pregnancy and parenting, public policy development.

Suzanne England, Professor and Dean; Ph.D., Illinois at Chicago. Community and program development, health promotion and disease prevention research, use of new media in professional education, assessment of learning outcomes, creating and managing change in social work education.

Trudy B. Festinger, Professor; D.S.W., Columbia. Foster care and child adoption, research as a basis for public policy.

Martha A. Gabriel, Associate Professor; Ph.D., Smith. Group practice, health care, gay and lesbian issues, HIV/AIDS, secondary trauma.

Daniel S. Gardner, Assistant Professor; Ph.D., Columbia. Aging and social gerontology; end-of-life and palliative care; health-care practice and policy; clinical practice with individuals, couples, and families; program evaluation.

Caroline Rosenthal Gelman, Assistant Professor; Ph.D., Smith. Geriatric social work, culturally sensitive practice, community mental health.

Susan Gerbino, Clinical Assistant Professor; Ph.D., NYU. Bioethics, palliative and end-of-life care, geriatric social work, clinical practice.

Eda G. Goldstein, Professor Emerita; D.S.W., Columbia. Clinical practice theory, contemporary psychodynamic developmental theories, borderline and narcissistic disorders, short-term treatment.

Gladys Gonzalez-Ramos, Associate Professor; Ph.D., NYU. Multicultural issues, school-based services, child abuse and neglect, Latino families.

Diane Grodney, Clinical Associate Professor; Ph.D., NYU. HIV/AIDS, substance abuse, bereavement.

Robert Leibson Hawkins, Assistant Professor; Ph.D., Brandeis. Family and children's policy analysis, welfare and poverty, program evaluation, quantitative and qualitative methods, survey design and implementation.

Gary Holden, Professor; D.S.W., Columbia. Applied research for practice, role of new information technologies in social work, psychosocial factors in health, social cognitive theory and self-efficacy, research methodology.

Mary Ann Jones, Associate Professor; D.S.W., Columbia. Child and family welfare, psychotherapy research, gay and lesbian issues, research methodology.

Gerald Landsberg, Professor; D.S.W., CUNY, Hunter. Violence, forensic mental health, mental health and managed care, services in naturally occurring retirement communities.

Yuhwa Eva Lu, Associate Professor; Ph.D. (joint degree), Claremont and San Diego State. Cross-cultural psychotherapy, clinical process and outcome research, social work with Asian clients.

Virgen Luce, Clinical Assistant Professor; M.S.W., CUNY, Hunter. Field education, HIV/AIDS, mental health, children and adolescents.

James I. Martin, Associate Professor; Ph.D., Illinois at Chicago. HIV prevention, gay and lesbian issues, self-psychology, short-term treatment, clinical practice with gay and lesbian clients.

Linda G. Mills, Professor; Ph.D., Brandeis. Domestic violence, law and social work, women's issues, program and policy research, child welfare training.

Diane Mirabito, Associate Professor; D.S.W., CUNY, Hunter. Adolescent health/mental health, community mental health, school social work.

Peggy Morton, Clinical Associate Professor; D.S.W., CUNY, Hunter. Reproductive health issues, school-based social services, geriatric social work.

Duy Nguyen, Assistant Professor; Ph.D., Columbia. Immigrant and refugee adults and elders, Asian-Americans with severe mental illness and their families, children with emotional and behavioral disorders.

Maryellen Noonan, Associate Professor; Ph.D., NYU. The difficult client, acting out adolescents, child welfare, homelessness.

Deborah Padgett, Professor; Ph.D., Wisconsin. Mental health services research, ethnicity and aging, women's mental health, quantitative and qualitative research methods.

Marjorie A. Rock, Associate Professor; Dr.P.H., Columbia. Chronic mental illness, public mental health, services for the aging, forensic mental health services.

Dina J. Rosenfeld, Clinical Associate Professor; D.S.W., Yeshiva. Adoption, Holocaust studies, hospice care, field instructor training.

Jeffrey Seinfeld, Professor; Ph.D., NYU. Application of object relations theory to populations with serious emotional/environmental disadvantages.

Judith Siegel, Associate Professor; Ph.D., Virginia Commonwealth. Couples and family therapy.

Victoria Stanhope, Assistant Professor; Ph.D, Pennsylvania. Mental health services research, recovery, cultural competence, practice-based research, mental health policy.

Shulamith Lala Straussner, Professor; D.S.W., Columbia. Substance abuse, mass violence and trauma, occupational social work (including employee assistance programs), women's issues, family dynamics, social work education, mental health, international social work.

Helle Thorning, Clinical Professor; Ph.D., NYU. Resilience, mental illness, psychoeducational interventions for immigrant communities dealing with community trauma.

Carol Tosone, Associate Professor; Ph.D., NYU. Grief and bereavement, women's issues, masochism, short-term treatment, medical social work.

Ellen Tuchman, Assistant Professor; Ph.D., NYU. The intersection of HIV/AIDS, substance abuse, and menopause; evidence-based practice.

Jerome C. Wakefield, Professor; Ph.D., D.S.W., Berkeley. Concept of mental illness, social work practice, philosophy of mind, sexual dysfunction.

Allison V. Werner-Lin, Assistant Professor; Ph.D., Chicago. Psychosocial oncology, genetic testing for hereditary disease, family development, clinical practice with children and families in health-care settings.

Alice K. Wolson, Clinical Associate Professor; D.S.W., Yeshiva. Supervision, work with the chronically ill, short-term treatment.

UNIVERSITY OF PENNSYLVANIA

School of Social Policy & Practice

Programs of Study

The School of Social Policy & Practice at the University of Pennsylvania offers the following degree programs: Master of Social Work (M.S.W.), Master of Science in Nonprofit/Nongovernmental Organization Leadership (MSNPL), Master of Science in Social Policy (MSSP), Clinical Doctorate in Social Work (D.S.W.), and Doctor of Philosophy (Ph.D.) in Social Welfare. In addition, students can combine the M.S.W. with the Master of Bioethics (M.S.W./M.B.E.), the Master of Business Administration (M.S.W./M.B.A.), the Master of City Planning (M.S.W./M.C.P.), the Master of Science in Criminology (M.S.W./M.S.), the Master of Science in Education (M.S.W./M.S.Ed.), the Juris Doctor (M.S.W./J.D.), the Master of Government Administration (M.S.W./M.G.A.), the Master of Science in nonprofit/nongovernmental leadership (M.S.W./ MSNPL), the Master of Public Health (M.S.W./M.P.H.), the Master of Science in Social Policy (M.S.W./MSSP), and the Doctor of Philosophy (M.S.W./Ph.D.) degree program. In addition, the School offers an M.S.W./Certificate in Jewish Communal Studies, an M.S.W./Certificate in Catholic Social Ministry, and an M.S.W./Certificate in Lutheran Social Ministries.

The School also offers an Advanced Standing (M.S.W.) program. This program is designed for exceptional B.S.W. students who have graduated from a CSWE-accredited B.S.W. program within the past five years. A limited number of students are accepted into this program. Students begin graduate studies in the summer, followed by two semesters of full-time study. After successful completion of the required two summer courses, plus a no-cost integrated practice seminar and field placement, students enter their advanced year of study.

The primary goal of the Master of Social Work program is to prepare social workers for leadership roles in developing and providing services to individuals, families, groups, communities, and organizations. Full-time (two-year) and part-time (three-year) courses of study are available.

The M.S. in Nonprofit/NGO Leadership program is a full-time, rigorous one-year program designed for professionals who wish to assume leadership positions in business, foundations, government, or nonprofit organizations dedicated to social change. This program does not accept applicants directly from undergraduate study (a minimum of 2 years of post-undergraduate professional or volunteer experience is required) and offers a part-time option in which students may complete the program requirements in five semesters or 2½ academic years.

The Master of Science in Social Policy program is designed to prepare students for leadership positions in analyzing and shaping social policy at the local, national, and international level. The MSSP program is a ten- to eleven-month program spanning three semesters of full-time study. Students may elect to extend the full-time program over a longer period of time, or choose to pursue a part-time option. Individualized educational plans are developed for each option.

The Clinical Doctorate in Social Work program is intended for clinicians with at least two years of post-M.S.W. experience. Penn's clinical D.S.W. program differs from most doctoral programs in that it is a professional-practice degree, designed to prepare students for advanced clinical practice and university-level teaching. This program is an intensive, accelerated program that enables students to satisfy all degree requirements—coursework and dissertation—in three years, without career disruption.

The Ph.D. in Social Welfare program prepares students to address a wide range of social problems related to human welfare. Most graduates of this doctoral program pursue leadership positions in public and private human services organizations or careers in postsecondary teaching and research.

Research Facilities

The School operates six research centers: the Cartographic Modeling Lab; the Center for High Impact Philanthropy; the Field Center for Children's Policy, Practice, and Research; the Center for Research on Youth and Social Policy; the Out-of-School Time Research Center; and the Program for Religion and Social Policy Research.

Financial Aid

Financial aid is based primarily on need. More than 85 percent of M.S.W. students receive financial aid. In addition, the School recognizes merit by offering a range of scholarships to those who qualify. Limited financial aid is available for the M.S. in Nonprofit/NGO Leadership and M.S. in Social Policy programs. The Ph.D. program provides aid in the form of merit fellowships and graduate assistantships, which enable students to gain teaching experience and to collaborate with members of the faculty on research projects. There is no financial aid available for the D.S.W. program.

Cost of Study

Tuition and fees for the full-time M.S.W. program (academic year 2010–11) are $37,232 per year, including student fees; for part-time students, the cost per course unit, including fees, is $4655. Tuition and fees for the MSNPL program (academic year 2010–11) are $45,860. Tuition and fees for the full-time MSSP program (academic year 2010–11) are $45,860; for part-time students, the cost per course unit, including fees, is $4655. Tuition for the clinical D.S.W. program is calculated on a per-course basis; students must complete fourteen courses and the dissertation. Students should expect that the per-course tuition will increase slightly for years two and three, as determined by the University. Tuition and fees per course are $4954. All students accepted into the Ph.D. program and who maintain their academic standing are eligible for financial support, including full-tuition scholarships as well as fellowships or research assistantships for the three years of course work.

Living and Housing Costs

The approximate annual cost of living, including room and board, books, and miscellaneous (e.g., health insurance), for a single student is $23,060 for academic year 2010–11. On-campus living accommodations are available in Sansom Place (graduate student housing).

Student Group

The student body is diverse, representing a wide range of age groups and educational, geographical, and ethnic backgrounds. The School is committed to recruiting a diverse student body. The following are student organizations within the School: Student Council, Active Minds, National Association of Black Social Workers, Women Organized for Social Change, United Community Clinic, Asian Social Work Council, Jewish Social Work Alliance, Latino Social Workers Alliance, Queer Social Workers and Allies at Penn, Social Welfare Action Alliance, Students for International Social Work, Social Workers for a Democratic Society, and Society of Part-Time Students.

Location

The campus of the University of Pennsylvania is located near central Philadelphia, a metropolitan area with a population of more than 5 million. The city of Philadelphia and the University both offer a variety of cultural, recreational, and educational opportunities. Excellent rail and bus services connect Philadelphia to the Washington, D.C. (2½ hours), and New York (2 hours) areas. Philadelphia also operates an international airport that serves all parts of the country and most parts of the world with direct airline service.

The University

The University of Pennsylvania is a private Ivy League university with a long and distinguished history of education in social work. The University was founded by Benjamin Franklin and is the oldest university in the country. Penn's social work program, one of the oldest in the country, was established in 1908. The University has pioneered in the development of many professional fields of higher education in addition to social work, including city planning, nursing, medicine, law, education, veterinary medicine, dentistry, and business.

Applying

Students are admitted to the School's M.S.W., MSNPL, MSSP, D.S.W., and Ph.D. programs once a year, in the fall. Students are admitted to the full-time Advanced Standing program in July.

Applications are accepted on a rolling basis for the M.S.W., MSSP, and MSNPL programs beginning in the fall. Each of these programs will continue accepting applications on a rolling basis until admissions goals for the academic year are met. However, it is important to apply early, as enrollment is limited. Applications received by April 15 will be given preference for admissions and tuition assistance. Applications are also accepted on a rolling basis for the M.S.W. Advanced Standing Program. The priority deadline for this program is March 1.

The Ph.D. and D.S.W. programs do not admit on a rolling basis. Applications for the Ph.D. program are accepted between September 15 and December 15. The deadline for D.S.W. applications is March 15.

Correspondence and Information

Office of Admissions
School of Social Policy & Practice
University of Pennsylvania
3701 Locust Walk
Philadelphia, Pennsylvania 19104-6214
Phone: 215-898-5511
Web site: http://www.sp2.upenn.edu

University of Pennsylvania

THE FACULTY AND THEIR RESEARCH

Joretha Bourjolly, Associate Professor and Associate Dean, Academic Affairs; Ph.D., Bryn Mawr, 1996. Effects of chronic illness on individuals and family members as well as the impact of racial and economic factors on the delivery of health care.

Ram A. Cnaan, Professor and Associate Dean, Research; Ph.D., Pittsburgh, 1981. Social work research methods, social policy, volunteerism and volunteer action, information technology applications.

Dennis Culhane, Associate Professor; Ph.D., Boston College, 1990. Homelessness, housing policy, policy analysis research methods.

Joan K. Davitt, Assistant Professor; Ph.D., Bryn Mawr, 2003. Gerontology, policy, health, and health-care outcomes for older adults and ethical issues in long-term care.

Ezekiel J. Dixon-Roman, Assistant Professor; Ph.D., Fordham, 2007. Sociology of education, marginalized groups, interaction of political economy and culture, stratification and mobility, supplementary education, cultural capital, quantitative methods.

Andrea M. Doyle, Assistant Professor; Ph.D., Washington (Seattle), 2003. Clinical social work, substance abuse, mental health, HIV/AIDS, women and group psychotherapy.

Jeffrey Draine, Assistant Professor; Ph.D., Pennsylvania, 1995. Mental health and the criminal justice system, the intersection of mental illness with the criminal justice system, how policy and practice impact community inclusion of people with mental illness who come in contact with the law.

Richard J. Estes, Professor; D.S.W., Berkeley, 1973. International and comparative social welfare, social indicators, mental health, evaluative research, computer technology.

Damon W. Freeman, Assistant Professor; J.D., Ph.D., Indiana, 2004. African American intellectual history, critical race theory, social policy and social movements.

Richard James Gelles, Professor and Dean; Ph.D., New Hampshire, 1973. Child welfare, family violence, child abuse.

Zvi D. Gellis, Associate Professor; Ph.D., Toronto, 1999. Mental health, gerontology, evidence-based practice.

Toorjo Ghose, Assistant Professor; Ph.D., UCLA, 2005. Substance abuse, HIV/AIDS in developing countries, mental health service provision, welfare policy.

Femida Handy, Associate Professor, Ph.D., York, 1995. Nonprofit entrepreneurship and volunteerism, comparative and international aspects of the nonprofit and voluntary sector and social accounting.

Roberta Rehner Iversen, Associate Professor; Ph.D., Bryn Mawr, 1991. Practice with children and families, research on women and poverty.

Steven Corey Marcus, Research Associate Professor; Ph.D., Pittsburgh, 1998. Psychiatric medical errors, mental health services.

Karin Rhodes, Assistant Professor; M.D., Chicago, 1983. Family violence; quality of emergency services; access to follow-up care; the intersection between acute care and the mental health, social services, and criminal justice systems.

Roberta G. Sands, Professor; Ph.D., Louisville, 1979. Mental health, women's issues, clinical social work practice, interprofessional communications, ethnographic sociolinguistic research.

Kenwyn K. Smith, Associate Professor; Ph.D., Yale, 1974. Group and intergroup relations, organizational change, organizational politics, conflict management, impact of organizational dynamics on the health of employees.

Phyllis Solomon, Professor; Ph.D., Case Western Reserve, 1978. Social work research methods, mental health policy and service delivery systems, severely mentally disabled persons and their families.

Susan Sorenson, Professor; Ph.D., Cincinnati, 1985. Public health; epidemiology and prevention of violence, including homicide, suicide, sexual assault, child abuse, battering, and firearms.

Mark J. Stern, Professor; Ph.D., York (England), 1980. Social welfare policy; social history and social welfare; poverty in the United States, 1900–present.

Yin-Ling Irene Wong, Associate Professor; Ph.D., Wisconsin, 1995. Social policy, homelessness, homelessness prevention and poverty research.

WASHINGTON UNIVERSITY IN ST. LOUIS

George Warren Brown School of Social Work

Programs of Study

The George Warren Brown School of Social Work (Brown School) at Washington University in St. Louis offers a curriculum leading to the degree of Master of Social Work (M.S.W.), Master of Public Health (M.P.H.), and, in collaboration with the Graduate School of Arts and Sciences, the degree of Doctor of Philosophy in social work. The School's strength lies at the intersection of social work, public health, and social and economic development. Students with superior academic preparation are encouraged to apply.

The Brown School's M.S.W. program is characterized by flexibility in the choice of courses, including the practicum, individually planned curricula, interdisciplinary collaboration, and the integration of evidence-based practice into its teaching, research, and service.

The M.S.W. curriculum prepares students for leadership positions in the fields of children, youth, and family; gerontology; health; mental health; and social and economic development. Specializations are available in management and research. The program involves 60 credit hours for graduation and ordinarily requires two academic years of full-time study for completion. Students with a B.S.W. from a CSWE-accredited school enroll in an advanced-standing program that permits them to earn up to 19 credits toward their M.S.W.

A special feature of the Brown School's M.S.W. program is the availability of dual-degree options in social work and architecture (M.S.W./M.Arch.), business administration (M.S.W./M.B.A.), divinity (M.S.W./M.Div.), Jewish studies (M.S.W./M.A.J.S.), law (M.S.W./J.D.), pastoral studies (M.S.W./M.A.P.S.), and public health (M.S.W./M.P.H.). In addition, students often enroll in courses in other graduate schools of the University.

The Brown School's M.P.H. program grounds students in the core competencies of public health, such as behavioral science, biostatistics, epidemiology, environmental health, and health policy. A centerpiece of the program's curriculum is a series of intensive, team-based, problem-solving courses designed to expose students to a variety of viewpoints including architecture, education, economics, law, medicine, public policy, and public affairs.

The M.P.H. program is a two-year, 45 credit-hour program. The program includes a student-selected practicum (field work) experience. Students may choose to complete their practicum in a local, national, or international setting. In addition to the M.S.W/M.P.H. dual degree, Washington University offers a public health and business dual degree (M.P.H./M.B.A).

Like the M.S.W. program, the M.P.H. program is rooted in interdisciplinary, evidence-based approaches.

The Ph.D. program is highly interdisciplinary and is designed to prepare graduates for teaching and research careers. The average time needed to complete all Ph.D. requirements is three years of full-time study for students with the M.S.W. degree and four to five years for those without it.

Research Facilities

The Brown School is housed in two connecting buildings that were built for teaching and research—Goldfarb Hall, opened in 1998, and Brown Hall, the first academic building dedicated to social work in the United States. A wide range of computing equipment and services is available for use by students for classroom instruction and research projects. Library holdings in the social and behavioral sciences and social welfare are strong and up to date. There are many opportunities for collaborative and interdisciplinary work throughout the University. Most of the faculty members have ongoing research projects in which M.S.W., M.P.H., and Ph.D. students participate. The School is home to twelve research centers and applied programs: the Alliance for Building Capacity, Center for Latino Family Research, Center for Mental Health Services Research, Center for Social Development, Center for Tobacco Policy Research, Gephardt Institute for Public Service, Health Communication Research Laboratory, Kathryn M. Buder Center for American Indian Studies, Center for Violence and Injury Prevention, Prevention Research Center in St. Louis, Program in Obesity Prevention and Policy Research, and a new systems dynamics simulation laboratory.

The Brown School Dean is the founding director of Washington University's new Institute for Public Health.

Financial Aid

More than 200 scholarships, five loan programs, college work-study arrangements, paid practicums, and part-time employment assistance are among the various types of financial aid administered by the Brown School in conjunction with Washington University's Office of Student Financial Services. The School considers all applicants for admission and financial aid without regard to age, color, creed, disability, sexual orientation, marital status, national origin, race, or sex. Ninety percent of M.S.W. and M.P.H. students receive financial aid.

Cost of Study

The tuition for master's degree students is $1048 per credit hour in 2010–11. Additional expenses, including the cost of health service, student activity fees, books, and supplies, are about $1900 per year.

Living and Housing Costs

Approximately $650 per month should be budgeted to provide for living costs. Most students prefer to rent an apartment near the School.

Student Group

In spring 2010, there were 439 full-time and 30 part-time students in the M.S.W. program. Forty-seven students were working toward the Ph.D. degree in social work. The M.P.H program enrolled a cohort of 45 students in fall 2009. Approximately 80 percent of students relocate to St. Louis to attend Brown. In addition, 20 percent of students are from outside the United States. Social work and public health students at Brown can join and participate in a wide range of student-led groups. These groups allow students to build connections with others who have similar interests. The groups also provide opportunities to build leadership skills.

Location

The St. Louis area offers a variety of musical, cultural, and sports events throughout the academic year. Washington University is contiguous with the city of St. Louis and adjoins its suburbs. There is a delightful potpourri of shops, ethnic restaurants, churches, bookstores, movie theaters, and art museums within a mile of the campus. In addition, St. Louis social agencies offer outstanding practicum opportunities to students.

The University and The School

The Brown School is ranked among the top schools of social work in the United States. It is one of the eight graduate and professional schools that constitute Washington University in St. Louis—a medium-sized, private, urban institution. The Brown School profits from all of the University's resources, including an outstanding and internationally recognized faculty, a diverse and talented student body, a superior library, and an overall environment of creative excellence. The School is one of the few social work programs in the country to have its own career services office for graduates. The M.S.W. program is fully accredited by the Council on Social Work Education. The M.P.H program is new and is an applicant for accreditation from the Council on Education for Public Health.

Applying

Prospective students are encouraged to apply online at http://www.gwbweb.wustl.edu/apply. Applicants must have an undergraduate degree or be in the process of obtaining one. No specific undergraduate major is required. Undergraduate performance should demonstrate intellectual capacity for graduate study, with a B average as the minimum requirement. Applicants are advised to apply as early as possible for scholarship consideration.

Correspondence and Information

For the M.S.W. and M.P.H. programs:
Richard Sigg
Director of Admissions
Brown School
Box 1196
Washington University in St. Louis
St. Louis, Missouri 63130
Phone: 314-935-6676
877-321-2426 (toll-free, North America)
Fax: 314-935-4859
E-mail: brownschool@wustl.edu
Web site: http://brownschool.wustl.edu

For the Ph.D. program:
Dr. Wendy Auslander
Chairperson, Ph.D. Program
Brown School
Box 1196
Washington University in St. Louis
St. Louis, Missouri 63130
Phone: 314-935-6605
877-321-2426 (toll-free, North America)
Fax: 314-935-8511
E-mail: phdsw@gwbmail.wustl.edu
Web site: http://brownschool.wustl.edu

Washington University in St. Louis

THE FACULTY AND THEIR RESEARCH
PROFESSORS

Wendy Auslander, Ph.D., Washington (St. Louis). Minority health/health promotion, families, and chronic illness, juvenile diabetes, AIDS prevention.

Ross Brownson, Ph.D., Colorado State. Chronic disease prevention, evidence-based public health, policy effects on physical activity.

Sarah Gehlert, Ph.D., E. Desmond Lee Professor of Racial and Ethnic Diversity, Washington (St. Louis). Transdisciplinary research, women's health, health disparities.

David F. Gillespie, Ph.D., Washington (Seattle). Disaster preparedness, organizational theory, interorganizational relations, measurement.

Debra Haire-Joshu, Ph.D., St. Louis. Health policy, obesity prevention.

Shanti K. Khinduka, George Warren Brown Distinguished University Professor; Ph.D., Brandeis. Social work education, international social development.

Matthew W. Kreuter, Ph.D., North Carolina at Chapel Hill. Health communications, cancer prevention.

Edward F. Lawlor, Ph.D., William E. Gordon Distinguished Professor, Brandeis. Health care reform, health care administration, policy for the aged and poor, Medicare policy.

Douglas Luke, Ph.D., Illinois. Public health program evaluation, tobacco control, community health.

Timothy McBride, Ph.D., Wisconsin–Madison. Rural health care, Medicare policy, health economics, state health policy.

Nancy Morrow-Howell, Ralph and Muriel Pumphrey Professor of Social Work; Ph.D., Berkeley. Gerontology, care for dependent elderly, hospital discharge planning for elderly.

Martha N. Ozawa, Bettie Bofinger Brown Distinguished Professor of Social Policy; Ph.D., Wisconsin–Madison. Policy analysis of social welfare programs, income support programs, social security, unemployment.

Enola K. Proctor, Frank Bruno Professor for Social Work Research; Ph.D., Washington (St. Louis). Mental health and health services; treatment planning in direct practice; evaluation of clinical social work; race, gender, and socioeconomic status.

Mark Rank, Herbert S. Hadley Professor of Social Welfare; Ph.D., Wisconsin–Madison. Poverty, social stratification, family, social policy, social justice.

Michael W. Sherraden, Benjamin E. Youngdahl Professor of Social Development; Ph.D., Michigan. Social policy and administration, youth policy.

Arlene Stiffman, Barbara A. Bailey Professor of Social Work; Ph.D., Washington (St. Louis). Child and adolescent mental health, high-risk behaviors.

Luis H. Zayas, Shanti K. Khinduka Distinguished Professor of Social Work; Ph.D., Columbia. Child socialization and parent interaction, child and adolescent mental health and treatment, ethnoracial minority mental health and intervention research.

Associate Professors

F. Brett Drake, Ph.D., UCLA. Social stress, substance abuse, child abuse and neglect, burnout of child welfare workers.

Tonya Edmond, Ph.D., Texas at Austin. Sexual abuse survivors, women's issues, domestic violence, clinical practice.

Melissa Jonson-Reid, Ph.D., Berkeley. Children and violence, child welfare/juvenile justice services outcomes, interagency school interventions.

Carolyn Lesorogol, Ph.D., Washington (St. Louis). International social development, cross-cultural research, land use.

Jack A. Kirkland, M.S.W., Syracuse. Community work, group relations, international social development, racism, social planning.

J. Curtis McMillen, Ph.D., Maryland, Baltimore. Child welfare, clinical social work practice, mental health.

Shanta Pandey, Ph.D., Case Western Reserve. Social policy, poverty, program evaluation.

Vetta Sanders Thompson, Ph.D., Duke. Racial identity, cultural competency, disparities in health and mental health care.

Renee M. Williams, Ph.D., Washington (St. Louis). Mental health, addictions, gambling.

Gautam N. Yadama, Ph.D., Case Western Reserve. International community development, rural farming and forestry.

Assistant Professors

J. Aaron Hipp, Ph.D., California, Irvine. Environmental change, ecological modeling, geographic information systems (GIS), environmental design.

Lora Iannotti, Ph.D., Johns Hopkins. Infant and child nutrition, maternal nutrition, infectious diseases, poverty.

Patricia Kohl, Ph.D., North Carolina at Chapel Hill. Child welfare, mental health assessments and evaluation.

Amanda Moore McBride, Ph.D., Washington (St. Louis). Service/civic engagement, program evaluation, social policy.

Juan Pena, Ph.D., Columbia. Mental health and Latino populations.

Ramesh Raghavan, M.D., Ph.D., UCLA. Access to mental health services, health insurance and managed care, childhood trauma.

Paul Shattuck, Ph.D., Wisconsin-Madison. Autism, health, developmental disabilities, health policy.

APPENDIXES

Institutional Changes
Since the 2010 Edition

Following is an alphabetical listing of institutions that have recently closed, merged with other institutions, or changed their names or status. In the case of a name change, the former name appears first, followed by the new name.

Agnes Scott College (Decatur, GA): no longer offers graduate degrees

American Graduate School of International Relations and Diplomacy (Paris, France): name changed to American Graduate School in Paris

Antioch University McGregor (Yellow Springs, OH): name changed to Antioch University Midwest

Arizona State University at the Downtown Phoenix Campus (Phoenix, AZ): will be included with main campus Arizona State University (Tempe, AZ) by request from the institution

Arizona State University at the Polytechnic Campus (Mesa, AZ): will be included with main campus Arizona State University (Tempe, AZ) by request from the institution

Arizona State University at the West campus (Phoenix, AZ): [will be included with main campus Arizona State University (Tempe, AZ) by request from the institution

Arkansas State University (State University, AR): name changed to Arkansas State University–Jonesboro

Asbury College (Wilmore, KY): name changed to Asbury University

Australasian College of Health Sciences (Portland, OR): name changed to American College of Healthcare Sciences

Baker College Center for Graduate Studies (Flint, MI): name changed to Baker College Center for Graduate Studies–Online

Baltimore Hebrew University (Baltimore, MD): now a unit of Towson University (Towson, MD)

Beacon University (Columbus, GA): closed

Belhaven College (Jackson, MS): name changed to Belhaven University

Beth Benjamin Academy of Connecticut (Stamford, CT): no longer offers graduate degrees

Bethel College (McKenzie, TN): name changed to Bethel University

Bridgewater State College (Bridgewater, MA): name changed to Bridgewater State University

British American College London (London, United Kingdom): name changed to Regent's American College London

The Chicago School of Professional Psychology: Downtown Los Angeles Campus (Los Angeles, CA): name changed to The Chicago School of Professional Psychology at Downtown Los Angeles

The Chicago School of Professional Psychology: Grayslake Campus (Grayslake, IL): name changed to The Chicago School of Professional Psychology at Grayslake

The Cleveland Institute of Art (Cleveland, OH): no longer offers graduate degrees

Coleman College (San Diego, CA): name changed to Coleman University

Columbia Union College (Takoma Park, MD): name changed to Washington Adventist University

Dell'Arte School of Physical Theatre (Blue Lake, CA): name changed to Dell'Arte International School of Physical Theatre

DeVry University (San Francisco, CA): closed

Fitchburg State College (Fitchburg, MA): name changed to Fitchburg State University

Framingham State College (Framingham, MA): name changed to Framingham State University

George Meany Center for Labor Studies–The National Labor College (Silver Spring, MD): name changed to National Labor College

Hebrew Theological College (Skokie, IL): no longer offers graduate degrees

International University in Geneva (Geneva, Switzerland): no longer accredited by agency recognized by USDE or CHEA

Joint Military Intelligence College (Washington, DC): name changed to National Defense Intelligence College

Kent State University, Stark Campus (Canton, OH): name changed to Kent State University at Stark

Lancaster Bible College (Lancaster, PA): name changed to Lancaster Bible College & Graduate School

Leadership Institute of Seattle (Kenmore, WA): is now part of Saybrook University (San Francisco, CA)

New England School of Law (Boston, MA): name changed to New England Law-Boston

Otterbein College (Westerville, OH): name changed to Otterbein University

Pepperdine University (Los Angeles, CA): will be included with Pepperdine University (Malibu, CA) by request from the institution

The Protestant Episcopal Theological Seminary in Virginia (Alexandria, VA): name changed to Virginia Theological Seminary

Reinhardt College (Waleska, GA): name changed to Reinhardt University

Robert Morris College (Chicago, IL): name changed to Robert Morris University Illinois

St. Petersburg Theological Seminary (St. Petersburg, FL): no longer accredited by agency recognized by USDE or CHEA

Saybrook Graduate School and Research Center (San Francisco, CA): name changed to Saybrook University

Shorter College (Rome, GA): name changed to Shorter University

Southeastern University (Washington, DC): closed

Southern New England School of Law (North Dartmouth, MA): is now part of University of Massachusetts Dartmouth (North Dartmouth, MA)

Trinity Episcopal School for Ministry (Ambridge, PA): name changed to Trinity School for Ministry

University of Missouri–Columbia (Columbia, MO): name changed to University of Missouri

University of Phoenix–Renton Learning Center (Renton, WA): name changed to University of Phoenix–Western Washington Campus

University of Phoenix–Wisconsin Campus (Brookfield, WI): now listed as University of Phoenix–Madison Campus (Madison, WI)

West Liberty State University (West Liberty, WV): name changed to West Liberty University

World Medicine Institute: College of Acupuncture and Herbal Medicine (Honolulu, HI): name changed to World Medicine Institute of Acupuncture and Herbal Medicine

Abbreviations Used in the Guides

The following list includes abbreviations of degree names used in the profiles in the 2011 edition of the guides. Because some degrees (e.g., Doctor of Education) can be abbreviated in more than one way (e.g., D.Ed. or Ed.D.), and because the abbreviations used in the guides reflect the preferences of the individual colleges and universities, the list may include two or more abbreviations for a single degree.

Degrees

A Mus D	Doctor of Musical Arts
AC	Advanced Certificate
AD	Artist's Diploma
	Doctor of Arts
ADP	Artist's Diploma
Adv C	Advanced Certificate
Adv M	Advanced Master
AGC	Advanced Graduate Certificate
AGSC	Advanced Graduate Specialist Certificate
ALM	Master of Liberal Arts
AM	Master of Arts
AMBA	Accelerated Master of Business Administration
AMRS	Master of Arts in Religious Studies
APC	Advanced Professional Certificate
App Sc	Applied Scientist
App Sc D	Doctor of Applied Science
Au D	Doctor of Audiology
B Th	Bachelor of Theology
CAES	Certificate of Advanced Educational Specialization
CAGS	Certificate of Advanced Graduate Studies
CAL	Certificate in Applied Linguistics
CALS	Certificate of Advanced Liberal Studies
CAMS	Certificate of Advanced Management Studies
CAPS	Certificate of Advanced Professional Studies
CAS	Certificate of Advanced Studies
CASPA	Certificate of Advanced Study in Public Administration
CASR	Certificate in Advanced Social Research
CATS	Certificate of Achievement in Theological Studies
CBHS	Certificate in Basic Health Sciences
CBS	Graduate Certificate in Biblical Studies
CCJA	Certificate in Criminal Justice Administration
CCSA	Certificate in Catholic School Administration
CCTS	Certificate in Clinical and Translational Science
CE	Civil Engineer
CEM	Certificate of Environmental Management
CET	Certificate in Educational Technologies
CGS	Certificate of Graduate Studies
Ch E	Chemical Engineer
CM	Certificate in Management
CMH	Certificate in Medical Humanities
CMM	Master of Church Ministries
CMS	Certificate in Ministerial Studies
CNM	Certificate in Nonprofit Management
CP	Certificate in Performance
CPASF	Certificate Program for Advanced Study in Finance
CPC	Certificate in Professional Counseling
	Certificate in Publication and Communication
CPH	Certificate in Public Health
CPM	Certificate in Public Management
CPS	Certificate of Professional Studies
CScD	Doctor of Clinical Science
CSD	Certificate in Spiritual Direction
CSS	Certificate of Special Studies

CTS	Certificate of Theological Studies
CURP	Certificate in Urban and Regional Planning
D Admin	Doctor of Administration
D Arch	Doctor of Architecture
D Com	Doctor of Commerce
D Div	Doctor of Divinity
D Ed	Doctor of Education
D Ed Min	Doctor of Educational Ministry
D Eng	Doctor of Engineering
D Engr	Doctor of Engineering
D Env	Doctor of Environment
D Env M	Doctor of Environmental Management
D Law	Doctor of Law
D Litt	Doctor of Letters
D Med Sc	Doctor of Medical Science
D Min	Doctor of Ministry
D Miss	Doctor of Missiology
D Mus	Doctor of Music
D Mus A	Doctor of Musical Arts
D Phil	Doctor of Philosophy
D Ps	Doctor of Psychology
D Sc	Doctor of Science
D Sc D	Doctor of Science in Dentistry
D Sc IS	Doctor of Science in Information Systems
D Sc PA	Doctor of Science in Physician Assistant Studies
D Th	Doctor of Theology
D Th P	Doctor of Practical Theology
DA	Doctor of Accounting
	Doctor of Arts
DA Ed	Doctor of Arts in Education
DAH	Doctor of Arts in Humanities
DAOM	Doctorate in Acupuncture and Oriental Medicine
DAST	Diploma of Advanced Studies in Teaching
DBA	Doctor of Business Administration
DBL	Doctor of Business Leadership
DBS	Doctor of Buddhist Studies
DC	Doctor of Chiropractic
DCC	Doctor of Computer Science
DCD	Doctor of Communications Design
DCL	Doctor of Civil Law
	Doctor of Comparative Law
DCM	Doctor of Church Music
DCN	Doctor of Clinical Nutrition
DCS	Doctor of Computer Science
DDN	Diplôme du Droit Notarial
DDS	Doctor of Dental Surgery
DE	Doctor of Education
	Doctor of Engineering
DED	Doctor of Economic Development
DEIT	Doctor of Educational Innovation and Technology
DEL	Doctor of Executive Leadership
DEM	Doctor of Educational Ministry
DEPD	Diplôme Études Spécialisées
DES	Doctor of Engineering Science
DESS	Diplôme Études Supérieures Spécialisées
DFA	Doctor of Fine Arts
DGP	Diploma in Graduate and Professional Studies
DH Ed	Doctor of Health Education
DH Sc	Doctor of Health Sciences
DHA	Doctor of Health Administration
DHCE	Doctor of Health Care Ethics
DHL	Doctor of Hebrew Letters
	Doctor of Hebrew Literature

DHS	Doctor of Health Science Doctor of Human Services		**EMPA**	Executive Master of Public Administration Executive Master of Public Affairs
DHSc	Doctor of Health Science		**EMS**	Executive Master of Science
Dip CS	Diploma in Christian Studies		**EMTM**	Executive Master of Technology Management
DIT	Doctor of Industrial Technology		**Eng**	Engineer
DJ Ed	Doctor of Jewish Education		**Eng Sc D**	Doctor of Engineering Science
DJS	Doctor of Jewish Studies		**Engr**	Engineer
DLS	Doctor of Liberal Studies		**Ex Doc**	Executive Doctor of Pharmacy
DM	Doctor of Management Doctor of Music		**Exec Ed D**	Executive Doctor of Education
DMA	Doctor of Musical Arts		**Exec MBA**	Executive Master of Business Administration
DMD	Doctor of Dental Medicine		**Exec MPA**	Executive Master of Public Administration
DME	Doctor of Manufacturing Management Doctor of Music Education		**Exec MPH**	Executive Master of Public Health
			Exec MS	Executive Master of Science
DMEd	Doctor of Music Education		**G Dip**	Graduate Diploma
DMFT	Doctor of Marital and Family Therapy		**GBC**	Graduate Business Certificate
DMH	Doctor of Medical Humanities		**GCE**	Graduate Certificate in Education
DML	Doctor of Modern Languages		**GDM**	Graduate Diploma in Management
DMM	Doctor of Music Ministry		**GDPA**	Graduate Diploma in Public Administration
DMP	Doctorate in Medical Physics		**GDRE**	Graduate Diploma in Religious Education
DMPNA	Doctor of Management Practice in Nurse Anesthesia		**GEMBA**	Global Executive Master of Business Administration
DN Sc	Doctor of Nursing Science		**GEMPA**	Gulf Executive Master of Public Administration
DNAP	Doctor of Nurse Anesthesia Practice		**GM Acc**	Graduate Master of Accountancy
DNP	Doctor of Nursing Practice		**GMBA**	Global Master of Business Administration
DNS	Doctor of Nursing Science		**GPD**	Graduate Performance Diploma
DO	Doctor of Osteopathy		**GSS**	Graduate Special Certificate for Students in Special Situations
DPA	Doctor of Public Administration			
DPC	Doctor of Pastoral Counseling		**IEMBA**	International Executive Master of Business Administration
DPDS	Doctor of Planning and Development Studies			
DPH	Doctor of Public Health		**IM Acc**	Integrated Master of Accountancy
DPM	Doctor of Plant Medicine Doctor of Podiatric Medicine		**IMA**	Interdisciplinary Master of Arts
			IMBA	International Master of Business Administration
DPPD	Doctor of Policy, Planning, and Development		**IMES**	International Masters in Environmental Studies
DPS	Doctor of Professional Studies		**Ingeniero**	Engineer
DPT	Doctor of Physical Therapy		**JCD**	Doctor of Canon Law
DPTSc	Doctor of Physical Therapy Science		**JCL**	Licentiate in Canon Law
Dr DES	Doctor of Design		**JD**	Juris Doctor
Dr PH	Doctor of Public Health		**JSD**	Doctor of Juridical Science Doctor of Jurisprudence Doctor of the Science of Law
Dr Sc PT	Doctor of Science in Physical Therapy			
DRSc	Doctor of Regulatory Science			
DS	Doctor of Science		**JSM**	Master of Science of Law
DS Sc	Doctor of Social Science		**L Th**	Licenciate in Theology
DSJS	Doctor of Science in Jewish Studies		**LL B**	Bachelor of Laws
DSL	Doctor of Strategic Leadership		**LL CM**	Master of Laws in Comparative Law
DSN	Doctor of Science in Nursing		**LL D**	Doctor of Laws
DSW	Doctor of Social Work		**LL M**	Master of Laws
DTL	Doctor of Talmudic Law		**LL M in Tax**	Master of Laws in Taxation
DV Sc	Doctor of Veterinary Science		**LL M CL**	Master of Laws (Common Law)
DVM	Doctor of Veterinary Medicine		**LL M/MBA**	Master of Laws/Master of Business Administration
EAA	Engineer in Aeronautics and Astronautics		**LL M/MNM**	Master of Laws/Master of Nonprofit Management
ECS	Engineer in Computer Science		**M Ac**	Master of Accountancy Master of Accounting Master of Acupuncture
Ed D	Doctor of Education			
Ed DCT	Doctor of Education in College Teaching			
Ed M	Master of Education		**M Ac OM**	Master of Acupuncture and Oriental Medicine
Ed S	Specialist in Education		**M Acc**	Master of Accountancy Master of Accounting
Ed Sp	Specialist in Education			
Ed Sp PTE	Specialist in Education in Professional Technical Education		**M Acct**	Master of Accountancy Master of Accounting
			M Accy	Master of Accountancy
EDM	Executive Doctorate in Management		**M Actg**	Master of Accounting
EDSPC	Education Specialist		**M Acy**	Master of Accountancy
EE	Electrical Engineer		**M Ad**	Master of Administration
EJD	Executive Juris Doctor		**M Ad Ed**	Master of Adult Education
EMBA	Executive Master of Business Administration		**M Adm**	Master of Administration
EMFA	Executive Master of Forensic Accounting		**M Adm Mgt**	Master of Administrative Management
EMHA	Executive Master of Health Administration		**M Admin**	Master of Administration
EMIB	Executive Master of International Business		**M ADU**	Master of Architectural Design and Urbanism
EML	Executive Master of Leadership		**M Adv**	Master of Advertising
			M Aero E	Master of Aerospace Engineering

M AEST	Master of Applied Environmental Science and Technology
M Ag	Master of Agriculture
M Ag Ed	Master of Agricultural Education
M Agr	Master of Agriculture
M Anesth Ed	Master of Anesthesiology Education
M App Comp Sc	Master of Applied Computer Science
M App St	Master of Applied Statistics
M Appl Stat	Master of Applied Statistics
M Aq	Master of Aquaculture
M Ar	Master of Architecture
M Arc	Master of Architecture
M Arch	Master of Architecture
M Arch I	Master of Architecture I
M Arch II	Master of Architecture II
M Arch E	Master of Architectural Engineering
M Arch H	Master of Architectural History
M Bioethics	Master in Bioethics
M Biomath	Master of Biomathematics
M Ch	Master of Chemistry
M Ch E	Master of Chemical Engineering
M Chem	Master of Chemistry
M Cl D	Master of Clinical Dentistry
M Cl Sc	Master of Clinical Science
M Comp E	Master of Computer Engineering
M Comp Sc	Master of Computer Science
M Coun	Master of Counseling
M Dent	Master of Dentistry
M Dent Sc	Master of Dental Sciences
M Des	Master of Design
M Des S	Master of Design Studies
M Div	Master of Divinity
M Ec	Master of Economics
M Econ	Master of Economics
M Ed	Master of Education
M Ed T	Master of Education in Teaching
M En	Master of Engineering Master of Environmental Science
M En S	Master of Environmental Sciences
M Eng	Master of Engineering
M Eng Mgt	Master of Engineering Management
M Engr	Master of Engineering
M Env	Master of Environment
M Env Des	Master of Environmental Design
M Env E	Master of Environmental Engineering
M Env Sc	Master of Environmental Science
M Fin	Master of Finance
M Geo E	Master of Geological Engineering
M Geoenv E	Master of Geoenvironmental Engineering
M Geog	Master of Geography
M Hum	Master of Humanities
M Hum Svcs	Master of Human Services
M IBD	Master of Integrated Building Delivery
M IDST	Master's in Interdisciplinary Studies
M Kin	Master of Kinesiology
M Land Arch	Master of Landscape Architecture
M Litt	Master of Letters
M Man	Master of Management
M Mat SE	Master of Material Science and Engineering
M Math	Master of Mathematics
M Med Sc	Master of Medical Science
M Mgmt	Master of Management
M Mgt	Master of Management
M Min	Master of Ministries
M Mtl E	Master of Materials Engineering
M Mu	Master of Music
M Mus	Master of Music

M Mus Ed	Master of Music Education
M Music	Master of Music
M Nat Sci	Master of Natural Science
M Oc E	Master of Oceanographic Engineering
M Pet E	Master of Petroleum Engineering
M Pharm	Master of Pharmacy
M Phil	Master of Philosophy
M Phil F	Master of Philosophical Foundations
M Pl	Master of Planning
M Plan	Master of Planning
M Pol	Master of Political Science
M Pr Met	Master of Professional Meteorology
M Prob S	Master of Probability and Statistics
M Psych	Master of Psychology
M Pub	Master of Publishing
M Rel	Master of Religion
M Sc	Master of Science
M Sc A	Master of Science (Applied)
M Sc AHN	Master of Science in Applied Human Nutrition
M Sc BMC	Master of Science in Biomedical Communications
M Sc CS	Master of Science in Computer Science
M Sc E	Master of Science in Engineering
M Sc Eng	Master of Science in Engineering
M Sc Engr	Master of Science in Engineering
M Sc F	Master of Science in Forestry
M Sc FE	Master of Science in Forest Engineering
M Sc Geogr	Master of Science in Geography
M Sc N	Master of Science in Nursing
M Sc OT	Master of Science in Occupational Therapy
M Sc P	Master of Science in Planning
M Sc Pl	Master of Science in Planning
M Sc PT	Master of Science in Physical Therapy
M Sc T	Master of Science in Teaching
M SEM	Master of Sustainable Environmental Management
M Serv Soc	Master of Social Service
M Soc	Master of Sociology
M Sp Ed	Master of Special Education
M Stat	Master of Statistics
M Sw En	Master of Software Engineering
M Sys Sc	Master of Systems Science
M Tax	Master of Taxation
M Tech	Master of Technology
M Th	Master of Theology
M Tox	Master of Toxicology
M Trans E	Master of Transportation Engineering
M Urb	Master of Urban Planning
M Vet Sc	Master of Veterinary Science
MA	Master of Administration Master of Arts
MA Comm	Master of Arts in Communication
MA Ed	Master of Arts in Education
MA Ed Ad	Master of Arts in Educational Administration
MA Ext	Master of Agricultural Extension
MA Islamic	Master of Arts in Islamic Studies
MA Military Studies	Master of Arts in Military Studies
MA Min	Master of Arts in Ministry
MA Miss	Master of Arts in Missiology
MA Past St	Master of Arts in Pastoral Studies
MA Ph	Master of Arts in Philosophy
MA Psych	Master of Arts in Psychology
MA Sc	Master of Applied Science
MA Sp	Master of Arts (Spirituality)
MA Strategic Intelligence	Master of Arts in Strategic Intelligence
MA Th	Master of Arts in Theology

MA-R	Master of Arts (Research)
MAA	Master of Administrative Arts
	Master of Applied Anthropology
	Master of Applied Arts
	Master of Arts in Administration
MAAAP	Master of Arts Administration and Policy
MAAE	Master of Arts in Art Education
MAAT	Master of Arts in Applied Theology
	Master of Arts in Art Therapy
MAB	Master of Agribusiness
MABC	Master of Arts in Biblical Counseling
	Master of Arts in Business Communication
MABE	Master of Arts in Bible Exposition
MABL	Master of Arts in Biblical Languages
MABM	Master of Agribusiness Management
MABS	Master of Arts in Biblical Studies
MABT	Master of Arts in Bible Teaching
MAC	Master of Accountancy
	Master of Accounting
	Master of Arts in Communication
	Master of Arts in Counseling
MACC	Master of Arts in Accountancy
	Master of Arts in Christian Counseling
	Master of Arts in Clinical Counseling
MACCM	Master of Arts in Church and Community Ministry
MACCT	Master of Accounting
MACE	Master of Arts in Christian Education
MACFM	Master of Arts in Children's and Family Ministry
MACH	Master of Arts in Church History
MACIS	Master of Accounting and Information Systems
MACJ	Master of Arts in Criminal Justice
MACL	Master of Arts in Christian Leadership
MACM	Master of Arts in Christian Ministries
	Master of Arts in Christian Ministry
	Master of Arts in Church Music
	Master of Arts in Counseling Ministries
MACN	Master of Arts in Counseling
MACO	Master of Arts in Counseling
MAcOM	Master of Acupuncture and Oriental Medicine
MACP	Master of Arts in Counseling Psychology
MACS	Master of Arts in Catholic Studies
MACSE	Master of Arts in Christian School Education
MACT	Master of Arts in Christian Thought
	Master of Arts in Communications and Technology
MAD	Master in Educational Institution Administration
	Master of Art and Design
MADR	Master of Arts in Dispute Resolution
MADS	Master of Animal and Dairy Science
	Master of Applied Disability Studies
MAE	Master of Aerospace Engineering
	Master of Agricultural Economics
	Master of Agricultural Education
	Master of Architectural Engineering
	Master of Art Education
	Master of Arts in Education
	Master of Arts in English
	Master of Automotive Engineering
MAECMS	Master of Aerospace Engineering in Composite Materials and Structures
MAEd	Master of Arts Education
MAEL	Master of Arts in Educational Leadership
MAEM	Master of Arts in Educational Ministries
MAEN	Master of Arts in English
MAEP	Master of Arts in Economic Policy
MAES	Master of Arts in Environmental Sciences
MAESL	Master of Arts in English as a Second Language
MAET	Master of Arts in English Teaching
MAF	Master of Arts in Finance
MAFE	Master of Arts in Financial Economics
MAFLL	Master of Arts in Foreign Language and Literature
MAFM	Master of Accounting and Financial Management

MAFS	Master of Arts in Family Studies
MAG	Master of Applied Geography
MAGU	Master of Urban Analysis and Management
MAH	Master of Arts in Humanities
MAHA	Master of Arts in Humanitarian Assistance
	Master of Arts in Humanitarian Studies
MAHCM	Master of Arts in Health Care Mission
MAHG	Master of American History and Government
MAHL	Master of Arts in Hebrew Letters
MAHN	Master of Applied Human Nutrition
MAHSR	Master of Applied Health Services Research
MAIA	Master of Arts in International Administration
MAIB	Master of Arts in International Business
MAICS	Master of Arts in Intercultural Studies
MAIDM	Master of Arts in Interior Design and Merchandising
MAIH	Master of Arts in Interdisciplinary Humanities
MAIPCR	Master of Arts in International Peace and Conflict Management
MAIR	Master of Arts in Industrial Relations
MAIS	Master of Arts in Intercultural Studies
	Master of Arts in Interdisciplinary Studies
	Master of Arts in International Studies
MAIT	Master of Administration in Information Technology
	Master of Applied Information Technology
MAJ	Master of Arts in Journalism
MAJ Ed	Master of Arts in Jewish Education
MAJCS	Master of Arts in Jewish Communal Service
MAJE	Master of Arts in Jewish Education
MAJS	Master of Arts in Jewish Studies
MAL	Master in Agricultural Leadership
MALA	Master of Arts in Liberal Arts
MALD	Master of Arts in Law and Diplomacy
MALED	Master of Arts in Literacy Education
MALER	Master of Arts in Labor and Employment Relations
MALM	Master of Applied Leadership and Management
	Master of Arts in Leadership Evangelical Mobilization
MALP	Master of Arts in Language Pedagogy
MALPS	Master of Arts in Liberal and Professional Studies
MALS	Master of Arts in Liberal Studies
MALT	Master of Arts in Learning and Teaching
MAM	Master of Acquisition Management
	Master of Agriculture and Management
	Master of Applied Mathematics
	Master of Arts in Management
	Master of Arts in Ministry
	Master of Arts Management
	Master of Avian Medicine
MAMB	Master of Applied Molecular Biology
MAMC	Master of Arts in Mass Communication
	Master of Arts in Ministry and Culture
	Master of Arts in Ministry for a Multicultural Church
MAME	Master of Arts in Missions/Evangelism
MAMFC	Master of Arts in Marriage and Family Counseling
MAMFCC	Master of Arts in Marriage, Family, and Child Counseling
MAMFT	Master of Arts in Marriage and Family Therapy
MAMM	Master of Arts in Ministry Management
MAMS	Master of Applied Mathematical Sciences
	Master of Arts in Ministerial Studies
	Master of Arts in Ministry and Spirituality
MAMT	Master of Arts in Mathematics Teaching
MAN	Master of Applied Nutrition
MANP	Master of Applied Natural Products
MANT	Master of Arts in New Testament
MAOM	Master of Acupuncture and Oriental Medicine
	Master of Arts in Organizational Management

MAOT	Master of Arts in Old Testament		**MATFL**	Master of Arts in Teaching Foreign Language
MAP	Master of Applied Psychology		**MATH**	Master of Arts in Therapy
	Master of Arts in Planning		**MATI**	Master of Administration of Information Technology
	Master of Public Administration		**MATL**	Master of Arts in Teaching of Languages
	Masters of Psychology			Master of Arts in Transformational Leadership
MAP Min	Master of Arts in Pastoral Ministry		**MATM**	Master of Arts in Teaching of Mathematics
MAPA	Master of Arts in Public Administration		**MATS**	Master of Arts in Theological Studies
MAPC	Master of Arts in Pastoral Counseling			Master of Arts in Transforming Spirituality
MAPE	Master of Arts in Political Economy		**MATSL**	Master of Arts in Teaching a Second Language
MAPL	Master of Arts in Pastoral Leadership		**MAUA**	Master of Arts in Urban Affairs
MAPM	Master of Arts in Pastoral Ministry		**MAUD**	Master of Arts in Urban Design
	Master of Arts in Pastoral Music		**MAURP**	Master of Arts in Urban and Regional Planning
	Master of Arts in Practical Ministry		**MAW**	Master of Arts in Worship
MAPP	Master of Arts in Public Policy		**MAWL**	Master of Arts in Worship Leadership
MAPPS	Master of Arts in Asia Pacific Policy Studies		**MAWSHP**	Master of Arts in Worship
MAPS	Master of Arts in Pastoral Counseling/Spiritual Formation		**MAYM**	Master of Arts in Youth Ministry
	Master of Arts in Pastoral Studies		**MB**	Master of Bioinformatics
	Master of Arts in Public Service		**MBA**	Master of Business Administration
MAPT	Master of Practical Theology		**MBA-EP**	Master of Business Administration–Experienced Professionals
MAPW	Master of Arts in Professional Writing		**MBAA**	Master of Business Administration in Aviation
MAR	Master of Arts in Religion		**MBAE**	Master of Biological and Agricultural Engineering
Mar Eng	Marine Engineer			Master of Biosystems and Agricultural Engineering
MARC	Master of Arts in Rehabilitation Counseling		**MBAH**	Master of Business Administration in Health
MARE	Master of Arts in Religious Education		**MBAi**	Master of Business Administration–International
MARL	Master of Arts in Religious Leadership		**MBAICT**	Master of Business Administration in Information and Communication Technology
MARS	Master of Arts in Religious Studies		**MBAPA**	Master of Business Administration–Physician Assistant
MAS	Master of Accounting Science		**MBATM**	Master of Business Administration in Technology Management
	Master of Actuarial Science		**MBC**	Master of Building Construction
	Master of Administrative Science		**MBE**	Master of Bilingual Education
	Master of Advanced Study			Master of Bioengineering
	Master of Aeronautical Science			Master of Biological Engineering
	Master of American Studies			Master of Biomedical Engineering
	Master of Applied Science			Master of Business and Engineering
	Master of Applied Statistics			Master of Business Economics
	Master of Architectural Studies			Master of Business Education
	Master of Archival Studies		**MBET**	Master of Business, Entrepreneurship and Technology
MASA	Master of Advanced Studies in Architecture		**MBiotech**	Master of Biotechnology
MASD	Master of Arts in Spiritual Direction		**MBIT**	Master of Business Information Technology
MASE	Master of Arts in Special Education		**MBL**	Master of Business Law
MASF	Master of Arts in Spiritual Formation			Master of Business Leadership
MASJ	Master of Arts in Systems of Justice		**MBLE**	Master in Business Logistics Engineering
MASL	Master of Arts in School Leadership		**MBMI**	Master of Biomedical Imaging and Signals
MASLA	Master of Advanced Studies in Landscape Architecture		**MBMSE**	Master of Business Management and Software Engineering
MASM	Master of Aging Services Management		**MBS**	Master of Behavioral Science
	Master of Arts in Specialized Ministries			Master of Biblical Studies
MASP	Master of Applied Social Psychology			Master of Biological Science
	Master of Arts in School Psychology			Master of Biomedical Sciences
MASPAA	Master of Arts in Sports and Athletic Administration			Master of Bioscience
MASS	Master of Applied Social Science			Master of Building Science
	Master of Arts in Social Science		**MBSI**	Master of Business Information Science
MAST	Master of Arts in Science Teaching		**MBT**	Master of Biblical and Theological Studies
MASW	Master of Aboriginal Social Work			Master of Biomedical Technology
MAT	Master of Arts in Teaching			Master of Biotechnology
	Master of Arts in Theology			Master of Business Taxation
	Master of Athletic Training		**MC**	Master of Communication
	Masters in Administration of Telecommunications			Master of Counseling
Mat E	Materials Engineer			Master of Cybersecurity
MATCM	Master of Acupuncture and Traditional Chinese Medicine		**MC Ed**	Master of Continuing Education
MATDE	Master of Arts in Theology, Development, and Evangelism		**MC Sc**	Master of Computer Science
MATDR	Master of Territorial Management and Regional Development		**MCA**	Master of Arts in Applied Criminology
				Master of Commercial Aviation
MATE	Master of Arts for the Teaching of English		**MCAM**	Master of Computational and Applied Mathematics
MATESL	Master of Arts in Teaching English as a Second Language		**MCC**	Master of Computer Science
MATESOL	Master of Arts in Teaching English to Speakers of Other Languages		**MCCS**	Master of Crop and Soil Sciences
MATF	Master of Arts in Teaching English as a Foreign Language/Intercultural Studies			

MCD	Master of Communications Disorders
	Master of Community Development
MCE	Master in Electronic Commerce
	Master of Christian Education
	Master of Civil Engineering
	Master of Control Engineering
MCEM	Master of Construction Engineering Management
MCH	Master of Chemical Engineering
MCHE	Master of Chemical Engineering
MCIS	Master of Communication and Information Studies
	Master of Computer and Information Science
	Master of Computer Information Systems
MCIT	Master of Computer and Information Technology
MCJ	Master of Criminal Justice
MCJA	Master of Criminal Justice Administration
MCL	Master in Communication Leadership
	Master of Canon Law
	Master of Comparative Law
MCM	Master of Christian Ministry
	Master of Church Music
	Master of City Management
	Master of Communication Management
	Master of Community Medicine
	Master of Construction Management
	Master of Contract Management
	Masters of Corporate Media
MCMS	Master of Clinical Medical Science
MCP	Master in Science
	Master of City Planning
	Master of Community Planning
	Master of Counseling Psychology
	Master of Cytopathology Practice
MCPC	Master of Arts in Chaplaincy and Pastoral Care
MCPD	Master of Community Planning and Development
MCRP	Master of City and Regional Planning
MCRS	Master of City and Regional Studies
MCS	Master of Christian Studies
	Master of Clinical Science
	Master of Combined Sciences
	Master of Communication Studies
	Master of Computer Science
	Master of Consumer Science
MCSE	Master of Computer Science and Engineering
MCSL	Master of Catholic School Leadership
MCSM	Master of Construction Science/Management
MCST	Master of Science in Computer Science and Information Technology
MCTP	Master of Communication Technology and Policy
MCTS	Master of Clinical and Translational Science
MCVS	Master of Cardiovascular Science
MD	Doctor of Medicine
MDA	Master of Development Administration
	Master of Dietetic Administration
MDB	Master of Design-Build
MDE	Master of Developmental Economics
	Master of Distance Education
	Master of the Education of the Deaf
MDH	Master of Dental Hygiene
MDM	Master of Digital Media
MDP	Master of Development Practice
MDR	Master of Dispute Resolution
MDS	Master of Dental Surgery
ME	Master of Education
	Master of Engineering
	Master of Entrepreneurship
	Master of Evangelism
ME Sc	Master of Engineering Science
MEA	Master of Educational Administration
	Master of Engineering Administration
MEAP	Master of Environmental Administration and Planning
MEBT	Master in Electronic Business Technologies
MEC	Master of Electronic Commerce

MECE	Master of Electrical and Computer Engineering
Mech E	Mechanical Engineer
MED	Master of Education of the Deaf
MEDS	Master of Environmental Design Studies
MEE	Master in Education
	Master of Electrical Engineering
	Master of Energy Engineering
	Master of Environmental Engineering
MEEM	Master of Environmental Engineering and Management
MEENE	Master of Engineering in Environmental Engineering
MEEP	Master of Environmental and Energy Policy
MEERM	Master of Earth and Environmental Resource Management
MEH	Master in Humanistic Studies
	Master of Environmental Horticulture
MEHS	Master of Environmental Health and Safety
MEIM	Master of Entertainment Industry Management
MEL	Master of Educational Leadership
	Master of English Literature
MELP	Master of Environmental Law and Policy
MEM	Master of Ecosystem Management
	Master of Electricity Markets
	Master of Engineering Management
	Master of Environmental Management
	Master of Marketing
MEME	Master of Engineering in Manufacturing Engineering
	Master of Engineering in Mechanical Engineering
MEMS	Master of Engineering in Manufacturing Systems
MENG	Master of Arts in English
MENVEGR	Master of Environmental Engineering
MEP	Master of Engineering Physics
MEPC	Master of Environmental Pollution Control
MEPD	Master of Education–Professional Development
	Master of Environmental Planning and Design
MEPM	Master of Environmental Protection Management
MER	Master of Employment Relations
MES	Master of Education and Science
	Master of Engineering Science
	Master of Environmenta and Sustainability
	Master of Environmental Science
	Master of Environmental Studies
	Master of Environmental Systems
	Master of Special Education
MESM	Master of Environmental Science and Management
MET	Master of Education in Teaching
	Master of Educational Technology
	Master of Engineering Technology
	Master of Entertainment Technology
	Master of Environmental Toxicology
Met E	Metallurgical Engineer
METM	Master of Engineering and Technology Management
MF	Master of Finance
	Master of Forestry
MFA	Master of Financial Administration
	Master of Fine Arts
MFAM	Master in Food Animal Medicine
MFAS	Master of Fisheries and Aquatic Science
MFAW	Master of Fine Arts in Writing
MFC	Master of Forest Conservation
MFCS	Master of Family and Consumer Sciences
MFE	Master of Financial Economics
	Master of Financial Engineering
	Master of Forest Engineering
MFG	Master of Functional Genomics
MFHD	Master of Family and Human Development
MFM	Master of Financial Mathematics
MFMS	Masters in Food Microbiology and Safety
MFPE	Master of Food Process Engineering

MFR	Master of Forest Resources
MFRC	Master of Forest Resources and Conservation
MFS	Master of Food Science
	Master of Forensic Sciences
	Master of Forest Science
	Master of Forest Studies
	Master of French Studies
MFSA	Master of Forensic Sciences Administration
MFST	Master of Food Safety and Technology
MFT	Master of Family Therapy
	Master of Food Technology
MFWB	Master of Fishery and Wildlife Biology
MFWCB	Master of Fish, Wildlife and Conservation Biology
MFWS	Master of Fisheries and Wildlife Sciences
MFYCS	Master of Family, Youth and Community Sciences
MG	Master of Genetics
MGA	Master of Governmental Administration
MGD	Master of Graphic Design
MGE	Master of Gas Engineering
	Master of Geotechnical Engineering
MGEM	Master of Global Entrepreneurship and Management
MGH	Master of Geriatric Health
MGIS	Master of Geographic Information Science
	Master of Geographic Information Systems
MGM	Master of Global Management
MGP	Master of Gestion de Projet
MGPS	Master of Global Policy Studies
MGS	Master of Gerontological Studies
	Master of Global Studies
MH	Master of Humanities
MH Ed	Master of Health Education
MH Sc	Master of Health Sciences
MHA	Master of Health Administration
	Master of Healthcare Administration
	Master of Hospital Administration
	Master of Hospitality Administration
MHAD	Master of Health Administration
MHB	Master of Human Behavior
MHCA	Master of Health Care Administration
MHCI	Master of Human-Computer Interaction
MHCL	Master of Health Care Leadership
MHE	Master of Health Education
	Master of Human Ecology
MHE Ed	Master of Home Economics Education
MHEA	Masters of Higher Education Administration
MHHS	Master of Health and Human Services
MHI	Master of Health Informatics
	Master of Healthcare Innovation
MHIIM	Master of Health Informatics and Information Management
MHIS	Master of Health Information Systems
MHK	Master of Human Kinetics
MHL	Master of Hebrew Literature
MHMS	Master of Health Management Systems
MHP	Master of Health Physics
	Master of Heritage Preservation
	Master of Historic Preservation
MHPA	Master of Heath Policy and Administration
MHPE	Master of Health Professions Education
MHR	Master of Human Resources
MHRD	Master in Human Resource Development
MHRIR	Master of Human Resources and Industrial Relations
MHRLR	Master of Human Resources and Labor Relations
MHRM	Master of Human Resources Management

MHS	Master of Health Science
	Master of Health Sciences
	Master of Health Studies
	Master of Hispanic Studies
	Master of Human Services
	Master of Humanistic Studies
MHSA	Master of Health Services Administration
MHSM	Master of Health Sector Management
	Master of Health Systems Management
MI	Master of Instruction
MI Arch	Master of Interior Architecture
MI St	Master of Information Studies
MIA	Master of Interior Architecture
	Master of International Affairs
MIAA	Master of International Affairs and Administration
MIAM	Master of International Agribusiness Management
MIB	Master of International Business
MIBA	Master of International Business Administration
MICM	Master of International Construction Management
MID	Master of Industrial Design
	Master of Industrial Distribution
	Master of Interior Design
	Master of International Development
MIE	Master of Industrial Engineering
MIH	Master of Integrative Health
MIHTM	Master of International Hospitality and Tourism Management
MIJ	Master of International Journalism
MILR	Master of Industrial and Labor Relations
MiM	Master in Management
MIM	Master of Industrial Management
	Master of Information Management
	Master of International Management
MIMLAE	Master of International Management for Latin American Executives
MIMS	Master of Information Management and Systems
	Master of Integrated Manufacturing Systems
MIP	Master of Infrastructure Planning
	Master of Intellectual Property
MIPER	Master of International Political Economy of Resources
MIPP	Master of International Policy and Practice
	Master of International Public Policy
MIPS	Master of International Planning Studies
MIR	Master of Industrial Relations
	Master of International Relations
MIS	Master of Industrial Statistics
	Master of Information Science
	Master of Information Systems
	Master of Integrated Science
	Master of Interdisciplinary Studies
	Master of International Service
	Master of International Studies
MISE	Master of Industrial and Systems Engineering
MISKM	Master of Information Sciences and Knowledge Management
MISM	Master of Information Systems Management
MIT	Master in Teaching
	Master of Industrial Technology
	Master of Information Technology
	Master of Initial Teaching
	Master of International Trade
	Master of Internet Technology
MITA	Master of Information Technology Administration
MITM	Master of International Technology Management
MITO	Master of Industrial Technology and Operations
MJ	Master of Journalism
	Master of Jurisprudence
MJ Ed	Master of Jewish Education
MJA	Master of Justice Administration

MJM	Master of Justice Management
MJS	Master of Judicial Studies
	Master of Juridical Science
MKM	Master of Knowledge Management
ML	Master of Latin
ML Arch	Master of Landscape Architecture
MLA	Master of Landscape Architecture
	Master of Liberal Arts
MLAS	Master of Laboratory Animal Science
	Master of Liberal Arts and Sciences
MLAUD	Master of Landscape Architecture in Urban Development
MLD	Master of Leadership Development
	Master of Leadership Studies
MLE	Master of Applied Linguistics and Exegesis
MLER	Master of Labor and Employment Relations
MLERE	Master of Land Economics and Real Estate
MLHR	Master of Labor and Human Resources
MLI	Master of Legal Institutions
MLI Sc	Master of Library and Information Science
MLIS	Master of Library and Information Science
	Master of Library and Information Studies
MLM	Master of Library Media
MLOS	Masters in Leadership and Organizational Studies
MLRHR	Master of Labor Relations and Human Resources
MLS	Master of Leadership Studies
	Master of Legal Studies
	Master of Liberal Studies
	Master of Library Science
	Master of Life Sciences
MLSP	Master of Law and Social Policy
MLT	Master of Language Technologies
MM	Master of Management
	Master of Ministry
	Master of Missiology
	Master of Music
MM Ed	Master of Music Education
MM Sc	Master of Medical Science
MM St	Master of Museum Studies
MMA	Master of Marine Affairs
	Master of Media Arts
	Master of Musical Arts
MMAE	Master of Mechanical and Aerospace Engineering
MMAS	Master of Military Art and Science
MMB	Master of Microbial Biotechnology
MMBA	Managerial Master of Business Administration
MMC	Master of Manufacturing Competitiveness
	Master of Mass Communications
	Master of Music Conducting
MMCM	Master of Music in Church Music
MMCSS	Masters of Mathematical Computational and Statistical Sciences
MME	Master of Manufacturing Engineering
	Master of Mathematics Education
	Master of Mathematics for Educators
	Master of Mechanical Engineering
	Master of Medical Engineering
	Master of Mining Engineering
	Master of Music Education
MMF	Master of Mathematical Finance
MMFT	Master of Marriage and Family Therapy
MMG	Master of Management
MMH	Master of Management in Hospitality
	Master of Medical Humanities
MMI	Master of Management of Innovation
MMIS	Master of Management Information Systems
MMM	Master of Manufacturing Management
	Master of Marine Management
	Master of Medical Management
MMME	Master of Metallurgical and Materials Engineering

MMP	Master of Management Practice
	Master of Marine Policy
	Master of Medical Physics
	Master of Music Performance
MMPA	Master of Management and Professional Accounting
MMQM	Master of Manufacturing Quality Management
MMR	Master of Marketing Research
MMRM	Master of Marine Resources Management
MMS	Master of Management Science
	Master of Management Studies
	Master of Manufacturing Systems
	Master of Marine Studies
	Master of Materials Science
	Master of Medical Science
	Master of Medieval Studies
	Master of Modern Studies
MMSE	Master of Manufacturing Systems Engineering
MMSM	Master of Music in Sacred Music
MMT	Master in Marketing
	Master of Management
	Master of Music Teaching
	Master of Music Therapy
	Masters in Marketing Technology
MMus	Master of Music
MN	Master of Nursing
	Master of Nutrition
MN NP	Master of Nursing in Nurse Practitioner
MNA	Master of Nonprofit Administration
	Master of Nurse Anesthesia
MNAL	Master of Nonprofit Administration and Leadership
MNAS	Master of Natural and Applied Science
MNCM	Master of Network and Communications Management
MNE	Master of Network Engineering
	Master of Nuclear Engineering
MNL	Master in International Business for Latin America
MNM	Master of Nonprofit Management
MNO	Master of Nonprofit Organization
MNPL	Master of Not-for-Profit Leadership
MNPS	Master of New Professional Studies
MNpS	Master of Nonprofit Studies
MNR	Master of Natural Resources
MNRES	Master of Natural Resources and Environmental Studies
MNRM	Master of Natural Resource Management
MNRS	Master of Natural Resource Stewardship
MNS	Master of Natural Science
MO	Master of Oceanography
MOD	Master of Organizational Development
MOGS	Master of Oil and Gas Studies
MOH	Master of Occupational Health
MOL	Master of Organizational Leadership
MOM	Master of Oriental Medicine
MOR	Master of Operations Research
MOT	Master of Occupational Therapy
MP	Master of Physiology
	Master of Planning
MP Ac	Master of Professional Accountancy
MP Acc	Master of Professional Accountancy
	Master of Professional Accounting
	Master of Public Accounting
MP Aff	Master of Public Affairs
MP Th	Master of Pastoral Theology
MPA	Master of Physician Assistant
	Master of Professional Accountancy
	Master of Professional Accounting
	Master of Public Administration
	Master of Public Affairs
MPAC	Masters in Professional Accounting
MPAID	Master of Public Administration and International Development

MPAP	Master of Physician Assistant Practice Master of Public Affairs and Politics	**MS Kin**	Master of Science in Kinesiology
		MS Acct	Master of Science in Accounting
MPAS	Master of Physician Assistant Science Master of Physician Assistant Studies Master of Public Art Studies	**MS Accy**	Master of Science in Accountancy
		MS Aero E	Master of Science in Aerospace Engineering
		MS Ag	Master of Science in Agriculture
MPC	Master of Pastoral Counseling Master of Professional Communication Master of Professional Counseling	**MS Arch**	Master of Science in Architecture
		MS Arch St	Master of Science in Architectural Studies
MPD	Master of Product Development Master of Public Diplomacy	**MS Bio E**	Master of Science in Bioengineering Master of Science in Biomedical Engineering
MPDS	Master of Planning and Development Studies	**MS Bm E**	Master of Science in Biomedical Engineering
MPE	Master of Physical Education Master of Power Engineering	**MS Ch E**	Master of Science in Chemical Engineering
		MS Chem	Master of Science in Chemistry
MPEM	Master of Project Engineering and Management	**MS Cp E**	Master of Science in Computer Engineering
MPH	Master of Public Health	**MS Eco**	Master of Science in Economics
MPHE	Master of Public Health Education	**MS Econ**	Master of Science in Economics
MPHTM	Master of Public Health and Tropical Medicine	**MS Ed**	Master of Science in Education
MPIA	Master of Public and International Affairs Master Program in International Affairs	**MS El**	Master of Science in Educational Leadership and Administration
MPM	Master of Pastoral Ministry Master of Pest Management Master of Policy Management Master of Practical Ministries Master of Project Management Master of Public Management	**MS En E**	Master of Science in Environmental Engineering
		MS Eng	Master of Science in Engineering
		MS Engr	Master of Science in Engineering
		MS Env E	Master of Science in Environmental Engineering
		MS Exp Surg	Master of Science in Experimental Surgery
MPNA	Master of Public and Nonprofit Administration	**MS Int A**	Master of Science in International Affairs
MPOD	Master of Positive Organizational Development	**MS Mat E**	Master of Science in Materials Engineering
MPP	Master of Public Policy	**MS Mat SE**	Master of Science in Material Science and Engineering
MPPA	Master of Public Policy Administration Master of Public Policy and Administration	**MS Met E**	Master of Science in Metallurgical Engineering
MPPAL	Master of Public Policy, Administration and Law	**MS Metr**	Master of Science in Meteorology
MPPM	Master of Public and Private Management Master of Public Policy and Management	**MS Mgt**	Master of Science in Management
		MS Min	Master of Science in Mining
MPPPM	Master of Plant Protection and Pest Management	**MS Min E**	Master of Science in Mining Engineering
MPPUP	Master of Public Policy and Urban Planning	**MS Mt E**	Master of Science in Materials Engineering
MPRTM	Master of Parks, Recreation, and Tourism Management	**MS Otal**	Master of Science in Otalrynology
MPS	Master of Pastoral Studies Master of Perfusion Science Master of Planning Studies Master of Political Science Master of Preservation Studies Master of Professional Studies Master of Public Service	**MS Pet E**	Master of Science in Petroleum Engineering
		MS Phys	Master of Science in Physics
		MS Phys Op	Master of Science in Physiological Optics
		MS Poly	Master of Science in Polymers
		MS Psy	Master of Science in Psychology
		MS Pub P	Master of Science in Public Policy
MPSA	Master of Public Service Administration	**MS Sc**	Master of Science in Social Science
MPSRE	Master of Professional Studies in Real Estate	**MS Sp Ed**	Master of Science in Special Education
MPT	Master of Pastoral Theology Master of Physical Therapy	**MS Stat**	Master of Science in Statistics
		MS Surg	Master of Science in Surgery
MPVM	Master of Preventive Veterinary Medicine	**MS Tax**	Master of Science in Taxation
MPW	Master of Professional Writing Master of Public Works	**MS Tc E**	Master of Science in Telecommunications Engineering
MQF	Master of Quantitative Finance	**MS-R**	Master of Science (Research)
MQM	Master of Quality Management	**MSA**	Master of School Administration Master of Science Administration Master of Science in Accountancy Master of Science in Accounting Master of Science in Administration Master of Science in Aeronautics Master of Science in Agriculture Master of Science in Anesthesia Master of Science in Architecture Master of Science in Aviation Master of Sports Administration
MQS	Master of Quality Systems		
MR	Master of Recreation Master of Retailing		
MRA	Master in Research Administration		
MRC	Master of Rehabilitation Counseling		
MRCP	Master of Regional and City Planning Master of Regional and Community Planning		
MRD	Master of Rural Development		
MRE	Master of Religious Education		
MRED	Master of Real Estate Development		
MREM	Master of Resource and Environmental Management	**MSA Phy**	Master of Science in Applied Physics
		MSAA	Master of Science in Astronautics and Aeronautics
MRLS	Master of Resources Law Studies	**MSAAE**	Master of Science in Aeronautical and Astronautical Engineering
MRM	Master of Resources Management		
MRP	Master of Regional Planning	**MSABE**	Master of Science in Agricultural and Biological Engineering
MRS	Master of Religious Studies		
MRSc	Master of Rehabilitation Science	**MSAC**	Master of Science in Acupuncture
MS	Master of Science	**MSACC**	Master of Science in Accounting
MS Cmp E	Master of Science in Computer Engineering	**MSaCS**	Master of Science in Applied Computer Science

MSAE	Master of Science in Aeronautical Engineering
	Master of Science in Aerospace Engineering
	Master of Science in Applied Economics
	Master of Science in Applied Engineering
	Master of Science in Architectural Engineering
	Master of Science in Art Education
MSAL	Master of Sport Administration and Leadership
MSAM	Master of Science in Applied Mathematics
MSANR	Master of Science in Agriculture and Natural Resources Systems Management
MSAPM	Master of Security Analysis and Portfolio Management
MSAS	Master of Science in Applied Statistics
	Master of Science in Architectural Studies
MSAT	Master of Science in Accounting and Taxation
	Master of Science in Advanced Technology
	Master of Science in Athletic Training
MSAUS	Master of Science in Architectural Urban Studies
MSB	Master of Science in Bible
	Master of Science in Business
MSBA	Master of Science in Business Administration
MSBAE	Master of Science in Biological and Agricultural Engineering
	Master of Science in Biosystems and Agricultural Engineering
MSBC	Master of Science in Building Construction
MSBE	Master of Science in Biological Engineering
	Master of Science in Biomedical Engineering
MSBENG	Master of Science in Bioengineering
MSBIT	Master of Science in Business Information Technology
MSBM	Master of Sport Business Management
MSBME	Master of Science in Biomedical Engineering
MSBMS	Master of Science in Basic Medical Science
MSBS	Master of Science in Biomedical Sciences
MSC	Master of Science in Commerce
	Master of Science in Communication
	Master of Science in Computers
	Master of Science in Counseling
	Master of Science in Criminology
MSCA	Master of Science in Construction Administration
MSCC	Master of Science in Christian Counseling
	Master of Science in Community Counseling
MSCD	Master of Science in Communication Disorders
	Master of Science in Community Development
MSCE	Master of Science in Civil Engineering
	Master of Science in Clinical Epidemiology
	Master of Science in Computer Engineering
	Master of Science in Continuing Education
MSCEE	Master of Science in Civil and Environmental Engineering
MSCF	Master of Science in Computational Finance
MSChE	Master of Science in Chemical Engineering
MSCI	Master of Science in Clinical Investigation
	Master of Science in Curriculum and Instruction
MSCIS	Master of Science in Computer and Information Systems
	Master of Science in Computer Information Science
	Master of Science in Computer Information Systems
MSCIT	Master of Science in Computer Information Technology
MSCJ	Master of Science in Criminal Justice
MSCJA	Master of Science in Criminal Justice Administration
MSCJS	Master of Science in Crime and Justice Studies
MSCL	Master of Science in Collaborative Leadership
MSCLS	Master of Science in Clinical Laboratory Studies
MSCM	Master of Science in Conflict Management
	Master of Science in Construction Management
MScM	Master of Science in Management
MSCM	Master of Supply Chain Management

MSCP	Master of Science in Clinical Psychology
	Master of Science in Computer Engineering
	Master of Science in Counseling Psychology
MSCPE	Master of Science in Computer Engineering
MSCPharm	Master of Science in Pharmacy
MSCPI	Master in Strategic Planning for Critical Infrastructures
MSCRP	Master of Science in City and Regional Planning
	Master of Science in Community and Regional Planning
MSCS	Master of Science in Clinical Science
	Master of Science in Computer Science
MSCSD	Master of Science in Communication Sciences and Disorders
MSCSE	Master of Science in Computer Science and Engineering
MSCTE	Master of Science in Career and Technical Education
MSD	Master of Science in Dentistry
	Master of Science in Design
	Master of Science in Dietetics
MSDD	Master of Software Design and Development
MSDM	Master of Design Methods
MSDR	Master of Dispute Resolution
MSE	Master of Science Education
	Master of Science in Economics
	Master of Science in Education
	Master of Science in Engineering
	Master of Science in Engineering Management
	Master of Software Engineering
	Master of Special Education
	Master of Structural Engineering
MSECE	Master of Science in Electrical and Computer Engineering
MSED	Master of Sustainable Economic Development
MSEE	Master of Science in Electrical Engineering
	Master of Science in Environmental Engineering
MSEH	Master of Science in Environmental Health
MSEL	Master of Science in Educational Leadership
	Master of Science in Executive Leadership
MSEM	Master of Science in Engineering Management
	Master of Science in Engineering Mechanics
	Master of Science in Environmental Management
MSENE	Master of Science in Environmental Engineering
MSEO	Master of Science in Electro-Optics
MSEP	Master of Science in Economic Policy
	Master of Science in Engineering Physics
MSEPA	Masters of Science in Economics and Policy Analysis
MSES	Master of Science in Embedded Software Engineering
	Master of Science in Engineering Science
	Master of Science in Environmental Science
	Master of Science in Environmental Studies
MSESM	Master of Science in Engineering Science and Mechanics
MSET	Master of Science in Education in Educational Technology
	Master of Science in Engineering Technology
MSETM	Master of Science in Environmental Technology Management
MSEV	Master of Science in Environmental Engineering
MSEVH	Master of Science in Environmental Health and Safety
MSF	Master of Science in Finance
	Master of Science in Forestry
MSFA	Master of Science in Financial Analysis
MSFAM	Master of Science in Family Studies
MSFCS	Master of Science in Family and Consumer Science
MSFE	Master of Science in Financial Engineering
MSFOR	Master of Science in Forestry
MSFP	Master of Science in Financial Planning

MSFS	Master of Science in Financial Sciences
	Master of Science in Forensic Science
MSFSB	Master of Science in Financial Services and Banking
MSFT	Master of Science in Family Therapy
MSGC	Master of Science in Genetic Counseling
MSGL	Master of Science in Global Leadership
MSH	Master of Science in Health
	Master of Science in Hospice
MSHA	Master of Science in Health Administration
MSHCA	Master of Science in Health Care Administration
MSHCI	Master of Science in Human Computer Interaction
MSHCPM	Master of Science in Health Care Policy and Management
MSHE	Master of Science in Health Education
MSHES	Master of Science in Human Environmental Sciences
MSHFID	Master of Science in Human Factors in Information Design
MSHFS	Master of Science in Human Factors and Systems
MSHI	Master of Science in Health Informatics
MSHP	Master of Science in Health Professions
	Master of Science in Health Promotion
MSHR	Master of Science in Human Resources
MSHRL	Master of Science in Human Resource Leadership
MSHRM	Master of Science in Human Resource Management
MSHROD	Master of Science in Human Resources and Organizational Development
MSHS	Master of Science in Health Science
	Master of Science in Health Services
	Master of Science in Health Systems
	Master of Science in Homeland Security
MSHT	Master of Science in History of Technology
MSI	Master of Science in Instruction
MSIA	Master of Science in Industrial Administration
	Master of Science in Information Assurance and Computer Security
MSIB	Master of Science in International Business
MSIDM	Master of Science in Interior Design and Merchandising
MSIDT	Master of Science in Information Design and Technology
MSIE	Master of Science in Industrial Engineering
	Master of Science in International Economics
MSIEM	Master of Science in Information Engineering and Management
MSIID	Master of Science in Information and Instructional Design
MSIM	Master of Science in Information Management
	Master of Science in International Management
	Master of Science in Investment Management
MSIMC	Master of Science in Integrated Marketing Communications
MSIR	Master of Science in Industrial Relations
MSIS	Master of Science in Information Science
	Master of Science in Information Systems
	Master of Science in Interdisciplinary Studies
MSISE	Master of Science in Infrastructure Systems Engineering
MSISM	Master of Science in Information Systems Management
MSISPM	Master of Science in Information Security Policy and Management
MSIST	Master of Science in Information Systems Technology
MSIT	Master of Science in Industrial Technology
	Master of Science in Information Technology
	Master of Science in Instructional Technology
MSITM	Master of Science in Information Technology Management
MSJ	Master of Science in Journalism
	Master of Science in Jurisprudence
MSJE	Master of Science in Jewish Education
MSJFP	Master of Science in Juvenile Forensic Psychology
MSJJ	Master of Science in Juvenile Justice
MSJPS	Master of Science in Justice and Public Safety
MSJS	Master of Science in Jewish Studies
MSK	Master of Science in Kinesiology
MSKM	Master of Science in Knowledge Management
MSL	Master of School Leadership
	Master of Science in Leadership
	Master of Science in Limnology
	Master of Strategic Leadership
	Master of Studies in Law
MSLA	Master of Science in Landscape Architecture
	Master of Science in Legal Administration
MSLD	Master of Science in Land Development
MSLS	Master of Science in Legal Studies
	Master of Science in Library Science
MSLSCM	Master of Science in Logistics and Supply Chain Management
MSLT	Master of Second Language Teaching
MSM	Master of Sacred Ministry
	Master of Sacred Music
	Master of School Mathematics
	Master of Science in Management
	Master of Science in Mathematics
	Master of Science in Organization Management
	Master of Security Management
MSMA	Master of Science in Marketing Analysis
MSMAE	Master of Science in Materials Engineering
MSMC	Master of Science in Mass Communications
MSME	Master of Science in Mathematics Education
	Master of Science in Mechanical Engineering
MSMFE	Master of Science in Manufacturing Engineering
MSMFT	Master of Science in Marriage and Family Therapy
MSMIS	Master of Science in Management Information Systems
MSMIT	Master of Science in Management and Information Technology
MSMM	Master of Science in Manufacturing Management
MSMO	Master of Science in Manufacturing Operations
MSMOT	Master of Science in Management of Technology
MSMS	Master of Science in Management Science
	Master of Science in Medical Sciences
MSMSE	Master of Science in Manufacturing Systems Engineering
	Master of Science in Material Science and Engineering
	Master of Science in Mathematics and Science Education
MSMT	Master of Science in Management and Technology
	Master of Science in Medical Technology
MSMus	Master of Sacred Music
MSN	Master of Science in Nursing
MSN-R	Master of Science in Nursing (Research)
MSNA	Master of Science in Nurse Anesthesia
MSNE	Master of Science in Nuclear Engineering
MSNED	Master of Science in Nurse Education
MSNM	Master of Science in Nonprofit Management
MSNS	Master of Science in Natural Science
	Master's of Science in Nutritional Science
MSOD	Master of Science in Organizational Development
MSOEE	Master of Science in Outdoor and Environmental Education
MSOES	Master of Science in Occupational Ergonomics and Safety
MSOH	Master of Science in Occupational Health
MSOL	Master of Science in Organizational Leadership

MSOM	Master of Science in Operations Management
	Master of Science in Organization and Management
	Master of Science in Oriental Medicine
MSOR	Master of Science in Operations Research
MSOT	Master of Science in Occupational Technology
	Master of Science in Occupational Therapy
MSP	Master of Science in Pharmacy
	Master of Science in Planning
	Master of Science in Psychology
	Master of Speech Pathology
MSPA	Master of Science in Physician Assistant
	Master of Science in Professional Accountancy
MSPAS	Master of Science in Physician Assistant Studies
MSPC	Master of Science in Professional Communications
	Master of Science in Professional Counseling
MSPE	Master of Science in Petroleum Engineering
MSPG	Master of Science in Psychology
MSPH	Master of Science in Public Health
MSPHR	Master of Science in Pharmacy
MSPM	Master of Science in Professional Management
	Master of Science in Project Management
MSPNGE	Master of Science in Petroleum and Natural Gas Engineering
MSPS	Master of Science in Pharmaceutical Science
	Master of Science in Political Science
	Master of Science in Psychological Services
MSPT	Master of Science in Physical Therapy
MSpVM	Master of Specialized Veterinary Medicine
MSR	Master of Science in Radiology
	Master of Science in Reading
MSRA	Master of Science in Recreation Administration
MSRC	Master of Science in Resource Conservation
MSRE	Master of Science in Real Estate
	Master of Science in Religious Education
MSRED	Master of Science in Real Estate Development
MSRLS	Master of Science in Recreation and Leisure Studies
MSRMP	Master of Science in Radiological Medical Physics
MSRS	Master of Science in Rehabilitation Science
MSS	Master of Science in Software
	Master of Social Science
	Master of Social Services
	Master of Software Systems
	Master of Sports Science
	Master of Strategic Studies
MSSA	Master of Science in Social Administration
MSSCP	Master of Science in Science Content and Process
MSSE	Master of Science in Software Engineering
	Master of Science in Space Education
	Master of Science in Special Education
MSSEM	Master of Science in Systems and Engineering Management
MSSI	Master of Science in Security Informatics
	Master of Science in Strategic Intelligence
MSSL	Master of Science in Strategic Leadership
MSSLP	Master of Science in Speech-Language Pathology
MSSM	Master of Science in Sports Medicine
MSSP	Master of Science in Social Policy
MSSPA	Master of Science in Student Personnel Administration
MSSS	Master of Science in Safety Science
	Master of Science in Systems Science
MSST	Master of Science in Security Technologies
MSSW	Master of Science in Social Work
MSSWE	Master of Science in Software Engineering

MST	Master of Science and Technology
	Master of Science in Taxation
	Master of Science in Teaching
	Master of Science in Technology
	Master of Science in Telecommunications
	Master of Science Teaching
MSTC	Master of Science in Technical Communication
	Master of Science in Telecommunications
MSTCM	Master of Science in Traditional Chinese Medicine
MSTE	Master of Science in Telecommunications Engineering
	Master of Science in Transportation Engineering
MSTM	Master of Science in Technical Management
MSTOM	Master of Science in Traditional Oriental Medicine
MSUD	Master of Science in Urban Design
MSW	Master of Social Work
MSWE	Master of Software Engineering
MSWREE	Master of Science in Water Resources and Environmental Engineering
MSX	Master of Science in Exercise Science
MT	Master of Taxation
	Master of Teaching
	Master of Technology
	Master of Textiles
MTA	Master of Tax Accounting
	Master of Teaching Arts
	Master of Tourism Administration
MTCM	Master of Traditional Chinese Medicine
MTD	Master of Training and Development
MTE	Master in Educational Technology
	Master of Teacher Education
MTESOL	Master in Teaching English to Speakers of Other Languages
MTHM	Master of Tourism and Hospitality Management
MTI	Master of Information Technology
MTIM	Masters of Trust and Investment Management
MTL	Master of Talmudic Law
MTM	Master of Technology Management
	Master of Telecommunications Management
	Master of the Teaching of Mathematics
MTMH	Master of Tropical Medicine and Hygiene
MTOM	Master of Traditional Oriental Medicine
MTP	Master of Transpersonal Psychology
MTPC	Master of Technical and Professional Communication
MTS	Master of Theological Studies
MTSC	Master of Technical and Scientific Communication
MTSE	Master of Telecommunications and Software Engineering
MTT	Master in Technology Management
MTX	Master of Taxation
MUA	Master of Urban Affairs
MUD	Master of Urban Design
MUEP	Master of Urban and Environmental Planning
MUP	Master of Urban Planning
MUPDD	Master of Urban Planning, Design, and Development
MUPP	Master of Urban Planning and Policy
MUPRED	Masters of Urban Planning and Real Estate Development
MURP	Master of Urban and Regional Planning
	Master of Urban and Rural Planning
MUS	Master of Urban Studies
MVM	Master of VLSI and microelectronics
MVP	Master of Voice Pedagogy
MVPH	Master of Veterinary Public Health
MVS	Master of Visual Studies
MWC	Master of Wildlife Conservation
MWE	Master in Welding Engineering

MWPS	Master of Wood and Paper Science
MWR	Master of Water Resources
MWS	Master of Women's Studies
MZS	Master of Zoological Science
Nav Arch	Naval Architecture
Naval E	Naval Engineer
ND	Doctor of Naturopathic Medicine
NE	Nuclear Engineer
Nuc E	Nuclear Engineer
OD	Doctor of Optometry
OTD	Doctor of Occupational Therapy
PBME	Professional Master of Biomedical Engineering
PD	Professional Diploma
PGC	Post-Graduate Certificate
PGD	Postgraduate Diploma
Ph L	Licentiate of Philosophy
Pharm D	Doctor of Pharmacy
PhD	Doctor of Philosophy
PhD Otal	Doctor of Philosophy in Otalrynology
Phd Surg	Doctor of Philosophy in Surgery
PhDEE	Doctor of Philosophy in Electrical Engineering
PM Sc	Professional Master of Science
PMBA	Professional Master of Business Administration
PMC	Post Master Certificate
PMD	Post-Master's Diploma
PMS	Professional Master of Science Professional Master's Degree
Post-Doctoral MS	Post-Doctoral Master of Science
PPDPT	Postprofessional Doctor of Physical Therapy
PSM	Professional Master of Science Professional Science Master's
Psy D	Doctor of Psychology
Psy M	Master of Psychology
Psy S	Specialist in Psychology
Psya D	Doctor of Psychoanalysis
Re Dir	Director of Recreation
Rh D	Doctor of Rehabilitation
S Psy S	Specialist in Psychological Services

Sc D	Doctor of Science
Sc M	Master of Science
SCCT	Specialist in Community College Teaching
ScDPT	Doctor of Physical Therapy Science
SD	Doctor of Science Specialist Degree
SJD	Doctor of Juridical Science
SLPD	Doctor of Speech-Language Pathology
SLS	Specialist in Library Science
SM	Master of Science
SM Arch S	Master of Science in Architectural Studies
SM Vis S	Master of Science in Visual Studies
SMBT	Master of Science in Building Technology
SP	Specialist Degree
Sp C	Specialist in Counseling
Sp Ed	Specialist in Education
Sp LIS	Specialist in Library and Information Science
SPA	Specialist in Arts
SPCM	Special in Church Music
Spec	Specialist's Certificate
Spec M	Specialist in Music
SPEM	Special in Educational Ministries
SPS	School Psychology Specialist
Spt	Specialist Degree
SPTH	Special in Theology
SSP	Specialist in School Psychology
STB	Bachelor of Sacred Theology
STD	Doctor of Sacred Theology
STL	Licentiate of Sacred Theology
STM	Master of Sacred Theology
TDPT	Transitional Doctor of Physical Therapy
Th D	Doctor of Theology
Th M	Master of Theology
VMD	Doctor of Veterinary Medicine
WEMBA	Weekend Executive Master of Business Administration
XMA	Executive Master of Arts
XMBA	Executive Master of Business Administration

INDEXES

Close-Ups and Displays

Directories and Subject Areas

Following is an alphabetical listing of directories and subject areas. Also listed are cross-references for subject area names not used in the directory structure of the guides, for example, "Arabic (*see* Near and Middle Eastern Languages)."

Graduate Programs in the Humanities, Arts & Social Sciences

Addictions/Substance Abuse Counseling
Administration (*see* Arts Administration; Public Administration)
African-American Studies
African Languages and Literatures (*see* African Studies)
African Studies
Agribusiness (*see* Agricultural Economics and Agribusiness)
Agricultural Economics and Agribusiness
Alcohol Abuse Counseling (*see* Addictions/Substance Abuse Counseling)
American Indian/Native American Studies
American Studies
Anthropology
Applied Arts and Design—General
Applied Economics
Applied History (*see* Public History)
Applied Social Research
Arabic (*see* Near and Middle Eastern Languages)
Arab Studies (*see* Near and Middle Eastern Studies)
Archaeology
Architectural History
Architecture
Archives Administration (*see* Public History)
Area and Cultural Studies (*see* African-American Studies; African Studies; American Indian/Native American Studies; American Studies; Asian-American Studies; Asian Studies; Canadian Studies; Cultural Studies; East European and Russian Studies; Ethnic Studies; Folklore; Gender Studies; Hispanic Studies; Holocaust Studies; Jewish Studies; Latin American Studies; Near and Middle Eastern Studies; Northern Studies; Pacific Area/Pacific Rim Studies; Western European Studies; Women's Studies)
Art/Fine Arts
Art History
Arts Administration
Arts Journalism
Art Therapy
Asian-American Studies
Asian Languages
Asian Studies
Behavioral Sciences (*see* Psychology)
Bible Studies (*see* Religion; Theology)
Biological Anthropology
Black Studies (*see* African-American Studies)
Broadcasting (*see* Communication; Film, Television, and Video Production)
Broadcast Journalism
Building Science
Canadian Studies
Celtic Languages
Ceramics (*see* Art/Fine Arts)
Child and Family Studies
Child Development
Chinese
Chinese Studies (*see* Asian Languages; Asian Studies)
Christian Studies (*see* Missions and Missiology; Religion; Theology)
Cinema (*see* Film, Television, and Video Production)
City and Regional Planning (*see* Urban and Regional Planning)
Classical Languages and Literatures (*see* Classics)
Classics
Clinical Psychology
Clothing and Textiles
Cognitive Psychology (*see* Psychology—General; Cognitive Sciences)

Cognitive Sciences
Communication—General
Community Affairs (*see* Urban and Regional Planning; Urban Studies)
Community Planning (*see* Architecture; Environmental Design; Urban and Regional Planning; Urban Design; Urban Studies)
Community Psychology (*see* Social Psychology)
Comparative and Interdisciplinary Arts
Comparative Literature
Composition (*see* Music)
Computer Art and Design
Conflict Resolution and Mediation/Peace Studies
Consumer Economics
Corporate and Organizational Communication
Corrections (*see* Criminal Justice and Criminology)
Counseling (*see* Counseling Psychology; Pastoral Ministry and Counseling)
Counseling Psychology
Crafts (*see* Art/Fine Arts)
Creative Arts Therapies (*see* Art Therapy; Therapies—Dance, Drama, and Music)
Criminal Justice and Criminology
Cultural Studies
Dance
Decorative Arts
Demography and Population Studies
Design (*see* Applied Arts and Design; Architecture; Art/Fine Arts; Environmental Design; Graphic Design; Industrial Design; Interior Design; Textile Design; Urban Design)
Developmental Psychology
Diplomacy (*see* International Affairs)
Disability Studies
Drama Therapy (*see* Therapies—Dance, Drama, and Music)
Dramatic Arts (*see* Theater)
Drawing (*see* Art/Fine Arts)
Drug Abuse Counseling (*see* Addictions/Substance Abuse Counseling)
Drug and Alcohol Abuse Counseling (*see* Addictions/Substance Abuse Counseling)
East Asian Studies (*see* Asian Studies)
East European and Russian Studies
Economic Development
Economics
Educational Theater (*see* Theater; Therapies—Dance, Drama, and Music)
Emergency Management
English
Environmental Design
Ethics
Ethnic Studies
Ethnomusicology (*see* Music)
Experimental Psychology
Family and Consumer Sciences—General
Family Studies (*see* Child and Family Studies)
Family Therapy (*see* Child and Family Studies; Clinical Psychology; Counseling Psychology; Marriage and Family Therapy)
Filmmaking (*see* Film, Television, and Video Production)
Film Studies (*see* Film, Television, and Video Production)
Film, Television, and Video Production
Film, Television, and Video Theory and Criticism
Fine Arts (*see* Art/Fine Arts)
Folklore
Foreign Languages (*see* specific language)
Foreign Service (*see* International Affairs; International Development)
Forensic Psychology
Forensic Sciences
Forensics (*see* Speech and Interpersonal Communication)
French
Gender Studies
General Studies (*see* Liberal Studies)
Genetic Counseling
Geographic Information Systems
Geography
German
Gerontology
Graphic Design
Greek (*see* Classics)

Health Communication
Health Psychology
Hebrew (*see* Near and Middle Eastern Languages)
Hebrew Studies (*see* Jewish Studies)
Hispanic Studies
Historic Preservation
History
History of Art (*see* Art History)
History of Medicine
History of Science and Technology
Holocaust and Genocide Studies
Home Economics (*see* Family and Consumer Sciences—General)
Homeland Security
Household Economics, Sciences, and Management (*see* Family and Consumer Sciences—General)
Human Development
Humanities
Illustration
Industrial and Labor Relations
Industrial and Organizational Psychology
Industrial Design
Interdisciplinary Studies
Interior Design
International Affairs
International Development
International Economics
International Service (*see* International Affairs; International Development)
International Trade Policy
Internet and Interactive Multimedia
Interpersonal Communication (*see* Speech and Interpersonal Communication)
Interpretation (*see* Translation and Interpretation)
Islamic Studies (*see* Near and Middle Eastern Studies; Religion)
Italian
Japanese
Japanese Studies (*see* Asian Languages; Asian Studies; Japanese)
Jewelry (*see* Art/Fine Arts)
Jewish Studies
Journalism
Judaic Studies (*see* Jewish Studies; Religion)
Labor Relations (*see* Industrial and Labor Relations)
Landscape Architecture
Latin American Studies
Latin (*see* Classics)
Law Enforcement (*see* Criminal Justice and Criminology)
Liberal Studies
Lighting Design
Linguistics
Literature (*see* Classics; Comparative Literature; specific language)
Marriage and Family Therapy
Mass Communication
Media Studies
Medical Illustration
Medieval and Renaissance Studies
Metalsmithing (*see* Art/Fine Arts)
Middle Eastern Studies (*see* Near and Middle Eastern Studies)
Military and Defense Studies
Mineral Economics
Ministry (*see* Pastoral Ministry and Counseling; Theology)
Missions and Missiology
Motion Pictures (*see* Film, Television, and Video Production)
Museum Studies
Music
Musicology (*see* Music)
Music Therapy (*see* Therapies—Dance, Drama, and Music)
National Security
Native American Studies (*see* American Indian/Native American Studies)
Near and Middle Eastern Languages
Near and Middle Eastern Studies
Near Environment (*see* Family and Consumer Sciences)
Northern Studies
Organizational Psychology (*see* Industrial and Organizational Psychology)
Oriental Languages (*see* Asian Languages)
Oriental Studies (*see* Asian Studies)
Pacific Area/Pacific Rim Studies
Painting (*see* Art/Fine Arts)
Pastoral Ministry and Counseling
Philanthropic Studies
Philosophy
Photography

Playwriting (*see* Theater; Writing)
Policy Studies (*see* Public Policy)
Political Science
Population Studies (*see* Demography and Population Studies)
Portuguese
Printmaking (*see* Art/Fine Arts)
Product Design (*see* Industrial Design)
Psychoanalysis and Psychotherapy
Psychology—General
Public Administration
Public Affairs
Public History
Public Policy
Public Speaking (*see* Mass Communication; Rhetoric; Speech and Interpersonal Communication)
Publishing
Regional Planning (*see* Architecture; Urban and Regional Planning; Urban Design; Urban Studies)
Rehabilitation Counseling
Religion
Renaissance Studies (*see* Medieval and Renaissance Studies)
Rhetoric
Romance Languages
Romance Literatures (*see* Romance Languages)
Rural Planning and Studies
Rural Sociology
Russian
Scandinavian Languages
School Psychology
Sculpture (*see* Art/Fine Arts)
Security Administration (*see* Criminal Justice and Criminology)
Slavic Languages
Slavic Studies (*see* East European and Russian Studies; Slavic Languages)
Social Psychology
Social Sciences
Sociology
Southeast Asian Studies (*see* Asian Studies)
Soviet Studies (*see* East European and Russian Studies; Russian)
Spanish
Speech and Interpersonal Communication
Sport Psychology
Studio Art (*see* Art/Fine Arts)
Substance Abuse Counseling (*see* Addictions/Substance Abuse Counseling)
Survey Methodology
Sustainable Development
Technical Communication
Technical Writing
Telecommunications (*see* Film, Television, and Video Production)
Television (*see* Film, Television, and Video Production)
Textile Design
Textiles (*see* Clothing and Textiles; Textile Design)
Thanatology
Theater
Theater Arts (*see* Theater)
Theology
Therapies—Dance, Drama, and Music
Translation and Interpretation
Transpersonal and Humanistic Psychology
Urban and Regional Planning
Urban Design
Urban Planning (*see* Architecture; Urban and Regional Planning; Urban Design; Urban Studies)
Urban Studies
Video (*see* Film, Television, and Video Production)
Visual Arts (*see* Applied Arts and Design; Art/Fine Arts; Film, Television, and Video Production; Graphic Design; Illustration; Photography)
Western European Studies
Women's Studies
World Wide Web (*see* Internet and Interactive Multimedia)
Writing

Graduate Programs in the Biological Sciences

Anatomy
Animal Behavior

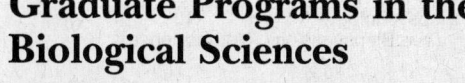

Bacteriology
Behavioral Sciences (see Biopsychology; Neuroscience; Zoology)
Biochemistry
Biological and Biomedical Sciences—General
Biological Chemistry (see Biochemistry)
Biological Oceanography (see Marine Biology)
Biophysics
Biopsychology
Botany
Breeding (see Botany; Plant Biology; Genetics)
Cancer Biology/Oncology
Cardiovascular Sciences
Cell Biology
Cellular Physiology (see Cell Biology; Physiology)
Computational Biology
Conservation (see Conservation Biology; Environmental Biology)
Conservation Biology
Crop Sciences (see Botany; Plant Biology)
Cytology (see Cell Biology)
Developmental Biology
Dietetics (see Nutrition)
Ecology
Embryology (see Developmental Biology)
Endocrinology (see Physiology)
Entomology
Environmental Biology
Evolutionary Biology
Foods (see Nutrition)
Genetics
Genomic Sciences
Histology (see Anatomy; Cell Biology)
Human Genetics
Immunology
Infectious Diseases
Laboratory Medicine (see Immunology; Microbiology; Pathology)
Life Sciences (see Biological and Biomedical Sciences)
Marine Biology
Medical Microbiology
Medical Sciences (see Biological and Biomedical Sciences)
Medical Science Training Programs (see Biological and Biomedical Sciences)
Microbiology
Molecular Biology
Molecular Biophysics
Molecular Genetics
Molecular Medicine
Molecular Pathogenesis
Molecular Pathology
Molecular Pharmacology
Molecular Physiology
Molecular Toxicology
Neural Sciences (see Biopsychology; Neurobiology; Neuroscience)
Neurobiology
Neuroendocrinology (see Biopsychology; Neurobiology; Neuroscience; Physiology)
Neuropharmacology (see Biopsychology; Neurobiology; Neuroscience; Pharmacology)
Neurophysiology (see Biopsychology; Neurobiology; Neuroscience; Physiology)
Neuroscience
Nutrition
Oncology (see Cancer Biology/Oncology)
Organismal Biology (see Biological and Biomedical Sciences; Zoology)
Parasitology
Pathobiology
Pathology
Pharmacology
Photobiology of Cells and Organelles (see Botany; Cell Biology; Plant Biology)
Physiological Optics (see Physiology)
Physiology
Plant Biology
Plant Molecular Biology
Plant Pathology
Plant Physiology
Pomology (see Botany; Plant Biology)
Psychobiology (see Biopsychology)
Psychopharmacology (see Biopsychology; Neuroscience; Pharmacology)
Radiation Biology
Reproductive Biology
Sociobiology (see Evolutionary Biology)

Structural Biology
Systems Biology
Teratology
Theoretical Biology (see Biological and Biomedical Sciences)
Therapeutics (see Pharmacology)
Toxicology
Translational Biology
Tropical Medicine (see Parasitology)
Virology
Wildlife Biology (see Zoology)
Zoology

Graduate Programs in the Physical Sciences, Mathematics, Agricultural Sciences, the Environment & Natural Resources

Acoustics
Agricultural Sciences
Agronomy and Soil Sciences
Analytical Chemistry
Animal Sciences
Applied Mathematics
Applied Physics
Applied Statistics
Aquaculture
Astronomy
Astrophysical Sciences (see Astrophysics; Atmospheric Sciences; Meteorology; Planetary and Space Sciences)
Astrophysics
Atmospheric Sciences
Biological Oceanography (see Marine Affairs; Marine Sciences; Oceanography)
Biomathematics
Biometry
Biostatistics
Chemical Physics
Chemistry
Computational Sciences
Condensed Matter Physics
Dairy Science (see Animal Sciences)
Earth Sciences (see Geosciences)
Environmental Management and Policy
Environmental Sciences
Environmental Studies (see Environmental Management and Policy)
Experimental Statistics (see Statistics)
Fish, Game, and Wildlife Management
Food Science and Technology
Forestry
General Science (see specific topics)
Geochemistry
Geodetic Sciences
Geological Engineering (see Geology)
Geological Sciences (see Geology)
Geology
Geophysical Fluid Dynamics (see Geophysics)
Geophysics
Geosciences
Horticulture
Hydrogeology
Hydrology
Inorganic Chemistry
Limnology
Marine Affairs
Marine Geology
Marine Sciences
Marine Studies (see Marine Affairs; Marine Geology; Marine Sciences; Oceanography)
Mathematical and Computational Finance
Mathematical Physics
Mathematical Statistics (see Applied Statistics; Statistics)
Mathematics
Meteorology
Mineralogy
Natural Resource Management (see Environmental Management and Policy; Natural Resources)
Natural Resources

Nuclear Physics (*see* Physics)
Ocean Engineering (*see* Marine Affairs; Marine Geology; Marine
    Sciences; Oceanography)
Oceanography
Optical Sciences
Optical Technologies (*see* Optical Sciences)
Optics (*see* Applied Physics; Optical Sciences; Physics)
Organic Chemistry
Paleontology
Paper Chemistry (*see* Chemistry)
Photonics
Physical Chemistry
Physics
Planetary and Space Sciences
Plant Sciences
Plasma Physics
Poultry Science (*see* Animal Sciences)
Radiological Physics (*see* Physics)
Range Management (*see* Range Science)
Range Science
Resource Management (*see* Environmental Management and
    Policy; Natural Resources)
Solid-Earth Sciences (*see* Geosciences)
Space Sciences (*see* Planetary and Space Sciences)
Statistics
Theoretical Chemistry
Theoretical Physics
Viticulture and Enology
Water Resources

Graduate Programs in Engineering & Applied Sciences

Aeronautical Engineering (*see* Aerospace/Aeronautical Engineering)
Aerospace/Aeronautical Engineering
Aerospace Studies (*see* Aerospace/Aeronautical Engineering)
Agricultural Engineering
Applied Mechanics (*see* Mechanics)
Applied Science and Technology
Architectural Engineering
Artificial Intelligence/Robotics
Astronautical Engineering (*see* Aerospace/Aeronautical Engineering)
Automotive Engineering
Aviation
Biochemical Engineering
Bioengineering
Bioinformatics
Biological Engineering (*see* Bioengineering)
Biomedical Engineering
Biosystems Engineering
Biotechnology
Ceramic Engineering (*see* Ceramic Sciences and Engineering)
Ceramic Sciences and Engineering
Ceramics (*see* Ceramic Sciences and Engineering)
Chemical Engineering
Civil Engineering
Computer and Information Systems Security
Computer Engineering
Computer Science
Computing Technology (*see* Computer Science)
Construction Engineering
Construction Management
Database Systems
Electrical Engineering
Electronic Materials
Electronics Engineering (*see* Electrical Engineering)
Energy and Power Engineering
Energy Management and Policy
Engineering and Applied Sciences
Engineering and Public Affairs (*see* Technology and Public Policy)
Engineering and Public Policy (*see* Energy Management and Policy;
    Technology and Public Policy)
Engineering Design
Engineering Management
Engineering Mechanics (*see* Mechanics)
Engineering Metallurgy (*see* Metallurgical Engineering and
    Metallurgy)
Engineering Physics
Environmental Design (*see* Environmental Engineering)

Environmental Engineering
Ergonomics and Human Factors
Financial Engineering
Fire Protection Engineering
Food Engineering (*see* Agricultural Engineering)
Game Design and Development
Gas Engineering (*see* Petroleum Engineering)
Geological Engineering
Geophysics Engineering (*see* Geological Engineering)
Geotechnical Engineering
Hazardous Materials Management
Health Informatics
Health Systems (*see* Safety Engineering; Systems Engineering)
Highway Engineering (*see* Transportation and Highway Engineering)
Human-Computer Interaction
Human Factors (*see* Ergonomics and Human Factors)
Hydraulics
Hydrology (*see* Water Resources Engineering)
Industrial Engineering (*see* Industrial/Management Engineering)
Industrial/Management Engineering
Information Science
Internet Engineering
Macromolecular Science (*see* Polymer Science and Engineering)
Management Engineering (*see* Engineering Management; Industrial/
    Management Engineering)
Management of Technology
Manufacturing Engineering
Marine Engineering (*see* Civil Engineering)
Materials Engineering
Materials Sciences
Mechanical Engineering
Mechanics
Medical Informatics
Metallurgical Engineering and Metallurgy
Metallurgy (*see* Metallurgical Engineering and Metallurgy)
Mineral/Mining Engineering
Nanotechnology
Nuclear Engineering
Ocean Engineering
Operations Research
Paper and Pulp Engineering
Petroleum Engineering
Pharmaceutical Engineering
Plastics Engineering (*see* Polymer Science and Engineering)
Polymer Science and Engineering
Public Policy (*see* Energy Management and Policy; Technology and
    Public Policy)
Reliability Engineering
Robotics (*see* Artificial Intelligence/Robotics)
Safety Engineering
Software Engineering
Solid-State Sciences (*see* Materials Sciences)
Structural Engineering
Surveying Science and Engineering
Systems Analysis (*see* Systems Engineering)
Systems Engineering
Systems Science
Technology and Public Policy
Telecommunications
Telecommunications Management
Textile Sciences and Engineering
Textiles (*see* Textile Sciences and Engineering)
Transportation and Highway Engineering
Urban Systems Engineering (*see* Systems Engineering)
Waste Management (*see* Hazardous Materials Management)
Water Resources Engineering

Graduate Programs in Business, Education, Health, Information Studies, Law & Social Work

Accounting
Actuarial Science
Acupuncture and Oriental Medicine
Acute Care/Critical Care Nursing
Administration (*see* Business Administration and Management;
    Educational Administration; Health Services Management and
    Hospital Administration; Industrial and Manufacturing

Management; Nursing and Healthcare Administration; Pharmaceutical Administration; Sports Management)
Adult Education
Adult Nursing
Advanced Practice Nursing (*see* Family Nurse Practitioner Studies)
Advertising and Public Relations
Agricultural Education
Alcohol Abuse Counseling (*see* Counselor Education)
Allied Health—General
Allied Health Professions (*see* Clinical Laboratory Sciences/Medical Technology; Clinical Research; Communication Disorders; Dental Hygiene; Emergency Medical Services; Occupational Therapy; Physical Therapy; Physician Assistant Studies; Rehabilitation Sciences)
Allopathic Medicine
Anesthesiologist Assistant Studies
Art Education
Athletics Administration (*see* Kinesiology and Movement Studies)
Athletic Training and Sports Medicine
Audiology (*see* Communication Disorders)
Aviation Management
Banking (*see* Finance and Banking)
Bioethics
Business Administration and Management—General
Business Education
Child-Care Nursing (*see* Maternal and Child/Neonatal Nursing)
Chiropractic
Clinical Laboratory Sciences/Medical Technology
Clinical Research
Communication Disorders
Community College Education
Community Health
Community Health Nursing
Computer Education
Continuing Education (*see* Adult Education)
Counseling (*see* Counselor Education)
Counselor Education
Curriculum and Instruction
Dental and Oral Surgery (*see* Oral and Dental Sciences)
Dental Assistant Studies (*see* Dental Hygiene)
Dental Hygiene
Dental Services (*see* Dental Hygiene)
Dentistry
Developmental Education
Distance Education Development
Drug Abuse Counseling (*see* Counselor Education)
Early Childhood Education
Educational Leadership and Administration
Educational Measurement and Evaluation
Educational Media/Instructional Technology
Educational Policy
Educational Psychology
Education—General
Education of the Blind (*see* Special Education)
Education of the Deaf (*see* Special Education)
Education of the Gifted
Education of the Hearing Impaired (*see* Special Education)
Education of the Learning Disabled (*see* Special Education)
Education of the Mentally Retarded (*see* Special Education)
Education of the Physically Handicapped (*see* Special Education)
Education of Students with Severe/Multiple Disabilities
Education of the Visually Handicapped (*see* Special Education)
Electronic Commerce
Elementary Education
Emergency Medical Services
English as a Second Language
English Education
Entertainment Management
Entrepreneurship
Environmental and Occupational Health
Environmental Education
Environmental Law
Epidemiology
Exercise and Sports Science
Exercise Physiology (*see* Kinesiology and Movement Studies)
Facilities and Entertainment Management
Family Nurse Practitioner Studies
Finance and Banking
Food Services Management (*see* Hospitality Management)
Foreign Languages Education
Forensic Nursing
Foundations and Philosophy of Education
Gerontological Nursing

Guidance and Counseling (*see* Counselor Education)
Health Education
Health Law
Health Physics/Radiological Health
Health Promotion
Health-Related Professions (*see* individual allied health professions)
Health Services Management and Hospital Administration
Health Services Research
Hearing Sciences (*see* Communication Disorders)
Higher Education
HIV/AIDS Nursing
Home Economics Education
Hospice Nursing
Hospital Administration (*see* Health Services Management and Hospital Administration)
Hospitality Management
Hotel Management (*see* Travel and Tourism)
Human Resources Development
Human Resources Management
Human Services
Industrial Administration (*see* Industrial and Manufacturing Management)
Industrial and Manufacturing Management
Industrial Education (*see* Vocational and Technical Education)
Industrial Hygiene
Information Studies
Instructional Technology (*see* Educational Media/Instructional Technology)
Insurance
International and Comparative Education
International Business
International Commerce (*see* International Business)
International Economics (*see* International Business)
International Health
International Trade (*see* International Business)
Investment and Securities (*see* Business Administration and Management; Finance and Banking; Investment Management)
Investment Management
Junior College Education (*see* Community College Education)
Kinesiology and Movement Studies
Laboratory Medicine (*see* Clinical Laboratory Sciences/Medical Technology)
Law
Legal and Justice Studies
Leisure Services (*see* Recreation and Park Management)
Leisure Studies
Library Science
Logistics
Management (*see* Business Administration and Management)
Management Information Systems
Management Strategy and Policy
Marketing
Marketing Research
Maternal and Child Health
Maternal and Child/Neonatal Nursing
Mathematics Education
Medical Imaging
Medical Nursing (*see* Medical/Surgical Nursing)
Medical Physics
Medical/Surgical Nursing
Medical Technology (*see* Clinical Laboratory Sciences/Medical Technology)
Medicinal and Pharmaceutical Chemistry
Medicinal Chemistry (*see* Medicinal and Pharmaceutical Chemistry)
Medicine (*see* Allopathic Medicine; Naturopathic Medicine; Osteopathic Medicine; Podiatric Medicine)
Middle School Education
Midwifery (*see* Nurse Midwifery)
Movement Studies (*see* Kinesiology and Movement Studies)
Multilingual and Multicultural Education
Museum Education
Music Education
Naturopathic Medicine
Nonprofit Management
Nuclear Medical Technology (*see* Clinical Laboratory Sciences/Medical Technology)
Nurse Anesthesia
Nurse Midwifery
Nurse Practitioner Studies (*see* Family Nurse Practitioner Studies)
Nursery School Education (*see* Early Childhood Education)
Nursing Administration (*see* Nursing and Healthcare Administration)
Nursing and Healthcare Administration
Nursing Education

Nursing—General
Nursing Informatics
Occupational Education (*see* Vocational and Technical Education)
Occupational Health (*see* Environmental and Occupational Health; Occupational Health Nursing)
Occupational Health Nursing
Occupational Therapy
Oncology Nursing
Optometry
Oral and Dental Sciences
Oral Biology (*see* Oral and Dental Sciences)
Oral Pathology (*see* Oral and Dental Sciences)
Organizational Behavior
Organizational Management
Oriental Medicine and Acupuncture (*see* Acupuncture and Oriental Medicine)
Orthodontics (*see* Oral and Dental Sciences)
Osteopathic Medicine
Parks Administration (*see* Recreation and Park Management)
Pediatric Nursing
Pedontics (*see* Oral and Dental Sciences)
Perfusion
Personnel (*see* Human Resources Development; Human Resources Management; Organizational Behavior; Organizational Management; Student Affairs)
Pharmaceutical Administration
Pharmaceutical Chemistry (*see* Medicinal and Pharmaceutical Chemistry)
Pharmaceutical Sciences
Pharmacy
Philosophy of Education (*see* Foundations and Philosophy of Education)
Physical Education
Physical Therapy
Physician Assistant Studies
Physiological Optics (*see* Vision Sciences)
Podiatric Medicine
Preventive Medicine (*see* Community Health and Public Health)
Project Management
Psychiatric Nursing
Public Health—General
Public Health Nursing (*see* Community Health Nursing)
Public Relations (*see* Advertising and Public Relations)
Quality Management
Quantitative Analysis
Radiological Health (*see* Health Physics/Radiological Health)

Reading Education
Real Estate
Recreation and Park Management
Recreation Therapy (*see* Recreation and Park Management)
Rehabilitation Sciences
Rehabilitation Therapy (*see* Physical Therapy)
Religious Education
Remedial Education (*see* Special Education)
Restaurant Administration (*see* Hospitality Management)
School Nursing
Science Education
Secondary Education
Social Sciences Education
Social Studies Education (*see* Social Sciences Education)
Social Work
Special Education
Speech-Language Pathology and Audiology (*see* Communication Disorders)
Sports Management
Sports Medicine (*see* Athletic Training and Sports Medicine)
Sports Psychology and Sociology (*see* Kinesiology and Movement Studies)
Student Affairs
Substance Abuse Counseling (*see* Counselor Education)
Supply Chain Management
Surgical Nursing (*see* Medical/Surgical Nursing)
Sustainability Management
Systems Management (*see* Management Information Systems)
Taxation
Teacher Education (*see* specific subject areas)
Teaching English as a Second Language (*see* English as a Second Language)
Technical Education (*see* Vocational and Technical Education)
Teratology (*see* Environmental and Occupational Health)
Therapeutics (*see* Pharmaceutical Sciences; Pharmacy)
Transcultural Nursing
Transportation Management
Travel and Tourism
Urban Education
Veterinary Medicine
Veterinary Sciences
Vision Sciences
Vocational and Technical Education
Vocational Counseling (*see* Counselor Education)
Women's Health Nursing

Directories and Subject Areas in This Book

NOTES

NOTES

NOTES

NOTES

NOTES

NOTES

NOTES

NOTES